The New Encyclopædia Britannica

Volume 25

MACROPÆDIA

Knowledge in Depth

FOUNDED 1768
15 TH EDITION

Encyclopædia Britannica, Inc.
Robert P. Gwinn, Chairman, Board of Directors
Peter B. Norton, President
Philip W. Goetz, Editor in Chief

Chicago
Auckland/Geneva/London/Madrid/Manila/Paris
Rome/Seoul/Sydney/Tokyo/Toronto

THE UNIVERSITY OF CHICAGO

"Let knowledge grow from more to more
and thus be human life enriched."

The *Encyclopædia Britannica* is published with the editorial
advice of the faculties of the University of Chicago.

Additional advice is given by committees of members drawn
from the faculties of the Australian National University,
the universities of British Columbia (Can.), Cambridge (Eng.),
Copenhagen (Den.), Edinburgh (Scot.), Florence (Italy), London
(Eng.), Marburg (W.Ger.), Oxford (Eng.), the Ruhr (W.Ger.),
Sussex (Eng.), Toronto (Can.), Victoria (Can.), and Waterloo
(Can.); the Complutensian University of Madrid (Spain);
the Max Planck Institute for Biophysical Chemistry (W.Ger.);
the New University of Lisbon (Port.); the School of Higher
Studies in Social Sciences (Fr.); Simon Fraser University (Can.);
and the State University of Leiden (Neth.).

First Edition	1768–1771
Second Edition	1777–1784
Third Edition	1788–1797
Supplement	1801
Fourth Edition	1801–1809
Fifth Edition	1815
Sixth Edition	1820–1823
Supplement	1815–1824
Seventh Edition	1830–1842
Eighth Edition	1852–1860
Ninth Edition	1875–1889
Tenth Edition	1902–1903

Eleventh Edition
© 1911
By Encyclopædia Britannica, Inc.

Twelfth Edition
© 1922
By Encyclopædia Britannica, Inc.

Thirteenth Edition
© 1926
By Encyclopædia Britannica, Inc.

Fourteenth Edition
© 1929, 1930, 1932, 1933, 1936, 1937, 1938, 1939, 1940, 1941, 1942, 1943,
    1944, 1945, 1946, 1947, 1948, 1949, 1950, 1951, 1952, 1953, 1954,
    1955, 1956, 1957, 1958, 1959, 1960, 1961, 1962, 1963, 1964,
    1965, 1966, 1967, 1968, 1969, 1970, 1971, 1972, 1973
By Encyclopædia Britannica, Inc.

Fifteenth Edition
© 1974, 1975, 1976, 1977, 1978, 1979, 1980, 1981, 1982, 1983, 1984, 1985,
    1986, 1987, 1988, 1989
By Encyclopædia Britannica, Inc.

© 1989
By Encyclopædia Britannica, Inc.

Printed in U.S.A.

Library of Congress Catalog Card Number: 87-83306
International Standard Book Number: 0-85229-493-X

CONTENTS

CONTENTS

Number Games
and Other Mathematical Recreations

Mathematical recreations comprise puzzles and games that vary from naive amusements to sophisticated problems, some of which have never been solved. They may involve arithmetic, algebra, geometry, theory of numbers, graph theory, topology, matrices, group theory, combinatorics (dealing with problems of arrangements or designs), set theory, symbolic logic, or probability theory. Any attempt to classify this colourful assortment of material is at best arbitrary. Included in this article are the history and the main types of number games and mathematical recreations and the principles on which they are based. Details, including descriptions of puzzles, games, and recreations mentioned in the article, will be found in the references listed in the bibliography.

At times it becomes difficult to tell where pastime ends and serious mathematics begins. An innocent puzzle requiring the traverse of a path may lead to technicalities of graph theory; a simple problem of counting parts of a geometric figure may involve combinatorial theory; dissecting a polygon may involve transformation geometry and group theory; logical inference problems may involve matrices. A problem regarded in medieval times—or before electronic computers became commonplace—as very difficult may prove to be quite simple when attacked by the mathematical methods of today.

Mathematical recreations have a universal appeal. The urge to solve a puzzle is manifested alike by young and old, by the unsophisticated as well as the sophisticated. An outstanding English mathematician, G.H. Hardy, observed that professional puzzle makers, aware of this propensity, exploit it diligently, knowing full well that the general public gets an intellectual kick out of such activities.

The relevant literature has become extensive, particularly since the beginning of the 20th century. Some of it is repetitious, but surprisingly enough, successive generations have found the older chestnuts to be quite delightful, whether dressed in new clothes or not. Much newly created material is continually being added.

This article is divided into the following sections:

History

EARLY HISTORY

People have always taken delight in devising "problems" for the purpose of posing a challenge or providing intellectual pleasure. Thus, many mathematical recreations of early origin that have reappeared from time to time in new dress seem to have survived chiefly because they appeal to man's sense of curiosity or mystery. A few survived from the ancient Greeks and Romans: little was known about them during the Dark Ages, but a strong interest in such problems arose during the Middle Ages, stimulated partly by the invention of printing, partly by enthusiastic writers of arithmetic texts, and partly by the rivalry and disputations among early algebraists and scholars. Such activities were most prominent on the Continent, particularly in Italy and Germany. Notable contributors included Rabbi ben Ezra (1140), Fibonacci (Leonardo of Pisa; 1202), Robert Recorde (1542), and Gerolamo Cardano (1545).

Kinds of problems. The problems in general were of two kinds: those involving the manipulation of objects, and those requiring computation. The first required little or no mathematical skill, merely general intelligence and ingenuity, as for example, so-called decanting and difficult crossings problems. A typical example of the former is how to measure out one quart of a liquid if only an eight-,

a five-, and a three-quart measure are available. Difficult crossings problems are exemplified by the dilemma of three couples trying to cross a stream in a boat that will hold only two persons, with each husband too jealous to leave his wife in the company of either of the other men. Many variants of both types of problems have appeared over the years.

Some examples. Problems involving computation also took on a variety of forms; some were as follows:

Finding a number. Think of a number, triple it, and take half the product; triple this and take half the result; then divide by 9. The quotient will be one-fourth the original number.

"God-Greet-You" problems. For example, in "God greet you, all you 30 companions," someone says: "If there were as many of us again and half as many more, then there would be 30 of us." How many were there?

The chessboard problem. How many grains of wheat are required in order to place one grain on the first square, 2 on the second, 4 on the third, and so on for the 64 squares?

The lion in the well. This is typical of many problems dealing with the time required to cover a certain distance at a constant rate while at the same time progress is hindered by a constant retrograde motion. There is a lion in a well whose depth is 50 palms. He climbs $1/7$ of a palm

Manipulation of objects and computation

daily and slips back $\frac{1}{9}$ of a palm. In how many days will he get out of the well?

Courier problems.   These are typified by the movements of bodies at given rates in which some position of these bodies is given and the time required for them to arrive at some other specified position is demanded.

PIONEERS AND IMITATORS

The 17th century produced books devoted solely to recreational problems not only in mathematics but frequently in mechanics and natural philosophy as well. The first important contribution was that of the Frenchman Claude-Gaspar Bachet de Méziriac, one of the earliest pioneers in this field, who is remembered for two mathematical works: his *Diophanti*, the first edition of a Greek text on the theory of numbers (1621), and his *Problèmes plaisans et delectables qui se font par les nombres* (1612). The latter passed through five editions, the last as late as 1959; it was the forerunner of similar collections of recreations to follow. The emphasis was placed on arithmetic rather than geometric puzzles. Among the outstanding problems given by Bachet were questions involving number bases other than 10; card tricks; watch-dial puzzles depending on numbering schemes; the determination of the smallest set of weights that would enable one to weigh any integral number of pounds from one pound to 40, inclusive; and difficult crossings or ferry problems.

In 1624 a French Jesuit, Jean Leurechon, writing under the pen name of van Etten, published *Récréations mathématiques*. This volume struck the popular fancy, passing through at least 30 editions before 1700, despite the fact that it was based largely on the work of Bachet, from whom he took the simpler problems, disregarding the more significant portions. Yet it did contain some original work, and it served as a model for others, including Mydorge and Schwenter. The first English edition (1633) bore the title: *Mathematicall Recreations, or a Collection of Sundrie Problemes, extracted out of the Ancient and Moderne Philosophers, as Secrets in Nature, and Experiments in Arithmeticke, Geometrie, Cosmographie, Horologographie, Astronomie, Navigation, Musicke, Opticks, Architecture, Staticke, Machanicks, Chimestrie, Waterworkes, Fireworks, etc. Not vulgarly made manifest until this Time . . . . Most of which were written first in Greeke and Latine, lately compiled in French, by HENRY VAN ETTEN Gent. And now delivered in the English Tongue with the Examinations, Corrections, and Augmentations* [translated by William Oughtred].

The rising tide of interest was exploited by French mathematicians Claude Mydorge, whose *Examen du livre des récréations mathématiques* was published in 1630, and Denis Henrion, whose *Les Récréations mathématiques avec l'examen de ses problèmes en arithmétique, géométrie, méchanique, cosmographie, optique, catoptrique,* etc., based largely upon Mydorge's book, appeared in 1659. Leurechon's book, meanwhile, had found its way into Germany: Daniel Schwenter, a professor of Hebrew, Oriental languages, and mathematics, assiduously compiled a comprehensive collection of recreational problems based on a translation of Leurechon's book, together with many other problems that he himself had previously collected. This work appeared posthumously in 1636 under the title *Deliciae Physico-mathematicae oder Mathematische und Philosophische Erquickstunden.* Immensely popular, Schwenter's book was enlarged by two supplementary editions in 1651–53. For some years thereafter Schwenter's enlarged edition was the most comprehensive treatise of its kind, although in 1641–42 the Italian Jesuit Mario Bettini had issued a two-volume work called *Apiaria Universae Philosophiae Mathematicae in Quibus Paradoxa et Nova Pleraque Machinamenta Exhibentur,* which was followed in 1660 by a third volume entitled *Recreationum Mathematicarum Apiaria Novissima Duodecim . . . .* And in 1665 one Johann Mohr in Schleswig published an imitation of Schwenter under the title of *Arithmetische Lustgarten.*

In England, somewhat belatedly, William Leybourn, a mathematics teacher, textbook writer, and surveyor, in 1694, published his *Pleasure with Profit: Consisting of Recreations of Divers Kinds, viz., Numerical, Geometrical, Mechanical, Statical, Astronomical, Horometrical, Cryptographical, Magnetical, Automatical, Chymical, and Historical.* The title page further states that the purpose of the book was to "recreate ingenious spirits and to induce them to make farther scrutiny into these sublime sciences, and to divert them from following such vices, to which Youth (in this Age) are so much inclined." Much of the volume is conventional textbook material, for most of Leybourn's published works grew out of his teaching.

18TH AND 19TH CENTURIES

The 18th century saw a continuation of this interest. Published in England were volumes by Edward Hatton, Thomas Gent, Samuel Clark, and William Hooper. In 1775 Charles Hutton published five volumes of extracts from the *Ladies' Diary* dealing with "entertaining mathematical and poetical parts." On the Continent there appeared several writers, including: Christian Pescheck, Abat Bonaventura, the Dutch writer Paul Halcken, and A.H. Guyot's four volumes of *Nouvelles Récréations physiques et mathématiques,* etc. (1769, 1786). But by far the outstanding work was that of Jacques Ozanam, the precursor of books to follow for the next 200 years. First published in four volumes in 1694, his *Récréations mathématique et physiques* went through many editions; based on the works of Bachet, Mydorge, Leurechon, and Schwenter, it was later revised and enlarged by Montucla, then translated into English by Charles Hutton (1803, 1814) and again revised by Edward Riddle (1840, 1844).

The first half of the 19th century produced only a moderate number of lesser writers on mathematical recreations, but the second half of the 19th century witnessed a crescendo of interest, culminating in the outstanding contributions of Édouard Lucas, C.L. Dodgson (Lewis Carroll), and others at the turn of the century. Lucas' four-volume *Récréations mathématiques* (1882–94) became a classic. The mathematical recreations of Dodgson included *Symbolic Logic* and *The Game of Logic; Pillow Problems* and *A Tangled Tale,* 2 vol. (1885–95).

20TH CENTURY

Among the more colourful figures at the turn of the 20th century were two Americans named Sam Loyd, father and son. Tremendously successful in making puzzles, the elder Loyd sold his weekly puzzle column to a national syndicate for years, and, in addition, created or adapted hundreds of mechanical puzzles fashioned of cardboard, wood, and metal that were also financially rewarding. When Loyd II died in 1934 at the age of 60, it was estimated that he had produced at least 10,000 puzzles.

In Germany, Hermann Schubert published *Zwölf Geduldspiele* in 1899 and the *Mathematische Mussestunden* (3rd ed., 3 vol.) in 1907–09. Between 1904 and 1920 Wilhelm Ahrens published several works, the most significant being his *Mathematische Unterhaltungen und Spiele* (2 vol., 1910) with an extensive bibliography.

Among British contributors, Henry Dudeney, a contributor to the *Strand Magazine,* published several very popular collections of puzzles that have been reprinted from time to time (1917–67). The first edition of W.W. Rouse Ball's *Mathematical Recreations and Essays* appeared in 1892; it soon became a classic, largely because of its scholarly approach. After passing through 10 editions it was revised by the British professor H.S.M. Coxeter in 1938; it is still a standard reference.

Outstanding work was that of Maurice Kraitchik, editor of the periodical *Sphinx* and author of several well-known works published between 1900 and 1942.

About the middle third of the 20th century, there was a gradual shift in emphasis on various topics. Up to that time interest had focussed largely on such amusements as numerical curiosities; simple geometric puzzles; arithmetical story problems; paper folding and string figures; geometric dissections; manipulative puzzles; tricks with numbers and with cards; magic squares; those venerable diversions concerning angle trisection, duplication of the cube, squaring the circle, as well as the elusive fourth dimension. By the middle of the century, interest be-

Books and collections

The work of Ozanam

Modern
shift in
emphasis

gan to swing toward more mathematically sophisticated topics: cryptograms; recreations involving modular arithmetic, numeration bases, and number theory; graphs and networks; lattices, group theory; topological curiosities; packing and covering; flexagons; manipulation of geometric shapes and forms; combinatorial problems; probability theory; inferential problems; logical paradoxes; fallacies of logic; and paradoxes of the infinite.

Types of games and recreations

ARITHMETIC AND ALGEBRAIC RECREATIONS

Number patterns and curiosities. Some groupings of natural numbers, when operated upon by the ordinary processes of arithmetic, reveal rather remarkable patterns, affording pleasant pastimes. For example:

$$1 \times 8 + 1 = 9 \qquad 3 \times 37 = 111 \qquad (1)^2 = \qquad 1$$
$$12 \times 8 + 2 = 98 \qquad 6 \times 37 = 222 \qquad (11)^2 = \qquad 121$$
$$123 \times 8 + 3 = 987 \qquad 9 \times 37 = 333 \qquad (111)^2 = \quad 12321$$
$$1234 \times 8 + 4 = 9876 \quad 12 \times 37 = 444 \quad (1111)^2 = 1234321$$
$$\text{etc.} \qquad\qquad \text{etc.} \qquad\qquad \text{etc.}$$

Another type of number pleasantry concerns multigrades; *i.e.*, identities between the sums of two sets of numbers and the sums of their squares or higher powers—*e.g.*,

$$1^n + 6^n + 8^n = 2^n + 4^n + 9^n \text{ (for } n = 1 \text{ or } 2).$$

An easy method of forming a multigrade is to start with a simple equality—*e.g.*, $1 + 5 = 2 + 4$—then add, for example, 5 to each term: $6 + 10 = 7 + 9$. A second-order multigrade is obtained by "switching sides" and combining, as shown below:

$$1^n + 5^n + 7^n + 9^n = 2^n + 4^n + 6^n + 10^n \, (n = 1 \text{ or } 2).$$

On each side the sum of the first powers (S_1) is 22 and of the second powers (S_2) is 156.

Ten may be added to each term to derive a third-order multigrade:

$$11^n + 15^n + 17^n + 19^n = 12^n + 14^n + 16^n + 20^n \, (n = 1 \text{ or } 2).$$

Switching sides and combining, as before:

$$1^n + 5^n + 7^n + 9^n + 12^n + 14^n + 16^n + 20^n$$
$$= 2^n + 4^n + 6^n + 10^n + 11^n + 15^n + 17^n + 19^n$$
$$(n = 1, 2, \text{ or } 3).$$

In this example $S_1 = 84$, $S_2 = 1,152$, and $S_3 = 17,766$.

This process can be continued indefinitely to build multigrades of successively higher orders. Similarly, all terms in a multigrade may be multiplied or divided by the same number without affecting the equality. Many variations are possible: for example, palindromic multigrades that read the same backward and forward, and multigrades composed of prime numbers.

Narcis-
sistic
numbers

Other number curiosities and oddities are to be found. Thus, narcissistic numbers are numbers that can be represented by some kind of mathematical manipulation of their digits. A whole number, or integer, that is the sum of the nth powers of its digits (*e.g.*, $153 = 1^3 + 5^3 + 3^3$) is called a perfect digital invariant. On the other hand, a recurring digital invariant is illustrated by:

$$55: \quad 5^3 + 5^3 \qquad = 250;$$
$$250: \quad 2^3 + 5^3 + 0^3 = 133;$$
$$133: \quad 1^3 + 3^3 + 3^3 = \quad 55.$$

(From *Mathematics on Vacation*, Joseph Madachy; Charles Scribner's Sons.)

A variation of such digital invariants is

$$165,033 = 16^3 + 50^3 + 33^3.$$

Another curiosity is exemplified by a number that is equal to the nth power of the sum of its digits:

$$81 = (8 + 1)^2 = 9^2;$$
$$4913 = (4 + 9 + 1 + 3)^3 = 17^3.$$

An automorphic number is an integer whose square ends with the given integer, as $(25)^2 = 625$, and $(76)^2 = 5776$. Strobogrammatic numbers read the same after having been rotated through $180°$; *e.g.*, 69, 96, 1001.

It is not improbable that such curiosities should have

suggested intrinsic properties of numbers bordering on mysticism.

Problem
of the
four *n*'s

Digital problems. The problem of the four *n*'s calls for the expression of as large a sequence of integers as possible, beginning with 1, representing each integer in turn by a given digit used exactly four times. The answer depends upon the rules of operation that are admitted. Two partial examples are shown.

For four 1s:

$$1 = 1 + \tfrac{1}{1} - 1$$
$$2 = 1 + 1 + 1 - 1$$
$$3 = 1 + 1 + \tfrac{1}{1}$$
$$4 = 1 + 1 + 1 + 1$$
$$5 = (1 + 1 + 1)! - 1$$
$$\text{etc.}$$

For four 4s:

$$1 = \left(\tfrac{4}{4}\right) \cdot \left(\tfrac{4}{4}\right)$$
$$2 = \tfrac{4}{4} + \tfrac{4}{4}$$
$$3 = \tfrac{4}{4} + 4/\sqrt{4}$$
$$4 = \sqrt{(4)(4)} \cdot \left(\tfrac{4}{4}\right)$$
$$5 = \sqrt{4} + \sqrt{4} + \tfrac{4}{4}$$
$$\text{etc.}$$

(In M. Bicknell & V. Hoggatt, "64 Ways to Write 64 Using Four 4's," *Recreational Mathematics Magazine*, No. 14, Jan.–Feb. 1964, p. 13.)

Obviously, many alternatives are possible; *e.g.*, $7 = 4 + \sqrt{4} + 4/4$ could also be expressed as $4!/4 + 4/4$, or as $44/4 - 4$. The factorial of a positive integer is the product of all the positive integers less than or equal to the given integer; *e.g.*, "factorial 4," or $4! = 4 \times 3 \times 2 \times 1$. If the use of factorial notation is not allowed, it is still possible to express the numbers from 1 to 22 inclusive with four "4s"; thus $22 = (4 + 4)/.4 + \sqrt{4}$. But if the rules are extended, many additional combinations are possible.

A similar problem requires that the integers be expressed by using the first m positive integers, $m > 3$ ("m is greater than three") and the operational symbols used in elementary algebra. For example, using the digits 1, 2, 3, and 4:

$$2 = 4 - 3 + 2 - 1$$
$$4 = \sqrt{4} + 3 - 2 + 1$$
$$6 = \sqrt{4} + 3 + 2 - 1$$
$$8 = \sqrt{4} + 3 + 2 + 1$$
$$9 = 4 + 3 + (2 \cdot 1).$$

Such problems have many variations; for example, more than 100 ways of arranging the digits 1 to 9, *in order*, to give a value of 100 have been demonstrated.

All of these digital problems require considerable ingenuity but involve little significant mathematics.

Cryptarithms. The term "crypt-arithmetic" was introduced in 1931, when the following multiplication problem appeared in the Belgian journal *Sphinx*:

$$\begin{array}{r} \text{ABC} \\ \underline{\text{DE}} \\ \text{FEC} \\ \underline{\text{DEC}} \\ \text{HGBC} \end{array}$$

The shortened word cryptarithm now denotes mathematical problems usually calling for addition, subtraction, multiplication, or division and replacement of the digits by letters of the alphabet or some other symbols.

An analysis of the original puzzle suggested the general method of solving a relatively simple cryptarithm:

1. In the second partial product $D \times A = D$, hence $A = 1$.
2. $D \times C$ and $E \times C$ both end in C; since for any two digits 1–9 the only multiple that will produce this result is 5 (zero if both digits are even, 5 if both are odd), $C = 5$.
3. D and E must be odd. Since both partial products have only three digits, neither D nor E can be 9. This leaves only 3 and 7. In the first partial product $E \times B$ is a number of two digits, while in the second partial product $D \times B$ is a number of only one digit. Thus E is larger than D, so $E = 7$ and $D = 3$.
4. Since $D \times B$ has only one digit, B must be 3 or less. The only two possibilities are 0 and 2. B cannot be zero because 7B is a two digit number. Thus $B = 2$.
5. By completing the multiplication, $F = 8$, $G = 6$, and $H = 4$.
6. Answer: $125 \times 37 = 4,625$.

(From *150 Puzzles in Crypt-Arithmetic* by Maxey Brooke; Dover Publications, Inc., New York, 1963. Reprinted through the permission of the publisher.)

Such puzzles had apparently appeared, on occasion, even earlier. Alphametics refers specifically to cryptarithms in which the combinations of letters make sense, as in one of the oldest and probably best known of all alphametics:

$$\begin{array}{r} \text{SEND} \\ + \text{MORE} \\ \hline \text{MONEY} \end{array}$$

Unless otherwise indicated, convention requires that the initial letters of an alphametic cannot represent zero, and that two or more letters may not represent the same digit. If these conventions are disregarded, the alphametic must be accompanied by an appropriate clue to that effect. Some cryptarithms are quite complex and elaborate and have multiple solutions. Electronic computers have been used for the solution of such problems.

Paradoxes and fallacies. Mathematical paradoxes and fallacies have long intrigued mathematicians. A mathematical paradox is a mathematical conclusion so unexpected that it is difficult to accept even though every step in the reasoning is valid. A mathematical fallacy, on the other hand, is an instance of improper reasoning leading to an unexpected result that is patently false or absurd. The error in a fallacy generally violates some principle of logic or mathematics, often unwittingly. Such fallacies are quite puzzling to the tyro, who, unless he is aware of the principle involved, may well overlook the subtly concealed error. A sophism is a fallacy in which the error has been knowingly committed, for whatever purpose. If the error introduced into a calculation or a proof leads innocently to a *correct* result, the result is a "howler," often said to depend on "making the right mistake."

Many paradoxes arise from the concepts of infinity and limiting processes. For example, the infinite series

$$1 + \tfrac{1}{2} + \tfrac{1}{4} + \tfrac{1}{8} + \ldots$$

has a continually greater sum the more terms are included, but the sum always remains less than 2, although it approaches nearer and nearer to 2 as more terms are included. On the other hand, the series

$$1 + \tfrac{1}{2} + \tfrac{1}{3} + \tfrac{1}{4} + \tfrac{1}{5} + \tfrac{1}{6} + \ldots$$

is called divergent: it has no limit, the sum becoming larger than any chosen value if sufficient terms are taken. Another paradox is the fact that there are just as many even natural numbers as there are even and odd numbers all together, thus contradicting the notion that "the whole is greater than any of its parts." This seeming contradiction arises from the properties of collections containing an infinite number of objects. Since both are infinite, they are for both practical and mathematical purposes equal.

Zeno's paradoxes The so-called paradoxes of Zeno (*c.* 450 BC) are, strictly speaking, sophisms. Thus, in the case of Achilles and the tortoise, Achilles, who could run 10 yards per second, competed with a tortoise that ran five yards per second; the tortoise was to have a handicap of 10 yards. Zeno claimed that Achilles could never catch the tortoise, his argument being based on the "fact" that whenever Achilles reached a point where the tortoise had just been, the tortoise would have moved ahead. Obviously, Zeno did not believe what he claimed; his interest lay in locating the error in his argument. The same observation is true of the three remaining paradoxes of Zeno, the *Dichotomy*, "motion is impossible"; the *Arrow*, "motionless even while in flight"; and the *Stadium*, or "a given time interval is equivalent to an interval twice as long." Beneath the sophistry of these contradictions lie subtle and elusive concepts of limits and infinity, only completely explained in the 19th century when the foundations of analysis became more rigorous and the theory of transfinite numbers had been formulated.

Common algebraic fallacies usually involve a violation of one or another of the following assumptions:

1. If $a = b$, then $a/k = b/k$, provided $k \neq 0$.
2. If $a > b$, then $ka > kb$, provided k is positive.
3. If a is nonnegative, then $\sqrt{a^2} = +a$.

Three examples of such violations follow:

A. Solve: $6x - 18 = 4x - 12$
   Factoring: $3(2x - 6) = 2(2x - 6)$
   Dividing by $(2x - 6)$: $3 = 2$
B. Since $+1/-1 = -1/+1$, then $\sqrt{+1}/\sqrt{-1} = \sqrt{-1}/\sqrt{+1}$, and so $(\sqrt{+1})(\sqrt{+1}) = (\sqrt{-1})(\sqrt{-1})$, hence $+1 = -1$
C. Given two positive numbers, a and b:

then,	also,
$a > -b$	$b > -a$
$b > -b$	$a > -a$
Multiplying: $ab > b^2$	$ab > a^2$
Or $a > b$	$b > a$

Thus a is both greater than b and less than b.

An example of an illegal operation or "lucky boner" is:

$$\tfrac{16}{64} = \tfrac{1\!\!/6}{6\!\!/4} = \tfrac{1}{4}.$$

Polygonal and other figurate numbers. Among the many relationships of numbers that have fascinated man are those that suggest (or were derived from) the arrangement of points representing numbers into series of geometrical figures. Such numbers, known as figurate or polygonal numbers, appeared in 15th-century arithmetic books and were probably known to the ancient Chinese; but they were of especial interest to the ancient Greek mathematicians. To the Pythagoreans (*c.* 500 BC) numbers were of paramount significance; everything could be explained by numbers, and numbers were invested with specific characteristics and personalities. Among other properties of numbers, the Pythagoreans recognized that numbers had "shapes." Thus the triangular numbers, 1, 3, 6, 10, 15, 21, etc., were visualized as points or dots arranged in the shape of a triangle.   **The "shapes" of numbers**

Square numbers are the squares of natural numbers, such as 1, 4, 9, 16, 25, etc., and can be represented by square arrays of dots, as shown in Figure 1. Inspection reveals that the sum of any two adjacent triangular numbers is always a square number.

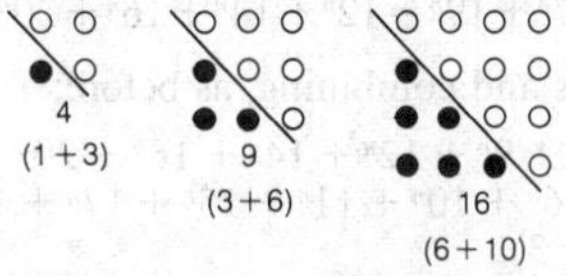

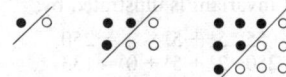

Figure 1: Square numbers shown formed from consecutive triangular numbers.

From *The Number of Things: Pythagoras, Geometry and Humming Strings* by Evans G. Valens, copyright © 1964 by Evans G. Valens; published by E.P. Dutton & Co., Inc., and used with their permission

Oblong numbers are the numbers of dots that can be placed in rows and columns in a rectangular array, each row containing one more dot than each column. The first few oblong numbers are 2, 6, 12, 20, and 30. This series of numbers is the successive sums of the series of even numbers or the products of two consecutive numbers: $2 = 1 \cdot 2$; $6 = 2 \cdot 3 = 2 + 4$; $12 = 3 \cdot 4 = 2 + 4 + 6$; $20 = 4 \cdot 5 = 2 + 4 + 6 + 8$; etc. An oblong number also is formed by doubling any triangular number (see Figure 2).

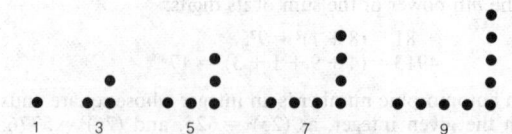

Figure 2: Oblong numbers formed by doubling triangular numbers.

From *The Number of Things: Pythagoras, Geometry and Humming Strings* by Evans G. Valens, copyright © 1964 by Evans G. Valens; published by E.P. Dutton & Co., Inc., and used with their permission

The gnomons include all of the odd numbers; these can be represented by a right angle, or a carpenter's square, as illustrated in Figure 3. Gnomons were extremely use-

Figure 3: Odd numbers shown as gnomons.

From *The Number of Things: Pythagoras, Geometry and Humming Strings* by Evans G. Valens, copyright © 1964 by Evans G. Valens; published by E.P. Dutton & Co., Inc., and used with their permission

ful to the Pythagoreans. They could build up squares by adding gnomons to smaller squares and from such a figure could deduce many interrelationships: thus $1^2 + 3 = 2^2$, $2^2 + 5 = 3^2$, etc. or $1 + 3 + 5 = 3^2$, $1 + 3 + 5 + 7 = 4^2$, $1 + 3 + 5 + 7 + 9 = 5^2$, etc. (see Figure 4). Indeed, it is

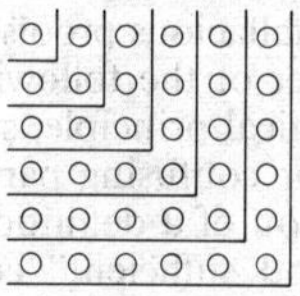

Figure 4: Addition of gnomons to squares to form larger squares.
From *The Number of Things: Pythagoras, Geometry and Humming Strings* by Evans G. Valens, copyright © 1964 by Evans G. Valens; published by E.P. Dutton & Co., Inc., and used with their permission

quite likely that Pythagoras first realized the famous relationship between the sides of a right triangle, represented by $a^2 + b^2 = c^2$, by contemplating the properties of gnomons and square numbers, observing that any odd square can be added to some even square to form a third square. Thus

$$3^2 + 4^2 = 5^2, \text{ where } 3^2 = 4 + 5;$$
$$5^2 + 12^2 = 13^2, \text{ where } 5^2 = 12 + 13,$$

and in general, $a^2 + b^2 = c^2$, where $a^2 = b + c$. This is a special class of Pythagorean triples (see below).

Besides these, the Greeks also studied numbers having pentagonal, hexagonal, and other shapes. Many relationships can be shown to exist between these geometric patterns and algebraic expressions.

Polygonal numbers constitute a subdivision of a class of numbers known as figurate numbers. Examples include the arithmetic sequences

and
$$1, 2, 3, 4, \ldots, r$$
$$1, 3, 5, 7, \ldots, (2r - 1).$$

When new series are formed from the sums of the terms of these series, the results are, respectively,

and
$$1, 3, 6, 10, \ldots$$
$$1, 4, 9, 16, \ldots$$

These series are not arithmetic sequences but are seen to be the polygonal triangular and square numbers. Polygonal number series can also be added to form three-dimensional figurate numbers; these sequences are called pyramidal numbers.

The significance of polygonal and figurate numbers lies in their relation to the modern theory of numbers. Even the simple, elementary properties and relations of numbers often demand sophisticated mathematical tools. Thus it has been shown that every integer is either a triangular number, the sum of two triangular numbers, or the sum of three triangular numbers; e.g., $8 = 1 + 1 + 6$; $42 = 6 + 36$; $43 = 15 + 28$; $44 = 6 + 10 + 28$.

Pythagorean triples. The study of Pythagorean triples as well as the general theorem of Pythagoras leads to many unexpected byways in mathematics. A Pythagorean triple is formed by the measures of the sides of an integral right triangle; i.e., any set of three positive integers such that $a^2 + b^2 = c^2$. If a, b, and c are relatively prime—i.e., if no two of them have a common factor—the set is a primitive Pythagorean triple.

A formula for generating all Pythagorean triples is

$$a = p^2 - q^2, b = 2pq, c = p^2 + q^2,$$

in which p and q are relatively prime, p and q are neither both even nor both odd, and $p > q$. By choosing p and q appropriately, for example, primitive Pythagorean triples such as the following are obtained:

p	q	(a) $p^2 - q^2$	(b) $2pq$	(c) $p^2 + q^2$
2	1	3	4	5
3	2	5	12	13

The only primitive triple that consists of consecutive integers is 3, 4, 5.

Certain characteristic properties are of interest:

1. Either a or b is divisible by 3.
2. Either a or b is divisible by 4.
3. Either a or b or c is divisible by 5.
4. The product of a, b, and c is divisible by 60.
5. One of the quantities a, b, $a + b$, $a - b$ is divisible by 7.

It is also true that if n is any integer, then $2n + 1$, $2n^2 + 2n$, and $2n^2 + 2n + 1$ form a Pythagorean triple.

Some of the properties of Pythagorean triples were known to the ancient Greeks; e.g., that the hypotenuse of a primitive triple is always an odd integer. It is now known that for an odd integer R to be the hypotenuse of a primitive triple, a necessary and sufficient condition is that every prime divisor of R be of the type $4k + 1$, in which k is a positive integer.

Perfect numbers and Mersenne numbers. Most numbers are either "abundant" or "deficient." In an abundant number, the sum of its proper divisors (i.e., including 1 but excluding the number itself) is greater than the number; in a deficient number, the sum of its proper divisors is less than the number. A perfect number is an integer that equals the sum of its proper divisors. For example, 24 is abundant, its divisors giving a sum of 36; 32 is deficient, giving a sum of 31. The number 6 is a perfect number, since $1 + 2 + 3 = 6$; so is 28, since $1 + 2 + 4 + 7 + 14 = 28$. The next two perfect numbers are 496 and 8,128. The first four perfect numbers were known to the ancients. Indeed, Euclid suggested that any number of the form $2^{n-1}(2^n - 1)$ is a perfect number whenever $2^n - 1$ is prime, but it was not until the 18th century that the Swiss mathematician Leonhard Euler proved that every even perfect number must be of the form $2^{n-1}(2^n - 1)$, where $2^n - 1$ is a prime.

A number of the form $2^n - 1$ is called a Mersenne number after the French mathematician Marin Mersenne; it may be prime (i.e., having no factor except itself or 1) or composite (composed of two or more prime factors). A necessary though not sufficient condition that $2^n - 1$ be a prime is that n be a prime. Thus, all even perfect numbers have the form $2^{n-1}(2^n - 1)$ where both n and $2^n - 1$ are prime numbers. Until comparatively recently only 12 perfect numbers were known. In 1876 the French mathematician Édouard Lucas found a way to test the primality of Mersenne numbers. By 1952 the U.S. mathematician Raphael M. Robinson had applied Lucas' test and, by means of electronic digital computers, had found the Mersenne primes for $n = 521$; 607; 1,279; 2,203; and 2,281, thus adding five more perfect numbers to the list. By 1974 there were 24 known perfect numbers.

It is known that to every Mersenne prime there corresponds an even perfect number and vice versa. But two questions are still unanswered: the first is whether there are any odd perfect numbers; and the second is whether there are infinitely many perfect numbers.

Many remarkable properties are revealed by perfect numbers. All perfect numbers, for example, are triangular. Also, the sum of the reciprocals of the divisors of a perfect number (including the reciprocal of the number itself) is always equal to 2. Thus

for 6: $\frac{1}{1} + \frac{1}{2} + \frac{1}{3} + \frac{1}{6} = 2$
for 28: $\frac{1}{1} + \frac{1}{2} + \frac{1}{4} + \frac{1}{7} + \frac{1}{14} + \frac{1}{28} = 2$

Fibonacci numbers. In 1202 the mathematician Leonardo of Pisa, also called Fibonacci, published an influential treatise, *Liber abaci*. It contained the following recreational problem: "How many pairs of rabbits can be produced from a single pair in one year if it is assumed that every month each pair begets a new pair which from the second month becomes productive?" Straightforward calculation generates the following sequence:

Month:	1 2 3 4 5 6 7 8 9 10 11 12
No. of pairs:	1 1 2 3 5 8 13 21 34 55 89 144

The second row represents the first 12 terms of the sequence now known by Fibonacci's name, in which each term (except the first two) is found by adding the two terms immediately preceding; in general, $x_n = x_{n-1} + x_{n-2}$, a relation that was not recognized until about 1600.

Over the years, especially in the middle decades of the 20th century, the properties of the Fibonacci numbers have been extensively studied, resulting in a considerable literature. Their properties seem inexhaustible; for example, $x_{n+1} \cdot x_{n-1} = x_n^2 + (-1)^n$. Another formula for generating the Fibonacci numbers is attributed to Édouard Lucas:

$$x_n = \frac{1}{\sqrt{5}} \left\{ \left(\frac{1+\sqrt{5}}{2}\right)^n - \left(\frac{1-\sqrt{5}}{2}\right)^n \right\}.$$

The Golden Section

The ratio $(\sqrt{5}+1):2 = 1.618\ldots$, designated as Φ, is known as the golden number; the ratio $(\sqrt{5}-1):2$, the reciprocal of Φ, is equal to $0.618\ldots$. Both these ratios are related to the roots of $x^2 - x - 1 = 0$, an equation derived from the Divine Proportion of the 15th-century Italian mathematician Luca Pacioli, namely, $a/b = b/(a+b)$, when $a < b$, by setting $x = b/a$. In short, dividing a segment into two parts in mean and extreme proportion, so that the smaller part is to the larger part as the larger is to the entire segment, yields the so-called Golden Section, an important concept in both ancient and modern artistic and architectural design. Thus, a rectangle the sides of which are in the approximate ratio of $3:5$ ($\Phi^{-1} = 0.618\ldots$), or $8:5$ ($\Phi = 1.618\ldots$), is presumed to have the most pleasing proportions, aesthetically speaking.

Raising the golden number to successive powers generates the sequence that begins as follows:

$$\begin{array}{ll} \Phi = (\sqrt{5}+1)/2 & \Phi^4 = (3\sqrt{5}+7)/2 \\ \Phi^2 = (\sqrt{5}+3)/2 & \Phi^5 = (5\sqrt{5}+11)/2 \\ \Phi^3 = (2\sqrt{5}+4)/2 & \Phi^6 = (8\sqrt{5}+18)/2 \end{array}$$

In this sequence the successive coefficients of the radical $\sqrt{5}$ are Fibonacci's 1, 1, 2, 3, 5, 8, while the successive second terms within the parentheses are the so-called Lucas sequence: 1, 3, 4, 7, 11, 18. The Lucas sequence shares the recursive relation of the Fibonacci sequence; that is, $x_n = x_{n-1} + x_{n-2}$.

If a golden rectangle ABCD is drawn and a square ABEF is removed, the remaining rectangle ECDF is also a golden rectangle. If this process is continued and circular arcs are drawn, the curve formed approximates the logarithmic spiral, a form found in nature (see Figure 5). The

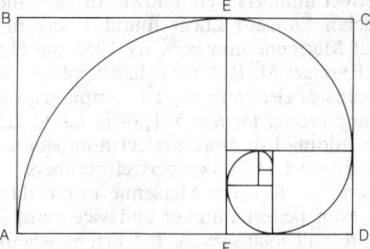

Figure 5: Golden rectangles and the logarithmic spiral.

logarithmic spiral is the graph of the equation $r = k^\Theta$, in polar coordinates, where $k = \Phi^{2/\pi}$. The Fibonacci numbers are also exemplified by the botanical phenomenon known as phyllotaxis. Thus, the arrangement of the whorls on a pinecone or pineapple, of petals on a sunflower, and of branches from some stems follows a sequence of Fibonacci numbers or the series of fractions

$$\frac{1}{1}, \frac{1}{2}, \frac{2}{3}, \frac{3}{5}, \frac{5}{8}, \frac{8}{13}, \text{ etc.}$$

GEOMETRIC AND TOPOLOGICAL RECREATIONS

Optical illusions. The creation and analysis of optical illusions may involve mathematical and geometric principles such as the proportionality between the areas of similar figures and the squares of their linear dimensions. Some involve physiological or psychological considerations, such as the fact that, when making visual comparisons, relative lengths are more accurately perceived than relative areas.

For treatment of optical illusions and their illusory effects, including unorthodox use of perspective, distorted angles, deceptive shading, unusual juxtaposition, equivocal contours or contrasts, colour effects, chromatic aberration, and afterimages, see the article PERCEPTION.

Geometric fallacies and paradoxes. Some geometric fallacies include "proofs": (1) that every triangle is isosceles (*i.e.*, has two equal sides); (2) that every angle is a right angle; (3) that if ABCD is a quadrilateral in which $\overline{AB} = \overline{CD}$, then AD must be parallel to BC; and (4) that every point in the interior of a circle lies on the circle.

The explanations of fallacious proofs in geometry usually include one or another of the following: faulty construction; violation of a logical principle, such as assuming the truth of a converse, or confusing partial inverses or converses; misinterpretation of a definition, or failing to take note of "necessary and sufficient" conditions; too great dependence upon diagrams and intuition; being trapped by limiting processes and deceptive appearances.

Impossible figures. At first glance, drawings such as those in Figure 6 appear to represent plausible three-dimensional objects, but closer inspection reveals that they

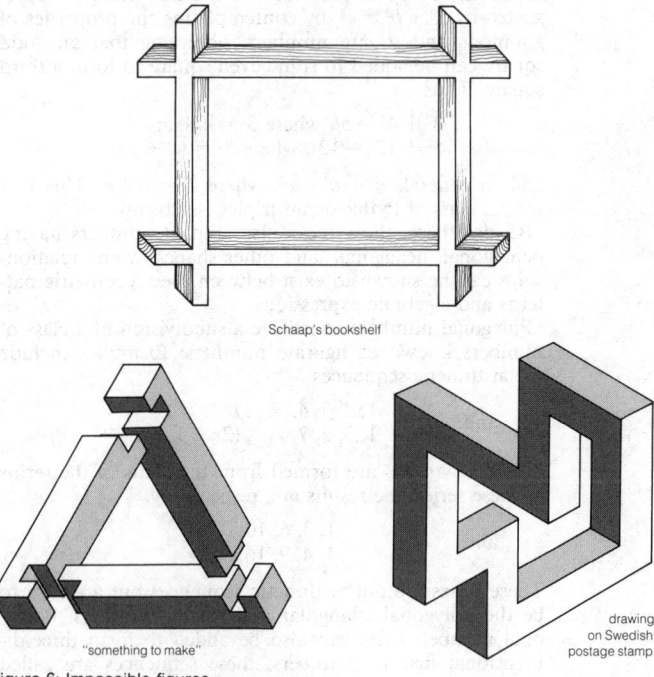

Schaap's bookshelf

"something to make"

drawing on Swedish postage stamp

Figure 6: Impossible figures.

cannot; the representation is flawed by faulty perspective, false juxtaposition, or psychological distortion. Among the first to produce these drawings—also called undecidable figures—was Oscar Reutersvard of Sweden, who made them the central features of a set of Swedish postage stamps.

In 1958 L.S. Penrose, a British geneticist, and his son Roger Penrose, a mathematical physicist, introduced the undecidable figures called strange loops. One of these is the Penrose square stairway (Figure 7), which one could apparently traverse in either direction forever without get-

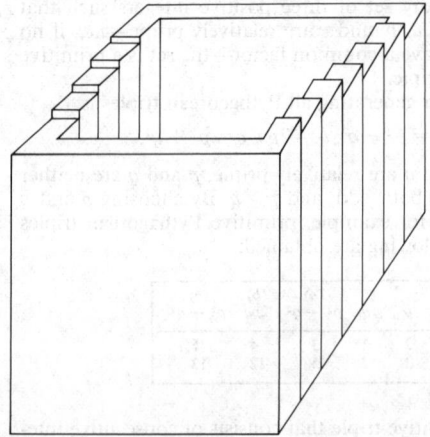

Figure 7: The endless stair.

ting higher or lower. Strange loops are important features of some of M.C. Escher's lithographs, including "Ascending and Descending" (1960) and "Waterfall" (1961). The concept of the strange loop is related to the idea of infinity and also to logical paradoxes involving self-referential statements, such as that of Epimenides (see below *Logical paradoxes*).

Pathological curves. A mathematical curve is said to be pathological if it lacks certain properties of continuous curves. For example, its tangent may be undefined at some—or indeed any—point; the curve may enclose a finite area but be infinite in length; or its curvature may be undefinable. Some of these curves may be regarded as the limit of a series of geometrical constructions; their lengths or the areas they enclose appear to be the limits of sequences of numbers. Their idiosyncrasies constitute paradoxes rather than optical illusions or fallacies.

Von Koch's snowflake curve, for example, is the figure obtained by trisecting each side of an equilateral triangle and replacing the centre segment by two sides of a smaller equilateral triangle projecting outward, then treating the resulting figure the same way, and so on. The first two stages of this process are shown in Figure 8. As the con-

Figure 8: Von Koch's snowflake curve.

struction proceeds, the perimeter of the curve increases without limit, but the area it encloses does approach an upper bound, which is $8/5$ the area of the original triangle.

In seeming defiance of the fact that a curve is "one-dimensional" and thus cannot fill a given space, it can be shown that the curve produced by continuing the stages in Figure 9, when completed, will pass through *every* point in the square. In fact, by similar reasoning, the curve can be made to fill completely an entire cube.

From E. Kasner and J. Newman, *Mathematics and the Imagination* (copyright © 1940 by Edward Kasner and James R. Newman); reprinted by permission of Simon and Schuster, Inc.

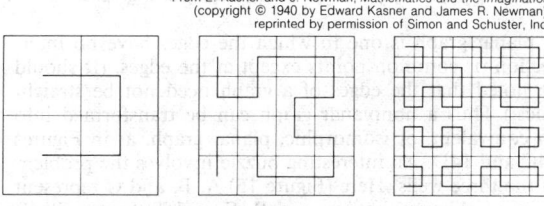

Figure 9: A space-filling curve (see text).

The Sierpinski curve, the first few stages of which are shown in Figure 10, contains every point interior to a square, and it describes a closed path. As the process of forming the curve is continued indefinitely, the length of the curve approaches infinity, while the area enclosed by it approaches $5/12$ that of the square.

A fractal curve, loosely speaking, is one that retains the same general pattern of irregularity regardless of how much it is magnified; von Koch's snowflake is such a curve. At each stage in its construction, the length of its perimeter increases in the ratio of 4 to 3. The mathematician Benoit Mandelbrot has generalized the term dimension, symbolized D, to denote the power to which 3 must be raised to produce 4; that is, $3^D = 4$. The dimension that characterizes von Koch's snowflake is therefore log 4/log 3, or approximately 1.26.

Beginning in the 1950s Mandelbrot and others have intensively studied the self-similarity of pathological curves, and they have applied the theory of fractals in modelling natural phenomena. Random fluctuations induce a statistical self-similarity in natural patterns; analysis of these patterns by Mandelbrot's techniques has been found useful in such diverse fields as fluid mechanics, geomor-

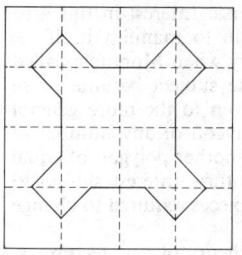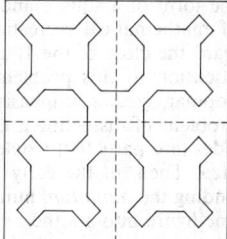
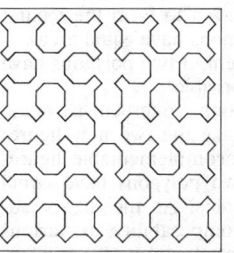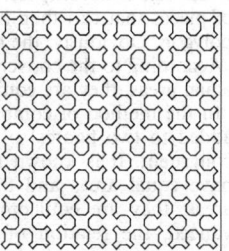

Figure 10: The Sierpinski curve.

phology, human physiology, economics, and linguistics. Specifically, for example, characteristic "landscapes" revealed by microscopic views of surfaces in connection with Brownian movement, vascular networks, and the shapes of polymer molecules are all related to fractals.

Mazes. A maze having only one entrance and one exit can be solved by placing one hand against either wall and keeping it there while traversing; the exit can always be reached in this manner, although not necessarily by the shortest path. If the goal is within the labyrinth, the "hand-on-wall" method will also succeed, provided that there is no closed circuit; *i.e.,* a route that admits of complete traverse back to the beginning (Figure 11).

From Martin Gardner, *The Second Scientific American Book of Mathematical Puzzles and Diversions* (copyright © 1961 by Martin Gardner); reprinted by permission of Simon and Schuster, Inc.

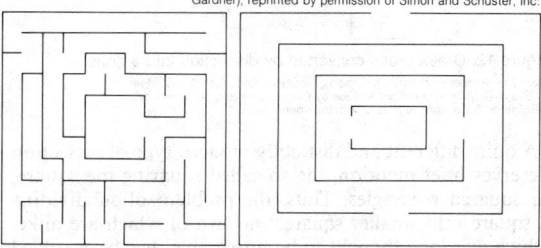

Figure 11: *Examples of mazes.*
(Left) "Simply connected" maze. (Right) "Multiply connected" maze (see text).

If there are no closed circuits—*i.e.,* no detached walls—the maze is "simply connected"; otherwise the maze is "multiply connected." A classic general method of "threading a maze" is to designate a place where there is a choice of turning as a node; a path or node that has not yet been entered as a "new" path or node; and one that has already been entered as an "old" path or node.

The procedure is as follows:

1. Never traverse a path more than twice.
2. When arriving at a new node, select either path.
3. When arriving at an old node or at a dead end by a new path, return by the same path.
4. When arriving at an old node by an old path, select a new path, if possible; otherwise, an old path.

Although recreational interest in mazes has diminished, two areas of modern science have found them to be of value: psychology and communications technology. The former is concerned with learning behaviour, the latter with improved design of computers.

Geometric dissections. Geometric dissection problems involve the cutting of geometric figures into pieces that can be arranged to form other geometric figures; for example, cutting a rectangle into parts that can be put together in the form of a square and vice versa. Interest in this area of mathematical recreations began to manifest itself toward the close of the 18th century when Montucla called attention to this problem. As the subject became more popular, greater emphasis was given to the more general problem of dissecting a given polygon of any number of sides into parts that would form another polygon of equal area. Then, in the early 20th century, interest shifted to finding the *minimum* number of pieces required to change one figure into another.

Theory of equi- decom- posable figures

According to a comprehensive theory of equidecomposable figures that was outlined in detail about 1960, two polygons are said to be equidecomposable if it is possible to dissect, or decompose, one of them into a finite number of pieces that can then be rearranged to form the second polygon. Obviously, the two polygons have equal areas.

According to the converse theorem, if two polygons have equal areas, they are equidecomposable.

In the method of complementation, congruent parts are added to two figures so as to make the two new figures congruent. It is known that equicomplementable figures have equal areas and that, if two polygons have equal areas, they are equicomplementable. As the theory advanced, the relation of equidecomposability to various motions such as translations, central symmetry, and, indeed, to groups of motions in general, was explored. Studies were also extended to the more difficult questions of dissecting polyhedra.

On the "practical" side, the execution of a dissection, such as converting the Greek cross into a square (Figure 12), may require the use of ingenious procedures, some of which have been described by H. Lindgren (see *Bibliography*).

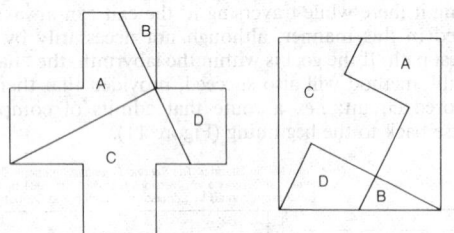

Figure 12: Greek cross converted by dissection into a square.

From *The Number of Things: Pythagoras, Geometry and Humming Strings* by Evans G. Valens, copyright © 1964 by Evans G. Valens; published by E.P. Dutton & Co., Inc., and used with their permission.

A quite different and distinctly modern type of dissection deserves brief mention, the so-called squaring the square, or squared rectangles. Thus, the problem of subdividing a square into smaller squares, no two of which are alike, which was long thought to be unsolvable, has been solved by the means of network theory. In this connection, a

From Martin Gardner, *The Second Scientific American Book of Mathematical Puzzles and Diversions* (copyright © 1961 by Martin Gardner); reprinted by permission of Simon and Schuster, Inc.

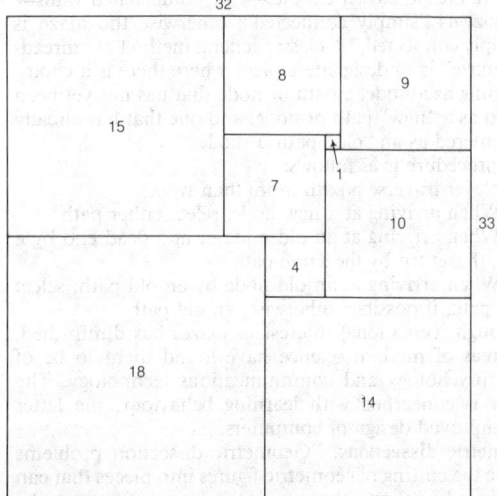

Figure 13: Squared rectangle (see text).

squared rectangle is a rectangle that can be dissected into a finite number of squares; if no two of these squares are equal, the squared rectangle is said to be perfect. The order of a squared rectangle is the number of constituent squares. It is known that there are no perfect rectangles of orders less than 9, and that there are exactly two perfect rectangles of order 9. (One of these is shown as Figure 13.) The dissection of a square into unequal squares, deemed impossible as early as 1907, was first reported in 1939.

Graphs and networks. The word graph may refer to the familiar curves of analytic geometry and function theory, or it may refer to simple geometric figures consisting of points and lines connecting some of these points; the latter are sometimes called linear graphs, although there is little confusion within a given context. Such graphs have long been associated with puzzles.

If a finite number of points are connected by lines (Figure 14A), the resulting figure is a graph; the points, or corners, are called the vertices, and the lines are called the edges. If every pair of vertices is connected by an edge, the graph is called a complete graph (Figure 14B).

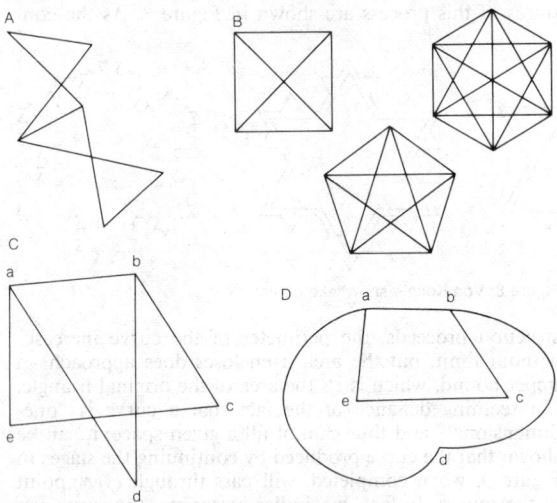

Figure 14: *Examples of linear graphs.*
(A) Graph. (B) Complete graphs. (C) Nonplanar graph. (D) Nonplanar graph of (C) changed to equivalent planar graph.

A planar graph is one in which the edges have no intersection or common points except at the edges. (It should be noted that the edges of a graph need not be straight lines.) Thus a nonplanar graph can be transformed into an equivalent, or isomorphic, planar graph, as in Figures 14C and 14D. An interesting puzzle involves the problem of the three wells. Here (Figure 15) A, B, and C represent three neighbours' houses, and R, S, and T three wells. It

From *Graphs and Their Uses*, by Oystein Ore. Copyright © 1963 by Yale University. Reprinted by permission of Random House, Inc.

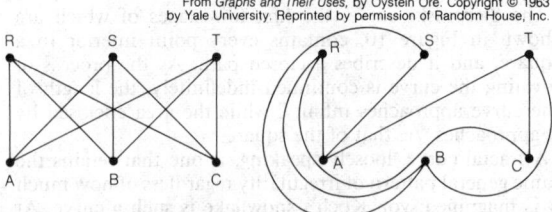

Figure 15: Three wells problem (see text).

is desired to have paths leading from each house to each well, allowing no path to cross any other path. The proof that the problem is impossible depends on the so-called Jordan curve theorem that a continuous closed curve in a plane divides the plane into an interior and an exterior region in such a way that any continuous line connecting a point in the interior with a point in the exterior must intersect the curve. Planar graphs have proved useful in the design of electrical networks.

Problem of the three wells

A connected graph is one in which every vertex, or point (or, in the case of a solid, a corner), is connected to every other point by an arc; an arc denotes an unbroken succession of edges. A route that never passes over an edge more than once, although it may pass through a point any number of times, is called a path.

Modern graph theory (in the sense of linear graphs) had its inception with the work of Euler in connection with the Königsberg bridge problem and was, for many years, associated with curves now called Eulerian paths; *i.e.,* figures that can be drawn without lifting the pencil from the paper. The city of Königsberg (now Kaliningrad) embraces the banks and an island of the forked Pregel (Pregolya) River; seven bridges span the different branches. The problem was: Could a person leave home, take a walk, and return, crossing each bridge just once? Euler showed why it is impossible.

Briefly stated, Euler's principles (which apply to any closed network) are as follows:

1. The number of even points—*i.e.,* those in which an even number of edges meet—is of no significance.

2. The number of odd points is always even; this includes the case of a network with only even points.

3. If there are *no odd points,* one can start at any point and finish at the same point.

4. If there are *exactly two odd points,* one can start at either of the odd points and finish at the other odd point.

5. If there are *more than two odd points,* the network cannot be traced in one continuous path; if there are $2n$ odd points and no more, it can be traced in n separate paths.

Thus Figures 16B and 16C can be traversed by Eulerian paths; Figures 16D and 16E cannot; Figure 16F shows a network corresponding to the Königsberg bridge problem, in which the points represent the land areas and the edges the seven bridges.

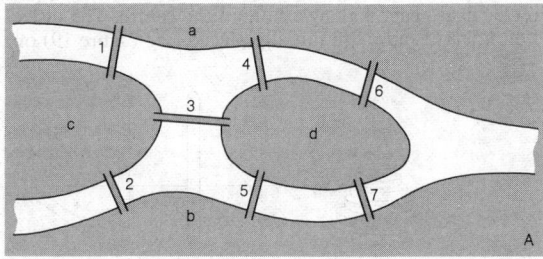

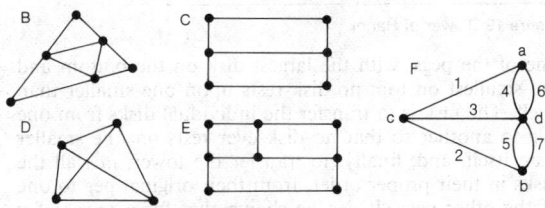

Figure 16: *Illustrations of Euler's principles.*
(A) Königsberg bridge problem. (B) and (C) Eulerian networks.
(D) and (E) Non-Eulerian networks. (F) Network corresponding to Königsberg bridge problem.

Networks are related to a variety of recreational problems that involve combining or arranging points in a plane or in space. Among the earliest was a puzzle invented by an Irish mathematician, Sir William Rowan Hamilton (1859), which required finding a route along the edges of a regular dodecahedron that would pass once and only once through every point. In another version, the puzzle was made more convenient by replacing the dodecahedron by a graph isomorphic to the graph formed by the 30 edges

The Hamilton circuit

of the dodecahedron (Figure 17). A Hamilton circuit is one that passes through each point exactly once but does not, in general, cover all the edges; actually, it covers only two of the three edges that intersect at each vertex. The route shown in heavy lines is one of several possible Hamilton circuits.

Graph theory, being a branch of mathematics known as combinatorial topology, lends itself to a variety of problems involving combinatorics: for example, designing a network to connect a set of cities by railroads or by telephone lines; planning city streets or traffic patterns; matching

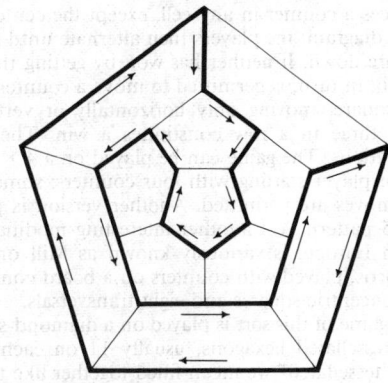

Figure 17: Hamilton circuit.
From Martin Gardner, *The Scientific American Book of Mathematical Puzzles and Diversions* (copyright © 1959 by Martin Gardner); reprinted by permission of Simon and Schuster, Inc.

jobs with applicants; arranging round-robin tournaments such that every team or individual meets every other team or individual.

Map-colouring problems. Although geographers have long known that maps depicting subdivisions of areas can be coloured in such a way that any two subdivisions having a common boundary show different colours and no more than four distinct colours need be used, the celebrated "four-colour map problem" bears little or no relation, historically, to cartography. The mathematical question was originally framed in 1850 and publicized in 1878. Essentially, the problem is: How many colours are needed to colour any map so that no two regions sharing a common border (edge) will have the same colour? Are four colours both necessary and sufficient? In short, is it possible to construct a map for which five colours are necessary? No one was sure until 1977, when a group of mathematicians proved that four colours are sufficient for every possible configuration. The proof occupied 170 pages of text and diagrams derived from more than 1,000 hours of calculations on a large electronic computer; it is treated in more detail in the article COMBINATORICS.

The four-colour problem

Flexagons. A flexagon is a polygon constructed from a strip of paper or thin metal foil in such a way that the figure possesses the property of changing its faces when it is flexed. First discussed in 1939, flexagons have become a fascinating mathematical recreation. One of the simplest flexagons is the trihexaflexagon, made by cutting a strip of suitable material and marking off 10 equilateral triangles. By folding appropriately several times and then gluing the last triangle onto the reverse side of the first triangle, the resulting model may be flexed so that one of the faces disappears and another face takes its place.

MANIPULATIVE RECREATIONS

Puzzles involving configurations. One of the earliest puzzles and games that require arranging counters into some specified alignment or configuration was Lucas' Puzzle: in a row of seven squares, each of the three squares at the left end is occupied by a black counter, each of the three squares at the right end is occupied by a white counter, and the centre square is vacant. The object is to move one counter at a time until the squares originally occupied by white counters are occupied by black, and vice versa; black counters can be moved only to the right and white only to the left. A counter may move to an adjacent vacant square or it may jump one counter of the other colour to occupy a vacant square. The puzzle may be enlarged to any number of counters of each colour. For n counters of each kind the number of required moves is $n(n + 2)$.

Lucas' Puzzle

A similar puzzle uses eight numbered counters placed on nine positions. The aim is to shift the counters so that they will appear in reverse numerical order; only single moves and jumps are permitted.

Well known, but by no means as trivial, are games for two players, such as Ticktacktoe and its more sophisticated variations, one of which calls for each player to begin with three counters (3 black, 3 white); the first

Ticktacktoe

player places a counter in any cell, except the center cell, of a 3×3 diagram; the players then alternate until all the counters are down. If neither has won by getting three in a row, each, in turn, is permitted to move a counter to an adjacent square, moving only horizontally or vertically. Achieving three in a row constitutes a win. There are many variations. The game can be played on a 4×4 diagram, each player starting with four counters; sometimes diagonal moves are permitted. Another version is played on a 5×5 pattern. Yet another interesting modification, popular in Europe, is variously known as Mill or Nine Men's Morris, played with counters on a board consisting of three concentric squares and eight transversals.

Another game of this sort is played on a diamond-shaped board of tessellated hexagons, usually 11 on each edge, where by "tessellated" we mean fitted together like tiles to cover the board completely. Two opposite edges of the diamond are designated "white"; the other two sides, "black." Each player has a supply of black or white counters. The players alternately place a piece on any vacant hexagon; the object of the game is for each player to complete an unbroken chain of his pieces between the sides designating his colour. Though the game does not end until one of the players has made a complete chain, it may meander across the board; it cannot end in a draw because the only way one player can block the other is by completing his own chain. The game was created by Piet Hein in 1942 in Denmark, where it quickly became popular under the name of Polygon. It was invented independently in the United States in 1948 by John Nash, and a few years later one version was marketed under the name of Hex.

In addition to the aforementioned varieties of a class of games that can be loosely described as "three in a row" or "specified alignment," many others also exist, such as three- and four-dimensional Ticktacktoe and even a computer Ticktacktoe. The game strategy in Ticktacktoe is by no means simple; an excellent mathematical analysis is given by F. Schuh (see *Bibliography*).

Chessboard problems. Recreational problems posed with regard to the conventional chessboard are legion. Among the most widely discussed is the problem of how to place eight queens on a chessboard in such a way that none of the queens is attacking any other queen; the problem interested the great German mathematician C.F. Gauss (*c.* 1850). Another group of problems has to do with the knight's tour; in particular, to find a closed knight's tour that ends at the starting point, that does not enter any square more than once, but that passes through all the squares in one tour. Problems of the knight's tour are intimately connected with the construction of magic squares. Other chessboard problems are concerned with determining the relative values of the various chess pieces; finding the maximum number of pieces of any one type that can be put on a board so that no one piece can take any other; finding the minimum number of pieces of any one type that can be put on a board so as to command all cells; and how to place 16 queens on a board so that no three of them are in a straight line.

The Fifteen Puzzle. One of the best known of all puzzles is the Fifteen Puzzle, which was invented by Sam Loyd the elder about 1878. It is also known as the Boss Puzzle, Jeu de Taquin, and Diablotin. It became popular all over Europe almost at once. It consists essentially of a shallow square tray that holds 15 small square counters numbered from 1 to 15, and one square blank space. With the 15 squares initially placed in random order and with the blank space in the lower right-hand corner, the puzzle is to rearrange them in numerical order by sliding only, with the blank space ending up back in the lower right-hand corner. It may overwhelm the reader to learn that there are more than 20,000,000,000,000 possible different arrangements that the pieces (including the blank space) can assume. But in 1879 two American mathematicians proved that only one-half of all possible initial arrangements, or about 10,000,000,000,000, admitted of a solution. The mathematical analysis is as follows. Basically, no matter what path it takes, as long as it ends its journey in the lower right-hand corner of the tray, any numeral must pass through an even number of boxes. In

Solving the Fifteen Puzzle

the normal position of the squares (Figure 18A), regarded row by row from left to right, each number is larger than all the preceding numbers; *i.e.,* no number *precedes* any number smaller than itself. In any other than the normal arrangement, one or more numbers will precede others smaller than themselves. Every such instance is called an inversion. For example, in the sequence 9, 5, 3, 4, the 9 precedes three numbers smaller than itself and the 5 precedes two numbers smaller than itself, making a total of five inversions. If the total number of *all* the inversions in a given arrangement is *even,* the puzzle can be solved by bringing the squares back to the normal arrangement; if the total number of inversions is *odd,* the puzzle cannot be solved. Thus, in Figure 18B there are two inversions,

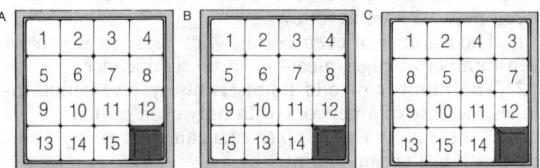

Figure 18: (A) Fifteen Puzzle with no inversions. (B) With two inversions. (C) With five inversions.

and the puzzle can be solved; in Figure 18C there are five inversions, and the puzzle has no solution. Theoretically, the puzzle can be extended to a tray of $m \times n$ spaces with $(mn - 1)$ numbered counters.

The Tower of Hanoi. The puzzle of the Tower of Hanoi is believed to have been originated in 1883 by Lucas, under the name of M. Claus. Ever popular, made of wood or plastic, it still can be found in toy shops. It consists essentially of three pegs fastened to a stand and of eight circular disks, each having a hole in the centre. The disks, all of different radii, are initially placed (see Figure 19) on

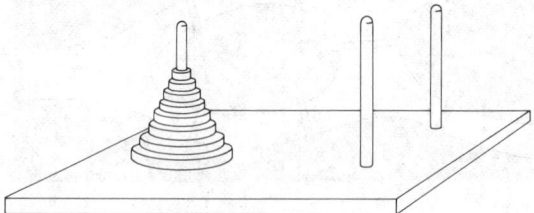

Figure 19: Tower of Hanoi.

one of the pegs, with the largest disk on the bottom and the smallest disk on top; no disk rests upon one smaller than itself. The task is to transfer the individual disks from one peg to another so that no disk ever rests on one smaller than itself, and, finally, to transfer the tower; *i.e.,* all the disks in their proper order, from their original peg to one of the other pegs. It can be shown that for a tower of n disks, there will be required $2^n - 1$ transfers of individual disks to shift the tower completely to another peg. Thus for 8 disks, the puzzle requires $2^8 - 1$, or 255 transfers. If the original "needle" (peg) was a tower with 64 disks, the number of transfers would be $2^{64} - 1$, or 18,446,744,-073,709,551,615; this is exactly the same number required to fill an 8×8 checkerboard with grains of wheat, 1 on the first square, 2 on the second, 4 on the next, then 8, 16, 32, etc.

Polyominoes. The term polyomino was introduced in 1953 as a jocular extension of the word domino. A polyomino is a simply connected set of equal-sized squares, each joined to at least one other along an edge. The simpler polyomino shapes are shown in Figure 20A. Somewhat more fascinating are the pentominoes, of which there are exactly 12 forms (Figure 20B). Asymmetrical pieces, which have different shapes when they are flipped over, are counted as one.

The number of distinct polyominoes of any order is a function of the number of squares in each, but, as yet, no general formula has been found. It has been shown that there are 35 types of hexominoes and 108 types of heptominoes, if the dubious heptomino with an interior "hole" is included.

Manipulating squares

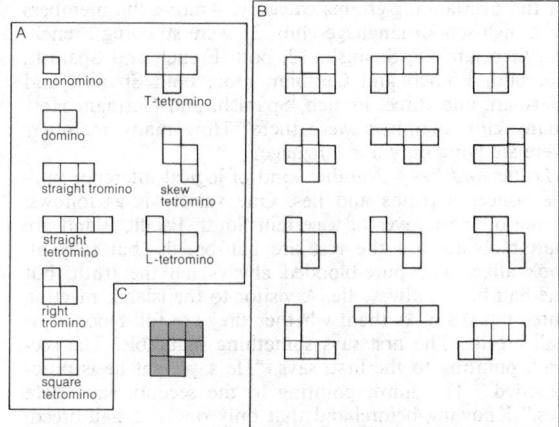

Figure 20: *Shapes made of squares.*
(A) Monomino with simple polyominoes. (B) Pentominoes.
(C) Heptomino with interior "hole."

Recreations with polyominoes include a wide variety of problems in combinatorial geometry, such as forming desired shapes and specified designs, covering a chessboard with polyominoes in accordance with prescribed conditions, etc. Two illustrations may suffice.

The 35 hexominoes, having a total area of 210 squares, would seem to admit of arrangement into a rectangle 3×70, 5×42, 6×35, 7×30, 10×21, or 14×15; however, no such rectangle can be formed.

Can the 12 pentominoes, together with one square tetromino, form an 8×8 checkerboard? A solution of the problem was shown around 1935. It is not known how many solutions there are, but it has been estimated to be at least 1,000. In 1958, by use of a computer, it was shown that there are 65 solutions in which the square tetromino is exactly in the centre of the checkerboard.

Soma Cubes. Piet Hein of Denmark, also known for his invention of the mathematical games known as Hex and Tac Tix, stumbled upon the fact that all the irregular shapes that can be formed by combining three or four congruent cubes joined at their faces can be put together to form a larger cube. There are exactly seven such shapes, called Soma Cubes; they are shown in Figure 21. No two shapes are alike, although the fifth and sixth are mirror images of each other. The fact that these seven pieces (comprising 27 "unit" cubes) can be reassembled to form one large cube is indeed remarkable.

Many interesting solid shapes can be formed from the seven Soma Cubes, shapes resembling, for example, a sofa, a chair, a castle, a tunnel, a pyramid, and so on. Even the assembling of the seven basic pieces into a large cube can be done in more than 230 essentially different ways.

As a recreation, the Soma Cubes are fascinating. With experience, many persons find that they can solve Soma problems mentally. Psychologists who have used them find that the ability to solve Soma problems is roughly correlated with general intelligence, although there are some strange anomalies at both ends of the distribution of intelligence. In any event, people playing with the cubes do not appear to want to stop; the variety of interesting structures possible seems endless.

Coloured squares and cubes. There is a wide variety of puzzles involving coloured square tiles and coloured cubes. In one, the object is to arrange the 24 three-colour patterns, including repetitions, that can be obtained by subdividing square tiles diagonally, using three different colours, into a 4×6 rectangle so that each pair of touching edges is the same colour and the entire border of the rectangle is the same colour.

More widely known perhaps is the 30 Coloured Cubes Puzzle. If six colours are used to paint the faces there result 2,226 different combinations. If from this total only those cubes that bear all six colours on their faces are selected, a set of 30 different cubes is obtained; two cubes are regarded as "different" if they cannot be placed side by side

so that all corresponding faces match. Many fascinating puzzles arise from these coloured squares and cubes; many more could be devised. Some of them have appeared commercially at various times under different names, such as the Mayblox Puzzle, the Tantalizer, and the Katzenjammer. Stimulating discussions may be found in books by MacMahon, Winter, and O'Beirne (see *Bibliography*).

A revival of interest in coloured-cube problems was aroused by the appearance of a puzzle known as Instant Insanity, consisting of four cubes, each of which has its faces painted white, red, green, and blue in a definite scheme. The puzzle is to assemble the cubes into a $1 \times 1 \times 4$ prism such that all four colours appear on each of the four long faces of the prism. Since each cube admits of 24 different orientations, there are 82,944 possible prismatic arrangements; of these only two are the required solutions.

This puzzle was soon superseded by Rubik's Cube, developed independently by Ernő Rubik (who obtained a Hungarian patent in 1975) and Terutoshi Ishigi (who obtained a Japanese patent in 1976). The cube appears to be composed of 27 smaller cubes, or cubelets; in its initial state, each of the six faces of the cube is made up of nine cubelet faces all of the same colour. In the commercial versions of the puzzle, an internal system of pivots allows any layer of nine cubelets to be rotated with respect to the rest, so that successive rotations about the three axes cause the cubelet faces to become scrambled. The challenge of restoring a scrambled cube to its original configuration

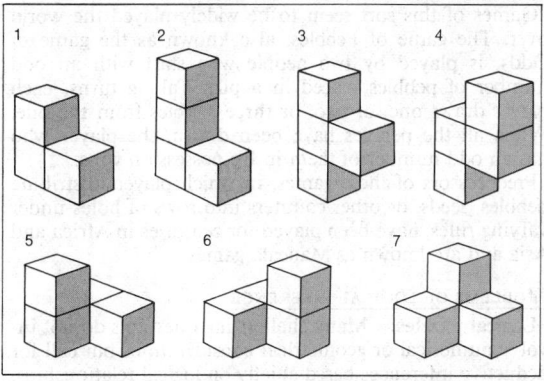

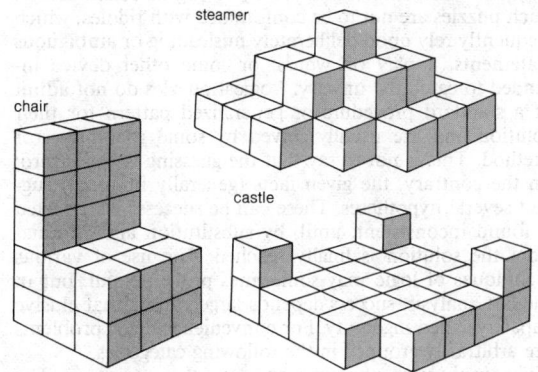

Figure 21: *Soma Cubes.*
(Top) The seven basic pieces. (Bottom) Examples of some of the shapes that can be built from Soma pieces.

is formidable, inasmuch as more than 10^{19} states can be reached from a given starting condition. A thriving literature quickly developed for the exposition of systematic solutions (based on group theory) of scrambled cubes.

Nim and similar games. A game so old that its origin is obscure, Nim lends itself nicely to mathematical analysis. In its generalized form, any number of objects (counters) are divided arbitrarily into several piles. Two people play alternately; each, in turn, selects any one of the piles and removes from it all the objects, or as many as he chooses, but at least one object. The player removing the last object wins. Every combination of the objects may be considered "safe" or "unsafe"; *i.e.*, if the position left by a player after his move assures a win for that player, the position

"Safe" and
"unsafe"
positions

is called safe. Every unsafe position can be made safe by an appropriate move, but every safe position is made unsafe by any move. To determine whether a position is safe or unsafe, the number of objects in each pile may be expressed in binary notation: if each column adds up to zero or an even number, the position is safe. For example, if at some stage of the game, three piles contain 4, 9, and 15 objects, the calculation is:

$$
\begin{array}{r}
4 \rightarrow 1\,0\,0 \\
9 \rightarrow 1\,0\,0\,1 \\
15 \rightarrow \underline{1\,1\,1\,1} \\
2\,2\,1\,2
\end{array}
$$

Since the second column from the right adds up to 1, an odd number, the given combination is unsafe. A skillful player will always move so that every unsafe position left to him is changed to a safe position.

A similar game is played with just two piles; in each draw the player may take objects from either pile or from both piles, but in the latter event he must take the same number from each pile. The player taking the last counter is the winner.

Games such as Nim make considerable demands upon the player's ability to translate decimal numbers into binary numbers and vice versa. Since digital computers operate on the binary system, however, it is possible to program a computer (or build a special machine) that will play a perfect game. Such a machine was invented by E.U. Condon and an associate; their automatic Nimatron was exhibited at the New York World's Fair in 1940.

Games of this sort seem to be widely played the world over. The game of Pebbles, also known as the game of Odds, is played by two people who start with an odd number of pebbles placed in a pile. Taking turns, each player draws one, or two, or three pebbles from the pile. When all the pebbles have been drawn, the player who has an odd number of them in his possession wins.

Predecessors of these games, in which players distribute pebbles, seeds, or other counters into rows of holes under varying rules, have been played for centuries in Africa and Asia and are known as Mancala games.

PROBLEMS OF LOGICAL INFERENCE

Solution
of logical
problems

Logical puzzles. Many challenging questions do not involve numerical or geometrical considerations but call for deductive inferences based chiefly on logical relationships. Such puzzles are not to be confounded with riddles, which frequently rely on deliberately misleading or ambiguous statements, a play on words, or some other device intended to catch the unwary. Logical puzzles do not admit of a standard procedure or generalized pattern for their solution and are usually solved by some trial-and-error method. This is not to say that the guessing is haphazard; on the contrary, the given facts (generally minimal) suggest several hypotheses. These can be successively rejected if found inconsistent, until, by substitution and elimination, the solution is finally reached. The use of various techniques of logic may sometimes prove helpful, but in the last analysis, success depends largely upon that elusive capacity called ingenuity. For convenience, logic problems are arbitrarily grouped in the following categories.

The brakeman, the fireman, and the engineer. The brakeman-fireman-engineer puzzle has become a classic. The following version of it appeared in O. Jacoby and W.H. Benson's *Mathematics for Pleasure* (1962).

The names, not necessarily respectively, of the brakeman, fireman, and engineer of a certain train were Smith, Jones, and Robinson. Three passengers on the train happened to have the same names and, in order to distinguish them from the railway employees, will be referred to hereafter as Mr. Smith, Mr. Jones, and Mr. Robinson. Mr. Robinson lived in Detroit; the brakeman lived halfway between Chicago and Detroit; Mr. Jones earned exactly $2,000 per year; Smith beat the fireman at billiards; the brakeman's next-door neighbour, one of the passengers, earned exactly three times as much as the brakeman; and the passenger who lived in Chicago had the same name as the brakeman. What was the name of the engineer?

Overlapping groups. The following problem is typical of the overlapping-groups category. Among the members of a high-school language club, 21 were studying French; 20, German; 26, Spanish; 12, both French and Spanish; 10, both French and German; nine, both Spanish and German; and three, French, Spanish, and German. How many club members were there? How many members were studying only one language?

Truths and lies. Another kind of logical inference puzzle concerns truths and lies. One variety is as follows: Some of the natives of a certain South Pacific island are pure-blooded and the rest are half-breeds, but they all look alike. The pure-blooded always tell the truth, but the half-breeds always lie. A visitor to the island, meeting three natives, asks them whether they are full-blooded or half-breeds. The first says something inaudible. The second, pointing to the first, says, "He says that he is pure-blooded." The third, pointing to the second, says, "He lies." Knowing beforehand that only one is a half-breed, the visitor decides what each of the three is.

In a slightly different type, four men, one of whom was known to have committed a certain crime, made the following statements when questioned by the police:

Archie: Dave did it.
Dave: Tony did it.
Gus: I didn't do it.
Tony: Dave lied when he said I did it.

If only one of these four statements is true, who was the guilty man? On the other hand, if only one of these four statements is false, who was the guilty man? (From *101 Puzzles in Thought and Logic* by C.R. Wylie, Jr.; Dover Publications, Inc., New York, 1957. Reprinted through the permission of the publisher.)

The smudged faces. The problem of the smudged faces is another instance of pure logical deduction. Three travellers were aboard a train that had just emerged from a tunnel, leaving a smudge of soot on the forehead of each. While they were laughing at each other, and before they could look into a mirror, a neighbouring passenger suggested that although no one of the three knew whether he himself was smudged, there was a way of finding out without using a mirror. He suggested: "Each of the three of you look at the other two; if you see at least one whose forehead is smudged, raise your hand." Each raised his hand at once. "Now," said the neighbour, "as soon as one of you knows for sure whether his own forehead is smudged or not, he should drop his hand, but not before." After a moment or two, one of the men dropped his hand with a smile of satisfaction, saying: "I know." How did that man know that his forehead was smudged?

The unexpected hanging. A final example might be the paradox of the unexpected hanging, a remarkable puzzle that first became known by word of mouth in the early 1940s. One form of the paradox is the following: A prisoner has been sentenced on Saturday. The judge announces that "the hanging will take place at noon on one of the seven days of next week, but you will not know which day it is until you are told on the morning of the day of the hanging." The prisoner, on mulling this over, decided that the judge's sentence could not possibly be carried out. "For example," said he, "I can't be hanged next Saturday, the last day of the week, because on Friday afternoon I'd still be alive and I'd know for sure that I'd be hanged on Saturday. But I'd known this *before* I was told about it on Saturday morning, and this would contradict the judge's statement." In the same way, he argued, they could not hang him on Friday, or Thursday, or Wednesday, Tuesday, or Monday. "And they can't hang me tomorrow," thought the prisoner, "because I know it today!"

Careful analysis reveals that this argument is false, and that the decree can be carried out. The paradox is a subtle one. The crucial point is that a statement about a future event can be known to be a true prediction by one person but not known to be true by another person until *after* the event has taken place.

Logical paradoxes. Highly amusing and often tantalizing, logical paradoxes generally lead to searching discussions of the foundations of mathematics. As early as the 6th century BC, the Cretan prophet Epimenides allegedly observed that "All Cretans are liars," which, in effect, means that "All statements made by Cretans are false." Since Epimenides was a Cretan, the statement made by him is false, so that all statements made by Cretans are *not* false. Thus the initial statement is self-contradictory. A similar dilemma was given by an English mathematician, P.E.B. Jourdain, in 1913, when he proposed the card paradox. This was a card on one side of which was printed:

"The sentence on the other side of this card is TRUE."

On the other side of the card the sentence read:

"The sentence on the other side of this card is FALSE."

The barber paradox The barber paradox, offered by Bertrand Russell, was of the same sort: The only barber in the village declared that he shaved everyone in the village who did not shave himself. On the face of it, this is a perfectly innocent remark until it is asked "Who shaves the barber?" If he does not shave himself, then he is one of those in the village who does not shave himself and so is shaved by the barber, namely, himself. If he shaves himself, he is, of course, one of the people in the village who is not shaved by the barber. The self-contradiction lies in the fact that a statement is made about "all" the members of a certain class, when the statement or the object to which the statement refers is itself a member of the class. In short, the Russell paradox hinges on the distinction between those classes that are members of themselves and those that are not members of themselves. Russell attempted to resolve the paradox of the class of all classes by introducing the concept of a hierarchy of logical types but without much success. Indeed, the entire problem lies close to the philosophical foundations of mathematics.

BIBLIOGRAPHY

General works: w.w. ROUSE BALL and H.S.M. COXETER, *Mathematical Recreations and Essays*, 12th ed. (1974); JOHN H. CONWAY, *On Numbers and Games* (1976); HENRY E. DUDENEY, *536 Puzzles and Curious Problems*, ed. by MARTIN GARDNER (1967); KOBON FUJIMURA, *The Tokyo Puzzles*, trans. from the Japanese, ed. by MARTIN GARDNER (1978); MARTIN GARDNER, more than a dozen collections of mathematical recreations, including *Mathematical Circus* (1979, reissued 1981) and *Wheels, Life and Other Mathematical Amusements* (1983); DOUGLAS R. HOFSTADTER, *Gödel, Escher, Bach: An Eternal Golden Braid* (1979, reprinted 1980); J.A.H. HUNTER, *Challenging Mathematical Teasers* (1980); J.A.H. HUNTER and JOSEPH S. MADACHY, *Mathematical Diversions*, rev. ed. (1975); DAVID A. KLARNER, ed., *The Mathematical Gardner* (1981), a tribute to Martin Gardner; BORIS A. KORDEMSKY, *The Moscow Puzzles*, trans. from the Russian by ALBERT PARRY, ed. by MARTIN GARDNER (1972); MAURICE KRAITCHIK, *Mathematical Recreations*, 2nd rev. ed. (1953); JOSEPH S. MADACHY, *Madachy's Mathematical Recreations* (1979); T.H. O'BEIRNE, *Puzzles and Paradoxes* (1965, reprinted 1984); HUBERT PHILLIPS ("CALIBAN"), *Question Time: An Omnibus of Problems for a Brainy Day* (1938); FREDERIK SCHUH, *The Master Book of Mathematical Recreations*, trans. from the Dutch, ed. by T.H. O'BEIRNE (1968); HUGO STEINHAUS, *Mathematical Snapshots*, 3rd U.S. ed. (1983; originally published in Polish, 1954).

Books on special topics: (*Cube puzzles*): JOHN EWING and CZES KOSNIOWSKI, *Puzzle It Out: Cubes, Groups, and Puzzles* (1982); P.A. MacMAHON, *New Mathematical Pastimes* (1921); JAMES G. NOURSE, *The Simple Solution to Cubic Puzzles* (1981); DON TAYLOR and LEANNE RYLANDS, *Cube Games* (1981); FERDINAND WINTER, *Das Spiel der 30 Bunten Würfel* (1934). (*Dissections*): V.G. BOLTYANSKII, *Equivalent and Equidecomposable Figures* (1963; originally published in Russian, 1956); HARRY LINDGREN, *Geometric Dissections* (1964). (*Fallacies*): V.M. BRADIS, V.L. MINKOVSKII, and A.K. KHARCHEVA, *Lapses in Mathematical Reasoning* (1963; originally published in Russian, 2nd ed., 1959); EDWIN A. MAXWELL, *Fallacies in Mathematics* (1959, reprinted 1969). (*Fibonacci numbers*): VERNER E. HOGGATT, JR., *Fibonacci and Lucas Numbers* (1969). (*Fractals*): BENOIT B. MANDELBROT, *The Fractal Geometry of Nature*, rev. ed. (1983). (*Graphs*): OYSTEIN ORE, *Graphs and Their Uses* (1963). (*Logical inference*): MAXEY BROOKE, *150 Puzzles in Crypt-Arithmetic*, 2nd rev. ed. (1969); HUBERT PHILLIPS ("CALIBAN"), *My Best Puzzles in Logic and Reasoning* (1961); RAYMOND M. SMULLYAN, *What Is the Name of This Book? The Riddle of Dracula and Other Logical Puzzles* (1978), and *This Book Needs No Title* (1980); GEORGE J. SUMMERS, *Test Your Logic: 50 Puzzles in Deductive Reasoning* (1972); CLARENCE R. WYLIE, *101 Puzzles in Thought and Logic* (1957). (*Manipulative puzzles and games*): MAXEY BROOKE, *Fun for the Money* (1963); SOLOMON W. GOLOMB, *Polyominoes* (1965); RONALD C. READ, *Tangrams: 330 Puzzles* (1965); T. SUNDARA ROW, *Geometric Exercises in Paper Folding*, 2nd ed. (1905, reprinted 1966); SID SACKSON, *A Gamut of Games* (1969, reissued 1982). (*Mazes*): WALTER SHEPHERD, *Mazes and Labyrinths: A Book of Puzzles*, rev. ed. (1961). (*Polytopes*): H.S.M. COXETER, *Regular Polytopes*, 3rd ed. (1973); H. MARTYN CUNDY and A.P. ROLLETT, *Mathematical Models*, 2nd ed. (1961, reprinted 1977); L. FEJES TÓTH, *Regular Figures* (1964). (*Probability*): WARREN WEAVER, *Lady Luck: The Theory of Probability* (1963, reprinted 1982).

Periodicals: *Journal of Recreational Mathematics* (quarterly; United States); *Pythagoras* (4 issues a year; The Netherlands, England, and the United States).

(W.L.S.)

Number Theory

Number theory is a branch of mathematics concerned with the properties of integers, or whole numbers, such as $0, \pm 1, \pm 2, \ldots$. These properties have been the object of fascination and investigation for thousands of years; interest in the natural numbers is as old as civilization itself. In this article some of the more elementary notions and examples are given first, the more sophisticated ideas following.

This article is divided into the following sections:

Elementary and algebraic number theory

ELEMENTARY THEORY OF NUMBERS

Divisibility and prime numbers. An integer a is said to be divisible by another integer b, not 0, if there is a third integer c such that $a = bc$. Thus 6 is divisible by 3 since the integer 2 exists for which $6 = 2 \cdot 3$. If this is the case, b is said to be a divisor or factor of a, and the fact is expressed by the notation $b \mid a$. If a and b are two integers, not both zero, the notation (a, b) is used for the greatest integer d that is a factor of both a and b. The integer d is known as the greatest common divisor of a and b. It was known to the 4th-century-BC Greek mathematician Euclid that integers x and y exist with the property that $ax + by = d$, d being the greatest common divisor of a and b.

An integer p that is greater than 1, but has no positive divisors other than 1 and p, is said to be prime. Thus the first few prime numbers are 2, 3, 5, 7, 11, 13, 17, ... An integer greater than one that is not prime is called composite. A fundamental theorem of arithmetic states that every integer greater than one may be written as a product of primes in a unique way (apart from rearrangements of the factors). Thus $666 = 2 \cdot 3 \cdot 3 \cdot 37$ but has no different expression as a product of other primes. This result is a simple consequence of another of Euclid's theorems: if a prime p divides ab, then either $p \mid a$ or $p \mid b$ can itself be deduced from the theorem of Euclid mentioned above.

Euclid also knew that there are infinitely many prime numbers, and his proof is much quoted as an example of mathematical reasoning and an example of mathematical beauty revealed in elegance and simplicity. It runs as follows: If it be supposed, on the contrary, that there is only a finite number of primes and they are denoted by $p_1, p_2, \cdots, p_n$, then the number N that is a product of primes plus 1 (see Box, equation 1) is not divisible by any p_i (for which the subscript i is a number between 1 and n, inclusive) and so must be divisible by a prime other than these (which may of course be N itself). This contradicts the hypothesis that there are no other primes.

The sieve of Eratosthenes. The first problem after the proof that infinitely many primes exist is that of finding a way to exhibit all primes up to any given number n.

About 250 BC, a contemporary of the Greek mathematician Archimedes named Eratosthenes of Cyrene proposed the following procedure, which is now called the sieve of Eratosthenes. If it is required to find all primes less than 200, all the numbers up to 200 are written down (see 2). Every second integer after 2 is not a prime, every third after 3 is not, every fifth after 5 is not a prime, and so forth; these are struck out (see 3). The striking out of every 2nd, 3rd, and 5th has been illustrated. On the face of it, this seems like a laborious task, but in fact, this sieving is surprisingly efficient. It is efficient because it is only necessary to sieve by primes 2, 3, 5, 7, 11, 13, because 13 is the largest prime that is less than or equal to the square root of the number 200. The reason for this is that in general any integer n which is not a prime must have a prime factor $\leq \sqrt{n}$.

This simple principle has been refined, modified, and generalized into an extremely powerful tool in the theory of numbers.

Definition of prime

Euclid's proof

(1) $N = p_1 p_2 \cdots p_r + 1$

(2) $2, 3, 4, 5, 6, 7, 8, 9, 10, 11, 12, \cdots, 197, 198, 199, 200$

(3) $2, 3, \cancel{4}, 5, \cancel{6}, 7, \cancel{8}, \cancel{9}, \cancel{10}, 11, \cancel{12}, 13, \cdots, \cancel{196}, 197, \cancel{198}, 199, \cancel{200}$

(4) $F_n = 2^{2^n} + 1$

(5) $\begin{cases} F_0 = 3, & F_1 = 5, & F_2 = 17, & F_3 = 257 \\ F_4 = 65,537 \end{cases}$

(6) $M_p = 2^p - 1$

(7) $\begin{cases} 6 = 1 + 2 + 3 \\ 28 = 1 + 2 + 4 + 7 + 14 \end{cases}$

(8) $2^{p-1}(2^p - 1)$

Fermat and Mersenne primes. The Fermat numbers F_n, for non-negative integer n, are defined by taking the 2^nth power of 2 and adding the number 1 (see 4). In 1640 a French mathematician, Pierre de Fermat, noted that the first five such numbers were all prime (see 5) and he was led to conjecture that F_n was prime for all n.

The 18th-century Swiss mathematician Leonhard Euler was able to show, however, that F_5 is composite. F_n is now known to be composite for all values of n from 5 to 16 and for several higher values. No further Fermat prime beyond F_4 has been discovered, and it is now thought that the total number of such primes is finite. The Fermat primes have an interesting connection with the classical problem of constructing a regular polygon by Euclidean methods (*i.e.*, by the use of straightedge and compass). The ancients knew that regular polygons of $2^k m$ sides could be constructed by such methods when $m = 3$ or 5. In 1796 the German mathematician Carl Friedrich Gauss proved—at the age of 18—that such constructions were possible if and only if m is a product of distinct Fermat primes.

The Mersenne numbers M_p are constructed from a prime p by taking the pth power of 2 and subtracting the number 1 (see 6). The French mathematician Marin Mersenne gave in 1644 a list of primes p for which he conjectured that M_p was prime. Several mistakes have been found in this conjecture, although it was not until 1886 that the first error was discovered. A few very large primes of this form are known. In particular, in 1971, it was demonstrated that $M_{19,937}$ is prime. Mersenne primes also have a connection with the ancient problem of perfect numbers. A number is said to be perfect if it is equal to the sum of its positive factors other than itself; examples are easily constructed (see 7). It was known to Euclid that if a number now called Mersenne is a prime then a certain power of two times this number is perfect (see 8). Euler showed that all even perfect numbers are of this type. Whether there exist any odd perfect numbers remains an unsolved problem.

Bernoulli numbers. The Swiss mathematician Jakob I Bernoulli introduced, in his *Ars conjectandi* (1713; "The Conjectural Arts"), an important sequence of numbers known as Bernoulli numbers. The nth Bernoulli number is denoted by the symbol B_n and the first few numbers are simply expressed (see 9). The numbers of odd orders, other than B_1, are zero. The numbers of even order, other than B_0, alternate in sign.

One definition of Bernoulli numbers is a symbolic one (see 10), in which after expansion of the nth power of the sum $(B + 1)$, powers of B are degraded into subscripts. Thus B_3 is obtained by expanding a 4th power (see 11). In this way B_3 is obtained in terms of Bernoulli numbers of lower order. This is only one example of a host of recursion formulas for generating these numbers.

Historically the first definition of Bernoulli numbers was that given by Bernoulli himself. Bernoulli's approach was to re-express the sum of a common power of a finite number of successive integers as a linear combination of successive powers of a common integer. Terms in the re-expression provided the Bernoulli numbers as coefficients (see 12). Another definition of B_n, given in terms of an explicit formula, is attributable to Euler, who made a striking independent discovery of the numbers in 1748 (see 13).

The Bernoulli numbers have several applications in number theory—in particular in work on Fermat's last theorem. Perhaps the most famous property of B_n is expressed in the Von Staudt-Clausen theorem (see 14) that expresses the $2n$th Bernoulli number as the difference between an integer and the sum of reciprocals of primes that exceed by 1 as divisor of $2n$. The 12th Bernoulli number provides an example (see 15).

Fermat's last theorem. Fermat's last theorem, an example of an unsolved theorem in number theory, concerns the equation (see 16) for which x, y, z, and n are nonzero integers. This is an example of a Diophantine equation (named after Diophantus of Alexandria, who lived about AD 250)—an equation the solutions of which are required to be integers.

$$(9) \quad \begin{cases} B_0 = 1, & B_1 = -\tfrac{1}{2}, & B_2 = \tfrac{1}{6} \\ B_3 = 0, & B_4 = -\tfrac{1}{30}, & B_5 = 0, & B_6 = \tfrac{1}{42} \\ B_7 = 0, & B_8 = -\tfrac{1}{30}, & B_9 = 0, & B_{10} = \tfrac{5}{66} \end{cases}$$

$$(10) \quad B_n = (B + 1)^n$$

$$(11) \quad (B + 1)^4 = B_4 + 4B_3 + 6B_2 + 4B_1 + B_0$$

$$(12) \quad \begin{cases} 1^k + 2^k + 3^k + \cdots + (N - 1)^k = \\ \qquad \dfrac{1}{k + 1}\left\{ B_0 N^{k+1} + B_1 \binom{k+1}{1} N^k + \cdots + \right. \\ \qquad\qquad\qquad \left. + B_k \binom{k+1}{k} N \right\} \\ \text{in which } \binom{n}{m} = \dfrac{n!}{m!(n-m)!} \end{cases}$$

$$(13) \quad B_{2n} = \frac{2(-1)^{n-1}(2n)!}{(2\pi)^{2n}}\left(1 + \frac{1}{2^{2n}} + \frac{1}{3^{2n}} + \frac{1}{4^{2n}} + \cdots\right)$$

$$(14) \quad B_{2n} = A_n - \frac{1}{p_1} - \frac{1}{p_2} - \cdots - \frac{1}{p_k}$$

$$(15) \quad B_{12} = -\frac{691}{2730} = 1 - \frac{1}{2} - \frac{1}{3} - \frac{1}{5} - \frac{1}{7} - \frac{1}{13}$$

$$(16) \quad x^n + y^n = z^n$$

$$(17) \quad x^l + y^l + z^l = 0$$

$$(18) \quad a = qm + r$$

$$(19) \quad \{1, a, a^2, \cdots, a^{\varphi(m) - 1}\}$$

The above equation can be solved when $n = 2$; for example, it is satisfied by the integers 3, 4, and 5 because $3^2 + 4^2 = 5^2$. Fermat's theorem states that if n is an integer greater than 2, there is no solution for this equation in nonzero integers. He wrote (*c.* 1637)—on the margin of his copy of the works of Diophantus—"I have discovered a truly remarkable proof which this margin is too small to contain." Although he proved it for $n = 4$, the general proof remains undiscovered. Leonhard Euler produced an incomplete proof for $n = 3$ in 1770, the missing steps being filled in by later mathematicians.

To prove Fermat's last theorem in general, it is sufficient to demonstrate the impossibility of a similar equation in which the common power is any odd prime greater than 3 (see 17). In 1823 Adrien-Marie Legendre of France showed that this was the case when the power is 5, and a countryman of Legendre's, Gabriel Lamé, in 1839 proved it for a power of 7. Many efforts were made to extend proofs to other powers, and in 1850 Ernst Eduard Kummer of Germany showed that the equation $x^p + y^p = z^p$ cannot be solved for positive integers x, y, and z if p is a prime that does not divide the numerators of B_2, B_4, ..., B_{p-3}, these being Bernoulli numbers. The criteria developed by Kummer have been used with a digital computer to show that Fermat's last theorem is true for all exponents less than 25,000. *Attempts to prove Fermat's last theorem*

Kummer's criteria

The theorem has been attacked by many mathematicians and has acquired a unique reputation because of the great difficulties it presents. Some mathematicians think that Fermat's statement was incorrect, though it may be that the theorem will never be proved or disproved.

Residue classes and congruence. If m denotes a given positive integer, every integer a can be written uniquely in the form (see 18) in which q, an integer, denotes the quotient of a on division by m, and r, the remainder, takes one of the m values 0, 1, 2, ..., $m - 1$. If two integers a and b have the same remainder on division by m, they are said to be congruent modulo m, written $a \equiv b$ mod m. This is equivalent to the assertion $m|(a - b)$. The set of integers congruent to a given integer modulo m is called a residue class. Clearly there are m such residue classes.

Euler introduced the symbol $\varphi(m)$ to denote that number of positive integers a not exceeding m that are such that $(a, m) = 1$; if $(a, m) = 1$, a and m are said to be relatively prime. It is possible to prove that if $(m, n) = 1$, $\varphi(mn) = \varphi(m)\varphi(n)$; and that if p is a prime, $\varphi(p^r) = p^{r-1}(p - 1)$. These facts enable the calculation of $\varphi(m)$ for any given m. If $a \equiv b$ mod m, $(a, m) = (b, m)$. In particular, an obvious meaning may now be attached to the term residue class modulo m, relatively prime to m. There are $\varphi(m)$ such residue classes.

Euler's theorem states that if $(a, m) = 1$, then $a\varphi^{(m)} \equiv 1$ (mod m). This generalized a theorem of Fermat, who found that if p is prime and does not divide a then $a^{p-1} \equiv 1$ (mod p).

It may happen that for a given number m there exists a number a with the property that the set of certain powers of number a (see 19) contains precisely one number from each of the $\varphi(m)$ relatively prime residue classes modulo m. In such a case a is said to be a primitive root modulo m. Gauss showed that primitive roots exist when (and only when) m is 2, 4, p^k, or $2p^k$ for some odd prime p.

Three further theorems concerning congruences may be mentioned: (1) The Chinese remainder theorem, so called from its having been known to the Chinese in the 1st century AD: If $m_1, \ldots, m_k$ are k positive integers, each pair of which are relatively prime, and if $r_1, r_2, \ldots, r_k$ are any k integers, then there exists an integer x satisfying the k congruences: $x \equiv r$ (mod m_1), ..., $x \equiv r_k$ (mod m_k). Moreover, any two such integers x are congruent modulo $m_1 \ldots m_k$. (2) Lagrange's theorem, named after the 18th-century French mathematician Joseph-Louis Lagrange: If p is a prime and $f(x)$ a polynomial of degree n with integer coefficients, then the congruence $f(x) \equiv 0$ mod p is satisfied by at most n incongruent integers x. (3) Wilson's theorem, named after the 18th-century English mathematician John Wilson: If p is a prime, then $1 \cdot 2 \cdot 3 \ldots (p - 1) \equiv -1$ (mod p).

Quadratic residues.   If m is a positive integer, then an integer a that is relatively prime to m is said to be a quadratic residue of m if there exists an integer x satisfying $x^2 \equiv a$ (mod m). The most interesting case is when m is an odd prime p. In this situation $(p - 1)/2$ of the positive integers not exceeding $p - 1$ are quadratic residues of p and the remaining $(p - 1)/2$ are not (they are known as quadratic non-residues). Numerous interesting results about quadratic residues are known; for example, -1 is a quadratic residue of an odd prime p if, and only if, $p \equiv 1$ mod 4; if $p \equiv 3$ mod 4, there are more quadratic residues in the first half of the interval from 1 to $p - 1$ than in the second. The most striking and important of such theorems, however, is the law of quadratic reciprocity, which was first proved by Gauss, although its truth had been conjectured both by Euler and Legendre. It may be stated simply as follows: if p and q are different odd primes, then p is a quadratic residue of q if, and only if, q is a quadratic residue of p, unless both p and q are congruent to 3 modulo 4, in which case p is a quadratic residue of q if, and only if, q is a quadratic non-residue of p. A more succinct statement of this important law may be obtained by employing Legendre's symbol $(a|p)$, which is defined to equal 1 if a is a quadratic residue of p, -1 if a is not a quadratic residue, and 0 if $p|a$ (see 20).

Continued fractions.   A continued fraction is an expression of a form composed of a number plus a fraction in which the denominator of the fraction is again a number plus a fraction (see 21), which may or may not terminate. If it does terminate, it has an obvious meaning. If not, and the sequence (see 22), obtained by cutting off the continued fraction at successive stages, converges to a limit V, the continued fraction is said to converge, and to have the value V. (Plainly, for this to happen, B_n must be non-zero for sufficiently large n.)

The continued fraction is said to be simple if each $a_i = 1$ and each b_i $(i > 0)$ is a positive integer (b_0 is allowed to be an integer).

Convergent fractions

$$(20) \quad (p|q)(q|p) = (-1)^{\frac{1}{2}(p-1)\frac{1}{2}(q-1)}$$

$$(21) \quad b_0 + \cfrac{a_1}{b_1 + \cfrac{a_2}{b_2 + \cfrac{a_3}{b_3 +}}}$$

$$(22) \quad \frac{A_0}{B_0} = \frac{b_0}{1}, \quad \frac{A_1}{B_1} = \frac{b_0 b_1 + a_1}{b_1}$$
$$\frac{A_2}{B_2} = \frac{b_0 b_1 b_2 + a_1 b_2 + a_2 b_0}{b_1 b_2 + a_2}, \quad \ldots$$

$$(23) \quad \xi = [\xi] + \cfrac{1}{[\xi_1] + \cfrac{1}{[\xi_2] + \cdots}}$$

A simple continued fraction is always convergent. Every real number has an expansion as a simple continued fraction. To obtain the continued fraction expansion of a real number, symbolized by the Greek letter xi, ξ, it is necessary to write $[\xi] + \theta_1$, in which $[\xi]$ denotes the greatest integer not exceeding ξ, and $0 \le \theta_1 < 1$. If $\theta_1 = 0$, the process terminates. Otherwise the proof continues with $\xi_1 = 1/\theta_1$ and then $\xi_1 = [\xi]_1 + \theta_2$ with $0 \le \theta_2 < 1$. If $\theta_2 = 0$, the process terminates. If not, $\xi_2 = 1/\theta_2$ and the process goes on as before. In this way an expansion for ξ (see 23) is obtained. It may be shown that the expansion terminates if, and only if, ξ is rational, and otherwise it is periodic if, and only if, ξ is a quadratic surd.   (Ed.)

ALGEBRAIC NUMBER THEORY

Whereas ordinary number theory is the study of the integers, $0, \pm 1, \pm 2, \ldots$, in algebraic number theory larger collections of numbers are studied. A number is algebraic if it is a root of a polynomial equation with rational coefficients; if the highest power of the variables has coefficient 1, the number is called an algebraic integer. For instance, $\sqrt{2}$ is an algebraic integer because it satisfies the equation $x^2 - 2 = 0$; so is $1 + \sqrt{3}$ in view of the equation $x^2 - 2x - 2 = 0$, which it satisfies; and the five roots of $x^5 - x + 2 = 0$ are all algebraic integers, although it is not possible to exhibit a simple formula for them.

Since about 1830, when the formal study of algebraic numbers began, evidence has multiplied that algebraic number theory is the best road to take in the search for a better understanding of ordinary numbers and a deeper insight into the mysteries they hold. In addition, algebraic number theory has been applied to nearly every other branch of mathematics.

Early history.   For brevity certain standard symbols are used in this article, beginning with Z, the symbol for the set of ordinary integers $0, \pm 1, \pm 2, \ldots$. Such integers belong to this set and are said to lie in Z.

The simplest system of algebraic numbers going beyond this set is the set of all numbers of the form $a + ib$, in which a and b are in Z (i.e., they are integers) and i is the square root of -1. These complex numbers are added and multiplied in the natural way, subject to the rule that $i^2 = -1$. For instance, $(2 + 3i) + (4 - 7i) = 6 - 4i$, and $(2 + 3i)(4 - 7i) = 8 - 14i + 12i - 21i^2 = 29 - 2i$. These numbers, first studied in depth in 1828 by Gauss, are called the Gaussian integers in his honour. The symbol $\mathfrak{G}$ is used for the set of Gaussian integers.

Gaussian integers

An illustration of the power of algebraic number theory lies in the proof that the equation $x^2 + 1 = y^3$ has in Z only the solution $x = 0$, $y = 1$. In other words, the only integers satisfying the equation are these values. This assertion was made by Euler in 1738 after he sketched a proof of a similar theorem. The first complete proof was given in 1875 by Pepin.

In the proof facts about $\mathfrak{G}$ are used to obtain information about Z, and the vital tool required for the proof is that in $\mathfrak{G}$, as in Z, numbers can be uniquely expressed as a product of primes. (Primes in $\mathfrak{G}$ may be defined in a similar way to primes in Z.) While this is true in $\mathfrak{G}$, it must be accompanied by a precaution concerning units (numbers that divide 1). In Z there are only two units, 1 and -1, and the ambiguity introduced is easily avoided by confining attention to positive numbers. On the other hand, in $\mathfrak{G}$, there are four units, ± 1 and $\pm i$, and it is necessary to accept the complication that primes of $\mathfrak{G}$ come in indistinguishable quadruplets. These primes are readily catalogued by observing the factors, lying in $\mathfrak{G}$, of primes in Z. Number 2, for example, becomes $i(1-i)^2$, with $1-i$ a prime.

If n is an integer, $1, 2, 3, \cdots$, then primes of Z that can be expressed in the form $(4n-1)$, such as $3, 7, 11, \cdots$, remain prime in $\mathfrak{G}$. Primes in Z of the form $(4n+1)$, such as $5, 13, 17, \cdots$, have factors in $\mathfrak{G}$ that are two primes. Thus $5 = (2+i)(2-i)$, etc.

In this way a neat proof may be obtained of the theorem that any prime in Z of the form $4n+1$ is uniquely expressible as a sum of two squares. This was stated by Fermat and proved by Euler.

The equation $x^2 + 1 = y^3$ has the form $(x+i)(x-i) = y^3$. It is first necessary to dispose of the possibility that $x+i$ and $x-i$ have a common factor. If this were the case, the common factor would divide their difference, $2i$, and it would follow that y is even and x is odd. This is quite impossible because $x^2 + 1$ would then be twice an odd number, whereas y^3 would be divisible by 8.

Unique factorization then yields the result that $x+i$ is a cube in $\mathfrak{G}$ (there is fortunately no difficulty with units, because the equation $i = (-i)^3$ shows that all units in $\mathfrak{G}$ are cubes). If $x+i = (a+bi)^3$, then the equations $x = a^3 - 3ab^2$ and $1 = b(3a^2 - b^2)$ follow. Thus $b = \pm 1$, $1 = \pm(3a^2 - 1)$, $3a^2 = 0$ or 2, $a = 0$, $x = 0$. A similar method will show that $x^2 + 2 = y^3$ has in Z only the solutions $x = \pm 5$, $y = 3$; this is historically interesting as one of a number of statements made without proof by Fermat; it was not until 1875 that a complete proof was given, again by Pepin. For this problem unique factorization for numbers of the form $a + b\sqrt{-2}$ is required.

The first substantial study of algebraic number theory was recorded by Gauss in the memoir of 1828 mentioned above. In it he used $\mathfrak{G}$, the Gaussian integers, to break into new territory in the study of biquadratic (fourth power) residues in Z. For instance, it may be asked when the integer 2 is a biquadratic residue of a prime p, this meaning that there exists x with $x^4 - 2$ divisible by p. The question is not an interesting one if p has the form $4n - 1$, for then any quadratic residue is a biquadratic residue. For p of the form $4n + 1$, Gauss discovered the following criterion: 2 is a biquadratic residue of p if, and only if, p can be expressed in the form $a^2 + 64b^2$. As an illustration, the first prime having this form is $73 = 3^2 + 64(1^2)$, and indeed $25^4 - 2 = 390,623$ is divisible by 73. Again, here is a theorem stated wholly within Z; Gauss proved it by a skillful, detailed development of the properties of $\mathfrak{G}$.

Kummer's attempt to prove Fermat's last theorem

The next major advance in algebraic number theory was achieved by Kummer in his investigation of Fermat's last theorem. The problem is to prove the impossibility of solving $x^n + y^n = z^n$ in Z for $n \geq 3$. Kummer's method was to rewrite the equation in the form $(x+y) \cdot (x+uy) \cdots (x+u^{n-1}y) = z^n$, in which $u = e^{2\pi i/n} = \cos(2\pi/n) + i\sin(2\pi/n)$ is a primitive nth root of unity. For instance, when $n = 3$, $u = (-1 + \sqrt{-3})/2$, and the equation reads $(x+y)(x+uy)(x+u^2y) = z^3$. The problems that must now be overcome are precisely those encountered above in the study of the equation $x^2 + 1 = y^3$—units, relative primeness, and unique factorization. The difficulties concerning units and relative primeness were formidable, but Kummer mastered them completely. In his first work, however, he overlooked the

need to prove unique factorization. The error was pointed out by the German mathematician Peter Gustav Lejeune Dirichlet. Because the first instance of non-uniqueness occurs at $n = 23$, it is not easy to exhibit the failure in connection with Fermat's last theorem. It is simpler to observe the phenomenon of non-uniqueness in an example in which the calculations are slight. The set of numbers $a + b\sqrt{-5}$ are considered in which a and b range over Z, the ordinary integers. There are two factorizations of 6 (see 24). It is easy to check that 2, 3, and $1 \pm \sqrt{-5}$ are all primes. Units play no role here because the only units are ± 1. Hence factorization is not unique in this case.

Despite the error that spoiled his proof, Kummer did not abandon the project. He had the novel, ingenious idea of restoring unique factorization by inventing additional "ideal numbers." By his new method Kummer made a great deal of progress on Fermat's last theorem, but did not arrive at a complete proof—nor did the numerous mathematicians who followed up his program. Computations based on Kummer's ideas, however, have shown $x^n + y^n = z^n$ to be impossible up to $n = 25,000$ (Richard M. Pollack and John L. Selfridge, 1964).

Foundations. In a systematic study of algebraic number theory, a basic role is played by the concept of a field (*i.e.,* a set of numbers in which the operations of addition, subtraction, multiplication, and division can be performed). The set $\mathfrak{H}$ of rational numbers forms a field. On adjoining to $\mathfrak{H}$ an algebraic number u, a typical algebraic number field, $\mathfrak{F} = \mathfrak{R}(u)$, is obtained. The set $\mathfrak{R}$ of algebraic integers lying in $\mathfrak{F}$ is a collection admitting addition, subtraction, and multiplication (but not division); such a set is called **Rings** a ring. In this ring uniqueness of factorization into primes may fail, as noted above in the case $\mathfrak{F} = \mathfrak{H}(\sqrt{-5})$. Unique factorization may be restored by a method of the German mathematician Richard Dedekind by introducing ideals. An ideal in $\mathfrak{R}$ is a subset of $\mathfrak{R}$ that is closed under addition

$$\text{(24)} \qquad 6 = 2 \cdot 3 = (1 + \sqrt{-5})(1 - \sqrt{-5})$$

$$\text{(25)} \qquad 6 = (2, 1 + \sqrt{-5})(2, 1 - \sqrt{-5}) \times$$
$$\times (3, 1 + \sqrt{-5})(3, 1 - \sqrt{-5})$$

and subtraction and, furthermore, admits multiplication by any element of $\mathfrak{R}$. The most obvious example of an ideal is a principal ideal $x\mathfrak{R}$, consisting of all multiples of an element x of $\mathfrak{R}$. If every ideal is principal, then factorization is unique and the introduction of ideals is superfluous: this is, for instance, the case for Z, the integers, and $\mathfrak{G}$, the Gaussian integers. When factorization is not unique, so that there exist nonprincipal ideals, something valuable has been accomplished by the introduction of ideals, for Dedekind proved that every ideal is uniquely a product of prime ideals. (In the ring $\mathfrak{R}$ of algebraic integers in an algebraic number field, a prime ideal $\mathfrak{B}$ can be defined very simply as one admitting no factorization into ideals except the trivial factorization $\mathfrak{B} = \mathfrak{B}\mathfrak{R}$.) In the example $6 = 2 \cdot 3 = (1 + \sqrt{-5}) \cdot (1 - \sqrt{-5}$ of nonunique factorization given above, uniqueness is restored when the factors are decomposed further into prime ideals (see 25). Here the notation $(2, 1 + \sqrt{-5}$ denotes the ideal generated by 2 and $1 + \sqrt{-5}$; *i.e.,* the set of all numbers $2x + (1 + \sqrt{-5})y$ with x and y in the ring.

Class group and class number. It is possible, in a useful way, to measure the extent of the departure from unique factorization by an invariant called the class number. Crudely speaking, the larger the class number, the greater the failure of factorization to be unique.

The class number is essentially a measure of the number of nonprincipal ideals. To state this precisely, it is convenient to use fractional ideals—*i.e.,* ideals that may contain algebraic numbers that are not integers. These fractional ideals form a group under multiplication, with the principal ideals as a subgroup. The quotient group is called the class group. (For basic information on group theory see ALGEBRA.) An important theorem of a Lithuanian-born mathematician, Hermann Minkowski, asserts that the class group is finite. The number of elements in the class group is the class number.

The class number is 1 precisely when unique factorization holds. Thus the class number of $\mathfrak{G}$ is 1, whereas the class number of $\mathfrak{H}\sqrt{-5}$ must exceed 1 (it can be shown to be 2). It is in general a difficult computation to find the class number of an algebraic number field, and its value oscillates unpredictably from one field to another. The case of quadratic field has been most thoroughly explored. (A quadratic algebraic number field $\mathfrak{H}(\sqrt{m})$ is one obtained from the rational numbers $\mathfrak{H}$ by adjoining a square root of a number m; m can be taken to be square-free [*i.e.*, to have no square factors other than 1], and the

Real and imaginary fields

field is called real or imaginary according as m is positive or negative.) In his *Disquisitiones Arithmeticae* ("Discussions on numbers") Gauss listed nine imaginary quadratic fields with class number 1, given by $-m = 1, 2, 3, 7, 11, 19, 43, 67,$ and 163. Gauss conjectured that these were all. There was no progress on this problem until 1934, when H. Heilbronn and E. Linfoot proved that there was at most one more. Computations by the U.S. mathematician D.H. Lehmer showed that a 10th field, if it existed, would have an enormous value for $-m$. Finally, in 1967 another U.S. mathematician, Harold M. Stark, proved that Gauss was right: the list of nine fields is complete. At about the same time, and independently, A. Baker developed methods that reduced the problem to a finite amount of computation. In retrospect it was recognized that in 1952 K. Heegner had made an attempt on the problem that could have been completed by techniques already known at that time.

This theorem of Heegner and Stark has an intriguing connection with an elementary question concerning primes. The question goes back to Euler, and the connection was observed by G. Rabinovich in 1911. Euler had asked: when is it true for a prime p that $x^2 + x + p$ is prime for all the values $0, 1, 2, \ldots, p - 2$? (It is fruitless to attempt to go higher than $x = p - 2$, for when x is set equal to $p - 1$, $x^2 + x + p$ takes the value p^2.) Euler gave the example 41, and there are five easily discovered smaller primes that work: 2, 3, 5, 11, and 17. If these six numbers are multiplied by 4 and 1 is subtracted, the numbers 7, 11, 19, 43, 67, and 163, the six largest values of $-m$ for fields of class number, are obtained. (The three values 1, 2, 3 are too small for there to be a connection with Euler's question.) It follows in fact from the theorem of Heegner and Stark that 41 is the last prime enjoying Euler's property.

For real quadratic fields (those of the form $\mathfrak{H}(\sqrt{m})$ with m positive) numerical evidence indicates that the class number 1 occurs with great frequency. Gauss conjectured that there are an infinite number of real quadratic fields with class number 1, but this remains unsettled.

It is known that the class number of an algebraic number field can be arbitrarily large. One way of exhibiting large class numbers appears in Gauss's *Disquisitiones*. It is a consequence of a theorem of his on duplication of genera that the class number of the field $\mathfrak{H}(\sqrt{m})$ is divisible by 2^{k-1} if the integer m has k or more distinct odd prime factors.

Dirichlet discovered a connection between the class numbers of certain quadratic fields and quartic fields. Given a square-free positive integer m, the quadratic fields $\mathfrak{H}(\sqrt{m})$ and $\mathfrak{H}(\sqrt{-m})$ can be formed, and in addition the field $\mathfrak{H}(\sqrt{m},\sqrt{-m})$ obtained by adjoining both $\sqrt{m}$ and $\sqrt{-m}$ to the rational numbers. Dirichlet's theorem asserts that the class number of $\mathfrak{H}(\sqrt{m},\sqrt{-m})$ is either the product of the class numbers of $\mathfrak{H}(\sqrt{m})$ and $\mathfrak{H}(\sqrt{-m})$ or else half that number. This result was the starting point for a considerable amount of subsequent research.

Units. In the ring $\mathfrak{R}$ of integers of an algebraic number field $\mathfrak{F}$, an element u of $\mathfrak{R}$ is called a unit if there exists an element v in $\mathfrak{R}$ with $uv = 1$. At least the numbers 1 and -1 are units; for some fields there are no other units. In a special category are those units u having the property that some power u^n is equal to 1; these are called roots of unity.

Dirichlet's unit theorem

In 1846 Dirichlet found a decisive theorem concerning the units of an arbitrary algebraic number field. This theorem gives a formula for the number of units, other than roots of unity, that are independent in a reasonable

sense. $\mathfrak{F}$ is allowed to equal $\mathfrak{H}(x)$ and is supposed to be n-dimensional over $\mathfrak{H}$ so that the irreducible equation for x has degree n. Of the n roots of this equation, some are real and some imaginary, the imaginary ones coming in pairs; r_1 is written for the number of real roots and r_2 for the number of pairs of imaginary ones, so that $n = r_1 + 2r_2$. Dirichlet's formula for the number of independent units is $r_1 + r_2 = 1$.

Quadratic fields furnish simple illustrations for Dirichlet's unit theorem. If the field is imaginary, then $r_1 = 0$ and $r_2 = 1$, so that $r_1 + r_2 - 1 = 0$ and there are no units other than roots of unity. If the field is real, then $r_1 = 2$ and $r_2 = 0$, so that $r_1 + r_2 - 1 = 1$. There is then one basic unit called the fundamental unit, and all others are powers of it or their negatives. Stated in direct terms, this is the assertion about the equation named after the 17th-century English mathematician John Pell, $x^2 - Dy^2 = 1$, with D a non-square positive number. There is a solution in integers other than the trivial ones $x = \pm 1$, $y = 0$, and all solutions are obtainable in a simple way from a certain basic solution. As an illustration, if $D = 2$, the basic solution of $x^2 - 2y^2 = 1$ is given by $x = 3$, $y = 2$. If x^*, y^* is any solution, then $x^* + y^*\sqrt{2} = \pm(3 + 2\sqrt{2})^m$ for some m. Dirichlet's theorem can be viewed as a far-reaching generalization of the theory of the Pell equation.

The discriminant. If $\mathfrak{F}$ is an n-dimensional algebraic number field and $\mathfrak{R}$ its ring of integers, then there exists for $\mathfrak{R}$ an integral basis over the ring Z of ordinary integers. This is a set $u_1, \ldots, u_n$ of elements of $\mathfrak{R}$ with the property that every element of $\mathfrak{R}$ is uniquely a linear combination of the u's with coefficients in Z. For example, the numbers $1, i$ form an integral basis for the Gaussian integers. Now every member of $\mathfrak{F}$ has n conjugates that do not necessarily lie in $\mathfrak{F}$. When $u_{i1}, \ldots, u_{in}$ is written for the conjugates of u_i, d is the n by n determinant formed from the n^2 elements u_{ij}. It can be seen that $D = d^2$ lies in Z and that D does not depend on the choice of the integral basis; D is called the discriminant of $\mathfrak{F}$. The discriminant plays an important role in determining the properties of $\mathfrak{F}$.

A quadratic field $(\mathfrak{H}\sqrt{m})$ serves as a simple illustration. If $m \equiv 2$ or $3 \pmod 4$, then an integral basis consists of 1 and $\sqrt{m}$ and $D = 4m$. If $m \equiv 1 \pmod 4$, the elements 1 and $(1 + \sqrt{m})/2$ form an integral basis, and D turns out to equal m.

Some facts about the discriminant follow. Of these, the first is due to the Swiss mathematician Ludwig Stickelberger, the second to Dedekind, the third to the 20th-century Norwegian-born U.S. mathematician Oystein Ore, and the remaining three to the 19th–20th-century Lithuanian-born mathematician Herman Minkowski. (1) $D \equiv 0$ or $1 \pmod 4$; (2) the only primes in Z that acquire as factors multiple powers of prime ideals in $\mathfrak{R}$ (they are called the ramified primes) are those that divide D; (3) $2D$ is a multiple of the number of roots of unity in $\mathfrak{F}$; (4) D is never equal to 1 or -1; (5) there are only a finite number of fields with a given discriminant; (6) D becomes large with n; for example, there exists an absolute constant c such that $D > e^{cn}$.

The Zahlbericht and Hilbert's problems. At the invitation of the German Mathematical Society, the German mathematician David Hilbert prepared a report on algebraic number theory, published in 1897 and reprinted in his collected works. While initially planned as a joint project with Minkowski, he completed it alone. It was really a full length treatise, and in a masterful way it covered virtually all work in the field up to that date. Known as the "Zahlbericht" (number report), it became the "Bible" for all workers in the field. It fixed the notation, the names for the main concepts, and the style of proof used.

Signifi-cance of the Zahlbericht

In 1900, at the International Mathematical Congress in Paris, Hilbert proposed 23 problems that he considered would be significant for research in the 20th century. The importance he attached to algebraic number theory is attested by three of the problems (the 9th, 11th, and 12th) being entirely in that field, and another (the 8th) partly so. These problems will be mentioned again below.

Hensel's p-adic numbers. As 20th-century work on algebraic number theory got under way, an important innovation was made by the German mathematician Kurt

Hensel. Inspired partly by congruences to powers of primes that abound in number theory, and partly by an analogy with the power series that occur in algebraic function theory (see below), he conceived the idea of forming power series in a prime p. A typical p-adic number formed in this way can be written as a sum of powers of p with coefficients a_k (see 26) in which each coefficient a_i lies in the range $0 \leq a_i \leq p-1$. If $a_{-1} = a_{-2} = a_{-3} = \ldots = 0$, the number is called a p-adic integer. This is just like a number written in the scale of p, except for the novelty that the digits are allowed to run on forever to the left. Addition and multiplication of p-adic numbers follow the usual rules of arithmetic. Such numbers could also be formed to the base 10, but there is then the serious disadvantage that divisors of zero occur—*i.e.,* there exist two non-zero 10-adic numbers the product of which is 0.

A simple illustration of the efficiency of using p-adic

$$(26) \quad \cdots + a_n p^n + \cdots + a_2 p^2 + a_1 p + a_0 + a_{-1} p^{-1} + \cdots + a_{-m} p^{-m}$$

$$(27) \quad \mathfrak{F} = \mathfrak{F}_0 \subset \mathfrak{F}_1 \subset \mathfrak{F}_2 \cdots$$

numbers is the statement that -1 has a square root in the $5 = $ adic numbers. It is easily proved by an approximation procedure that is systematized once for all in a lemma (auxiliary proposition) named after Hensel. From this an infinite number of statements about ordinary integers may be deduced: for every n there exists an integer x such that $x^2 + 1$ is divisible by 5^n.

Out of Hensel's p-adic numbers there developed a major branch of modern algebra called valuation theory.

Quadratic forms and the Hasse principle. A quadratic form is an expression of the form $\Sigma\, a_{ij} x_i x_j$, the x's being variables. The earliest work on quadratic forms concerned the case in which the coefficients a_{ij} were ordinary integers. Eventually it was realized that it clarifies matters to study first the case of rational coefficients. This was the subject of a brilliant paper by Minkowski in 1890 in which he gave a complete classification of rational quadratic forms, which took advantage of virtually everything that had been done during the 19th century on integral quadratic forms. With this triumph fresh in his mind, Hilbert thought it timely in his 11th problem to ask for a classification of quadratic forms over an arbitrary algebraic number field.

The solution to Hilbert's 11th problem

The solution was given by the German mathematician Helmut Hasse in 1923, and the method was an impressive application of Hensel's p-adic numbers. Hasse first recast Minkowski's theorem in a new, attractive way. The field $\mathfrak{H}$ of rational numbers can, for each prime p, be regarded as forming part of the field of p-adic numbers (say $\mathfrak{H}_p$), and also part of the field $\mathfrak{R}$ of real numbers. The theorem states that two quadratic forms over $\mathfrak{H}$ are equivalent (meaning that it is possible to pass from one to the other by a change of variable) if, and only if, they are equivalent over each $\mathfrak{H}_p$ and over $\mathfrak{R}$. In this form the result is ready for a natural generalization to any algebraic number field, a generalization that Hasse succeeded in proving by a method, called the Hasse principle, that is regarded as a passage from local to global data. For the field of rational numbers, the local information is given one prime at a time, the field of real numbers being treated as a prime "at infinity." For a general algebraic number field, the primes are replaced by prime ideals, and there are usually several primes at infinity.

The Hasse principle has had other successes (for instance, in associative algebras and in algebraic groups), but for polynomial equations of degree higher than two it may fail. A simple example was given by the Norwegian Ernst Selmer in 1951: the equation $3x^3 + 4y^3 + 5z^3 = 0$ admits a nontrivial solution over the p-adic numbers for every p and also a solution over the real numbers, but it has no solution over the rational numbers.

Class field theory and reciprocity. A portion of algebraic number theory unites virtually everything that is known into a highly sophisticated structure. Two algebraic

number fields $\mathfrak{F}$ and $\mathfrak{L}$ are studied, with $\mathfrak{L}$ an extension of $\mathfrak{F}$. Information is sought about how ideals behave in the passage from $\mathfrak{F}$ to $\mathfrak{L}$. The object is to classify the possibilities for $\mathfrak{L}$ in terms of readily computed objects in $\mathfrak{F}$. For a given $\mathfrak{F}$, there is a particularly important field $\mathfrak{L}$ that enjoys numerous special properties with respect to $\mathfrak{F}$: for instance, its dimension over $\mathfrak{F}$ is equal to the class number of $\mathfrak{F}$, and every ideal in $\mathfrak{F}$ becomes principal in $\mathfrak{L}$. The field $\mathfrak{L}$ is called the class field of $\mathfrak{F}$, the origin of the name class field theory.

There is a close relation between class field theory and reciprocity. In its original form, reciprocity referred to quadratic residues computed in the ring of ordinary integers and asserted the following: if p and q are odd primes, then p is a quadratic residue of q if, and only if, q is a quadratic residue of p, unless both p and q have the form $4n + 3$, in which case the behaviour is opposite. In his 9th problem, Hilbert asked for two advances to be made: squares were to be replaced by arbitrary nth powers, and the context was to be broadened to any algebraic number field.

Many mathematicians (including Hilbert himself) made partial contributions until the climax in 1927, when Austrian-born Emil Artin discovered a definitive version of reciprocity and was able to prove it in full generality. It is typical of the increasing sophistication and abstraction of modern mathematics that in the theorem powers and reciprocity are no longer visible (indeed, it requires a fair amount of effort to extract a conventional reciprocity statement from Artin's theorem). Instead, Artin constructed two groups and a function from the first to the second; his theorem asserts that this function is an isomorphism (that is, it is one-to-one, onto, and preserves the product laws of the groups).

Artin's reciprocity theorem

The class field tower. If $\mathfrak{F}$ be an algebraic number field and $\mathfrak{L}$ its class field, as described above, it is not necessarily the case that $\mathfrak{L}$ has class number 1; for, although every ideal in $\mathfrak{F}$ has become principal, some new ideals in $\mathfrak{L}$ may have arisen that are not principal. The process of passing to the class field can be iterated, resulting in the class field tower starting at $\mathfrak{F}$ and successively including other fields (see 27). It was an outstanding open question for many years whether, for any $\mathfrak{F}$, the class field tower had to end in a finite number of steps with a field having class number 1. Then, in 1964, the Russian mathematicians E.S. Golod and Igor Rostislavovich Shafarevich gave a counterexample. An explicit choice of a field $\mathfrak{F}$ having an infinite class field tower is $\mathfrak{H}(\sqrt{-30030})$.

Abelian fields and the Jugendtraum. If u is a primitive nth root of 1, the algebraic number field $\mathfrak{F} = \mathfrak{H}(u)$ is formed by adjoining u to the rationals; $\mathfrak{F}$ is called a cyclotomic field. It is known (by Galois theory: see the article ALGEBRA) that $\mathfrak{F}$ is normal over $\mathfrak{H}$ with a Galois group that is Abelian and has order $\varphi(n)$, in which φ is the Euler φ-function. If $\mathfrak{F}_0$ is any field between $\mathfrak{H}$ and $\mathfrak{F}$, then $\mathfrak{F}_0$ likewise is Abelian over $\mathfrak{H}$. In 1877 the German mathematician Leopold Kronecker proved the remarkable converse: any field Abelian over $\mathfrak{H}$ is a subfield of a suitable cyclotomic field. In a letter to Dedekind dated March 15, 1880, Kronecker said his *liebster Jugendtraum* ("dearest dream of youth") had been to prove an analogous theorem concerning Abelian extensions of imaginary quadratic fields. This was achieved by the German mathematician Heinrich Weber, whose result showed that they are generated by certain values of elliptic functions (see ANALYSIS: *Complex analysis*). Hilbert's 12th problem called for extensions of this work to arbitrary algebraic number fields. Only scattered results have been obtained. Possibly further extensive development of class field theory is needed to obtain the requisite insight.

The analogy with algebraic functions. In studying algebraic functions in one variable the process begins with a field k, called the constant field, adjoins a variable x to get the field $\mathfrak{F} = k(x)$, and then forms a finite-dimensional extension of $\mathfrak{F}$ to get a field $\mathfrak{L}$. $\mathfrak{F}$ may be thought of as being analogous to the field $\mathfrak{H}$ of rational numbers, and $\mathfrak{L}$ as being analogous to an algebraic number field. The ring $k[x]$ of polynomials in x is a subset of $\mathfrak{F}$; it is a principal ideal ring like the ring Z of integers. By taking appropriate integers inside $\mathfrak{L}$, a theory remarkably parallel to algebraic number theory is obtained. A great many theorems hold in both cases, and to a considerable extent a unified account covering both cases can be given. In particular, power series in x play a role quite similar to Hensel's p-adic numbers; in fact, they served to inspire him.

When the field k is finite, the analogy becomes closer still. All the major results of class field theory then hold, and there are perfect analogues of the unit theorem and the finiteness of the class number. Indeed, Artin and the U.S. mathematician George W. Whaples in 1945 set forth a simple set of axioms holding simultaneously for algebraic number fields and algebraic function fields over finite fields. The main axiom was the assertion of a neat product formula for valuations, asserting that certain infinite products are equal to 1. Arguing directly from their axioms, Artin and Whaples were able to give new unified proofs of the major theorems.

Dirichlet's two analysis theorems

Analytic methods. In 1840 Dirichlet initiated the use of analysis on a large scale to prove results in number theory. Among other things he proved two remarkable theorems. The first was the existence of an infinite number of primes in every nontrivial arithmetic progression (an arithmetic progression is a sequence of the form $a, a + d, a + 2d, \ldots$; it is nontrivial if a and d are relatively prime). The second was a class number formula. Since algebraic number theory had yet to be developed, Dirichlet's formula necessarily referred to binary quadratic forms. Translated into the language of algebraic number theory, his formula gave the class number of $\mathfrak{H}(\sqrt{-p})$, with p a prime. It is simplest if p has the form $8n + 7$, and then is the sum from $r = 1$ to $r = (p-1)/2$ of $(r|p)$, in which $(r|p)$ is the Legendre symbol, equal to 1 if r is a quadratic residue of p and -1 otherwise. For instance, if $p = 23$ the sum of $(1|p), \ldots$, $(11|p)$ is obtained. The numbers 1, 2, 3, 4, 6, 8, 9, are residues and 5, 7, 10, 11 are non-residues. Hence the class number of $\mathfrak{H}(\sqrt{-23})$ is $7 - 4 = 3$.

The modernization of this work operates in an arbitrary algebraic number field $\mathfrak{F}$. The number, say $Z(t)$, of ideals with norm less than a given number t is counted; the norm of an ideal is an integer formed in analogy to the assignment of the integer $a^2 + b^2$ to the Gaussian integer $a + bi$. As t goes to infinity, $Z(t)/t$ can be proved to have a definite limit given by a formula built out of the class number, the discriminant, and the units of $\mathfrak{F}$. This result is then used to study the Riemann zeta function that can be formed relative to $\mathfrak{F}$. The result is that much information is obtained about the class number and the existence of prime ideals satisfying various restrictions, as called for in Hilbert's 8th problem. (I.K.)

Analytic number theory

THE SCOPE OF ANALYTIC NUMBER THEORY

Analytic number theory is a branch of number theory concerned with the interaction of analysis and number theory. Analysis can be used to prove certain properties of ordinary and algebraic integers and to establish quantitative results. Similarly, arithmetic properties can be used to analyze and shed light on analytic questions.

Diophantine equations

Among the earliest problems in number theory upon which any sort of systematic study was brought to bear is the class of problems known as Diophantine equations, named after the Greek mathematician Diophantus of Alexandria, who lived during the third century of the Christian era. A Diophantine equation is an equation the solutions of which are required to be integers, the simplest example being the Diophantine equation involving first powers of x and y (see 28). The solution of these equations required the development of general properties of divisibility. The pursuit of Diophantine equations of higher degree led Gauss, in about 1820, to a study of a new set of integers, the Gaussian integers.

Properties of integers, whether ordinary or algebraic, may be of two types that are here characterized as qualitative, or descriptive, and quantitative. An example of the former is the question of whether, for a given integer n, he Diophantine equation that identifies n with a sum of second powers (see 29) has a solution in integers x_1, x_2, x_3, x_4.

$$(28) \quad ax + by = c$$

$$(29) \quad n = x_1^2 + x_2^2 + x_3^2 + x_4^2$$

$$(30) \quad 18 = 13 + 5, \qquad 30 = 23 + 7$$

$$(31) \quad \begin{cases} \text{The function } \pi(x) \text{ associated with the sequence:} \\ 2, 3, 5, 7, 11, 13, 17, 19, 23, \cdots . \\ \pi(x) = \text{number of primes} \leqslant x. \\ \pi(10) = 4, \qquad \pi(20) = 8, \qquad \pi(35) = 10, \qquad \cdots \end{cases}$$

$$(32) \quad \lim_{x \to \infty} \frac{\pi(x) \log x}{x} = 1$$

$$(33) \quad x_1^k + \cdots + x_s^k = n$$

$$(34) \quad \sum_{n=0}^{\infty} p(n)x^n = \prod_{n=1}^{\infty} (1 - x^n)^{-1}$$

$$(35) \quad n = p_1^{\alpha_1} p_2^{\alpha_2} \cdots p_r^{\alpha_r}$$

$$(36) \quad \begin{cases} d(n) = \text{number of divisors of } n \\ \tau(n) = \text{sum of the divisors of } n \\ \omega(n) = \alpha_1 + \alpha_2 + \cdots + \alpha_r \\ \Lambda(n) = \begin{cases} \log p \text{ if } r = 1 \\ 0 \text{ otherwise} \end{cases}, \text{ the von Mangoldt function} \\ \mu(n) = \begin{cases} 0 \text{ if } \alpha_i \geqslant 2 \text{ for some } i \\ (-1)^r \text{ if } \alpha_i = 1 \text{ for all } i \end{cases}, \text{ the Möbius function} \end{cases}$$

$$(37) \quad \begin{cases} x^m \cdot x^n = x^{m+n} \\ n^s \cdot m^s = (nm)^s \end{cases}$$

An example of the latter is the question of how many solutions this equation has.

In analytic number theory the problems investigated can be divided into three classes. The first class is that in which analysis is used to prove properties of integers, the statements of which can be formulated in terms of elementary concepts of mathematics. These are qualitative properties. One of the most noted examples is the Goldbach conjecture. This conjecture was made by the Prussian-born mathematician Christian Goldbach in 1742, and a related problem was partially solved by the Soviet mathematician Ivan Matveyevich Vinogradov in 1937. Goldbach conjectured that every even number greater than or equal to 4 can be expressed as a sum of two primes. For example, the numbers 18 and 30 may be so expressed (see 30). While this conjecture had not been settled by the early 1970s, Vinogradov did prove in 1937 that every sufficiently large odd natural number can be written as the sum of three primes. It is notable that the statements of the conjecture of Goldbach and result of Vinogradov do not involve any analytic notions, yet to date the result of Vinogradov cannot be proved without deep and intricate analytic methods and techniques.

Goldbach's conjecture

The second class of problem involves the use of analysis to establish quantitative results. Among the most important sequence of integers singled out for special study is the sequence of primes with which a function that indicates the number of primes less than or equal to x is associated (see 31).

Primes and $\pi(x)$ have been studied for many years, and one of the objectives was to find a simple formula for $\pi(x)$. This ambition was only partially realized when, in 1896, the French mathematician Jacques Hadamard and the Belgian mathematician Charles-Jean de la Vallée-Poussin independently proved that $\pi(x)$ is approximately $x/\log x$ in the precise sense that is expressed in terms of a limit (see 32).

The third class of problems makes use of arithmetic properties to analyze and shed light on analytic questions, the two interacting strongly.

Some problems dealt with under these three headings are given below. Qualitative problems include: (1) Various modifications of Goldbach's conjecture. (2) The 18th-century English mathematician Edward Waring's problem; *i.e.*, the solution of the Diophantine equation that identifies a sum of k powers with an integer n (see 33). (3) The existence of infinitely many primes in various sets, such as arithmetic progressions. (4) The existence of infinitely many pairs of primes differing by 2. (5) The existence of primes in various intervals—for example, the existence of a prime in the interval x to $x + x^{1/2}$. (6) The congruence properties of various functions, such as the partition function, coefficients of various modular functions. (7) The existence of solutions of Diophantine equations. (8) The properties of class numbers of algebraic number fields.

Quantitative problems include: (1) The prime factorization of an integer n (see 35). There are many functions associated with n such as the number of divisors of n (see 36). The behaviour of these functions and magnitude of their average values form part of the object of this study. (2) The number of primes in various sequences such as arithmetic progressions, etc. (3) The interval between successive primes. (4) The magnitude of various exponential sums, including character sums. (5) Applications to the determination of the least primitive root mod p. (6) The magnitude of the class number of algebraic number fields. (7) Numbers of solutions of Diophantine equations; *e.g.*, number of solutions of $n = x_1^2 + x_2^2 + x_3^2 + x_4^2$, number of solutions in Waring's problem. (8) The orders of magnitude of coefficients of various power series (see 34). (9) The number of lattice points in various domains; for example, the number of lattice points in a circle. (10) Dirichlet and other densities.

Examples of the third class of problem include the following: (1) Kronecker's limit formulas. (2) Abelian functions. (3) Complex multiplication. (4) Modular functions over rational and algebraic number fields. (5) The German mathematician Erich Hecke's operators.

METHODOLOGY

History. Historically the use of analysis in number theory started with Euler in 1742 and is based on two simple observations, one concerned with integer powers of x and the second concerned with s powers of integers (see 37). In the first case the variable is x and in the second case the variable is s. Moreover, in the first case the product involves the sums $m + n$ of the integers m and n, and in the second case the product mn. Thus, it is to be expected that the first will be used in additive problems and the second in multiplicative problems. These can be illustrated with examples. For the first the equation that identifies k with squares of integers (see 38) is considered. Then, the series for squared powers of x (see 39) are considered. Multiplying these together leads to a relationship between series (see 40 and 41) in which the coefficient of x^k is the number of ways in which k can be written as a sum of two squares counting order (see 42). Because x^3 does not occur, then 3 cannot be written as a sum of two squares and so forth. If $r(k)$ is the number of solutions of the equation that identifies with k a sum of two squares of integers (see 43), then if $f(x)$ is an infinite sum of squared powers of x, the square of f can be computed in terms of a series with coefficients $r(k)$ (see 44) with the convention that $r(0) = 1$.

To illustrate the second case, the function $d(n) =$ number of divisors of n is considered: $d(n) = \Sigma 1$, the summation extended over all divisions of n. The series expressed in reciprocals of a power of positive integers (see 45) are used. Multiplying these two together leads to a square of such series (see 46).

The term $1/2^s$ occurs twice, as $1 \times 1/2^s$, $1/2^s \times 1$, likewise with $1/3^s$; but $1/4^s$ occurs three times as $1 \times 1/4^s$, $1/4^s \times 1$, $1/2^s \times 1/2^s$.

In general, the question is how many times $1/k^s$ occurs, or, in other words, what the coefficient of $1/k^s$ is. If $k = mn$, then the terms $1/m^s \times 1/n^s = 1/(mn)^s$ contribute

$$(38) \quad k = m^2 + n^2$$

$$(39) \quad \begin{cases} \displaystyle\sum_{m=0}^{\infty} x^{m^2} = 1 + x + x^4 + x^9 + \cdots \\ \displaystyle\sum_{n=0}^{\infty} x^{n^2} = 1 + x + x^4 + x^9 + \cdots \end{cases}$$

$$(40) \quad \sum_{m=0}^{\infty} x^{m^2} \sum_{n=0}^{\infty} x^{n^2} = \sum_{m,n} x^{m^2+n^2}$$

$$(41) \quad \begin{aligned} &(1 + x + x^4 + x^9 + \cdots)(1 + x + x^4 + x^9 + \cdots) \\ &= 1 + 2x + x^2 + 2x^4 + 2x^5 + x^8 + 2x^9 + 2x^{10} + \cdots \end{aligned}$$

$$(42) \quad \begin{cases} 1 = 1^2 + 0^2 = 0^2 + 1^2 \\ 2 = 1^2 + 1^2 \\ 4 = 2^2 + 0^2 = 0^2 + 2^2 \\ 5 = 1^2 + 2^2 = 2^2 + 1^2 \end{cases}$$

$$(43) \quad k = m^2 + n^2$$

$$(44) \quad f^2(x) = \sum_{m=0}^{\infty} x^{m^2} \sum_{n=0}^{\infty} x^{n^2} = \sum_{k=0}^{\infty} r(k)x^k$$

$$(45) \quad \begin{cases} \displaystyle\zeta(s) = \sum_{n=1}^{\infty} \frac{1}{n^s} = 1 + \frac{1}{2^s} + \frac{1}{3^s} + \cdots + \frac{1}{n^s} + \cdots \\ \displaystyle\zeta(s) = \sum_{m=1}^{\infty} \frac{1}{m^s} = 1 + \frac{1}{2^s} + \frac{1}{3^s} + \cdots + \frac{1}{m^s} + \cdots \end{cases}$$

$$(46) \quad \begin{cases} \displaystyle\zeta^2(s) = \left(1 + \frac{1}{2^s} + \frac{1}{3^s} + \cdots\right)\left(1 + \frac{1}{2^s} + \frac{1}{3^s} + \cdots\right) \\ = 1 + \frac{2}{2^s} + \frac{2}{3^s} + \frac{3}{4^s} + \cdots \end{cases}$$

$$(47) \quad \zeta^2(s) = \sum_{k=1}^{\infty} \frac{d(k)}{k^s}$$

$$(48) \quad A = \{a(0), a(1), a(2), \cdots, a(n), \cdots\}$$

$$(49) \quad f(x) = \sum_{n=0}^{\infty} a(n)x^n$$

$$(50) \quad B = \{b(1), b(2), \cdots, b(n), \cdots\}$$

$$(51) \quad g(s) = \sum_{n=1}^{\infty} \frac{b(n)}{n^s}$$

$$(52) \quad n = n_1 + n_2 + \cdots + n_r$$

$$(53) \quad f_i(x) = \sum_{n_i \in A_i} x^{n_i}$$

$$(54) \quad f_1(x)f_2(x)\cdots f_r(x) = \sum_{n_1 \in A_1} x^{n_1} \sum_{n_2 \in A_2} x^{n_2} \cdots \sum_{n_r \in A_r} x^{n_r}$$

1 to the coefficient, and this happens for each decomposition; there are, however, as many decompositions as there are divisors of n. Hence, the coefficient of $1/k^s$ is $d(k)$ (see 47).

More generally, if any sequence of non-negative integers (see 48) is given, the function (in power series form with coefficients from the previous previous sequence; see 49) is called the generating function of the sequence. If a sequence of the form $b(k)$ is given (see 50) then the function that is formed from a series of reciprocals of s powers of integers, coefficients being selected from the given se-

The Dirichlet series

quence (see 51), is called the Dirichlet series associated with the sequence.

There are still other ways that a function can be associated with a given sequence, but attention is restricted for the time being to associations already given (see 49, 51). One association (49) is the more natural for additive problems, whereas another one (51) is more natural for multiplicative problems.

Classification and techniques. *Additive properties.* In the case of additive problems the general problem can be formulated as follows. It is required to write a natural number n as a sum of an element from a set A_1 plus an element from a set A_2 plus, etc. That is, it is required to determine whether an integer n can be written in the form of a sum of n_i (see 52) with $n_i \in A_i$ ($i = 1, 2, \ldots, r$), and the number $v(n)$ of such representations also is required. Evidently a representation exists if it can be shown that $v(n) \geq 1$.

As above, a sum of powers of x (see 53) is formed quite generally. Then it follows that a product of such sums is possible (see 54). Multiplying leads to another sum of powers of x (see 55). Setting n equal to a sum of integers (see 56), it follows that x^n occurs each time there is a representation in the form given by (52); that is, a sum of integer powers of x each power multiplied by a coefficient $v(n)$ (see 57). Naturally, the determination of $v(n)$ is by no means resolved without detailed analysis of the functions $f_1(x), \cdots, f_r(x)$. The function $f(x) = f_1(x), \cdots, f_r(x)$ is the generating function for $v(n)$.

Generating functions

As another example, the generating function for the number of unrestricted partitions $p(n)$ of a natural number n can be found. A partition of n is a decomposition into an unrestricted sum of natural numbers m_i (see 58). For example, if $n = 5$, then all the cases can be listed (see 59); therefore, $p(5) = 7$.

To obtain the generating function, the partition must be made more systematic; r_1 is the number of 1's, r_2 the number of 2's, r_3 the number of 3's, . . . , r_k the number of k's, occurring in a particular partition; so that n is a sum of products of integers times corresponding r_k (see 60). Thus a partition corresponds to a solution of an equation identifying n with a sum of integers, each integer in the sum belonging to a certain class (see 61). Therefore, the functions composed of sums of powers of x (see 62) are formed and the product is given by a general sum (see 63) with the convention that $p(0) = 1$. Noting that the expression for $f_k(x)$ is a geometric series, it follows that $f_k(x) = (1 - x^k)^{-1}$ and, therefore, that a product expression can be obtained (see 64). This is Euler's example. All questions of convergence have been ignored in this illustration.

Multiplicative properties. Here the problems dealt with are rooted in the multiplicative properties of integers. Let $a(1), a(2), \ldots, a(n), \ldots$ and $b(1), b(2), \ldots, b(m), \ldots$ be any two sequences. Guided again by the observation made earlier, the Dirichlet series is considered for each sequence (see 65). Then a product of sums can be reduced to a single sum (see 66).

Putting $mn = k$, the coefficient of k^{-s} is determined by a sum of terms $a(n)b(m)$, and $a(n)b(m)$ is part of the coefficient whenever $mn = k$. This is written succinctly as a sum over all integers nm whose product equals k (see 67) or equivalently as a sum (see 68), the sum being over all divisors of n.

As a further example, the Dirichlet series for the German mathematician Hans von Mangoldt's function may be found (see 69). If the f is set equal to a sum with typical term $\Lambda(n)$ divided by the s power of n, a moment's reflection shows that the sum of $\Lambda(d)$ over divisions d of n equals $\log n$ (see 70). Therefore $f(s) = -[\zeta'(s)/\zeta(s)]$, in which $\zeta'(s)$ is the derivative of $\zeta(s)$ (see 71).

SPECIFIC TOPICS IN NUMBER THEORY

The distribution of prime numbers. The earliest recorded fact about primes is Euclid's proof that the number of primes is infinite, occurring as proposition 20 in the 9th book of his *Elements*. The sieve of Eratosthenes, introduced about 250 BC, is a technique for exhibiting the primes below a certain number. The subject of primes and their distribution then lay dormant until 1640, when

$$(55) \quad f_1(x)f_2(x)\cdots f_r(x) = \sum_{\substack{n_1 \cdots n_r \\ n_i \in A_i}} x^{n_1 + n_2 + \cdots + n_r}$$

$$(56) \quad n = n_1 + n_2 + \cdots + n_r$$

$$(57) \quad f(x) = f_1(x)f_2(x)\cdots f_r(x) = \sum_{n=0}^{\infty} v(n)x^n$$

$$(58) \quad n = m_1 + m_2 + m_3 + \cdots + m_\ell$$

$$(59) \quad \begin{cases} 5 = 1+1+1+1+1 \\ = 1+1+1+2 \\ = 1+1+3 \\ = 1+2+2 \\ = 2+3 \\ = 1+4 \\ = 5 \end{cases}$$

$$(60) \quad n = 1r_1 + 2r_2 + \cdots + kr_k$$

$$(61) \quad \begin{cases} n = n_1 + n_2 + \cdots + n_k \\ n_1 \in A_1 = \{0, 1, 2, \cdots\} \\ n_2 \in A_2 = \{0, 2, 4, 6, \cdots\} \\ \cdot \\ \cdot \\ \cdot \\ n_k \in A_k = \{0, k, 2k, \cdots\} \end{cases}$$

$$(62) \quad \begin{cases} f_1(x) = \sum_{n_1=0}^{\infty} x^{n_1} \\ f_2(x) = \sum_{n_2=0}^{\infty} x^{2n_2} \\ \cdot \\ \cdot \\ \cdot \\ f_k(x) = \sum_{n_k=0}^{\infty} x^{kn_k} \end{cases}$$

$$(63) \quad \begin{cases} F(x) = f_1(x)f_2(x)\cdots f_k(x)\cdots \\ = \sum_{n_1, n_2, \cdots, n_k, \cdots} x^{n_1 + 2n_2 + \cdots + kn_k + \cdots} \\ = \sum_{n=0}^{\infty} p(n)x^n \end{cases}$$

$$(64) \quad \sum_{n=0}^{\infty} p(n)x^n = \prod_{k=1}^{\infty} (1 - x^k)^{-1} = F(x)$$

$$(65) \quad \begin{cases} f(s) = \sum_{n=1}^{\infty} \dfrac{a(n)}{n^s} \\ g(s) = \sum_{m=1}^{\infty} \dfrac{b(m)}{m^s} \end{cases}$$

$$(66) \quad f(s)g(s) = \sum_{n=1}^{\infty} \sum_{m=1}^{\infty} \frac{a(n)b(m)}{(nm)^s} = \sum_{k=1}^{\infty} \frac{c(k)}{k^s}$$

$$(67) \quad c(k) = \sum_{nm=k} a(n)b(m)$$

$$(68) \quad c(k) = \sum_{d|k} a(d)b\left(\frac{k}{d}\right) = \sum_{d|k} a\left(\frac{k}{d}\right)b(d)$$

Fermat wrote that he was "almost convinced" that numbers of a form $2^n + 1$ were prime if n was a power of 2. Euler showed that this is false for $n = 2^5$ because $2^{32} + 1$ is divisible by 641.

The next contribution of importance was made by Euler, in a paper, "Variae observationes circa series infinitas," published in the Petersburg Academy, 1742. Euler connected the harmonic series (see 72), being not too much concerned with convergence, with the sum of the reciprocals of the primes (see 73). This ushered a new era in the theory of prime numbers, and a study of the function composed of a sum of s powers of positive integers (see 74) was initiated.

The next contribution was due to the French mathematician Adrien-Marie Legendre. In *Essai sur la théorie des nombres* (1798), he proposed that for large x, $\pi(x)$ had a specific form expressed in terms of the log x (see 75) approximately in which $\pi(x)$, as above, is the number of primes $\leq x$. Legendre was unable to give a proof, and, as a matter of fact, later work shows that if for large x, $\pi(x)$ could be expressed in terms of A (see 76), then the best value of A is 1.

It was noted above that the primes appear to diminish in frequency, the number of primes in an interval of a given length getting steadily smaller as the beginning of the given interval is larger. In a letter to the German astronomer Johann Franz Encke, Gauss in 1792 suggested an explicit rate at which the frequency diminishes and proposed that the number of primes per unit interval beginning at x is $1/\log x$. Thus, he proposed a formula involving an integral of the reciprocal of a logarithmic function (see 77) approximately, the expression $\mathrm{li}(x)$ being an abbreviation for the integral.

The Russian mathematician Pafnuty Lvovich Chebyshev, in 1851, set out to prove that a certain limiting relation holds that involves the number of primes less than or equal to x (see 78). Although he did not succeed, he did at least establish the plausibility of this relation and, therefore, of those of Legendre and Gauss. He proved in particular that if the limit exists, then it must be 1.

Riemann's contribution

In 1859, the German mathematician Bernhard Riemann inaugurated a new era in the theory of distribution of primes. Returning to the function introduced by Euler, Riemann considered the same function, but now written as a sum of reciprocals of the s powers of the positive integers (see 79) with s a complex variable; that is, $s = \sigma + it$. This seemingly minor modification had a profound consequence. Using complex function theory, Riemann first derived a functional equation for $\zeta(s)$, expressed $\pi(x)$ in terms of $\zeta(s)$, wrote $\zeta(s)$ in terms of its zeros, and inferred the plausibility of the relation that the number of primes less than or equal to x is asymptotically the same as $\mathrm{li}(x)$ (see 80) in which the tilde sign is used and, in fact, gives a more precise statement. The $\sim$ sign is an abbreviation for the fact that the ratio of $\pi(x)$ to $\mathrm{li}(x)$ tends to 1. The completion of this proof was carried out independently and simultaneously by Hadamard and de la Vallée-Poussin in 1896.

In the 20th century much of the work centring on the distribution of primes has been concerned with the finer properties of their distribution. Having established that $\pi(x)$ is approximately $\mathrm{li}(x)$, it is natural to determine how accurately $\mathrm{li}(x)$ in fact represents $\pi(x)$. This problem is intimately connected with the Riemann zeta function and its zeros. If the series form of the function is given with complex argument (see 81), then the series converges for $\sigma > 1$, but there is an analytic continuation into the whole complex plane, and $\zeta(s)$ is meromorphic with a simple pole at $s = 1$ with residue 1. Instead of working with $\pi(x)$, it is more natural analytically to work with a function defined in terms of the logarithm and written ψ (see 82). The connection with $\pi(x)$ is: the statement that $\pi(x)$ is asymptotically equal to x divided by the logarithm of x (see 83) is equivalent to the statement that $\psi(x) \sim x$.

The advantage of working with $\Lambda(n)$ lies in the Dirichlet series associated with $\Lambda(n)$ (see 84) as contrasted with the more complicated series expressed as a sum of reciprocals of s powers of p (see 85). The starting point for studying $\psi(x)$, and hence $\pi(x)$, is the relation that expresses the

$$(69) \quad \Lambda(n) = \begin{cases} \log p & \text{if } n = p^k \\ 0 & \text{otherwise} \end{cases}$$

$$(70) \quad \begin{cases} f(s) = \sum_{n=1}^{\infty} \dfrac{\Lambda(n)}{n^s} \\ \sum_{d \mid n} \Lambda(d) = \log n \end{cases}$$

$$(71) \quad f(s) \cdot \zeta(s) = \sum_{n=1}^{\infty} \frac{\log n}{n^s} = -\zeta'(s)$$

$$(72) \quad \sum_{n=1}^{\infty} \frac{1}{n}$$

$$(73) \quad \sum_{p} \frac{1}{p}$$

$$(74) \quad \zeta(s) = \sum_{n=1}^{\infty} \frac{1}{n^s}$$

$$(75) \quad \pi(x) = \frac{x}{\log x - 1.08366}$$

$$(76) \quad \pi(x) = \frac{x}{\log x - A}$$

$$(77) \quad \pi(x) = \int_2^x \frac{dt}{\log t} = \mathrm{li}(x)$$

$$(78) \quad \lim_{x \to \infty} \frac{\pi(x) \log x}{x} = 1$$

$$(79) \quad \zeta(s) = \sum_{n=1}^{\infty} \frac{1}{n^s}$$

$$(80) \quad \pi(x) \sim \mathrm{li}(x)$$

$$(81) \quad \zeta(s) = \sum_{n=1}^{\infty} \frac{1}{n^s} \quad \text{with } s = \sigma + it$$

$$(82) \quad \begin{cases} \psi(x) = \sum_{n \leq x} \Lambda(n) \\ \Lambda(n) = \begin{cases} \log p & \text{if } n = p^k \\ 0 & \text{otherwise} \end{cases} \end{cases}$$

$$(83) \quad \pi(x) \sim \frac{x}{\log x}$$

$$(84) \quad \sum_{n=1}^{\infty} \frac{\Lambda(n)}{n^s} = -\frac{\zeta'(s)}{\zeta(s)}$$

$$(85) \quad \sum_{p} \frac{1}{p^s} = \sum_{n=1}^{\infty} \frac{\mu(n)}{n} \log \zeta(ns)$$

$$(86) \quad \psi(x) = \frac{1}{2\pi i} \int_{a-i\infty}^{a+i\infty} \left(-\frac{\zeta'(s)}{\zeta(s)} \right) \frac{x^s}{s} \, ds \qquad a > 1$$

$$(87) \quad |\Delta(x)| \leq A x^{\frac{1}{2}} \log^2 x$$

$$(88) \quad |\pi(x) - \mathrm{li}\, x| \leq B x^{\frac{1}{2}} \log x$$

function ψ as a line integral that involves the zeta function (see 86).

Cauchy's theorem is then used to move the line of integration past the pole of the integrand, but here is encountered a great difficulty because the poles of the integrand involve the zeros of $\zeta(s)$, the function $\zeta(s)$ occurring in the denominator.

The Riemann hypothesis

In a now famous memoir of 1859, Riemann proposed the conjecture that all of the complex zeros $\beta + i\gamma$ of $\zeta(s)$ had $\beta = \frac{1}{2}$. The complex zeros are known to satisfy $0 < \beta < 1$. This is the so-called Riemann hypothesis, which remains unproved. What can be proved is that if the Riemann hypothesis is true, then there exists a constant A such that if $\Delta(x) = \psi(x) - x$, then the absolute value of Δ has a bound that depends on A and the logarithm of x (see 87) and a corresponding result for $\pi(x)$: If $\pi(x) - \text{li } x = D(x)$, then the absolute value of $D(x)$ is bounded by a constant B times a function of x (see 88). By contrast the best result known to date is that there are constants c, A such that a bound for the absolute value of Δ as a function of x depends upon c, A, and a complicated function of x (see 89).

This result is due to A. Walfisz and is based on the work of Hermann Weyl, Godfrey Harold Hardy, John Edensor Littlewood, Ivan Matveyevich Vinogradov, and Nikolay Mikhaylovich Korobov.

In the opposite direction, Littlewood has proved that the error $\Delta(x)$ cannot be much different from that predicted by the Riemann hypothesis. More precisely, he has proved that for infinitely many values of x, there is for $c > 0$ a lower bound that depends on c as well as upon the logarithm of the logarithm of the logarithm of x (see 90) and for infinitely many values of x there is an upper bound for Δ of similar structure (see 91). Concerning the finer properties of the primes, there is the result of asymptotic nature concerning π as a function of x (see 92). Thus, if x is sufficiently large, there is a prime between x and $x + x^{5/8}$. Furthermore, it can be deduced that there is a constant A such that for every n an inequality holds for the absolute difference between adjacent primes (see 93). H.L. Montgomery, using sieving methods, has shown that $|p_{n+1} - p_n| \leq Ap_n^{3/5 + \varepsilon}$, and M.N. Huxley has made a further refinement of the index to $7/12 + \varepsilon$. This is to be contrasted with the inference to be drawn if the Riemann hypothesis is true (see 94). It is an unsolved problem whether for x sufficiently large a difference expression involving π as a function of x is positive (see 95). Much effort has been devoted to the Riemann hypothesis, but by the 1970s the best known about a region in the strip $0 \leq \sigma \leq 1$ in which the function has no zeros is that σ is greater than or equal to 1 minus a function that involves A and the logarithm of t (see 96), a result due to Korobov and Vinogradov and used to prove the above quoted result on $\Delta(x)$.

Other arithmetic functions. The analysis of other arithmetic functions such as those referred to above takes place by way of the Dirichlet series determined by them. For example, two summations are given, one of which involves the function μ and relates it to the ζ function, the other of which involves the function φ and relates it to the ζ function (see 97).

Typical results are Φ as a function of x expressed as a sum of φ as a function of n (see 98), in which $|\Delta(x)| \leq Ax \log x$. If $M(x) = \Sigma\mu(n)$, the summation for $n \leq x$, then the absolute value of M is bounded by a function expressed in terms of A and the exponential of a square root of the logarithm of x (see 99).

Primes in arithmetic progressions. If k and a be two relatively prime integers with $k \geq 2$ and the arithmetic progression, a sequence of integers beginning with a (see 100), is considered, then the questions raised by Legendre

Legendre's questions

in 1803 were these:

(i) Are there infinitely many primes in this progression; *i.e.*, are there infinitely many $p \equiv a \pmod{k}$?

(ii) If so, and $\pi(a, k, x)$ be the number of such primes $\leq x$, then if $(a_1, k) = (a_2, k) = 1$, is it true that a limiting expression for a ratio of functions π equals 1 (see 101)? That is, are the numbers of primes in the different residue classes modulo k equidistributed?

The example gives the progressions $1 + 4n$, and $3 + 4n$—

(89) $\quad |\Delta(x)| \leq Axe^{-c(\log x)^{3/5}(\log\log x)^{1/5}}$

(90) $\quad \Delta(x) > cx^{\frac{1}{2}} \log\log\log x$

(91) $\quad \Delta(x) < -cx^{\frac{1}{2}} \log\log\log x$

(92) $\quad \pi(x + x^{\frac{5}{8}}) - \pi(x) \sim \dfrac{x^{\frac{5}{8}}}{\log x}$

(93) $\quad |p_{n+1} - p_n| \leq Ap_n^{\frac{5}{8} + \varepsilon}$ for any $\varepsilon > 0$

(94) $\quad |p_{n+1} - p_n| \leq Ap_n^{\frac{1}{2}} \log p_n$

(95) $\quad \pi(x + x^{\frac{1}{2}}) - \pi(x) > 0$

(96) $\quad \begin{cases} \zeta(s) \neq 0 \quad \text{for} \\ \sigma \geq 1 - \dfrac{A}{(\log t)^\alpha} \quad \text{with } t \geq 3, \quad \alpha \geq 2/3 \end{cases}$

(97) $\quad \begin{cases} \displaystyle\sum_{n=1}^{\infty} \dfrac{\mu(n)}{n^s} = \dfrac{1}{\zeta(s)} \\ \displaystyle\sum_{n=1}^{\infty} \dfrac{\varphi(n)}{n^s} = \dfrac{\zeta(s-1)}{\zeta(s)} \end{cases}$

(98) $\quad \Phi(x) = \displaystyle\sum_{n \leq x} \varphi(n) = \dfrac{3}{\pi^2} x^2 + \Delta(x)$

(99) $\quad |M(x)| \leq Axe^{-c\sqrt{\log x}}$

(100) $\quad a, a + k, a + 2k, \cdots$

(101) $\quad \displaystyle\lim_{x \to \infty} \dfrac{\pi(a_1, k, x)}{\pi(a_2, k, x)} = 1$

(102) $\quad \begin{cases} 1, 5, 9, 13, 17, 21, \cdots \\ 3, 7, 11, 15, 19, 23, \cdots \end{cases}$

(103) $\quad \log \zeta(s) = \displaystyle\sum_p \dfrac{1}{p^s} + R(s)$

(104) $\quad \displaystyle\sum_p \dfrac{1}{p}$

(105) $\quad \varepsilon(n) = \begin{cases} 0 \quad \text{if } n \not\equiv a \pmod{k} \\ 1 \quad \text{if } n \equiv a \pmod{k} \end{cases}$

(106) $\quad \displaystyle\sum_p \dfrac{\varepsilon(p)}{p^s} = \displaystyle\sum_{p \equiv a \pmod{k}} \dfrac{1}{p^s}$

(107) $\quad \begin{cases} \chi(n) = \chi(m) \quad \text{if} \quad n \equiv m \pmod{k} \\ \chi(mn) = \chi(m)\chi(n) \\ \chi(n) = 0 \quad \text{if } (n, k) > 1 \\ \chi(n) \text{ is not identically } 0 \end{cases}$

i.e., two sequences, one beginning with 1 and one beginning with 3 (see 102). Are there as many primes in the first sequence as there are in the second in the sense of the limit of the ratio already given (see 101)? Dirichlet gave an affirmative answer to the first question in 1837 and laid the foundations for an affirmative answer to the second. In doing so, Dirichlet was guided by Euler's proof that $\pi(x) \to \infty$ and was led to the concept of a character. Euler had proved that the logarithm of the ζ-function can be expressed as a sum of reciprocals of s powers of primes plus a remainder (see 103) in which the first sum is over all primes and in which the term $R(s)$ remains bounded as $s \to 1$. It then followed that the sum of the reciprocals of the primes (see 104) diverged in view of the fact that $\zeta(s) \to \infty$ as $s \to 1$.

To duplicate the argument requires a function ε as a function of n being defined to take on values 1 or 0 on conditions that depend on $a \bmod k$ (see 105) and then requires that the sum over all primes of the ratio of $\varepsilon(p)$ to p^s (see 106) be expressed in terms of functions the properties of which lend themselves readily to investigation. To produce such a function, Dirichlet postulates the existence of a function χ for fixed $k \geq 2$ with specific properties (see 107). The following facts are then established: (a) Such a function does indeed exist, and there are $\varphi(k)$ distinct such characters in which $\varphi(k) =$ the number of integers less than k and having no factors in common with k, called the Euler φ-function. (b) The values of $\chi(n)$ that are different from 0 are $\varphi(k)$-th roots of unity; *i.e.*, satisfy the equation $x\varphi^{(k)} = 1$. (c) There is a character χ_1 the values of which are as follows: $\chi_1(a) = 1$ if $(a, k) = 1$, $\chi_1(a) = 0$ if $(a, k) > 1$; χ_1 is called the principal character. Two further conditions may be expressed symbolically (see 108). The Dirichlet L-series is now defined by a sum over positive integers of ratios of the function χ to s powers of the integers for s a complex number (see 109).

Some properties of these functions are displayed (see 110). The last relation is one of fundamental importance; much attention has been devoted to a proof, but no simple proof is known.

With the help of the various properties enumerated, it is now possible to show that if a^* is chosen such that $aa^* \equiv 1 \pmod{k}$, then an equality exists between sums that relates the function χ, the function L, the function φ, and certain primes (see 111) in which $R(s)$ remains bounded as $s \to 1$. It follows that the limit as s approaches 1 of a restricted sum of reciprocals of s powers of primes is infinity (see 112). Thus the sum with $s = 1$ diverges, and, hence, there are infinitely many $p \equiv a \pmod{k}$. In fact, the above argument shows that the limit as s approaches 1 of a ratio of sums involving reciprocals of s powers of primes is equal to the reciprocal of φ at k (see 113). Thus the proportion of primes $p \equiv a \pmod{k}$ does not depend upon a and is $1/\varphi(k)$ in the sense of the limit of a ratio (see 113). In general, A is any set of natural numbers and B any subset. Then, the following limit (if it exists): the limit as s approaches 1 of a ratio of sums of reciprocals of s powers (see 114) is called the Dirichlet density of the set B with respect to the set A.

Dirichlet density

On the other hand, if $A(x)$ is defined as the number of elements of A that are less than or equal to x and $B(x)$ is similarly defined, then the limit (if it exists) of the ratio of B as a function of x to A as a function of x as x approaches infinity (see 115) is called the natural density of the set B with respect to the set A.

It is known that if the natural density exists, then the Dirichlet density exists. It is a fundamental problem to decide when the converse is true.

Distributions of other arithmetic functions in arithmetic progressions are handled in analogy with the distributions among the entire set of natural numbers, the L-functions usually replacing the zeta function.

Much attention has been devoted to the question of the uniformity of the distribution of primes in arithmetic progressions. De la Vallée-Poussin provided an expression for π in terms of a function φ and a function of x (see 116). The problem of a uniform error $\Delta(x)$, uniform in the sense that it does not depend on k or a, has played an important role in various questions. Some results are formulated in terms of the function ψ equal to a restricted sum of Λ as a function m (see 117).

As a consequence of Siegel's theorem on the class number, Walfisz proved that if $k \leq (\log x)^N$, there exists a constant c depending only on N such that the absolute value of Δ is less than or equal to a function involving constants A, c, and the logarithm of x (see 118) uniformly in k. Vinogradov used this result in his proof of the 3-prime version of the Goldbach conjecture.

$$(108) \quad \begin{cases} (d) \displaystyle\sum_{a=1}^{k-1} \chi(a) = \begin{cases} \varphi(k) & \text{if } \chi = \chi_1 \\ 0 & \text{otherwise} \end{cases} \\[3ex] (e) \displaystyle\sum_{\chi} \chi(a) = \begin{cases} \varphi(k) & \text{if } a \equiv 1 (\bmod k) \\ 0 & \text{otherwise} \end{cases} \end{cases}$$

$$(109) \quad L(s, \chi) = \sum_{n=1}^{\infty} \frac{\chi(n)}{n^s} \qquad s = \sigma + it$$

$$(110) \quad \begin{cases} \text{(i) If } \chi = \chi_1 \text{ the principal character, then } L(s, \chi) \\ \quad \text{differs from } \zeta(s) \text{ by a simple factor.} \\ \text{(ii) If } \chi \neq \chi_1, \text{ then } L(s, \chi) \text{ converges for } \sigma > 0. \\ \text{(iii) } L(s, \chi) = \displaystyle\prod_p \left(1 - \frac{\chi(p)}{p^s}\right)^{-1} \text{ its "Euler product."} \\ \text{(iv) If } \chi \neq \chi_1, \text{ then } L(1, \chi) \neq 0. \end{cases}$$

$$(111) \quad \sum_{\chi} \chi(a^*) \log L(s, \chi) = \frac{1}{\varphi(k)} \sum_{\substack{p \equiv a \\ \bmod k}} \frac{1}{p^s} + R(s)$$

$$(112) \quad \lim_{s \to 1} \sum_{p \equiv a(\bmod k)} \frac{1}{p^s} \to \infty$$

$$(113) \quad \lim_{s \to 1} \frac{\displaystyle\sum_{p \equiv a(\bmod k)} \frac{1}{p^s}}{\displaystyle\sum_p \frac{1}{p^s}} = \frac{1}{\varphi(k)}$$

$$(114) \quad \lim_{s \to 1} \frac{\displaystyle\sum_{n \in B} \frac{1}{b^s}}{\displaystyle\sum_{a \in A} \frac{1}{a^s}}$$

$$(115) \quad \lim_{x \to \infty} \frac{B(x)}{A(x)}$$

$$(116) \quad \begin{cases} \pi(a, k, x) = \dfrac{1}{\varphi(k)} \dfrac{x}{\log x} + \Delta(x) \\ \text{in which} \\ |\Delta(x)| \leq A x e^{-c\sqrt{\log x}} \end{cases}$$

$$(117) \quad \psi(a, k, x) = \sum_{\substack{n \leq x \\ n \equiv a(\bmod k)}} \Lambda(n)$$

$$(118) \quad |\Delta(x)| \leq A x e^{-c\sqrt{\log x}}$$

$$(119) \quad \mathfrak{F}(x, k) = \max_a \Delta(x) \qquad (a, k) = 1$$

$$(120) \quad \mathfrak{F}^*(x, k) = \max_{y \leq x} \mathfrak{F}(y, k)$$

$$(121) \quad \mathfrak{F}(x) = \sum_{k \leq x} \mathfrak{F}^*(x, k)$$

$$(122) \quad |\mathfrak{F}(X)| \leq A x (\log x)^{-c_1}, \qquad X = x^{\frac{1}{2}} (\log x)^{-c_2}$$

Deeper results have been obtained by the mathematician E. Bombieri, which require sieving methods and estimates for the number of zeros of the L-functions. One result takes the following form. Let $\mathfrak{F}$ equal the maximum over a of Δ (see 119) and $\mathfrak{F}^*$ equal a certain maximum of $\mathfrak{F}$, the range considered being y less than or equal to x (see 120) and $\mathfrak{F}$ equal to a sum of $\mathfrak{F}^*$, the range of summation being k less than or equal to x (see 121). Then for any constant c_1 there exists a constant c_2 such that if $X = x^{1/2} (\log x)^{-c_2}$, the absolute value of $\mathfrak{F}$ is less than or equal to a function of x that includes constants A and c_1 also a functional expression X (see 122). The complexity of the result is in the nature of the subject because the primes are so irregularly distributed.

Other applications of L-functions. There is a close connection between class numbers (see above *Algebraic number theory*) and the *L*-functions of Dirichlet. In fact, let $\mathfrak{F} = \mathfrak{H}(\sqrt{d})$ be a quadratic extension of the rational field $\mathfrak{H}$, with class number h. Consider the case when $d < 0$ and $d \equiv 1 \pmod 4$ [similar results hold when $d \equiv 2, 3 \pmod 4$]. Then Dirichlet proved that the product πh divided by the square root of d is equal to L (see 123) in which $\chi(n) = (d/n)$ is the Kronecker symbol (an extension of the Legendre symbol) and is a character mod $|d|$. The series for $L(1, \chi)$ may be expressed as a finite sum. In the more general case, there is a constant, symbolized by the Greek letter alpha, α, depending on the field K, such that αh equals the residue of ζ at s equals 1 (see 124), the function $\zeta_K(s)$ being the Riemann zeta function defined by ζ_K at s equals a summation over the class $\mathfrak{U}$ of reciprocals expressed in terms of N (see 125) summed over all integral ideals $\mathfrak{U}$. In certain cases $\zeta_K(s)$ can be written as a product of Dirichlet *L*-functions and its residue computed in terms of *L*-functions. Siegel proved that for a quadratic field of discriminant d a ratio of logarithms involving α and h converges to 0 (see 126) as $|d| \to \infty$. This was generalized by the German-born U.S. mathematician Richard Brauer in 1947.

The circle method. The case of the partition function $p(n)$ was previously considered and its generating function determined. It was found that a power series with coefficients $p(n)$ equals a product over positive integers of the function of x, which in turn equals F (see 127).

In 1917, Hardy and the Indian mathematician Srinivasa Ramanujan obtained an asymptotic formula for $p(n)$ and laid the foundations for a method that was further developed by Hardy and Littlewood, which method has since been called the circle method. This method has been modified and refined by Vinogradov and has been widely used to derive results on additive problems in number theory. The method will be described briefly as it applies to $p(n)$. Using Cauchy's theorem p as a function of n equals an integral over C of a function involving F (see 128), C being a simple closed contour inside the unit circle D, containing the origin. The function $F(x)$ is analytic inside D, but on the boundary of D, $F(x)$ has a dense set of poles. Thus it is not possible to integrate past the poles but only to come close to these. A circle of radius $N < 1$ is chosen and cut in a prescribed manner into arcs, the Farey fractions being used to determine the arcs and the number of arcs depending on N and tending to infinity as N tends to 1. Moreover, the circle approaches the unit circle as $N \to 1$.

The function $F(x)$ is now approximated along each of the arcs. The success of the method depends upon the precision with which $F(x)$ may be approximated. In this special case $F(x)$ satisfies a functional equation, and the approximation is so effective that a rapidly convergent series for $p(n)$ can be derived, as was shown by the German-born U.S. mathematician Hans Rademacher in 1937.

Vino-
gradov's
modifi-
cation

Vinogradov's modification is as follows: If, for example, the Goldbach problem for three primes be considered, then $r(n)$ may be the number of solutions of n equal to a sum of three primes (see 129). By use of an idea previously stated (see above *Methodology*), it is readily seen that a power series with coefficients r equals a third power of a sum extended over primes (see 130) in which the summation on the right is over primes.

Vinogradov replaces the infinite series with a finite sum and, because x is then no longer required to be in absolute value < 1, replaces x by $\exp(2\pi i t)$, and integrates along the unit circle, which is then transformed into the unit interval or indeed any interval of length 1. If the function f equals a restricted sum of exponentials involving p and t (see 131), r as a function of n is an integral from zero to one of the third power of f times an exponential (see 132). The interval is now dissected into subintervals by analogy

$$(123) \qquad \frac{\pi h}{\sqrt{d}} = L(1, \chi)$$

$$(124) \qquad \alpha h = \text{residue of } \zeta_K(s) \quad \text{at } s = 1$$

$$(125) \qquad \zeta_k(s) = \sum_{\mathfrak{A}} \frac{1}{N(\mathfrak{A})^s}$$

$$(126) \qquad \frac{\log \alpha h}{\log \sqrt{|\alpha|}} \to 0$$

$$(127) \qquad \sum_{n=0}^{\infty} p(n)x^n = \prod_{k=1}^{\infty} (1 - x^k)^{-1} = F(x)$$

$$(128) \qquad p(n) = \frac{1}{2\pi i} \int_C F(x)x^{-n-1}\, dx$$

$$(129) \qquad n = p_1 + p_2 + p_3$$

$$(130) \qquad \sum_{n=0}^{\infty} r(n)x^n = \left(\sum_p x^p\right)^3$$

$$(131) \qquad f(t) = \sum_{p \leq N} e^{2\pi i p t}$$

$$(132) \qquad r(n) = \int_0^1 f^3(t)e^{-\pi i n t}\, dt$$

$$(133) \qquad r(n) = \int_I f^3(t)e^{-2\pi i n t}\, dt + \int_S f^3(t)e^{-2\pi i n t}\, dt = I_1 + I_2$$

$$(134) \qquad r(n) = (C(n) + \lambda(n)) \frac{n^2}{\log^3 n}$$

$$(135) \qquad n = x_1^k + \cdots + x_s^k$$

$$(136) \qquad \begin{cases} \text{If } s \geq [10k^2 \log k], \text{ then} \\ r(n) = C(n)\,\gamma(s, k) + \lambda(n)n^{s/(k-1)} \end{cases}$$

with the decomposition into Farey arcs. The intervals are in two classes, basic intervals and supplementary intervals. The basic intervals contribute the principal term. If the basic intervals are denoted by S, and the supplementary intervals by S, r as a function of n is a sum of two integrals, one extended over I and one extended over S, each with integrands of the type: third power of f times an exponential (see 133). After suitable approximation on I and S, respectively, the conclusion is reached that r as a function of n is a sum of two terms C and λ all multiplied by a function involving the third power of the logarithm of n (see 134) when $C(n)$ is positive if n is odd and $\lambda(n) \to 0$ as $n \to \infty$. The first term comes from I and the second from S.

It follows that if n is sufficiently large then $r(n) > 0$. The same method has been used to obtain a variety of results. For example, if $r(n)$ is the number of solutions of an equation giving n as a sum of s terms of the type x_1 raised to the kth power (see 135) if s is greater than or equal to a specific function of k involving a logarithm, then r as a function of n is a sum of two terms, one a product of C times γ, one a product of λ and a certain power of n (see 136), in which $C(n)\gamma(s, k) > 0$ and $\lambda(n) \to 0$ as $n \to \infty$. This was proved by Vinogradov.

In particular, the English mathematician Harold Davenport has proved that if $k = 4$, then $r(n) > 0$ if and only if $s \geq 16$. Yury Vladimirovich Linnik (Soviet) and George Leo Watson (English) have proved that for $k = 3$, $r(n) > 0$ if $s \geq 7$.

Although the Goldbach conjecture for even numbers has not been proved, it can be shown using the circle method that almost all even numbers are sums of two primes. This means that if $E(N)$ is the number of even integers, m, that are not the sum of two primes and $m \leq N$, then the limit, as N approaches infinity, of the ratio $E(N)/N$ is zero.

Exponential sums. It is significant that both in the distribution of primes and in additive problems, as well as in numerous other questions, the basic problems frequently reduce to the problem of estimating the size of the exponential sum E as a function of x. This is a sum over all values of n less than or equal to N of an exponential involving f (see 137), in which $f(y)$ is some function of y. In the case of the Goldbach problem, f as a function of y takes on one of two values 0 or 1, depending on whether y is not or is a prime (see 138). In the case of the zeta function $\zeta(s)$, $(s = \sigma + it)$, the estimates of $\zeta(s)$ can be reduced to a function $E(x)$ in which f as a function of y is expressed in terms of the logarithm of y (see 139). It is to be noted that because each of the terms in the sum has absolute value 1, then trivially the absolute value of E is less than or equal to N (see 140). The basic problem is to show that under suitable conditions on $f(y)$ and on x, the limit as N approaches infinity of the ratio of the absolute value of E to N is 0 (see 141), and the rate at which this takes place is an important part of the problem. A typical result due to Korobov and Vinogradov is the following: If a number of conditions are satisfied that involve r, w, t, M, M', and θ, then the absolute value of a sum of exponentials of the logarithm of m and w is less than or equal to a certain power of M (see 142). The complexity of the statement of the result is fairly typical and it is noted once again that this intricacy is in the nature of the subject.

Elliptic, theta, and modular functions. In addition to analysis of the partition function, Euler considered a function that makes $\theta(x)$ equal a product over all positive integers of the difference between 1 and integer powers of x (see 143) and proved the so-called pentagonal number theorem—i.e., θ as a function of x can be found by calculation to be 1 plus an infinite sum of positive and negative terms each being powers of x (see 144)— the name stems from the relation of the exponents to the pentagon.

(margin) **Pentagonal number theorem**

More important, however, is the fact that this function was the first example of a theta function. From this result and other related ones, interesting identities and relations involving partitions are proved. Theta functions appeared in the works of Bernoulli (1713), in Fourier's *Théorie analytique de la chaleur* (1822; *The Analytical Theory of Heat*, 1878), but were only systematically introduced and studied by the German mathematician Karl Gustav Jacob Jacobi in *Fundamenta nova Theoriae Functionum Ellipticarum* (1829; "New Foundations of the Theory of Elliptic Functions"). There are four types of theta functions; one is defined by θ as a function of z and q is equal to 1 plus twice the sum over all positive integers of a product involving a cosine function (see 145) with $q = \exp(\pi i \tau)$, im $\tau > 0$, which for $z = \pi$ takes the form θ as a function of π and q is equal to 1 plus twice the infinite sum over all positive integers of q raised to the squared power of an integer (see 146), a function useful for studying sums of squares.

Using the theory of θ-functions and their transformations, Jacobi proved several results on the numbers of representations of integers by sums of squares. In particular, he proved that the number $r_4(n)$ of representations of n as a sum of four squares is (i) 8 times the sum of the odd divisors of n when n is odd and (ii) 24 times the sum of the odd divisors of n when n is even.

Jacobi also proved the identity an infinite product extending over all positive integers is equal to an infinite sum extending over both negative and positive integers, the product expressed in three factors that involve x, z, and an integer, the sum involving two factors expressed in terms of z, x, and an integer (see 147) from which a number of results could be derived.

The introduction of modular forms and functions began a new era in the interplay between number theory and analysis.

(margin) **Modular transformations**

If $f(z)$ be a function of a complex variable z that is meromorphic in the upper half plane, then if a, b, c, d are integers with $ad - bc = 1$, the transformation w is a

$$(137) \qquad E(x) = \sum_{n \leq N} e^{2\pi i f(n) x}$$

$$(138) \qquad f(y) = \begin{cases} 0 & \text{if } y \text{ is not a prime} \\ 1 & \text{if } y \text{ is a prime} \end{cases}$$

$$(139) \qquad f(y) = t \log y$$

$$(140) \qquad |E(x)| \leq N$$

$$(141) \qquad \lim_{N \to \infty} \frac{|E(x)|}{N} = 0$$

$$(142) \qquad \begin{cases} \text{Let } r \geq 46, \quad 0 \leq w \leq 1, \quad t \geq 1 \\ M \leq M' \leq 2M, \qquad \theta = (266{,}000 r^2)^{-1} \\ t^{1/r} \leq M \leq t^{1/(r-1)} \quad \text{then} \\ \left| \sum_{m=M}^{M'} e^{ti \log(m+w)} \right| \leq M^{1-\theta} \end{cases}$$

$$(143) \qquad \theta(x) = \prod_{n=1}^{\infty} (1 - x^n)$$

$$(144) \qquad \begin{cases} \theta(x) = 1 + \sum_{n=1}^{\infty} (-1)^n \left(x^{\frac{n(3n-1)}{2}} + x^{\frac{n(3n+1)}{2}} \right) \\ = 1 - x - x^2 + x^5 + x^7 - x^{12} - x^{15} + \cdots \end{cases}$$

$$(145) \qquad \theta(z, q) = 1 + 2 \sum_{n=1}^{\infty} q^{n^2} \cos 2nz$$

$$(146) \qquad \theta(0, q) = 1 + 2 \sum_{n=1}^{\infty} q^{n^2}$$

$$(147) \qquad \prod_{n=1}^{\infty} (1 - x^{2n})(1 + z x^{2n+1})(1 + z^{-1} x^{2n-1}) = \sum_{k=-\infty}^{\infty} z^k x^{k^2}$$

$$(148) \qquad w = \frac{az + b}{cz + d}$$

$$(149) \qquad \begin{cases} w_1 = z + 1 \\ w_2 = -\dfrac{1}{z} \end{cases}$$

$$(150) \qquad f(z) = (cz + d)^{-2k} f\left(\frac{az + b}{cz + d} \right) \qquad (ad - bc = 1)$$

$$(151) \qquad G_k(z) = \sum_{m,n}' \frac{1}{(mz + n)^{2k}}$$

$$(152) \qquad \Delta(\tau) = (60 G_2)^3 - 27(140 G_3)^2$$

$$(153) \qquad \Delta(\tau) = (2\pi)^{12} q \prod_{n=1}^{\infty} (1 - q^n)^{24}$$

rational function of z with coefficients a, b, c, and d (see 148); this is called a modular transformation. The set of modular transformations forms a group generated by the particular transformations w_1 and w_2; these are each simple functions of z (see 149), and a modular transformation takes the upper half plane into itself. If f, as a function of z, is a factor raised to the $2k$ power times f, as a function of a rational function of z, the rational function involving coefficients a, b, c, and d that satisfy a simple condition (see 150), then $f(z)$ is called a modular form of weight (or dimension) $2k$. Examples of such modular forms are the Eisenstein series, G_k as a function of z, a restricted sum over two integer valued variables m and n of a simple function of two variables (see 151), in which m, n range over all integers except the pair (0, 0). The form Δ, as a function of τ, which is a difference of two terms, one term involving G_2, a second term involving G_3 (see 152), plays an important role in the theory. It is a modular form of weight 12. It turns out that Δ, as a function of τ, is a factor involving π and q multiplied by an infinite product over positive integers of a simple function of q and an integer (see 153), in which $q = \exp(2\pi i\tau)$. On the other hand, the function η, as a function of τ, that is the $^1/_{12}$ power of q times an infinite product extended over all positive integers of a simple function of q and an integer (see 154), appears in Riemann's works, and its properties were elucidated by Dedekind. It plays a fundamental role in the problem of partitions, and its relation with $\Delta(\tau)$ is immediate. The function j, as a function of τ, that is equal to a ratio of a third power involving g_2 to Δ, as a function of τ (see 155), is a modular form of weight 0; it is invariant under the complete modular group. Moreover, if $f(\tau)$ is any function meromorphic in the upper half plane and is a modular form of weight 0, then $f(\tau)$ is a rational function of $j(\tau)$; *i.e.*, the ratio of two polynomials in $j(\tau)$.

It is most remarkable that Abelian extensions of an imaginary quadratic field can be obtained as subfields obtained by adjoining values of $j(\tau)$ to the quadratic field. This settled the *Jugendtraum* of Kronecker. Abelian extensions of the rational field $\mathfrak{H}$ are subfields of fields obtained by adjoining to $\mathfrak{H}$ values of the exponential function e^x. Thus the relation between modular forms and algebraic number fields is very profound. Mention should be made of the connection between the zeta functions of algebraic number fields and elliptic functions, connections that were discovered by Kronecker in 1875. Extensions of these results were made by Erich Hecke (German-born), Carl L. Siegel (U.S.), and others.

These connections were used by the mathematicians K. Heegner in 1952 and Harold M. Stark in 1967 and others to determine all imaginary quadratic fields that have unique factorization. The problem had remained unsolved since 1933 when the mathematicians H. Heilbronn and E. Linfoot showed that there could be at most 10 such fields, nine of which were identified.

Another connection between modular forms and number theory was discovered by Hecke as follows: $f(\tau)$ may be expanded in a Fourier series in q such that f, as a function of q, is a power series with coefficients a_n, q being a complex exponential with variable τ (see 156). If $a_0 = 0$, then $f(\tau)$ is called a cusp form. Hecke proved that if $f(\tau)$ is a cusp form of weight $2k$, then the absolute value of a_n is less than or equal to a constant times the k power of n (see 157).

Ramanujan investigated in great detail the function that is a sum over positive integers of the function τ times q raised to an integer power and that is equal to q times a product of terms involving q and an integer (see 158). He conjectured that if $(m, n) = 1$, then $\tau(m)\tau(n) = \tau(mn)$, a fact proved by the U.S.-born mathematician Louis Joel Mordell. He was led to the conjecture that if p is prime, then the absolute value of τ as a function of p is less than a simple function of p (see 159). This conjecture remains unproved though a proof was reported in the 1970s.

RESULTS OBTAINABLE FROM ELEMENTARY METHODS

A great deal of attention has been paid to the question of whether the results of analytic number theory can be derived without the use of complex analytic machinery, especially such results as those of the Goldbach and Waring problems, the statements of which do not involve analytic concepts. In fact, a number of results have been proved without complex function theory. Several results that have been proved by elementary methods are enumerated below.

(i) The prime number theorem—proved by the Norwegian-born U.S. mathematician Atle Selberg and the Hungarian mathematician Paul Erdös with later refinements by Bombieri.

(ii) Solution to the Waring problem obtained by the Soviet mathematician Yury Vladimirovich Linnik.

(iii) Dirichlet's theorem on primes in an arithmetic progression, proved by the German-born Canadian mathematician Hans Zassenhaus and Atle Selberg.

$$(154) \qquad \eta(\tau) = q^{1/12} \prod_{n=1}^{\infty} (1 - q^n)$$

$$(155) \qquad j(\tau) = \frac{(720G_2(\tau))^3}{\Delta(\tau)}$$

$$(156) \qquad f(q) = \sum_{n=0}^{\infty} a_n q^n \qquad q = e^{2\pi i\tau}$$

$$(157) \qquad |a_n| \leqslant An^k$$

$$(158) \qquad \sum_{n=1}^{\infty} \tau(n)q^n = q\Pi(1 - q^n)^{24}$$

$$(159) \qquad |\tau(p)| < 2p^{\frac{11}{2}}$$

$$(160) \qquad f(s) = 1 - \frac{1}{2^s} + \frac{1}{3^s} - \cdots$$

$$(161) \qquad \left| \sum_{n \leqslant x} \mu(n) \right| \leqslant Ax^{1/2 + \varepsilon}$$

$$(162) \qquad K(a, b) = \sum_{\substack{n \bmod p \\ n\bar{n} \equiv 1(p)}} e^{\frac{2\pi i}{p}(an + b\bar{n})}$$

$$(163) \qquad |K(a, b)| \leqslant A\sqrt{p}$$

(iv) Calculation of the number of lattice points inside contours, performed by Vinogradov.

(v) Siegel's theorem on the class number of quadratic fields, proved by Linnik.

The term elementary is in some respects a misnomer. The methods are elementary primarily in avoiding the use of such results as Cauchy's theorem of complex function theory. In fact, they tend to be rather intricate.

Furthermore, there has also been a trend to avoid the use of analysis even in the statements of some of the theorems that on the face of it are analytic in character. For example, in the prime number theorem the function log x is replaced by $\ell(n) = \Sigma 1/k$, the summation for $k \leq n$, and then $\pi(n)/n$ is compared with $\ell(n)$: Thus, transcendental concepts are entirely removed.

SOME UNSOLVED PROBLEMS OF ANALYTIC NUMBER THEORY

1. The most famous is perhaps the Riemann hypothesis: If $s = \sigma + it$ and f as a function of s is equal to 1 plus negative and positive reciprocals of integers raised to the s power (see 160), which converges for $\sigma > 0$, then the Riemann conjecture is that if $f(s) = 0$, $0 < \sigma < 1$, then $\sigma = ^1/_2$. Again, if $\mu(n)$ is the Möbius function described above, then the Riemann hypothesis is equivalent to the statement that there exists a constant A such that the absolute value of the function μ with integer arguments is less than or equal to a constant A times the $^1/_2 + \varepsilon$ power of x (see 161), in which ε is any positive number.

2. The Goldbach conjecture for even integers: Every even integer $n \geq 4$ is the sum of two primes.

3. Hecke's hypothesis: If χ is a real character mod k, then $L(s,\chi) \neq 0$ if $0 < s < 1$.

4. Better estimates for exponential sums. In the case of K as a function of a and b—that is, a sum over integers defined in terms of p, summands being of exponential type (see 162)—the mathematician André Weil proved the Riemann hypothesis for function fields and using it showed that the absolute value of K is less than or equal to A times the square root of p (see 163).

Such sharp estimates in general are much to be desired.

5. The least quadratic non-residue. If p is a prime and $n(p)$ is the least quadratic non-residue, then the Riemann hypothesis implies, as shown by the mathematician N. Ankeny, that $| n(p) | \leq A \log^2 p$. The mathematician Burgess has shown that $| n(p) | \leq Ap^{1/4 \sqrt{e}}$.

Hecke's discovery

Avoidance of analysis

6. If $d > 0$, and $h(d)$ the class number of the quadratic field $\mathfrak{H}\sqrt{d}$, then is $h(d) = 1$ infinitely often as Gauss conjectured?

7. More generally, are there infinitely many algebraic number fields that have unique factorization; i.e., for which the class number is 1?

8. Are there infinitely many primes of the form $n^2 + 1$?

9. Artin's conjecture. Given an integer g, are there infinitely many primes p of which g is a primitive root?

10. Ramanujan conjectured that in $q (\prod_{n=1}^{\infty} (1 - q^n))^{24} = \Sigma \tau(k) q^k$, the summation for $k = 1$ to ∞, if p is a prime, then $| \tau(p) | \le 2p^{11/2}$. The mathematician Lehmer conjectured that for every n, $\tau(n) \ne 0$.

11. More general conjectures on coefficients of modular forms of a given weight.

12. Improvement of the error term in the prime number theorem is being sought.

13. Proofs of congruence properties of partitions; e.g., Ramanujan conjectured if $24k \equiv 1 \pmod{m}$, in which $m = 5^a 7^b 11^c$, the function p, with argument expressed in terms of m, n, and λ, is equivalent to $0 \pmod{m}$ (see 164). Some special cases of this are known. The mathematician A.O.L. Atkin proved some results for $m = 11^c$. The mathematician Sarvadaman Chowla pointed out that the conjecture is false for $m = 7^3$. It remains to determine what congruence properties are true.

14. If $d(n)$ is the number of divisors of n, and it is known that D, as a function of x, is a sum of two terms plus Δ, as a function of x, the first term involving the product $x \log x$, the second term involving γ and x (see 165), in which $\Delta(x)$ is an error term. Does there exist a constant A such that the absolute value of Δ is less than or equal to A times the $1/4 + \varepsilon$ power of x (see 166)? A similar conjecture for the number of lattice points in a circle.

15. Do there exist infinitely many Fermat primes; i.e., primes of the form $2^{2^k} + 1$?

16. Do there exist infinitely many regular primes; i.e., primes p such that if h is the class number of the field $\mathfrak{H}(\exp 2\pi i/p)$ then p is not a factor of h? This has a close connection with Fermat's last theorem.

17. Waring's problem. If $n = x_1^k + \ldots + x_S^k$, then it is known that if $s \ge 2^k + 1$, there exists n_0, such that if $n > n_0$ the equation has a solution in integers $x_1, x_2, \ldots, x_s$. What is the least value of s for which this statement remains valid; e.g., is $s \ge 4k$ sufficient?

18. Are there infinitely many twin primes; i.e., primes p such that $p + 2$ is also prime? (R.G.A.)

Geometric and probabilistic number theory

GEOMETRIC NUMBER THEORY

Primary concerns of geometric number theory

Geometric number theory, or, as it is sometimes misleadingly called, the geometry of numbers, is a branch of number theory that can be developed by the use of certain geometric methods. It centres on the arithmetical theory of quadratic and higher forms and the problems of the approximation of real numbers by rational numbers. If integers a, b, c satisfy the inequality $ac > b^2$, the (positive definite) binary quadratic form in x and y with coefficients a, b, and c (see 167) takes the value zero when the variables x, y are both zero, but takes only positive integral values for other integral values of the variables. A question of interest is what can be said about the positive integers that will be represented by the form, and, in particular, what will be the smallest positive value taken by the form for integral values of the variables. Lagrange developed an arithmetical technique for answering such questions in 1773, and, in particular, he proved that it is always possible to choose integers x, y such that a quadratic in x and y satisfies a double inequality, being greater than zero and less than a function of its coefficients (see 168). By 1831, the theory had been developed further, and the mathematician L.A. Seeber published an elaborate account of the corresponding arithmetical theory for ternary quadratic forms. In his review of Seeber's book, Gauss introduced a geometric point of view that greatly simplified the proofs of Seeber's results and led to a proof of an important conjecture of Seeber's. If Q as a function of x,

(164)	$p(mn + \lambda) \equiv 0 \pmod{m}$
(165)	$D(x) = x \log x + (2\gamma - 1)x + \Delta(x)$
(166)	$|\Delta(x)| \le Ax^{1/4 + \varepsilon}$
(167)	$ax^2 + 2bxy + cy^2 \quad (ac > b^2, \quad a > 0)$
(168)	$0 < ax^2 + 2bxy + cy^2 < [\frac{4}{3}(ac - b^2)]^{\frac{1}{2}}$
(169)	$Q(x, y, z) = ax^2 + by^2 + cz^2 + 2fyz + 2gzx + 2hxy$
(170)	$Q(x, y, z) = \xi_1^2 + \xi_2^2 + \xi_3^2$
(171)	$\begin{cases} \xi_1 = \alpha_1 x + \beta_1 y + \gamma_1 z \\ \xi_2 = \alpha_2 x + \beta_2 y + \gamma_2 z \\ \xi_3 = \alpha_3 x + \beta_3 y + \gamma_3 z \end{cases}$
(172)	$\begin{vmatrix} a & h & g \\ h & b & f \\ g & f & c \end{vmatrix} = \begin{vmatrix} \alpha_1 & \beta_1 & \gamma_1 \\ \alpha_2 & \beta_2 & \gamma_2 \\ \alpha_3 & \beta_3 & \gamma_3 \end{vmatrix}^2 > 0$
(173)	$T:(x, y, z) \rightarrow (\xi_1, \xi_2, \xi_3)$

y, and z, a ternary quadratic with six coefficients (see 169), is positive definite—i.e., if it takes no negative values, and only takes the value zero when the variables x, y, z are all zero—then it can be expressed, in many ways, as the sum (see 170) of the squares of the three linear forms that are written ξ_1, ξ_2, ξ_3 (see 171). The coefficients will satisfy a determinantal identity involving a third-order determinant that is positive with elements symmetric about the diagonal (see 172). Gauss recognized that as x, y, z vary independently over the integers, the corresponding points (ξ_1, ξ_2, ξ_3) will vary over the points of a regular discrete array of points, the points of a lattice. Indeed, the lattice is simply obtained by applying the linear transformation (see 173) already defined (see 171) to the standard lattice Λ_0 of all points (x, y, z) with integral coordinates. A previous formula (see 170) then expresses the value of the quadratic form when the variables x, y, z are integers, as the square of the Euclidean distance of the corresponding lattice point (ξ_1, ξ_2, ξ_3) from the origin. This very simple idea enabled Gauss to reinterpret much of Seeber's work geometrically and to simplify and extend it.

The lattices introduced here are essentially the same as the lattices used in crystallography but are quite distinct from the abstract mathematical structures that the U.S. mathematician Garrett Birkhoff named lattices later.

Although Dirichlet made some use of these geometrical ideas, the next major development was due to Minkowski, who published his *Geometrie der Zahlen* ("Geometry of Numbers") giving a detailed account of his methods in 1896.

Minkowski's application to a convex body

Minkowski introduced the idea of a convex body. A set K is said to be convex, if whenever A and B are points of K, the line segment AB is also in K. A set K is said to be a convex body if it is closed (i.e., contains all the points of its boundary or surface), bounded (i.e., does not extend to infinity), and contains an inner point (i.e., a point not on its boundary). A set is said to be symmetrical in the origin $O = (0, 0, 0)$ if, with each point A in the set, the reflection A' of A in O is also in the set. In three-dimensional space, Minkowski's first fundamental theorem, in its simplest form, asserts that if a convex body is symmetrical in the origin and has volume eight or more units, then it contains, in addition to the origin, a symmetrical pair of points (x, y, z), $(-x, -y, -z)$ with integral coordinates, not all zero. On applying the transformation T (see 171, 173) the general form is obtained: If a convex body K is symmetrical in the origin and has volume at least eight times the absolute value of the determinant Δ—that is, a determinant with columns composed of $\alpha_i \beta_j \gamma_k$ (see 174)—giving the volume of the unit cell of the lattice, then K contains, in addition to the origin, a symmetrical pair of points (ξ_1, ξ_2, ξ_3), $(-\xi_1, -\xi_2, -\xi_3)$ of the lattice defined by the transformation (see 171).

Applying this result to the cube of points (ξ_1, ξ_2, ξ_3), satisfying the condition that the absolute value of a typical variable ξ_i is less than or equal to the one-third power of the absolute value of Δ (see 175), Minkowski obtained Dirichlet's 1842 result on linear forms: given the forms referred to (see 171), there will always be integers x, y, z, not all zero satisfying the stated inequalities (see 175). This result leads quite simply to the result that, if θ, φ are any real irrational numbers, there are infinitely many pairs of rational numbers u/w, υ/w, u, υ, w being integers that are good simultaneous approximations to θ and φ in that the absolute differences between θ and the ratio u to w and between φ and the ratio υ to w are each less than or equal to a simple function of w (see 176).

Minkowski obtained many other important results, in particular, his second fundamental theorem, and his improvements of the French mathematician Charles Hermite's estimate for the arithmetic minima of positive definite quadratic forms. To discuss these results and the subsequent development of the subject the limitations of three-dimensional space must be discarded.

The 17th-century French mathematician René Descartes had revolutionized three-dimensional geometry by introducing a rectangular Cartesian coordinate system, so that each point of space is represented by a set of three coordinates, and by showing that the whole of geometry could be reduced to the algebra and analysis of the sets of coordinates. For example, if a and b are points with coordinates (a_1, a_2, a_3) and (b_1, b_2, b_3), the distance between these is the square root of the sum of squares of differences between b_i and a_i (see 177), and the points on the line segments joining a to b are those with coordinates forming a vector with three components, each of which is expressed in terms of θ and $\{a_k\}$ and $\{b_k\}$ (see 178) when $0 \le \theta \le 1$. Furthermore, $\mathbf{a} = (a_1, a_2, a_3)$, $\mathbf{b} = (b_1, b_2, b_3)$ are regarded as vectors, the distance between the points a and b is the distance between vectors $\mathbf{b}$ and $\mathbf{a}$ and is the square root of the sum of squares of differences of components (see 179) of the vector $\mathbf{b} - \mathbf{a}$, and the points on the line segments joining $\mathbf{a}$ to $\mathbf{b}$ are $(1 - \theta)\mathbf{a} + \theta\mathbf{b}$, with $0 \le \theta \le 1$.

When vector algebra was developed, partly as a result of the Irish mathematician Sir William Rowan Hamilton's attempts to develop applied mathematics in terms of quaternions, there were immediate advantages in developing an algebra for vectors with any arbitrary fixed number n of components. The basic formula for combination of vectors is that if $\mathbf{a} = (a_1, a_2, \ldots, a_n)$, $\mathbf{b} = (b_1, b_2, \ldots, b_n)$ are vectors, and λ, μ are scalars (in this context, just another name for real numbers), then $\lambda\mathbf{a} + \mu\mathbf{b}$ denotes the vector with n components each of which is expressed in terms of λ, μ and a_k and b_k with length of the vector $\mathbf{a}$ determined in the usual way (see 180). The geometrical term length has already been used to describe a purely algebraic object, the square root of the sum of the squares of the components of a vector, which has no realization in ordinary geometry. Mathematicians soon took this process much further, calling the vectors $\mathbf{x}$ that have n components (see 181) the points of n-dimensional Euclidean space, and using geometrical language to describe the vector algebra. For example, the distance between the points $\mathbf{a}$ and $\mathbf{b}$ is defined to be $\| \mathbf{b} - \mathbf{a} \|$, and the line segment joining the points $\mathbf{a}$ and $\mathbf{b}$ is defined to be the set of points $(1 - \theta)\mathbf{a} + \theta\mathbf{b}$ with $0 \le \theta \le 1$. While Descartes regarded the sets of coordinates and their algebra as a means of describing the geometric realities of space, the geometrical language used in the study of n-dimensional Euclidean space E^n is now regarded as describing the realities of the corresponding vector algebra of vectors with n real components.

The set Λ_0 of all points $\mathbf{x} = (x_1, x_2, \cdots, x_n)$ with integral coordinates is taken to be the standard lattice in E^n; the general lattice Λ in E^n is obtained by applying a nonsingular linear transformation to Λ_0, and so is the set of points possessing n coordinates ξ_i (see 182) with ξ_i a

The Cartesian coordinates

$$(174) \qquad \Delta = \begin{vmatrix} \alpha_1 & \beta_1 & \gamma_1 \\ \alpha_2 & \beta_2 & \gamma_2 \\ \alpha_3 & \beta_3 & \gamma_3 \end{vmatrix}$$

$$(175) \qquad |\xi_i| \le |\Delta|^{\frac{1}{3}}, \qquad i = 1, 2, 3,$$

$$(176) \qquad \left| \theta - \frac{u}{w} \right| \le \frac{1}{w^{3/2}}, \qquad \left| \varphi - \frac{\upsilon}{w} \right| \le \frac{1}{w^{3/2}}$$

$$(177) \qquad [(b_1 - a_1)^2 + (b_2 - a_2)^2 + (b_3 - a_3)^2]^{\frac{1}{2}}$$

$$(178) \qquad ((1 - \theta)a_1 + \theta b_1, (1 - \theta)a_2 + \theta b_2, (1 - \theta)a_3 + \theta b_3)$$

$$(179) \qquad \|\mathbf{b} - \mathbf{a}\| = [(b_1 - a_1)^2 + (b_2 - a_2)^2 + (b_3 - a_3)^2]^{\frac{1}{2}}$$

$$(180) \qquad \begin{cases} (\lambda a_1 + \mu b_1, \lambda a_2 + \mu b_2, \cdots, \lambda a_n + \mu b_n) \\ \text{further, the length of the vector } \mathbf{a} \text{ is} \\ \|\mathbf{a}\| = [a_1^2 + a_2^2 + \cdots + a_n^2]^{\frac{1}{2}} \end{cases}$$

$$(181) \qquad \mathbf{x} = (x_1, x_2, \cdots, x_n)$$

$$(182) \qquad \xi = (\xi_1, \xi_2, \cdots, \xi_n)$$

$$(183) \qquad \xi_i = \sum_{j=1}^{n} \alpha_{ij} x_j$$

$$(184) \qquad d(\Lambda) = |\det(\alpha_{ij})|$$

$$(185) \qquad \lambda_1^n V(K) \le 2^n d(\Lambda)$$

linear combination of x_j (see 183), $x_1, x_2, \cdots, x_n$ taking all integral values, and the determinant $\det(\alpha_{ij})$ of the coefficient matrix being nonzero. The determinant $d(\Lambda)$ of Λ is defined to be the absolute value of the determinant of the coefficients (see 184).

Using the natural generalizations of the ideas of a convex body symmetrical in $O = (0, 0, \cdots, 0)$, Minkowski's first theorem takes the form: If a convex body K in E^n is symmetrical in O and has volume $2^n d(\Lambda)$ or more, then K contains, in addition to the origin, a symmetrical pair of points of Λ.

Minkowski's second fundamental theorem is explained by introducing the successive minima of a convex symmetrical body for a lattice. For any set S of points and any positive number λ, the set of all points of the form $\lambda\mathbf{s}$ with $\mathbf{s}$ a point of S is called the expansion of S by the factor λ and is denoted by λS. The expansion of S will be a genuine expansion or enlargement of S from the origin if λ exceeds unity; but it will be a contraction or reduction of S toward the origin if λ is less than unity. The first minimum λ_1 of a convex body K in E^n, symmetrical in O, for a lattice Λ is defined to be the least positive number λ_1 such that the expanded body $\lambda_1 K$ contains points of Λ other than O. More generally, if $1 \le r \le n$, the rth minimum λ_r is defined to be the least positive number λ_r such that the set of points of Λ in $\lambda_r K$ does not lie in any substance of E^n of dimension less than r. It follows immediately from these definitions that $\lambda_1, \lambda_2, \cdots, \lambda_n$ is a nondecreasing sequence of positive numbers. Using $V(K)$ to denote the volume of the convex body, Minkowski's first theorem reduces to the inequality setting the nth power of λ_1 multiplied by $V(K)$ less than or equal to $d(\Lambda)$ times the nth power of 2 (see 185); his second theorem makes the stronger and more sophisticated assertion that there is a similar inequality involving the product of n of the $\{\lambda_k\}$ (see 186). While the first theorem is easy to prove, there is no very simple proof of the second theorem; the simplest is probably that due to the mathematician Harold Davenport (1939).

Minkowski's first fundamental theorem can be restated in yet another form. If K is any convex body symmetrical in O, there may exist a largest real number $\Delta(K)$ with the property that all lattices Λ with determinant $d(\Lambda)$ less than $\Delta(K)$ have a pair of symmetrical points, not O, in K. Minkowski's theorem asserts that there is such a number $\Delta(K)$ for each K, and that $\Delta(K) \geq 2^{-n}V(K)$. The number $\Delta(K)$ is called the critical determinant of K, and any lattice Λ with $d(\Lambda) = \Delta(K)$ and with no point, other than O, in the interior of K is called a critical lattice of K. These definitions of critical determinant and critical lattice extend immediately to the case in which K is replaced by a star-body S. A star-body is defined to be a closed set, not necessarily bounded, symmetrical in O, containing O as an inner point, and with the star property that, whenever a point X lies in S, then the line segment OX lies wholly in S. Although Minkowski's theorem does not apply, the critical determinant $\Delta(S)$ will exist as a positive real number or will have the conventional value plus infinity. In order to obtain refined applications to number theory, much effort has been devoted to determining or estimating the critical determinants of a whole range of convex bodies and of star-bodies. Although many of the most interesting star-bodies are of infinite volume, some, and in particular all the convex bodies, have finite volume. Minkowski stated that he had proved that, for any star-body S of finite volume $V(S)$, the critical determinant satisfies the inequality involving a function of n, the function being a sum over positive integers of reciprocals of nth powers of the integers (see 187). Minkowski never published a proof (except in the very special case of a sphere), and the first published proof was accomplished by the mathematician Hlawka in 1944.

Lattice packing

Minkowski's proof of his first theorem was based on the idea of a lattice packing. If K is a convex body (not necessarily symmetrical in O), then the system of translates $\{K + \mathbf{x}_i\}$, $i = 1$ to $i = \infty$, of K by a sequence of vectors $\{\mathbf{x}_i\}$, $i = 1$ to $i = \infty$, is said to be a packing of K, if no two of the translates have any point in common. The packing is said to be a lattice packing with lattice Λ if the sequence of vectors $\{\mathbf{x}_i\}$, $i = 1$ to $i = \infty$, is an enumeration of the vectors of the lattice Λ. The density of a packing is defined to correspond to the intuitive notion of that proportion of the whole of space covered by the sets of the packing. Minkowski gave a very simple proof, using only a few lines of vector algebra, that if K is a convex body symmetrical in O, and if Λ is a lattice, then the translates by the vectors of Λ of the contracted body $\frac{1}{2}K$ will form a packing, if, and only if, O is the only point of Λ in K. His first result follows immediately from this observation and the intuitively obvious remark that the density of a packing cannot exceed unity.

Densities of packing and lattice packings of convex bodies

The densities of packings and lattice packings of convex bodies have been extensively studied. The work of Lagrange, Seeber, and Gauss already implies that the densest lattice packings of circular disks in the plane and of spherical balls in 3-space are given by the hexagonal lattice and by the body centred cubic lattice. The densest lattice packings of spherical balls were determined by the Russian mathematicians Aleksandr Nikolayevich Korkin and Zolotarev in 1872 and 1877 for dimensions 4 and 5 and by the mathematician Blichfeldt in 1925, 1926, and 1934 for dimensions 6, 7, and 8. Although the densest lattice packings of spherical balls are not known in higher dimensions, some quite dense examples are known. In particular, the Canadian mathematician Harold Scott MacDonald Coxeter (1951) gives a dense packing of spherical balls in 12 dimensions and the U.S. mathematician Joseph Leech (1967) one in 24 dimensions. The mathematician Conway's study (1969) of the remarkable symmetry group of Leech's packing lattice led him to the discovery of three new large simple groups. Much less is known about general packings that are not necessarily lattice packings. The mathematician L. Fejes Tôth has developed a beautiful and almost completely satisfactory theory of the packing of convex domains in the plane. Very little is known, however, even in 3-space, in which mathematicians have been unable to show that the density of a non-lattice packing of spherical balls cannot exceed the density $0.7404\cdots$ of the densest lattice pack-

$$(186) \qquad \lambda_1 \lambda_2 \cdots \lambda_n V(K) \leq 2^n d(\Lambda)$$

$$(187) \qquad \begin{cases} \Delta(S) \leq \dfrac{1}{2\zeta(n)} V(S) \\ \text{with} \\ \zeta(n) = \displaystyle\sum_{r=1}^{\infty} \dfrac{1}{r^n} \end{cases}$$

$$(188) \qquad \frac{n+2}{2}\left(\frac{1}{\sqrt{2}}\right)^n$$

$$(189) \qquad \tau_n \sim \frac{n}{e\sqrt{e}}, \quad \text{as } n \to \infty$$

$$(190) \qquad n \log n + n \log \log n + 5n$$

$$(191) \qquad n^{\log_2 \log_e n + c}$$

ing, despite convincing physical evidence that this must be true. Blichfeldt in 1914 showed that in n-dimensions the density of a packing of spherical balls cannot exceed the bound composed of the product of one-half the quantity $n + 2$ multiplied by the nth power of the reciprocal of the square root of 2 (see 188), a bound that has only been very slightly improved since by the mathematician Rogers (1958). A very elementary argument shows that spheres, or indeed any symmetrical convex bodies, can be packed with density at least $(1/2)^n$, and this lower bound for the density has only been slightly improved by the mathematician Schmidt (1963). The factor of ignorance between the upper and lower bounds for the density of the densest packing, or lattice packing, of spherical balls remains essentially of the order $(\sqrt{2})^n$.

There is a parallel theory of coverings and lattice coverings of space with convex bodies. The condition that no two translates have any common point is dropped and replaced by the condition that each point of space is in at least one of the translates. The density of a covering is now the average number of times a point of space is covered by the system of translates. The thinnest, or least dense, lattice covering of n-dimensional space by spherical balls has been determined for $n = 2$ by the mathematician Kerschner (1939), for $n = 3$ by the mathematician Bambah (1954), and for $n = 4$ by the mathematicians Delauney and Rushkov (1963). Tôth has solved the general covering problem for symmetrical convex plane domains; but again there are virtually no precise results for general coverings in three or more dimensions. Coxeter, Few, and Rogers (1959) have shown that coverings of n-dimensional space by spherical balls must have density that is at least a certain bound τ_n; τ_n becomes asymptotically equal to a constant times n, as n approaches infinity, the constant being the reciprocal of the product of e and the square root of e (see 189). Rogers (1957, 1959) has shown that, for any convex body K, in n-dimensional space, there is a covering with K with density not greater than an expression composed of n times the logarithm of n and the logarithm of the logarithm of n (see 190) and that there is a lattice covering with K with density not greater than an expression involving n raised to a power, the log to the base two of the natural logarithm of n (see 191). Rogers' results, however, are nonconstructive, and there is no effective method of finding coverings with densities that are at all reasonably small.

Lattice coverings

The results about lattice packings of spherical balls can all be translated to yield results about the arithmetical minima of positive definite quadratic forms. The n linear forms are considered, each ξ_i being a linear combination of n variables such as x_j (see 192) with determinant having absolute value written Δ and being composed of coefficients $\alpha_{i,j}$ (see 193). For each n, there will be a least positive number γ_n such that the inequality, the sum of the squares of the $\{\xi_k\}$ being less than or equal to γ_n times a power of Δ (see 194), always has a solution in integers $x_1, x_2, \ldots, x_n$, not all zero. This constant γ_n was discussed by Hermite (1850) and is sometimes known as Hermite's constant. By the results quoted for the closest lattice packings of spherical balls, its precise value is known up to $n = 8$; for large values of n, it lies between the asymptotic bounds $n/(2\pi e)$ and $n/(\pi e)$. Many results of geometric number theory can be stated in terms of such inequalities. An early result of the Russian mathematician

(192)	$\xi_i = \sum_{j=1}^{n} \alpha_{ij} x_j$
(193)	$\Delta = \|\det(\alpha_{ij})\|$
(194)	$\xi_1^2 + \xi_2^2 + \cdots + \xi_n^2 \leqslant \gamma_n \Delta^{2/n}$
(195)	$\|\xi_1 \xi_2\| \leqslant \frac{1}{3}\Delta$
(196)	$\begin{cases} \|\xi_1 \xi_2 \xi_3\| & \text{Davenport (1939) has also discussed the} \\ \text{form } \|\xi_1\|(\xi_2^2 + \xi_3^2) \text{ and Oppenheim (1929, 1931) the} \\ \text{forms } \|\xi_1^2 + \xi_2^2 - \xi_3^2 - \xi_4^2\| \text{ and } \|\xi_1^2 - \xi_2^2 - \xi_3^2 - \xi_4^2\|. \end{cases}$
(197)	$\|\xi_1^2 - \xi_2^2 \pm \xi_3^2 \pm \xi_4^2 \pm \xi_5^2\| < \varepsilon \Delta^{\frac{2}{5}}$
(198)	$\Delta(K \cap (2\mathbf{a} - K)) \leqslant d(\Lambda)$
(199)	$\xi_i = \sum_{j=1}^{n} \alpha_{ij} x_j, \qquad i = 1, 2, \cdots, n$
(200)	$\Delta = \det(\alpha_{ij})$
(201)	$\|(\xi_1 + c_1)(\xi_2 + c_2) \cdots (\xi_n + c_n)\| \leqslant (\frac{1}{2})^n \|\Delta\|$
(202)	$\|(\xi_1 + c_1)(\xi_2 + c_2)\| < \frac{1}{128} \|\Delta\|$

Andrey Andreyevich Markov (1878) asserts that integers x_1, x_2, not both zero, can be found to satisfy the absolute value of the product of ξ_1 and ξ_2 being less than or equal to one-third of Δ (see 195), unless the ratios $\alpha_{11}/\alpha_{12}, \alpha_{21}/\alpha_{22}$ belong to a countable sequence of pairs of conjugate quadratic irrationals, and that in these cases only slightly weaker inequalities hold. Similar results, involving only a finite sequence of exceptions, have been obtained by Markov (1903) and by the mathematician Venkov (1945) for the quadratic form $\|\xi_1^2 - \xi_2^2 - \xi_3^2\|$ and by Davenport (1938, 1943) and Swinnerton-Dyer (1971) for the product of three linear forms (see 196). It is conjectured that for any $\varepsilon > 0$, it is always possible, for each choice of the $+$ and $-$ signs, to find integers x_1, x_2, x_3, x_4, x_5, not all zero, to satisfy the absolute value of certain sums and differences of squares of ξ_k being less than ε times a power of Δ (see 197), but this conjecture seems to be far beyond the reach of known methods. The best result in this direction is due to combined work of the mathematicians Bryan John Birch (English), Harold Davenport, and Ridout (1958) and asserts the corresponding result for indefinite quadratic forms in 21 or more variables.

Nonhomogeneous forms

The examples discussed so far all involve homogeneous forms. When lattice covering problems are expressed in terms of the theory of forms, they involve nonhomogeneous forms. There are a number of further results in geometric number theory that are of this nonhomogeneous nature. One of the few general results of the subject is the remarkable result of the mathematician Macbeath (1952) that: if a closed convex set K in n-dimensional space contains no complete straight line but does contain in its interior a point of a lattice Λ, then there is a point $\mathbf{a}$ of Λ that is reasonably close to the boundary of the convex set K, in that, the volume $V(K \cap (2\mathbf{a} - K))$ of the intersection $K \cap (2\mathbf{a} - K)$ of the convex body K with its

reflection $2\mathbf{a} - K$ in the point $\mathbf{a}$ does not exceed $2^n d(\Lambda)$; indeed, Macbeath proves the stronger inequality involving Δ, K, the vector $\mathbf{a}$, and $d(\Lambda)$ (see 198). A much more special nonhomogeneous problem stems from the work of Minkowski, who proved, in the case $n = 2$, and who conjectured, in general, that: given linear forms establishing ξ_i as a linear combination (see 199) of integral variables $x_1, x_2, \ldots, x_n$ with Δ being the determinant of the coefficients (see 200) and given real numbers $c_1, c_2, \ldots, c_n$, then there are integral choices for the variables that ensure that the absolute value of the product of n factors, each the sum of ξ_i and c_i, is less than or equal to the nth power of $1/2$ times the absolute value of Δ (see 201). The conjecture has been proved by R. Remak (1923) in the case $n = 3$ and by Freeman J. Dyson (1948) in the case $n = 4$. B.F. Skubenko (1973) proved it for $n = 5$. The mathematician N. Tschebotareff (1940), in the general case, proved that weaker inequality with $(1/2)^n |\Delta|$ replaced by $(1/2)^{n/2} |\Delta|$. The problem of deciding whether or not Minkowski's conjecture is true or false remains one of the most challenging problems of the subject. Davenport (1950), in the case $n = 2$, has proved a partial converse to Minkowski's result. He proves that, if the forms ξ_1, ξ_2 are given, then constants c_1, c_2 can be found, namely, the absolute value of products of two sums, each of a ξ_i with a c_i, is less than the reciprocal of 128 times the absolute value of Δ (see 202), has no solution in integers x_1, x_2. This enabled Chatland and Davenport (1950) to show that Euclid's algorithm holds in no real quadratic field beyond the last known example (that generated by $\sqrt{73}$). A little later Davenport (1950), by a refinement of his method, showed that Euclid's algorithm holds only a finite number of cubic fields with negative discriminant, and only in a finite number of complex quartic fields with complex conjugate fields.

The German-born mathematician Kurt Mahler has investigated the problems of geometric number theory from a general point of view. The formal definitions of critical determinant and critical lattice are his. By regarding the lattices in n-dimensional space as points of a larger space of n^2 dimensions and establishing the compactness of certain sets of lattices, Mahler (1946) was able to show that every star-body with finite critical determinant has at least one critical lattice. This general result at once enabled many difficult special results to be proved by rather simpler methods. Mahler's work also led to a much clearer understanding of the circumstances under which one can assert that infinitely many points of a lattice lie in a star-body. In the case of a convex body, symmetrical in O, Swinnerton-Dyer (1953) established the useful result that a critical lattice must have at least $n(n + 1)$ points on the boundary of the convex body.

Critical determinants and critical lattices

The classical applications of geometric number theory were mainly to the theory of algebraic numbers and included Dirichlet's theory of units and Minkowski's proof that the absolute value of the discriminant of an algebraic number field exceeds unity. Davenport's contribution to the problem of Euclid's algorithm has already been mentioned. Two striking applications are now mentioned. Davenport, partly in collaboration with Birch and Donald J. Lewis (U.S.), has used results of John William Scott Cassels (English) and Minkowski's successive minima results together with an extension of the Hardy–Littlewood–Vinogradov method to obtain striking new results about the values taken by quadratic and cubic forms with sufficiently many variables.

Schmidt (1971) has used results derived by Mahler on the geometric number theory of compound convex bodies, together with a method introduced by the English number theorist Klaus Friedrich Roth, to prove that if $\theta_1, \theta_2, \cdots, \theta_n$ are algebraic numbers and $1, \theta_1, \theta_2, \cdots, \theta_n$ are linearly independent over the rationals and ε is positive, then there is a constant k, depending only on n and ε, such that the inequalities composed by setting the absolute difference between θ_i and the ratio h_i to q less than an expression involving k, q, n, and ε (see 203) have only finitely many solutions in integers $h_1, h_2, \cdots, h_n, q$. The case $n = 1$ is an important theorem proved by Roth in 1955.

(C.A.Ro.)

$$(203) \qquad \left|\theta_i - \frac{h_i}{q}\right| < \frac{k}{q^{1+(1/n)+\varepsilon}}, \qquad i = 1, 2, \cdots, n$$

(204)

n	r(n)	n	r(n)	n	r(n)	n	r(n)	n	r(n)
1	0	8	1	15	2	22	2	29	1
2	1	9	1	16	1	23	1	30	3
3	1	10	2	17	1	24	2	31	1
4	1	11	1	18	2	25	1	32	1
5	1	12	2	19	1	26	2	33	2
6	2	13	1	20	2	27	1	34	2
7	1	14	2	21	2	28	2	35	2

$$(205) \qquad \frac{r(1) + r(2) + \cdots + r(N)}{N}$$

$$(206) \qquad \frac{r(1) + r(2) + \cdots + r(N)}{N} \approx \log \log N$$

(207)

Value	Frequency	Proportional Frequency
0	1	.01
1	35	.35
2	56	.56
3	8	.08

$$(208) \qquad \frac{r(n) - \log \log N}{\sqrt{\log \log N}}$$

PROBABILISTIC NUMBER THEORY

The theory of probability, conceived originally in connection with gambling, provides an insight into some remarkable multiplicative properties of the integers—properties that in the absence of probability theory would remain undiscovered or at best inexplicable. Probability illuminates aspects of arithmetic because certain divisibility phenomena reflect the probabilistic idea of independence.

The number of prime divisors. According to the fundamental theorem of arithmetic, each positive integer can be factored in just one way into a product of primes. From the multiplicative point of view then, an integer is built up of primes, and it is natural to ask how many of them it contains. Probability is useful here.

The number $r(n)$ is taken to be the number of distinct primes appearing in the factorization of n. For example, $r(12) = 2$ because $12 = 2 \cdot 2 \cdot 3$ contains the two prime divisors 2 and 3 (the divisor 2 is counted only once, even though it appears twice in the factorization). It is simple to list the values of $r(n)$ for, say, the first 35 values of n (see 204). The case $n = 1$ is special because 1 is not counted as a prime, $r(1) = 0$, whereas $r(n)$ is a positive integer in all other cases.

The number $r(n)$ grows very slowly. The smallest integer containing two distinct prime factors is $6 = 2 \cdot 3$; the smallest containing three of them is $30 = 2 \cdot 3 \cdot 5$; the smallest containing four is $210 = 2 \cdot 3 \cdot 5 \cdot 7$. On the other hand, the fact that there is an infinite number of primes implies that $r(n)$ takes on arbitrarily large values: $r(n) = k$ if n is the product of k distinct primes, and, however large k may be, there do exist k distinct primes. The same fact implies that $r(n)$ takes on the value 1 infinitely often: $r(n) = 1$ if n is a prime. As n increases $r(n)$ thus fluctuates irregularly.

In view of this irregularity, it is of mathematical interest to see how $r(n)$ behaves on the average and how its values are distributed. It is supposed that n varies from 1 through N, in which N is a large integer, and the average (see 205) of $r(n)$ over this range is considered. If $N = 100$, this av-

erage is 1.71: the typical integer under 100 has rather less than two prime divisors. If $N = 100,000,000$, the average is not much greater, being approximately 2.9: the typical integer under 100,000,000 has just under three prime divisors—remarkably few. Even for $N = 10^{100}$, sometimes called a googol, the average is only about 5.4. Still, the average does go to infinity with N—but very slowly indeed: if N is the 10^{100}-th power of 10, a considerable number called a googolplex, the average is around 231. Except for the case $N = 100$, these figures come from an approximation specifying that the arithmetic average of N values of r is asymptotically equal to the natural logarithm of the natural logarithm of N (see 206).

A more detailed description of the way in which the number of prime factors varies is provided by the complete distribution of the values of $r(n)$ as n runs from 1 to N. A sorting of all the cases for $N = 100$ gives the distribution (see 207). That is, of the integers up to 100, 35 contain exactly one prime factor, 56 contain two, and 8 contain three, the corresponding proportions thus being .35, .56, and .08 in a table relating integer values from zero to three (inclusive) with frequency and with proportional frequency (see 207).

The high frequencies are near the average, and they taper off on either side of this central value. The problem probability helps solve is that of describing this distribution in more detail—for large values of N, for which an actual counting out of cases would be impossible. The probabilistic analysis that follows reveals the striking fact that this distribution, when converted to the proper scale, approximately follows the normal law of errors; that is, the proportion of integers n—in the range $1 \le n \le N$—for which $r(n)$, properly scaled, lies between specified limits will be approximately the area between those limits under the standard normal density—the famous bellshaped curve that describes the distribution of various quantities (see PROBABILITY THEORY).

The appropriate scale is a ratio composed of $r(n)$ and the negative value of and the square root of the logarithm of the logarithm of N (see 208); the centre $\log \log N$ of the scale comes from the approximation (see 206) for the average value of $r(n)$, and the division by $\sqrt{\log \log N}$ properly counteracts the ever-increasing dispersion about this central value. The proportion of integers up to N for

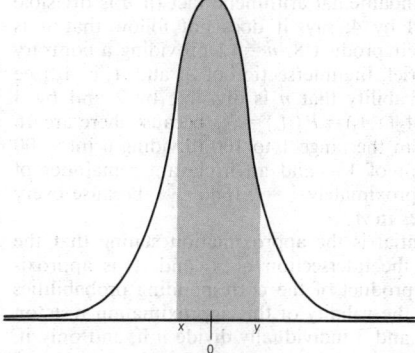

Figure 1: The normal distribution curve, showing two real values x and y and the corresponding shaded area beneath the curve that gives a proportion or a probability (see text).

which this ratio (see 208) lies between x and y is for large N approximately the area of the shaded region in Figure 1. For example, if $x = -.2$ and $y = +1.2$, this area is about .46. If N is a googol, so that $\log \log N \approx 5.4$, then the stated ratio lies between these two limits if $r(n)$ itself lies between 5 and 8. If N is a googolplex, so that $\log \log N \approx 231$, the ratio is in this range if $r(n)$ is between 228 and 249. Thus something like half the integers under a googol have 5 to 8 prime divisors, and something like half the integers under a googolplex have 228 to 249 prime divisors.

Independence. The right-hand column of the table constructed with the values 0, 1, 2, 3 and corresponding frequencies 1, 35, 56, 8 (see 207) can be viewed as a set of probabilities. If an integer is drawn at random from among the integers 1, 2, 3, · · · , 99, 100, each having probability $^1/_{100}$ of being drawn, then there is probability .56 that it has exactly two prime divisors. Probability theory applies, leading to the distribution law just described, not merely because proportional frequencies can be viewed as probabilities, but because it is possible to bring to bear one of the basic ideas of probability, that of independence.

If Peter throws a pair of balanced dice, there is probability $\frac{6}{36} = \frac{1}{6}$ that the total number of dots showing is seven. If Paul throws a pair, there is probability $\frac{4}{36} = \frac{1}{9}$ that his total is five. The probability that Peter throws a seven *and* that Paul throws a five is the product $\frac{1}{6} \cdot \frac{1}{9} = \frac{1}{54}$, and this is because the two events in question are independent.

Definition of independence

Mathematically, two events are independent if their probabilities satisfy this product rule, and the definition reflects a phenomenon common in nature: the occurrence of the one event has no influence on the occurrence of the other.

To see how independence ties in with the behaviour of $r(n)$, the set of multiples of k is considered for each integer k. If this set is denoted A_k, A_2 consists of even integers, A_3 consists of those divisible by 3, and so on. Of these sets (see 209), in which the subscript ranges over the primes, some contain a given integer n and some do not, and $r(n)$ is precisely the number of sets in the list (209) that do contain n. To ask after the statistical behaviour of $r(n)$ is to ask for the probability that $r(n)$ takes on a specified value, say 4, and this is to ask for the probability that n lies in exactly 4 of the sets in the list (209). This probability can in principle be computed and can in fact be understood via the probabilities that n lies in A_2, in A_3, in A_2 and A_3 simultaneously, in A_2 and A_5 and A_{11} simultaneously, and so on for all combinations.

If n is drawn at random from among 1, 2, 3, · · · , 99, 100, the probability that it lies in A_2 is $P(A_2) = \frac{50}{100} = \frac{1}{2}$, because there are 50 even integers up to 100. The probability that n lies in A_3 is $P(A_3) = \frac{33}{100}$ because there are 33 multiples of 3 up to 100. That $P(A_3)$ is approximately $\frac{1}{3}$ reflects the fact that every third integer is a multiple of 3; that $P(A_3)$ is not exactly $\frac{1}{3}$ is due to the fact that 3 does not divide evenly into 100.

Now n lies in the set $A_2 \cap A_3$ (the intersection of A_2 and A_3); that is to say, n lies both in A_2 and in A_3, when it is divisible both by 2 and by 3. And n is divisible both by 2 and by 3 exactly when it is divisible by their product 6; this is so because 2 and 3 have no common factor, and it represents a fundamental arithmetic fact (if n is divisible both by 2 and by 4, say, it does not follow that it is divisible by their product 8, $n = 12$ providing a contrary instance). In brief, the intersection of A_2 and A_3 is A_6 (see 210). The probability that n is divisible by 2 and by 3 is therefore $P(A_2 \cap A_3) = P(A_6) = \frac{16}{100}$, because there are 16 multiples of 6 in the range 1 to 100 (dividing 6 into 100 gives a quotient of 16—and an irrelevant remainder of 4); $P(A_6)$ is approximately $\frac{1}{6} = 0.1666 \cdots$ because every sixth integer lies in A_6.

What is essential is the approximation stating that the probability of the intersection of A_2 and A_3 is approximated by the product of the corresponding probabilities (see 211), and the validity of this approximation rests on the fact that 2 and 3 individually divide n if, and only if, their product 6 does, together with the fact that A_2, A_3, and A_6 have respective probabilities approximately $\frac{1}{2}$, $\frac{1}{3}$, and $\frac{1}{6}$. Now this approximation (see 211) can advantageously be viewed as asserting the approximate independence of two events: An integer is drawn at random between 1 and 100; the event that it is divisible by 2 is approximately independent of the event that it is divisible by 3.

The rest of the events in the list (209)—divisibility by 5, divisibility by 7, and so on—are also approximately independent of one another if n is chosen at random between 1 and a large integer N. This is the key idea of probabilistic number theory. Now $r(n)$, the quantity of interest, is the number among these events that actually occur, and it is just this kind of random quantity (mainly for cases in which the events in question are strictly independent) that has received much attention in the classical literature of probability. Under appropriate conditions, such a number of occurrences will, when measured on the proper scale, approximately follow the normal distribution curve, and

this is true of $r(n)$ rescaled as above (see 208). This theorem (it becomes a precise mathematical theorem, a form of the central limit theorem, when stated in terms of limits [see 216]) is plausible on probability grounds and can be given a rigorous proof by means of a proper combination of probability theory and number theory—there are difficulties, owing to the fact that the events in the list (209) are only approximately independent.

The Euler φ-function. A different application of probabilistic reasoning explains some properties of Euler's function, the number $\varphi(n)$ of integers less than or equal to n and relatively prime to n (that is, having no factors in common with n). The integers not exceeding 6 and relatively prime to 6 are 1 and 5, so that $\varphi(6) = 2$. The concern here is with $\varphi(n)/n$, the proportion of integers up to n that share no factors with it. It has a convenient expression as a product of factors of the form 1 minus the reciprocal of p (see 212).

Euler's function

The right side of this equation stands for the product of the factors $(1 - 1/p)$ for all primes p that divide n; if $n = 6$, for example, it is $(1 - \frac{1}{2})(1 - \frac{1}{3})$, which checks with $\varphi(6)/6 = 2/6$.

As before, n is chosen at random between 1 and N. If 3 divides n, it contributes to the product (see 212) the factor $(1 - \frac{1}{3})$; as indicated before, the probability of this is about $\frac{1}{3}$ for large N. If 3 does not divide n, then $(1 - \frac{1}{3})$ does not appear in the product (see 212), and in this case 3 may conveniently be regarded as contributing to the product the factor 1; the probability of this is about $\frac{2}{3}$. So the expected value of the factor contributed by 3, the amount 3 contributes on the average, is about 1 minus the reciprocal of 3 squared (see 213). The product of this and the analogous expected values for the other primes is an infinite product of factors of the type 1 minus the reciprocal of a prime squared (see 214), an infinite product known to have value $6/\pi^2$.

Now the expected value of a product of independent random factors is the product of their individual expected values; the random factors here are approximately independent (see 211). This is indeed true in the limit: the arithmetic average of N terms of the type $\varphi(k)$ divided by k converges to 6 over the square of π (see 215).

If m is chosen at random between 1 and n, the chance that it is relatively prime to n is $\varphi(n)/n$. And if n is chosen at random between 1 and N, and then m is chosen at random between 1 and n, the chance that m and n are relatively prime is the average referred to above (see 215). Because m and n play symmetric roles in this argument, it follows that, if m and n are chosen independently and randomly between 1 and N, the probability that they are relatively prime is near $6/\pi^2$ for large N.

In addition to its expected value, it is possible to describe

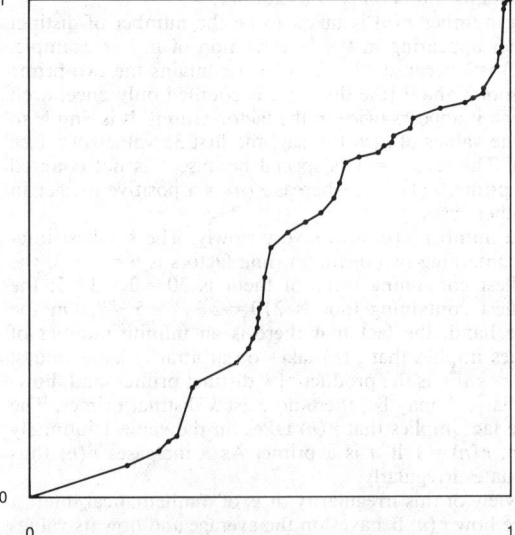

Figure 2: Probability distribution, such that the height of the curve over a given point x on the horizontal axis gives the proportion of n for which $\varphi(n)/n \leq x$.

the distribution of $\varphi(n)/n$. Figure 2 gives this distribution for $N = 100$. The height of the curve over a given point x on the horizontal scale gives the proportion of n, $1 \le n \le 100$, for which $\varphi(n)/n \le x$. (The distribution actually gives discrete points, linked in the diagram by line segments.) The curve is seen to be irregular, rising slowly over most of its range but very sharply in some places. A probabilistic analysis shows that the corresponding curve for general N tends, as N increases to infinity, toward a limiting curve that is very irregular indeed. The limiting curve has horizontal tangent at almost all (in the technical sense of measure theory) of its points, so that its rate of increase is zero almost everywhere, but it nonetheless contrives to climb continuously from 0 to 1 over its course (it represents what is called a singular function).

The theorems. The exact theorem governing the behaviour is of the above ratio (208) that identifies the limit of $P_N(A)$ as N approaches infinity as the integral of the normal density and in which $P_N(A)$ for a set A of integers is $1/N$ times the number of integers n that satisfy $1 \le n \le N$ and at the same time lie in A [P_{100} was denoted P above; in (216) $\{n : \cdots\}$ denotes the set of integers satisfying the condition following the colon].

It should be noted that the number of multiples of k up to N is $[N/k]$, the integer part of N/k, so that $P_N(A_k)$ is approximately the reciprocal of k (see 217), the approximation being valid for large N because the two quantities in question differ by less than $1/N$. It is a consequence of the fundamental theorem of arithmetic that distinct primes p and q each divide n if and only if their product does. Therefore, $A_p \cap A_q = A_{pq}$ and P_N of the intersection of A_p and A_q is approximately a product of two factors, one involving A_p and one involving A_q (see 218). If $\delta_p(n)$ is 1 if the prime p divides n, and 0 otherwise, then r as a function of n is the sum over primes of $\delta_p(n)$ (see 219). The approximation (218) shows that the summands here are approximately independent random variables if n is random, $n \le N$. The expected value of $r(n)$ is a sum of values of P_N that has two approximations (see 220), in which the first approximation comes from the chain of reasoning summarized above and the second is a basic fact of number theory (the combined error is bounded, so the percentage error goes to 0). The variance of $r(n)$ is essentially what it would be if the summands were truly independent, and this turns out to be asymptotically $\log \log N$ as well. The normalizing constants (see 216) are thus the asymptotic mean and standard deviation of the sum (see 219) and the summands behave sufficiently like independent random variables that the central limit theorem (see 216) does hold. This was first proved by sieve methods; simpler proofs based on the method of moments have since been found.

Error estimates for the central limit theorem (216) have been found; these coincide with the estimates for independent random variables.

It is a consequence of the central limit theorem that, if x_N goes to infinity faster than $\sqrt{\log \log n}$, then the limit, as N approaches infinity, of P_N is 1 when applied to the set of integers n for which the absolute difference between $r(n)$ and the $\log \log N$ is less than x_N (see 221). This stands to the previous result as the law of large numbers stands to the central limit theorem. From this limit (221) it follows that, for most values of n under N, $r(n)$ is near $\log \log N$; the central limit theorem (216) gives very detailed information about how $r(n)$ is distributed around this central value.

Additive functions

A function $f(n)$ of integers is called additive if $f(mn) = f(m) + f(n)$ whenever m and n are relatively prime, and it is called completely additive if, in addition, $f(p^\alpha) = f(p)$ for prime powers p^α. If f is completely additive, then it can be written as a sum over primes of products $f(p)\delta_p(n)$ (see 222), a special case of which was previously given (see 219)—$r(n)$ is completely additive with $r(p) = 1$. The summands (see 222) being approximately independent, as in the case of $r(n)$, it is possible to establish for completely additive functions a general central limit theorem, similar to the one that was already stated (see 216), under conditions that parallel those of the classical Lindeberg theorem. It is even possible to treat the

$$(209) \quad A_2, A_3, A_5, A_7, A_{11}, \cdots,$$

$$(210) \quad A_2 \cap A_3 = A_6$$

$$(211) \quad P(A_2 \cap A_3) = .16 \approx P(A_2) \cdot P(A_3) = .165$$

$$(212) \quad \frac{\varphi(n)}{n} = \prod_{p|n} \left(1 - \frac{1}{p}\right)$$

$$(213) \quad \frac{1}{3} \cdot \left(1 - \frac{1}{3}\right) + \frac{2}{3} \cdot 1 = 1 - \frac{1}{3^2}$$

$$(214) \quad \left(1 - \frac{1}{2^2}\right)\left(1 - \frac{1}{3^2}\right)\left(1 - \frac{1}{5^2}\right) \cdots$$

$$(215) \quad \frac{1}{N}\left(\frac{\varphi(1)}{1} + \frac{\varphi(2)}{2} + \cdots + \frac{\varphi(N)}{N}\right) \to \frac{6}{\pi^2}$$

$$(216) \quad \lim_{N \to \infty} P_N\left\{n : x \le \frac{r(n) - \log \log N}{\sqrt{\log \log N}} \le y\right\}$$
$$= \frac{1}{\sqrt{2\pi}} \int_x^y e^{-\frac{1}{2}u^2} \, du$$

$$(217) \quad P_N(A_k) = \frac{1}{N}\left[\frac{N}{k}\right] \approx \frac{1}{k}$$

$$(218) \quad P_N(A_p \cap A_q) = \frac{1}{N}\left[\frac{N}{pq}\right] \approx \frac{1}{pq} \approx \frac{1}{N}\left[\frac{N}{p}\right] \cdot \frac{1}{N}\left[\frac{N}{q}\right]$$
$$= P_N(A_p) \cdot P_N(A_q)$$

$$(219) \quad r(n) = \sum_p \delta_p(n)$$

$$(220) \quad \sum_p P_N(A_p) = \sum_{p \le N} \frac{1}{N}\left[\frac{N}{p}\right] \approx \sum_{p \le N} \frac{1}{p} \approx \log \log N$$

$$(221) \quad \lim_{N \to \infty} P_N\{n : |r(n) - \log \log N| < x_N\} = 1$$

$$(222) \quad f(n) = \sum_p f(p) \delta_p(n)$$

case in which the limiting normal distribution is replaced by a more general infinitely divisible distribution.

Similar results hold if $f(n)$ is additive but not completely additive. An example of such a function is the number of prime divisors of n with multiplicity counted, so that $f(12) = 3$ because 2 appears twice in the factorization $12 = 2 \cdot 2 \cdot 3$ and 3 appears once. The central limit theorem (216) is unaltered if $r(n)$ is replaced by this function.

The central limit theorem and the law of large numbers are represented in probabilistic number theory by the above limits (216) and (221) and their generalizations. There are also representatives of certain probability theorems that concern the convergence of random series, and the limit theorem for $\varphi(n)/n$ is one of these.

Convergence of random series

The logarithm of the ratio of $\varphi(n)$ to n is a sum over primes of products involving $\delta_p(n)$ and a logarithmic function (see 223), and this is a completely additive function. The $\delta_p(n)$ behave very much as do independent random variables that assume the values 1 and 0 with probabilities p^{-1} and $1 - p^{-1}$. If the $\delta_p(n)$ were exactly like such variables, it would follow from probability theory that, since $\sum_p p^{-1} \log(1 - p^{-1})$ converges, the series (see 223) converges with probability 1; moreover, the distribution function $F(x)$ of the total sum could be identified as the one having as characteristic function (Fourier transform; see 224) the product of the characteristic functions of the various summands. As N increases, the $\delta_p(n)$ mimic ever more closely the independent variables, and in the limit

(223) does have the distribution function $F(x)$ just derived (see 225). Results on random series imply $F(x)$ is a singular function; the curves corresponding to the one in Figure 2 converge to $F(\log x)$, which must also be singular.

A generalization of this result covers a broad class of completely additive functions for which the series $\Sigma_p \mid f(p) \mid /$

$$(223) \qquad \log \frac{\varphi(n)}{n} = \sum_p \delta_p(n) \log\left(1 - \frac{1}{p}\right)$$

$$(224) \qquad \int_{-\infty}^{\infty} e^{itx}\, dF(x) = \prod_p \left\{1 - \frac{1}{p} + \frac{1}{p} \exp\left[it \log\left(1 - \frac{1}{p}\right)\right]\right\}$$

$$(225) \qquad \lim_{N \to \infty} P_N\left\{n: \log \frac{\varphi(n)}{n} \le x\right\} = F(x)$$

$$(226) \qquad \lim_{N \to \infty} P_N\left\{n: \log \frac{\sigma(n)}{n} \le x\right\} = G(x)$$

$$(227) \qquad D\left\{n: \log \frac{\sigma(n)}{n} \le x\right\} = G(x)$$

p and $\Sigma_p \mid f(p) \mid ^2/p$ converge (if these diverge, as for $r(n)$, central limit theory applies instead). It is possible also to treat functions that are only additive (not completely additive), such as $\log \{\sigma(n)/n\}$, in which $\sigma(n)$ is the sum of all the divisors (prime or not) of n. In this case, as N increases, the distribution function converges to a function $G(x)$ whose characteristic function can be identified (see 226).

All these results can be restated in terms of density. A set A of integers has density d if $\lim_N P_N(A) = d$, which is expressed by $D(A) = d$. The limit relation that was just derived can be restated in terms of D (see 227). The distribution function $G(x)$ is continuous for all x, as follows from an analysis of its characteristic function, which is interesting because it shows that the set of deficient numbers (those satisfying $\sigma(n) < n$) and the set of abundant numbers (those satisfying $\sigma(n) > n$) have densities and that the set of perfect numbers (those satisfying $\sigma(n) = 2n$) has density 0 (it is conjectured that the last set is finite).

Except for one (see 215), all the results here were discovered in the present century. Hardy and Ramanujan proved the law of large numbers (see 221) in 1920 by nonprobabilistic methods, and Paul Turán in 1934 gave it a probabilistic proof. The mathematicians Paul Erdös (Hungarian) and Mark Kac (U.S.) proved the central limit theorem in 1939, extensions and refinements of which as well as other results (see 226) are associated with the names Davenport, Delange, H. Halberstam, J. Kubilius, I.J. Schoenberg, and A. Wintner.

(P.P.B.)

BIBLIOGRAPHY. The following works are concerned with elementary topics: HAROLD T. DAVIS (comp.), *Tables of the Higher Mathematical Functions*, vol. 2 (1935, reprinted 1963), contains extensive tabular and bibliographical material on Bernoulli numbers. Additional references on Bernoulli numbers include: H.S. VANDIVER, "An Arithmetical Theory of the Bernoulli Numbers," *Am. Math. Soc. Transl.*, 51:502–531 (1942); JAMES V. USPENSKY and MAXWELL A. HEASLET, *Elementary Number Theory*, ch. 9 (1939); ALAN FLETCHER, J.C.P. MILLER, and LOUIS ROSENHEAD, *An Index of Mathematical Tables*, pp. 40–80 (1946); and H.S. VANDIVER, "On Developments in an Arithmetic Theory of the Bernoulli and Allied Numbers," *Scr. Math.*, 25:273–303 (1961). For information on Fermat's last theorem, see LOUIS J. MORDELL, *Three Lectures on Fermat's Last Theorem* (1921); H.S. VANDIVER and G.E. WAHLIN, "Report of the Committee on Algebraic Numbers," *Bull. Natn. Res. Coun., Wash.*, no. 62, ch. 2 (1928); and H.S. VANDIVER, "Fermat's Last Theorem: Its History and the Nature of the Known Results Concerning It," *Am. Math. Mon.*, 53:555–578 (1946). Several treatises on algebra have chapters on the arithmetic theory of continued fractions. HUBERT S. WALL, *Analytic Theory of Continued Fractions* (1948, reprinted 1967), deals with questions of convergence and the function-theoretic aspects of continued fractions. The paper of J.S. MACNERNEY, "Investigation Concerning Positive Definite Continued Fractions," *Duke Math. J.*, 26:663–677 (1959), deals with continued fractions whose partial numerators and denominators are matrixes. See also IVAN M. NIVEN and H.S. ZUCKERMAN, *An Introduction to the Theory of Numbers* (1980).

The reader interested in algebraic number theory may wish to consult some of these works: DAVID HILBERT, *Die Theorie der algebräischen Zahlkörper* (*Jahresbericht der deutschen Mathematiker-Vereinigung*, vol. 4, 1897), reprinted in vol. 1 of Hilbert's *Gesammelte Abhandlungen;* this work (the *Zahlbericht*) is not available in English. It contains an extensive bibliography covering the literature up to 1897. The "Report of the Committee on Algebraic Numbers," *Bull. Natn. Res. Coun., Wash.*, no. 28 (1923), and no. 62 (1928), is an updating of the *Zahlbericht*. HARRY POLLARD, *The Theory of Algebraic Numbers* (1950), is a brief, elementary account in classical style. The following take the modern p-adic view: EMIL ARTIN, *Algebraic Numbers and Algebraic Functions* (1967); EDWIN WEISS, *Algebraic Number Theory* (1963); and Z.I. BOREVICH and I.R. SHAFAREVICH, *Number Theory* (1966; original published in Russian, 1964), also contains a good treatment of analytic number theory. The following also incorporate a treatment of class field theory: EMIL ARTIN and JOHN TATE, *Class Field Theory* (1967); J.W.S. CASSELS and ALBRECHT FROHLICH (eds.), *Algebraic Number Theory* (1967); SERGE LANG, *Algebraic Number Theory* (1970). ANDRE WEIL, *Basic Number Theory* (1967), also includes class field theory as well as some material on analytic number theory.

The following works are especially useful as references on analytic number theory. SARVADAMAN CHOWLA, *The Riemann Hypothesis and Hilbert's Tenth Problem* (1965); HAROLD DAVENPORT, *Multiplicative Number Theory* (1967); HELMUT HASSE, *Vorlesungen über Zahlentheorie*, 2nd rev. ed. (1963); KARL PRACHAR, *Primzahlverteilung* (1957); JEAN-PIERRE SERRE, *Cours d'arithmetique* (1970); CARL L. SIEGEL, *Analytische Zahlentheorie* (1963–64); EDWARD C. TITCHMARSH, *The Theory of the Riemann Zeta-Function* (1951); IVAN M. VINOGRADOV, *The Method of Trigonometrical Sums in the Theory of Numbers* (1954; originally published in Russian, rev. ed., 1953), are recent works, suitable for an introduction to topics in analytic number theory, and are by authors who have contributed significantly to the subject. Other good introductory works include RAYMOND AYOUB, *An Introduction to the Analytic Theory of Numbers* (1963); JOSEPH LEHNER, *A Short Course in Automorphic Functions* (1966); HANS RADEMACHER, *Lectures on Analytic Number Theory* (1954–55); and RICHARD E. BELLMAN, *Analytic Number Theory* (1980).

Some works concerning geometric number theory and related topics are J.W.S. CASSELS, *An Introduction to Diophantine Approximation* (1957) and *An Introduction to the Geometry of Numbers*, 2nd ed. (1971); L. FEJES TOTH, *Lagerungen in der Ebene auf der Kugel und im Raum* (1953) and *Regular Figures* (1964); CORNELIUS G. LEKKERKERKER, *Geometry of Numbers* (1969); HERMANN MINKOWSKI, *Geometrie der Zahlen* (1896, reprinted 1969), *Diophantische Approximationen* (1907, reprinted 1961), and *Gesammelte Abhandlungen*, 2 vol. (1911, reprinted 1967); and CLAUDE A. ROGERS, *Packing and Covering* (1964).

On probabilistic number theory, see GODFREY H. HARDY and EDWARD M. WRIGHT, *An Introduction to the Theory of Numbers*, 4th ed. (1960), an excellent introduction to the theory of numbers, touching incidentally on probabilistic number theory; MARK KAC, *Statistical Independence in Probability, Analysis and Number Theory* (1959), which contains a very readable introduction to probabilistic number theory and is highly recommended; and JONAS KUBILIUS, *Probabilistic Methods in the Theory of Numbers* (1964; Eng. trans. from the 2nd Russian ed., 1962), a full-scale treatment of the subject with a large bibliography.

Some additional references on various aspects of number theory are as follows: LEONARD E. DICKSON, *History of the Theory of Numbers*, 3 vol. (1919–23), a monumental topical history; and *Modern Elementary Theory of Numbers* (1939); H.J.S. SMITH, *Report on the Theory of Numbers* (1859–65, reprinted 1965); GEORGE B. MATHEWS, *Theory of Numbers* (1892); ROBERT D. CARMICHAEL, *The Theory of Numbers* (1914) and *Diophantine Analysis* (1915), reprinted together as *The Theory of Numbers and Diophantine Analysis* (1959); OYSTEIN ORE, *Number Theory and Its History* (1948); BURTON W. JONES, *The Arithmetic Theory of Quadratic Forms* (1950); TRYGVE NAGELL, *Introduction to Number Theory*, 2nd ed. (1964); WILLIAM J. LEVEQUE, *Elementary Theory of Numbers* (1962) and *Topics in Number Theory*, 2 vol. (1956); HAROLD DAVENPORT, *The Higher Arithmetic*, 3rd ed. (1968); HANS RADEMACHER and OTTO TOEPLITZ, *The Enjoyment of Mathematics: Selections from Mathematics for the Amateur* (1957); HANS RADEMACHER, *Lectures on Elementary Number Theory* (1964); ERNST TROST, *Primzahlen* (1953); and THEODOR ESTERMANN, *Introduction to Modern Prime Number Theory* (1952). See also HANSRAJ GUPTA, *Selected Topics in Number Theory* (1980), essays with an analytic approach.

(I.K./R.G.A./C.A.Ro./P.P.B.)

Numerical Analysis

Numerical analysis comprises three related activities: the study of a problem by the computation of numerical values that solve the mathematical equations (called mathematical models) describing the behaviour of some system, the development of methods (called numerical algorithms) for finding those values, and the analysis of the properties of those methods. The mathematical models are developed by professionals in various areas of application, that is, by scientists, engineers, or economists. A numerical analyst is a person who develops or analyzes methods for computing the numerical values.

Mathematical models are the starting point for the numerical analyst. Examples of models include an astronomer's mathematical description of the motion of a planet or a satellite (called its equations of motion), the equations used by a designer to describe the radioactivity in a nuclear reactor and the operation of its control system, the equations hypothesized by a research chemist to describe a chemical reaction, the equations used by government planners to express the relationships between economic and social indicators such as gross national product (GNP), prime rate, and unemployment rate, and the equations used in computer-aided tomography (CAT scans) to construct a view of the interior of a human body from an X-ray scan.

Among the uses of models are the following: prediction of future behaviour—for example, the determination of the future locations of the heavenly bodies (a matter of continuing interest in scientific calculation but of great concern in previous centuries because of its importance to navigation before the development of modern instruments); the selection of the best design—for example, the choice of the lowest cost nuclear reactor that meets the requirements of power output and safety; the comparison of computed values with experimental observations to test the validity of the theory represented by the model or to estimate the values of unknown constants that appear in the model—for example, the research chemist's effort to determine the rate at which materials react by comparing changes in chemical concentrations predicted from model equations with the values measured in the laboratory; and the determination of values that are not directly observable from other values that are—for example, in computer-aided tomography, the use of X-ray observations to provide the average density of a large set of narrow, pencil-shaped sections of the body, which then are used to construct a map of the density of the interior of the body.

Some problems are described by models so simple that they can be manipulated without numerical computation. For example, if a metal rod is subject to a stretching force (the stress, F) and it lengthens a certain amount (the strain, L), the stress-strain relationship might be modeled by the equation $L = \lambda F$, in which λ is a numerical constant. This says that the stretching is linearly proportional to the applied force, so that if the force is doubled, the stretching doubles. A person can understand this relationship and use it to solve problems such as "What force is needed to stretch the rod L millimetres?" in the symbolic or explicit form $F = L/\lambda$, so that it is unnecessary to compute actual values until they are needed in a design task. However, many models are so complex that it is not possible to solve problems explicitly or to understand the relationships expressed by the model. In that case, the model user turns to numerical methods, either to compute specific solutions or to study the behaviour of the model as it is changed.

The goal of numerical analysis is the efficient computation of accurate approximations of the values that satisfy mathematical equations. Two major problems confront the numerical analyst: the round-off errors that unavoidably arise during computation, and the representation of problems involving infinite amounts of information with the finite number of values that a person (or computer) can handle.

For coverage of related topics in the *Macropædia* and *Micropædia*, see the *Propædia*, section 10/23.

This article is divided into the following sections:

ERRORS

Most problems involve infinite sets of values, each of which can potentially require an infinite number of digits for exact representation. Digital computation, either human, mechanical, or electronic, is, by its very nature, finite: it involves a finite set of numerical values, each of which is represented in a finite set of digits. These two approximations of infinite quantities by finite ones lead to the two types of error in numerical computation, round-off and truncation error. A numerical analyst is interested in determining the size of possible errors in a calculation. Analysts try to find bounds on errors or estimates of errors. A bound is a value that the analyst can guarantee the error will not exceed. An estimate is a value that the analyst believes is an approximation of the error (error estimates typically vary from the true error by a factor of 2). The word *error* is unfortunate because it suggests a mistake or sin. Round-off and truncation errors are unavoidable: the

Bounds and estimates of errors

job of the numerical analyst is to find out how to compute accurately and efficiently in their presence.

Finite-precision errors: round-off. The precision of a value is indicated by the number of digits used in its representation. It is typically between seven and 15 decimal digits, depending on the type of computer and calculation. Finite precision means that most values cannot be represented exactly, but that there is some round-off error in the computed approximation. For example, if $4/3$ is represented by five significant decimal digits as 1.3333 (the most accurate possible using five digits), there is a round-off error of $0.0000333\ldots$ or $1/3 \times 10^{-4}$, as illustrated below:

	decimal representation
correct value	1.3333333...
5-digit representation	1.3333
round-off error	0.0000333...

All calculations are subject to the effects of round-off errors. Round-off errors, which are proportional to the size of the value containing the error when a fixed number of significant digits is used, can be as large as 5 in the first neglected place or one-half in the last retained place. When a value is added to a much smaller value, the round-off can be large relative to the smaller value. For example, if 23,456 is added to 10.518 in five digits, the result is 23,467, with a round-off error of −0.482. If 23,456 is subtracted from the answer, the result is 11. Thus, in five-digit arithmetic, (23,456 + 10.518) − 23,456 = 11.0, which has an error in the third place. After the addition, the error was less than one-half in the last place, but the subtraction removed the three leading digits, 234, moving this error to the third place. This phenomenon is called cancellation. It does not cause errors but makes the size of errors already introduced larger relative to the computed result. Thus, although round-off errors are small, their effect in the final answer can be large, so that one of the tasks of the numerical analyst is to devise or modify computational schemes to minimize the effect of these errors.

The effect of a change in the computational scheme is illustrated by a simple example related to an exterior ballistics problem. (Exterior ballistics deals with the trajectory of a projectile after it leaves the barrel of a gun. Much early numerical table building and computing was devoted to this problem, which is related to the orbit problem.) When a projectile is fired from ground level (that is, from an initial height, $h = 0$) and with an initial vertical velocity of v_0, its height, h, after t seconds is $h = tv_0 - t^2 g/2$, where g is the acceleration due to the force of gravity. The projectile will hit a target at height h_0 at a time that satisfies the quadratic equation

$$h_0 = tv_0 - t^2 \frac{g}{2}. \qquad (1)$$

This equation can be rewritten in the form of the standard quadratic equation $ax^2 + bx + c = 0$ whose roots, r, are given by the formula

$$r = \frac{-b \pm \sqrt{b^2 - 4ac}}{2a}.$$

Upon replacing a, b, and c by $g/2$, $-v_0$, and h_0, the roots of (1) are found to be

$$r = \frac{v_0 \pm \sqrt{v_0^2 - 2gh_0}}{g}.$$

For the case $v_0 = 500$, $h_0 = 75$, and $g = 9.82$, the two roots can be computed from

$$r = \frac{500 \pm \sqrt{250,000 - 2 \times 9.82 \times 75}}{9.82}.$$

The value of the quantity under the square root symbol is 248,527. If three-digit arithmetic is used, it becomes 249,000 (trailing zeros do not count as significant digits). The square root of 249,000 is 499 correct to three digits. Hence the two roots are computed as $(500 + 499)/9.82 = 102$ and $(500 - 499)/9.82 = 0.102$ to three digits. The correct solutions to three digits are 102 and 0.150. The 50 percent error in the smaller root occurs because the root is computed by the subtraction of the two nearly equal values 500 and 499. This illustrates the phenomenon of cancellation. Because of three-digit accuracy, each of these two values can be in error by as much as 0.5. In fact, to six digits the second value is 498.525 so that the approximation 499 is in error by 0.475. After subtraction, the computed result of $500 - 499$ is 1.0, instead of 1.475, and is in error in the second place. This large error can be avoided by computing the smaller root with a different version of the formula. It is easy to show (by dividing (1) by t^2 and solving for $1/t$) that the second root is given by

$$r = \frac{2h_0}{v_0 + \sqrt{v_0^2 - 2gh_0}},$$

from which the result, 0.150, can be computed using three-digit arithmetic. In the article "What Is a Satisfactory Quadratic Equation Solver?" George E. Forsythe discusses further the difficulties that can arise even in this simple problem.

The quadratic equation above is a problem whose solutions can be computed accurately if the calculation is organized correctly. Numerical analysis is used to investigate the errors that can arise in such computations. In some problems it is very difficult to compute accurate answers because a slight change in the problem can cause a large change in the answer. Such problems are said to be ill-conditioned. In some types of problems, an arbitrarily small change in the problem can lead to an arbitrarily large change in the answer. Such problems are said to be ill-posed. A properly posed problem is one in which bounded changes to the problem lead to bounded changes in the answer. A well-conditioned problem is one whose answers change only in a small way if the initial problem is changed in a small way. The equation

> **Ill-conditioned and ill-posed problems**

$$(x - 1.1)^4 = 0$$

has the answer $x = 1.1$ by inspection. When the expression on the left-hand side is multiplied out, the equation

$$x^4 - 4.4x^3 + 7.26x^2 - 5.324x + 1.4641 = 0 \qquad (2)$$

is obtained. In this form it is ill-conditioned. If five-digit arithmetic is used, the coefficients in (2) can be represented exactly. On the other hand, if four-digit arithmetic is used, the last coefficient would be represented as 1.464, to get the equation

$$x^4 - 4.4x^3 + 7.26x^2 - 5.324x + 1.464 = 0, \qquad (3)$$

which is the same as

$$x^4 - 4.4x^3 + 7.26x^2 - 5.324x + 1.4641 = 0.0001 = 10^{-4}. \qquad (4)$$

In this particular case, the roots of the changed equation can be computed exactly because it has the form $(x - 1.1)^4 = 10^{-4}$, of which one root is given by $(x - 1.1) = 10^{-1}$ or $x = 1.2$. Thus, a change in the fifth decimal place, or 0.01 percent, in the original problem (2) to get (3) has caused a change in the second place, or 10 percent, in the answer. Because this problem is ill-conditioned, no numerical method can avoid the fact that a slight change to the problem can cause a large change in the answer. Because round-off errors in the early stages of the calculation are indistinguishable from changes in the original problem, such problems are susceptible to large errors in their numerical answers, and a simple error analysis shows these errors.

A direct analysis of the effect of the errors on the answers is called a forward error analysis because it analyzes the effects of the errors as they propagate forward through the steps of the calculation to the final result. A forward analysis leads to the statement "Round-off errors have caused this much error in the answer." As illustrated above, a small round-off can cause a large error in the answer of an ill-conditioned problem. Another useful measure of the computational error is the amount by which the computed answer fails to satisfy the problem. This is called the residual. For example, if the computed answer of 1.2 is substituted into equation (2), the left-hand side is $(1.2 - 1.1)^4 = 10^{-4}$. Although the error in the answer is 0.1, the residual is 10^{-4}. In this example and in many others, the size of the residual can be estimated by a backward error analysis. This leads to the statement "Round-off errors can change the answers so that they are the exact answers of a problem that is different from the original problem by this much." A backward error analysis applied to a good method for the problem discussed above might show that the method solved a problem whose coefficients were within 0.01 percent of those in (2), so that (3) could have been the problem solved. Although the answers to the changed problem may be very different from those of the original, they are as good as can be expected from an ill-conditioned problem. A good method is one that has small backward errors or residuals: for a well-conditioned problem, such a method always gives accurate answers because, by definition, in a well-conditioned problem the answer changes by only a small amount when the problem changes by a small amount.

> **Forward and backward error analysis**

Finite-dimension errors: truncation. The types of problems discussed in the previous section are finite dimensional because only a finite number of values are involved:

the values of the unknown, x, and the coefficients. In many problems an infinite amount of information is inherently present, and the problem cannot be solved exactly by numerical methods that deal with only a finite number of values. This circumstance introduces a fundamental concept, that of a finite approximation to an infinite-dimensional object, which is illustrated by the approximation of a smooth graph of a function by a series of straight lines (a piecewise-linear approximation).

A function, $f(x)$, is a prescription of a value corresponding to each value of its argument, x. For example, $f(x) = 2 - x + x^2$ is a function whose value is 2 when $x = 0$, 2 when $x = 1$, 4 when $x = 2$, etc. A description of a function by a mathematical formula defines the value of the function for all values of its argument. The mathematical definition of a function is that it is a (possibly infinite) set of pairs of values, (x_i, y_i). A function of a single variable x can be represented graphically by placing a point at $[x, f(x)]$ for each value of x. If this is done for a few values of x, say five values, the set of points shown in Figure 1 is obtained. This graph can be described with just 10 numbers, $x_1, y_1, x_2, y_2, \ldots, y_5$, where $y_i = f(x_i)$. The members of each pair (x_i, y_i) are the coordinates of one of the points. These five points, however, do not prescribe the value of the function for other than the five given values of x. More pairs of values (x_i, y_i) could be added, but they cannot specify the value of the function for every value of x unless there is an infinite number of pairs of values. Hence, this graph needs infinitely much information if it is to describe the function completely. Thus, a general function is an infinite-dimensional object because it requires infinitely much information to specify it. If the graph is "smooth," however, it is reasonable to approximate it by joining a small set of points with a continuous line. If consecutive points are joined by a sequence of straight lines, as shown in Figure 2, a piecewise-linear approximation is obtained. Such an approximation requires the values of only a finite number of values, the values of the end points of each of the straight-line segments shown in Figure 2. The piecewise-linear approximation is a finite-dimensional approximation to an infinite-dimensional object. This is critically important in numerical computation by hand or computer because computers and people can deal only with finite amounts of information. More closely spaced points can be used in a piecewise-linear approximation to get a more accurate approximation, as also shown in Figure 2, but the additional points mean that more information is used to approximate the function.

The error caused by replacing an infinite-dimensional object by a finite-dimensional approximation is called truncation error. A large part of numerical analysis is

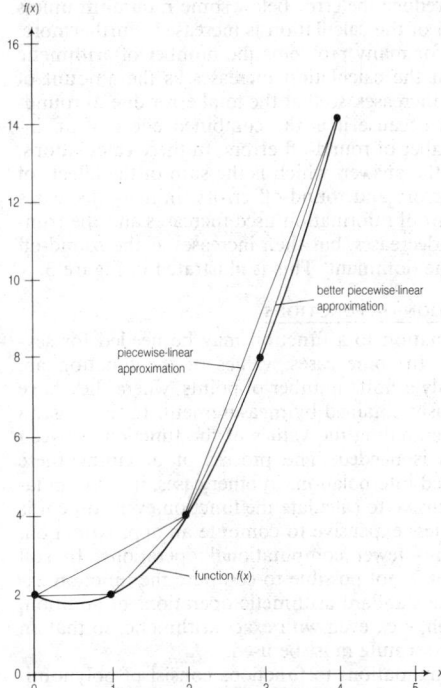

Figure 2: Piecewise-linear approximations to a continuous function (see text).

concerned with the accuracy of finite-dimensional approximations, examining questions such as "What type of approximation can be used?", "How much information is needed for a given accuracy?", and "Will the approximation become more accurate as more information is used?". As more information is used in an approximation, more computation is required to evaluate it, so that it is natural to expect more accuracy. A method that can achieve arbitrarily much accuracy by using sufficient information is said to be convergent. Most methods have one or a few parameters that determine the amount of information used in the approximation. For example, if, in the piecewise-linear approximation discussed above, the points x_i are equally spaced, that is, if $x_{i+1} - x_i = h$ for all i, where h is the mesh spacing, then the number of points used over a fixed interval, say $(0, 1)$, is determined by the parameter h. As h is reduced, the amount of information used to approximate the function increases, and it is visually obvious from Figure 2 that the approximation becomes more accurate. How much more accurate it becomes is typical of the questions that numerical analysts investigate. In this case it is relatively easy to show with calculus that if h is halved, the error decreases by a factor of approximately 4, provided that the function $f(x)$ is smooth enough, that is, if it is continuous and has no sharp turns in it, or, mathematically, if it has a second derivative. The relationship between the error and the mesh size for the piecewise-linear approximation is that the error is no larger than h^2 times a constant times the second derivative of the function. This method is said to have second-order convergence. (If a method depends on a parameter h and its error is proportional to h^p, it is said to have pth-order convergence.) Numerical analysts look for methods that have high orders of convergence because, as more information is used, their accuracy increases more rapidly than lower-order methods. Straightforward methods for simple problems, such as the approximation of functions, are usually convergent, but much care must be exercised in the choice of methods for complex problems to get convergence. A significant part of the theoretical work in numerical analysis is concerned with proofs of the convergence of methods.

In practical calculation, round-off errors are also present. As the amount of information is increased to decrease truncation error, the size of each round-off error, which is determined by the number of digits used in the calculation, remains constant. Hence, no amount of additional infor-

Convergent methods

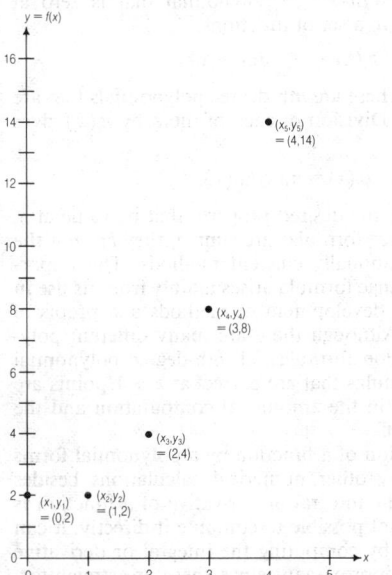

Figure 1: Graph of values of the function $y = f(x) = 2 - x + x^2$ for $x = 0, 1, 2, 3,$ and 4.

mation can reduce the error below some minimum unless the precision of the calculation is increased. Furthermore, in methods for many problems the number of arithmetic operations in the calculation increases as the amount of information increases, so that the total error due to round-off increases because it is the combined effect of an increasing number of round-off errors. In these calculations, the error in the answer, which is the sum of the effects of truncation errors and round-off errors, initially decreases as the amount of information used increases and the truncation error decreases, but then increases as the round-off errors become dominant. This is illustrated in Figure 3.

APPROXIMATION OF FUNCTIONS

An approximation to a function may be needed for several reasons. In some cases, values of the function are known at only a finite number of points, where they have been previously obtained by measurement. In that case, a method of estimating the values of the function between those points is needed. The process of obtaining these values is called interpolation. In other cases, it is computationally expensive to calculate the function every time it is needed, but less expensive to compute an approximation, which requires fewer computational operations. In still other cases, it is not possible to compute the function exactly with the standard arithmetic operations of addition, multiplication, etc., even with exact arithmetic, so that an approximate formula must be used.

Many approximations to functions consist of polynomials. A polynomial is a function of the form

$$P(x) = a_0 + a_1 x + a_2 x^2 + \cdots + a_n x^n. \qquad (5)$$

This polynomial has degree n. It can be evaluated using n multiplications and additions when written in the form

$$(\cdots((a_n \times x + a_{n-1}) \times x + a_{n-2}) \times x + \cdots + a_1) \times x + a_0.$$

A polynomial of degree n contains $n + 1$ coefficients a_i, $i = 0, 1, \ldots, n$, so that it has $n + 1$ degrees of freedom, or has dimension $n + 1$. It is formed as a linear sum of multiples of the $n + 1$ basis functions x^i, $i = 0, 1, \ldots, n$. These functions are independent, which means that no linear combination of them will be identically zero for all x. When an infinite-dimensional object has to be approximated by a finite-dimensional one, any set of independent functions can be used. If $\varphi_i(x)$, $i = 0, 1, \ldots, n$, are a set of $n + 1$ independent functions, they form a basis, and the approximation

$$f(x) \approx a_0\varphi_0(x) + a_1\varphi_1(x) + \cdots + a_n\varphi_n(x)$$

can be used. If the $\{\varphi_i(x)\}$, $i = 0, 1, 2, \ldots$, are an infinite set of independent basis functions that satisfy certain technical restrictions, they can be used to get arbitrarily accurate approximations by including enough of them. If the basis function $\varphi(x)$ is a polynomial of degree i, these technical restrictions are satisfied. The approximations generally have better properties if the basis functions are as different from one another as possible. In this respect, the functions x^i are not very good because, for example, the functions x^2 and x^4 are not greatly different in overall shape, as can be seen by drawing them. An important class of basis functions are those that are mutually orthogonal,

which is a mathematical prescription for requiring them to be as different as possible. (This use of orthogonal is related to its use in specifying directions that are at right angles, and thus very different, such as north and east.)

Polynomial interpolation. Interpolation is used to compute the approximate value of a function, given its values at a set of points. To approximate the function at a point whose value is not given, the value of a polynomial passing through a few neighbouring points is computed, as shown in Figure 4. Usually, the points with known values closest to the point of unknown value are chosen because the accuracy of interpolation is proportional to the distance of the unknown point from each of the known points. An important fact about polynomials is that a unique polynomial of degree n can be constructed to pass through any set of $n + 1$ points; that is, if (x_i, y_i), $i = 0, 1, \ldots, n$, are a set of points with all x_i different, there is a unique set of coefficients a_i such that $P(x)$ given by equation (5) satisfies $P(x_i) = y_i$ for $0 \le i \le n$. A different set of points, and hence a different polynomial, is used to interpolate for different regions of x values. For example, if a third-degree polynomial (a cubic) were to be used, four points would be needed. If the x_i are ordered, that is, if $x_0 < x_1 < x_2 < \ldots$, and x lies between, say, x_7 and x_8, the points x_6, x_7, x_8, and x_9 would be used, whereas if x lies between x_{15} and x_{16} the points x_{14}, x_{15}, x_{16}, and x_{17} would be used to construct the interpolating polynomial. The coefficients of that polynomial could be calculated for each interval, and then the value of $P(x)$ could be calculated from the polynomial. However, computational schemes have been devised to compute the interpolated value directly without finding the coefficients of the underlying polynomial. The user of such schemes is interested in rapid calculation with a minimum susceptibility to round-off error. The Lagrange formula is an important form of polynomial interpolation. To interpolate an nth-degree polynomial that matches the $n + 1$ points (x_i, y_i), $i = 0, 1, \ldots, n$, this formula incorporates the set of $n + 1$ polynomial basis functions, $\varphi_i(x)$, each of degree n, which are such that $\varphi_i(x)$ is zero at all of the $n + 1$ points except at x_i, where its value is 1. The interpolating polynomial can be written as

$$P(x) = y_0\varphi_0(x) + y_1\varphi_1(x) + \cdots + y_n\varphi_n(x).$$

This clearly satisfies the interpolation conditions: each of the basis functions is a polynomial of degree n, so their sum is also an nth-degree polynomial; when $x = x_i$, all of the terms in the sum vanish except for $y_i\varphi_i(x_i)$, which is just y_i. Definition of the $\varphi_i(x)$ is straightforward. On the basis of the function

$$\Pi(x) = (x - x_0)(x - x_1) \cdots (x - x_n),$$

which is an $(n + 1)$st-degree polynomial that is zero at $x = x_i$ for $0 \le i \le n$, a set of functions

$$\pi_i(x) = \Pi(x)/(x - x_i)$$

may be defined. These are nth-degree polynomials that are zero except at x_i. Division of each of them by $\pi_i(x_i)$ gives the functions

$$\varphi_i(x) = \pi_i(x)/\pi_i(x_i),$$

each of which has the desired property that its value at x_i is 1. Although these formulas are simple, they are not the basis for computationally efficient methods. The importance of the Lagrange formula arises mainly from its use in the mathematical development of methods and proofs of their properties. Although there are many different polynomial interpolation formulas, all nth-degree polynomial interpolation formulas that are correct at $n + 1$ points are equivalent except in the amount of computation and the effects of round-off.

The approximation of a function by a polynomial forms the basis of many other numerical calculations besides interpolation. If the integral or derivative of a function is needed and it is not possible to compute it directly, it can be approximated by computing the integral or derivative of a polynomial approximant since there are straightforward rules for evaluating the integral or derivative of a polynomial.

Lagrange formula

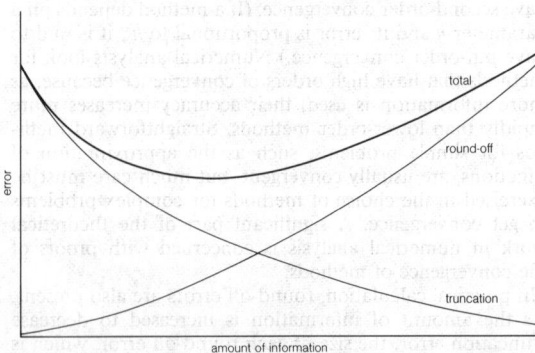

Figure 3: The effect of the amount of information on error in numeric computations.

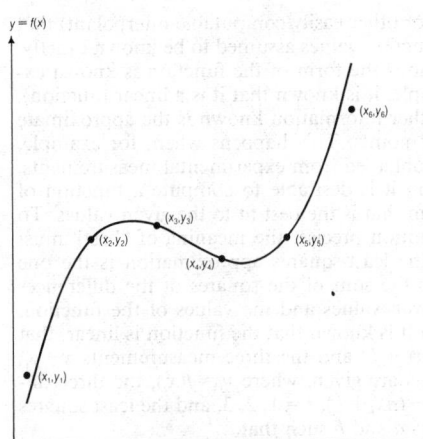

Figure 4: *Polynomial interpolation.*
The six points x_1, y_1, etc., represent values of an unknown function. A third-degree polynomial has been constructed so that four of its values match four of the values of the unknown function. Other third-degree polynomials could be made to match other sets of four values of the unknown function, or a polynomial of higher degree could be found to match all six.

Difference calculus. Differences are the basis for the development of many methods of polynomial approximation. If the values of a function $f(x)$ are given at a set of equally spaced argument values $x_0, x_1, x_2, \ldots$, where $x_n = x_0 + nh$, the forward difference of $f(x)$ at x_n, written as $\Delta f(x_n)$, is defined as $f(x_{n+1}) - f(x_n)$. Piecewise-linear interpolation between x_n and x_{n+1} is given by the formula

$$f(x) \approx f(x_n) + \frac{(x - x_n)}{(x_{n+1} - x_n)} \Delta f(x_n).$$

Since the spacing between the x_i's is h, this can be written as

$$f(x) \approx f(x_n) + s\Delta f(x_n),$$

where $s = (x - x_n)/h$. Higher degree polynomials can be used by using higher order differences. The second difference, written $\Delta^2 f(x_n)$, is defined as $\Delta f(x_{n+1}) - \Delta f(x_n)$, which can be rewritten as $f(x_{n+2}) - 2f(x_{n+1}) + f(x_n)$. In general, the mth-order difference is given by

$$\Delta^m f(x_n) = \Delta^{m-1} f(x_{n+1}) - \Delta^{m-1} f(x_n).$$

The polynomial of degree m passing through the points $x_n, x_{n+1}, \ldots, x_{n+m}$ can be written as

$$P(x) = f(x_n) + \frac{(x - x_n)}{(x_{n+1} - x_n)} \Delta f(x_n) + \frac{(x - x_{n+1})(x - x_n)}{(x_{n+2} - x_{n+1})(x_{n+2} - x_n)} \Delta^2 f(x_n)$$
$$+ \cdots + \frac{(x - x_{n+m-1}) \cdots (x - x_n)}{(x_{n+m} - x_n) \cdots (x_{n+1} - x_n)} \Delta^m f(x_n).$$

This can be rewritten as

$$f(x) \approx f(x_n) + s\Delta f(x_n) + \frac{s(s-1)}{2} \Delta^2 f(x_n)$$
$$+ \cdots + \frac{s(s-1) \cdots (s - m + 1)}{m!} \Delta^m f(x_n).$$

If the function is smooth, its differences get smaller as their order increases until round-off errors cause them to increase again. The point at which they become smallest gives a direct indication of how many differences can be used to achieve the maximum accuracy possible. A list of the differences of various orders can be easily computed and used for interpolation. An important property of differences is that if the function is a polynomial of degree m in x, the differences of order higher than m are zero and $\Delta^m f(x_n)$ is independent of n, that is, is a constant.

Difference calculus is a formal manipulation scheme for developing useful approximations. It uses the operators Δ (already introduced as the forward difference operator); E, which is defined as the step operator so that $Ef(x_n) = f(x_{n+1})$; and others. Because of the relationship

$$f(x_{n+1}) = f(x_n) + f(x_{n+1}) - f(x_n) = f(x_n) + \Delta f(x_n),$$

the formal relationship

$$E = 1 + \Delta$$

can be written. This can be squared to get

$$E^2 = (1 + \Delta)^2 = 1 + 2\Delta + \Delta^2.$$

This is the formal statement that

$$f(x_{n+2}) = f(x_n) + 2\Delta f(x_n) + \Delta^2 f(x_n),$$

whose truth can be verified by simple algebra. Since E^m is the equivalent of moving forward m values in the table, it seems reasonable that $E^{0.5}$ should be the equivalent of moving forward half a step in the table, that is, to interpolating for the value of $f(x)$ at $x_{n+1/2}$. Similarly, E^s should represent interpolation s steps forward for any s, whether integer or not. Formally, E^s can be rewritten as

$$E^s = (1 + \Delta)^s$$

and expanded according to the binomial expansion to get

$$E^s = 1 + s\Delta + \frac{s(s-1)}{2} \Delta^2 + \frac{s(s-1)(s-2)}{3!} \Delta^3 + \cdots.$$

When this is applied to $f(x_n)$ and the infinite series is terminated after $m + 1$ terms, the previous interpolation formula is obtained. Thus, difference calculus has provided a formal verification of the formula stated earlier.

To illustrate how differences can be used for many other approximations, it is convenient to define the operator D as differentiation. Formally,

$$Df(x) = \frac{d}{dx} f(x).$$

The Taylor's series approximation to a function states that

$$f(x + a) = f(x) + a\frac{d}{dx} f(x) + \frac{a^2}{2} \frac{d^2}{dx^2} f(x) + \frac{a^3}{3!} \frac{d^3}{dx^3} f(x) + \cdots.$$

This can be written in operator form as

$$E^{a/h} = 1 + aD + \frac{(aD)^2}{2} + \frac{(aD)^3}{3!} + \cdots.$$

The series on the right-hand side is the power-series expansion of the exponential function and is equal to e^{aD}. On the replacement $a = sh$ this relation becomes

$$E^s = e^{shD} = (e^{hD})^s.$$

This leads to $E = e^{hD}$, from which the relationship

$$hD = \log(E) = \log(1 + \Delta)$$

is obtained. Expansion of the logarithm then yields

$$hD = \Delta - \frac{\Delta^2}{2} + \frac{\Delta^3}{3} - \cdots,$$

which gives a numerical approximation for the derivative of a function in terms of its differences. If this relation is terminated after $m + 1$ terms, it is exactly equivalent to computing the derivative of a polynomial of degree m through $m + 1$ values of the function. This fact follows from the fact that the differences of order higher than m of an mth-degree polynomial are zero.

Difference calculus operates on data tabulated at equidistant points. If the mesh points x_i are unequally spaced, different formulas must be used. In this case, divided differences are a valuable tool. The first divided difference of a function $f(x)$ is the slope of the line through two points on the function. It is written as

$$f[x_n, x_{n+1}] = \frac{f(x_{n+1}) - f(x_n)}{x_{n+1} - x_n}.$$

Its value depends on the two points, x_n and x_{n+1}, that are used, but not on their order. That is, $f[x_n, x_{n+1}] = f[x_{n+1}, x_n]$. The mth-order divided difference on $m + 1$ points is defined as

$$f[x_n, x_{n+1}, \ldots, x_{n+m}]$$
$$= \frac{f[x_{n+1}, x_{n+2}, \ldots, x_{n+m}] - f[x_n, x_{n+1}, \ldots, x_{n+m-1}]}{[x_{n+m} - x_n]}.$$

If the points x_i are equally spaced with the distance between them equal to 1, then the mth-order divided difference is identical to the mth-order difference divided by $m!$. Polynomial interpolation by an mth-degree polynomial can be written as

$$f(x) \approx f(x_n) + (x - x_n)f[x_n, x_{n+1}] + \cdots$$
$$+ (x - x_n)(x - x_{n+1}) \cdots (x - x_{n+m-1})f[x_n, x_{n+1}, \cdots, x_{n+m}].$$

Computation of elementary functions. Elementary functions are functions that occur very frequently in scientific and engineering calculations. They are usually the solution of simple relations that cannot be expressed directly in terms of other, simpler operations or functions. Examples include sine, cosine, and exponential. The solutions to many problems can be written explicitly in terms of elementary functions. Many elementary functions can be expressed as power series, which are like polynomials but which have infinitely many terms. For example, the exponential function has the power series expansion

$$e^x = 1 + x + \frac{x^2}{2!} + \frac{x^3}{3!} + \frac{x^4}{4!} + \frac{x^5}{5!} + \cdots . \qquad (6)$$

This summation has the property that as more and more terms are included it converges; that is, its value comes closer and closer to the true value. If (6) is evaluated to seven-digit accuracy with $x = 0.1$ for a number of terms, the following results are obtained:

number of terms (n)	value of nth term	sum of n terms
1	1.000000	1.000000
2	0.100000	1.100000
3	0.005000	1.105000
4	0.000167	1.105167
5	0.000004	1.105171
6	0.000000	1.105171

Further terms would not change the seven-digit sum. The series provides a way of computing an approximation of e^x to any desired accuracy by adding enough terms. Many elementary functions are calculated in this way (although the minimax method described later can be used to reduce the amount of arithmetic and hence the time taken).

Spline approximation. In many applications the shape of an object is defined by the positions of a number of points on its surface, for example, the hull of a ship or the body of an automobile. The builder, to construct a smooth-surfaced object from this information, needs a mechanism for determining the position of any point on its surface. A simpler case of this problem is the construction of a smooth curve through a set of points—the problem solved by a drafter asked to draw a graph. The numerical problem is to approximate a function smoothly from the knowledge of a few of its points. Polynomial interpolation provides an interpolant, which is the approximating function, but it is not usually smooth because different polynomials are used between different pairs of points. Thus, a piecewise-linear interpolant has angles between the straight lines in adjacent regions, as shown in Figure 2.

A spline approximant is a piecewise polynomial interpolant with the property that it matches the function values at the given points, called the knots, and that it is smooth. The mathematical definition of a smooth function is that it has a certain number of continuous derivatives. The first derivative is the slope of the curve. If the slope is continuous, the curve has no angles, that is, no sudden changes in direction. The second derivative is related to the radius of curvature. In a surface such as that of an automobile body, the radius of curvature determines how reflections are magnified or reduced. A sudden change in the radius of curvature results in a surface that is not visually pleasing if it is supposed to be uniform—for example, the hood of an automobile might appear to have a crease in it. For this reason, curves and surfaces with continuous second derivatives are often desirable. A common spline approximation is a piecewise cubic with continuous second derivatives.

Least squares approximation. Interpolation approximates functions whose form is known approximately with a polynomial (or other easily computable interpolant) that matches the function values assumed to be known exactly. In some situations the form of the function is known exactly (for example, it is known that it is a linear function), but the only other information known is the approximate value at a few points. This happens when, for example, the values are obtained from experimental measurements. In this situation it is desirable to compute a function of the known form that is the best fit to the given values. To make this definition precise, the meaning of "best" must be specified. The least-squares approximation is the one that minimizes the sum of the squares of the differences between the given values and the values of the function. For example, if it is known that the function is linear, that is, that $f(x) = ax + b$, and the three measurements x_1, y_1; x_2, y_2; and x_3, y_3 are given, where $y_i \approx f(x_i)$, the three differences are $y_i - (ax_i + b)$, $i = 1, 2, 3$, and the least squares method chooses a and b such that

$$[y_1 - (ax_1 + b)]^2 + [y_2 - (ax_2 + b)]^2 + [y_3 - (ax_3 + b)]^2$$

is as small as possible. If at least two of the x_i are distinct, there is a unique set a and b that achieves a minimum of this expression. Formulas for the values of a and b can be derived by the use of calculus. The general linear least-squares problem, which is a least-squares problem in which the unknown parameters (a and b in the example) appear linearly in the original errors ($y_i - ax_i - b$ in the example), has the same properties: if there are n unknown parameters and there are at least n distinct points x_i, there is a unique minimum.

The calculation of the solution to a least-squares problem is a good example of the application of numerical analysis. Straightforward application of calculus to the problem of the least-squares nth-degree polynomial approximant leads to a system of linear equations whose solution is discussed below. For large n the system is very poorly conditioned, so that a poor numerical answer is obtained. This occurs when the polynomials x^i are used as a basis; the use of orthogonal polynomials as a basis leads to much better accuracy.

Minimax approximation. Minimax approximation is another example of choosing the best approximation from a set of possible approximations. A measure of the error in an approximation to a function is first defined as the size of the largest difference between the approximation and the function at any of the points of interest. The approximation that has the smallest error measure is the minimax approximant. For example, the minimax linear approximation to the three points (x_i, y_i), $i = 1, 2,$ and 3, is the line shown in Figure 5. It is equidistant from each of the points, as shown. Minimax approximations are related to least-squares approximations in that both are best approximations; in both approximations, "best" is defined as the minimum of some measure of error, but the measure of the error is different. In least squares, it is the sum of the squares of the errors; in the minimax case, it is the size of the largest error. (Both methods can be viewed as special cases of general minimum-error approximations.)

Minimax approximations are most frequently used to approximate one known function by another function that is less difficult to compute. For example, the sine function might be approximated by a polynomial in a computer program that computes a numerical value of $\sin(x)$ by

Measures of error

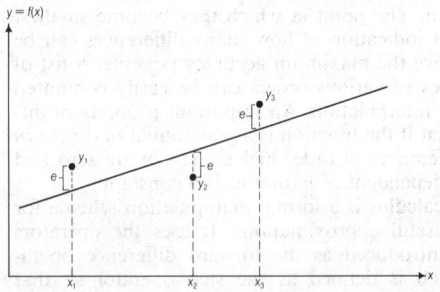

Figure 5: *Linear minimax approximation.*
The line has been drawn so that its vertical distance, *e*, is the same from each of the three points.

evaluation of the polynomial. In this approach, a polynomial that is the best approximation in the minimax sense is used. The minimax polynomial may require fewer terms to get a given accuracy than would be needed if the first few terms of the power series were used. Although it takes a large amount of computation to determine the minimax polynomial for a given accuracy, that computation can be carried out once, and then the resulting polynomial can be evaluated whenever an approximation to the function is needed.

The nth-degree minimax polynomial approximant to a function has the important property that the difference between the polynomial and the function (the error) reaches its maximum value at least $n + 2$ times, and the sign of the error has alternate signs at each extremum. Figure 5 illustrates this in the case $n = 1$. The Chebyshev orthogonal polynomials are a set of polynomials, $T_0(x)$, $T_1(x)$, $T_2(x), \ldots$, where $T_n(x)$ has degree n and is such that it has $n + 1$ equal and opposite extrema. The values of the extrema alternate between $+1$ and -1. These polynomials are effective as basis functions for the representation of minimax approximations.

SOLUTION OF EQUATIONS

An equation is a relation between two expressions, for example, $3z + 4 = (y - 2)^2$. The expressions may contain known values, such as the numbers in the example, and unknowns, such as z and y, for which values must be computed. An equation says that the values of the unknowns must be such that the values of the expressions on either side of the equal sign are the same. An unknown, say x, appears linearly in an expression if it appears only in the form ax, where a has a known value independent of x, after all terms in the expression have been multiplied out. Thus, z appears linearly in the above example, but y does not—because the right-hand side is $y^2 - 4y + 4$ and the term y^2 is nonlinear. A linear equation is one in which all unknowns appear linearly and each is multiplied only by a constant. Most phenomena that physicists and engineers model are nonlinear, so that the effective solution of nonlinear equations is important. Many of the models can be approximated by linear equations, however, so the efficient solution of linear equations is equally important. Indeed, the solution of nonlinear equations often involves the solution of linear equations within the process.

The first section below discusses the solution of linear equations. In addition to their importance in many problems, they also illustrate the problems of round-off errors, backward error analysis, and the difficulty of ill-conditioned problems. Linear equations have the property that they can be solved exactly using the usual arithmetic operations of addition, subtraction, etc., if no round-off is involved. Methods that solve a problem exactly in the absence of round-off are called direct methods because they lead directly to the solution. Nonlinear equations cannot be solved exactly; rather, their solution must be approximated. So-called iterative methods generate a sequence of closer and closer approximations called iterates.

Linear equations and direct methods. The standard linear-equation problem is a set of N linear equations in N unknown variables. An example of a simple system of two equations is

$$3x_1 + 6x_2 = 12 \qquad (7)$$
$$5x_1 - 3x_2 = 7. \qquad (8)$$

Gauss's procedure

These can be solved by the process of elimination and back substitution originated by the 19th-century German mathematician Carl Friedrich Gauss. In this process one of the equations is solved for a variable in terms of the other variables, and this variable is eliminated from the remaining equations to get a system of one fewer equations in one fewer unknowns. In the simple example above, equation (7) is divided by the coefficient of x_1, namely, 3, and rearranged to get

$$x_1 = 4 - 2x_2. \qquad (9)$$

This is substituted into equation (8) to get

$$5(4 - 2x_2) - 3x_2 = 7, \qquad (10)$$

which can be rearranged to get

$$-13x_2 = -13$$

or $x_2 = 1$. This result can now be substituted back into equation (9) to get $x_1 = 2$. The key idea is that, with each elimination step, the number of equations and number of unknowns involved is reduced by one. If there are initially N equations, $N - 1$ elimination steps reduce the system to one equation in one unknown, which can be solved directly. A system of N equations in N unknowns is usually written as

$$A_{i1}x_1 + A_{i2}x_2 + \cdots + A_{iN}x_N = b_i, \ i = 1, \cdots, N, \quad (11)$$

where the A_{ij} are the coefficients, the b_i are the right-hand side values, and the x_j are the unknowns to be computed. The first of these equations ($i = 1$) can be solved for x_1 to get

$$x_1 = (b_1 - A_{12}x_2 - \cdots - A_{1N}x_N)/A_{11} \qquad (12)$$

and this value of x_1 can be substituted into the remaining $N - 1$ equations, which will then involve only $N - 1$ unknowns. The same process can be repeated until a set of equations, each like equation (12) and each specifying an x_i in terms of x_j for $j > i$, is obtained. The Nth such equation specifies x_N directly. The value of x_N can then be substituted into the $(N-1)$st equation to get x_{N-1}, and so on. This is an entirely mechanical process that can be programmed easily for a computer. It is called an algorithm, a specification of a computational process that will determine the answer to a problem in a finite number of steps. It should be noted that if exact arithmetic could be used in this algorithm and if the division in equation (12) and subsequent divisions were possible (that is, if A_{11} and subsequent A_{ii} were not zero), the solution of the linear equations could be computed exactly.

In a practical computation, arithmetic cannot be performed exactly, so round-off errors will affect the answers. Their effect can be seen by considering a graphic interpretation of an equation: an equation of the form (7) represents a straight line on a graph relating x_1 and x_2, as in Figure 6. Any point on the line λ_1 shown has coordinates x_1 and x_2 that satisfy equation (7). Similarly, equation (8) represents another straight line shown as λ_2 in Figure 6. Any point on that line satisfies equation (8). Hence, the values of x_1 and x_2 that satisfy both (7) and (8) must lie on both lines, so that these values are the coordinates of the intersection of the two lines. If the lines are not parallel, they have a unique intersection, so that the equations have a unique solution.

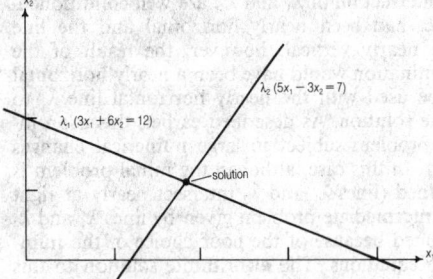

Figure 6: Graphic solution of a pair of linear equations (see text).

Round-off errors in the computation have an effect similar to that of changing the coefficients of the equations. Hence, in the presence of round-off errors, a computer will work with a narrow region that can be thought of as a "thick line," as shown in Figure 7, rather than an ideal line. The coordinates of any point inside the shaded region satisfy the equation of the line within the accuracy of the errors introduced into the coefficients. A pair of equations represents two thick lines within the accuracy of their coefficients, and the solution determined by the pair of equations lies somewhere within the intersection of the two thick lines, as shown in Figure 8.

If the equations represent a pair of lines that are nearly parallel, the numerical problem represented by the pair

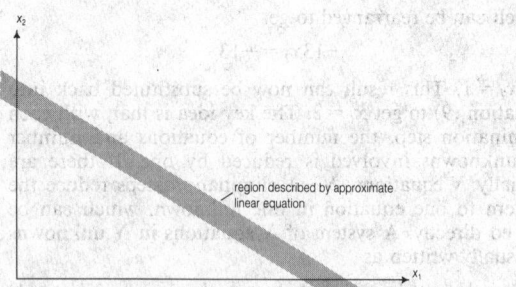

Figure 7: *Effect of round-off errors on the graphic representation of a linear equation.*
If the coefficients could be expressed exactly, the equation would be represented by an ideal line (having zero width), but because the coefficients can be expressed with limited accuracy, the line must be replaced by a band of finite width.

of thick lines in Figure 9 does not have an accurately determined answer because the region of intersection is large. The problem is said to be ill-conditioned. Any slight changes in the coefficients can cause large changes in the answer, so any round-off errors in the numerical procedure may cause large changes in the answer.

In the Gauss elimination–back substitution procedure described above, it was noted that it could always be completed unless one of the A_{ii} divisors was zero. If one of those divisors is very small, intermediate results may be very large, and the final answer may be obtained as the difference of two large numbers. This means that cancellation may occur so that there may be a large effect due to round-off. This effect can be seen in a graphic view of the process of Gaussian elimination. As described above, the equations represent a pair of lines. Dividing an equation by a number, as in dividing (7) by 3 to get (9), does not change the line the equation represents. Substituting one equation into another, as in substituting (9) into (8) to get (10), gives another equation that also represents a straight line, λ_4. Since the solution of the original equations lies on the new line, this new line must pass through the intersection of the two original lines. It should be noted that equation (10) does not involve x_1, so that line λ_4 is horizontal, as shown in Figure 10. The final step, the back substitution, evaluates x_2 from (10) and substitutes into (9)—which represents the same line as (7)—to get x_1. Thus, the solution is determined from lines λ_1 and λ_4. In Figure 6 they intersect nearly at right angles, as do λ_1 and λ_2. Hence, both the original problem of finding the intersection of λ_1 and λ_2, and the intermediate problem of finding the intersection of λ_1 and λ_4, are well-conditioned. If the line λ_1 had been nearly horizontal and the line λ_2 had been nearly vertical, however, the result of the Gaussian elimination would have been a nearly horizontal line, λ_4, to be used with the nearly horizontal line λ_1 to determine the solution. As described earlier, this is an ill-conditioned problem subject to large numerical changes in the answer. In this case, although the initial problem is well-conditioned (lines λ_1 and λ_2 intersect nearly at right angles), the intermediate problem given by lines λ_1 and λ_4 is ill-conditioned because of the poor choice of the numbering of the equations. The algorithmic solution to this

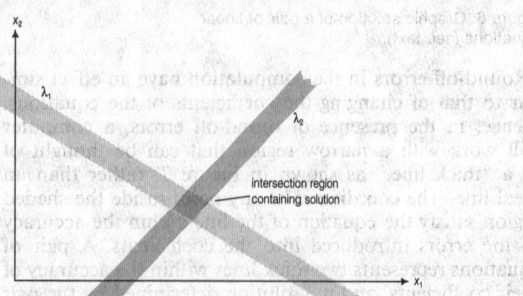

Figure 8: *Graphic solution of two linear equations, showing the effect of round-off error.*
Instead of two ideal lines intersecting in a single point, two narrow bands intersect in a region of finite area.

is to reorder the equations during the elimination process to ensure that the A_{ii} elements are large. This is called partial pivoting. Even with partial pivoting, solution errors for ill-conditioned problems can be large. A formal error analysis provides a pessimistic bound of the errors that can occur even for a well-conditioned problem, especially as the number of equations increases. Before the introduction of electronic computers this situation did not present a difficulty because large problems could not be tackled. Around 1950 it was thought unlikely that computers could produce accurate solutions of large systems of linear equations. The English mathematician J.H. Wilkinson and other researchers, who had been solving problems by hand methods, showed that problems could frequently be solved much more accurately than the conventional analysis predicted. Finally, Wilkinson's backward error analysis showed that the Gaussian elimination process would solve a system of equations with a residual or backward error that did not increase too rapidly as the size of the problem increased. Experience has confirmed Wilkinson's theoretical result: the error does not increase very much with the size of the problem. **Partial pivoting**

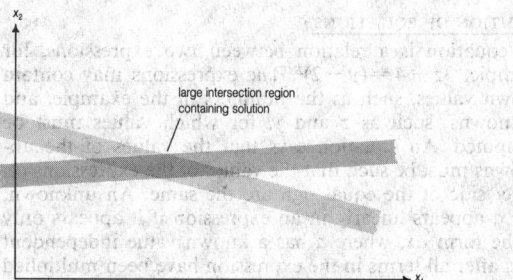

Figure 9: *Graphic solution of two linear equations for which the slopes of the lines are nearly the same.*
Because the region of intersection is large, the error in the solution is large.

Today it is common to solve sets of hundreds of thousands of linear equations on computers. There is major interest in ways in which such large problems can be solved rapidly. If the system is dense, which means that most of the coefficients, A_{ij}, are not zero, the Gaussian elimination process takes an amount of time equal to $aN^3 + bN^2 + cN + d$, where a, b, c, and d are constants that depend on the computer. As N gets large, the dominant term in the time is aN^3, and subsequent doublings in the problem size result in eightfold increases in the solution time. The method is said to have a running time asymptotic to N^3. The asymptotic behaviour of a method provides a measure of its speed for very large problems. For example, if a method has an asymptotic speed of $N^{2.5}$, it will execute more rapidly than one with asymptotic speed N^3 for very large N, although for small N it may not be faster. The asymptotically fastest method for linear equations is not known, and it is a question of considerable theoretical interest. It is known that they can be solved at asymptotic speeds close to $N^{2.5}$. For practical problems that will fit into computers, the Gaussian elimination technique remains the best method known for dense problems. **Comparing speeds of computations**

Many large problems are sparse; that is, most of the coefficients A_{ij} are zero (because each equation describes a small piece of the physical system being modeled, and each piece is influenced only by a few other pieces). In such cases, the numerical analyst is interested in methods that do not change many coefficients from zero to nonzero (called fill-in). Gaussian elimination can still be used, and the equations can be re-ordered to minimize fill-in. In many cases of large sparse problems, however, iterative methods (discussed below) are preferable.

Nonlinear equations and iterative methods. Most accurate models necessitate the solution of nonlinear equations. Only in a few cases is it possible to solve such equations explicitly. The example of the quadratic equation $ax^2 + bx + c = 0$ was used above. The roots of this can be written explicitly, but polynomial equations involving x^5 or higher powers cannot be solved explicitly. The general

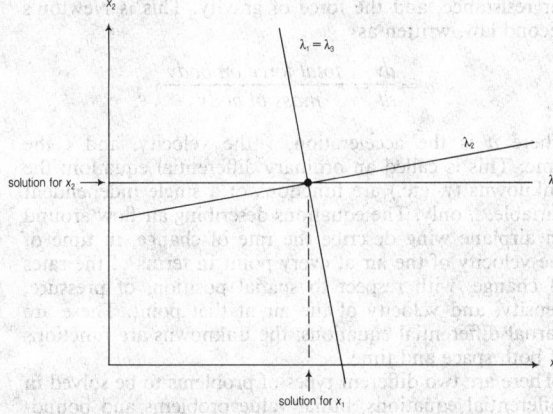

Figure 10: Graphic representation of the Gaussian elimination–back substitution procedure (see text).

problem is to find the value of x that gives a zero of a function $f(x)$, that is, to find a root of

$$f(x) = 0. \qquad (13)$$

Generally, the computational solution of this problem is possible only by approximating the function by one for which a zero can be computed. If the approximation is good enough, the zero of the approximate function may be a sufficiently accurate approximation to the desired zero. If not, another approximation is used to get a more accurate answer. Each repetition of this process is called an iteration. Iteration is an extremely important approach to the solution of nonlinear equations, and it also has applications to linear equations.

An iterative method can be described as one in which knowledge about each succeeding approximate solution is used to compute a better solution. This knowledge is used to get a better approximation to the function. To illustrate the principle, the simplest of iterative methods is considered here, even though it is of value only in very limited applications. If x is added to both sides of equation (13), it becomes

$$x + f(x) = x, \qquad (14)$$

an equation with the same roots as (13). It is now rewritten as

$$x = x - f(x). \qquad (15)$$

Equation (15) is no easier to solve than (13), but the nonlinear right-hand side can be replaced with an approximation. In the first method, it is replaced by the constant value obtained by replacing x with a known value, say, c, to get

$$x = c - f(c). \qquad (16)$$

This is certainly easy to solve for x since it is linear in x; in fact, it is necessary only to evaluate the right-hand side. This process can be turned into an iterative algorithm by taking the value computed for x and using it for the value of c in a second application of the process, and so on. An initial guess for the root is obtained somehow. (The problem solver will probably have some knowledge of an approximate value of the solution from experience. If not, any reasonable value, for example, $x = 0$, is chosen.) This initial guess is called $x^{(0)}$, and each new approximation is named $x^{(i)}$, $i = 1, 2, \ldots$. Then the relationship

$$x^{(n+1)} = x^{(n)} - f(x^{(n)}) \qquad (17)$$

is obtained. The values $x^{(0)}, x^{(1)}, x^{(2)}, \ldots$, form an infinite sequence. If they are such that $x^{(n+1)} = x^{(n)}$, it is clear that $x = x^{(n)} = x^{(n+1)}$ satisfies (15) and hence the original problem (13). This method is illustrated with the linear equation $f(x) = 0.9x - 1$ to keep the exposition simple (it is obvious that the zero of $0.9x - 1$ could be found directly with simple arithmetic). The iteration is

$$x^{(n+1)} = x^{(n)} - (0.9x^{(n)} - 1) = 1 + 0.1x^{(n)}. \qquad (18)$$

If $x^{(0)} = 0$, the following sequence of values for $x^{(n)}$ is obtained:

n	$x^{(n)}$
1	1.
2	1.1
3	1.11
4	1.111
5	$\ldots$

It is clear that $x^{(n+1)}$ will never equal $x^{(n)}$ mathematically because it will have one more digit, but each succeeding value is closer to the answer, $10/9 = 1.111 \ldots$. Thus, $x^{(n)}$ converges to the correct solution as n gets larger, although it never gets there. As much accuracy as is needed can be obtained by performing enough iterations.

The iterative process described above (which is called functional iteration) can be described graphically as follows: Figure 11 shows a simple function $f(x)$ with a zero at x^*. The current guess, $x^{(n)}$, is also shown along with $f(x^{(n)})$. The right-hand side of (17) can be constructed by drawing a 45° right-angle triangle as shown to get $x - f(x^{(n)})$ on the x-axis. This is the next iterate. In Figure 11 the graph of $f(x)$ has been approximated by a 45° line. This view suggests that a better approximation to the curve could be used. This is the basis of many methods, of which two will be described, the chord method and Newton's method.

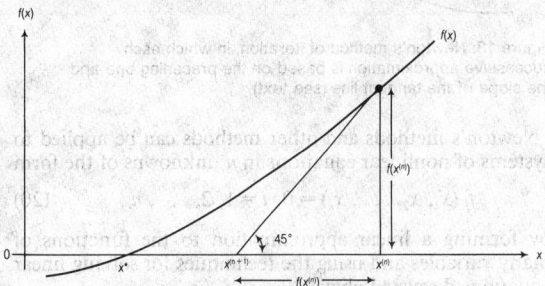

Figure 11: Functional iteration for successive approximations to x^*, the value of x for which $f(x)$ is zero (see text).

Chord method

In the chord method, two different values of x, $x^{(0)}$, and $x^{(1)}$, are selected, and a straight line is drawn through them to approximate the curve. The next point, $x^{(2)}$, is given by the intersection of this line with the x-axis, as shown in Figure 12. The process is repeated using $x^{(1)}$ and $x^{(2)}$ to get $x^{(3)}$, and so on. It is not difficult to construct examples for which the chord method will not converge, so many variants of the method have been devised in attempts to improve its performance. A particular variant, the method of false position, always finds an answer if the initial guesses are such that the values of the function at the two initial points, $f(x^{(0)})$ and $f(x^{(1)})$, have opposite signs. The method computes $x^{(2)}$ exactly as in the chord method, and it then uses $x^{(2)}$ and one of $x^{(0)}$ and $x^{(1)}$ as the starting point for the next iteration so that they also satisfy the opposite-sign criterion.

Newton's method

In Newton's method, the curve is approximated by the straight line tangent to the curve at the current point $x^{(n)}$, as shown in Figure 13. If s is the slope of the curve at the point x (s is the derivative $df(x)/dx$) and $s^{(n)}$ is its value at $x^{(n)}$, then the approximation is given by

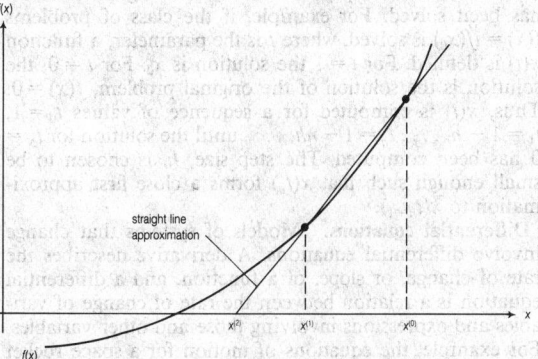

Figure 12: Chord method of iteration, in which each successive approximation is based on two previous approximations (see text).

$$f(x) \approx f(x^{(n)}) + s^{(n)}(x - x^{(n)}).$$

The zero of the approximation is computed to get the Newton formula

$$x^{(n+1)} = x^{(n)} - \frac{f(x^{(n)})}{s^{(n)}}. \qquad (19)$$

This is one of the fastest methods for finding zeros when the initial guess is fairly close to the answer, but $x^{(n)}$ may not converge to the root if the initial guess is far away.

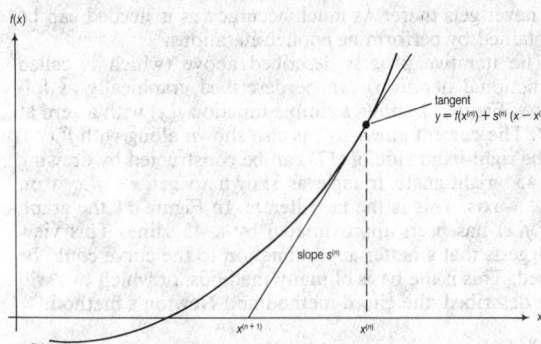

Figure 13: Newton's method of iteration, in which each successive approximation is based on the preceding one and the slope of the tangent line (see text).

Newton's methods and other methods can be applied to systems of nonlinear equations in n unknowns of the form

$$f_i(x_1, x_2, \ldots, x_n) = 0, \; i = 1, 2, \ldots, n, \qquad (20)$$

by forming a linear approximation to the functions of many variables and using the techniques for solving linear equations discussed above.

The first example of the iterative solution was devoted to a linear equation. Iterative methods are an efficient way to solve large, sparse linear systems.

General nonlinear equations can be very difficult to solve computationally, in part because it is not possible to know where a solution may exist from local knowledge of the functions. (Local knowledge means information derived from the values of the function at a few points near a particular x.) Methods that use a local approximation to estimate the solution may compute an approximant that is in error by more than the current best approximant, so that the approximants diverge. For this reason, many iterative methods work only if the initial approximant is near the solution. Continuation methods are ones that construct a class of problems based on a parameter such that problems with nearby values of the parameter have solutions that are close. Hence, if the solution for one value of the parameter is known, it forms a good initial guess to the solution for a nearby value of the parameter. After the problem has been solved for the nearby parameter value, the process can be repeated. If the process starts with a value of the parameter for which the solution is known, the solution can be computed for a sequence of other values of the parameter until the original problem has been solved. For example, if the class of problems $f(x) = tf(x_0)$ is solved, where t is the parameter, a function $x(t)$ is defined. For $t = 1$ the solution is x_0. For $t = 0$, the solution is the solution of the original problem, $f(x) = 0$. Thus, $x(t)$ is computed for a sequence of values $t_0 = 1$, $t_1 = 1 - h, \ldots, t_n = 1 - nh, \ldots$, until the solution for $t_N = 0$ has been computed. The step size, h, is chosen to be small enough such that $x(t_n)$ forms a close first approximation to $x(t_{n+1})$.

Differential equations. Models of systems that change involve differential equations. A derivative describes the rate of change, or slope, of a function, and a differential equation is a relation between the rate of change of variables and expressions involving those and other variables. For example, the equations of motion for a space rocket relate the rate of change of the velocity of the rocket (called its acceleration) and its mass, to the forces on the rocket due to the thrust from its engines, the drag due to air resistance, and the force of gravity. This is Newton's second law, written as

$$a = \frac{dv}{dt} = \frac{total \; force \; on \; body}{mass \; of \; body},$$

where a is the acceleration, v the velocity, and t the time. This is called an ordinary differential equation: the unknowns (v, etc.) are functions of a single independent variable, t, only. The equations describing air flow around an airplane wing describe the rate of change, in time of the velocity of the air at every point in terms of the rates of change, with respect to spatial position, of pressure, density, and velocity of the air at that point. These are partial differential equations: the unknowns are functions of both space and time.

There are two different types of problems to be solved in differential equations, initial value problems and boundary value problems. The former type arises when the values of the unknowns are given at a particular point, for example, at a given time, and the values at future times are to be computed. For example, the position of the rocket before launch may be known, and future values of its position and velocity are to be computed. The latter type arises when the values of the unknowns are given on the boundary of a region and the values in the interior of the region are to be computed. For example, the flow of air a great distance from the airplane wing may be known to be uniform with a specified velocity and pressure, and the flow near the wing is to be computed. The methods used for these two types of problems are somewhat different, but they share the most important feature: a differential equation describes an infinite-dimensional object, a finite-dimensional object must be chosen to represent the solution, and the value of that approximation must be computed.

There are two main forms of approximation: finite differences and finite elements. In finite difference methods, the solution is represented by its values at a finite number of points, called mesh points. For example, if the velocity of the space rocket is to be computed, its velocities v_n at the set of times $t_n = nh$, $n = 0, 1, \ldots, N$, where h is the mesh spacing, could be computed as an approximation. If a differential equation of the form

$$s = \frac{dy}{dt} = f(y, t)$$

is given, where s is the slope, or derivative, of the unknown function $y(t)$, s can be replaced with the slope of a polynomial through a few neighbouring points to get

$$slope \; of \; polynomial \; through \; \{y_{n+i}\} = f(y_n, t_n), \qquad (21)$$

where y_n is the computed approximation to $y(t_n)$. For example, if a straight-line approximation through points y_n and y_{n+1} is used, the approximate equation becomes

$$\frac{y_{n+1} - y_n}{t_{n+1} - t_n} = f(y_n, t_n).$$

This method is called Euler's method. It is usually written $y_{n+1} = y_n + hf(y_n, t_n)$. If y_0 is given as an initial value, this formula can be used to compute successive values of y_1, y_2, etc. Euler's method is the simplest of all methods but is seldom the most efficient.

In the finite element method, the region over which the solution is to be computed is divided up into a number of small subregions called elements. The unknown solution is expressed as a sum of basis functions $\varphi_i(x)$, which are polynomials in each of the elements, continuous across the boundaries of the elements (and possibly having continuous derivatives), and such that each is zero except in a very small number of elements. The simplest basis functions are the linear functions, which will be illustrated in one dimension. In this case, an interval (say, [0, 1]) of the real line is divided into a series of subintervals. These are called $[x_i, x_{i+1}]$ for $i = 0, 1, \ldots, N$, where $x_0 = 0$, $x_i < x_{i+1}$, and $x_{N+1} = 1$. The ith basis function is as shown in Figure 14. It is zero except in the intervals from x_{i-1} to x_{i+1}, where it rises to 1 linearly and then falls back to zero. It is known

Initial-value and boundary-value problems

Finite difference methods

Finite element methods

as a hat function. (The zeroth hat function is 1 at x_0 and falls to zero at x_1, while the $(N+1)$st rises from zero at x_N to 1 at x_{N+1}.) The unknown y is expressed as

$$y = a_0\varphi_0(x) + a_1\varphi_1(x) + \cdots + a_{N+1}\varphi_{N+1}(x). \quad (22)$$

This is a piecewise-linear function.

The next step in the finite element method is to use the differential equation to compute the unknown parameters a_i in (22). This function cannot satisfy the differential equation in general because the differential equation implies relations at all points in the interval. There are an infinite number of points, but there are only a finite number of parameters to be chosen. There are several ways to proceed. One is to apply the differential equation at a finite number of points only. This is called collocation and is applicable in some situations. Another way, valuable when the original problem satisfies a minimum-energy principle, is to seek the minimum-energy form of the approximation. This is an important method for many physical problems because they frequently satisfy a minimum-energy principle. For example, the shape assumed by a soap bubble is the one that has the least energy.

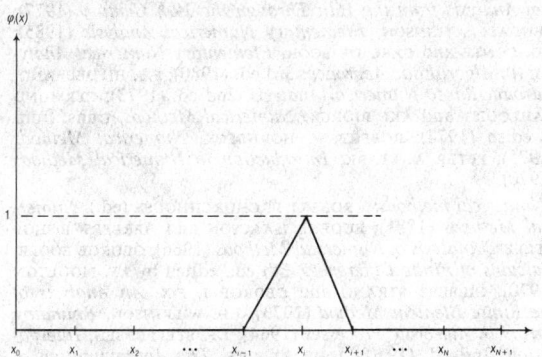

Figure 14: Example of a hat function used as a basis function in the finite-element method of finding approximate solutions of differential equations (see text).

As more points or elements are used, the mesh spacing diminishes, and the truncation error or residual in methods such as Euler's method becomes smaller. Methods for which these errors diminish as the mesh spacing is reduced are called consistent. Unfortunately, consistency alone is not enough to guarantee accuracy, because the number of mesh points or elements, and hence the number of equations such as (22), is increasing at the same time. Each of these approximate equations contributes a small error, and it is possible that the contribution of an increasingly large number of increasingly small errors could have a large effect. A critical property of methods is their stability. The technical definition of stability depends on the type of problem, but the essential idea is that as the number of mesh points (and approximate equations) increases, the effect of a single small error remains bounded. The so-called equivalency theorem for properly posed initial value problems in differential equations states that the consistency and stability of a method guarantee the convergence of the answer—that is, the errors in the answer shrink to zero as the mesh spacing is reduced.

Stability of methods (margin note)

APPLICATIONS AND IMPLEMENTATION

Methods for the numerical approximation and solution of equations are applied to complex problems that arise in the utilization of computers for a variety of tasks. The numerical solution of these problems requires their decomposition into sequences of subtasks that can be solved by standard methods. Many of these methods are made available to users through mathematical software that consists of programs organized to provide reliable solutions to large classes of problems on various types of computers. This section discusses two important applications and the implementation of methods in software for high-speed computation.

Numerical optimization. Many problems involve finding the best—in some defined respect—of many possible solutions. The best solution might be the one leading to the lowest cost, the largest profit, or the shortest journey. Such problems are ones of optimization. Because of their economic importance, their efficient computational solution is extremely important. The mathematical problem is to find a set of values x_i such that $\varphi(\{x_i\})$ is as small (or as large) as possible, where $\{x_i\}$ means the set of all x_i, $i = 1, 2, \ldots, n$. The function φ represents the cost, the profit, or other value to be optimized. It is called the cost function, or objective function, and the problem is usually defined so that the cost is to be minimized. In many problems, the variables, x_i, are subject to constraints. These can be equality or inequality constraints, or both. They take the form $f_j(\{x_i\}) = 0$, $j = 1, 2, \ldots, p$, for the equality constraints and $g_k(\{x_i\}) \geq 0$, $k = 1, 2, \ldots, q$, for the inequality constraints. Either or both of p and q can be zero, meaning that there are no constraints in that class. The cost function and the constraints may be linear or nonlinear. If both are linear, the problem belongs to the specialty called linear programming. For a discussion of this topic, see the article OPTIMIZATION, THE MATHEMATICAL THEORY OF.

Linear programming (margin note)

Linear programming problems can involve thousands of variables and require the solution of numerous linear equations at each step of an iterative process. Nonlinear optimization is an important problem that is computationally more difficult than linear programming. The simplest case is the minimization of a function of a single variable, $\varphi(x)$. If the function is as shown in Figure 15, the problem is to find the point marked **P**. At that point the curve has a horizontal tangent; that is, its derivative is zero. One method is to solve the nonlinear equation $d\varphi(x)/dx = 0$ using the methods discussed for nonlinear equations. This method, however, requires a technique for evaluating the derivative, which may not be convenient or possible in some applications. In such cases, the function $\varphi(x)$ may be evaluated at a number of points and this information used to construct an approximation to the function locally, usually as a quadratic function that has a minimum. This approximation, however, is not a reliable indicator of the minimum, and it is normally used to indicate in which direction to look for a smaller value of the function. In the case of a function of several variables ($n > 1$), the derivative or the function approximation indicates a direction in which to move, that is, a line in the space of x_i variables. The users of most optimization algorithms, in effect, search along that line for a smaller value of the cost function.

Because of the nonlinearities, these problems are very difficult, and it is not possible to develop methods that always work. Even in the simple example shown in Figure 15, a method might find the local minimum at **Q** instead of the global minimum at **P**.

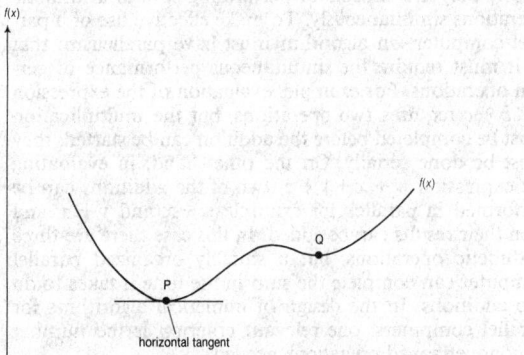

Figure 15: *Nonlinear optimization.*
In seeking the global minimum **P**, computational difficulties may lead the procedure to the local minimum **Q** (see text).

Inverse problems. An inverse problem takes the form: "Here is the answer, what was the question?" These problems arise when a person needs to determine some information, such as the density of different regions in the interior of a human head to check for medical problems, but it is not possible to gather all of the information needed by direct methods, as it clearly is not in this example. What the person can determine is information concerning the amount of X rays that can be transmitted along various line segments through the head. This information will give an estimate of the average density along the whole line but not at any specific interior point. The inverse problem in this example is to start with measurements along many different lines and with these data to calculate the density at all interior points.

Inverse problems are ill-posed because there are usually many different questions that could have yielded the same answer. This is simply illustrated in the interpolation and approximation problems discussed above. A function is infinite dimensional, so that if its values are given at a finite set of points, its values cannot be determined everywhere; in fact, there are infinitely many functions passing through any given set of points (as many different functions can be drawn as desired). In computing an approximation, assumptions are made concerning the nature of the function—for example, that it is a polynomial or has some other form. The same approach is taken to inverse problems: assumptions are made about the nature of the unknown function so that the finite amount of data in the observations is sufficient to determine that function. This is called regularization and converts the ill-posed problem into a properly posed one.

Large-scale scientific computation. The increasing speed of computers and advances in numerical methods have made it possible to solve most small problems rapidly by means of readily available software, and the attention of many numerical analysts has turned to the solution of problems so large that they require inordinate amounts of computer time. The use of the most efficient method has much greater importance in large problems than it does in small ones. In the latter the flexibility of human use of the program may be of much greater importance. One measure of the efficiency of a numerical method is the number of arithmetic operations needed to solve a problem. (Others include the amount of memory used and the order in which it is used, but these issues are more properly subjects of computer science.) Computational complexity is the study of the inherent computational cost (measured by number of operations) of solving a problem. The result of a complexity analysis is an estimate of how rapidly the solution time increases as the problem size increases. It can be used to analyze problems and assist in the design of algorithms for their solution.

Computational complexity

On a serial computer, which is one with a single processor capable of performing only one arithmetic operation at a time, the time needed to solve a problem is proportional to the number of operations, so that this is the number that the numerical analyst tries to reduce in algorithm design. Because parallel computers have more than one processor, they are capable of performing several arithmetic operations simultaneously. To make effective use of a parallel computer, an algorithm must have parallelism; that is, it must require the simultaneous performance of certain operations. For example, evaluation of the expression $a \times b + c$ requires two operations, but the multiplication must be completed before the addition can be started: they must be done serially. On the other hand, in evaluating the expression $w + x + y + z$, two of the additions can be performed in parallel, for example $w + x$ and $y + z$, and then their results can be added. In this case there are three arithmetic operations, but a suitably organized parallel computer can complete the sum in the time it takes to do two additions. In the design of numerical algorithms for parallel computers, one relevant criterion is the number of nonoverlapped operations needed.

Mathematical software. An important product of the numerical analyst's activity is mathematical software. It consists of computer programs designed to solve classes of numerical problems both automatically and reliably. Such software can be used by people with little knowledge of numerical techniques, and the programs themselves determine, on the basis of evaluations of the mathematical expressions provided by the user, the best method to use and the parameters of that method. For example, in software for differential equations, the program might decide which of several methods to use and what mesh spacing to use for the method chosen. Since there are infinitely many problems and a program can evaluate a function only at a finite number of points, it is possible for such software to make mistakes (but so can people who try to solve problems). Robust software is software that is not only reliable but that also attempts to determine when it has encountered an intractable problem and informs the user that an answer cannot be found, rather than returning an incorrect one. The oft-heard statement that "any answer is better than none" is not true for most computational problems, as any passenger on an airplane—pondering the amount of numerical computation used in its safe and efficient design—realizes. The challenge to numerical analysts is to develop methods that compute accurate results efficiently or to recognize that they cannot do so.

BIBLIOGRAPHY

General works: HERMAN H. GOLDSTINE, *A History of Numerical Analysis from the 16th Through the 19th Century* (1977); KENDALL ATKINSON, *Elementary Numerical Analysis* (1985); S.D. CONTE and CARL DE BOOR, *Elementary Numerical Analysis: An Algorithmic Approach,* 3rd ed. (1980); F.B. HILDEBRAND, *Introduction to Numerical Analysis,* 2nd ed. (1973); GERMUND DAHLQUIST and ÅKE BJÖRCK, *Numerical Methods,* trans. from Swedish (1974); ROBERT W. HORNBECK, *Numerical Methods* (1975); PETER A. STARK, *Introduction to Numerical Methods* (1970).

Numerical methods: ROBERT F. CHURCHHOUSE (ed.), *Numerical Methods* (1981); EUGENE ISAACSON and HERBERT BISHOP KELLER, *Analysis of Numerical Methods* (1966); GEORGE BOOLE, *Calculus of Finite Differences,* 5th ed., edited by J.F. MOULTON (1970); GILBERT STRANG and GEORGE J. FIX, *An Analysis of the Finite Element Method* (1973); J.H. WILKINSON, *Rounding Errors in Algebraic Processes* (1964); J.F. STEFFENSEN, *Interpolation,* 2nd ed. (1950); JOHN R. RICE, *The Approximation of Functions,* 2 vol. (1964–69); L. COLLATZ, *Functional Analysis and Numerical Mathematics* (1966; originally published in German, 1964); and E.W. CHENEY, *Introduction to Approximation Theory,* 2nd ed. (1982).

Solution of equations: J.H. WILKINSON and C. REINSCH, *Linear Algebra* (1971); BEN NOBLE and JAMES W. DANIEL, *Applied Linear Algebra,* 2nd ed. (1977); A.S. HOUSEHOLDER, *The Numerical Treatment of a Single Nonlinear Equation* (1970); J.E. DENNIS, JR., and ROBERT B. SCHNABEL, *Numerical Methods for Unconstrained Optimization and Nonlinear Equations* (1983); GEORGE E. FORSYTHE, "What Is a Satisfactory Quadratic Equation Solver?", pp. 53–61 in BRUNO DEJON and PETER HENRICI (eds.), *Constructive Aspects of the Fundamental Theorem of Algebra* (1969); J.M. ORTEGA and W.C. RHEINBOLDT, *Iterative Solution of Nonlinear Equations in Several Variables* (1970); J.F. TRAUB, *Iterative Methods for the Solution of Equations,* 2nd ed. (1982); A.M. OSTROWSKI, *Solution of Equations in Euclidean and Banach Spaces,* 3rd ed. (1973); L.M. MILNE-THOMSON, *The Calculus of Finite Differences,* 2nd ed. (1981); PETER HENRICI, *Discrete Variable Methods in Ordinary Differential Equations* (1962); G.D. SMITH, *Numerical Solution of Partial Differential Equations: Finite Difference Methods,* 3rd ed. (1985); C. WILLIAM GEAR, *Numerical Initial Value Problems in Ordinary Differential Equations* (1971); L.G. CHAMBERS, *Integral Equations: A Short Course* (1976); and GENE H. GOLUB and CHARLES F. VAN LOAN, *Matrix Computations* (1983).

Applications and implementations: G.M. PHILLIPS and P.J. TAYLOR, *Theory and Applications of Numerical Analysis* (1973); R.W. HAMMING, *Numerical Methods for Scientists and Engineers,* 2nd ed. (1973, reprinted 1987); CURTIS F. GERALD and PATRICK O. WHEATLEY, *Applied Numerical Analysis,* 3rd ed. (1984); CARL-ERIC FRÖBERG, *Numerical Mathematics: Theory and Computer Applications,* rev. ed. (1985; originally published in Swedish, 1962); GEORGE E. FORSYTHE, MICHAEL A. MALCOLM, and CLEVE B. MOLER, *Computer Methods for Mathematical Computations* (1977); BRUCE W. ARDEN (ed.), *What Can Be Automated?: The Computer Science and Engineering Research Study* (1980); and C. WILLIAM GEAR, "Numerical Software: Science or Alchemy?", *Advances in Computers,* 19:229–248 (1980).

(C.W.Ge.)

Nutrition

Nutrition is the process by which an organism absorbs and utilizes food substances. The study of nutrition involves the identification of individual nutrients essential for growth and for the maintenance of individual organisms; it includes the determination of interrelationships among nutrients within individual organisms, as well as the evaluation of the quantitative requirements of organisms for specific nutrients under various environmental conditions. Treated in this article are the identification and determination of the requirements of nutrients, the ways in which they vary from one organism to another, and the ways in which requirements for certain of them arose. Human nutritional requirements are then discussed, followed by a review of the diseases and disorders related to nutrition.

For coverage of related topics in the *Macropædia* and *Micropædia*, see the *Propædia*, sections 421, 422, and 423.

This article is divided into the following sections:

General features of nutrients and nutrition

FUNCTIONS OF FOOD

Food serves three functions in most living organisms. First, it provides materials that are metabolized either by oxidative or by fermentative processes to supply the energy required for the absorption and translocation of nutrients, for the synthesis of cell materials, for motility and locomotion, for excretion of waste products, and for all other activities of the organism. Second, food supplies the electron donors (reducing agents) required for the formation of the reduced coenzymes (enzyme components) necessary for the synthetic processes that occur within the cell. Third, food provides the materials from which all of the structural and catalytic components of the living cell can be assembled by processes sometimes called anabolism. The three roles of food are not mutually exclusive; energy-yielding substances in many organisms may function in all three ways, and essential nutrients, if present in excess, may frequently be metabolized to supply energy.

The essential precursors (*i.e.*, the substances from which other substances are formed) of cell materials can be divided into two groups—nonessential nutrients, which can be synthesized by the cell from other materials, and essential nutrients, which, because they cannot be synthesized by the cell, must be supplied in foods. All of the inorganic materials required for growth, together with an assortment of organic compounds whose number may vary from one to 30 or more, depending on the organism, fall into the latter category. Although organisms are able to synthesize nonessential nutrients, such nutrients are frequently utilized directly if present in food, thereby saving the organism the need to expend the energy required to synthesize them.

Nutritional patterns. One method of classifying living organisms on a nutritional basis centres on the way in which the functions of food are carried out. Thus, organisms such as green plants and some bacteria that need only inorganic compounds for growth are called autotrophic organisms; and organisms, including all animals, fungi, and most bacteria, that require both inorganic and organic compounds for growth are called heterotrophic. Although these general terms are widely employed, the classification has been broadened to describe various nutritional patterns that have been observed. In one scheme, organisms are classified according to the energy source they utilize. Phototrophic, or photosynthetic, organisms trap light energy and convert it to chemical energy in the form of an energy-rich compound, adenosine triphosphate (ATP); chemoautotrophic, or chemosynthetic, organisms utilize inorganic or organic compounds to supply their ATP requirements. An additional method of differentiation is based on the type of electron-donor material utilized to form the reduced coenzymes required for synthesis of cell

Anabolism

Autotrophic and heterotrophic organisms

constituents. If the electron-donor material consists of inorganic compounds, the organism is said to be lithotrophic; if organic, the organism is organotrophic. Combinations of these patterns may also be used to describe organisms; higher plants, for example, are photolithotrophic; *i.e.,* they utilize light energy, with the inorganic compound water serving as the ultimate electron donor. Certain photosynthetic bacteria that cannot utilize water as the electron donor and require organic compounds for this purpose are called photo-organotrophs. Animals, by this classification, are chemoorganotrophs; *i.e.,* they utilize chemical compounds to supply ATP and organic compounds as electron donors.

Despite wide variations in the nature of the external energy source utilized by various organisms, all organisms form from the external energy source the immediate intracellular source of energy, ATP, which is common to all cells. Through the breaking of the high-energy phosphate bonds of ATP and thus by its conversion to a less energy-rich compound, adenosine diphosphate (ADP), ATP provides the energy for the chemical and mechanical work required by an organism. The energy requirements of the organism can be measured in either joules or calories; the need for cell-precursor materials cannot be.

Chemo-
organo-
trophs

All animals, fungi, and most bacteria are chemoorganotrophs (*i.e.,* organic compounds supply both ATP and serve as electron donors). In these organisms the multiple roles played by foodstuffs are partially obscured because the carbon-containing compounds that serve as energy sources also serve as electron donors and provide intermediate compounds from which many cell materials are synthesized. Similarly, essential organic nutrients, when present in excess, may be utilized in part to provide the energy needs of the organisms.

Nutritional evolution of organisms. Little is known about the nutritional evolution of living organisms. Nucleic acids, proteins, carbohydrates, and fats, which are present in all living cells, are formed by specific reaction sequences from a limited number of smaller compounds, most of which are common to all living organisms and, according to current theories, were available on Earth before life arose. Since less complex metabolic organization and less energy are required to synthesize cellular proteins from preformed amino acids than from carbon dioxide and other precursors, it is assumed that the simplest early forms of life were heterotrophic organisms requiring many organic nutrients for growth and that they selected such nutrients from their surroundings. As the supply of these preformed substances was exhausted the organisms presumably developed the capacity to synthesize these preformed substances from simpler (precursor) materials present in the environment; in some organisms, this synthesizing capacity eventually evolved to the extent that carbon from carbon dioxide could be utilized to synthesize organic compounds.

At this point, autotrophy, as it now is known, became possible; autotrophy, in fact, may have evolved as a result of the exhaustion of the supply of preformed organic materials in the environment and the consequent necessity of organisms to synthesize the requirements themselves in order to survive. Implicit in this theory is the demonstrable assumption that autotrophic cells contain the most complex biosynthetic organization found in living things and that heterotrophic cells are simpler in that certain biosynthetic pathways do not occur. After the evolution of photosynthesis, a constantly renewable source of the organic compounds necessary for heterotrophic cell growth became available. It became feasible that those organisms whose environments provided a constantly available supply of a given compound could lose, through changes in their genetic material (mutations), the ability to synthesize that compound and still survive. Entire biosynthetic pathways may have been lost in this way; as long as such mutant organisms remained in an environment that supplied the necessary compound, the simplification in cellular organization and the energy saved by using preformed cell components would have given them a competitive advantage over the more complex parents from which they were derived and permitted stabilization of the mutation within

Effects of
mutation

the cell type. A theory that the requirements of modern organisms for essential organic nutrients arose through the loss of synthetic abilities present in more complex parent organisms was confirmed between 1940 and 1950 by the discovery that artificially produced mutant offspring of microorganisms can be readily obtained and may require the presence of one or more preformed organic compounds, which the parent microorganisms could synthesize.

Methods of ingestion or penetration of nutrients. Foodstuffs of chemoorganotrophs are composed chiefly of large molecules, such as nucleic acids, proteins, lipids, and carbohydrates, which are derived from other organisms. When these materials are eaten as food, they usually must be broken down into the low-molecular-weight substances from which they were formed (*e.g.,* purine and pyrimidine bases from nucleic acids, amino acids from proteins, fatty acids from fats, and simple sugars from carbohydrates) before they can be absorbed and utilized. The breakdown process is generally accomplished outside the cells (extracellularly) of both unicellular and multicellular organisms through hydrolysis (breakdown involving water), catalyzed by specific enzymes secreted for this purpose. Some unicellular organisms (*e.g.,* the protozoan genus *Amoeba*), however, engulf particulate matter and hydrolyze it intracellularly.

The organic products of digestion produced extracellularly, together with essential inorganic nutrients, must cross one or more cell membranes before they can be utilized for growth. When nutrient concentrations are high, some materials may diffuse through the cell membrane to enter the cell. Absorption of some materials can occur from an extracellular solution containing small quantities of the nutrients to an intracellular solution containing larger quantities (active transport) and is catalyzed within the cell membrane by systems that are specific for the type of compound being transported. Those catalysts best characterized involve either specific proteins with high affinity for the nutrient substance being transferred or enzymes that chemically modify the nutrient during its passage through the membrane or both.

Absorption
of nutrients

DETERMINATION OF ESSENTIAL REQUIREMENTS

It has been estimated that the approximate quantities of chemical elements in the human body (in percent of wet weight) are oxygen, 65; carbon, 18; hydrogen, 10; nitrogen, 3; calcium, 2; phosphorus, 1.1; sulfur, 0.25; potassium, 0.20; sodium, 0.15; chlorine, 0.15; magnesium, 0.05; iron, 0.004; copper, 0.00015; manganese, 0.00013; and iodine, 0.00004. Also present are traces of about 20 other elements—*e.g.,* zinc, cobalt, silicon, molybdenum, selenium, aluminum, arsenic, barium, boron, bromine, cadmium, chromium (Table 1). Analytical figures such as those for humans given above serve to distinguish between chemical elements that occur in relatively large amounts—oxygen, carbon, nitrogen, sulfur, and phosphorus—and the so-called trace elements, an obsolescent term applied to elements that are present in small amounts and that in the past could be detected in tissues but not analyzed accurately.

Trace
elements

The methods used to determine the pure substances necessary for growth are similar in principle for all organisms. Occasionally, crude diets lacking only one or a few nutrients result in some naturally occurring deficiency disease; the substance that cures such a condition can be determined directly by adding it to the diet. Certain vitamins were recognized in this way. In the absence of a deficiency condition, a crude nutrient medium (or diet) adequate for growth is selected for the organism to be studied, and attempts are then made to replace the various ingredients of the medium with purified materials and, finally, with substances of known composition. If replacement with substances of known composition permits growth, the added materials can be determined with relative ease; if the pure substances do not allow growth, however, chemical testing must be carried out to isolate and identify the substances in crude materials that permit growth. Detailed nutritional requirements of many organisms are known, and essentially all of the organic nutrients are available as pure compounds, so determination of the nutrient requirements of a previously unstudied organism is a comparatively easy task. Elucidation of trace-element requirements remains troublesome, however, because these substances occur commonly as contaminants in other materials.

ESSENTIAL INORGANIC NUTRIENTS

Table 1 is a list of inorganic elements (minerals) that are essential for the growth of living things, together with one or more examples of organisms that exhibit a requirement for them. The effects of certain mineral deficiencies on the development of higher plants and animals are illustrated by several photographs. Naturally occurring deficiencies of a number of different trace elements occur in various parts of the world in special types of soils and are therefore of tremendous economic and agricultural importance.

Specialized mineral requirements

Several examples of specialized mineral requirements are present in Table 1. Boron, for example, has been demonstrated to be required for the growth of many—perhaps all—higher plants but has not been implicated as an essential element in the nutrition of either microorganisms or animals. Trace amounts of fluorine (as fluoride) are certainly beneficial, and perhaps essential, for proper tooth formation in higher animals, but no essential role for fluorine in other organisms has been found. Similarly, iodine (as iodide) is required in animals for formation of thyroxine, the active component of an important regulatory hormone; it plays no known role in other organisms. Silicon (as silicate) is a prominent component of the outer skeletons of diatomaceous protozoans and similar organisms and is required in them for normal growth. In higher animals, the requirement for silicon is much smaller. A less obvious example of a specialized mineral requirement is provided by calcium, which is required by higher animals in comparatively large amounts because it plays a role in the formation of bone and eggshells (in birds); for other organisms, calcium is an essential nutrient but only as a trace element. Several additional examples of specialized requirements are evident from Table 1. Mineral elements in wide variety are present in trace amounts in almost all foodstuffs. It cannot be assumed that, because a given mineral element is nonessential, it plays no useful role in metabolism.

Antagonistic mineral nutrients

Important antagonistic relationships between certain mineral nutrients also are known. A large excess of rubidium, for example, interferes with the utilization of potassium in some lactic-acid bacteria; zinc can also interfere with manganese utilization in the same organism. In animal nutrition, excessive molybdenum or zinc (both of which are essential minerals) interferes with the utilization of copper, another essential mineral, and, in higher plants, excessive zinc can lead to a disorder that is known as iron chlorosis. Proper nutrient growth media for microorganisms and plants or diets for animals, therefore, require not only that the essential mineral elements be provided in sufficient amounts but also that they be used in the proper ratios to each other.

ESSENTIAL ORGANIC NUTRIENTS

Considered in this section is the nature of the essential organic nutrients, necessary building blocks of various cell components that certain organisms can no longer synthesize and therefore must be supplied to them preformed.

Essential compounds

These essential compounds include certain amino acids, which are the precursors of protein; purine and pyrimidine bases or their derivatives, which are the precursors of nucleic acids; fatty acids, which are precursors of fats and phospholipids; and, occasionally (in mutant organisms), simple sugars (e.g., glucose). Other essential organic nutrients include the vitamins, which are required in small amounts (relative to, for example, the amino acids), because of either the catalytic role or the regulatory role they play in metabolism.

Amino acid requirements. Proteins usually contain about 20 different amino acids or their derivatives, and there are organisms that require none, several, or most of them for growth. Many yeasts and bacteria (e.g., Escherichia coli) are able to synthesize all of their amino acids from other compounds (glucose and ammonium salts). Animals may require up to nine or 10 different

Table 1: Essential Inorganic Nutrients for Living Organisms*

element	utilizable ionic form	representative organisms exhibiting the requirement
Boron	$B_4O_7{}^{2-}$	certain vascular plants and algae; no evidence of an animal requirement
Calcium	Ca^{2+}	plants, animals, most microorganisms
Chlorine	Cl^-	higher animals; no evidence for requirement in plants
Chromium	Cr^{3+}	probably essential in higher animals
Cobalt	Co^{2+}	essential in ruminants; probably functions chiefly through microbial incorporation into vitamin B_{12}
Copper	Cu^{2+}	plants, animals, most microorganisms
Fluorine	F^-	highly beneficial to bone and tooth formation in animals, including humans
Iodine	I^-	higher animals; no evidence for requirement in plants or microorganisms
Iron	Fe^{2+}	animals, higher plants, most microorganisms
Magnesium	Mg^{2+}	animals, plants, microorganisms
Manganese	Mn^{2+}	animals, plants, microorganisms
Molybdenum	$MoO_4{}^{2-}$	animals, plants, nitrogen-fixing bacteria
Nitrogen	NO_3^-, NH_4^+	plants, microorganisms (animals derive nitrogen mostly from organic sources and utilize limited amounts of NH_4^+, but not NO_3^-)
Phosphorus	$PO_4{}^{3-}$	animals, plants, microorganisms
Potassium	K^+	animals, plants, microorganisms
Selenium	$SeO_4{}^{2-}$	higher animals
Silicon	$SiO_4{}^{4-}$	certain Protozoa and Porifera
Sodium	Na^+	animals, some plants, some marine bacteria
Sulfur	$SO_4{}^{2-}$	plants, many bacteria (animals derive sulfur mostly from organic sources)
Vanadium	$VO_4{}^{2-}$	various tunicates and holothurian echinoderms; some algae; possibly higher animals
Zinc	Zn^{2+}	all animals, plants, most microorganisms

*Carbon dioxide (CO_2) and water (H_2O), although not formally tabulated, are important nutrients for all organisms; external sources of carbon dioxide, however, are required for only a few heterotrophic organisms since it is a prominent waste product of energy metabolism in these organisms.

amino acids in their diets. Species of lactic-acid bacteria have been identified as requiring none (Streptococcus bovis), a few (Lactobacillus plantarum), or as many as 17 amino acids (Streptococcus equinus).

Purine and pyrimidine bases and related compounds. A large number of species of microorganisms require one or more of these substances as precursors for the synthesis of nucleic acids. All higher animals examined have retained the capacity to synthesize purine and pyrimidine bases. Certain compounds (putrescine, spermidine, spermine) that are closely associated with nucleic acids in living cells, although synthesized by most organisms, are required preformed by certain bacteria; e.g., Haemophilus parainfluenzae, Neisseria perflava.

Lipids and related compounds. Phospholipids are essential components of all cell membranes. Those organisms that have lost the ability to synthesize certain lipids (since they are supplied in their diets), require them as essential nutrients. Essential fatty acids for rats (and most vertebrates) include linoleic and arachidonic acids and, perhaps, linolenic acid as well. For many bacteria (e.g., Erysipelothrix rhusiopathiae, several species of lactic-acid bacteria), oleic acid is essential for growth, although it can be replaced in most cases by linoleic acid and by an unusual fatty acid called lactobacillic acid.

Choline, inositol, and cholesterol

Choline, a nitrogen-containing compound found in the phospholipid lecithin, is usually listed among the nutrients required by rats, although it can be synthesized by them if sufficient vitamin B_{12} is present. Choline is also required for growth of certain pneumococcal bacteria. Inositol, another structural component of certain lipids, is an essential nutrient for many yeasts but appears to be synthesized by most animals. Finally, the steroid cholesterol is an essential nutrient for a wide variety of protozoans and for the bacteria-like organisms known as mycoplasmas. Higher animals are able to synthesize this important cell constituent; it is not present in most bacteria.

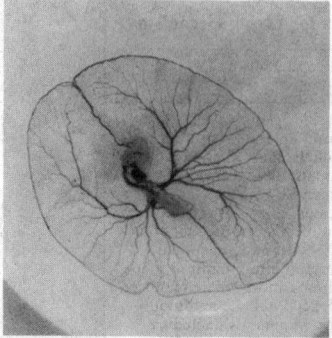
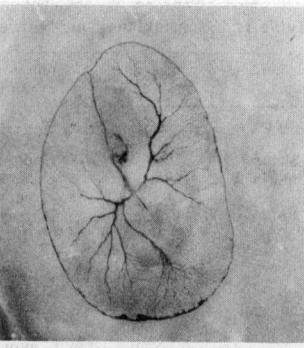

Effects of mineral deficiencies on the development of higher plants and animals.
(Top left) Normal 72-hour embryo from hen fed 10 parts per million of supplementary copper. (Top right) Anemic 72-hour embryo from hen receiving copper-deficient diet. (Centre) A normal chick, left, from hen receiving an adequate amount of zinc in its diet and two chicks from hens given zinc-deficient diets. (Bottom) Tomato leaves from plant grown in (left to right) copper-deficient soil, complete nutrient solution, and zinc-deficient soil.

By courtesy of (bottom) D. Arnon; from (top left, top right, centre)
J.E. Savage, *Federation Proceedings*, vol. 27, p. 927 (1968)

Vitamins. Vitamins may be defined as nutritionally essential organic substances that play a catalytic role within the cell, usually as components of coenzymes or other groups associated with enzymes. More than half of the water-soluble vitamins required by humans were discovered when they were found to be growth factors for microorganisms. Vitamin requirements are specific for each organism, and their deficiency may cause disease. Vitamin deficiencies in young animals usually result in growth failure, various symptoms whose nature depends on the vitamin, and eventual death. Certain vitamins (retinol, calciferol, tocopherol, and ascorbic acid) do not appear to play an essential role in unicellular organisms. Para-aminobenzoic acid is a vitamin for several bacteria only because it is an essential precursor of the vitamin folic acid, which, since it is unable to cross the bacterial cell membrane, must be synthesized from para-aminobenzoic acid. Heme and lipoic acid are typical vitamins for organ-

Para-
amino-
benzoic
acid

isms that cannot synthesize them, but they have a catalytic role in all organisms; they are synthesized by higher animals. A few bacteria have lost the ability to convert certain vitamins to their functional forms, the coenzymes; the preformed coenzymes (or intermediates in their synthesis) thus are vitamins for such organisms.

Interdependency of nutritional requirements. The effects of one mineral nutrient in reducing or increasing the requirement for another have been mentioned previously (see above *Essential inorganic nutrients*). Similar relationships occur among organic nutrients and originate for several reasons, the most common of which are discussed briefly below.

Competition for sites of absorption by the cell. Since absorption of nutrients frequently occurs by way of active transport within cell membranes, an excess of one nutrient (A) may inhibit absorption of a second nutrient (B), if they share the same absorption pathway. In such cases, the apparent requirement for nutrient B increases; B, however, can sometimes be supplied in an alternate form that is able to enter the cell by a different route. Many examples of amino acid antagonism, in which inhibition of growth by one amino acid is counteracted by another amino acid, are best explained by this mechanism. For example, under some conditions *Lactobacillus casei* requires both D- and L-alanine, which differ from each other only in the position of the amino, or NH_2, group in the molecule, and the two forms of this amino acid share the same absorption pathway. Excess D-alanine inhibits growth of this species, but the inhibition can be alleviated either by supplying additional L-alanine or, more effectively, by supplying peptides of L-alanine. The peptides enter the cell by a pathway different from that of the two forms of alanine and, after they are in the cell, can be broken down to form L-alanine. Relationships of this type provide one explanation for the fact that peptides are frequently more effective than amino acids in promoting growth of bacteria.

Amino
acid
antagonism

Competition for sites of utilization within the cell. This phenomenon is similar to that regarding competition for absorption sites, but it occurs inside the cell and only between structurally similar nutrients (*e.g.,* leucine and valine; serine and threonine).

Precursor-product relationships. The requirement of rats and humans for the essential amino acids phenylalanine and methionine is substantially reduced if tyrosine, which is formed from phenylalanine, or cysteine, which is formed from methionine, is added to the diet. These relationships are explained by the fact that tyrosine and cysteine are synthesized in animals from phenylalanine and methio-

By courtesy of The Upjohn Company, Kalamazoo, Mich.

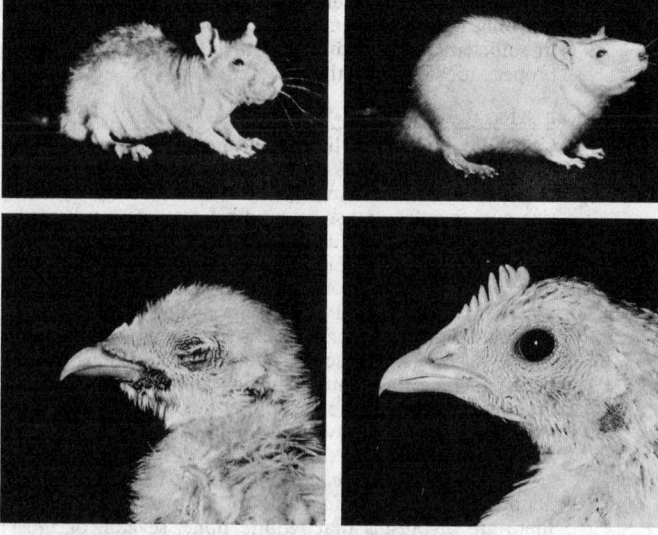

Effects of vitamin deficiencies in animals.
(Top) Rat fed biotin-deficient diet. Same rat after three months on a diet with an adequate amount of biotin. (Bottom) Chick fed a diet deficient in pantothenic acid. Same chick after three weeks on a diet sufficient in pantothenic acid.

nine, respectively. When the former (product) amino acids are supplied preformed, the latter (precursor) amino acids are required in smaller amounts. Several instances of the sparing of one nutrient by another because they have similar precursor-product relationships have been identified in other organisms.

Changes in metabolic pathways within the cell. Rats fed diets containing large amounts of fat require substantially less thiamine than do those fed diets high in carbohydrate. The utilization of carbohydrate as an energy source (*i.e.,* for ATP formation) is known to involve an important thiamine-dependent step, which is bypassed when fat is used as an energy source, and it is assumed that the lessened requirement for thiamine results from the change in metabolic pathways.

COMPARISON OF NUTRIENT REQUIREMENTS

Micro-
nutrients

Trace elements and vitamins are distinguished from other nutrients on the basis of the relatively smaller amounts required. For example, potassium, a mineral element present in comparatively large amounts in all organisms, is required by *Lactobacillus casei* in amounts more than 200 times greater than the requirement for manganese. The magnitude of the requirement for potassium is similar to that for the amino acid leucine. Nutrients such as manganese and the vitamins, which are required in small amounts, are sometimes referred to as micronutrients because of these quantitative relationships. For *Lactobacillus,* glucose is the energy source, and, to permit the amount of growth described, approximately 1,000 times more glucose is required than the nutrients potassium and leucine. These ratios are fairly representative of organoheterotrophs in general. Lactic-acid bacteria, however, form lactic acid from glucose; other organisms, which oxidize this substance to carbon dioxide and water, require only about 5 percent of the amount of glucose required by lactic-acid bacteria for equivalent ATP production and, hence, for equivalent growth.

SYNTROPHISM

Influence
of popula-
tions on
each other

Since the nutritional requirements and metabolic activities of organisms differ, it is clear that two or more different organisms growing relatedly may produce different overall changes in the environment. A rough example is provided by a balanced aquarium, in which aquatic plants utilize light and the waste products of animals—*e.g.,* carbon dioxide, water, ammonia—to synthesize cell materials and generate oxygen, which in turn provide the materials necessary for animal growth. Such relationships are common among microorganisms; *i.e.,* intermediate or end products of metabolism of one organism may provide essential nutrients for another. The mixed populations that result in nature provide examples of this phenomenon, which is called syntrophism; in some instances, the relationship may be so close as to constitute nutritional symbiosis, or mutualism. Several examples of this phenomenon have been found among thiamine-requiring yeasts and fungi, certain of which (group A) synthesized the thiazole component of thiamine molecule but require the pyrimidine portion preformed; for a second group (group B), the relationship is reversed. When group A and group B are grown together in a thiamine-free medium, both types of organisms survive, since each organism synthesizes the growth factor required by its partner; neither organism grows alone under these same conditions. Thus, two or more types of microorganisms frequently grow in situations in which only one species would not.

Such nutritional interrelationships may explain the fact that the nutritionally demanding lactic-acid bacteria are able to coexist with the nutritionally nondemanding coliform bacteria in the intestinal tracts of animals. It is known that the bacterial flora of the intestinal tract synthesize sufficient amounts of certain vitamins (*e.g.,* vitamin K, folic acid) so that detection of deficiency symptoms in rats requires special measures, and the role of rumen bacteria in ruminant animals (*e.g.,* cows, sheep) in rendering otherwise indigestible cellulose and other materials available to the host animal is well-known. These few examples indicate that syntrophic interrelationships are widespread in nature and may contribute substantially to the nutrition of a wide variety of species.   (E.E.Sn./A.S.T.)

Human nutrition and diet

The scope of human nutrition extends far beyond the classical study of the physiological and biochemical processes involved in nourishment; *i.e.,* how substances in food are converted into energy and body tissues. Human nutrition has come to involve all the effects on humans of any component found in food; these include most chronic degenerative diseases (dental decay, coronary heart disease, some cancers, etc.), which are now major targets of research activity. The scope of nutrition extends to the effects of food on human function; *e.g.,* mental function, athletic performance, resistance to infection, and fetal health and development. There is a growing interaction between nutritional science and genetics because of the diversity of human chemical make-up and because food components of which most people are unaware can have marked effects on some individuals. Last, nutrition also considers why people choose to eat the foods they do, even after they have been advised that doing so may be unhealthy. The study of food habits and people's attitudes, beliefs, likes, and dislikes overlaps with the social sciences of physiology, anthropology, sociology, and economics. Dietetics is the application of nutrition in the health sciences.

UTILIZATION OF FOOD BY THE BODY

The human body can be thought of as an engine that releases the energy present in the foods and utilizes it partly for the mechanical work performed by muscles and in secretory processes and partly for the work necessary to maintain its structure and functions. The performance of this work is associated with the production of heat; heat loss is controlled so as to keep body temperature within a narrow range. Unlike other engines, the human body is continually breaking down (catabolism) and building up (anabolism) its component parts. Certain foods supply nutrients essential to the manufacture of the new material and provide energy needed for the chemical reactions involved.

Measuring
energy
utilization

The supply of energy. The energy taken in food and that utilized in daily life can be measured. The measuring unit has been the kilocalorie (kcal), which is 1,000 gram calories; a gram calorie is the amount of heat required to raise one gram of water from 14.5° to 15.5° C at one atmosphere of pressure. Nutritionists are now coming into line with other branches of science and using joules as the unit of energy. One joule is the energy expended when one kilogram is moved one metre by a force of one newton. The amount of energy spent by the whole body and that present in foods are relatively large and are expressed as kilojoules ($kJ = 10^3$ J) or megajoules ($MJ = 10^6$ J). One kilocalorie is equivalent to 4.186 kilojoules.

The energy present in food can be determined directly by measuring the output of heat when the food is oxidized in a calorimeter. Heats of combustion of individual proteins, fats, and starches are about 5.4, 9.3, and 4.1 kilocalories (23, 39, and 17 kilojoules) per gram, respectively.

Not all of this energy is available to the body because some ingested material is not absorbed from the gut and is lost in the feces; further, the nitrogenous compounds are not completely combusted, and some of the energy in proteins is lost in the urine, mostly as urea. Corrections for these losses give physiological values for dietary protein, fat, and carbohydrate of approximately four, nine, and four kilocalories (17, 38, and 17 kilojoules) per gram, respectively. These are called the Atwater factors, after the American physiologist Wilbur Olin Atwater, who, between 1895 and 1905, calculated the quantitative aspects of energy exchanges. Tables of energy value and nutrient content of common foods provide background data for general dietetic advice (see Table 2).

Sources
of energy

Proteins, fats, and carbohydrates can, within wide limits, be interchanged as sources of energy. Among the members of prosperous communities most diets provide 12 percent of the energy as protein, about 40 percent as fat, and 48 percent as carbohydrate. In many poor agricultural soci-

Table 2: The Energy Value and Nutrient Content of Some Common Foods
(values per 100 g edible portion)

	energy		water (g)	carbo-hydrate (g)	protein (g)	fat (g)	alcohol (g)
	kcal	kJ					
Whole wheat flour	318	1,351	14	65.8	13.2	2.0	—
White bread	233	991	39	49.7	7.8	1.7	—
Rice, boiled	123	522	69.9	29.6	2.2	0.3	—
Milk, fresh, whole	65	272	87.6	4.7	3.3	3.8	—
Butter	740	3,041	15.4	trace	0.4	82.0	—
Cheese, Cheddar	406	1,682	37.0	trace	26.0	33.5	—
Beef steak, grilled	218	912	59.3	0	27.3	12.1	—
Tuna, canned in oil	289	1,202	54.6	0	22.8	22.0	—
Potatoes, boiled	80	343	80.5	19.7	1.4	0.1	—
Peas, frozen, boiled	41	175	80.7	4.3	5.4	0.4	—
Cabbage, boiled	9	40	95.7	1.1	1.3	trace	—
Orange, peel removed	35	150	86.1	8.5	0.8	trace	—
Apple, raw	46	196	84.3	11.9	0.3	trace	—
White sugar	394	1,680	trace	105.0	trace	0	—
Beer*, canned	32	132	96.1	2.3	0.3	trace	3.1
Spirits* (gin, whiskey 70 proof)	222	919	59.9	trace	trace	0	31.7

*Values per 100 ml.
Source: A.A. Paul and D.A.T. Southgate, McCance and Widdowson's *The Composition of Foods* (1978).

eties, for whom cereals provide most of the energy, the figures for the individuals' diets are 10 percent for protein, 10 percent for fat, and 80 percent for carbohydrate. Throughout most of the world, protein provides between 8 and 14 percent of the energy ingested. High-fat diets are associated with a high incidence of atherosclerosis (deposits of lipid material in the larger arteries). Wide variations in the proportions of fat and carbohydrate in the diet may, nevertheless, be compatible with good health, at least in the short term. Ethyl alcohol is another source of energy to the body. Only a small part of the alcohol intake, usually less than 5 percent, is excreted in the urine and expired air; most is oxidized in the liver, where it serves as a source of energy with a value of seven kilocalories (29 kilojoules) per gram (almost that of pure fat). Muscle cannot utilize alcohol, and alcohol intake reduces the use of fat and carbohydrate by the liver. In this way alcoholic drinks increase the energy value of a diet and often contribute to obesity and fat deposits in the liver.

Building and maintenance. The body of a young adult male weighing 65 kilograms (143 pounds) consists of some 11 kilograms of protein, nine of fat, one of carbohydrate, four of minerals, and 40 of water. During the first 20 years of life, an average of about 1.5 grams of protein and 150 milligrams of calcium must be retained from the diet every day in order to build soft tissues and skeleton. Tissues, however, are not static, and their components are being continually catabolized and replaced at varying rates. The inner epithelial lining of the gut is replaced every three or four days and red blood cells have a lifespan of only 120 days. On the other hand, collagen, a protein constituent of tendons, is turned over at intervals of a few years. Much of the material derived from the breakdown of tissues is reutilized, but new material is also required from food. Probably some 200 grams of tissue protein is replenished daily in an adult, but the minimal dietary requirement of protein is only about 40 grams per day.

Essential nutrients. The principal evidence that an organic compound is essential is that it consistently cures a specific deficiency disease. An inorganic element is essential if it regularly occurs in the body and is demonstrated to have a function (such as being an integral part of an enzyme). Humans require oxygen, water, food energy, protein, 14 other organic compounds (vitamins and essential fatty acids), and some 18 inorganic elements, as well as carbon, hydrogen, and nitrogen.

Protein. Growing children need more protein per kilogram of body weight than do adults. Protein requirement at all ages is increased by infections not only because there is an increased utilization of protein but also because illness usually impairs the appetite and thus reduces dietary intake of all substances, including protein. In many countries children are weaned on a diet of cereal paps with little or no supplement of milk or other protein-containing foods. Such a diet at the least retards growth and development. If a child on such a diet suffers from an

acute infection, notably measles or gastroenteritis, a severe illness, which may take several forms—known variously as protein-calorie malnutrition, kwashiorkor, or nutritional marasmus—may ensue. The death rate from protein-calorie malnutrition in many poverty-stricken communities is high. (See below *Energy* (*calories*), under the heading *Deficiency diseases*.) Primary protein deficiency is not common among adults, for whom cereals in general satisfy the protein requirement.

Foods vary in the quantity of proteins they contain per 100 grams (or per typical serving). They also vary in the nutritional value, or quality, of their protein. This is because of differences in the pattern of essential amino acids that they contain (see Table 3). Eight amino acids are essential (*i.e.*, required, but not produced, by the body) for humans: isoleucine, leucine, lysine, methionine (which can be partly replaced by cystine), phenylalanine (which can be partly replaced by tyrosine), threonine, tryptophan, and valine. Histidine appears to be essential as well in some situations. These amino acids are not all required in the same amount each day; for example, leucine is required most, and tryptophan least. Vegetable food proteins usually have lower nutritive values because they have suboptimal proportions of one or more essential amino acids, called the limiting amino acids; *e.g.*, lysine in wheat (see Table 3). When vegetable protein sources are combined, however, the amino acid pattern of the combination is usually improved.

Minerals. Iron is required for the synthesis of hemoglobin, the oxygen-binding pigment in red blood cells. Normally the iron liberated from old cells is retained and can be reutilized. When, however, there is chronic bleeding from wounds or there is severe and prolonged menstruation, the normal amount of dietary iron may be insufficient to replenish the body's supply. Losses of iron in the menses, the needs of a fetus, and the inevitable loss at labour and in the milk of a lactating woman increase the iron requirements of women during their reproductive life.

Most dietary iron is in a form that is poorly absorbed from the gut. Many diets contain about 12 milligrams of iron, of which less than 10 percent need be absorbed by a normal adult male. Absorption of iron in plant foods is usually less than 10 percent. The iron in meat is absorbed better and so is that in human milk. As body stores of iron become depleted, the efficiency of intestinal absorption is enhanced. If menstrual losses are large, iron-deficiency anemia follows unless the diet is supplemented with absorbable iron compounds.

Calcium is the most obvious and persistent of the mineral nutrients, yet it is more difficult to measure the adequacy of its intake than for other nutrients. More than 99 percent of the body's calcium is in the skeleton, where it not only provides structural support but also is a large reservoir for maintaining a constant calcium concentration in plasma. Several hormones, including parathormone, cal-

Protein deficiency

Turnover of body stores

Iron and calcium

Table 3: Essential Amino Acid Patterns in Proteins of Some Common Foods*

	human milk	cow's milk	beef muscle	hen's egg	wheat flour	cornmeal (maize)	soy-bean
Histidine	24	27	41	25	25	28	30
Isoleucine	47	53	48	55	39	39	51
Leucine	90	97	86	88	75	128	82
Lysine	60	81	95	72	(25)	(28)	68
Methionine + cystine	36	35	41	59	46	41	33
Phenylalanine + tyrosine	75	84	76	93	84	104	95
Threonine	39	41	49	46	30	40	41
Tryptophan	13	13	11	15	11	(6)	14
Valine	51	64	50	68	44	52	52

*Milligrams of amino acid per one gram of protein. In wheat flour, lysine (ringed) is the limiting amino acid; in cornmeal, lysine and tryptophan (ringed) are both limiting.
Source (except for cornmeal): Japanese Standard Tables of Amino Acid Composition of Foods, 1986, published by Resources Council, Science and Technology Agency.

citonin, and a derivative of vitamin D, are all involved in this regulation. The amount of calcium in the bones is nearly 30 grams at birth and builds up to about 1,200 grams in an adult. Hence, an average of 180 milligrams of calcium must be retained in the body throughout childhood, and the individual daily amounts should reach 400 milligrams during the adolescent growth spurt. Absorption of calcium, like that of many other metallic elements, is inefficient. The diet must therefore supply more calcium than the amount theoretically retained for skeletal growth. Three major questions about calcium are as yet not fully answered by nutritional science: (1) whether generous intakes of calcium during childhood and adolescence will lead to taller adults or heavier bones, (2) whether a generous intake of calcium from about 45 years of age will delay the progress of osteoporosis (thinning of the bones), which occurs in older people and is more likely to cause symptoms in women after menopause, and (3) what mechanisms enable people in Africa, for example, who grow up on cereal diets low in calcium, to retain enough calcium to achieve a skeleton of similar height to those in northern countries where milk and cheese (both rich in calcium) are staples in the diet.

Sodium and potassium
Sodium is present only in small quantities in most natural foods, but salt is added, often in large amounts, in food processing and by cooks to enhance flavour. Sodium is the predominant ion in extracellular fluid; an excess can cause edema (an accumulation of extracellular fluid), especially in conditions such as congestive heart failure. A low sodium intake leads to a lowering of the blood pressure and brings about diuresis, ridding the body of the excess extracellular fluid. There is now much evidence that excess dietary salt may contribute to high blood pressure in some individuals, but other factors are also responsible.

Potassium, present in all natural foods, is the predominant intracellular ion. Deficiency of it does not occur as a result of a primary dietary lack, but it may arise when there is chronic diarrhea or from repeated diuresis. All wasting diseases are associated with loss of potassium from the tissues. Potassium deficiency disturbs the excitability of tissues and leads to paralysis of muscle, including cardiac muscle. Sodium and potassium are two of the most important ions in maintaining the homeostatic equilibrium of the body fluids.

Other elements required by humans are magnesium, iodine, zinc, phosphorus (in the form of phosphate), sulfur (usually in the forms of the amino acids methionine and cystine), and chlorine (in the form of chloride, often combined with sodium). Other elements required in trace amounts are copper, chromium, molybdenum, selenium, cobalt (in the form of vitamin B_{12}), probably fluorine (in the form of fluoride), and possibly vanadium.

Vitamins. For normal nutrition and metabolism the body requires certain organic substances, called vitamins, which it cannot make for itself, at least in sufficient quantities. Many of them function as components of enzyme systems. Because they are required in such small quantities, vitamins do not contribute significantly to the energy needs of the body. In their absence, however, the carbohydrates, fats, and proteins required for energy production and tissue maintenance cannot be properly metabolized. Vitamins were originally identified by letters as each new one was discovered, but this method of nomenclature is being replaced as the vitamins become known by their chemical names (Table 4). For a detailed treatment of deficiency diseases, see below *Deficiency diseases: Vitamins.*

Vitamin deficiency diseases

The evidence that vitamins promote health in any way apart from preventing deficiency diseases is controversial and not established scientifically. The recommended intakes or allowances of vitamins (Table 5) carry a safety margin that allows for a wide range of individual needs, so there are usually no deficiency effects if the intake is only a small percentage below the recommended intake. High intakes are of no benefit and may be dangerous in the cases of the fat-soluble vitamins A and D and the water-soluble vitamin B_6.

CLASSES OF FOODS

The following set of 17 groups covers most of the nutritional differences between foods: (1) cereals and cereal products, (2) starchy roots, (3) legumes (pulses), (4) other vegetables, (5) fruits, (6) nuts and seeds, (7) sugars, syrups, sweets, and preserves, (8) meat, including poultry, and meat products, (9) seafood—finfish and shellfish, (10) eggs and roe, (11) milk, cream, and cheese, (12) fats and oils, (13) herbs and spices, (14) nonalcoholic, nondairy beverages, (15) alcoholic beverages, (16) dietetic preparations, (17) miscellaneous (*e.g.*, salt and vinegar).

Grouping of food

Cereals. Of the present world population, half lives in Asia and three-quarters in developing countries. In these areas cereals play the leading dietary role. On the whole, the carbohydrate-rich cereals compare favourably with the protein-rich foods in energy value; in addition they are significantly less expensive to produce. Therefore most of the world's diets are arranged to meet main calorie re-

Table 4: Nomenclature of Vitamins

name recommended by IUNS*	alternative name	usual pharmaceutical preparation
Vitamin A	Retinol	Retinol
Thiamin	Vitamin B_1	Thiamine hydrochloride
Riboflavin	Vitamin B_2	Riboflavin
Niacin	Nicotinic acid and nicotinamide	Nicotinamide
Vitamin B_6	Pyroxidine	Pyroxidine hydrochloride
Pantothenic acid		Calcium pantothenate
Biotin		Biotin
Folate	Folacin	Folic acid
Vitamin B_{12}	Cobalamin	Cyanocobalamin or hydroxocobalamin
Vitamin C	Ascorbic acid	Ascorbic acid
Vitamin D	Vitamins D_2 and D_3	(Ergo) calciferol
Vitamin E		α-Tocopherol
Vitamin K		Vitamin K_1

*International Union of Nutritional Sciences. Note that in some instances IUNS spelling differs from standard usage.
Source: A. Stewart Truswell *et al., ABC of Nutrition* (1986).

Table 5: Size of Adult Requirements for Essential Nutrients

adult daily requirement* in foods	nutrients
2–10 µg	vitamin D, vitamin B_{12}, vitamin K, chromium
100 µg	biotin, iodine, selenium
200 µg	folic acid, molybdenum
1–2 mg	{ vitamin A, thiamine, riboflavin, vitamin B_6, fluoride, copper
5–10 mg	pantothenate, manganese
15 mg	niacin, vitamin E, iron, zinc
50 mg	vitamin C
300 mg	magnesium
1 g	calcium, phosphorus (as phosphate)
1–5 g	sodium, chloride, potassium, essential fatty acids
50 g	protein (8–10 essential amino acids)
50–100 g	available carbohydrate
1 kg (litre)	water

*Figures are approximate and in places rounded. The range of size of requirements is about 10^9.
Source: A. Stewart Truswell et al., *ABC of Nutrition* (1986).

Forms of cereals

quirements from the cheaper carbohydrate foods, and the protein-rich foods are used sparingly to provide essential amino acids. Cereal products generally contribute a large proportion of the dietary protein of vegetable origin, in addition to their carbohydrate content.

Cereals are largely consumed as bread and to a lesser extent as cakes, crackers, and breakfast cereals. They are also consumed in other forms in some countries; e.g., boiled, crushed, or rolled, made into pasta, etc. There has been controversy as to the relative merits of white bread and bread made from whole wheat flour of much longer extraction, which is darker in colour. White flour consists of about 72 percent of the grain but contains little of the germ, or embryo, and of the outer coverings (bran). Since the B vitamins are concentrated mainly in the scutellum (covering of the germ), and to a lesser extent in the bran, the vitamin B content of white flour, unless artificially enriched, is much less than that of brown flour. The dietary fibre is mostly in the bran, and white flour contains only about one-third of that in whole wheat flour. White flour is routinely fortified with synthetic vitamins in a number of countries, including the United States and United Kingdom, so that the vitamin content is similar to that of the darker flours. In the United Kingdom white bread is also fortified with calcium carbonate.

Nutritional value

Table 6 shows the contribution of cereals to the intakes of a number of key nutrients in the United Kingdom. As a group they provide almost half the carbohydrate, one-quarter of the protein and calcium, more than one-third of the iron, and nearly half the thiamine. The protein of cereals does not have as high a nutritive value as that of many animal foods because of the low lysine content. It is possible to fortify bread with synthetic lysine. Corn has been altered to produce a higher lysine and tryptophan content than standard corn (see Table 3), but the yield is lower. The usual solution to the suboptimal amino acid pattern of cereals is to eat them mixed with other foods (legumes, animal foods) that have more than enough lysine. This is the traditional, intuitive way in which cereals have been eaten in settled communities in many different cultures. The amino acids of mixed protein foods tend to complement one another and increase the percentage of the limiting amino acid. In less developed countries, the contribution of cereals to the intake of nutrients is greater than in the United Kingdom, which is an example of an industrial country in which the cereal consumed by humans is predominantly wheat.

Wheat and rice are the two major cereals for human consumption; wheat in Europe, North America, and northern India, and rice in East and Southeast Asia. The nutritional weakness of rice is its low thiamine and riboflavin content when it is milled to polished rice. Beriberi was formerly common in poor Asian communities in which a large proportion of the diet consisted of polished rice. Beriberi has almost completely disappeared from Asia with the advent of greater availability of other foods, of better ways of handling the rice (e.g., parboiling), and, in some areas, of fortification with thiamine.

Corn differs from other cereals in that the yellow form contains carotenoids with provitamin A activity. Its other special feature is its low content of tryptophan. The niacin in corn is in a bound form that cannot be digested and absorbed by humans unless pretreated with lime (calcium hydroxide) or by roasting. Niacin is also formed in the body as a metabolite of the amino acid tryptophan, but this alternative source is not available when the tryptophan content is too low.

Niacin

Most cereals contain little fat, although oats contain 7 percent. Wheat contains a type of dietary fibre (arabinoxylan hemicellulose) that is particularly valuable for treatment and prevention of constipation. It increases the bulk of the feces and shortens the mouth-to-anus transit time. Bran is a concentrated source of the same dietary fibre.   (D.W.K.-J./A.S.T.)

Starchy roots. Potatoes, cassava, and yams are easily cultivated and are valuable as cheap sources of energy. Their nutritive value, in general, resembles that of cereals, but their protein content is lower. Protein deficiency may be common in tropical communities in which the staple food is cassava or yams. The potato, however, provides some protein—less than cereal does—but also contains some vitamin C, and sweet potatoes contain the pigment beta-carotene, convertible in the body into vitamin A. Although the quantity of protein in potatoes is only small (2 percent), its nutritive value appears to be high. Cassava contains half the protein of potatoes. There are toxic substances in, or adjacent to, some of the starchy root foods that have to be avoided or dealt with by careful preparation; e.g., solanine in the green sprouts of potatoes and a cyanide compound in the leaves and outer parts of the roots of cassava.

Legumes (pulses). Peas and beans, the seeds of Fabaceae, resemble the cereals in nutritive value but have a higher protein content and, since they are not subject to milling, are a good source of B vitamins. They are thus a valuable supplement to a cereal diet, especially in tropical or subtropical countries; moreover, they, particularly the soybean, are also valued for their taste. The soybean is especially rich in protein (38 percent) and is a major commercial source of edible oil.

Table 6: Percentage of Several Major Nutrients Supplied by Food Groups in the United Kingdom*

	energy	protein	fat	carbo-hydrate	iron	cal-cium	thi-amine	vitamin C	vitamin A
Milk, cream, and cheese	14	22	19	7	3	59	12	7	13.5
Meat	16	32	27	2	24	3	15	2	37
Fish	1	4.5	1	0.3	2	1	1	—	—
Eggs	2	4.5	3	—	5	1.5	2	—	3
Butter, margarine, and other fats	15.5	—	37	—	1	—	—	—	20
Sugar, syrups, preserves	9	—	—	20	1	—	—	—	—
Total vegetables	9	9.5	2	15	19	6	19	48	24
Total fruits	3	1	—	5	4	2	4	41	1
Total cereals	29	24	10	48	37	24	42	—	1
(Breads)	(13.5)	(14)	(2)	(24)	(17)	(12)	(21)	(—)	(—)

*From the Household Food Consumption Survey (1981). The figures for breads are in parentheses because they are part of the total for cereals.

Vegetables and fruits. Vegetables and fruits all have similar nutritive properties. Because 70 percent or more of their weight is water, they provide comparatively little energy or protein, but many contain vitamin C and carotene, two nutrients not found in cereals. Fresh fruits, particularly the citrus variety, and their juices are usually rich in vitamin C, but cooked vegetables are an uncertain source, as this vitamin is easily destroyed. Vegetables and fruits contain fibre, which adds bulk to the intestinal content and is useful in preventing constipation. Vegetables also provide calcium and iron but often in a form that is poorly absorbed.

Sugars, preserves, and syrups. In adults in the United States, the average intake of added sugars is 60 grams per day in males, or one pound per week. The sugars, mostly sucrose and high-fructose corn syrup, are added both in processing and at the table. Together sucrose and fructose provide 12 percent of the average total calories in adults and a little more in children. There are also naturally occurring sugars in foods (fructose, glucose, sucrose in fruits and some vegetables, and lactose in milk). The intake of these in the United States is about 8 percent of total caloric intake in adults and much more in young children (due to the lactose). Sugar, however, contains no protein, no minerals, and no vitamins and thus has been called a source of "empty calories."

Advantages and dis-advantages

Sugar is an excellent preservative because it adsorbs water and prevents the growth of microorganisms. Jams contain from 30 to 60 percent sugar, and honey and natural syrups (*e.g.*, maple) are composed of more than 75 percent sugar.

Meat, fish, and eggs. Meats generally consist of about 20 percent protein, 20 percent fat, and 60 percent water; the amount of fat present in a particular portion of meat varies greatly, not only with the kind of meat—pork, beef, lamb, etc.—but also with its quality; the "energy value" varies in direct proportion with the fat content. Meat is valuable for its protein, which is of high biological value. Meat also is an excellent source of B vitamins, including thiamine, one of the most important. Pork is the best source of thiamine, liver is next, and skeletal muscle, from any meat source, is third. Meat is also a good source of niacin, vitamin B_6, vitamin B_{12}, other vitamins of the B group, and the mineral nutrients iron, zinc, phosphorus, potassium, and magnesium. Liver is the storage organ for, and very rich in, vitamins A and B_{12}. It is also an excellent source of riboflavin and of folic acid.

Fish

The muscular tissue of fishes consists of 13–20 percent protein; varying amounts of fat, ranging from less than 1 to more than 20 percent; and 60–82 percent water, varying inversely with fat content. Exact proportions vary among different species, and seasonal and feeding variations result in differences among individuals of the same species. The fatty acids in fish are largely polyunsaturated. One of the major fatty acids, eicosapentaenoic acid, in large amounts reduces the tendency to thrombosis.

Eggs have a deservedly high reputation as a food. The white is protein and the yolk is rich in both protein and vitamin A. Eggs also provide calcium and iron; egg yolk, however, has a high cholesterol content.

Milk and milk products. The milk of each species of animal is a complete food for its young. One pint of cow's summer milk contributes about 90 percent of the calcium, 30 to 40 percent of the riboflavin, 25 to 30 percent of the protein, 10 to 20 percent of the calories and vitamins A and B, and up to 10 percent of the iron and vitamin D needed by an adult. Although human milk supplies a higher proportion of the daily needs of a five-year-old child for calories, protein, vitamin A, thiamine, and riboflavin, the contribution of calcium is reduced to about 70 percent because of the higher calcium requirements of a child.

The milks of mammals contain all essential nutrients. Human milk (Table 7) is the perfect food for infants, provided it comes from a healthy, well-nourished mother and the infant is full-term. Breast milk contains important antibodies, white cells, and nutrients, and, in communities where hygiene is poor, breast-fed babies have fewer infections than formula-fed babies.

Human versus cow's milk

Cow's milk (Table 7) is good food for human adults, but the cream (*i.e.*, fat) contains 52 percent saturated

Table 7: Some Nutrients in Milks			
	human* milk	whole cow's milk (full cream)	modified infant milk formula† (powder diluted as directed)
Energy (kilocalories)	70	67	69
Protein (total; g)	1.1	3.5	1.5
Casein (% protein)	40%	80%	40%
Lactose (g)	7.3	5.0	7.2
Fat (total; g)	4.0	3.7	3.6
Saturated fat (% fat)	46%	66%	44%
Linoleic acid (% fat)	7–11%	3%	17%
Sodium (millimoles)	0.7	2.2	0.71
Calcium (mg)	35	120	49
Phosphorus (mg)	15	95	30
Iron (mg)	0.075	0.050	0.9
Vitamin C (mg)	3.8	1.5	6.9
Vitamin D (µg)	0.8	0.15	1.1

*The composition of breast milk varies considerably with stage of lactation, between individuals, and with maternal nutrition.
†Mean of Cow and Gate Premium and SMA-S26 infant formula brands.
Source: A. Stewart Truswell *et al.*, *ABC of Nutrition* (1986).

fatty acids (longer than 10 carbon atoms in length) as compared to only 3 percent polyunsaturated fat. This fat raises the plasma cholesterol and is thought to be one of the dietary components that contributes to coronary heart disease, along with the same fat in concentrated forms (cream and butter). To circumvent this, the dairy industry has developed low-fat cow's milk (with 2 percent instead of almost 4 percent fat), very low-fat skim milk, or skim milk with extra nonfat milk solids (lactose, protein, and calcium), which gives more body to the milk.

Lactose, the characteristic sugar of milk, is a disaccharide made of the monosaccharides glucose and galactose. While these monosaccharides are easily absorbed, lactose is not. Lactose passes to the large intestine, where it is fermented by the resident bacteria to produce gas and sometimes diarrhea. Galactose is incorporated into the complex fatty substance ceramide, which is the major component of the myelin sheaths of nerves (the white matter of the central nervous system).

Lactose

In the late 1960s it was discovered that the adults of many ethnic groups cannot break down the lactose of large quantities of milk into galactose and glucose; they lose most of their intestinal lactase enzyme activity as they grow up (lactose intolerance). It is now recognized that such individuals share this deficiency with adults throughout the world, such as in Asia and Africa, and with most of the animal kingdom. People originating in northern Europe are the exception from the global viewpoint: they usually retain full intestinal lactase activity into adult life. People who have little of the enzyme lactase in their bodies can still take large amounts of milk if it has been allowed to go sour, if lactobacilli have split most of the lactose into lactic acid, or if the lactose has been treated with commercially available lactase.

The vitamin C present in milk is destroyed by heating (pasteurization), which in many countries is required to prevent the milk from spreading bacterial and other infections.

Cheese making is an ancient art formerly used on farms to convert surplus milk into a food that could be stored without refrigeration. Cheese is rich in protein and calcium and is a good source of vitamin A and riboflavin. Most cheeses, however, contain about 25 to 30 percent fat (constituting about 70 percent of the calories of the cheese), which is mostly saturated, and they are usually high in salt (sodium).

Cheese making

Fats and oils. The animal fats used by humans are butter, suet from beef, lard from pork, and fish oils. Important vegetable oils include olive oil, peanut (groundnut) oil, coconut oil, cottonseed oil, sunflower seed oil, soybean oil, safflower oil, rape oil, sesame (gingelly) oil, mustard oil, red palm oil, and corn oil. All these are high in calories. Only butter (other than the previously mentioned fish-liver oils) contains any of the vitamins A and D, but red palm oil does contain carotene, which is converted to vitamin A in the body. Vitamins A and D in controlled amounts are added to margarines.

Fatty acids

All natural fats and oils contain variable amounts of vitamin E, the fat-soluble vitamin antioxidant. They provide more calories per gram than any other food, and they contain no protein and few micronutrients.

The predominant substances in fats and oils are triglycerides, chemical compounds containing any three fatty acids combined with a molecule of glycerol. The fatty acids consist of a chain of carbon atoms with a carboxylic acid group (—COOH) at one end. The number of carbon atoms ranges from four to more than 22, but the most common chain length is 16 or 18. Because they are synthesized in the body from two-carbon units (acetyl coenzyme A), chain lengths are nearly always even numbers. Each carbon has four valences, or potential sites for bonding—two valences for the adjacent carbons and one for each hydrogen.

Butyric acid is an example of a saturated fatty acid. The four valences of each carbon atom are attached to two hydrogen atoms and to the two adjacent carbons:

$$-\overset{\displaystyle H}{\underset{\displaystyle H}{\overset{|}{\underset{|}{C}}}}-\overset{\displaystyle H}{\underset{\displaystyle H}{\overset{|}{\underset{|}{C}}}}-\overset{\displaystyle H}{\underset{\displaystyle H}{\overset{|}{\underset{|}{C}}}}-\overset{\displaystyle H}{\underset{\displaystyle H}{\overset{|}{\underset{|}{C}}}}-$$

When adjacent carbon atoms are linked by a double bond, each has only one valence available for hydrogen:

$$-\overset{\displaystyle H}{\underset{\displaystyle H}{\overset{|}{\underset{|}{C}}}}-\overset{\displaystyle H}{\overset{|}{C}}=\overset{\displaystyle H}{\overset{|}{C}}-\overset{\displaystyle H}{\underset{\displaystyle H}{\overset{|}{\underset{|}{C}}}}-$$

When no double bonds are present, the fatty acid is said to be saturated; with the presence of one (monounsaturated) or more (polyunsaturated) double bonds, the fatty acid is said to be unsaturated.

Fats with a high percentage of saturated fatty acids tend to be solid at room temperature; e.g., butter and lard. Those with a high percentage of unsaturated fatty acids are usually liquid oils; e.g., sunflower, safflower, and corn oils. The names and shorthand numbers for the principal fatty acids in foods are shown in Table 8. In this shorthand notation, the number to the left of the colon is the number of carbon atoms, and the number to the right of the colon represents the number of double bonds; e.g., 4:0 has four carbon atoms and no double bonds (i.e., is saturated). This is the shorthand notation for butyric acid.

Essential fatty acids

A small group of fatty acids are essential in the diet. They occur in body structures, especially the different membranes inside and around cells, and cannot be synthesized in the body from other fats. Linoleic acid (18:2) is the most important of these fatty acids because it is convertible to the other essential fatty acids. Linoleic acid has two double bonds and is a polyunsaturated fatty acid. As well as being an essential fatty acid it tends to lower the plasma cholesterol. Linoleic acid occurs in moderate

Table 8: Important Natural Fatty Acids

acids	shorthand
Saturated acids	
Butyric	4:0
Caproic	6:0
Caprylic	8:0
Capric	10:0
Lauric	12:0
Myristic	14:0
Palmitic	16:0
Stearic	18:0
Arachidic	20:0
Behenic	22:0
Monounsaturated acids	
Palmitoleic	16:1
Oleic	18:1
Erucic	22:1
Polyunsaturated acids	
Linoleic	18:2
Linolenic	18:3
Arachidonic	20:4
Eicosapentaenoic	20:5
Docosahexaenoic	22:6

to high proportions in many of the seed oils; e.g., corn, sunflower, cottonseed, and safflower oils. Some margarines (polyunsaturated margarines) use a blend of oils selected so that they have a moderately high linoleic acid content.

Edible fats and oils contain smaller amounts of other lipids as well as triglycerides (see below Habitual dietary pattern and disease: Diet and coronary heart disease).

Beverages. Although most adults drink one to two litres (about one to two quarts) of water a day, much of this is in the form of liquids such as coffee, tea, fruit juices, soft drinks, beer, wines, or spirits. In general, these are appreciated more for their taste or for their effects than for their nutritive value. Fruit juices are, of course, useful for their vitamin C content and good sources of potassium while low in sodium. Coffee and tea by themselves are of no nutritive value, except that coffee contains some niacin and tea contains fluoride and manganese, but they may be a vehicle for intakes of sugar, milk, or lemon. Beer contains 2 to 6 percent alcohol, natural wines 10–13 percent, and most spirits up to 40 percent. Since ethyl alcohol has an energy value of seven kilocalories per gram, very significant amounts of energy can be obtained from alcoholic drinks, and beer and wine contain natural sugars as well. With one or two exceptions, they contain no nutrients and are only a source of "empty calories." The only vitamin present in significant amounts in beer from a brewery is riboflavin. Wines are devoid of vitamins but sometimes contain large amounts of iron, probably acquired from iron vessels used in preparation, especially of cheap wine. It is possible for excess iron to be absorbed and stored in the liver where it may contribute to toxic manifestations.

Ethyl alcohol and "empty calories"

RECOMMENDED INTAKES OF NUTRIENTS

Some forty countries now have their own recommended intakes of nutrients. In addition, international recommendations are published jointly by the Food and Agricultural Organization (FAO) and the World Health Organization (WHO). Several names are used to describe these dietary standards, but recommended dietary allowance (RDA) is the most common. In general, RDAs can be defined as the levels of intake of essential nutrients considered, in the judgment of the (national or international) committee on dietary allowances, to be adequate to meet the known nutritional needs of practically all healthy persons. This means that the RDA for each nutrient (except calories) is set at the top end of the frequency distribution of experimentally determined individual requirements (Figure 1A). For energy (calories), the RDA is different (Figure 1B)—it should be set in the middle of the frequency distribution of individual calorie requirements so that the value is too little for half the population and too much for the other half; i.e., it is the mean for the group.

The RDAs have a number of uses. The prescriptive and original use of RDAs is for planning diets of groups or individuals. The RDAs have been used as well for planning national or regional food supplies. International agencies compare the RDAs of countries to see which has the greater need for aid because they are the fairest basis for calculating rations during food shortages or disaster. The RDAs provide a standard reference so that, when the food intake of groups or individuals is assessed, the relative levels of different nutrients can be seen in perspective. Since the RDA of each nutrient is enough for almost all healthy people, an intake just below the RDA may be quite adequate for a particular individual. If the intake of a whole group is below the RDA, however, the probability is high that some individuals in the group are eating a diet inadequate in that nutrient. Finally, RDAs can be used as a denominator for nutrition labeling of foods. Thus, rather than indicating the amount of nutrient available (e.g., 0.35 milligram of thiamine), the percentage relative to the RDA may be cited (e.g., percent of the RDA of thiamine).

The following information is required to work out the RDAs: (1) the level of nutrient intake at which a deficiency disease starts to occur in the community, (2) the least amount of nutrient required to cure clinical signs of deficiency, (3) the lowest intake of the nutrient that maintains chemical balance in the body over a long period, and

Uses of RDAs

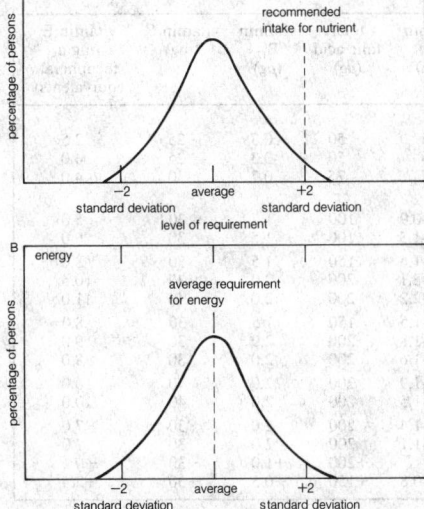

Figure 1: *Theoretical frequency distribution of individual requirements (same sex and age group) for (A) a typical essential nutrient and (B) energy. (A) The recommended dietary allowance is set at the upper end of the distribution. For a few nutrients— for example, iron in women—the frequency distribution of requirement is not Gaussian but skewed. (B) The recommended allowance is in the centre of the distribution—the mean or median—so that half of the population need more and half need fewer calories per day than the recommended daily allowance (RDA).*

(4) the minimum intake needed to give normal function tests for the nutrient or for tissue saturation (an index of adequacy for some of the vitamins).

Limitations   Most RDAs are for nutrients as eaten in foods after processing and cooking. They are for healthy people and do not allow for illnesses or major stresses in life, and they may be affected by a variety of medications, as well as smoking. The RDAs do not have to be reached every day, and a low intake on one day can be balanced by taking more than the recommendation the next day. They are more than enough for most people, and, although they should not be considered the upper limit, they do not (usually) indicate at what higher level toxic effects might start. The RDA assumes that enough of other major nutrients and energy are consumed. The RDAs are for standard body size (usually predefined) and for a usual range of exercise and assume a moderate or good nutritive quality, biological value, or availability of the nutrient to the body. They do not cover minor vitamins and minor trace elements and assume that adequate intakes of the main nutrients generally mean a mixed diet and an adequate intake of the minor nutrients. The RDAs cannot fully allow for the adaptation that can occur to high or low intake of some nutrients (*e.g.*, iron and calcium) and they do not allow for interactions between some of the nutrients.

The RDAs of the United States have been regularly revised about every five years since they first appeared in 1941. During the 1980s a proposal was made to bring the RDAs for vitamins A and C into line with the RDAs of most other countries. The British RDAs cover only about 10 nutrients as well as calories. As an example of a modern set of RDAs, the Australian recommendations (1982–88) are reproduced in Table 9.

Energy. The body needs dietary energy in amounts equal to the energy expended in the external work of daily physical activities, in the internal work of tissue maintenance, for repair in the case of disease or injury, and, in the case of children, for growth.

The French chemist Antoine-Laurent Lavoisier initiated the quantitative study of energy exchange in animals using a small calorimeter, which allowed the rates of oxygen utilization and carbon dioxide release to be measured. Lavoisier also measured the rate of oxygen consumption in humans and showed that it rose with exercise. It was

not until the end of the 19th century, however, that a calorimeter chamber was constructed in which a person could live for three or four days. During this 72–96-hour period all the energy expenditure could be measured as heat and equated with the net energy intake (energy in food minus energy in feces and urine). In this way the law of conservation of energy in humans was demonstrated. There is no doubt that the human body operates within the limits imposed by the law of conservation of energy. Energy output is related to the rate of oxygen utilization, with one litre of oxygen equivalent to approximately 4.8 kilocalories of energy.

Measurements of the heat output of humans, direct calorimetry, are difficult. By contrast, measurements of oxygen consumption by indirect calorimetry are relatively easy and can be made on humans in their normal day-to-day environment, at home, and at work in offices, factories, fields, and mines, and during recreations, including most sports.

The rate at which energy is expended for maintenance at rest, known as the basal metabolic rate (BMR), amounts to about 1.25 kilocalories per minute for a man weighing 65 kilograms (one kilogram = 2.2 pounds) and 0.90 kilocalorie per minute for a woman weighing 55 kilograms. The basal metabolism, if expressed per unit of body weight or per unit of surface area, as has been the tradition for a long time, appears higher in men than in women. This is so because women have relatively more fat (adipose tissue) and less muscle than men and because men tend to be much more active.   **Basal metabolism**

The metabolic rate is raised by as much as 30 percent after a meal. This is the thermic effect of meals and is due in part to the work of secretion of the digestive juices and in part to chemical processes, mainly in the liver, involved in the metabolism of amino acids and other absorbed products of digestion.

The metabolism of a seated person usually is not raised by more than 50 percent above the basal level (*i.e.*, $1.5 \times$ BMR). The arms are light, and little physical work is involved in writing or sewing. Although the metabolism of the brain is high and accounts for 20 percent of resting energy expenditure, it is not raised significantly by mental activity.

Energy expenditure is increased fourfold, up to about five kilocalories per minute, by a brisk walk and is usually between two and four times the resting rate during the accomplishment of such light work as most assembly-line labour in industry, domestic activities, painting, and carpentry and in participation in recreations such as golf or bowling.

An increase of up to sixfold, or 7.5 kilocalories per minute, constitutes moderate work and is characteristic of most manual labour, gardening, tennis, and bicycling. Work involving energy expenditures above this is graded as heavy. Although many jobs in coal mining, lumbering, and the steel industry involve periods of strenuous work, relatively few persons in a modern industrial society do significant amounts of continuous heavy work. Cross-country skiing is the recreation with one of the greatest demands for energy and involves rates of 15 kilocalories per minute, or even more, for long periods.

Most individuals in urban societies have their days divided into three eight-hour portions. Normally, one period is spent in bed and asleep, one at work, and one in recreation or in other nonoccupational activities. The period in bed at approximately basal rates involves about 500 kilocalories of energy. A rough guide for occupational work is as follows: sedentary (about 900 kilocalories per eight-hour period), including office workers, drivers, teachers, and shop workers; and moderately active (about 1,200 kilocalories per eight-hour period), including virtually all engaged in light industry and assembly plants, postal workers, most farm labourers, and construction labourers.   **Average daily energy expenditure**

A man's energy expenditure, however, is determined in an urban society more by how he uses his spare time than by the nature of his job. Nonoccupational activities may range from 800 to 1,800 kilocalories per eight-hour period. Energy requirements from food may vary from 2,200 kilocalories per day for sedentary activities to more than

Table 9: Recommended Dietary Intakes for Use in Australia*

group	age	vitamin A (µg retinol equivalents)	thiamine (mg)	riboflavin (mg)	niacin (mg niacin equivalents)	vitamin B_6 (mg)	total folic acid (µg)	vitamin B_{12} (µg)	vitamin C (mg)	vitamin E (mg a tocopheral equivalents)
Infants	0–6 months									
	breast-fed	425	0.15	0.4	4	0.25	50	0.3	25	2.5
	bottle-fed	425	0.25	0.4	4	0.25	50	0.3	25	4.0
	7–12 months	300	0.35	0.6	7	0.45	75	0.7	30	4.0
Children (male and female)	1–3 years	300	0.5	0.8	9–10	0.6–0.9	100	1.7	30	5.0
	4–7 years	350	0.7	1.1	11–13	0.8–1.3	100	1.5	30	6.0
Boys	8–11 years	500	0.9	1.4	14–16	1.1–1.6	150	1.5	30	8.0
	12–15 years	725	1.2	1.8	19–21	1.4–2.1	200	2.0	30	10.5
	16–18 years	750	1.2	1.9	20–22	1.5–2.2	200	2.0	40	11.0
Girls	8–11 years	500	0.8	1.3	14–16	1.0–1.5	150	1.5	30	8.0
	12–15 years	750	1.0	1.6	17–19	1.2–1.8	200	2.0	30	9.0
	16–18 years	750	0.9	1.4	15–17	1.1–1.6	200	2.0	30	8.0
Men	19–64 years	750	1.1	1.7	18–20	1.3–1.9	200	2.0	40	10.0
	64+ years	750	0.9	1.3	14–17	1.0–1.5	200	2.0	40	10.0
Women	19–54 years	750	0.8	1.2	12–14	0.9–1.4	200	2.0	30	7.0
	54+ years	750	1.0	1.0	10–12	0.8–1.1	200	2.0	30	7.0
Pregnant		+0	+0.2	+0.3	+2	+0.1	+200	+1.0	+30	+0
Lactating		+450	+0.4	+0.8	+5	+0.7–0.8	+150	+0.5	+30	+2.5

4,000 for the very active. These figures are generalities and cannot be applied to nonmechanized farming, still the way of life for the majority of the world's male population. There may be marked seasonal variations with men "very active" at seed and harvest time, and "sedentary" during some periods in between. Surveys in Africa and Asia indicate that a yearly average shows most farmers to be moderately active.

Corresponding figures for women show a total of about 2,200 kilocalories per day. The range of expenditure is not as wide as for men, and the great majority of women need food providing from 1,800 to 2,400 kilocalories per 24-hour period.

Much of the work done by humans consists in contracting muscles to move the body or its parts. Energy expenditure during exercise is directly related to body weight, and the basal metabolism is related to body size. In theory, then, large people should require more food than smaller people do. Activity level, however, is important, and some less physically active large men and women may have lower energy requirements than smaller persons. Exercise alone is not the most important factor in weight loss. The types and amounts of food consumed, as well as the balance of nutrients, play major roles as well. As age advances, physical activity is curtailed, lean body mass gradually declines, and the need for dietary energy is reduced.

(R.Pa./A.S.T.)

Protein. Protein constitutes the soft tissues of the lean body as well as the hundreds of enzymes involved in its activity. These proteins are continually broken down and replaced, some faster than others. In the process, proteins are converted to their constituent amino acids, some of which are deaminated in the liver and used up in energy production (*e.g.*, in the citric acid cycle). The amino groups are concentrated in urea and excreted in the urine (Figure 2). Because of this turnover, some protein is required in the adult diet. Additional protein is required in the growth of new tissues in children and pregnant women and for the secretion of milk in lactating women. Protein requirements vary with lean body mass, and they are usually expressed as the amount per kilogram of body weight.

Since the League of Nations nutrition committee first recommended one gram of protein per kilogram of body weight for adults in 1938, pronouncements on protein requirements by successive international (FAO/WHO) committees in 1957, 1965, 1973, and 1985 have fluctuated between recommending 0.66 and 0.89 grams per kilogram of body weight. In 1985 the international recommendation was 0.75 grams of good-quality protein per kilogram of body weight for adults. This is 52.5 grams for a 70-kilogram man and 41 grams for a 55-kilogram woman. For children, the recommendation starts at 1.85 grams per kilogram of body weight in young infants and falls to one gram per kilogram of body weight by the age of five years.

Proteins are made up of some 20 amino acids, at least eight of which are indispensible for humans. Their proportions vary from food to food (Table 3), and human requirements of individual amino acids range widely. The requirement for tryptophan is smallest. If tryptophan is taken as 1, the requirements for the others are approximately as follows: threonine, 2; valine, 3; isoleucine, 3; histidine, 3; lysine, 3.4; methionine + cystine (*i.e.*, total sulfur-containing amino acids), 3.7; leucine, 4; and phenylalanine + tyrosine, 4. (These requirement ratios are not related to molecular weights; they do not come closer if expressed in molar units.) Tryptophan has the highest molecular weight but the smallest requirement.

The reasons for the different requirements for individual amino acids are that they are present in different amounts in the major body tissues; *e.g.*, muscle (the most abundant tissue) contains about seven times as much leucine as tryptophan. There are differences as well in the rates of involvement of amino acids in different pathways of interconversion and metabolism.

If the diet is deficient in one of the essential amino acids, the protein requirement has to be adjusted upward. In practice, however, when protein foods are eaten together their amino acids complement one another. Mixtures of foods are less likely than single foods to have any individual amino acids far below the requirement.

Inorganic elements. Although requirements for nutrients are generally lower in women, who have lower lean body mass and eat less food, the RDA for iron is an exception. Women of reproductive age need about twice

Importance of protein

Relative requirements

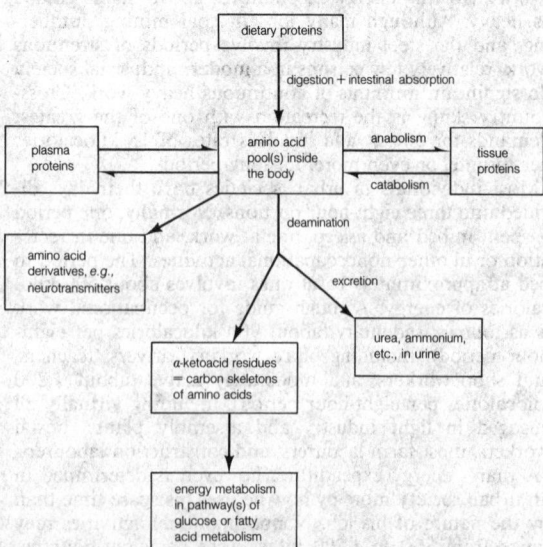

Figure 2: General scheme of protein and amino acid metabolism.

Table 9: Recommended Dietary Intakes for Use in Australia* (continued)

group	age	zinc (mg)	iron (mg)	iodine (µg)	magnesium (mg)	calcium (g)	phosphorus (mg)	selenium (µg)	sodium (mmol)	sodium (mg)	potassium (mmol)	potassium (mg)	protein g/kg body weight
Infants	0–6 months												
	breast-fed	3–6	0.5	50	40	300	150	10	6–12	140–280	10–15	390–580	—
	bottle-fed	3–6	3.0	50	40	300	150	10	6–12	140–280	10–15	390–580	2.0
	7–12 months	4.5–6	9.0	60	60	550	300	15	14–25	320–580	12–35	470–1,370	1.6
Children (male and female)	1–3 years	4.5–6	6–8	70	80	700	500	25	14–50	320–1,150	25–70	980–2,730	1.2
	4–7 years	6–9	6–8	90	110	800	700	30	20–75	460–1,730	40–100	1,560–3,900	1.0
Boys	8–11 years	9–14	6–8	120	180	800	800	50	26–100	600–2,300	50–140	1,950–5,460	1.0
	12–15 years	12–18	10–13	150	240	1,200	1,200	85	40–100	920–2,300	50–140	1,950–5,460	1.0
	16–18 years	12–18	10–13	150	320	1,000	1,100	85	40–100	920–2,300	50–140	1,950–5,460	1.0
Girls	8–11 years	9–14	6–8	120	160	900	800	50	26–100	600–2,300	50–140	1,950–5,460	1.0
	12–15 years	12–18	10–13	120	240	1,000	1,200	70	40–100	920–2,300	50–140	1,950–5,460	1.0
	16–18 years	12–18	10–13	120	270	800	1,100	70	40–100	920–2,300	50–140	1,950–5,460	1.0
Men	19–64 years	12–16	7	150	320	800	1,000	85	40–100	920–2,300	50–140	1,950–5,460	0.75
	64+ years	12–16	7	150	320	800	1,000	85	40–100	920–2,300	50–140	1,950–5,460	0.75
Women	19–54 years	12–16	12–16	120	270	800	1,000	70	40–100	920–2,300	50–140	1,950–5,460	0.75
	54+ years	12–16	5–7	120	270	1,000	1,000	70	40–100	920–2,300	50–140	1,950–5,460	0.75
Pregnant		+4–5	+10	+30	+30	+300	+200	+10	+0	+0	+0	+0	+6 g
Lactating		+6	+0	+50	+70	+400	+200	+15	+0	+0	+0	+0	+16 g

*Expressed as a mean daily intake. This table expresses the amounts of nutrients that should be available per head of population if the needs of practically all members of the population are to be met. All RDIs are based on estimates of requirements with a generous "safety factor" added. Recommendations for all nutrients were revised between 1982 and 1988. Recommendations for dietary intakes of Vitamin D were not considered necessary since the Vitamin D status of Australians is determined by exposure to sunlight. For people confined indoors, however, 10 µg per day is recommended.
Source: National Health and Medical Research Council, Canberra.

as much iron as men. Some degree of iron deficiency is a worldwide problem in women. In the Third World most of the iron in food is in vegetables, from which it is poorly absorbed. In affluent communities meat is available, but many women have low iron intakes because they restrict food consumption in order to lose weight. The RDA for iron in pregnant women (Table 9) may be considered very high, but it represents the upper end of the distribution of requirements, because some women who begin pregnancy with depleted body iron stores are likely to become anemic unless they take an iron supplement.

Calcium Requirements for calcium are difficult to determine because 99 percent of it in the body is in the bones. Any reduction of absorbed calcium is not evident in the plasma concentration because calcium loss increases the secretion of parathormone, which mobilizes some calcium from bones. In parts of the world without a dairy industry, adults appear to maintain strong bones on calcium intakes around 500 milligrams, while in industrial countries adults have been found to go into negative calcium balance on such low intakes.

The RDAs for zinc have only been considered and researched since the 1970s. Human zinc deficiency was not described until 1963, and it took an additional 10 years before it was confirmed and accepted that zinc is an important nutrient for humans. Although most reports agree with the RDA of 12–16 milligrams per day for adults in Table 9, more recent evidence suggests that the present RDAs are set too high.

Sodium levels are more than adequate in the great majority of human diets. Sodium chloride (common table salt) is added during processing to many foods, and smaller amounts of sodium bicarbonate and monosodium glutamate are also widely used as additives in food processing and preparation. The concern of nutritionists is not whether people are consuming enough sodium but whether they are consuming too much. This is why the Australian RDAs suggest an upper level of intake as well as a lower, but still generous, requirement.

Potassium Because it is the major cation inside all living cells, potassium is present in moderate amounts in most unrefined plant and animal foods (e.g., meat, fruits, vegetables). Potassium presents a problem only in people with a variety of diseases in which potassium intake must be carefully monitored. Potassium intake may need to be supplemented in people with chronic diarrhea and in those with heart disease or high blood pressure who take regular diuretic tablets. On the other hand, those with impaired kidney function (renal failure) may develop a blood potassium level that is too high, even while consuming an ordinary amount.

Magnesium and phosphorus (in the form of phosphate) are essential elements but few, if any, natural diets do not meet the requirements. Iodine deficiency is important in a number of underdeveloped inland and mountainous areas in the world. Intakes are adequate in nearly all the industrialized countries because foods come from a variety of places and so some at least have been grown in soils with adequate iodine. In addition, iodized salt is available and a few food additives contain iodine.

Vitamins. Table 4 shows the 13 vitamins essential for humans.

Vitamin A. A fat-soluble compound, vitamin A (retinol) is found in animal foods, especially in liver of land animals or fish, where it is stored and concentrated. Most of the world's population, however, derive most or all of their vitamin A from plant foods, many of which contain the yellow-orange pigment β-carotene. One molecule of β-carotene can be cleaved by an intestinal enzyme into two molecules of vitamin A. The pigment β-carotene occurs in fruits such as apricots, peaches, melons, mangoes, and pumpkins. It is also a companion of chlorophyll, the green pigment in leaves, so that green vegetables are good sources. Enough vitamin A is stored in the liver of a well-nourished adult to last about two years of deprivation. Vitamin A (not carotene) is one of the vitamins whose toxicity at doses 10 times the RDA or more is well established. It can lead to bone changes and fetal malformations and has been responsible for occasional fatalities.

Thiamine. Found in whole-grain cereals, meats, yeasts, and nuts, thiamine (a water-soluble vitamin) plays an indispensable role as cofactor for enzymes involved in the metabolism of carbohydrates, alcohol, and some amino acids. The requirement is therefore proportional to an individual's calorie intake from foods other than fats. There are hardly any stores of thiamine in the body, and it only takes about 30 days without thiamine intake before signs of deficiency appear, provided the calorie intake is maintained. Alcoholics are at special risk of thiamine deficiency because the more alcohol a person drinks, the less thiamine-containing food he consumes. Alcohol requires thiamine for its metabolism, and body stores of thiamine are smaller than for any other vitamin.

Thiamine deficiency

Riboflavin. Another of the water-soluble vitamins, riboflavin is unusual in that it has a fluorescent yellow-green colour. It too plays a vital role in intermediary metabolism, but deficiency disease is rare. In industrial countries this may be because milk is a good source.

Niacin. Niacin is a water-soluble vitamin that is also made in the human liver by the conversion of the amino acid tryptophan. If the protein intake is low, preformed niacin must be provided in the diet; if the protein intake is generous, niacin normally can be made by the body from the tryptophan. Some animals (such as cats) do not have this ability. One form of niacin (nicotinic acid) in doses about 200 times the RDA is used in medicine as a drug that lowers the cholesterol level in the plasma. This is an example of a pharmacological action of a nutrient.

Vitamin B₆. Vitamin B₆ is a water-soluble vitamin of the B group. The five closely related substances with B₆ activity, of which the best-known is pyridoxine, act as cofactors for the many enzymes involved in amino acid metabolism. Vitamin B₆ requirements, therefore, are proportional to the protein intake. Primary deficiency is rare but several drugs (*e.g.,* isoniazid) can produce secondary vitamin B₆ deficiency. Pyridoxine in megadoses (100 and more times the RDA of around two milligrams per day) has been taken to ameliorate the effects of premenstrual syndrome (prescribed or self-medication), but its efficacy has not been established. It is known that prolonged dosage of 500 milligrams and above causes damage to peripheral nerves, with a loss of sensation in legs and hands.

Folic acid. A number of related water-soluble compounds have folic acid activity. Because the main function of folic acid is in the synthesis of DNA, in folic acid deficiency replication of DNA and cell division are slowed or stopped. Cells that rapidly turn over, such as blood cells and epithelial cells lining the intestine, are affected first. The requirement for folic acid is notably increased in pregnancy. The name comes from Latin *folia* ("leaf"), but this vitamin is found in animal organs and whole-grain cereals, as well as vegetables. It is sensitive to heat and is mostly destroyed when vegetables are overboiled. Folic acid deficiency is common in a number of conditions encountered in hospital patients.

Function in DNA synthesis

Vitamin B₁₂. Vitamin B₁₂ was the last of the vitamins to be isolated (in 1948). It is water-soluble, has the highest molecular weight (1,355) of any vitamin, and is absorbed by a complex mechanism. Failure of absorption (pernicious anemia) is more common than dietary deficiency. Vitamin B₁₂ is found only in animal foods, so that vegans (pure vegetarians) are at risk of deficiency over the course of several years. The requirement of vitamin B₁₂ is (with vitamin D) the smallest of all the vitamins, only two micrograms per day, with liver stores usually enough to last for five years of deprivation. Vitamin B₁₂ participates with folic acid in DNA synthesis so its deficiency leads to a similar anemia. There is a separate effect of vitamin B₁₂ deficiency on the nervous system.

Results of deficiency

Vitamin C. Also water-soluble, vitamin C is the opposite of vitamin B₁₂ in that it is found in almost all plant foods but not in meat. It is a powerful antioxidant and is required for the formation of collagen; *i.e.,* in wound healing. The RDA of vitamin C in Table 9 is more than enough to prevent scurvy. It is not clear whether there is any advantage in larger intakes than 40 milligrams per day. Indirect epidemiological data suggest the possibility that generous intakes of salads and citrus fruits may reduce the chance of developing cancer of the stomach. Megadoses, 100 to 250 times RDA, have been claimed to prevent colds, but most controlled trials have shown that it does not. Like folic acid, vitamin C is easily destroyed by cooking. Large doses of vitamin C are well tolerated but they may contribute to the formation of kidney stones in the urinary tract.

Vitamin D. Vitamin D is fat-soluble, and cholecalciferol is the major active substance. Its main function is to stimulate the absorption of calcium. The natural source of vitamin D is from the action of short-wave ultraviolet light from the Sun on a derivative of cholesterol in the skin. Vitamin D also occurs in some foods. It is only when people live in high latitudes, consistently wear concealing clothes, and spend nearly all their time indoors, and when the sky is usually cloudy and smoky, that there is insufficient skin exposure to ultraviolet light to make the required amount of vitamin D. Under these conditions dietary intake becomes critical and cholecalciferol assumes the role of a vitamin. Overdose of vitamin D leads to an increased blood calcium concentration and symptoms such as vomiting.

Association with sunlight

Vitamin E. Eight chemically similar substances have vitamin E activity: *a*-tocopherol is the most active of these and the most abundant in most foods. Vitamin E is fat-soluble and an antioxidant that is present in cell membranes. Its requirement is increased by high intakes of polyunsaturated fats. Vitamin E deficiency that produces signs and symptoms is rare; it can occur in premature infants and in older individuals with chronic defects of fat absorption. It is possible that generous intakes protect cell membranes from oxidation damage and consequent degenerative diseases, but this is speculation. No controlled trial has been carried out. Dosages of vitamin E up to 20 times the RDA appear to be well tolerated.

Vitamin K. Vitamin K is a fat-soluble vitamin involved in the processes of coagulation. Although the alphabetical letters for most vitamins are arbitrary, the letter *K* came from the German *Koagulationsvitamin.* This activity is found in several chemically different substances. One (vitamin K₁) occurs in some plant foods; others (the vitamin K₂ group) are formed by bacteria in the large intestine. Some of this is absorbed by the host. In newborn infants the latter source has not yet come into operation, and transfer of vitamin K from the mother's blood across the placenta is evidently unreliable. Vitamin K₁ is commonly given to newborn babies to prevent the possibility of hemorrhagic disease. Vitamin K deficiency in older individuals can occur when fat absorption is defective. Oral anticoagulants (warfarin, etc.) act by antagonizing the action of vitamin K.

Biotin and pantothenic acid. Biotin and pantothenic acid are the last two of the established vitamins for humans. Spontaneous deficiency of biotin is extremely rare and that of pantothenic acid is unknown. They are, however, required in infant formulas and in fluids for total parenteral (intravenous) nutrition.

The following compounds are not vitamins required for humans, or in infant formulas or fluids for total parenteral nutrition: bioflavonoids, carnitine, inositol, orotic acid, para-aminobenzoic acid (PABA), "pangamic acid" (vitamin B₁₅), laetrile (vitamin B₁₇), and vitamin P.

Diet and diseases

SOURCES OF INFORMATION

Animal experiments. The results of studies on animals provide suggestive associations to humans, but for each nutritional biochemical process some or many animals may not be suitable models for humans. For example, rats do not need vitamin C in their diet because they synthesize it in their bodies from glucose. For a model of human scurvy, therefore, rats cannot be used. Only a very small number of higher animals are similar to humans in that they lack the enzyme to complete the synthesis of vitamin C. In 1907 it was discovered in Norway that guinea pigs must have vitamin C in their diets; research on vitamin C made rapid progress after this.

Animal models

Comparative and evolutionary studies. *Homo sapiens* and his predecessors have been on the Earth for at least 1,000,000 years. For 99 percent of this time they lived as hunter-gatherers; agriculture did not begin until 10,000 years ago. There has not been time for humans to evolve biochemical mechanisms to deal with the mixture of foods that has become usual in Western communities. Presumably human bodies are well adapted to the habits and diet of their hunter-gatherer forebears. There is some information about these diets (and a little about their effects) from archaeological records and some information from studies of the few isolated groups of hunter-gatherers remaining today.

Experiments of nature and travelers' tales. People in the United States and Britain cannot be persuaded to take an unfamiliar and unpleasant diet long-term in order to follow its effect on body functions. In other parts of the world, however, groups of people may be on restrictive diets due to reasons such as culture and the availability of food. Diets may consist of a lot of fatty fish, or of blood and sour milk, or of mostly starchy low-protein roots, or of food cooked in salt water. It may be no coincidence that many of the leading human nutritionists have worked in several different countries, returning with their experiences (the so-called travelers' tales). The trouble with such experiences is that the data are not very reliable.

Epidemiological studies. Epidemiology is the study of the distribution of disease in different sections of the population. Modern epidemiology is a more important tool for studying human nutrition than is animal nutrition. It has been particularly useful in finding which diets are associated with each of the chronic degenerative diseases—dental caries, coronary heart disease, high blood pressure, diverticulosis, and various cancers. Association, however, does not prove cause and effect.

Prospective studies
Prospective (or cohort) studies are more reliable than retrospective or cross-sectional ones. In a prospective study a large group of several thousand people in one place (a town or large firm) at risk of later developing a common disease have their medical histories taken and are examined, including laboratory tests (blood biochemistry, etc.). Their health is then monitored for a period of time, usually five years or longer. If one of the variables at the initial examination is significantly associated with early development of disease X, this is considered evidence that a high value of the variable is a "risk factor" for disease X. If the same association should hold up in other prospective studies made in different places, the evidence becomes very strong.

Clinical records. Measurements of the food intake of patients with deficiency diseases are an important part of the classic evidence about these diseases. Precise information has come from experiences with patients fed entirely with solutions given by vein (total parenteral nutrition). Patients with extensive disease of the small intestine can be kept alive in this way. When patients rely on this route for all their nutrients for weeks, months, or years, the essentiality of trace elements becomes obvious. If a particular nutrient is not included in the fluid for total parenteral nutrition, the patient develops specific symptoms, which are then corrected when that nutrient is supplied. The role of diet in treatment of diseases such as diabetes mellitus or kidney failure is important. The dietary changes that will give the lowest blood glucose or blood urea, respectively, is explored by the nutritionist.

Food composition analysis. The independent variables in nutritional epidemiology and in dietary treatment of diseases are food constituents (protein, vitamin C, iron, etc.). Foods keep changing because of new methods of production, different formulations of ingredients, and changing consumption patterns. To facilitate international sharing of the available food composition data, Infoods (International Network of Food Data Systems) was set up in 1983, with its secretariat at the Massachusetts Institute of Technology in Cambridge.

Human experiments and trials. There are many different types of human experiments and trials. They range in duration from hours to years and in number of subjects from a handful to thousands. The variables measured can be clinical symptoms; biochemical substances in any available body fluid or accessible tissue, including expiratory air; body composition (estimates of size of the different compartments of the body); or the chemical transformations of radioactively labeled nutrients. Such studies are usually performed on healthy subjects. Some examples illustrate the scope.

Depletion diets
The first type of study involves the depletion of a single nutrient in human volunteers under experimental conditions (with all other essential nutrients provided, either in the food or as supplements). Ethical considerations are important, so that subjects often have been the scientists themselves and numbers usually have been very small. Such experiments, however, have provided important information. Some experiments have been continued (under close supervision) until the first clinical signs of deficiency appear; this takes three or four months for vitamin C and folic acid and much longer for vitamin A (because of large stores in the liver). Other experiments have used indexes such as low blood levels as measures and have stopped before any symptoms or signs.

A second type of study, involving absorption and uptake studies using test meals, takes only a few hours to carry out. Many are needed, however, because humans digest and absorb nutrients in different amounts and at different rates, depending on the food. For example, measures of iron uptake vary considerably, and a number of tests have been done with radioactive isotopes of iron (short half-life) to find the effects of different foods on uptake of this nutrient element.

In a third type of trial, the metabolic study, the diet is usually changed in one way only, and the result is measured in a change in blood or excreta. One type of study is the balance experiment, where the intake of a nutrient is controlled and measured and its output (in urine, feces, etc.) is measured. Because of variability in defecation, measurements have to be made for a metabolic "period" of about a week. The amount of the nutrient measured can be changed (with time allowed for adjustment) and the effect of this on the balance determined. When, for example, the output of nitrogen exceeds intake, there is a negative nitrogen balance; when output is less than intake the balance is positive.

Another type of metabolic experiment measures the effect of a change of diet on plasma cholesterol. Such an effect takes 10 to 14 days to appear and requires control periods for comparison before and after the dietary change being examined. Whenever one component is added to, or removed from, a person's diet, another food must be removed or added to keep the calories and other important nutrients constant. That substitution may itself affect the variable under study.

Double-blind trials
In a fourth type of study, the double-blind trial, control groups receive identical-looking placebo tablets, and individuals are randomly allocated to experimental or control group by someone who is not going to assess the clinical results. The researchers also do not know who took which tablets. Controlled double-blind trials of vitamin C tablets during winter months to see if they prevent colds measured incidence, severity, duration, and type of respiratory symptoms. Most of the trials have shown no statistically significant reduction in the incidence of colds with the use of vitamin C.

A fifth type of trial, the prevention trial, measures the effects of one combination of foods versus another. It is not possible to achieve double-blind conditions, but the control group is kept separate from the experimental group and the emphasis is on objective rather than subjective changes, such as biochemical measurements on blood samples and electrocardiographic changes. For example, the effects of a low saturated-fat, increased polyunsaturated-fat diet were measured in half of 850 middle-aged male war veterans in Los Angeles. The other half (the control group) consumed their usual foods. Variables measured were blood lipids, tissue fatty acid patterns (reflecting compliance with the prescribed increase of polyunsaturated fat), electrocardiographic changes, and the incidences of coronary and other diseases.

Classification of nutritional disorders. *Undernutrition.* Undernutrition is a condition in which there is not enough food energy as measured in calories or kilojoules. Undernutrition usually means that not enough total food is consumed. The main characteristics are loss of body weight and wasting of body fat and later muscle. Severe forms are starvation in adults and marasmus in young children. Undernutrition may be due to a failure of the food supply or to deliberate fasting, or it may be secondary to prolonged disease. Epidemic failure of the food supply is called famine.

Malnutrition. Malnutrition covers at least 25 different deficiency diseases resulting from lack of one of the essential nutrients: protein, vitamins, essential fats, or nutrient elements. Kwashiorkor, rickets, and iron-deficiency anemia are examples of the results of malnutrition. Multiple deficiencies are more likely than single, though one type often predominates. The deficiency disorder may be subclinical (recognizable only by laboratory tests) and not show characteristic features.

Obesity. Obesity is an excess of fat in the body (subcutaneous or internal) that results from a prolonged net positive energy balance; *i.e.*, the energy (calories or joules) consumed has been greater than the energy expended. Obesity is the opposite of undernutrition. Any or all of the

Positive energy balance

proximate energy-yielding nutrients can be responsible: usually fat, carbohydrate, and/or alcohol.

Nutrient excess. Nutrient excess is due to too much of one nutrient. For many nutrients a very high intake in the short term or a high intake over a long period (chronic nutrient toxicity) can be harmful. The nutrient may be an essential one (*e.g.*, as in vitamin D intoxication and iron overload), or it may be a nonessential nutrient (*e.g.*, alcohol or saturated fat, resulting in raised blood cholesterol).

Effects of toxicants. Unless very refined, foods contain hundreds of substances other than the nutrients, most in tiny amounts. Some naturally occurring toxicants can cause illness if people rely too heavily on a single foodstuff—*e.g.*, lathyrism, a paralysis of both legs (which occurs in India) from eating too much of the pulse *Lathyrus sativus* (grass pea). Potatoes contain alkaloids, including solanine, mostly in the green sprouts, and occasionally cases are reported of vomiting and other symptoms attributed to solanine poisoning. Other substances affect only a few individuals who are hypersensitive to them—*e.g.*, celiac disease (from sensitivity to wheat gluten) and urticaria (from sensitivity to such substances as naturally occurring salicylates). (A.S.T.)

DEFICIENCY DISEASES

Deficiency diseases may best be considered under six main headings, according to the principal deficiency: water, energy (calories), proteins, vitamins, inorganic elements, and fats and carbohydrates. There is considerable overlap among these groups.

Water. Some 65 percent of a normal body consists of water distributed between three compartments: within the cells, between the cells, and within the circulatory system. A great variety of diseases disturb the water balance, but in healthy people dehydration and overhydration result *Dehydra-* from wrong intake of water. The prominent symptom of *tion and* dehydration is thirst, which develops quickly when water *over-* is unavailable. Dehydration becomes rapidly worse, and *hydration* death may ensue within two or three days. Water is lost from the body by evaporation from the lungs and skin, through the urine, and through the stools, a loss that can become serious in diarrhea. Lung and skin losses are increased by work that causes sweating, particularly in a hot, dry climate. The kidneys usually excrete between one and two litres of urine per day, but when dehydration threatens they can conserve water through concentration of the urine.

Overhydration from overdrinking is not a common occurrence in healthy people because the combined effects of excretion by the kidney and satiation, the opposite of thirst, are usually adequate even for the most enthusiastic drinker.

The distribution of water between the three compartments is largely determined by the ions sodium and potassium. The important positively charged ion, or cation, in the interstitial (between the cells) fluid is sodium. Mammals, which have acquired an energy-dependent mechanism for removing sodium from the individual cells, the sodium pump, have potassium as their principal cation within the cells. (The cell membrane is permeable to sodium ions, and the sodium concentration outside the cells is stronger than within, so that one would expect sodium to pass from the tissue fluids into the cells; its movement in the opposite direction requires energy. The process that involves this expenditure of energy is called the sodium pump.) Ion and fluid balance are both normally maintained by the regulatory power of the sodium pump and of the kidney tubules. Upset of the delicate ion and fluid balance may be aggravated by deficient or excess intake of water.

The most severe dehydration occurs from diarrhea, with or without vomiting, in undernourished infants in poor communities who develop gastroenteritis, and in adults with cholera. The most efficient lifesaving treatment is intravenous infusion of sterile water containing glucose, sodium chloride, and potassium chloride. Water is poorly absorbed when drunk, but a good first aid formula consists of sodium chloride, 3.5 grams; sodium bicarbonate, 2.5 grams; potassium chloride, 1.5 grams; glucose 20 grams (or sucrose 40 grams); and clean water up to one litre. The

glucose assists absorption of the sodium and vice versa, and as they are absorbed water is absorbed with them.

Energy (calories). Chemical energy in food, ultimately dependent on solar energy, occurs in carbohydrates, fats, and proteins (and alcohol). It is expended in mechanical work, in the work of the internal organs, in maintaining body temperature, and in growth. Undernutrition (calorie *Calorie* deficit) can result from (1) failure of the food supply, *deficit* (2) loss of appetite, (3) fasting and anorexia nervosa, (4) persistent vomiting or inability to swallow, (5) incomplete absorption, comprising a group of diseases (malabsorption syndrome) in which digestion and intestinal absorption are impaired and there is excess loss of nutrients in the feces, (6) increased basal metabolic rate, as in prolonged fever, overactivity of the thyroid gland, or some cancers, and (7) loss of calories from the body; *e.g.*, glucose in the urine in diabetes.

Cessation of growth is an early feature of undernutrition in children. There is otherwise little difference between starving adults and marasmic infants. Body tissues are used as energy reserves. Body fat (adipose tissue) is the largest and most concentrated energy store and it is used first and most. As energy deficit continues, the proteins in muscles are used as well. Typically there is a large loss (wasting) of subcutaneous fat and a smaller loss (wasting) of the muscles. Some compensatory changes reduce the rate of energy expenditure: reduced voluntary activity, thyroid secretion, basal metabolic rate, and heart rate.

Severity of undernutrition is usually graded by comparing actual weight to the standard weight for a certain height. In adults undernutrition is defined as mild when weight is *Under-* 81 to 90 percent of standard weight for the height; moder- *nutrition* ate when weight is 71 to 80 percent of standard weight for *defined* the height; and severe when weight is 70 percent or less of standard weight for the height. During famine people with mild starvation are in no danger; those with moderate starvation need extra feeding; those severely underweight need hospital care. Table 10 gives moderate (80 percent of standard weights) and severe (70 percent of standard) underweights for adults of different heights, and it can be used for men or women.

height		weight			
(m)	(in.)	80% of standard (kg)	(lb)	70% of standard (kg)	(lb)
1.45	57.1	38	84	33	73
1.48	58.3	39.5	87	34.5	76
1.50	59.1	40.5	89	35	77
1.52	59.8	41.5	91.5	36	79
1.54	60.6	42.5	94	37	82
1.56	61.4	44	97	38.5	85
1.58	62.2	45	99	39	86
1.60	63.0	46	101	40	88
1.62	63.8	47	104	41	90
1.64	64.6	48.5	107	42	93
1.66	65.4	49.5	109	43	95
1.68	66.1	50.5	111	44	97
1.70	66.9	52	115	45.5	100
1.72	67.7	53	117	47	104
1.74	68.5	54.5	120	48	106
1.76	69.3	56	123.5	49	108
1.78	70.1	57	126	50	110
1.80	70.9	58	128	51	112.5
1.82	71.7	60	132	52	115
1.84	72.4	61	134.5	53.5	118
1.86	73.2	62	137	54	119
1.88	74.0	63.5	140	55.5	122
1.90	74.8	65	143	57	126

Protein. Because children have higher protein requirements per calorie and are more at risk of being given a low-protein diet, protein deficiency is more prominent among them. In most malnourished children, calorie deficiency and protein deficiency are combined, and features of both are detectable. There is a spectrum that begins with marasmus at one end, showing severe wasting but no signs of protein deficiency, and kwashiorkor at the other end, showing edema, severe reduction of the major plasma protein (albumin), and usually little weight loss.

The most common severe form of protein-energy mal- *Nutritional* nutrition, nutritional marasmus usually occurs in the first *marasmus* year of life. The affected child is extremely underweight and has lost all subcutaneous fat. The body is wizened, the face gaunt, and the limbs like matchsticks. The cause is a diet very low in calories from all sources (including protein), often from early weaning to bottled formula diluted because of poverty. Poor hygiene leads to gastroenteritis and a vicious cycle of poor appetite and even more diluted formula. In turn further depletion leads to thinning of the inner lining of the intestine and reduction of its resistance to infection. In marasmus, the child's weight is 60 percent or less of standard weight for age (which is the median weight for healthy children in the United States). With such a large loss of tissue it takes about three months of good nutrition before the child's weight is normal, but the general condition is usually much improved after the first two weeks.

Kwash-iorkor In its fullest form, kwashiorkor is less common than marasmus. It was first described in Ghana in the 1930s, and the word kwashiorkor comes from the Ga language of that country. There is edema, with puffy feet or face, and patches of excess skin pigmentation and peeling. There may be little wasting or loss of weight. The hair is pale and thinned; the child is miserable and apathetic and will not eat. The liver is infiltrated with fat and the concentration of albumin in blood plasma is about one-quarter of the normal. While all agree that marasmus results from not enough food, the classical hypothesis of the pathogenesis of kwashiorkor—insufficient protein with adequate starchy food and sugar—is not fully accepted by all researchers. A major reason is that the dietary histories of children with kwashiorkor are inaccurate.

Treatment of mal-nutrition Treatment of protein-energy malnutrition is essentially the same whether it is marasmus or kwashiorkor. There are three phases to treatment. (1) Resuscitation is the correction of dehydration, deficiency of potassium, low blood sugar, and low body temperature and treatment of infections. (2) The cure is begun with mixed foods, usually including milk, providing increasing calories and protein per kilogram of body weight. Appetite may be poor and the child must be fed by hand. A multivitamin preparation and supplements of potassium, magnesium, and zinc are needed. (3) Rehabilitation takes place after about three weeks when the child usually has improved and has a good appetite, but is still underweight. It will take many weeks of good nutrition before catch-up growth is complete. If the home background is unfavourable because of poverty or social disorganization, the mother will need support as well as advice.

Other nutrients are often deficient in malnourished children: potassium, magnesium, zinc, folic acid, vitamin A, iron, and others that differ from one region (and staple diet) to another. Children malnourished for a long period in early childhood are likely to grow up to be short adults. A more serious and complex question is whether severe malnutrition impairs a child's mental ability. Malnourished children often come from an emotionally and educationally deprived home; however, the balance of evidence from psychological follow-up studies shows that children who have been malnourished have the potential to reach normal intellectual development, though they may not. The outcome is likely to be favourable if the child returns to an encouraging and stimulating home and unfavourable if the malnutrition was prolonged and occurred in the first year of life.

Mild mal-nutrition For every child in a developing country with marasmus, marasmic kwashiorkor, or kwashiorkor (the severe forms) there are likely to be about 10 with mild to moderate forms, the most useful sign of which is a low weight for age (between 61 and 80 percent of the normal standard). It has been estimated that around 2 percent of young children in Third World countries have severe malnutrition while about 20 percent show mild to moderate forms. Such children are not growing at their genetic potential, and they have an increased risk of severer attacks of the common infections of childhood (gastroenteritis, respiratory infections, measles, etc.). Two keys to recognizing mild to moderate protein-energy malnutrition are widespread inexpensive maternal and child health clinics, each with a weighing machine, and a clear and simple growth chart

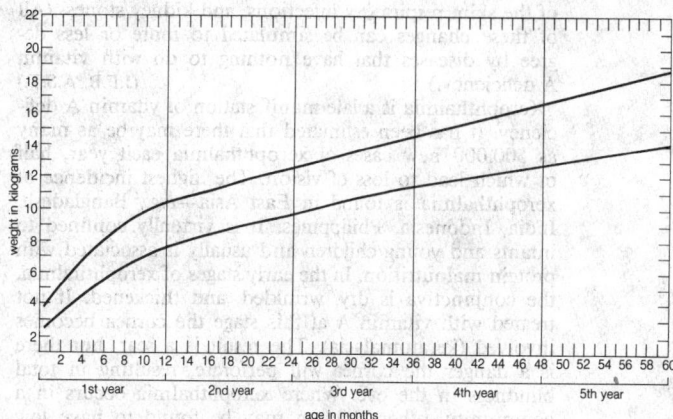

Figure 3: *Standard weights for children.*
The top line is the World Health Organization standard weight for age (the 50th percentile of the National Center for Health Statistics reference) and the bottom line is the 3rd percentile of the reference, close to 80 percent of the standard. In prosperous communities children's weights should be close to the top line. In poor communities they should not fall too far below the bottom line.
By courtesy of the World Health Organization

(Figure 3). Another simple measurement is the mid-upper arm circumference: from 12 to 60 months of age a measurement of 13.5 centimetres (or above) is normal, which remains the same for these four years. A circumference of 12.5 to 13.5 centimetres suggests mild malnutrition and under 12.5 centimetres indicates definite malnutrition.

Vitamins. Each of the vitamin-deficiency diseases is commonly attributed to a deficiency of a single vitamin, and many have been produced in animals and in human volunteers by diets apparently complete except for the vitamin under trial. In human experience, these supposed single-vitamin diseases usually arise from unhealthy and unbalanced diets that are also deficient in other vitamins or in nonvitamin nutrients. In these complex nutrient-deficiency states, the nutrient whose deficiency plays the largest part in the causation of symptoms is often referred to as the most limiting nutrient; *e.g.,* niacin is the most limiting nutrient in pellagra, but there are often deficiencies of other B vitamins, and protein deficiency is commonly present.

Scurvy A good example of a single-nutrient disease is scurvy, the scourge of mariners in the days of long ocean voyages. In 1754 a Scottish naval surgeon, James Lind, established the concept of deficiency diseases by showing that scurvy can be both cured and prevented by the use of orange and lemon juice. Scurvy is an eminently preventable disease, and it is now seen mainly at the extremes of life and where there is disregard of the principles of nutrition. At an early stage scurvy results in swelling and bleeding of the gums and bleeding into the skin. Bleeding into the muscles and under the periosteum, the membrane that covers the bones, in small children may also occur. It is probable that in the classical epidemics among mariners and in prisons the diet was unsatisfactory in many ways and that other deficiency states contributed to the more serious complications and to death, but experiments on human volunteers fed diets lacking in vitamin C but otherwise satisfactory have shown that scurvy can be and often is a single-nutrient-deficiency disease.

Vitamin A deficiency The earliest manifestation of vitamin A deficiency is night blindness, because the retinal pigment rhodopsin (visual purple) in the retina of the eye requires retinol (vitamin A) for its functioning. Retinol deficiency manifests itself as inability of the eyes to adapt in dim light. Moreover, epithelial cells throughout the body—the various cells covering or lining the body and its organs—degenerate in vitamin A deficiency. In the eyes, the conjunctiva and cornea undergo changes (xerophthalmia) that can lead eventually to breakdown and complete blindness. Other epithelial cells, including the skin and the mucous lining of the respiratory and urinary tracts, degenerate, with characteristic results such as hardening and drying of the skin, respiratory infections, and kidney stones. (All of these changes can be simulated to more or less degree by diseases that have nothing to do with vitamin A deficiency.) (J.F.B./A.S.T.)

Xerophthalmia is a late manifestation of vitamin A deficiency. It has been estimated that there may be as many as 500,000 new cases of xerophthalmia each year, half of which lead to loss of vision. The highest incidence of xerophthalmia is found in East Asia—*e.g.,* Bangladesh, India, Indonesia, Philippines. It is virtually confined to infants and young children and usually is associated with protein malnutrition. In the early stages of xerophthalmia, the conjunctiva is dry, wrinkled, and thickened. If not treated with vitamin A at this stage the cornea becomes involved (keratomalacia). The result is a scar, but there is a danger the cornea will perforate, resulting in total blindness in the eye. Where xerophthalmia occurs in a community, other children may be found to have low plasma levels of vitamin A. Children with mild eye signs (night blindness or early xerophthalmia) have an increased risk of acquiring severe measles and respiratory infections. These children develop vitamin A deficiency first because the mother was undernourished, so that they are born with small liver stores of vitamin A and their mother's milk has a low vitamin A content; second because they are given little or no dietary preformed vitamin A or β-carotene; and third because absorption of vitamin A is impaired in protein malnutrition. The World Health Organization has made prevention of xerophthalmia one of its priorities in nutrition. In the short term, the incidence of the disease is being reduced by giving young children a high-dose vitamin A capsule (50 times the adult RDA) every six months. The long-term solution is education, so that mothers and babies regularly eat foods rich in β-carotene, such as dark green leafy vegetables or pumpkin, squash, mangoes, pawpaw, even sweet potatoes and yellow corn, which all provide β-carotene.

Vitamin D deficiencies Vitamin D is involved in the absorption of calcium and, less important, phosphorus from the gastrointestinal tract. The process is affected by both the ratio of calcium to phosphorus and the amount of phytate in the diet. (Phytate, which is present in cereals, interferes with the availability of calcium.)

Whether formed in the skin from a derivative of cholesterol or taken from the diet (*e.g.,* in fatty fish and dairy products), vitamin D is changed in the liver to 25-hydroxyvitamin D. This is further changed in the kidney by an enzyme (regulated by parathormone) to 1,25-dihydroxyvitamin D (1,25-$(OH)_2$ vitamin D), the active form. The best-known action of activated vitamin D at the cellular level is to turn on synthesis of calcium transport protein in the cells lining the small intestine.

Vitamin D deficiency affects the bones. The signs and symptoms of rickets in growing children are different from those of osteomalacia in adults. Features of rickets vary with age, depending on which bones are growing fastest. In young infants there may be softening of the skull (craniotabes). At about one year the wrist bones are thickened and there is a line of beadlike bony nodules (the rachitic rosary) at the junctions of the ribs and the breastbone (sternum). When the child is walking, the growing bone ends (epiphyses) most affected are just above and just below the knee joints and there is either knock-knee or bowlegs. A complication of severe rickets in older children is a contracted pelvis, now rare, which later gives difficulty in childbirth. In adults with osteomalacia, in one or more of the large bones there are pain and tenderness, reduced bone density, and cracks.

Rickets and osteomalacia are rare in tropical countries unless infants or young women are by custom kept indoors or completely covered while outside. In the industrial countries these diseases have been eliminated largely by a combination of cleaner air, sunshine, fortification of some basic foods with vitamin D (margarine and infant formulas generally, milk for adults in North America and Sweden), and administration of cod-liver oil or low-dose vitamin D capsules prophylactically when required. Rickets remains a health problem in Asian people living in northern industrial cities in Britain, and osteomalacia is a possibility in housebound and institutionalized elderly people unless they are given a vitamin D supplement or regularly sit in the sunshine.

Vitamin E deficiency is rare and only known in two situations: in premature infants and in some prolonged cases of defective absorption; *e.g.,* cystic fibrosis. In the former only the earliest manifestation is seen, a mild hemolytic anemia. In the latter, where the deficiency is more chronic, parts of the spinal cord may be affected, with loss of position sense in the legs. Pure dietary deficiency has only been seen under experimental conditions in adults who were given a diet low in vitamin E for over a year; the effect was a mild hemolytic anemia. Vitamin E, like other fat-soluble vitamins, is transported with difficulty across the placenta to the fetus. In adults vitamin E is stored primarily in adipose tissue, and generally enough is stored to last about a year.

Vitamin K deficiency Vitamin K is necessary for the formation of prothrombin and other clotting factors in the liver. Vitamin K deficiency causes hemorrhagic disease in which there is excessive bleeding from a wound as well as internal bleeding that can occur anywhere in the body even without injury. Vitamin K deficiency occurs in four situations: (1) in hemorrhagic disease of the newborn, for which many obstetricians routinely give vitamin K to infants at birth; (2) in disorders of fat absorption (*e.g.,* biliary obstruction) and extensive intestinal disease since vitamin K is fat-soluble; (3) in patients who combine a restricted diet, lacking vegetable foods, with one of the antibiotics that destroys the normal bacterial flora in the large intestine—thus producing a situation in which dietary vitamin K_1 and colonic vitamin K_2 are both lacking; and (4) in therapy with anticoagulant tablets (*e.g.,* warfarin), prescribed to reduce clotting in veins, which antagonizes (or competes with) vitamin K and can be counteracted by an injection of vitamin K_1.

Thiamine deficiency When thiamine is deficient, the two most prominent biochemical abnormalities are (1) the accumulation of pyruvic acid, because the enzyme that processes pyruvic acid for entry into the tricarboxylic acid cycle cannot function without thiamine, and (2) disturbances in areas of the nervous system, a system highly dependent on glucose as fuel and thus requiring thiamine as an essential coenzyme for three steps in glucose metabolism. Thiamine deficiency can lead to beriberi, Wernicke's encephalopathy in association with Korsakoff's syndrome, or a peripheral neuropathy (a disorder of the peripheral nervous system). Beriberi is a high-output cardiac failure associated with general dilatation of small blood vessels in response to accumulation of pyruvic and lactic acids. It was formerly common in rice-eating peoples of East Asia but is now rare. It is occasionally seen in Western alcoholics. In Wernicke's encephalopathy the abnormalities are in the central part of the brain. There is progressive mental deterioration, disorientation, and a characteristic paralysis of eye movements. It is mostly seen in alcoholics but was reported in Japanese prisoner of war camps in World War II. Like beriberi it responds dramatically to injection of thiamine, but unlike beriberi there may be a residual abnormality of memory. Thiamine deficiency is one of many causes of peripheral neuropathy, generally involving an impairment of the sensory, motor, and reflex functions of the limbs. But other B-vitamin deficiencies and a number of toxins can produce a similar effect. Response to nutrient therapy always takes weeks and it is advisable to treat the disease with multiple B vitamins.

Pellagra Pellagra, before the 20th century, occurred in Italy (the name is Italian for "rough skin") and in the southern United States. It has now disappeared from Europe and North America but still occurs in Egypt and southern Africa. It affects poor people who subsist primarily on corn and little other food. In industrial countries it is occasionally seen in alcoholics. The principal nutritional deficiency in pellagra is of niacin. In corn the niacin is in bound form, not able to be broken down by humans unless prepared in a special way. In addition, unlike other cereals, corn is low in the amino acid tryptophan, a precursor of niacin. Pellagra is the disease of dermatosis, diarrhea, and dementia. The first clinical features of pellagra are demarcated, symmetrical areas of pigmentation and thickening and cracking of the skin where it is exposed to sunlight. The collar area is usually affected and provides a useful diagnostic sign ("Casal's collar"). In severer cases there are mental disturbances such as fatigue, depression, and progressive confusion. Gastrointestinal effects include diarrhea. Other B vitamins, especially riboflavin and vitamin B_6, are usually deficient, and complete treatment calls for multiple B vitamins (in diet or tablets), not just niacin.

Folic acid and vitamin B_{12} deficiencies
The major effect of deficiency of either folic acid or vitamin B_{12} is the failure of cell division because one of the family of folic acid compounds (5, 10-methyltetrahydrofolate) is required for addition of a methyl group to uracil to form thymine, one of the four bases of DNA. An important function of vitamin B_{12} involves interconversion of folic acid compounds. (When it is lacking, the methyltetrahydrofolate compound accumulates and the compound required for DNA synthesis is not made.)

Cells that turn over rapidly are most affected by deficiencies of folic acid and vitamin B: red blood cells, white blood cells, and platelets all decrease in number. Replacement of the lining cells of the intestine and formation of germ cells are also affected. In the bone marrow the red cell precursors are larger than normal, with an immature nucleus, called megaloblastic change. Thus folic acid deficiency and vitamin B_{12} deficiency each causes megaloblastic anemia.

Vitamin B_{12} plays another biochemical role, unrelated to folic acid, in the maintenance of myelin (the sheath that forms around a nerve fibre) in the nervous system. In vitamin B_{12} deficiency, unusual odd-numbered fatty acids appear in myelin, apparently because of the accumulation of three-carbon compounds instead of the usual two-carbon raw material for fatty acid synthesis. The usual symptom is subacute degeneration of both sensory and motor tracts in the spinal cord.

Folic acid deficiency can occur in late pregnancy, when the requirement is double that in other adults. It is also fairly common in patients with diseases in which cell division is increased; e.g., in blood diseases or cancer. The most common cause of vitamin B_{12} deficiency is pernicious anemia, in which absorption of the vitamin is defective because of the failure of the stomach to secrete a special protein (intrinsic factor) that assists absorption of vitamin B_{12} in the lower intestine. Dietary deficiency occurs in vegans, who eat no animal food. It takes five or more years of such a diet before symptoms appear because the stores of vitamin B_{12} in the liver, although only about 1.5 milligrams, are enough to last about five years with the daily requirement as small as one microgram.

Fats and carbohydrates. Most human diets contain between 10 and 15 percent of the total calories as protein. In poor communities this is mostly from vegetable foods; in rich communities it is more from animal foods. The rest of the dietary energy comes from carbohydrates, fats, and, in some people, alcohol. The proportion of calories from fats is only about 10 percent in poor communities, but it is 40 percent or even more in rich communities. Carbohydrates vary reciprocally: from 75 to 80 percent in poor communities to 45 percent in rich communities (Figure 4).

Humans are adaptable omnivores and survive on a greater variety of foods and metabolic fuels than many other animals. Adaptations occur to a low or high carbohydrate/fat ratio. Dietary carbohydrates can be considered for nutritional purposes in three groups: (1) metabolically available sugars, (2) starches, and (3) carbohydrates not absorbed in the small intestine (unavailable carbohydrates)—mostly cellulose, hemicelluloses, and pectin. These are the main types of dietary fibre. The minimum requirement for available carbohydrate is low, only about 50 grams for an adult. Below this intake ketosis occurs. In practice, few diets contain as few carbohydrates as this, except for discredited very-low-carbohydrate weight-loss diets.

Essential fatty acids
There is also a minimum requirement for fat—not for total fat, but only for a small group of fatty acids, of which linoleic acid is the most abundant and arachidonic acid and a-linolenic acid the only other important ones (see Table 8). The basic requirement for essential fatty acids to prevent deficiency is 1 to 2 percent of dietary energy;

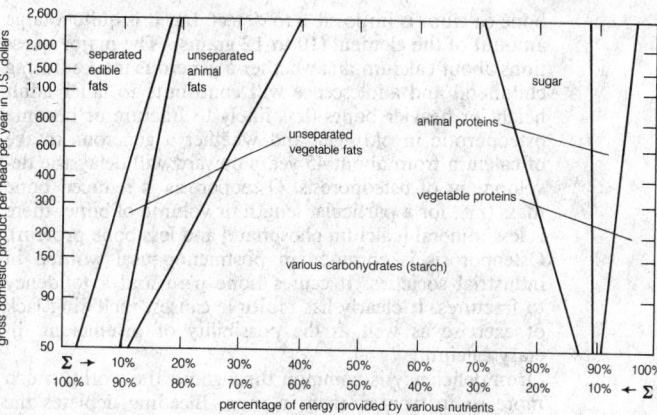

Figure 4: Dietary energy derived from fats, carbohydrates, and proteins as a percentage of total energy, related to the income or gross domestic product of 85 countries at 1962 values of money on a logarithmic scale.

From J. Perisse, F. Sizaret, and P. Francois, *Nutrition Newsletter* (1969); Food and Agriculture Organization

i.e., two to six grams of linoleic acid. The characteristics of essential fatty acid deficiency include a scaly dermatitis, poor wound healing, anemia, reduced platelet count, and fatty infiltration of the liver. Deficiency of essential fatty acids as a result of an inadequate diet is rare. Even if people do not eat separated fats (butter, oils, etc.), they usually obtain enough linoleic acid from the cell membranes of plant foods and meats. With total parenteral nutrition, however, essential fatty acid deficiency is well described. It will occur if this form of feeding is prolonged unless a lipid emulsion rich in linoleic acid (e.g., Intralipid) is added to the administered fluids. There is good evidence that amounts of linoleic acid several times the basic requirement can contribute to reducing the risk of coronary heart disease by different mechanisms, such as lowering the plasma cholesterol and reducing the tendency to thrombosis.

Inorganic elements. Twenty-two of the 103 chemical elements are required as nutrients by humans. Another three or four might yet be shown to be needed in minute amounts. Carbon, nitrogen, hydrogen, and oxygen make up the organic nutrients, and the latter two are also consumed as water. Cobalt is only required as vitamin B_{12} and sulfur as part of the essential amino acids methionine and cystine. Requirements for the rest range from 0.1 milligram or less for iodine, selenium, and chromium to up to one to five grams per day for sodium, chloride, and potassium. Elements required in minute amounts, usually present in food and body tissues in small amounts, were formerly called trace elements because analysts could only report presence of an amount too small to quantify. With modern methods, such as advanced atomic absorption spectrometry, extremely low concentrations can be accurately determined, and there is no reason to separate trace elements from minerals. Table 5 shows that there is no grouping of requirements for the inorganic elements.

Requirements

Sodium depletion
Sodium depletion occurs, usually with accompanying water loss, as a result of massive loss of fluids; e.g., diarrhea, vomiting, and excessive urination. Sodium is the major ion in the extracellular fluid, the total volume of which contracts as does the blood volume; the blood pressure falls and the heart rate increases. The patient is weak and exhausted. Sodium depletion occurs in a number of disease states, and chloride depletion usually accompanies it.

Potassium depletion occurs in similar situations and may become obvious if sodium and water, but not potassium, are replaced. Potassium loss is especially likely to occur with diarrhea or overuse of purgatives, with regular use of diuretic drugs, with corticosteroid treatment, and with wasting diseases. In potassium depletion the serum potassium level is low, there is weakness of voluntary muscles, intestinal peristalsis may stop, and an electrocardiograph shows low T waves.

Calcium depletion, unlike that of sodium and potassium, is difficult to recognize because 99 percent of the calcium in the body is in the bones. A 1 percent reduction of bone calcium is impossible to detect, but it is quite a large amount of the element (10 to 12 grams). The major questions about calcium are: whether a generous intake during childhood and adolescence will contribute to taller adult height or heavier bones (less likely to fracture or become osteoporotic in old age), and whether a generous intake of calcium from about 45 years onward will delay the development of osteoporosis. Osteoporosis is reduced bone mass (i.e., for a particular length or volume of bone, there is less mineral [calcium phosphate] and less bone protein). Osteoporosis is common in postmenopausal women in industrial societies. It causes bone pain and a tendency to fractures. It clearly has multiple causes, including lack of exercise as well as the possibility of insufficient dietary calcium.

Iron deficiency is common throughout the world, much more so in women than in men. Bleeding depletes the body of iron because each millilitre of blood contains 0.5 milligram of iron and the body does not actively excrete iron, so that excretion cannot be shut down to adapt to a negative iron balance. There are stores in the bone marrow and other tissues that are drawn on, and absorption of iron, which is always inefficient, becomes more efficient. The main function of iron is in the formation of hemoglobin, the red pigment of the blood that carries oxygen from the lungs to other tissues. When iron stores are empty there is anemia (reduced red blood cell count) with small cells containing less hemoglobin than normal (microcytic, hypochromic anemia).

Hemoglobin and anemia

Iodine deficiency is now rare in the industrial countries but is an important handicap to development in those inland and mountainous areas with poor transport. Iodine is necessary for the synthesis of the hormones of the thyroid gland. In the absence of adequate iodine, the thyroid enlarges because of increased secretion of pituitary thyrotrophin. It has come to be realized that where the frequency of endemic goitre is high, not only are occasional babies born with cretinism (a cause of mental defect and dwarfism), but a large percentage of apparently normal people in the community have minor abnormalities such as learning disabilities, deafness, and a higher rate of stillbirths and malformed babies. The World Health Organization is giving priority to reducing these iodine-deficiency disorders. It has been estimated that 400,000,-000 people may be affected to some degree. Iodized salt is effective only in developed communities. For remote, isolated communities the best method of prevention is an injection of two millilitres of iodized oil to all women of childbearing age.

Zinc deficiency has been described in its different manifestations since the late 1960s, although its frequency and importance have not been clearly defined. Zinc is often associated with protein in foods, and zinc status is low in protein-energy malnutrition. Zinc deficiency has been claimed in a number of circumstances; e.g., among adolescents in the Middle East, Australian Aborigines, alcoholics, those affected by chronic renal failure and anorexia nervosa, and possibly pregnant women. It is difficult to interpret the significance of moderate reductions of plasma zinc below the usual concentration. Some cases of deficiency have been validated; e.g., by the body's response to zinc supplementation. Some clear examples of zinc deficiency were encountered in patients given total parenteral nutrition before it became routine to include zinc in the regimen. Features of zinc deficiency in humans have been protean: various combinations of loss of taste, retarded growth, delayed wound healing, baldness, pustular skin lesions, impotence in males, infertility in females, and reduced immunity to infections.

Epidemiological studies in the United States in the 1930s and 1940s revealed an inverse relationship between the fluoride content of natural waters and the rate of dental caries. Fluoridation of water supplies at one part per million is safe, though it may be associated with mottled (not carious) teeth in hot, dry countries where large amounts of water are drunk. Wherever fluoridation has been introduced, the number of decayed, missing, and filled teeth in children has decreased, and where fluoridation has been subsequently stopped, the rate of caries has increased

Fluoridation

again. Fluoride is concentrated in the dental enamel and in bones. It increases the resistance of the enamel to erosion by acid. The chronic toxic dose of fluoride starts at intakes of about five milligrams per day; the first sign is mottling of the teeth. Above 10 milligrams per day bony outgrowths may occur (skeletal fluorosis). The only foods that contain appreciable amounts of fluoride are tea and fish. In communities and countries where the drinking water is not fluoridated many obtain some fluoride from toothpastes, a few give fluoride tablets to children prophylactically, and dentists apply fluoride solution directly to their patients' teeth periodically. The incidence of dental caries has fallen remarkably in most countries since the 1960s.

Selenium deficiency appears to be responsible for heart muscle disease (cardiomyopathy) in children in K'o-shan Hsien, a part of northeastern China where the soil has the lowest selenium content in the world. Deficiencies of phosphate, magnesium, copper, molybdenum, manganese, and chromium are rare because the levels in foods cover requirements in most situations.

Dietary fibre. Fibre is not a true nutrient in the classical sense. Dietary fibre is the natural packing of plant foods. It can be defined as those parts of foods that are not digested by human enzymes in the small intestine. The principal chemical classes of dietary fibre are cellulose, hemicelluloses, pectins, gums, and lignins. They are all polysaccharides (i.e., unavailable carbohydrates) except lignin, which occurs with cellulose in the structure of plants. Pectins and gums are not really fibrous; they are amorphous and viscous.

Some types of fibre, notably the hemicellulose of the outer layers of wheat, increase the water-holding capacity of the contents of the large intestine and so increase the bulk of the feces. This relieves simple constipation and probably reduces the likelihood of diverticula forming in the large intestine in older people. There is some evidence that fibre may reduce the chances of developing cancer of the large intestine. Other viscous, indigestible polysaccharides like pectin and guar gum, when isolated and in large doses, have more effect on the upper gastrointestinal tract. They tend to slow gastric emptying and contribute to satiety. They slow the rise of blood glucose after a carbohydrate meal, and they reduce the plasma cholesterol concentration.

Uses of dietary fibre

Dietary fibre is in fact partly digested in the large intestine. It is fermented by some of the resident bacterial flora (not by enzymes), resulting in the production of gas (hydrogen, methane, or carbon dioxide) in the form of flatus. A small quantity of volatile fatty acids (acetic, butyric, or propionic) is absorbed through the lining cells of the large intestine. Thus, some of the chemical energy in fibre does become available. Much of the pectins and hemicelluloses are metabolized by colonic fermentation and so is some of the cellulose. Lignin, however, resists even bacterial action. There are no official RDAs for dietary fibres because analyses for the different types in foods are not complete, but the average adult intake of about 15 to 20 grams per day in affluent countries is thought to be too low. Increased intake is likely to be most helpful in people confined to bed, in pregnant women, and in the elderly, three groups of people often troubled with constipation. The food sources of fibre are cereals (especially whole grain), vegetables, nuts, and fruits. A concentrated form of the fibrous type is found in wheat bran.   (A.S.T.)

OBESITY AND OTHER DISORDERS OF THE DIET

Obesity. By far the most common effect of continued overconsumption of calories is obesity, a state of excess accumulation of fat in and on the body. It is often wrongly defined as a state in which weight is in excess of a 10 percent margin allowed over standard weight tables for age, height, sex, and race. Fat on the body is easily seen and measured. It is assumed that if there is excess fat in the subcutaneous tissue, there is probably also excess fat inside the body. More accurately, the amount of fat in the body can be calculated from the specific gravity of the total body, which in turn is measurable by comparison of weight underwater with weight in air. The more fat there is, the lower is the body specific gravity. To describe weight in excess of 10 percent above standard weight as obesity is misleading, because a small minority of persons who have inherited a large frame and bulky muscles may be 20 percent or more in excess of standard weight without being obese. Nevertheless, weight is a valuable screening measure for obesity.

Theories concerning causes of obesity

Obesity is caused by consistent consumption of more calories than are required to meet energy expenditure. This simple explanation, however, conceals a great deal of difficult theory about causation. It is probably true that some persons put on fat more readily than others. This may have a simple double explanation: namely, that these people are more interested in food or that they expend less energy. This latter theory probably accounts for obesity in only a small minority. Overeating may be a habit culturally imposed by family custom, may be an occupational hazard (*e.g.,* of cooks), may follow immobilization, can be stimulated by certain drugs, or may be an expression of boredom or emotional frustration. Underexpenditure of energy may be determined by cultural family environment, sedentary life, or temperament. It has been shown that obese adolescents at summer camps expend less energy than their leaner friends, even when engaged in active games.

Obesity, like underweight, is a condition with multiple causes. Some people have a metabolic rate that is lower than average (they may feel the cold sooner than others). Whenever energy intakes have been measured over a week in a standardized group, some members are found to eat consistently less than others. They presumably adjust their energy intake to their lower energy expenditure. These efficient metabolizers would have a better chance of survival under conditions of chronic undernutrition. Certain ethnic groups have been noted to have a predisposition to obesity when food is plentiful—*e.g.,* the Pima American Indians, Micronesians (notably in Nauru), and probably Polynesians and Australian Aborigines. It is postulated that they have evolved as metabolically "thrifty genotypes" because their ancestors went through periods of starvation. In the few short-term studies of experimental overeating, some subjects have not put on as much weight as expected. It is suggested that this may be because they retain some brown adipose tissue, a specialized type of fat tissue present in newborns that is rich in mitochondria and which (when stimulated by norepinephrine) produces a large amount of heat and uses a large amount of energy. No solid evidence has been found for this in humans, however.

Brown adipose tissue

The effects of obesity can be stated with more certainty. Obese persons have a reduced life expectancy, and they suffer disproportionately from a number of diseases and disabilities. Diabetes of the middle-aged is strongly associated with obesity, and there is association of obesity in females with gallbladder disease. Contrary to general impression, coronary heart disease is not causally related to obesity, but in some communities it has been reported that those who put fat on their trunks are more likely to suffer coronary disease, while those who put fat on their hips or buttocks are not. Anyone with heart disease should maintain a standard weight because obesity increases the load on the heart. Obesity is a mechanical load on the lower spine and the major weight-bearing joints, the hips, knees, and ankles. Reduction of the weight of obese persons may mitigate the middle-aged tendency to degenerative diseases of the joints and muscular rheumatism. Obesity of the trunk may interfere seriously with breathing and may contribute to pulmonary heart disease. There is considerable association, both as cause and effect, between obesity and psycho-emotional disturbance. Many obese persons suffer a considerable sense of inferiority. Misdirected attempts at weight reduction may lead to deficiency disease and debility or, in a few persons, may go on to self-imposed starvation (anorexia nervosa). (J.F.B./A.S.T.)

The scientific principles of management of obesity stress prevention because prevention is easier than treatment of established obesity. The psychological aspects of weight management are more important than details of the diet, because, without the inner motivation to reduce weight, it is impossible to make it happen. Major aspects of the help

that doctors and dietitians can offer centre on building up the person's self-esteem and guiding the person in avoiding situations in which it is difficult to stop eating. Habits are more important than diets. Crash diets do not work and may be dangerous. A loss of about one kilogram (two pounds) per week is as much as can be expected; half of this is acceptable and all that some people can manage.

Importance of self-esteem

Weight management should fit the grade of the obesity. People with gross obesity (Table 11) require special medical treatment, and special surgical procedures, such as jaw wiring or gastric stapling, are often investigated for such individuals. It is more appropriate to treat people with moderate obesity using behaviour modification and a reduced-calorie diet.

Table 11: Guidelines for Body Weight in Adults

height without shoes		weight without clothes					
		acceptable		obese		grossly obese	
(m)	(ft, in.)	(kg)	(lb)	(kg)	(lb)	(kg)	(lb)
1.45	4,9	42–53	93–117	64	141	85	187
1.48	4,10	42–54	93–119	65	143	86	190
1.50	4,11	43–55	95–121	66	146	88	194
1.52	5,0	44–57	97–126	68	150	90	198
1.54	5,1	44–58	97–128	70	154	93	205
1.56	5,1	45–58	99–128	70	154	93	205
1.58	5,2	51–64	112–141	77	170	102	225
1.60	5,3	52–65	115–143	78	172	104	229
1.62	5,4	53–66	117–146	79	174	105	232
1.64	5,5	54–67	119–148	80	176	106	234
1.66	5,5	55–69	121–152	83	183	110	243
1.68	5,6	56–71	124–157	85	187	113	249
1.70	5,7	58–73	128–161	88	194	117	258
1.72	5,8	59–74	130–163	89	196	118	260
1.74	5,9	60–75	132–165	90	199	120	265
1.76	5,9	62–77	137–170	92	203	122	269
1.78	5,10	64–79	141–174	95	210	126	278
1.80	5,11	65–80	143–176	96	212	128	282
1.82	6,0	66–82	146–181	98	216	130	287
1.84	6,0	67–84	148–185	101	223	134	296
1.86	6,1	69–86	152–190	103	227	137	302
1.88	6,2	71–88	157–194	106	234	141	311
1.90	6,3	73–90	161–198	108	238	144	318
1.92	6,4	75–93	165–205	112	247	150	331

Partly based on Table I from Royal College of Physician's report *Obesity,* 1983, and J.S. Garrow, *Treat Obesity Seriously,* 1981.
Source: A. Stewart Truswell *et al., ABC of Nutrition* (1986).

The nutritional principles of weight reduction and management are to eat less—two-thirds or one-half of the food previously eaten, which corresponds to about 1,500 kilocalories for a man and 1,000 kilocalories for a woman. The foods that should be cut from the diet are the "empty calorie" foods—fats, alcohol, and sugars (in order of priority), which provide nine, seven, and four kilocalories per gram, respectively. Meals should not be missed and a variety of foods, including meat or fish, milk or cheese, bread or cereals, and vegetables and fruits should be eaten each day. Fatty foods and fried foods as well as "tempting foods" must be avoided. Foods vary considerably in calories per usual serving (Table 12).

Some of the techniques of behaviour modification include using a shopping list, purchasing only nonfattening foods (see Table 12), avoiding shopping when hungry, eating only in one room, eating slowly, avoiding distracting activities (except conversation) like watching television, and avoiding eating unnecessarily. A variety of low-calorie foods, like raw vegetables, should always be available to use as snacks. Other people can be recruited to help by reinforcing the positive benefits of not overeating. Nonedible rewards should be given for remaining on the program. Steps should be taken to minimize hunger, loneliness, depression, boredom, anger, and fatigue, each of which can set off a bout of overeating. Finally, the amount of exercise taken each day should be increased.

Anorexia nervosa. Anorexia nervosa is the opposite of obesity. It seems to occur only in societies where adequate food is taken for granted and where people may feel anxiety about avoiding obesity. In affluent communities many teenage girls and young women diet to stay slim or become slim, though their attempts may not be successful. The young woman with anorexia nervosa, on the other hand, does not talk about dieting but succeeds in losing

Societal influence

Table 12: Representative Energy Values of Some Common Foods

food	kilocalories	food	kilocalories	food	kilocalories
Cucumber (2 oz)	5	Bread (1 slice, 1 oz)	65	Carbonated soft drink (12-oz can)	155
Lettuce (1 oz)	5	Potatoes (new, boiled, 4 oz)	85	Peanuts (1 oz)	160
Cauliflower (4 oz, raw)	15	Egg (medium, boiled)	90	Cake, sponge (2 oz)	170
Tomatoes (4 oz)	15	Banana (1 fruit)	90	Chicken (meat only, roast, 4 oz)	170
Carrot (3 oz)	20	Wine (4 oz)	90	Cheese, Cheddar (1½ oz)	175
Grapefruit (½ fruit = 6 oz)	20	Beer (½ pint)	90	Avocado (½ fruit)	190
Milk (1 oz, in tea)	20	Butter (½ oz, for slice of bread)	105	Rice (2 oz before cooking)	205
Sugar (1 level teaspoon)	30	Cornflakes (1 oz)	105	Macaroni (2 oz before cooking)	210
Jam (½ oz)	35	Fish (cod, grilled, 4 oz)	110	Fish fried in batter (4 oz)	225
Orange juice (unsweetened, 4 oz)	45	Yogurt (low-fat, flavoured, 5 oz)	115	Beefsteak, grilled (4 oz)	250
Apple (one, 5 oz)	50	Dates (2 oz)	140	Pork chops (7 oz, grilled, fat cut off)	265
Peas (4 oz, boiled)	60	Baked beans (8 oz)	145	Cookies, chocolate (2 oz)	300
Whiskey (1 oz) and soda	65	Chocolate, milk (1 oz)	150	French fries (4 oz)	330

Source: A. Stewart Truswell *et al.*, *ABC of Nutrition* (1986).

the weight that the others talk about losing. She does have an appetite but it is strongly suppressed. By rigid control of her eating she avoids foods that she understands to be fattening. She has a phobia of being fat and often has a distorted body image, seeing herself in the mirror as fatter than she really is. Amenorrhea (cessation of menstruation) is an early characteristic. Before the loss of weight she was often a model of good behaviour, conformism, and achievement, though this probably concealed a sense of ineffectiveness and self-doubt. Up to one in 100 middle-class women from 15 to 25 years may be affected. Some women not only abstain; they have learned to induce vomiting or purging and may have eating binges in between. When habitual, this behaviour is called bulimia nervosa.

The physical effects of a young woman starving herself down to 90 pounds (45 kilograms) or less differ in several ways from those of famine. The young woman with anorexia nervosa usually eats adequate protein and micronutrients; she is restless and overactive. She denies that she is too thin or that she is not eating enough.

Treatment is easiest if the condition is recognized at an early stage. It is best managed by a specialized team, most often a psychiatrist with experience in anorexia nervosa, working with a dietitian. The principles of treatment are behavioral therapy, supervised eating, and supportive psychotherapy.

Nutrient excess. Ethyl alcohol is the only drug that provides calories, although meals of nonalcoholic foods have a gentle sedative effect. The acute effects of a large intake of alcohol are well known. Mental impairment starts when the blood concentration is about 0.05 percent. Levels of alcohol in the blood up to 0.15 percent are the maximum permitted for drivers in many countries. When ingested, alcohol is rapidly distributed throughout the entire body. A concentration of alcohol in the blood of 0.40 percent usually causes unconsciousness, and 0.50 percent can be fatal. The most dangerous effects of acute alcohol intoxication, however, are road accidents and violence. The many complications of chronically high intakes of alcohol include gastric ulcer, pancreatitis, cirrhosis of the liver, convulsions, delirium tremens, hypertension, several varieties of malnutrition, and fetal malformations. Malnutrition is avoided if a nutritious diet is consumed along with the alcohol, but this does not prevent the rise of blood pressure, which is seen from about four drinks per day. Cirrhosis of the liver takes years to develop. The lowest chronic intake of alcohol that can lead to cirrhosis is difficult to determine partly because heavy drinkers underestimate their consumption and partly because of the other causes of liver damage; *e.g.,* viral hepatitis may coexist in an alcoholic. Eight or more drinks per day over the course of many years is the typical pattern of an alcoholic. Women with smaller lean body mass are more susceptible to hepatic damage from alcohol. Fetal alcohol syndrome (a combination of malformations with characteristic facial appearance) has been reported with apparently quite low alcohol intakes in the first trimester of pregnancy. Delirium tremens is the withdrawal syndrome of tremor, agitation, and occasionally hallucinations that is seen when heavy chronic drinkers are removed from their supply.

In all biologic systems the dose of an added substance, including nutrients, determines the effect. Nutrients taken in amounts above the RDA can be toxic. The level at which the nutrient may exert toxic effects varies, and for some nutrients, such as vitamins A and D, iron, fluoride, selenium, and iodine, the level is much lower than for others. Among the vitamins, the rule that fat-soluble vitamins can be toxic but water-soluble vitamins are not cannot be relied upon because vitamin B_6 (water-soluble) has been found to cause peripheral neuropathy in doses at least 200 times the RDA, while no consistent side effect of large intakes of fat-soluble vitamin E has been shown. The toxic effects of vitamins A and D and of fluoride are described above.

Iron toxicity may be acute or chronic. Acute toxicity occurs if a number of sugar-coated iron tablets are accidentally swallowed; it can be fatal. Chronic iron intoxication occurs in persons who regularly consume acidic alcoholic drinks brewed in unlined iron vessels. Iron is dissolved in the drink and absorbed and deposited in the liver. The condition, hemosiderosis, has been reported in blacks in southern Africa and in some drinkers in Europe who consume large amounts of wine. Selenium toxicity occurs in animals grazing on selenium-rich soils (*e.g.,* in South Dakota). In humans it has occurred occasionally from industrial exposure and, rarely, from the diet (in an area of China) and following unintentional overdose of selenium supplement tablets. The clinical features are loss of hair and nails, skin lesions, gastrointestinal disturbances, lassitude, and polyneuritis.

There are two types of vitamin tablets: multivitamins and single vitamins. Multivitamin tablets are, in theory, harmless, though usually unnecessary. Most multivitamin preparations do not contain all 13 true vitamins, and the doses of vitamins they do contain usually deviate far from their RDAs. Single-vitamin preparations are more difficult to justify because it has been found that people often take the wrong supplements. In pregnancy, for example, the special need is for extra iron, folic acid, and calcium. Megadoses of vitamins carry the risk of toxic effects, especially for vitamins A, D, and B_6, and possibly for some of the other vitamins.

FOOD SENSITIVITY

Some foods and drinks are more likely to provoke sensitivity than others and people exhibit varying sensitivities to foods. The most common reactions are gastrointestinal, in the form of indigestion, vomiting, or diarrhea; urticaria and angioneurotic edema; eczema; asthma; and migraine. Gastrointestinal effects are the result of the irritant effect of one of the ingredients in food. In sensitive people, these ingredients might relax the cardiac sphincter at the lower end of the esophagus so that acid regurgitates from the stomach; they might stimulate gastric acid secretion; or they might increase the motility of the intestine.

When the onset of eczema is related to food it is the result of a true allergic mechanism, an abnormal immunological reaction by immunoglobulin E to one of the proteins of the food. Urticaria and asthma sometimes can be truly allergic reactions but it seems likely that other mechanisms are more usual. Urticaria in some people is due to naturally occurring salicylates in plant foods. It is thought that they act by inhibiting the enzyme cyclo-oxygenase and allowing more arachidonic acid to be converted to

Toxicity of nutrients

Alcohol

Common sensitivity reactions

leukotrienes by the action of the enzyme lipoxygenase. Whether hyperactivity in children (usually boys) is aggravated by naturally occurring food salicylates or by some artificial food colours is controversial. There is little objective confirmation of this belief.

A minority of sufferers from migraine are able to incriminate particular foods as provoking agents. Cheese, chocolate, citrus fruits, and alcoholic drinks are the most likely agents, possibly via pressor amines like tyramine and histamine, which tend to raise blood pressure.

Gluten sensitivity

There are other more specific examples of food sensitivity, the most important of which is celiac disease, or gluten enteropathy. There is malabsorption, fat in the feces (steatorrhea), weight loss, impaired growth in children, and other manifestations of malnutrition. Celiac disease is due to atrophy (flattening of the cells) of the inner lining of the small intestine. This condition was first described in 1888, but it was not until 1953 that doctors in The Netherlands discovered that a fraction of wheat, the gluten, acts as a toxin in these patients. When wheat is meticulously eliminated from the diet, patients recover. This is one therapeutic diet that is literally lifesaving.

When symptoms of food sensitivity are immediate, the individual himself makes the diagnosis. There are some people, for instance, whose lips swell the moment their mouth touches a peanut, and if by chance they should swallow some they will have several systemic symptoms—vomiting, urticaria, even asthma. When the symptoms are more delayed, diagnosis of the responsible food or food component requires more detective work. If the symptoms are chronic or recur frequently, they should disappear on an elimination diet, a diet of very few foods (lamb, rice, carrots, lettuce, refined seed oil, sugar, and water) that do not cause food sensitivity. Suspected foods then can be reintroduced one at a time. Skin tests are not very reliable.

Not all people who believe they are sensitive to a particular food really are. They may in fact dislike the food, or they may have eaten it coincidentally with the onset of an illness, or they may have been told by an unorthodox practitioner that their symptoms are due to a particular food.

HABITUAL DIETARY PATTERNS AND DISEASE

A major preoccupation of nutrition research and a theme of the public debate over nutrition in North America, Europe, and Australasia is the relationship between the usual diet and the chances of developing (prematurely) one of the prevalent chronic degenerative diseases—coronary heart disease, high blood pressure, cancer, diabetes mellitus, dental caries, gallstones, urinary tract stones, colonic diverticulosis, cirrhosis of the liver, etc. Only the first five of these will be discussed below.

Multiple causes

The causation of each of these degenerative diseases is multifactorial; there are several factors that act over a long period of time and interact with one another. There are protective factors as well as pathogenic factors; there are genetic, dietary, and non-dietary factors. Even in the diet there often appear to be multiple factors operating in different ways. The evidence for each disease comes from a variety of sources and several disciplines; from descriptive epidemiology—cross-sectional and retrospective; from prospective (cohort) epidemiological studies; from basic science (biochemistry, microbiology, pathology); from animal models; from human metabolic studies; and from prevention trials (primary or secondary).

Diet and coronary heart disease. In a prospective study, a large group of people at moderate risk of developing coronary heart disease (usually middle-aged Caucasian men) is examined and blood tests performed. The group is then followed up for five to 20 years, during which time some develop one of the manifestations of coronary heart disease, while most do not. Coronary heart disease may or may not show signs and symptoms of disease. When symptoms are present there are four possible manifestations: sudden cardiac death, myocardial infarction (the typical heart attack, requiring hospitalization and a period of time off of work), angina pectoris (heart pain on exertion), and cardiac failure with an electrocardiogram indicating that the cause is coronary artery insufficiency. Those who develop clinical coronary heart disease are

compared against the battery of findings at the initial examination to see which characteristics are "risk factors"; *i.e.*, strongly associated with the disease and appearing to be predictive. Over 20 prospective studies have been made on thousands of people in 14 countries. They have all found that the three biggest risk factors for coronary heart disease are a high plasma total cholesterol, cigarette smoking, and high blood pressure (hypertension).

Lipoproteins

Being lipid and nonpolar, cholesterol is totally insoluble in an aqueous solution. All cholesterol in blood plasma, therefore, is carried on lipoproteins. Low-density lipoprotein (LDL) cholesterol, which normally carries about three-fourths of the total cholesterol, is the risk factor; it can, in some situations, carry cholesterol into the inner lining of artery walls. High density lipoprotein (HDL) cholesterol, on the contrary, tends to act as a protective factor; it may be able to clear some of the cholesterol deposited in the periphery and carry it to the liver, where it can be excreted with the bile. Deposition of cholesterol on the inner aspect of the walls of arteries is part of the process of formation of atherosclerosis, the pathological basis of coronary heart disease. Plasma HDL cholesterol only makes up about one-quarter of normal total cholesterol concentration, and its level is higher in women than in men, but never very high. A total cholesterol that is high nearly always results from elevation of LDL cholesterol; when very high it is always due to raised LDL cholesterol. It is a little simpler and cheaper to measure total cholesterol than LDL cholesterol. When discussing elevation of cholesterol and its treatment the two terms are almost synonymous. A change of plasma total cholesterol means the same sort of change in LDL cholesterol.

Plasma (total or LDL) cholesterol may be raised as the inherited condition familial hypercholesterolemia, a condition with a tendency toward premature coronary heart disease. Plasma cholesterol is also raised secondary to certain diseases; *e.g.*, hypothyroidism, some types of kidney disease, bile duct obstruction, and diabetes mellitus. Finally, it is moderately raised by a diet rich in saturated fat and cholesterol, a phenomenon first demonstrated in rabbits just before World War I. From a global viewpoint such countries as Great Britain, Finland, Ireland, New Zealand, Czechoslovakia, Australia, Hungary, and the United States are high plasma cholesterol countries, consuming high-fat diets and experiencing high incidences of coronary heart disease. In residents of these countries plasma cholesterol (total and LDL) can be consistently reduced by combining the following dietary changes (listed in order of effectiveness): (1) reduce saturated fat as much as possible, (2) reduce energy intake if overweight, (3) increase consumption of vegetables, legumes, fruits, and cereals (preferably whole grain), (4) partly replace the reduced saturated fat with moderate increase of polyunsaturated and some monounsaturated oils, and (5) reduce dietary cholesterol. In practical dietetics these translate to avoiding butter, hydrogenated margarine, lard and suet, full-cream milk, cream, meat fat, frying, chocolate, and sausages; to restricting egg yolks, most cheeses, cakes, pastries, and cookies; and to eating more vegetables, legumes, fruits, bread, rice, pasta, breakfast cereals, polyunsaturated oils (*e.g.*, sunflower seed, safflower, corn oils), and skim or low-fat milk.

Reduction of plasma cholesterol

Plasma total (and LDL) cholesterol is related to the risk of coronary heart disease in a continuous gradient. The higher the plasma cholesterol above about 4.9 millimoles per litre (190 milligrams per 100 millilitres) the greater the chances of subsequent coronary heart disease (Figure 5). Trials in people starting with moderately elevated plasma cholesterol have shown that the amount of coronary heart disease is less in subsequent years in those given a cholesterol-lowering drug compared with untreated controls. A World Health Organization expert committee concluded in 1982 that there is a causal relationship between plasma total cholesterol and coronary heart disease. In high-incidence countries, the committee recommended lowering the whole population's plasma cholesterol distribution by progressive changes in eating patterns toward the sort of diet described in the preceding paragraph. The United States National Heart, Lung, and Blood Institute and the British

Cholesterol and heart disease

Department of Health, as well as heart associations or foundations in other countries, have reached essentially the same conclusions and recommendations. Several countries, notably the United States, Australia, New Zealand, Belgium, and Finland have seen important reductions in mortality from coronary heart disease since the mid-1960s. There, the amount of cigarette smoking is decreasing in men, hypertension is being treated, and there have been some dietary changes. Total fat intake has not come down in general but polyunsaturated fat intake has gone up and with it the ratio of polyunsaturated to saturated fats. In the same period, mortality from coronary heart disease has been increasing in the Soviet Union and other countries of eastern Europe. The incidence of coronary heart disease remains very low in Japan.

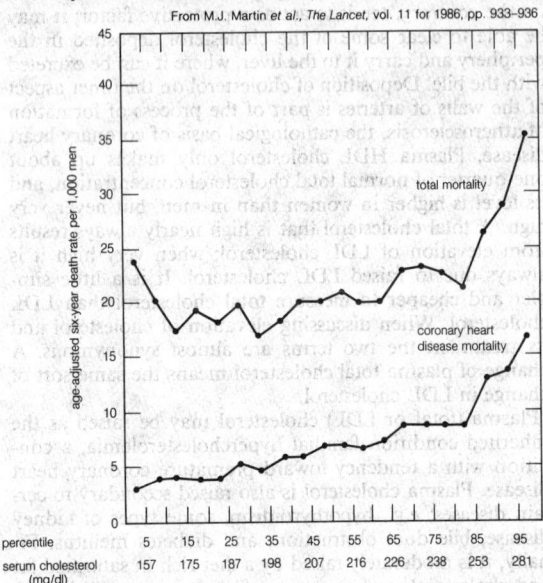

From M.J. Martin et al., *The Lancet*, vol. 11 for 1986, pp. 933–936

Figure 5: Relation between serum (total) cholesterol and subsequent death rate from coronary heart disease in a prospective study of more than 361,000 men screened.

Coronary atherosclerosis takes years to develop. What determines the onset of coronary heart disease in a middle-aged person with moderately narrowed coronary arteries appears to be the acute superimposition of thrombosis. Thrombosis is initiated when platelets adhere to the vessel wall and to one another. Four of the polyunsaturated fatty acids in Table 8 appear to reduce the tendency of platelets to stick together. Linoleic and linolenic acids are found in plant seed oils like safflower and sunflower seed oils; eicosapentaenoic (EPA) and docosahexaenoic acids (DHA) are found in fatty fish. Both EPA and DHA are probably more active inhibitors weight-for-weight, but it is easier to obtain more linoleic acid from the diet. A fish oil concentrate containing 30 percent EPA and DHA is available in capsules at pharmacies. It does not lower plasma cholesterol. Its effect on platelet aggregation is probably due to the fact that EPA is the parent substance for an unusual series of prostaglandins.

Diet and blood pressure. Arterial hypertension affects 10 to 15 percent of older adults in most countries. It can lead to strokes, heart failure, kidney disease, and aneurysms and contributes to coronary heart disease. It is usually treated with drugs, but these often have side effects. There are, however, some seven dietary factors now known to influence blood pressure. If several are changed in the appropriate directions their effects may enable mild hypertensives to cease using drugs and moderate hypertensives to reduce the number or dosage of drugs. The seven dietary factors are: (1) Blood pressure tends to be higher in obese people and to fall if they successfully lose weight. (2) Blood pressure is increased in people who regularly take more than three alcoholic drinks per day. (3) The great majority of people in developed and many developing countries eat much more sodium, in the form of table salt (NaCl) than is necessary. In the few isolated communities that do not have salt, hypertension is rare.

When people with hypertension reduce their intake of table salt, blood pressure falls, although in some people the salt intake must fall so low that the diet must be radically changed. There is, however, little correlation between salt intake and blood pressure among individuals. It would seem that either only some people are sensitive to salt (perhaps genetically determined) or high salt intake only affects blood pressure over a long time. (4) Vegetarians tend to have lower blood pressures. (5) Potassium is a natural antagonist of sodium, and in some trials potassium tablets have produced significant lowering of blood pressure. (6) A change of the dietary fat from mostly saturated to mostly polyunsaturated has usually resulted in a small reduction of blood pressure. (7) Calcium is being investigated for its postulated blood-pressure-lowering action. In some trials calcium tablets have lowered blood pressure but not in others.

Diet and cancer. First, the best indication that habitual diet is one of the multiple risk factors for some types of cancer is the large differences recorded in age-standardized incidence (or mortality) tables of different types of cancer between human populations. Genetic concentration cannot explain most of these large differences; they must be environmental, and there is patchy evidence of association between diet and certain types of cancer. Second, in experimental animals (mostly small rodents), induction of some types of tumours is influenced by the nature of the animals' rations. Third, almost all foreign substances that are able to enter the human body must do so via the alimentary canal; i.e., in food or drink. Substances that affect the pathogenesis of cancer work in one of two broad ways. They may initiate malignant change by gene toxicity, altering some of the DNA in the nucleus of a particular cell type: occasionally, one of these mutations results in unchecked growth of the cell. Alternatively, once tumour growth has started a substance may promote its growth or protect against its development.

There are three ways in which a person's usual diet may lead to cancer: (1) A carcinogenic (cancer-producing) substance in food (or drink) can come in contact with the epithelium (inner lining) of mouth, throat, esophagus, stomach, or, usually in chemically altered form, with the intestines, liver, or urinary bladder. Most such substances in food are only weakly carcinogenic and would have no effect taken once or twice, but they might lead to cancer if taken repeatedly over a long time. (2) The plane of nutrition (i.e., whether a person is a little overfed or a little underfed) may influence the incidence of endocrine-dependent cancers by altering hormone secretion or metabolism. Cancers thought to be in this category are those of the breast, uterus, or prostate. (3) Some nutrients may influence susceptibility to carcinogenesis at other sites. A major question about diet and cancer is whether intakes of some nutrients could act as protective factors at intakes above the RDA and below the start of toxic levels. According to the "free radical hypothesis," free oxygen radicals sometimes arise from chemical processes in cells and may produce damage to DNA. This increases the chance of a carcinogenic mutation. Generous intake of one or more of the nutrients with antioxidant properties—vitamin A, vitamin C, vitamin E, selenium—might reduce this risk. This hypothesis is theoretical; evidence supporting it is small and circumstantial at present.

In 1981 Sir Richard Doll estimated the proportions of deaths from cancer in the United States that could be attributed to environmental factors. Potentially, cancer mortality could be reduced by these estimated proportions if specific environmental factors were identified and avoided. The diet group of factors (not food additives) was thought to be more important than any other group, responsible for around 38 percent of cancer deaths. While there is strong but indirect epidemiological evidence that most of the common cancers could be made less common by suitable modifications of food habits, there is still no precise and reliable evidence as to exactly what dietary changes would be of major importance. There are many different types of cancer, and knowledge of the relation between diet and even the most common types is many years behind the body of knowledge about diet and coro-

Carcino-
genic
substances

Environ-
mental
factors

Dietary
factors

nary heart disease. Three major types illustrate that dietary factors differ for cancer in different sites.

Stomach cancer. Dietary factors associated with gastric cancer include dried salted fish, pickled foods, cured meats, high salt intake, and lack of domestic refrigerators. Foods that appear from surveys to be protective include salads and citrus fruits. The best-fitting hypothesis is that nitrates (in salts) form nitrites, which combine with secondary amines (derived from bacterial action on meat proteins) in the stomach to produce small amounts of potently carcinogenic nitrosamines. In people who secrete subnormal amounts of gastric acid (achlorhydria), bacteria can live in the stomach and produce more nitrites. Refrigeration reduces secondary amine production in protein-rich foods; vitamin C (in salads and citrus) tends to inhibit formation of nitrosamine. The incidence of gastric cancer is declining spontaneously in all industrial countries.

Pathogens

Large intestinal cancer. Several studies both within and between countries suggest a pathogenic association between total fat intake and cancer of the colon or rectum and that both wheat fibre and brassica vegetables may protect against it. Meat consumption is usually correlated with fat but is less consistently related to cancer of the large intestine. Some types of beer have been associated with cancer of the rectum (the lower end of the large intestine). There have, however, been variations and inconsistencies in all the epidemiological studies. Most cancers of the large intestine appear to originate in polyps (precancerous adenomas), which are often multiple.

Breast cancer. The range between countries with the lowest and those with the highest mortalities from breast cancer is only sevenfold, so the environmental influence must be smaller than with some other cancers. Two sets of data have suggested a relationship of breast cancer with dietary fat: it is seen in between-country correlations and in experimental mammary tumours in mice and rats. In several case-control and two prospective studies, however, the association with dietary fat has been unimpressive or absent. In animal experiments it now seems that the effect originally attributed to fat could have been due, at least in part, to increased calorie intake.

Diabetes. In terms of diabetes, there are two questions about habitual diet: (1) whether diet predisposes a person to the development of diabetes, and, if so, which diet, and (2) which diet is best for the treatment of patients who have established diabetes.

Types of diabetes

There are two basic types of diabetes: insulin-dependent and non-insulin-dependent. Insulin-dependent diabetes usually starts in younger people; their islets of Langerhans secrete little or no insulin and they must receive one or more injections of insulin each day to control their blood glucose. Development of this type of diabetes is not related to diet. It occurs throughout the world and is probably the result of a viral infection or autoimmune (self-imposed by the body's own cells) damage to the islets of Langerhans.

Non-insulin-dependent (NID) diabetes is the more common type in developed communities. In NID, which usually starts in middle age, the patient's islets of Langerhans secrete normal amounts of insulin, but the tissues are resistant to insulin so that the response of blood glucose to insulin is subnormal. The NID type of diabetes is closely linked to obesity. Comparisons between countries suggest that a diet high in fat is likely to lead to diabetes. Findings of a decrease in the incidence of diabetes in periods of shortages (*e.g.,* wartime) support this.

There is clearly a genetic predisposition to NID diabetes in those who become overweight or obese. This is seen most clearly in the Pima American Indians in Arizona and the Micronesians on the island of Nauru. When these people are obese the incidence of diabetes (in later life) is over 50 percent.

Changes in diet

The proportions of carbohydrate in the therapeutic diet prescribed for diabetes have changed greatly from that used before and shortly after the introduction of insulin in 1921. At that time patients were expected to take diets with as little as five percent total carbohydrate. This meant that they were eating a very high-fat diet. Modern dietary prescriptions emphasize weight reduction for obese patients and a generous carbohydrate intake be-

cause: (1) Western diabetics are now more likely to die of atherosclerotic diseases like coronary heart disease than of uncontrolled diabetes; a high-fat diet would be harmful because it would raise their plasma cholesterol. (2) In Asian countries, diabetics can manage relatively well and have fewer complications on high-carbohydrate (*e.g.,* rice) diets. It has been found that blood glucose is not as high after the ingestion of legumes, pasta, and many fruits and dairy products as after other carbohydrate foods like bread and potatoes.

Dental caries. Dental caries, or a hole in the enamel outer layer of the teeth, occurs all over the world. Ancient skeletons show that it has plagued humans for a long time. Its incidence is mostly in the first 25 years of life. Dental enamel is the hardest material in the body. Its weakness is that, because it is a form of calcium phosphate, it can be dissolved by acid. Three factors contribute to dental caries: the presence of a specific bacteria, sugars that these bacteria metabolize to lactic acid, and resistance of the enamel to bacterial colonization and carious attack.

A species of bacteria, *Streptococcus mutans,* is necessary for dental caries to occur. It is part of the bacterial population of most people's mouths, but some people harbour more than others. This organism not only metabolizes sucrose, glucose, fructose, or lactose to lactic acid, but it also converts them to sticky polymers (plaque) in which the bacteria are shielded from saliva and the tongue. Starches too, if they stay in the mouth, are split (depolymerized) by the amylase enzyme in saliva to glucose, which the streptococci can also use as substrate. Consumption of sugary or starchy foods between meals, especially if they are sticky, favours the development of caries.

Plaque

In the teeth the most susceptible surfaces are in the fissures and between the teeth, where plaque is least disturbed by saliva, chewing, the tongue, or toothbrush. A fluoride intake of one to three milligrams per day—as with fluoridated drinking water—increases the enamel's resistance to acid attack, especially if the fluoride is taken while the tooth's enamel is being formed in the jaws before the permanent teeth erupt.

DIETARY GUIDELINES

Dietary goals, or guidelines, are a more recent tool for nutritional advice than RDAs. They aim not to provide enough of the essential nutrients but to reduce the chances of developing chronic degenerative diseases. While there has never been more than one RDA committee and report in a country, there can be several sets of dietary guidelines.

Dietary guidelines start not from zero intake (as for RDAs) but from the present estimated national average diet. They deal not with energy requirements but with optimal proportions of the energy-yielding dietary components—how much carbohydrate and fat and what type. Dietary guidelines are not usually expressed as weight of nutrient per day but as percentage change of food components from the present average intake. They are targets for the community to aim for, not what people have to eat that week. The first set of dietary guidelines in the world appeared in 1968 in Scandinavia. The following is a summary of the dietary guidelines for Americans suggested by the United States Department of Agriculture and the United States Department of Health and Human Services.

Goals of the guidelines

The daily diet should contain a variety of foods in adequate amounts, including selections from the food groups discussed above. Ideally, an infant should be breast-fed unless there are special problems, and other foods should be delayed until a baby is four to six months old; salt or sugar should not be added to the food. A healthy weight should be maintained. Excessive amounts of fat and fatty foods, sugar and sweets, and alcoholic beverages should be avoided; pregnant women are advised to refrain from the use of alcohol. Physical activity should be increased.

Excess fat, saturated fat, and cholesterol should be avoided; instead lean meat, fish, poultry, and dry beans and peas should be used as protein sources. Skim or low-fat milk and milk products should be used. Egg yolks, organ meats, fats and oils (especially those high in saturated fat, such as butter, cream, lard, heavily hydrogenated fats, shortenings, and foods containing palm and coconut oils) should be avoided. Foods should be broiled (grilled), baked, or boiled rather than fried.

Foods with adequate starch and fibre should be part of the diet. The use of large amounts of sugars and foods containing large amounts of sugars should be avoided, as should large amounts of sodium. Food should be flavoured with herbs, spices, and lemon juice instead of salt.

Dietary guidelines will have to be amended, developed, and added to as knowledge of the relationship between habitual diet and disease grows by research. They should be modified based on age and sex, as well as for individuals who appear to be more or less sensitive to sodium, dietary cholesterol, and so on. They are, however, a valuable statement of consensus among a country's orthodox scientific nutritionists of the direction in which ordinary healthy people are advised to move their dietary habits to improve their chances of better health in the future—not to guarantee it.

BIBLIOGRAPHY

General works: Major journals covering general human and animal nutrition include *The Journal of Nutrition* (monthly); *The British Journal of Nutrition* (bimonthly); *Nutrition Abstracts and Reviews: Series A. Human and Experimental* (monthly); *Nutrition Abstracts and Reviews: Series B. Livestock Feeds and Feeding* (monthly); *The American Journal of Clinical Nutrition* (monthly); *European Journal of Clinical Nutrition* (monthly); *Journal of the American Dietetic Association* (monthly); *Nutrition Reviews* (monthly); and *Annual Review of Nutrition*.

Requirements for nutrients and nutrition: The nutritional requirements of microorganisms are detailed in BEVERLY M. GUIRARD and ESMOND E. SNELL, "Biochemical Factors in Growth," ch. 7, pp. 79–111, in PHILIPP GERHARDT (ed.), *Manual of Methods for General Bacteriology* (1981). Good sources on animal nutrition in general with information on particular animals, such as ruminants, include P. MCDONALD, R.A. EDWARDS, and J.F.D. GREENHALGH, *Animal Nutrition*, 4th ed. (1988); and D.C. CHURCH, *Digestive Physiology and Nutrition of Ruminants*, 2nd ed., vol. 2, "Nutrition" (1979). Most common (and some uncommon) animals are covered in "Nutrient Requirements of Domestic Animals," a multivolume series by the National Research Council (U.S.); as well as in "The Nutrient Requirements of Farm Livestock," a series by the British Agricultural Research Council. See also E.J. UNDERWOOD, *The Mineral Nutrition of Livestock*, 2nd ed. (1981); and WALTER MERTZ (ed.), *Trace Elements in Human and Animal Nutrition*, 5th ed., 2 vol. (1986–87), a classic text on inorganic micronutrients.

Human metabolism and nutrition: General comprehensive information is presented in GREAT BRITAIN. MINISTRY OF AGRICULTURE, FISHERIES, AND FOOD, *Manual of Nutrition*, 8th ed. (1976); ETHEL AUSTIN MARTIN and ARDATH ANDERS COOLIDGE, *Nutrition in Action*, 4th ed. (1978); and A. STEWART TRUSWELL et al., *ABC of Nutrition* (1986), a collection of articles from the *British Medical Journal*. *Nutrition Reviews' Present Knowledge in Nutrition*, 5th ed. (1984), is a major text providing broad coverage; as is *Davidson and Passmore Human Nutrition and Dietetics*, 8th ed., rev. by R. PASSMORE and M.A. EASTWOOD (1986). Special topics in human nutrition are studied in RICHARD B. LEE and IRVEN DeVORE (eds.), *Man the Hunter* (1969), and *Kalahari Hunter-Gatherers: Studies of the !Kung San and Their Neighbors* (1976), in which see especially A. STEWART TRUSWELL and J.D.L. HANSEN, "Medical Research Among the !Kung." See also M. ISABEL IRWIN et al., *Nutritional Requirements of Man: A Conspectus of Research* (1980); SAMUEL J. FOMON, *Infant Nutrition*, 2nd ed. (1974); DERRICK B. JELLIFFE and E.F. PATRICE JELLIFFE, *Human Milk in the Modern World: Psychosocial, Nutritional, and Economic Significance* (1978); and MARTHA L. HUTCHINSON and HAMISH N. MUNRO (eds.), *Nutrition and Aging* (1986).

Foods: The composition and nutritional value of foods, in tabular form, are presented in *McCance and Widdowson's The Composition of Foods*, 4th rev. ed., edited by A.A. PAUL and D.A.T. SOUTHGATE (1978); and in many issues of the *Agriculture Handbook* (irregular), published by the United States Department of Agriculture.

Nutrition recommendations: Recommended dietary allowances are studied in WORLD HEALTH ORGANIZATION, *Energy and Protein Requirements: Report* (1985); A. STEWART TRUSWELL, "Recommended Dietary Intakes Around the World," *Nutrition Abstracts and Reviews*, 53(11):940–1015 (November 1983), and 53(12):1075–1119 (December 1983); and NATIONAL RESEARCH COUNCIL (U.S.), *Recommended Dietary Allowances*, 9th rev. ed. (1980). See also ANTHONY R. LEEDS (ed.), *Dietary Fibre Perspectives: Reviews and Bibliography* (1985); LAWRENCE J. MACHLIN (ed.), *Handbook of Vitamins: Nutritional, Biochemical, and Clinical Aspects* (1984); and ARTEMIS P. SIMOPOULOS (ed.), "Diet and Health: Scientific Concepts and Principles," *American Journal of Clinical Nutrition*, Supplement, vol. 45, no. 5 (May 1987).

Nutrition and disease: Nutritional deficiency disorders are examined in ANCEL KEYS et al., *The Biology of Human Starvation*, 2 vol. (1950); W.R. AYKROYD, *The Conquest of Famine* (1974); DAVID GRIGG, *The World Food Problem, 1950–1980* (1985); MYRON WINICK (ed.), *Hunger Disease: Studies by the Jewish Physicians in the Warsaw Ghetto* (1979; originally published in Polish, 1946); ROBERT E. OLSON, *Protein-Calorie Malnutrition* (1975); and RICHARD A. WRIGHT and STEVEN HEYMSFIELD (eds.), *Nutritional Assessment* (1984). Nutrition problems other than hunger are the subject of AMERICAN ACADEMY OF ALLERGY AND IMMUNOLOGY, *Adverse Reaction to Foods* (1984); SARA GILBERT, *Pathology of Eating: Psychology and Treatment* (1986); PATRICIA HAUSMAN, *Jack Sprat's Legacy: The Science and Politics of Fat & Cholesterol* (1981); ALBERT J. STUNKARD (ed.), *Obesity* (1980); and J.S. GARROW, *Treat Obesity Seriously: A Clinical Manual* (1981). Nutritional aspects of other diseases and diet therapies are discussed in MAURICE E. SHILS and VERNON R. YOUNG (eds.), *Modern Nutrition in Health and Disease*, 7th ed. (1988); GREAT BRITAIN. PANEL ON DIET IN RELATION TO CARDIOVASCULAR DISEASE, *Diet and Cardiovascular Disease: Report* (1984); WORLD HEALTH ORGANIZATION, *Prevention of Coronary Heart Disease: Report* (1982); and NATIONAL RESEARCH COUNCIL (U.S.), *Diet, Nutrition, and Cancer* (1982).

(A.S.T.)

Occultism

Occultism encompasses a wide range of theories and practices involving a belief in and knowledge or use of supernatural forces or beings. Such beliefs and practices—principally magical or divinatory—have occurred in all human societies throughout recorded history, with considerable variations both in their nature and in the attitude of societies toward them. In the West the term occultism has acquired intellectually and morally pejorative overtones that do not obtain in other societies where the practices and beliefs concerned do not run counter to the prevailing worldview.

Occult practices centre on the presumed ability of the practitioner to manipulate natural laws for his own or his client's benefit; such practices tend to be regarded as evil only when they also involve the breaking of moral laws. Some anthropologists have argued that it is not possible to make a clear-cut distinction between magic—a principal component of occultism—and religion, and this may well be true of the religious systems of some nonliterate societies. The argument does not hold, however, for any of the major religions, which regard both natural and moral law as immutable.

Those aspects of occultism that appear to be common to all human societies—divination, magic, witchcraft, and alchemy—are treated in depth below. Features that are unique to Western cultures, and the history of their development, are treated only briefly.

The Western tradition of occultism, as popularly conceived, is of an ancient "secret philosophy" underlying all occult practices. This secret philosophy derives ultimately from Hellenistic magic and alchemy on the one hand and from Jewish mysticism on the other. The principal Hellenistic source is the *Corpus Hermeticum,* the texts associated with Hermes Trismegistos, which are concerned with astrology and other occult sciences and with spiritual regeneration.

The Jewish element is supplied by the Kabbala (the doctrine of a secret, mystical interpretation of the Torah), which had been familiar to scholars in Europe since the Middle Ages, and which was linked with the Hermetic texts during the Renaissance. The resulting Hermetic-Kabbalistic tradition, known as Hermetism, incorporated both theory and magical practice, with the latter presented as natural, and thus good, magic, in contrast to the evil magic of sorcery or witchcraft.

Alchemy was also absorbed into the body of Hermetism, and this link was strengthened in the early 17th century with the appearance of Rosicrucianism, an alleged secret brotherhood that utilized alchemical symbolism and taught secret wisdom to its followers, creating a spiritual alchemy that survived the rise of empirical science and enabled Hermetism to pass unscathed into the period of the Enlightenment.

During the 18th century the tradition was taken up by esoterically inclined Freemasons who could not find an occult philosophy within Freemasonry. These enthusiasts persisted, both as individual students of Hermetism and, in continental Europe, as groups of occult practitioners, into the 19th century, when the growth of religious skepticism led to an increased rejection of orthodox religion by the educated and a consequent search for salvation by other means—including occultism.

But those interested turned to new forms of occultism rather than to the Hermetic tradition: on the one hand to Spiritualism—the practice of alleged regular communication between the living and the spirits of the dead through a living "medium"—and on the other to Theosophy—a blend of Western occultism and Eastern mysticism that proved to be a most effective propagator of occultism but whose influence has declined markedly over the last 50 years.

Indeed, despite the 19th-century revival, occult ideas have failed to gain acceptance in academic circles, although they have occasionally influenced the work of major artists, such as the poet William Butler Yeats and the painter Wassily Kandinsky, and occultism in Europe and North America seems destined to remain the province of popular culture. (R.A.Gi.)

For coverage of related topics in the *Macropædia* and *Micropædia,* see the *Propædia,* Part Eight, Division I, Section 811; Division II, Section 829.

This article is divided into the following sections:

Alchemy

Alchemy was the name given, in Latin Europe, from the 12th century, to an aspect of thought that corresponds to astrology, which is apparently an older tradition. Both represent attempts to discover the relationship of man to the cosmos and to exploit that relationship to his benefit. The first of these objectives may be called scientific, the second technological. Astrology (see below) is concerned with man's relationship to "the stars" (including the members of the solar system); alchemy, with terrestrial nature. But the distinction is far from absolute, since both are interested in the influence of the stars on terrestrial events. Moreover, both have always been pursued in the belief that the processes human beings witness in heaven and on earth manifest the will of the Creator and, if correctly understood, will yield the key to the Creator's intentions.

NATURE AND SIGNIFICANCE

That both astrology and alchemy may be regarded as fundamental aspects of thought is indicated by their apparent universality. It is notable, however, that the evidence is not equally substantial in all times and places. Evidence from ancient Middle America (Aztecs, Mayans) is still almost nonexistent; evidence from India is tenuous and from ancient China, Greece, and Islāmic lands is only relatively more plentiful. A single manuscript of some 80,-000 words is the principal source for the history of Greek alchemy. Chinese alchemy is largely recorded in about 100 "books" that are part of the Taoist canon. Neither Indian nor Islāmic alchemy has ever been collected, and scholars are thus dependent for their knowledge of the subject on occasional allusions in works of natural philosophy and medicine, plus a few specifically alchemical works.

Nor is it really clear what alchemy was (or is). The word is a European one, derived from Arabic, but the origin of the root word, *chem,* is uncertain. Words similar to it have been found in most ancient languages, with different meanings, but conceivably somehow related to alchemy. In fact, the Greeks, Chinese, and Indians usually referred to what Westerners call alchemy as "The Art," or by terms denoting change or transmutation.

The chemistry of alchemy. Superficially, the chemistry involved in alchemy appears a hopelessly complicated succession of heatings of multiple mixtures of obscurely named materials, but it seems likely that a relative simplicity underlies this complexity. The metals gold, silver, copper, lead, iron, and tin were all known before the rise of alchemy. Mercury, the liquid metal, certainly known before 300 BC, when it appears in both Eastern and Western sources, was crucial to alchemy. Sulfur, "the stone that burns," was also crucial. It was known from prehistoric times in native deposits and was also given off in metallurgic processes (the "roasting" of sulfide ores). Mercury united with most of the other metals, and the amalgam formed coloured powders (the sulfides) when treated with sulfur. Mercury itself occurs in nature in a red sulfide, cinnabar, which can also be made artificially. All of these, except possibly the last, were operations known to the metallurgist and were adopted by the alchemist.

The alchemist added the action on metals of a number of corrosive salts, mainly the vitriols (copper and iron sulfates), alums (the aluminum sulfates of potassium and ammonium), and the chlorides of sodium and ammonium. And he made much of arsenic's property of colouring metals. All of these materials, except the chloride of ammonia, were known in ancient times. Known as sal ammoniac in the West, *nao sha* in China, *nao sadar* in India, and *nushādir* in Persia and Arabic lands, the chloride of ammonia first became known to the West in the *Chou-i ts'an t'ung ch'i,* a Chinese treatise of the 2nd century AD. It was to be crucial to alchemy, for on sublimation it dissociates into antagonistic corrosive materials, ammonia and hydrochloric acid, which readily attack the metals. Until the 9th century it seems to have come from a single source, the Flame Mountain (Huo-yen Shan) near T'u-lu-p'an (Turfan), in Central Asia.

Finally, the manipulation of these materials was to lead to the discovery of the mineral acids, the history of which began in Europe in the 13th century. The first was probably nitric acid, made by distilling together saltpetre (potassium nitrate) and vitriol or alum. More difficult to discover was sulfuric acid, which was distilled from vitriol or alum alone but required apparatus resistant to corrosion and heat. And most difficult was hydrochloric acid, distilled from common salt or sal ammoniac and vitriol or alum, for the vapours of this acid cannot be simply condensed but must be dissolved in water.

Goals. "Transmutation" is the key word characterizing alchemy, and it may be understood in several ways: in the changes that are called chemical, in physiological changes such as passing from sickness to health, in a hoped-for transformation from old age to youth, or even in passing from an earthly to a supernatural existence. Alchemical changes seem always to have been positive, never involving degradation except as an intermediate stage in a process having a "happy ending." Alchemy aimed at the great human "goods": wealth, longevity, and immortality.

Alchemy was not original in seeking these goals, for it had been preceded by religion, medicine, and metallurgy. The first chemists were metallurgists, who were perhaps the most successful practitioners of the arts in antiquity. Their theories seem to have come not from science but from folklore and religion. The miner and metallurgist, like the agriculturalist, in this view, accelerate the normal maturation of the fruits of the earth, in a magico-religious relationship with nature. In primitive societies the metallurgist is often a member of an occult religious society.

But the first ventures into natural philosophy, the beginnings of what is called the scientific view, also preceded alchemy. Systems of five almost identical basic elements were postulated in China, India, and Greece, according to a view in which nature comprised antagonistic, opposite forces—hot and cold, positive and negative, and male and female; *i.e.,* primitive versions of the modern conception of energy. Drawing on a similar astrological heritage, philosophers found correspondences among the elements, planets, and metals. In short, both the chemical arts and the theories of the philosophers of nature had become complex before alchemy appeared.

REGIONAL VARIATIONS

Chinese alchemy. Neither in China nor in the West can scholars approach with certitude the origins of alchemy, but the evidences in China appear to be slightly older. Indeed, Chinese alchemy was connected with an enterprise older than metallurgy—*i.e.,* medicine. Belief in physical immortality among the Chinese seems to go back to the 8th century BC, and belief in the possibility of attaining it through drugs to the 4th century BC. The magical drug, namely the "elixir of life" (elixir is the European word), is mentioned about that time, and that most potent elixir, "drinkable gold," which was a solution (usually imaginary) of this corrosion-resistant metal, as early as the 1st century BC—many centuries before it is heard of in the West.

Although non-Chinese influences (especially Indian) are possible, the genesis of alchemy in China may have been a purely domestic affair. It emerged during a period of political turmoil, the Warring States Period (from the 5th to the 3rd century BC), and it came to be associated with Taoism—a mystical religion founded by the 6th-century-BC sage Lao-tzu—and its sacred book, the *Tao-te Ching* ("Classic of the Way of Power"). The Taoists were a miscellaneous collection of "outsiders"—in relation to the prevailing Confucians—and such mystical doctrines as alchemy were soon grafted onto the Taoist canon. What is known of Chinese alchemy is mainly owing to that graft, and especially to a collection known as *Yün chi ch'i ch'ien* ("Seven Tablets in a Cloudy Satchel"), which is dated 1023. Thus, sources on alchemy in China (as elsewhere) are compilations of much earlier writings.

The oldest known Chinese alchemical treatise is the *Chou-i ts'an t'ung ch'i* ("Commentary on the *I Ching*"). In the main it is an apocryphal interpretation of the *I Ching* ("Classic of Changes"), an ancient classic especially esteemed by the Confucians, relating alchemy to the mystical mathematics of the 64 hexagrams (six-line figures used for divination). Its relationship to chemical practice is tenuous, but it mentions materials (including sal ammoniac) and implies chemical operations. The first Chinese alchemist who is reasonably well known was Ko Hung (AD 283–343), whose book *Pao-p'u-tzu* (pseudonym of Ko Hung) contains two chapters with obscure recipes for elixirs, mostly based on mercury or arsenic compounds. The most famous Chinese alchemical book is the *Tan chin yao chüeh* ("Great Secrets of Alchemy"), probably by Sun Ssu-miao (AD 581–after 673). It is a practical treatise on creating elixirs (mercury, sulfur, and the salts of mercury and arsenic are prominent) for the attainment of immortality, plus a few for specific cures for disease and such other purposes as the fabrication of precious stones.

Altogether, the similarities between the materials used and the elixirs made in China, India, and the West are more remarkable than are their differences. Nonetheless, Chinese alchemy differed from that of the West in its objective. Whereas in the West the objective seems to have evolved from gold to elixirs of immortality to simply superior medicines, neither the first nor the last of these objectives seems ever to have been very important in China.

Objective of Chinese alchemy

Chinese alchemy was consistent from first to last, and there was relatively little controversy among its practitioners, who seem to have varied only in their prescriptions for the elixir of immortality or perhaps only over their names for it, of which one Sinologist has counted about 1,000. In the West there were conflicts between advocates of herbal and "chemical" (*i.e.,* mineral) pharmacy, but in China mineral remedies were always accepted. There were, in Europe, conflicts between alchemists who favoured gold making and those who thought medicine the proper goal, but the Chinese always favoured the latter. Since alchemy rarely achieved any of these goals, it was an advantage to the Western alchemist to have the situation obscured, and the art survived in Europe long after Chinese alchemy had simply faded away.

Chinese alchemy followed its own path. Whereas the Western world, with its numerous religious promises of immortality, never seriously expected alchemy to fulfill that goal, the deficiencies of Chinese religions in respect to promises of immortality left that goal open to the alchemist. A serious reliance on medical elixirs that were in varying degrees poisonous led the alchemist into permanent exertions to moderate those poisons, either through variation of the ingredients or through chemical manipulations. The fact that immortality was so desirable and the alchemist correspondingly valued enabled the British historian of science Joseph Needham to tabulate a series of Chinese emperors who probably died of elixir poisoning. Ultimately a succession of royal deaths made alchemists and emperors alike more cautious, and Chinese alchemy vanished (probably as the Chinese adopted Buddhism, which offered other, less dangerous avenues to immortality), leaving its literary manifestations embedded in the Taoist canons.

Indian alchemy. The oldest Indian writings, the Vedas (Hindu sacred scriptures), contain the same hints of alchemy that are found in evidence from ancient China, namely vague references to a connection between gold and long life. Mercury, which was so vital to alchemy everywhere, is first mentioned in the 4th- to 3rd-century-BC *Artha-śāstra*, about the same time it is encountered in China and in the West. Evidence of the idea of transmuting base metals to gold appears in 2nd- to 5th-century-AD Buddhist texts, about the same time as in the West. Since Alexander the Great had invaded India in 325 BC, leaving a Greek state (Gandhāra) that long endured, the possibility exists that the Indians acquired the idea from the Greeks, but it could have been the other way around.

Medical and religious concerns of Indian alchemy

It is also possible that the alchemy of medicine and immortality came to India from China, or vice versa; in any case, gold making appears to have been a minor concern, and medicine the major concern, of both cultures. But the elixir of immortality was of little importance in India (which had other avenues to immortality). The Indian elixirs were mineral remedies for specific diseases or, at the most, to promote long life.

As in China and the West, alchemy in India came to be associated with religious mysticism, but much later—not until the rise of Tantrism (an esoteric, occultic, meditative system), AD 1100–1300. To Tantrism are owed writings that are clearly alchemical (such as the 12th-century *Rasārṇava*, or "Treatise on Metallic Preparations").

From the earliest records of Indian natural philosophy, which date from the 5th–3rd centuries BC, theories of nature were based on conceptions of material elements (fire, wind, water, earth, and space), vitalism ("animated atoms"), and dualisms of love and hate or action and reaction. The alchemist coloured metals and on occasion "made" gold, but he gave little importance to that. His six metals (gold, silver, tin, iron, lead, and copper), each further subdivided (five kinds of gold, etc.), were "killed" (*i.e.,* corroded) but not "resurrected," as was the custom of Western alchemy. Rather, they were killed to make medicines. Although "the secrets of mercurial lore" became part of the Tantric rite, mercury seems to have been much less important than in China. The Indians exploited metal reactions more widely, but, although they possessed from an early date not only vitriol and sal ammoniac but also saltpetre, they nevertheless failed to discover the mineral acids. This is the more remarkable because India was long the principal source of saltpetre, which occurs as an efflorescence on the soil, especially in populous tropical countries. But it lacks the high degree of corrosivity of metals possessed by the vitriols and chlorides and played a small part in early alchemy. Saltpetre appears particularly in 9th- to 11th-century-AD Indian and Chinese recipes for fireworks, one of which—a mixture of saltpetre, sulfur, and charcoal—is gunpowder. Saltpetre first appears in Europe in the 13th century, along with the modern formula for gunpowder and the recipe for nitric acid.

Hellenistic alchemy. Western alchemy may go back to the beginnings of the Hellenistic period (*c.* 300 BC–*c.* AD 300), although the earliest alchemist whom authorities have regarded as authentic is Zosimos of Panopolis (Egypt), who lived near the end of the period. He is one of about 40 authors represented in a compendium of alchemical writings that was probably put together in Byzantium (Constantinople) in the 7th or 8th century AD and that exists in manuscripts in Venice and Paris. Synesius, the latest author represented, lived in Byzantium in the 4th century. The earliest is the author designated Democritus but identified by scholars with Bolos of Mende, a Hellenized Egyptian who lived in the Nile Delta about 200 BC. He is represented by a treatise called *Physica et mystica* ("Natural and Mystical Things"), a kind of recipe book for dyeing and colouring but principally for the making of gold and silver. The recipes are stated obscurely and are justified with references to the Greek theory of elements and to astrological theory. Most end with the phrase "One nature rejoices in another nature; one nature triumphs over another nature; one nature masters another nature," which authorities variously trace to the Magi (Zoroastrian priests), Stoic pantheism (a Greek philosophy concerned with nature), or to the 4th-century-BC Greek philosopher Aristotle. It was the first of a number of such aphorisms over which alchemists were to speculate for many centuries.

The importance of the Physica et mystica

In 1828 a group of ancient papyrus manuscripts written in Greek was purchased in Thebes (Egypt), and about a half-century later it was noticed that among them, divided between libraries in Leyden (The Netherlands) and Stockholm, was a tract very like the *Physica et mystica*. It differed, however, in that it lacked the former's theoretical embellishments and stated in some recipes that only fraudulent imitation of gold and silver was intended. Scholars believe that this kind of work was the ancestor both of the *Physica et mystica* and of the ordinary artist's recipe book. The techniques were ancient. Archaeology has revealed metal objects inlaid with colours obtained by grinding metals with sulfur, and Homer's description (8th century BC) of the shield of Achilles gives the impression that the artist in his time was virtually able to paint in metal.

Democritus is praised by most of the other authors in the Venice–Paris manuscript, and he is much commented upon. But only Zosimos shows what had become of alchemy after Bolos of Mende. His theory is luxuriant in imagery, beginning with a discussion of "the composition of waters, movement, growth, embodying and disembodying, drawing the spirits from bodies and binding the spirits within bodies" and continuing in the same vein. The "base" metals are to be "ennobled" (to gold) by killing and resurrecting them, but his practice is full of distillation and sublimation, and he is obsessed with "spirits." Theory and practice are joined in the concept that success depends upon the production of a series of colours, usually black, white, yellow, and purple, and that the colours are to be obtained through *Theion hydōr* (divine or sulfur water—it could mean either).

Zosimos credits these innovations mainly to Maria (sometimes called "the Jewess"), who invented the apparatus, and to Agathodaimon, probably a pseudonym. Neither is represented (beyond Zosimos' references) in the Venice–Paris manuscript, but a tract attributed to Agathodaimon, published in 1953, shows him to be preoccupied with the colour sequence and complicating it by using arsenic instead of sulfur. Thus, the colour-producing potentialities of chemistry were considerable by the time of Zosimos.

Zosimos also shows that alchemical theory came to focus on the idea that there exists a substance that can bring about the desired transformation instantly, magically, or, as a modern chemist might say, catalytically. He called it "the tincture," and had several. It was also sometimes called "the powder" (*xērion*), which was to pass through Arabic into Latin as elixir and finally (signifying its inorganic nature) as the "philosopher's stone," "a stone which is not a stone," as the alchemists were wont to say. It was sometimes called a medicine for the rectification of "base" or "sick" metals, and from this it was a short step to view it as a drug for the rectification of human maladies. Zosimos notes the possibility, in passing. When the objective of alchemy became human salvation, the material constitution of the elixir became less important than the incantations that accompanied its production. Synesius, the last author in the Venice–Paris manuscript, already defined alchemy as a mental operation, independent of the science of matter.

Thus, Greek alchemy came to resemble, in both theory and practice, that of China and India. But its objectives included gold making; thus it remained fundamentally different.

Arabic alchemy. Arabic alchemy is as mysterious as Greek in its origins, and the two seem to have been significantly different. The respect in which *Physica et mystica* was held by the Greek alchemists was bestowed by the Arabs on a different work, the *Emerald Tablet* of Hermes Trismegistos, the reputed Hellenistic author of various alchemical, occult, and theological works. Beginning "That which is above is like to that which is below, and that which is below is like to that which is above," it is brief, theoretical, and astrological. Hermes "the thrice great" (Trismegistos) was a Greek version of the Egyptian god Thoth and the supposed founder of an astrological philosophy that is first noted in 150 BC. The *Emerald Tablet*, however, comes from a larger work called *Book of the Secret of Creation*, which exists in Latin and Arabic manuscripts and was thought by the Muslim alchemist ar-Rāzī to have been written during the reign of Caliph al-Ma'mūn (AD 813–833), though it has been attributed to the 1st-century-AD pagan mystic Apollonius of Tyana.

Some scholars have suggested that Arabic alchemy descended from a western Asiatic school and that Greek alchemy was derived from an Egyptian school. As far as is known, the Asiatic school was not Chinese or Indian. What is known is that Arabic alchemy was associated with a specific city in Syria, Harran, which seems to have been a fountainhead of alchemical notions. And it is possible that the distillation ideology and its spokeswoman, Maria—as well as Agathodaimon—represented the alchemy of Harran, which presumably migrated to Alexandria and was incorporated into the alchemy of Zosimos.

The existing versions of the *Book of the Secret of Creation* have been carried back only to the 7th or 6th century but are believed by some to represent much earlier writings, although not necessarily those of Apollonius himself. He is the subject of an ancient biography that says nothing about alchemy, but neither does the *Emerald Tablet* nor

The significance of Hermetic literature

the rest of the *Book of the Secret of Creation*. On the other hand, their theories of nature have an alchemical ring, and the *Book* mentions the characteristic materials of alchemy, including, for the first time in the West, sal ammoniac. It was clearly an important book to the Arabs, most of whose eminent philosophers mentioned alchemy, although sometimes disapprovingly. Those who practiced it were even more interested in literal gold making than had been the Greeks. The most well-attested and probably the greatest Arabic alchemist was ar-Rāzī (c. 850–923/924), a Persian physician who lived in Baghdad. The most famous was Jābir ibn Ḥayyān, now believed to be a name applied to a collection of "underground writings" produced in Baghdad after the theological reaction against science. In any case, the Jābirian writings are very similar to those of ar-Rāzī.

Ar-Rāzī classified the materials used by the alchemist into "bodies" (the metals), stones, vitriols, boraxes, salts, and "spirits," putting into the latter those vital (and sublimable) materials, mercury, sulfur, orpiment and realgar (the arsenic sulfides), and sal ammoniac. Much is made of sal ammoniac, the reactive powers of which seem to have given Western alchemy a new lease on life. Ar-Rāzī and the Jābirian writers were really trying to make gold, through the catalytic action of the elixir. Both wrote much on the compounding of "strong waters," an enterprise that was ultimately to lead to the discovery of the mineral acids, but students have been no more able to find evidence of this discovery in the writings of the Arabic alchemists than in those of China and India. The Arabic strong waters were merely corrosive salt solutions.

Ar-Rāzī's writing represents the apogee of Arabic alchemy, so much so that students of alchemy have little evidence of its later reorientation toward mystical or quasi-religious objectives. Nor does it seem to have turned to medicine, which remained independent. But there was a tendency in Arabic medicine to give greater emphasis to mineral remedies and less to the herbs that had been the chief medicines of the earlier Greek and Arabic physicians. The result was a pharmacopoeia not of elixirs but of specific remedies that are inorganic in origin and not very different from the elixirs of ar-Rāzī. This new pharmacopoeia was taken to Europe by Constantine of Africa, a Baghdad-educated Muslim who died in 1087 as a Christian monk at Monte Cassino (Italy). The pharmacopoeia also appeared in Spain in the 11th century and passed from there to Latin Europe, along with the Arabic alchemical writings, which were translated into Latin in the 12th century.

The dissemination of the pharmacopoeia

Latin alchemy. In the 12th century the Christian West began to shed its habit of indifference or hostility to the secular literature of ancient and alien civilizations. Christian scholars were particularly attracted to Muslim Spain and Sicily and there made translations from both Arabic and Greek works, many of which were in some degree familiar, but some of which, including the literature of alchemy, were new.

The Greek alchemy of the Venice–Paris manuscript had much less impact than the work of ar-Rāzī and other Arabs, which emerged among the voluminous translations made in Spain about 1150 by Gerard of Cremona. By 1250 alchemy was familiar enough to enable such encyclopaedists as Vincent of Beauvais to discuss it fairly intelligibly, and before 1300 the subject was under discussion by the English philosopher and scientist Roger Bacon and the German philosopher, scientist, and theologian Albertus Magnus. To learn about alchemy was to learn about chemistry, for Europe had no independent word to describe the science of matter. It had been touched upon in works concerned with other forms of change—*e.g.*, the motion of projectiles, the aging of man, and similar Aristotelian concepts. On the practical side there were also artists' recipe books; but for the first time in the works of Bacon and Albertus Magnus change was discussed in a truly chemical sense, with Bacon treating the newly translated alchemy as a general science of matter for which he had great hopes.

But the more familiar alchemy became, the more clearly it was understood that gold making was the almost exclusive objective of alchemy, and Europeans proved no more

The objective of European alchemy

resistant to the lure of this objective than their Arabic predecessors. By 1350, alchemical tracts were pouring out of the scriptoria (monastic copying rooms), and the Europeans had even taken over the tradition of anonymity and false attribution. One authority wrote at length about supposed disagreements between two Arabs, Iahiae Abindinon and Geber Abinhaen, who were probably two versions of the name of Jābir ibn Hayyān. The most famous Jābirian work in Europe, *The Sum of Perfection*, is now thought to have been an original European composition. At about this time personal reminiscences of alchemists began to appear. Most famous was the Paris notary Nicolas Flamel (1330–1418), who claimed that he dreamed of an occult book, subsequently found it, and succeeded in deciphering it with the aid of a Jewish scholar learned in the mystic Hebrew writings known as the Kabbala. In 1382 Flamel claimed to have succeeded in the "Great Work" (gold making); certainly he became rich and made donations to churches.

Alchemy and Kabbalistic speculation

By 1300 alchemists had begun the discovery of the mineral acids, a discovery that occupied about three centuries between the first evidence of the new strong water (aqua fortis—*i.e.,* nitric acid) and the clear differentiation of the acids into three kinds: nitric, hydrochloric, and sulfuric. These three centuries saw prodigious efforts in European alchemy, for these spontaneously reactive and highly corrosive substances opened a whole new world of research. And yet, it was of little profit to chemistry, for the experiments were inhibited by the old objectives of separating the base metals into their "elements," concocting elixirs, and other traditional procedures.

The "water of life" (aqua vitae; *i.e.,* alcohol) was probably discovered a little earlier than nitric acid, and some physicians and a few alchemists turned to the elixir of life as an objective. John of Rupescissa, a Catalonian monk who wrote *c.* 1350, prescribed virtually the same elixirs for metal ennoblement and for the preservation of health. His successors multiplied elixirs, which lost their uniqueness and finally simply became new medicines, often for specific ailments. Medical chemistry may have been conceived under Islām, but it was born in Europe. It only awaited christening by its great publicist, Paracelsus (1493–1541), who was the sworn enemy of the malpractices of 16th-century medicine and a vigorous advocate of "folk" and "chemical" remedies. By the end of the 16th century, medicine was divided into warring camps of Paracelsians and anti-Paracelsians, and the alchemists began to move en masse into pharmacy.

Paracelsian pharmacy was to lead, by a devious path, to modern chemistry, but gold making still persisted, though methods sometimes differed. Salomon Trismosin, purported author of the *Splendor solis,* or "Splendour of the Sun" (published 1598), engaged in extensive visits to alchemical adepts (a common practice) and claimed success through "kabbalistic and magical books in the Egyptian language." The impression given is that many had the secret of gold making but that most of them had acquired it from someone else and not from personal experimentation. Illustrations, often heavily symbolic, became particularly important, those of *Splendor solis* being far more complex than the text but clearly exercising a greater appeal, even to modern students.

MODERN ALCHEMY

The possibility of chemical gold making was not conclusively disproved by scientific evidence until the 19th century. As rational a scientist as Sir Isaac Newton (1643–1727) had thought it worthwhile to experiment with it. The official attitude toward alchemy in the 16th to 18th century was ambivalent. On the one hand, The Art posed a threat to the control of precious metal and was often outlawed; on the other hand, there were obvious advantages to any sovereign who could control gold making. In "the metropolis of alchemy," Prague, the Holy Roman emperors Maximilian II (reigned 1564–76) and Rudolf II (reigned 1576–1612) proved ever-hopeful sponsors and entertained most of the leading alchemists of Europe.

This was not altogether to the alchemist's advantage. In 1595 Edward Kelley, an English alchemist and companion

of the famous astrologer, alchemist, and mathematician John Dee, lost his life in an attempt to escape after imprisonment by Rudolf II, and in 1603 the elector of Saxony, Christian II, imprisoned and tortured the Scotsman Alexander Seton, who had been traveling about Europe performing well-publicized transmutations. The situation was complicated by the fact that some alchemists were turning from gold making not to medicine but to a quasi-religious alchemy reminiscent of the Greek Synesius. Rudolf II made the German alchemist Michael Maier a count and his private secretary, although Maier's mystical and allegorical writings were, in the words of a modern authority, "distinguished for the extraordinary obscurity of his style" and made no claim to gold making. Neither did the German alchemist Heinrich Khunrath (*c.* 1560–1601), whose works have long been esteemed for their illustrations, make such a claim.

Conventional attempts at gold making were not dead, but by the 18th century alchemy had turned conclusively to religious aims. The rise of modern chemistry engendered not only general skepticism as to the possibility of making gold but also widespread dissatisfaction with the objectives of modern science, which were viewed as too limited. Unlike the scientists of the Middle Ages and Renaissance, the successors of Newton and the great 18th-century French chemist Antoine-Laurent Lavoisier limited their objectives in a way that amounted to a renunciation of what many had considered the most important question of science, the relation of man to the cosmos. Those who persisted in asking these questions came to feel an affinity with the alchemists and sought their answers in the texts of "esoteric," or spiritual, alchemy (as distinct from the "exoteric" alchemy of the gold makers), with its roots in Synesius and other late Greek alchemists of the Venice–Paris manuscript.

This spiritual alchemy, or Hermetism, as its practitioners often prefer to call it, was popularly associated with the supposititious Rosicrucian brotherhood, whose so-called *Manifestoes* (author unknown; popularly ascribed to the German theologian Johann Valentin Andreä) had appeared in Germany in the early 17th century and had attracted the favourable attention not only of such reform-

Saturn, or *Mercurius senex,* being cooked in the bath until the spirit or white dove (*pneuma*) ascends. From Salomon Trismosin's *Splendor solis,* 1598. In the British Museum (MS, Harley 3469).

ing alchemists as Michael Maier but also of many prominent philosophers who were disquieted by the mechanistic character of the new science. In modern times alchemy has become a focal point for various kinds of mysticism. The old alchemical literature continues to be scrutinized for evidence, because alchemical doctrine is claimed to have on more than one occasion come into the possession of man but always again been lost. Nor is its association with chemistry considered accidental. In the words of the famous 19th-century English spiritual alchemist Mary Anne Atwood,

Association of alchemy with chemistry

> Alchemy is an universal art of vital chemistry which by fermenting the human spirit purifies and finally dissolves it. . . . Alchemy *is* philosophy; it is *the* philosophy, the finding of the Sophia in the mind.

ASSESSMENTS OF ALCHEMY

Accomplishments.   The most persistent goals of alchemy have been the prolongation of life and the transmutation of base metals into gold. It appears that neither was accomplished, unless one credits alchemy with the consequences of modern chemotherapy and the cyclotron.

It has been said that alchemy can be credited with the development of the science of chemistry, a keystone of modern science. During the alchemical period the repertoire of known substances was enlarged (*e.g.,* by the addition of sal ammoniac and saltpetre), alcohol and the mineral acids were discovered, and the basis was laid from which modern chemistry was to rise. Historians of chemistry have been tempted to credit alchemy with laying this base while at the same time regarding alchemy as mostly "wrong." It is far from clear, however, that the basis of chemistry was in fact laid by alchemy rather than medicine. During the crucial period of Arabic and early Latin alchemy, it appears that innovation owed more to nascent medical chemistry than to alchemy.

But those who explore the history of the science of matter, where matter is considered on a wider basis than the modern chemist understands the term, may find alchemy more rewarding. Numerous Hermetic writers of previous centuries claimed that the aims of their art could yet be achieved—indeed, that the true knowledge had been repeatedly found and repeatedly lost. This is a matter of judgment, but it can certainly be said that the modern chemist has not attained the goal sought by the alchemist. For those who are wedded to scientific chemistry, alchemy can have no further interest. For those who seek the wider goal, which was also that of the natural philosopher before the advent of "mechanical," "Newtonian," or "modern" science, the search is still on.

Interpretations.   Charlatanism was a prominent feature of European alchemy during the 16th century, and such monarchs as Rudolf II—even if they had mainly themselves to blame—were not entirely without reason in incarcerating some of their resident adepts. The picturesqueness of this era, which also saw the birth of the modern science of chemistry, has led many historians of chemistry to view alchemy in general as a fraud.

Other historians of chemistry have attempted to differentiate the good from the bad in alchemy, citing as good the discovery of new substances and processes and the invention of new apparatus. Some of this was certainly accomplished by alchemists (*e.g.,* Maria), but most of it is more justifiably ascribed to early pharmacists.

Modern Hermetic and psychological views

Scholars generally agree that alchemy had something to do with chemistry, but the modern Hermetic holds that chemistry was the handmaiden of alchemy, not the reverse. From this point of view the development of modern chemistry involved the abandonment of the true goal of the art.

Finally, a new interpretation was offered in the 1920s by the Swiss psychoanalyst Carl Jung, who, following the earlier work of the Austrian psychologist Herbert Silberer, judged alchemical literature to be explicable in psychological terms. Noticing the similarities between alchemical literature, particularly in its reliance on bizarre symbolic illustrations, and the dreams and fantasies of his patients, Jung viewed them as manifestations of a "collective unconscious" (inherited disposition). Jung's theory, still

largely undeveloped, remains a challenge rather than an explanation.   (R.P.M./R.A.Gi.)

Divination: astrology

Divination, the alleged art or science of foretelling the future by various natural, psychological, and other techniques, is a phenomenon found in all civilizations, both ancient and modern. In the context of ancient Latin language and belief, divination was concerned with discovering the will of the gods. Today, however, scholars no longer restrict the word to that earlier root meaning. Divinatory practices and the beliefs undergirding them are greater in scope than the ancient methods of discerning the will of the gods and the fatalistic view of the human condition that inspired so much of early Mediterranean religious thought. In some societies, in fact, divination is a practice to which many persons frequently resort, but never in terms of discovering the will of the gods. The idea of a godly providence controlling human affairs, in such societies, is unusual, although humbler spirits are often thought to intervene in troublesome ways.   (G.K.P.)

The most significant form of divination is astrology, defined as the science, or pseudoscience, of forecasting earthly and human events by means of observing and interpreting the fixed stars, the Sun, the Moon, and the planets. As a science, astrology has been used to predict or affect the destinies of individuals, groups, or nations by an assumed understanding of the influence of the planets and stars on earthly affairs. As a pseudoscience, astrology is considered to be diametrically opposed to the findings and theories of modern Western science.

NATURE AND SIGNIFICANCE

Astrology is a method of predicting mundane events based upon the assumption that the celestial bodies—particularly the planets and the stars considered in their arbitrary combinations or configurations (called constellations)—in some way either determine or indicate changes in the sublunar world. The theoretical basis for this assumption lies historically in Hellenistic philosophy and radically distinguishes astrology from the celestial *omina* ("omens") that were first categorized and cataloged in ancient Mesopotamia. Originally, astrologers presupposed a geocentric universe in which the "planets" (including the Sun and Moon) revolve in orbits whose centres are at or near the centre of the Earth, and in which the stars are fixed upon a sphere with a finite radius whose centre is also the centre of the Earth. Later, the principles of Aristotelian physics were adopted, according to which there is an absolute division between the eternal, circular motions of the heavenly element and the limited, linear motions of the four sublunar elements: fire, air, water, earth.

Special relations were believed to exist between particular celestial bodies and their varied motions, configurations with each other, and the processes of generation and decay apparent in the world of fire, air, water, and earth. These relations were sometimes regarded as so complex that no human mind could completely grasp them; thus, the astrologer might be readily excused for any errors. A similar set of special relations was also assumed by those whose physics was more akin to that of the Greek philosopher Plato. For the Platonic astrologers, the element of fire was believed to extend throughout the celestial spheres, and they were more likely than the Aristotelians to believe in the possibility of divine intervention in the natural processes through celestial influences upon the Earth, since they believed in the deity's creation of the celestial bodies themselves.

The role of the divine in astrological theory varies considerably. In its most rigorous aspect, astrology postulates a totally mechanistic universe, denying to the deity the possibility of intervention and to man that of free will; as such it was vigorously attacked by orthodox Christianity and Islām. For some, however, astrology is not an exact science like astronomy but merely indicates trends and directions that can be altered either by divine or by human will. In the interpretation of Bardesanes, a Syrian Christian scholar (154–*c.* 222)—who has often been identified as a

The role of the divine will

Gnostic (a believer in esoteric salvatory knowledge and the view that matter is evil and spirit good)—the motions of the stars govern only the elemental world, leaving the soul free to choose between the good and the evil. Man's ultimate goal is to attain emancipation from an astrologically dominated material world. Some astrologers, such as the Harranians (from the ancient Mesopotamian city of Harran) and the Hindus, regard the planets themselves as potent deities whose decrees can be changed through supplication and liturgy or through theurgy, the science of persuading the gods or other supernatural powers. In still other interpretations—*e.g.,* that of the Christian Priscillianists (followers of Priscillian, a Spanish ascetic of the 4th century who apparently held dualistic views)—the stars merely make manifest the will of God to those trained in astrological symbolism.

Significance of astral omens. The view that the stars make manifest the divine will is closest to the concept that lies behind the ancient Mesopotamian collections of celestial omens. Their primary purpose was to inform the royal court of impending disaster or success. These might take the forms of meteorological or epidemic phenomena affecting entire human, animal, or plant populations. Frequently, however, they involved the military affairs of the state or the personal lives of the ruler and his family. Since the celestial *omina* were regarded not as deterministic but rather as indicative—as a kind of symbolic language in which the gods communicated with men about the future and as only a part of a vast array of ominous events—it was believed that their unpleasant forebodings might be mitigated or nullified by ritual means or by contrary omens. The *bāru* (the official prognosticator), who observed and interpreted the celestial *omina,* was thus in a position to advise his royal employer on the means of avoiding misfortunes; the omens provided a basis for intelligent action rather than an indication of an inexorable fate.

Purposes of astrology. The original purpose of astrology, on the other hand, was to inform the individual of the course of his life on the basis of the positions of the planets and of the zodiacal signs (the 12 astrological constellations) at the moment of his birth or conception. From this science, called genethlialogy (casting nativities), were developed the fundamental techniques of astrology.

Principal subdivisions of astrology

The main subdivisions of astrology that developed after genethlialogy are general, catarchic, and interrogatory.

General astrology studies the relationship of the significant celestial moments (*e.g.,* the times of vernal equinoxes, eclipses, or planetary conjunctions) to social groups, nations, or all humanity. It answers, by astrological means, questions formerly posed in Mesopotamia to the *bāru.*

Catarchic (pertaining to beginnings or sources) astrology determines whether or not a chosen moment is astrologically conducive to the success of a course of action begun in it. Basically in conflict with a rigorous interpretation of genethlialogy, it allows the individual (or corporate body) to act at astrologically favourable times and, thereby, to escape any failures predictable from his (or its) nativity.

Interrogatory astrology provides answers to a client's queries based on the situation of the heavens at the moment of his posing the questions. This astrological consulting service is even more remote from determinism than is catarchic astrology; it is thereby closer to divination by omens and insists upon the ritual purification and preparation of the astrologer.

Other forms of astrology, such as iatromathematics (application of astrology to medicine) and military astrology are variants on one or another of the above.

HISTORICAL DEVELOPMENT

Astral omens in the ancient Middle East. The astral omens employed in Mesopotamian divination were later commingled with what came to be known as astrology in the strict sense of the term and constituted within astrology a branch described as natural astrology. Though lunar eclipses apparently were regarded as ominous at a somewhat earlier period, the period of the 1st dynasty of Babylon (18th to 16th centuries BC) was the time when the cuneiform text *Enūma Anu Enlil,* devoted to celestial *omina,* was initiated. The final collection and codification of this series, however, was not accomplished before the beginning of the 1st millennium BC. But the tablets that have survived—mainly from the Assyrian library of King Ashurbanipal (7th century BC)—indicate that a standard version never existed. Each copy had its own characteristic contents and organization designed to facilitate its owner's consultation of the omens.

The common categories into which the omens of *Enūma Anu Enlil* were considered to fall were four, named after the chief gods involved in the ominous communication: Sin, Shamash, Adad, and Ishtar. Sin (the Moon) contains omens involving such lunar phenomena as first crescents, eclipses, halos, and conjunctions with various fixed stars; Shamash (the Sun) deals with omens involving such solar phenomena as eclipses, simultaneous observations of two suns, and perihelia (additional suns); Adad (the weather god) is concerned with omens involving meteorological phenomena, such as thunder, lightning, and cloud formations, as well as earthquakes; and Ishtar (Venus) contains omens involving planetary phenomena such as first and last visibilities, stations (the points at which the planets appear to stand still), acronychal risings (rising of the planet in the east when the Sun sets in the west), and conjunctions with the fixed stars.

The four omen categories

Though these omens are often cited in the reports of a network of observers established throughout the Assyrian Empire in the 7th century BC, they seem to have lost their popularity late in the period of the Persian domination of Mesopotamia (ending in the 4th century BC). During the later period new efforts were made, in a large number of works called *Diaries,* to find the correct correlations between celestial phenomena and terrestrial events. Before this development, however, portions of the older omen series were transmitted to Egypt, Greece, and India as a direct result of the Achaemenid domination (a dynasty ruling in Persia 559–330 BC) of these cultural areas or of their border regions.

Astral omens in Egypt, Greece, India, China, and Islām. The evidence for a transmission of lunar omens to Egypt in the Achaemenid period lies primarily in a demotic papyrus based on an original of about 500 BC. A more extensive use of Mesopotamian celestial omens is attested by the fragments of a book written in Greek in the 2nd century BC and claimed as a work addressed to a King Nechepso by the priest Petosiris. From this source, among others, the contents of *Enūma Anu Enlil* were included in the second book of the *Apotelesmatika,* or "Work on Astrology" (commonly called the *Tetrabiblos,* or "Four Books"), by Ptolemy, a Greek astronomer of the 2nd century AD; the first book of an astrological compendium, by Hephaestion of Thebes, a Greco-Egyptian astrologer of the 5th century AD; and the *On Signs* of John Lydus, a Byzantine bureaucrat of the 6th century. Yet another channel of transmission to the Greeks was through the Magusaeans of Asia Minor, a group of Iranian settlers influenced by Babylonian ideas. Their teachings are preserved in several classical works on natural history, primarily that of Pliny the Elder (*c.* AD 23–79), and the *Geoponica* (a late collection of agricultural lore).

In various Middle Eastern languages there also exist many texts dealing with celestial omens, though their sources and the question as to whether they are directly descended from a Mesopotamian tradition or are derived from Greek or Indian intermediaries is yet to be investigated. Of these texts the most important are those ascribed to Hermes Trismegistos by the Harranians and now preserved in Arabic, the *Book of the Zodiac* of the Mandaeans (a Gnostic sect still existing in Iraq and Khuzistan), the *Apocalypse,* attributed to the Old Testament prophet Daniel (extant in Greek, Syriac, and Arabic versions), and *The Book of the Bee* in Syriac.

The transmission of Mesopotamian omen literature to India, including the material in *Enūma Anu Enlil,* apparently took place in the 5th century BC during the Achaemenid occupation of the Indus Valley. The first traces are found in Buddhist texts of this period, and Buddhist missionaries were instrumental in carrying this material to Central Asia, China, Tibet, Japan, and Southeast Asia. But the most important of the works of this In-

Introduction of Mesopotamian literature to India

dian tradition and the oldest extant one in Sanskrit is the earliest version of the as yet unpublished *Gargasaṃhitā* ("Compositions of Garga") of about the 1st century AD. The original Mesopotamian material was modified so as to fit into the Indian conception of society, including the system of the four castes and the duty of the upper castes to perform the *saṃskāra*s (sanctifying ceremonies).

There are numerous later compilations of omens in Sanskrit—of which the most notable are the *Bṛhatsaṃhitā,* or "Great Composition," of Varāhamihira (*c.* 550), the Jaina *Bhadrabāhu-saṃhitā,* or "Composition of Bhadrabāhu" (*c.* 10th century), and the *Pariśiṣṭa*s ("Supplements") of the Atharvaveda (perhaps 10th or 11th century)—though these add little to the tradition. But in the works of the 13th century and later, entitled *Tājika,* there is a massive infusion of the Arabic adaptations of the originally Mesopotamian celestial omens as transmitted through Persian (*Tājika*) translations. In *Tājika* the omens are closely connected with general astrology; in the earlier Sanskrit texts their connections with astrology had been primarily in the fields of military and catarchic astrology.

Astrology in the Hellenistic period (3rd century BC to 3rd century AD). In the 3rd century BC and perhaps somewhat earlier, Babylonian diviners began—for the purpose of predicting the course of an individual's life—to utilize some planetary omens: positions relative to the horizon, latitudes, retrogressions, and other positions at the moment of birth or of computed conception. This method was still far from astrology, but its evolution was more or less contemporary and parallel with the development of the science of genethlialogy in Hellenistic Egypt.

Equally obscure are those individuals who, living in Egypt under the Ptolemies (a Greek dynasty ruling 305–30 BC), mathematicized the concept of a correspondence between the macrocosm (larger order, or universe) and the microcosm (smaller order, or man) as interpreted in terms of Platonic or Aristotelian theories concerning the Earth as the centre of the planetary system. They conceived of the ecliptic (the apparent orbital circle of the Sun) as being divided into 12 equal parts, or zodiacal signs, each

The zodiac

of which consists of 30°; in this they followed the Babylonians. They further regarded each of these 12 signs as the domicile (or house) of a planet and subdivided each into various parts—decans of 10° each, *fines* ("bounds") of varying lengths, and *dōdecatēmoria* of 2°30′ each—each of which is also dominated by a planet. Scattered at various points throughout the ecliptic are the planets' degrees of exaltation (high influence), opposite to which are their degrees of dejection (low influence). Various arcs of the zodiac, then, are either primarily or secondarily subject to each planet, whose strength and influence in a geniture (nativity) depend partially on its position relative to these arcs and to those of its friends and enemies.

Furthermore, each zodiacal sign has a special relation with a part of the human body. The 12 signs are further divided into four triplicities, each of which governs one of the four elements. Numerous pairs of opposites (male–female, diurnal–nocturnal, hot–cold, and others), based on the speculations of the followers of Pythagoras, a Greek mystical philosopher of the 6th century BC, are connected with consecutive pairs of signs. Finally, a wide variety of substances in the elemental world and attributes of human character are more or less arbitrarily associated with the different signs. These lists of interrelationships provide the rationale for many of the astrologer's predictions.

The individual planet's influences are related both to its general indications when regarded as ominous in Mesopotamian texts and to the traits of its presiding deity in Greek mythology. But on them are also superimposed the system of the four elements and their four qualities, the Pythagorean opposites, and lists of sublunar substances. Furthermore, as in the omens, the modes of the planetary motions are carefully considered, since their strengths are partially determined by their phases with respect to the Sun. Also, they exert a mutual influence both by occupying each other's houses and by means of conjunction and aspects—opposition (to the seventh) and quartile (to the fourth or 10th) being generally considered bad, trine (to the fifth or ninth) and sextile (to the third or 11th) good.

Moreover, as the planetary orbits revolve from west to east, the zodiac rotates daily about the Earth in the opposite sense. From a given spot on the Earth's surface this latter motion—if the ecliptic were a visible circle—would appear as a succession of signs rising one after the other above the eastern horizon. The astrologers regard the one that is momentarily in the ascendant as the first place, the one to follow it as the second, and so on, with the one that rose immediately prior to the ascendant being the 12th. In genethlialogy each place in this *dōdecatropos* determines an aspect of the life of the native (one born under a particular sign); in other forms of astrology the place determines some appropriate aspect of the sublunar world.

The astrologer, then, casts a horoscope by first determining for the given moment and locality the boundaries of the 12 places and the longitudes and latitudes of the seven planets. He reads this horoscope by examining the intricate geometric interrelationships of the signs and their parts and of the planets of varying computed strengths with the places and each other and by associating with each element in the horoscope its list of sublunary correspondences. Any horoscopic diagram, of course, will yield a vast number of predictions, including many that are contradictory or extravagant. The astrologer thus must rely on his knowledge of his client's social, ethnic, and economic background and on his own experience to guide him in avoiding error and attaining credibility.

Horoscopes

Since about 100 BC the above method has been the essential procedure of astrology, though various refinements and additional devices occasionally have been introduced, including those associated with the Hermetic tradition of Hermes Trismegistos and with Dorotheus of Sidon, an influential astrological poet of the third quarter of the 1st century AD. One is the system of lots, which are influential points as distant from some specified points in the horoscopic diagram as two planets are from each other. A second is the prorogator, a point on the ecliptic that, traveling at the rate of one degree of oblique ascension a year toward either the descendant or ascendant, determines a person's length of life. Another is the method of continuous horoscopy, under which anniversary diagrams are compared with the base nativity to provide annual readings. And, finally, certain periods of life are appor-

Table 1: The Signs and Relationships of the Zodiac

sign	sex, nature	triplicity	house	decan Greek	decan Indian	exaltation
Aries	masculine, moving	fire	Mars	Mars Sun Venus	Mars Sun Jupiter	Sun (19°)
Taurus	feminine, fixed	earth	Venus	Mercury Moon Saturn	Venus Mercury Saturn	Moon (3°)
Gemini	masculine, common	air	Mercury	Jupiter Mars Sun	Mercury Venus Saturn	
Cancer	feminine, moving	water	Moon	Venus Mercury Moon	Moon Mars Jupiter	Jupiter (15°)
Leo	masculine, fixed	fire	Sun	Saturn Jupiter Mars	Sun Jupiter Mars	
Virgo	feminine, common	earth	Mercury	Sun Venus Mercury	Mercury Saturn Venus	Mercury (15°)
Libra	masculine, moving	air	Venus	Moon Saturn Jupiter	Venus Saturn Mercury	Saturn (21°)
Scorpio	feminine, fixed	water	Mars	Mars Sun Venus	Mars Jupiter Moon	
Sagittarius	masculine, common	fire	Jupiter	Mercury Moon Saturn	Jupiter Mars Sun	
Capricorn	feminine, moving	earth	Saturn	Jupiter Mars Sun	Saturn Venus Mercury	Mars (28°)
Aquarius	masculine, fixed	air	Saturn	Venus Mercury Moon	Saturn Mercury Venus	
Pisces	feminine, common	water	Jupiter	Saturn Jupiter Mars	Jupiter Moon Mars	Venus (27°)

**Table 2: Relationship of
Positions in the Zodiac to
Aspects of Life**

| place | dōdecatropos | |
	Greek	Indian
I	life	body
II	wealth	wealth
III	siblings	siblings
IV	parents	relatives
V	children	children
VI	health	enemies
VII	marriage	marriage
VIII	death	death
IX	travel, religion	religion
X	occupation, honors	occupation
XI	benefits, friends	gains
XII	losses, enemies	losses

tioned to their governing planets in a fixed sequence; these period governors in turn share their authority with the other planets by granting them subperiods. All of these complications serve, among other purposes, to provide the astrologer with convenient excuses for his inevitable errors.

Astrology after the Hellenistic period. *In India.* Greek astrology was transmitted to India in the 2nd and 3rd centuries AD by means of several Sanskrit translations, of which the one best known is that made in AD 149/150 by Yavaneśvara and versified as the *Yavanajātaka* by Sphujidhvaja in AD 269/270. The techniques of Indian astrology are thus not surprisingly similar to those of its Hellenistic counterpart. But the techniques were transmitted without their philosophical underpinnings (for which the Indians substituted divine revelation), and the Indians modified the predictions, originally intended to be applied to Greek and Roman society, so that they would be meaningful to them. In particular, they took into account the caste system, the doctrine of metempsychosis (transmigration of souls), the Indian theory of five elements (earth, water, air, fire, and space), and the Indian systems of values.

The Indians also found it useful to make more elaborate the already complex methodology of Hellenistic astrology. They added as significant elements: the *nakṣatra*s (or lunar mansions); an elaborate system of three categories of *yoga*s (or planetary combinations); dozens of different varieties of *daśā*s (periods of the planets) and *antardaśā*s (subperiods); and a complex theory of *aṣṭakavarga* based on continuous horoscopy. The number of subdivisions of the zodiacal signs was increased by the addition of the *horā*s (15° each), the *saptāṃśa*s ($4\frac{2}{7}$° each), and the *navāṃśa*s (3°20′ each); the number of planets was increased by the addition of the nodes of the Moon (the points of intersection of the lunar orbit with the ecliptic), and of a series of *upagraha*s, or imaginary planets. Several elements of Hellenistic astrology and its Sāsānian offshoot (see below *In Sāsānian Iran*), however—including the lots, the prorogator, the Lord of the Year, the triplicities, and astrological history—were introduced into India only in the 13th century through the *Tājika* texts. Besides genethlialogy, the Indians particularly cultivated military astrology and a form of catarchic astrology termed *muhūrta-śāstra* and, to a lesser extent, iatromathematics and interrogatory astrology.

In Sāsānian Iran. Shortly after Ardashīr I founded the Sāsānian Empire in AD 226, a substantial transmission of both Greek and Indian astrology to Iran took place. There were Pahlavi (Iranian language) translations of Dorotheus of Sidon, Vettius Valens, Hermes, and an Indian called (in the Arabic sources) Farmasp. Since the Pahlavi originals are all lost, these translations provided the only knowledge of the Sāsānian science. Genethlialogy in Iran was essentially an imitation of the Hellenistic (though without any philosophy), onto which were grafted some Indian features, such as the *navāṃśa*s and a Śaivite interpretation of illustrations of the Greco-Egyptian deities of the decans. The most influential and characteristic innovation of the Sāsānian astrologers was the development of the theory of

astrological history—that is, the writing of history, both past and future, on the basis of extensions of the techniques of the prorogator, the Lord of the Year, the planetary periods, and the continuous horoscopy employed in Hellenistic genethlialogy. This was done in conjunction with Zoroastrian millenarianism (the division of the finite duration of the material creation into 12 millennia).

In Islām. Astrology entered Islāmic civilization in the 8th and 9th centuries in three simultaneous streams—Hellenistic, Indian, and Sāsānian. Arabic translations from the Greek and Syriac represented the Hellenistic science, from Sanskrit the Indian version, and from Pahlavi the Sāsānian combination of the two. But to these influences Islāmic astrology, through the work of Abū Ma'shar, an astrologer of the 9th century, added the Harranian adaptation of the Neoplatonic definition of the mode of astral influences in terms of Aristotelian physics. Abū Ma'shar further elaborated Sāsānian astrological history and greatly expanded the number of lots that an astrologer had to take into consideration. Much attention was paid by the Muslims to catarchic and interrogatory astrology, but, under attack by the theologians for denying divine intervention in the world and man's free will, astrology rapidly declined in its appeal to Muslim intellectuals after the Mongol invasions of the 13th century, though not before its influence had spread in India, the Latin West, and Byzantium.

Significance of Arabic astrology

In Byzantium. During the last upsurge of paganism in the 5th and 6th centuries AD, Byzantium (the Eastern Roman Empire) boasted a host of astrologers: Hephaestion, Julian of Laodicea, "Proclus," Rhetorius, and John Lydus. Though their works are singularly unoriginal compilations, they remain the major sources for an understanding of earlier Hellenistic astrology. By the end of the 6th century, however, the general decline of the Byzantine Empire's intellectual life and the strong opposition of the church had combined to virtually obliterate astrology, though some practice of reading celestial omens survived in Byzantium as it did in western Europe. The science was revived only in the late 8th century and the 9th century under the impact of translations from Syriac and Arabic. The period from about 800 to 1200 was the most propitious for Byzantine astrology, though nothing was essentially added to astrological theories or techniques. This period was rivaled only by a last flowering of astrology in the late 14th century, when John Abramius and his students revised the older astrological treatises in Greek to provide the Renaissance with vulgate texts.

In western Europe. The astrological texts of the Roman Empire were written almost universally in Greek rather than in Latin; the only surviving exceptions are the poem *Astronomica* of Manilius (*c.* AD 15–20), the *Matheseos libri* ("Books on Astrology") of Firmicus Maternus (*c.* 335), and the anonymous *Liber Hermetis* ("Book of Hermes") from the 6th century. In the absence of astronomical tables in Latin, however, none of these was of any use, and astrology for all practical purposes disappeared with the knowledge of Greek in western Europe. It was revived only with the numerous translations of Arabic astrological and astronomical treatises executed in Spain and Sicily in the 12th and 13th centuries, supplemented by a few translations directly from the Greek. But the new astrology in the Latin-reading world remained essentially an offshoot of Islāmic astrology, gaining an adequate representation of its Hellenistic originals only in the 15th and 16th centuries. These two centuries also witnessed the fullest flowering of astrology in western Europe, frequently in conjunction with Neoplatonism and Hermetism. By the 17th century, however—with the displacement of the Earth from the centre of the universe in the new astronomy of Copernicus (1473–1543), Galileo (1564–1642), and Johannes Kepler (1571–1630), and with the rise of the new mechanistic physics of Descartes (1596–1650) and Newton (1643–1727)—astrology lost its intellectual viability and became increasingly recognized as scientifically untenable. Though Kepler attempted to devise a new method of computing astrological influences in the heliocentric (Sun-centred) universe, he did not succeed.

Effect of modern science on astrology

Astrology in modern times. In the West, Newtonian physics largely eradicated a belief in astrology among the educated, and the practice of what now degenerated into a pseudoscience became increasingly the province of the fraudulent fortune-teller. In countries such as India, however, where only a small intellectual elite has been trained in Western physics, it manages to retain here and there its position among the sciences. Some Indian universities offer advanced degrees in astrology.

Recently in the West, however, astrology has gained a large popular following, and there have been attempts to reestablish a firm theoretical basis for it, notably by the French psychologist Michel Gauquelin, although with results that are at best inconclusive. The divisions of the year governed by the 12 zodiacal signs (which are derived from Hellenistic astrology) as depicted in newspapers, manuals, and almanacs are as follows:

Aries, the Ram, March 21–April 19	Libra, the Balance, September 23–October 23
Taurus, the Bull, April 20–May 20	Scorpio, the Scorpion, October 24–November 21
Gemini, the Twins, May 21–June 21	Sagittarius, the Archer, November 22–December 21
Cancer, the Crab, June 22–July 22	Capricorn, the Goat, December 22–January 19
Leo, the Lion, July 23–August 22	Aquarius, the Water Carrier, January 20–February 18
Virgo, the Virgin, August 23–September 22	Pisces, the Fish, February 19–March 20

Attempts have been made to incorporate into the general astrological scheme the planets discovered since the Renaissance and to find some sort of statistical relation between planetary positions and human lives. None of these attempts appears to be at all convincing, however, and no serious explanation seems to exist regarding the alleged spheres of influence of the planets, the alleged nature of their influences, or the manner in which they are received. Nor has any modern astrologer proved that arbitrary arcs (houses or zodiacal signs) on a nonexistent circle (the ecliptic) are endowed with existence and with attributes, much less with the power to affect human lives. Moreover, since the phenomena of this world are now largely explicable by the hypotheses of modern science, it is difficult to understand how astrological influences can also be responsible for them. In short, modern Western astrology, though of great interest sociologically and popularly, generally is regarded as devoid of intellectual value.

(D.E.P./R.A.Gi.)

Divination: other forms

While divination is most commonly practiced in the modern Western world in the form of horoscopic astrology, other forms of divination were and are of equal importance for other cultures, both ancient and contemporary.

NATURE AND SIGNIFICANCE

Concerns of divination

Divination is universally concerned with practical problems, private or public, and seeks information upon which practical decisions can be made; but the source of such information is not conceived as mundane, and the technique of getting it is necessarily fanciful. The mantic (divinatory) arts are many, and a broad understanding can only emerge from a survey of actual practices in various cultural settings. A short definition, however, may be offered as a preliminary guide: divination is the effort to gain information of a mundane sort by means conceived of as transcending the mundane.

Though the act of divination is attended by respect and the attitude of the participants in the divinatory act may be religious, the subject matter of divination (like that of magic) is ephemeral—*e.g.,* an illness, a worrisome portent, a lost object. Divination is a consultative institution, and the matter posed to a diviner may range from a query about a few lost coins to high questions of state. The casual or solemn nature of the matter is normally matched by that of the diviner in terms of attitude, technique, and style. Where the diviner is a private practitioner, the elaborateness of the procedure may be reflected in the fee. In contrast to the worldly motives of some diviners, the calling of diviner-priest was seen by the ancient Etruscans in Italy and the Maya in Mexico as sacred; his concern

Barotse basket diviner. The diviner shakes various objects in the winnowing basket and by interpreting their final juxtaposition seeks to predict the outcome of an illness and to name the sorcerer responsible.
By courtesy of the Livingstone Museum, Republic of Zambia

was for the very destiny of his people. Divination has many rationales, and it is difficult to describe the diviner as a distinctive social type. He may be a shaman (private curer employing psychic techniques), a priest, a peddler of sorcery medicines, or a holy man who speaks almost with the voice of prophecy. To appreciate the significance of the diviner's art in any culture or era, one must be familiar with prevailing beliefs about man and the world. In Christian times Europe has moved from a horror of necromancy (conceived not as consultation with a ghost but as a literal "raising of the dead") to an amused tolerance (among the educated) of spiritualism as a sort of parlour game. To assert that European beliefs about God and man have remained the same throughout the Christian Era would be to ignore the impact of modern science and secularization. On the other hand, to suppose that divination has been doomed by science and secularism would be to ignore the abiding popularity of horoscopic astrology and recurrent fashions for other mantic disciplines—and perhaps to misjudge the security of "modern" beliefs.

THE STRUCTURE OF DIVINATION

Importance of world-views and philosophical under-girdings for divination

The extent to which a practice such as divination should be called a corollary of the beliefs entailed and the extent to which the opposite might be true (*i.e.,* the beliefs deriving from the practice as an after-the-fact explanation) is difficult to ascertain. Among the great cultures, the Chinese tradition has given the broadest scope to divination; yet there is no single Chinese religious cosmology, or theory on the ordering of the world, comparable to those of the Maya, Sanskritic (Hindu), or Judeo-Christian traditions, from which the variety of popular practice can be seen to derive. Sometimes, as with the flourishing business of astrology in Christian countries since the Renaissance, the metaphysical (transcendent) presuppositions of mantic practice may have been muted in order to minimize conflict with official religious and scientific doctrines. Generally, however, the philosophical underpinnings of divination need not be deep or well worked out, but, where they are, they will afford clues to fundamental beliefs about man and about visible or invisible nature. Some traditions of divination—such as astrology, geomancy (divination by means of figures or lines), or the Chinese divinatory disciplines—are so old and established that it is virtually impossible to discover their original contexts. Over the centuries such practices have survived many changes and have become perennial attempts to answer recurring questions about the human condition.

Established long ago in the hieratic (priestly) discipline of primitive theocracies, such a tradition still bears the marks of the specialists who worked out its systematic techniques. Since the practice is now observed only as a folk or popular tradition, however, it would be rash to suppose that any legitimate philosophical tradition undergirding divination survives. Only in the case of the *I Ching,* the Chinese "Classic of Changes," have scholarly commentaries of any great intellectual substance accumulated over the millennia. Systematic studies of geomancy are recent, and the literature of astrology is as perishable as it is massive. Babylonian astrology, from which later forms are derived, arose in an agrarian Mesopotamian civilization concerned the vicissitudes of nature and the affairs of state. The mercantile, seafaring, and individualistic Greeks absorbed the mantic system of the collectivistic floodplain civilization of Mesopotamia, elaborated on it by adding the horoscopic discipline, and transmitted it, through Hellenistic, Egyptian, and Islāmic science, to Europe. In the course of this transformation, a two-way relationship between a society's view of the world and its system may be seen. Various priests and scholars have made their contributions to the system; yet there also is a clear correspondence between the general character of a culture and the uses it finds for divination. That is, the worldview implicit in the divination system itself may reflect the historical rather than the current context of use. It requires only practical understanding to consult a ouija board or use a forked stick to decide where to drill for water. Hence, men of very different beliefs may adopt the same practices, and a full correspondence between practice and belief can only be expected where both have developed in the same cultural context. Where much of the popularity of the mantic art derives from its "exotic" flavour, its symbolism may be little understood. By its very nature, however, divination tends to develop as a discipline, becoming the tradition of an organized body of specialists. This is because the means to which the diviner must resort are conceived as setting him apart. That is the case even among such peoples as the Azande (adjective and singular noun form Zande) of the Nile-Congo divide in Africa, where the resort to divination is frequent, and the most common techniques utilized are recognized to be within the competence of ordinary men. There, on a sensitive or contentious issue, an extraordinary credibility is desired, and the ultimate reliability of an oracle reflects the political standing of its owner—the king's oracle, for example, is viewed as the final authority, and the royal court is scrupulously organized to guard this vessel of power (divinatory and other) from contamination. Few societies are as enthusiastically given to divination as the Azande, who routinely employ it to explore their thoughts and who will not consider any important undertakings without oracular confirmation in advance. Among the Azande, the ordinary man could be considered a divinatory specialist. Elsewhere, men are content to reserve divination for special crises, and consultation must be with a recognized expert in order to distinguish an authentic answer from a spurious one.

Types of divination. As schools of dramatic art range from those relying on explicit technique to those teaching intuitive identification with a role, mantic skills range from the mechanical to the inspirational but most often combine both skills in a unique, dramatically coherent format. The comparative study of divinatory practices is at least as old as the 1st-century-BC Roman orator and politician Cicero's treatise *De divinatione* (*Concerning Divination*), and the convenient distinction there drawn between inductive and intuitive forms designates the range. An intermediate class, interpretive divination, allows a less rigid classification, since many divinatory disciplines do not rely strongly either upon inductive rigour or upon trance and possession.

Inductive divination presupposes a determinative procedure, apparently free from mundane control, yielding unambiguous decisions or predictions. The reading of the "eight characters" of a Chinese boy and girl before proceeding to arrange a marriage—the year, month, day, and hour of birth of the two persons to be betrothed— illustrates this class of procedures. The "characters" are all predetermined by the accidents of birth date and hour, and it is supposed that all proper diviners would come to the same conclusions about them.

Interpretive divination requires the combination of correct procedure with the special gift of insight that sets a diviner apart from his fellows. The contemporary Maya diviner of Guatemala, seeking to diagnose an illness, will carefully pass a number of eggs over the patient's body in order to draw into them an essence of the affliction. The intact contents are then collected in water, and the diviner withdraws into a darkened corner to bend over the receptacle and read the signs of the eggs. His recitation then interprets the origin and nature of the disease.

Intuitive divination presupposes extraordinary gifts of insight or ability to communicate with beings in an extramundane sphere. The "Shaking Tent" rite of the Algonkian Indians of Canada illustrates the use of uncanny phenomena to lend credence to a mediumistic performance. The diviner, bound and cloaked, is no sooner placed in his barrel-like tent than the tent begins to shake with astonishing vigour and to fill the air with monstrous noises; and this continues with great effect until, all of a sudden, the communicating spirit makes his presence known from within the tent and undertakes to answer questions. It is difficult to explain away the phenomena of spirit possession as products of deliberate instruction.

The cosmological and psychological conditioning that affects divinatory practices within a cultural tradition will influence in a similar fashion all of its religious practices. The Greeks tended to the intuitive or "oracular" style, and the Etruscans, in contrast, elaborated upon the more systematic but less versatile inductive practice of Mesopotamia—developing an authoritative state religion in which the positions were monopolized by the ruling class. Greek divination was eccentric in that sanctuaries were located apart from the centres of political power; the Etruscan system, on the other hand, was concentric, focused at the summit itself. Rome eclectically incorporated both Greek and Etruscan elements, the ecstatic cult and the expert "reading" of livers—*i.e.,* haruspimancy. Rome, however, never allowed divination to become the central preoccupation of society as it had been for Etruria, nor did it become an autonomous force in society as it had been for the Greeks. In this, Rome represented a balance that is more congenial to modern Western thought. Throughout the ancient Mediterranean world, the notable exception being Egypt, divination was tied to expiation and sacrifice: fate was perceived as dire but not quite implacable, and the function of divination was to foresee calamity in order to forestall it. In trans-Saharan Africa, religion centres on expiation and sacrifice, and divination is a pivotal institution, but the Mediterranean notion of fate is not developed. Instead, the trouble of a person is attributed to witchcraft, sorcery, or ancestral vexation—all of which are believed to be arbitrary and morally undeserved. Divination is employed to discover the source of trouble in order to remove it, whether by sacrifice, countersorcery, or accusation and ordeal. The mind is turned to past events or hidden motives of the present time, however, and not to the future—that would be to borrow trouble.

The function of divination. The function of divination needs to be understood in its motivational context. It is not enough to say that information won from the diviner serves to allay uncertainty, locate blame, or overcome misfortune. Divination is motivated by the fact that information, whether spurious or true, will please a client. Unless one assumes that the information is usually accurate, one would expect clients to be displeased and subsequently skeptical. A careful assessment of the kinds of information that divinatory systems are required to yield is thus in order. The two main kinds are general information about the future and specific information about the past as it bears upon the future.

The first kind of information is yielded by horoscopic divination. It is usually so general that it cannot be properly tested. If such information were really specific, the prediction could interfere with its own fulfillment, acting as a warning or breeding overconfidence. The other kind of information demanded from diviners is specific enough to be tested and often is; but testing a particular diviner's competence is seldom seen as putting the institution to the test. Indeed, it is common in trans-Saharan societies for a troubled client to consult a series of diviners until he finds one who is convincing. Again, many systems of divination have a double check built into them: the question is posed first in the positive and then in the negative, and the oracle must (obviously without manipulation) answer consistently. The chances are actually even that any oracle will fail to do so, yet the credibility of such oracles seems not to be lost. Technically, this means that false information can be obtained by a client without weakening his belief in the source. Early students of divinatory practice concluded that clients must be gullible, superstitious, illogical, or even "prelogical"; *i.e.,* culturally immature. Ethnographic studies do not confirm this, suggesting rather that what a client seeks from the diviner is information upon which he can confidently act. He is seeking, in so doing, public credibility for his own course of action. Consistent with this motive, he should set aside any finding that he thinks would lead him into doubtful action and continue his consultations until they suggest a course that he can take with confidence. The diviner's findings are judged pragmatically.

Occasions of divinatory consultation Clients seek out a diviner when they are unsure how to behave—when there is illness, drought, death, or the fear of death; when there is suspicion of malevolence, theft, or breach of faith; when dreams or other symptoms are disturbing or the signs of the time seem bad. Divination serves the purpose of circumscription, of marking out and delimiting the area of concern: the nature of the crisis is defined, the source of anxiety is named. Concern becomes allegation, bafflement decision. The diviner may function as a stage manager, speeding up the action, rejecting false moves in advance, or indicating the secret fear or the hidden motive. Where divinatory practice is a recognized resource, a man who ignores it is considered arbitrary, and one who heeds it needs no further justification for his actions. In this sense, the ultimate function of divination is the legitimation of problematic decisions.

VARIETIES OF DIVINATION

Because dramatic effect is important, divination takes many forms and employs a wealth of devices. In a general way, it may be said that inductive divination employs nonhuman phenomena, either artificial or natural, as signs that can be unambiguously read. The prime condition is that the signs appear to be genuine, not manipulated. Interpretive divination commonly combines the use of nonhuman phenomena with human action, employing devices so complex, subtle, or fluid that the special gifts of the diviner seem required if the meaning is to be known. It is here that divination takes its most characteristically dramatic forms. Intuitive divination usually places little reliance upon artificial trappings, except for dramatic effect. The impressive performer may exhibit gifts like those that in a different context would have made him an effective actor, writer, or political leader. Where the diviner can produce voices other than his own, the impression is that the gods or spirits are speaking.

Inductive divination. To speculate that inductive divination from natural phenomena must be very old—*i.e.,* that it arose from early man's intimate acquaintance with nature—is tempting. In fact, however, evidence of an awareness of nature as a system among preliterate peoples is spotty, and this is particularly true in respect to astral observation. Divination from the skies is concerned preeminently with the future but presupposes a concern with cycles of time and history. Quite distinctive attitudes were taken toward the celestial clock by the ancient Maya astronomers and those of Mesopotamia; and distinct but related forms of astrology were developed in the Western, Indian, and Chinese civilizations. But the relation between astrology and scientific astronomy is quite apparent, and the two "sciences" were inseparable in the West until early modern times.

Forms of inductive divination Associated with the observation of the heavens is the reading of signs in the weather and the movement of birds. The interpretation of lightning as a decipherable message from the gods—not simply as an outburst of divine anger—was brought to the level of a pseudoscience by the Etruscans. Winds and clouds, being suited to less

exact observation, invited interpretive rather than inductive divination. Weather phenomena were also conceived of as in a special status relative to man, in that rain, drought, and natural disasters are forces that man seeks not simply to read but to control. Nonetheless, Hindu scripture discusses the art of interpreting "castles in the air"—celestial cities seen in towering clouds.

Augury, the art of interpreting omens, is the attempt to discover divine will in phenomena of animate nature. In Mesopotamia, augury was associated with sacrifice and perhaps developed from it. As the priests watched the rising smoke to divine the answer to a ritual query, they observed the movement of birds as auspicious or inauspicious. As a further augury the viscera of the sacrificial victim were examined, particularly the liver, which (rather than the heart) was conceived as the vital centre. The discipline of augury mapped cosmic space with the sacrificial altar at the centre, and each sector was assigned a definite meaning. Every event in the heavens could thus be charted and pondered. Similarly, haruspicy, the study

By courtesy of (bottom) the Museo Civico, Piacenza, Italy; from (top) O.W. von Vacano, *The Etruscans in the Ancient World*

(Top) Etruscan mirror showing a ritual scrutiny of a sacrificed liver. The various sections of the liver were believed to be a reflection of the divisions of heaven, each of which had a favourable or unfavourable meaning. The man (second from right) holds the liver so that the lobes can be examined and the details for foretelling the future are distinct. From Tuscania, Italy, 3rd century BC. In the Museo Archeologico, Florence. (Bottom) Bronze model of a sheep's liver used for divining. It is divided on its upper surface into about 40 sections, each with the name of an Etruscan divinity inscribed on it. From Piacenza, Italy, 4th–3rd century BC. In the Museo Civico, Piacenza, Italy.

of the liver, was developed by mapping it as a microcosm and reading it as one may read the palm.

Inductive divination from nature is associated with the reading of artificially contrived events, such as the movement of sacrificial smoke, the fall of an arrow shot upward, or the cast of dice or lots. A much-used natural–artificial technique consists in the braising of bone or shell to produce a system of signs. Scapulimancy—divination from a fire-cracked shoulder blade—was widespread in North America and Eurasia. The related but more elaborate Chinese technique of tortoiseshell divination was inspired by the idea of equating the carapace (back) and ventral (lower) shell with their view of a rounded sky over flat earth. Only the "earth" was inscribed and heated to produce signs. In general, however, artificial systems of signs are likely to be manipulatory, as they will be used in an artful way by the professional diviner—and in such cases interpretive techniques have to be taken into account.

Interpretive divination. Interpretive divination involves, in the main, the reading of portents, omens, or prodigies. To the scientifically minded, no event is without a cause. Yet, the apparently arbitrary event does occur in an ordered world and thus is subject to various interpretations. Manipulated events are an element of interpretive divination, but the less active forms depend upon projection, introjection, and free association—thus being associated, to some degree, with intuitive techniques.

Pyromancy, divination by fire, may be highly dramatic in a society dependent on fire for light and safety at night. In some trans-Saharan societies the diviner may test an accusation at a seance around the fire, which will suddenly explode upon the "guilty" one. Elsewhere, objects may be overtly cast into the fire and signs read in the reaction. Hydromancy, divination by water, is usually less dramatic, ranging from the reading of reflections in a shallow surface, in the manner of the crystal gazer, to construing the movements of floating objects, as in the reading of tea leaves.

A range of related mantic practices may be grouped under the terms cleromancy, divination by lots, and geomancy, which may involve the casting of objects upon a map or a figure drawn on the ground. Cleromantic practices in trans-Saharan Africa may rely on the supposedly magical— or indeed horrifying—qualities of objects in the diviner's bag or basket. When they are thrown, the proximity of one piece to another—for example, a dried bit of intestine from a murdered child and a man-eating animal's tooth— may be regarded as having meaning; or the position of a particular piece at the centre or apart from the others may be picked out. Often, the diviner must first prove his ability by discovering the client's problem, through a line of patter accompanying the throws—suggesting this, questioning that, leaping from one matter to another until the reactions of the client betray his interest. Here the diviner may be said to introject ideas and attitudes, while the lots act for the diviner and client alike as a projective device, the meaning of which is only half-formed in the objective pattern cast. A far more elaborate practice is the geomancy of West Africa, in which elegant equipment is combined with impressive erudition to produce a seance in which lots are used to select verses, wherein the client is expected to find his answers. The nature of the lots employed, the number lore on which the selection of verses is based, and the verses themselves are entirely distinct from their counterparts in the Chinese yarrow (an herb with finely dissected leaves) tradition embodied in the *I Ching*, but the general equivalence of the two elaborations is noteworthy. The parallel has perhaps been obscured by the use of "geomancy" in China to signify only a specialized art by which propitious locations are selected.

Sometimes a diviner can be said to interpret signs so characteristic of his client that the practice falls between interpretive and intuitive arts. Somatomancy, body divination, is clearly interpretive in most forms, whether in China or the West, though the system of signs employed comprises private attributes of the client's physique. Examples are phrenology, employing features of the head that are normally unnoticed; and the reading of moles, where the body is treated as a microcosm bearing astrological signs. But oneiromancy, dream interpretation, employs explicitly psychic phenomena; and here the diviner may be said to assist the intuition of meaning by his client as often as he can be said to introject. The Ojibwa and Bella Coola Indians of North America were characteristically preoccupied with the meanings of their dreams.

Intuitive divination. The prototype of the intuitive diviner is the occasional shaman or curer who uses trance states. These are achieved idiopathically (*i.e.,* arising from the self spontaneously) or induced by drugs or by autokinetic (self-energized) techniques, such as hand trembling among the Navajo, a large North American Indian tribe. As a mantic art, trance is associated with oracular utterance and spirit possession. An impressive performance will be taken to represent the actual voice of a god or spirit addressing the client directly; and divination in this mode is known from diverse religious traditions, including Christianity. The idea that the gods may be importuned to speak on a matter of temporal human concern seems to be very ancient. In early Egypt incubation was practiced— *i.e.,* sleeping in the temple in the hope of being inspired by the resident god. The idea behind Maya maiden sacrifice was the same: a number of maidens were cast into a sacred cenote or deep well, and those who survived after some hours were brought back to recite the messages received during their ordeal—a virtual enactment of the journey into the underworld. As oracular utterance became regular, special techniques or contraptions were developed for making the god's image show assent or denial or for amplifying the sound of an unseen priest's voice. In nomadic societies today, however, the diviner may still achieve personal authority by passing into a trance before his fellows, trembling and speaking "as if possessed"—that is, as if his own spirit had ceased to inhabit his body and had been replaced by another.

Related to possession is the conviction that malevolent persons are essentially unlike innocent ones, though not in outward appearance. When a test is devised for discovering malevolence, commonly conceived of as witchcraft or as a nonhuman force disguising itself in human form, the test takes the form of an ordeal. This may be a demonstration of invulnerability to harm, the presence of blessed qualities being viewed as inconsistent with malevolence; among the many types of ordeal are walking on coals and retrieving an object from boiling liquid. The ordeal may even involve death: in the ordeal by water, a witch was expected to float and so be spared for burning, but an innocent person would be accepted by the water and drown. In trans-Saharan poison ordeals the innocent person is expected to survive.

Intuitive divination may also be a wholly private affair. A Roman might hear a warning from the gods in a piece of conversation; the Aztec might discern a portent in an animal's howl. The North American Indian who sought a private vision through isolation, self-mutilation, and fasting would preserve the memory of that vision throughout life, turning to it as his unique guardian spirit.

Divination today. The immense popularity of horoscopes in the urban West today illustrates the almost exclusive concern with individual fortune-telling that characterizes divination in a mobile and competitive mass society. Chiromancy, Tarot (fortune-telling) cards, and crystal gazing represent respectively body divination, sortilege (divination by lots), and trancelike performance in styles suitable for what might be called a half-serious attempt to learn one's fate. Necromancy, in its modern spiritualist form, represents a slightly more serious and sustained effort to establish contact with extramundane beings. But astrology, in its various popular forms, is the form of divination best suited to mass consumption, since it is based on a well-articulated body of lore, touches matters of high destiny as well as individual fortune, and "personalizes" its introjective advice without the client's having to be interviewed. On the other hand, the more esoteric mantic arts have the appeal of discipline—an individual may enter into the lore deeply until it becomes a part of his own worldview. Study of the *I Ching* for divinatory purposes can involve this sort of commitment. (G.K.P./R.A.Gi.)

Forms of interpretive divination

Forms of intuitive divination

Popularity of horoscopic astrology

Magic

In the occult, magic comprises a wide range of phenomena, from the elaborate ritual beliefs and practices that are at the core of many religious systems, to acts of conjuring and sleight of hand for entertainment. Used in the former sense magic is a social and cultural phenomenon found in all places and at all periods, with varying degrees of importance.

NATURE AND SIGNIFICANCE

The term magic essentially refers to a ritual performance or activity that is thought to lead to the influencing of human or natural events by an external and impersonal mystical force beyond the ordinary human sphere. The performance involves the use of special objects or the recitation of spells (words with an innate power or essence) or both by the magician. The nature of magic is frequently misunderstood because of uncertainty as to its definition, its relationship to other religious behaviour and institutions, and its social and psychological functions.

Magic and religion

This uncertainty is largely a consequence of 19th-century views on cultural and historical evolution that set magic apart from other religious phenomena as being especially prevalent in archaic and primitive societies and as merely a form of superstition without cultural or theological significance. This view has led to magic's being considered as different and distinct from other religious rites and beliefs and the overlooking of its essential similarity and connection with them, since both magical and non-magical rites and beliefs are concerned with the effects on human existence of outside mystical forces. The frequently held view that magical acts lack the intrinsically spiritual nature of religious acts, comprising external manipulation rather than supplication or inner grace, and that they are therefore of a simpler and lower kind in theological terms, has compounded the misunderstanding. The definition given above recognizes a main point of distinction between magic and other religious phenomena, in that the latter are concerned with a direct relationship between men and spiritual forces, whereas magic is regarded as rather an impersonal or technical act in which the personal link is not so important or is absent, even though the ultimate force behind both religious and magical acts is believed to be the same. The distinction made by Émile Durkheim (1858–1917), a seminal French sociologist of religion (see below), that a religious practitioner has a congregation whereas a magician has a clientele, is also a meaningful one. The difficulty in defining magic and distinguishing it from religion is due largely to Western ethnocentric views. In Judeo-Christian belief it has been distinguished from other religious acts, but this distinction is not always found in other religious systems and in fact would appear to be unusual. Many writers have referred to "magico-religious" phenomena, a convenient blanket term.

Magic is often confused with witchcraft, especially in the history of European religions. Modern anthropologists, however, make the useful distinction between magic as the manipulation of an external power by mechanical or behavioral means to affect others, and witchcraft as an inherent personal quality motivated to the same ends. In this classification, the word sorcery is used for magic that aims to harm other people; that is, sorcery is "black" magic, whereas magic used for beneficent ends is "white" magic. This distinction does not always hold for specific societies but is a useful one in analysis. Divination, the skill of understanding mystical agents that affect people and events, should be distinguished from magic in that its purpose is not to influence events but rather to understand them. The ultimate mystical power of diviners, however, may be thought to be the same as that behind the forces of magic. In some societies, magicians act as diviners, but the two skills should be distinguished. Magicians are often confused with priests, shamans, and prophets, mainly because many of these practitioners' activities include acts that are traditionally defined as "magical"; *i.e.*, while essentially they are regarded as intermediaries between men and gods or spirits, in the sense of acting in a direct personal relationship, some of their acts are also imper-

sonal or "magical." It is often, perhaps usually, impossible clearly to distinguish between priests and magicians; any distinction lies in the kind of actions they perform in particular situations rather than in any true distinction between the kinds of practitioners themselves.

HISTORY AND DISTRIBUTION

Magic in one form or other appears to be a part of all known religious systems, at all levels of historical development, although the degree of importance given to it varies considerably. The term has been used loosely by many writers, especially when discussing European magic. Also the ethnographic accounts of small-scale preliterate societies vary in the degree to which they contain detailed descriptions even when magic is important in a particular culture. Thus the analyses of magic in its total cultural setting are remarkably few.

Knowledge of magic in prehistory is limited by lack of reliable data. Many cave paintings and engravings, from all parts of the world, have been claimed to represent figures practicing hunting magic and sorcery, but this is only conjecture. More certain information about magical phenomena is available for the ancient Middle Eastern and Greco-Roman cultures, Christian Europe, and contemporary preliterate societies.

Magic in the ancient world. There are many recorded texts of what appear to be magic spells and formulas from ancient Mesopotamia and Egypt. Most accounts of these cultures class almost all records of ritual as forms of magic and as examples of magical or mythopoeic ways of thought. This is usually because the writers themselves assumed that these cultures were examples of "prelogical" thought (as compared with the thought of civilized man), and so took any religious record as evidence of this. The pharaohs of Egypt, for example, were what are usually called "divine kings," and as such were believed to have the power to control nature and fertility. Many writers refer to their powers as magical, but the evidence is rather that they were expressions of royal omnipotence and contingent on their divine status. Examples of true magical spells and formulas are recorded from both Mesopotamia and Egypt; *e.g.*, spells to ward off witches and sorcerers. Spells addressed to gods, to fire, to salt, and to grain are recorded from Mesopotamia and Egypt, as are spells uttered by sorcerers and including necromancy or invocation of the spirits of the dead, who were referred to as a last resort against evil magic. Excellent examples of spells are recorded from the earliest times, and especially in Greco-Egyptian papyruses of the 1st to the 4th century AD. They include both magical recipes involving animals and animal substances, and also instructions for the ritual preparations and purification necessary to ensure the efficacy of the spells.

Magic in Egypt and Mesopotamia

In ancient Roman culture much importance was given to sorcery and counter-sorcery. These seem to have been associated with the development of new urban classes whose members had to rely on their own efforts in both material and magical terms to defeat their rivals and attain success. Spells are recorded to ensure victory in love as well as in business, games, and oratory. Along with these are counter-spells to defeat rival sorcerers.

Magic in Christian Europe. For the European Middle Ages and later periods there is a vast corpus of written records. As is known from recent anthropological and historical work on witchcraft, magic, and religious syncretism, magic is specially prevalent during periods of rapid social change and mobility, when new personal relations and conflicts assume greater importance than the traditional kin and family relations more typical of times of social stability. Europe appears to have been no exception, particularly when the church, struggling to assert or maintain hegemony, leveled accusations of magic against its opponents. There are three main aspects to the history of European magic, much of which is ill-described and almost always without adequate accounts of the full cultural setting. One is that of magic and sorcery in everyday relationships at the community level from the end of the classical world until recently, when beliefs in magic have in general become weakened. In most cases these beliefs were part of the culture of lowly rural people and records are scant. An exception was sorcery used by wealthier and urban people, especially in Italy and Spain from the 14th century onward, a concomitant of increased social mobility and growth of class hierarchies. A second aspect is the better known but frequently misunderstood belief in magic defined by the church as the heretical practice of making pacts with the devil and evil spirits. St. Augustine and other early Christian writers had considered magic to be a relic of paganism and removable by conversion and education. After a papal bull in 1320, magic, regarded as synonymous with witchcraft, came to be defined as heresy, and the Inquisition's records began to mention the Witches' Sabbath (midnight assembly in fealty to the devil) and the Black Mass (a travesty of the Christian mass) as forms of magic and witchcraft. They were defined as magic because of the supposed use of material objects, philtres, spells, and poisons. The spells included the perverted use of prayers and the use of sacred writings and objects for diabolical ends. This aspect of European magic has persisted into recent times in the activities of self-styled satanists.

Whereas these forms of magic were regarded as evil and tantamount to heresy, the third aspect has usually been considered as good, or "white," in intent. This is the use of magic as part of the Hermetic tradition. Followers of this tradition, who often practiced alchemy rather than magic, were sometimes considered to be evil magicians, acquiring their knowledge by a pact with the devil (as in the Faust legends), but most of them were tolerated in society because their practices, however strange, were perceived as being within the main Judaic and Christian Hermetic tradition. When their magical activities proved, or appeared, to be antisocial, the results were more often put down to simple trickery—as in the case of the 18th-century charlatan Alessandro, conte di Cagliostro (Giuseppe Balsamo)—than to supernatural agency.

"White" magic (margin note)

Magic in nonliterate societies. Most knowledge of magic in its social setting is derived from anthropological accounts of people of the non-Western world who today believe in magic. The importance of firsthand anthropological accounts, even though many anthropologists tend to make use of the ethnocentric distinction between religion and magic, is that they show how the people themselves actually regard magic and what they actually do with it and against it, rather than relying on the records of inquisitors and missionaries whose aim it was to stamp out magic. Detailed descriptions of magic come mostly from accounts of societies in Oceania and Africa; magic is also frequently reported from many Muslim societies where pre-Islāmic beliefs still exist, as in Malaysia and Indonesia. A difficulty in this respect is that accounts only rarely distinguish magic from witchcraft and divination, both of which are found in virtually every known Oriental society.

STRUCTURE AND FUNCTIONS

Structure. A general point to be made is that the frequent tales of peoples living in fear of evil magicians and black magic are merely fanciful travelers' stories. Magic is normally regarded as an everyday aspect of religion used to explain certain kinds of events and to help bring about desired eventualities. Like most religious phenomena, magic may be regarded with some sense of awe and mystery, but this is more often a sign of the importance given to it than of fear or terror. Typically people perform magical acts themselves or they go to a magician, an expert who knows how to observe the necessary ritual precautions and taboos, and who may be a professional consulted for a fee. Depending upon the beliefs of the particular culture, the skill may be transmitted by inheritance or bought from other magicians, or may be invented by the magician for himself. Magicians may be consulted for nefarious purposes, to protect a client from the evil magic of others, or for purely benevolent reasons. It seems universal that magic is morally neutral, although the emphasis in any particular society may be on either its good or its evil use.

In some religions, especially those of small-scale nonliterate societies, magic may be considered as important and even central to religious belief; whereas in others, especially in the main world religions, it may be unimportant, and often regarded as a mere superstition that is not acceptable to official dogma. It has often been maintained that magic is important in societies that possess a particular worldview or cosmology, in which a scientifically or empirically correct cause-effect relationship between human and natural phenomena is seen as a symbolic one. This view, which is associated particularly with the British anthropologist Sir James Frazer (1854–1941), is now viewed as being based on a misunderstanding of patterns of thought in prescientific cultures. It is true that these cultures may lack the scientifically accurate knowledge of Western industrial societies; they may use magical techniques (for example, rainmaking), whereas in an industrial society it is known that such techniques are instrumentally ineffective. But magic is also performed for expressive purposes; *i.e.,* stating and maintaining the formal culture and organization of the society, so that rainmaking magic has also the function of stressing the importance of rain and the farming activities associated with it.

The magical view (margin note)

There are usually considered to be three main elements in magic: the spell, the rite itself, and the ritual condition of the performer. This was first stated by the anthropologist Bronisław Malinowski (1884–1942) in his study of the Trobriand Islanders of Melanesia. With the spell may be included the use of material objects or "medicines.".

The spell. The importance of the spell or incantation is now thought to have been somewhat exaggerated by the influence of Malinowski's work. Among the Trobriand Islanders this aspect is extremely important: using the right words in the right way is regarded as essential to the efficacy of the rite. Among the Maori of New Zealand this element is thought so important that a mistake in the recitation of a spell would lead to the magician's own death. Frequently spells have an archaic or esoteric vocabulary that adds to the respect in which the rite is held. But in many societies the spell is of minimal importance, the magician using his own words and regarding the content as more significant.

Material objects or "medicines.". Equally widespread— perhaps more so than the use of spells—is the use of material objects, often known in the literature as "medicines" (hence the popular use of the term medicine man for magician). The nature of the medicines varies greatly. In some cases, medicines intended to cause harm are genuine poisons (some African peoples place poisons in rivers to stun and catch fish, but regard them as they do any other, less genuinely efficacious medicines). More usually the medicines do not empirically bring about the effect but in some way represent it; for example, it is common practice for a magician to try to harm another person by destroying something from his body (*e.g.,* hair or nail parings), or something that has been in contact with him (*e.g.,* a piece of clothing or other personal possession). Another kind of symbolism is exemplified by the Trobriand use of light vegetable leaves in rites to ensure a canoe's speed, symbolizing the ease with which it will glide over the water; the Azande of The Sudan place a stone in a tree fork to postpone the setting of the Sun; many Balkan peoples used to swallow gold to cure jaundice.

The rite. The significance of the magical rite itself is often overlooked by those who hold the view that magic is something apart from religion. But it seems universal that magic is practiced only in formal and carefully defined ritual situations. The rite itself may be symbolic, as with the sprinkling of water on the ground to make rain or the destruction of a waxen image to harm a victim.

Condition of the performer. The ritual nature of magical performances may also be seen in a third element, that of the condition of the performer. Even though regarded as an everyday and "natural" phenomenon, magic is nonetheless considered as potentially dangerous and polluting, as is any sacred or religious object or activity. Both the magician and the rite itself are typically surrounded by the observance of taboos, by the purification of the participants, and so on. The magician may observe restrictions on certain foods or on sexual activity, and he may be regarded as polluting to other people at these times.

Taboos, purifications, and precautions (margin note)

There are two obvious reasons: failure to observe such precautions nullifies the magic, and taking precautions indicates to the participants and others the importance of the rite itself and the ends desired. The precautions mark off the rite from ordinary and profane activities and invest it with sanctity.

Functions. The functions of magic are several, but there are two main aspects, the instrumental and the expressive. A basic feature of magical rites and beliefs is that the practitioners believe that these are instrumental; *i.e.,* they are designed to achieve certain ends in nature or in the behaviour of other people. This is usually the aspect most important for the people concerned as well as for past writers on the subject. The symbolic or expressive aspect is always present, however; it is because of its symbolic content that magic may best be understood as a part of a religious system.

Instrumental functions. Malinowski and his followers have distinguished three main instrumental functions: the productive, the protective, and the destructive. Productive magic is used to ensure a successful outcome to some creative or productive activity in terms of both human labour and natural bounty, such as a good harvest or hunt. Malinowski showed clearly how it may foster confidence where technology is weak or uncertain; his example of the Trobriand Islanders making magic when fishing in the open sea but not doing so when fishing in a calm and protected lagoon makes the point clearly. In addition, productive magic may also assist the efficient organization of labour and give greater incentive to those who feel confident of success. Protective magic aims to prevent or remove danger, to cure sickness, and to protect an individual or community from the vagaries of nature and the evil acts of others. Again, it may give people confidence to continue their normal activities. Destructive magic is sorcery, directed specifically to harm other people. The fear of this form of magic may reduce individual initiative since a successful or wealthy person in an egalitarian society may fear the sorcery of the envious. On the other hand, the use of counter-magic against sorcery rids a community of its internal fears and tensions.

Expressive functions. The expressive functions of magic are symbolic and usually latent in the sense that the performers may not themselves be immediately aware of them. They have largely to do with the effects of individual acts upon society at large. It is there that the part played by magic in a total system of religion may be seen.

MAGIC, RELIGION, AND SCIENCE

Magic and religion. The relationship of magic to other religious activities depends on three main considerations. The first is the nature of the power toward which the rites are directed. The eminent British anthropologist Sir Edward Burnett Tylor (1832–1917) and his successors distinguished a personal, conscious, and omnipotent spiritual being as the object of religious ritual; magical performances have no power in themselves but are usually thought by believers to be an expression of an external, impersonal force in nature, for which the Melanesian–Polynesian term mana has typically been used. A second consideration is the participants: the magician and those who go to him. As noted above, Durkheim pointed out that a priest has a congregation whereas the magician has a clientele. A religious ritual has as its principal function (in sociological terms) the maintenance of a sense of cohesion among the members of the church, whereas the magical rite lacks this function. This view has been influential in the past and has by now become part of general anthropological thinking, although some of its details have been rejected by recent researchers.

Distinctive functions of magic and religion

The third consideration is that of the function of magic and of other religious activities. The magician may see the overt function of his action as instrumental, as geared to a specific end; the external observer may accept this but also see a latent function. Malinowski, for example, maintained that much of Trobriand magic was performed as an extension of human ability, as a power beyond the normal or understood. It had as its most important function the instillation of confidence in situations where human knowledge and competence cease. In addition, the rite helps to throw the importance of a given activity and the cooperation needed for it into relief and thus helps maintain the high social value of cooperation in a small community beset by disruptive jealousies and competition over scarce and difficult resources. A.R. Radcliffe-Brown (1881–1955) pointed out in his work on the Andaman Islanders that their magical rites and precautions at childbirth and death may comfort those concerned, although they are also irksome, but that their main function is to highlight the social importance of birth and death and to bring to public notice the changes in patterns of local and kinship organization that follow them. Some of the hypotheses of Malinowski and Radcliffe-Brown are today regarded as questionable, but they have influenced subsequent studies in that they were concerned not only with the individual's belief in magic but also with the function of magic in the total social system.

In brief, it may be said that religious rites are ways of acting out beliefs about the relationships of man to God, man to man, and man to nature. In contrast, magic is a way of achieving certain ends beyond the knowledge and competence of ordinary people, especially in technologically limited societies, and of expressing their desires symbolically. Certain functions are common to both: the provision of explanation for the otherwise inexplicable; a means of coping with the unusual and mysterious; the enhancement of the social values of certain activities and situations and the coordination of socially valuable activities.

Magic, technology, and science. The problem of the relationship of magic to technical and scientific knowledge has concerned most writers on the subject. Magical rites have at least superficial similarities to nonmagical technical activities. In each the actor performs an action that he expects will have a certain consequence. The distinction between the two processes made by Tylor and Frazer (see below) was that the magician assumes a direct cause-effect relationship between the action and the subsequent event, whereas in empirical fact the relationship is one of the association of ideas only. Many writers have pointed out that magic is used when technical knowledge is missing or uncertain. This is not to say that magic is a substitute for technical knowledge but that its performance gives confidence to people aware of their technical limitations. The magician does not regard his magic as being the same kind of activity as weeding a field or sharpening a knife; the magical rite is of a different order, dealing with external and mystical forces.

To the scientific mind it is puzzling that people continue to believe in magic when it seems clear that there is empirically no cause-effect relationship between a magical rite and the desired consequence. The main purpose of magic, however, is not so much to achieve a certain technical end as to perform an act that has symbolic or psychological value. It is thus pointless to test it, in the same sense that a Christian does not test the efficacy of prayer. The problem was discussed by Tylor, who produced reasons why the failure of magic was not easily apparent to believers. The idiom of magic pervades all in contact with it and cannot be tested scientifically in its own terms, so that tests as to the magic's efficacy are not in fact tests at all but rational statements about commonsense experience.

THE MAIN THEORIES OF MAGIC

There is a voluminous literature on magic. The earliest studies were those of Judaic and Christian scholars concerned with the relationship of magic to their faiths, both as relics of paganism and as heresy. During the latter part of the 19th century, anthropologists entered the field with the aim of analyzing magic and its part in the evolution of the world's religions.

Anthropological. The first important figure in the anthropological consideration of the subject was Tylor, who, in his *Primitive Culture* (1871), regarded magic as a "pseudo-science" in which the "savage" incorrectly postulated a direct cause-effect relationship between the magical act and the desired event. Although Tylor regarded magic as "one of the most pernicious delusions that ever vexed mankind," he studied it not as a superstition or heresy but as a phenomenon based on the "symbolic principle of magic," a logical scheme of thought founded on a quite rational process of analogy. He also faced the question of why the believer in magic did not realize its inefficacy. His reasons included the frequent association of magic with empirical behaviour, nature often performing what the magician tries to do; the attribution of failure to the breaking of taboos or to hostile magic forces; the plasticity of the notions of success and failure; and the weight of cultural belief and authority behind the magician. He also realized that magic and religion are parts of a total system of thought; they are not alternatives but complementary, and thus not stages in the evolutionary development of mankind—although he considered that magic and animistic beliefs decreased in the later stages of history.

Frazer's theory In *The Golden Bough* (1890) Frazer refined Tylor's views on magical thought, discussed the relationship of magic to religion and science, and placed them all in a grandiose evolutionary scheme. He accepted Tylor's theory about the false cause-effect relationship between magical and natural events, calling magic a "spurious system of natural law," and analyzed the principles behind the false relationship. According to Frazer the principles were that "like produces like, or that an effect resembles its cause" (the Law of Similarity) and that things once in physical contact with each other later continue to act on each other at a distance (the Law of Contact or Contagion). Magic based on the former he called homeopathic magic, that based on the latter he called contagious magic. He added the notion of taboo as negative magic, acting on the same principles of association.

Frazer also developed an evolutionary scheme for magic and religion. He saw magic and religion as belonging to different stages in the development of human thought. Magic was prior because it seemed to him to be logically more simple, because he assumed (erroneously, as was shown later) that the Australian Aborigines, examples of an archaic people, believed in magic but not in religion, and because magic forms a substratum of superstition even in advanced societies. According to Frazer, individuals in the earliest cultures must have come to realize the inefficacy of magic and the powerlessness of men to control nature; from this they postulated the existence of omnipotent spiritual beings who required supplication in order to direct nature as men wanted. Thus there came into existence religion. The final stage in this schema began with the recognition of the existence of empirical natural laws, aided by the discoveries of alchemy and then of science proper. With this final development religion joined magic as superstition.

These writers, and their followers such as R. Ranulph Marett (1866–1943), regarded magic as essentially an individual and intellectual matter, one of the ways in which individuals think about the world. Another line of writers widened the discussion by regarding the problem as essentially one of the social function of magic. The first such writers of note were the French sociologists Marcel Mauss (1872–1950) and Émile Durkheim. Durkheim, in *The Elementary Forms of the Religious Life* (Eng. trans. 1915), considered that magical rites comprised the manipulation of sacred objects by the magician on behalf of individual clients; the socially cohesive significance of religious rites proper, by the priests, was therefore largely lacking. His views were followed by Radcliffe-Brown (*The Andaman Islanders*, 1922) and to a lesser extent by Malinowski (*Arg-*

Theories of Malinowski, Radcliffe-Brown, and Evans-Pritchard *onauts of the Western Pacific*, 1922, and various papers brought together as *Magic, Science and Religion*, 1925), the latter influenced more by Frazer and the early psychoanalysts. Radcliffe-Brown's main hypothesis has been mentioned above: the social function of magic was to express the social importance of the desired or protected event. Malinowski, on the other hand, regarded magic as being opposed to religion, and as directly and essentially concerned with the psychological needs of the individual. It acted to extend his normal knowledge and competence; to provide confidence in situations of technical uncertainty by "ritualizing optimism"; to express desires that are otherwise unrealizable in a small and technically limited community; and, as counter-magic, to explain failure. Ma-

linowski's influence has been marked, due largely to the fact that his was the first detailed and firsthand account of the actual working of an ongoing system of magic. Other writers, notably Marett in England and Robert Lowie and Alexander Goldenweiser in the United States, differed from Tylor and Frazer in voicing the opinion that the distinction between magic and religion reflects an ethnocentric distinction between the "natural" and the "supernatural" that is largely untenable.

More recently there have been many reports of the working of systems of magic, especially from Africa and Oceania. On the whole they have followed Malinowski and Radcliffe-Brown and have been based on the single most important work on the topic that has appeared since theirs, *Witchcraft, Oracles and Magic Among the Azande* (1937), by Sir Edward Evans-Pritchard (1902–73). Evans-Pritchard shows concisely how magic is an integral part of religion and culture, being used to explain events the normal understanding and control of which are beyond the technical competence of this southern Sudan people. The Azande accept magic, together with witchcraft and oracles, as a normal part of nature and society. These various phenomena form a closed logical system, each part of which buttresses the other and provides a rational system of causation for both natural order and social order as well as for disorder or coincidence.

Psychological. These various anthropological approaches to magic have had the advantage of regarding it as a social phenomenon rather than one of individual psychology. The views of Tylor and Frazer, however, are ultimately psychological, since they are based on their notions of individual ways of thought. Their work was based to a considerable extent on that of Herbert Spencer and Wilhelm Wundt and was followed by anthropologists with views on the psychological origins of magic and religion, such as Lowie, Paul Radin, and Goldenweiser, all of whom were concerned with the problem of the individual psychological status of believers. Much of Malinowski's work depends on providing psychological reasons for belief in magic. Sigmund Freud (*Totem and Taboo*, 1918) had at one time considerable influence with his view that magic, the earliest phase in the development of religious thought (following Frazer), was similar in its essential processes to the thought of children and neurotics. This view was based on his theory of the "Omnipotence of Thought," by which savages, children, and neurotics all assumed that wish or intention led automatically to the fulfillment of the desired end. This view has long been abandoned, due not so much to its inherent misunderstanding of the expressive nature of magical ritual as to the general recognition that the assumption of the similarity between primitive, infantile, and neurotic modes of thought is false; it arose largely from the ignorance about primitive culture that prevailed before the development of modern anthropological field researches.

Conclusion. The study of magic as a distinct cultural phenomenon has a long history in anthropological and historical studies. Although some distinctions between it and other religious activities may often be useful, it cannot be studied in isolation as was once the fashion. It is essentially an aspect or reflection of the worldview held by a particular people at a particular stage of development in scientific and technical knowledge. It is thus a part, although to the people concerned often a very important part, of their total system of religion and cosmology.

(J.F.M./R.A.Gi.)

Witchcraft

The term witchcraft commonly has referred to the supposed use of supernatural means for harmful or evil ends. In traditional and popular English usage it is practically synonymous with sorcery. Many anthropologists, however, distinguish between witchcraft, as involving an inherent mysterious power of certain weird, aberrant individuals, and sorcery, as the work of ordinary persons using deliberate techniques and external means familiar to other adult members of the community. Practitioners of both types aim to do harm to others, but, while the witch appears to **Witchcraft and sorcery** move through an obscure compulsion or spirit possession, the sorcerer seems to be moved by simple ill will. Although this distinction was originally discerned among the Azande people of Central Africa, it has been found applicable to many other tribal peoples in nonliterate cultures and also to some early modern European societies. On the other hand, students of such phenomena in Oceania use the term sorcery for all forms of destructive magic, whether for socially approved purposes (*e.g.,* to protect property) or not. To add to the complexity of terms and meanings, in some societies (*e.g.,* in medieval Europe) witches were believed occasionally to pursue beneficial aims, such as healing the sick—so-called white witchcraft.

In any case, belief in witchcraft, in its anthropological sense, has been widely distributed in human society. Records of such beliefs go back to the dawn of history and, if certain interpretations of rock paintings and other archaeological evidence are accepted, probably to the prehistoric period as well. Nevertheless, there are some peoples (*e.g.,* the Kalahari San and Andaman Islanders) among whom a belief in witchcraft does not exist; others (*e.g.,* the Javanese) believe in sorcery but not witchcraft in the technical sense above; and still others (*e.g.,* in Arab-Muslim cultures) believe in the Evil Eye, but do not believe in witchcraft.

NATURE AND SIGNIFICANCE

Witchcraft and magic. The term magic, as treated above, refers to human actions that are believed to influence human or natural events through supernatural power. For anthropologists it is a neutral term, though the actions involved may be classified as productive, protective, or destructive. Sorcery belongs to the category of destructive magic but does not encompass all of it, since certain socially approved forms of destructive magic (*e.g.,* to protect property or to prevent adultery) are not considered sorcery. Sorcery is destructive magic that is regarded as antisocial and illicit, the resort of misguided persons who should instead have used arbitration or litigation for settling the issues that have aroused their anger, envy, or malice. Thus, the practice of sorcery is destructive magic illicitly applied.

All magic, whether productive, protective, or destructive, licit or illicit, has four recurring elements: performance of rituals or prescribed formal symbolic gestures, use of material substances and objects that have symbolic significance, utterance of a closely prescribed spell or of a less formal address, and a prescribed condition of the performer (see above *Magic*).

Magic and witchcraft need to be considered together. Sorcery, the illicit form of destructive magic, is closely akin to witchcraft in the special sense, since the same moral status is accorded those who are believed to practice or to be involved in it. Beliefs in both sorcery and witchcraft involve magical methods of identifying the supposed sorcerer or witch; and it is permissible to apply destructive counter-magic against either sorcerers or witches. Moreover, both beliefs derive from the same worldview, or cosmology, one that has been described as the closed predicament (*i.e.,* one in which any alternatives to traditional beliefs are unthinkable) as opposed to the open one that is considered to prevail in more enlightened modern societies. The third of these similarities has made the study of witchcraft and sorcery relevant to the philosophy of science (see below *A coherent explanatory system*).

Structure and function. Beliefs in witchcraft in the generic sense are conspicuous in most small-scale communities (*e.g.,* in preliterate cultures), where interaction is based upon personal relationships that tend to be lifelong and difficult to break. In such societies belief in witches makes it possible for misfortunes to be explained in terms of disturbed social relationships; and the threat either of being accused of witchcraft or of being attacked by witches may well be a source of social control, making people more circumspect about their conduct toward others. Witches who are blamed for misfortunes, while often near kinsmen and neighbours, are conceived of as inhuman and beyond the pale of decent society. They are, thus, convenient scapegoats who are blamed for events

"Linda Maestra," by Francisco de Goya, showing a young witch being instructed by an experienced hag.
By courtesy of the trustees of the British Museum; photograph, J.R. Freeman & Co. Ltd

otherwise inexplicable in terms of the limited empirical knowledge prevailing in a society with a poorly developed technology—*e.g.,* events such as sudden death or persistent illness or even accidents.

This explanatory function of witchcraft is widespread. So too are some of the details of the witch's supposed habits and techniques, such as operating at night; flying through the air on broomsticks (in Europe) or saucer-shaped winnowing baskets (in Central Africa); employing animal familiars (assistants or agents), such as cats, dogs, and weasels in Europe, dogs and foxes in Japan, or hyenas, owls, and baboons in Africa; stealing or destroying property; and injuring people in a variety of ways, eating them while they are still alive (an African explanation for tropical ulcers), or killing them first and exhuming their corpses for ghoulish feasts.

Beliefs in witchcraft provide the mystical medium in which deep-lying structural conflicts, especially those not susceptible to rational adjustment by social intervention and arbitration, may be expressed and in some measure discharged. The inherent disharmonies in the social system are thus cloaked under an insistence that there is harmony in the values of the society, and the surface disturbances that they cause are attributed to the wickedness of individuals. This is why the witch and sorcerer become the villains of the society's morality plays (as personified vices), the ones to whom the most inhuman crimes and characteristics are attributed. So numerous and so revolting are the practices ascribed to witches that to accuse anyone of witchcraft is a condensed way of charging him with a long list of the foulest crimes—and much the same may be said of sorcery, except that the alleged sorcerer might find some room for defense in the ambiguity as to when the use of destructive magic is legitimate and when it is to be regarded as sorcery.

Because accusations of witchcraft, if they are successful, are devastating attacks on reputation, they punctuate the micropolitical processes relating to many forms of competition for some scarce status, power, resource, or personal affiliation. For example, among the matrilineal Cewa of east central Africa the generally accepted succession rule states that a headman's office should pass to his younger brothers in turn, followed by the eldest son of their eldest sister. In practice, however, the Cewa take personal qualifications into account and would not permit the succession of the rightful heir if his competence as a headman were seriously challenged by a convincing accusation of sorcery. The supposed victim of witchcraft or sorcery may also sometimes be regarded as getting his just deserts if he has, by tactless folly, incurred the wrath of powerful persons in the community.

Because in such belief systems the transgressors of a society's ideals are depicted with dramatic disapproval, witchcraft and sorcery are usually powerful brakes upon

Common details of witches' habits and techniques

social change. In many preliterate societies in modern times it is often those who have progressed economically and educationally who are most obsessed by fears of attack by witches and sorcerers or of accusation of employing witchcraft or sorcery. This is because they find themselves either out of line in social orders that economically at least are equalitarian or with a new-found status that lacks a niche in the traditional hierarchy; and their fears of the consequences of their eccentricity are expressed in beliefs that witches and sorcerers in the community will take their revenge or that they themselves will be accused of advancing their interests through mystical means at the cost of their kinsmen and neighbours.

On the other hand, belief in witchcraft may, under certain circumstances, have the effect of accelerating social change; *e.g.,* by facilitating the rupture of close relationships that have become redundant but are difficult to break off. In such a situation an accusation of witchcraft has the effect of making a public issue out of what started as a private quarrel.

Characteristics of the witch or sorcerer. There is no single description of the witch or the sorcerer that may be taken as an authoritative picture fitting all societies. In most the witch is characteristically depicted as female, but in many either sex may be conceived of as witches. In a single society the sex ratio may vary according to whether the accusations consist of broad, general statements, leading to the impression that most witches are women, or specific explanations of misfortune, which may designate most witches as men, since men are often more socially involved in a small-scale community.

In regard to other characteristics, the stereotype of the witch varies from one society to another. In Europe witches are pictured as thin and gaunt, whereas in Central Africa they are described as fat from eating human flesh, while their eyes may be bloodshot from pursuing in sleeping hours evil practices of which their everyday waking selves may not be aware. Witches' familiars or imps may be conceived of as simply aiding them in their nefarious practices or as personifying their addiction by relentlessly driving them on in their evil ways. In most societies in which belief in them occurs, witches are assumed to be members of the same local community as their accusers and supposed victims. Among the peoples of the Himalayan foothills and the Navajo of the U.S. Southwest, however, witches are believed to attack people outside their own community. This is also commonly reported of sorcerers in Oceania, who, however, may be considered as legitimately employing destructive magic against an outside enemy rather than practicing sorcery in the antisocial sense of the term.

In many societies witches are believed to be slaves of aberration and addiction. Thus considered, they are weird, sometimes tragic, characters in the human drama. Sorcerers, on the other hand, are regarded as ordinary people driven by understandable, even if deplorable, urges, such as malice, envy, or revenge, which are a part of everyone's experience. The propensity to be a witch is usually attributed to heredity or at least is considered constitutional in the sense of having been implanted at an early age through one's mother's milk or, as among the Cewa of east central Africa, through a child's having been magically inoculated by an adult, such as his grandparent, against the skin rash believed to result from eating human flesh, an activity attributed to Cewa witches. Sorcery, on the other hand, usually demands no special personal attributes and is believed to be practiced by anyone who can acquire the necessary magical substances (especially in Africa) or the appropriate magical spells (especially in Oceania).

Occasions of witchcraft. The envisioned relationships between the alleged witch and his believed victim, as well as the observable ones between him and his accuser (who may be the victim himself or a close relative or friend), are conceived of as tense because of the problems of close living or because of competition between them for social honour and prestige. In most instances people are believed to resort to witchcraft when the tension they feel toward those with whom they have quarreled or competed is not subject to arbitration by the society's normal

machinery of tension management, such as courts and similar assemblies.

Although the members of small-scale societies, both contemporary ones described by anthropologists and past ones reconstructed by historians, have tended to attribute a large proportion of their misfortunes to the evil actions of sorcerers and witches in their own communities, this does not necessarily mean that people in such societies are continuously involved in the rituals of sorcery or are frequently preoccupied with the possibility that they are exerting the mysterious, evil influences of witchcraft; nor does it mean that those who believe themselves to be the victims of sorcery or witchcraft are continuously obsessed by fears of them. People seem to learn to live with the threat of witchcraft and sorcery just as members of modern societies learn to live with the threat of automobile or airplane accidents.

A coherent explanatory system. Perhaps the most interesting feature of systems of belief involving witchcraft, sorcery, and divination is the consistency and harmony with which they bring together their constituent elements. This is the main message of the classic study *Witchcraft, Oracles and Magic Among the Azande,* by Sir Edward Evans-Pritchard. The Azande are shown to attribute virtually all their misfortunes to witchcraft and sorcery, and their conceptions of these entirely or largely imagined activities—along with beliefs in the general efficacy of their divinatory techniques—provide them with an explanatory frame of reference. Such a frame of reference removes uncertainties and prescribes steps for the management of tensions, steps that, though to the modern Western mind unrelated to the causes of their misfortunes, are nevertheless of psychological value to the believer and tend to reinforce and harmonize the circular belief system. For example, someone falls ill or has an accident; the poison oracle points to the witch responsible and is confirmed by superior oracles; the alleged witch is induced to withdraw his witchcraft; the patient gets better—as most patients do anyway. If he should not, however, the predictive failure of the oracle is easily explained away by the secondary elaborations that tend to develop as supports to the basic belief in divination; for example, the oracle poison used was of the wrong kind, or stale, or the oracle was upset by someone's use of witchcraft.

Michael Polanyi, a contemporary Hungarian-British philosopher, has analyzed Zande beliefs relating to witchcraft and found them to be characterized by the circularity just illustrated, by what he calls "epicyclical elaboration" (*i.e.,* secondary beliefs that explain away predictive failure), and by what he terms "suppressed nucleation" (*i.e.,* objections to the theory that explains misfortunes in terms of witchcraft are met and explained away one by one, so that they can never cluster into a rival explanatory system that can displace the belief in witchcraft). These three features, circularity, epicyclical elaboration, and suppressed nucleation, Polanyi maintains, are also characteristic—at least in the short run—of modern scientific theories, assuring their maintenance against contradictory experience and data. Another contemporary thinker, Thomas S. Kuhn, contends that scientific paradigms (*i.e.,* prevailing theoretical systems) tend to outlast the observed anomalies that, logically speaking, should destroy them; and that they are abandoned less often by a change of heart on the part of the scientific establishment than by the entry into the field of a new generation of scientists uncommitted to the prevailing paradigm.

Theories of witchcraft. Various theories have been put forward to account for the existence of witch beliefs. Among those advanced to account for their occurrence in early modern Europe is that of Margaret Murray, a British Egyptologist, who considered the witches of western Europe to be the lingering adherents of a once general pagan religion displaced by Christianity. Most contemporary scholars in witchcraft reject this theory as unfounded historically. A more recent theory relating to the so-called European witch mania lasting from the mid-15th to the mid-18th century is that of the British historian Hugh R. Trevor-Roper. He views witchcraft as an outgrowth of the systematic "demonology" that the medieval church constructed out of the scattered folklore of peasant superstitions and that acquired a momentum of its own in the centuries of political and religious strife that transformed Europe from the so-called Dark Ages to the modern period.

Theories of more general applicability include the diffusionist, psychological, and sociological theories of various anthropologists and historians. Diffusionist theories are concerned with accounting for the distribution, either at present or in historical times, of beliefs and practices relating to witchcraft; *e.g.,* viewing Pueblo witch beliefs as an amalgam of Spanish and Indian influences. Psychological theories stem ultimately from Freud's doctrine of the displacement of affect (that emotions repressed in one situation find an outlet in another), as exemplified in the theory of Malinowski, who regarded magic (including sorcery) as institutionalized "substitute activity" resorted to when urges for survival or for revenge are blocked by the inadequacies of technology or (following Clyde K.M. Kluckhohn's development of the theory) are limited by the closeness of social relationships that can be ended only with great difficulty.

Sociological theories of witchcraft stem from Evans-Pritchard's work among the Azande and illuminate two fields, the sociology of knowledge (the social conditions of knowledge and explanation) and the study of the micropolitical processes, already noted above. Although Evans-Pritchard's book was a study in the sociology of knowledge in a particular society, it contained several acute insights into the links between social structure and belief that led other investigators to consider applying them in their studies of other societies. As a result there has emerged a body of theory that takes the relative frequency of accusations or supposed instances of witchcraft or sorcery to be social strain gauges that reveal which roles and relationships in a social system are especially subject to tensions—tensions for which articulation and periodic discharge must be provided if the structure is to survive.

WITCHCRAFT IN HISTORICAL CULTURES

Ancient Middle East and Europe. Belief in magical practices was apparently widespread in the cultures of the ancient Middle East. Magical power to heal sickness and other acts of white witchcraft or sorcery are ascribed to gods, heroes, and men in the extant literature of ancient Mesopotamia, Egypt, and Canaan. There was also a fear of malevolent magic or sorcery, especially in Mesopotamia, and a search for counteraction. According to the biblical record, the ancient Hebrews, as well as their pagan neighbours, were conversant with these practices, fears, and avoidances. It is disputable whether any of the Hebrew terms rendered "witch" or "sorcerer" in various translations refer to witchcraft in the special modern sense. Very often they have to do with mediums and necromancers applying certain techniques of divination. The so-called witch of Endor used by King Saul, according to the story in the First Book of Samuel, is a good example of this; actually the King James Version calls her "a woman that hath a familiar spirit," and the Revised Standard Version, "a medium." On the other hand, a passage in the Book of Ezekiel referring to certain women who, through the use of "magic bands" and veils, control the souls of other persons seems clearly to refer to sorcery. Such women are castigated as vainly going against God and his power. Sorcerers and magicians in general are denounced frequently in the Old Testament as antisocial as well as anti-God, and their offenses are punishable by death. The vehemence and frequency of the denunciations indicate that some such practices were prevalent; the New Testament writers also denounced them as immoral and idolatrous.

In ancient Greece and Rome only magical practices intended to do harm were condemned and punished; beneficent sorcery was approved and even official. It was believed that certain persons could do harm to others in their economic, political, athletic, and amorous endeavours and even cause their death. Such activities were often ascribed to the gods themselves, who, unlike the Judeo-Christian God, were not purely good and were, moreover, subject to the same impulses as human beings (and also to human sorcery). Certain goddesses—*e.g.,* Diana, Selene, or Hecate—were associated with the performance of malevolent magic that took place at night and according to a fixed ritual, with various paraphernalia and spells. A story recounted by Apuleius in *The Golden Ass* (2nd century), probably reflecting popular belief, centres on the alleged tendency of the witches of Thessaly (a region notorious for its witches) to gnaw off bits of a dead man's face and their power to assume various animal forms to carry out their ghoulish purpose.

Among the Germanic peoples, who spread throughout Europe during the decline and fall of the Roman Empire, fear of witches was widespread. Here, too, the gods were sponsors and practitioners of sorcery, as well as subject to its power, while kings practiced and suffered from malevolent magic. Types of witchcraft were assigned to whole social classes or families. As in the Greco-Roman world, such powers were especially attributed to women, and the old-woman witch type that was to become central in later European witch scares was a frequent figure in literature. Similar themes appear in the literature of the ancient Slavic peoples.

Western Christendom. Laws, both civil and ecclesiastical, against witchcraft practices and beliefs were enacted quite early in ancient Spain and Gaul in the early Christian Era. Charlemagne and other Frankish rulers condemned such practices and beliefs as evil and superstitious and passed severe laws against them, involving the death penalty. Church councils and leaders sometimes inveighed against belief in witchcraft as mere superstition and illusion, a contemptible relic of paganism; at other times they declared its practice was an actual evil that must be suppressed.

On the whole, though, with a few notable exceptions, such as Augustine and Thomas Aquinas, the ancient and medieval church attempted to wean its adherents from folk beliefs in witchcraft and magic. This skepticism, maintained by such influential figures as St. Boniface and St. Agobard, was officially embodied in canon law, which was comparatively moderate and lenient in its measures against witches and witchcraft.

Between the 12th and 15th centuries a decisive transformation occurred in the church's attitude. Contact with Arabic culture in the 12th century introduced studies such as alchemy and astrology that evoked a new interest in what has been called "natural magic," which, quite apart from the weapon it provided against heresy, could no longer be dismissed as peasant superstition. It was, however, agitation against heretics that finally caused a change in official church policy. In 1484 two Dominican friars, Heinrich Kraemer and Johann Sprenger, induced Pope Innocent VIII to issue a bull authorizing them to extirpate witchcraft in Germany; and two years later these two men published the *Malleus maleficarum* (*The Witches' Ham-*

Devil and witches trampling a cross, from *Compendium maleficarum*, 1608.

Frontispiece to *The Discovery of Witches*, a pamphlet prepared in 1647 by Matthew Hopkins, English witchfinder, in which he explained his methods. Hopkins is shown with two of the women he accused and the familiars he claimed were theirs. The woman on the left names Sir John Holt, chief justice of England, who did not believe Hopkins' evidence of witchcraft was genuine. In the British Museum.

By courtesy of the trustees of the British Museum; photograph, J.R. Freeman & Co. Ltd.

mer), a work that became the authoritative encyclopaedia of demonology throughout Christendom. It was a synthesis of folk beliefs that had hitherto been manifested in local outbursts of witchfinding. Its authority lasted for nearly three centuries, during the time of the European witch mania.

The demonology that the *Malleus* enshrined became an established and systematized theory attributing witches' powers to their special links with the devil, especially their sexual relationships with him as incubus (embodiment in masculine form) if they were women or as succubus (embodiment in feminine form) if they were men. Though witches in other societies personify evil in general, in European history they became specifically identified as the earthly representatives of the Prince of Evil.

The campaign against the devil's earthly representatives was waged long and unrelentingly. The biblical injunction "You shall not permit a sorceress to live" was observed repeatedly. The fomenting of the witch mania cannot be attributed exclusively to either Roman Catholic or Protestant leaders. Although launched by Roman Catholic evangelists, it was revived and extended by their Protestant counterparts and further cultivated during the Counter-Reformation. Although throughout the centuries of its sway there were skeptics who opposed its fundamental tenets, the mania did not decline until the whole medieval cosmology was displaced by that of the less theocratic and more secular frame of reference of the modern world. A.D.J. Macfarlane, a modern British historian of witchcraft during the Tudor and Stuart eras in England, has used the insights of modern Africanist anthropology to demonstrate the link between the witch mania and the broader social changes in which it was set. This he has done by reviewing more than 1,200 cases gleaned from court records and contemporary pamphlets relating to the English county of Essex in the 120 years following 1560. The most frequent kind of accusation of witchcraft was the one in which someone who had repudiated a neighbour, usually an old woman seeking a favour, subsequently attributed some misfortune befalling him to her anger at being refused and thus to her witchcraft. Macfarlane links

this typical instance with the wider changes taking place from a neighbourly, highly integrated, mutually dependent village society to a more individualistic one of the kind now prevalent. In this general setting, the belief in witchcraft provided a means, though not necessarily one consciously employed, of sundering a close but redundant relationship.

The famous Salem witch trials of 1692 may be regarded as one of the last fitful flares of the witch mania. They have been studied anew by Chadwick Hansen, an American historian, who concluded that witchcraft was practiced in Salem, that it did harm to persons claimed to be victims, and that it posed a real threat to the community. The indiscriminate accusations that resulted in the execution of innocent people were the result of a general public panic in response to the psychosocial situation, not to the exhortations of clerical bigots. This fear sprang from a system of beliefs held by most Westerners at the time and also accounted for the harm done to the "afflicted" persons. Witchcraft worked in Salem because the persons involved believed in it.

The modern, secular world. During the following centuries cultural, social, economic, and technological developments resulted in the modern secular worldview in which belief in witchcraft has no place but instead appears as sheer superstition. Yet modern societies, too, have been beset by mass obsessions that in many respects resemble the witch manias of earlier times; the equivalent of satanic power and evil is sometimes ascribed to political and social deviants who are publicly accused, condemned, and suppressed. Moreover, reports of witchcraft practices and beliefs in the traditional sense still occur today in Western societies.

The term witchcraft is currently applied to two types of phenomena in modern societies, correctly to one but erroneously to the other. The authentic use of the term refers to cases in which persons believed to have harmed others by witchcraft are physically attacked or perhaps even lynched. Such cases usually occur in peasant communities in which old traditions are preserved and in which social mobility is slight; hence they resemble instances of witchcraft in nonliterate societies. In such communities people are living in close association with kinsmen and neighbours and cannot easily escape from the social networks that hold them; consequently, interpersonal tensions build up until the flash point of an accusation is reached.

The incorrect use of the term refers to persons claiming to be witches and reported to belong to covens, who assemble on appropriate calendrical occasions for sabbaths at which they perform rituals according to a tradition that the coven leaders claim descends from earlier witches. This kind of "witchcraft," judging by the way in which its participants freely acknowledge their adherence, seems highly respectable compared with the activities of the despised and hated miscreants of earlier periods in our own society or of contemporary nonliterate or peasant communities. These so-called witches claim to be adherents of an ancient religion, the one to which Christianity is regarded as a counter-religion, and in this way they seek to secure public recognition of their eccentric activities by appealing to the cherished modern value of religious toleration.

These practitioners usually turn out to be entirely sincere but misguided people who have been directly or indirectly influenced by Margaret Murray's article "Witchcraft," published in the 14th edition of *Encyclopædia Britannica* (1929), which put forth in its most popular form her theory that the witches of western Europe were the lingering adherents of a once general pagan religion that has been displaced, though not completely, by Christianity. This highly imaginative but now discredited theory gave a new respectability to witchcraft and, along with the more practical influence of such modern practitioners as Aleister Crowley and Gerald Gardner, contributed to the emergence of self-styled witches that are sometimes featured in the sensationalist press.

WITCHCRAFT IN NONLITERATE SOCIETIES

Knowledge of the nature and functions of witchcraft has probably been advanced most by anthropological studies

Witchcraft today—authentic and inauthentic

of nonliterate societies, as in the classic study by Evans-Pritchard of the Azande, already noted.

In 1831–32 A.C.P. Gamitto, a young Portuguese army officer, on an expedition to the interior of the African continent, made some remarkably full and objective notes on the witch beliefs of the Maravi and Ceŵa peoples on the plateau between the Zambezi River and its tributary, the Luangwa. His notes describe the measures taken against persons who were suspected of witchcraft, such as the administration of the poison ordeal—according to which innocence was believed to result in the vomiting of the poison and guilt was believed to result in its retention with consequent purging or death—and the execution of a witch by burning.

In their monumental works, published at the turn of this century, on the peoples of central Australia, Sir Baldwin Spencer and F.J. Gillen made frequent references to the Aborigines' belief in the power of sorcerers, who, by pointing with a charmed bone or stick, were believed to kill their enemies at a distance. According to the later studies (1937) of W. Lloyd Warner, the Murngin people of northern Australia believe that sorcerers by performing operations on their victims cause them to die later without knowing what has befallen them.

Reo Fortune's study (published in 1932) of Tewara, an island in the western Pacific near Dobu, revealed a small community riven by tension, hostility, and anxiety, one in which misfortunes and failures were constantly attributed to the sorcery of men and the witchcraft of women. To elucidate the tangled social relationships ultimately blamed for their frustrations and disappointments, the Dobuans resort to elaborate forms of divining, including water gazing, crystal gazing, and bending the supposed victim's middle finger and noting whether or not this causes the tip of it to flush.

Clyde Kluckhohn's study of the Navajo, published in 1946, included a systematic examination of the occasions on which Navajo believe witchcraft to be employed, the various forms it is believed to take, and the measures taken to detect and combat it. Kluckhohn interprets Navajo witchcraft as providing a psychological safety valve for the tensions that develop from living in small groups at close quarters with kinsmen with whom one must cooperate in order to survive. He also sees witch beliefs as important instruments of social control in that they check wide divergences from economic and social norms. J.D. and E.J. Krige, working among the Lovedu of South Africa, adopted a psychological approach similar to that of Kluckhohn. Among their conclusions are (1) that "witchcraft and sorcery provide avenues of vicarious achievement to those who, because of their aggressive temperaments or disharmonious conditioning, find it impossible or extremely irksome to conform [to the Lovedu society's ideal] pattern of co-operativeness and reciprocity" and (2) that "witchcraft is a reflection, not of tensions as such, whether open or repressed, but of tensions within the framework of cultural mechanisms for avoiding their being projected as witchcraft."

The study of witchcraft and sorcery as a means of elucidating micropolitical processes is a field to which several anthropologists working in Africa have contributed. Monica Wilson and S.F. Nadel have each made comparative studies of witch beliefs, showing how they are related to the social structures of the societies in which they occur. Clyde Mitchell among the Yao and Victor Turner among the Ndembu, in 1956 and 1957, respectively, have shown how accusations of witchcraft punctuate the periodic crises in the development of the social relationships enmeshing a village community. Max Marwick has shown how accusations of sorcery among the Ceŵa precipitate the periodic divisions of local village communities as they grow in size beyond the limits of administrative convenience and of local resources. Other writers have noted the changes in beliefs accompanying urbanization and similar modern developments. For instance, Clyde Mitchell and Marc Swartz have observed a decline among urban Africans in the tendency to explain misfortunes in terms of witchcraft. They attribute this to the fact that, because in modern towns there is a preponderance of strangers

not linked intimately or emotionally, it is often possible for tensions resulting from the normal frustrations of living to be expressed openly rather than supernaturally and that, when tension between intimate associates develops, it is easier in an urban setting for them to break off their relationship than it would be were they living in a small-scale rural community. These developments observed in African cities since the mid-20th century may well parallel those that finally emancipated the Western world from a universal belief in witchcraft.

Among the numerous accounts that have been published on modern movements in Africa, concerned with the extirpation of witchcraft, Roy Willis' study (1968) of the Kamcape movement among the Fipa of southwestern Tanzania broke new theoretical ground, for it showed that the movement had quasi-revolutionary overtones. The witch beliefs and the community's epidemic reaction to them facilitated a redistribution of power between generations, a kind of change the analysis of which is likely to increase understanding of the politics of developing countries. Willis pointed to the importance in the theory of social change of what he referred to as "proto-institutions," such as anti-witch cults, in which a general discontent with the strains of culture contact takes the form of organized rejection of traditional belief systems.

(M.G.Ma./R.A.Gi.)

BIBLIOGRAPHY

General: RICHARD CAVENDISH (ed.), *Man, Myth, & Magic: The Illustrated Encyclopedia of Mythology, Religion, and the Unknown,* new ed. edited and comp. by YVONNE DEUTCH, 12 vol. (1983), profusely illustrated and generally reliable; JAMES G. FRAZER, *The Golden Bough: A Study in Magic and Religion,* 3rd ed. rev. and enlarged, 12 vol. (1911–15, reprinted 1955), the classic anthropological study; WILLIAM A. LESSA and EVON Z. VOGT (eds.), *Reader in Comparative Religion: An Anthropological Approach,* 4th ed. (1979), a collection of essays, including articles on divination, magic, and witchcraft; JOSEPH NEEDHAM, *Science and Civilisation in China* (1954–), a multi-volume history of science in China, including substantial sections covering astrology and alchemy, with much comparative material relevant to Europe—6 vol. in 14 parts had appeared to 1986; LESLIE SHEPARD (ed.), *Encyclopedia of Occultism & Parapsychology,* 2nd ed., 3 vol. (1984–85); and LYNN THORNDIKE, *A History of Magic and Experimental Science,* 8 vol. (1923–58, reissued from various printings, 1964), a monumental study, concerned with Europe from the period of the Roman Empire to the end of the 17th century.

Hermetism: HERBERT LEVENTHAL, *In the Shadow of the Enlightenment: Occultism and Renaissance Science in Eighteenth Century America* (1976), a detailed study of nonrational thought in colonial North America; A.D. NOCK (ed.) and A.-J. FESTUGIÈRE (trans.), *Corpus Hermeticum,* 4 vol. (1945–54, reprinted 1980); WALTER SCOTT (ed. and trans.), *Hermetica: The Ancient Greek and Latin Writings Which Contain Religious or Philosophic Teachings Ascribed to Hermes Trismegistus,* 4 vol. (1924–36, reissued 1985); WAYNE SHUMAKER, *The Occult Sciences in the Renaissance: A Study in Intellectual Patterns* (1972, reprinted 1979), an analysis of alchemy, astrology, Hermetism, magic, and witchcraft during the Renaissance of the 16th century; ARTHUR EDWARD WAITE, *The Brotherhood of the Rosy Cross: Being Records of the House of the Holy Spirit in Its Inward and Outward History* (1924, reissued 1973), the only satisfactory study of Rosicrucianism to cover both its early and later periods; JAMES WEBB, *The Occult Underground,* rev. ed. (1974), and *The Occult Establishment* (1976, reissued 1981), studies of occultist movements in Europe during the 19th and 20th centuries; EDGAR WIND, *Pagan Mysteries in the Renaissance,* rev. and enlarged ed. (1968, reissued 1980), the influence of Neoplatonic and esoteric thought on the arts of the Renaissance; and FRANCES A. YATES, *Giordano Bruno and the Hermetic Tradition* (1964, reprinted 1979), *The Rosicrucian Enlightenment* (1972, reissued 1978), and *The Occult Philosophy in the Elizabethan Age* (1979, reissued 1983), the most important of the author's studies of the Hermetic-Kabbalist tradition and of its place in 16th- and 17th-century thought in Europe.

Alchemy: JOHN FERGUSON, *Bibliotheca Chemica: A Catalogue of the Alchemical, Chemical and Pharmaceutical Books in the Collection of the Late James Young of Kelly and Durris,* 2nd ed., 2 vol. (1954), the most important bibliography of alchemy, carefully and copiously annotated; ALAN PRITCHARD, *Alchemy: A Bibliography of English-Language Writings* (1980), a comprehensive work, valuable for its listing of secondary material; M. BERTHELOT and CH.-ÉM. RUELLE (eds.), *Collection des anciens alchimistes grecs,* 3 vol. (1887–88, reprinted 1967), the principal source for all studies of Hellenistic alchemy, although its accuracy has often been impugned; TITUS BURCKHARDT, *Alchemy: Science of the Cosmos, Science of the Soul* (1967; originally published in German, 1960); C.A. BURLAND, *The Arts of the Alchemists* (1967), a valuable source for the iconography of alchemy; MIRCEA ELIADE, *The Forge and the Crucible,* 2nd ed. (1978; originally published in French, 1956), a comparison of alchemy with the practices of the primitive metallurgist; RICHARD RUSSELL (trans.), *The Works of Geber* (1678, reprinted 1928; originally published in Latin, 1545), the most famous and important medieval Latin work on alchemy; E.J. HOLMYARD, *Alchemy* (1957, reprinted 1968), a general history; C.G. JUNG, *Psychology and Alchemy,* 2nd rev. ed. (1968, reprinted 1980; originally published in German, 2nd rev. ed., 1952), the classic statement of the psychological interpretation of alchemy; JACK LINDSAY, *The Origins of Alchemy in Graeco-Roman Egypt* (1970), a popular work but with a detailed consideration of occult ideas of the Hellenistic period; ROBERT P. MULTHAUF, *The Origins of Chemistry* (1967), a discussion of Greek, Arabic, and European alchemy, with an extensive bibliography of the sources; PRAPHULLA CHANDRA RAY, *A History of Hindu Chemistry from the Earliest Times to the Middle of the Sixteenth Century, A.D.,* 2 vol. (1902–09), a valuable study not yet replaced; HERBERT SILBERER, *Problems of Mysticism and Its Symbolism* (1917, reprinted 1971 as *Hidden Symbolism of Alchemy and the Occult Arts;* originally published in German, 1914), the earliest psychological interpretation of alchemy, from the standpoint of a Freudian psychoanalyst; NATHAN SIVIN, *Chinese Alchemy: Preliminary Studies* (1968); H.E. STAPLETON, "The Antiquity of Alchemy," *Ambix,* 5(1 and 2):1–43 (October 1953), a discussion of the relationship between Greek and Arabic alchemy; F.S. TAYLOR, "A Survey of Greek Alchemy," *The Journal of Hellenic Studies,* 50:109–139 (1930), an excellent English-language summary of the subject; ARTHUR EDWARD WAITE, *The Secret Tradition in Alchemy: Its Development and Records* (1926, reprinted 1969), the spiritual interpretation of alchemy; and *Ambix* (3 times per year), the journal of the Society for the History of Alchemy and Early Chemistry, and the principal source of new research in the history of alchemy.

Divination: (Astrology): F. LEIGH GARDNER, *A Catalogue Raisonné of Works on the Occult Sciences,* vol. 2, *Astrological Books* (1911), far from comprehensive but useful for European astrology; J.C. HOUZEAU and A. LANCASTER, *Bibliographie générale de l'astronomie,* 2 vol. in 3 (1880–89, reprinted 1964), including in vol. 1 an important listing of some 2,500 works on astrology; DAVID AMAND (EMMANUEL AMAND DE MENDIETA), *Fatalisme et liberté dans l'antiquité greque: recherches sur la survivance de l'argumentation morale antifataliste de Carnéade chez les philosophe grecs et les théologiens chrétiens des quatre premiers siècles* (1945, reprinted 1973), a discussion of the philosophical criticisms of astrology developed in antiquity; AUGUSTE BOUCHÉ-LECLERCQ, *L'Astrologie grecque* (1899, reprinted 1979), the fundamental work on Greek astrology; JEAN-LOUIS BRAU, HELEN WEAVER, and ALLAN EDWARDS, *Larousse Encyclopedia of Astrology* (1980, reissued 1982; originally published in French, 1977), a useful compendium of knowledge about modern astrology; FRANZ CUMONT, *Astrology and Religion Among the Greeks and Romans* (1912, reprinted 1960), a review of the position of astrology in the pagan religions; ROBERT EISLER, *The Royal Art of Astrology* (1946), an excellent critical history; EUGENIO GARIN, *Astrology in the Renaissance: The Zodiac of Life* (1983; originally published in Italian, 1976), the relationship of astrology to other aspects of Hermetism; MICHEL GAUQUELIN, *The Scientific Basis of Astrology: Myth or Reality* (1969; originally published in French, 1964), an attempt to provide a scientific justification for astrology; HILAIRE DE WYNGHENE, *Les Présages astrologiques* (1932), a survey of astrology in ancient Mesopotamia; ELLIC HOWE, *Urania's Children: The Strange World of the Astrologers* (1967), the history of astrology in England and Germany in the 19th and 20th centuries; E.S. KENNEDY and DAVID PINGREE, *The Astrological History of Māshā' allāh* (1971), Arabic text and English translation dealing with Sāsānian astrology and its application to history; HANS LEWY, *Chaldaean Oracles and Theurgy: Mysticism, Magic and Platonism in the Later Roman Empire,* new ed. by MICHEL TARDIEU (1978), the role of astrology in other divinatory practices; CARLO ALFONSO NALLINO, "Astrologia e astronomia presso i Musulmani. 1. Astrologia," in his *Raccolta di scritti editi e inediti,* ed. by MARIA NALLINO, vol. 5, *Astrologia, astronomia, geografia,* pp. 1–41 (1944), the best discussion of astrology in Islam; DAVID PINGREE, *Census of the Exact Sciences in Sanskrit,* 4 vol. (1970–81), a detailed account of Indian astrologers; and G.J. TOOMER (trans.), *Ptolemy's Almagest* (1984), the most important classical astronomical text and the source of all subsequent astrological theory.

(Other forms): WILLIAM BARRETT and THEODORE BESTERMAN, *The Divining Rod: An Experimental and Psychological Investigation* (1926, reissued 1968), a detailed study with an important

bibliography of water divining; WILLIAM BASCOM, *Ifa Divination: Communication Between Gods and Men in West Africa* (1969), a detailed study of West African geomancy; AUGUSTE BOUCHÉ-LECLERCQ, *Histoire de la divination dans l'antiquité,* 4 vol. (1879–82, reprinted 1975), a classic and fundamental work; HENRY CALLAWAY, *The Religious System of the Amazulu* (1870, reissued 1970), with an analysis of their divinatory practices; ANDRÉ CAQUOT and MARCEL LEIBOVICI, *La Divination: études recueillies,* 2 vol. (1968), a comprehensive survey by specialists in many fields; GEORGES DUMÉZIL, *Archaic Roman Religion,* 2 vol. (1970; originally published in French, 1966), with an appendix on the religion of the Etruscans; ROBERT FLACELIÈRE, *Greek Oracles,* 2nd ed. (1976; originally published in French, 1961); WILLIAM A. LESSA, *Chinese Body Divination: Its Forms, Affinities and Functions* (1968); MICHAEL LOEWE and CARMEN BLACKER (eds.), *Divination and Oracles* (1981), nine studies covering the ancient and Oriental worlds; RENÉ DE NEBESKY-WOJKOWITZ, *Oracles and Demons of Tibet: The Cult and Iconography of the Tibetan Protective Deities* (1956, reprinted 1976); VICTOR W. TURNER, *Ndembu Divination: Its Symbolism & Techniques* (1961, reprinted 1969), an ethnographic study; EVON Z. VOGT and RAY HYMAN, *Water Witching, U.S.A.,* 2nd ed. (1979), an ethnographic study of water divining; and HELMUT WILHELM, *Change: Eight Lectures on the I-Ching* (1960, reprinted 1973; originally published in German, 1944), studies of Chinese divination.

Magic: CAMPBELL BONNER, *Studies in Magical Amulets: Chiefly Graeco-Egyptian* (1950), an important source for the study of Greco-Egyptian magic; E.M. BUTLER, *The Myth of the Magus* (1948, reprinted 1979), and *Ritual Magic* (1949, reissued 1986), studies of European magic and its sources; ÉMILE DURKHEIM, *The Elementary Forms of the Religious Life* (1915, reprinted 1976; originally published in French, 1912), the classic statement of the sociological approach to magic; E.E. EVANS-PRITCHARD, *Witchcraft, Oracles and Magic Among the Azande* (1937, reprinted 1968), an essential study of African magic and witchcraft; SIGMUND FREUD, *Totem and Taboo: Some Points of Agreement Between the Mental Lives of Savages and Neurotics* (1950, reissued 1983; originally published in German, 1912–13), the psychoanalytic interpretation of magic; MARCEL MAUSS, *A General Theory of Magic* (1972, reissued 1975; originally published in French, 1902–03), an important early anthropological study; ELIPHAS LÉVI (ALPHONSE LOUIS CONSTANT), *The History of Magic: Including a Clear and Precise Exposition of Its Procedure, Its Rites, and Its Mysteries,* 4th ed. (1948, reprinted 1982; originally published in French, 1860), and *Transcendental Magic: Its Doctrine and Ritual,* rev. ed. (1923, reissued 1984; originally published in French in 2 vol., 1854–56), historically unreliable but important as sources of most of modern occultist theory; JOHN MIDDLETON (ed.), *Magic, Witchcraft, and Curing* (1967, reprinted 1979), a collection of essays; A.R. RADCLIFFE-BROWN, *The Andaman Islanders* (1922); FRANZ STEINER, *Taboo* (1956, reprinted 1967); KEITH THOMAS, *Religion and the Decline of Magic: Studies in Popular Beliefs in Sixteenth and Seventeenth Century England* (1971, reissued 1978), a study based on anthropological theory; R. CAMPBELL THOMPSON, *Semitic Magic: Its Origins and Development* (1908, reprinted 1976), ancient Hebrew and Assyrian magic; JOSHUA TRACHTENBERG, *Jewish Magic and Superstition: A Study in Folk Religion* (1939, reissued 1984), medieval Jewish magic of eastern Europe; BRIAN VICKERS (ed.), *Occult and Scientific Mentalities in the Renaissance* (1984); D.P. WALKER, *Spiritual and Demonic Magic: From Ficino to Campanella* (1958, reprinted 1976), magical theory of the Renaissance; MURRAY WAX and ROSALIE WAX, "The Notion of Magic," *Current Anthropology,* 4(5):495–518 (December 1963); and HUTTON WEBSTER, *Magic: A Sociological Study* (1948, reprinted 1973).

Witchcraft: ROSSELL HOPE ROBBINS, *The Encyclopedia of Witchcraft and Demonology* (1959, reprinted 1984), concerned solely with European and North American witchcraft, with a valuable bibliography, and *Witchcraft: An Introduction to the Literature of Witchcraft* (1978), a bibliographical study based on the major collection at Cornell University Library; JULIO CARO BAROJA, *The World of the Witches* (1964, reprinted 1973; originally published in Spanish, 1961), the history of continental European witchcraft; GEORGE LINCOLN BURR (ed.), *Narratives of the Witchcraft Cases, 1648-1706* (1914, reprinted 1975), documents relating to North American witchcraft, especially the Salem affair; NORMAN COHN, *Europe's Inner Demons: An Enquiry Inspired by the Great Witch-Hunt* (1975, reissued 1977), an original study on a socio-historical basis; J.R. CRAWFORD, *Witchcraft and Sorcery in Rhodesia* (1967), a study based on cases coming before the Rhodesian courts; C. L'ESTRANGE EWEN (comp. and ed.), *Witch Hunting and Witch Trials: The Indictments for Witchcraft from the Records of 1373 Assizes Held for the Home Circuit A.D. 1559-1736* (1929, reprinted 1971), and C. L'ESTRANGE EWEN, *Witchcraft and Demonianism: A Concise Account Derived from Sworn Depositions and Confessions Ob tained in the Courts of England and Wales* (1933, reprinted 1984), pioneering studies of English case records of the 16th and 17th centuries; CLYDE KLUCKHOHN, *Navaho Witchcraft* (1944, reprinted 1962), an important modern anthropological analysis; HENRY CHARLES LEA (comp.) and ARTHUR C. HOWLAND (ed.), *Materials Toward a History of Witchcraft*, 3 vol. (1939, reissued 1957), a valuable documentary source for European witchcraft; ALAN MACFARLANE, *Witchcraft in Tudor and Stuart England: A Regional and Comparative Study* (1970), a most carefully researched study; LUCY MAIR, *Witchcraft* (1969), a popular work, largely of anthropological studies and concentrating on Africa; M.G. MARWICK, *Sorcery in Its Social Setting:*

A Study of the Northern Rhodesia Cewa (1965, reprinted 1970); M.G. WARWICK (ed.), *Witchcraft and Sorcery: Selected Readings*, 2nd ed. (1982), a collection of extracts and papers from ancient to modern times on the sociology of witchcraft and sorcery; EDWARD PETERS, *The Magician, the Witch, and the Law* (1978), evidence for the relationship between magicians and witches; and JEFFREY BURTON RUSSELL, *Witchcraft in the Middle Ages* (1972, reprinted 1984), and *A History of Witchcraft: Sorcerers, Heretics and Pagans* (1980, reprinted 1983), describing the social dynamics of witchcraft from ancient to modern times.

(R.P.M./D.E.P./G.K.P./J.F.M./ M.G.Ma./R.A.Gi.)

Occupational Diseases and Disorders

Occupational diseases and disorders are those associated with a particular occupation or industry. They result from a variety of biological, chemical, physical, and psychological factors that are present in the work environment or are otherwise encountered in the course of employment. Occupational medicine is concerned with the effect of all kinds of work on health and the effect of health on a worker's ability and efficiency.

Occupational diseases are essentially preventable and can be ascribed to faulty working conditions. The control of occupational health hazards decreases the incidence of work-related diseases and accidents and improves the health and morale of the work force, leading to decreased absenteeism and increased worker efficiency. In most cases the moral and economic benefits far outweigh the costs of eliminating occupational hazards.

This article discusses general occupational health hazards and the disorders they cause, as well as the role of occupational health services. More detailed information about specific disorders can be found in the articles dealing with human diseases and the structures of the human body, such as CANCER; INFECTIOUS DISEASES; and RESPIRATION AND RESPIRATORY SYSTEMS.

For coverage of related topics in the *Macropædia* and *Micropædia*, see the *Propædia*, section 424.

The article is divided into the following sections:

HISTORICAL OVERVIEW

The preindustrial era. The first recorded observation of an occupational disease may be a case of severe lead colic suffered by a worker who extracted metals. It is described in the third book of *Epidemics*, attributed to Hippocrates, the Greek physician of the 4th century BC. Other early writers also recognized the association between certain disorders and occupations. The Roman scholar Pliny, in the 1st century AD, described mercury poisoning as a disease of slaves because mines contaminated by mercury vapour were considered too unhealthy for Roman citizens and thus were worked only by slaves. In general, however, physicians of antiquity were not concerned with the health of workers.

During the Middle Ages the rise of metalliferous mining in central Europe inspired the German mineralogist Georgius Agricola to make a detailed study of gold-and silver-mining operations. In his *De Re Metallica*, published posthumously in 1556, Agricola described the primitive methods of ventilation and personal protection in use, common mining accidents and disasters, and such miners' occupational diseases as the "difficulty in breathing and destruction of the lungs" caused by the harmful effects of dust inhalation.

A more comprehensive account of occupational disorders was written by Bernardino Ramazzini, a professor of medicine first at the University of Modena and later at the University of Padua. His *De Morbis Artificum Dia-*

triba (1700; *Diseases of Workers*) contains descriptions of the diseases associated with 54 different occupations, from the mercury poisoning of Venetian mirror makers to the diseases afflicting learned men. Ramazzini believed that a physician must determine the patient's occupation in order to discover the cause of the patient's disorder. He is generally regarded as the father of occupational medicine.

The industrial era. The Industrial Revolution of the 18th century had a profound impact on occupational diseases. Rapid technological progress and industrial growth had led to crowded, unsanitary working and living conditions, with a corresponding rise in the number of accidents and deaths caused by the new machinery and exposure to toxic materials. In 1775 Percivall Pott, a London surgeon, linked the frequent occurrence of scrotal cancer among chimney sweeps to the soot ingrained into their skin by prolonged exposure to flue dusts. Charles Turner Thackrah, a Leeds physician, further advanced the study of occupational medicine in Britain with his *The Effects of the Principal Arts, Trades and Professions . . . on Health and Longevity . . .* (1831), which described lung diseases caused by dust that commonly afflicted miners and metal grinders. In 1895 Britain introduced a statutory notification system that required medical personnel to report all occurrences of certain diseases to the chief inspector of factories. Other industrial nations followed Britain's lead, and legal provisions for the health of the worker continued to be instituted throughout the 19th and 20th centuries.

The father of occupational medicine

The 20th century. Although such classic occupational diseases as lead poisoning and anthrax have declined in incidence in industrialized countries, none have been eradicated. Furthermore, new diseases continue to develop as a result of advances in technology. X rays were discovered in 1895, and 20 years later nearly 100 radiologists were estimated to have died as a result of occupational exposures. Asbestos-related disease was first reported in the first half of the 20th century, and in 1974 hemangiosarcoma, a rare malignant tumour of the liver, was discovered among workers involved in the polymerization of vinyl chloride monomer. Other occupational diseases related to the introduction of industrial processes and materials may well be recognized in the future.

Paralleling the development of new technology and occupational hazards has been the development of occupational health services. No longer concerned primarily with the prevention of industrial accidents and diseases among manual workers, industrial medicine now aims to protect and improve the health of all classes and kinds of workers. In 1950 a joint committee of the International Labour Organisation and the World Health Organization (ILO/WHO) defined the concerns of occupational health as:

The ILO/ WHO definition of occupational health

the promotion and maintenance of the highest degree of physical, mental and social well-being of workers in all occupations; the prevention among workers of departures from health caused by their working conditions; the protection of workers in their employment from risks resulting from factors adverse to health; the placing and maintenance of the worker in an occupational environment adapted to his physiological equipment and, to summarise, the adaptation of work to man and of each man to his job.

In most countries in the West the responsibility for health and safety at work is placed on the employer, although the government may establish safety standards. Occupational health services are provided as benefits by employers and generally are separate from other community health services. In the Soviet Union and other eastern European countries, occupational health and hygiene are given high priority and are fully integrated in the general medical care system. In the developing and Third World countries, many of which are undergoing rapid industrialization, the importance of occupational health is increasingly realized. The problems of exposure to occupational hazards, however, are frequently compounded by preexisting malnutrition and a high incidence of infectious disease. Occupational health services in these countries are often most practical and cost-effective, therefore, when combined with primary health care delivery.

AIMS AND FUNCTIONS OF OCCUPATIONAL HEALTH SERVICES

The primary concerns of occupational health services remain those specified by the ILO/WHO in 1950, although work-related diseases are now considered as well as purely occupational diseases. The actual services offered are essentially preventive in nature and are summarized below.

Job placement. People with certain preexisting medical conditions may be at a disadvantage in some jobs. A pre-employment health questionnaire or medical examination can be of great value in such cases by determining job unsuitability before training time and expense have been incurred. Job suitability may also need to be regularly monitored in order to assure employee health and ability. Airline pilots, for example, undergo regular medical checkups because a pilot with failing vision or one who suffers from an undetected heart condition that can lead to a heart attack could endanger many lives. The health service can also give valuable advice with regard to alternative employment when a worker is found to be unfit for a particular job.

Safety training. An occupational health service has a responsibility to keep all employees informed about hazards in the workplace. The measures taken to protect employee health should be thoroughly explained so that workers understand the necessity of complying with such irksome or unpleasant restrictions as the wearing of protective clothing and face masks. First aid facilities should be organized and employees instructed about first aid procedures in case of accidental injuries or other emergencies.

Supervision of high-risk groups. Exposure levels considered safe for a young male worker may be hazardous for a pregnant woman (the fetus, especially during the first three months of development, is particularly sensitive to environmental toxic agents). Pregnant women, as well as such other vulnerable groups as the very young, the elderly, and the disabled, therefore require appropriate medical surveillance and advice about specific precautionary measures they can take.

Control of recognized hazards. A complex system of environmental and biological monitoring has been developed for the control of known hazards at work. Occupational health practice is concerned with monitoring the concentration of toxic substances in the environment, determining safe exposure levels, suggesting procedures to limit worker exposure, and monitoring workers for signs of overexposure. Occupational health specialists can also contribute to the prevention of health risks by assisting in the planning and design of new equipment and factories.

Identification of unrecognized hazards. Occupational health services can play a major role in the detection of new health hazards of all types. Clinical observation and study may reveal a causal relationship between patterns of sickness or mortality in groups of workers and their occupational exposure. Examples of hazards identified in this manner include lung and nasal cancer among nickel workers, lung cancer in asbestos workers, and coronary heart disease among workers exposed to carbon disulfide (used in the manufacture of rayon).

Treatment. Quick, on-site treatment of work injuries and poisonings can prevent complications and aid recovery. Such treatment can also be economically beneficial by saving traveling and waiting time. Furthermore, physicians and nurses who are unfamiliar with their patients' working conditions may keep workers with minor injuries away from work longer than necessary. An occupational treatment service offers opportunities for specialized counseling and health education.

General health education and surveillance. Occupational health services may have to provide general medical care for workers and their families in developing countries with inadequate community health services. Even when general health care is provided elsewhere, an occupational health service can offer an effective and often economically advantageous program of health education and counseling. By advising employees on such topics as smoking, alcohol or drug abuse, exercise, and diet, the occupational health service can improve worker health and efficiency and reduce illness and absenteeism. The health service is also in a position to organize employee health surveillance programs for the early diagnosis of disease.

DISORDERS DUE TO CHEMICAL AGENTS

Hazardous chemicals can act directly on the skin, resulting in local irritation or an allergic reaction, or they may be absorbed through the skin, ingested, or inhaled. In the workplace ingestion of toxic chemicals is usually accidental and most commonly results from handling contaminated food, drink, or cigarettes. Substances that occur as gases, vapours, aerosols, and dusts are the most difficult to control, and most hazardous chemicals are therefore absorbed through the respiratory tract. If inhaled, airborne contaminants act as irritants to the respiratory tract or as systemic poisons. Toxicity in such cases depends on the contaminant's concentration, particle size, and physicochemical properties, particularly its solubility in body fluids. An individual's reaction to any hazard depends primarily on the length, pattern, and concentration of exposure but is also affected by such factors as age, sex, ethnic group, genetic background, nutritional status, coexistent disease, concomitant exposure to other toxic agents, life-style, and history of previous exposure to the agent in question. The wide range of both naturally occurring and synthetic chemical compounds that can give rise to adverse health effects can be roughly organized into four major categories: gases, metals, organic compounds, and dusts.

Exposure to hazardous chemicals

Gases. Gases may act as local irritants to inflame mucous surfaces. Examples include sulfur dioxide, chlorine, and fluorine, which have pungent odours and can severely irritate the eyes and the respiratory tract. Some gases, such as nitrogen oxides and phosgene, are more insidious. Victims may be unaware of the danger of exposure because the immediate effects of these gases may be mild and overlooked. Several hours after exposure, however, breathlessness and fatal cardiorespiratory failure due to pulmonary edema (collection of fluid in the lungs) may develop.

Asphyxiants

Gases that interfere with oxygen supply to the tissues are known as asphyxiants and are of two principal types. Simple asphyxiants are physiologically inert gases that act by diluting atmospheric oxygen. If the concentration of such gases is high enough, hypoxia (deficiency of oxygen reaching the tissues of the body) results. Victims of mild hypoxia may appear to be intoxicated and may even resist rescue attempts. Common examples of simple asphyxiants are methane and carbon dioxide.

In contrast to simple asphyxiants, chemical asphyxiants, such as carbon monoxide and hydrogen sulfide, are highly reactive. They cause a chemical action that either prevents the blood from transporting oxygen to the tissues or interferes with oxygenation in the tissues. For example, carbon monoxide, a frequently encountered gas produced by incomplete combustion, combines with hemoglobin in the blood and reduces its oxygen-carrying capacity. In low concentration carbon monoxide poisoning can cause symptoms of fatigue, headache, nausea, and vomiting, but heavy exposure leads to coma and death. It is especially dangerous because it is both colourless and odourless. Hydrogen sulfide, however, can be recognized by its characteristic smell, suggestive of rotten eggs. It is produced when sulfur compounds decompose and acts by inhibiting the respiratory enzyme cytochrome oxidase, thus giving rise to severe tissue hypoxia. In addition to its asphyxiant properties, hydrogen sulfide also acts as an irritant to the eyes and mucous membranes.

Preventing gas poisoning involves preventing exposure. Workers should never enter enclosed spaces that have suspect atmospheres alone; workplaces should provide adequate ventilation, and air should be regularly tested for contamination. If exposure does occur, treatment involves the removal of the victim from the contaminated atmosphere, artificial respiration, and administration of oxygen or recommended antidotes. Victims exposed to gases with insidious delayed effects should be kept under medical observation for an appropriate period.

Metals. Metals and their compounds are among the poisons most commonly encountered in the home and workplace. Even metals essential for life can be toxic if they are present in excessive amounts. Iron, for example, is an essential element and is sometimes given therapeutically; if taken in overdose, however, it can be lethal.

Mercury poisoning

Mercury poisoning, one of the classic occupational diseases, is a representative example of metal poisoning. Exposure to mercury can occur in many situations, including the manufacture of thermometers, explosives, fungicides, drugs, paints, batteries, and various electrical products. The disorders it can cause vary depending on the type of mercury compound and the method of exposure.

Ingestion of mercury salts such as mercuric chloride (corrosive sublimate) leads to nausea, vomiting, and bloody diarrhea. Kidney damage resulting in death may follow in extreme cases. Inhalation or absorption through the skin of mercury vapour causes salivation, loosening of the teeth, and tremor; it also affects the higher centres of the brain, resulting in irritability, loss of memory, depression, withdrawal, anxiety, and other personality changes. This mental deterioration, known as erethism, led to the well-known saying "mad as a hatter," because, in the past, hatters commonly became ill when they used mercury salts to make felt out of rabbit fur. Poisoning with organic mercury compounds (used in fungicides and pesticides) results in severe, permanent neurological damage and can be fatal.

Other hazardous metals commonly encountered in industry include arsenic, beryllium, cadmium, chromium, lead, manganese, nickel, and thallium. Some have been shown to be carcinogenic, including certain compounds of nickel (linked to lung and nasal cancer), chromium (lung cancer), and arsenic (lung and skin cancer).

Organic compounds. The organic compounds that pose the greatest occupational hazards are various aromatic, aliphatic, and halogenated hydrocarbons and the organophosphates, carbamates, organochlorine compounds, and bipyridylium compounds used as pesticides.

Pesticides

Pesticides are used the world over; and, even though precautionary measures (such as using protective clothing and respirators, monitoring contamination of equipment and clothing, keeping workers out of recently sprayed areas, and requiring workers to wash thoroughly after exposure) can be instituted, poisoning not infrequently occurs in agricultural communities. The organophosphates and the generally less toxic carbamates exert their effects by inhibiting cholinesterase, an enzyme that prevents stimulation from becoming too intense or prolonged by destroying the acetylcholine involved in the transmission of impulses in the autonomic nervous system. Cholinesterase inhibitors allow the accumulation of acetylcholine, causing symptoms related to parasympathetic overactivity, such as chest tightness, wheezing, blurring of vision, vomiting, diarrhea, abdominal pain, and in severe cases respiratory paralysis. Atropine and certain oximes counteract their effects.

Paraquat and diquat, the bipyridylium compounds, are deadly if ingested. Skin contact or inhalation of a concentrate of paraquat can cause fatal lung damage. Because no specific antidote is known, treatment consists of minimizing the body's absorption of the poison.

The organochlorine compounds, such as DDT, are being progressively phased out of use. Because they are fat-soluble and very stable, they accumulate and remain in the fatty tissues of the body for prolonged periods. Symptoms of poisoning include nausea, irritability, weakness, muscle tremors, and convulsions. There is no specific antidote.

Other groups of pesticides that are used less frequently or are less hazardous include the organomercury compounds (see above *Metals*); the dinitro and arsenic compounds; and nicotine.

Hydrocarbons

Hydrocarbons are used industrially in the derivation of other compounds and in solvents, degreasing agents, refrigerants, fire extinguishers, dry cleaning agents, paint removers, and other products. Many are volatile and can be absorbed by inhalation; some are fat-soluble and can be readily absorbed following spills on the skin.

Gasoline, fuel oils, and other petroleum products are common examples of aliphatic hydrocarbons. If they are ingested or inhaled, dizziness, weakness, nausea, or irritation of the lungs may follow. In very severe cases victims may become unconscious or experience convulsions. Direct contact causes skin irritation and dryness. Prolonged exposure to certain petroleum oils may result in skin cancer.

The aromatic hydrocarbon benzene provides the basis for the synthesis of many other organic compounds. It is rapidly absorbed following inhalation or skin contact. Symptoms from mild exposure include dizziness, headache, euphoria, confusion, and nausea. Long-term exposure may be followed by bone marrow depression, anemia, spontaneous bleeding, and leukemia. Several aromatic hydrocarbons are known to be carcinogens. Particularly hazardous are naphthylamine, benzidine, and 4-amino diphenyl, which cause bladder cancer. Previously used in the synthetic dye, synthetic rubber, cable-making, and chemical industries, they have been banned in a number of countries.

When aliphatic and aromatic hydrocarbons have hydrogen atoms in their structure replaced by halogens (often chlorine), they are known as halogenated hydrocarbons. In general, increasing the chlorination of aliphatic hydrocarbons increases their toxicity, while the reverse is true of the aromatic series. Many chlorinated hydrocarbons, including chloroform and trichloroethylene, act as depressants on the central nervous system, producing anesthetic or narcotic effects that may be abused. Occupational exposure to many solvents may act synergistically with alcohol, resulting in more damage than either agent could produce on its own. Some halogenated hydrocarbons cause extensive disorders in addition to their common narcotic effect. Inhaling or ingesting the solvent carbon tetrachloride, for example, leads to liver damage; and exposure to vinyl chloride causes Raynaud's phenomenon (spasms in the small arteries that cause the extremities to become pale and cold, as well as painful), necrosis of the small bones of the hand, liver damage, and a rare, highly malignant tumour of the liver.

Workers exposed to hydrocarbons should wear protective clothing or masks when appropriate, moderate alcohol consumption, and verify that work areas are well ventilated and that recommended exposure levels are not exceeded.

Dusts. The inhalation of a variety of dusts is responsible for a number of lung and respiratory disorders, whose symptoms and severity depend on the composition and size of the dust particle, the amount of dust inhaled, and the length of exposure. The lung diseases known as the pneumoconioses result when certain inhaled mineral dusts are deposited in the lungs, where they cause a chronic fibrotic reaction that leads to decreasing capacity for exercise and increasing breathlessness, cough, and respiratory difficulty. No specific treatment is known, but as with all respiratory disorders patients are urged to quit smoking, which aggravates the condition. Suggested measures for limiting exposure include using water and exhaust ventilation to lower dust levels and requiring workers to wear respirators or protective clothing, but such procedures are not always feasible. Coal worker's pneumoconiosis, silicosis, and asbestosis are the most common pneumoconioses.

As its name suggests, coal worker's pneumoconiosis (also known as black lung) occurs most frequently among coal miners and workers involved in the transporting or processing of coal. It is generally benign in its early stages, but after a variable number of years of exposure to coal dust, progressive massive fibrosis may develop, ending in cardiorespiratory failure. Miners and quarry workers are the people most likely to suffer from silicosis. Because silica is found in many rocks and is used in a variety of industries, workers involved in stonecutting, grinding, drilling, foundry work, sandblasting, pottery making, and the manufacture of abrasives are also at risk. Silicosis is an aggressive form of pulmonary fibrosis that speeds the progress of tuberculosis. Routine chest X rays can aid early diagnosis by revealing abnormal shadowing. Asbestosis is more difficult to detect in the early stages because chest X rays usually reveal little until the disease is advanced. From onset asbestosis progresses more rapidly than the other pneumoconioses and can result from relatively low exposure. Asbestos is the general term for a number of fibrous silicates that are used primarily in various fireproofing, insulation, and cement products. In addition to pulmonary fibrosis, inhaling asbestos fibres has also been shown to cause lung and other cancers.

Prolonged exposure to certain plant and animal dusts can cause asthma, even in people without a predisposition for allergies. Specific hazards include dusts from flour, grains, and wood and wood products. Cotton workers and others handling hemp or flax may develop a condition known as byssinosis, similar to asthma. The group of diseases known as farmer's lung, malt worker's lung, bird fancier's lung, and so forth are caused by an allergic inflammatory reaction to the fungal spores present in moldy hay or barley, bird droppings, feathers, and a variety of other organic materials. Symptoms initially resemble those of influenza or pneumonia, but repeated episodes eventually lead to pulmonary fibrosis with chronic respiratory impairment. The only treatment for these disorders is avoiding exposure to the dusts.

DISORDERS DUE TO PHYSICAL AGENTS

Temperature. When working in a hot environment, humans maintain normal body temperature by perspiring and by increasing the blood flow to the surface of the body. The large amounts of water and salt lost in perspiration then need to be replaced. In the past, miners who perspired profusely and drank water to relieve their thirst experienced intense muscular pain—a condition known as miner's cramps—as a result of restoring their water but not their salt balance. When salt in the requisite amount was added to their drinks, workers no longer developed miner's cramps. Heat exhaustion is characterized by thirst, fatigue, giddiness, and often muscle cramps; fainting can

also occur. Heatstroke, a more serious and sometimes lethal condition, results when prolonged exposure to heat and high humidity prevents efficient perspiration (by preventing evaporation of sweat), causing the body temperature to rise above 106° F (41° C) and the skin to feel hot and dry. If victims are not quickly cooled down, coma, convulsions, and death can follow. To prevent heat exhaustion or heatstroke, workers unaccustomed to high temperatures should allow adequate time (ranging from days to weeks) for their bodies to become acclimatized before performing strenuous physical tasks.

Work in cold environments may also have serious adverse effects. Tissue damage that does not involve freezing can cause inflammatory swelling known as chilblains. Frostbite, or the freezing of tissue, can lead to gangrene and the loss of fingers or toes. If exposure is prolonged and conditions (such as wet or tight clothing) encourage heat loss, hypothermia, a critical fall in body temperature, may result. When body temperature falls below 95° F (35° C), physiological processes are slowed, consciousness is impaired, and coma, cardiorespiratory failure, and death may ensue. Workers exposed to extreme cold require carefully designed protective clothing to minimize heat loss, even though a degree of acclimatization occurs with time.

Atmospheric pressure. Decompression sickness (caisson disease) can result from exposure to high or low atmospheric pressure. Under increased atmospheric pressure (such as that experienced by deep-sea divers or tunnel workers), fat-soluble nitrogen gas dissolves in the body fluids and tissues. During decompression the gas comes out of solution and, if decompression is rapid, forms bubbles in the tissues. These bubbles cause pains in the limbs (known as the bends), breathlessness, angina, headache, dizziness, collapse, coma, and in some cases death. Similarly, the gases in solution in the body tissues under normal atmospheric pressure form bubbles when pressure rapidly decreases, as when aviators in unpressurized aircraft ascend to high altitudes too quickly. Emergency treatment of decompression sickness consists of rapid recompression in a compression chamber with gradual subsequent decompression. The condition can be prevented by allowing sufficient decompression time for the excess nitrogen gas to be expelled naturally.

Noise. Exposure to excessive noise can be unpleasant and can impair working efficiency. Temporary or permanent hearing loss may also occur, depending on the loudness or intensity of the noise, its pitch or frequency, the length and pattern of exposure, and the vulnerability of the individual. Prolonged exposure to sound energy of intensity above 80 to 90 decibels is likely to result in noise-induced hearing loss, developing first for high frequencies and progressing downward. The condition can be prevented by enclosing noisy machinery and by providing effective ear protection. Routine audiometry gives an indication of the effectiveness of preventive measures.

Vibration. Whole-body vibration is experienced in surface and air transport, with motion sickness its most familiar effect. A more serious disorder, known as Raynaud's syndrome or vibration white finger (VWF), can result from the extensive use of vibratory hand tools, especially in cold weather. The condition is seen most frequently among workers who handle chain saws, grinders, pneumatic drills, hammers, and chisels. Forestry workers in cold climates are particularly at risk. Initial signs of VWF are tingling and numbness of the fingers, followed by intermittent blanching; redness and pain occur in the recovery stage. In a minority of cases the tissues, bones, and joints affected by the vibration may develop abnormalities; even gangrene may develop. VWF can be prevented by using properly designed tools, avoiding prolonged use of vibrating tools, and keeping the hands warm in cold weather.

Other mechanical stresses. Muscle cramps often afflict workers engaged in heavy manual labour as well as typists, pianists, and others who frequently use rapid, repetitive movements of the hand or forearm. Tenosynovitis, a condition in which the sheath enclosing a tendon to the wrist or to one of the fingers becomes inflamed, causing pain and temporary disability, can also result from prolonged repetitive movement. When the movement involves the

Pneumoconioses

Asthma

Decompression sickness

rotation of the forearm, the extensor tendon attached to the point of the elbow becomes inflamed, a condition commonly known as tennis elbow.

Ionizing radiation. Ionizing radiation damages or destroys body tissues by breaking down the molecules in the tissues into positively or negatively charged particles called ions. Radiation that is capable of causing ionization may be electromagnetic (X rays and gamma rays) or particulate (radiation of electrons, protons, neutrons, alpha particles, and other subatomic particles) and has many uses in industry, medicine, and scientific research.

Ionizing radiation injury is in general dose-dependent. Whole-body exposure to doses in excess of 1,000 rads results in acute radiation syndrome and is usually fatal. Doses in excess of 3,000 rads produce cerebral edema (brain swelling) within a matter of minutes, and death within days. Lesser doses cause acute gastrointestinal symptoms, such as severe vomiting and diarrhea, followed by a week or so of apparent well-being before the development of the third toxic phase, which is characterized by fever, further gastrointestinal symptoms, ulceration of the mouth and throat, hemorrhages, and hair loss. There is an immediate drop in the white-cell elements of the blood, affecting the lymphocytes first and then the granulocytes and platelets, with a slower decline in the red cells. If death does not occur, these symptoms may last for many months before slow recovery begins.

Carcino-genic effects of exposure to radiation

Delayed effects of exposure to radiation include the development of leukemia and other cancers. Examples include the skin cancers that killed many of the pioneering scientists who worked with X rays and radioactive elements; the lung cancer common among miners of radioactive ores; and the bone cancer and aplastic anemia that women who painted clock dials with a luminous mixture containing radium and mesothorium developed as a result of ingesting small amounts of paint when they licked their paintbrushes to form a point.

Nonionizing radiation. Nonionizing forms of radiation include electromagnetic radiation in the radio frequency, infrared, visible light, and ultraviolet ranges. Exposure to radiation in the radio frequency range occurs in the telecommunications industry and in the use of microwaves. Microwaves produce localized heating of tissues that may be intense and dangerous. Various other disorders, mainly of a subjective nature, have been reported in workers exposed to this frequency range. Infrared radiation can be felt as heat and is commonly used in industry in drying or baking processes. Prolonged exposure to the radiation can result in severe damage to the skin and especially to the lens of the eye, where cataracts may be produced. Working under poor lighting conditions can adversely affect worker efficiency and well-being and may even cause temporary physical disorders, such as headache or dizziness. Proper lighting should provide adequate, uniform illumination and appropriate contrast and colour, without any flickering or glare. Exposure to ultraviolet radiation from the Sun or such industrial operations as welding or glassblowing causes erythema of the skin (a condition familiarly known as sunburn), skin cancer, and inflammation of the conjunctiva and cornea. Pigmentation offers natural protection against sunburn, and clothing and glass can also be used as effective shields against ultraviolet radiation. Lasers emit intense infrared, visible, or ultraviolet radiation of a single frequency that is used in surgery, for scientific research, and for cutting, welding, and drilling in industry. Exposure to these beams can burn the skin and cause severe damage to the eye.

DISORDERS DUE TO INFECTIOUS AGENTS

A large number of infectious diseases are transmitted to humans by animals. Many such diseases have been largely eliminated, but some still pose hazards. Anthrax, for example, can be acquired by workers handling the unsterilized hair, hide, and bone of infected animals; and slaughterhouse workers, farmers, veterinarians, and others in contact with infected animals, milk, and milk products still frequently contract brucellosis.

Contact with contaminated water is another common method of acquiring infectious diseases. Many workers are infected by organisms that thrive in the puddles or stagnant water found in sewers, canals, paddies, slaughterhouses, irrigation projects, and mines.

Laboratory workers, nurses, surgeons, and other health care workers may contract infectious diseases such as tuberculosis in the course of their work. To help prevent infection, these workers should wear appropriate protective clothing and exercise care when handling contaminated needles or other equipment. Contaminated material should be appropriately bagged, labeled, and disposed.

DISORDERS DUE TO PSYCHOLOGICAL FACTORS

Psychological factors are important determinants of worker health and well-being. Studies have shown that workers who feel satisfied and stimulated by their jobs, who maintain good relationships with their employers or supervisors and with other employees, and who do not feel overworked have lower rates of absenteeism and job turnover and higher rates of output than average.

Bore-dom and mental stress

The two psychological hazards commonly encountered at work are boredom and mental stress. Workers who perform simple, repetitive tasks for prolonged periods are subject to boredom, as are people who work in bland, colourless environments. Boredom can cause frustration, unhappiness, inattentiveness, and other detriments to mental well-being. More practically, boredom decreases worker output and increases the chances of error and accident. Providing refreshment and relaxation breaks or other outside stimulus can help relieve boredom.

Mental stress often results from overwork, although nonoccupational factors, such as personal relationships, life-style, and state of physical health, can play a major role. Job dissatisfaction, increased responsibility, disinterest, competition, feelings of inadequacy, and bad working relationships can also contribute to mental stress. Stress affects both mental and physical health, causing anger, irritation, fatigue, aches, nausea, ulcers, migraine, asthma, colitis, or even breakdown and coronary heart disease. Moderate exercise, meditation, relaxation, and therapy can help workers to cope with stress.

BIBLIOGRAPHY. GEORG AGRICOLA, *Georgius Agricola De Re Metallica,* translated by HERBERT CLARK HOOVER and LOU HENRY HOOVER (1912, reprinted 1950; originally published in Latin, 1556), an illustrated 16th-century study of working conditions in the mines of central Europe; BERNARDINO RAMAZZINI, *Diseases of Workers,* translated and revised by WILMER CAVE WRIGHT (1940, reprinted 1983; originally published in Latin, rev. ed., 1713), a classic; H.E. SIGERIST, "Historical Background to Industrial and Occupational Diseases," *Bulletin of the New York Academy of Medicine,* 12:597–609 (November 1936), a brief account of the recognition of occupational disease; DONALD HUNTER, *The Diseases of Occupations,* 6th ed. (1978), a historical overview of occupational medicine; R.S.F. SCHILLING (ed.), *Occupational Health Practice,* 2nd ed. (1981), a detailed account of industrial hygiene and disease prevention practices; and LUIGI PARMEGGIANI (ed.), *Encyclopaedia of Occupational Health and Safety,* 3rd rev. ed. (1983), a comprehensive reference source prepared under the auspices of the International Labour Organisation. Other comprehensive works include MARCUS M. KEY *et al.* (eds.), *Occupational Diseases: A Guide to Their Recognition,* rev. ed. (1977); LINDA ROSENSTOCK and MARK R. CULLEN, *Clinical Occupational Medicine* (1986); and JOHN C. BARTONE, *Occupational Diseases: International Survey with Medical Subject Directory and Bibliography* (1983).

Specific problems are studied in G. KAZANTZIS and L.J. LILLY, "Mutagenic and Carcinogenic Effects of Metals," in vol. 1 of LARS FRIBERG, GUNNAR F. NORDBERG, and VELIMIR B. VOUK (eds.), *Handbook on the Toxicology of Metals,* 2nd ed., 2 vol. (1986); W. KEITH C. MORGAN and ANTHONY SEATON, *Occupational Lung Diseases,* 2nd ed. (1984); DAVID F. GOLDSMITH, DEBORAH M. WINN, and CARL M. SHY (ed.), *Silica, Silicosis, and Cancer: Controversy in Occupational Medicine* (1986); MICHAEL ALDERSON, *Occupational Cancer* (1986); ARTHUR F. DiSALVO (ed.), *Occupational Mycoses* (1983); RICHARD R. WEEDEN, *Poison in the Pot: The Legacy of Lead* (1984); A.J. BRAMMER and W. TAYLOR (eds.), *Vibration Effects on the Hand and Arm in Industry* (1982); and DIANA CHAPMAN WALSH and RICHARD H. EGDAHL (eds.), *Women, Work, and Health: Challenges to Corporate Policy* (1980). *Preventing Illness and Injury in the Workplace* (1985), is a survey on the prevention and control of occupational disease in the United States prepared by the Office of Technology Assessment.

(G.Ka.)

Oceanic Arts

Art is an imprecise concept, especially if the economic connotations that accompany it in a given culture are not regarded. In the West, indeed, anything sold as art is considered such, especially whatever sells best. Well-known "aestheticians" have treated the bark paintings of Arnhem Land (Figure 1) as mere commercial objects and yet regard as "art" certain pieces that had lost their colour but acquired an "admirable" patina after being waxed.

Some art historians have tried to understand Oceanic art—like other supposedly "primitive" arts that now look so modern and sophisticated—as rising from the same kind of inspiration that gave birth to Western and other cultures. They have spoken of magical art, then of religious art, using concepts and connotations—positive or negative, black or white—that properly belong to the religious and theological universe of the Western world. It is better to discard such hand-me-down ideas and to look at the way each piece of Oceanic art—including those objects that the West regards as beautiful and, also, those that the Oceanic peoples themselves appreciate as such—finds its place within the specific society and culture. Within the concept of Oceanic art is included not only the plastic works—sculpture, painted plaques, and monumental structures—but also any object in daily use that has received a finished or intentionally fashioned form (Figure 2). It likewise includes the vocal arts, with all the forms and uses of a construed sentence, music of all types, and many of the elaborate formal gestures of the dance.

The article is divided into the following major sections:

General considerations

THE SOCIAL MILIEU

The influence of the social milieu on art is a constantly recurring problem in aesthetic studies, perhaps because the meaning of the term social milieu is so elusive. It is, indeed, better to question how aesthetic expression is introduced into and operates within the social group, from which it can only be detached for the sake of convenience and in formal terms; for there can be no aesthetic manifestation unless there is at least one person to serve as the public. There is, however, a permanent and balanced relationship between art and society in the sense that, while aesthetic expression profits from an organization that ensures its reproduction or transmission, the artist derives advantages that do not belong solely to the level of art: prestige or gain, if not both of them together.

Commercial values. A discovery of recent decades is that among the Oceanian peoples art has its commercial value and is bought and sold. The Melanesians, at any rate, have a system that, for want of a better term, might be called "copyright." This system is as complicated as that in the West, with both negative and positive aspects. It is forbidden under pain of supernatural punishment to take that which does not belong to one, and this extends to the arts: all stylistic elements, whether plastic forms, painted decoration, musical themes, poems, or sequences of dance steps are copyrighted. The usual owner is the local group or clan attached to a given area, and the group is represented by some chosen dignitary. Ownership may be by inheritance, the result of an expensive purchase, or both. Literature sells least well. This is because sung verse usually embodies the myth of a particular clan, and the recitation of a myth to which one has no right is considered theft—it is seen as an attempt to deprive the owners of their land. One does, however, come across song texts with the original music, either in the original language or in that of the borrowers, sometimes paired and sometimes not. (Chants can also be transmitted from one place to another without an accompanying translation and without the new singers necessarily knowing the meaning of the words.) Dance steps can also be borrowed and used with a different chant. The important thing is to pay for what is taken and (so that there can be no misunderstandings about this) to pay in public—ritually and with goods whose

The Oceanic conception of ownership

Figure 1: X-ray-style bark painting of kangaroos, earth pigments on eucalyptus bark. From Arnhem Land, Australia. In the Metropolitan Museum of Art, New York City. Height 1.03 m.

value is undisputed, such as pigs or traditional treasures.

A work of plastic art may also be sold, but the sale need not be of the piece itself. It may be one or other of its elements that provides the attraction—an outstanding portion, an astute technique, an aspect of decoration, or a combination of all. Each legitimately bought element can be combined with others obtained elsewhere to produce a new artifact that will appeal to the customs and fashions of society.

Art and social institutions. Aesthetic expression is thus influenced by society in a very wide sense and makes use of its institutions and forms of control, but there is hardly any evidence to suggest that a mode of government can have been the originating force of any particular aesthetic tradition. The combined nuances within an organized society can exert such a force, however, and a good example of how they do so is found at the level of the organization of trade. Craftsmen specialize by village in the Admiralty Islands, making a specific category of goods, and this ensures a stability of form, with variations occurring only in the fine detail. Individual gifts and abilities, therefore, are not especially important. On the other hand, societies that offer a premium to initiative or to individual inspiration (such as in Middle Sepik, a region of central New Guinea) foster the means to maximum creative power, and the importance of individual talent in this situation becomes paramount.

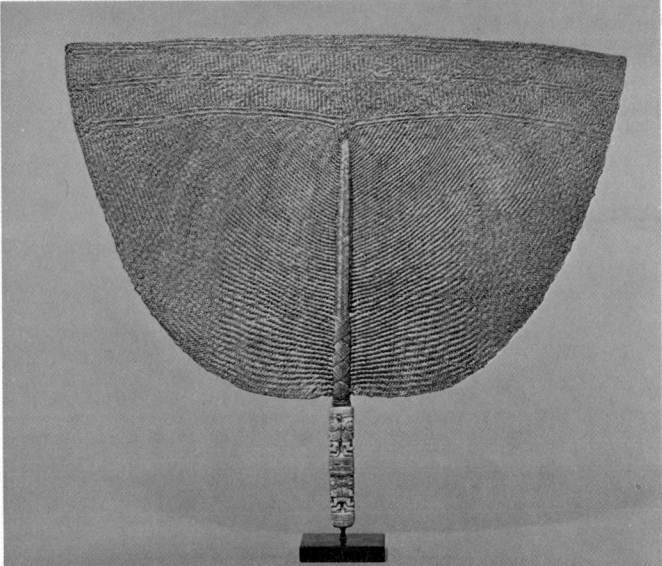

Figure 2: Fan, pandanus and whale ivory. From the Marquesas Islands, Polynesia. In the collection of Mr. and Mrs. R. Wielgus, Tucson, Arizona. Height 46.4 cm.

This factor alone, however, does not seem to account for the comparative artistic richness of certain areas as opposed to others. Such factors as wide circulation of information and the buying or selling of artistic ideas and elements are equally important and favour those places where ideas and themes are most readily interchanged. Another essential factor in the situation is competition for prestige among individuals (Middle Sepik) or among groups (New Hebrides, New Ireland), which, it is generally agreed, results in some of the finest art forms of all. Where there is a frozen hierarchy of power and prestige, such as there is in Tonga, a sophisticated theological structure has evolved, but a diversity of art forms has not (though some does exist). The complex theogonies of the Maoris, for example, were not the inspiration behind sculptures and bas-reliefs of New Zealand (Figure 3); the fact that rival schools of sculpture flourished there offers a better explanation for their exuberant form.

Sexual attitudes seem to have had little connection with artistic productiveness: the New Caledonians, who are sexually reserved, have created many interesting works of sculpture; on the other hand the inhabitants of the Loyalty Islands, who are sexually permissive, have a very

Figure 3: Maori (Polynesian) wall panel from a meeting house, wood and reeds. From New Zealand. In the Museum für Völkerkunde, Hamburg. Height 21.6 cm.

developed art of chanting and dancing (but know almost nothing of sculpture), whereas the Trobriand Islanders, also permissive, have not developed these arts. (The traditional cultures of Oceania are discussed in detail in the article PACIFIC ISLANDS.)

DEMOGRAPHIC INFLUENCES

Coastal populations seem to be more productive than those of the interior. This is especially true of New Guinea,

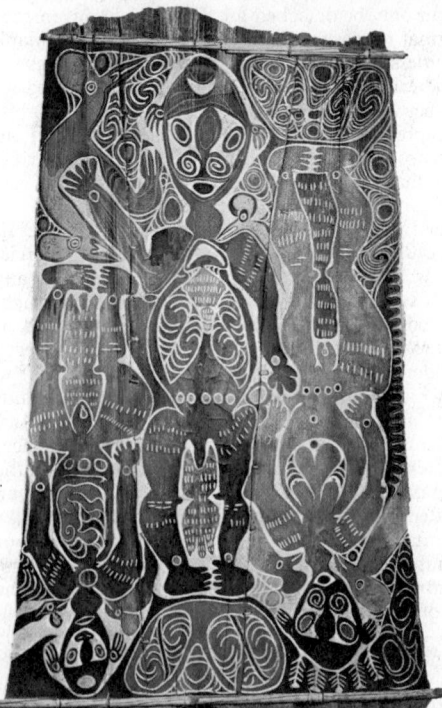

Figure 4: Vegetable panel, sago spathe, bamboo, earth pigments. From the Lower Sepik area, New Guinea, Melanesia. In the Metropolitan Museum of Art, New York City. Height 1.02 m.

where distance from the coast can mean virtual isolation. Being by necessity involved in coastal trade and therefore well placed for cultural interchanges, the seafarers all knew some kind of sculpture, though of widely differing forms. But this is not a hard and fast rule. The people living inland in New Guinea, known for convenience under the designation of Middle Sepik, achieved the highest artistic levels, for instance, and the inhabitants of the highlands often produced forms, motifs, and colours of great interest. Their work, however, was either deliberately destroyed after ritual use or else decayed very quickly, for they used mainly fragile vegetable materials (Figure 4).

Works that were made to be destroyed

Works gathered by European collectors were usually taken from the coastal regions, and even these were those pieces that were most easily transported. Very little is known, therefore, about the interior from an aesthetic standpoint, and problems of transport still present a formidable obstacle in the way of learning very much more.

Isolation. The state of isolation, when it truly exists, inevitably works against inventiveness and encourages stereotyped repetition. Actually, only cases of relative isolation are known: even the people of Tikopia, for instance, travelled far in their boats, or "pirogues" as their crafts are called, along routes established by tradition, and they reached some destination. The extent to which harsh climatic conditions inhibit artistic expression is not known, if indeed they do at all—the abstract art engraved on stone plaques by aborigines of the inhospitable central Australian desert is, for example, especially fine. Nor is there much evidence that the rough or elaborate aspect of wood sculpture (Figure 5) has any relation to technological backwardness or otherwise: the basic technique of cutting wood (which is prepared by slow, controlled firing) with a stone hatchet is everywhere the same, and only the finishing tools—splinters of jade or obsidian, shells, dog incisors, and the like—vary.

By courtesy of (left) the Museum für Völkerkunde und Schweizerisches Museum für Volkerkunde Basel, Switzerland, (right) the Peabody Museum, Harvard University, Cambridge, Massachusetts; photograph, (left) Hans Steiner

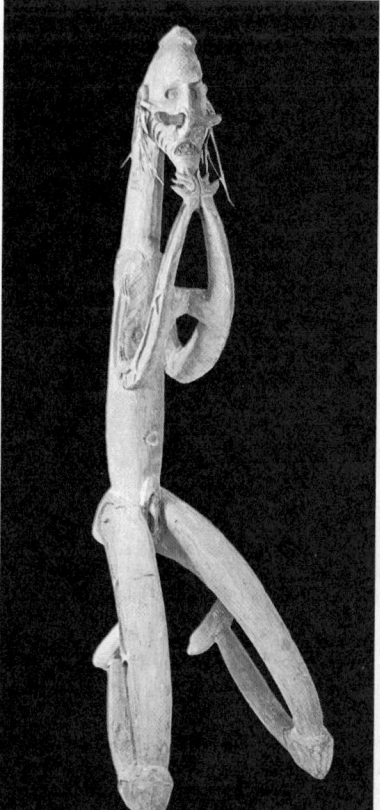 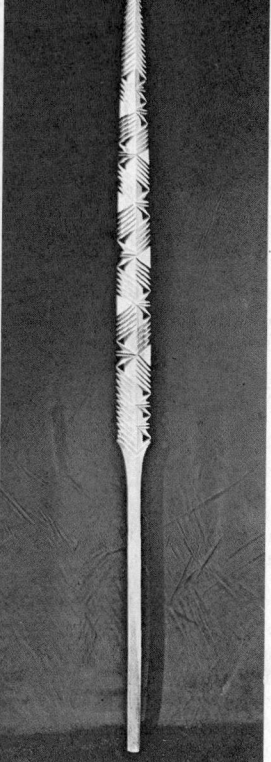

Figure 5: *Rough and elaborate styles of woodcarving.*
(Left) Canoe prow from the Asmat area, New Guinea, Melanesia. In the Museum für Völkerkunde und Schweizerisches Museum für Volkerkunde Basel, Switzerland.
(Right) Spear from the Samoa Islands, Polynesia. In the Peabody Museum, Harvard University. Length 1.88 m.

Intercultural borrowings. It is the element of complexity and number of intergroup relations that seem to provide conditions that are most clearly favourable to aesthetic production in Oceania. Essentially the same thing can be gleaned from studying the 2,000 years of Western history. Objects are "borrowed" by one culture from another, but the object borrowed does not always retain its original significance. The society borrowing, stealing, or plundering the object attributes to it the connotations that suit it, those that are available at the moment. A mask, for example, acquires quite a different significance from one place to another (Figure 6): it may be an object used in theatrical games, with the laughing participation of women and children; another group may use it as a symbol for the initiation of young men, with the appropriate respect (even if the oldest women know which man is hidden under the disguise); somewhere else it represents a returning ancestor and is therefore invested with the appropriate emotion; and yet elsewhere it serves as the public symbol of an institution, guaranteeing a form of social control and serving to support the proclamation of decrees concerning public order. It never has the same connotations in one place as it has in another; as a result generalizing discourses on the mask, as a subject, have little basis in fact.

Western influence. The effect of the West on Oceanic culture after two centuries has been both overestimated and underestimated. During the 18th century, through the intelligence or determination of the parties concerned, the relationship between the two was much more equal than is generally believed, though this equality was achieved at the cost of many human lives. The artistic traditions of Oceania were not stifled; indeed, when the European policy of conquest was abandoned, largely because of the territories' lack of useful natural resources, many societies underwent an aesthetic flowering (particularly in the visual arts) that has not always been appreciated. To a great extent this took place because metal tools had been introduced—bringing about more efficient techniques in carving wood—but it occurred also because new leisure time had been created, which had to be filled by a kind of ritual explosion and in which invention was given free rein (though the resultant themes were, nevertheless, drawn from tradition).

In the 19th century, however, conversion to Christianity and forced colonialization brought about the progressive disappearance of all indigenous visual arts. The musical arts and the dance resisted better: despite the quickly adopted Western techniques, they displayed much originality in their reinterpretation. Some of the most modern experiments in rhythm in the 20th century, for example, were foreshadowed in the orchestras of unknown villages in the mid-Pacific, where the players used instruments that consisted of no more than a string stretched across an empty gasoline can.

Effects of Christianity on Oceanic art

HISTORICAL PERSPECTIVES

Oceania does not lack historical depth, though knowledge of it is not consistent, even among the people of the region: the great and ancient Tonga lineages stretch back for some 40 generations, whereas some groups have difficulty in tracing themselves back more than two. Tonga is also exceptional in that its dynamism was turned outward, for it built up a maritime empire. But usually, within an insular society's stable population and fixed habitat, the complexities of family relationship were of major importance—particularly when determining an inheritance. Often the relationships worked out were not accurate, but this need not, in fact, have hindered the actual working of a system based on genealogical reference. In New Guinea, on the other hand, where a sustained population movement had been in existence for more than 1,000 years (the movement was partly from west to east and partly from the high, overpopulated mountain valleys to the less healthy coastal areas), the permanence of land tenure was never guaranteed, and the peoples there did not favour the father-to-son pattern of inheritance. As a result, it is very important that notions of patrimony and inheritance pertaining to other cultures be very carefully reviewed

Figure 6: *Melanesian masks.*
(Top left) Helmet mask, tapa (bark) cloth, bamboo,
fibre, earth pigments. From the Gulf of Papua, New
Guinea. In the Metropolitan Museum of Art, New York
City. Height 1.31 m. (Bottom left) Face mask, tapa
cloth stretched on a rattan frame. From New Ireland.
In the Ethnographical Museum, Budapest. (Right)
Helmet mask, tree fern wood painted with earth
pigments. From south Malekula, New Hebrides. In
the Museum für Völkerkunde und Schweizerisches
Museum für Volkskunde Basel, Switzerland. Height
1.20 m.

By courtesy of (top left) the Metropolitan Museum of Art, New York City, The
Michael C. Rockefeller Memorial Collection of Primitive Art, bequest of Nelson A.
Rockefeller, 1979, (bottom left) the Ethnographical Museum, Budapest, (right) the
Museum fur Volkerkunde und Schweizerisches Museum fur Volkskunde Basel,
Switzerland; photographs, (top left) Lisa Little, (right) Hans Hinz, Basel

and corrected before being attributed to Oceanic societies.
Even the most specialized Western observers, in studying
this phenomenon, have too often been coloured by value
systems belonging to their own society.

Continuity of tradition.   There has been a tendency to
treat the Oceanian peoples a little as though they belong
to fairy tales. The societies they constructed and made
function were considered by ethnologists to be as fragile as they were precious. They were supposed to have
operated rigorously and unchangingly over thousands of
years until the days of European colonialism, which the
specialist considered a noxious and disruptive influence
with an impact that inevitably destroyed the existing society. It is true that the West and Christianity made
such a crushing advance that Oceanic societies appeared
to be delicate structures, as easily broken as a fine bone
china teacup. No one in the West imagined that they
had adopted tactical, collective decisions in the face of
the invader. These tactics were aimed at saving the essential structure of their society, while letting go of the
superfluous—the visual appearances that the observer so
often regarded as basic. This fact helps to explain how,
at different periods, mass conversions to Christianity (the
missionaries' efforts being supported from afar and close
at hand by irresistible naval forces) were followed after
50 years or so by an easy return to paganism (except

where, disconcertingly to Western observers, the natives
hurled themselves headlong into some kind of messianic
movement). That societies, weak in the sense of lacking
armed strength, might adopt tactical compromises when
faced by a superior force ought not to be surprising, for it
is a recurring feature of behaviour throughout the history
of the world; Oceanian peoples, like all others, are part
of the evolutionary pattern. Delicate and supple social
structures can be destroyed, however, and it is little short
of miraculous that Oceanic societies should still be alive
and thriving, capable of independent life while preserving
a cultural heritage sufficient to maintain their cohesion.

Such a capacity for life implies that, before the arrival
of Europeans, the people in Oceanic societies had a broad
vision of the world that could accommodate any new
situation they faced. It is not always easy to rediscover
this vision through the distorting prism that now exists
because of the mistaken conceptions of the first European
observers and the considerable caution of their Oceanic
informants. They were conscious that if they were to
protect themselves, it was necessary for them to comprehend and assimilate the white man's concepts and way of
thinking. The great gift of the Oceanic person for psychological penetration and his capacity for adaptation are thus
largely responsible for the inadequate and untrustworthy
evidence that stems from that time. This is especially true

The
Oceanic
worldview

of the Polynesians, who quickly learned how to present themselves to romantically minded navigators as representatives of a classical culture like that of the Celts, a society with bards and hierarchies of kings and priests. As a result, they were often able—with the exception of Hawaii—to retain more of their land and to avoid collective conscription for forced labour. The explanation of this capacity for adaptation should be sought in the very heart of traditional structures, in their permanent receptivity to any external contribution, and in their tradition of welcoming the newcomer and providing him, in the form of land, spouse, and social status, with the means of becoming assimilated as a part of society. The entry of European elements must also have been facilitated in many areas by a long-standing preeminence given to light skins—girls of high station were kept in the shade, for example. The Europeans were therefore looked on favourably as possible fathers. The symbolic contrast between black (accentuated in time of war by means of various vegetable pigments) and white (the colour of mourning, obtained by coating oneself with ashes or lime on the hair and upper part of the body) has played a constant role in the relations between Europeans and Melanesians. Esteemed like the dead, that is to say like gods, because of the colour of their skins, the Europeans benefitted from the prestige that this gave them until events proved that they were mortal and fallible; after this initial acceptance they came to be dreaded instead for their intentions and material strength. There was a later attempt to place the phenomenon of the white man's arrival within the context of destiny. Various explanations emerged, turning around a confusion of such ancient themes and biblical outlines as the departure of a Melanesian or Papuan Noah in a pirogue, or canoe, carrying with him the elements of power that would one day be restored to his people or the idea of the "cargo," material wealth that had been sent by the dead to their descendants, in chests whose labels were changed by the whites so that they could usurp the contents.

The Old World vision first gave way before the arrival and entry of outside elements, both from the sea in pirogues and from inland by migrations that drove the people of New Guinea from west to east and from the high, overpopulated mountain valleys toward the coast. Consequently, groups now became defined socially in terms of their physical—that is, topographical—position within the general system. The universe, broken down and divided into elements that could be listed, was apportioned among the various groups. Each group had symbolic control of its part of the known world—its animals, vegetable life, atmospheric elements, mythological figures—and located on its own territory fixed spots from which this control was asserted. Thus, the soil itself was of prime importance, and it is very important to understand that in societies without writing systems this should be so. For the soil offers subsistence and is literally the basis of social and religious rites—it supports communication routes and provides the sacred spots (ritual or mythological or both) among the areas assigned to lie fallow or to be cultivated, to be given over to hunting or the gathering of fruit and vegetables. This fact of the soil's importance cannot be neglected in favour of an arrangement of concepts more in line with the intellectual habits of other cultures. In order to begin understanding Oceanic culture, it is essential to realize that its peoples symbolically express their very society in what may seem to others no more than a dry list of topographical detail. The "list" is an embodiment of their basic myth, and the native inherits, as it were, a "key" to its interpretation.

Culture and tradition. There is an often bewildering multiplication of languages spoken in Oceania; there are several hundred separate tongues spoken in New Guinea alone and scores spoken in each of the Melanesian archipelagoes. In contrast, the Polynesian languages are more obviously similar, a fact that may be connected with man's comparatively late arrival there. The languages of Oceania are divided into two large groupings. One is called, at present, Austronesian, which is considered to be of relatively recent origin and which includes Indonesian, certain Madagascan, Melanesian, Polynesian, and

Micronesian languages. Formerly this grouping was designated as Malayo-Polynesian. The other group, called Non-Austronesian, is considered to be older than Austronesian and includes many of the languages of New Guinea, of New Britain, and a few isolated languages in New Ireland and the Solomon Islands. In older terminology these Non-Austronesian languages were subsumed under the general term Papuan. While the Austronesian languages seem to be historically related, the Non-Austronesian group serves as a convenient catch-all grouping, the constituent languages of which are not necessarily related to each other. The presence of such a large number of the older Non-Austronesian languages in Melanesia makes this region an important one for research into historical linguistic relationships between older and newer language manifestations prevalent in Oceania.

Symbolism, imagery, and the aesthetic tradition. It is difficult to pinpoint any common general elements within the great variety of symbolic systems that the Oceanian peoples have built up. The bird symbol appears to be the one most frequently used, as much in speech, myth, dance, and song as in visual art. It seems to represent the political group, power, high social status, and also virility. Often it is a small sea eagle, common in coastal regions, or some other sea bird, such as the frigate bird. But the symbolic meaning is attached to the species rather than to the genus. A predatory bird of the fields, the sultana hen, for example, supplies a female connotation—it is the symbol of illicit love. Therefore one should not invoke the whole order of flying creatures to explain the above series of symbols, inasmuch as the large fruit-eating bat that feeds on the same fruits as the sultana hen is both a male symbol and a representation of life; the lizard, the water snake, and the shark (Figure 7) have the same connotations, and those of the shark can vary to the point of overlapping those of the sea eagle. The explanation of this apparent discrepancy lies in the division between, and the appropriation by, the different groups constituting a society of the whole of the known elements of the universe. The specific significance of the recourse to such a symbol will only be understood in terms of the whole symbolic lexicon and, simultaneously, of the overall aspects and details of its adaptation.

Figure 7: Carving of a shark, blackened wood with inlaid decoration of mother-of-pearl. From San Cristobal Island, Solomon Islands, Melanesia. In the Museum für Völkerkunde und Schweizerisches Museum für Volkskunde Basel, Switzerland. Length 57.8 cm.

It is, likewise, difficult to extract from the overall culture anything that might be called a common aesthetic tradition. Landscape architecture might constitute one, for it is everywhere methodically planned and executed, though with quite different aims from one archipelago to another. Here, one will find a compact, close-cropped lawn around the houses; there, everything that encroaches on the black, lustreless, volcanic soil has been carefully uprooted. Here, the hierarchy of constructions will be organized vertically

Language groupings

as a function of their attributes; there, grassy open spaces will be used to distinguish large categories of huts. The most elaborately worked of these glades, in terms of the techniques of arboriculture used to provide shade, will be the one that contains no huts, being used as a common dancing ground by several groups.

CONTEMPORARY FEATURES

It has been suggested above that most Oceanic cultures, despite their confrontation by Western colonialists and missionaries, retained much more life and cohesion than observers generally supposed. It is, however, a fact that the expression of their culture was seen as a manifestation of godlessness by the white overlord and could not be maintained. Much opprobrium has since fallen on those missionaries who compelled the suppression of chants and dances and still more on those who burned the idols (Figure 8). But a great many Polynesian sculptures were also

Figure 8: Wooden image of the war god Kukailimoku, one of the Polynesian works of art that escaped destruction by missionaries. From the Hawaiian Islands. In the British Museum. Height 76.8 cm.

destroyed by isolated Polynesian evangelists and their converts, who were eager to demonstrate their changed lives and often were motivated further by the hope of attaining the evident wealth and power of the white man. Traditional dances and chants were generally condemned by Catholic and Protestant missionaries alike, but the extent to which they survived depended upon the proximity of the missionary station and the zeal of its local representative. Many songs and dances were, in fact, preserved, often because European dignitaries expressed an interest: official ceremonies that they attended would incorporate music and dance. Tourists were also interested in folklore, and their patronage helped to keep alive some parts of it as well as to encourage pale copies and complete invention. But a tradition can only be maintained if the principals involved really desire it. Once the ritual itself has been abandoned, everything related to it has the greatest difficulty in retaining anything but a residual or revised function.

It is, however, astonishing to discover how much was not destroyed but lay dormant, eventually to emerge from an oblivion that might have been thought final as Christianity began to suffer a relative loss of prestige. Complex texts and ceremonies have been built in a way that reveals how retentive is the collective memory. The plastic arts, on the other hand, have largely succumbed to a process

of commercialization whereby an ever greater number of objects—mostly of poor quality—are needed to supply the needs of a greatly expanded export market that is controlled by a class of, usually, European middlemen of extraordinary rapacity. The manufacture of ritual and utilitarian objects for overseas sale as artworks has necessarily affected not only the quality but also the aesthetic characteristics of the objects. *Commercialization*

Literature

GENERAL CHARACTERISTICS

Oceanic literature is oral. Its existence was discovered about two centuries ago in Polynesia, when European observers realized that complex cosmogonies and theological formulations, embodied in astonishingly long and complicated texts, were committed to memory by what they thought of as bards and priests. For a long time, however, no one felt any call to take this discovery further. The prevailing strain of European pre-Romanticism—and, later, Romanticism itself—which then tinged the outlook of most observers, unfortunately resulted in intellectual scruples being abandoned when they came face to face with attractively exotic Oceanic situations; they produced a flood of literary reconstruction, giving current European ideas free rein, so that the genuine Polynesian literary tradition was quickly swamped. To construct a "Polynesian" text it was enough to sprinkle it with proper names and a few other words or phrases borrowed from the language. Those who did not invent did translations, and the translated texts were even more dangerous because of innumerable misinterpretations and small mistakes. Few authors supplied the Polynesian text alongside their translation, a course that would be expected if the work were one of the genuine scholarship (although an early effort by serious scholars did succeed in organizing the body of New Zealand's vernacular, unexpurgated texts, presenting them in a line-by-line translation, with an arsenal of notes and commentaries, in such a way that the text could be both understood and critically appreciated). A properly serious and scientific approach to textual criticism was, on the whole, reserved to the classical and sacred texts of other cultures.

The rise of anthropological studies toward the end of the 19th century ought to have brought with it a new interest in Oceania's oral literature. But however much conditions varied from country to country, anthropology was never practically influenced by the methods of classical philology, the rigorous discipline of which it admits with the greatest reluctance even today. Vernacular vocabularies did become an object of sustained attention for certain scholars, but they were basically seeking to describe normative and conceptual systems; as a result, they preserved very little apart from those phrases that aptly served to demonstrate the truth of their own arguments and theories. The methodical collecting of documents was scarcely begun, and the task has now become one of extreme urgency before texts are completely forgotten. It is, moreover, the sort of work in which linguists and anthropologists ought to collaborate.

It is not easy for scholars belonging to other cultures to describe the content of Oceanic literature because their understanding of it is so limited. There are, however, one or two pointers. First of all, it must be reiterated that the purpose of literature is to communicate: it therefore demands an audience. In the case of an oral literature, communication depends first on memory, and this usually means that such memory aids as rhythm and stock formulas and phrases are an important element of all texts. The majority of Oceanic texts keep closely to traditional forms and appear to be committed to memory and then are communicated in a strictly unvarying manner. This is, however, only approximately the case because the various techniques of formalization can allow for a rather fluid text. The tradition can be made evident at the lexical level, with the possibility of a great freedom of syntax. It only prevents prosodic elements from taking on primary importance. But it is these that have been studied last by modern linguistics. *Traditional forms of oral literature*

Types. The literary occasions of the Oceanian peoples are, as in other cultures, reflected in sacred literature, political literature, and frivolous—even erotic—texts. This division, however, should not be taken to represent an attempt at classification; any such pigeonholing would be inconvenient, indeed, because such a large number of texts defy neatness and straddle two categories. But there are certainly two poles between which the various forms of literary expression can be placed. On the one hand, there is a body of works that appeals to Western readers and is made accessible to them by its use of the poetic image. On the other hand, there are many texts, often brief, in which each word is frequently a complete image. This kind of text is part and parcel of the culture that has produced it and requires a veritable arsenal of commentaries of others to interpret the key words and to unravel its significance to nonnative readers. Texts are, basically, of two kinds: (1) recitatives, whose form is rigid; they can be expanded but not transformed; in this category belong all the songs or chants that accompany dances—whether the performers be standing or seated—funeral chants, songs that accompany children's games, and those with an erotic significance; and (2) public orations, in which the elements are formally but roughly organized, giving the speaker the right to vary the presentation within certain limits established for this literary genre. Such discourses, which can aptly be delivered as a high-level political oration and as a funeral eulogy or remembrance speech, can also, in a more simple form, commemorate such events as a birth or a marriage.

Themes. The themes are those that appear in other literatures of the world: love and death, defiance and hatred, nostalgia for the past, and the pleasure of the moment. Nature provides the necessary images. There is a barrier between Oceanic literature and that of other cultures because, although it presents a familiar mental universe, it does so in what is often an allusive manner that demands an intimate knowledge of local place-names, local political geography, and land division before its meaning can be understood: the owl, for example, is symbolic of a given place, the lizard of some other, and the sea eagle associated with a third.

Although there is no specific body of Oceanic literature, there are fragments of different kinds that, once gathered, suggest a cultural coherence: definite conclusions cannot be drawn, but lines for further research are indicated. Even small texts, which have frequently been overlooked because they did not seem sufficiently elevated—such as those that were spoken by a man and accompanied by a flute or a stringed instrument as part of individual rites for the purpose of securing a woman's favours—contribute to the total picture.

Importance of small texts

MELANESIAN LITERATURES

Melanesian literatures are better known to contemporary scholarship than are Polynesian because they remained untampered with over a longer period by Western anthropologists and scholars and were, therefore, not distorted by them. Because of this, they are of great interest, although they are only just being recovered. Great pioneering work was done by Maurice Leenhardt into the literature of New Caledonia, but it has scarcely been followed up. A prime difficulty is that of method. Leenhardt trained a few Melanesians, teaching them to read and write their own language after inventing for them a system of transcribing their verbal utterances. Thus, he provided for himself scribes—and even authors—in the local language that he had chosen for study. The body of literature he assembled in this way, since published only in part, is the most complete available to date. Leenhardt's method (which had in fact been previously employed half a century earlier by British clergyman Robert Henry Codrington [1830–1922], who did not, however, leave to posterity the literature of the Mota language that had been given him by his pupils) makes it possible to obtain texts of very high quality over a long period. Written out by the trained student himself, who has had the opportunity to re-read and check for accuracy in the quiet of his hut, the method avoids the psychological tension that inevitably results from a

dictation session. The results make for more confident study afterward, and the method is still the only sound one. Texts taken down directly on a tape recorder can too easily be garbled or abridged unless the informants are especially trained to use the machine by a linguist, so as to avoid a psychological block when faced by it.

Two generations of researchers have succeeded Maurice Leenhardt and have been working in the same region as he did. They have amassed a complementary body of literature that is astonishingly rich and have been able to establish just what the function of each text was in the life of the society they studied. The results of their work have obliged scholars to re-examine their conceptions of the oral literary tradition. It now emerges that not even words, symbols, or places have any fixed significance: the vocabulary is at once coherent and diversified, for it is used in a way that takes into account the momentary interest of the parties present.

The traditional speech. A traditional speech may be "hurled" at the crowd by a speaker perched on a flimsy platform; the crowd responds with a muffled cry at the end of each "sentence"; it is the quality of accord reached between the crowd and the speaker that comprises the "new content" of the familiar, traditional speech (henceforth becoming part of its tradition), while the accord also conveys what other cultures would call the "message"—the new stage in a rising political career, perhaps, or a declaration denoting peace between combatants or the beginning of a war. Anyone analyzing the speech itself has to search for and consider carefully all the possible interpretations and temporal conditions it might have. The traditional form of the speech is respected all the more because it allows this variation of content—within acceptable limits—to be conveyed by nuances that may easily escape observers from other cultures.

The form of the speech also presents a somewhat thorny problem. On the surface, it is a simple enumeration of the local groups and their symbols (that is, the portion of the land that is theirs, together with its animals, plants, weather conditions, and so on). The recitation of these physical realities is an affirmation of their very society, and they are stated one after the other, linked by some stock connecting phrase. Each listed item is given its precise geographical location; of special importance are the names of special places where authority is exercised or where rites are practiced. The whole constitutes a world vision, or system, in which the individual society and its members have their place. The native audience is perfectly familiar with the spatial affirmation of their society contained in the speech, and, from the dry enumeration of its components, they are able to supply for themselves a history of alliances and wars and to remodel the traditional text until it fits the conditions of the present. The orator's delivery, the nuances he maintains or introduces into the speech, are a sign of his success.

The myth. Another kind of literature, less easily defined, is the one commonly understood as myth (a term that smacks of Western classical culture and thus carries overtones that are irksome from the scientific point of view). Involved here are all formalized recitatives, straightforwardly delivered, made up of narrative with pleasing scenes interpolated, whose apparent aim is to give the account of a rite, for example, or to describe the situation of some group of family lineage (perhaps in connection with land ownership or political status) or to tell of the origin of man and his culture. The recitative may involve as little as 10 lines, or it may take three hours to dictate. In any given local culture, the rules that govern the way in which the texts' content is formalized and those that govern the way in which they are recited are consistent. The symbolic vocabulary, formally identical with that used in public speeches, carries elaborate but acknowledged references. A text may be established on the basis of a single symbol, but in general the symbolic pattern is so complex that other cultures have great difficulty in understanding it. Indeed, it is only possible to decipher its meaning if the cultural significance of every place mentioned in the text is understood, if it is known what creature or being is worshipped where and to the benefit of which group, and often only if the intineraries that are the subject of a majority of the myths are entirely familiar to the interpreter, so that old place-names—and thus their meaning—that are referred to in the text can be identified.

POLYNESIAN AND MICRONESIAN LITERATURES

Similarity of Polynesian and Micronesian literatures

Problems of interpretation. Polynesian and Micronesian literatures are similar in structure, but they vary in detail from island to island. Little is known about the Micronesian texts, however, and work on the interpretation of Polynesian literature has been hindered—first by the excesses of European Romanticism and its flights of fancy, then for nearly two centuries by well-intentioned amateurism. Authentic texts were not collected when the opportunity was at hand, and it is now often too late to do so because the traditions—especially of religion—that maintained them have not survived. A great body of mythological material was gathered in the 19th century, but it has still not been critically edited, and it cannot be overemphasized that nothing like a properly established record of their myths has yet been produced. Polynesian "priests" have been likened to those of ancient Egypt, their recitatives treated as theological monuments—interpretations that distort the situation entirely. Such textual interpretation must, in any case, be demonstrated scientifically; since the commentaries published to date do not attempt to do this, the serious investigator is suspicious also of the soundness of their attendant translations. These translations, on the slightest pretext, indulge in lyrical flights of fancy that seem to have been inspired by old memories of Sir Walter Scott or the poets of the French Parnassian school. Editions of Polynesian texts are published by the Bernice Pauahi Bishop Museum in Honolulu, and, though interesting in the absence of any other methodical work, these, too, are open to criticism. Their translations are never literal but attempt some kind of free translation, as though dating from a period when translations aspired primarily to literary beauty.

As a result, the theogonies that have been published (supplied with diagrams indicating the superposition of the heavens) are engaging, but little more. They are no more than easy summaries for the casual reader, lacking any explanation of the texts on which they are based. Because they are simplicity itself, they enjoy much popularity, even in Polynesian circles, but they are of no scientific help to the serious modern investigator. He, nonetheless, must all too often fall back on such a summary simply because nothing else exists to help him.

The scholar must be on guard against an outstanding storyteller. He must take the events narrated, put them into their proper place and space, and compare them with what else is known in as complete a way as possible so that contradictions in the fabric are revealed. Such contradictions, subtle but evidently present, indicate that an entire population has sided with the storyteller to disguise the real truth, which is in itself an interesting phenomenon for study.

The legendary cycles. There are few comparative studies of Polynesian and Micronesian literatures. The methods they employ are not always impressive—only authentic texts should be used for comparison, not simplified summaries—but they do give a glimpse of how widespread certain legendary cycles were, the most frequently recurring, from a geographical point of view, being that of the trickster figure, Maui-tiki-tiki, who was a fisherman of the islands and who discovered fire. He can be recognized, on the fringes of the Polynesian area, as the god of the first fruits of the yam harvest on this or that island, sometimes revered under a symbolic manifestation or sometimes as a less abstract figure. Indications of his variety of function over such a large area make the loss, sustained over two centuries of interpretation willfully blind to the true Polynesian cultural phenomenon, all the more frustrating.

The "trickster" figure in legend

The few scraps of knowledge available about the indigenous literatures of Australia and Micronesia, as well as those of Polynesia, indicate that the figures of their great mythological cycles were simultaneously general symbols and local divinities. The people saw no contradiction in this double manifestation: great cultural heroes were naturally assigned to a specific place when an individual within that culture would establish a reverential dialogue with any one of them.

(J.Gt.)

The performing arts: music and dance

THE ROLE OF MUSIC AND DANCE

Music and dance in Polynesia and Micronesia are audible and visual extensions of poetry, whereas in Melanesia they are more aimed at spectacular display during times of life crises and secret-society rituals. The differences between Melanesian and Polynesian music and dance can be related to a basic differentiation in political types that reflects differences in social structure that have been characterized as "bigmen" societies and chiefdoms.

Melanesia. The leader, or bigman, in many Melanesian and New Guinea societies is often a self-made man; he becomes a leader by creating followers, succeeding because he possesses skills that command respect in his society, such as oratory, bravery, gardening prowess, and magical powers. He amasses goods and has great public giveaways, often in connection with the erection of a bigman's dwelling or a men's house, the purchase of higher grades of rank in secret societies, the sponsorship of funeral or other religious ceremonies, or the erection and consecration of slit-gongs (or slit-drums, percussion instruments made from hollowed-out logs or living tree trunks). These ceremonies occasion spectacular displays of the visual and performing arts.

There are basically two kinds of dance in these Melanesian ceremonies: dances of impersonation (Figure 9) and dances of participation (Figure 10). In the first type, the dancer impersonates mythical or ancestral beings; the dance–actor becomes someone else, and his attire is usually distinctly unhuman or supernatural—consisting often of huge masks and a full otherworldly costume. The dance movements are dictated by the two considerations that the dancers are not human and that their attire is difficult to move in. Thus the movements are those of legs and swaying bodies; the arms are often covered and frequently used to steady the costume and mask or perhaps hold a drum to accompany the dance. The movements do not interpret recited poetry; however, the voices of these supernatural beings may be heard in the sounds of musical instruments.

Impersonation of otherworldly beings

Kal Muller—Woodfin Camp

Figure 9: Melanesian dance of spirit impersonation, Ambrim Island, New Hebrides, Melanesia.

The dances of participation are often extensions of these dramatic ceremonies, for individuals who do not impersonate spirits often join in and dance with them, imitating the steps of the supernatural. In dances celebrating headhunting, warfare, funeral rites, or fertility—in which everyone participates—the same movements are used, often to the accompaniment of drumming and communal singing. The dances have a character of spontaneity and

Figure 10: *Melanesian dances of participation.*
(Left) Dancers celebrating a good yam harvest, Tana Island, New Hebrides. (Right) Mudmen
of the Asaro River area, New Guinea, performing a dance in which they reenact their
ancestors' defeat of their enemies.

(Left) Kal Muller—Woodfin Camp; (right) © Axel Poignant

do not require long and arduous training. Their aim is
not the simultaneous flawless execution of music and
intricate movements but, rather, the creation of a mass
rhythmic environment that might be characterized as a
visual extension of rhythm. If words are associated, they
are repetitious and seem not to tell a story; they may even
be unintelligible. Although the specific structure of any
single dance tradition in Melanesia is not yet known, it
seems probable that the isolated units of movement would
be primarily those of legs and body.

Polynesia. The entirely different world of Polynesia
stands in contrast. Polynesian dance is a visual extension
of poetry that uses chant or heightened speech as a vehicle for the praise and honour of high-ranking chiefs or
visitors (Figure 11). In Polynesia power resides in chiefly
office, and texts tell of a chief's deeds and his descent
from the gods. Genealogical rank is a distinctive feature of
Polynesian societies, and music and dance pay allegiance
to the rank-based sociopolitical structure, reflecting and
validating the system of social distinctions and interpersonal relationships. In these societies, where power resides
in the office and the regime is long and enduring, specialists compose poetry, add music and movement, and
rehearse the performers for many months before a public ceremony. Movements are primarily those of hands
and arms, and interpretation is that of a storyteller. The

dancer does not become a character in a drama, and his
stylized gestures do not correspond to words or ideas as
they do in literature-inspired dance traditions of Indonesia
and Southeast Asia. In Polynesia the dancer interprets a
story orally, usually chanting or reciting metred poetry,
and accompanies the words with actions. The presentation is not dramatic in the Western sense of the word,
for there is no conflict. Instead, the dancer is storyteller
par excellence, audibly and visually telling *about* a person,
place, event, or emotion, Yet, although Polynesian dance
texts are based on traditional stories, legends, or myths, a
story is not "told" in the usual sense: traditional literature
is referred to in a roundabout way, but the poetry is often
the vehicle for saying something else, usually something
relevant for the occasion at which it is presented. In addition, the order of the dances and the choice and placement
of the dancers often supply further information about the
social structure.

The structure is known for at least two Polynesian dance
traditions—Tongan, in western Polynesia, and Hawaiian—and the basic units of movement are primarily those
of the arms. The only Polynesian dance tradition, however, that has been thoroughly studied is the Tongan.
Tongan dance is a visual extension of poetry and is closely
intertwined with social organization. This sung poetry is a
series of references to mythology, chiefly genealogies, fa-

© Axel Poignant

Figure 11: Welcome dance performed as a mark of respect to visitors, Viti Levu Island,
Fiji Islands, Polynesia.

Figure 12: Festival dance, Yap, Caroline Islands, Micronesia.
Burt Glinn—Magnum

mous scenic places, and contemporary events. The dances, which are performed either standing or sitting, interpret selected words of the text with hand and arm movements. The distinguishing characteristics of Tongan dance are the emphasis on the rotation of the lower arm and the flexion and extension of the wrist, as well as a quick sideward tilt of the head. The legs are used mainly to keep time with sideward stepping movements, and there is a marked absence of hip or torso movement. In pre-European times the most important dance was the *me'etu'upaki*—a paddle dance performed by a large group of men in accompaniment to singing and a slit-gong, which was often played by a high-ranking chief. This dance is still performed today. Group dances called *me'elaufola* were performed by men or women separately in accompaniment to singing, long bamboo stamping tubes, and percussion sticks. The evolved form of this dance, which flourishes today, the *lakalaka*, is performed by men and women together in accompaniment to sung poetry only. Solo and small group dances performed by one, four, or eight women often follow the large group dances and are more concerned with beautiful movements than with interpretation of poetry, although the same movements are used. In the 20th century Polynesian dances are classified into six genres, three of which have survived from pre-European times. The most acculturated dance type, the *tau'olunga*, is a combination of Tongan and Samoan movements and accompanies Western-style singing in conjunction with stringed instruments.

Micronesia.   Music and dance in Micronesia, though certainly not the same as their Polynesian counterparts, are closely related to them. With the exception of Truk in the central Carolines, which displays traits of Melanesian and possibly Indonesian influence, the music structure of all parts of Micronesia is predominantly word determined, as is that of Polynesia. Dance movements are mainly of hands and arms in accompaniment to poetry. In some islands, such as Yap (in the western Carolines) and the Gilberts, there is a similar concern for rank in the placement of dancers, as well as the emphasis on rehearsed execution of songs and movements. But, although movements and types of dance have a superficial similarity to Polynesia, there are differences. In the Yap Empire, for example, dances were given as tribute to Yap by Ulithi, Woleai, and other islands, and the dance texts were in languages not intelligible to the Yapese dancers—the function of movements was not to illustrate a story but to decorate it (Figure 12). Instead of acknowledging a chief's deed or genealogy, the Yapese dancers demonstrated the overlordship of Yap to the other islands. Even in Ifalik, where texts were in their own language, the movements did not interpret poetry but were apparently abstractly decorative. The same is true for the Gilbert Islands. Thus Polynesian dance could be characterized as illustration of

Dance as ornament to poetry

poetry and Micronesian dance as decoration of poetry, while music in both areas serves as an elevated form of audible performance for poetry.

In many parts of Micronesia, dance and music were associated with tattooing, and with the decline of tattooing has come the virtual demise of these genres. The importance and dependence of the Micronesians on the sea is illustrated in poetry, music, and dance. In some areas dances were performed on a platform of canoes; canoelike paddles were used in other dances, and in some areas canoe head ornaments were worn by the performers. A study of the influence of the sea on Micronesian music and dance would reveal a great deal about the underlying value systems.

Again, the specific structure of any of the Micronesian dance traditions is not known, but apparently the basic units are primarily those of hands and arms and, if early descriptions are to be believed, the head.

Australia.   Music and dance of Australian Aborigines are important elements of sacred ceremonies that reenact mythological origins of the tribes and ensure the continued supply of foods through the propitiation of totemic plants and animals. Little is known about the internal structure or basic movements of the various Aboriginal dance traditions; however, in general terms there are often mimetic movements that involve the entire body to add a visual interpretative extension to the oral literature of the tribe.

MUSICAL INSTRUMENTS

Oceanic cultures have developed a large variety of sound-producing instruments. Some are unique, such as the friction blocks of New Ireland: three to four plaques carved out of a wooden block are rubbed with the hands to produce shrieking or hollow-resonant sounds, depending on size (eight to 80 inches for the entire instrument). Many instruments are used not in musical contexts but for other purposes—for example, to produce the voices of supernatural beings (in Melanesia), as lures (shark rattles), as toys, and for communication.

Musical instruments proper generally lack provisions for musical efficiency and easy handling. Flutes have no or few finger holes and no air ducts. Tuning devices with drums are rare, as are fixed resonators with chordophones (stringed instruments), which are represented only by simple types of musical bows and zithers. In general, instrumental music is culturally less important than vocal music, and in some areas it is absent altogether. In some other areas, however, such as the Solomon Islands, there are highly developed pan-flute orchestras.

Although some types of instruments—*e.g.*, conch trumpets and slit-drums—can be found in many parts of Oceania (excepting Australia), others occur only locally or are distinguishing features of certain musical areas. Open, hourglass-shaped drums with one membrane are typical of

New Guinea and Melanesia, while Polynesians use cylindrical drums. Flutes of various types are usually blown with the mouth in Melanesia, with the nose in Polynesia (nose flutes), and both ways in western Micronesia. In contrast to their simple technical structure, which is the more demanding on the skills of the player, some instruments display elaborate ornamentation related to their function as cult objects in Melanesia, or they may be highly carved and finished befitting their function of honouring gods and chiefs in Polynesia.

REGIONAL STYLES AND TRADITIONS

Melanesia. Melanesia—including New Guinea—houses a multitude of regional musical styles, few of which have been thoroughly investigated. The diversity, which parallels the linguistic situation, is assumed to be a result both of migrations and the relative isolation of ethnic groups due to geographic conditions. Intergroup contacts, including European influences, mostly since the late 19th century, have had a clear influence on present styles.

Generally speaking, Melanesian music tends to be less word determined than Polynesian and Micronesian music. Melody, rhythm, and form appear to be shaped by intrinsically musical principles rather than by text structure and meaning. Song texts often use archaic or foreign languages and are thus frequently unintelligible to all participants in a performance.

Melodic characteristics. Musical scale and melodic movement have been primary criteria in the analysis of Melanesian music. The main types of melodic form are triadic, in which the melody moves exclusively or predominantly on the steps of a triad (three tones, each a third apart, as C-E-G); and pentatonic, which uses five steps within an octave, the melodic structure typically emphasizing seconds, fourths, and fifths. Other types include "narrow," in which melodic movement is restricted to an ambit (range) of a third; and "tiled," in which the melody consists of a sequence of short narrow phrases on different tonal levels, always in a descending order.

Several attempts have been made to link these types of melodic form with specific cultures within Melanesia. The Dutch scholar Jaap Kunst attributed the tiled type found in the interior of western New Guinea, the Torres Strait, and Australia to "a people who, without doubt, emigrated from Asia to Australia—where the majority of them finally settled—by way of New Guinea and Torres Strait." Triadic melody style has been connected with speakers of non-Austronesian (Papuan) languages in New Guinea and elsewhere in Melanesia, while pentatonic structure is described as an element of Austronesian culture in Melanesia. But, whenever new data become available, previous hypotheses on the distribution of stylistic characteristics and their attribution to ethnic and cultural groupings usually have to be revised.

Also, rarely is the music of an ethnic group found to be based on one single principle of melodic structure. There is usually a mixture of several principles apparent, with one or the other prevailing.

Musical style and cultural context. This mixture of musical structures holds true for the three New Guinea groups whose music has been studied in its cultural context: the Monumbo, the Kate, and the Watut. A more detailed discussion of Kate music will illustrate the stylistic heterogeneity of the Kate, who live in the hinterland of the Huon Peninsula of northeast New Guinea and speak a non-Austronesian (Papuan) language, while some of their neighbours on the coast and on adjacent islands speak Austronesian (Melanesian) languages. A Lutheran mission was established in that area in 1886.

Before the mission terminated their non-Christian religious activities, the Kate shared with their neighbours, specifically the Melanesian-speaking Jabem, Bukawa, and Tami, a secret initiation cult that provided for an exchange of music and dances among participants. The mission introduced "Christian songs" with texts in Kate language and European church tunes; but missionaries also created "Christian" adaptations of traditional Kate melodies, which were more readily acceptable than Lutheran hymns.

By about 1910 the Kate experienced a twofold cultural change resulting from the continuing contact with their Melanesian-speaking neighbours and from the impact of European colonial culture. But many aspects of their precolonial culture were then still functioning or in fresh memory.

Music and dance activities were connected with childbirth, children's games, initiation, hunting, agriculture, ceremonial bartering of pigs, warfare, and death—the latter occasion being the only one to prohibit dancing. Consequently, initiation ceremonies, which usually extended over two years, had to be interrupted whenever a death occurred.

In addition to music and dance in ceremonial context, there were songs for entertainment and expression of individual sentiments or experiences. Most of the common social dances and dance songs were adopted from the off-coast Siassi Islands, including texts that were unintelligible to the Kate.

Structural characteristics of Kate music include triadic and pentatonic melody, both pure and in various degrees of blending; monophony (music having a single voice part); reverting and progressive strophes (stanzas) of varying lengths; basically isorhythmic organization (*i.e.,* using recurring rhythmic patterns); and a wide range of tempi. Analysis of stylistic characteristics in relation to context and historical data revealed that triadic melody and short progressive strophes are associated with the old, non-Austronesian (Papuan) stratum of Kate culture. Pentatonic melody and longer, reverting strophes seem to represent Melanesian influence, while a specific melody style characterized by the use of several pentatonic modes in succession ("modulating pentatony"), very wide ambit, and extended strophic form can be attributed to European culture contact.

The Solomon Islands. While the music of New Guinea and western Melanesia—particularly the Bismarck Archipelago—is predominantly vocal and monophonic, the music of the Solomon Islands is largely determined by use of highly developed panpipes. These instruments have three to nine closed tubes, usually doubled by open tubes that sound the higher octave. New instruments are tuned by comparison with old "masters," at the occasion of special ceremonies. Panpipes are used in orchestras alone and in conjunction with song. Vocal melodic style, which is characterized by triadic structure, wide melodic leaps, elaborate polyphony (several simultaneous voice parts), a specific timbre, or tone colour, and frequent change of register, is apparently an imitation of panpipe music. Types of polyphony include parallel melodic movement a third or a sixth apart, a practice most likely a result of overblowing the double panpipes, which may produce such parallels automatically.

The triadic melody style of the Solomon Islanders seems to have spread into adjacent western Polynesia, where similar melodic types are found in the Ellice Islands and Futuna.

Micronesia. From the Carolines in the west to the Gilberts in the east, most traditional music is accompanied by dancing in standing or sitting posture. Group singing with rhythmic accompaniment by body and ground beats or concussion sticks is the prevailing type of musical performance. Purely instrumental music was performed on nose and mouth flutes in the Carolines and Marianas.

Except in the central Carolines (Truk), where musical influences from Melanesia and eastern Indonesia are prominent, elements of chanting and metred declamation are the most conspicuous characteristics of musical structure, underlining the importance of poetry versus intrinsically musical principles. Vocal polyphony takes the forms of drone (sustained note heard against a melody) and parallel movement in a variety of intervals, with fourths most common.

Micronesia is the least known part of Oceania, as far as music and dance are concerned. On some of the Gilbert atolls, consecrations of assembly halls, races of boat models, and meetings between local groups were or still are connected with performances of dances in which both women and men participated. Active participation and choreographic role are determined by individual profi-

The triadic and pentatonic forms

Music of the Kate people of New Guinea

Panpipe ensembles

ciency as dancer and singer and by social rank. The *ruoia* is a sequence of standing dances in which movements are slow and mainly those of the arms and hands. In introductory and main dances, up to six leading dancers, male or female, pose as "gliding frigate birds" in front of the other dancers, who are lined up according to status in their patriclans (kinship groups). All dancers participate in chanting long poems that are rehearsed beforehand. Endings of dance songs are frequently shouted, and texts of the final dance in a sequence are recited in heightened speech throughout. There are also sitting dances, with arm and hand movements similar to those of the standing dances, and stick dances. Dance gestures are not illustrative of the song texts, which are not generally understood by performers or audience.

The texts of traditional dance songs were "received" by composers from ancestor spirits (*anti*) in special rituals and probably in trance. Since the early 20th century, multipart singing of European church tunes has spread throughout the area. In consequence of a general culture change, social dances based on traditional movement patterns but accompanied by adaptations of Western music have become dominant.

Polynesia. Since the second half of the 18th century, all parts of Polynesia have undergone a drastic culture change that affected music and dance traditions severely. At present, adaptations of Western musical forms are predominant throughout the area. Both European church singing introduced by various missions and secular styles, ranging from the whalers' chanties to modern international entertainment music, have participated in this process. Yet, remnants or elements of precontact Polynesian music have survived almost everywhere, either alongside of or within acculturated styles—because of a marked traditionalism, as in Hawaii and New Zealand, or because of a delayed acculturation process, as in many of the smaller and remoter islands.

Common traits. The first useful descriptions of Polynesian music and dance come from Capt. James Cook and his companions on his exploration voyages (1768–80). Such reports of early travellers agree with 20th-century research in suggesting that, despite regional variance, the concepts and structural characteristics of music and dance are highly similar throughout Polynesia. Music serves as a vehicle for Polynesian poetry, as dance is its illustration. The central role of the word explains why Polynesian music is primarily vocal. The only noteworthy traditional instruments used independently from song are the nose flute and the musical bow. Accompaniment of song includes body percussion (*e.g.,* slaps, claps), drums, and various idiophones (instruments the bodies of which vibrate to produce sound, such as rattles and slit-drums).

The most obvious stylistic characteristics of songs, common to all parts of Polynesia, result from word orientation. Most traditional songs can be classified as chant, as recitation in heightened speech, or as a blending of both. In some areas—for example, the Ellice Islands—the same text may be performed in either style. Chanting uses a limited number of tone levels, mostly a third or a fourth apart, and numerous tone repetitions. Rhythmic organization varies from recitative bound to the accents of the words to strict repetition of rhythmic patterns. Vocal polyphony is widespread throughout Polynesia and undisputedly indigenous. It was described by 18th-century explorers when foreign influence could hardly have affected the style of music. The most common form of polyphony, reported from almost all Polynesian groups with the marked exception of the Maori (of New Zealand) and Hawaiians, is drone produced by a second part that follows the melody rhythmically while repeating one—usually the basic—tone. All authorities agree that pure drone is a precontact element of Polynesian music. Other forms of polyphony occur locally and are believed to be a result of European influence; especially notable among these is imitational counterpoint (simultaneous, interwoven melodies using melodic imitation among the voice parts).

Beyond these basic common traits, Polynesian peoples have developed musical forms and stylistic characteristics that are distinctive for individual groups of islands.

Hawaii. What is generally known as "Hawaiian music" is the result of the acculturation that began in the early 19th century and that was greatly enhanced by the introduction (*c.* 1820) of Christian hymn tunes. The ukulele, so closely connected with this almost entirely Western style of singing, is a local adaptation of the Portuguese *bragha,* a small guitar imported to Hawaii about 1879. The Hawaiian guitar is a way of playing the European instrument by stopping the strings with a metal bar.

Despite the predominance of Western—and, more recently, Asian—influences, some evolved forms of precontact Hawaiian music and dance have been preserved. Their stylistic characteristics fall well within the limits of what has been described as common Polynesian elements.

The Society Islands. The inhabitants of the Society Islands, whose ritual and profane dances accompanied by polyphonic chanting, nose flute, and drum playing were admired by 18th-century explorers, experienced a particularly rapid and thorough Westernization of their music. A visitor to Tahiti, the largest of the Society Islands, stated in 1838: "If they ever had any native music, it has long been forgotten and no other singing is now heard but hymns and sailors' songs . . ." (Capt. Charles Wilkes, U.S. Navy; see Burrows, 1934). Still, the modern Tahitian *himene,* contrapuntal compositions in as many as six voices, retain some indigenous elements of music structure derived from polyphonic chant. These *himene,* which deal with various subjects besides the Christian sentiments (from which their name is adopted), represent a highly developed form of a hybrid Polynesian-European music style.

The Maori. The Maori of New Zealand have lost most of their instrumental music in the process of acculturation but have preserved many of their traditional chants and dances. Traditional chants and dances are classified according to function and contents of the text. Among the more prominent types are the lullabies (*oriori*), the laments (*tangi*), the incantations (*karakia*), the love songs (*waiata aroha*), the historical or genealogical recitations (*patere*), and the dance songs (*haka*). They are either recited in heightened speech or sung on narrow melodic lines undulating around a central tone, *oro.* Rhythm is largely word-bound. Any polyphony is considered a fault of performance. One important aesthetic concept requires a performance to be uninterrupted even by breaks for breathing. Consequently, chants are usually performed by two or more singers who take breaths at different moments. As in all of Polynesia the younger generations favour adaptations of Western music.

Western archipelagoes. Very little is published on the music of the large archipelagoes of western Polynesia such as Tonga and Samoa, whereas for some of the smaller groups—Uvéa, Futuna, and the Ellice Islands—published studies are available.

Before Western contact, music on the Ellice Islands was closely connected with social rank, religion, and magic. There are no detailed descriptions of dances; vocal styles included recitation in heightened speech and chant with drone polyphony (common to most of Polynesia) and triadic melodies resembling those of the Solomons. The Samoan emissaries of the London Missionary Society who converted the Ellice Islanders to Christianity (1861–76) destroyed the traditional social hierarchy and suppressed dances and songs either related to non-Christian beliefs or simply not fitting for their concepts of morality. They introduced pentatonic Christian songs characterized by two-part contrapuntal polyphony resulting from overlapping antiphony (contrasting groups of singers). This "pentatonic antiphony" is believed by some authorities to have developed in Samoa under European influence. By 1900, it seems to have become the predominant musical style on the Ellice Islands for both religious and secular topics. Since 1914, church hymns and school songs in four-part European harmony began to replace "pentatonic antiphony" as the favourite style. By 1960, four-part harmony was the almost exclusive style of church, school, and dance tunes. International "Hawaiian" music is gradually penetrating the islands as mass media and Western musical instruments such as guitars and ukuleles become available. Remnants of the earlier traditions persist only

Margin notes:

Polynesian songs

The Tahitian *himene*

with members of the older generations, although outside interest has stimulated a modest revival movement.

STUDY AND EVALUATION

Music. Although valuable descriptions of music and dance date back to the three voyages of Captain Cook (1768–80) and other early explorers, systematic studies of music structure were hardly possible before the introduction of the phonograph as an anthropological and musicological research tool. The Austrian anthropologist Rudolf Pöch was the first to record Oceanic music during his field research in New Guinea (1904–06). He was followed by many anthropologists, mostly German, who visited Melanesia, western Micronesia, and Samoa during the next 10 years. Similar recording activities began in eastern Polynesia only in the 1920s. Proper ethnomusicological evaluation of these early recordings began only much later and is still far from advanced.

The first comprehensive study of one Oceanic music culture (*i.e.,* music, underlying concepts, social role) based on a musicologist's own fieldwork is Helen H. Roberts' 1926 study of Hawaiian music, followed in 1945 by Edwin G. Burrows' study of Uvéa and Futuna. Almost all other musicological descriptions and analyses are based on archive materials rather than the authors' own field research. Only in most recent years have ethnomusicologists resumed direct investigations in Oceania, allowing studies to extend in scope beyond solely musical analysis.

Dance. Even fewer scholarly significant descriptions and analyses of Oceanic dance exist. For some island groups, reports from the voyages of Cook and other early explorers furnish largely untapped raw materials for studies in the ethnohistory of dance as well as for culture change. Much of this early journal material on dance has been extracted and included by Johannes C. Andersen in his 1933 study of Maori music. Some of the Micronesian literature was reviewed by Mary Browning in 1970 (in *Dance Perspectives*). Nothing comparable has been done for Melanesia or Australia. Scattered references can be found in the "classic" ethnographic studies, such as the Thilenius Expedition for Micronesia, John Layard for Malekula, and Margaret Mead on Samoa.

It was only in the 1960s that a few adequate, systematic studies and film documentations began to appear. Several excellent films of Australian Aboriginal dance in its ceremonial context have been produced by the Institute of Aboriginal Studies, Canberra, Australia. The only scholarly study of dance in Melanesia is Allison Jablonko's 1968 study of the Maring people of New Guinea, accompanied by a film, *Maring in Motion*. There are also dance films and descriptions for the Gilbert and Ellice Islands by Gerd Koch. On Polynesian dance, two excellent films of Hawaiian dances have been produced, and the structures of Hawaiian and Tongan dances have been analyzed by Adrienne Kaeppler. On the whole, both systematic documentation and penetrating interpretation of Oceanic music and dance still remain promising fields for future research.

(Di.C./A.Ka.)

The visual arts

GENERAL CHARACTERISTICS

Form and technology. It has often been suggested that the arts of Oceania go back to the cut or polished tool phases of the Stone Age. There is every reason to regard this as an untenable approximation. An early hypothesis that the Polynesians, for example, or at least certain components of their population, were descended from a society that had known metals is not at all unlikely. Oceanic solutions to technological problems in no way suggest the residue of a prehistoric age. On the contrary, they appear to be the result of rational choice, aiming at efficiency and economy. The "progressive" methods later brought by Europeans all too often proved to be clumsy, costly, and deceptive as far as the organization of daily life and agricultural production were concerned. There are many convincing examples of the Oceanians' capacity for scientific reflection and deliberate experimentation, such

as their adaptation of traditional fighting techniques in order to resist the Europeans and their organization of efficient methods of cultivation without the slightest assistance from their conquerors.

Materials. Oceanic art was largely governed by what material means were at hand (Figure 13). In a physical environment whose vegetation, though not luxuriant, was thoroughly understood and utilized, the people there developed a variety of working textures such as Western industrial society, for example, cannot match. Locally established Westerners have turned with immense satisfaction to the materials available there, adopted them as their own, and even transformed them into luxury items. Both as working materials and as a source of colour, the vegetable compounds available to the Oceanian artist could satisfy all of his creative requirements (especially if it is borne in mind that his artifact was never intended to stand in a home with central heating). Contemporary Western experiments in new means of artistic expression do not rival the multiplicity and complexity of Oceanic art. Today in the West, for instance, works of art are being produced by a collage of nonmetallic materials—a process long familiar to the Oceanic artist, who knew how to combine a wide variety of materials using special vegetable glues. These artists discovered many techniques for physically transforming plant materials, including pounding, chewing, and cooking. The soft paste they obtained was used to remedy any deficiencies on the surface of the principal support (which might be wood, stone, tree fern, rattan basketwork), and it also furnished an absorbent surface to receive vegetable pigment (Figure 6). The form of the finished work was thus not determined by the size of the wood or piece of stone; the work could be extended in any or all of its dimensions to whatever proportions were required to harmonize with, for example, the architecture of the great ceremonial houses.

Techniques of transforming plant materials

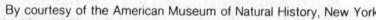
By courtesy of the American Museum of Natural History, New York

Figure 13: Variety of materials used in Oceanic art exemplified by a Melanesian decorated flute figure, wood, snail and cowrie shells, fibre, feather, opossum fur. From the Sepik area, New Guinea, Melanesia. In the American Museum of Natural History, New York City. Height 68.6 cm.

MELANESIAN VISUAL ARTS

Knowledge of metals. The Melanesians have long suffered from a prejudice whereby people who only wish to remain themselves are thought of as barbarians. Their determination, however, kept their culture alive—at least until the mid-20th century, for now it is being swept away by an accelerated process of economic development imposed and controlled by foreigners. This longer duration (outlasting traditional Polynesian art by a century) has allowed observers to discover some perhaps unexpected factors concerning the Melanesians—for example, their adaptation to iron, introduced by Europeans at the end of the 18th century. Hoops from empty barrels, which had contained wine or salted meat, were collected and cut up; the pieces were sharpened and made into carpenters' adzes. These homemade tools were distributed more widely than the "proper" axes sold at a higher price by the crews of Western warships. The technique and form of wood carving was not fundamentally affected, but the results were. First of all, the slow, carefully controlled process of firing green wood to produce a material that could be carved easily was no longer necessary: with the metal axes, wood fibres could now be cut cleanly. Next, there was the new possibility of achieving a right angle—or even an acute one—instead of being obliged to have only obtuse angles (as had previously been the case, at least in the larger works; small pieces, which could be carried by hand, might always be shaped as desired by using stone splinters or animal teeth).

Although this theory of the introduction of metal seems attractive by reason of its neatness, and the cultural area in question has enough consistency to lend itself to a linear analysis of its development, it is probably advisable to proceed with some caution. The coastal populations adapted with suspicious speed to the relatively massive introduction of metal at this time, and it is important to remember that the whole area of Serera (Geelvink) Bay, New Guinea, could not have been totally unaware of metals (indeed, bronze blades have occasionally been unearthed there, which indicates a lengthy period of contact with metal). European sailing vessels during the 17th and 18th centuries took on fresh water and provisions there; some of them must also have been shipwrecked, and the debris washed ashore would undoubtedly contain pieces of metal. Earlier still, Malay *proas* (boats) and even Chinese junks had sailed along the coasts of New Guinea; and the extent to which the trading in objects of Chinese origin was carried (it occurred principally along the northern coast of western New Guinea, from Indonesia) is not known. The

Polynesians, at least, seem to have been already familiar with metal by the time of its "introduction" around the end of the 18th century.

Diversity and range. It is impossible to define "Melanesian art." It must be remembered that Melanesia is a geographical concept only, designating an arc of islands—thousands in number—between New Guinea and New Zealand. Its cultural diversity is extraordinary and absolutely defies classification. Its art is no exception. Distinct regions must be treated separately; for local artists, like those of other cultures, have different ways of transforming various components into an original work. Even in the interior of one island there may be numerous quite different plastic traditions, though of course, there may also be elements in common, such as the *uli* and *malanggan* carving traditions of New Ireland (Figure 14). Aesthetic elements are absorbed and diffused so quickly that an alteration of the distribution map of themes and methods would be necessary at least every 50 years. Striking similarities in palette and the use of comparable vegetal materials—as used, for example, in Papua and Arnhem Land (northern Australia)—have not led to a similarity of artifact or style. Even if an influence of one on the other or even an interchange of cultural elements can be supposed as taking place between New Guinea and the area of Australia opposite, the artistic products of each side have no need of this proximity to explain their own existence. Ignorance on the matter is, indeed, considerable, because no one observed the technology behind the production of these objects at the time they were being made, and there is no museum equipped for the scientific study of this essential aspect. The efforts that have been made to understand everything about easel painting have not yet been extended to what is called primitive art.

If, however, the plastic art of Melanesia is to be characterized on the basis of very slim knowledge, attention might first be called to its wide range, which takes in the most durable, finished stone sculptures as well as pieces so delicate that they could be rightly called arachnidean, for they actually use cobwebs as material. Broadly speaking, however, there are two tendencies to be distinguished. One leads to stereotyped art in which the individual variations of each piece lie in the small detail, discernible only on careful examination. The other favours a form of continuous creation, much of it achieved by wholly original

Cultural diversity of Melanesian art

By courtesy of the Museum fur Volkerkunde und Schweizerisches Museum fur Volkskunde Basel, Switzerland; photograph, Hans Hinz, Basel

Figure 14: Cult house with *malanggans* from Medina, New Ireland. The house is made of wood, bamboo, small palm leaves, and croton leaves. The figures are carved in wood and painted with earth pigments and yellow oil colour. The house was erected to commemorate 14 deceased persons from the village. In the Museum für Völkerkunde und Schweizerisches Museum für Volkskunde Basel, Switzerland.

plastic innovation, the rest by a double process of first analyzing existing formal elements and then constructing new ensembles by a partial or total regrouping of these same elements.

Stereotyped art. The first tendency can operate best within the framework of a society itself unconcerned with innovation, whose local artists specialize in a way that makes it possible instantly to recognize a piece of their work, regardless of where it may be found. This specialization need not be artistic so much as a matter of craftsmanship. The Tami Islands in the Huon Gulf and the island of Tami and the Admiralty Islands, especially, have organized specialization by village for the production of a wide variety of useful articles, which include ladders, house posts, bedsteads, mortars and pestles and spatulas for preparing and spreading lime, and obsidian dagger handles and spear points, wood and coconut-shell spoons, amulets of war or the dance, pirogue (canoe) prows, and

By courtesy of the Ethnographical Museum, Budapest

Figure 15: *Melanesian articles of everyday use.*
(Left) Wooden lime spatula. From the Trobriand Islands, New Guinea. In the Ethnographical Museum, Budapest. Length 30.5 cm. (Right) Spoon fashioned from a coconut shell. From the Admiralty Islands. In the Ethnographical Museum, Budapest. Height 21.9 cm.

platters of various sizes (Figure 15). Each individual member of the given society is a more or less skillful producer of one category of objects.

Innovative art. Sometimes the specialization is a prerogative of individuals because of heredity (as in the case of Big Nambas, the sculptor of tree-fern ridgepieces, or *ponarat,* of North Malekula in the New Hebrides), and sometimes because of a personal vocation (as on Ambrim in the New Hebrides). In these cases, products, though less numerous, become more accessible to classical aesthetic analysis—because of their artistic coherence and style rather than their finish. It also becomes less difficult to attempt tracing a chronology of these works with the help of the oral tradition and, sometimes, of archaeological discovery.

There are many obstacles to be overcome in analyzing the aesthetics of Melanesian art. There is not even a documentary language adequate to describe the human body, so often the essential theme of plastic representation. A simple description of an object has no value at the level of scientific interpretation unless it is closely linked to the most exhaustive iconography possible. The more prominent characteristics of a work cannot meaningfully be isolated from the piece as a whole. The terms of the art historian's vocabulary have proved inadequate to convey the inventiveness and refinement of these artists. The eye, framed by some orbital motif—circular, oval, lozenge-shaped, double- or triple-comma-shaped—is a character-

Individual specialization (margin note)

istic of the area that includes the Sepik Valley and the northeast coast of New Guinea (Figure 16). But the variations are countless; and the only scientifically useful definition of them would be a list of every known case, with statistics of each variation and a comprehensive index. The result would be unreadable and probably useful only in the task of settling the origin of pieces that, stylistically, might belong to more than one region.

Classification by natural materials. It is perhaps the factors of environment that offer the best means of classification. There are, for example, elements common to all the areas forming the immense marshy stretches of New Guinea: palm leaves, interlaced and stitched together, are used as a surface to be painted (Figure 17); trees, whose outer wood at least offers enough resistance to the chisel, are used by sculptors such as those of the Asmat coast (Figure 5, left); beds of coloured clay along the raised banks of the rivers provide a plentiful supply of pigments. There are, of course, local variations of material and technique. In Papua the bark of the mulberry tree is treated and used to make masks, both secular and ceremonial (Figure 6, top left), whereas this material is not seen in works from Sepik and the Asmat coast. The bark, however, is again used for masks made in the mountainous regions toward the northern coast of New Guinea, as well as on the islands between that coast and New Britain, and also in the Walonga (Baining) masks of northern New Britain itself (Figure 17, right).

Perishable art of New Guinea. The high plateau and mountain valleys of the New Guinea interior have yielded so little that they might seem to constitute an aesthetic void. Such a judgment does not, however, take into account some fragile, perishable works that are made to be destroyed immediately after use. Beyond the fact that such objects are indeed made, little else is known about them.

The archipelagoes. More information about the archipelagoes—which are, properly speaking, Melanesian—awaits proper research into a number of historical collections, especially that of the British Museum. Representations of human, beast, and fish figures from the Solomon Islands (Figure 7), notable for their austere, stylized simplicity, suggest an area of common influence that includes Merat Island (north of western New Guinea); the Huon Gulf and Tami; the Massim area; and the Admiralty Islands, even extending to western Polynesia (including Fiji) and central Polynesia. The figures also have features in common with some that have been dug from peat bogs in New Zealand.

Limited knowledge of art in the New Guinea interior (margin note)

Holle Bildarchiv, Baden-Baden, West Germany

Figure 16: Mask with orbital motif, rattan painted with earth pigments. From the southern Maprik area, New Guinea, Melanesia. In the Museum für Völkerkunde und Schweizerisches Museum für Volkskunde Basel, Switzerland. Height 54.6 cm.

Figure 17: *Natural materials used by Melanesian artists.*
(Left) Painted plaques made of interlaced and stitched palm leaves. From the southern
Maprik area, New Guinea. In the Museum für Völkerkunde und Schweizerisches Museum für
Volkskunde Basel, Switzerland. Height 78.1 cm. (Right) Tapa (bark) cloth mask made by the
Walonga (Baining) tribe of northern New Britain, New Guinea. In the Museum für Völkerkunde
und Schweizerisches Museum für Volkskunde Basel, Switzerland. Height 79.4 cm.

By courtesy of the Museum fur Volkerkunde und Schweizerisches Museum fur Volkskunde Basel, Switzerland; photographs, Hans Hinz, Basel

Southern Melanesia. At the southern end of the Melanesian arc, however, from New Caledonia to the New Hebrides, there exists the familiar contrast between some areas, where there is an established and stable tradition of sculptors specializing in one or another type of mask or in monumental decorative pieces for the large clan house, such as doorjambs (Figure 18) and lintels, posts, ridge pieces; and other areas where there is an inventive culture whose aesthetic coherence is closely connected with public or partly esoteric rituals and where the art of carving is linked to a right that is sold and bought rather than being inherited. Technological ingenuity, using earth and vegetal elements, is greatest in the New Hebrides, especially in south Malekula (Figure 6, right). In the Loyalty Islands, however, and in the southern New Hebrides (Aneityum, Tana, Eromanga) there is little of interest offered other than examples of monumental architecture (Loyalty Islands), weapons for close combat, plaited articles, and various elements of body decoration.

MICRONESIAN VISUAL ARTS

Micronesia is culturally an area of transition in every way. Known facts and common sense link Micronesia—with the exception of such Polynesian islands as Kapingamarangi, or the southern Gilberts, and the Ellice Islands, where there is Samoan influence—with the aboriginal cultures of Taiwan, the Philippines, and the islands situated off the northern coast of New Guinea, with which there were continuing relations in both peace and war. Micronesian pirogues reached the Solomon Islands (especially the "Polynesian outliers," where Micronesian components form an important part of the basic population) and the northern New Hebrides. Little is known of the travel between Micronesia and Indonesia, though Spanish archives give some account of these contacts.

Because this was a warrior civilization, living in fear of powerful enemies likely to come from the east and either expecting or actively preparing for warlike expeditions within their perimeter, art tended toward the monumental (raised stones, monumental doorways) rather than the figurative. The technique in wood was, however, that of cabinetmakers, and household articles, such as the platters and stools used when grating coconuts, show modern functional forms. The artists knew how to work with mother-of-pearl inlay (Palau Islands), and their technique of plaiting ribbons cut out of pandanus leaves resulted in a delicacy of work that has something in common with certain Indonesian fabrics. The large gable figures of the Caroline Islands representing the human face (Figure 19, left) and the standing *tino* statuettes (Figure 19, right) seem, by their perfection, to be the result of a long cultural development. In the final period, the Micronesians devoted their energies and ingenuity to organizing complex political systems, establishing a hierarchy of their islands, so that there was perhaps no longer a place for artistic creativity.

Figure 18: Wooden doorjamb. From Ouebia, New Caledonia,
Melanesia. In the Museum für Völkerkunde und
Schweizerisches Museum für Volkskunde Basel,
Switzerland. Height 1.65 m.

Holle Bildarchiv, Baden-Baden, West Germany

Figure 19: *Micronesian art.*
(Left) Wooden gable-end ornament. From Mortlock Island, Caroline Islands. In the Museum für Völkerkunde, Hamburg. Height 45.1 cm. (Right) Wooden *tino* figure. From the Caroline Islands. In the Musée de l'Homme, Paris. Height 33 cm.

POLYNESIAN VISUAL ARTS

General characteristics. Polynesia is a world that ought to be better understood than it is. The West, for instance, has been aware of it since the 18th-century voyages of Capt. James Cook and Louis-Antoine de Bougainville. But it is difficult to sort out from old documents what is useful information and what stems from the romantic imaginations of 19th-century observers. Later research, such as that undertaken by the renowned Bernice P. Bishop Museum in Honolulu, though seriously intended,

too often produces only unrelated items of information, bits and pieces of folklore, which never cast much steady light on how the society under consideration functions.

In addition, much essential information was early destroyed, partly by Western missionaries, some of whom were bigots, and partly by the Polynesians themselves, who gave way with such alacrity before the power and wealth of the West that they became iconoclasts, destroying their own culture. An early 19th-century missionary, John Williams, managed to preserve some of their reli-

Figure 20: *Hawaiian wickerwork.*
(Left) War god Kukailimoku, wicker framework covered with netting into which feathers are knotted. In the British Museum. Height 81.3 cm. (Right) Royal cloak, wicker covered with netting into which feathers are knotted. In the British Museum. Height 1.75 m, overall diameter 2.89 m.

gious sculptures by hanging them from the yards of his ship, as "testimony" to the destruction of the devil's reign, so that the Polynesian evangelists would agree to spare the "pagan idols" from the pyre they had already prepared. These sculptures are now in London (Figure 8). But many specimens of plastic art did not escape. There is no way of knowing whether what has been preserved is wholly representative, or, if so, of what.

Making do with what is known and awaiting the publication of scientifically inferred catalogs, it is possible to advance the idea cautiously that Polynesia offers the most stereotyped—and in many ways the least colourful—visual arts culture of the whole Oceanic area. There are striking exceptions: Hawaiian wickerwork (either hard, to make representations of gods, or supple, to provide royal cloaks), with its outer covering of coloured feathers, displays an extraordinary iridescence (Figure 20).

New Zealand. Violent colours—red, black, jade green—are also employed in the indigenous art of New Zealand but with little subtlety. Their function is rather to provide a coloured background or even to protect perishable surfaces such as wood or interwoven reeds.

Protective function of violent colour

Using hardwoods and volcanic stone—materials that would not so easily be destroyed by time—and patiently carrying out the arduous task of carving with their inadequate tools, the Maori became meticulous sculptors (Figure 3). They showed a preference for squat human figures approximating the fetal position, whose faces, with their globular eyes, recall the people's dread of miscarriage and were indeed a reverent symbol of that to which life has been denied. These works display an astonishing mastery of technique: the Maori sculptor, for example, passing from the representation of the face to that of the profile in the bas-reliefs adorning the great reception houses; found a technical solution to the problem more advanced than that of the ancient Egyptian sculptor. Maori art remained alive the longest, though basic changes and innovations were produced by the introduction of iron. Thanks particularly to the results of a half century of local archaeology, Maori art is perhaps the best documented in the Oceanian area.

Marquesas Islands. Like New Zealand, the Marquesas Islands offer both monumental sculptures and small objects, the latter often more valuable for the study of style. Nothing like the exquisite boxes for feathers or the votive statuettes of the Maori are to be found there; but the minute scenes that are represented in filigree on ear ornaments and, with less animation, on Marquesan tortoise-shell plaques or fan handles (Figure 2), are most attractive. Also of great interest is the art of tattooed body decoration practiced there. Decoration may cover the whole body, especially the man's, with contrasting light and dark lines and bands and elaborate designs. Stone sculpture is not used so much to represent gods as to elaborate the main structural points of an open architecture consisting of terraces that are raised one above the other.

Easter Island. Easter Island will always arouse astonishment for the ingenuity of a people on a barren windswept island who, by managing volcanic tufa and utilizing the strength of hundreds of men, erected huge, heavy sculptures (Figure 21). Many of them are adorned with tufa hats, and their angular faces top bodies that were unknown for a long time afterward because they were buried in the Earth. The Easter Islanders also carved twisted forms from the branches of the only available shrubs. The forms are human representations that reflect the harsh conditions of life in a climate in which men are poised between life and death each time a prolonged dry spell scorches all cultivation, leaving only seafood as possible nourishment—and this only on days when rough seas do not make fishing an impossibility. The peoples of this inhospitable island also produced ideographic signs that are still in the process of being deciphered.

Tahiti and the surrounding islands. In eastern Polynesia, Tahiti experimented in nonfigurative art: a bundle of coconut fibres, with shell pendants, would represent the figure of the god; tapa cloth, obtained from the bark of the mulberry tree, would be given a thin wash of colour obtained from fern leaves and enjoyed simply for its decorative value (Figure 22). Art in the surrounding islands, and

Nonfigurative art of Tahiti

Figure 21: Sculptures cut from volcanic rock, Easter Island, Polynesia.
Shostal—Ernest Manewal

also in the Îles Tubuai (Austral) group, is related to that of the Cook Islands, where many of the people claim to have come from the Society Islands. Sculptures of humans are not common; but the decoration of fan handles (Huahine), of votive axes (Mangaia in the Cook Islands), of ceremo-

Holle Bildarchiv, Baden-Baden, West Germany

Figure 22: Detail of a tapa cloth printed with stamps and painted. From the Hawaiian Islands, Polynesia. In the Sammlungen des Instituts für Völkerkunde der Universität, Göttingen, West Germany. Size of detail 47 cm x 64.1 cm.

nial ladles and vertical drums (Îles Tubuai) displays great subtlety. Designs, both engraved and in relief, are made up of repeated, stylized representations of a figure with outstretched arms and legs. The statuettes of Rarotonga (representing the god Te Oro and his sons) or the representation of Tangaroa (Figure 23) creating mankind from the human forms that burgeon from his own body show the mastery of relief that Polynesian sculptors achieved, especially considering the limits that were imposed by the myth itself on its plastic representation. The perfection of form and decoration of ordinary objects—pestles to crush the taro root in preparing poi, or the countless fishing weights bearing a human face or fish form—ought also to be noted.

Figure 23: Wooden image of the god Tangaroa creating man and lesser gods. From Rurutu, Îles Tubuai (Austral Islands), Polynesia. In the British Museum. Height 1.11 m.

AUSTRALIAN VISUAL ARTS

In many parts of Australia man has had to make a great effort to survive, especially when faced by the desert conditions of the centre or the semidesert conditions to the north during the dry season. Iron was not known, and the camel was introduced only in relatively recent times. Incomparable walkers, their naked bodies tough and resistant to hardship, the Australian Aborigines strove to maintain their culture against colonial contempt and the repugnance of Christian missionaries, with the result that much more is known today about them than about the Polynesians, who were treated infinitely better by the European colonialists of their island.

Since Sir Baldwin Spencer and F.J. Gillen in the late 19th and early 20th centuries, a host of researchers have carried out a thorough survey of the aboriginal cultures. Although not as much attention has been paid to material culture and art as to other aspects of their societies, local museums display rich collections, both old and new, which are somewhat better documented than in other cases. A substantial amount of work remains to be done, but there are qualified informants still living who could give more information. It has been possible, however, thanks to the persevering efforts of Karel Kupka, to discover that colours and motifs were appropriated by certain social groups (the Dua and Yiritya dualities). But the superposition on this normative framework of systems of relations and interpersonal exchanges, implying, from one bark painter to another, prestations in the form of license to use colours and themes belonging to others, means that no work is strictly what it should be and that to decipher it a researcher must be familiar with the men and groups involved (Figure 1).

Abstract art of the central desert. Similarly, it is known that in central Australia the engraved decorations to be found on stone plaques (*tjurunga*) served the Aborigines as an aid in reciting their myths of origin. The art is abstract, and the various elements—stippled decoration, half circles, concentric circles, and parallel lines—can be understood to represent specific themes, such as seated man, tree, footprints, water hole, mythological figure, and so forth. It does not, however, represent a coherent ideographic language that can be deciphered without consulting those Aborigines who inherit a knowledge of its significance. *The tjurunga*

Ritual structures. An important part of Australian Aboriginal art consists of ritual structures, usually planted in the soil, made from a wooden framework on which strands of human hair are strung, stuck on with human blood often drawn from the male sex organ. Other works, using the same materials, were laid out over the surface of especially prepared ground. Both kinds of art were destined to be destroyed immediately after the rite, and only rare examples are known.

Rock art. Australian rock art is certainly the richest in Oceania, perhaps because ecological conditions, including the dryness of the climate, have ensured a better state of preservation for these works (Figure 24). Another factor, this time a ritual one, explains this good state of preservation. It is now known that, in a great many cases, paintings that are to be seen in caves and rock shelters are restored each year at the end of the dry season on the occasion of what is known as a multiplication rite. To retrace the outlines of the figures, say, of a kangaroo, ensures the multiplication of that species and thus a fruitful hunt during the rainy season—the season of full stomachs. The same is true of other animal figures, including human representations, as an assurance that the group will not be in danger of extinction.

(J.Gt.)

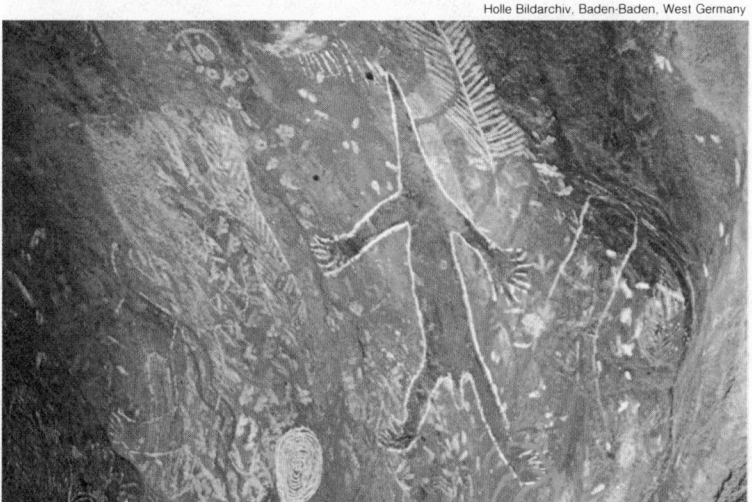

Figure 24: Rock painting of a lizard-like animal, Hawker, South Australia.

BIBLIOGRAPHY

Literature: There are no comprehensive surveys of the literature of the Oceanian peoples. The following are representative of the types of works available: JOHANNES C. ANDERSEN, *Myths and Legends of the Polynesians* (1928, reprinted 1969); CARL STROVEN (ed.), *The Spell of the Pacific: An Anthology of Its Literature* (1949); PHILIP SNOW (comp.), *Best Stories of the South Seas* (1967); JAMES NORMAN HALL, *The Forgotten One, and Other True Tales of the South Seas* (1950); WILLIAM ARMAND LESSA, *Tales from Ulithi Atoll: A Comparative Study in Oceanic Folklore* (1961); JOHN FRANCIS STIMSON, *Songs and Tales of the Sea Kings: Interpretations of the Oral Literature of Polynesia* (1957); BACIL F. KIRTLEY, *A Motif-Index of Traditional Polynesian Narratives* (1971); INEZ HANES, *Folk Tales of the South Pacific* (1969).

Music: WILLIAM P. MALM, *Music Cultures of the Pacific, the Near East and Asia* (1967), a general survey useful as an introduction; HANS FISCHER, *Schallgeräte in Ozeanien* (1958), the only comprehensive study of sound instruments in Oceania. (*Melanesia*): JAAP KUNST, *Music in New Guinea* (1967), three authoritative studies covering western New Guinea (West Irian); DIETER CHRISTENSEN, *Die Musik der Kate and Sialum* (1957), a treatise on the music of two northeastern New Guinea tribes, based on data collected 1908–10; HERBERT HUEBNER, *Die Musik im Bismarck-Archipel* (1938), the only extensive study of Melanesian music styles outside New Guinea, but the approach and conclusions are now obsolete. (*Polynesia*): JOHANNES C. ANDERSEN, *Maori Music with Its Polynesian Background* (1934), covers Polynesia in general, with an emphasis on the Maoris of New Zealand—a useful compilation of relevant excerpts from the travelogs of 18th- and 19th-century witnesses; HELEN H. ROBERTS, *Ancient Hawaiian Music* (1926, reprinted 1967), a thorough, comprehensive study; EDWIN G. BURROWS, *Native Music of the Tuamotus* (1933), a study of Tuamotu chant in its cultural context, and *Songs of Uvea and Futuna* (1945), a study of the music cultures of two small West Polynesian islands, based on the author's field work in 1932; DIETER CHRISTENSEN and GERD KOCH, *Die Musik der Ellice-Inseln* (1964), a study of the music history of this West Polynesian archipelago, is based on field research conducted in 1960–63. See also JAAP KUNST, *Ethnomusicology,* 3rd ed. (1959, with suppl. 1960), the largest and most comprehensive ethnomusicological bibliography, which contains several indexes and covers Oceania very well.

Dance: GERD KOCH, in the *Encyclopaedia Cinematographica* (E-415–418, 915–920, 1962–68), dance films and descriptions of Gilbert and Ellice Islands groups; MARY BROWNING, *Micronesian Heritage* (1970), a review of early descriptions of and writings on Micronesian dance.

Visual arts: GILBERT ARCHEY, "South Sea Folk," *Handbook of Maori and Oceanic Ethnology,* 2nd ed. (1949), and "Sculpture and Design: An Outline of Maori Art," *Handbook of the Auckland War Memorial Museum* (1955); TERRY BARROW, "Maori Decorative Carving: An Outline," *Journal of the Polynesian Society,* 65:305–331 (1956); TIBOR BODROGI, *Oceanian Art* (Eng. trans. 1959) and *Art in Northeast New Guinea* (1961 Eng. trans.); ALFRED BUHLER, TERRY BARROW, and CHARLES P. MOUNTFORD, *Ozeanien und Australien: Die Kunst der Sudsee* (1961; Eng. trans., *Oceania and Australia,* 1962); STEPHEN CHAUVET, *Les Arts indigènes en nouvelle Guinée* (1930) and *L'Île de Pâques et ses mystères* (1935); B.A.L. CRANSTONE, *Melanesia: A Short Ethnography* (1961); DANIEL SUTHERLAND DAVIDSON, *A Preliminary Consideration of Aboriginal Australian Decorative Art* (1937); ADOLPHUS PETER ELKIN and CATHERINE and RONALD BERHDT, *Art in Arnhem Land* (1950); JEAN GUIART, *Océanie* (1963); KAREL KUPKA, *Un Art à l'état brut: peintures et sculptures des aborigènes d'Australie* (1962; Eng. trans., *Dawn of Art: Painting and Sculpture of Australian Aborigines,* 1965); MAURICE LEENHARDT, *Arts de l'Océanie* (1947; Eng. trans., *Arts of the Oceanic People,* 1950); RALPH LINTON and PAUL S. WINGERT, *Arts of the South Seas* (1946); DOUGLAS NEWTON, *Art Styles of the Papuan Gulf* (1961); GLADYS AMANDA REICHARD, *Melanesian Design: A Study of Style in Wood and Tortoise Shell Carving,* 2 vol. (1933); ADRIAN A. GERBRANDS, *Wow-ipits: Eight Asmat Woodcarvers of New Guinea* (1967); T. P. VAN BAAREN, *Korwars and Korwar Style: Art and Ancestor Worship in North West New Guinea* (1968).

(J.Gt./Di.C./A.Ka.)

Oceans

The oceans and smaller seas cover about 71 percent of the Earth's surface and constitute its most conspicuous feature. These waters, together with the relatively small amount that occurs in the form of rivers, lakes, ice, and groundwater, are called the Earth's hydrosphere. The other physical spheres of the Earth are the atmosphere and the rocky lithosphere.

The oceans and seas form an integrated unit and together may properly be called the World Ocean. The Caspian Sea and the Dead Sea, however, are generally considered to be salty lakes. The exact boundaries between the various seas and oceans are arbitrarily defined and have been fixed by convention.

For many years, five oceans were accepted, namely the Atlantic, Pacific, Indian, Arctic, and Antarctic oceans. After the work of Otto Krümmel (*Handbuch der Ozeanographie* 1897), however, it became common practice to recognize only three oceans, the Atlantic, Pacific, and Indian. The Arctic Ocean is now regarded by many researchers as part of the Atlantic Ocean; this is a not unreasonable view, because it is a marginal sea of the Atlantic. The Bering Strait, which divides the Arctic from the Pacific Ocean, is only 58 kilometres (36 miles) wide and 58 metres (190 feet) deep.

Much of this article is devoted to a general discussion of the World Ocean. The chemical and physical properties of seawater are reviewed, and the interactions of the atmosphere and oceans that produce waves, currents, and other movements of oceanic waters delineated. The ocean floor and the continental terrace are also dealt with. The final sections of the article focus on the three principal oceans of the world, treating their distinctive physiographic, geologic, climatic, and hydrologic features. Other points of coverage include the economic resources of the oceans—both realized and potential.

For specifics concerning the relationship of the oceans to the other components of the Earth's hydrosphere, see HYDROSPHERE. See also ECOSYSTEMS for coverage of the life forms that populate the marine environment. Information about the nature, scope, and methods of oceanography is provided in EARTH SCIENCES.   (Ed.)

This article is divided into the following sections:

Ratio of land to water

General considerations. The oceans predominate over land areas in the Southern Hemisphere far more than they do in the Northern Hemisphere; the ratio of water to land area is roughly 4:1, 81:19 in the Southern Hemisphere and roughly 3:2, 61:39 in the Northern. Considering zones, or belts, on the Earth's surface at intervals of five degrees latitude, land predominates only between 45° and 70° N, where the Eurasian continent lies, and between 70° and

90° S, which is the location of Antarctica. Everywhere else the oceans predominate; indeed, between about 84° and 90° N there is no land at all, and from 45° to 66° S only a very small fraction of the surface is land. The areas of the Atlantic, the Indian, and the Pacific oceans, including their marginal seas, are roughly in the proportion of 10:7:17, respectively. More accurate figures are given in Table 1, which also shows the areas of various marginal seas.

In shape, the Atlantic Ocean is distinctly oblong in a north–south direction and is much more irregular than the other two oceans. It narrows between the eastern tip of Brazil and the western bulge of Africa, and this aspect of its shape is striking. On both sides of the North Atlantic but especially on the eastern side, large marginal seas and bays occur; the Mediterranean and Black Sea, the Bay of Biscay, the North Sea, the Baltic Sea, all on the eastern side, Baffin Bay, Hudson Bay, the Gulf of Mexico, and the Caribbean Sea on the western side are examples. By contrast, the configuration of the South Atlantic is much smoother, as is the eastern littoral (coastal region) of the Pacific Ocean from north to south. The western border of the Pacific, however, is indented considerably by adjacent seas such as the Sea of Okhotsk, the Sea of Japan, the East China Sea, the Yellow Sea, the South China Sea, and the seas of the Indonesian archipelago. Finally, in the Indian Ocean, only a few seas of significance occur along its northern margin, namely the Red Sea, the Persian Gulf, the Arabian Sea, and the Bay of Bengal (see Figure 1).

The Atlantic Ocean has the greatest length of coastline because of its irregular shape; the length is greater than that of the Indian and Pacific oceans combined. Another distinctive feature of the Atlantic Ocean is that the majority of major continental rivers discharge into it. Because navigation has played an important part in the history of civilization, the presence of irregular coastlines with many marginal seas, shielded bays, and river mouths, which provide excellent natural harbours, has contributed to the development and spread of culture. The lands bordering the Mediterranean Sea and western Europe and the coastal regions of India, China, and Japan have been so favoured.

Table 1 shows the horizontal dimensions of the oceans and seas and, in addition, gives their average depths and volumes.

The average depth of all the seas has been estimated at 3,790 metres (12,430 feet), a figure considerably larger than that of the average elevation of the land above the sea level, which is 840 metres (2,760 feet). If the average depth is multiplied by its respective surface area, the volume of the World Ocean is 11 times the volume of the land above sea level. The maximum depth of the ocean, 11,034 metres (36,200 feet), occurs in the Mariana Trench, halfway between the islands of Guam and Yap in the Pacific Ocean. This depth exceeds the height of Mt. Everest, which is 8,848 metres (29,028 feet).

Table 2 shows the areas that are occupied by various ocean depth zones in relation to total area of the sea surface, as a percentage. Because the 0–200-metre (660-

Depths of water

By courtesy of the International Hydrographic Organization

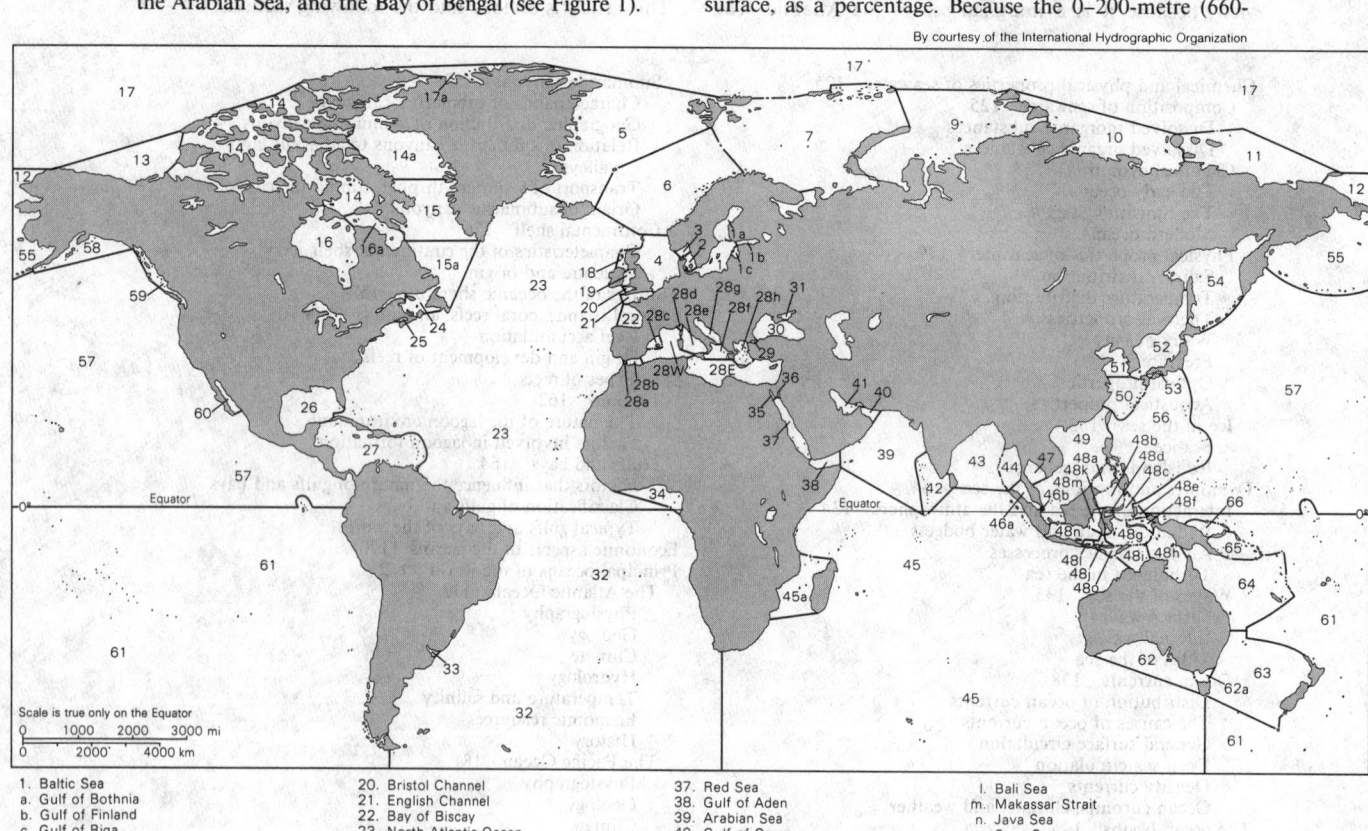

1. Baltic Sea	20. Bristol Channel	37. Red Sea	l. Bali Sea
a. Gulf of Bothnia	21. English Channel	38. Gulf of Aden	m. Makassar Strait
b. Gulf of Finland	22. Bay of Biscay	39. Arabian Sea	n. Java Sea
c. Gulf of Riga	23. North Atlantic Ocean	40. Gulf of Oman	o. Savu Sea
2. Kattegat, Sound and Belts	24. Gulf of St. Lawrence	41. Persian Gulf	49. South China Sea
3. Skagerrak	25. Bay of Fundy	42. Laccadive Sea	50. East China Sea
4. North Sea	26. Gulf of Mexico	43. Bay of Bengal	51. Yellow Sea
5. Greenland Sea	27. Caribbean Sea	44. Andaman Sea	52. Sea of Japan
6. Norwegian Sea	28W. Mediterranean Sea (Western Basin)	45. Indian Ocean	53. Inland Sea
7. Barents Sea	28E. Mediterranean Sea (Eastern Basin)	a. Mozambique Channel	54. Sea of Okhotsk
8. White Sea	a. Strait of Gibraltar	46. Malacca and Singapore straits	55. Bering Sea
9. Kara Sea	b. Alboran Sea	a. Strait of Malacca	56. Philippine Sea
10. Laptev Sea	c. Balearic Sea	b. Singapore Strait	57. North Pacific Ocean
11. East Siberian Sea	d. Ligurian Sea	47. Gulf of Thailand	58. Gulf of Alaska
12. Chukchi Sea	e. Tyrrhenian Sea	48. East Indian Archipelago (Indonesia)	59. Coastal waters of Southeast Alaska and British Columbia
13. Beaufort Sea	f. Ionian Sea	a. Sulu Sea	60. Gulf of California
14. Northwestern Passages	g. Adriatic Sea	b. Celebes Sea	61. South Pacific Ocean
a. Baffin Bay	h. Aegean Sea	c. Molucca Sea	62. Great Australian Bight
15. Davis Strait	29. Sea of Marmara	d. Gulf of Tomini	a. Bass Strait
a. Labrador Sea	30. Black Sea	e. Halmahera Sea	63. Tasman Sea
16. Hudson Bay	31. Sea of Azov	f. Ceram Sea	64. Coral Sea
a. Hudson Strait	32. South Atlantic Ocean	g. Banda Sea	65. Solomon Sea
17. Arctic Ocean	33. Río de la Plata	h. Arafura Sea	66. Bismarck Sea
a. Lincoln Sea	34. Gulf of Guinea	i. Timor Sea	
18. Inner Seas (off the west coast of Scotland)	35. Gulf of Suez	j. Flores Sea	
19. Irish Sea and St. George's Channel	36. Gulf of Aqaba	k. Gulf of Boni	

Figure 1: Boundaries of the world's oceans and seas.

Table 1: Surface Area, Volume, and Average Depth of Oceans and Seas

	area		volume		average depth	
	000,000 sq km	000,000 sq mi	000,000 cu km	000,000 cu mi	m	ft
Atlantic Ocean						
without marginal seas	82.440	31.830	324.600	77.900	3,930	12,890
with marginal seas	106.460	41.100	354.700	85.200	3,330	10,920
Pacific Ocean						
without marginal seas	165.250	63.800	707.600	169.900	4,280	14,040
with marginal seas	179.680	69.370	723.700	173.700	4,030	13,220
Indian Ocean						
without marginal seas	73.440	28.360	291.000	69.900	3,960	10,040
with marginal seas	74.920	28.930	291.900	70.100	3,900	12,790
Arctic Ocean	14.090	5.440	17.000	4.100	1,205	3,950
Mediterranean Sea and Black Sea	2.970	1.150	4.200	1.000	1,430	4,690
Gulf of Mexico and Caribbean Sea	4.320	1.670	9.600	2.300	2,220	7,280
Australasian Central Sea	8.140	3.140	9.900	2.400	1,210	3,970
Hudson Bay	1.230	0.470	0.160	0.040	128	420
Baltic Sea	0.420	0.160	0.020	0.005	55	180
North Sea	0.570	0.220	0.050	0.010	94	310
English Channel	0.075	0.029	0.004	0.001	54	180
Irish Sea	0.100	0.040	0.006	0.001	60	200
Sea of Okhotsk	1.530	0.590	1.300	0.300	838	2,750
Bering Sea	2.270	0.880	3.300	0.800	1,440	4,720
The World Ocean	361.100	139.400	1,370	329	3,790	12,430

foot) depth zone corresponds to the continental shelf, it covers an area almost as large as the zone with depths of 200–2,000 metres (660–6,600 feet), where the steeper continental slope occurs; on the other hand, depths of more than 6,000 metres (19,700 feet) cover only a very small part of the ocean bottom, in contrast to 3,000–6,000-metre (9,850–19,700 feet) depths.

The relatively shallow, submerged platform bordering the continents, called the continental shelf, slopes gently seaward to the shelf break, where an increase in gradient leads to the continental slope. (The shelf and the slope comprise the continental terrace.) Conventionally, the edge of the shelf has been placed at the 100-fathom (180-metre [about 600-foot]) depth line, although the water depth at the shelf break is more nearly 85 fathoms. The width of the continental shelf varies enormously, from nearly zero along parts of the west coast of North and South America to more than 1,000 kilometres (620 miles) off the north coast of Siberia. The average width is 75 kilometres (47 miles), and the average slope is 1.7 metres per kilometre (0.1°). The continental slope extends downward to a depth of about 4,000 metres (13,000 feet).

Its average slope near the shelf is some 70 metres per kilometre, or 370 feet per mile (4°) over a width of 20–100 kilometres (12–62 miles), and farther out to sea it gradually becomes gentler. The third zone, which may vary in width from 0 to 600 kilometres (400 miles), is called the continental rise. It merges with the deep-sea abyssal plain at an average depth of about 4,000 metres (13,100 feet).

Continental rise

Table 2: Depth Zones of the World Ocean and Their Extent

depth of zones		extent of zones		percentage of total surface of the sea
m	ft	000,000 sq km	000,000 sq mi	
0–200	660	2.74	1.06	7.6
200–1,000	660–3,300	15.5	6.0	4.3
1,000–2,000	3,300–6,600	15.2	5.9	4.2
2,000–3,000	6,600–9,800	24.5	9.5	6.8
3,000–4,000	9,800–13,100	70.8	27.3	19.6
4,000–5,000	13,100–16,400	119.1	46.0	33.0
5,000–6,000	16,400–19,700	84.1	32.5	23.5
6,000–7,000	19,700–23,000	4.0	1.5	1.1
over 7,000	23,000	0.4	0.2	0.1

CHEMICAL AND PHYSICAL PROPERTIES OF SEAWATER

Composition of seawater

The constituents of seawater include dissolved inorganic substances (such as salts), dissolved gases, and dissolved organic substances. Apart from these dissolved substances, seawater contains widely varying concentrations of particulate matter in suspension. This particulate matter, nonliving and living (such as plankton, floating forms of marine organisms), can influence certain properties of seawater, but the discussion at this point will be confined primarily to inorganic components. See below *Dissolved organic substances* for a discussion of organic constituents.

DISSOLVED INORGANIC SUBSTANCES

Table 3 shows the principal inorganic constituents of seawater other than gases. Excluding water, the constituents are listed not as chemical compounds but rather as ions, the electrically charged parts of compound molecules that dissociate because of the electrolytic action of the water in which they are dissolved. The last column, in addition, gives the percentage occurrence of constituents relative to their total mass.

Sodium and chloride ions predominate in seawater; together they form more than 85 percent by weight of the total amount of dissolved salts. The last column of the table indicates that, although the total amount of these dissolved substances may vary from place to place and

from time to time, the relative proportions of the components are remarkably constant. The total salt content may vary, because seawater can be diluted by additions of precipitation in the form of rain or snow, fresh river water, or meltwater from icebergs. At other times or places, seawater may become more saline because of evaporation of water. In both cases, the proportions of the salt constituents remain the same. The middle column of Table 3 shows the amounts of the various components relative to the amount of seawater, as parts per thousand by weight, or pro mille (grams per kilogram of seawater). These figures are only illustrative, because the total salt content may vary.

Because the total volume of the oceans and seas is 1,370,000,000 cubic kilometres (329,000,000 cubic miles), and the average total concentration of salt in the seawater amounts to about 0.036 kilograms per litre, the total amount of salt in the sea may be computed to be roughly 5×10^{19} kilograms, or 50,000,000,000,000,000 tons. Dried and spread over the whole Earth, this would produce a layer 45 metres (150 feet) thick.

The list of components given here is not complete. Although they account for virtually the entire weight of the dissolved substances, there are other trace elements (minute quantities of matter) in seawater that may be of essential importance to the economy of the sea and to life for certain organisms. Chemical analyses of seawater have revealed traces of iodine, which is an important constituent

Table 3: Principal Constituents of Seawater
(of 19 parts per thousand chlorinity)

constituent	g/kg of seawater	proportion of total salt content (percent)
Chloride (Cl⁻)	18.980	55.044
Sulfate (SO₄²⁻)	2.649	7.682
Bicarbonate (HCO₃⁻)	0.140	0.406
Bromide (Br⁻)	0.065	0.189
Fluoride (F⁻)	0.001	0.003
Boric Acid (H₃BO₃)	0.026	0.075
Sodium (Na⁺)	10.556	30.613
Magnesium (Mg²⁺)	1.272	3.689
Calcium (Ca²⁺)	0.400	1.160
Potassium (K⁺)	0.380	1.102
Strontium (Sr²⁺)	0.013	0.038
Total	34.482	100.000
Water (with traces of other substances)	965.518	
Total	1,000.000	

of some seaweeds, and of copper, which occurs in the blood of crabs. Several chemical elements were found in marine organisms before their identification in seawater. Because rivers continuously carry products of the Earth's crust from the land to the sea, the sea should contain all the elements that are found on the lands. Radioactive matter also occurs naturally in the sea, albeit in exceedingly minute concentrations. Uranium, in concentrations of about three milligrams per cubic metre, and radium, in concentrations of 0.03–0.15 milligram per 1,000,000 cubic metres, generally increase in concentration with water depth. In addition, there are such isotopic constituents as the radioactive isotope of potassium (potassium-40), which has an abundance of 0.0118 percent of the total potassium content and which constitutes by far the largest single source of radioactivity in the ocean. The radioactive isotopes of carbon (carbon-14) and hydrogen (tritium, hydrogen-3) play an important role in estimating the "age" of deep-water masses in the oceans (*i.e.,* the time elapsed since these waters were in contact with the atmosphere).

Salinity and chlorinity of seawater

Salinity is used by oceanographers to characterize the total salt content of a sample of seawater. It is defined as the total amount of solid material (in grams) that is in solution in one kilogram of seawater, when the bromine and iodine content have been replaced theoretically by an equivalent amount of chlorine, when all the carbonate has been converted to oxide, and when all the organic matter has been completely oxidized. This definition arises partly from certain considerations in analytical chemistry. With respect to the major dissolved constituents, seawater has a composition relatively constant enough so that any single major element can be selected for use as a measure of other elements and of salinity. The standard method of analysis determines the chlorinity of the sample; in effect, bromine and iodine present in the seawater are replaced by an equivalent amount of chlorine, because those two elements are precipitated by silver nitrate as well as the chlorine. The chlorinity, expressed in grams per kilogram of seawater, is identical with the number of grams of silver that is just necessary to precipitate the halogens in 0.3285233 kilogram of the seawater sample. The empirical relation between salinity (S) and chlorinity (Cl), which has been used since the standardization of the method of chlorinity determination, is that salinity equals 0.03 more than 1.805 times the chlorinity, written $S = 1.805$ Cl + 0.03. Most salinity determinations currently are made from measurements of electrical conductivity. The conductivity–chlorinity relationship has been internationally established on the basis of analyses of samples from all the seas of the world, and the chlorinity–salinity relation adopted is written $S = 1.80655$ Cl.

Both salinity and chlorinity are written as pro mille; that is, as parts per thousand (‰, or grams per kilogram).

In the vast majority of places in the oceans, the salinity lies between 34 and 37 parts per thousand. The horizontal and vertical distribution of salinity will be discussed later (see below *Physical properties of seawater: Salinity distribution*).

Dissolved gases

Because the sea is continually in contact with the atmosphere, the gases that occur in the atmosphere are also found in seawater, in concentrations depending upon their solubilities and on the chemical and biochemical reactions in which they are involved.

The solubilities of nitrogen (N_2), oxygen (O_2), and carbon dioxide (CO_2) differ greatly. They are present in air in proportions of 78 percent, 21 percent, and 0.03 percent by volume, respectively, but their saturation concentrations in seawater of 19 parts per thousand chlorinity at a temperature of 12° C (54° F), in contact with air of one atmosphere pressure, are 11.1, 6.2, and 0.3 millilitres of gas per litre of seawater. The solubility of oxygen considerably exceeds that of nitrogen, and carbon dioxide is much more soluble than either of these gases. The value given for carbon dioxide here includes carbonic acid, the compound formed by reaction of carbon dioxide with water. The solubility of gases decreases with increasing temperature.

Nitrogen is of little importance to life in seawater, with the exception of certain bacteria living on or near the bottom that manufacture ammonium salts and nitrates from nitrogen.

Oxygen is derived from the atmosphere and from marine plants that use sunlight to manufacture carbohydrates from water and carbon dioxide by photosynthesis, by which process oxygen is released. Both sources exist near the surface of the sea; at greater depth it is too dark for photosynthesis by green plants to take place. On the other hand, oxygen is consumed everywhere, even at the greatest depths, because organisms that use oxygen live there. Moreover, oxygen is consumed by combination with organic waste products when the dead remains of organisms sink to the bottom and decompose. Hence, near the surface there is overproduction of oxygen, and at greater depths there is overconsumption. In between there is a level at which production and consumption are just balanced (called the compensation depth), which may vary between one metre and 100 metres (about three to 330 feet), depending on the amount of sunlight available at the sea surface, the transparency of the water, and the abundance of plant life—which in its turn depends on available nutrients. Because oxygen is subject to consumption at all depths, it might be thought that no oxygen exists at great depths, where the production of oxygen is essentially zero, but water refreshment is brought about by the slow, continual, large-scale, water circulation within the World Ocean. At high latitudes the very heavy coldwater masses sink toward the bottom and spread to lower latitudes through the entire deep-sea layers. In the area between the upper layers of the sea, where oxygen is naturally abundant, and the deep layers, where oxygen is supplied by the oceanic circulation, a layer having a minimum oxygen concentration often occurs.

Oxygen-deficient environments

In some seas that are nearly enclosed, ventilation is lacking, and oxygen is completely absent in the stagnating deep water. Part of the Black Sea bottom waters, some Norwegian fjords with high sills (shallow inlets), and the Kau Bay of Halmahera (Indonesia) are examples. In such cases, there is a lack of horizontal communication with outside deep waters, but, in addition, stable water stratification prevents mixing of the upper and lower layers. Anaerobic bacteria (those in reducing, or oxygen-deficient, environments) produce much hydrogen sulfide (H_2S) in such water.

Apart from the fact that carbon dioxide (CO_2) is highly soluble in seawater and combines with water to give carbonic acid, the latter dissociates partly to give bicarbonate (HCO_3^-) and carbonate (CO_3^{2-}) ions, and it also reacts with calcium and magnesium to form calcium and magnesium carbonate and bicarbonate. All these reactions are reversible and may proceed in either direction, depending on the amount of carbon dioxide that is available. Because of this reversibility, the sea has a large buffering capacity (storing and regulating capacity) with respect to processes involving carbon dioxide in the atmosphere and in the sea, including those pertinent to plant life and photosynthesis. The whole system of reactions in which carbon dioxide is involved, however, is extremely complex.

DISSOLVED ORGANIC SUBSTANCES

Seawater contains a diversity of dissolved organic compounds that originate from the decomposition of organisms after their death. The amount of total dissolved organic carbon in the open ocean varies from 0.2 to 2.5 milligrams per litre. Higher values are found in landlocked areas, such as the Black Sea and the Baltic; the shallow water of the Dutch Waddenzee may contain as much as eight milligrams per litre. The highest organic-carbon concentrations are in waters of high phytoplankton (floating forms of small marine plants) productivity. In deeper water, the products of decomposition of organisms that sink toward the bottom tend to be released in the lower layers, beneath the zone where they might serve as nutrients for phytoplankton. From those depths, they may again be brought up by the water-circulation systems and by upwelling along certain coastal regions.   (P.Gr./Ed.)

Chemical evolution

The chemical history of the oceans has been divided into three stages. The first is an early stage in which the Earth's crust was cooling and reacting with volatile or highly reactive gases of an acid, reducing nature to produce the oceans and an initial sedimentary rock mass. This stage lasted until about 3,500,000,000 years ago. The second stage was a period of transition from the first to essentially modern conditions, and it is estimated to have ended 1,500,000,000 to 2,000,000,000 years ago. Since that time it is likely that there has been little change in ocean-water composition.

THE EARLY OCEANS

The initial accretion of the Earth by agglomeration of solid particles occurred about 5,000,000,000 years ago. Heating of this initially cool, unsorted conglomerate by the decay of radioactive elements and the conversion of kinetic and potential energy to heat resulted in the development of a liquid iron core and the gross internal zonation of the Earth (see EARTH). It has been concluded that formation of the Earth's core took about 500,000,000 years. It is likely that core formation resulted in the escape of an original primitive atmosphere and its replacement by one derived from loss of volatile substances from the Earth's interior (see ATMOSPHERE). Whether most of this degassing took place during core formation or soon afterward or whether there has been significant degassing of the Earth's interior throughout geologic time is uncertain. Recent models of Earth formation, however, suggest early differentiation of the Earth into three major zones (core, mantle, and crust) and attendant early loss of volatile substances from the interior. It is also likely that the Earth, after initial cold agglomeration, reached temperatures such that the whole Earth approached the molten state. As the initial crust of the Earth solidified, volatile gases would be released to form an atmosphere that would contain water (H_2O), later to become the hydrosphere; carbon gases, such as carbon dioxide (CO_2), methane (CH_4), and carbon monoxide (CO); sulfur gases, mostly hydrogen sulfide (H_2S); and halogen compounds, such as hydrochloric acid (HCl). Nitrogen also may have been present plus minor amounts of other gases. Gases of low atomic number, such as hydrogen and helium, would escape the Earth's gravitational field. Substances degassed from the Earth's interior have been called excess volatiles because their masses cannot be accounted for simply by rock weathering. An estimate of the masses of the various volatiles degassed throughout geologic time is given in Table 4.

At an initial crustal temperature of about 600° C (1,100° F), almost all of these compounds, including H_2O, would be in the atmosphere. The sequence of events that occurred as the crust cooled is difficult to construct. Below 100° C (212° F) all of the H_2O would have condensed, and the acid gases would have reacted with the original igneous crustal minerals to form sediments and an initial ocean. There are at least two possible pathways by which these initial steps could have been accomplished.

One pathway assumes that the 600° C atmosphere contains, together with other compounds, H_2O, CO_2, and HCl

Earth formation and gases released

Table 4: Estimate of "Excess Volatiles" (units of 10^{20} grams)	
Water	16,600
Total carbon as carbon dioxide	910
Sulfur	22
Nitrogen	42
Chlorine	300
Hydrogen	10
Boron, bromine, argon, fluorine, etc.	4

Source: W.W. Rubey (1951).

in the ratio of 20:3:1 and would cool to the critical temperature of H_2O. The H_2O therefore would have condensed into an early hot ocean. At this stage, the hydrochloric acid would be dissolved in the ocean (about 1 mole per litre), but most of the CO_2 would still be in the atmosphere with about 0.5 mole per litre in the ocean water. This early acid ocean would react vigorously with crustal minerals, dissolving out silica and cations and creating a residue that consisted principally of aluminous clay minerals that would form the sediments of the early ocean basins. This pathway of reaction assumes that reaction rates are slow relative to cooling. A second pathway of reaction, which assumes that cooling is slow, is also possible. In this case, at a temperature of about 400° C (752° F) most of the H_2O would be removed from the atmosphere by hydration reactions with pyroxenes and olivines. Under these conditions H_2O would not condense until some unknown temperature was reached, and the Earth might have had at an early stage in its history an atmosphere rich in CO_2 and no ocean: the surface would have been much like that of Venus today.

The pathways described are two of several possibilities for the early surface environment of the Earth. In either case, after the Earth's surface had cooled to 100° C, it would have taken only a short time geologically for the acid gases to be used up in reactions involving igneous rock minerals. The presence of bacteria and possibly algae in the fossil record of rocks greater than 3,000,000,000 years old attests to the fact that the Earth's surface had cooled to temperatures lower than 100° C by this time and that the neutralization of the original acid gases had taken place. If most of the degassing of primary volatile substances from the Earth's interior occurred early, the chloride released by reaction of HCl with rock minerals would be found in the oceans and seas or in evaporite deposits, and the oceans would have a salinity and volume comparable to those that they have today.

This conclusion is based on the assumption that there has been no drastic change in the ratios of volatiles released through geologic time. The overall generalized reaction indicative of the chemistry leading to formation of the early oceans can be written in the form: Primary igneous rock minerals + acid volatiles + H_2O → sedimentary rocks + oceans + atmosphere. Notice from this equation that if all the acid volatiles and H_2O were released early in the history of the Earth and in the proportions found today, then the total original sedimentary rock mass produced would be equal to that of today, and ocean salinity and volume would be near that of today. If, on the other hand, degassing were linear with time, then the sedimentary rock mass would have accumulated at a linear rate, as would oceanic volume. However, the salinity of the oceans would remain nearly the same if the ratios of volatiles degassed did not change with time. The most likely situation is that presented here, namely, that major degassing occurred early in Earth's history, after which minor amounts of volatiles were released episodically or continuously for the remainder of geologic time. The salt content of the oceans based on the constant proportions of volatiles released would depend primarily on the ratio of sodium chloride ($NaCl$) locked up in evaporites to that dissolved in the oceans. If all the $NaCl$ in evaporites were added to the oceans today, the salinity would be approximately doubled. This value gives a sense of the maximum

Early salinity and volume

Production
of oxygen

salinity the oceans could have attained throughout geologic time.

One component missing from the early Earth's surface was free oxygen, because it would not have been a constituent released from the cooling crust. Early production of oxygen was by photodissociation (separation due to the energy of light) of water in the Earth's atmosphere as a result of adsorption of ultraviolet light. The reaction is $2H_2O + hv \rightarrow O_2 + 2H_2$ in which hv represents photon of ultraviolet light. The hydrogen produced would escape into space, and the O_2 would react with the early reduced gases by reactions such as $2H_2S + 3O_2 \rightarrow 2SO_2 + 2H_2O$. Oxygen production by photodissociation gave the early reduced atmosphere a start toward present-day conditions, but it was not until the appearance of photosynthetic organisms approximately 3,000,000,000 years ago that it was possible for the accumulation of oxygen in the Earth's atmosphere to proceed at a rate sufficient to lead to today's oxygenated environment. The photosynthetic reaction leading to oxygen production may be written $6CO_2 + 6H_2O + hv \rightarrow C_6H_{12}O_6 + 6O_2$, in which $C_6H_{12}O_6$ represents sugar.

THE TRANSITION STAGE:
3,500,000,000–1,500,000,000 YEARS AGO

The nature of the rock record from the time of the first sedimentary rocks (about 3,500,000,000 years ago) to about 1,500,000,000 to 2,000,000,000 years ago suggests that the amount of oxygen in the Earth's atmosphere was significantly lower than today and that there were continuous chemical trends in the sedimentary rocks formed and, more subtly, in oceanic composition. The source rocks of sediments during this time were likely to be more basaltic than would later ones; sedimentary detritus was formed by the alteration of these rocks in an oxygen-deficient atmosphere and accumulated primarily under anaerobic marine conditions. The chief difference between reactions involving mineral-ocean equilibria at this time and today was the role played by ferrous iron. The concentration of dissolved iron in today's oceans is low because of the insolubility of oxidized iron oxides. During the period 1,500,000,000–3,500,000,000 years ago, oxygen-deficient environments were prevalent; these favoured the formation of minerals containing ferrous iron (reduced state of iron) from the alteration of basaltic rocks. Indeed, the iron carbonate siderite and the iron silicate greenalite, in close association with chert and the iron sulfide pyrite, are characteristic minerals that occur in middle Precambrian iron formations. The chert originally was deposited as amorphous silica; equilibrium between amorphous silica, siderite, and greenalite at 25° C (77° F) and one atmosphere total pressure requires a CO_2 pressure of about $10^{-2.5}$ atmosphere, or 10 times today's value.

The oceans at this time can be thought of as the solution resulting from an acid leach of basaltic rocks, and because the neutralization of the volatile acid gases was not restricted primarily to land areas as it is today, much of this alteration may have occurred by submarine processes. The atmosphere at the time was oxygen deficient; anaerobic depositional environments with internal CO_2 pressures of about $10^{-2.5}$ atmosphere were prevalent, and the atmosphere itself may have had a CO_2 pressure near $10^{-2.5}$

The pH of
seawater

atmosphere. If so, the pH of early ocean water was lower than that of modern seawater, the calcium concentration was higher, and the early ocean water was probably saturated with respect to amorphous silica (about 120 parts per million [ppm]).

To simulate what might have occurred, it is helpful to imagine emptying the Pacific Basin, throwing in great masses of broken basaltic material, filling it with HCl so that the acid becomes neutralized, and then carbonating the solution by bubbling CO_2 through it. Oxygen would not be permitted into the system. The HCl would leach the rocks, resulting in the release and precipitation of silica and the production of a chloride ocean containing sodium (Na), potassium (K), calcium (Ca), magnesium (Mg), aluminum (Al), iron (Fe), and reduced sulfur species in the proportions present in the rocks. As complete neutralization was approached, Al could begin to precipitate

as hydroxides and then combine with precipitated silica to form cation-deficient aluminosilicates. The aluminosilicates, as the end of the neutralization process was reached, would combine with more silica and with cations to form minerals like chlorite, and ferrous iron would combine with silica and sulfur to make greenalite and pyrite. In the final solution, chlorine (Cl) would be balanced by Na and Ca in roughly equal proportions, with subordinate K and Mg; Al would be quantitatively removed, and silicon (Si) would be at saturation with amorphous silica. If this solution were then carbonated, Ca would be removed as calcium carbonate ($CaCO_3$), and the Cl balance would be maintained by abstraction of more Na from the primary rock. The sediments produced in this system would contain chiefly silica, ferrous iron silicates, chloritic minerals, calcium carbonate, calciummagnesium carbonates, and minor pyrite.

If the HCl added were in excess of the CO_2, the resultant ocean would have a high content of calcium chloride ($CaCl_2$); but the pH would still be near neutrality. If the CO_2 added were in excess of the Cl, Ca would be precipitated as the carbonate until it reached a level approximately that of the oceans today, namely, a few hundred parts per million.

If this newly created ocean were left undisturbed for a few hundred million years, its waters would evaporate and be transported onto the continents (in the form of precipitation); streams would transport their loads into it. The sediment created in this ocean would be uplifted and incorporated into the continents. Gradually, the influence of the continental debris would be felt and the pH might shift a little. Iron would be oxidized out of the ferrous silicates to make iron oxides, but the water composition would not vary a great deal.

The primary minerals of igneous rocks are all mildly basic compounds. When they react in excess with acids such as HCl and CO_2, they produce neutral or mildly alkaline solutions plus a set of altered aluminosilicate and carbonate reaction products. It is improbable that ocean water has changed through time from a solution approximately in equilibrium with these reaction products, which are clay minerals and carbonates.

MODERN OCEANS

It is likely that the oceans achieved their modern characteristics 1,500,000,000 to 2,000,000,000 years ago. The chemical and mineralogical compositions and the relative proportions of sedimentary rocks of this age differ little from their Paleozoic counterparts. Calcium sulfate deposits of late Precambrian age testify to the fact that the acid sulfur gases had been neutralized to sulfate by this time. Chemically precipitated ferric oxides in late Precambrian sedimentary rocks indicate available free oxygen, whatever its percentage. The chemistry and mineralogy of middle and late Precambrian shales is similar to that of Paleozoic shales. Thus, it appears that continuous cycling of sediments like those of today has occurred for 1,500,-000,000 to 2,000,000,000 years and that these sediments have controlled oceanic composition.

Salt
content of
the oceans

It was once thought that the saltiness of the modern oceans simply represents the storage of salts derived from rock weathering and transported to the oceans by fluvial processes. With increasing knowledge of the age of the Earth, however, it was soon realized that, at today's rate of delivery of salts to the ocean or even at much reduced rates, the total salt content and the mass of individual salts in the oceans could be attained in geologically short-time intervals compared to Earth's age. The total mass of salt in the ocean can be accounted for at today's rates of stream delivery in about 12,000,000 years. The mass of dissolved silica in ocean water can be doubled in only 20,000 years by addition of stream-derived silica; to double sodium would take 70,000,000 years. It then became apparent that the oceans were not simply an accumulator of salts, but as water evaporated from the oceans, along with some salt, the introduced salts must be removed in the form of minerals. Thus, the concept of the oceans as a chemical system changed from that of a simple accumulator to that of a steady-state system, in which rates of inflow of materials into the oceans equal rates of outflow. The steady-state concept permits influx to vary with time, but it would be matched by nearly simultaneous and equal variation of efflux. Calculations of rates of addition of elements to the oceanic system and removal from the system show that for at least 100,000,000 years the oceanic system has been in a steady state with approximately fixed rates of major element inflow and outflow and, thus, fixed chemical composition.

In recent years it has been shown that not only is the oceanic system steady state but that its composition is probably controlled by chemical equilibria involving seawater and minerals found in marine sediments. In 1961, L.G. Sillén published a paper on *The Physical Chemistry of Sea Water,* in which he showed that the chemical composition of seawater is approximately that of a theoretical solution brought to chemical equilibrium with the minerals quartz, illite, montmorillonite, chlorite, kaolinite, calcite, and phillipsite, and the atmosphere. He pointed out that in his model the ratios of the major chemical species would be fixed but that their absolute concentrations could increase or decrease with changes in the concentration of NaCl. Sillén's model further implies that even if the rates of addition of feed material to the oceanic system are changed or the proportions of minerals in the feed, the chemical composition of seawater will be invariant.

Equili-
brium with
silicate
minerals If seawater maintains near equilibrium with the detrital silicates that have been falling through it for billions of years, its composition should correspond to that predicted by thermodynamic calculations of the composition of an aqueous solution in equilibrium with those phases. It is impossible, of course, for ocean water to have one equilibrium composition, a balance that depends upon temperature and pressure, among other factors, because its temperature ranges from 0° to 35° C (32° to 95° F) and its pressure from 1 to 1,000 atmospheres. Moreover, it cannot be in equilibrium simultaneously with all the minerals being delivered. Gibbsite and feldspar, for example, are incompatible because if placed together in a solution they would react: one would disappear and the other would be left with the final solution and an intermediate phase.

Figure 2 shows the phases that would be in equilibrium with present-day seawater at 25° C and 0° C (77° F and 32° F), respectively. The stability fields of the phases are shown as functions of pH and dissolved silicon dioxide (SiO_2). The shaded areas denote the range of seawater compositions. Gibbsite, kaolinite, montmorillonite, K-feldspar, and illite all can be stable species within the commonly observed range of seawater composition. At a P_{CO_2} near that of today's atmosphere, calcite is also a stable phase. This relation does not prove that these minerals are the cause of seawater composition, but it does show that if a mixture of these minerals were placed in a NaCl solution with the same Cl as seawater, maintained in equilibrium with the atmosphere, and allowed to come to equilibrium with the final solution, no matter which of the various coexisting mineral assemblages remained, it would fall within the typical range of composition of seawater.

The chemical equilibrium relations predict that present-day seawater has a chemical composition that is compatible with that expected for a solution continuously reacting with the great variety of minerals being added to it. Of these minerals, it is nearly in equilibrium with the typically detrital clay minerals and is out of equilibrium with most of the primary igneous rock minerals such as plagioclase feldspar, pyroxenes, and olivines. This situation may be transient and but an instant in a long-term chemical trend. On the other hand, it is compatible with continuous control of seawater by the synthesis and dissolution of a few silicate phases, resulting in seawater that never deviates far from saturation. (F.T.M./Ed.)

Physical properties of seawater

SALINITY DISTRIBUTION

In the example given in Table 3, the calculated salinity is 34.48 parts per thousand. The salinity generally varies in open seas within rather narrow limits; it is between 34 and 37 parts per thousand in most places (Figure 3). It

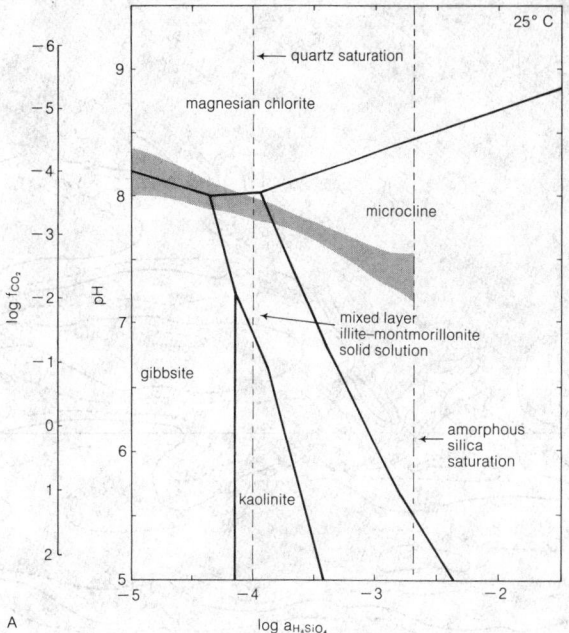

A

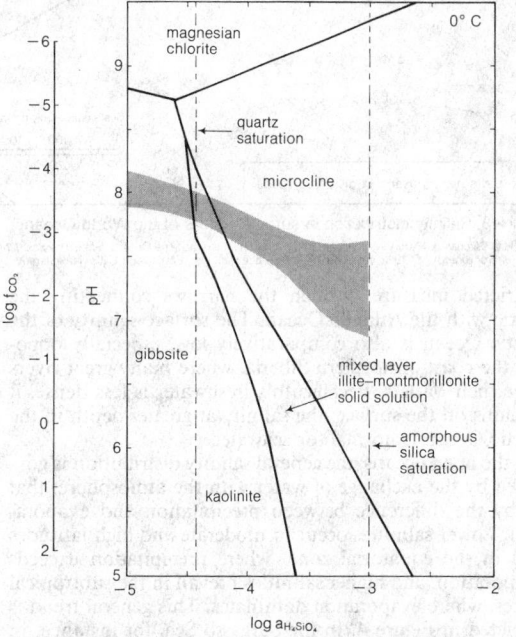

Figure 2: Stability of aluminosilicates as a function of pH and the activity of dissolved silica drawn for seawater of present composition, one atmosphere total pressure, unit activity of H_2O, at (A) 25° C and (B) 0° C (see text).

is lowest wherever there is much rainfall or where there is an influx of freshwater from many large rivers that empty into the sea. In regions receiving much freshwater in this way, particularly if they are somewhat divorced from the open ocean, salinities may be less than 34 parts per thousand as in coastal lagoons and shallow isolated areas, such as the Waddenzee behind the Frisian Islands. The salinity also is less than 34 parts per thousand in the vicinity of Newfoundland, not only because freshwater is discharged to the sea by the St. Lawrence River and the rivers of Labrador but also because pack ice and icebergs float down from the north and release their meltwater. Meltwater generally contains less salt than ocean water, and in the case of icebergs it contains no salt at all. Another example is the Baltic, where the salinity is as low as 10 parts per thousand or less in many places; in the Gulf of Bothnia and the Gulf of Finland, it is as low as 5 parts per thousand. This low salinity is caused by the great freshwater discharge of many rivers in the area and by the fact that saline ocean water can enter only in very

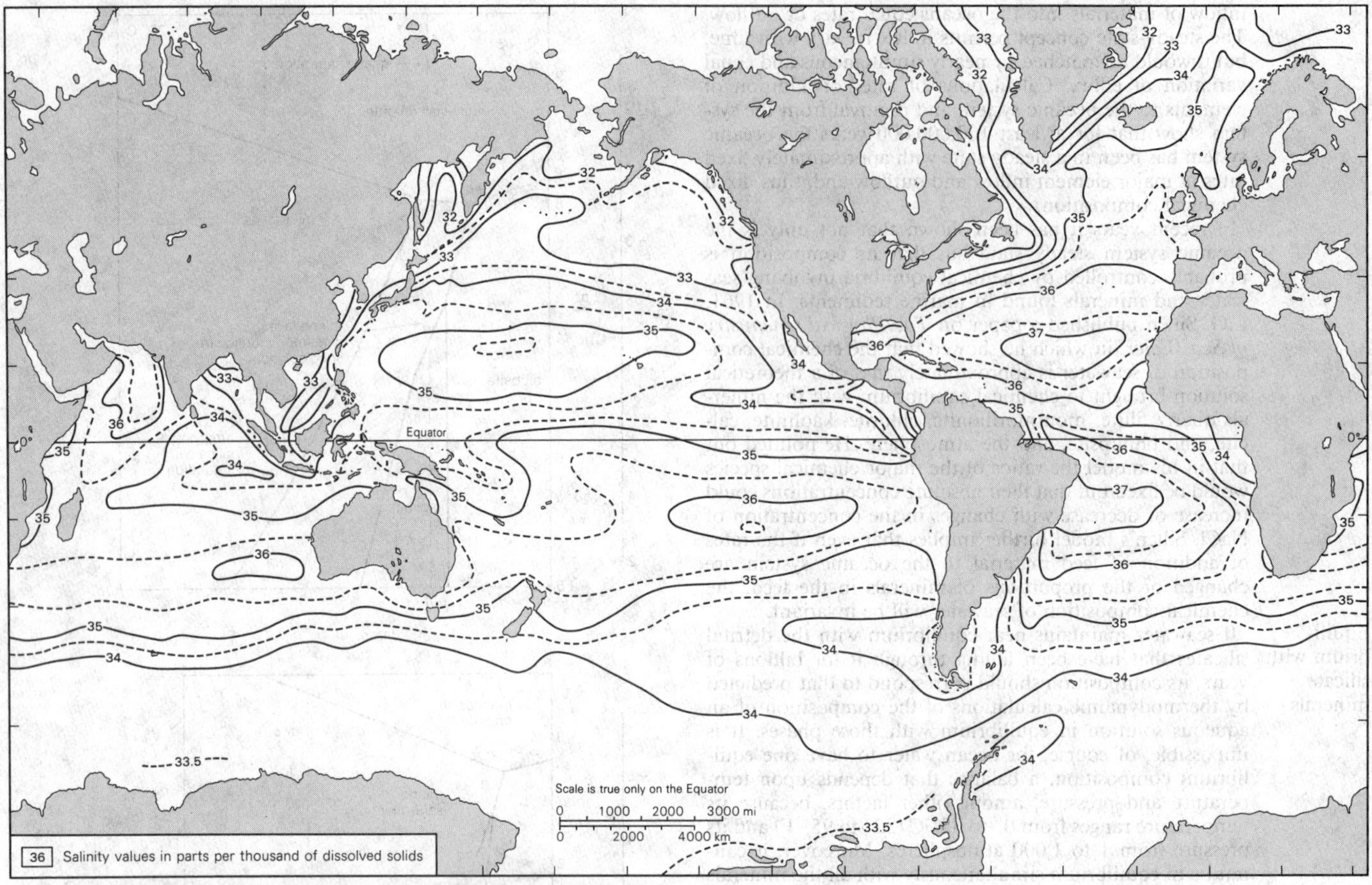

Figure 3: Salinity distribution in surface waters of the World Ocean.

From H.U. Sverdrup, Martin W. Johnson, and Richard H. Fleming, *The Oceans: Their Physics, Chemistry, and General Biology,* © 1942, renewed 1970; Prentice-Hall, Inc., Englewood Cliffs, New Jersey

restricted measure through the narrows connecting the Baltic with the Atlantic Ocean. The surface salinity of the Arctic Ocean is also comparatively low, especially opposite the coast of northern Siberia, where many great rivers have their outlets. Because this freshwater is less dense, it remains on the surface; the salinity at greater depth in the Arctic Ocean is normal for seawater.

Governing factor

In the open oceans, the general salinity distribution is governed by the exchange of water with the atmosphere; that is, by the difference between precipitation and evaporation. Lower salinities occur in moderate and high latitudes and in the equatorial zone, where precipitation exceeds evaporation, and higher salinities prevail in the subtropical zones, where evaporation dominates. This general trend is depicted in Figure 4. In the Sargasso Sea, for instance, in the middle of the Atlantic Ocean at about latitude 25° N, the salinity in summer is more than 37 parts per thousand. Salinity is still higher in the Mediterranean (38 parts per thousand) and the Red Sea (41 parts per thousand). These high salinities are the result of the small amounts of freshwater received by such seas and the high prevailing evaporation rates. Furthermore, because the water bodies are almost enclosed, they have poor communication with the open ocean. Communication of the Mediterranean Sea with the Atlantic Ocean, for example, is maintained through the narrow Strait of Gibraltar. There, water flows in from the Atlantic Ocean, notably in the upper layers, and at greater depths a countercurrent carries more saline water of the Mediterranean Sea over the sill of the strait into the Atlantic (see below *Density currents*).

Differences in salinity in the deep sea are smaller than those at the surface, ranging from 34.5 to 35.0 parts per thousand. Very exceptional conditions have been found in a few places on the floor of the Red Sea, where salinities in small bottom depressions are as high as 256 parts per thousand. These values are accompanied by temperatures as high as 60° C (140° F). It is believed that mineral salts have been extracted directly from the underlying crust in these restricted pockets.

TEMPERATURE DISTRIBUTION

The temperature of the surface waters of the oceans and seas varies greatly in different parts of the world. It may be −1.9° C (29° F) in the polar seas and may rise to as much as 30° C (86° F) in such subtropical waters as the

Surface temperatures

As adapted in *The Encyclopedia of Oceanography,* edited by Rhodes W. Fairbridge, © 1966 by Litton Educational Publishing, Inc., by permission of Van Nostrand Reinhold Company, from A. Defant, *Physical Oceanography* (© 1961); Pergamon Press Ltd., reprinted with permission

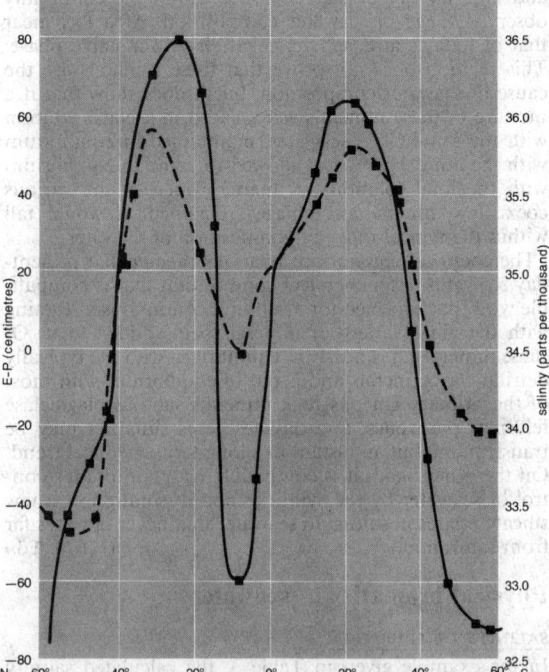

Figure 4: Mean meridional distribution of evaporation precipitation (E-P; solid line) and surface salinity (dashed line) for the entire ocean.

South China Sea and the Gulf of Mexico; temperatures may be higher still in such restricted marginal seas as the Persian Gulf, where 33° C (91° F) is not exceptional. Figure 5 shows mean annual temperatures of the ocean surface waters for the several latitudes, averaged along circles of latitude, together with the approximate annual temperature range. For the sea, the coldest and warmest

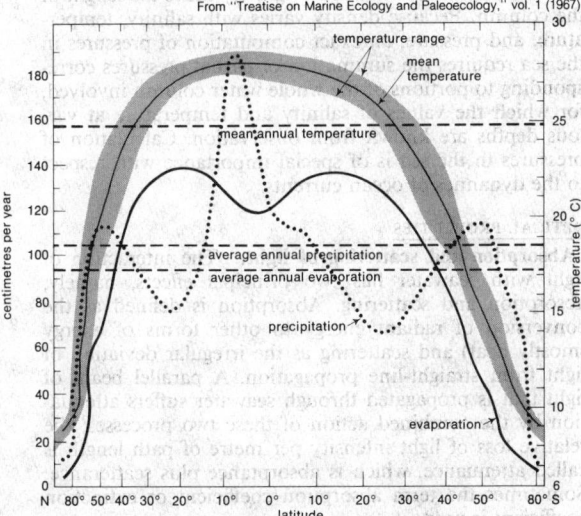

From "Treatise on Marine Ecology and Paleoecology," vol. 1 (1967)

Figure 5: Distribution of temperatures of oceanic surface waters and variation of water gains (precipitation) and losses (evaporation) with respect to latitude. The latitude scale has been adjusted for ocean area to reflect the greater water expanse in the Southern Hemisphere.

months are usually February and August in the Northern Hemisphere, outside the equatorial belt, and the reverse in the Southern Hemisphere. In tropical seas and in the polar regions, the annual range is small, about 1° to 2° C (1.8° to 3.6° F). It is largest, as far as the open ocean is concerned, between latitudes 40° and 45° N in the North Atlantic Ocean, where it is roughly 8° to 9° C (about 14° to 16° F), and in the North Pacific, where it is about 9° to 10° C (16° to 18° F). In these regions, especially on the western sides of oceans, the annual range is increased by cold offshore winds in winter that lower the winter temperatures of the sea. There is scarcely anything of this kind in the Southern Hemisphere, where the largest annual temperature range, roughly 5° to 6° C (about 9° to 11° F), occurs between latitudes 30° and 40° S. In shallow marginal seas, the annual range will generally be greater than it is in the open ocean because of the influence of neighbouring land areas.

With increasing depth beneath the surface, the annual temperature variations become smaller. In general, they may be perceptible down to 300 metres (1,000 feet), but often these temperature variations extend downward no farther than about 100 metres (330 feet).

There are certain zones of significant temperature changes over a short distance in the general pattern of horizontal temperature distribution at the ocean surface, giving the appearance of a front. Such is the case on the left-hand side of the Gulf Stream, east of the northern United States and Newfoundland, where cold waters from the north meet the warm Gulf Stream waters and partly dive under it. The boundary here is called the Arctic Polar Front, or Arctic Convergence. In the Pacific, a similar phenomenon occurs to the northeast of Japan, where the cold waters of the Oyashio meet the warm Kuroshio, or Japan Current. In the Southern Hemisphere, there is the Antarctic Convergence, winding as a closed line around the globe between latitudes 50° and 60° S, along which cool waters from higher latitudes meet warmer waters from mid-latitudes; this meeting causes the surface temperature to jump two or three degrees within a short distance.

Subsurface temperatures

Temperatures generally decrease with increasing depth, except in the polar water masses, where temperatures are low from the surface to the bottom. The vertical temperature decrease often shows a jump, above which the water

often is more or less isothermal; that is, it has the same temperature at different depths. This phenomenon may be caused by wind mixing or, in the cold season, by cooling from above, which induces vertical circulation (convection), or by both. These factors tend to make the mixed layer attain its greatest depth (to 100 metres) in winter and in spring. The jump also may be absent, particularly after a period of heating from above, or may be broken into sublayers. The drop in temperature found beneath the mixed layer is called the thermocline.

Beneath this thermocline, the decrease in temperature is more gradual, down to very low temperatures; even in tropical regions, temperatures of less than 1° C (34° F) have been found at depths of 5,000 metres (16,400 feet) or more, and the temperature already is 3.5° C (38.3° F) or less in most places at depths of 2,000 metres (6,600 feet). The cause of these low temperatures is the slow deep-sea circulation, referred to earlier in connection with the oxygen content of these deep waters. These cold-water masses are of polar or subpolar origin, and the very coldest have come from the Antarctic. In order to have a true circulation, the water must, of course, eventually come up again from these great depths. This rise does occur, but it takes place in a diffuse manner and is extremely slow everywhere in the World Ocean. This deep-sea circulation, fed by cold polar and subpolar water masses, has its place mainly within the deep part of the body of the World Ocean. It is the colder part, the other part being the warm and moderately warm upper waters of tropical and subtropical regions. These warm waters form a layer several hundred metres thick, situated roughly between latitudes 45° S and 45° to 55° N; the boundary at the surface is not sharply defined, certainly not in the eastern part of the North Atlantic Ocean, which receives the Gulf Stream waters. The lower boundary of the warm layer also is not well defined. It is usually placed at the isothermal level of approximately 10° C (50° F). The two layers may be called the thermosphere (warm sphere) and the cryosphere (cold sphere), but the important point is that the thermosphere has a circulation of its own; the two circulations are associated, however, and water may pass sometimes from one layer into the other.

There are places in the deep sea where at some depth the temperature stops falling and then rises slightly at greater depth. Such temperature inversions occur in certain deep basins and troughs, particularly in the Moluccan seas, where the bottom water enters across a shallow sill and then flows downward for a considerable vertical distance. In flowing down, it is subjected to compression, which increases with depth, and this causes adiabatic heating— heating without any heat exchange with surrounding water.

THERMAL PROPERTIES

The adiabatic temperature change just mentioned is a consequence of the fact that water is compressible. An increase in pressure causes the volume to decrease slightly so that work is performed on the water, and, if this takes place adiabatically, then the energy gained causes a rise in temperature. For example, if seawater of 35 parts per thousand salinity and a temperature of 18° C (64° F) is lowered adiabatically from the surface to 1,000 metres depth (3,300 feet), the temperature increases by 0.18° C (0.32° F); for seawater of 2° C (36° F), the rise in temperature would be 0.06° C (0.1° F); taken down to 10,000 metres (33,000 feet) depth, the water would undergo a temperature increase of 1.3° C (2.3° F). These effects depend on the compressibility and the thermal-expansion coefficient of seawater, which have different values at different temperatures and pressures. They also depend, of course, on the specific heat (heat capacity) of seawater. If water is raised from a lower to higher level, the adiabatic temperature change has the same numerical value but is negative, which means a temperature decrease. In this connection, the concept of potential temperature must be mentioned. This is the calculated temperature that a quantity of water would assume if it were brought to a certain standard level of pressure adiabatically—for instance, to the sea surface. If water is actually lowered or raised, the actual temperature will change, but the potential temperature will not. The latter, called a conservative property, can therefore be used to trace water masses in the deep sea.

Specific heat of seawater

The specific heat of seawater is the amount of heat required to raise the temperature of one kilogram (2.2 pounds) of seawater by 1° C (1.8° F) under constant pressure or with constant volume. It is somewhat smaller in value than the specific heat of pure water at the same temperature. At a temperature of 17.5° C (63.5° F), it is 1,000 calories per kilogram for pure water (under constant pressure of one atmosphere), whereas it is 932 calories per kilogram for seawater of 35 parts per thousand salinity. Specific heat decreases slightly with increasing temperature and with increasing pressure.

The freezing point of saltwater is lower than that of freshwater. For various salinity values the freezing point is as follows:

salinity (parts per thousand)	0	10	20	30	35
freezing point	0.00	−0.53	−1.08	−1.63	−1.91° C

WATER DENSITY

The density of seawater is the mass per unit volume, expressed in kilograms per cubic metre. It increases with increasing salinity and pressure and decreases with increasing temperature.

The dependency on salinity is exemplified by the following figures: at a temperature of 0° C (32° F), under atmospheric pressure, pure water has a density of 999.9 kilograms per cubic metre. Seawater of 20 parts per thousand and 35 parts per thousand salinity has a density of 1,016.1 and 1,028.1 kilograms per cubic metre, respectively. The effect of pressure becomes apparent from the following figures for seawater of 0° C and 35 parts per thousand salinity at various depths:

depth (metres)	0	1,000	2,000	10,000
density (kg/m³)	1,028	1,033	1,037.5	1,071

Dependence on temperature

The dependence of density on temperature deserves some special attention. Unlike freshwater, seawater attains its maximum density not at 4° C (39° F) but at a lower temperature. The higher its salinity, the lower the temperature at which its density is a maximum; and, if its salinity is 24.7 parts per thousand or more, seawater continues getting heavier with decreasing temperature until the freezing point is reached. This fact is of special importance in connection with the freezing over of seawater. If the sea is cooled from above, and the surface water thus becomes colder than the water underneath, it will sink downward, and water from below will take its place. For this reason, the surface water cannot drop to freezing temperature as long as the water beneath is not almost equally cold. This phenomenon explains why, apart from the lower freezing temperature, the sea does not freeze over as readily as freshwater, which remains at the surface when cooled below 4° C. The fact that the coldest seawater is the heaviest, provided its salinity is not less than 24.7 parts per thousand, also has an important bearing on global deep-sea circulation, which is driven by the sinking of ice-cold polar water masses.

The figures below give some values of the density of seawater of 35 parts per thousand salinity, for various temperatures, at atmospheric pressure (in oceanographic literature it is customary to use a quantity called sigma [σ], which is equal to density in kilograms per cubic metre minus 1,000; for the density as a function of temperature at atmospheric pressure, the symbol sigma-t [σ_t] is in use):

temperature	0	10	20	25	30° C
density (kg/m³)	1,028.1	1,027.0	1,024.8	1,023.4	1,021.75
σ_t	28.1	27.0	24.8	23.4	21.75

PRESSURE

The pressure on water in the sea is expressed in a unit called the bar, which is equal to 10^5 newton per square metre, the newton being the physical unit of force according to the international system of units. The practical unit is the decibar, which equals 0.1 bar. One decibar corresponds approximately to the pressure of one metre of seawater of normal salinity. The exact pressure exerted by a column of seawater depends on its density. If it is in equilibrium with the force of gravity, the pressure difference between the top and the bottom of a column of seawater is equal to density times acceleration of gravity times the height of the column. Because density varies with salinity, temperature, and pressure, an exact computation of pressures in the sea requires the summation of partial pressures corresponding to portions of the whole water column involved, for which the values of salinity and temperature at various depths are known from observation. Calculation of pressures in the sea is of special importance with respect to the dynamics of ocean currents.

OPTICAL PROPERTIES

Absorption and scattering of light. The interaction of light with seawater has two principal effects, namely, absorption and scattering. Absorption is defined as the conversion of radiant energy to other forms of energy (mostly heat) and scattering as the irregular deviation of light from straight-line propagation. A parallel beam of light that is propagated through seawater suffers attenuation by the combined action of these two processes; the relative loss of light intensity per metre of path length is called attenuance, which is absorptance plus scatterance. Sometimes the term absorption coefficient or extinction coefficient is used.

The absorption and scattering of light in seawater are caused by four constituents, namely, water, dissolved salts, dissolved organic substances, and suspended particles. Sea salts have negligible effect on attenuation. For pure seawater, Table 5 shows values of attenuance, scatterance, and absorptance for various wavelengths. Seawater is most transparent to blue light, and red light is strongly absorbed (infrared even more). The scattering produced by the water molecules is inversely proportional to the fourth power of the wavelength. Of the organic substances dissolved in seawater, a yellow substance, mainly carbohydrate-humic acids, especially adds significantly to the absorption of light, particularly in the shorter wavelengths. The substance is formed by decomposition of organic particulate matter and is especially abundant in northern coastal waters.

Table 5: Light Attenuance in Pure Seawater

wavelength (micron)	attenuance (percent per m)	scatterance (percent per m)	absorptance (percent per m)
0.375	4.4	0.7	3.7
0.400	4.2	0.5	3.7
0.450	1.9	0.3	1.6
0.500	3.5	0.2	3.3
0.550	6.7	0.1	6.6
0.600	16.7	0.1	16.6
0.650	25.0	0.1	24.9
0.700	39.3	0.0	39.3

Suspended particles in the sea are responsible for absorption as well as scattering. The absorption is generally stronger for short wavelengths of light than for longer waves. Scattering, on the other hand, is virtually independent of wavelength. Table 6 shows some values of the attenuance for various wavelengths in different types of seawater.

Colour and transparency of seawater. The colour of sea-

Table 6: Loss of Light (Percent) in One Metre of Seawater*

	violet		blue	green		yellow	orange	red
Wave length (micron)	0.30	0.40	0.46	0.50	0.54	0.58	0.64	0.70
Oceanic water, most transparent	16%	4%	2%	3%	5%	9%	29%	42%
Oceanic water, least transparent	57%	16%	11%	10%	13%	19%	36%	55%
Coastal water, average		63%	37%	29%	28%	30%	45%	74%

*According to Jerlov.

water depends on the spectral distribution of attenuance. It is blue for clear ocean water and shifts toward greater wavelengths for less transparent (more turbid) waters, in accordance with the shift of the spectral-attenuation minimum.

The intensity of underwater light derived from the sunlight falling on the sea surface depends on the amount of reflection at the sea surface and on the depth and transparency of the intervening layer of water. The reflection from a smooth sea surface with the Sun at various elevations in a clear sky varies from 3 percent for a high Sun to very high values for a low Sun, as is shown by the following data:

Sun's elevation (degrees)	90	50	40	30	20	10	5
reflectance (percent)	3	3	4	6	12	27	42

If the sea surface is rough because of wave action, the reflectance is decreased at low elevations and increased at higher elevations of the Sun. Also, with an overcast sky, the differences of reflectance for different elevations of the Sun become smaller.

The transparency of the sea for daylight is usually smallest in the topmost few metres of water, because of the presence of small-sized drifting material and air bubbles (foam). The amount of light reaching various depths is, of course, different for different wavelengths. For average ocean water, the following values provide an example of the relative downward light intensities, expressed in percentage of the light intensity immediately below the sea surface:

depth (m)	0	10	20	50	130	200
relative intensity (percent)	100	9.5	3.7	0.31	5×10^{-4}	2×10^{-6}

Various instruments are used to measure optical properties of the sea, the most common being the transparency meter and the Secchi disk. The principal parts of the former, also called the turbidity meter, are a light source that emits a directed beam of light and a photoelectric cell placed at some fixed distance. The cell measures the intensity of the light transmitted through the intervening column of water. The Secchi disk, about 30 centimetres (12 inches) in diameter, painted white or yellow, is lowered into the sea, and the depth at which it vanishes from sight is taken as a measure of the transparency of the water.

ACOUSTICAL PROPERTIES

Velocity of sound

The velocity of sound in seawater varies from about 1,450 to 1,570 metres (4,760 to 5,150 feet) per second; it increases with temperature at a rate of about 4.5 metres per second per degree C (8.2 feet per second per degree F), and it increases with salinity at a rate of 1.3 metres (4.3 feet) per second per part per thousand of salinity. The increase with depth (pressure) is at a rate of 1.7 metres (5.6 feet) per second per 100 metres (330 feet). At the sea surface, in water of 35 parts per thousand salinity and a temperature of 10° C (50° F), the velocity is 1,501 metres (4,923 feet) per second. A typical sound-velocity profile along a vertical in the ocean generally shows a decrease of velocity with increasing depth down to about 1,500 metres (4,900 feet), caused by the dominating effect of the temperature decrease, which is followed by a steady increase of velocity with greater depths. This velocity increase results from the effect of increasing pressure.

In the topmost 10 to 100 metres (33 to 330 feet) of the sea, a slight increase of sound velocity with depth may occur because of the pressure effect if this top layer is a mixed layer with constant temperature and salinity.

The differences in sound velocity at different depths give rise to refraction, or bending, of the sound rays. When velocity decreases with increasing depth, a downward bending occurs; when it increases with depth, there is an upward bending of the sound rays. Refraction of sound gives rise to such phenomena as shadow zones and sound channels. A shadow zone is produced when a layer with downward increase of sound velocity occurs above a layer with downward decrease of sound velocity. If a sound projector, as used in underwater acoustic detection,

is in the upper layer, one gets a shadow zone as depicted in Figure 6.

A sound channel is caused by a sound-velocity minimum in the velocity profile, such as that mentioned above. Along the axis of the velocity minimum, sound rays are refracted successively upward and downward and essentially are trapped. The sound is focussed in the channel, and loss of intensity is minimized. Small charges exploded at the right depth (about 1,500 metres) produce sounds that may be detected by hydrophones placed in the channel many thousands of miles from the source. This phenomenon is the principle of the SOFAR, sound fixing and ranging system used to locate positions at sea.

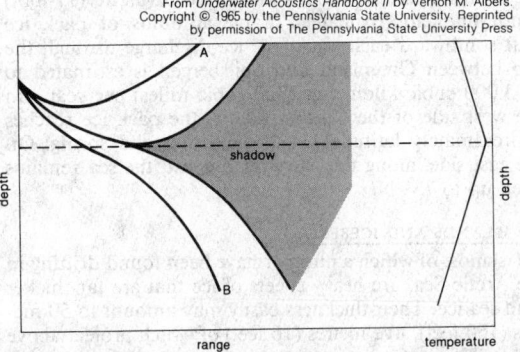

Figure 6: Acoustical properties of seawater: shadow zone formation that occurs when a positive temperature gradient lies above a negative temperature gradient. The sound projector is located within the positive gradient, and AB indicates boundaries of the sound channel (see text).

Ice in the sea

There are two types of ice in the seas: sea ice, which is ice formed by the freezing of seawater, and ice that has come from land, such as icebergs and ice islands.

SEA ICE

From an initial stage of so-called frazil crystals (floating needles and platelets) and sludge composed of them, sea ice grows to a compact aggregate of crystals of pure ice with pockets of seawater entrapped between them. Because of this composition, the salinity of sea ice is lower than that of the seawater from which it has grown. The initial sea-ice salinity may vary between 20 and two parts per thousand; the more rapid the freezing, the saltier the ice. After sea ice has formed, a process of salt removal by drainage of part of the enclosed brine sets in, because the cells in which it is contained are not completely isolated. Old ice has very low salinity, on the order of one part per thousand or less.

Growth rate of sea ice

The growth rate of sea ice depends on surface temperature, the depth of snow cover, and the heat flux in the underlying water. In the central Arctic, the thickness of an ice cover formed in one growing season is about two metres (six and one-half feet). If the ice is not broken up, it finally reaches an equilibrium thickness of about three to four metres (10 to 13 feet) in five to eight years, when the annual ablation (loss by any means) at the top and the bottom equals the annual growth. In the Antarctic, perennial sea ice is found only in the Weddell Sea and a narrow strip around the continent. Most of the Antarctic sea ice is seasonal and reaches a thickness of about 1.5 metres (five feet) by the end of October.

The drastic change of reflectivity that occurs when the sea freezes over (from 5 to 10 percent to 80 percent) makes sea ice an important factor in the heat budget of the ocean. The boundaries of the sea ice are highly variable. In the Norwegian and Greenland seas, deviations of 300 kilometres (200 miles) north or south of the average position are not uncommon. The estimated mean areas of sea ice at the end of the summer and at the end of the winter in the Arctic are 9,000,000 square kilometres (3,500,000 square miles) and 12,000,000 square kilometres (4,600,000 square miles), respectively. In the Antarctic, the corresponding values are 4,000,000 square kilometres (1,500,000 square miles) and 20,000,-000 square kilometres (8,000,000 square miles). The mean total volume of sea ice on Earth is 40,000 to 50,000 cubic kilometres (9,600 to 12,000 cubic miles), and the total amount of freezing and melting that occurs each year has been estimated at 30,000 cubic kilometres (7,200 cubic miles).

In the Arctic, it is possible to distinguish three regimes of sea ice: the great inner core, the permanent polar cap of sea ice (the Arctic pack), which covers about 6,000,000 square kilometres (2,300,000 square miles); around this the true drift ice or pack ice; and the landfast ice, which is present during nine months of the year, when it fringes the shores of the Arctic Sea out to the 22-metre (72-foot) depth line, approximately. Large amounts of pack ice drift southward each year. The ice discharge through the gap between Greenland and Spitsbergen is estimated to be 3,000 cubic kilometres (720 cubic miles) per year. On the west side of the North Atlantic, the pack ice reaches approximately latitude 45° N in winter and spring. On the east side, along the Norwegian coast, the sea remains open up to 73° N.

ICE ISLANDS AND ICEBERGS

Ice islands, of which a number have been found drifting in the Arctic Sea, are heavy sheets of ice that are far thicker than sea ice. Their thickness easily may amount to 50 metres (160 feet), five metres (16 feet) of which project above water. The surface area of the largest known ice island is approximately 1,000 square kilometres (400 square miles), but others are far smaller. Ice islands consist of a kind of glacier-like snow ice. The majority of them probably have been formed by the breaking of the shelf ice that borders the north coast of Ellesmere Island. The first ice island reported has undergone little change in configuration since its detection in 1946.

Icebergs are formed by the calving (detaching of parts) of glaciers or of inland ice that reaches the sea. The main sources of icebergs in the northern seas are the valley glaciers of Greenland, which produce some 12,000 to 15,-000 sizable icebergs annually. Almost as many are calved by the glaciers reaching the sea on the eastern seaboard as by those on the west coast, but the icebergs deriving from the east side do not travel much farther south than Kap Farvel, the southern tip of Greenland. The icebergs of the west coast, on the other hand, after travelling northward and across to the other side of Baffin Bay, are carried far south, along Baffin Island and Labrador, by the Labrador Current. It is estimated that about one in every 20 icebergs derived from west Greenland ends up south of Newfoundland (48° N), the greatest numbers arriving there in April, May, and June.

The icebergs of the Antarctic derive from an ice barrier, or shelf ice, a layer of ice that stretches out from the inland ice into the sea. It rests on the bottom near shore, but farther out to sea it floats on the water. Because of their origin, the Antarctic icebergs are very much longer than they are high, occasionally measuring some tens of kilometres in length. For this reason they are called table bergs.

The frequency with which icebergs occur in the Southern Ocean does not vary much with the season, in contrast to the North Atlantic occurrences. Generally speaking, October and November are the months in which they are most numerous in the south because of the release of the bergs from the pack ice in the southern spring. They reach farthest north from November to February. The average northern boundary for icebergs is about 40° S in the Atlantic Ocean, between 40° and 50° S in the Indian Ocean, and about 50° S in the Pacific. At least several thousands of them are adrift every year in the southern seas (see also ICE AND ICE FORMATIONS).

DYNAMICS AND MOTIONS OF THE SEA

Interaction of the sea and the atmosphere

RADIATION, HEAT, AND WATER BUDGETS

Energy gains and losses. Incoming sunlight is the primary source of energy for the atmosphere, the oceans, and the land. The heat flow from the interior of the Earth through the sea bottom is approximately 0.1 watt per square metre (see EARTH). The supply of energy to the oceans by direct and scattered solar radiation, averaged over all seas and for the entire year, has been estimated at 150 watts per square metre, or 3.5 kilowatt hours per day per square metre, less than half of the incoming solar radiation at the top of the atmosphere, which averages 350 watts per square metre. The loss is due to backscattering and absorption by the air, reflection by clouds, and reflection by the surface of the sea. Besides this shortwave primary radiation, there is a considerable supply of infrared heat radiation from the atmosphere, derived from the clouds, the water vapour, and, to a small extent, from carbon dioxide. This radiation from the atmosphere is quite variable, depending on the water-vapour content, the temperatures in the lower layers of the atmosphere, and, particularly, on the cloud cover. Averaged over the whole World Ocean, it amounts to some 235 watts per square metre. On the other hand, the Earth's surface loses heat by radiation, by evaporation, and by direct conduction through contact with the atmosphere. The loss by radiation at any place is proportional to the fourth power of the absolute temperature of the Earth's surface at that place. For the whole World Ocean, the average outgoing radiation is estimated at 300 watts per square metre. The average heat loss by evaporation is estimated at 75 watts per square metre, and the average heat conduction to the overlying air is about ten watts per square metre. Thus, the total heat gains and heat losses both amount to 385 watts per square metre. The considerable effect of the atmospheric down radiation upon the temperatures of the Earth's surface is called the greenhouse effect of the atmosphere.

Heat losses by evaporation and by conduction vary greatly from place to place and from time to time. They may even be negative, because there may be a gain of heat by condensation on the sea surface instead of evaporation at certain places. Often there is conduction of heat from the air to the seawater if the seawater is colder, as is usually the case in summer and in regions of cold ocean currents. In general, evaporation is greatest in winter, when the seawater is usually warmer than the overlying air.

Although taken as a whole there is a balance between the thermal gains and losses of the oceans of the world, this need not be the case for any particular area, because transport of heat within the oceans occurs by current action. In the northeastern part of the Atlantic Ocean to the west of Norway, expenditure in the form of heat transfer to the atmosphere and upward radiation exceeds the incoming radiation. This deficit is balanced, however, by the internal transfer of heat carried through the ocean by the Gulf Stream system. The reverse occurs in the northwestern part of the Atlantic, where cold water carried down by the Labrador Current with its burden of ice fields balances out the surplus of heat received from above.

Water budget. The annual water budgets of the oceans and the lands are approximately as follows:

	oceans	lands
evaporation km³/year	360,000	70,000
precipitation km³/year	330,000	100,000
runoff km³/year	30,000	−30,000

Stated differently, the values are

	oceans	lands
evaporation m³/sec	11.4×10^6	2.2×10^6
precipitation m³/sec	10.4×10^6	3.2×10^6
runoff m³/sec	1.0×10^6	-1.0×10^6

The annual precipitation averaged over all the oceans and seas and expressed as the height of a water column amounts to 91 centimetres (36 inches). All these figures are estimates and incorporate a considerable degree of uncertainty, but they reflect one important aspect of atmosphere–ocean interaction (see also HYDROSPHERE).

AIR–SEA TRANSFER PROCESSES

Horizontal and vertical transport

The upward or downward transport of water vapour and heat from or toward the sea surface was referred to above in relation to the energy exchange of the sea with the air. This transport is performed by fluctuating vertical motions of the air immediately above the water surface. Except within about one millimetre (0.04 inch) of the interface, where molecular processes are of importance, turbulence is responsible for the vertical transport of matter and heat. Another property that is important in connection with transport is horizontal momentum. Momentum per unit mass is velocity, the rate of supply of momentum is force, and the rate of transfer of horizontal momentum per unit area of the surface is force per unit area, which is a stress exerted through the surface. A downward transfer of horizontal momentum across the sea surface means that a wind stress is exerted on the water.

The rate of turbulent transfer of any property depends on spatial differences of that property—that is, on its gradient (difference per unit distance)—and on the magnitude of the turbulent velocities. The definition and significance of turbulent velocity will be considered later in connection with turbulence in the sea. If in the lowest layers of air there is an upward gradient of horizontally averaged value of any mass property (Q)—e.g., heat content, water-vapour content, or momentum per unit volume—a parcel of air moving downward at a certain level is liable to carry a higher value of Q with it than does an upward moving parcel of air at the same level; statistically, then, there will be a net downward flux of the corresponding quantity (heat, water vapour, momentum). Thus, the direction of flux is opposite to the direction of the gradient of Q and this is also the case with ordinary molecular diffusion. The relationship between flux and gradient is often written as

$$\text{flux} = -A \times \text{gradient of } Q,$$

in which A is the turbulent exchange (or Austausch) coefficient. Instead of A, it is customary to write $A = K \times$ density (of air), in which K is the turbulent, or eddy, diffusivity for the property concerned. In contrast to molecular diffusivity, K is not a constant characteristic of the air but is dependent upon the intensity of the turbulence and on the distance from the boundary surface. In the case of air over water, for example, it depends on the height above the water surface. In general, it will also depend on the property concerned; that is, it may be different for the exchange of water vapour, heat, and momentum. In the case of momentum transfer, K is called the eddy viscosity.

For practical purposes, instead of using the local gradient Q for determining the corresponding flux, the difference of Q between two levels is often used. For instance, the difference between the value at the sea surface and the value at some standard level, usually chosen to be 10 metres (33 feet) above sea level, can substitute for the gradient of Q. The relationship used is then: upward flux $= -D$ ($Q_1 - Q_0$), in which D is the eddy diffusion factor for the property concerned. Empirically, this factor has been shown to be roughly proportional to the wind velocity (U_1) at standard height, at least if the air is not too unstable or too stably stratified. The formula for the flux then becomes: upward flux $= -CU_1$ ($Q_1 - Q_0$), in which the factor C represents a nondimensional quantity (a pure number), which depends on what meaning has been assigned to Q.

In the case of wind stress, which is a downward transfer of momentum, Q means density times wind velocity, so that, if the wind velocity at the very sea surface is supposed to be zero, the above formula becomes:

$$\text{wind stress} = C_1 \rho U_1{}^2,$$

in which rho (ρ) equals air density. C_1, called the drag coefficient, depends on the height of the standard level chosen and on the roughness of the sea surface or the small corrugations of that surface and consequently is not a true constant. Empirically, it has been shown to have values of about 0.001 to 0.002 for wind velocities of at least seven metres per second. It increases somewhat with increasing wind velocity. Also, it tends to be greater for pronounced instability of the air and to be smaller for pronounced stability.

Three types of movements of seawater may be distinguished, namely, oscillating and rotating movements, as in water waves and tides; regular, or direct, currents; and irregular eddying movements, or turbulence that is superposed on waves or ocean currents as a form of "noise" (secondary or background disturbance).

Three movements of seawater

TURBULENCE IN THE SEA

The distinction between regular currents and turbulence is not absolute, because a varying current system of restricted dimensions within the framework of a larger current system may be looked upon as an element of turbulence with respect to that larger system. It may also be considered as a regular, though not constant, current system of its own with respect to still smaller eddies, with its own field of superposed turbulence. If, then, the turbulent velocity is defined as the momentary velocity at a certain point minus the average velocity of the current (the average being taken over a certain area), the outcome of this definition depends on the scale of averaging.

The effect of turbulent motions is to bring about an exchange of mass, heat, and momentum in much the same way as molecular motions bring about molecular diffusion, heat conduction, and viscosity. The flux, or the net amount of substance, heat, or momentum that passes per unit time through a surface of unit area by turbulence, is proportional to the gradient of mean mass of the substance concerned per unit volume. The coefficient of proportionality, called eddy diffusivity, eddy conductivity, or eddy viscosity, respectively, is not a physical constant (as is molecular diffusivity, conductivity, or viscosity) but depends on the nature of the turbulent motion and on the scale of averaging. It depends on the scale of the phenomenon under consideration and, consequently, it may have much larger values for horizontal than for vertical exchange. On the whole, it may vary from 0.1 to 10^9 square centimetres per second, increasing with increasing scale of the phenomenon. It has the same order of magnitude for the exchange of mass, heat, and momentum. Vertically, it also depends on the stability of the stratification; pronounced stability tends to counteract the development of turbulence. In the ideal case of statistical equilibrium between the eddies of different sizes, eddy diffusivity has been shown to be proportional to the 4/3rd power of the scale involved. As a consequence, the horizontal spreading of a patch of matter (suspended particulate matter or a dissolved substance) goes on at a rate that increases in time with the dimensions of the patch; indeed, as the patch becomes larger, ever larger eddies participate in spreading it; as long as the patch is of a smaller size, a larger eddy only displaces it, the spreading being left to the smaller eddies.

Effect of turbulent motions

Eddy viscosity, concerned with momentum, is of paramount importance for the dynamics of currents in the sea, particularly for wind-driven currents. In the neighbourhood of boundaries, its value decreases with decreasing distance to the boundary (e.g., bottom or sea surface) and depends on its roughness.   (P.Gr.)

Waves of the sea

Waves of the sea are of many different kinds, and only gravity waves, of which gravity is the stabilizing factor, will be considered here. Gravity waves may be surface waves or internal waves; and, in either case, a further distinction can be made between running waves and standing waves.

The tides are essentially gravity waves that are running, standing, or in an intermediate state. The tides may be termed forced waves, because they have fixed, prescribed periods that are strictly determined by the relative movements of Moon, Earth, and Sun. Sometimes the word tide is used in a wider, somewhat loose sense, including such phenomena as surges, which are called storm tides, or meteorological tides. Also, the term tidal wave is sometimes used in a general sense to denote very long gravity waves; that is, waves whose wavelength is very much greater than the depth of the sea. In the following discussion the use of the words tide and tidal will be restricted to the tides of astronomic origin and the forces and phenomena connected with them.

SURFACE WAVES

Of the nontidal kinds of running surface waves, three types may be distinguished, namely, wind waves and swell, wind surges, and sea waves of seismic origin (tsunamis).

Wind waves and swell. Wind waves are the wind-generated waves that are controlled and strengthened by the wind or wind field that made them. Afterward, when the wind has abated or shifted or when the waves have left the wind field, they run on independently as swell.

The dependence of the sizes of the waves on the wind field is a complicated one. A general impression of this dependence is given by the descriptions of the various states of the sea corresponding to the scale of wind strengths known as the Beaufort scale (Table 7), after the British admiral Sir Francis Beaufort, who drafted it in 1808, using as his yardstick the surface of sail that a fully rigged warship of those days could carry in the various wind forces. In the list given in Table 7, each Beaufort number is accompanied by a brief description of the appearance of the sea, on the lines adopted by the German sailing-ship captain Peterson. These descriptions were approved by the World Meteorological Organization for use at sea to determine the force of the wind. The Beaufort wind force is followed by the name given to such a wind at sea, and the next column gives the range of wind speeds.

Table 7: The Beaufort Scale

Beaufort number	name of wind	wind speed knots	wind speed km/hr	description of sea surface
0	calm	<1	<1	like a mirror
1	light air	1–3	1–5	ripples with the appearance of scales are formed, but without foam crests
2	light breeze	4–6	6–11	small wavelets, still short but more pronounced; crests have a glassy appearance and do not break
3	gentle breeze	7–10	12–19	large wavelets; crests begin to break; foam of glassy appearance, perhaps scattered white horses
4	moderate breeze	11–16	20–28	small waves, becoming longer; fairly frequent white horses
5	fresh breeze	17–21	29–38	moderate waves, taking a more pronounced long form; many white horses are formed (chance of some spray)
6	strong breeze	22–27	39–49	large waves begin to form; the white foam crests are more extensive everywhere (probably some spray)
7	moderate gale	28–33	50–61	sea heaps up and white foam from breaking waves begins to be blown in streaks along the direction of the wind
8	fresh gale	34–40	62–74	moderately high waves of greater length; edges of crests begin to break into spindrift; the foam is blown in well-marked streaks along the direction of the wind
9	strong gale	41–47	75–88	high waves; dense streaks of foam along the direction of the wind; crests of waves begin to topple, tumble and roll over; spray may affect visibility
10	whole gale	48–55	89–102	very high waves with overhanging crests; the resulting foam, in great patches, is blown in dense white streaks along the direction of the wind; on the whole the surface of the sea takes a white appearance; the tumbling of the sea becomes heavy and shock-like; visibility affected
11	storm	56–65	103–117	exceptionally high waves (small and medium-sized ships might be for a time lost to view behind the waves); the sea is completely covered with long white patches of foam lying along the direction of the wind; everywhere the edges of the wave crests are blown into froth; visibility affected
12–17	hurricane	above 65	above 117	the air is filled with foam and spray; sea completely white with driving spray; visibility very seriously affected

When considering the descriptions, it must be remembered that the size of the waves depends not only on the strength of the wind but also on its duration and its fetch; that is, the length of its path over the sea. Moreover, the waves are liable to be modified considerably by tidal currents; the sea is affected by precipitation (rainfall, snow, hail); and at moderate and high latitudes, at the same wind speed at observation level, the motion of the sea is higher in an air mass colder than the water than it is in one that is warmer.

Wave characteristics and motion

The theory of waves starts with the concept of simple waves, those forming a strictly periodic pattern with one wavelength and one wave period and propagating in one direction; but real waves always have a more irregular appearance. They may theoretically be described as composite waves, in which a whole spectrum of wavelengths, or periods, is present and which have more or less diverging directions of propagation. In reporting observed wave heights and periods (or lengths) or in forecasting them, one height or one period is mentioned as the height or period, however, and some agreement is needed in order to guarantee uniformity of meaning. The height of simple waves means the elevation difference between the top of a crest and the bottom of a trough. The significant height, a characteristic height of irregular waves, is by convention the average of the highest one-third of the observed wave heights. Period, or wavelength, can be determined from the average of a number of observed time intervals between the passing of successive well-developed wave crests over a certain point, or of observed distances between them.

Wave period and wavelength are coupled by a simple relationship: wavelength equals wave period times wave speed, or $L = TC$, when L is wavelength, T is wave period, and C is wave speed.

The wave speed of surface gravity waves depends on the depth of water and on the wavelength, or period; the speed increases with increasing depth and increasing wavelength, or period. If the water is sufficiently deep, then the wave speed equals the wave period times the acceleration caused by gravity, divided by two pi, or the square of the wave speed equals the wavelength times the acceleration caused by gravity, divided by two pi; these relations may be expressed as:

$$C = gT/2\pi \text{ or } C^2 = gL/2\pi,$$

in which C is wave speed, g is the acceleration caused by gravity (9.8 metres per second squared), and T and L are again wave period and length. In this case, the depth does not appear explicitly in the formula. Here, deep and shallow have only a relative meaning, denoting the ratio of depth to wavelength. In practice, for the water to be called deep and the above formula applied, it is sufficient if the depth is more than half the wavelength. A few examples are listed below, giving the period in seconds, the wavelength in metres, and wave speed in metres per second:

period T (seconds)	1	2	4	8	16
wavelength L (m)	1.56	6.2	25.0	100	400
wave speed in deep water (m/sec)	1.56	3.1	6.2	12.5	25.0

For waves in very shallow water, another simple formula holds, one in which wavelength and period do not appear explicitly. It is: wave speed squared equals the depth times the acceleration caused by gravity, or:

$$C^2 = gD,$$

in which D means depth. In practice, this formula may be applied if the depth is less than $\frac{1}{25}$ of the wavelength or if L is more than 25 times the depth. Instead of denoting this expression as one for waves in very shallow water, it often is considered to be for long waves, both expressions meaning the same thing.

Wave trains and group velocity

Waves often appear in groups as the result of interference of wave trains of slightly differing wavelengths. A wave group as a whole has a group speed that generally is less than the speed of propagation of the individual waves; the two speeds are equal only when the waves are in very shallow water. For deep-water waves, the group velocity (V) is half the wave speed (C). In intermediate cases, V has a value from 0.5 C to C. In the physical sense, group velocity is the velocity of propagation of wave energy. From the dynamics of the waves, it follows that the wave energy per unit area of the sea surface is proportional to the square of the wave height, except for the very last stage of waves running into shallow water, shortly before they become breakers.

The height of wind waves increases with increasing wind speed and with increasing duration and fetch of the wind. Together with height, the dominant wavelength also increases. Finally, however, the waves reach a state of saturation, because they attain the maximum significant height to which the wind can raise them, even if duration and fetch are unlimited. For instance, winds of five metres (16 feet) per second, 15 metres (50 feet) per second, and 25 metres (80 feet) per second may raise waves with significant heights up to 0.5 metre (1.6 feet), 4.5 metres (15 feet), and 12.5 metres (41 feet), respectively, with corresponding wavelengths of 16 metres (53 feet), 140 metres (460 feet), and 400 metres (1,300 feet), respectively.

After becoming swell, the waves may travel thousands of kilometres over the ocean, particularly if the swell is from the great storms of moderate and high latitudes, whence it easily may travel into the subtropical and equatorial zones, and the swell of the trade winds, which runs into the equatorial calms. In travelling, the swell waves gradually become lower; energy is lost by internal friction and air resistance and by energy dissipation because of some divergence of the directions of propagation (fanning out). With respect to the energy loss, there is a selective damping of the composite waves, the shorter waves of the wave mixture suffering a stronger damping over a given distance than the longer ones. As a consequence, the dominant wavelength of the spectrum shifts toward the greater wavelengths. Therefore, an old swell must always be a long swell.

When waves run into shallow water, their speed of propagation and wavelength decrease, but the period remains the same. Eventually, the group velocity, the velocity of energy propagation, also decreases, and this decrease causes the height to increase. The latter effect may, however, be affected by refraction of the waves, a swerving of the wave crests toward the depth lines and a corresponding deviation of the direction of propagation. Refraction may cause a convergence or divergence of the energy stream and result in a raising or lowering of the waves, especially over nearshore elevations or depressions of the sea bottom.

In the final stage, the shape of the waves changes, and the crests become narrower and steeper until, finally, the waves become breakers (surf). Generally, this occurs where the depth is 1.3 times the wave height.

Wind surges. Running wind surges are long waves caused by a piling up of the water over a large area through the action of a travelling wind or pressure field. Examples include the surge in front of a travelling storm cyclone, particularly the devastating hurricane surge caused by a tropical cyclone, and the surge occasionally caused by a wind convergence line such as a travelling front with a sharp wind shift.

Genera-
tion of
tsunamis

Waves of seismic origin. A tsunami (Japanese *tsu*, "harbour," and *nami*, "sea") is a very long wave of seismic origin that is caused by a submarine or coastal earthquake, landslide, or volcanic eruption. Such a wave may have a length of hundreds of miles and a period of the order of a quarter of an hour. It travels across the ocean at a tremendous speed; to a depth of 4,000 metres (13,000 feet), for instance, the corresponding wave speed is about 200 metres per second, or 720 kilometres per hour (450 miles per hour). In the open ocean the height of tsunamis may be only a foot or two and they pass unnoticed. As they approach a continental shelf, however, their speed is reduced and their height increases dramatically. Tsunamis have caused enormous destruction of life and property, piling up in coastal waters at places thousands of kilometres away from their point of origin, particularly in the Pacific Ocean.

A freestanding wave may arise in an enclosed or nearly enclosed basin as a free swinging of the whole water mass. Such a standing wave is also called a seiche, after the name given to the oscillating movements of the water of Lake Geneva, where this phenomenon first was studied seriously. The period of oscillation is independent of the force that first brought the water mass out of equilibrium (and that is supposed to have ceased after that) but depends only on the dimensions of the enclosing basin and on the direction in which the water mass is swinging. Assuming a simple rectangular basin of constant depth and supposing the most simple lengthwise oscillation, the period of oscillation (T) is equal to two times the length of the basin divided by the wave speed computed from the shallow-water formula above. This relationship may be written: $T = L/C$, in which L equals two times the length of the basin and C is the wave speed found from the formula, using the known depth of the basin. Besides this fundamental tone (or response to stimuli), the water mass may also swing according to an overtone, showing one or more nodal lines across the basin.

The water in an open bay or marginal sea may also perform such a free oscillation as a standing wave, the difference being that in an open bay the greatest horizontal displacements are not in the middle of the bay but at the mouth. For the fundamental period of oscillation, the formula given above is used with a wavelength equal to four times the length (from the mouth to the closed end) of the bay. In practice, of course, it is more difficult than that, because the form of a bay or marginal sea is irregular, and the depth differs from place to place. The North Sea has a period of lengthwise swinging of about 36 hours. The cause of such free oscillations may be a temporary wind or pressure field, which brought the sea surface out of its horizontal position and which afterward ceased to act more or less abruptly, leaving the water mass out of equilibrium.

(P.Gr./R.A.R.T./Ed.)

INTERNAL WAVES

Role of
density
differences

Waves that have their maximum energy at some depth rather than at the surface are called internal waves. They are carried by an interface, or layer, separating lighter water above from heavier water below; the difference in density is caused either by a difference in salinity or by a difference in temperature. Internal waves manifest themselves by a regular rising and sinking of the water layers around which they centre, whereas the height of the sea surface is hardly affected at all. Because the restoring force, excited by the internal deformation of the water layers of equal density, is much smaller than in the case of surface waves, internal waves are much slower than the latter. Given the same wavelength, the period is much longer (the movements of the water particles being much more sluggish), and the speed of propagation is much smaller; the formulas for the speed of surface waves include the acceleration of gravity (g), but those for internal waves include the gravity factor times the difference between the densities of the upper and the lower water layer divided by their sum.

The cause of internal waves may lie in the action of tidal forces (the period then equalling the tidal period) or in the action of a wind or pressure fluctuation. Sometimes, a ship may cause internal waves (dead water) if there is a shallow, brackish upper layer.

TIDES OF THE SEA

The tides may be considered as a kind of forced waves, partially running waves, partially standing waves. They are manifested by vertical movements of the sea surface (the height maximum and minimum are called high water [HW] and low water [LW]) and in alternating or rotating horizontal movements of the water, the tidal currents. The words ebb and flow or flood are used to designate the falling tide and the rising tide or the tidal currents accompanying the falling tide and the rising tide, respectively.

Tide-generating forces. The forces that cause the tides are called the tide-generating forces. A tide-generating force is the resultant force of the attracting force of the Moon or the Sun and the force of inertia (centrifugal force) that results from the orbital movement of the Earth around the common centre of gravity of the Earth–Moon or Earth–Sun system.

Considering the Earth–Moon system, at any time the tide-generating force is directed vertically upward at the two places on the Earth where the Moon is in the vertical (on the same and on the opposite side of the Earth); it is directed vertically downward at all places (forming a circle) where the Moon is in the horizon at that moment; at all other places, the tide-generating force also has a horizontal component. Because this pattern of forces is coupled to the position of the Moon with respect to the Earth and because for any place on the Earth's surface the relative position of the Moon with respect to that place has, on the average, a periodicity of 24 hours 50 minutes, the tide-generating force felt at any place has that same periodicity. When the Moon is in the plane of the Equator, this force runs through two identical cycles within this time interval, because of the symmetry of the global pattern of forces described above. Consequently, the tidal period is 12 hours 25 minutes in this case; it is the period of the semidiurnal lunar tide. The fact that the Moon is alternately to the north and to the south of the Equator causes an inequality of the two successive cycles within the time interval of 24 hours 50 minutes. The effect of this inequality is formally described as the superposition of a partial tide called the diurnal lunar tide, with the period of 24 hours 50 minutes, on the semidiurnal lunar tide.

In the same manner, the Sun causes a semidiurnal solar tide, with a 12-hour period, and a diurnal solar tide, with a 24-hour period. In a complete description of the local variations of the tidal forces, still other partial tides play a role, because of further inequalities in the orbital motions of the Moon and the Earth.

The interference of the solar-tidal forces with the lunar-tidal forces (the lunar forces are about 2.2 times as strong) causes the regular variation of the tidal range between spring tide, when it has its maximum, and neap tide, when it has its minimum.

Although the tide-generating forces are very small in comparison with the force of gravity of the Earth (the lunar tidal force at its maximum being only 1.14×10^{-7} times the force of gravity), their effects upon the sea are considerable, especially because of their horizontal component. Because the Earth is not surrounded by an uninterrupted envelope of water but shows a very irregular alternation of sea and land, the mechanism of the response of the oceans and seas to the tidal forces is extremely complex, a further complication being brought about by the deflecting force of the Earth's rotation (Coriolis force).

In the Southern Ocean, the tide is propagated east–west around the world as a running wave, but it manifests itself between the continents—for instance, in the Atlantic Ocean—partly as a north-going running wave and partly as an east–west swinging standing wave; both wave movements are modified by the action of the Coriolis force. In gulfs and bays, the tide is generated by the tide of the open ocean as a forced standing wave to which the Coriolis force adds a swinging cross component, and both oscillations together result in a rotating tide. In such nearly enclosed seas as the Mediterranean, the Black, and the Baltic, a standing wave is generated by the direct action of the local tidal forces.

In these seas, the tidal range of sea level is only on the order of centimetres (2.5 centimetres equals one inch). In the open ocean, it generally is on the order of tens of centimetres. In bays and adjacent seas, however, the tidal range may be much greater, because the shape of a bay or adjacent sea may favour the development of the tide inside; in particular, there may be a resonance (large co-oscillation) of the basin concerned with the tide. The largest known tides occur in the Bay of Fundy, where spring tidal ranges up to 15 metres (50 feet) have been measured.

Tidal bores. Tidal bores form on rivers and estuaries near a coast where there is a large tidal range and the incoming tide is confined to a narrow channel. They consist of a surge of water moving swiftly upstream headed by a wave or series of waves. Such bores are quite common.

There is a large one, known as the *mascaret* on the Seine, which forms on spring tides and reaches as far upriver as Rouen. There is a well-known bore on the Severn, in England, and another forms on the Petitcodiac River, which empties into the Bay of Fundy in New Brunswick. The classical example is the bore on the Chian Tang Kiang described by Commander W. Usborne Moore of the British navy in 1888 and 1892. He reported heights of 2.5 to 3.5 metres (eight to 11 feet).

When a tidal bore forms in a river the direction of flow of the water changes abruptly as the bore passes. Before it arrives the water may be still or, more usually, a small freshwater current is flowing outward toward the sea. The tide comes in as a "wall of water" that passes up the river. Behind the wall or bore, the current flows upriver. At the division between the moving water behind the bore and the still water in front, there is a wave, the water surface behind being higher than it is in front.

This wave must travel more quickly than the water particles behind it, because as the advancing water travels upriver it collects the still water in front and sets it in motion. Upriver, the advancing tide will consist not of salt water from the sea, but of freshwater that has passed farther down and been collected and returned in front of the incoming tide. It is therefore necessary to distinguish between the velocity of the advancing wave and that of the water particles just behind it.　　(P.Gr./R.A.R.T.)

Current flow and the "wall of water"

Ocean currents

The great water masses of the Earth are interconnected by a rather orderly system of ocean currents. The driving forces for this water motion are wind friction at the sea surface and horizontal and vertical differences in the density of seawater. Differential heating and cooling, precipitation, and evaporation produce differences of water density at the sea surface. Overturning of water masses, vertical convection, and mixing provide the mechanisms for distributing density differences from the sea surface into deeper layers. This creates horizontal density differences and, consequently, horizontal pressure differences and currents at all depths in the oceans. As far as the driving forces are concerned, a distinction is made between these two components of the general oceanic circulation (wind friction and differential density); they are not independent of each other, however.

Because the oceanic circulation is so closely linked to the atmosphere and its behaviour, the great oceanic current systems cannot be as stable or as steady as might be expected. The usual charts depicting ocean currents show only the prevailing current directions and speeds, not their variability. Such charts represent the average trend of water displacements and are comparable to climatic wind charts.

DISTRIBUTION OF OCEAN CURRENTS

Charts that show the horizontal distribution of ocean currents are based on a large number of direct and indirect current observations. Most of the data are obtained from ship drifts, however. If careful record of the course and speed of the ship is made then a "dead reckoning position" is established. This would be the true position if no drift by currents has affected the course and speed of the ship. The difference between dead reckoning and the actual position as determined by astronomical or electronic means indicates the average current. Whenever possible, these differences are determined at least 24 hours apart.

The general pattern of currents throughout the world's oceans is shown in Figure 7 for the Northern Hemisphere winter. More detailed maps are available for individual oceans or for parts of the oceans, and the adjacent seas. Figure 7 shows that the distribution of currents in the upper strata of the oceans tends to coincide with the prevailing winds of the world. It should be recognized, however, that this smooth, average representation of the oceanic circulation only outlines the general trend of horizontal water movements.

Because ocean currents are three-dimensional water displacements, the vertical components of currents are also of

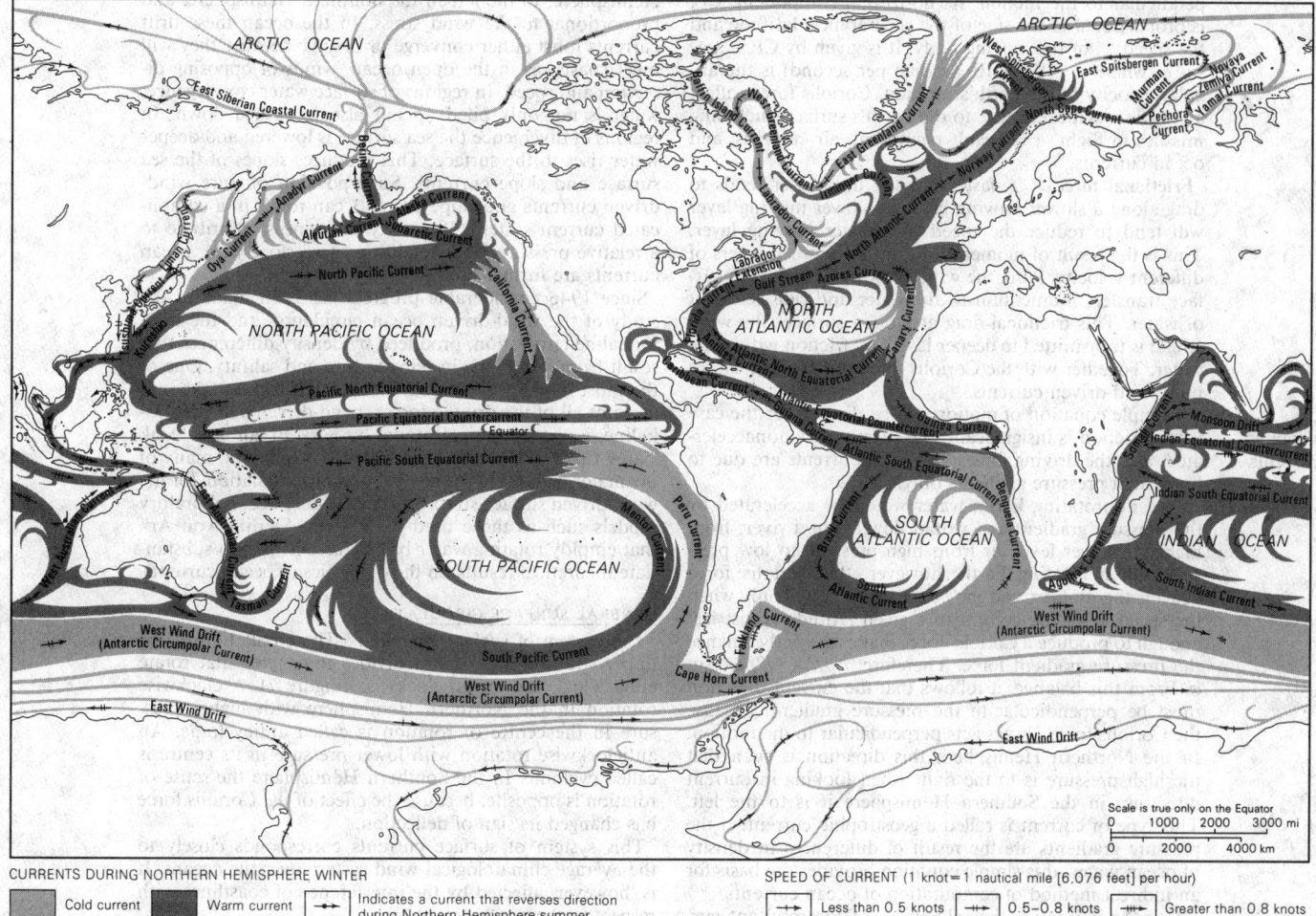

Cold current	Warm current	→←→ Indicates a current that reverses direction during Northern Hemisphere summer

SPEED OF CURRENT (1 knot = 1 nautical mile [6,076 feet] per hour)

→→ Less than 0.5 knots	→+→ 0.5–0.8 knots	→#→ Greater than 0.8 knots

Figure 7: Major ocean current systems of the world.

Vertical components of currents   interest. In general, vertical speeds are much smaller than horizontal speeds. Nevertheless, vertical motions are important for an accurate description and explanation of the oceanic circulation system. Significant vertical branches in the current structure occur mainly where horizontal currents either diverge or converge. The phenomenon of upwelling water in the surface strata of the oceans is caused by diverging surface currents in the open ocean, or near the coasts of continents where a supply of water from deeper layers is required to compensate for the seaward motion of surface currents. The formation and spreading of water masses in the deep sea also depends upon vertical branches in the current system for explanation.

THE CAUSES OF OCEAN CURRENTS

The equations of motion in hydrodynamics make use of one of Newton's fundamental laws of mechanics when applied to a continuous volume of water. They state that the product of mass and current acceleration equals the vector sum of all forces that act upon the mass.

Besides gravity, the most important forces that cause and affect ocean currents are horizontal pressure gradient forces, the Coriolis forces, and frictional forces.

Pressure gradients. The hydrostatic sea pressure, p, at any depth below the sea surface is given by the product $p = g\rho z$, where g is the acceleration of gravity, ρ is the density of seawater, and z the depth below the sea surface. Because differences in density at any fixed depth are due to differences in temperature and salinity, the sea pressure, p, will vary correspondingly from region to region. This part of the total internal pressure field in the oceans is called the relative field of pressure.

In a homogeneous ocean of constant potential density, horizontal pressure differences are possible only if the sea surface is tilted against level surfaces. Level surfaces are everywhere perpendicular to the force of gravity. In this case, surfaces of equal pressure, called isobaric surfaces, are also tilted against level surfaces in the deeper layers. This part of the internal pressure field is called the slope field. Thus, the total oceanic pressure field is composed of two parts: the relative field and the slope field. The slope field of pressure can be the result of the wind, for example, when wind-driven surface currents pile up water against a coastline or between opposing winds in the open sea.

The rate of change of pressure, Δp, along a horizontal distance, Δn, is called the horizontal pressure gradient, $\Delta p/\Delta n$. Although much smaller than the vertical pressure gradient, $\Delta p/\Delta z$, the horizontal pressure gradient nevertheless is most important with respect to ocean currents.

Coriolis effect. To an observer in space a moving body would continue to move in a straight line unless the motion were acted upon by some other force. To an earth-bound observer, however, this motion cannot be along a straight line because the reference system of coordinates is fixed to the rotating Earth. This is similar to the effect that would be experienced by an observer standing on a large turntable if an object moved over the turntable in a straight line. An apparent deflection of the path of the moving object would be seen. If the turntable rotated clockwise, this apparent deflection would be to the left, relative to an observer looking in the direction of the motion.

Because the Earth rotates from west to east about its axis, an observer in the Northern Hemisphere would notice a deflection of any moving body to the right. In the Southern Hemisphere this deflection would be to the left. At the Equator there would be no apparent horizontal deflection but only a vertical deflection for zonal currents. This most remarkable effect of the Earth's rotation, the Coriolis effect, is named after Gaspard Coriolis, a 19th-century French mathematician.

It can be shown that the Coriolis force always acts perpendicular to the motion. Its horizontal component, CF, is proportional to the sine of the geographical latitude and the speed, c, of the moving body. It is given by $CF = 2\omega c \sin\varphi$, where ω (7.29×10^{-5} radian per second) is the angular velocity of the Earth's rotation. Coriolis forces affect all motions with reference to the Earth's surface, including missiles in flight, a Foucault pendulum, air currents, and ocean currents.

Frictional forces. A faster moving fluid layer tends to drag along a slower moving layer. A slower moving layer will tend to reduce the speed of a faster moving layer. This is the result of momentum transfer between layers of different velocity. Also, the wind blowing over the sea surface transfers momentum to the water and causes a drift of water. This frictional drag at the sea surface (the wind stress) is transmitted to deeper layers by friction within the water. Together with the Coriolis force this friction causes pure wind-driven currents.

Geostrophic currents A simple equation of motion can be derived for the case where friction is insignificant, the currents are nonaccelerated, and the driving forces for ocean currents are due to horizontal pressure gradients only.

On a nonrotating Earth, water would be accelerated by the pressure gradient and would flow, as in a river, from higher to lower level, or from high pressure to low pressure. On a rotating Earth, however, the Coriolis force deflects the motion, and the acceleration ceases only when the speed, c, of the current in a given latitude is just fast enough to produce a Coriolis force that can exactly balance the pressure gradient force. Therefore: $\Delta p/\Delta n = 2\rho\omega c \sin\varphi$. From this balance, it follows that the current direction must be perpendicular to the pressure gradient, because the Coriolis force always acts perpendicular to the motion. In the Northern Hemisphere this direction is such that the high pressure is to the right when looking in current direction, in the Southern Hemisphere it is to the left. This type of current is called a geostrophic current. If the pressure gradients are the result of differences in density of ocean water, this simple equation provides the basis for an indirect method of computation of ocean currents.

If $\Delta p/\Delta n$ is known, the velocity, c, of the resultant current can be computed. Because $\Delta p/\Delta n = g\rho(\Delta z/\Delta n)$, where $\Delta z/\Delta n$ is the slope of an isobaric surface, the speed, c, of the current is obtained from $c = g(\Delta z/\Delta n)/2\omega \sin\varphi$.

Across the Gulf Stream, the slope of the sea surface over a distance of 100 kilometres is about one metre, thus $\Delta z/\Delta n = 10^{-5}$. With $g = 9.8$ metres per second squared and $2\omega \sin\varphi = 10^{-4}$ in middle latitudes, it follows that $c = 0.98$ metre per second, or about one metre per second. This is a reasonable average surface speed of the Gulf Stream. Because the Gulf Stream often is less wide and somewhat "streaky," however, its speed in some parts of its course can be higher.

The frictional drag of the wind at the water surface, and between layers of water, sets ocean water in motion. If a steady wind blows long enough over a large ocean, pure wind-driven currents are the result. They show some remarkable properties. The currents do not follow the wind direction, but are deflected at the sea surface by 45° to the right in the Northern Hemisphere, and to the left in the Southern Hemisphere. With increasing depth this deflection increases while the current speed decreases. At a certain depth, roughly around 75 or 100 metres (246 or 330 feet) in middle latitudes, the current even flows against the surface current; however, its speed has reduced to about $1/23$ of its surface speed.

Wind-driven currents In 1902 the Swedish oceanographer V. Walfrid Ekman deduced these results in a theoretical model. He considered a homogeneous ocean where frictional forces are balanced by Coriolis forces, and where resulting currents are nonaccelerated. His results show that the end points of the current vectors from surface to bottom, when vertically projected on a horizontal plane, produce a logarithmic spiral, now termed the Ekman spiral.

Pure wind-driven currents of this type do not penetrate deeply into the ocean. Essentially, they occupy a surface layer called the Ekman layer, about 100 metres deep. The average total water transport in the Ekman layer is 90° to the right of the wind direction in the Northern Hemisphere, to the left in the Southern Hemisphere, and proportional to the wind stress. In the ocean these drift currents must either converge or diverge because they will meet coasts or, in the open ocean, winds of opposing direction and speed. In regions of surface water convergence, water is not only piled up but also is pushed down. In regions of divergence the sea surface is lowered and deeper water rises to the surface. This produces slopes of the sea surface and slope currents. Superposition of pure wind-driven currents and slope currents can result in a complicated current system. If density differences contribute to a relative pressure field in addition to a slope field, ocean currents are further modified.

Since 1946 considerable progress has been made in the study of the wind-driven ocean circulation and the thermohaline circulation, produced by density differences that result from variations in temperature and salinity. One of the most modern theoretical models that tries to take into account all of the driving forces, wind-driven and thermohaline, is the numerical model by Kirk Bryan and Doak Carey Cox (1967). It has succeeded in explaining many of the major features of the general oceanic circulation, for the wind-driven surface strata and for the deep sea. Laboratory models such as those used by William Sterling von Arx that employ rotating water basins have helped to substantiate theoretical results on the dynamics of ocean currents.

GENERAL SURFACE CIRCULATION

The system of surface currents. The circulation of the upper strata of the oceans divides into gyres that rotate either clockwise or anticlockwise (Figure 7). A clockwise rotation in the Northern Hemisphere with higher pressure in the centre of rotation is called anticyclonic. An anticlockwise rotation with lower pressure in its centre is called cyclonic. In the Southern Hemisphere the sense of rotation is opposite, because the effect of the Coriolis force has changed its sign of deflection.

This system of surface currents corresponds closely to the average climatological wind system over the oceans. It is, however, affected by the interference of coastlines with respect to the winds.

The tendency of ocean currents in big, elongated, anticyclonic gyres is to displace their centres of rotation to the west, and to form strong western boundary currents like the Gulf Stream and the Kuroshio. This westward intensification of ocean currents was explained by Henry Melson Stommel (1948) as a result of the fact that the horizontal Coriolis force increases with increasing latitude. *Westward intensification of currents*

Walter Heinrich Munk (1950) and others explained theoretically many of the major features of the wind-driven ocean circulation by using the mean climatological wind stress distribution at the sea surface as a driving force.

Effects of bottom topography or of a restricted vertical extent of wind-driven currents by strong vertical density gradients in the oceans have not been considered in these models, however. These additional effects may help to explain why the westward intensification of ocean currents is not equally strong in the Southern Hemisphere.

Western and eastern boundary currents. Individual branches of the surface current pattern are indicated by their geographical names in Figure 7. The poleward flow on the western side of the great subtropical gyres in the North Atlantic and North Pacific, the western boundary currents, is fast, narrow, and deep; whereas the return flow toward the Equator, the eastern boundary currents, is slower, broader, and less deep. In the Southern Hemisphere, however, western boundary currents like the Brazil Current and the East Australian Current are not as strongly developed as their Northern Hemisphere counterparts.

Western and eastern boundary currents associated with subtropical gyres in the world's oceans are listed in Table 8.

The best explored western boundary currents are the Gulf Stream and the Kuroshio. The Gulf Stream system is composed of the Florida Current, the Gulf Stream proper between Cape Hatteras and the Grand Banks, and the North Atlantic Current. The corresponding divisions of the Kuroshio system are the Kuroshio, south of 35° N, the Kuroshio Extension, and, farther east, the North Pacific Current. *Gulf Stream and Kuroshio currents*

Table 8: Western and Eastern Boundary Currents of the World's Oceans				
boundary currents	Atlantic Ocean		Pacific Ocean		Indian Ocean

boundary currents	north	south	north	south	Indian Ocean
Western	Gulf Stream	Brazil Current	Kuroshio	East Australian Current	Somali Current Mozambique Current Agulhas Current
Eastern	Canary Current	Benguela Current	California Current	Peru Current	West Australian Current

The Gulf Stream and Kuroshio are usually sharply defined by an oceanic front along their continental side that marks a transition between the warm and more saline water masses of these currents and the cooler, less saline water of coastal regions. This front, often called the cold wall, is distinguished by a sudden change in temperature and sea colour.

Recent observations have shown that both currents are much narrower and faster than previously supposed. Sometimes they break up into two or more streaks that are considerably variable in their position and speed, often forming meanders and eddies that may detach from the main current.

Eastern boundary currents are relatively shallow and often indicate the presence of numerous eddies and countercurrents. These currents are closely connected with the process of upwelling water in coastal regions. Outstanding areas for this phenomenon are the coasts of northwest Africa, southwest Africa, California, and northern Chile and Peru. The upwelling water is usually restricted to the upper layer of 200 metres or 300 metres (660 or 980 feet) depth.

The equatorial current system. The circulation of the upper ocean strata in tropical and subtropical regions is dominated by the North and South Equatorial currents, Equatorial countercurrents, Equatorial undercurrents, and in some parts by Monsoon currents. Pronounced seasonal variations of the equatorial current system are the result of strong seasonal changes of the wind system, particularly in the Indian Ocean. This wind system is governed essentially by the trade winds and in some areas by monsoon winds. Between the fairly steady trade winds of both hemispheres a more or less broad belt of light variable winds or calms develops, often called the doldrums.

Equatorial countercurrents — Among the outstanding branches of the equatorial current system are the Equatorial countercurrents. The most impressive is the North Pacific Equatorial Countercurrent. The Equatorial Countercurrent of the Atlantic is fully developed only during the Northern Hemisphere summer when it extends from about 50° W longitude into the inner Gulf of Guinea. During winter (Figure 7), it occupies only the eastern part of the tropical Atlantic.

In the Indian Ocean, during the time of the northeast monsoon (Northern Hemisphere winter), a strong countercurrent is found between about 2° S and 8° S, embedded in the westward flowing North and South Equatorial currents. During this season, the Somali Current, near the African coast, flows southward, where at about 7° S it feeds part of its water into the countercurrent (see Figure 7). During the Indian southwest monsoon (Northern Hemisphere summer), however, currents have completely reversed their direction in the tropical western and northern part of the Indian Ocean. The Equatorial Countercurrent has disappeared and the Somali Current has reversed its direction and flows northeastward, sometimes even faster than the Gulf Stream. This remarkable current now feeds its water masses into the eastward flowing Southwest Monsoon Current in the northern Indian Ocean.

The doldrums — The locations of the Equatorial countercurrents are closely related to the locations of the doldrums. A qualitative explanation of the tropical current system for the case where doldrums occupy latitudes between 5° and 10° N is as indicated in Figure 8. Wind-driven water transport in

the Ekman layer leads to convergences and divergences of surface water between the major winds and to a piling up or depression of the sea surface, respectively. The resulting slopes of the sea surface in a meridional section from about 25° N to 10° N are downward. Between 10° N and 5° N it must be upward because of the convergence at 5° N. Near the Equator is a region of divergence and, therefore, the sea surface must rise from the Equator not only toward 25° S but also toward 5° N.

These slopes of the sea surface produce horizontal pressure gradients and slope currents that superpose the pure wind-driven currents. Because the resultant currents must always flow in such a direction that the higher pressure is to the right in the Northern Hemisphere and to the left in the Southern Hemisphere, westward flowing currents must occur between 25° N and 10° N, and between 5° N and 25° S. These currents represent the North and South Equatorial currents. The surface slope in the doldrums belt between 10° N and 5° N, however, requires a narrow, eastward flowing current, the Equatorial Countercurrent.

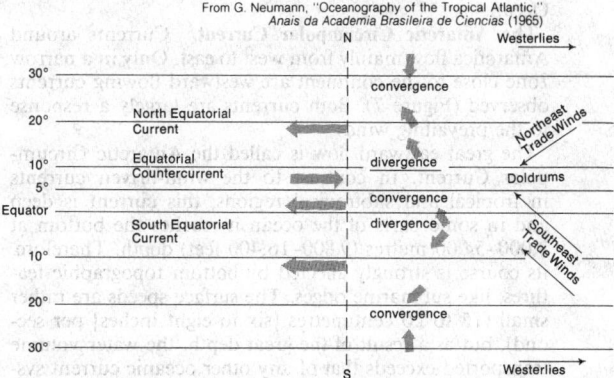

From G. Neumann, "Oceanography of the Tropical Atlantic," *Anais da Academia Brasileira de Ciencias* (1965)

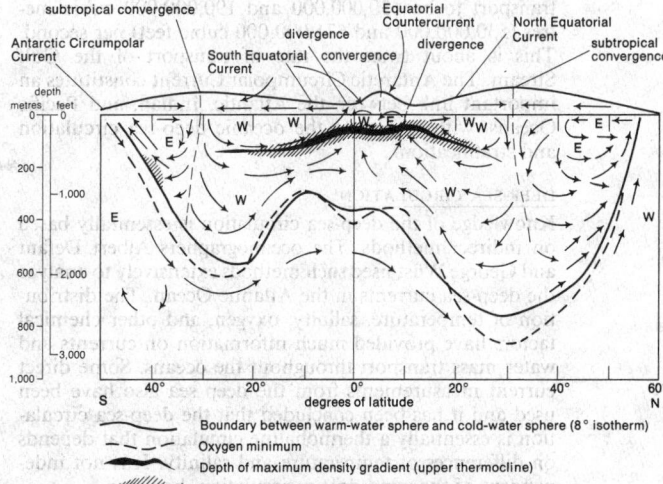

Boundary between warm-water sphere and cold-water sphere (8° isotherm)
Oxygen minimum
Depth of maximum density gradient (upper thermocline)
Subsurface salinity maxima in warm-water sphere

Figure 8: (Top) Explanation of equatorial and subtropical current system. (Bottom) Cross-sectional view of warm-water sphere (equatorial and subtropical regions) showing meridional circulation by arrows and zonal currents by W and E, respectively. Main features of stratification as related to currents are also shown.

Equatorial Undercurrent and the Cromwell Current — The Equatorial Undercurrent is another extremely narrow, eastward setting current branch in the equatorial current system. It is centred on the Equator with a width of about 200 to 300 kilometres (320 to 480 miles) and a vertical extent of 200 to 300 metres. Most often, it does not reach the sea surface and is, therefore, not represented in surface current charts. Maximum eastward speeds of 100–150 centimetres (40–60 inches) per second may occur at depths between about 50 and 150 metres (160 and 490 feet), while at the sea surface westward setting currents are observed. This current was first extensively studied in the Pacific Ocean where it is named the Cromwell Current. During recent years, oceanographic work in equatorial regions has established the worldwide existence of this

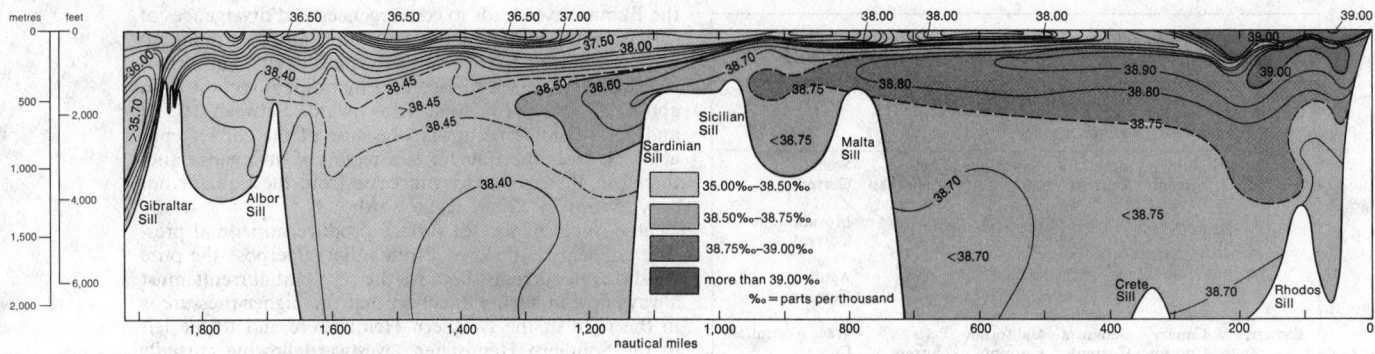

Figure 9: Longitudinal sections of summer salinity in the Mediterranean Sea along the axis
of the Levantine Intermediate Water, showing the origin of the water that forms the so-called
Upper Deep Water in the Atlantic Ocean.

From Wüst (1961) in G. Neumann and W.J. Pierson, Jr., *Principles of Physical Oceanography* (1966); Prentice-Hall, Inc.

remarkable current. In 1960 G. Neumann pointed out evidence for an Equatorial Undercurrent in the Atlantic Ocean.

The Antarctic Circumpolar Current. Currents around Antarctica flow mainly from west to east. Only in a narrow zone close to the continent are westward flowing currents observed (Figure 7). Both currents are largely a response to the prevailing winds.

The great eastward flow is called the Antarctic Circumpolar Current. In contrast to the wind-driven currents in tropical and subtropical regions, this current is deep and in some parts of the ocean it reaches the bottom at 3,000–5,000 metres (9,800–16,400 feet) depth. Therefore, its course is strongly affected by bottom topographic features, like submarine ridges. The surface speeds are rather small (15 to 20 centimetres [six to eight inches] per second), but as a result of the great depth, the water volume transported exceeds that of any other oceanic current system. V.G. Kort (1962) estimated the Antarctic Current transport to be 150,000,000 and 190,000,000 cubic metres (530,000,000 and 671,000,000 cubic feet) per second. This is about twice the rate of transport of the Gulf Stream. The Antarctic Circumpolar Current constitutes an important link between the Atlantic, Indian, and Pacific Oceans, with respect to the oceanic deep-sea circulation and stratification.

DEEP-SEA CIRCULATION

Knowledge of the deep-sea circulation is essentially based on indirect methods. The oceanographers Albert Defant and George Wüst used such methods extensively to analyze the deep-sea currents in the Atlantic Ocean. The distribution of temperature, salinity, oxygen, and other chemical factors have provided much information on currents and water mass transport throughout the oceans. Some direct current measurements from the deep sea also have been used and it has been concluded that the deep-sea circulation is essentially a thermohaline circulation that depends on differences of temperature and salinity. It is not independent of the wind-driven circulation, however.

Influence of highly saline waters Compared to the Pacific and Indian oceans, the vertical structure of temperature, salinity, and oxygen in the Atlantic is more differentiated. This is because the exchange of water with the Arctic Ocean is many times greater than that of the Pacific. Moreover, the Atlantic is bordered by a number of adjacent seas, among which the Mediterranean Sea is the most important. Small, but continuous, intrusions of Mediterranean water of high salinity and relatively high temperature through the Strait of Gibraltar create a special "climate" in the Atlantic deep sea.

The Mediterranean Sea, in general, is located in an arid climate zone. Evaporation exceeds precipitation, and this causes an increase of surface salinity, especially in its eastern parts. This high salinity water near Asia Minor sinks into subsurface layers because of its higher density. From there, it moves with subsurface currents at about 500 metres (1,600 feet) depth westward and, finally, flows through the Strait of Gibraltar into the Atlantic Ocean (Figure 9). This Mediterranean water sinks quickly to about 1,500 to 2,500 metres (4,900 to 8,200 feet) depth and spreads out

into the Atlantic (see below *Density currents*). It can be traced across the Equator as far south as the Antarctic Ocean, where it is entrained in the Antarctic Circumpolar Current. Along its path this water mass, termed Upper Deep Water, gradually decreases in salinity while mixing with less saline water above and below its level of spreading. In the Indian Ocean a similar water mass originates in the Red Sea and the Persian Gulf, whereas it is missing in the Pacific Ocean.

A schematic block diagram (Figure 10) for the western part of the Atlantic Ocean summarizes knowledge of its surface currents and deep-sea circulation. The spreading of the Mediterranean water from about 30° N and 1,500 metres depth is indicated.

Middle and Lower Deep Water masses Other important deep-sea movements from north to south are associated with the spreading of Middle and Lower Deep Water masses. These water masses originate near Greenland. They are cooler (3°–4° C [about 5°–7° F]) than the Upper Deep Water and can be traced by their higher oxygen content while spreading southward between about 2,500 and 4,000 metres (8,200 to 13,100 feet) depth. Wüst estimated current speeds of 10 to 15 centimetres (four to six inches) per second at about 3,000 metres (9,800 feet) depth in western equatorial regions. There seems to be no source of cold deep water in the North Pacific.

Deepwater movements from north to south in the Atlantic are sandwiched between water masses that spread northward with relatively low salinities (less than 34.85 parts per thousand; see Figure 10). The upper water mass is called the Antarctic Intermediate Water. It is formed at the sea surface near the Polar Front, or Antarctic Convergence, around 50° S. From there it spreads northward at about 700 or 1,000 metres (2,300 or 3,300 feet) depth, mainly in the western part of the Atlantic, where it is characterized by low salinities. It can be traced as far north as 25°–30° N.

Antarctic Bottom Water The deepest water mass of all, Antarctic Bottom Water, originates on the shelf of the Antarctic continent. Because of its high density, it slides down to the ocean bottom and then spreads northward and eastward. Its movements are channelled by submarine ridges and troughs, and it spreads mainly along the western half of the Atlantic (West Atlantic Trough), crossing the Equator while passing some of its water through a narrow pass (the Romanche Trench) in the Mid-Atlantic Ridge. Average velocities of 10–15 centimetres per second near South America have been obtained from geostrophic current computations. Bottom-water current speeds can be more than twice as great on occasion, however. Relatively strong bottom-current speeds, up to 60 centimetres (24 inches) per second, have been inferred by marine geologists from ripple marks, scour marks, and rock outcrops beneath the Antarctic Bottom Water, in the Drake Passage south of Cape Horn, and in other parts of the oceans, including the Pacific Ocean. (G.N.)

DENSITY CURRENTS

Density currents are currents that are kept in motion by the force of gravity acting on a relatively small density differ-

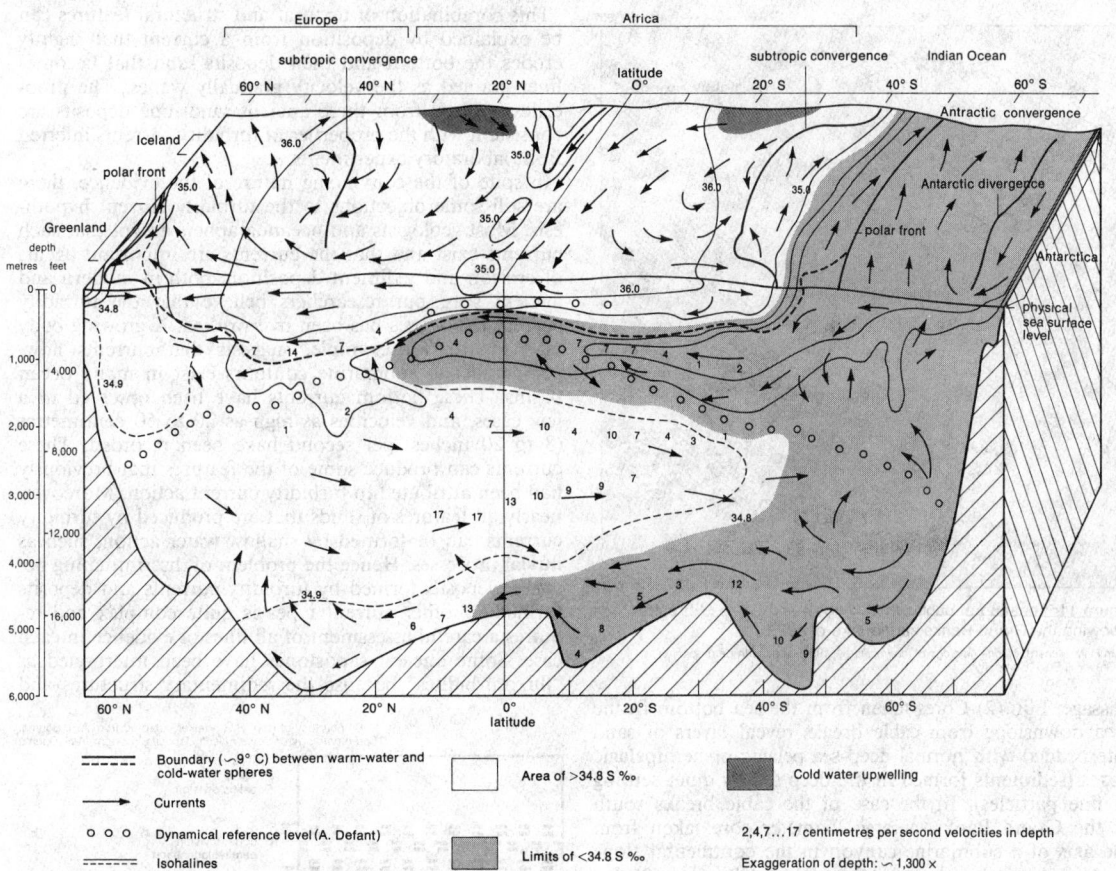

Figure 10: Essential aspects of deep-sea circulation and spreading of water masses in the Atlantic Ocean.

From Wüst (1961) in G. Neumann and W.J. Pierson, Jr., *Principles of Physical Oceanography* (1966); Prentice-Hall, Inc.

ence caused by variations in salinity, temperature, or sediment concentration. As noted above, salinity and temperature variations produce stratification in oceans. Below the surface layer, which is disturbed by waves and is lighter than the deeper waters because it is warmer or less saline, the oceans are composed of layers of water that have distinctive chemical and physical characteristics, which move more or less independently of each other and which do not lose their individuality by mixing even after they have flowed for hundreds of kilometres from their point of origin.

An example of this type of density current, or stratified flow, is provided by the water of the Mediterranean Sea as it flows through the Strait of Gibraltar out into the Atlantic. Because the Mediterranean Sea is enclosed in a basin that is relatively small compared with the ocean basins and because it is located in a relatively arid climate, evaporation exceeds the supply of fresh water from rivers. The result is that the Mediterranean contains water that is both warmer and more saline than normal deep-sea water, the temperature ranging from 12.7 to 14.5° C (55 to 58° F) and the salinity from 38.4 to 39.0 parts per thousand. Because of these characteristics, the Mediterranean water is considerably denser than the water in the upper parts of the North Atlantic, which has a salinity of about 36 parts per thousand and a temperature of about 13° C (55° F). The density contrast causes the lighter Atlantic water to flow into the Mediterranean in the upper part of the Strait of Gibraltar (down to a depth of about 200 metres [660 feet]) and the denser Mediterranean water to flow out into the Atlantic in the lower part of the strait (from about 200 metres to the top of the sill separating the Mediterranean from the Atlantic, at a depth of 320 metres [1,050 feet]). Because the strait is only 20 kilometres (12 miles) wide, both inflow and outflow achieve relatively high speeds. Near the surface the inflow may have speeds as high as two metres (6.6 feet) per second and the outflow reaches speeds of over one metre (3.3 feet) per second at a depth of about 275 metres (900 feet). One result of the high current speeds in the strait is to cause a considerable amount

of mixing, which reduces the salinity of the outflowing Mediterranean water to about 37 parts per thousand. The outflowing water sinks to a depth of about 1,500 metres or more, where it encounters colder, denser Atlantic water. It then spreads out as a layer of more saline water between two Atlantic water masses.

Density currents caused by suspended sediment concentrations in the oceans are called turbidity currents. They appear to be relatively short-lived, transient phenomena that occur at great depths. Turbidity currents are thought to be caused by the slumping of sediment that has piled up at the top of the continental slope, particularly at the heads of submarine canyons. Slumping of large masses of sediment creates a dense sediment–water mixture, or slurry, that then flows down the canyon to spread out over the ocean floor and deposit a layer of sand in deep water. Repeated deposition forms submarine fans, which are analogous to the alluvial fans found at the mouths of many river canyons. Sedimentary rocks that are thought to have originated from ancient turbidity currents are called turbidites.

Although large-scale turbidity underflows have never been directly observed in the oceans, there is much evidence supporting their occurrence. This evidence may be briefly summarized: (1) Telegraph cables have been broken in the deep sea in a sequence that indicates some disturbance at the bottom moving from shallow to deep water at speeds of the order of 10 to 40 knots (11 to 46 miles per hour). The trigger for this phenomenon is commonly, though not exclusively, an earthquake near the edge of the continental slope. The only disturbance that seems capable of being transmitted downslope at the required speed is a large turbidity current. The best known example of such a series of cable breaks took place in the North Atlantic following the 1929 earthquake under the Grand Banks of Newfoundland (Figure 11), but other examples have been described from the Magdalena River Delta (Colombia), the Congo Delta, the Mediterranean Sea north of Orléansville and south of the Straits of Messina, and Kandavu

Evidence for currents

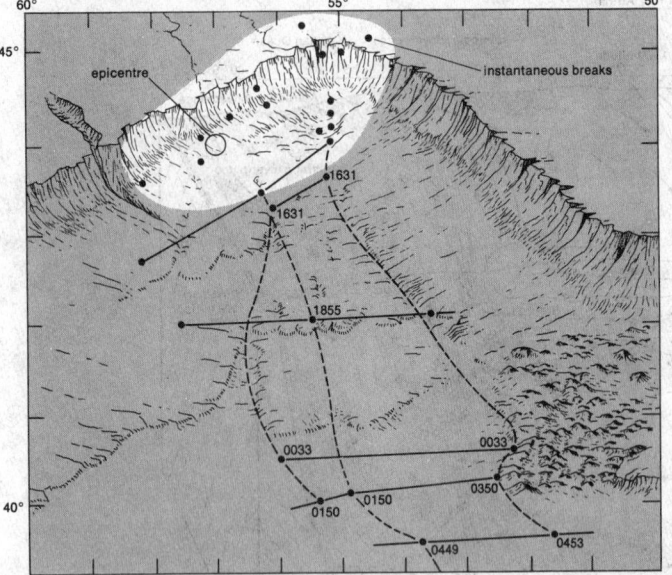

Figure 11: Location of cables (heavy lines) and times of breaks following the Grand Banks earthquake of 1929.

From H.W. Menard, *Marine Geology of the Pacific* (© 1964); used with permission of McGraw-Hill Book Company

This combination of textural and structural features can be explained by deposition from a current that slightly erodes the bottom and then deposits sand that becomes finer grained as the velocity gradually wanes. The properties inferred from these ancient sandstone deposits are consistent with the properties of turbidity currents inferred from laboratory experiments.

In spite of the convincing nature of the evidence, there are still some objections to the turbidity current hypothesis. Most geologists and oceanographers accept that such currents exist and that the currents are important agents of erosion and sediment deposition, both in modern and ancient seas, but researchers believe that the turbidity current hypothesis has been overworked. A growing body of evidence, for example, suggests that currents flowing parallel to submarine contours exist in many ocean basins. These bottom currents have been observed in a few cases, and velocities as high as 20 to 50 centimetres (8 to 20 inches) per second have been recorded. These currents can produce some of the features that previously had been attributed to turbidity current action. Moreover, nearly all features of sands that are produced by turbidity currents can be formed by shallow water action, such as fluvial processes. Hence the problem of discriminating between deposits formed by turbidity currents and deposits formed by other current types is quite complex and requires a careful assessment of all lines of evidence in each case. Some ancient sandstones have been interpreted as "fluxoturbidites" because the sedimentary structures and

By courtesy of (top) R.G. Walker, adapted from A.H. Bouma, *Sedimentology of Some Flysch Deposits*; (bottom) A.H. Bouma

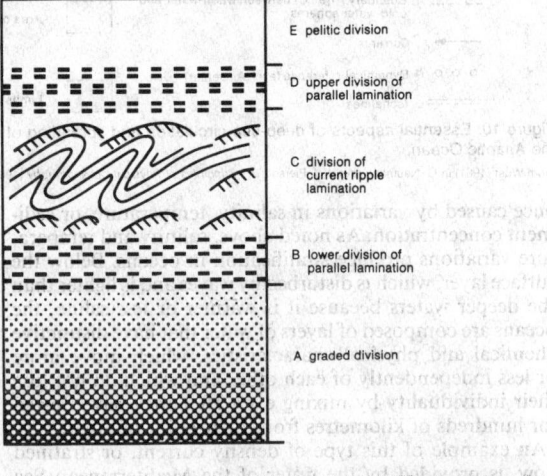

E pelitic division

D upper division of parallel lamination

C division of current ripple lamination

B lower division of parallel lamination

A graded division

Figure 12: *Beds deposited by turbidity currents—turbidites.*
(Top) Ideal sequence of sedimentary structures deposited in a bed by a turbidity current. (Bottom) Radiograph of a turbidite off southern California showing sequence of sedimentary structures. (A) Graded division. (B) Lower division of parallel lamination. (C) Division of current ripple lamination.

Passage, Fiji. (2) Cores taken from the sea bottom in the area downslope from cable breaks reveal layers of sand interbedded with normal deep-sea pelagic or hemipelagic oozes (sediments formed in the deep sea by quiet settling of fine particles). In the case of the cable breaks south of the Grand Banks, a large diameter core taken from the axis of a submarine canyon in the continental slope contained one centimetre (about 0.5 inch) of gray clay underlain by at least 20 centimetres (eight inches) of gray pebble and cobble gravel. Cores farther south showed a graded layer, about one metre thick, of coarse silt and fine sand. The presence of these gravel and sand layers is consistent with the hypothesis that they were deposited by the turbidity current that broke the cables. (3) Coring has revealed layers of fine-grained sand or coarse silt at many other localities in the abyssal plains of the oceans. These layers are generally moderately well sorted and contain microfossils characteristic of shallow water that are also size sorted. In some cases the layers are laminated and arranged in a definite sequence (Figure 12). It is clear that the sand forming these layers has been moved down from shallow water, and in many cases the only plausible mechanism appears to be a turbidity current. (4) At the base of many submarine canyons there are very large submarine fans. Deep-sea channels on the fan surfaces extend for many tens of kilometres and have depths of over a hundred metres and widths of a kilometre or more. Submarine levees are a prominent feature, and these project above the surrounding fan surface to elevations of 50 metres (160 feet) or more. The gross characteristics of such channels suggest that they were formed by a combination of erosion and deposition by turbidity currents. (5) Thick deposits of interbedded graded sandstones and fine-grained shales are common in the geological record. In some cases there is good fossil evidence that the shales were deposited in relatively deep water, perhaps as much as several thousand metres deep. Relatively deepwater deposition is also suggested by the absence of sedimentary structures characteristic of shallow water. The interbedded sandstones, however, contain shallow-water fossils that are sorted by size, have a sharp basal contact with the shale below and a transitional contact with the shale above, and display a characteristic sequence of sedimentary structures (Figure 12). The structures include erosional marks made originally on the mud surface but now preserved as casts on the base of the sandstone bed (sole marks) and internal structures including some or all of the following: massive graded unit, parallel lamination, ripple cross-lamination or convolute lamination, and an upper unit of parallel lamination.

Ocean floor sediments

Turbidites

other properties suggest a transporting agent intermediate between turbidity currents and large-scale slumping and sliding of sediment. Future studies will no doubt resolve many of the problems connected with turbidity current deposits and will provide further insight into the hydrodynamics of density flows.

(G.V.M./Ed.)

OCEAN CURRENTS, CLIMATE, AND WEATHER

The mutual influence of atmosphere and ocean manifests itself in climate and weather phenomena, as well as in the circulation and stratification of the oceans. Ocean currents are largely responsible for the temperature distribution at the sea surface, which, in turn, affects the overlying atmosphere. The difference between the temperature of the air and water basically determines evaporation rates, atmospheric humidity, precipitation, and the vertical stability of air masses moving over the ocean surface. As air cools when flowing over a cold ocean current, fog is likely to form. When cool air flows over a warm current, the air is heated from below and may rise. This leads to condensation of water vapour in the rising air, cloud formation, and often precipitation. Such atmospheric convection processes can sometimes be violent, forming towering cumulonimbus clouds and thunderstorms.

Interaction of atmosphere and ocean

Meteorological consequences of the interaction of atmosphere and ocean are obvious in regions of upwelling water near the west coasts of the continents. The upwelling water is accompanied by relatively cool sea surface temperatures. Because the air is cooled and stabilized over these regions, the climate is cool, with haze or fog, but little or no precipitation. From the biological point of view, these coastal regions offer a striking contrast between land and sea. Off the coast of northern Chile and southern Peru, for example, the land is barren, dry, and almost wholly infertile (Atacama desert); the sea, however, teems with sea life of every type. Its cool waters provide some of the world's best fishing grounds, because water from deeper layers with a high nutrient content is brought up to the sea surface by the upwelling process.

The oceanic circulation also supports the atmospheric circulation in equalizing temperature differences between the tropics and the poles. The oceans can store great amounts of heat because of the great specific heat of water. The heat stored in tropical regions is transported over great distances, especially by western boundary currents. It is released to the atmosphere in higher latitudes chiefly as latent heat of evaporation. The fact that northwest Europe has such an agreeable climate is ultimately the result of the Gulf Stream system, a warm-water heating system that is supported by, and mutually related to, a warm-air heating system that is provided by the prevailing winds. In the Pacific Ocean, the Kuroshio Current system plays a similar role with respect to the climate of the northwestern part of North America.

Disturbances of the oceanic current system and its associated heat transport can produce far-reaching effects that are reflected in climatological anomalies; droughts or floods, abnormally cold and severe winters, or extremely mild ones are examples. Attempts at long range weather forecasting depend largely on the general oceanic circulation, its variation through time, and its effect on physical conditions at the air–sea interface. (G.N.)

THE OCEAN BASINS

The ocean basins and the continents constitute the largest relief features on Earth, with the ocean basins, covering three-fifths of the Earth's surface, dominant. Water actually covers 71 percent of the Earth, but only 60 percent of this overlies the deep ocean basins, which occur below the 2,000-metre (6,600-foot) contour line. The average depth of the sea is 3,790 metres (12,430 feet), whereas the average height of the continents is 840 metres (2,760 feet). Thus, the total relief contrast is 4,630 metres (15,190 feet).

The distribution of ocean basins and continents is asymmetrical. Continents are generally antipodal (diametrically opposed) to ocean basins. The antipodal position of Australia, for example, is within the North Atlantic Basin, and Antarctica opposes the Arctic Basin. The ocean basins lie principally in the Southern Hemisphere, and the Antarctic Basin encircles the Earth. In a sense, the three major oceanic basins (Pacific, Atlantic, and Indian) may be regarded as huge gulfs that extend off the Antarctic Basin, with the Arctic Basin being a secondary northward extension of the Atlantic. Thus, unlike the separated and isolated continents, the ocean basins are all interconnected, so that there is really only one worldwide ocean basin. This ocean basin is subdivided into a number of individual ocean basins largely as a matter of convenience.

Results of modern research. A classical view of natural philosophers held the oceans to be as deep as the mountains are high, which is roughly correct if only the greatest mountains are considered. The first deep-sea sounding was made in the central South Atlantic in 1840; a heavy plummet was lowered 2,425 fathoms (4,435 metres [14,500 feet]) on the end of a long line. The first generalized map of the ocean basins was fashioned in 1895, using the 7,000 oceanic soundings deeper than 2,000 metres (6,600 feet) that were then available. The advent of the echo sounder in 1920, with which precisely timed pulses of sound are bounced off the bottom and compared with their echoes, revolutionized deep-sea soundings. A modern survey ship can obtain a sounding every second along its track. The problem of obtaining accurate position control, or fixes, under all conditions of weather and in any part of the world was solved recently through satellite navigation, determination of fixes continuously from low-orbited satellites. Since the early 1970s the bathymetry of the entire ocean floor has rapidly been revealed and charted with literally millions of soundings.

Before about 1930 the ocean floor was regarded as a flat, monotonous, and generally featureless surface. Increasingly since then charts show a topography remarkably varied in both shape and relief. Some seamounts (isolated more or less conical submarine peaks) and escarpments (steep slopes) are much higher and more rugged than any on land. The abyssal (deep-sea) plains, on the other hand, are the levelest surfaces on the face of the globe. It has also been learned that the ocean floor, like the surface of the Moon, is a distinct geomorphic domain (*i.e.,* occupied by distinctive landforms); constructional and depositional physiography are quite unlike that on land. Erosional landforms on the continents are sculptured by wind, ice, and running water, but only sluggishly moving water modifies the features on the deep ocean floor. Terrestrial stream action is imitated beneath the sea by turbidity currents, the mud-laden tongues of water that periodically pour down the continental shelves and slopes to the ocean floor. Weathering (rock disintegration by chemical and mechanical processes), as well as erosion, proceeds extremely slowly beneath the sea, so that the sea-floor morphology (fault scarps, volcanic knolls, and other features) tends to retain a pristine appearance.

Varied topography of the ocean floor

Undersea constructional topography commonly differs from that on land. There is, for example, no undersea equivalent of folded sedimentary mountains. The major features of the ocean floor are deep-sea trenches, ridges with deep steep-sided valleys called rifts, and fracture zones that are created by the interaction along their boundaries of shifting rigid crustal plates. The giant volcanic cones that create seamounts are especially spectacular. The smaller features represent a variety of volcanic topographic forms, related mainly to fissure eruptions (along linear cracks rather than through a central vent) and rifting of the ocean floor.

The oceanic crust. The oceanic crust contrasts sharply with the granitic crust that makes up the continental blocks. The ocean floor is separated from the Earth's upper mantle (zone beneath the crust) by three distinct layers, which have been revealed by seismic refraction studies. These are: Layer 1 (zero–two kilometres [0–1.2 miles] thick), consisting of unconsolidated sediments that have been derived from the remains of marine organisms as well as from the rock materials of the continents by submarine density currents or surface transport; Layer 2, comprising Layer 2a (0.5 kilometre [0.3 mile] thick), consisting of pillow lava, a submarine form produced by the

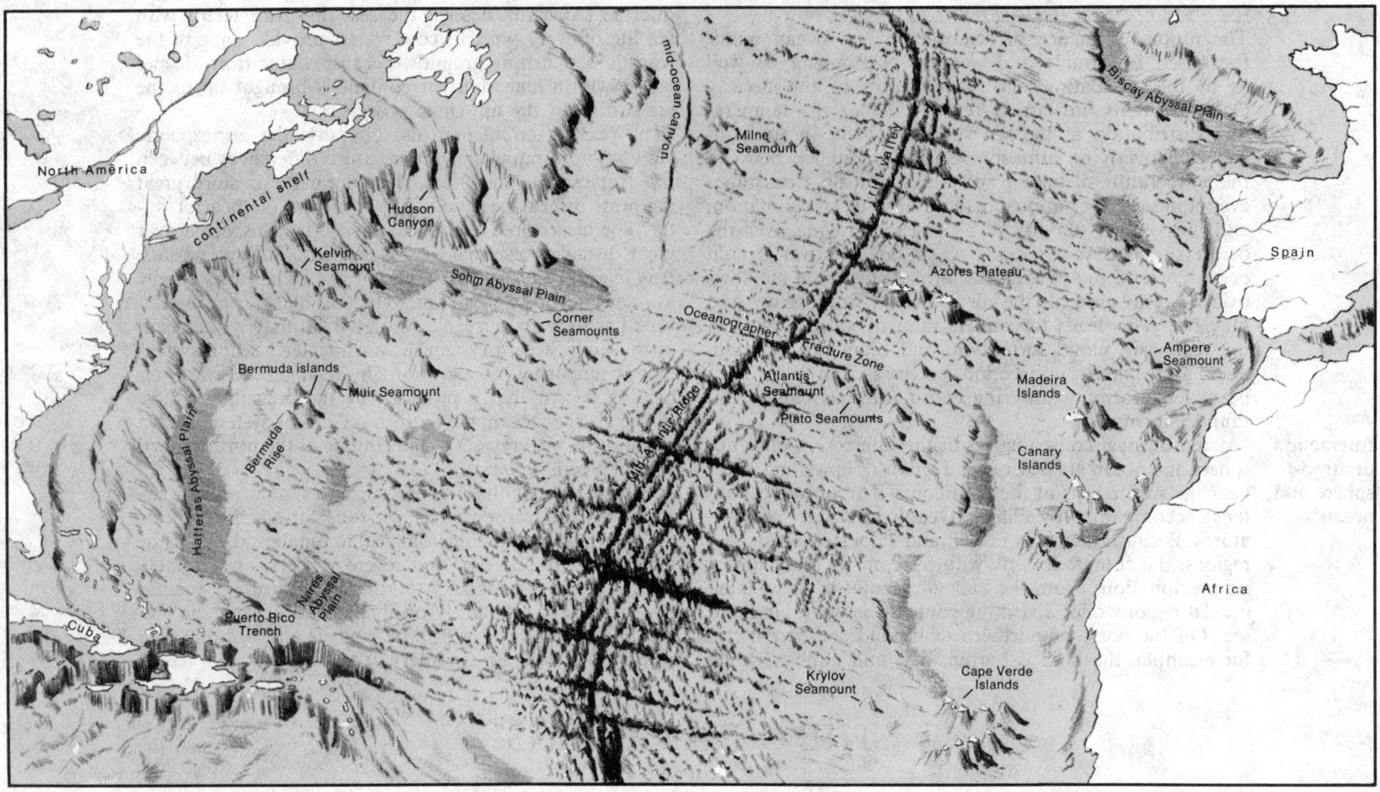

Figure 13: Midocean ridge, fracture zones, and sea-floor topography of the North Atlantic.
Drawing by E. Derdeyn

rapid quenching of lava as it poured from fissures onto the ocean floor, and Layer 2b (two kilometres thick), a series of feeder dikes (dikes are solidified sheets of lava that intrude pre-existing rocks) that originally provided passages for the lavas onto the ocean floor; and Layer 3 (five kilometres [three miles] thick), consisting principally of gabbro, a coarse, crystalline, basic intrusive rock, a form of olivine basalt. Unlike the sediments that are added by deposition from above, these igneous rocks are all injected from below. They are derived by the partial melting of the primitive iron- and magnesium-rich rock of the upper mantle.

Relation of rocks and features to plate tectonics

The nature of the igneous crustal layers found below the sediments is in accord with the concept of sea-floor spreading (see below). As 100-kilometre- (60-mile-) thick lithospheric plates move apart at midocean rifts, mantle rock moves up from below to fill the void. Much of this injection takes place by viscous-solid flow, but there is also some molten rock present that is squeezed to the top. Outpouring of lava onto the sea floor is quickly chilled into bolster-shaped pods with glassy surfaces that are called pillow lavas (Layer 2a). Below these pillow lavas are feeder dikes, along which the lava rose to the sea floor. With sea-floor spreading these dikes are pulled apart and injected with new dikes, forming a complex system of dikes (Layer 2b). These dikes are derived from an underlying layer of magma that cools slowly and crystallizes to form gabbro (the intrusive equivalent of olivine basalt) and associated suites of rocks.

This interpretation of the oceanic crust is not fully agreed upon by all authorities. According to this interpretation, however, all of the oceanic crustal rocks have the general composition of olivine basalt.

Major geologic and geographic features

The most significant features within the ocean basins are the oceanic ridges, particularly those classified as midocean ridges, fracture zones, and trenches. These grand features are related, because they are all associated with the boundaries of the Earth's major crustal plates. These boundaries almost invariably lie within the ocean basins rather than on the continents. The trenches mark zones of underthrusting associated with the descent of the crust into the mantle; the midocean ridge forms along the pull-apart zones; and the fracture zones reflect lines of crustal disruption associated with great shearing action where one crustal plate has slid past its neighbour. Thus, the concept of plate tectonics (that the Earth's surface consists of a small number of crustal plates the boundaries of which are sites of major deformation) accounts for these three major types of features that dominate the ocean basins.

(R.S.D./Ed.)

OCEANIC RIDGES AND FRACTURE ZONES

Types of oceanic ridges. Oceanic ridges can be classified into a few types on the basis of their properties and their relationships to one another and to the adjacent continents. The most important question is whether or not a ridge is active; that is, whether earthquakes occur along its axis. This distinction, combined with the delineation of submarine topography, suffices to provide a classification that is confirmed by other geophysical and geological properties. Only the midocean ridge system and the island arcs of the world are active; all others are aseismic or quiescent.

The midocean ridge system. In 1956 the U.S. scientists Maurice W. Ewing and Bruce C. Heezen proposed that the several great sections of the known active ridges might form a continuous system. In support of this proposition it was pointed out that earthquake focuses in the southern Atlantic, Pacific, and Indian oceans join together and might mark the course of connections that had not been detected because of the paucity of soundings in Antarctic waters.

Scientific expeditions sent for the purpose soon confirmed the hypothesis that the midocean ridge is indeed continuous and that it winds for 60,000 kilometres (37,000 miles) through all the world's oceans. The midocean ridge extends down the axis of the entire Atlantic Ocean, passes midway between the continents of Africa and Antarctica, and turns north to the centre of the Indian Ocean, where it branches, the main ridge continuing midway between Australia, New Zealand, and Antarctica to cross the east side of the Pacific Basin, running all the way to the mouth of the Gulf of California.

Continuity and dimensions

Because the system is so large and the behaviour and properties of different sections vary, several sections have separate names, such as the Mid-Atlantic Ridge, the Carlsberg Ridge, or the Albatross Cordillera (East Pacific Rise). Nevertheless, the system has an essential unity and is called the midocean ridge because of its generally axial position. Seismically active branches of the ridge system join the Azores to Gibraltar, the centre of the Indian Ocean to the Gulf of Aden, and other points on the crest to New Zealand and to Chile. A few short sections occur independently, for example, off the coast of Oregon.

The essential characteristic of the midocean ridge is that it is a broad and enormous uplift along the axis of the ocean floors. The floors slope up from depths of over 6,000 metres (20,000 feet) in marginal basins to the crest of the ridge, which is almost everywhere less than 4,000 metres (13,100 feet) in elevation, with crestal mountains commonly rising to depths of 2,000 to 3,000 metres (6,600 to 9,800 feet) and sometimes reaching above sea level.

Profiles of the Albatross Cordillera show that the central portion is fairly smooth. In contrast, in the North Atlantic Ocean the crest is marked by a rift valley averaging 30 kilometres (20 miles) in width and up to 1,500 metres (4,900 feet) deep, and the inner flanks are rough and block faulted. The crest is, of course, the highest part of the ridge, but it does not lie at a uniform depth; rather, it rises towards a number of well-separated peaks or domes. In the Atlantic the crest rises above the sea to form seven groups of islands, of which Iceland and the Azores are conspicuous examples.

At the crest the basalt floor is everywhere exposed, but sediments increase steadily in thickness down the flanks and fill depressions until only abyssal (deep-sea) hills project, and finally all the bedrock is hidden beneath flat abyssal plains (see below). But the essential structure of the ridge continues beneath the sediments to continental margins or to boundary ridges.

Fractures and earthquakes

At intervals the ridge is crossed, usually at right angles, by large horizontal lineations of high and rugged topography called fracture zones. These are long, narrow ridges and depressions that usually separate oceanic ridges of different depth. The fracture zones may be as much as 100 kilometres (60 miles) wide and 2,000 kilometres (1,000 miles) long. The first to be described was the Mendocino Fracture Zone, extending westward for 3,300 kilometres (2,100 miles) from Cape Mendocino, California. Subsequently, three other almost parallel extensive fracture zones have been surveyed off western North America—namely, the Murray, Molokai, and Clarion fracture zones. These appear to be scarps associated with offsets of a former extension of the Albatross Cordillera, which was overridden by the westward drift of North America. In the Atlantic Basin there are also numerous fracture zones that offset the axial rift of the Mid-Atlantic Ridge. These fracture zones also extend far beyond the limits of the offsets (commonly called transform faults) and, in some cases, can be traced nearly to Africa or North America before their trace is lost beneath the thick-lying blanket of sediments along the continental margins.

Earthquake activity indicates that these fracture zones are actively shearing (moving) today only where they connect segments of actively spreading ridges or where they connect a rift to a trench. The extensions of the fracture zones onto the adjacent segments of the ocean floor are dead (immobile), although the rugged relief along their trends remains as evidence of earlier faulting and crustal slippage.

The midocean ridge system is the largest feature of the Earth's surface after continents and ocean basins. Its volume exceeds 100,000,000 cubic kilometres (25,000,000 cubic miles), and, if it did not exist, sea level would occur at more than 250 metres (800 feet) lower than it does.

Gravity measurements show that the midocean ridge is in isostatic equilibrium—*i.e.,* its height above the seabed must be held up by lighter material below. Seismic refraction studies show that the upper mantle (zone immediately beneath the Earth's crust), to depths of 100 or more kilometres beneath the crest, has low seismic velocities (speed of travel of earthquake waves) of about 7.6 kilometres (4.7 miles) per second, compared with normal values of

about 8.2 kilometres (5.1 miles) per second. Velocities measured perpendicular to the rise are as much as 8 percent higher than those measured parallel to it. Other measurements show that the heat flow along the crest is higher than normal. To explain these observations it has been proposed that hot matter from the deeper mantle is upwelling toward the surface (the ocean floor) along the axis of the ridge.

Another remarkable geophysical feature of the ridge is that everywhere along it a pattern of magnetic anomalies occurs as long strips, each a few kilometres wide and parallel to the axis. This can be explained if the lava in successive strips on the sea floor is alternately normally and reversely magnetized. It has been proposed that along the locus of the crest of the midocean ridge the ocean floor has been spreading apart and that the natural reversals that occur in the Earth's magnetic field cause the pattern of alternating strips of magnetic anomalies. This proposal fits the assumption that hot material is welling up under the ridge.

Other types of ridges. Aseismic ridges that extend wholly or partly from uplifted islands on the axis of the midocean ridge to coasts of adjacent continents are called lateral ridges. Usually they occur in pairs and are perpendicular ("normal") to or make large angles with the midocean ridge. For example, broad ridges whose crests are everywhere less than 2,000 metres (6,600 feet) deep extend in opposite directions from Iceland to the coast of Greenland and to the continental shelf of Europe near the Faeroes and Scotland. Also, the Walvis Ridge and Rio Grande Rise make a nearly complete chevron-shaped pattern about the Tristan da Cunha group, in the South Atlantic Ocean.

Lateral ridges

Nearly straight ridges that terminate at one end in a young or active volcanic island are called linear chains. The other islands of the chain appear to get steadily older away from the volcanic end. Except for local earthquakes connected with volcanism, these chains are aseismic. The Hawaiian Islands are an excellent example.

Linear chains

In the Atlantic Ocean the midocean ridge system lies near the centre of the ocean, except in the Arctic Ocean, where its continuation is much closer to the Siberian coast than to North America. On the other hand, the ridge does occupy a symmetrical position halfway between the Siberia coast and the Lomonosov Ridge. The latter is a great submarine mountain system that cuts right across the Arctic Ocean from north of Greenland and Ellesmere Island to the delta of the Lena River. It is generally supposed that this aseismic ridge marks the boundary of the present Atlantic system with an older section of sea floor north of Alaska. As a consequence, the ridge is often called a boundary ridge.

Boundary ridges

The Seychelles archipelago in the Indian Ocean resembles a continent in everything but size. The rocks of these islands are Precambrian (older than 570,000,000 years) gneisses (metamorphic rocks, formed under high temperatures and pressures); the crust beneath them is thick and continental, and the flora and fauna are of continental rather than insular types. There is complete agreement that this archipelago constitutes a microcontinent. There is also good evidence from deep-sea drilling and geophysical investigations that some submarine rises, notably the Rockall Bank, off the British Isles, are also submerged microcontinents, and many other banks and islands, including the Lomonosov and Walvis ridges and Kerguelen Island, have also been considered to be continental, but the evidence in many cases is still uncertain.

Micro-continents

(J.T.W./R.S.D./Ed.)

OCEANIC TRENCHES AND ISLAND ARCS

Characteristics of trenches. Oceanic trenches are long, narrow, arcuate depressions in the ocean floor. They occur principally around the periphery of the Pacific Basin, but examples are also found in both the Atlantic and Indian oceans. Individual trenches have lengths of thousands of kilometres, widths of roughly 100 kilometres (60 miles), and depths of two to four kilometres (one to two miles) below the adjacent ocean floor. Nearly all of the hadal regions, which are those deeper than 6,000 metres (20,000 feet), lie within trenches. Their continuity is remarkable—

9,000-metre- (30,000-foot-) deep Tonga Trench is about five kilometres (three miles) wide, but it is continuous for 700 kilometres (400 miles). Typically, trenches have an asymmetrical V shape with a steeper slope toward land and a gentle slope toward the ocean basin; a low arch sometimes intervenes before the normal deep ocean floor is attained. Trenches and their associated island arcs, surmounted by explosive volcanoes, are the most active geological features on the face of the Earth. The great earthquakes and tsunamis generated from them are invariably associated with trenches.

Greatest
ocean
depths

The greatest depths are found in trenches and so are near continental margins or island arcs rather than in the middle of the ocean basins. The deepest depression is the 11,034-metre (36,200-foot) Challenger Deep, discovered by HMS "Challenger II" in 1948, in the Mariana Trench not far from Guam. Some greater depths for this deep have been claimed, but they remain unsubstantiated. The oceanographers Jacques Piccard and Don Walsh descended to the bottom of the Challenger Deep in 1960 aboard the bathyscaphe "Trieste," a feat comparable to the ascent of Mt. Everest. Some other great deeps of the Pacific are Tonga Trench, 10,882 metres (35,702 feet); Kermadec Trench, 10,047 metres (32,962 feet); and Philippine Trench, 10,497 metres (34,439 feet). The greatest depth in the Atlantic Ocean is 9,219 metres (30,246 feet), found in the Puerto Rico Trench, just north of that island.

It is now commonly agreed that trenches are subduction zones—that is, zones where the outer, 100-kilometre-thick outer shell of the Earth plunges into the mantle at angles from 30° to nearly vertical. The bending of this rigid crustal plate in adapting to the spherical geometry of the Earth is the cause of the arcuate shape of the trench. The descending lithospheric plate contains numerous rock types that are unstable in the regime of high pressures and temperatures that exists in the mantle. Hence, they cannot be consumed and are melted and returned to the surface as magmas and lavas that build up the arc behind the trenches. The Aleutians–Alaska Arc, which lies behind the Aleutian Islands, is a prime example; the Kuril and Mariana arcs are others.

Typical features of island arcs. Above the surface of the water, a typical island arc (Figure 14) consists of two parallel, curved chains of islands, convex toward the deep ocean and concave toward the nearest continent. The outer row of islands is nonvolcanic and may partly consist of deep-sea sediments that have been raised far above the ocean floor. The inner arc is a site of active volcanism of the hazardous explosive type; classical volcanoes of conical shape and with relatively frequent eruptions occur on

this chain. New "islands" occasionally appear in this row, although historically, they subsequently have been quickly eroded away. Beneath the level of the water the typical arc shows the following features, beginning at the normal deep ocean floor and progressing across the trench and the arc: (1) a gentle topographic rise of the order of a few hundred metres with slopes normally less than 1 percent; (2) a reversal in slope followed by a zone of increasing depth and slope; the greatest slope ranges from a few percent to 10 percent at the outer wall of the trench, and in many trenches topographic depressions corresponding to the surface expressions of down-dropped blocks, or grabens, are observed here; (3) the floor of the trench, which is usually flat over the deepest portion as a result of partial filling by sediments; (4) a zone of decreasing depth, the inner wall of the trench, with slopes generally steeper than those of the outer wall with slopes frequently exceeding 10 percent. The inner wall sometimes has one or more prominent benches that sometimes dam or pond sediments, and the walls in general become less steep above the benches; (5) a ridge overlain by relatively shallow water, normally less than a kilometre or two in depth, from which the two rows of nonvolcanic and volcanic islands protrude, with the volcanic islands farthest from the trench; (6) an interarc basin characterized by rugged topography and water of intermediate depths, perhaps two to three kilometres (1.2 to 1.9 miles). (7) A "third" arc with the same general trend as the main arc, shallow-water depths and, rarely, a few islands. This "third arc" is prominent in a few cases such as the Tonga-Kermadec Arc and the Mariana Arc but may not be perceived so readily in many arcs.

All arcs depart to some degree from the simple description given above. Many vary markedly in curvature along their course. Some arc segments, such as a large part of the Tonga-Kermadec Arc and the Chilean portion of the South American Arc are not true arcs at all in the strict sense because these two segments are best approximated by straight lines. These two zones have many of the other characteristics outlined above, however, and so are appropriately classed as arcs in this geological sense.

Variation of characteristics along the trend of an arc is quite common. At its western end the Aleutian Arc consists largely of islands whose volcanoes are inactive at present. Near the middle section of the arc the island chain consists primarily of active volcanoes. Near its eastern end the Aleutian Arc becomes double and then changes from an island arc to an arc that is continental as it merges into the Alaskan peninsula. The Aleutian Trench, some 4,000 kilometres (2,480 miles) in length, is, in common with most trenches, narrow and usually flat bottomed as a result of sediment accumulation. In general, the depths of the floors vary throughout their length; elongated basins of somewhat different depths are isolated from one another by sills. The Aleutian Trench has depths over 6,500 metres (21,300 feet) near its western end and deepens to well over 7,500 metres (24,600 feet) along the central portion of the arc. It shoals to the east until, southeast of the Alaskan peninsula, the trench is filled with sediments derived primarily from the Alaska mainland and is no longer apparent in the morphology of the ocean floor. Proximity to a rich sediment source thus appears to account, at least partly, for one of the characteristics of this trench. Comparable phenomena can be seen in other trenches. The Kuril Trench, for example, also shoals toward the north opposite the Kamchatka peninsula. The land elevations of the Aleutian Arc partially mimic the ocean depths, increasing some 2,000 metres (6,600 feet) from Attu on the west to Mt. Spurr on the Alaskan peninsula.

The
Aleutian
Trench

The Aleutian Trench, in common with several other trenches, such as the Philippine Trench, the Peru-Chile Trench, and the Java Trench, has a pronounced bench on its landward flank at a depth of about 2,000–2,500 fathoms (3,650–4,570 metres). This bench is generally continuous along most of the arc's length but is interrupted where the Adak Canyon crosses and apparently offsets it. The canyon may mark a fault that intersects the arc at a high angle. The northern slope of the Aleutian ridge is steep, indicative, according to one view, of normal faulting along the inner margin of the arc. Behind the Aleutian-Alaskan

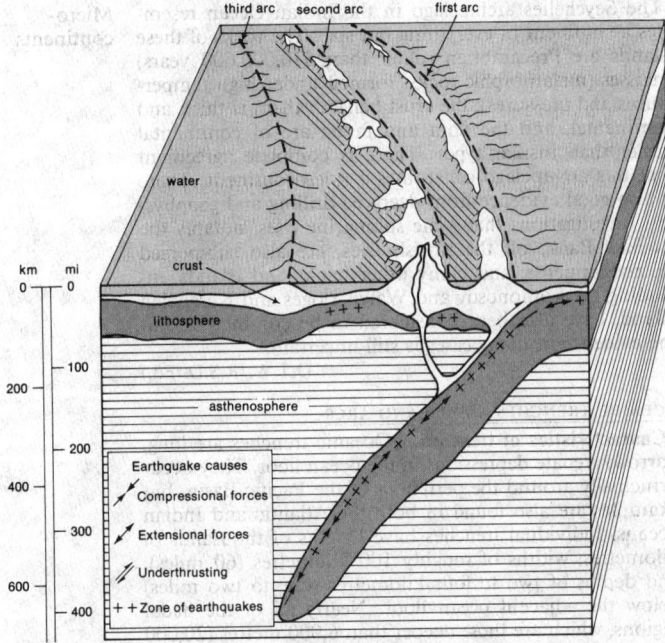

Figure 14: Typical island arc (see text).

Arc, the Bering Sea is largely underlain by continental shelf to the east and by deep sea to the west. Within this western portion, beginning at about Amchitka Island and curving gently to the north and then west, is an arcuate submarine feature called Bowers Bank. This feature complicates the bathymetry and suggests the presence of an ancient arc because no modern seismic activity or volcanism is known to be associated with it.

No general description of arcs would be complete without special mention of the linked arcs of New Britain, the Solomons, and the New Hebrides. These arcs are exceptional in that they are convex toward the continental area and the trenches are on the side of the arc nearest the continent (Australia). Other asymmetric features of these arcs also are oriented oppositely to those of most arcs. The zone of deep earthquakes dips away from the continent, and the volcanoes are seaward of the trenches. The bathymetry is further complicated in this region by the occurrence of a system of trenches that includes the Cape Johnson and the Vityaz trenches on the concave side of the Solomon and New Hebrides arcs.

Thus, the remarkable first-order similarity of the physiography of the island arcs and their associated submarine features is most impressive; so too, is the great variety of second-order or subsidiary features. (R.S.D./J.E.O.)

OTHER SIGNIFICANT TOPOGRAPHIC FEATURES

Mountains beneath the sea

Seamounts and guyots. A seamount is a mountain beneath the sea, generally in the form of an isolated, conical elevation of the sea floor at least one kilometre (0.6 mile) high. Seamounts are the most prominent and striking features on the ocean floor. More than 2,000 seamounts have been reported, and many more await future discovery. There remains no doubt that seamounts are nearly all volcanoes (mostly extinct), because when dredged the bedrock is always basalt, and their shapes and slopes are like that of a volcano on land. They are composed of alkaline basalts derived from depths of 150 kilometres (about 90 miles) or more within the deep portion of the upper mantle.

The Northeast Pacific Basin is especially rich in seamounts that commonly trend northwest to southeast in long festoons. Many of these chains are entirely submerged, such as the Magellan Seamount Group in the far western Pacific. Others, such as the Hawaiian chain, are mixed groups of islands, banks, and seamounts. Forming an extension of this chain is the giant, deeply submerged Emperor Seamount Chain off Japan. Each of these seamounts is named after a semi-mythical Japanese emperor.

Oceanic islands, those rising from the deep ocean bed beyond the continental shelves, may be classified as either high islands or low islands. High islands are simply the tops of giant seamounts that are both tall enough to pierce the surface and young enough not to have been eroded away by wave action. These are nearly all active, dormant, or recently extinct volcanoes, because erosion reduces an island to a shallow bank after a few million years. Strings of islands, such as the Hawaiian chain, may be formed when the Earth's outer crust drifts over a deep, stationary lava pipe. Thus, the volcanically active island always lies at one end of the chain. Low oceanic islands, those lying essentially at sea level, generally are coral atolls in tropical latitudes. As Darwin surmised about the mid-19th century, these atolls have formed by the deposition of limestone upon a subsiding, extinct volcano. The upward growth by corals and lime-secreting algae offsets subsidence and maintains the atoll precisely at sea level, so that these limestone edifices are "the gravestones of departed volcanic islands."

Some large, deeply submerged seamounts, especially in the central North Pacific, are flat-topped and are termed guyots, after Arnold Henry Guyot, a 19th-century Swiss–U.S. geologist. An especially large cluster of guyots is that of the Mid-Pacific Mountains, which stretch from west of Hawaii to Wake Island.

Because truncation of a seamount can occur only by wave action at sea level, guyots are thought to be drowned ancient islands that have subsided one or more kilometres beneath the sea surface. They are found in regions un-

favourable to coral growth, so that no atoll was built up to offset their subsidence. This sinking usually is largely a result of regional subsidence of the ocean floor and of the horizontal drift of the seamount as the ocean crust moves down the flank of a rise. Local subsidence, or foundering, caused by the load emplaced on the crust by a volcanic seamount, may also play a role, but sinking caused by a relative rise of sea level (addition of new water to the oceans) apparently is not important. Although the oceans probably are growing deeper with time as new water is squeezed out of the Earth's mantle, this deepening is exceedingly slow, probably not more than a few centimetres per million years.

Abyssal hills and plains. Hills and knolls on the ocean floor are termed abyssal; they are protuberances smaller than seamounts, rising to heights from a few tens to several hundred metres above the ocean floor in regions largely devoid of sediment. Extensive regions of chaotic roughness especially characterize the Pacific floor along the flanks of the midocean ridges. Where careful surveys have been made, these hills commonly display an elongate form. They are caused by faulting of the oceanic crust, volcanic extrusions, and other kinds of deformation.

Featureless plains on the sea floor

Extensive regions of the ocean floor are abyssal plains, flat, featureless, sedimentary plains with slopes of less than one part in 1,000. Over broad reaches these plains will not vary in depth by as much as one metre (3.3 feet), and they are the levelest regions on the face of the Earth. This nearly perfect flatness is derived by the long-continued deposition of sediments by muddy bottom flows, which pond in the deepest hollows, burying any existing irregularities. These plains are found in all ocean basins but are best developed near continental margins and in the Atlantic Ocean, where deposition rates are high. Fine examples off the eastern United States are the Hatteras and Nares plains, lying at 5.5 kilometres (3.4 miles) depth, which have been developed by sediments shed from North America. The world's greatest abyssal plain is probably that underlying the Bay of Bengal, which has been built up by the muddy Ganges and Irrawaddy rivers.

SEDIMENTS OF THE OCEAN FLOOR

Types of sediments. The ocean floor is blanketed in most places with a sedimentary cover. Two basic types are recognized: namely, terrigenous sediments (sands, silts, and clays) that are shed from the continents or from islands and pelagic, or open-sea sediments—the finely suspended clays and remains of pelagic (floating-form) plants and animals that "rained" gently on the bottom.

Wherever biogenic constituents exceed 30 percent of the total, deep ocean sediments are said to be oozes. The most abundant of the biogenic constituents are the carbonate minerals calcite and aragonite, which are precipitated by many protozoans and other organisms to form their shells. Calcareous or foraminiferal muds cover about 48 percent of the deep-ocean bottom. Another important biogenic constituent is opal, a glasslike silicate formed by diatoms (algae) and radiolarians (protozoans). Where diatom growth is luxuriant, the sediments consist largely of their remains and are termed diatomaceous muds. Radiolarians are especially abundant in the equatorial waters of the eastern Pacific Ocean, where they form radiolarian muds (or oozes). Siliceous muds cover 14 percent of the deep-ocean floor.

The terrigenous sediments generally are deposited near the base of the continental slope as sedimentary fans or aprons. They are mostly turbidites laid down by turbidity currents, and they attain great thickness. Although covering a larger area, the pelagic oozes form a thinner blanket (zero–two kilometres thick). The most common is globigerina ooze, composed of minute calcium carbonate shells of protozoans, mostly of the genus *Globigerina*. This ooze covers vast expanses of the Atlantic and Indian oceans. Calcium carbonate dissolves in the deeper portions of the oceans so that in much of the central Pacific Basin calcareous oozes are replaced by red clay. The rates of sedimentation of red clay, however, are quite low, of the order of one or two millimetres (0.04 or 0.08 inch) per 1,000 years. Deep-sea trenches are generally well below the carbonate level, but the sediments found in them do not consist solely of red clay. Because of their exceptional depths, and in many cases their proximity to sources of abundant sediments from the continents, the trenches serve as traps for such terrigenous sediments.

Marine sedimentary rocks. Sediments are lithified or transformed into sedimentary rocks by several processes. These include compaction—the expulsion of water and reduction of pore space, which is especially important in muds and other fine-grained sediments; cementation—the precipitation of minerals in pores or at points of grain contact, which is important in many sediments and is quite conspicuous in sands; and diagenesis—the reactions that take place within the sediment between the contained minerals and the interstitial fluids. Solutions may bring in new materials from outside the sediment, thus precipitating new minerals and changing the chemical composition of the sediment as it lithifies.

Studies of these processes in deep-ocean sediments have been handicapped by difficulties and the expense of obtaining samples of ancient sediments far below the deep-ocean bottom. Deep-ocean drilling has provided limestones and siliceous rocks in various cores. Recovery of rocks containing unusual minerals, including zeolites, clays, and carbonate minerals, show that diagenetic alteration of sediments occurs in the deep ocean. Igneous activity at or below the ocean bottom produces fluids that react with sediments to cause diagenesis. The nature of sediment diagenesis involves the consideration of geochemical equilibria at low temperatures and pressures.

Most sedimentary rocks now exposed on the continents were originally deposited in shallow water when the ocean covered continental areas. Sedimentary rocks formed from deep-ocean sediment are rare, but some do occur in regions of crustal instability where mountain building has been active. Uplifted deep-ocean sediments are found on the islands of Timor in the Indonesian region, Barbados in the West Indies, and in the Alps.

Thickness of sediments
The thickness of sediment deposits in the ocean can be determined directly by drilling from specially constructed and equipped vessels, or indirectly by geophysical techniques. The latter, which have been used most extensively include seismic reflection and refraction techniques. Reflection techniques utilize an explosion to generate a sound signal that bounces off successive sediment layers. Precise determinations of the time elapsed between sending the signal and receiving the echo permit calculations of the layer thickness.

Seismic refraction techniques also utilize an explosion to generate a signal but employ a second station at some distance to receive the signal transmitted through the ocean bottom. Sound travels at different velocities in the various layers. Precise timing of the signal arrival from the various layers provides information about layer thickness and sound velocities in each layer. Sound velocity in turn provides information about physical properties of layers that cannot be obtained from reflected signals.

Using these techniques, geophysicists have shown that marine sediments are several kilometres thick near continents; more than three kilometres (two miles) thick, for instance, in the Argentine basin off South America. Away from continents, sediments are 200 to 300 metres (660 to 980 feet) thick in the Pacific and about a kilometre thick in the Atlantic. Deep-ocean deposits average about 450 metres (1,500 feet) thick, lying on about 1.8 kilometres of consolidated sediments or volcanic rocks (Layer 2a) and under that, about five kilometres (three miles) of basalt, in part altered (Layer 3). Layer 3 makes up the lowest part of the oceanic crust, which lies above the Earth's mantle region.

Sea-floor spreading effects
As previously mentioned, the deep-ocean bottom seems to be constantly renewed through sea-floor spreading. In this process, overlying sediments are carried along passively as the oceanic crust moves away from midocean ridges toward the trenches, changing both depth and position relative to the ridge crest. This affects both the type of sediment deposited and the rate at which it accumulates. Volcanic or igneous activity near ridge crests produces lithogenous material and causes a locally increased rate of

sediment accumulation. Rough topography on the ridges also forms small protected areas in which these sediments collect; sediment can neither enter these small depressions at a later time nor readily escape from them. Furthermore, the shallowness of the ocean bottom near the ridges favours development of carbonate-rich sediments. Foraminiferal muds are common on the Mid-Atlantic Ridge; it is also one of the few areas where pteropods, delicate shells of planktonic gastropods, accumulate.

As the crust moves away from ridges through time, the sediment deposits are moved to greater depths where carbonate solution is most intensive, so that the most recently deposited sediment is less carbonate-rich than the older underlying sediment. The ridge topography is gradually covered by sediment accumulations. As the ocean bottom becomes deeper, turbidity currents may eventually reach the area, further changing the type of sediment deposited. Where the ocean bottom approaches a continent, the sediment deposits become thicker. Island arcs or ridges along the continental margins, as in the western Pacific Ocean, may trap sediment locally and cause an immense thickness of sediment to accumulate, up to 15 kilometres (nine miles) in some of the Asiatic basins. In such cases, virtually no sediment escapes to be deposited in the trench or on the deep-ocean floor seaward of the island arc.

(R.S.D./M.G.G./Ed.)

Origin of ocean basins

The concepts of plate tectonics and sea-floor spreading have worked a revolution in the Earth sciences. Among other things, the concepts provide an adequate explanation for the origin of ocean basins. The theory holds that the Earth's outer shell is broken into about eight large, rigid, spherical caps, plus many small subplates. Except for the Pacific plate, which includes much of the Pacific Ocean, each major plate contains a separate continent embedded within it. An ideal plate may be envisioned as being rectilinear. Along one edge, where the plate is heavy, it dives into the Earth's mantle along a trench called a subduction zone. Opposing this zone of lithospheric descent, a rift is formed. As the rift grows larger, the void left behind is constantly healed by the upwelling of mantle rock. The midocean ridge system and its branches mark boundaries along which upwelling is splitting the crest and creating new ocean crust along the trailing edges of both plates. This growth, which occurs equally on both sides, causes the plates to move apart.

New ocean crust is presently being generated at about 1.5 square kilometres (0.6 square mile) per year, a rate sufficient to repave the entire ocean basin in 200,000,000 years. To accommodate this spreading of the sea floor, the rift and the trench are connected by large zones of shear or slippage called transform faults. Thus, crust is consumed at the trenches, created at the rifts, and conserved along the transform faults. The crustal plates and the continents embedded within them undergo drift, and this condition provides the mechanism for continental drift (see PLATE TECTONICS). Typical drift rates range from one to several centimetres a year, a remarkably rapid geologic process.

Formation of ocean basins between the continents
To understand why the Earth has ocean basins, the origin of continents must be considered, because the ocean basins are simply those depressed crustal regions that lie between the isolated continents. The continental plateaus are slabs of granitic rock or sial (siliceous or acid igneous rock), and they literally float in the Earth's denser mantle like blocks of wood floating in water. Following the principle of Archimedes, the continents adjust themselves to a level at which the weight of the mantle rock displaced is equivalent to their own weight, which is called isostatic (equal-weight) equilibrium. The 35-kilometre (22-mile) thickness of the continents and their density contrast with sima (mantle rock) is such that a five-kilometre (three-mile) relief results between oceanic and continental levels.

The generation of the granitoid rocks that form the continents requires at least two stages of melting and gravitational differentiation (separation according to density differences) of the low-density rock from the heavier rock. First, as the midocean rifts pull apart, new oceanic basalt fills in the void, repaving the ocean floor. This basalt is a partial melt or differentiate of the primitive, heavy, ultrabasic material of the Earth's mantle. Because of crustal drift this basalt is eventually consumed within trenches, subduction zones that carry the crust downward into the hot regime of the upper mantle. There the oceanic basalt is remelted, giving off sialic (lighter) rock that rises up to the surface as lava or granitic intrusions. This new rock generally forms an island arc that ultimately becomes accreted to the margin of a continent. In this manner the continents grow and the regions between these sialic plateaus become the ocean basins.   (R.S.D./Ed.)

BASIN BOUNDARIES

Continental slopes

The outer edge of the continental slope, which comprises the lower part of the continental terrace, is marked by an abrupt brink where the sea floor plunges three to five kilometres (two to three miles) to join the abyssal floor. The continental slopes are the longest, highest, and straightest boundary walls in the world. Only the lofty Himalayan rampart facing India attains the scale of a continental slope. If the ocean waters were removed, the continents would stand as pedestals everywhere. The continental slopes are the margins of the continents and, hence, are the boundaries of the ocean basins.

CHARACTERISTICS OF THE CONTINENTAL SLOPE

The gradient varies between 1° and near vertical, but the average is just over 4° for the first 2,000 metres (6,600 feet). Most slopes are steepest at the top but a few are precipitous in the deeper portion. The total length of the continental slope is 300,000 kilometres (200,000 miles), almost eight times the circumference of the Earth. The junction with the deep-sea floor or with a continental rise on the floor is usually indistinct.

In addition to being deeply indented by the numerous submarine canyons (see below), the slope is diversified by the presence of broad plateaus and other features. The Blake Plateau, at a depth of about 800 metres (2,600 feet) off the southeastern corner of the U.S., is an example of a major submarine plateau. Elsewhere, mounds and dents cause irregularities in the topography. The most typical continental borderland occurs off southern California, where a dozen basins of about 1,000 square kilometres (400 square miles) each are separated by submarine ranges, some topped by islands.

Salient to-
pographic
features

Most of the continental slope is covered by fine mud, consisting of clay and silt with a variable admixture of volcanic ash or shelly materials. But in areas where the declivity exceeds about 10°, the underlying rock bottom normally is exposed. Either hard rock (granite, basalt, consolidated sediment, reef rock, etc.) or semiconsolidated terrace sediments are most common.

On the continental rise and particularly on subsea fans, large corers often cut through sandy beds that are interstratified with normal deep-sea deposits. The structures and components show that these beds have been deposited by turbidity currents (see above). These density currents clean out the canyons and sweep the slopes at intervals of centuries or thousands of years. Within the confines of submarine canyons the deposits usually are coarse-grained. It is understandable that typical turbidity current deposits are missing there, because such flows are too mobile and competent to lose sediment in a steep gorge. The deposits that do occur represent the remainder of abortive turbidity currents—that is to say slides—and creeping beds modified by bottom currents that move independent of any sedimentary load.

ORIGIN OF THE CONTINENTAL SLOPE

Several origins are invoked for the continental slope. One possibility already mentioned is downwarping beyond a hinge line that would increase the slope. Another is subsidence of a subaerial slope together with the hinterland. This seems likely for the west coast of Corsica because the subaerial valleys continue all the way down to the deep floor of the Mediterranean without change in character. The likelihood of this subsidence is augmented by the presence of great volumes of quartz sand in Tertiary beds situated in southern France and the Apennines. This sand came from a former land area situated in the present Mediterranean, where the depth to the old land surface is now 3,000 metres (9,800 feet).

Some slopes have been built out, as shown by their internal structure. Other slopes show outcrops of older rocks that evidently have been truncated on their seaward end. Erosion of the slope by turbidity currents, especially during low sea levels, and slumping of subaqueous landslides have both played a part in slope creation. Where the beds thicken seaward from a point far inland of the coastline, there must be a slight tilting of the continental border toward the deep sea. Extremely precipitous slopes such as the one to the west of Florida into the Gulf of Mexico are obviously enormous fault scarps. The consequences of several possible processes and events on terrace structure are shown in Figure 15.

Slope
configura-
tions

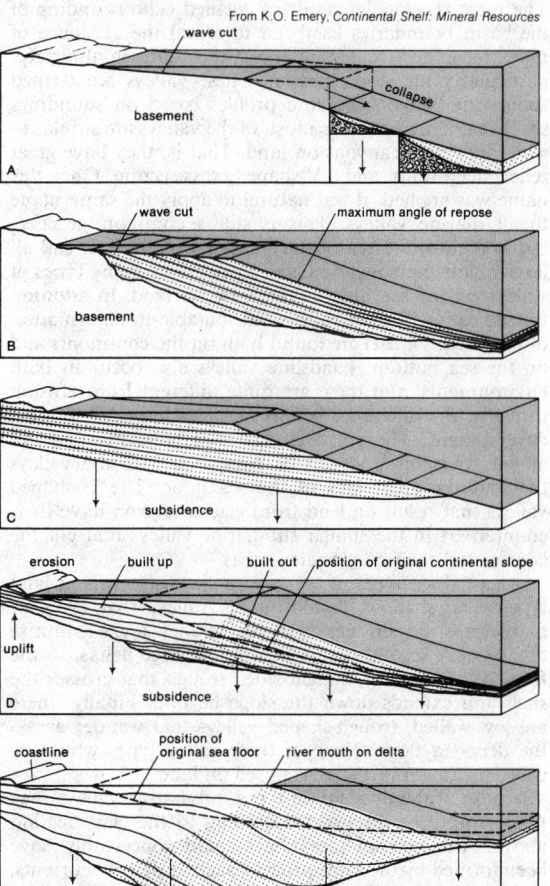

Figure 15: *Various types of continental terrace structures.* Structures resulting from (A) faulting and marine erosion, (B) outbuilding, (C) upbuilding in subsiding area, (D) combination of (B) and (C), (E) the same, but with great delta building by large river, and (F) tectonic dams and basins in a region of slumping.

A special case is formed by the steep slope to the east of Florida. Deepwater drilling has revealed that the adjoining Blake Plateau is underlain by shallow water sediments and subsidence evidently has occurred. But the Gulf Stream has prevented sediment accumulation and it still sweeps the bottom clean.

A recent investigation of the continental margin of Europe has shown that three major events have occurred. In the course of the Mesozoic Era the margin developed by faulting and subsidence of an old land surface. During the Cretaceous a thick mass of sediment accumulated. Upbuilding amounted to a maximum of four kilometres (2.5 miles) and outbuilding to many kilometres. An episode of erosion followed at the close of the Mesozoic, and this resulted in turbidite deposition in the deep ocean and an unconformity within the terrace with respect to the later Tertiary sediment. The northern and western margin of Iberia were produced by faulting, but there appears to have been little terrace building.

A second erosional episode of faulting, slumping, and canyon cutting occurred at the end of the Tertiary. Possibly it was induced by glacial lowering of sea level. Since then, accumulation has again predominated, but a renewed advance of the ice would tip the balance in the opposite direction again.   (P.H.K./Ed.)

Submarine canyons

The most spectacular result of detailed echo sounding of the basin boundaries has been to reveal the existence of many huge, deep valleys that gash the continental terrace, particularly the slope portion. These valleys are termed submarine canyons because profiles based on soundings show that many, perhaps most, of the valleys are similar to what are called canyons on land. That is, they have great relief, steep walls, and a V-shaped cross section. Once this name was applied, it was natural to apply the same name to all marine valleys. This is still a common practice, but it is no more reasonable than it would be to call all land valleys canyons. Actually, there are as many types of valleys on the sea floor as there are on land. In addition to true canyons, fault valleys (attributable to deformation of the Earth's crust) are found both on the continents and on the sea bottom. Landslide valleys also occur in both environments, and these are quite different from erosion canyons, the difference being catastrophic versus gradual development. The small elongated depressions that cut alluvial fans on land can be compared with the valleys that cut the great fans of the sea floor. The U-shaped valleys that result on land from glacial erosion have their counterpart in the similar submarine valleys that cut the continental shelf off glaciated areas.

At least three types of sea valleys are distinct from land types. The shallow, discontinuous valleys that cross or partly cross the continental shelves in a few areas comprise one type. A second occurs near a few large deltas, in the form of a relatively straight-sided trough that crosses the shelf and extends down the slope beyond. Finally, there are low-walled, trough-shaped valleys that wander across the deep-sea floor. None of these valley types would be called a canyon if it were exposed on land.

Because of the diversity of types, submarine valleys may most simply be discussed according to the classification above. Although all the valleys could conceivably have been formed by the same process, such as density currents, their origins were likely more diverse.

CHARACTERISTICS OF SUBMARINE CANYONS

The best known and probably the most common type of ocean-floor valley can properly be called the submarine canyon. These formations have an extraordinary resemblance to river-cut land canyons. In addition to their V-shaped cross sections, their floors slope outward as continuously as do land canyons. They have many entering tributaries that form the dendritic (branching) pattern characteristic of land canyons. Their steep walls frequently have rock outcrops, although a sediment cover is more common than in land canyons, and most of the sea canyons have similar winding courses.

The vertical dimensions of submarine canyons are surprising. Most of them have walls thousands of metres high, and the highest, in the Bahamas, rises almost five kilometres (three miles) from the canyon floor—dwarfing, by comparison, the walls of the Grand Canyon that are only about 1.6 kilometres (one mile) high. Some canyons have been traced for slightly more than 320 kilometres (200 miles) in length, but most extend less than 48 kilometres (30 miles). Usually they can be traced as far as the base of the steep part of the continental slopes, often more than 1.6 kilometres in depth. Their width varies in the same manner as that of land valleys. A narrow gorge off La Jolla, California, is as deep as it is wide, but the more typical canyons have widths of many kilometres. A five-kilometre-deep canyon in the Bahamas, for example, is 37 kilometres (23 miles) wide at its deepest point. By comparison, the Grand Canyon is about 19 kilometres (12 miles) wide. In both cases, the average slope is small, but photographs show vertical rock walls in the Bahama Canyon, and the Grand Canyon has vertical walls interspersed with terraces and pyramidal buttes (flat-topped and steep-sided hills). The seaward gradients of the canyon floors are generally steeper than those of land canyons. The average floor slope is about 57 metres per kilometre (300 feet per mile), but the numerous canyons that closely approach the coastline have high gradients at their heads, sometimes as great as 45°. The gradients almost always decrease in the outer portions.

The appearance of the canyons has been ascertained in recent years both by lowering cameras to the bottom and by observation from deep-diving vehicles. The dives, which have penetrated to depths of more than 2,100 metres (roughly 7,000 feet) within a canyon, have been particularly useful in describing physical features. They have indicated that vertical or even overhanging walls are commonplace, and that canyon walls often are grooved or polished as if they had been smoothed by a glacier. The floors, while generally covered with cobbles and other coarse sediment, are locally bare rock. Some have ripple-marked surfaces, which have been shown by remote camera pictures to occur at depths of more than three kilometres (two miles). The floors may vary considerably in gradient, ranging from a gentle slope to a steep drop-off, with the latter often occurring where boulders, fallen from the walls, have allowed sediments to build up above this obstruction.

All of the preceding features suggest that canyons are subject to active marine processes and are by no means mere remnants of long past erosional processes. Further evidence that conditions are far from static comes from

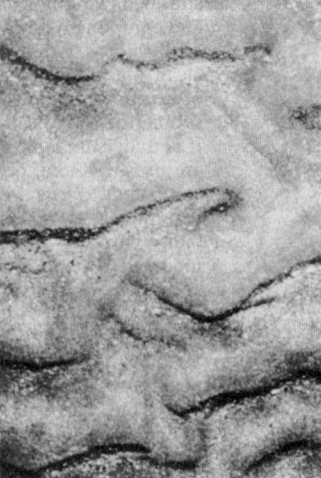

Figure 16: *Submarine canyon floors.*
(Left) Wall rock and cobbles in the Grand Bahama Canyon, at a depth of 3,523 metres, or 11,560 feet. (Right) Current ripples in Mera Canyon near Tokyo Bay, at a depth of 510 metres, or 1,673 feet.

Vast dimensions

Major physical features

repeated soundings taken along the same ranges at the canyon heads. It has been known since the mid-20th century that the profiles sometimes undergo radical changes. Apparently depth increases very suddenly, but shoaling occurs at a more gradual pace. This sudden deepening has broken cables—notably off the Congo, where a canyon extends seaward for 193 kilometres (120 miles). Piers and jetties built into submarine canyon heads have collapsed from the sudden removal of sediment on which they were resting.

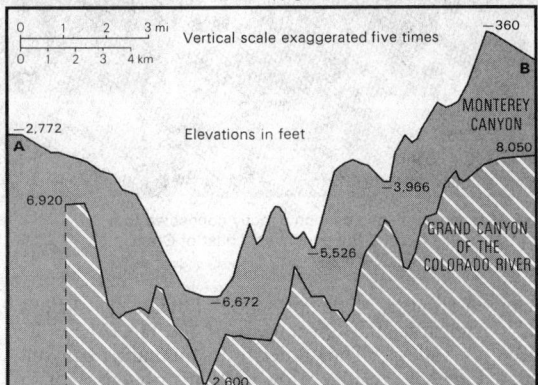

Figure 17: Profile comparison of the Grand Canyon of the Colorado River and the Monterey Canyon. The location of the Monterey Canyon profile is shown by the line A–B in Figure 20.

The nature of the rocks on the canyon walls has been determined by dredging and by observation from deep-diving vehicles. Most of it has proved to be relatively soft and hence rather easily eroded, but there are some canyons that have been cut through very hard rock, even quartzite. Granite walls have been found in several places, and one vertical granite cliff was discovered in a vehicle dive to 1,265 metres (4,150 feet) off the tip of Baja California. There, both walls of the canyon were granite; in some areas only one of the walls is hard rock, whereas the other wall is relatively soft.

GEOGRAPHIC DISTRIBUTION
OF SUBMARINE CANYONS

Submarine canyons are found along most continental slopes, although they have not yet been discovered around Antarctica nor along the slope into the Arctic off northern Europe and Asia, where soundings are spotty because of ice packs. Canyons are cut into the slopes off the Hawaiian Islands and possibly a few other oceanic islands. Soundings on these insular slopes are generally too incomplete to determine whether or not canyons are present. Along some slopes, canyons are as common as on typical mountain fronts, but elsewhere the slopes appear to be free from any canyons for many miles. In general, canyons

are scarce wherever the upper continental slopes are very gentle, as south of Cape Hatteras and around Antarctica. A surprising concentration of canyons is found around Sri Lanka, the tip of Baja California, the east coast of the U.S. north of Cape Hatteras, and along the northwest coast of the Mediterranean. There appears to be little if any relationship between canyons and latitude. The Sri Lanka canyons and the Congo Canyon are near the Equator, but the longest and largest canyons in the world are in the Bering Sea. The oceanic slopes that are not bordered by either continents or large islands appear to lack submarine canyons, but most of these slopes are not yet sufficiently well explored to make the conclusion certain. Off New England, the oceanic slope with many canyons is separated from the land valley by a shallow bank and a deep gulf inside, but the canyons may have been cut before the inner shelf was deepened by glaciation.

Concentrations of canyons

RELATION OF SUBMARINE CANYONS
TO ADJACENT LAND VALLEYS

From a worldwide point of view, it is difficult to generalize about the relationship between sea canyons and the river valleys on adjacent land areas. The canyons, such as those off the east coast of the U.S., head far out from the land and, as most of them lack connecting shelf valleys, it is not known whether they are related to the adjacent land valleys and to the estuaries at the valley mouths. When the canyons occur near the coast, it is easier to determine such a relationship. In a study of 57 submarine canyons that come close to the coast, it was determined that 46 (81 percent) were located directly off river valleys, and the remainder had no river valley inside the canyon head. At least one of the latter group, located in northern California, may have been connected with a land canyon before the faulting along the San Andreas Rift shifted the sea floor to the northeast, so that it is now located off a land cliff between canyons. Elsewhere, the shift of a stream mouth after the canyon had been cut may account for the lack of any connection, as at Cap Breton in southwest France, where the Adour River changed its course in the 15th century.

The mouths of many streams were drowned by the relatively recent rise of sea level, which accompanied the melting of the great ice sheets of the Pleistocene Epoch (began about 2,500,000 years ago and ended about 10,000 years ago). The relationship of such bays to canyon heads can be compared. In a study of 77 submarine canyons, 13 were found to enter drowned valleys, 25 to lie outside broad embayments that are not clearly drowned valleys, and 39 to occur either off long straight beaches or relatively straight sea cliffs.

Pleistocene drainage and changes of sea level

Another important consideration is the comparison between the type of land valley with the adjacent canyon on the sea floor. In almost all cases the characteristics of marine canyons are very different from those of land canyons, which usually have much lower gradients, much gentler side slopes, and much broader floors. The clos-

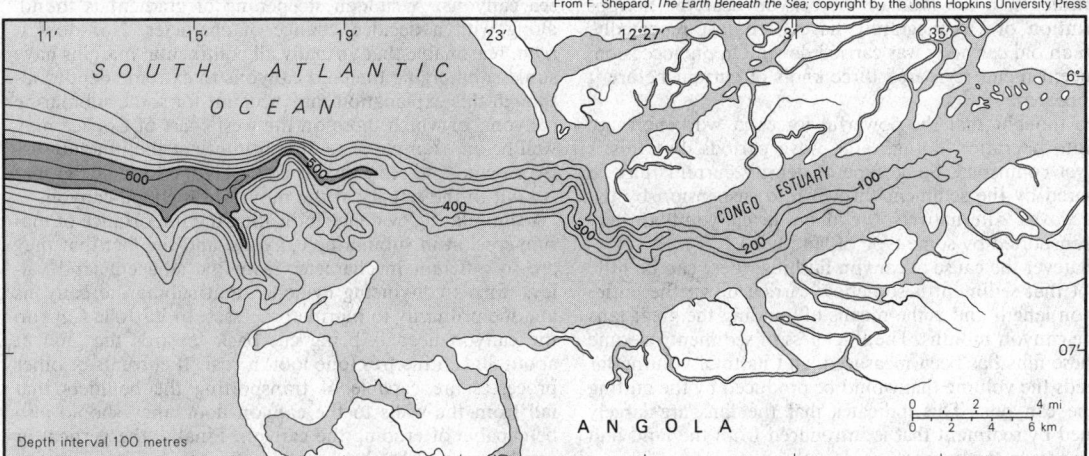

Figure 18: The topography of the Congo Canyon at the mouth of the Congo River.

est resemblance of land canyons to adjacent sea canyons is along the west coast of Corsica, but even there, the land valley mouths have low gradients and wide floors compared to the high gradients and narrow floors of the submarine canyon heads.

The drainage pattern of the land valleys also differs from the adjacent submarine canyons. The submarine canyons have a considerable number of tributaries at their heads, which makes them comparable to the land canyons, but in general the land valleys have more tributaries in their lower courses than do submarine canyons. An exception is the large Monterey Submarine Canyon, which has a fine display of tributaries along its entire course.

TRANSPORT OF SEDIMENT THROUGH SUBMARINE CANYONS

Streams carry large quantities of sand to the coast, and wave erosion adds to the supply. Along relatively straight coasts, like those of California, the diagonal approach of water waves causes the transport of this sediment along the shore in the direction in which the waves are approaching.

When canyon heads extend across the continental shelf to, or almost to, the coast, they have an enormous effect on sediments being carried along the coast by longshore currents. This sediment, consisting largely of sand, is carried in short jumps, in a process called saltation. Once the sediment has passed the lip of the canyon and falls on the steep sides, there is little chance for the currents, which are induced mostly by waves, to lift it clear. As it piles up on the walls, the sediment becomes unstable and slumps to the canyon floor. Repeated depth measurements across the canyons show that this process would soon fill the heads level with the surrounding shelf if there were no means of carrying the sediment down the canyon. Thus a fill of three metres (10 feet) in a period of a few months is not uncommon, but ordinarily within about a year the canyon head has somehow been flushed and the sediment must have moved seaward.

The cause of canyon flushing is still somewhat uncertain. Sand flows have been observed in places along the canyon walls where the slopes have become oversteep, but these flows do not take place at slope angles of less than about 30°. There are currents that alternately move up and down the canyon floors with velocities of up to one mile an hour. Such velocity is sufficient to transport sand. The available evidence indicates that the currents moving downcanyon are the strongest. This is supported by ripple markings observed on canyon floors, most of which indicate a downcanyon movement. These ordinary currents, however, are in almost constant operation; so if they were the sole cause of canyon flushing, the long periods of canyon-head filling could not occur. Apparently, some more powerful process operates from time to time to reverse this tendency to fill. Furthermore, cobbles are transported down the canyon floors, and these relatively weak currents are certainly not the cause of their movement. Fairly substantial evidence indicates that large rocks that have fallen from the walls are eventually carried away. Instruments in the head of the canyon near the Scripps Institution of Oceanography have been lost repeatedly. Even an old car body was carried down. On one occasion, a current meter registered three knots of current before it disappeared.

It is thought that the powerful forces at work here are set into operation during large wave periods, but this is not yet confirmed. Some type of density current may be triggered by the sediment thrown into suspension by the large waves. Alternatively, the fill on the canyon floor may be transported by some type of landslide.

Whatever the cause of canyon flushing, there can be little doubt that sediment is somehow carried down the entire canyon length and is the means of building the great fans at the canyon mouths. The thickness of sediment in some of these fans has been measured, and its total volume far exceeds the volume that would be produced by the cutting of the canyons. This indicates that the fans are largely formed by sediment that is introduced from the land and moves down the canyon.

One of the interesting features of the submarine fans

Evidence of canyon flushing

Figure 19: Prominent land canyon directly connected to a submarine canyon along the southwest coast of Crete.
By courtesy of Scripps Institution of Oceanography, University of California, San Diego

at canyon mouths is the presence of relatively shallow valleys truncating the upper beds of the fan. These are called "fan valleys." They differ from submarine canyons because they have relatively low walls, distributaries rather than tributaries (channels that transport water and sediment away from, not toward, the main canyon), and are usually bordered by levees, comparable to the levees on the sides of channels that cross river deltas (see RIVERS). These levees sometimes occur 30 metres (100 feet) or more above the channel floors, and they may rise seven metres (20 feet) above the general level of the adjacent fan. They apparently result from deposition of the overflow of currents moving down the fan valley.

Many of the fans are not cut by valleys. However, it is possible that fans can be built upward while valleys cut through them during the process. Recent evidence indicates that the fan valley outside La Jolla Submarine Canyon has been cut by a change from depositional processes to those of erosion. The fan valley outside Monterey Canyon has developed a meander comparable to those of rivers flowing in a flood plain.

Presence of "fan valleys"

ORIGIN OF SUBMARINE CANYONS

The discussion of the character of these canyons has provided much of the basis for the discussion of their origin. The resemblance of the canyons on the sea floor to those on land is, of course, an argument favouring a common origin. Also, the location of most known canyons off river valleys adds weight to the argument. If, however, submarine canyons are simply the submerged lower portions of land canyons, there should be a closer relationship between the submerged and the emerged portions. As A.O. Woodford has emphasized, the profiles of the land valleys show a sharp break when they are continued into the sea canyons. A sudden steepening of gradient is found, along with a decided change of character. Nor does it seem reasonable that virtually all continental margins have sunk, submerging the land canyons to extreme depths, although this explanation may account for some submarine canyons, of which those on the west coast of Corsica may well be an example. The discontinuity at the juncture between land and sea canyons could be due to the delta that is built in the estuary at the mouth of the land canyon.

Accumulating evidence indicating the importance of marine erosion in submarine canyons, and the fact that they are so different in character from the adjacent land valleys, forms convincing evidence that submarine canyons are due primarily to marine processes. In La Jolla Canyon the canyon head is being cut back towards the land at about 30 centimetres (one foot) a year. If currents or other processes are capable of transporting the boulders that fall from the walls to the canyon floor, they should also be capable of eroding the canyon. Finally, the vertical or overhanging walls that occur in the canyons seem to be proof of active erosion. If these walls had been cut long

Importance of marine processes

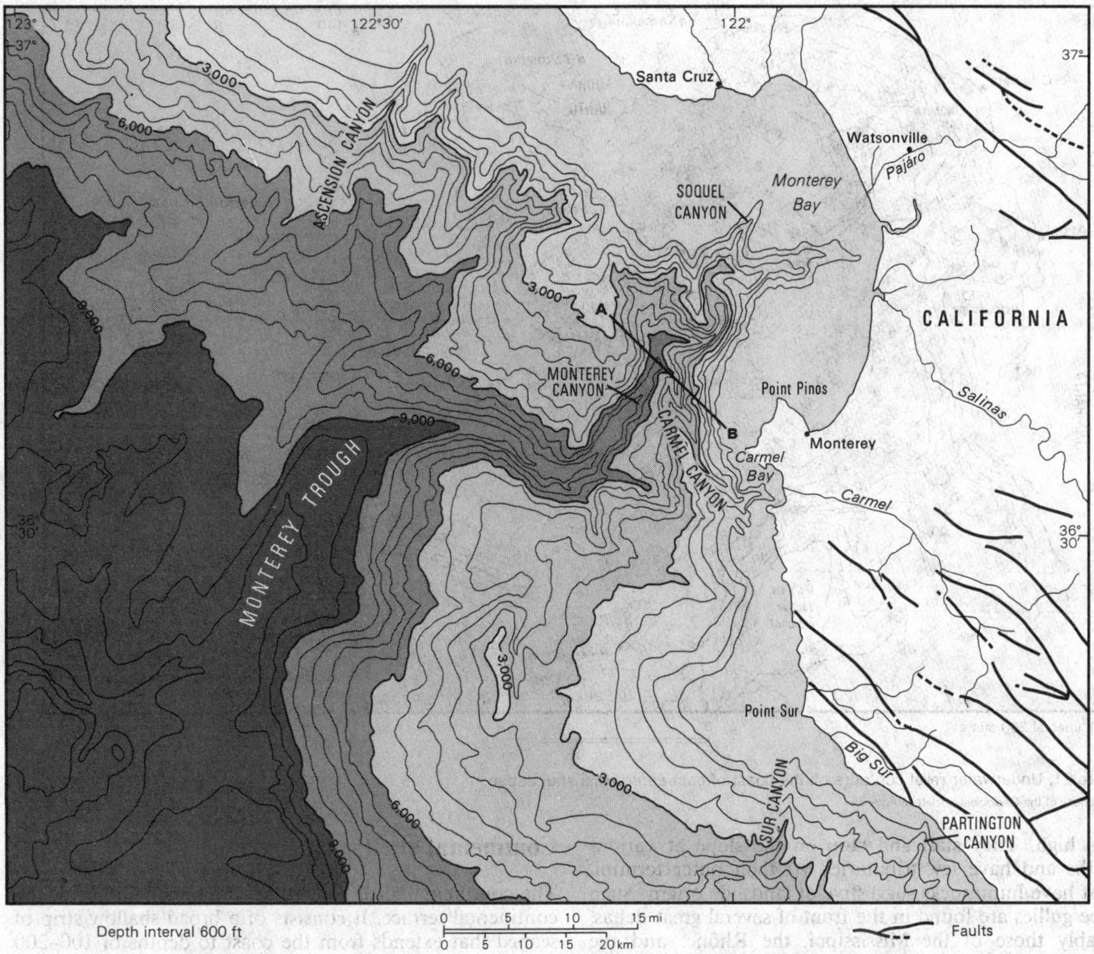

Figure 20: Ocean floor off the coast of Monterey, California. Profile along line A–B is shown in Figure 17.
From F. Shepard, *The Earth Beneath the Sea;* copyright by the Johns Hopkins University Press

ago, the action of organisms that live on them and the erosive effect of sediments sliding down from the shelf into the canyon should have greatly reduced the declivities. There must be active erosion along the canyon floors and lower walls to maintain the steep slopes.

Creeping action is occurring in the sediment at the head of La Jolla Canyon. A series of stakes driven in a line across the floor of this canyon by Robert Dill, an American marine geologist, show that the stakes in the centre move faster than those on the sides, as in a glacier. Also, an occasional major disturbance carries away all the stakes. Some stakes have been bent downcanyon because the sediment at the surface creeps forward at a faster rate than that beneath. Even in the fan valley beyond the canyon off La Jolla, the fill shows cracks and steps that suggest a creeping movement.

On the other hand, it does not seem likely that the major transfer of sediment down the canyons, nor their cutting, are due principally to creeping action. Cores taken in the canyon floor have rather well-preserved stratification. If the sediment was creeping continuously down the canyon, this stratification would be much disturbed and would show many drag folds (bending of strata due to the dragging of one bed over and past another) oriented downcanyon. Therefore, it seems likely that the major erosion and transportation of sediments downcanyon is the result of currents which are generally thought to be density currents, even though positive proof is still lacking.

Ages of submarine canyons. Little is known about the age of the existing submarine canyons. Some geologists have thought that they were cut during low sea-level stages of the glacial period, but the huge size of the fans found beyond the canyons means that they probably have been developing for several million years. This would imply an age that antedates the glacial period. Furthermore, geologists have found many features in ancient rocks that

appear to represent old submarine canyons subsequently filled with sediments. Lowered sea levels would have helped the movement of sediments onto the continental slopes because of the exposure of the shelves. Canyons certainly are forming, and there is little reason to confine their origin to the short periods when the shelves were laid bare by lowered sea level. These episodes must have been too brief for marine processes to excavate the huge gorges out of granite.

The investigations of a huge canyon in the Bahamas has shown that it was probably in existence in the Pliocene, a period prior to glaciation. It is quite probable that this canyon has been forming for millions of years, while the Bahama limestone banks grew upward, keeping pace with the sinking of the sea floor. Deep wells show that Cretaceous rocks underlie the younger formations in the Bahamas at depths of 1,830 to 2,135 metres (6,000 to 7,000 feet). So far as is known, these all were deposited in shallow water, whereas deep-water formations are found along the walls of the submarine canyon.

Submarine fault valleys. Blocks of the Earth's crust can drop between upraised masses and can produce valleys in this way. Death Valley in California, the Jordan Valley in the Near East, and the rift valleys of Africa are examples of land valleys in earthquake belts. Most of these valleys have relatively flat floors, straight steep walls, basin depressions, developing lakes, and they lack tributaries. Using the same criteria, fault valleys can be identified on the sea floor. The valley of this type that extends down Sagami Bay in Japan was the locus of the 1923 earthquake that destroyed much of Tokyo and Yokohama. Various sea-floor valleys in the earthquake belts south of the Aleutian Islands also appear to be fault valleys. Some of them are V-shaped but otherwise suggest fault origin.

Slope gullies. Many submarine slopes have a valley with low walls that are rarely more than 30 metres (100

Pre-Pleistocene and present formation

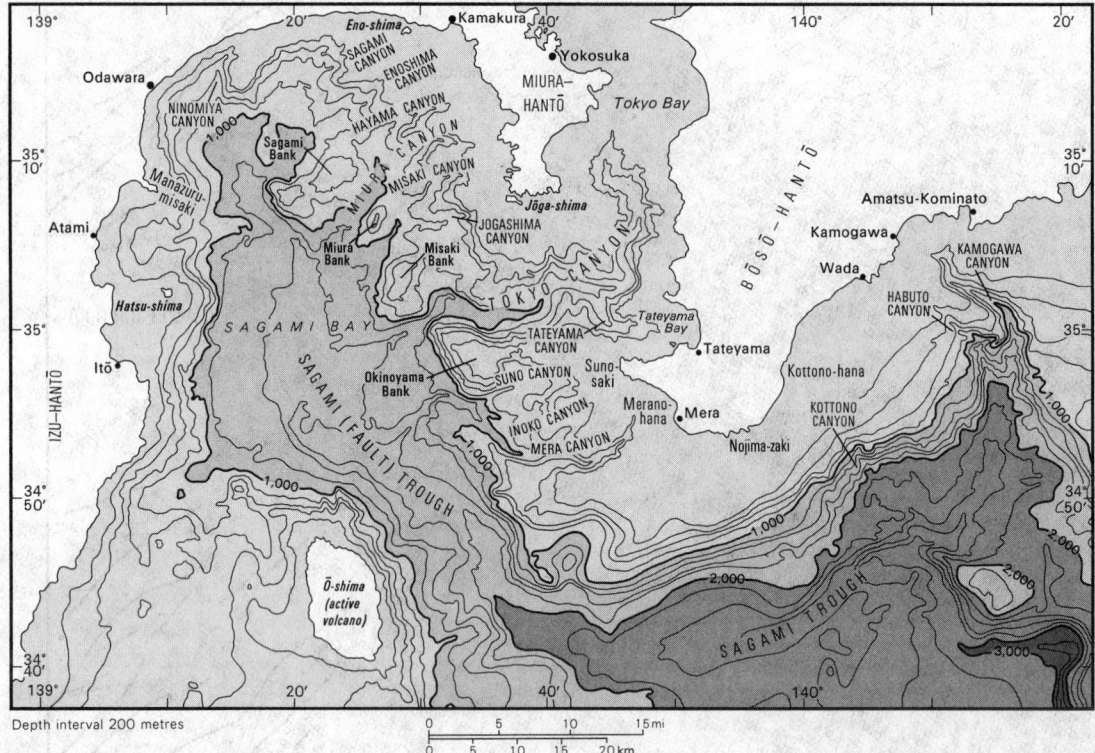

Figure 21: Underwater relief contours off the coast of east central Honshu, Japan.
By courtesy of the Geological Society of America

Depth interval 200 metres

feet) high. They start and stop on the slope at various depths and have few tributaries. At their outer termini, most have hummocks suggestive of landslide origin. Such slope gullies are found in the front of several great deltas, notably those of the Mississippi, the Rhône, and the Fraser. They change position as the delta builds forward, as shown by comparing old and new surveys. They are the result of slumping of recent sediment.

Delta-front troughs. Beyond the broad deltas of the Ganges and Indus, broad-floored valleys extend across the shelf and down the adjacent floor. These valleys seem to be related to the delta building. They differ from submarine canyons in their broad trough shape, absence of entering tributaries, and their relatively straight course, in contrast to the winding courses of the canyons. Outside these troughs are great fans cut by fan valleys, much the same as those outside submarine canyons.

At present, there is not sufficient information to fully understand the origin of the delta-front troughs. Apparently, sediment moves out along them, as along submarine canyons. Off the Mississippi, the head of a delta-front trough has been filled for 48 kilometres (30 miles); but a typical trough occurs beyond that distance, and the filled portion of the trough was only discovered by borings and seismic reflection profiling across the shelf.

Role of turbidity currents

Deep-sea channels. The existence of very long channels cutting the deep-sea floor of both the Atlantic and Pacific has been well established. They are cut to depths of as much as a few hundred metres below the surrounding sea floor. They have relatively flat floors that are several kilometres across and, so far as is known, they slope continuously in one direction. Some of them have entering tributaries. Sediments from the channel floors include sand, indicating that strong currents are operating along them. Some of the channels extend out beyond the continental slopes, but others run essentially parallel to the base of the slopes. These channels have been attributed by B. Heezen and others to turbidity currents, but there is no clear evidence. Some valleys may represent shallow fault troughs that have been the locus of turbidity currents coming out from the continental slopes.

(F.P.S./Ed.)

Continental shelf

The continental shelf constitutes the upper surface of the continental terrace. It consists of a broad shallow strip of seabed that extends from the coast to depths of 100–200 metres (330–660 feet). Some authors include the coastal plain on the landward side, but the shore represents a reasonable limit. The breadth of the shelf and the depth of its outer margin vary greatly. Beyond the shelf is the continental slope, which was described above. The relationship between the shelf and slope is shown in Figure 22.

CHARACTERISTICS OF THE CONTINENTAL SHELF

The shelf begins at the low-water line, but there is uncertainty whether to include estuaries, tidal flats, or shallow lagoons (see below *Lagoons*). There is less reason to exclude barrier-reef lagoons, and it can be argued that atoll lagoons and banks of the same depth as shelves also are part of the system (*e.g.*, the Bahama Banks). A similar problem is whether shallow inland seas should also be incorporated. The difficulty is that there are many transitions between enclosed seas such as Hudson Bay, and shelves with a few minor islands such as the Farilhões off Portugal or Sable Island opposite Nova Scotia.

The outer margin of the shelf formerly was defined as the 100-fathom (180-metre) line. A much better limit now

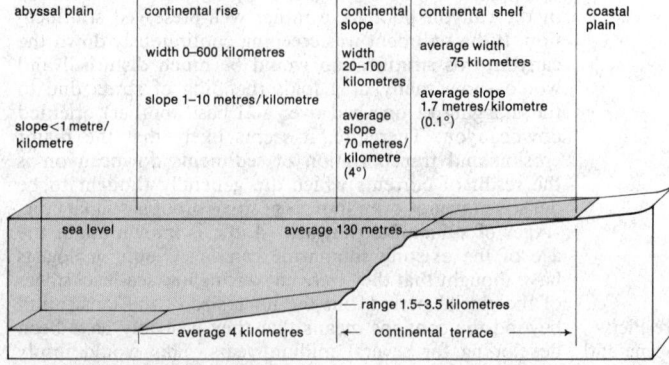

Figure 22: The configurations and general dimensions of the continental shelf and slope regions.

can be set by the break in slope, or shelf break, between the nearly horizontal platform and the much steeper continental slope, which nearly always starts abruptly. The depth at this break averages 130 metres (430 feet), but it may be less than 40 metres (130 feet) or as much as 500 metres (1,600 feet). There are areas, however, where no distinct break in slope exists and the 180-metre line must be adopted for a limit.

Shelf topography, valleys, and river deltas. The average slope is about one-tenth of a degree; near shore it normally is slightly steeper. The average width is 75 kilometres (45 miles). There is practically no shelf off Miami, Florida, or the French Riviera, but, in contrast, the Atlantic shelf off Patagonia is 500 kilometres (300 miles) wide. The surface of the shelf may be remarkably smooth or may consist of rocky or sandy shoals, depressions, or channels, one or two terrace-like features, and a gradual or abrupt longitudinal slope. In fact, the topography of continental shelves is at least as diversified as that of coastal plains.

Submarine valleys on the shelf are of several distinct types. Some are broad with a fairly flat bottom and occur only in high latitudes. These evidently were scoured out by Pleistocene glaciers. Some valleys actually form the continuation of fjords onto the shelf. Others are more isolated, like the huge Cabot Strait Trough between Nova Scotia and Newfoundland, which is 500 metres deep and almost 100 kilometres (60 miles) wide. There also are many instances of glacial troughs parallel to the coast, exemplified by the trench curving around the southern extremity of Norway, which is up to 800 metres (2,600 feet) deep, 800 kilometres (500 miles) long and 80 kilometres (50 miles) wide.

A different kind of sea valley results from the action of tidal scour. It occurs when restrictions force tidal currents to sweep with extra force over the seabed—as between the Frisian Islands of the southeastern North Sea, for example.

Another type of submarine valley results from the drowning of a river valley. The Hudson Channel, extending from New York harbour to the outer margin of the shelf, and the "Sunda River," a dendritic system of valleys between Sumatra, Malay Peninsula, and Borneo, are examples of this phenomenon. No sharp distinction can be made between valleys and oblong depressions of tectonic origin that may be modified by external processes.

Delta types River deltas form on the shelf. Some, like the Rhône Delta, appear to pinch out on top of the shelf. Other deltas, such as those of the Nile and Niger rivers, have built out the continental slope so that the terrace locally bulges seaward. The Mississippi Delta is a multiple feature. The present bird-foot set of distributaries has built out onto the shelf and has reached the edge of the continental slope at one point. Similar structures of greater age overlap each other and have disappeared by subsidence and marine attack. Thin sediments have contributed to the construction of the continental terrace off Louisiana.

The great South American rivers, notably the Paraná and Amazon, have large estuaries and do not appear to have extended the shelf seaward. The same lack of outbuilding characterizes the Orinoco Delta, which is situated partly behind the island of Trinidad. This may be due to strong tidal currents and the preponderance of fine sediment that is washed away by currents, partly in a lateral direction along the coast and partly into the deep sea. Many great rivers such as the Irrawaddy and Indus appear to have filled sinking trenches but have not extended the land onto the terrace. Others, including the Euphrates and Po, have built deltas with sufficient rapidity to prevent inundation by the sea due to land subsidence.

The actions of water waves and ocean currents have combined to throw up sandy barriers on some shelves that are approximately parallel to the coast and separated from the mainland by a lagoon. One of the most spectacular examples is Pamlico Sound, where Cape Hatteras extends out into the Atlantic halfway across the shelf. Sedimentation and plant growth will reclaim these lagoons, thus adding large areas to the land. In tidal flats the struggle between destructive and constructive forces is in full swing.

Sea-level fluctuation **Influence of the Ice Age.** During the Pleistocene Epoch sea level was lowered considerably during each major advance of the ice caps; the last such lowering amounted to about 100 metres (330 feet). Ice advances occurred about a half a dozen times in the course of the last 2,500,000 years. During intervening interglacial intervals sea level was equal to or higher than its present elevation.

The influence on the shelf has been dramatic. The breaker zone and its rough turbulence has passed down the shelf surface and back again, disturbing the deposits of sedimentary material and winnowing out the finer particles. Exposure of the shelf by the lowering of sea level resulted in weathering and overall degradation in some areas and deltaic deposition by minor rivers elsewhere. The larger rivers flowed down to the new coast on much steeper gradients than are usual in their unaffected lower courses. This tended to cause erosion of gorges on the exposed shelf. Vast amounts of sediment were brought to the outer edge of the shelf as a consequence of this process. The deposited material served partly to prograde the shelf; it also passed down submarine canyons and greatly stimulated the action of turbidity currents. Most estuaries are the result of postglacial submergence of river valleys scoured out during stages of lowered sea level. They serve as sediment traps today and hence reduce present deposition on the shelves.

Since the end of the last glacial interval sea level has risen 100 to 120 metres (330 to 390 feet) in about 12,000 years, or about one centimetre (0.4 inch) per year. Over the last 5,000 years sea level has fluctuated slightly around its present stand (elevation).

Sea level was depressed approximately by the same amount over the entire globe, and the lowering was at least of the same order of magnitude for the major ice advances. The growth and waning of the ice sheets and glaciers was irregular, and periods of stagnation or temporary reversal occurred. As a result, sea level sometimes remained almost stationary for longer periods, and this resulted in the cutting of terraces that are still preserved at various altitudes above and below sea level. But worldwide correlation is rendered difficult by local crustal movements.

Although the reality of all these effects of the Ice Age has been demonstrated, the configuration of the continental terraces before the Ice Age is not yet clear. At present, there is a thin veneer of shallow-water and reworked beach deposits between 150-metre (490-foot) depth and the shoreline (Figure 23). This cover rests on a lower

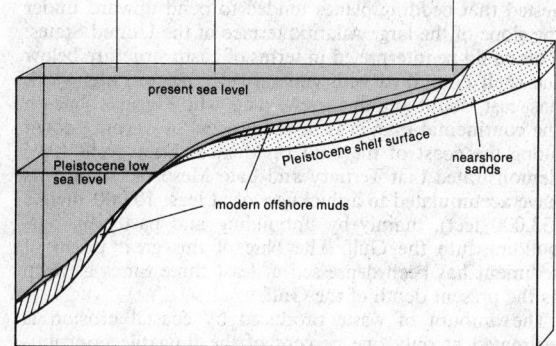

Figure 23: Idealized model of sediment deposition, showing effects of sea-level rise since Pleistocene on distribution of surface sediments.

veneer of earlier marine deposits or lowland formations (fluviatile deposits, marshes, dunes, boulder clay, etc.) of Pleistocene age that have been partly altered by weathering. This in turn is underlain by undisturbed preglacial shelf deposits. It is not unlikely that this picture is more complex where similar remnants of the earlier Pleistocene low levels have been partially preserved. A third veneer is now forming on the sea floor, consisting of sand (partly of organic origin) in very shallow water and mud farther offshore, out to a distance of a few dozen kilometres.

Beyond this recent covering deposit, the rock or coarse-grained Pleistocene formations have not been buried.

These barren stretches of the shelf evidently are unsuitable for mud accumulation. The reason must be the action of incoming waves and currents, two factors that presumably act energetically near the slope break but are damped off towards the coast. Not until the surf zone is approached does wave energy on the seabed increase again.

A complicating factor is the presence of bottom-dwelling animals—worms, bivalves, sea urchins, and others—that filter clay from the water and add it to the bottom as pellets. By burrowing and ploughing they also mix the sand with some fine-grained material deposited during periods of quiet.

STRUCTURE AND ORIGIN

It is obvious that the two main processes fashioning the shelf are deposition and erosion. On cliffed coasts wave action and currents are visibly making inroads on the terrestrial material. The retreat of an exposed coastline that is composed of unconsolidated sediments can be many metres per year, whereas in hard rock it is so slow that rates of retreat are very slight.

It once was assumed that waves eroded to depths of 100 metres, but it is now well established that they cannot attack hard rock at depths below a dozen metres. They can prevent sediment from accumulating at much greater depths, however. Because a wide, shallow platform of rock will effectively damp and absorb wave energy, marine erosion will have more influence when sea level changes with relation to the land than under stable conditions. The contribution from sedimentation is most readily demonstrated where the shelf bordering a delta has been built out into the deep-sea realm (*e.g.*, the Niger Delta).

Other possible origins are the subaerial development of a coastal plain, followed by subsidence beneath the sea. The elevation of a deeper zone to produce a shelf is less likely. It also has been postulated that the continental margin is due to down flexure beyond a hinge line that must evidently coincide with the break in slope. The precipitous slope south of the Riviera and its dendritic system of steep rocky valleys is considered to be an example. Most geologists assume that the location and shape of the break in slope was caused by the lowering of glacial sea level.

Terrace structures   **Geophysical evidence.** Geophysical investigations have demonstrated a variety of internal structures. Shelves bordered on the oceanic side by hard rock are thought to be infilled lagoons behind barrier reefs, rocky basins containing accumulated sediment, or an erosional platform that has been veneered with sediment except at its rim.

The first seismic reconnaissance of terrace structure suggested that bedding planes tended to bend upward under the slope of the large Atlantic terrace of the United States. This could be interpreted in terms of basin structure below the shelf combined with general subsidence. Later work has cast doubt on this view. The whole crust beneath the continental margin is in the process of warping down along the coast of the Gulf of Mexico. Deep wells have demonstrated that Tertiary and Late Mesozoic sediments have accumulated to a thickness of at least 10,000 metres (33,000 feet), mainly by upbuilding and partly by outbuilding into the Gulf. The base of this great prism of sediment has been depressed at least three times as deep as the present depth of the Gulf.

The amount of waste produced by coastal erosion is estimated at only one percent of the fluviatile contribution to marine sedimentation. This accords very well with the finding that the dominant terrace structure is constructional and is the result of upbuilding combined with outbuilding. Details of the structure of many sections suggest the following development. Subsidence rapidly occurs over the area of the shelf and presumably part of the slope. Then, during the following period of crustal stability, sedimentation builds out from the landward side with a relatively steep dip slope, in some cases continuing beyond the break in slope and thus extending the slope into deep water. The cycle is then repeated. The subsidence is attributable in part to the weight of the new sediment, which causes compaction of buried deposits and downwarping of the Earth's crust, and in part to consolidation of deeper layers, crustal thinning under tension, and loss of light material from below the crust by processes within the Earth's mantle.

Relation to continental drift   **Geological relationships.** The continental shelves obviously have a bearing on the theory of continental drift and sea-floor spreading (see PLATE TECTONICS). The strongest case for drift is evidence that the Atlantic Ocean constitutes a rift that opened in the course of the Mesozoic between the Americas and Europe–Africa. This dovetails neatly with the Early Cretaceous age of the continental shelves on both sides that must have been constructed since the break. The theory originated from the good fit between the opposite margins of the Atlantic. But the most convincing proof of the rift is now supplied by paleomagnetism, deep-ocean drilling, geological fitting, the relics of the Permian Ice Age, and paleo-biogeography. It has become obvious that the shelf break is hardly better than the coastline or the margin of the continental rise as a feature by which to test the claim of a fit between the opposite coasts. The shelf edge came into being long after the rift, and the original continental margins appear to have been spread out and attenuated by loss of lateral support. The split off of the Rockall and Porcupine banks and the rotation of Iberia have caused deformations. Alpine mountain building has distorted the blocks themselves. Volcanism and delta building have inserted new masses. In spite of all these alterations the fit, whatever system of comparison is taken, is remarkably good. It is still a strong point in favour of the drift theory.

The origin and age of the Atlantic terraces and of the other margins created by continental rifting thus can be reasonably well accounted for. The younger ones of deep inland seas can be explained along the same lines; they developed after subsidence of their floors. But there remain the Pacific margins and a few others that have fronted the presumably primordial oceanic basin for a dozen times as long. These terraces are not more voluminous as one would expect but tend to be of modest size. It has been suggested that the continent has actively overridden the ocean floor and terrace or passively has allowed the ocean crust to be carried obliquely beneath them by mantle currents. The coastal ranges of continents could be tectonically compressed former terraces, but this would imply a radically different origin for all the great mountain chains crossing the continents, a consequence that is most unsatisfactory.

Even in broad view, the question of how the continental terrace has come into being requires a complex answer. Some coastal erosion is involved, but upbuilding and outbuilding on a subsiding margin are more important, and faulting and submarine erosion are also implicated. Sea level basically has had a unifying influence. The shallow inland seas are not genetically related to the terrace and they can be considered as typical continental areas that happen to have been flooded. Deep inland seas are widely considered to be foundered continental areas, in which chasms opened by continental drift. But in spite of the insight obtained, the origin and obliteration of many terraces remain obscure, especially those of the Pacific.

(P.H.K./Ed.)

FEATURES OF THE OCEANIC SHORELINE

Coral islands, coral reefs, and atolls

The outer margin of the continental shelf sustains islands or shallow banks. The most extreme examples occur where coral reefs have developed barrier reefs and atoll rims.

Coral reefs are masses of carbonate of lime built up from the sea floor by the accumulation of the skeletons of a profusion of animals and algae; eventually they rise to the surface of the water.

Reef buildingcorals, chiefly the stony corals or Sclerac-

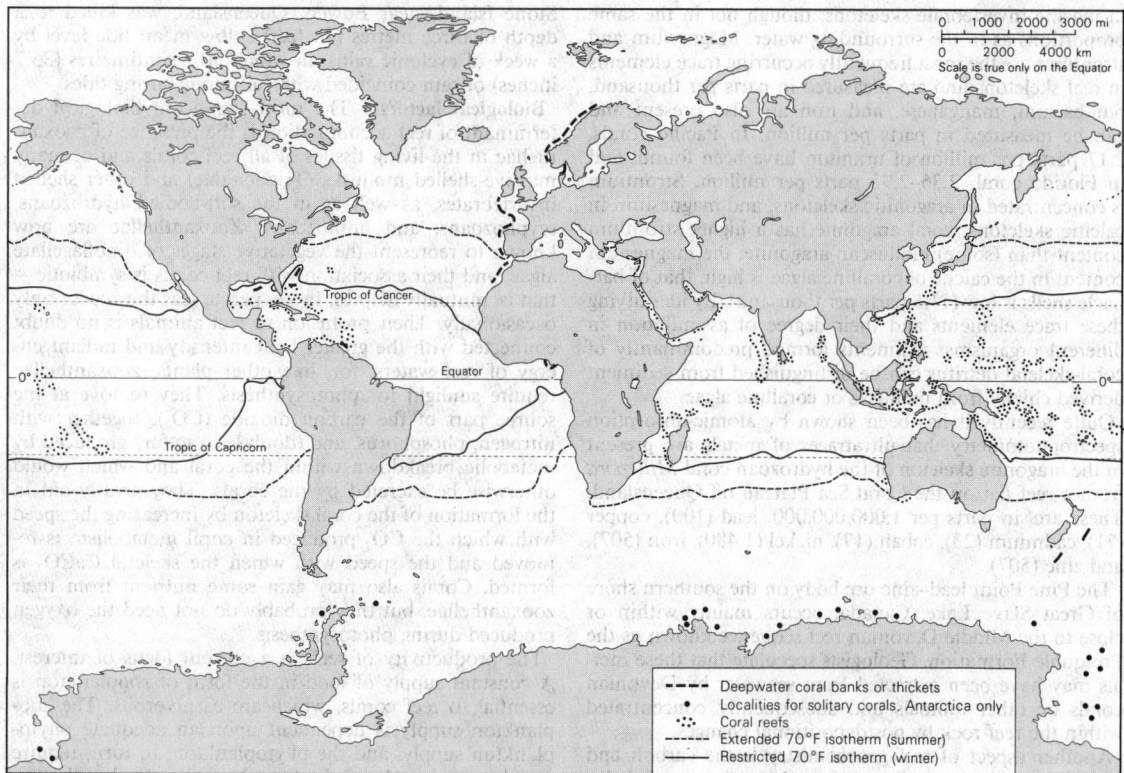

Figure 24: Distribution of coral reefs and their relation to controlling sea-surface temperature.
By courtesy of the Geological Society of America

tinia, grow best in shallow, sunlit water, between the low-water mark and a depth of six fathoms (11 metres), but they can still construct reefs in water as deep as 22 fathoms (40 metres), and they may have a sparse existence between 22 and 30 fathoms (40 and 55 metres). These corals prefer water of normal salinity and with an annual maximum temperature above 22° C (72° F) but below 28° C (82° F); but their reef-building activities may be carried on in waters whose minimum temperature in winter is not less than 15° C (59° F).

A second group of corals in present-day seas grow in thickets and coppices that develop banks rather than reefs on the outer, deeper, colder, and darker parts of continental shelves and platforms. These organisms flourish in water with a winter minimum temperature ranging between about 4° and 15° C (39° and 59° F) at depths of about 33 fathoms to 110 fathoms (60 to 200 metres). In any one thicket there are commonly only two genera of delicately branching corals involved. Such coral banks are known along the eastern Atlantic shelf edge (or continental slope) from Norway to the Cape Verde Islands and again off the Niger River Delta and in the west Atlantic around the Gulf of Mexico, the Bahamas, and the Orinoco River Delta. Off New Zealand such banks have been recognized on the Campbell Plateau and the Chatham Rise; they also occur in the northwest Pacific near Japan.

The third coral assemblage of the modern seas is associated with even colder or deeper seas; it consists of small, solitary corals of relatively few genera, known from the abyssal floors of the oceans and from the shelves around Antarctica, Patagonia, and the Falkland Islands in waters 2° to 6° C (35° to 43° F) in temperature.

Fossil reefs   Buried fossil reefs on ancient continental shelves are targets for petroleum-exploration companies. The porosity of reefs and the characteristic curvature of nonporous enclosing sediments cause them to be prospective reservoirs for oil and gas. The rich oil fields of Alberta, for example, are associated with Devonian reefs (about 345,000,000 to 395,000,000 years old). Fossil reefs recently have become targets for metal prospecting because some corals contain small percentages of metals such as zinc and copper, selectively incorporated from seawater. A living coral reef may also have economic potential, in that it constitutes a major tourist attraction.

REEF ACCUMULATION

Tropical water conditions.   Water conditions favourable to the growth of reefs exist in tropical or near-tropical surface waters. Regional differences may result from the presence or absence of upwelling currents of colder waters or from the varying relation of precipitation to evaporation.

Tropical seas are well lit, the hours of daylight varying with the latitude. Light intensity and radiant energy also vary with the depth. Thus, at latitude 32°44′ N (Madeira Island) the "day" in March has a length of 11 hours at a depth of 20 metres (70 feet), five hours at 30 metres (100 feet), and only about a quarter of an hour at 40 metres (130 feet). Nearer the pole these figures decrease further. Light intensity has a profound effect on the growth of the individual reef-coral skeleton, because of the symbiont zooxanthellae of reef corals (see below *Biological factors*). The number of species present on a reef may also be related to light intensity and radiant energy.

Effects of light, turbidity, and nutrients

Turbidity may be high in lagoons, where shallow water lies over a silt-covered sea floor and where storms and windy periods cause considerable disturbance of the bottom silt. The average transparency may be low (about 12 metres [39 feet]), and light penetration is reduced.

Inside the Great Barrier Reef, on the shallow continental shelf of Queensland, the oxygen content of the water is high, exceeding 90 percent saturation most of the time; in deeper water, during the calm periods of the rainy season, the saturation may fall to about 80 percent. Plant nutrients such as phosphate and nitrate show no seasonal change in quantity; both are present in very small quantities throughout the year. Constant mixing of the shallow sea prevents any stratification of the nutrients. As a result, growth of phytoplankton is possible and almost uniform throughout the year, providing a constant supply of food for the zooplankton which in turn form the chief food supply of the corals. Some nutrients enter the lagoonal waters with the oceanic water that flows through the reef openings, but the dissolved phosphates in the lagoons are probably derived chiefly from bacterial decomposition of the organic matter on the sea-bottom, as well as from detritus swept in from the reef surfaces. This environmental pattern is typical of many atoll lagoons.

Geochemistry of reefs.   Minute quantities of metallic elements are present in solution in seawater and also occur

Trace
elements
in reef
skeletons

in marine invertebrate skeletons, though not in the same proportions as in the surrounding water. Magnesium and strontium are the most frequently occurring trace elements in reef skeletons and are measured in parts per thousand, but barium, manganese, and iron are also present and can be measured in parts per million. In Pacific corals, 2.17 parts per million of uranium have been found; and in Florida coral, 2.36–2.95 parts per million. Strontium is concentrated in aragonitic skeletons, and magnesium in calcitic skeletons; coral aragonite has a higher strontium content than (some) molluscan aragonite; the magnesium content in the calcite of coralline algae is high; that of barnacle shells is low (11.5 parts per thousand). By identifying these trace elements and their degree of assimilation in different organisms, sediments formed predominantly of coral-skeletal detritus can be distinguished from sediment derived chiefly from mollusks or coralline algae.

Quite recently it has been shown by atomic-absorption spectrophotometry that ultratraces of metals are present in the aragonite skeleton of the hydrozoan coral *Millepora* from a reef flat on the Coral Sea Plateau off Queensland. These are, in parts per 1,000,000,000: lead (100), copper (71), cadmium (23), cobalt (17), nickel (1,480), iron (507), and zinc (507).

The Pine Point lead–zinc ore body on the southern shore of Great Slave Lake, Canada, occurs mainly within or close to the Middle Devonian reef sequence known as the Presqu'ile Formation. Geologists speculate that these metals may have been extracted from seawater by Devonian corals or other animals and subsequently concentrated within the reef rock by postdepositional changes.

Another aspect of reef geochemistry is the carbon and oxygen isotopic composition of coral skeletons and shells. Determination of the number of carbon isotopes present provides a method of assessing the age of a sample, and determinations of oxygen isotopes present are useful in indicating water-temperature changes that occurred during the period of growth of the reef.

Winds, currents, temperature, and salinity. Winds and currents are important in shaping individual reefs and in determining the orientation, shape, and position of the coral sand cays, or "low islands," that develop on reefs. Currents are primarily those generated by the prevailing winds, but, in areas where the tidal range is great, tidal effects may become paramount.

Cays may be round; oval, or boat-shaped; or irregular in outline. They originate when sediment is lifted from the reef surface and carried leeward by waves or tidal currents and then deposited where the water velocity is reduced abruptly. Thus, they commonly form on the more protected leeward end of the reef. Wind action at low tide on these deposits may build dunes above the high-water mark. Beach rock may form by carbonate cementation of grains in deposits lying between tide levels; it then acts as a stabilizing factor. Storm waves may drive forward coral fragments derived from "stag-horn" corals growing on the windward slopes of the reef, forming shingle banks; successive, superposed banks may thus be formed. The shingle on the banks may become cemented and thus add considerable stability to the cay, as does the growth of vegetation. Hurricanes, however, may carve back the shorelines of even stabilized cays. Huge, isolated boulders of coral or coral limestone are fairly common along reef margins. Some may be remnants of a once-emergent reef platform; others are hurricane or storm jetsam.

Restric-
tions
on reef
formation

Coral reefs are best developed where the mean annual surface-water temperatures are approximately 23° to 25° C (73° to 77° F); no significant reefs occur where such temperatures fall below about 18° C (64° F), although a few reef-coral species can exist in temperatures considerably below this. Seasonal temperature differences on any one reef are usually slight, as are differences due to depths of water or situation on the reef.

Seawater of normal oceanic salinity (between 30 and 40 parts per thousand), to which corals are restricted, is normally supersaturated in calcium carbonate ($CaCO_3$), so that adequate ionized calcium (Ca^{2+}) is available for the skeleton-forming process. Floods of freshwater may destroy life on inshore fringing reefs. A luxuriant reef on

Stone Island, near Bowen, Queensland, was killed to a depth of three metres (10 feet) below mean tide level by a week of cyclonic rains, in which 90.7 centimetres (35.7 inches) of rain coincided with full-moon spring tides.

Biological factors. The most significant biological determinant of reef accumulation is the presence of zooxanthellae in the living tissues of all reef corals and of many massive-shelled mollusks (Tridacnidae) and other shelled invertebrates, as well as in the soft-bodied hydrozoans, scyphozoans, and anthozoans. Zooxanthellae are now known to represent the vegetative stages of dinoflagellate algae, and their association with reef corals is symbiotic—that is, mutually helpful. In temperate seas they occur only occasionally. Their profusion in reef animals is no doubt connected with the greater light intensity and radiant energy of reef waters, for, like other plants, zooxanthellae require sunlight for photosynthesis. They remove at the source part of the carbon dioxide (CO_2), together with nitrogen, phosphorus, and (doubtless) sulfur, produced by metabolic breakdown within the coral and which would otherwise be excreted by the corals. They greatly aid in the formation of the coral skeleton by increasing the speed with which the CO_2 produced in coral metabolism is removed and the speed with which the skeletal $CaCO_3$ is formed. Corals also may gain some nutrient from their zooxanthellae, but they probably do not need the oxygen produced during photosynthesis.

The productivity of reefs is a current focus of interest. A constant supply of food in the form of zooplankton is essential to reef corals, which are carnivorous. The zooplankton supply is dependent upon an adequate phytoplankton supply, and the phytoplankton, in turn, require an adequate supply of plant nutrients dissolved in the water. An atoll in the open ocean may be compared with an oasis in a desert, as a localized centre of high productivity. In the warm, well-lit, and well-mixed lagoon waters there is a rapid turnover of the endemic planktonic (floating or swimming) and benthic (bottom-dwelling) population, perhaps 12.5 times per year. Carbonate skeletal matter is accumulated perhaps 1,000 times faster on the summit of an atoll than in the surrounding deeps.

Certain biological factors may contribute to the destruction of coral reefs; the fish and invertebrates that feed on the soft tissues of reef builders and the organisms that bore into coral rock. Of the former, the most destructive such enemy yet known is *Acanthaster planci,* the crown-of-thorns starfish, which, during the 1960s multiplied spectacularly and removed the soft tissues from large areas of many reefs in the southwest Pacific. *A. planci* feeds by everting its stomach and liquifying and absorbing the tissues of the corals. By the late 1970s it had become apparent, however, that the sudden spread of *A. planci* was part of the organism's natural life cycle and that the coral reefs could regenerate rapidly after such an infestation. Coral-rock borers include boring algae, boring sponges (of great significance), various polychaete and sipunculid worms, and many bivalves and a few gastropods. These organisms usually penetrate the rock mechanically but in some cases do so chemically. Extensive damage is caused both by their own activities and by the assistance they give to the erosive action of the sea.

The
menace of
the crown-
of-thorns
starfish

ORIGIN AND DEVELOPMENT OF REEFS

The English evolutionist Charles Darwin concluded in 1842 that barrier reefs began as reefs fringing the land around which they now form a barrier, and that oceanic atoll reefs began as reefs fringing a volcanic island. Subsidence of the land fringed was thought to allow the reef to grow upward (and outward over its own forereef debris). Maximum growth would occur at the seaward edge, and lagoons would develop between the ascending barrier, or atoll, reef and the land or volcanic cone. When the volcanic cone became completely submerged, the atoll lagoon would contain only coral islands. Fundamentally, Darwin's concept is still valid, although many consider submergence by the rise of sea level, following melting of Pleistocene ice sheets, to be a better explanation of the latest upward growth of many reefs, particularly on continental shelves. A reef whose surface lies above high-tide

Darwin's
theory of
atolls

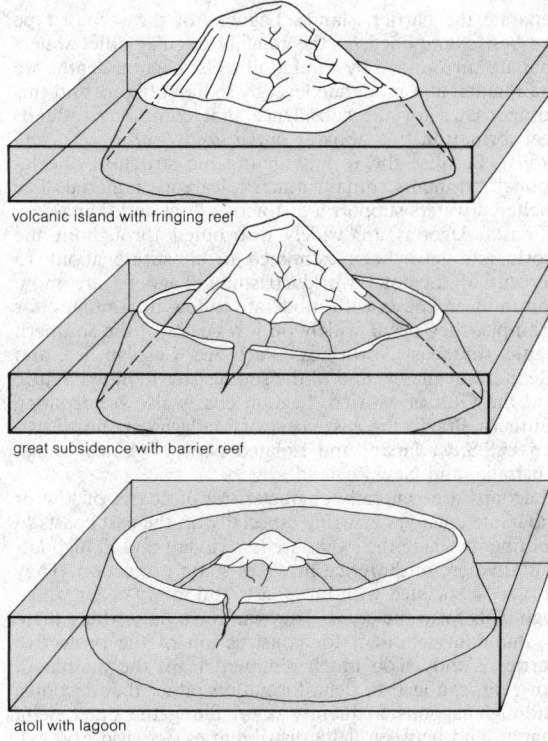

volcanic island with fringing reef

great subsidence with barrier reef

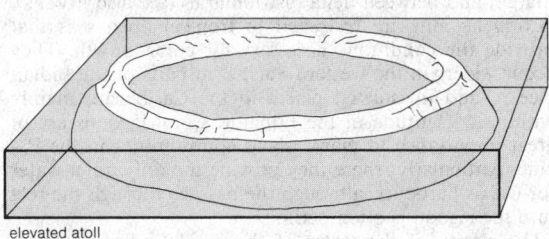

atoll with lagoon

elevated atoll

Figure 25: Stages in reef development on a subsiding island.
From *Geomorphology* by A. Lobeck. Copyright 1939. Used with
permission of McGraw-Hill Book Company

mark, either by uplift or by eustatic regression of the sea (that determined by ice sheet–sea level relations), is subject to planing by marine erosion. If planing off is complete, a flat-topped submerged platform results; if subsidence or eustatic submergence intervenes, a wave-cut terrace is left around the reef. Terraces that may have formed in this way are known around many reefs. Some annular reefs may develop without relation to subsiding volcanic cones. When reef platforms have been uplifted above sea level, they are subjected to subaerial erosion. Surface slope, or gradient, determines the amount of runoff and is a prime factor in this erosion. Two secondary processes also are involved: (1) case hardening of steep, bare limestone surfaces by recrystallization caused by alternate wetting and drying, so that walls or knife edges result from weathering; and (2) continuous subsoil solution, if surfaces are nearly horizontal and runoff is diminished. These processes combine to produce a prominent rim and a saucer-shaped interior in emerged limestone islands. With submergence, algal and coral growth resumes, the fastest growth being on the rim and on any pinnacles that may be left. Thus an atoll or annular reef may develop along the rim around the lowlying central region, which becomes a lagoon, and coral knolls grow on former pinnacles in the lagoonal area.

TYPES OF REEFS

Fringing reefs. Fringing reefs form a veneer in the shallow water near or at the shore of the mainland or of islands. On shorelines where bays receive large quantities of terrestrial mud, sand, and freshwater, fringing reefs are intermittent and are restricted to promontories. Along limestone coasts, however, coastal erosion is by solution, little mud or sand is supplied, and coral growth may be almost continuous along the shore. Fringing reefs may extend as far as 1,500 metres (4,900 feet) from shore;

they show ecological zonation parallel to the shore. Along mainland shores with easily eroded rocks, mudbanks may be washed into the reef flat and colonized by mangroves. Inner parts of reef flats may show low mesas of middle Holocene (perhaps 5,000 years old) and even Pleistocene emergent reefs that have not been quite planed off by marine abrasion. Geomorphological features peculiar to raised fringing reefs have been described for the Solomon Islands, and there the complex problem of dead reefs and dead patches on reefs arises. The surface of the reef flat is mostly of dead coral, but pools occur in which live coral colonies flourish. An algal rim formed by growing red calcareous algae may develop on a fringing-reef margin if the reef faces strong waves and swells the year around. This rim is commonly less spectacular than the algal ridge of the windward edge of Pacific oceanic atolls and may be developed merely as an algal platform, or pavement, on which algal encrustation over corals is thin. The seaward slope of a fringing reef, like the seaward slope of an atoll reef, is characterized by a zone of grooves and spurs to a depth of perhaps 15 metres (50 feet), and it is in this zone that vigorous growth occurs. Under stable shelf conditions, the fringing reef will extend outward as the spurs elongate and the grooves fill or roof over with coral and algal growth. In tectonic belts (zones of uplift and deformation), fringing reefs may be uplifted intermittently, resulting in parallel, stepped subaerial terraces such as those of the Finsch Coast of New Guinea.

Platform and patch reefs. Platform and patch reefs are characteristic of continental shelves; they may or may not lie behind a barrier reef. Reefs grow actively outward as well as upward, especially in the stable conditions of a continental shelf. Any given reef, having depth and temperature fixed by its location, will have its shape determined by the direction and force of the water currents that bring food and by the shape of the base on which it grows. Where the forces of growth are equal in all directions, radial expansion results in platform-like reefs. With further radial growth, lagoonal platform reefs develop. If the reef grows on a sand bank, elongation may result. The shape of an elongated platform reef may be determined by the orientation of rising and falling tidal currents; these may be directly opposed to each other. The boat-shaped reefs of Torres Strait, between Australia and New Guinea, apparently developed in such a pattern. Where wave-generated currents are asymmetric, horseshoe reefs develop, with convexity facing the current and the leeward ends curving round to partly surround a lagoon. Low Islets, made famous by the Great Barrier Reef Expedition of 1928–29, is the best known example of this type. A sand cay (or cays) commonly develops on one or both of the leeward wings. Those parts of Pacific platform reefs that face strong and persistent currents characteristically have a low algal rim from which radiate grooves and spurs.

Barrier and ribbon reefs. Barrier reefs commonly present to the ocean and the trade winds a steep wall, in some dropping abruptly 1,000 to 5,000 metres (3,300 to 16,400 feet). On the lagoon side they grade off gently with a wedge of sediment dotted by small patch reefs, coral knolls, and coral heads; depths in the lagoon may reach 50 to 80 metres (165 to 260 feet). According to the strength of surf and swell, an algal ridge, rim, platform,

From *Encyclopedia of Geomorphology* by R. Fairbridge,
copyright © 1968 by Litton Educational Publishing, Inc.; and C.
Yonge, *Advances in Marine Biology*, Vol. 1 (1963), Academic Press

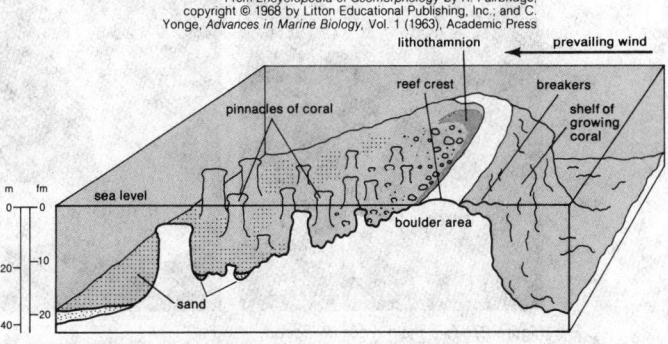

Figure 26: Section of an outer barrier reef, showing the
relation of form to prevailing winds.

or pavement develops and is commonly emergent at low water. The seaward slope has radial grooves and spurs, the grooves forming surf channels and imparting great wave resistance. Ecological zonation on the seaward slope is difficult to study because of the dangers of surf and swell. Zonation on the reef flat, parallel to the wall, is dependent mainly upon depth.

A characteristic form in a barrier reef system is the wall, or ribbon, reef, emergent at low tide, such as Yonge Reef, Queensland. A ribbon reef flat is commonly only 300 to 450 metres (1,000 to 1,500 feet) wide from the seaward wall to its lagoonward edge; its ends may curve leeward and border the passages between it and the next reefs in line. Rarely, there may be an unvegetated sand cay. A wall reef may develop irregular leeward prongs normal (perpendicular) to its axis by vigorous coral growth favoured by augmented turbulence associated with a high tidal range. The open leeward zone may be very wide (three kilometres or two miles) and support large, scattered reef clumps that are always submerged.

Association with volcanic cones
Atolls. The oceanic atoll reefs of the Pacific Ocean rise from volcanic cones that have subsided, probably intermittently, in areas of oceanic deeps. According to the Darwinian subsidence theory, the annular atoll reefs extend and grade downward into barrier reefs. The theory suggests that these barrier reefs originated as reefs that fringed the volcanic cone. On the other hand, the compound atoll reefs of the Indian Ocean, such as the Maldive Islands and Laccadives, and of the Coral Sea Plateau of the Pacific Ocean, are believed to have grown above foundered continental (rather than oceanic) crustal segments. The Nicaraguan atolls rise from a sea floor of 1,000 metres (3,300 feet) or more, in a volcanic province. (D.Hi./Ed.)

Lagoons

Lagoons are, as indicated above, areas of relatively shallow water situated in a coastal environment and having access to the sea but separated from the open marine conditions by a barrier. The barrier may be either a sandy or shingly wave-built feature, or it may be a coral reef. Thus, there are two main types of lagoons, namely, elongated or irregular stretches of water that lie between coastal barrier islands and the shoreline, and circular or irregular stretches of water surrounded by coral atoll reefs or protected by barrier coral reefs from direct wave action. Lagoons of the first type are characterized by quiet water conditions, fine-grained sedimentation, and, in many cases, brackish marshes. Water movements are related to discharge of river flow through the lagoon and to the regular influx and egress of tidal waters through the inlets that normally

separate the barrier islands. Lagoons of the second type are best exemplified by the roughly circular quiet waters that are surrounded by coral atoll reefs. Lagoon depths are maintained at a moderate level by sedimentation, and this compensates for the subsidence that commonly attends reef formation (see above *Coral islands, coral reefs, and atolls*). Because the reef is an organic structure, the lagoonal sediments contain much calcareous material. The sheltered waters support a distinctive flora and fauna.

Coastal lagoons are widely distributed throughout the world and have been estimated to constitute about 13 percent of the total world coastline. Lagoons are more common on coasts with moderate to low tidal ranges; for example, they occur widely on low coasts of the southern Baltic, southeast North Sea, Black Sea, Caspian Sea, and Mediterranean Sea, and of the southeastern United States, and the Gulf of Mexico. Lagoon coasts also occur along southern Brazil; the east coast of Madagascar; northeastern U.S.S.R.; Japan; and isolated parts of Africa, India, Australia, and New Zealand.

Typical sites
Lagoons are generally characteristic of coasts of low or moderate energy, occurring especially on the east coasts of continents where the swells are less violent and in high latitudes where offshore ice provides some protection. They also are associated with low coasts and rarely occur where high cliffs form the coast. They can form only where there is abundant sediment for construction of the protective barrier islands. Too much sediment from the mainland, however, can lead to delta formation rather than lagoons, although lagoons frequently occur along the outer delta margin and between delta distributaries (see also RIVERS).

Coral lagoons are restricted to tropical open seas that provide the conditions necessary for coral growth. They occur widely in the western Pacific, in parts of the Indian Ocean, and in isolated places in the Caribbean, mainly within 25° latitude of the Equator. Coral lagoons are of great importance to many island communities in the Pacific, particularly where they provide the only quiet water for use as harbours, although the passage through the reef into the lagoon is often perilous.

The clarity of the water of the coral lagoon contrasts with the considerable amount of fine sediment in barrier island lagoon water. The extensive growth of salt marsh in such lagoons often detracts from or precludes their use as harbours, but where the water is deep enough these lagoons provide sheltered anchorage and good conditions for small-boat sailing in quiet water.

THE NATURE OF THE LAGOON ENVIRONMENT

Dimensions. Coral lagoon dimensions range from small atolls to those so wide that the coral reefs on the far side

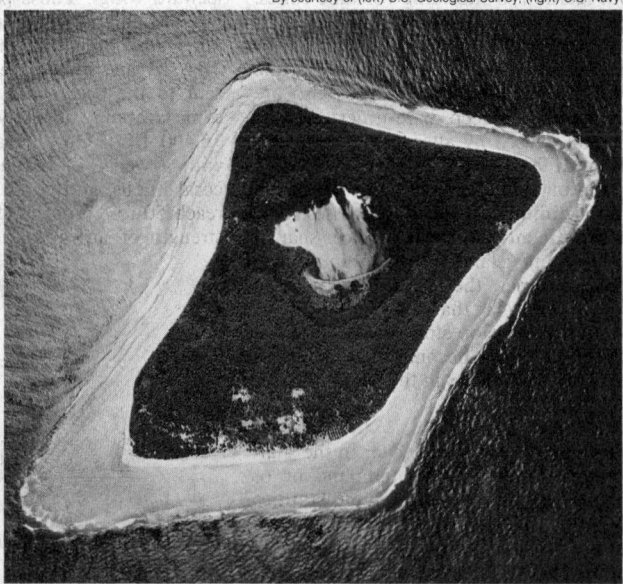

Figure 27: *Two main types of lagoon.*
(Left) Barrier island lagoon at Westhampton, Long Island, New York. (Right) Coral lagoon surrounding Lib Island, Kwajalein area, Marshall Islands.

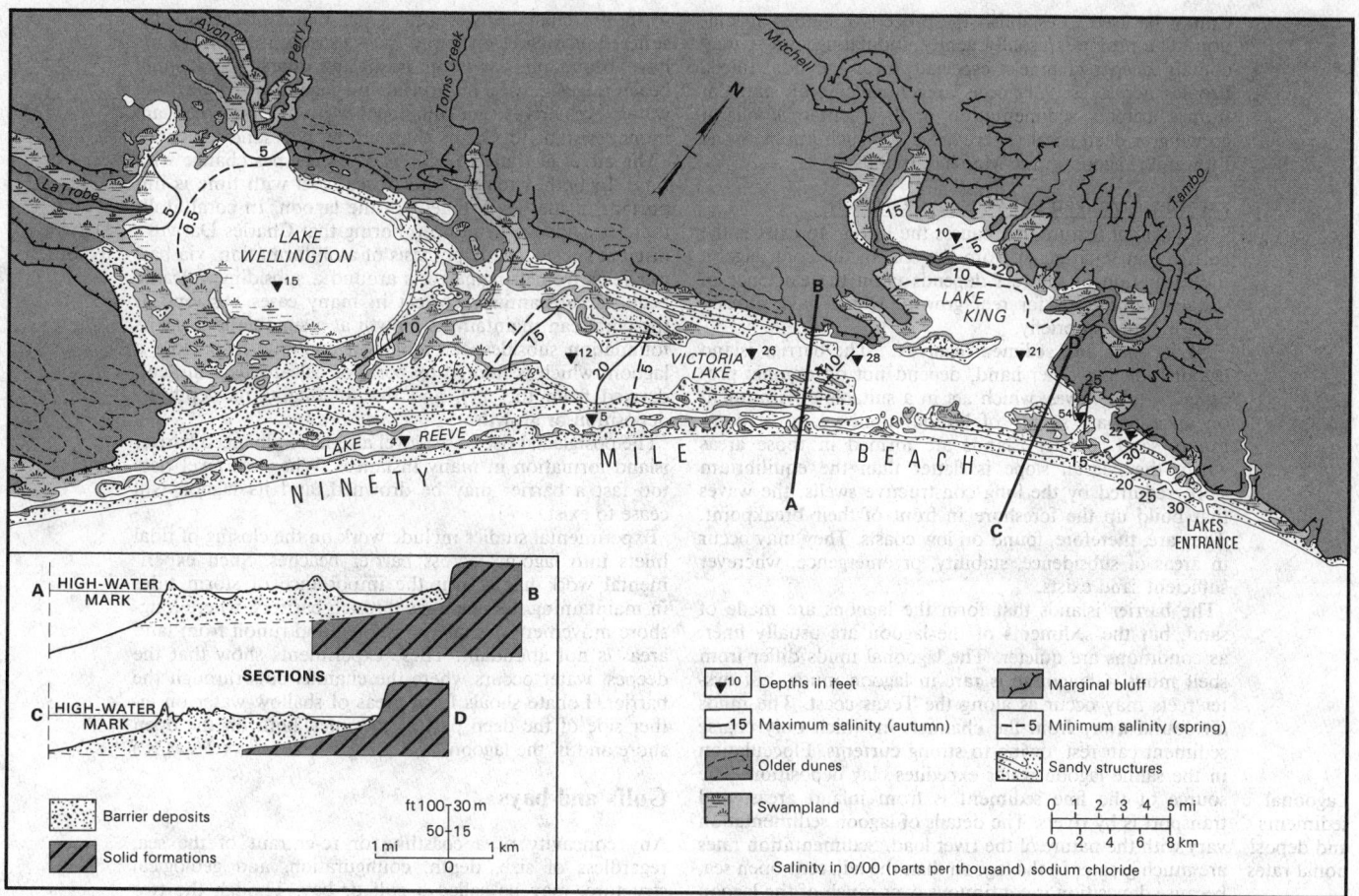

Figure 28: Sandy coastal barriers enclose the Gippsland Lakes, a lagoon region in the state of Victoria, Australia.

Current velocities

cannot be seen across the lagoon. Atoll widths range from about 2.5 to nearly 100 kilometres (1.6 to 62 miles), but the mean value is about 20 kilometres (12 miles). Depths rarely exceed 60 metres (200 feet) and many are shallower, usually less than 20 metres (65 feet) deep. The lagoon of Mayotte Island in the Comoro Archipelago in the Indian Ocean attains a maximum depth of about 92 metres (300 feet) but generally is shallower, and it is about 16 kilometres (10 miles) in width at its widest point; this lagoon lies behind a barrier reef that encircles the island, forming an atoll about 55 kilometres (34 miles) in diameter.

Barrier island lagoons are usually elongated, though irregular ones may occur where river estuaries flood behind the barriers. This occurs on the east coast of the U.S., where lagoons extend intermittently for nearly 1,500 kilometres (930 miles) along the coast. The Gippsland Lakes in Victoria exemplify a complex lagoon system formed behind the 149-kilometre (90-mile) beach (Figure 28). Elongated lagoons up to 64 kilometres (40 miles) in length lie behind the beach barrier, and larger lagoons, such as Lake Wellington, lie behind the southwestern end. Postglacial subsidence has flooded the lowland in this area. The lagoons are shallow; Lake Wellington is less than 3.5 metres (11 feet) deep and much of King Lake is less than 6 metres (20 feet) deep. Scour holes as deep as 16.5 metres (54 feet) do occur, however. The elongated lagoon behind the barrier is only 1 to 1.5 metres (3.3 to 5 feet) deep, typical of barrier island lagoons.

Water circulation. The degree of water circulation depends on the width of the tidal inlets, the tidal range, and on the amount of runoff from adjacent land areas. Maximum velocities are attained at the points where the water passes through the barriers. In the entrance to the Gippsland lagoons, tidal currents reach three knots, but river floods that escape to the sea can raise the velocity to seven knots. Water may be blown into the lagoon by strong winds; the increased level results in an outflowing current when the wind drops. Seiches can be created in this way. Small waves can be generated within lagoons

when the wind blows along their maximum dimension. These may reach 1.25 metres (4 feet) in height and 1.5 to 9 metres (5 to 30 feet) in length in the Gippsland lagoons. In coral atoll lagoons there is little or no runoff; and seawater moves in and out through the passes, where tidal currents reach their maxima. Velocities of 10 to 12 knots (19 to 22 kilometres per hour) have been recorded in the Hao Channel of the Tuamotu Island.

Water temperature and salinity. In the Mayotte Lagoon the water has the same properties as the upper layers of the open sea; the salinity is close to 35 parts per 1,000, and the temperature varies between 27° and 24° C (81° and 75° F). This is typical of coral lagoons, but the temperature and salinity of barrier island lagoons are more variable because of their wider climatic range. Because they are shallow, lagoon waters approximate the air temperature: colder than the open sea in winter, warmer in summer.

Salinities decrease as a function of the amount of runoff entering the lagoon in relation to the tidal influx. Lagoons may be considered brackish, marine, or hypersaline. Brackish lagoons receive much runoff, and salinity increases toward the tidal inlets. The Gippsland lagoons exemplify this type. The salinity at the inner end varies from 0.50/00 to 50/00 parts per thousand according to season, and central values vary between 50/00 and 200/00. Hypersaline lagoons occur where evaporation exceeds inflow. Laguna Madre in Texas and Sivash Lagoon in the Black Sea have salinities of 65 and 1320/00 parts per thousand, respectively. Salt deposits may form in these conditions. The denser saline water tends to lie beneath the fresher water where mixing is not severe.

Equilibrium bottom profiles. Lagoons behind coastal barriers normally are zones of fine sedimentation. Their bottom profiles, therefore, build up gradually with time. Typical depths of the Texas lagoons vary between 1.25 and 3.5 metres (4 and 11 feet), and their floors are flat. Early theories that attempted to relate the form of the offshore and lagoon profile are no longer held; and because the lagoon profile changes with continued deposition, it cannot be used to establish the process of lagoon formation. The profile is usually gently undulating, but it may contain deeper channels, especially near the tidal inlets. Profiles across coral lagoons are either smooth and flat from calcareous sedimentation, or they contain knolls of growing or dead coral. There are 2,300 such knobs in the Eniwetok Lagoon in the Marshall Islands.

FACTORS INVOLVED IN LAGOON FORMATION

The essential feature that causes the lagoon to exist is the barrier that separates it from the sea. In the coral lagoon the formation of the reef depends upon the existence of suitable conditions for reef growth, which have already been mentioned briefly.

Barrier bars and sediment sources. The barrier island lagoons, on the other hand, depend not on organic processes but on waves, which act in a suitable environment on an adequate supply of bottom material, most commonly sand. Barrier islands are formed in those areas where the coastal slope is flatter than the equilibrium slope required by the long constructive swells, the waves that build up the foreshore in front of their breakpoint. They are, therefore, found on low coasts. They may occur in areas of subsidence, stability, or emergence, wherever sufficient sand exists.

The barrier islands that form the lagoons are made of sand, but the sediments of the lagoon are usually finer, as conditions are quieter. The lagoonal muds differ from shelf muds. Glauconite is rare in lagoon muds, but oyster reefs may occur as along the Texas coast. The muds are found away from the channels in which only coarse sediment can rest, owing to strong currents. Flocculation in the saline lagoon water expedites clay deposition. The source of the fine sediment is from inland areas, and transport is by rivers. The details of lagoon sedimentation vary with the nature of the river load. Sedimentation rates are much greater in the lagoon than the adjacent open sea, because deposition is continuous over much of the lagoon and is often aided by flocculation and vegetation. In the Texas lagoons from 1875 to 1936, 20 centimetres (eight inches) of deposition occurred, despite 30 centimetres (12 inches) of subsidence; the sedimentation rate, therefore, was about one metre (3.3 feet) in 100 years.

Lagoonal sediments and depositional rates

Waves, tides, and surf. The barrier islands are formed by the waves, which build up their equilibrium profile by deposition on a gradient that is too flat. The level of the growing accumulation may be raised by the wind, forming dunes. Where the land behind the growing barrier is low, it will become flooded to form a lagoon if sea level rises slowly. Such a rise of sea level has occurred during the last 20,000 years. As long as the barrier island can maintain its level above the sea, as sea level rises, the lagoon will exist until it is filled with sediment. Not all lagoons and barrier island complexes have formed during rising sea-level conditions, but where there is evidence that no open sea foreshore sediments lie on the land side of the barrier this hypothesis seems likely. In some barriers, however, outbuilding of material by glacial outwash streams or rivers may provide a suitably low gradient and enough sediment to form a barrier, as along the south coast of Iceland. In other areas material carried alongshore to form a spit may develop into a bay-mouth barrier, enclosing a lagoon. Such features can be of sand or shingle. The Fleet behind Chesil Bank in southern England is an example of the latter type.

Waves within the lagoon may develop cuspate spits along the land side of the barrier and the inner edge of the lagoon. These features may eventually break the lagoon into almost circular or oval water bodies. Examples occur on the Chukchi Sea lagoons in the U.S.S.R. and elsewhere where vegetation does not form marshland.

Storms and catastrophic events. Storms or tsunamis exert an effect on lagoons when they breach or overtop the barriers around the lagoon by raising the water level temporarily. Major changes in configuration can occur in a short time. Hurricanes, for instance, can cause serious effects on the coast of Texas, along which lagoons are common. Padre Island was lowered to below mean low tide at its southern end by one storm in 1919, and several washover channels were cut. The mainland shore also suffered erosion. Deposition may also occur; saline marls have been laid down on freshwater marsh, and small beach ridges may be built inside the lagoon where the high water level drives sand inland over mud. Coral reefs are more resistant to storms than are mobile sandy barriers.

The effect of time. Lagoons of both types change with time. In both a relative rise of sea level with time is important in the development of the lagoon. In coral atolls there is evidence from deep boring that Charles Darwin's original subsidence hypothesis of atoll formation, via barrier reefs from fringing reefs around a subsiding volcanic peak, is substantially correct in many cases. As long as the coral can maintain its growth at a suitable level as its foundation subsides, the atoll will continue to enclose a lagoon, which is floored by coral or calcareous sediment, derived from the reef, and that maintains its depth by deposition or growth.

Darwin's hypothesis

The postglacial rise of sea level also has influenced barrier island formation in many instances. When sea level rises too fast a barrier may be drowned, and its lagoon will cease to exist.

Experimental studies include work on the closing of tidal inlets into lagoons across barrier beaches. Such experimental work has shown the importance of storm tides in maintaining the openings through barriers, where longshore movement of material is great and runoff from land areas is not abundant. These experiments show that the deepest water occurs where the channel cuts through the barrier. Lobate shoals form areas of shallow water on either side of the deep part of the inlet, both on the open shore and in the lagoon. (C.A.M.K.)

Gulfs and bays

Any concavity of a coastline or re-entrant of the sea, regardless of size, depth, configuration, and geological structure, may be called a gulf or bay. Though the two terms are not strictly defined, the term gulf usually refers to large water bodies. Some large gulfs and bays preserve local names such as bight (Australia), channel (England), firth (Scotland), sound (U.S.), fjord (Norway), fjörd (Sweden), fjördhur or *floi* (Iceland), *zaliv* or *guba* (U.S.S.R.), ria or *río* (Iberian peninsula and South America), and *wan* (China and Japan). A number of pronounced concavities of oceanic margins have no proper name at all.

The problem of terminology extends to the difference between gulfs and seas. There are many small seas, such as the Sea of Marmara (11,000 square kilometres [4,250 square miles]) and the Sea of Azov (38,000 square kilometres [14,670 square miles]), which, strictly speaking, are really gulfs of the ocean or other seas (the Sea of Azov is a gulf of the Black Sea). The Gulf of Aden (about 270,000 square kilometres [104,200 square miles]), another example, is part of the Arabian Sea and these water bodies have a common regime (similar tides, precipitation, evaporation, etc.). The narrow sound of Bab el-Mandeb connects the gulf with the vast Red Sea (438,100 square kilometres [169,200 square miles]) and exhibits a number of specific geomorphic features. The Red Sea, in turn, has two small gulfs to the north, namely, those of Suez and Aqaba.

The Bay of Bengal and the Arabian Sea are approximately the same size and have the same monsoonal water circulation. The Bay of Bengal is, in fact, the largest of the gulfs and bays, with a surface area of 2,172,000 square kilometres (838,610 square miles) and a length of 1,850 kilometres (1,150 miles; see Table 9). The width of a gulf may exceed its length. The Great Australian Bight has the widest mouth (2,800 kilometres [1,740 miles]). The Gulf of Guinea is deepest; its maximum depth (6,363 metres [20,880 feet]) exceeds that of the Bay of Bengal by more than 1,000 metres (3,280 feet).

The shape and bottom topography of gulfs and bays are amazingly diverse. They depend on the geological structure and development of the region. Homogeneous bedrock of low strength or resistance results in simple shapes and shallow depths. The Gulf of Riga (at the Baltic Sea) is a possible example of the type. Long narrow arms with approximately parallel shores of the south Kara Sea extend inland for about 800 kilometres (500 miles). They occupy troughs that originated by erosion during a period of lower sea level (Baidaratskaya Guba, Obskaya Guba with Tazovskaya Guba tributary, Yenisey Bay, Gydanskaya Guba). Deep, angular gulfs, on the other hand, are created along fractures, faults, and rifts (*e.g.,* Varanger Fjord); they usually have irregular bottom topography. Parallel fractures form very deep, narrow gulfs with parallel shores, such as the Gulf of California. Genuine fjordgulfs are notable for their very high length to width ratios (up to 50:1). In regions that have undergone nonuniform deformation and uplift, gulfs and bays of complicated and irregular shape and bottom topography are consequently formed; the Gulf of St. Lawrence is an example.

Gulfs are connected with the sea by means of one or more straits. Sometimes there may be an archipelago in the mouth of the gulf as in the Gulf of Bothnia. There are some gulfs that open into the sea or into another gulf on opposite sides (Baffin Bay, Gulf of Aden, and the Gulf of Oman).

Single gulfs usually are formed along linear shores of the continent. If the shoreline is irregular and has a complex geological structure, groups of gulfs of a similar nature may occur. Most shorelines have small reentrants of various size that are called bays. These features are strongly influenced by local conditions, and they are not described or classified within the context of this section, which treats major water bodies of the world. For additional information on the dynamics of water within gulfs and bays, see above *Waves of the sea* and *Ocean currents.*

FACTORS THAT INFLUENCE
THE NATURE OF GULFS AND BAYS

Gulfs and bays may differ from the adjacent sea by virtue of water properties and dynamics and processes of sedimentation. Such differences are determined by the size and the shape of a given gulf, by the depth and bottom topography, and to a considerable extent by the degree of isolation from the ocean. Climatic conditions also are important. Isolation from an adjacent sea or ocean depends on the ratio of width of mouth to total surface area of a gulf or on the cross section of the mouth to total water volume. If there is a sill, the ratio of depth above the sill to the depth of the gulf is of great importance. No extensive comparisons of these ratios have been made to date; hence analysis of controlling variables must remain somewhat qualitative.

Climates, sills, and river runoff

A high sill hampers the water exchange between an ocean and gulf and may lead to stagnation (oxygen deficiency) as is found in some fjords of Norway, in the Red Sea, and, particularly, in the Black Sea. Also, the presence of a sill causes independent circulation of gulf waters, created by local winds and the runoff of rivers. Sills are not indispensable for the formation of an independent circulation, however. A narrow mouth, as in the Gulf of Bothnia, leads to the same result.

In humid climates, the waters of gulfs are freshened by river runoff. Salinity is particularly low in the gulfs of the Baltic Sea and along the southern coast of the Kara Sea. Water becomes almost fresh in their heads, especially in the spring when snow begins to thaw. Gulfs of the arid zone suffer from intensive evaporation and receive little river runoff. Thus, salinity increases markedly in this climatic regime—up to 60 parts per thousand in the Persian Gulf and up to 350 parts per thousand in the Kara-Bogaz-Gol (a gulf of the Caspian Sea). In addition to its effect on salinity, river runoff delivers organic matter and nutrient salts that may determine the specific features of life in the gulfs. The number of genera and species of organisms is small, but the organisms present tend to develop in quantities. That is why shrimp, oyster, and other fisheries are concentrated in many gulfs.

Funnel-shaped gulfs, in which the depth gradually decreases headward, usually have resonant tides. The tidal range at the head of such gulfs is several times greater than that in the open sea (Bristol Channel, Río de la Plata, Mezenskaya Guba, Zaliv Shelikhova, etc.). The world maximum tidal range has been registered in the Bay of Fundy (18 metres [59 feet]). The regularity (magnitude and frequency) of the flood tide may be distorted in such instances and the duration of the flood tide may become much shorter than that of the ebb tide. This may cause the phenomenon of tidal bore, in which a steep wave will move rapidly upstream for dozens of kilometres.

Gulfs of simple shape with narrow mouth and a high degree of isolation from the ocean commonly are subject to seiches. These free oscillations can result from rapid changes of atmospheric pressure and, of course, from tectonic movements such as earthquakes. Seiches gradually decrease but some oscillation continues long after their cause disappears. A high rise of the water (storm surge) occurs in long and shallow gulfs if winds from the sea are protracted. Such phenomena are difficult to predict, and the high water levels may cause floods. Seiches often occur at the heads of Helgoländer Bay in the North Sea and in the Gulf of Finland.

Occurrence of seiches

Certain aspects of sedimentation are affected by the isolation of gulfs from the sea and river runoff. The rate of sediment accumulation in gulfs of limited area may be very high. This, of course, is a function of river discharge; sediment composition is usually similar to that of the load transported by entering rivers. Deposition of calcium carbonate often occurs in shallow gulfs in the arid zones where few if any perennial streams exist. The bottoms of long gulfs (or gulfs having sills) are usually covered with silt even at the shallowest depths (*e.g.,* Hudson Bay, the Po Hai [Gulf of Chihli], the inlets or *gubas* of the Kara Sea, the Gulf of Riga). Only strong tidal currents can prevent this siltation and, in some cases, cause the opposite phenomenon of bottom erosion. Currents maintain the existence of or actively deepen bottom troughs in narrow-mouthed gulfs whose depths are over 200 metres (660 feet), whereas depths of adjacent parts of the open sea are only on the order of some dozens of metres.

Waves of the open sea either do not penetrate into comparatively isolated gulfs or, if they do, they become greatly reduced after entry. Small local waves that are related to gulf size prevail there. This tends to make gulfs quite navigable, and seaports and harbours have generally been situated on them.

CLASSIFICATION OF GULFS AND BAYS

The geological structure and developmental history of gulfs and bays are as varied as are those of the continents or oceans proper. The factors discussed above influence the morphological peculiarities of gulfs, and the latter, in turn, permit some general division or classification of these features to be made. The several groups in one possible scheme will be discussed here using typical gulfs and bays of each group as examples (Table 9).

Areas situated in open concavities of the continental coast (Gulf of Alaska, Bay of Biscay, Gulf of Guinea, Great Australian Bight, Bay of Bengal, Gulf of Tehuantepec, etc.) are classified as the A_1 group. The depth of these gulfs in the region of the mouth usually is on the order of kilometres. The continental shelf and slope are generally pronounced. The general shape of such gulfs is simple; width of mouth usually exceeds its length. Water circulation and its physical properties are similar to those of the ocean. The character of the marine faunas does not differ from that of oceanic areas.

Open concavities and isolated areas

Large areas considerably isolated from the ocean, such as the Gulf of Mexico and Baffin Bay, are designated as group A_2 (Table 9). The former includes a geosynclinal hollow, founded in Mesozoic time and finally shaped during the Tertiary Period (2,500,000 to 65,000,000 years ago). It is connected with the ocean by the narrow and relatively shallow straits of Florida and Yucatan. Baffin Bay is a rift hollow that is connected by straits with the Atlantic and the Arctic oceans.

Ocean gulfs, such as the Gulfs of Oman, California, Aden, and some others have smaller areas and are isolated to a lesser degree. These gulfs and bays, in group A_3, have shapes that are determined by young faults and fractures. Depths in these gulfs generally exceed one kilometre. Unlike the previous group, in which gulfs might be of composite geological structure, these occupy areas that have undergone only a single episode of deformation.

Table 9: Physical-Geographical Features of Some Gulfs and Bays*

names of gulfs and bays	surface area (10⁶ sq km)	volume (10⁶ cu km)	length in kilometres	width in kilometres		depth in metres			tidal range in metres	surface water temperature (Celsius)		surface salinity (parts per thousand)		river runoff
				max	mouth	max	mean	sill		max	min	max	min	
A₁ Group														
Gulf of Alaska	1.327	3.226	325	1,650	1,650	5,659	2,431	none	12.0†	12	<0	33	32	small
Bay of Bengal	2.172	5.616	1,850	1,720	1,720	5,258	2,586	none	10.7	27	25	34	18	large
Bay of Biscay	0.194	0.332	400	500	500	5,120	1,715	none	6.7	20	5	35.5	34	medium
Gulf of Guinea	1.533	4.592	540	1,900	1,900	6,363	2,996	none	2.7	27	25	35	31	large
A₂ Group														
Baffin Bay	0.689	0.593	>1,000	600	340‡	>2,300	861	466‡	4.2	5	<0	33.5	30	none
Gulf of Mexico	1.543	2.332	1,330	1,780	445	4,029	1,512	800	1.7	29	17	36.7	33	large
A₃ Group														
Gulf of Aden	...	...	900	335	335	3,328	...	none	2.9	>30	25	36.5	36	none
Gulf of California	0.177	0.132	1,200	200	200	3,660	813	none	5.2§	30	16	35.5	35	medium
Gulf of Oman	...	...	450	330	325	3,474	...	none	3.5	32	22	38	37	none
B Group														
Bay of Fundy	...	...	300‖	100	100	214	75	none	18.0	17	2	32	30	medium
Hudson Bay	0.819	0.092	1,560	1,140	190	274	112	none	7.9	14	<0	28.5	23	large
Río de la Plata	...	...	220	95	95	10	5–7	6	1.0	21	11	33	20	large
Gulf of St. Lawrence	0.238	0.030	¶	¶	¶	530	127	none	5.9	20	−1.8	32	26	large
C₁ Group														
Gulf of Aqaba	...	...	180	28	6	1,828	...	462	0.7♀	26	24	42	41	none
Sirt Gulf	...	...	200	450	450	1,627	...	none	0.3	27	14	38	38	none
C₂ Group														
Anadyrsky Zaliv	...	...	350	460	460	110	60–70	none	3.0	14	<0	30	28	medium
Persian Gulf	0.241	0.010	1,000	350	56	170	40	71	4.7	33	15	60δ	30	small
Gulf of Suez	...	...	325	58	58	82	40–60	none	1.8	28	23	43	41	none
Zaliv Shelikhova	...	...	750	300	190	495	100–150	none	12.9	14	<0	33	31	small
Gulf of Thailand	...	...	830	550	370	83	45.5	58	0.8□	31	27	32.5	30.5	large
D Group														
Gulf of Bothnia	0.117	...	668	240	155°	294	21	none	0.6	14	0	5.5	1	medium
Gulf of Chihli	0.0827	0.0017	480▲	285	105	38	15–20	none	4.4	28	<0	31	22	large
Gulf of Carpentaria	0.4116	...	675	650	530	70	40–50	none	3.6	29	23	35.5	35	small
Mezenskaya Guba	...	...	105	97	97	31	10–20	none	10.0	16	<0	32	15	large
Obskaya Guba	...	...	800	90	60	18	10–12	7	0.7	14	0	15	1	large
Gulf of Finland	0.030	...	420	125	70	110	50–60	86	0.1	17	0	5	2	medium

*Data in this table may differ from those given elsewhere in set for some features because of differing definitions of geographical limits of each feature. Data adapted in part from Kossina (1921, 1933) and Lyman (1961).   †Cook Inlet's head.   ‡Davis Strait.   §Up to ten metres at the Colorado River mouth.   ‖Up to the Minas Bay head.   ¶Not given because of the complicated outlines.   ♀The value for the Red Sea's head.   δIn shallow parts along the south coast.   □Up to 4 metres at the Mae Nam Chao Phraya.   °South Quarken Strait—40 kilometres.   ▲From the Laichow Wan head to Liao-tung Wan's head.

Gulfs situated on the oceanic shelf, such as the Bay of Fundy, Hudson Bay, Río de la Plata, Golfo San Matías (off Argentina), and others, are in group B. The depth of such gulfs is up to 200 metres or more, and their configuration is determined by geological conditions. Because shelf areas repeatedly became dry land when the sea level fell during the ice ages, these gulfs received their final shape during the Pleistocene Epoch. The Gulf of St. Lawrence is included in this group (Table 9), though it is really intermediate between groups A₃ and B. It contains both a pronounced shelf and a long trough up to 530 metres (1,740 feet) deep.

Marginal and shelf areas

Gulfs of intercontinental and marginal seas are considered to be a third category. These may be divided into group C₁, which consists of gulfs of basin seas, including the deepwater part only (Aqaba) or both the deepwater and the shelf parts (the Gulf of Honduras), and group C₂, the shelf gulfs of the same seas (the Persian Gulf, Gulf of Suez, Anadyrsky Zaliv, Bristol and Norton channels, Zaliv Shelikhova, etc.).

Finally, there are the gulfs of the shelf seas (*gubas* of the Arctic seas of the U.S.S.R., gulfs of the Baltic and White Seas, the Gulf of Carpentaria, the Po Hai [Gulf of Chihli], and many others), which are placed in group D (Table 9). The shallow character of the shelf seas influences the water dynamics of the gulfs. Water exchange is weakened, and sediments may accumulate in the gulf mouths, thus forming submarine barriers and further reducing exchange.

Certain characteristic features of these groups of gulfs and bays are enumerated in Table 9. Some additional group characteristics can best be seen by describing in greater detail selected typical gulfs and bays exhibiting common and distinctive features.

TYPICAL GULFS AND BAYS OF THE WORLD

Gulf of Alaska.   The Gulf of Alaska is a wide concavity of the North American Pacific coast. Its water properties and circulation are those of the ocean. Along its entire shore there are mountains and fractures that form fjord type bays and mountainous islands. The continental shelf in this area is rather broad to the north and west of the gulf, but it is dissected by troughs and contains other depressions. The main elements of coastal relief and continental shelf are of tectonic origin (related to earth deformation), but they received a final molding during the last glaciation. Glaciers still flow down into the heads of some bays and form icebergs. The shore of the gulf has high seismicity and is part of the Pacific earthquake belt.

Diatomaceous ooze (muds composed of unicellular organisms termed diatoms) is widespread in the deeper part of the gulf. An important peculiarity of the bottom topography of the Gulf of Alaska is the occurrence of submarine mountains with flat tops (guyots). These are ancient volcanoes that were abraded and planed off at or near sea level. Subsequently, these volcanoes were submerged and their present depth is as much as 1,000 metres (3,280 feet) or more.

Bay of Bengal.   The Bay of Bengal is part of the Indian Ocean. It washes the Indian and Sri Lanka (formerly Ceylon) shores in the west and borders on Burma and a chain of the Andaman and Nicobar islands in the east. Its basin occupies a tectonically stable area. It has a flat bottom and steep continental slopes. The shelf is narrow though developed all along the continental coast. It is fairly wide at the head of the bay where a broad delta of the Ganges and the Brahmaputra rivers is situated. A large submarine canyon begins at the mouth of the Ganges, which almost crosses the entire shelf. Submarine canyons of smaller size were discovered recently along the coasts of India and Sri Lanka. The Indian coast is relatively flat and is bordered with broad sand beaches. Coral reefs are developed along the Sri Lanka shores and those of the Andaman and Nicobar Islands.

Deltas, coral reefs, and submarine canyons

The water of the bay has certain oceanic features, but

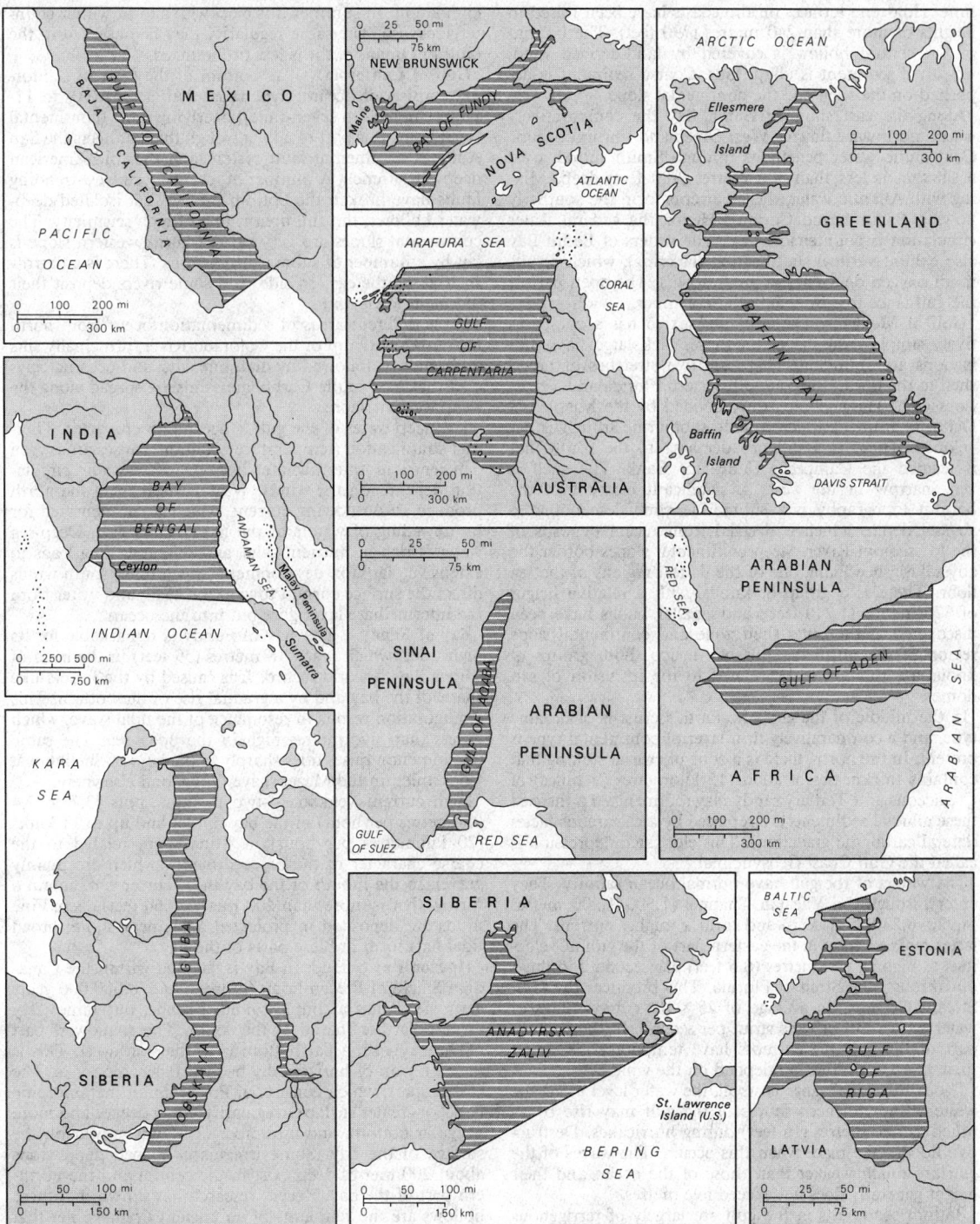

Figure 29: Plans of typical gulfs and bays.

its salinity is somewhat lower. It exhibits a seasonally fluctuating circulation that changes with the monsoons. In spring the current moves clockwise with a velocity of three to five knots (5.6 to 9 kilometres per hour) along the Indian coast. Subsequently, a counterclockwise and weaker circulation appears. During this period the salinity of the water falls sharply because the rainy season begins. During the dry season an upwelling of deep water takes place along the Indian coast (Waltair), the content of oxygen falls, and that of nutrient salts (phosphates and nitrates) rises.

The prevailing sediment of the deep part of the bay is Globigerina ooze. Alluvial mud accumulates in the head of the bay at a very high rate of deposition. There is a zone of shell-sediment and calcium carbonate concretions along the outward part of the Indian shelf.

Baffin Bay. Baffin Bay is a deep, elongated basin stretching in a northwestern direction between Greenland and the islands of the North Canadian Archipelago. It is connected by Smith, Jones, and Lancaster sounds with the Arctic Ocean and by the much broader Davis Strait with the Atlantic Ocean.

The flat bottom of Baffin Bay originated as a result of sinking (possibly along faults) that took place during pre-Quaternary time (more than 2,500,000 years ago). Its coasts consist of igneous and metamorphic rocks. They are mountainous and are cut by numerous fjords of glacial origin. In the northern part of the bay the shores are formed by the Greenland Icecap.

The bottom of Baffin Bay near its margins is of discontinuous character; broad troughs that continue the trends of the largest fjord systems occur there. Apparently these were molded by ice during periods of low sea level of Pleistocene time. It is possible that sounds of the Canadian Archipelago are ancient river valleys that were deepened by as much as 600 metres (2,000 feet) in pre-Quaternary

Ice molding and Holocene terraces

time. Holocene terraces on the coasts have been raised to heights of more than 240 metres (790 feet). The bottom of the central hollow is covered by land-derived mud; ice-rafted sediment is ubiquitous. Coarse sediment is deposited on the shelf and the continental slope.

Along the east shore of Baffin Bay the comparatively warm, northward flowing West Greenland Current occurs. Cold arctic water penetrates through Smith sound, over a sill that is less than 300 metres (980 feet) deep. Mixing with Atlantic water, these currents form the southerly flowing Baffin Island Current. Hence the general water circulation is counterclockwise. The waters of Baffin Bay also exhibit vertical stratification (layering), which results in an oxygen deficiency at great depths. The open part of the gulf is ice-free from July to September.

Gulf of Mexico. The Gulf of Mexico has a comparatively simple oval shape. Its shores lack large bays, but lagoons are abundant. There are two stretches of broad shelf to the north; these are off western Florida and Texas-Louisiana. The shelf areas are divided by the Mississippi Delta, in front of which a wide submarine trough is developed. There is a still broader area to the south that is termed the Campeche (Yucatán) Bank. The shelf is very narrow in the west. A significant element of the bottom topography is a submarine cone descending to abyssal depth, which is derived from recent deposits of the Mississippi River. Steep continental slopes border the abyssal Sigsbee Plain, one of the flattest regions of the sea floor. There is a group of knolls, with a relative height of 370 metres (1,210 feet), and smaller knolls have been discovered at the outer shelf zone and continental slope region of the northern Gulf of Mexico. Both groups of knolls are thought to be related to the intrusion of salt domes.

Knolls of the Sigsbee Plain

In the middle of the gulf, the Earth's crust is of oceanic type, and a comparatively thin layer of continental type is present. In the north, there is a zone of crustal sinking that contains thicknesses of about 15 kilometres (9 miles) of Cretaceous and Tertiary sandy-clay sediments. To the east these alluvial sediments are replaced by a calcareous facies (lateral carbonate gradation). This elongated depression is called the Gulf Coast Geosynclinal.

The waters of the gulf have normal ocean salinity. They enter through the Yucatan Channel (1,500–1,900 metres [4,920–6,230 feet] deep) and form a mighty current. The latter makes a loop in the eastern part of the gulf at velocities as high as two metres (6.6 feet) per second and flows out through the Strait of Florida. This produces the Gulf Stream Current; an average of 25×10^6 cubic metres of water passes through the strait per second. In the western part of the gulf the currents have temporary character; their speed and direction depend on the winds.

Though the tidal range is small, the water level along the western and northern shores of the gulf may rise by as much as five metres (16 feet) during hurricanes. Destructive floods take place when this occurs. The waves of the gulf are much weaker than those of the ocean and their height generally does not exceed five metres.

Bottom sediments in the gulf are largely of terrigenous origin; silt occurs on the continental shelf and slope, and clay in the central parts of the gulf. A thin layer of carbonate sediments has been deposited on the shelves of Florida and Campeche. These rest upon a limestone surface of Quaternary and Tertiary age, which exhibits karst topography (pitted with caverns and sinks). The latter was formed during the Pleistocene lowerings of sea level.

Gulf of Oman and Gulf of Aden. The gulfs of Oman and Aden open into the Arabian Sea and exhibit similar physicogeographical conditions. They are fairly deep and are nearly equal in width, but the Gulf of Aden is twice as long as the Gulf of Oman. The salinity and the temperature of their waters are very high. The basins of both are of tectonic origin; they are related to the fracture system of the northwestern part of the Indian Ocean. Both gulfs have very narrow shelves and steep continental slopes, and the bottoms of their central parts are irregular.

Water circulation of the gulfs, connected with that of the ocean, depends on the changes of the monsoon regime. In the Gulf of Aden there is an established surface-water

circulation. In summer it is clockwise and in winter counterclockwise. The same regularity may be observed in the Gulf of Oman, but it is less pronounced.

Gulf of California. The bottom of the Gulf of California consists of oceanic type crust with a thin (10- to 11-kilometre [six- to seven-mile]) overlying sialic (continental type) layer. It is part of a long trough that connects the San Andreas continental fault system and the mid-American deepwater trench. A number of recent, northwest-trending faults have broken the bottom into several isolated deepwater hollows; the gulf area is one of high seismicity. The continental slopes are very steep and the western slope is cut by a number of submarine canyons. There is a narrow shelf along the eastern side, and some rivers deposit their sediment loads on it.

Relation to the San Andreas fault

Three different areas of sedimentation occur from north to south. Alluvium of the Colorado River, principally silts and sands, is followed by diatomic silts, and oceanic clays occur farthest south. Carbonate sands are spread along the steep western shore.

The deep water of the gulf is oceanic in character. Thermal stratification (temperature zonation) causes an oxygen deficiency in intermediate layers. Surface-water circulation depends on the winds. Winter winds from the north produce an outflowing current, which is compensated for by upwelling of waters at the head of the gulf. Deep-sea water is rich in nutrient salts, and this upwelling leads to extensive plankton development. In summer, south winds direct the surface current toward the head, and water from the intermediate layer goes out into the ocean.

Bay of Fundy. The Bay of Fundy is remarkable for its high tides, which reach 18 metres (59 feet) in the head of Minas Bay, a world record. It is caused by the funnel-like shape of the bay and by a gradual rise of the bottom. This configuration results in resonance of the tidal wave, which is less than five metres high in the open sea. The same phenomenon raises tides sharply in the bays of Shelikhova, Cook Inlet, in the Mezenskaya Guba, and elsewhere.

High current velocities—two to four knots (3.7 to 7.4 kilometres per hour) in the bay proper and up to 11 knots (20 kilometres per hour) in Minas—are related to the coarse character of the bay sediments, which are mainly gravel. In the mouth of the bay these currents maintain a furrow that is more than 200 metres (660 feet) deep. Fine muds are deposited in protected areas near shore; broad tidal flats form in these parts of the bay.

Hudson Bay. Hudson Bay is situated within the Canadian Shield of Precambrian (more than 570,000,000 years ago) age. It has a simple rounded shape, but James Bay extends farther inland at the south. The shallowest part of the bay with a flat bottom is to the southwest. This is in the region of horizontally bedded Paleozoic rocks. The eastern part, which consists of Precambrian metamorphic rocks of greater surface irregularity, has a deeper and more irregular bottom, and a number of islands appear on the surface of the bay. Some irregularly shaped depressions about 200 metres deep exist in the central and the northern part of the bay. Recent research has shown that these hollows are the remnants of an ancient drainage net that led to the ancestral Hudson Strait. This strait connects Hudson Bay to the Atlantic Ocean today.

Drainage and Quaternary history

Coarse sand and gravel and much ice-rafted material are deposited in shallow places near shore. In the open part of the bay, to the west, the sediment is coarser (silt) in comparison to that in the east (silty clay). Sediment cores of the deep part of the bay reveal the presence of varved clays and till. This proves that the bottom of the bay was not submerged during the Quaternary regressions of the sea. During late phases of the glacial period, the area of Hudson Bay was one of the centres from which ice spread radially in all directions. Recently (during the last 8,000 years, approximately) the shores of the bay were subjected to isostatic uplift as a consequence of removal of the overburden of ice.

Hudson Bay receives a number of rivers, and its character is somewhat estuarine; pronounced water stratification exists in summer. Water coming through the Hudson Strait is of about 33.5 parts per thousand salinity, whereas the surface water is comparatively fresher. General water circulation is counterclockwise but this changes during periods of intensive river runoff. Hudson Bay is ice-free for only a few months a year, and the surface water is always very cool.

Gulf of St. Lawrence. The Gulf of St. Lawrence is situated between the crystalline rocks of the Canadian Shield and the folded Paleozoic rocks of the Appalachians. Its complicated shape and bottom topography are strongly determined by faults. The gulf is connected with the ocean by the Cabot Strait. Another narrow strait is called Belle Isle and is situated to the north of Newfoundland. A comparatively deep and smoothly curved trench leads from Cabot Strait to the mouth of the St. Lawrence River. It has some branches to the north of Anticosti Island and in the direction of Belle Isle. The southern part of the gulf (between Cape Breton and the Gaspé Peninsula) is quite flat and shallow.

The Earth's crust is up to 45 kilometres (28 miles) thick in the Gulf of St. Lawrence. The bottom topography of the gulf and its hilly shores received their modern shape through the influence of Quaternary glaciers. It is thought that a glacier excavated the comparatively deep furrows along the axis of the gulf. The northern shores of the gulf have undergone isostatic uplift at a rate of 40 centimetres (16 inches) per 100 years. The rate of uplift is zero in the direction of the southern shore, however.

The water of the cold Labrador Current penetrates the gulf, and St. Lawrence River water is mixed with this, reducing its salinity and raising its temperature (in summer). The general surface circulation is counterclockwise. Oceanic water forms the bottom layer with a salinity of 34 parts per thousand. The water stratification is subjected to seasonal changes. Ice cover is present from November through April in the western part of the gulf and until June in the eastern part.

Persian Gulf. The Persian Gulf is situated in a pronounced depression and is connected with the Gulf of Oman through the Strait of Hormuz. The Arabian shore on the south consists of crystalline rocks of the Arabian Shield, upon which sedimentary rocks rest. This shore is fairly high but is bordered by a low-lying plain. Lagoons and small coral islands are present.

Topography, currents, and salinity

The Zagros Mountains extend along the northern shore. They were formed during Tertiary episodes of folding, and the thickness of rocks in the Zagros is over 12 kilometres (seven miles). The Persian Gulf depression was created as a result of mountain-building processes. Salt plugs may be observed at the bottom and on the shores of the gulf, and there is some evidence of recent submergence in the deltaic area, while, to the south, there are uplifted terraces on both shores.

The bottom topography of the gulf is rather discontinuous, save for its northern and southern parts. Bottom deposits form three different regions, or zones. There is a thick layer of sand and clay with up to 20 percent calcium carbonate in the head of the gulf. In the centre, calcareous sediments of chemical and biogenic origins prevail. Coarse carbonate sands are deposited in shallow parts of the gulf, especially along its southern shore. These sands contain shell fragments, corals, and organic remains in general. Windblown material from the adjoining deserts is present everywhere.

Due to strong evaporation in the Persian Gulf, the surface waters of Oman penetrate the gulf waters as a compensation current. As their salinity increases, they become denser and flow back to the Gulf of Oman along the bottom. Strong tidal (up to four knots in the Strait of Hormuz) and wind currents are superimposed on these salinity currents. Distinct vertical stratification probably does not exist because of strong currents and the shallowness of the gulf.

Zaliv Shelikhova. The Zaliv Shelikhova is an enlarged copy of the Bay of Fundy. The resonance of its tidal wave raises water levels in its forked head (Penzhinskaya Guba) by almost 13 metres (43 feet). Tidal currents determine the coarseness of the bottom sediments, and a trough over 400 metres (1,300 feet) deep, stretching from the Sea of Okhotsk into the gulf, also is related to these tidal currents.

Zaliv Shelikhova is frozen for some months. In summer the upwelling of its deep cold waters takes place near the mouth, and the surface circulation is counterclockwise.

The Gulf of Thailand and the Gulf of Carpentaria. These gulfs have much in common. Both are vast shelf areas with rectangular contours (determined by tectonics) that open widely into the sea. The Gulf of Thailand is in the humid tropical zone, however, and the Gulf of Carpentaria, in the arid tropical zone.

The water of the South China Sea penetrates into the Gulf of Thailand at its bottom, and the freshwater of the Mae Nam Chao Phraya (Chao Phraya River) is spread on the surface. This forms stratification of estuarine character. The surface water circulation, depending on the monsoons, is clockwise in autumn and winter and counterclockwise in summer. Upwelling of bottom water of high salinity (up to 34 parts per thousand) takes place in areas of divergent currents. Muddy alluvium of the Mae Nam Chao Phraya covers the entire gulf bottom, and a considerable part of its low shores with mangrove swamps were similarly derived.

Water circulation and swamp occurrences

The Gulf of Carpentaria extends into the northern shore of Australia. Its flat basin is bordered by faults that separate Precambrian rocks of the western coast from Mesozoic and Tertiary rocks of the east. These rocks are not visible everywhere because the low shore is bordered by mangrove swamps. The gulf was not filled by seawater until Holocene time.

Mezenskaya Guba. This bay is distinguished from other gulfs and bays of the White Sea by the high tides at its head. In this respect it is similar to the Bay of Fundy. Because of the strong currents, the flat bottom of the bay is covered by coarse gravel and exposed outcrops of Permian carbonate rocks. Clay and peat shores of the bay retreat at a rate of up to 10 metres (33 feet) a year. This is due to the influence of drift ice (the bay is frozen for some months) and melting of the permafrost within the shores. Muddy tidal flats, many kilometres in width, exist in estuaries of Mezenskaya Guba and in some open areas. These flats also constitute a characteristic physical feature of the area.

Obskaya Guba. The longest inlet of the southern shore of the Kara Sea is the Obskaya Guba. It receives the runoff of the Ob and Taz rivers, and its currents tend to have runoff characteristics. In summer, water emerging from the *guba* is six to eight degrees warmer than that in the adjoining part of the sea.

The shores of the *guba* consist of loose Quaternary alluvium. They are precipitous on the west, where they are being attacked and destroyed by the sea. On the east they are mainly low-lying.

Po Hai (Gulf of Chihli). This gulf is noteworthy because it receives the water of the Yellow River, which has the largest sediment discharge in the world (up to $1,380 \times 10^6$ tons a year). The flat bottom of the gulf is covered by yellowish mud, which is derived from erosion of the loess of China. The southern and the western shores of the gulf are also muddy because the mouth of the Yellow River has repeatedly migrated through time.

The turbid water of the gulf is warmed down to the bottom by strong tidal currents, and productivity (fish, shrimp, and oyster) is high. The Río de la Plata of South America is quite similar; this gulf is in a basin that is completely filled by alluvium of the Paraná River.

Gulf of Bothnia and Gulf of Finland. These gulfs of the tideless Baltic Sea have much in common. They receive the runoff of many rivers and their turbid waters are especially freshened at the basin heads. Local, unstable circulations that depend on the winds and river floods are characteristic of both of them. Fluctuations of water level due to seiches are peculiar. In the Gulf of Finland these reach a height of 120 centimetres (47 inches), and high storm surges (up to 375 centimetres [148 inches]) at its head can cause disastrous floods. In winter both gulfs are frozen for some months.

During the last glaciation the basins of both gulfs were filled with ice. When glacial retreat and ice melting occurred, fresh glacial lakes were formed in this region. Subsequently, as the world sea level rose and the isostatic uplift of Fennoscandia (Norway, Sweden, and Finland) occurred, the shape, water composition, and marine pop-

Ice retreat and isostatic uplift

ulation of the gulfs changed several times. A complicated history has been deciphered from study of terrace altitudes and ancient deposits of the shores and the bottom of the gulfs. The shores are still rising today. In the head of the Gulf of Bothnia the rate of uplift is over one metre a century. This diminishes to the south and is essentially zero in the head of the Gulf of Finland.

The mouth of the Gulf of Bothnia is partitioned off by the Åland Skerries Archipelago, and it is only to the west that a deep strait remains. The hollows of the two gulfs occupy ancient depressions of the crystalline Baltic Shield. There also are pre-Paleozoic fractures along some parts of the shores that may have undergone renewed movement dur-

ing the Tertiary Period. The southern shore of the Gulf of Finland is formed by horizontal layers of Paleozoic rocks. The basins of the gulfs were considerably influenced by glaciers, and moraine ridges are still preserved at the bottom of the Gulf of Finland. The northern shore of the Gulf of Finland and the whole of the southern part of the Gulf of Bothnia are strongly dissected by *fjärds* and skerries islands.

The sediments of the central part of the Gulf of Bothnia consist of terrigenous muds that overlie varved glacial clays and till. Sediments of the Gulf of Finland are coarser, and in many places sands are deposited on its bottom. There is an admixture of ice-rafted stones in the sediments of both gulfs.

(V.P.Z.)

ECONOMIC ASPECTS OF THE OCEANS

The sea is generally accepted by scientists as the place where life began on Earth. Without the sea, life as it is known today could not exist. Among other functions, it acts as a great heat reservoir, levelling the temperature extremes that would otherwise prevail over the Earth and expand the desert areas. The oceans provide the least expensive form of transportation known to man, and the margins of the sea serve as one of his major sites of recreation. The sea is a major source of food and a dumping ground for many wastes. And the sea is a major potential source of protein, minerals, and power, all of which are required in ever-increasing quantities by all industrialized societies.

Transport and communications. From the beginning of recorded history, man has used the sea as a means of transport, first for himself, and then as a means of distributing products throughout the world. The bulk of the tonnage of products transported throughout the world today is moved in ocean vessels. The size of these vessels ranges from small boats capable of carrying a few tons to bulk carriers capable of transporting more than 500,000 tons of oil. The cost of transporting goods on the ocean depends on the product, the form of shipment, and the type of vessel. Probably the cheapest form of transportation known to man is that of the great oil carriers in which a ton of oil may be shipped for an average cost of hundredths of a cent per ton mile. This cost is about 100 times cheaper than shipping such material on land, if the use of pipelines is excluded. As the per capita consumption of materials increases, the outlook for marine transportation is one of ever-increasing tonnages and size of carrying vessels, not only in conventional vessels but also in ground-effect vessels (already in commercial operation in Europe) and in bulk-carrying submarines to pass beneath the polar ice cap.

Since the laying of the trans-Atlantic cable in the 19th century, the oceans have served as a major means of communication between continents and islands. Hundreds of sea-floor cables connect all major centres of world population. With the development of satellite communications, ocean-floor cables as a means of communication may tend to decrease in importance, but they will continue to carry information for many decades to come.

In addition to communications, cable and pipes laid on the ocean floor carry electrical energy, oil, and other commodities in many parts of the world.

Food and water. *Fishing.* Man extracts about 70,000,000 tons of food from the ocean annually by fishing. The food-producing potential of the sea, however, is several hundreds of times the present rate of production. The methods by which man takes food from the sea are inefficient, and the fact that he takes only certain choice species of fish makes fishing in the ocean doubly inefficient. The development of a process to extract protein concentrates from all types of fish might rectify this shortcoming. This protein concentrate could be stored, transported, and utilized very efficiently. It has been estimated that the daily protein requirements for a human being can be produced from fish for less than a penny. It is estimated that, by efficient harvesting of all the fish of the sea, the ocean could produce a sustained yield of about 2,000,000,000 tons of

food annually, but it must be noted that such utilization requires, in many instances, a change in human attitudes. In many parts of the world, wheat has proved to be an unacceptable substitute for rice where rice is a customary, integral part of the diet of the inhabitants.

The Japanese have instituted a substantial program of studies of continental shelf development to further the eventual farming of adequate supplies of fish and edible plants there. While Japan has farmed oysters in its oceanic bays for many years, its fishermen have been active around the world's oceans in the manner of those from other countries. With that activity seemingly at a point of diminishing returns, Japan has thus turned to home waters.

Fish need not be fenced in to be farmed. They will stay where the food supply is. By creating an artificial food supply in a given location, fish can be kept where they are wanted. Creating a food supply for the fish need not mean the adding of fish nutrients to the sea but the development of some means of mixing the nutrient-rich bottom layers of water in the ocean with the life-rich upper layers of water. Wherever a natural upwelling of the bottom layers of water occurs, such as off Peru, a tremendous fish population also is found. By encouraging such an upwelling artificially, the fish population could be greatly increased at some more convenient point rather than at the location nature has provided. Developing this technique could probably increase the potential yield of the ocean by 10 times or so over the present potential productive capacity of the ocean. The energy for sustaining this upwelling in the ocean can be produced by several sources; for example, by nuclear reactors on the bottom of the ocean. The development of this or any other means of producing upwelling, however, will probably await economic necessity, if not actual crisis; reactors on the sea floor do not appear to be likely in the immediate future.

Desalination. Although springs of freshwater issuing on the ocean floor are known to occur in water depths as great as 1,000 metres (3,300 feet), these springs never will prove to be a major source of freshwater for the world. Of greater interest is the prospect of desalting seawater itself. Throughout the world, hundreds of desalination units, producing from a few thousand to 37,900,000 litres (10,000,000 gallons) or more per day, already are in operation. In general, the desalination plants in production are in areas where the population has outstripped the on-shore water supply and where high-cost desalinated water can be afforded. This situation tends to arise in coastal-desert areas, or on densely populated islands because the costs of pumping water through pipelines to interior areas would add prohibitively to the basic cost—at the sites of desalination.

A population usually can afford to pay about 10 times as much for water for domestic purposes as it does for agricultural water. Proposals for large-scale nuclear desalination facilities, when constructed, promise to lower the cost of desalinated water at the desalination sites to a level that most industries and a few agricultural enterprises can afford.

The bulk of the water produced from seawater is produced by some form of evaporation and condensation. Al-

Fish-
farming

though the principle of this technique is quite simple, the mechanics of achieving high efficiencies can become quite complicated. Superheated water and multiple evaporation and condensation units, operating at varying temperatures and pressures, are employed in a number of these facilities. The choice of construction materials is quite important, because the brines produced in extracting pure water can be corrosive.

Other processes under consideration as potential economic methods of desalting seawater are freezing, reverse osmosis, ionic processes, electrodialysis, and techniques that change the physical or chemical properties of water itself so that it can be separated from the salts in seawater. In the future, it can be expected that the ocean will become an increasingly important source of freshwater. If production and transportation costs can be lowered sufficiently, it may be possible to produce freshwater to irrigate large areas that border the oceans in many parts of the world.

Energy resources. There are a number of recognized techniques by which energy can be extracted from the sea. The major problem in taking energy resources from the sea is that they tend to be diffused over a large lateral area. A point-concentration energy source is necessary if it is to be exploited economically.

Power generation. Although energy presently is extracted from the tides of the ocean, it is unlikely that man will develop a technique for extracting efficiently large amounts of energy from such sources as the waves of the sea. Another potential power source in the ocean, however, is the temperature differential between the surface layers and the lower layers of water; it can be as large as 50 degrees over vertical distances of as little as 90 metres (300 feet) in some areas of the ocean. For many years, the French have experimented with techniques of using this temperature differential to generate electricity. The processes they used were a technical success; but they were not economic, mainly because the plant was located on land, and most of the energy obtained from this system was used in pumping the seawater into and out of the plant. Pilot plants utilizing this technique, built in the late 1970s in French Polynesia and Hawaii, however, tested the technology for much larger facilities.

A group in the United States has developed a system whereby the energy can be extracted by a floating power plant that eliminates the pumping problem. Propane or some similar fluid that will boil at the temperature of the surface layer of water is used, the gaseous phase then being released to a turbogenerator to manufacture the power. After the gas is condensed to a liquid in the cooler, lower layers of water, it is pumped to a surface boiler to be recycled. To be economically practical, the temperature differential should be several tens of degrees, and major markets for the energy created should not be more than a few hundred miles from the power plant. The areas of the ocean in which it would be most efficient to operate such a plant, normally in the tropics, are not near major markets.

Some techniques were developed in the 1970s for handling liquid hydrogen and liquid oxygen on a large scale. If power generated in remote areas of the ocean were used to reduce seawater to hydrogen and oxygen, these gases might be utilized economically in shoreside thermal power plants. This procedure is, admittedly, hypothetical. Followed to its logical though futuristic conclusion, it suggests that oceanic thermal power plants may someday be used to power the artificial upwelling previously mentioned.

A conservative estimate of the energy resources presently available in the ocean is several thousands of years, at present rates of world energy consumption. Even more significant, however, is the fact, that because this thermal differential is generated by the Sun, it is renewing itself about 100 times as fast as it could be used to provide the whole world with its present total energy consumption. Man could take from the sea about 200,000,000 megawatt hours of energy each day. There are, of course, no fuel costs involved in generating power in the sea, and the estimated plant operational and capital costs indicate an overall power-production cost substantially lower than that of power generated from conventional sources.

Petroleum. In the mid-1950s, the production of oil and gas from oceanic areas was negligible. By the early 1980s, about 14,000,000 barrels per day, or about a quarter percent of the world's production, came from ocean wells. More than 500 offshore drilling and production rigs were at work in the 1980s, at more than 200 offshore locations throughout the world drilling, completing, and maintaining offshore oil wells (see FUELS). Estimates have placed the potential offshore oil resources at about 2,000,000,-000,000 barrels, or about half of the presently known onshore potential oil sources.

It was once thought that only the continental-shelf areas contained potential petroleum resources, but discoveries of oil deposits in deeper waters of the Gulf of Mexico (about 3,000 to 4,000 metres [9,800 to 13,-100 feet]) have led to a revision of this idea. It is now believed that the continental slopes and neighbouring ocean-floor areas will contain large oil deposits, thus enhancing potential petroleum reserves of the ocean bottom.

Minerals. The rivers of the world dump billions of tons of material into the sea each year. Sea-floor springs and volcanic eruptions also add many millions of tons of elements. Even the winds contribute solid materials to the sea in appreciable quantities. Most of these sediments rapidly settle to the sea floor in nearshore areas, in some cases forming potentially valuable placer mineral deposits. The dissolved load of the rivers, however, mixes with seawater and is gradually dispersed over the total oceanic envelope of the Earth. Because of the nature of the minerals and their mode of formation, it is convenient to consider the occurrence of sea deposits in several environments, namely marine beaches, seawater, continental shelves, sub-sea-floor consolidated rocks, and the marine sediments of the deep-sea floor. Minerals are mined from all of these environments except for the deep-sea-floor area, which was only in the 1970s recognized as a repository for mineral deposits of unbelievable extent and significant economic value.

Minerals that resist the chemical and mechanical processes of erosion in nature and that possess a density greater than that of the Earth's common minerals have a tendency to concentrate in gravity deposits known as placers. During the ice ages (about 10,000 to 2,500,000 years ago), sea level was appreciably lowered as the ocean water was transferred to the continental glaciers. Because of the cyclical nature of the ice ages and the intervening warm periods, series of beaches were formed in near-shore areas both above and below present sea level. Also, when sea level was lowered in past ages, the streams that now flow into the sea coursed much further seaward, carrying placer minerals to be deposited in channels that are now submerged. With geophysical-exploration techniques, these channels and beaches can be easily delineated, even though these features are totally covered by Recent or Holocene sediments; that is, those deposited during the last 10,000 years.

Sand and gravel, mined from a number of offshore locations around the world, generally with hydraulic dredges, are used mainly for construction purposes or for beach replenishment or nearshore fills.

Sulfur, which is taken from salt domes in the Gulf of Mexico, is mined by a process in which pressurized hot water is pumped into the sulfur-containing cap of the dome, melting the sulfur and forcing it to the surface. Compressed air is also used to pump sulfur to the surface; the still-molten sulfur is then pumped ashore through insulated pipelines.

Of considerable interest are the sea-floor phosphorite deposits on the coastal shelves of many nations. The phosphorite off California occurs as nodules that vary in shape from flat slabs, a few metres across, to small spherical forms termed oölites. The nodules commonly are found as a single layer at the surface of coarse-grained sediments. Phosphorite composition from the California offshore area is surprisingly uniform and contains potentially economically attractive amounts of phosphorus.

Another type of phosphate deposit has been found off the west coast of Mexico, namely, a fine-grained, uncon-

Utilization of temperature differentials

Placer and nearshore deposits

Deep-sea
deposits

solidated deposit in about 50 metres (160 feet) of water. It contains as much as 40 percent apatite (common phosphate mineral), and it is speculated that there is as much as 20,000,000,000 tons of recoverable phosphate rock in this deposit.

Mineral deposits of monumental size and potential economic significance are found in the deep-sea areas of the ocean. Minerals formed in the deep sea are frequently found in high concentrations, because there is relatively little clastic material generated in these areas to dilute the chemical precipitates.

An estimated 10^{16} tons of calcareous oozes, formed by the deposition of calcareous shells and skeletons of planktonic (floating) organisms, cover some 130,000,000 square kilometres (50,000,000 square miles) of the ocean floor. In a few instances, these oozes, which occur within a few hundred kilometres of most nations bordering the sea, are almost pure calcium carbonate; but they often show a composition similar to that of the limestones used in the manufacture of portland cement.

Covering about 39,000,000 square kilometres (15,000,000 square miles) of the ocean floor in great bands across the northern and southern ends of the Pacific Ocean and across the southern ends of the Indian and Atlantic oceans are other oozes, consisting of the siliceous shells and skeletons of plankton animals and plants. Normally these oozes could serve in most of the applications for which diatomaceous earth is used, for fire and sound insulation, for lightweight concrete formulations, as filters, and as soil conditioners.

An estimated 10^{16} tons of red clay covers about 104,000,000 square kilometres (40,000,000 square miles) of the ocean floor. Although compositional analyses are not particularly exciting, red clay may possess some value as a raw material in the clay-products industries, or it may serve as a source of metals in the future. The average assay for alumina is about 15 percent, but red clays from specific locations have assayed as high as 25 percent alumina; copper contents as high as 0.20 percent also have been found. A few hundredths of a percent of such metals as nickel and cobalt and a percent or so of manganese also are generally present in a micronodular fraction of the clays and probably can be separated and concentrated from the other materials by screening or by some other physical method.

Underlying the hot brines in the Red Sea are basins containing metal-rich sediments that potentially may prove to be one of the great metal-deposit discoveries of all time. It has been estimated that the largest of several such pools, the Atlantis II Deep, contains over $2,000,000,000 worth of copper, zinc, silver, and gold values in relatively high grades. These pools lie in about 2,000 metres (6,600 feet) of water, midway between The Sudan and the Arabian Peninsula. Because of their gel-like nature, pumping these sediments to the surface should prove relatively uncomplicated. These deposits are forming today under present geochemical conditions, and they are similar in character to certain major ore deposits on land.

Manganese
nodules

From an economic standpoint, the most interesting oceanic sediments are manganese nodules—small, black to brown, friable lumps found to be widely distributed throughout the three major oceans in the late 19th century by the famous "Challenger" and "Albatross" expeditions. Many theories have been proposed to account for the

formation of manganese nodules, the best probably being that the ocean is saturated at its present state of acidity–alkalinity in iron and manganese. For this reason, these elements precipitate as colloidal particles that gradually increase in size and filter down to the sea floor. Colloids of manganese and iron oxides collect many metals and bear an electrical charge; they tend to agglomerate as nodules at the sea floor rather than settle as particles in the general sediments.

An estimated 1,500,000,000,000 tons of manganese nodules are on the Pacific Ocean floor alone, and they are estimated to be forming at an annual rate of about 10,000,000 tons. Averaging about four centimetres (1.6 inches) in diameter and found in concentrations as high as 38,600 tons per square kilometre (100,000 tons per square mile), these manganese nodules contain as much as 2.5 percent copper, 2.0 percent nickel, 0.2 percent cobalt, and 35 percent manganese. In some deposits, the content of cobalt and manganese is as high as 2.5 percent and 50 percent, respectively. Such concentrations would be considered high-grade ores if found on land, and, because of the large horizontal extent of the deposit, they are a potential source of many important industrial metals.

Relatively simple mechanical cable bucket or hydraulic dredges with submerged motors and pumps can effect the mining of the nodules at rates as high as 10,000 to 15,000 tons per day, from depths as great as 6,000 metres (20,000 feet). The estimated costs to mine and process the nodules indicate that copper, nickel, cobalt, and other metals can be economically produced from this source.

Waste disposal.   One of the least known but most important uses of the sea is as a garbage dump. In the past, the ocean was capable of assimilating the wastes of societies without noticeable pollution effects. Because society is becoming increasingly affluent, however, the dumping of wastes into the ocean is overwhelming the ocean's capacity to digest them. Great marginal areas of the world's oceans have been heavily polluted by many forms of man's wastes, the most obvious of which is sewage. Less apparent forms of pollution are nuclear wastes, chemical wastes, trash and oil spills from vessels, oil spills from offshore wells, and heat. Great power plants are generally located along coastlines to reduce the costs involved in cooling their condensers by water-circulation systems. Although the whole of the ocean never will be affected by the waste heat dissipated by these plants, great environmental effects can be caused in the immediate area of the power-plant outfall. Crude oil from leaking offshore oil wells, from sinking tankers, and from bilges pumped by practically all vessels using oil for power have polluted countless beaches throughout the world. Lead, which is highly toxic to life, is being added to the ocean in great quantities by fallout from internal-combustion exhausts, which enters the Earth's atmosphere and ultimately precipitates and reaches the seas. Pollution by mercury, another highly toxic substance, became of great concern around 1970 after analyses revealed its presence in marine and freshwater fish. The effects of dumping these wastes into the ocean are becoming great enough to pollute the entire ocean in some manner. Man can continue to use the ocean as a dumping ground for his wastes, but he must control the form and point of dumping into the ocean so that the pollution effects are reduced to an acceptable level.

(J.L.M.)

PRINCIPAL OCEANS OF THE WORLD

The Atlantic Ocean

The Atlantic Ocean is the name given to that vast stretch of the World Ocean that separates the continents of Europe and Africa from those of North and South America. The term, derived from Greek mythology, means the Sea of Atlas. It is second in size only to the Pacific Ocean.

The Atlantic is, generally speaking, S-shaped and narrow in relation to its length. The area of the Atlantic without its dependent seas is 82,440,000 square kilometres (31,-830,000 square miles), and with them, 106,460,000 square kilometres (41,100,000 square miles).

Although not the largest of the world's oceans, the Atlantic, as noted earlier, has by far the largest drainage area. The continents on both of its sides tend to slope toward it, so that it receives the waters of a large proportion of the great rivers of the world, including the St. Lawrence, the Mississippi, the Orinoco, the Amazon, the Río de La Plata, the Congo, the Niger, the Loire, the Rhine, the Elbe, and the great rivers of the Mediterranean and the

The
ocean's
drainage
area

Baltic. The total area of land draining to the Atlantic and the Arctic Sea is nearly 43,229,700 square kilometres (16,-691,000 square miles), almost four times the area draining to the Pacific Ocean, and almost exactly four times the area draining to the Indian Ocean.

PHYSIOGRAPHY

Extent. The Arctic Basin, which stretches from the Bering Strait across the North Pole to Spitsbergen and Greenland, connects with the Atlantic Ocean by way of the narrow, but deep, straits between Spitsbergen and Greenland. In the south, the Atlantic extends to the shores of the Antarctic continent. The Atlantic Ocean has, therefore, a share in both the seas of ice.

In contrast to the South Atlantic, the North Atlantic is rich in islands, in the variety of its coastline, and in tributary seas. The latter include the Caribbean Sea, the Gulf of Mexico, the Gulf of St. Lawrence, Hudson Bay, and Baffin Bay on the west, and the Mediterranean Sea, Black Sea, North Sea, and Baltic Sea on the east. Between Spitsbergen and Novaya Zemlya, on the one hand, and the Murmansk coast, on the other, lies the Barents Sea; between Greenland, Iceland, the Faeroes, Shetlands, Norway, and Spitsbergen lies the Norwegian–Greenland Sea. Hudson Strait in the northwest is 103 kilometres (64 miles) wide; Davis Strait to the north of it 320 kilometres (200 miles); and Denmark Strait, between east Greenland and Iceland, 256 kilometres (159 miles) across. The passage between Iceland and northern Scotland is 833 kilometres (518 miles) wide.

Margin note: Tributary seas

In the South Atlantic, on the other hand, between Cape Horn and South Africa, the ocean approaches Antarctica on a 6,380-kilometre (3,965-mile) front and is much colder and rawer than the North Atlantic.

From east to west, the ocean's breadth varies considerably. From Newfoundland to Ireland it is 3,313 kilometres (2,059 miles); further south it widens to over 4,825 kilometres (3,000 miles), before narrowing again so that the distance from Cabo São Roque, Brazil, to Cape Palmas, Liberia, is only 2,846 kilometres (1,769 miles). Southward, it again becomes broader and is bordered by simple coasts almost without islands.

Relief of the ocean floor. The foundations of knowledge of the Atlantic floor were laid in the last century when the practical needs of telegraphic engineers and the curiosity of natural scientists led to the first explorations of the abyss. Though soundings were taken by lead line or wire, real comprehension of sea floor topography was not possible until the development of continuously recording precision echo sounders after World War II. The detailed profiles produced by these instruments allowed a realistic appraisal of the ocean floor, which made the earlier probings seem vague and almost dream-like.

Margin note: The Mid-Atlantic Ridge

The outstanding feature of the Atlantic floor is the Mid-Atlantic Ridge, an immense median mountain range extending throughout the length of the Atlantic, claiming the centre third of the ocean bed, and reaching 1,600 kilometres (1,000 miles) in breadth. This feature, though of tremendous proportions, is but the Atlantic portion of the world-encircling midocean ridge (see above).

In some places the Mid-Atlantic Ridge reaches above sea level. The Azores, Ascension, St. Helena, Tristan da Cunha, Gough, and Bouvet—all volcanic islands—rise from its flank; Iceland, which rises from its crest, is rent by an extension of the median rift valley. East and west of the ridge, 3,660 to 5,500 metres (12,000 to 18,000 feet) below sea level, lie basins which seem on first inspection to present a rather even profile. Study reveals, however, that parts of the basin floor are as mountainous as the Mid-Atlantic Ridge, while other parts are extremely smooth. The former are rocky abyssal hills; the latter are the abyssal plains that form the upper surface of great ponds of mud which fill many of the broad depressions. Large ancient volcanoes are found singly or in rows in the basins; these rise to form seamounts and occasionally islands. As the continents are approached and the rugged Mid-Atlantic Ridge is left behind, the echo-sounding profile of a survey vessel will first reveal an abyssal plain and then the smooth, undulating surface of the continental rise.

These broad embankments, which lie at depths of 2,440 to 4,570 metres (8,000 to 15,000 feet) at the foot of continents, reach in widths of over 480 kilometres (300 miles) off Northwest Africa, Angola, Argentina, and the eastern seaboard of the United States. In other areas they are exceedingly narrow. The continental rise is in fact an immense refuse heap of sediments eroded from the continents through geologic time. Here, in all probability—within the 3,050- to 15,240-metre- (10,000- to 50,000-foot-) thick accumulations—lie the largest potential reserves of petroleum on Earth.

The Caribbean Islands and the South Sandwich Islands form great unstable island arcs, where the greatest depths of the Atlantic are found in steep-sided, narrow gashes that drop to over 9,140 metres (30,000 feet) below sea level, and over 3,050 metres below the floors of adjacent basins.

Margin note: Unstable island arcs

The North Polar Basin and the intervening Norwegian Basin are separated from the open Atlantic by a shallow ridge extending from Greenland to Scotland upon which Iceland and the Faeroe Islands rise above sea level. The maximum depths in Denmark Strait, between Greenland and Iceland, and over the Wyville-Thompson Ridge, between the Faeroes and Scotland, are only about 490 metres (1,600 feet). Lowering the sea level about 490 metres would expose a land bridge from North America to Europe and would completely isolate the waters of the Polar Basin from both the Atlantic and the Pacific. In the North Polar Basin relatively few soundings were made until a Russian expedition (1937–38), which landed by plane on the ice within 97 kilometres (60 miles) of the pole. After that time numerous soundings were made from the ice floes and ice islands throughout the basin. The basin, roughly elliptical, is divided into two parts by the Lomonosov Ridge, having a sill depth of about 1,525 metres (5,000 feet), which runs from the continental shelf north of Ellesmere Island through a position of 89° N 180° W, then south near the meridian of 140° E toward the New Siberian Islands. The depression on the right looking north from Ellesmere Island is smaller, but deeper—over 4,880 metres—whereas, depths in the larger basin to the left (toward Alaska) approach 3,960 metres (13,000 feet). There are two lobes in the larger basin and some evidence of a second ridge roughly parallel to the Lomonosov Ridge. Between Greenland and Spitsbergen the sill depth is about 450 metres (1,500 feet), and in the Norwegian Basin the greatest depth is about 3,660 metres (12,000 feet).

Depths greater than 3,960 metres occur in the Caribbean Basin and in the Mediterranean Sea. The former has numerous shallow and several deep connections with the open ocean, but the Mediterrean communicates with the Atlantic only through the Strait of Gibraltar, which is about 19 kilometres (12 miles) wide and where the maximum depth on the sill is only 305 metres (1,000 feet). The partial isolation of the large adjacent seas has a profound effect on the conditions in the seas and also upon those in the open ocean.   (B.C.H./Ed.)

Islands. Among purely oceanic islands without any foundation of continental rock, usually the result of volcanic action, there are Jan Mayen, Iceland, the Azores, Ascension, St. Helena, Tristan de Cunha, and Bouvet (latitude 54° 26′ S), which rise from the Mid-Atlantic Ridge, and the Canaries, Madeira, the Cape Verdes, and Fernando de Noronha (near Cabo de São Roque), rising from the continental margins of Africa and South America. Volcanic islands of a different sort are those of the two great arcs, the Lesser Antilles and the South Sandwich. Partly continental and partly oceanic are the Greater Antilles in the Caribbean, and South Georgia and the South Orkneys in the Scotia Sea. Purely continental are Spitsbergen and the Bear Islands, the British Isles, Newfoundland, and the Falkland Islands.   (J.O.Fl./Ed.)

GEOLOGY

Origin and development. The Atlantic is the youngest of the oceans. Its origin and development are now accounted for by the theory of continental drift, according to which a vast "proto-continent," Pangaea, which once "floated" on the Earth's liquid mantle, broke up in the

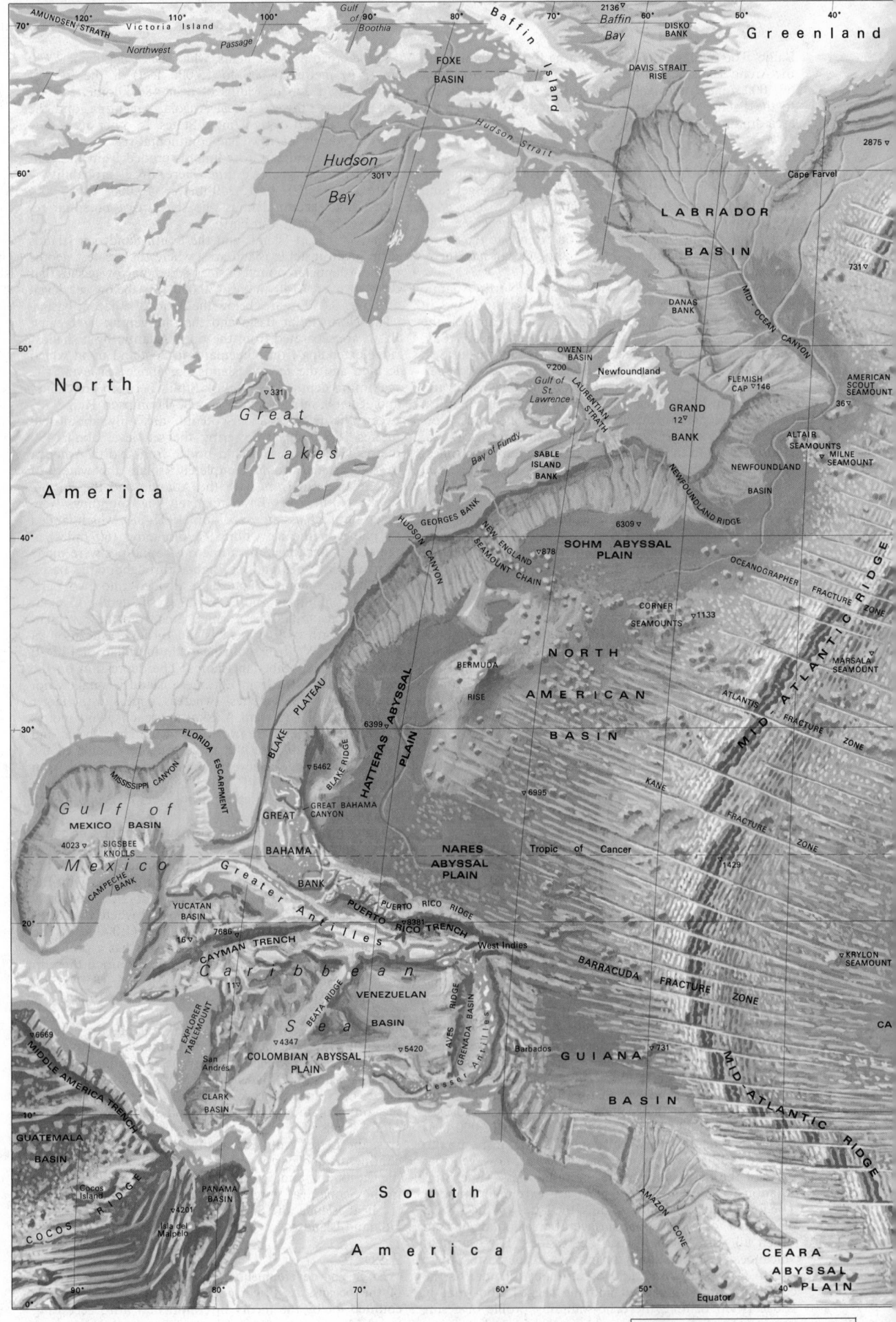

70° 120° Victoria Island 110° 100° Gulf 90° 80° Baffin 70° Baffin 2136▽ 60° DISKO Greenland
AMUNDSEN STRATH of Bay BANK 50° 40°
Northwest Passage Boothia Island
FOXE DAVIS STRAIT
BASIN RISE

Hudson Strait 2875 ▽

Hudson
60° Bay 301▽ LABRADOR 731▽
BASIN

DANAS
BANK

MID-OCEAN CANYON
OWEN
BASIN
50° ▽200 FLEMISH AMERICAN
North Newfoundland CAP ▽146 SCOUT
Gulf of SEAMOUNT
St. GRAND 36▽
▽ 331 Lawrence 12 BANK ALTAIR
Great ▽ SEAMOUNTS
MILNE
Lakes NEWFOUNDLAND SEAMOUNT
Bay of Fundy BASIN
America SABLE
ISLAND NEWFOUNDLAND RIDGE
40° GEORGES BANK BANK 6309 ▽
NEW ENGLAND SOHM ABYSSAL
HUDSON CANYON SEAMOUNT CHAIN PLAIN OCEANOGRAPHER FRACTURE ZONE

▽878 N O R T H
CORNER
SEAMOUNTS ▽1133
BERMUDA A M E R I C A N
BLAKE PLATEAU RISE MARSALA
HATTERAS ABYSSAL PLAIN SEAMOUNT
30° B A S I N ATLANTIS
6399 ▽ FRACTURE
▽ 5462 BLAKE RIDGE KANE ZONE
FLORIDA ESCARPMENT GREAT BAHAMA ▽ 6895
MISSISSIPPI CANYON CANYON FRACTURE 1479
Gulf of ZONE
MEXICO BASIN GREAT Tropic of Cancer
4023▽ SIGSBEE BAHAMA NARES
KNOLLS BANK ABYSSAL KRYLON
M e x i c o PLAIN ▽ SEAMOUNT
CAMPECHE Greater Antilles PUERTO RICO RIDGE
BANK PUERTO RICO TRENCH
YUCATAN West Indies BARRACUDA FRACTURE ZONE
20° BASIN ▽8381
16 ▽ 7686▽ C a r i b b e a n
CAYMAN TRENCH CA
11▽ S e a VENEZUELAN RIDGE ▽ KRYLON
EXPLORER BEATA RIDGE BASIN GRENADA BASIN Barbados ▽731 MID
TABLEMOUNT ▽ 4347 AVES G U I A N A ATLANTIC
▽6669 San Andrés ▽ 5420
COLOMBIAN ABYSSAL Lesser Antilles
MIDDLE AMERICA TRENCH PLAIN B A S I N
10° CLARK
GUATEMALA BASIN
BASIN
Cocos PANAMA
Island BASIN S o u t h
COCOS ▽ 4201 AMAZON CONE
Isla del RIDGE
Malpelo A m e r i c a CEARA
ABYSSAL
0° 90° 80° 70° 60° 50° Equator 40° PLAIN

NORTHERN ATLANTIC OCEAN   Depths in metres

Colours used are thought to be those of the
various rocks and sediments on the sea floors.
Differences in relief are shown by relief shading.

NANSEN CORDILLERA

Jan Mayen

LOFOTEN
BASIN

Novaya
Zemlya

Barents Sea

30° 20° 10° 0° 10° 20° 30° 40° 50° 60° 70°

GREENLAND-
ICELAND RISE

SOUTH JAN MAYEN RIDGE

NORWEGIAN
BASIN

Arctic Circle

Gulf
of
Bothnia

REYKJANES RIDGE

Iceland

Norwegian
Sea

▽3970

▽3008

Rockall
RISE

Faeroe Islands

FAEROE ICELAND RIDGE

Shetland
Islands

WYVILLE THOMPSON RIDGE

NORWEGIAN TRENCH

91▽

Baltic
Sea

60°

GIBBS FRACTURE ZONE

Rockall

ROCKALL TROUGH

North

DEVILS
239▽ HOLE

DOGGER
BANK
▽18

Sea

British
Isles

50°

HECATE
SEAMOUNT

▽3412

PORCUPINE
BANK

▽155

FARADAY
SEAMOUNT
GROUP

66▽ GREAT
SOLE
BANK

English Channel

Europe

TREVELYAN ESCARPMENT

WEST

BISCAY
ABYSSAL PLAIN

EUROPEAN

▽676

BASIN

▽4693

IBERIAN
ABYSSAL
PLAIN

Black Sea

▽51

▽2211

AZORES

Azores

ADRIATIC
▽1183
ABYSSAL
PLAIN

40°

PLATEAU

AZORES GIBRALTAR RIDGE

▽5402

▽20

ALGERIAN

2866 ▽

3630▽

TYRRHENIAN
ABYSSAL
PLAIN

AMPERE
SEAMOUNT

BASIN

Mediterranean

Aegean
Sea

ATLANTIS
SEAMOUNT

▽148

Strait of Gibraltar

MEDITERRANEAN RIDGE

MALTA
RISE

5121▽

Madeira

Sea

CRUISER
TABLEMOUNT

CANARY
BASIN

MESSINA
ABYSSAL
PLAIN

LEVANTINE
BASIN

GREAT ▽269
METEOR
TABLEMOUNT

▽6293

3174▽

30°

Canary
Islands

CANARY RIDGE

CAPE VERDE BASIN

261▽ ECHO
SEAMOUNT

20°

▽3164

TROPIC
SEAMOUNT ▽

CAPE VERDE
TERRACE

Cape
Verde
Islands

▽7292

Cape
Verde

Africa

10°

VERDE

BASIN

10°

GUINEA FRACTURE ZONE

SIERRA LEONE RISE

▽6040

118
▽

Rochedos São Pedro
e São Paulo

ROMANCHE FRACTURE ZONE

GUINEA
5212 ▽ BASIN

São Tomé

NIGER FAN

© Rand McNally & Co.
A-513800-957 -1 -1 -1 -1

0°

30° 20° 10° 0° 10° 20° 30° 40° 50° 60°

0   200 400 600 800 1000 km

0   200   400   600   800 mi

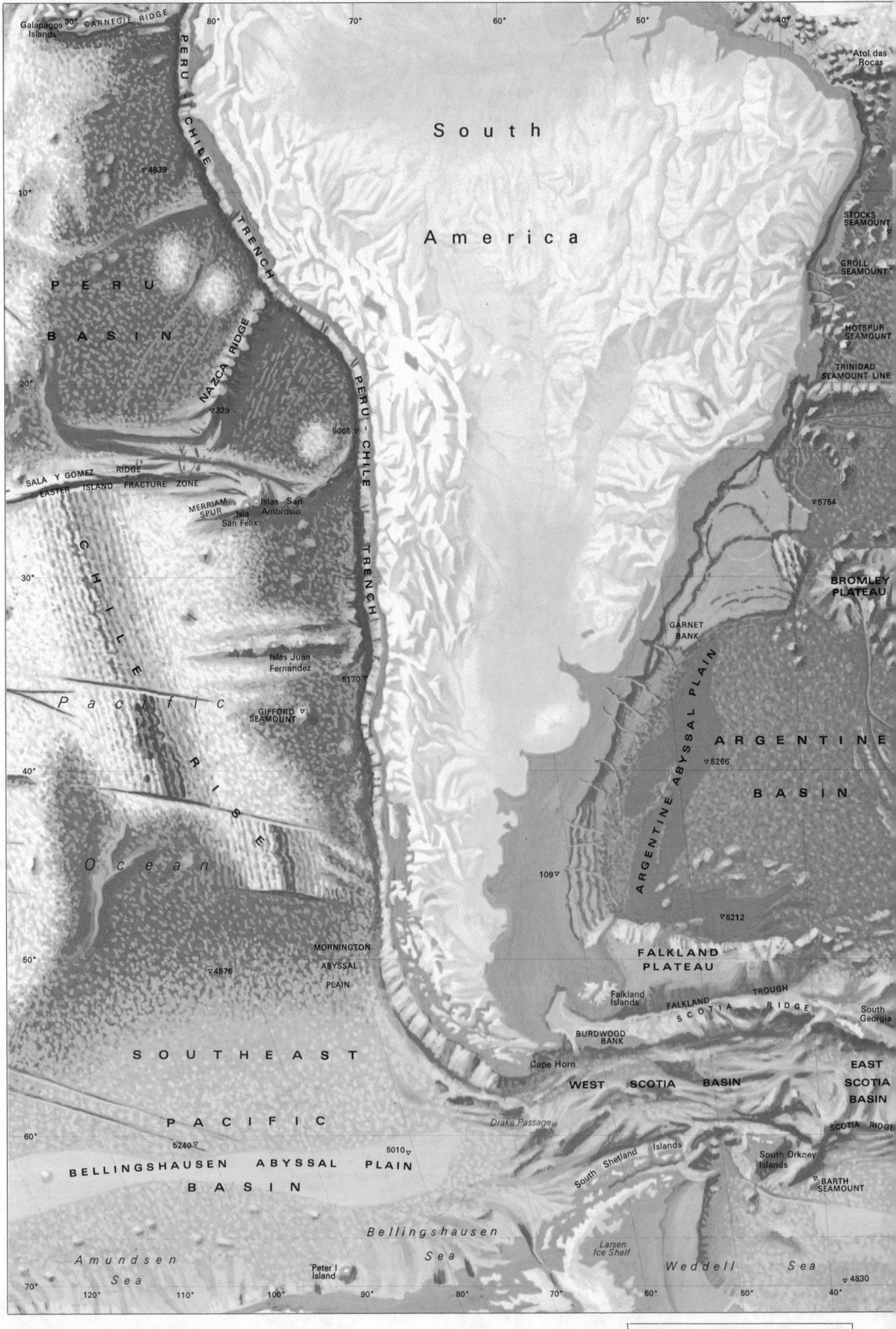

Galapagos 90° CARNEGIE RIDGE 80° 70° 60° 50° 40°
Islands

▽4839

10°

S o u t h

A m e r i c a

Atol das
Rocas

P E R U

B A S I N

STOCKS
SEAMOUNT ▽

GROLL
SEAMOUNT ▽

▽ 7329

HOTSPUR
SEAMOUNT ▽

20°

NAZCA RIDGE

TRINIDAD
SEAMOUNT LINE

8066 ▽

SALA Y GOMEZ RIDGE
EASTER ISLAND FRACTURE ZONE

MERRIAM
SPUR

Islas San
Ambrosio
Isla
San Felix

▽5754

30°

C
H
I
L
E

Islas Juan
Fernandez

5170 ▽

GARNET
BANK

ARGENTINE ABYSSAL PLAIN

BROMLEY
PLATEAU

P a c i f i c

GIFFORD
SEAMOUNT ▽

R
I
S
E

A R G E N T I N E

B A S I N

40°

O c e a n

▽ 5266

MORNINGTON
ABYSSAL

PLAIN

109 ▽

▽ 6212

50°

▽4876

FALKLAND
PLATEAU

S O U T H E A S T

Falkland
Islands

Falkland

SCOTIA
RIDGE

TROUGH

South
Georgia

P A C I F I C

BURDWOOD
BANK

EAST
SCOTIA

BASIN

60°

5240 ▽

Cape Horn

WEST SCOTIA BASIN

SCOTIA RIDGE

5010 ▽

Drake Passage

South Shetland Islands

South Orkney
Islands

B E L L I N G S H A U S E N   A B Y S S A L   P L A I N

B A S I N

South Shetland

▽ BARTH
SEAMOUNT

B e l l i n g s h a u s e n

Larsen
Ice Shelf

W e d d e l l   S e a

A m u n d s e n

S e a

Peter I
Island

S e a

▽ 4830

70°
120° 110° 100° 90° 80° 70° 60° 50° 40°

SOUTHERN ATLANTIC OCEAN   Depths in metres

Colours used are thought to be those of the
various rocks and sediments on the sea floors.
Differences in relief are shown by relief shading.

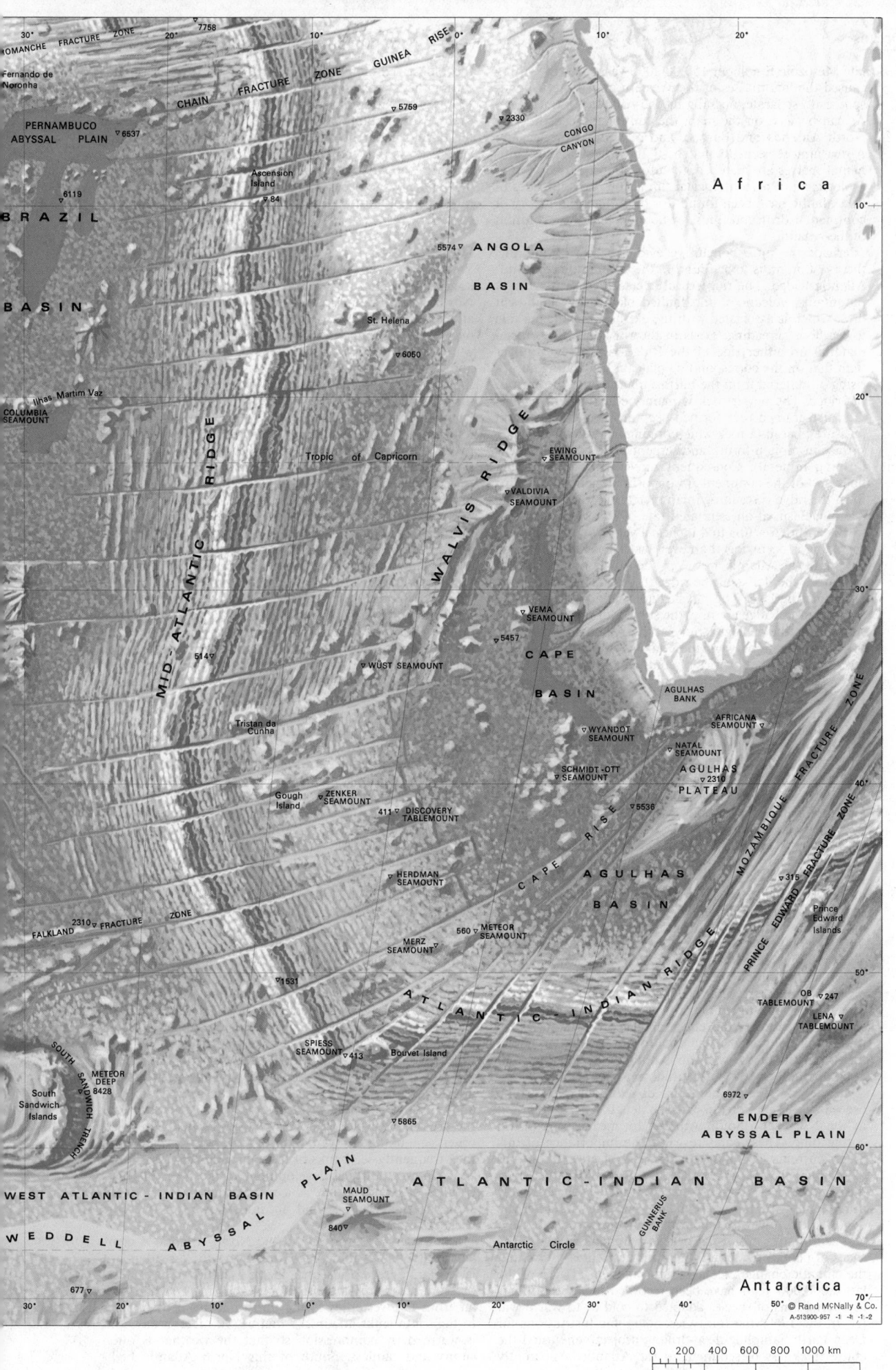

ROMANCHE FRACTURE ZONE
Fernando de Noronha
PERNAMBUCO ABYSSAL PLAIN ▽6537
6119 ▽
B R A Z I L
B A S I N
Ilhas Martim Vaz
COLUMBIA SEAMOUNT

7758
20°
10°
CHAIN FRACTURE ZONE
GUINEA RISE
▽5759
Ascension Island ▽84

M I D - A T L A N T I C   R I D G E

Tropic of Capricorn

514 ▽

Tristan da Cunha

Gough Island ▽ ZENKER SEAMOUNT

411 ▽ DISCOVERY TABLEMOUNT

▽ WÜST SEAMOUNT

HERDMAN SEAMOUNT

2310 ▽ FRACTURE ZONE
FALKLAND

MERZ SEAMOUNT

▽1531

SPIESS SEAMOUNT ▽413

SOUTH SANDWICH
METEOR DEEP 8428
South Sandwich Islands
SOUTH SANDWICH TRENCH

▽5865

WEST ATLANTIC - INDIAN BASIN

W E D D E L L   A B Y S S A L   P L A I N

677 ▽

30°
20°
10°

10°
▽2330
CONGO CANYON

A f r i c a

10°

5574 ▽ A N G O L A
B A S I N

St. Helena
▽6050

20°

W A L V I S   R I D G E

EWING ▽ SEAMOUNT
▽ VALDIVIA SEAMOUNT

30°

▽ VEMA SEAMOUNT
▽5457

C A P E
B A S I N

AGULHAS BANK
AFRICANA SEAMOUNT ▽

▽ WYANDOT SEAMOUNT

NATAL SEAMOUNT
A G U L H A S
▽2310
P L A T E A U

40°

SCHMIDT -OTT ▽ SEAMOUNT

C A P E   R I S E
▽5536

A G U L H A S
B A S I N

560 ▽ METEOR SEAMOUNT

A T L A N T I C - I N D I A N   R I D G E

Bouvet Island

MAUD SEAMOUNT
840 ▽

A T L A N T I C - I N D I A N

Antarctic   Circle

30°
20°
10°
0°
10°
20°
30°

M O Z A M B I Q U E   F R A C T U R E   Z O N E

P R I N C E   E D W A R D   F R A C T U R E   Z O N E
▽315
Prince Edward Islands

50°
OB TABLEMOUNT ▽247
LENA ▽ TABLEMOUNT

6972 ▽

E N D E R B Y
A B Y S S A L   P L A I N
60°

B A S I N
GUNNERUS BANK

Antarctica
40°
50°
70°

© Rand McNally & Co.
A-513900-957 -1 -h -1 -2

0   200 400 600 800 1000 km
0   200   400   600   800 mi

late Mesozoic Era about 150,000,000 years ago; the rifting caused the landmasses of the Western and Eastern hemispheres to separate, opening up the Atlantic Ocean Basin. As can be seen on the map, the continental coastlines of North America and Europe, and of South America and Africa almost seem to match. If the edges of the continental shelves are matched, the fit is almost perfect. Other geological and paleontological similarities on both sides of the Atlantic have been found to substantiate the theory of continental drift and, thus, to help explain the evolution of the Atlantic.

Perhaps the most conclusive evidence bearing out this theory of origin is to be found in the existence of the Mid-Atlantic Ridge. The ridge is, in effect, a long rift zone of mountains, volcanoes, and faulted plateaus. A high-heat flow, which is associated with the extrusion of magna due to sea-floor spreading, exists in the rift zone. The crustal material on either side of the Ridge is notably younger than that on the corresponding plateaus, indicating an uprising of material from the Earth's mantle onto the crest of the ridge. The newer rock is mainly composed of gabbro (a coarse-grained rock formed deep down under heat and pressure), basalt (a rock which originally poured out at the surface in molten form), and serpentine (a common rock-forming mineral). Consequent movement of the ocean floor and of the continents in opposite directions outward from the ridge is resulting in an increasing widening of the Atlantic Basin at an estimated rate of from less than one to 10 centimetres (0.5 to 4 inches) a year. A corresponding spreading is occurring at an even faster pace in the Pacific Ocean; in the Atlantic, however, the slower rate of spreading causes the flanks of the ridge to be built up steeply by accumulating lava. The physiography and geology of the Mid-Atlantic Ridge are now the subject of much scientific study, as is the geologic study of the Atlantic as a whole. Such investigations were undertaken only comparatively recently, since the theories of continental drift and of sea-floor spreading were not generally accepted until the later 1960s. (I.M.J.)

Bottom deposits. The greater part of the bottom of the Atlantic between the Arctic and the Antarctic circles is covered with globigerina ooze. At depths greater than 5,000 metres (16,400 feet) the calcium carbonate content decreases, and the calcareous deposits give way to red clay. On submarine ridges the finer material is lacking, and the shells of pteropod gastropods (mollusks of the gastropod class comprising the snails) may be sufficiently abundant to characterize the deposits as pteropod ooze. Diatom ooze (formed from microscopic unicellular algae having cell walls consisting of or resembling silica) is the most widespread deposit in the high southern latitudes but, contrary to conditions in the Pacific, is not found in northern latitudes. The bottom itself is covered with mud (oozes, globigerina, etc.), 60 percent; sand, 25 percent; and rock, gravel, and shells, 15 percent. Airborne material is abundant off the west coast of Africa where dry offshore winds carry material from the desert regions. In high latitudes ice-rafted detritus, including rock fragment, sometimes showing the effect of glacial abrasion, is an important component. The calcium carbonate content of the sediments of the Atlantic is notably greater than that at comparable depths and latitudes in the Pacific.

After World War II thousands of sediment cores, some exceeding 20 metres (66 feet) in length, were collected in the North and South Atlantic by means of a piston coring tube. These cores revealed the importance of turbidity currents (see above) as carriers of great quantities of sediment to the greatest depths in the Atlantic. Since the last ice age, turbidity currents have been relatively infrequent, with the consequence that the characteristic deposits laid down by them are as a rule covered by several centimetres of normal pelagic sediment. Study of the shells of planktonic foraminifera in these cores shows that the climatic changes, ice ages, and interglacial ages of the last 2,000,000 years have been recorded in the sediments as alternations of species adapted to cold or to warm water. In the 1960s the Joint Oceanographic Institutions for Deep Earth Sampling deep-drilling project penetrated the entire thickness of sediment in the Atlantic. Apparently

the oldest sediments in the Atlantic Basin accumulated during the Mesozoic Era (from 65,000,000 to 225,000,000 years ago). Dating of sediment layers by radioactive decay or by examination of the traces in rocks of reversals of the Earth's magnetic poles (which occur every few million years) shows that the rate of accumulation of pelagic sediment in the Atlantic is between one and two centimetres (0.4 and 0.8 inch) per 1,000 years. Locally, however, the rate is much faster because of deposition by turbidity currents. (D.B.E.)

CLIMATE

Weather over the North Atlantic is largely determined by large-scale wind currents and air masses emanating from North America. In winter the Prevailing Westerly Winds at levels of 3,050 to 12,200 metres (10,000 to 40,000 feet) over North America meander in such a way that a northward bulge (ridge) is generated by and over the Rockies and a southward bulge (trough) over the eastern half of the continent. This geographically forced flow pattern sets the stage for the frequent deployment of cold air masses from Canada and Alaska to the Atlantic seaboard. Large temperature contrasts are thereby frequently set up between the polar outbreaks and mild air from the Pacific or tropical air from the Gulf of Mexico or Gulf Stream. Along these zones of contrast, which are called fronts, wave cyclones (low pressure areas) are formed, and these develop into strong vortices as they move toward Newfoundland and Iceland. Their growth rate largely depends on the temperature contrast, so that winter storms usually become appreciably stronger than summer storms in terms of low pressure, wind, and severe weather.

These cyclonic storms carry heat, moisture, and momentum northward from the tropics and thereby siphon off the excess heat constantly generated by solar heating in the tropics. They also contribute a large share of the energy required to maintain the Prevailing Westerlies of midlatitudes, which are found to be one-half as strong and about 10° further north over the North Atlantic in summer than in winter.

Since even in winter the temperatures of air masses along the eastern seaboard vary considerably from one week to another, the number of coastal storms, their growth rate, and even their paths may vary. Thus, despite the underlying fixed geography, the North Atlantic average pressure distribution, on which the prevailing winds depend, may show large differences from one January to another. In some winters, Iceland may be dominated by prevailing high pressure in contrast to the normally low pressure, and in this case storms leaving the North American coast are blocked and shunted into the Davis Strait and to the Azores. When this happens, warm maritime air masses that normally flow into Europe and account for its mild climate are replaced by cold air from the European Arctic and from Siberia.

Thus, it is not surprising that in winter tremendous amounts of heat are extracted from the western North Atlantic by overflowing cold air masses. Although the transfer of real (sensible) heat is large, the transfer of heat by evaporative losses into the cold, dry air is about three times larger. The oceanic heat losses are soon restored by the flow of warm water associated with the Gulf Stream and other currents. The net effect of the increase in heat and moisture off the east coast is to further stimulate the growth of cyclonic storms. In the United States, an observer looking eastward from a high point over Boston may frequently see banks of large cumulus clouds (clouds showing great vertical development in the form of heaps or piles of cloud) at sea as a manifestation of rapid offshore heating when a cold air mass flows out over the warmer seas.

In latitudes 15° N to 30° N the North Atlantic is characterized by prevailing high pressure with an attendant lack of intense storms and severe weather. These high-pressure areas are part of a globe-encircling belt in which air from the westerlies to the north and from the tropics to the south sinks about 275 metres (900 feet) a day, and is warmed by compression so that the weather is often sunny and rainless. South of this North Atlantic high-

Movement of the ocean floor

Storm patterns

pressure zone the Northeast Trade Winds blow with characteristic steadiness.

Although low latitudes of the North Atlantic are usually storm free, there are notable exceptions during later summer and early fall, when wavy patterns in the east winds occur and occasionally develop into tropical storm vortices or hurricanes. The hurricanes grow by the liberation of vast amounts of heat released when vapour evaporated from the warm ocean is lifted and condensed to bands of heavy showers. Hurricanes may live more than a week, travelling as severe wind vortices steered by upper air currents. Thus they frequently move clockwise around the periphery of the North Atlantic high-pressure belt and into the Prevailing Westerlies, often ending up in the Icelandic area. They have, however, occasionally struck England, and even the Azores, in modified form with abnormal upper-air wind patterns.

Hurricanes

Over the South Atlantic the belt of Prevailing Westerlies extends from about 40° S almost to Antarctica, and the South Atlantic high-pressure area is centred around 30° S. This anticyclone (circulation of winds around a central region of high atmospheric pressure) leads to Southeast Trade Winds on its north side, since the rotation of wind around the high-pressure area is opposite to that in the Northern Hemisphere, due to the Coriolis force (the effect caused by the Earth's rotation). The Southeast Trades meet the Northeast Trades in the zone roughly centring on the Equator called the doldrums or intertropical convergence. Here heavy showers result from ascending warm, moist air that is being continually replaced by moistened trade wind air.

As in the North Atlantic, the weather is usually settled and fine in the latitudes of the high pressure but is unsettled and stormy in the higher latitudes of the Westerlies. The great storminess of the Southern Hemisphere Westerlies largely derives from the temperature contrast set up by the cold Antarctic continent and the adjacent open sea, rather than the west–east contrast described in connection with the North Atlantic storms.

While many regional weather peculiarities may be found over the Atlantic, one of the most interesting, especially to the jet-age traveller, is the large amount and variety of cloud in the Westerlies. These clouds are continually being generated by the large cyclonic storm systems, by warm, moist air masses condensing while moving northward over colder water (in advance of storms), and by rapid vertical ascent (convection) produced by cold air streaming over warm water. Extensive fog banks may frequently be seen in summer off the Grand Bank, when heated air from the continent is forced to flow over the cold Labrador Current.

(J.Na.)

HYDROLOGY

Surface currents. The surface currents of the Atlantic Ocean primarily correspond to the system of prevailing winds with such modifications as are imposed upon the movement of the water by land boundaries. Other factors that influence the currents are regional excesses of evaporation or precipitation, regional differences in cooling or heating, friction, and the Earth's rotation. In the North Atlantic the Trade Winds maintain a fairly steady current from east to west, partly by the direct action of the wind and partly by maintaining an accumulation of warm water on the northern side of the current. A great bulk of water carried by this current continues into the Caribbean Sea and through the Strait of Yucatán into the Gulf of Mexico from which it flows out as a warm and swift current through the Strait of Florida. This current, reinforced by water which has flowed on the eastern side of the Antilles, forms the Gulf Stream off the American east coast. The Gulf Stream follows the coast closely as far as Cape Hatteras; continues at some distance from the coast; and turns more and more toward the east, flowing due east to the south of the Grand Banks of Newfoundland in latitude 40° N. In its further course, the Gulf Stream loses its identity as a well-defined current. The warm surface waters turn to the right and form part of the big eddy circulating around the Sargasso Sea (an area of the North Atlantic between the West Indies and the Azores, charac-

The Gulf Stream

terized by relatively still waters and containing gulfweed [*sargassum*] and specialized marine animals). Somewhat colder water continues toward the European coast as the North Atlantic Current. One diffuse branch turns south, and another branch turns north and splits up still more. One part, the Irminger Current, turns northwest, washes the southeast coast of Iceland and continues past the southern cape of Greenland. The waters of this current become gradually mixed with cold low-salinity water from the Arctic Ocean, but the last traces of Gulf Stream water are still found in latitude 65° N off western Greenland. Another branch of the Gulf Stream system enters the Norwegian Sea to the north of Scotland. One small portion turns south into the North Sea, but the major part follows the coast of Norway to North Cape and continues to Spitsbergen, sending minor branches into the Barents Sea. North of Spitsbergen the current submerges below the less saline waters of the Arctic and continues as a subsurface current clear across the Arctic Ocean where traces of Gulf Stream water of temperature slightly above 0° C (32° F) are found to the north of the New Siberian Islands (north of Siberia, separating the Laptev and East Siberian seas).

The surface layer of the Arctic Ocean, throughout the year, is at a temperature close to the freezing point (at −1.6° C [29° F]) but is of relatively low density because the salinity has been reduced by runoff from the great Siberian rivers. This cold, low-salinity water flows out from the Arctic Ocean along the east coast of Greenland where it is gradually mixed with Atlantic water. It continues around the south cape of Greenland, Cape Farvel; flows north along the west coast of Greenland; turns around again; and, after addition of cold water from Baffin Bay, flows south as the cold Labrador Current. To the south of the Grand Bank of Newfoundland, where this cold water meets the warm waters of the Gulf Stream, it is deflected toward the east and mixes with the Atlantic water. In winter this mixed water, with a salinity of almost 35 parts per thousand, is cooled to a temperature of nearly 3° C (37° F), whereby it attains a density high enough to make it sink to the bottom and spread to the south. On an average for the whole year, 3,999,000 cubic metres (5,230,000 cubic yards) of water sink every second. Similarly, bottom water is formed in winter to the north of Iceland, but this has a considerably lower temperature, about −1° C (30° F). It fills the deep basin of the Norwegian Sea but is prevented from returning directly into the Atlantic Ocean by the submarine ridge that extends from Scotland to Iceland and from Iceland to Greenland; after some intermixing, the Norwegian Basin water eventually crosses the ridge to the Atlantic.

In the southeast part of the North Atlantic, surface water flows into the Mediterranean and high-salinity Mediterranean deep water flows out along the bottom of the strait and spreads over wide areas. Along the west coast of northwest Africa, the Canary Current flows to the southwest and continues across the southern part of the North Atlantic as part of the North Equatorial Current. Low temperatures prevail on the African coast.

The currents of the South Atlantic correspond in many respects to those of the North Atlantic. The Southeast Trade Winds maintain the South Equatorial Current that flows toward the west where it divides into two branches, one that continues to the Northern Hemisphere and enters the Caribbean together with water from the North Equatorial Current, and one which turns south as the Brazil Current, a weak counterpart of the Gulf Stream. Between the Equatorial currents, the Equatorial Countercurrent flows toward the east and is particularly well-developed off Ghana, where it is known as the Guinea Current. To the south of the high-pressure area of the South Atlantic the current flows to the east and turns toward the Equator when reaching the African coast. There the Benguela Current is more pronounced than its northern counterpart, the Canary Current, and is characterized by lower temperatures near the coast, caused by more intense upwelling. Further south the Antarctic Circumpolar Current enters the Atlantic Ocean through Drake Passage, sending one branch, the Falkland Current, a counterpart of the Labrador Current, along the east coast of Argentina. The

African coastal currents

major branch of the Antarctic Circumpolar Current continues to the east into the Indian Ocean, sending another branch to the south and feeding a large clockwise eddy in the Weddell Sea.

Deepwater currents. The deep and bottom water of the North Atlantic, as already stated, consists of surface water sinking between Iceland and Greenland and in the Labrador Sea, from where it spreads to the south. At depths between 910 and 1,980 metres (3,000 and 6,500 feet) the water that flows out from the Mediterranean spreads and can be recognized by an intermediate salinity maximum. With increasing distance from the Mediterranean the salinity decreases because of mixing with other water masses, but traces of Mediterranean water are found as far south as latitude 40° S.

In the Antarctic, bottom water with a temperature of about −0.6° C (31° F), and salinity of 34.65 parts per thousand, is formed by sinking of water from the continental shelf. The temperature of this water is so low that its density is higher than that of the North Atlantic deep water. This water flows toward the north and can be traced as bottom water to 40° N. Surface water sinks at the Antarctic Convergence in about latitude 50° S and spreads to the north as low-salinity water. This Antarctic intermediate water also crosses the Equator and can be traced to about 20° N. Large amounts of the Antarctic bottom water and intermediate water mix with the North Atlantic deep water, return to the south, and rise toward the surface between 50° and 60° S latitude. In rising, the deep water brings quantities of plant nutrients, including phosphates, to the surface layers, and the oceanic circulation therefore accounts for the high productivity of the Antarctic waters.

The deep and bottom waters of the Atlantic are characterized by a high oxygen content because there exists a fairly rapid circulation. The waters have sunk from the surface where they became saturated with oxygen by contact with the air.

TEMPERATURE AND SALINITY

Temperature. The distribution of the sea-surface temperature is closely related to the character of the currents. The waters of the North Equatorial Currents spread to the north and those of the South Equatorial Current spread both north and south when reaching the east coasts of North and South America and, correspondingly, the region of high surface temperature is wide off the American east coasts but narrow off the African coast, where the Canary Current and the Benguela Current carry cold water toward the Equator. Therefore, in latitudes about 10° S to 30° S and 10° N to 30° N the sea surface is warmer off the eastern coast than off the western, but poleward of 30° this feature is reversed. This reversal is barely evident in the South Atlantic, where the Falkland Current carries cold water up to about latitude 30° S (in August to 25° S), but is conspicuous in the North Atlantic. There the
The
Labrador
Current
Labrador Current brings cold water to latitude 40° N, whereas the extreme branches of the Gulf Stream system carry warm water along the coast of Norway where ports remain ice-free even in latitude 71° N. The contrast between the South and the North Atlantic is related to the surface currents, which in turn reflect the action of the prevailing winds and the effect of the shape of the coasts. Where the Falkland Current meets the Brazil Current, and where the Labrador Current meets the Gulf Stream, the surface temperature changes rapidly within a very short distance. The change is particularly striking when passing from the Gulf Stream to the Labrador Current where the interface is called "the cold wall."

In the Tropics the surface temperature is controlled by climatological factors to such an extent that it is nearly uniform, and differences related to currents do not appear. Such differences are very marked, however, at a depth of about 200 metres (650 feet), where in latitude 6° to 7° N the temperature is 10° C (50° F), whereas it is 20° C (68° F) in latitude 20° N. The existence of the cold water at shallow depths to the north of the Equator should not be interpreted as showing that deep water rises to the surface. The temperature distribution is directly related to

the existence of Equatorial currents—which flow toward the west, and within which the warm water must be to the right in the Northern Hemisphere and to the left in the Southern Hemisphere.

The distribution of temperature at greater depths has already been touched upon when discussing the deep water circulation. In the North Atlantic, the temperature decreases slowly toward the bottom from a value of about 5° C (41° F) at 910 metres to about 2.5° C (36.5° F) at the bottom. In the South Atlantic, up to latitude 40° S, the temperature first decreases to a minimum between 910 and 1,220 metres, increases again and reaches a maximum of 2° to 4° C (36° to 39° F) at about 1,980 metres, indicating the flow of North Atlantic deep water, and then decreases to less than 1° C (34° F) at the bottom where Antarctic bottom water is encountered. To the south of 40° S low temperatures prevail throughout, and near Antarctica a large body of water has a temperature below 0° C.

Salinity. The surface waters of the North Atlantic Ocean have a higher salinity than those of any other ocean, reaching values exceeding 37 parts per thousand in latitudes 20° to 30° N. The salinity distribution is also related to the currents but is greatly influenced by evaporation and precipitation. It has been shown that for each ocean the average surface salinity can be taken as equal to a constant basic value plus a correction that is directly proportional to the difference between evaporation and precipitation.
Evapora-
tion and
precipita-
tion
The basic salinity value differs from one ocean to another and is highest for the North Atlantic. It is 35.5 parts per thousand for the North Atlantic and 34.5 for the South Atlantic. This difference can be explained as the effect of the intense evaporation in the Mediterranean and the outflow from that sea of high-salinity water that maintains the salinity of the North Atlantic at a higher level than that characteristic of any other ocean. On an average for every latitude range, say 0° to 5° N, and so on, the deviations from the basic value are proportional to the difference between evaporation and precipitation. Near the Equator precipitation dominates, and surface salinities of about 35 parts per thousand are encountered; but in latitudes 20° to 25° N and about 20° S evaporation greatly exceeds precipitation, and over large areas the surface salinity is above 37 parts per thousand. Proceeding poleward precipitation again becomes greater than evaporation, and, correspondingly, the surface salinity decreases, in large areas to values below 34 parts per thousand. Superimposed upon these general features are the effects of currents, which again are more striking in the North Atlantic where Atlantic water of salinity exceeding 35 parts per thousand is carried as far north as Spitsbergen in latitude 78° N, and Arctic water of salinity below 34 parts per thousand is carried south to nearly 45° N off Newfoundland. North of 40° N the sea-surface isohalines (lines of equal salinity) run nearly in a north–south direction, whereas south of 45° S they run east–west. In adjacent seas the salinity depends also upon the runoff from rivers. In the Mediterranean and the Red Sea, where the runoff is small and evaporation is great, high salinities prevail; in the Black Sea and in the Baltic, where large rivers empty, the salinity is low. In the inner part of the Gulf of Bothnia between Sweden and Finland, the water is nearly fresh. The surface water of the Polar Sea has a salinity of 30 to 33 parts per thousand because of admixture of freshwater from the great Siberian rivers.
(H.U.S./R.H.Fl./C.A.B.)

ECONOMIC RESOURCES

Biological resources. The Atlantic Ocean contains six of the world's 14 major fishing grounds. They are roughly
Principal
fishing
grounds
situated in the northwest, northeast, west central, east central, southwest, and southeast Atlantic.

Regions of high fertility, supporting large quantities of marine life, lie along the Atlantic seaboard of the North and South American continents. The waters of the Grand Bank off Newfoundland are among the most populous fishing grounds in the world. Here, where the waters of the Gulf Stream and Labrador Current merge, herring and menhaden (a fish resembling a shad but with a more compressed body) thrive in great numbers. The northeast Atlantic and North Sea have long been traditional fishing grounds, but are in danger of being overfished. Since the 1950s, fishing has increased south of the Equator, with large quantities of tuna, hake, and herring being caught. The waters off the Florida Keys, especially Key West, abound in shrimp and sponges. The calm Sargasso Sea, bounded on the east by the Canary Current and on the west by the Gulf Stream, is the breeding ground of all the migratory eels of both Europe and North America. Clams, lobsters, crabs, and octopus are other important biological resources.

Mineral resources. Ever since the British "Challenger" Expedition conducted a pioneering oceanographic survey from 1872 to 1876, it has been known that the Atlantic Ocean contains large stores of manganese nodules. These nodules are distributed most abundantly in the red clay bottom deposits throughout 10 percent of the pelagic (oceanic) area. Their composition is roughly 24 percent manganese and 14 percent iron; the nodules are formed of concentric layers, anywhere from several micrometres (a micrometre is a millionth part of a metre) in size to large slabs.

Large diamond deposits have also been located off the coast of South West Africa/Namibia: the diamonds were washed into the ocean millions of years ago. The diamond-iferous sediments vary in thickness from 1.8 to 9 metres (6 to 30 feet); the stones are almost all of gem quality, and few industrial diamonds are found among them. The richest area so far located is along the southwest African coastline between Hottentotbaai and Oranjemund.

Petroleum, natural gas, and sulfur are found in the Gulf of Mexico and off the west central coast of Africa. Petroleum and gas represent 90 percent of the Atlantic's available mineral resources; they occur in the sediments of the continental rise.

Petroleum and gas reserves

Smaller deposits of coal and tin are found in sediments off the British Isles. Salt occurs along most of the Atlantic seaboard, and 70 percent of the world's bromine is extracted from the ocean waters. The water of the ocean itself, in desalinated form, constitutes a potential, though still extremely expensive, resource.

Resource exploitation. Exploitation in the second half of the 20th century has produced a dangerous shortage of many species of fish in several of the traditional fishing grounds. The Atlantic at the present time yields 40 percent of the world's catch of fish. The situation is most serious in the North Atlantic, where several varieties of fish, including flounders, ocean perch, cod, hake, herring, and tuna, are being overfished. South of the Equator, the yield, except for tuna and pilchard, is not yet in danger. Tuna has been the most exploited species, and, as a result, yields are becoming more and more meagre not only in the Atlantic but also in other oceans.

No comparable problem, however, faces the mining industry. A single diamond dredge, for instance, sweeps up by suction roughly $420,000 worth of diamonds off the coast of South West Africa/Namibia every day, and the resources are just beginning to be tapped. There seems to be an almost unlimited reserve of manganese nodules, but they have as yet been little exploited because it is still far more expensive to reclaim them from the sea than to mine manganese on land. Petroleum and natural gas reserves are being exploited off the coast of southern United States in the Gulf of Mexico, and petroleum resources are also being tapped in European and African territorial waters.

HISTORY

Exploration. The story of the surface exploration of the Atlantic is well known. Centuries before the age of Columbus, the Vikings in their 11th-century wooden ships charted the waters around Greenland, Iceland, and northeastern North America. After the Portuguese discovery of Madeira and the Azores in the 15th century, and the transatlantic voyage of Christopher Columbus in 1492 to 1493, Europeans of many nationalities joined in the exploration of the lands bordering the Atlantic's western shores. Not much scientific attention, however, was paid to the Atlantic until 1842, when a pioneering oceanographic study of the Atlantic and the Pacific was made by Lieutenant Matthew Fontaine Maury of the United States Navy. Maury compiled charts on winds and

currents, collected other data, and prepared an extensive treatise on the Gulf Stream, thus paving the way for the further studies of the Atlantic. A Scottish naturalist, Sir C. Wyville Thomson, discovered the Mid-Atlantic Ridge on the "Challenger" expedition already mentioned, using temperature variations as indicators that a vast barrier existed below the surface. His findings were substantiated by a German expedition of 1925–27, which verified the presence of a distinct mountain range.

Exploration was not, however, conducted solely from the surface. As interest in oceanography increased, such deep-sea vehicles as Trieste I, a deep-sea bathyscaph built for Jacques Piccard, a member of a well-known Swiss family of scientists and explorers, were constructed, and used to obtain further information about the ocean's depths. Many different types of submarine have also been used to gather information.

New methods of underwater research

The "Glomar Challenger," a United States deep-sea drilling ship, made extensive surveys of Atlantic and adjacent waters; in 1970 it discovered a vast oil field 3,660 metres (12,000 feet) below the Gulf of Mexico. Yet another technique is to establish an underwater habitat in order to study marine environments for an extended period. One such habitat, the United States Sealab, housed four aquanauts for three weeks in waters off Bermuda, enabling them to study marine life in its natural environment.

Naval predominance. Following early Portuguese and other explorations, Spain became the dominant naval power in the Atlantic in the 16th century. Later, Spain's naval supremacy was challenged by French, British, and Dutch ships. In the 19th century, Britain established a naval supremacy that endured until the first half of the 20th century, during which United States seapower developed. At the present time both the United States and the Soviet Union have powerful naval forces in Atlantic waters, and are competing with each other in oceanographic research and its applications.

Navigation. The areas of congested sea traffic all lie in the North Atlantic. As ice conditions occur at certain times of the year, the International Convention for the Safety of Life at Sea was adopted in 1948 in order to systematize and regulate use of shipping lanes. Each lane is designated for use at a certain time of year. Countries are also assigned their own routes in order to relieve traffic congestion; for instance, the United States is assigned a route far to the south only when extreme ice conditions occur. An International Ice Patrol, formed and operated by the United States Coast Guard, maintains surveillance of icebergs. The United States Navy and the Royal Canadian Air Force fly air reconnaissance flights over both the Atlantic and Arctic oceans for the same purpose, while certain European nations maintain surveillance in the Baltic and North seas. The Soviet northern sea route, where many icebergs are to be found, is also kept under close observation. Hardly any regular ice reconnaissance flights are flown south of the Equator, but satellite observations of Antarctic ice limits have been recorded since the 1970s.

Among the many harbours on the Atlantic, the port of Amsterdam, used by ships from all over the world, is perhaps the busiest. Punta Arenas in Chile is the southernmost port in the South Atlantic, and Archangel in the Soviet Union is the northernmost North Atlantic port.

(I.M.J./Ed.)

The Pacific Ocean

Of the three oceans that extend northward from the Antarctic continent, the Pacific, occupying about a third of the surface of the terrestrial globe, is by far the largest. Its area, excluding adjacent seas, encompasses about 165,-250,000 square kilometres (63,800,000 square miles). It has double the area and more than double the water volume of the Atlantic—the next largest division of the hydrosphere. Its area exceeds that of the whole land surface of the globe, Antarctica included, with Africa counted twice. The Pacific stretches from the shores of Antarctica to the Bering Strait through 135° of latitude, or for 15,500 kilometres (9,600 miles). Its greatest longitudinal extent measures 21,300 kilometres (13,235 miles) along the par-

Extent of the Pacific

allel of 5° N, between the coasts of Colombia in South America and the Malay Peninsula in Asia. The mean depth of the Pacific (excluding adjacent seas) is 4,280 metres (14,050 feet). Its greatest known depth is 11,034 metres (36,200 feet)—in the Mariana Trench.

The Pacific and Arctic systems mingle their waters in the Northern Hemisphere at the shallow Bering Strait, and in the Southern Hemisphere the Pacific and Atlantic mix in the relatively narrow Drake Passage between Tierra del Fuego in South America and Graham Land in Antarctica. The separation between the Pacific and Indian oceans is less distinct; here, it is considered to lie along the line of islands extending eastward from Sumatra, through Java to Timor, thence across the Timor Sea to Cape Londonderry in Australia. To the south of Australia the boundary extends across the Bass Strait and thence from Tasmania to Antarctica.

Because of the pattern of major mountain systems of the globe, a relatively small proportion (one-seventh) of the total continental drainage enters the Pacific—*i.e.,* a total drainage area of not more than about three times that of Australia. Of the rivers that drain into the Pacific, those of China and Southeast Asia are of the greatest importance; the basins of these rivers support more than one-quarter of the world's population.

The eastern boundary of the Pacific is associated with the American Cordilleran mountain system, which stretches from Alaska in the north to Tierra del Fuego in the south. Except for its extreme northern and southern sections, which are characterized by fjords and their numerous offlying islands, and except for the deeply indented Gulf of California, the coastal boundary is relatively regular and the continental shelf narrow. The western, or Asiatic, coastal boundary, in contrast, is irregular. Although the mountain systems there lie roughly parallel to the coast, as they do on the eastern Pacific coastlands, the western Pacific is noted for its many peripheral seas. From north to south they include the Bering Sea, Sea of Okhotsk, the Sea of Japan, the Yellow Sea, the East China Sea, and the South China Sea. Their eastern boundaries are formed by southward-jutting peninsulas or by island arcs or both. It is of oceanographic significance that the great rivers of eastern Asia—including the Amur, the Yellow River, the Yangtze, the Hsi Chiang, and the Mekong—enter the Pacific indirectly by way of peripheral seas.

PHYSIOGRAPHY

Relief. The Pacific Basin may conveniently be divided into three major physiographic regions, the eastern, western, and central Pacific regions.

Eastern region. The eastern region, which extends southward from Alaska to Tierra del Fuego, is relatively narrow and is associated with the American Cordilleran system of almost unbroken mountain chains, the coastal ranges of which rise steeply from the western American shores. The continental shelf, which runs parallel to it, is steep and comparatively narrow. Significant oceanic trenches in this region are the Acapulco and Guatemala trenches in the North Pacific and the Peru–Chile Trench in the South Pacific.

Western region. The second physiographic province is the western region, the seaward boundary of which is marked by a broken line of oceanic trenches, extending from the Aleutian Trench in the north through the Kuril and Japan trenches and southward to the Tonga and Kermadec trenches, terminating close to the southeast of North Island, New Zealand. The western region has a structure more complex than that of the eastern region. Characteristically associated with the ocean trenches of the western region are festoons either of peninsulas or islands or both. The islands, which include those of Japan as well as numerous small islands, represent the upper parts of mountain systems that rise abruptly from the deep ocean floor. The island clusters of the western Pacific form the boundaries of the several wide and deep continental seas of the region.

Central Pacific region. The third province is the central Pacific region lying between the boundaries of the eastern and western regions. The largest and the most geologically

stable of the structural provinces of the Earth's crust, it is characterized by expansive areas of low relief, lying at a general depth of about 4,570 metres (15,000 feet) below the surface.

Principal ridges and basins. To the east of the meridian of 150° W the relief of the ocean floor is considerably less pronounced than it is to the west. In the eastern Pacific the Cocos Ridge extends southwestward from the Central American isthmus to the Galápagos Islands. To the southwest of the Galápagos lies the Southeast Pacific Basin, which is separated by the extensive Sala y Gomez Ridge from the Southeast Pacific Basin, which, in turn, is separated from the Southwest Pacific Basin by the indeterminate Pacific-Antarctic Ridge, which runs from the Southeastern Pacific Plateau to Antarctica in the vicinity of 150° W.

Extending southward from the Tasman Basin (between New Zealand and East Australia) is the Macquarie Ridge, which forms a significant boundary between the deep waters of the Pacific and Indian oceans. The Hawaiian Ridge extends westward from Hawaii to the meridian of 180°.

The submerged parts of the series of ridges that are capped by the island archipelagoes of the western Pacific are continuous and are to be found at depths of less than about 610 metres (2,000 feet). These ridges include the Aleutian ridge in the northwest Pacific; the series of ridges extending southward through the Kurils, Bonin, Marianas, Yap, and Patou; those extending eastward from Patou including the Bismarck, Solomons, and Santa Cruz ridges; and finally the ridges extending southward from which rise the Samoan islands, Tonga, Kermadec, Chatham, and Macquarie.

Islands. The islands of the western region—including the Aleutians, Kurils, Ryukyus, Taiwan, the Philippines, Indonesia, New Guinea, and New Zealand—are continental in character. Geologically they consist, in part, of sedimentary rocks, and their structures are not dissimilar to those of the coastal mountain ranges of the adjacent continent. Most are sufficiently large for oceanic climatic influences not to be pervasive.

A geologically important boundary between the continental, or "high" islands, and the numerous truly oceanic, or "low" islands, of the Pacific is the Andesite Line. In the north and west Pacific the Andesite Line follows close to seaward the trend of the island arcs from the Aleutians southward to the Yap and Patou arcs, thence eastward through the Bismarcks, Solomons, and Santa Cruz, and thence southward through Samoa, Tonga, Chatham, and Macquarie to Antarctica. Within that boundary, islands are essentially of basalt, a basic igneous rock characteristic of ocean basins; basalt contrasts with the more acid igneous rocks associated with volcanic activity in continental areas.

The numerous "oceanic" islands of the Pacific are unevenly distributed. They lie, in the main, between the Tropics of Cancer and of Capricorn and occur in great numbers in the western Pacific. The northernmost chain of oceanic islands is associated with the Hawaiian Ridge. The Hawaiian archipelago consists of about 2,000 islands, although the term Hawaiian Islands is usually applied to the small group that lies at the eastern end of the archipelago.

The numerous small islands of Micronesia lie mainly north of the Equator and to the west of the 180th meridian. Nearly all are coralline; the principal groups are the Marianas, the Marshalls, the Carolines, and the Gilbert and Ellice Islands.

To the south of Micronesia lie the islands of Melanesia, most of which are small coral islands. The region's physiography is dominated by a group of large continental islands, however, including New Guinea. The principal groups of the Melanesian islands are the Bismarck Archipelago, the Solomons, the New Hebrides, New Caledonia, and Fiji.

The immense triangular area, with Hawaii in the north, Easter Island in the southeast, and New Zealand in the southwest is peppered with the multitude of islands known as Polynesia. The main Polynesian groups are the Phoenix Islands, Samoa, Tonga, the Cook Islands, Society Islands, Tuamotu, and the Marquesas.

Margin notes:

Oceanic trenches

"High" islands and "low" islands

GEOLOGY

Tectonic processes and features. Corroboratory evidence drawn from various geophysical fields—seismology, volcanology, gravimetry (the measurement of weight or density), and paleomagnetism (the study of the traces of magnetic polarization of rocks from previous eras)—points to the general validity of the theory of continental drift (see above).

Formation of the Pacific island arcs

The Pacific island arcs, or epicontinental (*i.e.,* near-continental) islands as they are sometimes called, are believed to have originated in the lateral thrusting of the Asian continental crust toward and over the Pacific floor, the shapes of the island arcs corresponding to the intersections of the thrust planes with the spherical Earth's surface. The intense folding and faulting along the volcanic zone of the western Pacific provide unmistakable evidence of orogenic (mountain-building) forces at work. The deep basins that lie between the Asian continent and the island arcs were evidently caused by the local downfolding of the Earth's crust; the island arcs themselves, along the line of which volcanic and seismic activity are pronounced, are the result of weakening of crustal strata by strong upfolding. On the oceanic side of the island arcs, intense downfolding has resulted in the formation of the deep trenches that fringe the line of the island arcs.

The character of the eastern marginal physiographic region of the Pacific suggests a lateral movement of the North American and South American continents westward over the Pacific floor. The floor of the northeastern Pacific is remarkable for its several major fracture zones, which extend east and west and which, in some instances, are identifiable over distances of thousands of miles.

Formation of oceanic islands. Of great geological interest are the guyots and the oceanic islands of the Pacific. The numerous tropical islands of the Pacific are mainly coralline. The three principal types of coral reef—fringing, barrier, and atoll, as well as the flat-topped guyots, which are abundant on the ocean floor in extratropical latitudes within the Pacific—are explained by the slow subsidence theory advanced by the English naturalist Charles Darwin during the 19th century (see above).

Bottom deposits. Apart from the narrow coastal zone of the eastern region and the broad continental seas of the western region, the Pacific is floored with pelagic (*i.e.,* oceanic) material derived from the remains of marine organisms that once inhabited the waters lying above. Red or brown radiolarian ooze is found along the zone of the North Equatorial Current, east of the meridian of 170° W, and on the floors of some deep Indonesian basins. A belt of diatom ooze occurs between the parallels of 45° and 60° S and across the northern Pacific, between Japan and Alaska. *Globigerina* ooze occurs in the shallower parts of the South Pacific, the dissolving power of the sea water at great depths being sufficient to dissolve calcareous material to such an extent that calcareous oozes are not generally found at depths in excess of about 4,570 metres. Silica-containing material, such as radiolarian and diatom ooze, is found at greater depths, but even these siliceous remains are dissolved at very great depths, where the characteristic deposit is red clay. Red clay, which covers no less than half the Pacific floor, is believed to be formed of colloidal (very finely divided) clays derived essentially from the land.

Among the many different forms of land-derived muds (formed by the erosive action of rivers, tides, and currents) that floor the continental shelves and slopes of the Pacific, the yellow mud of the Yellow Sea is of particular interest. The mud is conveyed to the sea bed by the Huang Ho that drains a vast area of North China blanketed with loess, a fine-grained soil.

Occurrences of ocean-floor ooze

CLIMATE

The wind and pressure systems of the Pacific conform closely with the so-called planetary system—*i.e.,* the pattern of air pressure and the consequent wind pattern that develops when the Earth's surface (land or sea) is smooth. This conformity is partly a consequence of the great extent of the Pacific and the comparative uniformity of its surface. Climatic conditions in the South and East Pacific,

where the steadiness of the Trade Winds and the Westerlies is remarkable, are the most uniform on the globe. In the North Pacific, however, conditions are not so uniform, particularly the considerable climatic differences between the eastern and western regions in the same latitude. The rigour of the winters off the east coast of the Soviet Union, for instance, contrasts sharply with the relative mildness of winters in the region of British Columbia.

Uniformity of climate

The Trade Winds. The Trade Winds of the Pacific represent the eastern and equatorial parts of the air-circulation system; they move around the subtropical high-pressure zones centred, respectively, over the northeast and southeast Pacific between the 30th and 40th parallels N and S. The obliquity of the ecliptic (the term used to denote the angle, approximately 23$^{1}/_{2}$°, contained between the planes of the Earth's rotation on its axis and its revolution around the Sun) limits the seasonal shifting of the Pacific Trade-Wind belts to about 5° of latitude. The Easterly Winds in between the two subtropical zones form the intertropical air flow, which is most pronounced in the eastern Pacific.

The Trade Winds, especially in the eastern Pacific, convey relatively cool air toward the Equator; in moving, the air comes in contact with the sea and thus becomes increasingly humid and warm, and high lapse rate (the term used to denote the rate of change of air temperature with increasing height above sea or land surface) result. The average wind speed of the Pacific Trade Winds is about 13 knots (24 kilometres per hour). The weather in the Trade-Wind belts is normally fine, with relatively little cloud; such cloud as there is characteristically takes the form of broken cumulus (small piles of cloud with flat bases) at about 610 metres above sea level. Precipitation, usually in the form of light showers, is slight; visibility is generally excellent.

Off the west coasts of the American continent in the Trade-Wind belts, upwelling of cold, subsurface water results in the overlying air being cooled below its dew point (the air temperature below which vapour condenses as dew), with the consequent formation of widespread and low, thick clouds. Fog in these regions is not uncommon.

The equatorial region, in which the Trade Winds of the Northern and Southern hemispheres converge, is the region of calms or light variable breezes and is known as the doldrums.

Tropical storms. Although, in general, the climatic conditions of the Trade-Wind belts are characteristically regular and uniform, storms of great violence do originate there. In such storms, winds of exceptionally great force blow around a centre of exceedingly low sea-level air pressure. These are the tropical storms known in the western Pacific as typhoons. The mechanism that operates to trigger a tropical storm is not understood completely, but the energy required to engender and sustain a storm is undoubtedly related to the enormous quantity of latent heat associated with tropical maritime air.

Typhoons of the western Pacific

Ideal conditions for the development of tropical storms occur in the western Pacific between the parallels of 5° and 25° N during late summer and early autumn. The regions to the east of the Philippines and in the South and East China seas are notorious for these storms, which imperil shipping and often cause severe coastal flooding, accompanied by loss of life and property.

The Westerlies. Within the belts of the Westerly Winds, cold Easterly Winds from polar regions meet the warm Westerly Winds of the middle latitudes, causing the formation of the travelling depressions characteristic of middle latitudes. The zone of convergence, or polar front, is most strongly developed in winter when the contrast in temperature and humidity of the air between the converging flows is greatest.

The Westerlies in the Southern Hemisphere are steady and strong, and "brave west winds" is an apt name. The gales that accompany the depressions have led to the term roaring forties named for the latitudinal zone in which the storm winds are of greatest frequency.

The monsoon regime. The western Pacific is subject to a seasonal climatic regime, which replaces the planetary system. This is the regime of the monsoon (rain-bearing winds), which is associated with the heating of the Asian

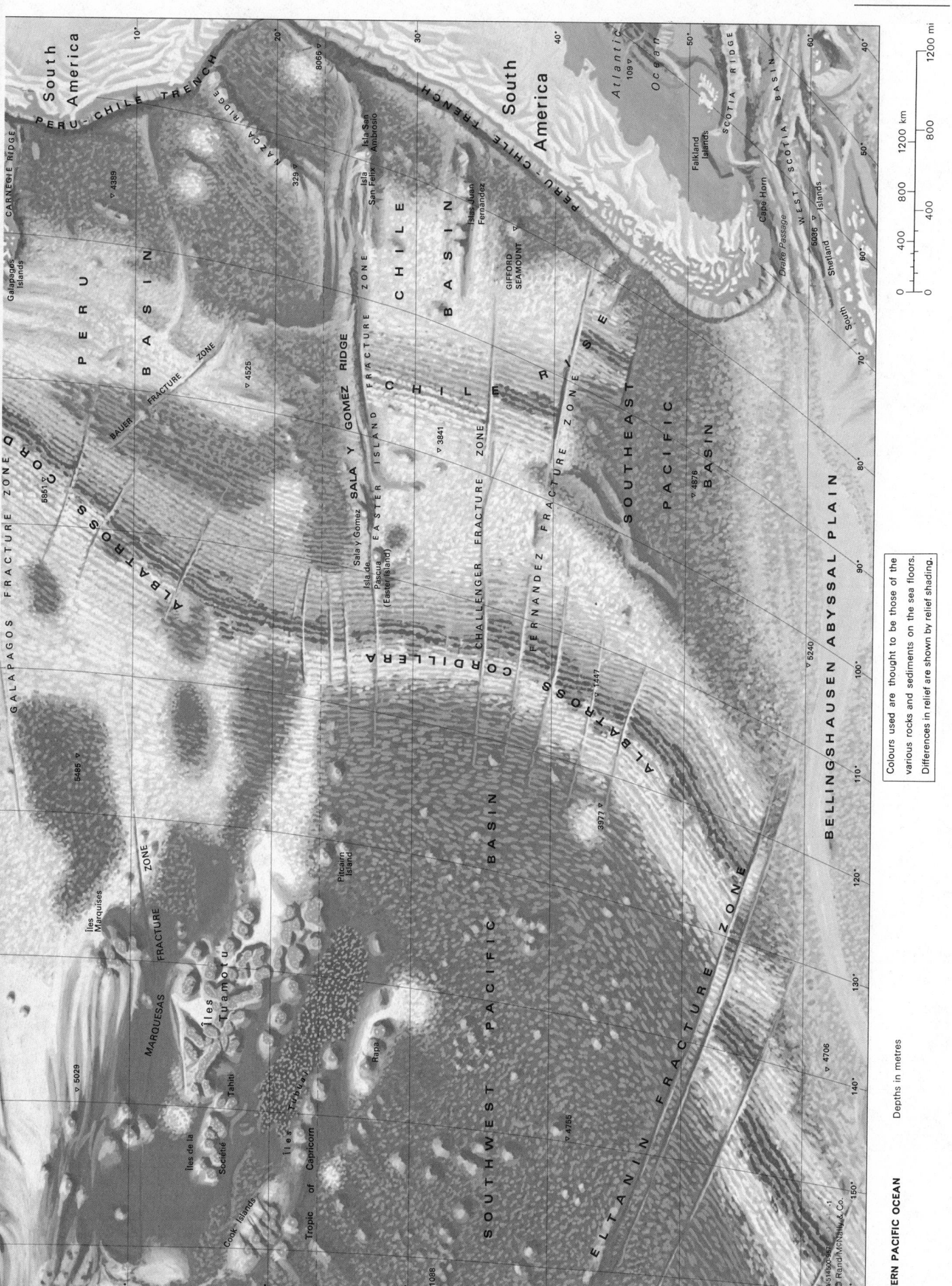

South America

PERU-CHILE TRENCH

CARNEGIE RIDGE

Galapagos Islands

NAZCA RIDGE

▽ 4389

329 ▽

8066 ▽

P E R U   B A S I N

Isla San Felix

Isla San Ambrosio

GALAPAGOS FRACTURE ZONE

BAUER FRACTURE ZONE

FRACTURE   ZONE

▽ 4525

5851 ▽

SALA Y GOMEZ RIDGE

EASTER ISLAND FRACTURE ZONE

FRACTURE ZONE

C H I L E   B A S I N

GIFFORD SEAMOUNT

Islas Juan Fernandez

PERU CHILE TRENCH

South America

Atlantic   Ocean

109 ▽

SCOTIA RIDGE

Falkland Islands

Cape Horn

Drake Passage

5086 ▽

SCOTIA RIDGE

South Shetland Islands

WEST SCOTIA

SCOTIA BASIN

C O R D I L L E R A

Sala y Gomez

Isla de Pascua (Easter Island)

▽ 3841

CHALLENGER FRACTURE ZONE

FERNANDEZ FRACTURE ZONE

FRACTURE ZONE

S E

S O U T H E A S T   P A C I F I C

B A S I N

▽ 4876

▽ 5240

A L B A T R O S S

A L B A T R O S S   C O R D I L L E R A

1347 ▽

3977 ▽

B E L L I N G S H A U S E N   A B Y S S A L   P L A I N

Îles Marquises

FRACTURE   ZONE

MARQUESAS FRACTURE ZONE

5485 ▽

5029 ▽

Îles Tuamotu

Tahiti

Îles de la Société

Cook Islands

Tropic   of   Capricorn

Rapa

Pitcairn Island

▽ 4755

▽ 4706

S O U T H W E S T   P A C I F I C   B A S I N

E L T A N I N   F R A C T U R E   Z O N E

1098 ▽

Îles Tubuai

A51H000-367
© Rand McNally & Co.

160°

150°

140°

130°

120°

110°

100°

90°

80°

70°

60°

50°

40°

30°

20°

10°

EASTERN PACIFIC OCEAN

Depths in metres

Colours used are thought to be those of the various rocks and sediments on the sea floors. Differences in relief are shown by relief shading.

0   400   800   1200 km

0   400   800   1200 mi

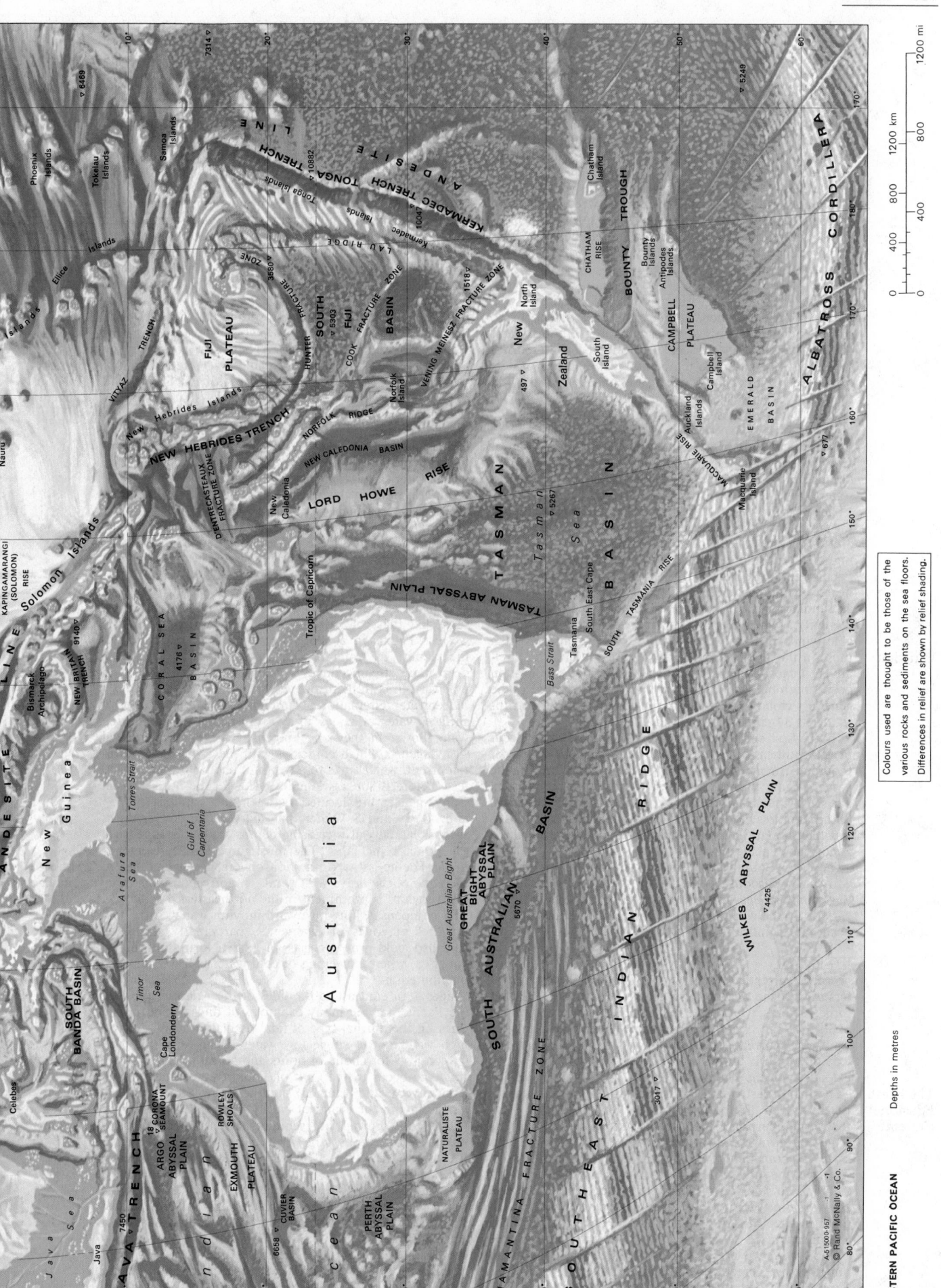

Phoenix Islands

Tokelau Islands

Samoa Islands

▽6469

7314 ▽

Ellice Islands

Islands

Nauru

VITYAZ TRENCH

FIJI PLATEAU

New Hebrides Islands

NEW HEBRIDES TRENCH

D'ENTRECASTEAUX FRACTURE ZONE

HUNTER

FRACTURE ZONE

3580 ▽

SOUTH FIJI
▽5303

COOK FRACTURE ZONE

BASIN

LAU RIDGE

Tonga Islands

▽10882

TONGA TRENCH

Kermadec Islands

10047 ▽

KERMADEC TRENCH

A N D E S I T E

L I N E

Chatham Island

Chatham Rise

BOUNTY TROUGH

Bounty Islands

Antipodes Islands

CAMPBELL PLATEAU

Campbell Island

EMERALD BASIN

▽677

ALBATROSS CORDILLERA

VENING MEINESZ FRACTURE ZONE 1518 ▽

New
Zealand

497 ▽

Norfolk Island

NORFOLK RIDGE

New Caledonia BASIN

New Caledonia

LORD HOWE RISE

T A S M A N

North Island

South Island

Auckland Islands

MACQUARIE RISE

RISE

Tasman Sea

▽5267

Macquarie Island

A N D E S I T E

L I N E

KAPINGAMARANGI (SOLOMON) RISE

Solomon Islands

Bismarck Archipelago

NEW BRITAIN TRENCH 9140 ▽

CORAL SEA

4176 ▽

BASIN

Tropic of Capricorn

TASMAN ABYSSAL PLAIN

T A S M A N

S E A   B A S I N

South East Cape

SOUTH TASMANIA RISE

Celebes

SOUTH BANDA BASIN

JAVA TRENCH

7450

ARGO ABYSSAL PLAIN

18 CORONA SEAMOUNT

ROWLEY SHOALS

EXMOUTH PLATEAU

6658 ▽ CUVIER BASIN

PERTH ABYSSAL PLAIN

New Guinea

Arafura Sea

Timor Sea

Torres Strait

Gulf of Carpentaria

Cape Londonderry

A u s t r a l i a

Great Australian Bight

GREAT AUSTRALIAN BIGHT

GREAT AUSTRALIAN ABYSSAL PLAIN

5670 ▽

SOUTH AUSTRALIAN BASIN

NATURALISTE PLATEAU

DIAMANTINA FRACTURE ZONE

S O U T H E A S T

I N D I A N

R I D G E

WILKES ABYSSAL PLAIN

▽4425

3017 ▽

F R A C T U R E   Z O N E

▽ –1

Bass Strait

Tasmania

J a v a
S e a

Java

I n d i a n

O c e a n

▽5249

S o u t h E a s t

WESTERN PACIFIC OCEAN

A-515000-957

© Rand McNally & Co.

Depths in metres

Colours used are thought to be those of the various rocks and sediments on the sea floors. Differences in relief are shown by relief shading.

1200 mi

1200 km

0   400   800

0   400   800

landmass in summer and its intense cooling in winter. The heating of tropical Asia in summer initiates a low-pressure system, which becomes the focal point of the Trade Winds of both hemispheres. The doldrums, therefore, do not exist in the western Pacific during northern summer because of the large-scale flow of maritime air into the Asian low-pressure zone. The cooling of the continent in winter results in the development of the Asian high-pressure system, which leads to a strengthening of the Trade Winds of the Northern Hemisphere.

As a result of seasonal changes in pressure and wind circulation, marked seasonal contrast between continental and maritime influences—the first associated with drought and cold and the second with moisture and heat—is to be found in the whole of the western Pacific from the Sea of Japan southward.

TEMPERATURE AND SALINITY

Temperature. As noted earlier, the oceans tend to be stratified, with the densest water lying at the bottom and the least dense at the surface. The principal factor in establishing this pattern is temperature; the bottom waters of the deep parts of the ocean are intensely cold, with temperatures only slightly above freezing.

Ocean temperatures in the North Pacific tend to be higher than those experienced in the South Pacific because the ratio of land to sea areas is larger in the Northern Hemisphere than it is in the Southern Hemisphere and because the ice continent of Antarctica also influences water temperature.

The mean position of the thermal Equator (the line on the Earth on which the highest average air temperatures are found; the line migrates latitudinally with the changing angular distance from the equator of the Sun) in the Pacific, although it lies in the Northern Hemisphere, is nearer to the geographical Equator than in the Atlantic and Indian oceans.

Variation   **Salinity.** The waters within the belt of calms and variable winds near the Equator have lower salinities than those in the Trade-Wind belts. In the equatorial belt, relatively large amounts of rain fall and little evaporation occurs both because of low windspeeds and because of the generally cloudy skies; salinity in the equatorial belt runs as low as 34 parts per thousand.

The highest surface salinities in the open Pacific occur in the southeastern area, where they reach 37 parts per thousand; in the corresponding Trade-Wind belt in the North Pacific the maximum salinity seldom reaches 36 parts per thousand. Pacific waters near Antarctica have salinities of less than about 34 parts; the lowest salinities—less than about 32 parts—occur in the extreme northern zone of the Pacific.

The heavy rainfall of the western Pacific, associated with the monsoons of the region, gives rise to relatively low salinities. Seasonal variations there, as well as in the eastern Pacific where seasonal changes in surface currents occur, are significant.

HYDROLOGY

Surface currents. Pacific Trade Winds drive surface waters toward the west to form the North and South Equatorial currents, whose axes coincide, respectively, with the parallel of 15° N and the Equator. Squeezed between the Equatorial currents is a well-defined countercurrent, the axis of which is always north of the Equator and which extends from the Philippines to the shores of Ecuador.

The North Equatorial Current   The major part of the North Equatorial Current swings northward in the vicinity of the Philippines to form the warm Kuroshio Current. To the east of Japan the Kuroshio swings eastward to form the Kuroshio Extension. The branching of this current in the region of 160° E results in the movement known as the North Pacific Drift. A branch of the warm Kuroshio Current passes through the Tsushima Strait to form the Tsushima Current, which flows in a northward direction on the eastern side of the Sea of Japan.

The surface waters of the Bering Sea circulate in an anticlockwise direction. The southward extension of the Kamchatka Current forms the cold Oya-shio, which flows

to the east of Honshu to meet the warm Kuroshio waters in the vicinity of 36° N.

The California Current forms the eastern branch of the main circulation system of the North Pacific. Having a great east–west extent, its surface-water movement is very slow.

The South Equatorial Current, on reaching the Solomon Islands, swings southward to form the East Australian Current, which links with the southern line of the main South Pacific circulation system, which, in turn, reaches the South American coast in the region of 45° S. One branch flows northward to form the Peru (Humboldt) Current, and a second branch flows southward to pass through the Drake Passage.

Between January and February—but sometimes as late as March, or even April—the axis of the Equatorial Countercurrent is displaced southward of its mean position, north of the Equator, so that warm saline waters reaching the coast of Ecuador swing southward to merge with the relatively cold northward-flowing waters of the Peru Current south of the Equator. The warm south-flowing current is called El Niño ("The Child")—a reference to the infant Christ. The strong development of El Niño, which may extend to 14° S, causes destruction (due to changes in temperature and salinity) of vast numbers of marine planktonic life and of fish and other higher marine life-forms that feed on the plankton. Mass starvation of birds that rely on the fish of these waters for food follows.   *Effects of El Niño Current*

Deepwater circulation. Observations of temperature and salinity at different levels in the ocean reveal well-defined layers, each forming a water mass distinguished by its own temperature and salinity characteristics.

It appears that the most important influence on the vertical circulation of the Pacific is the cold water generated around the Antarctic continent. This dense circumpolar water sinks and then spreads northward to form the bottom layer of the greater part of the Pacific. It has been suggested that cold, deep water flows northward in the western Pacific in a relatively well-defined current from the vicinity of Antarctica to Japan. Branches from this deep main stream convey cold water eastward and then poleward in both hemispheres.

Deepwater circulation is influenced by the descent of surface water at zones of convergence of neighbouring water flows. In the zone known as the Pacific Tropical Convergence, which coincides with the Equatorial Countercurrent, water sinks to a depth of about 90 metres (300 feet) before it spreads laterally. The Pacific Sub-Tropical Convergences are located between the parallels of 35° and 40° N and S. Water that sinks at the convergences spreads laterally at increasing depths as the distance from the Equator increases. The most important convergence in the Pacific is the Antarctic Convergence, which lies in the zone of the brave west winds. A corresponding Arctic Convergence is prominent in the northeastern Pacific.   *The Antarctic Convergence*

To compensate for downward-moving water, some water rises at zones of divergence, particularly along the so-called cold water coasts of both North and South America, where upwelling of cold water is a well-marked phenomenon.

Tides. In contrast to the tides of the Atlantic, those of the Pacific include many examples of diurnal and mixed tides. In the diurnal type of tidal oscillation, only a single high water and a single low water occur each tidal day (which lasts for about 24 hours and 50 minutes). Tides of this type occur in the Gulf of Tonkin in Southeast Asia, Vancouver Island (Canada), and the Torres Strait (between Australia and the island of New Guinea). Mixed tides, in which both diurnal and semidiurnal oscillations appear, are characterized by large inequalities in successive high (or low) water heights. This type of tide is prevalent along the Pacific coast of the United States. At certain places in the South Pacific the natural period of oscillation of the sea accentuates the solar tidal oscillation. At these places the time of the AM (or PM) high (or low) water, instead of getting later each day by about 50 minutes (as is generally the case), occurs at about the same time for several days in succession. The tide at Tahiti, for example, follows the Sun and not the Moon—the time of high water occurring, day after day, at about midnight and noon, and that of low water at about 6 AM and 6 PM.

In general, tidal ranges within the Pacific are small. That at Tahiti is about 0.3 metre (one foot); at Honolulu it is about 0.6 metre (two feet); at Yokohama, the port for Tokyo, it seldom exceeds 1.5 metres (five feet); and at Cape Horn it is never more than about 1.5 metres. In the upper reaches of the Gulf of California and the Gulf of Korea, however, large tidal ranges of more than 12 metres (40 feet) are common.

ECONOMIC RESOURCES

Biological resources. The resources of the Pacific include large quantities of fish, mammals, crustaceans, and mollusks. The northeast Pacific is noted for its salmon fisheries based on the Skeena, Fraser, and Columbia rivers. The fisheries of the northwest Pacific, especially in the seas of Japan and Okhotsk, harvest great quantities of herring, cod, tunny, bonito, crab, lobster, shrimp, and prawn. More fishermen find employment in these waters than in any other fishing ground, and the annual catch of Japan exceeds in value that of any other nation. The waters off the South American coasts are rich in marine life; the growth of the Peruvian anchoveta fishery—anchoveta are a species similar to anchovy—has been phenomenally rapid since 1957. The greater proportion of Peru's catch is converted into fishmeal for cattle and other domestic animals.

Mineral resources. The mineral resources of the waters of the ocean are vast and virtually inexhaustible. But apart from the extraction of sea salt, magnesium, and bromine, the Pacific's mineral resources for economic reasons remain untapped. The mineral deposits of the sea beds, especially on the continental shelves, however, are being increasingly exploited. Sea-bed oil prospecting started as far back as 1891 when a well was drilled beneath the shallow waters off the southern California coast. Sea-bed surveys in the Yellow Sea and East China Sea since the 1960s indicated that the continental shelf there may contain one of the most extensive and richest petroleum reserves in the world. Petroleum and natural gas exist in continental shelves adjacent to Alaska, Washington, Oregon, California, Central America, Ecuador, and Peru, as well as in the western Pacific off China, Japan, Indonesia, Australia, and New Zealand.

During the scientific voyage of the British naval vessel HMS "Challenger" in the 1870s, nodules of concretions of manganese compounds and minerals were discovered on the floors of the ocean basins. Considerable economic interest was aroused during the International Geophysical Year (1957 to 1958) when scientists discovered huge quantities of nodules on the Pacific floor, off the coast of California as well as in other localities. Research into economical methods of dredging and extracting the valuable metallic nodules continues.

Resource exploitation. In exploiting the resources of the sea, men require knowledge as well as tools and machines. Prospects for making optimum use of the resources of the sea, therefore, depend upon improved technology. No Pacific nation is more aware of this need than Japan, which dominates the commercial fishing of the Pacific.

The sophisticated oceangoing factories of the Japanese fishing fleet are capable of remaining at sea for long periods of time and thus are taking an increasingly important role in Pacific fishing. Fish canneries have been established in American Samoa, the New Hebrides, and Fiji; and these, together with older established factories in Hawaii and the Galápagos Islands, are supplied with tuna and bonito caught by Japanese fishermen.

The formerly prosperous whaling and pearling industries of the Pacific have dwindled to negligible proportions. Pearling for pearls and shell used to be important in many parts of Micronesia and Polynesia, but overgathering has reduced production to insignificance. Fishpond culture and oyster farming are practiced, techniques that may grow in economic importance.

It is worthy of note that the sea and lagoons play a relatively important role in Pacific island life; Polynesian food gatherers learned long ago the art of tending reef "gardens" in order to obtain food from the sea.

Minerals of the ocean floor

HISTORY

Exploration and mapping. Although the peoples of the western Pacific coastlands formed flourishing civilizations in very early times, they appear to have made no attempt to explore the Pacific beyond their coastal waters. Direct contact between Europe and the Pacific dates from the 16th century, when the exploration of the Pacific began in earnest. The initial European explorations of the Pacific were designed to open up oceanic trade routes to link Europe with the spiceries of the Far East. Later, attention was given to the discovery of Terra Australis. These explorations brought the peoples of western Europe into direct contact with the world of the Pacific islands.

Eight years after the Spanish conquistador Vasco Núñez de Balboa had sighted the "peaceful sea" from a peak in Darien in the Isthmus of Panama in 1513, the ship of Ferdinand Magellan, the Portuguese navigator, voyaged across the Pacific. Subsequent Spanish voyages led to the European discovery of the Moluccas, the Carolines, Papua, the Hawaiian Islands, and the Solomons. From the beginning of the 17th century, Pacific voyages of discovery were dominated by the Dutch, and credit is due to the Dutch navigator Abel Tasman for his significant discoveries of Tasmania, New Zealand, and Fiji.

A later major period of Pacific exploration is marked by the 18th-century voyages of the English navigator James Cook, the French navigator Louis-Antoine de Bougainville, and others who made possible the accurate mapping of the whole of the Pacific.

In the 19th century, the English naturalist Charles Darwin sailed on the British naval vessel HMS "Beagle," which circumnavigated the globe between 1831 and 1836. Growing interest, at that time, in the physical and biological problems of the ocean paved the way for the many oceanographic voyages made later in that century. These were initiated by the previously mentioned "Challenger" expedition.

The voyage of USS "Tuscarora," from 1874 to 1875, contributed significantly to oceanographic discovery in the northern Pacific; scientists aboard the German research vessel "Gazelle" in its 1874–76 voyage added considerably to knowledge of oceanic physics. During the International Geophysical Year the Soviet vessel "Vityaz" carried out detailed soundings of the deep trenches of the western Pacific. In the same year the United States bathysphere "Trieste" descended to the bottom of the Mariana Trench, reaching the greatest known depth of 11,034 metres (36,-200 feet).

Eras of naval predominance. The European intrusion into the Pacific resulted in the establishment of the first Spanish colony in the Philippines, in 1564. The 17th century witnessed the rise of Dutch naval power in the East Indies. From the beginning of the 19th century onward, the Pacific became the scene of a struggle for colonies and coaling stations by the maritime powers of western Europe.

The history of modern naval strategy in the Pacific dates from 1894, when Japan defeated the Chinese navy. Ten years later Japan destroyed the Russian Far East fleet and became ruler of the western Pacific, from its own shores to the Philippines. To safeguard British interests in the Pacific an alliance between Great Britain and Japan was concluded in 1902.

After World War I Japan acquired former German Pacific islands, thus strengthening its naval influence. Although the opening of the Panama Canal in 1914 allowed the United States to operate its fleet in the Pacific, Japanese control of the western Pacific remained unchallenged. World War II committed the major part of the British fleet to the Atlantic, and in 1941 significant U.S. naval forces were transferred to the Atlantic from the Pacific. Nevertheless, Japan, despite its military successes in Asia, failed to establish control of the eastern Pacific. By degrees the United States wrested command of the western Pacific from Japan and, since World War II, has been master of the whole of the Pacific. The South Pacific remains a sphere of influence in which Great Britain, Australia, and New Zealand are important naval powers.

Trade and communications. Although Thor Heyerdahl, the Norwegian author and anthropologist, has amply

Dutch voyages of discovery

The rise of Japan's naval dominance

demonstrated the possibility that at least some Pacific islands may first have been inhabited by peoples from South America, the weight of anthropological evidence suggests that the indigenous peoples of the Pacific islands originated in Asia and that the peninsulas of Southeast Asia were the principal centres from which Polynesian, Micronesian, and Melanesian settlement spread out. The European impact on the Pacific, which began in the early 16th century when the Spanish entered Central America, did not become significant until about 1800, when local Pacific economies were severely disrupted by European exploitation of the resources of the Pacific islands. This epoch was marked by the arrival of numerous planters, traders, and missionaries, and the introduction into the Pacific islands of relatively large numbers of Indian, Chinese, and Japanese labourers. The native populations decreased sharply as a result of diseases introduced by Europeans, the introduction of slavery, and the more lethal local warfare caused by the availability of guns.

The development of the North American west coast during the early 19th century, and the concomitant extension of United States trade into the Pacific, ushered in a period of profitable trading in which manufactures were exported from North America in exchange ultimately for silks, spices, and other products of the Far East and Oceania.

Since the beginning of the 20th century, Japan's influence in the Pacific has increased. After World War II, when Japan's economic power was temporarily eclipsed, Australia, New Zealand, France, The Netherlands (which later withdrew), the United States, and the United Kingdom were instrumental in establishing the South Pacific Commission, with headquarters initially in Australia and afterward in Nouméa, New Caledonia. The commission aims to encourage and coordinate research into the economic and social problems of the region.

The South Pacific Commission

The major trading patterns of the Pacific are essentially determined by political factors. Strong trading links have long existed between Hawaii (which achieved statehood in 1959) and the United States; between Great Britain and France and their respective scattered colonial Pacific islands; and between Australia and New Zealand and their dependent territories.

Communications across the Pacific are better than they are between island communities within the Pacific. Regular ocean-freight and passenger services connect North America with Japan and the Philippines; and Honolulu, the capital of Hawaii, serves as an important port of call. The Panama Canal provides a sea-trade route linking Atlantic and Pacific ports. The principal focal point of air and shipping services in the Far East is Japan; from there, routes lead southward to Australasia and, by way of the Strait of Malacca, to the Indian and Atlantic oceans. Important airports providing calling points in an increasingly complex network of air services include Honolulu (Hawaii), Papeete (Tahiti), Pago Pago (American Samoa), Nandi (Fiji), and Guam.

(C.H.C./Ed.)

The Indian Ocean

The Indian Ocean is that part of the World Ocean that lies south of Asia and between Africa and Australia, extending south to Antarctica. Although it stretches for more than 10,000 kilometres (6,200 miles) between the southern tips of Africa and Australia and although—after the Pacific and Atlantic—it is the third largest ocean of the world, it comprises only about 20 percent of the total ocean area. Without its marginal seas, the Indian Ocean is estimated to have an area of about 73,440,000 square kilometres (28,360,000 square miles).

The ocean is bounded by Bangladesh, India, Pakistan, and Iran to the north; the Arabian Peninsula and Africa to the west; Australia, the Sunda Islands of Indonesia, and the Malay Peninsula to the east; and Antarctica to the south. In the southwest it joins the Atlantic Ocean south of the southern tip of Africa, and to the east and southeast its waters mingle with those of the Pacific. For the most part, it lies in the Southern Hemisphere; for that reason and because its maritime trade routes cross through the tropical zone, it is often thought of as a tropical sea, despite the fact that it extends south to Wilkes Land in Antarctica. Its northernmost extensions—the Red Sea and the Persian Gulf—reach to 30° N.

As noted above, the question of defining the oceanic limits of the Indian Ocean is complicated and remains unsettled. The clearest border and the one most generally agreed upon is that with the Atlantic Ocean: it runs from Cape Agulhas, at the southern tip of Africa, due south along the 20° E meridian to the shores of Antarctica. The border with the Pacific Ocean to the southeast is usually drawn from South East Cape on the island of Tasmania, south along the 147° E meridian to Antarctica. Bass Strait, between Tasmania and Australia, is considered by some researchers as part of the Indian Ocean, by others as part of the Pacific. The northeastern border is the most difficult to define. Some consider it to run across the Torres Strait between Australia and the island of New Guinea, and then from the island of Adi, off the western New Guinea coast, along the southern shores of the Lesser Sunda Islands and the island of Java, thence across the Sunda Strait to the shores of Sumatra. Other researchers, however, consider the Arafura Sea and even the Timor Sea as parts of the Pacific and not the Indian Ocean. Between the island of Sumatra and the Malay Peninsula the boundary is sometimes drawn at Singapore and sometimes from Cape Pedro to the northeast, thus making the Strait of Malacca a part of the Pacific.

Boundaries with other oceans

In comparison with the other oceans, the Indian Ocean has the fewest seas. To the north are the inland seas—the Red Sea and the Persian Gulf; the marginal seas are the Arabian Sea to the northwest, the Andaman Sea to the northeast, and the Timor and Arafura seas to the east. The large gulfs of Aden and Oman are to the northwest, the Bay of Bengal to the northeast, and the Gulf of Carpentaria off the north coast of Australia, and the Great Australian Bight off the south coast of the continent; to the south is Antarctica—with the Rüser–Larsen Sea, Sea of the Cosmonauts, Commonwealth Bay, Davis Sea, Mouson Sea, d'Urville Sea—and bays such as Prydz Bay and others.

PHYSIOGRAPHY AND GEOLOGY

Shores and islands. The shores of the Indian Ocean are multiform. Wave-eroded and sedimentary coastlines are widely represented; they are indented and levelled, with eroded cliffs. The sedimentary coasts are alluvial, lagoonal, and deltaic. Some are coral, some caused by faults, and some, in Antarctica, glacial. The shoreline is gently indented with the exception of the northern part of the ocean where the seas and bays cut deeply into the land.

The Indian Ocean has few islands; the large ones, such as Madagascar, Socotra, and Sri Lanka (formerly Ceylon), are continental—as are also the Seychelles. The volcanic islands of Kerguelen, Crozet, Prince Edward, Nouvelle (New) Amsterdam and Saint-Paul lie to the south. Coral atolls, which predominate in the tropical reaches, include the Laccadive, Maldive, Amirante, Farquhar, and Cocos islands and the Chagos Archipelago. Volcanic islands, ringed by coral reefs, are also encountered: notably the Mascarenes, the Comoro Islands, and others.

Submarine features. The floor of the Indian Ocean can be divided into four major topographical features—the continental margin, the island arc, the ocean basin floor, and the mid-ocean ridge.

The continental margin. The Indian Ocean continental shelf essentially consists of a narrow, flat surface up to 97 kilometres (60 miles) wide, broadening to a width of between 193 and 290 kilometres (120 and 180 miles) in the Arabian and Andaman seas as well as in the Bay of Bengal and, northward of the Great Australian Bight, spreading to 965 kilometres (600 miles) between Australia and New Guinea. The outer edge of the shelf lies mainly at depths of 46 to 183 metres (150 to 600 feet), but off northwestern Australia the depths reach 275 to 365 metres (900 to 1,200 feet). The Antarctic shelf has acquired a more complex structure because of ice action. The shelf is divided into two parts, outer and inner, by an abrupt underwater cliff, or scarp, with a longitudinal depression at the base in some places; the levelled portion of the outer shelf is submerged to a depth of 365 to 457 metres (1,200 to 1,500 feet), while the inner shelf lies from 137 to 183 metres (450 to 600 feet) deep. In addition, the Antarctic shelf is intersected by deep transverse depressions, which are glacial troughs. In the tropical zone, coral reefs are widespread—as fringing reefs, barrier reefs, and atolls. Channels, banks, shoals, sandwaves, and dunes also have been created by the flow of the currents in the straits of Malacca, Singapore, and Bass; in the gulfs of Cambay and Kutch; and near the mouths of the Ganges, Irrawaddy, and Shatt al-Arab rivers.

Beyond the shelf edge, the continental slope of the Indian Ocean is represented, for the most part, by steep scarps, with slopes of from 10° to 30°, which are complicated in places by marginal plateaus (Western Australia) or which are dissected by valleys and canyons (Indus, Ganges, Trincomalee, Perth, and others).

The Sunda arc. In the northeastern Indian Ocean the Sunda arc (most of Indonesia and other islands) extends for more than 5,150 kilometres (3,200 miles) from Burma to Australia. Along more than half of its length lies the Java (or Sunda Double) Trench, the deepest place in the Indian Ocean, reported at 7,450 metres (24,442 feet)—a figure, however, that has not been confirmed by Soviet investigations, which have established a flat bottom there at 7,130 metres (23,392 feet). The Sunda arc is divided into two chains: (1) an inner ridge of islands consisting of the volcanic chain of the Greater and Lesser Sunda islands (Sumatra, Java, Timor, and others) and (2) an outer ridge, an uplift consisting of the Andaman, Nicobar, and Mentawai islands and the submerged Bali Ridge.

Ocean basin floor. The bed of the Indian Ocean is separated by a system of midocean ridges into three parts or segments—African, Australasian, and Antarctic—that in turn are subdivided by ridges, plateaus, rises, and chains of seamounts into basins extending from about 320 kilometres (Comoro and North Australian basins) to 9,000 kilometres (South Indian, or Australian Antarctic, Basin).
Basins and plains Some basins—the Arabian, for example—are surrrounded by uninterrupted high ridges, and others, such as the Mid-Indian Basin, have in some places low barriers; a third type—the Crozet and Atlantic-Indian basins—are unobstructedly connected by wide, deep gaps.

Two types of topography dominate the bottoms of the oceanic basins; smooth topography (abyssal plains) occurring near the continents in areas where sediment is abundantly spread out, and rough or uneven topography (abyssal hills) occurring in the central part of the ocean where a very thin sedimentary layer is deposited. Deep-sea channels—elongated depressions a few kilometres across but up to 2,410 kilometres (1,500 miles) long with low rises (levees) along the banks and maximum wall heights of 180 metres—are one of the common features of the abyssal plains. As they approach the continents, the plains are transformed into abyssal fans (cones), such as the Indus and Ganges fans, or into marginal inclined planes (the lower continental rise), as occurs off the coast of Equatorial Africa. Along the periphery of the abyssal cones and inclined planes, the flattest surfaces of the bottom occur; they are called abyssal plains, such as the Ceylon and Somali plains. The rough topography of the basin is characterized by widespread development of hills and volcanic seamounts. The hills usually have conical profiles up to 460 metres in height (higher ones are considered low mountains), distributed individually or in groups over the whole basin bed. Flat-topped hills with steep sides are also encountered.

Mountains and fracture zones Among the ridges of the Indian Ocean, the Ninety east Ridge (the East Indian Ridge) is distinguished by its straightness and length (approximately 4,990 kilometres [3,100 miles]). It was discovered in 1962. It is connected on the south, at a right angle, to the Broken (or West Australian) Ridge.

Large ridges stretch to the south from the Hindustān Peninsula, from the island of Madagascar, and from the eastern shore of South Africa. In the south the massive Kerguelen Plateau runs from northwest to southeast. Trenches occur at the foot of a number of the ridges;

these include the East-Indian, Chagos, Ob', and Amirante trenches. The large aseismic (earthquake-resistant) ridges and plateaus (Madagascar, Seychelles, Mauritius, Agulhas, Kerguelen, and West Australian) represent a considerable thickness of the Earth's crust; sometimes, when formed of a continental type of rock, they are called microcontinents.

Large fractures, called fracture zones, have been discovered on the ocean bottom. The Diamantina, Mascarene, and other fracture zones form narrow strips from about 48 to 145 kilometres (30 to 90 miles) wide and up to nearly 2,900 kilometres (1,800 miles) long, with severely disrupted relief that consists of deep trenches, ridges, mountains, and scarps. Volcanoes with conical peaks are widely represented on the ocean basin floor, forming large groups with massive structures, such as that culminating in the Farquhar Islands, or ranges found here and there to the east of the Cocos (Keeling) Islands and to the north of Madagascar.

The midocean ridges. The midocean ridges form an enormous mountain system made up of three sections diverging from the centre of the ocean: one toward the north (the Carlsberg, or Arabian-Indian, Ridge), the second toward the southwest (the West-Indian and Atlantic-Indian, and Southwest Indian ridges), and the third toward the southeast (the Mid-Indian Ridge and the Southeast Indian Rise or Australian Antarctic Ridge). The first two branches represent a complex mountain structure 400 to 970 kilometres (250 to 600 miles) in width and from 1,830 to 3,050 metres (6,000 to 10,000 feet) in height, with the most rugged topography occurring along the crest, and characterized by the occurrence of a rift valley surrounded by rift mountains. The third, southeastern, branch of the midocean ridge to the east of New Amsterdam (Amsterdam) Island is lower (920 metres [3,000 feet]) and wider (1,450 kilometres [900 miles]), with a severely but not deeply dissected surface, and is usually devoid of rift valleys. The midocean ridges of the Indian Ocean are intersected by numerous fracture zones, some of which are large, such as the Owen Fracture Zone, which extends into the bottoms of the Arabian and Somali basins. Horizontal displacement of the bottom was found for 320 kilometres along the Owen Fracture Zone.

Bottom structures. Stable crustal structures are predominant in the Indian Ocean, both on the bed and on the periphery (continental platforms). The actively developing structures—recent geosynclines (depressions) such as the Sunda Islands arc and rift formations—occupy a Actively developing structures smaller area and are extensions of the corresponding land structures (the Alpine ranges of Burma and the rifts of East Africa). The volcanic mountain ranges on the ocean floor are usually crowned with coral islands (the Maldive and Amirante islands and the southern part of the Mascarene Ridge). Developing sea-bottom structures include trench fractures (Chagos, Ob'), fracture zones (Owens, Diamantina, Mauritius), rift zones and scarps, all formed by movements of the Earth's crust. The microcontinents (small continental platforms) are stable aseismic features, such as ridges and plateaus (the Madagascar, Kerguelen, West Australian, Crozet, and other features).

Sediments and bottom rocks. The greatest thicknesses (up to 1,980 metres [6,500 feet]) of bottom sediments in the Indian Ocean are near the continents. In the centre the sediments are thin (approximately 90 metres [300 feet]), and in areas of rough topography their distribution is intermittent. Most widely represented are: calcareous remains of foraminifera (one-celled protozoans) found on the continental slopes, on the ridges, and in the majority of the basin bottoms to depths up to 4,270 metres (14,000 feet); the siliceous shells of diatom algae (between the 50th parallel and Antarctica); the minute, opaline silica shells of radiolaria near the Equator; and the coral sediments. Red clays are distributed south of the Equator at depths of from three to more than six kilometres (two to four miles); terrigenous (land-derived) sediments predominate on the continental shelves and upper parts of the continental slopes. Deposits formed by chemical action are represented by phosphorite and manganese nodules. In the rift zone of the mid-oceanic range a special type of sediment occurs; it is formed by the disintegration of the intrusive

A s i a

South China Sea

MACCLESFIELD BANK

South China Sea

Kalimantan (Borneo)

Java Sea

JAVA TRENCH

ARGO ABYSSAL PLAIN

CORONA SEAMOUNT

ROWLEY SHOALS

EXMOUTH

110°

100°

Gulf of Siam

Malay Peninsula

Sumetera

Djawa

ROO RISE

7450

Christmas Island

KARMA RISE

CHRISTMAS RISE

WHARTON BASIN

W E S T

Gulf of Siam

MENTAWEI TROUGH

MENTAWEI RIDGE

C O C O S

B A S I N

ANDAMAN BASIN

Nicobar Islands

▽ 65

Andaman Islands

▽ 2095

Cooks Islands

▽ 6335

90°

Bay of Bengal

GANGES CANYON

▽ 2359

EAST RIDGE

N I N E T Y

NIKITIN (AFANASIY) SEAMOUNT

▽ 5243

1549 ▽

Ceylon Abyssal Plain

M I D -

I N D I A N

B A S I N

R I D G E

▽ 6090

India

GANGES FAN

Ceylon

80°

Equator

▽ 3244

▽ 5408

CHAGOS-LACCADIVE PLATEAU

Laccadive Islands

Maldive Islands

Chagos Archipelago

70°

Arabian Sea

INDUS CANYON

ARABIAN BASIN

INDIA ABYSSAL PLAIN

▽ 3858

▽ 5870

CARLSBERG RIDGE

▽ 1755

YEMI TRENCH

▽ 6227

60°

3694 ▽

INDUS FAN

▽ 5115

SEYCHELLES-MAURITIUS PLATEAU

SAYA DE MALHA BANK

▽ 618

NAZARETH BANK

Seychelles

Coetivy Island

Agalega Islands

Tromelin

Cargados Carajos Shoals

MASCARENE BASIN

Persian Gulf

▽ 5143

Suqutra

Gulf of Aden

CHAIN RIDGE

▽ 846

SOMALI ABYSSAL PLAIN

S O M A L I

B A S I N

▽ 5340

Amirante Islands

Farquhar Group

AMIRANTE TRENCH

Madagascar

Mozambique Channel

50°

40°

RED SEA RIFT

Aldabra Islands

Comoro Islands

COMORO RIDGE

30°

A f r i c a

20°

10°

0°

10°

20°

10°

0°

10°

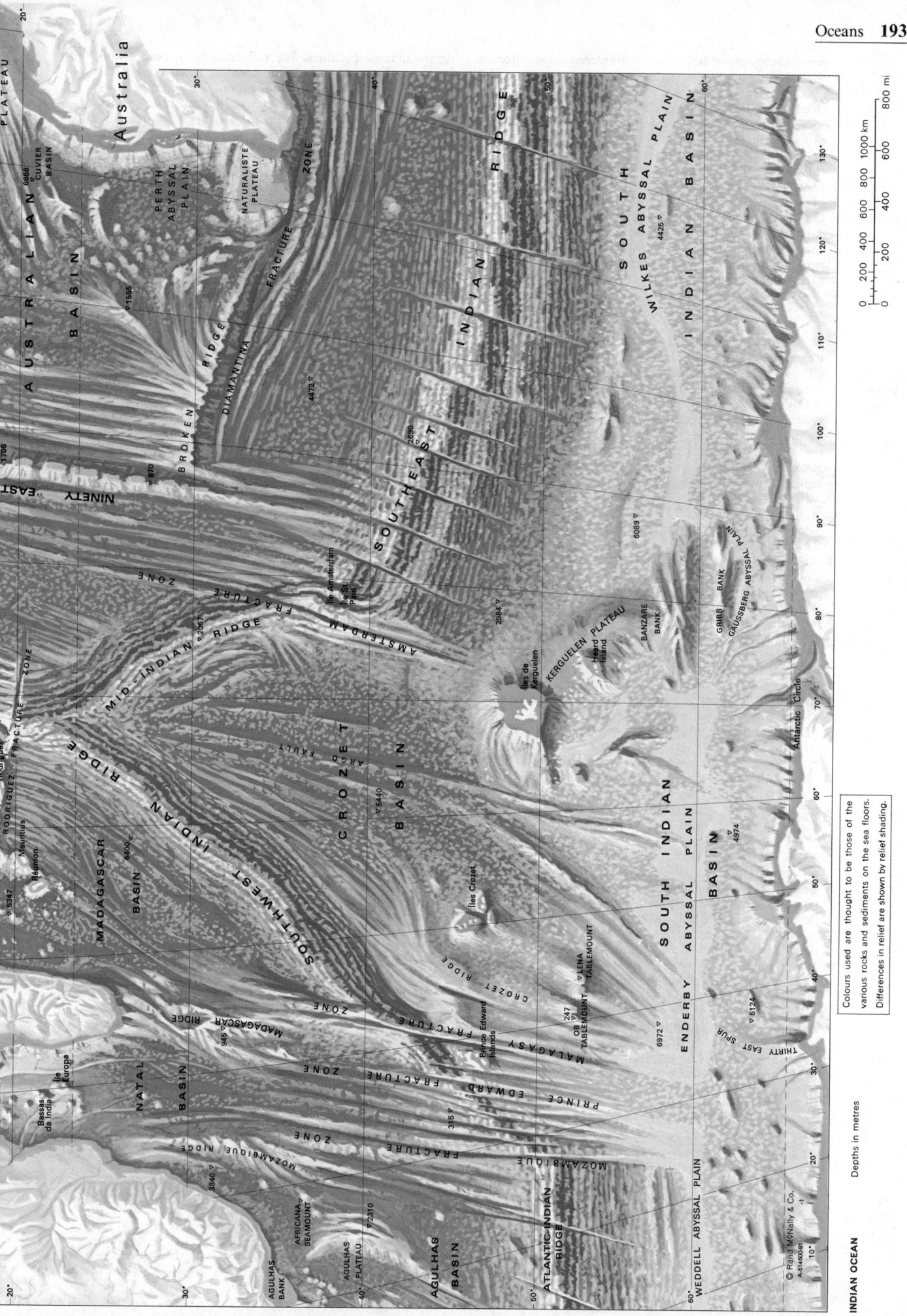

Australia

PLATEAU

6668 CUVIER
BASIN
1556

PERTH
ABYSSAL
PLAIN

NATURALISTE
PLATEAU

AUSTRALIAN

BASIN

FRACTURE ZONE

DIAMANTINA

RIDGE

BROKEN

1706

870

NINETY EAST

2067

ZONE

FRACTURE

AMSTERDAM

Île Amsterdam
Île St.
Paul

4472

2890

SOUTHEAST

INDIAN

RIDGE

SOUTH

WILKES ABYSSAL PLAIN

4425

INDIAN BASIN

6089

2984

KERGUELEN PLATEAU

Îles de
Kerguelen

BANZARE
BANK

Heard
Island

GRIBB
BANK

GAUSSBERG ABYSSAL
PLAIN

Antarctic Circle

MID-INDIAN RIDGE

CROZET

ARGO FAULT

BASIN

5440

SOUTHWEST INDIAN RIDGE

Rodriguez

RODRIGUEZ FRACTURE ZONE

Mauritius
5347
Réunion

MADAGASCAR

BASIN

6400

945

MADAGASCAR RIDGE

ZONE

FRACTURE

EDWARD

PRINCE

ZONE

3840

MOZAMBIQUE RIDGE

AFRICANA-
SEAMOUNT

AGULHAS
PLATEAU

2310

AGULHAS
BANK

NATAL

BASIN

Île
Europa

Bassas
da India

AGULHAS
BASIN

ATLANTIC-INDIAN
RIDGE

Îles Crozet

CROZET RIDGE

LENA
TABLEMOUNT
247
80
TABLEMOUNT

Prince Edward
Islands

MALAGASY FRACTURE

315

ZONE

MOZAMBIQUE

PLAIN

WEDDELL ABYSSAL PLAIN

SOUTH INDIAN

BASIN

4974

ENDERBY ABYSSAL PLAIN

6972

5124

THIRTY EAST SPUR

© Rand McNally & Co.
A-614600-91

INDIAN OCEAN

Depths in metres

Colours used are thought to be those of the
various rocks and sediments on the sea floors.
Differences in relief are shown by relief shading.

| 0 | 200 | 400 | 600 | 800 | 1000 km |

| 0 | 200 | 400 | 600 | 800 mi |

rock. Outcrops of bedrock—encountered most often on the continental slopes (sedimentary and metamorphic), on the mountains (basalt), and on the midoceanic ridges (basalt and also peridotite, cherzolite, and other rocks)—represent little changed substances from the upper mantle of the Earth.

Genesis. According to many scholars, the genesis of the Indian Ocean Basin occurred during the Mesozoic Era (225,000,000 to 65,000,000 years ago) with the breakup of an ancient continent in the Southern Hemisphere—Gondwanaland—into huge blocks (South America, Africa, Australia, Antarctica, Madagascar, and India) that subsequently drifted to their present positions. Future submarine drilling in the Indian Ocean should permit a more exact answer to this question. (V.F.K./Ed.)

CLIMATE

The Indian Ocean can be roughly subdivided into four basic latitudinal climatic zones according to the special characteristics of atmospheric circulation.

Four basic climatic zones

The first zone, extending north from 10° S, has a monsoon climate (characterized by rain-bearing winds). Atmospheric circulation in summer (May to October) is determined by the counterclockwise movement of the South Asiatic cyclone, and in winter (October to April) by the clockwise circulation of the Asiatic anticyclone. A seasonal alteration occurs in the direction of the prevailing winds, which in summer blow strongly from the southwest at speeds of up to 24 knots (12 metres per second) and in the winter gently from the north and northeast. The average annual precipitation in the eastern part of the Arabian Sea and in the Bay of Bengal exceeds 1,016 millimetres (40 inches). Some western areas have less than 254 millimetres (10 inches), and the equatorial regions average approximately 1,778 millimetres (70 inches). Air temperature in the summer is 25° to 28° C (77° to 82° F), but along the northeast coast of Africa it drops to 23° C (73° F) as a result of the upwelling of the cold, deep waters of the Somali Current. The winter air temperature drops to 22° C (72° F) in the northern ocean, remaining almost unchanged along and south of the Equator. Cloudiness is 60 to 70 percent in summer and 10 to 30 percent in winter in the monsoon region.

The second zone, that of the Trade Winds, lies between 10° and 30° S. Here very steady southeasterly trade winds prevail in the tropical and subtropical latitudes. The prevailing air mass is tropical sea air, which forms in the South Indian anticyclone. In the northern part of the zone the summer air temperature averages 25° C and slightly higher in winter; along the 30th parallel it is 16° to 17° C (61° to 63° F) in summer and 20° to 22° C (68° to 72° F) in winter. Because of warm ocean currents the air temperature is 2° to 3° C (4° to 6° F) higher in the western Trade-Wind zone than in its eastern portion. Precipitation distribution is zonal. The annual precipitation decreases from 203 millimetres (eight inches) in the north to 102 millimetres (four inches) in the south. Hurricanes occur in the summer and autumn in the western Trade-Wind zone.

The third zone lies in the subtropical and temperate latitudes of the Southern Hemisphere, between 30° and 45° S. The dynamic system of the zone is shaped by the influence of the South Indian anticyclone situated at approximately 35° S. In the northern part of the zone the prevailing winds are light and variable; in the southern area, moderate to strong westerly winds prevail. Throughout the entire year the average air temperature decreases continuously with increasing south latitude: from 20° to 22° C down to 10° C (50° F) in winter, and from 16° to 17° C to 6° to 7° C (43° to 45° F) in summer. The uniformly distributed average precipitation is about 100 centimetres (40 inches).

Antarctic influences

Finally, the fourth, or subantarctic and Antarctic, zone occupies the wide belt between 45° S and the continent of Antarctica. The atmospheric circulation over the ocean in this region is determined by the interaction of the Antarctic low-pressure belt and the subtropical belt of high atmospheric pressure. Steady westerly winds prevail, reaching gale force at times with their passage through the

deep Antarctic cyclones. The influence of the continental ice upon the wind regime is evident in a narrow coastal belt where strong easterly winds prevail. The average summer (December, January, February) air temperature varies from 6° to 7° C in the north to −16° C (3° F) near the continent. The corresponding winter temperatures vary within the limits of 10° to −4° C (50° to 25° F). The precipitation varies from 100 to 50 centimetres (40 to 20 inches) southward. The annual range of air-temperature variations is not large, approximately 5° to 6° C (9° to 11° F), over most of the ocean waters, except in the south where it exceeds 15° C (27° F).

HYDROLOGY

The hydrological characteristics of the Indian Ocean depend not only on the atmospheric circulation described above but also on the complex interaction with and absorption of the waters of the Red Sea and of the Atlantic, Pacific, and Antarctic oceans.

Water temperatures. A zonal asymmetry is noted in the surface-water temperature distribution in summer, north of 20° S. Summer surface temperatures are higher in the eastern part of this region than in the western. In the Bay of Bengal the maximum temperature is around 28° C. The minimum temperature is about 22° C in the area of Cape Guardafui, and is associated with the upwelling of cold, deep water off the African coast north of the Equator. South of 20° S the temperature of the surface waters decreases at a uniform rate with increase of latitude, from 22° to 24° C (72° to 75° F) to −1° C (30° F) near Antarctica.

Zonal and seasonal variations

Near the Equator, winter surface temperatures in excess of 28° C are encountered in the eastern part of the ocean. Winter surface-water temperatures are around 22° to 23° C in the northern portion of the Arabian Sea, and 25° C in the Bay of Bengal. At 25° S the temperature is about 25° to 27° C; at the 40th parallel, 14° to 16° C (57° to 61° F); and at the coast of Antarctica, 0° to −1° C. The annual variation in surface-water temperatures over the major portion of the Indian Ocean is approximately 4° to 5° C (7° to 9° F). In the eastern equatorial region and south of 60° S, the annual variation is less than 2° C; in the south-Indian high-pressure region it may reach 10° C (18° F); and in the peripheral seas of the northern Indian Ocean it corresponds to that of the air temperature (in the Persian Gulf the annual variation exceeds 14° C [25° F]).

Salinity. The salinity of Indian Ocean surface waters varies within the limits of 32 to 37 parts per 1,000. The Red Sea and Persian Gulf are the sources of the high salinity in the northwestern part of the ocean. There, between the Equator and the Arabian Peninsula, maximum salinity exceeds 37 parts per 1,000, while in the northeast the salinity drops to 34 parts and even to 32 parts per 1,000 as the result of the considerable drainage from rivers and of greater precipitation. From 40° S to the shores of Antarctica the salinity gradually decreases from 35 to 33.5 parts per 1,000 as a result of the erosion and thawing of the Antarctic continental and pack ice. Surface salinity in the remaining waters of the ocean slightly exceeds 35 parts per 1,000 on the average.

Surface water density. As previously mentioned, temperature has a decisive influence on water density in the open ocean; the surface-water density shows the same distribution characteristics as the temperature. The lowest density in the northern portion of the Indian Ocean is found on the surface of the Bay of Bengal, where it is 1.022 grams per cubic centimetre (0.591 ounces per cubic inch). The highest density, in the western Arabian Sea, is approximately 1.025 grams per cubic centimetre (0.593 ounces per cubic inch). Density distribution in the southern half of the ocean is zonal, increasing gradually from 1.023 grams per cubic centimetre (0.592 ounces per cubic inch) at the Equator to 1.027 grams per cubic centimetre (0.594 ounces per cubic inch) in the Antarctic region.

Vertical structure of the water. A usual characteristic of seawater is its decrease in temperature and salinity and increase in density with increased depth. In the Antarctic region of the Indian Ocean, from 45° to 50° S, the temperature does not follow this pattern. Instead, a layer of relatively warm water of subtropical origin is distributed at a depth of from 460 to 2,740 metres (1,500 to 9,000 feet) beneath the cold surface waters. North of 40° S a layer of lower salinity water of Antarctic origin is everywhere found at intermediate depths (460 to 920 metres).

North of 10° S the effect of the highly saline waters of the Red Sea and of the diluted waters from the Bay of Bengal cause local maximums and minimums of salinity to occur in the uppermost 460 metres of water. Fundamental changes in temperature, salinity, and density of the ocean are concentrated, as a rule, in the uppermost 1,100- to 1,370-metre (3,600- to 4,500-foot) layer of water. At this layer the average water temperature is 4° to 6° C (39° to 43° F), salinity is 34.6 to 34.7 parts per 1,000, and density is 1.027 to 1.028 grams per cubic centimetre (about 0.594 ounces per cubic inch). Water temperatures on the bottom are 1° to 2° C (34° to 36° F) and drop to −1° C (30° F) in the Antarctic region. Below 1,370 metres (4,500 feet) the salinity and density do not vary materially.

Ice. In the Indian Ocean, ice is formed in the south polar region during the Antarctic winter. The coastal ice is packed solid and reaches a thickness of 1.8 to 3.7 metres (six to 12 feet). The outer edge of the ice pack may extend for tens of kilometres from the shore. Between January and February the melting coastal ice is broken up by severe storms and, in the form of large blocks and broad floes, Floating ice and icebergs carried away by wind and currents to the open ocean. In some coastal areas the tongues of ice-shelf glaciers break off to form icebergs. West of the 90° E meridian in the Indian Ocean the northern limit for floating ice lies close to 65° S. To the east of that meridian, however, floating ice is commonly encountered to 60° S; large icebergs are sometimes carried as far north as 40° S.

Tidal range. In the open areas of the Indian Ocean the tidal range is small and is basically semidiurnal. Tides along the coasts average 46 to 137 centimetres (1.5 to 4.5 feet). In certain areas, however, such as the bays of northern Australia, tides vary from six to nine metres (20 to 30 feet). Similarly, a large tidal range is found also in some coastal regions of the Arabian Sea and the Bay of Bengal.

Currents. Surface-water movement is determined by the prevailing winds. Under the influence of the monsoon winds the currents change from season to season north of 10° S. During the winter there is a counterclockwise circulation in the Arabian Sea, where the currents have an average velocity of 30–50 centimetres per second (12–20 inches per second). In summer the current reverses its Reversing and shifting currents direction. A counterclockwise rotation with average velocities of 20–30 centimetres per second (8–12 inches per second) is maintained throughout the year in the Bay of Bengal. Under the influence of southwesterly winds, blowing in summer, the Monsoon (North Equatorial) Current flows within a 10° zone along both sides of the Equator, the water moving from west to east at a speed of approximately 40 centimetres (16 inches) per second.

In winter the Monsoon Current changes its direction to west-northwest and no longer flows to the east of the Maldive Ridge. During this period an equatorial countercurrent develops in the equatorial zone, flowing in the opposite direction to the prevailing wind.

Southward from the Equator the currents are virtually constant throughout the year. This system of currents is composed of the Tradewind (or South Equatorial) Current, the Cape Needle (or Agulhas) Current, the South Indian Ocean Current, and the West Australian Current. All these currents together form a southern tropical anticyclonic circulation pattern.

Between 40° S and 60° to 65° S the belt of the Antarctic Circumpolar Current moves eastward under the influence of the westerly winds, and near Antarctica there is a chain of local clockwise currents. Their southern portions are known as the East Wind Drift.

The characteristic pattern of the horizontal structure of the surface currents is maintained to a depth of about 460 metres in the northern part of the ocean. In the deeper layers, where the seasonal changes do not penetrate, a westerly movement with an average velocity of several centimetres per second prevails in the open ocean to the north of 30° S. The eastward movement of the Antarctic Circumpolar Current remains unchanged right to the very bottom of the ocean. On the edges of currents moving in opposite directions and in regions of abrupt changes in their velocities there are zones of maximum vertical movement of the water. An upwelling of the water occurs along 5° S in the area of the subequatorial divergence (division of the current); and downwellings occur both in the south-tropical and subtropical convergence (30° to 10° S) and by the cold waters in the area of the Antarctic Convergence Zone (50° to 55° S). The upwelling and downwelling in these zones play an important role in the generation of water masses in the Indian Ocean. (V.G.N.)

Mineral resources. There are many minerals on the bottom of the Indian Ocean: petroleum and gas on the continental shelves (Persian Gulf, Red Sea, Bass Strait, Western Australia, and elsewhere); rutile and zircon (Northwestern Australia); the rare-earth mineral monazite in beach sands (India); diamonds, phosphorite nodules (Agulhas Bank); and coralline limestones. Sediments that contain enormous amounts of iron, copper, manganese, and other metals have been discovered in the Red Sea; and chrome ores have been found in the rift zone of the mid-oceanic ridge. Huge accumulations of manganese nodules containing numerous metals, some of them rare, lie on the ocean bed.

Biological resources. The greater part of the water area of the Indian Ocean lies within the tropical and temperate zones. The shallow waters of the tropical zone are characterized by numerous corals and other organisms capable of building, together with calcareous red algae, coral islands and atolls. These coralline structures shelter a thriving marine animal life consisting of sponges, worms, crabs, mollusks, sea urchins, brittle stars, starfish, and small but exceedingly brightly coloured coral fish. The major portion of the tropical coasts is covered with mangrove thickets with an animal life specific to that environment.

The small crustaceans, including more than 100 species of minute copepods, form the bulk of the animal life, followed by small mollusks, jellyfish, and polyps, and other invertebrate animals ranging from single-celled radiolaria to large Portuguese man-of-war jellyfish, which attain a size of several feet. The squid form large schools. Of the fishes, the most abundant are several species of flying fish, luminous anchovies, lantern fish, large and small tunnies, sailfish, and various types of sharks. Here and there are found sea turtles and large marine mammals, such as dugongs, or sea cows, toothed and baleen whales, dolphins, and seals. Among the birds the most common are the albatross and frigate birds, but there also are several species of penguins populating the Antarctic coast and the islands lying in the ocean's temperate zone.

Early exploration. Study of the Indian Ocean began long ago. The Egyptians, Phoenicians, and Indians made long journeys in the northern portion of it during the 1st millennium BC, as did Chinese and Arabic seafarers from the middle of the 1st millennium AD onward. The Early seafarers and explorers writings of medieval Arab and Persian pilots from the 9th to the 15th centuries include detailed sailing instructions and information on navigation, winds, currents, coasts, islands, and ports from Sofala in East Africa to China. It was on an Indian trading vessel that the Russian voyager Afanasy Nikitin sailed to India in 1469. Vasco da Gama, sailing around Africa in 1497, signed on an Arabian pilot at Malindi before he crossed the Indian Ocean to reach the western shores of India.

The Dutch, English, and French followed the Portuguese to the Indian Ocean. In 1521 the Spanish navigator Juan Sebastián de Elcano crossed the central part of the ocean, continuing the first voyage of circumnavigation of the globe after the death of the original commander, Ferdinand Magellan, in the Philippine Islands. The Dutch navigator Abel Tasman, pursuing voyages of discovery in the eastern Indian Ocean from 1642 to 1644, explored the northern coast of Australia and discovered the island of Tasmania. The southern waters of the Indian Ocean were explored by Captain James Cook in 1772. Beginning in 1806 the Indian Ocean was crossed repeatedly by Russian ships commanded by Adam Johann Krusenshtern, Otto von Kotzebue, and others.

Between 1819 and 1821 the expedition of the Russian explorer Fabian Gottlieb von Bellingshausen that circumnavigated Antarctica penetrated the Indian Ocean south of the 60th parallel. A number of important voyages to Antarctica followed, led by the explorers Lieut. Charles Wilkes (American), Jules Sébastien César Dumont d'Urville (French), James Ross (Scottish), Jean-Baptiste Charcot (French), and others.

Systematic investigations. The famous round-the-world expedition of the British naval vessel "Challenger," which began in 1872, marked the beginning of systematic investigation of the oceans, including the Indian Ocean. Thereafter, there were numerous expeditions.

Circumnavigational voyages following World War II were made by the Danish "Galathea," the Swedish "Albatross," and the English "Challenger II," which explored the northern portion of the Indian Ocean. During the preparation and execution of the International Geophysical Year (1957 to 1958) and in subsequent years systematic explorations of the southern Indian Ocean were carried out by Australian, New Zealand, Soviet, French, Japanese, and other expeditions. The International Indian Ocean Expedition, from 1960 to 1965, was a cooperative effort by more than 20 research ships of many countries. Similar studies of the ocean are continuing. (V.F.K./Ed.)

BIBLIOGRAPHY

Physical and chemical aspects of the oceans: The interested reader should not fail to consult the classics by M.F. MAURY, *The Physical Geography of the Sea* (1855, reprinted 1963); J. MURRAY and J. HJORT, *The Depths of the Ocean* (1912); and O. KRUMMEL, *Handbuch der Ozeanographie,* 2 vol. (1907–11). Recent texts on oceanography that are both readable and comprehensive include G.L. PICKARD, *Descriptive Physical Oceanography,* 2nd ed. (1966); G. NEUMANN and W.J. PIERSON, JR., *Principles of Physical Oceanography* (1966); P. GROEN, *De wateren der wereldzee,* 2nd ed. (1961; Eng. trans., *The Waters of the Sea,* 1967); and P.K. WEYL, *Oceanography: An Introduction to the Marine Environment* (1970). In this same vein, no list of general texts would be complete without citing H.U. SVERDRUP, M.W. JOHNSON, and R.H. FLEMING, *The Oceans* (1942), which was in many ways the forerunner of all modern general texts; it covers biological aspects as well as the physics and chemistry of the oceans. More mathematical treatment of oceanography is provided by J. PROUDMAN, *Dynamical Oceanography* (1953); A. DEFANT, *Physical Oceanography,* 2 vol. (1961); and the collection of papers on selected topics edited by M.N. HILL, *The Sea: Ideas and Observations on Progress in the Study of the Seas,* 3 vol. (1962–63). *The Encyclopedia of Oceanography,* ed. by R.W. FAIRBRIDGE (1966), contains many readable articles on specific water bodies as well as on general oceanographic topics; DONALD G. GROVES and LEE M. HUNT, *Ocean World Encyclopedia* (1980), is an introductory level reference work for the general reader.

(P.Gr.)

Dynamics and motions of the sea: V. CORNISH, *Waves of the Sea and Other Waves* (1910), an old but readable account of sea waves, including an additional note by Sir Harold Jeffreys dealing with his sheltering theory of wave generation, group velocity, the transport of sediment by streams and waves, the formation of sand dunes and sand ripples, and tidal bores; D.E. CARTWRIGHT, "Modern Studies of Wind-Generated Waves," *Contemp. Phys.,* 8:171 183 (March 1967), a semipopular account of the results of recent research; R.A.R. TRICKER, *Bores, Breakers, Waves and Wakes: An Introduction to the Study of Waves on Water* (1965), contains a description of tidal bores in several rivers, together with an elementary account of their causes, and several chapters on the generation and properties of shallow-water and ocean waves. W. HANSEN, "Tides," in M.N. HILL (ed.), *The Sea: Ideas and Observations on Progress in the Study of the Sea,* vol. 1 (1962), is a summary of modern research on tides. Specialized textbooks on currents are H. STOMMEL, *The Gulf Stream: A Physical and Dynamical Description,* 2nd ed. (1965); L.M. FOMIN, *The Dynamic Method in Oceanography* (1964); and G. NEUMANN, *Ocean Currents* (1968), with an extensive bibliography. D.R.F. HARLEMAN, "Stratified Flow," in V.L. STREETER (ed.), *Handbook of Fluid Dynamics* (1961), a review article on the hydraulics of density currents; H.W. MENARD, *Marine Geology of the Pacific,* ch. 9 (1964), a review of turbidity currents, written from the point of view of marine geology; "Symposium on Density Currents," *Proc.*

Int. Ass. Hydraul. Res., 8th Congr., vol. 2 (1959), many technical papers on the hydraulics of density currents; A.H. BOUMA and A. BROUWER (eds.), *Developments in Sedimentology,* vol. 3, *Turbidities* (1964), symposium with extensive bibliography on sediments deposited by turbidity currents; CHIA-SHUN YIH, *Dynamics of Nonhomogenous Fluids* (1965), an advanced text on theoretical aspects of density currents; ALFRED C. REDFIELD, *Introduction to Tides* (1981), a study of the waters of New England and New York.

(R.A.R.T./G.N./G.V.M.)

Ocean basins: The literature on the ocean basins is extensive and is growing at a rapid rate. Some general nontechnical discussions about the ocean floor are: B.C. HEEZEN and C.D. HOLLISTER, *The Face of the Deep* (1971), a magnificent monograph of deep sea photos with explanatory text; F.P. SHEPARD, *The Earth Beneath the Sea* (1959), which emphasizes the geomorphology of the ocean floor; D.H. and M.P. TARLING, *Continental Drift* (1971), summarizes the now accepted concept of drifting continents in terms of plate tectonics; H.W. MENARD, *Anatomy of an Expedition* (1969), tells how a modern scientific expedition is organized to study a portion of the Pacific Basin. Some popular books that deal with the oceans generally are: J. DUGAN, *Man Under the Sea,* rev. ed. (1965), which concerns man's entry into the subsurface world; and J. PICCARD and R.S. DIETZ, *Seven Miles Down* (1961), a documentary account of the bathyscaphe "Trieste" and its ultimate dive to the bottom of the Challenger Deep. An excellent treatment of the Pacific is presented by H.W. MENARD in *Marine Geology of the Pacific* (1964). F.P. SHEPARD, *Submarine Geology,* 2nd ed. (1963); and P.H. KUENEN, *Marine Geology* (1950), discuss the ocean floor generally. See also JAMES P. KENNETT, *Marine Geology* (1982). Charts of the coastal regions of the United States may be obtained from National Oceanic and Atmospheric Administration (NOAA), National Ocean Survey, Washington, D.C.; chart and bathymetric maps for other countries are issued by the Naval Oceanographic Office, Washington, D.C. Physiographic maps of the Atlantic, Pacific, Arctic, and Indian oceans may be obtained from the National Geographic Society; and original oceanographic data for selected regions is available from NOAA, Environmental Data Service, National Oceanographic Data Center, Rockville, Maryland.

(R.S.D.)

Basin boundaries: T.H. VAN ANDEL and G.G. SHOR (eds.), *Marine Geology of the Gulf of California* (1964), see esp. J.R. CURRAY and D.G. MOORE, "Pleistocene Deltaic Progradation of Continental Terrace, Costa de Nayarit, Mexico," pp. 193–215; J.R. CURRAY and R.D. NASON, "San Andreas Fault North of Point Arena, California," *Bull. Geol. Soc. Am. 78,* pp. 413–418 (1967); G.W. DEAN, "A Pragmatic Look at the Ocean's Mineral Resources," *Trans. N.Y. Acad. Sci.,* ser. 2, 31:731–736 (1969); K.O. EMERY, *The Sea off Southern California* (1960), an authoritative text on the continental borderland off southern California; *The Continental Shelf and Its Mineral Resources* (1967), and "Shallow Structure of Continental Shelves and Slopes," *Seast. Geol.,* 9:173–194 (1968), an up-to-date review; J.R. CURRAY, "Continental Terrace," in *Encyclopedia of Oceanography,* pp. 207–214 (1966); A.H. STRIDE et al., "Marine Geology of the Atlantic Continental Margin of Europe," *Phil. Trans. R. Soc.,* ser. A, 264:31–73 (1969), historical development admirably elucidated; W.F. WHITTARD and R. BRADSHAW (eds.), *Submarine Geology and Geophysics* (1965), several papers treating recent advances. See also GILBERT BOILLOT, *Geology of the Continental Margins* (1981; originally published in French, 1978).

An attempt to synthesize the rapidly growing information on submarine canyons is found in F.P. SHEPARD and R.F. DILL, *Submarine Canyons, and Other Sea Valleys* (1966).

(P.H.K./F.P.S.)

Features of the ocean shoreline: CHARLES DARWIN, *The Structure and Distribution of Coral Reefs* (1842, reprinted 1962); A.P. ORR and F.W. MOORHOUSE, "Variations in Some Physical and Chemical Conditions On and Near Low Isles Reef," *Sci. Rep. Great Barrier Reef Expedition,* 2:87–98 (1933); T.A. STEPHENSON et al., "The Structure and Ecology of Low Isles and Other Reefs," *ibid.,* 3:17–112 (1931); C.M. YONGE, "The Biology of Coral Reefs," in F.S. RUSSELL (ed.), *Advances in Marine Geology,* vol. 1, pp. 209–260 (1963); "Living Corals," *Proc. Roy. Soc.,* Ser. B, 169:329–344 (1968); JOHN L. DAVIES, *Geographical Variation in Coastal Development,* 2nd ed. (1980), a text in geomorphology.

Useful references on barrier island lagoons include: K.O. EMERY, R.E. STEVENSON, and J.W. HEDGPETH, "Estuaries and Lagoons," in *Treatise on Marine Ecology and Paleoecology,* ch. 23, pp. 673–749 (1957); A. GUILCHER, *Coastal and Submarine Morphology* (1958; orig. pub. in French, 1954); V.P. ZENKOVICH, *Processes of Coastal Development* (1967; orig. pub. in Russian, 1962). H.G. GIERLOFFEMDEN, "Nehrungen und Lagunen," *Petermanns Geogr. Mitt.,* 105:81–92, 161–176 (1961), deals in detail with early theories of lagoon formation and includes a map of lagoon and barrier shorelines of the world. A more detailed study of one lagoon is E.C.F. BIRD, "Coastal Lagoons of Southeastern Australia," in J.N. JENNINGS and J.A. MABBUTT (eds.), *Landform Studies from Australia and New Guinea*, pp. 365–385 (1967).

Information on the properties and general characteristics of large gulfs and bays of the world may be found in R.W. FAIRBRIDGE (ed.), *The Encyclopedia of Oceanography* (1966). A.J. HUXLEY (ed.), *Standard Encyclopedia of the World's Oceans and Islands* (1962), contains abbreviated information on numerous gulfs and bays, including some of the smaller ones. For morphometric and physical-geographical data on some of the larger gulfs and bays, see E. BRUNS, *Oceanologie*, vol. 1 (1958). Modern monographs on particular gulfs and bays include: F.P. SHEPARD *et al.* (eds.), *Recent Sediments, Northwest Gulf of Mexico* (1960), a summary of all aspects of the Gulf of Mexico as known through the late 1950s; T.H. VAN ANDEL and G.G. SHOR (eds.), *Marine Geology of the Gulf of California* (1964); and V.P. ZENKOVICH (ed.), *Tikhiy okean: berega Tikhogo okeana* (1967), a fairly detailed description of geological and geomorphological conditions in most of the gulfs and bays of the Pacific Ocean region (in Russian); J.R. SCHUBEL, *The Living Chesapeake* (1981), covering the geologic history and life cycles of many of its inhabitants.

(D.Hi./C.A.M.K./V.P.Z.)

Economic aspects of the oceans: J.H. and J.H. ANDERSON, "Power from the Sun by Way of the Sea?" *Power* 109:64–65 (1965), the original paper describing a method of extracting power from the thermal differential of the ocean using a floating power plant; J.E. BARDACH, "Aquaculture," *Science*, 161:1098–1106 (1968), a comprehensive review on growing food in bodies of water; J.L. BISCHOFF and F.T. MANHEIM, "Economic Potential of the Red Sea Heavy Metal Deposits," in E.T. DEGANS and D.A. ROSS (eds.), *Hot Brines and Recent Heavy Metal Deposits in the Red Sea*, pp. 535–541 (1969), a paper dealing with the economic potential of the heavy metal deposits underlying the

Red Sea brines; R.H. CHARLIER, "Harvesting the Energies of the Ocean," *MTS Journal*, 3:13–32 (1969), a comprehensive paper dealing with the techniques of extracting power from the tides and waves of the ocean; J.L. MERO, *The Mineral Resources of the Sea* (1965); J. MURRAY and A.F. RENARD, *Report on Deep-Sea Deposits Based on the Specimens Collected During the Voyage of H.M.S. Challenger* (1891), two classic references on the mineralogy of deep-sea deposits; D.F. OTHMER, "Desalination of Seawater," in F.C. FIRTH (ed.), *The Encyclopedia of Marine Resources*, pp. 162–169 (1969), a review article on the techniques of desalting seawater; L.A. WALFORD, *Living Resources of the Sea* (1958), a classic; L.G. WEEKS, "The Ocean's Resources," *Offshore*, 28:39–48, 87–88 (1968), a comprehensive review of the petroleum resources of the sea; LESLEY MARX, *The Oceans* (1981), argues against use of ocean minerals and other resources; AUGUSTA GOLDIN, *Oceans of Energy* (1980), an argument for exploitation of the ocean for energy.

(J.L.M.)

Principal oceans of the world: M.N. HILL, (ed.), *The Sea*, 3 vol. (1962–63), oceanographical articles for the specialist by experts in their respective fields; J. SCOFIELD, "The Lower Keys, Florida's Out Islands," *Natn. Geogr. Mag.*, 139: 72–93 (1971); O.W. FREEMAN (ed.), *Geography of the Pacific* (1951), a standard geographical text; H.W. MENARD, *Marine Geology of the Pacific* (1964), a general and very readable account; P.L. BEZRUKOV and V.F. KANAEV, *Principal Features of the Structure of the Bottom of the North-Eastern Part of the Indian Ocean* (Eng. trans. from the Russian, 1963); M. EWING *et al.*, "Sediment Distribution in the Indian Ocean," *Deep Sea Res.*, 16:231–248 (1969); V.G. NEYMAN, *The New Current Charts of the Indian Ocean* (Eng. trans. from the Russian, 1970); D.J. ROCHFORD, *Hydrology of the Indian Ocean*, 3 vol. (1961–64); E. WENK, "Physical Resources of the Oceans," *Scient. Am.*, 221:166–176 (1969), a paper on resource discoveries in the Atlantic, Pacific, and Indian oceans.

(I.M.J./C.H.C./V.F.K./Ed.)

Olympic Games

Just how far back in history organized athletic contests were first held remains a matter of doubt, but it is reasonably certain that they occurred in Greece, at least, some 3,500 years ago.

However ancient in origin, by the end of the 6th century BC at least four of the Greek sporting festivals, sometimes known as classical games, had achieved major importance. They were the Olympic Games, held at Olympia; the Pythian Games at Delphi; the Nemean Games at Nemea; and the Isthmian Games at Corinth. Later, similar festivals were held in nearly 150 cities as far afield as Rome, Naples, Odessus, Antioch, and Alexandria.

The Olympic Games in particular were to become famous throughout the Greek world. There are records of the champions at Olympia from 776 BC to AD 217. The Games, held every four years, were abolished in AD 393 by the Roman emperor Theodosius I, probably because of their pagan associations. For the first 100 or 200 years, Olympic champions came from a dozen or more Greek

cities, the majority from Sparta and Athens, but in the next three centuries, athletes were drawn from 100 cities in the Greek empire. And in the final 100 years or so before the games were discontinued, champions came from as far from Olympus as Antioch, Alexandria, and Sidon.

In 1887 the 24-year-old Baron Pierre de Coubertin conceived the idea of reviving the Olympic Games and spent seven years preparing public opinion in France, England, and the United States to support his plan. At an international congress in 1894, his plan was accepted and the International Olympic Committee was founded. The first modern Olympic Games were held in Athens in April 1896, with 13 nations sending nearly 300 representatives to take part in 42 events and 10 different sports. The revival of the Olympic Games led to the formation of many international bodies controlling their own amateur sports and to the creation of National Olympic Committees in countries throughout the world.

This article is divided into the following sections:

EARLY HISTORY

Greece. Of all the games held throughout Greece, those staged at Olympia in honour of Zeus are the most famous. Held every four years between August 6 and September

19, they occupied such an important place in Greek life that time was measured by the interval between them— an Olympiad. Although the first Olympic champion listed in the records was one Coroebus of Elis, a cook, who won

The first Olympic champion

the sprint race in 776 BC, it is generally accepted that the Games were probably at least 500 years old at that time. According to one legend they were founded by Heracles, son of Alcmene. The Games, like all Greek games, were an intrinsic part of a religious festival. They were held at Olympia in the city-state of Elis, on a track about 32 metres (35 yards) wide. The racing length was one stade, a distance of about 192 metres (210 yards). In the early Olympics a race, called a stade, covered one length of the track. Horse racing, which became part of the ancient games, was held in the hippodrome, south of the stadium.

At the meeting in 776 BC, there was apparently only one event, the stade, but other events were added over the ensuing decades. In 724 BC a two-length race, *diaulos,* roughly similar to the 400-metre race, was included, and four years later the *dolichos,* a long-distance race possibly to be compared to the modern 1,500- or even 5,000-metre event, was added. Wrestling and the pentathlon were introduced in 708 BC. The latter was an all-around competition consisting of five events—the long jump, javelin throw, discus throw, foot race, and wrestling.

Boxing was introduced in 688 BC, and in 680 a chariot race. In 648 the pancratium (Greek *pankration*), a kind of all-strength, or no-holds-barred, wrestling, was included. Kicking and hitting were allowed; only biting and gouging (thrusting a finger or thumb into an opponent's eye) were forbidden. Between 632 and 616 BC events for boys were introduced. And from time to time further events were added, including contests for fully armed soldiers, for heralds, and for trumpeters. The program must have been as varied as that of the modern Olympics, although the athletics (track and field) events were limited; there was no high jumping in any form and no individual field event, except in the pentathlon.

Until the 77th Olympiad (472 BC) all of the contests took place on one day; later they were spread, with, perhaps, some fluctuation, over four days, with a fifth devoted to the closing-ceremony presentation of prizes and a banquet for the champions. Sources generally agree that women were not allowed as competitors or, except for the priestess of Demeter, as spectators. In most events, the athletes participated in the nude.

The Olympic Games were originally restricted to freeborn Greeks. The competitors, including those who came from the Greek colonies, were amateur in the sense that the only prize was a wreath or garland. The athletes *Early* underwent a most rigorous period of supervised training, *profes-* however, and eventually the contestants were true profes-*sionalism* sionals. Not only were there substantial prizes for winning, but the Olympic champion also received adulation and unlimited benefits from his city. Athletes became full-time specialists—a trend that in the modern games has caused a long and bitter controversy over amateurism.

Rome. Greece lost its independence to Rome in the middle of the 2nd century BC, and the support for the competitions at Olympia and other places fell off considerably in the next century. The Romans looked on athletics with contempt—to strip naked and to contend in public was degrading in the eyes of the Roman citizen. The Romans realized the value of the Greek festivals, however, and Augustus, who had a genuine love for athletics, staged athletic games in a temporary wooden stadium erected near the Circus Maximus. Nero was also a keen patron of the festivals in Greece. By the 4th century AD, Rome, with its population of more than 1,000,000, had well over 150 holidays for games. There was chariot racing in the hippodrome and horse racing in the Circus Maximus, with room for more than 250,000 spectators. In an amphitheatre with accommodation for 50,000, animals and human beings were maimed and slaughtered in the name of sport.

Indeed, public games were held in abundance, but for the Romans athletic events occupied a secondary position. The only ones that really interested them were the fighting events—wrestling, boxing, and the pancratium. The main difference between the Greek and Roman attitude was that the Roman festivals were described as *ludi* (games), the Greek as *agōnes* (contests). The Greeks originally organized their games for the competitors, the Romans for the public. One was primarily competition, the other

entertainment; and it is not unreasonable to suggest that the Greeks took an "amateur" view of sport, the Romans a professional one.

REVIVAL OF THE OLYMPICS

The architect of the modern Olympics was Baron Pierre de Coubertin, born in Paris on New Year's Day, 1863. As a young man he was intensely interested in literature and in education and sociology. Family tradition pointed to an army career or possibly politics, but at the age of 24 Coubertin decided that his future lay in education. At the same time he had the idea of reviving the Olympic Games, and he propounded his desire for a new era in international sport when on November 25, 1892, at a meeting of the Union des Sports Athlétiques in Paris, he said:

> Let us export our oarsmen, our runners, our fencers into other lands. That is the true Free Trade of the future; and the day it is introduced into Europe the cause of Peace will have received a new and strong ally. It inspires me to touch upon another step I now propose and in it I shall ask that the help you have given me hitherto you will extend again, so that together we may attempt to realise, upon a basis suitable to the conditions of our modern life, the splendid and beneficent task of reviving the Olympic Games.

The speech did not produce any appreciable activity, but Coubertin was not fainthearted. At a conference on international sport in Paris in June 1894 at which Coubertin raised the possibility of the revival of the Olympic Games, there were 79 delegates representing 49 organizations from nine countries. Coubertin himself wrote that except for his co-workers Dimítrios Vikélas of Greece, who was to be the first president of the International Olympic Committee, and Professor William M. Sloane of the U.S. from the College of New Jersey (later Princeton University), no one had real interest in the revival of the Games. Nevertheless, and to quote Coubertin again, "a unanimous vote in favour of revival was rendered at the end of the Congress chiefly to please me."

It was at first agreed that the Games should be held in Paris in 1900. Six years seemed a long time to wait, however, and it was decided to change the venue—what better site than Athens, the capital of Greece—and the date, to April 1896. A great deal of indifference, if not opposi- *First* tion, had to be overcome, including a refusal by Athens *games* to stage the Games at all. But Coubertin and his newly *of the* elected International Olympic Committee of 14 members *modern* won through, and the Games were opened by the King of *cycle* Greece in the first week of April 1896.

ORGANIZATION OF THE MODERN OLYMPICS

The International Olympic Committee. At the Congress of Paris in 1894, the control and development of the modern Olympic Games was entrusted to the International Olympic Committee (IOC; Comité International Olympique), with headquarters to be established in Switzerland. It is responsible for maintaining the regular celebration of the Olympic Games; seeing that the Games are carried out in the spirit that inspired their revival; and promoting the development of amateur sport throughout the world. The original committee in 1894 consisted of 14 members and Coubertin, and membership since then has been self-perpetuating.

Convinced that the downfall of the ancient Olympic Games had been caused by outside influences that undermined the spirit of the Games, Coubertin felt that the revived Games would go the same way unless they were in the hands of people whose concern was to keep the *Indepen-* spirit of amateur sport alive and who were responsible in *dence of* no way to any outside influences. Thus IOC members are *Interna-* regarded as ambassadors from the IOC to their national *tional* sports organizations. They are in no sense delegates to the *Commit-* committee and may not accept from the government of *tee* their country, or from any organization or individual, any *members* instructions that in any way affect their independence.

The IOC is a permanent organization that elects its own members. Each member—the present membership is about 70—must speak French or English and be a citizen of or reside in a country that has a National Olympic Committee. With a very few exceptions, there is only one member from any one country. Members were originally elected for life, but anyone elected after 1965 must retire at 75.

Presidents of the IOC   The IOC elects its president for a period of eight years, at the end of which he is eligible for reelection for further periods of four years each. Juan António Samaranch (Spain) was elected in 1980. Previous presidents were Dimítrios Vikélas (1894–96, Greece), Baron Pierre de Coubertin (1896–1925, France), Count Henri de Baillet-Latour (1925–42, Belgium), J. Sigfrid Edström (1946–52, Sweden), Avery Brundage (1952–72, U.S.), and Michael Morris, Lord Killanin (1972–80, Ireland).

The executive board of 11 members holds periodic meetings with the international federations and National Olympic Committees. The IOC as a whole meets annually, and a meeting can be convened at any time that one-third of the members so request.

National Olympic committees.   Each country that desires to participate in the Olympic Games must have an Olympic committee accepted by the IOC. By 1984 there were 160 such committees.

A National Olympic Committee is composed of at least five national sporting federations, each affiliated to an appropriate international federation. The ostensible purpose of these National Olympic Committees is the development and promotion of the Olympic movement and of amateur sport. National Committees arrange to equip, transport, and house their country's representatives at the Olympic Games. According to the rules of the committee, they must be not-for-profit organizations; must not associate themselves with affairs of a political or commercial nature; and must be completely independent and autonomous and in a position to resist all political, religious, or commercial pressure.

A person who has ever competed in sports as a professional, who has ever coached sports competitors for payment, or who is engaged in or connected with sport for personal profit is not eligible to serve on a national committee. The rules provide that

exceptions to these categories may be made by the Executive Board of the I.O.C. on the recommendation of the National Olympic Committee concerned.

National Olympic Committees that do not conform to IOC rules and regulations forfeit their recognition and their right to send participants to the Olympic Games.

IOC awards.   In individual Olympic Games events, the award for first place is a gold (silver-gilt, with six grams of fine gold) medal, for second place a silver medal, and for third place a bronze medal. Solid gold medals were last given in 1912. Diplomas are awarded for fourth, fifth, sixth, seventh, and eighth places. All competitors and officials receive a commemorative medal.

The IOC presents two noncompetitive awards, the Olympic Cup and the Olympic Order. The former was instituted by Baron de Coubertin in 1906. It is awarded to an association or institution that has a general reputation for merit and integrity, that has eminently served the cause of amateur sport, and that has made a substantial contribution to the Olympic movement. The first recipient of the Olympic Cup was the Touring Club de France.

Olympic Order   The Olympic Order, created in 1974, is intended for living persons, excluding active members of the IOC. There are two degrees of award—gold and silver—to be made "to any person who has illustrated the Olympic ideal through his action, has achieved remarkable merit in the sporting world, or has rendered outstanding services to the Olympic cause, either through his own personal achievement or his contribution to the development of sport." The first gold medal was awarded posthumously to Avery Brundage, for 20 years president of the IOC. Among the silver awards that have been made were those to Jesse Owens, winner of four gold medals at the 1936 Olympics, and to Dan Ferris, for more than 50 years a prominent administrator in U.S. and world track and field. Bronze medals had also been awarded but were discontinued in 1981.

Five previous awards were suspended in 1974: the Olympic Diploma of Merit, first awarded in 1905; the Sir Thomas Fearnley Cup and the Mohammed Taher Trophy, first awarded in 1951; the Count Alberto Bonacossa

Trophy, established in 1955; and the Tokyo Trophy, first awarded in 1967.

The Games and participants.   The Olympic Games (Summer) are held every four years. There is no age limit for competitors, unless one has been established by a sport's international federation. No discrimination is allowed on grounds of race, religion, or political affiliation. The Games are contests between individuals and not between countries. Separate Winter Games have been held since 1924.

The Olympic Games celebrate an Olympiad, or period of four successive years. The first Olympiad of modern times was celebrated in 1896, and subsequent Olympiads are numbered consecutively, even though no Games take place (as was the case in 1916, 1940, and 1944).

The period of the Summer Games and the Winter Games must not exceed 15 days each.

The maximum number of entries permitted for individual events is three per nation. The number is fixed (but can be varied) by the IOC in consultation with the international federation concerned. In team events, only one team per country is allowed. In general, a National Olympic Committee may only enter a citizen of the country concerned.

Problems of eligibility.   To be allowed to compete, a competitor must meet the eligibility rules as defined by the international body of the particular sport and also by the rules of the IOC.

IOC rule changes   The IOC rules were substantially changed in 1976 and now provide that a competitor must not have received any financial reward or material benefit in connection with his or her sports participation except as permitted by the IOC bylaws. These bylaws permit the athlete to receive personal sports equipment and clothing, travelling and hotel expenses, and compensation (authorized by a National Olympic Committee or a National Federation). Compensation may be given in case of necessity to cover financial loss resulting from absence from work or basic occupation because of preparation for, or participation in, the Olympic Games and international sports competitions.

This wide concession for payment, known as "broken time," in effect authorizes a competitor (subject, of course, to the rules of each individual International Federation, or of any national controlling body) to devote as much time as he or she wishes to training and competitions and to be recompensed to the full for any loss of earnings. The only limitation is that "in no circumstances shall payment made exceed the sum which the competitor would have earned in the same period." In the extreme, therefore, a competitor may abandon his or her normal occupation and engage primarily in sport.

It now appears to some of those who have been closely associated with the Games that they have become too vast, too nationalistic, too expensive, and too commercial. It is felt that no longer is the important thing "to take part," but that winning a gold medal is the only thing that matters. The primary consideration appears no longer to be the competitors, more than 95 percent of whom cannot win gold medals, but the public. Entertainment now seems to supersede the enjoyment of competition, and the demand for entertainment may well be the death of amateur sport.

Programs and events.   An official Summer Olympic program must include at least 15 of the following sports: archery, athletics (track and field), basketball, boxing, canoeing, cycling, diving, equestrian sports, fencing, field hockey, football (soccer), gymnastics, handball (team handball), judo, modern pentathlon, rowing, shooting, swimming, table tennis, tennis, volleyball, water polo, weight lifting, wrestling, and yachting. Women can participate in all of the sports except boxing, football, judo, modern pentathlon, water polo, weightlifting, and wrestling. An Olympic program may also include up to two demonstration sports and in addition must include national exhibitions and demonstrations of fine arts (architecture, literature, music, painting, sculpture, photography, and sports philately).

The Olympic sports   The particular events included in the different sports are a matter for agreement between the IOC and the international federations. For many years there were 24 events for men in track and field. In 1976, however, the men's 50,000-metre walk was excluded (on the grounds that the total number of competitors in the Games must be reduced), while women's rowing events were included for the first time. It appears that although the IOC feels that in some way there must be a limit placed upon the total number of competitors, it is unwilling to take the severe action of excluding certain sports.

The Olympic Village. The Olympic Village was first introduced at Los Angeles in 1932. The organizing committee provides the village so that competitors and team officials can be housed together and fed at a reasonable price. The villages are located as close as possible to the main stadium and other facilities and have separate accommodations for men and women. Only competitors and officials may live in the village, and the number of team officials is limited.

Ceremonies. *The Olympic flag.* In the stadium and its immediate surroundings, the Olympic flag is flown freely together with the flags of the nations taking part. The Olympic flag presented by Baron Coubertin in 1914 is the prototype: it has a white background and in the centre there are five interlaced rings—blue, yellow, black, green, and red. The blue ring is on the left next to the pole. These rings represent the five continents joined together in the Olympic Movement. The Olympic motto is *Citius—Altius—Fortius* ("Faster—Higher—Stronger").

The opening ceremony. The form of the opening ceremony is laid down by the IOC in great detail, from the moment when the chief of state of the host country is received by the president of the IOC and the organizing committee at the entrance to the stadium, to the end of the proceedings when the last team files out. The rules provide that participants are not permitted to carry cameras into the arena, but this provision is always ignored.

When the head of state has reached his place in the tribune, he is greeted with the national anthem of his country, and the parade of competitors begins. The Greek team is always the first to enter the stadium, and, except for the host team, which is always last, the other nations follow in alphabetical order as determined by the language of the organizing country. Each contingent, dressed in its official uniform, is preceded by a shield with the name of its country, while an athlete carries its national flag. At the 1980 games, some of the countries protesting the Soviet Union's involvement in Afghanistan carried the Olympic flag in place of their national flag. The competitors march around the stadium and then form up in the centre of the ground facing the tribune.

The president of the organizing committee then delivers a brief speech of welcome, followed by another brief speech from the president of the IOC, who asks the chief of state to proclaim the Games open.

A fanfare of trumpets is sounded as the Olympic flag is slowly raised; pigeons are released, symbolically to fly to the countries of the world with the news that the Games are open.

The Olympic flame is then carried into the stadium by the last of the runners who have brought it from Olympia, Greece. The runner circles the track, mounts the steps, and lights the Olympic fire that burns night and day during the Games. In 1968 a woman carried the flame into the stadium, and in 1976 the flame was borne jointly by a male and a female athlete. In 1984, at the Games in Los Angeles, a female runner brought the flame into the stadium but passed it to a male, who ran up the steps to light the Olympic fire.

Victory ceremony. Medals are presented during the Games at the various venues and usually soon after the conclusion of the event. The competitors who have won the first three places proceed to the rostrum, with the winner (gold medalist) in the centre, the silver medalist on his or her right, and the bronze medalist on the left. The medals, attached to a chain or ribbon, are hung around the necks of the winners by a member of the IOC, and the flags of the nations concerned are raised to the top of the flagpoles while an abbreviated form of the national anthem of the winner is played. The spectators

Margin note: The Olympic flame

are expected to stand and face the flags, as do the three successful athletes.

Closing ceremony. The closing ceremony takes place after the final event, which is usually the equestrian Prix des Nations. Since the Melbourne Olympics in 1956, the closing ceremony has been a less formal affair, and after certain formalities have been observed, the athletes taking part stage their own demonstrations.

The ceremonies include a parade of athletes, six from each nation, marching eight or 10 abreast without distinction of nationality, and signifying the friendly bonds of Olympic sport. The president of the IOC calls the youth of the world to assemble in four years to celebrate the Games of the next Olympiad. A fanfare is sounded, the Olympic fire is extinguished, and to the strains of the Olympic anthem the Olympic flag is lowered and the Games are over.

The awarding of the Olympic Games. The honour of holding the Olympic Games is entrusted to a city and not to a country. The choice of the city lies solely with the IOC. Application to hold the Games is made by the chief authority of the city, with the support of the national government.

Applications must state that no political meetings or demonstrations will be held in the stadium or other sports grounds or in the Olympic Village, and it must be promised that every competitor shall be given free entry without any discrimination on grounds of religion, colour, or political affiliation. This involves the assurance that the national government will not refuse visas to any of the competitors. At the Montreal Olympics in 1976, however, the Canadian government refused visas to the representatives of Taiwan because they were unwilling to forgo the title of the Republic of China, under which their National Olympic Committee was admitted to the IOC. This Canadian decision, in the opinion of the IOC, did great damage to the Olympic Games, and it was later resolved that any country in which the Games are organized must undertake strictly to observe the rules. Enforcement would be difficult and even the use of severe penalties by the IOC might not guarantee elimination of infractions.

HISTORY OF THE MODERN GAMES

Since the revival of the Games, growth in the numbers of competitions, of competitors, and of participating countries has been almost continuous. The history of the modern Games may be conveniently divided into four periods: (1) from the revival in 1896 to the outbreak of World War I, (2) the period between the two World Wars, (3), from the resumption of the Games in 1945 through the 1968 Games, and (4) from the 1972 games onward.

First period: 1896–1912. It took some time for the Games to find their continuing pattern. Of the five celebrations in the first period, the first three, Athens in 1896, Paris in 1900, and St. Louis, Missouri, in 1904, were somewhat haphazard affairs. The entries were unlimited and hardly ever "national" in the sense of representing each nation's best performers. The actual events included varied considerably, and it is not possible to determine with any degree of confidence which of the events were really of Olympic significance. Women competed at golf and lawn tennis in the Paris Games and at archery in the St. Louis Games.

The Games of 1908 in London were the first to be organized by the various sporting bodies concerned and were not regarded as an appendage to a world fair and controlled by the promoters. Though the holding of a Franco-British Exhibition at Shepherd's Bush, London, made possible the construction of a new stadium—the famous White City, with a capacity of 66,000—the governing bodies of sport were in control. Twenty-two nations sent more than 2,000 athletes (but only 36 women) to compete in more than 100 events in 17 different sports. Archery and lawn tennis were included in the 1908 program.

Margin note: London, 1908

At Stockholm in 1912, the number of nations increased to 28, the number of competitors exceeded 2,500, and for the first time three swimming events for women were included. Because of World War I, no Games were held in 1916.

Second period: 1920–36. This period saw the golden

age of athletes—from the Finnish domination of middle- and long-distance running to the performances in the sprints, especially that of Jesse Owens. In this period, too, there were five celebrations. In less than two years after the Armistice in November 1918, Belgium organized the first post-World War I Olympics, opened at Antwerp by King Albert I. Twenty-nine nations, including many new ones, sent more than 2,500 competitors to take part in more than 150 events in 19 sports. Women competitors were still a mere handful (about 60). Four years later, in Paris, the number of countries increased to 44, with more than 3,000 competitors for 137 events, a decrease because of a reduction in the excessive number of shooting and yachting events. More than 100 women took part, competing in fencing as well as swimming and lawn tennis. After 1924 a question of eligibility in lawn tennis caused the IOC to omit the sport from future Games.

Increase of women's events

In 1928 in Amsterdam, women's track and field competitions (five events) and one event for women in gymnastics were introduced. Again there were 3,000 athletes, from 46 countries, but the number of women (290) was more than double that at Paris (136). Four years later the Games for the second time crossed the Atlantic, to Los Angeles, and there was a falling off in the number of competitors— less than 1,500 from 37 countries. The long journey from Europe and the heavy cost during a major depression were responsible for the decreases. The return to Europe for the Berlin Games produced 4,000 athletes in 1936.

Third period: 1948–68. In this period there was a significant rise in the number of women competitors and the number of events open to women. Sports other than track and field, such as swimming, came into prominence. Most of all an increase in television coverage of both Winter and Summer Games increased the audience. Because of World War II, no Games were held in 1940 or 1944. London was given the task of organizing the first postwar Games in 1948 with a bare three years available. This was accomplished despite difficult postwar conditions, with rationing of various materials and supplies still in effect and with expenditures limited. The number of competing countries was 59, with 4,000 competitors of whom 385 were women. Track and field events for women were increased to nine by the addition of the 200-metre run, the broad (now long) jump, and the shot put.

Finland was host to the 1952 Games, at Helsinki. The number of countries participating rose to 69, competitors totalled within 100 of 6,000, and women topped the 500 mark. In 1956 for the first time the venue was in the Southern Hemisphere. The Games in Melbourne were celebrated in November and December, and for the first time one of the sports had to take place in another country. Because of quarantine regulations that prohibited the importation of horses to Australia, the equestrian events were decided in Stockholm. Again the distance from Europe reduced the competitors in Melbourne by 1,500.

In Rome four years later, however, the number of competitors passed the 5,000 mark, the number of nations rose to more than 80, and of events to 150. Originally Rome was to have staged the 1908 Games.

First Asian Games

The Games were in Asia for the first time in 1964, at Tokyo, again in a city where the previous award (in 1940) had not been fulfilled. Once more there were record figures: 94 countries; 162 events; and 5,500 competitors.

There was considerable criticism when Mexico City was awarded the 1968 Games. Controversy surrounded charges that the altitude, more than 2,300 metres (7,500 feet), would adversely affect the majority of distance runners, who would not have been able to spend many months living in a comparably rarefied atmosphere. The number of competitors rose to more than 6,500 from 125 countries. Women numbered 800, the total events 172.

Fourth period: 1972 onward. This period has been marked by political violence and dissension. In Munich in 1972 there were nearly 200 different events, with 8,000 competitors from 124 countries. Tragedy struck the Games when Arab (Palestinian) terrorists invaded the Olympic Village and killed two and seized nine Israeli athletes as hostages for the release of 200 Arab prisoners in Israel; all nine, five of their captors, and a West German policeman were slain when police rescue attempts failed.

The Munich tragedy

In Montreal in 1976 the number of entries exceeded those of Munich, but the last minute withdrawals by countries protesting the presence of the New Zealand team because of their rugby affiliation with South Africa, whose apartheid policies were held to be objectionable, reduced the actual competitors by more than 400.

The games of the XXII Olympiad at Moscow in 1980 were marred by the lack of participation by some 60 eligible nations in protest against the Soviet Union's invasion of Afghanistan in December 1979. A total of 5,923 competitors representing 81 nations did take part, but the Games were further diminished by the intrusion of two other issues—alleged bias in judging by eastern European officials and the use of anabolic steroids by athletes to improve performance. The latter issue was exacerbated just before the Games when seven athletes caught using the drugs in 1979 were made eligible for the Olympics against the rules of the International Amateur Athletic Federation.

Moscow Games boycott

Preparations for the 1984 Games at Los Angeles were complicated by the fears of some over the physiological effects of the infamous Los Angeles smog on athletes; by jurisdictional disputes over security by various law enforcement agencies; by legal suits over scheduling of endurance events for women athletes; and by the decision of the Soviet Union and a number of its allies not to send teams to participate in the games.

The 1988 Olympics were scheduled for Seoul.

The Winter Olympic Games. While some skating events were included in the 1908 and 1920 Games, the Winter Games were accepted as a celebration comparable to the Summer Games and given the official blessing of the IOC in 1924. The first Winter Games were held at Chamonix, France, and consisted of 16 events. There were 16 participating countries, and the participants numbered less than 300. Subsequent Winter Games were held at St. Moritz, Switzerland (1928); Lake Placid, New York (1932); Garmisch-Partenkirchen, Germany (1936); St. Moritz (for a second time; 1948); Oslo (1952); Cortina d'Ampezzo, Italy (1956); Squaw Valley, California (1960); Innsbruck, Austria (1964); Grenoble, France (1968); Sapporo, Japan (1972); Innsbruck (for a second time; 1976); Lake Placid (for a second time; 1980); and Sarajevo, Yugoslavia (1984). The 1988 Winter Olympics were scheduled for Calgary, Alberta.

BIBLIOGRAPHY. H.A. HARRIS, *Greek Athletes and Athletics* (1964, reissued 1979); E. NORMAN GARDINER, *Greek Athletic Sports and Festivals* (1910, reissued 1970), and *Athletics of the Ancient World* (1930, reprinted 1980); and MOSES I. FINLEY and H.W. PLEKETT, *The Olympic Games: The First Thousand Years* (1976), are histories of ancient games. BARON PIERRE DE COUBERTIN, *Olympic Memoirs* (1979; originally published in French, 1931); BILL HENRY and PATRICIA H. YEOMANS, *An Approved History of the Olympic Games* (1984); JOHN KIERAN, A. DALEY, and PAT JORDAN, *The Story of the Olympic Games, 776 B.C. to 1976*, rev. ed. (1977); and NICHOLAS M. YALOURIS, *Eternal Olympics* (1979), are reports of the Games up to modern times. JOHN L. MACALOON, *The Great Symbol: Pierre de Coubertin and the Origins of the Modern Olympic Games* (1981), is a scholarly biography. There are official reports of every celebration since 1904. PETER LOVESEY and T. MCNAB, *The Guide to British Track and Field Literature from 1275–1968* (1969), includes 50 works on the Olympic Games.

(H.M.A./Ed.)

Principles of Optics

Kepler's
theory

O riginally, the term optics was used only in relation to the eye and vision. Later, as lenses and other devices for aiding vision began to be developed, these were naturally called optical instruments, and the meaning of the term optics eventually became broadened to cover any application of light, even though the ultimate receiver is not the eye but a physical detector, such as a photographic plate or a television camera. Within the present century optical methods have been applied extensively to regions of the electromagnetic radiation spectrum not visible to the eye, such as X-rays, ultraviolet, infrared, and microwave radio waves, and to this extent these regions are now often included in the general field of optics.

In the present article the image-forming properties of lenses, mirrors, and other devices that make use of light are considered. The wave and quantum nature of light, its velocity, wavelength, polarization, diffraction, and interference may be found in LIGHT. The interrelations between light and electricity, which are involved in light sources and detectors, are treated in ELECTRONICS: *Electron tubes*. The analysis of light into its component colours by prisms and gratings forms the basis of the extensive field of spectroscopy, the principles of which are discussed in ANALYSIS AND MEASUREMENT: *Spectroscopy*. For information about the reception of light by the retina of the eye and the interpretation of images by the brain, see SENSORY RECEPTION: *Vision*.

This article is divided into the following sections:

Geometrical optics

GENERAL CONSIDERATIONS

The optical image.   An optical image may be regarded as the apparent reproduction of an object by a lens or mirror system, employing light as a carrier. An entire image is generally produced simultaneously, as by the lens in a camera, but images may also be generated sequentially by point-by-point scanning, as in a television system or in the radio transmission of pictures across long distances in space. Nevertheless, the final detector of all images is invariably the human eye, and, whatever means is used to transmit and control the light, the final image must either be produced simultaneously or scanned so rapidly that the observer's persistence of vision will give him the mental impression of a complete image covering a finite field of view. For this to be effective the image must be repeated (as in motion pictures) or scanned (as in television) at least 40 times a second to eliminate flicker or any appearance of intermittency.

Historical background.   To the ancients, the processes of image formation were full of mystery. Indeed, for a long time there was a great discussion as to whether, in vision, something moved from the object to the eye or whether something reached out from the eye to the object. By the beginning of the 17th century, however, it was known that rays of light travel in straight lines, and in 1604 Johannes Kepler, a German astronomer, published a book on optics in which he postulated that an extended object could be regarded as a multitude of separate points, each point emitting rays of light in all directions. Some of these rays would enter a lens, by which they would be bent around and made to converge to a point, the "image" of the object point whence the rays originated. The lens of the eye was not different from other lenses, and it formed an image of external objects on the retina, producing the sensation of vision.

There are two main types of image to be considered: real and virtual. A real image is formed outside the system, where the emerging rays actually cross; such an image can be caught on a screen or piece of film and is the kind of image formed by a slide projector or in a camera. A virtual image, on the other hand, is formed inside an instrument at the point where diverging rays would cross if they were extended backward into the instrument. Such an image is formed in a microscope or telescope and can be seen by looking into the eyepiece.

Kepler's concept of an image as being formed by the crossing of rays was limited in that it took no account of possible unsharpness caused by aberrations, diffraction, or even defocussing. In 1957 the Italian physicist Vasco Ronchi went the other way and defined an image as any recognizable nonuniformity in the light distribution over a surface such as a screen or film; the sharper the image, the greater the degree of nonuniformity. Today, the concept of an image often departs from Kepler's idea that an extended object can be regarded as innumerable separate points of light, and it is sometimes more convenient to regard an image as being composed of overlapping patterns of varying frequencies and contrasts; hence, the quality of a lens can be expressed by a graph connecting the spatial frequency of a parallel line object with the contrast in the image. This concept is investigated fully under *Optics and information theory* below.

Optics had progressed rapidly by the early years of the 19th century. Lenses of moderately good quality were being made for telescopes and microscopes, and in 1841 the great mathematician Carl Friedrich Gauss published his classical book on geometrical optics. In it he expounded the concept of the focal length and cardinal points of a lens system and developed formulas for calculating the position and size of the image formed by a lens of given focal length. Between 1852 and 1856 Gauss's theory was extended to the calculation of the five principal aberrations of a lens (see below), thus laying the foundation for the formal procedures of lens design that were used for the next 100 years. Since about 1960, however, lens design has been almost entirely computerized, and the old methods of designing lenses by hand on a desk calculator are rapidly disappearing.

By the end of the 19th century numerous other workers had entered the field of geometrical optics, notably an English physicist, Lord Rayleigh (John William Strutt), and a German physicist, Ernst Karl Abbe. It is impossible to list all their accomplishments here. Since 1940 there has been a great resurgence in optics on the basis of information and communication theory, which is treated at length below.

Light rays, waves, and wavelets. A single point of light, which may be a point in an extended object, emits light in the form of a continually expanding train of waves, spherical in shape and centred about the point of light. It is, however, often much more convenient to regard an object point as emitting fans of rays, the rays being straight lines everywhere perpendicular to the waves. When the light beam is refracted by a lens or reflected by a mirror, the curvature of the waves is changed, and the angular divergence of the ray bundle is similarly changed in such a way that the rays remain everywhere perpendicular to the waves. When aberrations are present, a convergent ray bundle does not shrink to a perfect point, and the emerging waves are then not truly spherical.

In 1690 Christiaan Huygens, a Dutch scientist, postulated that a light wave progresses because each point in it becomes the centre of a little wavelet travelling outward in all directions at the speed of light, each new wave being merely the envelope of all these expanding wavelets. When the wavelets reach the region outside the outermost rays of the light beam, they destroy each other by mutual interference wherever a crest of one wavelet falls upon a trough of another wavelet. Hence, in effect, no waves or wavelets are allowed to exist outside the geometrical light beam defined by the rays. The normal destruction of one wavelet by another, which serves to restrict the light energy to the region of the rectilinear ray paths, however, breaks down when the light beam strikes an opaque edge, for the edge then cuts off some of the interfering wavelets, allowing others to exist, which diverge slightly into the shadow area. This phenomenon is called diffraction, and it gives rise to a complicated fine structure at the edges of shadows and in optical images (see LIGHT).

The pinhole camera. An excellent example of the working of the wavelet theory is found in the well-known pinhole camera. If the pinhole is large, the diverging geometrical pencil of rays leads to a blurred image, because each point in the object will be projected as a finite circular patch of light on the film. The spreading of the light at the boundary of a large pinhole by diffraction is slight. If the pinhole is made extremely small, however, the geometrical patch then becomes small, but the diffraction spreading is now great, leading once more to a blurred picture. There are thus two opposing effects present, and at the optimum hole size the two effects are just equal. This occurs when the hole diameter is equal to the square root of twice the wavelength (λ) times the distance (f) between the pinhole and film—i.e., $\sqrt{2\lambda f}$. For $f = 100$ millimetres and $\lambda = 0.0005$ millimetre, the optimum hole size becomes 0.32 millimetre. This is not very exact, and a 0.4-millimetre hole would probably be just

as good in practice. A pinhole, like a camera lens, can be regarded as having an *f*-number, which is the ratio of focal length to aperture. In this example, the *f*-number is 100/0.32 = 310, designated *f*/310. Modern camera lenses have much greater apertures, in order to achieve light-gathering power, of around *f*/1.2–*f*/5.6.

Resolution and the Airy disk. When a well-corrected lens is used in place of a pinhole, the geometrical ray divergence is eliminated by the focussing action of the lens, and a much larger aperture may be employed; in that case the diffraction spreading becomes small indeed. The image of a point formed by a perfect lens is a minute pattern of concentric and progressively fainter rings of light surrounding a central dot, the whole structure being called the Airy disk after George Biddell Airy, an English astronomer, who first explained the phenomenon in 1834. The Airy disk of a practical lens is small, its diameter being approximately equal to the *f*-number of the lens expressed in microns (0.001 millimetre). The Airy disk of an *f*/4.5 lens is therfore about 0.0045 millimetre in diameter (ten times the wavelength of blue light). Nevertheless, the Airy disk formed by a telescope or microscope objective can be readily seen with a bright point source of light if a sufficiently high eyepiece magnification is used.

The finite size of the Airy disk sets an inevitable limit to the possible resolving power of a visual instrument. Rayleigh found that two adjacent and equally bright stars can just be resolved if the image of one star falls somewhere near the innermost dark ring in the Airy disk of the other star; the resolving power of a lens can therefore be regarded as about half the *f*-number of the lens expressed in microns. The angular resolution of a telescope is equal to the angle subtended by the least resolvable image separation at the focal length of the objective, the light-gathering lens. This works out at about four and a half seconds of arc divided by the diameter of the objective in inches.

The Rayleigh limit. As noted above, when a perfect lens forms an image of a point source of light, the emerging wave is a sphere centred about the image point. The optical paths from all points on the wave to the image are therefore equal, so that the expanding wavelets are all in phase (vibrating in unison) when they reach the image. In an imperfect lens, however, because of the presence of aberrations, the emerging wave is not a perfect sphere, and the optical paths from the wave to the image point are then not all equal. In such a case some wavelets will reach the image as a peak, some as a trough, and there will be much destructive interference leading to the formation of a sizable patch of light, much different from the minute Airy disk characteristic of a perfectly corrected lens. In 1879 Rayleigh studied the effects of phase inequalities in a star image and came to the conclusion that an image will not be seriously degraded unless the path differences between one part of the wave and another exceed one-quarter of the wavelength of light. As this difference represents only 0.125 micron (5×10^{-6} inch), it is evident that an optical system must be designed and constructed with almost superhuman care if it is to give the best possible definition.

REFLECTION AND REFRACTION

Reflection. The use of polished mirrors for reflecting light has been known for thousands of years, and concave mirrors have long been used to form real images of distant objects. Indeed, Isaac Newton greatly preferred the use of a mirror as a telescope objective to the poor-quality lenses available in his time. Because there is no limit to the possible size of a mirror, all large telescopes today are of this type.

When a ray of light is reflected at a polished surface, the angle of reflection between ray and normal (the line at right angles to the surface) is exactly equal to the angle of incidence. It can be seen that a convex mirror forms a virtual image of a distant object, whereas a concave mirror forms a real image. A plane mirror forms a virtual image of near objects, as in the familiar looking glass. Plane mirrors are often used in instruments to bend a beam of light into a different direction.

Marginalia (left column):
Lens theories

Marginalia (right column):
Airy disk

Law of reflection

The law of refraction. When a ray of light meets the surface of separation between two transparent media, it is sharply bent or refracted. Because rays are really only directions and have no physical existence, the passage of light waves through a surface must be considered if refraction is to be understood. Refraction effects are based on the fact that light travels more slowly in a denser medium. The ratio of the velocity of light in air to its velocity in the medium is called the refractive index of the medium for light of a particular colour or wavelength. The refractive index is higher for blue light than for light at the red end of the spectrum.

In Figure 1, AA' represents a plane wave of light at the instant that A' meets the plane refracting surface $A'B$ separating two media having refractive indices n and n', respectively. During the time taken by the light to travel from A to B in material n, light travels from A' to B' in material of refractive index n', forming the new wave BB' in the second material, proceeding in direction BC. Hence, the relationship $n'/n = AB/A'B'$ can be obtained; and dividing numerator and denominator by BA' gives

$$\frac{n'}{n} = \frac{AB/BA'}{A'B'/BA'} = \frac{\sin I}{\sin I'} . \qquad (1)$$

The angles I and I' are called the angle of incidence and angle of refraction between the refracting surface and the incident and refracted waves, respectively.

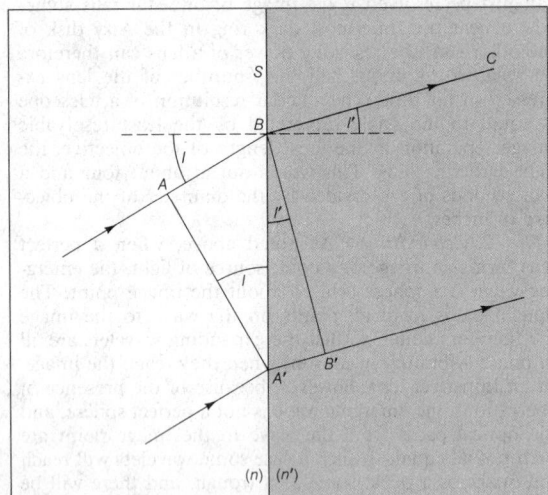

Figure 1: The law of refraction. Plane light wave at position AA' in medium of index n and BB' in medium of index n' (see text).

Returning now to the convention of considering the movement of light in terms of rays because entering and emerging rays are always perpendicular to the light waves they represent, angles I and I' also denote the angles between the entering and emerging rays and the normal (perpendicular) line to the refracting surface at B.

Equation (1), known as the law of refraction, is generally written: $n' \sin I' = n \sin I$.

Dispersion. The difference between the refractive indices of a transparent material for a specific blue light and a specific red light is known as the dispersion of the material. The usual choices of blue and red lights are the so-called "F" and "C" lines of hydrogen in the solar spectrum, named by Fraunhofer, with wavelengths 4861 and 6563 angstroms (the angstrom unit, abbreviated Å, is 10^{-8} centimetre), respectively. It is generally more significant, however, to compare the dispersion of the material for some intermediate colour such as the sodium "D" Fraunhofer line of wavelength 5893 angstroms. The dispersive power (w) of the material is then defined as the ratio of the difference between the "F" and "C" indices and the "D" index reduced by 1, or,

Dispersive power

$$w = \frac{n_F - n_C}{n_D - 1} .$$

Hundreds of different types of optical glass are currently available from manufacturers. These may be represented

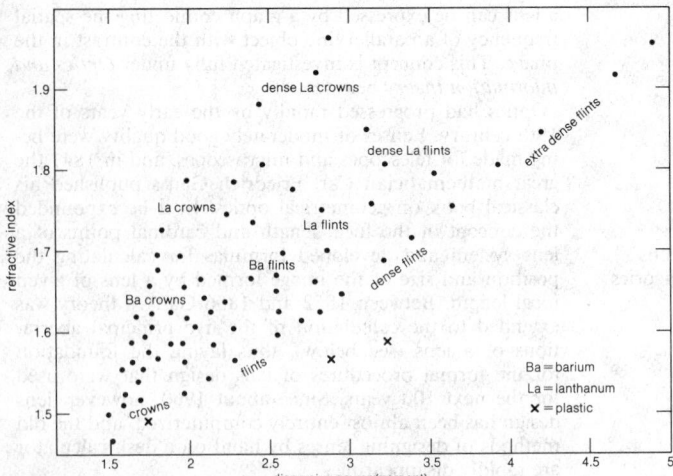

Figure 2: Relationships between refractive indices and dispersive powers of several representative optical glasses and plastics.

graphically on a plot of mean refractive index against dispersive power (Figure 2).

At first lenses were made from selected pieces of window glass or the glass used to make blown tableware. In the early 1800s, the manufacture of clear glass that was intended specifically for lenses began in Europe. The glass was slowly stirred in the molten state to remove striations and irregularities, and then the whole mass was cooled and broken up into suitable pieces for lens making. Subsequently, the pieces were placed in molds of the approximate size of the lens, slowly remelted to shape, and carefully annealed; *i.e.,* allowed to cool slowly under controlled conditions to reduce strains and imperfections. Various chemicals were added in the molten state to vary the properties of the glass: addition of lead oxide, for example, was found to raise both the refractive index and the dispersive power. In 1884 it was discovered that barium oxide had the effect of raising the refractive index without increasing the dispersion, a property that proved to be of the greatest value in the design of photographic lenses known as anastigmats (lenses devoid of astigmatic aberration). In 1938 a further major improvement was achieved by the use of various rare-earth elements, and since 1950 lanthanum glass has been commonly used in high-quality photographic lenses.

The cost of optical glass varies considerably, depending on the type of glass, the precision with which the optical properties are maintained, the freedom from internal striae and strain, the number of bubbles, and the colour of the glass. Many common types of optical glass are now available in quite large pieces, but as the specifications of the glass become more stringent the cost rises and the range of available sizes becomes limited. In a small lens such as a microscope objective or a telescope eyepiece, the cost of the glass is insignificant, but in large lenses in which every millimetre of thickness may represent an additional pound in weight, the cost of the glass can be very high indeed.

Lenses can be molded successfully of various types of plastic material, polymethyl methacrylate being the most usual. Even multi-element plastic lenses have been manufactured for low-cost cameras, the negative (concave) elements being made of a high-dispersion plastic such as styrene.

Plastic lenses

Total internal reflection. When a ray of light emerges obliquely from glass into air, the angle of refraction between ray and normal is greater than the angle of incidence inside the glass, and at a sufficiently high obliquity the angle of refraction can actually reach 90°. In this case the emerging ray travels along the glass surface, and the sine of the angle of incidence inside the glass, known as the critical angle, is then equal to the reciprocal of the refractive index of the material. At angles of incidence greater than the critical angle, the ray never emerges, and total internal reflection occurs, for there is no measurable loss if the glass surface is perfectly clean. Dirt or dust on the surface can cause a small loss of energy by scattering some light into the air.

Light is totally internally reflected in many types of reflecting prism and in fibre optics, in which long fibres of high-index glass clad with a thin layer of lower index glass are assembled side-by-side in precise order. The light admitted into one end of each fibre is transmitted along it without loss by thousands of successive internal reflections at the interlayer between the glass and the cladding. Hence, an image projected upon one end of the bundle will be dissected and transmitted to the other end, where it can be examined through a magnifier or photographed. Many modern medical instruments, such as cystoscopes and bronchoscopes, depend for their action on this principle. Single thick fibres (actually glass rods) are sometimes used to transmit light around corners to an otherwise inaccessible location.

RAY-TRACING METHODS

Graphical ray tracing. In 1621 Willebrord Snell, a professor of mathematics at Leiden, discovered a simple graphical procedure for determining the direction of the refracted ray at a surface when the incident ray is given. The mathematical form of the law of refraction, equation (1) above, was announced by the French mathematician René Descartes some 16 years later.

Snell's construction is as follows: The line AP in Figure 3A represents a ray incident upon a refracting surface at P, the normal at P being PN. If the incident and refracted rays are extended to intersect any line SS parallel to the normal, the lengths PQ and PR along the rays will be

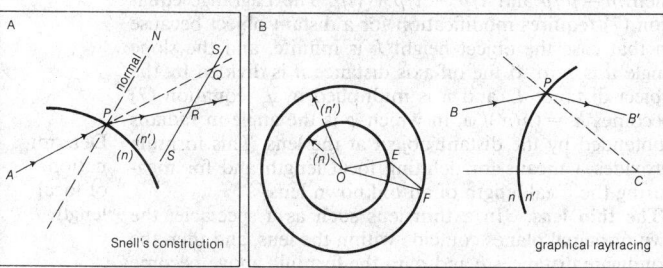

Figure 3: Graphic refraction procedures (see text).

Snell's
construc-
tion

proportional to the refractive indices n and n'. Hence, if PQ and the indices are known, PR can be found and the refracted ray drawn in.

A convenient modification of Snell's construction can readily be used to trace the path of a ray through a complete lens. In Figure 3B, the incident ray BP strikes a refracting surface at P. The normal to the surface is PC. At any convenient place on the page two concentric circles are drawn about a point O with radii proportional to the refractive indices n and n', respectively. A line OE is now drawn parallel to the incident ray BP extending as far as the circle representing the refractive index n of the medium containing the incident ray. From E a line is drawn parallel to the normal PC extending to F on the circle representing the refractive index n'. The line OF then represents the direction of the desired refracted ray, which may be drawn in at PB'. This process is repeated successively for all the surfaces in a lens. If a mirror is involved, the reflected ray may be found by drawing the normal line EF across the circle diagram to the incident-index circle on the other side.

Trigonometrical ray tracing. No graphical construction can possibly be adequate to determine the aberration residual of a corrected lens, and for this an accurate trigonometrical computation must be made and carried out to six or seven decimal places, the angles being determined to single seconds of arc or less. There are many procedures for calculating the path of a ray through a system of spherical refracting or reflecting surfaces, the following being typical: The diagram in Figure 4 represents a ray lying in the meridian plane, defined as the plane containing the lens axis and the object point. A ray in this plane is defined by its slope angle, U, and by the length of the

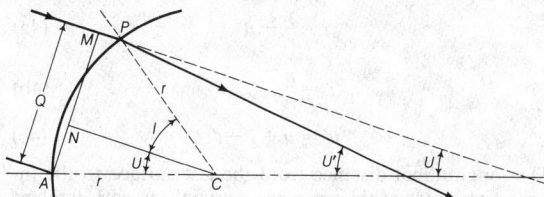

Figure 4: Trigonometrical ray tracing (see text).

perpendicular, Q, drawn from the vertex (A) of the surface on to the ray. By drawing a line parallel to the incident ray through the centre of curvature C, to divide Q into two parts at N, the relation is stated as $AN = r \sin U$, and $NM = r \sin I$. Hence

$$Q = r (\sin U + \sin I). \qquad (2)$$

From this the first ray-tracing equation can be derived,

$$\sin I = \frac{Q}{r} - \sin U. \qquad (3a)$$

Applying the law of refraction, equation (2), gives the second equation

$$\sin I' = \frac{n}{n'} - \sin I. \qquad (3b)$$

Because the angle $PCA = U + I = U' + I'$, the slope of the refracted ray can be written as

$$U' = U + I - I'; \qquad (3c)$$

and, lastly, by adding primes to equation (2),

$$Q' = r (\sin U' + \sin I').$$

Having found the Q' of the refracted ray, transfer to the next surface can be performed by

$$Q_2 = Q'_1 - d \sin U'_1,$$

in which d is the axial distance from the first to the second refracting surface. After performing this calculation for all the surfaces in succession, the longitudinal distance from the last surface to the intersection point of the emergent ray with the lens axis is found by

$$L' = \frac{Q'}{\sin U'}.$$

Corresponding but much more complicated formulas are available for tracing a skew ray, that is, a ray that does not lie in the meridian plane but travels at an angle to it. After refraction at a surface, a skew ray intersects the meridian plane again at what is called the diapoint. By tracing the paths of a great many (100 or more) meridional and skew rays through a lens, with the help of an electronic computer, and plotting the assemblage of points at which all these rays pierce the focal plane after emerging from the lens, a close approximation to the appearance of a star image can be constructed, and a good idea of the expected performance of a lens can be obtained.

PARAXIAL, OR FIRST-ORDER, IMAGERY

In a lens that has spherical aberration, the various rays from an axial object point will in general intersect the lens axis at different points after emerging into the image space. By tracing several rays entering the lens at different heights (*i.e.,* distances from the axis) and extrapolating from a graph connecting ray height with image position, it would be possible to infer where a ray running very close to the axis (a paraxial ray) would intersect the axis, although such a ray could not be traced directly by the ordinary trigonometrical formulas because the angles would be too small for the sine table to be of any use. Because the sine of a small angle is equal to the radian measure of the angle itself, however, a paraxial ray can be traced by reducing the ray-tracing formulas to their limiting case for small angles and thus determining the paraxial intersection point directly. When this is done, writing paraxial-ray data with lowercase letters, it is found that the Q and Q' above both become equal to the height of incidence y, and the formulas (3a), (3b), and (3c) become, in the paraxial limit:

Paraxial
rays

$$i = \frac{y}{r'} - u \qquad (4a)$$

$$i' = \frac{n}{n'} i \qquad (4b)$$

$$u' = u + i - i'. \qquad (4c)$$

The longitudinal distance from the last surface to the intersection point of the emerging paraxial ray with the lens axis becomes $l' = y/u'$.

Because all paraxial rays from a given object point unite at the same image point, the resulting longitudinal distance (l') is independent of the particular paraxial ray that is traced. Any nominal value for the height of incidence, y, may therefore be adopted, remembering that it is really an infinitesimal and y is only its relative magnitude. Thus, it is clear that the paraxial angles in equation (4) are really only auxiliaries, and they can be readily eliminated, giving the object–image distances for paraxial rays:

$$n'(l' - r)u' = n(l - r)u \qquad (5)$$

and

$$\frac{n'}{l'} = \frac{n}{l} + \frac{n' - n}{r}. \qquad (6)$$

Magnification: the optical invariant. It is frequently as important to determine the size of an image as it is to determine its location. To obtain an expression for the magnification—that is, the ratio of the size of an image to the size of the object—the following process may be used: If an object point B lies to one side of the lens axis at a transverse distance h from it, and the image point B' is at a transverse distance h', then B, B', and the centre of curvature of the surface, C, lie on a straight line called the auxiliary axis. Then, by simple proportion,

$$m = \frac{h'}{h} = \frac{l' - r}{l - r} = \frac{nu}{n'u'}.$$

Hence,

$$h'n'u' = hnu, \qquad (7)$$

and the product (hnu) is invariant for all the spaces between the lens surfaces, including the object and image spaces, for any lens system of any degree of complexity. This theorem has been named after the French scientist Joseph-Louis Lagrange, although it is sometimes called the Smith-Helmholtz theorem, after Robert Smith, an English scientist, and Hermann Helmholtz, a German scientist; the product (hnu) is often known as the optical invariant. As it is easy to determine the quantities h, n, and u for the original object, it is only necessary to calculate u' by tracing a paraxial ray in order to find the image height h' for any lens. If the lens is used in air, as most lenses are, the refractive indices are both unity, and the magnification becomes merely $m = u/u'$.

The Gauss theory of lenses. In 1841 Gauss published a now famous treatise on optics in which he demonstrated that, so far as paraxial rays are concerned, a lens of any degree of complexity can be replaced by two principal, or nodal, points and two focal points, the distances from the principal points to their respective focal points being the focal lengths of the lens, and, furthermore, that the two focal lengths are equal to one another when the refractive indices of object and image spaces are equal, as when a lens is used in air.

The principal and focal points may be defined as follows: Figure 5 shows a lens system of any construction, with a bundle of rays entering from the left in a direction parallel to the lens axis. After refraction by the lens each ray will cross the axis at some point, and the entering and

emerging portions of each ray are then extended until they intersect at a point such as Q. The locus of all the points Q is a surface of revolution about the lens axis known as the equivalent refracting locus of the lens. The point where this locus crosses the axis is called the principal point, P_2, and the central portion of the locus in the neighbourhood of the axis, which is virtually a plane perpendicular to the axis, is called the principal plane. The point where the emerging paraxial ray crosses the axis is called the focal point F_2, the distance from P_2 to F_2 being the (posterior) focal length f'. A similar situation exists for a parallel beam of light entering from the right, giving the anterior principal point P_1, the anterior focal point F_1, and the front focal length f. For a lens in air it can be shown that the two focal lengths are equal in magnitude but opposite in direction—i.e., if F_2 is to the right of P_2, then F_1 must lie to the left of P_1, as in the case of an ordinary positive lens (one that gives a real image). In a negative lens (one that gives a virtual image), F_2 lies to the left of P_2, and the posterior focal length f' is negative.

The relation between the distances of object and image from a lens can be easily stated if the positions of the two principal points and the two focal points are known. (In using these expressions, distances are considered positive or negative depending on whether they are measured to the right or to the left from their respective origins.) For a lens in air: (a) If the conjugate distances measured from the respective focal points are x and x', and if m is the image magnification (height of image divided by height of object), then $m = -x'/f' = f'/x$ and $xx' = -f'^2$. (b) If the conjugate distances measured from the respective principal points are p and p' and if m is the image magnification, then $m = p'/p$ and $1/p' = 1/p + 1/f'$. The Lagrange equation (7) requires modification for a distant object because in that case the object height h is infinite, and the slope angle u is zero. If the off-axis distance h is divided by the object distance L, and u is multiplied by L, equation (7) becomes $h' = (n/n')f'\varphi$, in which φ is the angle in radians subtended by the distant object at the lens. This formula provides a means for defining focal length and for measuring the focal length of an unknown lens.

The thin lens. In a thin lens such as a spectacle, the two principal planes coincide within the lens, and then the conjugate distances p and p' in the formula above become the distances of object and image from the lens itself.

The focal length of a thin lens can be computed by applying the surface-conjugate formula (6) to the two surfaces in succession, writing the l of the first surface as infinity and the l of the second surface equal to the l' of the first surface. When this is done, the lens power (P) becomes

$$P = \frac{1}{f'} = (n - 1)\left(\frac{1}{r_1} - \frac{1}{r_2}\right).$$

If a number of thin lenses are assembled together in contact, assuming that the combination is still virtually a thin lens, then the power $(1/f')$ of the combination will be equal to the sum of the powers of the separate lenses. Thus, if a thin negative lens is placed in close contact with a thin positive lens of equal power, the combination will have zero power and will no longer act like a lens. This is the basis of a process used by optometrists to ascertain the power of an unknown lens by combining it with one of a series of known lenses from a trial case.

Chromatic aberration. Because the refractive index of glass varies with wavelength, every property of a lens that depends on its refractive index also varies with wavelength, including the focal length, the image distance, and the image magnification. The change of image distance with wavelength is known as chromatic aberration, and the variation of magnification with wavelength is known as chromatic difference of magnification, or lateral colour. Chromatic aberration can be eliminated by combining a strong lens of low-dispersion glass (crown) with a weaker lens made of high-dispersion (flint) glass. Such a combination is said to be achromatic. This method of removing chromatic aberration was discovered in 1729 by Chester Hall, an English inventor, and it was exploited vigorously in the late 18th century in numerous small telescopes. Chromatic variation of magnification can be eliminated by

Lagrange theorem (margin note, left)

Determination of focal length (margin note, right)

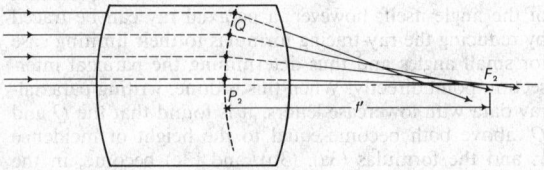

Figure 5: The Gauss theory (see text).

achromatizing all the components of a system or by making the system symmetrical about a central diaphragm. Both chromatic aberration and lateral colour are corrected in every high-grade optical system.

Longitudinal magnification. If an object is moved through a short distance δp along the axis, then the corresponding image shift $\delta p'$ is related to the object movement by the longitudinal magnification $(\overline{m})$. Succinctly,

$$\overline{m} = \delta p'/\delta p = m^2 ,$$

in which m is the lateral magnification. The fact that the longitudinal magnification is equal to the square of the transverse magnification means that $\overline{m}$ is always positive; hence, if the object is moved from left to right, the image must also move from left to right. Also, if m is large, then $\overline{m}$ is very large, which explains why the depth of field (δp) of a microscope is extremely small. On the other hand, if m is small, less than one as in a camera, then $\overline{m}$ is very small, and all objects within a considerable range of distances (δp) appear substantially in focus.

Limita-
tion on
depth of
field

Image of a tilted plane. If a lens is used to form an image of a plane object that is tilted relative to the lens axis, then the image will also be tilted in such a way that the plane of the object, the plane of the image, and the median plane of the lens all meet. This construction can be derived by the use of the lateral and longitudinal magnification relations just established above. With a tilted object the magnification at any point is given by the ratio of the distances of image and object from the lens at that point in the image, and, consequently, m varies progressively from one end of the image to the other. This arrangement is frequently used in view cameras equipped with "swings" to increase depth of field and in enlargers to rectify the convergence of parallel lines caused by tilting the camera, for example, in photographing tall buildings. The rule finds extensive application in photogrammetry and in the making of maps from aerial photographs.

OPTICAL SYSTEMS

System components. An optical system consists of a succession of elements, which may include lenses, mirrors, light sources, detectors, projection screens, reflecting prisms, dispersing devices, filters and thin films, and fibre-optics bundles.

Lenses. All optical systems have an aperture stop somewhere in the system to limit the diameter of the beams of light passing through the system from an object point. By analogy with the human eye, this limiting aperture stop is called the iris of the system, its images in the object and image spaces being called the entrance pupil and exit pupil, respectively. In most photographic lenses the iris is inside the objective, and it is often adjustable in diameter to control the image illumination and the depth of field. In telescope and microscope systems the cylindrical mount of the objective lens is generally the limiting aperture or iris of the system; its image, formed behind the eyepiece where the observer's eye must be located to see the whole area being observed, called the field, is then the exit pupil.

Entrance
and exit
pupils

The pupils of a lens system can be regarded as the common bases of oblique beams passing through the system from all points in an extended object. In most systems, however, the mounts of some of the lens elements cut into the oblique beams and prevent the beams from being perfectly circular, and the pupils are then not fully filled with light. This effect is known as vignetting and leads to a reduction in illumination in the outer parts of the field of view.

A common feature of many optical systems is a relay lens, which may be introduced to invert an image or to extend the length of the system, as in a military periscope. An example of the use of a relay lens is found in the common rifle sight shown diagrammatically in Figure 6. Here the front lens A is the objective, forming an inverted image of the target on the cross wire or reticle at B. The light then proceeds to the relay lens C, which forms a second image, now erect, at D. Beyond this image is the eyepiece E to render the light parallel so that the image may be seen sharply by the observer. Unfortunately, the oblique beam from the objective will usually miss the relay lens, and so a field lens must be inserted at or near the first image B to bend the oblique beams around and redirect them toward the relay lens. The power of the field lens is chosen so that it will form an image of the objective lens aperture on the relay lens aperture. The iris and entrance pupil of this system coincide at the objective; there is an internal pupil at the relay lens, and the exit pupil lies beyond the eyepiece as shown in Figure 6.

Mirrors. Mirrors are frequently used in optical systems. Plane mirrors may be employed to bend a beam of light in another direction, either for convenience or to yield an image reversed left for right if required. Curved mirrors, concave and convex, may be used in place of lenses as image-forming elements in reflecting telescopes. All of the world's largest telescopes and many small ones are of the reflecting type. Such telescopes use a concave mirror to produce the main image, a small secondary mirror often being added to magnify the image and to place it in a convenient position for observation or photography. Telescope mirrors are commonly made parabolic or hyperbolic in section to correct the aberrations of the image. Originally telescope mirrors were made from polished "speculum metal," an alloy of copper and tin, but in 1856 Justus von Liebig, a German chemist, invented a process for forming a mirror-like layer of silver on polished glass, which was applied to telescope mirrors by the German astronomer C.A. von Steinheil. Today most mirrors are made of glass, coated with either a chemically deposited silver layer or more often one made by depositing vaporized aluminum on the surface. The aluminum surface is as highly reflective as silver and does not tarnish as readily.

Use in
reflecting
telescopes

A large astronomical mirror presents many problems to the optical engineer, mainly because even a distortion of a few microns of the mirror under its own weight will cause an intolerable blurring of the image. Though many schemes for supporting a mirror without strain have been tried, including one to support it on a bag of compressed air, the problem of completely eliminating mirror distortion remains unsolved. A metal mirror, if well ribbed on the back, may be lighter than a glass mirror and therefore easier to handle, but most metals are slightly flexible and require just as careful support as glass mirrors. Since temperature changes can also cause serious distortion in a mirror, astronomers try to hold observatory temperatures as constant as possible.

Light sources. Many types of optical instruments form images by natural light, but some, such as microscopes and projectors, require a source of artificial light. Tungsten filament lamps are the most common, but if a very bright source is required, a carbon or xenon arc is employed. For some applications, mercury or other gas discharge tubes are used; a laser beam is often employed in scientific applications. Laser light is brilliant, monochromatic, collimated (the rays are parallel), and coherent (the waves are all in step with each other), any or all of these properties being of value in particular cases.

Detectors. The image formed by an optical system is usually received by the eye, which is a remarkably adaptable and sensitive detector of radiation within the visible region of the electromagnetic spectrum (see LIGHT). A photographic film, another widely used detector, has the advantage of yielding a permanent record of events. Since about 1925 many types of electrical detectors of radiation, both within the visible region and beyond it, have been developed. These include photoelectric cells of various kinds in which either a voltage or a resistance is modified by light falling on the device. Many new types of detectors are sensitive far into the infrared spectrum and are used to detect the heat radiated by a flame or other hot object. A number of image intensifiers and converters, particularly for X-ray or infrared radiation, which have appeared

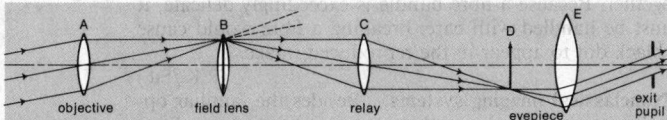

Figure 6: Operating principle of the telescopic rifle sight (see text).

since World War II, embody a radiation detector at one end of a vacuum tube and an electron lens inside the tube to relay the image on to a phosphor screen at the other end. This arrangement produces a visible picture that may be observed by eye or photographed to make a permanent record.

Television camera tubes detect real images by electronic scanning, the picture on the viewing tube being a replica of the image in the original camera. The combined application of electronics and optics has become common (see below). An extreme example of electro-optics appears in some space cameras, in which the film is exposed, processed, and then scanned by a tiny point of light; the light passing through the film is picked up by a photocell and transmitted to Earth by radio, where it is made to control the brightness of another point of light scanning a second piece of film in exact synchronism with the scanning spot in the camera. The whole system thus produces a picture on Earth that is an exact replica of the picture photographed in space a few minutes earlier.

Projection screens. The simplest screen for the projection of slides or motion pictures is, of course, a matte white surface, which may be on a hard base as in outdoor theatres or on a stretched cloth indoors. A theatre screen is often perforated to transmit sound from loudspeakers placed behind it.

Improved screen materials have been developed to increase the brightness of the picture to suit the particular shape of the auditorium. A screen covered with tiny beads tends to send the light back in the general direction of the projector, and is suitable for use at one end of a long, narrow auditorium. Another type of screen is covered with fine embossed vertical grooves; this tends to distribute the light in a horizontal band across the audience with little or no vertical spread. A real advantage of these highly reflective screens is that they tend to reflect ambient room light away from the viewer as by a mirror, so that the pictures appear almost as bright and clear by day as in a darkened room.

Reflecting prisms. Reflecting prisms are pieces of glass bounded by plane surfaces set at carefully specified angles. Some of these surfaces transmit light, some reflect light, while some serve both functions in succession. A prism is thus an assembly of plane reflectors at relatively fixed angles, which are traversed in succession by a beam of light.

The simplest prism is a triangular block of glass with two faces at right angles and one at an angle of 45°. The face at 45° deflects a beam of light through a right angle. The common Porro prism used in a pair of binoculars contains four 45° reflecting surfaces, two to reverse the beam direction in the vertical plane and two in the horizontal plane (Figure 7). These reflecting faces could be replaced by pieces of mirror mounted on a metal frame,

Prism binoculars

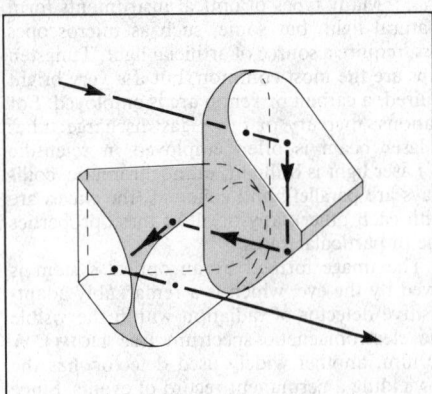

Figure 7: Porro prism.

but it is hard to hold mirrors rigidly and harder still to keep them clean. Some microscopes are equipped with a 45° deflection prism behind the eyepiece; this prism may provide two or three reflections depending on the type of image inversion or left-for-right reversal required.

Prisms containing a semireflecting, semitransmitting surface are known as beam splitters and as such have many uses. An important application is found in some colour television cameras, in which the light from the lens is divided by two beam splitters in succession to form red, green, and blue images on the faces of three image tubes in the camera.

Dispersing devices. There are two forms of dispersing element used to spread out the constituent colours of a beam of light into a "spectrum," namely a prism and a grating. The prism, known to Newton, is the older; it separates the colours of the spectrum because the refractive index of the glass is lowest for red light and progressively increases through the yellow and green to the blue, where it is highest. Prism spectroscopes and spectrographs are made in a variety of forms and sizes, but in all cases the blue end of the spectrum is greatly spread out while the red end is relatively compressed.

Prism and grating

A diffraction grating is a ruled mirror or transparent plate of glass having many thousands of fine parallel grooves to the inch. It separates the colours of the spectrum by a process of diffraction. Each groove diffracts, or scatters, light in all directions, and in the case of light of one particular wavelength, there will be one direction in which the light wave from one groove lags behind the light wave from the next groove by precisely one or more whole wavelengths. This results in a strong beam of diffracted light in that direction and darkness in all other directions. Since each spectral colour corresponds to a different wavelength, the grating spreads out the spectrum into a fan where it can be observed or photographed. The red rays are bent most and the blue rays least, the opposite of the situation with a prism.

Although a prism or grating is the essential dispersing element in a spectrograph, a fine slit and additional lenses or focussing mirrors must be used to form a sharply defined spectrum. Prism spectroscopes are, of course, limited to those wavelengths for which the prism material is transparent; a reflecting grating can be used for any wavelength that the material will reflect.

Filters and thin films. A colour filter is a sheet of transparent material that modifies a light beam by selective absorption of some colours in relation to others. A neutral filter absorbs all wavelengths equally and merely serves to reduce the intensity of a beam of light without changing its colour.

Filters may be made from sheets of coloured glass, plastic, or dyed gelatin, and in some cases glass cells filled with liquid have been used. Since World War II, another type of filter depending on the interference of light has been developed in which one or more metallic or other types of films of controlled thickness have been deposited on a glass plate, the layers being so thin as to cause selective interference of some wavelengths in relation to others and thus act as a nonabsorbing filter. In this case the rejected colours are reflected instead of being absorbed.

Polarizing filters have the property of transmitting light that vibrates in one direction while absorbing light that vibrates in a perpendicular direction. These filters are used extensively in scientific instruments. In sunglasses and when placed over a camera lens, polarizing filters reduce unwanted reflections from nonmetallic surfaces. Polarizing spectacles have been used to separate the left-eye and right-eye beams in the projection of stereoscopic pictures or movies.

Fibre-optics bundles. As noted earlier, a thin rod or fibre of glass or other transparent material transmits light by repeated internal reflections, even when the rod is somewhat curved. An ordered bundle of rods or fibres is thus capable of taking an image projected upon one end of the bundle and reproducing it at the other end. A fibre-optics bundle can be fused together into a rigid channel, or it may be left flexible, only the ends being rigidly fastened together. Because a fibre bundle is exceedingly delicate, it must be handled with care; breaking a fibre would cause a black dot to appear in the reproduced image.

(R.K./Ed.)

Nonclassical imaging systems. Besides the familiar optical systems cited above, there are many nonclassical optical elements that are used to a limited extent for special purposes. The most familiar of these is the aspheric (non-

Aspheric surfaces

spherical) surface. Because plane and spherical surfaces are the easiest to generate accurately on glass, most lenses contain only such surfaces. It is occasionally necessary, however, to use some other axially symmetric surface on a lens or mirror, generally to correct a particular aberration. An example is the parabolic surface used for the primary mirror of a large astronomical telescope; another is the elliptic surface molded on the front of the little solid glass reflector units used on highway signs.

Another commonly used optical surface is the side of a cylinder. Such surfaces have power only in the meridian perpendicular to the cylinder axis. Cylindrical lenses are therefore used wherever it is desired to vary the magnification from one meridian to a perpendicular meridian. Cylindrical surfaces are employed in the anamorphic lenses used in some wide-screen motion-picture systems to compress the image horizontally in the camera and stretch it back to its original shape in the projected image.

To correct astigmatism in the eye, many spectacles are made with toric surfaces—*i.e.*, with a stronger curvature in one meridian than in the perpendicular meridian, like the bowl of a teaspoon. These surfaces are generated and polished by special machines and are made by the million every year.

Another nonclassical optical system is the bifocal or trifocal spectacle lens. They are made either by forming two or three separate surfaces on a single piece of glass or obtaining additional power by fusing a piece of high-index glass on to the front of the main lens and then polishing a single spherical surface over both glasses.

Two French scientists, Georges-Louis Buffon and Augustin-Jean Fresnel, in the 18th century suggested forming a lens in concentric rings to save weight, each ring being a portion of what would normally be a continuous spherical surface but flattened out. On a large scale, Fresnel lenses have been used in lighthouses, floodlights, and traffic signals, and as cylindrical ship's lanterns. With fine steps a few thousandths of an inch wide, molded plastic Fresnel lenses are often used as condensers in overhead projectors and in cameras as a field lens in contact with a ground-glass viewing screen.

Lenses have occasionally been made with one surface taking the form of a flattened cone. Such lenses produce a long, linear image of a point source, lying along the lens axis; for this reason they are commonly referred to as axions. They have been used to produce a straight line of light in space for aligning machines and shafting, but since about 1965 the beam from a gas laser has generally been used instead.

Axicons

LENS ABERRATIONS

Seidel sums. If a lens were perfect and the object were a single point of monochromatic light, then, as noted above, the light wave emerging from the lens would be a portion of a sphere centred about the ideal image point, lying in the paraxial image plane at a height above the axis given by the Lagrange theorem. In practice, however, this condition is most unlikely to occur; it is much more probable that the emerging wave will depart slightly from a perfect sphere, the departure varying from point to point over the lens aperture. This departure is extremely small, being of the order of the wavelength of light that is only half a micron, so it would be impossible to show this departure on a drawing. It can be represented mathematically, however, in the following way: The coordinates of a point in the exit-pupil aperture will be represented by x_0 and y_0, the y_0 coordinate lying in the meridian plane containing the object point and the lens axis. The departure of the wave from the ideal sphere is generally called OPD, meaning optical path difference. It can be shown that OPD is related to x_0 and y_0 by five constants S_1 through S_5, and the quantity h'_0,

$$\text{OPD} = S_1(x_0^2 + y_0^2)^2 + S_2 y_0(x_0^2 + y_0^2)h'_0 +$$
$$+ S_3(x_0^2 + 3y_0^2)h_0'^2 + S_4(x_0^2 + y_0^2)h_0'^2 + S_5 y_0 h_0'^3 .$$

Each of these five terms is considered to be a separate "aberration," the coefficients $S_1, \ldots S_5$, being called Seidel sums after the 19th-century German scientist L.P. Seidel, who identified the imperfections. These aberrations

are respectively spherical, coma, astigmatism, Petzval field curvature, and distortion. The symbol h'_0 refers to the height of the final image point above the lens axis, and hence it defines the obliquity of the beam.

The five Seidel sums can be calculated by tracing a paraxial ray from object to image through the lens and by tracing also a paraxial principal ray from the centre of the aperture stop outward in both directions toward the object and image, respectively. The angle of incidence i and the ray slope angle u of each of these paraxial rays at each surface are then listed and inserted into the following expressions for the five sums. The angle u'_0 represents the final emerging slope of the paraxial ray.

Calculation of Seidel sums

The calculation starts by determining the radius A of the exit pupil by $A = \sqrt{x_0^2 + y_0^2}$ and also the quantity K at each surface by

$$K = \tfrac{1}{2} y\, n \left(\frac{n}{n'} - 1\right)(i - u').$$

The corresponding K_{pr} for the paraxial principal ray is also determined at each surface. Then, the five aberrations may be written

$$S_1 = \frac{1}{4A_4} \sum K i^2 \qquad S_2 = \frac{1}{A^3 h'_0} \sum K i i_{pr}$$

$$S_3 = \frac{1}{2A^2 h_0'^2} \sum K i_{pr}^2 \qquad S_4 = \frac{u_0'^2}{4A^2} \sum \frac{n - n'}{nn'\, r}$$

$$S_5 = \frac{1}{A h_0'^3} \sum \left[K_{pr} i i_{pr} + \tfrac{1}{2} h'_0 u'_0 (u_{pr}'^2 - u_{pr}^2) \right].$$

To interpret these aberrations, the simplest procedure is to find the components x', y' of the displacement of a ray from the Lagrangian image point in the paraxial focal plane, by differentiating the OPD expression given above. The partial derivatives $\partial \text{OPD}/\partial x_0$ and $\partial \text{OPD}/\partial y_0$ represent respectively the components of the slope of the wave relative to the reference sphere at any particular point (x_0, y_0). Hence, because a ray is always perpendicular to the wave, the ray displacements in the focal plane can be found by

$$x' = f\frac{\partial \text{OPD}}{\partial x_0} \qquad \text{and} \qquad y' = f\frac{\partial \text{OPD}}{\partial y_0},$$

in which f is the focal length of the lens. The aggregation of rays striking the focal plane will indicate the kind of image that is characteristic of each aberration.

This procedure will be applied to each of the five aberration terms separately, assuming that all the other aberrations are absent. Obviously, in a perfect lens x' and y' are zero because OPD is zero. It must be remembered, however, that by using rays instead of waves, all fine-structure

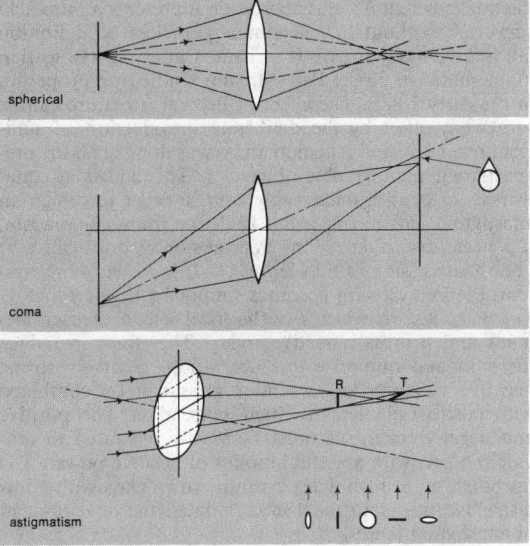

Figure 8: Lens aberrations.

effects caused by diffraction will be lost, and only the macroscopic image structure will be retained.

Spherical aberration. The first term in the OPD expression is OPD $= S_1(x_0^2 + y_0^2)^2$. Hence

$$x' = f\frac{\partial \text{OPD}}{\partial x_0} = 4fA^2S_1 \cdot x_0 \quad \text{and} \quad y' = f\frac{\partial \text{OPD}}{\partial y_0} = 4fA^2S_1 \cdot y_0.$$

These displacements can both be eliminated simultaneously by applying a longitudinal shift L to the focal plane. This changes x' by $-Lx_0/f$ and y' by $-Ly_0/f$; hence, if L is made equal to $4fA^2S_1$, both ray displacements vanish. The aberration, therefore, represents a condition in which each zone of the lens has a different focus along the axis, the shift of focus from the paraxial image being proportional to A^2. This is known as spherical aberration (see Figure 8).

Coma. The S_2 term in the OPD expression represents the aberration called coma, in which the image of a point has the appearance of a comet. The x' and y' components are as follows:

$$x' = fh_0'S_2(2x_0y_0)$$
$$y' = fh_0'S_2(x_0^2 + 3y_0^2).$$

When this aberration is present, each circular zone of the lens forms a small ringlike image in the focal plane, the rings formed by successive concentric zones of the lens fitting into two straight envelope lines at 60° to each other (Figure 8). Because the brightness of this image is greatest at the tip, coma tends to form a one-sided haze on images in the outer parts of the field.

Astigmatism. If only the S_3 term is present, then

$$x' = 2fh_0'^2S_3(x_0)$$
$$y' = 2fh_0'^2S_3(3y_0).$$

For any one zone of the lens, x' and y' describe a vertical ellipse with major axis three times the minor axis. The images formed by all the smaller zones of the lens fit into this ellipse and fill it out with a uniform intensity of light. If the image plane is moved along the axis by a distance L, as in focussing a camera, then, at $L = 2f^2h_0'^2S_3$, the ellipse shrinks to a radial focal line (R). Twice this displacement yields a circle; three times this L gives a tangential focal line (T), which is followed by an ellipse with its major axis in the x direction, as in Figure 8, bottom. The usual effect of astigmatism in an image is the appearance of radial or tangential blurring in the outer parts of the field.

Petzval curvature. For the S_4 term taken alone,

$$x' = 2fh_0'^2S_4 \cdot x_0$$
$$y' = 2fh_0'^2S_4 \cdot y_0.$$

The image of a point is now a small circle that contracts to a point at a new focus situated at a longitudinal distance $L = 2f^2h_0'^2S_4$ from the paraxial image. As the longitudinal displacement of the focus is proportional to the square of the image height h_0', this aberration represents a pure field curvature without any accompanying loss of definition (all lines remain sharp). It is named after the Hungarian mathematician József Petzval, who studied its properties in the early 1840s. The effect of Petzval curvature can be somewhat offset by the deliberate introduction of sufficient overcorrected astigmatism, as was done in all the pre-anastigmat photographic objectives. This added astigmatism is, of course, undesirable, and in order to design an anastigmat lens having a flat field free from astigmatism, it is necessary to reduce the Petzval sum S_4 drastically.

For a succession of thin lenses (1, 2, 3, ... etc.) in a system, the Petzval sum becomes simply $1/f_1n_1 + 1/f_2n_2 + 1/f_3n_3 + \ldots$ etc., in which f is the focal length of each element and n is its refractive index. Therefore, to reduce the sum and minimize this aberration, relatively strong negative elements of low-index glass can be combined with positive elements of high-index glass. The positive and negative elements must be axially separated to provide the lens with a useful amount of positive power. The introduction of high-index barium crown glass with a low dispersive power in the 1880s initiated the development of anastigmat lenses.

Distortion. For the S_5 aberration,

$$x' = 0$$
$$y' = fh_0'^3S_5.$$

When this aberration is present, the entire image point is displaced toward or away from the axis by an amount proportional to the third power of the transverse distance h_0' of the image from the axis. This leads to the formation of an image of a square that is either a barrel-shaped or a cushion-shaped figure.

It is to be noted that the five Seidel aberrations represent the largest and most conspicuous defects that can arise in an uncorrected optical system. Even in the best lenses in which these five aberrations have been perfectly corrected for one zone of the lens and for one point in the field, however, there will exist small residuals of these aberrations and of many other higher order aberrations, also, which are significantly different from the classical types just described. The typical aberration figures shown in Figure 8 are, of course, grossly exaggerated, and actually it requires some magnification of a star image to render these appearances clearly visible. Nevertheless, they are important enough to require drastic reduction in high-quality lenses intended to make sharp negatives capable of considerable enlargement.

Other aberrations

IMAGE BRIGHTNESS

General relations. All photometric concepts are based on the idea of a standard candle, lamps having accurately known candle power being obtainable from the various national standards laboratories. The ratio of the candle power of a source to its area is called the luminance of the source; luminances range from about 2,000 candles per square millimetre at the surface of the Sun down to about $3 + 10^{-6}$ candle per square centimetre ($3 + 10^{-6}$ stilb) for the luminous paint on a watch dial. Ordinary outdoor scenes in daylight have an average luminance of several hundred candles per square foot. The quantity of light flux flowing out from a source is measured in lumens, the lumen being defined as the amount of flux radiated by a small "point" source of one candle power into a cone having a solid angle of one steradian. When light falls upon a surface it produces illumination (i.e., illuminance), the usual measure of illuminance being the foot-candle, which is one lumen falling on each square foot of receiving surface.

It is often important to be able to calculate the brightness of an image formed by an optical system, because photographic emulsions and other light receptors cannot respond satisfactorily if the light level is too low. The problem is to relate the luminance of an object with the illuminance in the image, knowing the transmittance and aperture of the optical system. A small area A of a plane object having a luminance of B candles per square unit will have a normal intensity of AB candles. This source radiates light into a cone of semi-angle U, limited, for example, by the rim of a lens. The light flux (F) entering the cone can be found by integration to be

$$F = \pi AB \sin^2 U \text{ lumens}.$$

If the object luminance is expressed as B_L lamberts, the lambert being an alternative luminance unit equal to $1/\pi$ (i.e., 0.32) candle per unit area, the flux (F) is

$$F = AB_L \sin^2 U \text{ lumens},$$

because there are π times as many lamberts in a given luminance as there are candles per unit area.

A fraction t of this flux finds its way to the image, t being the lens transmittance, generally about 0.8 or 0.9 but less if a mirror is involved. The area of the image is Am^2, in which m, the magnification, is given by

$$m = \frac{\sin U}{\sin U'}.$$

Hence, the image illuminance (E) is

$$E = (t\pi AB \sin^2 U) \div (A \sin^2 U/\sin^2 U') = t\pi B \sin^2 U' \quad (8)$$

or

$$E = tB_L \sin^2 U'.$$

The image illuminance thus depends *only* on the luminance of the source and the cone angle of the beam proceeding from the lens to the image. This is a basic and most important relation underlying all calculations of image illuminance.

It is often more convenient to convert the angle U' into other better known quantities, such as the *f*-number of the lens and the image magnification. The relation here is

$$\sin U' = \frac{1}{2(f\text{-number})(1 + m/m_p)}. \tag{9}$$

Definition of *f*-number

The *f*-number of the lens is defined as the ratio of the focal length to the diameter of the entrance pupil; m is the image magnification; and m_p is the pupil magnification—*i.e.*, the diameter of the exit pupil divided by the diameter of the entrance pupil. Combining equations (8) and (9) gives

$$\text{Image illuminance} = E = \frac{\pi t B}{4(f\text{-number})^2(1 + m/m_p)^2}.$$

As an example in the use of this relation, if it is supposed that an $f/2$ lens is being used to project an image of a cathode-ray tube at five times magnification, the tube luminance being 5,000 foot-lamberts (1.7 candles per square centimetre), the lens transmittance is 0.8, and the pupil magnification is unity. Then the image illuminance will be

$$E = \frac{0.8 \times 5,000}{4 \times 4 \times 36} = 6.9 \text{ foot-candles.}$$

The image is very much less bright than the object, a fact that becomes clear to anyone attempting to provide a bright projected image in a large auditorium.

Distribution of illumination over an image. So far only the illumination at the centre of an image has been considered, but the distribution of illumination over a wide field is often important. In the absence of any lens, the small plane source already considered radiates in a direction inclined at an angle φ to the axis with an intensity $AB \cos \varphi$. This light has to travel farther than the axial light to reach a screen, and then it strikes the screen at another angle φ. The net result is that the oblique illumination on the screen is smaller than the axial illumination by the factor $\cos^4 \varphi$.

The same law can be applied to determine the oblique illumination due to a lens, assuming a uniform extended diffusing source of light on the other side of the lens. In this case, however, the exit pupil will not in general be a perfect circle because of possible distortion of the iris by that part of the optical system lying between the iris and the image. Also, any mechanical vignetting in the lens will make the aperture noncircular and reduce still further the oblique illumination. In a camera this reduction in oblique illumination results in darkened corners of the picture, but, if the reduction in brightness is gradual, it is not likely to be detected because the eye adapts quickly to changing brightness as the eyes scan over the picture area. Indeed, a 50 percent drop in brightness between the centre and corners of an ordinary picture is scarcely detectable.

Visual brightness. The apparent brightness of things seen by the eye follows the same laws as any other imaging system, because the apparent brightness is measured by the illuminance in the image that is projected on the retina. The angle U' in equation (8) inside the eye is determined by the size of the pupil of the eye, which varies

Retinal illuminance

from about one millimetre to about eight millimetres, depending on the brightness of the environment. Apart from this variation, retinal illuminance is directly proportional to object luminance, and objects having the same luminance appear equally bright, no matter at what distance they are observed.

From this argument, it is clear that no visual instrument, such as a telescope, can possibly make anything appear brighter than when viewed directly. To be sure, a telescope having a large objective lens accepts more light from an object in proportion to the area of the lens aperture, but it magnifies the image area in the same proportion; so the increased light is spread over an increased area of the retina, and the illuminance remains unchanged. Actually,

the telescopic view is always dimmer than the direct view because of light losses in the telescope due to glass absorption and surface reflections and because the exit pupil of the telescope may be smaller than the pupil of the eye, thus reducing the angle U'.

The case of a star being observed through a telescope is quite different, because no degree of magnification can possibly make a star appear as anything other than a point of light. Hence, star images appear brighter in proportion to the area of the telescope objective (assuming that the exit pupil is larger than the eye pupil), and the visibility of a star against the sky background is thus improved in proportion to the square of the diameter of the telescope objective lens.

Optics and information theory

GENERAL OBSERVATIONS

A new era in optics commenced in the early 1950s following the impact of certain branches of electrical engineering—most notably communication and information theory. This impetus was sustained by the development of the laser in the 1960s.

The initial tie between optics and communication theory came because of the numerous analogies that exist between the two subjects and because of the similar mathematical techniques employed to formally describe the behaviour of electrical circuits and optical systems. A topic of considerable concern since the invention of the lens as an optical imaging device has always been the description of the optical system that forms the image; information about the object is relayed and presented as an image. Clearly, the optical system can be considered a communication channel and can be analyzed as such. There is a linear relationship (*i.e.*, direct proportionality) between the intensity distribution in the image plane and that existing in the object, when the object is illuminated with incoherent light (*e.g.*, sunlight or light from a large thermal source). Hence, the linear theory developed for the description of electronic systems can be applied to optical image-forming systems. For example, an electronic circuit can be characterized by its impulse response—that is, its output for a brief impulse input of current or voltage. Analogously, an optical system can be characterized by an impulse response that for an incoherent imaging system is the intensity distribution in the image of a point source of light; the optical impulse is a spatial rather than a temporal impulse—otherwise the concept is the same. Once the appropriate impulse response function is known, the output of that system for any object intensity distribution can be determined by a linear superposition of impulse responses suitably weighted by the value of the intensity at each point in the object. For a continuous object intensity distribution this sum becomes an integral. While this example has been given in terms of an optical imaging system, which is certainly the most common use of optical elements, the concept can be used independent of whether the receiving plane is an image plane or not. Hence, for example, an impulse response can be defined for an optical system that is deliberately defocussed or for systems used for the display of Fresnel or Fraunhofer diffraction patterns. (Fraunhofer diffraction occurs when the light source and diffraction patterns are effectively at infinite distances from the diffracting system, and Fresnel diffraction occurs when one or both of the distances are finite.)

Temporal frequency response. A fundamentally related but different method of describing the performance of an electronic circuit is by means of its temporal frequency response. A plot is made of the response for a series of input signals of a variety of frequencies. The response is measured as the ratio of the amplitude of the signal obtained out of the system to that put in. If there is no loss in the system, then the frequency response is unity (one) for that frequency; if a particular frequency fails to pass through the system, then the response is zero. Again, analogously the optical system may also be described by defining a spatial frequency response. The object, then,

The optical system as a communication channel

to be imaged by the optical system consists of a spatial distribution of intensity of a single spatial frequency—an object the intensity of which varies as $(1 + a \cos \omega x)$, in which x is the spatial coordinate, a is a constant called the contrast, and ω is a variable that determines the physical spacing of the peaks in the intensity distribution. The image is recorded for a fixed value of a and ω and the contrast in the image measured. The ratio of this contrast to a is the response for this particular spatial frequency defined by ω. Now if ω is varied and the measurement is repeated, a frequency response is then obtained.

Nonlinear optical systems. The analogies described above go even further. Many optical systems are nonlinear, just as many electronic systems are nonlinear. Photographic film is a nonlinear optical element in that equal increments of light energy reaching the film do not always produce equal increments of density on the film.

A different type of nonlinearity occurs in image formation. When an object such as two stars is imaged, the resultant intensity distribution in the image is determined by first finding the intensity distribution formed by each star. These distributions must then be added together in regions where they overlap to give the final intensity distribution that is the image. This example is typical of an incoherent imaging system—*i.e.,* the light emanating from the two stars is completely uncorrelated. This occurs because there is no fixed phase relationship between the light emanating from the two stars over any finite time interval.

A similar nonlinearity arises in objects illuminated by light from the Sun or other thermal light source. Illumination of this kind, when there is no fixed relationship between the phase of the light at any pair of points in the incident beam, is said to be incoherent illumination. If the illumination of the object is coherent, however, then there is a fixed relationship between the phase of the light at all pairs of points in the incident beam. To determine the resultant image intensity under this condition for a two point object requires that the amplitude and phase of the light in the image of each point be determined. The resultant amplitude and phase is then found by summation in regions of overlap. The square of this resultant amplitude is the intensity distribution in the image. Such

Nonlinear
optical
systems a system is nonlinear. The mathematics of nonlinear systems was developed as a branch of communication theory, but many of the results can be used to describe nonlinear optical systems.

This new description of optical systems was extremely important to, but would not alone account for, the resurgence of optical research and development. This new approach resulted in the development of whole new branches of study, including optical processing and holography (see below). It also had an effect, together with the development of digital computers, on the concepts and versatility of lens design and testing. Finally, the invention of the laser, a device that produces coherent radiation, and the development and implementation of the theory of partially coherent light gave the added impetus necessary to change traditional optics into a radically new and exciting subject.

IMAGE FORMATION

Impulse response. An optical system that employs incoherent illumination of the object can usually be regarded as a linear system in intensity. A system is linear if the addition of inputs produces an addition of corresponding outputs. For ease of analysis, systems are often considered stationary (or invariant). This property implies that if the location of the input is changed, then the only effect is to change the location of the output but not its actual distribution. With these concepts it is then only necessary to find an expression for the image of a point input to Intensity
distribution develop a theory of image formation. The intensity distribution in the image of a point object can be determined by solving the equation relating to the diffraction of light as it propagates from the point object to the lens, through the lens, and then finally to the image plane. The result of this process is that the image intensity is the intensity in the Fraunhofer diffraction pattern of the lens aperture function (that is, the square of the Fourier transform of the

lens aperature function; a Fourier transform is an integral equation involving periodic components). This intensity distribution is the intensity impulse response (sometimes called point spread function) of the optical system and fully characterizes that optical system. Figure 9 shows the impulse response for a perfect optical system (no aberration) that is limited only by its aperture.

With the knowledge of the impulse response, the image of a known object intensity distribution can be calculated. If the object consists of two points, then in the image plane the intensity impulse response function must be located at the image points and then a sum of these intensity distributions made. The sum is the final image intensity. If the two points are closer together than the half width of the impulse response, they will not be resolved. For an object consisting of an array of isolated points, a similar procedure is followed—each impulse response is, of course, multiplied by a constant equal to the value of the intensity of the appropriate point object. Normally, an object will consist of a continuous distribution of intensity, and, instead of a simple sum, a convolution integral results.

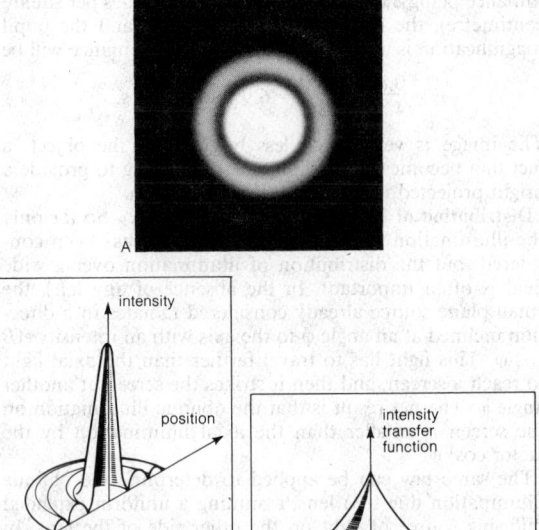

Figure 9: *The intensity impulse response of a perfect (i.e., no aberrations) optical system.*
(A) Photograph; (B) plot; (C) the transfer function of the same aberration-free system.

Transfer function. The concept of the transfer function of an optical system can be approached in several ways. Formally and fundamentally it is the Fourier transform of the intensity impulse response. The transfer function for the optical system for Figure 9B is shown in Figure 9C. Because the impulse response is related to the lens aperture function, so is the transfer function. In particular, the transfer function can be obtained from a knowledge of the aperture function by taking the function and plotting the resultant overlapping areas as the aperture function is slid over itself (*i.e.,* the autocorrelation of the aperture function). Auto-
correlation

Conceptually, however, the transfer function is best understood by considering the object intensity distribution to be a linear sum of cosine functions of the form $(1 + a \cos 2\pi\mu x)$, in which a is the amplitude of each component of spatial frequency μ. The image of a cosine intensity distribution is a cosine of the same frequency; only the contrast and phase of the cosine can be affected by a linear system. The image of the above object intensity distribution can be represented by $[1 + b \cos (2\pi\mu x + \varphi)]$, in which b is the amplitude of the output cosine of frequency μ and φ is the phase shift. The transfer function, $\tau(\mu)$, for that frequency is then given by the ratio of the amplitudes:

$$\tau(u) = \frac{b}{a} \, e^{j\varphi(\mu)}.$$

If μ is now varied, the spatial frequency response of the system is measured by determining $\tau(\mu)$ for the various values of μ. It should be noted that $\tau(\mu)$ is in general complex (containing a term with $\sqrt{-1}$), although in the example of Figure 9 it is real and positive [$\varphi(\mu) = 0$ for all μ].

The transfer function, like the impulse response, fully characterizes the optical system. To make use of the transfer function to determine the image of a given object requires that the object be decomposed into a series of periodic components called its spatial frequency spectrum. Each term in this series must then be multiplied by the appropriate value of the transfer function to determine the individual components of the series that is the spatial frequency spectrum of the image—a transformation of this series will give the image intensity. Thus, any components in the object spectrum that have a frequency for which $\tau(\mu)$ is zero will be eliminated from the image.

PARTIALLY COHERENT LIGHT

Image formation is concerned above with incoherent object illumination, which results in an image formed by the addition of intensities. The study of diffraction and interference, on the other hand, requires coherent illumination of the diffracting object, the resulting diffracted optical field being determined by an addition of complex amplitudes of the wave disturbances. Thus, two different mechanisms exist for the addition of light beams, depending upon whether the beams are coherent or incoherent with respect to each other. Unfortunately, this is not the whole story; it is not sufficient to consider only the two situations of strictly coherent and strictly incoherent light. In fact, strictly incoherent fields are only approximately obtainable in practice. Furthermore, the possibility of intermediate states of coherence cannot be ignored; it is necessary to describe the result of mixing incoherent light with coherent light. It was to answer the question How coherent is a beam of light? (or the equivalent one, How incoherent is a beam of light?) that the theory of partial coherence was developed. Marcel Verdet, a French physicist, realized in the 19th century that even sunlight is not completely incoherent, and two objects separated by distances of over approximately $^1/_{20}$ millimetre will produce interference effects. The eye, operating unaided in sunlight, does not resolve this separation distance and hence can be considered to be receiving an incoherent field. Two physicists, Armand Fizeau in France and Albert Michelson in the United States, were also aware that the optical field produced by a star is not completely incoherent, and hence they were able to design interferometers to measure the diameter of stars from a measurement of the partial coherence of the starlight. These early workers did not think in terms of partially coherent light, however, but derived their results by an integration over the source. At the other extreme, the output from a laser can produce a highly coherent field.

The concepts of partially coherent light can best be understood by means of some simple experiments. A circular uniform distant source produces illumination on the front of an opaque screen containing two small circular apertures, the separation of which can be varied. A lens is located behind this screen, and the resultant intensity distribution in its focal plane is obtained. With either aperture open alone, the intensity distribution observed is such that it is readily associated with the diffraction pattern of the aperture, and it may thus be concluded that the field is coherent over the dimensions of the aperture. When the two apertures are opened together and are at their closest separation, two-beam interference fringes are observed that are formed by the division of the incident wave front by the two apertures. As the separation of the apertures increases, the observed interference fringes get weaker and finally disappear, only to reappear faintly as the separation is further increased. As the separation of the apertures is increased, these results show that (1) the fringe spacing decreases; (2) the intensities of the fringe minima are never zero; (3) the relative intensity of the maxima above the

minima steadily decreases; (4) the absolute value of the intensity of the maxima decreases and that of the minima increases; (5) eventually, the fringes disappear, at which point the resultant intensity is just twice the intensity observed with one aperture alone (essentially an incoherent addition); (6) the fringes reappear with a further increase in separation of the aperture, but the fringes contain a central minimum, not a central maximum.

If the intensities of the two apertures are equal, then the results (1) through (5) can be summarized by defining a quantity in terms of the maximum intensity (I_{max}) and the minimum intensity (I_{min}), called the visibility (V) of the fringes—i.e., $V = (I_{max} - I_{min})/(I_{max} + I_{min})$. The maximum value of the visibility is unity, for which the light passing through one aperture is coherent with respect to the light passing through the other aperture; when the visibility is zero, the light passing through one aperture is incoherent with respect to the light passing through the other aperture. For intermediate values of V the light is said to be partially coherent. The visibility is not a completely satisfactory description because it is, by definition, a positive quantity and cannot, therefore, include a description of item (6) above. Furthermore, it can be shown by a related experiment that the visibility of the fringes can be varied by adding an extra optical path between the two interfering beams.

The key function in the theory of partially coherent light is the mutual coherence function $\Gamma_{12}(\tau) = \Gamma(x_1,x_2,\tau)$, a complex quantity, which is the time averaged value of the cross correlation function of the light at the two aperture points x_1 and x_2 with a time delay τ (relating to a path difference to the point of observation of the interference fringes). The function can be normalized (i.e., its absolute value set equal to unity at $\tau = 0$ and $x_1 = x_2$) by dividing by the square root of the product of the intensities at the points x_1 and x_2 to give the complex degree of coherence, hence

$$\gamma_{12}(\tau) = \frac{\Gamma_{12}(\tau)}{\sqrt{I(x_1)I(x_2)}}.$$

The modulus of $\gamma_{12}(\tau)$ has a maximum value of unity and a minimum value of zero. The visibility defined earlier is identical to the modulus of the complex degree of coherence if $I(x_1) = I(x_2)$.

Often the optical field can be considered to be quasi-monochromatic (approximately monochromatic), and then the time delay can be set equal to zero in the above expression, thus defining the mutual intensity function. It is often convenient to describe an optical field in terms of its spatial and temporal coherence by artificially separating out the space- and time-dependent parts of the coherence function. Temporal coherence effects arise from the finite spectral width of the source radiation; a coherence time Δt can be defined as $1/\Delta\nu$, in which $\Delta\nu$ is the frequency bandwidth. A related coherence length Δl can also be defined as $c/\Delta\nu = \lambda^2/\Delta\lambda^2$, in which c is the velocity of light, λ is the wavelength, and $\Delta\lambda$ the wavelength bandwidth. Providing that the path differences in the beams to be added are less than this characteristic length, the beams will interfere.

The term spatial coherence is used to describe partial coherence arising from the finite size of an incoherent source. Hence, for the equipath position for the addition of two beams, a coherence interval is defined as the separation of two points such that the absolute value $|\gamma_{12}(0)|$ is some prechosen value, usually zero.

The mutual coherence function is an observable quantity that can be related to the intensity of the field. The partially coherent field can be propagated by use of the mutual coherence function in a similar way to the solution of diffraction problems by propagation of the complex amplitude. The effects of partially coherent fields are clearly of importance in the description of normally coherent phenomena, such as diffraction and interference, but also in the analysis of normally incoherent phenomena, such as image formation. It is notable that image formation in coherent light is not linear in intensity but is linear in the complex amplitude of the field, and in partially coherent light the process is linear in the mutual coherence.

Partial coherence

Fringe visibility

The mutual coherence function

OPTICAL PROCESSING

Coherent optical systems. Optical processing, information processing, signal processing, and pattern recognition are all names that relate to the process of spatial frequency filtering in a coherent imaging system—specifically, a method in which the Fraunhofer diffraction pattern (equivalently the spatial frequency spectrum or the Fourier transform) of a given input is produced optically and then operated upon to change the information content of the optical image of that input in a predetermined way.

The idea of using coherent optical systems to allow for the manipulation of the information content of the image is not entirely new. The basic ideas are essentially included in Abbe's theory of vision in a microscope first published in 1873; the subsequent illustrative experiments of this theory, notably by Albert B. Porter in 1906, are certainly simple examples of optical processing.

Abbe's ideas can be interpreted as a realization that image formation in a microscope is more correctly described as a coherent image-forming process than as the more familiar incoherent process. Thus, the coherent light illuminating the object on the microscope stage would be diffracted by that object. To form an image, this diffracted light must be collected by the objective lens of the microscope, and the nature of the image and the resolution would be affected by how much of the diffracted light is collected. As an example, an object may be considered consisting of a periodic variation in amplitude transmittance—the light diffracted by this object will exist in a series of discrete directions (or orders of diffraction). This series of orders contains a zero order propagating along the optical axis and a symmetric set of orders on both sides of this zero order. Abbe correctly discerned what would happen as the microscope objective accepted different combinations of these orders. For example, if the zero order and one first order are collected, then the information obtained will be that the object consisted of a periodic distribution, but the spatial location of the periodic structure is not correctly ascertained. If the other first order of diffracted light is included, the correct spatial location of the periodic structure is also obtained. As more orders are included, the image more closely resembles the object.

Coherent optical data processing became a serious subject for study in the 1950s, partly because of the work of a French physicist, Pierre-Michel Duffieux, on the Fourier integral and its application to optics, and the subsequent use of communication theory in optical research. The work was initiated in France by André Maréchal and Paul Croce, and today a variety of problems can be attempted by the technique. These include removal of raster lines (as in a TV picture) and halftone dots (as in newspaper illustration); contrast enhancement; edge sharpening; enhancement of a periodic or isolated signal in the presence of additive noise; aberration balancing in which a recorded aberrated image can be somewhat improved; spectrum analysis; cross correlation of data; matched and inverse filtering in which a bright spot of light in the image indicates the presence of a particular object.

Filtering. The basic system required for coherent optical processing consists of two lenses (Figure 10). A collimated beam of coherent light is used to transilluminate the object. The first lens produces the characteristic Fraunhofer diffraction pattern of the object, which is the spatial frequency distribution associated with the object. (Mathematically, it is the Fourier transform of the object amplitude distribution.) A filter that consists of amplitude (density) or phase (optical path) variations, or both, is placed in the plane of the diffraction pattern. The light passing through this filter is used to form an image, this step being accomplished by the second lens. The filter has the effect of changing the nature of the image by altering the spatial frequency spectrum in a controlled way so as to enhance certain aspects of the object information. Maréchal gave the descriptive title double diffraction to this type of two-lens system.

The filters can be conveniently grouped into a variety of types depending upon their action. Blocking filters have regions of complete transparency and other regions of complete opacity. The opaque areas completely remove

Examples of data processing

Blocking filters

certain portions of the spatial frequency spectrum of the object. The removal of raster lines and halftone dots is accomplished with this type of filter. The object can be considered as a periodic function the envelope of which is the scene or picture—or equivalently the periodic function samples the picture. The diffraction pattern consists of a periodic distribution with a periodicity reciprocally related to the raster periodicity. Centred at each of these periodic locations is the diffraction pattern of the scene. Hence, if the filter is an aperture centred at one of these locations so that only one of the periodic elements is allowed to pass, then the raster periodicity is removed, but the scene information is retained (see Figure 10). The problem of

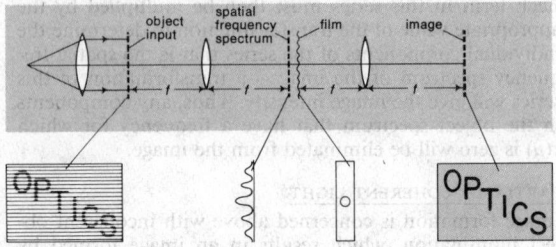

Figure 10: Two-lens coherent optical processing system, showing how the raster periodicity is removed but the scene information is retained (see text).

the removal of halftone dots is the two-dimensional equivalent of the above process. Because the two-dimensional spatial frequency spectrum of an object is displayed in a coherent optical processing system, it is possible to separate out information by means of its orientation. Other applications of blocking filters include band-pass filters, which again have a direct relationship to the band-pass filters in electronic circuits.

A second type of filter is an amplitude filter that will consist of a continuous density variation. These filters can be produced to achieve the enhancement of contrast of the object input or the differentiation of the object. They are often constructed by controlled exposure of photographic film or evaporation of metal onto a transparent substrate.

Certain optical processing techniques require that the phase of the optical field be changed, and, hence, a filter with no absorption but varying optical thickness is required. Usually, both the amplitude and the phase have to be modified, however, thus requiring a complex filter. In simple cases the amplitude and phase portions can be made separately, the phase filter being manufactured by using an evaporated layer of transparent material, such as magnesium fluoride. Current practice is to fabricate the complex filter by an interferometric method in which the required complex amplitude function is recorded as a hologram (see below).

The phase-contrast microscope can be considered to be an example of an optical processing system, and the concepts understood by reference to Figure 10. Only the simplest form will be considered here. The spatial frequency spectrum of the phase object is formed and the phase of the central portion of that spectrum changed by $\pi/2$ or $3\pi/2$ to produce positive or negative phase contrast, respectively. To improve the contrast of the image an additional filter covering the same area as the phase filter is used that is partially absorbing (i.e., an amplitude filter). The restriction on this process is that the variations of the phase $\varphi(x)$ are small so that $e^{i\varphi(x)} \cong 1 + i\varphi(x)$. With incoherent light, phase information is not visible, but many biological samples consist only of variations of refractive index, which results in optical path and hence phase, differences. The image in the phase-contrast microscope is such that the intensity in that image relates linearly to, and hence is a display of, the phase information in the object—e.g., $I(x) \propto 1 \pm 2\varphi(x)$ for positive and negative phase contrast, respectively.

One of the important motivations for the study of optical processing methods is to achieve some correction of aberrated images. Considerable technological advantage can be gained if photographs taken with an aberrated optical system in incoherent light can be corrected by subsequent processing. Within definable limits this can be

Amplitude filters

Correction of aberrated images

accomplished, but the impulse response or the transfer function of the aberrated system must be known. The recorded image intensity distribution is the convolution of the object intensity with the intensity impulse response of the aberrated system. This record is the input to the coherent optical processing system; the diffraction pattern formed in this system is the product of the spatial frequency spectrum of the object and the transfer function of the aberrated system. Conceptually, the filter has to be the inverse of the transfer function in order to balance out its effect. The final image would then ideally be an image of the object intensity distribution. It is critical, however, that the transfer function has a finite value over only a limited frequency range, and only those frequencies that are recorded by the original aberrated system can be present in the processed image. Hence, for these spatial frequencies that were recorded, some processing can be carried out to get a flatter effective transfer function; both the contrast and the phase of the spatial frequency spectrum may have to be changed because the transfer function is, in general, a complex function. Prime examples are for images aberrated by astigmatism, defocussing, or image motion.

HOLOGRAPHY

Theory. Holography is a two-step coherent image-forming process in which an intermediate record is made of the complex optical field associated with the object. The invention of the wave-front reconstruction process (now called holography) was first described in 1948 by Dennis Gabor, a Hungarian-born physicist, with a specific application in mind—to attempt to improve the resolution of images formed with electron beams. The technique has, however, had most of its success to date when light beams are employed particularly in the visible part of the spectrum. The first step in the process is to record (often *Steps in* on high-resolution film) the interference pattern produced *the* by the interaction of the light diffracted by the object of *holography* interest and a coherent background or reference wave. In *process* the second step, this record, which is the hologram, is illuminated coherently to form an image of the original object. In fact, two images are usually formed—a real image (often called the conjugate image) and a virtual image (often called the primary image). There are two basic concepts that underlie this process: first, the addition of a coherent background (or reference) beam. Two optical fields may be considered, the complex amplitudes of which vary as the cosine of an angle proportional to the space coordinate and as the modulus (absolute magnitude) of the cosine of the angle, respectively. From a measurement of the intensity of these fields it is impossible to distinguish them because both vary as the cosine squared of the space coordinate. If a second coherent optical field is added to each of these two fields, however, then the resultant fields become $(1 + \cos x)$ and $(1 + |\cos x|)$, respectively. The measured intensities are now different, and the actual fields can be determined by taking the square root of the intensity. The amplitude transmittance of a photographic record is, in fact, the square root of the original intensity distribution that exposed the film. In a more general sense, an optical field of the form $a(x) \exp [i\varphi_1(x)]$, in which $a(x)$ is the amplitude and $\varphi_1(x)$ is the phase, can be distinguished from a field $a(x) \exp [i\varphi_2(x)]$ by adding a coherent background; the phases $\varphi_1(x)$ and $\varphi_2(x)$ are then contained as cosine variations of intensity in the resulting pattern. Hence, the problem of recording the phase information of the optical field is circumvented. When the hologram is illuminated, however, the optical field that originally existed in that plane is recreated. To apply the second basic concept—that of an image-forming property—it is necessary to determine what the hologram of a point object is—in actuality it is a sine-wave zone plate or zone lens. If a collimated beam of light is used to illuminate a zone lens, then two beams are produced; the first comes to a real focus, and the other is a divergent beam that appears to have come from a virtual focus. (By comparison, the more classical zone plate has a multitude of real and virtual focuses, and a real lens has but one.) When the object is other than a point, the zone lens is modified by the diffraction pattern of the object; *i.e.*, each

point on the object produces its own zone lens, and the resultant hologram is a summation of such zone lenses.

In Gabor's original system the hologram was a record of the interference between the light diffracted by the object and a collinear background. This automatically restricts the process to that class of objects that have considerable areas that are transparent (see Figure 11A). When the hologram is used to form an image, twin images are formed, as illustrated in Figure 11B. The light associated with these images is propagating in the same

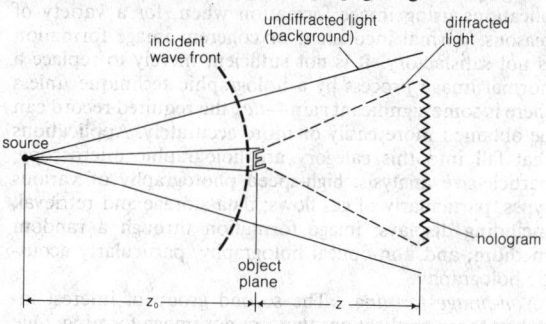

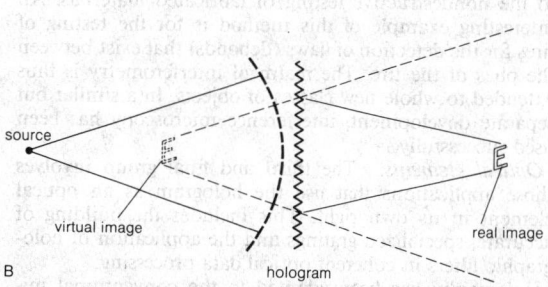

Figure 11: *Holography.*
(A) Formation of a hologram by light diffracted by an object with collinear background (Gabor's original method). (B) Image formation by illumination of the hologram.

direction, and hence in the plane of one image light from the other image appears as an out-of-focus component. This type of hologram is usually referred to as an in-line Fresnel hologram because it is the pattern of the object that interferes with the collinear coherent background. The deleterious effects of the second image can be minimized if the hologram is made in the far field of the object so that it is a Fraunhofer diffraction pattern of the object that is involved. This latter technique has found significant application in microscopy, particularly in the measurement of small particles, and in electron microscopy.

A more versatile method of recording the hologram is to add a second beam of light as a reference wave to produce the hologram. The hologram is now the record of the interference pattern produced by the light diffracted by the object and this separate reference wave. The reference wave is usually introduced at an angle to the diffracted beam, hence this method is often called off-axis (or sideband) holography. When the hologram is illuminated, the image-forming beams do not propagate in the same direction but are inclined to each other with an angle twice that between the diffracted beam and the original reference beam. Hence, the light associated with an image is completely separated from the other image.

A further technique that has some value and relates to the earlier discussion of optical processing is the production of the so-called generalized or Fourier transform *The* hologram. Here the reference beam is added coherently to *general-* a Fraunhofer diffraction pattern of the object or formed *ized* by a lens (as in the first stage of Figure 10). *hologram*

The process described so far has been in terms of transmitted light through the object. The methods involving the separate reference beam can be used in reflected light, and the virtual (primary) image produced from the hologram has all the properties of an ordinary image in terms of three-dimensionality and parallax. Normally, a recorded image is only a two-dimensional representation of the object. Full-colour holograms can be recorded by essentially recording three holograms simultaneously—one in red light, one in blue, and one in green.

Applications. *Image forming.* The applications mentioned here are in three groups: image-forming applications, non-image-forming applications, and the hologram as an optical element. It is notable that all three groups relate to the basic use of the process rather than specific holographic techniques. The first group involves those applications using image formation when, for a variety of reasons, normal incoherent or coherent image formation is not satisfactory. It is not sufficient merely to replace a normal image process by a holographic technique unless there is some significant gain—*i.e.,* the required record can be obtained more easily or more accurately. Applications that fall into this category are holographic microscopy; particle-size analysis; high-speed photography of various types, particularly of gas flows; data storage and retrieval, including displays; image formation through a random medium; and non-optical holography, particularly acoustic holography.

Non-image forming. The second group of interest involves those applications that are not image forming. One of the very real and exciting applications of holography is to the nondestructive testing of fabricated materials. An interesting example of this method is for the testing of tires for the detection of flaws (debonds) that exist between the plies of the tire. The realm of interferometry is thus extended to whole new classes of objects. In a similar but separate development, interference microscopy has been used successfully.

Optical elements. The third and final group involves those applications that use the hologram as an optical element in its own right. This includes the building of accurate, specialized gratings and the application of holographic filters in coherent optical data processing.

Holography has been adapted to the conventional microscope, which is modified by the inclusion of a separate reference beam so that the light diffracted by the object in the microscope is made to interfere with the light from the reference beam. An increase in the depth of field available is achieved by this type of recording process. The image is produced when the hologram is illuminated again by a coherent beam.

The application of holography to particle-size analysis (*e.g.,* to determine the size distribution of dust and liquid droplets) was really the first of the modern-day applications. In a sense, this, too, can be thought of as microscopy. The principles of Fraunhofer holography were developed

Transient holograms

to solve this particular problem. Because the particles are in motion, a hologram must be made instantaneously. A pulsed-ruby laser technique is therefore used. The hologram is formed between the light diffracted by the particles or droplets and the coherent background light that passes directly through the sample. In reconstruction, a series of stationary images are formed that can be examined at leisure. Hence, a transient event has been transformed into a stationary image for evaluation.

Data storage and retrieval is perhaps one of the more important applications of holography, which is in the process of development and refinement. Because the information about the image is not localized, it cannot be affected by scratches or dust particles. Recent advances in materials, particularly those that might be erasable and reusable, have added further interest in holographic optical memories.

Among the non-image-forming applications are interferometry, interference microscopy, and optical processing. Holographic interferometry can be done in several ways. The basic technique involves recording a hologram of the object of interest and then interfering the image produced from this hologram with the coherently illuminated object itself. A variation on this technique would be to form two holograms at different times of the same object as it undergoes testing. The two holograms can then be used together to form two images, which would again interfere. The interference fringes seen would be related to the changes in the object between the two exposures. A third technique uses a time-average hologram, which is particularly applicable to the study of vibrating objects.

There are two applications that come under the heading holographic optical elements—the use of holographic gratings and the use of holographic filters for coherent optical data processing.

NONLINEAR OPTICS

Nonlinear effects in optics are now quite readily observable using the highly coherent and highly energetic laser beams. These effects occur when the output of a system is not linearly related to the input (*e.g.,* a nonlinear electronic amplifier can be built with a gain that increases with signal intensity). The most important nonlinear effect is probably frequency doubling. Optical radiation of a given frequency is propagated through a crystalline material and interacts with that material to produce an output of a different frequency that is twice the input frequency. For example, the 10,600 angstroms infrared output of a neodymium laser can, under suitable conditions, be converted into green light at 5300 angstroms in a crystal of barium strontium niobate.

(B.J.T.)

BIBLIOGRAPHY. There are many journals and hundreds of books covering the general field of optics; some of the more familiar books include A.C. HARDY and F.H. PERRIN, *The Principles of Optics* (1932); and F.A. JENKINS and H.E. WHITE, *Fundamentals of Optics,* 3rd ed. (1957). At a more advanced level are R.S. LONGHURST, *Geometrical and Physical Optics,* 2nd ed. (1967); L.C. MARTIN, *Technical Optics,* 2 vol. (1960–61); and MAX BORN and EMIL WOLF, *Principles of Optics,* 2nd ed. (1964). In the purely geometrical field, the following can be recommended: W.T. WELFORD, *Geometrical Optics* (1962), which is fairly elementary and provides an excellent introduction to the subject; and L.C. MARTIN, *Geometrical Optics* (1956), which is somewhat more advanced. Other useful works include R. KINGSLAKE (ed.), *Applied Optics and Optical Engineering,* 5 vol. (1945–69), a definitive work, with the first three volumes treating optical devices and theory and the remaining two volumes giving detailed treatment of the principal types of optical instruments; and A.E. CONRADY, *Applied Optics and Optical Design,* 2 vol. (1957–60), a full description of the theory and practice of lens design, providing detailed instructions for the design of many types of optical systems.

Recommended books on the subject of information theory are EDWARD L. O'NEILL, *Introduction to Statistical Optics* (1963); JOSEPH W. GOODMAN, *Introduction to Fourier Optics* (1968); ARNOLD R. SCHULMAN, *Optical Data Processing* (1970); KENDALL PRESTON, *Coherent Optical Computers* (1972); HENRY LIPSON (ed.), *Optical Transforms* (1972); GEORGE W. STROKE, *An Introduction to Coherent Optics and Holography,* 2nd ed. (1969); JOHN B. DEVELIS and GEORGE O. REYNOLDS, *Theory and Applications of Holography* (1967); and ROBERT J. COLLIER, CHRISTOPH B. BURCKHARDT, and LAWRENCE H. LIN, *Optical Holography* (1971). For particular topics, reference should be made to the *Journal of the Optical Society of America* (monthly); *Applied Optics* (monthly); and EMIL WOLF (ed.), *Progress in Optics* (1961–).

(R.K./B.J.T./Ed.)

The Mathematical Theory of Optimization

Optimization is a technique for improving or increasing the value of some numerical quantity that in practice may take the form of temperature, air flow, speed, pay-off in a game, political appeal, destructive power, information, monetary profit, and the like. Techniques of optimization assume such varied forms that no one general description is possible. With the advent of modern technology more and more emphasis has been placed on optimization of various types, and special thinking has developed to the extent that it is meaningful to speak of a mathematical theory of optimization. Computer technology has been critically important in practical applications, such as in the optimal control of rockets. Further advances in the optimization and control of complex systems will probably depend more on mathematical theory than on technological invention.

Optimization includes linear and nonlinear programming, cybernetics, and control theory, the various aspects of which are treated in this article. Game theory is often included as well, since early work on optimization was extended by the development of that branch of mathematics. For information about its basic concepts and methodology, see GAME THEORY. The present article is divided into the following sections:

Linear and nonlinear programming (mathematical programming)

GENERAL OBSERVATIONS

Mathematical programming may be described in terms of its mathematical structure and computational procedures or in terms of the broad class of important decision problems which can be formulated as the minimization (maximization) of a function of several variables that are subject to a system of side constraints. For example, a linear program is defined as the minimization of a linear "objective" function whose variables satisfy a system of linear inequalities.

The scope of mathematical programming

In practice, mathematical programming usually refers to such linear programs, the general study of nonlinear programs (those in which either the objective function or at least one of the constraint functions is nonlinear), integer programs (that is, linear programs with the additional restriction that some or all of the variables must be integer valued), stochastic programs (those programs involving random variables), and network flow theory (transportation or flow through networks). As such, mathematical programming overlaps, has contributed to, and has been influenced by operations research, mathematical economics, control theory, dynamic programming, and combinatorial theory.

The term programming had its origin in programming (*i.e.*, planning, scheduling) the quantity and timing of the various activities of an organization such as a factory, an airline, the defense establishment, the national economy, or world trade. (It is not to be confused with "programming" as used for the task of preparing a sequence of instructions for a computer.) The goal is to find an optimum schedule.

A simple example, "the assignment problem," illustrates the essential difficulty. A factory has 70 men with different qualifications and it is desirable to assign them to 70 jobs. If a "value" can be attached to assigning a particular man to a particular job, then the problem becomes one of selecting out of 70! (which is the product of integers from 1 to 70) possible ways of permuting the assignments the one that yields the maximum total value to the factory. Because 70! is approximately 10^{100}, it would take an electronic computer executing 1,000,000 operations per second over 10^{87} years (or many times the projected life of the universe) to examine all the permutations. Such decision problems are common and have resulted in the development of clever formulation of the mathematical models, powerful mathematical methods of solution, and efficient computer algorithms (step-by-step procedures). The solution of linear programs is said to constitute 25 percent of all the time used by computers to solve scientific problems.

ORIGINS AND INFLUENCES

Although widely used now to solve everyday decision problems, linear programming was comparatively unknown before 1947. No work of any significance was carried out before this date, even though the French mathematician Jean-Baptiste-Joseph Fourier seemed to be aware of the subject's potential as early as 1823. A Russian mathematician, Leonid Vitalyevich Kantorovich, who published an extensive monograph in 1939, *Matematicheskie metody organizatsi i planirovaniya proizvodstva* ("Mathematical Methods for Organization and Planning of Production"), is credited with being the first to recognize that certain important broad classes of scheduling problems had well-defined mathematical structures. Unfortunately his proposals remained unknown both in the Soviet Union and elsewhere for nearly two decades. Meanwhile, linear programming had developed considerably in the United States and Western Europe. In the period following World War II, officials in the United States government felt that efficient coordination of the energies of a whole nation in the advent of atomic war would require the use of scientific planning techniques. The advent of the computer made such an approach feasible.

Intensive work began in 1947 in the United States Air Force. The linear programming model was proposed because it is simple, practical, and yet provided a sufficiently general framework for representing interdependent activities that must share scarce resources. The system (*e.g.*, national economy) is viewed as made up of various activities (*e.g.*, production, training, shipping, disposal, and storing).

The first linear programming model

Each activity is assumed to require a flow of inputs and outputs of various types of items (*e.g.*, men, materials) proportional to the level of the activity. Activity levels are assumed to be representable in terms of positive numbers or zero. The revolutionary feature of the approach, however, was the expressing of the goal, as that of minimizing (maximizing) an objective function (*e.g.*, maximizing sorties in the case of the air force or maximizing profits in industry). Before 1947 all practical planning was characterized by a series of authoritatively imposed rules of procedure and priorities. General objectives were never stated, probably because of the impossibility of performing the calculations necessary to minimize an objective function under constraints. In 1947 a method composed of successive tests for optimality at extreme points and intervening linear movement along polygonal edges called the simplex computational method was introduced which turned out to be indeed efficient. Interest in linear programming grew rapidly and by 1951 its use spread to industry. Today, it is almost impossible to name an industry that is not using mathematical programming in some form, although its use varies greatly, even within the same industry.

The current interest in linear programming by economists appears to be an anachronism. The French economist François Quesnay's attempt in his *Tableau économique* (1758) to interrelate the role of the landlord, the peasant, and the artisan was a crude example of a linear programming model. Léon Walras, another French economist, in 1874 proposed a sophisticated approach that had as part of its structure fixed technological coefficients (as assumed in linear programs). Oddly enough, until the 1930s, the linear-type model was little exploited.

Von Neumann in a 1937 paper analyzed a steadily expanding economy based on alternative methods of production and fixed technological coefficients. As far as mathematical history is concerned, the study of linear inequality systems excited virtually no interest before 1936. In 1911 a vertex-to-vertex movement along edges of a polyhedron (as is done in the simplex method) was suggested as a way to solve a problem that involved optimization, and in 1941 movement along edges was proposed for a problem involving transportation. Credit for laying much of the mathematical foundations should probably go to von Neumann. In 1928 he published his famous paper on *Game theory*. In 1947 he conjectured the equivalence of linear programs and matrix games, introduced the important concept of duality, and made several proposals for the numerical solution of linear programming and game problems. Serious interest by other mathematicians began in 1948 with the rigorous development of duality and related matters.

The general simplex method, already mentioned (see above *Origins and influences*) and to be discussed in detail (see below *The simplex method*), was first programmed in 1951 for the United States Bureau of Standards SEAC computer. Starting in 1952, the simplex method was programmed for use on various models of IBM (International Business Machines) computers and later for those of other companies. These programs turned out to be practical. As a result, commercial applications of linear programs in industry and government grew rapidly. New computational techniques and variations of older techniques continued to be developed.

At the present time there is much interest in solving large linear programs with special structures, for example, corporate models and national planning models that are multistaged, dynamic, and exhibit a hierarchical structure. It is estimated that certain underdeveloped countries have the potential of increasing their GNP (gross national product) anywhere from 10 to 15 percent per year if detailed growth models of the economy could be constructed, optimized, and implemented.

LINEAR PROGRAMMING THEORY

Linear programming in factory production

Basic ideas. A simple problem in linear programming is one in which it is necessary to find the maximum (or minimum) value of a simple function, such as $x_1 + 2x_2$, subject to certain constraints. An example of its application might be that of a factory producing two commodities.

In any production run, it produces x_1 of the first type and x_2 of the second. If the profit on the second type is twice that on the first, then $x_1 + 2x_2$ represents the total profit. The function $x_1 + 2x_2$ is known as the objective function.

Clearly the profit will be highest if the factory devotes its entire production capacity to making the second type of commodity. In a practical situation, however, this may not be possible; a set of constraints is introduced by such factors as availability of machine time, manpower, or raw materials. For example, if the second type of commodity requires a raw material that is limited so that no more than five can be made in any batch, then x_2 must be less than or equal to five; *i.e.*, $x_2 \leq 5$. If the first commodity requires another type of material limiting it to eight per batch then $x_1 \leq 8$. If 1 and 2 take equal times to make and the machine time available allows a maximum of ten to be made in a batch, then $x_1 + x_2$ must be less than or equal to 10; *i.e.*, $x_1 + x_2 \leq 10$.

Two other constraints are that x_1 and x_2 must each be greater than or equal to zero, because it is impossible to make a negative number of either; *i.e.*, $x_1 \geq 0$ and $x_2 \geq 0$. These conditions result in a simple linear program that can be stated in concise algebraic form. The problem is to find the values of x_1 and x_2 for which the profit is a maximum. Any solution can be denoted by a pair of numbers (x_1, x_2); for example, if $x_1 = 3$ and $x_2 = 6$, the solution is $(3, 6)$. These numbers can be represented by points plotted on two axes; in Figure 1 the distance along

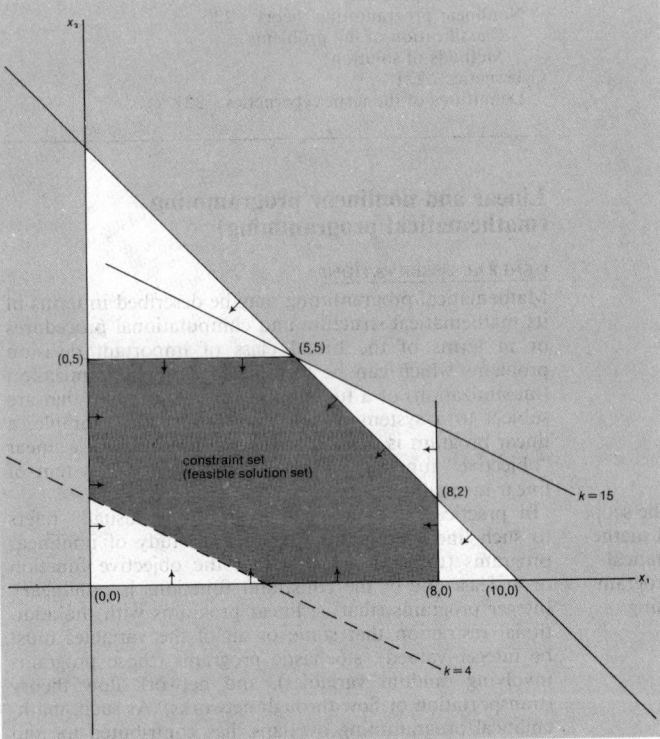

Figure 1: Constraint set bounded by the five lines $x_1 = 0$, $x_2 = 0$, $x_1 = 8$, $x_2 = 5$, and $x_1 + x_2 = 10$. These enclose an infinite number of points that represent feasible solutions.

the horizontal axis represents x_1 and that along the vertical represents x_2. An infinite number of points exist corresponding to an infinite number of solutions, but because of the constraints the feasible solutions must lie within a certain region. For example, the constraint $x_1 \geq 0$ means that points representing feasible solutions lie on or to the right of the x_2 axis. The constraint $x_2 \geq 0$ means that they also lie on or above the x_1 axis. Application of all the constraints leads to the result that points representing solutions lie within the shaded area bounded by a polygon formed by intersection of the lines $x_1 = 0$, $x_2 = 0$, $x_1 = 8$, $x_2 = 5$, and $x_1 + x_2 = 10$. These form the constraint set. For example, to make three items of commodity 1 and four of 2 is a feasible solution since the point $(3, 4)$ lies in this region. To find the best solution, the objective function $x_1 + 2x_2 = k$ is plotted on the graph for some value of k, say $k = 4$. This value is indicated by the broken line in Figure 1. As k is increased, a family of parallel lines are produced and the line for $k = 15$ just touches the constraint set at the point $(5, 5)$. If k is increased further, the values of x_1 and x_2 lie outside the set of feasible solutions. Thus the best solution is that in which equal quantities of each commodity are made. The points $(0, 0)$, $(0, 5)$, $(5, 5)$, $(8, 2)$, and $(8, 0)$ are the extreme points of the constraint set, and the problem involves finding the extreme point the coordinates of which yield the largest value for k.

The standard form of a linear program is expressed as an instruction to maximize (or minimize) a linear expression in n nonnegative variables, $\{x_i\}$, subject to m linear equations (see 1). In applications, the equations correspond to material balance of various items and the variables to levels of various activities (*e.g.*, production processes). Any system of linear inequalities can be reduced to this standard form by simple substitutions.

Definition of a feasible solution A set of x_j values that is nonnegative and satisfies the equations is a "feasible" solution and corresponds to a feasible but not necessarily optimal program. Such a solution is viewed as a point in n-dimensional space.

The constraint set—*i.e.*, the set of feasible solutions—has a property known as convexity. In general, a set S is convex if and only if it contains the entire line segment between any two of its elements. An element of a convex set S is called an extreme point if it does not lie on the line segment joining two other points of S. A line segment

in S is called an edge if no point on it lies also on a line segment in S that crosses it. The constraint set of a linear program has only a finite number of extreme points.

If a linear programming problem has a unique optimal feasible solution, then it is at an extreme point; if not unique, there is an optimal solution at an extreme point. Thus, the optimal feasible solution is within a finite set of extreme points.

The simplex method. There are certain difficulties involved in the simple graphical approach to solutions. First, the graphical method of solution illustrated by the figure is useful only for systems of inequalities involving two variables. Practical problems often involve hundreds of equations, thousands of variables, however, and a computer is required. Second, the number of extreme points can be quite large. For example, for n equal to 2,000 and a constraint set defined by restricting the sum of x_j and y_j to be 1 for all nonnegative values of the variables and for all n values of j (see 2), there are 2^n, or about 10^{600}, extreme points. It is thus necessary to restrict the number of extreme points to be examined. This is done by using the simplex method. It works in the following way. It is assumed that an extreme point is known. (If no extreme point is given, a variant of the simplex method, called Phase I, is used to find one or determine that there are no feasible solutions.) Using the algebraic specification of the problem, it is easy to test whether that extreme point is optimal. If the test for optimality is not passed, then a movement along some edge to an adjacent extreme point is sought along which the value of the objective function increases at the fastest rate. Sometimes one can move along an edge and make the objective function value increase without bound. If this occurs, the procedure terminates with a prescription of the edge along which the objective goes to positive infinity. If not, a new extreme point is reached having at least as high an objective function value as its predecessor. The sequence described is then repeated. Termination occurs when an optimal extreme point is found or the unbounded case occurs.

The simplex method solves the numerical example given above in the following way: The problem is put into canonical form by converting the linear inequalities into equations by introducing slack variables $x_3 \geq 0$, $x_4 \geq 0$, $x_5 \geq 0$, and the variable x_0 for the value of the objective **Slack variables** function; the problem may then be restated as that of finding nonnegative quantities $x_1, \cdots, x_5$ and the largest possible x_0 satisfying the resulting equations (see 3). One obvious solution of the resulting system of equations is found by setting $x_1 = 0$, $x_2 = 0$ (see 4), which corresponds to the extreme point at the origin in the figure. If x_1 (or x_2) were increased from zero while the other one x_2 (or x_1) is fixed at zero, the values of x_0, x_3, x_4, x_5 could be made to satisfy the equations, and the objective value x_0 would increase as desired. The variable x_2 produces the largest increase of x_0 per unit change; so it is used first. Its increase is limited by the nonnegativity requirement on the variables. In particular, if x_2 were increased beyond 5, x_4 would become negative.

At $x_2 = 5$, this situation produces a new solution (see 5) and corresponds to the extreme point $(0, 5)$ in the figure. The system of equations is put into equivalent form (see 6) by solving for the variables x_0, x_2, x_3, x_5, which are nonzero in the above solution in terms of those variables now at zero; *i.e.*, x_1 and x_4. It is now apparent that an increase of x_1 while holding x_4 equal to zero will produce a further increase in x_0. The nonnegativity restriction on x_3 prevents x_1 from going beyond 5. The new solution (see 7) corresponds to the extreme point $(5, 5)$ in the figure. Solving for x_0, x_1, x_2, x_3 in terms of the variables x_4, x_5 (which are currently at zero value) yields a final equivalent system of equations (see 8). It is to be noted that no variable can be changed from its present value and yield a feasible solution with a higher value than $x_0 = 15$ (see 9). Hence, an optimal solution is determined (see 10).

The dual problem. Associated with each linear programming problem is a second linear programming problem known as its dual. In this association, the original problem is referred to as the primal. Von Neumann provided a

$$(1) \quad \begin{cases} \text{maximize } p_1 x_1 + \cdots + p_n x_n \\ \text{subject to } a_{11}x_1 + \cdots + a_{1n}x_n = b_1 \geq 0 \\ \qquad\quad a_{21}x_1 + \cdots + a_{2n}x_n = b_2 \geq 0 \\ \qquad\qquad\qquad \vdots \\ \qquad\quad a_{m1}x_1 + \cdots + a_{mn}x_n = b_m \geq 0 \\ \qquad\quad x_1 \geq 0, \cdots, x_n \geq 0 \end{cases}$$

$$(2) \quad x_j + y_j = 1, \qquad x_j \geq 0, \qquad y_j \geq 0 \quad \text{for } j = 1, \cdots, n$$

$$(3) \quad \begin{cases} -x_0 + x_1 + 2x_2 & = 0 \\ \quad x_1 \quad + x_3 & = 8 \\ \quad x_2 \quad + x_4 & = 5 \\ \quad x_1 + \ x_2 \quad + x_5 & = 10 \end{cases}$$

$$(4) \quad \begin{cases} x_0 = 0, \ x_1 = 0, \ x_2 = 0, \ x_3 = 8 \\ x_4 = 5, \ x_5 = 10 \end{cases}$$

$$(5) \quad (x_0, x_1, x_2, x_3, x_4, x_5) = (10, 0, 5, 8, 0, 5)$$

$$(6) \quad \begin{cases} -x_0 + x_1 \quad -2x_4 & = -10 \\ \quad x_1 + x_3 & = 8 \\ \quad x_2 \ + x_4 & = 5 \\ \quad x_1 \quad - x_4 + x_5 & = 5 \end{cases}$$

$$(7) \quad (x_0, x_1, x_2, x_3, x_4, x_5) = (15, 5, 5, 3, 0, 0)$$

$$(8) \quad \begin{cases} -x_0 \qquad\quad - x_4 - x_5 = -15 \\ \qquad x_3 + x_4 - x_5 = 3 \\ \quad x_2 \ + x_4 \quad = 5 \\ \quad x_1 \quad - x_4 + x_5 = 5 \end{cases}$$

$$(9) \quad x_4 \geq 0, \ x_5 \geq 0, \ x_0 = 15 - x_4 - x_5 \leq 15$$

$$(10) \quad x_1 = 5, \ x_2 = 5, \ x_3 = 3, \ x_4 = x_5 = 0$$

form for the primal problem (see 11) that yields an elegant statement of the dual problem (see 12).

An intimate relationship exists between a linear program and its dual. For any vector x^0 (see ANALYSIS: *Vector and tensor analysis*) satisfying the constraints of the primal and any vector y^0 satisfying the constraints of its dual, the primal objective value is never greater than the dual objective value, namely, $px \leq yb$. One implication of this relationship is that when the dual problem possesses at least one feasible vector, the primal objective function is bounded from above.

If the objective values satisfy $px^0 = y^0b$, then it is easy to show that x^0 and y^0 if feasible are optimal solutions of the primal and dual programs. If a vector x^0 is an optimal solution of the primal problem, there exists an optimal solution of the dual problem such that px^0 equals y^0b. Moreover, if $v^0 = b - Ax^0$ and $u^0 = p - y^0A$, then for optimal primal and dual feasible vectors x^0 and y^0, the relations $y_i^0 v_i^0 = 0$ for $i = 1, \cdots, m$ and $x_j^0 u_j^0 = 0$ for $j = 1, \cdots, n$ hold and are referred to as complementary slackness conditions. Thus, if x_j^0 is positive in an optimal solution, then the jth inequality constraint of the dual holds as an equality; *i.e.*, its slack, measured by u_j^0, satisfies $u_j^0 = 0$.

Complementary slackness conditions

NONLINEAR PROGRAMMING THEORY

A mathematical programming problem is nonlinear if the objective function $f(x)$ to be minimized, in which x is a vector, or any of the constraint functions are nonlinear.

Classification of the problems. One broad class of non-

linear programming problems is that concerning minimizing $f(x)$ subject to no constraints (the unconstrained problem); another is the linearly-constrained nonlinear programs that include as a special subclass quadratic programs concerned with the minimization of a quadratic function (see 13) subject to linear constraints. Another is the chemical equilibrium problem in which the Gibbs function, a measure of the free energy of a chemical system (see 14), is to be minimized subject to (linear) mass-balance equations (see 15) and nonnegativity conditions (see 16). The x_j in the problem represent the unknown number of molecules of different types in a system under constant temperature and pressure. In the mass-balance equations the b_i are the given number of atoms of various types; the a_{ij} are the number of atoms of type i in a single molecule of type j. The c_j in the Gibbs function are related to the constants in the law of mass action and are considered as constants only for dilute solutions.

Classes of nonlinear programming problems

Nonlinear programs are also classified according to whether defining functions have the appropriate convexity property. A function $F(x)$ defined on a convex set S is convex if (and only if) the set of points lying on or above its graph is convex. In analytic terms, convexity is equivalent to an inequality relation (see 17). The function $G(x)$ on S is concave if and only if $F(x) = -G(x)$ is convex. A useful property of any convex function $F(x)$ defined on the convex set S is that the set of all points in S such that $F(x) \leq 0$ is a convex set. (But the set of vectors x, such that $F(x) = 0$, is not necessarily convex.)

When a quadratic function has the property that its quadratic part (see 18) is nonnegative for all choice of values for x_i, x_j, then $Q(x)$ is a convex function. Linear functions are both convex and concave.

If $f(x)$ and $h_1(x), \cdots, h_l(x)$ are convex functions, defined for each vector x appearing as the argument of the functions, then the problem of minimizing $f(x)$ subject to $h_j(x) \leq 0 (j = 1, \cdots, l)$ is called the convex programming problem. One important property of convex functions is the sufficiency of local conditions for identifying a minimum. If f is a convex function on the convex set S and x^0 is a point of S such that $f(x^0) \leq f(x)$ for all x in S that are sufficiently close to x^0, then x^0 is also a (global) minimum of f on S; that is, $f(x^0) \leq f(x)$ for all x in S. This property can be exploited in computational procedures aimed at calculating optimal solutions of convex programming problems.

Convex programming problem

Methods of solution. The question of identifying optimal solutions of nonlinear programs is often discussed assuming that the constituent functions are differentiable. The simplest such case is the unconstrained minimization of a differentiable function $f(x)$. If $x^0 = (x_1, \cdots, x_n)$ is an optimal solution, then the gradient vector of f at x^0 vanishes (see 19). Geometrically, this means that the tangent plane to the graph of f at the point $[x^0, f(x^0)]$ is horizontal. For a convex function f, the vanishing of the gradient is enough to guarantee that the point x^0 is a (global) minimum of f. But in general, the vanishing of the gradient can occur at points that are not even local minima, namely, at saddle points and local maxima.

The equality-constrained minimization problem is of the form: minimize $f(x)$ subject to $g_i(x) = 0$ for $i = 1, \cdots, m$ and $m < n$. If the functions $f, g_1, \cdots, g_m$ are differentiable, the attempt to isolate a (local) minimum point x^0 for this problem by finding numbers

$\lambda_1, \cdots, \lambda_m$ such that $\nabla f(x^0) = \sum_{i=1}^{m} \lambda_i \nabla g_i(x^0)$ is called the

method of Lagrange multipliers (see 20). In this approach, one looks for unconstrained (local) minima of an associated Lagrangian function (see 21).

When all the constituent functions are differentiable, there is an analogous result on the necessary conditions of optimality for inequality-constrained minimization problems (see 22). These necessary conditions are closely related to the Kuhn-Tucker conditions. The mathematicians H.W. Kuhn and A.W. Tucker of the United States showed in a now classic, nonlinear programming paper that if a certain regularity condition holds, a relation is true between the gradient of f and the gradients of subsidiary

$$(11) \quad \begin{cases} \text{PRIMAL: Maximize } px \text{ subject to } x \geq 0, Ax \leq b \\ \text{in which } A = [a_{ij}] \text{ is an } m \times n \text{ matrix,} \\ x = (x_1, x_2, \cdots, x_n)^T, p = (p_1, p_2, \cdots, p_n) \\ \text{and } b = (b_1, b_2, \cdots, b_m)^T. \end{cases}$$

$$(12) \quad \begin{cases} \text{DUAL: Minimize } yb \text{ subject to } y \geq 0, yA \geq p, \\ \text{in which } y = (y_1, y_2, \cdots, y_m). \end{cases}$$

$$(13) \quad Q(x) = \sum_{j=1}^{n} c_j x_j + \tfrac{1}{2} \sum_{i=1}^{n} \sum_{j=1}^{n} d_{ij} x_i x_j$$

$$(14) \quad F(x) = \sum_{j=1}^{n} c_j x_j + \sum_{j=1}^{n} x_j \log\left(x_j \Big/ \sum_{j=1}^{n} x_j\right)$$

$$(15) \quad \sum_{j=1}^{n} a_{ij} x_j = b_i, \qquad i = 1, \cdots, m$$

$$(16) \quad x_j \geq 0, \qquad j = 1, \cdots, n$$

$$(17) \quad \begin{cases} F(\lambda x + \mu y) \leq \lambda F(x) + \mu F(y) \quad \text{for all } x \in S, y \in S \\ \text{and } \lambda \geq 0, \mu \geq 0 \text{ such that } \lambda + \mu = 1. \end{cases}$$

$$(18) \quad \sum_{i=1}^{n} \sum_{j=1}^{n} d_{ij} x_i x_j$$

$$(19) \quad \nabla f(x^0) = \left[\frac{\partial f(x^0)}{\partial x_1}, \cdots, \frac{\partial f(x^0)}{\partial x_n}\right] = (0, \cdots, 0)$$

(20) If f and g_i are differentiable and the m gradient vectors $\nabla g_1(x^0), \cdots, \nabla g_m(x^0)$ are independent, then there exist numbers $\lambda_1, \cdots, \lambda_m$ such that the vector relation

$$\nabla f(x^0) = \lambda_1 \nabla g_1(x^0) + \cdots + \lambda_m \nabla g_m(x^0)$$

holds. The numbers $\lambda_1, \cdots, \lambda_m$ are known as Lagrange multipliers.

$$(21) \quad L(x, \lambda) = f(x) + \lambda_1 g_1(x) + \cdots + \lambda_m g_m(x)$$

functions h_j at an optimal solution x^0. In particular, if f and the functions h_j are convex, then a solution x^0 that satisfies stated conditions for some vector λ of multipliers is a global minimum.

Convex quadratic programming problems

Some methods for solving convex quadratic programming problems are closely related to the simplex method for linear programming and share with it the feature of terminating after only a finite number of iterations. Most of these methods make use of the Kuhn-Tucker conditions because the differentiability and regularity requirements are automatically satisfied. These characteristics are seldom found in nonlinear programming procedures in general. Instead of leading in a finite number of steps to an exact solution, they (at best) yield a point close to a point at which a local minimum is attained.

One of the historically important ancestors of nonlinear programming methods is the method of steepest descent due to the 19th-century French mathematician Augustin-Louis Cauchy. Its original application was to solving systems of nonlinear equations. For example, to solve the system of simultaneous equations $g_i(x) = 0$, $(i = 1, \cdots, m)$ a sum of squares of the functions appearing in the equations can be formed (see 23). An attempt can be made to obtain its unconstrained minimum. For every vector x, the functional value $f(x)$ is nonnegative because it is the sum of squares. Consequently, x^0 is a solution if and only if $f(x^0) = 0$.

The method is easily stated: From a starting point (trial solution) $x^{(1)}$, compute the direction of steepest descent, $-\nabla f(x^{(1)})$. Using a fixed step size, symbolized by the Greek letter sigma, σ, minimize the function f along the line segment of length σ issuing from $x^{(1)}$ in the direction of steepest descent. The point $x^{(2)}$ that minimizes $f(x)$ along this line segment becomes the new trial solution. In general, the preceding step is repeated from at each trial solution $x^{(k)}$ to obtain the next one $x^{(k+1)}$.

The method of steepest descent is valid under the assumption that the function f is continuously differentiable, and all points satisfying $f(x) \leq f(x^{(1)})$ lie within a fixed finite distance from the origin. The aim of the procedure is actually to locate a point x^* satisfying the necessary local conditions of optimality: $\nabla f(x^*) = 0$. Because such a point might be reached only in a limiting sense, it is customary to terminate the computational process when a point $x^{(k)}$ is reached at which the absolute value $|\partial f(x^{(k)})/\partial x_j|$ is less than a prescribed value for $j = 1, \cdots, n$. If the function f being minimized is convex, a point x^* at which $\nabla f(x^*)$ is zero must be a global minimum.

Another method deals with the linearly-constrained nonlinear programming problem: Minimize $f(x)$ subject to $Ax = b$, $x \geq 0$ in a manner that uses both linear programming and the Kuhn-Tucker conditions. It is assumed that the objective function $f(x)$ is continuously differentiable. It is then natural to replace f by its linear approximation at a feasible point and solve the associated linear program. For example, if $x^{(k)}$ is a feasible point, f can be replaced by its linear approximation (see 24). Assuming that $y^{(k)}$ is the solution of this linear program, a search can then be performed to minimize f along the line joining $x^{(k)}$ to $y^{(k)}$. The point $x^{(k+1)}$ at which the latter minimum is attained becomes the new trial solution at which the linear approximation to f can be formed for the repetition of the process. The computation can be interrupted if a point x^0 is reached at which the solution point y^0 of the associated

linear programming problem satisfies $\nabla f(x^0)(y^0 - x^0) \geq 0$. It can be shown that the point x^0 must be optimal when the objective function f is convex.

Generalized reduced-gradient method

Of the many algorithms for the solution of nonlinear programming problems, none is known to be superior to the generalized reduced-gradient method. Its roots lie in the reduced-gradient method (for linearly-constrained nonlinear programs) and ultimately in the simplex method itself.

(G.B.D./R.W.Co.)

Cybernetics

The presentation to follow deals only with the principles of cybernetics and includes reference to mathematical aspects such as information theory, automata theory, and cybernetic systems. The technological aspects of cybernetics are multifold and can be found in INFORMATION PROCESSING AND INFORMATION SYSTEMS and AUTOMATION.

DEFINITIONS OF THE TERM CYBERNETICS

The term cybernetics comes from the ancient Greek word *kybernētikos* ("good at steering") referring to the art of the helmsman. In the first half of the 19th-century, the French physicist André-Marie Ampère, in his classification of sciences, suggested that the still nonexistent science of the control of governments be called cybernetics. This term was soon forgotten until used by the United States mathematician Norbert Wiener as the title for his book published in 1948. In that book Wiener made reference to an 1868 article by the British physicist James Clerk Maxwell on governors and pointed out that "governor" is derived, via Latin, from the same Greek word that gives rise to the term "cybernetics." The date of Wiener's publication is generally accepted as the date of the birth of cybernetics as an independent science. Wiener defined cybernetics as "the science of control and communications in the animal and machine." This definition relates cybernetics closely first of all with the theory of automatic control and with physiology, particularly the physiology of the nervous system. Subsequently, the computer and the areas of mathematics related to it (*e.g.*, mathematical logic) had a great influence on the development of cybernetics. The reason is that the computer can be used not only for automatic calculation, but also for all conversions of information, including various types of information processing used in control systems. This ability made two different views of cybernetics possible. The narrower view, common in the Western countries, defines cybernetics as the science of control of complex systems of various types (technical, biological, and social). In many countries (for example, in the United States), particular emphasis is given to those aspects of cybernetics that are used in the generation of control systems in technology and in living organisms. In addition to cybernetics, the science of computers and the general rules of information processing is being developed in the Western countries (English—computer science; French—*informatique*).

The broader interpretation of the subject of cybernetics common in the Soviet Union includes not only control but all forms of information processing. This definition includes therefore the Western computer science as one of the component parts of cybernetics.

PRINCIPLES

Information theory. It should be emphasized that the concept of information and its conversion is an important first concept of cybernetics no matter how its subject is defined. Information arises with any act of selection or limitation of possibilities of selection. For example, if it is known that a room can contain 100 men, then the message that the room at a given moment contains 50 men or that the number of people in the room is less than 40 carries information. The message that the number is less than 200 carries no information, because the first, fixed selection is in no way thus limited. In developing the principle of limitation of selection, Claude E. Shannon, an electrical engineer in the United States, introduced the method of changing the quantity of information.

Information is transmitted by signals. In pure cybernetics,

$$(22) \quad \begin{cases} \text{Minimize } f(x) \text{ subject to } h_j(x) \leqslant 0 \text{ for } j = 1, \cdots, l. \\ \text{Then } x^0 \text{ is a locally minimizing solution only if there} \\ \text{exist multipliers } \lambda_0, \lambda_1, \cdots, \lambda_l \text{ not all zero such that} \\ \lambda_0 \nabla f(x^0) = \lambda_1 \nabla h_1(x^0) + \cdots + \lambda_l \nabla h_l(x^0) \text{ and} \\ h_j(x^0) \leqslant 0, \quad \lambda_j \geqslant 0, \quad \lambda_j \cdot h_j(x^0) = 0 \text{ for } j = 1, \cdots, l. \end{cases}$$

$$(23) \quad f(x) = [g_1(x)]^2 + \cdots + [g_m(x)]^2$$

$$(24) \quad F(y) = f(x^k) + \nabla f(x^k)(y - x^k)$$

The nature
and types
of signals

the physical nature of the signals is completely disregarded. It is important only that the signals can be differentiated from each other. The form of the set of possible signals and the nature of their changes are also significant. For example, a signal carrying information on the number of persons in a room cannot take on fractional values. The values of these signals change in jumps. On the other hand, a signal giving information of the temperature of the air in the room cannot change its value, say from 19° C to 20° C, without passing through all intermediate values. Signals of the first type are called discrete and of the second type, continuous. The same terms are used in relation to the information represented by these signals.

In describing continuous information within a certain accuracy, it can always be reduced to discrete information. The usual method of representation of discrete information is as a finite sequence of signals selected from a certain fixed finite set of signals called the (abstract) alphabet, for example the set of letters in the Latin alphabet, the set of decimal numbers, etc. One important but simple fact is the possibility of representing any discrete information in the form of sequences of signals of only two different types, as is done, for example, in the dots and dashes of the well-known Morse telegraph code. Problems of various forms of representation of discrete information make up the subject of a special division of theoretical cybernetics called encoding theory.

Automata as information converters. Encoding is the simplest form of information conversion. In the general case, these conversions are performed by so-called information converters, or data processors. An information converter, referred to in cybernetics as a machine or automaton (see AUTOMATA THEORY), is a device that converts a certain set of signals called the input signals to another set, the set of output signals. The input signals arrive at the converter through the input channels, the output signals leave through the output channels. Furthermore, in the general case, the processor can store signals in the form of a certain set of parameters, the different values of which determine the internal state of the processor, that is, the condition of its memory.

A processor is called continuous if all of the parameters that define it (memory, input, and output signals) are continuous. In the case of discrete processors, all of these signals must be discrete. Processors dealing both with continuous and with discrete signals are called hybrid processors.

The changes in output signals and in the internal state of any processor depend generally both on the input signals and on the internal state of the processor at a given time. For a processor without memory, the values of the output signals at any moment in time depend only on the values of the input signal at the same moment in time. If all of these dependences are fixed by fully defined, unambiguous functions (*e.g.*, single-valued), the processor is called deterministic. If there are random dependences, the processor is called probabilistic.

Information processors in which no functional components and no internal structural parts other than those described above can be distinguished are called elementary. Nonelementary processors, also called cybernetic systems, consist of networks composed of elementary (or in any case simpler) processors. A network is constructed by connecting some (or all) of the output channels of the processors composing the network to some (or all) of their input channels. A portion of the input and output channels of the elementary processors may be appropriately connected to the input and output signals of the entire system.

The concept of elementariness or nonelementariness of a processor is relative and depends on the depth of penetration into the subject. For example, if interest is confined to the functions of the brain, not in its structure, it can be analyzed as an elementary processor (although it is characterized by a tremendous number of parameters). It is known, however, that the brain is an extremely complex system, composed of more elementary processors, the neurons. In turn, upon transition to the molecular level, the neurons themselves can be regarded as extremely complex cybernetic systems.

Study of systems. The study of systems and particularly of the complex probabilistic systems is one of the most important tasks in cybernetics. The specific feature of the cybernetic approach to the study of systems is that it abstracts itself from the actual nature of the elements of the system and the signals circulating in it. This allows a general mathematical apparatus and general methods of investigation to be developed, suitable for systems of varying nature and purpose. In the study of continuous cybernetic systems, a system of ordinary differential equations is particularly significant.

The
cybernetic
approach
to systems
study

Theory of algorithms. In the discrete case, the modus operandi is the so-called theory of algorithms. An algorithm is an arbitrary, finite system of rules of any nature, allowing expressions in any alphabet to be converted to new expressions in the same (or any other) alphabet. So-called algorithmic languages are used for precise descriptions of the rules for these conversions (see AUTOMATA THEORY: *Classification of automata*).

It is extremely important that the presence in an algorithmic language of a relatively small number of means of expression can give it the property of universality. Universality of an algorithmic language means the possibility of expressing in this language any conversion of discrete information that can be defined using a finite number of rules, that is, expressed as a certain algorithm in any other algorithmic language.

The fact of existence of universal algorithmic languages means that it is possible to construct universal discrete information processors. To do this, it is sufficient to fix upon some concrete alphabet and to construct a memory device capable of storing any word (expression) in the alphabet and a device capable of performing all of the elementary rules of a certain universal algorithmic language.

Universal digital computers are such universal information processors if the limitations resulting from their finite memory volume are not considered. Until computers appeared, the only universal data processor was the natural information processor, the human brain.

The availability of technical universal data processors is highly significant for the development of cybernetics in at least two ways. First of all, this fact opens unlimited possibilities for the automation not only of the physical, but also of the mental activity of man, and this automation does not require that new technical devices be invented for each case. It is sufficient to study and describe the rules defining the type of activity to be automated and to program them; *i.e.*, express them in one of the algorithmic languages used in existing computers.

Mathematical modelling. Second, the use of universal data processors—computers—gives cybernetics a method of scientific investigation of systems that is new in principle—so-called mathematical modelling. Until this method appeared, scientists actually had only two different methods of study: experimental and theoretical. In the former, experiments were performed only with the system itself, or with an actual, physical model of the system. In the second, it was necessary to be able to solve equations describing the system.

Mathematical modelling occupies an intermediate position between these two methods: there is no necessity to construct an actual physical model of the system. It is replaced by a mathematical model; *i.e.*, a description of the system in some algorithmic language. There is also no need to solve complex mathematical problems related to this description (*i.e.*, to solve systems of differential equations). The description of the system is simply entered into a computer that models the behaviour of the system (*i.e.*, provides precise descriptions of the system) under various conditions defined according to the purpose of the research assignment.

This method allows the scientist to produce a full description of complex systems, the individual parts of which are studied by different people or even in different sciences. One example is the human organism. Its individual parts (circulatory system, digestive system, nervous system, glandular system, etc.) are studied by different specialists, even though the parts are closely related to each other.

To produce a mathematical model of the organism, first

Modelling
the human
organism

of all it must be divided into individual parts and the state of each part described by some system of parameters. Among these parameters might be continuous quantities (for example, the percent content of sugar in the blood) or discrete quantities (for example, qualitatively differing levels of secretory function of the liver). The next step is description of the relationships between the separate parts. One of the most typical forms of relationship for this example is expressed by a sentence such as: When organ A shifts from state m_1 to state m_2, and organ B shifts from state n_1 to state n_2 after k days (weeks, months), organ C will change its state from l_1 to l_2 with probability p. The specialists must describe all of the relations of this type with which they are familiar (called simple relationships) to form the required mathematical model. Operations with this model in the computer permit the establishment of the complex relationships (*i.e.*, the influence of organs on other organs not directly, but through still other organs). This type of model can be used to study versions of the development of various diseases, various methods of treatment, etc.

Mathematical modelling can in principle be performed in any universal data processor, including the human brain. The brain, however, being a very complex system itself, is comparatively poorly suited for such routine but laborious work as the modelling of complex systems. Consequently, only the appearance of the computer provided a qualitative jump and made it possible to perform effective study of really complex systems in various areas of knowledge. Actually, the concern is with coarse qualitative criteria, differentiating simple systems from complex; if the structure and behaviour of a system can be studied by a single man in a reasonable time, the system is called simple. If the efforts of many persons and the use of special technical equipment (computers) are required to draw the whole picture, the system is called complex.

Cybernetic systems. *Self-teaching mechanisms.* Complex tasks arise in so-called self-teaching systems, in which attempts to achieve a certain final goal lead to changes in the methods of its attainment, and the setting of various intermediate goals. One of the simplest examples of this type of system is the so-called Shannon's mouse. It is a moving automaton placed in a maze. The final purpose of the automaton is to find the "food" placed at some point in the maze.

Shannon's mouse

At first, the mouse uses a simple trial and error algorithm, bumping into the walls until an exit is found. During the process of this type of search, it "learns" and memorizes the plan of the maze. After once reaching the goal (by chance), the mouse will use an entirely different, much more economical, and seemingly "intelligent" algorithm for reaching the goal in a subsequent experiment, based on "knowledge" of the layout of the maze.

Self-teaching is one type of self-improvement of control systems. In this case, the improvement occurs without changing the structure of the system. It is also possible, however, that the upper levels of a system may change the structure of lower levels in order to improve their functioning. This type of self-improvement is naturally called self-development.

Methods have been designed for the quantitative definition of self-improvement. In this case, in pure theory, the boundary between self-teaching and self-development disappears. In practice, however, the difference between these types of self-improvement is usually rather clear.

Biocybernetics. Many control systems in biology are constructed according to the principles of self-teaching and self-development. For example, in all probability, only a small portion of the organization of the human brain is determined genetically. Everything else is produced as a result of the effects of many, rather effective, mechanisms of self-improvement.

Highly complex examples of self-development can be found in the processes of biological evolution, as well as various social processes.

For systems of the high degree of complexity characteristic of living organisms and human society, an ever greater role is played not just by control processes, but by cognition processes. These systems have highly perfected systems of sensors and effectors (for example, the eye and the hand), capable of recognizing complex patterns and performing widely varied actions. The central portion of the system has a multilevel structure; the upper links of the structure develop abstract concepts and recognize the deeper regularities existing both in the system itself and in its surroundings.

By the last quarter of the 20th century, cybernetics had achieved significant success in the solution of the problem of pattern recognition, automation (by computer) of the processes of logical conclusion, formation of new concepts, and other problems. This success has allowed the creation of universal robots controlled by computers and imitating rather complex forms of conscious behaviour. (Ed.)

Control theory

GENERAL BACKGROUND

As long as human culture has existed, control has always meant some kind of power over man's environment. Cuneiform fragments suggest that the control of irrigation systems in Mesopotamia was a well-developed art at least by the 20th century BC. There were some ingenious control devices in the Greco-Roman culture, the details of which have been preserved. Methods for the automatic operation of windmills go back at least to the Middle Ages. Large-scale implementation of the idea of control, however, was impossible without a high-level of technological sophistication, and it is probably no accident that the principles of modern control started evolving only in the 19th century, concurrently with the Industrial Revolution. A serious scientific study of this field began only after World War II and is now a major aspect of what has come to be called the second industrial revolution.

Although control is sometimes equated with the notion of feedback control (which involves the transmission and return of information)—an isolated engineering invention, not a scientific discipline—modern usage tends to favour a rather wide meaning for the term; for instance, control and regulation of machines, muscular coordination and metabolism in biological organisms, prosthetic devices; also, broad aspects of coordinated activity in the social sphere such as optimization of business operations, control of economic activity by government policies, and even control of political decisions by democratic processes. Scientifically speaking, modern control should be viewed as that branch of system theory concerned with changing the behaviour of a given complex system by external actions. (For aspects of system theory related to information, see below.) If physics is the science of understanding the physical environment, then control should be viewed as the science of modifying that environment, in the physical, biological, or even social sense.

Examples of feedback control

Much more than even physics, control is a mathematically-oriented science. Control principles are always expressed in mathematical form and are potentially applicable to any concrete situation. At the same time, it must be emphasized that success in the use of the abstract principles of control depends in roughly equal measure on the status of basic scientific knowledge in the specific field of application, be it engineering, physics, astronomy, biology, medicine, econometrics, or any of the social sciences. This fact should be kept in mind to avoid confusion between the basic ideas of control (for instance, controllability) and certain spectacular applications of the moment in a narrow area (for instance, manned lunar travel).

EXAMPLES OF MODERN CONTROL SYSTEMS

To clarify the critical distinction between control principles and their embodiment in a real machine or system, the following common examples of control may be helpful. There are several broad classes of control systems, of which some are mentioned below.

Machines that cannot function without (feedback) control. Many of the basic devices of contemporary technology must be manufactured in such a way that they cannot be used for the intended task without modification by means of control external to the device. In other words, control is introduced after the device has been built; the same effect cannot be brought about (in practice and sometimes even in theory) by an intrinsic modification of the characteristics of the device. The best known examples are the vacuum-tube or transistor amplifiers for high-fidelity sound systems. Vacuum tubes or transistors, when used alone, introduce intolerable distortion, but when they are placed inside a feedback control system any desired degree of fidelity can be achieved. A famous classical case is that of powered flight. Early pioneers failed, not because of their ignorance of the laws of aerodynamics, but because they did not realize the need for control and were unaware of the basic principles of stabilizing an inherently unstable device by means of control. Jet aircraft cannot be operated without automatic control to aid the pilot, and control is equally critical for helicopters. The accuracy of inertial navigation equipment (the modern space compass) cannot be improved indefinitely because of basic mechanical limitations, but these limitations can be reduced by several orders of magnitude by computer-directed statistical filtering, which is a variant of feedback control.

The role of computers in feedback control

Control of machines. In many cases, the operation of a machine to perform a task can be directed by a human (manual control), but it may be much more convenient to connect the machine directly to the measuring instrument (automatic control); *e.g.,* a thermostat (temperature-operated switch) may be used to turn on or off a refrigerator, oven, air-conditioning unit, or heating system. The dimming of automobile headlights, the setting of the diaphragm of a camera, the correct exposure for colour prints may be accomplished automatically by connecting a photocell or other light-responsive device directly to the machine in question. Related examples are the remote control of position (servomechanisms), speed control of motors (governors). It is emphasized that in such case a machine could function by itself, but a more useful system is obtained by letting the measuring device communicate with the machine in either a feedforward or feedback fashion.

Control of large systems. More advanced and more critical applications of control concern large and complex systems the very existence of which depends on coordinated operation using numerous individual control devices (usually directed by a computer). The launch of a spaceship, the 24-hour operation of a power plant, oil refinery, or chemical factory, the control of air traffic near a large airport, are well-known manifestations of this technological trend. An essential aspect of these systems is the fact that human participation in the control task, although theoretically possible, would be wholly impractical; it is the feasibility of applying automatic control that has given birth to these systems.

Biocontrol. The advancement of technology (artificial biology) and the deeper understanding of the processes of biology (natural technology) has given reason to hope that the two can be combined; man-made devices should be substituted for some natural functions. Examples are the artificial heart or kidney, nerve-controlled prosthetics, and control of brain functions by external electrical stimuli. Although definitely no longer in the science-fiction stage, progress in solving such problems has been slow not only because of the need for highly advanced technology but also because of the lack of fundamental knowledge about the details of control principles employed in the biological world.

Robots. On the most advanced level, the task of control science is the creation of robots. This is a collective term for devices exhibiting animal-like purposeful behaviour under the general command of (but without direct help from) man. Industrial manufacturing robots are already fairly common, but real breakthroughs in this field cannot be anticipated until there are fundamental scientific advances with regard to problems related to pattern recognition and the mathematical structuring of brain processes.

PRINCIPLES OF CONTROL

The scientific formulation of a control problem must be based on two kinds of information: (A) the behaviour of the system (*e.g.,* industrial plant) must be described in a mathematically precise way; (B) the purpose of control (criterion) and the environment (disturbances) must be specified, again in a mathematically precise way.

Information of type A means that the effect of any potential control action applied to the system is precisely known under all possible environmental circumstances. The choice of one or a few appropriate control actions, among the many possibilities that may be available, is then based on information of type B; and this choice, as stated before, is called optimization.

The task of control theory is to study the mathematical quantification of these two basic problems and then to deduce applied-mathematical methods whereby a concrete answer to optimization can be obtained. Control theory does not deal with physical reality but only with its mathematical description (mathematical models). The knowledge embodied in control theory is always expressed with respect to certain classes of models, for instance, linear systems with constant coefficients, which will be treated in detail below. Thus control theory is applicable to any concrete situation (*e.g.,* physics, biology, economics) whenever that situation can be described, with high precision, by a model that belongs to a class for which the theory has already been developed. The limitations of the theory are not logical but depend only on the agreement between available models and the actual behaviour of the system to be controlled. Similar comments can be made about the mathematical representation of the criteria and disturbances.

Basic task

Once the appropriate control action has been deduced by mathematical methods from the information mentioned above, the implementation of control becomes a technological task, which is best treated under the various specialized fields of engineering. The detailed manner in which a chemical plant is controlled may be quite different from that of an automobile factory, but the essential principles will be the same. Hence further discussion of the solution of the control problem will be limited here to the mathematical level.

To obtain a solution in this sense, it is convenient (but not absolutely necessary) to describe the system to be controlled, which is called the plant, in terms of its internal dynamical state. By this is meant a list of numbers (called the state vector) that expresses in quantitative form the effect of all external influences on the plant before the present moment, so that the future evolution of the plant can be exactly given from the knowledge of the present state and the future inputs. This situation implies, in an intuitively obvious way, that the control action at a given time can be specified as some function of the state at that time. Such a function of the state, which determines the control action that is to be taken at any instant, is called a control law. This is a more general concept than the earlier idea of feedback; in fact, a control law can incorporate both the feedback and feedforward methods of control.

In developing models to represent the control problem, it is unrealistic to assume that every component of the state vector can be measured exactly and instantaneously. Consequently in most cases the control problem has to be broadened to include the further problem of state determination, which may be viewed as the central task in statistical prediction and filtering theory. Thus, in principle, any control problem can be solved in two steps: (1) Building an optimal filter (so-called Kalman filter) to determine the best estimate of the present state vector; (2) determining an optimal control law and mechanizing it by substituting into it the estimate of the state vector obtained in step 1.

In practice, the two steps are implemented by a single unit of hardware, called the controller, which may be viewed as a special-purpose computer. The theoretical formulation given here can be shown to include all other previous methods as a special case; the only difference is in the engineering details of the controller.

The mathematical solution of a control problem may not always exist. The determination of rigorous existence conditions, beginning in the late 1950s, has had an important effect on the evolution of modern control, equally from the theoretical and the applied point of view. Most important is controllability; it expresses the fact that some

Controllability

kind of control is possible. If this condition is satisfied, methods of optimization can pick out the right kind of control using information of type B.

CONTROL OF LINEAR SYSTEMS

Systems with constant coefficients. The preceding considerations may be illustrated much more directly by taking the special case of linear systems with constant coefficients. The point of view and most of the results described below originated after 1950, but the beginnings of the theory are more than 100 years old dating from Maxwell's work published in 1868. In fact, this class of models is the only one for which a reasonably complete mathematical theory of control exists so far.

One may denote by $y(t)$ the number giving the value of the output of the plant at time t; similarly, the number $u(t)$ denotes the value of the input to the plant at the same time. A classical way to describe the behaviour of the plant (information of type A) is to assume that the input and output are related by a linear differential equation with constant coefficients $\alpha_1, \cdots, \alpha_n$ (see 25), which is called the open-loop equation of the plant. In this case the state vector is the list $(y(0), \cdots, y^{(n-1)}(0))$ consisting of the output at time $t = 0$ and the first $n - 1$ derivatives with respect to time of the function $y(t)$ at $t = 0$. Under these circumstances, the control law is a linear combination of the state variables, with coefficients $\beta_1, \cdots, \beta_n$ (see 26).

The fact that this control law is linear in the state is an assumption needed to assure the manageability of mathematical machinery for the problem. It is desirable to assume also that the coefficients $\beta_1, \cdots, \beta_n$ are all constants so that the same formula can be used at any time. [A minus sign in the control law (26) expresses the classical idea of negative feedback; in the general theory, this has become merely a notational convention.]

Substitution of the control law into the linear differential equation of the plant (25) leads to the closed-loop differential equation for the controlled output of the plant (see 27). Here the coefficients γ_i are the differences $\alpha_i - \beta_i$. So the effect of control is to replace the coefficients α_i of the open-loop equation with the γ_i of the closed-loop equation. Since the β_i in the control law are arbitrary, it follows that arbitrary changes can be effected in the dynamical behaviour of the plant by means of control. In particular, it is possible to make a plant stable by means of the control law because the criterion for stability is given by the positiveness of the Routh–Hurwitz determinants (see 28). These conditions can of course always be met since the γ_i can be arranged to have any values.

It is necessary to comment on this seemingly overly general (but indeed correct) result from two points of view First the result assumes that the plant description (see 25) is exactly true and that the state list $(y(t), \cdots, y^{(n-1)}(t))$ is known at every time t. These assumptions are never exactly correct, but they can be approximated in many cases with sufficient accuracy by restricting the output $y(t)$ to small deviations about a given steady-state value and by constructing a statistical filter to estimate the derivatives of the function $y(t)$ with respect to t. Second, the model (see 25) does not represent the most general linear system with constant coefficients; in fact, this model, because of its special form, implicitly possesses the property of controllability that may not hold for the general model in the linear, constant coefficient class.

The most general system of this class (with one input and one output) is given by a pair of state-vector equations (see 29); the symbol x denotes the state vector (a list of n arbitrary numbers), F is an $n \times n$ matrix, g is an n-vector, h is an n-vector, and $<, >$ is the inner product; the symbols $u(t)$ and $y(t)$ have the same meaning as above. The equations of the plant discussed above (see 25) can always be transformed into the general case (see 29), but not necessarily vice versa.

Transforming the plant equations discussed above to the general form gives the canonical matrices F, g (shown in 30). If these expressions are substituted into the controllability criterion (see 31) for the general system (29), it is seen that the special model for the plant that was used above (25) is always controllable. Thus, it is clear that the true significance of the celebrated controllability concept can be grasped only after the control problem has been formulated in the state-vector style. In the classical development of control theory, too much emphasis was placed on special models for the plant (25); the advances since 1950 to a large extent resulted from a recognition that the most general model corresponding to the basic restrictive hypotheses of linearity and constant coefficients is given by the state-vector equations (29); this recognition eventually led to the discovery that for the general class there is a nontrivial controllability condition (31).

The explicit form of the controllability condition is of great practical and philosophical importance. It is a generic condition: it is satisfied by almost all systems of the linear, constant-coefficient class. Because the state-vector equations (29) accurately represent most physical systems making only small deviations about their steady-state behaviour, it follows further that in the natural world control in the small is, in principle, almost always possible. This fact of nature is the theoretical basis of practically all the presently existing control technology. On the other hand, little is known at present, in the scientific sense, about the ultimate limitations of control when the models in question are not linear. In particular, it is not known under what conditions control is possible in the large; that is, for arbitrary deviations from existing conditions. This lack of scientific knowledge should be kept in mind in assessing often exaggerated claims by economists and sociologists in regard to a possible improvement in human society by governmental control.

Optimal control. To reduce the arbitrariness of the control law (see 26), it is necessary to use information of type B. This is done, conceptually, in the following way. It is assumed (after a change of variables, if necessary) that the state $x = 0$ represents the ideal condition of the plant to be controlled. Any given state $x(0)$ not equal to zero at time $t = 0$ is regarded as an undesirable deviation, attributed to unavoidable disturbances acting on the system. The task of control is to restore the ideal condition $x(t) = 0$ in the best possible way. The specification of a suitable optimality criterion is frequently dictated by mathematical expediency.

The long mathematical history of the calculus of variations has suggested that the most natural criterion to consider is the minimization of an integral from zero to infinity, which measures the deviation of $x(t)$ from zero as

The criterion for stability

Control limitations in nonlinear modelling

(25) $$\frac{d^n y}{dt^n} + \alpha_1 \frac{d^{n-1} y}{dt^{n-1}} + \cdots + \alpha_n y = u(t)$$

(26) $$-u(0) = \beta_n y(0) + \beta_{n-1} \dot{y}(0) + \cdots + \beta_1 y^{(n-1)}(0)$$

(27) $$\frac{d^n y}{dt^n} + \gamma_1 \frac{d^{n-1} y}{dt^{n-1}} + \cdots + \gamma_n y = 0$$

(28) $$\gamma_1 > 0, \quad \begin{vmatrix} 1 & \gamma_2 \\ \gamma_1 & \gamma_3 \end{vmatrix} > 0, \cdots$$

(29) $$\frac{dx}{dt} = Fx + gu(t), \quad y(t) = \langle h, x(t) \rangle$$

(30) $$F = \begin{bmatrix} 0 & 1 & 0 & \cdots & 0 \\ 0 & 0 & 1 & \cdots & 0 \\ \cdot & \cdot & \cdot & & \cdot \\ \cdot & \cdot & \cdot & & \cdot \\ \cdot & \cdot & \cdot & & \cdot \\ 0 & 0 & 0 & \cdots & 1 \\ -\alpha_n & -\alpha_{n-1} & -\alpha_{n-2} & \cdots & -\alpha_1 \end{bmatrix}, \quad g = \begin{bmatrix} 0 \\ 0 \\ \cdot \\ \cdot \\ \cdot \\ 0 \\ 1 \end{bmatrix}$$

(31) $$\det[g \quad Fg \quad F^2 g \quad \cdots \quad F^{n-1} g] \neq 0$$

well as the cost of control. For example, the coefficients in the control law may be explicitly determined by minimizing a quadratic integral (see 32) by the choice of the function $u(t)$ with respect to solutions of the open-loop differential equation (see 25). The applied-mathematical technique for solution is well developed and requires the solution of a nonlinear differential equation of the Riccati type, which can be conveniently carried out by digital computer. It can be shown also that this general procedure includes older techniques based on semi-quantitative engineering analyses, for instance, the idea of maximizing the loop gain.

In many respects, optimization theory represents a satisfactory solution of the control problem (in some cases even outside the linear case), but basic difficulties remain in regard to the appropriate choice of the criterion represented by the quadratic forms in the performance index (see 32).

Optimal filtering and state estimation. At least in the linear case, the solution of the state-estimation problem can be accomplished by methods similar to that for optimal control; this follows from the well-known Duality Principle which states that the dual equations (matrices

$$(32) \qquad \int_0^\infty [Q(x(t)) + R(u(t))]\,dt \qquad (Q, R \text{ are quadratic forms})$$

and vectors replaced by their transposes) of control optimization are the equations for state estimation. The optimal filter is then a dynamical system similar to (25), in which the principal task is to determine a dual control law similar to (26).

In practice, the state estimation problem is much more important than the control problem; approximately 90–95 percent of practical controllers are devoted to state estimation, only about five percent being required for the implementation of the control law.

NONLINEAR CONTROL SYSTEMS

Whenever the controlled variable $y(t)$ is allowed to have large deviations from the steady state, the linear constant-coefficient model will cease to represent the plant accurately because of intrinsic nonlinearities involved in the description of most natural dynamical phenomena. Equally important are intentionally introduced nonlinearities that result from reasons of economy, simplicity and reliability of engineering, or from ignorance of the fact that the savings achieved by nonlinear control devices may be negated by factors resulting from the greater intrinsic difficulty of control. A good example of unavoidable nonlinearities in the object to be controlled is a space vehicle whose rockets, at the current state of technology, can only be controlled by turning them on or off. Continuously variable control action (which is desirable) in this case is technologically impossible; the high cost of rocket engines, however, justifies extremely sophisticated computer-based technology to achieve optimal control. The purpose of the computer is then simply one of switching the rockets on or off; the difficulty of the control lies in the extreme precision with which the time must be determined when this takes place.

Example of a non-linearity

When the basic mathematical data can be stated in the conventional optimization framework, effective methods are available for solving the optimal control problem even in the nonlinear case. The methods for doing this are an extension of the classical methods of the calculus of variations. These methods, however, have yielded little theoretical insight and their straightforward application becomes prohibitively expensive for large-scale systems.

Even less satisfactory is the status of the nonlinear optimal filtering and state estimation problem, which, as has been noted, is a critical part of the general solution of the control problem. Because of nonlinearity, the Duality Principle no longer applies; even the formulation of the problem is controversial.

Nonlinear systems do not represent a special case, but simply everything that is not subjected to the special assumption of linearity; in a sense "nonlinear" is synonymous with "unknown." Scientific progress will undoubtedly occur by singling out special classes of systems subject to restrictive structural assumptions other than linearity.

(R.E.K.)

BIBLIOGRAPHY

Linear and nonlinear programming: The history, theory, and applications of linear programming may be found in GEORGE B. DANTZIG, *Linear Programming and Extensions* (1963); see also GEORGE HADLEY, *Linear Programming* (1962). For the classic work on the subject, see LESTER R. FORD and D.R. FULKERSON, *Flows in Networks* (1962). An alternate source is T.C. HU, *Integer Programming and Network Flows* (1967). LEON S. LASDON, *Optimization Theory for Large Systems* (1970), deals with linear and nonlinear programming problems. One of the pathbreaking books on linear and nonlinear programming is G. ZOUTENDIJK, *Methods of Feasible Directions* (1960). OLVI L. MANGASARIAN, *Nonlinear Programming* (1969), deals exclusively with theory; while WILLARD I. ZANGWILL, *Nonlinear Programming* (1969), is concerned primarily with algorithms. From various conferences have come J. ABADIE (ed.), *Nonlinear Programming* (1967) and *Integer and Nonlinear Programming* (1970); and GEORGE B. DANTZIG and ARTHUR F. VEINOTT, JR. (eds.), *Mathematics of the Decision Sciences,* 2 vol. (1968)—all feature papers on a wide range of subjects.

Cybernetics: NORBERT WIENER, *Cybernetics,* 2nd rev. ed. (1961), a very general discussion; and VIKTOR GLUSHKOV, *Introduction to Cybernetics* (1966). See also STAFFORD BEER, *Cybernetics and Management* (1959); and JIRI KLIR and MIROSLAV VALACH, *Kybernetické modelování* (1965; Eng. trans., *Cybernetic Modelling,* 1967).

Control theory: Among good books on modern control and system theory, see RICHARD E. BELLMAN, *Dynamic Programming* (1957). More mathematical treatments are L.S. PONTRYAGIN et al., *The Mathematical Theory of Optimal Processes* (1962); and E.B. LEE and L. MARKUS, *Foundations of Optimal Control Theory* (1967). Control theory in the wider context of system theory is treated in R.E. KALMAN et al., *Topics in Mathematical System Theory* (1969), see especially Chapter 2. ROGER W. BROCKETT, *Finite-Dimensional Linear Systems* (1970), surveys the fundamental problems of description and optimization of linear, constant-coefficient systems. A historical overview of feedback devices may be found in OTTO MAYR, *The Origins of Feedback Control* (1970). For information on biocontrol, see DOUGLAS and K. STANLEY-JONES, *The Kybernetics of Natural Systems* (1960).

(G.B.D./R.W.Co./R.E.K./Ed.)

Plant and Animal
Organs and Organ Systems

An organ is composed of various tissues, not necessarily similar but related in a structural and functional unit. This article is concerned with the evolution of organs and their integration into the highly specialized complexes known as organ systems.
The article is divided into the following sections:

ANIMAL BODIES AT THE ORGAN AND ORGAN SYSTEM LEVEL OF DEVELOPMENT

The bodies of multicellular animals are generally organized on the basis of tissues, organs, and organ systems. Larger and more complex animals have distinct but related organs, which may cooperate as a functional complex. Such a complex is called an organ system. Ten highly specialized organ systems make up the bodies of advanced animals; lower forms usually are not as complex in structure. For a depiction of many of the organs of the human body, shown in relation to each other, see the colour Trans-Vision in the *Propædia*: Part Four, Section 421.

Organs and organ systems

SPECIALIZED ORGAN SYSTEMS

Integumentary system. The integument, or outer covering of the body, is often called the skin in higher forms. The integument and its derivatives make up the integumentary system, which functions as a protective covering that resists harmful substances and organisms and prevents excessive water loss. All animals have an outer covering, the nature of which varies. In protozoans, the simplest animals, it consists of a fine membrane or a firm, elastic film. In certain more advanced invertebrates, inhabiting an aquatic or moist environment, the integument consists of a single layer of cells; in others, the outer cells secrete a noncellular, waxy substance called a cuticle. The cuticle may be hard enough to form a shell, as in the case of snails, or a protective exoskeleton, as in the case of insects. The periodic shedding of this outer layer is known as molting, or ecdysis. In vertebrates, the integument consists of an outer layer, the epidermis, and an underlying layer, the dermis. These layers vary in structure in different parts of the body (see INTEGUMENTARY SYSTEMS).

Skeletal system. The framework of the vertebrate body is the skeleton. Vertebrates have a jointed internal skeleton (endoskeleton), composed of cartilage, bone, or both, that supports the rest of the body, serves as an attachment for muscles, and protects delicate vital organs. In a few forms, such as turtles and armadillos, skeletal elements may also be present in the dermis of the skin, making up the dermal skeleton. Among certain lower animals (*e.g.,* many protozoans, coelenterates, flatworms, and slugs), no skeletal system exists. As stated above, the cuticle derived from the integument may, in some animals, form an exoskeleton that provides support and protection and serves for muscle attachment. It may be composed of calcareous (containing calcium carbonate), siliceous (containing

silica), or organic substances, and it is either rigid, as in corals and mollusks, or jointed, as in certain echinoderms and arthropods. Exoskeletons of arthropods must be shed periodically in order to permit growth (see SUPPORTIVE AND CONNECTIVE TISSUES: *Animal skeletal systems*).

Muscular system. In all but the simplest organisms, specialized muscle cells perform the function of converting chemical energy into mechanical energy. The actual contractile machinery of muscle resides in long, threadlike filaments of molecular dimensions called myofilaments. The combination of muscle cells into large, organized groups—*i.e.,* tissues—that act together is called a muscle. Two types of muscle tissue are found in animals: striated, or striped, muscle and smooth muscle.

Striated muscle fibres are found in a great variety of both vertebrates and invertebrates. Some coelenterates and rotifers and all arthropods have striated muscle, which is rare in worms and mollusks. All muscles of arthropods, in fact, are striated and thus function as both visceral and skeletal muscles. Striated muscle is found in the entire skeletal, or voluntary, muscular system of vertebrates, and a special type of striated muscle, called cardiac muscle, is found in the heart. Striated muscle is capable of rapid motions (*e.g.,* the flight muscles of an insect can contract and relax more than 100 times per second) or slow motion (*e.g.,* the heart muscle of some large mammals may contract only one or two times a second); most striated muscles function between the two extremes.

Smooth muscles vary widely in structure among animals; some have spiral or ribbon-shaped units (myofibrils); others have no recognizable structural units. Smooth muscle is found in all animal phyla. In most worms, the body and visceral movements are dependent on smooth muscle. Smooth muscle is found in the feet of many mollusks. Smooth muscle forms the greater part of the visceral musculature of vertebrates and forms coats around the alimentary canal and certain associated structures. In general, smooth muscle fibres act more slowly than do striated ones (see MUSCLES AND MUSCLE SYSTEMS).

Nervous system. Nervous tissue possesses the properties of irritability (the ability to respond to stimuli) and conductivity (the ability to conduct a signal). In Protozoa with minute hairlike structures called cilia, a specialized region (motorium) serves to coordinate and relay impulses from small filaments (fibrils) connecting the bases of the cilia. Many Protozoa also possess organelles; that is, cell parts analogous to organs specialized for stimulus

Types of integuments

Striated and smooth muscle

reception, such as eyespots or sensory bristles. Sponges lack definite nerve cells, but all animal groups above the level of sponges have some form of nervous system. Coelenterates have a diffuse nerve net within the cell layer known as the epithelium but no central ganglion, or nerve cluster. Flatworms have two anterior ganglia with nerves to the head region and two separate nerve cords joined by cross connectives. Mollusks, annelid worms, and arthropods have paired anterior ganglia above and below the esophagus, joined by connecting nervous tissue. The echinoderms possess a radially arranged nervous system.

Compo-
nents
of the
vertebrate
nervous
system

The vertebrate nervous system is divided into two main parts: (1) the central nervous system, composed of brain and spinal cord, and (2) the peripheral nervous system, made up of cranial nerves and spinal nerves. Part of the peripheral system, consisting of portions of cranial nerves and spinal nerves, as well as outlying ganglia, controls involuntary functions, such as muscular contraction of the intestinal wall, and is called the autonomic system (see NERVES AND NERVOUS SYSTEMS).

Endocrine system. The endocrine system consists of a number of ductless glands that secrete chemical substances called hormones. These substances are carried by the circulating fluid to all parts of the body and exert highly specific effects on various tissues. In invertebrates, there is evidence of hormones in nematodes, mollusks, annelids, and arthropods. In crustaceans, a substance produced in the sinus gland influences the chromatophores—specialized pigment cells—so that the animal's body colour more closely resembles that of its environment. Endocrine glands in vertebrates include the pituitary, thyroid, parathyroid, adrenals, gonads, islets of Langerhans in the pancreas, and parts of the gastric and intestinal mucosa. In some mammals, the placenta, a structure through which the unborn animal is nourished, functions as an endocrine gland (see ENDOCRINE SYSTEMS; BIOCHEMICAL COMPONENTS OF ORGANISMS: *Hormones*).

Digestive system. The function of the digestive system is to procure and process, or metabolize, nutrients. The nutritional requirements and the basic processes of digestion are essentially similar in all animals; however, the body plan of animals varies so greatly that the structures involved are often different. *Amoeba*, a protozoan, lacks a permanent structure for digesting or ingesting food. Pseudopodia, temporary extensions of the body mass, are used to surround the food, which then becomes a bubble-like food vacuole in the body. *Paramecium*, however, another protozoan, has a permanent structure, the ciliated oral groove, into which food passes before forming a food vacuole. Sponges capture food by means of collar cells equipped with flagella, long whiplike structures. Coelenterates have a central saclike digestive pocket, the gastrovascular cavity, which has only one opening and functions as both mouth and anus. In flatworms, the mouth opens into a muscular pharynx that leads to an extensively branched gastrovascular cavity. Animals above the level of coelenterates and flatworms have a complete digestive system—i.e., one with two openings, a mouth and an anus. Food is passed in one direction through a tubular system that may have distinct sections, each specialized for a different function (see DIGESTION AND DIGESTIVE SYSTEMS).

Respiratory system. If nutrient materials are to be completely metabolized to carbon dioxide and water, oxygen is essential. One of the basic tasks of the organism, then, is the procurement of oxygen and the elimination of carbon dioxide. Gas exchange between a living cell and its environment always takes place by diffusion across a

Mecha-
nisms
for gas
exchange

moist membrane. In protozoans, sponges, coelenterates, and flatworms, most of which are aquatic, each cell is in direct contact with the surrounding medium or is only a few cells removed from it. These animals, therefore, have not evolved special respiratory devices.

With few exceptions, the respiratory systems of higher multicellular aquatic animals involve evaginated (outpocketed) exchange surfaces, usually known as gills. Gills are found in such diverse groups as annelids, mollusks, arthropods, and vertebrates. Most terrestrial animals have evolved invaginated (infolded) respiratory systems. These systems are of two principal types: lungs, found in land snails and the higher vertebrates; and tracheae, found in most terrestrial arthropods (see RESPIRATION AND RESPIRATORY SYSTEMS).

Circulatory system. Since every cell of an animal must obtain nutrients and oxygen and rid itself of carbon dioxide and nitrogen-containing wastes, some mechanism is needed for transporting these substances. In protozoans, such transport occurs by the flow, or streaming, of cytoplasm within the cell. In multicellular types such as sponges, coelenterates, flatworms, and roundworms, these substances are transported by simple diffusion between the external environment and internal organs. In higher metazoans (many-celled animals except sponges), most of the body cells are far removed from the external environment; a circulatory system for internal transport, therefore, has developed. Mollusks (except cephalopods) and arthropods have an open circulatory system with dorsal (back-side) three-chambered hearts; the annelids have a closed system with dorsal and ventral (belly-side) vessels and cross-connective vessels. In vertebrates, the highly specialized system is composed of integrated vascular networks for the separate transport of blood and lymph, which are carried directly to tissues (see CIRCULATION AND CIRCULATORY SYSTEMS).

Excretory system. Excretion is the process by which waste products of metabolism are removed from an organism. Excretory mechanisms also help to regulate water and salt balance. Special excretory structures are absent in many unicellular and simple multicellular animals, such as sponges and coelenterates. Some protozoans, however, have a special excretory organelle, or organ-like structure, the contractile vacuole. Flatworms possess a primitive, so-called flame-cell excretory system. This consists of two or more long, branching tubules, one end of which opens on the body surface through numerous excretory pores, the other ends of which are ciliated hollow bulbs—the flame cells. The arthropods possess Malpighian tubules, tiny pockets in the walls of the digestive tract. They collect wastes from the body fluids and pass them into the lower end of the gastrovascular cavity (hindgut) for excretion. In the earthworm, an annelid, each body segment has a pair of excretory organs called nephridia that consist of an open ciliated funnel, a coiled tubule, an enlarged bladder, and a pore (nephridiopore) leading to the outside. The excretory organs of vertebrates consist of paired kidneys, each with a separate duct (see EXCRETION AND EXCRETORY SYSTEMS).

Specialized
excretory
structures

Reproductive system. Reproduction is essential if a species is to survive. Both asexual and sexual reproduction occur among animals. Asexual, or agamic, reproduction does not involve the transfer of sex cells between individuals and occurs in members of the lower animal phyla. Some protozoans reproduce by dividing into "twin" cells, after which each develops into the original form. Budding, which occurs in coelenterates, is a process by which a new individual arises from an outgrowth, or bud, of an older animal. Some flatworms reproduce by fragmentation of their own bodies; each fragment then develops into a complete animal.

Asexual
and
sexual
repro-
duction

Sexual reproduction is the method of propagation common to all but the lower animal phyla. Gametes—i.e., egg cells, or ova, and sperm cells, or spermatozoa—are formed in the reproductive organs, or gonads—ovaries in the female, testes in the male. If both male and female systems are in one individual, as in flatworms and earthworms, the animal is termed monoecious. In nematodes, arthropods, various other invertebrates, and practically all vertebrates, each individual is either male or female; the sexes thus are separate, and such animals are termed dioecious (see REPRODUCTION AND REPRODUCTIVE SYSTEMS).

INTERRELATIONSHIPS BETWEEN ORGAN SYSTEMS

Functional interdependence. An understanding of the complexity of life functions and of the intricacy with which these functions are interwoven has gradually emerged from investigations of the various aspects of the biology of organisms. This complexity is not restricted to multicellular organisms, with their many cooperating cells, tissues, organs, and organ systems; it also characterizes unicellular organisms, which are known to be far from simple. Each cell of a living organism requires an environment that is dependent upon the interrelationships of cellular structure, metabolism, nutrient procurement, gas exchange, internal transport, regulation of levels of salts and other substances, and excretion. Homeostasis, or the state of equilibrium between the internal and external environments, is brought about by the functional interdependence of organelles, in unicellular animals, and of organ systems, in multicellular animals. This is demonstrated by the inability of one organ system to function without the assistance of another.

Coordination of regulatory functionsThat living organisms function in an orderly fashion despite their immense complexity shows clearly that control mechanisms are at work. Coordination of the regulatory functions and all the myriad other functions of an organism depends upon two principal types of control mechanisms: chemical control mechanisms, which are found in all organisms, and nervous control mechanisms, which, in the strict sense, are found only in multicellular animals.

Since the multicellular organism is characterized by a division of labour among its parts, it is not unexpected that evolution has led to specialization of certain cells or tissues as producers of chemical controls, usually hormones. These substances often have important control functions in parts of the body far removed from the sites of synthesis and are transported in higher animals from sites of production to sites of action through the blood circulatory system. Chemical controls are produced by specialized tissues or organs, exert highly specific effects on other tissues of the body, and are effective in very low concentrations. Hormonal control, however, is a relatively slow process, there being an appreciable delay between the release of the hormone and its arrival at the target organ. Slow chemical control is compatible with normal activity when instantaneous response is not needed, as in control of digestion, salt and water balance, metabolism, and growth. When rapid response is required, however, nervous control is essential. A nerve impulse can travel several hundred feet per second, thus reducing the interval between stimulus and response to milliseconds.

In vertebrates, the autonomic nervous system plays a large role in the maintenance of homeostasis and provides a fine control of the visceral, or internal, functions of the body. The autonomic system is generally involuntary and acts on the internal effectors such as smooth muscle, cardiac muscle, exocrine glands (glands with ducts), and endocrine glands (glands without ducts). The autonomic nervous system is the structural pathway linking the control centres in the brain with the internal organs. Physiological control of visceral functions includes sensors and nerve pathways as well as central control.

Specialized nerve cells, found in both external and internal receptor organs, are the organism's principal means of obtaining information. External sense organs are those stimulated by environmental changes. They include organs for the senses of sight, hearing, smell, taste, touch, pressure, temperature, and pain. Internal sense organs, affected by stimuli arising within the body, include proprioceptors (sensors of body movement and position), deep pain receptors, interoceptors—for such internal sensations as hunger, thirst, and nausea—and sensors of salt balance and carbon dioxide level in the blood plasma. Receptor organs are capable of responding to stimuli by initiating impulses that are transmitted by nerve fibres to the central nervous system for interpretation as sensations. The central nervous system may then send appropriate signals to muscles, glands, or other effector systems for response to the stimuli.

Feedback mechanisms. Since homeostatic mechanisms act to minimize the difference between the actual and optimal response of a system, they may be considered Examples of negative feedbackas biological examples of negative feedback control. In systems of this type, the level of the controlled variable is sensed, and action is taken to oppose change from the desired level. If the response increases, a negative, or inhibitory, signal is fed back to an effector mechanism so that the subsequent response is reduced. On the other hand, a decrease in response elicits a subsequent increase. The interaction between the anterior pituitary gland and

the thyroid gland is an example of negative feedback control. Thyrotropic hormone, released by the pituitary when the concentration of thyroxine in the blood is low, stimulates increased production of the thyroxine by the thyroid. When the rising concentration of thyroxine in the blood reaches a certain level, the secretion of more thyrotropic hormone by the pituitary is inhibited. There is thus a feedback of information from the thyroid to the pituitary. The pituitary exerts control over the thyroid, and the thyroid in turn exerts some control over the pituitary. A similar relationship exists between the pituitary and the other endocrine glands.

The nervous control of the rate of the heartbeat provides a good example of autonomic nervous system feedback control. When the heart is engorged with blood, stretch receptors in the wall of the upper right portion (right atrium) send impulses to the accelerating centre in the brain. The impulses from the stretch receptors stimulate the accelerating centre to send, via the autonomic nervous system, excitatory impulses to the S-A (sino-atrial) node, or "pacemaker," thereby causing the heart to beat faster. As the blood pressure rises, however, pressure receptors in the wall of the aorta (the blood vessel that conveys blood to the body) begin sending impulses to the inhibiting centre in the brain, stimulating it to send inhibitory impulses, via the autonomic nervous system, to the S-A node, with the effect of slowing the heart.

Embryonic development of organ systems

ORIGINS OF INDIVIDUAL SYSTEMS

Germ-layer concept. During embryonic development the cells making up the so-called germ layers—ectoderm, endoderm, and mesoderm—are said to be undifferentiated; *i.e.,* they do not possess distinctive or individual characteristics. Further development of an embryo entails, among other things, a differentiation or specialization of various groups of cells to form the several types of tissues and organs that make up an organism. Growth of the embryo and differentiation of organs from germ layers begin even before the germ layers are completely formed. The entire process of development is gradual, and, although the various phases occur in a step-by-step order, they are not in themselves distinct but are merged imperceptibly with each other. In all vertebrates the different germ layers and structures arising from them are considered to be homologous, or similar in origin. The germ-layer concept is of importance chiefly because it furnishes a convenient method of classifying organs according to their embryonic derivation.

The ectoderm gives rise to three main structural groups and their derivatives: (1) the epidermis of the skin and its derivatives, including the skin glands, hair, feathers, nails, claws, hoofs, horns, epidermal scales, and the coverings of external gills; (2) the lining of the mouth and related structures, including enamel of teeth, glands of the mouth, covering of the tongue and lips, and anterior and intermediate lobes of the pituitary gland; (3) the nervous system, consisting of the brain and spinal cord, cranial and spinal nerves, autonomic portion of the peripheral nervous system, sensory parts of all sense organs, inner region (medulla) of the adrenal gland, infundibulum (structure connecting the pituitary gland to the brain), and the posterior lobe of the pituitary gland.

The endoderm develops into the epithelial lining of the following: (1) the alimentary canal, which includes pharynx, esophagus, stomach, intestine, liver, pancreas, and most of the cloaca (a cavity at the posterior end of the body); (2) the pharyngeal derivatives, consisting of the larynx, trachea, lungs, gills of the internal type, middle ear, eustachian tube, tonsils, thyroid, parathyroids, and thymus; (3) miscellaneous structures, including the urinary bladder, its canal to the outside of the body (urethra), and two embryonic structures—allantois and yolk sac.

The mesoderm differentiates into (1) the muscles, including smooth, skeletal, and cardiac; (2) the skeleton, composed of cartilage, bone, and other connective tissue; (3) the excretory organs, including the kidneys and their ducts; (4) the reproductive organs; (5) the circulatory system, composed of the heart, blood vessels, blood, spleen, lymphatics, and blood-forming tissues; and (6) miscellaneous tissues, including dentine of teeth, dermis of skin, outer region (cortex) of the adrenal glands, lining of body cavities, mesenteries (tissues supporting the viscera), and portions of the eye.

Appearance of organ systems during development. Organ systems of the vertebrate body make their appearances at precise stages of embryonic development. The human ovum is normally fertilized in the upper fallopian tube, which leads from the ovary to the uterus. At the end of the first week, it becomes implanted in the uterine wall.

Summary of embryonic development

After two weeks the embryo consists of a flat disk, in the centre of which are the primitive streak, which later becomes the mesoderm, and the first rudiments of the nervous system, the neural plate, and the neural groove. A head process and rudiments of the heart may be present. No endodermal derivatives are yet present.

By the end of the third week the neural groove is complete and closes to form the neural tube; the optic vesicles (rudimentary eyes), auditory placodes (rudimentary ears), and ganglia are present; and the oral membrane may rupture to form the mouth. In addition, the separation of the body from the yolk sac produces the foregut and hindgut, antecedents of the pharynx and lower parts of the digestive tract. The visceral pouches and visceral arches—which both develop into parts of the jaw and throat—and the lung and liver pouches appear. Blood vessels containing blood cells develop and connect with an S-shaped heart, in which pulsations begin. The pronephros, an early stage of the kidney, and its ducts grow posteriorly, or downward.

After four weeks the body has a C shape. The neural tube has entirely closed, the three primary brain sections have formed, and the spinal and cranial nerves are developing. In the endoderm, paired lung buds grow posteriorly; the stomach, liver, pancreas, and intestines are defined. Paired limb buds and primitive vertebral organization are apparent. Abundant blood is forming and circulating, and the heart is tubular. The pronephros degenerates and is replaced by subsequent stages of the embryonic kidney, the mesonephros and the metanephros.

At the end of the fifth week the embryo has a temporary tail. The face is assuming a characteristic appearance with jaws, and the brain has five sections. The trunk and appendage muscles develop, and bone-forming centres arise. The circulatory system is extensively developed, and the heart begins its final divisions.

After six weeks of development, the heart is the four-chambered organ of the adult; undifferentiated gonad primordia are prominent. By the seventh week, the eye and pituitary gland are well developed, as are the lungs and the components of the digestive system. The body muscles are becoming organized; cartilage formation is extensive; and the jaws, vertebrae, and ribs are becoming bony.

Fetal development

After eight weeks, the embryo, now termed a fetus, has a recognizable form. Muscles of the body are differentiated and innervated to allow movement. The blood-vascular system is complete; the mesonephros degenerates as the metanephros grows; and sex differentiation begins. During the ninth week nails and hair follicles form, and the metanephric kidney becomes functional. By the tenth week, the brain is essentially developed, the lungs are almost complete, and the smooth muscle of the entire gut is organized.

By the 14th week, the head, until now large with respect to the body, and the body approach normal proportions. Most of the bones are present in some degree, allowing spontaneous movements. After 18 weeks, the body proportions approach those of the newborn. The cerebral hemispheres of the brain become convoluted and creased; the retina of the eye becomes sensitive to light, and the sex organs have developed. (For a specific account of human prenatal development, see GROWTH AND DEVELOPMENT: Human embryology.)

EVOLUTION OF ORGAN SYSTEMS

Organelles. Unicellular animals are found only among the Protozoa; all other animals are multicellular. The individual protozoan, however, should not be regarded as equivalent to a single cell of a more complex animal but as a complete organism with the same properties and characteristics of a multicellular animal. Protozoans lack tissues and organs, since such parts are defined as aggregations of differentiated cells, but they do have functionally equivalent subcellular structures called organelles, which are analogous to multicellular organs. Some protozoans digest food in food vacuoles. No special organelles exist for gas exchange, the general cell membrane serving as the gas exchange surface. Many freshwater protozoans possess contractile vacuoles, which function primarily in the regulation of osmotic pressure, thus controlling the internal concentration of salts and water; nitrogen-containing wastes may also be expelled through these vacuoles. Locomotion is performed by formation of pseudopodia or with beating cilia or flagella. Although an individual protozoan has many cilia, cilial action is coordinated by a system of fibrils connecting so-called basal bodies of the cilia.

Multicellularity. Members of the animal kingdom possessing a multicellular plan of structure constitute the subkingdom Metazoa. The body structure of a typical metazoan involves more than just a multicellular condition, however; the specialization of cells for different functions produces an interdependency of cells. Cell specialization has in turn led to the development of tissues consisting of similar cells organized in sheets and layers. In lower metazoans, development of tissues is relatively primitive; in higher groups tissues have become organized to form organs.

Zoologists agree that metazoans evolved from unicellular organisms. There are three theories concerning the nature of the ancestral form and the mode of origin. The first is the syncytial theory, which holds that multicellular animals arose from a primitive group of unicellular, ciliated animals having more than one nucleus. The ancestral metazoan, at first syncytial (i.e., with more than one nucleus within a single mass of cytoplasm) in structure, later became compartmented or cellularized by the development of cell membranes, thus producing a typical multicellular condition. Because many ciliates tend toward bilateral symmetry—that is, similar left and right sides comprise the body—proponents of the syncytial theory maintain that the ancestral metazoan was bilaterally symmetrical and gave rise to the acoel flatworms (lacking a digestive cavity with definite walls). The fact that these flatworms, thought to be the most primitive living metazoans, are about the same size as the ciliates, have bilateral symmetry and cilia, and tend towards a syncytial condition is regarded as evidence in support of the syncytial theory. That it requires acoels to be the most primitive living metazoans is regarded as an objection to the theory; a ciliate ancestry, moreover, does not explain the general occurrence of flagellated sperm in metazoans. Opponents of the syncytial theory further point out that the developmental patterns among the lower metazoans are not comparable.

Nature of ancestral forms

The second theory of the origin of metazoans is the colonial theory, which states that the origin of multicellular animals is from a spherical, hollow, colonial, flagellated organism. Proponents of the colonial theory regard the following as evidence: (1) flagellated body cells commonly occur among lower metazoans; (2) sperm and eggs as clearly definable entities have evolved in the phytoflagellates, organisms with flagella and the ability to photosynthesize; (3) in some forms of flagellates that live in colonies, a differentiation between reproductive cells and somatic (nonreproductive) cells has occurred. The colonial theory holds that through the migration of cells into the interior of the colony, the originally hollow sphere became a solid, ovoid mass, with similar parts arranged radially around a central axis (radially symmetrical) and with the exterior cells flagellated. Since this hypothetical organism is very similar to an immature coelenterate form called a planuloid larva, it is called the planuloid ancestor of the lower metazoans. The bilateral symmetry of the flatworms would then represent a later modification in symmetry. The principal weakness of the colonial theory is that the extant colonial phytoflagellates are plantlike and possess cellulose walls with chlorophyll. An alternative explana-

Colonial theory

tion is that metazoans arose from some group of extinct flagellates that did not have these typical plant features.

The third theory of the origin of metazoans, the theory of polyphyletic origin, proposes that the sponges and coelenterates evolved from colonial flagellates, ctenophores, and flatworms by way of the ciliates.

The colonial theory, despite certain weaknesses, appears to be the most compatible with evidence relating to the subsequent evolution of metazoans. The problem of the planuloid ancestor shifting from a radial to a bilateral symmetry is not difficult if it is assumed that the ancestral planuloid stock lived on the ocean bottom and, as a result, developed a creeping mode of movement over rocks. This type of movement would lead to a differentiation between dorsal and ventral (top and bottom) surfaces; bilateral symmetry would result. The free-living flatworms demonstrate the transition from a bilateral planuloid ancestor to a more complex form.

Flatworm evolution

A hypothetical ancestral flatworm may be described from the various primitive features of living flatworms. A marine animal, it was dorsal-ventrally flattened, with a single layer of ciliated epidermal cells, the bases of which contained contractile extensions that formed a muscle layer.

An otocyst, or hearing organ, and a light-sensitive pigment spot may have been present. The otocyst, near the front end, may have been covered by a delicate network of nerve cells. Possibly a midventral mouth opened into a syncytial network of nutritive cells and a meshwork of reproductive cells.

In subsequent evolution of the flatworms, a number of fundamental changes appear that foreshadow the structure exhibited by most higher bilateral animals: (1) the separation of the contractile function from the epidermis to form a distinct muscle layer; (2) the reorganization of a nerve net contiguous with the body surface into a series of deeper, radially arranged, longitudinal nerve cords; (3) the concentration of nervous tissue around the statocyst (an organ of equilibrium) to form a brain; (4) the development of a cup-shaped eye with pigment cells from flattened pigment spots; (5) the formation of a rudimentary digestive system with inturning of the epidermis around the mouth to form a short pharynx; (6) the formation from mesenchyme of a rudimentary reproductive system with structures for conducting, transmitting, and receiving sperm.

(C.K.W./K.W.K./M.S.K.)

PLANT BODIES AT THE ORGAN AND ORGAN SYSTEM LEVEL OF DEVELOPMENT

Plant organs include such structures as individual leaves, stems, roots, flowers (or parts of flowers, such as the male or female reproductive structures), fruits, and other units of vegetation depending upon the level of organization chosen to delimit them. Plant organ systems, like those of animals, are groups of mutually functioning organs. Such structures and interrelated systems are the means by which plants exploit the environment; they are the products of successful evolutionary advances over geological time.

Development of plant organs

Very early in its development, the body of a plant exhibits a polarized (*i.e.,* directional with definite shoot and root ends) differentiation into an axis composed of three organs: stem, leaf, and root. This differentiation occurs as the fertilized egg develops into the embryo and, in the seed plants, is evident long before the seed is mature (see GROWTH AND DEVELOPMENT: *Plant development*). Although each of these organs differs significantly in structure and function, all are similar in important ways. They have a common origin in the young embryo. The tissues of each organ merge imperceptibly, an arrangement facilitating the performance of joint functions—*e.g.,* the movement of water, dissolved minerals, and food longitudinally from one part of the plant body to another (see TISSUES AND FLUIDS). In addition, the stem and root actually constitute one continuous structure, exhibiting basically a cylindrical or rodlike form. These two organs also possess similarities in their method of growth from the meristems, the regions of cell division in shoot and root tips. During plant evolution, the stem, leaf, and root have arisen from a common structure.

THE STEM

Description.   The stem is normally a cylindrical, rodlike axis that supports the food-producing leaves and connects them with the anchoring and absorbing roots. The stem also produces the cones, flowers, fruits, and other reproductive structures. In addition, the growth pattern and structure of the stem determine the habit or form of the plant.

At its apex, the stem possesses a bud, a juvenile and incompletely developed structure. The bud contains the microscopically small apical meristem, which gives rise by cell division to new cells and tissues, thereby increasing the height of the stem. During seasons of the year unfavourable to plant growth (winter or dry seasons), the delicate meristem tissue is often protected from desic-

cation by small modified leaves known as bud scales. During the growing season, the apical meristem is usually protected by a covering of young leaves. Some buds give rise only to new stem and leaves, while others produce only flowers; still others develop leaves and flowers. When the bud develops into a new stem and leaves, the bud scales fall away, leaving several closely crowded bud scale

Structure and contents of buds

(Left, centre right) from W.W. Robbins, T.E. Weir, and C.R. Stocking, *Botany, An Introduction to Plant Science,* 3rd ed. (1964); John Wiley & Sons, Inc. (Top right) *Biology,* 3rd ed., by Willis H. Johnson, Richard A. Laubengayer, Louis E. DeLanney and Thomas A. Cole; copyright © 1966 by Holt, Rinehart and Winston, Inc.; copyright © 1956 and 1961 by Holt, Rinehart and Winston, Inc., under the title *General Biology;* reprinted by permission of Holt, Rinehart and Winston, Inc. (Bottom right) Kimball, *Biology,* 2nd ed. (1968); Addison-Wesley Publishing Company, Reading, Mass.

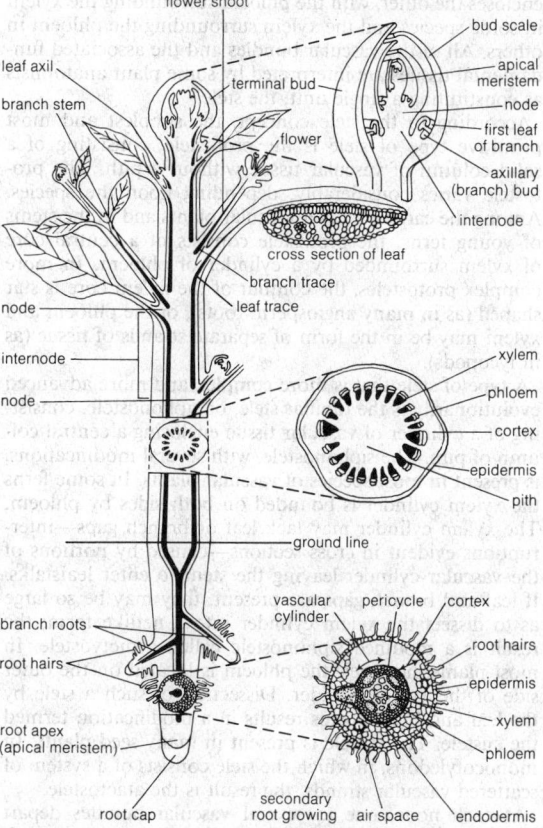

Figure 1: Principal organs and tissues of the body of a seed plant.

scars on the stem. Embryonic leaves formed by the apical meristem develop at regions of the stem called nodes; the intervening portion of the stem between two nodes is the internode. Depending upon the species, the internodes may be long and distinct or very short and indistinct. In trees and shrubs, the division of the stem into nodes and internodes eventually becomes obscured because of growth in thickness of the stem caused by the cambium, a layer of dividing cells just under the bark. Eventually the leaves are shed from the plant, leaving leaf scars on the stem. Within each leaf scar may be seen one or more vascular-bundle scars produced at the location of the water- and food-conducting tissues (vascular bundles) that enter the leaf from the stem. Each node on the stem, therefore, may have a variety of features: there may be one or more leaves, each usually with a bud in the leaf axil, the upper angle between the leafstalk (petiole) and the stem.

Tissue organization.   After being produced by the apical meristem, the cells of the young stem differentiate gradually into the three main tissues: protective (epidermis, the "skin"), fundamental or ground (cortex, pith), and vascular (phloem and xylem). There is considerable diversity among plants in the patterns exhibited by these tissues.

Among the lycopods (club mosses), ferns, and some aquatic angiosperms, the centre of the stem is occupied by a solid rod of xylem, specialized water-conducting tissues made of hollow cells. In most plants, however, the vascular tissue is arranged in a cylinder or as a complex of interconnected strands arranged either as a cylinder or scattered in bundles throughout nearly all of the stem. The region between the vascular tissue and the epidermis is occupied by the cortex, one of the fundamental tissues. The interior of stems in which the vascular tissue is arranged as a cylinder is filled with the pith.

Each strand of the primary (*i.e.*, derived from the apical meristem) vascular tissue is a vascular bundle. Within each vascular bundle, the xylem and phloem are arranged in characteristic patterns. In the collateral pattern, the phloem lies on only one side of the xylem, usually toward the stem exterior, whereas in bicollateral vascular bundles, the phloem is located on both sides of the xylem. In concentric bundles, one type of vascular tissue completely encloses the other, with the phloem surrounding the xylem in some species and the xylem surrounding the phloem in others. All of the vascular bundles and the associated fundamental tissues are interpreted by some plant anatomists as constituting a single unit, the stele.

According to the stele concept, the simplest and most primitive type of stele is the protostele, consisting of a solid column of vascular tissue without a pith. The protostele varies considerably, depending upon the species. Among the earliest known vascular plants and in the stems of young ferns, the protostele consists of a central core of xylem surrounded by a cylinder of phloem. In more complex protosteles, the contour of the xylem core is star shaped (as in many angiosperm roots), or the phloem and xylem may be in the form of separate strands of tissue (as in lycopods).

A type of stele that is more complex and more advanced evolutionarily is the tubular stele, or siphonostele, consisting of a cylinder of vascular tissue enclosing a central column of pith. The siphonostele, with several modifications, is present in most species of vascular plants. In some ferns the xylem cylinder is bounded on both sides by phloem. The xylem cylinder may lack leaf or branch gaps—interruptions evident in cross sections—caused by portions of the vascular cylinder leaving the stem to enter leafstalks. If leaf and branch gaps are present, they may be so large as to dissect the xylem cylinder into a netlike form; the result is a modified siphonostele called a dictyostele. In most plants, however, the phloem is located on the outer side of the xylem cylinder. Dissection of such a stele by the leaf and branch gaps results in a modification termed the eustele. The eustele is present in many seed plants. In monocotyledons, in which the stele consists of a system of scattered vascular strands, the result is the atactostele.

At each node, one to several vascular bundles depart from the stem vascular system and enter the leaf; each such bundle is a leaf trace. The xylem and phloem of the leaf traces are continuous with the xylem and phloem in the stem. In the region of the vascular cylinder, immediately above the point of departure of the leaf trace out into the leaf, is a gap in the vascular tissue. Within this gap, parenchyma (cells of an undifferentiated, roughly globular form, usually with thin walls) tissue develops instead of vascular tissue, producing a region known as a leaf gap. Leaf gaps are often very conspicuous, especially in the stems of herbaceous plants from which the cortex, phloem, and pith have rotted away. The xylem tissue, more resistant to decay, remains, and the leaf gaps can be seen as holes through the xylem cylinder.

Axillary buds are also served by strands of vascular tissue departing from the vascular system of the stem. The bundles leading to the buds are called bud traces. Just as with the leaf trace, immediately above each bud trace is a region of parenchyma tissue, the bud gap. Bud traces are conspicuous parts of the stem anatomy and also appear as large holes in the vascular cylinder of rotted herbaceous stems.

All plants increase the height of their stems through the production of new cells and tissues, called primary tissues, by the apical meristem. In the young plant, only a small amount of conducting and strengthening tissue is present, the stem and roots being thin and fairly delicate. Many species, especially among the dicotyledons (broad-leaved flowering plants such as roses, woody trees and shrubs, members of the pea family, and others) and gymnosperms, possess the ability to produce additional conductive, fundamental, and protective tissues (secondary tissues) by means of lateral meristems—the vascular cambium and the cork cambium (see TISSUES AND FLUIDS). The great bulk of a tree or shrub, therefore, consists of secondary tissues, especially of xylem, produced by the lateral meristems. The xylem formed by the vascular cambium accumulates year after year, with each year's accumulation forming a layer, the annual, or growth, ring. The phloem produced by the vascular cambium usually functions for only one or two seasons and is progressively crushed and destroyed as the new xylem presses outward. The tree does not become devoid of phloem, however, because the cambium is constantly producing new phloem cells during each growing season.

The vascular cambium in the stems of most gymnosperms and dicotyledons originates as a cylinder between the primary xylem and phloem. As long as the plant is alive, the vascular cambium occupies this same relative position, producing secondary xylem toward the stem centre and secondary phloem toward the stem surface. Secondary growth by the vascular cambium modifies the primary body of the plant in various ways. The secondary tissues usually cover the primary xylem and the pith, and the cells in these tissues eventually die. The primary phloem soon becomes nonfunctional and is destroyed as the stem increases in diameter. The cortex and epidermis are eventually replaced by the development of periderm (bark).

Periderm usually forms in the stems (and roots) of trees and shrubs and may be produced by the older parts of herbaceous dicotyledons. The outer portion of the periderm, the outer bark or cork, may be relatively thin, giving the trunk a smooth surface, or it may be thick, producing a cracked and fissured surface. The bark may develop as wings, projecting from the surface, as large scales or plates, or as long strips. Clearly defined, wartlike lenticels (pores) occur here and there in the cork. Each lenticel is a mass of loosely arranged cells protruding above the stem surface through a crack in the periderm. Each lenticel usually forms just beneath a stoma-guard cell apparatus in the epidermis. A stoma, or stomate, is a tiny opening or pore in a leaf or stem surface, usually flanked by two liplike cells called guard cells. Like the stomata, lenticels are believed to function in the movement of gases into and out of the stem.

Types of stems.   *Life-span categories.* The type of stem is related to the life-span of the plant. Many long-lived plants increase the rigidity of their stems (and often their roots also) by the production in the vascular cambium of hard, mechanically strong xylem tissue; such plants are called either trees or shrubs. Trees are characterized by a

Arrangement of vascular tissue

Leaf traces

Production of annual growth rings

stem that grows to become a conspicuous trunk; shrubs usually have several stems, which arise near the ground. Many species of plants are relatively short-lived and consequently possess weak stems, with only a little woody tissue at the base or without any woody tissue at all. Such herbaceous plants are of diverse types. In shrubby herbs, the upper portions of the stems are herbaceous, and the lower parts are woody; the herbaceous portions die during the winter. Perennial herbs possess a very short woody crown stem, which may continue to produce new herbaceous stems for many years. Biennial herbs live only two years, the lower portion of the stem persisting through the winter and giving rise the next spring to an erect stem. After producing flowers and seeds the second year, the entire plant dies. Finally, annual herbs live for only a single growing season, completing their entire life cycle during this brief period.

Perennial, biennial, and annual plants

Woody stems. When the trunk of a tree is sawed in half, the bark and the wood are easily distinguished. The bark, usually much darker in colour than the wood, can be separated fairly easily from the wood, especially in the spring and early summer, because the cells of the vascular cambium have thin delicate walls that are readily broken. Microscopically, the bark can be seen to be composed of all of the tissues outside the vascular cambium, including the phloem and the periderm.

To the interior of the vascular cambium lies the wood or secondary xylem. A conspicuous feature of the wood is the concentric layers, the annual increments, or growth rings, especially in trees of temperate climates. The outer portion of the trunk may be a light-coloured zone of sapwood; the inner part may be differentiated into a generally darker region of heartwood. The sapwood is the younger tissue, and it functions in the conduction of water and dissolved minerals (*i.e.,* "sap") and in the storage of food. As the tree ages, the sapwood is gradually transformed into heartwood. During this process, many by-products of cell metabolism (*e.g.,* oils, tannins, resins, pigments, phenols) are transported away from the living cells of the phloem, cambium, and xylem in the direction of the inner sapwood, where they are stored in the cells. The formation of heartwood in trees is the result of such deposition of the plant's waste products. As the waste materials accumulate in the cells of the inner sapwood, a toxic level is finally reached, the xylem parenchyma cells die, and another cylinder or ring of heartwood is produced. In this manner, the sapwood-heartwood boundary moves outward as the diameter of the tree increases.

Herbaceous stems. The stem anatomy of herbaceous plants varies considerably. Some perennial herbs possess small amounts of secondary growth, especially in the lower portion of the stem and in the root. The stems of many biennial and annual herbs may lack secondary growth entirely because of the absence of a vascular cambium. Externally, the stems of these herbs resemble closely those of the young twigs of a woody plant, except that typical winter buds are not formed. Apical growth, nodes, internodes, and lateral branches are usually present in herbaceous stems. Internally, the vascular bundles are usually arranged in a single ring. This basic pattern of stem anatomy may be variously modified, especially in those stems functioning as food- and water-storing organs. In such stems, extensive parenchyma is often present.

Plants without secondary growth

The stems of most monocotyledons (flowering plants with parallel-veined leaves, such as grasses, orchids, and palms) lack a vascular cambium and do not have secondary growth. Palms and other treelike monocotyledons do, however, possess a means of thickening the trunk through the activity of a primary thickening meristem located beneath the embryonic leaves at the stem apex. In herbaceous monocotyledons such as the grasses, the stem-tissue arrangement features numerous vascular bundles scattered throughout the stem, as in corn (maize), or in two circles near the periphery, as in wheat. Just beneath the epidermis is (usually) a continuous cylinder of sclerenchyma (thick-walled cells) that functions in support of the stem. In some grasses, the stem centre is occupied by a pith, which may break down in the internodes during growth, leaving a hollow pith cavity. At the base of each internode in grasses is a region of cell division called the intercalary meristem, which adds new cells to the internode.

THE LEAF

The leaf is the principal photosynthetic (food-producing) organ of the plant. Although the leaf normally differs significantly, especially in form, from the stem, both of these organs are actually part of the same unit, the shoot. Both the stem and the leaf arise in the bud from the apical meristem. When fully developed, the tissues of the stem merge with those of the leaf. The leaf possesses basically the same tissues as the stem, with an epidermis forming the outermost layer, vascular tissues arranged in veins, and photosynthetic tissue occupying the same region as does the cortex in the stem.

Form and structure. The leaf is highly variable in its form and internal structure, and, accordingly, several kinds of leaves can be distinguished. The most familiar type is the foliage leaf, usually consisting of a thin, flattened,

From (top) Adams, Baker, and Allen, *The Study of Botany* (1970), Addison-Wesley, Reading, Massachusetts; (bottom) Kimball, *Biology*, 2nd ed. (1968), Addison-Wesley

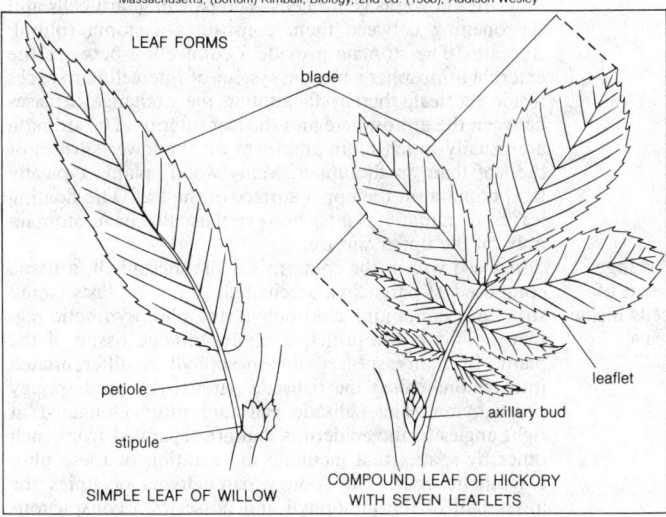

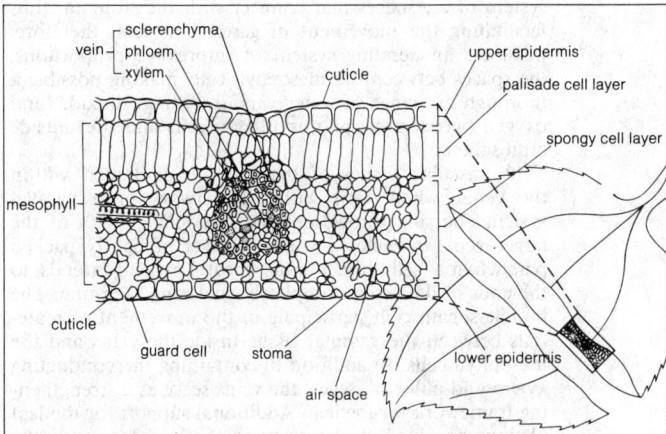

Figure 2: (Top) Leaf forms. (Bottom) Internal organization of a leaf shown in cross section.

green blade, which, in many species, is attached to the stem by a stalk, the petiole. The base of the leaf in many monocotyledons and some dicotyledons is differentiated into a sheath, which encircles the stem. The leaf base of some species possesses leaflike outgrowths, the stipules, which function in protecting the young leaf before it unfolds. The stipules are often inconspicuous and fall away early in leaf development. If only a single leaf blade is present, the leaf is simple. The simple leaves of species such as maples may be deeply lobed. A compound leaf has two or more blades, the leaflets. The leaf margins of some species are smooth, or entire, while the margins of others may be finely or coarsely indented. Only one vascular bundle or vein may be present, as in conifers, but leaves of most ferns and angiosperms have numerous

Leaf venation

veins. In many dicotyledons, the veins form a reticulate, or netted, pattern. The leaves of many monocotyledons have veins that run essentially parallel throughout most of the blade. In both types of venation, the veins join with one another at intervals, forming a closed system. The venation of many ferns, *Ginkgo,* and a few dicotyledons consists of repeatedly forked, or dichotomous, veins.

Internal structure. Internally, foliage leaves are constructed of three main tissues: epidermis, mesophyll, and vascular tissue. The epidermis, a single layer of living cells, forms a protective layer on both surfaces of the leaf. The outer walls of the epidermal cells are covered by a delicate film, the cuticle, composed of a waxy material, cutin, which enables the leaf to resist excessive evaporation of water. In many plants the waxy cuticle forms a light-gray "bloom" that can be easily wiped off, as in the leaves of red cabbage. A distinctive feature of the epidermis is the conspicuous pairs of usually bean-shaped cells with a small opening between them. Since the size of the opening can vary through changes in the shape of the pair of cells, they are known as guard cells. The pair of guard cells and the opening between them constitutes a stoma (plural: stomata). The stomata provide a connection between the external atmosphere and the system of intercellular spaces inside the leaf, thereby facilitating the exchange of gases between the atmosphere and the leaf interior. The stomata are usually much more abundant on the lower surface of the leaf than on the upper. Many woody plants typically lack stomata on the upper surface of the leaf. The floating leaves of aquatic plants, however, usually have stomata only on the upper surface.

Enclosed within the epidermis is the mesophyll, a tissue composed of parenchyma cells rich in chloroplasts (small structures containing chlorophyll, the photosynthetic pigment). This is the principal photosynthetic tissue of the plant. In many species, the mesophyll is differentiated into regions called the palisade parenchyma and spongy parenchyma. The palisade cells are more elongated at right angles to the epidermis and are separated from each other by spaces that facilitate the aeration of these photosynthetic cells. The spongy parenchyma occupies the lower half of the mesophyll and possesses a conspicuous system of air spaces that connect with the stomata, thus facilitating the movement of gases. The leaf, therefore, possesses an aerating system of impressive proportions, the spaces between the mesophyll cells making possible a thorough exchange of water vapour, carbon dioxide, and oxygen between the photosynthetic cells and the outside atmosphere.

The vascular tissues of the leaf are contained within the veins, which form either a network or a parallel system coursing throughout the mesophyll. Each of the larger veins is enclosed within a layer of tightly packed parenchyma cells, the bundle sheath, which extends to the ends of the veins, completely enclosing each one. The bundle-sheath cells participate in the movement of materials between the vascular tissue inside the veins and the mesophyll cells. In addition to containing the conducting xylem and phloem tissues, the veins serve as a strengthening framework for the leaf. Additional support for the leaf blade is provided by the pressure of the water inside the mesophyll cells. The epidermis also affords much support for the leaf because of the compact arrangement of its cells and the strength of the cuticle layer. Collenchyma cells (cells with thickened walls) and sclerenchyma fibres may also be present beneath the epidermis or in close association with the veins, an arrangement that provides additional support for the leaf blade.

Kinds of leaves. In addition to the more familiar foliage leaves, plants usually possess one or more of the following kinds of leaves: cotyledons, scale leaves, and bracts. Cotyledons are the first leaves to be formed, arising early in the development of the embryo inside the seed. During germination the cotyledons in some species remain enclosed within the seed coat and hidden beneath the soil surface. In other species the cotyledons break through the seed coat and appear on the young seedling above the ground surface, where they become green and carry on photosynthesis for a time, just as do foliage leaves. Scale

leaves occur as bud scales, where they function in protecting the young developing leaves and apical meristem inside the bud. Scale leaves are the only type of leaf produced by underground stems, or rhizomes; they are usually small and short-lived. Bracts are often associated with the flowers, where they serve to protect the young developing flower. Sometimes the bracts are brightly coloured (as in the poinsettia) and function as petals in the attraction of prospective pollinators (bees, butterflies, birds, etc.; see RE-PRODUCTION AND REPRODUCTIVE SYSTEMS: *Pollination*).

Leaf fall. Leaves are relatively short-lived organs and sooner or later are shed from the plant, leaving leaf scars on the stem marking their former locations at the nodes. In evergreen species, such as conifers, and many broadleaved angiosperms, the leaves may be retained on the tree for two or three years, after which they fall irregularly. In deciduous plants, the leaves function for only a single growing season and fall completely, usually in the autumn or at the beginning of the dry season. The fall of leaves of perennial and woody plants is a complex phenomenon involving the separation of the leaf from the stem without undue damage to the newly exposed living tissues. Preceding the fall of the leaves from the tree, a special group of cells known as the abscission layer differentiates across the petiole near its base. Through chemical changes in their walls, the cells in this abscission layer become softened until the leaf finally breaks away and falls to the ground. On the stem side of the abscission layer, a healing layer develops, closing the wound with a corky tissue, which forms the leaf scar. The abscission process involves complex biochemical processes that are, in turn, influenced by various environmental factors such as day length, temperature, availability of oxygen, water, and mineral nutrients, and even attacks by insects or fungi. Various chemical sprays are often used in agriculture and in warfare to promote leaf abscission.

Leaves of many species have undergone various modifications during the course of evolution. Their form and structure have become conspicuously adapted in varying degrees to their environment. The leaves of plants in very dry habitats may be very small in blade area, or they may die quickly; in such plants the photosynthetic function is performed mainly by the stem, as in the cacti. In species such as *Acacia,* the leaf blade has disappeared, and the petiole has become flattened and leaflike (a phyllode). Many plants of deserts and other dry habitats possess pointed, awl-shaped spines, which are, in many cases, evolutionary derivatives of leaves. The leaves of other desert plants are very thick and fleshy, with abundant water-storage capacity; such plants are known as succulents.

Climbing plants often possess elongated, threadlike, branched or unbranched organs known as tendrils, which wrap themselves around nearby stems, thereby anchoring the plant. In many species tendrils are evolutionary modifications of leaves or leaf parts. In cucumbers and melons, for example, the tendrils have evolved from the midribs of leaves, whereas in peas the tendrils originated from a leaflet of a compound leaf.

Highly bizarre leaf modifications are present in carnivorous plants. The leaf of the sundew plant (*Drosera*) has tentacles resembling the "horns" of a snail. These tentacles excrete a sticky fluid attractive to insects, which become firmly caught and are eventually digested by the leaf. The leaves of the Venus's-flytrap function as mechanical traps, capturing insects with amazing rapidity. The leaves of *Sarracenia* and *Nepenthes* are modified into hollow, trumpet- or jug-shaped, brightly coloured structures containing a watery fluid attractive to animals. Upon entering the leaf, the animals (usually insects) slide into the fluid and are unable to escape. Subsequently, their bodies are digested and the dissolved materials used in the plant's own nutrition.

THE ROOT

Form and growth. The root is generally the underground portion of the plant body and functions primarily as an anchoring and absorbing organ. Some subterranean structures are actually modified stems. The root, however, differs from such underground stems by always lacking leaves and buds and by having its growing tip protected by a root cap. The root cap consists of short-lived parenchyma cells. A short distance behind the root tip, where the cells have reached their maximum length, root hairs occur. Each root hair, a tubular outgrowth of a single epidermal cell, greatly increases the surface area of the root, thereby facilitating absorption of water and dissolved minerals from the soil. Root hairs usually live only a few days but are rapidly replaced by new ones, which form just back of the growing root apex. Root hairs are usually lacking in plants living in aquatic habitats.

Primary roots

The first root of a plant, the primary root, develops from the root end of the embryo (the radicle) during seed germination. In gymnosperms and dicotyledons, the primary root usually develops into the root system of the plant through the formation of branch or secondary roots from the pericycle tissue, a special layer of cells surrounding the vascular bundle, or stele, in the interior of the root. In monocotyledons, however, the primary root commonly dies while the plant is still very small. In these plants adventitious roots, roots that grow in other than the usual place on a plant, develop from the stem, usually close to the nodes. Adventitious roots are also produced on the creeping and underground stems (rhizomes) of many dicotyledons.

Internal structure. Internally, the root possesses a definite pattern of tissues. Three main regions are discernible: epidermis, cortex, and vascular cylinder. The epidermis is composed of tightly packed cells and typically lacks a cuticle. Root hairs occur in the region near the root tip. The cortex consists mostly of parenchyma cells that are characteristically separated from each other by spaces of various sizes. The cortex functions in the movement of water and dissolved minerals across the root from the epidermis to the xylem and also stores food molecules transported downward from the leaves. The innermost layer of the cortex usually differentiates as an endodermis, composed of a cylinder of cells, each of which develops a narrow, waterproof band, the Casparian strip, around all but the innermost- and outermost-facing cell walls. The Casparian strip serves as a barrier to the free movement of water and minerals between the cells, thus requiring all such materials to enter the central stele through the membranes of the living endodermis cells.

Interior to the endodermis is the vascular cylinder, which begins with one or more layers of parenchyma cells, the pericycle, immediately inside the endodermis. Cells of the pericycle retain the ability to undergo cell division, thereby giving rise to branch or secondary roots. On the inner surface of the pericycle are the vascular tissues, which, in many species, are arranged in a star-shaped pattern. Comprising the core of this star is the xylem tissue. The phloem tissue is located in small groups between the points of the star. Usually the phloem is separated from the xylem by a cambium layer, which, in those species whose roots undergo an increase in thickness, produces both secondary xylem and phloem. In most monocotyledons and some herbaceous dicotyledons, the central core of the stem consists of pith tissue.

Secondary growth in roots

In many plants the roots undergo increase in thickness through the production of secondary growth by the vascular cambium, just as does the stem. In fact, the old roots of trees may reach several inches in diameter and exhibit numerous annual rings similar to those in the wood of the stem. As the root increases in thickness, a secondary covering of periderm (bark or cork) similar to that of the stem replaces the epidermis as a protective covering. Externally, therefore, the older root can hardly be distinguished from an older stem, especially when erosion has removed the soil cover, exposing the root to weathering. Internally, the woody root can hardly be distinguished from the woody stem.

Modifications of the root. During the course of evolution, roots of many species have become modified and specialized with reference to particular functions. The root may function as a food-storage organ, becoming enlarged and swollen, as in the carrot, turnip, radish, or sweet potato. Roots may serve as supporting structures, as in mangrove and corn (maize) plants. In plants of swamps and marshes, branch roots may grow above the mud into the atmosphere and function as aerating organs (pneumatophores) for the entrance of oxygen into the root system. In some palms the roots become modified into thorns. Many species of vines and epiphytes (plants that are supported on the branches of trees rather than being rooted in soil) form aerial roots that hang freely in the air. In many trees and shrubs, the absorptive roots are short and thick and are enclosed within a dense network of fungus hyphae (filaments). The fungus enters the root cortex, producing a condition known as mycorrhiza. The mycorrhizal association of root and fungus takes the place of root hairs in the absorption of water and dissolved minerals. The roots of the mistletoe plant, a partial parasite on trees, enter the stem cortex of the host, where they absorb water and dissolved minerals (see ANGIOSPERMS: *Santalales*). In Spanish moss, an epiphyte, roots are absent, and the leaves function in the absorption of water and minerals by means of special absorptive hairs.

Mycorrhizal fungi

Physiology of the plant organs

The external and internal morphology of the organs of the plant body can be understood simply by viewing them as adaptations facilitating the way the green plant makes its living as an autotrophic (*i.e.,* self-feeding—plants manufacture their own food by photosynthesis) organism. Although it is convenient for botanists to describe the plant in terms of three organs (stem, leaf, root), the plant must be viewed as a whole functional organism in which the cells, tissues, and organs work together to carry out an integrated series of activities. Only when the individual organs of the plant body are viewed in relation to the whole can the intricate mechanisms by which the living plant maintains itself begin to be understood.

During the course of plant evolution, there has been considerable selective value in the development by the green plant of light-accessible surfaces: the erect stem with many branches carrying numerous flattened leaves. It has also been of great selective value for the green plant to develop an underground portion highly efficient in both anchoring the plant and in absorbing water and dissolved minerals from the soil; hence, the root with its many branches and numerous root hairs has developed.

Green plants require three classes of materials from their environment: water, minerals, and the gases carbon dioxide and oxygen. To be used by the plant, however, these materials must be moved from the environment into the plant body.

WATER ABSORPTION BY ROOTS

Nearly all of the water for the plant is absorbed by the roots, especially through the root hairs. In the soil surrounding the root hairs, water is usually present in high concentration. Inside the root cells, water is generally in much lower concentration because of the dissolved sugars, salts, and other substances present in living cells. Water molecules, therefore, move into the root cells by the process of osmotic diffusion, the movement of water across cell membranes (which prevent the passage of sugars, salts, and many other substances) from regions of high water concentration to regions of lower water concentration. There is also evidence suggesting that some of the water absorption by the root requires the expenditure of energy by the root cells.

Considerable amounts of water may enter the root and move across the epidermis and cortex by diffusing through the cell walls, never actually entering the living cells. To move into the vascular cylinder, however, the water molecules must move across the membranes of the endodermis cell layer. The water is channelled in its movement through the endodermal-cell membranes by the bandlike layer of waxy thickening (Casparian strip) in some of the walls of the endodermis.

In addition to water entering the root through the root-hair region of young roots, considerable absorption of water has been found to take place in roots old enough to possess a corky bark. Since as much as 95 percent of the root surface of a tree or shrub consists of bark-covered roots, it is most likely that the major portion of the water and mineral absorption occurs not through the root hairs but through lenticels and cracks in these older roots.

Roots also absorb the mineral elements necessary for plant growth. These elements enter the root cells as ions; *i.e.*, atoms or groups of atoms bearing an electric charge. Phosphorus, for example, is absorbed as phosphate ions (PO_4^{-3}), nitrogen as nitrate ions (NO_{3-}) or ammonium ions (NH_{4+}), and potassium in the form of potassium ions (K^+). There is good evidence that the root cells must expend energy to absorb mineral ions from the soil; that is, the absorption process is an active transport phenomenon. Water and minerals may also be absorbed through the stems and leaves. It is common practice, for example, to apply iron and other minerals to shrubs and trees by spraying them on the leaves.

GASEOUS EXCHANGE IN LEAVES

The gases, carbon dioxide and oxygen, enter the plant by diffusion whenever the stomata of the leaves are open. Experiments have demonstrated that, while the open stomata constitute only 1 to 2 percent of the epidermal surface, they possess, nonetheless, the capacity to permit the passage of gases from the atmosphere into the interior of the leaf to a degree far greater than that required by the plant. It seems very likely that the stomatal complex of guard cell, stoma, and intercellular-space system of the leaf evolved primarily as an adaptive device facilitating the absorption of the carbon dioxide required for photosynthesis and the oxygen necessary for respiration. Once inside the intercellular-space system of the leaf mesophyll, carbon dioxide and oxygen become dissolved in the thin film of water that encloses the mesophyll cells and then diffuse into the interior of the cells.

It has been known at least since the late 17th century that plants not only absorb but also lose large amounts of water from their leaves. The corn plants on a single acre (1 acre = 0.4047 hectare), for example, have been shown to lose some 324,000 gallons (1 gallon = 3.7854 litres) of water during one growing season. When glass containers are placed over a leafy shoot, water will soon condense on the container walls. The process of water loss involves evaporation from the mesophyll cells into the intercellular spaces. The diffusion of this water vapour to the exterior of the leaf is controlled by the behaviour of the guard cells enclosing the stomata. Since the loss of water in gaseous form from the leaves differs in this respect from ordinary evaporation, the term transpiration is used for this process.

Transpiration, the loss of water from the leaf in vapour form, is, therefore, one of the normal functional processes of plants. The plant can do little to stop this water loss. The stomata are an adaptation for the movement of carbon dioxide and oxygen from the atmosphere into the leaf. Both gases are absolutely necessary for the continued life of the plant. A structure that is an excellent adaptation for the entrance of gases is also an efficient device for the loss of water vapour from the leaf interior. In fact, the entire leaf structure is highly favourable for the loss of water by transpiration. Whenever the stomata are open, there is a direct pathway from the surface of the mesophyll cells in the leaf interior out through the stomata into the atmosphere. There is some evidence that the loss of water from the leaf by transpiration is of some value in cooling the plant. On the other hand, when plants are transpiring rapidly, as in the middle of a hot, dry summer day, they may lose so much water that the cells of the leaves and young stems lose turgor (internal water pressure), causing these structures to wilt. If the wilting is severe, the leaves and young stems may droop, and the leaves become rolled. Little harm is done to the plant if these tissues recover their turgidity at night, but, if the loss of water has been too great, the plant may not recover and may eventually die from dehydration.

If water is being lost from the plants by transpiration from the leaves and if water is being absorbed from the soil by the roots, then there must be some mechanism for the transportation of water from the root tissues upward through the xylem of the stem into the veins of the leaves. Many explanations have been proposed to account for this water movement upward in plants; none is completely sat-

isfactory. Various experiments have clearly demonstrated that water is actually being pulled upward in the plant by forces acting in the leaves. It has been shown that the water in the xylem cells is actually under tension; *i.e.*, it is being pulled much in the way a rubber band is stretched.

In addition to the transport of water and dissolved minerals in the xylem, there is also movement through the phloem of sugars, hormones, and vitamins. Much is known about the phloem-transport process, yet no single explanation yet proposed has been able to account for all the various observations about conduction of materials through the phloem. It is known that the phloem cells are alive, unlike the cells of the xylem, which are dead at functional maturity. The rate of movement of materials through the phloem is relatively rapid, although much slower than movement through the xylem. (Xylem and phloem are examined in detail in the article TISSUES AND FLUIDS: *The tissues and fluids of plants.*)

Patterns of differentiation

THE ORGAN SYSTEMS OF VASCULAR PLANTS

Variability of growth forms. The body of a vascular plant consists basically of the three organs: stem, leaf, root. Any individual plant, however, may possess several to many stems (and stem branches), numerous leaves, and many roots. It is convenient for descriptive purposes to speak of the stem with its many branches and numerous leaves as comprising the shoot system and all of the roots as the root system. The shoot system and the root system form one continuous structure and function together in a remarkably integrated, harmoniously interacting organization, the whole plant body.

Vascular plants exist in a remarkable array of diverse forms and sizes. Among the angiosperms, the plant body ranges from giant *Eucalyptus* trees of over 300 feet (91.44 metres) in height to the minute floating aquatic herb *Wolffia,* with a body so tiny that it can be more easily felt between the fingers than seen with the unaided eye. This amazing diversity presented by vascular plants is the result of the working-out in detail during evolution of a scheme of construction that is in itself unlimited. Any plant has the fundamental architectural potential to attain indefinite size, even the smallest herbs (through the activity of the meristems).

The unlimited scheme of growth exhibited by plants becomes evident very early in the development of the embryo. As the embryo grows, the production of new cells and tissues gradually becomes limited to certain regions of the embryonic axis, the meristems. The meristems remain permanently embryonic. Thus, unlike an animal, which usually completes the construction of all its tissues and organs during an early period of embryonic development, a plant body is partially embryonic and partially adult throughout its entire life. In a plant body, therefore, additional organs (*e.g.,* leaves) are formed throughout the life-span of the individual, while, in the animal body, the number of organs is fixed at a certain definite number early in embryo development.

The shoot system. *Branching habits.* The shoot system consists of the stem, its branches, and the leaves. During its development, the shoot system may attain considerable complexity due to branching. In lycopods and some ferns, the growing shoot subdivides or dichotomizes into two more or less equal apices. Each of these sister apices grows individually for a time and then may dichotomize once again. Dichotomous branching is considered to be the most primitive type of ramification in the vascular plants.

The shoot system in the vast majority of vascular plants consists of a main shoot axis or stem from which lateral branches develop from buds in the leaf axils; this is monopodial or lateral branching. The lateral branches may themselves branch and rebranch, producing an intricate shoot system. In some species, one of the axillary buds near the apex of the main stem may grow vigorously, soon overtopping the main stem, producing an apparent monopodial condition that actually consists of a series of lateral branches. This is sympodial branching.

The lateral branches of the main stem may grow into

long shoots with widely spaced internodes and numerous leaves. In some species, however, most of the lateral branches are short shoots with crowded internodes and only a few leaves. In pines, most of the leaves are borne on short shoots. The flowers and fruits in many plants occur only on short shoots. Short shoots are apparently caused by growth-inhibiting hormones produced by the long-shoot tissues.

The tree—a model shoot system. Perhaps the tree is the most familiar type of shoot system. Trees vary considerably in both external form and in internal construction. In the tree ferns, much of the trunk thickness is caused by a thick sheath of intertangled adventitious roots that arise close to the shoot apex and grow downward through the trunk. At the base of the trunk, a dense mat of these roots forms a buttress that aids in supporting the tree trunk. Another type of tree construction occurs in palms and other, arborescent (treelike) monocotyledons. In these plants, the stem apex of the seedling enlarges rapidly just below the apical meristem. Cells in the region below the embryonic leaves function as a primary thickening meristem, which enlarges the stem of the young palm to almost the full diameter it is destined to have. Only after this dramatic increase in thickness does the stem begin to increase markedly in length. Thus the stout trunk is a primary construction of the stem apex and involves no secondary tissues of the kind produced by the vascular cambium of dicotyledons.

Increase in stem thickness among palms

The most common type of tree construction is that characteristic of the conifers and angiosperms. In these plants the original stem is produced by the apical meristem. Later, the stem becomes thicker by the activity of a lateral meristem, the vascular cambium. The vast bulk of a coniferous or angiospermous tree, therefore, is a secondary construction of the cambium, not the apical meristem.

In addition to variations in their internal anatomy, trees also exhibit a wide range of external forms. At one extreme is the short, unbranched or sparsely branched tree with a stout trunk supporting an umbrella-like crown, or rosette, of large compound leaves. Some of these umbrella, or rosette, trees have soft trunks with only weak secondary thickening; *e.g.,* the papaya *(Carica).* Other species—*e.g.,* the cycads and palms—exhibit the same general form but possess much more secondary thickening and much stouter trunks. At the other extreme is the lofty canopy tree with an immense crown consisting of thousands of small leaves borne on hundreds of twigs on the lateral branches. The canopy tree is well developed in the tropical rain forests. Between these extremes are various types of trees with diverse combinations of branching pattern, leaf types, sizes, and wood and bark development.

The shrub and other shoot systems. Another familiar type of shoot system is the shrub. The shoot system of a shrub is characterized by extensive branching, usually from or near the ground level. The buds in the lower portion of the main stem tend to develop instead of those higher up the principal axis. The shrubby shoot system generally is much shorter than that of the tree, and the life-span of the shrub is usually much less than that of the tree.

The shoot system of some species is well adapted for climbing up on other plants, thereby bringing the leaves into the sunlight. Such climbing plants are called vines or lianas and are very abundant in the tropical rain forests, often weaving the canopy into a continuous web. The stem of many species of vines is a long, flexible woody structure which resembles a rope or cable. Internally, the secondary xylem is often arranged in bands, furrows, or discrete cylinders or bundles. Many species possess special structures that facilitate climbing. The shoots of roses *(Rosa)* and blackberries *(Rubus)* possess sharp, curved epidermal outgrowths which are called prickles. Other plants *(e.g., Bougainvillea)* have hooklike thorns. Climbing plants such as grape *(Vitis)* have tendrils that wrap around the stems of other plants.

Lianas

Shoot adaptations. The shoot systems of many species exhibit various modifications enabling the plant to be better adapted to its environment. Perennial herbs, for example, may have slender stems that grow horizontally along the soil surface or just beneath the ground level;

these horizontal stems are known as stolons or runners. In other plants the underground horizontal stem may be a thick structure with short internodes and much-reduced, colourless scale leaves. These are rhizomes, the "root" of *Iris* being a familiar example. Adventitious roots usually arise from the nodes. These subterranean stems or rhizomes function as food-storage organs. Rhizomes usually continue growth for several years, giving rise each growing season to new, aboveground portions of the shoot. Other plants produce short thick stems or parts of stems in which food is stored but that persist only from one growing season to the next. These structures, known as stem tubers, may be formed entirely from the hypocotyl (the root end of the embryo), as in the radish and beet, or they may arise at the tips of underground stolons, as in the potato. The depressions ("eyes") on a potato tuber are the locations of lateral buds and small scalelike leaves (visible in the young potato tuber). After the tubers are produced, the parent plant dies. In such species as crocus and gladiolus, the lower portion of the main shoot itself may develop into another kind of thickened underground stem known as the corm. Thin, membranous scale leaves cover the solid, essentially round stem. Another type of shoot modification is the bulb, consisting of an underground, very short stem from which arise thick, fleshy scale leaves in which food is stored. Bulbs are characteristic of onions, tulips, hyacinths, and leeks.

Stem tubers

The root system. Just as the shoot system becomes more complex through the production of lateral branches, the root system increases in surface area by branching. In the lycopods, dichotomous branching of the root occurs. In most vascular plants, root branching is lateral. Unlike the lateral branches of the shoot, however, the lateral roots arise at some distance back of the growing apex in a region where the tissues are fully matured. In addition, lateral roots originate from tissues deep within the parent root, usually the pericycle of the vascular cylinder in the seed plants, and they must penetrate the cortex tissue of the parent root in their growth outward into the soil. Usually the lateral roots are more slender than the parent root, and they are usually arranged more or less at right angles to the main root. Most trees and shrubs and many herbs have a root system consisting of a radially symmetrical taproot that grows straight downward into the soil. From this taproot, lateral or branch roots develop in sequence, the youngest near the growing root tip, and spread out horizontally or obliquely into the soil. In turn, these branch roots give rise to smaller lateral roots. The result is an extensively branched root system that is especially effective in both the absorption of water and dissolved minerals and in anchoring the plant. The taproots of many species may be especially adapted for the storage of food; *e.g.,* the carrot. The lateral roots of some species (*e.g., Dahlia*) develop into thick, fleshy tubers, which, like the stem tubers they resemble, serve as food-storage structures. The root system of grasses, sedges, and most ferns is a fibrous system composed of numerous roots arising from the stem, all of about the same size. Although fibrous root systems do not anchor plants in the ground as well as do taproot systems, they are well adapted for absorbing water near the surface. In ferns and in many monocotyledons, most of the root system is adventitious, with the roots developing from the stem nodes. This type of root system is well illustrated by corn and grasses.

Root systems of grasses

Transition between the root and shoot systems. Usually there is a transition between the root system and the shoot system near the soil level. This transition is marked externally in the young plant by a rapid abrupt change in coloration from the pale colour of the root to the green colour of the stem. In woody plants with secondary growth, the change in external appearance is less pronounced since the bark extends over both the stem and older roots. In the embryo, the connection between the root and shoot systems is accomplished by the embryo axis or hypocotyl. Internally, the transition between the two parts of the plant body involves changes in the arrangement of the primary vascular tissues. The vascular tissue, which in the root is essentially a single central core or bundle with discrete strands of phloem lying adjacent to the central core of xylem, is gradually changed so that, in the stem, the xylem and phloem tissues assume characteristic positions within the several vascular bundles. Once cambial activity begins, however, the secondary xylem and phloem form continuous tissues between the root and the stem, thus obscuring the initial differences in the structure of the root–shoot transition region.

The reproductive system. Both the shoot and the root systems of the plant may participate in reproduction. The shoot system is involved in the formation of flower clusters or inflorescences; the inflorescence is a part of the branching system of the stem with flowers at the tips. Inflorescences vary greatly in size, form, and in flower number; various types have been distinguished. For more information on flowers, seeds, and fruit, see REPRODUCTION AND REPRODUCTIVE SYSTEMS: *Plant reproduction: Seed and fruit*.

Asexual reproduction

Both the shoot and the root systems are involved in vegetative or asexual reproduction. The shoot system exhibits diverse modifications facilitating reproduction. Some plants—*e.g.,* the aquatic plant *Anacharis canadensis* (elodea)—multiply largely by fragmentation of the plant body. Gardeners and horticulturists propagate plants by inducing cuttings from the parent plant to produce adventitious roots. In many plants, specialized portions of the plant body known as propagules are produced. The propagule may be a stolon or runner, which gives rise to new plants at the nodes, as in the strawberry. In species such as iris and canna, the propagule is a rhizome, which forms a new plant at the growing tip. The corm is utilized as a propagule in species such as crocus and gladiolus, while bulbs serve the same function in onions, tulips, and many other plants. Stem tubers are used to propagate potatoes; the tuber is cut into pieces, each of which gives rise to a new plant. Many aquatic plants, such as *Utricularia,* develop special buds called turions that overwinter in the bottom mud and germinate the following spring to produce new plants. Small, fully formed plantlets are formed on the leaf margins of many ferns and angiosperms such as *Bryophyllum*. These eventually fall to the ground and grow into new plants.

Like the shoot system, the root system also participates in asexual reproduction through the production of a diversity of structures. Species of *Cyrilla* and *Hypericum* develop new plants at irregular intervals along roots that grow just beneath the soil surface; these are "root sprouts." Many perennial and biennial herbs form root tubers; *e.g., Dahlia* and many terrestrial orchids. See also REPRODUCTION AND REPRODUCTIVE SYSTEMS: *Plant reproduction*.

THE ORGANS OF NONVASCULAR PLANTS

Differentiation of the plant body into organs has occurred also in various kinds of multicellular nonvascular plants, including mosses, liverworts, and algae. Much of the vegetative body of mosses and most liverworts is constructed very similarly to that of the vascular plants; that is, there is an aerial, shootlike portion attached to a subterranean rootlike portion. The leafy shootlike gametophyte (*i.e.,* one of the two main phases in the life cycle of lower plants—in mosses and liverworts it is the conspicuous leafy growth form) of mosses exhibits differentiation into three tissue regions: epidermis, cortex, and central conducting strand. While the conducting tissue is composed of phloemlike cells, there are no tracheids (elongate overlapping water-conducting cells that communicate by lateral pores) or vessel elements (more advanced tubular hollow cells with open ends) such as those of vascular plants. The leaves are usually one-cell-layer thick, except over the midrib, and typical mesophyll is lacking. The rootlike underground portion has filamentous structures called rhizoids, but these serve mainly to anchor the plant in the soil. The gametophyte body of some liverworts consists of a flat, ribbonlike, often dichotomously branched, green structure with filamentous rhizoids on its lower surface. Both mosses and liverworts are largely restricted to moist habitats.

Among the algae are many species that exhibit bodies remarkably similar to those of vascular plants, at least in external appearance. The stoneworts *Chara* and *Nitella*

Lower plant structures compared to vascular plants

have an upright, green, shootlike portion with whorls of branches at the nodes and very long internodes. The plants are anchored to the mud in the bottom of ponds and streams by colourless, branched filamentous rhizoids that arise from the nodes near the base. Among the brown algae (Phaeophyta) are many species with bodies composed of leafy shootlike portions anchored to the rocks by means of rootlike holdfasts; *e.g.,* the giant kelps *Nereocystis* and *Macrocystis*. Some of these large brown algae even have food-conducting cells remarkably similar in structure and function to the sieve cells (a type of phloem cell) of vascular plants. Various members of the red algae (Rhodophyta) also display leaflike and stemlike bodies very similar in external appearance to the leaves and stems of vascular plants. The internal anatomy of these highly organized algal bodies is much less complex than that of the vascular plants, however. (See PROTOPHYTES: *Algae*.) Among the green algae (Chlorophyta), the genus *Fritschiella* has a multicellular body consisting largely of parenchyma tissue differentiated into an erect, aerial system anchored to the mud by a prostrate system of rhizoids. In fact, these features make *Fritschiella* an attractive model for a possible ancestor of green land plants.

EVOLUTION OF PLANT ORGANS AND ORGAN SYSTEMS

Functional evolution. The great diversity of organs and organ systems among the numerous species of plants is the result of evolution by natural selection. These structures enable the plant to be better adapted to its environment. The origin and diversification of multicellular plants with complex organs and organ systems have long been a subject of intense interest among plant evolutionists. The fossil record indicates that simpler plants originated earlier in geological time than the more complex plants. It is consistent with the concept of evolution by natural selection to assume that plants received some selective advantage in becoming more complex.

Advantages of complex multicellular structure

What advantages may have accrued to plants by the adoption of the more complex multicellular state? The multicellular condition enables cell and tissue specialization, a division of labour among the parts of the whole plant body. Some cells and tissues can become specialized for capturing sunlight and synthesizing food, others anchor the plant body, while still others play a role in reproduction. The result is a corresponding increase in the ability of the plant to exploit its environment and increase its chances for survival.

The fossil record. The time of origin of the multicellular plant body can be estimated from the earliest occurring fossils presently known. Filamentous structures identified as blue-green algae have been discovered in rocks calculated as being about 2,000,000,000 years in age. Multicellular bodies differentiated into organs had evolved among the green algae and possibly also among the red algae and brown algae by the beginning of the Ordovician Period, some 500,000,000 years ago.

The earliest known fossil land plants (*i.e.,* vascular plants with an erect aerial photosynthesizing system and a horizontal underground anchoring and absorbing system) are found in rocks formed during the Upper Silurian and Early Devonian periods, around 395,000,000 years ago. Geological evidence suggests that, during this time, many regions of the Earth's surface may have been subjected to prolonged seasonal droughts. During some portions of the year, rainfall would be abundant (as today in some tropical regions); at other times, the rains would cease, and the water level in the larger bodies of water would decrease drastically, while that of many smaller ponds and lakes might dry up altogether. Under these conditions of intermittent drought, the evolutionary migration of plants to the land is thought to have occurred.

Proposed conditions leading to land-plant evolution

Once the transition to full-time land existence had been accomplished, the stage was then set for the relatively rapid adaptive radiation of plants into all suitable habitats. This radiation produced several evolutionary lines of vascular plants as well as of the mosses and liverworts. The invasion of the land by photosynthetic plants also created a new environment—one in which fungi and animals could compete successfully for the necessities of life.

Indeed, clear evidence that fungi were in existence during the Early Devonian Period is provided by the discovery of fungal hyphae in the fossilized remains of vascular plants that lived during that time. Fossil remains of land-dwelling invertebrate animals, which lived during this time, have also been discovered.

(P.Ad.)

BIBLIOGRAPHY

Animal organs and organ systems: c.k. weichert, *Anatomy of the Chordates,* 4th ed. (1970); and r.d. barnes, *Invertebrate Zoology,* 2nd ed. (1968), are detailed references describing animal organ systems and their evolution. The former deals primarily with vertebrates, the latter with invertebrates. See also w.t. keeton, *Biological Science* (1967), a thorough biology textbook, with several chapters concerning the interrelationships of organ systems; e.e. selkurt (ed.), *Physiology,* 2nd ed. (1966), a complete account of mammalian physiology; and r. rugh, *Vertebrate Embryology* (1964), which presents the normal sequence of events of vertebrate development.

(C.K.W./K.W.K./M.S.K.)

Plant organs and organ systems: e. strasburger, *Lehrbuch der Botanik für Hochschulen,* 28th ed. (1962; Eng. trans., *Textbook of Botany,* 1965), a comprehensive college-level botany textbook and reference work (a classic since 1894, periodically revised by outstanding authorities); k. esau, *Plant Anatomy,* 2nd ed. (1965), a splendid, well-illustrated, college-level textbook of seed plant anatomy by a foremost plant anatomist; a.j. eames, *Morphology of the Angiosperms* (1961), an excellent college-level textbook that brings together both factual material and theories on the morphology and phylogeny of the angiosperms; t.e. weier, *et al., Botany,* 4th ed. (1970), an introductory college-level botany textbook with excellent coverage of plant morphology and well illustrated with many photographs and drawings; e.j.h. corner, *The Life of Plants* (1964), a highly original story of important events in the evolution of plants from single cells to forest trees (well illustrated, especially with examples from the tropics); h.p. banks, *Evolution and Plants of the Past* (1970), a short, well-illustrated, college-level book on fossil plants by one of the foremost researchers in Devonian paleobotany; a.s. foster and e.m. gifford, jr., *Comparative Morphology of Vascular Plants* (1959), a well-written and illustrated college-level textbook of vascular plant morphology; p. adams, *et al., The Study of Botany* (1970), a college-level botany textbook, with emphasis on the thought processes of plant scientists, containing chapters on the evolutionary aspects of plant anatomy and morphology; a.f. hill, *Economic Botany* (1937), an old but still useful college-level textbook describing the uses of plants and plant products; f.o. bower, *Plants and Man* (1925), an old but still excellent, relatively nontechnical discussion by a recognized authority on the life of plants, especially those aspects of interest to the layman; p.r. bell and c.l.f. woodcock, *The Diversity of Green Plants* (1968), a well-illustrated college-level textbook on the morphology of autotrophic plants; f.b. salisbury and r.v. parke, *Vascular Plants: Form and Function,* 2nd ed. (1970), a well-written college-level discussion of plant anatomy in relation to plant physiology; m. richardson, *Translocation in Plants* (1968), a succinct discussion of the movement of water, minerals, and metabolites within the xylem and phloem tissues of the plant body; a. cronquist, *The Evolution and Classification of Flowering Plants* (1968), a unique, advanced level book presenting major new concepts about flowering plant taxonomy and evolution; a. takhtajan, *Flowering Plants: Origin and Dispersal* (1969; Eng. trans. from the 2nd Russian edition, 1961), an advanced level treatment of the problems of the origin and dispersal of the flowering plants by a recognized Russian authority in plant evolution.

(P.Ad.)

Ōsaka–Kōbe Metropolitan Area

The Ōsaka–Kōbe metropolitan area is the second largest urban and industrial agglomeration in Japan. It is located on Ōsaka Bay at the eastern end of the Inland Sea. The cities of Ōsaka and Kōbe are at the centre of what is called by geographers the Hanshin Industrial Zone; as a result of the expansion of the urban area along the Inland Sea and northeast toward the city of Kyōto, the region is now included in the larger Keihanshin Industrial Zone. Neither of these zones is a political entity, but the larger of the two corresponds to the Kansai, one of Japan's traditional cultural areas. The Kansai, a region of ancient cities, is the birthplace of the earliest Japanese state. It is an area of historically dense population that until well into the 20th century was the most industrialized and economically advanced part of Japan.

Ōsaka is the capital of Ōsaka *fu* (urban prefecture), an administrative division that includes the city of Ōsaka and large urban and rural areas. Kōbe is the capital and largest city of Hyōgo *ken* (prefecture) and one of Japan's chief ports. There are many satellite industrial and residential cities around the two central cities.

This article is divided into the following sections:

Physical and human geography

THE LANDSCAPE

River deltas and uplands

The city site. The city of Ōsaka is situated on the delta of the Yodo River. To the east of the central city, Ōsaka Castle, originally built by Toyotomi Hideyoshi, stands on a northern extension of the upland (about 65 feet [20 metres] above sea level) that rises in the southern part of Ōsaka urban prefecture to more than 3,000 feet. The metropolitan area spreads over the deltas of the Yodo, Yamato, and other rivers and into their diluvial uplands. The area is bounded by the Ikoma Mountains in the east, the Izumi Mountains in the south, and the Rokkō Mountains in the northwest. The southwestern boundary of Ōsaka Bay is formed by Awaji Island. On the northwestern shore of the bay is Kōbe, above which rises the granite peak of Mount Rokkō (3,058 feet). The coastline between the two cities has been altered by reclamation for port facilities and industries. Along the coast and in the uplands are the best residential areas of Kōbe and the cities of Ashiya, Nishinomiya, Ikeda, Itami, and Toyonaka. On the delta of the Kanzaki River, just west of Ōsaka, is the city of Amagasaki, a centre of heavy industry. To the north of Ōsaka are the cities of Toyonaka, Suita, and Ibaraki. Above them, on Senri Hill, are new towns developed since the 1960s. Northeast of Ōsaka, along the Yodo River, are the industrial and residential cities of Takatsuki, Moriguchi, Neyagawa, and Hirakata. To the east of Ōsaka are the cities of Kadoma, Higashiōsaka, and Yao. To the southeast are Fujiidera, Tondabayashi, Matsubara, and others, most of them old historical towns. To the southwest, on the coastal plain, are Sakai, Izumi-Ōtsu, Kaizuka, Kishiwada, and Izumi-Sano, some of them industrial and others residential. Urbanization extends to Nara, 25 miles (40 kilometres) east of Ōsaka, and to Kyō-to, 25 miles northeast. A dense network of railways and roads winds throughout the area.

Climate. The region has a temperate climate. The annual mean temperature is about 60° F (16° C), and the annual rainfall averages 54 inches (1,370 millimetres). The temperature in August is often 86° F (30° C) or more, with no breeze from the sea at night. The January mean is about 40° F (4° C), and snow falls several times in winter. The rainy seasons are in June–July and September–October. In September the region is usually struck by one or two typhoons. The greatest typhoon disaster in the area's history occurred in 1934, when 3,000 people were killed. During the rainy season of June–July 1938, huge landslides from the Rokkō Mountains buried wide areas of Kōbe, and floods took the lives of 870 persons.

The citizens of Ōsaka once took pride in its smoky atmosphere as a mark of industrial progress, calling it the "Capital of Smoke" ("Kemuri no miyako"); but by the mid-1970s the city's smog and air pollution were seen as harmful, and during the 1980s improvement of air quality became a priority. Other environmental problems receiving attention include water pollution and subsidence (sinking) of the earth in the Amagasaki region.

Street patterns

The city layout. The streets of central Ōsaka are laid out on a grid plan, but the rest of the city is a patchwork of planned grids and rambling streets. The north–south axis is Midō-suji ("Midō Street"), connecting Ōsaka railway station in the north and Namba station in the south. The east–west axis is Chūō Ōdōri ("Central Boulevard"), running from the Central Pier of the Port of Ōsaka in the west to the foot of the Ikoma Mountains in the east. Parallel to Midō-suji is the narrow Shinsaibashi-suji, the central shopping district. Dotombori, at the south end of Shinsaibashi-suji, is a crowded theatre and restaurant area.

The central business district is the northern part of the downtown area. Nakanoshima, an island formed by arms

Lawrence Smith—Photo Researchers

Ōsaka Castle.

of the Yodo River, contains City Hall, the Central Civic Hall, the Bank of Japan, and the headquarters of the Asahi Press and of a number of other large businesses. Until World War II, the traditional commercial centres had been Semba and Shimanouchi streets, where old-style white-walled shops with family quarters behind them had continued for centuries.

There are two large *sakariba* (amusement districts) in the city. Kita ("The North") is located just south of Ōsaka railway station, where the city's highest-priced land is found. Kita has a complex of high-rise office buildings and a large underground shopping centre. Minami ("The South") has many theatres and restaurants. Ōsaka's industrial areas are on the lower Yodo delta and in the eastern and northeastern parts of the city.

The street pattern of Kōbe is governed by its location between the mountains and the shore. Main streets run east and west, crossed by short north–south streets and occasional longer streets going up into the hills. The central shopping street, Motomachi, runs between the Sannomiya and Kōbe railway stations. The central business district is near the harbour.

Burial mounds and housing developments

The Ōsaka area has been settled and built upon since prehistoric times; kitchen middens and pottery shards have been found dating to at least 7000 BC. There are many ancient burial mounds from the Tumulus period (c. AD 250–c. 600), and the contents of some of these have helped document the presence of settlers from the Korean peninsula. The ancient villages of the rice farmers were on the marshy plains, while the palaces, shrines, and temples were located on higher ground. Medieval settlements were in the uplands. Some modern residential areas are on the sites of several former settlements. Thus, Tezukayama, a residential development in Ōsaka south of the old castle, is built over a number of ancient mounds.

The central part of Ōsaka is now primarily commercial; since 1920 there has been a migration from the city to the suburbs, helped along by private railway companies that have made suburban building land available along their rights-of-way. The Hankyū Electric Railway was particularly instrumental in developing the city of Toyonaka northwest of Ōsaka. Two of the large postwar housing developments are Senri New Town and Senboku New Town, started in 1961 and 1965, respectively.

About two-thirds of Ōsaka urban prefecture's dwellings are apartment houses. Much of Ōsaka and nearly all of Kōbe were destroyed during World War II, and inner-city areas are now occupied mostly by Western-style multistoried buildings; traditional architectural styles can still be seen, however, in the Tekijuku, a school of foreign studies (18th century), and the Kōnoike (1708; rebuilt 1853) in Ōsaka, as well as in some residential houses in Kōbe. Examples of early Western-influenced architecture survive on Nakanoshima, including the Bank of Japan building (1903) and the Ōsaka Prefectural Library (1904). The redevelopment of the central business districts of both cities since the 1960s has produced many large, modern, and architecturally innovative buildings: notable examples include the office and hotel complex in front of Ōsaka railway station; the Semba Centre Building, which although only four floors in height extends about three-fifths of a mile along Chūō Ōdōri and is constructed under an elevated expressway and over a subway; and the convention centre built on the man-made Port Island in Kōbe Harbour.

THE PEOPLE

Demographic trends in the Ōsaka–Kōbe metropolitan region parallel two major national trends: sustained urban population growth through rural–urban migration and suburbanization. Thus, the region's population has been swelled for more than a century by a continuous stream of people moving in from rural areas; but the population of the city of Ōsaka—after reaching a peak of about 3,150,000 in the mid-1960s—has declined, as people have migrated from the city to the suburbs. In addition, the city's highest density is not in the centre but in the peripheral wards, because the population decrease has been greatest in the central wards. By contrast, the population

Central Kōbe and Rokkō Mountains, seen from Port Island.
Kurt Scholz—Shostal Associates

of the city of Kōbe has increased steadily, although, like Ōsaka, there has been a loss of population in the inner city and high increases in peripheral wards.

The population of the Ōsaka–Kōbe metropolitan area—like the Kansai region in general—is the most ethnically diverse of Japan. Included are the country's largest concentrations of ethnic Koreans, most of whom are descendants of Koreans who migrated to Japan during the period (1910–45) when Korea was a Japanese colony and who retain Korean nationality; Okinawans, who legally are Japanese but who are treated as internal aliens; and *burakumin,* the term being a euphemism for descendants of an outcaste group that was once legally, though not genetically, distinct from the general Japanese population. All three groups are subject to discrimination in education, employment, marriage, and housing. In Kōbe there are also sizable communities of Chinese, Indians, and Westerners, whose presence contributes an international flavour to the city's culture.

THE ECONOMY

Industry. Ōsaka was once known as the Manchester of the Orient because of its great textile industry; now, however, its leading industries are the manufacture of iron and steel, fabricated metals, electric machinery, machinery, and chemicals. Between Ōsaka and Kōbe are several other industrial cities. The largest, Amagasaki, is a centre of machinery, metallurgy, chemicals, cement, and paper production. The major industries in Kōbe are shipbuilding and steel production. Heavy industry and chemical plants are situated along the shore of Ōsaka Bay, while light industry and assembly plants are inland.

Commerce. In the past the merchants of Ōsaka greeted one another in the mornings with the query, "Are you making money?" Contemporary merchants and executives continue to greet each other by asking about the state of their businesses. The salutations reflect the traditional importance of commercial enterprise in Ōsaka. The city holds about one-seventh of the nation's wholesale trade.

Ōsaka is Japan's second largest financial centre. Together with Kōbe it is the leading port for foreign trade, handling about one-fifth of all exports.

Transportation. Ōsaka is an important junction point Railways of the national railway network, handling traffic between the Tokyo region to the northeast and regions farther west and south. Following the privatization of the formerly government-controlled Japanese National Railways (JNR) in 1987, Ōsaka became the headquarters of the West Japan Railway Company (JR Nishi Nihon), which operates passenger service in western Honshu. The region is also served by Shinkansen "bullet" express trains and the national freight rail system, both of which also have become private entities. In addition, there are other privately owned railroads that provide suburban commuter and regional interurban passenger service between Ōsaka and Kōbe and their suburbs and to other major cities in

central Honshu, particularly Kyōto and Nagoya. Rail lines also run inland from Kōbe to rural areas of Hyōgo prefecture north of the city. Ōsaka's subway system, started before World War II, underwent great expansion in the late 1960s and was expanded again in the early 1980s; Kōbe's first subway line was opened in the mid-1980s.

Because of heavy automobile traffic, Ōsaka's main streets are one-way. A network of surface and elevated expressways runs through the central parts of Ōsaka and Kōbe, linking the two cities together as well as joining them to the national expressway system. Ordinary highways also span the whole region. Kōbe and Ōsaka are both international and domestic ports; passenger ships, freighters, and car ferries sail to the islands of Shikoku and Kyushu and to various ports of the Inland Sea. Air service is provided by the Ōsaka International Airport, located north of the city near Itami. A considerable increase in both domestic and international air travel since the mid-1970s led to the need for a second regional airport; construction of the new facility—on a man-made island in Ōsaka Bay—began in 1987.

ADMINISTRATION AND SOCIAL CONDITIONS

Government. The city of Ōsaka is the capital of Ōsaka urban prefecture, which consists of 31 cities and 13 towns and villages. It is also the centre of the Kinki District (Kinki-chihō), which consists of the seven prefectures of Ōsaka, Kyōto, Hyōgo, Nara, Wakayama, Shiga, and Mie. Various prefectural and regional institutions have their main offices in Ōsaka.

Public utilities. Ōsaka's main source of water is the Yodo River; Kōbe has several reservoirs on the slope of the Rokkō Mountains. Sewage services are adequate in the central urban areas. Electricity is available everywhere, and gas is available in most city areas.

Health. Medical care in Ōsaka centres on the hospitals of Ōsaka University and of the Ōsaka City University and on several other medical institutions. Other hospitals and health centres are distributed throughout the region.

Education. In Ōsaka and Hyōgo prefectures there are more than 100 universities and junior colleges. Ōsaka University, Ōsaka University of Foreign Studies, Ōsaka University of Education, Kōbe University, and Hyōgo University of Education are national universities. Public municipal institutions include Ōsaka City University and the University of Ōsaka Prefecture. Kansai University in Ōsaka and Kwansei Gakuin University in Nishinomiya are the oldest and largest private universities in the area.

CULTURAL LIFE

Ōsaka and Kyōto have long been leading centres of culture—Ōsaka, famous for its cuisine, has a more bustling, democratic tone than Kyōto, which is one of the great centres of Japanese culture. The difference is expressed in the popular sayings: "Kyōto dandies; Ōsaka gourmands" (*Kyō no kidaore; Ōsaka no kuidaore*).

Traditional and modern Japanese drama and music are performed at theatres and halls in the metropolitan area, as are Western music, operas, and plays. There are numerous museums, galleries, and libraries. Ōsaka is the home of two national newspapers, the *Asahi* and the *Mainichi*.

Green space in the city of Ōsaka is scarce, but recreational opportunities abound. The important parks include Nakanoshima, Ōsaka Castle, Tsurumi Ryokuchi, Nagai, and Tennoji, the latter with a zoo and botanical gardens. The suburbs have many historical sites and large recreation areas. Beside the spacious man-made Hattori Ryokuchi and Meiji no Mori Minoo parks, there are the recreational areas of the Kii Peninsula on the Pacific, the beaches of the Inland Sea, the historical towns of Nara and Kyōto, and beautiful Lake Biwa, near Kyōto. At Kōbe, Mount Rokkō can be ascended by road or by cable car; there is a golf course at the top and ponds for swimming. There are four professional baseball teams in the metropolitan area, and the national high school baseball championships are played in the summer in Nishinomiya. The town of Takarazuka, northwest of Ōsaka, has been developed as an amusement centre; it houses the Girls Opera and Dancing Theatre. In 1970 the Japan World Exposition (Expo 70) was held near Senri New Town; Expo Memorial Park now holds the National Museum of Ethnology, the National Museum of Art, and a recreation area.

History

ŌSAKA

Ōsaka's ancient origins

The plain of Ōsaka was settled in Paleolithic times and by *c.* AD 300 was a political centre. Among the many ancient burial mounds in the Ōsaka area is that ascribed to the semilegendary emperor Nintoku; the largest tomb of the Tumulus period, the 5th-century structure is surrounded by three moats and occupies some 80 acres (32 hectares). Ancient Naniwa—in what is now Ōsaka—was the site of palace or capital complexes intermittently from the early 5th to the mid-7th century, but in 710 it lost its position to Nara, the first "permanent" national capital.

When Kyōto became the Imperial capital in 794, land and water routes between Ōsaka and Kyōto were improved. The reclamation of the delta of the Yodo River allowed the building of new settlements, including Watanabe, which became a provincial capital and port during the Middle Ages. South of Ōsaka, on the eastern shore of the bay, is Sakai, which had emerged as a port town by the 14th century. There is evidence that, like some medieval European towns, it was self-governing in the 15th and 16th centuries, run by its leading merchants until they capitulated to the warlord Oda Nobunaga in 1569. These merchants grew wealthy from Sakai's lucrative domestic and foreign trade; under their patronage Sakai became a centre of the arts after Kyōto was devastated in the Ōnin War (1467–77). Sakai was also a centre of Christian proselytizing in the late 16th and early 17th centuries; the accounts of Jesuit missionaries tell of the wealth and cosmopolitan flavour of the city at that time.

In 1496—in the midst of a century of civil war—Rennyo, chief priest of the militant True Pure Land (Jōdo Shin) sect of Buddhism, selected a site near the mouth of the Yodo River for a fortress temple. Completed in 1532, this temple, Ishiyama Honganji, became the nucleus of a major town that was destroyed in 1580 by Oda Nobunaga, after a siege of many years. Oda's successor, Toyotomi Hideyoshi, built a great castle on the site with massive stone walls and broad moats; the castle town that developed around it was the origin of present-day Ōsaka. From this base Hideyoshi brought the whole of Japan under his control, and Ōsaka was the seat of national power until his death in 1598.

The castle and town were badly damaged and depopulated during Tokugawa Ieyasu's siege of 1614–15, in which he eliminated Hideyoshi's heir and consolidated his power as shogun. Succeeding shoguns rebuilt the castle and town, and during the rest of the Tokugawa period (1603–1867) Ōsaka was a directly administered shogunal city. Unlike other towns of the period, Ōsaka was not a political centre and therefore was not dominated by the samurai (warrior) class. Instead, it became the country's main commercial city; feudal lords from all Japan established warehouses for their tax rice along the city's canals, and rice was traded actively. Many other goods were traded in Ōsaka—which had some 380 wholesale houses by 1679—and the city became an expanding commercial and manufacturing centre. These activities stimulated the rapid monetization of the regional economy.

As it grew more prosperous, Ōsaka became a centre of the cultural renaissance of the Genroku period (late 17th–early 18th century). New dramatic forms such as *bunraku* (puppet theatre) and Kabuki were created, and new genres of prose fiction arose, the styles and themes of which catered to the tastes of urban commoners and marked a shift in cultural arbitration away from the samurai class. During the 18th century, however, Ōsaka's position as cultural leader was lost to Edo (now Tokyo), but the city remained an educational centre, with schools in classical studies and in medicine. In the mid-19th century, when Japan was still closed to most Westerners, the Dutch language and Western science were studied by the Japanese in Ōsaka.

Ōsaka remained preeminent both as a port and as a centre of industry until World War II. Much of the city was destroyed by aerial bombardment during the war, however, and postwar economic growth was focused largely in the Tokyo–Yokohama metropolitan area. The revolution in China deprived Ōsaka of its important China trade until the early 1970s, while the increasing economic role of the national government tended to encourage industrial location in the Tokyo–Yokohama area.

KŌBE

The history of Kōbe is as old as that of Ōsaka. In ancient times the name Kōbe was applied to a small fishing village separated by the Minato River from the town of Hyōgo, the chief port of the area. Hyōgo, also known as Ōwada and Muko, was an important port for trade with China and Korea as early as the 8th century. For many centuries it continued to be Japan's chief port for foreign trade, prospering especially during the 15th and 16th centuries, and the government maintained patrol boats there to control pirates in the Inland Sea. For a brief period during the 12th century Taira Kiyomori made it the capital instead of Kyōto.

During the Tokugawa period, Hyōgo served as the outer port of Ōsaka until in 1868 it was reopened to foreign trade. Soon it was outstripped and absorbed by Kōbe, which has a deeper harbour. The combined ports have been called the port of Kōbe since the establishment of the Kōbe customhouse in 1872. Hyōgo and Kōbe were incorporated as the city of Kōbe in 1889. The many foreigners who settled there in the 19th century gave it an international and cosmopolitan atmosphere.

Incorporation of Kōbe

The size of the city increased in the late 19th and early 20th centuries through the absorption of adjacent communities. During World War II, air raids destroyed much of the city. It was rebuilt quickly after the war, its size again increasing by annexation. Kōbe has become one of the largest cities in Japan. Its port facilities, which have undergone tremendous expansion since the war, have been combined administratively with those of Ōsaka since the early 1970s.

BIBLIOGRAPHY. Two publications by the Association of Japanese Geographers are useful: *Japanese Cities: A Geographical Approach* (1970), for the academic study of postwar urban Japan; and *Geography of Japan* (1980), especially ch. 12–18, which contains scholarly analyses of contemporary Japanese urban development. WILLIAM B. HAUSER, *Economic Institutional Change in Tokugawa Japan: Ōsaka and the Kinai Cotton Trade* (1974), analyzes Ōsaka's premodern economic role. *Osaka and Its Technology* (semiannual) includes essays on urban development and public works. A novel by JUNICHIRŌ TANIZAKI, *The Makioka Sisters* (1957, reissued 1983; originally published in Japanese, 3 vol., 1949), provides an excellent if romanticized view of life in the Ōsaka–Kōbe region before World War II. PAT TUCKER SPIER (ed.), *The River Without Bridges: An Encounter with the Japanese Buraku* (1986), discusses the civil rights of the *burakumin* in Ōsaka.

(S.K./R.P.T.)

Pacific Islands

The Pacific Islands is an expression commonly accepted as including all of those islands in the Pacific Ocean that are collectively referred to as Melanesia, Micronesia, and Polynesia, also sometimes known as Oceania. This usage rules out the Australian island continent, the Asia-related Indonesian, Philippine, and Japanese archipelagoes, and the Ryukyu, Bonin-Volcano, and Kuril island arcs that project seaward from Japan. Neither does the term encompass the Aleutian chain connecting Kamchatka and Alaska nor such isolated islands as Juan Fernández off the coast of South America.

Although the Pacific Ocean makes up nearly one-third of the Earth's surface, the Pacific Islands discussed in this article add up to a little less than 500,000 square miles (1,300,000 square kilometres) of land area. New Guinea, the largest island in the world after Greenland, represents 70 percent of this total, and New Zealand accounts for 20 percent. The remaining 10 percent of the land area of the Pacific is divided among more than 10,000 islands. The Pacific Islands lie mainly in the area bounded by latitudes 23° north and 27° south and longitudes 130° east and 125° west. Exceptions to this are New Zealand, which lies in the southern temperate zone, and Easter Island, which stands in isolation at longitude 109° west, almost halfway to South America. (Australia and New Zealand are treated in separate articles, and Hawaii is treated in the article UNITED STATES OF AMERICA.)

This article is divided into the following major sections:

THE REGION

For convenient reference, the Pacific Islands are customarily divided into three ethnogeographic groupings. The great arc of islands located north and east of Australia and south of the Equator is called Melanesia (from the Greek words *melas,* "black," and *nēsos,* "island") after the predominantly dark-skinned peoples of New Guinea, the Bismarcks, Solomon Islands, Vanuatu (formerly the New Hebrides), New Caledonia, and Fiji. North of the Equator and east of the Philippines is another island arc that ranges from Palau (Belau) and the Marianas in the west through the Carolines and Marshalls all the way to Kiribati (formerly the Gilbert Islands). This is Micronesia, so named because of the smaller size of these islands and atolls. In the eastern Pacific, and largely enclosed within a huge triangle formed by Hawaii in the north, New Zealand to the south, and Easter Island far to the east, are the "many" (poly) islands of Polynesia. Other components of this widely scattered collection are Samoa, Tonga, French Polynesia (including the Society, Tuamotu, and Marquesas Islands), and the Cook Islands. In this, the last section of the Pacific Ocean to be inhabited, the islanders share a cultural tradition that relates them closely to many Fijians. Fiji, indeed, is actually a transitional territory between Melanesia and Polynesia.

Since the 16th century the Western world has shown an interest in the Pacific Islands that has been expressed in the activities of explorers, scientists, artists and writers, missionaries, commercial entrepreneurs, and imperialistic statesmen. The variety of the Pacific's environments, both physical and biotic, continues to be a laboratory for experimenting in social and cultural adaptation. Though insularity has often dominated this process, its effect has been offset by the opportunities for human contact and exchange in many directions across the ocean's expanse. In the 20th century the islands and their inhabitants have continued to attract international interest, although for new reasons, such as their strategic significance in the relationships of the world powers in Europe, Asia, and America. Attention has also centred on the problems created for Pacific islanders by nature's limitation of land and resources in the face of expanding populations and rising standards of living.

Physical and human geography

THE LAND

The island ecosystem. To know what it is like to live on a Pacific island, the intermixture of physical and biologic characteristics of the particular island must be considered. Each of the myriad ecological systems in the Pacific is a unique complex of living organisms and their nonliving environment. Each is a functional system of interacting components that tends toward an equilibrium that is never quite achieved. The limited size of most Pacific islands makes it probable that almost any change, whether by human action or by some natural agency, will have repercussions elsewhere within the ecosystem. The landform, climate, soils, vegetation, and animal life all are elements to which people who live on an island must relate, for they, too, occupy a niche in the total ecological scheme.

Relief. The islands may be classified as either continental or oceanic. The former are associated with the ancient continental platforms of Asia and Australia, now partially submerged. Oceanic islands, located eastward in the deeper Pacific basin, are differentiated as high volcanic-based islands or low coral islands and atolls. A coral island may be single, or two or more coral islets may be part of an atoll if connected by a reef ringing a lagoon. The "high–low" distinction is misleading as the two types occur in many combinations, and some coral islands have been elevated considerably by changes in the ocean level.

Continental islands. The islands of the broad western Pacific margin, formed mainly of metamorphosed rocks, sediments, and andesitic volcanic material, are separated

Continental and oceanic islands

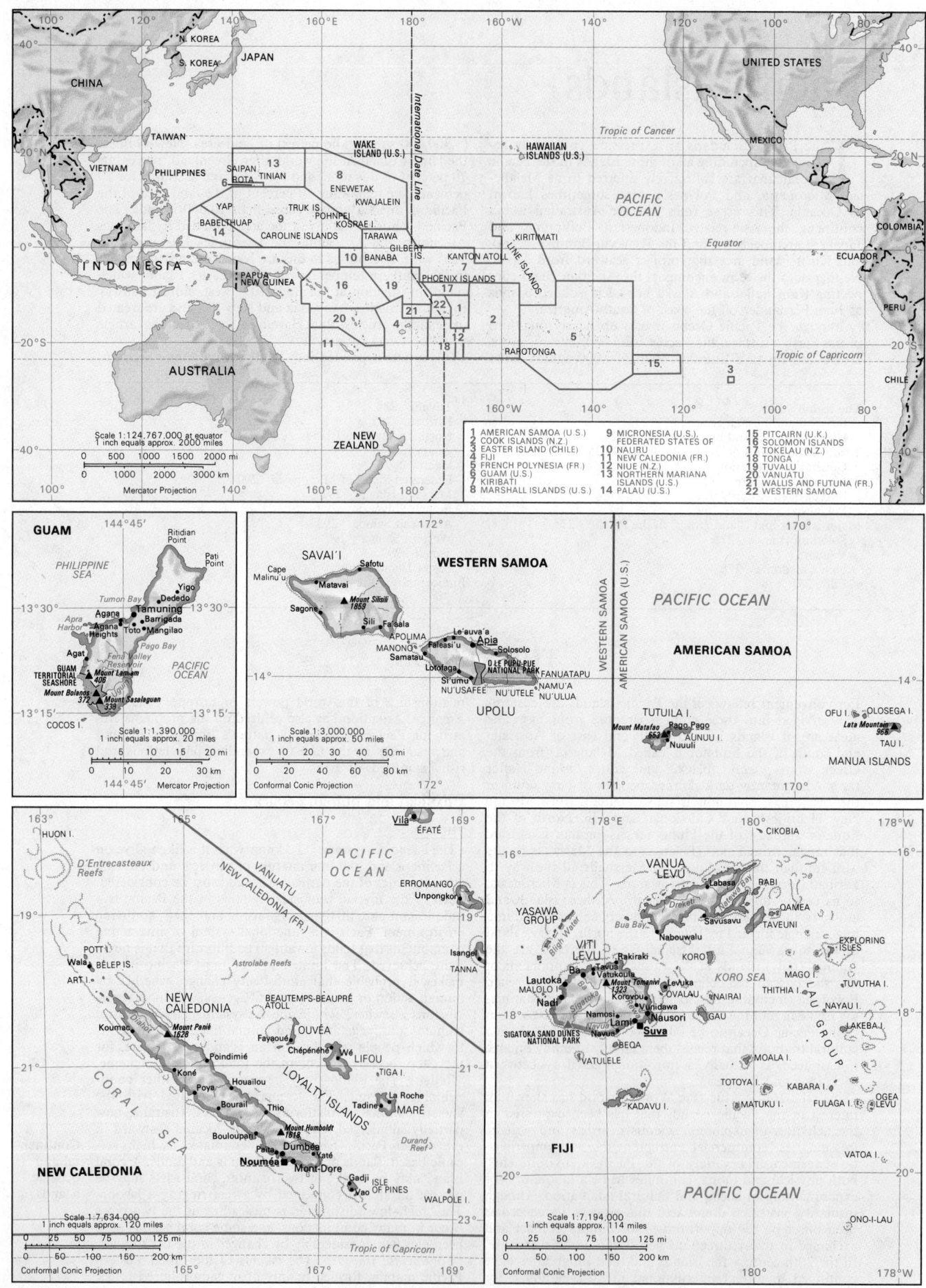

GUAM

PHILIPPINE SEA

Ritidian Point
Pati Point
Yigo
Tumon Bay
Dededo
Tamuning
Agana
Barrigada
Agana Heights
Toto
Mangilao
Apra Harbor
Agat
Fena Valley Reservoir
Pago Bay
PACIFIC OCEAN
GUAM TERRITORIAL SEASHORE
▲ Mount Lamlam 406
Mount Bolanos 372 ▲ ▲ Mount Sasalaguan 338
COCOS I.

Scale 1:1,390,000
1 inch equals approx. 20 miles
0   5   10   15   20 mi
0   10   20   30 km
Mercator Projection

WESTERN SAMOA

SAVAI'I
Cape Malinu'u
Safotu
Matavai
Mount Silisili ▲ 1859
Sagone
Sili
Fa'aala
APOLIMA
MANONO
Faleasi'u
Le'auva'a
Samatau
Apia
Solosolo
Lotofaga
SI'UMU
O LE PUPU-PUE NATIONAL PARK
FANUATAPU
NU'USAFEE
NU'UTELE
NAMU'A
NU'ULUA
UPOLU

Scale 1:3,000,000
1 inch equals approx. 50 miles
0   10   20   30   40   50 mi
0   20   40   60   80 km
Conformal Conic Projection

WESTERN SAMOA
AMERICAN SAMOA (U.S.)
PACIFIC OCEAN

AMERICAN SAMOA

TUTUILA I.
Mount Matafao 653 ▲
Pago Pago
AUNU'U I.
Nuuuli
OFU I.
OLOSEGA I.
Lata Mountain 966 ▲
TAU I.
MANUA ISLANDS

1   AMERICAN SAMOA (U.S.)
2   COOK ISLANDS (N.Z.)
3   EASTER ISLAND (CHILE)
4   FIJI
5   FRENCH POLYNESIA (FR.)
6   GUAM (U.S.)
7   KIRIBATI
8   MARSHALL ISLANDS (U.S.)
9   MICRONESIA (U.S.), FEDERATED STATES OF
10   NAURU
11   NEW CALEDONIA (FR.)
12   NIUE (N.Z.)
13   NORTHERN MARIANA ISLANDS (U.S.)
14   PALAU (U.S.)
15   PITCAIRN (U.K.)
16   SOLOMON ISLANDS
17   TOKELAU (N.Z.)
18   TONGA
19   TUVALU
20   VANUATU
21   WALLIS AND FUTUNA (FR.)
22   WESTERN SAMOA

Scale 1:124,767,000 at equator
1 inch equals approx. 2000 miles
0   500   1000   1500   2000 mi
0   1000   2000   3000 km
Mercator Projection

NEW CALEDONIA

HUON I.
D'Entrecasteaux Reefs
PACIFIC OCEAN
Vila
ÉFATÉ
VANUATU
NEW CALEDONIA (FR.)
ERROMANGO
Unpongkor
POTT I.
Wala
BÉLEP IS.
ART I.
Astrolabe Reefs
Isangel
TANNA
NEW CALEDONIA
BEAUTEMPS-BEAUPRÉ ATOLL
Koumac
▲ Mount Panié 1628
Diahot
OUVÉA
Fayaoué
Chépénéhe
Wé
LIFOU
Poindimié
Koné
TIGA I.
Poya
Houailou
La Roche
Bourail
Thio
Tadine
MARÉ
LOYALTY ISLANDS
Bouloupari
▲ Mount Humboldt 1618
Paita
Dumbéa
Yaté
Nouméa
Mont-Dore
CORAL SEA
Gadji
Vao
ISLE OF PINES
WALPOLE I.
Durand Reef

Scale 1:7,634,000
1 inch equals approx. 120 miles
0   25   50   75   100   125 mi
0   50   100   150   200 km
Conformal Conic Projection

FIJI

CIKOBIA
VANUA LEVU
Labasa
RABI
YASAWA GROUP
Dreketi
QAMEA
TAVEUNI
Nabouwalu
Bua Bay
Savusavu
EXPLORING ISLES
Bligh Water
VITI LEVU
Rakiraki
KORO
MAGO I.
KORO SEA
Lautoka
Ba
Tavua
▲ Mount Tomanivi 1323
Levuka
OVALAU
THITHIA I.
TUVUTHA I.
MALOLO I.
Vatukoula
Korovou
NAIRAI
NAYAU I.
Nadi
Namosi
Vunidawa
GAU
LAKEBA I.
Sigatoka
Lami
Nausori
Navua
Suva
SIGATOKA SAND DUNES NATIONAL PARK
BEQA
LAU GROUP
VATULELE
MOALA I.
KADAVU I.
TOTOYA I.
KABARA I.
MATUKU I.
FULAGA I.
OGEA LEVU
VATOA I.
ONO-I-LAU
PACIFIC OCEAN

Scale 1:7,194,000
1 inch equals approx. 114 miles
0   25   50   75   100   125 mi
0   50   100   150   200 km
Conformal Conic Projection

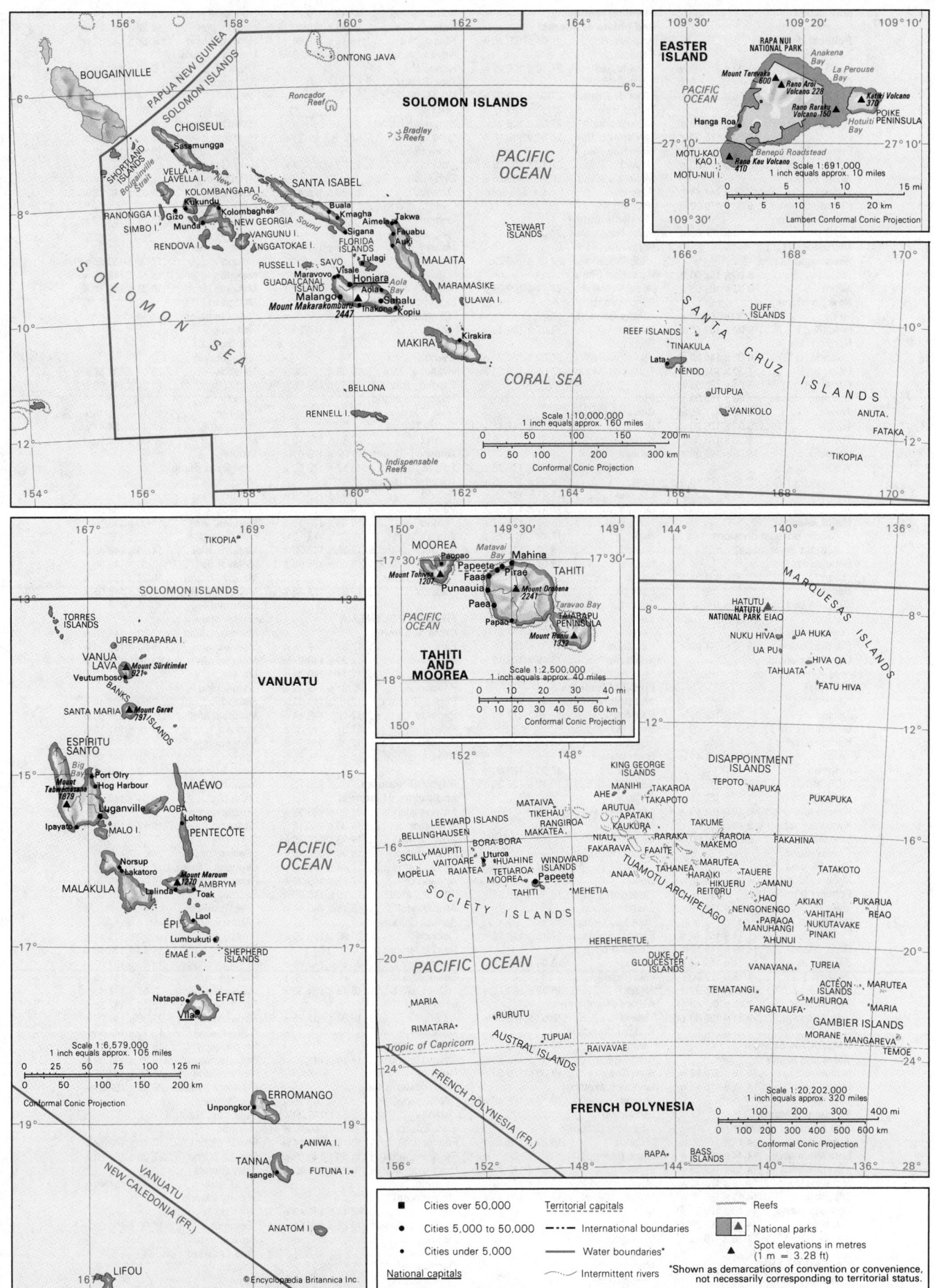

SOLOMON ISLANDS

BOUGAINVILLE

PAPUA NEW GUINEA

ONTONG JAVA

CHOISEUL

Sasamungga

SHORTLAND ISLANDS

VELLA LAVELLA I.

KOLOMBANGARA I.

Kukundu

RANONGGA I.

SIMBO I.

Gizo

Munda

NEW GEORGIA

VANGUNU I.

RENDOVA I.

NGGATOKAE I.

SANTA ISABEL

Buala

Kmagha

Takwa

Aimela

Sigana

Fauabu

Auki

FLORIDA ISLANDS

Tulagi

MALAITA

RUSSELL I.

Maravovo

Visale

Honiara

GUADALCANAL ISLAND

Malango

Aola

Aola Bay

Sahalu

Kopiu

MARAMASIKE

Mount Makarakomburu 2447

Inakona

ULAWA I.

Kirakira

MAKIRA

REEF ISLANDS

Lata

NENDO

TINAKULA

Bradley Reefs

Roncador Reef

STEWART ISLANDS

PACIFIC OCEAN

DUFF ISLANDS

SANTA CRUZ ISLANDS

UTUPUA

VANIKOLO

ANUTA

FATAKA

TIKOPIA

CORAL SEA

BELLONA

RENNELL I.

Indispensable Reefs

SOLOMON SEA

Scale 1:10,000,000
1 inch equals approx. 160 miles

0 50 100 150 200 mi
0 50 100 200 300 km

Conformal Conic Projection

EASTER ISLAND

RAPA NUI NATIONAL PARK

Anakena Bay

La Perouse Bay

Mount Terevaka ~600

Rano Aroi Volcano 228

Rano Raraku Volcano 150

Katiki Volcano 370

POIKE PENINSULA

Hotuiti Bay

Hanga Roa

PACIFIC OCEAN

MOTU-KAO KAO I.

Rano Kau Volcano 410

Benepú Roadstead

MOTU-NUI I.

Scale 1:691,000
1 inch equals approx. 10 miles

0 5 10 15 mi
0 5 10 20 km

Lambert Conformal Conic Projection

VANUATU

TIKOPIA

SOLOMON ISLANDS

TORRES ISLANDS

UREPARAPARA I.

VANUA LAVA

Mount Sürétiméat 921

Veutumboso

BANKS ISLANDS

SANTA MARIA

Mount Garet 797

ESPIRITU SANTO

Big Bay

Mount Tabwemasana 1879

Port Olry

Hog Harbour

Luganville

Ipayato

MALO I.

AOBA

MAÉWO

Loltong

PENTECÔTE

Norsup

Lakatoro

AMBRYM

Mount Maroum 1270

MALAKULA

Lalinda

Toak

ÉPI

Laol

Lumbukuti

ÉMAÉ I.

SHEPHERD ISLANDS

Natapao

ÉFATÉ

Vila

PACIFIC OCEAN

Scale 1:6,579,000
1 inch equals approx. 105 miles

0 25 50 75 100 125 mi
0 50 100 150 200 km

Conformal Conic Projection

ERROMANGO

Unpongkor

ANIWA I.

TANNA

Isangel

FUTUNA I.

ANATOM I.

NEW CALEDONIA (FR.)

VANUATU

LIFOU

© Encyclopædia Britannica Inc.

TAHITI AND MOOREA

MOOREA

Paopao

Matavai Bay

Mahina

Papeete

Faaa

Pirae

TAHITI

Mount Tohivea 1207

Punaauia

Paea

Mount Orohena 2241

Taravao Bay

Papao

TAIARAPU PENINSULA

Mount Roniu 1332

PACIFIC OCEAN

Scale 1:2,500,000
1 inch equals approx. 40 miles

0 10 20 30 40 mi
0 10 20 30 40 50 60 km

Conformal Conic Projection

FRENCH POLYNESIA

KING GEORGE ISLANDS

DISAPPOINTMENT ISLANDS

MANIHI

TAKAROA

TAKAPOTO

TEPOTO

NAPUKA

PUKAPUKA

MATAIVA

AHE

TIKEHAU

ARUTUA

APATAKI

KAUKURA

TAKUME

LEEWARD ISLANDS

BELLINGHAUSEN

RANGIROA

MAKATEA

NIAU

RARAKA

RAROIA

FAKAHINA

SCILLY

MAUPITI

BORA-BORA

FAKARAVA

FAAITE

MAKEMO

MARUTEA

TATAKOTO

MOPELIA

Uturoa

VAITOARE

HUAHINE

WINDWARD ISLANDS

TAHANEA

HARAIKI

TAUERE

AMANU

RAIATEA

TETIAROA

MOOREA

ANAA

HIKUERU

REITORU

AKIAKI

PUKARUA

TAHITI

Papeete

HAO

NENGONENGO

VAHITAHI

REAO

MEHETIA

PARAOA

NUKUTAVAKE

MANUHANGI

PINAKI

AHUNUI

HEREHERETUE

DUKE OF GLOUCESTER ISLANDS

VANAVANA

TUREIA

MARIA

TEMATANGI

ACTÉON ISLANDS

MARUTEA

MURUROA

RIMATARA

RURUTU

FANGATAUFA

MARIA

GAMBIER ISLANDS

MORANE

MANGAREVA

TUPUAI

AUSTRAL ISLANDS

RAIVAVAE

TEMOE

Tropic of Capricorn

FRENCH POLYNESIA (FR.)

RAPA

BASS ISLANDS

SOCIETY ISLANDS

TUAMOTU ARCHIPELAGO

MARQUESAS ISLANDS

HATUTU

HATUTU NATIONAL PARK

EIAO

NUKU HIVA

UA HUKA

UA PU

HIVA OA

TAHUATA

FATU HIVA

PACIFIC OCEAN

Scale 1:20,202,000
1 inch equals approx. 320 miles

0 100 200 300 400 mi
0 100 200 300 400 500 600 km

Conformal Conic Projection

■ Cities over 50,000

● Cities 5,000 to 50,000

• Cities under 5,000

National capitals

Territorial capitals

-·-·- International boundaries

——— Water boundaries*

~~~ Intermittent rivers

Reefs

National parks

▲ Spot elevations in metres
(1 m = 3.28 ft)

*Shown as demarcations of convention or convenience, not necessarily corresponding to territorial status.

Small offshore coral atoll at the eastern end of Guadalcanal Island, Solomon Islands.
© Michael McCoy/Australasian Nature Transparencies

from the basaltic volcanic islands of the central and eastern Pacific by deep ocean trenches along the eastern borders of Japan, the Marianas, New Guinea, Solomon Islands, Fiji, and New Zealand, a demarcation that is commonly called the Andesite Line. These continental islands, faulted and folded in mountainous arcs, tend to be higher and larger than those farther east and have rich soils that support almost every kind of vegetation. New Guinea, 1,500 miles long and with a maximum width of nearly 500 miles, is a good example. Its snowcapped mountains rise to about 16,400 feet (5,000 metres), its interior is dissected by high plateaus and extensive river systems, and its slopes and coastal margins contain dense forests and vast swamps.

High oceanic islands. Extensive volcanic mountain ranges in the central and eastern Pacific rise abruptly from the ocean deep, their cores of dense black basalt built up from lava flows from the fractured seafloor. Where summits stand in high relief above sea level, they represent most of the islands that constitute Polynesia and Micronesia. Small to intermediate in land area, nowhere do they match the extent of continental islands. Hawaii's snow-topped Mauna Kea reaches 13,796 feet, though most oceanic islands have peaks of somewhat less than 5,000 feet. Topography is extremely rugged, with sharp ridges, deep canyons, high cliffs, and waterfalls abounding. Human communities occupy the more congenial lower slopes, floodplains, and wide strands. The islands, rich in iron and magnesium oxides, are densely forested.

Low coral islands. Most Pacific islands are coral formations, although all rest on volcanic or other cores. In the shallow waters of the tropics, both continental and oceanic islands attract coral growth in the form of fringing reefs, partially submerged platforms of consolidated limestone, with coral organisms at the ocean edge feeding on materials carried in by waves and currents. Coral-building polyps and algae secrete calcium carbonate from seawater, forming skeletal frameworks that adhere to land surfaces or to the rock remains of coralline ancestors. Many islands have been gradually submerged through a combination of sinking, caused by geologic action, and flooding, caused by the melting of ice caps. As islands were flooded, coral growth continued outward, producing barrier reefs farther from shore and separated from it by a lagoon.

A coral atoll results when still further flooding reduces an island to a submarine condition. The usually irregular reef continues to build up in the warm shallows. It encircles a clear-surfaced lagoon of moderate depth and in time supports a number of islets, known locally as motu, built up from reef debris to 20 or 30 feet above sea level. Atolls exist in all shapes and sizes. Kwajalein Atoll in the Marshalls is the world's largest, being about 80 miles long and 20 miles wide, with a lagoon area of 655 square miles. Openings, or passages, which commonly occur on the leeward side of Pacific atolls, permit access to the lagoon by ocean shipping. The only source of fresh water is rain.

Successive elevations of an island above sea level by geologic action have created a variety of "raised" coral formations. The northern half of Guam, for example, is a coralline limestone plateau rising to 850 feet, while the mountains in the southern half of the island, formed by volcanic activity, reach elevations up to 1,300 feet. Nauru and Banaba (Ocean Island) are raised coral islands that stand at elevations of about 210 and 265 feet, respectively. They have deeper soil and a more adequate water supply than atoll islets.

Soils. Pacific island soils develop through the action of temperature, rainfall, and organic matter on the original rock materials. This process is further influenced by factors of time and land relief. Coral island soils are the least mature and are deficient in organic materials and low in fertility. The mineral-bearing soils of the continental islands are more complex and, being favoured by a longer period of weathering, are richer than those of the volcanic-based high islands. The most productive soils on high islands occur in the lower valley slopes, alluvial floodplains, and deltas, and in some instances are further enriched by

Coral atolls

© Nicholas DeVore III/Bruce Coleman Inc.

Volcanic peaks of Bora-Bora, a high volcanic island surrounded by a lagoon, Society Islands, French Polynesia.

volcanic ash deposits of recent age. Tropical temperatures and rainfall have produced laterite soils from which nutrients have been leached. These soils, of only moderate fertility, decline rapidly after two or three years of crop use. Fertilizers must then be added, or else the land must be abandoned to allow it to recover by natural processes.

Climate. To describe the climate as tropical and oceanic is to stress the influence of the lower latitudes and the tremendous expanse of the sea. Humidity and temperature tend to be high and are generally uniform throughout the year. Regional differentiation in climate is linked principally to rainfall patterns. Here, factors of altitude and longitude, as well as latitude, come into play as they relate to the various systems of air circulation prevailing in the Pacific.

Across the eastern and central Pacific, air currents, moving from the north and south toward the Equator, trend westward and form the northeast and southeast trade winds. These brisk winds bring light to moderate showers interspersed with brief downpours or clear skies. The windward sides of high islands are cloudier and wetter than the drier leeward coasts. Seasonal shifts in wind direction frequently presage stormy weather. Where the trade winds meet near the Equator lie the doldrums, a region often of little or no wind, considerable clouds, and high humidity. The trade winds merge or give way to the monsoon winds in the far western Pacific, where the alternate cooling and heating of continental Asia produces a seasonal reversal of winds. From about November to March, the northwest monsoon from Asia brings rain to the northerly slopes of the western Carolines, New Guinea, and the Solomons. In summer the southeast monsoon reverses the process.

Monsoon winds

Typhoons, or hurricanes, occur frequently in western Micronesia from July to November and are active south of the Equator from Australia to the Society Islands four to six months later. These winds of gale force are accompanied by torrential rains and high waves and cause extensive damage to crops and buildings, especially on low-lying coral islands. Atolls in the equatorial region, however, have suffered droughts lasting as long as two or three years. In 1982–83 the entire western Pacific was devastated by extreme aridity caused by a meteorological and oceanographic phenomenon known as El Niño, which at the same time caused extensive flooding in the easternmost parts of the Pacific Basin.

Plant and animal life. Most island vegetations reveal Asian ancestries stemming from Indonesia and New Guinea. Generic variety declines eastward across the Pacific, providing evidence that seeds and fruits carried by ocean currents, birds, winds, and island voyagers encountered mounting obstacles to acceptance. The easternmost islands were host to limited plant dispersal movement from South America. Plant adaptation to local differences in moisture, soil, salinity, and temperature resulted in countless new, endemic species. Plant introductions from other world sources during the past century have, however, markedly altered island vegetations.

The seacoast, or strand, vegetation is the most widespread of Pacific zonal types. Depending on the availability of moisture, this setting supports shrubs, herbs, woody vines, and trees that have a high tolerance for the salt spray that is borne by ocean winds. Mangrove thickets proliferate in brackish swamps. On coral islands coconut and pandanus trees flourish. Breadfruit, banana, and papaya may also be grown farther inland, as may marsh taro (*Cyrtosperma*), a root crop cultivated in pits dug to groundwater level and enriched with plant debris.

On high islands primary forests still survive in valley bottoms, on intermediate slopes, and on lowland plains. The ever-present rain forest is a community of huge trees that overlook smaller trees and shade-tolerant ferns, vines, and shrubs. Species differentiate enormously. Yam, taro (*Colocasia*), cassava (manioc), and sweet potato, in addition to those crops already noted, are important staples in high-island economies. Secondary forests and grasslands have replaced virgin forests destroyed by fire and by shifting cultivation. Grasslands are also associated with areas of poor soil and little rain, as on leeward slopes.

Bats, rats, and, in New Guinea, wallabies, flying opossums, and spiny anteaters were the only mammals to precede humans into the Pacific, after which pigs, dogs, poultry, goats, deer, and cattle were introduced. Most islands have some snakes and lizards, but crocodiles are restricted to the west. Seabirds, such as terns, frigates, albatrosses, petrels, and boobies, supplemented by migratory ducks, plovers, and curlews, are found almost everywhere. While oceanic islands support only a few land birds, New Guinea has unusual species such as the cockatoo, hornbill, bird of paradise, and cassowary.

Unusual bird species

The abundant marine life is infinitely valuable for human subsistence. Reefs and lagoons provide fish, lobsters, shrimps, clams, oysters, snails, eels, octopuses, and turtles. In deeper waters beyond the reefs are found skipjack and yellowfin tuna (which are fished commercially), swordfish, marlin, and many other sport fishes. Sharks predominate as predators. Schools of whales and porpoises are seen frequently at sea. Insects are the most numerous of island fauna; the more pestiferous include centipedes, cockroaches, lice, houseflies, and the malaria-carrying *Anopheles* mosquito, which exists in Melanesia from coastal New Guinea to Vanuatu. Scorpions are also found.

THE PEOPLE

Humans in the Pacific have had to adapt to island environments just as other species have done. The technologies and organizational systems introduced into the Pacific by migrants were established in habitats that varied from receptive to hostile. The earliest arrivals, as food-gathering peoples, probably provoked little disruption of the environment. Their successors, practiced in horticulture and skilled in sea transport, were more able to fashion and control local environmental conditions after their own customs. Later, Western practices, part of an advanced technology and civilization, threatened the balance of the inherently vulnerable island ecosystems.

Aboriginal groupings. Natives of the Pacific tend to identify themselves by their home island or their mother tongue, saying, for example, that they are from Nauru, or that they speak Fijian. Occasionally, however, they may invoke another, and larger, identity, claiming to be Polynesian, Micronesian, or Melanesian. As a geographic designation this representation has value, but as a mark of racial, linguistic, or cultural affiliation it is apt to be misleading. While Melanesians appear to be more Australoid and Micronesians more Mongoloid, with Polynesians demonstrating characteristics of both physical types, a great deal of racial intermixture has taken place throughout the Pacific since the first immigrants arrived in the southwestern islands. The linguistic pattern is also complex. Some valid generalizations about the three regions may nevertheless be made, although it must be remembered that overlap among the areas is common and that there are exceptions to every statement.

Generalizations about the traditional regions

Polynesia. Polynesians are the most homogeneous in speech, custom, and physical appearance, although western Polynesians (Samoans and Tongans) are moderately distinct from the rest. Accomplished as cultivators and fishermen, they have directed their principal energies to nonmaterial pursuits. Epic mythology, copious genealogies, sophisticated social etiquettes, hereditary aristocracies, and elaborated religious formality, with varying degrees of emphasis, characterized society in pre-European Polynesia. A kinship system that recognized the worth of both maternal and paternal family ties supported group solidarity in community enterprises. Secular leaders, regarded as lineal descendants of deified ancestors, served gods and humans alike. The social–religious–political hierarchies encouraged and rewarded aesthetic creativity in wood and stone sculpture, featherwork, tapa (barkcloth), and tattooing, according privileges to the artists commensurate with those accorded warriors, navigators, herbalists, and seers.

Micronesia. Eight or 10 cultural–linguistic areas in Micronesia attest to its greater heterogeneity. Palau, Yap, and the Mariana Islands, in western Micronesia, suggest affinities with Melanesia, Indonesia, and the Philippines. The customary siting of island farmsteads and hamlets near the shore reflects the prevailing interest in fishing, canoeing, and interisland trade. Except in Kiribati (the

Gilbert, Phoenix, and Line Islands), matrilineal clans and lineages, requiring marriage outside each group, influence property inheritance, succession to traditional titles, and intracommunity competition. Local political autonomy was formerly overshadowed by loose confederations and tribute allegiance in western Micronesia, as well as in Pohnpei, Kosrae, and the Marshall Islands, where class stratification is still observed. Indigenous religions lacked formality and were largely of personal or family concern. Art is mainly decorative and is manifest in mat work, shell ornaments, loom weaving, tattooing, and functionally crafted wood and shell artifacts.

Melanesia. This is a region of unending contrast. "Beach" populations, who maintain advantages from coastal trading and cultural exchanges, may be compared with more traditional and isolated "bush" populations in the interiors of the larger islands. Polynesian influence touches Fiji and a few outlying islands to the northwest. The massive extent of New Guinea, with its thousands of indigenous tribes, requires separate consideration.

Melanesians are all cultivators, with a penchant for pig raising. Descent groups, usually patrilineal, are the basis for community organization. In most Melanesian societies, leadership depends on the local "Big Man," who, aided by his many relatives, gains support within his own village and enhances his influence in others nearby by hosting more and bigger feasts than his rivals and amassing wealth through ceremonial exchanges of valuable goods. Opportunities for upward mobility are better for the sons of an established "Big Man," assuming they can prove themselves. Head-hunting and raiding of neighbouring tribes continue in the interior of New Guinea. The animistic religion of Melanesians, a mixture of magic, sorcery, totemism, and ancestor worship, is dominated by elaborate initiations, secret societies, and men's clubhouses. Although males dominate most cultural activities, the roles of women are substantial in certain religious and exchange systems. Art forms associated with these activities include dance masks, sculptured figures, and body scarification.

For a detailed treatment of these cultural areas, see below *Traditional cultures of the Pacific Islands.*

Interaction with Western societies. During almost five centuries of contact with, first, Europeans and, then, Americans and Asians, island societies fluctuated between change and disorganization on the one hand and stability and reintegration on the other. Relatively balanced ecosystems of prehistoric times were disrupted when islanders, reacting to the novelty and authority of Western civilization, redirected traditional skills to serve new economies and, under pressure from missions and alien governments, adopted practices and beliefs that were strange to them. From this initial confusion there emerged reasonably stabilized island societies that, while preserving the traditional ethos, reflected a fusion of specific elements from both cultures. European, American, and Asian residents continued to maintain their own cultural identities in social enclaves. Meanwhile, influence toward change was exercised by an increasing mixed-blood population, reflecting the needs of culturally marginal individuals.

The direct impact of World War II stimulated many island communities to seek greater participation in Western society. Their efforts were expressed in chiefly two ways. The first was in a proliferation of mystical cults. Occurring principally in Melanesia, where they are called cargo cults, these cults blended traditional and Christian elements in systems aimed at materialistic bounty, but they provided solutions largely in fantasy. The second, a more rational effort toward economic betterment and political nationalism, was promoted by both native and part-native persons, many of whom had been educated overseas and who lived in the more urbanized island centres. Opposed to assimilation, most islanders retained pride in their island origins and argued for more independent status within the structure of a westernized "Pacific way."

Killing epidemics of introduced diseases contributed to population decline until around 1900, when they were checked by modern medical treatment and health education. Many island populations almost trebled during the next five decades. Family planning programs and economic pressures have not been very effective in slowing the rate of population growth. Many islanders have migrated to the port towns and island capitals, reacting to overpopulation in the smaller outlying islands or, more often, seeking gainful employment or further education. The urban centres are built around business, school, hospital, mission, and administration facilities; government is the largest single employer.

In some island states more than half of the population live in the towns. Poor housing and sanitation, underemployment, scarcity of land for residential use, and decline of the extended family structure are common features of island urbanism. Alcoholism and crime are widespread, and suicide among young men has increased. Meanwhile, communities in the outer islands are less able to function, depleted as their populations are by the exodus of able-bodied adults who have left for the towns. The urban centres link the hinterland communities by sea and air transport and by radiotelephone networks; they also serve as a point of departure for overseas destinations where employment opportunities in the private sector are greater. Although most of those who migrate are unskilled, a significant number have technical and professional talents that are needed in the island centres, and their migration constitutes an undesirable drain on their communities.

Emigration to ports and overseas

THE ECONOMY

Agriculture and natural resources. Coconut products, including copra, from which oil is extracted, form the principal export from most islands. Agricultural production depends as much on native family enterprise as it does on plantation systems, which predominate in the larger islands. Perishable fruits, such as pineapples, bananas, and citrus fruits, require markets close at hand unless they are locally processed or can be assured of prompt delivery to overseas destinations. Sugar, exported mainly from Hawaii and Fiji, requires careful management, costly machinery, and specialized labour. Experiments in growing coffee, cacao, spices, and other cash crops have been undertaken to stimulate diversification and to minimize the hazards of a one-crop economy. Timber and wood by-products are processed commercially on some islands.

Marine resources, although almost unlimited, require skilled labour and capital facilities for commercial exploitation. Deep-sea fishing, mostly for tuna, is conducted throughout the Pacific, mainly by Korean, Taiwanese, Japanese, and American fishing fleets. Canneries employing islanders are operated in American Samoa, Fiji, and Solomon Islands. Local cooperatives have been successful in marketing fresh fish.

Fiji, Papua New Guinea, Irian Jaya (a province of Indonesia comprising the western half of the island of New

Bob and Ira Spring

Open-pit nickel mine on mainland New Caledonia.

Guinea and its offshore islands), and Solomon Islands have profited from either gold or gold and copper discoveries, and New Caledonia is rich in nickel ores. Oil reserves and their exploitation are restricted to Irian Jaya, although prospecting in Papua New Guinea and Solomon Islands is encouraging. Natural phosphates on Nauru continue to be mined, but those on Banaba were depleted in 1979. In 1979 the South Pacific Forum, an organization of independent and self-governing countries, established the Forum Fisheries Agency (FFA) to facilitate mutual cooperation and assistance in fisheries and policing the 200-nautical-mile Exclusive Economic Zone (EEZ) of each member state. This group of 16 entities in 1987 concluded a multilateral treaty with the United States, whereby the United States agreed to pay $60,000,000 in license fees and assistance to the fishing industry in return for permission for American fishing fleets to operate in the EEZs of the FFA member states. The latter are free to negotiate further agreements with other nations on the Pacific Rim.

Trade. Pacific islanders, as producers of agricultural, marine, and mineral commodities, face problems of market demand, labour supply, management skills, and transport that restrict them to an insignificant role in world export trade. Neither do the small, scattered populations present an attractive consumer market to overseas entrepreneurs. The combination of limited exportable products, heavy dependency on food imports, high cost of fuel imports, and overreliance on foreign aid makes each island state's economy extremely vulnerable.

Economic handicaps

More than half of the exports from the Pacific Islands are sent to Japan, the United States, Australia, New Zealand, and members of the European Economic Community (EEC). Imports are received mainly from the United States, Australia, New Zealand, France, Japan, and Singapore. Almost all island groups import far more, in dollar amounts, than they export. External financial aid for economic development is received primarily from Australia, New Zealand, the United States (for Guam, American Samoa, and the U.S. interests in Micronesia), France (for New Caledonia, Wallis and Futuna, and French Polynesia), and from international organizations (the Asian Development Bank, the United Nations Development Programme, and the European Economic Community). Most grants-in-aid are made on a bilateral basis.

In the 1970s tourism opened up new employment opportunities and sources of revenue. By 1980 Guam, the Northern Marianas, Fiji, French Polynesia, and New Caledonia, among others, had followed Hawaii's earlier lead in attracting visitors by air and sea to enjoy the tropical scenery, handicrafts, and friendly hospitality of the Pacific Islands. Australians made up the largest group of tourists traveling to destinations south of the Equator, while Japanese made up the majority of vacationers to the north. However, the increasing ability of international airlines to bypass midway island stops, the devastation of hotel facilities by more frequent hurricanes, the fluctuating currency values in Pacific Rim countries, and political disorders in Fiji and New Caledonia slowed the growth of the tourist industry. In some cases island labour was mostly restricted to the menial services, and management posts and industry profits were more often enjoyed by expatriate personnel and foreign-based corporations. The degree of government and private involvement and investment in tourist accommodations and entertainment varied with each island state. Some island populations, indeed, were more concerned with safeguarding their traditional cultures than deriving income from their commercialization.

Transportation and communication. Most islanders, by resorting to some combination of road, canoe, motorboat, interisland freighter, local air service, or international airline, can travel within a week or two to such distant cities as Sydney, Auckland, San Francisco, Vancouver, Tokyo, Manila, Hong Kong, or Singapore. Because of infrequent or irregular travel schedules, inhabitants of more remote islands may need two months or more to make such a journey. More than a score of shipping and airline companies offer carriers to move outbound and inbound cargo and passengers through such island centres as Guam, Port Moresby, Honiara, Nouméa, Suva, Pago Pago, Papeete,

and Honolulu. This readier access, in both directions, has developed largely because islanders have demanded better facilities for travel and commercial expansion.

Radio, radiotelephone, cable, and satellite services have greatly improved communications. Two-way radio transmission is used, even in distant islands, to inform central authorities of emergencies and other critical needs. Radio broadcasts and news publications in English, French, and indigenous languages keep the island public informed about local and world events. Commercial television or videotaped programs from the metropolitan nations are available in urbanized centres.

Communications systems

ADMINISTRATIVE INSTITUTIONS

By the mid-20th century overpopulation in a region of fragmented land areas, widely scattered communities, poor communications, inadequate resources, and rising costs of living posed a fundamental dilemma. Political responsibility for the situation rested largely with the five metropolitan nations (Australia, France, New Zealand, the United Kingdom, and the United States) administering the possessions, protectorates, and trusteeships that perpetuated a colonial heritage that was no longer popular. The amelioration of social and economic conditions seemed to await changes in the political environment, while the question of the five nations' willingness to share their territorial interests with the emerging native elites remained undecided.

Changing administrations. Two United Nations trust territories were the first to achieve sovereignty as independent nations—Western Samoa in 1962 and Nauru in 1968. The first continued to rely on New Zealand in foreign affairs, while Nauru ended its trusteeship ties with Australia, New Zealand, and the United Kingdom. New Zealand, a Commonwealth member with a self-conscious Maori Polynesian population surviving inside its borders, continued an active relationship with other Polynesian groups—the Cook Islands, Niue, and Tokelau. Cook Islanders in 1965 and Niueans in 1974 became self-governing in free association with New Zealand, from which they required only support in certain aspects of external affairs and financial aid.

United Nations trust territories

In 1975 Australia, a Commonwealth country with territorial interests in Melanesia, relinquished its hold on Papua, which it had acquired from Great Britain in 1906, and its trusteeship in northeastern New Guinea, which the United Nations had granted in 1946. The fully independent nation of Papua New Guinea was thereby created. British Fiji and Tonga gained their independence from the United Kingdom in 1970. Other British colonies achieved freedom in subsequent years—the Solomon Islands in 1978; the Ellice Islands, renamed Tuvalu, also in 1978; the Gilbert Islands in 1979, which then became Kiribati; and the New Hebrides, which Britain administered jointly with France until 1980, when the island group assumed nationhood as Vanuatu.

France is represented in the Pacific by three overseas territories—French Polynesia, New Caledonia, and Wallis and Futuna. Each of these territories enjoys a degree of local autonomy and is represented in the French parliament by elected delegates. Popular movements toward greater self-government or independence are active in both French Polynesia and New Caledonia.

The United States dominates the Pacific region north of the Equator. Hawaii, formerly a territory, became the 50th U.S. state in 1959. Other U.S. territories are Guam and American (Eastern) Samoa, both of which have been under civilian administration since 1950–51, after a half-century of naval rule. The Trust Territory of the Pacific Islands, covering much of Micronesia, was granted to the United States in 1947 as a strategic-area trusteeship. Micronesians in the trust islands have negotiated in separate groups with the United States about their status. In 1975 the Northern Mariana Islands elected commonwealth status with the United States, and the commonwealth took partial effect in 1976. A constitution became effective two years later. Three other political entities have emerged in the remaining islands—the Republic of Palau (Belau), the Federated States of Micronesia (Kosrae, Pohnpei, Truk, and Yap), and the Republic of the Marshall Islands. Constitutional governments were established in the Federated States of Micronesia and the Marshall Islands in 1979, and Palau followed suit in 1981. Each of these has negotiated a Compact of Free Association with the United States, which in 1986 proclaimed that the trusteeship was terminated for the Republic of the Marshall Islands, the Federated States of Micronesia, and the Commonwealth of the Northern Mariana Islands. The U.S. government notified the United Nations Security Council of this action, but by the end of 1987 no response had come from the council. Neither, by that date, had the compact with the Republic of Palau been approved by the required majority of Palauans.

Two Pacific island territories are politically peripheral to contemporary Oceania. Western New Guinea, which was formerly a part of the Dutch East Indies, became a province of Indonesia in 1963 and was called Irian Barat until 1973, when it was renamed Irian Jaya. Easter Island has been a dependency of Chile since 1888, and development of its Polynesian population is strongly oriented toward the interests of Chile.

Regional cooperation. The average Pacific island state is too small and limited in human and natural resources to function well on the world stage and has sought the advantages of joint action through regional cooperation among governments, churches, educational institutions, businesses, workers' unions, and cultural organizations. The total number of regional bodies in the Pacific Islands is over 200. The first significant attempt at regional cooperation came in 1947, when the major powers that had dependencies in the region agreed to form the South Pacific Commission (SPC) to provide research and consultative services in health, social, and economic development to island governments. Members now include the five metropolitan powers—Australia, France, the United Kingdom, New Zealand, and the United States—and 22 island states and dependent territories.

The South Pacific Commission

Proposals to add a political dimension to the SPC's activities have never been approved, and by the mid-1980s its image as a metropolitan body had seriously weakened its impact in the region. In part to meet this political need, the South Pacific Forum was organized in 1971 by leaders of the independent and self-governing island countries, including Australia and New Zealand; it was essentially an association of Pacific states in the British Commonwealth. In 1973 the forum established the South Pacific Bureau for Economic Cooperation (SPEC) to promote regional alliances in trade, shipping and air services, telecommunications, and external aid. The SPEC has also provided liaison with other regional organizations, such as the EEC and the United Nations Economic and Social Commission for Asia and the Pacific. The forum has taken strong positions in support of the Law of the Sea and its 200-nautical-mile Exclusive Economic Zone concept and of the acceleration of the decolonization process in French Polynesia and New Caledonia, and in 1985 at its annual meeting in Rarotonga its members adopted the South Pacific Nuclear Free Zone Treaty.

By the late 1970s Australia and New Zealand had become the primary sources of regional aid, while France and the United States pursued their strategic interests in the Pacific. Regional cooperation has depended to a great extent on the pragmatic advantages to be gained by the smaller independent states made vulnerable by limited resources.

For coverage of related topics in the *Macropædia* and *Micropædia*, see the *Propædia*, sections 967 and 977.

(L.E.M.)

History and cultural development

The prehistory of the Pacific Islands, the period before written materials begin, extends back at least 33,000 years, a date provided in 1985 by sites in the Bismarck Archipelago. It is probable that human settlement significantly antedates the limit of radiocarbon determination of 40,000 years. Migration extended into the 2nd millennium AD and led to the populating of every habitable island. Since the arrival of Europeans in the early 16th century, the prehistoric world has been transformed, to varying

extents, at first by contact with passing explorers and then, from the late 18th century, by the influence of more permanent visitors: castaways, beachcombers, missionaries, and traders. In the 19th and 20th centuries settlers, labourers and other immigrant communities (predominantly Indian and Chinese), and European administrators arrived. Missionaries, settlers, and immigrants remain significant segments of the population in the islands today, even though European governments, with the exception of the French, have withdrawn from the region.

Both the prehistorical and historical periods present problems in the evidence of human activity. Archaeology has provided dates for the earliest settlement, but, until more sites are uncovered, sampling error makes certainty difficult. Linguistics, using a chronology of sound changes, traces the time and place of dispersion of language groups; but many of the languages of Oceania are as yet unstudied and unclassified. Genetics, using the distribution of leukocyte antigens in present blood-group samples, can establish, between contemporary human groups, connections that reveal past migrations, but systematic sampling has not yet been carried out. So, although the broad picture seems clear, much detail has yet to be filled in.

The period of Oceanic history for which documentary evidence is available also presents difficulties. The documents are chiefly of European origin and are, therefore, the products of people who may not accurately have recorded a culture different from their own—a culture they perceived and understood only imperfectly. This distortion can be corrected to some extent by using the findings of social anthropology and the oral traditions of the Pacific island people, but these sources are difficult because, by definition, they are contemporary. They may not describe the past accurately because they serve contemporary purposes; they do not record the past for its own sake. But the main historiographic problem of Oceania is its diversity. Some 10,000 islands scattered across 500,000 square miles of ocean, a variety of cultures, hundreds of mutually unintelligible languages, and diverse historical experiences make it hard to generalize.

The distortion of later Oceanic history

PREHISTORIC TIMES AND THE PROLIFERATION OF CULTURE

The influence of physical geography. The physical diversity means that contact between islands has never been easy because of the distances involved; it also means that the physical environment is not only isolated but varied. The large continental islands of Melanesia—such as New Guinea, New Caledonia, and Viti Levu (Great Fiji)—have a different physical basis of life and a wide variation in climate and fertility; moreover, their rugged terrain has made for social isolation. The smaller volcanic high islands, such as Samoa and Tahiti, have greater homogeneity and are very fertile, supporting life well above the subsistence level. The coral atolls, the low islands of Oceania, support a narrower range of vegetation; they are

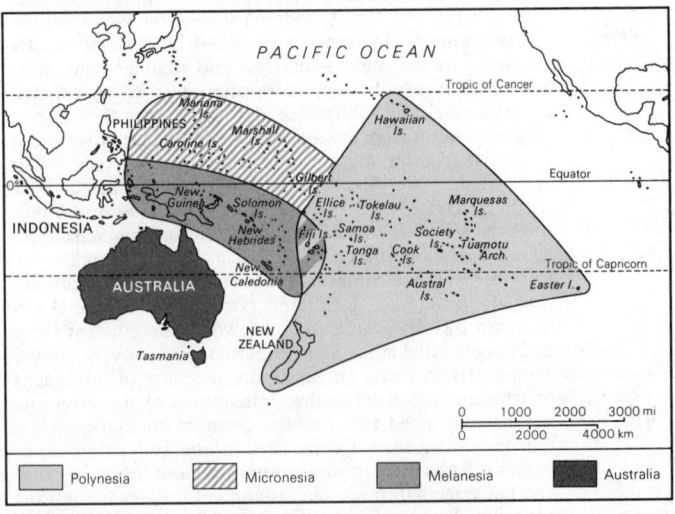

The culture areas of the Pacific.

more exposed to bad weather and support an existence closer to subsistence, except for the rich marine life in the lagoons.

Physical environment does not determine the kind of society that exists, but it does set limits to it. The large islands of Melanesia produce marked differences between people of the coast and those of the interior. Their long coastlines have acted as a filter for many different arrivals in Oceania. The valleys have perpetuated differences. Thus Melanesia is characterized by many small groups of people, divided from each other by language and custom. Political and social organization has been small in scale. The margin above subsistence has not been great enough to allow for elaborate ceremonial. The high volcanic islands of Polynesia offered no such barriers to social and political unity. Their fertility allowed the development of elaborate social, religious, and political ceremonial. The low islands also allowed homogeneity and wide social groupings, but their land resources offered no great margin for ceremonial life. These contrasts within Oceania were obvious to early European visitors, but they conceal a similarity: whether small, with leadership a matter of acquiring influence rather than hereditary position, or larger, with chiefs surrounded with awe and reverence, Oceanic societies all rested on the principle of reciprocity. Every gift or service had to be returned.

Origins of Oceanic peoples. Jules-Sébastien-César Dumont d'Urville, an early 19th-century French navigator and explorer, classified the islanders as Melanesian, Micronesian, and Polynesian. The apparent differences among the islanders were regarded as evidence of separate waves of ethnically different people out of Southeast Asia (a discredited variant theory traced the Polynesians to South America). Recent research suggests that the differences arose within the islands themselves, through the intermixture of an original settlement of non-Austronesian-language speakers from Southeast Asia with a later wave of Austronesian speakers. The earlier wave of settlement occurred in Melanesia at least 33,000 years ago and probably, since New Guinea and Australia were then linked by land, at dates contemporaneous with Australian dates of settlement, extending back to the limit of radiocarbon determination of 40,000 years. Secure dates in the interior of New Guinea approach 30,000 years ago.

The later Austronesian speakers, who are associated with the pottery called Lapita ware (from the site at which it was first discovered in New Caledonia), established themselves in the Bismarck Archipelago about 4,000 years ago and then spread to Fiji, Tonga, and Samoa, which have been regarded as the Polynesian homeland. They then dispersed to Micronesia and eastern Polynesia. New evidence, however, has led to disagreement among prehistorians about the Lapita complex: it may have arrived in Fiji with a later wave of seafaring immigrants. There is also disagreement about the speed with which the Lapita culture, distinctively linked with the Polynesians, moved from Southeast Asia through Melanesia into Fiji and thence to eastern Polynesia; the theory of rapid spread has been challenged on the basis of the length of time needed for a Polynesian homeland to develop in the Fiji-Samoa-Tonga region. Nevertheless, the known evidence of the Lapita culture outside the Bismarcks is dated after 3,500 years ago. In Fiji and western Polynesia the date is before 1000 BC; in eastern Polynesia it is about 500 BC. Allowing for new evidence to appear and for arguments as to its significance, there are still grounds for supposing that, from a Polynesian homeland region (Fiji-Samoa-Tonga), eastern Polynesia was settled by the Lapita culture bearers. It is possible that the Marquesas were settled as early as the 2nd century BC, rather than AD 300, a date at which settlements may have occurred in Hawaii. The Society Islands were occupied by at least the 9th century AD.

DEVELOPMENT OF DISTINCTIVE CULTURES

Oceanic societies, at the time of European discovery, were Neolithic. They had developed a technology based on stone, bone, and shell; they cultivated tubers and tree fruits, all of which were of Southeast Asian origin, with the exception of the sweet potato, which derives from South America and which culture had spread through most of Polynesia in pre-European times but only marginally into Melanesia. This Neolithic cultivation was associated with three domesticated animals: the pig, dog, and chicken, also of Asian ancestry. The coastal people had developed techniques of fishing and considerable skills as sailors; navigation between the closer islands was well-developed. Some skills were lost: pottery, for example, disappeared in the Samoas and the Marquesas shortly after initial settlement. And with the control of the environment that Oceanic technology offered, there is evidence of overpopulation, settlement spreading into less-favoured areas of the islands and being fortified, as in the Marquesas. (For a further discussion of the indigenous cultures, see below *Traditional cultures of the Pacific Islands.*)

THE PERIOD OF EUROPEAN EXPLORATION

The 16th and 17th centuries. The Oceanic world was not a static one, but changes were slow compared with those that attended European discovery. Vasco Núñez de Balboa was the first European to sight the Pacific, in 1513; seven years later Ferdinand Magellan rounded South America and sailed across the ocean, missing the main island groups but probably encountering Pukapuka in the Tuamotu Islands and Guam. After his death in the Philippines, his expedition encountered some of the Carolines. These northern islands were further explored by the Spaniards as they established a galley trade between Manila and Acapulco. The next major Spanish discoveries were made by Álvaro de Mendaña de Neira and Pedro Fernández de Quirós. In 1567 the former set out from Peru to discover the great southern continent that was believed to exist in the South Pacific. He found the Solomons but failed to find them again on his second journey, during which he died. In 1606 his chief pilot, Quirós, after finding part of the Tuamotu Archipelago, found the northern Cooks, Tikopia, and the New Hebrides. One of his companions, Váez de Torres, found southeastern New Guinea and then the strait (later named for him) between that island and Australia, although the discovery was unknown to later sailors. These Spanish expeditions were motivated by the search for riches, by zeal to extend religion, and, in the case of Quirós, by an interest in discovery for its own sake. But with the voyage of Váez de Torres, the Spanish effort was ended.

Thereafter, the Dutch, who were already established in Indonesia, entered the Pacific. They too looked for a southern continent. In 1615–16 the Dutch navigator Jacques Le Maire came from the east through the Tuamotus to find Tonga, New Ireland, and New Hanover. In 1642 Abel Janszoon Tasman, sailing from Batavia (now Jakarta), the Dutch headquarters in the East Indies, saw New Zealand, Tonga, some of the Fijis, and New Britain. The Dutch were primarily interested in commerce; they found none. Tasman thought that New Zealand was part of the great southern continent. The effect of these visitors on Oceania was transitory. They stayed for periods of at most a few months. Their contacts with the islanders were those of simple barter, but the demands they made upon food supplies often caused hostilities in which some European and many islanders' lives were lost, as on Guadalcanal and in the Marquesas during Mendaña's visits.

The 18th century. During the early 18th century the extent of Oceania was further revealed. The English pirate William Dampier visited New Hanover, New Britain, and New Ireland in command of a Royal Navy ship. Dampier was the forerunner of scientific exploration, and he proved that those islands were separated from each other and from Australia. In 1722 the Dutch admiral Jacob Roggeveen crossed the Pacific from east to west on a voyage of exploration that also had commercial objects. He found Easter Island, more of the Tuamotu Archipelago, the northern islands of the Society group, and some of the Samoan islands. These voyages were not essentially different from earlier ones, but they foreshadowed the scientific interest of the later 18th century. The execution of that interest was delayed by European wars. But in 1765 the English admiral John Byron (grandfather of the poet), who was sent by the British Admiralty in search of the supposed

Sighting by Balboa

southern continent, found more of the Tuamotus and the southern Gilberts. In 1767 Samuel Wallis and Philip Carteret followed, but their ships were separated as they entered the Pacific. Wallis found Tahiti, more of the Tuamotus, and the Society Islands, while Carteret found Pitcairn and rediscovered the Solomons of Mendaña, although he did not so identify them. This was left to the French following Louis-Antoine de Bougainville's visit in 1768, during which he also found some of the New Hebrides and Rossel Island in the Louisiade Archipelago.

The explorers contributed greatly to Europe's knowledge of the Pacific. Dampier's *A New Voyage Round the World* and Bougainville's description of the "noble savage" in Tahiti were particularly influential. The interest their journeys created was in part responsible for the instructions given to the greatest of all 18th-century explorers of Oceania, James Cook. After three voyages he left others little to do but fill in occasional details of Oceania. Cook was sent in 1769 to observe the transit of Venus at Tahiti and then to search for the great southern continent. Cook found some of the Society Islands, but he also circumnavigated New Zealand, and he defined the limits of eastern Australia. During his second voyage (1772–75), he proved that there was no southern continent, but he also made further discoveries in Oceania: in the Tuamotus, the Cooks, the Marquesas, Fiji, New Caledonia, the New Hebrides, and Norfolk Island. His third voyage (1776–79) was mainly concerned with the North Pacific, during which he found some of the Tongan group, Christmas Island, and Hawaii. He had completed the main work of discovery with an exactitude thitherto unknown. Although his contacts with islanders were not in essence different from those of his predecessors, his relations with them were nevertheless more prolonged and more humane. And his exploration of eastern Australia, through the account of his naturalist, Joseph Banks, was of great importance in Oceania, for it led to European settlement close to the islands.

Importance of Cook's travels

EARLY EUROPEAN SETTLEMENT

Itinerants. With the establishment in 1788 of the Australian settlement, Oceania became a source of supply. In 1793 pigs from Tahiti were landed at Sydney, and until 1826 the trade, although subject to fluctuations due to the competition of other cargoes and Tahitian wares, was important. The competition among Europeans for sandalwood, pearl shell, and bêche-de-mer (sea cucumber), valuable cargoes that attracted ships from the Australian colony, further involved Oceania with the European world. In 1804 sandalwood was found in Fiji, and for the next 10 years it attracted European traders. The sealing industry drew seal hunters to New Zealand, and fur traders, in the 1790s, wintered in Hawaii. All of these contacts began to affect Oceanic societies because they were sustained and prolonged. Together with the castaways and beachcombers who had begun to live in the islands from the days of first European contact and who increased in numbers with commercial shipping, these European contacts began to transform Oceania. Castaways, such as HMS *Bounty* mutineers who went to Tahiti in 1789, began to alter the political state of the islands they lived in by supporting with their muskets the chiefs who befriended them.

The Bounty mutineers

Missionary activity. Such Europeans had an important effect, but they were dependent upon the people they lived with for their survival. Very different were the missionaries, who traveled to Oceania with the deliberate intention of changing Oceanic society. In 1797 the London Missionary Society (LMS), now the Congregational Council for World Mission, sent a party to Tahiti. After some vicissitudes the missionaries converted the chief Pomare II, who controlled the area of Matavai Bay, where Europeans had called since Wallis' discovery. The LMS failed in its first attempts in Tonga and the Marquesas, although it was more successful in Huahine, the Tuamotus, the Cook Islands, and later in Samoa. Other missionary societies followed. In 1822 the Methodists began to work in Tonga; in 1835 they went to Fiji. In the 1840s Roman Catholic missionaries began working in New Caledonia, and the Church of England began to penetrate into Oceania from New Zealand. These missionaries encountered societies in Polynesia that already had a problem of law and order from the influence of European beachcombers and traders. Its solution was to create missionary kingdoms, in the case of British missionaries, or the establishment of direct political control, in the case of the French.

In Tahiti, Hawaii, and Tonga, native chiefs whose power was established by their access to European arms and support not only became kings but took missionary advisers and missionary-designed codes of law. In 1819 Pomare II of Tahiti promulgated such a code. In Tonga, Taufa'ahau took the name of George in 1833, and in 1845, when he took the Tongan title of Tu'i Kanokupolu, he became "king" of Tonga; in 1862, under the influence of the Rev. Shirley Baker, he adopted a constitution. By attempting to enforce a scriptural code of law, these missionary kingdoms were an answer to the problems of European lawlessness in the islands. If the missionaries could not prevent the sale of arms, they could at least make sure that these passed into the hands of friendly chiefs. But the authority of these "kings" was challenged from two sides. By becoming Christian they had cut themselves off from the mana (a Polynesian religious concept sometimes described as an all-pervasive energy) that came from the old gods, and this produced nativist reactions. In Tahiti there was a revolt against the new Christian order by supporters of the old ways in 1830; in Tonga there was a similar reaction in 1831. In Samoa, where the holder of the Malietoa (district chief) title had embraced Christianity from Tahitian missionaries, there were heretical movements. If traditional beliefs thus resisted the chiefs and their missionary supporters, the European traders also resisted the political authority of the kings. Dissidents and heretics looked to these Europeans for leadership, and these Europeans looked to their own national governments for protection.

Missionary kingdoms

In Melanesia the story is somewhat different. In Fiji the missionaries who landed in 1835, accompanied by an envoy from George of Tonga, made no headway with the rising chief Cakobau, who was not converted until 1854, when his fortunes were at a low ebb and he needed Tongan support. Elsewhere in Melanesia, the absence of chiefs meant that missionary work had to be conducted with small groups of people and repeated every few miles. There was no wholesale conversion of the kind that had happened in Polynesia. The attempt of the LMS in the New Hebrides in the 1840s came to nothing. The Anglican Melanesian mission in the Solomons made slow progress in the 1850s. In New Guinea, mission work, divided into four spheres of influence in Papua, did not begin systematically until the 1870s. Micronesia was a backwater. The Spaniards had established missionaries in the Marianas in 1668, but the missionaries in the Carolines were killed in 1733. The main effort came from the Hawaiian Evangelical Mission in the 1850s. The general effect of mission activity was, nevertheless, the same as it was in Polynesia. It dissolved the old ties of society by attacking the supernatural sanctions that supported leadership and social mores. It altered the political structure of Oceanic societies. It incidentally introduced both European goods and the desire for them. The missionaries themselves acted as intermediaries between Oceanic societies and other Europeans—as political advisers, as agents, and as interpreters.

Growth of trading communities. Beachcombers and castaways preceded missionaries in many of the islands, but the growth of trading communities was in part the result of the missionaries' work in restraining native violence. Those traders were initially pork traders in Tahiti, but European captains followed valuable cargoes from island to island. When the supply of sandalwood was depleted in Fiji by 1813, the traders then found it in Hawaii in the 1820s, in the New Hebrides in 1825, and in New Caledonia in 1840. Pearl shell attracted traders to the Tuamotus in 1807. The sandalwood trade declined as supplies were exhausted. Pearling declined as the native inhabitants took reprisals for the atrocities that had accompanied both trades. The demands of the Oceanians also changed the character of trade. Once native polities were established, the demand for muskets fell off; under missionary influence, the demand for alcohol was limited.

What the islanders now wanted was clothing and hardware. The exchange traders were not guilty of the cruelties that those looking for sandalwood or pearls were apt to perpetrate, and exchange trading encouraged the growth of resident agents in the islands, a development that met the needs of the whalers who came ashore to refit their vessels. After 1840 it also met the needs of the staple trade of the islands—coconut oil, used for soap and candles. Copra trading, from which the oil came, became the mainstay of European trade because even islands that had no other resources had coconut palms.

European trade centres

Such commerce promoted the growth of the port towns and of resident trading communities. Papeete in Tahiti, Apia in Samoa, and Levuka in Fiji became European centres, including not only respectable traders but also lawless men who might be escaped convicts from New South Wales (Australia) or others escaping from the rules of settled societies. These were frontier towns and could be regulated only with difficulty by native kings or by visiting European captains.

Establishment of plantation societies. The problem became more urgent with the advent of permanent European settlers. In Fiji, for example, after Cakobau's first offer to cede the islands to Great Britain in 1858, Europeans arrived to establish plantations, at first of coconuts, then, during the U.S. Civil War, of cotton, and, afterward, of sugar. The development in Samoa was similar. But planters needed land on a much larger scale than traders, and they needed labour in much greater quantities to work the plantations. Both land sales and labour recruitment caused friction, for "ownership" was not an Oceanic concept; thus, land titles were disputed or resented, and the recruitment of labour often caused the breakup of traditional societies if too many males left their communities and the creation of immigrant labour communities if they did not. By 1870 there were 2,000 such permanent European residents in Fiji. Politically the settlers had an interest in stability, and economically they needed security of title to land and a supply of labour. Neither requirement was satisfied by the missionary kingdoms. Nor was it satisfied by native governments that were not guided by missionaries. In Tahiti, Tonga, Samoa, and Fiji no native authority was able to keep order in the novel circumstances created by European enterprise; in any case, the native kings were themselves open to challenge within their own societies. Pomare II encountered revolt in Tahiti, Samoan politics were always a matter of rivalry between chiefs, and Cakobau's government was threatened by the Tongan chief Ma'afu, who had established his own confederacy in the Lau Islands of the Fiji group.

COLONIAL RULE

Involvement of foreign governments. Eventually the unstable internal conditions in the Pacific began to draw in European governments, all of which acknowledged some responsibility for the protection of their nationals and their property. The French government was the first to intervene, after the expulsion of two Roman Catholic missionaries from Tahiti in 1836. In the same year two more were deported from Hawaii. In 1839 the Archbishop of Chalcedon suggested regular association between the Roman Catholic missions and the French navy, but the French government was also aware of the need for a good naval station for the fleet and for French commerce and for a place of penal settlement. Abel DuPetit-Thouars thus took possession of Tuahata and the southeast Marquesas in 1842 and in the same year persuaded the Tahitians to ask for a French protectorate, which was formally granted in 1843. In 1853 the presence of French missionaries in New Caledonia led to French annexation, possibly for fear of British action, certainly to establish a penal colony (to which convicts were transported until 1897). Other European nations intervened for different reasons. In 1857 August Unshelm, as agent for J.C. Godeffroy and Son, set up the company's depot at Apia, and Samoa became the greatest trading centre in the islands; and even when Godeffroy failed in 1879, the Deutsche Handel und Plantagengesellschaft (German Trading and Plantation Company) took over, and Samoa remained the favourite colony

Naval stations and penal colonies

of the colonial party in German politics. British nationals had trading and plantation interests in the islands; to give some protection to these interests, the British government had appointed consuls to those islands governed by recognizable rulers, but their powers to maintain order were limited and, except for the visits of warships, unenforceable. The United States also appointed consuls.

The rivalry between these officers and between European entrepreneurs, and the involvement of both in the internal politics of Oceanic societies, merely emphasized to metropolitan governments the disordered condition of the islands. In Tahiti the problem was resolved by French annexation. In Samoa, after a tripartite supervision set up by the Samoa Act of 1889 came to grief in European rivalries and Samoan factionalism over chieftainships, an agreement of 1899 divided the Samoa group between Germany and the United States; Britain received compensation elsewhere. Britain's main concern was in fact with the activity of its nationals: in Fiji, where it accepted the offer of cession of 1874, it did so primarily because native authority had broken down. But Britain also had been concerned with the labour trade by which the Queensland (Australia) plantations took islanders, who were sometimes recruited under doubtful or brutal conditions. In the 1860s this trade flourished in the New Hebrides, and violence there led the missionaries to protest. Then the labour trade moved north to the Solomons, where again there was violence, including the murder of the Anglican bishop in the Santa Cruz group, from which five men had been taken by recruiters. The British solution was the Western Pacific Order in Council (1877), which empowered the governor of Fiji to exercise authority over British nationals and vessels in a wide area of the western Pacific. The problem still remained, however, of non-British nationals in islands that had neither native kings nor European governors, especially those of Melanesia.

European government, like both mission and commercial enterprise, had been slower to penetrate Melanesia. Missionary activity did not begin in New Guinea until 1873. There was not much labour recruiting. The first main activity was the gold rush of 1877, but German traders had arrived on the northern coast in 1873, followed by the firm of Hernsheim (general trade) in 1875. Such foreign interest produced a demand in the Australian colonies for annexation for reasons quite unconnected with the internal situation in the islands. German interests were marked in Micronesia, French in the New Hebrides. A number of groups in Australia also looked on New Guinea as a rich possession. But the British government, notwithstanding Queensland's abortive attempt at annexation in 1883, would not annex unless the Australian colonies paid the cost of administration, the same argument it was applying to New Zealand's interest in the Cook Islands. When the Australian colonies agreed to pay, the British government acted. Southeast New Guinea was declared a protectorate in 1884 and annexed four years later; the Cooks became a protectorate in 1888 and were annexed in 1901. Germany annexed northeast New Guinea in 1884, including some of the Solomons; and the British established a protectorate over the rest of the Solomons in 1893. In Micronesia the Germans, after an attempt to annex the Spanish possession of the Carolines in 1885, finally bought them from Spain with the Palaus and the Marianas (excepting Guam) in 1899. They had annexed the Marshalls in 1885 and, under a convention with Britain of 1886, the phosphate-rich island of Nauru. By that convention Britain's interest in the Gilberts was recognized, although no protectorate was declared until 1892. The Ellices were added to it, the group becoming the Gilbert and Ellice Islands. France declared a protectorate over Wallis and Futuna in 1887, and in the same year a convention set up a mixed British and French naval commission in the New Hebrides. Its authority was limited, and in 1906 a Condominium was agreed upon by which such difficult legal questions as land title were settled and a joint administration set up. The process of partition was completed by the United States, which took Guam in the Spanish–American War (1898), annexed the republic of Hawaii that same year, and obtained American (eastern) Samoa by agreement

The annexation of Melanesian islands

with Germany and Great Britain in 1899 and by deeds of cession (1900, 1904) from island chiefs.

Patterns of colonial administration. With the exception of Tonga, which remained an independent kingdom under British protection (from 1900) with a consul who was not to interfere in internal affairs, almost the whole of Oceania passed under the control of European powers and the United States between 1842 and the end of the century. Having acquired colonies, these powers governed Oceania with metropolitan institutions modified to a degree by local circumstances. Thus Britain reproduced in the islands the pattern of crown colony government, which derived from its own political development: a governor who represented the king; an executive council of senior officials; and, where the European population justified it, a legislative council to advise the governor. Within this form of government, administration was adapted to local conditions. Thus, Sir Arthur Gordon, the first governor of Fiji, set up a system of native administration that incorporated the chiefs: the island was divided into provinces and districts that, on the information available to him, represented the old divisions of Fiji, and over each he tried to select the chief to take administrative office. Even in Melanesia, where chieftainship was not highly developed, the British attempted to appoint chiefs who were men of influence. The first administrator of British New Guinea was a former officer in Gordon's government, William MacGregor, who first tried appointed chiefs and then settled for village constables. The Australians, who took over British New Guinea in 1906 and rechristened it Papua, followed the British pattern. The first Australian governor, Sir Hubert Murray, although he introduced measures of native development, still preserved the British pattern of colonial government, as did New Zealand in the Cook Islands. Beneath the governor, district administration tried to incorporate both native leadership and the technical and professional direction of specialized departments (such as agriculture and health), as well as those departments that dealt with the questions raised by European settlement (such as land and labour).

Other nations had different patterns. The Germans, if only because domestic German politics made colonies an incident of European policy, tried to administer their colonies through commercial companies. In northeastern New Guinea, the German New Guinea Company was commissioned to administer the colony as a commercial enterprise. Only when it failed did the imperial government assume responsibility (1899). In the Marshalls, the German firms known as the Jaluitgesellschaft became a chartered company under a government commissioner in 1885. In Western Samoa, in the first decade of the 20th century, the governor Wilhelm Solf attempted to control the importation of Chinese labour for the plantations and tried to enlist Samoan interest for the government, but he was subject to the pressure commercial interests were able to exert in Germany itself. In the French territories, colonial rule meant assimilation to French institutions. The governor was analogous to the prefect of a French *département,* assisted by an administrative council and from time to time by a general council drawn from French citizens. Where such a council existed, its powers were limited to an optional section of the budget, the rest of which was obligatory. In effect, the governor ruled by administrative decree. In the U.S. territories there was also a marked assimilation to U.S. metropolitan forms of government. When Hawaii was annexed in 1898, the president of the republic became a U.S. governor. When eastern Samoa was given to the United States under the convention of 1899, President William McKinley, in 1900, placed it under the authority of the Department of the Navy, the commanding officer of the station also becoming governor and administering the islands with the help of his technical officers and the advice of a Samoan *fono,* or legislature. These colonial governments were adapted to local circumstances. In the Polynesian islands and in Fiji, Britain and Germany attempted to incorporate the authority of the chiefs into their governments, both as advisers and as local officials in the districts, as did the United States in American Samoa. But in both Hawaii and Tahiti the

The British system

The Germans in Samoa

old system of rank had broken down under the impact of missionaries, traders, and settlers, so that it could not be used for administrative purposes but had to be replaced by appointed local officials. In Melanesia, where there was in general no chiefly authority that could be used because influence was acquired by criteria that made it fleeting, the colonial powers had no choice but to use appointed local headmen. The Germans and the British used appointed headmen in New Guinea and the Solomons and the system was supervised by a patrol of European officers with an escort of armed native police. The patrols were brief and infrequent, however, and their effect was limited.

Colonial rule after World War I. This pattern of colonial rule in Oceania was altered by the outbreak of World War I in 1914. An Australian force took German New Guinea, and a New Zealand force took German (Western) Samoa; Japan took the Carolines, the Marshalls, the Palaus, and the Marianas. At the end of the war these German territories, together with Nauru, were retained by the occupying powers as mandates under the League of Nations. The professed aim of the administrators was to help the people of these territories to stand on their own feet under the strenuous conditions of the modern world.

This stress on Oceanic interests was not new, but it became an international standard. Still, the first step was the establishment of government control and of law and order before any other measures could be taken. In New Guinea, in the Solomons, and in many parts of Melanesia, the interior was rarely known, let alone controlled. So the attention of colonial government was concentrated on opening the interior. The government-sponsored exploration in 1933 of the grass valleys of New Guinea, which had been known for a decade by missionaries and miners, presented the Australian administration with the problem of 750,000 new people. Australia's resources for administering New Guinea were spread thinly. Health and education were left to the missions. By contrast, Fiji was more developed. With the importation of labourers from India to work the sugar plantations from 1879, and with the reforms in the indenture system (which came after a commission of 1909), the large Indian population of Fiji received the attention of the government in education and health matters, but the increase in this population raised the difficult question of the Fijians' future. They played a minor part in the economic life of the colony, and the trend of official policy was to preserve them within their villages under a separate system of administration, which was reorganized in 1944 as the Fijian Administration—to be virtually a state within a state. But the government's resources were not enough to introduce welfare measures, nor was it able to promote development on any great scale. A good deal depended on the missions and other private organizations. In Samoa, where the old society had retained its organization, there was resistance to change. The New Zealand administration of Western Samoa had begun with the objective of promoting the welfare of the native race, which meant health, education, and better use of the land. By recognizing Samoan councils it tried to ensure Samoan support, but the policies broke down in execution. In American Samoa the U.S. Navy provided welfare services as part of its routine work but could do little more than that when its principal concern had to be the smooth running of the naval base. In French Polynesia native policy aimed at making the people French citizens. The welfare services were directed from Paris, but they were limited by the resources available.

The role of the missions

WORLD WAR II AND THE POSTWAR ERA

Impact of the war. Such limited resources and the competition between different objectives of colonial policy plainly restricted what could be done. The islands were affected directly by external events such as the Great Depression and the fluctuations in world markets for copra, sugar, and other products of Oceania. The principal achievements of the colonial powers were to check population decline by control of the introduced European diseases that had ravaged the islands and by increasing control of endemic diseases (such as malaria in Melanesia) and to hold a rough balance between European and indigenous interests. But welfare policies and island administration were both interrupted by World War II. The Japanese had been established in the north of Oceania, where they had treated their mandates as part of Japan itself. In 1941 they advanced into the rest of Oceania, reaching and controlling most of New Guinea as well as much of the Solomons at the peak of their advance. New Caledonia, the New Hebrides, Fiji, and the islands of Polynesia were not occupied but the effects of the war made colonial government there secondary to military operations. After the war the Trusteeship Council of the United Nations replaced the mandates; all of the colonial powers accepted that independence or self-government was the aim of their rule. The Oceanians themselves had been exposed to a more intensive European (and Japanese) impact; their horizons had widened. The colonial powers felt a greater urgency to promote development and to make available greater resources to achieve it.

Beginnings of self-government. Politically, colonial governments were reorganized to give indigenous people a part in government. In Western Samoa in 1947 the Legislative Council was given a Samoan majority and considerable powers. In American Samoa naval rule was replaced in 1951 by civilian control, and a legislature of two houses was set up, which by 1960 became a lawmaking body of Samoans. In French Polynesia and New Caledonia, elected assemblies were given considerable local autonomy in 1956; both territories chose to stay within the French Community in 1958. The trend toward a limited degree of internal autonomy and increased political participation by native residents continued in the 1960s in Fiji, the Cook Islands, and other Pacific dependencies.

THE INDEPENDENCE MOVEMENT

With the exception of some French, American, and Chilean territories, most of the Pacific Islands had achieved independence by 1980. Although most of these newly independent territories remained within the British Commonwealth, they represented a sizable addition to the ranks of microstates.

The speed of political development in the Pacific Islands was partly a matter of external pressure in the United Nations; but the colonial governments, with the exception of the French, were already moving toward self-government or independence. There were no mass nationalist movements, as in Africa and Asia, to whose demands colonial governments responded. The reaction to European rule usually took the form of nativistic movements or cargo cults in which rituals attempted to secure "cargo" diverted by Europeans. Occasionally, as with the Mau ("Strongly Held View") movement in Western Samoa in the 1920s and '30s, there was more overtly political action. In the French territories of French Polynesia and New Caledonia, for example, European-style political parties have demanded greater local autonomy and, as a minority, independence. In Fiji and Papua New Guinea, political parties formed when electoral machinery was established. The absence of mass nationalist movements owed something to the policies of colonial governments, which on the whole maintained the paramountcy of Oceanic interests in the face of European pressures; but it owed even more to the nature of Oceanic societies, in which kinship ties and a preference for consensus as "correct" behaviour led to "the Melanesian way" or "the Pacific way" as a style of politics. (F.J.W.)

TRADITIONAL CULTURES OF THE PACIFIC ISLANDS

General considerations

INDIGENOUS PEOPLES

Archaeological research has been undertaken in the Pacific Islands to trace the region's migration and settlement patterns. The region is vast, however, and understanding is both incomplete and uneven, despite collaboration among archaeologists, linguists, and physical anthropologists.

Earliest occupation dates

The area first penetrated by human immigrants was limited to New Guinea, Australia, and Tasmania, which are thought to have been connected in the Pleistocene Epoch (10,000–1,700,000 years ago) in what has been called the Greater Australian continent. Excavations in southeastern Australia reveal that people of modern type, *Homo sapiens sapiens,* had arrived there by 40,000 years ago. Migration eastward from New Guinea began by the end of the Pleistocene, but movement beyond the Melanesian region required sophisticated watercraft and did not occur until 3,000 to 4,000 years ago. Then, generations of voyagers ranged eastward into Polynesia (Fiji, Tonga, Samoa) and northward into eastern Micronesia, bearing with them distinctive physical, cultural, and linguistic characteristics.

Racial groups. The reconstruction of the racial history of Oceanian peoples has produced many theories and explanations. The opportunities for breeding groups to develop in isolation and evolve adaptive responses to special conditions were numerous, and just as important to the racial diversity of the area is the hybridization produced by centuries of ebb and flow of migrating peoples. Such diversity is certainly the combined result of isolation or its lack, adaptation to differing environments, mating patterns, and natural selection.

Authorities disagree over whether early hominid forms known from fossil finds to have inhabited Indonesian, Melanesian, and Australian areas were progenitors of peoples found there in recent times. There is similarly a great diversity of opinion on just which groups may have been antecedent—the Australoid, Veddoid, or Negritoid peoples found in the insular projection of lands south of Asia. Some specialists once proposed commonality of origin or at least some link between the Negroid peoples of Africa and the darkly pigmented, sometimes frizzy-haired groups

found in Melanesia. Blood-group research studies, however, show no evidence for such claims. In general, notions of a series of massive migrations, of relatively "pure" racial types from the Asian continent, and their miscegenation with antecedent peoples, seem to most specialists to be simplistic. Blood-group genetic research has contributed to a better understanding of certain populations, however, particularly the Negritos of the Philippines, who are thought by some researchers to be descended from late Pleistocene peoples who inhabited the islands of Southeast Asia and who are called Proto-Malays.

Main racial elements

The racial composition of Pacific peoples is a composite of Mongoloid, Caucasoid, and Negroid elements; Negrito peoples have survived or been reported in remote areas of Melanesia, Australia, and Tasmania in addition to the Philippines. The Australian Aborigines may be described as a subcontinental isolate, although there is some evidence of genetic markers that point to ancient ties with New Guinea populations. Generalizations about the normative racial type of a particular culture area may be misleading. There are general tendencies, of course, but there are also such ranges of characteristics within virtually all areas that a representative of one area could easily be assimilated in one or more other areas.

Hair form among certain Melanesians is kinky, and many Polynesians have wavy to straight hair; but kinky hair is also to be found in Polynesia, as is curly to straight hair in Melanesia. The epicanthic eye fold, which distinguishes Mongoloids, is found in abundance in Micronesia, but it occurs elsewhere as well. Recognizing the difficulties of generalization, then, it may still be noted that Tongans, Fijians, Samoans, and Hawaiians are often tall and inclined to corpulence. Pigmentation generally tends to be darker among Melanesian groups than is normal in Polynesia or Micronesia. In some of the Melanesian islands, such as the Solomons and New Britain, colour is virtually blueblack in some individuals. The ruggedness of Australian Aborigine facial characters exceeds that of other regions of the Pacific Islands. The people of the New Guinea highlands are of relatively short stature and have facial features of distinctive quality.

Migration sequences. The influxes of population into

Australia and Tasmania continued until at least the final phase of the Pleistocene (10,000 to 12,000 years ago). Tasmania was then cut off by the rise in sea level as the polar ice caps partially melted and Bass Strait was formed. New Guinea, because of its size and location, continued to receive migrants well past the end of the last ice age. Migration to Micronesia and Polynesia appears not to have begun until 3,000 to 4,000 years ago: the islands of these areas were thus the last habitable portions of the Earth to be populated.

Chronological sequences based on pottery styles, types of fishhooks, and other dating techniques suggest that human presence in Micronesia was earlier than the oldest radioactive-carbon date yet found there of approximately 3,500 years ago. The evidence points to the entry of people into central Polynesia from eastern Melanesia. In due course, migrations radiating from both western and eastern central Polynesian island groups are thought to have settled the more distant reaches of Polynesia. The Marquesas were reached by people from Samoa as early as AD 300. Some authorities have suggested that settlement may have been even earlier. Hawaii was first reached midway to late in the 1st millennium AD by voyagers from the Marquesas, who were followed several centuries later by those from the Societies. The Societies also appear to have been the point of origin for the Polynesians who settled the Cook Islands, and people from either the Society or Marquesas islands reached New Zealand prior to AD 1000. Although the validity of the radioactive-carbon dates that have been recorded for Easter Island, indicating human presence by 400, has been questioned, the dates are in accord with the time of settlement of the Marquesas (whence Easter Island probably was reached).

The watercraft used by the ancient migrants from Asia were probably crude rafts or coracles; it is likely that the highly sophisticated sailing vessels so distinctive of the cultures of the islands developed over a long period of time. However simple the early craft, those that were used thousands of years later to explore and settle the far reaches of Micronesia and Polynesia were impressive indeed. These were great double-hulled vessels capable of carrying a hundred or more voyagers and their provisions for a voyage lasting a month or longer, as well as carrying domesticated animals and plants for propagation in a new homeland.

The issue of deliberate versus accidental voyages of discovery in the Pacific has prompted an impressive array of arguments from specialists on both sides. There is considerable evidence that some islands were, indeed, populated by seafarers who, because of a storm or mere random sailing, came unexpectedly upon their new home. There is also a great deal of evidence, however, of the navigational skills and abilities of Oceanian peoples and of certain deliberate voyages of discovery. It is also clear that return voyages were made to points of origin.

Language groups. The study of Oceanian languages sometimes requires generalizations that are no more than statements of probabilities. Many of the languages have yet to be studied, and some are beyond study because they are extinct. Nevertheless, linguists offer the following characterization.

Two major language classifications

The languages of Polynesia, Micronesia, Melanesia, and Indonesia may be divided into two major groups: the Austronesian (sometimes called Malayo-Polynesian) and the non-Austronesian (also called Papuan). Virtually all of the latter group are found on New Guinea and islands to the east and west of it. Some 750 or more Papuan languages have been identified. The number of Austronesian languages probably exceeds 600. Their geographic distribution extends from Easter Island to Madagascar and from Hawaii and Taiwan to New Zealand, and they are spoken in New Guinea, except for the south coast area. There are even some Austronesian languages found in Southeast Asian mainland communities.

Most of the more than 200 languages of Australia, although in some instances quite different from each other, are thought to be related to one another—more than 85 percent being closely related. Common structural features strongly suggest a single original linguistic stock. Attempts to trace the Australian languages to those of other areas, even to contiguous ones, have proved fruitless; this probably indicates the great antiquity of the languages of Australia and the long isolation of the Aboriginal population (see also LANGUAGES OF THE WORLD: *Austronesian languages; Papuan languages;* and *Australian Aboriginal languages*).

Effect of European contact on population trends. The nature and number of the various island peoples at the time of the arrival of Europeans are uncertain. The period of European exploration was spread over several hundred years, beginning in the 16th century and becoming intense by the 18th and 19th. It was 1788, for example, before colonists from Europe settled in Australia. The number of Aborigines at that time is not known, and their widely dispersed and seminomadic hunting and gathering groups are estimated to have been organized into several hundred to nearly a thousand tribes. Tribal groups were generally associated with a given territory in which they eked out an existence from a relatively inhospitable land. Theirs was a simple yet highly functional material culture, which contrasted with a complex social system and a rich ceremonial life, featuring ancestor worship and totemic beliefs. They had rudimentary, impermanent shelters, went unclothed but for personal adornment, and foraged, hunted, and fought with simple but efficient implements and weapons. Some have estimated an Australian Aborigine population of 300,000 at time of European contact, but this is at best a guess. It is thought that the population had over time stabilized in relation to the ecology of the subcontinent and that, as a food-gathering and hunting culture, it was in balance with the environment. Like many other Oceanian peoples, the Australian Aborigines suffered severe population loss as a result of contact with the Western world.

Precolonial Aborigine culture

DIVERSITY OF PACIFIC CULTURE PATTERNS

The people and cultures of present-day Oceania differ greatly from those of the days when the areal classification into Polynesia, Melanesia, Micronesia, and Australia was devised. The Aborigines of Australia are few in number and many are of mixed race. The Tasmanian Aborigines fared even worse and became extinct in the late 19th century. Other Pacific peoples, such as those living in the Mariana Islands and on Easter Island, often are more Spanish and Chilean, respectively, than they are Micronesian or Polynesian. On some islands there are substantial populations of East Indian, Chinese, Japanese, or European-North American origin. With few exceptions, such as

© Gary & Robyn Wilson/Australasian Nature Transparencies

Pandanus growing in the ash plain at the base of Mount Yasur, an active volcano on Tanna, Vanuatu; at right, Lake Siwi.

in remote areas of New Guinea, the peoples of the Pacific Islands have been exposed intensively to Western civilization and have adapted their ways to it either by choice or by necessity. Only certain features of their traditional cultures remain. There are, in greatly varying numbers, native inhabitants of all regions who manifest the physical types commonly associated with their culture areas. In some places, however, the native population is in the minority. It is, therefore, no longer accurate to say that the people of the Hawaiian Islands possess a Polynesian culture or that those of New Caledonia are Melanesian culturally. Nevertheless, the fourfold typology of Oceanian peoples and their cultures continues to be used with reference to the contemporary inhabitants as well as to the traditional people of Oceania and their ways of life.

Mana and tapu

Social structure. Highly stratified social structures are typical of the aboriginal cultures of Polynesia and Micronesia. Hereditary chieftainship was closely related to supernatural beliefs that incorporated concepts of power (mana) and avoidance (tapu). Features of these two culture areas include an elaborate mythology; specialist craftsmen; distinctive artistic styles produced in part by isolation; pandemic and sometimes savage warfare; strong bonds of kinship and a related emphasis on genealogies; and, in places, strong trading or tributary relationships between island communities.

Melanesian societies are, because of their great diversity, less easily characterized. They were in general less concerned with social rank based on birth than with prestige gained through manipulation of resources. Root-crop agriculture (principally yams, sweet potatoes, and taro) was practiced as in many parts of Micronesia and Polynesia, and the resources of the sea were widely exploited. Ancestor worship and a rich ceremonial life were combined to produce a wealth of religious practices; they marked life crisis situations and incorporated both venerative and propitiative behaviour. In many areas complicated and highly ritualistic trading relationships were developed, and there were usually distinct differences between coastal and inland societies. Personal adornment was often elaborate; warring raids, in which heads were taken and cannibalism was sometimes practiced, were common; stone tools were polished; and animism was featured in supernatural beliefs. Melanesia's domesticated animals were those found elsewhere in the Pacific region, but pigs were vastly more important in the pursuit of personal prestige.

Technological development. Most of the people of the Pacific, prior to contact with the Western world, were at the Neolithic stage of technological development; that is, they worked stone by grinding rather than by chipping and flaking as in the Paleolithic stage. Some areas also had various other cultural features of the Neolithic such as agriculture, animal husbandry, pottery, and watercraft.

Seashells were used generally both as ornaments and as cutting tools. Shark, snake, and lizard skins were used as heads for drums. Bird, whale, and human bone, as well as fish vertebrae, were used for ornamental purposes and for tools, implements, and weapons. Basalt, obsidian, jadeite, chalk, coral stone, and other lithic materials are irregularly distributed throughout the Pacific Islands. Where these materials were available craftsmen produced a bounty of objects—adz blades, ornaments, images, and weapons—by skillfully chipping and grinding. Native woods of both hard and soft varieties were used to produce finely executed weapons, drums, masks, images, and building ornamentation. Great logs of pine were felled in New Zealand to produce flotillas of war vessels that could carry more than 100 men. Other islanders, without suitable timber for such canoes, scoured the beaches for driftwood logs or devised canoes from smaller trees, fastening planks together with cordage and caulking the seams with gum. Polynesian ironwood provided a source for some of the most intricately carved and heaviest of weapons. Ebony, bamboo, tree fern, and palm all added to the lumber supply of the carver. Feathers of colourful birds were woven into garments and effigies in some places. Headdresses of feathers appeared in many parts of the Pacific region, but only the Hawaiians devised beautiful feather helmets. The kiwi, the tropic bird, the parrot, and the cassowary

were but a few of the birds that added their plumage to the artisan's kit. Fibres and barks were used abundantly, particularly orchid fibre, hibiscus, banana, flax, pandanus and ti leaves, and coconut-husk fibre. Pigments such as turmeric were obtained from plants. Earth and burned coral provided others. Pacific island craftsmen also used resins, gums, seaweed, spider webs, flying-fox fur, human hair, dog skin, kangaroo fur, boar tusks, vegetable seeds, shells, and teeth from humans, dogs, fish, and fruit bats (see also OCEANIC ARTS).

Environmental limitations

The environment in which the traditional island native lived provided the setting for his culture. If there was little suitable land for agriculture, he had only tree crops such as coconut or pandanus; yam growing could thus not become a factor in social prestige nor could tapa making become a fine art. Although environment did not absolutely determine the nature of the culture that evolved in a given location, it served as a limiting factor; the technology of a people was in direct consonance with the surrounding region. The peoples who lived on continental islands (that is, on islands geomorphologically connected with a continent) had at their disposal a variety of minerals, a diversified flora and fauna, and, usually, a good freshwater supply. By contrast, the resident of a small coral atoll was preoccupied with securing an adequate supply of potable water and had fewer species of plants and animals. The type of island, its age, composition, and elevation, as well as its location and climate were vital factors in the development of a particular culture. Oceanian peoples had to adapt to a broad range of extremely diversified environments—tiny Micronesian atoll, humid New Guinea forest, or arid Australian desert. (R.W.Fo.)

Melanesian cultures

Melanesian is an old anthropological category that has been rendered somewhat obsolete by developments in prehistory and linguistics. It groups together the dark-skinned, frizzy-haired populations of the southwestern Pacific and characterizes them culturally in terms of Neolithic root-crop economies, highly developed systems of exchange, generally small-scale and nonhierarchical polities, and diversity in social structure. As a culture area, Melanesia can be reexamined in the light of modern evidence.

The vast continental island of New Guinea and the islands that form an arc from its eastern end down toward the southeast—the Bismarck Archipelago, the Solomon Islands, the New Hebrides (the state of Vanuatu), and New Caledonia—represent a meeting ground of two cultural traditions and populations. The earliest, for which the term Papuan provides the best label, is ancient: Papuans occupied the Sahul continent (now partly submerged) at least 40,000 years ago. As hunting-and-gathering peoples whose ways of life were adapted to tropical rain forest, they occupied the equatorial zone that, after sea levels rose at the end of the Pleistocene glacial period, became the vast island of New Guinea.

Modern descendants of these early populations speak languages belonging to a number of different families. They are categorized as Papuan (see LANGUAGES OF THE WORLD: *Papuan languages*).

Perhaps partly through indirect contact with developments in Southeast Asia, Papuan peoples developed one of the earliest agricultural complexes in the world (perhaps 9,000 years old, contemporaneous with the dawn of agriculture in the Middle East). Evidence indicates that they domesticated root crops and sugarcane and may have kept domestic pigs. By 5,000 years ago agricultural production in parts of the New Guinea highlands was marked by systems of water control in agriculture and associated pig husbandry, both of which became intensified over subsequent millennia.

About 4,000 years ago seafaring peoples bearing a Southeast Asian cultural tradition must have been moving in areas north of New Guinea; by 3,500 years ago they had occupied parts of the islands of the Bismarck Archipelago. Their presence is marked by the appearance of the distinctive pottery and associated tools and ornaments of shell that define the Lapita culture. They apparently spoke a language of the Austronesian family (see LANGUAGES OF THE WORLD: *Austronesian languages*) related to languages of the Philippines and the Indonesian archipelago. This early language is labeled Proto-Oceanic: from it are descended the languages of central and eastern Micronesia and Polynesia; the languages of the Solomons, Vanuatu, and New Caledonia; and many of the languages of coastal eastern New Guinea, adjacent islands, and much of the Bismarck Archipelago.

The speakers of Proto-Oceanic, with a maritime orientation and sophisticated seagoing technology, probably had a system of hereditary chiefs with political-religious authority and elaborate cosmogonies and religious systems, not unlike those recorded in western Polynesia.

Earliest Melanesian settlement

The Bismarck Archipelago east of New Guinea was already occupied by speakers of Papuan languages (whose earliest settlement has been dated as far back as 30,-000 years). The dark-skinned, woolly-haired populations anthropologists have classed as Melanesian that now occupy the Bismarck Archipelago and the arcs of islands extending to the southeast (the Solomons, Vanuatu, New Caledonia) represent the mixing of cultural traditions and biologic heritages of Papuan and Austronesian peoples. The mixing may have taken place largely within the zone of the Bismarcks prior to the settlement of the islands to the southeast (although the exact process and relative contributions of these historical populations is debated). A great deal of economic interchange took place between a Southeast Asian complex based on root- and tree-crop cultivation and on maritime technology, and the already well-developed Papuan agricultural and technological systems. It is probable that an interchange of other cultural traditions, from social organization to religion, took place as well. Some Austronesian-speaking communities—perhaps ones that retained their maritime orientation—appear to have remained relatively isolated from intermarriage and cultural interchange.

Linguistically, in the interchange between Papuan and Austronesian peoples the latter were clearly dominant. Almost all languages spoken by dark-skinned peoples in the Pacific east of the Bismarcks are classed as Oceanic Austronesian, although some (especially those of the eastern tip of New Guinea and adjoining islands, but perhaps also those of the Santa Cruz Islands, southern Vanuatu, New Caledonia, and the Loyalty Islands) reflect extensive Papuan borrowings. The languages spoken by dark-skinned peoples of the southeastern Solomons and northern and central Vanuatu are closely related to the languages of Polynesia and central and eastern Micronesia.

The zone east of New Guinea can be characterized as island, or seaboard, Melanesia, to contrast it with the Papuan-speaking zone of the continental island of New Guinea itself. "Melanesian" has sometimes been used in a narrow sense to label the dark-skinned peoples speaking Austronesian languages, in contrast to "Papuans." More commonly, "Melanesian" has been used in a more inclusive sense, to label both.

Little evidence has been found to identify the earliest settlers of the zone of island Melanesia south and east of the Bismarcks. It seems likely that the Solomons chain was settled by Papuan-speaking populations following the early occupation of the Bismarcks. The islands to the southeast of the Solomons—the Santa Cruz group, Banks Islands, New Hebrides, New Caledonia, and the Loyalties—are separated by much larger gaps of open sea, and they may well have been unoccupied prior to the arrival of Austronesian-speaking peoples in the Bismarcks. The pioneer settlers of large zones of island Melanesia may have been speakers of Austronesian languages who represented the genetic and cultural fusion described above, and others, contemporaneous with them, who had remained relatively isolated from intermarriage and cultural interchange with Papuan speakers. In the period from 3,500 to 3,000 years ago the latter established coastal communities and associated trade systems in the southeastern Solomons, New Hebrides, New Caledonia, and Fiji. Long-distance trade, particularly of shell ornaments and obsidian, suggests that these widely spread communities characterized by the Lapita pottery tradition were linked politically. The

Long-distance trade

settlement of eastern Micronesia by speakers of Oceanic languages, perhaps from the Solomons, apparently took place in this period. Fiji apparently was initially colonized by Lapita-making peoples and later was settled by dark-skinned, culturally Melanesian peoples after Fiji had been a springboard to the settlement of western Polynesia. The spread of this Lapita tradition from Fiji into Samoa and Tonga fits closely with the evidence of the initial breakup of a linguistically reconstructed Proto-Polynesian.

Although the prehistory of most of island Melanesia remains little-documented, some evidence suggests that the cultural, linguistic, and political fragmentation that prevailed at the time of European penetration, with a half-dozen languages and cultures often represented on a single island, is partly a product of devolution in the past 2,000 years. More hierarchical regional political systems and concomitant trade systems seem to have fragmented and devolved, with progressive involution, the replacement of trade by exchange, the disappearance of political hierarchy (except in some coastal zones), and the separation of language or dialect groups as results. The causes of these transformations, perhaps including internecine warfare and the spread of diseases (of malaria in particular), remain unclear. These changes were accelerated by European penetration, which further disrupted trade systems, intensified intercommunity warfare by supplying firearms, thinned populations by introducing diseases and indentured labour, and eroded traditional authority systems. The island Melanesia described by anthropologists reflects both long-term devolution and recent disruption.

Although the mix of Austronesian and Papuan cultural elements varies in different parts of island Melanesia, in many ways the classification of these peoples and their cultures along with Papuan-speakers as Melanesians—in contrast to the Micronesians and Polynesians—does violence to the ethnological, linguistic, and archaeological evidence. The Melanesians of northern New Hebrides and the southeastern Solomons speak languages very closely related to those of Polynesia and eastern Micronesia. Culturally, they are in many ways more closely related to these other Austronesian-speaking peoples than to the Papuans of interior New Guinea. The Melanesians' religious systems, for example, incorporate such concepts as mana and, in the Solomons, tapu.

A further complexity is that the region has emerged not only into the modern world but also into the community of nations: Papua New Guinea, Solomon Islands, Vanuatu, and Fiji constitute separate nation-states; western New Guinea (Irian Jaya) is a province of Indonesia; and the indigenous peoples of New Caledonia and the Loyalty Islands are locked in a struggle for independence with French settlers and the French government.

SOCIAL AND POLITICAL LIFE

Settlement patterns. In many areas, local groups were not concentrated in villages but were dispersed through territories in scattered homesteads and hamlets. In many cases these were occupied for short periods until the groups moved on to follow cultivation cycles. Where communities were in danger of surprise attack, they tended to cluster more closely; in interior areas they were usually sited on ridges and peaks.

In parts of the Sepik plains of New Guinea, huge villages (some with populations of more than 1,000 people) represented the aggregation of descent-based local groups. In the agricultural heartland of northern Kiriwina, in the Trobriands (Massim), villages of up to 200 people were arrayed around a central dance ground; villages at least as large were packed together on coral platforms in the lagoons of northern Malaita (Solomons). In general, larger villages settled over a span of generations were characteristic of coastal environments, and smaller, shifting settlements were characteristic of interior areas.

Residential separation of the sexes was common. Men's clubhouses, a focus of ritual and military solidarity, were common in many areas of New Guinea and island Melanesia. The men's huge cult-houses of the Sepik River basin and on the southern Papuan coast are examples. In the montane, sparsely settled interior zone of New Guinea, men's longhouses were built as defenses against the threat of raiding and as centres of cult activities. Women and children occupied domestic dwellings; in some regions women were isolated during menstruation and childbirth.

Gender relations. In many parts of New Guinea and island Melanesia male–female relationships were polarized. In New Guinea a zone of extreme polarization extended from the Papuan coast (Marind Anim, Asmat) along the southern face of the highlands (Anga speakers, Papuan plateau) and the high central mountains (Mountain Ok peoples) down into the Sepik. Men's cult secrecy, ritualized male homosexuality, elaborate men's initiation rituals, and the celebration of warfare were accompanied by belief in the dangers emanating from women's bodies and by separation of the sexes. Peoples throughout this zone were preoccupied with growth and with the physical fluids and substances (menstrual blood, semen, vaginal fluids) that are agents of reproduction and growth, all regarded as sources of power and danger.

These concerns were echoed in the eastern highlands with a physical separation of the sexes, men's initiations and cult rituals, the use of sacred flutes, ritualized nose- or penis-bleeding (ostensibly in imitation of menstruation), and accompanying myths of an ancient female power that fell into the hands of men. In the Sepik basin complexes of what has been called "pseudo-procreative" ritual accompanied male cult activities.

In the central and western highlands, where populations were dense and sweet potato and pig production were intensive, the risk of pollution by the female body and the array of male ritual activities were subordinated to the politics of extracting female labour, acquiring prestige and power through exchange, and mobilizing armed strength. Although cosmological beliefs reinforced the separation of male and female realms, women were actually a danger more as potential spies from enemy groups than as sources of polluting substances and essences.

In the Massim, in contrast, the powers of women, reproductive and productive, were represented both in the realities of social relations and in ideologies of descent and cosmic processes. In the Trobriands, women played prominent parts in some rituals. Matrilineages (in much of the Massim called *susu*, meaning "breast" or "breast milk") provided symbols of cosmic reproduction as well as physical and social reproduction.

While some polarization of the sexes emerges in accounts from the Solomons and Vanuatu, sexual segregation and concerns with pollution by females seem to have more to do with the preservation of symbolic boundaries than the inherent dangers of women's bodies and essences. In everyday domestic politics, women had relatively high status in many island Melanesian communities. Their complementary but central role was widely given cultural recognition. In many areas both paternal and maternal links provided bases of ritual status or local group affiliation, and women were accorded importance in ritual and as healers, elders, and ancestors.

Kinship and local groups. The societies of precolonial New Guinea and island Melanesia were characteristically organized in local groups based on kinship and descent and linked together by intermarriage. In the usual absence of centralized political institutions, such local groups were relatively autonomous political units. In most areas the local groups were relatively small, with between 20 and 100 members; in densely settled areas of the New Guinea highlands, and parts of the Sepik plains, kinship- and descent-based local groups were considerably larger.

Although domestic groups or individuals held rights over gardens and cultivated trees, in transmission, alienability, and the distribution of rights, the dominant pattern was the holding of corporate title to land by a local group. That is, title to land was inherited and held collectively by (some of) the descendants of those who initially cleared it. Use rights might then be extended to others. In patrilineal systems, for example, rights might be given to individuals related to the land through mothers or grandmothers, or to outsiders. In coastal zones, corporate title might be held to reefs or fishing grounds.

In many areas the relationship between people and land

[margin: Extreme sexual polarization]

[margin: Land-holding]

was conceptualized in terms of chains of descent—in male line (patrilineal descent), female line (matrilineal descent), or some combination of male and female links (cognatic descent)—from founding ancestors. Patrilineal descent systems prevail in most of lowland New Guinea; matrilineal descent systems, in much of the Massim and the Bismarck Archipelago and in much of the Solomons and the Banks Islands. The northern New Hebrides and New Caledonia have primarily patrilineal descent systems. Considerable variation is found within these areas, however.

Societies of the central and western highlands of New Guinea have been described as segmentary patrilineal descent systems. While some of them emphasize chains of descent connecting the living to ancestors, most seem unconcerned with such connections. They use father–son links as the main mechanism of group recruitment but are open to the attachment of refugees and individuals connected through women. The segmentary structures (of phratries, or clans above the level of local groups) characteristically use brother–brother and father–son links to represent what were once in fact relatively unstable political alliances. With intergroup warfare, the sheer size of local groups was a key to survival, and groups crystallized and dispersed according to the tides of warfare.

In patrilineal (and highlands filiation-based) systems, political leadership within local groups, expressed in warfare and exchange, provided an arena for competition among men. Where matrilineal descent systems had developed, arenas for men's assertion of and competition for leadership and status parallel to the descent-based local groups tended to develop: examples are the secret societies of New Britain and the Banks Islands and the overseas exchange systems of the Massim.

The matrilineally organized societies of island Melanesia represent several variations on the themes of descent and residence. In parts of the Bismarck Archipelago, matrilineal moieties were localized on the basis of uxorilocal postmarital residence (that is, residence with the wife's kin after marriage), with communities containing members of each moiety. In parts of the Massim, matrilineal clans or subclans were at least partly localized on the basis of avunculocal postmarital residence: after childhood in his father's settlement, a boy moved to his mother's brother's village, where he later lived with his wife. In other parts of the Massim, notably Dobu, postmarital residence alternated between the husband's matrilineage village and the wife's matrilineage village. In other areas (such as parts of the Solomons), postmarital residence lay with the husband's kin, so that matrilineages were only indirectly localized by virtue of coresidence of several lineages in the same village. (Such a juxtaposition of two or more matrilineages or matriclans in the same village, or contiguous villages, is common in matrilineal descent systems in Melanesia; in patrilineal descent systems, local communities more commonly comprised members of a single descent group and in-marrying wives.)

Ties of intermarriage were important in creating and maintaining connections between descent- or kinship-based local groups. Marriages negotiated with enemies made at least temporary allies of them. Particularly where marriage entailed a transfer to her husband's group of rights to a wife's fertility as well as to her labour, these transfers of rights were validated by bridewealth in the form of valuables or pigs or both. (The custom is resilient in much of modern Melanesia despite Christianity and capitalist economic relationships.) Polygyny was relatively widespread, at least for prominent leaders, who could use the productive and reproductive labour to accumulate surplus pigs and root crops. In some areas, as in the Trobriands, polygynous marriages of high-ranking leaders were instruments of political alliance and of tributary relationships between descent-based local groups. (In the Trobriands, because a matrilineal subclan was obligated to cultivate and ceremonially present yams for the husbands of its absent female members, a leader with many wives became a centre of yam distribution.) Where polygyny was not practiced, leaders could use the financing of the bridewealth of followers to create a labour force for productive enterprises.

[margin: Matrilineal descent patterns]

The stability of marriage bonds varied widely from society to society. The dissolution of marriages was constrained, particularly in patrilineally structured societies, by rights acquired through bridewealth. Marriage tended to be less stable in some matrilineally organized societies.

Ties of kinship created through marriage alliances between local groups crosscut and were complementary to divisions based on unilineal descent. In the patrilineally organized societies of lowland New Guinea and island Melanesia, a person's connection to the mother's group and ancestors was often recognized in acts of kinship support, in ritual, and in the parts played by the groups in marriages, mortuary ceremonies, and other exchanges. In the matrilineally organized societies of island Melanesia, ties to the father's matrilineal relatives were similarly expressed. The complementary parts played by maternal and paternal subclans in Trobriand (Massim) mortuary rites were particularly complex. In some areas, secondary land rights were extended on the basis of such "complementary filiation" (so that a person could acquire interests in, or cultivate, land of the father's matrilineage or mother's patrilineage). Such secondary ties could be the basis for succession to corporate title when groups died out, dwindled, or were dispersed by warfare.

Throughout Melanesia, obligations toward kin constituted the ultimate moral imperative. Systems of exchange were constructed out of kinship obligation. Rights deriving from birth commonly had to be validated by prestations or the fulfillment of obligations. One case was the payment of a midwife by a father in matrilineally organized Mota (Banks Islands): unless he paid the fee, and thus validated his status as father, the person who paid in his stead acquired rights over the child.

Warfare and feuding. Large-scale armed confrontations between warriors was common in parts of New Guinea and some parts of island Melanesia. Ethnographers have often stressed the pageantry and ritual posturing involved and have inferred that few lives were lost; these accounts also often emphasize that territory was not gained or lost. But further evidence from the New Guinea highlands and other parts of the island suggests that warfare, or in some areas clandestine raiding, had a high cost of human life (among the Mae Enga of the western highlands, as many as 15 percent of male deaths occurred in war, and even today a resumption of armed combat takes a substantial toll of life). Moreover, it is now clear that victorious groups often did displace their enemies from territories, as in many parts of New Guinea (such as the Sepik and the southern and eastern highlands). Homicidal raiding of neighbouring peoples was widespread and was associated with headhunting in such regions as the southern New Guinea coast (Asmat, Marind Anim) and the western Solomons (Roviana, Vella Lavella) and with cannibalism in others (southern Massim, New Caledonia). The cultural orientations of many Papuan and island Melanesian peoples were shaped by a warrior ethic—an ethos of bravery and violence, vengeance and honour—and by the religious imperatives that promoted aggression.

In other areas, such as Malaita in the Solomons and much of Vanuatu, large-scale combat was rare, but blood feuding was endemic. Where deaths were attributed to sorcery, a common pattern in both Papuan- and Austronesian-speaking areas, accusations of sorcery commonly triggered vengeance murders. So, in some areas, did seduction, adultery, theft, or ritual insult. Chains of blood feuding led neighbouring villages or clans into vengeance killings; feuding was laid to rest only when murders were finally balanced out or death compensation was paid.

Political leadership. Both in Papuan-speaking New Guinea and Austronesian-speaking island Melanesia, leaders of local groups characteristically emerged on the basis of success in prestige economy, warfare, or both. This mode of leadership, based on status achieved through entrepreneurial success and the influence and obligations attendant to it, has been elevated in anthropological stereotypes of the "Big Man" as prototypical Melanesian leader. The stereotype needs critical examination. With warfare and feuding endemic in much of precolonial Melanesia, the importance of warrior leaders in many societies

had waned or been eclipsed by leadership in competitive feasting and other exchange by the time anthropologists arrived. A second problem in the stereotype, at least for Austronesian-speaking Melanesia, is that it seems likely that early Oceanic-speaking peoples had hereditary chiefs. Thus, the emergence of entrepreneurial (or warrior) leaders to whom others deferred by virtue of their deeds, not their rank, may well have been a concomitant of the process of political devolution.

The most serious problem in the Big Man stereotype is that in many parts of island Melanesia, at the time of first European penetration, societies were led by hereditary chiefs. This was true of parts of Austronesian-speaking coastal New Guinea (e.g., Mekeo, Motu), parts of the Solomons (e.g., Buka, Shortlands, Small Malaita), parts of Vanuatu (Aneityum), and most of New Caledonia. In other areas leadership was based on conceptions of rank but with succession to leadership based on a complex relation between hereditary right and demonstrated ability (indeed, such a relation was important in much of Polynesia as well). Bronisław Malinowski's "Paramount Chief" in northern Kiriwina, in the Trobriands, has become recognized as a hybrid figure, not quite a chief in a classical sense but of an exalted rank that set him apart from the *mumi* of the Siuai of Bougainville or the *ngwane-inoto* of northern Malaita, on whom the Big Man stereotype was modeled. In much of precolonial island Melanesia, particularly in coastal areas, leaders seem to have fallen into this middle zone, with rank and achievement operating together to confer leadership and each reinforcing the other. The power of such local leaders depended partly on monopolies over trade or prestige exchange systems, or regional domination based on war, both of which were disrupted by European penetration. The stereotypical image of the Big Man is partly a result of the fact that ethnographic accounts were gathered in the colonial period and by observers operating in a tradition that discounted and disguised historical processes.

ECONOMIC SYSTEMS

Production and technology. The ancient root-crop cultivation systems of Papuan and Austronesian cultural traditions depended on swidden horticulture, a practice of shifting cultivation whereby rain-forest gardens are cleared, planted, harvested, and then left fallow for periods of up to a generation. Ground stone tools (and in some coral-island areas, shell tools) and fire were used to clear forest; digging sticks were used for cultivation.

The primary plant domesticates were taro and yams (*Dioscorea*), with plantains, sago, pandanus, leafy greens such as *Hibiscus manihot,* and sugarcane being other important domesticates. In swampy areas of New Guinea, sago production continues to support dense populations. Sweet potatoes, a New World domesticate that reached New Guinea through the Moluccas no earlier than the 16th century, allowed an intensification of production and dense settlement of higher altitudes (where *Pueraria*—a root vegetable—and taro had been cultivated earlier). The progressive expansion of intensified cultivation in the great highland valleys of New Guinea, accelerated in recent centuries, has resulted in the progressive transformation of montane forest hunting territories (also used for foraging and swidden cultivation) into *Imperata* grass, further accelerating reliance on pig husbandry and intensified production, particularly of sweet potatoes.

In island Melanesia either yams or taro typically has been the major staple crop. The two have quite different productive regimens (as well as symbolic meanings), and focus on one or the other (which often is difficult to account for on ecological grounds) tends to structure community life. Yams are planted and harvested seasonally, and the tubers, if unblemished and dry, keep for several months. Hence, communities that focus on yam production tend to have an annual cycle and to emphasize communal labour and common enterprise. Taro corms rot quickly after harvest, and taro has no seasonal cycle; the shoots are replanted after the corms have been cut off, so that both harvest and planting are continuous throughout the year. Cultivation by individual families, and more flexible

Marginal notes:

"Complementary filiation"

Endemic blood feuding

Problems of anthropological stereotype

Results of intensified cultivation

local group structures, are promoted by the regimen of taro production.

In New Guinea and parts of island Melanesia agriculture was intensified by water control, mounding and composting, or terracing. Terraced and irrigated taro fields were found in parts of the New Hebrides and New Caledonia; the mounded and composted gardens of parts of highland New Guinea, associated with water control, allowed intensification of production and continuous use of land.

Root- and tree-crop production was augmented by the raising of domestic pigs, fishing (on coasts or in interior rivers, lakes, and streams), and hunting of marsupials and birds (and, sometimes, gathering of insects and grubs). Gathering of wild vegetable foods, including tubers, greens, nuts (notably the canarium almond, which was extremely important in areas such as northern Malaita in the Solomons), and fruits, augmented diets or provided emergency rations. Food crops were complemented by a range of cultigens used for purposes other than food. The areca nut and accompanying betel pepper, for example, were widely chewed as a stimulant and were a crucial medium of sociality in large zones of Melanesia; kava (*Piper methysticum*) served a similar purpose in parts of Vanuatu and in Fiji; and plants such as ginger and *Cordyline fruticosa* were used in ritual, magic, and medicine.

Although swidden horticulture typified the region, many peoples of montane New Guinea relied heavily on hunting and gathering and had low-intensity food production systems. Competition for hunting territories was apparently a major factor in warfare and raiding, particularly among the peoples of the ecologically marginal zones of the southern regions of the highlands.

In island Melanesia, coastal zones offered rich environments for the exploitation of fish, shellfish, and sea turtles. As sources of shell used for valuables and ornaments, of salt and lime, and of marine food products, the coastal zones contributed goods that coastal dwellers could trade and barter with peoples of the interior. In some areas, trade of root crops for marine products was institutionalized. In northern Malaita, in the Solomons, the coastal dwellers, who lived on islets and coral platforms dredged from the lagoon floor, bartered fish for root vegetables at regular markets. Other Solomons coastal communities specialized in manufacturing and exporting shell beads, which were widely used as valuables. Similar arrangements occurred in the Admiralty Islands and other areas of island Melanesia.

In addition to manufacturing ground stone adzes and axes, peoples of New Guinea and the islands to the east commanded a broad range of Neolithic technology. Bags and nets for fishing, hunting, and trapping were made from bush fibres, and bark cloth was widely manufactured. Giant bamboo served a multitude of purposes, providing cooking vessels, water containers, torches, and carving knives. Canoes, ranging from small dugouts to elaborate composite seagoing canoes, were manufactured. Weapons included bows and arrows, spears, and clubs.

Although this technology was virtually universally distributed through the zone, particular peoples specialized in particular forms of production. Specialization in part followed the distribution of resources, such as clay for pottery, chert or greenstone for tool blades, or trees for canoes or weapons. But systems of trade and regional exchange seem to have depended on political and cultural imperatives as well as resources.

Trade and exchange systems. The regional trading systems of the islands around the eastern end of New Guinea were particularly elaborate. In the Massim—what is now Milne Bay province of Papua New Guinea (taking in the D'Entrecasteaux islands, the Louisiades, and nearby islands)—the trade of pottery from the Amphletts, canoe timber and greenstone blades from Murua (Woodlark), carved platters and canoe prow boards, and other specialized products was complemented by a flow of yams and pigs from resource-rich areas to smaller, ecologically less favoured islands. Some islanders, such as those from Tubetube in the southern Massim, did little producing and specialized instead as middlemen and traders. Similar interdependencies and specializations, with some communities acting as export traders and middlemen, occurred

in the Vitiaz Straits between New Guinea and New Britain. Through chains of intermediary trading partnerships among neighbouring peoples, trade systems in New Guinea connected communities that were separated by scores of miles of rugged mountains. Such networks carried salt, shell, and other objects from coasts to interiors and forest products, such as blackpalm, from interiors to coasts. They connected specialist communities, such as those extracting salt, collecting ochre, or making blades, to communities far away.

Both Papuan-speaking and Austronesian-speaking zones of Melanesia had highly elaborated exchange systems, in which surpluses of pigs and root crops were used in prestige feasts and ceremonial valuables (usually shell beads or other shell objects, but also including dolphin and dog teeth and a range of other material objects) were exchanged. Elaborations of ceremonial exchange, in mortuary feasts and homicide-compensation payments, bridewealth presentations, and various forms of competitive feasting, were foci of community production, social cooperation, status rivalry, and political conflict. In some areas, at least, competitive exchanges were a surrogate for warfare (and in some instances they seem to have grown out of homicide compensation).

In New Guinea the most highly developed exchange systems were those of the western highlands: the Enga *tee,* the Hagen *moka,* and other mass exchanges of pigs and shell. Cycles of pig production were orchestrated so that vast surpluses of sweet potatoes were required to feed expanded herds; mass pig kills, or the presentation of live pigs to the leaders of rival clans, were a focus of political rivalry and community productive labour.

In island Melanesia the best-known prestige exchange system was the *kula* of the Massim, documented by Malinowski. As he described it, the *kula* entailed the endless circulation of valuables through a network of communities on islands forming a giant ring. Through the network passed intrinsically useless valuables: shell-bead necklaces passed around the ring in a clockwise direction and were exchanged for arm shells, which moved counterclockwise. The exchanges were made between partners in neighbouring communities, or, in the most exciting, dangerous, and prestigious exchanges, between neighbouring islands. Research in different parts of the *kula* zone has shown the exchange to have been considerably more complex than Malinowski was able to see from his vantage point in the Trobriands (as well as highly resilient in the face of westernization and economic change). Early European penetration did much to change the nature of exchanges and to stabilize a system that was highly unstable because of intercommunity warfare.

Complex systems of prestige feasting, often with a strong competitive element, have been described for many parts of island Melanesia, including Goodenough Island (in the Massim) and the Solomons (Bougainville, Malaita). In precolonial northern New Hebrides, status rivalry was played out through complex graded societies in which men moved to progressively higher grades by sponsoring feasts and presenting valuables and pigs.

Although strung shell beads and other valuables were best known as exchange tokens in the prestige economy, in some parts of Melanesia they served very much like money—as media of economic value and exchange. They were used to buy and sell pigs, fish, craft products, and even land. The *tambu* of the Tolai of New Britain are well known, and similar valuables were used on Malaita and in some other areas as generalized instruments of value, with standard "denominations" and standard "prices" for commodities.

RELIGION

In Austronesian-speaking Melanesia a strong orientation to ancestors and the past was common, but it was a past manifested in the present, with ancestral ghosts and other spirit beings as everyday participants in social life. (While beliefs in gods and powerful spirits were held in the region, such beings figured more in myths than in everyday life and practical religion.)

Human effort in the uncertain projects of war, gardening,

Exploitation of the coastal zone

Trade networks

The past in the present

and the pursuit of prestige was thought to succeed only when complemented by support from invisible beings and forces, which were manipulated by magical formulas and elicited through prayer and sacrifice. The presence and effects of invisible ghosts and spirits were manifested in dream, revealed in divination, and inferred from human success or failure, prosperity or disaster, health or death. In such a world, religion was not a separate sphere of the transcendental but a part of everyday life; and religion and magic were not clearly distinguishable. The most sacred rituals often entailed the performance of magic, and performance of magic for personal, manipulative ends might be accompanied by prayer or even sacrifice. Although ghosts and spirit beings were not usually moral agents in their intervention in human life, there were some well-documented exceptions (such as Manus, in the Admiralties). Spirit beings were viewed in parts of island Melanesia as policing the punctilious observance of rules regarding pollution or exogamy and the correct performance of ritual. The concepts of tapu (sacred, forbidden, off-limits) and mana (efficacy or potency), well known for Polynesia, are fairly widely distributed in Oceanic Austronesian-speaking island Melanesia: mana is found in many Solomons languages and some languages of northern Vanuatu, and tapu or tabu is found widely in the Solomons and the Austronesian languages of the New Guinea area.

Island Melanesian societies lacked full-time religious specialists, so those who acted as priests or officiants or as community magicians, intermediating with ghosts and spirits, were in everyday life indistinguishable from their fellows. Some forms of everyday magic—for gardening, fishing, attracting valuables or lovers—were widely known, although knowledge of magic often constituted a form of property. Other forms, for powers of fighting or theft, tended to be closely guarded, and malevolent magic for destructive ends was secretly held and generally used in clandestine fashion (although in a few cases, as among the Mekeo of coastal New Guinea, sorcerers acted as agents of chiefs). In many Melanesian societies sorcery was seen as the major cause of death or illness. Belief in witchcraft occurred in some areas.

Diversity in New Guinean religions Religions of Papuan-speaking New Guinea remain diverse. In much of New Guinea, ghosts and other spirit beings are much less important participants in everyday life than among Austronesian speakers, although there are many exceptions. Thus, the vast *tambaran* houses of the Sepik, with their elaborate rituals and developed beliefs in spirit beings (as described for such peoples as Abelam and Plains Arapesh) contrast sharply with the relatively secular pragmatism of much of the highlands. Among such montane peoples as Telefol, Bimin Kuskusmin, and Baktamin, highly complex male initiatory cults progressively reveal cosmic secrets to initiates. In New Guinea as in island Melanesia, fear of sorcery is widespread; and among such peoples as the Fore of the highlands, accusations of sorcery are a major cause of hostility between groups and of blood feuding. Some highland peoples, such as Chimbu, Kuma, and Hewa, believe that witches—humans acting in the grip of forces or agencies beyond their conscious control—prey on the living, taking possession of them or draining their bodily substances.

In some areas, such as the Sepik and the lagoons of northern Malaita in the Solomons, where traditional religious systems and associated cult practices remain, the old religions are giving way under the combined pressures of Christianity and capitalist development. A striking phenomenon of the early colonial period was the emergence of cargo cults in coastal New Guinea and island Melanesia. The movements, such as the Vailala Madness of the Gulf Division and the cargo cults of the Rai coast, were based on the revelations of local prophets that the ancestors were withholding European material goods from indigenous peoples. Cult doctrines included the iconoclastic destruction of old ceremonial objects and the moral, social, and logistical preparation for the arrival of vast quantities of Western "cargo," expected to be delivered by ship or plane. Cargo cults were widespread in New Guinea, the Bismarcks, and parts of the Solomons and New Hebrides (the John Frum Movement of Tanna is well

known). Some of the movements were highly political and explicitly anticolonial in character, with a spectrum connecting millenarian movements, such as the Vailala Madness, at one end and political movements with mystical overtones, such as the postwar Maasina Rule movement in the Solomons, at the other.

ART

Melanesian art is highly varied. In much of highland New Guinea the body itself becomes a focus for art, with face and body painting, wigs and headdresses, and elaborate costumes. In lowland New Guinea, ebullient art traditions like the painting and carvings of such Sepik peoples as Iatmul and Abelam have become widely known. The curvilinear art of the Massim, of which Trobriand prow **The art of the Massim** boards and dancing shields are examples, has also attracted interest. The *malanggan* carvings of New Ireland are equally spectacular and well-known and are relatively well-documented anthropologically. The latter, in contrast to the Sepik and Massim carvings, are ephemeral art; the fretwork *malanggan,* like some of the fern bole carvings of Vanuatu, were created for ceremonies and abandoned or destroyed afterward.

In some cultural traditions of Melanesia, carvings and other art forms had strong religious significance. Masks were a focus of creativity in several regions; they were often used in elaborate ceremonials, with masked figures impersonating mythical beings or perpetuating or dramatizing cult secrets. Many peoples, however, as in the Solomons, the Huon Gulf, and the Admiralties, decorated virtually every object not immediately discarded, however utilitarian.

Music and dance have been less well-documented, partly because (until the era of tape recording and film) they were less easy to preserve than material objects, and partly because Christianization of much of the area led to the early abandonment of many forms of music and dance. Although it is difficult to generalize, dancing often was focused primarily on displaying the bodies and costumes of the dancers (and sometimes the collective strength of the group they represented). Complex dance forms have been recorded from some areas, however. Music ranges from dirges at wakes and love songs to highly complex forms such as the polyphonic panpipe music, with as many as eight contrapuntal voices, played by orchestras on Malaita in the Solomons. Also characteristic of the region are the genres of epic narrative, myth, folktales, and oratory, redolent with metaphor and mythic allusion. These traditions, too, have often been lost because of the incursions of Christianity and the unavailability, until modern times, of effective recording devices.

EFFECTS OF EUROPEAN CONTACT

The indigenous peoples of much of the Melanesian region are now part of the world economic system and are subjected to pressures of Christianization and westernization. In some areas such forces have operated for more than a century. In some interior areas, however, particularly in New Guinea, Western penetration came much later—in the 1930s or even after. But today the most remote regions have become accessible, and they have been transformed.

Papua New Guinea, Solomon Islands, and Vanuatu are now sovereign states and members of the United Nations; the indigenous Kanak peoples of New Caledonia have become a minority in a French overseas territory, battling for independence. The indigenous peoples of western New Guinea (Irian Jaya), since incorporation into Indonesia, have been subjected to massive disruption, dislocation, political repression, and the forced accommodation of large settler populations under national transmigration policies.

With Melanesians now serving as diplomats, businessmen, bishops, doctors, lawyers, and professors, many generalizations about Melanesia as a region marked by "primitive societies" have become anachronistic. Some general observations still seem possible, however. One is **Newly class-stratified societies** that classless societies have become class-stratified societies, with politicians, public servants, and entrepreneurs constituting an emerging elite. Moreover, at least in the English-speaking areas, the elites increasingly share a common (westernized and consumerist) culture and common political and economic interests and ideologies that cut across boundaries not only between cultures and language groups but also between nations.

Internally, the countries of modern Melanesia show increasing polarization between metropolitan centres and village hinterlands. Squatter settlements on urban peripheries and movement into towns are increasingly found, and both serve as links between the villages and urban life. The more remote villages are poor and have little access to the educational, medical, and economic services of the state. It is in the marginal areas that the traditional culture tends to be the most resilient.

Cash cropping and various modes of capitalist enterprise, as well as dependence on imported goods, have penetrated ever farther into the Melanesian village hinterlands, with some areas (notably parts of highland New Guinea) attaining a measure of prosperity by Western standards through the production of coffee or other high-value crops. Roads and airfields now connect once-isolated hinterlands to regional networks.

Among the new elite, cultural nationalist ideologies have tended to focus on "custom" and "the Melanesian way"; cultural revivalism has become a prominent theme. Art festivals, cultural centres, and ideologies of *kastom* have cast in a more positive light the traditional cultural elements, such as ceremonial exchange, dance and music, and oral traditions, that had long been suppressed by the more conservative and evangelistic forms of Christianity. The emphasis on traditional cultures as sources of identity has been expressed in the perpetuation or revival of old genres of exchange. In Papua New Guinea, the *kula* exchange of arm shells and necklaces continues in the Massim, carried on through the medium of air travel and among politicians, professionals, and public servants as well as by villagers in canoes. Members of the new elite conspicuously pay bridewealth in shell valuables.

Christianity has been a powerful force of change within the region for many decades. Much of island Melanesia and coastal New Guinea has been Christianized for two or three generations or longer. In the colonial period, missions were a major force of education and local economic change. Many of the leaders of postcolonial Melanesia have come from mission schools and backgrounds, and some have been trained as ministers or evangelists. In terms of their orientations and their leaders, the Melanesian postcolonial states are among the most Christian nations on earth.

Different Christian denominations, and even individual missionaries, have in varying degrees been sympathetic to and knowledgeable about local languages and cultures. Missionary work, in conjunction with the imposition of colonial rule, has helped Melanesians to transcend and to liberate themselves from customary practices that exacted a heavy cost in violence, cruelty, and exploitation; but it has also destroyed much cultural richness, and the process continues in remote regions of Papua New Guinea.

(R.M.Ke.)

Micronesian cultures

Diversity of the Micronesian peoples

Seven major high-island cultures can be distinguished in Micronesia: those of the Chamorros, most of whom live on the four southern islands of the Marianas; the Palauans; the Yapese; the Trukese, inhabiting about 12 high islands of varying size in the large Truk Lagoon; the Pohnpeians; the Kosraeans; and some of the inhabitants of the isolated island of Nauru, which is geologically a raised atoll (without exposed volcanic rock).

The inhabitants of most of the low islands or atolls in Micronesia are culturally distinct from the high islanders, though in contact with them. In the east are found two culturally distinctive groups of atolls, the Marshalls and the Gilberts (politically constituted as the Republic of the Marshall Islands and the republic of Kiribati, respectively), ranging from the northwest to the southeast over about 1,400 miles. The culture of Banaba (formerly Ocean Island), a raised atoll, is quite similar to that of the Gilberts and will be treated herein as a variant of Gilbertese culture.

Three atolls within sailing distance of Pohnpei—Mokil, Pingelap, and Ngatik—show closer cultural relationships to the people of Pohnpei than to any other large population but are clearly distinct from them. The Hall Islands, atolls to the north of Truk, and the Mortlock (Nomoi) Islands, atolls to the south, are culturally closest to Truk. The remaining low islands to the west of Truk also show linguistic and cultural relationships to Truk, with the differences becoming more and more marked as distance increases. The low islands between Namonuito and Yap were once part of a ceremonial exchange system called the Yapese Empire by anthropologists. Linguistically and culturally, however, these low-island people were closer to the Trukese than to the Yapese.

The cultural diversity of Micronesia is indicated by the number of mutually unintelligible languages in the area. The following all have mutually unintelligible languages: Nauru, the Gilberts, the Marshalls, Kosrae, Pingelap, Mokil, Pohnpei, Ngatik, the Mortlocks, Truk, the Puluwat area, the Woleai area, Yap, the Palaus, and the Marianas. The languages of the islands from the Marshalls and the Gilberts through the Woleai area in the above list appear to be somewhat more closely related to each other than to the remaining languages and have been referred to as Nuclear Micronesian. The languages of the Palaus, Yap, and the Marianas are relatively distinct from each other and from other Micronesian languages, although they are clearly Austronesian in their general affiliation. The Chamorro language, spoken in the Marianas, has undergone much influence from Spanish and probably also from the Philippine Tagalog language after more than four centuries of Western contact.

Traditional Micronesian cultures were characterized by a belief in the stability of society and culture. People suffered occasional natural disasters, such as typhoons or droughts, but their goal after encountering one of these was to reconstitute the previous state of affairs. Wars occurred in most areas from time to time, mainly at the instigation of competing chiefs. At stake was the control of land (a very limited resource in the tiny islands of Micronesia) and followers, but there were usually few casualties.

Living in small communities on small territories, Micronesians learned to adjust to their neighbours and remain on good terms with most of them most of the time and to develop techniques of reconciliation when fights did break out. In general, Micronesians valued good manners. Even today, Micronesian adults and children are likely to impress the outsider as unusually quiet, polite people.

Local loyalties

Micronesians traditionally depended on the cultivation of plant crops and on fishing in shallow reef waters. Because both arable land and reef were in short supply for the relatively dense population, the Micronesian had a strong practical basis for his attachment to his locality and lands. Land rights were usually held through some sort of lineage or extended family group, often backed up by traditions of ancestral origins on the land.

The strong local loyalties of the Micronesians may also be partly explained by the difficulty of traveling to any place very far from home, especially for the high islanders who lacked oceangoing canoes. Of the high-island peoples, only the Yapese practiced very much navigation in the open seas at the time of their discovery by Europeans, sailing to Palau and to some of the atolls in the central Carolines. The remaining high-island peoples mostly sailed around their home islands without losing sight of land, although they were visited from time to time by low islanders. The low islanders had reason to visit the high islands, with their more fertile soil and greater elevation; they could obtain food and other items not found on their home islands or seek refuge after a typhoon or drought. Low islanders also had reason to visit other low islands in search of mates outside the limits of the incest taboo and for help after typhoons. Some of the low islanders, especially in the storm-swept central Carolines area between Truk and Yap and in the Marshalls, were skilled navigators of oceangoing canoes.

The populations of the Micronesian islands appear to have been in good balance with the natural resources at the time of their discovery by the Europeans. Because the climate is equable and varies little during the year, moderate amounts of labour were sufficient for comfortable survival, and much leisure was available for activities such as dancing, feasting, romantic affairs, and visiting friends and relatives. Some kinds of subsistence activities, especially fishing, were regarded as something like play. The period of youth was often prolonged, since the older people could afford to indulge their children. This positive attitude toward the enjoyment of leisure was especially characteristic of the high islanders, with their more fertile soil and more secure life.

SOCIAL AND POLITICAL LIFE

Settlement patterns and housing. Micronesians preferred to live in dispersed, extended-family homesteads, in contrast to some Melanesians and Polynesians. In atolls the inhabitants generally preferred the lagoon side of the larger islands for ease in launching canoes and for protection from typhoons. On the high islands, people again wanted access to the lagoon, although easily defensible sites were sometimes also preferred, such as the top of a steep, cleared slope.

The "Venice" of Pohnpei

One ancient "city" in Micronesia is the archaeological site of Nan Matol or Metalanim on Pohnpei. This is a sort of tiny Venice, containing about 100 artificial islands, separated by shallow canals, covering one-third of a square mile in all, including water. The islands were used for royal, priestly, and noble residence and for ritual, and the total population may have been several hundred to 1,000. There is a similar site on the islet of Lelu (Lele) in Kosrae.

The typical Micronesian community had one or more meetinghouses. These served both as social gathering places and as places to plan community affairs. The number and elaborateness of the meetinghouses are greatest in Yap and Palau. Palauan meetinghouses were built by the men's clubs, suggesting some Melanesian influence. In Palau, Yap, and the western atolls, meetinghouses were used mostly by men, while farther east, women and children also entered them freely much of the time.

Houses in most areas were built on slightly raised platforms made of coral rock and gravel on the low islands and volcanic rock and dirt on the high islands. They generally had thatched roofs with low eaves and poor ventilation. The smoke from a small hearth may have been used to control mosquitoes, although plaited mosquito sleeping bags were also used at times. This form of construction may have also provided good protection against heavy rainstorms. Some of the houses in the Marianas appear to have been constructed on stone pillars. The *latte* stones of this area—double rows of stone pillars with capstones—are now thought to have been piles for raised houses, perhaps for chiefs and wealthy men, since the *latte* sites are relatively few for the reported population. Other houses may have been built on wooden piles that have since disappeared.

Canoe houses were another important form of building throughout Micronesia. Those big enough to store the larger canoes were on the scale of meetinghouses and often were used as such in some areas.

Small buildings for the isolation of menstruating women were common in the western Carolines and continued in use in Yap until recent times.

Family and kinship. The majority of Micronesians before European contact lived in some form of extended-family group. In most areas the organization of this group probably had considerable flexibility, some newlywed couples living with the husband's family, others with the wife's relatives. Major determinants in the choice of residence were the relative availability of agricultural land and the need for additional labourers on one or the other side of the family. In much of the area the wife's family was considered the ideal place of residence; but frequently exceptions were allowed in practice, and children often had rights to use land on their father's mother's side. In Yap, on the other hand, patrilocal residence and patrilineal inheritance of land were considered ideal.

As in other parts of Oceania, the adoption of children of relatives was frequent. This was, in part, a way of caring for illegitimate and orphaned children; in part, a way of relieving young adults of the chores of child care and providing old people with young children to do minor work for them; in part, a way of insuring more equitable distribution of land rights; and, in part, a way of providing heirs for specialized knowledge when the proper natural heir was lacking or unsatisfactory.

Matrilineages existed in most of Micronesia, with the exception of Yap, and they were traditionally exogamous— *i.e.,* members did not marry within the same lineage. While matrilineage membership was considered basically unalterable in some communities, there was probably some flexibility everywhere. If a lineage grew too large, it tended to split into two parts, one of which would adopt a new name and no longer observe exogamy with the other. If outsiders came into a community, they would often be taken into an existing lineage as honorary or fictive members and eventually might merge with the patron group and observe rules of exogamy with them.

Descent based on matrilineage

Marriage in Micronesia varied in formality. In the west, in Palau and Yap, marriages were marked by formal payments from the groom's family to the bride's. In the area from the central Carolinian atolls to the Marshalls, marital relationships were usually rather loose and informal, although people of high rank may have had public ceremonies with some exchange of wealth. In this area considerable premarital and extramarital sex was traditionally expected; marriage for ordinary people consisted simply of openly living together and being spoken of by the community as spouses. Apparently, there was more formality to marriage and more control of premarital sex in the Gilberts. Polygyny was generally permitted to some extent in Micronesian societies, although it was not very common. It was more likely to be practiced by high-ranking men, and in eastern Micronesia it may have been restricted to chiefs.

Birth order has traditionally been widely important in Micronesian societies. The seniority of the eldest child is recognized in representing the family or lineage in public and in inheriting political office. The eldest child generally directs the use of lineage or family lands. Younger siblings generally exhibit formal respect to older siblings.

Brother–sister avoidance relationships are well developed in parts of Micronesia, perhaps most strongly in the central Carolines from Truk through the atolls to the west. In this area women were traditionally expected to avoid speaking to their brothers, to crouch in their presence, and in other ways to show respect. In Pohnpei, farther to the east, a similar relationship existed between a man and his next younger sister but did not extend with the same force to other sisters.

A certain amount of hereditary social stratification was found universally in Micronesia, but its degree varied considerably from some of the smaller Carolinian atolls, which had nominal hereditary chiefs with little special power or wealth, to the high island of Yap, which had several ranked endogamous castes. Other cultures that showed relatively marked social stratification were Palau, Pohnpei, Kosrae, the Marshalls, and the Gilberts. It seems likely that the Marianas may have also had distinct social classes before the Spanish conquest. In all the above areas there appear to have been some chiefs who were supported principally by tribute from their subjects; who were the object of considerable deference; who could punish offenses (especially against themselves and their own relatives) by fines, destruction of property, or death; and whose principal wives were chosen mostly from other high-ranking families. In these areas the high chiefs also had subordinate chiefs and officials.

Social stratification

The hierarchical principle was not well-developed in most of these societies. The notion of crime to be punished by the state was weakly developed. Palau and Pohnpei had an abundance of nominal political titles, the principal significance of which might be called recreational and dramatic. In both these societies individuals were able to rise above their initial hereditary status through personal achievement, thus introducing much flexibility into the system of social stratification.

On the high islands of Truk and on many low islands, especially in the central Carolines and the smaller communities in the Marshalls and Gilberts, social relationships were egalitarian. The local chief was expected to work for his living like anyone else. He received ceremonial deference but traditionally had little power to order people to do anything or punish them for offenses. His principal function was to preside at meetings and define and state the community consensus as it developed.

Social hierarchy and political organization. Throughout most of Micronesia the maximum independent autonomous political unit was the high island or the atoll, often subdivided into more than one unit. Satawan atoll in the Mortlocks had four separate communities aboriginally, each with its own chief; sometimes they fought each other. The Palaus had two confederations of villages or districts aboriginally, each independent of the other, and the villages themselves had considerable autonomy. Pohnpei had five petty states at the time of first European contact, although there were traditions of a unified rule for the whole island at an earlier period. Truk was extremely fragmented politically, with several independent communities on each of the six larger high islands. The Marshalls and the Gilberts had larger political units, integrating groups of separate atolls under a high chief, although the fullest development of these expansionist states was achieved after the introduction of firearms by Europeans.

The low islands between Truk and Yap have been described as belonging to the "Yapese Empire." The so-called empire consisted mainly of a chain of trading and ceremonial relationships with one of the petty states of Yap. The Yapese exerted no military force against the low islanders but did claim the ability to punish them by sending typhoons, disease, and famine if they should fail to fulfill their obligations. According to widely accepted myths, the low islanders originated from the Yapese, although they are culturally and linguistically closer to the Trukese.

In most of the area from the Palaus in the west to the Marshalls in the east, the community was considered to be owned in some sense by a clan, the head of which was also the chief of the community. Other clans had land rights by their relation to former chiefs or to the men of the ranking clan: their women had married men of the chiefly clan, or their men had rendered the chiefly clan service in the past. The chiefly clans in some cases claimed their position by virtue of ancient military conquest and in others by virtue of being the first human beings to occupy the land. The aboriginal pattern of political and community organization in the Marianas has been obscured by the early Spanish conquest, which exterminated most of the population and concentrated the remainder under close Spanish military and religious control. Chieftainship in the Gilberts was by patrilineal succession.

Socialization and education. Micronesians were indulgent with infants. Children were inducted into adult life gradually through observation and participation; there was little in the way of formal schooling or initiation ceremonies in most of the Micronesian societies. Several forms of bodily ornamentation by mutilation were practiced, mostly performed around puberty or in early adulthood. The most widespread of these was tattooing, practiced by both sexes. This and other forms of bodily mutilation were generally done on individual initiative, to demonstrate bravery and increase sexual attractiveness.

Training in cultural specialties, such as medicine, magic, esoteric mythology, canoe and house building, and navigation, was often delayed until young adulthood or middle age. It was usually given by an older relative, although sometimes outsiders could receive it by payment of food and goods. The most formal training in esoteric knowledge appears to have been given by the specialists known as *itang* (in Truk). Each *itang* had himself been trained under an older expert adept in traditional history, oratory, war strategy and tactics, and magic. At the end of his training he was formally awarded the title or degree of *itang* and thenceforth could serve as an orator, ambassador, counselor, and executive officer for a chief.

ECONOMIC SYSTEMS

Production and technology. The islands of Micronesia were probably first settled by small groups of immigrants with few technical specialists among them. The prehistoric Micronesians had basically a subsistence technology with a few part-time specialists producing luxury items, such as personal ornaments and the shell and stone valuables that were used, mostly in the western Carolines, for ceremonial payments.

Subsistence everywhere was based primarily on fishing and horticulture, with fishing somewhat more important in the low islands and horticulture more important in the high islands. Domestic animals were limited to dogs and chickens, found only in some areas.

Rice was grown in the Marianas but later was largely replaced by corn (maize), introduced from Mexico by the Spanish conquerors. Coconuts and coconut palms were used everywhere, both as food and for other purposes, such as thatch, lumber, and cordage. Some form of taro, either the true taro (*Colocasia*) or the giant swamp taro (*Cyrtosperma*), was probably cultivated everywhere except on some of the drier low islands in the east, where the groundwater tended to be too brackish. The breadfruit tree, which produces a large starchy fruit in abundance in the early summer, was also widely distributed. Bananas were an important food crop on the high islands. Tropical yams (*Dioscorea*), which produce large starchy tubers, are found today on a number of the high islands but are of greatest importance as a cultivated crop on Pohnpei, where they have high prestige and provide an important source of food in the winter. The sweet potato and cassava, introduced by Europeans, now serve as alternate subsistence foods on some of the high islands. On some of the drier atolls in the Marshalls and the Gilberts, the pandanus tree is a major subsistence crop. The edible fruit of some cultivated varieties contains starch and sugar that can be made into a flour and stored. Other varieties have large edible nuts. Some varieties of pandanus are cultivated for their leaves, used principally in making plaited mats and sometimes for thatch.

Many kinds of fishing were practiced traditionally. Often there was a division of labour, with men using techniques requiring canoes in deep water, such as seines and line fishing, and women wading in the waters of the fringing reefs. Deep-sea trolling with sailing canoes was practiced mostly by low islanders. The low islanders also at times made expeditions to certain small, uninhabited reefs and low islands to fish and collect turtle and seabird eggs.

Cutting tools were made from stone and shell. Iron was introduced by Europeans, although some iron tools may have been obtained from Oriental sources in western Micronesia.

Simple pottery has been found only in the western high islands of Micronesia: the Marianas, Palau, and Yap. Suitable clay apparently exists in Truk, Pohnpei, and Kosrae, but if pottery was ever introduced to these islands, it was not widely used.

All Micronesians, even the high islanders, relied often on water travel, although the high islanders used canoes principally in the sheltered coastal waters of their home islands. Micronesian canoes had a single hull with one outrigger. Canoes used in protected waters were often simple dugout canoes, but the oceangoing canoes, found especially in the central Carolinian atolls, the Marshalls, and the Gilberts, had sides built up of irregular planks that were caulked and sewn together with cord made from coconut-husk fibre.

Some of the atoll dwellers regularly went on trips requiring several nights in the open sea. Extra provisions were usually taken along as gifts and for emergency needs if the canoe were blown off course. In historic times vessels blown off course have ended up in a variety of islands inside and outside of Micronesia. Conversely, vessels from other areas of the Pacific and from the Orient have been blown to Micronesia. It seems clear that, prehistorically, there was communication in chain fashion from the Ellice Islands (now the state of Tuvalu) and western Polynesia through the Gilberts, the Marshalls, and the Carolines to Palau and the southeast atolls and beyond them into the northern Moluccas in Indonesia. Probably there was also deliberate communication across the larger gap between the central Carolinian atolls and the Marianas; in the

[margin: The Yapese Empire]

[margin: Fishing and horticulture]

[margin: Travel on the open sea]

Islanders of Satawal Island, Federated States of
Micronesia, sailing a hand-hewn outrigger canoe.
© Nicholas DeVore III/Bruce Coleman Inc.

latter there is a long-established population of cultural
Carolinian immigrants retaining their original language.

Property and exchange. The most important property
among the Micronesians was land. Land-tenure customs
varied considerably from island to island, even among
those with related cultures. Land was owned primarily by
extended-family groups or lineages. Individuals acquired
use rights to particular plots through their kin connections,
acknowledging the rights of the group by periodic offerings
of first fruits to the kin-group head. Often a community
chief and sometimes a superior chief received offerings
from each household or larger kin group holding land
under his jurisdiction. In some areas, especially in eastern
Micronesia, strong chiefs confiscated land from those who
fell out of their favour, awarding it to loyal followers.

Because land was a scarce resource in much of Micronesia, various mechanisms developed to govern its distribution. In most areas matrilineal inheritance of land rights
was practiced, and, if necessary, children of the men of the
lineage could also inherit use rights to the land worked by
their fathers or receive a share outright if the lineage had
more than it needed. In general, land was not sold, but
it might be given in payment for medicine and nursing
services or as compensation for an injury.

In the larger high islands, interior areas not under regular cultivation were considered community property and
were used for collecting wild food and for temporary gardens. In the atolls all land was owned by one or another
family group, even the smallest islets with only a few
coconut trees.

Feasts as
exchange
rituals

Large feasts were common throughout Micronesia. The
people assembled large quantities of food and offered it
to the chief, and he in turn redistributed much of it to
the people. Sometimes kin groups or communities held
alternating semicompetitive feasts in which each tried to
outdo the other. Feasts were held to commemorate important transitions in the life cycle, especially marriage
and death. A kind of delayed exchange might take place
at these feasts, certain relatives being obliged to make
presentations of food and goods in return for past or anticipated services.

Substantial payments were sometimes made to practitioners of traditional medicine, especially when the practitioner was not a close relative. Such payments consisted of
food and other goods. The precise amount was generally
left to the family of the patient, with the understanding
that a stingy family might not get the most energetic and
effective treatment.

In Palau and Yap, shell and stone valuables were used
in transactions at life crises and for certain other specific
compensations, such as payment for injuries. These are
often called money, but their use was much more limited
and specific than that of most money. The best known of
them were the large stone disks that the men of Yap manufactured on Palau and carried home in sailing canoes.

A certain amount of trade developed between the low
islanders and high islanders, the low islanders providing
handicraft products that the high islanders could have
made if they had needed to, and the high islanders providing things obtained more easily there. This trade was
especially well developed between the low islanders of the
central Carolines and the high islanders of Yap and Truk.
The most important high-island export was turmeric, used
for medicinal and cosmetic purposes, which formed a
bright orange body paint when mixed with coconut oil.
The low islanders provided shell beads, plaited pandanus
mats, and coarse cloth woven from banana or wild hibiscus fibre and used for women's wraparounds and for
men's loincloths. Trade was often with particular partners
who regarded themselves as distant relatives. An important function of the trade was to provide the low islanders
with aid and a temporary dwelling place when their islands were devastated by the periodic typhoons.

RELIGION AND ART

After 1900 Christianity became well established in most
major centres in Micronesia. Traditional religions were no
longer practiced in their full original form, although in
Yap and some atolls of the central Carolines, traditional
religion continued to be practiced until the middle of the
20th century. Missionaries and travelers have left descriptions of certain aspects of the island religions, but there is
no complete and systematic account.

The basic patterns of religion were probably similar
throughout most of Micronesia. The Micronesians were
polytheists, believing in several high gods, a large number
of spirits attached to specific localities or performing specific functions, and a number of ancestors and deceased
neighbours who could sometimes make contact with their
living descendants and friends. Practices connected with
these three major categories of supernatural beings tended
to be distinct and to be handled by different specialists,
although a figure might gradually shift from one category
into the other.

Micronesians generally believed in at least three vertically arranged levels of the universe: the earth proper,
the underworld, and heaven or the sky world. Some Micronesians may have believed in multiple heavens, as did
people in Polynesia and Indonesia, but the details of their
beliefs are now unclear.

Micronesian origin myths generally tell of the origin of
particular islands or descent groups or the initial discovery
or later conquest of an island by the ruling descent group.
The notion of the supernatural creation of the whole human species or of the whole world is either not found or
little emphasized in Micronesian mythology.

Ceremonies for the high gods appear to have been principally seasonal offerings of first fruits, performed often
in private by a specialist priest with a few helpers. Special appeals to the high gods were probably also made at
times of community crisis, such as wars or typhoons, but
human sacrifice apparently was not practiced. The priests
were very likely relatives of the ruling chiefs. The lesser
spirits were called on by magicians for specific purposes,
most notably for the diagnosis and cure of disease but also
for such purposes as success in fishing, control of weather,
success in love, and prowess in athletic contests, battle,
canoe building, and other difficult pursuits.

Ancestral spirits were often contacted in dreams and in
the trances of spirit mediums, as were the high gods and
other nonhuman spirits. They would give people information about the causes of disease, deaths, and other misfortunes and would sometimes prescribe new medicines
or new varieties of magic. At times, the spirit mediums
would also order their human protégés to perform songs

Communi-
cation
with
spirits

and dances for the entertainment of the spirits, to win their goodwill and insure the prosperity of the community.

Micronesia has little permanent visual art. The best known consists of the painted bas-relief scenes on the timbers and gables of the men's houses in Palau. Stylized wooden masks and human figures have been found in the Mortlock Islands, southeast of Truk. Decorative lashings of light and dark sennit twine are found in important buildings. Painting and decoration of canoes is common, following traditional patterns for each island. Patterns were woven into clothing. Wooden bowls were carved and painted with aesthetic intent.

Much of the most-developed traditional art of Micronesia was ephemeral: body painting and ornamentation with garlands of flowers, singing, dancing, and the recital of myths, tales, and poetry. Oratory was also an important traditional art and still survives. A good orator was expected to make mythological and historical allusions and to use special figures of speech. (J.L.Fi./R.C.Ki.)

EFFECTS OF EUROPEAN CONTACT

Micronesia has the most complicated colonial history in the Pacific. Guam, the southernmost of the Mariana Islands, became the first inhabited Pacific island to be visited by a European when Ferdinand Magellan landed there in 1521, and the Marianas became the first European colony when Spain took control of the island chain in 1668. In 1670 the indigenous Chamorro people rebelled, and a quarter-century of sporadic warfare followed. That conflict, along with diseases introduced by Europeans, reduced the local population from perhaps as many as 100,000 to 4,000. Most of the Chamorro people were moved to Guam. Much of Chamorro culture was destroyed, but the language survived.

Spain attempted to expand its rule as far east as Pohnpei but did not succeed. The Germans claimed the Marshall Islands in 1885 and the island of Nauru in 1888. In 1892 Britain entered the scene in eastern Micronesia and added the Gilbert Islands to its colonial empire.

The Spanish–American War brought an end to Spain's presence in the Pacific. Upon Spain's defeat in 1898 the United States seized Guam because of the strategic coaling station that Spain had developed there. In the following year Germany purchased Spain's claims to the Caroline Islands (Palau, Yap, Pohnpei, Truk, and Kosrae) and the northern Marianas. The copra industry was greatly expanded under German rule, and its administration was one of indirect rule.

Micronesia and the League of Nations

World War I changed the face of Micronesia. Japan replaced Germany in the northern Marianas, the Carolines, and the Marshall Islands. In 1920 the islands became a mandated territory under the authority of the League of Nations. Japan initiated an aggressive program of economic development, and Japanese, Okinawan, and Korean immigrants eventually came to outnumber the islanders by a ratio of two to one. Sugar, fishing, and other industries were developed, and the copra industry was greatly expanded.

After World War I Nauru, which had been held by Germany, also became a League of Nations mandate, with Australia having administrative responsibility. Guam remained under the firm direct rule of the U.S. Navy, and the Gilberts continued as part of the larger British crown colony of the Gilbert and Ellice Islands with a system of indirect rule.

World War II again altered the political map of Micronesia. After its attack on Pearl Harbor in late 1941, Japan occupied the Gilberts, Guam, and Nauru, and for the only time in its history all of Micronesia was under one colonial master. The war inflicted great suffering, and major military engagements took place between Japanese and American forces in parts of the Gilberts, the Marshalls, Truk, Palau, Guam, and the northern Marianas. At the end of the war the economy was a shambles, a great amount of property had been destroyed, there were food shortages, and many people had been displaced.

After the war Guam was returned to the United States, and British colonial rule was resumed for the Gilberts. Nauru became a trust territory of the United Nations,

similar to the old mandate system, and Australia resumed administrative responsibility. The United States replaced Japan in the former mandated islands, and this portion of Micronesia became the United Nations' Trust Territory of the Pacific Islands (TTPI).

The decolonization of the Pacific began when the Polynesian state of Western Samoa became independent in 1962. Nauru was the first Micronesian country to become a sovereign nation when it gained independence in 1968. Because of its rich phosphate deposits, its people have one of the highest per capita incomes in the world. Large sums are invested in trust funds around the world in preparation for the eventual exhaustion of its mineral wealth, which is expected to occur before the turn of the century. Nauruans are almost totally dependent on imports. Little traditional culture remains; housing, foods, and clothing are almost entirely Western.

The Gilbert Islands, along with Kiritimati (formerly Christmas) Island, Banaba (formerly Ocean) Island, and most of the Line Island and Phoenix Island groups, now form the nation of Kiribati, having gained independence in 1979. The Gilberts form the core of the nation and have the vast majority of its population. Outside of Tarawa Atoll, the site of the nation's capital, much of the traditional culture and life-style prevails. Subsistence agriculture and fishing remain the mainstays of the outer island economy, and most buildings and dwellings are of traditional designs and materials.

Negotiations regarding the future political status of the TTPI began in 1969, and it soon became clear that the peoples with such diverse cultures and languages did not feel any real sense of kindred or national unity. Three island groups had strategic value to the United States and used it to their advantage to demand separate negotiations with the United States.

Strategic islands

The northern Mariana Islands were the first to break away. The highly westernized Chamorro peoples had little in common with other Micronesians, and in 1975 they voted to become the Commonwealth of the Northern Mariana Islands, an integral part of the United States. The islands have a well-developed tourist trade and a sophisticated economy. With commonwealth status, the Chamorros became American citizens, and the population is highly urbanized and concentrated on the island of Saipan, the capital.

Palau and the Marshall Islands became republics, and the remaining islands of the TTPI formed the Federated States of Micronesia (composed of the four states of Yap, Truk, Pohnpei, and Kosrae). Each approved a Compact of Free Association under which the United States handles matters of defense, and strategic access is denied to all other nations. In return, the United States provides substantial subsidies to the nations, and their citizens have the legal status of "habitual resident," allowing them the right to live in and seek employment in the United States. The compacts have been approved by the United States for the Federated States of Micronesia and the Republic of the Marshall Islands.

Each of the Micronesian entities has its own capital and urban area, and in the case of the Federated States of Micronesia there is a capital in each constituent state. Approximately one-half of all islanders in the former trust territory are urban dwellers today. They are heavily dependent on imports, and, except on the outer islands, much of traditional life has been lost. (R.C.Ki.)

Polynesian cultures

The physical environment of the islands of the Polynesian triangle is not as favourable for human habitation as it might at first seem and certainly presented difficulties when the ancestors of the Polynesians entered the area from the west, well before the beginning of the Christian Era. The islands were devoid of much that was needed for human habitation. Most of the food and useful plants and all of the domestic fowl and animals had to be transported by the settlers. Since that time, the physical environment has continued to exert a marked influence on the nature and extent of the evolution of Polynesian cultures.

The popular image of Polynesian cultures suggests an almost blissfully simple and easy way of life, devoid of harsh extremes of any type, played out on islands of great beauty and natural abundance. But the image, a product of popular literature and the motion-picture and tourist industries, is wide of the mark. Traditional Polynesian cultures were complex, highly specialized, and diversified, and the environment was not always benign.

The principal characteristic of Polynesian cultures is an effective adaptation to and mastery of the ocean environment in which they have flourished. This mastery did not extend merely to the technology involved in ship building, to the techniques of navigation, and to other obvious nautical aspects of the culture but permeated social organization, religion, food production, and most other facets of the culture. The Polynesians could not only sail the seas, but socially they could cope with the human problems of shipwreck, split families, and the sudden loss of large portions of the social group. In short, the cultures were well equipped to handle the numerous hazards that they had to face in the beautiful but actually quite hostile Pacific environment.

Polynesian conservatism

Another important characteristic of Polynesian cultures was a high degree of conservatism and traditional orientation and the rather detailed structuring that placed every person in a well-defined relationship to society and to the universe. This conservatism is apparent even in a rapid examination of Polynesian materials from islands separated by hundreds or thousands of miles, whose populations had been separated from the common Polynesian stock two or three millennia in the past. The similarity between such items as stone adzes and fish hooks is most remarkable. The same is true for kinship terms, plant names, and much of the rest of the technical vocabulary of the cultures, as well as for art motifs and medical preparations. The ornate and voluminous genealogies, chants, legends, songs, and spells that were passed down and elaborated through the generations show a profound reverence for the past.

The traditions of Polynesian cultures provided a definition of an individual's relation to his society and to all of nature. The creation myths told of the origin of the world, setting forth the order of precedence of Earth, sky, and sea and all the phenomena thereof, including man and woman. The genealogies fixed the individual tightly into the typically aristocratic Polynesian social order. Other legends interpreted natural phenomena, while historical accounts often described, with varying amounts of mythological embroidery, the migrations of a people before they arrived at the island on which they were located, their adventures on the way, and the development of the culture following settlement.

The Polynesians were unusually well oriented, as would be expected of a nautical culture, to the entirety of nature. Their languages abound with terminology for stars, currents, winds, landforms, and directions and include a large number of grammatical elements indicating, for example, direction of motion implied by verbs, including movement toward or away from the speaker, relative positions of objects with reference to the speaker, and direction of movement along a seashore–inland axis.

Polynesian cultures displayed a thoroughly realistic and practical exploitation of the environment but at the same time exhibited a profound interest in the supernatural. This interest was directly related to the general interest in systematization and structure, the supernatural being for the Polynesian another portion of reality, albeit less manageable, that had to be structured and coped with.

Violence and cruelty were ever-present elements of Polynesian cultures. This is reflected in their oral literature and in all aspects of traditional life. Custom controlled and repressed direct physical expression of aggression within the kin group and the tribe up to a point, but there were definite limits beyond which only violence could restore status or assuage injured pride. Punishments for transgressing rules of behaviour toward chiefs and high priests or for violating various rituals incorporated ritual sacrifice and cannibalism as major features. Intertribal warfare was extemely common, particularly when population pressure had built up and land and resources were limited.

Perhaps the most publicized, and accordingly overrated, aspect of Polynesian culture is its sensuality: as in many other aspects of life, the Polynesians generally took a very direct, realistic, and quite physical approach to gratification of the senses. But there was no abnormal focus or concentration on any aspect of sensual gratification such as is seen in many other cultures where, for example, eating, drinking, or sex have become the object of great cultural elaboration. This lack of elaboration may be due in part to limitations imposed by the environment. The flora of Polynesia did not, for example, provide a very good basis for elaboration of cuisine, as the number of edible plants was rather restricted, and there was a dearth of spices. In general, however, this balanced approach to sensual gratification seems to be just another reflection of the Polynesian straightforward approach to the world.

Sexual mores

Polynesian culture, for example, is generally thought to have been characterized by extreme sexual promiscuity, but such is not the case. Definite restrictions were placed on sexual behaviour, though the limits of acceptable behaviour were indeed wider than in many other cultures of the world. Children were permitted freedom of sexual expression; from puberty on, sexual activity was strongly encouraged, limited only by incest restrictions (which were not stringent) and considerations of social prestige. Parents would become concerned if daughters were not sought after for sexual favours, and premarital pregnancy only enhanced a girl's attractiveness. Public intercourse was engaged in during certain religious festivals and crisis rite ceremonies as a means to promote general fertility. There was, however, no pathological elaboration of sex for its own sake. Polynesian art, for example, is strikingly devoid of sexual content. There are occasional references made to sexual activity in native Polynesian oral literature, but many of these have to do with creative acts of the Polynesian gods, for the Polynesians saw the process of the creation of the universe as having taken place in a manner similar to human procreation. There is no corpus of Polynesian literature analogous to pornography.

SOCIAL AND POLITICAL LIFE

Settlement patterns and housing. Two major settlement patterns were present in Polynesia prior to European contact: the hamlet and the village. Their origin and development may depend to a large extent on geographic factors, such as the distribution of food-crop resources, on defense considerations, and on social organization.

The hamlet settlement pattern was found in the larger volcanic islands, where food resources were diversified and scattered over the range of environmental zones that developed on such islands. A typical hamlet settlement pattern was often found in the Marquesas Islands. There, in prehistoric times as at present, the population spread over the floors and up the sides of the deep and narrow Marquesan valleys in clusters of perhaps four to five houses, often with gardens, taro patches, coconut trees, and breadfruit clustered in the immediate vicinity. The Marquesan houses were built on rectangular platforms, the height and composition of which depended on the prestige of the owner. Individuals of lower status might have a simple paved rectangle no more than a few inches high, while warriors, priests, or chiefs might live in houses perched on platforms seven to eight feet high and containing stones of several tons in weight. The house itself was built on a kind of a step running across the rear of the platform. Composed of a lashed and fitted wooden framework and with a thatched roof, the typical house was open all the way across the front and had square ends. The roof sloped from the high ridgepole directly to the platform floor in the rear. Inside, a polished coconut log often ran the length of the house, serving as a kind of community pillow. The floors were covered with mats, shredded leaves, or bark. Belongings were suspended in bundles from the rafters. Most of the household activity took place on the "veranda," or unroofed front portion of the platform, which was paved with smooth basalt stones from streambeds. Houses of chiefs and other individuals of high status often made use of cut stone slabs for decorating the platform. Many also had rectangular pits in the platforms for storing fermenting breadfruit paste (an important delicacy) and small caches in which were interred the carefully cleaned and packaged bones of important family members.

Among the clusters of houses in each major valley section was a large rectangular ceremonial plaza, or *tohua,* which served as the focal point for all tribal or subtribal ceremonies, as well as a point for daily social gatherings. This complex of structures, often 600 feet (200 metres) or more in length, was generally built upon a huge artificial terrace carved out of a slope. Surrounding the plaza atop the terrace were the houses of the tribal chiefs and priests, temples and other sacred structures, and long sheds for spectators. At one end was usually found a temple with a sacred banyan tree in which were suspended the packaged bones of the illustrious dead of the tribe.

In Samoa, on the other hand, the village settlement pattern was followed after AD 1000 or so. There, fortified villages, consisting of 30 or more houses arranged in a network of paths, grew up along the coast. The houses at the time of European contact were built on oval mounds faced with rough stone slabs, although earlier houses had been built on rectangular platforms much like those of the Marquesas. The typical Samoan house was and is today a large shedlike structure without walls, oval in floor plan, with a beehive-shaped, thatched roof supported by a series of stout wooden pillars. Rolled mats along the eaves were let down to protect the inhabitants from sun, rain, or the night air. These houses, arranged in orderly fashion along the paths and sunken roadways that crosscut the villages, were surrounded by a fortification wall of stone or by wooden palisades.

Maori fortified villages The Maori of New Zealand constructed large and impressive fortified villages (*pa*) on hilltops, surpassing those of all other Polynesian cultures. These forts were protected by ditches, palisades, trenches, and terraces. The interiors were partitioned off by additional defensive works so as to facilitate battle even after the outer defenses had been penetrated by an enemy assault. The houses within were of timber, rectangular in plan, and generally dug about one foot into the earth surface.

Other, unfortified Maori villages consisted of loose collections of houses arranged around a level area where ceremonies and meetings might take place. Forts were usually constructed in the vicinity of such villages for the use of inhabitants in time of war.

Family and kinship. The typical Polynesian family was extended, that is, it consisted of three or more generations, and it centred around a descent group. The extended family and the descent group were not the same. In most cases descent was preferably traced through males, with both females and males belonging to their father's descent group, and the extended family consisted of a senior male, his sons and grandsons, and their spouses and unmarried children of both sexes. Residence was usually virilocal; females left their family of birth and joined their husbands' families upon marriage. Polynesian societies were noted for their flexibility, however, and there were many variations in the system of descent. In Hawaii, Tahiti, and elsewhere, and especially if it were to one's advantage, descent could be traced through females and one could become a member of one's mother's descent groups. Thus, while descent through males was preferred, the descent system was actually bilateral (through either parental sex). Adoption was very common and added to the flexibility of the social system. Siblings and cousins frequently adopted one another's children, and grandparents sometimes adopted their own grandchildren. These children behaved toward their adopted parents as they would their own.

The basic Polynesian kinship pattern is a very simple one: it distinguishes among generations, as might be expected in a society so strongly oriented on tradition and genealogy. There are sets of terms for the grandparents' generation, distinguishing by sex only; parents' generation, in which parents are distinguished from various categories of aunt and uncles; members of a person's own generation, in which the terms permit identification by sex, relative age, and sometimes marital potential (marriage of certain cousin categories is preferred in some Polynesian societies); and, finally, children's generation, in which age and sex are again distinguished.

In general, the kinship terminologies in use in the various societies in eastern and marginal Polynesia are relatively simpler than those in the west.

Social hierarchy and political organization. The two major types of settlement in Polynesian cultures—hamlet and village—were bound together by a web of kinship and territorial ties of varying degrees of importance.

There were two main and probably related types of kinship-based descent groups prevalent in Polynesian society. By far the most common and perhaps the most like the ancestral form of Polynesian social organization was the "ramage" type, in which the whole society might be represented in the form of a multibranched tree. There was a senior line of descent, in which descent passed from firstborn son to firstborn son and was traceable back to the mythological past. Branches off this main line were founded by junior sons, and these branches in turn produced further branches. Because the main line was the direct line to the gods and therefore carried the maximum traditional prestige and sanctity, it followed that each of the branches was ranked in terms of its proximity to the main line, and each individual in each branch could place himself in a prestige-ranking scale relative to other members of his household settlement and kin group.

"Ramage"-type descent

The levels of the branches off the main line assumed different levels of importance in various Polynesian societies. In New Zealand, for example, four levels were recognized: (1) The *waka* were a group descended on both maternal and paternal sides (male preferred) from the crew of one of the original canoes in the traditional Maori migration to New Zealand. They occupied a given territory and had a chief who functioned only in times of crisis and members who recognized their common tradition and interest. (2) The *iwi* were component parts of the *waka* but were made up of individuals tracing descent from a single occupant of one of the canoes, through either maternal or paternal line (again, the male line was the prestige line). The *iwi* had a chief and was a more tightly knit kinship group occupying a defined section of land within the *waka* territory. (3) The *hapu,* a component unit of the *iwi,* was the principal Maori descent group, consisting of all descendants of a given ancestor, usually sited in a particular village and controlling the farming land around the village. The *hapu* had a chief responsible for all economic and civil affairs. (4) The *whanau,* or households of the *hapu,* formed the lowest unit within Maori society and usually consisted of three to four generations.

Each of the hierarchical kinship segments just mentioned could be ranked relative to the others, with the exception of the *iwi.* The *hapu* could all be ranked within any given *iwi* on the basis of their chiefs' ancestry. Within the *waka,* each *iwi* could also be ranked in terms of the distance of its founding ancestor from the chief of the canoe.

This form of hierarchical branching-descent-group organization with territorial overtones was found in most Polynesian societies, with appropriate variations for local environmental conditions and cultural history.

The other major form of kinship-based descent group found in Polynesia is that known as the "descent line." Descent-line organization appears to be the result of a breakdown in genealogical ties between the lower levels of a ramage organization. The descent line in Samoa, for example, consists of a group of people tracing descent in the male line from a common mythical ancestor. This group was known as a *sa.* There was no concern for genealogical relationship of one descent line to another, nor was there any concern for ranking based on distance from or proximity to any particular male line of descent. What were passed down through the descent line were titles, each of which had rank and prestige attached to it. Each descent line held a number of these titles, which enabled it to participate in certain ways in the village council (*fono*). A number of descent lines were represented in each village council, and each descent line was spread through a number of villages in a given area. Within a given village, the senior title, determined by mythological connections, gave its holder the position of chief.

"Descent-line" kinship groups

A characteristic of the descent-line system is its flexibility. Depending so heavily on myth and tradition for validation of status and title, it was only natural that ambitious titleholders could advance the prestige of their titles at the expense of others by various kinds of prestige behaviour, such as displays of wealth and power. The traditions governing title seniority could then be judiciously tampered with to produce the realignment that would allow the advance in status to occur. New descent lines might also be founded with similar "rewriting" of oral tradition.

Stratification. The tendency toward social stratification is perhaps inherent in Polynesian society, with its great interest in and emphasis on status and the indicators and prerogatives thereof. There seems to have been a process of social evolution occurring in Polynesia that tended to be somewhat unidirectional, leading toward more sharply defined differences in status and development of social classes that were clearly defined in terms of rights, duties, behaviour, and general life-style.

The chief in ancient Polynesian society was the person of highest status, yet he was regarded by his people and generally conducted himself as merely "first among equals." In most of the more traditional of the societies, the chief could not appropriate the land of his followers, nor did he appear to be too interested in increasing his own group's holdings at the expense of neighbouring groups. In terms of his clothing and behaviour, there was little to distinguish him from other males. Nevertheless, he was the repository of sacred power for the group, a symbol of its tie with the past, and the vehicle whereby this tie would be perpetuated for coming generations. Even in the traditional Polynesian societies, however, it was possible for a man to rise in prestige by various achievements; by giving gifts, holding feasts, or displaying military prowess, for example. These activities seem to have contained the seed of change in the traditional social order.

Warfare. There was a group of Polynesian societies in
which the more traditional social order, when breaking
down, gave way to one in which chiefs and other individuals of high status no longer held office on the traditional
genealogical basis but by virtue of having taken it, often by
force, or as a result of some act that raised their prestige
higher than that of the actual chief. In these societies the
chiefs behaved more autocratically and set themselves off
from the rest of the population by various kinds of privileges and behaviour. Changes in leadership were frequent, and kinship groups were split internally and reorganized in the course of internecine wars. Finally, out of this dynamic social situation emerged the most socially and politically advanced Polynesian societies (Hawaii, Tahiti, Tonga), with clear-cut social stratification and concentration of all power at the apex of the social pyramid—the paramount chief—below whom were several levels of nobility usually selected on genealogical relationship to the chiefly line. The paramount chiefs and upper classes had absolute powers over the commoners, inflicting cruel physical punishments, such as human sacrifice, for all manner of affronts to their dignities (touching a chief's shadow, for example). Warfare was frequent, well organized, and marked by acts of great cruelty. Religious and political powers were closely linked, with religious concepts and the gods themselves mirroring the cruelty and viciousness of the societies that had produced them.

Socialization and education. The Polynesian child was generally born into a large and warm family environment. Even before the child could walk, it was turned over for care to the other children of the household (siblings, cousins), who generally associated in a kind of amorphous play group with children of other families. It was in this context that the Polynesian child received a great deal of its socialization, first carried piggyback by an older sister and then running with a crowd. A particularly warm relationship existed between a child and its grandparents, often taking the form of rather gross bantering but providing the vehicle for inculcation of traditional lore, technical training, and even sexual advice.

There was little by way of formal education in Polynesian society, except for the training in special crafts and skills, such as tattooing, and the sacred academies for training

the priest-bards who were the repositories of the society's traditions, mythology, and genealogies.

Rites of passage varied in type and importance from society to society, but there were several that were generally held throughout Polynesia. The birth of a child was a matter of great significance, particularly if the child happened to be a firstborn son of a high-status descent group. Various procedures were called for to announce the birth to the community, to the ancestors, and to the gods, and to care for the welfare (both physical and supernatural) of the infant and mother by application of medical and magical techniques.

Circumcision was a major event in the male life cycle and was marked by elaborate rituals, which increased in importance with the status of the male. Polynesians generally have an unusual abhorrence of the uncircumcised, to the extent that in some societies it was believed such people would go to a very unpleasant netherworld after death. Although no such rite involving mutilation is reported for girls, some societies, such as the Marquesas, had orgiastic ceremonies in which adolescent girls made a more or less public debut, in a sexual sense.

There were other milestones in life that were marked with ceremonies in Polynesian cultures, such as the formal presentation of a royal heir, the completion of a tattooing operation or ear piercing in a high-status child, and the formal investiture of a priest or chief. The observances of these milestones were marked with a variety of rituals and quite often included human sacrifice, wanton killing of members of the population who might happen into the path of the ceremonial party, or killing of those who made mistakes in performance of the rituals.

Death, the terminal milestone, was universally celebrated with extravagant behaviour, increasing in extravagance in direct proportion to the status of the deceased. In many societies these ceremonies were marked by violence, with mourners mutilating themselves and others, and by human sacrifices, obtained from within the social group or without. Feasts were also common, as was orgiastic behaviour. The extravagance of funeral rites was surpassed, in some societies, by ceremonies to deify a departed chief or priest. These went on for prolonged periods, involving prodigious feasting and drinking, violence, and sexuality.

ECONOMIC SYSTEMS

Production and technology. The Polynesians were above all mariners, but among the many seafaring peoples of the world they were quite unusual, for, far from having a disdain for the land and all that it involves, they were capable of and devoted to horticulture and arboriculture.

The sea provided most of the protein in the Polynesian diet. Fishing was carried on not only on an individual basis, with spear, line, or net, but on a group basis with large numbers of men spreading and drawing in huge nets in bays or lagoons or driving fish toward shore, where they could be captured in nets held in shallow water. In some Polynesian societies (Marquesas and Samoa, for example) there were specialists who directed the mass fishing efforts and the elaborate religious rituals that went along with them. Sea mammals (porpoises and whales) were also taken, the former often being driven into shore by means of large, well-organized drives: when a school of porpoises was sighted in a bay, a fleet of canoes would seal off the bay entrance, and crew members would leap into the water carrying stones in their hands, which they beat together as they swam slowly toward shore. The sounds terrified the porpoises, and they beached themselves in a frenzy.

The Polynesian fishermen's exploits were not, however, confined to coastal waters, for they were just as much at home on the high seas. The waters around their island homes were explored for miles in all directions. The Easter Islanders, for example, used to travel east to Sala y Gómez reef to fish—a journey of some 300 miles (500 kilometres). Good fishing waters were located by reference to land bodies if visible or just by dead reckoning. Line fishing to depths of 90 feet was not uncommon to take the grouper. School tuna were taken in large quantities on the high seas by means of shiny pearl shell lures with bone points. The flesh of sharks and rays were delicacies.

The breakdown of traditional social order

Distinctive rites of passage

Mollusks and crustaceans were important as food, and mollusks also provided the shells from which a wide variety of tools and ornaments were made. Clams, cowries, and various snails and conches were collected, generally by women and children, along the reefs or shorelines and in the shallows. Shrimps were netted with fine nets, while lobsters were collected by men who dove and pried their spiny prey loose from underwater crannies. The octopus was lured from its hiding place by an ingenious lure made of leopard cowrie shells. Various types of seaweeds and algae were also collected and were highly prized for their salty taste. There was, in short, nothing edible in the sea that was not food for the Polynesians.

Horti-
cultural
practices
Gardens and groves produced the staples of the Polynesian diet and most of the condiments. The major native Polynesian crops were yams, sweet potatoes, taro, breadfruit, bananas, sugarcane, coconuts, and Tahitian chestnuts (*Inocarpus edulis*). These crops achieved different levels of importance in various Polynesian societies, depending on cultural factors and environmental conditions. The Hawaiians, for example, relied heavily on taro, building extensive irrigation systems to grow the variety that requires muddy soil and planting the "dry" variety in the uplands. Breadfruit was not of great importance in Hawaii, however. In the Marquesas and Tahiti, on the other hand, breadfruit was the major staple, although taro was by no means neglected. In these islands breadfruit was allowed to become overripe and was then beaten into a pulp and stored in large, well-drained pits in the ground, in neat hibiscus-leaf bundles. The breadfruit paste thus stored would ferment but remain edible and nutritious for years, its sour taste being highly prized for imparting flavour to the rather bland fresh breadfruit paste.

In the subtropical climate of Easter Island and in temperate New Zealand, the most important Polynesian food plants could not survive. On Easter Island, for example, the coconut did not survive, although legends maintain that germinating coconuts were brought by the earliest settlers. This deprived the Easter Islanders not only of a variety of condiments and a rich source of vitamins but also of the leaves that were used elsewhere in Polynesia for thatch and baskets and of the husk fibres that were used to make fishing line and netting. In New Zealand it was not only the coconut but also breadfruit, yams, and bananas that did not survive. The radically different flora and fauna of New Zealand, however, offered foods to replace, at least partially, those that it would not support.

Not only the coconut but most food plants in Polynesia also provided materials for other purposes. The breadfruit furnished wood for the hulls of dugout canoes, and the milky sap of the fruit itself was used in caulking the gaps between the planks of larger canoes. The black mud of the taro patches was used to stain wood and stone carvings. The pandanus fruit was highly prized as a kind of chewing gum, as well as a major component of floral necklaces and headpieces, to which it contributed its strong and pleasant colour. Pandanus leaves, when bleached, became the raw material for fine mats. The candlenut was used for torches, its oil was a cathartic, and its wood furnished certain canoe parts.

Polynesian technology can be circumscribed by five items: wood, stone, vegetable fibre, shell, and bone. The canoes, houses, domestic utensils, weapons, religious sculpture, and a host of other incidental tools were fashioned from wood with stone or shell adzes; stone-flake knives; files made of coral, sea urchin, or rough stone; and drills of bone, stone, or shells. Fine carving was done with stone, shell, or animal teeth, particularly those of rats or sharks. Stone, generally fine-grained basalt, was the hardest material available to the Polynesians and was used to produce a variety of adzes.

The
absence of
metal
The absence of metal for use in attaching or clamping wooden parts posed no obstacle to Polynesian construction. Wooden components were skillfully fitted together and lashed with cordage made of various types of vegetable fibre, such as hibiscus bark, pandanus-leaf fibre, coconut fibre, or banyan bark. Huge double canoes 100 to 150 feet in length, for example, were built of numerous small wooden components all held together only by fitting and lashing, yet they were able to withstand the pounding of wind and wave for thousands of miles.

Vegetable material also furnished a major source of clothing in the form of the beaten bark (tapa) of the paper mulberry tree or the banyan. This material was beaten out into small sheets that could then be assembled to produce loincloths, capes, skirts, and headdresses. Bark cloth was decorated by painting and water marking and by attaching feathers, shells, teeth, and other ornaments. Fine mats were also used as apparel in western Polynesia.

Home furnishings also consisted mainly of vegetable material in the form of mats for sleeping and sitting, as well as for protection from the weather, and of baskets for holding personal belongings and food. Coconut shells and bottle gourds provided handy, durable containers for various items.

Pottery was in use in western Polynesia at the time of European contacts. It had been in use earlier in the Marquesas Islands, at the extreme eastern edge of Polynesia, but had disappeared from the technology.

Craft organizations are an interesting aspect of Polynesian culture. These organizations provided for the training of specialists in tasks requiring special knowledge and higher levels of manual skills—canoe construction, wood carving, and adz making, for example, as well as complicated operations, such as fishing and tattooing. When specialist groups existed, they were usually designated by name and would ply their craft for pay in the form of goods and services, as well as support for the period of their service.

Property and exchange.   Personal property was a well-developed concept in prehistoric Polynesia. Each individual, regardless of rank, had his own tools, small canoes, clothing, ornaments, trophies, weapons, and other items and was generally free to dispose of them as he wished. Other types of property, however, were owned by extended families or descent groups in common and used for the common good. These included items too large to be produced or managed by a single man alone, such as a large double canoe or a fishing net several hundred feet in length, as well as facilities and land intended directly for community use, such as a tribal ceremonial ground, a refuge fortification, or a large breadfruit-paste storage pit.

The matter of ownership of land and the means of production were complicated and varied among Polynesian cultures depending on the type of social organization that they developed. In Polynesian societies of the more traditional type, land was vested in a corporate descent group. Among the Maori this group was the *hapu,* and its members usually inhabited one or a few villages located in close proximity to each other. The land of the *hapu* was viewed as being symbolic of the *hapu* chief's sanctity and power and as almost a literal extension of his body. Yet, the land was apportioned out to the various family groups within the *hapu* and worked by them. The chief, regardless of his prestige (stemming from a close family tie to the tribe's mythological ancestors), could not evict a family of nonproducers or in any way cut them off from their source of livelihood. He could invoke supernatural powers in the form of a curse or of a ritual prohibition, but expropriation was quite uncommon. In return for this essentially inalienable right to his land, the good Maori was expected to provide certain quantities of produce for the chief on various occasions and also for the chief of the next highest element in Maori social organization, the *iwi.* If his offerings were not of sufficient size and quality, the Maori risked punishment and possibly even death in extreme cases but not expropriation. If the food offered was acceptable, however, the offerer would be assured of an appropriate amount of food of other types in return, demonstrating the chief's desire to live up to his own obligations.

Maori
land-
holding
practices

A number of Polynesian societies were essentially similar to the Maori in their land-holding practices, including those of the Tikopia, Pukapuka, Futuna, and Uvea; but in others, evolutionary changes in social organization began to exert pressure on the basic land-holding descent group (as exemplified by the Maori *hapu*), which seems to have been the basic building block of Polynesian society. As a result, the descent group ultimately lost control of all rights to land, surrendering it to increasingly powerful and autocratic chiefs. Thus, in Hawaii, perhaps the most sociopolitically evolved of all the Polynesian societies, there was a large mass of completely landless commoners dwelling in territorial districts, each of which ran from the seashore to the island's centre, thus including a segment of each of the island's ecological zones. Each of these districts was ruled by a chief, somewhat like a lord in medieval Europe, who was responsible to the paramount chief of the island for supervising, among other things, the production of that district. The district chief or the paramount chief was free to shift at will the population of commoners within the district, regardless of their kin affiliation, although the chief and nobles themselves still relied heavily on their own kinship affiliations and prerogative. The district chief saw to the production of each household in his district and could evict the unlucky farmer who failed to meet his quota. Both he and the paramount chief could also make a variety of arbitrary demands from which the commoners had little or no protection, except to leave the district and submit to the authority of another district chief. The commoners were responsible for producing certain specified quantities of food at certain times, which was collected and passed up to the district chiefs and ultimately to the paramount chief. At that level, certain types of food reserved for chiefs only would be set aside, and a redistribution of the remaining food would take place, with portions being passed back down the same channels that had been used to collect the food in the first place. Kinship groupings, consisting of all individuals related through both male and female lines, still existed to be sure, but their main functions seem to have been to serve as a channel for low-level exchange of food and other commodities and to assist in the organization of the massive food collections held periodically throughout the year for the nobility.

Economic redistribution in Hawaii

The Polynesian system of exchange of goods and services may be summarized by two terms: redistribution and reciprocity, both already mentioned in connection with the discussion of the land-holding systems. The redistributive system was essentially a vertical system with goods moving up from the lower strata of the society to the chiefs and other high-ranking persons and then being apportioned and redistributed, so that all would share in more equal fashion in the productivity of every kinship group or region. This system involved a complex, shifting web of reciprocal obligations, which is very much at the heart of Polynesian culture, even today. Goods and services rendered, even if not requested, necessarily give rise to an obligation for a return in kind. There were no markets in Polynesian cultures, nor was there any standard medium of exchange. All exchange was in the form of barter, often under the general supervision of some senior family or kin-group member. Thus, for example, a portion of the fish catches made on a minor fishing expedition by coastal residents would be passed inland to residents at central villages, who might return dry taro for the fish at some fixed ratio of units of taro to units of fish. The services of any of the numerous specialists in Polynesian cultures (tattooists, fishermen, wood-carvers, for example) was also paid for by barter, usually over and above the cost of the specialist's keep during his period of service. Early European visitors to Polynesia who were able to analyze the importance of reciprocal exchange and put it to their own use generally fared quite well among the Polynesians, although they sometimes found themselves overwhelmed by the increasing size of the obligations they had undertaken. Captain David Porter of the U.S. Navy, for example, in 1813 won the friendship of the chief of Taiohae, Nuku Hiva, with a gift of sperm whales' teeth but within a few months found himself fighting a tribal war essentially on behalf of the same chief, in order to live up to his obligations.

RELIGION AND ART

Religion and magic pervaded all aspects of Polynesian culture. All things, animate and inanimate, were believed to be endowed to a greater or lesser degree with mana, or sacred supernatural power. This power could be nul-

lified by various human actions. Polynesian chiefs had great mana, so great, in fact, that in some islands if a commoner touched the chief's shadow the injury to the chief's mana could only be compensated by the death of the commoner. In many Polynesian cultures even today, it is still considered to be in very poor taste to step over a person's legs, pass one's hand over a person's head, or stand with one's head higher than that of a person of high rank. These actions are believed to sap a person's mana, rendering him profane.

It was not only people who had mana, however, but buildings, stones, tools, canoes, and all things. Polynesian life was infused with a wide variety of complicated rules designed to prevent damage to the mana inherent in various things. Groves, trees, temples, or tracts of land were considered sacred and could not be entered by ordinary people because they were pervaded by the mana of a high-status person or god. If anyone inadvertently stepped over a tool left on the ground, it was thus rendered profane and would often be discarded. Women were not permitted in canoes under normal conditions in the Marquesas because their presence defiled the canoe. In many societies, men preparing for war or for any other hazardous or demanding undertaking had to avoid the company of women, eat certain foods only, and often go into seclusion so as to protect their powers from defilement. Some chants and songs were so sacred that every syllable had to be pronounced correctly. The penalty for major violations of these tapu, or prohibitions, was often death, swiftly executed and gruesome. Violations of lesser tapu, such as trespassing in a sacred grove or disturbing the bones of the dead, were believed to be visited with supernatural punishment in the form of illness, bad luck, or debilitation.

The sacred power of places

Mana was not the only force that the Polynesian had to be wary of, however. The universe, in their beliefs, was peopled with spiritual beings of various types, many of whom were malevolent. In addition, there was a host of gods of various degrees of importance, ranging from the great gods of the Polynesian pantheon, such as Tangaroa, Tu, and Lono, to strictly local gods who were deified priests or chiefs of great renown. All of these gods had to be worshiped in their own way, the most important by full-time priests of highest status, those of lesser importance by part-time priests. Worship of the gods involved sacrifices (including humans), chants and recitations, feasting (often with great prodigality), sexual orgies (to promote fertility), and elaborate rituals, often preceded by long fasting and abstinence.

Magic flourished in Polynesian society, with everyone practicing various rituals for success in love, war, planting, or fishing, or to bring misfortune to rivals. There were also magical specialists who could be resorted to when the problem at hand was too great or complicated to be solvable by ordinary magic. Such magical practices have survived in Polynesian cultures right down to the present time.

The numerous restrictions and demands placed upon the average Polynesian by religion and the supernatural were in many cases seen as oppressive by the Polynesians themselves, and, in one case, the whole system was simply abolished. This occurred in Hawaii in 1819, when the young king, Kamehameha II, assisted by the high priest, his adviser, and other leaders of the court, publicly and intentionally broke the main food and eating tapu at a festival, after which the high priest desecrated the images of the gods and burned the temple. While many factors played a part in the prelude to this dramatic act (not the least of which were the presence of Europeans and the desires of the royal women to be free from the burden of tapu), the principal factor motivating Kamehameha II seems to have been a real impatience and frustration at an increasingly constricting system that provided little obvious benefit in return for the great inconvenience. Although no other islands in Polynesia followed the Hawaiian example, there is evidence that the religious system was viewed as extremely frustrating in many other Polynesian cultures.

Polynesian art was highly developed and brilliant, but little of what is known to have existed has survived down to the present day. This is mainly due to the perishability of much of the material (bark cloth, basketry, feather-work) and the dispersion that took place during the era of European contact, when such items were bartered for firearms, liquor, iron tools, or trinkets.

Each Polynesian society developed its own particular area of artistic endeavour—monumental stone sculpture on Easter Island and the Marquesas; highly decorated bark cloth in western Polynesia; fine mats in Tonga. In this development, a vocabulary of art motifs, styles, and artistic principles was elaborated, which also differ somewhat from culture to culture. Certain types of motifs nevertheless are widely distributed in Polynesia. For example, a number of small geometric decorative elements, such as a toothed pattern or units of diagonally sloping lines, are found in most cultures in many media. Stylized floral and animal elements are also widely distributed. In eastern and marginal Polynesia, an anthropomorphic figure and an often grotesque anthropomorphic face with bulging eyes and protruding tongue are prominent in all types of plastic art, as well as in tattooing.

Architecture was developed almost everywhere in Polynesia, but only the ruined stone structures of the eastern Polynesian islands remain to bear witness to the Polynesians' considerable skill. The stone temples of the Society Islands, Easter Island, and the Marquesas, even in their ruined state, display striking proportions and design; clever use of stones of different colours, shapes, and textures; and the evidence of sound combination of practical engineering with artistic objectives. (R.C.Su./R.C.Ki.)

EFFECTS OF EUROPEAN CONTACT

Polynesian cultures have been radically altered by contact with the Western world. European explorers navigated much of the area in the latter quarter of the 18th century, and the first missionaries arrived in the late 1700s and early 1800s. The colonial partitioning began in 1842 when France annexed Tahiti. Eventually, Chile, Germany, New Zealand, the United Kingdom, and the United States held territory in the area. Germany lost its interests in the islands as a consequence of World War I.

The period between the two world wars was tranquil, although there was some open resistance to New Zealand's administration of Western Samoa under a League of Nations mandate. The missions' influence on the Polynesian peoples increased, and Christianity became an integral part of the islanders' lives. In many areas Christianity in turn was influenced by local traditions and customs. Quite commonly, villages competed to build larger and more elaborate churches, and first-time visitors to Polynesia are often surprised at the intensity of the islanders' commitment to Christianity. Many Polynesians were recruited to missionize other parts of the Pacific.

After World War II sentiments for decolonization began to spread, and Western Samoa became the first independent Pacific nation when it gained sovereignty from New Zealand in 1962. Tonga freed itself as a protectorate of the United Kingdom in 1970, and the Ellice Islands, in the Gilbert and Ellice Islands Colony of Great Britain, achieved independence as Tuvalu in 1978. Ironically, the conservatism of Polynesian cultures is most manifest in

these three independent nations. Of the three island groups that had been monarchies—Tonga, Tahiti, and Hawaii—monarchy survives only in Tonga, although Tonga also has a British-style parliament that gives special status to traditional nobles. Having been a mandate of New Zealand, a Commonwealth nation, Western Samoa also has a parliamentary system, but only traditional chiefs (*matai*) may vote and run for election. Tuvalu also follows the parliamentary style of government. In Tonga, Samoa, and Tuvalu, the vast majority of people live in subsistence-based villages, where much of traditional culture survives.

The Cook Islands and its former colonial authority created a new political status in 1965 when the Cooks became self-governing in free association with New Zealand. In this innovative arrangement, the Cooks became self-governing with regard to internal affairs, and New Zealand agreed to manage external affairs as requested. New Zealand provides the government of the Cook Islands with a financial subsidy, and Cook Islanders enjoy dual citizenship. As the relationship has subsequently evolved, the Cook Islands has assumed control of most of its external or foreign affairs. Niue Island, another former dependency of New Zealand, followed suit in 1974 when it also became self-governing in free association with the former colonial power. Many of the people of the Cook Islands and Niue have become very westernized, and many of their citizens as well as those of Western Samoa have immigrated to New Zealand. Indeed, Auckland, N.Z., has the largest concentration of Polynesians of any city or place in the world.

Six other Polynesian entities remain parts of or are territories of four Western powers. Of these, two—French Polynesia and Wallis and Futuna—are integral parts of France and vote in French national elections. French Polynesia includes several island groups, but a large majority of the people live in or near the capital city of Papeete on the island of Tahiti and are quite urbanized. Wallis and Futuna is small and remote, and much of its traditional culture survives in a diluted form. Tokelau, New Zealand's last dependency in the Pacific, has small islands and a very small population. Like Wallis and Futuna, it is remote, and much of its former way of life remains.

Two island groups are American: Hawaii and American Samoa. Hawaii is the 50th state of the United States. The city of Honolulu, with its large, Western-style commercial district and sprawling suburbs, dominates the island of Oahu, has most of the state's population, and has much in common with cities on the U.S. mainland. American Samoa is a territory of the United States, and it is far less traditional than Western Samoa. The capital town of Pago Pago is a blend of both American and Samoan life-styles. Rural villages, however, have much in common with their counterparts in Western Samoa.

Easter Island is the anomaly of the area. The aboriginal population was decimated by European-introduced diseases and by slavers in the 1860s and almost became extinct. In 1888 Easter Island was annexed by Chile, and its people are the only Pacific Islanders controlled by a Latin-American power. Little remains of the traditional culture. The indigenous Polynesian language survives, but most people also speak Spanish. About one-third of Easter Island's small population is from Chile. (R.C.Ki.)

MAJOR ISLANDS AND ISLAND GROUPS OF THE PACIFIC

(As mentioned at the beginning of this article, Australia and New Zealand are treated separately, and Hawaii is treated in the article UNITED STATES OF AMERICA. Other political and geographic units of the Pacific not covered below are treated individually in the *Micropædia*.)

Solomon Islands

Solomon Islands, an independent country in the southwestern Pacific Ocean, consists of a double chain of volcanic islands and coral atolls in Melanesia, occupying a total land area of 10,954 square miles (28,370 square kilometres). Buka and Bougainville islands, at the northwest-

ern end of the Solomons chain, form the North Solomons province of Papua New Guinea. Honiara, on Guadalcanal Island, is Solomon Islands' capital and largest city.

PHYSICAL AND HUMAN GEOGRAPHY

The land. The main islands of the group are large and rugged, rising to 8,028 feet (2,447 metres) at Mount Makarakomburu (Makarakombou) on Guadalcanal. They lie in two parallel chains: the western includes Vella Lavella, Kolombangara, New Georgia, and Guadalcanal; the eastern, Choiseul Island, Santa Isabel, and Malaita. The chains converge on Makira (San Cristóbal) Island. Geologically, they are part of the volcanic arc extending from New Ireland, in Papua New Guinea, to Vanuatu.

The climate is tropical oceanic; that is, hot and humid, but relieved by cool winds and abundant, year-round rainfall. Temperatures seldom exceed 90° F (32° C) and rainfall generally averages 120–140 inches (3,000–3,500 millimetres) a year. Heavily wooded, mountainous terrain is characteristic and, although there are extensive plains, only those on the northern side of Guadalcanal have been developed for large-scale agriculture. As in most island groups, animal life is limited. There are hot springs on Savo, where a volcano last erupted in the 1840s. Solomon Islands has a number of other volcanoes. Tinakula in the Santa Cruz group and Kavachi, a submarine volcano near New Georgia, for example, have erupted regularly every few years, and Simbo Island has a solfatara (a volcanic area or vent that yields only hot vapours and sulfurous gases). Earthquakes and destructive cyclones also occur regularly.

The people. Most of the population is Melanesian. Polynesians, forming a small minority, live mainly on outlying atolls, principally Ontong Java, Rennell and Bellona, the Reef Islands, Sikaiana, Tikopia, and Anuta. There are also Gilbertese from Micronesia, who were resettled there between 1955 and 1971, and small numbers of Chinese and Europeans. Anglican, Roman Catholic, South Sea Evangelical, United (a union of Methodists and Congregationalists), and Seventh-day Adventist denominations exist in Solomon Islands, and almost all of the islanders are Christian. More than 60 languages and dialects are spoken. English is the official language, but Pijin, an English-based pidgin, is the one most widely used and understood. Most of the people live in small rural villages. They engage mainly in subsistence gardening, pig raising, and fishing.

The economy. Solomon Islands' main resources, fish and timber, have been exploited excessively, with little regard for their depletion. Its other export products are derived from plantation crops: palm oil from oil palms, copra from coconuts, and cocoa from the cacao plant. Japan, Thailand, and Australia are the major customers. The chief imports are machinery, fuels, manufactured goods, and food, and Australia is the main supplier. A government plan to reduce food imports was scuttled in 1986 when a cyclone destroyed the rice cultivations on Guadalcanal.

The islands have significant reserves of bauxite (on Rennell Island) and phosphates (on Bellona Island), and some gold has been extracted on Guadalcanal. Manufacturing includes fibreglass products, boat building, batteries, and clothing, in addition to fish freezing and canning. Traditional handicrafts, including woodwork, shell-inlay, mats, baskets, and shell jewelry, are made both for the tourist market and for export. Indigenous currencies such as shell money (from Malaita) and red-feather money (from Santa Cruz) are also made for use in customary transactions. Henderson Field, near Honiara, is the principal international airport, although airfields at Munda, Nusatupe (at Gizo), and Graciosa Bay (at Santa Cruz) may also serve as international points of entry. Solomon Islands Airlines, which is owned by the government, provides domestic air service. Ports handling overseas cargoes include Honiara, Tulagi (the prewar capital), and Gizo. Interisland shipping is operated both privately and by the government.

Traditional handicrafts

Administration and social conditions. Solomon Islands is an independent parliamentary state and a member of the Commonwealth. As established by the constitution of 1978, the British monarch is the head of state and is represented by a governor general who is appointed by the monarch upon recommendation by Parliament. The governor general must be a citizen of Solomon Islands. Parliament, which is elected every four years by universal adult suffrage, is composed of 38 members. Executive power is exercised by a prime minister chosen by and from Parliament and a cabinet of 12 ministers (also members of Parliament). Although political parties exist in name, their organization and discipline tend to be loose. Political loyalties are based on personal and local factors rather than on broad class interests or ideology. As a result, the prime minister rarely commands a clear majority in Parliament, and so he owes his position to the sometimes shaky support of a coalition of parties or factions. In 1981

considerable decentralization occurred with the establishment of seven provincial bodies that assumed control of matters regarding transportation, economic development, health, and education.

Before World War II schooling was solely the concern of the missions. Since then the government has become involved. Primary education was provided mostly by subsidized mission schools until 1974, when local government authorities assumed responsibility. There are several secondary schools, a multi-faculty college of higher education, and a branch (1971) of the University of the South Pacific. Some students study overseas, especially in Fiji and Papua New Guinea. There is a well-equipped hospital at Honiara.

Much of traditional culture endures. Crafts are promoted by the Solomon Islands National Museum, established in 1969 in Honiara, and dances and music are regularly performed. Panpipes and percussive "bamboo bands" are popular. Since the 1970s an indigenous literary movement has developed. The writing is in English and mostly published in Solomon Islands.

For statistical data on the land and people of Solomon Islands, see the *Britannica World Data* section in the BRITANNICA WORLD DATA ANNUAL.

HISTORY

The Solomon Islands were initially settled by at least 2000 BC—well before the archaeological record begins—probably by people of the Austronesian language group. Lapita pottery was in use in Santa Cruz and the Reef Islands about 1500 BC. Material radiocarbon dated to about 1000 BC has also been excavated at Vatuluma Cave (Guadalcanal), Anuta, Santa Ana, and Tikopia.

The first European to reach the islands was the Spanish explorer Álvaro de Mendaña de Neira, in 1568. Subsequently, unjustified rumours led to the belief that he had not only found gold there but had discovered where the biblical King Solomon obtained the gold for his temple in Jerusalem. The islands thus acquired the name Islas de Solomón. Later Spanish expeditions to the southwest Pacific, in 1595 and 1606, were unable to confirm the discoveries reported by Mendaña. Geographers came to doubt the existence of the group, and it was not until the late 18th century, after further sightings by French and English navigators, that the Solomons were accurately charted. After the settlement by the English of Sydney in 1788, naval and commercial shipping began increasingly to pass through the Solomons' waters.

The naming of the Solomons

Roman Catholic missionaries in the 1840s failed to establish a settlement but did so in 1898. Anglican missionaries, who had been taking islanders to New Zealand for training since the 1850s, began to settle in the Solomons in the 1870s. Other missions arrived later.

By the late 19th century the islands were being exploited for labour to work the plantations of Fiji and other islands and of Queensland, Australia. About 30,000 labourers were recruited between 1870 and 1910. To protect their own interests Germany and Britain divided the Solomons between them in 1886; but in 1899 Germany transferred the northern islands, except for Buka and Bougainville, to Britain (which already claimed the southern islands) in return for recognition of German claims in Western Samoa and parts of Africa. The British Solomon Islands Protectorate was declared in 1893, partly in response to abuses associated with labour recruitment and partly to regulate contacts between islanders and European settlers, but mainly to forestall a threat of annexation by France. Colonial rule began in 1896. Although generally humane, administrators were more concerned with promoting the interests of European traders and planters than with those of the islanders, and islanders were punished harshly for offenses against colonial law and order. The murder of government tax collectors on Malaita in 1927 was answered with a savage punitive expedition, backed by an Australian warship. Together with some of his associates, Basiana, the leader of the assassins, was later hanged, and his young sons were forced to witness the execution.

With the outbreak of World War II in the Pacific, the Japanese began occupying the protectorate early in 1942, but their advance farther southward was stopped by U.S. forces, who invaded on August 7. Fighting in the Solomons over the next 15 months was some of the most bitter in the Pacific; the long struggle on Guadalcanal was the crucial battle of the Pacific war. Throughout the campaign the U.S. forces and their allies were strongly supported by the islanders. At the end of the war, because of the proximity of an airfield and the availability of flat land and of the military's buildings, Honiara on Guadalcanal became the new capital, replacing Tulagi.

Another result of the war was to stimulate political consciousness among the islanders and so inspire a nationalist movement known as Maasina Rule, which lasted from 1944 to 1952. Subsequently, in response to the worldwide movement for decolonization, the Solomons set out on the path of constitutional development. The nation was formally renamed Solomon Islands in 1975, and independence was attained on July 7, 1978.

For later developments in the history of the Solomon Islands, see the *Britannica Book of the Year* section in the BRITANNICA WORLD DATA ANNUAL. (H.M.La.)

Vanuatu

Vanuatu is a republic consisting of a chain of 13 principal and many smaller islands in the southwestern Pacific Ocean, 500 miles (800 kilometres) west of Fiji and 1,100 miles east of Australia. The islands extend from north to south for 400 miles in an irregular Y shape and have a total area of 4,707 square miles (12,190 square kilometres); they include Vanua Lava and Gaua (Santa Maria) in the Banks and Torres groups; and Espíritu Santo, Aoba, Maéwo, Pentecôte (Pentecost), Malakula, Ambrym, Épi, Éfaté, Erromango, Tanna, and Anatom. Formerly the jointly administered Anglo-French condominium of the New Hebrides, Vanuatu achieved independence in 1980. The capital, largest city, and commercial centre of the republic is Vila, on Éfaté Island.

PHYSICAL AND HUMAN GEOGRAPHY

The land. A diverse relief—ranging from rugged mountains and high plateaus to rolling hills and low plateaus, with coastal terraces and offshore coral reefs—characterizes the islands. Sedimentary and coral limestones and volcanic rock predominate; frequent earthquakes indicate structural instability. Active volcanoes are found on several islands, including Mount Séré'ama on Vanua Lava, Mount Garet on Gaua, Mount Benbow and Mount Marum on Ambrym, and Mount Yasur on Tanna. There are also several submarine volcanoes in the group, and some islands have solfataras or fumaroles. The highest point is Mount Tabwémasana, 6,165 feet (1,879 metres), on Espíritu Santo, the largest island. The climate divides into two seasons—hot and wet from November to April and cooler and drier from May to October. The southeast trades are the prevailing winds, although northerlies during the hot season provide most of the heavy rainfall. Rainfall varies from 80 inches (2,000 millimetres) in the south to 160 inches in the northern islands. Much of the group is covered by dense rain forest, but drier regions have patches of savanna grassland. Abundant bird and insect life contrasts with the sparse fauna. Of the 11 types of bats found in Vanuatu, three are found only there.

Volcanoes

The people. The indigenous population, called ni-Vanuatu, is overwhelmingly Melanesian, though some of the outlying islands have Polynesian populations. More than 100 local Melanesian languages and dialects are spoken; Bislama, an English-based pidgin, is the national language and, along with English and French, is one of three official languages. Religions include Christianity, traditional ancestor worship, and cargo cults.

The economy. Subsistence agriculture has traditionally been the economic base of Vanuatu, together with an elaborate exchange network within and between islands. Economic changes occurred with the development of European plantations in the island group after 1867: cotton was the initial crop, followed by corn (maize), coffee, cocoa beans, and coconuts (for copra). Cattle ranching was instituted later. By the 1880s French planters had reversed the initial British domination of the plantation sector, though they too found it increasingly difficult to compete with ni-Vanuatu producers, who could fall back on subsistence agriculture in times of economic downturn. French hopes of economic hegemony, based on high world prices for copra and the importation of Vietnamese labour in the 1920s, were dashed by the worldwide depression of the 1930s. By 1948 most of the copra in the island group was being produced by the ni-Vanuatu themselves, though it was not until the development of cooperatives in the 1970s that they were finally able to assume control of the trade.

Copra, cocoa, fish, and beef remain the most important exports. Imports, of food and manufactured goods, come principally from Australia. Though Vanuatu looks toward large-scale agricultural development for its long-term economic growth, since independence tourism has emerged as the largest earner of foreign income.

On most of Vanuatu's islands, roads link coastal settlements; there are few interior roads. Interisland transportation is by boat or airplane. Bauerfield airport, near Vila, and Pékoa airport, near Luganville on Espíritu Santo, are international airports, and many smaller airfields are scattered throughout the islands.

Administration and social conditions. The constitution of 1980 provides for a president, elected to a five-year term by an electoral college comprising the parliament and the presidents of the Regional Councils. Members of the parliament are elected to four-year terms on the basis of universal franchise. The parliament elects the prime minister from among its members, and the prime minister then appoints the Council of Ministers from among members of the parliament. The constitution also provides for a National Council of Chiefs, composed of "custom chiefs," which is concerned with matters relating to custom and tradition. Island government councils have taken the place of the Regional Councils proposed in the constitution. The Supreme Court hears and determines civil and criminal proceedings.

The education system

Although attempts have been made since independence to institute a single, and English-speaking, education system, much French economic aid has been channeled into the maintenance of the Francophone school system, and thus French aid has ensured that the 25 percent of ni-Vanuatu children who are French-speaking attend French-language schools. Only a small proportion of ni-Vanuatu children undertake post-primary education, but with more than 300 primary schools, the nation's elementary school attendance is one of the highest in the Pacific.

Health care in Vanuatu consists of two hospitals in Vila supplemented by smaller hospitals, clinics, and dispensaries on the other islands. Malaria, tuberculosis, hookworm, and gastroenteritis are the most common diseases.

Cultural life. The overwhelming majority of ni-Vanuatu are subsistence agriculturalists, living in small rural villages where activities revolve around the land. The constitution has guaranteed that land cannot be alienated from its "indigenous custom owners," or traditional owners, and their descendants. More than an economic resource, land is the physical embodiment of the metaphysical link with the past, and identification with a particular tract of land (expressed by the Bislama phrase *man ples*) remains one of the fundamental concepts governing ni-Vanuatu culture. On many islands the men of a clan still gather nightly at their local *nakamal* to drink kava and communicate with the spirits of their ancestors, whose bones typically are buried nearby. Through magic stones they will contact and try to control the all-pervasive spiritual realm. Among the vast majority of rural dwellers *kastom* (custom), along with Christianity, continues to guide daily life.

For statistical data on the land and people of Vanuatu, see the *Britannica World Data* section in the BRITANNICA WORLD DATA ANNUAL.

HISTORY

Archaeological evidence indicates that by 1300 BC islands in northern Vanuatu were settled by the makers of the distinctive Lapita pottery from Melanesian islands to the west. Since then, there have been successive waves of migrants, including people of Polynesian origin on the southern islands of Futuna and Aniwa. Around AD 1200, a highly stratified society developed in central Vanuatu with the arrival (from the south, according to tradition) of the great chief Roy Mata (or Roymata). His death was marked by an elaborate ritual that included the burying alive of one man and one woman from each of the clans under his influence. European contact began with the Portuguese explorer Pedro Fernández de Quirós (1606), followed by the French navigator Louis-Antoine de Bougainville (1768) and the British captain James Cook (1774). Cook mapped the group and named it the New Hebrides. European missionaries and sandalwood traders settled on the fringes of islands from the 1840s, but their impact on the indigenous people was minimal. Significant cultural change occurred only after the 1860s, as thousands of ni-Vanuatu men and women who had been indentured to work on plantations in Fiji and New Caledonia, and in Queensland, Australia, began to return to their homes. Many established new forms of political influence within the network of Protestant (mainly Presbyterian) missions or successfully competed against European traders and planters in the group. To protect the interests of the mainly British missionaries and mainly French planters, the British and French governments established rudimentary political control with a Joint Naval Commission in 1887. This was succeeded in 1906 by an Anglo-French condominium, under which resident commissioners in the capital, Vila, retained responsibility over their own nationals and jointly ruled the indigenous people. This clumsy administrative arrangement had only a slight impact, however, on most ni-Vanuatu, whose chief European contact continued to be with either missionary or planter. The islands became a major Allied base during World War II, when the spectacle of free-spending black American troops inspired the development of the John Frum cargo cult on Tanna into an important anti-European political movement. After the war, local political initiatives originated in concern over land ownership, more than one-third of the New Hebrides then being owned by foreigners.

The return of indentured workers

Independence was agreed upon at a 1977 conference in Paris attended by British, French, and New Hebrides representatives. Elections were held and a constitution was drawn up in 1979. Despite an unsuccessful attempt in mid-1980 by Jimmy Stevens, the Na-Griamel Party leader, to establish Espíritu Santo Island as independent from the rest of the group, the New Hebrides became independent within the Commonwealth under the name of the Republic of Vanuatu ("Our Land Forever") on July 30, 1980.

For later developments in the history of Vanuatu, see the *Britannica Book of the Year* section in the BRITANNICA WORLD DATA ANNUAL.   (R.Ad.)

New Caledonia

New Caledonia (official name Territoire de la Nouvelle-Calédonie et Dépendances, or Territory of New Caledonia and Dependencies) is a French overseas territory in the southwest Pacific Ocean, about 900 miles (1,500 kilometres) east of Australia. It includes the island of New Caledonia (the Grande Terre, or mainland), where the capital, Nouméa, is situated; the Loyalty Islands; the Bélep Islands; and the Isle of Pines. These islands, which form more than 99 percent of the total land area of about 7,300 square miles (19,000 square kilometres), lie between latitudes 18° and 23° S and longitudes 163° and 169° E. The territory also includes a number of far-flung uninhabited islets: Huon and Surprise islands in the D'Entrecasteaux Reefs, the atolls of the Chesterfield Islands and Bellona Reef, Walpole Island, Beautemps-Beaupré Atoll, and Astrolabe Reefs. France also claims Hunter and Matthew islands, but the claim is disputed by Vanuatu. Although New Caledonia has a relatively small population, it has acquired significance as a remaining outpost of European sovereignty in a largely decolonized region.

The main island, with an area of 6,500 square miles, is by far the largest island and contains about 90 percent of the population. It is surrounded by a coral reef that extends from the Huon Islands in the north to the Isle of Pines in the south. Except for the central part of the west coast, which is bordered only by a fringing reef, it is a true barrier reef enclosing a large lagoon. There are numerous passages in the reef, usually at the mouths of rivers.

Relief and drainage. Rugged mountain ranges, consisting principally of metamorphic rock formations, divide the island into an east coast, which in many places descends precipitously to the sea, and a west coast, which contains flat, undulating land. Ultrabasic, serpentine rock forms a continuous plateau over most of the southern third of the island, rising to a height of 5,308 feet at Mount Humboldt, and continues along the west coast as a series of discrete massifs. Outcrops from this formation form the islands of Art and Pott in the Bélep archipelago in the north and, in the south, the central part of the Isle of Pines, which is bordered by an emerged coral platform. These rocks have weathered to form the striking *terre rouge* (i.e., red soils that overlay the island's extensive deposits of nickel, chrome, and cobalt ore). In the northeast an outcrop of gneiss forms a 40-mile-long mountain range that includes the territory's highest mountain, Mount Panié, 5,341 feet. Elsewhere, the northern half of the island consists mainly of an irregular series of ranges formed from schists. Sedimentary rocks are limited to a narrow zone extending along much of the west coast inland between the serpentine massifs and the northern schist formations. They have weathered to produce broad, undulating plains with some steep-sided hills.

Metamorphic rock formations

Numerous streams descend from the central mountain chain to the lagoon, often flooding rapidly after rainfall and drying out in dry weather, especially on the west coast. The Diahot River, the longest river in the territory, flows for about 60 miles toward the northern tip of the island along the western escarpment of the Mount Panié range.

The Loyalty Islands consist of three main islands—Ouvéa, Lifou, and Maré—and numerous small islands, the most important being Tiga. The Loyalty Islands form more than 10 percent of New Caledonia's total land area, and about 10 percent of the population lives there. In contrast to the mainland, these islands are raised coral plateaus, nowhere rising more than 330 feet above sea level. Surface water is lacking because of the porous nature of the calcareous rock formation.

Climate. The climate is subtropical with a year-round rainfall. The rainfall is higher on the east coast, where at higher elevations more than 120 inches (3,000 millimetres) may fall annually. On the west coast the rainfall is regularly less than 40 inches. The period from December to March is particularly rainy because of equatorial depressions, including frequent cyclones. Another period of heavy rainfall occurs in July and August; the driest months are September through November. Winds bearing northeast to southeast, including trade winds, predominate throughout the year and relieve temperatures in the hot season, which begins in November. Cyclonic winds are frequent late in the hot season.

The mean annual temperature at sea level ranges between 71° F (22° C) and 75° F (24° C). In the south of the mainland there are very few days when the temperature rises above 86° F (30° C), but their frequency increases to the north. The lowest temperature recorded in Nouméa is 55° F (13° C), but farther north on the west coast temperatures as low as 41° F (5° C) have been known to occur.

Plant and animal life. Geographic isolation, contrasting soils, and a wide range in altitudes have produced a rich indigenous flora. *Terre rouge* soils support a highly original maquis in which sclerophyllic (resistant to drying) shrubs with spectacular coloured flowers are dominant. Different forms of rain forest range from those growing on coral platforms, as in the Loyalty Islands, to montane forests above 3,000 feet on the mainland. The savanna woodlands of the west coast are dominated by a ti tree, the ubiquitous niaouli (*Melaleuca quinquenervia*), which is highly fire-resistant and the spread of which is stimulated by bushfires. Although it grows best in wet soils up to an altitude of 2,000 feet, it extends also onto well-drained slopes and crests and forms the dominant species of closed swamp forests growing on the seaboard plains of the Diahot valley. A once-widespread dry sclerophyll forest, dominated by the guaiacum (*Acacia spirorbis*),

The influence of red soils on flora

growing at low altitudes on the west coast, is now confined to relict sites. Mangrove swamps proliferate on the highly indented west coast.

Except for several species of bat, which were present before the arrival of Europeans, mammals are absent from the native fauna. There are no frogs and no venomous land reptiles, although scorpions and centipedes are present. There are no endemic malaria-carrying mosquito species. The kagu, a flightless bird, is the most unusual of some 100 endemic bird species and is now rare. A wide range of marine life is present in the lagoon.

Settlement patterns. About three-fifths of the population live in Nouméa, which since 1965 has expanded to embrace the adjacent municipalities of Dumbéa, Mont-Dore, and Païta. Nouméa has the facilities of a French provincial city, including numerous bars and restaurants, modern shops and supermarkets, a hospital, schools, a local newspaper, and radio and television facilities. About four-fifths of people of migrant origin, including Europeans, Polynesians, and Asians, live there as compared with one-quarter of the Melanesian population. About three-quarters of the Melanesians live outside Nouméa in small, widely dispersed villages with few modern facilities. They engage chiefly in subsistence agriculture based on the cultivation of the yam, taro, sweet potato, and banana. The population is almost entirely Melanesian in the Loyalty Islands, the Isle of Pines, and the Béleps and on the east coast and in the mountain ranges of the mainland.

The people. Melanesians and Europeans are the two principal ethnic groups, forming 43 and 37 percent of the population, respectively. Their differing cultures have given rise to two distinct ways of life, known as *kanak* and *caldoche;* people of mixed descent tend to ascribe to one or the other. The *kanak* identity is based on clan membership, a network of family alliances and specific land rights. The *caldoche* way of life is essentially integrated into a cash economy. The Polynesian minority comprises Wallis and Futuna Islanders (9 percent) and Tahitians (4 percent). Descendants of Indonesian and Vietnamese migrant workers form 4 and 2 percent of the population, respectively, and are essentially an urban group.

French is the official language but is not the mother tongue of most Melanesians and Polynesians. Some 30 Melanesian languages are spoken, most Melanesians being proficient in more than one.

Religions

The Roman Catholic Church claims about two-thirds of the population as adherents, including almost all European, Wallisian, and Vietnamese and half of the Melanesian and Tahitian minorities. Two Protestant churches, the Evangelical Church in New Caledonia and the Loyalty Islands (Église Evangélique en Nouvelle-Calédonie et Îles Loyauté) and the Free Evangelical Church (Église Libre), serve one-fifth of the population. Their memberships are almost entirely Melanesian. There are also numerous minor Christian sects and small numbers of Muslims.

The Melanesian population is widely believed to have declined rapidly in the 19th century, but estimates for the period, including that for the 1887 census, were so poorly based that this remains an impressionistic view. In the 20th century the figure for Melanesians was fairly stable up to 1939 but doubled in the 40 years following World War II. Migration into and out of the territory plays an important role in determining the numbers of the non-Melanesian communities. The birth rate is higher among Melanesians and Wallisians than among other groups, but infant mortality is high among Melanesians, and life expectancy is relatively low.

The economy. New Caledonia's economy is highly dependent on France. Exports, which consist largely of partly refined nickel and nickel ore, cover less than half the cost of imports but vary with the world market price of nickel. Half of the territory's trade is with France; other important trade partners are Japan, the United States, and Australia. The trade deficit is made up by the transfer of funds from France, chiefly as grants to the territorial budget and expenditures for health, education, and the maintenance of military and security forces, which accounts for about one-third of the gross domestic product (GDP). The administration, commerce, and transport

and services sectors contribute three-quarters of the GDP, compared with 9 to 12 percent for mining and 2 percent for agriculture. Efforts to diversify the economy beyond the commercial and administrative sectors have met with little success. There is, however, considerable potential for tourism, relying on tourists from Australia, New Zealand, and Japan. Import replacement industries have had little impact on the economy because of the small local market.

Although the per capita GDP is one of the highest in the countries of the South Pacific, distribution between ethnic groups is unequal, Melanesian household revenues being on average only about one-quarter of that of European households. The distribution of land resources on the mainland also is very uneven. Although some 35,000 Melanesians live by cultivating the land, two-thirds of the land is in the hands of European families, very few of whom are engaged in agriculture or cattle raising.

Europeans also dominate trades, businesses, and professions and hold most of the high-ranking administrative posts in the government. Among the official unemployed, Melanesians are twice as numerous as Europeans; figures do not include the considerable number of "hidden" unemployed who have returned to their villages.

Taxes in the territory consist primarily of duties on imported goods, sales taxes, and taxes on business revenues. An income tax was introduced in 1982 but has been maintained at a deliberately low level. More than 90 percent of the total tax receipts come from within Nouméa.

Resources. The weathering of serpentine rock provides the territory with 20 percent of the world's known reserves of nickel ore, as well as large deposits of chromium, cobalt, iron, and magnesium. The export of nickel ore, which has been mined since 1875, and of partly refined nickel from the Société Le Nickel (SLN) foundry on the outskirts of Nouméa, is subject to cycles of booms and depressions determined by the needs of the world steel industry and competition from other producers. It is a large industry by world standards. A large chromium mine at Tiébaghi in the north of the mainland was reopened in 1982 after a long period of inactivity to export ore to China and the United States. Cobalt and iron-ore deposits, as well as deposits of gypsum on the west coast and of phosphates on outlying islands, are no longer worked. Noncommercial deposits of coal are found on the west coast. The search for oil has not been successful. Hydroelectric power from Yaté and Néaoua provides nearly half of the territory's energy needs; the remainder of the territory's power is produced with imported fuel oil. More than three-quarters of the energy produced is used in the refining of nickel.

Mineral reserves

Agriculture. Local agricultural products meet barely half of the territory's needs for meat, vegetables, and fruit. Commercial agriculture has not succeeded despite efforts to establish sugarcane, cotton, rice, coffee, and copra industries. The production of coffee and copra that began in the 19th century was kept going after World War II chiefly through the efforts of Melanesian subsistence farmers to diversify into the cash economy, but very little is now exported. A project began in 1982 to restart a coffee industry chiefly on Melanesian land by using varieties of coffee plants that are tolerant to sunlight. In the late 1970s reforestation projects, consisting mainly of plantings of Caribbean pine, were established on Melanesian land on the Isle of Pines and on the mountains inland from Koné on the west coast of the mainland. Similar projects have not been continued. Cattle raising is important to the economy; pigs and horses also are raised but rarely for commercial purposes. Fishing and timber resources have not been extensively exploited.

Transportation. The main island of New Caledonia and the inhabited outer islands are ringed by roads. Virtually the entire coast of the island of New Caledonia may be traveled by road, and crossroads penetrate the centre of the island.

The port of Nouméa handles the majority of ocean traffic; a new deep-water harbour was completed in 1974. Regular service is available for cargo and passengers.

The domestic airline, Air Calédonie, provides internal air service from Magenta Airport near Nouméa to the main and outer islands, as well as to France and other countries.

French authority

Administration and social conditions. As a French overseas territory, New Caledonia is fully integrated into the French Republic, is subject to its laws, and sends parliamentary representatives to Paris. Special legislation is required, however, to introduce laws for the government of the territory and in areas such as education, health, and labour. Authority over defense, internal security, immigration, justice, radio and telecommunications, and secondary and higher education is retained by the French government and is administered by its appointed representative, the high commissioner. The administration of health, social security, transportation, industry, and infrastructure is shared by the high commissioner and locally elected representatives. Municipal and regional government is administered by the state.

Health and educational facilities of a high standard are in principle available to all but are of a higher standard in Nouméa than elsewhere. The school system closely follows the syllabus of schools in France, and students of non-European origin tend to progress more slowly than children of French origin. Although all attend school, attendance being compulsory until the 16th birthday, relatively few non-Europeans gain higher qualifications. French is the only language of instruction in state-supported schools.

Cultural life. Nouméa, with its bars, restaurants, cinemas, an excellent library and museum, good bookshops, and radio and television, offers a touch of Europe. For the Europeans, sports tend to be closely related to the sea and include boating, fishing, windsurfing, and swimming or sunbathing at the city beaches of Anse Vata and the Baie de Citron; tennis and cycling are also popular. Although big-league soccer in France is closely followed, soccer playing has virtually been appropriated by Melanesian men and a version of cricket (first introduced by early British missionaries in the Loyalty Islands) by Melanesian women. Melanesian soccer and cricket teams compete annually in territory-wide competitions.

In many areas, Melanesian custom remains strong, particularly in relation to clan and family ties and obligations. Almost without exception Melanesians, regardless of their education or urbanization, return to their villages to take part in elaborate ceremonies and gift exchanges on such occasions as births, marriages, and deaths. "Tradition" has, of course, been modified, an important inclusion now being Christian ceremonies. In rural areas, women still tend to carry out the daily agricultural round of planting, weeding, and harvesting, as well as their domestic tasks of cooking, cleaning, and child rearing. Men perform the heavier tasks of clearing the ground for new gardens. All take part in the annual yam planting and harvesting, which is still something of a ceremonial and social occasion, and these events also sometimes draw urban workers back to their villages for a short period.

Local languages remain surprisingly strong, despite the fact that, through the educational system, French has become the lingua franca. In the 1980s, due to increasing nationalist feeling, there has been a revival of interest among Melanesians in the traditional arts of sculpture, mat and basket weaving, singing, dancing, and wood carving. This has been encouraged by the French government.

State-owned radio and television stations relay programs to all parts of the territory. In Nouméa there are also several privately owned radio stations. There is one daily newspaper, *Les Nouvelles Calédoniennes.*

For statistical data on the land and people of New Caledonia, see the *Britannica World Data* section in the BRITANNICA WORLD DATA ANNUAL.

HISTORY

Melanesians settled the territory more than 3,000 years ago and, except for rare Polynesian voyagers, probably were cut off from outside contact until the late 18th century. In 1774 Captain James Cook landed at Balade, on the east coast of the mainland, and he named the island New Caledonia for his native Scotland. Cook was followed there by the French navigator Antoine de Bruni, chevalier d'Entrecasteaux, in 1793. Regular contact with Europeans began in 1841 when sandalwood traders from Australia introduced islanders to the use of iron. The arrival of a Protestant mission from the London Missionary Society in the Loyalty Islands in 1841 and a Marist mission, which was set up at Balade with the aid of the French navy in 1843, marked the beginning of the Protestant and Roman Catholic churches in the territory.

The French claim

France took possession of most of present-day New Caledonia in 1853 in ceremonies at Balade and the Isle of Pines with the aim of reserving the territory as a possible site for a penal colony. The French flag was not run up in the Loyalty Islands until 1864.

From the time of colonial settlement until as late as 1917, Melanesian uprisings were common and were constantly feared by the settlers and authorities alike. The insurrection of 1856–59 near Nouméa and the uprising of 1878–79, which extended along the west coast from Bouloupari to Poya, seriously endangered French occupation. Grievances centred around the confiscation of Melanesian lands, the foraging of settlers' cattle on the Melanesians' produce gardens, and, in 1917, the head tax, which had been imposed by the colonial government in 1899. The French suppressed each uprising (with the help of indigenous auxiliaries) by destroying villages and crops and demanding unconditional surrender, and insurgents were punished by deportation or execution and further confiscation of their lands. By 1860 French authority had been established over the southern third of the mainland, and in the next decade policies for the disposal of indigenous land, the regrouping of tribes, and the appointment of a system of tribal chiefs to represent the administration were established. By the end of the 19th century large areas of Melanesian land had been alienated and the inhabitants relegated to reserves. Forced labour, limitations on travel, and curfews were imposed from the early days of colonial rule and became the basis of a system of administrative law codified in 1887 as the *indigénat* ("native regulations"). In 1899 a head tax was levied on male Melanesians to oblige them to obtain employment with settlers and the government and, like the *indigénat,* remained in force until 1946.

Although the prime concern of the early colonial administration was the reception and control of about 22,000 French convicts sent to New Caledonia between 1864 and 1897, the need to attract free settlers and to provide a supply of cheap labour also were continuing preoccupations. Between 1864 and 1939 some 60,000 indentured labourers, as well as the convicts, were imported to construct public works and to work on plantations, ships, wharves, and mines and in commerce and domestic service. These included ni-Vanuatu and Solomon Islanders (1865–1920), Vietnamese (1891–1939), Javanese (1896–1939), and Japanese (1892–1921). Only a small percentage of the survivors of these workers remained in the colony after the expiry of their contracts, and, although few ex-convicts left the territory, not many established families. New Caledonia was also the unlikely home of 4,000 *déportés,* political exiles of the 1871 uprising of the Paris Commune, but few of the survivors stayed after being granted amnesty. Most of the free white settlers were either former members of the French administration and armed forces, settlers from Australia and New Zealand, or former sugar planters from Réunion. Two later waves of free settlers in the 1890s and 1920s were encouraged to migrate to help establish coffee and cotton industries, respectively. By 1936, however, there were only 15,000 residents of European origin among 29,000 native Melanesians. After World War II the European population gradually increased by migration, but the main influx of white and Polynesian settlers occurred in the years leading up to and including the nickel boom of 1969–72. For the first time the Melanesians became a minority in their own country, although they still were the largest single ethnic group.

The main influx of settlers

Since the beginning of French settlement, political debate among the white settlers revolved around the rights of residents to administer their own affairs without endangering the flow of French financial aid. Between 1885 and 1956 a locally elected general council advised the governor on territorial affairs and voted a local budget. By 1953 French citizenship had been granted to all, regardless of ethnic origin. Melanesians then formed a coalition with Europeans to bring the party, the Caledonian Union (Union Calédonienne), to power on a ticket of full self-government in local affairs. Progress toward self-government was made in 1957 when a Territorial Assembly was created with powers to elect an executive to administer, under the presidency of a high commissioner, the affairs of the territory. In the 1970s the Caledonian Union became an increasingly Melanesian party as Europeans deserted it. Many Melanesians also left to form parties that campaigned in support of independence. In 1979 the Caledonian Union, which had converted to the cause of independence, formed an Independence Front in coalition with several minority Melanesian parties. The Socialist French government of 1981 took many steps to stem the growing political polarization and granted complete self-government in territorial affairs under the Lemoine Statute of 1984. The statute was rejected, however, by the Independence Front, which reconstituted itself as the Kanak Socialist National Liberation Front (Front de Libération Nationale Kanake et Socialiste; FLNKS) and boycotted the elections held under the statute in November of that year. In the weeks following the elections the FLNKS used roadblocks to take control of most of the territory outside Nouméa. Peace was gradually restored as the government proposed to grant the Melanesians independence in association with France in an arrangement through which French citizens would retain residential and other rights. The European community, with the strong support of non-Melanesian ethnic groups, vigorously rejected this proposal.

In 1985 the French government transferred most of the powers of self-government to four regional councils. In elections held in September 1985 the FLNKS won a majority of seats in all except the Nouméa region, which was won by the settler-dominated party, the Rally for Caledonia in the Republic (Rassemblement pour la Calédonie dans la Republique; RPCR). In 1986 France reduced the powers of the regional councils and held a referendum. The referendum was boycotted by the FLNKS and produced a large majority for continued ties with France. It was followed by a new statute for self-government, which altered the regional boundaries to limit FLNKS successes to the principal concentrations of Melanesians in the Loyalty Islands and on the east coast of the mainland.

For its part the FLNKS demonstrated its ability to direct the votes of the great mass of Melanesian voters in four electoral consultations since 1984. With the aid of the independent countries of the South Pacific that form the South Pacific Forum, the question of New Caledonia was listed on the agenda of the United Nations Committee of Decolonization. The lack of consensus on the subject among political circles in France was paralleled by the increasing polarization along ethnic lines within the territory. (D.L.Sh.)

For later developments in the history of New Caledonia, see the *Britannica Book of the Year* section in the BRITANNICA WORLD DATA ANNUAL.

Fiji

Fiji is an independent nation consisting of an archipelago surrounding the Koro Sea in the South Pacific Ocean, about 1,300 miles (2,100 kilometres) north of Auckland, N.Z. It forms part of the Melanesian cultural area.

The archipelago consists of some 300 islands and 540 islets scattered over about 1,000,000 square miles (3,000,-000 square kilometres). Of the 300 islands, about 100 are inhabited. The total land area is 7,056 square miles. The capital, Suva, is on the southeast coast of the largest island, Viti Levu ("Great Fiji"). Fiji includes within its borders Rotuma, an island of 18 square miles located 440 miles north of Suva; Rotuma has a Polynesian population and was administered from Fiji in colonial times.

PHYSICAL AND HUMAN GEOGRAPHY

The land. *Relief.* Fiji has a complex geologic history. Based on a submerged platform of ancient formation, the Fiji islands are largely the product of volcanic action, sedimentary deposit, and formations of coral. Viti Levu, the largest island, has an area of about 4,000 square miles and

accounts for more than half of Fiji's land. A jagged dividing range running from north to south has several peaks above 3,000 feet (914 metres), the highest being Mount Tomanivi (formerly Mount Victoria) at 4,341 feet (1,323 metres). The main river systems—the Rewa, Navua, Sigatoka, and Ba—all have their headwaters in the central mountain area. To the southeast and southwest, and to the south where the range divides, the mountains give way to plateaus, then lowlands. The coastal plains in the west, northwest, and southeast account for only 15 percent of Viti Levu's area but are the main centres of agriculture and settlement.

Vanua Levu, the second largest island, has an area of about 2,140 square miles. It is divided along its length by a mountain range with peaks rising to more than 3,000 feet. On the island's northern coast, away from the mouth of the Dreketi River, the coastal plains are narrow. Most of the other islands, including the Lomaiviti, Lau, and Yasawa groups, are volcanic in origin, but, like the major islands, they are bounded by coral reefs, offshore rocks, and shoals that make the Koro Sea hazardous for navigation.

Climate. At Suva the average summer high temperature is 85° F (29° C) and the average winter low is 68° F (20° C); temperatures typically are lower in elevated inland areas. All districts receive the greatest amount of rainfall in the season from November through March, during which time hurricanes are also experienced perhaps once every two years. While rainfall is reduced in the east of the larger islands from April to October, giving an annual average of 120 inches (3,050 millimetres) per year, it virtually ceases in the west, to give an annual rainfall of 70 inches, thus making for a sharp contrast in both climatic conditions and agriculture between east and west. ~Rainy season~

Plant and animal life. Almost half of Fiji's total area remains in forest, while dry grasslands are found in western areas of the large islands. Coconut palms are common in coastal areas, and almost all tropical fruits and vegetables can be grown. Much of the shoreline is composed of reefs and rocks, while mangrove swamps are found on eastern coasts. There are few white-sand swimming beaches and, because of the encircling reef, little surf.

Most animals, including pigs, dogs, cattle, and a few horses, are domesticated. Mongooses, introduced to prey on snakes and rats, are often seen.

The people. While the indigenous Fijian people are usually classified as Melanesian, they are larger in stature than Melanesians from Vanuatu, Solomon Islands, or New Guinea; their social and political organization is closer to that of Polynesia; and there has been a high level of intermarriage between Fijians from the Lau Islands of eastern Fiji and the neighbouring Polynesian islands of Tonga. Almost all indigenous Fijians are Christian, mostly Methodist and Roman Catholic.

Since World War II, indigenous Fijians have been outnumbered by Indians, most of whom are descendants of indentured labourers brought to work in the sugar industry. A few, particularly in commerce and the professions, are descended from free migrants. Most of the Indians are Hindus, though a significant number are Muslims.

There are also significant minorities of Europeans, part-Europeans, Chinese, and Pacific islanders from outside Fiji. In the last group are the Polynesian population of Rotuma and the Banabans, who were forced to leave Banaba after destruction in World War II made it uninhabitable. Many Banabans settled on Rabi Island in Fiji.

English is the official language. The widely used Fijian language has many dialects; the one most commonly used is known as Bauan Fijian and comes from Bau, the district that enjoyed political supremacy at the advent of colonial rule. Most people speak at least two languages, including English and the language of their own racial community.

There is very little intermarriage between racial communities. The relative proportions of Fijians and Indians in the population have been changing in recent years because the Fijian birth rate is higher than the Indian and because of the accelerating outward migration of Indians, especially to Canada, Australia, and New Zealand. While Suva has a very mixed population, the sugar regions of Viti Levu and Vanua Levu have predominantly Indian ~Indian settlements~

Indian farmers transporting a load of sugarcane near Natandola, Viti Levu, Fiji.
© S. Chester/Comstock

populations. On the smaller islands, and in less developed rural areas of the larger islands, Fijians live in traditional villages. The two largest urban centres are on Viti Levu: Suva, in the southeast, which has about one-fifth of the total population, and Lautoka in the northwest, which is the centre of the sugar industry and has a major port. Labasa on Vanua Levu is a centre for administration, services, and sugar production.

The economy. Fiji has an agriculture-based market economy, including a substantial subsistence sector dominated by indigenous Fijians who earn a supplementary cash income from copra, cocoa, kava, *dalo* (taro), pineapples, cassava, or bananas, or from fishing. The commercial sector is heavily based on sugar, which, for the most part, is produced by independent Indian farmers. Sugar production is concentrated on the western side of Viti Levu and in the area around Labasa. The Fiji Sugar Corporation has a monopoly on milling and marketing. Sugar is by far Fiji's largest export and accounts for more than one-half of all exports.

Except for a few years early in the 20th century, the alienation of native land has been prohibited since 1874, thus leaving 83 percent of all land under Fijian ownership. Farmers of other races operate on leaseholds of up to 30 years under the Agricultural Landlord and Tenant Act. Fijian land ownership is in the hands of *mataqali,* or clan groups, but may be administered through the Native Lands Trust Board.

Tourism is almost as large an earner of foreign exchange as sugar. Fiji is strategically located for air travelers from Australia, New Zealand, the United States, and Japan and is a major destination for tourist cruises. Tourism is based on the attractions of duty-free shopping and colourful handicraft markets as well as the usual attractions of tropical islands.

The third major export earner, though well behind sugar and tourism, is gold, which is mined at Vatukoula in northern Viti Levu. Copper deposits are known to exist at Namosi, inland from Suva, but mining is not viable.

Since large-scale systematic planting of pine forests began in the 1960s, a timber industry has developed for domestic use and export. Development plans have emphasized the need to reduce dependence on imported food, especially rice, meat, fish, and poultry products. There is substantial hydroelectricity generation, but fuel remains a major import together with manufactured goods (many for resale to tourists), machinery, and food. Australia, New Zealand, Japan, and the United States are the major sources of imports.

The economy has a strong service and light industrial component serving small neighbouring countries as well as Fiji; activities range from boat building (especially fishing boats and pleasure craft) to brewing and paint manufacture. The government offers incentives (including residence) for investors but insists on potential for job creation and training programs for local employees.

Sugar is sold on long-term contracts to New Zealand, Malaysia, and Singapore and, under the Lomé Convention (which gives former overseas territories access to the European market), to the European Economic Community. Regional trading agreements give Fiji special access to markets in Australia and New Zealand.

The larger islands, and many smaller ones, are served by domestic air services. International airports are located at Nausori, near Suva (mostly for regional flights), and Nadi, on the western side of Viti Levu. A coastal highway circles Viti Levu, and minor roads to the interior give access to most areas of settlement. For many villagers, however, river punts with outboard motors provide the most efficient form of transport, while from more remote areas it may still be simplest to transport produce to market by floating it downriver on bamboo rafts. Regular bus services operate within and between the major towns. *(Trans-portation)*

Administration and social conditions. *Government.* Until the coup d'état of May 1987, Fiji was a dominion, a member of the Commonwealth, and a parliamentary democracy, acknowledging the British sovereign, through a governor general, as head of state. There was a bicameral legislature of a Senate and a House of Representatives. Eight members of the Senate were appointed by the Great Council of (Fijian) Chiefs, seven by the prime minister, six by the leader of the opposition, and one by the Rotuman council. The House of Representatives had 52 members, 27 of whom were elected by adult suffrage by and from the separate racial communities. A further 25 members (10 Fijian, 10 Indian, and five General [those of other ethnic origin]) were elected by all voters combined on a national electoral roll. The leader of the majority party became the prime minister.

In October 1987 Fiji officially left the Commonwealth and became a republic. The coup leader, then-Lieutenant Colonel Sitiveni Rabuka, appointed a civilian government headed by a president with a largely ceremonial role. The government was composed of a prime minister and cabinet of appointed members, almost all of whom are ethnic Fijians.

Local government reflects the plurality of Fiji's social structure. There are elected multiracial councils in the larger towns, a separate Fijian administration incorporating a hierarchy of chiefs and councils for the control of rural Fijians, and direct administration elsewhere.

Before the first of two coups in 1987, Fijian military forces had a largely ceremonial role, though they bore much of the burden of rebuilding and organizing after natural disasters and of civilian development projects. Military forces continued to perform these services after the coup, with the added role of agricultural distribution, together with their major preoccupation with the enforcement of internal security policies.

Education and medical facilities. While the government provides some primary and secondary education, most schools are controlled through local committees run by and for a single racial or religious community. Entry to secondary schools is by competitive examination. Students pay fees but not the full cost of their education, which is subsidized by the government. The University of the South Pacific, near Suva, is a regional institution; Fiji and other Pacific Islands governments fund the budget, and foreign aid meets the costs of buildings and capital development. To extend the reach of the university, lessons are broadcast to distant regional centres by a satellite network. Fiji also provides for its own technical, agricultural, and medical education and teacher training. There are private medical practitioners in all large towns, a national network of clinics and small hospitals, and major hospitals in Suva, Lautoka, and Labasa. *(The University of the South Pacific)*

Effects of urbanization. Rapid urbanization, especially on the fringes of Suva, has seen the emergence of squatter settlements and has caused some social problems. The disparities of income between urban and rural workers, contrasting life-styles within the urban areas, and high urban unemployment can be related to an escalating rate of crime and to the rapid growth of a trade union movement.

Cultural life. Fiji's mixed racial background contributes to a rich cultural heritage. Many features of traditional Fijian life survive; they are most evident in the elaborate investiture, marriage, and other ceremonies for high-ranking chiefs. These provide a focus for the practicing of traditional crafts, such as the manufacture of *masi*, or tapa cloth, made from the bark of the paper mulberry; mat weaving; wood carving; and canoe making. Drinking of *yaqona* (kava, made from the root of *Piper methysticum*) is a part not only of important ceremonies but of everyday life. Displays of "traditional" Fijian culture, music, and dancing make an important contribution to tourism; model villages and handicraft markets are popular.

Most Indian women continue to wear the sari together with traditional jewelry in gold and silver. Traditional marriage ceremonies are practiced, as are customs such as fire walking and ritual self-torture as part of important religious ceremonies. Cinemas showing imported Indian films are popular. Dīwālī, the Hindu Festival of the Lights, is celebrated every October and is a public holiday.

Fiji has two daily newspapers and a multilingual public radio broadcasting system. Videocassette players are common in the towns (many villages have no electricity).

For statistical data on the land and people of Fiji, see the *Britannica World Data* section in the BRITANNICA WORLD DATA ANNUAL.

HISTORY

Two types of settlement

When Fiji's first settlers arrived from island Melanesia at least 3,500 years ago, they carried with them a wide range of food plants, the pig, and a style of pottery known as Lapita ware. This pottery is generally associated with peoples who had well-developed skills in navigation and canoe building and were horticulturists. From Fiji the Lapita culture was carried to Tonga and Samoa, where the first distinctively Polynesian cultures evolved. Archaeological evidence suggests that two other pottery styles were subsequently introduced into Fiji, though it is not clear whether these represent major migrations or simply cultural innovations brought by small groups of migrants. In most areas of Fiji the settlers lived in small communities near ridge forts and practiced a slash-and-burn type of agriculture. In the fertile delta regions of southeast Viti Levu, however, there were large concentrations of population. These settlements, which were based on intensive taro cultivation using complex irrigation systems, were protected by massive ring-ditch fortifications.

Traditional Fijian society was hierarchical, with tribal groups led by chiefs chosen according to rank based on descent as well as personal achievement. Tribes were divided into *mataqali*, or clans, and residential subclans. By alliance or conquest tribes might form confederations led by paramount chiefs; warfare was common.

The first Europeans to sight the Fiji Islands were Abel Janzsoon Tasman, who passed the northeast fringe of the group in 1643, and Captain James Cook, who passed the southeastern islands in 1774. Captain William Bligh passed through the group in his open longboat after the mutiny on HMS *Bounty* in 1789 and returned to explore it in 1792.

Commercial interest in the group began with the discovery of sandalwood at the beginning of the 19th century, leading to a rush to Bua Bay at the southwestern end of Vanua Levu. A few beachcombers, useful as armourers and interpreters, were adopted by influential chiefs from this time. Within little more than a decade the accessible, commercial stands of sandalwood were depleted, but by the 1820s traders were again visiting the group to trade for edible varieties of the marine invertebrate called the sea cucumber, also known as bêche-de-mer or trepang. Whereas most of the sandalwood had been cut by gangs of foreigners, the bêche-de-mer harvest involved large numbers of Fijians in gathering, cleaning, and drying and in the provision of food and firewood. These opportunities for new wealth and power, symbolized by the acquisition of muskets, intensified political rivalries and hastened the

rise of the confederation of Bau, led first by Naulivou, then by his nephew Cakobau. Bau is a tiny island off the southeast coast of Viti Levu, but by the 1850s it dominated western Fiji. Cakobau's main rival was the Tongan chief, Ma'afu, who led an army of Christian Tongans and their allies from eastern Fiji. After a short-lived alliance with Ma'afu, Cakobau became a Christian in 1854, thus bringing most Fijians under the influence of Methodist missionaries. Roman Catholic and Anglican missionaries arrived later but did not enjoy the same success.

By the 1860s Fiji was attracting European settlers intent on establishing plantations to capitalize on a boom in cotton prices caused by the American Civil War. The consequent disputes over land and political power within and between European and Fijian communities, and problems with labour introduced from other Pacific islands, contributed to violent confrontations and exacerbated the implicit instability of Fijian society and ensured that no Fijian chief could impose his rule on the whole group. European attempts at government were doomed by the greed and factionalism of their members and by the interference of European governments and consuls. Imperial intervention thus became inevitable. On Oct. 10, 1874, after negotiations had led to an offer of unconditional cession, Fiji became a British crown colony. The policies of the first governor, Sir Arthur Gordon, were decisive in shaping the history of Fiji. Gordon saw himself as the protector of the Fijian people and thus initiated policies that limited their involvement in commercial and political developments. Sales of Fijian land were banned; the Fijians were taxed in agricultural produce, not cash; and they were governed through a system of indirect rule based on the traditional political structure.

Crown colony status

In order to maintain these policies yet encourage the economic development of the new colony, Gordon promoted the introduction of indentured Indian labourers and investment by the Colonial Sugar Refining Company to establish sugar plantations and processing mills. Indian migrants were encouraged to become permanent settlers at the conclusion of their contracts, even though little land was available for sale and the migrants' political rights were circumscribed. After the termination of the indenture system in 1920, Indian agitation over political and economic grievances caused strikes and continual discontent and challenged the commercial and political domination of the small European community in the islands.

During World War II Fiji was occupied by Allied forces, and a battalion of Fijians saw service as scouts in the campaign for the Solomon Islands. Indians refused to serve because they were not offered the same wages and conditions as Europeans. Indians also refused to cut their cane at the low prices offered. These actions led to the taint of disloyalty being applied to Indians by the other races, and to the army, which was retained after the war, remaining exclusively Fijian except for a handful of European officers. Incipient racial awareness was heightened by the realization that from 1943 Fijians were outnumbered by Indians. As one response to perceived stagnation in Fijian society, the colonial authorities restructured the Fijian administration, reinforcing chiefly leadership and thus consolidating the conservatism of Fijian society.

Constitutional development toward independence, which began in the 1960s, was more a response to international and British pressures than to any demand from within Fiji. The steps taken were, in practice, a compromise between the principles of parliamentary democracy and the racial divisions within the country. The franchise, previously exercised by Europeans and some Indians, was extended to adults of all races, including Fijians, who until then had been represented by their chiefs. Fijian land rights, guaranteed by the Deed of Cession in 1874, were given constitutional protection, while Fijian chiefs were given an effective veto on all important matters affecting the status of Fijians and on changes to the constitution itself. Facing political reality, Indian leaders relinquished their earlier demands for improved access to freehold land and accepted the communal and cross-voting system, thus giving away the common electoral roll that they had sought since the 1930s.

The effect
of the con-
stitution

The effect of the constitution was to give power to Fijian politicians so long as they remained in partnership with the General voters and, critically, so long as the Fijian vote remained unified. Despite race riots during by-elections in 1968, independence was achieved in a spirit of cooperation on Oct. 10, 1970, the 96th anniversary of cession.

From that time until April 1987, Fiji was governed by the Alliance Party, which was pledged to policies of multiracialism. Its electoral supremacy was challenged only briefly in 1977, when Fijian votes were attracted by Fijian nationalist candidates campaigning under a slogan of "Fiji for the Fijians"; only factionalism prevented the formation of an Indian-led government.

In 1987, however, the Indian-dominated National Federation Party joined in coalition with the new Labour Party (led by a Fijian, Timoci Bavadra), which had strong support from Fijian and Indian trade unionists. The coalition was successful in elections held in April. The new government, which had a majority of Indian members in the legislature, was greeted with widespread Fijian protest. After only a few weeks the new government's leaders were arrested and deposed in a coup d'état led by Lieutenant Colonel Sitiveni Rabuka, who demanded greater protection for Fijian rights and an entrenched Fijian dominance of any future government. The governor general declared a state of emergency and assumed control of the government. With political leaders he then negotiated a compromise that would have maintained civilian rule pending a constitutional revision and new elections. The compromise prompted Rabuka to lead a second coup in September and reimpose military rule. Toward the end of 1987 he declared Fiji a republic and appointed a new civilian government with Ratu Sir Kamisese Mara, prime minister from 1970 to 1987, as prime minister.

For later developments in the history of Fiji, see the *Britannica Book of the Year* section in the BRITANNICA WORLD DATA ANNUAL.

Tuvalu

Tuvalu, an independent nation composed of nine small coral islands, lies south of the equator in the central Pacific Ocean. The islands are scattered in a chain lying approximately northwest to southeast over a distance of some 420 miles (676 kilometres). The islands are small; Tuvalu has a land area of less than 10 square miles (26 square kilometres). The capital is Fongafale, on Funafuti Atoll. Tuvalu was formerly called Ellice Islands and with colonial Kiribati formed the unit known as Gilbert and Ellice Islands Colony.

PHYSICAL AND HUMAN GEOGRAPHY

The land. The group includes both atolls and reef islands. The atolls—Nanumea, Nui, Nukufetau, Funafuti, and Nukulaelae—have islets encircling a shallow lagoon; the reef islands—Nanumanga, Niutao, Vaitupu, and Niulakita—are compact with a fringing reef. The islands are low-lying, most being 13 to 16 feet (4 to 5 metres) above sea level. There are no rivers; rain catchment and wells provide the only fresh water. Rainfall averages 100 inches (2,500 millimetres) in the north and 125 inches in the south. The prevailing winds are southeast trades; westerly storms occur from November to February but hurricanes are rare. Daytime temperatures range from 80° to 85° F (27° to 29° C).

Porous
soils

Because the soils are porous, agriculture is limited. Coconut palms thrive, and breadfruit trees and pandanus are grown. Taro and bananas can be grown in pits. Pigs and chickens are raised, and seabirds, fish, and shellfish are caught for food. The islands are increasingly dependent on imported food.

The people. The Tuvaluans are Polynesian, and their language, called Tuvaluan, is closely related to Samoan. The major exception is Nui, which was heavily settled in prehistoric times by Micronesians from the Gilbert Islands (now Kiribati). English is taught in the schools and widely used. Almost all of the population belongs to the Church of Tuvalu (the former Ellice Islands Protestant Church). Although most people live on the outer islands in extended family households clustered into villages, about one-third of the population lives on Funafuti, the centre of government and commerce. Population growth has been slowed by family planning; life expectancy at birth is about 60 years. About 10 percent of the population lives overseas, either pursuing education, working in the Nauru phosphate industry, or working on merchant ships.

The economy. Most Tuvaluans are subsistence farmers and are aided by remittances from relatives working overseas. A small quantity of copra is produced for export, the sale of stamps accounts for modest earnings, and fees are collected from foreign fishing fleets, but the country depends heavily on foreign aid. It imports most of its food, fuel, and manufactured goods. Retailing is handled by community-based cooperative societies. Tuvalu uses Australian currency but also issues its own coinage. There is a single bank, a joint government–commercial venture.

Tuvalu has air links with Kiribati and Fiji; for international shipping, it depends on irregular regional services. Seaplanes have been used for interisland travel, but generally the outer islands depend on a single government vessel. Motorcycles are common on Funafuti, but there are few automobiles.

Administration and social conditions. Tuvalu is a constitutional monarchy within the Commonwealth, with the British sovereign (through a governor general) as head of state. The government is a parliamentary democracy with a unicameral legislature elected by universal adult suffrage. There are no political parties: the prime minister is chosen by and from the legislature. Tuvalu is a member of the South Pacific Forum.

The government provides universal primary education and, under a joint arrangement with the Church of Tuvalu, secondary education to school certificate level for selected pupils. A few are sent overseas for further education and training. Medical facilities are centralized on Funafuti, but all other islands have clinics with trained medical staff.

Cultural life. The Tuvaluan life-style has been westernized to an extent, but Western-style amenities are few. Only Funafuti has a regular electricity supply; the government publishes a brief news sheet but there is no newspaper; a few motion pictures are shown but there is no television; and there is only a single radio station. Most Tuvaluans live in villages of a few hundred people, tend their gardens, and fish from handcrafted canoes. Traditional music and dancing still enjoy a strong following, along with Western forms. Volleyball, soccer, and cricket are popular. Tuvaluan life, despite urbanization and modernization, still rests on a firm traditional base.

Mixture of
traditional
and West-
ern ways

For statistical data on the land and people of Tuvalu, see the *Britannica World Data* section in the BRITANNICA WORLD DATA ANNUAL.

HISTORY

The first settlers were from Samoa and probably arrived in the 14th century AD. Smaller numbers subsequently arrived from Tonga, the northern Cook Islands, Rotuma, and the Gilbert Islands. Niulakita, the smallest and southernmost island, was uninhabited before European contact; the other islands were settled by the 18th century, giving rise to the name Tuvalu, or "Cluster of Eight."

Europeans first discovered the islands in the 16th century through the voyages of Álvaro de Mendaña de Neira, but it was only from the 1820s, with visits by whalers and traders, that they were reliably placed on European charts. In 1863 labour recruiters from Peru kidnapped some 400 people, mostly from Nukulaelae and Funafuti, reducing the population of the group to less than 2,500. A few were later recruited for plantations in Fiji; Samoa; Queensland, Australia; and Hawaii. Concern over labour recruiting and a desire for protection helps to explain the enthusiastic response to Samoan pastors of the London Missionary Society who arrived in the 1860s. By 1900, Protestant Christianity was firmly established.

With imperial expansion the group, then known as the Ellice Islands, became a British protectorate in 1892 and part of the Gilbert and Ellice Islands Colony in 1916. There was a gradual expansion of government services, but most administration was through island governments supervised by a single district officer based in Funafuti. Ellice Islanders sought education and employment at the colonial capital in the Gilbert group or in the phosphate industry at Banaba or Nauru. During World War II, U.S. forces were based on Nanumea, Nukufetau, and Funafuti but hostilities did not reach the group.

From the 1960s, racial tension and rivalries over employment emerged between Gilbertese and Ellice Islanders. Ellice Islanders' demands for secession resulted in a referendum in 1974, transition to separate colonial status between October 1975 and January 1976, and independence as Tuvalu in 1978. After independence the main priorities were to establish the infrastructure for a separate, if small, nation, and to seek foreign assistance to match political independence with economic viability.

For later developments in the history of Tuvalu, see the *Britannica Book of the Year* section in the BRITANNICA WORLD DATA ANNUAL.

Kiribati

Kiribati is a republic of low-lying coral islands in the central Pacific Ocean. Of its 33 islands, only 20 are inhabited. The population is concentrated in the 16 Gilbert Islands, which straddle the Equator. From the Gilbert Islands, Kiribati extends 250 miles (400 kilometres) to the west to Banaba (formerly Ocean Island), and 1,800 miles to the east, to the Line Islands, three of which are inhabited. In between lie the islands of the Phoenix group, which have no permanent population. The capital is at Bairiki on Tarawa atoll in the northern Gilberts. Kiribati and Tuvalu were formerly joined as the Gilbert and Ellice Islands Colony.

PHYSICAL AND HUMAN GEOGRAPHY

The land. A few of the islands are compact with fringing reefs, but most are atolls. The largest atoll (and one of the largest in the world) is Kiritimati (Christmas Island) in the Line group, which has a land area of 150 square miles (388 square kilometres) and accounts for about one-half of the country's total. Kiritimati was used for U.S. and British nuclear testing in the 1960s; it now has a large coconut plantation and fish farms. Banaba rises to 265 feet; its rich layer of phosphate was exhausted by mining from 1900 to 1979. It is sparsely inhabited. Average rainfall in the Gilbert group ranges from 120 inches (3,000 millimetres) in the north to 20 inches in the south. Most rain falls in the season of westerly winds, from November through March; from April to October, northeast trade winds prevail. Temperatures are usually in the range of 75° to 85° F (27° to 33° C).

The importance of coconuts

Coconut palms dominate the landscape on each island. With the products of the reef and the ocean, coconuts are the major contributors to village diet—not only the nuts themselves but also sap tapped from the fruit-bearing spathes. The resulting "toddy" is used in cooking and as a sweet beverage; fermented, it becomes a powerful intoxicant. Breadfruit and pandanus also are grown. *Cyrtosperma chamissonis,* a coarse tarolike plant, can be cultivated in pits, but plants such as taro, bananas, and sweet potatoes are scarce. Pigs and chickens are raised.

The people. The people are Micronesian and speak a single language, which has 13 sounds; "ti" is pronounced as "s" or "see"; thus Kiribati, pronounced "Kiri-bas," is the local rendition of "Gilberts." English is widely spoken, especially on Tarawa. Half of the population is Roman Catholic, and most of the rest is Congregational Protestant.

For many years the population of most islands has remained static because of migration to the rapidly growing urban centres of South Tarawa, where one-third of the population now lives. Betio, the port and commercial centre, has a population density of 13,000 per square mile (5,000 per square kilometre), most living in single-story accommodation. The rural population lives in villages dominated by Western-style churches and large open-sided thatched meetinghouses. Houses of Western-style construction are seen on outer islands and are common on Tarawa.

The economy. Until 1979, when Banaba's phosphate deposit was exhausted, Kiribati's economy depended heavily on the export of phosphate. Before the cessation of mining a large reserve fund was accumulated; the interest now contributes to government revenue. Other revenue earners are copra, mostly produced in the village economy, and license fees from foreign fishing fleets. An Exclusive Economic Zone of 1,350,000 square miles is claimed. Kiribati depends on foreign aid for most capital and development expenditure. Food accounts for one-third of all imports. The main shipping links are with Australia and Fiji. While South Tarawa has an extensive wage economy, most of the people living on outer islands are subsistence farmers with small incomes from copra, fishing, or handicrafts. These are supplemented by remittances from relatives working elsewhere. Interisland shipping is provided by the government, and most islands are linked by a domestic air service. Tarawa and Kiritimati have major airports.

Administration and social conditions. Kiribati is a member of the Commonwealth. It has a president chosen by national election from among four candidates chosen by and from members of the legislature (who are also popularly elected, for a four-year term). The president chooses his ministers from the legislature, and they remain responsible to it. One seat is reserved for the people of Banaba, who have been resettled in Fiji. Local government is through elected island councils.

Primary education is compulsory, and selected pupils attend government- or church-run secondary schools. Kiribati conducts its own technical and teacher training, but other higher education is by overseas scholarship. Tarawa has two hospitals, and there are clinics on all of the inhabited islands.

Cultural life. Kiribati society remains conservative and resistant to change; ties to family and traditional land remain strong, and conspicuous displays of individual achievement or wealth are discouraged. The building and racing of sailing canoes is a popular pastime. Musical composition and dancing in customary styles are regarded as art forms and are the basis of widespread competition. Volleyball and soccer are now widely played.

For statistical data on the land and people of Kiribati, see the *Britannica World Data* section in the BRITANNICA WORLD DATA ANNUAL.

HISTORY

The first settlers in the Gilbert Islands and Banaba came from Southeast Asia, by way of Micronesia, some 4,000–5,000 years ago. About the 14th century AD the southern islands received an influx of Samoans, and soon thereafter the islanders adopted a gerontocratic style of government (based on rule by elders). The Line and Phoenix islands had no prehistoric population.

Rule by elders

Spanish explorers sighted some of the islands in the 16th century, but most did not appear on charts until the early 19th century, when first whalers and then coconut-oil traders reached the islands. From the mid-19th century, labour was recruited in the Gilberts for plantations elsewhere in the region.

The Gilbert Islands became a British protectorate in 1892, and Banaba was annexed in 1900 after the discovery of its rich phosphate deposits. Both were linked with the Ellice Islands as the Gilbert and Ellice Islands Colony from 1916; the colony subsequently was extended to include most of the Phoenix and Line groups and, for a time, Tokelau. Administration was through island governments, which sometimes became enmeshed in sectarian rivalries between Roman Catholics and Protestants. As a response to drought and perceived overpopulation in the 1930s, a resettlement scheme was initiated for the Phoenix Islands; a later scheme saw other Gilbertese resettled in the Solomons.

During World War II the Gilberts were occupied by the Japanese and later liberated by American forces. The colony had few services until aid-funded development programs were introduced after the war. An elected House of Representatives was established in 1967. The subsequent emergence of racial tensions led to the division of the colony in 1975–76. In 1976 the British High Court rejected Banaban claims for massive compensation over mining issues. The Gilbert Islands achieved independence as Kiribati in 1979.

After independence a high priority was given to economic development, especially the exploitation of marine resources. Kiribati belongs to the South Pacific Forum and the Commonwealth. (B.K.M.)

For later developments in the history of Kiribati, see the *Britannica Book of the Year* section in the BRITANNICA WORLD DATA ANNUAL.

Northern Mariana Islands

The Northern Mariana Islands, a self-governing commonwealth in political union with the United States, is composed of 22 islands and islets in the western Pacific. It is a part of the Mariana Islands, a chain of volcanic mountain peaks and uplifted coral reefs extending from latitude 12° to 21° N and longitude 144° to 146° E. (The Marianas chain also includes the politically separate island of Guam.) The Northern Marianas has a land area of 184 square miles (477 square kilometres). Saipan (47 square miles), Tinian (39 square miles), and Rota (33 square miles) are the principal islands and, together with Alamagan and Agrihan, are inhabited. Another island, Pagan, was evacuated in 1981 after a severe volcanic eruption.

PHYSICAL AND HUMAN GEOGRAPHY

The land. Rota, the southernmost island, consists of a volcanic base capped with coral limestone, giving it a terraced appearance. Four southern islands (Farallon de Medinilla, Saipan, Tinian, and Aguijan) are composed of limestone and have gently rolling elevations and few mountains. The islands farther north are volcanic peaks. Mount Pagan erupted in 1922 and again in 1981, 1983, and 1988; Farallon de Pajaros (also called Urucas), the northernmost of the Marianas, and Asuncion are also active volcanoes. Agrihan volcano, the highest of the Northern Mariana group, rises to 3,165 feet (965 metres). Besides Guam, the nearest neighbours are the Bonin Islands (north) and the Federated States of Micronesia (southeast).

Tropical climate

The climate is tropical, with average yearly temperatures on Saipan ranging between 79° F (26° C) and 82° F (28° C) and annual rainfall averaging about 70 inches (1,800 millimetres). Typhoons strike the islands periodically. Rainfall is significantly less on the northernmost islands. The four limestone islands have tropical or scrub forests at higher elevations and coconut palms and casuarina trees along the coast, with the exception of Farallon de Medinilla, which is barren. Where level or gently sloping areas occur, cattle are grazed. The steep slopes of the volcanic islands from Guguan northward are mostly barren. Their soils are generally shallow and low in fertility.

The people. The native people of the Northern Mariana Islands are Micronesians. Three-fifths of the population are Chamorros, descendants of the original inhabitants, who intermingled with Spaniards, Mexicans, Filipinos, and various other Europeans and Asians. About 14 percent of the population is Filipino. About 12 percent of the population are Carolinians, descendants of people who migrated from the central Carolines during the 19th century. There are small numbers of Europeans and Asians (other than Filipinos) as well.

Having lost most of their original Pacific Islands culture, the people of the Northern Mariana Islands have a mode of life that is Spanish Roman Catholic but is influenced by American culture. Saipan has more than 85 percent of the commonwealth's total population. Chamorro, related to Indonesian, is the principal language; English is the official language, and Japanese is widely used.

The economy. Tourism is the principal economic activity. Saipan and Rota are the main tourist centres and offer luxury hotels. The tourists are mainly Japanese and Americans. Subsistence farming, including the cultivation of taro, cassava, yams, breadfruit, vegetables, and bananas, is practiced extensively by many islanders to supplement their cash income. Copra production, fishing, pig and cattle raising, truck farming, and handicrafts have dwindled in recent years. Small manufacturing industries were introduced from Korea, China, and the Philippines, and such

economic activity, with the continuing rise in tourism, has encouraged much immigration from Asia.

Saipan, Tinian, and Rota have paved roads. Transportation between the islands is largely by air, with some boat traffic primarily for cargo. Saipan is the largest port, followed by Tinian and Rota. Saipan has an international airport.

Administration and social conditions. Part of the Trust Territory of the Pacific Islands granted to the United States by the United Nations in 1947, the Northern Marianas voted in plebiscite for status as a U.S. commonwealth in 1975. Some aspects of the commonwealth status were implemented in 1976, and the full commonwealth became effective upon the dissolution of the Trust Territory for the Marianas by the U.S. government in 1986. Eligible residents of the commonwealth became U.S. citizens at that time.

U.S. citizenship

According to the constitution of 1978, residents elect a governor, a lieutenant governor, and a bicameral legislature made up of nine senators and 14 representatives. The administrative headquarters of the commonwealth is at Chalan Kanoa on Saipan.

All inhabited islands have primary schools and hospitals. There are public and church-run secondary schools on Saipan. The College of the Northern Marianas, a public junior college, was established in 1976.

Cultural life. In recent years there has been an increase in the cultural diversity of the Northern Marianas. There are growing Filipino, Chinese, and Korean communities, although none of these has political representation. The Carolinian community, which has lived at Saipan for more than 100 years, is represented in the legislature. The local Chamorro population, with its tradition of extended families, is dominant. A local arts council has promoted folk arts and cultural events in the community, and a small museum and library have been established. Public beach parks and preserves as well as two large golf courses provide recreation. American national holidays and several local holidays are celebrated. Two local weekly newspapers are supplemented by the Guam daily newspaper, which provides some local coverage; all are published in English. There are several radio and television stations.

HISTORY

Archaeological evidence at Chalan Piao on Saipan indicates that the Northern Marianas were settled by an insular people originating in Southeast Asia. They made a distinctive red-slipped ware, sometimes incised with lime-filled decoration, closely related to Philippine wares. By AD 800 a plain, unslipped ware was in use and stone architecture had developed. Parallel rows of upright pillars topped with hemispheric capstones (*halege*) were erected. According to early Spanish accounts, the pillars were supports for structures called *latte* (after which term the culture is named), which may have served as men's houses or as canoe sheds. Each village had from one to several *latte* structures. Stone and shell tools were used and the betel nut was chewed, as shown by extended burials most often located between the rows of *latte*.

Ferdinand Magellan was the first to open the Marianas to the West when he stopped there briefly during his first circumnavigation in 1521. There is some historical question as to which island he actually visited, but Magellan named the islands the Ladrones (Spanish: "Thieves") because while he was there some of the islanders took a small skiff that he had trailing behind one of his ships.

In 1565 Miguel López de Legazpi landed at Umatac, Guam, and proclaimed Spanish sovereignty over the Ladrones; some priests went ashore to say the mass. No colonies were started at that time, however, because the Spanish were more interested in conquests in the Americas, the Philippines, and the Moluccas. The British adventurer Thomas Cavendish was the next to visit the Marianas, in 1588 aboard the *Desire*. He traded briefly, and as he left he ordered his men to open fire from the rear of the ship to discourage the islanders from following.

The early explorers and those who followed took mixed blessings to the islands. On the one hand they provided ironware and cloth, which was traded for fresh produce.

Effects of early explorers

On the other hand they introduced infectious diseases, including influenza, smallpox, leprosy, venereal diseases, and tuberculosis, which severely depleted the indigenous population.

The permanent colonization of the islands began with the arrival of Father Diego Luis de Sanvitores in 1668. With him were priests, laymen, women, and some Filipino soldiers. Mariana of Austria, the regent of Spain, financed his mission, and he renamed the islands the Marianas in her honour. Sanvitores and his colonists established churches and religious schools. A series of revolts attended these efforts, since the islanders resisted conversion to a religion that did not fit traditional beliefs. The Spanish during this time, in order to control the islanders more effectively, moved the population of the Marianas into enclaves and segregated the people into villages. Many islanders were killed in the process of relocation. Others died during their adjustment to new social environments, and the population was further decreased.

In 1680 the Spanish sent reinforcements led by Don José Quiroga, who was interim governor of the Marianas from 1680 to 1696. He subdued the islanders after a series of revolts, sieges, murders of missionaries, and burnings of churches that was known as the "Chamorro wars" and that resulted in many islanders fleeing to the hills. In reprisal, the entire native population was relocated from Saipan and Rota in the northern Marianas to the island of Guam. Finally, the Chamorro people took the oath of allegiance to the king of Spain, accepted Spanish customs, and began to wear Western-style clothes, cultivate corn, and learn to eat meat. Artisans were sent to the villages to teach sewing, spinning, weaving, tanning, iron forging, stone masonry, and other crafts. By 1698 the subjugation of the Marianas was complete.

The Spanish branched out from the Marianas into the rest of Micronesia, meeting only mild resistance. Guam became a regular stop for the Spanish galleons traveling between the Philippines and Mexico. By the 19th century the Marianas had become involved in European colonial rivalries. The Germans as well as the British began to encroach on the Spanish claims in Micronesia, and difficulties were averted in 1886 by the mediation of Pope Leo XIII, whose efforts in this regard prevented war between Germany and Spain. But Spain's empire was weakening, and by 1898 war with the United States was at hand. After American naval forces under the command of Commodore George Dewey defeated the Spanish fleet in the Philippines and took Guam, Spain made the decision in 1899 to withdraw entirely from the Pacific and sold its possessions—including all of the Marianas except Guam, which the Americans still held—to Germany.

German administration

The Germans promptly established an administrative centre at Saipan, which had served as the seat of the Spanish administration after the Americans captured Guam in 1898. This period marked the permanent division between Guam and the northern Marianas. Schools, a hospital, and other public buildings were erected in the northern Marianas, and colonists were encouraged to immigrate from Germany. Large coconut plantations were started, as were other agricultural projects. Copra production was the main German agricultural interest.

German control in the northern Marianas ended abruptly with the outbreak of World War I. In October 1914 the Japanese navy took possession of the northern Marianas and the rest of Micronesia. Japan's authority for this seizure was based upon several secret agreements with the British designed to keep the peace in Asia in the event of war. After World War I Japan received the northern Marianas by the terms of the Treaty of Versailles on June 28, 1919, and then later as a mandate under the League of Nations on Dec. 17, 1920. The United States, which continued to hold Guam, recognized this mandate on Feb. 11, 1922.

Japanese rule in the northern Marianas was direct and allowed the islanders little part in local government. The basic laws of Japan were extended to the islands with only such modifications as were needed to meet local conditions. Formal educational facilities were restricted, emphasis being placed upon learning the Japanese language. Public health conditions, however, were improved, and hospitals were established. Economic development was Japan's main interest, and large sugar plantations and refineries were started at Saipan and Rota. Large amounts of labour and capital were made available. There was full employment, and the islanders were made more productive than they had been before.

When World War II began the Japanese immediately took Guam from the United States and made their domination of the Marianas complete. The larger islands of Saipan, Tinian, Rota, Pagan, and Agrihan, along with Guam, became bases for Japanese expansion to the south and east. In 1943, U.S. forces began to reduce Japanese strength in Micronesia, and in June–July 1944 the Marianas were neutralized with the recapture of Saipan, Tinian, and Guam. The three islands then became Allied bases for the bombing of the Japanese home islands; the atomic bombs dropped on Hiroshima and Nagasaki were flown from a base at Tinian. Most of the individual islands of the Marianas were bypassed, and with most of these communication was not reestablished until the war was over.

U.S. invasion

The U.S. invasion of the Marianas during World War II completely destroyed the Japanese-created economy in the islands. The United States began the task of rebuilding. President Harry S. Truman signed a Trusteeship Agreement with the United Nations for the administration of the northern Marianas as a district within the Trust Territory of the Pacific Islands in Micronesia on July 18, 1947, and delegated responsibility for the civil administration to the U.S. Navy. Then, on July 1, 1951, following the signing of the peace treaty with Japan and the renouncing of all Japanese claims to the northern Marianas, U.S. administrative responsibility under the UN Trusteeship was transferred to the secretary of the interior. A special designation of "strategic" trusteeship was made, which placed the ultimate jurisdiction of the Marianas under the United Nations Security Council. The other Micronesian island groups of the Marshalls and the Carolines were also covered under this Trusteeship Agreement.

The United States pledged to "promote development . . . towards self-government or independence as may be appropriate." In 1969 political status talks began between the Micronesians from the entire Trust Territory and U.S. representatives. In 1973 the northern Marianas began separate negotiations with the United States that led to a plebiscite in 1975 in which the people approved a commonwealth status in association with the United States. The new government began operations under its own constitution and an elected governor, who was installed in January 1978. Eligible residents of the Northern Marianas became U.S. citizens. The United States declared the trusteeship officially ended on Nov. 4, 1986.

Guam

Guam, the largest, most populous, and southernmost island of the Mariana Islands and an unincorporated territory of the United States, lies in the Pacific Ocean about 5,800 miles (9,300 kilometres) west of San Francisco and 1,600 miles east of Manila. The total land area is 209 square miles (541 square kilometres). Agana is the capital. The most populous settlements are Tamuning, Apra Harbor, and Mangilao.

PHYSICAL AND HUMAN GEOGRAPHY

The land.   The island is sharply divided into a northern limestone plateau with a general elevation of about 500 feet (150 metres) and an area of higher, volcanic hills to the south. The plateau is covered with a thick growth of jungle; the volcanic hills support mainly sword grass. The hills rise more than 1,000 feet above sea level, and their lower slopes to the east (and also in part to the west) are covered with younger limestones, generally similar to those of the northern limestone plateau. The higher hills are Mount Lamlam, which rises to an elevation of 1,332 feet (406 metres); Mount Bolanos (1,220 feet); and Mount Sasalaguan (1,109 feet).

Guam has a pleasant tropical climate. Temperatures range from 70° to 90° F (21° to 32° C) and are fairly even throughout the year. Average annual rainfall is about 95 inches (2,400 millimetres), three-fourths of which falls during the wet season, generally starting in May or June and lasting through November. The even climate is punctuated by destructive typhoons that occur at irregular intervals.

The people. The native Guamanians, ethnically called Chamorros, are basically of Malayo-Indonesian descent with a considerable admixture of Spanish, Filipino, Mexican, and other European and Asian influences. Their vernacular, called the Chamorro language, is a distinct language with its own vocabulary and grammar mixed with many Spanish words. The word Chamorro is derived from Chamorri, or Chanioli, the ancient name for chief. English and Chamorro are the official languages; although Chamorro is still used in many homes, English is the language of education and commerce. The predominant religion is Roman Catholicism.

Fiesta tradition

Before World War II the villages were the main social and economic units, preserving customs and traditions similar to those of 19th-century Spain. The fiesta held in memory of a patron saint was the great social and religious event of the year for each village, and it brought together people from other villages. Fiesta customs are still observed in modern Guam. Changes in the social life and institutions of Guamanians, however, have come about with economic improvement and increasingly international contacts.

The economy. The development of Guam into an important U.S. military base brought about profound changes in the island's agricultural patterns after World War II. Foodstuffs were imported in increasing amounts, discouraging the cultivation of many formerly important truck crops. Guam now imports most of its food.

All branches of the U.S. armed forces are represented at military facilities on Guam. Andersen Air Force Base, at the northern end of Guam, is a part of the U.S. Strategic Air Command; the armed forces also operate a naval station with a ship repair yard, a naval air station, a communications station, and a hospital. The availability of work at the military facilities has drawn many islanders from their former lives of subsistence agriculture and fishing.

Tourism is the most prominent component of the economy after the military, with more than half a million tourists visiting from Japan alone in 1987. There are several luxury hotels along Tumon Bay, which has been highly developed as a tourist area. A modern international airport links Guam with Japan, Hawaii, the U.S. west coast, the Philippines, Australia, and other parts of Asia. Guam is a duty-free port, and this status has attracted a number of small manufacturing companies from countries in Asia and has also prompted some immigration. In the 1970s poultry farming, garment-finishing plants, and an oil refinery were established. Major imports are petroleum products, machinery, automobiles and transport vehicles, manufactures, and food.

Administration and social conditions. Guam is an unincorporated territory of the United States governed under the Organic Act of Guam, passed by the U.S. Congress and approved by the president on Aug. 1, 1950. The Organic Act made all Chamorros U.S. citizens, but they were not given the right to vote in national elections.

The act was amended in 1968 to provide for the popular election of a governor and lieutenant governor for four-year terms. All persons 18 years of age or older are permitted to vote. The legislature is a unicameral body with 21 senators directly elected at large for a term of two years. Guam has no constitution. The people of Guam, in seeking to improve their political relationship with the United States, voted in 1982 in favour of pursuing a commonwealth relationship similar to that established in the Northern Marianas. A draft Commonwealth Act was approved by the people in 1987 and was presented by the governor to the U.S. Congress on Feb. 23, 1988.

The judiciary consists of the Federal District Court of Guam, whose judge is appointed by the U.S. president for a term of eight years. There are two levels of local trial courts: the Superior Court of Guam, for criminal and civil cases, and the traffic, juvenile, and small-claims courts. Judges are appointed by the governor with consent of the legislature and are reconfirmed by majority public vote every four years. Appeals may be made to the U.S. Court of Appeals for the Ninth Circuit and to the U.S. Supreme Court.

Village commissioners

Each of the island's villages is headed by a popularly elected commissioner. A chief commissioner, elected by the commissioners, acts as liaison between the governor and the districts.

Education is compulsory between the ages of six and 16. The University of Guam, opened in 1952, is a four-year institution with colleges of agriculture, business and public administration, arts and sciences, and education. Graduate programs at the master's level are also available. Health facilities include public, private, and military hospitals and local clinics.

Cultural life. Guam is culturally diverse, with Chinese, Japanese, Filipino, Korean, and other Asian communities of significant size in addition to its indigenous and mainland U.S. populations. As a centre of transportation and communication for the island region it also has sizable numbers of islanders from various parts of Micronesia, such as Palau, Yap, Truk, Pohnpei, Kosrae, and the Marshall Islands. The extended family is the main social unit for most groups on Guam, although many of the younger members travel and live in the United States. Folk arts and handicrafts of Guam have enjoyed a revival in recent years with the advent of various public and private groups that have promoted music, dance, and other cultural arts for the benefit of both the local community and tourists. U.S. national holidays are celebrated, as are several significant local dates such as Discovery Day, March 6, which commemorates the arrival of Ferdinand Magellan in 1521. The museum and library on Guam have active programs for the community, and the university is also a promoter of regional arts and culture. There are daily and semi-weekly newspapers and quarterly and monthly magazines, and several radio and television stations broadcast local and international news and features daily.

HISTORY

Guam, like the other Mariana Islands, was settled before the second quarter of the 2nd millennium BC by an Indonesian–Filipino people. Archaeological research shows that by AD 800 they had developed a complex society that erected elaborate stone pillars (*halege*), which served as supports for communal houses (*latte*).

Ferdinand Magellan probably landed on Guam in 1521. The island was officially claimed by Spain in 1565, and there was no attempt to conquer it until the latter part of the 17th century. After an uprising in 1670 and 25 years of intermittent warfare, the Spanish subdued the population with considerable bloodshed. Disease, particularly smallpox and influenza, also played an important role in the decimation of the population. Typhoons in 1671 and 1693 caused further destruction and loss of life. Guam remained a Spanish possession until 1898, when, in the course of the Spanish–American War, the U.S. warship *Charleston* steamed into the harbour of Apra and shelled the old fort. Guam was ceded to the United States, and the other islands of the Marianas were sold by Spain to Germany in 1899. From that time until 1950 (excepting World War II) the governor of the island was a naval officer appointed by the president of the United States.

During World War I Japan occupied Germany's island possessions north of the Equator, and after the war Japan received the Marianas (except Guam) and the Caroline and Marshall groups as a mandate under the League of Nations. Japan retained possession of the islands even after it withdrew from the League in 1933.

In World War II the Japanese landed on Guam just after the attack on Pearl Harbor and occupied the island by Dec. 12, 1941. U.S. forces retook Guam by Aug. 10, 1944. It was a major air and naval base for the squadrons of bombers that attacked Japan near the end of the war. Under the jurisdiction of the U.S. Navy, it was made a territory (1950) that was administered by the U.S. Department of the Interior (from 1973, by the Office of Territorial Affairs, within that department). Guam remains the site of major U.S. naval and air bases; about one-third of the land in Guam is owned by the U.S. armed forces.

In the 1970s Guam gradually began to move toward representative self-government. The first popularly elected governor ran for office in 1970, and in 1972 Guam was given the right to send one nonvoting delegate (entitled to vote in committees, however) to the U.S. House of Representatives. In 1978 the U.S. Senate accorded Guam the right to adopt a territorial constitution. In 1982, in a referendum offering six options, the option of commonwealth status won a plurality (48 percent) of votes.

(D.A.B.)

Palau

The Republic of Palau (Palauan: Beluu era Belau) is an internally self-governing republic. It consists of about 340 coral and volcanic islands perched on the Kyushu-Palau Ridge in the western Pacific. The Palau archipelago lies in the southwest corner of Micronesia with the Philippines 550 miles (885 kilometres) to the west, New Guinea 400 miles to the south, and Guam 830 miles to the northeast. It reaches from latitude 2°55′ to 8°12′ N and from longitude 131°05′ to 134°44′ E. A huge barrier-reef system, continuous on the west and broken on the east, encircles most of the archipelago's 188 square miles (488 square kilometres) of land: its major populated islands are Babelthuap (Babeldaob), Koror, Malakal, Arakabesan, and Peleliu. The sparsely populated Kayangel atoll to the north of Babelthuap and the raised coral islands of Angaur, Sonsorol, Pulo Anna, and Tobi south of Peleliu lie outside the barrier-reef system. Koror Island, rising to 2,061 feet (628 metres) just south of Babelthuap, is the provisional capital and largest population centre.

Palau was a member of the UN Trust Territory of the Pacific Islands established in 1947 and administered by the United States. When the U.S. government dissolved the trusteeship in 1986, a compact of free association between Palau and the United States was pending, and the United States retained responsibility as the administering authority.

PHYSICAL AND HUMAN GEOGRAPHY

The land. *Relief and drainage.* All but six of Palau's islands lie within an expansive lagoon, enclosed by the barrier reef, that stretches northeast to southwest for almost 70 miles. Babelthuap, the largest island (153 square miles), is volcanic, mainly andesite, and is bounded by thick mangrove forests broken occasionally by sandy beaches on the east coast. Its highest point, Rois Ngerekelehuus, in the northwest, is 794 feet (242 metres) high. Babelthuap is essentially a rolling upland, part grassland and part jungle, that has been incised by stream action to form a well-developed drainage system of three rivers. With 150 inches (3,800 millimetres) of rain annually, considerable erosion has taken place on Babelthuap in spite of the stability provided by laterite soils, clays, and vegetation. The Palauan practice of burning the grassy upland areas during the dry season has contributed to erosion.

Mangrove forests [margin note]

Since 1977 Babelthuap has been connected by a concrete bridge to the 3.6-square-mile Koror, which, in turn, is linked by causeway to Malakal island, the site of Palau's deepwater port, and Arakabasan island. The combined area of the three smaller linked islands is 7 square miles. All are of volcanic origin. Beginning adjacent to southern Babelthuap and eastern Koror, however, and filling the huge lagoon for 28 miles south to Peleliu, are 320 green velvet "rock" islands. These are uplifted reef structures of coralline limestone, each deeply undercut at sea level. Some of the islands are large, towering 600 feet, and have interior brackish lakes that are connected to the lagoon by subterranean channels. Plant growth is thick on the rock islands and, together with the chemical action of heavy rains, has sculpted and broken the surfaces, producing razor-sharp edges and points and broken rubble. The limestone islands have rich deposits of phosphate, and the more accessible ones have been mined.

The inhabited coral islands outside of Palau's reef–lagoon–island system sit on volcanic substructures and consist of Kayangel atoll, 25 miles north of Babelthuap; and Angaur, six miles south of Peleliu, which was heavily mined for its phosphate first by the Germans and later by the Japanese. Sonsorol, Pulo Anna, and Tobi, all with areas of less than one square mile, are 180 miles southwest of the Palau archipelago. All are flat platform structures with fringing reefs.

Climate. Palau's climate is tropical. Rainfall varies from 120 to 160 inches per year. Humidity is fairly constant, ranging from 77 to 84 percent, and temperatures vary not more than 10° F (5.5° C) diurnally, monthly, or annually, from a mean of 81° F (27° C). Northeast trade winds prevail from December to March and southwest monsoons from June to October. Prevailing oceanic currents offshore are the North Equatorial Current and the Equatorial Countercurrent. Geologically, Palau sits on the Philippine Sea Plate only 30 miles west of the 26,200-foot-deep Palau Trench, the western boundary of the upthrusting Pacific Plate. Despite its close proximity to this subduction zone, Palau rarely experiences earthquake activity.

Palau's marine environment exhibits a rich fauna balanced by an abundant terrestrial flora. This richness derives from Palau's close proximity to Indonesia, New Guinea, and the Philippines. Palau has more species of marine life than any other area of similar size in the world; corals, fish, snails, clams, sea cucumbers, starfish, sea urchins, sea anemones, jellyfish, squid, and feather worms exist in profusion and variety. Common flora are the beach morning glory, Polynesian ironwood tree, pandanus, and various species of palm and fern. The birds of Palau are abundant and colourful and many migrate to or through Palau twice annually. A few species of reptile and amphibian live in Palau, including a unique frog that gives birth to live young. Insects are also abundant. The accidentally introduced coconut rhinoceros beetle did enormous damage to coconut palms until it was brought under control by the parasitic scolia wasp.

Unique frog species [margin note]

Emperor angelfish (*Pomacanthus imperator*) swimming among the corals in the barrier-reef channel of Aulong Island, Palau.

The people. Palau's people are generally of medium height with diverse skin tones and facial types. The islands were inhabited from 2,000 to 3,000 years ago by successive waves of Malays from Indonesia, Melanesians from New Guinea, Philippine natives, and some Polynesians from outlying Polynesian islands in Micronesia, who formed the basic genetic stock. During the past two centuries Europeans, Japanese, and Americans have made genetic contributions. The southwest islanders, culturally and linguistically distinct from the Palauans, are the only minority group; they trace their origin to a group of ancestral survivors of one or more canoes that drifted to Sonsorol from Ulithi Atoll, northeast of Yap. Palauan is a Western Austronesian language and is very complex in that it has many irregularities that make formulation of grammatical and lexical rules difficult.

The indigenous Palauan religion of powerful ancestral and nature spirits was supplanted by Christianity. The only remnant of past belief systems is the Modekngei religion, which developed as a syncretic movement in response to colonial pressure. In addition to the well-established Roman Catholic, Lutheran, and Seventh-day Adventist churches, missionaries of the Jehovah's Witness, Mormon, Bahā'ī, and Assemblies of God faiths have carried their message to Palau.

Palauans are atypical Micronesians in their desire to migrate overseas. There are substantial Palauan communities on Guam, in Hawaii, and on the U.S. west coast. This movement and the apparent decline in birth rates have resulted in a small negative population growth rate.

The economy. Since the end of World War II, the major employer in Palau has been government—first the U.S. Navy, then the Trust Territory of the Pacific Islands, and finally the government of Palau. Nevertheless, in the rural areas outside Koror the subsistence economy is active. Women gather and cultivate wet taro, sweet potato, and cassava, and men fish and tend pigs, which are used at customary feasts. Tourism has grown considerably.

With the majority of Palau's population in Koror, that island has a good system of paved roads. There are stretches of paved road on Babelthuap, and the roads built in 1944–46 by U.S. military forces on Peleliu and Angaur are still usable. Transportation between islands is by boat or airplane. There is regular commuter service from Koror to Peleliu and Angaur, and trips by speedboat to coastal villages on Babelthuap can be completed in a few hours.

Near-shore reef fishing is carried out on a subsistence and small-venture basis, but it does not generate significant government revenue. Offshore tuna fishing by foreign vessels provides a small amount of government revenue through the sale of licenses.

Administration and social conditions. The constitution of the Republic of Palau established a presidential form of government, which was installed in 1981. The executive consists of separately elected offices of president and vice president, a Council of Chiefs to advise the president on traditional laws and customs, and a Cabinet. The National Congress consists of a Senate and a House of Delegates. Both executive and legislative branches are elected for four-year terms. The Palau judiciary consists of a Supreme Court and a National Court of Common Pleas with both trial and appellate divisions. At the local level, each of the 16 traditional settlement areas comprises a state with an elected governor and legislature. Palau has no armed forces.

Each of the rural states has an elementary school. Three church-run high schools and a public high school take most of those who complete the eighth grade. The Micronesian Occupational College on Koror was established in 1969 and was reaccredited in 1987.

Health care is provided by the hospital on Koror and dispensaries in each rural state. The incidences of mental illness, suicide, and alcoholism in Palau are higher than in most countries.

Adaptation to occupation **Cultural life.** Pragmatic adaptation, persistence of wealth-exchange customs, and competition characterize Palauan society. Palauans adapted to a century of colonial intrusion—Spanish, German, Japanese, and American—by viewing reality as something imposed from the outside to which one must adjust quickly if it is to be manipulated. Reciprocity and redistribution customs carried out between clans exchange food and services for money and gifts at births, house completions, and funerals. Women are the strength of society and control land, money, and titles. Men, previously occupied as fishermen and warriors, continue their traditional tasks in the rural areas and, as an adaptation to modern society, compete for elected office, in business, and in baseball. Traditional art forms persist in chants and storyboards, which are now made for tourists. The Palau National Museum in Koror has a small but instructive collection of artifacts.

HISTORY

Large hillside terraces, numerous stone ruins, and megaliths on Babelthuap give evidence of a vital pre-contact culture. The first extensive contact of Palauans with Westerners took place after the shipwreck of the East India Company's packet *Antelope* in 1783. George Keate's *An Account of the Pelew Islands* (1788), which recounted the friendship and high adventure found in Palau, served to fuel the European myths of the noble savage and island paradise. The first 70 years of the 19th century were punctuated by the occasional visits of whalers and traders, who left beachcombers and firearms behind. Imported diseases led to the deaths of many islanders, and firearms were prized for intervillage warfare, which was ended in 1883 through the peaceful intervention of Captain Cyprian Bridge of HMS *Espiégle.* Spanish and German colonial influence was expressed through Roman Catholic missionaries. The Japanese navy expelled the Germans at the beginning of World War I, and, although the Japanese period is locally remembered as one of economic development and order, the Palauans were a marginal minority by 1936. Japan lost Palau in World War II in a struggle that was socially destabilizing and confusing to the Palauans.

After a short period of administration by the U.S. Navy, Palau became part of the United Nations Trust Territory of the Pacific Islands under U.S. administration in 1947. A constitution was adopted in 1981 (following two prior referendums), and elections were held in the same year. The country became internally self-governing in 1981. Palau signed a Compact of Free Association with the United States in 1982. The compact requires that the United States remain responsible for external security and defense and that it provide financial assistance for Palau. Its articles provide for Palau to become fully independent or to alter its status with the United States at any time, based upon approval of such changes through plebiscite. The compact was endorsed by a majority of Palauan voters in 1983. It was not passed by the U.S. Congress, however, because the United States maintained that it could not carry out its defense obligations without removal of Palau's constitutional prohibition on the operation of U.S. nuclear-powered or nuclear-armed vessels and aircraft within the jurisdiction of Palau. According to the terms of the compact, the United States reserves this right as well as the right to neither confirm nor deny the presence or absence of such weapons in Palau. Several attempts were made to revise the constitution, revise the compact agreement, and secure Palauan approval, but the issue remained unresolved when the United States dissolved the trusteeship in 1986. *Nuclear weapons controversy*

In 1985 volatile internal politics resulted in the assassination of the first president, Haruo I. Remeliik. In August 1985 Lazarus E. Salii was elected to serve out the four-year term begun by Remeliik in January 1985, but Salii himself met a violent death in August 1988.

(D.R.Sh.)

Federated States of Micronesia

The Federated States of Micronesia is an internally self-governing country in the western Pacific Ocean. It is composed of more than 600 islands and islets in the Caroline Islands archipelago and is divided, roughly along cultural and linguistic lines, into the states of Yap, Truk, Pohnpei, and Kosrae. The total land area is about 270 square miles (435 square kilometres). The capital is Kolonia, on the island of Pohnpei. To the west of the Federated States of Micronesia lies the Republic of Palau, also in the Caroline archipelago, and to the east is the Republic of the Marshall Islands. These two nations, together with the Commonwealth of the Northern Marianas and the Federated States of Micronesia, were administered by the United States as the Trust Territory of the Pacific Islands from 1947 to 1986.

PHYSICAL AND HUMAN GEOGRAPHY

The land. The islands are of two general types: high volcanic islands that support a large variety of plant forms and low-lying coral atolls with poorer soil. The main landmass in Yap is distinctive in that it was formed by folds in the Earth's crust and is continental in geologic composition. Each of the four states has as its population centre an elevated landmass of fairly large extent. These range in size from Pohnpei, with an area of 129 square miles, to Yap and Truk, each with 39 square miles. The volcanic islands of Truk are an anomaly in the Pacific since they are encircled by a reef but have not yet subsided beneath sea level to become a classic atoll. Yap Island and six islands in the Truk group rise to more than 500 feet (150 metres), and Kosrae and Pohnpei islands have peaks of 2,061 feet (628 metres) and 2,593 feet (790 metres), respectively. The coral atolls consist of groups of small islands, formed atop a coral reef enclosing a lagoon.

The climate is tropical, with high humidity and a mean annual temperature of 81° F (27° C). There is little seasonal variation in temperature. Rainfall averages 120 inches (3,000 millimetres) per year throughout the area, although Pohnpei receives more than 200 inches yearly. There are distinct rainy and dry seasons, the latter occurring during the height of the northeasterly trade-wind season between December and April. Yap, which alone is situated in the monsoon area, has westerly winds for part of the year. Numerous typhoons originate in the east each year, usually spinning off to the northwest toward Yap and the Mariana Islands and seldom striking any of the other islands.

On the high islands, mangrove swamps grow along the shore, and grassland or scrub ascends to tropical rain forests in the interior mountain areas. Settlements are almost without exception located near the coast. Volcanic islands, with their richer soil, support many different species of plant life. On coral atolls the predominant forms of vegetation are the coconut palm and pandanus and breadfruit trees. Atoll dwellers typically locate their houses on the lagoon side of the island.

The people. The native people of the Federated States, while generally classified as Micronesian, are very diverse in physical types, cultures, and languages. The people of Yap Island have Melanesian-like features and speak a language only distantly related to the other languages of the area. Inhabitants of the coral atolls in Yap state are similar in language and culture to the people of Truk, although their languages are not mutually intelligible. Both Truk and Pohnpei contain several dialects, and the inhabitants of Kapingamarangi and Nukuoro, two atolls in the southwestern portion of Pohnpei state, are Polynesians and speak languages unrelated to Pohnpeian. Only Kosrae has complete ethnic and linguistic unity. Altogether eight local languages are recognized as distinct, and dialectal differences in the outlying atolls add further variety.

Almost half of the total population lives in Truk. Pohnpei has about 30 percent, and Yap and Kosrae have about 10 percent and 7 percent, respectively. In recent years there has been some migration to the towns for employment and education, and the four main towns—the capitals of each state—now contain about one-quarter of the total population. The birth rate remains high and mortality rates have been sharply reduced. The population is growing by about 3 percent yearly. Almost the entire population is Christian. English is spoken widely in commerce and government throughout the nation.

The economy. Subsistence farming and fishing are the principal economic activities. The main staples are breadfruit, taro, coconuts, and bananas, but yams, cassava, and sweet potatoes also are grown on some of the high islands. Poultry, pigs, and dogs are sometimes also raised for food. The main source of revenue is U.S. government grant aid, which continues under the Compact of Free Association signed in 1982 and which accounts for an estimated 70 percent of the gross national product. Government employment is by far the major source of income, and this in turn supports the service industries that make up the private sector. Exports, which account for less than 5 percent of the gross national product, include copra, a few marine products, black pepper, and handicrafts. Additional income is derived from the sale of fishing rights and from a slowly expanding tourist industry. Local commercial fishing is developed only on a small scale, and large-scale agriculture has repeatedly proved a failure. Much of the Federated States' food and almost all manufactured goods and fuel oil must be imported.

Interisland and international transportation are by air or ocean freighter. The major commercial ports are at Takatik near Pohnpei, Kosrae, Colonia on Yap, and Moen. International airports are located on Yap, Pohnpei, and Moen. Smaller ships operated by the government provide service to the outlying atolls in each state. Some of the atolls are also linked by weekly flights on smaller planes. On major islands all villages are connected by a road system, and main roads in the commercial centres are paved.

Administration and social conditions. Under the 1979 constitution, the government of the Federated States of Micronesia consists of a president and vice president elected by the unicameral National Congress, made up of one at-large senator from each state, with four-year terms, and single-district senators (elected on the basis of population), with two-year terms, including one each from Yap and Kosrae, three from Pohnpei, and five from Truk. Each of the four local state governments has a popularly elected governor and a unicameral legislature. There are no political parties. The judicial system consists of the Supreme Court of the Federated States of Micronesia, state courts in each of the four states, and municipal courts in each political subdivision of each state. Recognized customary law is in force wherever it does not conflict with constitutional law.

There are elementary schools on every island, and each state has at least one public high school. The Community College of Micronesia, with its main campus on Pohnpei and extension programs in other states, is the only institution for higher education in the Federated States of Micronesia, but several U.S. universities offer extension programs for teacher training. A hospital is maintained in each of the state capitals, and dispensaries have been built on all major islands. Local healers continue to practice massage and other traditional medical skills.

Cultural life. Although only the people of Yap and a few of the outlying atolls in Truk still wear traditional dress (loincloths for men and grass skirts or lavalavas for women), most villagers live much as their ancestors did. They support themselves by subsistence farming and fishing, use traditional food preparation techniques, and gather in community meetinghouses for ceremonies and leisure activities. The seamanship of the islanders is probably their most remarkable achievement and has astonished Westerners since initial contact. Wood carving, which was originally practiced for religious purposes, has become a commercial enterprise. Women in some of the islands still weave lavalavas on traditional belt looms, and nearly everywhere large sleeping mats are plaited of pandanus leaves. Tattooing, once used widely to indicate social status, is seldom practiced today, but the traditional dances remain a favourite form of entertainment.

HISTORY

The eastern Caroline Islands, like the Marshall and Gilbert islands, were probably first settled from the New Hebrides–Fiji area in the millennium before the Christian Era. Archaeological and linguistic evidence suggests that the earliest migrants worked their way up the chain of islands to the east and gradually spread westward from the Marshalls. Pottery dating to the beginning of the Christian Era has been found in Truk, and artifacts of similar antiquity have been unearthed in other islands in the east. The languages of the area, with the exception of the two Polynesian outliers and Yap, are closely related to one another and show striking similarities to Vanuatuan tongues. The high island of Yap appears to have been settled from the west, probably from the Philippines or Indonesia. Pottery and shell adzes found there date from the 2nd century AD and show a resemblance to types discovered in the Marianas. Yap's caste system and other features of its social organization are unparalleled elsewhere in the area. The renowned Yapese stone money was quarried in nearby Palau and the Marianas. In later centuries a reciprocal tribute and trade system was evolved with the surrounding coral atolls, sometimes termed the Yap Empire or Yapese Empire. In the eastern islands of Pohnpei and Kosrae, some seven centuries ago, a major social upheaval occurred, possibly under the impact of invasion from the

Coastal settlements

Absence of political parties

Yap's atypical social organization

south. Fortified settlements were built of huge basaltic logs, their ruins still visible today, and political authority over each island was centralized even as the society became more stratified.

The islands were visited occasionally during the 16th century by Spanish navigators and were later named for the Spanish king Charles II. During the 19th century European naval ships followed whalers and traders to the islands, and the inhabitants experienced their first intensive contact with foreigners and their wares. In 1886 Spain finally colonized the Carolines, but its short rule was ended in 1899 when the islands were sold to Germany at the conclusion of the Spanish–American War. Germany, in turn, yielded the islands at the outbreak of World War I to Japan, which gained formal title to them in 1920 as a League of Nations mandate. At first Japan attempted to develop a solid economy; later it used the islands as an outlet for surplus population; and finally it fortified them just before World War II. In July 1947 the Carolines, together with the Marshalls and northern Marianas, became a United Nations trust territory under U.S. administration. They were designated as a strategic area to allow the United States to set up military bases as deemed necessary; consequently, ultimate responsibility for the Trust Territory of the Pacific Islands rested in the UN Security Council rather than in the UN General Assembly, as was the case with other trust territories.

Micronesian leaders began negotiations with the United States for full self-government in 1969. The constitution that was drafted in 1975 became the basis for the federated government that went into effect in 1979. By that time, however, the Marianas, the Marshalls, and Palau had voted to separate from the proposed federation; this left only the "inner states" of Yap, Truk, Kosrae, and Pohnpei to compose the new political entity. In a 1983 plebiscite, voters approved a Compact of Free Association with the United States. The compact provides for internal self-government for the Federated States of Micronesia, while requiring that the United States remain responsible for defense and external security and that it provide financial assistance. The articles of the compact provide for the Federated States of Micronesia to become fully independent and alter its status with the United States at any time, providing this change of status is approved in plebiscites. The compact has a 15-year duration but is renewable by mutual consent.   (F.X.H.)

Marshall Islands

The Republic of the Marshall Islands, a self-governing republic, consists of some of the easternmost islands of Micronesia. The Marshalls are composed of two parallel chains of coral atolls, the Ratak, or Sunrise, to the east and the Ralik, or Sunset, to the west. The chains lie about 125 miles (200 kilometres) apart and extend some 800 miles northwest to southeast. The islands and islets number more than 1,200 and have a total land area of 70 square miles (181 square kilometres). Majuro Atoll is the capital of the republic.

The Marshalls were administered by the United States as part of the U.S. Trust Territory of the Pacific Islands from 1947 to 1986, when the Trust Territory was dissolved by the U.S. government.

PHYSICAL AND HUMAN GEOGRAPHY

The land. None of the 29 low-lying coral atolls and the five coral islands in the Marshall group rises to more than 20 feet (six metres) above high tide. The islands are coral caps set on the rims of submerged volcanoes rising from the ocean floor. The island units of the Marshalls are scattered over about 180,000 square miles of the Pacific. The largest atoll in the group and in the world is Kwajalein, which has a land area of only six square miles but surrounds a 655-square-mile lagoon. The Marshall Islands' nearest neighbours are Wake Island (north), Kiribati and Nauru (south), and the Federated States of Micronesia (west).

The climate is tropical, with a mean annual temperature for the entire group of 82° F (28° C). Annual rainfall

Scattered island group

varies from 20 to 30 inches (500 to 800 millimetres) in the north to 160 inches in the southern atolls. The wettest months are October and November. Several of the northern atolls are uninhabited due to insufficient rainfall. Most of the Marshall Islands are true atolls, consisting of an irregular, oval-shaped coral reef surrounding a lagoon; the islets lie along the coral reef. The islands and islets of the Ratak chain tend to be more heavily wooded than those of the Ralik. Coconut and pandanus palms and breadfruit trees are the principal vegetation. Soils are generally sandy and low in fertility.

The people. The native people of the Marshalls are Micronesians. The most populous atolls are Majuro and Kwajalein, which offers employment at the U.S. missile testing range; together they have more than two-thirds of the country's total population. The remaining one-third of the population lives in traditional villages on the outer islands away from the two urban centres. The American missionary effort began in the Marshalls in the 1850s and was very successful. The Marshallese today are predominantly Christian. The Marshallese and English languages are spoken, but only a minority are fluent in the latter.

The economy. Substantial U.S. subsidies to the Republic of the Marshall Islands under the Compact of Free Association (see below) and the leasing of land for the U.S. missile testing range on Kwajalein are the main sources of revenue for the nation. Employment and modern amenities at both Majuro and Kwajalein serve as magnets that draw people to the two urban centres.

On the outer islands, subsistence farming, fishing, and the raising of pigs and poultry are the principal economic activities. Coconut, pandanus, breadfruit, and taro are the major food crops. The production of copra is the main source of income for the outer islands. The chief import is processed foods. Other major imports include machinery and transport equipment, manufactured goods, and fuels, mainly from the United States, Japan, and Australia.

Transportation among the atolls and islands is by boat or air. Government-owned ships make scheduled trips among the islands. Several commercial cargo lines also serve the islands. Majuro has a commercial dock complex, and many of the atolls have good anchorage within their lagoons. Majuro and Kwajalein have international airports, and domestic and regional flights link some of the other atolls and islands.

Administration and social conditions. Under the constitution adopted in 1979, the government consists of a president elected by a unicameral, 33-member parliament known as the Nitijela. The Council of Iroji (Chiefs) has mainly a consultative function, concerned with traditional laws and customs.

A hospital on Majuro, a small sub-hospital on Ebeye (part of Kwajalein atoll), and dispensaries on other islands provide health care. There are primary schools, both public and church-run, on the inhabited islands and islets. Majuro and Jaluit atolls each have a public secondary school. Majuro is also the site of a centre for continuing education operated by the Federated States of Micronesia's College of Micronesia.

Education

HISTORY

The Marshall Islands were settled initially around the beginning of the Christian Era by Micronesians who may have been influenced by early Polynesian (Lapita) culture. Radiocarbon dates from earth-oven charcoal samples that were excavated in Laura village on Majuro yielded dates of about 30 BC and AD 50. The early Marshall Islanders were skilled navigators and made long canoe voyages among the atolls.

Sighted in 1529 by the Spanish navigator Álvaro Saavedra, the Marshalls lacked the wealth to encourage exploitation or mapping. The British captain Samuel Wallis chanced upon Rongerik and Rongelap atolls while sailing from Tahiti to Tinian. The British naval captains John Marshall and Thomas Gilbert partially explored the Marshalls in 1788, but much of the mapping was done by Russian expeditions under Adam Johann Krusenstern (1803) and Otto von Kotzebue (1815 and 1823). U.S. whalers frequented the islands from the 1820s, and U.S.

and Hawaiian Protestant missionaries began efforts to convert the islanders in the 1850s. Germany established a coaling station on Jaluit Atoll by treaty with island chiefs and in 1886, by agreement with Great Britain, established a protectorate over the Marshalls. Japan seized the islands in 1914 and later (after 1919) administered them as a League of Nations mandate. Occupied by the United States in World War II, following heavy fighting at Kwajalein and Enewetak, the Marshall Islands were made part of the United Nations Trust Territory of the Pacific Islands under jurisdiction of the United States in 1947. After their populations were removed to other atolls, Bikini and Enewetak served as an official testing ground for U.S. nuclear bombs (1946–58). The tests stopped in 1958 and cleanup efforts began in the late 1960s. During the trial resettlement of the Bikinians, however, their atoll was found to be too contaminated for permanent habitation, and by the late 1970s the people had to be evacuated once again. The Enewetak people were returned to their homeland, and a program to monitor Bikini was put in place.

After voting to separate from the other entities of the Trust Territory of the Pacific Islands, in 1978, the Marshall Islands drew up a constitution that was approved by the voters in 1979. It formed the republic and brought internal self-government. In 1982 the government signed the Compact of Free Association with the United States. This agreement was subsequently approved by the voters in 1983. The compact requires that the United States remain responsible for defense and external security and that it provide financial assistance for the republic. The compact entitles the United States to use the missile testing range on Kwajalein atoll. The compact's articles provide for the republic to become fully independent and to alter its status with the United States at any time, subject to approval of the residents through plebiscites. In 1983 the islanders reopened negotiations on the compact's provision regarding compensation for the people of the four atolls affected by the U.S. nuclear tests. The United States agreed to set up a separate fund for the people of the four atolls and established an open-ended fund to cover personal injury claims among the islanders; it also agreed to set up a joint U.S.–Marshallese claims tribunal. A further agreement set up a fund to improve living conditions on Ebeye atoll, where all Micronesians working on the Kwajalein missile range and base resided. The Trust Territory was dissolved in 1986 by the U.S. government with the approval of the UN Trusteeship Council. (R.C.Ki.)

Compact of Free Association

French Polynesia

French Polynesia (French: Polynésie Française) comprises about 130 islands with a total land area of some 1,550 square miles (4,000 square kilometres) scattered over an area of the south central Pacific between latitudes 7° to 27° S and longitudes 134° to 155° W. The islands are administered as an overseas territory of France.

PHYSICAL AND HUMAN GEOGRAPHY

The land. *Relief.* There are five distinct groups of islands, all protrusions of parallel submarine ridges trending from the northwest to the southeast.

The Society Islands are the most westerly of the group and the most important in terms of land area (40 percent) and population (85 percent). Except for a few small atolls, the Society Islands are of the high-island type, their formation having resulted from the emergence of underwater volcanoes. The volcanic cones are highly eroded and cut up into high crests and deep, radiating valleys. The often lushly vegetated mountains drop abruptly to narrow coastal strips or directly into lagoons or the sea. The islands are protected from the force of the sea by almost completely encircling barrier reefs.

Tahiti and Moorea

The most highly populated of the Society Islands are Tahiti and its neighbour, Moorea, both situated in the eastern Windward Group, or Îles du Vent. Tahiti, formed of two ancient volcanic cones, is particularly striking because of its dramatic silhouette, which rises 7,352 feet (2,241 metres) above sea level. The mountains are empty of all human settlement, habitation and planting being entirely limited to the coastal strip and valley outlets of the island. Moorea, separated from Tahiti by a channel 8½ miles (14 kilometres) wide, is also a high island and is encircled with very white coral sand beaches. It is well connected to Tahiti by boat and taxi planes—a consequence of the booming tourist industry.

Some 75 miles to the west of Tahiti are the Leeward Islands, or Îles sous le Vent, made up of five high islands and four atolls. They closely resemble the Windward Islands in appearance. Raiatea, a double island group, is the largest and most densely populated of the Leeward Group. Separated by a channel that is about two miles wide, Raiatea and its northern neighbour, Vaitoare, are located on the same mountain mass and lie within a single barrier reef. Both have coastal plains suitable for growing coconut palms and raising stock. The growing of vanilla, once an important crop, declined in the 1970s. The Leeward Group's port is Uturoa, located on Raiatea. To the east of Raiatea is the picturesque island of Huahine, a volcanic structure bisected by a shallow arm of the sea.

The decline of vanilla growing

Finally, to the west of Raiatea lies the beautiful little island named Bora-Bora. It is formed from two volcanic peaks rising to 2,385 feet and 2,169 feet and dropping abruptly to the lagoon. Bora-Bora is one of the centres of the tourist trade in French Polynesia.

The Tuamotu Archipelago, lying to the east of the Society Islands, has an area of 280 square miles and consists of some 80 islands. These are low, flat islands or atolls of coral origin, surrounding a lagoon. Their size varies greatly: the largest ones, such as Rangiroa, reach 29 square miles; the smallest are made up of a few acres of land barely protruding above the surface of the sea. With only porous, coral-based soils and with no permanent streams, they have no agricultural potential aside from the ever-present coconut trees. The lagoons, however, are a source of fish, pearls, and mother-of-pearl shell. Only Rangiroa, with its airport, is in close contact with Tahiti. Elsewhere, living conditions are difficult, and many people emigrate to Tahiti. French nuclear installations are situated in the Tuamotus; test sites are on Mururoa and Fangataufa, both ceded to France in 1964.

Morphologically different, the Îles Gambier (Mangareva) lie at the southern extremity of the Tuamotu Archipelago and include four large, high islands and a few islets (14 square miles). The main island is Mangareva.

The 14 islands of the Marquesas group lie 900 miles to the northeast of Tahiti. They have a land area of 405 square miles. Some of them are high islands (over 4,000 feet), with sharp and twisting contours. Unlike the Society Islands, they are not protected from the sea by a barrier reef, with the result that they lack a coastal plain. Approaching the islands from the sea is difficult. People live exclusively in the valleys, where they engage in farming.

The Austral Islands, or Îles Tubuai, situated 450 miles south of Tahiti, make up the southernmost part of the territory. This chain of four islands, with the addition of the isolated island of Rapa in the southeast and the uninhabited Marotiri and Maria islands, covers 57 square miles. All of the islands are of volcanic origin but are relatively low (270 to 1,440 feet) and have unpronounced contours. Income is derived from agriculture (taro, arrowroot, copra, market vegetables) and pandanus plaiting.

Like the Marquesas and the Tuamotu-Gambiers, the Austral Islands have poor connections with Tahiti. As elsewhere, the hard living conditions cause many people to migrate to Tahiti and Papeete.

Climate. The climate is tropical—warm and humid. A warm rainy season lasts from November until April and is followed by a relatively cool dry season from May until October. The dispersion of the islands through 20 degrees of latitude, however, results in local and regional climatic variation. Except in the Marquesas and the northern Tuamotus, rainfall is abundant, falling in violent showers. As much as 120 inches (3,050 millimetres) falls on the coastal areas. There are local variations due to differing exposures; on average, the coasts exposed to the winds receive more precipitation.

Abundant rainfall

The temperature varies only slightly throughout the year. At Papeete the average annual temperature is 79° F (26°

C); the high average is 91° F (33° C) in March and the low average 70° F (21° C) in August. The Austral Islands, farther south, enjoy a cooler climate; the low average can go down to 64° F (18° C) in September. The relative humidity is always high—80 to 90 percent on the average. The high areas are continually enveloped in a heavy cloud formation.

The territory is in the trade-wind zone. The dominant winds thus blow from the north and northeast, but they tend toward the southeast between May and October. There are long periods of calm (April, May, June) but with occasional typhoons. During occurrences of El Niño Current the territory is frequently in danger of typhoons.

Plant and animal life. Because of the recent origin and the isolation of the islands, there is little variety in terrestrial flora and fauna. Most of the plant species were introduced by the first Polynesians, and others were introduced by Europeans.

The vegetation's appearance varies with the ecological conditions. On the limestone soils of the atolls, it has a pronounced xerophilous (desert-plant-type) character. On the high volcanic islands it is more diversified; ferns have often conquered the hills and plateaus, whereas rain forests are established in the upper valley areas. On coastal plains coconut, breadfruit, and various fruit trees flourish.

The land fauna is especially limited, and most of the species have been introduced. No mammals are indigenous to the islands; there are feral goats, pigs, horses, cattle, and rats. A fish, called *nato,* and a variety of shrimp are found in the islands' freshwater streams. The marine life in the lagoons and surrounding seas is rich.

Patterns of settlement. On the high islands, homes are scattered through the coconut groves along the coastal roads. Villages are spaced two to three miles apart and typically have a church, government house, school, shop, pastor's home, and a few residences. The contemporary rural house is of concrete construction in a yard shaded by fruit trees, with a separate kitchen made from traditional materials (palm, bamboo) where food is prepared and eaten. On the atolls, the population is usually grouped together in villages located close to the passes through the surrounding reefs. Population and business activity tend to concentrate in the Papeete area. The town consists of the old colonial city (still the business centre), residential areas (often on the heights), and an excellent harbour.

The people. Most of the people throughout the islands may be classed as Polynesian, speaking eastern Polynesian languages (although intermixture has left few pure Polynesians). There are minorities of Chinese, Europeans, and Americans. About 95 percent of the population is Christian. More than one-half is Protestant, about 40 percent is Roman Catholic, and the remainder belongs to various other Christian denominations. The Evangelical Church of French Polynesia is the dominant church.

The economy. Many resources are used for local subsistence, including fruits, products from fishing and planting, and materials for the construction of traditional types of houses and canoes. Pigs, cattle, and chickens are raised for food. The traditional exports—copra and vanilla—have greatly declined, but this loss of revenue has been partially compensated for by the development of fishing, especially with the extension of territorial waters to 200 miles offshore in 1978. Shrimp and oysters are farmed; and the cultured-pearl industry is important, especially on the Tuamotu and Gambier island groups.

Manufactured products include coconut oil, processed foods, printed textiles, construction materials, copper wares, beer and soft drinks, sandals, traditional handicrafts, and boats. Hydroelectric power plants on Tahiti began service in the early 1980s.

Revenue has been greatly increased by tourism and by an influx of French military personnel to support the nuclear testing facilities in the Tuamotus. Logistical support activities on Tahiti and Hao atoll have created additional employment.

There have been considerable developments in transportation facilities since the early 1960s, including the construction of a modern port in Papeete, construction of an international airport at Faaa, and development of air

The development of fishing

services with some of the outlying islands: Moorea, the Leewards, the western Tuamotus, the Marquesas, and the Australs. There is scheduled shipping to other regions in the Pacific, but interisland shipping remains largely dependent on local unscheduled schooner sailings. The road network has been increased to several hundred miles of paved or stone-surfaced roadway.

Administration and social conditions. Represented in the French parliament by two deputies and a senator and placed under French law, the territory is administered locally under the statutes of 1977 and 1984. These provide for a popularly elected territorial assembly, a high commissioner appointed by the French government, and a president and Cabinet selected from the assembly.

Schooling is compulsory to the end of primary school and is conducted largely in government schools, supplemented by mission schools.

Cultural life. Polynesia's cultural and artistic traditions have been misrepresented and to an extent have been reduced to a sort of folklore by the romantic image that Europeans adopted. A local ethnographic museum and a local learned society have contributed to efforts to preserve the territory's cultural heritage. The absence of newspapers in Polynesian languages, the small amount of broadcasting in the Tahitian language, and the nonrecognition of vernacular languages as official languages all threaten what survives of Polynesian culture.

For statistical data on the land and people of French Polynesia, see the *Britannica World Data* section in the BRITANNICA WORLD DATA ANNUAL.

HISTORY

Archaeological evidence suggests that the Marquesas Islands may have been settled in about 200 BC from western Polynesia. In subsequent dispersions, Polynesians from the Marquesas migrated to the Hawaiian Islands in about AD 300 and reached the Society Islands by about the 9th century AD. Large chieftainships were formed on Tahiti, Bora-Bora, and Raiatea. Teriaroa, north of Tahiti, was a royal retreat, and Taputapuatea, on Raiatea, was the most sacred shrine in the islands.

European contact with the islands of French Polynesia was gradual. The Portuguese navigator Ferdinand Magellan sighted Pukapuka in the Tuamotu group in 1521. The southern Marquesas Islands were discovered in 1595. The Dutch explorer Jacob Roggeveen in 1722 discovered Makatea, Bora-Bora, and Maupiti. Captain Samuel Wallis in 1767 discovered Tahiti, Moorea, and Maiao Iti. The Society Islands were named after the Royal Society, which sponsored the expedition under Captain James Cook that observed from Tahiti the 1769 transit of the planet Venus. Tubuai was discovered on Cook's last voyage, in 1777.

Sighting by Magellan

The history of the Society Island groups is virtually that of Tahiti, which was made a French protectorate in 1842 and a colony in 1880. French missionaries went to the Gambier group in 1834, and in 1844 a French protectorate was proclaimed, followed by annexation in 1881. The Austral Islands were also evangelized from Tahiti, and as late as 1888 Rimatara and Rurutu sought British protection, which was refused. They were placed under the French protectorate in 1889 and annexed in 1900. The Tuamotus were part of the kingdom of the Pomare family of Tahiti, which came originally from Fakarava. These islands were claimed as dependencies of Tahiti within the protectorate by France in 1847 and became part of the colony in 1880. In the Marquesas, Nuku Hiva was annexed to the United States in 1813 by Captain David Porter of the frigate *Essex,* but the annexation was never ratified. French occupation of the group followed the landing of forces from a French warship, requested by the chief of Tahuata (near Hiva Oa). Soon after there was a quarrel with the French; in 1842 the chiefs ceded sovereignty to France.

The islands were administered as the French Colony of Oceania. The colony was ruled by a naval government until 1885, when an organic decree provided for a French governor and Privy Council and for a General Council, representing the islands, that had some control over fiscal policies. The powers of the General Council, however, were cut back in 1899, and in 1903 it was replaced by an advisory council, the function of which was purely administrative. In 1940 the voters on the islands chose to side with the Free French Government of Charles de Gaulle, and many islanders fought alongside Allied armies during World War II. French Polynesia was made an overseas territory of France in 1946. It was provided with a territorial assembly and was allowed to elect one representative to the French National Assembly and one to the French Senate.

In 1957 the French government extended the powers of the local Territorial Assembly. In 1958 Pouvanaa a Oopa, vice president of the Council of Government, announced a plan to secede from France and form an independent Tahitian republic. He was subsequently arrested; the movement collapsed, and local powers were again curtailed. France issued new statutes granting more local autonomy in 1977, but the pro-independence and pro-autonomy parties continued to call for popular election of the president and either more autonomy or outright independence.

Nuclear testing

In 1963 the French government began the nuclear testing program on Mururoa atoll. Mururoa and neighbouring Fangataufa were ceded to France by the territorial assembly in 1964. In response to worldwide pressure the tests were moved underground on Fangataufa in 1975. In the mid-1980s political parties and environmental-protection and human rights groups united to protest France's continued nuclear testing. In 1985 world attention focused on the area when the French secret service blew up a yacht owned by the Greenpeace environmental group as it was preparing to lead a protest near Mururoa atoll.

For later developments in the history of French Polynesia, see the *Britannica Book of the Year* section in the BRITANNICA WORLD DATA ANNUAL. (F.J.W.)

American Samoa

American Samoa, a territory of the United States, consists of the eastern part of the Samoan archipelago. It is situated in the central Pacific Ocean about 1,600 miles (2,600 kilometres) northeast of New Zealand and 2,200 miles southwest of the Hawaiian Islands. The territory includes the six Samoan islands east of the 171° W meridian and is part of Polynesia. Western Samoa, its closest neighbour and a self-governing nation, consists of the nine Samoan islands west of that meridian.

American Samoa, with a total land area of 77 square miles (199 square kilometres), includes the inhabited islands of Tutuila, Tau, Olosega, Ofu, and Aunuu and an uninhabited coral atoll named Rose Island. Swains Island (inhabited), a coral atoll 280 miles northwest of Tutuila and geographically not a part of the archipelago, was made a part of American Samoa in 1925. The capital of American Samoa is Pago Pago, on Tutuila.

PHYSICAL AND HUMAN GEOGRAPHY

The land. *Relief.* Except for the coral atolls, the islands of American Samoa were formed within the past 7,000,-000 years by volcanic activity; their interiors are high and rugged. The main island of Tutuila, with an area of 53 square miles, rises steeply above deep inlets, of which the most notable is Pago Pago Harbor, which almost divides the island in two. Its highest peak is Mount Matafao (2,141 feet [653 metres]). The Manua island group (Tau, Olosega, and Ofu islands), situated about 60 miles east of Tutuila,

Presence of coral reefs

constitutes the second largest island area. Coral reefs are common to the extremities of the islands, particularly Tutuila; some of the reefs form barriers that enclose lagoons.

Climate. The climate is tropical and rainfall is ample. Pago Pago receives about 200 inches (5,000 millimetres) annually. Most streams carry greater volumes of water in the highlands than near the sea and do not reach the ocean; rather, they filter into the porous basalt rocks. Hence, coastal wells provide much of the water supply. Temperatures are unusually constant; average temperatures range from 68° F to 90° F (21° C to 32° C). Average humidity is 80 percent. The moderate southeast trade winds prevail, but severe storms can occur during the wet season, from November to March.

Plant and animal life. Rain forests with tall ferns and trees cover the mountainous interiors of the islands. Plantations of taro, coconut, and other food crops are located on the coasts. Although the islands are not rich in animal life, some of their bird species—such as the rare tooth-billed pigeon—are unique. Wildlife includes the flying fox, lizards, rats, harmless snakes, and pigs. The islands also have a rich insect life.

Settlement patterns. Most people live in coastal villages. Pago Pago, the only town, is the main port and administrative and commercial centre. Since the mid-20th century many American Samoans have migrated to the United States, with the result that there are more American Samoans abroad than on the islands.

The people. The Samoans are a Polynesian people closely related to the native peoples of New Zealand, Tahiti, Hawaii, and Tonga. The Samoan way of life, or *fa'a Samoa,* is communal. The basic unit of social organization is the extended family (*aiga*). These extended families are arranged in villages, which are grouped into districts. The extended families are headed by chiefs (*matai*), who are selected by their extended families on the basis of consensus. Most chiefs' titles are very old. The village chiefs together make up a village council (*fono*), which controls and runs village affairs. Even after decades of foreign influence, most Samoans still live according to *fa'a Samoa,* and nearly all of them are fluent in the Samoan language. Most of the American Samoans, nonetheless, also speak English. The Congregational Christian Church has the largest following among religious institutions; most of the remaining population is either Roman Catholic or Methodist.

Fa'a Samoa

The economy. *Industry and agriculture.* The U.S. administration is the main employer. Tuna canning (by American-owned canneries) and tourism are major industries. Agriculture is organized on a semicommercial basis for the production of taro, bananas, tropical fruits, and vegetables. Traditional family gardens produce coconuts, breadfruit, and yams. Production nearly meets domestic needs, and the U.S. government has implemented programs to increase production to self-sufficiency levels.

Social legislation ties American Samoa more closely to U.S. costs of living than its South Pacific neighbours.

Transportation. A major public works program on American Samoa has increased paved road mileage, most of which is located on Tutuila. Pago Pago is the only port of note. An international airport is located on Tutuila, and smaller airstrips operate from the islands of Tau and Ofu.

Administration and social conditions. *Government.* American Samoa is an unincorporated, unorganized territory, the people of which are U.S. nationals but not citizens. The territory's chief executive, according to the constitution of 1967, is the governor. Until 1977 the governor was appointed by the U.S. Department of the Interior; in response to a referendum of 1976, however, the offices of governor and lieutenant governor are filled by popular election. Elections are to be held every four years. The minimum voting age is 18. The Fono (bicameral legislature) is autonomous in its disposition of local revenues and is the sole law-making body, subject to the governor's approval. The 21 members of the House of Representatives are elected by universal suffrage; one is a nonvoting delegate elected from Swains Island. The 18 senators are chosen by councils of chiefs, in accordance with Samoan custom. In 1981 the first official delegate from American Samoa to the Congress of the United States was elected. Apart from Swains Island, the islands are divided into three administrative districts (each with an appointed district governor), which are subdivided into a total of 14 counties. Chiefs representing each family form village and district councils. This autonomous village control is linked with the central government through three district governors appointed by the governor. Each village has a village court with authority to adjudicate on minor misdemeanours.

Village courts

Education. Education is compulsory between the ages of six and 18 in American Samoa. Televised instruction, given mainly in English and mostly by teachers and technicians from the United States, is available to local schools. The American Samoan Community College offers vocational training and nursing programs, with university education available from universities in Hawaii or the U.S. mainland. (P.R.C./A.We.)

The Samoan islands were settled by Polynesians (probably from Tonga) in about 1000 BC. By about AD 200 Samoa had become the centre of much of the settlement of Eastern Polynesia.

The Dutch navigator Jacob Roggeveen sighted Samoa in 1722, and other European explorers, beachcombers, and traders followed. The London Missionary Society sent its first missionaries to the islands in the 1830s. More missionaries traveled to the islands as missionary influence spread to Tutuila and later the Manua Islands. In 1878 the United States signed a treaty for the establishment of a naval station in Pago Pago Harbor, and in 1899 eastern Samoa was annexed by the United States.

By 1904 the eastern islands had all been ceded to the United States, but the U.S. Congress did not formally accept the deeds of cession until Feb. 20, 1929. Under the administration of the U.S. Navy (1900–51) American Samoa became a strategic naval base, but the Samoan leaders had little administrative power. In 1951 control of the territory was transferred to the Department of the Interior. The U.S. government appointed a governor who had full powers to administer the territory. He appointed political advisers and senior civil servants from the United States to help him. The Samoans agitated for control of their country's affairs, and in 1977 Peter Coleman, a Samoan, became the territory's first elected governor. Since then, all members of the territory's House of Representatives have been elected by the citizens. Except for defense, the governor and the Fono run American Samoa's affairs. American Samoans are U.S. nationals and can move freely between their country and the United States. (A.We.)

Western Samoa

Western Samoa, a former United Nations trust territory and a self-governing nation since 1962, consists of the western part of the Samoan archipelago. Its islands, situated in the south-central Pacific Ocean about 2,700 miles (4,300 kilometres) east of Australia and 2,200 miles southwest of the Hawaiian Islands, are among the westernmost islands of Polynesia. Western Samoa consists of nine islands west of the 171° W meridian. American Samoa, its closest neighbour and a territory of the United States, consists of the six Samoan islands east of that meridian in addition to Swains Island, a coral atoll 280 miles to the north.

Western Samoa has a total land area of 1,093 square miles. It includes the inhabited islands of Upolu, Savai'i, Manono, and Apolima and the uninhabited islands of Fanuatapu, Namu'a, Nu'utele, Nu'ulua, and Nu'usafee. The capital of Western Samoa is Apia, on Upolu.

The land. *Relief.* The islands of Western Samoa are rocky and were formed by volcanic activity that progressed from east to west within the past 7,000,000 years. The largest island of Western Samoa is Savai'i (659 square miles); its highest peak is Silisili (6,099 feet [1,859 metres]). There have been two eruptions from Savai'i volcanoes in historic times, the more recent in 1911. The other large island is Upolu (432 square miles), which has five uninhabited, offshore islets. Manono and Apolima are smaller islands that lie between the two main islands.

Except where the shorelines are marked by cliffs formed by recent lava flows, all of the islands are ringed by coral reefs and shallow lagoons. The volcanic soils are easily exhausted by farming but support lush vegetation, which varies from plantations of taro, coconuts, and other food crops on the coast to rain forest and mountain rain (or mist) forest farther inland.

Climate. The climate is tropical. Rainfall varies from more than 100 inches (2,540 millimetres) on the northern and western coasts to 300 inches inland, but porous soils and rocks make water supplies unreliable. Hence,

Volcanic eruptions (margin note)

coastal wells are the only water source for much of the rural population. Temperatures are unusually constant, the monthly mean varying only 1.2° F (0.7° C) from an average of 79° F (26° C). The southeast trade winds prevail, varying occasionally to northerlies during the wet season, from November to March, when severe storms are liable to occur.

Animal life. The islands are not rich in animal life. Nevertheless, of the 53 species of birds, at least 16 are unique, including a rare tooth-billed pigeon. The only native mammals are the flying fox and smaller bats. There are several species of lizards and two harmless snakes of the boa family. Rats, wild cattle, and pigs have been introduced. There are centipedes and millipedes, scorpions, spiders, and a rich insect life.

Settlement patterns. Most people live in coastal villages. Apia, on the northern coast of Upolu Island, is the nation's only town. It is the main port and administrative and commercial centre and has grown rapidly because it offers employment opportunities. Since World War II many Western Samoans have migrated to the United States and New Zealand.

A typical village features *fale*—traditional oval-shaped houses with thatched or corrugated tin roofs and open sides—clustered around the village green, or *malae,* but these are giving way to rectangular timber or concrete-block houses with walls and windows.

The people. The Samoans are of eastern Polynesian stock. Their language, believed to be the oldest of the Polynesian tongues, is closely related to the Maori, Tahitian, Hawaiian, and Tongan languages. English is also widely spoken. Within the villages, close kinship ties have traditionally bound individuals into a sternly collectivist society. Elected family leaders called *matai* form village or district councils to administer group affairs. Extended blood ties traditionally have linked family or village groups; beyond the social framework of well-regulated village life a network of allegiances arose, with the major families striving for supremacy and regularly plunging the islands into warfare. The material culture was utilitarian, and most artifacts are unadorned. There appears to have been no dominant priestly class; family elders performed the rituals of a pantheistic religion.

Village life and culture (margin note)

While European contact and a cash economy have produced some changes in values and traditional authority, preservation of the culture has become an important goal among Western Samoan leaders; many outward features of rural life have thus remained virtually unchanged. The Christian churches were easily absorbed into the village social structure; some of the remotest villages have churches of cathedral proportions. The Congregational Christian Church in Samoa (formerly the London Missionary Society) is predominant, followed by the Roman Catholic and Methodist faiths and smaller groups of the Church of Jesus Christ of Latter-day Saints and Seventh-day Adventists.

The economy. *Agriculture and industry.* Copra and cocoa account for a majority of the exports, followed by bananas, taro, coffee, and other fruits. Growing fishery and lumber industries have made increasingly large economic contributions. In the manufacturing sector Western Samoa has diversified beyond the traditional coconut and handicrafts to produce clothing and footwear, animal feed, tropical beverages, beer, and coconut by-products. Electrical energy production has shifted away from thermal generation, which requires imported fuels, and toward hydroelectric generation.

Transportation. About one-fifth of all roadways in Western Samoa are paved. Regular shipping services link the main islands with ports abroad; international airlines operate flights to and from American Samoa, Fiji, New Zealand, and Australia. The principal trade and transport links are with Hawaii and California to the north and Fiji, New Zealand, and Australia to the south.

Administration and social conditions. *Government.* In 1962 Western Samoa became the first independent Polynesian state, and in 1970 it joined the Commonwealth. The constitution provides for parliamentary government but blends Samoan and English traditions. There were originally two heads of state, with the provision that when

Cluster of traditional *fale* and a present-day rectangular house with walls and windows in the village of Papa, Savai'i, Western Samoa.
© Nicholas DeVore III/Bruce Coleman Inc.

one died (which happened in 1963) the other would continue as sole head of state for life, after which the head of state would be elected by Parliament for a five-year term from among the four "royal son" titleholders. The prime minister is elected by Parliament and appoints a Cabinet of eight other ministers from elected members.

The Parliament has 47 members. Two represent the Individual Voters, the population of mixed-blood citizens, who vote by universal suffrage. The remaining 45 are Samoan *matai,* who alone are eligible as candidates or voters; but they in their turn have been chosen by consensus of their entire family. In each village, *matai* form a council to run their own affairs.

Education. Education in Western Samoa is optional, but most children attend school. Selected pupils receive higher education at government- or mission-run secondary, vocational, or teacher-training institutions. The University of the South Pacific has its School of Agriculture at Alafua. Western Samoa has established its own university, the National University of Samoa, but most high school graduates go overseas for their university education.

(P.R.C./A.We.)

HISTORY

Polynesians settled in the Samoan islands in about 1000 BC, as indicated by shards of decorated Lapita ware found in Mulifanua Lagoon on Upolu. Characteristics of the Samoan language indicate that the settlers probably came from Tonga. Pottery manufacture ceased by about AD 200, by which time Samoa had become the centre of much of the settlement of eastern Polynesia. Contact between Samoans, Tongans, and Fijians continued and is recorded in hundreds of legends and genealogies.

Europeans began to arrive in the first half of the 18th century, and the Samoans welcomed them at first for the technology and goods they brought. John Williams, a member of the London Missionary Society, arrived to establish a Christian mission in 1830. He converted Malietoa Vainu'upo, who had just conquered all of Samoa, and the entire population soon converted. By the 1850s a foreign settlement had sprung up around Apia Harbour. As more settlers arrived from the United States, Great Britain, and Germany and tried to persuade their respective govern-

Settlers in Western Samoa

ments to annex Samoa, the Samoans began to resist. Rival Samoan leaders played the foreign powers against each other in pursuit of their factional wars. Urged on by their nationals in Samoa, the three powers became more embroiled in Samoa's affairs. They frustrated attempts by the Samoans to establish a national government. In 1878 the United States signed a treaty for the establishment of a naval station in Pago Pago Harbor. Great Britain and Germany signed similar agreements the following year. War between the three powers in 1889 was prevented only by a great hurricane, which sank six of their warships. They signed the Berlin Act to provide for the neutrality of the islands and to avoid further conflict. Finally, in 1899, eastern Samoa was annexed by the United States and the western region, by Germany. The Samoan people were not consulted, and many resented it deeply.

In Western Samoa the drive for political independence began in 1908 with the Mau a Pule, a movement led by the orator chief, Lauaki Namulau'ulu, during the German administration. The Samoan leaders were dissatisfied with the German governor's attempts to change the *fa'a Samoa* (the Samoan way of life) and centralize all authority in his hands. The governor called in warships, and Lauaki and nine of his leading supporters surrendered. They were tried and exiled to Saipan in the Mariana Islands.

On Aug. 30, 1914, New Zealand troops occupied Western Samoa and met no resistance from the Germans. For the next few years the Samoans did not resist New Zealand rule. The influenza epidemic of 1918, however, which killed more than 20 percent of the population, prompted accusations of official negligence and united most of the people against the New Zealand administration. In 1920 the League of Nations granted New Zealand a mandate over Western Samoa. When the New Zealand-appointed governor tried to further undermine the power of the *matai* leadership and that of the local business community, an organized political movement emerged. The movement, called the Mau ("Strongly Held View"), was led by O.F. Nelson, whose mother was Samoan. New Zealand claimed that part-Europeans such as Nelson were misleading the Samoans, and the Mau was outlawed. New Zealand troops were sent in, and Nelson was exiled to New Zealand. On Dec. 28, 1929, during a peaceful Mau demonstration in Apia, Tupua Tamasese Lealofi III, one of the Mau leaders, and other Mau supporters were shot by New Zealand troops. This only strengthened the Mau's determination to win their struggle.

In 1935 the first Labour government came to power in New Zealand, and it recognized the Mau as a legal political organization. The Samoan independence movement continued until 1962, when Western Samoa regained its political independence.

(A.We.)

Tonga

Tonga is a constitutional monarchy and a member of the Commonwealth. Its official name is Pule'anga Fakatu'i 'o Tonga, or Kingdom of Tonga. Situated in the southwestern Pacific, it consists of 169 islands divided into three main island groups: Tongatapu in the south, Ha'apai in the centre, and Vava'u in the north. Isolated islands include Niuafo'ou, Niuatoputapu, and Tafahi in the far north and 'Ata in the far south. Tonga's total land area of 290 square miles (750 square kilometres) is dispersed between latitudes 15° to 23° S and longitudes 173° to 177° W. The capital, Nuku'alofa, on the island of Tongatapu, is approximately 1,245 miles (2,000 kilometres) northeast of Auckland, N.Z.

PHYSICAL AND HUMAN GEOGRAPHY

The land. *Relief.* The summit of volcanic undersea mountains forms the two roughly parallel chains of the Tongan islands. Most of the islands of the western chain are classified as high islands because they have been raised well above sea level by repeated volcanic activity. Four of them are still active volcanoes. Some of the islands composed of lava formed by shield volcanoes, such as Late and Kao, have a cone-shaped, hard surface that is not easily eroded. Others, such as Fonuafo'ou (Falcon Island), were formed by more explosive volcanoes, and their surfaces, composed of ash and pumice, have eroded readily.

The low islands of the eastern chain have been capped by coral polyps and foraminifera (marine organisms that have calcareous shells), which build coral rock and limestone reefs. The continuing growth of coral counteracts the sea's erosion of the reefs and the islands enclosed by them. A protective reef surrounds Tongatapu Island; many islands in the Vava'u group lack such protection and are shrinking.

Tongatapu Island, a raised atoll in the Tongatapu group, is the largest island in Tonga, with an area of 99 square miles, and is the most densely populated. The highest point in Tonga, 3,380 feet (1,030 metres), is on Kao Island in the Ha'apai group. 'Eua Island (Tongatapu group) has an old volcanic ridge rising to 1,078 feet above sea level. The Vava'u group has hills ranging from 500 to 1,000 feet, and Vava'u Island has a fine, large landlocked harbour. The effects of natural erosion are particularly vivid in Vava'u. Rainwater reacting with the carbon dioxide in vegetation acquires acidic properties and dissolves coral and limestone rock, thereby forming caves. The sheer cliffs and sandspits of Vava'u and Nuku'alofa have been caused by the constant action of the waves. There are no rivers in Tonga. There are creeks, however, on 'Eua and on Niuatoputapu, one of the far northern islands. The geologic subsidence of Vava'u, followed by two phases of uplift, resulted in the formation of the Ano Lagoon.

Climate. Tonga has a semitropical climate except in the northernmost islands, where a truly tropical climate prevails. Temperatures range from 60° to 70° F (16° to 21° C) in June and July to 80° F (27° C) in December and January. The mean annual humidity is 77 percent. The mean annual rainfall varies from 63 inches (1,600 millimetres) in Tongatapu to 87 inches in Vava'u; on Niuatoputapu the annual rainfall averages 101 inches. Humidity is higher as the distance from the Equator lessens. The northern islands, which are closest to the Equator, are particularly vulnerable to typhoons, which generally occur between December and April.

Plant and animal life. The well-drained, fertile soils of 'Eua, Kao, Tofua, Late, and the slopes and hilltops of Vava'u support original forests. 'Eua has the greatest number and variety of trees, and the ridge on the eastern side is a forest reserve. Some of the more significant are the hiapo, or paper mulberry, the fau (*Hibiscus tiliaceaus*), the coconut, the ngatata, and the toi and tavahi, which constitute a majority of the trees on 'Eua. The sandy, rocky, dry soils of the coasts and the direct exposure to strong winds and salty spray create unfavourable conditions for coastal vegetation. To conserve moisture, plants near the shore have small, waxy, or hairy leaves. Tidal sand and mud flats have swampy areas that support mangroves.

Tonga's land birds include doves, rails, starlings, kingfishers, owls, cuckoos, shrikes, bulbuls, purple swamp hens, and swiftlets. The red-breasted musk parrot and the blue-crowned lory, considered by some to be the most beautiful birds in the Pacific, inhabit 'Eua. Among the native birds of Niuafo'ou Island is the incubator bird. The common reef heron is a native shore bird. Transient species include the golden plover, wandering tattler, long-billed curlew, and bar-tailed godwit. Tongan waters attract several varieties of seabirds such as noddies, terns, frigate birds, and mutton birds. The village of Kolovai on Tongatapu Island is the home of the fruit bat (often called "flying fox" because of its appearance). The fruit bat clings to large trees by day and flies at night to forage for food.

Human settlement. About three-quarters of the Tongan population live in the three major island groups and nearly two-thirds live on Tongatapu Island. The urban population has been steadily growing and now accounts for more than a third of the total population. Many Tongans migrate overseas, to the United States and New Zealand in particular.

The majority of the population live in villages. Traditional structures are called *fale;* they are rectangular in shape and have thatched or corrugated tin roofs and sides made of woven coconut leaves, reeds, or timber. Some Tongans reside in South Seas colonial-style wooden homes

with gingerbread trim and outside walls in pastel shades.

Nuku'alofa, the name of which signifies "Abode of Love," has all the amenities of a capital city. It is also a major port of entry and has several wharves and piers. Much of Nuku'alofa's economic activity revolves around coconuts and coconut products. Other ports and commercial centres are Neiafu in the Vava'u group and Pangai in the Ha'apai group.

The people. Tongans are closely related to Samoans and other Polynesians in culture, language, and racial makeup. More than 90 percent of the population claims an original Polynesian ancestry. Contact with Fiji has resulted in the transference of some Melanesian physical characteristics. Intermarriage with Europeans has become more common, especially as a result of the increasing outmigration of Tongans since the 1970s. Religion is an important aspect of Tongan society, and most Tongan families are members of a church. About 47 percent belong to the Free Wesleyan Church; 16 percent are Roman Catholics; 14 percent belong to the Free Church of Tonga; 9 percent are Mormon; and the remainder belong to smaller denominations. The Tongan language is taught in primary schools and is the official language, in addition to English, which is studied as a second language.

The economy. Agriculture is the mainstay of the Tongan economy. Coconuts, bananas, and vanilla beans constitute the main cash crops, and other important crops include yams, taro, cassava, corn (maize), watermelons, pineapples, and tomatoes. All land is essentially owned by the Crown, but large estates have been divided among the nobles of Tonga. Land is parceled out to peasant proprietors: every male aged 16 or over is entitled to an allotment of 7.5 acres (three hectares) of land for cultivation. Timber production, livestock raising, and fishing also contribute to Tonga's economy.

Manufacturing industries include a plant that produces plastic pipe; several charcoal-producing plants, which export charcoal to New Zealand; canning and corrugated-iron-rolling factories; small handicraft enterprises; and other manufacturing concerns established by local and foreign investors. Crop processing has been undertaken by cooperative societies; the Tonga Feeds Manufacturing Society procures stock feed, and vanilla is processed by the Leimatu'a Vanilla Society located in the Vava'u group. Remittances from Tongans working overseas—especially in New Zealand, the United States, and Australia—and tourism have both contributed significantly to the growth of the Tongan economy.

Overseas workers

More than half of Tonga's road network is all-weather roads, almost all of which are located on the two largest islands. Tonga has no railroad. Nuku'alofa and Neiafu

© L. Zann/Australasian Nature Transparencies

Coconuts germinating on a copra plantation on Lifuka in the Ha'apai Group, Tonga.

Margin notes (left column):
Erosion and coral growth

The "flying fox," or fruit bat

(Vava'u) are ports used for external shipping. Copra and bananas are exported from Pangai (Ha'apai group). Regular international air service to New Zealand, Fiji, Western and American Samoa, and Niue is available from Fua'amotu Airport on Tongatapu. Domestic flights are serviced by airports on 'Eua, Ha'apai, Vava'u, Niuafo'ou, and Niuatoputapu.

Administration and social conditions. Tonga's constitution, granted in 1875 by King George Tupou I and amended only slightly since, establishes a constitutional monarchy. The chief executive is the monarch, who appoints a Privy Council. The council consists of the monarch and the Cabinet. The Cabinet has a prime minister, deputy prime minister, six other ministers, and the governors of Ha'apai and Vava'u. The unicameral legislature consists of a speaker, the members of the Cabinet, nine nobles selected by the 33 nobles of Tonga, and nine representatives elected for three-year terms by literate taxpaying males and literate females aged 21 and over. Popularly elected town and district officials are the only form of local government; town officials represent villages, and district officials have authority over groups of villages. The most important administrative divisions are the three island groups.

Education is free for all Tongans and attendance is compulsory between the ages of six and 14. The government runs primary, secondary, and vocational training schools, including a teacher-training college. Some primary and secondary schools as well as vocational institutions are run by churches. Tongans receive free dental and medical treatment. Although the general health of the population is adequate, several communicable diseases, such as influenzas, typhoid, filariasis, and tuberculosis, exist. Family planning aids are disseminated with the help of the United Nations and New Zealand.

Cultural life. Despite Western influence, certain Tongan rituals and art forms survive. For example, Tonga shares with Fiji, Samoa, and parts of French Polynesia the elaborate ritual surrounding the drinking of *kava*. The drink, prepared from the root of a pepper plant, has the properties of a mild narcotic.

Carving was traditionally done by men, but the craftsmanship was inferior to that of other Polynesians, such as the Maori. Carving and other traditional crafts of higher quality have been produced, however, in response to the demands of the tourist market. Women manufacture tapa cloth from bark and weave mats and baskets from several varieties of pandanus leaves. Traditional dancing is an important part of national ceremonies and local village festivities. In the popular paddle dance, called *me'etu'upaki,* dancers carry paddle-shaped boards painted or carved with abstractions of the human body. Other popular dances include the *kailao,* a war dance; the *lakalaka,* a group action song performed while standing; the *ma'ulu'ulu,* an action song performed while seated; and the *tau'olunga,* an individual dance accompanied by singing. An oral tradition persists in Tongan villages in the form of proverbs, religious epics, genealogies, poetry, fables, and myths.

For statistical data on the land and people of Tonga, see the *Britannica World Data* section in the BRITANNICA WORLD DATA ANNUAL.

HISTORY

Tonga was first inhabited about 3,000 years ago by Austronesian-speaking people, who made elaborately decorated Lapita ware. From at least the 10th century AD Tonga was ruled by a line of sacred kings and queens, the Tu'i Tonga. About 1470 the reigning Tu'i Tonga transferred his temporal powers to his brother under the title of Tu'i Ha'a Takalaua. A similar transfer of power about 1600 resulted in the creation of a third line of monarchs, the Tu'i Kanokupolu, who eventually became the rulers.

Although some islands were visited by the Dutch navigators Jakob Le Maire and Abel Tasman in 1616 and 1643, respectively, effective European contact dates from Captain James Cook's visits between 1773 and 1777. Cook called the Tonga islands the Friendly Islands because the native inhabitants had provided him with necessary supplies and had given him a warm welcome. The Lon-

don Missionary Society and a mission of Methodists made unsuccessful attempts to introduce Christianity to Tonga in 1797 and 1822, respectively. A renewed attempt by the Methodist mission in 1826 was successful, and a Roman Catholic mission was established by the Marists in 1842. Between 1799 and 1852 Tonga went through a period of war and disorder. This was finally ended by Taufa'ahau, who had been converted to Christianity in 1831 by the Methodist missionaries. He became Tu'i Kanokupolu and subsequently took the title King George Tupou I in 1845. During his long reign (1845–93) Tonga became a unified and independent nation with a modern constitution (1875), legal code, and administrative structure. With Taufa'ahau as its most important convert, Christianity spread rapidly. In separate treaties, Germany (1876), Great Britain (1879), and the United States (1888) recognized Tonga's independence. George I was succeeded by his great-grandson George II, who died in 1918. During his reign the kingdom became a British protectorate (1900) to discourage German advances. Under the treaty with Great Britain (amended in 1905), Tonga agreed to conduct all foreign affairs through a British consul, who had veto power over Tonga's foreign policy and finances. George II was followed by Queen Salote Tupou III, who ruled from 1918 to 1965. She was succeeded by her son Prince Tungi, as Taufa'ahau Tupou IV. In 1970 Tonga regained full control of domestic and foreign affairs and became a fully independent nation within the Commonwealth. (Si.L.)

For later developments in the history of Tonga, see the *Britannica Book of the Year* section in the BRITANNICA WORLD DATA ANNUAL.

Easter Island

Easter Island (Isla de Pascua), a Chilean dependency in the eastern Pacific Ocean, famous for its giant stone statues, represents the easternmost outpost of the Polynesian island world. It stands in isolation 1,200 miles (1,900 kilometres) east of lonely Pitcairn Island and 2,200 miles west of Chile. Forming a triangle 14 miles long by seven miles wide, the island has an area of 63 square miles (163 square kilometres); its highest point, Mount Terevaka, is 1,969 feet (600 metres) above sea level. To its original inhabitants the island is known as Rapa Nui ("Great Rapa") or Te Pito te Henua ("Navel of the World"); its first European visitors, the Dutch, named it Paaseiland ("Easter Island") in memory of their own day of arrival. Its mixed population is predominantly of Polynesian descent; almost all live in the village of Hanga Roa on the sheltered west coast. The island is a province that is administratively part of the region of Valparaíso, Chile.

PHYSICAL AND HUMAN GEOGRAPHY

The land. *Relief.* The small and hilly island is not part of a sunken landmass but is a typical oceanic high island formed by volcanoes rising from the seafloor. Geologic and oceanographic evidence shows that no perceptible emergence or submergence of the island's coastline has taken place since the last fall in sea level, which occurred less than 10,000 years ago. Three extinct volcanoes chiefly composed of tuff (a rock formed of compacted volcanic fragments) and joined by their own lava flows give the island its characteristic triangular shape. Parasitic tuff craters and cones (*i.e.,* craters and cones formed on the side of, or near, volcanoes after the original vent has become plugged up) are interspersed in the landscape, which is otherwise dominated by eroded lava fields. Most of these fields are thickly packed with both large and small lumps of cellular and tuffaceous lava that is either black or rusty in colour. Stoneless surface soil is sparse; it is suitable for extensive cultivation mainly in the Hanga Roa and Mataveri area in the southwest, at Vaihu and on the plain southwest of the volcano Rano Raraku, and on the prehistorically cleared Poike peninsula in the eastern corner of the island. Rain collects in the partly bog-covered crater lakes of the volcanoes Rano Kao, Rano Raraku, and Rano Aroi. One intermittent stream, fed by the Rano Aroi crater lake, flows down Mount Terevaka's slopes before disappearing into the porous soil. Water from the extremely deep crater

Tongan dance forms

Formed by three extinct volcanoes

of Rano Kao, which is about 3,000 feet wide, is piped to Hanga Roa. The coast is formed by soft, eroded, ashy cliffs, with a vertical drop of about 500 to 1,000 feet; the cliffs are intercepted by long stretches of low, hard, and rugged lava formations. There is no natural harbour, but anchorage is found off Hanga Roa on the west coast; off Vinapu and Hotu-Iti on the south coast; and off Anakena and in the Bahía la Perouse on the north coast. Notable among the few small offshore islets are Motu-Nui, Motu-Iti, and Motu-Kaokao (which figured in a local bird cult) near the southwest cape. The only true sand beach is at Anakena; most other beaches are of gravel. Caves abound, many consisting of subterranean rooms joined by narrow tunnels extending far into the lava beds.

Climate. The climate is subtropical. The warmest months are January through March, when the average temperature is 73° F (23° C), and the coolest months are June through August, when the average temperature is 64° F (18° C). Average annual precipitation is about 49 inches (1,250 millimetres) but with considerable annual variation. September is the driest month, and the heaviest rainfall occurs in June and July. Winds in June and August are irregular; during the rest of the year trade winds from the east and southeast are dominant. From September through March the Peru (or Humboldt) Current, which has an average temperature of about 70° F (21° C), flows against the island.

Plant and animal life. Indigenous plants and animals are few. At the time of European arrival the toromiro tree, endemic to the island, was the only wild tree and the Carolina wolfberry the only wild shrub, the vegetation being predominantly herbaceous. The toromiro tree was overexploited by the island wood carvers, and the last local specimen died in the 1950s. The species was saved from extinction, however; the Norwegian Archaeological Expedition collected seeds and planted them in the Gothenburg Botanical Garden, and saplings from the garden were reintroduced to Easter Island in 1988. Analysis of pollen deposits has revealed that other trees and shrubs, among them the giant Chile palm, were formerly present on the island until exterminated by extensive fires occurring at the time of aboriginal human settlement. Today only 31 wild flowering plants, 14 ferns, and 14 mosses are reported. Grass and small ferns dominate the barren landscape, whereas the boggy crater lakes are thickly covered by two imported American species, the totora reed (an important building material) and *Polygonum acuminatum* (a medicinal plant). A number of cultivated species of plants were also introduced partly from America and partly from Polynesia before the arrival of Europeans; of these the principal species was the sweet potato, which was cultivated in extensive plantations and formed the staple diet. Bottle gourds, sugarcane, bananas, taro, yams, and two useful trees (*i.e.,* the Asiatic paper mulberry, with bark used for cloth manufacture, and the American *Triumfetta semitriloba,* with bark used for rope making) were of aboriginal importation, as also probably were the husk-tomato, a small variety of pineapple, and the coconut.

Before the arrival of human beings, the only vertebrates were either fish or seabirds capable of long flights. The animal life on land was otherwise restricted to a very few species of isopods (an order of crustaceans), spiders, insects, worms, a snail, and a centipede. Vast quantities of flies, large cockroaches, and a small scorpion were introduced recently. A small, long-legged chicken reported to have laid blue eggs was introduced in pre-European times but later interbred with European varieties. The aboriginal edible Polynesian rat was subsequently replaced by larger European species. Sheep, horses, cattle, and pigs were introduced by the missionaries who established themselves ashore in 1864. Sheep were especially numerous for almost a century after foreign ranchers began commercial ranching in 1870; sheep ranching came to an end in the mid-1980s, but cattle ranching was enhanced. A large wild cat, living in caves, is of unknown introduction. A Chilean partridge, a quail, and a small hawk have been added to the wildlife since 1880. Sea turtles and seals are now rare curiosities, but crayfish and various coastal and deep-sea fishes abound around the coast.

The people. The island's population represents the easternmost settlement of a basically Polynesian subgroup that probably derived from the Marquesas group. The original Rapa Nui vocabulary has been lost except for some mixed Polynesian and non-Polynesian words recorded before the Tahitian dialect was introduced to the decimated population by missionaries in 1864. Today Spanish is generally spoken. In their traditions, the islanders consistently divide themselves into descendants of two distinct ethnic groups, the "Long-Ears" and the "Short-Ears" (see below). Intermarriage is common, and an influx of foreign blood has become increasingly dominant in recent years.

The economy. Whereas the aboriginal economy was based on the cultivation of sweet potato, chicken raising, and coastal fishing, the island has shifted to a cash economy based on tourism. The opening of an airport near Hanga Roa has permitted an increasing influx of tourists since the 1960s, and a few small hotels have been built in the village area, where many islanders and settlers from continental Chile also have accommodations in their homes. The ties to continental Chile are strengthened through twice-weekly flights from Santiago and the building of schools, hospitals, and a large community hall for sports and performances. A well-organized Chilean national park system provides guided tours and security for the unique archaeological monuments. Reforestation projects have been successfully initiated, including eucalyptus plantations at Vaitea and coconut groves in Anakena Bay.

HISTORY

The first European to land on Easter Island was the Dutch admiral Jacob Roggeveen, who paid it a single day's visit in 1722. He and his crew found a population that they described as being of mixed physical types who worshiped huge standing statues with fires while they prostrated themselves to the rising Sun. Some of them, said to be "white men," had their earlobes slit and hanging to their shoulders, a distinctly non-Polynesian custom.

An expedition dispatched by the Spanish viceroy of Peru rediscovered the island in 1770. The Spanish spent four days ashore and were the first to report that the aborigines had their own local form of script. They estimated a population of some 3,000 persons.

A civil war seems to have raged on the island before the arrival of the British navigator Captain James Cook in 1774; a decimated, poverty-stricken Polynesian population of only about 600 or 700 men and fewer than 30 women was found by the Englishmen, who also observed that the large statues were no longer venerated, most of them having been deliberately overthrown. In 1786 the French navigator Jean-François de Galaup, comte de La Pérouse, arrived and found some 2,000 people on the island; he tried in vain to introduce domestic animals. A number of sailing vessels, including whalers, visited the island from 1792 onward. By 1860 the population was about 3,000, but a major slave raid launched from Peru in 1862, followed by smallpox epidemics, reduced the population to 111 in 1877. At the end of the 19th century it began to increase once more. In 1864 Brother Eugène Eyraud, a French Catholic missionary, became the first foreigner to settle on the island; as a result, the population became converted to Christianity by 1868. Settlers from Tahiti began to raise sheep in 1870. In 1888 the island was annexed by Chile, which leased nearly all its territory for sheep raising; in 1954 the Chilean navy administration took over the sheep range. In 1965 a civilian governor was appointed by the Chilean government, and the islanders became full Chilean citizens. Within a single generation the Easter Islanders successfully responded to a complete acculturation to continental standards without losing their pride in their own ancestors and their skills and customs. Annually in February old and young of both sexes meet in contests to revive the arts and practices of the island's past, including carving, tattooing, reed-boat building, and traditional singing and dancing.

Archaeology. The island is famous for its gigantic stone statues, of which there are more than 600, and for the ruins of giant stone platforms (*ahus*) with open courtyards on their landward sides, some of which show masterly

Reintroduction of the toromiro tree

Chilean national park system

The stone statues

The tallest standing Easter Island stone statue (about 37 feet [12 metres] high) after being excavated by Thor Heyerdahl (top right, leaning against statue); it was subsequently partially buried again.

By courtesy of Thor Heyerdahl; photograph, Walter Leonardi

construction. Archaeological surveys were carried out in 1886, 1914, and 1934; archaeological excavations were initiated in 1955. The excavations revealed that three distinct cultural periods are identifiable on the island. The early period is characterized by *ahu*s at Tahai, Vinapu, and Anakena, carbon dated to *c.* AD 700–850. The first two were admired and described by Captain Cook; the wall in Anakena remained hidden below ground until it was excavated archaeologically in 1987. The excavations in Anakena have revealed that a variety of statues were carved in the early period, among them a smaller prototype of the middle-period busts, which mainly differ from the latter by their rounded heads and stubby bodies. Another type was a realistic sculpture in full figure of a kneeling man with his buttocks resting on his heels and his hands on his knees, in one case with his ribs exposed, all features characteristic of pre-Inca monuments at Tiahuanaco in South America. In the middle period, *c.* 1050–1680, statues were deliberately destroyed and discarded, and all *ahu*s were rebuilt with no regard for solar orientation or masonry fitting. The sole desire seems to have been to obtain strong platforms capable of supporting ever taller and heavier busts, the classical *moai* of the middle period.

Burial chambers also were constructed within the *ahu*s in the middle period. The sizes of the statues made were increased until they reached stupendous dimensions; the slim and lofty busts also had huge cylindrical *pukao* (topknots) of red tuff placed on top of their slender heads. Most middle-period statues range from about 10 to 20 feet in height, but the biggest among those formerly standing on top of an *ahu* was about 32 feet tall, consisted of a single block weighing about 82 tons (74,500 kilograms) and had a *pukao* of about 11 tons balanced on its apex. The largest statue still standing partly buried in the deep silt below the quarries is about 37 feet tall, and the largest unfinished one with its back attached to the rock is about 68 feet tall. Traditions, supported by archaeology, suggest that the images represented important personalities who were deified after death.

Statues of the middle period were all quarried from the special yellow-gray tuff found in the crater walls of Rano **Unfinished** Raraku. Inside and outside the crater bowl numerous un-**carvings** finished statues and thousands of crude stone picks are scattered about, bearing witness to a sudden interruption of the sculptors' work. The unfinished images show that each statue had its front and sides completed to a polish before the back was detached from the bedrock. The image

was then slid away to be raised at random in the rubble below the quarries to have the back finished before being moved to some distant *ahu.* Eye cavities and topknots were added only after the monument was erected; recent discoveries have revealed that these concavities had inlaid eyes of white coral with a dark stone disk as pupil. From one to a dozen completed statues would stand in a row on a single *ahu,* always facing inland.

Experiments based on island traditions in 1955–56 showed that the numerous basalt picks left in the quarries were perfectly suitable for carving the hard tuff. Reenactments showed that 12 islanders were able to lift a 25-ton statue about 10 feet off the ground and to tilt it on end on top of an *ahu;* this work took 18 days with no tools other than two wooden logs that were used as levers. Stones of all sizes were wedged under the statue one by one to form a slowly rising cairn in order to lift the giant monoliths upright. Tradition claimed that the statues had "walked" across the terrain to their distant destinations, but in the experiment 180 islanders were able to pull a medium statue over the ground. A renewed experiment in 1986 revived the tradition and discovered that 15 men sufficed to move a medium-sized statue over the ground in upright position by jerking it ahead with a system of ropes.

The middle-period busts clearly evolved from a local prototype and have no counterpart elsewhere. Also peculiar to the middle period was a bird cult with attendant birdman rites that survived into the third, or late, period. Its ceremonial centre was the village of Orongo, on top of Rano Kao, which consisted of stone houses with roof vaults built as false arches. These houses and contiguous circular masonry dwellings with roof entrances are characteristic of the early and middle periods on the island; while unknown elsewhere in Polynesia they are common in the adjacent area of South America.

Traditional culture. The late-period Easter Islanders dwelt in boat-shaped pole-and-thatch houses or in caves. This period was marked by internal wars, general destruction, and cultural decadence. The *mataa,* or obsidian spearpoint, which was mass-produced, is the characteristic artifact of this period. Wood carving and small crude stone figurines replaced monumental art. Written wooden tablets covered with incised signs (called *rongo-rongo*) placed in boustrophedon (a method of writing in which the lines run alternately from right to left and from left to right) were copied from earlier specimens merely for ritual purposes; their proper reading was forgotten, and—despite many claims—modern attempts at deciphering them have failed. During this period art treasures were hidden in secret family caves, while the upright *ahu* images were successively overthrown. Silt from the abandoned quarries descended to the chests of the blind and unfinished busts standing at the foot of the volcano, rendering their overthrow impossible and thus securing for posterity the eyeless heads that have given the island its fame.

Tradition maintains that destruction began after a period of peaceful coexistence between two people of different culture and language—the Long-Ears and the Short-Ears. The latter, tired of toiling for the former, all but exterminated them in a pyre along an ancient ditch at Poike on the far northeastern coast. Carbon dating and genealogies concur in placing this event and the beginning of the late period at about AD 1680. The original construction of the artificial Poike ditch, according to carbon dating, took place in about AD 380.

The First International Science Congress convening on Easter Island in 1984 agreed on a resolution defining the island as the site of a pre-European civilization. The recent excavations, which reveal that the earliest settlers arrived with previously developed architectural concepts and a highly specialized megalithic masonry technique, support island traditions, which claim that the first ancestors arrived in an organized party of emigrants and not merely as casually wind-driven fishermen. (Th.H.)

BIBLIOGRAPHY

Physical and human geography: RON CROCOMBE, *The South Pacific* (1983); and FREDERICA M. BUNGE and MELINDA W. COOKE (eds.), *Oceania, a Regional Study,* 2nd ed. (1985), provide comprehensive information. Large-scale maps are found in *Atlas of the South Pacific,* 2nd ed. (1986), published by the New Zealand government. HEROLD J. WIENS, *Atoll Environment and Ecology* (1962), explores the physical characteristics of Pacific Islands environments. The classic demographic study is NORMA MCARTHUR, *Island Populations of the Pacific* (1967, reprinted 1983); see also VERN CARROLL (ed.), *Pacific Atoll Populations* (1975). On physical anthropology, see WILLIAM HOWELLS, *The Pacific Islanders* (1973). F.R. FOSBERG (ed.), *Man's Place in the Island Ecosystem* (1963), is a collection of ecological, cultural, and anthropological research. DOUGLAS L. OLIVER, *The Pacific Islands,* rev. ed. (1961, reprinted 1975), is a popular introduction to the anthropology and history of Pacific Islands societies. UNIVERSITY OF THE SOUTH PACIFIC. INSTITUTE OF PACIFIC STUDIES, *Pacific Tourism, as Islanders See It* (1980), analyzes the impact of tourism. Current writings about the area are found in *Pacific Islands Business* (monthly, Fiji); *Pacific Magazine* (bimonthly, Hawaii); and *Pacific Islands Monthly* (Australia). JOHN CARTER (ed.), *Pacific Islands Yearbook,* 15th ed. (1984), is a detailed reference work on contemporary conditions and events. For further research, see C.R.H. TAYLOR, *A Pacific Bibliography: Printed Matter Relating to the Native Peoples of Polynesia, Melanesia, and Micronesia,* 2nd ed. (1965); and *Bibliographie de l'Océanie,* published irregularly by the Société des Océanistes in Paris.

History: The best general history of the precolonial Pacific is K.R. HOWE, *Where the Waves Fall: A New South Sea Island History from First Settlement to Colonial Rule* (1984). For early periods, see JOHN TERRELL, *Prehistory in the Pacific Islands: A Study of Variation in Language, Customs, and Human Biology* (1986), a general treatment; PATRICK VINTON KIRCH (ed.), *Island Societies: Archaeological Approaches to Evolution and Transformation* (1986), a collection of articles; PETER BELLWOOD, *Man's Conquest of the Pacific: The Prehistory of Southeast Asia and Oceania* (1978), a documentation of human origins and migrations, and *The Polynesians: Prehistory of an Island People,* rev. ed. (1987); JANET DAVIDSON, *The Prehistory of New Zealand* (1984), a regional study; and M.P.K. SORRENSON, *Maori Origins and Migrations: The Genesis of Some Pakeha Myths and Legends* (1979). ROBERT D. CRAIG and FRANK P. KING (eds.), *Historical Dictionary of Oceania* (1981), is a comprehensive reference source. For current writings, see *Journal of Pacific History* (semiannual, Australia).

The following histories focus on special topics: FRANCIS X. HEZEL, *The First Taint of Civilization: A History of the Caroline and Marshall Islands in Pre-Colonial Days, 1521–1885* (1983); JOHN GARRETT, *To Live Among the Stars: Christian Origins in Oceania* (1982); and F.J. WEST, *Political Advancement in the South Pacific: A Comparative Study of Colonial Practice in Fiji, Tahiti, and American Samoa* (1961, reprinted 1984). Biographies that date from European contact can be found in J.W. DAVIDSON and DERYCK SCARR (eds.), *Pacific Islands Portraits* (1970); and DERYCK SCARR (ed.), *More Pacific Islands Portraits* (1978).

The development of Pacific trade and the establishment of exploitative industries are discussed in DOROTHY SHINEBERG, *They Came for Sandalwood* (1967), the first full-length study of trade in the Pacific; H.E. MAUDE, *Of Islands and Men: Studies in Pacific History* (1968); O.H.K. SPATE, *The Spanish Lake* (1979), *Monopolists and Freebooters* (1983), and *Paradise Found and Lost* (1989), on the European exploration and subsequent exploitation of the area; MASLYN WILLIAMS and BARRIE MACDONALD, *The Phosphateers: A History of the British Phosphate Commissioners and the Christmas Island Phosphate Commission* (1985); K. BUCKLEY and K. KLUGMAN, *The History of Burns Philp: The Australian Company in the South Pacific* (1981); PETER CORRIS, *Passage, Port, and Plantation: A History of Solomon Islands Labour Migration, 1870–1914* (1973); and MICHAEL MOYNAGH, *Brown or White?: A History of the Fiji Sugar Industry, 1873–1973* (1981).

Politics is studied in PETER LARMOUR and ROPATE QALO (eds.), *Decentralization in the South Pacific: Local, Provincial, and State Government in Twenty Countries* (1985), on the growth of local governments in the postcolonial period; UENTABO FAKAOFO NEEMIA, *Cooperation and Conflict: Costs, Benefits, and National Interests in Pacific Regional Cooperation* (1986), on local agencies and the economic aspects of national self-realization; LEONARD MASON and PATRICIA HERENIKO (eds.), *In Search of a Home* (1987), reports by island authors on problems of immigrants in urban centres; HARUHIRO FUKUI (ed.), *Political Parties of Asia and the Pacific,* 2 vol. (1985), an encyclopaedic source; FRANK P. KING (ed.), *Oceania and Beyond: Essays on the Pacific Since 1945* (1976); and DIRK ANTHONY BALLENDORF and FRANK P. KING (eds.), *Oceania Today: Towards New Directions and Political Self-Actualization* (1980). See also STEWART FIRTH, *Nuclear Playground* (1987).

Traditional cultures: ANDREW P. VAYDA (ed.), *Peoples and Cultures of the Pacific: An Anthropological Reader* (1968), a collection of articles; ROBERT KIRK and EMÖKE SZATHMARY (eds.), *Out of Asia: Peopling the Americas and the Pacific* (1985), which explores the demography and language; and LYNDALL RYAN, *The Aboriginal Tasmanians* (1981). Cultural life, beliefs, and customs are examined in LENORE MANDERSON (ed.), *Shared Wealth and Symbol: Food, Culture, and Society in Oceania and Southeast Asia* (1986). Other works include WILLIAM A. FOLEY, *The Papuan Languages of New Guinea* (1986), a treatment of the most complex linguistic area of the world; EMILIANA AFEAKI, RON CROCOMBE, and JOHN MCCLAREN (eds.), *Religious Cooperation in the Pacific Islands* (1983), descriptions of contemporary religious bodies in the area; A.C. HADDON and JAMES HORNELL, *Canoes of Oceania* (1975); and BEN R. FINNEY (comp.), *Pacific Navigation and Voyaging* (1976), on Oceanic maritime technology. The arts are surveyed in SIDNEY M. MEAD (ed.), *Exploring the Visual Art of Oceania: Australia, Melanesia, Micronesia, and Polynesia* (1979); ADRIENNE L. KAEPPLER, *Artificial Curiosities: Being an Exposition of Native Manufactures Collected on the Three Pacific Voyages of Captain James Cook, R.N.* (1978); and ROLAND W. FORCE and MARYANNE FORCE, *The Fuller Collection of Pacific Artifacts* (1971). MILES M. JACKSON (ed.), *Pacific Island Studies: A Survey of the Literature* (1986), is a guide to the literature on Pacific peoples.

Melanesian cultures: H.C. BROOKFIELD, *Melanesia: A Geographical Interpretation of an Island World* (1971), is a comparative survey of geography. R.J. MAY and HANK NELSON (eds.), *Melanesia, Beyond Diversity,* 2 vol. (1982), presents information on everything from linguistics to archaeology and history. An excellent summary, in the light of findings in early history and linguistics, is ANN CHOWNING, *An Introduction to the Peoples and Cultures of Melanesia,* 2nd ed. (1977). On material culture, B.A.L. CRANSTONE, *Melanesia: A Short Ethnography* (1961), remains useful. A fine study of a particular people is MARIE REAY, *The Kuma: Freedom and Conformity in the New Guinea Highlands* (1959). Syntheses and collections of papers on aspects of society and culture in New Guinea include PAULA BROWN, *Highland Peoples of New Guinea* (1978); PAULA BROWN and GEORGEDA BUCHBINDER (eds.), *Man and Woman in the New Guinea Highlands* (1976); ANDREW STRATHERN (ed.), *Inequality in New Guinea Highland Societies* (1982); JERRY W. LEACH and EDMUND LEACH (eds.), *The Kula: New Perspectives on Massim Exchange* (1983); R.M. GLASSE and M.J. MEGGITT (eds.), *Pigs, Pearlshells, and Women: Marriage in the New Guinea Highlands* (1969); GILBERT H. HERDT (ed.), *Rituals of Manhood: Male Initiation in Papua New Guinea* (1982), and *Ritualized Homosexuality in Melanesia* (1984); DAN JORGENSEN (ed.), *Concepts of Conception: Procreation Ideologies in Papua New Guinea* (1983); PAULA G. RUBEL and ABRAHAM ROSMAN, *Your Own Pigs You May Not Eat: A Comparative Study of New Guinea Societies* (1978); and C.A. GREGORY, *Gifts and Commodities* (1982). Other works include MICHELE STEPHEN (ed.), *Sorcerer and Witch in Melanesia* (1987); L.L. LANGNESS and JOHN C. WESCHLER (eds.), *Melanesia: Readings on a Culture Area* (1971); MARILYN STRATHERN (ed.), *Dealing with Inequality: Analysing Gender Relations in Melanesia and Beyond* (1987); P. LAWRENCE and M.J. MEGGITT (eds.), *Gods, Ghosts, and Men in Melanesia: Some Religions of Australian New Guinea and the New Hebrides* (1965); and PETER WORSLEY, *The Trumpet Shall Sound: A Study of "Cargo" Cults in Melanesia,* 2nd ed. (1968).

Micronesian cultures: A general overview is offered in WILLIAM H. ALKIRE, *An Introduction to the Peoples and Cultures of Micronesia,* 2nd ed. (1977). JOHN L. FISCHER, *The Eastern Carolines* (1957, reprinted 1966), is a regional study. Special topics are discussed in MARK R. PEATTIE, *Man'yō: The Rise and Fall of the Japanese in Micronesia, 1885–1945* (1988); DONALD F. MCHENRY, *Micronesia, Trust Betrayed: Altruism vs Self Interest in American Foreign Policy* (1975); and DAVID NEVIN, *The American Touch in Micronesia* (1977). A good island history is DAVID HANLON, *Upon a Stone Altar: A History of the Island of Pohnpei to 1890* (1988). For further study, see MAC MARSHALL and JAMES D. NASON, *Micronesia, 1944–1974: A Bibliography of Anthropological and Related Source Materials* (1975).

Polynesian cultures: The following works treat the development of Polynesian cultures: IRVING GOLDMAN, *Ancient Polynesian Society* (1970); JESSE D. JENNINGS (ed.), *The Prehistory of Polynesia* (1979); ROBERT BOROFSKY, *Making History: Pukapukan and Anthropological Construction of Knowledge* (1987); PATRICK VINTON KIRCH, *The Evolution of the Polynesian Chiefdoms* (1984); and ANTONY HOOPER and JUDITH HUNTSMAN (eds.), *Transformations of Polynesian Culture* (1985).

Major islands and island groups: (Solomon Islands):   PATRICK VINTON KIRCH and D.E. YEN, *Tikopia: The Prehistory and Ecology of a Polynesian Outlier* (1982); JUDITH A. BENNETT, *Wealth of the Solomons: A History of a Pacific Archipelago, 1800–1978* (1987); DAVID HILLIARD, *God's Gentlemen: A History of the Melanesian Mission, 1849–1942* (1978); ROGER M. KEESING and

PETER CORRIS, *Lightning Meets the West Wind: The Malaita Massacre* (1980); HUGH LARACY, *Marists and Melanesians: A History of Catholic Missions in the Solomon Islands* (1976); HUGH LARACY (ed.), *Pacific Protest: The Maasina Rule Movement, Solomon Islands, 1944–1952* (1983); and DEBORAH WAITE, *Art of the Solomon Islands: From the Collection of the Barbier-Müller Museum* (1983). For further study, see SALLY EDRIDGE (comp.), *Solomon Islands Bibliography to 1980* (1985).

(*Vanuatu*): The standard bibliography is PATRICK O'REILLY, *Bibliographie méthodique, analytique et critique des Nouvelles-Hébrides* (1958); his *Hébridais: répertoire bio-bibliographique des Nouvelles-Hébrides* (1957), provides short sketches of some of the persons (principally European) in Vanuatu's colonial past. See also JOSÉ GARANGER, *Archaeology of the New Hebrides: Contribution to the Knowledge of the Central Islands* (1982; originally published in French, 1972), an account of the excavation of Roy Mata's burial site; MICHAEL ALLEN (ed.), *Vanuatu: Politics, Economics, and Ritual in Island Melanesia* (1981), comparative ethnographic studies; UNIVERSITY OF THE SOUTH PACIFIC. INSTITUTE OF PACIFIC STUDIES, *Vanuatu* (1980), with contributions by leading ni-Vanuatu figures; JEREMY MAC-CLANCY, *To Kill a Bird with Two Stones: A Short History of Vanuatu* (1981), a survey; RON ADAMS, *In the Land of Strangers: A Century of European Contact with Tanna, 1774–1874* (1984), an account of the first hundred years of European contact; and JEAN GUIART, *Un Siècle et demi de contacts culturels à Tanna, Nouvelles-Hébrides* (1956), on the origins and development of the John Frum cargo cult.

(*New Caledonia*): OFFICE DE LA RECHERCHE SCIENTIFIQUE ET TECHNIQUE OUTRE-MER, *Atlas de la Nouvelle-Calédonie et dépendances* (1981), gives an account of the natural, human, economic, and urban development, with detailed maps. *Comptes économiques* (annual), and INSTITUT NATIONAL DE LA STATISTIQUE ET DES ÉTUDES ÉCONOMIQUES. FRANCE, *Résultats du recensement de la population de la Nouvelle Calédonie* (1984), are useful official publications. Political and social affairs are the subject of VIRGINIA THOMPSON and RICHARD ADLOFF, *The French Pacific Islands: French Polynesia and New Caledonia* (1971); MYRIAM DORNOY, *Politics in New Caledonia* (1984); and ALAN WARD, *Land and Politics in New Caledonia* (1982). Sociological studies include J.M. KOHLER, *Colonie ou Democratie* (1987); J.M. KOHLER and P. PILLON, *Impact de l'opération café en milieu Mélanésien* (1982); J.M. KOHLER and LOÏC J.D. WACQUANT, *L'École inégale: éléments pour un de sociologie de l'école en Nouvelle-Calédonie* (1985); and K.R. HOWE, *The Loyalty Islands: A History of Culture Contacts, 1840–1900* (1977). ALAIN SAUSSOL, *L'Héritage: essai sur le problème foncier mélanésien en Nouvelle-Calédonie* (1979); and PIERRE GASCHER, *La Belle au bois dormant: regards sur l'administration coloniale en Nouvelle-Calédonie de 1874 à 1894* (1974), provide accounts of French settlement. The most comprehensive history is JOHN CONNELL, *New Caledonia or Kanaky?: The Political History of a French Colony* (1987).

(*Fiji*): On geography and demography, see R. GERARD WARD, *Land Use and Population in Fiji* (1965). Socio-economic aspects are studied in CYRIL S. BELSHAW, *Under the Ivi Tree: Society and Economic Growth in Rural Fiji* (1964); H.C. BROOKFIELD, F. ELLIS, and R.G. WARD, *Land, Cane, and Coconuts* (1985); and R.F. WATTERS, *Koro: Economic Development and Social Change in Fiji* (1969). Traditional Fijian society and 20th-century change are discussed in R.R. NAYACAKALOU, *Leadership in Fiji* (1975); JOHN NATION, *Customs of Respect: The Traditional Basis of Fijian Communal Politics* (1978); and G.K. ROTH, *Fijian Way of Life*, 2nd ed. (1973). R.A. DERRICK, *History of Fiji* (1946), is a pioneering study and an excellent introduction. DERYCK SCARR, *Fiji, a Short History* (1984), gives a general account. PETER FRANCE, *The Charter of the Land: Custom and Colonization in Fiji* (1969), deals with the foundations of colonial policy. BRUCE KNAPMAN, *Fiji's Economic History, 1874–1939: Studies of Capitalist Colonial Development* (1987), examines the colonial economy. On the history of Indians in Fiji, see K.L. GILLION, *Fiji's Indian Migrants: A History to the End of Indenture in 1920* (1962), and *The Fiji Indians: Challenge to European Dominance, 1920–1946* (1977). See also ADRIAN C. MAYER, *Peasants in the Pacific: A Study of Fiji Indian Rural Society*, 2nd ed. (1973). The political situation is outlined in BRIJ V. LAL (ed.), *Politics in Fiji: Studies in Contemporary History* (1986); and the coup is discussed in BRIJ LAL, *Power and Prejudice: The Making of the Fiji Crisis* (1988).

(*Tuvalu*): AUSTRALIAN MUSEUM. SYDNEY, *The Atoll of Funafuti, Ellice Group: Its Zoology, Botany, Ethnology, and General Structure Based on Collections Made by Mr. Charles Hedley*, 10 pt. (1896–1900), is a broad scientific survey. On village economy and general socioeconomic conditions, see ANNE CHAMBERS, *Nanumea Report: A Socio-Economic Study of Nanumea Atoll, Tuvalu* (1975, reissued as *Nanumea*, 1984). DONALD GILBERT KENNEDY, *Field Notes on the Culture of Vaitupu, Ellice Islands*

(1931), surveys the traditional material culture. HUGH LARACY (ed.), *Tuvalu: A History* (1983), provides an introduction. BARRIE MACDONALD, *Cinderellas of the Empire: Towards a History of Kiribati and Tuvalu* (1982), is a comprehensive account.

(*Kiribati*): TONY WHINCUP, *Nareau's Nation: A Portrait of the Gilbert Islands* (1979), offers insights into modern life. ROSEMARY GRIMBLE (ed.), *Migrations, Myth, and Magic from the Gilbert Islands: Early Writings of Sir Arthur Grimble* (1972), gives an account of myth, legends, and traditions. On material culture, see GERD KOCH, *The Material Culture of Kiribati* (1986; originally published in German, 1965). See also ALAIMA TALU et al., *Kiribati: Aspects of History* (1979). ALBERT F. ELLIS, *Ocean Island and Nauru: Their Story* (1935), explores the history of the island's phosphate trade. See also the work by Barrie Macdonald cited above under *Tuvalu*.

(*Northern Mariana Islands*): For information on the Northern Mariana Islands, see the works by Francis X. Hezel, Frank P. King, and Dirk Anthony Ballendorf, cited above under *History*, and the works by Mark R. Peattie, Donald F. McHenry, and David Nevin, under *Micronesian cultures*.

(*Guam*): LAURA THOMPSON, *Guam and Its People*, 3rd rev. ed. (1947, reprinted 1969), remains a valuable source. An overview of economics, politics, and industry is given in WILLIAM LUTZ, *Guam* (1987). For history, see PAUL CARANO and PEDRO C. SANCHEZ, *A Complete History of Guam* (1964); TIMOTHY P. MAGA, *Defending Paradise: The United States and Guam, 1898–1950* (1988); and ROBERT F. ROGERS, *Guam's Commonwealth Effort 1987–1988* (1988). Guam in World War II is discussed in TONY PALOMO, *An Island in Agony* (1984).

(*Palau*): DOUGLAS FAULKNER, *This Living Reef* (1974), is an illustrated survey of the marine environment. The islands themselves are explored in DOUGLAS OSBORNE, *The Archeology of the Palau Islands: An Intensive Survey* (1966); and GEORGE J. GUMERMAN, DAVID SNYDER, and W. BRUCE MASSE, *An Archaeological Reconnaissance in the Palau Archipelago, Western Caroline Islands. Micronesia* (1981). R.E. JOHANNES, *Words of the Lagoon: Fishing and Marine Lore in the Palau District of Micronesia* (1981), examines the peoples' knowledge of fish behaviour and the ocean. ROLAND W. FORCE and MARYANNE FORCE, *Just One House: A Description and Analysis of Kinship in the Palau Islands* (1972); and H.G. BARNETT, *Being a Palauan* (1959, reissued 1979), are anthropological accounts. DANIEL J. PEACOCK, *Lee Boo of Belau: A Prince in London* (1987), is the story of the first Palauan to visit the West. EDWARD C. BARNARD, *Naked and a Prisoner: Captain Edward C. Barnard's Narrative of Shipwreck in Palau, 1832–1833*, ed. by KENNETH R. MARTIN (1980), is a personal account of a stay in Palau by a European.

(*Federated States of Micronesia*): For a geographic survey, see KENNETH BROWER, *Micronesia, the Land, the People, and the Sea* (1981); and WILLIAM H. STEWART, *Explorer's Atlas of Tourist Maps for the Federated States of Micronesia, Pacific Ocean: Kosrae, Ponape, Truk, and Yap* (1982). Other sources include STEVEN C. SMITH, *The Federated States of Micronesia: An Emerging Nation: An Overview for Peace Corps Volunteers* (1986); and AUSTIN RANNEY and HOWARD R. PENNIMAN, *Democracy in the Islands: The Micronesian Plebiscites of 1983* (1985).

(*Marshall Islands*): ALEXANDER SPOEHR, *Majuro: A Village in the Marshall Islands* (1949, reprinted 1973); and ROBERT C. KISTE, *The Bikinians: A Study in Forced Migration* (1974), describe the ethnology, anthropology, and social conditions of the area.

(*French Polynesia*): BENGT DANIELSSON, *Work and Life on Raroia: An Acculturation Study from the Tuamotu Group, French Oceania* (1956); and F. ALLAN HANSON, *Rapan Lifeways: Society and History on a Polynesian Island* (1970, reprinted 1983), study society and culture. See also DOUGLAS L. OLIVER, *Ancient Tahitian Society*, 3 vol. (1974), a classic treatment of ethnography, social relations, tribal polity, and the power elite. For history, see ROBERT LANGDON, *Tahiti, Island of Love*, 5th ed. (1979); COLIN NEWBURY, *Tahiti Nui: Change and Survival in French Polynesia, 1767–1945* (1980); and PIERRE-YVES TOULLELAN, *Tahiti Colonial* (1984). Other studies include WILLIAM TAGUPA, *Politics in French Polynesia, 1945–1975* (1976); VIRGINIA THOMPSON and RICHARD ADLOFF, *The French Pacific Islands* (1971); and PAUL HODÉE, *Tahiti, 1834–1984: 150 ans de vie chrétienne en eglise* (1983).

(*American Samoa and Western Samoa*): LOWELL D. HOLMES, *Samoan Village* (1974); MARGARET MEAD, *Coming of Age in Samoa: A Psychological Study of Primitive Youth for Western Civilization* (1928), available also in later editions; and DEREK FREEMAN, *Margaret Mead and Samoa: The Making and Unmaking of an Anthropological Myth* (1983), explore the traditional heritage and its interpretations. Effects of modernization are studied in PAUL T. BAKER, JOEL M. HANNA, and THELMA S.

BAKER (eds.), *The Changing Samoans: Behavior and Health in Transition* (1986). GEORGE TURNER, *Samoa, a Hundred Years Ago and Long Before* (1884, reprinted 1984), remains a valuable historical study. J.W. DAVIDSON, *Samoa mo Samoa: The Emergence of the Independent State of Western Samoa* (1967); and R.P. GILSON, *Samoa 1830 to 1900: The Politics of a Multi-Cultural Community* (1970), are classic histories. A modern survey is offered in FRED HENRY, *Samoa, an Early History* (1980). For further research, see LOWELL D. HOLMES (comp.), *Samoan Islands Bibliography* (1984). The best sources for a discussion of the political development of Western Samoa include MALAMA MELEISEA and PENELOPE SCHOEFFEL MELEISEA (ed.), *Lagaga: A Short History of Western Samoa* (1987); and MALAMA MELEISEA, *The Making of Modern Samoa* (1987).

(*Tonga*): JOHN CONNELL, *Migration, Employment, and Development in the South Pacific: Country Report* (1983), vol. 18, *Tonga*, studies the effects of internal and external migration. ELIZABETH BOTT, *Tongan Society at the Time of Captain Cook's Visits: Discussions with Her Majesty Queen Sālote Tupou* (1982), is a standard historical reference. SIONE LĀTŪKEFU, *Church and State in Tonga: The Wesleyan Methodist Mission-aries and Political Development, 1822–1875* (1974), is a detailed history. A.H. WOOD, *A History and Geography of Tonga* (1943), is a brief but excellent introduction; and NOEL RUTHERFORD, *Friendly Islands: A History of Tonga* (1977), provides comprehensive coverage of social, economic, political, and religious aspects of life.

(*Easter Island*): A comprehensive introduction is provided in NORWEGIAN ARCHAEOLOGICAL EXPEDITION TO EASTER ISLAND AND THE EAST PACIFIC. 1955–1956, *Reports*, 2 vol. (1961–65). History and culture are outlined in GRANT MCCALL, *Rapanui: Tradition and Survival on Easter Island* (1981). See also THOR HEYERDAHL, *Aku-Aku: The Secret of Easter Island*, trans. from Norwegian (1958, reprinted 1988), an account of an archaeological expedition, *Sea Routes to Polynesia* (1968), a report on modern knowledge of pre-European activities, *Art of Easter Island* (1975), a survey of art in collections throughout the world, with more than 300 plates of photographs, and *Easter Island—a Mystery Solved* (1989).

(L.E.M./F.J.W./R.W.Fo./R.M.Ke./
R.C.Ki./H.M.La./R.Ad./D.L.Sh./B.K.M./
D.A.B./D.R.Sh./F.X.H./A.We./Si.L./Th.H.)

The Art of **Painting**

The art of painting is the expression of ideas and emotions, with the creation of certain aesthetic qualities, in a two-dimensional visual language. The elements of this language—its shapes, lines, colours, tones, and textures—are used in various ways to produce sensations of volume, space, movement, and light on a flat surface. These elements are combined into expressive patterns in order to represent real or supernatural phenomena, to interpret a narrative theme, or to create wholly abstract visual relationships. The artist communicates his visual message in terms of the sensuous qualities and expressive possibilities and limitations of a particular medium, technique, and form.

Earlier cultural traditions—of tribes, religions, guilds, royal courts, and states—largely controlled the craft, form, imagery, and subject matter of painting and determined its function, whether ritualistic, devotional, decorative, entertaining, or educational. Painters were employed more as skilled artisans than as creative artists. Later, the Far East and Renaissance Europe saw the emergence of the fine artist, with the social status of scholar and courtier, who signed his work, who decided its design and often its subject and imagery, and who established a more personal, if not always amicable, relationship with his patron.

During the 19th century the painter in Western societies began to lose his social position and secure patronage. Generally, he can now reach an audience only through commercial galleries and public museums, although his work may be occasionally reproduced in art periodicals. He may also be assisted by financial awards or commissions from industry and the state. He has, however, gained the freedom to invent his own visual language and to experiment with new forms and unconventional materials and techniques. The restless endeavour to extend the boundaries of expression in Western art produces continuous international stylistic changes. The often bewildering succession of new movements in painting is further stimulated by the swift interchange of ideas by means of international art journals, travelling exhibitions, and art centres.

This article is concerned with the elements and principles of design in painting and with the various mediums, forms, imagery, subject matter, and symbolism employed or adopted or created by the painter. For the history of painting in the West, see PAINTING, THE HISTORY OF WESTERN. For treatment of painting as practiced in non-European cultures, see AFRICAN ARTS; AMERICAN INDIANS; CENTRAL ASIAN ARTS; EAST ASIAN ARTS; EGYPTIAN ARTS AND ARCHITECTURE; ISLĀMIC ARTS; OCEANIC ARTS; PREHISTORIC PEOPLES AND CULTURES; SOUTH ASIAN ARTS; SOUTHEAST ASIAN ARTS.

The article is divided into the following sections:

ELEMENTS AND PRINCIPLES OF DESIGN

The design of a painting is its visual format: the arrangement of its lines, shapes, colours, tones, and textures into an expressive pattern. It is the sense of inevitability in this formal organization that gives a great painting its self-sufficiency and presence.

The colours and placing of the principal images in a design may be sometimes largely decided by representational and symbolic considerations. Yet it is the formal interplay of colours and shapes that alone is capable of communicating a particular mood, producing optical sensations of space, volume, movement, and light and creating forces

Formal
interplay
of colours
and shapes

Figure 1: *Linear design.*
(Top) The linear design of Georges Seurat's oil painting "La Parade," 1887–88, composed of ovals and rectangles arranged in an overall grid pattern, based on the Golden Mean system of proportions. In the Metropolitan Museum of Art, New York City. 1 m × 1.5 m. (Bottom) The interwoven, linear pattern of Leonardo da Vinci's panel painting "Virgin and Child with St. Anne," c. 1501–12. In the Louvre, Paris. 1.68 m × 1.3 m.

By courtesy of (top right) the Metropolitan Museum of Art, New York, bequest of Stephen C. Clark, 1961; photograph, (bottom right) Giraudon—Art Resource

of both harmony and tension, even when a painting's narrative symbolism is obscure.

Elements of design. *Line.* Each of the design elements has special expressive qualities. Line, for example, is an intuitive, primeval convention for representing things; the simple linear imagery of young children's drawings and prehistoric rock paintings is universally understood. The formal relationships of thick with thin lines, of broken with continuous, and of sinuous with jagged are forces of contrast and repetition in the design of many paintings in all periods of history. Variations in the painted contours of images also provide a direct method of describing the volume, weight, spatial position, and textural characteristics of things. The finest examples of this pictorial shorthand are found in Japanese ink painting, where an expressive economy and vitality of line is closely linked to a traditional mastery of calligraphy.

In addition to painted contours, a linear design is composed of all of the edges of tone and colour masses, of the axial directions of images, and of the lines that are implied by alignments of shapes across the picture. The manner in which these various kinds of line are echoed and repeated animates the design (Figure 1). The artist, whether acting consciously or intuitively, also places them in relationship to one another across the picture, so that they weave a uni-fying rhythmic network throughout the painting (Figure 1).

Apart from the obvious associations of some linear patterns with particular actions—undulating lines suggesting buoyant movement, for instance—emotive sensations are produced by certain linear relationships. Thus, lines moving upward express feelings of joy and aspiration, those directing the eye downward evoke moods of sadness or defeat, while lines at angles opening to the right of a design are more agreeable and welcoming than those spreading outward to the left.

Shape and mass. Shape and mass, as elements of design, include all areas of different colour, tone, and texture, as well as individual and grouped images.

Children instinctively represent the things they see by geometrical symbols. Not only have sophisticated modern artists, such as Paul Klee and Jean Dubuffet, borrowed this primitive imagery, but the more arresting and expressive shapes and masses in most styles of painting and those to which most people intuitively respond will generally be found to have been clearly based on such archetypal forms. A square or a circle will tend to dominate a design and will therefore often be found at its focal centre— the square window framing Christ in Leonardo da Vinci's "Last Supper," for example, the hovering "sun" in an Adolph Gottlieb abstract, or the halo encircling a Chris-

Response to archetypal forms

tian or Buddhist deity. A firmly based triangular image or group of shapes seems reassuring, even uplifting, while the precarious balance implied by an inverted triangular shape or mass produces feelings of tension. Oval, lozenge, and rectangular forms suggest stability and protection and often surround vulnerable figures in narrative paintings.

There is generally a cellular unity, or "family likeness," between the shapes and masses in a design similar to the visual harmony of all units to the whole observed in natural forms—the gills, fins, and scales in character with the overall shape of a fish, for example.

The negative spaces between shapes and masses are also carefully considered by the artist, since they can be so adjusted as to enhance the action and character of the positive images. They can be as important to the design as time intervals in music or the voids of an architectural facade.

Colour. In many styles and periods of painting, the functions of colour are primarily decorative and descriptive, often serving merely to reinforce the expression of an idea or subject communicated essentially in terms of line and tone. In much of modern painting, however, the full-spectrum range of pigments available has allowed colour to be the primary expressive element.

The principal dimensions of colour in painting are the variables or attributes of hue, tone, and intensity. Red, yellow, and blue are the basic hues from which all others on the chromatic scale can be made by mixtures. These three opaque hues are the subtractive pigment primaries and should not be confused with the behaviour of the additive triads and mixtures of transparent, coloured light. Mixtures of primary pairs produce the secondary hues of orange, violet, and green. By increasing the amount of one primary in each of these mixtures, the tertiary colours of yellow-orange, orange-red, red-violet, violet-blue, blue-green, and green-yellow, respectively, are made. The primary colours, with their basic secondary and tertiary mixtures, can be usefully notated as the 12 segments of a circle (Figure 2). The secondary and tertiary colour segments between a pair of parent primaries can then be seen to share a harmonious family relationship with one another—the yellow-orange, orange, and orange-red hues that lie between yellow and red, for example.

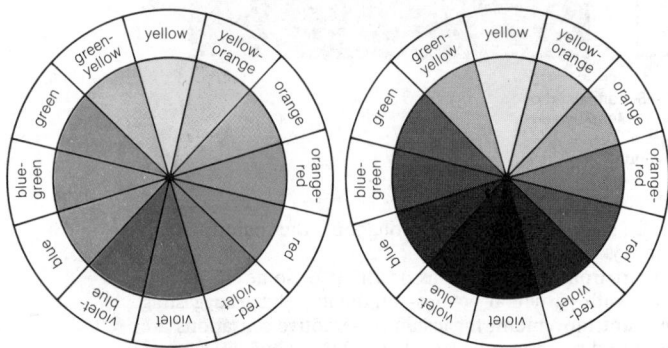

Figure 2: *Colour.*
(Left) Colour wheel made up of the primary colours and their basic secondary and tertiary mixtures. (Right) Colour wheel with approximate, inherent tonal values.

Local hues are the inherent and associative colours of things. In everyday life, familiar things are described by particular colours, and these often are identified by reference to familiar things; the green of grass and the grass green of paint, for instance. Although, as the Impressionists demonstrated, the inherent colours of forms in the real world are usually changed by effects of light and atmosphere, many of the great primitive and classical styles of representational painting are expressed in terms of local hues.

Tone is a colour's relative degree, or value, of lightness or darkness. The tonal pattern of a painting is shown in a monochrome reproduction. A painting dominated by dark colours, such as a Rembrandt, is in a low tonal key, while one painted in the pale range of a late Claude Monet is said to be high keyed. The tonal range of pigments is too

Tonal
pattern of
a painting

Figure 3: An example of the early oil method of (left) colour glazing a (right) monochrome painting.

narrow for the painter to be able to match the brightest lights and deepest darks of nature. Therefore, in order to express effects of illumination and dense shadow, he must lower the overall tonal key of his design, thus intensifying the brightness value of his lightest pigment colours.

The Greco-Roman, Renaissance, and Neoclassical method of representing volume and space in painting was by a system of notated tonal values, the direction of each plane in the design being indicated by a particular degree of lightness or darkness. Each tonal value was determined by the angle at which a plane was meant to appear to turn away from an imaginary source of light. The tonal modelling, or shading, of forms was often first completed in a monochrome underpainting. This was then coloured with transparent washes of local hues, a technique similar to that of colour tinting a black-and-white photograph (Figure 3).

Each hue has an intrinsic tonal value in relation to others on the chromatic scale; orange is inherently lighter than red, for instance, and violet is darker than green (Figure 2). Any reversal of this natural tonal order creates a colour discord. An optical shock is therefore produced when orange is juxtaposed with pink (a lighter tone of red) or pale violet is placed against dark green. Such contrasts as these are deliberately created in paintings for the purpose of achieving these dramatic and disturbing effects.

The intensity of a colour is its degree of purity or hue saturation. The colour of a geranium, therefore, is said to be more intense, more highly saturated with pure orange-red than is mahogany. The pigment vermilion is orange-red at maximum intensity; the brown earth pigment burnt sienna is grayer and has a lower degree of orange-red saturation.

Intense hues are termed chromatic colours. The achromatic range is made up of hues reduced in intensity by the addition of white, making the tints, or pastel colours, such as cream and pink; or of black, producing the shades, or earth colours, such as mustard and moss green; or of both white and black, creating the neutralized hues, or colour-tinged grays, such as oatmeal and charcoal.

An achromatic colour will seem more intense if it is surrounded by neutralized hues or juxtaposed with its complementary colour. Complementaries are colour opposites. The complementary colour to one of the primary hues is the mixture of the other two; the complementary to red pigment, for example, is green—that is, blue mixed with yellow. The colour wheel (Figure 2) shows that the tertiaries also have their colour opposites, the complementary to orange-red, for instance, being blue-green. Under clear light the complementary to any chroma, shade, or tint can be seen if one "fixates," or stares at, one colour intently for a few seconds then looks at a neutral, preferably white, surface. The colour afterimage will appear to glow on the neutral surface (Figure 4). Mutual enhancement

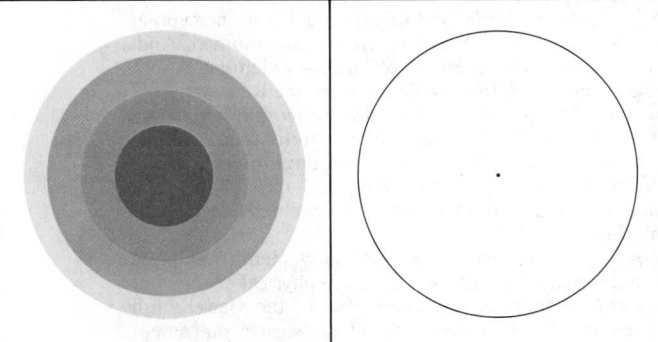

Figure 4: Coloured afterimages: if a person stares for about 30 seconds at the coloured disk under a clear light and then fixes upon the empty space of the adjacent circle, coloured afterimages will appear.

Enhance-
ment of
colour
intensity

of colour intensity results from juxtaposing a complementary pair, red becoming more intensely red, for instance, and green more fiercely green when these are contiguous than either would appear if surrounded by harmonious hues. The 19th-century physicist Michel-Eugène Chevreul referred to this mutual exaltation of opposites as the law of simultaneous contrast. Chevreul's second law, of successive contrast, referred to the optical sensation that a complementary colour halo appears gradually to surround an intense hue. This complementary glow is superimposed on surrounding weaker colours, a gray becoming greenish when juxtaposed with red, reddish in close relationship with green, yellowish against violet, and so on (Figure 5).

Hues containing a high proportion of blue (the violet to green range) appear cooler than those with a high content of yellow or red (the green-yellow to red-violet range). This difference in the temperature of hues in a particular painting is, of course, relative to the range and juxtaposition of colours in the design. A green will appear cool if surrounded by intense yellow, while it will seem warm against blue-green (Figure 5). The optical tendency for warm colours to advance before cold had been long exploited by European and Oriental painters as a method of suggesting spatial depth. Changes in temperature and intensity can be observed in the atmospheric effects of nature, where the colours of distant forms become cooler, grayer, and bluish, while foreground planes and features appear more intense and usually warmer in colour.

The apparent changes in a hue as it passes through zones of different colour has enabled painters in many periods to create the illusion of having employed a wide range of pigment hues with, in fact, the use of very few. And, although painters had applied many of the optical principles of colour behaviour intuitively in the past, the publication of research findings by Chevreul and others stimulated the Neo-Impressionists and Post-Impressionists and the later Orphist and Op Art painters to extend systematically the expressive possibilities of these principles in order to create illusions of volume and space and vibrating sensations of light and movement. Paul Cézanne, for example, demonstrated that subtle changes in the surface of a form and in its spatial relationship to others could be expressed primarily in facets of colour, modulated by varying degrees of tone, intensity, and temperature and by the introduction of complementary colour accents.

While the often-complex religious and cultural colour symbologies may be understood by very few, the emotional response to certain colour combinations appears to

be almost universal. Optical harmonies and discords seem to affect everyone in the same way, if in varying degrees. Thus, an image repeated in different schemes of colour will express a different mood in each change (Figure 6).

Texture. Pointillism was a term given to the Neo-Impressionist system of representing the shimmer of atmospheric light with spots of coloured pigment. This technique produced an overall granular texture. As an element of design, texture includes all areas of a painting enriched or animated by vibrating patterns of lines, shapes, tones, and colours, in addition to the tactile textures created by the plastic qualities of certain mediums. Decorative textures may be of geometrical repeat patterns, as in much of Indian, Islāmic, and medieval European painting and other art, or of representations of patterns in nature, such as scattered leaves, falling snow, and flights of birds.

Volume and space. The perceptual and conceptual methods of representing volume and space on the flat surface of a painting are related to the two levels of understanding spatial relationships in everyday life.

Perceptual space is the view of things at a particular time and from a fixed position. This is the stationary window view recorded by the camera and represented in the later periods of ancient Greek and Roman paintings and in most Western schools of painting since the Renaissance. Illusions of perceptual space are generally created by use of the linear perspectival system, based on the observations that objects appear to the eye to shrink and parallel lines and planes to converge as they approach the horizon, or viewer's eye level (Figure 7).

Young children and primitive artists, however, do not understand space in this way and represent it conceptually. Their paintings, therefore, show objects and surroundings independently of one another and from the views that best present their most characteristic features. The notion of scale in their pictures is also subjective, the relative size of things being decided by the artist either by their degree of emotional significance for him or by their narrative importance in the picture (interest perspective).

The conceptual, polydimensional representation of space has been used at some period in most cultures. In much of ancient Egyptian and Cretan painting, for example, the head and legs of a figure were shown in profile, but the eye and torso were drawn frontally. And in Indian,

Perceptual
and
conceptual
levels of
under-
standing
spatial
relation-
ships

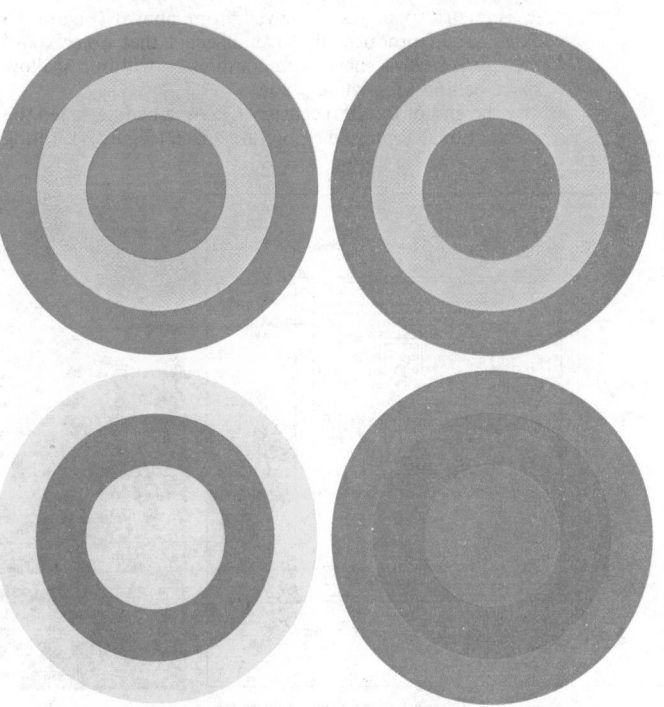

Figure 5: *Optical colour change.*
(Top) By complementary action, the same gray pigment will appear greenish when adjacent to red but reddish if adjacent to green. (Bottom) A green hue will seem cool if surrounded by yellow but warm when surrounded by blue-green.

Figure 6: Emotive colour relationships: an identical pattern of shapes may express a different emotional mood through each colour variation.

Islāmic, and pre-Renaissance European painting, vertical forms and surfaces were represented by their most informative elevation view (as if seen from ground level), while the horizontal planes on which they stood were shown in isometric plan (as if viewed from above) (Figure 7). This system produces the overall effect that objects and their surroundings have been compressed within a shallow space behind the picture plane.

By the end of the 19th century Cézanne had flattened the conventional Renaissance picture space (Figure 7), tilting horizontal planes so that they appeared to push vertical forms and surfaces forward from the picture plane and toward the spectator (Figure 8). This illusion of the picture surface as an integrated structure in projecting low relief was developed further in the early 20th century by the Cubists. The conceptual, rotary perspective of a Cubist painting shows not only the components of things from different viewpoints but presents every plane of an object and its immediate surroundings simultaneously. This gives the composite impression of things in space that is gained by having examined their surfaces and construction from every angle.

In modern painting, both conceptual and perceptual methods of representing space are often combined. And, where the orbital movement of forms—which has been a basic element in European design since the Renaissance—was intended to hold the spectator's attention within the frame (Figure 7), the expanding picture space in late 20th-century mural-size abstract paintings directs the eye outward to the surrounding wall, and their shapes and colours seem about to invade the observer's own territory (Figure 9).

Time and movement. Time and movement in painting are not restricted to representations of physical energy, but they are elements of all design. Part of the viewer's full experience of a great painting is to allow the arrangement of lines, shapes, and accents of tone or colour to guide the eye across the picture surface at controlled tempos and rhythmic directions. These arrangements contribute overall to the expression of a particular mood, vision, and idea.

Centuries before cinematography, painters attempted to produce kinetic sensations on a flat surface. A mural of 2000 BC in an Egyptian tomb at Beni Hasan, for instance, is designed as a continuous strip sequence of wrestling holds and throws, so accurately articulated and notated that it might be photographed as an animated film cartoon. The gradual unrolling of a 12th-century Japanese hand scroll produces the visual sensation of a helicopter flight along a river valley, while the experience of walking to the end of a long, processional Renaissance mural by Andrea Mantegna or Benozzo Gozzoli is similar to that of having witnessed a passing pageant as a standing spectator.

In the Eastern and Western narrative convention of continuous representation, various incidents in a story were depicted together within one design, the chief characters in the drama easily identified as they reappeared in different situations and settings throughout the painting. In Byzantine murals and in Indian and medieval manuscript paintings, narrative sequences were depicted in grid patterns, each "compartment" of the design representing a

Kinetic sensations on a flat surface

Figure 7: *Perceptual and conceptual space.*
(Left) Perceptual space: the illusion of an interior space as it might be recorded by a camera and as it is represented by the optical laws of Renaissance perspective. (Centre) Example based on Jan Vermeer's oil painting "The Music Lesson," *c.* 1660. In Buckingham Palace, London. 74 cm × 64 cm. (Right) Conceptual space: how the same subject might be represented by polydimensional and "interest" perspectival systems.

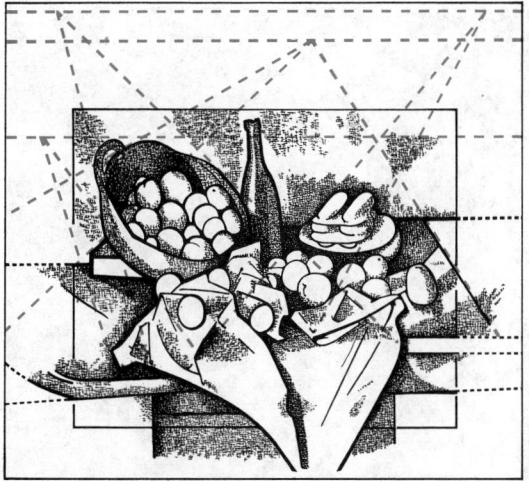 

Figure 8: *Simultaneous viewpoints.*
(Left) Paul Cézanne's method of representing things in a painting as if seen from different directions and at varying eye levels over a period of time. In contrast to the receding planes of Vermeer's design (Figure 7), the illusion is created, by tone and colour contrasts, that planes and forms are advancing toward the spectator. (Right) Example based on Cézanne's oil painting "The Basket of Apples," 1890–94. In the Art Institute of Chicago. 65 cm × 81 cm.

visual chapter in a religious story or a mythological or historical epic.

The Cubists aimed to give the viewer the time experience of moving around static forms in order to examine their volume and structure and their relationships to the space surrounding them. In paintings such as "Nude Descending a Staircase," "Girl Running on a Balcony," and "Dog on Leash," Marcel Duchamp and Giacomo Balla combined the Cubist technique of projected, interlocking planes with the superimposed time-motion sequences of cinematography. This technique enabled the artists to analyze the structural mechanics of forms, which are represented as moving in space past the viewer.

Principles of design. Because painting is a two-dimensional art, the flat pattern of lines and shapes is an important aspect of design, even for those painters concerned with creating illusions of great depth. And, since any mark made on the painting surface can be perceived as a spatial statement—for it rests upon it—there are also qualities of three-dimensional design in paintings composed primarily of flat shapes. Shapes in a painting, therefore, may be balanced with one another as units of a flat pattern and considered at the same time as components in a spatial design, balanced one behind another. A symmetrical balance of tone and colour masses of equal weight creates a serene and sometimes monumental design, while a more dynamic effect is created by an asymmetrical balance.

Geometrical shapes and masses are often the basic units in the design of both "flat patterns," such as Byzantine and Islâmic paintings, and "sculptural compositions," such as Baroque and Neoclassical figure tableaux. The flat, overlapping squares, circles, and triangles that create the pattern of a Romanesque mural, for example, become the interlocking cubic, spherical, and pyramidal components that enclose the grouped figures and surrounding features in a Renaissance or a Neoclassical composition (Figure 10).

An emphasis upon the proportion of the parts to the whole is a characteristic of Classical styles of painting. The Golden Mean, or Section, has been used as an ideal proportion on which to base the framework of lines and shapes in the design of a painting. The Renaissance mathematician Lucas Pacioli defined this aesthetically satisfying ratio as the division of a line so that the shorter part is to the longer as the longer is to the whole (approximately 8 to 13). His treatise (*Divina proportione*) influenced Leonardo da Vinci and Albrecht Dürer. The Neo-Impressionists Georges Seurat (Figure 1) and Paul Signac based the linear pattern of many of their compositions upon the principle of this "divine proportion." Golden Mean proportions can be discovered in the design of many other styles of paint-

ing, although often they may have been created more by intuitive judgment than by calculated measurement.

Tension is created in paintings, as it is experienced in everyday life, by the anticipation of an event or by an unexpected change in the order of things. Optical and psychological tensions occur in passages of a design, therefore, when lines or shapes almost touch or seem about to collide, when a harmonious colour progression is interrupted by a sudden discord, or when an asymmetrical balance of lines, shapes, tones, or colours is barely held.

Tension in paintings

Contrasts in line, shape, tone, and colour create vitality; rectilinear shapes played against curvilinear, for instance, or warm colours against cool. Or a painting may be composed in contrasted overall patterns, superimposed in counterpoint to one another—a colour scheme laid across contrasting patterns of lines and tones, for example (Figure 11).

Design relationships between painting and other visual arts. The philosophy and spirit of a particular period in painting usually have been reflected in many of its other visual arts. The ideas and aspirations of the ancient cultures, of the Renaissance, Baroque, Rococo, and Neoclassical periods of Western art and, more recently, of the 19th-century Art Nouveau and Secessionist movements were expressed in much of the architecture, interior design, furniture, textiles, ceramics, dress design, and handicrafts, as well as in the fine arts, of their times. Following the Industrial Revolution, with the redundancy of handcraft-

Figure 9: Opening out the picture space: the movement of shapes in Morris Louis' acrylic painting "Alpha-Phi," 1961, directs the spectator's eye outside the picture surface. In the Tate Gallery, London. 2.59 m × 4.58 m. In contrast, Vermeer's design (Figure 7) is contrived to hold the spectator's attention within the frame.

Figure 10: *Principles of design.*
(Left) The flat pattern design of the anonymous Spanish panel painting "Virgin and Child,"
12th century. In the Museo Arqueológico Artístico Episcopal, Vich, Spain. (Right) The
three-dimensional design of interlocking pyramids of Andrea del Sarto's panel painting
"Madonna of the Harpies," 1517. In the Uffizi, Florence. 2.07 m × 1.78 m.

(Left) Archivo Mas, Barcelona, (right) SCALA—Art Resource

manship and the loss of direct communication between
the fine artist and society, idealistic efforts to unite the
arts and crafts in service to the community were made
by William Morris in Victorian England and by the
Bauhaus in 20th-century Germany. Although their aims
were not fully realized, their influences, like those of the
short-lived de Stijl and Constructivist movements, have
been far-reaching, particularly in architectural, furniture,
and typographic design.

Michelangelo and Leonardo da Vinci were painters,
sculptors, and architects. Although no artists since have
excelled in so wide a range of creative design, leading 20th-
century painters have expressed their ideas in many other
mediums. In graphic design, for example, Pierre Bonnard,
Henri Matisse, and Raoul Dufy produced posters and illustrated books; André Derain, Fernand Léger, Marc Chagall, Mikhail Larionov, Robert Rauschenberg, and David
Hockney designed for the theatre; Joan Miró, Georges
Braque, and Chagall worked in ceramics; Braque and
Salvador Dalí designed jewelry; and Dalí, Hans Richter,
and Andy Warhol made films. Many of these, with other
modern painters, have also been sculptors and printmak-
ers and have designed for textiles, tapestries, mosaics, and
stained glass, while there are few mediums of the visual
arts that Pablo Picasso did not work in and revitalize.

In turn, painters have been stimulated by the imagery,
techniques, and design of other visual arts. One of the
earliest of these influences was possibly from the theatre,
where the ancient Greeks are thought to have been the
first to employ the illusions of optical perspective. The
discovery or reappraisal of design techniques and imagery in the art forms and processes of other cultures
has been an important stimulus to the development of
more recent styles of Western painting, whether or not
their traditional significance have been fully understood.
The influence of Japanese woodcut prints on Synthetism
and the Nabis, for example, and of African sculpture on
Cubism and the German Expressionists helped to create
visual vocabularies and syntax with which to express new
visions and ideas. The invention of photography introduced painters to new aspects of nature, while eventually
prompting others to abandon representational painting altogether. Painters of everyday life, such as Edgar Degas,

*Influence
of photog-
raphy*

Henri de Toulouse-Lautrec, Édouard Vuillard, and Bonnard, exploited the design innovations of camera cutoffs,
close-ups, and unconventional viewpoints in order to give
the spectator the sensation of sharing an intimate picture
space with the figures and objects in the painting.

TECHNIQUES AND METHODS

Whether a painting reached completion by careful stages or
was executed directly by a hit-or-miss alla prima method
(in which pigments are laid on in a single application)
was once largely determined by the ideals and established
techniques of its cultural tradition. For example, the medieval European illuminator's painstaking procedure, by
which a complex linear pattern was gradually enriched
with gold leaf and precious pigments, was contemporary
with the Sung Chinese Zen practice of immediate, calligraphic brush painting, following a contemplative period
of spiritual self-preparation. More recently, the artist has
decided the technique and working method best suited to
his aims and temperament. In France in the 1880s, for
instance, Seurat might be working in his studio on drawings, tone studies, and colour schemes in preparation for a
large composition at the same time that, outdoors, Monet
was endeavouring to capture the effects of afternoon light
and atmosphere, while Cézanne analyzed the structure of
the Montagne (mountain) Sainte-Victoire with deliberated
brush strokes, laid as irrevocably as mosaic tesserae (small
pieces, such as marble or tile).

The kind of relationship established between artist and
patron, the site and subject matter of a painting commission, and the physical properties of the medium employed
may also dictate working procedure. Peter Paul Rubens,
for example, followed the businesslike 17th-century custom of submitting a small oil sketch, or *modella,* for his
client's approval before carrying out a large-scale commission. Siting problems peculiar to mural painting, such as
spectator eye level and the scale, style, and function of
a building interior, had first to be solved in preparatory
drawings and sometimes with the use of wax figurines or
scale models of the interior. Scale working drawings are essential to the speed and precision of execution demanded
by quick-drying mediums, such as buon' fresco (see below *Mediums: Fresco*) on wet plaster and acrylic resin

Figure 11: *Visual counterpoint in design.*
(Left) Linear arabesques drawn across (centre) patterns of tone and colour. (Right) Example
based on Henri de Toulouse-Lautrec's oil paint on cardboard painting "At the Nouveau
Cirque: Five Stuffed Shirts," 1891. In the Philadelphia Museum of Art. 119 cm × 87 cm.
(Right) By courtesy of the Philadelphia Museum of Art, John D. McIlhenny Fund

Preservation of a painting

on canvas. The drawings traditionally are covered with a network of squares, or "squared-up," for enlarging on the surface of the support. Some modern painters prefer to outline the enlargement of a sketch projected directly onto the support by epidiascope (a projector for images of both opaque and transparent objects).

In Renaissance painters' workshops, pupil assistants not only ground and mixed the pigments and prepared the supports and painting surfaces but often laid in the outlines and broad masses of the painting from the master's design and studies.

The inherent properties of its medium or the atmospheric conditions of its site may themselves preserve a painting. The wax solvent binder of encaustic paintings (in which after application, the paint is fixed by heat [see below *Mediums*], for example) both retains the intensity and tonality of the original colours and protects the surface from damp. And, while prehistoric rock paintings and buon' frescoes are preserved by natural chemical action, the tempera pigments thought to be bound only with water on many ancient Egyptian murals are protected by the dry atmosphere and unvarying temperature of the tombs. It has, however, been customary to varnish oil paintings, both to protect the surface against damage by dirt and handling and to restore the tonality lost when some darker pigments dry out into a higher key. Unfortunately, varnish tends to darken and yellow with time into the sometimes disastrously imitated "Old Masters' mellow patina." Once cherished, this amber-gravy film is now generally removed to reveal the colours in their original intensity. Glass began to replace varnish toward the end of the 19th century, when painters wished to retain the fresh, luminous finish of pigments applied directly to a pure white ground. The air-conditioning and temperature-control systems of modern museums make both varnishing and glazing unnecessary, except for older and more fragile exhibits.

The frames surrounding early altarpieces, icons, and cassone panels (painted panels on the chest used for a bride's household linen) were often structural parts of the support. With the introduction of portable easel pictures, heavy frames not only provided some protection against theft and damage but were considered an aesthetic enhancement to a painting, and frame making became a specialized craft. Gilded gesso moldings (consisting of plaster of paris and sizing that forms the surface for low relief) in extravagant swags of fruit and flowers certainly seem almost an extension of the restless, exuberant design of a Baroque or Rococo painting. A substantial frame also provided a proscenium (in a theatre, the area between the orchestra and the curtain) in which the picture was isolated from its immediate surroundings, thus adding to the window view illusion intended by the artist. Deep, ornate frames are

unsuitable for many modern paintings, where the artist's intention is for his forms to appear to advance toward the spectator rather than be viewed by him as if through a wall aperture. In contemporary Minimal paintings, no effects of spatial illusionism are intended; and, in order to emphasize the physical shape of the support itself and to stress its flatness, these abstract, geometrical designs are displayed without frames or are merely edged with thin protective strips of wood or metal.

MEDIUMS

By technical definition, mediums are the liquids added to paints to bind them and make them workable. They are discussed here, however, in the wider meaning of all the various paints, tools, supports, surfaces, and techniques employed by painters. The basis of all paints is variously coloured pigment, ground to a fine powder. The different expressive capacities and characteristic final surface texture of each medium are determined by the vehicle with which it is bound and thinned, the nature and surface preparation of the support, and the tools and technique with which it is handled.

Pigments are derived from various natural and artificial sources. The oldest and most permanent pigments are the blacks, prepared from bone and charcoal, and the clay earths, such as raw umber and raw sienna, which can be changed by heating into darker, warmer browns. In early periods of painting, readily available pigments were few. Certain intense hues were obtainable only from the rarer minerals, such as cinnabar (orange-red vermilion), lapis lazuli (violet-blue ultramarine), and malachite (green). These were expensive and therefore reserved for focal accents and important symbolic features in the design. The opening of trade routes and the manufacture of synthetic substitutes gradually extended the range of colours available to painters.

Sources of pigments

Tempera. A tempera medium is dry pigment tempered with an emulsion and thinned with water. It is a very ancient medium, having been in constant use in most world cultures, until in Europe it was gradually superseded, during the Renaissance, by oil paints. Tempera was the original mural medium in the ancient dynasties of Egypt, Babylonia, Mycenean Greece, and China and was used to decorate the early Christian catacombs. It was employed on a variety of supports, from the stone stelae (or commemorative pillars), mummy cases, and papyrus rolls of ancient Egypt to the wood panels of Byzantine icons and altarpieces and the vellum leaves of medieval illuminated manuscripts.

True tempera is made by mixture with the yolk of fresh eggs, although manuscript illuminators often used egg white and some easel painters added the whole egg.

Other emulsions have been used, such as casein glue with linseed oil, egg yolk with gum and linseed oil, and egg white with linseed or poppy oil. Individual painters have experimented with other recipes, but few of these have proved successful; all but William Blake's later tempera paintings on copper sheets, for instance, have darkened and decayed, and it is thought that he mixed his pigment with carpenter's glue.

Distemper is a crude form of tempera made by mixing dry pigment into a paste with water, which is thinned with heated glue in working or by adding pigment to whiting, a mixture of fine-ground chalk and size. It is used for stage scenery and full-size preparatory cartoons for murals and tapestries. When dry, its colours have the pale, mat, powdery quality of pastels, with a similar tendency to smudge. Indeed, damaged cartoons have been retouched with pastel chalks.

Egg tempera is the most durable form of the medium, being generally unaffected by humidity and temperature. It dries quickly to form a tough film that acts as a protective skin to the support. In handling, in its diversity of transparent and opaque effects, and in the satin sheen of its finish, it resembles the modern acrylic resin emulsion paints.

Traditional process of tempera painting Traditional tempera painting is a lengthy process. Its supports are smooth surfaces, such as planed wood, fine set plaster, stone, paper, vellum, canvas, and modern composition boards of compressed wood or paper. Linen is generally glued to the surface of panel supports, additional strips masking the seams between braced wood planks. Gesso, a mixture of plaster of paris (or gypsum) with size, is the traditional ground. The first layer is of gesso grosso, a mixture of coarse, unslaked plaster and size. This provides a rough, absorbent surface for ten or more thin coats of gesso sotile, a smooth mixture of size and fine plaster previously slaked in water to retard drying. This laborious preparation results, however, in an opaque, brilliant white, light-reflecting surface, similar in texture to hard, flat icing sugar.

The design for a large tempera painting traditionally was executed in distemper on a thick paper cartoon. The outlines were pricked with a perforating wheel so that when the cartoon was laid on the surface of the support, the linear pattern was transferred by dabbing, or "pouncing," the perforations with a muslin bag of powdered charcoal. The dotted contours traced through were then fixed in paint. Medieval tempera painters of panels and manuscripts made lavish use of gold leaf on backgrounds and for symbolic features, such as haloes and beams of heavenly light. Areas of the pounced design intended for gilding were first built up into low relief with gesso duro, the harder, less absorbent gesso compound used also for elaborate frame moldings. Background fields were often textured by impressing the gesso duro, before it set, with small, carved, intaglio wood blocks to create raised, pimpled, and quilted repeat patterns that glittered when gilded. Leaves of finely beaten gold were pressed onto a tacky mordant (adhesive compound) or over wet bole (reddish-brown earth pigment) that gave greater warmth and depth when the gilded areas were burnished.

Colours were applied with sable brushes in successive broad sweeps or washes of semitransparent tempera. These dried quickly, preventing the subtle tonal gradations possible with watercolour washes or oil paint; effects of shaded modelling had therefore to be obtained by a crosshatching technique of fine brush strokes. According to the Italian painter Cennino Cennini, the early Renaissance tempera painters laid the colour washes across a fully modelled monochrome underpainting in terre vert (olive-green pigment), a method developed later into the mixed mediums technique of tempera underpainting followed by transparent oil glazes.

The luminous gesso base of a tempera painting, combined with the accumulative effect of overlaid colour washes, produces a unique depth and intensity of colour. Tempera paints dry lighter in value, but their original tonality can be restored by subsequent waxing or varnishing. Other characteristic qualities of a tempera painting, resulting from its fast drying property and disciplined technique,

are its steely lines and crisp edges, its meticulous detail and rich linear textures, and its overall emphasis upon a decorative flat pattern of bold colour masses.

The great Byzantine tradition of tempera painting was developed in Italy in the 13th and 14th centuries by Duccio di Buoninsegna and Giotto. Their flattened picture space, generously enriched by fields and textures of gold leaf, was extended by the Renaissance depth perspectives in the paintings of Giovanni Bellini, Piero della Francesca, Carlo Crivelli, Sandro Botticelli, and Vittore Carpaccio. By that time, oil painting was already challenging the primacy of tempera, Botticelli and some of his contemporaries apparently adding oil to the tempera emulsion or overglazing it in oil colour.

Following the supremacy of the oil medium during succeeding periods of Western painting, the 20th century saw a revival of tempera techniques by such U.S. artists as Ben Shahn, Andrew Wyeth, and George McNeil and by the British painter Edward Wadsworth. It would probably have been the medium also of the later hard-edge abstract painters had the new acrylic resin paints not proved more easily and quickly handled. 20th-century revival of tempera techniques

Fresco. Fresco (Italian: "fresh") is the traditional medium for painting directly onto a wall or ceiling. It is the oldest known painting medium, surviving in the prehistoric cave mural decorations and perfected in 16th-century Italy in the buon' fresco method.

The cave paintings are thought to date from about 20,000–15,000 BC. Their pigments probably have been preserved by a natural sinter process of rainwater seeping through the limestone rocks to produce saturated bicarbonate. The colours were rubbed across rock walls and ceilings with sharpened solid lumps of the natural earths (yellow, red, and brown ochre). Outlines were drawn with black sticks of wood charcoal. The discovery of mixing dishes suggests that liquid pigment mixed with fat was also used and smeared with the hand. The subtle tonal gradations of colour on animals painted in the Altamira and Lascaux caves appear to have been dabbed in two stages with fur pads, natural variations on the rock surface being exploited to assist in creating effects of volume. Feathers and frayed twigs may have been used in painting manes and tails.

These were not composite designs but separate scenes and individual studies that, like graffiti drawings, were added at different times, often one above another, by various artists. Paintings from the Magdalenian period (c. 10,000 BC) exhibit astonishing powers of accurate observation and ability to represent movement. Women, warriors, horses, bison, bulls, boars, and ibex are depicted in scenes of ritual ceremony, battle, and hunting. Among the earliest images are imprinted and stencilled hands. Vigorous meanders, or "macaroni" linear designs, were traced with fingers dipped in liquid pigment.

Fresco secco. In the fresco secco, or lime-painting, method, the plastered surface of a wall is soaked with slaked lime. Lime-resistant pigments are applied swiftly before the plaster sets. Secco colours dry lighter than their tone at the time of application, producing the pale, mat, chalky quality of a distempered wall. Although the pigments are fused with the surface, they are not completely absorbed and may flake in time, as in sections of Giotto's 14th-century S. Francesco murals at Assisi. Secco painting was the prevailing medieval and early Renaissance medium and was revived in 18th-century Europe by artists such as Giovanni Battista Tiepolo, François Boucher, and Jean-Honoré Fragonard.

Buon' fresco. Buon', or "true," fresco is the most durable method of painting murals, since the pigments are completely fused with a damp plaster ground to become an integral part of the wall surface. The stone or brick wall is first prepared with a brown trullisatio scratch coat, or rough-cast plaster layer. This is then covered by the arricciato coat, on which the linear design of the preparatory cartoon is pounced (see above *Tempera*) or engraved by impressing the outlines into the moist, soft plaster with a bone or metal stylus. These lines were usually overworked in reddish sinopia pigment. A thin layer of fine plaster is then evenly spread, allowing the linear design to show Arricciato coat through. Before this final intonaco ground sets, pigments thinned with water or slaked lime are applied rapidly with calf-hair and hog-bristle brushes; depth of colour is achieved by a succession of quick-drying glazes. Being prepared with slaked lime, the plaster becomes saturated with an aqueous solution of hydrate of lime, which takes up carbonic acid from the air as it soaks into the paint. Carbonate of lime is produced and acts as a permanent pigment binder. Pigment particles crystallize in the plaster, fusing it with the surface to produce the characteristic lustre of buon' fresco colours. When dry, these are mat and lighter in tone. Colours are restricted to the range of lime-resistant earth pigments. Mineral colours such as blue, affected by lime, are applied over earth pigment when the plaster is dry.

The intonaco coat is laid only across an area sufficient for painting before the plaster sets. The joins between each successive "day piece" are sometimes visible. Alterations must be made by immediate washing or scraping; minor retouching to set plaster is possible with casein or egg tempera, but major corrections necessitate breaking away the intonaco and replastering. The swift execution demanded stimulates bold designs in broad masses of colour with a calligraphic vitality of brush marks.

No ancient Greek buon' frescoes now exist, but forms of the technique survive in the Pompeian villas of the 1st century AD and earlier, in Chinese tombs at Liao-yang, Manchuria, and in the 6th-century Indian caves at Ajantā. Among the finest buon' fresco murals are those by Michelangelo in the Sistine Chapel and by Raphael in the Stanze of the Vatican. Other notable examples from the Italian Renaissance can be seen in Florence: painted by Andrea Orcagna in the Museo dell'Opera di Sta. Croce, by Gozzoli in the chapel of the Palazzo Medici-Riccardi, and by Domenico Ghirlandajo in the church of Sta. Maria Novella. Buon' fresco painting is unsuited to the damp, cold climate of northern countries, and there is now some concern for the preservation of frescoes in the sulfurous atmosphere of even many southern cities. Buon' fresco was successfully revived by the Mexican mural painters Diego Rivera, José Orozco, and Rufino Tamayo.

Sgraffito. Sgraffito (Italian *graffiare*, "to scratch") is a form of fresco painting for exterior walls. A rough plaster undercoat is followed by thin plaster layers, each stained with a different lime-fast colour. These coats are covered by a fine-grain mortar finishing surface. The plaster is then engraved with knives and gouges at different levels to reveal the various coloured layers beneath. The sintered-lime process binds the colours. The surface of modern sgraffito frescoes is often enriched with textures made by impressing nails and machine parts, combined with mosaics of stone, glass, plastic, and metal tesserae.

Sgraffito has been a traditional folk art in Europe since the Middle Ages and was practiced as a fine art in 13th-century Germany. It has been recently revived in northern Europe.

Oil. Oil paints are made by mixing dry pigment powder with refined linseed oil to a paste, which is then milled in order to disperse the pigment particles throughout the oil vehicle. According to the 1st-century Roman scholar Pliny the Elder, whose writings the Flemish painters Hubert and Jan van Eyck are thought to have studied, the Romans used oil colours for shield painting. The earliest use of oil as a fine-art medium is generally attributed to 15th-century European painters, such as Giovanni Bellini and the van Eycks, who glazed oil colour over a glue-tempera underpainting. It is also thought probable, however, that medieval manuscript illuminators had been using oil glazes in order to achieve greater depth of colour and more subtle tonal transitions than their tempera medium allowed.

Oils have been used on linen, burlap, cotton, wood, hide, rock, stone, concrete, paper, cardboard, aluminum, copper, plywood, and processed boards, such as masonite, pressed wood, and hardboard. The surface of rigid panels is traditionally prepared with gesso and that of canvas with one or more coats of white acrylic resin emulsion or with a coat of animal glue followed by thin layers of white-lead oil primer. Oil paints can be applied undiluted to these prepared surfaces or can be used thinned with

Earliest use as a fine-art medium

pure gum turpentine or its substitute, white mineral spirit. The colours are slow drying; the safest dryer to speed the process is cobalt siccative.

An oil glaze is a transparent wash of pigment, traditionally thinned with an oleoresin or with stand oil (a concentrate of linseed oil). Glazes can be used to create deep, glowing shadows and to bring contrasted colours into closer harmony beneath a unifying tinted film. Scumbling is the technique of scrubbing an undiluted, opaque, and generally pale pigment across others for special textural effects or to raise the key of a dark-coloured area.

Hog-bristle brushes are used for much of the painting, with pointed, red sable-hair brushes generally preferred for outlines and fine details. Oils, however, are the most plastic and responsive of all painting mediums and can be handled with all manner of tools. The later works of Titian and Rembrandt, for example, appear to have been executed with thumbs, fingers, rags, spatulas, and brush handles. With these and other unconventional tools and techniques, oil painters create pigment textures ranging from delicate tonal modulations to unvarying, mechanical finishes and from clotted, impasto ridges of paint to barely perceptible stains.

The tempera-underpainting-oil-glaze technique was practiced into the 17th century. Artists such as Titian, El Greco, Rubens, and Diego Velázquez, however, used oil pigments alone and, employing a method similar to pastel painting, applied them directly to the brownish ground with which they had tinted the white priming. Contours and shadows were stained in streaks and washes of diluted paint, while lighter areas were created with dry, opaque scumbles, the tinted ground meanwhile providing the halftones and often remaining untouched for passages of local or reflected colour in the completed picture. This use of oil paint was particularly suited to expressing atmospheric effects and to creating chiaroscuro, or light and dark, patterns. It also encouraged a bravura handling of paint, where stabs, flourishes, lifts, and pressures of the brush economically described the most subtle changes of form, texture, and colour according to the influence exerted by the tinted ground through the varying thicknesses of overlaid pigment. This method was still practiced by the 19th-century painters, such as John Constable, J.M.W. Turner, Eugène Delacroix, and Honoré Daumier. The Impressionists, however, found the luminosity of a brilliant white ground essential to the alla prima technique with which they represented the colour intensities and shifting lights of their plein air (open air) subjects. Most oil paintings since then have been executed on white surfaces.

The rapid deterioration of Leonardo's 15th-century "Last Supper," which was painted in oils on plaster, possibly deterred artists from using the medium directly on a wall surface. And the likelihood of eventual warping also prohibited using the large number of braced wood panels required to make an alternative support for an extensive mural painting in oils. Canvas, however, can be woven to any length, and, since an oil-painted surface is elastic, mural paintings could be executed in the studio and rolled and restretched on a wooden framework at the site or marouflaged (fastened with an adhesive) directly onto the wall surface. In addition to the immense studio canvases painted for particular sites by artists such as Jacopo Tintoretto, Paolo Veronese, Delacroix, Pierre-Cécile Puvis de Chavannes, and Monet, the use of canvas has made it possible for mural-size, modern oil paintings to be transported for exhibition to all parts of the world.

The tractable nature of the oil medium has sometimes encouraged slipshod craftsmanship. Working over partly dry pigment or priming may produce a wrinkled surface. The excessive use of oil as a vehicle causes colours to yellow and darken, while cracking, blooming, powdering, and flaking can result from poor priming, overthinning with turpentine, or the use of varnish dryers and other spirits. Colour changes may also occur through the use of chemically incompatible pigment mixtures or from the fading of fugitive synthetic hues, such as the crimson lakes used by Pierre-Auguste Renoir.

Watercolour. Watercolours are pigments ground with gum arabic and gall and thinned with water in use. Sable

Deterioration of Leonardo's "Last Supper"

and squirrel ("camel") hair brushes are used on white or tinted paper and card.

Three hundred years before the late 18th-century English watercolourists, Albrecht Dürer had anticipated their technique of transparent colour washes in a remarkable series of plant studies and panoramic landscapes. Until the emergence of the English school, however, watercolour became a medium merely for colour tinting outlined drawings or, combined with opaque body colour to produce effects similar to gouache (see below) or tempera, was used in preparatory studies for oil paintings.

The chief exponents of the English method were Thomas Girtin, John Sell Cotman, John Robert Cozens, Richard Parkes Bonington, David Cox, and Constable. Their contemporary J.M.W. Turner, however, true to his unorthodox genius, added white to his watercolour and used rags, sponges, and knives to obtain unique effects of light and texture. Victorian watercolourists, such as Birket Foster, used a laborious method of colour washing a monochrome underpainting, similar in principle to the tempera-oil technique. Following the direct, vigorous watercolours of the French Impressionists and Postimpressionists, however, the medium was established in Europe and America as an expressive picture medium in its own right. Notable 20th-century watercolourists have been Wassily Kandinsky, Paul Klee, Dufy, and Georges Rouault; the U.S. artists Thomas Eakins, Maurice Prendergast, Charles Burchfield, John Marin, Lyonel Feininger, and Jim Dine; and the English painters John and Paul Nash, Eric Ravilious, Edward Bawden, Edward Burra, and Patrick Procktor.

The "pure" water-colour technique

In the "pure" watercolour technique, often referred to as the English method, no white or other opaque pigment is applied, colour intensity and tonal depth being built up by successive, transparent washes on damp paper. Patches of white paper are left unpainted to represent white objects and to create effects of reflected light. These flecks of bare paper produce the sparkle characteristic of pure watercolour. Tonal gradations and soft, atmospheric qualities are rendered by staining the paper when it is very wet with varying proportions of pigment. Sharp accents, lines, and coarse textures are introduced when the paper has dried. The paper should be of the type sold as "handmade from rags"; this is generally thick and grained. Cockling is avoided when the surface dries out if the dampened paper has been first stretched across a special frame or held in position during painting by an edging of adhesive tape.

Ink. Ink is the traditional painting medium of China and Japan, where it has been used with long-haired brushes of wolf, goat, or badger on silk or absorbent paper. Oriental black ink is a gum-bound carbon stick that is ground on rough stone and mixed with varying amounts of water to create a wide range of modulated tones or applied almost dry, with lightly brushed strokes, to produce coarser textures. The calligraphic brush technique is expressive of Zen Buddhist and Confucian philosophies, brush-stroke formulas for the spiritual interpretation of nature in painting dictating the use of the lifted brush tip for the "bone," or "lean," structure of things and the spreading belly of the hairs for their "flesh," or "fat," volumes. The Far Eastern artist poises the brush vertically above the paper and controls its rhythmic movements from the shoulder. Distant forms represented in landscapes painted on silk were sometimes brushed on from the reverse side.

In the Western world, ink has been used rather more for preparatory studies and topographical and literary illustrations than as a medium for easel paintings. Western artists have generally combined ink washes with contours and textures in quill or steel pen. Among the finest of these are by Rembrandt, Nicolas Poussin, Francisco Goya, Samuel Palmer, Constable, and Édouard Manet. Claude Lorrain, Turner, and Daumier and, in the 20th century, Braque, Picasso, Reginald Marsh, Henri Michaux, and John Piper are some of those who have exploited its unique qualities. Modern artists also use ballpoint and felt pens.

Gouache. Gouache is opaque watercolour, known also as poster paint and designer's colour. It is thinned with water for applying, with sable- and hog-hair brushes, to white or tinted paper and card and, occasionally, to silk. Honey, starch, or acrylic is sometimes added to retard its quick-drying property. Liquid glue is preferred as a thinner by painters wishing to retain the tonality of colours (which otherwise dry slightly lighter in key) and to prevent thick paint from flaking. Gouache paints have the advantages that they dry out almost immediately to a mat finish and, if required, without visible brush marks. These qualities, with the capacities to be washed thinly or applied in thick impasto and a wide colour range that now includes fluorescent and metallic pigments, make the medium particularly suited to preparatory studies for oil and acrylic paintings. It is the medium that produces the suede finish and crisp lines characteristic of many Indian and Islāmic miniatures, and it has been used in Western screen and fan decoration and by modern artists such as Rouault, Klee, Dubuffet, and Morris Graves.

Medium particularly suited to preparatory studies

Encaustic. Encaustic painting (from the Greek: "burnt in") was the ancient method, recorded by Pliny, of fixing pigments with heated wax. It was probably first practiced in Egypt about 3000 BC and is thought to have reached its peak in Classical Greece, although no examples from that period survive. Pigments, mixed with melted beeswax, were brushed onto stone or plaster, smoothed with a metal spatula, and then blended and driven into the wall with a heated iron. The surface was later polished with a cloth. Leonardo and others attempted unsuccessfully to revive the technique. North American Indians used an encaustic method whereby pigments mixed with hot animal fat were pressed into a design engraved on smoothed buffalo hide.

A simplified encaustic technique uses a spatula to apply wax mixed with solvent and pigment to wood or canvas, producing a ridged, impasto surface. This is an ancient and most durable medium. Coptic mummy portraits from the 1st and 2nd centuries AD retain the softly blended, translucent colouring typical of waxwork effigies. In the 19th century, Vincent van Gogh also used this method to give body to his oil pigment; the Neo-Impressionist artist Louis Hayet applied encaustic to paper, and it was used by the U.S. painter Jasper Johns for his Pop art canvases. Coloured wax crayons have also been used by modern painters such as Picasso, Klee, Arshile Gorky, and Hockney (see above *Mediums: Fresco*).

Casein. Casein, or "cheese painting," is a medium in which pigments are tempered with the gluey curd of cheese or milk precipitate. For handling, an emulsion of casein and lime is thinned with water. The active element of casein contains nitrogen, which forms a soluble caseate of calcium in the presence of lime. It is applied in thin washes to rigid surfaces, such as cardboard, wood, and plastered walls.

Casein colours dry quickly, although lighter in tone than when first applied. Since they have more body than egg-tempera paints, they can be applied with bristle brushes to create impasto textures not unlike those of oils. Casein paints were used in ancient Rome. They are now available ready-made in tubes and have been used by such modern artists as Robert Motherwell and Claes Oldenburg.

Casein is also an ingredient of some charcoal and pastel fixatives and was a traditional primer for walls and panels.

Synthetic mediums. Synthetic mediums, developed by industrial research, range from the Liquitex fabric dyes used on canvas by the U.S. abstract painter Larry Poons to the house enamel paints employed at times by Picasso and Jackson Pollock.

The most popular medium and the first to challenge the supremacy of oils is acrylic resin emulsion, since this plastic paint combines most of the expressive capabilities of oils with the quick-drying properties of tempera and gouache. It is made by mixing pigments with a synthetic resin and thinning with water. It can be applied to any sufficiently toothed surface with brush, roller, airbrush, spatula, sponge, or rag. Acrylic paints dry quickly, without brush marks, to form a mat, waterproof film that is also elastic, durable, and easily cleaned. They show little colour change in drying, nor do they darken in time. While they lack the surface textural richness of oil or encaustic, they can be built up with a spatula into opaque impastos or thinned immediately into transparent colour glazes. Polyvinyl acetate (PVA) is applied for priming, although it is claimed that acrylic paints can be safely applied directly

Acrylic resin emulsion

Tempera

"Wind from the Sea," egg tempera painting by Andrew Wyeth, 1947.
In a private collection. 47 × 70 cm.

"Christ Discovered in the Temple," panel painting in
egg tempera with gold leaf by Simone Martini, 1342.
In the Walker Art Gallery, Liverpool. 49.5 × 35 cm.

"King Khusrau Seated upon His Throne," Persian
miniature in glue tempera from the *Khamsa of
Nizami,* 1524–25. In the Metropolitan Museum of Art,
New York City. 32 × 23 cm.

A leaf from the *Calendar of a Book of Hours (April),*
manuscript illumination in egg tempera by Simon Bennick,
early 16th century. In the Victoria and Albert Museum,
London. 14 × 9.6 cm.

Plate 2   Painting, The Art of

Fresco of a court scene from the *Mahājanaka Jataka*, Cave I, Ajantā, India, 600–700.

Frescoes by Giovanni Battista Tiepolo, 1750–52, decorating the Kaisersaal Residenz, Würzburg, West Germany, designed by Balthasar Neumann, 1719–44.

"Fowling in the Marshes," detail of a wall painting from the tomb of Nebamun, Thebes, Egypt, c. 1450 BC, XVIII dynasty. In the British Museum.

"The Creation of Adam," detail of the ceiling fresco in the Sistine Chapel, Vatican, by Michelangelo, 1508–12.

Wall painting

Frescoes by José Clemente Orozco, 1938–39, decorating the ceiling and drum of the dome of the Hospicio Cabañas, Guadalajara, Mexico.

Fresco cycle depicting scenes from the life of the Virgin and the life of Christ by Giotto in the Arena Chapel, Padua, Italy, c. 1305–09.

Folk art fresco on the Adam and Eve house, Ardez, Switzerland, 1647.

Plate 4 Painting, The Art of

Oil and encaustic

"Salisbury Cathedral," oil painting by John Constable, c. 1825. In the National Gallery, London. 53 × 77 cm.

"Smaragd Red and Germinating Yellow," oil painting by Hans Hofmann, 1959. In the Cleveland Museum of Art. 1.4 × 1 m.

Detail from "Water Lilies," oil on canvas by Claude Monet, 1904. In the Musée de Jeu de Paume, Paris. Entire painting 90 × 92 cm.

"Venus and the Lute Player," oil painting by Titian, c. 1560. In the Metropolitan Museum of Art, New York City. 1.7 × 2.1 m.

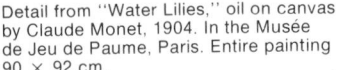

Detail from ''The Bridal Couple,'' oil painting by Rembrandt,
c. 1665. In the Rijksmuseum, Amsterdam. Entire
painting 1.2 × 1.7 m.

Detail from ''The Annunciation,'' oil painting by
Jan van Eyck, c. 1434/36. In the National
Gallery of Art, Washington, D.C. Entire
painting 93 × 36.5 cm.

Portrait of a boy, encaustic painting
from al-Fayyūm, Egypt, probably 2nd
century. In the Metropolitan Museum
of Art, New York City. 33 × 18.5 cm.

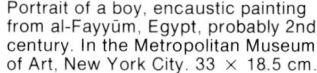

Detail from ''Quos Ego'' (''Neptune Calming the Tempest''), oil painting by
Peter Paul Rubens, c. 1635. In the Fogg Art Museum, Harvard University.
Entire painting 49 × 64 cm.

Plate 6 Painting, The Art of

"The Burning of the Houses of Parliament," watercolour painting by J.M.W. Turner, 1834. In the British Museum. 23.4 × 32.4 cm.

Ink, gouache, and watercolour

"A Young Man Among Roses," watercolour miniature by Nicholas Hilliard, c. 1588. In the Victoria and Albert Museum, London. 13.4 × 7.4 cm.

"The Annunciation," anonymous Austrian or Swabian woodcut, hand-coloured with watercolour, 1450–70. In the National Gallery of Art, Washington, D.C. 27.3 × 19.2 cm.

"The Monumental Turf," watercolour painting by Albrecht Dürer, 1503. In the Albertina, Vienna. 41 × 31.5 cm.

onto unprepared raw canvas or cotton. The wide range of intense hues is extended by fluorescent and metallic pigments. Polymer paints are particularly suitable for the precise, immaculate finish demanded by Op art, Minimalist, and Photo-realist painters such as Bridget Riley, Morris Louis, Frank Stella, and Richard Estes.

Other mediums. *French pastels.* French pastels, with the sharpened lumps of pigment used by Ice Age artists, are the purest and most direct painting materials. Pastel pigments are mixed only with sufficient gum to bind them for drying into stick molds. Generally, they are used on raw strawboard or on coarse-grained tinted paper, although vellum, wood, and canvas have been also employed. These colours will not fade or darken, but, since they are not absorbed by the surface of the support, they lie as pigment powder and are easily smudged. Unfortunately, pastel colours lose their luminosity and tonality if fixed with a varnish and so are best preserved in deep mounts behind glass. Degas often overcame the fragile nature of true pastel painting by the unorthodox method of working on turpentine-soaked paper, which absorbed the powdery pigment.

Eighteenth-century portrait pastellists, such as Maurice-Quentin de La Tour, Jean-Baptiste Peronneau, Jean-Étienne Liotard, and Anton Raphael Mengs, blended the pigment with coiled paper stumps so the surface resembled that of a smooth oil painting. Later pastel painters, such as Degas, Toulouse-Lautrec, Mary Cassatt, Everett Shinn, Odilon Redon, and Arthur Dove, contrasted broad masses of granular colour, spread with the side of the stick, with broken contours and passages of loose cross-hatching and smudging. They often used the tinted ground as a halftone, and, according to the amount of manual pressure exerted on the chalk, they varied the degree of pigment opacity to extract a wide range of tints and shades from each pastel colour.

Oil pastels. Oil pastels are pigments ground in mastic with oil of turpentine, spermaceti, and poppy oil. They are used in a similar way to that of French pastels but are already fixed and harder, producing a permanent, waxy finish. Oil-pastel paintings are generally executed on white paper, card, or canvas. The colours can be blended if the surface of the support is dampened with turpentine or if they are overworked with turpentine. They are popular for small preparatory studies for paintings.

Glass paintings. Glass paintings are executed with oil and hard resin or with watercolour and gum on glass sheets. These have been a folk art tradition in Europe and North America and, from the 15th to the 18th century, were regarded as a fine art in northern Europe, where they have been more recently revived by such painters as Willi Dirx, Ida Kerkovius, Lily Hildebrandt, Klee, Oskar Schlemmer, and Heinrich Camperdonck. Colours are applied from the back in reverse order. Unpainted areas of glass are often coated with mercury, providing a mirror background to the coloured images; this creates the kind of illusionary, bizarre spatial relationship between the viewer and picture space sought by the modern artist Michelangelo Pistoletto with his use of photographic images fixed to a polished steel sheet. The colours seen through glass appear translucent, jewel-like, and, since they cannot be touched, even magical.

Ivory painting. Ivory painting was practiced in the 18th and 19th centuries in Europe and America for portrait miniatures. These were generally oval-shaped and designed as keepsakes, lockets, and mantle pictures. They were painted under a magnifying glass in fairly dry watercolour or tempera stippling, with sable- or marten-hair brushes on thin, semitranslucent ivory pieces. Corrections were made with a needle. The velvet quality of their colours was enhanced, on the thinner ivories, by the glow produced by a gold leaf or tinted backing.

Lacquer. Lacquer has been a traditional Chinese medium for more than 2,000 years. It combines painting with intaglio relief. Linen-covered wood panels are coated with chalk or clay, followed by many thin layers of black or red lacquer-tree resin. The surface is polished and a design engraved, which is then coloured and gilded or inset with mother-of-pearl. Layers of compressed paper

Folk art tradition

or molded papier-mâché have also provided supports. In China and Japan, lacquer has been used principally for decorating shrine panels, screens, caskets, panniers (large baskets), and musical instruments.

Sand, or dry, painting. Sand, or dry, painting is a traditional magic art of the North American Indians; it is still practiced in healing ceremonies among the Navajos of New Mexico and Arizona. Ground sandstone, natural ochres, mineral earths, and powdered charcoal are sprinkled onto a pattern marked into an area covered with yellow-white sand. The patient sits in the centre of this vivid symbolic design of coloured figurative and geometrical shapes. Following the ritual, the painting is destroyed. These "floor" pictures influenced Jackson Pollock in his horizontally spread "action paintings."

Paper. From the end of the 18th century, profiles and full-length group portraits were cut in black paper, mounted on white card, and often highlighted in gold or white. A silhouette ("shade") might be first outlined from the sitter's cast shadow with the aid of a physionotrace.

Collage. Collage was the Dada and Synthetic Cubist technique of combining labels, tickets, newspaper cuttings, wallpaper scraps, and other "found" surfaces with painted textures simulating wood graining and marbling. Among the most lyrical and inventive works in this magpie medium are the so-called *Merz* collages by Kurt Schwitters. Frottage was Max Ernst's method of taking paper rubbings from surfaces, unrelated to one another in real life, and combining them to create fantasy landscapes. Cut paper shapes, hand coloured in gouache, were used by Matisse for his monumental last paintings; Piet Mondrian composed his famous "Victory Boogie Woogie" (1942–43) in coloured-paper cutouts.

Mechanical mediums. The use of mechanical mediums in painting has run parallel to similar developments in modern music and drama. In the field of cybernetics, painters have programmed computers to permutate drawings, photographs, diagrams, and symbols through sequences of progressive distortion; and light patterns are produced on television screens by deliberate magnetic interference and by sound-wave oscillations. Artists have also explored the expressive and aesthetic possibilities of linear holograms, in which all sides of an object can be shown by superimposed light images. Painters are among those who have extended the boundaries of filmmaking as an art form. Following the Surrealist film fantasies created by Berthold Bartosch, Jean Cocteau, Hans Richter, and Salvador Dalí, by Schlemmer's filmed ballets and Norman McLaren's hand-painted abstract animations, some painters and other graphic artists are now experimenting with video cassettes for television.

For some Conceptual artists the typewriter is the only equipment used when visual ideas are expressed in the form of instruction sheets alone. For example, typed proposals for defining the real space of an exhibition area with painted lines might invite the active participation of visitors (see below *Forms of painting: Modern forms*).

Mixed mediums. Some pictures are first painted in one medium and corrected or enriched with colour and texture in another. Examples of this kind of mixed mediums are the Renaissance tempera-oil technique, William Blake's relief etchings colour-printed in glue tempera and hand-finished in watercolour, and Degas's overpainted monotypes and his combinations of pastel, gouache, and oil. More recent examples are Richard Hamilton's photographs overpainted in oil colour, Dubuffet's patchwork assemblages of painted canvas and paper, and Klee's alchemy in mixing ingredients such as oil and distemper on chalk over jute and watercolour and wax on muslin stuck on wood.

FORMS OF PAINTING

Mural painting. Mural painting has its roots in the primeval instincts of people to decorate their surroundings and to use wall surfaces as a form for expressing ideas, emotions, and beliefs. In their universal manifestation in graffiti and in ancient murals, such as Ice Age cave paintings and protodynastic Egyptian frescoes, symbols and representational images have been spread freely and indiscriminately across walls, ceilings, and floors. But, in more disciplined attempts to symbolize the importance and function of particular buildings through their interior decoration, murals have been designed for the restricted framework of specific surface areas. They therefore have to be painted in close relationship to the scale, style, and mood of the interior and with regard to such siting considerations as light sources, eye levels, the spectators' lines of sight and means of approach, and the emotive scale relationship between spectators and the painted images.

Early mural decorations for tombs, temples, sanctuaries, and catacombs were generally designed in horizontal divisions and vertical axes. These grid patterns were in harmony with the austere character of the interiors, and their geometrical plan enabled the artist to depict clearly the various episodes and symbols of a narrative subject. In these early traditions of mural design, in China, India, Mexico, Egypt, Crete, and Byzantium, no illusionary devices were used to deny the true flatness of the wall surface; images were silhouetted against a flatly painted ground framed by decorative dadoes (the decoration adorning the lower part of an interior wall) of stylized motifs in repeat patterns. By the early Renaissance, however, innovators such as Giotto, Masaccio, and Fra Angelico were placing figures within architectural and landscape settings, painted as if extensions to the real dimensions of the interior. The peak of technical skill and artistic expression was reached in the 15th and 16th centuries with the frescoes of Piero della Francesca, Michelangelo, and Raphael. The irregular shapes of wall areas and the distortions produced by convex surfaces were inventively exploited in the design. Intruding doors and windows, for example, were skillfully circumvented by sweeping pattern rhythms or were incorporated as features in the painting, and figures were foreshortened so as to appear to float across or to rise into cupolas (rounded vaults that form ceilings), lunettes (rounded spaces over doors or windows), and apses (domed projections of a church, usually at the east end or altar), the curving surfaces of which might be painted to simulate celestial skies. Existing structural wall features provided the divisions between narrative episodes. These were often supplemented by trompe l'oeil ("deceive the eye") columns, pilasters, arcading, balustrading, steps, and other architectural forms that also served to fuse the painted setting with the real interior.

With the increasing dependence upon tapestry hangings and stained glass as primary forms of interior decoration, mural painting suffered a decline in the Western world. Except for those given to Rubens, Tiepolo, Delacroix, and Puvis de Chavannes, there were relatively few important mural commissions in the period following the High Renaissance. In the 20th century, however, enlightened patronage has occasionally enabled leading modern artists to execute paintings for specific sites: Monet's "Water-Lilies" series for the Paris Orangerie, for example, and other murals in France by Vuillard, Matisse, Léger, Chagall, and Picasso; in Mexico and the United States by Orozco, Rivera, Tamayo, and David Siqueiros, and also in the U.S. by Matisse, Shahn, and Willem de Kooning; in Britain by Sir Stanley Spencer and Bawden; in Norway by Edvard Munch; in Holland by Karel Appel; and in Italy by Afro Basaldella.

Easel and panel painting. The easel, or studio, picture was a form developed during the Renaissance with the establishment of the painter as an individual artist. Its scale and portability enabled European artists to extend the range of themes, previously restricted to those suitable to mural decoration. Easel and panel forms include still life, portraiture, landscape, and genre subjects and permit the representation of ephemeral effects of light and atmosphere that the more intimate forms of Oriental art had already allowed the painters of scrolls, screens, and fans to express. Although easel paintings are occasionally commissioned for a special purpose, they are generally bought as independent art objects and used as decorative focal features or illusionary window views in private homes. They are also collected as financial investment, for social prestige, for the therapeutic escapism their subject may provide, or purely for the aesthetic pleasure they afford.

Panel paintings, by strict definition, are small pictures designed for specific sacred or secular purposes or as part of a functional object. Although these wooden boards are sometimes categorized as a form of "decorative" rather than "fine" art, the best examples justify their place in museums alongside great easel paintings. Among the functions they originally served were as predellas (the facings to altar-step risers); devotional and ceremonial icons; portable, folding diptych and triptych altarpieces; shop and tavern signboards; mummy cases; and panel decorations of carriages, musical instruments, and cassoni. Many of them were painted by acknowledged masters, such as Fra Angelico, Paolo Uccello, and Antoine Watteau, as well as by anonymous folk artists.

Miniature painting. Miniature painting is a term applied both to Western portrait miniatures and to the Indian and Islāmic forms of manuscript painting discussed below. Portrait miniatures, or limnings, were originally painted in watercolour with body colour on vellum and card. They were often worn in jewelled, enamelled lockets. Sixteenth-century miniaturists, such as Hans Holbein, Jean Clouet, Nicholas Hilliard, and Isaac Oliver, painted them in the tradition of medieval illuminators. Their flat designs, richly textured and minutely detailed, often incorporated allegorical and gilded heraldic motifs. In 17th- and 18th-century Western portrait miniatures, the two-dimensional pattern of rich colours was developed by atmospheric tonal modelling into more naturalistic representations; these were sometimes in pastel and pencil or painted in oils on a metal base. Pantographs (reducing and enlarging copying instruments made on the lazy-tongs lever principle) might be used to transfer a drawing. Among the exponents of this naturalistic style were Francisco Goya, Fragonard, Samuel Cooper, John Hoskins, François Dumont, and the U.S. miniaturists Robert Field and Edward Green Malbone. The introduction of painted ivory miniatures was followed, in the 19th century, by a decline in aesthetic standards, although a classical simplicity was achieved by unsophisticated itinerant limners and by the German miniaturist Patricius Kittner. The painted miniature was eventually superseded by the small, hand-tinted photograph (see above *Mediums: Ivory painting*).

Manuscript illumination and related forms. Among the earliest surviving forms of manuscript painting are the papyrus rolls of the ancient Egyptian Book of the Dead, the scrolls of Classical Greece and Rome, Aztec pictorial maps, and Mayan and Chinese codices, or manuscript books. European illuminated manuscripts were painted in egg-white tempera on vellum and card. Their subjects included religious, historical, mythological, and allegorical narratives, medical treatises, psalters, and calendars depicting seasonal occupations. In contrast to the formalized imagery of Byzantine and early Gothic manuscript painters, Celtic illuminators developed a unique, abstract style of elaborate decoration, the written text being overwhelmed by intricate latticework borders, with full-page initial letters embraced by interlacing scrolls. The medieval Gothic style of illumination, in sinuous, linear patterns of flattened forms isolated against white or gilded grounds, had developed, by the end of the 15th century, into exquisitely detailed, jewel-like miniatures of shaded figures and spatial landscapes. These were often framed by gilded initial letters as vignettes or by margin borders in simulated half relief. With the advent of printing in the 15th century and a final, brilliant period of Flemish and Italian illumination, European manuscript painting survived only in official documents, maps, and in the form of hand-coloured, block-printed pages. Pennsylvanian-German birth and baptismal certificates in the U.S. and William Blake's hand-coloured engravings to the Bible and to his own poems were isolated revivals of those forms.

Indian and Islāmic miniature painting, however, was practiced into the 19th century; and 11th-century Oriental albums of poem paintings in ink, on leaves of silk or paper, represent a tradition that was continued into modern times. The subjects of Near Eastern miniatures included religious and historical narrative, cosmic maps, and medical, palmistry, and astrological charts, as well as illustrations to poems, songs, and romantic epics. These

"Kirkstall Abbey, Yorkshire—Evening,"
watercolour painting by Thomas Girtin,
1801. In the Victoria and Albert
Museum, London. 30.4 × 51 cm.

"Landscape," detail of a Japanese handscroll,
ink on paper by Sesshū (1420–1506). In the
National Museum, Tokyo. Dimensions of entire
scroll 147.3 × 35.6 cm.

French fan, gouache on paper, sticks of carved mother-of-pearl
inlaid with gilt and set with pastes, c. 1750. In the Victoria and
Albert Museum, London.

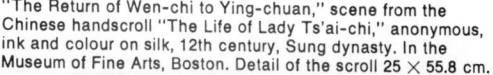

"The Return of Wen-chi to Ying-chuan," scene from the
Chinese handscroll "The Life of Lady Ts'ai-chi," anonymous,
ink and colour on silk, 12th century, Sung dynasty. In the
Museum of Fine Arts, Boston. Detail of the scroll 25 × 55.8 cm.

Plate 8 Painting, The Art of

"Union I," epoxy paint and fluorescent
alkyd painting by Frank Stella, 1966.
In the Detroit Institute of Arts.
2.6 × 4.5 m.

Modern forms

"First Landing Jump," combine painting by Robert
Rauschenberg, 1961. In the Museum of Modern Art, New York
City. 2.3 × 1.8 m.

"Breakfast," pasted paper, crayon, and oil paint collage by
Juan Gris, 1914. In the Museum of Modern Art, New York
City. 81 × 60 cm.

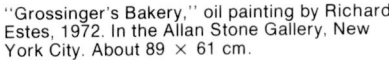

"Grossinger's Bakery," oil painting by Richard
Estes, 1972. In the Allan Stone Gallery, New
York City. About 89 × 61 cm.

were generally painted in gouache on paper, with occasional gold- or silver-leaf embellishment. The linear design was first drawn with a brush in delicate contours and soft shading. Landscape and architectural detail was as well observed as in that of the principal figures.

The rapprochement established between text, painted borders, margin spaces, and illustration is characteristic of both Eastern and Western manuscript paintings. In Indian and Islāmic miniatures, for example, the panels of decorative script are integrated within the overall pattern as areas of textural enrichment; and, with the margin and inset frames, these panels serve also as concrete screens and prosceniums to the action depicted, the participants in the narrative episode making their exits and entrances across or behind them.

Scroll painting. Hand scrolls, traditional to China and Japan, are ink paintings on continuous lengths of paper or silk. They are unrolled at arm's length and viewed from right to left. These generally represent panoramic views of rivers, mountain and urban landscapes, and domestic interiors. They also illustrate romantic novels, Taoist and Buddhist themes, and historical and genre subjects. Narrative poetic commentaries were included as integral textures in the flowing design. The scrolls are remarkable for their vitality, the lyrical representation of atmospheric space, and for the rising and dipping viewpoints that anticipate the zooming motion-picture camera. The earliest surviving scrolls, such as Ku K'ai-chih's "Admonitions of the Instructress to the Court Ladies," date from the 4th century AD. Oriental hanging scrolls and Indian and Tibetan temple banners are forms similar to those of Western easel and panel paintings. Their subjects range from the seasons, domestic interiors, landscapes, and portraits to Vishnu epics, mandalas (symbolic diagrams of the universe), and temple icons. They are painted in ink or gouache on silk and paper and are usually mounted on embroidered or block-printed silk. The dramatic interplay of bold, flattened images against the open space of an unpainted or gilded ground influenced 19th-century Western Art Nouveau decoration.

Hanging scrolls and temple banners

Screen and fan painting. Folding screens and screen doors originated in China and Japan, probably during the 12th century, and continued as a traditional form into the 20th. They are in ink or gouache on plain or gilded paper and silk. Their vivid rendering of animals, birds, and flowers and their atmospheric landscapes brought nature indoors. In some screens each panel was designed as an individual painting, while in others a continuous pattern flowed freely across the divisions. Japanese screens were often painted in complementary Yin and Yang pairs. Large 12-panel Chinese coromandel lacquer screens were imported into Europe during the 17th and 18th centuries. French Rococo boudoir screens depicting *fêtes champêtres* (townspeople enjoying rural surroundings) and toile de Jouy (landscape or floral) pastoral themes were painted on silk or on wood panels in a flamboyantly scrolled, gilded framework. The designs of Art Nouveau screens were inspired by the Japanese tradition. Sidney Nolan's screens on Greek themes and the pastiches of Victorian paper-scrap screens by Pop art painters are recent Western revivals. Traditional to the Greek and Russian Orthodox churches is the iconostasis screen, which stands between the nave and sanctuary and displays icon panel paintings representing the Virgin, the saints, and narrative subjects.

Rigid fans are depicted in the paintings and reliefs of ancient Egypt, Assyria, Greece, and Rome, but the oldest surviving specimens are the round and folding fans from Japan and China. These were painted in India ink and colour on paper, card, and silk, the ground often sprinkled with gold dust or laid with gold or silver leaf. Spread freely across the mount, a calligraphic design depicted seasonal landscapes, genre scenes, and bird, flower, and animal motifs, with accompanying poems and commentaries. Leading Oriental painters produced much of their finest work in this form. In Europe, however, where fan painting had been rarely practiced until the 17th century, it was considered a minor art, and designs were often based on frescoes and easel paintings. The richest and most elegant of these were painted in France and Italy during the 18th century. Watercolour and gouache paintings and hand-coloured engraved designs were made on paper, card, kid, and gauze. Allegories and romantic pastoral landscapes were frequently designed as separate vignettes, linked by floral swags and border scrolls. Both sides of the mount might be painted. The guards and sticks of the spoke framework were in delicately carved wood or ivory, inlaid with gold leaf or mother-of-pearl. Round hand-screens of parchment, mounted on handles like lollipops, were popular in early 19th-century English society. Charles Conder was a notable fin de siècle ("end of the century," characterized by effete sophistication) fan painter, and, more recently, Oskar Kokoschka decorated a lively set of fans on an autobiographical narrative theme.

Round hand-screens

Panoramas. Panoramas were intended to simulate the sensation of scanning an extensive urban or country view or seascape. This form of painting was popular at the end of the 18th century. Notable examples are "The Battle of Agincourt" (1805), by R.K. Porter, and "Scheveningen," by Hendrik Willem Mesdag. Panoramas might be compared to Cinerama films and enjoyed as a stimulating optical entertainment, along with cyclorama drums (large pictorial representations encircling the spectator), trompe l'oeil diorama peep shows, and the show box, for which Thomas Gainsborough painted glass transparencies. More serious forms of panoramic painting are exemplified in Chinese Buddhist sanctuary frescoes, Oriental hand scrolls, Dürer's watercolour townscapes, Andrey Rublyov's 14th-century mural of Moscow, and Uccello's original sequence of three panels depicting the Battle of San Romano.

Modern forms. The concept of painting as a medium for creating illusions of space, volume, texture, light, and movement on a flat, stationary support has been challenged by many modern artists. Some recent forms, for example, have blurred the conventional distinctions between the mediums of sculpture and painting. Sculptors such as David Smith, Eduardo Paolozzi, and Philip Sutton have made multicoloured constructions; painters such as Jean Arp and Ben Nicholson have created abstract designs in painted wood relief, and Richard Smith has painted on three-dimensional canvas structures the surfaces of which curl and thrust toward the spectator. And, rather than deny the essential flatness of the painting support by using traditional methods of representing volume and texture, Robert Rauschenberg and Jim Dine have attached real objects and textures to the painted surface, and Frank Stella and Kenneth Noland have designed their irregularly shaped canvases to be seen as explicitly flat art objects. Rejecting earlier painting methods of reproducing effects of light with tonal contrasts and broken pigment colour, some artists have made use of neon tubes and mirrors. Instead of simulating sensations of movement by optical illusion, others have designed kinetic panels and boxes in which coloured shapes revolve under electric power. The traditional definition of painting as a visual, concrete art form has been questioned by recent aspects of Conceptual art, in which the painter's idea might be expressed only in the form of documented proposals for unrealized and often unrealizable projects. In "performance art" and "happenings," which employ techniques akin to those used in theatre, the artists themselves become a kind of medium.

IMAGERY AND SUBJECT MATTER

The imagery and subject matter of paintings in early cultures were generally prescribed by tribal, religious, or dynastic authorities. In some Eastern countries, traditional models survived into the 18th century and even later. With the Renaissance, however, images and themes in Western painting, reflecting the new spirit of Humanistic, objective curiosity and scientific research, came to be decided by the artist and his patron and, in more recent periods, by the artist alone.

Kinds of imagery. Within the various cultures the art of representing things by painted images has rarely shown a continuously developing pattern toward greater realism. More often, religious and philosophical precepts have determined the degree of naturalism permitted. Rules governing portrayals of the human figure have been particularly stringent in certain traditions of representational painting,

Attitudes toward the cosmic significance of man

reflecting different attitudes to the cosmic significance of man. For example, a belief in the inferiority of man in relation to an almighty deity is expressed in the faceless figures in early Jewish painting and in the dehumanized stylizations of Byzantine imagery; and his insignificance against the dynamic forces of nature is symbolized in Chinese landscape paintings by his puny scale within a monumental setting. An earlier view, which instead sought to glorify the spiritual, intellectual, and physical attributes of mankind, is typified in the noble figures of Greco-Roman art and in the renewed celebration of human physical beauty in the Renaissance and subsequent Neoclassical styles. The uniqueness of man among living things and the expression of his individual physical and emotional characteristics are exemplified in Japanese and northern European narrative and genre painting. Concomitant with the antipathy toward figurative representation in some cultures was a general distaste for the portrayal of all things of the exterior world, animals, landscape features, and other natural forms rarely appearing except as stylized images signifying spiritual forces of good and evil. The representational imagery of modern painting borrows freely from ancient and contemporary sources such as primitive and child art, Classical mythology, commercial advertising, press photography, and the allegories and fantasies of the motion picture and the comic strip. Nonrepresentational imagery is not restricted to modern painting but appears also in earlier forms such as Aurignacian (Paleolithic) decorative meanders, the scrollwork of Celtic illuminations, and the patterns of Islāmic Kūfic calligraphy (an angular variety of the Arabic alphabet). And the abstraction of natural forms into rudimentary symbols, characteristic of modern painting, is echoed in the "pin-men" conventions of Magdalenian caves, in Aztec pictograms, and Indian and Tibetan cosmic-diagram paintings.

Kinds of subject matter. *Devotional.* The range and interpretation of subjects in different forms of devotional painting express a particular attitude to the relationship between man and his deity. Early Christian and Buddhist murals, for example, portrayed an all-powerful, remote, and mysterious being, painted as a flat, formalized head or figure whose stern gaze dominated the interiors of temples, churches, and sanctuaries. Christian Last Judgments and Oriental hell paintings were intended to frighten the believer, while subjects such as the Virgin enthroned, the Assumption, and Buddha descending from Paradise sustained his faith with hopes for salvation and rewards of blissful immortality.

Narrative. When the autocratic ecclesiastical control over Western painting weakened under Renaissance Humanism, the religious narrative picture became a window onto a terrestial rather than a celestial world. Both emotional and physical relationships between the figures depicted were realistically expressed, and the spectator was able to identify himself with the lifelike representation of a worldly space inhabited by Christ, his disciples, and saints, wearing updated dress and moving naturally within contemporary settings. This kind of narrative interpretation persists in the modern religious paintings of Sir Stanley Spencer, where biblical environments are represented by the clipped hedgerows, the churchyards, and the front parlours of his neat, native English village of Cookham.

Allegorical narrative subjects

Allegorical narrative subjects might exalt the sensuous arts, as in the symbolic muses portrayed by Poussin and Luca Signorelli and the paradisiac gardens of 15th-century French illuminated manuscripts. But they might also carry warnings. In the 16th century, Pieter Bruegel the Elder, for example, combined overt and often grotesque symbols with subtle visual metaphors to point stern morals in such paintings as "The Triumph of Death" (alluding to the "wages of sin"), "The Land of Cockaigne" (attacking gluttony and sloth), and "Mad Meg" (ridiculing covetousness). Even Bruegel's apparently straightforward genre subjects, such as "The Peasant Dance" and the festival of "The Fight Between Carnival and Lent," conceal parables on man's follies and sins, while Hieronymus Bosch introduced abstruse, allegorical phantasmagoria into such traditional narratives as "The Temptation of St. Antony" and "The Prodigal Son" and made his "Garden of De-

lights" an expression of disgust rather than of joy. Botticelli's late paintings, probably produced under the influence of the 15th-century Italian monk and reformer Girolamo Savonarola, are other savagely pessimistic allegories: "The Story of Virginia Romana" and "The Tragedy of Lucretia," representing virtue upheld only by death, and "The Calumny of Apelles," in which envy, suspicion, deceit, guile, repentance, and truth are identified, like medieval mummers, by their costume, pose, and gesture. Rubens, however, found in allegorical symbolism a means of dramatizing mundane state commissions, such as "The Union of Scotland and Ireland" and "The Bounty of James I (Triumphing over Avarice)." Among famous 19th-century allegories are Delacroix's "Liberty Leading the People" and Pierre-Paul Prud'hon's "Crime Pursued by Vengeance and Justice."

Possibly the highest achievements in narrative illustrations to poetry and literature are found in Eastern miniatures and Oriental scrolls, such as the Persian paintings of Ferdowsī's 11th-century national epic poem, the *Shāhnāmeh,* and the 12th-century Japanese scrolls of the *Genji monogatari* and the *Story of Ben Dainagon.* An example of modern literary painting is Sidney Nolan's narrative series portraying the Australian folklore hero Ned Kelly.

Ancient Greek and Roman mythologies have provided Western artists with rich sources of imagery and subject matter and with opportunities for painting the nude. Historical narrative painting includes Classical mythology and heroic legend, as well as the representation of contemporary events; examples include Benjamin West's "Death of Wolfe," Théodore Géricault's "Raft of the Medusa," and Goya's "The 3rd of May in Madrid."

Portraiture. The earliest surviving portraits of particular persons are probably the serene, idealized faces painted on the front and inside surfaces of dynastic Egyptian sarcophagi. The human individuality of the Roman mummy portraits of the 1st and 2nd century AD, however, suggests more authentic likenesses. Although portraits are among the highest achievements in painting, the subject poses special problems for the artist commissioned to paint a notable contemporary. The portraits of patrons by artists such as Raphael, Rubens, Hyacinthe Rigaud, Antoine-Jean Gros, Jacques-Louis David, and Sir Thomas Lawrence were required to express nobility, grace, and authority, just as the sultans and rajahs portrayed on frontispieces to Persian and Indian illuminated books and albums had understandably to be flattered as benevolent despots. Such concessions to the sitter's vanity and social position seem to have been disregarded, however, in the convincing likenesses by more objective realists such as Robert Campin, Dürer, Jan van Eyck, Velázquez, Goya, and Gustave Courbet. Probably the finest are the self-portraits and studies of ordinary people by Rembrandt and Van Gogh, where psychological insight, emotional empathy, and aesthetic values are fused. A more decorative approach to the subject is seen in the flattened portraits by Holbein, the Elizabethan and itinerant naïve U.S. limners, and the Far Eastern paintings of ancestors, poets, priests, and emperors. Like these paintings, the full-length portraits by Boucher, Gainsborough, Kees van Dongen, and Matisse display as much regard for the texture and form of their sitters' dress as for their facial features.

Since the development of photography, however, portraiture has been rarely practiced for its own sake as a serious art form, except where artists such as Cézanne and Braque have used it as a subject for structural research or—like Amedeo Modigliani, Chaim Soutine, and Francis Bacon—for the expression of a personal vision beyond the scope of the camera.

Photographs and painted portraits

Genre. Genre subjects are scenes from everyday life. Hunting expeditions and tribal rituals figure in prehistoric rock paintings. Domestic and agricultural occupations, with banquet scenes of feasting, dancing, and music, were traditional subjects for ancient Egyptian tomb murals. Far Eastern hand scrolls, albums, and screens brilliantly describe court ceremonies, the bustle of towns, and the hardships of the countryside. The depiction of earthly pursuits was forbidden under the strict iconography prescribed by the early Christian Church, but the later illuminated Books of Hours provide enchanting records of the festivals and occupations of northern European communities. In Renaissance painting, genre subjects were generally restricted to background features of portraits and historical narratives. Domestic scenes, however, not only provided Bruegel with subjects for moral allegories but, as with Rembrandt, were used to counterpoint the emotional intensity of a dramatic religious theme. The withdrawal of religious patronage in northern Europe directed painters toward secular subjects. The rich period of genre painting in 17th-century Holland is represented by the interiors, conversation pieces, and scenes of work and play by David Teniers the Younger, Frans Hals, Jan Steen, Gerard Terborch, Pieter de Hooch, Adriaen van Ostade, and, the finest, by Jan Vermeer. Pictures of rustic life had a special appeal for collectors in 18th-century France and England; these were the somewhat picturesque representations of peasant life painted by Jean-Baptiste Greuze, Boucher, George Morland, and Gainsborough. Jean-Baptiste-Siméon Chardin's paintings of servants and children, however, exhibit a timeless dignity and grandeur. The harsher realities of working life were depicted by Jean-François Millet, Daumier, Courbet, Van Gogh, and Degas; the robust gaiety of cafés and music halls was captured by Toulouse-Lautrec, John Sloan, Everett Shinn, and Walter Richard Sickert; and intimate domestic scenes were recorded by Bonnard and Vuillard. Modern genre movements have included the American Scene painters, the Ashcan and Kitchen Sink schools (represented by such painters as George Wesley Bellows, Jack Smith, and Derrick Greaves), the Camden Town and Euston Road groups (Frederick Spencer Gore, Sir William Coldstream, and Victor Pasmore), and the Social Realists in England and in the United States (Robert Henri, Stuart Davis, and Maurice Prendergast).

Landscape. Idealized landscapes were common subjects for fresco decoration in Roman villas. Landscape painting (as exemplified by a Chinese landscape scroll by Ku K'ai-chih dating from the 4th century) was an established tradition in the Far East, where themes such as the seasons and the elements held a spiritual significance. In Europe, imaginary landscapes decorated 15th-century Books of Hours. The first naturalistic landscapes were painted by Dürer and Bruegel. Landscapes appeared in most Renaissance paintings, however, only as settings to portraits and figure compositions. It was not until the 17th-century Dutch and Flemish schools—of Rembrandt, Jacob van Ruisdael, Meindert Hobbema, Aelbert Cuyp, Rubens, and Hercules Seghers—that they were accepted in the West as independent subjects. The most significant developments in 19th-century painting, however, were made through the landscapes of the Impressionists and the Neo-Impressionists and Postimpressionists. Styles in landscape painting range from the tranquil, classically idealized world of Poussin and Claude, the precise, canal topography of Francesco Guardi and Canaletto, and the structural analyses of Cézanne to the poetic romanticism of Samuel Palmer and the later Constables and Turners and the exultant pantheism of Rubens and Van Gogh. Modern landscapes vary in approach from the Expressionism of Oskar Kokoschka's cities and rivers, Maurice de Vlaminck's wintry countrysides, and John Marin's crystalline seascapes to the metaphysical country of Ernst, Dalí, and René Magritte and the semi-abstract coastlines of Nicolas de Stael, Maria Helena Vieira da Silva, and Richard Diebenkorn.

Still life. The earliest European still-life painting is usually attributed to Jacopo de' Barbari (*i.e.,* "Dead Bird," 1504). In Western paintings, still life often appears as a minor feature of the design; but until the 17th century it was not generally painted for its own sake, although it was already traditional to Far Eastern art. The subject is particularly associated with northern European painting, and the choice of objects very often has a religious or literary significance: wine, water, and bread symbolizing the Passion; skulls, hourglasses, and candles, the transience of life; and selected flowers and fruits, the seasons. Flower painting, especially, held a spiritual and emotional meaning for Japanese artists and for 19th-century European painters, such as Odilon Redon, Paul Gauguin, and Van

Gogh. Still life has been expressed in many different ways: Giuseppe Arcimboldo's witty arrangements of fruit, flowers, and vegetables made into fantastic allegorical heads and figures; the sensuous representation of food by Frans Snyders, Goya, and William Merritt Chase; the trompe l'oeil illusionism of François Desportes and William Harnett; the formal decoration of folk artists or primitives such as Henri Rousseau and Séraphine and of modern painters such as Matisse, Dufy, and Pat Caulfield; the semi-abstract designs of Picasso, Gris, and William Scott; and, probably at its highest level of expression, the majestic still lifes of Chardin, Cézanne, and Giorgio Morandi.

Other subjects. Since ancient times, animals and birds have provided the primary subject matter of a painting or have been included in a design for their symbolic importance. In the paintings of prehistoric caves and dynastic Egyptian tombs, for example, animals are portrayed with a higher degree of naturalism than human figures. Their texture, movement, and structure have provided some artists with a primary source of inspiration: the classical, anatomical grace of a George Stubbs racehorse and a more romantic interpretation in the ferocious energy of a Rubens and Géricault stallion; the vivid expression of rhythmically co-ordinated movements of deer by Tawaraya Sotatsu and Antonio Pisanello; the weight and volume of George Morland's pigs and Paul Potter's cows; the humanized creatures of Gothic bestiaries and of Edward Hicks's "Peaceable Kingdom"; and, finally, Dürer's "The Hare," which is possibly as famous as Leonardo's "Mona Lisa."

Increasing interest is shown in notable painters' versions of other artists' works. These are not academic copies (such as the study made by Matisse, when a student, of Chardin's "La Raie"), but creative transcriptions. Examples that can be appreciated as original paintings are those by Miró of Sorgh's "Lute Player"; by Watteau of Rubens' "Apotheosis of James I"; by Degas of Bellini's "Jealous Husband"; by Caulfield of Delacroix's "Greece Expiring on the Ruins of Missolonghi"; by Larry Rivers of Jean-Auguste-Dominique Ingres's "Mlle Rivière"; and by Picasso of Manet's "Déjeuner sur l'herbe," Velázquez' "Las Meñinas," and Delacroix's "Woman of Algiers" (which produced Roy Lichtenstein's "Femmes d'Alger, After Picasso, After Delacroix"). Picasso has also painted free versions of works by El Greco, Lucas Cranach, Poussin, and Courbet, as Rubens had of Mantegna and Titian, Rembrandt of Persian and Indian miniatures, Cézanne of Rubens and El Greco, and Van Gogh of Millet, Gustave Doré, and Delacroix.

In an abstract painting, ideas, emotions, and visual sensations are communicated solely through lines, shapes, colours, and textures that have no representational significance. The subject of an abstract painting may be therefore a proposition about the creative painting process itself or exclusively about the formal elements of painting, demonstrating the behaviour of juxtaposed colours and shapes and the movements and tensions between them, their optical metamorphosis and spatial ambiguities. Many abstracts, however, are more than visual formal exercises and produce physical and emotional reactions in the spectator to illusions of shapes and colours that appear to rise and fall, recede and advance, balance and float, disintegrate and re-form; or of moods created of joy, sadness, peace, or foreboding; or of effects produced by light or by flickering or throbbing movement. Some abstracts evoke the atmosphere of a particular time, place, or event; and then their titles may be significant: "Pancho Villa, Dead and Alive" (Robert Motherwell); "Late Morning" (Bridget Riley); "Broadway Boogie Woogie" (Mondrian); "Gold of Venice" (Lucio Fontana); "Capricious Forms" (Kandinsky).

SYMBOLISM

Most early cultures developed iconographic systems that included prescriptions for the site, design, function, form, medium, subject matter, and imagery of their painting. The siting of early Byzantine murals, for instance, echoed the symbolic, architectural planning of the basilica. Thus, a stylized, linear image of Christ, surrounded by heavenly

Subject matter of still lifes

The subject of an abstract painting

hosts, occupied the central dome; the Virgin was represented in the apse; and stiff figures of apostles, prophets, martyrs, and patriarchs occupied the aisle walls. The format of early devotional paintings was also prescribed, Christian and Buddhist deities being placed in the focal centre of the design, above the eye level of the audience and larger than surrounding figures. And, in the conventional arrangement of a Christian subject such as the Holy Trinity, a central, bearded, patriarchal God, flanked by archangels, presented Christ on the cross; between them was a dove, representing the Holy Spirit. In a rendering of the risen Christ, the Son faced the audience, with the Virgin Mother on the left and St. John on the right of the design. In the Far East a traditional format depicted Buddha on a lotus throne or in a high chariot drawn by oxen across clouds, surrounded by figures representing the planets. Deities generally appear against undefined grounds of white (signifying eternity or nothingness), blue (the celestial vaults), or gold (representing heavenly light by radiating lines or the spiritual aura by a nimbus). The elaborate surface preparation of supports and the painstaking execution with the finest materials symbolized the intention that paintings dedicated to a deity should last forever. The imagery, subject matter, and form might also have a mystical function: the realistic rendering of animals in contrast to the perfunctory human representations in Ice Age rock paintings, thought to signify a wishful guarantee for success in hunting; the earthly pleasures depicted on ancient Egyptian tomb murals intended to secure their continuance for the deceased; and the North American Indian sand paintings designed for magic healing ceremonies and the Tantric (relating to Tantrism, a school of Mahāyāna Buddhism) mandalas used for meditation and enlightenment.

Symbolism in Eastern painting—intended to deepen the experience of a picture's mood and spirituality—is more generalized and poetic than in Western art. Both the execution and the subject matter of Buddhist Chinese and Japanese painting have a religious or metaphysical significance: the artist's intuitive, calligraphic brush movements symbolizing his mystical empathy with nature and his cyclic landscape and flower subjects expressing his belief in the spiritual harmony of natural forms and forces. Much of Indian symbolism is visually emotive, images such as snakes, plantain leaves, twining creepers, and rippling water being overtly sexual. And, although symbolic attributes and colour codes identify Indian mythological characters (for example, the four arms of the terrible goddess Kālī and the blue skin of the divine lover Krishna), the formal character and colour scheme of settings generally reflect the narrative's emotional mood (for example, vibrant, dark-blue, cloudy skies and embracing, purple-black glades evoking amorous anticipation and red grounds expressing the passions of love or war).

Western symbolic systems

Western symbolic systems, however, are more intellectually directed, their imagery having precise literary meanings and their colour codes intended primarily for narrative or devotional identification. The iconographic programs of the early Christian churches, for example, laid down complex formulas for the viewpoints, gestures, facial expressions, and positions of arms, hands, and feet for religious figures. An elaborate Ethiopian Christian iconographic system was followed until very recently, and elsewhere traditional methods survive of identifying archangels and saints by their attributes and by the symbols of martyrdom that they display: distinguishing white-bearded St. Peter from black-bearded St. Paul, for example, and portraying St. Catherine with a wheel and St. Bartholomew with a knife and skin. Christian iconography adopted and elaborated Greco-Roman and Jewish symbolic imagery: the pagan signs of the vine and the fish, for example, and the image of Christ as the Good Shepherd based on the Greek Hermes Kriophoros. Medieval and Renaissance writings define an immense vocabulary of symbolic images, such as the crescent, sea urchin, and owl signifying heresy, the toad and jug representing the devil, and the egg and bagpipes as erotic symbols (all of which appear in Hieronymus Bosch's 15th-century narrative moralities). Angels and devils, hellfire and golden

paradise, heavenly skies and birds in flight representing spirituality and rebirth are examples of the similarity of symbolic meaning for many religious, mythological, and allegorical traditions. The significance of images common to several cultures, however, may also be very different: the dragon representing avarice in European medieval allegory symbolizes friendliness in Japanese Zen painting; and the snake, symbol of temptation and eroticism in the West, signifies, by its skin shedding, the renewal of life in Far Eastern iconography.

BIBLIOGRAPHY

General reference: Both KIMBERLEY REYNOLDS with RICHARD SEDDON, *Illustrated Dictionary of Art Terms* (1981, reissued 1984); and RALPH MAYER, *A Dictionary of Art Terms and Techniques* (1969, reissued 1981), include modern art references. Two works by HAROLD OSBORNE (ed.), *The Oxford Companion to Art* (1970), and *The Oxford Companion to Twentieth-Century Art* (1981), provide extensive bibliographies. Also see RENÉ HUYGHE (general ed.), *Larousse Encyclopedia of Prehistoric and Ancient Art*, rev. ed. (1966, reissued 1981); *Larousse Encyclopedia of Byzantine and Medieval Art*, rev. ed. (1966, reissued 1981); *Larousse Encyclopedia of Renaissance and Baroque Art* (1964, reissued 1981); and *Larousse Encyclopedia of Modern Art* (1965, reissued 1981).

Design: Good surveys of the subject include FREDERICK MALINS, *Understanding Paintings: The Elements of Composition* (1981); and JOHANNES ITTEN, *Design and Form: The Basic Course at the Bauhaus*, rev. ed. (1975; originally published in German, 1963). Works on colour include JOSEF ALBERS, *The Interaction of Color* (1963, reissued with rev. plate section, 1975); JOHANNES ITTEN, *The Art of Color* (1961, reissued 1973; originally published in German, 1961); FABER BIRREN, *Creative Color* (1961), and (ed.), *A Grammar of Color: A Basic Treatise on the Color System by Albert H. Munsell* (1969); ROBERT L. HERBERT, *Neo-Impressionism* (1968); WILLIAM INNES HOMER, *Seurat and the Science of Painting* (1964, reprinted 1978); and BARBARA ROSE, "The Primacy of Color," *Art International*, 8:22–26 (1964). The influence of photography on painting is examined in AARON SCHARF, *Art and Photography* (1968, reissued 1974); and KAREN TSUJIMOTO, *Images of America: Precisionist Painting and Modern Photography* (1982).

Mediums: Standard works on most painting materials, supports, surfaces, and techniques include RALPH MAYER, *The Artist's Handbook of Materials and Techniques*, 4th rev. ed. (1982), with extensive bibliography; HILAIRE HILER, *The Painter's Pocket Book of Methods and Materials*, 3rd ed. rev. by COLIN HAYES (1970); KURT HERBERTS, *The Complete Handbook of Artist's Techniques* (1958; trans. from the German); MARIA BAZZI, *The Artist's Methods and Materials* (1960; originally published in Italian, 1956), with a bibliography of important treatises on mediums and techniques; FREDERIC TAUBES, *A Guide to Traditional and Modern Painting Methods* (1963); and MAX DOERNER, *The Materials of the Artist and Their Use in Painting*, rev. ed. (1949, reprinted 1969; originally published in German, 4th ed., 1933). For discussion of tempera, see the appropriate sections in DANIEL V. THOMPSON, *The Materials of Medieval Painting* (1936; reprinted as *Materials and Techniques of Medieval Painting*, 1956). Watercolour painting is treated in WALTER KOSCHATZKY, *Watercolor: History and Technique* (1970; originally published in German, 1969). For treatment of ink painting, see FEI CH'ENG WU, *Brush Drawing in the Chinese Manner* (1957); and OSVALD SÍREN, *Chinese Painting: Leading Masters and Principles*, 7 vol. (1973). FRED GETTINGS, *Polymer Painting Manual* (1971), is a thorough and well-illustrated guide to acrylic painting. Works on other mediums include JEAN GUICHARD-MELLI, *Matisse Paper Cutouts* (1984; originally published in French, 1983); and HARRIET JANIS and RUDI BLESH, *Collage*, rev. ed. (1967).

Forms: WILLIAM G. ARCHER, *Indian Miniatures* (1960), and *Indian Paintings from the Punjab Hills: A Survey and History of Pahari Miniature Painting* (1973); MARK ZEBROWSKI, *Deccani Painting* (1983); JANET WOODBURY ADAMS, *Decorative Folding Screens: In the West from 1600 to the Present Day* (U.S. title: *Decorative Folding Screens: 400 Years in the Western World*, 1982); ELISE GRILLI, *The Art of the Japanese Screen* (1971); ROSELEE GOLDBERG, *Performance: Live Art, 1909 to the Present* (1979); and ADRIAN HENRI, *Environments and Happenings* (U.S. title: *Total Art: Environments, Happenings, and Performance*, 1974).

Imagery: E.H. GOMBRICH, *Art and Illusion*, 4th ed. (1972); GYORGY KEPES (ed.), *Sign, Image, Symbol* (1966); LEON M. ZOLBROD, *Haiku Painting* (1983); LUCY R. LIPPARD et al., *Pop Art* (1966, rev. ed. 1970); and J.H. MATTHEWS, *Eight Painters: The Surrealist Context* (1982).

Subject matter: HOWARD DANIEL, *Encyclopedia of Themes and Subjects in Painting* (1971), a concise survey of Western mythological and religious subjects; DAVID ROSAND, *Painting in Cinquecento Venice* (1982); SVETLANA ALPERS, *The Art of Describing: Dutch Art in the Seventeenth Century* (1983); NORMAN BRYSON, *World and Image: French Painting of the Ancient Régime* (1982); MICHAEL LEVEY, *The Painter Depicted: Painters as a Subject in Painting* (1982); JOHN POPE-HENNESSY, *The Portrait in the Renaissance* (1966, reissued 1979), includes interpretive discussions of the works and extracts from the artists' letters; KENNETH CLARK, *Landscape into Art* (1949, reissued 1975); A. RICHARD TURNER, *The Vision of Landscape in Renaissance Italy* (1966, reprinted 1974); JOSEPH S. CZESTOCHOWSKI, *The American Landscape Tradition* (1982); ROGER BOULET, *The Canadian Earth: Landscape Paintings by the Group of Seven* (1982); MICHAEL JACOBS, *Nude Painting* (1979); and KENNETH CLARK, *The Nude: A Study of Ideal Art* (1976).

Symbolism: ERWIN PANOFSKY, *Studies in Iconology* (1939, reissued 1972), and *Meaning in the Visual Arts* (1955, reprinted 1982); F.D.K. BOSCH, *The Golden Germ* (1960); CARL G. JUNG et al., *Man and His Symbols* (posthumous ed. 1964, reprinted 1979), with excellent illustrations; RUDOLF WITTKOWER, *Allegory and the Migration of Symbols* (1977), includes Eastern imagery; PAUL FRANKL, *The Gothic: Literary Sources and Interpretations Through Eight Centuries* (1960); GEORGE FERGUSON, *Signs and Symbols in Christian Art* (1954, reprinted 1973); JOAN EVANS, *Monastic Iconography in France: From the Renaissance to the Revolution* (1970); and JITENDRA NATH BANERJEA, *The Development of Hindu Iconography*, 2nd rev. ed. (1956, reprinted 1974).

Writings: IRMA A. RICHTER (ed.), *Selections from the Notebooks of Leonardo da Vinci* (1952, reprinted 1977), illustrated; GIORGIO VASARI, *Vasari on Technique*, ed. by G. BALDWIN BROWN, trans. by LOUISA A. MACLEHOSE (1907, reprinted 1961); *The Mustard Seed Garden Manual of Painting, 1679–1701,* included in MAI-MAI SZE, *The Tao of Painting*, 2nd ed., 2 vol. (1963); ELIZABETH G. HOLT (ed.), *A Documentary History of Art*, 2nd ed., 3 vol. (1957–65); JOHN REWALD (ed.), *Cézanne's Letters*, 5th ed. (1982); VINCENT VAN GOGH, *The Complete Letters of Vincent van Gogh*, 2nd ed., 3 vol. (1978); FERNAND LÉGER, *Functions of Painting*, ed. by EDWARD F. FRY (1973; originally published in French, 1965); ROBERT DELAUNAY and SONIA DELAUNAY, *The New Art of Color*, ed. by ARTHUR A. COHEN (1978); ROBERT MOTHERWELL (ed.), *The Dada Painters and Poets: An Anthology*, 2nd ed. (1981); MARCEL JEAN (ed.), *The Autobiography of Surrealism* (1980); WASSILY KANDINSKY, *Kandinsky, Complete Writings on Art*, 2 vol., ed. by KENNETH C. LINDSAY and PETER VERGO (1982), with the original illustrations; PAUL KLEE, *Pedagogical Sketchbook* (1953, reprinted 1977; originally published in German, 1925), *On Modern Art* (1948, reprinted 1966; originally published in German, 1945), *The Thinking Eye*, ed. by JÜRG SPILLER (1961, reprinted 1969; originally published in German, 1956), and *The Diaries of Paul Klee, 1898–1918*, ed. by FELIX KLEE (1964, reissued 1968; originally published in German, 1957); MARCEL DUCHAMP, *The Essential Writings of Marcel Duchamp: Salt Seller*, ed. by MICHEL SANOUILLET and ELMER PETERSON (1975; originally published in French, 1958), and *Marcel Duchamp, Notes*, ed. by PAUL MATISSE (1983); HENRI MATISSE, *Notes of a Painter*, included in ALFRED H. BARR, *Matisse: His Art and His Public* (1951, reprinted 1966); EDWARD F. FRY, *Cubism* (1966, reprinted 1978; trans. from the French and German); PIERRE DAIX, *Cubists and Cubism* (1982; originally published in French, 1982); PABLO PICASSO, *Picasso on Art: A Selection of Views*, comp. by DORE ASHTON (1972); KATHARINE KUH, *The Artist's Voice: Talks with Seventeen Artists* (1962); and *The New York School*, foreword by MAURICE TUCHMAN (1970), with an extensive bibliography.

(P.D.O.)

The History of Western Painting

Painting, the execution of forms and shapes on a surface by means of pigment (but see also DRAWING for discussion of depictions in chalks, inks, pastels, and crayons), has been continuously practiced by humans for some 20,000 years. Together with other activities that may have been ritualistic in origin but have come to be designated as artistic (such as music or dance), painting was one of the earliest ways in which man sought to express his own personality and his emerging understanding of an existence beyond the material world. Unlike music and dance, however, examples of early forms of painting have survived to the present day. The modern eye can derive aesthetic as well as antiquarian satisfaction from the 15,000-year-old cave murals of Lascaux—some examples testify to the considerable powers of draftsmanship of these early artists. And painting, like other arts, exhibits universal qualities that make it easy for viewers of all nations and civilizations to understand and appreciate.

The major extant examples of early painting anywhere in the world are found in western Europe and the Soviet Union. But some 5,000 years ago, the areas in which important paintings were executed shifted to the eastern Mediterranean Sea and neighbouring regions. For the purposes of this article, therefore, Western painting is to be taken as signifying painting not only in Europe but also in regions outside Europe that share a European cultural tradition—the Middle East and Mediterranean Basin and, later, the countries of the New World.

Western painting is in general distinguished by its concentration on the representation of the human figure, whether in the heroic context of antiquity or the religious context of the early Christian and medieval world. The Renaissance extended this tradition through a close examination of the natural world and an investigation of balance, harmony, and perspective in the visible world, linking painting to the developing sciences of anatomy and optics. The first real break from figurative painting came with the growth of landscape painting in the 17th and 18th centuries. The landscape and figurative traditions developed together in the 19th century in an atmosphere that was increasingly concerned with "painterly" qualities of the interaction of light and colour and the expressive qualities of paint handling. In the 20th century these interests contributed to the development of a third major tradition in Western painting, abstract painting, which sought to uncover and express the true nature of paint and painting through action and form.

For coverage of related topics in the *Macropædia* and *Micropædia*, see the *Propædia*, section 628.   (Ed.)

This article is divided into the following sections:

European Stone Age

Upper Paleolithic. During the Upper Paleolithic Period, just before the final retreat of the glaciers at the end of the last Ice Age (15,000–10,000 BC), much of Europe was peopled by small bands of nomadic hunters preying on the migratory herds of reindeer, cattle, bison, horses, mammoth, and other animals whose bodies provided them with food, clothing, and the raw materials for tools and weapons. These primitive hunters decorated the walls of their caves with large paintings of the animals that were so important for their physical well-being. Most surviving examples of such murals have been found in France and Spain (see PREHISTORIC PEOPLES AND CULTURES), but similar figures from caves in the Ural Mountains in the Soviet Union may indicate that the practice was more widespread than has been supposed.

Ever since the first examples of these paintings came to light in the late 19th century, they have excited admiration for their virtuosity and liveliness. The simplest figures are mere outline drawings, but the majority combine this technique with sophisticated shading and colour washes that modulate the surface and suggest the differing textures of pelts, horn, and bone. Volume is indicated by carefully controlled changes in the thickness of brushstrokes, and the astonishingly advanced draftsmanship conveys a considerable sense of movement and life. Most of the animals were originally depicted as individual figures without narrative import, and what appear to the modern observer to be sophisticated groupings of figures are, in reality, the end result of a long additive process.

The lack of a clear narrative element in these paintings has caused problems in their interpretation. Man is seldom portrayed, and depictions of human figures unambiguously interacting with the numerous animal figures are rare. One of the few exceptions to this rule is a scene at Lascaux in southern France depicting a bison butting a falling male figure. The "Sorcerer" at Les Trois Frères, also in southern France, is more characteristic. Although he is draped in the skin of an animal and seems to be engaged in stalking or a ritual dance, his complete isolation from any other figure leaves his exact significance unclear. It is also interesting that, in contrast to the obvious care taken in the detailed portrayal of animals, the few human figures are usually executed in a perfunctory and schematized fashion. Sometimes the only hint of man is provided by depictions of darts wounding or killing a few of the animal figures. These projectiles have been interpreted as exercises in sympathetic magic designed to induce success in a future hunt. Conversely, they might just as easily commemorate past kills. But certain features suggest that such simple explanations do not tell the whole story: first, such portrayals are rare (in inverse proportion to the amount of scholarly discussion they have engendered) and, second, the beasts that are shown as wounded—indeed the vast majority of the species depicted on the cave walls—were not significant items in the diet of the cave artists. Contemporary habitation deposits indicate that most of the meat consumed came from reindeer, and reindeer appear almost as infrequently as man himself among the surviving paintings. One fact is clear: individual initiative seems paramount, both in the execution of the animal figures and in the recording of the activities of the isolated humans. Any hint of social interaction is absent, and it has been assumed that society as such existed at a relatively low level. Nature provided the impetus for change, and in the art of the following period man finally emerged as part of a community.

Mesolithic. At the end of the Ice Age the great herds that had provided sustenance for the Paleolithic hunters disappeared from France and Spain. Forests cloaked the landscape and harboured much smaller groups of deer and related species. These were fleet and elusive and, in consequence, much more difficult to hunt and kill. Thus, although the climate was warmer than before, it was much harder to live by hunting alone. Man had to modify his hunting techniques and forage for the seeds and fruits that the forests provided, or the fish and shellfish that he could find in rivers or on the coasts. Cooperation was essential, and the new situation is clearly reflected in the art of the period.

In the southern and eastern parts of what is now Spain, small bands of such hunter-gatherers left a record of their activities in the rock shelters where they camped periodically. In some ways the new paintings resemble the old. Although a simple silhouette technique for the most part replaced the outline and shading techniques of the Paleolithic style, facility of brushwork and accuracy of observation continued to imbue the new creations with a vivacity and sense of movement similar to those of their predecessors. There are obvious conceptual differences between the two artistic complexes, however. The new paintings constitute the first real compositions having a clear narrative meaning, and man finally emerges as the chief actor in the dramas played out on the rock walls. At Remigia three hunters are depicted stalking a leaping ibex, while at Los Caballos a line of archers fires arrows into a small herd of panic-stricken deer, presumably driven into the ambush by beaters. Scenes of battle or groups of dancers also occur, while social status is implied in a carefully executed archer found at Santolea: he is dressed in painstakingly portrayed finery and is flanked by two other figures. This emphasis on man is new, but even more significant is the element of cooperation as part of a group whose social cohesion in warfare, hunting, or ritual was probably necessary if the group was to survive and prosper.

Social status implied

Neolithic. The subsequent Neolithic Period saw the introduction from western Asia of farming and the raising of domesticated animals. The new way of life appeared in the Balkans sometime before 6000 BC and rapidly spread across Europe. For the first time man was able to live a relatively settled village life and accumulate a wide range of household goods. So far as large-scale painting is concerned, however, this period is something of a disappointment. Thus far, there is no evidence that the farming communities decorated their house walls with painted designs, in this at least failing to imitate their Asiatic mentors whose walls, as in the shrines at Catalhüyük in Turkey, were often embellished with ambitious decorative schemes. In different places and at different times the European farmers did indeed indulge their aesthetic drive by producing highly decorated painted pottery whose patterns reflect contemporary basketwork or textiles. Few of these styles include human or animal figures and, despite their undoubted charm, these vases are the products of craft traditions that have little to do with large-scale art.

Aegean and eastern Mediterranean Metal Age

In Greece and the Aegean, influence from the adjacent areas of western Asia helped promote the rise of small towns by about 3000 BC. The cultural development is usually divided into three separate strands: Minoan on Crete, Cycladic on the islands of the central Aegean, and Helladic on the Greek mainland. A fourth area, Cyprus, is often included in this development, though its culture was closer to those of Syria and Asia Minor and it was only during the 13th century BC that Greek invaders brought Cyprus fully into the Aegean orbit. (P.J.C.)

The Metal Age in Europe started in the early 3rd millennium BC, when the peoples around the Aegean Sea began to work copper, under the influence of the neighbouring peoples of western Asia. By 2500 BC coppersmiths were also active across the Alps. Bronze began to be used in Europe at the beginning of the 2nd millennium BC, and iron was used in Greece by the 11th century BC and north of the Alps by the 8th century BC. Bronze was always a luxury item because the sources of its constituent metals, tin and copper, occurred in scattered deposits, often far from the producing centres. Its use, therefore, encouraged trade. But iron, when it came into use, was cheaper and easier to work; moreover, the ore lodes were often close at hand. Its use, especially for agricultural implements, allowed more intensive exploitation of the countryside, especially those areas where heavy soils had precluded farming with more primitive tools. The end of this period is usually placed at the point where written records supplement the archaeological record. In Greece and Italy this happened during the 8th century BC or a little later, whereas in northwestern Europe the Celtic and Germanic peoples had to wait for the Roman conquests of the 1st century BC before emerging into history. Beyond the imperial frontiers old patterns continued longer. Throughout this long period it was the Mediterranean, with its flourishing towns and cities, that produced major works of painting.

(O.K.-J./P.J.C.)

EARLY BRONZE AGE (3000–2000 BC)

Early Minoan. In Crete the Early Minoan peoples lived in small towns and villages with a basically agricultural economy. Although traces of their houses have been preserved, it is clear that they did not paint their walls with decorative designs. The fine plaster introduced at this time, however, did provide the basis for later developments. Their pottery was at first plain or decorated with simple, arresting patterns of straight lines. (Pottery is an important source for modern knowledge of painting in the last three millennia BC because, although fired clay objects—even when decorated—may be broken, they are not easily pulverized, so many fragments have survived.) In the following phase (2500–2200 BC) a similar style flourished, though other vases with a mottled surface imitating variegated stones were produced. During the third phase (2200–2000 BC) most fine vases were decorated with designs in white or cream paint on a dark ground. Elegant running spirals and other curvilinear motifs, as well as the occasional use of other colours, revolutionized the style and paved the way for the greater advances of the Middle Minoan period.

Running spirals and other curvilinear motifs

Early Cycladic. In the islands there was little interest in painted designs. Most decoration consisted of incised or impressed geometric schemes, though there were some vases with similar designs in paint. The typical pottery of the second and third phases (2500–2000 BC) was decorated in semilustrous paint, either as an allover wash or in angular patterns.

Early Helladic. On the Greek mainland there was a similar lack of interest in painted decoration on pots. Although monumental buildings have been found in the Peloponnese dating to the Early Helladic II period (2500–2200 BC), none of these had decorated walls. New settlers arrived about 2200 BC and destroyed the old centres of power. Their houses were primitive affairs and only a few of their finer vases bore painted designs, these being of straight lines or other simple patterns.

MIDDLE BRONZE AGE (2000–1600 BC)

Middle Minoan. The Middle Minoan period saw the evolution of a monarchical society based on palaces situated in the most fertile districts of Crete. There were undoubtedly frescoes in these large buildings before 1600 BC, but little survived the disastrous earthquake of about 1700 BC, and once again it is the pottery that gives the best idea of contemporary aesthetics. The decorative style is basically a development of the previous period's. Curvilinear patterns in white, yellow, and red swirl around the surfaces of these bulbous vases. The latest Middle Minoan style is similar, but its static formality seems better suited to wall decoration, and it is likely that monumental frescoes from the old palaces influenced the vase painter. The combination of modeled flowers and animals with painted motifs on the vases certainly reflects similar developments in wall painting, where stucco reliefs were combined with simple painted backgrounds.

Middle Cycladic and Middle Helladic. On the mainland and in the islands, native styles of plain or simply painted pottery continued to be executed, but Cretan influence was felt toward the end of the period in both areas, and they began to be drawn into the wider cultural orbit characteristic of the following period.

LATE BRONZE AGE (1600–1100 BC)

Wall paintings. The three separate areas of the Aegean were brought into intimate contact during the Late Bronze Age; indeed the whole eastern Mediterranean saw intense cross connections and cultural diffusion. Great palaces arose on the Greek mainland and Crete and even on some of the lesser islands. Although there were probably differences in the natures of the societies that built them (resulting in fortified structures on the Greek mainland and unfortified ones on Crete), the palaces and great houses were decorated with complex frescoes whose style was based on Cretan models. Many of the figured scenes are merely decorative and depict landscapes with birds and animals or figures gathering flowers. Others show ceremonies connected with a cult or the court (Plate 1, "The Toreador Fresco") and were probably useful in bolstering the power of the royal or priestly classes. The style is a combination of dark outline drawing, to delimit the object shown, and solid painted areas within it. On some birds and animals the feathers or pelts are imitated by slightly more impressionistic brushstrokes. Most of these frescoes are in fragmentary condition, but a better idea of what they must once have looked like can be gained from the house walls at Akrotíri on Thera (one of the Cyclades of the southern Aegean). Thera was destroyed by volcanic eruption during the 15th century BC and is often referred to as the Greek Pompeii. The wall paintings there were heavily influenced by those of Crete, both as to style and subject matter, though the popularity of outline figures on a pale background stemmed from the local pottery tradition. One of the most exciting discoveries is a long frieze depicting a fleet of gaily decorated ships sailing against a backdrop of hilly islands with towns, shepherds, and hunters scattered along the shores or set upon the forested peaks among gushing streams. Another painting shows a group of women at a religious festival and—in the first known instance at this period—ordinary people: two boys boxing and a fisherman proudly displaying his catch (Plate 1). These paintings decorated well-to-do houses. In the great palaces of Crete and on the Greek mainland many of the scenes are rather more formal. At Knossos on Crete there are long lines of offering bearers in the vestibule leading to the state rooms. The throne in one ritual chamber is flanked by fresco paintings of griffins whose presence must have had a protective value. Griffins also flank the throne at Pylos in Greece, and the same site has produced fragments of another fresco showing battle scenes. Mycenae (also on the Greek mainland) possesses a small sanctuary whose walls are decorated with ritual episodes, and religious ceremonies do indeed appear to have been an important part of the wall painters' repertoire. There are, however, none of the historical or annalistic scenes so characteristic of the palaces and temples of western Asia and Egypt. In particular there are no depictions of investitures or battles with accompanying inscriptions; in short, Aegean paintings are far less bombastic than their Middle Eastern equivalents. This is not to say that the visitor would have been less impressed by the ruler's power in these first great European civilizations, merely that the iconographic emphases were different. (P.J.C.)

Differences between Asia and Europe

Vase paintings. *Late Minoan.* The light-on-dark style of pottery was by now replaced by dark-on-light ornamentation. At first (roughly 1600–1500 BC), curvilinear patterns and simple designs of vegetation predominated. Between 1500 and about 1450 BC, however, there flourished the Marine style, possibly the most successful of all Minoan pottery styles (Figure 1). Nearly every form of marine life is accurately reproduced in a riotous allover arrangement: octopuses, argonauts, dolphins, and fish, against a background of rocks and waves. In the 70 or 80 years after 1450 BC, the spontaneity of the early Marine style degenerated into a rigid formality. Subsequently, Late Minoan pottery became little more than a provincial version of Mycenaean ware.

Late Mycenaean. For about two and a half centuries after around 1600 BC, Mycenaean pottery painting echoed Minoan. After the eclipse of Knossos, however, Minoan influence declined, and Mycenaean potters fell back on their own resources. Minoan plant and marine motifs became simpler until virtually unrecognizable as representations of anything in real life. A figure style also developed. Adapted at first from frescoes and later from textiles, this style is seldom successful, however. Unlike the classical Greeks who came later, the Mycenaean potters were not

Figure 1: The "Octopus Vase," Marine style vessel from Palaíkastron, Crete, c. 1500 BC. In the Archaeological Museum, Iráklion. Height 27.9 cm.

From *Crete and Mycenae* published by Thames & Hudson, London, and Harry N. Abrams, New York; photograph, Hirmer Fotoarchiv, Munchen

able to adapt their fresco style so as to form a convincing figure style for vases.

Late Cypriot. The Cypriot pottery of the Late Bronze Age is of three main kinds: (1) a handmade ware with a glossy brown surface called base-ring ware, vases and statuettes of humans and animals being the most common examples of this type, (2) white-slip ware, in which handmade vases of a leathery appearance are decorated with patterns in black on a white slip (slip is liquid clay covering the pottery body), and (3) local imitations, made on the wheel, of imported Mycenaean pottery, which was evidently popular. (R.A.Hi./P.J.C.)

Ancient Greek

At the root of Greek art was the desire to explore man and the nature of his experience. Even divine subjects were cast in terms of human behaviour, and both gods and epic heroes could at times stand as representations of and models for contemporary political achievement. The seemingly naturalistic outward forms characteristic of Greek art have continued to fascinate Western artists to the present day, and the history of Western painting is full of classical revivals that have aimed at recapturing the spirit of the Greek original. Art, however, is deeply rooted in the society that creates it, and these classical revivals usually say more about those who are attempting the revival than they do about the Greek art that served as the model. Attempts to re-create the spirit and form of antique art do serve, however, as a reminder that a mere description of form does not reveal the whole truth about the art of an ancient culture. This section defines, therefore, the reasons for certain developments as well as the technical advances themselves.

A major stumbling block has been the difficulty in defining the ancient Greek attitude to art. Certainly it is clear that there was no concept of "art for art's sake" before the Hellenistic period (roughly the last three and a quarter centuries BC). Great works of art were functional: they served as gifts to the gods, monuments to the dead, or commemorations of events in the life of a city. The Greek language itself made no distinction between art and craft: both were called *technē*; a great work of art was simply an exceptional piece of workmanship (*aristourgēma*). This lack of linguistic variety should not be made too much of, however, for the actions of the artists indicate that they were exceptionally proud of their work. For the first time in the history of art, painters signed their works, and both painters and sculptors explored new means of expression. The greatest sculptors sometimes wrote books detailing

their philosophy of art, and there was obviously a body of philosophical thought behind the more important advances in the painter's technique during the 5th and 4th centuries BC. By the late 5th century BC this became a basis for discussion by the philosophers themselves, indicating that, by then at least, a theory of art coexisted with the corpus of workshop techniques that might reasonably be called the practice of art. (P.J.C.)

Paintings on wall plaster, wood, and marble panels are easily eradicated, and most ancient paintings were destroyed long ago. Many fine examples, some of the highest quality, have survived, however. These are the funerary paintings on stelae (decorated stone slabs) or burial chamber walls in northern Greece and Macedonia, whose rich kings and nobles could afford the best talents from the southern cities. Contemporary vase paintings—so long as vase painting continued—often depict the same subjects and sometimes faintly reflect the style and composition of monumental frescoes, but they were in no sense accurate or even deliberate copies. The paintings on vases, now the main evidence for the development of Greek draftsmanship, were hardly mentioned by ancient writers and, although in great demand, were evidently not considered important works of art. (B.As./P.J.C.)

DARK AGES (1200–900 BC)

During the 13th century BC the great palatial centres of the Aegean world came to a violent end. Both internal dissension and foreign invasion seem to have played a part in this development, and, if the exact course of events is still obscure, the end result is quite clear: Greece was severely depopulated and impoverished. The small, scattered settlements that took the place of the great Mycenaean and Minoan kingdoms were not able to support the luxury arts that had flourished in the Bronze Age palaces. No wall paintings are known from this period, and the sophisticated Bronze Age aesthetics was lost. Before the end of the 11th century BC Greece began a steady recovery, and a secure basis was laid for all future developments. At Athens, a city that had won a position of importance in Greece only at the end of the Bronze Age, the potters invented a new painted style, which has been called the Protogeometric. Old Bronze Age shapes persisted, but they became tauter and better proportioned. In addition, the old patterns were executed with a new finesse, aided by improved equipment—a multiple brush and compasses. Using these, the painter decorated selected zones of the vase with distinctive concentric circles and semicircles, simple zigzags, and wavy lines. The vases were well potted and restrained and successful in their decoration. The simple precision of their patterns is a quality that remained dominant in Greek vase painting as well as in the other arts. Other Greek cities besides Athens adopted the Protogeometric style as well. [Proto-geometric patterns]

GEOMETRIC PERIOD (C. 900–700 BC)

The Geometric style arose in Athens about 900 BC. It built upon the foundations of the previous period, though the area covered by painted patterns expanded and new motifs were incorporated into the painters' repertoire. The meander, swastika, and crenellation (battlement) patterns were prominent and, together with the older concentric circles, were used by the painters to push back the large areas of solid black characteristic of Protogeometric vases and to create a pleasing halftone decorative effect. A few human and animal figures were introduced into this otherwise severely geometric scheme, but it was not until about 760 BC that a renewed interest in figures became paramount. The major achievement in this development was that of the Dipylon Master, who specialized in monumental vases used as markers over the graves of rich Athenians (Figure 2). These vases incorporated scenes with animal and human figures: funerals, battles, and processions as well as files of deer or goats. The figures were not conceived in realistic terms; rather, they were formalized into geometric shapes whose schematic appearance did the least possible damage to the overall decorative pattern. That this was deliberate is indicated by the fact that newly introduced types, such as sows and piglets, are more naturalistic at

Figure 2: Attic Geometric amphora with *prothesis* (scene depicting the dead lying in state with mourners), 8th century BC. In the National Archaeological Museum, Athens. Height 1.55 m.
Alison Frantz

the time of their first appearance than in their subsequent development, when the artists learned how to cast them in a more formalized mold. Nevertheless, the introduction of schemes involving figures marked the beginning of the end for the Geometric style, for later painters became more and more fascinated with this aspect of decoration, and the older pattern work languished. By the end of the 8th century BC the figures had become much more naturalistic and were joined by floral patterns introduced from western Asia, leading to the rise of new styles in which men and gods occupied the most important positions.

The reasons for the introduction of figures, even the exact significance of such decoration, are problematic. On the simplest level, the subject matter is a factor: battles and funerals can be related to the lives of the aristocratic patrons whose graves were marked out by the Dipylon

Anderson—Alinari from Art Resource/EB Inc.

Figure 3: The "Chigi Vase" with battle, procession, and hunting scenes, Proto-Corinthian, c. 640 BC. In the National Museum of Villa Giulia, Rome. Height 26.2 cm.

vases. Some scholars believe, however, that the figured scenes include episodes from the heroic past or that the whole of the new iconography was cast in a heroic mold, indicating a basic identification between the aristocrats of the 8th century BC and their epic forebears. Athens in the Geometric period remained the centre from which the vase-painting studios of other cities took their inspiration.

ORIENTALIZING PERIOD (C. 700–625 BC)

About 700 BC important changes took place in vase painting. Floral motifs, animals, and monsters borrowed from the art of Syria and Phoenicia delivered the coup de grace to an already debased Geometric style. In Athens the new style is called Proto-Attic and includes, for the first time, scenes referring unambiguously to Greece's heroic past. The exploits of Heracles, Perseus, and other heroes were painted, often on large vases used as burial containers. The bodies of men and animals were depicted in silhouette, though their heads were drawn in outline; women were drawn completely in outline. The brushwork is bold, even sloppy on occasion, and the general effect is monumental and very impressive.

At Corinth, painting followed a different course during the 7th century BC. Corinthian painters also borrowed Oriental motifs, but their predilection for small vases, whose surfaces were divided into horizontal registers and covered with numerous tiny and beautifully drawn figures, created a miniaturist style called Proto-Corinthian (Figure 3). By the end of the century human or mythological figures were rare, and the backgrounds of the animal and narrative scenes were filled with incised floral rosettes. Corinthians introduced the black-figure technique, which, although seeming to owe something to Asian influence, is essentially native to Greece. In black-figure technique figures were painted on the naturally pale clay surface of the vase in a lustrous black pigment and then incised to indicate details of anatomy and drapery. Added colours enhanced the liveliness of these scenes. The high quality of these Proto-Corinthian vases led to a flourishing export trade, and in the later 7th century BC they were exported throughout the Mediterranean.

ARCHAIC PERIOD (C. 625–500 BC)

Corinth remained the leading exporter of Greek vases until about 550 BC, though mass production quickly led to a drop in quality. These later vases were decorated with unambitious and stereotyped groups of animal or human figures; there was little or no interest in narrative. By the late 7th century BC Athenian artists had adopted many of the stylistic features of Corinthian pots, as well as the black-figure technique. Files of animals became popular at Athens, but the artists always maintained an interest in the narrative scenes that had been so popular in the Proto-Attic style. The finest example of the marriage of Corinthian discipline and Attic invention is the François vase (in the Archaeological Museum in Florence), produced about 570 BC and exported to Etruria in Italy. Its surface is divided into horizontal friezes containing hundreds of carefully drawn, tiny figures showing episodes from Greek myth. The professionalism of the Attic masters, so clearly displayed on this and other contemporary vases, contrasted with the laziness of the Corinthian painters, and it is hardly surprising that the Attic products soon captured the foreign markets.

The first generation of Athenian painters after 500 BC concentrated on large-scale narrative scenes. One, Exekias, was fond of heroes. His superb draftsmanship and sense of the monumental was emphasized by exceedingly detailed use of incision to indicate the patterns on drapery, weapons, and anatomy (Figure 4). The Amasis Painter, on the other hand, preferred the wild cavortings of the wine god, Dionysus, and his band of drunken followers.

In general, many old conventions were retained. Men were still painted in black on the red ground of the vase; women had white skins. But some of the work of the Amasis Painter and his contemporaries used an outline technique for women and certain other figures, and it must soon have become obvious that the brush allowed greater freedom than the graver. By about 530 BC several

Important changes in vase painting

Many old conventions retained

Figure 4: Amphora with Ajax and Achilles playing a board game, painted by Exekias, c. 550–540 BC. In the Vatican Museum. Height 61 cm.

Hirmer Fotoarchiv, Munchen

painters took the momentous decision to dispense with the old black-figure technique entirely and show all their figures in outline, the details being indicated only with the brush. The background of the vase was now painted solid black and the figures stood out dramatically against this sombre field. This is called the red-figure technique, and, in the hands of artists such as Euthymides and Euphronius, the style rapidly gained ground. It had several advantages over black-figure. Incising the older decoration was painfully laborious, and it was almost impossible to vary the thickness or intensity of the incised lines. The painted line, however, could be made thicker or thinner depending on the amount of pressure applied and the amount of paint on the brush; it could also be made lighter by diluting the glaze. Red-figure artists took advantage of all these tricks and found that it was possible to depict complicated groups of overlapping figures or incidents involving violent action. Cities other than Athens and Corinth had studios producing black-figure vases; of these the most distinguished were in Sparta and eastern Greece. By the end of the Archaic period, however, only Athens was producing and exporting finely decorated pottery in any quantity.

It has always been assumed that vase painting in the Orientalizing and Archaic periods mirrored developments in monumental art, and to a certain extent this seems to be true. Not many paintings on monuments survive, but a sufficient number exist to give a general idea of their form and technique. Temple models of the late Geometric and Orientalizing periods are decorated in a way that suggests that temples had paintings on their walls; fragments of such paintings have actually been found at the temple of Poseidon at the Isthmus of Corinth. The earliest reasonably well-preserved temple decoration, however, comes from the temple of Apollo at Thermon, in central Greece, and dates from the later 7th century BC. The temple roof was decorated with a series of square terra-cotta frieze plaques, called metopes, bearing mythological scenes. Although there are several similarities to contemporary vases, there are also important differences: black-figure incision is confined to relatively minor details of drapery, and the figures themselves are drawn in outline, the women then being overpainted in white. Among vases of this period, only the brightly painted drinking cups from the island of Chios seem at all similar in technique. Other terra-cotta plaques painted in a similar, though more developed, style have been found in Italy at Caere (where they decorate the interior walls of a temple) and on the Acropolis, at Athens, indicating that there was probably a continuous tradition in this technique.

More important, because more numerous, are the many paintings on stucco. These are found in Italy and Asia Minor, as well as in Greece. They were painted by Greeks or artists working under intense Greek influence. At Pitsa,

near Corinth, votive plaques covered in stucco and then painted have been found. There was a flourishing school of Greek painters who decorated tombs in the colonies of southern Italy. In Asia Minor, two tombs dating from the Late Archaic period have been found near Elmalı, in ancient Lycia (what is now southwestern Turkey). Although depicting scenes from the life of a Lycian prince, they were certainly painted by Greeks. With the exception of the plaque from Pitsa, a minor work, all these paintings come from provincial areas of the Greek world and probably do not represent the very finest of paintings then in existence, but many are highly competent pieces of work and they do give some idea of the state of monumental painting at the time. As on the vases, the greatest emphasis was on finely controlled line. Colours were applied in flat, undifferentiated masses, and there was no attempt at shading, perspective, or illusionistic treatment. At Karaburun, near Elmalı, variety was introduced by the use of finely detailed motifs on the clothing of the prince, an effect closer to the work of Exekias than to the practices of the early red-figure vase painters.

CLASSICAL PERIOD (C. 500–323 BC)

Early Classical (c. 500–450 BC). The Early Classical period is deemed to have begun after Athens' double defeat of the Persian invaders in 490 and 479 BC, but a new feeling of self-confidence was already in the air about 500 BC, possibly as a result of the firm establishment of democracy in Athens 10 years earlier. By now the Archaic colour and pattern were gone from vase painting, to be replaced by sobriety and dignity. The artist's ability to render anatomy in line had reached the point where he could accurately indicate the roundness of a figure without shading. The artist was still bound, however, to a strict profile view of heads, with few frontal, and even fewer three-quarter, views of the features. The vase painters of the first quarter of the 5th century BC included some of the finest Athens was ever to produce. One, the Cleophrades Painter, has often been called the "painter of power" since his intense, majestic subjects are rich in psychological insight. Although not all his vases concern scenes of violence, perhaps the vase that captures his spirit best is the kalpis, or wine jar, depicting the sack of Troy. It has been suggested that the extreme cruelty and tragedy present in this scene may well reflect Greek shock at the brutal sack of Miletus by Persian troops in 494 BC.

Another artist of this period was the Berlin Painter. His finest vases are almost completely covered in black glaze. Isolated or small groups of overlapping figures of extreme delicacy are posed on each side of the vases. The brushwork is exceptionally fine, and in these vases there is a sombre mood of introspection that also characterizes many contemporary sculptures. The work of this fine artist, though, is a relatively isolated phenomenon, except in funerary art where inaction and otherworldliness are appropriate. Most vase painters preferred a more narrative approach, and these narratives often reflected contemporary political developments. In 510 BC the tyranny (a tyrant at that time was a ruler, not necessarily brutal, who ruled unconstitutionally) of the Peisistratids had been overthrown in Athens, and the new democratic rulers, seeking among the heroes of the past a suitable patron, chose Theseus, an ancient king of Athens who had been credited with the union of the whole of Attica under the rule of its chief city. The new democracy fought off attempts to reinstate the tyrants, as well as defeating the two Persian invasions. It is therefore hardly surprising that the vase painters responded to the general enthusiasm and civic pride by adopting Theseus as a frequent subject. This development was reflected in monumental painting. About 460 BC the Painted Stoa at Athens was decorated with a series of paintings representing famous battles, including both legendary and historical events involving Athenians. Thus, probably for the first time in Greek history, painters placed their talents at the service of the state—moreover, a state that used them to decorate purely secular buildings. Panaenos, the brother or nephew of the sculptor Phidias, executed a picture of the Battle of Marathon for the Painted Stoa and, sometime later, included a painting of

Stucco
paintings
more
numerous

Exceptionally fine
brushwork

Greece and Salamis personified on the throne for the cult statue of Zeus at Olympia. This brought the depiction of political achievement into the very temples of the gods.

None of the Early Classical architectural paintings has survived, but a reasonable idea of what they might have looked like may be gleaned from the work of various vase painters who seem to have been working under the influence of the monumental artists. The great wall painter Polygnotus is said to have depicted figures at different depths in his compositional field, and similar compositions occur in the work of the Niobid Painter (Figure 5), although the lack of scope for such compositions on vases generally makes this something of an isolated example. Micon was another celebrated wall painter; both he and Polygnotus worked in Athens and Delphi. Ancient descriptions of their work dwell on features and moods that are easy to envisage in the light of extant contemporary vase painting and the Olympia sculptures, to which they seem to have been similar in spirit. The effect of wall paintings on white plaster may also be imagined by examining various white-ground vases intended for the tomb, where there is a concentration on calligraphic line and colour applied in flat areas without any use of shading. In other words, for all its achievements, Greek painting was still closer to drawing than anything that might today be regarded as exhibiting true painterly qualities.

Figure 5: Calyx krater showing unidentified subjects with Heracles and Athena, by the Niobid Painter, c. 455–450 BC. In the Louvre, Paris. Height 54 cm.

High Classical (c. 450–400 BC). Because Greek vase painting consists essentially of the delineation of form by line, it could not follow monumental wall or panel painting once the latter began to depart significantly from their common traditions. This happened during the second half of the 5th century BC, and vase painting, while surviving for a time by looking to sculpture as a source of inspiration, went into a swift decline from about 400 BC.

There were certainly revolutionary changes in monumental painting technique. The Athenian painter Apollodorus introduced *skiagraphia* (literally "shadow painting"), or shading technique. In its simplest form this consists of hatched areas that give the illusion of both shadow and volume. A few of the white-ground vases exhibit this technique in a discreet fashion, but its true potentialities may be seen in the great cycle of wall paintings that decorate the small royal tomb at Vergina, in Macedonia. The paintings (Plate 2), executed in the 4th century BC, represent the abduction of Persephone by Hades. The figures are defined less by an outline technique than by complicated patterns of shading and contour lines. Another technique that also may have been included within the concept of *skiagraphia* by the ancient Greeks can be found in the treatment of Persephone's drapery: the reddish pink mantle is overlaid with slabs of darker red to create realistic patterns of light and shade, and then still darker lines are used to indicate the folds. This tomb is of the utmost importance for understanding the development of Greek painting, since it contains the earliest first-rate monumental wall painting to have survived. It indicates, among other things, how rash it is to generalize about the state of painting at that time

from either vase painting or later Roman works, which, it has been argued, were based on Greek originals.

Late Classical (c. 400–323 BC). All authorities agree that the Late Classical period was the high point of ancient Greek painting. Within its short span many famous artists were at work, of whom Zeuxis, Apelles, and Parrhasius were the most famous. Considerable advances in technique were made at this time. Zeuxis built on the discoveries of Apollodorus, and his pupil Apelles, who lived in the later 4th century BC, worked along the same lines but achieved even greater fame. They appear to have added the concepts of highlighting and subtle gradations of colour. Late Classical monuments such as the Great Tomb at Leukadia, in Macedonia, suggest that one of the means at their disposal was the juxtaposition of lines of different colours to create optical fusion; in other words, a true painterly style in the modern sense of the term. Parrhasius, in contrast, was a conservative and insisted on the priority of something called linear style, which is assumed to be closer to drawing than painting. His influence has been detected in the figure of Hermes at Leukadia and in the Lion Hunt and Dionysus mosaics at Pella, also in Macedonia.

In Athens, red-figure vase painting was in decline, and the majority of vases were painted with showy scenes, using much added colour and gilding. Occasionally there is a glimpse of brilliant line drawing, but the technique barely survived the century.

HELLENISTIC PERIOD (C. 323–1ST CENTURY BC)

The Hellenistic period began with the incorporation of the Persian Empire into the Greek world, and specifically with the death of Alexander the Great (323 BC). In art history terms, however, a new relationship of painter and patron had begun slightly earlier. Apelles executed works depicting the tyrant of Sicyon and was later court painter to Alexander the Great. His career, in fact, spans the division between the two periods. The major monument for the new period is the Great Tomb at Vergina, whose exact date should lie between the death of Philip II of Macedon, in 336 BC, and the death of his son Philip III, in 317 BC. The facade of the tomb is decorated with a large wall painting depicting a royal lion hunt. The background was left white, landscape being indicated by a single tree and the ground line. The figures themselves were painted in the fashion Apelles is assumed to have introduced, and there are sophisticated examples of optical fusion and light and shadow. Very similar in style is the famous Alexander mosaic from Pompeii, almost certainly a copy of an original painting executed about the same time as that at Vergina. Apart from the interesting developments in technique discernible during the 4th century BC, an important change in patronage and choice of subject matter occurred. The great patrons were kings and tyrants, and many paintings exalted their claims to rule. After the 4th century BC there were few advances until the Roman period. One Demetrius of Alexandria is said to have specialized in "topographic" paintings, but the exact meaning of this word remains unclear. All other surviving Hellenistic works are of low quality.   (Jo.Bo./P.J.C.)

Western Mediterranean

In the Metal Age, western Mediterranean cultures were similar at many points. The area occupied by them extended from Illyria (an area roughly the same in extent as modern Yugoslavia) in the east to the Atlantic shores of the Iberian Peninsula in the west, and from the shores along the Gulf of Lion and the Ligurian Sea (*i.e.,* the coasts of what are now southern France and northwestern Italy) and the top of the Adriatic in the north to a line stretching from Sicily to Gibraltar in the south. Of the earliest painting in classical antiquity, however, little remains except the frescoes on the tombs of the Etruscans.   (R.Bl./P.J.C.)

ETRUSCAN

During the 8th and 7th centuries BC the Greeks founded many colonies in southern Italy, partly in order to ex-

High point of ancient Greek painting

Change in patronage and subject matter

pand their trade with the native peoples of Etruria, who controlled rich mineral deposits. In the Archaic period (6th century BC) these native settlements, scattered across the landscape of present-day Tuscany and Lazio in the area north of Rome, evolved into flourishing city-states whose culture was heavily dependent on influences from Greek art. More in the way of Etruscan painting has survived than in the case of Greek painting. The Etruscans buried their dead in large chamber tombs cut into bedrock; in many of these, especially in central Italy at Tarquinii (modern Tarquinia), Clusium (modern Chiusi), and Caere (modern Cerveteri), the walls of the tomb chambers were covered with plaster, and lively scenes were painted on them. Although some of these frescoes show scenes from Greek mythology, the overwhelming majority depict events in the lives of the Etruscans themselves. Funeral games were very popular subjects; perhaps the best-known depictions are those on the Tomb of the Augurs at Tarquinii, with its scenes of wrestlers, dancers, musicians, and a banquet. These paintings date from the late 6th century BC and, although the style of painting changed somewhat in later periods, the types of scene represented remained standard. The Archaic period saw the gradual evolution of an Etruscan style of wall painting whose inspiration is probably to be found in the Ionian colonies of southern Italy. By the early 5th century BC, however, the Athenian style began to predominate, and it ushered in the Classical period as well. There are many classical tombs at Clusium, including the Tomb of the Monkey.

Clusium's cultural lead This inland city seems to have taken a cultural lead during the 5th century BC; certainly it contains competently executed works that made use of the new stylistic discoveries of mainland Greece—shading, hatching, and simple dimensional effects. There are few surviving later classical monuments in Etruria, and they seem to add little to the style established during the 5th century BC. It was only with the advent of Roman political and cultural influence during the Hellenistic period that an Etruscan renaissance in painting took place. The earliest examples of the new style are the Orcus tomb at Tarquinii and the Golinia tombs at Orvieto (south of Clusium), where there is some use of chiaroscuro effects as well as simpler means of shading. Tombs in Vulci and Tarquinii of the 1st century BC carry the development of these techniques even further. In the François Tomb at Vulci there is a celebrated fresco known as the "Sacrifice of the Trojan Prisoners." It is next to a historical scene showing wars between Etruscan and Roman princes during the Archaic period. This renewed interest in mythological or legendary equivalents of actual historical events is yet another hint that the Greek Hellenistic allegorical tradition was beginning to take hold. The same sacrificial scene and others depicting the deaths of the Theban princes during the war of the Seven Against Thebes were extremely popular on the ash urns that were used as burial jars by the late Etruscans, and it may very well have been through them that a taste for myth allegory was imparted to the Romans at this time.

ROMAN

Pagan. During the Archaic period Rome was ruled by Etruscan and Etruscanized kings. The city's temples were built and decorated in the Etruscan manner and most features of Etruscan culture were present. Although the Romans did not build painted tombs for their dead, they may have employed Etruscan artists to decorate the painted walls of the temples. When the republic was founded at the end of the 6th century BC, much of this Etruscan influence Etruscan influence survived, especially the tendency to use painting for political purposes. Accounts of temple decoration during the 4th and 3rd centuries BC mention depictions of triumphal processions. The probable style of these is visible in the contemporary tombs of Tuscany. It was to Greek artists that the Romans turned when, in the 3rd century BC, they first came into contact with the flourishing Greek cities of southern Italy and the eastern Mediterranean. Contact was usually in the form of war, and soon Greek works of art were being brought to Rome as booty in order to decorate the temples set up as memorials to victorious campaigns. Greek artists followed the works of art as it became

increasingly clear that Rome offered the best and most consistent source of patronage. In 168 BC Lucius Aemilius Paullus, the victor over the Macedonian king Perseus at the Battle of Pydna, employed Metrodorus, an Athenian painter, to execute panels depicting events in his victorious campaign. It is significant, perhaps, that Metrodorus was a philosopher as well as a painter and that he was also employed by Paullus in educating his children. Tradition states that Demetrius, an Alexandrian "place painter" (*topographos*), was working in Rome by 164 BC. The exact meaning of his title is problematic, but it could mean that he painted landscapes, later to become a favourite motif in the decoration of Roman houses. Some Alexandrian tombs of the 2nd century BC do indeed represent gardens and groves as seen through colonnades or windows in the wall of the tomb chamber. A late Hellenistic version of the type is preserved on floor mosaics from Pergamum in Asia Minor and from Italy itself. Paintings on Delos show floral motifs in an illusionistic style against a dark ground. This was later to become the Roman garden scene, usually set against a cool, dark background, that is found so often in the colonnades of Pompeian courtyards. (P.J.C.)

Wall paintings of the Roman period, for instance those from Pompeii, vary so much in their treatment of any one subject that it is hazardous to conjecture which version is likely to be closest to any earlier Greek painting, even supposing there was definite copying. With the exception of the Alexander mosaic already mentioned (see above *Hellenistic period*)—evidently a direct copy of a painting of the 4th century BC—there is nothing in painting to correspond to the straightforward copying of Greek statues that was apparently so abundant under the Roman Empire.

(B.As./P.J.C.)

Virtually the only example of painting in Rome and Latium to have survived from before the 1st century BC is a fragment of a historical tomb painting with scenes from the Samnite Wars, found in a family tomb on the Esquiline and probably dating from the 3rd century BC (Palazzo dei Conservatori, Capitoline Museums, Rome). In addition to Metrodorus and Demetrius, ancient writers mention the names of three painters, each of whom worked in a temple: Fabius Pictor, in the Temple of Salus in Rome at the end of the 4th century; Pacuvius, a dramatist and native of Brundisium, in the Temple of Hercules in the Forum Boarium in Rome during the first half of the 2nd century; and Lycon, an Asiatic Greek, in the Temple of Juno at Ardea in the late 3rd or early 2nd century. Nothing is known about the work of these artists.

At Pompeii during the 2nd century BC the interior walls of private houses were decorated in a so-called Incrustation, or First, style; that is, the imitation in painted stucco of veneers, or *crustae* ("slabs"), of coloured marbles. But in the second half of the 1st century BC, there suddenly appeared in Rome and in the Campanian cities (the most famous of which is probably Pompeii) a brilliant series of domestic mural paintings of the so-called Second style, the aim of which was to deny the walls as solid surfaces confining the room space. This was sometimes done by covering the whole area of the walls with elaborate landscapes, in which depth, atmosphere, and light are rendered in a highly pictorial, illusionistic manner. Such are the *Odyssey* paintings (Plate 1) found in a Roman house on the Esquiline (now in the Biblioteca Apostolica Vaticana, Vatican City), which consist of a continuous flow of episodes that unfold, filmlike, beyond a colonnade of pilasters, with vertical, bird's-eye-view perspective and human figures strictly subordinated to their settings. Other wall paintings, such as those in a room from Livia's Villa at Prima Porta (transferred to the Museo Nazionale Romano), represent a great park or garden filled with trees, shrubs, flowers, and birds, with no pilasters in the foreground to interrupt the prospect and no human figures to distract attention.

The possibility of Hellenistic models for this type of painting has already been mentioned, though the surviving Hellenistic precursors were no preparation for the important Roman developments. Most examples of the type, which survived into the Fourth style, have been found on the back walls of the colonnades running around real gardens. The cool painted scenes would have given the illusion that an idler in this part of the house was surrounded by shrubs or groves of trees. Another type of landscape combined sacred and idyllic features and was often placed as though behind elaborate stage buildings. These monotone compositions held sacred columns or rustic shrines and were closely related to other illusionistic scenes peopled with little figures whose antics, the written sources make clear, were a source of endless amusement for the householder and his guests.

Frieze in the Villa of the Mysteries
A celebrated frieze of life-size figures, depicting Dionysiac initiation rites and the prenuptial ordeals of a bride, in the so-called triclinium of the Villa of the Mysteries (or Villa Item) outside the Herculaneum gate of Pompeii, also belongs to the Second style (Plate 2). There the walls are denied by the device of substituting for them a narrow stage on which the figures carry out the ritual before a drop scene of continuous painted panels. But the most common Second-style paintings are known as Architectural and show a threefold horizontal division of the wall into dado, central area, and cornice, combined with a triple vertical scheme of design that consists of a large central panel (in the main, intermediate horizontal area), framed by flanking columns and a pediment, and two smaller panels on either side. The central panel and often the lateral panels as well are views seen through windows that break through the walls and link the spectator with the world outside, as in the house of Augustus on the Palatine in Rome.

In the Third style, which covers most of the Augustan period, the central panel picture on a wall is no longer thought of as a scene through a window but as a real picture hung on or inserted into a screen or woven into a tapestry, which partially conceals an architectural vista behind it. The columns, entablatures, and so on are completely unreal and so complicated that this Third style is sometimes dubbed Ornate.

The Fourth style, which runs from the close of the Augustan Age to the destruction of Pompeii and its fellow Campanian cities in AD 79, is less homogeneous than its predecessors and exhibits three main variants: first, an architectural design soberer and more realistic but still with a central screen or tapestry partly covering a retreating vista; second, an architectural layout that imitates a *scaena* ("stage background"); and third, a method (sometimes known as "intricate") by which the whole surface of the wall is covered with a flat, white, neutral ground painted with an allover, latticelike pattern of fantastic architectural elements, arabesques, grotesques, small figure motifs, or small panels containing pictures. This third type of Fourth-style painting came into vogue at Pompeii between an earthquake of AD 63 and the catastrophic volcanic eruption of 79, and one of its most impressive exponents is the Golden House of Nero in Rome.

The subjects of the panel pictures of the Second, Third, and Fourth styles are for the most part drawn from Greek mythology. Some of them recall literary descriptions of famous classical Greek and Hellenistic paintings or show motifs that suggest their originals were painted on the Greek mainland or in Asia Minor. It is certain that many masterpieces of Greek painting did make their way to Rome as the booty of Roman generals of republican days, and wall painters could have studied them at first hand. But often those artists must have had to rely only on sketches of the celebrated pictures, and it is not known how faithfully the Roman and Campanian murals reproduce the prototypes. Other panel pictures present scenes from contemporary religious ritual, and a few show themes from Roman legend. Frequently, in the case of the Greek mythological subjects and those taken from rustic religious cults, the artist produced landscape with figures, as in the *Odyssey* frescoes (Plate 1), not figures with landscape, as on Trajan's Column. These late republican

Late republican and early imperial set pieces
and early imperial set pieces are competently executed, remarkably vivid, and extremely naturalistic. But, with a few exceptions, they reveal that the principles of a single vanishing point and unified lighting from a single source of illumination either were not understood by Roman painters or did not interest them.

The flat, uniform background of the last phase of the Fourth style remained a constant feature of mural painting in houses, tombs, temples, and other religious shrines throughout the 2nd, 3rd, and 4th centuries. The decoration, which stands out against that ground, takes any of several forms: (1) latticelike, allover patterns, as in many pagan tombs; (2) small groups of figures or figure panels spread out at intervals across the field, as in the Christian catacombs of Rome; (3) a mixture of large human figures and extensive scenes with small-scale figures, as in the early 3rd-century Hypogeum of the Aurelii on the Viale Manzoni in Rome, the interesting painted content of which is Gnostic or crypto-Christian; or (4) large scenes with relatively large figures, such as a group of marine deities in a 2nd-century Roman house under the Church of SS. John and Paul on the Caelian, a late 2nd- or early 3rd-century leopard hunt on the south wall of the frigidarium of the hunting baths at Leptis Magna (on the coast of modern Libya), or the early 3rd-century biblical scenes from a baptistery at Doura-Europus, an important archaeological site on the Euphrates in what is now Syria.

In the case of the Roman tombs, cross- or barrel-vaulted ceilings, where preserved, normally carry out the painted decoration of the walls, showing either a latticelike pattern or a series of small, spaced-out, figured panel pictures. At Trier (in what is now West Germany) remains have been found of a flat, coffered ceiling with panels of painted plaster from an early 4th-century imperial hall destroyed to make room for a Christian basilica. Large portions of eight painted panels are preserved. Four depict female busts—three of them with nimbi—which may be either personifications or portraits of members of the imperial family; the other four show pairs of dancing or sporting cupids. As the skillful modeling and lively naturalism of these figures show, late Roman painting could reach high standards.

Roman portrait painting comes only a short way behind portrait sculpture in technical skill and realism. One of the earliest extant examples is a group of Terentius Neo and his wife, from Pompeii (National Archaeological Museum, Naples). Both figures recall mummy portraits in Egypt, being painted in encaustic (a technique by which colours are mixed with liquid wax and fixed by heat) and ranging in date from the Flavian period to the 3rd century. A circular portrait group of frontal figures painted on wood, probably in Egypt (now in the Staatliche Museen Preussischer Kulturbesitz, West Berlin), seems to have originally depicted the emperors Septimius Severus and Caracalla, Julia Domna (Septimius Severus' wife), and Geta (Caracalla's brother); but Geta (so it seems) was subsequently washed out (perhaps most consequent upon his murder by Caracalla). Particularly attractive are the portraits done on gold-glass medallions, which in the exquisite refinement of their treatment may be compared to 16th-century European miniatures. A medallion in the Museum of Christian Antiquities, Brescia, dating from the 3rd century and carrying a portrait group, is a veritable masterpiece (Plate 2).

Gold-glass medallions

(J.M.C.T./P.J.C.)

Early Christian. It is customary to distinguish early Christian painting of the West or Latin part of the late Roman Empire from the Christian painting of regions dominated by the Greek language and to consider the latter as proto-Byzantine. The Western strain of early Christian painting may be said to have ended with the collapse of the empire in the West at the end of the 5th century. In the East, until the 6th and even the 7th century, painting in many regions followed the paths traced by Christian painting at its beginnings. Exceptions to the above schematization are Doura-Europus and early Christian paintings in Egypt (see below).

Early Christian painting did not have a distinct existence until about the end of the 2nd century AD. There are several reasons for this. First, there can have been few, if any, monumental churches before that time capable of taking decoration showing Christian themes. Second, Christianity did not at first make great headway among those able to afford large painted tombs where examples of Christian iconography might be expected to appear. Third, early Christianity was much closer to Judaism than in later years and may have retained the Judaic distaste for the painted image, especially if it referred to the Godhead. Lastly, even Christians prized classical education, which was, after all, the only sound basis for a public career, and they could appreciate classical works of art even if they rejected pagan subject matter. This was made easier for them by the concept of myth as allegory, according to which depictions of mythological scenes were not so much statements of a religious position as moral lessons whose messages could be appreciated by any educated man. Because most surviving early Christian painting is funerary, it is hardly surprising that purely Christian subjects at first made little headway in a field already crowded with edifying moral messages based on the Greek myths. These may have been pagan, but they did emphasize the common belief in life beyond the grave. It was only in the 3rd century AD, when the idea of Judaic or Christian allegories gained legitimacy, that any real development could begin. Even so, some rather odd compromises took place: representations of Christ as the victorious Sun God or as a philosopher occur in early Christian tomb paintings. Even the emperor Constantine, who by the Edict of Milan (AD 313) established toleration for Christianity throughout the Roman Empire and who himself professed Christianity, seems to have worshiped both in his lifetime.

The new elements, then, consisted not of form but of content. As the power of the church over public and private life grew, these new elements tended to gain in importance, but they never quite ousted the pagan scenes. The latter were often drawn undiminished from plays or epics whose prestige remained long after Christianity became the official religion of the Roman Empire.

With the growth of Christian communities, the catacombs—underground burial places—became veritable subterranean cities, their rooms linked by corridors. The most important extant examples are in Rome, with others in Naples, Sicily, Malta, North Africa (specifically in what is now Tunisia), and Egypt. Pictorial decoration of the catacombs, limited to only a few rooms, followed pagan models. Delicate lines on the ceilings and walls trace circles and squares in which decorative motifs are inserted: garlands, birds, four-legged animals, cupids, images of the seasons, and figures of ambiguous significance (pagan or Christian)—praying figures and a shepherd carrying a sheep on his shoulders, generally called "The Good Shepherd" (Figure 6).

As early as the first half of the 3rd century, however, scenes of purely Christian meaning were added to these neutral subjects. The oldest are located in Rome in the cemeteries of Domitilla (the gallery of the Flavians), of

Priscilla (the Greek Chapel), and of Calixtus (the Chapel of the Sacrament). Stories from the Old Testament are joined by stories from the Gospels. These images present examples of the succour brought to the faithful by God the Father and Christ the Son. Even the baptism and the adoration of the Magi can be interpreted in this manner; as revelations of Christ's divinity, they announce man's salvation.

The style and quality of these paintings vary. Some of those from the beginning of the 3rd century are light in touch and charmingly elegant (e.g., gallery of the Flavians), comparable to the best pagan paintings. In others (e.g., cemetery of Priscilla, mid-3rd century) there is a somewhat heavier element, with a passion of expression that seems to match the aspirations of the new faith. In the 4th century the style becomes firmly contoured.

The frescoes in the baptistery of Doura-Europus, executed between 230 and 240, differ only in style from those of the catacombs in the West. Scenes from the Old and New Testaments are used to explain the significance of baptism: the death of the old Adam and his rebirth to a new life through the baptismal bath. The back wall of the baptismal pool bears the images of Adam and Eve, recalling the Fall, as well as that of the Good Shepherd (who in this case is Christ, Saviour of souls). Illustrations on the longitudinal walls are of David fighting Goliath and of incidents from the Gospels—Christ walking on water, the healing of the paralytic, the holy women at the tomb, and Christ and the Samaritan—and were probably inspired by readings that accompanied the rite of baptism. Stylistic elements that recall the paintings in the Roman catacombs are the juxtaposition of scenes without apparent connection and the conciseness of the narrative.

Among the latest examples of early Christian funerary art are paintings dating from the 5th century in the tomb of el-Bagaouat at al-Khārijah, in Egypt.

(He.S./P.J.C./Ed.)

Book illustration in antiquity. That book illustration existed as far back as the late Hellenistic world can be inferred from some of the so-called Megarian bowls, imitations in clay of gold or silver vessels that date from the 3rd century BC to the 1st century AD. They often bear on their exteriors scenes in relief from literary texts that are sometimes accompanied by Greek quotations. They must, in part at least, have served as models for Roman artists. Book illustration is known to have existed in Rome comparatively early—examples include 700 pictures illustrating the early 1st-century-BC scholar and satirist Marcus Terentius Varro's 15 books of *Hebdomades vel de imaginibus* and a portrait of Virgil prefixed to an edition of

Myth as allegory (margin note)

Catacomb paintings and the beginnings of Christian iconography (margin note)

By courtesy of Pontifica Commissione di Archaeologia Sacra, Rome

Figure 6: "The Good Shepherd," painted ceiling in the catacomb of SS. Pietro e Marcellino, Rome, beginning of 4th century AD.

his poems. Miniatures in the codex of the *Iliad* in the Biblioteca Ambrosiana, Milan, were painted probably at the end of the 5th or beginning of the 6th century AD but reflect pictures of the 3rd, 2nd, and even 1st centuries AD, as do those of the Codex Virgilius Vaticanus in the Biblioteca Apostolica Vaticana (No. 3225), written around 400. Miniatures in the second great illustrated Codex Virgilius Romanus in the Biblioteca Apostolica Vaticana (No. 3867), written around 500, are still Roman in spirit, if less classical in style; the tenacious influence of Greco-Roman painting can be clearly traced in the illustrations of certain early Byzantine books. A most remarkable, if aesthetically crude, mid-4th-century mosaic pavement, found in a Romano-British villa at Low Ham, Somerset, and showing scenes from the first and fourth books of the *Aeneid,* is undoubtedly based on the copybook illustrations used for some Virgilian codex. (J.M.C.T.)

The only Christian illuminated manuscript surviving from before the 6th century is a fragment of the Book of Judges from Quedlinburg (Staatsbibliotek Preussischer Kulturbesitz, West Berlin). (He.S./Ed.)

Eastern Christian

A new artistic centre was created in the eastern Mediterranean with the foundation in the early 4th century AD of Constantinople (modern Istanbul) on the site of Byzantium. The term Byzantine is normally used to identify the art of this city and of the Orthodox Christian empire that was controlled from it and that survived from 330 until its capture in 1453 by the Ottoman Turks. From the reign of Justinian I (527–565) there were relatively clear political and ecclesiastical differences between the Byzantine world and the West, and the term Byzantine art from this period onward broadly reflects these differences. In practice, the division of Mediterranean art into two polarities is not always easy to maintain, as artistic contacts were frequent and each "sector" influenced the other. For instance, by the 12th century Byzantine influence had made itself felt outside the empire, as, for example, in the mosaics of Sicily and Venice; and the Byzantine style had been adopted by the Orthodox states that were growing up in Russia, Bulgaria, and the western Balkans. During the first half of the 13th century, when Constantinople was in Latin crusader hands, it was in these outlying areas that the most important developments in painting took place. Once the Greek emperors had returned to Constantinople in 1261, developments there began anew, and fine Byzantine mosaics and paintings date from this last phase. In the study of Byzantine art, mosaics are frequently included with painting, but here painting is treated alone; for mosaics, see DECORATIVE ARTS AND FURNISHINGS.

By 1460 or a short while after, the little that remained of the empire following Constantinople's fall in 1453, together with the independent Orthodox states (except Russia), was in Turkish hands. Nevertheless, painting in the Byzantine tradition continued in Greece, the western Balkans, and Bulgaria, for Orthodox Christian art was not banned by the new Muslim rulers. Indeed, works of great technical sophistication were still produced, and a number of painters of icons and church paintings are known through signed and dated works. In Russia a national art of great quality saw continuous development from a Byzantine basis throughout the Middle Ages and up to the end of the 17th century, when Peter I the Great imposed western fashions.

In general, Byzantine painters may perhaps have retained Greco-Roman traditions more faithfully than did medieval painters in the West. There is so much variation of expression in the history of Byzantine painting, however, that it would be misleading to describe it as a "style"; the term is better seen as the label for a period and for the patronage of an Orthodox Christian society. Because most surviving work is religious in content, Byzantine painting does have some distinctive features. Icons, or painted panels depicting holy figures, were a major item of production, and the most important churches have their walls decorated in mosaic. On the other hand, the production of illuminated books was limited. The range of subject matter in

Byzantine works is more restricted than that of the medieval West; scenes and figures from the New Testament and the history of the early church are perhaps the most popular choices.

Subject matter

Byzantine painting was a highly effective Christian art, expressing a new view of the divine and a new spirituality. On the whole, Byzantine emphasis concentrated less on presenting a naturalistic narrative than on suggesting the existence of a supernatural and timeless Christian realm; painters retained the pictorial devices of classical antiquity, even if they aimed at portraying a more abstract version of the world. It has been felt that Byzantine art as a result always contains a tension between naturalistic and abstract modes of expression.

EARLY BYZANTINE PERIOD (330–717)

Icons. Until quite recently very little was known about the icons of this age, but due to the cleaning of several in Rome and to the discovery of hundreds in the monastery of St. Catherine on Mount Sinai, much material is now available for study. Enough examples are now known for it to be possible to prove how important icons were at this time.

Early importance of icons

The icons in Rome (large cult images such as that of the Virgin from the Pantheon) represent Christian images at their most formal and monumental. The Sinai icons are more intimate, and many must have been intended for private devotions as well as church display. Among the finest are icons that represent Christ, St. Peter, and the Virgin and saints.

Illuminated manuscripts. It is now thought that illuminated manuscripts were relatively few in number even at the time they were produced. Certainly very few religious or classical texts survive. Of the latter, a copy of the pharmacological treatise *De materia medica* by Pedanius Dioscorides, a Greek physician of the 1st century AD, is certainly Constantinopolitan; it was done for Juliana Anicia, the founder of the church of St. Polyeuktos, and is dated 512. A copy of the *Iliad* at Milan may perhaps have been copied and illustrated in a Byzantine scriptorium. Of the religious manuscripts, the most important is a copy of the book of Genesis (known as the Vienna Genesis) at the Österreichische Nationalbibliothek, Vienna (Plate 3); there is a fragmentary copy of the Gospels in the Bibliothèque Nationale—usually known as the Sinop fragment, for it came from Sinop, in Turkey—and another at Rossano, in southern Italy. There is also another copy of Genesis, the Cotton Genesis, in the British Museum, but it was

Figure 7: Miniature of the Ascension from the Rabula Gospels, copied at Zagba, Syria, 586. In the Biblioteca Medicea-Laurenziana, Florence. 35.5 × 25.5 cm.

severely damaged by the fire that destroyed part of the Cotton Collection. There has been dispute as to where these manuscripts were written and painted, but either Constantinople or Syria is the normal attribution. A fifth religious manuscript, the Rabula Gospels, whose text is framed in elaborate architectural and floral motifs (Figure 7), was copied at Zagba, in Syria, in the year 586 and was executed in a more sketchy, informal style.

ICONOCLASTIC AGE (717–843)

By the early 8th century so great an importance had accrued to the depiction of the saintly and divine forms that one body of opinion in the state feared the population was in danger of lapsing into idolatry. As a countermeasure, a decree forbidding representation of saintly or divine forms in religious art was promulgated, and from about 717 until 843 there reigned emperors who are called Iconoclasts. To most of them, representation of the saintly or divine in religious art was genuinely anathema. In spite of the ban, pictorial decoration was not in itself forbidden. The church of Ayía Sophia (literally "Divine Wisdom") at Salonika (modern Thessaloníki, Greece) was decorated under the patronage of Constantine VI (780–797); his monogram survives, and in the apse there are indications that there was a great cross like that which is preserved in the Church of St. Irene (Eirene) at Constantinople and which dates from the 740s. The survival of the 6th- and 7th-century figural mosaics in St. Demetrius at Salonika suggests that the ban was not strictly enforced everywhere. In any case, it was strongly opposed in the monasteries. But in Constantinople the ban seems to have been universal, and religious mosaics and paintings in all the churches were removed, including all those in Hagia Sophia.

Figural church decoration

MIDDLE BYZANTINE PERIOD (843–1204)

"Icon lovers"

Icons. With the return to power of the "icon lovers," as they were called, in 843, figural art once more became important in the churches. Elaborate representational decorations in mosaic were set up in the more important buildings, painted ones in the poorer. The next two or three centuries were an age of great brilliance and represent the acme of Byzantine culture. The empire's frontiers were far-flung, its wealth was enormous, and its general culture was far in advance of the rest of Europe. After the death of Basil II (976–1025), a slow decline set in.

Icons were regularly produced throughout this period. The largest number are to be found in the Sinai monastery. These were mostly for Orthodox use but include a 12th- and 13th-century group done in a mixed East-West style by Western painters who were active in the Latin crusader kingdoms of the region and who copied Byzantine models. Others exist in various museums in the Soviet Union, where they were brought from provincial Russian churches and monasteries for cleaning and conservation. Some of these were imported from Constantinople; one of the finest, an icon of the Virgin known as "Our Lady of Vladimir" (Plate 3), was painted for a Russian patron about 1130. It is of considerable importance in the history of painting, for it not only is a work of outstandingly high quality but also is in a new, more human style, anticipating the late style that flourished between 1204 and 1453. It was at this time that the cult of the icon really came into its own, partly because richer materials became rare but mostly because the interior decoration of churches changed with the introduction of a screen called an iconostasis (*i.e.,* a screen that was to be covered in icons).

Wall painting. Wall paintings were important during this period, but only one decoration by trained artists in a larger building is known, namely that in the Church of St. Sophia at Ohrid, Macedonia (Yugoslavia). The majority of the scenes that survive were drawn from the Old Testament. They date from about 1050. More numerous are the paintings that decorate numerous rock-cut chapels in Cappadocia (in what is now Turkey); these were executed by lay painters for the monks who lived there alone or in small communities. This material is most important for understanding the character and varieties of Byzantine painting and for giving records of the near-complete decoration of churches. Some churches (such as the 10th-century Tokalı kilise in the Göreme Valley, in central Turkey) represent the best achievements of the period. Some artists who painted the Cappadocian churches must have traveled out from Constantinople or other cities; others probably made their living locally. All levels of quality were found there; indeed Cappadocia contains a whole range of the subjects depicted in Byzantine painting of this period.

Illuminated manuscripts. Two magnificent manuscripts of this period survive: the Paris Psalter (Figure 8) and a book of sermons (*Homilies of St. Gregory of Nazianzus*), both in the Bibliothèque Nationale, Paris. The former contains 14 full-page miniatures in a grand, almost classical style, which led scholars at one time to date it to the earliest Byzantine period. The miniatures in the other book are more varied in style, some of them recalling the narrative art of Cappadocia, but this latter book represents nevertheless the grandest type of Byzantine manuscript of the age. It was done for Basil I about 880. During the following centuries many illuminated psalters, octateuchs (the first eight books of the Old Testament), homilies, and copies of the Gospels were produced. (Gospels formed the most numerous category.) Notable examples include the Bible of Leo and the Mēnologion (a liturgical book

Grandest type of Byzantine manuscript of the age

Hirmer Fotoarchiv, Munchen

Figure 8: David composing psalms, miniature in the Paris Psalter (Gr. 139), 10th century. In the Bibliothèque Nationale, Paris. 26.0 × 35.9 cm.

relating lives of saints) of Basil II (976–1025), both in the Vatican, a psalter done for the same emperor and now in the Biblioteca Nazionale Marciana at Venice, and *The Homilies of St. John Chrysostom* in the Bibliothèque Nationale. A few of them contain many small-scale illustrations, as in a famous set of the Gospels in the Biblioteca Medicea-Laurenziana at Florence. The most common type of Gospel book had only a few illustrated scenes or only portraits of the Evangelists. The work is usually of high quality. Some psalters contained marginal illustrations referring to contemporary events (*i.e.,* the Iconoclastic Controversy). The 10th-century Joshua Roll (Figure 9) is interesting as an example of Byzantine illuminated manuscript that shows the tenacious influence of Greco-Roman painting.

In 1204 Constantinople was sacked by crusaders, its treasures were destroyed or dispersed, and the brilliant middle period of Byzantine art was brought to an end.

LATE BYZANTINE PERIOD (1204–1453)

Icons. Painted panels assumed a new importance in the last phase of Byzantine art. The most sophisticated work was done at Constantinople, some of it for patrons from elsewhere (notably Russia), and a number of icons survive

Figure 9: The attack on Ai, from the Joshua Roll (Josh. 7:3–5), Byzantine, 10th century. In the Biblioteca Apostolica Vaticana.
By courtesy of the Biblioteca Apostolica Vaticana

that can be associated with Constantinople on the basis of literary evidence or inscriptions. A particularly fine double-sided icon, with the Virgin on one face and the Annunciation on the other, now in the museum at Skopje, Yugos., was brought from Constantinople about 1300.

At this period the Russian school was the most important outgrowth of Byzantine icon painting; after the 13th century the influence of Byzantine models continued to be felt more in Russian icons than in the frescoes, but both wall and icon painting were showing local characteristics as early as the 13th century itself. The rigid Byzantine patterns, the dark colours, and the austere lines gradually became graceful, bright, and less solemn. Novgorod's style of icon painting, for example, gradually strengthened and took shape: the severity of faces was softened, composition was simplified, the silhouette became bold and increasingly important, and the palette was lightened by bright cinnabar, snow-white, emerald-green, and lemon-yellow tones.

Icons were produced in numerous other places, notably at Salonika, on Mount Athos, and in many other centres in what are now Bulgaria, Greece, Yugoslavia, and the Soviet Union. In a few instances icons can be assigned to a definite centre, thanks to inscriptions or other records, but the study of these panels has not progressed far enough to permit any reliable classification under localities on the basis of style alone. After the Turkish conquests of the mid-15th century, icons continued to be painted in large numbers in every part of the Orthodox world. In the 16th century Crete became an important centre, and many Cretan painters worked also in Venice, where there was a large Greek colony; many of the products of this school are to be found there today in the museum attached to the Church of St. George of the Greeks.

Wall painting. The last phase really began in the 12th century with the decoration at Nerezi in Macedonia (1164). It was done for a Byzantine patron and is in the same emotional style as "Our Lady of Vladimir." Work in a similar style is to be found in Russia from the late 12th century, and these models were followed by local craftsmen. In the 13th century new styles predominated in such paintings as those at Mileševa (1235) and Sopoćani (c. 1265), in what is now Yugoslavia, and in the church of Hagia Sophia at Trebizond (c. 1260; Trabzon), on the Black Sea.

It is probable that artists who had fled the capital after 1204 established themselves in a number of different areas and that wall paintings such as those mentioned above were the work of men they had trained. By the end of the century one can begin to speak of local art in the Byzantine Empire, as, for example, the regional art of Salonika. Examples of this last school are found in the Chapel of St. Eugenius, attached to the Church of St. Demetrius at Salonika, in the Protaton (i.e., the First Church, in the

sense of the first in rank, c. 1300), at Kariaí (Karyaes) on Mount Athos, on the north coast of the Aegean, and in some of the monasteries there, as well as in a number of churches in Serbia and Macedonia decorated under the patronage of King Stephen Uroš II Milutin at the end of the 13th and in the early years of the 14th century. There has been some dispute among authorities as to whether King Milutin's painters were Greeks from Salonika or local Slavs. Throughout the 14th century a great deal of work was done by painters in what is now Yugoslavia and in Greece. Somewhat similar work was done in Bulgaria.

In Russia the Mongol invasion about the middle of the 13th century disrupted previous centres of production, such as Kiev and Vladimir-Suzdal. Only in the northern regions of Russia—particularly in the Novgorod district—did painting continue to develop. The city of Novgorod had as early as the second half of the 12th century developed an individual style, combining Byzantine severity with a folk art picturesqueness. (Examples are the frescoes in the Church of St. George in Staraya Ladoga [c. 1180] and the Church of Nereditsa.) Novgorod escaped damage by the Asiatic hordes and became virtually the metropolis and cultural centre of old Rus after the fall of Kiev (1240). Together with the city of Pskov and other northwestern Russian population centres, it harboured many Greek artists, who continued to work in the traditions of Byzantium.

A prominent figure in Russian painting was Theophanes the Greek, a native of Constantinople who moved to Russia after about 1370. His paintings, though closely adhering to Byzantine styles, show distinctive Russian features, notably elongated proportions and delicacy of detail. Such features can be seen in his Novgorod frescoes and especially in the central part of the iconostasis in the Cathedral of the Annunciation in the Moscow Kremlin.

Among the immediate followers and collaborators of Theophanes was Andrey Rublyov, whose religious types are imbued with a fresh spirituality. His best-known work is the icon "The Old Testament Trinity" (c. 1410), painted for the Trinity-St. Sergius Monastery at Zagorsk. The subject—popular in Byzantine iconography—is the visit of three angels to Abraham and Sarah. But the severe symbolism of the old Byzantine tradition is transformed into something more human. It is one of the great creations of medieval Russian painting.

Another inspired Novgorod painter of the 15th century was Dionisi, whose art is marked by the extreme elongated stylizing of his figures as well as a subtle and glowing colour scheme. He and his predecessor Rublyov succeeded in expressing the aura of spirituality that is the essence of the Russian icon.

At Constantinople some paintings of outstanding quality were executed at the Monastery of the Chora, now known as Kariye Cami (Plate 3), and it is known from the

Continuity in northern regions

Elongated stylizing

texts that similar paintings existed in a number of other churches there. Several were painted in the third quarter of the 14th century by Theophanes the Greek before he went to Russia. The same style was also introduced to Mistrás, in the Peloponnese, and there the wall paintings of the Brontocheion (early 14th century), the Church of the Peribleptos (c. 1350), and the Pantanassa (1428) are all of high quality. Paintings in the monasteries of the Morava Valley (in what is now Yugoslavia) done at the end of the 14th and beginning of the 15th centuries are in the same refined style.

Illuminated manuscripts. Illuminated manuscripts of the last Byzantine age are not as numerous as those of the middle period, but their quality is often just as high. A few seem to have been produced during the 13th century, both at Constantinople and in the cities where Orthodox nobles established themselves while the Latin crusaders were in possession of the capital, notably Nicaea and Trebizond. After the return to Constantinople in 1261 the noble families seem to have played a greater role than the emperors as patrons of all arts, and many of the more important works of art of the age were produced on their behalf. A copy of a work attributed to the 5th-century-BC Greek physician Hippocrates, now in the Bibliothèque Nationale, was made for the high admiral Alexius Apocaucos (Plate 3), and a beautiful copy of the Gospels in the same library was made for the emperor John VI Cantacuzenus between 1347 and 1355. Manuscripts were, of course, also copied and illuminated in the monasteries, and this process continued until printing made it obsolete. Few of the later ones contain illuminations of great quality. In the Slavic lands, however, fine work continued, and in Romania excellent manuscripts were executed in the 16th century.   (A.Vo./D.T.R./R.S.Co.)

POST-BYZANTINE RUSSIA

In the 15th century major changes began to take place in Russian icon painting, leading to the birth of what may justifiably be called a national art. This evolution first became noticeable in the gradual elimination of the Mediterranean setting depicted in the background of icons, notably landscape and architecture. Greek basilicas with their porticoes and atria (patios or courts) were replaced by Russian churches with their cupolas and *kokoshniki* (literally "women's headdresses," but here, by extension, "gables"). Russian saints and episodes from their lives furnished subjects for the Russian artists; Muscovite types and native costumes began to appear in icon painting. The colours were extraordinarily brilliant, and there was particular emphasis on outline.

Many of the great icon and fresco painters in the 16th century worked first at Novgorod and later at Moscow, thus linking Novgorod and Moscow closely in artistic terms, and in particular introducing to Moscow features characteristic of the Byzantine and Novgorodian traditions. The literary movement of the 16th century strongly influenced contemporary painting, and artists looked to new subjects. Some illustrated church preoccupations and prayers or expressed the rites of the church in symbolic images; others represented parables and legends.

At the end of the 16th century the Stroganov school made its appearance in Moscow, introducing a small-scale manner of icon painting. The masters of the Stroganov school became famous for the elegant attitudes of their figures, their Eastern choice of colours, and their elaborate detail. Some of them—Prokopy Chirin, Nikifor, and Istoma Savin—were later to join the ranks of the icon-painting studios in the Kremlin armory in Moscow.

Rapid spread of Western influences

Moscow icons of the 17th century constitute the last authentically Russian painting. As early as 1650 much of their Russian character had disappeared. From the end of the century, western European influences spread rapidly.
(A.Vo./R.S.Co.)

REGIONAL VARIATIONS IN EASTERN CHRISTIAN PAINTING

Georgia. Christian painting in Georgia dates from the 4th century and shows both Eastern and Western influences owing to the position of the region as a crossroads of trade between Europe and India. From the beginning of the 5th century the Georgian church approved the representation of the human form in religious painting. Accordingly Georgia was not affected by the wave of iconoclasm in the 8th and 9th centuries—a period that inhibited figural representation in most of Eastern Christendom for more than a century. In addition to a Christian tradition, Georgian painting also drew on a pagan one.

Until the 9th century, mosaics—more or less Byzantine in technique and design—were frequently used in the decoration of Georgian churches. By the 11th century the entire interior of Georgian churches was usually covered with frescoes instead. Many well-preserved examples survive from this period. Although following the Eastern Orthodoxy's general theological interest in church decoration, the Georgian murals deviated somewhat from Byzantine style and iconography, notably in extensive ornamentation between individual scenes.

The art of manuscript illumination flourished in Georgia from the 6th century onward, and numerous examples survive from all periods. Characteristic of the early works are two Gospel books, the Adishi Gospels (897) and the first set of Gospels of Dzhruchi (936–940). These are distinguished by their decorative treatment of draperies and their excellent drawing.

At the end of the 10th century Byzantine influence became strong in Georgia, and until the end of the 15th century Georgian manuscripts generally followed Byzantine models, differing only in an independent approach to the use of colour. These illuminations are of very high quality.

Byzantine influence strengthens

In the 16th century Persian influence from the East transformed Georgian manuscript illuminations. Ornamentation abounded, and the representation of figures and scenes was flat, decorative, and highly skillful.   (Ed.)

Armenia. What little remains of the pagan art of Armenia strongly resembles late Greco-Roman art. With the establishment of Christianity as the official religion in the first years of the 4th century, however, a truly national art developed.

From an early period the interiors of Armenian churches were adorned with frescoes and mosaics showing scenes from the Gospels and images of Christ, the Virgin, and saints. Surviving examples are less plentiful than illustrated manuscripts, however. Important specimens of the latter exist in an almost uninterrupted series ranging from the late 9th to the 17th century. They are executed in ornamental designs of great richness and diversity. Floral, geometric, and animal motifs are painted in vivid colours on a gold background around the canon tables of the Gospel manuscripts (concordances of the four Gospels), on the headpieces, and in the margins and are ingeniously adapted to the capital letters.

As regards iconography, the Gospel scenes follow early Christian and Byzantine models, but the Armenian painters, especially those of the medieval kingdom of Little Armenia, often displayed a marked independence and interpreted traditional formulas in a more lively or dramatic manner. Two artistic trends can be discerned in manuscript painting: one, more Eastern in character, tends to simplify the human form and subordinate it to ornamental interest; the other, under Byzantine influence, shows a subtle blending of naturalism and stylization. This latter trend was predominant in Little Armenia, where a flourishing school of painting developed under the patronage of the court and the church. The 13th-century manuscripts, in particular, belong in the first rank of medieval illumination. Through contacts with the crusaders and the Mongols, the painters of this period became acquainted with the art of the Latin West and of the Far East, and as a result they produced richly imaginative works.

Manuscripts continued to be illustrated throughout the Middle Ages in Armenian monasteries and in the various centres outside the area of Little Armenia where Armenians had settled after the destruction of the kingdom in 1375. These works are often inferior to those of the earlier period, but some original schools developed—for instance, in the area of Lake Van, especially at Khizan and on Aghthamar (modern Akdamar).   (S. Der N./R.S.Co.)

Coptic Egypt. Coptic painting—strictly speaking, that practiced by Christians in Egypt from the time when

Christianity first took hold there—consists primarily of wall paintings in monasteries, the earliest foundations of which date from the 4th and 5th centuries.

Stylistically, Coptic painting differs from that of pagan Egypt in its emphasis on animal and plant ornamentation; less naturalistic rendering of the human form; simplified outline, colour, and detail; and increasingly monotonous repetition of a limited number of motifs.

In content, the wall paintings resemble other Christian examples of the genre around the eastern Mediterranean. The most usual theme is a frieze of saints with an enthroned figure of Christ or the Virgin. There is little variety of pose, though the features of individual saints are distinguishable. An unusually lively piece is a fragment from Wādī Sarga (now in the British Museum) depicting the Old Testament story of the three Hebrews in the fiery furnace; the Hebrews are dressed in Eastern garb and Phrygian hats and are shown as being protected from death by an angel (Figure 10). A celebrated set of wall paintings are those from Bāwīt, now in the Coptic Museum at Cairo.

Figure 10: "The Three Hebrews in the Fiery Furnace"; fragment of a wall painting from a Coptic monastery at Wādī Sarga, Egypt, 6th century AD. In the British Museum, London.

Despite the 7th-century Muslim invasion of Egypt, there was no sudden break in the Coptic tradition. Indeed, some of the most notable surviving examples of manuscript illumination were produced during the first five centuries of Islāmic rule. It was only during the later Middle Ages that specifically Coptic painting ceased as Islāmic culture increasingly predominated.   (A.F.Sh./R.S.Co.)

Western Dark Ages and medieval Christendom

DARK AGES

Ancient Roman civilization in western Europe foundered and fell apart in the second half of the 6th century, and the changes that took place between late antiquity and the succeeding period, the Dark Ages, were fundamental and catastrophic. Urban life collapsed, patronage of the arts all but ceased, and the centuries-old Mediterranean traditions of artistic training and production died out almost everywhere. It was only in a few places in Italy that artistic production continued unbroken, albeit much reduced. Increasingly the cultural fabric of northern Europe was determined by the various tribal peoples—Franks, Vandals, Goths, Angles, and Saxons—who migrated into the western provinces of the old Roman Empire during the 4th to 6th centuries and who established new patterns of settlement and centres of authority. Painting was not one of the traditional arts of these newcomers, though their craftsmen were expert workers of fine metals, leather, wood, and semiprecious stones (known as hardstones) such as garnet.

The reappearance of painting in northern Europe in the late 7th century was determined by two overriding factors. The first was the conversion of these peoples to Christianity. By the 6th century the Christian church had developed an extensive iconographic repertory, and Christian images were in use everywhere: both as icons, which functioned as focal points of worship, and as symbolic and narrative compositions, which proclaimed the mysteries of the faith and instructed the unlettered in the stories of sacred scripture. Painted images had become an indispensable apparatus of orthodox Christianity, and for the newly converted they would have been one of its most arresting and tangible features. The second factor that induced the new masters of Europe to develop the art of painting and figural imagery was their fascination with, and desire to emulate, the culture of the late Roman world, in which painting had been widely employed.

Apart from a small number of images on wooden panels, two kinds of painting have survived from the early Middle Ages: large-scale painting on the walls of buildings and small-scale painting in manuscripts. These two genres involved differing techniques and, to a large extent, constituted separate artistic traditions. Only a tiny percentage has survived of the wall paintings originally to be found in almost every church and in many public buildings throughout the West. Exposed to the destructive agencies of light, moisture, fire, general wear and tear, and changes in fashion, paintings on walls have little chance of surviving for more than a few hundred years. Illuminated books of this period, on the other hand, have come down in large numbers. Made of resilient animal skin and protected by stout wooden boards, they last almost indefinitely, and their decoration usually remains in a remarkably good state of preservation. It is fortunate that book production and decoration were a major concern of the early medieval church. Christianity was the religion of the Book; the words of Jesus Christ, the Gospel, were written down in this book, which Christ, the Logos (literally the "Word"), and his saints are often represented as holding in their hands. Artists in the Middle Ages expended some of their greatest efforts on the illumination and embellishment of the Gospels, the books of the Old Testament, and the other liturgical, devotional, and instructional texts that the church required.

The history of early medieval painting in the West is best examined in the art produced in five areas: Italy, the British Isles, France, Germany and Austria, and Spain.

Rome and Italy, c. 600–850. Rome, the seat of the pope, was one place in the West where an unbroken tradition of artistic patronage and production endured from late antiquity into the high Middle Ages and beyond. This was of inestimable importance for the history of the period from about 600 to 850, since it was to Italy and to Rome that the people of northern Europe looked for direction and for example. Rome's unbroken tradition of patronage

The antique tradition of illusionistic naturalism continued in painting in Rome through the early Christian period; but toward 600 it weakened, and figures became flat and insubstantial. Increasingly, Jesus Christ, the Virgin, and the martyred saints of the church are represented alone or in groups, in strict hieratic frontality (in which the figures are arranged facing forward), gazing out to catch the eye of the onlooker. This development accompanied and served the growing cult of saints and the widespread practice of addressing images as focuses of prayer and veneration.

In the 7th and early 8th centuries successive waves of Byzantine influence dominated Roman patronage and artistic production. Rome at this time was still under the rule of the Byzantine emperor, and contacts with the Eastern capital were close. Various distinct Eastern pictorial traditions seem to have flourished side by side: hieratic figures and strictly symmetrical compositions in mosaic at the church of Sant'Agnese (625–638) and the chapel of San Venanzio at the Lateran Baptistery (642–649); faces carefully and vividly modeled to achieve astonishingly lifelike appearances at Santa Maria Antiqua (e.g., the "Pompeian" Annunciation and St. Anne, early 7th century); and elsewhere in the same church figures fleetingly but effectively rendered in delicate washes of colour, so that they seem to scarcely materialize out of a dense, light-suffused atmosphere (*e.g.,* Eleazar and Solomone and her seven sons, early 7th century).

Another strong and distinctive Byzantine wave hit Rome during the short papacy of John VII (705–707). Under his direct patronage, Eastern artists introduced an iconographic repertory new to the West, compositional schemes that were to endure for more than a century, and a vigorous new figural style (Figure 11).

Figure 11: St. Andrew, wall painting in the presbytery of Santa Maria Antiqua, Rome, 705–707.

In the late 8th century a highly effective technique for representing the human figure was developed, in which modeling was almost completely eschewed and an eloquent system of brightly coloured lines was employed to define the clothed body. Examples include the painting of the Ascension (*c.* 850) in San Clemente, Rome, and the crypt (*c.* 830) of San Vincenzo al Volturno, in central Italy. In this technique wall painting was often used in conjunction with elaborate systems of white highlighting (*e.g.,* the Harrowing of Hell in the lower church of San Clemente and paintings [*c.* 870] in the Temple of Fortuna Virile).

Some of the finest work in Italy of the 8th and the first half of the 9th century was done in the north. At Castelseprio, north of Milan, a Byzantine artist painted a wonderfully light and vigorous cycle of the early life of Mary and the Nativity of Christ in a manner that bafflingly recalls the fluid impressionistic painting of early imperial Rome. Other wall paintings of this time, by native Italian masters, are at Cividale del Friuli, in San Salvatore in Brescia, and at Müstair. Contemporary paintings in the south show clear connections with this new Byzantine-influenced art of northern Italy (*e.g.,* San Vincenzo al Volturno, early 9th century).

England and Ireland, c. 650–850. It is recorded that Roman missionaries, who played a major role in the conversion of England to Christianity in the early 7th century, brought painted images with them; but next to nothing is known about painting on panels or walls in the British Isles during the Dark Ages. There is, however, a good deal of information about the illumination of manuscripts.

In the 6th and 7th centuries monasteries were founded and prospered, first in Ireland, later in England. In their scriptoria (writing rooms) manuscripts were written and decorated in increasingly elaborate fashion. In the Northumbrian double monastery of Monkwearmouth and Jarrow, Italian books and their illustrations were imitated extraordinarily faithfully (*e.g.,* the Codex Amiatinus, a great Bible, *c.* 700). But artists in other Northumbrian centres in the late 7th century began to adapt the standard decorative apparatus of late antique Italian manuscripts to very different effect. Portraits of the Evangelists became brilliant symbols, their bodies and clothes radically abstracted and brightly coloured; and, in the earliest books, they are sometimes shown in the guise of the four apocalyptic beasts, the man, the lion, the bull-calf, and the eagle, which represented the transcendental, celestial aspects of the four authors of the Gospels (*e.g.,* the Durrow Gospels, *c.* 680; the Echternach Gospels, *c.* 700). Artists in the British Isles also introduced other new elements, the most striking being richly ornamented cross-pages, commonly called "carpet pages," filled with ribbon interlace and wonderfully intertwined beasts, and large initial letters. The great full-page initial letters in Gospel books of the British Isles, besides articulating the text, serve as images, almost as icons, of the Word of God (Plate 4). These manuscripts are distinguished by their extraordinary ornamental repertory, drawn from the native Celtic tradition, from the Mediterranean, and from the tradition of fine metalworking introduced by Anglo-Saxon settlers in Britain in the 6th century.

In the 8th century there were flourishing scriptoria also in the south of England, and several manuscripts prepared at Canterbury have been identified (*e.g.,* the Vespasian Psalter, *c.* 730–740; the Stockholm Codex Aureus, or "Golden Gospels," *c.* 750). In early 9th-century books from the south, formal and iconographic elements introduced from Frankish scriptoria across the Channel are in evidence.

It is not yet possible to distinguish between different Irish schools of illumination. The outstanding manuscripts are the St. Gall Gospels (*c.* 750), the great Book of Kells (*c.* 800), the Gospels of Macregol (early 9th century), and a group of little "pocket Gospel books."

The innovations of these early Irish and English scribes and artists left a lasting imprint on the subsequent development of book decoration throughout Europe. The elaborate initial letters that are found in nearly all later decorated manuscripts were first devised in the British Isles, and the decorative vocabulary of later continental illumination owed much to English and Irish invention.

Merovingian Gaul. It was only in the first half of the 8th century that manuscripts began to be elaborately decorated in the Frankish kingdom (an area roughly comprising northern France and southwestern Germany as far as the Rhineland). This production is known as Merovingian, after the Frankish dynasty that ruled, in name at least, until 751. In its subject matter, early Frankish illumination is decorative and symbolic rather than narrative. The idea of stressing the initial letters of a text was adopted from the British Isles, but the results were rather different. The strokes of letters are shaped like doves and fish with swelling bodies, or they are filled with simple ornamental motifs. A favoured frontispiece is a large cross standing within an arch, incorporating or surrounded by animals and birds of all kinds (*e.g.,* the Gelasian Sacramentary [Figure 12]; St. Augustine, *Quaestiones in Heptateuchon,* Laon, *c.* 750). The rare instances of figural composition from mid-8th-century France are usually rather ungainly copies of late antique prototypes (*e.g.,* the Gospels of Gundohinus, Laon, 754). It was only in the second half of the century, probably as a result of English influence, that figure drawing was subjected to a controlled linear discipline (as in the Flavigny Gospels). This development culminated about 800 in the wonderfully inventive historiated (decorated with figures of men or animals) initials in the Corbie Psalter.

EARLY MIDDLE AGES

Carolingian Empire. In the mid-8th century a new Frankish dynasty came to power. Under Charlemagne, whose long reign lasted from 768 to 814 and who was crowned the first emperor of the Romans in 800, a new courtly culture was created to rival those of late antique Rome and of contemporary Byzantium. The achievements of two groups of artists, members of both of which worked for the Emperor and his court, were to determine the overall development of painting in northern Europe for the next three centuries. One group, the so-called Court school, produced a series of splendidly rich Gospel books.

Figure 12: Frontispiece and initial page from the Gelasian Sacramentary, northern France, c. 750. In the Biblioteca Apostolica Vaticana, Vatican City (MS. Vat. Reg. Lat. 316, fol. 131v–132r). 26 × 17.1 cm.

Biblioteca Apostolica Vaticana, Vatican City

Their decoration is extremely inventive, even witty, and the figures, with carefully modeled limbs issuing from dense carapaces of brilliantly coloured, elaborately folded drapery, show a completely new mastery of the human form (Plate 4). The second group concentrated on figures dressed in archaic white garments, with faces and limbs modeled in dramatic chiaroscuro (contrasts of light and shade)—a conscious and very successful evocation of the painting of antiquity (e.g., the Coronation Gospels in Vienna, c. 795–800).

During the years from about 815 to 835 an extremely active and inventive scriptorium flourished at Rheims, under the patronage of the archbishop, Ebbo. Inspired by the masters of the Coronation Gospels, the Rheims artists aimed at producing work intentionally reminiscent of the art of classical antiquity. However, an extraordinary new spirit of linear excitement pervades their compositions, in such works as the Gospels of Ebbo, the Utrecht Psalter, and the Physiologus at Bern. These are some of the most vital and ecstatic creations of the early Middle Ages.

Leading schools of later Carolingian illumination were located at Tours, Saint-Amand (in what is now Belgium), Metz, St. Gall, and at an unidentified scriptorium from which Charlemagne's grandson, Charles the Bald, commissioned a number of extraordinarily lavishly decorated manuscripts in the 860s and 870s.

The early Carolingian artists reintroduced figurative painting and pictorial narrative to northern Europe. To achieve this, they studied monuments and manuscripts surviving from late antiquity and contemporary works from Italy, the British Isles, and Byzantium. They borrowed freely and exuberantly, but they were rarely mere copyists. Vitality and invention were always paramount. This remarkable achievement was the result of determined and demanding patronage and of intense creative effort.

The 10th century. The late 9th and the first half of the 10th century had been a time of economic depression, social upheaval, and political reorganization throughout western Europe. There had followed a period of reconstruction, with new ruling dynasties emerging and consolidating their power. Although production of wall paintings and manuscripts had continued, the energies of patrons had been directed elsewhere, and there had been a distinct decline in production. Only in the third quarter of the 10th century did renewed patronage lead to an outburst of artistic activity and invention.

Late Anglo-Saxon England. In England a coherent and magnificent style of book illumination was developed in the 960s in the scriptorium at Winchester. Narrative compositions and initial letters are framed in arched and rectangular bossed (articulated with circular and square ornamental motifs) trellises of golden bars filled with rampant foliage; figures are clothed in shells of brittle broken drapery, with elaborate zigzagged contours and fluttering hems (e.g., King Edgar's Charter to the New Minster, Winchester, 966; the Benedictional [a book of episcopal Eucharistic blessings] of St. Ethelwold, 971–984 [Plate 4]). During the following century scriptoria in southern England produced a considerable number of books of this kind, filled with flickering colour and glinting gold and intended for ceremonial liturgical use. Behind this initiative in lavish book production lay a movement of religious reform, instituted by the leading churchmen of the realm and supported by the king.

In the scriptoria at Glastonbury and Canterbury a lively tradition of expressive outline drawing developed, and some of the most arresting Anglo-Saxon works of the period are filled with animated figures in flying ruffled drapery (e.g., the Leofric Missal, 970s; Harley Psalter, early 11th century).

English artists of this time delighted in iconographic invention. The results were sometimes startling, and the innovations often endured: the horns of Moses (for example, see Plate 5, although this is a much later work) and Christ disappearing into clouds at his Ascension were both English inventions of the early 11th century.

France. Continuing Carolingian traditions of illumination can be traced in many centres in France, but it is only at the very end of the 10th century that a new energy is apparent in scriptoria in the north, reflecting a reforming spirit in the church. At Fleury, Saint-Bertin, and Saint-Vaast at Arras, imported works from England and the presence of English artists gave a fresh impetus to manuscript illumination. Spirited outline drawings, inspired by English example, were set alongside frames and initial letters of Carolingian ancestry (e.g., the Psalter and Gospels of Odbert of Saint-Bertin, c. 1000; Bible of Saint-Vaast, early 11th century).

Ottonian Germany. In Germany, now under the Saxon Ottonian dynasty, concerted royal and ecclesiastical patronage also brought about a great revival in the arts. As in England, this revival followed a reform movement that touched all the leading monastic communities and revitalized religious life throughout the land.

Ottonian art, like Anglo-Saxon, was solidly based on earlier Carolingian invention; and the illustrations in one of the earliest Ottonian books, the Gospel Lectionary (a book of Gospel lessons for the church year) of Gero (c.

960), were copied line for line from a manuscript of Charlemagne's Court school. The dominant figure in the late 10th century was an artist known as the Master of the Registrum Gregorii, who seems to have been based at Trier. Drawing inspiration from both early Christian and Carolingian manuscripts, he developed a new manner of painting, in which meticulously detailed, smoothly modeled figures are placed in elaborate and precisely calculated spatial settings. In his work, volume and planar design interact in dynamic tension (as in the Letters of Gregory the Great, c. 983; the Gospel Lectionary of Egbert of Trier, from the 980s; and the Gospels of Sainte-Chapelle, c. 1005).

In about 1000, younger contemporaries of this man who had learned much from his art produced, on royal commission, a series of magnificently illuminated books in which brilliantly lighted figures move with a supernatural grandeur against golden grounds and bands of colour (examples include the Gospel Books of Otto III in Aachen and Munich, c. 1000; the Gospel Lectionary of Henry II, 1002–14; and the Apocalypse and Commentaries on Daniel and Isaiah, early 11th century). The portraits of the Evangelists and the imperial images in these books are remarkable for their formal subtlety and iconographic ingenuity (Plate 4).

During the first half of the 11th century, manuscript illumination flourished in various monastic scriptoria in Germany. The inventions and example of the Master of the Registrum Gregorii largely determined developments at Echternach and Cologne. At Cologne, Eastern painted books must also have been available as models, since the wonderfully fluid painterly compositions of the early works of the school appear to have been inspired by contemporary Byzantine painting (as in the Gospels of Abbess Hitda of Meschede, early 11th century). At Regensburg the splendid house style was based largely on one grand Carolingian book, the golden Gospels of Charles the Bald, in the possession of the Abbey of St. Emmeram. In this scriptorium, illustrations became vehicles for elaborate theological arguments, laid out in complex schematic compositions and glossed with explanatory inscriptions (e.g., the Sacramentary [a service book typically containing the celebrant's part of the mass together with various prayers] of Henry II, 1002–14; the Gospels of Abbess Uta, early 11th century). At Corvey, on the other hand, book illumination was ornamental and largely aniconic. The ornamentation consisted chiefly of darkly brilliant initial pages, with large gilded capital letters set on densely patterned purple grounds (as in the Wernigerode Gospels, c. 970).

From literary sources and fragmentary remains it is known that wall painting was common in Germany during this period. But only one extensive program survives, in the Church of St. George on the island of Reichenau, in Lake Constance. This dates from the late 10th century and consists of a sequence of the miracles of Christ's ministry, narrated with great drama and psychological intensity.

ROMANESQUE

In the second half of the 11th century in many parts of Europe new energies and new initiatives are apparent in painting, sculpture, and architecture. It is impossible to categorize these changes fully or to reduce them to a common denominator, but in many places there was a tendency toward greater schematization and bold configurations in design, in which strong and abstract structures of line and colour predominate. The surfaces of clothed bodies are enlivened by intricate schemes of folds and pleats and highlights in regular patterns of reiterated parallel and converging lines. These developments are partly explained by the arrival in the West of examples of recent Byzantine painting, with its elaborate patterned highlighting. Another factor seems to have been an aesthetic that defined beauty in terms of symmetry and order and the juxtaposition of pure, bright saturated colours.

Italy.   In Italy the critical role played by Byzantine art is clearest of all. It is evident both in the north, particularly in Venice, and in the south at Montecassino, where Byzantine artists were summoned by the abbot Desiderius

in the 1060s to work on the decoration of his new abbey church. The wall paintings commissioned by the same Desiderius at Sant'Angelo in Formis, near Capua, are the outstanding surviving example of the consequent fusion of Eastern and Western traditions (Plate 5). In Rome and central Italy in the first decades of the century, the dominant fashion was for figures whose garments hung in a multitude of fine parallel pleats (as in the triptych of the Redeemer in the cathedral at Tivoli and in the wall paintings at Castel Sant'Elia di Nepi and in Santa Pudenziana in Rome). In the 12th century Italian artists took an increasing interest in ancient Roman art, nowhere more so than in Rome itself, where there was a veritable renaissance of classical and early Christian compositional formulas, motifs, and even styles.

France.   An early Romanesque art emerged in scriptoria throughout France in the late 11th century—at Saint-Omer in the north, at Mont-Saint-Michel in the northwest, at the abbey of Saint-Aubin at Angers in the west, at Limoges in central France, and at Toulouse in the south.

In the early 12th century, major schools of painting flourished in Burgundy, at the great Benedictine abbey of Cluny, and at the newly founded Cistercian house   Cluny
of Cîteaux. From Cluny there is a lectionary in which Byzantine influence is strong and a copy of St. Ildefonsus' treatise on the virginity of Mary, with stiff, gorgeously coloured and gilded compositions owing more to late Ottonian examples than to Byzantium. There are also wonderful wall paintings in the Cluniac chapel at Berzé-la-Ville, where the various compositions are filled with energy and colour, and a tumult of fine sweeping folds and flickering highlights plays over the surface of the drapery. At Cîteaux the early manuscripts show evidence of strong Norman and English influence in their decoration and a satirical delight in observation (as in Gregory the Great's Moralia in Job, 1111). Later, in a group of manuscripts of the second quarter of the century, the illustrations are colour-washed drawings with slender, lyrically conceived figures whose drapery falls in cascades of parallel rounded pleats, apparently inspired by contemporary southern Italian work (e.g., St. Jerome's Commentary on Isaiah, the Cîteaux Lectionary).

The most complete surviving set of early Romanesque wall paintings in France is in the church of Saint-Savin-sur-Gartempe, where the compositions show great narrative vigour and inventiveness. Quite startling formal mannerisms sometimes occur in provincial French painting of the first half of the 11th century. Two examples are the wonderfully highlighted and emphatically banded and pleated figures at Vicq-sur-Saint-Chartrier and the violently expressive gesturing figures on the vaults of the crypt of Saint-Nicolas at Tavant. In general, wall painters in the early Middle Ages had very limited means at their disposal, and it is remarkable how skilled artists were able to deploy three or four colours to impressive and unifying effect. An example of this is at Montcherand, in the Swiss Jura, where simple hues of brown, ochre, dull blue, and white have been used to depict ecstatically disputing Apostles beneath a huge Christ in Majesty, in a composition of bright abstract subtlety and strength.

England.   In the 1120s in England artists at the abbey of St. Albans, drawing on earlier English traditions and Ottonian painting from Germany, devised cycles of full-page scenes with large, emphatically gesturing figures set off against rectangular panels of colour, often within architectural settings. In structural density, in their use of accumulated motifs and bright areas of colour, and in the intensity of their storytelling, these images (e.g., the Psalter in St. Godhard, Hildesheim, and the Life of St. Edmund) have few parallels in earlier English art.

In the second quarter of the century acquaintance with contemporary Byzantine painting—probably via illuminated manuscripts—and recent developments on the Continent led English artists to a more organic, if expressively attenuated, conception of the human body. Drapery is now stretched and gathered, with sinuous folds isolating curving islands of taut cloth (so-called damp-fold drapery) to describe three-dimensional forms in torsion. Faces are more heavily modeled than before, and glances and gestures are even more piercing and insistent. This is first seen about 1130 in the great Bible of the Abbey of St. Edmund at Bury (Plate 5); later stages of the development can be traced in a series of magnificent manuscripts from southern English scriptoria (*e.g.,* the Dover Bible, the Lambeth Bible, the Psalter of Henry of Blois, and the Bodleian Terence) and in the wall painting of St. Paul and the viper in St. Anselm's Chapel in Canterbury cathedral (1160s).

In the late 11th century in southern England and in northern France a type of initial letter emerged in which men, monsters, beasts, and birds climb and struggle in "tanglewoods" of rinceaux (ornamental motifs consisting of sinuous and scrolling foliate branches). These ingenious constructions, full of movement and variety, fired the imaginations of artists throughout Europe. On the surface they are an expression of that love of joyously outlandish, grotesque, and even warring imagery that is a ubiquitous feature of 12th-century art; but at a deeper level they are concerned with man's unending conflict with sin and the Devil (Figure 13).

The Bodleian Library, Oxford

Figure 13: Initial letter U to the Book of Job in a Bible from Winchester, *c.* 1160. In the Bodleian Library, Oxford (MS. Auct. E. Infra I, fol. 304r). 14.3 × 14 cm.

Spain. An extraordinary and idiosyncratic tradition of manuscript illumination evolved in Spain in the 10th and 11th centuries. The chief vehicle for this art was the commentary on the book of Revelation of Beatus of Liebana, a text that seems to have been taken by contemporaries as a symbol of Christian resistance to the Muslim Arabs who dominated much of the Iberian Peninsula in the early Middle Ages. The Arab cultural presence in Spain was all-pervasive, and—even if it did not account for the strongly patterned, sometimes barbaric compositions and for the brilliant jarring use of colour—it was responsible for particular motifs adopted by these illuminators (such as the horseshoe arch) and for the common practice of recording in a manuscript's colophon the scriptorium, the scribe and artist, and the date of the manuscript itself.

Northern Spain also produced some of the most splendid Romanesque wall paintings. Spanish artists favoured formal symmetrical and hieratic compositions and strong, barely modulated colours. The human form and the stiff, banded drapery that encases it are consistently more idealized and abstracted than in other European painting of the time. At their finest, these works possess a hypnotic numinous power (Plate 5).

The Meuse Valley. The results of the great increase in artistic production, the sudden intensification of patronage, and the wealth of artistic invention found throughout Europe in the late 11th and early 12th century are nowhere

more clear than in the valley of the Meuse, in what is now eastern Belgium. One of the leading centres of artistic production was the abbey of Stavelot. The decoration of the outstanding early manuscript from its scriptorium, the Stavelot Bible, of about 1094–97, is the work of various hands and is a perfect microcosm of the influences and interests that gave rise to the first Romanesque painting. The majestic enthroned Christ clearly has his ancestry in Ottonian compositions from the nearby scriptorium at Echternach. Some of the historiated initials are inhabited by delicately drawn figures that seem to stem from the old English tradition of outline drawing. Others incorporate large, darkly modeled figures that look strikingly Byzantine. And the great initial of the book of Genesis has a complex program in which scenes from the Old and New Testaments are juxtaposed in a tree of medallions to demonstrate the scheme of Redemption. The concept of expounding a theological argument in a composition of diagrammatic complexity is something that was dear to the 12th century.

Germany and Austria. Full-page compositions of complex iconography in elaborate formal settings are also a characteristic of north German manuscripts of the 12th century. They are found above all in a group of books associated with the all-powerful duke of Saxony Henry the Lion (1142–95) and prepared in the abbey of Helmarshausen on the Weser River. This scriptorium's masterpiece is a Gospel book presented by Henry and his wife Matilda to Brunswick cathedral in 1173–75. The illumination is extraordinarily rich and dense, with a solemn and magisterial palette of gold, purple, dark green, azure, ochre, and white. The elaborate iconographies are glossed in long scrolls, which form undulating accents across the pages (Plate 5).

A very different art was practiced in the southeast, where Salzburg was the leading centre. A strong Italian element is detectable in the illustrations in books of the first half of the 12th century, such as the giant Bible at Michaelbeuern and the Admont Bible of 1140–50. The latter manuscript—which features large, full-page compositions dominated by tall turning figures, unreal landscapes, and bright colours—is a parallel phenomenon to the great contemporary English books, such as the Lambeth Bible and the Psalter of Henry of Blois. Each shows a preoccupation with Byzantine models for figures and faces. But the strong Italian influence in the Salzburg scriptorium ensured that the German figures are calmer and more solid than their exuberant English cousins. In the middle of the century a wonderfully elegant art of pen drawing emerged at Salzburg, with expressive swaying and gesticulating figures set against backgrounds of blue and green (the Antiphonary of St. Peter's at Salzburg).

A number of early wall paintings survive in Austria and Germany, but many of those in Germany have suffered disastrously from over-restoration. In Austria the major monument is the late 11th-century Christological cycle in the west choir of the abbey Church at Lambach, apparently by artists from Salzburg. This work was strongly influenced by the contemporary Byzantinizing art of the Veneto. Salzburg painting of the 1150s can be seen in a lyrical female figure personifying the Third Hour, in the monastic Church of St. Peter.

In Germany well-preserved paintings of the early 12th century at Idensen, in lower Saxony, have strong four-square compositions and clearly contoured, stern-faced figures, which stem from late Ottonian tradition. Half a century later, on the lower Rhine, a new spirit and mentality were expressed in two splendid but drastically repainted cycles at Schwarz Rheindorf and at Brauweiler, near Cologne, where elegantly drawn figures play against panels and frames of blue and green, illustrating recondite and complicated iconographic programs.

LATE 12TH CENTURY

In the late 12th century two broad developments took place in wall painting and manuscript illumination throughout the West. On the one hand, forms became smoother and more fluent, and a less abstract and less aggressively patterned interpretation was put on nature. On the other hand, the perennial interest that Western artists had shown in contemporary Byzantine art grew more intense, and this sometimes led to the opposite extremes of turbulent and mannered design. Both of these tendencies probably aimed at representing human actions and interactions with greater conviction and increased psychological power.

In England a new soft style is apparent in the later hands responsible for illuminating the great Winchester Bible in the 1170s. There, all traces of the elaborately patterned damp-fold drapery of mid-century painting have vanished, to be replaced by material that falls in tiny ripples and soft irregular undulations to reveal firm limbs beneath. A later, simplified, mannered, and frenzied version of this style is found in the illustrations of a bestiary from the Midlands of soon after 1200 (Figure 14). But the rounded, billowing drapery of the enthroned Christ in the contemporary Westminster Psalter seems to have left the 12th century far behind. This is pure Early Gothic painting.

Figure 14: "The Unicorn," miniature from an English Bestiary, early 13th century. In the Bodleian Library, Oxford (MS. Ashmole 1511, fol 14v). 10.4 × 11.5 cm.

A similar evolution can be traced in northern France, in books such as the Capucin's Bible from Champagne and in the Souvigny Bible from central France, in which Byzantine influence is strong. A variation, which originated in the Meuse Valley, was the so-called *Muldenfaltenstil,* named after the small, troughlike folds into which drapery breaks (*e.g.,* the Psalter of Queen Ingeborg, northern France, *c.* 1200). In Germany this style is found in manuscripts made on the middle Rhine and at Regensburg.

The other major factor in European art around 1200 was a widespread interest in Byzantium. Byzantine mosaicists in the late 12th century undertook vast commissions in Venice and Sicily, and these provided Western artists with the opportunity of studying monumental Byzantine art of the finest quality at first hand. Imported Byzantine illuminated manuscripts and panel paintings, enamels, and ivory carvings were also available as models. The purest and most striking instances of Byzantinizing painting are found in Italy. In Venice local craftsmen, trained by Byzantine masters, designed and laid mosaics that are almost indistinguishable from genuine Byzantine work; and in the cathedral at Aquileia the standing prophets and saints painted on the vaults of the crypt look as if they had walked straight out of an Eastern atelier. In Rome and its environs, too, the development of painting in the first half of the 13th century was determined largely by the extensive new programs of mosaics in Norman Sicily, at Palermo, Cefalù, and Monreale.

This swirling, contrived Byzantine art of the middle to late 12th century gave rise to many experiments in

northern Europe. It strongly affected artists at Salzburg (*e.g.,* the drawing of Christ in Majesty in Vienna, Österreichisches Nationalbibliothek, MS. 953) and on the upper Rhine (*e.g.,* the Gospel Lectionary from Speyer of 1196, in Karlsruhe), and it underlies the many figures in the great Tree of Jesse on the ceiling of the Church of St. Michael at Hildesheim, figures conceived in elaborate three-dimensional attitudes, with angular broken drapery. Finally, the *Zackenstil*—the new, elegant, early Gothic, jagged style of early 13th-century Germany, most magnificently exemplified in the Saxon Gospels in Goslar—was directly inspired by contemporary Byzantine painting.

In the early Middle Ages, wall painters had largely been laymen, whereas the illumination of manuscripts had been practiced almost exclusively in monastic scriptoria. In the late 12th century the production of books began to be taken up by lay scribes and painters working in their own shops. At the same time, illuminated books of private devotion and both religious and secular illustrated texts became increasingly popular. This process continued in the 13th century, when growing literacy and learning among laymen and the rise of the universities created a demand for illuminated and illustrated texts of all kinds. (Jo.B.M.)

GOTHIC

Gothic is the term generally used to denote the style of architecture, sculpture, and painting that developed from the Romanesque during the 12th century and became predominant in Europe by the middle of the 13th century. The many variations within the style are usually distinguished by the use of chronological or geographical terms (for example, early, high, Italian, International, and late Gothic).

Early Gothic. One of the moves away from Byzantine influence took the form of a softer, more realistic style, whose general characteristics survived until the middle of the 13th century. In France the style is particularly noticeable in a series of magnificent Bibles Moralisées (books of excerpts from the Bible accompanied by moral or allegorical interpretations and illustrated with scenes arranged in eight paired roundels, resembling stained glass windows) done probably for the French court *c.* 1230–40. In England the new style appears in numerous manuscripts; for instance, the psalter done for Westminster Abbey (British Museum, London; Royal MS. 2a XXII) and the Amesbury Psalter (*c.* 1240; All Souls College, Oxford). A particularly individual application of it is found in the manuscripts attributed to the chronicler Matthew Paris and in a series of illustrated manuscripts of the Apocalypse (Plate 6).

Pictorial style

In Germany the graceful pictorial style did not become popular. Instead the successor to the Byzantine conventions of the 12th century was an extraordinarily twisted and angular style called the *Zackenstil.* In the Soest altar (*c.* 1230–40; now in the Staatliche Museen Preussischer Kulturbesitz, West Berlin), for example, the drapery is shaped into abrupt angular forms and often falls to a sharp point, like an icicle.

High Gothic. Certain characteristics of high Gothic sculpture spread to influence painting about 1250–60. Probably the first place where this became evident was Paris, where Louis IX (St. Louis) was a leading patron (Plate 6). In an evangelary (a book containing the four Gospels) prepared for use at the Sainte-Chapelle (Louis IX's palace chapel), one can see the early Gothic pictorial style superseded quite abruptly by a drapery style incorporating the large, rather angular folds of the Joseph Master (Bibliothèque Nationale). Combined with this style was a growing emphasis on minute detail almost as an end in itself; faces, in particular, became tiny essays in virtuoso penmanship.

Although details such as faces and hands continued to be described chiefly by means of line, in a subsequent development drapery and other shapes were modeled in terms of light and shade. This "discovery of light," partial and piecemeal as it was, began around 1270–80 but is particularly associated with a well-known Parisian royal illuminator called Master Honoré, who was active about 1288–1300 or later.

It is possible that this new use of light was stimulated

New use
of light

by developments in Italian painting. However that may be, Italian influence emerged quite clearly in the second quarter of the 14th century, in the workshop of the Parisian artist Jean Pucelle (Plate 6). More than a dozen books have been associated with this artist; most show an awareness of the recent Italian discovery of perspective in the portrayal of space and some an awareness of Italian iconography.

The French style was introduced fairly rapidly into England. Although Henry III apparently was not a bibliophile, various manuscripts executed for his immediate family contain echoes of the dainty and minute style of Louis IX's artists. Some large-scale paintings that demonstrate similar stylistic traits, notably the "Westminster Retable," survive in Westminster Abbey.

Subsequent changes in English painting involved greater decorative elaboration. A number of large psalters, such as the Queen Mary Psalter (in the British Museum), survive from the first half of the 14th century, many of them done for East Anglian patrons and almost all laying heavy emphasis on marginal decoration. Although some books with elaborate border decorations date from as early as the 13th century, such decorations became much more lavish in the 14th. There are occasional indications of Italian influence in figure poses and compositions but nothing really comparable to that found in books from Jean Pucelle's Parisian workshop.

Italian influence reached other European countries. An Italianate style of painting developed in Spain in the 14th century and, to a lesser extent, parts of German-speaking Europe—in Austria, for instance, paintings in the Italianate style were added around 1324–29 to make up the present Klosterneuburg altarpiece.

Italian Gothic. In the 13th century both Rome and Tuscany had flourishing pictorial traditions, and both, until the middle of the century, were strongly influenced by Byzantine art. The transitional period 1250–1300 is poorly documented. Since much of the Roman work was subsequently destroyed, evidence for what was happening in Rome must be sought outside the city. The most important location where such evidence exists is Assisi, where the upper church of St. Francis was decorated by Roman-trained fresco painters between about 1280 and 1300. In Tuscany the stylistic changes are probably best revealed by Duccio di Buoninsegna's "Maestà" (1308–11), formerly the high altarpiece of Siena cathedral.

As with all Gothic decorative art, the changes are in the direction of greater realism. By the end of the 13th century, painters in Rome, such as Pietro Cavallini and probably Duccio in Tuscany, had discovered, like their contemporaries in Paris, the use to which light could be put in figure modeling. The Italian painters also made sudden and unexpected advances in the manipulation of perspective to describe the space of the scenes they were painting. More than this, the best painters developed an extraordinary ability to create figures that really look as if they are communicating with each other by gesture and expression; the work of the Isaac Master in the upper church at Assisi is an especially good example.

How far the Italian tradition of painting on a large scale magnified problems such as perspective, it would be hard to say. The survival of a large-scale mural tradition certainly marks Italy off from the north. Italian mural paintings were executed with a technique involving pigment applied to, and absorbed by, lime plaster that was still fresh (hence the name of this type of painting—fresco). It was with work in this medium as much as in tempera (a substance binding powdered pigments, usually made from egg at this date) on panel that artists in Italy won their reputations. The typical subjects of fresco painting were series of biblical or hagiographic narratives. The painting of such fresco narratives (in Italian, *istorie*, hence "history painting") was to be regarded in the 15th century as the most important part of an artist's work by Leon Battista Alberti, an architect, painter, sculptor, and the founder of "modern" or "Renaissance" art theory. In making such claims, Alberti had in mind the work of the painter Giotto di Bondone, better known as simply Giotto, of the late 13th to early 14th century.

Trained in Rome, Giotto executed his first important surviving work for the papal financier Enrico Scrovegni at the latter's family palace in Padua. The palace chapel, called the Arena Chapel (decorated *c.* 1305–13), is a masterpiece in which all the lessons of Roman mural painting were translated into a narrative sequence of great economy and expressiveness. In spite of the apparent realism of Giotto's work, however, the Byzantine past makes itself felt in the extremely strong sense of pattern and design noticeable throughout the compositions.

Giotto

In Tuscany somewhat similar developments took place. Duccio's altarpiece, the "Maestà," contains a large number of small narrative scenes reminiscent of Giotto's fresco paintings. The figures, which have firmly modeled faces and expressive gestures, are arranged in buildings or landscapes that convincingly enclose them. Duccio's interest in realistic space, however, was much weaker than Giotto's. Although Duccio's scenes feature a variety of action and wealth of detail that, on the whole, is lacking in Giotto's early work, they do not make the same simple but dramatic impact.

These conflicts are inherent in all realistic painting. In Giotto's work a shift in the balance between the two conflicting elements takes place. He completed two chapels in Santa Croce, Florence (*c.* 1315–30), of which one, the Bardi Chapel, is smaller but not unlike the Arena Chapel. The other, the Peruzzi Chapel, tends toward greater detail and less stability in the settings.

Subsequent Florentine and Sienese painters also moved in this direction. Of the Sienese, Simone Martini was probably the most famous, since he worked outside Italy at the papal court in Avignon and was a friend of the great Italian poet Petrarch. His painting has strong suggestions of northern influence in its elegance and grace, but his care over detail is reminiscent of Duccio, and the careful structure of his setting recalls Giotto and the Roman painters. His major surviving work is now in Siena and Assisi, but some impressive remains have been recovered at Avignon (Plate 6).

Among other Tuscan painters were the brothers Pietro and Ambrogio Lorenzetti, who worked for almost their entire lives in that part of Italy. Their major works are in Siena, but, again, there are important frescoes at Assisi, where, probably, it was Pietro Lorenzetti and his workshop who decorated a transept in the lower church (*c.* 1330). Ambrogio Lorenzetti is especially famous for an enormous landscape, illustrating the effect of good government, painted in the Palazzo Pubblico Siena (1338–39). Historically, it is the first large, realistic landscape in which Byzantine conventions were entirely discarded. It had strangely few imitators, suggesting that the process of discarding convention and using the evidence of the eye is a slow one.

The
Lorenzetti
brothers

By the middle of the 14th century, Italian painters had achieved a unique position in Europe. They had made discoveries in the art of narrative composition that set them quite apart from painters anywhere else. Their achievements in capturing reality were not easily ignored. Many subsequent changes in northern painting consist of the adaptation of Italian compositional realism to northern purposes.

International Gothic. The style of European painting prevalent during the last half of the 14th century and the early years of the 15th is frequently called International Gothic. There were certainly at that time features common to European painting generally. In particular, figures were elegant and graceful, yet at the same time there was a certain artificiality about such figures, and a taste grew for realism in detail, general setting, and composition. The degree of internationalism about this phase of Gothic painting owes something to the fact that much of the most important work was executed under court patronage, and most European royal families were closely linked by marriage ties. Local idiosyncrasies, however, persisted; seldom can the art of Paris, for example, be mistaken for that of Lombardy.

The main European courts were those of the Holy Roman emperors (who had nominal suzerainty over central Europe and who at this time had their capital at Prague), the Visconti of Milan, the Valois of France, and the Plantagenets of England. But other sources of patronage existed—in Florence, for example, where the art of Lorenzo Ghiberti and Lorenzo Monaco merged with that of the early Renaissance. And an extraordinary number of important painters were associated about 1350–1400 with the linguistic area of Low Germany—the Low Countries and Westphalia especially—and the Rhineland.

The patronage of Charles IV
Under the Holy Roman emperor Charles IV and his son Wenceslas, Prague was the seat of a flourishing and enlightened court for about 60 years. Brought up in Paris, Charles had also traveled in Italy. Indeed, his main palace chapel at Karlštejn Castle near Prague, which is the chief monument to Charles's patronage, had an altarpiece by an Italian painter called Tommaso da Modena. The chapel itself was decorated chiefly by a local painter called Theodoric of Prague, whose work is Italianate. A group of his panel paintings, especially the altar of Vyšší Brod (c. 1350), shows a curiously Sienese character, though he did not achieve the delicacy associated with paintings from Siena. The emphasis instead is on heavily modeled faces and thick, heavy drapery. Theodoric's style seems to have initiated the "soft style" that remained a part of German painting well into the 15th century. He certainly determined the character of Bohemian panel painting up to the outbreak of the disastrous Hussite wars (1419).

Charles IV apparently did not collect manuscripts. His ministers and courtiers, however, stimulated an important school of manuscript painting, influenced by French and Italian styles but with distinctive decorative characteristics. Two of the more important manuscripts were a missal (a book containing the office of the mass) done for the chancellor Jan of Streda (c. 1360; Prague, National Museum Library, MS. XIII. A. 12) and a huge Bible begun for Charles's son Wenceslas (1390s; Vienna, Österreichische Nationalbibliothek, Cod. 2759–2764).

Styles similar to this Bohemian painting soon appeared elsewhere—the paintings of Master Bertram of Minden at Hamburg (c. 1380), for example.

In Paris a style appeared that had some of the characteristics of Bohemian work, especially a strong emphasis on faces and facial expression. An early example, probably executed before 1364, is a portrait of John II (Louvre, Paris), which is firmly modeled in a rather Italianate manner. More important, however, is the workshop of the master of the "Parement de Narbonne" (1370s; Louvre; Figure 15), an altar hanging (*parement*) found at the Cathedral of St. Justin Narbonne. These artists, who were active c. 1370–1410, worked in a very distinctive style: their figures, while graceful, have markedly heavy heads and expressive faces. That some interest in settings had developed is suggested by the care that must have been taken to render them reasonably three-dimensional. In this respect the works have much in common with earlier Italian painting.

An interest in the settings of paintings was shared by panel painters such as Melchior Broederlam, who executed the Dijon altar wings (1390s; Museum of Fine Arts, Dijon). The interest quickly spread during the early 15th century to the manuscript painters, who produced a series of extremely impressive landscape and architectural settings. Especially fine are the so-called Brussels Hours (Brussels, The Belgian National Library, MS. 11060–1) and the *Hours of the Maréchal de Boucicaut* (Jacquemart-André Museum, Paris). The best of the manuscript painters worked for the royal family, among whom Jean, duc de Berry, the brother of King Charles V of France, has achieved permanent fame as a patron. The most notable painters who enjoyed his patronage were Pol de Limburg and Pol's two brothers. Their illuminations are frequently reminiscent of contemporary Italian painting.

The *Très Riches Heures du duc de Berry*
The largest and most sumptuous work, the *Très Riches Heures du duc de Berry* (left unfinished in 1416, Condé Museum, Chantilly, Fr.), includes calendar pictures representing each month in terms of the seasonal activities of nobility and peasants (Plate 7). At least one Italian artist—identified tentatively as Zebo da Firenze—was painting in Paris at this period (c. 1405). Manuscripts associated with him are usually sumptuously, if erratically, decorated. In-

Figure 15: Detail from the "Parement de Narbonne," scenes of the Passion of Christ, with portraits of Charles V of France and his queen, brush drawing in grisaille on a white-silk hanging, 1370s. In the Louvre, Paris. 77.5 cm × 2.86 m.
J.E. Bulloz

deed, in the matter of erratic decoration they seem to have had a baleful influence. The border decoration of Parisian manuscripts c. 1410–25, such as those of the artist called the Master of the Duke of Bedford, often seems to run wild and to lack the restraint characteristic of Parisian painting up to this date.

The most eminent Italian artist of this period was perhaps Gentile da Fabriano. Trained probably in Venice, he painted there in the Doges' Palace (first decade of the 15th century) and also at Brescia. Subsequently he moved to Florence and thence to Rome, where he died. Most of his north Italian work has been destroyed, and his style must be assessed chiefly by the work done in Tuscany (Plate 7), the "Adoration of the Magi" altar (1423; Uffizi, Florence). His faces and drapery tend to have a soft, rounded modeling, somewhat reminiscent of the northern "soft style." The subject matter of his painting includes detailed studies of birds, animals, and flowers.

His style forms an interesting contrast to that of Lorenzo Monaco in Florence, who, though equally an International Gothic artist, tended to draw figures with finer, more incisive lines. In many ways Gentile's style resembles painting done at the Milanese court during this period. Many illustrated manuscripts survive, giving an impression of a transition about 1370–1410 from a strongly traditional Lombard style to something that has much in common with northern work. In particular, Michelino da Besozzo seems as court artist to have worked in a soft style similar to that of Gentile. Also dating from around 1400 is a distinguished group of illuminated manuscripts including the Book of Hours of Gian Galeazzo Visconti (Plate 7), herbals (manuals containing botanical drawings), and a famous sketchbook (c. 1395) containing a large number of drawings of animals (Bergamo, Municipal Library, Δ VII 14) from the workshop of an earlier court artist, Giovannino de' Grassi.

In England the decoration of the royal Chapel of St. Stephen's (c. 1360) was apparently, for the period, outstandingly Italianate. (Surviving fragments are in the British Museum, London.) Subsequently, however, in the Chapter House of Westminster Abbey (probably executed c. 1370) there was strong Germanic influence, which has been tentatively compared with the work of Master Bertram at Hamburg.

The court style of the second half of the 14th century is

best illustrated by a series of manuscripts done for members of the Bohun family and by a sumptuous missal given to Westminster Abbey by its abbot, Nicholas Litlington, in 1383–84. The work is decoratively lavish, but the figure style conveys only distant reflections of Italian painting. A great change in English manuscript painting occurred about 1400 and is associated with an artist named Herman Scheerre, who seems to have come from the region of Cologne. His figures have a rather plump softness that brings them into line with stylistic developments elsewhere; he also had a command of perspective and compositional structure lacking in the work of most previous artists in England. The style of John Siferwas, another painter active during this period, is similar, but his page decoration is usually more lavish; he produced a series of beautiful bird studies reminiscent of Lombard work. It should be noted, however, that this sort of realistic observation had long been a feature of English work—in the 14th-century East Anglian manuscripts, for example, and in English embroidery from about 1300.

In view of the number of good painters who came from the region of the Low Countries, Westphalia, and the Rhineland, it is puzzling that these areas should themselves have produced little important painting from the period about 1350–1410. Judging from the surviving works, easily the most distinguished of the painters active in this part of Europe was the Duke of Burgundy's painter, Melchior Broederlam, who lived and worked at Ypres. Other artists, such as Konrad von Soest, who executed the "Niederwildungen Altar" about 1403, seem to have reflected developments elsewhere without pioneering anything strikingly new. It was not until the 1420s that the Low Countries became the centre of intense pictorial development.

Late Gothic. The key to much 15th-century painting in northern Europe lies in the Low Countries. The influence of Paris and Dijon decreased, partly because of the renewal of the Hundred Years' War between England and France and partly because of the removal of the Burgundian court, after the mid-1420s, from Dijon to Brussels, which subsequently became the centre of an extensive court patronage.

The founder of the Flemish school of painting seems to have been Robert Campin of Tournai. The works of Campin, his pupil Rogier van der Weyden, and Jan van Eyck remained influential for the whole century. One of the most important discoveries of the period of about 1430—especially in the work of van Eyck—was the multifarious effects a painter can achieve by observing the action of light (Plate 8). These early Flemish artists found that light can define form, shape, and texture and that, when captured in a landscape, it can help convey a mood. Rogier van der Weyden also explored the problems of conveying emotion (Plate 8). A development in the rendering of the drapery—the so-called crumpled style of hard angular folds—is particularly clear in the paintings of Campin. Portraiture made dramatic progress during this period. Portraits were obviously not new; sculptors were already experimenting in the 14th century with life—and death—masks. But the brilliant use of lighting gives the portraits of Jan van Eyck, for instance, a vivid life hitherto quite unknown.

A great deal of later 15th- and 16th-century Flemish painting seems to play variations on these themes. Although there were painters with distinctly individual styles, such as Hugo van der Goes, with his highly accomplished technique and somewhat contemplative depictions, Hans Memling was more typical (despite having been born in the Rhineland).

The influence of van Eyck's paintings was felt to a limited extent outside the Low Countries; for example, by Konrad Witz of Basel, Switz., by the Master of the Aix Annunciation (1442) of Aix-en-Provence, Fr., and by the Neapolitan artist Colantonio and his illustrious pupil Antonello da Messina. In the course of the century, however, the style of Rogier van der Weyden and his immediate successors, such as Dirck Bouts, became more influential, being felt in Germany, England, Spain, and Portugal. Evidence of Rogier van der Weyden's influence can be seen

in the works of Hans Pleydenwurff of Nürnberg, in the wall paintings in Eton College Chapel (c. 1480), and in the paintings of Nuno Gonçalves in Portugal. This new "international style" also influenced the great German engraver Martin Schongauer and, ultimately, the outstanding representative of the German Renaissance school of painting, Albrecht Dürer.

Any individualists at this time were usually painters who chose to go to the extreme of emphasizing the bizarre or the horrifying. Hugo van der Goes veered in this direction. Much more disquieting is the painting of Hiëronymus Bosch, whose strange scenes still puzzle and perplex (Plate 8). The work of Matthias Grünewald, whose main surviving work is the altarpiece for a monastery at Isenheim, Ger. (Unterlinden Museum, Colmar, Fr.; Plate 8) is grotesque and horrifying.

A very different sort of extreme individuality is found in the work of the Tirolean painter and sculptor Michael Pacher. His pictorial work is so strongly marked by a concern with the structure of the composition and with effects of perspective—particularly foreshortening—that it seems clear he knew the work of Andrea Mantegna of Padua. Although virtually free of antique motifs, Pacher's painting demonstrates the growing fascination of Italian Renaissance art for northern artists.

Rather different were the French painters of the 15th century (Plate 7). Court art revived, especially during the reign of Louis XI (1461–83), as exemplified by the illuminated manuscript *Le Livre du coeur d'amours éspris* (1465; Österreichische Nationalbibliothek, Vienna). The most interesting painter was probably Jean Fouquet, who, apparently early in his career, visited Italy. Italian details certainly appear in his work, but, as is evident in the *Hours of Étienne Chevalier* (Condé Museum, Chantilly) and the "Melun Diptych" (now divided between the Staatliche Museen Preussischer Kulturbesitz, West Berlin, and the Museum of Fine Arts, Antwerp), he still painted within the northern tradition. The restrained and somewhat reticent character of much French painting is interestingly similar to much of the sculpture. (A.Ma./Ed.)

Renaissance

The term Renaissance was first used by French art historians of the late 18th century in reference to the reappearance of antique architectural forms on Italian buildings of the early 16th century. The term was later expanded to include the whole of the 15th and 16th centuries and, by extension, to include sculpture, painting, and the decorative arts. There is still considerable disagreement among art historians as to whether the term should be restricted to a phenomenon that had its origins in Italy and then spread through western Europe (the point of view taken here) or whether directly contemporary developments north of the Alps, and especially in the Low Countries, should be included on an equal footing with what was happening in Italy.

The controversies that raged after the publication of Jacob Burckhardt's *Civilization of the Renaissance in Italy* (English translation, 1878) have abated, and the time span of the Renaissance is generally accepted as the period from roughly 1400 to about 1600, although certain geographical areas and certain art forms require greater latitude. This period is characterized as a rebirth or, better, the birth of attitudes and aims that have their closest parallel in the art of classical antiquity. Classical literature and, less often, classical painting were invoked as a justification for these new aims. The theoretical writings on art from the period indicate that man was the dominant theme. In religious painting, drama and emotion are expressed in human terms. From the late Middle Ages the theme of the Madonna enthroned with Christ Child is presented in an earthly setting peopled by mortals. This strongly humanistic trend serves to explain, at least in part, the development of portraiture as an independent genre and the ever-increasing number of profane, usually classical mythological, subjects in the art of the Renaissance. The painting of landscapes, as the earthly setting of man's activity, has its first modest beginnings in this period.

The role of art and of the artist began to take on modern form during the Renaissance. Leon Battista Alberti's *De pictura* (*Della pittura*), a treatise on the theory of painting, as opposed to the techniques of preparing and applying colours, appeared in Florence in 1435–36. The directions that art and art theory were to follow for the next 470 years are already present in this little book. The artist is considered to be a creator rather than a technician because he uses his intellect to measure, arrange, and harmonize the elements of his creation. The intellectual activity of art is demonstrated, by a series of comparisons, to be equivalent to that of the other liberal arts. Influences such as Alberti's book led to a new evaluation of the artist, with painters and their works being sought after by the rulers of Europe (Michelangelo and Titian were actually ennobled); the result was that great collections containing the works of major and minor masters were formed. At the same time the artist slowly began to free himself from the old guild system and to band together with his colleagues, first in religious confraternities and later in academies of art, which, in turn, were to lead to the modern art school. During the Renaissance, practitioners of all the arts evolved from anonymous craftsmen to individuals, often highly respected ones. Painting became more intellectual, sometimes to its own disadvantage, and changed from serving as a vehicle for didacticism or decoration to becoming a self-aware, self-assured form of expression.

For the sake of convenience, painting of the Renaissance is divided into three periods, although there is considerable overlap depending upon the painter and the place. The early Renaissance is reckoned to cover the period from about 1420 to 1495. The High Renaissance, or classic phase, is generally considered to extend from 1495 to 1520, the death of Raphael. The period of Mannerism and what has more recently been called late Renaissance painting is considered to extend from the 1520s to approximately 1600.

EARLY RENAISSANCE IN ITALY

The early Renaissance in Italy was essentially an experimental period characterized by the styles of individual artists rather than by any all-encompassing stylistic trend as in the High Renaissance or Mannerism. Early Renaissance painting in Italy had its birth and development in Florence, from which it spread to such centres as Urbino, Ferrara, Padua, Mantua, Venice, and Milan after the middle of the century.

The political and economic climate of the Italian Renaissance was often unstable; Florence, however, did at least provide an intellectual and cultural environment that was extremely propitious for the development of art. Although the direct impact of humanist literary studies upon 15th-century painting has generally been denied, three writers of the 15th century (Alberti, Filarete, and Enea Silvio Piccolomini, later Pope Pius II) drew parallels between the rebirth of classical learning and the rebirth of art. The literature of antiquity revealed that in earlier times both works of art and artists had been appreciated for their own intrinsic merits. Humanist studies also fostered a tendency, already apparent in Florentine painting as early as the time of Giotto, to see the world and everything in it in human terms. In the early 15th century Masaccio emphasized the human drama and emotions in his painting "The Expulsion" (Brancacci Chapel, Santa Maria del Carmine, Florence) rather than the theological implications of the act portrayed. Masaccio in his "Trinity" (Santa Maria Novella, Florence) and Fra Angelico in his San Marco altarpiece seem to be much more concerned with the human relations between the figures in the composition than with the purely devotional aspects of the subject. In the same way, the painter became more and more concerned with the relations between the work of art and the observer. This latter aspect of early 15th-century Florentine painting relies in great part on the invention of the one-point perspective system, which derives in turn from the new learning and the new vision of the world. The empirical system devised through mathematical studies by the architect Filippo Brunelleschi was given theoretical form and universal application by Alberti in *De pictura.*

Invention of a perspective system

In this system all parts of the painting bear a rational relation to each other and to the observer, for the observer's height and the distance he is to stand from the painting are controlled by the artist in laying out his perspective construction. By means of this system the microcosm of the painting and the real world of the observer become visually one, and the observer participates, as it were, in what he observes. To heighten the illusion of a painting as a window on the world, the Italian artists of the early 15th century turned to a study of the effects of light in nature and how to represent them in a painting, a study of the anatomy and proportions of man, and a careful observation of the world about them. It is primarily these characteristics that separate early Renaissance painting from late medieval painting in Italy.

Masaccio has rightly been called the father of Renaissance painting, for every major artist of the 15th and 16th centuries in Florence began his career by studying Masaccio's murals in fresco. Masaccio is the artistic heir of Giotto, yet there is no indication of direct borrowing from the older master. He was also a friend of Brunelleschi and from him may have learned perspective and the concept of a clear and rationally articulated space. He was a friend, too, of the Florentine sculptor Donatello and may have learned from him the effectiveness of simple drapery folds over a full and powerful figure. Whatever his artistic sources, Masaccio's extant work reveals a concern with large and simple figures clad in simple draperies. He was concerned with light and the way it gives the illusion of solidity to the painted figure. He created a deep and clearly articulated space in his paintings, and he was above all concerned with his actors as humans carrying out some purposeful human activity. The only extant work by Masaccio that can be clearly dated is the Pisa altarpiece of 1426 (the central panel depicting the Madonna enthroned with Christ Child and angels, now in the National Gallery, London, is the largest surviving section). Although Masaccio continued the medieval tradition of using a gold background, the architectural elements of the throne indicate his awareness of the influence of Roman antiquity on the architecture of his friend Brunelleschi. The Madonna is no longer an elegant queen of heaven but an earthly mother with a human child on her lap. The figure of the Christ Child is a clear demonstration for future generations of the way light and shade can be manipulated in a painting to give the illusion of a solid three-dimensional body. In this painting Masaccio laid the foundations for one major current in all Florentine painting. His concern with the sculpturally conceived figure, bathed in light and presented in a strong and simple manner, created a work of quiet dignity and great monumentality in that it appears to be larger than it really is.

Father of Renaissance painting

Masaccio's great fresco series in the Brancacci Chapel of Santa Maria del Carmine in Florence adds yet another dimension to early Renaissance painting. In this narrative sequence devoted to the life of St. Peter, he chose the most important moment in the narrative and then emphasized the drama by the human reactions to it. "The Tribute Money" is a simple yet powerful illustration of Christ's words, in which each apostle reacts individually to the tax collector's claim and Christ's reply (Plate 9). In this same chapel Masaccio also demonstrated his awareness of the real world, for the light of the paintings, indicated by the cast shadows, is the same as the natural light falling into the chapel.

Masaccio's awareness of the real world

"The Trinity" in Santa Maria Novella, Florence, provides a summary of Masaccio's brief career and indeed of the aesthetic principles of early Renaissance painting generally. The simple sculptural figures have acquired even greater dignity. The drama and emotion are presented in touching human terms as the Madonna turns to the observer to point out her crucified Son. In addition to the use of light to unite the space of the painting with the space of the observer, Masaccio also employed what appears to be the earliest practical example of the one-point perspective system, later to be formulated in words by Alberti. All the highest aims of early Renaissance painting are here: simplicity, strength, monumentality; man as observer, as actor, and as participant in the work of art.

Masaccio had no true followers or successors of equal stature, though there was a group of other Florentine painters who were about the same age as Masaccio and who followed in his footsteps to a greater or lesser degree: Fra Filippo Lippi, Fra Angelico, and Paolo Uccello.

Fra Filippo Lippi was a Carmelite monk who spent his youth and early manhood at Santa Maria del Carmine, where Masaccio's work was daily before his eyes. His earliest datable work, the "Madonna and Child" (1437) from Tarquinia Corneto, relies on the Madonna from the Pisa altarpiece, but in his Christ Child Fra Filippo already reveals an earthiness and sweetness unlike anything by Masaccio. "The Madonna and Child with Two Angels" (Uffizi, Florence)—with its urchin-angels, lumpy Christ Child, and elegant Madonna—is perhaps one of his best-known late works; the placement of the Madonna before an open window is one of the key sources for later Renaissance portraiture, including Leonardo da Vinci's "Mona Lisa," while the elegance and sweetness of the Madonna were to have their greatest reflection in the work of Fra Filippo Lippi's student, Botticelli.

Born about the same time as Masaccio, Fra Angelico was a Dominican monk who lived at Fiesole (just outside Florence) and at San Marco in Florence. His earliest documented work, the "Linaiuoli Altarpiece" (Museum of San Marco, Florence) of 1433, continues much that is traditional to medieval art, although the male saints in the wings (side pieces of a composite painting, typically a tripartite altarpiece) already reveal the influence of Masaccio. The altarpiece that he executed between 1438 and 1440 for the high altar of San Marco is one of the landmarks of **Introduction of the *sacra conversazione*** early Renaissance art. It is the first appearance in Florence of the *sacra conversazione,* a composition in which angels, saints, and sometimes donors occupy the same space as the Madonna and Christ Child and in which the figures seem to be engaged in conversation. In addition to inaugurating a new phase of religious painting, the altarpiece reveals the influence of Masaccio in the sculptural treatment of the figures and an accurate awareness of the perspective theories of painting expressed by Alberti in his treatise. At about the same date, Fra Angelico was commissioned to decorate the monks' cells in San Marco. The nature of the commission—traditional devotional images whose execution required assistants—apparently turned Fra Angelico toward the religious and didactic works that characterize the end of his career; *e.g.,* the Chapel of Nicholas V in the Vatican.

Paolo Uccello's reputation as a practitioner of perspective is such that his truly remarkable gifts as a decorator tend to be overlooked. Studies of his extant works suggest that he was more interested in medieval optics than in the rational perspective system of Alberti and Brunelleschi. His earliest documented work, the "Sir John Hawkwood" fresco of 1436 in Florence cathedral, is a decorative work of a very high order and one that respects the integrity of the wall to which it is attached. Uccello is perhaps best known for the three panels depicting "The Battle of San Romano," executed about 1456 for the Medici Palace (now in the National Gallery, London; the Louvre, Paris; and the Uffizi). The paintings were designed as wall decoration and as such resemble tapestries. Uccello is concerned only with creating a small boxlike space for the action, for he closes off the background with a tapestry-like interweaving of men and animals. His primary concern is with the rhythmic disposition of the elements of the composition across the surface, an emphasis that he reinforces with the repetition of arcs and circles. Uccello's concern with the decorative and linear properties of painting had a great impact on the cassone (chest) painters of Florence and found its greatest reflection and refinement in the work of Botticelli.

Masaccio's greatest impact can be seen in the works of three younger painters, Andrea del Castagno, Domenico Veneziano, and Piero della Francesca. Castagno was the leader of the group. His "Last Supper" of about 1445, in the former convent of Sant'Apollonia in Florence, reveals the influence of Masaccio in the sculptural treatment of the figures, the painter's concern with light, and his desire to create a credible and rationally conceived space. At the same time Castagno betrays an almost pedantic interest in antiquity, which roughly parallels a similar development in letters, by the use of fictive marble panels on the rear wall and of sphinxes for the bench ends, both of which are direct copies of Roman prototypes. In the last years of his life, Castagno's style changed abruptly; he adopted a highly expressive emotionalism that paralleled a similar development in the work of his contemporaries. His "The Trinity with Saints" in the church of the Santissima Annunziata, Florence, was originally planned with calm and balanced figures, as the underpainting reveals. In the final painting, however, the figures, though sculpturally conceived, project an agitation heightened by the emaciated figure of St. Jerome and the radically conceived figure of the crucified Christ. The optimism, rationality, and calm human drama of earlier Renaissance painting in Florence were beginning to give way to a more personal, expressive, and linear style. **Expressive emotionalism among Florentine painters**

One aspect of this new direction is met in the work of the enigmatic Domenico Veneziano, the second of the three principal painters who looked to Masaccio. His name indicates that he was a Venetian, and it is known that he arrived in Florence about 1438. He was associated with Castagno, and perhaps Fra Angelico, and helped to train the somewhat younger Piero della Francesca. His St. Lucy altarpiece of about 1445–50 (Uffizi) is an example of the *sacra conversazione* genre and contains references to the painting of Masaccio and the early 15th-century sculpture of the Florentine Nanni di Banco. The colour, however, is Domenico's own and has no relation to the Florentine tradition. His juxtaposition of pinks and light greens and his generally blond tonality point rather to his Venetian origins. In the painting he has lowered the vanishing point in order to make the figures appear to tower over the observer, with the result that the monumentality of the painting is enhanced at the expense of the observer's sense of participating in the painting. **Domenico Veneziano's unique use of colour**

Piero della Francesca received his early training in Florence but spent the active part of his career outside the city in such centres as Urbino, Arezzo, Rimini, and his native Borgo San Sepolcro, in Umbria. His "Flagellation of Christ" (late 1450s), in the National Gallery of the Marches, Urbino, is a summary of early 15th-century interest in mathematics, perspective, and proportion (Plate 9). The calm sculptural figures are placed in clear, rational space and bathed in a cool light. This gives them a monumental dignity that can only be compared to early 5th-century-BC Greek sculpture. Much the same tendency can be seen in Piero's great fresco cycle in the church of San Francesco in Arezzo.

A hiatus occurred in Florentine painting around 1465–75. All the older artists had died, and the men who were to dominate the second half of the century were too young to have had prolonged contact with them. Three of these younger artists, Antonio Pollaiuolo, Sandro Botticelli, and Andrea del Verrocchio, began their careers as goldsmiths, which perhaps explains the linear emphasis and sense of movement noticeable in Florentine painting of the later 15th century.

As well as being a goldsmith, Antonio Pollaiuolo was a painter, sculptor, engraver, and architect. His work indicates his fascination with muscles in action, and he is said to have been the first artist to dissect the human body. In the altarpiece "The Martyrdom of St. Sebastian" (1475; National Gallery, London) he presents the archers from two points of view to demonstrate their muscular activity. His painting (formerly in the Uffizi but now lost) and small sculpture (Bargello, Florence) of "Hercules and Antaeus," like the engraving of "The Battle of the Nudes," depict struggle and violent action. "The Rape of Deianira" (Yale University Art Gallery, New Haven, Conn.) emphasizes yet another new element in Florentine painting, the landscape setting, in this case a lovely portrait of the Arno Valley with the city of Florence in the background. **Pollaiuolo's concern with anatomy**

A similar concern with moving figures, a sense of movement across the surface of the panel, and landscape is found in the earlier works of Sandro Botticelli. In his well-known painting "The Primavera" (Uffizi) he uses line in depicting hair, flowing draperies, or the contour of an arm

Minoan and Greek painting

Youthful fisherman with his catch, fresco on the wall of the West House at Akrotíri, Thera, Greece, 15th century BC.

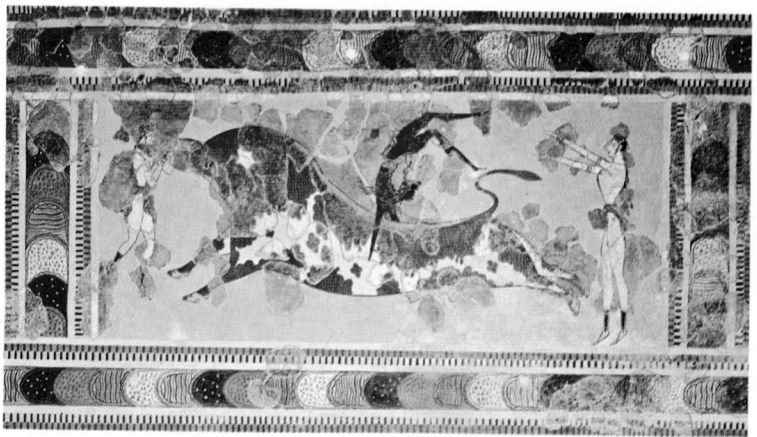

"The Toreador Fresco," restored wall painting from the Palace at Knossos, Crete, c. 1550 BC. In the Archaeological Museum, Iráklion, Crete. Height (including borders) 81 cm.

"Three Companions of Odysseus Encountering the Daughter of Antiphatis, King of the Laestrygones," Roman Second-style wall painting from a house on the Esquiline Hill, Rome, possibly based on a Hellenistic painting, c. 1st century BC. In the Biblioteca Apostolica Vaticana, Vatican City. Height 1.4 m.

Plate 2 Painting, The History of Western

Greek and Roman painting

Hades abducting Persephone, wall painting in the small royal tomb at Vergina, Macedonia, 4th century BC.

The family of Vunnerius Keramus, medallion of gold and glass, c. AD 250. In the Museum of Christian Antiquities, Brescia, Italy. Diameter 6 cm.

Dionysiac initiation rites and prenuptial ordeals of a bride, wall painting, Second style, c. 50 BC. In the Villa of the Mysteries, Pompeii, Italy.

''Anastasis'' (''Christ Ascending from Hell''), apse fresco, *c.* 1320. In the Church of St. Saviour at the Monastery of the Chora (Kariye Cami), Istanbul.

Rebekah at the well, illuminated miniature from the Vienna Genesis, 6th century. In the Österreichische Nationalbibliothek, Vienna (Cod. theol. graec. 31, fol. 7).

''Our Lady of Vladimir,'' tempera on wood, from Constantinople, *c.* 1130. In the State Tretyakov Gallery, Moscow. 78 × 55 cm.

Byzantine painting

Portrait of the high admiral Alexius Apocaucos, illuminated manuscript page from the Hippocrates Manuscript, *c.* 1342. In the Bibliothèque Nationale, Paris (Cod. Gr. 2144). 41.5 × 35 cm.

Plate 4 Painting, The History of Western

St. Mark, illuminated manuscript page from the Gospel Book of the Court school of Charlemagne, c. 810. In the Stadtbibliothek, Trier, W.Ger. (Cod. 22, fol. 59v). 36.6 × 24.5 cm.

Nativity, Benedictional of St. Ethelwold, Winchester, Hampshire, 971–984. In the British Library, London (Add. MS. 49598, fol. 15v). 29.3 × 22.5 cm.

Early Medieval and Romanesque painting

Liber Generationis, initial page from the beginning of St. Matthew in the Lindisfarne Gospels, c. 700. In the British Library, London (Cotton MS., Nero D.IV, fol. 27r). 34 × 24.5 cm.

St. Luke, illuminated manuscript page from the Gospel Book of Otto III, school of Reichenau, c. 1000. In the Bayerische Staatsbibliothek, Munich (CLM. 4453, fol. 139v). 24 × 19 cm.

Ascension, illuminated manuscript page from the Gospels of Henry the Lion, from the abbey of Helmarshausen, c. 1173–75. In the Herzog August Bibliothek, Wolfenbüttel, W.Ger. 34.2 × 25.5 cm.

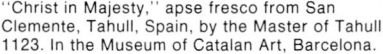

"Christ in Majesty," apse fresco from San Clemente, Tahull, Spain, by the Master of Tahull, 1123. In the Museum of Catalan Art, Barcelona.

Moses expounding the law of the unclean beasts, illuminated manuscript page from the Bury Bible, about 1130. In Corpus Christi College, Cambridge (MS. 2, fol. 94r). 51 × 35.7 cm.

Jesus at Bethany in the house of Simon the leper, detail of a fresco in Sant'Angelo in Formis, near Capua, Italy, second half of the 11th century.

Plate 6   Painting, The History of Western

David before Saul, page from the Belleville Breviary, illuminated manuscript attributed to Jean Pucelle, *c.* 1325. In the Bibliothèque Nationale, Paris (MS. lat. 10 483, fol. 24v). 24 × 18 cm.

Gothic painting in Italy, France, and England

Joshua bidding the Sun stand still, illuminated miniature from the Psalter of St. Louis, *c.* 1260. In the Bibliothèque Nationale, Paris (MS. lat. 10 525, fol. 46). 12 × 9 cm.

Angel blowing the trumpet, illuminated miniature from the Douce Apocalypse, *c.* 1270. In the Bodleian Library, Oxford (Douce MS. 180, p. 26). 15 × 11 cm.

"Annunciation," tempera on wood by Simone Martini, 1333 (saints on either side of the central panel by Lippo Memmi). In the Uffizi, Florence. 3.1 × 2.7 m.

October, from the *Très Riches Heures du duc de Berry*, illuminated manuscript page by the Limburg brothers, *c.* 1416. In the Condé Museum, Chantilly, Fr. (fol. 10v). 29 × 21 cm.

"Adoration of the Magi," tempera on wood by Gentile da Fabriano, 1423. In the Uffizi, Florence. 3 × 2.8 m.

Initial letter of the Magnificat, from the Book of Hours of Gian Galeazzo Visconti, illuminated manuscript page by Giovannino de' Grassi, *c.* 1385. In the Biblioteca Nazionale Centrale, Florence (Fondo Landau-Finaly MS. 22, fol. 147v).

Cuer reading the inscription on the magic fountain, page from *Le Livre du coeur d'amours éspris*, illuminated manuscript attributed to René of Anjou, 1465. In the Österreichische Nationalbibliothek, Vienna (MS. 2597, fol. 15r). 29 × 21 cm.

Plate 8   Painting, The History of Western

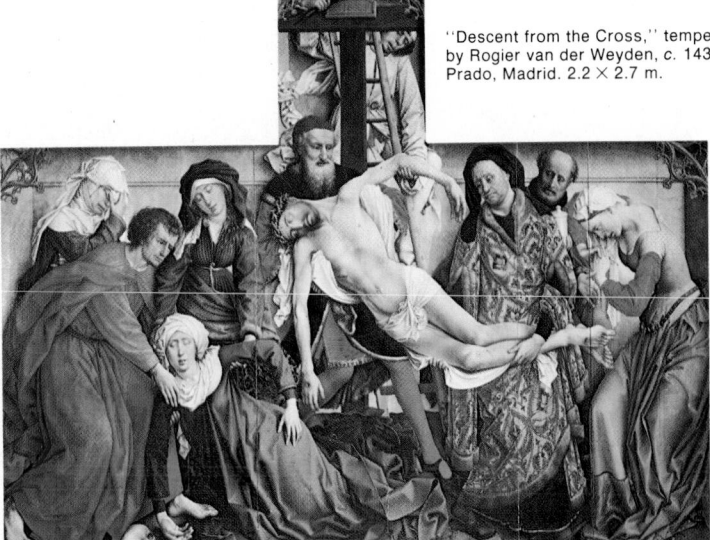

"Descent from the Cross," tempera on wood
by Rogier van der Weyden, c. 1435–40. In the
Prado, Madrid. 2.2 × 2.7 m.

**Gothic painting in
Germany and the
Low Countries**

"The Resurrection," open right panel of the
"Isenheim Altarpiece," oil on wood by Matthias
Grünewald, completed before 1516. In the
Unterlinden Museum, Colmar, Fr. 2.7 × 1.4 m.

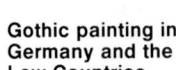

"Madonna with Chancellor Rolin," oil on wood by Jan van Eyck,
c. 1435. In the Louvre, Paris. 66 × 82 cm.

"Hell," open right panel of the "Garden of Delights" triptych, oil
on wood by Hiëronymus Bosch, c. 1505–10. In the Prado, Madrid.
2.2 m × 97 cm.

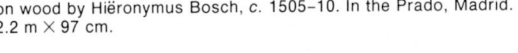

Plate 8: By courtesy of (top left) the Museo del Prado, Madrid; photographs, (top right, bottom right) SCALA/Art
Resource—EB Inc., (bottom left) Archivo Mas, Barcelona

"Flagellation of Christ," oil on wood by Piero della Francesca, late 1450s. In the National Gallery of the Marches, Urbino, Italy. 59.5 × 82 cm.

"Arrival of Cardinal Francesco Gonzaga," fresco by Andrea Mantegna, completed 1474. In the Camera degli Sposi, Palazzo Ducale, Mantua, Italy.

Renaissance painting of the 15th century in Italy

"The Tribute Money," fresco by Masaccio, 1425. In the Brancacci Chapel, Santa Maria del Carmine, Florence. 2.5 × 6m.

"The Primavera," tempera on wood by Sandro Botticelli, 1477–78. In the Uffizi, Florence. 2.1 × 3.2 m.

Plate 10 Painting, The History of Western

"The Bacchanal," oil painting by Titian, 1518–19. In the Prado, Madrid. 1.8 × 1.9 m.

"The Tempest," oil painting by Giorgione, c. 1505. In the Gallerie dell'Accademia, Venice. 77 × 74 cm.

"Madonna of the Meadows," oil on wood by Raphael, 1505. In the Kunsthistorisches Museum, Vienna. 1.1 m × 87 cm.

"The Last Supper," fresco by Leonardo da Vinci, 1495–97. In the refectory of the convent of Santa Maria delle Grazie, Milan. 8.8 × 4.6 m.

"The Last Judgment," fresco by Michelangelo, 1533–41. In the Sistine Chapel, Vatican, Rome. 14.5 × 13.5 m.

"Assumption of the Virgin," oil painting by El Greco, 1577. In the Art Institute of Chicago. 4 × 2.3 m.

Renaissance painting of the 16th century in Italy and Spain

"The Last Supper," oil painting by Tintoretto, 1594. In the chancel, S. Giorgio Maggiore, Venice. 3.5 × 5.6 m.

"Madonna dal Collo Lungo" ("Madonna of the Long Neck"), oil on wood by Parmigianino, c. 1535. In the Uffizi, Florence. 2.2 × 1.3 m.

Plate 12 Painting, The History of Western

"Peasant Dance," oil on wood by Pieter Bruegel the Elder, *c.* 1568. In the Kunsthistorisches Museum, Vienna. 1.1 × 1.6 m.

Renaissance painting of the 16th century in Germany and the Low Countries

"Four Apostles," oil on two wood panels by Albrecht Dürer, 1526. in the Alte Pinakothek, Munich. Each panel 2.2 m × 77 cm.

"Venus in a Landscape," oil on wood by Lucas Cranach the Elder, 1529. In the Louvre, Paris. 38.1 × 25.9 cm.

"Portrait of the Merchant Georg Gisze," oil and tempera on wood by Hans Holbein the Younger, 1532. In the Staatliche Museen Preussischer Kulturbesitz, West Berlin. 96.3 × 86 cm.

Elegance and grace of Botticelli's works

to suggest the movement of the figures (Plate 9). At the same time the pose and gesture of the figures set up a rising and falling linear movement across the surface of the painting. Botticelli's well-known paintings of the Madonna and Child reveal a sweetness that he may have learned from Fra Filippo Lippi, together with his own sense of elegance and grace. A certain nervosity and pessimistic introspection inherent in Botticelli's early works broke forth about 1490. His "Mystic Nativity" of 1501 (National Gallery, London) is even, in one sense, a denial of all that the Renaissance stood for. The ambiguities of space and proportion are directed toward the unprecedented creation of a highly personal and emotionally charged statement.

Florentine painters active in the closing decades of the 15th century include Andrea del Verrocchio, who is best known as the master of Leonardo da Vinci and Perugino. There was also Filippino Lippi, who was apparently apprenticed to Botticelli when his father, Fra Filippo Lippi, died; he painted a group of madonnas that are easily confused with Botticelli's early work. By 1485, however, he had developed a somewhat nervous and agitated style that can be seen in the highly expressive "Vision of St. Bernard" in the Badia, Florence. His last works, such as the series of frescoes he painted in Santa Maria Novella (1502), reveal a use of colour and distortion of form that may have influenced the later development of Mannerism in Florence a generation or so later. Another painter active at this time was Domenico Ghirlandajo, whose artistic career was spent as a reporter of the Florentine scene. The series of frescoes on the "Life of the Virgin" in Santa Maria Novella (finished 1490) can be viewed as the life of a young Florentine girl as well as a religious painting. His art was already old-fashioned in his own time, but he provided a large number of Florentine artists, among them Michelangelo, with training in the difficult art of fresco painting.

Diffusion of the innovations of the Florentine school

The discoveries and innovations of the early 15th century in Florence began to diffuse to other artistic centres by mid-century. Siena painters in general continued the traditions of the 14th century except for such artists as Matteo di Giovanni, Neroccio di Bartolomeo, and Vecchietta, who alone in that city were to a certain degree under Florentine influence. In Ferrara, Cosimo Tura, Francesco del Cossa, and Ercole de' Roberti felt the influence of Florence as transmitted by Piero della Francesca. Only in Padua and Venice, however, did painters arise who could actually challenge the preeminence of Florence.

Andrea Mantegna was influenced by the sculpture executed by Donatello in Padua, the art of antiquity around him, and the teaching of his master, Francesco Squarcione. The frescoes he completed in 1455 in the Ovetari Chapel of the Eremitani Church in Padua (destroyed in World War II) grew out of the traditions of Florence, traditions to which Mantegna gave his own special stamp, however. His space is like that devised by the Florentines except that he lowers the horizon line to give his figures greater monumentality. His sculptural and often stony figures descend from Donatello and from ancient Roman models. His use of decorative details from antiquity reveals the almost archaeological training that he had received from Squarcione. By 1460 Mantegna had moved to Mantua, where he became court painter for the Gonzaga family, executing a number of family portraits (Plate 9) and pictures depicting ancient myths. His altarpieces, interpretation of antiquity, and engravings made him preeminent in northern Italy and a strong influence on his contemporaries and successors.

The Bellini family

The Bellini family of Venice forms one of the great dynasties in painting. The father, Jacopo, who had been a student of Gentile da Fabriano, adopted a style that owed something to both that prevailing in the Low Countries and that in Italy; he also compiled an important sketchbook (British Museum; Louvre). A daughter of Jacopo's was married to Mantegna, and the two sons—Gentile and, more especially, Giovanni Bellini—dominated Venetian painting until the first decade of the 16th century. Gentile followed more closely in his father's footsteps and is perhaps best known for his portraits of doges and sultans of Constantinople and his large paintings of Venetian reli-

gious processions. Giovanni early fell under the influence of Mantegna. The paintings each executed of "The Agony in the Garden" (both in the National Gallery, London) indicate how close they were stylistically and also their common reliance on Jacopo Bellini's sketchbook. At an unknown point in his career, Giovanni was in addition introduced to Flemish painting. These different influences permitted him about 1480 to evolve a highly personal style that greatly influenced the work of subsequent Venetian painters. This style consists above all of a softly diffused Venetian light that can only be achieved in an oil medium. Giovanni's work in the traditional medium for painting on panels—egg tempera—retains the crispness of contour and tightness of composition that the medium seems to require. The oil paintings, however, emphasize by their use of light the textures of the objects represented, softening the outlines and creating an elegiac mood. The "Madonna and Child with Saints" of 1488, in Santa Maria dei Frari, Venice, derived its composition from the Florentine *sacra conversazione* and two earlier altarpieces by Mantegna in which the Madonna and attendant saints are located in a unified but compartmentalized architectural setting. Giovanni's greatest innovation is the way in which the soft light suffuses the entire space, an effect particularly remarkable where it strikes the golden half dome of the apse and the ample draperies of the figures, which seem almost palpable. The "Enthroned Madonna from San Giobbe" (Gallerie dell'Accademia di Venezia) of about the same date goes even further in defining a composition and a way of painting that endured in Venice for centuries. The painting of "St. Francis in Ecstasy" (c. 1480; Frick Collection, New York City) adds yet another dimension to Giovanni's art. The observer's eye tends to wander from the saint and his cell into the distant landscape, for Giovanni was one of the greatest 15th-century masters of landscape painting. Figures, animals, trees, and buildings provide a series of guideposts leading the eye back into space. Giovanni influenced several Venetian painters: Lorenzo Lotto and Vittore Carpaccio and also, more importantly, Giorgione and Titian.

The richness, the variety, and even the inherent contradictions of 15th-century Florentine painting are both embodied and transformed in the art and the person of the multifaceted genius Leonardo da Vinci. Although he devoted a great deal of his career to a theoretical treatise on the art of painting, he was above all interested in the appearance of things and in the way they operated. This curiosity led him to a study of the flight of birds, the movement of water, the features of the land, the mechanical advantage obtainable in gears and gear trains, the growth of plants, the anatomy of man, and many other things. His consummate skill as a draftsman made it possible for him to record these discoveries as no man before him had done. All the knowledge that he gained was directed toward enriching his art, for Leonardo thought of himself primarily as a painter.

Leonardo's interest in the appearance and operation of nature

As a youth Leonardo was apprenticed to Verrocchio, in whose shop he learned to draw, prepare and mix colours, and paint. He probably also learned how to model in wax and clay and how to cast bronze. He may even have been introduced to the art of sculpting in marble, although he clearly stated in his writings that he did not relish this difficult craft. Leonardo's genius is already apparent in his collaboration with Verrocchio in the "Baptism of Christ" (c. 1474–75; Uffizi), in which his contributions to the landscape and his figure of an angel clearly reveal his superiority. The unfinished "Adoration of the Magi" (Uffizi) for the monastery of San Donato a Scopeto outside the walls of Florence, together with the preparatory drawings (Louvre; Uffizi), is at once a summary of 15th-century Florentine painting and a forecast of the High Renaissance style. In his studies Leonardo reveals his debt to Pollaiuolo and Botticelli and his awareness of the rational compositions of the first half of the century, with their strong sense of perspective. In the painting, however, he makes a synthesis of these divergent tendencies and creates a composition that is at once ordered and free, calm and full of movement, simple and varied. Pose, gesture, and glance in the attendant figures create a movement leading toward and coming to rest in the figure of the Madonna and Christ Child. The figures are placed in a free yet ordered space that gives a sense of grandeur and expansion, the expansion in turn being balanced by the concentration of the group around the Madonna. The appearance of the finished painting and the final direction Leonardo's planning would have taken can only be guessed, yet the nature of the composition and the preparatory underpainting of the figures and landscapes clearly demonstrate that Leonardo had advanced so far beyond his contemporaries that his innovation would only be comprehended by the group of younger painters who emerged some 20 or 25 years later.   (J.R.Sp./Ed.)

In 1481 Leonardo wrote a famous letter to the Duke of Milan offering his services. The offer was accepted, and for the next 18 years he remained in Milan, where he executed a number of paintings and innumerable drawings, worked on a never-completed equestrian monument to the Sforza dynasty, planned additions to the canal systems of the city, designed costumes for ducal entertainments, and wrote extensively. "The Virgin of the Rocks" (Louvre), painted in Milan about 1483, stands at the threshold of the High Renaissance. In this painting Leonardo introduced the pyramidal composition that was to become a hallmark of the High Renaissance. The placement of the Madonna, the Christ Child, the young St. John the Baptist, and the angel creates a movement that the eye willingly follows, yet the movement is contained within the implied pyramid, giving a sense of stability and calm grandeur to the composition. The mysterious landscape that surrounds them implies adequate space in which the figures can exist and move and an extension into depth that the eye cannot follow. The light that falls on the figures delicately models them in a subtle juxtaposition of light and shade. The contours of the figures seem to dissolve into the background, and the light seems to flow gently over a surface. The subtle and delicate modeling and the suggestive smoky atmosphere are known as sfumato and were much imitated, but what was more important and eventually more influential was Leonardo's use of light and shade as a unifying compositional factor. This was unprecedented in painting. It was achieved by the tonal continuity of the shadows—a tonal continuity conditional upon a severe restriction of local colour.

These effects, as well as the softly diffused light characteristic of Venetian painting, were only possible in the oil medium, which, because of its lengthy drying period, enables all parts of a painting to be advanced and adjusted together and the transparent glazes of which make possible unity of atmosphere and chiaroscuro. The rich effects of impasto (deliberately rough and thick paint textures) were also made possible in oil and were particularly exploited in Venice, where the use of canvas as a support first became truly popular. But there is no doubt that oil painting is a technique that originated in the Low Countries.
                              (J.R.Sp./N.B.P.)

Leonardo's attempts to transfer this new concept of painting to the difficult genre of murals led to the triumph and the tragedy of "The Last Supper." Because the traditional technique of fresco painting was too final for Leonardo's method of working, he invented a new technique—still not fully understood—that permitted him to revise in the manner of oil painting. The technique was not permanent, and the painting began to deteriorate in Leonardo's own lifetime. Despite its deterioration the painting stands as one of man's greatest achievements. All elements of the painting lead the eye to the calm and pyramidal figure of Christ. The room is depicted according to the rules of perspective, with all the direction implied by the lines of the architecture meeting at the vanishing point in the head of Christ. In this painting Leonardo has combined the sense of drama of the groups of disturbed apostles, the sculptural figure of Christ, and the rationally constructed space of the first half of the 15th century with the movement and emotion of the second half, achieving a new synthesis that goes far beyond anything his predecessors had dreamed was possible. Leonardo's "The Last Supper" marks the actual beginning of the High Renaissance in Italy (Plate 10).

Introduction of the pyramidal composition

"The Last Supper"

HIGH RENAISSANCE IN ITALY

In painting, the style called High Renaissance or classic is, in a sense, the culmination of the experiments of the 15th century, for it is above all characterized by a desire to achieve harmony and balance. Movement is important and necessary, yet the eye is always given a point of focus and rest. The composition is self-contained and conforms to Alberti's definition of beauty as "that harmony of parts to which nothing can be added or taken away without destroying the whole." Although there is movement implied in the poses of the figures and movement across the surface of the composition, it is always dignified movement, giving the impression of calm. The style exhibits variety and richness, yet maintains simplicity and unity. It is never as self-conscious as 15th-century painting had been, nor is it as laboured as much of Mannerist painting. It is frequently compared to Greek art of the 5th century BC for its calm and monumentality. Its greatest practitioners were the Florentines Leonardo da Vinci (although Leonardo's earlier work is usually assigned to the early Renaissance) and Michelangelo, the Urbino-born Raphael, and the Venetian Titian. Other artists, such as Andrea del Sarto and Fra Bartolomeo in Florence, Correggio in Parma, and Giovanni Bellini and Giorgione in Venice, were more or less attracted to the style at some point in their careers.

The new style of painting that Leonardo had invented in Milan was continued with modifications by Bernardino Luini and others. It had no immediate repercussions in his native Florence, although the example of his unfinished "Adoration" remained there. It is true that Botticelli, Ghirlandajo, and Filippino Lippi borrowed the broad outlines of the composition, but they did not penetrate completely to the innovational features inherent in it. The full impact of Leonardo's art was felt only upon his return to Florence in 1500. Crowds flocked to the church of the Santissima Annunziata to see his cartoon (a full-scale study for a finished painting) of "The Virgin and Child with St. Anne." Leonardo's great mural of the "Battle of Anghiari" (1503–06) pitted him against his rival Michelangelo in a competition to record the history of the city in the seat of city government. Neither painting was finished. Yet, despite the inconclusive nature of the works partially executed during his brief Florentine stay, Leonardo left a deep impression on that city. The "Mona Lisa" (Louvre) revolutionized portrait painting. Leonardo's drawings encouraged fellow artists to make more and freer studies for their paintings and encouraged connoisseurs to collect those drawings. Through the drawings his Milanese works were made known to the Florentines. Finally, his reputation and stature as an artist and thinker spread to his fellow artists and assured for them a freedom of action and thought similar to his own.

The painter who benefited most from the example of Leonardo was undoubtedly Raphael. Born Raphael Sanzio, he was as a youth under the influence of Perugino. He was already a successful and respected artist when, at the age of 21, he came to Florence only to discover that all he had learned and practiced was old-fashioned and provincial. He immediately set about learning from the Florentines. His drawing style changed from the tight contours and interior hatching he had learned from Perugino toward the freer, more flowing style of Leonardo. From Leonardo's "Virgin of the Rocks" he evolved a new Madonna type seated in a soft and gentle landscape, such as "The Madonna of the Goldfinch" in the Uffizi or those in the Louvre and the Kunsthistorisches Museum, Vienna (Plate 10). He adopted the "Mona Lisa" format for his portraits, and he also studied closely the sculpture of Michelangelo. By 1509, when he departed for Rome, Raphael had assimilated all Florence had to offer and was ready to make his own unique statement.

The Stanza della Segnatura (the first of a series of rooms in the Vatican constituting Pope Julius II's apartments), particularly the "School of Athens," which Raphael painted between 1508 and 1511, is one of the clearest and finest examples of the High Renaissance style. In the "School of Athens" Raphael, like Leonardo before him, made a balance between the movement of the figures and the ordered

Alberti's definition of beauty

Evolution of the Raphael type of Madonna

and stable space. He peopled this space with figures in a rich variety of poses yet controlled poses and gestures to make one group lead to the next in an interweaving and interlocking pattern, bringing the eye to the central figures of Plato and Aristotle at the converging point of the perspective construction. The unity, variety, and harmony of High Renaissance felicitously combine in the frescoes that decorate the Stanza della Segnatura.

At about the same time Raphael was working in the papal apartments in the Vatican, Michelangelo had undertaken the formidable task of decorating the ceiling of the Sistine Chapel (1508–12), also for Pope Julius II. In 1481–82 under Pope Sixtus IV, the uncle of Julius, the chapel had been completed and the walls decorated with frescoes depicting scenes from the life of Moses and the life of Christ executed by Botticelli, Ghirlandajo, Perugino, and others. Against his will Michelangelo was assigned to paint in fresco scenes from the creation. Although he had been trained in fresco painting in the shop of Ghirlandajo and although he had already executed a few paintings of considerable power, Michelangelo thought of himself as a sculptor. He engaged a group of his former colleagues from the shop of Ghirlandajo and with them began to paint the "Drunkenness of Noah" above the entrance to the chapel. Michelangelo had little patience with his less gifted associates, dismissed them, and executed the entire ceiling alone. The scenes were painted in reverse chronological order, beginning with the "Drunkenness of Noah" over the door and ending with the act of creation over the altar. In the first three frescoes Michelangelo seems to be feeling his way. With the second three—"Temptation and Expulsion," "Creation of Eve," "Creation of Adam"—he returns to the models of his youth (Masaccio for the "Expulsion" and Jacopo della Quercia for the "Creation of Eve") to create a powerful High Renaissance composition. The balance between the kinetic energy of God the Creator with his whirlwind of figures around him and the flaccid lifeless form of Adam comes to a focus in the two hands and the significant void between them. In the final three scenes of creation, Michelangelo moves beyond his contemporaries to a highly personal statement without parallel in the art of the 16th century. The Sistine ceiling was recognized as a masterpiece in its own time. The artist was judged to be a superhuman being and earned the title "the divine Michelangelo." Contemporaries spoke of the *terribilità*, or awesome power, of the frescoes and their creator. Michelangelo, Leonardo, and Raphael raised the artist and his art to a position of esteem perhaps never enjoyed (or deserved) either before or since. Certainly their soaring levels of achievement made it difficult for succeeding artists to follow in their footsteps and impossible to surpass them. Hence, the "anticlassic style," as it has been called, emerged in their own lifetime—even in some of Raphael's late works—and provided one of the sources of Mannerism.

By 1513, when Julius II died and Leo X was elected pope, the three great painters of the Florentine-Roman High Renaissance style became involved in projects that diverted them from the paths they had hitherto been following. Leonardo had been since 1506 at the French court in Milan, where he continued to refine his portrait of "Mona Lisa" and where he devoted a great deal of time to his treatises and his projects for the French king. Michelangelo returned to the sculpture of the tomb of Julius II and in 1516 began to work in Florence on a number of architectural and sculptural projects for its Medici rulers. Raphael became more and more involved with purely administrative duties as architect in charge of the new St. Peter's and as surveyor of antiquities. The great number of commissions he received led him more and more to rely on talented assistants, such as Giulio Romano, and on the workers in the shop for the actual execution of his later works. In the few works in which Raphael's hand clearly appears, he seems to be moving away from the "School of Athens" toward a new style that had not completely developed at the time of his death in his 37th year.

Raphael's frescoes (1512–14) in the Stanza d'Elidoro ("Heliodorus Room," the second of the rooms in Julius II's apartments) already reveal Mannerist tensions in "The Expulsion of Heliodorus from the Temple" and an almost Baroque concern with light and shade in the "Liberation of St. Peter." The succeeding rooms were largely decorated by assistants. It is only in such works as the "Triumph of Galatea" (1511; Villa Farnesina, Rome), the "Sistine Madonna" (1513?; Gallery of Old Masters, Staatliche Kunstsammlungen Dresden, E.Ger.), or Raphael's final unfinished work, the "Transfiguration" (1517; Vatican Museum), that he can be seen to move toward a nascent Mannerism and then away from it toward a more relaxed, more personal, and deeply moving reconsideration of High Renaissance ideals.

When Michelangelo returned to painting in 1534, he had already had some experience of Mannerism in Florence. The past few years had not been entirely a matter of aesthetic enrichment, however, for they had witnessed the sack of Rome and the siege of Florence. Some of the horror of those events emerges in "The Last Judgment," painted in fresco on the altar wall of the Sistine Chapel (Plate 11). Commissioned by Pope Clement VII, the work was executed during the pontificate of Paul III. The Christ in Judgment is a thundering god in the way the pagan supreme god of the Romans, Jupiter, was, rather than a Christian saviour, more concerned with damning the human race than in welcoming the blessed into heaven. The figures falling into hell and the torments of the damned attract the eye by their power and the emotions they reveal. It is as though a new Dante had been born to depict hell with a brush rather than a pen. Though the fresco met with strong but mixed reactions when it was unveiled in 1541, Pope Paul was pleased enough to commission two frescoes representing the "Conversion of St. Paul" and the "Crucifixion of St. Peter" for his own private chapel, the Pauline Chapel. Since this chapel has never been open to the general public, and since Michelangelo had already moved into his highly personal late style, these frescoes had little impact on the painting of the time.

The ideals of the High Renaissance as it appeared in the works of Leonardo, Raphael, and Michelangelo continued to develop independently in areas outside Rome and Florence. In Parma the painter Antonio Allegri, better known as Correggio, formed his art under the influence of Mantegna and Leonardo's Milanese followers. His "Rest on the Flight into Egypt" (Uffizi) and the "Madonna of the Bowl" (c. 1525; National Gallery, Parma) are clearly painted in the High Renaissance idiom. Yet Correggio is perhaps best known for his frescoes at Parma in the cathedral and in the church of San Giovanni Evangelista, which seem to prefigure the style of painting found in the Baroque, and for his late series of sensuous paintings on the loves of Jupiter, all executed between about 1530 and 1534, consisting of "Danae" (Borghese Gallery, Rome), "Leda" (Staatliche Museen Preussischer Kulturbesitz, West Berlin), and "Jupiter and Io" and "The Rape of Ganymede" (Kunsthistorisches Museum, Vienna).

In the late 15th century, painting in Venice traveled much the same paths toward the High Renaissance as in Florence, while still maintaining a purely Venetian flavour. Giovanni Bellini's Madonnas of 1505–10 (Pinacoteca di Brera, Milan; and the National Gallery, London) are stylistically similar to the Madonnas that Raphael was painting in Florence at about the same time. The San Zaccaria altarpiece ("Enthroned Madonna with Four Saints") of 1505 carries the *sacra conversazione* fully into the High Renaissance. Inasmuch as Giovanni Bellini dominated Venetian painting, his style influenced the younger painters Giorgione and Titian, yet he was receptive enough to learn in turn from them and inventive enough to maintain his position of dominance.

Giorgione, having learned from Bellini, then went beyond his master to bring to Venetian painting a treatment of landscape that can only be compared to pastoral poetry. In his brief career (all his extant paintings date from the last five years of his life) this highly inventive young artist taught his contemporaries and successors how to exploit the medium of oil paint to create the illusion of textures, light, and air in their paintings. His earliest known painting, the "Madonna and Child with SS. Francis and Liberale" (c. 1504; Castelfranco cathedral, Italy), derives from the style of the mature work of Bellini. In only a few years Giorgione passed from this style of painting, through the turbulence of the dramatic landscape with storm clouds of "The Tempest" (c. 1505; Gallerie dell'Accademia di Venezia; Plate 10), to the dreamy landscape of the "Pastoral Concert" (c. 1510; Louvre). In the latter, Giorgione reveals the Venetians' love of textures, for he carefully renders almost palpable the appearance of flesh, fabric, wood, stone, and foliage. The soft, typically Venetian diffused light, together with the landscape, its hills stretching into the distance and all harsh or sharp contours removed (whether of landscape or figures), creates a gently pastoral mood. The use of landscape to create a mood and the use of figures in the landscape to reflect or intensify that mood is an innovation characteristic of Venetian painting of the 16th century and one of great importance to the development of Baroque art.   (J.R.Sp./Ed.)

Whatever the significance of the figures in Giorgione's painting "The Tempest," it is certain that the picture soon came to be regarded merely as a landscape, and it is one of the first European paintings, certainly the first by a great artist, to make this sort of "background" material its subject matter. Landscape painting was to become a specialization of artists only toward the close of the 16th century, and even then chiefly in northern Europe.

(N.B.P.)

The impact of Giorgione on Venetian art was immediate and direct. Bellini's last works, such as "The Feast of the Gods" (National Gallery of Art, Washington, D.C.), owe much to Giorgione, but Giorgione's greatest impact was on Titian (Tiziano Vecelli). Although Titian was never a student of Giorgione, he worked with him on one project and finished a number of his paintings. The so-called "Sacred and Profane Love" of 1512–15 (Borghese Gallery, Rome) is, in a sense, Titian's trial piece in which he shows himself capable of rivaling and surpassing Giorgione in Giorgione's own terms. The influence of Giorgione is especially marked in the profane paintings just as the religious paintings are marked by the influence of Bellini, Titian's teacher and rival until his death, when Titian himself emerged as the leader of Venetian painting.

Titian's reputation as Bellini's successor Titian's great masterpiece, the "Assumption of the Virgin" (1516–18; Santa Maria dei Frari, Venice), established his reputation as Bellini's successor. In the painting he exhibits the Venetians' love of colour and texture, but he succeeds in achieving a balanced and moving composition that can only be compared to Raphael's "School of Athens" in its grandeur. The environment is both earth and heaven, yet it is created and defined by light and atmosphere in a typically Venetian way, rather than by architecture, as would have been more common in Florence. This painting, together with the "Sacred and Profane Love," "Entombment" (Louvre), and the "Pesaro Madonna" (1519–26; Santa Maria dei Frari), typifies Titian's contribution to the High Renaissance.

Upon the completion of the "Assumption" Titian undertook to execute a series of paintings on mythological themes for the court of Ferrara. "The Bacchanal" (1518–19; Prado, Madrid) was soon joined by the "Worship of Venus" (1518–19; Prado) and "Bacchus and Ariadne" (1520–23; National Gallery, London). In "The Bacchanal" Titian reveals his mastery in treating mythological subjects (Plate 10). The bacchants are disposed about the miraculous stream of wine that flows through an island, dancing, singing, and drinking. The movement of the figures, the juxtaposition of nude and clothed, of male and female, creates a revel in which even the landscape seems to participate—only a Venetian could have created such a pagan, earthy, and hedonistic glorification of life.

On a trip to Rome in 1545 Titian succeeded in rivaling Raphael's "Portrait of Leo X with Cardinals Giulio de' Medici and Luigi de' Rossi" (Uffizi) and Michelangelo's "Leda and the Swan" (copy; National Gallery, London), while demonstrating that Venetian painting in its own unique way was the equal of the Florentine-Roman tradition. The portrait of "Pope Paul III and His Grandsons Ottavio and Cardinal Alessandro Farnese" (1546; Museo e Gallerie Nazionali di Capodimonte, Naples) is a free variation on Raphael's "Leo X," but Titian altered the composition and introduced a narrative dimension more dramatic and compelling than that in any of his earlier portraits. The "Danae with Nursemaid" (1553–54; Prado), from the same period, poses the colourism and sensuousness of Venetian painting against the sculptural and restrained tradition of Michelangelo for succeeding centuries to judge.

Titian's use of the oil medium In his late works Titian carried the oil medium to new heights. He used loosely juxtaposed patches of colour, sometimes allowing the prepared canvas to show through. He applied paint freely and loosely with the brush and sometimes reworked it with his fingers. Although his paintings have a fresh quality that makes them appear to have been painted quickly in the heat of inspiration, it is known from his biographers and friends that each work had been carefully studied, criticized, and reworked before the artist was satisfied.

Two works from this late period reveal the scope of Titian's genius. The "Martyrdom of St. Lawrence" (Church of the Jesuits, Venice) was begun about 1548 after his return from Rome and before a trip to Augsburg and the court of the Holy Roman emperor Charles V. Although Titian was nearly 60, he painted with all the enthusiasm of youth. There is a certain amount of Mannerist foreshortening and exaggeration, but Titian used these aspects of Mannerist vocabulary, together with the Venetians' skill in the use of light, to emphasize the dramatic and emotional content of the painting. Drama, light, and colour were used in the late "Rape of Europa" (c. 1559–62; Isabella Stewart Gardner Museum, Boston) in a way that prefigured the work of Rubens and the Baroque.

Titian's genius, given full rein in his long and productive career, deeply influenced Venetian painting. The two most outstanding painters of the end of the 16th century, Veronese and Tintoretto, each took a different aspect of Titian's style and developed it. Paolo Caliari, called **Veronese as a rich colourist** Veronese (he was born in Verona), is best known for the rich colour and interweaving compositions he learned from Titian. His frescoes at the Villa Barbaro at Maser northwest of Venice are important for Venetian Mannerism and for landscape painting, but the richness of his palette is best seen in the mythologies, such as "Mars and Venus United by Love" (Metropolitan Museum of Art, New York City), or the "Marriage of St. Catherine" (Gallerie dell'Accademia di Venezia). With Tintoretto he decorated the chambers of the Doges' Palace in Venice, partially supplanting the aging and busy Titian as official painter of the city; his "Apotheosis of Venice" (c. 1585) in the Sala del Maggior Consiglio in the Doges' Palace is a bold and successful use of dramatic foreshortening and rich colour to express the vigour and vibrancy of Venice. Splendid also are his extremely large paintings crowded with figures, such as the "Feast in the House of Levi" (1573; Gallerie dell'Accademia di Venezia).

Jacopo Robusti, called Tintoretto, was most interested in Titian's use of dramatic light and heightened emotion. **Tintoretto's use of dramatic light** By 1548 he had established his reputation as a leading artist of the younger generation with his "San Marco Freeing the Slave" (Gallerie dell'Accademia di Venezia). He decorated several chambers of the Doges' Palace with a number of inventive mythological scenes. A great part of his career and energy was devoted to the decoration of the Great School of San Rocco, Venice (1564–c. 1588). Perhaps the crowning achievement of his career can be found in "The Last Supper" of 1594, painted for the church of San Giorgio Maggiore, Venice (Plate 11). In this painting Tintoretto made use of all the rapidly receding diagonals and dramatic foreshortenings of the Mannerist vocabulary, but he brought to the painting the Venetians' love of light effects to define the forms and heighten the drama. The head of Christ is bathed in light that is repeated in the smoky lamps so that its true source cannot be known. Light is used, as in the work of Titian, to pick out certain forms, throw others into darkness, and create a sense of movement within the composition. The comparison of this painting with Leonardo's "Last Supper" of 100 years earlier reveals the differences between the High Renaissance and the late 16th century.

With the death of Titian, Tintoretto, and Veronese, Venice became a school for 17th-century painters, where great works of the past were studied but few great works were produced until the 18th century. The influence of 16th-century Venetian painting on such diverse Baroque artists as Annibale Carracci, Peter Paul Rubens, and Nicolas Poussin was not negligible, but they came to Venice only to learn; they made their major contributions in other centres. (J.R.Sp./Ed.)

ITALIAN MANNERISM AND LATE RENAISSANCE

The first reaction against Leonardo, Michelangelo, Raphael, and Andrea del Sarto occurred in Florence between 1515 and 1524, during which time the painters Giovanni Battista (called Rosso Fiorentino) and Jacopo Carucci Pontormo decisively broke away from the harmony and naturalism of the High Renaissance style. Their movement, particularly what might be called their aesthetic anarchy, attracted the sympathetic attention of some 20th-century art historians, largely because of affinities such art historians saw between their work and modern trends, particularly Expressionism. After the lead given by the German art historian Max Dvořák in his book *Über Greco und der Manierismus* (1921), these 16th-century nonconformists came to be known as Mannerists. Recent historians have suggested, however, that the term Mannerism can more accurately be applied to a very different style initiated in Rome about 1520. Roman Mannerism, which subsequently spread throughout Europe, is characterized by a display of the artificiality of art, a thoroughly self-conscious cultivation of elegance and facility, and a sophisticated delight in the bizarre.

The term Mannerism is ultimately derived from the Italian word *maniera* (literally "style"). It was in the 16th century that *maniera* was first consistently used in art criticism to indicate a definable quality—that of stylishness. Giorgio Vasari, who is known chiefly for his biographies of artists (some of whom were his contemporaries) but who was also an architect and painter, indeed a Mannerist himself, attributed this absolute quality of stylishness to Leonardo, Michelangelo, and Raphael, and, above all, to artists of his own day who had learned their styles from studying these great masters. Standing at the head of the enormous representational discoveries of the Renaissance and with an increased knowledge of antiquity, Vasari was convinced that his contemporaries were in a position to understand the secret of true artistic style. This was the *maniera*.

Taking Vasari's quality of *maniera* as the key to Mannerism, it is possible to outline some of its hallmarks. In figure style, the standard of formal complexity had been set by Michelangelo and that of idealized beauty by Raphael. In the art of their followers, obsession with style in figure composition often outweighed the importance of the subject matter. The highest value was placed upon the apparently effortless solution of considerable artistic problems, such as the portrayal of the nude figure in complex poses. Specifically, the finished work was not supposed to betray signs of the labour that lay behind it.

While depending heavily upon ancient Roman art for many of its decorative motifs and for many of its standards of design, Mannerist style commonly exploited a certain degree of license within the classical vocabulary—what Vasari and contemporary literary theorists called "a departure from the normal usage."

It was in the intellectualizing atmosphere of the Italian courts that Mannerism met with the greatest favour. There the conscious intricacies of Mannerist compositions and the eloquent quotations from antiquity were well appreciated; court literature of this period displayed many analogous features. Mannerism was first and foremost a connoisseur's art—certainly not one that appealed to a churchman. It is not surprising that the later Mannerist painters were censured by the church during the Counter-Reformation for painting altarpieces that were intended to demonstrate the virtuosity of their creators rather than illustrate a religious story. Even Michelangelo was attacked, one critic calling him "the inventor of obscenities, who cultivated art at the expense of devotion."

Factors such as these caused the style to fall into general disrepute, and, when in 1662 the French writer on architectural theory Fréart de Chambray coined the word *Maniériste* (translated six years later as "Mannerist" by the English diarist John Evelyn), he applied it in disparaging fashion to Vasari and his contemporaries, the practitioners of the *maniera*. If, therefore, Mannerism is identified with the *maniera*, it can be historically related to a particular 16th-century style; but if it is applied strictly to early Rosso and Pontormo, as it was by Dvořák, it has no firm grounding in the way people in the 16th century thought about painting.

During the second decade of the 16th century, Andrea del Sarto had emerged as the foremost practitioner of High Renaissance naturalism in Florence. The subtle and ambiguous emotional tension present beneath the harmony of Andrea's forms and colours was greatly accentuated by one of his pupils, Jacopo da Pontormo. In Pontormo's Visdomini altarpiece (1518), the tension approaches the breaking point; the composition is vertical and lacking in a sense of space; and a host of similar but clashing centres of action create an impression of agitation. Pontormo persisted with this expressive style, becoming increasingly influenced by the angular forms of Albrecht Dürer's German engravings and by the more tortured aspects of Michelangelo's figure style. Vasari made it quite clear that Pontormo's development was in direct contradiction to the later ideals of Mannerism.

The second of Andrea's important pupils, Rosso Fiorentino, began in a not dissimilar spirit of expressive rebellion. His highly unconventional "Madonna with SS. John the Baptist, Anthony Abbot, Jerome and Stephen" for Santa Maria Nuova (1518; Uffizi) displays an aesthetic anarchy bolder than anything by Pontormo, and by the 1520s he was creating works of savage emotionality (*e.g.,* the Volterra "Deposition," 1521). In 1523 Rosso journeyed to Rome. There he was overwhelmed by three experiences: Michelangelo's ceiling in the Sistine Chapel, the late style of Raphael, and the art of the newly arrived Parmigianino.

Parmigianino brought with him from Parma three sample pictures to display his virtuosity to Roman patrons. His style, based originally upon that of Correggio, already possessed much of the attenuated elegance for which he became famous (Plate 11). In Rome Parmigianino was hailed as the new Raphael and specifically as a painter capable of reproducing the sophisticated grace of Raphael's late "St. Michael" (Louvre). Raphael had died in 1520, but his most authoritative late work in the Vatican *stanze* (papal apartments) was continued and developed by his foremost pupils, Giulio Romano (who left for Mantua in 1524) and Perino del Vaga. Their Roman styles rely upon a direct though refined use of the art of classical antiquity as a source of inspiration and upon an ingenious exploitation of different levels of pictorial reality within a single decorative scheme. The underlying artificiality of their manner was reinforced by the latent academicism of Michelangelo's Sistine ceiling nudes.

Rosso's encounter with the latest painting Rome offered resulted in a radical realignment of his style. His "Dead Christ with Angels" (*c.* 1526; Museum of Fine Arts, Boston), a subject that he would earlier have been inclined to treat with exceptional angularity of form, is executed with a new feeling for rarefied beauty. Emotion is now expressed less overtly, and his handling of paint is less aggressive. Rosso, Parmigianino, and Raphael's pupils undoubtedly influenced each other during the mid-1520s, but in 1527 Rome was sacked, and the artists of Pope Clement VII's court became scattered. Parmigianino fled to Bologna, returning after four years to his native Parma, where he continued to develop his personal form of mannered beauty (*e.g.,* "Madonna of the Long Neck," Uffizi). Perino found employment with the ruling family at Genoa, and Rosso visited a number of Italian cities before settling in France.

The sophisticated Mannerism that evolved in Rome before 1527 became the chief formative influence upon the styles of a number of important younger artists. Vasari and Francesco Salviati had passed their period of ap-

Artistic dispersion resulting from the sack of Rome

prenticeship in Andrea del Sarto's Florence. They parted in 1527 but resumed their close acquaintance in Rome (1531), and it was the Roman style that influenced their subsequent development. Vasari, Salviati, and Jacopino del Conte, who worked with Salviati on the frescoes for San Giovanni Decollato, Rome, attempted to combine the formal and narrative artifice of the late Raphael decorations with the complex figure style of Michelangelo. The result in Vasari's case is undeniably eclectic, but Salviati created an individual *maniera* of enormous facility and inventiveness (*e.g.*, "Peace," Palazzo Vecchio, Florence). The Raphaelesque element in the Roman style was reinforced by Perino's return to Rome in about 1538.

Salviati's career was unsettled—he worked in Florence, Rome, Venice, and France—but Vasari returned to Florence to the court of the Medici duke Cosimo I, who had replaced in 1537 the unpopular (and assassinated) Alessandro de' Medici. Cosimo and his Spanish wife, Eleonora de Toledo, whose formal Iberian tastes influenced the artistic life of the court, shrewdly embarked on an ambitious series of propagandistic projects to consolidate his political position. Vasari became the "stage manager" for much Medicean propaganda. His success as a painter and architect after 1555 was considerable, but his most important contribution to Mannerism was undoubtedly his advocacy of Mannerist ideals in his *Lives,* first published in 1550 and revised and extended in 1568. As Vasari realized, the most important painter in Cosimo's court was Il Bronzino, a pupil of Pontormo.

Aloof formality of Bronzino's portraits

Bronzino had, from the first, reduced the emotional content that had been an important feature of Pontormo's style, and, during the 1530s in Florence, he began to establish a reputation as a court portrait painter. His mature portraits are elegant, perfectly finished, ingenious in detail, and aloofly formal, reflecting the Spanish etiquette of Cosimo's court. Bronzino was adopted as favourite artist by Eleonora, receiving the commission to decorate her small private chapel in the Palazzo Vecchio. The resulting frescoes are in no sense spiritually expressive, but they are brilliantly stylish, with references to antiquity, which displayed the erudition of both artist and sitter, and to Raphael and Michelangelo. Bronzino was later influenced by the teachings of the Counter-Reformation, adopting a more modest narrative style, but his underlying aesthetic art remained a sense of *maniera.*

A number of later Mannerists responded similarly to the Counter-Reformation—Santi di Tito is particularly important in this respect—but it was only with Federico Barocci that the ideals of Mannerism were abandoned in favour of an all-pervasive piety in religious painting. Barocci's attractively fluent and softly coloured style, based largely upon Correggio, may be considered as an exceptional precursor of the Baroque style. Barocci abandoned his Roman Mannerism as early as 1575, but the majority of his contemporaries in Rome and Florence continued to develop the eclectic aspects of the original *maniera.* Daniele da Volterra and Pellegrino Tibaldi painted in an explicitly Michelangelesque manner, while Cavaliere d'Arpino (Giuseppe Cesari) and Federico Zuccari, at the end of the century, investigated the complex intellectual conceits of the Raphael studio style. Zuccari—a painter, designer, and theorist—is the most representative figure of this late phase, and his travels (to Rome, Venice, Spain, England, France, and Antwerp) underline the internationalism of late Mannerist style.

Spreading influence of Mannerism

Outside Florence and Rome, many of the major Italian cities succumbed to the spreading influence of Mannerism after 1527. Siena, under the lead of Domenico Beccafumi, developed a bizarre form of emotional Mannerism, but only Venice maintained a steady, independent Mannerism. Venice was certainly receptive to Mannerist influence—as seen in the works of Titian after 1530, Tintoretto, and Veronese—but, with the exception of Andrea Meldolla (Schiavone), Venetian painting continued to be dominated by non-Mannerist ideas in colouring and expression. Vasari's disparaging remarks about Tintoretto's lack of good design show clearly that the differences between Romano-Florentine and Venetian painting remained fundamental.

The early and High Renaissance style as developed in Italy did not immediately dominate all European painting. A few northern artists adopted Renaissance motifs but used them in a piecemeal manner without full comprehension of Italian compositional methods. After 1520, however, northern and Spanish artists came increasingly to understand and adopt Mannerist ideas, and highly individual schools of Mannerism began to appear in various centres outside Italy. Regional styles of considerable decorative flamboyance resulted from the fusion of the intricacies of the late Gothic style with the complexities of Mannerism.

RENAISSANCE OUTSIDE ITALY

France. Francis I, despite his military reverses in Italy, was enamoured of all things Italian. He commissioned the celebrated goldsmith Benvenuto Cellini to execute both tableware and sculpture and prevailed upon friendly rulers in Italy to send him works by Titian and Bronzino and casts of sculpture. He also imported Italian artists to design, build, and decorate his palaces, the Château de Madrid and Fontainebleau, both outside Paris. Rosso arrived in France in 1530, followed two years later by his fellow Italian, the Mannerist Francesco Primaticcio. In the gallery of Francis I at Fontainebleau, Rosso initiated a new and intricate decorative system in which stucco and painting form a richly luxuriant complex—the plastic realization of the late Raphaelesque decorative manner. Primaticcio, who had been trained by Giulio Romano at Mantua and influenced by Parmigianino, took over Rosso's leading position on the latter's death in 1540. His Ulysses Gallery at Fontainebleau continued and refined Rosso's elaborate system of painted narratives surrounded by convoluted strapwork, elegant figures, and swags in stucco. French artists at the court, such as the two Jean Cousins and Antoine Caron, quickly adopted aspects of Italian Mannerism to create a style of painting characterized as the school of Fontainebleau. Less of a tendency to mimic the fashion was noticeable in Corneille de Lyon and Jean and François Clouet, whose portraits, while exhibiting some Mannerist qualities, recalled 15th-century court portraiture.   (M.J.Ke./Ed.)

Spain. During the first decade of the 16th century, Fernando Yáñez, who may have assisted Leonardo da Vinci on the "Battle of Anghiari" in 1505, executed works showing a good knowledge of Italian Renaissance developments. Further Italianate tendencies emerged strongly in the Valencian works of Juan de Macip and his son Juan de Juanes. Full-fledged Mannerism made its appearance in the Seville cathedral in the "Descent from the Cross" (1547) by Pedro Campaña (Pieter de Kempeneer), an artist from Brussels, and subsequently in the refined court portraiture of Anthonis Mor (Sir Anthony More) and Alonso Sánchez Coello, whose royal portraits possess an elegance reminiscent of Bronzino's Florentine style. Although Campaña's paintings are Mannerist in composition, they also foreshadow the expressiveness characteristic of Spanish style in the hands of Luis de Morales and El Greco.

From 1546 until his death in 1586, Morales remained almost exclusively in the provincial isolation of Badajoz, developing a highly individual art of great spiritual intensity, radically separated from the Mannerist mainstream. El Greco, though born in Crete, was more fully conversant with Italian painting, having studied with Titian in Venice and later residing in Rome for two years. His Spanish paintings exploit the anatomical attenuations of Roman Mannerism, but the vividly emotional qualities of his colour and paint handling depend almost entirely upon Venetian precedents—Tintoretto and Jacopo Bassano in particular. Under the influence of Counter-Reformation mysticism in Toledo after 1575, he developed an increasingly personal and nonrealistic manner, indulging in space and supernatural light effects (Plate 11). The narrative fervour of his style stands in sharp contrast to the stylish formalism of international Mannerism.

El Greco's exploitation of anatomical attenuations

Germany. Albrecht Dürer was the first important German artist who displayed a profound understanding of Italian Renaissance art and theory. Trained in Nürnberg in the late Gothic tradition, he had ambitions even as a youth far beyond the narrow confines of his native city and the late medieval style. He traveled to Switzerland and the Rhine Valley and may have been in the Low Countries. Shortly after his marriage in 1494 he made a brief trip to Italy, where he studied the works of Mantegna and the Venetians. In 1505–07 he was again in Italy and was on intimate terms with Giovanni Bellini. Dürer was

interested in what he felt to be the "secrets" of Italian art and in the new humanism carried north by such friends as the German humanist Willibald Pirkheimer. As a result, his paintings maintain the northerners' love of detail, rendered meticulously in oil, but he joined to it the Italian interest in broadly conceived compositions. In "The Paumgärtner Altarpiece" of 1502–04 (Alte Pinakothek, Munich), for example, the saints in the wings are depicted with the scrolls and a complexity of composition more reminiscent of a heraldic achievement, while the broad planes of the architecture and the large, simple figures of the adoration shown on the central panel suggest an Italianate conception. The "Four Apostles" (Alte Pinakothek) of 1526 (Plate 12) ultimately derives from the wings of Bellini's Frari altarpiece. Dürer's close association with the Venetian painter and admiration for his art can be seen in the broad simple folds of the drapery, the breadth of handling of the heads, and the quality of the light depicted.

Although he executed a large number of important paintings, Dürer is perhaps best known for his woodcuts and engravings, by which he raised printmaking from a minor to a major art (see PRINTMAKING). Dürer's prints, paintings, and writings had such a profound influence on 16th-century art in Germany that it is sometimes difficult to realize that he died in 1528.

In the 16th century the Renaissance as far as German painting was concerned tended to follow the lines established by Dürer. Two artists of note do emerge, but their styles are so individual that they do not represent a national school.

Lucas Cranach the Elder was deeply influenced by Dürer and the Danube school, an early 16th-century tradition of landscape painting that was in some ways a transition between the styles of Gothic and Renaissance painting. By 1505 he had moved to Wittenberg and become court painter to the electors of Saxony. There his style changed radically, epitomizing the dichotomy that existed in 16th-century northern European painting. He developed in Wittenberg the full-length portrait in which the sitter is rendered with consummate skill and fidelity. Cranach was a personal friend of Martin Luther and is probably best known for his portraits of the great reformer. At the same time his "Reclining River Nymph at the Fountain" of 1518 (Museum of Fine Art, Leipzig) illustrates his knowledge of Giorgione and Venetian painting and points the way to the group of highly erotic female nudes of his later works (Plate 12).

Hans Holbein the Younger was trained by his father in Augsburg but took up residence in Basel, Switz., around 1515. He early developed a portrait style that was greatly sought after by the burghers of Basel. His portraits of Burgomaster Meyer and his wife (1516; Kunstmuseum-Öffentliche Kunstsammlung Basel) or of Bonifacius Amerbach (1519; Kunstmuseum-Öffentliche Kunstsammlung Basel) show his gift for characterization. In 1526 he made

his first trip to London, where he painted "Sir Thomas More with His Household" (1527). In 1532 religious troubles in Basel were so intense that he accepted a position at the English court and left the city forever. He is perhaps best known for his portraits of Henry VIII, Henry's bride Anne of Cleves (1539; Louvre), and Christina of Denmark (1538; National Gallery, London), at one time considered by the King as a possible bride. "Jean de Dinteville and Georges de Selve" ("The Ambassadors," 1533; National Gallery, London), which depicts two French ambassadors to the English court, is probably the greatest tour de force of his years in England. The two sitters are rendered faithfully in a well-defined room and are surrounded by the trappings of 16th-century humanism—*e.g.,* books, globes, musical instruments. Holbein's portraits were all painted with a great understanding of the sitter and often have a note of Italian elegance. His surfaces tend to be tight and

hard, yet there is a certain expansiveness created by the positioning within the frame (Plate 12). He established a portrait tradition in England and also contributed to the popularity of the miniature in that country.

Low Countries. In the Low Countries there emerged early in the 16th century a group of painters misleadingly lumped together as the Antwerp Mannerists. Their exaggerated and fanciful compositions descend in great part from the decorative excesses of late Gothic art, generally with some Italianate details probably transmitted by architects' and goldsmiths' pattern books.

Jan Gossaert, called Mabuse, visited Rome in 1508. At first he continued his ornate late Gothic style, but by 1514 he began to adopt the great innovations occurring in Italian painting. His mythological paintings, such as the "Neptune and Amphitrite" (Staatliche Museen Preussischer Kulturbesitz, West Berlin) of 1516, indicate that he was able to understand only the superficialities and not the motivation and *terribilità* of Michelangelo's nudes. Bernard van Orley remained in Brussels and learned of Italy through Raphael's cartoons, which were sent to Brussels to be woven into tapestries. Before the end of the century, painters such as Jan van Scorel, Maerten van Heemskerck, and Sir Anthony More (a Utrecht-born portraitist knighted by Queen Mary I of England) were absorbing Italian influences, in van Scorel's case a specifically Venetian influence, yet creating an art that was their own. Joachim Patinir's depiction of the world around him, particularly of landscape, parallels Italian developments in northern terms and greatly influenced Pieter Bruegel the Elder.

Pieter Bruegel the Elder visited Italy in 1551–53 but was more influenced by the Italian and particularly Alpine landscape than by Italian painting. His two-dimensional sources are to be found rather in the popular prints of the time, the landscapes of Patinir, and the fantasies of Bosch. He was also a great observer of peasant life. Bruegel spent his adult life in the company of learned humanists, yet he showed no real interest in classical mythological subjects or antiquity. His paintings illustrating Low Countries' proverbs, children's games, or "The Fight Between Carnival and Lent" (1559; Kunsthistorisches Museum, Vienna) reveal an interest in popular themes and common life, rather than in the pedantic Romanizing compositions of some of his contemporaries. This choice of subject matter, latent from the early 15th century in the Low Countries, was given new dimensions by Bruegel. His series of depictions of the months is at once a revival of the labours of the months found in the portal sculptures of Gothic cathedrals and medieval books of hours and at the same time a new treatment of rural landscape and the peasants who work the land. His "Harvesters" (1565; Metropolitan Museum of Art, New York City) displays a remarkable sensitivity to colour and pattern. The intense golden yellow of the ripe wheat sets up a bold pattern across the lower half of the picture and contrasts with the cool greens and blues of the limitless plain stretching off into the distance. Some figures move across a lane cut through the wheat, while others cut into what seems a solid space. The sleeping peasants resting after their noon meal are disposed in patterns and poses that make one feel the heat and calm of the summer's day. This sympathetic view of peasant life, with its bold geometric patterns, runs throughout the series of the months and recurs in "The Wedding Dance" (1566; Detroit Institute of Arts) and "Peasant Dance" (Plate 12) and "Peasant Wedding" (both in the Kunsthistorisches Museum, Vienna).

Bruegel brought to an end the 16th century in the north and prepared the way for the Baroque. His sons and grandsons were important painters who helped to train some of the leading artists of the 17th century in the Low Countries. It was the elder Bruegel, however, who made landscape and peasant life an accepted subject for painting in the Renaissance. (J.R.Sp.)

The Mannerist style was not comprehended as soon in the 16th century in the Low Countries as it had been in France or Spain. With the notable exception of Frans Floris, it was not until the generation of artists born during the middle years of the century that Mannerism was fully assimilated. This generation of Flemish and Dutch Mannerists was influenced chiefly by the Italian Mannerists of the second half of the century: Frederik Sustris studied with Vasari; Hendrik Goltzius was an associate of Taddeo Zuccari, Federico's older brother; Johann von Aachen remained in Rome between 1574 and 1588; and Bartholomaeus Spranger collaborated with Federico Zuccari. Haarlem and Amsterdam became the early centres for northern Mannerism. Spranger's style was diffused throughout Europe by the engravings of his colleague Goltzius. Finally, as a late flowering of international Mannerism, Carel van Mander founded a Vasarian academy in Haarlem, in 1604 publishing his biographies of Netherlandish artists in direct emulation of Vasari.

Dutch centres of Mannerism

(M.J.Ke./Ed.)

Bohemia. By far the most ambitious patron of Mannerist art in Europe north of Italy was the Holy Roman emperor Rudolf II, who in the late 1570s established his court at Prague. Between the end of the 16th century and the beginning of the 17th, Rudolf employed architects, sculptors, and painters to create impressive artistic works for his court, much as Cosimo de' Medici had done in Florence. Spranger's "Allegory of Rudolf II" indicates the quality of Rudolf's court art and its clear Mannerist sympathies—sensually graceful figures clad in the dress of classical antiquity and a cultivated facility in composition and execution. (J.R.Sp./Ed.)

Baroque

Baroque is a term loosely applied to European art from the end of the 16th century to the early 18th century, with the latter part of this period falling under the alternative stylistic designation of Late Baroque. The painting of the Baroque period is so varied that no single set of stylistic criteria can be applied to it. This is partly because the painting of Roman Catholic countries such as Italy or Spain differed both in its intent and in its sources of patronage from that of Protestant countries such as Holland or Britain, and it is partly because currents of classicism and naturalism coexisted with and sometimes even predominated over what is more narrowly defined as the High Baroque style.

The Baroque style in Italy and Spain had its origins in the last decades of the 16th century when the refined, courtly, and idiosyncratic style of Mannerist painting had ceased to be an effective means of artistic expression. Indeed, Mannerism's inadequacy as a vehicle for religious art was being increasingly felt in artistic circles as early as the middle of that century. To counter the inroads made by the Reformation, the Roman Catholic Church after the Council of Trent (1545–63) adopted an overtly propagandistic stance in which painting and the other arts were intended to serve as a means of extending and stimulating the public's faith in the church and its doctrines. The church thus adopted a conscious artistic program, the products of which would make an overtly emotional and sensory appeal to the faithful. The Baroque style of painting that evolved from this program was paradoxically both sensuous and spiritual; while naturalistic treatment rendered the painted religious image more readily comprehensible to the average churchgoer, dramatic and illusory effects were used to stimulate piety and devotion. This appeal to the senses manifested itself in a style that above all emphasized movement and emotion. The stable, pyramidal compositions and the clear, well-defined pictorial space that were characteristic of Renaissance paintings gave way in the Baroque to complex compositions surging along diagonal lines. The Baroque vision of the world is basically dynamic and dramatic; throngs of figures possessing a superabundant vitality energize the painted scene by means of their expressive gestures and movements. These figures are depicted with the utmost vividness and richness through the use of rich colours, dramatic effects of light and shade, and lavish use of highlights. The ceilings of Baroque churches thus dissolved in painted scenes that presented convincing views of the saints and angels to the observer and directed him through his senses to heavenly concerns. (Ed.)

EARLY AND HIGH BAROQUE IN ITALY

By the last decades of the 16th century the Mannerist style had ceased to be an effective means of expression. Indeed, in Florence a conscious reassessment of High Renaissance painting had taken place as early as mid-century. This tendency gathered momentum in the last decades of the century, particularly with the Bolognese painters Lodovico Carracci and his cousin Annibale. The Roman Catholic Church's reaction to the Reformation, known as the Counter-Reformation, reaffirmed the old medieval concept of art as the servant of the church, adding specific demands for simplicity, intelligibility, realism, and an emotional stimulus to piety. For the zealots of the Counter-Reformation, works of art had value only as propaganda material, the subject matter being all important; and in Rome there was as a result a sharp decline in artistic quality. Under austere Counter-Reformation popes such as Paul IV and Pius V, most official patronage favoured the dry and prosaic; this late 16th-century style is best called Counter-Reformation Realist. A similar process took place in Florence, where a strong movement away from Mannerist conventions is seen in the paintings of Ludovico Cigoli, and in Milan, where the dominant artistic personalities were the painters Giovanni Crespi (known as Il Cerano) and Pier Francesco Mazzucchelli, known as Il Morazzone.

Effects of the Counter-Reformation

In contrast, late 16th-century Venetian painting was as little influenced by the Counter-Reformation as it had been by Mannerism; and the workshops of Tintoretto, Paolo Veronese, and Palma Giovane remained active until the plague of 1629–30.

Michelangelo Merisi, better known by the name of his birthplace, Caravaggio, a small town near Milan, was active in Rome by about 1595. His earliest paintings are conspicuous for the almost enamel-like brilliance of the colours, the strong chiaroscuro called Tenebrism, and the extraordinary virtuosity with which all the details are rendered. But this harsh realism was replaced by a much more powerful mature style in his paintings for San Luigi dei Francesi, Rome, begun in 1597, and Santa Maria del Popolo, Rome, executed about 1601 (Plate 13). His selection of plebeian models for the most important characters in his religious pictures caused great controversy, but the utter sincerity of the figures and the intensity of dramatic feeling are characteristic of the Baroque. Although Caravaggio had no direct pupils, "Caravaggism" was the dominant new force in Rome during the first decade of the 17th century and subsequently had enormous influence outside Italy.

Parallel with Caravaggio's was the activity of Annibale Carracci in Rome. During Annibale's years in Bologna, his brother and cousin had joined with him in pioneering a synthesis of the traditionally opposed Renaissance concepts of *disegno* ("drawing") and *colore* ("colour"). In 1595 Annibale took to Rome his mature style, in which the plasticity of the central Italian tradition is wedded to the Venetian colour tradition. The decoration of the vault of the gallery in the Palazzo Farnese, Rome (1597–1604), marks not only the high point in Annibale's career but also the beginning of the long series of Baroque ceiling decorations. The third important painter active in Rome during the first decade of the 17th century was the Low Countries' painter Peter Paul Rubens, who became court painter to the duke of Mantua in 1600. He came under the influence of Raphael and Titian, as well as that of Caravaggio, during a journey to Spain in 1603. The rich colours and strong dramatic chiaroscuro of his altarpieces for Santa Maria in Vallicella (New Church), Rome (1606–07), show how much he contributed to the evolution of Italian Baroque painting.

The Carracci synthesis of drawing and colour

Just as the first decade tended to be dominated by the "Caravaggist" painters, the second decade in Rome was the heyday of the Bolognese classicist painters headed by Guido Reni (Plate 13), Domenichino, and Francesco Albani, all of whom had been pupils of the Carracci. The crucial developments that brought the High Baroque into being took place in the third decade.

The little church of Santa Bibiana in Rome harbours three of the key works that ushered in the High Baroque, all executed in 1624–26: Gian Lorenzo Bernini's facade and the marble figure of Santa Bibiana herself, over the altar, and Pietro da Cortona's series of frescoes of Bibiana's life, painted on the side wall of the nave. The rich exuberance of the compositions is a prelude to the gigantic "Allegory of Divine Providence and Barberini Power," which Pietro was to paint on the vault of the Great Hall of the Palazzo Barberini, Rome (1633–39). Pietro continued with this style of monumental painting for the remainder of his career, and it became the model for the international grand decorative style, which by the close of the 17th century was to be found in Madrid, Paris, Vienna, and even London.

Controversy between the Baroque and classicism

Despite the continued triumph of High Baroque illusionism and theatricality in the hands of Bernini and Pietro da Cortona from the 1630s, the forces of classicism, now headed by the painter Andrea Sacchi and the Flemish-born sculptor François Duquesnoy, gained the upper hand in the 1640s after the death of Pope Urban VIII; and for the remainder of the century the Baroque-versus-classicism controversy raged in the Academy in Rome. Sacchi and the classicists, including the Frenchman Nicolas Poussin, held that a scene must be depicted with a bare minimum of figures, each with its own clearly defined role, and compared the composition to that of a tragedy in literature. But Pietro and the Baroque camp held that the right parallel was the epic poem in which subsidiary episodes were added to give richness and variety to the whole, and hence the decorative richness and profusion of their great fresco cycles. The lyrical landscapes of the French painter Claude Lorrain are among the finest expressions of High Baroque classicism; and they exerted a continual influence throughout the 18th century, particularly in Britain. Even in Rome itself, however, a number of painters of importance succeeded in remaining more or less independent of the two main camps. Sassoferrato (1609–85), for example, painted in a deliberately archaizing manner, carefully reproducing Raphaelesque formulas. The cryptically romantic movement, centred on Pier Francesco Mola, Pietro Testa, and Salvator Rosa, was more important and, together with the landscapes of Gaspard Dughet, was to have considerable repercussions in the 18th century. Claude Lorrain also adopted an independent stand, despite the highly developed classicism of his poetic landscapes and seascapes (Plate 17), both of which, but especially the latter, featured much splendid architecture.

The first two-thirds of the 17th century in Italy were dominated by the Roman Baroque, and few painters elsewhere provided serious competition. Reni, who returned to Bologna from Rome in 1614 and remained there until his death in 1642, remained the strongest artistic personality in that northern city but steadily abandoned the strong plasticity of the Carracci for a much looser style with a pale tonality (Plate 13). When Guercino, in turn, left Rome in 1623, he returned to his native Cento, just north of Bologna, and not until the death of Reni did he decide to settle in Bologna. Guercino's early, fiery style slowly gave way to a much more calm and classical outlook. Venetian painting took a new direction with the rich colours and free brushwork of Domenico Fetti, who had worked in Mantua before moving to Venice. In the hands of Johann Liss (or Jan Lys) the groundwork was laid for the flowering of the Venetian school of the 18th century. Venetian painting was also enriched by the pale colours and flickering brushwork of Francesco Maffei from Vicenza, whereas Bernardo Strozzi in 1630 carried to Venice the saturated colours and vigorous painterly qualities of the Genoese school. Giovanni Benedetto Castiglione also began his career in Genoa and, after a period in Rome, worked from 1648 as court painter in Mantua, where his brilliant free etchings and brush drawings anticipated the Rococo. Naples, under its Spanish viceroys, remained strongly influenced by the "Caravaggesque" tradition, particularly in its best-known painter, a Spaniard, José de Ribera, who settled there in 1616; the two most important native painters of the period, Massimo Stanzione and Bernardo Cavallino, both died in the disastrous plague of 1654.

New currents of painting in Venice

The most conspicuous aspect of the last phase of the High Baroque in Italy is provided by the series of great fresco cycles, which were executed in Rome during the last decades of the 17th century. Pietro da Cortona's decoration of Santa Maria in Vallicella (1647–55) is the link with the earlier phase of the Baroque, and his decoration of the gallery of the Palazzo Pamphili in Rome (1651–54) points the way to the decorations of Giovanni Coli and Filippo Gherardi in the Palazzo Colonna (1675–78) and to those of the vault of the gallery of the Palazzo Medici-Riccardi in Florence by Luca Giordano (1682). Bernini's dynamic and theatrical schemes of decoration reached their climax in the nave vault of the Gesù, Rome, painted in 1674–79 by Giovanni Battista Gaulli (Baciccia) under the direct tutelage of Bernini. The fresco bursts out of its frame and creates an overwhelming dramatic effect, with painted figures flooding over the gilt stucco architectural decoration of the ceiling into the space of the church (Plate 13). After this, the "Allegory of the Missionary Work of the Jesuits," painted by Andrea Pozzo on the nave vault of San Ignazio, Rome (1691–94), seems almost an anticlimax, despite its gigantic size and hypertrophic illusionism. Concurrently, the Baroque-versus-classicism controversy took on a new lease on life, with Gaulli heading the Baroque party in opposition to Sacchi's pupil Carlo Maratta. By the last decades of the century the Baroque was triumphant, and Maratta's Baroque classicism appears almost to be a compromise between Pietro da Cortona and Sacchi. Maratta's style, however, was to provide one of the most important sources for the grand manner of the 18th century.

The essential characteristics of Late Baroque painting can be identified first in the frescoes (1661) of Mattia Preti at the Palazzo Pamphili, Valmontone (southeast of Rome); but the transition between the High Baroque and the Late Baroque was a continuous process and occurred at different dates with different artists. At Valmontone the sense of dynamic structure characteristic of the High Baroque frescoes of Pietro da Cortona yields to a more decorative scheme in which the figures are scattered across the ceiling, giving the painting an overall unity without identifying any specific area as the focal point. Francesco Cozza used this scheme in the Pamphili Library, Rome (1667–73), but among the finest Late Baroque decorations of this type are ceilings painted in Genoa by Gregorio de' Ferrari and Domenico Piola, while Giordano took the style to Spain. The breakdown of any sense of direction in the composition is paralleled by a loosening in the design of individual figures; once again the unity is decorative rather than structural.

Transition between High and Late Baroque

LATE BAROQUE AND ROCOCO

Symptomatic of the changing status of the papacy during the 17th century was the fact that the Thirty Years' War was ended by the Peace of Westphalia in 1648 without papal representation in the negotiations. Concurrently, the influence of Spain also declined. The commencement of the personal rule of Louis XIV in 1661 marked the beginning of a new era in French political power and artistic influence, and the French Academy in Rome (founded 1666) rapidly became a major factor in the evolution of Roman art. Late Baroque classicism, as represented in Rome by Maratta, was slowly transformed into a sweet and elegant 18th-century style by his pupil Benedetto Luti, while Francesco Trevisani abandoned the dramatic lighting of his early paintings in favour of a glossy Rococo classicism. In the early 18th century, Neapolitan painting under Francesco Solimena developed from the brilliant synthesis of Pietro da Cortona's grand manner and Venetian colour that Giordano had evolved in the late 17th century. The impact, also, of Preti is revealed by his predilection for brownish shadows; but, compared to the pupils and followers of Maratta in Rome, Solimena's style has a greater strength and vitality despite the characteristic Late Baroque fragmentation of the composition. He himself supplied large paintings to patrons all over Europe, and his pupils occupied key positions in the mid-18th century. Francesco de Mura took the style to Turin, where he was court painter; Corrado Giaquinto, as court painter in Madrid, turned increasingly toward the Rococo, and Sebastiano Conca worked in Rome, falling increas-

Coexistence of Late Baroque classicism and the Rococo

ingly victim to the academic classicism dominant there. Anton Domenico Gabbiani practiced a particularly frigid classicism in Florence, and it was mainly in Bologna and Venice that real attempts were made to break away from the confines of Late Baroque classicism.

Giuseppe Maria Crespi (called Lo Spagnolo, "The Spaniard") turned instead toward the early paintings of Guercino and evolved a deeply sincere style, remarkable for its immediacy and sensibility. In Bologna he had no real successors, but in Venice his work provided one of the bases for the brilliant flowering of Venetian painting in this period. While Giovanni Battista Piazzetta looked toward Crespi for the basis of his expressive Tenebrist style, Sebastiano Ricci took his cue from Giordano. The brilliant lightness and vivacity of his frescoes in the Palazzo Marucelli-Fenzi, Florence, mark the beginning of a great tradition of Venetian decorative painting, a tradition that was to be carried all over Europe by Giovanni Antonio Pellegrini, Giambattista Pittoni, and, above all, Giovanni Battista Tiepolo. The vast majority of the finest decorations (*e.g.*, frescoes) carried out by the Venetian 18th-century painters were executed outside the Veneto (the region of which Venice is the principal city), but the opposite is true of the flourishing Venetian school of landscape, *vedute* ("views"), and genre painters. Giovanni Antonio Canal, called Canaletto, developed the views of Venice painted by Luca Carlevaris into an industry almost entirely dependent upon foreign tourists; and his nephew Bernardo Bellotto spent most of his career painting views in central Europe. Francesco Guardi avoided the cool precision of the *vedute* of Canaletto and Bellotto and instead evolved a much lighter and more lyrical Rococo style with a strong sense of the picturesque (Plate 13) and, occasionally, the bizarre. In Rome a similar contrast existed between the brilliant, precise *vedute* of Giovanni Paolo Pannini and the strange, almost Romantic *vedute* in the form of etchings by Giovanni Battista Piranesi.

Spain and Portugal. Two fundamental and ostensibly opposed streams permeate Spanish painting and separate it from that of the rest of Europe—ecstatic mysticism and sober rationalism. These qualities are essentially Gothic in spirit, and the Iberian Peninsula is remarkable for the tenacity with which Gothic ideas were retained and for the relatively small influence of Renaissance humanist ideas. The early 17th-century still lifes of Sánchez Cotán, with their strong realism and harsh, mysterious lighting, illustrate these contrasts admirably, whereas Luis Tristán abandoned the Mannerist style of his master El Greco for a much more careful realism. Francisco Pacheco, the teacher and father-in-law of Velázquez, was a more important writer than painter, and his writings laid down a theoretical basis for the Spanish approach to spirituality through naturalism. The early works of José de Ribera show a synthesis of Spanish realism and ideas drawn from both Annibale Carracci and Caravaggio; the fierce darkness of these paintings formed the basis of the Tenebrist style that dominated Neapolitan painting during the first half of the 17th century. Ribera himself, however, developed away from this style in his later paintings and moved toward a softer and more even handling of light (Plate 18). Francisco de Zurbarán was active mainly in Seville until his removal to Madrid in 1658, and unlike Ribera he painted throughout his life in the stark Spanish realist style. The massive solemnity of his figures and simple, clear-cut compositions are wholly in sympathy with the demands of the Counter-Reformation, and only in Madrid did he come under substantial Italian influence (Plate 18).

Diego Velázquez was almost the exact contemporary of Zurbarán, but, unlike Zurbarán, who spent almost all his life in the company of monks in the provinces, Velázquez' time from 1623 was spent in the Spanish court in Madrid. His early *bodegones* (scenes of daily life with strong elements of still life in the composition) were painted in Seville and belong to the Spanish realist tradition, but at court he saw the Titians collected by Philip II and also Rubens' paintings. After he visited Italy in 1629–31, there was greater freedom in the way he handled paint, more interest in colour, and increased depth to his analyses of character (Plate 18).

The early works of the Seville painter Bartolomé Esteban Murillo again follow the Spanish realist tradition in their cool detachment, but in his late works his style softened and sweetened into a sentimentality that proved immensely popular (Plate 18). Alonso Cano formed his early painting style in Seville on the simple monumentality of Zurbarán, but after he moved to Madrid in 1638 his paintings took on a new elegance and gracefulness. (Cano was also active as a sculptor and architect in Granada [1652–57]). Antonio del Castillo and Juan de Valdés Leal were the most important painters active in Andalusia after Murillo, and the works of both reveal that liveliness of handling, with accents of strong local colour, which replaced the sober realism popular in the first half of the century.

Portugal was ruled by Spain until 1640, when John IV was proclaimed king. But economic conditions hampered serious patronage of the arts until the reign of John V, when the most distinguished painter was Francisco Vieira de Matos. Unfortunately, the Lisbon earthquake of 1755 destroyed much of the best art collected in the Portuguese capital at that time.

Low Countries. *The Spanish Netherlands.* The year 1566 saw the Netherlands in open revolt against Philip II of Spain, and, inasmuch as this revolt had a Protestant as well as a nationalist aspect, a wave of iconoclasm swept across the area. By 1600 the area had become divided into the Spanish-dominated, Catholic, southern provinces— broadly modern Belgium—and the independent, predominantly Calvinist United Provinces of the north—broadly the modern Netherlands, or colloquially Holland; the boundary between the two remained fluid, however. In the southern provinces throughout the 16th to 18th centuries Brussels, headed by viceroys, remained the centre of court patronage, while Antwerp, with its great patrician families, was the commercial centre.

Painting in the southern provinces before 1610 was intensely conservative; the Mannerist conventions were never accepted as fully as in the north. Instead, Italianate ideas were joined with the late Gothic tradition.

Peter Paul Rubens arrived back in Antwerp from Italy late in 1608. In the following year he was appointed court painter to the archduke Albert and the archduchess Isabella, with special permission to reside in Antwerp, to help repair damage caused by the iconoclasm of 1566. The necessary ingredients were present for a brilliant flowering of the Baroque art that Rubens had evolved in Italy, and his studio became an artistic centre not only for the Netherlands but for England, Spain, and central Europe as well. The monumentality of Rubens' forms, with their impulsive drawing, restless movement, and dramatic lighting, provided the touchstone for the High Baroque in the Catholic areas of northern Europe (Plate 14). By Rubens' death, Philip IV of Spain had acquired more than 130 paintings by him. A diplomatic visit to England (where he found so much favour with Charles I that the latter knighted him) in 1630 had resulted in the commission to decorate the ceiling of the Banqueting Hall in Whitehall, one of the most monumental commissions of Rubens' last period.

Anthony Van Dyck, a pupil and assistant of Rubens, was a much less forceful personality than his master; and this is reflected in the quieter, more introspective note characteristic of his paintings. His greater sympathy for the sitter made him the most successful portrait painter of his time. Between 1625/26 and 1632 he was active, mainly as a portrait painter, in the entourage of Rubens, but the last years of his life (1632–41) were spent in England as court painter to Charles I, from whom he, too, received a knighthood (Plate 15). The elegant, relaxed, aristocratic portrait style he introduced was outstandingly successful and rendered obsolete the stiff portraits of Daniel Mytens and the straightforward, unpretentious portraits of Cornelius Johnson, two other painters of Low Countries origin active in England at this time. Van Dyck's death coincided with the outbreak of the Civil War in England; and the portraitists William Dobson and Robert Walker, in the troubled years 1641–60 the only painters of note active in England, reveal a considerable debt to him. Jacob Jordaens also worked as an assistant in Rubens' workshop in Antwerp and took it over after his death. His handling of the Rubensian idiom moved increasingly away from the control of Rubens himself toward a much more boisterous and vulgar style with an emphasis on large genre scenes populated with rough plebeian types.

The remaining members of Rubens' studio, such as Cornelis de Vos and Caspar de Crayer, were much weaker artistic personalities, and one of the few painters of genius relatively independent of Rubens was Adriaen Brouwer, who painted in the tradition of Pieter Bruegel the Elder. Best known for his low-life pictures (Plate 14), Brouwer also painted very expressive landscapes; his work is characterized by the sensitive use of a heavily loaded brush. In comparison, David Teniers the Younger was a minor master, and with him the influence of Dutch painting became increasingly strong. The impact of Rubens' landscape style is felt in the paintings of Jan Wildens and Lucas van Uden, while in contrast Jan Brueghel the Younger turned the making of copies and pastiches of his father's works into something approaching an industry. Still-life and animal painting reached new heights in the works of Frans Snyders as a result of the influence of Rubens, and in a much quieter vein Snyders' pupil Jan Fyt continued the tradition, which was to last into the 18th century. Jan Davidsz de Heem was also active in Holland, but he is important as one of the creators of the elaborate, fully developed Baroque still life, and as such he had a host of followers and imitators.

The United Provinces. Dutch painting of the 17th century shares roots with that of the Spanish Netherlands. Holland, however, was independent, rapidly prospering, and almost entirely Protestant. In the last decades of the 16th century the great port of Haarlem was the most active artistic centre, and the remarkable flowering of Mannerist painting there, as exemplified by Cornelis van Haarlem and Hendrik Goltzius, is without a parallel south of the border. In the later pictures of Abraham Bloemaert, Mannerism gave way to the much more straightforward realist style characteristic of the earliest phase of Dutch 17th-century painting. The influence of the figure paintings of Adam Elsheimer on this generation of artists was considerable; his particularly Italianate style, with sharply delineated forms painted in rich, deep colours and with a pronounced element of fantasy, is reflected by the early paintings of Leonard Bramer and, even more importantly, Pieter Lastman, the master of Rembrandt. Elsheimer's poetic little landscapes were also extremely important for the group of Dutch artists active in Rome about 1620. This group was headed by Cornelis van Poelenburgh and Bartolomeus Breenbergh, and back home it provided an additional source of Italian influence. The most striking influence of Italy was provided, however, by the Dutch followers of Caravaggio, who had seized eagerly upon the harsh dramatic lighting and coarse plebeian types they had seen in his paintings during their stays in Italy and brought the style to the north to form the so-called Utrecht school. Gerrit van Honthorst, Hendrik Terbrugghen (Plate 15), and Dirck van Baburen were leading champions of this style, but after 1628 Honthorst turned away in the direction of Van Dyck.

Frans Hals was born in Antwerp, but almost all of his life was spent in Haarlem, where he evolved his characteristic bravura style of portraiture (Plate 15). The stiff solemnity of earlier Dutch portraits gave way to the capture of fleeting changes of expression and superb textural effects, though Hals never succeeded in attaining the degree of psychological penetration characteristic of the portraits painted by Rembrandt.

The early works of Rembrandt van Rijn, painted in Leiden (1625–31), show a progressive lessening of the influence of Lastman, and Rembrandt, together with his associate Jan Lievens, evolved an increasingly Baroque style, with strong contrasts of light and shade derived from the "Caravaggists." After he moved to Amsterdam in 1631, these tendencies developed to an opulent and highly Baroque climax in the late 1630s. Following the death of his first wife, Saskia, in 1642, difficult times and the changing tastes of art collectors culminated in

his bankruptcy in 1656. In his later works the dramatic Baroque panache gives way to a deep introspection and sympathy for his subjects (Plate 15), and his series of about 60 self-portraits reveals this process in intimate detail. Parallel to his development as a painter is that of his style as an etcher; Rembrandt is considered by many to be the greatest etcher of all time (see PRINTMAKING). During the years of his financial success, Rembrandt had the largest and most successful painting and printmaking studio in Holland.

The increasing use at this time of portable easel paintings as domestic ornaments, many of them made for sale by dealers rather than on commission by the consumer, is related to the extraordinary range of subjects in which Dutch painters specialized. Nevertheless, certain basic changes in style and taste occurred during the course of the 17th century, and, although many painters long persisted in outdated styles, the same fundamental changes can be traced in the various specialities. The earliest phase of simple realism held sway until the early 1620s; and the characteristic bright local colours, lack of spatial unity, sudden transition between different planes, and tendency toward high viewpoints are to be found in the genre paintings of Willem Buytewech, flower pieces of Jacob II de Gheyn and Roelant Savery, and marine paintings of Hendrick Cronelisz Vroom and Adam Willaerts. This gave way to a much more limited palette in the early 1620s when, by reducing the strength and range of the colours, an atmospheric unity was obtained. In landscapes and marine paintings the horizon tended to drop, and a continuous and coherent recession into depth was attained, particularly in the paintings of Esaias van de Velde, Jan van Goyen, Hercules Seghers, and Jan Porcellis. The same change is seen in still lifes by Pieter Claesz and Willem Claesz Heda, in which the colours are almost monochrome (Plate 14). Atmospheric unity having been mastered, the change to the heroic classical phase of the middle of the 17th century was gradual, but there was a tendency toward ever-increasingly dramatic Baroque contrasts, be they the leaden skies or great oaks of Jacob van Ruisdael (Plate 14), the vast panoramas of Philips de Koninck, the luminous pastures of Aelbert Cuyp, or the heavy gray seas of Simon de Vlieger. The monumentality of these scenes is paralleled by the rich splendour of the still lifes of Jan Davidsz de Heem, Abraham van Beyeren, and Willem Kalff and the classical calm and simplicity of the scenes by Jan Vermeer (Plate 14) and Pieter de Hooch painted in Delft. In the landscapes of Meindert Hobbema, Claes Berchem, and Adam Pijnacker the majesty of Jacob van Ruisdael's landscapes gives way to a much lighter, more picturesque style. Similarly, the vigorous social realism of Adriaen van Ostade yields to a much lighter and more frivolous treatment in the paintings of his younger brother Isack and Jan Steen and the elegant hunting scenes of Philips Wouwerman.

With the French invasion of 1672 and the subsequent Dutch economic collapse, the demand for paintings dropped heavily, and in the last decades of the 17th century many Dutch painters either stopped painting or, like the van de Veldes Willem I and Willem II, left the country to work in England or Germany. Late 17th- and 18th-century taste tended toward the almost enamel-like brilliancy and intricate detail of the still lifes by Rachel Ruysch and Jan van Huysum; the same slightly dated flavour is characteristic of the marine paintings of Ludolf Backhuysen and of the hard figure subjects of Willem van Mieris and Adriaan van der Werff.

France. French-speaking painters continued the Mannerist conventions even later than did those at Haarlem, and at Nancy (capital of the independent duchy of Lorraine before 1633 and again from 1697 to 1766) a group of artists around Jacques Bellange and Jacques Callot was responsible for the last great flowering of the Mannerist style in Europe. By comparison, painting in Paris during the first decades of the 17th century was relatively insignificant, with the exception of that of Claude Vignon, who exchanged his Mannerist training for a style based on Elsheimer and to a lesser extent Lastman, and who in the 1620s revealed a remarkable knowledge of the earli-

Decline of
the Dutch
school

est paintings of Rembrandt. The return of Simon Vouet to Paris, however, marked the arrival of the Baroque in France. The earliest paintings from his stay in Rome are strikingly vigorous essays in the "Caravaggesque" style, but by 1620 he was painting in an eclectic, classicizing style based on the early Baroque painters active there, including Giovanni Lanfranco and Guido Reni. This style he brought back to France, enjoying until his death an immense success in Paris as a decorator and painter of large-scale altarpieces; even the return of Nicolas Poussin failed to shake his position. Poussin's activity in Paris is of relatively little importance compared with the remainder of his career in Rome, but the large number of works commissioned by French patrons then and subsequently was an important factor in the formation of the French predilection for classicism (Plate 16).

The influence of the highly Baroque paintings depicting the life of Marie de Médicis that Rubens had executed for the Luxembourg Palace in Paris was small. But Philippe de Campaigne evolved a grave and sober Baroque style that had its roots in the paintings of Rubens and Van Dyck rather than in Italy. Clear lighting and cool colours with an austere naturalism provided an alternative to the intellectual and archaeological classicism of Poussin. Georges de La Tour, a painter who had affinities with the Dutch "Caravaggists" of Utrecht, was active in Lorraine; but although he exploited the Caravaggist system of lighting, his figures became increasingly detached and simplified, leading to an uncomfortable hardness (Plate 16). The paintings of the Le Nain brothers—Antoine, Louis, and Mathieu—again look to Dutch painting for their inspiration (Plate 17). Eustache Le Sueur began painting under the influence of Vouet, but after Poussin's brief return to Paris (1640–42) he turned to a much more rigorous classical style influenced by Raphael's tapestry designs, whereas Sébastien Bourdon was capable of painting in almost any current style on request.

In the reorganization of the Academy of Painting and Sculpture in 1648, Charles Le Brun was appointed director and given the position of virtual dictator of the arts in France. An imaginative painter and designer, Le Brun was **Creation of** also a brilliant organizer, and the creation of the Louis XIV **the Louis** style, as exemplified by the Palace of Versailles, was above **XIV style** all due to him. The particular Baroque style that emerged was based on the Roman High Baroque but was purged of all theatricality and illusionism and modified to conform to the classical canons of French taste; this compromise solution struck the keynote for the frescoes of Le Brun and Pierre Mignard. The more full-blooded Baroque style of Pierre Puget received little official recognition, and his attempts to obtain major commissions at Versailles were thwarted, probably because of his difficult nature. During the last decades of the century, the full Baroque style took on a new lease on life, and the decorative paintings of Charles de La Fosse and Antoine Coypel clearly reveal the influence of Rubens. Even more Baroque are formal portraits by Hyacinthe Rigaud and Nicolas de Largillière, in which the strong contrapposto (twisting of the figure so that one half is in opposition to the other), rich settings, and floating masses of drapery reflect the pomp and swagger of this era—which, significantly, came to be known as the Grande Époque.

The great formal portraits of Largillière and Rigaud are entirely Baroque in their approach, but in the late informal portraits of these masters a new atmosphere prevails. This atmosphere goes by the name of Rococo. The turn of the century marks the victory of Rubens' influence over the severe classicism of Poussin. The evolution of the Rococo style of decoration has been traced from its emergence at the beginning of the 18th century, and it must be emphasized that the Rococo is fundamentally a decorative style. It made relatively little impact on religious painting in France, and painters such as Pierre Subleyras continued to work in a Baroque idiom until the arrival of Neoclassicism in the second half of the century. It took the genius of Antoine Watteau to put together all the ideas current in Paris and to create the new style of painting. Rubens (in particular his oil sketches), the brush drawings and etchings of Castiglione, the naturalism of the Dutch

painters, and the fantasy of the French artist Claude Gillot all provided important source material for early Rococo painting. The delicate sketchlike technique and elegant figures of Watteau's wistful fantasies, called *fêtes galantes* (Plate 16), provided the models for the paintings of Jean-Baptiste Pater and Nicolas Lancret, both of whom conveyed a delicately veiled eroticism. Eroticism was more explicit in the sensuous nudes, both mythological and pastoral, of François Boucher (Plate 16). Another painter with whom amorous dalliance is a hallmark was Jean-Honoré Fragonard, in whose soft landscapes flirtation and even seduction are conducted with gallantry. Such paintings formed an intimate part of the decoration of Rococo interiors, and more than any earlier secular paintings they were intended as a kind of two-dimensional furniture. **Fantasy and eroticism**

The furniture role also applies to the paintings of dead game and live dogs by François Desportes and Jean-Baptiste Oudry. But in the still lifes and tranquil scenes of domestic life painted by Jean-Baptiste-Siméon Chardin there is a sobriety of colour and composition (although great richness in the handling), an often relatively homely subject matter, and a concern to order the mind rather than dazzle the eye (Plate 17). Some of Chardin's subjects—the labours of the servant class, the care of children—were shared by Jean-Baptiste Greuze, who was, however, more interested in narrative and sentiment. Unlike Dutch painters of lower-class life, Greuze endowed his peasants with the sensibility of their social superiors. The edifying moral sympathy he intended to inculcate was, however, often subverted by a sly erotic interest he could not resist giving expression to.

Despite his great success, Greuze was judged to have failed in his attempt at painting heroic narrative from ancient history. But then it is true that the "higher" class of painting was generally less successfully practiced in France than were the "lower" genres in the 18th century. The mythologies and altarpieces of the Coypel family, Jean-François de Troy, or Jean-Marc Nattier may have been underestimated, but their names are not as familiar as those of still-life and genre painters such as Watteau or Chardin or even those of such accomplished painters of capricious ruin pieces or of landscapes and seascapes as Hubert Robert and Claude-Joseph Vernet.

The middle decades of the 18th century saw more accomplished portrait painters flourishing in France than perhaps ever before in any country. Yet it is the informal, the convivial, and the intimate that are associated with the portraiture of Jacques-André-Joseph Aved, François-Hubert Drouais, Louis Tocqué, Louis-Michel Van Loo, or Étienne Aubry. The heroic was seldom attempted and never achieved.

Britain. *The 17th century.* English painting during the 17th century had been dominated by a series of foreign-born practitioners, mostly portraitists (*e.g.,* Rubens and Van Dyck), even before the Civil War. Sir Peter Lely and Sir Godfrey Kneller continued this trend after the Restoration. The vast majority of the painting executed by native artists remained thoroughly provincial. Lely began **English** his activity in England during the Civil War, probably in **portraiture** 1641, but his portraits of the members of the court of **in the 17th** Charles II set the pattern for English portraiture of the **century** second half of the 17th century. British patrons in the 18th century sometimes collected paintings on religious or mythical themes by foreign artists, but at home they rarely commissioned anything other than portraits, landscapes, and marine paintings, although there was in the early 18th century a vogue for grand allegorical decorations in aristocratic houses. The Protestant church, however, did little to encourage painting. In fact, the preponderance of portraits is the most distinctive characteristic of old British collections. Gerard Soest, Jacob Huysmans, and Willem Wissing were also active in England as portrait painters close in style to Lely, whereas Jan Siberechts and Robert Streeter painted "portraits" of English country houses. The most distinguished painters to settle in England during this period were the van de Veldes, from whom the tradition of British marine painting descends, headed by Peter Monamy and Samuel Scott.

The Glorious Revolution of 1688 was followed by a brief

flowering of decorative painting under Sir James Thornhill, which was the closest that Britain ever approached to the developed Baroque style of the Continent. This process was in part due to the influx, following the end of the War of the Spanish Succession, of Italian painters, including the Venetians Giovanni Antonio Pellegrini and Jacopo Amigoni, and French ones, such as Charles de La Fosse. The German-born Kneller succeeded Lely as court portrait painter, but, although his portraits often have a certain liveliness, his rather heavy use of studio assistants resulted in a tendency to monotony.

Hogarth

The 18th century. Thornhill's son-in-law William Hogarth was, despite his chauvinism and virulently anti-French sentiments, heavily influenced by the continental Rococo style. Early in his career he succeeded in breaking away from the straitjacket of portraiture, and his moralizing paintings are superb evocations of life in the England of George I and George II (Plate 17). His rich, creamy paint handling and brilliant characterization of textures have a freshness and vitality unequaled in the work of any of his contemporaries. He invented a new form of secular narrative painting that imparts a moral. These paintings were often tragicomedies, although dependent upon no texts, and Hogarth's series of such works were always intended to be engraved for a large public as well as seen in a private picture gallery (just as plays were intended to be performed as well as read).

Despite Hogarth's considerable knowledge of and borrowings from continental old masters, he remained in the last analysis English through and through. This, however, was not the case with all the next generation of painters; and the Scottish-born Allan Ramsay studied in Rome and Naples in 1736–38 before settling in London in 1739. Until the return of Joshua Reynolds from Italy in 1752, Ramsay held undisputed sway as the most successful portrait painter in London; and to him must be given the credit for the initial marriage of the Italian "grand style" to English portraiture. Ramsay visited Italy again in 1755–57, and on his return his portraits took on a new delicacy and elegance and a silvery tonality. Reynolds possessed great ambitions and a more profound acquaintance with the old masters than any of his contemporaries. His colouring and handling can be compared with Rembrandt, Rubens, and Veronese, and his poses are indebted to the sculpture of antiquity and to Michelangelo. The *Discourses* that he delivered to the Royal Academy (founded in 1768 with Reynolds as its first president) are the most impressive statement in English of the central ideas of European art theory from the time of Leon Battista Alberti's treatise. Reynolds' own painting gained a genuine heroic power and elevated grace from his frustrated ambition to be a history painter, although for that very reason he occasionally tumbled into bathos.

Wilson's Italianate landscapes

The third major British painter of the period to study in Italy was a Welshman, Richard Wilson, who worked there from 1750 to about 1757 before settling in London. His landscape style was formed on Claude, Gaspard Dughet, and Cuyp; but the clear golden lighting of his Italian landscapes carries the conviction of an artist saturated with the Mediterranean tradition. A cooler clarity and classical simplicity pervade his northern landscapes; and, despite the uneven quality of his work, Wilson was the first British painter to lift the pure landscape above mere decorative painting and topography.

Thomas Gainsborough was in every way the antithesis to Reynolds. Trained entirely in England, he had no wish to visit Italy. Instead of the "grand style," his tastes in portraiture lay in the delicate flickering brushwork and evanescent qualities of the Rococo (Plate 17). He preferred landscape painting to portraiture, and the strong Dutch influence in his earliest works later gave way to spontaneous landscapes composed from models.

In the 1760s Francis Cotes was the most important fashionable London portrait painter after Reynolds and Gainsborough, a position succeeded to by George Romney, who, on returning to London from Italy in 1775, took over Cotes's studio. Romney's portraits deteriorated sadly in quality during the 1780s when the young Sir Thomas Lawrence began to make his mark.

Throughout the 18th century, portraiture remained the most important genre of British painting, despite the efforts of Reynolds and Gainsborough in their "fancy pictures." Even the taste for large-scale scenes illustrating Shakespeare and other themes—which were commissioned toward the end of the century from James Barry, James Northcote, and Edward Penny, among others—never spread far beyond a few patrons. Sporting and animal painting took on an entirely new dimension in the work of George Stubbs. Joseph Wright of Derby was active outside London and, apart from his romantic portraits, is important for his series of paintings of scientific and industrial subjects with strong light effects. Johann Zoffany was born in Germany but moved to Britain about 1761 and became a founder-member of the Royal Academy, specializing in elaborate group portraits and theatrical scenes.

During the second half of the 18th century the evolution of British oil painting was to a great extent paralleled by the extraordinary flowering in watercolours. The early topographical drawings of Paul Sandby gave way to the delicate linear drawings of Francis Towne, with their patches of colour resembling maps, and, at the close of the century, to the atmospheric unity of the landscapes of John Robert Cozens.

Colonial Americas. *North America.* Painting in the Dutch and English colonies of North America reflected generally the portrait styles of the mother countries, though with a note of provinciality. In the late 17th and early 18th centuries the Dutch colony of New Amsterdam (New York) had painters whose names today are forgotten. Their work lives on, however, and is signified by names such as the Master of the De Peyster Boy. Gustavus Hesselius, Swedish born, was painting in Maryland, and Jeremiah Theüs, a Swiss, was at work in South Carolina. Peter Pelham and John Smibert arrived from England and in the second quarter of the 18th century were painting portraits in Boston, Mass. These two self-taught itinerant artists were succeeded by John Wollaston and Joseph Blackburn. Robert Feke, a native American painter, realized his forms more solidly and with greater originality than his predecessors had. Another native American, John Singleton Copley, worked in Boston until 1774, when he went to live permanently in England, and was responsible for the finest painting produced in the American colonies. Benjamin West, another important native figure in the history of American painting, was born in Pennsylvania but settled in London in 1763, where he became the second president of the Royal Academy. Although domiciled in London, he helped to mold the styles of two generations of American painters.

Central and South America. Baroque painting in Central and South America is basically an extension of that of Spain and Portugal, and even the best rarely rises to the general standard of the European schools. Important paintings and sculptures tended to be imported from Europe, and Zurbarán was particularly active in producing works for export, while local productions were more or less heavily influenced by the Indian traditions.

Central Europe. In central Europe the Mannerist tradition remained dominant until the Thirty Years' War (1618–48), particularly in Bohemia and Bavaria, where Italian influence was perhaps strongest.

Influence of Rubens

The Rubensian Baroque became dominant after mid-century, and here the lead was taken by Silesia and Bohemia. Michael Willmann, originally from Königsberg (modern Kaliningrad) on the southeastern Baltic coast, developed a highly charged, emotional Baroque style, based on Rubens, at Lubiąż (modern Dorf Leubus, northwest of Wrocław) from 1661 to 1700 and at Prague after 1700. In Karel Škréta Šotnovoský, Bohemia possessed a painter of European stature; his sombre portraits and religious scenes are filled with a deeply serious mystical fervour. The frescoes by Johann Michael Rottmayr in the castle of Vranov in Moravia (1695) and in Breslau (now Wrocław; 1704–06) constitute a prelude to the great development of Baroque painting in the Habsburg domains. There the vigorous and extremely colourful frescoes are closely integrated with the architecture. The vast majority of the best central European Baroque painting outside portraiture is monumental in scale, and the concept of the *Gesamtkunstwerk* ("total work of art")—where painting, sculpture, and architecture are combined together into a single, unified, and harmonious ensemble—is of overwhelming importance.

Painting in Austria flourished, and Franz Anton Maulbertsch is arguably the greatest painter of the 18th century in central Europe. The vast majority of his brilliant fresco cycles are located in relatively inaccessible areas of Bohemia, Moravia, and northern Hungary. But the mystical intensity of his religious scenes and the joyous abandon of his secular subjects form a triumphant closing chapter to 18th-century central European painting. Maulbertsch's last frescoes at Strahov, Prague (1794), reveal, nevertheless, the impact of the Neoclassicism that descended in the last decades on all Austrian painters, including Troger's pupil Martin Knoller. But Austrian monumental painting remained fully Baroque in the hands of Daniel Gran, Paul Troger, and Bartholomäus Altomonte; and it was not until the latter part of the century that the Rococo made its impact.

Independent development of Bohemian painting
During the first four decades of the 18th century, Bohemian Baroque painting developed almost independently of Vienna, where the Habsburg rulers of Bohemia had their capital. The impetuous work of Jan Petr Brandl and the powerful realism of the portraitist Jan Kupecký, who worked in Rome, Venice, Vienna, and Nürnberg, always remained Bohemian in spirit. The frescoes of Wenzel Lorenz Reiner, however, show more Italian influence. One of the few important Baroque frescoes of the second half of the century is that by Jan Lucaš Kracker in St. Nicholas, Malá Strana ("Lesser Quarter"), Prague. The influence of Bohemian Baroque painting is frequently underestimated. Apart from Vienna and the surrounding area, it was dominant in Silesia and strong later in the century in Franconia.

After the death of Cosmas Damian Asam in 1739, Johann Baptist Zimmermann became the most important fresco painter in the Munich area; his lyrical handling of pale colours is typical of the Rococo period. Christian Wink continued to paint in the same style until the close of the century. In Georg Desmarées the court at Munich gained a painter in whose Rococo portraits there is more than a hint of decadence.

The centre of south German painting had by the late 1730s shifted from Munich to Augsburg in Swabia, where Johann Georg Bermüller became the director of the Academy in 1730; but his frescoes, as well as those of Franz Joseph Spiegler and Gottfried Bernhard Goetz, are perhaps more representative of the Late Baroque than the Rococo. The frescoes of Matthäus Günther, who became director of the Augsburg Academy in 1762, show a steady evolution from his early Baroque compositions, through the much lighter asymmetrical Rococo compositions, to the strongly sculptural quality of his late works, which reveal the onset of Neoclassicism.

In Franconia and the middle Rhineland the most important painters were Johann Zick and Carlo Carlone. Zick's frescoes at Würzburg (1749) had not been entirely successful, and in 1750 he was supplanted by Tiepolo; but at Bruchsal he produced one of the most brilliant series of Rococo frescoes in Germany (now destroyed). His son Januarius began painting in the Rococo style but under the influence of Anton Raphael Mengs produced some late frescoes that were strongly classical.

Prussian Rococo
The French tastes of Frederick I of Prussia at Berlin led him in 1710 to summon Antoine Pesne to court, where Pesne continued for the remainder of his life to paint in an entirely French Rococo style. The homely intimacy of the paintings of Daniel Chodowiecki, however, have a sensitivity and refinement more comparable to Chardin's.

Saxony under Augustus III produced few painters of real importance except Mengs, who rapidly turned from the Rococo to the Neoclassicism propounded by the influential art historian and classical archaeologist Johann Winckelmann.

Poland. King Władysław IV Vasa (reigned 1632–48) assembled an important collection of Italian and Flemish Baroque paintings, but these promising developments were cut short by the destruction of the Swedish Wars in the middle of the 17th century. Under John III Sobieski (reigned 1674–96), a cultivated man, there was a considerable revival, and, although two of the painters active in Poland—Claude Callot and Michelangelo Palloni—were foreign-born and foreign-trained, native talent flowered with the work of Jerzy Eleuter Szymonowicz-Siemiginowski and Jan Tretko. In 1697 the crowns of Poland and Saxony were united under Augustus II, and he and his son Augustus III ruled over Poland until 1763. During this period, Polish painting formed part of the Saxon tradition, but during the reign of the last king of Poland, Stanisław II August Poniatowski (reigned 1764–95), Warsaw quickly became a centre of European importance. Although inclined to Neoclassicism in architecture, Stanisław's taste in painting was more conservative. Accordingly it is the late Rococo portraits of Marcello Bacciarelli that are particularly important. A nephew and pupil of Canaletto, Bernardo Bellotto, settled in Warsaw in 1767 and executed for Stanisław the great series of 26 views of the city that were intended to hang in the Royal Castle.   (P.C.-B./Ed.)

Russia. The Baroque in Russia was imported from western Europe and outside court circles made little impact. Indeed the traditional production of icons for the Orthodox church by artists of the Novgorod and Moscow schools continued throughout the Baroque period. Nevertheless the foundation of St. Petersburg (1703) by Peter I the Great marked the beginning of the substitution of Western influence for Byzantine, an important change. During Peter's reign foreign painters began to go to Russia in increasing numbers; conversely, groups of young Russians were sent to Italy, France, Holland, and England to study painting. Western influence determined the character of Russian painting for more than two centuries.

Influx of foreign painters

The art of Peter's age shows almost no trace of Byzantine influence. Only in iconography did the old style persist for some time. Early in the 18th century, religious painting began to give way to secular painting, and the church prohibition of sculpture became ineffective. Dmitry Levitsky stands out as the only important Russian painter of the 18th century to work in the Western style.

Further westernizing occurred under the empress Elizabeth (reigned 1741–62), who had French tastes. A great number of vast and luxurious Rococo-style palaces were built, and painting was primarily concerned with their interior decoration—ceilings and walls. The work was carried on chiefly by Italians and Frenchmen.

In 1757 the Academy of Fine Arts was founded in St. Petersburg, and foreign artists—mostly French—were invited to direct the new school. These trained some remarkable native portraitists, such as Ivan Argunov, Anton Losenko, and Fyodor Rokotov. Their works reflected the ceremonial character of Elizabeth's tastes and showed little evidence of native Russian sensibility.   (A.Vo./Ed.)

Scandinavia. In the 17th century, Scandinavian painting derived from traditions of the Low Countries and northern Germany. The works of art carried off as loot from Prague by Swedish soldiers during the Thirty Years' War might conceivably have broadened the outlook of Swedes at home, but the best of them were taken to Rome by Queen Christina when she abdicated in 1654. A generation later, under the influence of the fashionable Venetian woman pastelist Rosalba Carriera, a school of Rococo portraitists flourished in Scandinavia. One such portraitist was Carl Gustav Pilo, who, though trained in Stockholm, executed many frankly Venetian portraits during his years as court painter in Copenhagen. Another was Lorentz Pasch the Younger, who trained under Pilo in Copenhagen, although he subsequently worked mainly in Sweden. Other painters of Swedish origin were Alexander Roslin, who worked throughout Europe, and Georg Desmarées, who settled in Bavaria. The Scandinavian Rococo has a distinctive flavour that is also detectable in the work of two important miniaturists of the period, Niclas Lafrensen and Cornelius Höyer. At the close of the century the paintings of Jens Juel in Denmark bridge the transition from Rococo to Neoclassicism.

Neoclassical and Romantic

NEOCLASSICISM

Neoclassicism was a widespread and influential movement in painting and the other visual arts that began in the 1760s, reached its height in the 1780s and '90s, and lasted until the 1840s and '50s. In painting it generally took the form of an emphasis on austere linear design in the depiction of classical themes and subject matter, using archaeologically correct settings and costumes.

Neoclassicism arose partly as a reaction against the sensuous and frivolously decorative Rococo style that had dominated European art from the 1720s on. But an even more profound stimulus was the new and more scientific interest in classical antiquity that arose in the 18th century. Neoclassicism was given great impetus by new archaeological discoveries, particularly the exploration and excavation of the buried Roman cities of Herculaneum and Pompeii (the excavations of which began in 1738 and 1748, respectively). And from the second decade of the 18th century on, a number of influential publications by Bernard de Montfaucon, Giovanni Battista Piranesi, the Comte de Caylus, and Robert Wood provided engraved views of Roman monuments and other antiquities and further quickened interest in the classical past. The new understanding distilled from these discoveries and publications in turn enabled European scholars for the first time to discern separate and distinct chronological periods in Greco-Roman art, and this new sense of a plurality of ancient styles replaced the older, unqualified veneration of Roman art and encouraged a dawning interest in purely Greek antiquities. The German scholar Johann Joachim Winckelmann's writings and sophisticated theorizings were especially influential in this regard. Winckelmann saw in Greek sculpture "a noble simplicity and quiet grandeur" and called for artists to imitate Greek art. He claimed that in doing so such artists would obtain idealized depictions of natural forms that had been stripped of all transitory and individualistic aspects, and their images would thus attain a universal and archetypal significance.

Neoclassicism as manifested in painting was initially not stylistically distinct from the French Rococo and other styles that had preceded it. This was partly because, whereas it was possible for architecture and sculpture to be modeled on prototypes in these media that had actually survived from classical antiquity, those few classical paintings that had survived were minor or merely ornamental works—until, that is, the discoveries made at Herculaneum and Pompeii. The earliest Neoclassical painters were Joseph-Marie Vien, Anton Raphael Mengs, Pompeo Batoni, Angelica Kauffmann, and Gavin Hamilton; these artists were active during the 1750s, '60s, and '70s. Each of these painters, though they may have used poses and figural arrangements from ancient sculptures and vase paintings, was strongly influenced by preceding stylistic trends. An important early Neoclassical work such as Mengs's "Parnassus" (1761; Villa Albani, Rome) owes much of its inspiration to 17th-century classicism and to Raphael for both the poses of its figures and its general composition. Many of the early paintings of the Neoclassical artist Benjamin West derive their compositions from works by Nicolas Poussin, and Kauffmann's sentimental subjects dressed in antique garb are basically Rococo in their softened, decorative prettiness. Mengs's close association with Winckelmann led to his being influenced by the ideal beauty that the latter so ardently expounded, but the church and palace ceilings decorated by Mengs owe more to existing Italian Baroque traditions than to anything Greek or Roman.

A more rigorously Neoclassical painting style arose in France in the 1780s under the leadership of Jacques-Louis David. He and his contemporary Jean-François-Pierre Peyron were interested in narrative painting rather than the ideal grace that fascinated Mengs. Just before and during the French Revolution, these and other painters adopted stirring moral subject matter from Roman history and celebrated the values of simplicity, austerity, heroism, and stoic virtue that were traditionally associated with the Roman Republic, thus drawing parallels between that time and the contemporary struggle for liberty in France. David's history paintings of the "Oath of the Horatii" (1784; Louvre, Paris) and "Lictors Bringing to Brutus the Bodies of His Sons" (1789; Louvre) display a gravity and decorum deriving from classical tragedy, a certain rhetorical quality of gesture, and patterns of drapery influenced by ancient sculpture. To some extent these elements were anticipated by British and American artists such as Hamilton and West, but in David's works the dramatic confrontations of the figures are starker and in clearer profile on the same plane, the setting is more monumental, and the diagonal compositional movements, large groupings of figures, and turbulent draperies of the Baroque have been almost entirely repudiated. This style was ruthlessly austere and uncompromising, and it is not surprising that it came to be associated with the French Revolution (in which David actively participated).

Neoclassicism as generally manifested in European painting by the 1790s emphasized the qualities of outline and linear design over those of colour, atmosphere, and effects of light. Widely disseminated engravings of classical sculptures and Greek vase paintings helped determine this bias, which is clearly seen in the outline illustrations made by the British sculptor John Flaxman in the 1790s for editions of the works of Homer, Aeschylus, and Dante. These illustrations are notable for their drastic and powerful simplification of the human body, their denial of pictorial space, and their minimal stage setting. This austere linearity when depicting the human form was adopted by many other British figural artists, including the Swiss-born Henry Fuseli and William Blake, among others.

Neoclassical painters attached great importance to depicting the costumes, settings, and details of their classical subject matter with as much historical accuracy as possible. This worked well enough when illustrating an incident found in the pages of Homer, but it raised the question of whether a modern hero or famous person should be portrayed in classical or contemporary dress. This issue was never satisfactorily resolved, except perhaps in David's brilliantly evocative portraits of sitters wearing the then-fashionable antique garb, as in his "Portrait of Madame Récamier" (1800; Louvre).

Classical history and mythology provided a large part of the subject matter of Neoclassical works. The poetry of Homer, Virgil, and Ovid, the plays of Aeschylus, Sophocles, and Euripides, and history recorded by Pliny, Plutarch, Tacitus, and Livy provided the bulk of classical sources, but the most important single source was Homer. To this general literary emphasis was added a growing interest in medieval sources, such as the pseudo-Celtic poetry of Ossian, as well as incidents from medieval history, the works of Dante, and an admiration for medieval art itself in the persons of Giotto, Fra Angelico, and others. Indeed, the Neoclassicists differed strikingly from their academic predecessors in their admiration of Gothic and Quattrocento art in general, and they contributed notably to the positive reevaluation of such art.

Finally, it should be noted that Neoclassicism coexisted throughout much of its later development with the seemingly obverse and opposite tendency of Romanticism. But far from being distinct and separate, these two styles intermingled with each other in complex ways; many ostensibly Neoclassical paintings show Romantic tendencies, and vice versa. This contradictory situation is strikingly evident in the works of the last great Neoclassical painter, Jean-Auguste-Dominique Ingres, who painted sensuous Romantic female nudes while also turning out precisely linear and rather lifeless historical paintings in the approved Neoclassical mode.

Britain. Hamilton—Scottish painter, archaeologist, and dealer—spent most of his working life in Rome, and his paintings include two series of large and influential canvases of Homeric subjects. West and the Swiss-born Kauffmann were the most consistent exhibitors of history pieces in London during the 1760s. James Barry and Fuseli also were important. Blake, poet and painter, was a Neoclassicist to some extent.

France. As well as being a painter, Vien was a friend of the archaeologist Caylus and a director of the French

Academy in Rome. This generation also included Jean-Baptiste Greuze, who painted a few classical history subjects as well as the scenes from contemporary life for which he is best known; Jean-Jacque Lagrenée the Elder, like Vien a director of the French Academy in Rome; and Nicolas-Guy Brenet.

David's role in French Neoclassical painting

The outstanding and most influential of all French Neoclassicists and one of the major artists in Europe was Vien's pupil Jacques-Louis David. David's early works are essentially Rococo, and his late works also revert to early 18th-century types; his fame as a Neoclassicist rests on paintings of the 1780s and 1790s. After winning the Prix de Rome of the French Academy in 1774 (important in the history of French painting because it awarded a stay in Rome, where winners studied Italian paintings at first hand), he was in that city in 1775–81, returning there in 1784 to paint "Oath of the Horatii." David's contemporaries, or near-contemporaries, included Jean-Germain Drouais, whose history paintings almost equaled David's own in severity and intensity.

The slightly younger generation of painters included Jean-Baptiste Regnault, Louis-Léopold Boilly, and Louis Gauffier. They were followed by a more important group that included Pierre-Paul Prud'hon. Prud'hon blended in his paintings a mild classicism and the lyrical mood and soft lights of Correggio; he was patronized by the empresses Josephine and Marie-Louise. Baron Pierre-Narcisse Guérin painted in a style close to the Neoclassicism of David, although he was not one of his pupils.

David's pupils

Of David's pupils, three became well-known and one became very famous. Baron François-Pascal-Simon Gérard had a high reputation as a portraitist under both Napoleon and Louis XVIII. Antoine-Jean Gros executed many large Napoleonic canvases and after David's death was the leading Neoclassicist in France. Anne-Louis Girodet de Roucy, known as Girodet-Trioson, won a Prix de Rome but stopped painting after 1812 when he inherited a fortune and turned to writing. The famous pupil was Ingres, who was important as a Neoclassicist in his subject paintings but not in his portraits.

Germany and Austria. Mengs was born in Aussig in Bohemia (modern Ústí nad Labem, Czech.) in 1728, the son of the court painter there. He was himself appointed Dresden court painter in 1745. In 1755 he met Winckelmann and subsequently he became a prominent figure in Roman Neoclassical circles. Mengs is important both as a painter and as a theorist. Apart from him, Germany's and Austria's main contribution to Neoclassicism was theoretical, not practical, however. The early Neoclassicists included Cristoph Unterberger; Anton von Maron, who married Mengs's sister; and Friedrich Heinrich Füger. After Unterberger, the most interesting painter was Johann Heinrich Wilhelm Tischbein, who executed both portraits and subject pieces. He was a director of the art academy in Naples and supervised the publication of engravings of the Greek vases in the collection of Sir William Hamilton, the British ambassador to Naples, who was a notable connoisseur.

The German painter Asmus Jacob Carstens worked in Berlin and was a professor at the Berlin Academy. Members of his artistic circle included the painters Karl Ludwig Fernow, Eberhard Wächter, Joseph Anton Koch (who was the most outstanding of this German group), and Gottlieb Schick.

Italy. One of the earliest Neoclassicists and one of the foremost painters of his generation in Italy was Batoni. His style blends Rococo with Neoclassical elements, and his work includes classical subject pieces as well as portraits in contemporary dress, the sitter posing with antique statues and urns, and sometimes amid ruins. The painter Domenico Corvi was influenced by both Batoni and Mengs and was important as the teacher of three of the leading Neoclassicists of the next generation: Giuseppe Cades, Gaspare Landi, and Vincenzo Camuccini. These artists worked mostly in Rome, the first two making reputations as portraitists, Landi especially being noted for good contemporary groups.

Rome was indeed the city where the principal Italian painters of this period were mostly active. One such was

Felice Giani, whose many decorations include Napoleonic palaces there and elsewhere in Italy (especially Faenza) and in France.

Major Italian Neoclassicists outside Rome

Important painters outside Rome include Andrea Appiani the Elder in Milan, who became Napoleon's official painter and executed some of the best frescoes in northern Italy. He was also a fine portraitist. One of his pupils was Giuseppe Bossi. Another leading Lombard painter was Giovanni Battista dell'Era, whose encaustic paintings were bought by Catherine the Great and others. Other good examples of Neoclassical decorative schemes outside Rome are in Florence (Pitti Palace) by the Florentine Luigi Sabatelli and by Pietro Benvenuti, who was born at Arezzo, and in Venice (Palazzo Reale) by Giuseppe Borsato, who was born in that city and was both painter and architect. Another painter of the time, though only given to a mildly Neoclassical style, was Domenico Pellegrini, born near Bassano, who traveled widely. The principal Neoclassicists in the south were the Sicilians Giuseppe Velasco, who did important frescoes in palaces in Palermo, and Giuseppe Errante.

Other countries. The main Danish painter who produced original Neoclassical works was Nicolai Abraham Abildgaard. Other Danish painters include Abildgaard's and David's pupil Christoffer Wilhelm Eckersberg. David was very influential in Brussels, where he retired late in life. The paintings of his Belgian pupil François-Joseph Navez, for example, are pure French Neoclassicism. The two main Neoclassical artists in The Netherlands were Humbert de Superville and Jan Willem Pieneman. The principal Neoclassicist in Spain was José de Madrazo y Agudo.   (D.I./Ed.)

ROMANTICISM

Romanticism is a term loosely used to designate numerous and diverse changes in the arts during a period of more than 100 years (roughly, 1760–1870), changes that were in reaction against Neoclassicism (but not necessarily the classicism of Greece and Rome) or against what is variously called the Age of Reason, the Augustan Age, the Enlightenment, or 18th-century materialism. In the sense of a personal temperament Romanticism had always existed, but in the sense of an aesthetic period it meant works of art whose prime impulse and effect derived from individual rather than collective reactions. Romanticism can generally be said to have emphasized the personal, the subjective, the irrational, the imaginative, the spontaneous, the emotional, and even the visionary and transcendental in works of art. The Romantic movement first developed in northern Europe with a rejection of technical standards based on the classical ideal that perfection should be attained in art.

It was writers and poets who gave initial expression to Romantic ideas; painters, while subject to similar feelings, acquired fundamental inspiration from the literature of the period. There was an increasing awareness generally of the way the various arts interacted. The Frenchman Eugène Delacroix and the German Philipp Otto Runge explored the implications of musical analogies for painting, and everywhere writers, artists, and composers could be found in close association.

Romantic critics agreed that experience of profound inner emotion was the mainspring of creation and appreciation of art. Received ideas, and especially aesthetic values sanctioned by the authority of official institutions, were distrusted, and the individual was pitted against society. The artist asserted the right to evolve his own criteria of beauty and in so doing encouraged a new concept of artistic genius. The genius whom the Romantics celebrated was one who refused to conform, who remained defiantly independent of society, and whose chief virtues were novelty and sincerity. This sometimes led to bizarre and extravagant projects in which the intention to shock, excite, and involve struck a melodramatic, almost hysterical note that failed to convince by its very lack of restraint.

As in the literature of the period, tragic themes predominated in Romantic painting, and interest turned sharply from classical history and mythology to medieval subjects, although an interest in the primitive was sometimes common to both. The fascination with the Middle Ages combined with strong nationalist tendencies, disposing artists to a concern with the history and folklore of their own countries. At the same time they often sought themes or styles that were distant in place as well as time. Accounts of foreign travel and the literary works of Dante, Shakespeare, Byron, Goethe, Sir Walter Scott, and the supposed Celtic bard Ossian greatly influenced painters. Study of medieval culture imbued some painters with a Christian ideal of simplicity and moral integrity.

A salient feature of Romantic sensibility was awareness of the beauties of the natural world. Artists identified their personal feelings with nature's changing aspects. An almost reverential affection, animated by the belief that the divine mind was immanent in nature, engendered at times a Christian or theistic naturalism. The artist was seen as the interpreter of hidden mysteries, to which end imaginative insight must combine with absolute fidelity and sincerity. In Britain and Germany especially, the moral implications inherent in the appreciation of natural or artistic beauty tended to outweigh aesthetic considerations. Interest in transitory phenomena led painters to devote themselves to an accurate study of light and atmosphere and their effects on the landscape. Concern to preserve the spontaneity of the immediate impression brought about a revolution in painterly technique, with the rapid notation of the sketch carried into the final conception. Whether emphasizing expressive or purely visual considerations, the landscape paintings of the period display dazzling colour.

Curiosity about the external world and a spirit of what might be called scientific inquiry led many painters to explore the minutiae of nature. Technological advance also excited artistic interest, though painting was affected less than architecture and the decorative arts; and the humanitarian sympathy and generosity so vital to the Romantic spirit gradually effected a reconciliation between art and life. The political and social upheavals of the 19th century involved many painters in revolutionary movements and stimulated a solicitude toward the helpless and downtrodden that found most passionate and powerful expression in the works executed during and immediately after the Revolutions of 1848.

Britain. In the late 1760s and '70s a circle of British painters in Rome had already begun to find academic precepts inadequate. James Barry, the brothers John and Alexander Runciman, John Brown, George Romney, and the Swiss-born Henry Fuseli favoured themes—whether literary, historical, or purely imaginary—determined by a taste for the pathetic, bizarre, and extravagantly heroic. Mutually influential and highly eclectic, they combined, especially in their drawings, the linear tensions of Italian Mannerism with bold contrasts of light and shade. Though never in Rome, John Hamilton Mortimer had much in common with this group, for all were participants in a move to found a national school of narrative painting. Fuseli's affiliations with the German Romantic *Sturm und Drang* writers predisposed him, like Flaxman, toward the "primitive" heroic stories of Homer and Dante. Flaxman himself, in the two-dimensional linear abstraction of his drawings, a two-dimensionality implying rejection of Renaissance perspective and seen for instance in the expressive purity of "Penelope's Dream" (1792–93), had important repercussions throughout Europe.

William Blake absorbed and outstripped the Fuseli circle, evolving new images for a unique private cosmology, rejecting oils in favour of tempera and watercolour, and depicting, as in "Pity" (1795; Tate Gallery, London), a shadowless world of soaring, supernatural beings (Plate 19). His passionate rejection of rationalism and materialism, his scorn for both Sir Joshua Reynolds and the Dutch Naturalists, stemmed from a conviction that "poetic genius" could alone perceive the infinite, so essential to the artist since "painting, as well as poetry and music, exists and exults in immortal thoughts." The spiritual, symbolical expression of Blake's complex sympathies, his ability to recognize God in a single blade of grass, inspired Samuel Palmer, who, with his friend Edward Calvert, extracted from nature a visionary world of exquisite, though short-lived, intensity.

British early Romantic painters in Rome

Blake

Empiricism and acceptance of the irrational, however, were not mutually exclusive, and each profoundly affected attitudes toward nature. Susceptible to the ideas of Blake and other radical theorists and animated by a growing spirit of inquiry into natural phenomena, painters slowly abandoned the picturesque desire to compose and became willing to be moved, awestruck, and terrified by nature unadorned. Early artists of the sublime, such as Alexander Cozens or Francis Towne, worked largely in watercolours and solved the problem of scale by abstraction—use of broad areas of colour to suggest the vast scope of natural forces—an approach developed by Thomas Girtin and John Sell Cotman.

By the early 19th century, the watercolourist John Varley was echoing current practice when he told his pupils John Linnell, William Mulready, and William Henry Hunt: "Go to nature for everything." But already two outstanding British landscape painters, John Constable and J.M.W. Turner, were going still further. Both men, while admiring the classical landscapes of Claude Lorrain and Poussin, believed that personal feeling was the mainspring of artistic activity and felt an almost mystical sympathy for the natural world. They made atmosphere almost palpable and painted everything from clouds to lichens with astonishing technical diversity. Constable considered himself before all else a "natural" painter and sought, in his own words, to capture "light—dews—breezes—bloom—and freshness" with scientific precision and deepest affection. For Constable, light clarified and enlivened, and his nostalgia for the Suffolk countryside is personal and explicit (Plate 20). With Turner, light increasingly diffused the objects illuminated, and only a more literary expression satisfied his concept of the sublime, drawing him to mountain grandeur, raging seas, storms, and conflagrations (Plate 21). The technical innovations of these two men were better understood in France than in Britain; even John Ruskin's passionate defense of Turner, with its emphasis on absolute fidelity to nature, helped deflect Turner's and Constable's successors onto a very different course.

Constable considered a "natural" painter

George Stubbs's anatomical studies and accurate delineations of animals were echoed a generation later by Thomas Bewick's bird studies, themselves harbingers of the drawings of Edwin Landseer and Ruskin's closely observed renderings of naturalistic detail. Stubbs's empathy for the animal world reemerged in the work of James Ward, together with an exultation in the power of nature, shared by Philip James de Loutherbourg. Demand for information about distant places partially superseded the taste for picturesque European scenes, and following William Hodges, who accompanied Captain James Cook's second voyage (1772–75), such painters as Richard Parkes Bonington, Samuel Prout, John Frederick Lewis, and Edward Lear traveled widely, recording scenes of historic or exotic interest.

In portraiture an interest in extremes of mood found most eloquent expression in the work of Sir Thomas Lawrence, who combined in portraits such as those of Richard Payne Knight (1794; Whitworth Art Gallery, Manchester) and Pope Pius VII (1819; Royal Collection, Windsor Castle) brilliant freedom of handling, at times approaching exhibitionism, with dramatic expression and setting, at times almost melodramatic.

History painting, too, was transformed: Bonington's "Henri III and the English Ambassador" (1827–28; Wallace Collection, London), while testifying to a sustained delight in the medieval world, already betrays commensurate interest in period detail and the finer points of human insight. The authentic, domestic treatment of biblical themes at the hands of William Dyce and the Pre-Raphaelites (see below) contrasts sharply with the earlier apocalyptic fantasies of John Martin and Francis Danby. Inspired by David Wilkie's mellow, unassuming representation of country life subject matter, William Mulready turned to contemporary scenes of daily life, adopting the brilliant palette that distinguished British painting for the next half-century. The high Victorian Age saw much narrative painting, a genre that was practiced with accurate and sympathetic observation, from the panoramic activ-

History painting

ity of William Powell Frith's "Derby Day" (1858; Tate Gallery) to such intimate glimpses of reality as "The Travelling Companions" (1862; City Museum and Art Gallery, Birmingham), by Augustus Egg. Painting as a vehicle for social or moral comment was provided by Sir Luke Fildes and Frank Holl, in whose work a tendency to sentimentality is redeemed by a genuine regard for the sufferings of the poor. In the 1850s the Pre-Raphaelites gave expression to the painting of contemporary life with such memorable images as "The Blind Girl" (1856; City Museum and Art Gallery, Birmingham), by John Everett Millais, or "The Stonebreaker" (1857–58; Walker Art Gallery, Liverpool), by John Brett.

The Pre-Raphaelite movement
The Pre-Raphaelite movement, echoing that of the Nazarenes (a group of religiously minded painters who sought to revive medieval workshop practices; see below), reiterated many earlier Romantic ideals. Literary inspiration and a passion for the Middle Ages were tempered for the Pre-Raphaelites by a moral outlook that recoiled from sophistication and virtuosity and demanded rigorous studies from natural life. These painters handled literary, historical, biblical, and contemporary themes with the same sincerity and fidelity that yielded the sparkling precision of Pre-Raphaelite landscape. Their earnest pursuit of truth, whether in depicting painful social realities or concentrating on the foreground blades of grass in a landscape, entailed a denial of many orthodox artistic pleasures. Together with Ford Madox Brown, the Pre-Raphaelites sustained the devotion to colour and light in painting that underlies the finest endeavours of English Romanticism.

Germany. In Germany also there was a reaction against classicism and the academies, and, as elsewhere, it involved all aspects of the arts. Again, as elsewhere, theory preceded practice: *Herzensergiessungen eines kunstliebenden Klosterbruders* ("Effusions of an Art-Loving Monk"), by Wilhelm Heinrich Wackenroder, had an immediate and widespread influence upon its publication in 1797. Wackenroder advocated a Christian art closely related to the art of the early German masters and provided the artist with a new role as interpreter of divine inspiration through his own feelings.

The painter Philipp Otto Runge had been reared on 17th-century German mysticism, and he proved susceptible to the ideas of writers such as Wackenroder when introduced to them in Dresden at the very end of the 18th century. In Dresden he formed a close association with the leading German landscape painter Caspar David Friedrich (Plate 21). Like Friedrich he was fascinated with the potential symbolic and allegorical power of landscape, which he used as a vehicle for religious expression. His vision of nature was pantheistic (as was Friedrich's), and in his portraits his aim was to capture the soul of the individual as part of the universal soul of nature. "The Artist's Parents and Children" (1806; Hamburger Kunsthalle, Hamburg) reflects not only his constant search for truth but also his admiration for the early German masters, through whose work he was made aware of the expressive power of line and colour. His interest in the German past, including folklore and fairy tales, was reflected in a bizarre fairylike quality in much of his work (*e.g.,* "Night," 1803), and it was this quality that was taken up and popularized by his two most important followers, Moritz von Schwind and Adrian Ludwig Richter, in whose hand the intensity of the first generation declined into popular genre paintings (usually small pictures depicting everyday life, as opposed to some idealized existence) and the comfortable Romanticism of the Biedermeier period (1815–48).

Friedrich was a deeply religious man whose vision demanded complete subjection to the spirit of God in nature; in suggesting through landscape the eternal presence of the Creator, he intended to induce in the beholder a state of religious awe. Among his pupils was Carl Gustav Carus, a physician, philosopher, and self-taught painter, whose chief contribution was as a theorist; *Neun Briefe über Landschaftsmalerei* (1831; "Nine Letters on Landscape Painting") elucidates and expands the ideas of Friedrich, adding Carus' own more-scientific approach to natural phenomena. Also influenced by Friedrich were Ernst Ferdinand Oehme, a landscape painter, and Georg Friedrich Kersting, who captured in his stark interiors something of the master's atmosphere of silent worship. Two other pupils of Friedrich subsequently abandoned tragic landscapes; one, the Norwegian Johan Christian Dahl, reverted to naturalism; the other, Karl Blechen, joined the Romantic realists.

Whereas Runge, Friedrich, and their followers interpreted Wackenroder in a highly personal way, others were inspired to communal activity. A number of young painters in Vienna founded in 1809 a group they called the Guild of St. Luke. The founding members were Johann Friedrich Overbeck (their leader), Franz Pforr, Joseph Wintergerst, Joseph Sutter, and Georg Ludwig Vogel. In 1810 they moved to Rome, where they were soon joined by Peter von Cornelius, Julius Schnorr von Carolsfeld, Friedrich Olivier, the brothers Philipp and Johannes Veit, Wilhelm von Schadow, Johann Evangelist Scheffer von Leonhartshoff, and Josef von Führich. Their semi-monastic existence occasioned the nickname Nazarenes.

The Guild of St. Luke

In general, their highest aspirations—toward monumental history painting—produced the least successful results, and they came closest to realizing their intentions on a small scale in highly finished watercolours and drawings, as in Overbeck's "The Raising of Jairus' Daughter" (1814). Only Joseph Anton Koch and Cornelius, who were both older and more experienced, achieved great vigour in their history paintings, combining medievalizing tendencies with the powerful classicism of Carstens (see above *Neoclassicism: Germany and Austria*), as seen in Cornelius' "The Recognition of Joseph by His Brethren" (1815–16; National Gallery, West Berlin). Even Overbeck, an articulate leader and a lucid draftsman, could not escape, in his "Joseph Being Sold by His Brethren" (1816–17; National Gallery, West Berlin), the self-conscious naïveté common to many of the Nazarenes. This naïveté is also noticeable in Pforr's "The Entry of the Emperor Rudolf of Habsburg into Basel in 1273" (*c.* 1809; Städelsches Kunstinstitut, Frankfurt am Main) and Schnorr's "The Procession of the Three Magi" (1819; Museum of Fine Art, Leipzig). Alfred Rethel, a late arrival, however, manages to avoid such an effect in his haunting "King David with His Harp" (*c.* 1831; Museum of Art, Düsseldorf). Not long afterward there was a move toward the more dramatic, though no less nostalgic, approach of von Schadow and his pupil Karl Friedrich Lessing.

Portraiture required less self-consciousness than history painting, and there are a number of highly sensitive portraits, mainly of their friends, by Overbeck, Schnorr, Scheffer von Leonardshoff, and Carl Philipp Fohr ("Portrait of Wilhelm von Schadow" [1818; Museum of the Palatinate, Heidelberg]). The Nazarenes' greatest contribution, however, was to landscape painting: inspired by the heroic landscapes of Koch (*e.g.,* "Bernese Oberland" [1816; Gallery of Modern Paintings, Staatliche Kunstsammlungen Dresden]), by the German "primitives," and by their own concept of truth to nature, they renounced the conventional Italianate solution and turned instead to the countryside around them and to memories of Germany and German painting. As the movement gathered momentum, the possibilities for development expanded, and the Nazarene landscape was valuable to later painters of the Biedermeier period and to painters of naturalistic landscape, Romantic realism, and secular historical subjects.

France. The French Revolution greatly stimulated interest in the depiction of contemporary events, although richly documented and highly detailed paintings of topical patriotic events were being painted in London by West and John Singleton Copley even before the Revolution. Encouraged by David's example, however, painters in France sought to represent authentically the crucial moments of their own time. Napoleon I enthusiastically endorsed this awareness of modern heroism and demanded pictorial celebration of the glorious achievements of the empire. David recorded the ceremonies of the imperial court with scrupulous precision. Napoleon's potent hold on the artistic imagination is well illustrated by Gros's "Napoleon Visiting the Pesthouse at Jaffa" (1804; Louvre), where he

Depiction of contemporary events

is endowed with godlike authority and the humanitarian sensibility of the true Romantic hero. At the same time, other artists—such as Gérard, Girodet-Trioson, and Ingres—readily responded to the Emperor's admiration for the stories of Ossian. After the fall of Napoleon few were disposed to depict contemporary subjects. Théodore Géricault was something of an exception, but he was separated from his immediate predecessors both by temperament and by the sincerity of his approach. Individual suffering rather than collective drama is vividly portrayed in "The Raft of the Medusa" (c. 1819; Louvre; Plate 21). This, Géricault's masterpiece, echoes in its strenuous forms the school of Caravaggio in the 17th century. His studies of the poor, aged, and insane are realistically observed and have a sympathetic intensity unmatched before the generation of Honoré Daumier and Gustave Courbet.

The paintings of Delacroix frequently disrupted the salons of the 1820s and '30s with their tumultuous colour and emotive energy. To many young men after 1815, France appeared to settle into a bourgeois respectability that implicitly disparaged the exhilarating years of the republic and the empire. In consequence, the art of the period often seems melancholic and introverted, the discontent expressing itself in historical and exotic themes or in a passionate concern with the humble and rejected members of society. Delacroix has justly been acclaimed the leader of the Romantic school in France. His fertile imagination, embracing a novel range of literary and historical themes and fastening with a characteristic sense of the sadness of life on moments of death, defeat, and suffering, together with his prodigious technical resources exemplify Romanticism in its most obvious aspects. His vigorous handling of paint and expert use of colour values for both description and expression were important for the later development of French painting. "The Massacre at Chios" (1824; Louvre) transposes contemporary events into a realm of tragic fiction soon established unrestrainedly with such melodramatic works as "The Death of Sardanapalus" (1827; Louvre), a riot of brilliant colour and ebullient forms (Plate 20).

Exoticism
of setting Delacroix's Moroccan paintings released a flood of North African subjects, although, in the hands of lesser artists—such as Eugène Fromentin, Ary Scheffer, and Eugène Devéria—the treatment is less effective. Alexandre-Gabriel Decamps, whose small canvases have a delicate, jewellike quality, provided the most refreshing variations on the theme. But Delacroix was not the first to handle Oriental subjects; Ingres had already done so with a reticence that belies the sensuous delight in "Valpinçon Bather" (1808; Louvre; Plate 19) and in "La Grande Odalisque" (1814; Louvre). Early in his career Ingres made notable contributions to the historical genre with episodes from medieval French history painted in a style of linear purity that parallels the methods of Flaxman and Blake in Britain and the Nazarenes in Germany. Under the spell of Raphael he returned to the academic fold, but his portraits always retained that trenchant simplicity and lucid insight that make him such a memorable exponent of lyric realism. The career of Ingres and in a converse sense that of Paul Delaroche well illustrate the imprudence of too readily distinguishing between academic and Romantic artists. Delaroche, perhaps the most popular representative of the Romantic school, specialized in highly charged narratives with royal and child characters, of which "The Children of Edward" (c. 1830; Louvre) is a typical example, being executed with a flatness that lacks either linear or colouristic inspiration. In comparison, the work of Théodore Chassériau is animated by powerful emotional overtones reminiscent of Delacroix. "The Cossack Girl Finding the Body of Mazeppa" (1851; Museum of Fine Art, Strasbourg) shows a similarly expressive use of paint, together with poignant imagery, both characteristic of his regrettably slender oeuvre. At the end of the century, Gustave Moreau and Odilon Redon transformed these features, along with others in Louis Boulanger's work, into whimsical, haunting fantasies that delighted the Symbolist poets.

In the 1830s and '40s it was Honoré Daumier, more than any other artist, who portrayed relatively lowly members of society, expressing in numerous drawings and paint-ings their patient resignation (Plate 20). In contrast, his truly excoriating depiction of the weaknesses and vices of the privileged classes, particularly officialdom, often displeased authority, which had long identified Romanticism with liberalism—and with good reason. A strain of poetic realism in the 1840s, essentially Romantic in approach, gathered sudden momentum with the Revolution and short-lived republic of 1848. Jean-François Millet and Gustave Courbet depicted peasant life, investing it with a certain timeless quality. Courbet's "Stone-Breakers" (1849; destroyed during World War II) and Millet's harrowing "Quarriers" (c. 1847; Toledo Museum of Art, Ohio) powerfully express their creators' concern for the poor. Courbet created a sombre monument to his own village in "Burial at Ornans" (1849; Louvre), and Millet succeeded in conferring an epic grandeur on scenes of rural life. Strain of
poetic
realism

A new approach to the familiar and unsophisticated occurs in the landscape painting of the 1830s and '40s; for, although French Romanticism produced no Turner, it did give rise to the Barbizon school, a group of naturalist painters who were particularly active in the forest of Fontainebleau. In this period the charm of the spontaneous sketch as opposed to the finished study was recognized: painters readily set up their easels in the open air and scrutinized the scene before them. A direct approach to nature and an interest in transitory moments, especially the changing effects of light, were features common to Romantic landscape painters throughout Europe and the United States. Paul Huet, a friend of Delacroix and Bonington and a painter closely associated with the Romantic school, represented dramatic, stormy scenes of solitude; yet, though scarcely a naturalist, he was deeply impressed by the works of Constable, several of which he copied and which inspired him to adopt a broken style of brushwork with dabs of bright pigment. The changed attitude to landscape is aptly expressed in the words of Théodore Rousseau, the most controversial representative of the new school: "Our art can only attain pathos through sincerity." Rousseau attempted to render nature as he found it, though his melancholic temperament is inevitably reflected in the desolate panoramas and gloomy sunsets in which he expressed an almost pantheistic feeling for the natural world. At the same time, his close attention to detail and painstaking accuracy in the delineation of plants and grasses betray the scientific concern shared by many Romantic artists. A similar penetration informed his studies of light, and both he and Charles-François Daubigny repeated virtually the same subjects under different weather conditions in order to capture the ephemeral effects of light and atmosphere. The freedom and freshness of Constable's handling is echoed in Daubigny's flickering treatment of sunset and light over water. A particularly poetic insight into nature was that of Narcisse-Virgile Diaz de La Peña and Constant Troyon. The work of Camille Corot, despite the restrained classicism of his style, is similarly enlivened by an instinctive feeling for naturalistic landscape (Plate 20). For, while they laid the foundation for the painterly revolution of the Impressionists, the Barbizon painters always retained the generous appreciation of natural beauty and emotional involvement with their subject that everywhere distinguish the Romantic temperament. Barbizon
school

United States. American Romantic painters were largely influenced by trends in late 18th-century Europe, especially Britain, but the absence of an indigenous artistic tradition permitted a much more intuitive development. At the same time, their work, like that of the early French Romantics, is closely associated with the new spirit fostered by a national revolution. The American Revolution, by reinforcing the democratic ideal, inspired a unique brand of Romantic realism that was a strong force in American painting from the late 18th century onward and that anticipated the emergence in Europe by a whole generation. Benjamin West, in addition to his contribution to Neoclassicism, developed a style of narrative painting with dramatic subjects taken from contemporary life; while he painted his most significant work in Britain, it was on American rather than English artists that it made the most impact. John Trumbull undertook a series of 12 scenes Influence
of the
American
Revolution
on
Romantic
realism from the American Revolution, in which careful studies of the principal participants were incorporated into colourful, baroque compositions. At their best, these works, for example "Sortie from Gibraltar" (1789; Museum of Fine Arts, Boston), carry great conviction, even if they tend to be somewhat theatrical. In 1784 one of the most candid portraitists of the period, Charles Willson Peale, completed a similarly ambitious project in his paintings of the leading figures of the Revolution. A more limited enthusiasm for precise naturalistic study informs the work of Alexander Wilson, whose devoted love of birds emerges in the freshness and simplicity of the plates to his *American Ornithology* (9 volumes; 1808–14). His achievement has been overshadowed by his greater successor, John James Audubon, who combined scientific precision with a delight in his specimens that transforms his watercolour drawings of birds into works of rare and delicate beauty.

Develop-
ment of an
American
style of
portraiture
At the beginning of the Romantic period, artists were still influenced by British painting, but this influence grew less and less perceptible as the 19th century progressed. For instance, the portrait of "Colonel Thomas Handasyd Perkins" (1831–32; Boston Athenaeum), by Thomas Sully, the leading exponent of a new portraiture supposedly expressive of mood, has touches of Sir Thomas Lawrence in the delicately brushed surface, strong contrasts of light and dark, and exquisite elegance of pose. But though Samuel F.B. Morse, Samuel Waldo, William Page, and others also practiced an emotive style, portraits of the 19th century increasingly tended to endorse the native tradition of solid characterization.

The career of the landscape painter Washington Allston reflects the development of American painting in his lifetime. Absorbed by German and English Romantic poetry, he began on a note of high drama, moving in cosmopolitan artistic circles in Rome and producing a number of early landscapes that seem to have played a part in winning the friendship of the English Romantic poet Samuel Taylor Coleridge. At this point, what was obviously an impetuous and brooding strain in Allston's temperament found expression by depicting nature in the darker, more destructive moods dear to Turner. "The Deluge" (1804; Metropolitan Museum of Art, New York City) is a typical macabre invention, with bodies in a raging tempest swept ashore to where wolves and serpents lurk. On his return to the United States, however, his work assumed a quieter, more pensive aspect. "The Flight of Florimell" (1819; Detroit Institute of Arts) illustrates this later style.

An uncomplicated love for their own natural scenery emerges in the work of a succession of landscape painters who frequently strike a contemplative, lyrical note. Thomas Cole reverently recorded scenes in the valley of the Hudson River that echo the loneliness and mystery of the North American forests. With his generous humanitarian sympathies, Asher B. Durand gave a serene and artless account of nature. His feeling for space and finely diffused light renders "Kindred Spirits" (1849; New York Public Library) a touching tribute to the friendship of Cole with the American Romantic poet William Cullen Bryant. An interest in light and atmosphere was shared by George Loring Brown, FitzHugh Lane, Frederick Edwin Church, and George Harvey; all followed Durand and painted in the open. Simplicity and reticence distinguish the landscapes of Thomas Doughty, who concentrated on painting the Hudson River valley as he knew and loved it. The details of country life that fill the stories of Washington Irving are portrayed with affection by William Sidney Mount, who in "Eel Spearing at Setanket" (1845; New York State Historical Association, New York City) transcends the merely anecdotal. George Caleb Bingham approached the life of

Painters of
the frontier
the frontier without the passionate concern that motivated many contemporary French artists. Solemn and severe in style and glowing with colour, his "Fur Traders Descending the Missouri" (c. 1845; Metropolitan Museum of Art) captures the silence and solitary grandeur of frontier life. The wildness of the frontier caught the imagination of many 19th-century artists: George Catlin, Seth Eastman, John M. Stanley, Alfred Jacob Miller, and Karl Bodmer all discovered a picturesque drama and excitement in Indian life. The Romantic period witnessed the emergence

of a truly national school of painting in the United States, where events and scenery provided a constant source of stimulation for artists content to distill their own poetry from the world around them.   (S.E.B./Ed.)

Russia.   Napoleon's invasion of Russia (1812) had far-reaching consequences. It marked the revival of national consciousness and the beginning of a widespread cult of Russian separateness from Europe, thus precipitating the long controversy between "Westerners" and "Slavophiles" that ran through so much of Russian 19th-century literature and thought. At the same time, Russia shared in the Romanticism that during the era of the Napoleonic Wars gripped Europe in the shape of France and Germany. This is reflected in the paintings of Orest Kiprensky and Vasily Tropinin. The most notable contribution to the Romantic spirit, however, was made by Karl Pavlovich Bryullov, with his monumental painting "The Last Days of Pompeii" (1830–33; State Russian Museum, Leningrad). A completely different trend appears in the work of Aleksandr Ivanov, the first Russian painter to express religious emotions in a western European manner. Other outstanding artists of that period were Aleksey Venetsianov and Pavel Fedotov, the forerunners of Realist painting in Russia.

The second half of the 19th century saw the maturing of Realism in Russia. A sympathetic attitude toward the hard life of the people is reflected in the works of most of the painters and sculptors of that time. The new trend in art had as its basis the populist revolutionary ferment prevalent toward the end of the 1850s and the beginning of the 1860s, much of it inspired by the writers Nikolay Dobrolyubov and Nikolay Chernyshevsky. Chernyshevsky's dissertation *Esteticheskiye otnosheniya iskusstva k deystvitelnosti* (1855; "The Aesthetic Relations of Art to Reality"), the main thesis of which was that art must not only reflect reality but also explain and judge it, provided a starting point for contemporary artists.

From the last third of the 19th century onward, the history of Russian art is the history of a series of school struggles: the Slavophiles against the Westerners; the Academy against the Peredvizhniki ("Wanderers"); and later the joint effort of the last two against a new movement, born in the 1890s and directed by the art review *Mir Iskusstva* ("The World of Art").

The Pere-
dvizhniki
society
The Peredvizhniki was a society formed in 1870 by a group of essentially Romantic artists who, however, regarded themselves as Realists. They seceded from the Academy in 1863 in protest against alien dogmatic formulas and the constricting programs of the Academy's annual competitions. Most prominent among the Peredvizhniki were Ivan Kramskoy, Ilya Repin, Vasily Ivanovich Surikov, Vasily Perov, and Vasily Vereshchagin. The society attached far more importance to the moral and literary aspects of art than to aesthetics. Its artistic creed was realism, national feeling, and social consciousness. Art was to be placed at the service of humanitarian and social ideals; it was to be brought to the people. Accordingly the society organized mobile (*peredvizheniye*) exhibitions—hence the name.

The influence of the Peredvizhniki spread throughout Russia and was dominant for nearly 30 years. But, by the end of the century it had greatly declined.   (A.Vo./Ed.)

Modern

The term modern art has come to denote the innovating and even revolutionary developments in Western painting and the other visual arts since the second half of the 19th century. It embraces a wide variety of movements, styles, theories, and attitudes, the modernity of which resides in a common tendency to repudiate past conventions and precedents in subject matter, mode of depiction, and painting technique alike. Not all the painting of this period has made such a departure; representational work, for example, has continued to appear, particularly in connection with official exhibiting societies. Nevertheless, the idea that some current types of painting are more properly of their time than others, and for that reason are more interesting or important, applies with particular force to the painting of the last 150 years.

By the mid-19th century, painting was no longer basically in service to either the church or the court but rather was patronized by the upper and middle classes of an increasingly materialistic and secularized Western society. This society was undergoing rapid change due to the growth of science and technology, industrialization, urbanization, and the fundamental questioning of received religious dogmas. Painters were thus confronted with the need to reject traditional, historical, or academic forms and conventions in an effort to create an art that would better reflect the changed social, material, and intellectual conditions of emerging modern life. Another important, if indirect, stimulus to change was the development from the early 19th century on of photography and other photomechanical techniques, which freed (or deprived) painting and drawing of their hitherto cardinal roles as the only available means of accurately depicting the visual world. These manually executed arts were thus no longer obliged to serve as the means of recording and disseminating information that they once had been and were eventually freed to explore aesthetically the basic visual elements of line, colour, tone, and composition in a nonrepresentational context. Indeed, an important trend in modern painting has been that of abstraction—*i.e.,* painting in which little or no attempt is made to accurately depict the appearance or form of objects in the realm of nature or the existing physical world. The door of the objective world was thus closed, but the inner world of the imagination offered seemingly infinite possibilities for exploration, as did the manipulation of pigments on a flat surface for their purely intrinsic visual or aesthetic appeal.

The beginnings of modern painting cannot be clearly demarcated, but it is generally agreed that it started in mid-19th-century France. The paintings of Gustav Courbet, Edouard Manet, and the Impressionists represent a deepening rejection of the prevailing academic traditions of Neoclassicism and Romanticism and a quest for a more truthful naturalistic representation of the visual world. These painters' Postimpressionist successors—notably Paul Cézanne, Vincent van Gogh, Edgar Degas, and Paul Gauguin—can be viewed as more clearly modern in their repudiation of traditional subject matter and techniques and in their assumption of a more subjective and personal vision. From about the 1890s a succession of varied styles and movements arose that are the core of modern painting and are also one of the high points of the history of the Western visual arts in general. These modern movements include Neo-Impressionism, Symbolism, the Nabis, Fauvism, Cubism, Expressionism, Futurism, the Ashcan School, Suprematism, Constructivism, Orphism, Metaphysical painting, de Stijl, Purism, Dada, Surrealism, Social Realism, Abstract Expressionism, Pop Art, Op Art, Minimalism, and Neo-Expressionism.   (F.W.W.-S./Ed.)

ORIGINS IN THE 19TH CENTURY

As long ago as 1846 the qualities proper to a specifically modern art were discussed by the French writer Charles Baudelaire in an essay on the French Salon. He argued that colour would be foremost among these modern qualities (a prediction that subsequent events confirmed), but he still saw the new art in the context of the Romantic movement. Subsequent modernity came to be seen as necessitating not only a new style but also contemporary subject matter, and in 1863 Baudelaire praised the draftsman Constantin Guys as "le peintre de la vie moderne" ("the painter of modern life"). In 1862, with Baudelaire's support, the French painter Édouard Manet brought together a subject from contemporary social life and an unconventional style in "Concert in the Tuileries Gardens" (National Gallery, London). This painting, though rather isolated in his work of the time, was influential in establishing a new outlook. Another literary figure whose critical writings were influential was the French novelist Émile Zola, though Zola had limited sympathy for what he called the "new manner in painting" of Manet; nevertheless he contributed from 1866 onward to the emergence of the Impressionist group. The first appearance of the phrase "modern art" in the relatively permanent form of a book title was in 1883, when it was used by the French

writer Joris-Karl Huysmans, a friend of Zola's, to describe the theme of various reviews of painters' work he had collected. Other books on the subject followed, such as the Anglo-Irish novelist George Moore's *Modern Painting* (1893). It was about this time that the term avant-garde was introduced by the critic Théodore Duret, who used it of certain young painters. From then on, modernity was to be a recurrent concern of artists and critics. Public acceptance of the new standpoint was slow, however. The first museums dedicated specifically to modern art grew out of the fervour of individual collectors—*e.g.,* the Folkwang Museum at Essen, W.Ger., and the Kröller-Müller State Museum at Otterlo, Neth., both largely consisting of collections built up before 1914. The Museum of Modern Art in New York City, the outstanding public collection in the field, was founded in 1929, and the Western capital that lacks a museum explicitly devoted to modern art is rare.

The conflict between the new forces and the established academic tradition in France came into the open in 1863. The jury of the official Salon, which had long exercised great despotism in matters to do with painting, rejected more than 4,000 canvases—an unusually high figure. The resulting outcry prompted the emperor Napoleon III to order that the rejected works, if the painters agreed, be shown in a special exhibition known as the Salon des Refusés. The exhibition included works by Manet; Johan Barthold Jongkind, an older Dutch painter who was working in a tonal and summary style from nature; Camille Pissarro and Paul Cézanne, who had met two years before at the Académie Suisse; Armand Guillaumin; James McNeill Whistler; and others. One of the greatest scandals was caused by Manet's painting "The Luncheon on the Grass" (Louvre, Paris), which was considered an affront to decency as well as taste. The younger painters became aware of their common aims. Claude Monet, whose landscape style had been influenced from the outset by the atmospheric sketches of the Channel coast of Eugène Boudin, as well as by Jongkind (whom he described to Boudin, as "quite mad"), had met Pierre-Auguste Renoir, Alfred Sisley, and Jean-Frédéric Bazille studying in the studio of Charles Gleyre. Abandoning academic study, they worked together outdoors in the forest of Fontainebleau, where contacts with the Barbizon painters Narcisse-Virgile Diaz de La Peña and Charles-François Daubigny strengthened their direction.

The implicit acceptance of the visual scene on which the new style was based owed something to the example of Courbet, who influenced Renoir in particular in the next few years. The plein air ("open-air") paintings of the Barbizon painters also had an effect, but the suggestion of an art based on the notation of pure colour was suggested by several sources. The example of Eugène Delacroix had a deep significance for the 19th century in France, and the reliance on separate, undisguised touches of the brush in the form that became characteristic of Impressionism is perhaps first apparent in sketches of the sea at Dieppe painted by Delacroix in 1852. The economy of Manet's touch in the 1860s was affected by Spanish and Dutch examples as well as by Delacroix, but his seascapes and racecourse pictures of 1864 are also important. The full Impressionistic style did not develop until the end of the 1860s.

Though the figurative aims of Impressionism can be regarded as the conclusion of 19th-century Realism, the method, which made no attempt to hide even the most basic means of preparing a finished painting, was an original one. Brushstrokes did not pretend to be anything but dashes of paint, thus conveying their coloured message without any disguise or effect at individual illusion. It was in this respect and in the all-embracing unity of colour and handling that resulted, rather than its realism, that Impressionism founded modern painting. Other developments in the 1860s had no immediate sequels in Impressionism. The presentation of some of Manet's figures, such as "The Fifer" (Louvre) of 1866, as vignettes or decorative designs shading into virtually blank backgrounds was a radical departure from the coherent pictorial construction of Western tradition since the Renaissance; it is the first

[margin notes:]

Salon des Refusés

Influences on the development of the new style

Unconventional principles of design

sign of the form built outward from a central nucleus without reference to the classic frame that has appeared repeatedly in modern art. Honoré Daumier is supposed to have said that "The Fifer" reduced painting "to faces on playing cards," and in 1865 Courbet compared Manet's "Olympia" (1863; Louvre) to "the Queen of Spades after a bath." The possibility of making an image out of the bare, almost heraldic juxtaposition of flat colours was neglected while the complex notation of Impressionism held sway, but it came to be regarded with interest as Impressionism receded. Other unconventional principles of design—suggested equally by Japanese prints, such as those that Manet placed in the background of his portrait of Zola (Louvre) in 1868, and by the chance arrangements of photography—appeared in the work of Edgar Degas, who sympathized with the aims of the new group, associating himself with them in seven of their eight exhibitions, which he largely helped to organize.

Other qualities that Baudelaire in 1846 had specified as the qualities of modern art—spirituality and aspiration toward the infinite—evolved quite apart from Impressionism. The visionary implications of Romantic painting were explored by Gustave Moreau, whose elaborate biblical and mythological scenes, weighed down with sumptuous detail, gave colour an imaginative and symbolic richness. His example had a special value to the next generation. The imagination of Pierre Puvis de Chavannes was of the opposite order, preserving the large-scale clarity of mural painting, a policy that made him appreciated when a reaction against Impressionism set in.

Another possibility of Romanticism was pursued in isolation by the Marseille painter Adolphe Monticelli. The richness of his colour is thought to have contributed something crucial to Cézanne's development. The counterpart of Moreau in Britain was Sir Edward Burne-Jones. The intricate and perverse linear formulations that he developed from the Pre-Raphaelites greatly influenced the international Symbolist style of the last decades of the century.

Early developments in Britain and Germany

The influence of the trend in the direction of the modern in France, together with its controversial element, was introduced to Britain by Whistler, whose concern was narrowly aesthetic rather than analytic. The harmonies he developed were close to being monochromatic; his use of Spanish and Japanese elements had little of the radical originality of Manet and Degas. His influence dominated and also limited the development of avant-garde painting in Britain for many years. John Singer Sargent, like Whistler an American who came to live in Britain, popularized a less-discriminating version of the Impressionistic style.

In Germany a Romantic strain coexisted with a Realistic style that remained unaffected by the most advanced French painting. Anselm Feuerbach, one of the Romantics, was influenced by Delacroix. In 1855 he went to Italy where the effect of the 16th century came to predominate in his work. The landscapes of Hans von Marées were also essentially Romantic. He had visited France but spent most of his working life in Italy; the frescoes he executed in Naples echo Puvis de Chavannes in their style. Realism found exponents in Wilhelm Leibl and Hans Thoma. In Italy the reaction against the academies was centred in Florence, where a group known as the Macchiaioli (from *macchia,* "patch") worked from 1855, producing landscapes, genre paintings, and Romantic costume pieces executed in the highly visible brushstrokes that gave the group its name.

The beginning of modern art in the United States

In the United States, Thomas Eakins developed a broadly handled, powerful Realist style that became almost Expressionistic in his later years (Plate 21). He had visited Paris in 1866, and the influence of Manet can be detected in his paintings. His interest in anatomy and perspective gave him a role analogous to that of Degas. The early development of Winslow Homer, who was in France a year later, ran parallel to Monet's style in the 1860s. The work of Albert Pinkham Ryder was, by contrast, introverted and visionary. He was among the artists who adapted the Romantic vocabulary to the symbolic purposes of modern art.

In France in the mid-1860s Monet produced a series of large-scale open-air conversation pieces in which elements derived from Courbet and Manet were fused with a wholly original expression of dappled light in solid paint. The approach of Pissarro, who had arrived in Paris from the West Indies in 1855, was more delicate; influenced by Camille Corot as well as Courbet, he recorded pure landscape motives in a limited range of tones, though with a natural lyricism of feeling. The starting point of Cézanne was, by contrast, vigorous to the point of violence. In 1866 he evolved a style in which paint was applied in thick dabs with a palette knife; this combined a handling (a technical term in painting meaning the individual's manipulation of materials in the execution of a work; it has been likened to a person's signature in handwriting) derived from Courbet with the gray tonality of Manet; its rough-hewn crudity has a consistency that was essentially new. His alternative style in the 1860s, with curling brushstrokes related to Daumier, is equally virile and was often applied to subjects of violent eroticism. The unbridled force of Cézanne's early work gave the first sign of qualities that were to become characteristic of modern painting. Though exceptional, it was not unique; in Italy during the 1860s the Russian painter of historical and scriptural themes, Nikolay Nikolayevich Ge, produced sketches with loose, expressive brushwork sometimes resembling Cézanne's.

The prelude to French Impressionism

Impressionism. The first steps toward a systematic Impressionist style were taken in France in Monet's coast scenes from 1866 onward, notably the "Terrace" (1866; Metropolitan Museum of Art, New York City), in which he chose a subject that allowed use of a full palette of primary colour. The decisive development took place in 1869, when Monet and Renoir painted together at the resort of La Grenouillère on the Seine River. The resulting pictures suggest that Monet contributed the pattern of separate brushstrokes, the light tonality, and the brilliance of colour; Renoir the overall iridescence, feathery lightness of touch, and delight in the recreation of ordinary people. Working at Louveciennes from 1869, Pissarro evolved the drier and more flexible handling of crumbly paint that was also to be a common feature of Impressionist painting.

It was in the environs of Paris after the Franco-Prussian War that there developed the fully formed landscape style that remains the most popular achievement of modern painting. An exhibition held in the studio of the photographer Nadar (Gaspard-Félix Tournachon) in 1874 included Monet's picture "Impression: Sunrise" (Marmottan Museum, Paris; Plate 23), and it was this work that, by being disparaged as mere "impressionism," gave a name to an entire movement. The exhibition itself revealed three main trends. The Parisian circle around Monet and Renoir had developed the evanescent and sketchlike style the furthest. The vision of those working near Pissarro in Pontoise and Auvers was in general more solid, being firmly rooted in country scenes. A relatively urbane, genrelike trend was detectable in Degas's picture of Paul Valpinçon and his family at the races called "Carriage at the Races" (1870–73; Museum of Fine Arts, Boston) and Berthe Morisot's "The Cradle" (1873; Louvre). Manet himself was absent, hoping for academic success; his "Gare Saint-Lazare" (1873; National Gallery of Art, Washington, D.C.), influenced by the Impressionist palette, was accepted at the Salon. Modeling himself on Pissarro, Cézanne sublimated the turbulent emotions of his earlier work in pictures that were studied directly and closely from nature; he followed the method for the rest of his life.

The first Impressionist exhibition

The experiment of an independent exhibition was repeated in 1876, though with fewer participants. Monet now began to make studies of the Gare Saint-Lazare. Renoir used effects of dappled light and shadow to explore genre subjects such as "Le Moulin de la galette" (1876; Louvre; Plate 23). In 1877 only 18 artists exhibited. The major painters began to go their separate ways, particularly as there were disputes about whether to continue with the independent exhibitions. Cézanne, who did not exhibit with the Impressionists again, was perhaps the first to realize that a critical stage had been reached. For the first time, a style had been based on the openly individual character of a technique rather than on the form of a particular subject or the way it was formulated. A style that admits to painting as being only a matter of paint raises in a peculiarly acute form the question of how far the qualities of art are intrinsic. Impressionism in the 1870s was inseparable from heightened visual experience of a sensuously satisfying world. But the blocklike shapes in Cézanne's pictures, such as the portrait of his patron Victor Chocquet (c. 1877; Columbus Museum of Art, Ohio), suggest that for him the relationship between the colour patches on his canvas was equally important. In the years that followed, he systematized his technique into patterns of parallel brushstrokes that gave a new significance to the pictorial surface. An unassuming series of still lifes and self-portraits by Cézanne were painted in 1879–80, and these, when they became known, profoundly impressed the younger generation, who reckoned them to be as monumental as the great art of the past, yet in a subtly different way that was inherent in the actual manner of painting.

The style of the 1870s was formless from a traditional standpoint, and at the beginning of the next decade Renoir decided that he had gone to the limit with Impressionism and "did not know either how to paint or draw." Following a trip to Italy, he set about acquiring a wiry, linear style that was the direct opposite of his relaxed, freely brushed manner of earlier years.

The appearance of a new generation posed a fresh challenge. Georges Seurat was moving away from the empirical standpoint of Impressionism toward a technique (Pointillism) and a form that were increasingly deliberately designed. Paul Gauguin, taking his starting point from Cézanne's style of about 1880, passed from a capricious personal type of Impressionism to a greater use of symbols. He exhibited with the Impressionists from 1880 onward, but it was soon evident that group shows could no longer accommodate the growing diversity. In 1884, after the Salon jury had been particularly harsh, the Société des Artistes Indépendants was formed. The last The last Impressionist exhibition Impressionist group show was held in 1886. Only Monet and Armand Guillaumin, to whose efforts the group owed much of its eventual recognition, were now in the strict sense Impressionists. Monet, who had exhibited only once since 1879, continued to build on the original foundation of the style, the rendering of visual impression through colour in paintings that studied a single motif in varying lights. For him the formlessness and the homogeneity of Impressionism were its ultimate virtues. In his last series of "Water Lilies," painted between 1906 and 1926, the shimmering of light eventually lost its last descriptive content, and only the colour and curling movement of his brush carried a general all-pervading reference to the visual world. Renoir's later work was equally expansive; his sympathetic vision of humanity revealed its own inherent breadth and grandeur.

Impressionism, in one aspect, continued the main direction of 19th-century painting, and after 1880 the movement was an international one, taking on independent national characteristics. Russia produced an exponent in Isaak Ilich Levitan, and Scotland one in William MacTaggart. In Italy Telemarco Signorini and in the United States such painters as Childe Hassam developed modified forms of the style. In France, and to some extent in Germany with Max Liebermann, Impressionism provided a basis for the styles that followed.

Symbolism. During the decades before 1900, the Symbolists were the avant-garde, and one of quite a new kind, influencing not only the arts but also the thought and spirit of the epoch. Maurice Denis, their theoretician, enunciated in 1890 the most famous of their artistic principles:

Remember that a picture—before being a war-horse, a nude or an anecdote of some sort—is essentially a flat surface covered with colours assembled in a certain order.

The Nabis Such ideas inspired a group of young painters, among whom was Denis himself, to call themselves Nabis (from the Hebrew word for "prophet"). They were in revolt against the faithfulness to nature of Impressionism; in addition, largely because they were in close touch with Symbolist writers, they regarded choice of subject as important. They included Paul Ranson, who gave the style a decorative and linear inflection; Pierre Bonnard; and Édouard Vuillard.

Other than the Nabis, one of the chief Symbolists was Odilon Redon, who moved from the same starting point as the Impressionists—the landscape style of the Barbizon school—but in precisely the opposite direction. Redon's visionary charcoal drawings (which he called his black pictures) led to successive series of lithographs that explored the evocative, irrational, and fantastic orders of creation that Impressionism excluded. Redon later wrote:

Nothing in art can be done by will alone. Everything is done by docile submission to the coming of the unconscious . . . for every act of creation, the unconscious sets us a different problem.

Redon established one of the characteristic standpoints of modern art, and his influence on the younger Symbolists was profound. In 1888 Gauguin, already affected by a trip to Martinique, settled at Pont-Aven in Brittany. The influential style he developed there was based on the juxtaposition of flat areas of colours enclosed by black contours, the total effect suggesting cloisonné enamel (a technique in which metal strips differentiate the colour areas of the design, thereby creating an outline effect), hence the name Cloisonnisme used to describe this style. Cloisonnisme The spirit in which Gauguin rendered Breton scenes was mystical. He wrote:

Do not copy nature too much. Art is an abstraction; derive this abstraction from nature while dreaming before it, but think more of creating than of the actual result.

At Pont-Aven, Gauguin was joined by Émile Bernard and Louis Anquetin, who had lately begun to work in a similar way. Paul Sérusier painted under Gauguin's direction a little sketch entitled "Bois d'amour" that appeared more independent of appearances and bolder in its synthesis of pattern than anything that had been seen before; it became known in Paris as "The Talisman." The liberation of Synthetism, as the new style was called, indeed worked like a charm, and after the Café Volpini exhibition of 1889 it spread rapidly. The movement was linked with literature and, in particular, with drama; it inspired its own periodical, *La Revue Blanche,* and Le Théâtre de l'Oeuvre (both founded in Paris in 1891); there were exhibitions twice a year at a Paris gallery, Le Barc de Boutteville, from 1891 to 1897.

The decorative style known as Art Nouveau, or Jugendstil, spread across Europe and the Americas in the 1890s. The pursuit of natural and organic sources for form still further alienated art from the descriptive purpose that had been the basis of figurative style, and an artistic movement without taint of historicism that molded the fine arts, architecture, and craftsmanship in a single, consistent taste recovered the creative unity that had been lost since the early 18th century. In The Netherlands the fin de siècle ("end of the century"; specifically the end of the 19th century, and a phrase that has overtones of a rather precious sophistication and world-weariness) style and sense of purpose appeared in the paintings of Johan Thorn Prikker and Jan Toorop. The Viennese Gustav Klimt made bolder and more arbitrary use of pattern (Plate 22). In Russia the demonic genius of Mikhail Aleksandrovich Vrubel had points of contact with the Art Nouveau style. It even affected Seurat and his circle, who were known as the Neo-Impressionists; the popular imagery of Seurat's later works, such as "The Circus" (1890–91; Louvre), was expressed in sinuous rhythms not far from Art Nouveau, and the Belgian Henry van de Velde passed from Neo-Impressionism by way of fin de siècle decorations that were near abstraction to a place among the founders of 20th-century architecture. A strange and beautiful blend of Symbolism with an alpine clarity of colour close to Neo-Impressionism appeared in compositions such as "The Unnatural Mothers" by the Italian Giovanni Segantini.

The end of the 19th-century tradition. Until Seurat no painter had expressly founded a style on the intrinsic reactions of colour to colour and a codified vocabulary of expressive forms. The consistent granulation of colour in Seurat's work from 1885 onward was specific to the picture, not to the sensation or the subject (Plate 22). The coherent images of space and light that he made out of this granulation ended with him. Seurat's followers, grouped as Neo-Impressionists under the leadership of Paul Signac,

Neo-
Impres-
sionists

developed his technique rather than his vision. Seurat's influence was nonetheless widespread and fertile; his system in itself supplied a clarity that painters needed. It was Neo-Impressionism that was in the ascendant when the Dutch painter Vincent van Gogh arrived in Paris in 1886. The emotional travail evident in van Gogh's early work was marvelously lightened in the new aesthetic climate. But in his hands the dashes of pure colour turned and twisted, trading invisible and unstable lines of force. They were woven into rhythmical and convulsive patterns reflecting the mounting intensity of his own feelings. Such patterns converted the Neo-Impressionist style into something quite different—a forerunner of what was to be known as Expressionism (Plate 22). Other painters were less radical in their approach. Pissarro assimilated the Neo-Impressionist method to the vision of the older generation; Henri-Edmond Cross and Maximilien Luce gave it the characteristic economy of the age that followed. Henri Matisse's repeated experiments with it, culminating in his contact with Signac and Cross in 1904, finally converted the pure colour of Impressionism to the special purposes of 20th-century art.

In the meantime, the older Impressionists were producing the broadly conceived works that crowned their artistic achievement and formed, as it seems in retrospect, the great traditional masterpieces of modern art. Degas's lifelong absorption in the human body as a subject led him to produce a series of bathing scenes and drawings from the nude in which the form expanded to an amplitude that filled the picture. Fullness of form was an effect that Renoir also achieved. Cézanne announced a determination "to do Poussin over again from nature" and was reckoned to have fulfilled that aim with his "Great Bathers" and the series of landscapes of Mont Sainte-Victoire (Plate 22). In the pictures of Henri de Toulouse-Lautrec, the style and standpoint derived from Degas, but his graphic work reflected the aims of the Symbolist generation. The most original contribution of Édouard Vuillard lay in the evocative patterning of the little pictures that he painted before 1900. The art of Pierre Bonnard, on the other hand, developed throughout his life. His subjects and his method remained, on the surface, those of the Impressionist tradition, but they were re-created from memory and imagination; Bonnard's pictures have the quality of a cherished private order of experience.

Develop-
ments
outside
France

Developments outside France were not of comparable importance. In Britain in the 1880s, Philip Wilson Steer painted a small group of landscapes with figures that were among the earliest and loveliest examples of the fin de siècle style. The work of Walter Sickert revolved around an idiosyncratic fascination with the actual touch of a brush on canvas. His affinities remained essentially with the tonal Impressionism of the earliest stages of the modern movement rather than with the art of colour that developed from it, though he eventually made the transition in old age. In Germany the artists of the Postimpressionist generation, such as Lovis Corinth and Max Slevogt, working with the peculiar recklessness that is endemic to German painting, laid the technical foundations of Expressionism. Ferdinand Hodler in Switzerland developed a painterly Symbolist style in the 1890s. The Belgian painter James Ensor abandoned Impressionism at the end of the 1880s for a bitter and fantastic style that was a pioneer example of extreme expressive alienation.

The most remarkable painter of the fin de siècle outside France, however, was the Norwegian Edvard Munch. "The Cry" (Nasjonalgalleriet, Oslo; Plate 23), the famous picture in which the rhythms of Art Nouveau were given a hysterical expressive force with hardly a vestige of the Impressionist description of nature, was painted in 1893. For many years before a breakdown interrupted his development in 1907, he worked abroad. He was particularly influential in Germany.

In the United States, Maurice Prendergast transformed Impressionism into pattern. In Russia the fin de siècle styles of Léon Bakst and the Mir Iskusstva ("World of Art") group, as well as a vivid revival of folk decoration, flourished, later becoming known internationally through their connection with the Russian ballet.

THE 20TH CENTURY

By 1903 the impetus of Symbolism was expended and a new and enigmatic mood was forming. The new attitude drew on a vein that was comic, poetic, and fantastic, exploring an irrational quality akin to humour inherent in the creative process itself, as well as on a reserve of ironic detachment. The new painters drew strength from unexpected sources. The work of Henri Rousseau, a former clerk in the Paris municipal customs service who was known as "Le Douanier" accordingly, and who had exhibited at the Indépendants since 1886, attracted attention. The apparent innocence of his pictures gave them a kind of imaginative grandeur that seemed beyond the reach of any art founded on sophistication (Plate 25).

The
attraction
of naive
and
"primitive"
painting

The art of supposedly primitive peoples had a special appeal in the early years of the 20th century. Gauguin, who had made direct contact with it in his last years, proved prophetic not only in the forms he adopted but in the spirit of his approach (Plate 23). Maurice de Vlaminck and André Derain, who met in 1900, evolved a style together based on crude statements of strong colours. Matisse had been moving more circumspectly in the same direction (Plate 25). The apparent ferocity of the works that the three exhibited in 1905 earned them the nickname of the Fauves ("Wild Beasts"). It appears that Matisse was responsible for introducing Pablo Picasso to African sculpture. Picasso had already shown signs of dissatisfaction with existing canons; his use of fin de siècle styles in his earliest works has a quality close to irony. Primitive art, both African and Iberian, provided him with an austerity and detachment that led after 1906 to a radical metamorphosis of the image and style hitherto habitual in European art. In 1904 Ernst Ludwig Kirchner, at Dresden, discovered the art of the Pacific Islands as well as African art. His first reflection of the primitive spirit was parallel to that of the Fauves and may have depended on them, if only partially.

The idea of art, first and last, as a matter of expression (in contrast to Impressionism) was common to Germany and France in the first decade of the 20th century; it appears in Matisse's *Notes of a Painter,* published in 1908. Matisse, in fact, hardly differentiated expression from decoration; his ideal of art as "something like a good armchair in which to rest" explicitly excluded the distortion and disquiet that earned the style of Kirchner and Die Brücke ("The Bridge") group, which was founded in 1905, the label of Expressionism. The worldly subjects of Kirchner represented only one aspect of the group; the earthy Primitivism of Emil Nolde and the emphatic pictorial rhetoric of Karl Schmidt-Rottluff are more typical. Both Nolde and Max Pechstein (another member of the group) traveled to the Pacific. The development of the Austrian Oskar Kokoschka, who was influenced by members of Die Brücke, spanned the first two-thirds of the 20th century; the tempestuous emotion of his finest pictures places them among the masterpieces of painting of the German-speaking world in his time.

Concept
of art as
expres-
sion

The transformation of painting after 1907 was particularly apparent in works executed in Germany. Wassily Kandinsky had come to Munich from Moscow at the age of 30 in 1896. His earliest mature works were painted in a jewellike, fairy-tale Cloisonniste style. He later told how one evening in his studio he came upon "an indescribably beautiful picture, drenched with an inner glowing . . . of which I saw nothing but forms and colours . . ." (from R.L. Herbert [ed.], *Modern Artists on Art,* 1965). It was one of his own works, standing on its side, so that its content was incomprehensible. Kandinsky's first nonfigurative watercolour was painted in 1910, and in the same year he wrote much of *Concerning the Spiritual in Art,* which converted the aesthetic doctrines of Goethe to the purposes of the new art. The series of "Improvisations" that followed preserved reminiscences of figuration, made illegible by the looseness of the pictorial structure; their diffuse and amorphous consistency had little connection with the main objectives of painting at the time (Plate 24). In the first decade of the 20th century, the idea of painting implied by Postimpressionism and that of a reasoned structure analogous to the structure of nature, if not to

Develop-
ment
of non-
figurative
painting

"Aurora," ceiling fresco by Guido Reni,
1613–14. In the Casino Rospigliosi, Rome.

Baroque painting in Italy

"View of the Lagoon," oil painting by
Francesco Guardi (1712–93). In the Museo
di Castelvecchio, Verona, Italy. 33 × 51 cm.

"The Conversion of St. Paul," oil painting by Caravaggio
(1573–1610). In Sta. Maria del Popolo, Rome. 2.3 × 1.8 m.

"The Triumph of the Name of Jesus," ceiling fresco by
Giovanni Battista Gaulli (Baciccia), 1674–79. In the Gesù,
Rome.

Plate 14   Painting, The History of Western

"Young Woman with a Water Jug," oil painting by Jan Vermeer, c. 1658–60. In the Metropolitan Museum of Art, New York City. 46 × 41 cm.

" Still Life," oil on wood by Willem Claesz Heda, 1634. In the Museum Boymans-van Beuningen, Rotterdam. 43 × 57 cm.

"The Rape of the Daughters of Leucippus," oil painting by Peter Paul Rubens, 1617. In the Alte Pinakothek, Munich. 2.2 × 2.1 m.

"The Smokers," oil on wood by Adriaen Brouwer, c. 1630. In the Metropolitan Museum of Art, New York City. 46 × 38 cm.

"Waterfall," oil painting by Jacob van Ruisdael, c. 1670? In the Uffizi, Florence. 52.3 × 61.7 cm.

"Calling of St. Matthew," oil painting by Hendrik Terbrugghen, c. 1617. In the Centraal Museum, Utrecht, The Netherlands. 1 × 1.4 m.

"Portrait of Charles I Hunting," oil painting by Sir Anthony Van Dyck, 1635. In the Louvre, Paris. 2.8 × 2.2 m.

Baroque painting in the Low Countries

"Gypsy Girl," oil on wood by Frans Hals, c. 1628–30. In the Louvre, Paris. 57.8 × 52.1 cm.

"Jacob Blessing the Sons of Joseph," oil painting by Rembrandt, 1656. In the Staatliche Kunstsammlungen, Kassel, West Germany. 1.8 × 2.1 m.

Plate 16 Painting, The History of Western

"La Partie Quarrée," oil painting by Antoine Watteau, 1713–14. In the collections of the Fine Arts Museums of San Francisco. 50 × 65.2 cm.

"St. John on Patmos," oil painting by Nicolas Poussin, 1645–50. In the Art Institute of Chicago. 1 × 1.4 m.

"The Lamentation over St. Sebastian," oil painting by Georges de La Tour, 1645. In the Staatliche Museen Preussischer Kulturbesitz, West Berlin. 1.6 × 1.3 m.

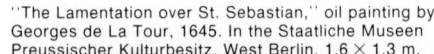

"Cupid a Captive," oil painting by François Boucher, 1754. In the Wallace Collection, London. 1.7 m × 85 cm.

"The Embarkation of the Queen of Sheba," oil painting by Claude Lorrain, 1648. In the National Gallery, London. 1.5 × 1.9 m.

"Mrs. Sheridan," oil painting by Thomas Gainsborough, c. 1785. In the National Gallery of Art, Washington, D.C. 2.2 × 1.5 m.

Baroque painting in France and Britain

"The Countess's Morning Levée," oil painting, part of the "Marriage à la Mode" series, by William Hogarth, 1743–45. In the National Gallery, London. 69 × 90 cm.

"Family of Country People," oil painting by Louis Le Nain, c. 1640. In the Louvre, Paris. 1.1 × 1.6 m.

"The Grace," oil painting by J.-B.-S. Chardin, 1740. In the Louvre, Paris. 48 × 40 cm.

Plate 18   Painting, The History of Western

"The Holy House of Nazareth," oil painting by Francisco de Zurbarán, c. 1630. In the Cleveland Museum of Art. 1.7 × 2.2 m.

Baroque painting in Spain

"Infanta Margarita," oil painting by Diego Velázquez, 1660. In the Prado, Madrid. 2.2 × 1.5 m.

"Boys Eating Grapes and Melon," oil painting by Bartolomé Esteban Murillo, c. 1650. In the Alte Pinakothek, Munich. 1.5 × 1 m.

"The Martyrdom of St. Bartholomew," oil painting by José de Ribera, 1630/39. In the Prado, Madrid. 2.4 × 2.4 m.

"Pity," colour print finished in pen and watercolour by William Blake, 1795. In the Tate Gallery, London. 44 × 55 cm.

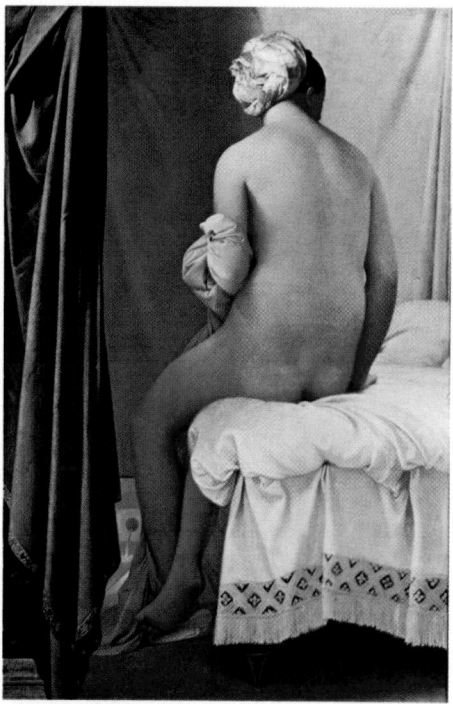

"Valpinçon Bather," oil painting by Jean-Auguste-Dominique Ingres, 1808. In the Louvre, Paris. 1.4 m × 99 cm.

Neoclassical and early Romantic painting

"Goethe in the Campagna," oil painting by Johann Heinrich Wilhelm Tischbein, 1787. In the Städelsches Kunstinstitut, Frankfurt am Main, Germany. 1.6 × 2 m.

"Oath of the Horatii," oil painting by Jacques-Louis David, 1784. In the Louvre, Paris. 4.3 × 3.4 m.

Plate 20 Painting, The History of Western

"Boatbuilding near Flatford Mill," oil painting by John Constable, 1815. In the Victoria and Albert Museum, London. 50.8 × 61.6 cm.

"The Third-Class Carriage," oil painting by Honoré Daumier, c. 1862. In the Metropolitan Museum of Art, New York City. 65 × 90 cm.

"The Death of Sardanapalus," oil painting by Eugène Delacroix, 1827. In the Louvre, Paris. 3.7 × 4.9 m.

"Souvenir de Mortefontaine," oil painting by Camille Corot, 1864. In the Louvre, Paris. 64 × 90 cm.

**Romantic
and Realist painting**

"The Raft of the Medusa," oil painting by Théodore Géricault, c. 1819. In the Louvre, Paris.
5 × 7.2 m.

"Man and Woman Gazing at the Moon," oil painting by Caspar David
Friedrich, c. 1824. In the Nationalgalerie, West Berlin. 34 × 44 cm.

"The Gross Clinic," oil painting by Thomas Eakins, 1875. In
the Jefferson Medical College, Thomas Jefferson University,
Philadelphia. 2 × 2.5 m.

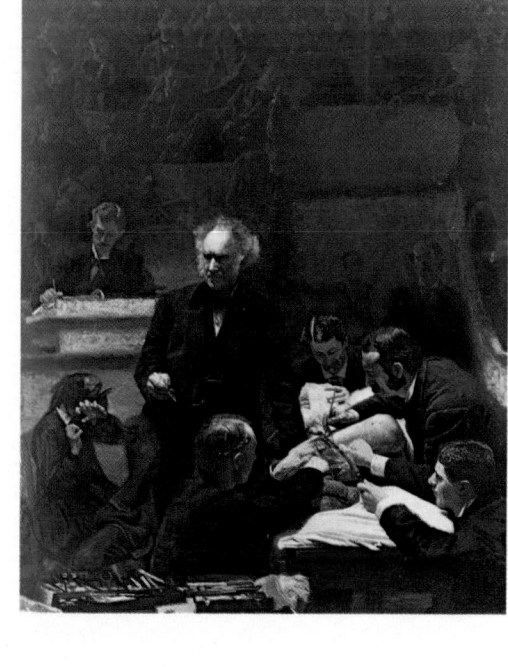

"Snow Storm—Steam-Boat off a Harbour's Mouth . . . ,"
oil painting by J.M.W. Turner, 1842. In the Tate
Gallery, London. 92 cm × 1.1 m.

Plate 22   Painting, The History of Western

**Impressionism,
Postimpressionism,
and Art Nouveau**

"The Starry Night," oil painting by Vincent van
Gogh, 1889. In the Museum of Modern Art, New York
City. 74 × 92 cm.

"Mont Sainte-Victoire," oil painting by Paul Cézanne, 1904. In the
Philadelphia Museum of Art. 72 × 93 cm.

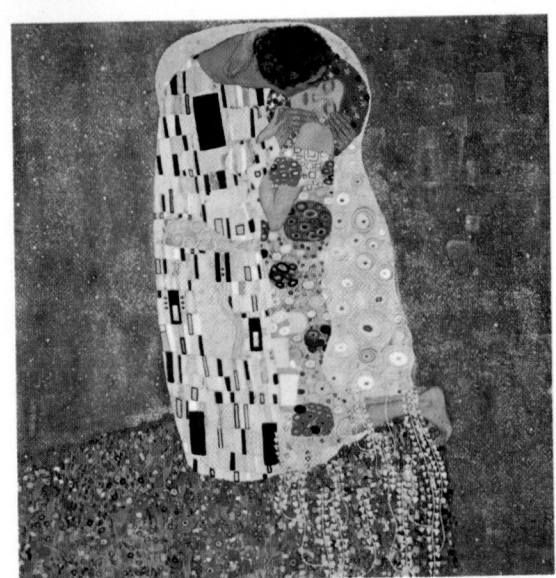

"The Kiss," oil painting by Gustav Klimt, 1908. In the
Österreichische Galerie, Vienna. 1.8 × 1.8 m.

"Sunday Afternoon on the Island of La Grande Jatte," by Georges
Seurat, 1884–86. In the Art Institute of Chicago. 2.1 × 3.1 m.

"Impression: Sunrise," oil painting by Claude Monet, 1872. In the Marmottan Museum, Paris. 50 × 67 cm.

"Le Moulin de la galette," oil painting by Pierre-Auguste Renoir, 1876. In the Louvre, Paris. 1.3 × 1.8 m.

"The Cry," oil and tempera on wood by Edvard Munch, 1893. In the Nasjonalgalleriet, Oslo. 91 × 74 cm.

"Te Rerioa" ("The Dream"), oil painting by Paul Gauguin, 1897. In the Courtauld Institute Galleries, London. 96 cm × 1.3 m.

Plate 24   Painting, The History of Western

"Violin and Palette," oil painting by Georges Braque, 1910. In the Solomon R. Guggenheim Museum, New York City. 93 × 43 cm.

"Composition," oil painting by Joan Miró, 1933. In the Wadsworth Atheneum, Hartford, Connecticut. 1.3 × 1.6 m.

"Improvisation No. 30," oil painting by Wassily Kandinsky, 1913. In the Art Institute of Chicago. 1.1 × 1.1 m.

"Departure," oil on canvas triptych by Max Beckmann, 1932–33. In the Museum of Modern Art, New York City. Centre panel 2.2 × 1.1 m, each side panel 2.2 × 1 m.

"Portrait of Madame Matisse," oil painting by Henri Matisse, 1905. In the Statens Museum for Kunst, Copenhagen. 40.5 × 32.5 cm.

"The Persistence of Memory," oil painting by Salvador Dali, 1931. In the Museum of Modern Art, New York City. 24 × 33 cm.

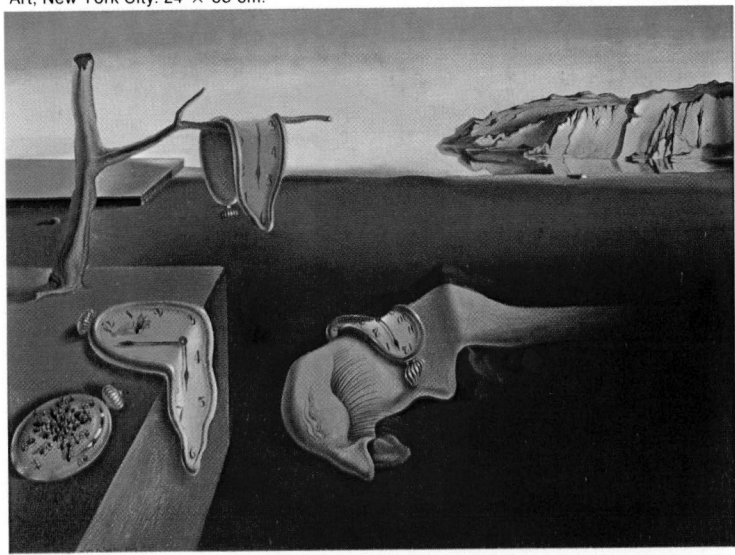

"Composition," oil painting by Piet Mondrian, 1929. In the Solomon R. Guggenheim Museum, New York City. 45.5 × 45.5 cm.

Painting 1900–45

"I and the Village," oil painting by Marc Chagall, 1911. In the Museum of Modern Art, New York City. 1.9 × 1.5 m.

"The Snake-Charmer," oil painting by Henri Rousseau, 1907. In the Louvre, Paris. 1.7 × 1.8 m.

Plate 25: By courtesy of (top left) the Royal Museum of Fine Arts, Copenhagen, with permission of Mme Marguerite Duthuit, permission S.P.A.D.E.M. 1973 by French Reproduction Rights, Inc., (top right, centre right) the Museum of Modern Art, New York, (centre right) Mrs. Simon Guggenheim Fund, (centre left) the Solomon R. Guggenheim Museum, New York, gift, Katherine S. Dreier Estate; photograph, (bottom left) Marc Garanger

Plate 26 Painting, The History of Western

Contemporary painting

"Whaam," oil on two canvas panels by Roy Lichtenstein, 1963.
In the Tate Gallery, London. 1.7 × 4.1 m.

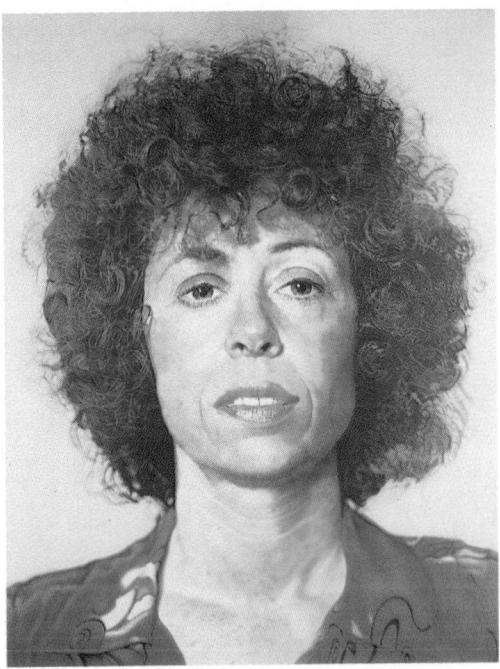

"Linda," acrylic on canvas by Chuck Close, 1975–76.
In the Pace Gallery, New York City. 2.7 × 2.1 m.

"Orange and Yellow," oil painting by Mark Rothko,
1956. In the Albright-Knox Art Gallery, Buffalo, New
York. 2.3 × 1.8 m.

"Autumn Rhythm," oil painting by
Jackson Pollock, 1950. In the
Metropolitan Museum of Art, New
York City. 2.7 × 5.3 m.

appearances, were far from exhausted. The influence of Kandinsky's "Improvisations" from 1911 onward, though delayed, was nonetheless great and pointed in a direction that abstract painting was to take 40 years later.

The Munich group Der Blaue Reiter ("The Blue Rider"), named after one of Kandinsky's earlier pictures, was formed in 1911 to represent the new tendencies when Kandinsky and Franz Marc withdrew from the heterogeneous Neue Künstlervereinigung ("New Artists' Association"). The group soon became, in its turn, a broadly based assembly of the international avant-garde artists of the day, although the stylizations of Marc himself now appear commonplace. Among the early members of the group, the Russian Alexey von Jawlensky evolved a structured form of Expressionism that culminated in the 1930s in a series of abstractions of a head, but the chief importance of the group was as a stage in the development of the Swiss painter Paul Klee.

Cubism and its consequences. Picasso's Primitivism, joined to the influence of Cézanne's "Great Bathers," culminated in 1907 in the enigmatic and famous picture "Les Demoiselles d'Avignon" (Museum of Modern Art, New York City). Those who saw it were astonished and perplexed, not only by the arbitrary disruption in the right-hand part of the picture of the continuity that had always united an image but also by the defiant unloveliness, which made it plain that the traditional beauties of art, the appeal of the subject, and the credibility of its imitation were now, at any rate to Picasso, finally irrelevant. "What a loss to French art!" a Russian collector said, and Picasso himself was not sure what to think of the picture; it was not reproduced for 15 years or publicly exhibited for 30. Nevertheless, the effect on his associates was profound. Matisse and Georges Braque, who, unlike Picasso, had been experimenting with Fauvism, immediately started painting female nudes of similar stridency. Subsequently, however, Matisse turned back toward relatively traditional forms and the flooding colour that chiefly concerned him. Braque, on the other hand, became more and more closely associated with Picasso, and Cubism, as the new style was labeled by one of Braque's hostile critics in the following year, was the result of their collaboration. In the first phase, lasting into 1909, the focus of their work was the accentuation and disruption of planes (Plate 24). In the next two years Braque went to paint at Cézanne's old sites, and the inspiration of Cézanne's style at this stage is indubitable. In the second phase, from 1910 to 1912, the irrelevance of the subject, in any integral form, became evident. It was no longer necessary to travel in search of a motif; any still life would do as well. The essence of the picture was in the treatment. If Analytical Cubism, as this phase is generally labeled, analyzed anything, it was the nature of the treatment. The great Cubist pictures were meditations on the intrinsic character of the detached Cézannesque facets and contours, out of which the almost-illegible images were built. Indeed, the objects were not so much depicted as denoted by linear signs, a spiral for the scrolled head of a violin or the trademark from a label for a bottle, which were superimposed on the shifting, half-contradictory flux of shapes. The element of paradox is essential; even when it approaches monumental grandeur, Cubism has a quality that eludes solemn exposition. Subtle and elegant geometric puns build up into massive demonstrations of pictorial structure, demonstrations that its complex parallels and conjunctions build nothing so firmly and so memorably as the picture itself. This proof that figurative art creates an independent reality is the central proposition of modern art, and it has had a profound effect not only on painting and sculpture, as well as on the arts of design that depend on them, but also on the intellectual climate of the age.

The experimental investigation of what reality meant in artistic terms then took a daring turn that was unparalleled since pictorial illusion had been isolated five centuries earlier. The Cubists proceeded to embody real material from the actual world within the picture. They included first stenciled lettering, then pasted paper, and later solid objects; the reality of art as they saw it absorbed them all. This assemblage of material, called collage, led in 1912

to the third phase of the movement, Synthetic Cubism, which continued until 1914. The textured and patterned planes were composed into forms more like pictorial objects in themselves than recognizable figurations. In the later work of Picasso and Braque, it is again possible to construe their pictorial code as referring plainly to the objective world—in the case of Braque, to still life chosen with an appreciation of household things and, with Picasso, to emotive yet enigmatic human subjects as well. The message of Cubism remained the same: meaning had been shown to reside in the structure of the style, the basic geometry implied in the Postimpressionist handling of life. The message spread rapidly.

The first theoretical work on the movement, *On Cubism,* by the French painters Albert Gleizes and Jean Metzinger, was published in 1912. It was argued that geometric and mathematical principles of general validity could be deduced from the style. An exhibition in the same year represented all Cubism's adherents except the two creators. The exhibition was called the Section d'Or ("Golden Section"), after a mathematical division of a line into two sections with a certain proportion to each other. Among the exhibitors were the Spaniard Juan Gris and the Frenchman Fernand Léger, who in their subsequent work were both concerned with combining the basic scheme of Synthetic Cubism with the renewed sense of a coherent subject. Cubism stimulated parallel tendencies in The Netherlands, Italy, and Russia. In The Netherlands, Piet Mondrian, on the basis of Cézanne and the Dutch painters of the fin de siècle, had reached a very simple, symbolic style analogous to the Dutch landscape. He first saw Cubist paintings in 1910 and moved to Paris two years later. The subsequent resolution of his sense of natural conflict into increasingly bare rectangular designs balancing vertical against horizontal and white against areas of primary colour is one of the achievements of modern art (Plate 25). In 1917 the de Stijl movement formed in The Netherlands around him, with lasting consequences for the architecture, design, and typography of the century.

In Italy in 1909 a program for all the arts was issued by the poet Filippo Marinetti, who called his exercise the Futurist manifesto. He rejected the art of the past and exalted energy, strength, movement, and the power of the modern machine. In painting, his ideas were taken up by Carlo Carrà. Umberto Boccioni, the most talented of the group, pursued its ideas not only in painting but also in sculpture. The most memorable serial images of movement were those of Giacomo Balla; they reveal that, under its vivid fragmentation, the vision of Futurism was not far from the photographic. Its imperative mood and disruptive tactics nonetheless had their effect, finding an echo in Britain in the Vorticist circle around Wyndham Lewis. Lewis' analytical intelligence and the toughness of his artistic temper marked equally his near-abstract early works and the incisive classical portraits he painted later. Among his early associates, David Bomberg developed from the Cubist idiom in 1912–13 images of a striking clarity and force; and William Roberts combined a Cubist formulation with social commentary analogous to that of the 18th-century painter William Hogarth.

In Russia, where Western developments were well known, the avant-garde, with its own roots in primitive art, had already evolved a simplified Expressionistic style. Kazimir Malevich produced formalized images of peasants at work that anticipated the later style of Léger. The strip-like and often abstract formulations of Mikhail Larionov and Natalya Gontcharova, to which they gave the name of Rayonism, date from 1911. In 1912 Malevich exhibited his first "Cubo-Futurist" works, in which the figures were reduced to dynamic coloured blocks, and in 1913 he followed these with a black square on a white background. This increasing tendency to abstraction reached its culmination in 1915 with the arrival of what he called Suprematism, in which simple geometric elements provided the whole dynamic force. The Russian movement, complicated by its own politics, was both accelerated and eventually broken by the Revolution, which gave it, for a time, a social function that the avant-garde has hardly achieved elsewhere. The Russian artists dispersed after

Early Cubism: 1907–10

Analytical Cubism: 1910–12

Synthetic Cubism: 1912–14

The Section d'Or group

Italian Futurists

1922, however, and their legacy, the tradition of Constructivism, was transmitted to western Europe by El Lissitzky, Antoine Pevsner, and the latter's brother, Naum Gabo.

Prismatic colour, the element in Cézanne that the Cubists had neglected in dismantling his style, was taken up by Robert Delaunay. Delaunay's variety of Cubism was named Orphism, after Orpheus, the poet and musician of ancient Greek myth. The essential discovery of Orphism was proclaimed as a realization that "colour is both form and subject." After an exquisite series of "Windows," Delaunay freed himself from representation and based his designs on the effects of simultaneous colour contrast. These dictated the concentric patterns of his "Discs" and "Cosmic Circular Forms," which occupied him and his wife, Sonia, thenceforward. The Czech František Kupka painted his first totally abstract work at about the same time. Even the simplest of his subsequent works never quite lost the rhythms of the fin de siècle style. Delaunay realized that a new order of painting was beginning, but his immediate influence was strongest abroad. Two American followers, Stanton Macdonald-Wright and Morgan Russell, exhibited as "Synchromists" in 1913. The Munich group Der Blaue Reiter was in touch with Delaunay, who exhibited with them, and the subsequent development of Klee was founded on his conversion to Delaunay's ideal of colour.

Fantasy and the irrational. The identity of a work of art as a thing in itself, independent of representation, was on the way to general recognition when the outbreak of war in 1914 interrupted artistic life throughout most of Europe. The activities of a group of painters, writers, and musicians who sought refuge in Zürich reflected the disorientation and disillusion of the time. Dada, as the movement was called, owed much to the iconoclasm of the Cubists and to the polemical tactics of the Futurists. Nonetheless its attack on art was fundamentally artistic; one wing of the avant-garde has owed allegiance to the Dadaist tradition ever since. As well as the need continually to attack the limits of the fine arts, it was felt important to "épater ["shock"] les bourgeois." The Dadaists enlarged the field open to artists in three ways. They questioned the idea that some subjects were simply not relevant to painting, a question that had been hovering over art for some time, by the simple expedient of arguing that anything and everything was fair game. The repetitive and amorphous trends of Impressionism had in fact already given grounds for such a supposition. The next step was to make a reluctant public accept that any object was a work of art if an artist chose to proclaim it one. In 1914 Marcel Duchamp, the exhibitor of serial images of movement in the Section d'Or, produced a bottle rack bought in a Paris store. Better and more *épatant* still, he submitted a urinal to a New York exhibition under a pseudonym in 1917. Duchamp did not paint again, and this is perhaps the single Dadaist gesture that time has failed to reconcile with art. It was also the Dadaists who posed the question, if art (as Redon had realized) is not within the reach of will, how is it different from chance? Jean Arp made collages and then reliefs from random shapes obtained "according to the laws of chance." Of all modern artists, he examined most closely the side of art akin to humour. Similarly, the Dadaists explored such elements as incongruity and dissociation, a process that led the way to Surrealism. Finally and almost incidentally, they asked, if the presentation of movement is proper to art, why not movement itself? Viking Eggeling and Hans Richter, with animated drawings and film, made the first works in a kinetic tradition that even by the late 1980s showed no sign of abating.

The painter who, more than any other, focused on incongruity—a feature that in painting involves the reinstatement of the subject, rather than its treatment, at the centre of art—was Giorgio de Chirico, an Italian born in Greece. De Chirico, rooted in the Mediterranean world, created from 1910 onward unforgettable images of its dereliction (Figure 16). In the immediate postwar years, he pioneered a style of emblematic, half-abstract still life called *pittura metafisica* ("metaphysical painting"), but by 1924, when the Surrealists began to work a similar vein

of fantasy, de Chirico had changed; and in later life he disavowed his early achievement. Metaphysical painting had one unexpected sequel, the serene realism of Giorgio Morandi. Meanwhile, Kurt Schwitters in Germany developed the mediums of collage and assemblage in the new spirit. Francis Picabia, who was associated with Duchamp in the United States during the war, joined forces with the Swiss Dadaists in 1918; his contribution was an epigrammatic elegance of style. The German Max Ernst was the most resourceful pictorial technician of the movement and a continually fertile inventor.

Figure 16: "The Rose Tower," by Giorgio de Chirico, 1913. In the Solomon R. Guggenheim Museum, New York City: The Peggy Guggenheim Collection, Venice. 73 × 100 cm.

It was in 1917 that the term Surrealism was coined, when the poet Guillaume Apollinaire described the style of the ballet *Parade,* for which Picasso had painted the sets, as:

> a sort of sur-realism in which I see a point of departure for a series of manifestations of that New Spirit which . . . promises to transform arts and manners from top to bottom with universal joy.

The manifesto of the Surrealist movement, which was composed by the poet André Breton, did not appear until 1924, however. Surrealism meant different things in different people's hands, but a common feature was absorption in the fantastic and irrational. The questions posed by Dada also preoccupied Surrealists, but for them the problem of the involuntary, fortuitous element in art, for example, was clearly open to psychological solution. The Surrealists demanded "pure psychic automatism"; the automatic drawings that the French artist André Masson made from 1925 onward and, on a more mechanical level, the frottage ("rubbing") devices of Ernst, which added to painting the evocative effect of fortuitously dappled textures, introduced an element that flourished even more fully 20 years later. Another discovery made in the wake of Dada was similarly delayed in its full impact: *Parade* had been the culmination of a series of musical compositions by Erik Satie that were based on ironic quotations of popular material. In the early 1920s the Americans Stuart Davis and Man Ray made paintings out of the designs on commercial packaging, foreshadowing the Pop Art of the 1950s.

The greatest achievement of Surrealist painting, however, was the invention of a new genre: fantastic realism— the prosaic, indeed quasi-photographic, rendering of the forms of fantasy and dream. The invention was the work, after de Chirico, of the Frenchman Yves Tanguy and the Spaniard Salvador Dalí. In the pictorial world of Dalí, everyday things undergo a transformation (Plate 25) that can be almost disturbing; in that of Tanguy, forms are more suggestive than related to actual objects. A different aspect of this dream realism, one that is particularly disturbing, was shown by the Belgian René Magritte.

In the years after 1918, a mood of classical consolidation affected some painters. In Germany a "New Objectivity"

Figure 17: "Guernica," oil on canvas by Pablo Picasso, 1937. In the Prado, Madrid. 3.51 × 7.82 m.

(Die Neue Sachlichkeit) was imposed on Expressionism; the eventual synthesis appeared in the brutal paintings of Max Beckmann (Plate 24). In France the Italian-born Amedeo Modigliani, affected by the simplicity of the Romanian-born sculptor Constantin Brancusi, arrived at a delicate linear realism, the last of the great Postimpressionist styles.

The Expressionist tradition was developed to an extreme of agonized distortion by Chaim Soutine. Another Russian-born member of the school of Paris, Marc Chagall, who had been influenced both by Cubism and the Russian avant-garde, discovered in the 1920s an individual and inconsequent vein of pictorial fancy (Plate 25). The sombre and devotional art of the Frenchman Georges Rouault bore the marks of his training with Gustave Moreau and as a stained-glass maker. Its crude force had been developed in the context of Fauvism, but the vision was one of refined introspection. The vigour and freedom of Fauvism was developed in the opposite direction in the decorative, extrovert style of another French painter, Raoul Dufy. The classicizing trend of the 1920s had a remarkable sequel in the work of the mural painters of Mexico. One such, Diego Rivera, had learned the formal lessons of Cubism in Paris; José Clemente Orozco was more dependent on the folk art of his country. Their frescoes combined grandeur with a legibility and social awareness rare in modern art.

The greatest imaginative achievements between World Wars I and II were, however, again those of Picasso. In the years immediately following World War I he had painted a series of solidly modeled yet oddly ironic figure pictures. Then his mood changed, and in 1925 "The Three Dancers" (Tate Gallery, London) reintroduced an anarchic and convulsive quality. The ambiguities and transformations of his art, both in painting and sculpture, have an emotional character that is entirely his own, but the enlargement of the artistic language greatly influenced others. The metamorphosis of natural shape into abstracted forms that nevertheless curve and bulge with their own life, a metamorphosis initiated by Picasso, became the international style of the early 1930s. The Spaniard Joan Miró gave it his own clarity and gaiety (Plate 24). Biomorphic abstraction, in essence the method of Tanguy, extended the resources of Surrealism, and the Chilean Roberto Matta Echaurren, who began painting in 1938, used it with dramatic effect. A poetic version of the style, rooted in an emotional response to landscape, was evolved in England by Graham Sutherland. In the later 1930s, with "Guernica" (1937; Prado, Madrid; Figure 17) and other pictures, Picasso responded to specific events. Around 1940, two painters in the United States, Arshile Gorky and Willem de Kooning, gave the biomorphic style a new character: relaxed, diffuse, and clear.

The development of abstract painting between the wars was comparatively slow. Klee (in 1921) and Kandinsky (in 1922) gravitated to the Bauhaus, the school in Germany whose work at Weimar and later at Dessau deeply influenced architecture and design as well as basic teaching. Oskar Schlemmer, whose simplified manner paralleled the Italian metaphysical painters, and Lyonel Feininger, an American-born painter working in a style developed from Cubism, were already teaching there. Kandinsky was concerned with refining the geometric ingredient of his work. Klee developed the poetic and fantastic elements of his art with an inconsequent fertility (Figure 18). The systematic purity of the Bauhaus approach survived longest in the work of Josef Albers, who moved to the United States in 1933. In 1940 Mondrian moved to New York City, and his last dynamic pictures reflect the new environment. Mondrian's work was appreciated by only a small circle, although a similar strength of purpose with a delicate re-

Mural painters of Mexico

Abstract painting between the wars

Figure 18: "Twittering Machine," mixed media (watercolour and pen and ink) by Paul Klee, 1922. In the Museum of Modern Art, New York City. 41.3 × 30.5 cm.

sponsiveness to a broader range of forms appeared in the work of the British painter Ben Nicholson. In the 1930s some paintings were executed by artists who formed themselves into groups, such as Abstraction-Création in Paris, Unit One in London, and the Association of American Abstract Artists in New York City. The work of these groups attained wider recognition only after World War II.

After 1945. The postwar work of Braque developed a few basic themes. The space and content of "The Studio" series of five paintings were formulated in vertical phases of varying sombreness; a mysterious bird that featured in this series was a symbol expressive of aspiration. Nicolas de Stael, a friend of Braque who was born in St. Petersburg, reached in 1950 a style in which lozenges of solid paint were built into structures of echo and correspondence. Colour in itself provided the substance, and de Stael's influence was considerable. The painterly and basically traditional vein of abstraction pursued in Paris by such painters as Alfred Manessier remained at root decorative. In Italy, traditional trends in sculpture are reflected in the brilliant accomplished modeling of Giacomo Manzù; Marino Marini, devoting himself almost entirely to the single theme of horse and rider, gave a bald realistic style an oddly apocalyptic force.

The "Cobra" group

The Expressionist tradition was revived in the new spirit by the "Cobra" group of painters from Copenhagen, Brussels, and Amsterdam who came together in Paris in 1948. In the work of Asger Jorn and Karel Appel, the image springs as if by chance from the free extempore play of brushstrokes. Surrealism proved remarkably durable. Among its adherents, the American Joseph Cornell had been evolving from the techniques of collage and assemblage a personal and evocative form of image; the Pole Hans Bellmer and the German Richard Lindner, working in Paris and New York, respectively, explored private and obsessive themes; they were recognized as among the most individual talents of their generation. In general, the most idiosyncratic and anarchic qualities of art were being developed as a new tradition, while geometric abstraction was seen to be the natural basis for the arts that are public and communal in purpose. Victor Pasmore in Britain, for instance, abandoned his earlier Postimpressionist standpoint to start afresh with constructional and graphic symbols deriving from Klee and Mondrian.

The presence of a number of the pioneer Surrealists in the United States during World War II affected later developments there. Surrealism's element of psychic automatism, particularly the spontaneous calligraphy of Masson, was particularly influential. The possibilities had, in fact, been implicit in modern painting for at least two decades; in Paris in the 1920s Jean Fautrier was already basing pictures on spontaneous and informal gestures with paint. In the United States in the 1940s, however, fresh impetus came from the impulsive play of colour in the work of the influential teacher Hans Hofmann. The movement that became known as Abstract Expressionism represented a decisive departure from its European sources, not only because the homogeneous consistency of a painted surface in itself took on a new meaning in the expansive U.S. conditions but at least equally because of the exceptional personality of Jackson Pollock. The style Pollock adopted in 1947 reflected an original involvement in the act of painting that transcended deliberation or control (Plate 26). The influential critic Harold Rosenberg wrote in 1952:

Abstract Expressionism

> At a certain moment the canvas began to appear to one American painter after another as an arena in which to act—rather than as a space in which to reproduce, redesign, analyze or "express" an object, actual or imagined. What was to go on the canvas was not a picture but an event.
>
> *(The Tradition of the New)*

In contrast to Pollock's work, that executed at the time by Willem de Kooning, though equally sweeping and ungovernable, showed a recurrent figurative reference; his series of alarming variations on the theme "Woman" began in 1950. Another Abstract Expressionist, Franz Kline, claimed, in executing his shapes like huge black and white ideograms, to be in some sense depicting figurative images. Rosenberg dubbed the group "action painters." In the course of the 1950s their influence was felt in almost

"Action painting"

every country. The climate of artistic opinion that spread outward from New York made possible flamboyant gesture paintings such as those of the French-born Georges Mathieu.

The idea of painting as a homogeneous allover fabric led at the same time to other quite separate developments. Prompted by the primitive and psychotic imagery that he called *l'art brut* ("raw art"), Jean Dubuffet embarked on an extraordinarily resourceful series of experiments in translating the raw material of the world into pictures. The energy that fills the works of the American painter Mark Tobey is by comparison gentle and lyrical and much influenced by East Asian art. Dubuffet's example inspired the abstract "matter" painting that developed in several countries around 1950. At its best, as in the work of the Catalan Antonio Tapies, this style conveys a strong sense of natural substance.

L'art brut

New forms. In painting generally a new directness was strikingly combined with a new simplicity. Beginning at the age of 80, in the five years before his death in 1954, Henri Matisse made a series of large gouaches *découpées* in which the increasingly abstract images were created solely by the juxtaposition of sharply cut patches of brilliant colour. Their influence was widespread and by no means confined to painters, such as the American Ellsworth Kelly, who developed the vibrant interaction of hard-edge colour areas. Even from other starting points, painters were reaching similar conclusions. The very simple yet resonant colour combinations of the New York painter Mark Rothko (Plate 26) or the grand severity of another American, Barnett Newman, furnish examples.

New directness and simplicity

Abstract painting was revealing far wider potentialities than had been apparent between World Wars I and II, but figurative styles showed a new freedom as well. The Swiss Alberto Giacometti, who had worked as a Surrealist, evolved in both sculpture and painting his sensation of the visual impact of figures in space. Francis Bacon in Britain uncovered unexpected and startling connotations in the apparition of a human likeness on canvas.

Painting in the 1960s not only sought originality; it took up a deliberately extreme position that may have seemed almost to pass the bounds of art. Paintings might be extremely large. Alternatively, they might be extreme in some other respect, such as the canvases of the Frenchman Yves Klein, which showed only a plain, arresting blue colour, or the black pictures of the American Ad Reinhardt, with variations so slight as to be hardly perceptible. The element of apparent chance in action painting explained the way the stains of colour in the work of the American painter Morris Louis appeared to flow and soak across the canvas as if of their own accord.

The tradition of Dada and its skepticism regarding what had once been the received definition of art prompted continual experiment with the techniques of assemblage. Robert Rauschenberg in the United States sought to place his subtly calculated "combine paintings" (collections of contrasting objects joined to make an ensemble) in the gap between reality and art, contrasting the significance of paint with the borrowed imagery and objects juxtaposed with it. Jasper Johns, an associate of Rauschenburg's, worked with preexisting designs such as targets and the U.S. flag, giving them an ironic look when subjected to incorporation in his works. In the borrowed imagery and popular quotations, on which much painting was based in the years that followed, the irony was intensified to the point of ceasing to be irony at all. Roy Lichtenstein took strip cartoons and other banal (even banally artistic) imagery as the motifs for pictures (Plate 26). Another American, Claes Oldenburg, began by reconstructing common things out of the random pictorial substance of Abstract Expressionism; his later reconstructions of the rigid furniture of everyday life are tailored out of limp plastic sheeting.

Pop Art and hard-edge painting

There is nothing random about the typical art of the 1960s. On the contrary, it was planned exactly and normally carried out by an efficient, almost mechanical-seeming system. Hard-edge painting developed into a wide range of planar styles having in common only their exploitation of optical reactions and the element of shock that is the visual concomitant of sharp contrast. The spread of this idiom was particularly influenced by the Hungarian-born Victor Vasarely, who worked in France; its most personal development was in the largely monochromatic work of Bridget Riley in Britain (Figure 19). Again, the initial tendency was to exclude such sensations from the aesthetic canon, but in the event a whole region of visual meaning, void for uncertainty since abstraction began, was reclaimed for painting. Optical art, or Op Art, emphasizes movement, whether potential, actual, or relative, and such effects have been ingeniously investigated by the *Groupe de Recherche d'Art Visuel* ("Group for Visual Research"), founded in Paris in 1960, and the Zero group in Düsseldorf, W.Ger. In the reliefs of the Venezuelan Jesús Raphael Soto, shifting vision is given a delicate order.

Op Art

Figure 19: "Fall," by Bridget Riley, 1963. In the Tate Gallery, London. 1.41 × 1.41 m.

Other developments have proved more fertile. In the hands of the American painters Kenneth Noland and Frank Stella, painting discovered new shapes, both within the rectangular canvas and beyond it. The new value given to the painted plane did not benefit painting only. The British painter Richard Smith deployed it in three dimensions in painted constructions that re-create impressions of commercial packaging in terms of the spatial imagination of the arts.

Minimal art

The extreme in this reduction of means and sophistication of aesthetics was perhaps reached when a group of sculptors in the United States and England turned to investigate the possibilities of minimal and primary forms, normally the simplest geometric solids, alone or arranged in baldly repetitive series. Here, it is the spectator (as perhaps in a sense it always is) who brings the interpretation and supplies the art. The proposition had the apparent preposterousness expected of avant-garde art, yet it seemed likely, in its turn, to shed light on problems that are very much older. It is characteristic of sculpture and painting in the 20th century to deal more and more consciously and directly with the ultimate definition of art. The perennial compulsion to reverse previously accepted definitions has threatened ever more directly the recognizable identity of art. At the end of the 1960s the tendency to emphasize the systems and attitudes of art rather than its product led to a move in several countries to deny the validity of the art object. Instead artists prepared written specifications for ideal, imaginary art, the fulfillment of which was superfluous, or self-sufficient programs for performances paradoxically analogous to some aspect of the more familiar artistic acts. Conceptual art has opened the way to activities notable in their defiance of conventional expectations. The designs of earth art or earthworks are fulfilled by moving large amounts of soil, preferably in inaccessible places, perhaps in token of the potency of

traditional art to impose its shape on the world. Activities of this order may appear to belong as much to theory as to artistic creation itself; in the 1970s these distinctions, with other familiar cornerstones of artistic thought, were held to have lost their validity. (La.G./Ed.)

In the 1970s critical and public interest centred on the reductive constructions of Minimalism and the nihilistic questioning of conceptual art. The late 1970s and early 1980s, however, witnessed a resurgence of excitement in painting and a return to figurative representation. A new movement called Neo-Expressionism arose in New York City and in the art capitals of western Europe, especially in West Germany, combining the heavy paint surfaces and dynamic brushstrokes of Abstract Expressionism with the emotional tone of early 20th-century German Expressionism. The new movement's subject matter ranged from basically literal, though self-consciously primitive, treatments of the human figure to a range of imaginary subjects indicative of modern urban life, particularly its glamour, alienation, and menace. A notable characteristic of Neo-Expressionism was the newly prominent role played in its commercial acceptance by gallery owners and art dealers who adroitly publicized the movement's artists. Indeed, Neo-Expressionism's sudden success was an indication of the growing commercialization of the avant-garde and its unhesitating acceptance by wealthy, influential collectors and progressive-minded museum curators. Some critics voiced doubts over what they saw as the reflexive pursuit of artistic novelty under the influence of commercial pressures, and some even asserted that critical and public acclaim had to some extent become divorced from the goals of finding and patronizing painters whose works had lasting artistic significance. (Ed.)

BIBLIOGRAPHY

General: Among the standard surveys of the history of Western art are HELEN GARDNER, *Gardner's Art Through the Ages,* 8th ed., edited by HORST DE LA CROIX and RICHARD G. TANSEY (1986); H.W. JANSON, *History of Art,* 3rd ed., revised and expanded by ANTHONY F. JANSON (1986); and DAVID M. ROBB and J.J. GARRISON, *Art in the Western World,* 4th ed. (1963). Among the major standard reference works are the *Encyclopedia of World Art,* 16 vol. (1959–83); ULRICH THIEME and FELIX BECKER (eds.), *Allgemeines Lexikon der bildenden Künstler von der Antike bis zur Gegenwart,* 37 vol. (1907–50, reprinted 1970–71); *McGraw-Hill Dictionary of Art,* edited by BERNARD S. MYERS, 5 vol. (1969); HAROLD OSBORNE (ed.), *The Oxford Companion to Art* (1970, reprinted 1984); and the *Praeger Encyclopedia of Art,* 5 vol. (1971). See also ARNOLD HAUSER, *The Social History of Art,* trans. from German, 4 vol. (1962); ELIZABETH G. HOLT (ed.), *A Documentary History of Art,* 3 vol. (1957–66, vol. 1 and 2 reprinted in 1982); PETER MURRAY and LINDA MURRAY, *A Dictionary of Art and Artists,* 4th ed. (1976); and E.H. GOMBRICH, *The Story of Art,* 14th rev. ed. (1984). An extensive bibliography may be found in E. LOUISE LUCAS, *Art Books: A Basic Bibliography on the Fine Arts* (1968). Later reference works include the *Larousse Dictionary of Painters* (1981; originally published in French, 1976); and DAVID PIPER (ed.), *The Random House Library of Painting and Sculpture,* 4 vol. (1981). F. DAVID MARTIN, *Sculpture and Enlivened Space: Aesthetics and History* (1981), examines the comparative importance of painting and sculpture in Western art.

European Metal Age cultures: STUART PIGGOTT, *Ancient Europe, from the Beginnings of Agriculture to Classical Antiquity* (1965); and WALTER TORBRUGGE, *Prehistoric European Art,* (1968; originally published in German, 1968), provide general surveys. There is a vast literature on the Aegean and eastern Mediterranean, including SPYRIDON MARINATOS, *Crete and Mycenae* (1960; originally published in Greek, 1959), photographs by MAX HIRMER; REYNOLD HIGGINS, *Minoan and Mycenaean Art,* rev. ed. (1981); and SPYRIDON MARINATOS, "Life and Art in Prehistoric Thera," *Proceedings of the British Academy,* vol. 57 (1972). SIR ARTHUR EVANS, *The Palace of Minos: A Comparative Account of the Successive Stages of the Early Cretan Civilization as Illustrated by the Discoveries at Knossos,* 4 vol. in 6 (1921–35, reissued 1964), is a classic work but is superseded in part by RICHARD W. HUTCHINSON, *Prehistoric Crete* (1962, reprinted 1968); SINCLAIR HOOD, *The Minoans: The Story of Bronze Age Crete* (1971); and KEITH BRANIGAN, *The Foundations of Palatial Crete* (1970). For Helladic art, the best works are GEORGE E. MYLONAS, *Mycenae and the Mycenaean Age* (1966); and LORD WILLIAM TAYLOUR, *The Mycenaeans,* rev. ed. (1983). For Cyprus, see VASSOS KARAGEORGHIS, *Cyprus* (1969), with a useful bibliography. Among the numerous works on the western Mediterranean are the following: ANTONIO ARRIBAS, *The Iberians* (1964); L. BERNABÒ BREA, *Sicily Before the Greeks* (rev. ed., 1966; originally published in Italian, 1966); DAVID H. TRUMP, *Central and Southern Italy Before Rome* (1966); DAVID RANDALL-MacIVER, *The Iron Age in Italy: A Study of Those Aspects of the Early Civilization Which Are neither Villanovan nor Etruscan* (1927, reprinted 1974) and *Villanovans and Early Etruscans: A Study of the Early Iron Age in Italy as It Is Seen near Bologna, in Etruria and in Latium* (1924); MARIO MORETTI and GUGLIELMO MAETZKE, *The Art of the Etruscans* (1970; originally published in Italian, 1969); P.J. RIIS, *An Introduction to Etruscan Art* (1953; originally published in Danish, 1948); RAYMOND BLOCH, *The Etruscans* (1958; originally published in French, 1958); MASSIMO PALLOTINO, *Etruscan Painting*, trans. from French (1952), and *Art of the Etruscans*, trans. from French (1955); MARGARET GUIDO, *Sardinia* (1964); and JOHN D. EVANS, *Malta* (1959). For northern European art, see PAUL JACOBSTHAL, *Early Celtic Art*, 2 vol. (1944, reprinted 1970). See also JOHN E. PFEIFFER, *The Creative Explosion: An Inquiry into the Origins of Art and Religion* (1982); ANDRÉ LEROI-GOURHAN, *The Dawn of European Art: An Introduction to Palaeolithic Cave Painting* (1982; originally published in Italian, 1981); and PIERRE AMIET *et al., Art in the Ancient World: A Handbook of Styles and Forms*, trans. from French (1981).

Ancient Greek: Important general works include JOHN D. BEAZLEY and BERNARD ASHMOLE, *Greek Sculpture and Painting to the End of the Hellenistic Period* (1932, reprinted 1966); JOHN BOARDMAN, *Greek Art*, new rev. ed. (1985); JOHN BOARDMAN *et al., Greek Art and Architecture* (1967; originally published in German, 1966), with photographs by MAX HIRMER; RHYS CARPENTER, *The Esthetic Basis of Greek Art of the Fifth and Fourth Centuries B.C.*, rev. ed. (1959); GISELLA RICHTER, *A Handbook of Greek Art*, 8th ed. (1983), and *Archaic Greek Art Against Its Historical Background* (1949); GEORGE BOAS (ed.), *The Greek Tradition* (1939), a collection of essays published in connection with an exhibition and accompanied by its catalog, GEORGE BOAS *et al., The Greek Tradition in Painting and the Minor Arts* (1939); BERNHARD SCHWEITZER, *Greek Geometric Art* (1971; originally published in German, 1969); and VINCENT J. BRUNO, *Form and Color in Greek Painting* (1977). Among the standard studies on vase painting are PAOLO E. ARIAS, *A History of 1000 Years of Greek Vase Painting* (1962; originally published in Italian, 1960), with photographs by MAX HIRMER; JOHN D. BEAZLEY, *The Development of Attic Black-Figure* (1951, reprinted 1986), *Potter and Painter in Ancient Athens* (1944), *Attic Black-Figure Vase-Painters* (1956, reprinted 1978), and *Attic Red-Figure Vase-Painters*, 2nd ed., 3 vol. (1963, reissued 1984); ERNST BUSCHOR, *Greek Vase Painting* (1921, reprinted 1971; originally published in German, 1913); JOSEPH V. NOBLE, *The Techniques of Painted Attic Pottery* (1965); and MARTIN ROBERTSON, *Greek Painting* (1959; reissued 1979). See also MANOLIS ANDRONIKOS, *Vergina: The Royal Tombs and the Ancient City* (1984; originally published in Greek, 1984). MARTIN ROBERTSON, *A Shorter History of Greek Art* (1981), is an excellent condensed study of Greek art from the Geometric through the Hellenistic periods.

Roman: General surveys include GEORGE M.A. HANFMANN, *Roman Art: A Modern Survey of the Art of Imperial Rome* (1964, reissued 1975); HEINZ KÄHLER, *The Art of Rome and Her Empire* (1963; originally published in German, 1962); GERMAN HAFNER, *Art of Rome, Etruria, and Magna Graecia*, trans. from German (1969); G.A. MANSUELLI, *The Art of Etruria and Early Rome*, trans. from Italian (1965); JOCELYN M.C. TOYNBEE, *Art in Roman Britain* (1962); and SIR MORTIMER WHEELER, *Roman Art and Architecture* (1964, reissued 1985). More detailed information on painting may be found in AMEDEO MAIURI, *Roman Painting*, trans. from French (1953); and WLADIMIRO DORIGO, *Late Roman Painting* (1971; originally published in Italian, 1966). BERNARD ANDREAE, *The Art of Rome* (1978; originally published in German, 1973), is a comprehensive survey; and OTTO J. BRENDEL, *Prolegomena to the Study of Roman Art* (1979), includes criticism of previous writings on the subject.

Early Christian, Byzantine, Armenian, Georgian, and Coptic: VIKTOR LAZAREV, *Storia della pittura bizantina* (1967; originally published in Russian, 2 vol., 1947–48), is a well-annotated general survey, now seriously out of date but still useful. Good coverage is provided by a combination of two books: BEAT BRENK (ed.), *Spätantike und frühes Christentum* (1977); and WOLFGANG F. VOLBACH and JACQUELINE LAFONTAINE-DOSOGNE, *Byzanz und der christliche Osten* (1968). See also WOLFGANG F. VOLBACH, *Early Christian Art*, with photographs by MAX HIRMER (1962; originally published in German, 1958); and D. TALBOT RICE, *Byzantine Art*, rev. ed. (1968); THOMAS F. MATHEWS, *The Byzantine Churches of Istanbul: A Photographic Survey* (1976); and CYRIL MANGO, *The Art of the Byzantine Empire, 312–1453: Sources and Documents* (1972, reprinted 1986). A number of books consider the art of the period as a whole

and propose various ways of interpreting the material: ANDRÉ GRABAR, *Christian Iconography: A Study of Its Origins* (1968, reprinted 1980; originally published in French, 1957; 2nd rev. French ed., 1984), *The Beginnings of Christian Art, 200–395* (1967; originally published in French, 1966), *Byzantium: From the Death of Theodosius to the Rise of Islam*, trans. from French (1967), and *Byzantine Painting: Historical and Critical Study*, trans. from French (1953, reissued 1979); ERNST KITZINGER, *Byzantine Art in the Making: Main Lines of Stylistic Development in Mediterranean Art, 3rd–7th Century* (1977); CLIVE FOSS and PAUL MAGDALINO, *Rome and Byzantium* (1977); and CYRIL MANGO, *Byzantium, the Empire of New Rome* (1980). HENRY MAGUIRE, *Art and Eloquence in Byzantium* (1981), discusses art as influenced by sermons and other theological writings; alternatively, ROBIN CORMACK, *Writing in Gold: Byzantine Society and Its Icons* (1985), interprets Byzantine art as a major element in the Byzantine outlook.

A number of helpful publications cover some of the specialist areas: KLAUS WESSEL, *Coptic Art* (1965; originally published in German, 1963); GUISEPPE BOVINI, *Ravenna: Its Mosaics and Monuments* (1956, reissued 1970; originally published in Italian, 1956); HEINZ KÄHLER, *Hagia Sophia* (1967; originally published in German, 1967); ANTHONY BRYER and JUDITH HERRIN (eds.), *Iconoclasm* (1977); KURT WEITZMANN, *The Icon: Holy Images—Sixth to Fourteenth Century* (1978); and KURT WEITZMANN *et al., The Icon* (1982; originally published in Italian, 1981).

Early medieval and Romanesque: The most satisfactory survey of the whole period is provided in ANDRÉ GRABAR and CARL NORDENFALK, *Early Medieval Painting from the Fourth to the Eleventh Century*, trans. from French and German (1957), and *Romanesque Painting from the Eleventh to the Thirteenth Century*, trans. from French and German (1958). The most exhaustive study on wall painting is still EDGAR W. ANTHONY, *Romanesque Frescoes* (1951, reprinted 1971). For manuscript illumination, see ALBERT BOECKLER, *Abendländische Miniaturen bis zum Ausgang der romanischen Zeit* (1930); a stimulating discussion by OTTO PÄCHT, *Book Illumination in the Middle Ages: An Introduction* (1986; originally published in German, 1984); and a survey by CHRISTOPHER DE HAMEL, *A History of Illuminated Manuscripts* (1986). An excellent short introduction to the subject is contained in ERNST KITZINGER, *Early Medieval Art, with Illustrations from the British Museum and British Library Collections*, rev. ed. (1983). The 9th through 12th centuries are covered in JOHN BECKWITH, *Early Medieval Art: Carolingian, Ottonian, Romanesque*, rev. ed. (1969, reprinted 1985); and C.R. DODWELL, *Painting in Europe, 800 to 1200* (1971). The most comprehensive modern overview of Dark Age and early medieval painting is CARLO BERTELLI, "Traccia allo studio delle fondazioni medievali dell'arte italiana," in *Storia dell'arte italiana*, part 2, *Dal medioevo al novecento*, vol. 1, *Dal medioevo al quattrocento*, pp. 3–163 (1983). For Rome, see RICHARD KRAUTHEIMER, *Rome, Profile of a City, 312–1308* (1980). The best survey of early Anglo-Saxon art is still T.D. KENDRICK, *Anglo-Saxon Art to A.D. 900* (1938, reprinted 1972). For book illumination in Britain and Ireland, see J.J.G. ALEXANDER, *Insular Manuscripts, 6th to the 9th Century* (1978); CARL NORDENFALK, *Celtic and Anglo-Saxon Painting: Book Illumination in the British Isles, 600–800* (1977); FRANÇOISE HENRY, *Irish Art in the Early Christian Period, to 800 A.D.* (1965), *Irish Art During the Viking Invasions, 800–1020 A.D.* (1967), and *Irish Art in the Romanesque Period, 1020–1170 A.D.* (1970; originally published in French together in a set of 3 vol., 1963–64).

Merovingian illumination is discussed in JEAN HUBERT, JEAN PORCHER, and WOLFGANG F. VOLBACH, *Europe in the Dark Ages* (1969; U.S. title, *Europe of the Invasions;* originally published in French, 1967). There are several good surveys of Carolingian painting: WOLFGANG BRAUNFELS, *Die Welt der Karolinger und ihre Kunst* (1968); JEAN HUBERT, JEAN PORCHER, and WOLFGANG F. VOLBACH, *Carolingian Art* (1970; U.S. title, *The Carolingian Renaissance;* originally published in French, 1968); and FLORENTINE MÜTHERICH and JOACHIM E. GAEHDE, *Carolingian Painting* (1976). Excellent particular studies can be found in WOLFGANG BRAUNFELS and HERMANN SCHNITZLER (eds.), *Karolingische Kunst* (1965). Late Anglo-Saxon art is considered in ELZBIETA TEMPLE, *Anglo-Saxon Manuscripts, 900–1066* (1976); JANET BACKHOUSE, D.H. TURNER, and LESLIE WEBSTER (eds.), *The Golden Age of Anglo-Saxon Art, 966–1066* (1984); and C.R. DODWELL, *Anglo-Saxon Art: A New Perspective* (1982). HANS JANTZEN, *Ottonische Kunst* (1947, reissued 1963), is an excellent review of Ottonian art; and ADOLPH GOLDSCHMIDT, *German Illumination*, vol. 2, *Ottonian Period* (1929, reprinted as part of a 1-vol. edition, 1970; originally published in German, 1928), is still valuable. A brief survey is LOUIS GRODECKI *et al., Le Siècle de l'an mil* (1973). C.R. DODWELL and D.H. TURNER, *Reichenau Reconsidered: A Re-assessment of the Place of Reichenau in Ottonian Art* (1965), offers a stimulating but contested examination of late 10th-century Ottonian illumination. The Romanesque period is surveyed in FRANÇOIS AVRIL, XAVIER BARRAL I ALTET, and DANIELLE GABORIT-CHOPIN, *Le Temps des Croisades* (1982), and *Les Royaumes d'Occident* (1983); HANNS SWARZENSKI, *Monuments of Romanesque Art: The Art of Church Treasures in North-Western Europe*, 2nd ed. (1967, reissued 1974); OTTO DEMUS and MAX HIRMER, *Romanesque Mural Painting* (1970; originally published in German, 1968); and WALTER CAHN, *Romanesque Bible Illumination* (1982). The best study of French Romanesque illumination is JEAN PORCHER, *Medieval French Miniatures* (1960; U.K. title, *French Miniatures from Illuminated Manuscripts;* originally published in French, 1959).

For England, there is an excellent survey of manuscripts: C.M. KAUFFMANN, *Romanesque Manuscripts, 1066–1190* (1975); and a later discussion in the exhibition catalog, GEORGE ZARNECKI, JANET HOLT, and TRISTRAM HOLLAND (eds.), *English Romanesque Art, 1066–1200* (1984). The standard work on early Spanish illumination, in English, is J. DOMÍNGUEZ BORDONA, *Spanish Illumination* (1930, reissued 1969; originally published in Spanish, 1930); see also JOHN WILLIAMS, *Early Spanish Manuscript Illumination* (1977). Illumination in northwest Germany is surveyed in two exhibition catalogs, *Rhein und Maas, Kunst und Kultur, 800–1400*, 2 vol. (1972–73); and ANTON LEGNER (ed.), *Ornamenta ecclesiae: Kunst und Künstler der Romanik*, 3 vol. (1985). The Gospels of Henry the Lion are discussed in *The Gospels of Henry the Lion, Count of Saxony, Duke of Bavaria* (1983), an auction catalog of Sotheby Parke Bernet Inc.; and HORST FUHRMANN and FLORENTINE MÜTHERICH (eds.), *Das Evangeliar Heinrichs des Löwen und das mittelalterliche Herrscherbild* (1986). The standard work on Salzburg illumination is still the masterly GEORG SWARZENSKI, *Die Salzburger Malerei von den ersten Anfängen bis zur Blütezeit des romanischen Stils: Studien zur Geschichte der deutschen Malerei und Handschriftenkunde des Mittelalters*, 2nd ed., 2 vol. (1969). The best survey of the art of the late 12th century is found in the three volumes of *The Year 1200*, a set published in conjunction with an exhibition: vol. 1, *A Centennial Exhibition at the Metropolitan Museum of Art: A Catalog*, edited by K. HOFFMANN (1970); vol. 2, *A Background Survey*, edited by F. DEUCHLER (1970); and vol. 3, *A Symposium*, texts by FRANÇOIS AVRIL *et al.* (1975). OTTO DEMUS, *Byzantine Art and the West* (1970), discusses the influence of Byzantine art on western Europe throughout the Middle Ages.

Gothic: General social and intellectual studies of Gothic art include JOAN EVANS (ed.), *The Flowering of the Middle Ages*, new ed. (1985); and JOHAN HUIZINGA, *The Waning of the Middle Ages: A Study of the Forms of Life, Thought and Art in France and the Netherlands in the XIVth and XVth Centuries* (1924, reprinted 1985; originally published in Dutch, 1919). See also ANDREW MARTINDALE, *Gothic Art* (1967, reprinted 1985); GEORGE HENDERSON, *Early Medieval* (1972), and *Gothic* (1967); EMILE MALE, *Religious Art in France, the Thirteenth Century: A Study of Medieval Iconography and Its Sources* (1984; originally published in French, 9th rev. ed., 1958), and *Religious Art from the Twelfth to the Eighteenth Century* (1949, reprinted 1970; originally published in French, 1945); TERESA G. FRISCH, *Gothic Art 1140–c. 1450* (1971); and JACQUES DUPONT and CESARE GNUDI, *Gothic Painting* (1954, reissued 1979; originally published in French, 1954).

For a discussion of Italian Gothic painting, see EVE BORSOOK, *The Mural Painters of Tuscany: From Cimabue to Andrea del Sarto*, 2nd rev. ed. (1980); MILLARD MEISS, *Painting in Florence and Siena After the Black Death* (1951, reprinted 1978); JOHN WHITE, *Art and Architecture in Italy, 1250–1400* (1966), and *The Birth and Rebirth of Pictorial Space*, 2nd ed. (1967); and FREDERICK ANTAL, *Florentine Painting and Its Social Background: The Bourgeois Republic Before Cosimo de'Medici's Advent to Power, XIV and Early XV Centuries* (1948, reprinted 1986). CHARLES D. CUTTLER, *Northern Painting from Pucelle to Bruegel: Fourteenth, Fifteenth, and Sixteenth Centuries* (1968), is an introductory work. No adequate monograph on International Gothic art exists, but, for France, see MILLARD MEISS, *French Painting in the Time of Jean de Berry: The Late Fourteenth Century and the Patronage of the Duke*, 2 vol. (1967), *French Painting in the Time of Jean de Berry: The Limbourgs and Their Contemporaries*, 2 vol. (1974), and *French Painting in the Time of Jean de Berry: The Boucicaut Master* (1968).

For late Gothic art, French painting is surveyed in GRETE RING, *A Century of French Painting, 1400–1500* (1949, reprinted 1979). Netherlandish painting is dealt with in MAX J. FRIEDLÄNDER, *Early Netherlandish Painting*, 14 vol. (1967–76; originally published in German, 1924–37); the best monograph on this early period is ERWIN PANOFSKY, *Early Netherlandish Painting, Its Origins and Character*, 2 vol. (1953, reprinted 1971). ANNE SHAVER-GRANDELL, *The Middle Ages* (1982), is an introduction to medieval art intended for the general reader; WALTER OAKESHOTT, *The Two Winchester Bibles* (1981), is a scholarly

study of 12th-century painting; RICHARD I. ABRAMS and WARNER A. HUTCHINSON, *An Illustrated Life of Jesus* (1982), includes an analysis of 94 paintings from the collection of the National Gallery of Art in Washington, D.C., with background notes on the artists; and PETER S. BEAGLE, *The Garden of Earthly Delights: Illustrations Taken from the Paintings of Hieronymus Bosch* (1982), is a creative and entertaining introduction to the artist's works.

Renaissance: (*Italy*): General works include CREIGHTON GILBERT, *History of Renaissance Art: Painting, Sculpture, Architecture Throughout Europe* (1973); MICHAEL LEVEY, *Early Renaissance* (1967, reprinted 1979), and *High Renaissance* (1975); and ROBERT KLEIN and HENRI ZERNER, *Italian Art, 1500–1600: Sources and Documents* (1966). A useful introduction to the theorists of the period is provided by SIR ANTHONY BLUNT, *Artistic Theory in Italy, 1450–1600* (1940, reprinted 1982). See also SYDNEY J. FREEDBERG, *Painting of the High Renaissance in Rome and Florence*, new rev. ed., 2 vol. (1985), and *Painting in Italy, 1500 to 1600*, 2nd ed. (1983), a fine survey of the often-complex movements in 16th-century Italian painting; JAMES BECK, *Italian Renaissance Painting* (1981), a historical survey of works of individual masters; and BRUCE COLE, *The Renaissance Artist at Work: From Pisano to Titian* (1983).

(*Northern Renaissance*): OTTO BENESCH, *Art of the Renaissance in Northern Europe: Its Relation to the Contemporary Spiritual and Intellectual Movements*, rev. ed. (1965), and *German Painting, from Dürer to Holbein*, trans. from German (1966); WOLFGANG STECHOW, *Northern Renaissance Art, 1400–1600: Sources and Documents* (1966); and ALBERT CHÂTELET, *Early Dutch Painting: Painting in the Northern Netherlands in the Fifteenth Century* (1981; originally published in French, 1980). (*France*): SIR ANTHONY BLUNT, *Art and Architecture in France, 1500 to 1700*, 4th ed. (1980), is an authoritative survey. (*Spain and Portugal*): GEORGE KUBLER and MARTIN SORIA, *Art and Architecture in Spain and Portugal and Their American Dominions, 1500 to 1800* (1959), is the only scholarly study in English. (*Central Europe and Russia*): G.H. HAMILTON, *The Art and Architecture of Russia*, 3rd ed. (1983), is a survey of all the arts of Russia.

Many studies have been done since the 1960s dealing exclusively with Mannerism. The most coherent view as a whole is JOHN SHEARMAN, *Mannerism* (1967). See also FRANZSEPP WÜRTENBERGER, *Mannerism: The European Style of the Sixteenth Century* (1963; originally published in German, 1962); and GIULIANO BRIGANTI, *Italian Mannerism* (1962; originally published in Italian, 1961).

Baroque and Rococo: The classic study of Baroque art, HEINRICH WÖLFFLIN, *Renaissance and Baroque* (1964, reprinted 1984; originally published in German, 1888), remains an important basic study. MICHAEL KITSON, *The Age of Baroque* (1966), provides an excellent modern summary. JOHN RUPERT MARTIN, *Baroque* (1977), is a fuller survey. GERMAIN BAZIN, *Baroque and Rococo*, trans. from French (1964, reprinted as *Baroque and Rococo Art*, 1974), covers the entire period in less detail, but it has in no way replaced the basic study by FISKE KIMBALL, *The Creation of the Rococo* (1943, reprinted as *The Creation of the Rococo Decorative Style*, 1980). ARNO SCHÖNBERGER and HALLDOR SOEHNER, *The Age of Rococo* (1960; U.S. title, *The Rococo Age: Art and Civilization of the 18th Century;* originally published in German, 1959), has excellent illustrations and detailed notes. Patronage during the period has been analyzed in depth by FRANCIS HASKELL, *Patrons and Painters: A Study in the Relations Between Italian Art and Society in the Age of the Baroque*, rev. ed. (1980). (*Italy*): DENIS MAHON, *Studies in Seicento Art and Theory* (1947, reprinted 1971), is of fundamental importance for an understanding of Baroque art in Italy. RUDOLF WITTKOWER, *Art and Architecture in Italy, 1600 to 1750*, 3rd rev. ed. (1973, reprinted with corrections 1980), surveys the 17th century with clarity and includes a massive bibliography. ELLIS WATERHOUSE, *Italian Baroque Painting*, 2nd ed. (1969), provides an introduction to the principal painters and stylistic movements of the time; a similar role is performed by MICHAEL LEVEY, *Painting in Eighteenth-Century Venice*, 2nd rev. ed. (1980). (*Latin America*): PAL KELEMEN, *Baroque and Rococo in Latin America*, 2nd ed., 2 vol. (1967), is an introduction to the art of the 17th and 18th centuries, with an exhaustive bibliography. (*Flanders*): The only comprehensive introduction to this period available in English is provided by HORST GERSON and E.H. TER KUILE, *Art and Architecture in Belgium, 1600 to 1800* (1960; originally published in German, 1942). (*Holland*): JAKOB ROSENBERG, SEYMOUR SLIVE, and E.H. TER KUILE, *Dutch Art and Architecture, 1600 to 1800*, 3rd ed. (1977), provides an excellent survey of the period and a large bibliography; while WOLFGANG STECHOW, *Dutch Landscape Painting of the Seventeenth Century*, 2nd ed. (1968, reprinted 1981), is a particularly detailed and valuable study of this important facet of Dutch painting. INGVAR BERGSTRÖM, *Dutch Still-Life Painting in the Seventeenth Century* (1956, reprinted 1983; originally published in Swedish, 1947), provides a survey of this group of paintings. (*France*): Important surveys are WEND GRAF KALNEIN and MICHAEL LEVEY, *Art and Architecture of the Eighteenth Century in France* (1972); and PHILIP CONISBEE, *Painting in Eighteenth-Century France* (1981). (*England*): ELLIS WATERHOUSE, *Painting in Britain, 1530 to 1790*, 4th ed. (1978); and MARGARET WHINNEY and OLIVER MILLAR, *English Art, 1625–1714* (1957), are both well-illustrated and include bibliographies. (*Central Europe*): The best introduction to Baroque art in central Europe, available in English, is undoubtedly EBERHARD HEMPEL, *Baroque Art and Architecture in Central Europe: Germany, Austria, Switzerland, Hungary, Czechoslovakia, Poland*, trans. from German (1965). (*Scandinavia*): Most of the information available on Scandinavian art of the 17th and 18th centuries is to be found in museum and exhibition catalogs devoted to wider subjects, but the monograph by GUNNAR W. LUNDBERG, *Roslin: Liv och verk*, 3 vol. in 2 (1957), is available, together with the relevant sections in TORBEN HOLCK COLDING, *Aspects of Miniature Painting: Its Origins and Development* (1953).

Neoclassicism, Romanticism, and Realism: Important works on the period in general are WALTER FRIEDLAENDER, *David to Delacroix*, trans. from German (1952, reprinted 1980); and FRITZ NOVOTNY, *Painting and Sculpture in Europe, 1780–1880*, 2nd ed. (1971, reissued 1980). Among the many general studies of Neoclassical art are HUGH HONOUR, *Neo-classicism* (1968, reprinted 1977), a sound introduction; ROBERT ROSENBLUM, *Transformations in Late Eighteenth Century Art* (1967), one of the best studies of the period; and DAVID IRWIN, *English Neoclassical Art: Studies in Inspiration and Taste* (1966), a book dealing exclusively with Neoclassical painting and sculpture in Britain. Among the most important works covering Romanticism are MARCEL BRION, *Art of the Romantic Era: Romanticism, Classicism, Realism* (1966; originally published in French, 1963); WERNER HOFMANN, *The Earthly Paradise: Art in the Nineteenth Century* (1961; originally published in German, 1960); FRANCIS D. KLINGENDER, *Art and the Industrial Revolution*, rev. ed., edited by ARTHUR ELTON (1968); EDGAR P. RICHARDSON, *The Way of Western Art, 1776–1914* (1939, reprinted 1969); FREDERICK ANTAL, *Classicism and Romanticism, with Other Studies in Art History* (1966); T.J. CLARK, *The Absolute Bourgeois: Artists and Politics in France, 1848–1851* (1973, reprinted 1982), and *Image of the People: Gustave Courbet and the 1848 Revolution* (1973, reprinted 1982); ALBERT BOIME, *The Academy and French Painting in the Nineteenth Century* (1971); HUGH HONOUR, *Romanticism* (1979); and MICHEL LE BRIS, *Romantics and Romanticism*, trans. from French (1981). LINDA NOCHLIN, *Realism and Tradition in Art, 1848–1900: Sources and Documents* (1966), and *Realism* (1971), are provocative studies. See also BARBARA NOVAK, *American Painting of the Nineteenth Century: Realism, Idealism, and the American Experience*, 2nd ed. (1979).

Modern: Among the numerous surveys of modern art are H.H. ARNASON, *History of Modern Art: Painting, Sculpture, Architecture, Photography*, 3rd rev. ed., updated by DANIEL WHEELER (1986); JOHN CANADAY, *Mainstreams of Modern Art*, 2nd ed. (1981); JEAN CASSOU, EMILE LANGUI, and NIKOLAUS PEVSNER, *Gateway to the Twentieth Century: Art and Culture in a Changing World* (1962); SAM HUNTER, *Modern American Painting and Sculpture* (1959), *Modern French Painting, 1855–1956* (1956), and *American Art of the 20th Century: Painting, Sculpture, Architecture* (1973); SAM HUNTER and JOHN JACOBUS, *Modern Art: Painting, Sculpture, Architecture*, 2nd ed. (1985); MARCEL BRION *et al.*, *Art Since 1945* (1958); and ROBERT L. HERBERT (ed.), *Modern Artists on Art* (1964). See also BEVERLY WHITNEY KEAN, *All the Empty Palaces: The Merchant Patrons*

of Modern Art in Pre-Revolutionary Russia (1983), an original study of important developments in the history of European art; and SIEGFRIED WICHMANN, *Japonisme: The Japanese Influence on Western Art in the 19th and 20th Centuries* (1981; originally published in German, 1980), a broad study including treatments of individual artists.

Important works dealing with modern painting include: WERNER HAFTMANN, *Painting in the Twentieth Century*, 2nd ed., 2 vol. (1965; originally published in German, 1965); BERNARD S. MYERS, *Mexican Painting in Our Time* (1956); GUIDO BALLO, *Modern Italian Painting: From Futurism to the Present Day* (1958; originally published in Italian, 1956); ALAN GOWANS, *The Restless Art: A History of Painters and Painting, 1760–1960* (1966); and HERBERT READ, *A Concise History of Modern Painting*, 3rd rev. ed. (1975). See also PAUL VOGT, *Expressionism: German Painting, 1905–1920* (1980; originally published in German), and *Contemporary Painting* (1981; trans. from German), a survey of international painting mostly of the 1950s and 1960s; GEORGE H. ROEDER, JR., *Forum of Uncertainty: Confrontations with Modern Painting in Twentieth-Century American Thought* (1980); JOHN RUSSELL, *The Meanings of Modern Art*, rev. ed. (1981); FRANK H. GOODYEAR, JR., *Contemporary American Realism Since 1960* (1981); and ABRAHAM A. DAVIDSON, *Early American Modernist Painting, 1910–1935* (1981).

(*Pre-Raphaelites*): CHRISTOPHER WOOD, *The Pre-Raphaelites* (1981); and *Pre-Raphaelites and Academics* (1981), a catalog of the exhibition organized in celebration of the publication of Wood's work. (*Impressionism and Postimpressionism*): LINDA NOCHLIN (ed.), *Impressionism and Post-Impressionism, 1874–1904: Sources and Documents* (1966); HORST KELLER, *Watercolors and Drawings of the French Impressionists and Their Parisian Contemporaries* (1982; originally published in German, 1980); JOHN REWALD, *The History of Impressionism*, 4th rev. ed. (1973, reprinted 1980), and *Post-Impressionism, from van Gogh to Gauguin*, 3rd rev. ed. (1978). (*Fauvism*): GEORGES DUTHUIT, *The Fauvist Painters* (1950; originally published in French, 1949). (*German Expressionism*): PETER SELZ, *German Expressionist Painting* (1957, reprinted 1974). (*Cubism*): JOHN GOLDING, *Cubism: A History and an Analysis, 1907–1914*, 2nd ed. (1968); CHRISTOPHER GRAY, *Cubist Aesthetic Theories* (1953); and ROBERT ROSENBLUM, *Cubism and Twentieth-Century Art*, rev. ed. (1966, reissued 1976). (*Futurism*): MARIANNE W. MARTIN, *Futurist Art and Theory, 1909–1915* (1968, reprinted 1978). (*Suprematism and Constructivism*): CAMILLA GRAY, *The Russian Experiment in Art, 1863–1922*, rev. ed., edited by MARIAN BURLEIGH-MOTLEY (1986). (*De Stijl and Neoplasticism*): H.L.C. JAFFÉ, *De Stijl, 1917–1931: The Dutch Contribution to Modern Art* (1956, reprinted 1986); and MILDRED FRIEDMAN (ed.), *De Stijl: Visions of Utopia* (1982), an exhibition catalog. (*Dada and Surrealism*): ROBERT MOTHERWELL (ed.), *The Dada Painters and Poets: An Anthology*, 2nd ed. (1981); HANS RICHTER, *Dada: Art and Anti-Art* (1966, reprinted 1978; originally published in German, 1964); WILLIAM S. RUBIN, *Dada, Surrealism, and Their Heritage* (1968, reprinted 1982); PATRICK WALDBERG, *Surrealism*, trans. from French (1962, reissued 1978); and HERBERT S. GERSHMAN, *The Surrealist Revolution in France* (1969, reprinted 1974). (*Abstract Expressionism*): BARBARA ROSE, *American Art Since 1900*, rev. and expanded ed. (1975). (*Pop Art and Op Art*): MARIO AMAYA, *Pop Art and After* (1965, reprinted 1972; U.K. title, *Pop as Art: A Survey of New Super Realism*); LUCY R. LIPPARD, *Pop Art* (1966); and JOHN RUSSELL and SUZI GABLIK (compilers), *Pop Art Redefined* (1969).

(P.J.C./R.S.Co./Jo.B.M./N.B.P./Ed.)

Pakistan

Pakistan (the Islāmic Republic of Pakistan, Urdu Islāmī Jamhūriya-e Pākistān) is a country in South Asia. It is bounded to the west by Iran, to the north by Afghanistan and the Soviet Union, to the northeast by China, to the east and southeast by India, and to the south by the Arabian Sea. The territory has an area (excluding the Pakistani-held part of Jammu and Kashmir) of 307,-374 square miles (796,095 square kilometres). The capital of the country is Islāmābād.

Pakistan was brought into being at the time of the Partition of British India in 1947 in order to create a separate homeland for India's Muslims in response to the demands of Muslim nationalists. From independence in 1947 until 1971, Pakistan (both de facto and in law) consisted of two regions—West Pakistan in the Indus River Basin, and East Pakistan, located more than 1,000 miles (1,600 kilometres) away in the Ganges River Delta. In response to grave internal political problems, however, an independent state of Bangladesh was proclaimed in East Pakistan in 1971.

Since 1947 the territory of Jammu and Kashmir, along the western Himalayas, has been disputed between Pakistan and India, with each holding sectors. The territory is treated both in the article INDIA and in the section below on Azad Kashmir.

Throughout the republic of Pakistan there is a high degree of concentration of landownership, although successive governments have pledged themselves to land reform. There is an even greater concentration of ownership of industry among a few.

The article is divided into the following sections:

Physical and human geography

THE LAND

Relief. Pakistan is situated at the western end of the Indo-Gangetic Plain, which is bounded to the north by the mountain wall of the Great Himalayan mountain ranges and their offshoots. It is situated in the northwestern part of the southern Asian subcontinent and may be subdivided into six natural regions—the northern mountains, the submontane plateau, the Indus Plain, the Baluchistan Plateau, the western bordering mountains, and the desert areas.

The northern mountains. The western ranges of the Himalayan mountains occupy the entire northern end of Pakistan, extending about 200 miles into the country; they are among the youngest mountains on Earth, having attained their present elevation only within the last 1,-000 years. Four of the peaks exceed an elevation of 26,000 feet (8,000 metres) and most rise to heights of more than 15,000 feet. These include such towering peaks as Nānga Parbat (26,660 feet [8,126 metres]) and K2, also called Godwin Austen (28,251 feet [8,611 metres]). Beyond the Karakoram Range in the extreme north lies the Chinese autonomous region of Sinkiang Uighur; to the northwest, beyond the Hindu Kush, are the Pamirs—the "Roof of the World"—where only a narrow strip of Afghan territory separates Pakistan from the Soviet Union. The Himalayan massif (mountainous mass) that isolates the South Asian subcontinent from Soviet and Chinese Central Asia was

The Himalayan sector

pierced in 1970 when a road was completed across the Karakoram Range, linking the town of Gilgit in Pakistan with Kashgar in Sinkiang Uighur, China.

The northern mountain barrier influences the rainfall pattern in Pakistan by intercepting monsoon (rain-bearing) winds from the south. Melting snow from the mountains also feeds rivers, including the mighty Indus, which emerge from the east–west aligned ranges to flow southward.

The population in this inhospitable region is generally sparse, although in a few favoured places it is dense. In most of the tiny settlements of this region, the usual crop is barley; fruit culture, especially of apricots, is of special importance. Timber, mainly pine, is found in some parts, but its occurrence varies with rainfall and altitude. Many slopes have been denuded of cover by excessive timber felling and overgrazing. The whole region in itself is of less significance than in its relation to the plains to the south.

The submontane plateau. Lying below the Himalayas, the submontane plateau has four distinct divisions—the Trans-Indus plains, the Potwar Plateau, the Salt Range, and Siālkot district.

The Trans-Indus plains, west of the Indus, comprise the hill-girt plateaus of the Vale of Peshāwar, Kohāt, and Bannu, which are oases in the arid, scrub-covered landscape of the North-West Frontier Province. Of these, the Vale of Peshāwar (consisting of Peshāwar and Mardān districts) is the most fertile. It was once a flourishing centre of Greco-Buddhist culture. Much of the area is covered by gravelly or clayey alluvial detritus. Rainfall is

The Vale of Peshā-war

generally only between 10 and 15 inches (250 and 380 millimetres) but is higher in Mardān district. Most of the cultivated area in the Vale of Peshāwar is irrigated from canals. Kohāt is, comparatively, less developed. Rainfall is about 16 inches. Only a small percentage of the cultivated area is canal irrigated. Nor is its groundwater adequately exploited, although the water table is generally high. Much of the area consists of scrub and poor grazing land. The region is much broken by limestone ridges, and the uneven limestone floor is variously filled with lacustrine clays, gravel, or boulders. In Bannu, soils are in general sandy or gravelly, except for rich silts that occur in places. About one-quarter of the cultivated area is irrigated. Rainfall is low, amounting to about 11 inches. In both Kohāt and Bannu fat-tailed sheep, camels, and donkeys are extensively reared; wool is an important cash crop.

The Potwar Plateau lies at a height of 1,200 to 1,900 feet and covers an area of about 5,000 square miles east of the Indus, in the Punjab. It is an open, undulating country developed on the Siwālik Range, which is mainly of sandstone and is covered by varying thicknesses of loess (a loamy deposit formed by the wind), which erodes easily. Rainfall is between 15 and 20 inches, being higher in the northwest; the southwest is very arid. The landscape is dissected and eroded by streams that, during the rains, cut into the land and wash away the soil. The streams are generally deep set and are of little or no use for irrigation. It is generally a poor agricultural area, with an excessive pressure of population upon its resources.

The Salt Range lies at the southern edge of the Potwar Plateau and has an average height of 2,200 feet, the highest peak being at Sakesar (4,992 feet); it is an extremely arid territory that sharply marks the boundary between the submontane region and the Indus Plain to the south. The Salt Range is of interest to geologists, as it contains the most complete geologic sequence in the world, in which rocks from the Cambrian Period (from 500,000,000 to 570,000,000 years old) to the Pleistocene Epoch (from 10,000 to 2,500,000 years old) are represented.

Siālkot district is a narrow submontane region in the northeast; unlike the Potwar Plateau, it is a rich agricultural region. Rainfall varies from 25 to 35 inches (650 to 900 millimetres), and the water table is high, facilitating well (and tube-well) irrigation; the soil is heavy and very fertile. The population distribution is dense; the land is divided into small farms on which intensive cultivation is practiced.

The Indus Plain. The Indus Plain, which covers an area of about 200,000 square miles, is the most prosperous agricultural region in Pakistan. It is an unrelieved featureless plain of fertile alluvium extending for 650 to 700 miles from the rim of the Potwar Plateau southward to the Arabian Sea. Its northern zone comprises the province of Punjab (literally, Five Waters) and is enclosed by the Indus and its five lower tributaries (the Jhelum, the Chenāb, the Rāvi, the Beās, and the Sutlej)—the tributaries converging to their confluence with the Indus at Mithankot. It is divided into several interfluves (lands situated between streams) called *doāb*s, the largest but the poorest of them being the Sind Sāgar Doāb, situated between the Indus and the Chenāb rivers, which is mostly a desert. The *doāb*s that lie to the east of it, however, are the richest agricultural lands in the country. Until the advent of irrigation, at the end of the 19th century, much of the area was a desolate waste, for there is little rainfall. But irrigation has been a mixed blessing; it has also caused waterlogging and salinity in some places.

The *doāb*s

In the southern zone of the Indus Plain lies the province of Sind, which is named after Sindhu (the Indus River). There, the size of the Indus—its waters augmented by the contribution of its five lower tributaries—is very great; its average annual discharge at Sukkur, in northern Sind, is more than 5,000,000,000,000 cubic feet (140,000,000,000 cubic metres), including nearly 10,000,000,000 cubic feet of water-borne silt. The land in Sind, consisting of alluvial sands and clays, tends to give way before the Indus flood, and the river frequently changes course. Manchhar, a marshy lake west of the Indus, has an area of 14 square miles at low water but extends for no less than 200 square

miles when full; on such occasions, it is one of the largest freshwater lakes in South Asia. The quality of groundwater in the Indus Plain varies, that in the southern zone (Sind) being mostly saline and unfit for agricultural use. Extensive areas in both the northern and southern zones of the Indus Plain have been affected by waterlogging and salinity. In the south the Indus Delta (in marked contrast to the Ganges Delta) is a wild waste. When high tides and Indus floods coincide, the littoral is flooded for 20 miles inland.

The Baluchistan Plateau. The Baluchistan Plateau extends westward, averaging more than 1,000 feet in elevation, with many ridges running across it from northeast to southwest; it is separated from the Indus Plain by the Sulaimān and Kīrthar ranges. It has a remarkable indigenous method of irrigation called the *kārez,* which consists of underground channels and galleries that collect subsoil water at the foot of hills and carry it to the fields and villages. The water is drawn from the channels through shafts that are sunk into the ground, at suitable intervals, in the fields. Because the channels are under ground, the loss of water by evaporation is minimized. The plateau is an extremely arid country and is the most sparsely populated region in Pakistan. Pastoral activity supplements a primitive form of agriculture. True pastoral nomadism survives in the northwest. Goats and fat-tailed sheep account for the majority of the stock, and much of the local traffic consists of camels and donkeys, although trucks and buses are in use on the new roads.

The western bordering mountains. These mountains run south from the Hindu Kush, in several parallel ranges, outside the path of the monsoons. Elevations in the Hindu Kush exceed 24,000 feet, but peaks become less lofty in the south. Rainfall is low, and there is little vegetation. Occasional heavy rain in the mountains results in destructive torrents, washing away the soil. Some cultivation is practiced beside streams and along riverbanks or (wherever conditions permit) by terracing hillsides. Three minor ranges run south from the Hindu Kush to the Kābul River, south of which lies the famous Khyber Pass, at the frontier with Afghanistan. Farther south the Sulaimān Range, with peaks averaging 6,000 to 7,000 feet, runs southward for about 300 miles, after which the generally lower Kīrthar Range, ranging from 4,000 to 8,000 feet, runs down to the coast. These hills separate the Indus Plain from Baluchistan. The people of these arid hills are tribal. The area in general is extremely poor; only a minimum of crops are grown in favoured valleys, which are generally malarial. Large numbers of sheep and goats are kept. The mule is the main beast of burden in this broken country.

The desert areas. The desert areas include firstly the dreary steppes of the Sind Sāgar Doāb (at the centre of it the Thal, which has true desert conditions) and secondly Cholistan in Bahāwalpur (Punjab), which is known as the Nāra or Registān in Khairpur (Sind) and farther south as the Thar Desert in the Thar Parkar District of Sind. All these areas are extensions of the Thar Desert of western India.

Soils. The soils of Pakistan are classfied as pedocals, which comprise a dry soil group having a high content of calcium carbonate and a low content of organic matter; they are characteristic of a land with low and erratic rainfall. The soils of the Indus Plain consist of alluvium, old and new, whereas in the desert areas and most of Baluchistan they consist either of windblown deposits known as loess or else of loess mixed with alluvium. The soils of the Thar Desert area are, for the most part, sandy loams with patches of clay and larger areas of pure sand. Some of the virgin soils respond generously to irrigation, and an extensive reclamation scheme has made much progress in the Thal region.

Climate. As Pakistan is located on a great landmass, north of the Tropic of Cancer (between latitudes 24° and 37° N), it has a continental type of climate characterized by extreme variations of temperature, both seasonally and daily. Very high altitudes modify the climate in the cold snow-covered northern mountains; temperatures on the Baluchistan Plateau are somewhat higher. Along the coastal strip, the climate is modified by sea breezes. In the

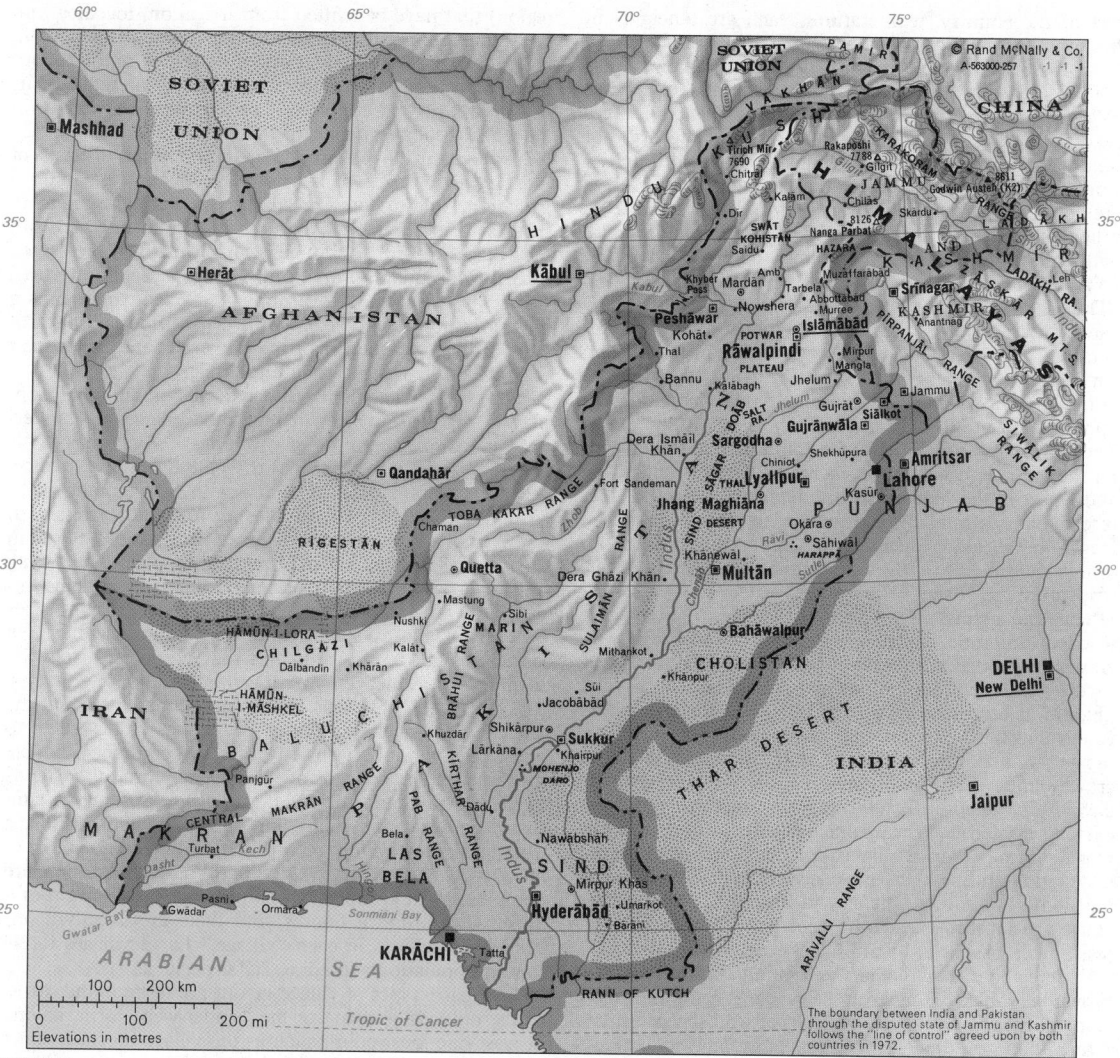

rest of the country, temperatures reach great heights in
the summer; the highest temperatures exceed 117° F (47°
C) in the plains and the mean temperature during June is
100° F (38° C) in the plains. In the summer, hot winds
called *loo* blow across the plains during the day. Trees
shed their leaves to avoid loss of moisture. The dry, hot
weather is broken ocasionally by dust storms and thunderstorms that temporarily lower the temperature. Evenings
are cool; the diurnal variation in temperature may be as
much as 20° to 30° F (11° to 17° C). Winters are cold,
with minimum mean temperatures of about 40° F (4°
C) in January.

The characteristics of different regions are determined by
variations in rainfall and irrigation rather than by temperature. Although the country is dominated by monsoon
winds, it is extremely arid, except for the southern slopes
of the Himalayas and the submontane tract, which have a
rainfall of from 30 to 35 inches (750 to 900 millimetres).
The 20-inch (500-millimetre) precipitation line, which runs
northwest from near Lahore, marks off the Potwar Plateau
and a part of the Indus Plain in the northeast; these areas
receive enough rainfall for dry cropping (farming without
irrigation by taking measures to conserve water). South
of this region, cultivation was confined mainly to riverine
strips until the advent of irrigation.

Plant and animal life.   Natural vegetation, except for
wooded mountain slopes, is largely limited to tough wiry
grass and stunted bushes, with only a few scattered trees,
except for a few plantations in forest reservations and
ubiquitous orchards of fruit trees. In Baluchistan the Salt
Range and the western-bordering-mountains vegetation is
mostly limited to xerophytic plants (plants adapted for
growth under dry conditions). The deserts are virtually
devoid of vegetation. The Indus Plain when watered, however, is very fertile. Wheat is the principal winter crop, the
main summer crops being cotton and rice. Widespread
installation of tube wells, especially in the Punjab, is bringing about substantial changes in cropping patterns, encouraging substitution of wheat for less valuable drought-
resisting crops, such as gram (chickpea).

Wildlife abounds in the northern mountains and includes
brown bear, black Himalayan bear, leopard, the rare snow
leopard, Siberian ibex, and varieties of wild sheep. Buffalo
rather than cows are kept as milch cattle, and bullocks
are employed for plowing, although occasionally camels
are also used for that purpose. Donkeys are the beasts of
burden. The Manchhar Lake in Sind has an abundance
of water birds, including mallards, teals, shovellers, spot
bills, geese, pochards, and wood ducks; desert gazelles are
also found in the region. Crocodiles, pythons, and wild
boars are found in the delta area. Jackals, foxes, wild cats,
and a variety of rodents and reptiles are found throughout
the country.

Settlement patterns.   *Traditional regions.*   The traditional regions of Pakistan, shaped by ecological factors
and historical evolution, are reflected in the administrative division of country into the four provinces of Sind,
Punjab, the North-West Frontier Province, and Baluchistan. The encroachment of the Cholistan Desert and of
the western bordering mountains narrows down the Indus
Plain below Mithankot, thus separating the destinies of
Sind and Punjab, each of which has a distinct language,
culture, and history. Until 1937 Sind was a part of the
Bombay Presidency, and it had no administrative links
with the Punjab. Baluchistan and the North-West Frontier
Province are separate, both linguistically and culturally;
they are distinguished by tribal societies subsisting on precarious agriculture, supplemented by pastoralism. In the
Punjab, until the advent of irrigation, the bulk of the
population was restricted to the *bārānī* ("land dependent
on rainfall for cultivation") region—the Potwar Plateau
and the Upper Indus Plain—which receives more than 20
inches of rainfall.

The Canal Colony districts of southern Punjab were
large tracts of uncultivated land in the Indus Plain that
were irrigated by canals and populated by colonists drawn
from every part of the Punjab. They now form the richest
agricultural region of the country. Agricultural wealth is
concentrated in districts of Lahore Division (in the *bārānī*

region) that have benefitted from irrigation, together with
the Canal Colony districts and Sind. These areas contain
most of the rural population of Pakistan and produce
more than half of its wheat crop and virtually all of its
cotton and rice. Landholdings are comparatively larger in
the Canal Colony districts of the Punjab and in Sind.

Elsewhere, in the overpopulated and poor districts of
the *bārānī* region, which moreover do not benefit from
irrigation, holdings are exceedingly small and fragmented.
In these districts there is a great pressure to migrate from
the villages to find employment in towns or in the armed
forces. Consequently, unlike the richer agricultural areas,
this impoverished and overpopulated region maintains a
close symbiotic relationship with urban economy and society. Educational levels in these districts are higher than
they are in the richer agricultural areas.

Rural settlement.   The vast majority of the rural population of Pakistan lives in nucleated villages or hamlets
(*i.e.,* in compact groups of dwellings). Sometimes, as is
generally the case in the North-West Frontier Province,
the houses are placed in a ring with blank outer walls,
so that each complex resembles a protected fortress with
a few guarded entrances. Dispersed habitation patterns in
the form of isolated single homesteads are rare, occurring
only in a few mountainous areas. But it is not uncommon to find numerous satellite hamlets of varying sizes
near larger villages; such hamlets are occupied either by a
landlord, with his servants and sharecroppers, or else by
members of a lineage living together in adjoining houses.
The spread of tube wells in the Punjab has increased the
tendency for such dispersal, for people often prefer to
live near their tube wells in order to guard the valuable
machinery. The concept of village, therefore, often tends
to be equivalent to that of the *mawzaʿ* (an area of land
that, together with a village and its satellite hamlets, forms
a unit in land-revenue records). It is difficult to speak of
an average size of village, for patterns of habitation are
complex. Most groups of dwellings have a minimum of a
dozen or a score of houses, and there are usually a few
hundred dwellings in each "village." Large villages rarely
have a population exceeding 2,500 persons.

Three basic types of village layout are to be found. Most
of the older villages are of the "spider-web" form, having
at least one focal point, such as the village mosque, some
shops, or a well from which lanes radiate. A few villages
follow the contours of hill slopes and other natural features. Finally, in the Canal Colony areas, villages are of
a regular rectangular pattern, with a well, a mosque, and
a school, as well as the house of the village headman, at
the centre, and with the houses being arranged in a series
of concentric rectangles. Houses are built from available
local materials; the vast majority are of mud, a material
that is not only cheap and reasonably durable in the dry
climate but also provides better insulation from extremes
of heat and cold than brick or stone. Houses usually have
walled courtyards where animals are tethered and where
people sleep in the open in the hot summer.

Urban settlement.   The urban population of Pakistan
represents about a quarter of the total. Two cities have
a dominating position—Karāchi and Lahore. Since the
1960s, government policy has been directed toward the
dispersal of industry, which had become heavily concentrated in Karāchi. As a consequence, urban growth
has been more evenly distributed among several cities.
Karāchi, the principal port and centre of commerce and
industry, was also the national capital until 1966, when
the new capital at Islāmābād, 750 miles to the northeast,
began to function.

Rapid and unplanned urban expansion has been paralleled by a deterioration in living conditions, particularly
in the housing conditions of lower income groups. Many
urban households are unable to pay rent for the cheapest
form of available housing and live in makeshift shacks.
Water supply and sewerage systems are inadequate, and
in many areas residents have to share communal water
taps. Inadequate urban transport is also a major problem.
After Karāchi and Lahore, the principal cities are Faisalābād (called Lyallpur until 1979), Rāwalpindi, Hyderābād,
Multān, Gujrānwāla, Peshāwar, Siālkot, Sargodha, Quetta,

Islāmābād, Jhang, Sukkur, Bāhāwalpur, Kasūr, Sahiwal, Mardān, and Wah. Karāchi is the provincial capital of Sind, Lahore of Punjab, Peshāwar of the North-West Frontier Province, and Quetta of Baluchistan. The new capital city of Islāmābād adjoins Rāwalpindi, where the army's general headquarters and the offices of the president of Pakistan are located.

THE PEOPLE

Ethnic groups. Race as such plays little part in defining regional or group identity in Pakistan, and no ideal racial type is accepted by all Pakistanis. The population is a complex mixture of indigenous peoples, many racial types having been introduced by successive waves of migrations from the northwest, as well as by internal migrations across the subcontinent of India. Aryans, Persians, Greeks, Pashtuns (Pathans), and Mughals came from the northwest and spread across the Indo-Gangetic Plain, while the Arabs conquered Sind. All left their mark on the population and culture of the land. During the long period of Muslim rule, immigrants from the Middle East were brought in and installed as members of the ruling oligarchy. It became prestigious to claim descent from them, and many members of the landed gentry and of upper class families are either actually or putatively descended from such immigrants. In 1947, when Pakistan and India became independent, there was another massive migration, of a different character, when millions of Muslim refugees were uprooted from different parts of India and settled in Pakistan; an equal number of Hindus were uprooted from Pakistan and driven across to India. This development further complicated the racial mixture of the population of the various regions of Pakistan.

Ethnic antecedents

Of the earlier people, almost the only known skeletal remains of much significance are those associated with the Indus civilization that flourished 5,000 years ago. Human skeletons and skulls found among the ruins at Mohenjo-daro in Sind reveal firstly that at least four racial types were present in that area in about 2500 BC—Mediterranean and Alpinoid (both Europoid), Proto-Australoid (Veddoid), and Mongoloid—and secondly that there was much racial mixture. The Indo-Aryans, who predominate in contemporary Pakistan, arrived between about 1500 and 1200 BC. In the 6th century BC the Persian Empire was extended to the Indus Valley, and in the 4th century BC Alexander the Great and his armies passed through the region. The region subsequently became a melting pot for diverse races and cultures that came not only from outside the Indian subcontinent but also as a result of internal movements, such as the expansion of the Mauryan Empire over northern India. These variegated influences and associated migrations render any attempt to identify racial origins of people in different parts of Pakistan somewhat arbitrary.

Racial types to be seen in Pakistan include the tall, fair-skinned, and blue-eyed type; the olive-skinned, fine-boned, hawk-nosed "Iranian" type; smaller, dark-skinned types of "Dravidian" and "Australoid" origin; wheaten-skinned, dark-eyed "Indo-Aryan" types; short-headed and long-headed Mongoloid peoples; and, in Baluchistan, the broad-headed Europoid type of stocky build, reminiscent of the Alpine type in Europe.

Regionally, the population is sometimes grouped into four types by racial origin as follows—(1) the "true" Mediterranean type, found in the Punjab; (2) the "Oriental" Mediterranean type, found in the Punjab and Sind, characterized by an unusually long and often convex nose and lighter skin colour but otherwise similar to the first type; (3) the Pashtuns of the North-West Frontier Province; (4) the brachycephalic (short-headed) Baluchi type, which derives from Iranian stock.

Attitudes to racial types vary. In Baluchistan, the short Iranian head is admired, so that the three major tribes of the region sometimes bind their daughters' heads. In other areas, longheadedness is valued. Elsewhere, again, the shape of the head is a matter of indifference. There is, however, a general prejudice in favour of fair rather than dark skin colour.

Linguistic groups. Pakistan is in general linguistically heterogeneous, and no single language can be said to be common to the whole population. Each of its principal languages has a strong regional focus, although statistics show some languages to be distributed between various provinces because administrative boundaries cut across linguistic regions. The picture is also complicated by the fact that, especially in Sind, there are substantial numbers of Urdu- and Punjabi-speaking immigrants who have moved from the place of their origin and have settled on the land or taken up urban employment. The languages claimed as mother tongue include Urdu, Punjabi, Sindhi, Pashto, Baluchi, and Brahui.

Urdu is the youngest of the nation's languages, and is not indigenous to Pakistan; it is very similar to Hindi, an official language of India. Although the two languages have a common base, in its literary form Urdu emphasizes words of Persian and Arabic origin, whereas Hindi emphasizes words of Sanskrit origin. Urdu is written in a modified version of the Persian script (written from right to left), whereas Hindi is written in Devānagari script from left to right. Because it is preeminently the language of the educated Muslims of northern India, including the Punjab, Urdu has strong associations with Muslim nationalism; hence the ideological significance of Urdu in Pakistan politics.

The 1956 constitution prescribed the use of English for official purposes for 20 years, and the 1962 constitution made the period indefinite. The 1973 constitution, however, designated a 15-year transition period to Urdu, after which English would no longer be used for official purposes. English is spoken by only a small percentage of the people. Urdu is the mother tongue of only a small percentage of the population of Pakistan; it is taught in the schools of the provinces along with the regional languages.

Punjabi has its own script called Gurmukhi, but this is mainly used in India. In Pakistan, Punjabi is mainly spoken rather than written; it is also a predominantly rural rather than an urban language. Urdu, rather than Punjabi, is the first language taught in schools in Punjab, so that every educated Punjabi reads and writes Urdu. There was, however, a movement for the promotion of the Punjabi language in the late 20th century, and some Punjabi literature is being published using the Urdu script; among the works published are Punjabi classics that have hitherto been available in Gurmukhi script or preserved in oral tradition.

Sindhi is derived from the Virachada dialect of Prākrit; it has fewer dialects than Punjabi. It is written in a special variant of the Arabic script. Most of the educated middle class in Sind were Hindu, and their departure to India in 1947 had a traumatic effect on Sindhi culture. Vigorous efforts were therefore directed toward a recovery and preservation of the rich Sindhi literary and cultural heritage. Large numbers of Urdu-speaking refugees settled in Sind and constitute the majority of the population of its larger towns. As a consequence, the movement for promotion of Sindhi language and culture was sometimes expressed as opposition toward Urdu.

Pashto, the language of the Pashtuns (Pakhtuns, or Pathans) of the North-West Frontier Province, has no written literary traditions although it has a rich oral tradition. There are two major dialect patterns within which the various individual dialects may be classified; these are Pakhto, which is the northern (Peshāwar) variety, and the softer Pashto spoken in southern areas. As in the Punjab, Urdu is the language taught in schools, and educated Pashtuns read and write Urdu. Again, as in the case of Punjabi, there was a movement for developing the written language in Persian script and increasing the usage of Pashto.

Pashto

The two main spoken languages of Baluchistan are Baluchi and Brahui. Makrani is an important dialect of Baluchi; it is spoken in Makrān, the southern region of Baluchistan, bordering on Iran.

Religions. Almost all the people of Pakistan are Muslims. Most of them belong to the Sunnī, the major branch of Islām, with a significant representation among the small but equally important Shī'ī branch. There is also a very small, though influential, sect called Aḥmadīyah, or Qadianis, which does not regard the prophet Muḥammad as

Muslim sects

being the final prophet, a basic tenet of Islām. The majority of Pakistani Sunnīs belong to the orthodox Ḥanafī school, which is one of four schools or subsects of Sunnīs. Shī'ites are also divided into numerous subsects; among them are Ismā'īlīs (the followers of the Aga Khan), as well as The Twelvers (Ithnā 'Asharīs) and Bohrās, which are prominent communities in commerce and industry. The principal business communities among Sunnīs are Gujarati Memons and Chiniotis from Punjab.

With the exception of some sects, such as Dawoodi Bohrās, there is generally no ordained priesthood among Pakistan's Muslims. Anyone may be appointed *imām* who leads prayers in mosques. Those who are trained in theology are given the title of mullah or *mawlānā*s or, collectively, *'ulamā'*. There are, however, powerful networks of "holy men" called *pīr*s, who receive great reverence, as well as gifts in cash or kind from a multitude of followers. They constitute a hierarchy in one of four Ṣūfī (Muslim mystic) orders. An established *pīr* may pass on his spiritual powers and sanctified authority to one or more of his *murīd*s ("disciples"), who may then operate as a *pīr* in his own right. There are also many self-appointed *pīr*s who practice locally without being properly inducted into one of the four orders. *Pīr*s who occupy high positions in the *pīr* hierarchy wield great power and play an influential role in public affairs.

The number of Hindus in Pakistan was greatly reduced as a consequence of the exodus of refugees to India in 1947. Both Hindus and Christians constitute only a tiny percentage of the population.

Demography. The rate of population growth is extremely high and primarily results from natural increase. As mentioned, the 1947 influx of Muslim refugees from India was balanced by an exodus of Hindu refugees to India. Refugees entering what was then West Pakistan numbered about 6,500,000, or about 20 percent of the population of the territory at that time. Minor migrational shifts occurred between India and West Pakistan in the wake of the 1965 border hostilities. Following the founding of Bangladesh, thousands of non-Bengali Muslims emigrated from Bangladesh to Pakistan and an almost equal number of Bengalis were repatriated to Bangladesh from Pakistan. A second major influx of Muslim immigration commenced when thousands began to flee Afghanistan, occupied by the Soviet Union in 1979, to live in camps and settlements along the Pakistani border.

Regional distribution of the population is uneven, being dense in the fertile Indus Valley, especially in the extreme northeast, in Lahore district. By contrast, in the vast expanse of Baluchistan, the population densities are relatively low.

Estimates of fertility levels (and changes) vary widely and are unreliable. It is generally believed, however, that the birth rate will remain almost constant for some time, that the death rate will decline because of improving health facilities, and that growth in population will therefore persist unless the fertility rate can be brought down drastically. But the achievements of the family-planning program have not been commensurate with the scale on which it has been operated. A high incidence of infant and maternal mortality is a result of maternal malnutrition.

A trend toward greater urbanization has been accompanied by a relatively faster growth of the larger cities as compared to smaller ones; this has reflected the influence of industrial location as a new factor in the pattern of urban growth.
(H.A.A.)

Regional population distribution

THE ECONOMY

The relative prosperity of the industrialized regions around Karāchi and Lahore contrasts sharply with the poverty of the semiarid Baluchistan province and the North-West Frontier. The economy still relies heavily on the agricultural sector, mainly cotton. The combination of occasional crop failures because of unfavourable weather and weak trends in world commodity prices is a major problem. At the same time, there has been a relentless increase in population, so that, notwithstanding a real growth in the economy, output per head rises slowly. Nevertheless, Pakistan's economic performance compares favourably with that of many other developing countries. Real progress has been made in reducing the dependence on agriculture and in the diversification of the manufacturing sector. In this, foreign aid has played an important part.

The gradual structural change in the economy is reflected in the composition of foreign trade. Although as a trading nation Pakistan is among those nations with the lowest

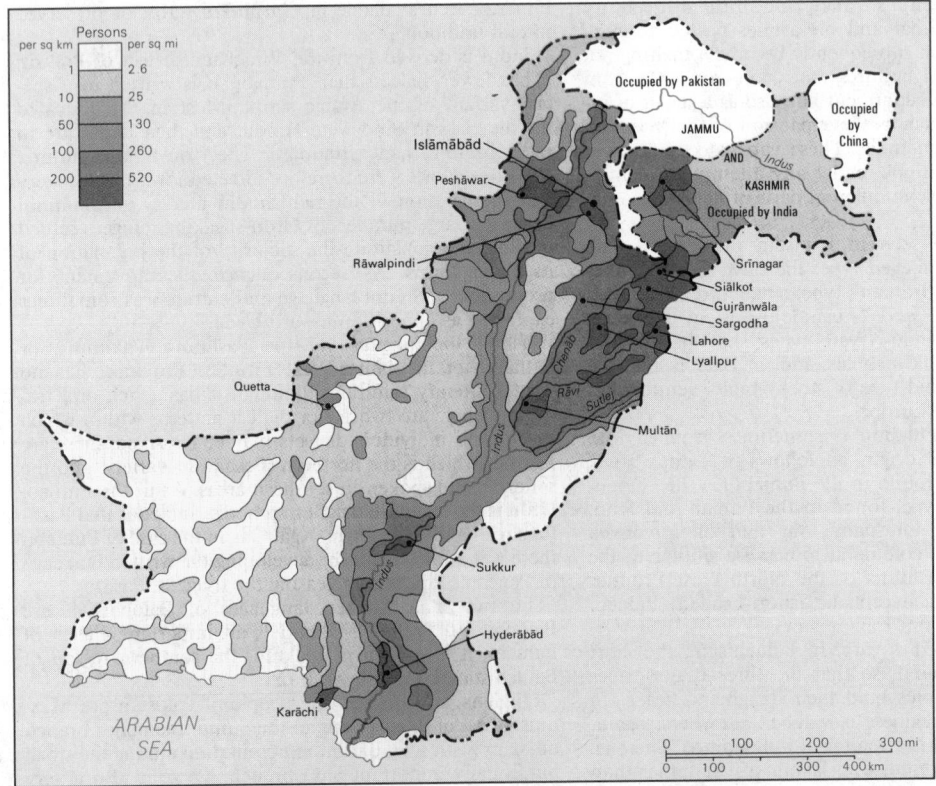

Population density of Pakistan and disputed areas. Data not available for areas occupied by China and Pakistan.

imports and exports per head, it is among the principal raw-cotton exporters. Pakistan has also managed to become a leading world exporter of cotton yarn and cloth. Pakistan was once an area supplying raw materials to the processing industries situated in what is now India; it now has evolved into a more integrated economy processing and manufacturing its own raw materials both for export and for the home market.

During the late 20th century a movement toward an "Islāmic economy" was announced by the Pakistani government. This movement involved the purging of economic practices outlawed by Muslim theology, such as *riba* (interest), and the mandatory reinstatement of the *zakat* (a tax on several types of personal financial assets) and the *ushr* (the *zakat* on land), which had not been universally adhered to but remained central tenets of Islāmic law.

Resources. *Mineral resources.* The exploration of Pakistan's mineral wealth is far from complete, but more than 20 different types of minerals have been located. Coal mining is one of the country's oldest industries. The quality of the coal is poor, and the mines are working below capacity because of the lack of demand. Iron-ore deposits are also mostly of poor quality. The most extensive known reserves are situated in the Kālābāgh region in western Punjab. Other low-grade ore reserves have been found in Hazāra in the North-West Frontier Province. Small reserves of high-grade iron ore have been identified in Chitrāl and in the Chilghāzi area (located in the Chagai district of Baluchistan province), also in the North-West Frontier Province. Deposits of copper ore, equalling or surpassing the reserves of iron ore, have been located, but most sites remain relatively unexploited. There are enormous reserves of easily exploited limestone that form the basis of a growing cement industry. Other minerals that are being exploited include chromite (mostly for export), barite (a white, yellow, or colourless mineral resembling marble), bauxite, celestite (strontium sulphate), antimony, aragonite (a mineral resembling calcite [calcium carbonate]), gypsum, rock salt, and marble. Radioactive minerals have been found in the Dera Ghāzi Khān district in the Punjab.

Oil and natural gas
Pakistan also has small quantities of oil and some very large natural-gas fields. The first oil discovery was made in 1915. By the late 20th century, several more fields had been found, none of them very important. Oil, however, fulfills a substantial portion of Pakistan's energy requirements, and the search for new and richer fields has continued. The largest natural-gas deposits are at Sūi (on the border between Baluchistan and the Punjab), discovered in 1953. A smaller field, at Māri, in the northwest of Sind province, was found in 1957. A network of gas pipelines links the fields with the main consumption areas: Karāchi, Lahore, Multān, Faisalābād (Lyallpur), and Islāmābād.

Biological resources. The variety of climates and soils has given rise to a wide diversity in biological resources. As Baluchistan is mostly desert, only in the small areas of intensive cultivation do crops and orchards thrive. In Sind and Punjab, where the annual rainfall is also low, most of the vegetation is basically xerophilous, except for the riverine forests along the Indus and its tributaries. The coastal region has mangrove forests. Regular rain and snow in the Himalayan foothills of the north have given them a variety of vegetation and animal life ranging from the Mediterranean to the Alpine types. There is a fishing industry centred on Karāchi, and part of the lobster and other shellfish catch is exported.

Pakistan's wildlife, already described, is varied. There are no game reserves, and indiscriminate hunting is threatening the survival of several animal species.

Hydroelectric and other power resources. Although Pakistan is poorly endowed with water resources, great progress has been made with the development of its hydroelectric potential. A giant hydroelectric plant is in operation at the Mangla Dam on the Jhelum River in Azad Kashmir. Another such source is the giant Tarbela Dam on the Indus River. Hydroelectric power surpasses thermal electric power in total generating capacity. Despite these advances in hydroelectric power, the majority of Pakistan's energy requirements continued to be fulfilled by oil, mostly imported, and natural gas. Nuclear power provides a small percentage of the total energy needs, primarily to Karāchi.

Agriculture, forestry, and fishing. Agriculture, forestry, and fishing provide employment for at least one-half of the official labour force and a livelihood for an even larger proportion of the population. A land-reform program has dealt with the dual problem of large-scale, often absentee ownership and the excessive fragmentation of small holdings by introducing maximum and minimum area limits.

Changes in agricultural techniques
The attention given to the agricultural sector in development plans has brought about some radical changes in centuries-old farming techniques. The construction of tube wells for irrigation and salinity control, the use of chemical fertilizers and scientifically selected seeds, and the gradual introduction of farm machinery—all have contributed to the notable increase in productivity. Early on, one of the prime objectives of agricultural development programs was self-sufficiency in wheat; this was so successful that by the early 1970s Pakistan was disposing of surpluses.

Pakistan experienced a "green revolution" during the late 20th century. In this period wheat production increased dramatically, leaving a surplus over domestic consumption that was partly shipped to East Pakistan (Bangladesh) and partly exported. Cotton production rose. Yields remained low by international standards, but increasing amounts were being processed locally; also, about one-half of Pakistan's edible oil was produced from cottonseed. Rice was the second major food staple and one of the country's important export crops. Large domestic sugar subsidies have been the main cause for the increase in sugarcane production.

Animal husbandry is a significant activity within the agricultural sector, providing important domestic and export products. Apart from the supply of meat and dairy products for local consumption, it includes production of wool for the carpet industry and for export and of hides and skins for the leather industry.

The contribution of forestry to national income remains negligible, but that of fisheries has been rising.

Industry. Mining and quarrying account for a small percentage of gross domestic product and of total employment. Manufacturing, however, accounts for a healthy proportion. The beginning of the main industrialization effort dates back to the Korean War boom and to the early 1950s. Initially, it was based on the processing of domestic agricultural raw materials for the home market and for export. This led to the setting up of cotton textile mills—an industry that accounts for a large part of the total employment in industry. Woollen textiles, sugar, paper, tobacco, and leather industries provide many jobs in the industrial labour force. The growing trade deficit in the mid-1950s compelled the government to cut down on imports. This encouraged the implantation of a number of import-substitution industries. At first, they produced mainly consumer goods, but, gradually, they came to produce intermediate goods and a range of capital goods, including chemicals, fertilizers, and light engineering products. Nevertheless, Pakistan still has to import a large proportion of the capital equipment and raw materials required by industry. In the late 20th century Pakistan began producing steel products for domestic use and export. Notwithstanding the diversification in the industrial sector, cotton textiles still account for a major share of total output.

Industrialization

Although energy production has risen faster than the economy as a whole, it has not kept pace with demand, and consequent shortages of fuel and electric power inhibit industrial growth. The exploitation of domestic natural-gas resources has been a major breakthrough, while heavy expenditure on thermal plants and hydroelectric resources has greatly increased electricity generating capacity.

Finance. Pakistan has a fairly well developed system of financial services. The State Bank of Pakistan has overall control over the banking sector, which consists of a number of commercial banks and specialist credit institutions. The State Bank acts as banker to the central and provincial governments and administers official monetary and credit policies, including exchange controls. It has sole currency-issuing rights and has custody of the country's

Banking and credit

gold and foreign exchange reserves. Pakistan has a number of scheduled banks subject to strict State Bank requirements as to paid-up capital and reserves. They account for the bulk of total deposits, collected through a network of branch offices. A few specialist financial institutions provide medium- and long-term credit for industrial, agricultural, and housing purposes and include the Pakistan Industrial Credit and Investment Corporation (PICIC), the Industrial Development Bank of Pakistan (IDBP), the Agricultural Development Bank of Pakistan (ADBP), and the House Building Finance Corporation. The Karāchi and Lahore stock exchanges deal in stocks and shares of registered companies. The Investment Corporation of Pakistan (ICP) and the National Investment Trust have helped to channel domestic savings into the capital market.

As part of the return to an "Islāmic economy," interest-free banking and financing practices have been instituted.

Trade. Although there was a trend toward increasing exports during the late 20th century, overall trade has generally remained heavily in deficit. Over the years some important changes have taken place in the composition of foreign trade. In particular, while the proportion of total export from primary commodities, including raw cotton, has fallen, the share of manufactures has greatly increased. But the bulk of the manufactured products coming into the export trade consists of cotton goods, so that Pakistan remains as dependent as ever on its leading cash crop. The other manufactures exported come mostly from industries based on agriculture, such as leather and leather goods and carpets. The shift toward manufactured agricultural exports, which have a higher added value content than the primary commodities, has been strongly encouraged by the government. The trade deficits and the shortages of foreign exchange have made it necessary for the government to restrict imports and to provide financial incentives to promote export trade.

Management of the economy. *The private sector.* The government has traditionally supported a system of free enterprise and has encouraged private domestic and foreign capital investment within the framework of the development plans. The policy has been comparatively successful. At the time of partition, in 1947, numbers of Muslim businessmen from what was to become secular India moved to Lahore and Karāchi and set up the nucleus of a new industrial and financial society. They were helped by the strong bias in favour of the manufacturing sector maintained by the government in its foreign-exchange allocation policy, particularly in the early 1950s. The availability of imported machinery and raw materials helped to promote a process of fairly diversified industrialization. Overall, private enterprise in the manufacturing and financial sectors has been concentrated in the hands of a small number of family cartels. This has been one of the big grievances nursed by the trade unions and left-wing political groups, which have sometimes contributed to social unrest.

In an effort to remedy this situation, the government in the early 1970s introduced a program of economic reforms that placed control over a number of key industries, such as iron and steel, chemicals, and cement, as well as the insurance sector, in the hands of the state. Many of these nationalized industries were returned to the private sector a few years later.

Foreign investment

Foreign private investors have been attracted to Pakistan by favourable investment incentive schemes, including tax holidays, long-term credit facilities from local industrial-financing institutions, and repatriation guarantees for capital and profits. United Kingdom investors account for the largest share of the total as a result of their predominant pre-independence position; but United States, German, and Japanese investments also gained in importance.

The public sector and the role of government. Investment by the public sector has been concentrated on social programs (education, health, etc.) and on the infrastructure (transport, communications, and power), leaving agriculture and industry to the private sector. Even in these sectors, however, when private investment would not or could not fulfill the set development targets, the government has stepped in. The development targets themselves have been spelled out in a series of five-year plans that have given the economy its general direction, but the government has also made use of a number of other methods to make short-term changes. Thus, the biannual foreign-trade policy could liberalize or restrict imports at short notice, while manipulations of bonus rates proved to be a flexible way of promoting selected exports. Subsidies, price controls, and tariff protection have all been used with varying degrees of success.

Taxation. Taxation accounts for more than three-quarters of government revenue, and government expenditures exceed revenues by a large amount. Income tax rates have been comparatively high, but the tax base has been so small that individual and corporate income tax revenues have remained substantially less than excise, sales, and other indirect taxes. The government has not made much use of internal deficit financing, primarily because of the high rate of consumption and low level of savings exhibited by most households. The government has been able to maintain heavy expenditure on development and defense because of the inflow of foreign aid. In doing this, however, the country has accumulated an enormous foreign debt, the financing of which has been a major problem.

The central-government budget is divided into a revenue budget, which deals with current expenditure, and a capital budget, covering development expenditure under the five-year plan. Taxation yields most of the revenue receipts—largely in excise duties and customs duties. Less than one-quarter of current revenue comes from income and corporation taxes. About half of the capital-budget receipts come from foreign aid. The provincial governments draw up their own budgets along lines similar to those adopted by the central government. Revenue consists of a share of the central government's tax receipts and of local taxes levied by the provincial governments themselves. Capital receipts are almost entirely made up of loans from the central government.

Sources of revenue

Defense has absorbed a great portion of the central government's current expenditure, but an even larger portion has been spent each year on development through the capital budget.

Trade unions and employer associations. The trade-union movement dates back to the late 19th century, but, because Pakistan's industrial sector (inherited at independence) was so small, organized labour as a proportion of total employment is still in a minority. This has not prevented it from becoming an important political force. Before the 1971 civil war, there were well over 1,000 registered unions, most of them organized within individual establishments. Countrywide unions based on a common craft or industry were very few. Most of the unions were situated in the urban centres and were affiliated to one of three national labour confederations. After the civil war and the emergence of Bangladesh the number of unions declined to a few hundred, affiliated to one umbrella organization, the Pakistan National Federation of Trade Unions. Because of the high rates of unemployment, employers remained in a strong position, and many of them were able to bypass working agreements and laws. Only the unions in the bigger industries (*e.g.,* cotton textiles) had the necessary coherence to fight back. The resulting wave of strikes and the rise in industrial costs slowed growth in the manufacturing sector.

Transportation. The dominant role of rail as the principal long-distance carrier has been displaced by the bus and truck. Motor trucks and tractor-drawn trailers are also displacing the traditional bullock cart for local transport of produce to markets.

The main arterial road, which runs from Karāchi to Peshāwar via Lahore and Rāwalpindi, is 1,080 miles (1,740 kilometres) long. The main rail route runs more than 1,000 miles north from Karāchi to Peshāwar, via Lahore and Rāwalpindi. Another main line branches northwest-ward from Sukkur to Quetta.

Pakistan International Airlines (PIA), established in 1955, is the sole carrier of internal air traffic. PIA also runs international flights to Europe, the Middle East, Africa, the Far East, and China, as well as to neighbouring Afghanistan.

The principal airports are at Karāchi, Lahore, Rāwalpindi, and Peshāwar. Karāchi is the principal ocean port.

ADMINISTRATIVE AND SOCIAL CONDITIONS

Government. The political system of Pakistan has undergone several far-reaching changes since independence; in 1971, its turbulent politics culminated in the secession of its eastern region (having more than 54 percent of the total population at that time), which established itself as the independent state of Bangladesh. In the aftermath of that event, in 1972, Pakistan (now reduced to what was previously West Pakistan) faced a number of political and economic problems and uncertainties about its future.

Political stresses

Three distinct sets of conflicts have left their mark on the politics of Pakistan. The first of these, initially obscured by the paraphernalia of a parliamentary form of government but later made manifest by overt seizure of power by men at the head of the military and bureaucratic establishment, was a continuing struggle between political leadership and a military-bureaucratic oligarchy for supremacy and authority in the state; ideologically, this struggle was expressed as a struggle for democracy. A second and a quite distinct conflict was a struggle between regional groups. Because it was directed against centralized authority, it merged with the democratic struggle. But its express aims were focussed on securing greater regional representation in the bureaucratic and military establishment, especially in the higher echelons, as well as achieving effective decentralization of powers within a federal governmental structure by emphasizing regional autonomy. A third set of conflicts concerned the allocation of economic resources and burdens and the distribution of a greater share of the benefits of development among the more deprived regions and strata of the population. In particular, a small number of business families controlled the bulk of the industrial wealth of the country. Agricultural wealth was concentrated in the hands of the landlords, especially of the Canal Colonies of the Punjab and of Sind.

These regional and class conflicts exploded into violence and death for hundreds of persons following accusations of vote fraud in the 1977 national and provincial elections. Martial law was imposed and the 1973 constitution was put into abeyance. Rather than acquiesce to the demands of factions, the government embarked on a program to unite Pakistan under the banner of Islām and restore Muslim teachings to the political, social, and economic spheres of Pakistan.

The constitutional framework. The task of framing a constitution for independent Pakistan was entrusted in 1947 to a Constituent Assembly that was also to function as the country's interim legislature under the Government of India Act (1935 [as adapted]), which was to be the interim constitution. It was federal in form, with the Constituent Assembly and a governor general at the centre and with provincial assemblies with governors of provinces on the regional level. Government was to be under Cabinets responsible to the central assembly and the provincial assemblies, respectively. Extraordinarily wide powers were, however, vested in the governor general, which were to prove decisive in establishing the power relationship between the bureaucratic and military establishment and the political leadership.

Pakistan's first constitution was enacted by the Constituent Assembly in 1956. It followed the form of the Government of India Act (1935), allowing the president far-reaching powers to suspend federal and provincial parliamentary government. The 1956 constitution also included the "parity formula," by which representation in the National Assembly for East and West Pakistan would be decided on a parity, rather than population, basis. (A major factor in the political crisis of 1970–71 was abandonment of the "parity formula" and adoption of representation by population, giving East Pakistan an absolute majority in the new National Assembly.)

In 1958 the constitution was abrogated and martial law was instituted. A new constitution, promulgated in 1962, provided for the election of the president and National and provincial assemblies by an electoral college composed of members of local councils. Although a federal form of government was retained, the assemblies had little power, which was, in effect, centralized through the authority of governors acting under the president. In April 1973 the third constitution in Pakistan's 25-year history was adopted by the National Assembly. The constitution lasted but four years before being suspended in 1977. In March 1981 a Provisional Constitutional Order was promulgated, providing a framework for government under martial law. Four years later a process was initiated for reinstating the constitution of 1973. By October 1985 a newly elected National Assembly had passed an amended constitution, and in late December of that year the end of martial law was proclaimed.

Political parties. The role of Islām in the political and cultural unification of Pakistan has been a controversial topic. Some factions have argued that Islāmic ideology was the only cement that could bind together its culturally diverse peoples. Opposing factions argued equally that it was the insistence on Islāmic ideology, in opposition to regional demands expressed in secular and cultural idiom, that progressively alienated regional groups and eroded national unity.

The Mus-lim League

The Muslim League, the party of Muslim nationalism in India, the aspirations of which were fulfilled by the creation of Pakistan, had by 1947 pushed all other political parties into insignificance. It had put forward the "two nation theory," which declared that Indian Muslims were a separate nation from other Indians. But its political idiom was not theological. It was the party of "Muslim modernists," the educated Muslim middle classes who aspired to more secure and more privileged positions in the worlds of government and public service and in business. The Muslim theocratic parties, however, such as the Jamī'at-e Islāmī or the Jamī'at-e 'Ulamā'e Hind, were opposed to the creation of Pakistan.

After independence the Muslim League was rapidly fragmented, and the fragments developed into rival political parties. The rump of the Muslim League allied itself closely with the bureaucratic-military establishment, and, reluctant to face an electorate in elections, it was willing to submit to the bureaucratic-military establishment as a price for holding office. To oppose regionalist and democratic demands against centralized authority, the Muslim League, to an extent that it had never done before, began to stress Islāmic ideology, which it advocated as the only basis for the unity of Pakistan in opposition to regionalist secular politics, thus further alienating regional sentiment.

Local government and administration. The basic administrative structure has remained virtually unchanged since the colonial period, despite all the constitutional upheavals and changes at the national and provincial levels. Provinces are subdivided into divisions, districts, and *tahsils* (district subdivisions), which are run by a hierarchy of administrators, such as the divisional commissioner, the deputy commissioner (in the district), and the subdivisional magistrate, subdivisional officer, or *tahsildār* at the *tahsil* level. The key level is that of the district, where the deputy commissioner controls all branches of government, being directly in charge of the administration of revenue and having judicial functions as the district magistrate; he also controls the police.

Local self-government in the form of district boards has existed since colonial times. In 1959, however, these were transformed into district councils with the deputy commissioner as chairman instead of having an elected chairman; they were also made a part of a hierarchy of councils, which were set up at the divisional as well as at the *tahsil* level. The councils were subject to extremely close control and regulation by administrative officers. The system fell into disrepute because of corruption as well as because of authoritarian control, and there was a public demand to disband them; the system has been moribund since 1969.

District councils

Following the suspension of the constitution, martial law was extended to provincial, division, and district government levels. Deputy commissioners and their division-level superiors (commissioners) were made accountable to a provincial martial law administrator. Executive and legislative functions were fulfilled by martial law cabinets and advisory councils. In 1985 new provincial assemblies were elected, and after martial law was ended civilians were again appointed to top administrative posts.

Justice. There is a formal division between the judiciary and the executive branches of government. The judiciary consists of the Supreme Court, the provincial high courts, and (under their jurisdiction and supervision) district courts that hear civil cases and sessions courts that hear criminal cases. There is also a magistracy that deals with cases brought by the police. The district magistrate (who, as deputy commissioner, also controls the police) hears appeals from magistrates under him; appeals may go from him to the sessions judge. The Supreme Court is a court of record. It has original, appellate, and advisory jurisdictions and is the highest court in the land. At the time of independence, Pakistan inherited legal codes and acts that remain in force, subject to amendment.

The judicial system also began a reorientation to Islāmic tenets and values designed to make legal redress inexpensive and accessible to all persons. A complete code of Islāmic laws was instituted.

Education and welfare. The literacy rate for Pakistan is substantially lower than that of other developing nations; only about one-quarter of all adults are literate. A significant percentage of those who are literate, however, have not had any formal education. Educational levels for women have been much lower than those for men. The share of females in educational levels progressively diminishes above the primary school level.

Since independence Pakistan has increased the number of primary and secondary schools and the number of students enrolled has risen dramatically. Teacher training has been promoted by the government and by international agencies. Higher education is available at vocational schools, technical schools, and colleges throughout the country. Each province, as well as Azad Kashmir, has a provincial university, and universities specializing in agricultural technology and engineering are located in Lahore, Faisalābād, and Karāchi. The oldest university in Pakistan is the University of the Punjab, established in 1882, and the largest universities are Allama Iqbal Open University and the University of Karāchi. Universities established during the late 20th century include the University of Azad Jammu and Kashmir (1980), the North-West Frontier Province Agricultural University in Peshāwar (1981), the Islāmic University in Islāmābād (1980), and the Aga Khan University in Karāchi (1983). Most university classes are taught in Urdu or English.

Welfare services are inadequately developed in relation to needs. There are insufficient numbers of doctors and nurses. Annual expenditure on education, health, and social welfare pales into insignificance beside the annual defense expenditure.

The *zakat* has been used by the government to provide social welfare funds. Mandatory and voluntary *zakat* collections are distributed to provincial, division, and district *zakat* committees for final distribution among organizations and religious orders engaged in social welfare activities or directly to needy persons. *Zakat* funds also contribute to provincial scholarship funds.

CULTURAL LIFE

Pakistan shares influences that have shaped the cultures of the peoples of South Asia. There are thus wider regional similarities extending beyond the national boundaries. On the other hand, the specific regional cultures of Pakistan present a picture of rich diversity. It is difficult, therefore, to speak of a single Pakistani culture.

Family organization is strongly patriarchal, as in most agrarian societies, and most people live in large extended families. A woman's place in society is low, and she is restricted to the performance of domestic chores and to fulfilling the role of a dutiful wife and mother. In wealthy peasant and landowner households and in urban middle-class families, women are kept in seclusion (*pardah*); on the rare occasions on which they set foot outside their houses, they must be veiled. Among poor peasants, women have duties on the farm as well as in the house and do not observe *pardah*. In the Punjab, cotton picking is exclusively a woman's job, and women keep the money thus

The literacy rate

The status of women

earned for their own purposes. Houses of those who practice *pardah* have a men's section (*mardānah*) at the front of the house, so that visitors do not disturb the women, who are secluded in the women's section (*zanānah*).

Among the very rich, Western education and modes of living have eliminated *pardah,* but, in general, even among this group, attitudes toward women in society and the family are akin to those of Victorian England. Change is coming most rapidly among the urban lower middle income group, in which women are forced to seek employment under the pressure of economic necessity; *pardah* is then cast off and the education of women encouraged. In consequence, some women have gained distinction in the professions; significantly, some of the country's leading trade unionists are women.

Social organization revolves around kinship rather than caste. *Berādarī* (patrilineage) is the most important social institution. A preferable marriage for a man is with his father's brother's daughter, and among many groups marriages are invariably within the *berādarī.* The lineage elders constitute a council that adjudicates disputes within the lineage and acts on behalf of the lineage with the outside world—for example, in determining electoral allegiances.

Pakistan claims a cultural heritage dating back more than 5,000 years, to the epoch of the Indus civilization. But the emphasis on Islāmic ideology has brought about a strong romantic identification with Islāmic culture—not only that of the Indian subcontinent but of the whole of the Islāmic world. *Qawwālī,* a form of devotional singing, is very popular. Poetry is also a popular rather than an esoteric art, and public poetry recitations called *mushā'irah*s are organized like musical concerts. Urdu, Sindhi, and Pashto poets are regional and national heroes. Literary tradition is the richest of all Pakistani art forms. Music and, especially, dancing are comparatively less developed arts. The visual arts, too, play little part in popular folk culture. Painting and sculpture, however, have made considerable progress as expressions of an increasingly sophisticated urban culture.

The cinema is now the most popular form of entertainment. Many feature films are produced each year, mostly in Urdu. The songs and music used in the films have a distinctive character and are often reproduced on phonograph records and broadcast on the radio.

Radio and television have been used in an attempt to harness folk cultural traditions (especially in song, music, and drama) for political and nonpolitical propaganda purposes. Censorship of broadcasting and of the press has been imposed at various times, but it has more usually been replaced by what is euphemistically called a "press-advice" system by which the ministry of information gives guidance to the press. (H.A.A./Ed.)

For statistical data on the land and people of Pakistan, see the *Britannica World Data* section in the BRITANNICA WORLD DATA ANNUAL.

History

BACKGROUND TO PARTITION

The Muslim League and Mohammed Ali Jinnah. The movement among the Muslim population of the India–Pakistan subcontinent that culminated in the creation of Pakistan stemmed from the historical fact that, for more than six centuries before the effective domination of the British in India, Muslim soldiers and administrators had controlled a population in which Hindus were a numerical majority, although mass conversions to Islām in economically backward areas like East Bengal (Bangladesh) produced local Muslim majorities. When the British replaced Muslim domination by their own, the tradition of rule prevented the Muslims from adapting themselves to the new situation as readily as the Hindus; but the failure of the risings of 1857 dashed Muslim hopes of a restoration of their authority. Later, while Hindus were pressing for constitutional reform through the Indian National Congress, the Muslims sought various guarantees to safeguard their minority position and finally founded their own political organization, the All-India Muslim League, at Dacca in 1906. For a more complete discussion of

Pakistan under British rule and the history of Pakistan before British domination see INDIA: *History.*

The gradual clarification of the British intention to grant self-government to India along the lines of British parliamentary democracy aroused Muslim apprehensions regarding ultimate political subjection to the Hindu majority of the population. Mohammed Ali Jinnah, as eager as any Hindu nationalist to bring British rule to an end, was at length driven to the conclusion, which the renowned poet-philosopher Muḥammad Iqbāl had already expressed, that the only way to preserve Indian Muslims from complete political, economic, and cultural subordination to the Hindus was to establish a separate Muslim state. By 1940, the demand for Pakistan had been formally endorsed by the Muslim League under his leadership.

British policy, supported by the whole weight of the Hindu nationalist movement, laboured hard to avoid disrupting the economic and political unity built up during the period of British rule. None of the many suggested alternatives to separation of Pakistan commended themselves to Jinnah, whose leadership of the bulk of the community was unchallenged, and without his cooperation—of which the price was Pakistan—Indian independence was impracticable. His courage and implacable determination triumphed in the end.

Birth of the new state. The new state came into existence as a dominion within the Commonwealth in August 1947, with Jinnah as its first governor general and his ablest colleague, Liaquat Ali Khan, as its first prime minister. With West and East Pakistan separated by more than 1,000 miles of Indian territory, and with the major portion of the wealth and resources of the British heritage passing to India, Pakistan's survival seemed to hang in the balance. Of all the well-organized provinces of British India, only the comparatively backward areas of Sind, Baluchistan, and the North-West Frontier came to Pakistan intact. The Punjab and Bengal were divided, and Kashmir became disputed territory. Economically, the situation seemed almost hopeless; the new frontier cut off Pakistani raw materials from the Indian factories, disrupting industry, commerce, and agriculture. The partition and the movement of refugees were accompanied by terrible massacres for which both communities were responsible. India remained overtly unfriendly; its economic superiority expressed itself in a virtual blockade. The dispute over Kashmir brought the two countries to the verge of war; and India's command of the headworks controlling the water supplies to Pakistan's eastern canal colonies gave it an additional economic weapon. The resulting friction, by obstructing the process of sharing (according to plans previously agreed) those assets inherited from the British raj, still further handicapped Pakistan in solving its problems.   (Ed.)

ISLĀMIC REPUBLIC OF PAKISTAN

India, too, received the advantage of Jawaharlal Nehru's leadership for almost two decades; Mohammed Ali Jinnah, however, died in September 1948, within 13 months of independence. The leaders of the new Pakistan were mainly lawyers, with a strong commitment to parliamentary government. They had supported Jinnah in his struggle against the Congress not so much because they desired an Islāmic state as because they had come to regard the Congress as synonymous with Hindu domination. They had various degrees of personal commitment to Islām. To some it represented an ethic that might (or might not) be the basis of personal behaviour within a modern, democratic state. To others it represented a tradition, the framework within which their forefathers had ruled India. But there were also groups that subscribed to Islām as a total way of life, and these people were said to wish to establish Pakistan as a theocracy (a term they repudiated). The members of the old Constituent Assembly, elected at the end of 1945, assembled at Karachi, the new capital.

Jinnah's lieutenant, Liaquat Ali Khan, inherited the task of devising an acceptable formula. Himself a moderate (he had entered politics via a landlord party), he subscribed to the parliamentary, democratic, secular state. But he was conscious that he possessed no local or re-

Ambivalent attitudes toward Islām

gional power base. He was a "refugee"; he came from the United Provinces, the Indian heartland, whereas most of his colleagues and potential rivals drew support from their own people in Punjab or Bengal. Liaquat Ali Khan therefore deemed it necessary to gain the support of the religious spokesmen (the *mullahs* or, more properly, the *'ulamā'*). He issued a resolution on the aims and objectives of the constitution, which began, "Sovereignty over the entire universe belongs to Allāh Almighty alone" and went on to emphasize Islāmic values. This led to protests from Hindu members of the old Constituent Assembly; Islāmic states had traditionally distinguished between the Muslims, as full citizens, and *dhimmī*s, nonbelievers who were denied certain rights and saddled with certain additional obligations.

Political decline. Liaquat Ali Khan fell to an assassin's bullet in October 1951. Into his place as prime minister stepped Khwaja Nazimuddin, the leading member of the family of the Nawab of Dacca. He was a Bengali aristocrat and a man of extreme personal piety. Nazimuddin had followed Jinnah as governor general under the interim constitution (virtually the 1935 Government of India Act). He was succeeded as governor general by Ghulam Mohammad, a Punjabi, so that the twin pillars of power represented the two main regional power bases in West Pakistan and East Pakistan.

With Nazimuddin in office, militant Muslims, led by the Ahrars, a puritanical political group, called for the purification of national life. In 1953 they demanded that the Aḥmadīyah sect should be outlawed from the Islāmic community. Nazimuddin temporized, and rioting and arson enveloped Lahore and other Punjabi towns. The secretary of defense, Col. Iskander Mirza, a former political officer, pressed the Cabinet into sanctioning the promulgation of martial law in Lahore, and order was restored. Ghulam Mohammad decided that Nazimuddin must go, although he enjoyed the support of the Constituent Assembly. The dismissal was effected, and a new prime minister from Bengal was found in Mohammad Ali Bogra.

Without a constitution, the legislative assemblies, both national and provincial, were replenished ad hoc. But in March 1954 a general election was held in East Bengal (East Pakistan) to choose a new provincial legislature. The contest was between the official Muslim League and a "United Front" of parties from the extreme right (orthodox religious) to extreme left (quasi-Marxist). There was a landslide defeat for the Muslim League. At the head of the victorious opposition stood two politicians who had previously kept one foot in the Muslim League and the other in the camp of the Congress and regional politics; these were the aged Fazl ul-Haq, with his Krishak Sramik (Workers and Peasants) Party, and Hussein Shaheed Suhrawardy, with a new party, the Awami League. The result was a dramatic demonstration of the gulf between West and East Pakistan.

Electoral defeat of the Muslim League (1954)

The Constituent Assembly reflected the new political mood by attempting to curb the powers of the governor general, who retaliated by proclaiming the dissolution of that body. Ghulam Mohammad's action was validated by the Supreme Court, with the rider that a new assembly must be convened. This was produced by a system of indirect election. The ministry of Mohammad Ali Bogra was completely reorganized, with three newcomers introduced as strong men from outside politics: these were Maj. Gen. Iskander Mirza, as minister of the interior, Gen. Mohammad Ayub Khan, commander in chief, as minister of national defense, and Chaudhri Mohammad Ali, a senior civil servant, as minister of finance. Mohammad Ali Bogra had little support in the new assembly, and he was replaced by Chaudhri Mohammad Ali.

Ghulam Mohammad, whose health had broken down, was replaced as governor general in August 1955 by Iskander Mirza. The latter had no regional power base and little in common with any of the politicians. Mirza insisted that his fellow administrator Chaudhri Mohammad Ali remain prime minister, and Chaudhri was able to succeed in one objective over which his three predecessors had failed: he induced the politicians to agree to a constitution (February 1956). In order to create a better balance between the West and East wings, the provinces and parts of West Pakistan were amalgamated into one administrative unit.

The constitution of 1956 embodied the Islāmic provisions of the "aims and objectives" resolution of 1949 and declared Pakistan to be an Islāmic republic. The national parliament was to comprise one house of 300 members, equally representing East and West. Ten seats were reserved for women. In constitutional theory the prime minister and Cabinet were to govern according to the will of the parliament, with the president exercising only reserve powers.

Khan Sahib, a former premier of North-West Frontier Province, was invited by the Muslim League to become the chief minister of the new "one unit" of West Pakistan. Soon after taking office, Khan Sahib was faced with a revolt against his leadership in the Muslim League, but he adroitly turned the tables by forming a new group, the Republican Party, out of dissident Muslim League assemblymen. In the National Assembly also, members adopted the Republican ticket, and Prime Minister Chaudhri Mohammad Ali found himself without a majority. He resigned in September 1956.

Iskander Mirza, then president, was compelled to accept an Awami League government headed by Suhrawardy but dependent on Republican support to retain office. For a time the combination worked, but the flimsy consensus of Pakistan politics soon began to dissolve into factionalism, regionalism, and sectarianism. Khan Sahib found his hold over the West Pakistan legislature slipping, and he asked the President to suspend the constitution. The East Pakistan legislature voted unanimously for autonomy in all matters except foreign affairs, defense, and currency. The country was to hold its first complete general election in 1958, but a dispute over the basis of the constituencies led to Suhrawardy's resignation. His successors proved ineffective, and the legislative process came to a halt.

Military government. President Mirza had made no secret of his dissatisfaction with the working of parliamentary democracy in Pakistan. He therefore came to a decision to put an end to politics. On October 7, 1958, a presidential proclamation announced that the political parties were abolished, the constitution abrogated, and the country placed under martial law, with Gen. Mohammad Ayub Khan as chief martial law administrator. Mirza announced that the martial law period would be brief and that a new constitution would be drafted. On October 27 he swore in his new Cabinet.

General Ayub became prime minister, and three lieutenant generals were named to the Cabinet. The eight civilian members included businessmen and lawyers, one being a young newcomer, Zulfikar Ali Bhutto. That same evening the new military ministers called on the President, with contingents of armed soldiers, and informed him that he was to resign. After a short interval, Mirza was exiled to London. A proclamation issued by Ayub announced his assumption of the presidency.

Martial law lasted 44 months. During that time a number of army officers took over vital civil-service posts. A number of politicians were excluded from public life under the Electoral Bodies (Disqualification) Order, or EBDO. A similar purge took place among civil servants.

Ayub had long pondered the problem of creating political institutions that would express Islāmic ideals and foster national development. He came forward with a plan for "basic democracies," directly elected by the people, as local units of development. Elections for the basic democracies took place in January 1960. The Basic Democrats, as they became known, were at once asked to endorse Ayub's presidency and to give him a mandate to frame a constitution. Of the 80,000 Basic Democrats, 75,283 gave him affirmative votes (February 1960). A constitutional commission was asked to advise on a suitable form of government. Ayub accepted some of its proposals and substituted some of his own, aiming, he said, for "a blending of democracy with discipline." In the early days of Ayub's regime there were notable reform measures, such as the Muslim Family Laws Ordinance of 1961, restricting polygamy, but later the President found it necessary to make concessions to Muslims in order to bolster his regime.

One feature of the Ayub regime was the quickening pace of economic growth. During the initial phase of independence, the growth rate was less than 3 percent per annum and scarcely moved ahead of the rate of population growth. During the mid-1950s even this rate declined, but from 1960 to 1965 the rate advanced to more than 6 percent per annum. Development was particularly vigorous in the manufacturing sector.

There was considerable imbalance between East and West; during the 1950s East Pakistan was becoming poorer in per capita terms every year, whereas the West was achieving positive growth. A continuing grievance was the contribution made by East Pakistan to foreign exchange by the export of jute and tea, from which it was felt the West reaped more advantage; the West was also the major beneficiary of foreign aid.

The outstanding example of favoured treatment for the West was the great Indus Basin scheme for hydroelectric development. Pakistan skillfully negotiated for assistance from the World Bank, the United States, and other friends. In addition to economic aid, Pakistan also received immense military aid from the United States.

The war over Kashmir in 1965 had more far-reaching effects on Pakistan than on India. Ayub received a new mandate from the Basic Democrats in January 1965, when he won decisively against a spirited challenge from Fatima Jinnah, the sister of Mohammed Ali Jinnah. In the early days of his presidency Ayub had moved freely among the rural people, talking to them face to face. After the war he withdrew behind a curtain of dictatorship, becoming a remote figure in a bulletproof limousine. Bhutto, the chief exponent of struggle against India, was relieved of office in 1966. Mujibur Rahman (Sheikh Mujib), who had inherited the leadership of the Awami League, the major force in East Pakistan, was arrested and accused of conspiring with India.

Ayub's autocratic position was suddenly challenged in the autumn of 1968; an unsuccessful attempt on his life was followed by the arrest of Bhutto and other opposition leaders. Ayub attempted to stem the mounting protest by summoning a conference of opposition leaders and by withdrawing the state of emergency under which Pakistan had been governed since 1965. These concessions failed to conciliate the opposition, and in February 1969 Ayub announced that he would not contest the presidential election due in 1970. Protests and strikes flared everywhere, being especially militant in Bengal. At length, on March 25, 1969, Ayub resigned, handing over responsibility for governing to the commander in chief, Gen. Agha Mohammad Yahya Khan. Once again the country was placed under martial law. Yahya assumed the title of president as well as chief martial law administrator. He made it clear that his aim was an early general election, which took place in December 1970.

Civil war. The success of the Awami League in East Pakistan surprised even its friends. Sheikh Mujib emerged with a majority at his command among the membership of the new assembly (167 of the 300 total). But what upset all predictions was the victory in West Pakistan of Bhutto's Pakistan People's Party (PPP), which won particularly heavily in Punjab and gained a clear majority (83) of the representation from the West. Yahya's plan provided that when the new assembly met it must produce a constitution within 100 days. Mujib, however, stood out for complete independence for East Pakistan, except for foreign policy, though the East wanted to make its own aid, trade, and defense agreements. Bhutto rejected these terms and refused to bring his party to Dacca to participate in the assembly. On March 1, 1971, President Yahya announced that the National Assembly would be suspended indefinitely. Sheikh Mujib replied by ordering a boycott and general strike throughout East Pakistan. Bowing to the inevitable, Yahya proceeded to Dacca in mid-March to negotiate a compromise that would concede the substance of Mujib's demands while retaining tenuous ties that might still preserve the name of Pakistan. But compromise proved impossible. President Yahya denounced Mujib and his men as traitors and launched a drive to "reoccupy" the East with West Pakistan troops.

Warfare between government troops and supporters of the Awami League broke out in the East in March. Sheikh Mujib and many of his colleagues were arrested, while others escaped to India, proclaiming East Pakistan an independent state under the name Bangladesh (Bengal Land). As fighting continued, the number of refugees crossing the border into India grew into the millions. In December 1971 India successfully invaded East Pakistan. The establishment of a Bangladesh government with Mujib as prime minister followed in January 1972.

Bhutto's regime. Accepting responsibility for the defeat and breakup of Pakistan, President Yahya resigned on December 20, 1971, and Bhutto became the undisputed leader of former West Pakistan. He secured another election victory for the PPP, opposition being largely confined to the North-West Frontier Province and Baluchistan. Bhutto's declared policy of Islāmic Socialism brought few tangible changes, but his populism was undeniably successful. He became increasingly autocratic, however, suppressing criticism, jailing opponents, and employing militant methods against the restive Pashtuns and Baluchs. A new constitution was adopted on April 10, 1973, and Bhutto became prime minister of Pakistan.

In January 1977 Bhutto announced that elections would be held within two months, unfolding a national charter of peasant reform. Nine opposition parties hastily patched together the Pakistan National Alliance (PNA) and launched a demand for the Islāmic way of life in Pakistan. The campaign was marked by violence, with opposition candidates complaining of brutal discrimination. The results were a sweeping victory for Bhutto's PPP, although they were denounced as fraudulent by the PNA. Mounting protest soon brought chaos to Karāchi and other major cities, where Bhutto was compelled to call out the army and proclaim martial law. He tried to buy peace by offering concessions to the PNA leaders (most of whom were under arrest), but they would accept nothing short of a new election.

Zia ul-Haq's regime. To avoid total chaos, the chief of staff of the army, Gen. Mohammad Zia ul-Haq, took over as chief administrator of martial law on July 5, 1977. His early efforts to create an acceptable political alternative had only limited success. He announced that elections would be held in 90 days, but it was clear that Bhutto was the only politician of mass appeal. In early September Bhutto was arrested and charged with attempted murder (he was sentenced to death the following March), and on September 16 Zia was proclaimed president of Pakistan.

By this time the PNA was split, with most elements forming an opposition that demanded early elections, withdrawal of the army from Baluchistan, and the introduction of a full Islāmic code of laws. A zealous Muslim, Zia had already imposed Islāmic criminal punishments, such as flogging and maiming, which were formally enacted as law in February 1979. Bhutto was hanged on April 4, 1979, following a Supreme Court review of his case. In October elections were postponed indefinitely, political parties and strikes were banned, and the press was submitted to strict censorship.

The invasion of Afghanistan by the Soviet Union in December 1979 became central to Pakistan's internal and foreign affairs. Zia embarked upon a military buildup supported by the United States and by other Islāmic countries and opposed by India. The influx of millions of refugees from Afghanistan led Zia also to acquire foreign economic aid. In March 1981 Zia announced a provisional constitutional order that allowed the government to be kept under martial law indefinitely and that gave the president power to amend the constitution. Periodic outbursts of religious and political violence added to domestic tensions and increased in intensity during the 1980s.

Partisan political activity was allowed to resume gradually, but it remained subject to official censure. A referendum held in December 1984 confirmed Zia's Islāmization policy, although the results were sharply contested by opposition groups. In February 1985 elections were held for both the National and local assemblies; by October an amended version of the 1973 constitution had been reinstated, and at the end of the year Zia officially declared the end of martial law. (H.R.T./Ed.)

Death of Bhutto

For later developments in the history of Pakistan, see the *Britannica Book of the Year* section in the BRITANNICA WORLD DATA ANNUAL.

For coverage of related topics in the *Macropædia* and *Micropædia,* see the *Propædia,* sections 935, 936, 968, and 976.

Azad Kashmir

The quasi-state of Azad (Free) Kashmir—along with three federally administered agencies, the Diāmir Agency, the Gilgit Agency, and the Baltistān Agency—constitutes that part of the disputed states of Jammu and Kashmir (see INDIA: *Jammu and Kashmir*) that is under Pakistan's control. Azad Kashmir consists of an arc-shaped stretch of territory bordering the Indian-held state of Jammu and Kashmir on the east, the Pakistani states of Punjab on the south and southwest and North-West Frontier Province on the west, and the Diāmir and Baltistān agencies on the north. The combined area of Azad Kashmir and the three agencies is 32,358 square miles (83,806 square kilometres).

Azad Kashmir is neither a province nor an agency but has a government of its own that is regarded by Pakistan as "independent," even though it is protected by and economically and administratively linked to Pakistan.

PHYSICAL AND HUMAN GEOGRAPHY

The Pakistani portion of Jammu and Kashmir has a relief that ranges from the inhabitable highlands of Azad Kashmir to the huge area of rugged and inhospitable terrain in the Gilgit and Baltistān agencies bordering on the People's Republic of China. The northern terrain consists of spurs of the Karakoram Range, the Pamirs, and the Hindu Kush. Throughout the region, most elevations are higher than 8,000 feet (2,500 metres); about half are above 15,000 feet; and several peaks exceed 22,000 feet. There are, nevertheless, several fertile valleys and upland pastures.

Terrain

In these northern highlands, winters are extremely cold and summers only mild. Annual mean rainfall there is high for Pakistan, exceeding 40 inches (1,000 millimetres) or even 60 inches in most areas except in the very highest elevations, where precipitation is low.

Whereas India's state of Jammu and Kashmir has several million inhabitants, Pakistan's Azad Kashmir has fewer than a million, and the Diāmir, Gilgit, and Baltistān agencies have only a few score thousand.

The government of Azad Kashmir, with headquarters at Muzaffarābād, was first set up in 1947. It is under a president, assisted by a State Council of 12. The quasi-state has its own High Court. Pakistan maintains overall control through the Ministry of Kashmir Affairs. Azad Kashmir is divided administratively into four districts: Mīrpur, Kotli, Pūnch, and Muzaffarābād. Although the three agencies are administered by the government of Pakistan, they are governed as separate units because of the difficult mountain terrain and the lack of communications between them. Gilgit town is the headquarters of the Gilgit Agency, Chilās that of Diāmir, and Skārdu that of Baltistān.

In its land reforms the Pakistani government has abolished all types of *jagir* (assignment of land and its revenues to privileged individuals) and conferred proprietary rights on occupancy tenants. Education at its lower levels is free.

HISTORY

The state of Jammu and Kashmir was first created by the British in 1846, with a maharaja as its head. Although the successive maharajas were Hindu, the great majority of the people were Muslim (except in Jammu, where Hindus and Sikhs were in a majority, and in Ladākh, which was predominantly Buddhist).

After the partition of the Indian subcontinent in 1947 Jammu and Kashmir became a bone of contention between India and Pakistan. On October 22, 1947, tribesmen from the northwest frontier of Pakistan invaded Kashmir and advanced on its capital, Srīnagar. The Maharaja appealed to India for help and executed an instrument of accession to the Indian Union. On October 27, with the accession of the state completed, a contingent of Indian troops was airlifted to Srīnagar, and the tribesmen failed to capture the city. Fighting continued, and in January 1948 India brought the case before the UN Security Council on the grounds that Pakistan was assisting the invaders. Pakistan denied the charge but later admitted that its regular troops were sent into Kashmir. A UN Commission for India and Pakistan arranged a cease-fire and provided for the future of the state to be decided by a plebiscite. Its resolutions of August 13, 1948, and January 5, 1949, accepted by India and Pakistan, prescribed a procedure for the withdrawal of all Pakistani troops from Kashmir to be followed by the withdrawal of the bulk of Indian forces in order to facilitate the holding of a plebiscite. The cease-fire agreement came into force on January 1, 1949, but all efforts of the Security Council and its representatives between 1950 and 1952 failed to bring about a permanent solution. India maintained that instead of withdrawing all its troops from Kashmir, Pakistan had built up its armed strength and consolidated its hold over the area under its occupation. Pakistan, on the other hand, asserted that India's refusal to withdraw its forces rendered an impartial plebiscite impossible. In 1953 and 1954 the prime ministers of India and Pakistan made an unsuccessful attempt to reach a solution by direct negotiations. In 1953 Sheikh Mohammed Abdullah, prime minister of Indian-held Jammu and Kashmir, was arrested for opposing complete integration of his state in the Indian Union. (He was held in detention·in India, with two short intervals, until 1968.) In 1957 the question was again referred to the Security Council, but further UN mediation proved fruitless. The Security Council again discussed the problem in 1962 and 1964. Direct Indo-Pakistan negotiations between December 27, 1962, and May 16, 1963, also yielded no result.

In 1963 the government of India declared its portion of Jammu and Kashmir to be a state, with a status equal to that of other Indian states, and further declared that its integration into the Union of India was complete and irrevocable. Pakistan rejected such a resolution.

Meanwhile, in 1959 it became known that Chinese forces had seized a protion of Ladākh in northeast Kashmir and had built a road across the occupied territory to connect Sinkiang with Tibet. An Indian reconnaissance patrol was attacked by Chinese troops and suffered casualties. In reply to Indian protests the Chinese government claimed the area in dispute as Chinese territory and refused to withdraw its forces. When the border conflict broke out again, in October 1962, Chinese troops forced the evacuation of key Indian military posts guarding the Karakoram Pass and overran defense positions in the Pangong Lake area 100 miles (161 kilometres) to the northeast. On November 21 the Chinese suddenly announced a unilateral cease-fire, which by implication suggested that, although they were prepared to withdraw to the McMahon Line at the eastern (North-East Frontier Agency) end of the Himalayan frontier, they intended to hold the gains of about 14,000 square miles (36,260 square kilometres) of territory in the northern Ladākh area. In March 1963 China and Pakistan signed an agreement defining a border 300 miles (483 kilometres) long along the northern area of Kashmir under Pakistani control.

In the later 1960s and in the early 1970s there were clashes along the India–Pakistan cease-fire line, with outright warfare occurring in 1965 and 1971.

The political turmoil and subsequent institution of martial law in Pakistan during the late 1970s also affected the government of Azad Kashmir. The Azad Kashmir Assembly was dissolved in 1977, and the following year Pakistan's President Zia dismissed Azad Kashmir's president, Sadar Mohammad Ibrahim Khan. Mohammad Hayat Khan was appointed by Zia as the new president.

Baluchistan

Baluchistan (or Balūchestān) is the westernmost province of Pakistan. It is bordered on the west and northwest by Iran and Afghanistan; on the north and east by the Pakistani provinces of North-West Frontier Province, Punjab, and Sind; and on the south by the Arabian Sea. With an area of 134,050 square miles (347,188 square kilo-

Efforts to decide the status of Jammu and Kashmir

metres), it is the largest Pakistani province, but it is the least developed and most sparsely populated. The provincial capital of Quetta is located in the north.

The name Baluchistan is derived from the words Baluch and *estān* and literally means "place, or abode, of the Baluch people," who inhabited most of the contemporary provincial area by the end of the 15th century. Baluchistan as the name of the area was in use in the 15th century, but it was not the official designation of the region until the 19th century.

PHYSICAL AND HUMAN GEOGRAPHY

The land. *Relief.* Baluchistan can be divided into four physical regions. The upper highlands of the central and northeastern regions are traditionally known as the Khorāsān country. The area is bounded by the Sulaimān Range to the east and the Toba Kākar Range to the northwest. To the north of the central Sulaimān Range is an oblong massif known as Kaisargarh (Kasi-barh) that reaches an altitude of 11,290 feet (3,441 metres). A series of hills curve westward from the Sulaimān Range to the broad mountain arc that abuts the Quetta-Pishīn uplands. Peaks in this region include Khalifat, which rises to 11,434 feet (3,485 metres) south of Ziārat, and Zarghūn, which attains 11,738 feet (3,578 metres) northeast of Quetta.

The great break in the mountains formed by the Bolān and Khojak passes separates the upper highlands from the lower highlands. The lower highlands include the eastern slopes of the Sulaimān Range; the lower ranges of Makrān, Khārān, and Chāgai on the west; and the Pab and Kīrthar ranges on the southeast.

The third region consists of the extensive flat plains along the coast that extend northward into the mountains. In the east, the plain stretches along the eastern slopes of the Kīrthar Range as far north as Sibi. The fourth region, in the northwest, consists of the arid deserts of Chāgai, Khārān, and Makrān and the swamps of Lora and Māshkel.

Drainage. The upper highlands drain into the Indus River, while the lower highlands drain northward into the swamps or southward to the Arabian Sea. The main rivers are the Zhob in the northeast; Bala Nāri and Bolān in the southeast; Māshkel, Rakhshān, Nihing, and Dasht in the west, and Hingol, Porāli Nai, and Hab in the southwestern Las Bela district.

Soils. Saline soils are found along the coast, around the swamps and lakes, and in some of the low-lying arid areas. Sandy soils occur in the three main desert areas and in parts of the plains. The valleys of the lower and upper highlands contain soft rocky soils, while stony soils dominate the vast waterless flats between the hills. There are deep deposits of alluvial soils in the plains of Sibi, Kachhi, and Las Bela.

Climate. There are three climatic zones. The climate is temperate along the coast, with a mean annual temperature of 86° F (30° C). The inland deserts and arid zones are hot, with a mean annual temperature of 98° F (37° C), while the submountainous region is cold, with a mean of 76° F (24° C). Outside the influence of the monsoon, most of the province is dry and experiences the extremes of heat and cold. The plains become extremely hot during the long summer from April to September, with temperatures at Sibi rising to 122° F (50° C). The plateaus of Kalāt and Quetta-Pishīn receive some snowfall and experience severe cold during winter from October to March, the temperature falling to several degrees below freezing. Rainfall is irregular and scanty; it ranges from an average of four to 11 inches (102 to 280 millimetres) on the coast to between six and 16 inches (152 to 406 millimetres) in the hilly region.

Plant and animal life. The upper highlands of Kalāt, Quetta-Pishīn, and Ziārat support such trees as the juniper, pistachio, olive, ash, edible pine, poplar, and willow. The flats remain covered with saxual and sagebrush, while the mountain valleys have a variety of fruit trees. The hillsides abound in herbaceous and bulbous plants, and the Ziārat and Kalāt uplands support such plants of economic value as cumin, hyssop (a European mint), and licorice. The perennial herb that is the source of asafetida occurs in Koh-i-Sultān, and wild rhubarb is found in the Khwāja

Four physical regions

Vegetation and animal life

Amrān Range. Dwarf palms grow in the hilly tracts, and tamarisk, acacia, and wild caper (a low prickly shrub) occur on the plains. The valley of the Dasht River abounds in date-palm trees of the best variety, and the grasses in the Khārān region yield seeds that have long been used as food during periods of famine.

The straight-horned markhor (a wild goat) and mountain sheep are found in the higher hills and the Sind ibex (a wild goat) in the lower highlands. Leopards and black bears are occasionally found in the western hilly regions, while the wild ass, the Persian gazelle, and the wolf occur in the deserts. The jackal, fox, and hyena are more common. Baluchistan has been a natural habitat for various breeds of sheep, cattle, and horses.

Typical game birds are the *chikōr* (a colourful bird of the partridge family) and *sisi* (of the same family, but smaller and dusty brownish in colour). The black and white *shakūk* (a larger bird with a longer tail) struts around in summer. There are waterfowl, bustards, and other migratories, while the raven, lammergeier (a large bird of prey), and golden eagle are among the permanent bird population. The deserts and plains abound in a vast variety of reptiles and insects. The horned snake, *kingarmār*, is typical of the Khārān region. The tortoise is common, and the skink (a lizard) occurs in the sandhills of Chāgai. Crocodiles are found in the Hingol River, and the coastal belt is rich in fish and mollusks. A large variety of marine fish include shark and skate, as well as pomfret, sole, and sardine.

The people. The Baluch and Pashtun (Pathan) peoples constitute the two major and distinct ethnic groups; the mixed ethnic stock, mainly of Sindhian origin, forms the third major group. There are minor ethnic communities of Meds along the coastal belt, Lurs in the predominantly Baluchi areas, and Jāts in the Sibi, Kachhi, and Las Bela districts.

The Pashtuns, divided into a number of subgroups, are **The** believed to be of Turko-Iranian origin. Pashtun tradition **Pashtun** claims northern Baluchistan immediately west of the Su- **and Baluch** laimān Range to be their ancient home, and the Pashtuns **peoples** are still concentrated in the contemporary Zhob, Loralai, and Quetta-Pishīn districts.

The Baluch are concentrated in the Kalāt Division and in the Sibi and eastern Loralai districts of the Quetta Division. Their tradition, irrespective of the languages spoken by the various subgroups, traces their origin back to the ancient Babylonian homeland of Aleppo, Syria. Baluchi tradition and scholarship support the theory that the Baluch are Chaldean descendants of Belus, identified as the Babylonian king Nimrod.

Baluchistan is a multilinguistic region; a majority of its inhabitants are bilingual, and there is a sizable trilingual population. Baluchi, Brahui, Pashto, Sindhi, and Seraiki are the main languages. Baluchi has eastern and western dialects, and Pashto is spoken in its southern dialect as distinct from the northern Pashto of North-West Frontier Province. Sindhi has four dialects, and Seraiki has two dialects. Persian, in the Dehwari dialect, is spoken by the Dehwar communities of Kalāt and Mastung, and a mixed dialect, the Mokaki, is spoken by the Lurs in the Kalāt Division. Punjabi is spoken by the settlers from Punjab, mainly in the urban areas, while Urdu is used as a lingua franca.

The Baluch and Pashtuns are mostly Sunnī Muslims, although some communities profess the Shī'ah doctrine. Some of the Baluchi communities and peoples of Makrān and Las Bela districts profess to be the followers of the 16th-century messiah Mīrān Muḥammad Mahdī of Jaunpur and constitute a sect by themselves. Hindus, Parsis (Zoroastrians), and Christians constitute minority communities, the latter two living mainly in Quetta city.

Settlement The vast rural areas are mostly barren, and semiarid **patterns** lands are visited by nomads in the rainy season. The few green areas have pastoral concentrations, while the coastline has clusters of fishing villages. Though some mining settlements have sprung up in the interior, the bulk of the rural population remains nomadic. Since 1947, however, the process of urbanization has increased in response to industrialization and the greater educa-

tional and employment opportunities in urban areas. The major towns, aside from Quetta city, are Zhob (formerly Fort Sandeman), Hindubāgh, Chaman, Mastung, Mach, Jhatpat, Osta Muhammad, Sibi, Kalāt, Khuzdār, Panjgūr, Turbat, Bela, Sonmiāni, Pasni, and Gwādar. Since 1951 there has been a marked increase in the urban population, but the number of urban dwellers has remained less than one-fifth of the provincial population. Immigration from other Pakistani provinces has also been responsible for this increase, particularly in Quetta city.

The economy. *Resources.* Baluchistan's major economic potential lies in its mineral wealth, marine fisheries, livestock, fruit farming, irrigated agriculture, and scope for industrial growth. Development costs of water and power resources and communication facilities, however, remain prohibitive.

The province has proved reserves of coal, chromite, sul- **Mineral** fur, marble, limestone, gypsum, emery stone, magnesite **wealth** (magnesium carbonate), natural gas, barite (barium sulfate), fluorite, onyx, and manganese. There are deposits of copper, bauxite, lead, antimony, iron ore, laterite, and brucite. Several of these minerals, such as coal, chromite, marble, sulfur, limestone, gypsum, barite, emery, and magnesite, are mined for export. The natural gas found in 1952 at Sui has produced almost half the nation's electric power.

The coastal belt has large fishing potential. Fishing cooperatives are supplied with motor launches, and curing yards have been established at Gwādar, Ormāra, Pasni, and Jīwani. Refrigerated storage facilities are at Gwādar and Pasni.

Agriculture. The sheep industry engages most of the population and utilizes most of the provincial acreage. The sheep raised produce high-quality wool, part of which is exported. Cattle and other animals yield hides and skins for the local leather industry and export.

Crop raising has remained limited for want of water, power, and adequate transportation facilities. Extension of irrigation acreage from the Gudu Barrage (dam) on the Indus has only marginally increased irrigated acreage. The principal crop is wheat, about half of which is irrigated, followed by jowar (sorghum), and rice; most of the production is for local consumption. The chief cash crops are fruits that are exported to other parts of Pakistan.

Industry. The province contains a small percentage of Pakistan's industry, virtually all of it small-scale. The major industries include cotton and woolen milling, food processing, carpet making, textile and leather embroidery, light engineering, one large pharmaceutical plant, and various handicraft shops.

Transportation. Modest fair-weather roads connect the important towns with one another. A small number of roads and highways link the province with Iran, Afghanistan, and Karāchi and Lahore. A route that links Quetta and Karāchi is part of an international highway connecting Pakistan, Iran, and Turkey.

The railway system radiates from Quetta to Zāhedān, **The** Iran; Chaman on the Afghanistan border; Sibi through **railway** the Bolān Pass to Karāchi and Lahore; Zhob in the **system** north; and Loralai in the northeast. Pakistan International Airlines provides daily domestic services between Quetta, Karāchi, Lahore, and Rāwalpindi. There are also air links between Pasni, Jīwani, Gwādar, and Panjgūr. Small ships, launches, and boats ply along the coast, linking the ports of Sonmiāni, Jīwani, Pasni, and Gwādar with Karāchi and the Persian Gulf.

The expansion of transport facilities is basic to future economic development. The mining centre of Spezand is linked by road and rail with Quetta; the industrial and administrative centre of Uthal is similarly linked with Karāchi.

Administrative and social conditions. *Government.* The province is headed by a governor, who is appointed by the federal government. Each of its four divisions of Quetta, Sibi, Kalāt, and Makrān is under a commissioner. The divisions are subdivided into 16 districts, which are headed by deputy commissioners, political agents, or deputy commissioner-cum-political agents, depending upon the degree of political control exercised by them within their jurisdiction. The districts are subdivided into *tahsil*s headed by *tahsildār*s, and the *tahsil* is further subdivided for purposes of revenue into *ḥalqah* and *maḥāl,* the smallest administrative unit, headed by a revenue officer.

Health. Health facilities, though inadequate, have been extended to the whole province. There are district hospitals, rural health centres, dispensaries, and mobile dispensaries. There are also tuberculosis clinics. Medical personnel include doctors, specialists, health visitors, and nurses. The major health problems are infant mortality, eye diseases and blindness, and stomach troubles and kidney stones.

Education. Traditional education includes an indigenous community-supported Islāmic system of *maktabs* (primary schools) and *madrasahs* (secondary and higher institutions) in towns and larger settlements. Classes are taught in Persian and Arabic, and religious studies are the main educational objective. Western education was introduced in 1882, when the first government school was established by the British in Quetta. There are more male than female students, although several colleges are especially for women. The University of Baluchistan in Quetta was established in 1970.

Welfare. A social-welfare program commenced in 1970, and there were many urban–rural community development projects. A provincial council distributes *zakat* revenues to local committees for disbursement to needy persons directly or through voluntary social-welfare agencies. Among the projects run by the agencies are homes for industrial workers, orphanages, schools for the deaf and dumb, clinics and health centres, social services, and vocational training centres.

Rural development is geared to the overall economic goal of increasing production. It includes the expansion of employment opportunities and the creation of new sources of income. As a measure against drought, a food-storage scheme has been devised to construct grain-storage facilities in central areas. Such facilities have been developed at Quetta, Chaman, Nushki, Mastung, Mach, and Turbat.

Cultural life. The Baluch and Pashtun peoples are organized on the basis of *qawm* or *qabīlah,* "community" or "tribe." Depending upon its strength and standing, a community headed by a *sardār* or *khān* may be composed of various divisions and groups, each with its own headman. The nucleus of a Pashtun community is characterized by blood bonds and homogeneity, while that of a Baluch community is characterized by "common weal and woe" and heterogeneity. In the Marri community of the Baluch, land is the common property of all and is divided among the three main clans every 10th year. *Riwāj* ("custom"), specific to each community, has served the function of unwritten law. The Balūchī Dīwān serves as a legislative assembly for the Baluch, while the *jirgah* serves as a judicial tribunal among both the Baluch and Pashtun communities. *Mayār* or *nang* is the traditional Baluch code of honour, based on blood feud and chivalry. Marri society includes the *rāhzan,* who conducts the attack in war, and the *rhezwār shā'ir,* or community poet laureate.

Horse racing, wrestling, religious holidays, *melās* (fairs), and marriage feasts are the main festivals. Baluch communities have professional minstrels who sing from *Balūchī daptar,* known as the great epic of the 30-year Rind–Lāshār War, and there are numerous regional folk songs. Among the Pashtuns, the *landai* form of folk song in the *kākarrī* style is the most popular singing style, and the Kākar community has a rich variety of folk songs.

The Baluchi Academy, the Brahui Adabī Dīwān, and the Pashto Academy—all centred in Quetta—are engaged in the investigation and preservation of the Baluchi, Brahui, and Pashto cultural and literary traditions of Baluchistan.

HISTORY

Archaeological remains have confirmed that prehistoric Baluchistan passed through the Stone and Bronze ages. The materials of the Quetta, Togho, Kulli, and Nal sites represent a fairly widespread level of cultural achievement and indicate that Baluchistan served as an intermediary link between the cultures of South Asia and the Middle East. Little is known of the region's early history, but it may have been subject to the Assyrians and the Medes. It

was subjugated and annexed as part of the 14th satrapy of the Persian Empire under Darius I (522–486 BC); but, with the defeat of Darius III by Alexander the Great in 330 BC, the area came under Greek supremacy.

The chronology of the succeeding powers suggests that, after Alexander's death, the territories of Baluchistan became a part or were under the political influence of the empires of Seleucus I Nicator and Candragupta Maurya (305 BC), the Indo-Greeks and the Parthians (3rd–2nd century BC), the Scythians (100 BC–AD 200), and the Sāsānids (3rd–7th century AD). The Hephthalite Turks controlled central and northeastern Baluchistan from AD 470 to 520, leaving the southern coastal area to the Sāsānids. As Sāsānid power weakened during the 7th century, the Brahmin rulers of Sind extended their influence into western Baluchistan.

Baluchistan emerges into recorded history with the advance of the Arab armies in the 7th century. With the final conquest by Muḥammad ibn al-Qāsim in 711, most of Baluchistan became part of the Sind province of the Umayyad and the 'Abbāsid empires. From the 11th century, the region fell under the control of various powers and formed part of the Mughal Empire from about 1595 to about 1638. Arab invasions of the 7th century

The first Baluch people to arrive in Baluchistan were mainly of the Brahui group. They set up the principality of Kalāt in the central portion of the region in the 14th century. In the 15th century, Kalāt was overrun by the last great migrating body of the Rind–Lāshār Baluch. Naming the new ruler of Kalāt, the Rind and the Lāshār moved onward; the former founded the principality of Sibi with its capital at Fatehpur and the latter the principality of Kachhi with its capital at Gandāvā. After the Rind–Lāshār War (c. 1490–1520), most of the Rind and Lāshār migrated to the Punjab, Sind, and Gujarāt.

The Brahui regained control of their principality, and the khanate of Kalāt, which became the future nucleus of Baluch power, was founded in 1666. Nasīr Khān (1750–93) welded together the region's different ethnic groups, organized the military and sociopolitical institutions of the Baluch, aligned himself with Nāder Shāh of Iran and Aḥmad Shāh Durrānī of Afghanistan, and succeeded in creating a political unit independent of neighbouring Sind, Iran, and Afghanistan.

The British influence in Baluchistan commenced with the mission of the British administrator Sir Robert Sandeman to Kalāt in 1875 and the subsequent occupation of Quetta in 1877. By the Treaty of Gandamak with Afghanistan in 1879 and other treaties with the *khāns* of Kalāt, the territories acquired were constituted into British Baluchistan Province and Tribal Areas by 1896, while Kalāt became a protected princely state. Baluchistan Province became part of Pakistan in 1947, and Kalāt state acceded to Pakistan one year later. The various parts of the former British Baluchistan Province (settled districts, native states, and tribal areas) became a more integrated single administrative unit after 1947. In 1955, Baluchistan was merged into the newly created "Province of West Pakistan," but Baluchistan was reestablished as a separate province in 1970.

In 1976 the Pakistani government abolished the *sadari* system in which local tribal chiefs exercised considerable authority over members of their tribes, including the right to administer justice, collect taxes and dues, and control armies. The abolition of the *sadar*'s authority ignited a rebellion and led to heavy fighting between army forces and tribesmen opposed to abolishment of tribal autonomy. Heavy casualties were suffered by both sides before the fighting decreased, but hostility among the tribesmen of Baluchistan toward the federal government persisted into the 1980s.

(N.A.B.)

North-West Frontier Province

North-West Frontier Province, the northernmost province of Pakistan, covers an area of 39,283 square miles (101,743 square kilometres), including 10,510 miles of Federally Administered Tribal Areas; it is bounded by Afghanistan to the west and north, Jammu and Kashmir to the north-

Educational facilities

east, Punjab Province to the southeast, and Baluchistan Province to the southwest.

This rugged, mountainous land is noted for the fierce independence and ethnic pride of its Pashtun population, especially those who live within the tribal areas and are not subject to Pakistani law. It is a hard land, poor in natural resources, and unsuited to extensive agriculture. The region is strategically important because it contains the Khyber Pass, an historic gateway through which invading armies from the north have marched several times on their way to conquer the Indian subcontinent.

PHYSICAL AND HUMAN GEOGRAPHY

The land. *Relief and drainage.* The terrain comprises mountain ranges, undulating dissected submontane areas, and plains surrounded by hills. In the north the general orientation of the ranges is longitudinal, while it is transverse south of the Kābul River, which runs from west to east. The Hindu Kush region in the northern part of the province is divided by the Kunar River into two distinct ranges—northern Hindu Kush and the Hindu Rāj. Tirich Mīr rises to 25,230 feet (7,690 metres) and is the highest peak of the northern Hindu Kush. The highest peak of the Hindu Rāj is Shāh Dok at 20,737 feet (6,321 metres). East of Tirich Mīr, the Hindu Kush is extensively covered with snow and lofty glaciers.

To the south of the Hindu Rāj is the rugged country of the Pānjkora, Swāt, and Kandia river basins. Hazāra District in the east contains the Lesser Himalayas and the sub-Himalayas, which form definite ranges broken by hilly country and small plains. The transverse arrangement of the ranges south of the Kābul is markedly represented by the Safed Koh, whose highest peak, Sakaram, rises to 15,620 feet (4,761 metres). This southern area is traversed by the Kurram, Tochi, and Gumal rivers.

Topography

The fertile Vale of Peshāwar, with less than one-tenth of the province's area and about one-half of its population, is covered with alluvial sediments that have been subjected to erosion. The tableland in the Kohāt area south of Peshāwar is rugged and cut by streams; the borders of the Bannu Plain southwest of Peshāwar are hilly. Topography has resulted in the development in some places of fascinating examples of the trellis pattern of drainage. In the area of Dera Ismāīl Khān, the land is mostly a dry plain intersected by torrents and bordered on the east by the *kachī*, the narrow Indus riverine tract.

Soils. The northern ridges are generally associated with the Himalayan territory; they contain gneiss and granite in upper Chitrāl. The transverse hills are mostly formed of nummulitic limestone (formed during the Eocene Epoch between 54,000,000 and 38,000,000 years ago) and sandstone. Much of the Vale of Peshāwar is covered with surface gravels and alluvium, while the rocks of Kohāt are mostly sandstones surrounding outcrops of nummulitic limestones. The Bannu Plain is mostly composed of soft sandstones and conglomerates; the greater part of the Dera Ismāīl Khān plain is covered with gravels, alluvium, and limestone.

Climate. The climate is highly diversified according to altitude. While the northern mountains have snowy winters and cool summers, the mean annual temperature increases markedly toward the south, rising from 73° F (23° C) at Peshāwar to 77° F (25° C) at Dera Ismāīl Khān. Precipitation falls in winter and spring. The mean annual rainfall is about 25 inches (635 millimetres) at Drosh, 14 inches (356 millimetres) at Peshāwar, and 10 inches (254 millimetres) at Dera Ismāīl Khān. The rainiest season is usually from January to April, but precipitation is generally variable, and droughts may occur in either summer or winter.

Plant life. In the far north of the province, where there are extremes of altitude and climate, the higher mountains are bare and rocky. Elsewhere in the north, the mountain slopes bear stands of evergreen oak and pine; and broadleaved deciduous trees such as the plane and poplar grow on the warmer, sunnier slopes. There are also extensive mountain grasslands. The hills to the south are sparsely covered with bushes, acacia, and grasses. About one-tenth of the uncultivated area of the province is forested.

The people. Muslims constitute virtually all of the population. Pashto is the predominant language, except in Hazāra and Dera Ismāīl Khān districts, where Punjabi predominates. The province is inhabited by numerous Pashtun tribes and *khēl*s, or clans, each taking great pride in its genealogy. The major tribes are the Yūsufzay, Utmān Khēl, Mahmand, Afrīdī, Ōrakzay, and Wazīrī. Others include the Mohammadzay, Shinwārī, Bangash, Khatak, Banūchī, and Mahsūd.

The Pashtuns

Only a small percentage of the overall population is urban. Urban growth is generally slower in the North-West Frontier Province than in Pakistan as a whole. The province has two cities, Peshāwar and Mardān; but there are a few large towns with populations of more than 25,000. There is a generally low percentage of migrants, except in Peshāwar District.

The economy. The province is poor in natural resources but receives developmental allocations from the central government. The development strategy of the provincial government has been to concentrate on productive short-term schemes, and the main emphasis has been on housing, education, transport and communications, health, and agriculture. Emphasis has also been placed on the improvement of rural roads, sanitation facilities, and irrigation systems.

Agriculture. The economy is essentially agricultural. Agriculture contributes about two-fifths of the total gross provincial product and employs about four-fifths of the population either directly or indirectly.

Irrigation is carried out on about one-third of the cultivated land. Wheat, corn (maize), sugarcane, and tobacco are the major crops. Other crops include millet, barley, rice, and cotton. Wheat production is highest in Peshāwar, Bannu, and Mardān districts, and Hazāra, Mardān, and Peshāwar districts are important corn-producing areas. Peshāwar and Mardān are also important regions of production of sugarcane and tobacco.

Principal crops

Industry. There is little industry; the province contains only a small percentage of the manufacturing industries located in Pakistan. Industries in the province include the manufacture and refining of sugar, the canning and preservation of fruits and vegetables, tobacco processing, and the manufacture of arms and accessories. Other products are cotton textiles, cement, ghee (clarified butter), nonmetallic mineral products, furniture, and milled grains. Minerals such as iron ore, chromite, gypsum, and magnesite are found in the province.

Transportation. In view of the strategic importance of the region, the British government constructed railways and roads across it, despite tribal opposition and the difficult nature of the terrain. Since independence these facilities have been improved to help promote economic growth.

Administrative and social conditions. *Government.* The province is divided into Malakand, Hazāra, Peshāwar, and Dera Ismāīl Khān divisions, which are further subdivided into a number of districts. Each of these districts is broken down into several *tahsils* (smaller administrative units). Between the settled districts to the south and the Afghan border is the tribal area, whose inhabitants enjoy a large measure of independence. The tribal area is divided into the Bājaur (Malakand), Mohmand, Khyber, Kurram, North Wazīristān, and South Wazīristān agencies, each of which is headed by a political agent. There also are tribal areas administered by Peshāwar, Kohāt, Dera Ismāīl Khān, and Bannu districts.

The governor is the chief executive. In the directly administered areas, the provincial secretariat is headed by a chief secretary. A commissioner is in charge of each division, and the districts are headed by deputy commissioners. At the district level, judicial functions are performed by district and sessions judges, civil judges, and magistrates. Magistrates also perform some executive functions. In each *tahsil* an official called the *tahsildār* collects revenue and discharges judicial and executive functions.

The tribal areas. In the tribal areas the people are free to rule themselves according to their own customs. Political and military agents have power to award or withhold subsidies and to control entry into and departure from the tribal areas. The agent—aptly described as "half ambassador and half governor"—reports to the divisional commissioner and the Ministry of State and Frontier Regions of the central government. Much of the local power of the *sadar*, or tribal chief, was abolished in the province in the late 1970s.

Counselling, judicial functions, intertribal liaisons, and communal dealings with the political agent are performed by the *jirgah* or council of elders. The selection of the *jirgah*'s members is based on tradition; their decisions are unanimously arrived at by consensus.

Education. The tribal order is inherently resistant to social change, and educational progress is quite slow. The literacy rate among the total population is lower than that of Pakistan.

There are primary and middle schools, high schools and colleges, and the university at Peshāwar, together with its constituent professional colleges. There are far fewer female than male students.

Health and welfare. Health facilities are inadequate. Among preventive schemes, the greatest emphasis is placed on malaria eradication. A family-planning program was started on a large scale in 1965.

The social welfare development program of the government is financed primarily by *zakat* revenue distributed to the province and is implemented by provincial, division, and district committees. The program aims at inculcating among the people a spirit of self-help, at developing leadership qualities, and at promoting the acquisition of skills within the context of Islāmic teachings and values.

Cultural life. The Pashtuns have a rich cultural heritage in which they take great pride. *Pakhtūnwalī,* or *Pashtūnwalī* (Way of the Pashtuns), constitutes a code of honour that imposes three chief obligations—*badal,* or revenge, the most important and binding aspect of *pakhtūnwalī; nanawātai,* the right to seek asylum; and *maelmastyā,* which entitles a stranger or even an enemy to hospitality.

The Pashtuns are an intensely religious people who uphold a long tradition of preserving their freedom. Their council of elders, the *jirgah,* settles disputes and maintains high standards of justice. In the tribal order the position of the *malik,* or *khān,* the head of the tribe, is most distinguished. Each village has at least one guest house, *ḥujrah,* which also serves as a club or town hall. Their festivals are mostly of a religious nature, but entertainments such as tent pegging and the whirling Khaṭak dance demonstrate the people's martial spirit. Folklore is generally related to the theme of Pashtun bravery or to other traditional characteristics and often strikes an ethical note. The everyday dress of the Pashtuns consists of a long shirt, waistcoat, *salwār* (trousers), and turban. Pashtuns often carry firearms, and women usually remain secluded from public view.

HISTORY

The early period. The early history of the province is related to the ancient state of Gandhāra, which comprised the Vale of Peshāwar and adjoining areas. The kingdom was important because of its strategic location at the end of the Khyber Pass, the most direct and easily negotiable route to Afghanistan, Iran, and Central Asia. Gandhāra was annexed by the Persian Achaemenid Empire in the early 6th century BC, and it remained a Persian satrapy until 327 BC. The region then passed successively under Greek, Indian, Indo-Bactrian, Śakan, Parthian, and Kushān rule.

Muslim administration was first brought to the region by the Turks, whose ruler, Sebüktigin, gained control of Peshāwar by AD 988. His son, Maḥmūd of Ghazna, invaded northern India several times between 1001 and 1027, bringing a large area of the present province, excluding Hazāra, into the boundaries of his Ghaznavid empire. In 1779 Muʿizz-ud-Dīn Muḥammad of Ghūr captured the Vale of Peshāwar, which remained under his rule until his death in 1206. After the decline of the Ghūrids, the region was held first by the Muslim Afghan dynasties and then by the Mughals. After the invasion of the Persian ruler Nāder Shāh in 1738, the territory remained under a loose form of Afghan Durrānī rule.

Foreign conquests

The Sikh invasions from the Punjab region of India began in 1818, after which the Sikhs increasingly made themselves the masters of the frontier territory until the coming of the British in 1849.

The British period. The northwestern frontier areas were annexed by the British after the Second Sikh War of 1849. They formed a part of the Punjab (including what is now the Indian state of Punjab) until North-West Frontier Province was created in 1901. The new province was administered from Peshāwar by a chief commissioner and agent to the governor general. The territory was not granted the measure of self-rule given to the other Indian provinces in 1919. In 1935, however, the Government of India Act raised its status to that of a governor's province and allowed provincial autonomy.

Independence. After independence in 1947 the region continued to exist as a separate province. The feudal states of Phūlra and Amb were merged with the province in 1950. In 1955, North-West Frontier Province, along with other provinces, was amalgamated into West Pakistan province. After the dissolution of West Pakistan province in 1970, the region regained its former provincial status, and the states of Swāt, Dīr, and Chitrāl were added to its territory. During the late 1970s and early 1980s the province was innundated by refugees from Afghanistan seeking asylum from Soviet occupation.

(K.U.K./Ed.)

Punjab

The province of the Punjab in Pakistan lies between the Himalayan foothills and the Indian state of Rājasthān and has an area of 79,284 square miles (205,345 square kilometres), excluding the 906 square miles of the Federal Capital Territory of Islāmābād. Punjab means "five waters," or "five rivers," and signifies the land drained by the Jhelum, Chenāb, Rāvī, Beās, and Sutlej.

The land was once unfavourable for settlment, but its character changed after the building of an extensive irrigation network at the beginning of the 20th century. The area of settlement, which had formerly been limited to the north and northeast, was enlarged to include the whole province. The irrigated areas are laid out in rectangular blocks, or *chaks*. The more recently established villages and towns have a gridiron pattern, with an open square in the centre, contrasting with the older settlements of the province.

PHYSICAL AND HUMAN GEOGRAPHY

The land. *Relief and drainage.* The province of Punjab lies on an alluvial plain formed by the Indus system of rivers. To the north are the hills of Murree and Rāwalpindi and the Pabbi hills of Gujrāt, forming part of the sub-Himalayas. The highest of these hills, Murree, has an altitude of 7,445 feet (2,269 metres). Potwar Plateau, in the far north, is a maze of uplands and small, alluvial, loessial flats, ranging in height from 1,000 to 2,000 feet (305 to 610 metres) above sea level. It is drained by the Haro and Soān rivers.

The plain of the Punjab has a compound slope. The general tilt of the land is from northeast to southwest, with an average gradient of one foot to the mile, but it rises in the areas between rivers. The plain has a diversity of landforms: an active floodplain, which is inundated by a river almost every rainy season and contains changing river channels; a meander floodplain, adjacent to the active floodplain and containing old channels; a covered floodplain, with deposits resulting from sheetflooding; a scalloped interfluve highland area between rivers comprising older alluvium and with practically no relief. The deserts are studded with sand dunes.

Climate. Punjab lies on the margin of the monsoon climate. The temperature is generally hot, with marked variations between summer and winter. The hottest month is June; the coldest is January. The average maximum and minimum temperatures of the hill station of Murree for June are 81° F (27° C) and 60° F (16° C), respectively; those for January are 45° F (7° C) and 31° F (−0.5° C). In the plain the mean June temperature is 97° F (36°

Climatic variation

C) at Multān and 93° F (34° C) at Lahore. The mean January temperature of those stations is, respectively, 56° F (13° C) and 54° F (12° C). Average annual rainfall is low, except in the sub-Himalayan and northern areas. It decreases markedly from north to south or southwest: 32 inches (810 millimetres) at Siālkot, 23 inches (580 millimetres) at Lahore, and seven inches (180 millimetres) at Multān.

Plant and animal life. The Murree hills carry subtropical and temperate forests. In the plain the natural vegetation consists of tough, wiry grass or dry stunted bushes, with few large trees. A small percentage of the uncultivated area of the province is under forests. Wild animal life is scanty.

The people. Punjab is the most populous province of Pakistan, containing well over half the nation's population and several of the major cities: Faisalābād (Lyallpur), Multān, Rāwalpindi, Gujrānwāla, Siālkot, and Sargodha. There is considerable rural–urban migration, particularly to the larger centres.

In religion, the province is almost entirely Muslim. A small percentage of the population is Christian, and a still smaller number practice other religions.

Punjabi is the mother tongue of 90 percent of the population in all districts. The main written language is Urdu, followed by English. The dominant ethnic groups, which have inhabited the Punjab throughout recorded history, are Jats, Rājputs, Arain, Gūjars, and Awan. The caste system is gradually becoming blurred as a result of increasing social mobility, intercaste marriages, and changing opinion.

The economy. *Agriculture.* Agriculture accounts for more than a third of the Punjab's gross provincial product. The Punjab's chief crops are wheat and cotton. Other crops include rice, grain, sugarcane, millet, corn (maize), oilseeds, pulses, fruits, and vegetables. About three-quarters of the cultivated land is irrigated. Livestock and poultry products make up about one-quarter of the output of the agricultural sector.

Industry. The Punjab is one of the more industrialized regions of Pakistan. The more important industries are textiles, machinery, electrical appliances, surgical instruments, metal industries, bicycles and rickshas, floor-covering, and food industries.

Transportation. Road transport has been growing at a rapid rate. The growth of road transport was at the expense of the railroads, which increased their traffic very little in the late 20th century.

Cultural life. Martial traditions, rural romanticism, and religion form the basis of Punjabi culture. These are reflected in Punjabi literature, particularly in the folklore. The oft recited folk romances *Heer Rānjhā, Sohnī Māhīwal,* and *Mirzā Ṣāḥibān* form the basis of Punjabi mystic poetry.

Marriages are generally arranged by parents. While marriage is a social contract between the bride and groom, it is also considered a tie between families and a source of prestige. Punjabi parents, therefore, attach high importance to making good marriages for their children. The custom of dowry is also important, particularly in the opulent sections of the society.

The practice of *vartan bhanjī,* the exchange of gifts, favours, and services, is widespread on ceremonial occasions. A woman's rights of *vartan bhanjī,* or visits to her parental home for receiving gifts, are almost continuous. The system is essentially a device for distributing gifts and money at times when they are most needed.

Dress commonly consists of a long shirt and *shalwār,* trousers or *lungī* (unstitched cloth tied around the waist in place of trousers), and a turban. Women generally wear a veil.

Administrative and social conditions. *Government.* The provincial capital is Lahore. The chief executive is a governor, who is appointed by the president of Pakistan. The province prepares its own budget, based on provincial receipts and central grants. The governor is assisted by the provincial secretariat, headed by a chief secretary. Civil servants are recruited on the basis of merit.

The judicial function is vested in the High Court of the province. Its decisions can be appealed to the Supreme Court of Pakistan.

The province is divided for administrative purposes into five divisions, 21 districts, and 75 *tahsil*s. A division is headed by a commissioner, a district by a deputy commissioner, and a *tahsil* by a *tahsildār.*

Education. The literacy rate in the Punjab is somewhat low; and the percentage of females who are literate is much lower than that of males. Since 1961 the number of educational institutions has increased considerably, particularly at primary, middle, and secondary levels. A number of vocational and commercial institutes and professional colleges have been added.

Health. Health facilities, though undergoing improvement, are still inadequate. Small gains were made in health and medical treatment with the completion of several hospitals on the district and *tahsil* levels. There was an acute housing shortage in urban centres, and severe overcrowding was common in Lahore and other cities.

Literacy and education

HISTORY

Archaeological excavations indicate that an urban civilization existed in this area from about 2500 BC to 1500 BC, when, it is believed, Aryan incursions brought it to an end. Of the following 1,000 years little is known. The early recorded history of the region begins with the annexation of Punjab and Sind to the Persian Empire by Darius I (*c.* 518 BC). Alexander descended on the Punjāb in the spring of 326 BC to establish his transient rule; the Greek withdrawal was completed by about 317 BC. Candragupta incorporated the states of the Punjab into his Indian empire, which reached its zenith in the reign of his grandson Aśoka (ruled *c.* 265–238 BC). The Greeks of Bactria (northern Afghanistan) extended their rule to parts of the Punjab in the last decade of the 2nd century BC.

The 1st century BC and the first two centuries AD were marked by political chaos resulting from the incursions of the Sakas, the Parthians, and the Kushans. In the first half of the 3rd century AD, the Kushans yielded to the Sāsānians. Punjab formed a part of the Gupta domain, which established in the middle of the 4th century and which in turn was shattered by the invasions of the Hephtalites in the third quarter of the 5th century. During a long period of anarchy, the Punjab changed hands between Kashmiri, Kābulī, and Hindu Shāhīs rulers.

The first Muslims to penetrate into northern India were the Arabs, who in 712 conquered the lower Punjab. The rest of the Punjab was conquered (1007–27) by Maḥmūd of Ghazna. From 1027 until the victories of Muʿizz-ud-Dīn Muḥammad of Ghūr between 1176 and 1193, this part of the Indian subcontinent remained fragmented. In 1206 Punjab came under the Sultanate of Delhi. It was then successively ruled by the Khaljīs (1290–1320), the Tughluqs (1320–98), the Sayyids (1414–50), and the Lodīs (1451–1526). The Mughals made their entry with the victory of Bābur at Pānīpat on April 21, 1526. Under the Mughals the province enjoyed peace and prosperity for more than 200 years. The Mughals, who had strong artistic and cultural traditions, also made wide social reforms. Their power declined after 1738, and in 1747 Lahore fell to Afghan troops. The Afghan hold remained quite weak, giving rise to lawlessness and disorder. The religious sect called the Sikhs rose to power in the latter part of the 18th century.

The Punjab came under British occupation in 1849, after the British victory over Sikhs in the battles of Chiliānwāla and Gujrāt. After the British annexation of the territory, the Punjab was incorporated into a province that included areas northwest of the Jumna River extending to the Indo-Afghan border. There were later territorial adjustments. The North-West Frontier Province was separated from the Punjab in 1901, as was the Delhi enclave in 1902. The province of Punjab was given autonomy, together with other provinces, in accordance with the Government of India Act of 1935.

When the Indian subcontinent received its independence in 1947, the British Indian province of Punjab was divided into West and East Punjab, which later became known, respectively, as Punjab (Pakistan) and Punjab (India). The

Period of Mughal rule

boundary was drawn in such a way as to achieve, among other things, contiguous Muslim and non-Muslim majority areas; thus it lacked any physical or geographical basis. Preservation of some irrigation and communication systems was attempted, at a loss to Punjab (Pakistan) of areas in which there were Muslim majorities. Punjab (Pakistan) was part of the single province of West Pakistan from 1955 to 1970, when it was reconstituted as a separate province; it also included the former princely state of Bahāwalpur. During the period from the early 1970s to the early 1980s the population of Punjab increased by more than one-quarter. (Ed.)

Sind

Sind (or Sindh) is the southeastern province of Pakistan. Bounded by the neighbouring Pakistani provinces of Punjab and Baluchistan on the north and west and India on the east and southeast, it extends along 150 miles (240 kilometres) of the Arabian Sea coast on the southwest and covers an area of 54,407 square miles (140,913 square kilometres).

Sind is essentially part of the Indus River Delta and has derived its name from that river, which has been known to the people as the Sindhu. The province of Sind was established in 1970, with the integration of Hyderābād and Khairpur Divisions and the District of Karāchi. The city of Karāchi is the provincial capital.

PHYSICAL AND HUMAN GEOGRAPHY

The land. *Relief.* From north to south, Sind assumes a pattern of three parallel belts—a central stretch of rich alluvial plain bisected by the long, winding, silvery line of the Indus, flanked on the west by the rocky range of the Khīrthar Range and bounded on the east by a sandy desert belt.

The Khīrthar Range consists of three parallel tiers of ridges. The easternmost section is steep on the west but has a long gradient to the east. The central ridge has flat tops and rounded sides broken by deep ravines and fissures, whereas the westernmost tier consists of a vast plateau or tableland with some peaks rising above 7,000 feet (2,100 metres). This mountainous belt has little soil and is mostly dry and barren. The easterly desert region first appears in the north as low dunes and vast flats. Continuing southward, the Achhrro Thar (White Sand Desert) occurs in the middle of the belt and is followed by the Thar Desert in the southeast.

The central riverine belt—360 miles (580 kilometres) long and about 20,000 square miles in area—constitutes the Valley of the Indus. The fertile plain, gradually sloping down from north to south, in its long gradient forms the three flat regions known as *siro* (the upper), *vichole* (the middle), and *larr* (the lower). The variety of soils includes *pakki,* or *patt,* the flat level land of old alluvium forming the northern strips of the Sukkur, Jacobābād, and Lārkāna districts; *reti-wari,* the soft reddish rocky soil of the belt skirting the northwesterly rocky range; *kacho,* the fertile silt alluvium in the narrow inundated belt of the Indus; *wariasi,* an admixture of soft clay and sand; *chiki,* the composite fine clay and soft sand on both sides of the inundated belt; and *kalar,* or alkaline soil, found mostly in the *larr* region.

Climate. A subtropical region, Sind is hot in summer and cold in winter. Temperatures frequently rise above 115° F (46° C) between May and August, and the average low temperature of 36° F (2° C) occurs during December and January. The annual rainfall averages about seven inches (180 millimetres), falling mainly during July and August. The southwesterly monsoon wind begins to blow in mid-February and continues until the end of September, whereas the cool northerly wind blows during the winter months from October to January.

Plant and animal life. Except for the irrigated Indus Valley, the province is arid and has scant vegetation. The dwarf palm, *kher* (*Acacia rupestris*), and *lohirro* (*Tecoma undulata*) trees are typical of the western hill region. In the central valley, the babul tree is the most dominant and occurs in thick forests along the Indus banks. The *nīm*

(*Azadirachta indica*), *bēr* (*Zizyphus vulgaris*) or *jujuba, lai* (*Tamarix orientalis*), and *kirirr* (*Capparis aphylla*) are among the more common trees. Mango, date palms, and the more recently introduced banana, guava, orange, and chiku are the typical fruitbearing trees. The coastal strip and the creeks abound in semiaquatic and aquatic plants, and the inshore Indus deltaic islands have forests of *timmer* (*Avicennia tomentosa*) and *chaunir* (*Ceriops candolleana*) trees. Water lilies grow in abundance in the numerous lakes and ponds, particularly in the lower Sind region.

Among the wild animals, the *sareh* (Sind ibex), *urial* or *gadh* (wild sheep), and black bear are found in the western rocky range, where the leopard is now rare. The *pirrang* (large tiger cat or fishing cat) of the eastern desert region is also disappearing. Deer live in the lower rocky plains and in the eastern region, as do the *charakh* (striped hyena), jackal, fox, porcupine, common gray mongoose, and hedgehog. The *Sindhi phekari* (red lynx, or caracal cat) is encountered in some areas. *Pharrho* (hog deer) and wild boar occur particularly in the central inundation belt. There is a variety of bats, lizards, and reptiles, including the cobra, *lundi* (viper), and the *Peean,* the mysterious Sind krait of the Thar region, which is supposed to suck the victim's breath in his sleep. Crocodiles are rare and inhabit only the backwaters of the Indus and its eastern Nāra channel. Besides a large variety of marine fish, the plumbeous dolphin, the beaked dolphin, rorqual, or blue whale, and a variety of skates frequent the seas along the Sind coast. The Pallo (sable fish), though a marine fish, ascends the Indus annually from February to April to spawn and returns to the sea in September. The *bulhan* (Indus dolphin) breeds in the Rohri-Sukkur section of the river.

The people. Although the population is of mixed ethnic origins, the background of many groups remains visible. The Indus Valley of Sind has been the terminal for sizable migrations, particularly from the west. Of the more ancient groups of Panyas, Takkas, and Mēds, only the progeny of the Mēds has survived as the Mehs, or Muhannas—the professional fishermen living along the Indus and its channels, around the lakes, and in the southern deltaic region. Among the other ethnic groups who form the bulk of the indigenous population are the Sammas and the related Lākhās, Lohānās, Nigamarās, Kākās, and Channās; the Sahtās, Bhattīs, and Thakurs (the present Sodhās of Tharpārkar) of Rājput origin; and the Jāts and Lorras, both admixtures of the ancient Scythian and the later Baluch peoples. The Jokhia, Burfat, and other sizable ethnic groups inhabiting the western rocky region also appear to be the remnants of early indigenous groups. With the advent of Islām (711), a number of groups of Arab, Persian, and Turkish origin settled in Sind, the most numerous of whom were the Baluch who, beginning in the 13th century, migrated to Sind and made it their second homeland after Baluchistan.

A great change occurred in the composition of the population with the influx of Muslim refugees from India after the partition of the subcontinent in 1947. As early as 1951, more than four persons in every 10 in Karāchi and more than one in every 10 in the rest of Sind were refugees from India. Earlier, since the opening of irrigation barrages on the Indus in the 1930s, there had also been a regular flow of settlers from the other present-day Pakistani provinces. Thus, the ethnographic pattern of Sind continues to undergo a change that is marked and visible.

Sindhi, Seraiki, and Baluchi are the main indigenous languages spoken in Sind. Besides the standard Sindhi speech of the middle Sind region, Sindhi is spoken in five main dialects. Brahui is spoken in the northwestern districts by the migrating communities from Baluchistan; and Dhātki—a mixed dialect of Rajasthani and Sindhi—is spoken in southeastern Tharpārkar District. With the entry of numerous linguistic groups from India, varieties of languages have come to be spoken in the urban areas. Of these, the most common is Urdu, followed by Punjabi, Gujarati, Rajasthani, and Pashto. Urdu is the official language taught in the schools along with Sindhi. English is taught as a foreign language in upper grades in schools and is spoken by most educated adults.

Most of the population is Muslim. The Hindus of Thar-

Linguistic patterns

pārkar District and the Christians and Parsis (Zoroastrians) of the city of Karāchi constitute the province's minority religious groups.

The ever-increasing population, large-scale immigration, and the process of agricultural development and industrialization have changed the settlement pattern in both rural and urban areas. The population has increased radically since 1947 and is concentrated in the cities and the irrigated central valley. With the extension of the irrigation system of the Indus, areas formerly barren have come under cultivation, and the seminomadic way of life has changed to that of permanent settlement. In 1947, some 15 percent of the population was urban; by the late 20th century the percentage had increased to more than 40. This trend towards urbanization is part of the historic process, but agricultural development since the 1930s and rapid industrial expansion since the 1950s have lent momentum to it.

Urban and industrial growth

The process of industrial growth has entailed alterations in the population's occupational structure, whereas large-scale movements have tended to accentuate local inequalities in the scope of social and economic development.

A number of urban areas have grown significantly, while a few rural areas have been consistently shrinking. Of the largest cities in Pakistan, Karāchi and Hyderābād are in Sind.

The economy. *Agriculture, fishing, and forestry.* The mainstay of Sind's economy is agriculture. Production increased substantially after 1961 because of the advance in agricultural research and extension services, use of inorganic fertilizers, development of agricultural engineering, and construction of surface drains to counter the effects of waterlogging and salinity. Major crops include cotton, wheat, rice, sugarcane, corn (maize), millet, and oilseeds. Fruit orchards have been extended, and a substantial increase has been achieved in the production of mangoes and bananas. Fruit-bearing date palms are also important.

Livestock includes cattle, buffalo, sheep, goats, camels and poultry. The Red Sindhi and Tharee cows are the best dairy animals, and the Sakrai and Dia-ee are the best camel breeds for transport. The potential for animal husbandry for commercial production has not been fully exploited. The government maintains livestock farms that are engaged primarily in experimentation and research.

With its 150 miles (240 kilometres) of coastline and hundreds of square miles of inshore backwaters, Sind has a high potential for marine fishing. The varieties found in abundance include prawns and shrimp, pomfrets, *palla* (shad), and *khagga* (catfish). The Indus and its deltaic branches, abandoned beds (*dhoras*) and irrigation canals, and the numerous freshwater lakes (*dhandhs*) constitute a rich reservoir for the breeding and production of freshwater fish, such as *kurirro* (*Cyprinus denticulatus*) and *thelhi* (*Catla buchanani*).

Sind has more than 2,655,000 acres (1,074,000 hectares) of forests managed by the Forest Department and the Agricultural Development Bank of Pakistan. The productive areas are exploited for both timber and firewood.

Mining and quarrying. The few known metallic minerals include celestite, laterite, and bauxite. Clays, gypsum, anhydrite (a mineral of calcium sulfate), limestone, chalk, dolomite (a mineral of calcium magnesium carbonate), silica sand, bentonite (a clay mineral), sulfur, flint, and lake salt all are available in large quantities. Coal, gas, and petroleum also occur. The resources exploited include coal, china clay, clay, chalk, fuller's earth, gravel, lake salt, limestone, and silica sand.

Petroleum products are produced in Sind. Most of the province's total energy is provided by oil and gas. All the transmission and distribution mains for the supply of gas are based on the Sūi gas field of Baluchistan.

Water and power development. The Pakistan Water and Power Development Authority was established to unify and coordinate the development of resources in Pakistan. Among the authority's main water-development schemes in Sind are the Gudu Barrage for irrigation; the Karachi Irrigation Project for irrigation and for supply of water for industrial and domestic use; the North Rohri Fresh Groundwater Project, involving the construction and elec-

Water-development projects

trification of tubewells; and the salinity control and reclamation projects in Khairpur, Lārkāna, and Shikārpur. The Gudu Barrage is administered by the Irrigation Department and the Agricultural Development Bank. Thermal and hydroelectric power are used to generate electricity in Sind. Electricity has been extended on an annual basis to many villages.

Industry. Sind is a highly industrialized area. It accounts for one-third of the entire cotton production of the country and contains almost half of the country's cotton textile mills. Several large cement factories turn out much of the country's cement products, and the country's first steel plant began operation in the early 1980s. There is also a sugar industry with a number of large mills. Pakistan's first automobile assembly plant opened in Karāchi during the early 1980s.

Sind Industrial Trading Estates Ltd. has developed industrial parks, or estates, at Karāchi, Kotri, Hyderābād, and Tando Ādam. The Pakistan Industrial Development Corporation has several industrial projects in Sind. The Pakistan Small Industries Corporation promotes cottage and other small industries and has many projects in the public sector, including a few small-industry developments, or estates, some service centres, an artisans' workshop, a handicraft development centre, a few handicraft sales centres, and an artisans' gallery.

Transportation. Communications are by road, rail, water, and, to a small extent, air. Two major highways traverse the province from south to north; the National Highway runs on the eastern bank of the Indus and leads to Multān and Lahore in the Punjab; and the Indus Highway, along the western bank of the Indus, leads to Sibi and Quetta in Baluchistan. The Karāchi-Hyderābād limited access highway runs for 97 miles (156 kilometres). Numerous feeder roads connect townships in the interior with the main roads.

The Pakistan Western Railway system starts at Karāchi and bifurcates at Kotri on the Indus into two main lines. The Hyderābād–Nawābshāh–Rohri line leads to Lahore, and the Kotri-Sehwān–Lārkāna–Jacobābād line leads to Quetta. A main-line connection from Hyderābād runs eastward through Mīrpur Khās to the Indian border at Khokhropār. There are also several different link and loop sections extending to some 600 miles (965 kilometres). In the city of Karāchi, there is the Karāchi Circular Railway.

The railway system

The Indus and some of its channels, particularly in the lower delta, have served as the main waterways since time immemorial. Country boats continue to ply the Indus, transporting grain, hay, timber, and firewood. Along the 150 miles (240 kilometres) of seacoast and the numerous creeks and abandoned mouths of the Indus, country boats and launches transport fish, grain, firewood, and other supplies.

Karāchi Airport maintains both domestic and international services. Within Sind, air services are in a preliminary stage of development. Hyderābād, 120 miles (193 kilometres) from Karāchi, is connected by flights from Karāchi en route to Quetta and Lahore.

Administrative and social conditions. *Government.* The head of the province is the governor, who is appointed by the president of Pakistan. The province has an elected legislature called the Sind Assembly. The majority party, with the chief minister as the leader, forms the government. Sind province consists administratively of the three divisions of Karāchi, Hyderābād, and Sukkur, which are divided into 15 districts. A district is divided into *taluka*s, each headed by a *mukhtīārkār;* a *taluka* is further divided into *tappa*s and a *tappa* into *deh*s, which are the smallest revenue units in the province. Law and order are maintained by an inspector general of police. For dispensation of justice and recruitment to government service, Sind has its own High Court and Public Service Commission.

Health. The provincial government has a permanent department of health, which is responsible for the organization and expansion of health services administered through the Directorate of Health. Along with the modern allopathic system, which alone is public supported, the age-old indigenous *ṭibbī* (traditional) system is also widely practiced by private *ḥakīm*s (professional doctors of this system). Since 1947, medical facilities have been extended to all parts of the province. Besides a number of private hospitals and clinics, there are several civil hospitals, dispensaries, rural health centres, and tuberculosis sanitariums; there is also an epilepsy hospital, a mental hospital, and a number of tuberculosis and dental clinics. In addition, there are child-health centres, midwifery and maternity services, mobile health units, and facilities for the training of nurses.

Health problems

Despite considerable progress, medical facilities remain inadequate, particularly in the rural areas. The problem of educating the general public to adopt preventive measures and seek timely medical advice needs to be tackled more effectively. The developmental health program centres upon the provision of curative facilities, the prevention and control of epidemics, the checking of adulteration of food and drugs, the eradication of malaria, the strengthening of tuberculosis control projects, the extension of school health services, and the improvement of facilities for treatment in the medical colleges and their attached hospitals.

Education. The provincial department of education is responsible for policy and planning; except for the universities, which are virtually autonomous, all educational institutions are under departmental control.

Primary school education is of five years duration, middle school of three years, and high school of two years. Primary schools have been extended to village areas, middle schools to bigger villages and small townships, high schools to the *taluka* towns, and colleges to the district headquarters. There are also teacher-training schools and technical, vocational, and commercial institutes. The institutions of higher education include colleges for secondary-teacher training, for medicine, agriculture, and engineering, as well as the University of Karāchi in Karāchi, the University of Sind in Hyderābād, and an institute of education.

Welfare. During the 1950s and for about two decades afterward welfare work was organized and extended to a number of selected rural and urban areas through a system of community development projects. The program was administered by the provincial directorate of social welfare. Vocational training was one of the projects' significant activities; they were also designed to serve religious and recreational needs. Some special institutions, such as a socio-economic centre, a home for the destitute, and orphanages, were established on a permanent basis. Beginning in 1980 much of the provincial social welfare work was financed by *zakat* revenues under division and district supervision.

The Sind family-planning program

The provincial Sind Family-Planning Board administers the family-planning program. Clinics and sales agents bring supplies and services within the reach of all, while family-planning workers, the lady health visitors, and other paramedical staff provide the necessary motivation and advice.

The Directorate of Labour Welfare maintains industrial relations conducive to higher productivity and promotes the welfare of all the workers employed in industrial establishments, factories, mines, docks, and other utilities by insuring their health and safety and improving their employment conditions. Employment exchange agencies and vocational guidance units render job-finding and job-placement services to the unemployed.

The Sind Employees' Social Security Institution, established in 1965, is an autonomous organization the governing body of which includes representatives of both employees and the government. It administers relief in the form of maternity, sickness, and injury benefits; total or partial disablement gratuities and pensions; and death grants and survivor's pensions. Nonmonetary benefits include medical care through social security dispensaries and polyclinics.

Cultural life. Separated from the rest of the subcontinent by a vast desert belt on the east, by ocean on the south, mountain ranges on the west, and a bottleneck of the Indus on the north, Sind long remained an isolated and self-contained region. With comparatively less borrowing from the outside, Sind has therefore stamped its arts and crafts, games and sports, music, and folklore with

a typical originality. The continuity of the ancient artistic tradition is manifest today in superb pottery; in work with glazed tile, lacquer, leather, and straw; and in carpetmaking, needlework, embroidery, quilt making, the making of hand prints, and the designing of textiles.

Melas (fairs) and *malakharas* (wrestling festivals) are the most popular recreation. *Malh* is the distinctive style of Sindhi wrestling, and the training of horses and camels to run in different styles is typical of Sindian riding and sport. Falconry is a time-honoured pastime. The method of catching the *palla* fish in the Indus by floating on an earthen pot is the distinctive technique of Sindhi fishermen. Bullock-cart racing and cockfighting are popular in some areas.

The music tradition in Sind goes back to early times. Its early professional minstrels, the Loras, carried Sindian music to ancient Iran, where it flourished as Luryan music; and the large variety of musical instruments confirms the existence of a long-standing musical tradition. The renowned poet Shāh 'Abd-ul-Laṭīf of Bhit (died 1752) founded a new music tradition of *Shāh jō rāga* in which thematic music primarily based on popular themes was interpreted by folk melodies.

The literary tradition has been influenced by the region's history of disastrous floods and storms. The story of *Dodo-Chanēsar* is the theme of a great epic of the Sūmra period. *Mōmul-Rāno, Nūrī-Jām tamachi, Suhnī-Mehar, Līlan-Chanēsar,* and *Sassī Punnūn* are among the famous age-old romances of Sind. The story of *Umar-Mārui* represents the lofty character of a village girl who prefers the company of her own simple people to the comforts of a king's palace and resists the temptation to leave her poor family to become a queen. The story of *Sōrath-Rai Daiāch* demonstrates the generosity of a munificent king and his love and appreciation of music, for which he lays down his life.

Traditional culture is greatly strained under the impact of modern development. It is mainly in the vast rural countryside and its more isolated areas where traditions have been perpetuated, although in a much diluted form. Unless sociocultural institutions attempt to preserve the traditional culture, it is likely to succumb to the growing impact of such developments as modern education and Westernization, agricultural development, industrialization, the extension of transport and communications, the use of mass communication, continued immigration, and urbanization.

Cultural institutions

The Sindhi Adabi (literary) board, functioning at Hyderābād, has published more than 200 works in Sindhi, Persian, Arabic, Urdu, and English, covering Sindhi language, literature, folklore, history, and lexicography. The Shāh 'Abd-ul-Laṭīf Cultural Centre at Bhit Shāh, 35 miles (56 kilometres) north of Hyderābād, has conducted research and published works on the life, music, and poetry of Shāh 'Abd-ul-Laṭīf. The preliminary development of the Sind-Provincial Museum and Library, both located at Hyderābād, was completed by the early 1970s. The Mehran Arts Council at Hyderābād is concerned with the development of the fine arts, crafts, and general culture and has published useful monographs on the traditional arts and crafts, early musical tradition, and musical instruments of Sind.

HISTORY

The Indus Valley civilization

The Indus Valley civilization, represented by the archaeological findings at Mohenjo-daro, Amri, and Kot Diji, existed from 2300 to 1750 BC, after which there is a gap of more than a millennium before its earliest recorded history began, with Sind's annexation to the Persian Empire under Darius I (reigned 522–486 BC). Nearly two centuries later, Alexander the Great stormed through the region in 326 and 325 BC. After Alexander's death, Sind came under the domination of the empires of Seleucus I Nicator, Candragupta Maurya (c. 305 BC), the Indo-Greeks and Parthians (3rd–2nd century BC), and the Scythians and the Kuṣāṇas (100 BC–AD 200). Under the Kuṣāṇa emperor Kaniṣka (c. AD 78–103), Sind embraced Buddhism. From the 3rd to the 7th century, the area remained under the Sāsānids, and Sind came to be ruled by the Samma chiefs of the local Rai Dynasty as feudatories of Persia. A Brahmin priest subverted Samma rule in 622 and brought Sind under Brahmin rule, which ended with the Arab conquest in 712.

The Arab conquest

The Arab conquest of Sind heralded the entry of Islām into the subcontinent. The region known as as-Sind included the present Sind, Baluchistan, and southern Punjab; it became an administrative province of the Umayyad and 'Abbāsid empires from 712 to c. 900, with its capital at al-Manṣūrah, 45 miles (72 kilometres) northeast of Hyderābād. With the weakening of central authority in Baghdad, the Arab governors in as-Sind established their own dynastic rule during the 10th century. The first Sindian dynasty of the Sūmras was established between 1058 and 1348 and was followed by the Samma Chiefs of Sind from 1349 to 1520.

Over the next two centuries Sind came under the outside domination of the Arghūns (1520–56), the Tarhāns (1556–96) and the Mughals (1591–1700), followed by the independent Sindhian dynasties of the Kalhōrās (1700–82) and the Tālpur Baluch (1782–1843), who lost Sind to the British in 1843. Except for the princely state of Khairpur, all of Sind was annexed to the Bombay Presidency. In 1937 it was established as a separate province; but after Pakistani independence, it was integrated into the province of West Pakistan from 1955 to 1970, together with Khairpur state. Upon dismemberment of the province of West Pakistan in 1970, Sind was reestablished as a separate province.

(N.A.B.)

BIBLIOGRAPHY

Physical and human geography: M.L.P. PATTERSON and R.B. INDEN, *South Asia: An Introductory Bibliography* (1962), cites more than 4,000 entries on Pakistan with emphasis on history, culture, and politics. BASIL LEONARD CLYDE JOHNSON, *Pakistan* (1979), is a useful introduction to the people and land of Pakistan. SHAUKAT ALI and GARTH N. JONES, *Pakistan Government and Administration: A Comprehensive Bibliography,* 2 vol. (1970–71), is exhaustive. O.H.K. SPATE and A.T.A. LEARMONTH, *India and Pakistan: A General and Regional Geography,* 3rd ed. (1967), is comprehensive and authoritative; KAZI S. AMMAD, *A Geography of Pakistan* (1964), is conveniently brief. K.U. KURESHY, *A Geography of Pakistan* (1977), is a concise geography of the country. ALOYS A. MICHEL, *The Indus Rivers* (1967), is concerned with development and with the dispute with India over allocation of river waters. W. CANTWELL SMITH, *Modern Islam in India* (1947), is as yet unsurpassed as an introductory account of the Muslim intellectual and political movements that culminated in the creation of Pakistan. ANWAR H. SYED, *Pakistan: Islam, Politics, and National Solidarity* (1982), is a thoughtful discussion in the 1980s. LAWRENCE ZIRING, *Pakistan: The Enigma of Political Development* (1980), discusses the quest for democracy and strong leaders by Pakistan's people. G.W. CHOUDHURY, *Constitutional Development in Pakistan* (1959) and *Democracy in Pakistan* (1963), is strongly oriented towards the "Muslim League" point of view, whereas TARIQ ALI, *Pakistan: Military Rule or People's Power?* (1970), offers a left-wing analysis. G.W. CHOUDHURY (ed.), *Documents and Speeches on the Constitution of Pakistan* (1967), is useful. RALPH BRAILBANTI, *Research on the Bureaucracy of Pakistan* (1966), is a comprehensive survey of the literature; and H.F. GOODNOW, *The Civil Service of Pakistan: Bureaucracy in a New Nation* (1964), is a valuable study of the structure of the bureaucracy and its role in public life. H.N. GARDEZI (comp.), *Sociology in Pakistan* (1966); and A.S. DIL (ed.), *Perspectives on Pakistan* (1965), contain essays by Pakistani scholars; STANLEY MARON (ed.), *Pakistan: Society and Culture* (1957), contains essays on history and rural social organization. FREDRIK BARTH, *Political Leadership Amongst Swat Pathans* (1959), is a classic study in political anthropology. S.K. CHATTERJI, *Languages and the Linguistic Problem,* 3rd ed. (1945), summarizes the *Linguistic Survey of India,* ed. by GEORGE A. GRIERSON, 11 vol. (1903–28); the *Census of Pakistan* (1951), but not that of 1961, briefly outlines the subject. B.S. GUHA, *Racial Elements in the Population* (1944), synthesizes the most widely accepted classifications of races of South Asia. V.G. KIERNAN, *Poems from Iqbal* (1955) and *Poems by Fraiz* (1971); H.T. SORLEY, *Shah Abdul Latif of Bhit* (1940, reprinted 1966); and G. ALLANA (ed.), *Presenting Pakistani Poetry* (1961), are some examples of poetry from Pakistan available in English translation.

History: KHALID BIN SAYEED, *Pakistan: The Formative Phase, 1857–1948,* 2nd ed. (1968), a searching description of events to 1948, *Politics in Pakistan: The Nature and Direction of Change* (1980), a discussion of political events since partition, and *The Political System of Pakistan* (1967); SHAHID JAVED BURKI, *Pakistan under Bhutto: 1971–1977* (1980), an insightful analysis of this leader's rise and fall. CHAUDHRI MUHAMMAD ALI, *The Emergence of Pakistan* (1967, reissued 1973), a senior Muslim administrator's account; HUGH TINKER, *Experiment with Freedom: India and Pakistan, 1947* (1967); HENRY V. HODSON, *The Great Divide: Britain, India, Pakistan* (1969), the definitive account of events from 1930 onward, especially with reference to Mountbatten's viceroyalty. LEONARD BINDER, *Religion and Politics in Pakistan* (1961), an analysis of religious complexities and contradictions; IAN STEPENS, *Pakistan,* 3rd ed. (1967), combines shrewdness and romantic feeling; MOHAMMAD AYUB KHAN, *Friends Not Masters* (1967), the political testament of the man who ruled Pakistan for 11 years; G.W. CHOUDHURY, *The Last Days of United Pakistan* (1975), in which a participant narrates the sequence of events leading to the breakup of Pakistan and emergence of Bangladesh.

Baluchistan: ARRIAN, *Anabasis,* ed. by A.G. ROOS (1907) and *Indica,* ed. by RUDOLF HERCHER (1885), contain an account of Alexander's conquests in India; the *Futûḥ al-Buldân,* by AHMAD IBN YAHYA, AL-BALADHURI, is available in translation but the original Arabic text edited by M.J. DE GOEJE (1866) gives an early and most authentic account of the Arab conquest. For discussions of the origin and history of the Baluch people, see M.K.B. MARRI BALOCH, *The Balochis Through Centuries: History Versus Legend* (1964) and *Search Lights on Baloches and Balochistan* (1974 and 1977); M.S. KHAN, *History of the Baluch Race and Baluchistan* (1958), and *A Literary History of Baluchistan: The Classical Period (1450–1650 A.D.),* vol. 1 (1977). An account of the Brahui and their language is contained in SIR DENYS DE SAUMAREZ BRAY, *The Brahui Language,* pt. 1, *Introduction and Grammar* (1909), pt. 2, *The Brāhūī Problem,* and pt. 3, *Etymological Vocabulary* (1934). SELIG S. HARRISON, *In Afghanistan's Shadow: Baluch Nationalism and Soviet Temptation* (1980), discusses the antecedents of this nationalistic movement and the potential consequences. For economic material see the various reports of the government of Baluchistan; and for additional bibliography, see DILAWAR KHAN, *Baluchistan: A Select Bibliography* (1977).

North-West Frontier Province: Numerous works, principally by British writers, emphasizing strategic aspects include: W.P. ANDREW, *Our Scientific Frontier* (1880); T.H. HOLDICH, *The Indian Borderland, 1880–1900,* 2nd ed. (1909), and *The Gates of India* (1910); A. VINCENT, *The Defence of India* (1922); and C.C. DAVIES, *The Problem of the North-West Frontier, 1890–1908* (1932). General treatment of the area, as a part of the Indo-Pakistan subcontinent, occurs in E.J. RAPSON (ed.), *The Cambridge History of India,* vol. 1 (1922, reprinted 1935); and O.H.K. SPATE and A.T.A. LEARMONTH, *India and Pakistan,* 3rd ed. (1967). The Imperial Gazetteer of India, Provincial Series, North-West Frontier Province (1908), is a reference work on the region. DAVID DICHTER, *The North-West Frontier of West Pakistan* (1967), provides useful geographical coverage. An informative work on landforms and land use in Pakistan is the COLOMBO PLAN COOPERATIVE PROJECT, *Landforms, Soil and Land Use of the Indus Plain* (1958).

Punjab: General works on the Indo-Pakistan subcontinent and the undivided British province of the Punjab include: *Gazetteer of the Punjab,* "Provincial Series" (1889); S.M. LATIF, *History of the Punjab* (1891, reprinted 1964); H.K. TREVASKIS, *The Land of Five Rivers* (1928) and *The Punjab of Today: An Economic Survey of the Punjab in Recent Years (1890–1925),* 2 vol. (1931–32); D.N. WADIA, *Geology of India,* 3rd ed. rev. (1961); M.L. DARLING, *The Punjab Peasant in Prosperity and Debt,* 2nd ed. (1928); K. DAVIS, *The Population of India and Pakistan* (1951); and O.H.K. SPATE and A.T.A. LEARMONTH, *India and Pakistan,* 3rd ed. rev. (1967). Some of the more important publications on Pakistan and West Pakistan, containing useful information relating to the Punjab, are: the *Pakistan Year Books; Twenty Years of Pakistan* (1967); R.R. PLATT (ed.), *Pakistan: A Compendium* (1961); the *Five Year Plans of Pakistan;* and the *Food and Agriculture Commissions Report* (1960). Z.S. ELGAR, *A Punjabi Village in Pakistan* (1960), is a study in the cultural life of a village community of the Punjab. The periodical, *Pakistan Geographical Review,* contains useful articles on the subject.

Sind: Two travel accounts of Sind are: HENRY POTTINGER, *Travels in Beloochistan and Sinde* (1816, reprinted 1976); and DAVID ROSS, *The Land of the Five Rivers and Sindh: Sketches Historical and Descriptive* (1883, reprinted 1976). SIR MORTIMER WHEELER, *The Indus Civilization,* supplementary volume to the *Cambridge History of India,* 3rd ed. (1968); F.A. KHAN, *The Indus Valley and Early Iran* (1964); and FAIZ MOHAMMAD SOOMRO, *Cultural History of Sind* (1977) are among the more recent works that deal with the beginning, development, and external relationships of the Indus Valley civilization. H.T. LAMBRICK, *Sind: A General Introduction,* 2nd ed. (1975), details the ancient history, though the more significant contribution lies in his delineation of the characteristic features of physical geography; MANECK BENJANJI PITHAWALLA, *A Physical and Economic Geography of Sind, (the Lower Indus Basin)* (1959), gives greater details of physiography, geology, hydrography of the Indus, climatic conditions, vegetation and animal life. H.M. ELLIOT, *The History of India As Told by Its Own Historians,* ed. by JOHN DOWSON, vol. 1 (1867–77, reprinted 1966), provides in English translation the more significant but copious extracts from the native histories in Persian and other sources. M.R. HAIG, *The Indus Delta Country* (1894, reissued 1972), is a scholarly monograph that remains unsurpassed in its discussion of the changing courses of the Indus, particularly in the lower deltaic region. SIR RICHARD FRANCIS BURTON, *Sindh and the Races That Inhabit the Valley of the Indus* (1851, reprinted 1973), contains general information on the ethnology and sociocultural conditions in Sind in the mid-19th century; while S.S. ANSARI, *Short Sketch, Historical and Traditional of the Musalman Races Found in Sind, Baluchistan, and Afghanistan* (1901),

gives in alphabetical order a brief account (sometimes based on hearsay) of the different Muslim groups, communities, tribes, and racial stocks of Sind. H.T. SORLEY, *Shah Abdul Latif of Bhit* (1940, reprinted 1966), in dealing with the poetry and biography of the renowned poet, Shāh ᶜAbd-ul-Laṭif, presents a study of the literary, social and economic conditions in 18th-century Sind. N.A. BALOCH, *Musical Instruments of the Lower Indus Valley of Sind* (1966), examines Sindhi folklore; and ETHEL-JANE W. BUNTING, *Sindhi Tombs and Textiles* (1980), is an illustrated introduction to various arts and crafts employed in early Sind. H.T. SORLEY, *The Gazetteer of West Pakistan: The Former Province of Sind Including Khaipur State* (1968/69); and the *Sind Annual,* provide the latest information and statistical data on administrative and developmental aspects. SYED ABDUL QUDDUS, *Local Self Government in Pakistan* (1981), offers documents pertaining to local administration in Sind. GEORGE L. ABERNETHY (comp.), *Pakistan: A Selected, Annotated Bibliography,* 4th ed., rev. and enlarged (1974), contains books and articles for the general reader.

Palestine

Palestine is a small region of the eastern Mediterranean comprising parts of modern Israel and Jordan. The area is also known as the Holy Land and is held sacred among Christians, Jews, and Muslims. In the 20th century it has been the object of conflicting claims between Jewish and Arab national movements, and the conflict has led in several instances to warfare.

Palestine was named after the Philistines, who occupied a small pocket of land on the southern coast, between modern Tel-Aviv–Yafo and Gaza, in the 12th century BC. The area, first called Philistia, gave its name in the 2nd century AD to Syria Palaestina, the southern portion of the Roman province of Syria. The name Palestine was revived as an official title when the British were given a mandate for the government of the country after its release from Ottoman rule in World War I. It is still in popular use as a general term to define a traditional region, but this usage does not imply precise boundaries. In the modern period, the area of Palestine may perhaps best be defined, therefore, as extending from the Mediterranean on the west roughly to the Jordan River on the east and from Israel's international border with Lebanon in the north to its southernmost city, Elat.

Its area is small, about 280 miles (450 kilometres) long and a maximum of 80 miles wide, but its strategic im-

portance is immense, as through it pass the main roads from Egypt to Syria and from the Mediterranean to the hills beyond the Jordan River. On a broad view, Palestine incorporates a part of the high edge of the Arabian Plateau, and its chief physical features are the outcome of the following processes: uplift and moderate folding that have raised the main hill masses; fracture and subsidence, producing the deep rifts and clefts that have severed these hills into their present partitions; the eruption of lava in certain districts; and the silting of the maritime plain with sediment borne by the current that sweeps round from the mouths of the Nile. Palestine consequently includes regions of very distinct geographic character.

Settlement is closely dependent on water, which is almost never abundant. The rainfall, which arrives in the cool half of the year, decreases in amount in general from north to south and from the coast inland. Perennial rivers are few, and the shortage of water is aggravated by the porous nature of the limestone rocks over much of the country.

For further reading on the political units most closely associated with Palestine, see the *Macropædia* articles EGYPT; ISRAEL; JORDAN; and LEBANON. For coverage of related topics in the *Macropædia* and *Micropædia,* see the *Propædia,* sections 911, 922, 96/11, and 978.

This article is divided into the following sections:

Physical and human geography

THE LAND

Of the coastal lowlands the most northerly is the Plain of ᶜAkko (Acre), which extends with a breadth of five to nine

miles for about 20 miles from the Nāqūrah Headland in Lebanon in the north to the Carmel promontory, in Israel, in the south, where it is a mere 600 feet (180 metres) wide. Farther southward it opens out rapidly into the Plain of Sharon, about eight miles wide and extending south to the

Palestine as defined in modern times, showing the boundaries of the State of Israel and territory occupied by Israel.

latitude of Tel-Aviv–Yafo. Once heavily forested in some sections and ill-drained and covered with marshes in others, the Sharon plain was reclaimed in the post-Exilic and Hellenistic period and is now a settled area. Fields and fruit groves are laid out between scattered sandstone ridges, on

which villages have grown up. South of the spur of low hills that approaches the coast about Yafo, the maritime plain widens into the fertile region of Philistia, a district of orange groves, irrigated orchards, and fields of grain.

The Plain of Esdraelon ('Emeq Yizre'el), formed by subsidence along lines of faults, separates the hills of southern Galilee from the mountains of Samaria. The plain, 16 miles wide at most, narrows to the northwest, where the Qishon River breaks through to the Plain of 'Akko, and to the southeast, where the river (the modern Harod), which rises at the Well of Harod ('En Harod), has carved the plain into the side of the Jordan Valley. Covered with rich basaltic soils washed down from the Galilean hills, Esdraelon is important both for its fertility and for the great highway it opens from the Mediterranean to the lands across the Jordan. The maritime plain connects with Esdraelon by the pass of Megiddo and several lesser routes between the mountain spurs of Carmel and Gilboa'.

The hill country of Galilee is better watered and more thickly wooded than that of Samaria or Judaea. North of the Plain of Asochis, Upper Galilee, with heights of 4,000 feet, is a scrub-covered limestone plateau and is thinly peopled. To the south, Lower Galilee, with its highest mountain, Tabor (1,929 feet), is a land of east–west ridges enclosing sheltered vales like that of Nazareth (Nazerat), with rich basaltic soils.

Samaria, the region of the ancient kingdom of Israel, is a hilly district extending from the Plain of Esdraelon to the latitude of Ramla. Its mountains, Carmel, Gilboa', Ebal, and Gerizim, are lower than those of Upper Galilee, while its basins, notably those of the 'Arrābah Plain and Nābulus (Shekhem), are wider and more gently contoured than their equivalents in Judaea. Samaria is easily approached from the coast over the hills of Ephraim and from the Jordan by the Fāri'ah Valley. The city of Jerusalem has expanded rapidly along the mountain ridges.

From Ramla in the north to Beersheba in the south, the high plateau of Judaea is a rocky wilderness of limestone, with rare patches of cultivation, as around al-Bīrah and Mt. Hebron (al-Khalīl). It is separated from the coastal plain by a longitudinal fosse and a belt of low hills of soft chalky limestone, about five to eight miles wide, known as ha-Shefela. The Judaean plateau falls abruptly to the Jordan Valley, which is approached with difficulty along the wadis Kelt and Mukallik.

The Jordan Valley is a deep rift valley that varies in width from 1.5 to 14 miles. In its northern section the bed of the drained Lake Hula and Lake Tiberias (the Sea of Galilee) are blocked by natural dams of basalt. Descending to about 1,310 feet below sea level, the valley is exceedingly dry and overheated, and cultivation is restricted to irrigated areas or rare oases, as at Jericho or at 'En Gedi by the shore of the Dead Sea.   (W.C.B./W.L.O.)

THE PEOPLE

The social geography of Palestine in the 20th century has been greatly affected by the dramatic political changes and wars that have brought this small region to the attention of the world. Since 1948 and the end of the British mandate, about three-fourths of geographic Palestine has been part of the State of Israel. Arabs constitute a minority of the population of Israel (about one-sixth in the late 1980s), while Jews constitute the rest of the citizenry. Hebrew is the predominant language, although Arabic is also an official language that can be used in government. The Jewish majority is increasingly composed of persons born in Israel itself, although hundreds of thousands of immigrants have arrived since independence. The Arab minority is descended from Arabs who lived in the area during the mandate period and, in most cases, for centuries before that time. A majority of both Jews and Arabs are now urbanized.

According to Jewish nationalists (Zionists), Judaism constitutes a basis for both religious and national (ethnic) identity. Arab Palestinian nationalists usually emphasize that their shared national identity or Arabness transcends the religious diversity of their community: Muslim Arabs are about 14 percent of the Israeli population, and Christian Arabs about 3 percent.

Topography

Farmland and mountain range near Nazareth, in Lower Galilee.
A.L. Goldman—Rapho/Photo Researchers

The other one-fourth of geographic Palestine not gained by Israel in 1948 was occupied by its forces in the Arab–Israeli war of 1967. The Arab majority resident in these territories—the West Bank, west of the Jordan River, and the Gaza Strip, along the Mediterranean coast—and the still larger number of Arab Palestinians living outside geographic Palestine (many in nearby countries such as Lebanon), have strongly opposed Israeli control and what they fear will be eventual annexation of these areas by Israel. Most Jewish Israeli settlers living in the occupied territories would like to have this annexation take place; they think the land ought to be part of Israel proper.

Both Zionists and Palestinian Arab nationalists have at various times in recent history claimed rightful possession of all of geographic Palestine. The rivalry between the two groups and their claims have been major causes of the numerous Arab–Israeli wars and the continuing crises in the region. Some members of each group still make such sweeping and mutually exclusive claims to complete control of Palestine, while others are now more willing to seek a peaceful compromise solution. (W.L.O.)

History

STONE AGE AND CHALCOLITHIC

The Paleolithic era of Palestine was first fully examined by the archaeologist Dorothy Garrod in her excavations of caves on the slopes of Mt. Carmel in 1929–34. The finds showed that at this stage Palestine was culturally linked with Europe, and human remains were recovered showing that the inhabitants were of the same group as the Neanderthal inhabitants of Europe. The Mesolithic period is best represented by a culture called Natufian, known from excavations at 'Ain Mallāha and Jericho. The Natufians lived in caves, as did their Paleolithic predecessors, but there is a possibility that they were experimenting in agriculture, for the importance to them of the collection of grain is shown by the artistic care that they lavished on the carving of the hafts of their sickles and in the provision of utensils for grinding. During the subsequent Neolithic period humans gradually undertook the domestication of animals, the cultivation of crops, the production of pottery, and the building of towns (*e.g.*, Jericho by 7000 BC). Excavations also have provided a picture of events in Palestine in the 5th–4th millennium BC, during which the transition from the Neolithic to the Chalcolithic (the first

Natufian culture

period of the Bronze Age) took place. It was probably in the 4th millennium that the Ghassulians immigrated to Palestine. Their origin is not known; they are called Ghassulians because the pottery and flints characteristic of their settlements first attracted attention in the excavations of Tulaylāt al-Ghassūl in the Jordan Valley. There was a permanent village site, with several successive layers of occupation, and the site probably was associated with reasonably efficient agriculture. The phase can be called Chalcolithic, since copper axes were found at Tulaylāt al-Ghassūl, and this is confirmed by the finds at sites near Beersheba, with pottery and a flint industry allied to those of Tulaylāt al-Ghassūl but not identical with them. At Beersheba there was a copper-working industry, which, presumably, imported ore from Sinai, and there was also evidence of an ivory-working industry, both proving the growth of a class of specialist craftsmen. Discoveries near 'En Gedi have revealed a shrine of this period, and basketry, ivory, leather, and hundreds of copper ritual objects were found in the Naḥal Mishmar caves of the Judaean desert.

The region in which the Ghassulian settlements have been found is mainly in the south of Palestine, with an extension up the coastal plain and its fringes. These settlements seem to have died out and disappeared in the last centuries of the 4th millennium, at about the same time as a new population immigrated, probably from the north. Thereafter, the composite elements in Palestine consisted of the indigenous Neolithic-Chalcolithic population, the Ghassulians, and these latest immigrants; in time the peoples were amalgamated into what was to become the sedentary urban population of the Early Bronze Age in the 3rd millennium.

Palestine dating is henceforth linked to Egyptian dating down to the time of the Hebrew monarchy; the interpretation of Egyptian dates in Rolf Krauss's *Sothis- und Monddaten* (1985) is followed in this article.

THE BRONZE AGE

Early Bronze Age. It was in the Early Bronze Age that most of the towns that are known in historic times came into existence. The growth of these towns can be approximately correlated chronologically with the development of the Old Kingdom in Egypt, Early Bronze I corresponding to the Late Predynastic period and Early Bronze II being cross-dated by finds to the time of the 1st dynasty, *c.* 2925 BC. Evidence of the early phases of the Early Bronze Age comes mainly from Megiddo, Jericho, Tell el Far'ah, Bet She'an, Khirbet Kerak, and Ai. All these sites are in northern or central Palestine, and it was there that the Early Bronze Age towns seem to have developed. The towns of southern Palestine, for instance Tell ed Duweir, Tell Beit Mirsim, and Tell el Hesi, seem only to have been established in Early Bronze III. The town dwellers, identified as the original Semitic population, can, for the sake of convenience, be called Canaanites, although the term is not attested before the middle of the 2nd millennium BC.

In the course of the 3rd millennium, therefore, walled towns begin to appear throughout Palestine. There is no evidence that the next step of unification under the leadership of a single town took place in Palestine, as it had in Mesopotamia and Egypt; Palestine's towns presumably remained independent city-states, except insofar as Egypt may at times have exercised a loose political control. By about the 23rd century BC, the whole civilization had ceased to be urban. The next phase was pastoral and was influenced by the settlement of nomads probably from east of the Jordan River. Among the nomads, Amorites from the Syrian desert may have predominated. It is not yet fully understood how these events are related to the creation of the Akkadian empire in Mesopotamia under Sargon of Akkad and his grandson Naram-sin (24th and 23rd centuries BC) and to the latter's destruction of the powerful kingdom of Ebla (modern Tall Mardīkh) in neighbouring Syria, nor is the extent of Eblaite and Akkadian hegemony over Palestine in this period known. It does, however, seem reasonable to associate the incursion of nomads from the east with the invasions of Asiatics into Egypt that brought the Old Kingdom to an end. An initial date of 23rd–22nd century BC, depending on the interpretation of the Egyptian evidence, and a final date of the 20th century BC seem probable.

The picture of Palestine at this period is thus unequivocally that of a country occupied by a number of allied tribes; between them there are many features in common, but there are also many differences. The most significant point is that, with the possible exception of the northern group, they made no contribution at all to town life. The different groups had tribal centres, but they were essentially seminomadic pastoralists. This description fits well that in the Book of Joshua of the Amorites who lived in the hill country, as opposed to the Canaanites who lived in the plains and on the coast—areas favourable to agriculture.

Middle Bronze Age. It was, in fact, the next period—the Middle Bronze Age—that introduced the Canaanite culture as found by the Israelites on their entry into Palestine. The Middle Bronze Age (c. 2000–c. 1550 BC) provides the background for the beginning of the story of the Old Testament. The archaeological evidence for the period shows new types of pottery, weapons, and burial practices. Once more an urban civilization based on agriculture was established. It is not entirely clear whether the wave of urban development after the 20th century BC was the work of a new immigrant people accustomed to dwell in towns or of the local inhabitants themselves, some of whom may have adopted a sedentary life-style and begun, as in Mesopotamia and Syria, to establish dynasties. But where they settled, there grew up towns of the widespread Middle Bronze Age civilization of Palestine. This civilization was intimately connected with that of the towns of the Phoenician–Canaanite coast. Extant Egyptian documents provide valuable information about Palestine in the period of the Egyptian 12th dynasty (1938–1756 BC) and argue for significant Egyptian interest and influence in Palestine at this time. (Most notable are the popular literary work known as the *Story of Sinuhe,* detailing the hero's exile in the Palestinian region, and the 20th–19th-century "Execration Texts," inscriptions of names of Egypt's enemies on pottery, which was ceremonially broken to invoke a curse.) The culture introduced at this stage was essentially the same as the culture found by the Israelites who moved into Palestine later, in the 14th and 13th centuries BC.

A large repertory of new forms in pottery arose, and for the first time in Palestine it was turned entirely on a fast wheel. Comparisons of Palestinian early Middle Bronze pottery forms with metallic and ceramic forms at Byblos, dated by Egyptian contacts, suggest that these forms were brought to Palestine around the 19th century from coastal Syria. Bronze weapons of a distinctive type, paralleled also on the Syrian coast, are found at Megiddo, Jericho, and Tell el 'Ajjul. Town life in Palestine gradually expanded after the mid-19th century BC, but the material culture was essentially a direct development from the preceding stage. Several towns of Middle Bronze Age Palestine were defended by plaster-faced ramparts (clearly discernible at Jericho and many other sites), an imported method of fortification giving evidence of a new and alien influence superimposed upon the existing Canaanite culture. These were probably introduced by the Asiatic Hyksos, possibly related to the Amorites, who secured control of northern Egypt in about 1630. The Hyksos may have included elements of a grouping of people, largely Semitic, called the Habiru, or Hapiru (Egyptian 'Apiru). (The term Habiru, meaning "outsiders," was applied to nomads, fugitives, bandits, and workers of inferior status; the word is etymologically related to "Hebrew," and the relationship of the Habiru [and aforementioned Hyksos] to the Hebrews has long been debated.) The Habiru appear to have established a military aristocracy in Palestine, bringing to the towns new defenses and new prosperity (as well as many Egyptian cultural elements) without interrupting the basic character of the local culture; this was to survive the destruction of Megiddo, Jericho, and Tell Beit Mirsim that followed the Egyptians' expulsion of the Hyksos into Palestine at the end of the Middle Bronze Age (c. 1550).

(K.M.K./G.R.B.)

Late Bronze Age. There was no sharp break between the Middle and the Late Bronze ages in Palestine. Shortly before the death of Ahmose I (1514 BC), the first native pharaoh of the New Empire, the Egyptian armies began to conquer Palestine, probably completing their task during his successor's reign. Under Queen Hatshepsut (1479–58), Palestine revolted against Egyptian domination, but the rebellion was put down firmly by her successor, Thutmose III, who established a stable administration, maintained through the reigns of his immediate successors. Egyptian administrative documents excavated in both Egypt and Palestine show in considerable detail how the provincial government was organized and even how it operated during the century 1450–1350 BC. Documents show, for example, that the land of Retenu (Syria-Palestine) was divided into three administrative districts, each under an Egyptian governor. The third district (Canaan) included all of Palestine from the Egyptian border to Byblos. This period is often known as the Amarna Age and is vividly illustrated by several hundred cuneiform letters found in Egypt at Tell el Amarna, site of the capital of the "heretic king" Akhenaton. The unusual concern of the pharaohs with the affairs of Palestine was chiefly a result of the fact that control of it was necessary for the defense of Phoenicia and southern Syria, menaced by Mitanni down to c. 1375 and by the Hittite Empire after that date. *Egyptian conquests of Palestine*

In about 1292 BC the increasingly weak rule of the last pharaohs of the 18th dynasty was replaced by the strong arm of the second and third kings of the 19th dynasty, Seti I and Ramses II (1279–13 BC). These kings blunted the southward thrust of the Hittites and consolidated the crumbling Egyptian Empire. The exactions of foreign bureaucrats, however, combined with internal decay, had so enfeebled the Canaanite vassal princes of Palestine that it was comparatively easy for the incoming Israelites to occupy most of the hill country of both Transjordan and western Palestine in the course of the closing decades of the 13th century BC. Archaeological evidence suggests that the Israelite settlement in Palestine was much more complex and disconnected than the biblical accounts indicate. During a short interlude of anarchy that followed the last weak kings of the 19th dynasty, Egyptian rule was completely extinguished, and the ephemeral victories of Ramses III in the early decades of the 12th century scarcely affected Palestinian history.

THE IRON AGE

The Israelites in Palestine. Though the Israelite tribes entered Palestine before the end of the Late Bronze Age, they did not become firmly established in their new home until the early decades of the 12th century. Their number was increased greatly during the settling of Canaan by seminomadic Hebrew tribes already in Palestine, as well as by many settled Canaanites (*e.g.,* the Gibeonites), who joined the invaders against their sedentary neighbours. Excavation has made it clear that the Israelites began building amid the ruins of their precursors and that new settlements sprang up rapidly all through the hill country. Had events followed their normal course, the resurgent Canaanites, who had not been driven from the coastal plain or the Plain of Esdraelon, might have overwhelmed the scattered and unorganized Israelite clans, but this was prevented by the great invasion of the Sea Peoples in the time of Ramses III, in the early decades of the 12th century BC. Among the invaders from the Aegean basin were the Philistines, who were to conquer much of the region within a century and a half after their settlement in the southern coastal plain. (The Philistines have been identified with the so-called Peleset, who were used as garrison troops and mercenaries by Ramses III.) Meanwhile, three other peoples were settling down in southern Transjordan: the Edomites in the south, the Moabites east of the Dead Sea, and the Ammonites on the edge of the Syrian Desert east of Gilead. Considered by the Israelites as fellow Hebrews, these peoples had begun to settle down before the Israelite invasion, and they remained polytheists until the end of the Old Testament period.

The early Israelites possessed a strong centralizing force in their monotheistic faith, combined with a stern code of ethics, which set them apart from all their neighbours. *Centralization among the Israelites*

The Mosaic tradition of the covenant between Yahweh and Israel, made concrete by the tabernacle and its ritual, bound the tribes together in a cultic bond resembling the later Greek amphictyonies. Characteristic of all these organizations was a central sanctuary, surrounded by its worshipers. Straining against this religious bond were disruptive tribal forces held in leash by a loose alliance between the tribes, which was often severed by civil war. But for the constant attacks launched by its neighbours, Israel would perhaps never have attained any political solidarity. As it was, salvation from its foes lay only in union, and after abortive attempts had been made at one-man rule, Saul became king of all Israel (c. 1020 BC).

He defeated the Ammonites and the Philistines but was killed in battle against the latter in about 1000 BC and was succeeded by David. King David crushed the Philistines (c. 990) and conquered the three Hebrew states of Transjordan, after which the intervention of the Aramaeans from Syria forced him to defeat and annex the states of Aram as far north as the borders of Hamath on the Orontes. Farther east he established some sort of control over the nomadic tribes of the Syrian Desert as far as the Euphrates, though it is scarcely probable that Israelite domination was very effective. At home David organized a stable administration based largely on Egyptian models and, according to tradition, carried out a census of the population. He died before he could complete his plans, but they were put into effect by his successor, Solomon.

The reign of Solomon (mid-10th century) represents the culmination of Israelite political history. Though he gradually lost control over outlying territories conquered by David, he was extraordinarily successful in organizing the economic life of the country. He joined forces with Hiram of Tyre, who was leading the Phoenicians toward the exploitation of Mediterranean trade. Expeditions to Ophir, a region probably in either East Africa or India, brought rich products such as gold, peacocks, and sandalwood to Palestine. At the same time the Israelite king entered into trade relations with the Arabs as far south as Sheba (Yemen). These activities would have been impossible but for the development of new principles in shipbuilding and for the recent domestication of the Arabian camel and its use in caravans. Among other undertakings of the King was his construction of a fortress or storehouse at a site near the head of the Gulf of Aqaba. The modern site, Tall al-Khalifah, may have been the biblical Ezion-geber. Most of the kingdom's wealth was spent in elaborate building operations, which included the Temple and royal palace in Jerusalem, as well as numerous fortified towns. The best-known of these were Megiddo, Hazor, and Gezer. But royal activities on such a vast scale cost more than was produced by foreign trade and the tribute of vassal states, and the Israelites themselves were forced to submit to conscription in royal labour gangs as well as to heavy levies of various kinds. It is not surprising that the people of northern Israel revolted after the great king's death, thus disrupting the united monarchy.

The rump kingdom of Israel lasted for two full centuries, sharing the worship of Yahweh and the Mosaic tradition with its smaller southern neighbour, Judah. After a period of intermittent warfare between Judah and Israel, King Asa of the former entered into an alliance with the growing kingdom of Damascus by which the latter attacked northern Israel, thus relieving pressure on Judah. This move cost Israel its Transjordan territory north of the Yarmuk River and ushered in a long series of wars between Israel and Damascus, which did not end until the capture of Damascus by the Assyrians in 732.

The best-known phase of Israelite history is the period during which the great prophets, Elijah and Elisha, flourished, under the Omrides of the 9th century. Omri himself, founder of the dynasty, selected Samaria as his capital and began the construction of elaborate defenses and royal buildings, which have been uncovered by excavations. His son Ahab was alternately hero and villain of the principal stories of the prophets; he became involved in complex international maneuvers, which ended with his ignominious death at Ramoth-Gilead. The dynasty of Omri closed amid torrents of blood (c. 841 BC); it was followed by the

The dynasty of Omri

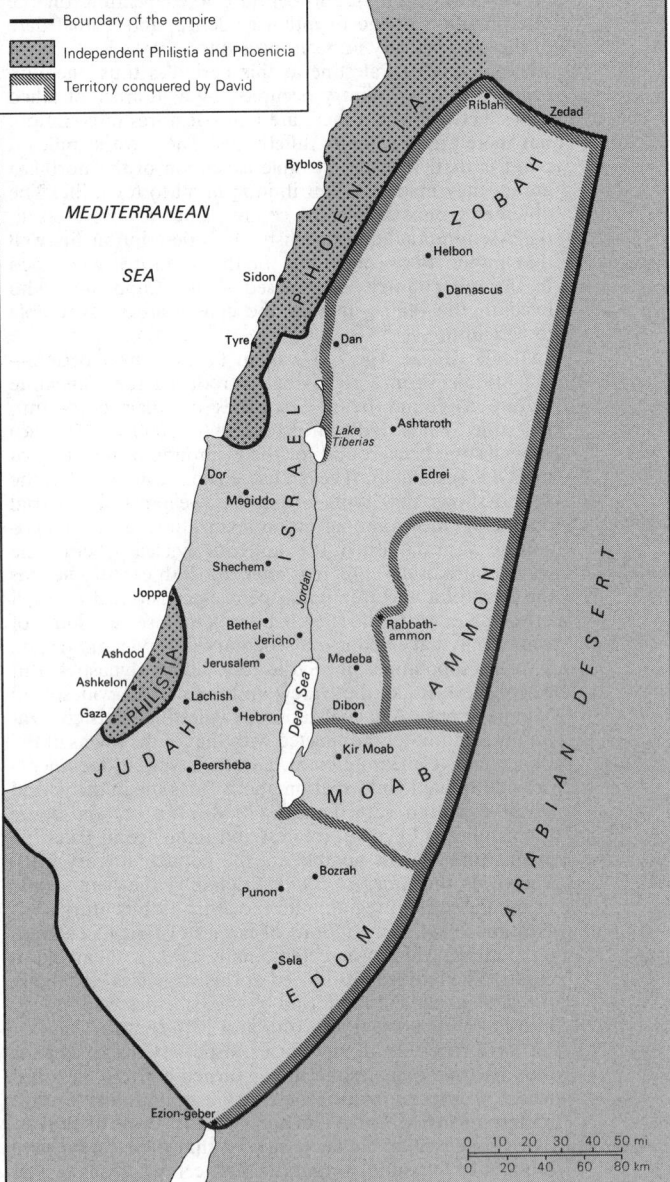

Palestine during the time of David and Solomon.

Adapted from *The Westminster Historical Atlas to the Bible,* revised edition, copyright 1945, by the Westminster Press; copyright 1956, by W.L. Jenkins. Edited by George Ernest Wright and Floyd V. Filson

dynasty of Jehu, which lasted for nearly a century. This was a period of extreme oscillations, from the catastrophic defeat of Israel (c. 815 BC) and the destruction of its army by Hazael, king of Damascus, to the triumphs of Jeroboam II (c. 786–746 BC). Meanwhile, Judah also oscillated between periods of prosperity and weakness; when it was strong it controlled Edom and the caravan routes of the south from Midian to the Mediterranean; when it was feeble it shrank behind its own narrow boundaries. Great kings like Asa, Jehoshaphat, and Uzziah alternated with weak kings.

In 741/740 the death knell of western independence was sounded by the capture of Arpad in northern Syria by the Assyrian king Tiglath-pileser III. Events followed with dizzying speed. In 738 Israel and Judah paid tribute to Assyria for the first time in decades; in 733 the Assyrians devastated Gilead and Galilee, turning the entire land into Assyrian provinces except for the territory of two tribes, western Manasseh and Ephraim; in 732 Damascus was captured and Aram ceased to exist as a state; in 725 the siege of Samaria began. Finally, in the first months of 722, Samaria was taken and Israel became politically extinct.

Assyrian and Babylonian rule.   Judah was left the sole heir of the glories of David and Solomon. Hezekiah (c.

715–c. 686), lured by promises of Egyptian aid, attempted to resist Assyria but was defeated and compelled to pay a crushing tribute. It is possible that only the timely intervention of an epidemic that decimated the Assyrian army of Sennacherib saved Judah from total devastation. The eloquent guidance of Isaiah restored the morale of the people, and even the weakness of Hezekiah's son Manasseh did not bring complete ruin. Another strong king, Josiah (c. 640–609), arose in time to restore the ebbing fortunes of Judah for a few years, during which much of the ancient territory of united Israel was brought back under the rule of the Davidic dynasty. Assyria was rapidly declining in power, and in 612 its hated capital, Nineveh, was destroyed by the Medes. Josiah's successful rebellion ended when he fell in battle against a more powerful contender for the Assyrian succession, Necho of Egypt.

Meanwhile, the Chaldean kings of Babylonia were rapidly gaining strength. Nabopolassar of Babylon and Cyaxares of Media divided the old Assyrian Empire between them, and the former's son, Nebuchadrezzar, gained control of Syria and Palestine in swift campaigns. The defeated Egyptians, however, continued to intrigue in Palestine, whose native states repeatedly joined anti-Babylonian coalitions, all of which collapsed of themselves or were crushed by the Chaldean armies. Jerusalem was twice besieged, in 597 and after 589. Finally, about 587, it was stormed and destroyed. The prophet Jeremiah, who had foreseen the tragic denouement and had repeatedly warned his people against their suicidal policy, died in Egypt. Judah was devastated and almost depopulated.

The Persian Empire. In 539 Cyrus II of Persia followed up his triumph over Media by conquering Lydia and Babylonia, thus making himself ruler of the greatest empire thitherto known. In the administrative reforms implemented by Darius I (reigned 522–486 BC), Phoenicia, Palestine-Syria, and Cyprus constituted the fifth province (satrapy) of the Persian empire (Herodotus, *The History,* 3.91).

One of Cyrus' first acts was to decree (c. 538) the restoration of Judah and the rebuilding of the First Temple of Jerusalem. A large number of Jewish exiles in Babylonia returned to Jerusalem, and work on the Second Temple was begun. The political situation was extremely unfavourable, however, since Judah south of Hebron had been occupied by Edomites escaping from Arab pressure, while the tiny remainder north of Hebron had passed under the control of the governor of Samaria. In spite of political intrigues to prevent completion of the work of rebuilding the Temple, the Jews took advantage of the civil wars and rebellions that racked the empire after the accession of Darius I to press forward with the work. They were urged on by the fiery prophets Haggai and Zechariah. In 515 BC the Second Temple was finished, but the Jews had meanwhile aroused the suspicion of the Persian authorities, and further efforts to improve their situation were discouraged.

Completion of the Second Temple

Matters rested in this unsatisfactory state until about 445 BC, when the Jewish royal favourite, Nehemiah, deeply stirred by reports of the sorry condition of Judah and Jerusalem, succeeded in obtaining the Persian ruler's support for a mission to Palestine. Under Nehemiah's leadership Jerusalem's walls were rebuilt. Knowledge of the exact sequence of events is complicated by the confused state of the documentary sources, and the chronology of events in the time of Nehemiah and Ezra, who became a leader of the Jews who had returned to Jerusalem from Babylonia, is not certain. There is good evidence to suggest that Ezra's return to Jerusalem should be dated to 398 BC, early in the reign of the Persian king Artaxerxes II. The mention of Persian intervention in the priestly affairs of the high priest Johanan can reasonably be associated with Ezra's reform activities. In any event, Nehemiah and Ezra were able to establish both the religious autonomy of Judah and the practice of normative Judaism so firmly that they continued with little change for several centuries.

Information concerning the history of Palestine in the period following the age of Nehemiah and Ezra is very scanty. It is known that the province of Judah continued to be administered by high priests who struck their own

coins and that the provinces of Samaria and Ammon remained under governors of the houses of Sanballat and Tobiah. In 343 Artaxerxes III Ochus is said to have devastated parts of Palestine in connection with his reconquest of Egypt. Eleven years later the country passed into Macedonian hands after Alexander's conquest of Phoenicia.

(W.F.A./G.R.B.)

FROM ALEXANDER THE GREAT TO AD 70

To Alexander, Palestine was, as to many before him, a corridor leading to Egypt, the outlying Persian province. Consequently, in his attack on that province after the Battle of Issus (333), he confined his attention, in his passage southward, to reducing the coastal cities that might form bases for the Persian fleet. The Jews he left undisturbed in their religion and customs. The high priest remained the head of the Jewish state, perhaps assisted by a council of elders.

The Ptolemies. After the death of Alexander in 323, Palestine, with much of Syria and Phoenicia, fell to Ptolemy, who established himself as satrap in Egypt in 323 BC and adopted the title of king by 304. (After the death of Ptolemy, the Ptolemaic dynasty ruled Egypt for 300 years.)

The successors of Alexander, including Ptolemy and Seleucus, defeated Antigonus Monophthalmus, one of Alexander's generals, who had almost succeeded in recreating under his sole rule Alexander's great empire, at Ipsus in Phrygia in 301 BC. This victory confirmed Ptolemy in his possession of his territory, although he had arrived too late for the battle, and Seleucus, whose participation in it had been decisive, at first disputed Ptolemy's claim to Syria and Phoenicia and actually occupied northern Syria. This early dispute laid the foundations of a century of bitter antagonism between the House of Ptolemy and that of Seleucus, an antagonism that led to war five times within a century and was finally stilled only by Palestine's passing in 200 BC into the hands of the Seleucid dynasty. The northern boundary of the kingdom established by Ptolemy I lay apparently slightly north of the modern Tripoli, perhaps on the course of the Kabīr River (ancient Eleutherus), and there are no signs of any important change in this frontier throughout the next century.

Of Ptolemaic rule in the southern part of this territory, Palestine, little is known. What little can be discovered, mainly from writers of a later period, especially the author of the First Book of Maccabees and Josephus, suggests that, unlike the northern region, known as Syria and Phoenicia, the area was left in much its previous state, with considerable power and authority in the hands of the native chieftains.

More is known of taxation than of administration. A story preserved by Josephus (*The Antiquities of the Jews,* xii, § 154 ff.) indicates that tax farming, whereby the right to collect taxes was auctioned or was awarded to privileged persons, was employed for the collection of local taxes. It seems likely that there were additional extraordinary taxes levied by edict from Egypt.

Knowledge of the economic and commercial life of Palestine in the middle of the 3rd century is, on the other hand, fuller and more reliable. It is drawn from the dossier of letters received and written by Zenon, the confidential business manager of the chief minister of Ptolemy II Philadelphus (285–246), who in 259 was sent to Palestine and Syria, where his master had commercial interests. These letters speak particularly of a trade in slaves, especially of young girls for prostitution, in whom there appears to have been a brisk trade, with export to Egypt. Zenon's records also testify to a considerable trade in cereals, oil, and wine. Inevitably, like all imports to Egypt, Palestinian exports worked under state monopoly, without which the internal monopolies of Egypt would have been undermined. Palestine, like Egypt and Syria, seems to have had no economic freedom under Ptolemaic rule; in all transactions the hand of the government's agents is clearly visible.

Zenon's records of life in Palestine

Of the material culture of Palestine in the Ptolemaic period, far less is known. The population seems, as in Syria, to have been divided between the Hellenized cities (*poleis*) of the coast, notably Ascalon and Joppa, and the rural population living in villages (*komai*). The fact that several cities had Ptolemaic dynastic names (Philadelphia, Philoteria, Ptolemais) must not lead to overemphasis of the desire of the early Ptolemies to urbanize and raise the standard of living of the people of Palestine. It seldom appears that they did more than rename a previously existing city (*e.g.*, Scythopolis for Bet She'an)—a practice not uncommon in the Hellenistic world. In fact, unlike the Seleucids, the Ptolemies do not appear to have been great city builders. Nor do they appear to have encouraged the outward forms of independence in local government. It seems likely from the story of the Phoenician tax farmers mentioned above that considerable authority lay in the hands of the wealthy, yet the fact that both Ascalon and Joppa issued Ptolemaic regal coinage, but apparently no autonomous bronze coinage, suggests a rigid control. The absence of epigraphical evidence from the cities of Ptolemaic Palestine, however, renders any judgment about the conditions of the cities hazardous. Archaeology, too, helps but little, inasmuch as the buildings of Roman Palestine have swamped most of the Hellenistic remains. One exception must be noted: the tombs of the Hellenized Sidonian military settlers at Marisa in Idumaea, the walls of which are decorated with frescoes of fine hunting scenes, indicate that Hellenic civilization had penetrated deep into the non-Greek population in this period.

The chronic state of hostility between Egypt and the Seleucid house, which in much of the 3rd century BC had been concerned with the coastal regions of western Asia Minor, received a new impetus with the accession to the Seleucid throne of the energetic Antiochus III the Great (223–187), who aimed to win southern Syria and Palestine from Egypt, now weakly governed, and thereby establish the frontier to which Seleucus I had unwillingly renounced his claim in 301 BC. After his severe defeat by Ptolemy IV at Raphia in 217, however, Antiochus was for several years occupied with internal troubles, and it was therefore not until about 200 BC that he could think again of an attack on Egypt. There, a child—Ptolemy V Epiphanes—had recently ascended the throne, and the government was in the hands of overpowerful ministers who were more concerned with feathering their own nests than with preserving the integrity of the kingdom. At Panion, on the northern boundary of Galilee, the armies of Antiochus and Ptolemy met, and Ptolemy was defeated. Thus, the Ptolemaic possessions north of the Sinai desert, including Palestine, passed into the hands of the House of Seleucus.

The Seleucids. The Seleucids brought to the problem of the administration of Palestine a different tradition from that which had been behind Ptolemaic rule. The latter was based on that careful exploitation of territory that was possible in a small and closely knit land like Egypt and had thence been extended to the Ptolemaic provinces. This had never been possible for the Seleucids, who had always been masters of regions so vast as to render a unified and absolute control impossible. There is no sign of oppression in Seleucid government of the native peoples—they seem, on the contrary, to have aimed at improving the natives' status as far as possible, largely through bringing them into contact with Greek modes of urban existence.

It might then be supposed that Seleucid rule would have been popular in Palestine. In fact, however, it was under Seleucid rule that the great uprising of the Jewish people, the revolt of the Maccabees, occurred. The explanation of this paradox is perhaps twofold. First, the Seleucids were in need of money, and second, the throne, at a critical time, was occupied by a tactless and neurotic king. Knowledge of Seleucid rule in Palestine before the accession of Antiochus Epiphanes is slight. The years from 188 BC onward were lean years for the dynasty, because the war with Rome, which had ended (in 189) in a complete Roman victory, had cost it not only almost the whole of Asia Minor but also a yearly indemnity of 15,000 talents. It is therefore not surprising that the first glimpse of Seleucid rule in Palestine tells of an attempt by Heliodorus, the leading minister of Seleucus IV (187–175), to deprive the Temple in Jerusalem of its treasure. His failure was soon ascribed to divine protection.

With the accession of Antiochus Epiphanes in 175 BC,

relations rapidly deteriorated. Antiochus appears to have aimed at a wholesale restoration of the Seleucid Empire in the east, including an occupation of Egypt, as a counter to the loss of the western province occasioned by the Peace of Apamea. He made an unwise beginning in Palestine by establishing a philhellene high priest, and it is clear from this and from his whole subsequent policy that he wished to extirpate Jewish religion from its central stronghold (there is no indication that he persecuted Jews of the Diaspora living in the cities of his kingdom). Antiochus Epiphanes

Antiochus invaded Egypt in 170 or 169 BC, returning to Syria by way of Jerusalem, where he and his army despoiled the Temple of all its wealth. Two years later, after his humiliating expulsion from the gate of Egypt by the Roman legate, he sent a financial official to exact taxes from the cities of Judaea. Antiochus' official attacked the city of Jerusalem by guile and largely destroyed it. He then built a fortified position on the citadel, called by the Greeks the Akra. This became the symbol of Judah's enslavement, though in itself the presence of a royal garrison in a Hellenistic city was by no means unusual. Its imposition was followed by an open attack on religious practice, many of the rites of which were forbidden. Noncompliance with the order, which contained many items calculated to raise the bitterest resistance in the hearts of law-abiding Jews, such as the prohibition of circumcision and the abolition of the observance of the Sabbath, was punishable by death. Finally, on the 25th day of the Hebrew month Kislev (December), 168 BC, the "abomination of desolation," namely the altar of Zeus, was set up in the Temple in Jerusalem. It was this above all that summoned forth the resistance of the sons of the aged priest Mattathias led by Judas Maccabeus so began the Maccabean Revolt.

The resistance, it must be emphasized, came from only a section of the population. The century and a half of Greek rule had Hellenized much of the upper class of Jerusalem, and some of the characteristic features of Greek city life, such as the ephebic institute, for the training of young men, and the gymnasia, had been established on the initiative of this section of the ruling class, which was able to accept a less radical observance of Judaism and combine it with loyalty to the throne. Throughout the revolt, and indeed until the closing days of the Hasmonean dynasty established by the Maccabeans, this Hellenized element had to be taken into account.

Judas Maccabeus proved himself a leader of high quality. He successfully resisted the weak forces sent by the Seleucid authorities, and after three years of intermittent warfare he succeeded in purifying the Temple (165 BC), though the Akra remained in Seleucid hands until 141 BC.

After the death of Antiochus Epiphanes in 164 BC, the numbers of claimants to the Seleucid throne made a continuous policy toward Palestine impossible, because each claimant felt the need to seek support wherever it might be found. Thus, Jewish high priests were bought and bribed by the kings and dynasts of Syria. This development enabled Judas and those who succeeded him to hold their own and eventually to establish a hereditary dynasty, known as the Hasmonean for their ancestor Hasmoneus. Soon after Antiochus Epiphanes' death, an agreement was reached with the Seleucid regent Lysias (who feared the appearance of a rival in Syria), through which the Jews received back their religious liberty. But at the same time the regular practice of pagan worship, beside the Jewish, was established, and a Seleucid nominee was appointed high priest. Thus were laid the seeds of fresh revolt.

Almost immediately Judas again took the field and scored a considerable victory over Nicanor, the Seleucid general, in which Nicanor was killed. Within two months, however, Demetrius I, the Seleucid king, sent Bacchides to take up a position near Jerusalem, and in the engagement that followed Judas lost his life (160).

The Hasmonean priest-princes. In the following years, dynastic disputes within the Seleucid Empire prevented a succession of rulers from settling the Palestinian question. These circumstances allowed first Jonathan (160–143), the brother and successor of Judas and then his brother Simon (143–134) to attain power. In 153 one of the Seleucid pretenders, Alexander Balas, in order to outplay the legitimate king, Demetrius I, granted Jonathan the office of high priest and gave him the Seleucid rank of a courtier, thereby legitimizing his position. When Simon succeeded Jonathan, he acquired the status of a recognized secular ruler; the year of his assumption of rule was regarded as the first of a new era, and official documents were dated in his name and by his regnal year. He secured from the new Seleucid monarch, Demetrius II, exemption from taxation for the Jews.

In 142–141 Simon forced the Syrian garrison on the Akra to surrender, and the Jews passed a decree in his honour, granting the right of permanent incumbency to Simon and to his successors, until "an accredited prophet" should arise. It was thus in Simon's reign that the rule of the priest-prince was transformed into a secular hereditary rule. The Seleucid king recognized this, granting Simon the right to issue his own coins.

Simon's son, John Hyrcanus I (134–104), suffered an initial setback at the hands of the last great Seleucid king, Antiochus VII Sidetes, who set out to reconquer Palestine, but at the latter's death John renewed his father's expansionist program, resulting in the conquest and destruction of Samaria. In internal policy, however, he made the grave error of quarreling with one of the two main Jewish ecclesiastical parties, the Pharisees, who followed the Law with great strictness and with whom the Maccabean movement had in origin close affinity, and siding with their opponents, the more liberal Sadducees. This is an early instance of that denial of the revolutionary origin of the movement that became very obvious in the reign of Alexander Jannaeus. Hyrcanus I was succeeded by Aristobulus I (104–103), who extended Hasmonean territory

northward and is said to have assumed the title of king (basileus), though on his coins he appears, like Hyrcanus I, as high priest.

The reign of his brother and successor, Alexander Jannaeus, was long (103–76) and largely filled with wars. He imposed his rule rigorously over an increasingly large area, including both Transjordan and the cities of the coast. Still more clearly than Hyrcanus I he attests the change in direction and aim of the Hasmonean house. He was the bitter enemy of the Pharisees, his coins bear Greek as well as Hebrew legends, and his title on them is simply "King Alexander." He was succeeded by his widow, Salome Alexandra, who reversed his policy and was guided by powerful religious advisers, members of the Pharisaic movement. After her death in 67 BC her two sons Aristobulus II and Hyrcanus II fought for the succession. Hyrcanus was defeated but was encouraged to reassert his rights by Antipater, an Edomite, son of the governor of Idumaea and father of the future Herod the Great.

At this stage the Romans appeared on the scene. Pompey the Great, during his reorganization of the lands of the newly conquered Seleucid kingdom, also arranged the affairs of Palestine (63 BC). He attempted to arbitrate between the brothers and eventually, after he had laid siege to and captured Jerusalem, appointed Hyrcanus II as high priest without the title of king adopted by his predecessors. He also imposed taxes on the Jews and curtailed Jewish dominions, granting virtual autonomy to a group of 10 or 11 Hellenized cities in Syria and Palestine, thenceforth to be known as the Decapolis, and placing them under the jurisdiction of the newly appointed governor of Syria. Pliny the Elder lists these cities as Damascus, Philadelphia (modern Amman, Jordan), Raphana, Scythopolis, Gadara, Hippos, Dion, Pella, Gerasa, and Canatha. On the basis of evidence in inscriptions, Abila can be added to the list. Thus, despite the name Decapolis, the actual number appears to have been 11. All of these cities, except for Scythopolis, are located east of the Jordan River, extending from Damascus in the north to Philadelphia in the south. Except for Damascus, all the other cities lie immediately to the west of Galilee, Samaria, and Judaea. Whether the Decapolis geographically belonged to Syria; to Coele Syria ("Hollow Syria"; *i.e.,* the southernmost region of Syria, which may include Palestine and is sometimes mistakenly limited to the modern al-Biqā' valley); or to Arabia, often identified as the land east of the Jordan River, is not clear, especially in the ancient geographers. In any event, the Decapolis ended as a political entity when Arabia was annexed in AD 106; the cities were distributed among the three provinces of Arabia, Judaea, and Syria. It appears that Philadelphia, Gerasa, and probably Dion went to Arabia, Damascus certainly to Syria, and the rest to Judaea or Syria.

After the death of Pompey, however, the power of Antipater and his family greatly increased. Hyrcanus II became a figurehead of no importance, and Antipater himself, in return for services to Julius Caesar, received Roman citizenship and was awarded the title of "procurator of Judaea," while his sons Phasael and Herod became governors (strategoi) of Jerusalem and Galilee, respectively. The unexpected occupation of Palestine by Parthian troops in 40 BC altered the situation. Antigonus, the son of Aristobulus and therefore a legitimate Hasmonean, won the favour of the Parthians and was established by them as king and high priest of Jerusalem. Phasael was reported to have committed suicide, while his brother Herod escaped to Rome.

The Herodian house and the Roman procurators. Herod, in Rome, was recognized by the Senate, with the approval of Octavian and Mark Antony, as king of Judaea (40 BC) and returned to Palestine in 39 BC. Shortly afterward Roman troops expelled the Parthians, whose popularity in Palestine had been and subsequently remained considerable. After struggles against Antigonus, the Parthian nominee, in which he was assisted by Roman troops, Herod eventually captured Jerusalem. At about the same time he married a niece of Antigonus, thus probably consoling those who remained loyal to the memory of the almost defunct Hasmonean house. Antigonus, when he

Pompey the Great

Jewish State under Judas

Additions under Jonathan

Additions under Simon

Additions under John Hyrcanus

Additions under Aristobulus I

Additions under Alexander Jannaeus

Palestine during the Maccabean period.

fell into the hands of his enemies, was executed by order of Mark Antony.

Herod's reign

The accession of Herod, the Roman protégé and an Edomite, brought to Palestine the peace that in the years of independence it had often lacked. His long reign (37–4 BC) was marked by general prosperity; his new city of Caesarea Maritima received lavish praise from Josephus for its spectacular port and sewer system. Between 31 and 20 Augustus restored to him the Jewish territories that Pompey had taken away, and in this enlarged kingdom he created a sound administrative system of Hellenistic type. Toward the end of his life the complex demands of a vast family (he had 9 wives at least) led him into difficulties regarding the succession, and it was then that he developed into the gruesome and vicious figure that Christian tradition has made so familiar. He had Mariamne and several of his sons put to death to prevent them from succeeding him; and on his death in 4 BC the country again entered a period of divided rule, which led to the reestablishment of direct Roman government. Augustus decided later that year, in the presence of three surviving sons of Herod, that Archelaus should rule Judaea, Samaria, and Edom (i.e., central and southern Palestine); Herod Antipas rule Galilee and Peraea (Transjordan); and Philip rule Trachonitis, Batanaea, and Auranitis (the area between the Decapolis and Damascus).

The fate of the rulers (of whom Philip and Herod Antipas were called tetrarchs, Archelaus ethnarch) and their territories was different. Philip, the most peaceable of the three, ruled the northern area until his death in AD 34. Antipas reigned in Galilee and Peraea until AD 39 but was then banished by Caligula on the ground that he had parleyed with Rome's enemies. Archelaus reigned for 10 years only; he was removed at the request of his subjects in AD 6. The region under Archelaus' rule (i.e., Judaea, Samaria, and Edom) became the province of Judaea and passed to a series of undistinguished Roman prefects, the last of whom (Pontius Pilate, AD 26–36, under whom Jesus was crucified) lost office for the unnecessary massacre of some Samaritans. Palestine finally was united under

the emperor Caligula's protégé, Herod Agrippa I, who succeeded Philip in the north in AD 37. The tetrarchy of Antipas was added soon after his removal in 39 and the territories of Judaea, Samaria, and Edom in 41, so that from 41 to his death in 44, Agrippa ruled the kingdom of his grandfather, Herod the Great, from Jerusalem. In 44 the entire kingdom passed under Roman rule and was reconstituted as the procuratorial province of Judaea.

Disturbances in the early years of procuratorial rule were frequent and largely caused by maladministration. Serious trouble arose under Ventidius Cumanus (48–52), and under his successor, the imperial freedman Felix (52–60), rebellion was open though sporadic. The incompetence and anti-Jewish posture of Gessius Florus, procurator 64–66, led in 66 to the decisive and final outbreak. Florus, the heir to a long tradition of hostility between the large Hellenized populations of Palestine and the Jews (also a problem in the Diaspora, most notably at Alexandria during the reign of Caligula), allowed the Greek population of Caesarea Maritima to massacre the Jews of that city with impunity. Greeks in other towns of Palestine repeated the assault. In turn, the Jews responded by slaughtering Gentiles in Samaria, Galilee, the Transjordan, and elsewhere. Soon Florus had lost control of the situation.

The organization of the Jews was better than it had previously been, and they were successful in an early engagement against the governor of Syria, who had advanced to Palestine with two legions to assist the hard-pressed procurator.

In 67, however, Vespasian, the future emperor, with his son Titus, arrived with a force of about 60,000 men, and the war became increasingly bitter. By the end of 67 Galilee was captured, and Judaea was reduced in three campaigns, which ended with the fall of Jerusalem in AD 70. The Temple was destroyed, though tradition recorded that Titus gave orders that it was to be spared, and the city became the permanent garrison town of a Roman legion. By AD 73 all resistance had ceased. (P.M.F./G.R.B.)

ROMAN PALESTINE

After the destruction of Jerusalem a legion (X Fretensis) was stationed on the site, and the rank of the provincial governor was raised from *procurator* to *legatus Augusti*, signifying a change from equestrian to senatorial rank. Caesarea Maritima, the governor's residence, became a Roman colony, and as a reward for the loyalty of the Greeks in the revolt a new pagan city, Neapolis (modern Nablus), was founded at Shechem, the religious centre of the Samaritans. Another new city was founded at Joppa (Jaffa) on the coast.

The Jews, deprived of the Temple, founded a new religious centre in the rabbinical school of Jamnia (Jabneh). A Jewish revolt broke out in AD 115 and the Roman emperor Trajan responded by appointing the first consular legate of Judaea, Lucius Quietus, to put it down. The rank of the legate confirms that two legions were stationed in Judaea, one at Jerusalem, the other at Caparcotna in Galilee, and thenceforth the province must have held consular status.

In AD 132 the emperor Hadrian decided to build a Roman colony, Aelia Capitolina, on the site of Jerusalem. The announcement of his plan, as well as his ban on circumcision (revoked later, but only for the Jews), provoked a much more serious revolt, led by Bar Kokhba. It was ruthlessly repressed by Julius Severus; almost 1,000 villages were destroyed and more than half a million people killed, according to certain accounts. In Judaea proper the Jews seem to have been virtually exterminated, but they survived in Galilee, which, like Samaria, appears to have held aloof from the revolt. Tiberias in Galilee became the seat of the Jewish patriarchs. The province of Judaea was renamed Syria Palaestina (later simply called Palaestina), and, according to Eusebius (*Historia Ecclesiastica* iv. 6), no Jew was thenceforth allowed to set foot in Jerusalem or the surrounding district. This prohibition apparently was relaxed some time later to permit Jews to enter Jerusalem on one day a year, a Day of Mourning. While this ban was officially still in force as late as the 4th century AD, there is some evidence that from the Severan period onward (after

Bar Kokhba's revolt

Adapted from A.H.M. Jones, *The Herods of Judaea*, The Clarendon Press, Oxford

Palestine during the time of Herod the Great and his sons.

AD 193) Jews visited the city more frequently, especially at certain festival times, and even that there may have been some Jews in residence. Around the time the Bar Kokhba revolt was crushed (AD 135), Hadrian proceeded to convert Jerusalem into a Greco-Roman city, with a circus, an amphitheatre, baths, and a theatre and with streets conforming to the Roman grid pattern. He also erected temples dedicated to Jupiter and himself (Aelia was his clan name) on the very site of the destroyed Temple of Jerusalem. To repopulate the city, Hadrian apparently brought in Greco-Syrians from the surrounding areas and even perhaps some legionary veterans. The urbanization and Hellenization of Palestine was continued by the emperor Septimius Severus (reigned AD 193–211), except in Galilee, where the Jewish presence remained strong. New pagan cities were founded in Judaea at Eleutheropolis and Diospolis (formerly Lydda) and at Nicopolis (formerly Emmaus) under one of Severus' successors, Elagabalus (reigned AD 218–222). In addition, Severus issued a specific ban against Jewish proselytism.

With the conversion of Constantine I to Christianity early in the 4th century, a new era of prosperity began for Palestine. The Emperor himself built a magnificent church on the site of the Holy Sepulchre, the most sacred of Christian holy places; his mother, Helena, built two others—at the place of the Nativity at Bethlehem and of the Ascension in Jerusalem—and his mother-in-law, Eutropia, built a church at Mamre. Palestine began to attract floods of pilgrims from all parts of the empire. It also became a great centre of the eremitic life; men flocked from all quarters to become hermits in the Judaean wilderness, which was soon dotted with monasteries. Constantine added the southern half of Arabia to the province, but in 357–358 (or perhaps as late as the 390s) the addition was made a separate province under the name of Palaestina or Salutaris (later Palaestina Tertia). At the end of the 4th century, an enlarged Palestine was divided into three provinces: Prima, with its capital at Caesarea; Secunda, with its capital at Scythopolis (Bet She'an); and Salutaris, with its capital at Petra or possibly for a time at Elusa. It is clear that the province of Palaestina underwent several territorial changes in the 4th century AD, but the details and the chronology remain obscure. The governor of Prima bore the high rank of proconsul from 382 to 385 and again from 535 onward. A dux of Palestine commanded the garrison of all three provinces.

The bishop of the civil capital, Caesarea, was, according to the usual rule, metropolitan of the province, but the bishops of Jerusalem were claiming special prerogatives as early as the Council of Nicaea. Eventually, Juvenal, bishop of Jerusalem from 421 to 458, achieved his ambition and was recognized by the Council of Chalcedon (451) as patriarch of the three provinces of Palestine.

There was a revolt of the Jews in Galilee in 352, which was suppressed by the Caesar Gallus. Under Marcian (reigned 450–457) and again under Justinian I (reigned 527–565) the Samaritans revolted. Palestine, like Syria and Egypt, was also troubled by the Monophysite controversy, a debate among Christians who disagreed with the Council of Chalcedon's assertion that the Person of Jesus Christ comprised two natures, human and divine. When Juvenal returned from Chalcedon, having signed the Council's canons, the monks of Palestine rose and elected another bishop of Jerusalem, and military force was required to subdue them. Gradually, however, the Chalcedonian doctrine gained ground, and Palestine became a stronghold of orthodoxy. Apart from these disturbances the country enjoyed peace and prosperity until 611, when Khosrow II, king of Persia, launched an invasion. His troops captured Jerusalem (614), destroyed churches, and carried off the True Cross. In 628 the Byzantine emperor Heraclius recovered Palestine, and he subsequently restored the True Cross to Jerusalem, but 10 years later Jerusalem fell to the Arabs.   (A.H.M.J./G.R.B.)

FROM THE ARAB CONQUEST TO AD 1900

The rise of Islām.   The successful unification of the Arabian Peninsula by the first caliph, Abū Bakr (AD 632–Aug. 23, 634), made it possible to channel the expansion of the

Arab Muslims into new directions. Abū Bakr, therefore, summoned the faithful to a holy war (jihad) and quickly amassed an impressive army. He dispatched three detachments of about 3,000 (later increased to about 7,500) men each to start operations in southern and southeastern Syria. He died, however, before he could witness the results of these undertakings. The conquests he started were carried on by his successor, the caliph 'Umar I (634–644).

The first battle took place at Wadi al-'Arabah, south of the Dead Sea. The Byzantine defenders were defeated and retreated toward Gaza but were overtaken and almost annihilated. In other places, however, the natural advantages of the defenders were more effective and the invaders were hard pressed. Khālid ibn al-Walīd, then operating in southern Iraq, was ordered to the aid of his fellow generals on the Syrian front, and the combined forces won a bloody victory on July 30, 634, at a place in southern Palestine that the sources call Ajnadain. All of Palestine then lay open to the invaders.

In the meantime, the emperor Heraclius was mustering a large army and in 636 dispatched it against the Muslims. Khālid concentrated his troops on the Yarmuk, the eastern tributary of the Jordan River. The decisive battle that delivered Palestine to the Muslims took place on Aug. 20, 636. Only Jerusalem and Caesarea held out, the former until 638, when it surrendered to the Muslims, and the latter until October 640. Palestine, and indeed all of Syria, was then in Muslim hands. After the surrender of Jerusalem, 'Umar divided Palestine into two administrative districts (jund), similar to the Roman and Byzantine provinces: they were Jordan (al-Urdunn) and Palestine (Filasṭīn). Jordan included Galilee and Acre and extended east to the desert; Palestine, with its capital first at Lydda and later at Ramlah (after 716), covered the region south of the Plain of Esdraelon.

'Umar lost no time in emphasizing Islām's interest in the holy city of Jerusalem as the first qibla toward which Muslims turned their faces in prayer and as the third holiest spot in Islām. On visiting the Temple area and finding the place suffering from neglect, he and his followers cleaned it with their own hands and declared it a sacred place of prayer.

Under the Umayyads, a Muslim dynasty that gained power in 661 from the Meccans and Medinans who had initially led the Islāmic community, Palestine formed, with Syria, one of the main provinces of the empire. Each jund was administered by an emir assisted by a financial officer. This pattern continued, in general, up to the time of Ottoman rule.

For various reasons, the Umayyads paid special attention to Palestine. The process of Arabization and Islāmization was gaining momentum there. It was one of the mainstays of Umayyad power and important in their struggle against both Iraq and the Arabian Peninsula. The caliph 'Abd al-Malik ibn Marwān (685–705) erected the Dome of the Rock in 691 on the site of the Temple of Solomon, which the Muslims believed had been the halting station of the Prophet on his nocturnal journey to heaven. This magnificent structure represents the earliest Muslim monument still extant. Close to the shrine to the south, 'Abd al-Malik's son, al-Walīd I (705–715), built the Aqṣa mosque. The Umayyad caliph 'Umar II (717–720) imposed humiliating restrictions on his non-Muslim subjects, particularly the Christians. Conversions arising from convenience as well as conviction then increased. These conversions to Islām, together with a steady tribal inflow from the desert, changed the religious character of Palestine's inhabitants. The predominantly Christian population gradually became predominantly Muslim and Arabic-speaking. At the same time, during the early years of Muslim control of the city, a small permanent Jewish population returned to Jerusalem after a 500-year absence.

'Abbāsid rule.   Umayyad rule ended in 750. Along with Syria, Palestine became subject to 'Abbāsid authority, based in Baghdad, and, like Syria, it did not readily submit to its new masters. Unlike the Umayyads, who leaned on the Yemeni (south Arabian) tribes, the 'Abbāsids, in Syria, favoured and indeed used the Qays (north Arabian) tribes. Enmity between the two groups was, therefore, intensified

Construc-
tion
of the
Dome
the Rock

and became an important factor in Palestinian politics. Pro-Umayyad uprisings were frequent and received Palestinian support. In 840/841 Abū Ḥarb, a Yemenite, unfurled the white banner of the Umayyads and succeeded in recruiting a large number of peasant followers, mainly among the Palestinians, who regarded him as the saviour whose appearance was to save the land from the hated ʿAbbāsids. Though the insurrection was put down, unrest persisted.

Under the ʿAbbāsids, the process of Islāmization gained momentum. The ʿAbbāsid rulers encouraged the settlement and fortification of coastal Palestine so as to secure it against the Byzantine enemy. During the second half of the 9th century, however, signs of internal decay began to appear in the ʿAbbāsid Empire. Petty states, and some indeed not so petty, mushroomed in different parts of the realm. One of the first to affect Palestine was the Tūlūnid dynasty (868–905) of Egypt, which marked the beginning of the disengagement of Egypt and, with it, of Syria and Palestine from ʿAbbāsid rule. During this period Palestine also experienced the destructive operations of the Qarmatians, an Ismāʿīlī Muslim sect that launched an insurrection in 903–906. After a brief restoration of ʿAbbāsid authority, Palestine came under Ikhshīdid rule (935–969).

The Fāṭimid dynasty. In the meantime the Shīʿite Fāṭimid dynasty was rising to power in North Africa. It moved eastward to seize not only Egypt but also Palestine and Syria and to threaten Baghdad itself. The Fāṭimids seized Egypt from the Ikhshīdids in 969 and in less than a decade were able to establish a precarious control over Palestine, where they faced Qarmaṭian, Seljuq, Byzantine, and periodic Bedouin opposition. Palestine was thus often reduced to a battlefield. The country suffered even greater hardship, however, under the Fāṭimid caliph al-Ḥākim (996–1021), whose erratic behaviour was at times extremely harsh, particularly on his non-Muslim subjects. He reactivated earlier discriminatory laws imposed upon Christians and Jews and added new ones. In 1009 he ordered the destruction of the Church of the Holy Sepulchre.

In 1071 the Seljuqs captured Jerusalem, which prospered as pilgrimages by Jews, Christians, and Muslims increased despite political instability. The Fāṭimids recaptured the city in 1098 only to deliver it a year later to a new enemy, the crusaders of western Europe.

The Crusades. A year after the capture of Jerusalem by the crusaders, the Latin kingdom of Jerusalem was established (Christmas day, 1100). Thereafter, there was no effective check to the expansion of the crusaders' power until the capture of their stronghold at Edessa (modern Urfa, Tur.) by the atabeg of Mosul, ʿImād ad-Dīn Zangī ibn Aq Sonqur, in 1144. Zangī's anticrusader campaign was carried on after his death by his son Nureddin (Nūr ad-Dīn Maḥmūd) and, more effectively, by the sultan Saladin, a protégé of the atabeg's family. After consolidating his position in Egypt and Syria, Saladin waged relentless war against the "infidel" Franks. On July 4, 1187, six days after the capture of Tiberias, he dealt the crusaders a crushing blow at the decisive battle of Hattin (Hittin). Most of Palestine was once again Muslim. Further attempts by the crusaders to regain control of Palestine proved ineffective, primarily because of incessant quarrels among the crusaders themselves. Ironically, it was left to an emperor of dubious Christian standing, Frederick II, to negotiate in 1229, while under excommunication, a 10-year treaty temporarily restoring Jerusalem, Nazareth, and Bethlehem to the Christians. In 1244, however, the Ayyūbid sultan aṣ-Ṣaliḥ Ayyūb definitively restored Jerusalem to Islām.

While the Ayyūbids of Saladin's house were losing ground to the Turkish-speaking Mamlūks in Egypt, the Mongol sweep westward continued, placing the crusaders, as it were, between two fires. To make matters worse, the crusaders themselves were hopelessly riddled with dissension. In 1260 the Mamlūk leader Baybars emerged as a champion of Muslim resurgence. After taking part in the defeat of the Mongols at ʿAyn Jalut in Palestine, he became sultan; in the years 1263 to 1271 he carried out annual raids against the harassed Franks. His task was resumed by the sultan al-Ashraf, during whose reign the last of the crusaders were driven out of Acre (May 18, 1291). A

Saladin's wars against the crusaders

chapter in the history of Palestine thus came to an end. The Mamlūks and subsequent Muslim regimes ruled the area with only brief interruptions for the next 600 years.

Palestine under the Mamlūks in the 14th century saw a period of prosperity for some; this was especially notable in Jerusalem, where the government sponsored an elaborate program of construction of schools, lodgings for travelers and Muslim pilgrims, and renovation of mosques. Tax revenues, collected mainly from the villages, were spent largely on support of religious institutions. Palestine formed a part of the district of Damascus, second only to Egypt in the Mamlūk domains. The region suffered the ravages of several epidemics, including the great pestilence, the same Black Death that in 1347–51 devastated Europe. The fall of the Baḥrī Mamlūks and the rise of the Burjī Mamlūks (1382–1517) ultimately helped lead to a deterioration in security and the economy. During the reign of the second Burjī sultan, Naṣīr Faraj (1398–1405), the last onslaught of the Mongols, which made the name of Timur (Tamerlane) a synonym of destruction and plunder, took place. Although Palestine was spared the pillage of his hordes, it could not escape its disastrous repercussions as the Mamlūks moved through in a vain attempt to defend Damascus against the invader. The death of Timur in 1405, and the weakness of Iran in the ensuing century, pitted the Mamlūks against the rising power of the Ottoman Turks for the control of western Asia. Hostilities broke out when Sultan Qait Bey contested, in 1486, with Bayezid II the possession of some border towns. The climax came three decades later on Aug. 24, 1516, when the Ottoman sultan, Selim I, routed the Mamlūk armies. Palestine began its four centuries under Ottoman domination.

Ottoman rule. Under the Ottoman Turks, Palestine continued to be linked administratively to Damascus until 1830, when it was placed under Sidon; then under Acre; then once again under Damascus until 1887–88, at which time the administrative divisions of the Ottoman Empire were settled for the last time. The geographic region of Palestine was divided into the *mutasarrifiyah*s of Nablus and Acre, both of which were linked with the vilayet of Beirut, and the autonomous *mutasarrifiyah* of Jerusalem, which dealt directly with Istanbul. With varying fortunes often accompanied by revolts, massacres, and wars, the first three centuries of Ottoman rule isolated Palestine from and insulated it against most outside influences. The prosperity of 16th-century Ottoman Palestine was followed by an economic and political decline in the 17th century. Ottoman control in the 18th century was indirect. Ḍāhir al-ʿUmar (c. 1737–75) dominated the political life of northern Palestine for nearly 40 years. Aḥmad al-Jazzār, the Ottoman governor of Acre, had control of most of Palestine, and in 1799, with English and Ottoman help, he successfully defended Acre against Napoleon.

Both Ḍāhir and al-Jazzār presided over a tightly controlled Palestine, where trade with Europe as well as taxation were both growing. They used their new wealth from these sources to gain influence in Istanbul, which allowed them to gain local autonomy and even intermittent control of many areas outside Palestine.

This period came to an end with Napoleon's abortive attempt (1798–1801) to carve for himself a Middle Eastern empire. Egypt, always a determining factor in the fortunes of Palestine, was placed, after the French withdrawal, under the rule of the viceroy Muḥammad (Meḥmet) ʿAlī, who soon embarked upon a program of expansion at the expense of his Ottoman overlord. In 1831 his armies occupied Palestine, and for nine years he and his son Ibrāhīm gave it a centralizing and modernizing administration. Their rule increasingly opened the country to Western influences and enabled Christian missionaries to establish many schools; at the same time, however, taxes were increased, and urban rebellions broke out against the harshness of the regime. When in 1840 the British, the Austrians, and the Russians came to the aid of the Ottomans, the Egyptians were forced to withdraw and Palestine reverted to the Ottoman Empire. Increased European interest, however, led to the establishment of consulates by the powers in Jerusalem and in the ports.

After 1840 the reforms the Sultan promulgated gradually took effect in Palestine. Increased security in the countryside and the Ottoman Land Law of 1858 encouraged the development of private property, agricultural production for the world market, the decline of tribal social organization, growth of the population, and the enrichment of the notable families. As the Ottomans extended the central government's new military, municipal, judicial, and educational systems to Palestine, the country also witnessed a marked increase in foreign settlements and colonies, French, Russian, and German. By far the most important, *Zionism* in spite of their initial numerical insignificance, were the Zionist agricultural settlements, which foreshadowed later Zionist endeavours for the establishment of a Jewish national home and still later a Jewish state in Palestine. The earliest of these settlements was established by Russian Jews in 1882. In 1896 Theodor Herzl issued a pamphlet entitled *Der Judenstaat* (*The Jewish State*) and advocated an autonomous Jewish state, preferably in Palestine. Two years later, he himself went to Palestine to investigate its possibilities and, possibly, to seek the help of the German emperor William II, who was then making his spectacular pilgrimage to the Holy Land.   (N.A.F./W.L.O.)

FROM 1900 TO 1948

In the last years of the 19th century and the early years of the 20th the Palestine Arabs shared a general Arab renascence. Palestinians found opportunities in the service of the Ottoman Empire, and Palestine deputies sat in the Ottoman parliament of 1908. Several Arabic newspapers appeared in the country before 1914. They showed in their pages that Arab nationalism and opposition to Zionism were strong among some sections of the intelligentsia even before World War I. The Arabs sought an end to Jewish immigration and to land purchases by Zionists. The number of Zionist colonies, however, mostly subsidized by Baron Edmond de Rothschild, rose from 22 in 1900 to 47 in 1918, even though the majority of the Jews were town-dwelling. The population of Palestine, predominantly agricultural, was about 690,000 in 1914 (535,000 Muslims; 70,000 Christians, most of whom were Arabs; and 85,000 Jews). Population decreased during the war.

World War I and after. Palestine was hard hit by the war, for to the destruction caused by the fighting were added famine, locusts, epidemics, and the punitive measures of the Ottomans against Arab nationalists. Major battles took place at Gaza before Jerusalem was captured by British and Allied forces under the command of General Sir Edmund (later Field Marshal Viscount) Allenby in December 1917. The rest of the country was occupied by the British by October 1918. The Arabs maintained that Palestine was included in the area the independence of which Britain promised in the exchange of correspondence in July–October 1915 between Sir Henry McMahon, high commissioner of Egypt, and Ḥusayn ibn 'Alī, then emir of Mecca. By May 1916 Britain, France, and Russia had reached an agreement according to which, inter alia, the bulk of Palestine was to be internationalized. In November 1917 Arthur Balfour, the British secretary of state for for- *The* eign affairs, addressed a letter to Lord Rothschild promis- *Balfour* ing British support for the establishment in Palestine of a *Declara-* national home for the Jewish people on the understanding *tion* that "nothing shall be done which may prejudice the civil and religious rights of existing non-Jewish communities in Palestine. . . ."

Britain's first postwar problem in Palestine was to secure international sanction for the continued occupation of the country in a manner consistent with its conflicting and ambiguous wartime commitments. A British military administration was set up after the capture of Jerusalem, and a general international framework existed for Britain in Article 22 of the Covenant of the League of Nations signed in June 1919. This article recognized the provisional independence of the former Ottoman Arab provinces, subject to the assistance of a mandatory power in whose selection the wishes of the communities themselves were to be consulted.

In July 1919 a general Syrian congress held at Damascus and attended by Palestinian delegates passed a resolution rejecting the Balfour Declaration and electing Fayṣal— son of Ḥusayn ibn 'Alī, who ruled the Hejaz—king of a united Syria (including Palestine). In April 1920, however, at the Conference of San Remo, the Allies divided the former territories of the defeated Ottoman Empire. Of the Ottoman provinces in the Syrian region, the northern half (Syria and Lebanon) was mandated to France, and the southern half (Palestine) was mandated to Great Britain. The French forced Fayṣal to give up his newly founded kingdom of Syria in July 1920. Thus the Arabs' hope for a united greater Syria under the Hāshimite dynasty— descending from the Prophet Muḥammad—was at least temporarily thwarted. Uncertainty over the disposition of Palestine affected all its inhabitants and increased political tensions.

In April 1920 anti-Zionist riots in Palestine resulted in five Jews being killed and 200 wounded. A British commission of inquiry attributed the riots to Arab disappointment at the nonfulfillment of the promises of independence and to their fear of economic and political subjection to the Zionists. In July the military administration was ended and Sir Herbert (later Viscount) Samuel was appointed the first high commissioner of a new civilian administration.

The mandate. The terms of the mandate had yet to be settled, and both Britain and the Zionists worked for the incorporation of the Balfour Declaration into the mandate instrument. Although the mandate was not approved by the League of Nations until July 1922, the administration in Palestine proceeded with the implementation of the Balfour Declaration and in August 1920 announced a quota of 16,500 Jewish immigrants for the first year. This announcement aroused Arab opposition, which was organized in the form of Christian–Muslim associations throughout the country. In May 1921 anti-Zionist riots resulted in 46 Jews being killed and 146 wounded. A commission of inquiry attributed the riots to Arab fear of Jewish immigration. Impressed by Arab opposition, the British government issued a White Paper in June 1922 *The British* containing an interpretation of its concept of a Jewish *White* national home. The intention was not that Palestine as a *Paper* whole should be converted into a Jewish national home *of 1922* but that such a home should be established in Palestine. Immigration would not exceed the economic absorptive capacity of the country, and steps would be taken to set up a legislative council. These proposals were rejected by the Arabs, both because they had a large majority of the total population of the mandate and therefore wished to dominate the instruments of government and rapidly gain independence and because, they argued, the proposals allowed Jewish immigration, which had a political objective, to be regulated by an economic criterion.

In July 1922 the mandate instrument for Palestine was approved by the League council, its preamble incorporating the Balfour Declaration and stressing the Jewish historical connection with Palestine. Article 2 made the mandatory (*i.e.,* the holder of the mandate) responsible for placing the country under such "political, administrative and economic conditions as will secure the establishment of the Jewish National Home . . . and the development of self-governing institutions." Article 4 allowed for the establishment of a Jewish agency to advise and cooperate with the Palestine administration in matters affecting the Jewish national home. Article 6 required that the Palestine administration, "while ensuring that the rights and position of other sections of the population are not prejudiced," under suitable conditions would facilitate Jewish immigration and close settlement of Jews on the land. Although Transjordan, all of which lay east of the Jordan River, was included in the British mandate of Palestine, under protest from the Zionists it was excluded from the clauses covering the establishment of a "Jewish national home." On Sept. 29, 1923, the mandate came officially into force.

The Jewish national home. Several Arab organizations in the 1920s opposed Jewish immigration. These included the Palestine Arab Congress, Muslim–Christian associations, the Arab Executive, and the National Defense Party. Most Arab groups were led by the strongly anti-British Ḥusaynī family, while the National Defense Party was under the control of the more accommodating Nashashibi family. (The Ḥusaynīs and Nashashibis were prominent Jerusalem notables, long resident in the area, who had held numerous government posts in the late Ottoman period.)

During 1923 the British high commissioner tried to win Arab cooperation by the offer first of a legislative council and then of an Arab Agency. Both offers were rejected by the Arabs as falling far short of their national demands. The years 1923–29 were relatively quiet; Arab passivity was partly due to the drop in Jewish immigration in the years 1926–28. In 1927 Jewish emigrants exceeded the immigrants, and in 1928 there was a net Jewish immigration of only 10 persons. Nevertheless, the national home continued to consolidate itself in terms of urban, agricultural, social, cultural, and industrial development. Large amounts of land were purchased from Arab owners, often from absentee landlords. In August 1929 negotiations were concluded for the formation of an enlarged Jewish Agency to include non-Zionist Jewish sympathizers throughout the world.

This last development, while accentuating Arab fears, gave the Zionists a new sense of confidence. In the same month a dispute in Jerusalem concerning religious practices at the Western Wall—sacred to Jews as the only remnant of the Second Temple of Jerusalem—flared up into communal clashes in which 133 Jews were killed and 339 wounded, the Arab casualties, mostly at the hands of the military, being 116 killed and 232 wounded. The report of a commission of inquiry attributed the clashes to the fact that "the Arabs have come to see in Jewish immigration not only a menace to their livelihood but a possible overlord of the future." In October a technical report by Sir John Hope Simpson established that there was at that time no margin of land available for agricultural settlement by new immigrants. These reports raised in an acute form the question of where Britain's duty lay if its specific obligations to the Zionists under the Balfour Declaration clashed with its general obligations to the Arabs under Article 22 of the Covenant of the League of Nations.

Arab grievances. A statement of policy made by the colonial secretary in October 1930 accorded some priority to Britain's obligations to the Arabs. This was seen by the Zionists to cut at the root of their program, for if the right of the Arab resident were to gain priority over that of the Jewish immigrant, whether actual or potential, the Jewish national home would come to a standstill. In February 1931 the British prime minister, Ramsay MacDonald, addressed an explanatory letter to Chaim Weizmann, president of the Jewish Agency, which was virtually a return to the 1922 White Paper policy. This letter convinced the Arabs that recommendations in their favour made on the spot could be annulled in London by Zionist influence at the centre of power. In December 1931 a Muslim congress at Jerusalem was attended by delegates from 22 countries to warn against the danger of Zionism.

In the early 1930s a boycott of Zionist and British goods was proclaimed. At the same time the Nazi accession to power in Germany and the widespread persecution of Jews throughout central and eastern Europe gave a great impetus to Jewish immigration, which jumped to 30,000 in 1933, 42,000 in 1934, and 61,000 in 1935. The Arab population of Palestine also increased rapidly, largely because of a decrease in infant mortality. Most of the Arabs continued to be engaged in agriculture, despite successive crop failures. In November 1935 the Arab political parties collectively demanded the cessation of Jewish immigration, the prohibition of land transfer, and the establishment of democratic institutions. In December the British administration offered a legislative council of 28 members on which the Arabs (both Muslim and Christian) would have 14 seats and the Jews eight. Although not represented in the council in proportion to their numbers, some of the Arabs were willing to consider the proposal, but the Zionists criticized it bitterly as an attempt to freeze the national home through a constitutional Arab stranglehold. The failure of the council proposal, the example of rising nationalism in neighbouring Egypt and Syria, increasing unemployment in Palestine, and a poor citrus harvest touched off the long-smoldering Arab rebellion.

Increase in Jewish immigration to Palestine

The Arab rebellion. In April 1936 the Arab political parties formed an Arab High Committee presided over by Amīn al-Ḥusaynī, who was mufti of Jerusalem from 1921 and president of the Supreme Muslim Council. Nationalistic sentiment had grown rapidly in the Arabic press, schools, and literary circles. The Arab High Committee called for a general strike, which was maintained for six months (although it did not include Arabs who were government employees). Simultaneously with the strike, Arab rebels, joined by volunteers from neighbouring Arab countries, took to the hills, and by the end of the year the movement assumed the dimensions of a national revolt of the Arab peasantry. The strike was called off in October at the request of the heads of the neighbouring Arab states, but the armed rebellion continued.

A royal commission of inquiry presided over by Lord Peel published its findings in July 1937. It attributed the revolt to the Arab desire for independence and fear of the Jewish national home. It declared the mandate unworkable and Britain's obligations to Arabs and Jews mutually irreconcilable. It therefore recommended the partition of the country.

The Peel Commission

The Zionist attitude to partition was ambivalent. For the first time a British official body explicitly spoke of a Jewish state: the area allotted to this state was immensely larger than the existing Jewish landholdings; and the commission had gone to the extent of recommending the forcible transfer of the Arab population from the proposed Jewish state. But the Zionists still needed mandatory protection for their further development and left the door open for an undivided Palestine. The Arabs were horrified by the idea of the dismemberment of the country and particularly at the suggestion of their forcible transfer. As a result the momentum of the revolt increased during 1937 and 1938, in spite of extensive British military operations and the outlawing in October 1937 of the Arab High Committee, most of the members of which (except Amīn al-Ḥusaynī and a few others who escaped arrest) were deported to the Seychelles Islands.

In September 1937 the League council authorized the mandatory to prepare a detailed partition plan. A technical commission entrusted with this task reported in November 1938 against the Peel Commission's plan, largely on the ground that the number of Arabs in the proposed Jewish state would be almost equal to the number of Jews, and put forward alternative proposals that drastically reduced the areas and sovereignty of the proposed states.

A British statement of policy announced the impracticability of partition and called for a round-table conference in London. Although the Arab revolt continued well into 1939, its casualties were high and it gradually lost its vigour under firm British measures. The Arabs of Palestine were unable to recover from their sustained effort of defiance of the British administration.

The White Paper of 1939. No agreement was reached at the London conference held during February–March 1939, and the British government in a White Paper in May 1939 made a unilateral statement of policy based upon the assumption that the Jewish national home pledge had already been substantially fulfilled. Within the next five years 75,000 Jews would be allowed into the country; thereafter, Jewish immigration would be subject to Arab "acquiescence." Land transfer would be allowed only in certain areas in Palestine, and an independent Palestinian state would be considered within 10 years. The Arabs, although in favour of the new policy, could not agree to it, largely because of mistrust of Britain and the provision for the extension of the mandate beyond the 10-year period. The Zionists were shocked by the statement, which they considered a deathblow to their program and to Jews who desperately sought refuge in Palestine from the persecution they endured in Europe. Britain was accused by the Zionists of callously appeasing the Arabs of the Middle East and of protecting its own strategic interests in the face of the deterioration of the international situation. The 1939 White Paper marked the end of the Anglo-Zionist entente.

The Jewish national home had, however, made remarkable progress since 1918. Although the majority of the Jewish population was urban, rural Zionist colonies had increased from 47 to about 200. Between 1922 and 1939 Jewish landholdings had risen from 148,500 acres to 383,350 acres and the Jewish population from 83,790 to 445,457 (almost 30 percent of the total population). Tel Aviv had developed into an all-Jewish city of 150,000 inhabitants, and £80,000,000 of Jewish capital had been introduced into the country. The Jewish literacy rate was high, schools were expanding, and the Hebrew language had become widespread. Despite the split in 1935 between the main-line Zionists, who were led by David Ben-Gurion, and the radical Revisionists, led by Vladimir Jabotinsky (who advocated the use of force to establish the Zionist state), Zionist institutions in Palestine became stronger in the 1930s and helped create the preconditions for the establishment of a Jewish state.

World War II. The Zionists found themselves in World War II in the paradoxical position of having to fight the 1939 White Paper policy while rallying to Britain's side against Germany, the common enemy. Publication in February 1940 of the new land transfer regulations and announcement in November 1940 of Britain's decision to accommodate illegal Jewish immigrants for the duration of the war outside Palestine caused a recrudescence of the activities of the Zionist underground organizations. Before the war the Haganah, a self-defense organization founded by Jabotinsky and sponsored by the Jewish Agency, practiced restraint, but the Irgun Zvai Leumi, a dissident group formed in 1931 and reorganized in 1936 by members of the Revisionist Party, had gone into action against the Arabs. After the battles of el-Alamein, and as news of the terrible tragedy that was befalling European Jewry percolated to the outside world, tension mounted in Palestine. The Irgun joined hands during 1944 with the Stern Gang, a splinter group, in widespread attacks, culminating in the murder of Lord Moyne, British minister of state in Cairo, in November 1944.

During the war years the Palestine Jewish community was vastly strengthened. The moderate Jewish community supported the British: in September 1944 a Jewish brigade attached to the British 8th Army was formed, a total of 27,000 Jews having enlisted in the British forces. Jewish industry in general was given immense impetus, and a Jewish munitions industry developed that manufactured antitank mines for the British forces. Equally important was the support won by the Zionists in the United States, to which they had shifted their major political effort after 1939. In May 1942, at a Zionist conference held at the Biltmore Hotel in New York City, David Ben-Gurion gained support for a program demanding unrestricted immigration and a Jewish army and the establishment of Palestine as a Jewish commonwealth. An increasing number of pro-Zionist statements were elicited from U.S. congressmen and politicians. In August 1945 President Harry S. Truman requested Clement Attlee, the British prime minister, to facilitate the immediate admission of 100,000 Jews into Palestine, and in December the U.S. Senate and House of Representatives asked for unrestricted Jewish immigration to the limit of the economic absorptive capacity of Palestine. This contributed to the internationalization of the question of Palestine, already under way with the involvement of the Arab states since the 1930s.

The Arabs of Palestine had remained largely quiescent throughout the war, although some supported the Axis powers and others enlisted in the British forces. Increases in agricultural prices benefited the Arab peasants, who began to pay accumulated debts. Amīn al-Ḥusaynī had fled, by way of Iraq, Iran, Turkey, and Italy, to Germany, from which he broadcast appeals to his fellow Arabs to ally with the Axis powers against Britain and Zionism.

After the war the neighbouring Arab countries began to take a more direct interest in Palestine. In March the covenant of the League of Arab States was drawn up with an annex emphasizing the Arab character of Palestine. In December the Arab League declared a boycott of Zionist goods. The pattern of the postwar struggle for Palestine was emerging unmistakably.

Proposal for partition. In November 1945, in an effort to secure U.S. co-responsibility for a Palestine policy, Ernest Bevin, the British secretary of state for foreign

affairs, announced the formation of an Anglo-American commission of inquiry. Pending the report of the commission, Jewish immigration would continue at the rate of 1,500 persons per month beyond the 75,000 limit set by the 1939 White Paper. A plan of provincial autonomy for Arabs and Jews was worked out in an Anglo-American conference in 1946, which became the basis for discussions in London between Britain and the representatives of Arabs and Zionists.

In the meantime Zionist pressure in Palestine was intensified by the unauthorized immigration of refugees on a thitherto unprecedented scale and by closely coordinated attacks by all Zionist underground forces. Jewish immigration was impelled by the burning memories of the Holocaust, the chaotic post-war conditions in Europe, and the growing possibility of the attainment of a Jewish state, where the victims of persecution could guarantee their own safety. The underground's attacks culminated in Jerusalem on July 22, 1946, when a part of the King David Hotel containing British government and military offices was blown up, with the loss of 91 lives. On the Arab side a meeting of Arab kings and heads of state at Inshās in Egypt in May 1946 reaffirmed the Arab character of Palestine, and at a meeting of the Arab League in Bludan, Syria, in June, secret resolutions were adopted threatening British and U.S. interests in the Middle East if Arab rights in Palestine were disregarded. With the failure of the London conference in February 1947, Britain, weakened by the world war and anxious to decrease its costly military presence, referred the Palestine question to the United Nations. A UN commission of inquiry recommended on August 31 in a majority report the partition of the country into Arab and Jewish states, which should retain an economic union. Jerusalem and its environs were to be international. These recommendations were substantially adopted by a two-thirds majority of the General Assembly in a resolution dated November 29, partly because of the agreement of the United States and the Soviet Union on partition and partly because of pressure on some small states by Zionist sympathizers in the United States. All the Islāmic Asian countries, however, voted against partition, and an Arab proposal to query the International Court of Justice on the competence of the General Assembly to partition a country against the wishes of the majority of its inhabitants (there were 1,269,000 Arabs and 678,000 Jews in Palestine in 1946) was narrowly defeated.

The Zionists welcomed the proposed partition because of its recognition of a Jewish state and because 55 percent of Palestine was alloted to the Jewish state. As in 1937 the Arabs were violently opposed to partition both in principle and because a substantial minority of the population of the Jewish state would be Arab. Britain was unwilling to implement a policy that was not acceptable to both sides and refused to share the administration with the UN Palestine Commission, which was to supervise the transitional period. Britain set May 15, 1948, as the date of the end of the mandate.

Civil war. Soon after the UN resolution communal fighting broke out in Palestine. The Zionists mobilized their strength and redoubled their efforts to bring in immigrants. In December 1947 the Arab League pledged its support to the Palestinian Arabs and organized a force of 3,000 volunteers. Civil war spread and external intervention increased as the dismantling of the British administration progressed, and by mid-January 1948 some 2,000 casualties had resulted from the fighting.

Early in March 1948 the United States expressed its opposition to a forcible implementation of partition, and on March 16 the UN Palestine Commission reported its inability to implement partition because of Arab resistance and the attitude of the British administration.

On March 19 the United States called for the suspension of the efforts of the UN Palestine Commission and on March 30 for the declaration of a truce and the further consideration of the problem by the General Assembly.

The Zionists, insisting that partition was binding and anxious about the change in U.S. policy, made a major effort to establish their state. Operations "Nachshon" and "Jephtha" were launched on April 1 and 18, respectively.

The Haganah and the Irgun Zvai Leumi

Arab resolutions

The success of these offensives coincided with the failure of an Arab attack on the Zionist settlement of Mishmar Haemek; the death in battle of an Arab national hero, 'Abd al-Qādir al-Ḥusaynī, in command of the Jerusalem front; and the massacre by Irgunists of 250 civilian inhabitants of the Arab village of Deir Yāsīn. On April 22 Haifa fell to the Zionists, and Jaffa, after severe mortar shelling, surrendered on May 13. Simultaneously with their military offensives the Zionists launched a campaign of psychological warfare. The Arabs of Palestine, badly led and reliant on the regular armies of the Arab states, collapsed.

Collapse of the Arab forces

On May 14 the last British high commissioner, General Sir Alan Cunningham, left Palestine. On the same day the State of Israel was proclaimed and within a few hours won de facto recognition from the United States. Early on May 15, units of the regular armies of Syria, Transjordan, Iraq, and Egypt crossed the frontiers of Palestine.

(W.A.K./W.L.O.)

In a series of campaigns alternating with truces between May and December 1948, the Arab units were routed. By the summer of 1949 Israel had concluded armistices with its neighbours. It had also been recognized by more than 50 governments throughout the world, had joined the United Nations, and had established its sovereignty over about 8,000 square miles of mandated Palestine west of the Jordan River. The remaining 2,000 square miles were divided between Transjordan and Egypt. Transjordan retained the lands on the west bank of the Jordan River, including East Jerusalem, which were all formally annexed in 1950. The name of the expanded country was changed to the Hashemite Kingdom of Jordan. Egypt retained control of, but did not annex, the Gaza Strip. "Palestine" ceased to exist.

PALESTINIANS AFTER 1948

If one element in the post-1948 pattern was embattled Israel and a second the unremitting hostility of its Arab neighbours, a third was the Palestinian refugees. The violent birth of Israel led to a mass exodus of Palestine Arabs. Between December 1947 and January 1949 some 700,000 took refuge in neighbouring Arab countries. Thenceforth, Palestinian Arabs lived in three different sets of circumstances, and their history began to diverge according to their location. Most lived in nearby Arab countries, usually as stateless persons, while a minority lived in Israel as citizens of the Jewish state and others went to the Persian Gulf states, far removed from what had been Palestine.

The Palestinian refugees were recipients of UN aid and were a source of cheap labour in the "host" countries. Their cause was argued for them by others, and such political activity as they evinced was in relationship with one or another of the Arab states or leaders.

Palestinians constituted about two-thirds of the population of Jordan, where they were given citizenship as of 1949. One-half of the seats in the Jordanian Chamber of Deputies were reserved for the West Bank, but this measure and similar attempts to integrate the West Bank with the area lying to the east of the Jordan River were made difficult by the significant social, economic, educational, and political differences between the residents of each. Most Jordanian Palestinians, other than the notable families favoured by the King, tended to support the radical pan-Arab and anti-Israeli policies of Egypt's president, Gamal Abdel Nasser, rather than the more cautious and conciliatory position of Jordan's King Hussein. The successes of Nasser and the pan-Arab nationalist Ba'th Party of Syria and Iraq in the late 1950s and early 1960s encouraged Palestinians everywhere to fix upon them their hopes for return to their homeland and for the establishment of an independent Palestine. Those Palestinians who continued to live in refugee camps, often in conditions of extreme deprivation, felt a greater sense of alienation and anomie than the more fortunate who found jobs and housing and who became integrated into the national economies of the countries in which they resided. In Syria, Iraq, Lebanon, and the Persian Gulf states, Palestinians found employment, but only a few were able to become citizens. Often they were the victims of discrimination and were closely supervised by the respective governments so as to limit their political activities. In Israel most Israeli Arabs, while citizens of the state, were cut off from trends and events that affected their former compatriots and remained politically quiescent, although some accepted Zionist Israel as a reality and sought to ameliorate their circumstances by electoral participation, education, and economic integra-

Palestine

Partition plan approved by UN General Assembly on Nov. 29, 1947

▨ Jewish State

▦ Arab State

▧ Jerusalem district

United Nations partition plan for Palestine adopted in 1947.

tion. Egypt ruled the crowded Gaza Strip harshly, and the Palestinians living there were stateless (*i.e.*, not citizens of any nation) and had little real control over local administration. The rate of unemployment was high; many of the Palestinians there lived in refugee camps under the supervision of the United Nations Relief and Works Agency for Palestine Refugees in the Near East.

Some Gaza Strip Palestinians were able to leave the territory and gain education and employment elsewhere, but most had no alternative but to stay in the vicinity, despite its lack of natural resources and jobs. Egypt controlled Amīn al-Ḥusaynī's short-lived Government of All Palestine, which had been established in Gaza in 1948. The failure of this government, and the discrediting of al-Ḥusaynī because of his collaboration with the Axis powers during World War II, did much to weaken Palestinian Arab nationalism in the 1950s.

The Palestine Liberation Organization In 1964, however, an Arab summit meeting led to the formation of a Palestine Liberation Organization (PLO). Some time earlier, Palestinians had formed a secret organization called the Palestine Liberation movement (Taḥrīr Filasṭīn), known from a reversal of its Arabic initials as al-Fatah. Both the PLO and al-Fatah undertook the training of guerrilla units for raids on Israel.

The Palestine National Council was established as the supreme body of the PLO, while an executive committee was formed to manage PLO activities. Aḥmad Shuqairi, a protégé of Egypt, became the first leader of the PLO. The National Council initially consisted of civilian representatives from various areas, including Jordan, the West Bank, the Gulf States, and other countries, and in 1968 representatives of guerrilla organizations were added. Al-Fatah was the largest and most influential group, while other major guerrilla organizations that emerged in the late 1960s were the Popular Front for the Liberation of Palestine (PFLP); the Popular Front for the Liberation of Palestine-General Command (PFLP-General Command, a splinter group from the PFLP); al-Saiqa (Vanguard of the Popular Liberation War), backed by Syria; the Democratic Front for the Liberation of Palestine (DFLP); and the Popular Struggle Front (PSF). These groups joined forces inside the PLO despite their differences in ideology and tactics. In 1969 Yāsir 'Arafāt, leader of al-Fatah, became chairman of the PLO's executive committee and thus the chief of the Palestinian national movement.

The guerrilla organizations rejected any political settlement that did not include the total liberation of Palestine and the return of the refugees to their homeland, which was to be achieved through armed struggle. Palestinian spokesmen claimed, however, that while they aimed at dismantling Israel they had no intention of destroying or expelling the Jews but sought rather to establish a nonsectarian state in which Jews, Christians, and Muslims could live in equality. Most Israelis doubted the sincerity or practicality of this goal and viewed the PLO as terrorists who wished to destroy not only the Zionist state but also Israeli Jews.

The Arab–Israeli War of 1967 devastated the Arab nations. In six days in June, Israel not only dispatched the combined forces of Egypt, Syria, and Jordan but also overran vast tracts of Arab territory, including East Jerusalem, the West Bank (known to Israelis as Judea and Samaria), and Gaza—all of which had formerly been part of mandated Palestine. About 200,000 Arabs fled from the West Bank to eastern Jordan. Only about 1,000 East Jerusalem Arabs applied for Israeli citizenship, while the rest retained Jordanian passports, and the Arabs of the West Bank remained citizens of Jordan. More than 1,000,000 Arabs came under Israeli rule (in addition to the 350,000 already living in the state of Israel).

As the Arab states' total defeat demonstrated the hollowness of pan-Arabism and the inefficacy of revolutionary governments in Syria and Egypt, all the Arabs, both Palestinians and others, turned to the Palestinian commandos, who emerged as a new element of major importance in the Middle East. They raised the morale of all the Arabs after their humiliating defeat. When Israel launched one of its heavy reprisal raids against their bases in the Jordan Valley in March 1968, they fought back and inflicted heavy casualties on the Israelis. Within Jordan, militant Palestinians seemed to be forming a state within a state. An understanding was reached whereby the royal government allowed the commandos independent control of their own bases in the Jordan Valley, but relations between the government and the commandos remained uneasy. The commandos suspected Jordan's king Hussein—who had to face the damage inflicted upon his country by Israeli raids—of preparing to reach a direct settlement with Israel at their expense.

The escalation of an internal conflict between the Jordanian Army, loyal to King Hussein, and the Palestinian guerrilla movement led in 1970 to a brief but bloody civil war. On September 6–9 the PFLP hijacked to a Jordanian airstrip three airliners (U.S., Swiss, and British) with more than 300 people aboard. PFLP representatives threatened to destroy the aircraft, with the passengers aboard, unless Arab commandos detained in Europe and Israel were released. All the passengers were freed by September 30 when the PFLP secured its main demands (after destroying the airliners). This episode made civil war inevitable, since the PFLP hijackers had defied the Jordanian army's authority.

By September 17 the army was fighting the guerrillas in Amman and in northern Jordan, where the guerrillas were reinforced by Syrian armoured units that crossed the border. Formal hostilities ended on September 25, and the guerrillas were still in control of their northern strongholds. Total casualties were variously estimated at 1,500–5,000 killed and up to 10,000 injured. In 1971, however, the fighting resumed, and the Jordanian army established full control over the whole country and crushed the Palestinian military. From that point on, the King and the PLO were deeply suspicious of each other, while the majority of Palestinian Jordanians, especially those living under Israeli control, became highly critical of the King and his policies.

Driven from Jordan, the Palestinians intensified their activities in Lebanon. The presence of Palestinians was a source of tension and conflict in Lebanon, as it had been in Jordan. Palestinian activity against Israel was countered with Israeli raids, primarily into southern Lebanon. In December 1968 Israel launched a major attack on the Beirut International Airport and blew up most of the Lebanese commercial airfleet. This precipitated efforts by the government in 1969 to restrict the activities of the Palestinian guerrillas, which led to sporadic fighting between the Lebanese Army and the guerrillas. In November 1969 a cease-fire agreement between the Lebanese government and al-Fatah allowed the guerrillas limited freedom of operation in exchange for a promise not to interfere in Lebanese politics. During the early 1970s the Palestinian guerrillas continued to carry out attacks against Israel.

In 1973 the Palestinian movement suffered a severe blow in an Israeli commando attack on Beirut on April 10 that killed three of its leaders. During the year, several prominent Palestinians were assassinated in various European capitals by what were assumed to be Israeli counterterrorist agents.

Following the Israeli attack, the Lebanese Army attacked guerrilla bases and refugee camps throughout the country. An agreement was reached requiring the Palestinians to limit their activities in border areas near Israel and in refugee camps near urban centres.

In the war of October 1973 the Palestinians acknowledged that they were not directly involved because Egypt's and Syria's objectives were declared limited to recovering their own lost territory. Egyptian president Anwar el-Sādāt's insistence, however, that they be represented at any subsequent peace negotiations, as well as the growing world opinion that they must be a party to any settlement, sparked off a debate within the movement. Some of the guerrilla groups, called the "rejection front," who were supported by Iraq and Libya, continued to reject any suggestion of Israel's right to exist, but others, realizing that they were in danger of being isolated and abandoned if Egypt, Syria, and Jordan all subscribed to a peace settlement, were prepared to consider taking part in negotiations. The guerrillas did not, however, take part in the peace conference in Geneva in December; Israel would not deal with them.

After 1973 many Palestinians from Lebanon and Jordan moved to the increasingly prosperous and labour-hungry Arab oil states, such as Kuwait and Saudi Arabia. Israeli Arabs began to recover from their long period of inactivity and, following the 1973 war, took a greater part in Israeli institutions while also intensifying contacts with the Arabs of the West Bank and Gaza Strip. The latter were spurred to action by the increasing number and size of Israeli Jewish settlements in the occupied territories. The settlements were viewed by the Arabs as the prelude to Israeli annexation of the land and the permanent denial of the opportunity for the Arabs to determine their own national future.

In its international relations the PLO made important gains in the 1970s. By the end of the decade the organization had representatives in more than 80 countries. On Sept. 22, 1974, the UN General Assembly, overriding strong Israeli objections, included on its agenda for the first time "the Palestine question" as a subject for debate rather than as part of the general question of the Middle East. On November 13 the Assembly heard 'Arafāt, the head of the PLO, plead for the Palestinian people's national rights.

International recognition of the PLO had an important effect on the Arab summit conference held in Rabat, Mor., on Oct. 26–28, 1974. The chief item on the agenda was Palestinian representation at peace talks. Jordan had previously given notice that, if other Arab states decided to recognize the PLO as representing the Palestinians of the West Bank, it would consider itself released from all responsibility for negotiating an Israeli withdrawal. At Rabat, however, King Hussein came under the combined pressure of all the Arab states to accept the PLO's right to represent the Palestinians in any liberated territory. King Fayṣal of Saudi Arabia carried special weight with his argument that the Arabs could hardly do less than the United Nations. Finally, Hussein accepted a resolution that said that any liberated Palestinian territory "should revert to its legitimate Palestinian owners under the leadership of the PLO." The Rabat decision was denounced by the "rejection front," composed of the PFLP, the PFLP-General Command, the pro-Iraq Arab Liberation Front, and the Front for the Popular Palestinian Struggle. Although the decision was recognized as enhancing the position of the moderate PLO elements led by 'Arafāt, the United States and Israel continued adamantly to refuse to recognize or deal with the PLO.

In 1975 Palestinian guerrilla activity against Israel was largely confined to the Lebanese border area, where it provoked heavy Israeli reprisals from air, land, and sea against Palestinian refugee camps that the Israelis alleged were used as guerrilla bases. Israeli raids, however, were overshadowed by the civil strife in Lebanon that developed along Muslim–Christian lines, with the Palestinians ultimately aligning with the Muslim leftists. The presence of some 400,000 stateless Palestinian Arabs was a contributing factor to the civil war.

Lebanon had to choose a policy on the PLO, either to repress it, as most of the rightist Christians wished, or to support it, as the leftists preferred. The PLO initially tried to stay out of the fighting, but by the end of 1975 groups within the overall organization, particularly the "rejection front" groups, were being drawn into an alliance with the Muslim leftists. During the first half of January 1976 there was fighting throughout the country as the Phalangist right-wing Christian forces blockaded the Palestinian refugee camps and the leftist Palestinian forces responded by attacking Christian villages on the coast. Syria, which had sworn to prevent Lebanon's partition by force if necessary, intervened by allowing Palestine Liberation Army forces (belonging to the PLO) under its control to enter the country. Syrian troops entered Lebanon in early April 1976 and supported the Lebanese right wing because of fears that a left-wing victory would result either in partition of Lebanon or in a Palestinian-dominated state, both of which would result in Israeli intervention. Christian forces besieged Palestinian refugee camps in June, and one of

them, Tel az-Zaatar in eastern Beirut, became a symbol of Palestinian resistance. This fell on August 12–13, after seven weeks of siege and heavy loss of life. Heavy fighting continued until a peace agreement was negotiated in October 1976. It provided for the creation of a 30,000-member Arab Deterrent Force (ADF), a cease-fire throughout the country and withdrawal of forces to positions held before April 1975, and implementation of a 1969 agreement that limited Palestinian guerrilla operations in Lebanon.

Although the Palestinian guerrillas suffered heavy losses in the war, they continued to wage their war of attrition against Israel in the late 1970s. They operated primarily from Lebanon, and Israel again responded with raids into southern Lebanon. In September 1977 Israeli troops crossed the border into southern Lebanon to support right-wing Christian forces opposing the Palestinians. On March 11, 1978, Palestinian guerrillas raided Israel, leaving 37 dead and 82 wounded, a move that was followed by the invasion of southern Lebanon by Israel on March 14.

On March 19 the UN Security Council passed Resolution 425, calling for an Israeli withdrawal and establishment of the UN Interim Force in Lebanon (UNIFIL). The Israelis withdrew in stages and had evacuated Lebanese territory by mid-June. They had been only partly successful in their aim of destroying Palestinian guerrillas and their bases south of the Litani River. Several hundred Palestinians were killed, but the bulk of them escaped northward.

The late 1970s were a period of more active negotiation on Arab–Israeli disputes. The Arab states supported Palestinian participation in an overall settlement providing for Israeli withdrawal from areas occupied since the 1967 war and establishment of a Palestinian state on the West Bank and the Gaza Strip. In March 1977, however, the Palestine National Council specifically rejected UN Security Council Resolution 242 of Nov. 22, 1967, which called for Israel's withdrawal from occupied territories but referred to the stateless Palestinians as a "refugee problem," not as a national group.

The U.S. position toward the Palestinians was changing. In March 1977 President Jimmy Carter spoke of the need for a Palestinian homeland, and he later stated that it was essential for the Palestinians to take part in the peace process. The Israeli Cabinet continued to reject the participation of the PLO in the peace process but agreed not to look too closely at the antecedents of Palestinians who might be involved as members of delegations from Arab countries.

In November 1977 President Sādāt traveled to Israel to address Israel's parliament, the Knesset. His visit initiated peace negotiations that led to the Camp David accords of 1978 and the Egyptian–Israeli peace treaty signed on March 26, 1979. Provisions of the accords included: the establishment of a self-governing authority in the West Bank and the Gaza Strip and a transitional period of not more than five years, in which time the inhabitants would become autonomous; and negotiations within three years of the beginning of the transitional period to determine the status of the West Bank and the Gaza Strip and to conclude a peace treaty between Israel and Jordan. The PLO and Jordan rejected the agreements: in their view Egypt was abandoning the Palestinian cause so as to regain Egyptian territory, while Israel maintained control of the remaining occupied territories. **Camp David accords**

During the Camp David process the Soviet Union recognized the PLO as the sole legitimate representative of the Palestinians, and in 1981 the Soviet Union extended formal diplomatic recognition. The PLO continued to seek U.S. diplomatic recognition, but the Carter administration honoured the secret commitment made by the former U.S. secretary of state Henry Kissinger to Israel not to deal with the PLO. In June 1980 the European Economic Community announced its support of PLO participation in peace negotiations.

The influence of the PLO was increasingly felt in the occupied territories, where PLO-supported candidates won the municipal elections of 1976, and separate Israeli and Jordanian attempts to encourage alternatives to the PLO failed in the 1980s. Active opposition to Israeli control in the West Bank spread, while frequent demonstrations, strikes, and other incidents occurred, particularly among students. A cultural renascence among the Palestinians living under Israeli control and in exile was especially visible in the works of Maḥmūd Darwīsh and Ghassān Kanafānī, who wrote nationalistic exhortations to remember the lost land. Israeli Arabs began on March 30, 1976, an annual observance of the "Day of the Land" to demonstrate their objections to Zionist appropriation of land in Israel and the occupied territories.

As Israeli occupation of the West Bank solidified, many Palestinians feared that their chances of regaining even part of their homeland were lessening. By the early 1980s the dominant factions inside the PLO favoured the creation of a "national authority," that is, a mini-state, perhaps linked to Jordan in some fashion. The possibility of peace and compromise was viewed with suspicion and disdain by the Likud party government of Israel, which, instead of adopting a policy of conciliation, chose to invade Lebanon on June 6, 1982, so as to crush the PLO and encourage the installation of a Lebanese government that would be friendly to Israel. The PLO and Syrian forces were defeated by Israeli troops, and the remaining PLO forces were contained in West Beirut. After a lengthy siege and bombardment by Israel, in late August some 11,000 Palestinian fighters were allowed to leave Beirut for various destinations, under international guarantees for their own safety and that of their civilian dependents. Despite these guarantees, after Israeli troops occupied West Beirut the Lebanese rightist allies of the Israelis massacred hundreds of Palestinian civilians in the refugee camps.

Israel in 1982 destroyed the PLO infrastructure in southern Lebanon, but it was unable to force all PLO guerrillas from the country, and, ultimately, the new government of Lebanon came under the sway of Syria. Syria sought to dominate but not annex Lebanon and, as a way of achieving this goal, ensured that no single Lebanese faction would triumph completely over the other groups. By 1985 Israel and its backer, the United States, saw their Lebanon policy as a failure.

While Israel's military victory in Lebanon was not in the end decisive, the dispersal of the PLO did significantly weaken that group's military strength and political militancy. It was unable to operate freely from any of the nations bordering Palestine. U.S. President Ronald Reagan's peace proposal of September 1982 recognized the "legitimate rights of the Palestinians," but not the PLO, and Reagan urged a solution that would, in effect, restore Jordanian control to the West Bank. 'Arafāt and the other PLO leaders were also threatened by the emergence of a faction within al-Fatah encouraged by Syria. 'Arafāt was driven out of northern Lebanon in December 1983 by the Syrians and their protégés inside the PLO. As a result, the majority of the PLO turned to Egypt and Jordan for support against Syria and sought to use King Hussein of Jordan as an intermediary for negotiations with the United States and Israel that might lead to a ministate and confederation with Jordan. This policy was seen most concretely in the meeting of the Palestine National Council in Amman in November 1984, the first time it had met there since Jordan crushed the PLO armed forces in 1970. The PLO–Jordan option, however, was hindered by doubt among many Palestinians that King Hussein was willing to see an independent political choice made by them; the fear of most Israelis that a Jordanian–PLO delegation in an international peace conference would involve unacceptable demands and risks; the reluctance of the United States to see the Soviet Union, a supporter of the PLO, have a major voice in the settlement; and PLO reluctance or inability to unite on a policy sufficiently accommodating to meet Israeli and American demands.

Instead of peace talks, violence escalated. West Bank Arabs rioted and engaged in strikes in 1982, before the invasion of Lebanon, and again in late 1986. Lebanese Shī'ites fought the PLO to stop its reemergence as an armed rival for supremacy in the chaotic situation prevalent in West Beirut and southern Lebanon. Palestinian guerrillas hijacked airliners and even a passenger cruise ship to publicize their cause. On Oct. 1, 1985, Israel bombed the PLO headquarters near Tunis.

In Israel itself several new developments seemed to strengthen Arab feelings of alienation from the Jewish majority. The Knesset approved a bill in 1985 banning any political party that endangered state security—*i.e.,* any party that was anti-Zionist. This reinforced the long-standing situation whereby most Israeli Arabs found that no legal political party could adequately reflect their national, economic, and political views. Equally frustrating for those Palestinians inside and outside Israel who wished to see a compromise peace was the Israeli rejection of a joint Jordanian–Palestinian delegation, whose membership had been approved by the United States in July 1985. Israelis in turn became more antagonistic toward Palestinians as armed attacks against Israel and Israelis living abroad increased in number.

The United States continued to support Israel fully but at the same time attempted to improve relations with some Arab states, such as Jordan, and to gain acceptance as an informal mediator from those Palestinians who were prepared to listen, despite the seemingly one-sided position of the United States in the Arab–Israeli dispute. The Reagan administration talked of improving the quality of life for Arabs living in the occupied territories and supported Jordan's announced plans to bring this about. In 1988 a new peace initiative was begun by U.S. Secretary of State George Shultz. The United States strongly opposed the PLO, however, and ordered that its offices in the United States be closed.

'Arafāt condemned U.S. policy, while officially disclaiming responsibility for attacks on Israeli civilians. He said that Syria and Libya (and the Palestinians the latter supported) were sponsoring such attacks to prevent a negotiated settlement with Israel. Aerial attacks by Israel on Palestinian guerrilla bases in Lebanon escalated.

In the middle and late 1980s the two chief Israeli political parties that dominated the Cabinet clearly reflected differing positions on the future of the Palestinians in the occupied territories. The Likud party wished ultimately to annex the land, but not necessarily the people living thereon, fearing their voting power if they were to participate in Israeli elections. The Labour Party was willing to return some of the occupied territories to Jordan in return for full peace. Because the two parties could agree neither on goals nor on methods (such as the advisability of an international peace conference involving the nations permanently holding seats on the United Nations Security Council), no action was taken, and the status quo endured.

The PLO was also divided, despite the surface unity achieved in April 1987 when the mainline and radical pro-Syrian factions formally accepted a common program.

In the occupied territories small-scale Arab Palestinian demonstrations; university closings, arrests, and deportations by the Israeli authorities; riots; and occasional violence directed against Israelis ensued throughout 1987 as the Arabs saw no improvement in effective support of their aspirations from outside and no likely favourable change coming from the Israelis. Attacks by Arabs on Israeli settlers and by Israeli settlers on Arabs mounted, as the 20th year of Israeli occupation passed with no signs of significant change. Large-scale riots and demonstrations broke out on Dec. 9, 1987, and continued for months thereafter. When demonstrations turned to throwing stones at Israeli troops, the soldiers responded by shooting and arresting demonstrators. Many were killed, hundreds more were wounded, and some demonstrators were tortured by the Israeli armed forces. The persistent disturbances were initially spontaneous, but ultimately they came under the leadership of the United National Command of the Uprising, which may be linked to the PLO and to Islāmic fundamentalists inside Gaza.

Tactics followed by the demonstrators were highly sophisticated. Strikes, commercial boycotts and closures, and demonstrations would be carried out in one part of the territories and then, after Israel reestablished its local power there, would be transferred to a previously unengaged area. Palestinian refugee camps provided major centres for the resistance, but Palestinian Arabs living in more affluent circumstances also participated, and some Israeli Arabs also showed their sympathy with the goals of

Israel's invasion of Lebanon

the uprising. For the first time since Israel gained control of East Jerusalem in 1967, a general curfew was imposed by the Israeli authorities in some Arab sections of the city. The Arabs in the occupied territories killed some of their compatriots whom they accused of being collaborators with Israel; Arab police employed by Israel were required by public pressure of their fellow Arabs to resign from their posts.

Despite the yearning for a peaceful resolution of the turbulent history of the Palestinian people, the apparent failure of the American peace initiative early in 1988 implied a bleak future. As for the chief representative of the Palestinian Arabs, the PLO, the gains of the 1970s have not been completely lost. Arafāt showed considerable endurance, being widely regarded as the only Palestinian Arab figure who could command general support among his people. The PLO continued to be recognized widely, in the United Nations and elsewhere, as the legitimate voice of Palestinian nationalism. More importantly, international recognition of a separate Palestinian identity, and the growth of the Palestinian population worldwide to more than 4,000,000, showed continued vitality. The military and political strength of Israel, however, also increased. While some Israelis were prepared to accept to a limited degree Palestinian autonomy, most Israelis and Palestinians remained deeply reluctant to acknowledge the legitimacy of each other's claims. For Israel, to acknowledge Palestinian nationalism would cast doubt on the moral basis of the whole Zionist enterprise. For the Palestinian Arabs, to recognize Israel's right to exist would mean condemning their own nation to a small fraction of the former homeland.   (W.L.O.)

BIBLIOGRAPHY. For the geography of the area, see *Atlas of Israel: Cartography, Physical and Human Geography,* 3rd ed. (1985; originally published in Hebrew, 3rd ed., 1985); *Geography* (1973), compiled from material originally published in the *Encyclopaedia Judaica;* and W.B. FISHER, *The Middle East: A Physical, Social, and Regional Geography,* 7th ed. rev. (1978).

For an authoritative survey of all periods of antiquity, see the relevant sections of the multivolume *Cambridge Ancient History.*

For prehistory and early history, see JACQUES CAUVIN, *Les Premiers Villages de Syrie-Palestine du IXᵉ au VIIᵉ millénaire avant J.C.* (1978); LORENZO VIGANÒ, "Literary Sources for the History of Palestine and Syria: The Ebla Tables," *Biblical Archaeologist,* 47(1):6–16 (March 1984); J. PERROT, A. KEMPINSKI, and M. AVI-YONAH, *Syria-Palestine,* 2 vol. (1979; originally published in French, 2 vol., 1978–80); A.T. OLMSTEAD, *History of Palestine and Syria to the Macedonian Conquest* (1931, reprinted 1972); MICHAEL GRANT, *The History of Ancient Israel* (1984), a good general account; JOHN BRIGHT, *A History of Israel,* 3rd ed. (1981); KATHLEEN M. KENYON, *Archaeology in the Holy Land,* 4th ed. (1979, reprinted 1985); JEROME MURPHY-O'CONNOR, *The Holy Land: An Archaeological Guide from Earliest Times to 1700,* 2nd ed. rev. and expanded (1986), a handbook for travelers; TRUDE DOTHAN, *The Philistines and Their Material Culture,* trans. from Hebrew, rev. ed. (1982); and F.E. PETERS, *Jerusalem: The Holy City in the Eyes of Chroniclers, Visitors, Pilgrims, and Prophets from the Days of Abraham to the Beginnings of Modern Times* (1985).

For Hellenistic and Roman Palestine, see VICTOR TCHERIKOVER, *Hellenistic Civilization and the Jews,* trans. from Hebrew (1959, reprinted 1975); M. ROSTOVTZEFF, *The Social & Economic History of the Hellenistic World,* 3 vol. (1941, reprinted 1986); and A.H.M. JONES, *The Herods of Judaea* (1938, reprinted 1967). The most valuable general modern work is EMIL SCHÜRER, *The History of the Jewish People in the Age of Jesus Christ (175 B.C.–A.D. 135),* rev. ed., trans. from German (1973–   )—3 vol. of which had appeared by 1987. See also

E. MARY SMALLWOOD, *The Jews Under Roman Rule: From Pompey to Diocletian* (1976, reprinted 1981); M. AVI-YONAH, *The Jews of Palestine: A Political History from the Bar Kokhba War to the Arab Conquest,* trans. from Hebrew (1976, reprinted with title *The Jews Under Roman and Byzantine Rule,* 1984); M. ROSTOVTZEFF, *The Social & Economic History of the Roman Empire,* 2nd ed. rev. by P.M. FRASER, 2 vol. (1957, reprinted 1979); HILDEGARD TEMPORINI and WOLFGANG HAASE (eds.), *Politische Geschichte: Provinzen und Randvölker: Syrien, Palästina, Arabien* (1977), part of the series "Aufstieg und Niedergang der römischen Welt"; F.M. HEICHELHEIM, "Roman Syria," in TENNEY FRANK (ed.), *An Economic Survey of Ancient Rome,* vol. 4 (1938, reprinted 1975), pp. 121–257; A.H.M. JONES, "Syria," in *The Cities of the Eastern Roman Provinces,* 2nd ed. rev. by M. AVI-YONAH et al. (1971, reprinted 1983), pp. 226–294; and GAALYAH CORNFELD (ed.), *The Historical Jesus: A Scholarly View of the Man and His World* (1982).

For the periods of Muslim rule before 1516, see GUY LE STRANGE (trans.), *Palestine Under the Moslems: A Description of Syria and the Holy Land from A.D. 650 to 1500* (1890, reprinted 1975), a collection of medieval Arabic sources; SHLOMO D. GOITEIN, "Jerusalem in the Arab Period (638–1099)," *The Jerusalem Cathedra,* 2:168–196 (1982); and AMNON COHEN and GABRIEL BAER (eds.), *Egypt and Palestine: A Millennium of Association (868–1948)* (1984).

Among many recent works on Ottoman Palestine the following are the broadest and most valuable: MOSHE MA'OZ (ed.), *Studies on Palestine During the Ottoman Period* (1975); AMNON COHEN, *Palestine in the 18th Century: Patterns of Government and Administration* (1973); DAVID KUSHNER (ed.), *Palestine in the Late Ottoman Period: Political, Social, and Economic Transformation* (1986); and NEVILLE J. MANDEL, *The Arabs and Zionism Before World War I* (1976, reprinted 1980).

Some useful general studies that cover the 20th century are FRED J. KHOURI, *The Arab-Israeli Dilemma,* 3rd ed. (1985); HOWARD M. SACHAR, *A History of Israel,* 2 vol. (1979–87); BRUCE R. KUNIHOLM and MICHAEL RUBNER, *The Palestinian Problem and United States Policy: A Guide to Issues and References* (1986), with an extensive bibliography; and PAMELA ANN SMITH, *Palestine and the Palestinians, 1876–1983* (1984).

The period of the British mandate is covered by TARIF KHALIDI, "Palestinian Historiography: 1900–1948," *Journal of Palestine Studies,* 10(3):59–76 (Spring 1981); ADNAN MOHAMMED ABU-GHAZALEH, *Arab Cultural Nationalism in Palestine During the British Mandate* (1973); ANN MOSELY LESCH, *Arab Politics in Palestine, 1917–1939: The Frustration of a Nationalist Movement* (1979); Y. PORATH, *The Emergence of the Palestinian-Arab National Movement, 1918–1929,* trans. from Hebrew (1974), and *The Palestinian Arab National Movement: From Riots to Rebellion, 1929–1939,* trans. from Hebrew (1977); KENNETH W. STEIN, *The Land Question in Palestine, 1917–1939* (1984); DAN HOROWITZ and MOSHE LISSAK, *Origins of the Israeli Polity: Palestine Under the Mandate* (1978; originally published in Hebrew, 1977); and WM. ROGER LOUIS and ROBERT W. STOOKEY (eds.), *The End of the Palestine Mandate* (1985).

For coverage from 1948 to the present, publications of the Israeli government and the Palestine Liberation Organization (PLO) should be supplemented by articles drawn from the *Journal of Palestine Studies* (quarterly); and *The Jerusalem Quarterly.* Among the many studies on the Palestinian Arabs, the following are particularly worth consulting: HELENA COBBAN, *The Palestinian Liberation Organisation: People, Power, and Politics* (1984); SHAUL MISHAL, *The PLO Under 'Arafat: Between Gun and Olive Branch* (1986); DON PERETZ, *The West Bank: History, Politics, Society, and Economy* (1986); BARRY RUBIN, *The Arab States and the Palestine Conflict* (1981); EDWARD SAID, CHRISTOPHER HITCHENS, et al., *Blaming the Victims: Spurious Scholarship and the Palestinian Question* (1987); and two articles from the *Journal of Palestine Studies*—PAMELA ANN SMITH, "The Palestinian Diaspora, 1948–1985," 15(3):90–108 (Spring 1986); and RASHID KHALIDI, "The Palestinian Dilemma: PLO Policy After Lebanon," 15(1):88–103 (Autumn 1985).

(G.R.B./W.L.O.)

Paraguay

Paraguay is an independent republic of South America, located in the south central part of the continent. A landlocked country, it is dwarfed by the larger bordering countries of Bolivia to the northwest and north; Brazil to the east; and Argentina to the southeast, south, and west. It has an area of 157,048 square miles (406,752 square kilometres). The national capital of Asunción is located on the east bank of the Paraguay

River opposite the mouth of its chief western tributary, the Pilcomayo River. Rivers play a vital role in the nation's economic life, providing the country with access to the distant Atlantic Ocean and with sites for hydroelectric power plants. Indeed, the name of the country is said to derive from the Guaraní Indian word that means "place with a great river."

The article is divided into the following sections:

Physical and human geography

THE LAND

Relief. The Paraguay River, which runs through the country from north to south, divides Paraguay into two distinct geographical regions—the Región Oriental (Eastern Region) and the Chaco Boreal (Northern Chaco), the latter officially comprising the Región Occidental (Western Region).

The Región Oriental, with an area of about 61,700 square miles, is an extension of the Brazilian Plateau and varies in elevation from about 165 feet (50 metres) above sea level at the southwestern corner of the country to a few hills that rise to about 2,500 feet. The Cordillera de Amambay (Amambay Mountains) runs approximately north to south along part of the border with Brazil and then runs eastward as the Cordillera de Mbaracayú. From the northeast, other ranges extend roughly southward toward Encarnación, diminishing to hills in the south. To the east of these mountains lies the Alto Paraná (Upper Paraná) River Valley. To the west lies the broad valley of the Paraguay River. The area from Encarnación northward to the Brazilian border, comprising one-third of eastern Paraguay, is generally called the Paraná Plateau. The western part of the Región Oriental and the Alto Paraná Valley north and east of Encarnación are the areas most favourable to human settlement.

The Chaco Boreal, which covers more than 95,000 square miles, about two-thirds of the country, forms the northern part of the Gran Chaco, a flat and largely featureless tropical region that also extends into Bolivia and Argentina.

Drainage. Four-fifths of the country's perimeter is traced by the Paraguay, Apa, Alto Paraná, and Pilcomayo rivers. The Alto Paraná forms both the eastern and southern borders of the country. Multiple tributaries cross the eastern and central regions. The mountain ranges of Amambay and Mbaracayú form the watershed between the Paraguay

and the Alto Paraná rivers, which join to form the Paraná at the country's southwestern corner. Important eastern tributaries of the Paraguay River include, from north to south, the Apa, Aquidabán, Yapané, Jejuí, and Tebicuary. Except for the Río Monday and Río Acaray systems, the rivers that flow into the Alto Paraná have little economic significance. The only important tributary flowing from the west is the unnavigable, poorly defined Pilcomayo, which joins the Paraguay just below Asunción. Rising to the northwest in Bolivia, the Pilcomayo forms the southern border of the Chaco Boreal. Other Chaco rivers are slow, sluggish, intermittent streams that drain into swamps or disappear during dry periods.

Paraguay has only two lakes of consequence. The largest, the swampy Lake Ypoá, which begins about 40 miles (65 kilometres) south of Asunción, merges into the Laguna Verá; it is drained by various channels of the Tebicuary and feeds the marshes of the Ñeembucú Plain. Lake Ypacaraí, about 18 miles east of Asunción, has a favourite summer resort at San Bernardino, a town founded in 1881 by German agricultural colonists.

Soils. A large part of eastern Paraguay is covered by a residual soil mantle so deep that bedrock is rarely exposed. This soil is generally red and sandy and is low in nitrogen and other basic plant foods. About 40 percent of eastern Paraguay, in a belt running from the Brazilian border south to the Tebicuary and including the Asunción area, is covered by soils underlain by sandstone. Soils from basaltic lava, which generally are the most fertile, cover the Paraná Plateau. Transported soils cover a band along the Paraguay River, extending from the Río Apa to the southern border and covering the Ñeembucú Plain. Soils of the Chaco are largely alluvial mud, clay, and sand that have been transported from the Bolivian highlands.

Climate. Paraguay's climate is subtropical, with most of eastern Paraguay lying south of the Tropic of Capricorn and most of the Chaco north. Masses of humid air blan-

Región Oriental and the Chaco Boreal

The river systems

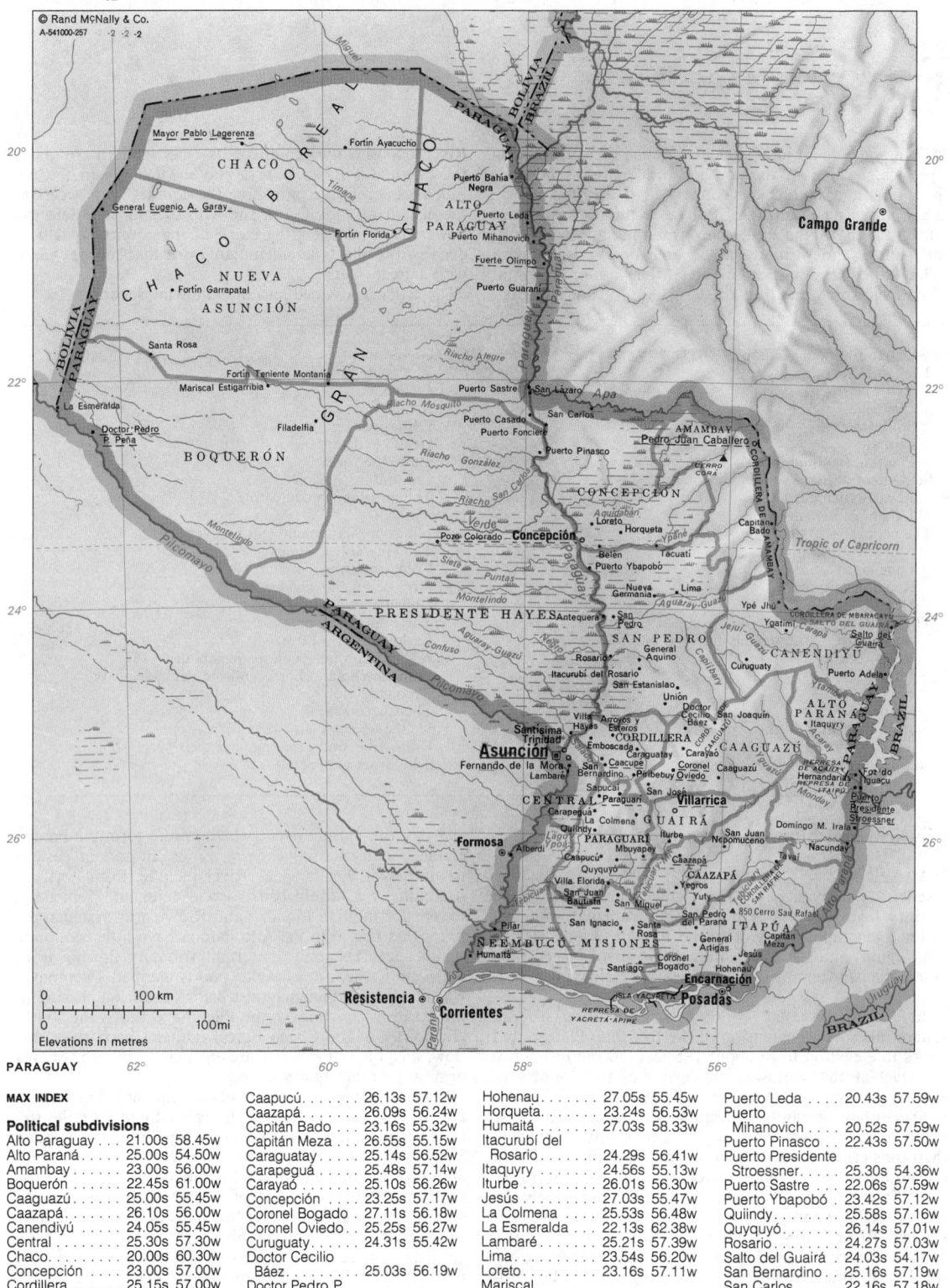

ket the country in the summers, and cold southern winds can make the winters miserable. Summer temperatures between October and March generally range between 77° F and 104° F (25° C and 40° C). Winter temperatures usually range between 50° F and 68° F (10° C and 20° C), although extremes of 30° F and 90° F (−1° C and 32° C) are not uncommon. Frost occurs every year somewhere in the country, but it is most common on the Paraná Plateau. The annual average rainfall in eastern Paraguay varies from 67 inches (1,700 millimetres) in the southeast to 55 inches along the Paraguay River. It diminishes gradually westward across the Chaco, averaging about 23 inches on the western border.

The entire country is subject to periodic floods and droughts, both of which cause severe agricultural losses. Plagues of locust frequently follow droughts.

The tropical forests

Plant and animal life. About two-fifths of the Eastern Region and more than one-half of the Chaco are forested. More than 500 species of hardwoods have been identified, among which are the urunday, peterebi, curupay, lapacho, and many kinds of palms. This wealth of forest resources has made Paraguay a world leader in the export of forest products, most of which go to Argentina. The supply of cedars has been exploited extensively for furniture, boxes, and general use. Large stands of native yerba del Paraguay (*Ilex paraguayensis*) occur in many areas. Marshes in the river valleys, especially in the southwest, are covered with tall grasses. Forest resources of the Chaco include many species of hardwoods that yield tannin, of which the red quebracho (*quebracho colorado*) is the most important. Numerous palms, such as the caranday, are commercially useful. The very hard palo santo ("holy wood") yields a valuable oil. Much of the Chaco is covered by cacti and a thorny scrub growth similar to the *caatinga* of Brazil's northeast. Medicinal plants abound in Paraguay and formerly were the basis of an extensive native pharmacopeia. The wild pineapple is native to eastern Paraguay, as is the bitter orange, which grows in wild profusion. The sweet orange, introduced by Spaniards, produces such huge quantities of fruit as to be worth only a pittance.

The name Chaco means "hunting ground," and the area, like eastern Paraguay, teems with wildlife. The jaguar, locally known as the *tigre*, lives among herds of wild boar, capybara (water hog), and deer and ranges over both parts of the country. The armadillo and anteater are common in the Chaco as is the otter and the coypu, a South American aquatic rodent. The varied birdlife includes ibis, herons, toucans, muscovy ducks, doves, partridges, parakeets, and parrots. Insect life is extensive and includes the deadly tarantula spider, as well as huge swarms of mosquitoes.

Animal life in the east is similar to that of Brazil and Argentina. There are various monkeys, tapirs, peccaries, puma, *tigres*, and deer. The more than 400 species of birds include eagles, falcons, partridges, pigeons, and herons. The waters of both regions abound with crocodiles, caymans, and a large variety of fish.

SETTLEMENT PATTERNS

Rural settlement. The principal areas of rural settlement are located in the east. There has been considerable development of agricultural colonies west of Puerto Presidente Stroessner and in the far northeast near Pedro Juan Caballero. Settlement in the Chaco is sparse. Except for the small town of Villa Hayes and a few ports serving industrial enterprises, there were no significant interior settlements to disturb the nomadic Indians until several Mennonite colonies were established about 120 miles west of Puerto Casado in the 1920s and 1930s.

Urban settlement. The largest urban concentration is found in the national capital, Asunción, and its suburbs. Puerto Presidente Stroessner, Fernando de la Mora, and Pedro Juan Caballero are the next largest centres of population, followed by Encarnación, Caaguazú, Pilar, Concepción, Villarrica, Coronel Oviedo, and Hernandarias.

THE PEOPLE

Ethnic composition. Paraguay has the most homogeneous population of any South American country. The vast majority of inhabitants are native Paraguayans; they pride themselves on their Guaraní descent, although the admixture of European strains is prominent.

The immigrant population is small. Immigrants have come largely from western Europe, principally Spain, but Japan, Korea, and Australia are also represented. Except in the case of Japanese immigrants, who have settled in such thriving agricultural colonies as La Colmena, most have been assimilated. Assimilation also has been resisted by the colonies of Mennonites and Hutterites, Christian sects that stress life-styles considerably different from those prevailing in Paraguay. These sects have received special privileges from the government, especially exemption from military service.

The religious colonies

There is a small Indian population living in Paraguay, nearly all in the Chaco, where there are small groups of Toba, Maskoy, Tapieté, Nanaiguá, Mataco, Lengua, Chamacoco, Zamuco (Moro), and Chulupí, among others. Despite efforts of the National Indian Institute, these survivors from the Stone Age have, at times, been forcibly relocated and threatened with extinction.

Language groups. The constitution recognizes both Spanish and Guaraní as national languages, but Spanish is the official language. Spanish is the medium of instruction and is used in business and government, whereas Guaraní is mainly the language of the home. Most of the population is bilingual.

Religious groups. Roman Catholicism is the official religion, and its adherents constitute all but a small minority of Paraguayans. There is tolerance for other Christian sects, as well as for other religions that are practiced by the population.

Demography. Population estimates for Paraguay have always been the despair of demographers. The best available estimates place the population at about 400,000 in 1864; at 176,000 in 1872, after the Paraguayan War; and, a century later in 1972, at about 2,400,000. Although about one-half of the population is rural, migration to the cities has accelerated. There is a slight majority of females. Life expectancy at birth is higher than the average Latin-American country. The population is young, with the majority under 30 years of age. Infant mortality has decreased, but it remains high.

Distribution of persons is not uniform, with the highest density in the Asunción metropolitan area.

The rate of emigration has fluctuated, but it has been

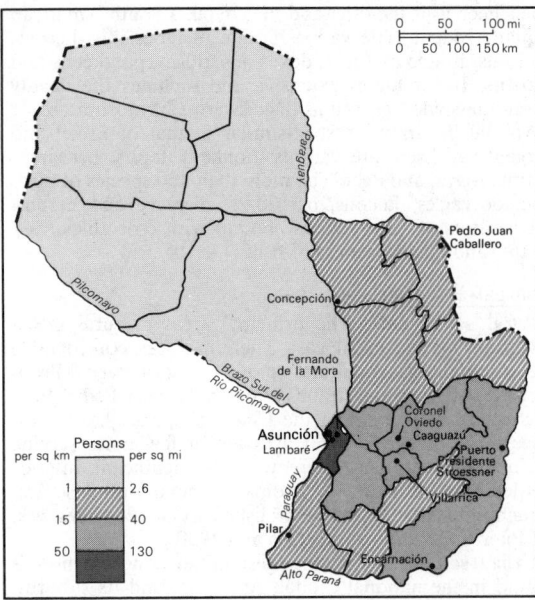

Population of Paraguay.

relatively high since 1870, especially among males seeking work in neighbouring countries. It is estimated that several hundred thousand Paraguayans have emigrated since 1940.

THE ECONOMY

Agriculture, cattle raising, forestry, and fishing. Agriculture, the most common economic activity, employs more than one-half of the population on a very small percentage of the arable land. The Rural Welfare Institute, through a program to legalize land tenancy, has greatly reduced the number of squatters. The overwhelming majority of farm units are occupied by owners, although small groups of tenant farmers and squatters still exist.

Land ownership

The average farm is about 100 acres (40 hectares), although most of the arable land is held in very large units. A national agency provides short-term credit for agricultural production, while the Rural Welfare Institute gives aid and guidance to hundreds of government agricultural colonies and several private ones. Large-scale agriculture is in its infancy, since most of the land is used for grazing. Agriculture suffers several problems, including the high price of fertilizer and petroleum, and a relatively low price for many farm products. The most important crops are cassava, sugarcane, corn (maize), soybeans, and cotton, and among other crops are rice, wheat, coffee, tobacco, tung oil, and peanuts (groundnuts).

Some pigs, sheep, chickens, and horses are raised, but cattle are the most important livestock. Cattle raising is a traditional activity that contributes to both domestic consumption and to the export trade. Cattle are raised in the southern part of eastern Paraguay, in the Concepción area, and in the eastern and northeastern Chaco. Almost all cattle are raised for slaughter or for export. Contrary to popular belief, Paraguayans, unlike Argentines, are not great consumers of beef.

Forestry products

Forest products account for a significant portion of exports, and Argentine investment in the timber industry, as well as in cattle raising, is extensive. Many of the agricultural colonies have been carved out of heavily forested land, however, and there has been little effort to reforest denuded areas with desirable species.

There is no organized fishing industry, although the rivers teem with fish. Especially popular are the *surubí* and dorado, while other species provide the basis for a small commercial industry.

Resources. *Mining and quarrying.* Most mineral deposits are found east of the Paraguay River. Manganese is located near Emboscada; malachite and azurite (copper ores) near Caapucú, Encarnación, and San Miguel; feldspar and mica near Concepción; and talc and *piroflita* (hard, iron-bearing flagstone) near Caapucú and San Miguel.

Ochre is found in the Cordillera region, and gypsum and limestone near the Paraguay River; there is some peat near Pilar. Other minerals include marble, clay (kaolin), and salt, and uranium ores have been reported. Extensive drilling in the Paraguayan Chaco has failed to find any hydrocarbons.

Despite the varied mineral resources, mining and quarrying are the least developed economic activities. Limestone, cement, and lime are produced for the building trades, and clay (kaolin) and sand are quarried for use in ceramics and in glass. The government promotes electricity-intensive industries, including expansion of the cement industry.

Energy. Most electricity in Paraguay came from wood- and oil-burning thermoelectric plants in Asunción until the Acaray hydroelectric power plant began operating in 1968. The plant's capacity was expanded to 190,000 kilowatts. Paraguay's total production increased more than 20-fold from 1954 to 1984. Nearly all of this increase came from hydroelectric sources. Distribution of electricity is controlled by the National Electricity Administration, which was created in 1949.

Itaipú hydroelectric project

A dramatic and far-reaching economic event in Paraguay's history was the construction of the hydroelectric project at Itaipú on the Alto Paraná, about 10 miles north of the International Friendship Bridge at Puerto Presidente Stroessner. Under a 1973 treaty a major portion of the cost was borne by Brazil. It was agreed that Paraguay would receive one-half of the electricity generated and would sell its excess power to Brazil. The United States supplied most of the equipment for the gigantic project. Financing, provided by both private and international banks, reached about $20,000,000,000.

Work was completed in 1982 on the main gravity dam, 620 feet high and 4,045 feet long, spanning the Alto Paraná. The reservoir created by the dam covers about 870 square miles of Paraguayan and Brazilian territory. The dam is one of the largest in the world and has one of the world's highest planned generating capacities, greater than Grand Coulee Dam. Construction stimulated land investment, expanded banking and financial services, and created a shortage of workers elsewhere as labourers flocked to Itaipú.

The joint Paraguayan–Argentine hydroelectric project in the Yacyretá–Apipé islands zone of the Alto Paraná is smaller but still important, with a planned capacity of 3,700,000 kilowatts. Corpus, in the Itacus area, was designated in 1979 as the site for another Paraguayan-Argentine project. The supply of electricity will provide Paraguay with a basis for transforming and modernizing its economy.

Industry. Paraguay is one of the most industrially undeveloped countries in South America. Manufacturing includes the production of tannin extract, vegetable oils, petitgrain oil, ginned cotton, maté, and soybean meal. Other industries, encouraged by the Banco Nacional de Fomento (National Development Bank), include textiles, shoes, sugar, soap, furniture, plywood, matches, leather products, ice, and soft drinks. Large quantities of alcoholic beverages, especially *caña* and beer, are produced locally. The meat-packing industry is very dependent on foreign markets.

Finance. The main banking establishments are the Banco Central del Paraguay, which handles all monetary and foreign exchange functions, and the Banco Nacional de Fomento and Banco de Desarollo del Paraguay, which grant credits to agricultural and industrial enterprises and conduct normal banking functions. There are also branches of other Latin-American, European, and U.S. banks. Foreign exchange reserves are limited, but generous loans are obtained from international development banks and associations.

Trade. The principal exports—cotton, soybeans, forest products, vegetable oils, and meat products—are chiefly marketed in Argentina, western Europe, Brazil, Japan, and Uruguay. Cotton and soybeans are the most important agricultural exports. Paraguay has become one of the world's largest producers and exporters of soybeans, which are grown mostly in the Itaipú and Alto Paraná departments.

The main sources of imports—the United States, West Germany, and France—provide Paraguay with transportation equipment, fuel, heavy machinery, motors, chemicals, pharmaceuticals, foodstuffs, lubricants, and iron and iron products. Paraguay is a member of the Latin American Integration Association (LAIA; formerly the Latin American Free Trade Association [LAFTA]). An elaborate system of subsidies, surcharges, and multiple exchange rates prevents Paraguay's unfavourable balance of trade from becoming excessive.

Administration of the economy. Although private initiative is encouraged, the government plays an important role in planning economic activities. It defines economic and social policy and participates directly in business life. The government holds a monopoly on the production of alcohol and operates a cement plant.

The government's role in the economy

Taxation. Most of Paraguay's revenue is derived from customs duties and indirect taxes, and from income, sales, and service taxes. Profits derived from commerce, industry, finance, ranching, farming, and real estate are taxable, but income from rents, securities, and pensions is exempt.

Trade unions. There is one large, government-recognized trade union—the Confederation of Paraguayan Workers. There are other, smaller labour unions, some of which represent rural workers and farmers. The right to join unions is guaranteed by law. Strikes are prohibited until compulsory arbitration before the Permanent Board of Conciliation and Arbitration is exhausted, and then are allowed only with strict limitations.

Economic policies and problems. Economic policy became inseparable from political policy under Pres. Alfredo Stroessner. The objectives of the Colorado Party, under Stroessner's control, were carried out to a remarkable degree, while political opposition was crushed or bypassed. Rather than impose the high taxes needed to finance development, the government preferred to borrow. Still, the public debt was kept within manageable limits, and the *guaraní* became one of the more stable Latin-American currencies.

Transportation. *Roads.* The enormous economic transformation in Paraguay has been aided tremendously by construction of a sizeable road network equipped with adequate bridges. Paraguay's major highway connects Asunción with Puerto Presidente Stroessner, where the International Friendship Bridge spans the Alto Paraná and carries the highway into Brazil. This paved road continues to the port of Paranaguá, from which Paraguay exports most of its soybeans. Another major paved highway joins Asunción with Encarnación. A suspension bridge, part of the Pan-American Highway, links Asunción and Clorinda, Argentina. The Chaco is served by a paved highway that runs northwest from Villa Hayes through the Mennonite colonies and on to the Bolivian border. Other unpaved routes connect Asunción with the principal interior cities.

Railways. Most of the railway system is made up of the Ferrocarril (Railway) Presidente Carlos Antonio López, which runs for 274 miles from Asunción southeastward to Encarnación, where it connects with a train ferry to Posadas, Argentina. The Ferrocarril del Norte operates between Concepción and Horqueta. Short, privately owned narrow-gauge railways connect Chaco industries with ports on the Paraguay River.

Water transport. The chief method of transportation in Paraguay is by water. The Paraguay and Alto Paraná carry much international traffic. Paraguay's merchant fleet, the Flota Mercante del Estado, which was created in 1945, runs many cargo vessels and also has tankers, passenger ships, ferries, and a training ship. Ocean shipping is handled by the Compañia de Ultramer.

Air services. Air transport is provided by the government-owned national airline, Líneas Aéreas Paraguayas, which has greatly expanded its services since its creation in 1962. Líneas Aéreas de Transporte Nacional serves interior cities. An international airport at Asunción has greatly expanded service for Paraguay's rapidly increasing tourist and commercial traffic. There are domestic airports at major interior cities.

ADMINISTRATIVE AND SOCIAL CONDITIONS

Government. *Constitutional framework.* The Constitution of 1967, amended in 1977, is the basic charter of Paraguay. The president is elected by direct vote for a five-year term and must be a Roman Catholic, a Paraguayan by birth, and more than 40 years of age. The prohibition on being reelected more than once was removed in 1977 to permit President Stroessner's reelection. The president has the usual powers of appointment, conducts foreign affairs, and may declare a state of siege and dissolve Congress, enact laws by decree, and mobilize the army. Stroessner's role as actual, but not titular, head of the Colorado Party gives him complete political control of the country.

The presidency

The Council of State is an advisory body appointed by the president. Its members include the Council of Ministers, as well as representatives of agriculture, manufacturing, and commerce; other members include the archbishop of Asunción, the rector of the National University, the presidents of the Banco Central and of the Banco Nacional de Fomento, and one retired officer from each of the three armed services. The council's functions include approval of measures proposed by the president.

The Congress is composed of the Chamber of Deputies and the Senate, all elected by popular vote for five-year terms. Congress can initiate legislation and may override a presidential veto by a two-thirds majority in each house.

Citizens and foreigners enjoy basic civil liberties, including freedom of expression, freedom of religion, and freedom to engage in professions and trades.

Local government. The country is divided into two provinces—the Occidental, to the west of the Paraguay River, and the Oriental, to the east. Occidental Province is divided into five departments; Oriental Province is divided into 14 departments and the federal district. Each department is further divided into *partidos,* or rural districts, that are controlled by the central government. *Partidos* are composed of units called *compañías,* which often correspond to areas inhabited by kin groups. The *compañías* often have Guaraní names. Areas with a minimum population of 3,000 and a central urban community may qualify as *municipios.*

The political process. *Elections.* Voting is compulsory for all men and women who are 18 years of age and older, excepting those in military service. Resident aliens are also allowed to vote in municipal elections. Elections for the executive and legislative branches of the central government are held every five years. If the president dissolves Congress, elections must be held within two months.

Political parties. Paraguay is constitutionally a multi-party state. Parties are legally free to organize, but they are closely regulated by the executive branch of the government. Between 1947 and 1962 only the Colorado Party was legally recognized. No party dedicated to the overthrow of republican representative democracy can be organized. No party may be subordinate to, or receive aid from, foreign sources, and parties may not boycott elections. To be recognized as a party, an organized group must have at least 10,000 affiliates.

The political process is, in effect, controlled by the party of the chief executive. Other parties are recognized, however, in the composition of the legislature. The party that wins a simple majority is awarded two-thirds of the seats of both houses, and the rest of the seats are proportionately distributed among the minority parties. While giving nominal recognition to the legal existence of other organizations, this process ensures executive control of the political life of the country.

Justice. The judicial system is headed by a Supreme Court of five members appointed by the president and confirmed by the Senate. Judges of lower courts and magistrates are appointed by the president with the approval of the Supreme Court. The judiciary is supervised by the Ministry of Justice, and judges can be tried by Congress.

The Supreme Court

Armed forces. Although Paraguay's armed forces are not large, military service is compulsory. A disproportionately large part of the budget, about 15 percent, is allocated to the police and armed forces, which also have received significant aid from the United States.

Education. Elementary education is free and compulsory for children between the ages of seven and 14. Despite large enrollments, the dropout rate is high, but it has been falling. The 3,500 elementary schools are supplemented by some 500 secondary schools, and there are centres for adult education in all departments. A school in Asunción prepares students for further training as secondary teachers. The two universities—the National University of Asunción (1890) and the private Catholic University (1960)—are located in Asunción; attendance is free at the National University. Paraguay also has schools of agriculture and veterinary science, as well as scientific institutes.

Health and welfare. The Ministry of Public Health and Social Welfare works to promote public health and to establish hospitals or clinics in the various parts of the country. There are also district and departmental health centres; clinics serve the rural population. In an effort to reduce the infant death rate, attention has been given to maternal and child care. The central government also has attempted to improve municipal water supplies. Except for Asunción, water and sewage services are inadequate in urban centres and are nonexistent in the countryside.

The police. Police chiefs, or *comisarios*, are appointed by the president and are important in maintaining his rule. The police in Asunción are responsible for the maintenance of dossiers on the country's citizens, for the prevention and investigation of crime, and for the maintenance of prisons. A secret Department of Investigations guards against subversive activities.

Wages and costs of living. Minimum wages were introduced by the Ministry of Labour in 1961. Per capita income figures are deceptive because so many subsistence farmers do not participate in the cash economy. Per capita income increased considerably in the late 20th century, however, although the cost of living also increased. More than one-third of the population is in the labour force. Nevertheless, the typical Paraguayan worker has not noticeably improved his standard of living.

Communications. The National Telecommunications Administration provides telephone service to Asunción and the other major cities. A satellite telephone system serves both domestic and international traffic. There is dependable telephone, telegraph, and telex service between Asunción and major cities in North and South America and in Europe. The domestic and international postal service is dependable and reasonably priced.

Health conditions. Heart diseases, infections, and lung diseases are the major causes of death. Inadequate shelter during the winter months is the chief factor in the prevalence of influenza, pneumonia, and tuberculosis. There is some malaria and leprosy.

CULTURAL LIFE

Guaraní and Spanish traditions

The main characteristic of Paraguayan culture is its fusion of both the Guaraní and Spanish traditions. Folklore, the arts, and literature reflect this dual origin. The country's outstanding handicraft is the production of ñandutí lace, which is thought to represent a combination of 16th-century needlepoint lacemaking techniques from Europe with Guaraní traditions.

Cultural institutions. Paraguay's principal cultural institutions are located in Asunción. There are learned societies concerned with Paraguayan and Guaraní history and culture, as well as various other societies and research institutes. The Normal School of Music, the Conservatory of Music, the National Academy of Fine Arts, and the Asunción Symphony Orchestra are major arts organizations. Paraguay has museums of ethnography, natural history, and military history, as well as museums with collections of the work of Paraguayan artists and private collections of national memorabilia.

Library services are centred in Asunción. The largest collections are in the National Library and Archive and the Museum of Natural History and Ethnography; other government libraries include the Public Library of the Ministry of Defense and the Library of the Ministry of Foreign Affairs. The American Library is attached to the Godoi Museum. Scientific materials are collected by the Library of the Museum of Natural History and Ethnography and the Library of the Paraguayan Scientific Society.

The press and broadcasting. Although Paraguay's constitution guarantees freedom of the press, the public media exercises self-restraint in criticism of the government since censorship is used periodically. All newspapers and periodicals are published in Spanish. The most interesting newspapers are *ABC Color* (1967) and *La Tribuna* (1925), which, along with *Ultima Hora* (1977) and *Hoy* (1977), have the largest circulations. The Colorado Party publishes *Patria* (1946), and the Roman Catholic Church publishes *Comunidad.*

The National Telecommunications Administration oversees radio and television broadcasting. Radio Nacional is the government network, but there are many privately operated stations. Privately owned commercial television networks transmit from Asunción, Encarnación, and Puerto Presidente Stroessner. For statistical data, see the "Britannica World Data" section in the current *Britannica Book of the Year.* (J.P.P./H.G.W.)

History

EXPLORATION, SETTLEMENT, AND INDEPENDENCE

The Guaraní. Indian tribes speaking the Guaraní language occupied the region between the Paraguay and Paraná rivers long before the arrival of Europeans in the area. They were members of the Tupian language stock, which was widespread in South America, and in most respects resembled the other Indian tribes of the tropical forests. The women cultivated maize, manioc, and sweet potatoes, and the men hunted and fished. They were warlike, seminomadic people who lived in large thatched dwellings grouped in villages, and each village was surrounded by a large defensive palisade of upright logs. In the 15th century raiders from the poorer Gran Chaco region made frequent attacks upon Guaraní tribes. The Guaraní retaliated, crossing the Paraguay River, and subdued their enemies, carrying the conflict into the margins of the Inca Empire. They were, therefore, the natural allies of early European explorers who were seeking short routes to the mineral wealth of Peru. Alejo García, making his way from the Brazilian coast in 1524, and Sebastian Cabot, sailing up the Paraná in 1526, were the earliest of these explorers to reach the area.

Colonial period. The first colonial settlements were established by Domingo Martínez de Irala in the period 1536–56. The first Spanish colonists, unsuccessful in their search for gold, settled peacefully among the Guaraní in the region of Asunción, the present capital of Paraguay. These first settlers established their notorious "harems" of Guaraní women. Their racially mixed descendants gradually grew into the rural population of modern Paraguay, which still considers itself to be Guaraní in custom and habit. With Asunción as his principal base Irala laid the foundations of Paraguay and made it the centre of Spanish power in southeastern South America. From Asunción were founded such cities as Santa Fé, Corrientes, and Buenos Aires. Irala's colonization policy involved the delimitation of the boundary with Brazil by a line of forts against Portuguese expansion, the foundation of villages, the reduction of the Guaraní to provide food, labour, and soldiers, and extensive Guaraní–Spanish intermarriage. Rapidly a national and fairly homogeneous amalgam of Indian and Spanish cultures came into being.

From early in the 17th century, for more than 150 years, Jesuit communal missions in the Alto Paraná and Uruguay basins of southeastern Paraguay governed the lives of 100,000 Indians in 32 *reducciones.* These were centres of religious conversion, agricultural and pastoral production, and manufacturing and trade, which served also as strategic outposts against Portuguese expansion from southern Brazil. Isolated from the heart of Paraguay, which centred on Asunción, the mission became an autonomous military, political, and economic "state within a state," which increasingly excited the envy of the Spanish landowners in the Asunción area. In the period 1721–35 the latter waged a struggle to overthrow the Jesuit monopoly of Indian trade. Unaided, the *reducciones* had to defend themselves also against slave raiders from São Paulo and, in 1754–57, a combined Spanish-Portuguese attack designed to enforce

Jesuit missions to the Indians

a territorial partition of the mission settlements. Defiance of such powerful groups paved the way for the expulsion of the Jesuits in 1767. The *reducciones* were abandoned; the Indians were absorbed either by the landed estates or the jungle; the settlements fell into ruin; economic activity ceased; and little permanent result survived of this period of Paraguayan history.

In 1776 the new Viceroyalty of Río de la Plata was created with its capital in Buenos Aires. This effectively made Asunción and all of Paraguay dependent on Buenos Aires, thus ending the region's colonial dominance.

Struggle for independence. As the power of Buenos Aires grew, the leaders of Paraguay began to resent the decline in their province's significance, and, although they had early challenged Spanish authority, they refused to accept the declaration of Argentine independence in 1810 as applying to Paraguay. Nor could an Argentine army under Gen. Manuel Belgrano enforce Paraguayan acceptance, as Paraguayan militia repulsed Belgrano's forces in 1811. Later, however, when the Spanish governor sought assistance from the Portuguese in defending the colony from further attacks from Buenos Aires, he underestimated the national spirit of the Paraguayans. Under the leadership of captains Pedro Juan Cabellero and Fulgencio Yegros, they promptly deposed the governor and declared their independence on May 14, 1811.   (E.R.Se./G.J.B./Ed.)

ESTABLISHMENT OF THE NATION

The Francia regime. A governing junta was soon established, led by Yegros but in reality dominated by a civilian lawyer, José Gaspar Rodríguez de Francia. Francia proposed the idea of a confederation of equals to Buenos Aires, which, hoping for eventual domination, settled for a vague military alliance, signed in October 1811. This constituted de facto recognition of Paraguayan independence, and when Buenos Aires attempted to use the alliance to acquire Paraguayan troops for its own interprovincial quarrels, the accord became void. Buenos Aires' response was to blockade Paraguay. In the face of regional fragmentation, Buenos Aires sent Nicolás de Herrera to Asunción to frighten, bluff, or bribe Paraguay into a union of unequals. Francia responded by convening a congress, which on October 12, 1813, formally declared Paraguay an independent republic and rejected further treaties with Buenos Aires. A consulate of two men, Yegros and Francia, was established to rule the nation for a year, and it was soon clear that the superpatriot Francia was the guiding force of the government.

At the end of that year, a new congress met and proclaimed Francia supreme dictator of the republic for a period of five years without a constitution or check and balance to restrain him. In 1816 a third congress made him perpetual dictator, and his will was to be the law in Paraguay for a further 24 years. El Supremo, as he was known, prohibited any political activity, stripped the church of its holdings and power, confiscated the wealth of the small Spanish elite and forbade its members to marry within their own clique, abolished the municipal government of Asunción, and generally isolated Paraguay from its rather hostile neighbours. Some Paraguayans objected, and in 1820 El Supremo discovered a plot to depose him and restore the native elite to power. Hundreds of arrests were made, and in the following year at least 68 men of the traditional Paraguayan aristocracy (including Fulgencio Yegros) were executed. Their wealth in land and slaves became part of the national patrimony, and well before Francia's death (1840) the state owned a vast proportion of the nation. With the borders sealed, Paraguay became, of necessity, almost self-sufficient; and only a small, carefully regulated commerce was permitted with Argentina and Brazil. Uninvited foreigners were often held for years under loose arrest in the interior. Several governments and even the Great Liberator, Simon Bolívar himself, attempted to gain the release of a celebrated French scientist, Aimé Bonpland; but Francia failed to respond, only voluntarily releasing the scientist in 1831, after 10 years of detention.

Carlos Antonio López. When Francia died, he left behind a quietly prosperous nation that had adjusted well to what amounted to state socialism, but he also left a nation of rustics with no political experience and a strong tradition of dictatorial rule. In 1841 a second consulate, reminiscent of the Francia–Yegros consulate, emerged from the chaos in the figures of a civilian, Carlos Antonio López, and a soldier, Mariano Roque Alonso. It was soon clear that López was the true ruler of Paraguay, and in 1844 a congress named him president. The same congress promulgated a constitution, notable for the extremely great powers accorded the president and the absence of the word liberty from its entire text. López was basically a good ruler for Paraguay, devoting much of his two decades in power to opening the country slowly to the wider world and to modernization. Doing so caused international crises on an unprecedented scale, and it was not until after the fall of the Argentine dictator Juan Manuel de Rosas in 1852 that Argentina recognized Paraguayan sovereignty and eased its stranglehold on the rivers leading to the sea.

PARAGUAY'S CONFLICTS WITH ITS NEIGHBOURS

While he was "opening" his nation, López also had to handle border crises with ever-expanding Brazil and Argentina. These crises convinced López that Paraguayan modernization should proceed along military avenues. Thus hundreds of foreign engineers, medical men, scientists, machinists, and advisers were put to work on essentially military projects. Iron foundries that cast enormous cannon and naval gear, a shipyard that turned out advanced, semimilitary vessels, railroad and telegraph systems, military clinics, a large arsenal, and the huge fortress complex of Humaitá, which dominated a bend of the Paraguay River—all these were constructed rapidly. López was threatened by a major Brazilian naval expedition on the Paraná River in 1855; in 1858 a large flotilla of the U.S. Navy appeared to force a solution to a complex diplomatic issue; and finally British war vessels captured and held for a time the flagship of the small Paraguayan Navy. In most of these contretemps, López was forced to give in, and the consequent humiliation lent greater urgency to his desire to strengthen Paraguay's defenses. By the time of his death, in September 1862, he had created a major regional military machine. A cautious man, however, he warned his eldest son, Francisco Solano López, who was to succeed him, not to use the new military might capriciously but to settle disputes through diplomacy and negotiation.

Francisco Solano López and the Paraguayan War. Francisco Solano López in 1862 was the inexperienced, spoiled son of an iron-willed dictator. He overestimated the military strength of his nation, and this led him to believe that Paraguay should have a larger voice in the affairs of the region. Thus, when Uruguay, the subcontinent's other buffer state, wracked by civil war, was threatened with intervention by Brazil, López in 1863 and 1864 took an increasingly bellicose position. When Brazil ignored his warnings and ultimatums and invaded Uruguay in August 1864 to support a pro-Brazilian faction in the civil war, López decided to use the strength of his military machine. In November he ordered the capture of a Brazilian war steamer and sent units of his army and navy north to invade the Mato Grosso, simultaneously preparing a larger army corps to strike south to destroy the Brazilian army in Uruguay. When Argentina denied his request for transit of a Paraguayan army, he made the fatal decision to declare war on Argentina as well, in March 1865. In May, as Paraguayan troops were approaching, a puppet Uruguayan government signed, with Brazil and Argentina, the Treaty of the Triple Alliance, committing all three to the war against Paraguay.

The Paraguayan force heading southward was destroyed at Uruguaiana, in Brazil, and a strike into northeast Argentina resulted in heavy Paraguayan casualties and the virtual destruction of López' fleet in 1865. Much of the rest of the war was fought in southwestern Paraguay, near and around Humaitá. In May 1866 López threw the cream of his army into suicidal attacks against allied forces at Tuyutí, losing almost 20,000 of his best men. Other lost battles in 1866–68, reinforced by widespread epidemics of Asiatic cholera, devastated the population of the country.

Modernization of the military forces

Diplomatic and economic isolation

Destruction in the Paraguayan War

In 1869 and 1870 the tragedy was completed as López, pursued by large allied forces, retreated through the interior of his nation with a shattered army and thousands of civilian refugees, dragging famine, disease, and death in his wake. Perhaps at this point unhinged, he ordered the executions of hundreds of people, including his own two brothers and two brothers-in-law and scores of his officer corps. Finally, on March 1, 1870, his last camp was attacked at Cerro Corá by Brazilian cavalry and López died in combat. His country by then lay in ruins, with half of its former population of 450,000 dead. A Brazilian occupation army remained, further draining the country, until 1876. This Paraguayan War, or War of the Triple Alliance, was the bloodiest in Latin-American history.

Reconstruction. Under a liberal constitution promulgated in 1870, Paraguay began a painful reconstruction. Only the mutual jealousies of Brazil and Argentina prevented the country from losing much of its territory. As a result, Brazil gained no lands that it had not actually occupied before the war, and Argentina's claims to most of the Chaco were reduced considerably when, in arbitration, U.S. Pres. Rutherford B. Hayes decided one important boundary issue in 1878 in favour of Paraguay. When the army of occupation was removed in 1876, it left a crowd of Paraguayan politicians known best for their corruption and drive for power. In 1887 Paraguay's two major political parties, the Liberales and the Colorados, were born. The Colorados were in power from 1887 until a Liberal revolt unseated them in 1904, and the Liberales, in their turn, dominated the presidency for the next 30 years.

Formation of major political parties

The Chaco War. Paraguay's reconstruction was complicated by a dispute with Bolivia concerning boundaries in the Chaco. The dispute was exacerbated when in the 1880s Bolivia lost its seacoast in the War of the Pacific with Chile and, seeing the Chaco as a possible outlet to the sea via the Paraná River, began to penetrate it with soldiers and colonists. By the 1920s, armed clashes began to take place as Paraguay moved into the region in greater force. As Paraguay was frantically trying to arm itself, a Bolivian force stormed a Paraguayan fort on June 15, 1932, and the war began. Paraguayan president Eusebio Ayala gave a military carte blanche to Gen. José Félix Estigarribia, who used his smaller army to gradually push the Bolivians back until they were almost entirely ejected from the Chaco. Through foreign mediation, a cease-fire was attained on June 12, 1935, and a peace treaty was signed three years later. By its terms, Paraguay retained at least three-quarters of the Chaco.

SINCE THE CHACO WAR

In February 1936, Ayala and Estigarribia were imprisoned following a military coup, the Febrerista revolt, conducted by radical officers. The inept new government soon fell, however, and Estigarribia was elected president in 1939.

Estigarribia and Morínigo and their successors. On September 7, 1940, before he could actually implement a new constitution that gave him great authoritarian powers, Estigarribia was killed in an air crash. He was replaced by Gen. Higinio Morínigo, a harsh opportunist, who immediately began to persecute the Liberales and reward the Colorados. A revolt of Liberales and other groups in 1947 again devastated the land and left thousands dead. Morínigo was deposed by the Colorados themselves in 1948. In the next six years, Paraguay had six weak presidents, and then, in 1954, Gen. Alfredo Stroessner, supported by both Colorados and the army, seized power.

The Stroessner regime. The authoritarian Stroessner, with considerable aid from the U.S. and later Brazil, managed to stabilize one of the world's least stable currencies, attract foreign investment, and embark on large public works projects, such as a highway network to link the towns and villages of his nation with one another and with Argentina and Brazil. Paraguayan isolation was broken down. Very harsh rule was relaxed somewhat after 1960, and elections on all levels were permitted; however, the Colorado Party never lost, and Stroessner was duly reelected every five years. The church alone continued to raise a voice of objection to the repressive aspects of the regime, such as treatment of the Indian minority and censorship. Relations with the U.S. steadily deteriorated throughout the 1970s, and U.S. aid was much reduced. Partly because of this, the Stroessner government aligned itself closely with the authoritarian regime in Brazil, which offered aid and political support. The two nations cooperated in the building of the Itaipú hydroelectric plant on their shared border. As a result of this project, the national economy briefly improved, but it took a downturn in the early 1980s, bringing some protests against the Stroessner regime. The government showed little tolerance for opposition to its policies, however, quickly clamping down on any movement before it could develop; most of the main opposition leaders were being kept forcibly in exile. Such repression focussed international attention on Paraguay for human rights violations, further hampering the country's foreign relations and intensifying economic stagnation. The aging Stroessner, who had been elected in 1983 for a seventh term, also had to deal with concerns in his own Colorado Party, where dissension was growing over the succession to the presidency.

For later developments in the political history of Paraguay, see the *Britannica Book of the Year* section in the BRITANNICA WORLD DATA ANNUAL.

For coverage of related topics in the *Macropædia* and *Micropædia*, see the *Propædia*, Part Nine, Division VI, Sections 964 and 966; and Division VII, Section 974.

(J.H.Wi./Ed.)

BIBLIOGRAPHY

Physical and human geography: Although dated, general surveys of Paraguayan history, economics, and politics include: ADOLF N. SCHUSTER, *Paraguay, Land, Volk, Geschichte, Wirtschaftsleben und Kolonisation* (1929); HARRIS GAYLORD WARREN, *Paraguay, An Informal History* (1949); PHILIP RAINE, *Paraguay* (1956); EFRAÍM CARDOZO, *Paraguay independiente* (1949); and PAUL H. LEWIS, *Socialism, Liberalism, and Dictatorship in Paraguay* (1982). The best bibliography is DAVID LEWIS JONES, *Paraguay, A Bibliography* (1979). HENRY D. CEUPPENS, *Paraguay año 2000* (1971), is accurate and perceptive. JOSEPH PINCUS, *The Economy of Paraguay* (1968), is the best general survey in English. GEORGE PENDLE, *Paraguay: A Riverside Nation*, 3rd ed. (1967), is brief but informative. For agriculture, see ADLAI F. ARNOLD, *Foundations of an Agricultural Policy in Paraguay* (1971); and CARLOS PASTORE, *La lucha por la tierra en el Paraguay*, 2nd ed. (1972). The best work on General Stroessner is PAUL H. LEWIS, *Paraguay under Stroessner* (1980). For social conditions and culture, see PAN AMERICAN UNION, *Paraguay* (1965); and CARLOS R. CENTURIÓN, *Historia de la cultura paraguaya*, 2 vol. (1961). *Revista paraguaya de sociología* (triennial) is indispensable.

History: General treatments include EFRAÍM CARDOZO, *El Paraguay independiente* (1949) and *Breve historia del Paraguay* (1965); CARLOS R. CENTURIÓN, *Historia de la cultura paraguaya* (1961); and HARRIS G. WARREN, *Paraguay: An Informal History* (1949), with a useful bibliography. The best treatment of the independence epoch is FULGENCIO R. MORENO, *Estudio sobre la independencia del Paraguay* (1911). Also useful is RAFAEL ELADIO VELAZQUEZ, *El Paraguay en 1811* (1965). On the Francia period see JULIO CESAR CHAVES, *El supremo dictador*, 4th ed. (1964), and JOHN HOYT WILLIAMS, *The Rise and Fall of the Paraguayan Republic, 1800–1870* (1979), which also deals with the two Lópezes. The first López and his modernization of Paraguay are well handled in JUAN F. PEREZ ACOSTA, *Carlos Antonio López, obrero máximo, labor administrativa y constructiva* (1948); and JULIO CESAR CHAVES, *El Presidente López*, 2nd. ed. (1968), permits a glimpse of a remarkable man. The War of the Triple Alliance is treated in EFRAÍM CARDOZO, *Vísperas de la guerra del Paraguay* (1954), and his day-by-day chronicle of the war years, *Hace cien años* (1964–73); AUGUSTO TASSO FRAGOSO, *História da guerra entre a Tríplice aliança e o Paraguai* (1934), a five-volume account; and HARRIS G. WARREN, *Paraguay and the Triple Alliance: The Postwar Decade, 1869–1878* (1978). For the postwar era, see JOSE RODRIGUEZ ALCALA, *El Paraguay moderno* (1915); and HIPOLITO SANCHEZ QUELL, *El caricaturista Miguel Acevedo y su época* (1974). Coverage of the Chaco War can be found in DAVID H. ZOOK, JR., *The Conduct of the Chaco War* (1960); and ROBERTO QUEREJAZU CALVO, *Masamaclay* (1965).

(J.H.Wi./J.P.P./H.G.W.)

Paris

Paris is the capital of France and one of Europe's largest conurbations. The city was founded more than 2,000 years ago on an island in the Seine River, some 233 miles (375 kilometres) upstream from the river's mouth on the English Channel. The modern city has spread from the island (the Île de la Cité) and far beyond both banks of the Seine. The City of Paris itself covers an area of 41 square miles (105 square kilometres); the Greater Paris conurbation, formed of suburbs and other built-up areas, extends around it in all directions to cover approximately 890 square miles. Paris occupies a central position in the rich agricultural region known as the Paris Basin, and it constitutes one of eight *départements* of the Île-de-France administrative region.

This article is divided into the following sections:

Physical and human geography

CHARACTER OF THE CITY

For centuries Paris has been one of the world's most important and attractive cities. It is appreciated for the opportunities it offers for business and commerce, for study, for culture, and for entertainment: its gastronomy, haute couture, painting, literature, and intellectual community especially enjoy an enviable reputation. Its sobriquet "the City of Light" (la Ville Lumière), earned during the Enlightenment, remains appropriate, for Paris has retained its importance as a centre for education and intellectual pursuits.

Paris' site at a crossroads of both water and land routes significant to Europe as well as to France has had a continuing influence on its growth. Under Roman administration, in the 1st century BC, the original site on the Île de la Cité was designated the capital of the Parisii tribe and territory. The Frankish king Clovis took Paris from the Gauls by AD 494 and later made his capital there. Under Hugh Capet (ruled 987–996) and the Capetian dynasty the preeminence of Paris was firmly established, and Paris became the political and cultural hub as modern France took shape. France has long been a highly centralized country, and Paris has come to be identified with a powerful central state, drawing to itself much of the talent and vitality of the provinces.

The three main parts of historical Paris are defined by the Seine. At its centre is the Île de la Cité, which is the seat of religious and temporal authority (the word *cité* connotes the nucleus of the ancient city). The Seine's left bank (*rive gauche*) has traditionally been the seat of intellectual life; and its right bank (*rive droite*) contains the heart of the city's economic life, but the distinctions have become blurred in recent decades. The fusion of all these functions at the centre of France and, later, at the centre of an empire, resulted in a tremendously vital environment. In this environment, however, the emotional and intellectual climate that was created by contending powers often set the stage for great violence in both the social and political arenas (the years 1358, 1382, 1588, 1648, 1789, 1830, 1848, and 1870 being notable for such events).

In its centuries of growth Paris has for the most part retained the circular shape of the early city. Its boundaries have spread outward to engulf the surrounding towns (*bourgs*), usually built around monasteries or churches and often the site of a market. From the mid-14th to the mid-16th century the city's growth was mainly eastward; since then it has been westward. It comprises 20 *arrondissements* (municipal districts), each of which has its own mayor, town hall, and particular features. The numbering begins in the heart of Paris and continues in the spiraling shape of a snail shell, ending to the far east. Parisians refer to the *arrondissements* by number as the first (*premier*), second (*deuxième*), third (*troisième*), and so on. Adaptation to the problems of urbanization, such as immigration, housing, social infrastructure, public utilities, suburban development, and zoning, has produced the vast urban agglomeration.   (Ed.)

THE LANDSCAPE

The city site: Paris and its river. Paris' city proper is small; no corner is farther than six miles from the square in front of Notre-Dame cathedral. The city occupies a depression hollowed out by the Seine, and the surrounding heights have been respected as the limits of the city. Elevation varies from 430 feet (130 metres) at Montmartre to 85 feet at Grenelle. The river flows for eight miles through the centre of the city and 10 of the 20 *arrondissements*. It enters the city at the southeast corner, flows northwestward, and turns gradually southwestward, eventually leaving Paris at the southwest corner. As a result, what starts out as the stream's east bank becomes its north bank and ends as the west bank, and the Parisians

The Eiffel Tower, from the Centre Beaubourg on the Right Bank, looking westward over the rooftops of the city.

Nancy Cohen—Black Star

The river bank

therefore adopted the simple, unchanging designation of Right and Left Bank (when facing downstream). Specific places are usually indicated by *arrondissement* or by quarter (*quartier*).

At water level, some 30 feet below street level, the river is bordered—at least on those portions not transformed into expressways—by cobbled quays graced with trees and shrubs. From street level another line of trees leans toward the water. Between the two levels, the retaining walls, usually made of massive stone blocks, are decorated with the great iron rings once used to moor merchant vessels, and some are pierced by openings left by water gates for old palaces or inspection ports for subways, sewers, and underpasses. At intermittent points the walls are shawled in ivy.

The city is ringed with great forests of beech and oak; they are called the "lungs of Paris," for they help to purify the air in the heavily industrialized region. Paris' position at the centre of the Île-de-France region, bordered by the Seine, Oise, and Marne rivers, has long made it the dominant settlement.

Climate. In its location on the western side of Europe and in a plain relatively close to the sea, Paris benefits from the balmy influences of the Gulf Stream and has a fairly temperate climate. The weather can be very changeable, however, especially in winter and spring, when the wind can be sharp and cold. The annual average temperature is 53° F (12° C); the July average is about 67° F (19° C), and the January average is about 38° F (3° C).

The temperature drops below freezing about 35 days a year, and snow falls on an average of 15 days. Since the 1950s the city has taken measures to decrease air pollution, and a system of water purification has made tap water safe for drinking.

NEIGHBOURHOODS AND SIGHTS

Paris' many old buildings, monuments, gardens, plazas, boulevards, and bridges compose one of the world's grandest cityscapes. An impressive spot from which to view the city is the Chaillot Palace, which stands on a rise on the Right Bank of the Seine to the west, where the river begins its southwestward curve.

The Chaillot Palace. The Chaillot Palace dates from the International Exposition of 1937. It replaced the Trocadéro Palace, a structure left over from the 1878 International Exposition. The Chaillot Palace is made up of two separate pavilions, from each of which extends a curved wing. The Musée de l'Homme, the Naval Museum, the Museum of French Monuments, and the Cinema Museum are located there. Under the terrace that separates the two sections are two theatres, the National Theatre of Chaillot and a small hall that serves as one of the two motion-picture houses of the national film library.

The terrace, which is lined by statues, gives a splendid view across Paris. The slope descending to the river has been made into a terraced park, the centre of which is alive with fountains, cascades, and pools. The Trocadéro Aquarium is in a grotto a few steps away in the park.

From the bottom of the slope the five-arched Jena Bridge (Pont d'Iéna) leads across the river. It was built for Napoleon in 1813 to commemorate his victory at the Battle of Jena in 1806. On the Left Bank rises the Eiffel Tower, an unclad metal truss tower designed by Gustave Eiffel. The tower was built for the International Exposition of 1889, against the strident opposition of national figures who thought it unsafe or ugly or both. When the

The Eiffel Tower

exposition concession expired in 1909, the 984-foot (300-metre) tower was to have been demolished, but its value as an antenna for radio transmission saved it. Additions made for television transmission have added 56 feet to the height. From the topmost of the three platforms the view extends for more than 40 miles.

From the two-acre base of the tower the Champ-de-Mars ("Field of Mars"), an immense field, stretches to

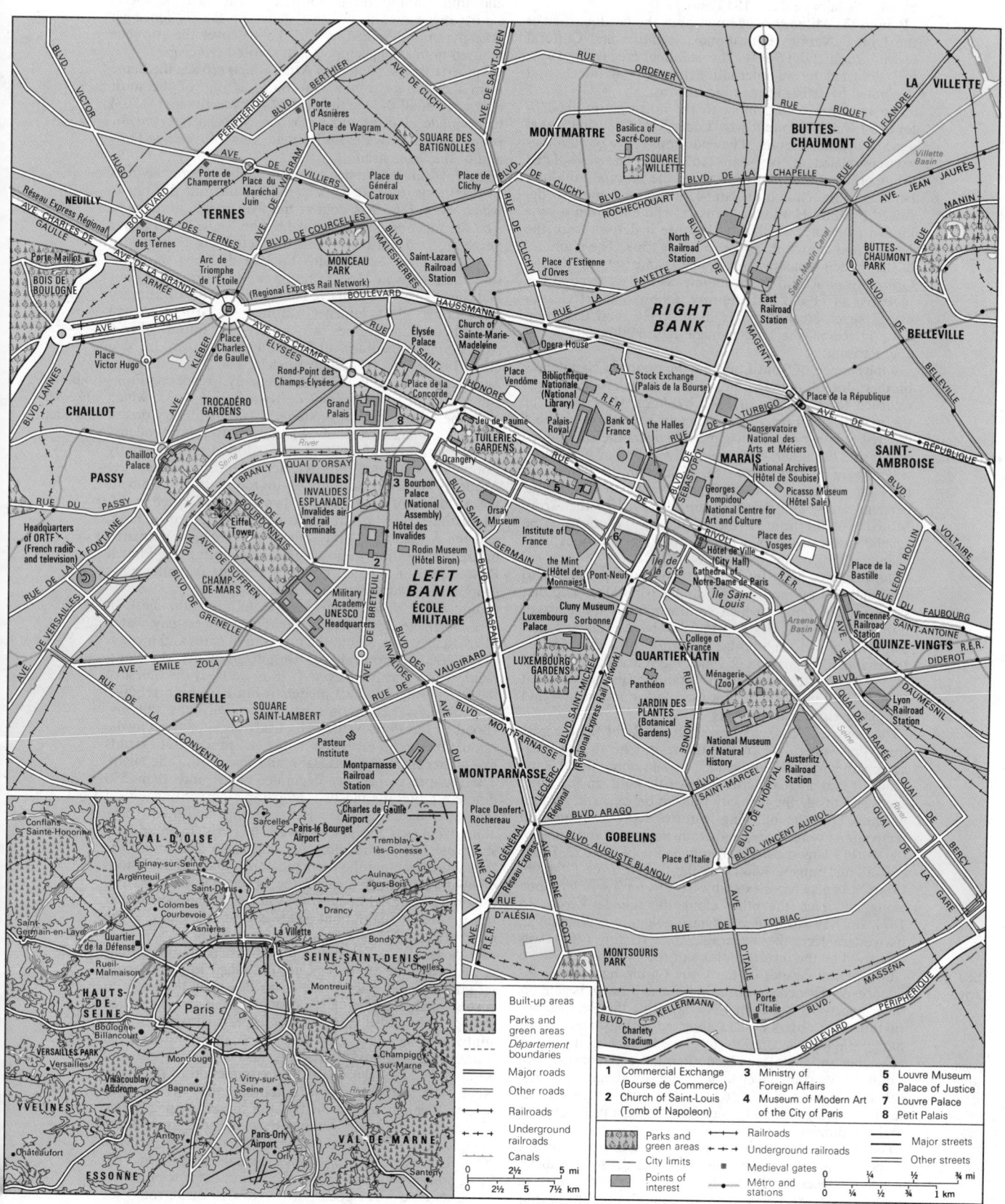

The city of Paris and (inset) its metropolitan area.

1 Commercial Exchange (Bourse de Commerce)
2 Church of Saint-Louis (Tomb of Napoleon)
3 Ministry of Foreign Affairs
4 Museum of Modern Art of the City of Paris
5 Louvre Museum
6 Palace of Justice
7 Louvre Palace
8 Petit Palais

the Military Academy (École Militaire), which was built from 1769 to 1772 and is still used by the War College (École Supérieure de Guerre). The Champ-de-Mars, which originally served as the school's parade ground, was the scene of two vast rallies during the French Revolution: that of the Federation (1790) and that of the Supreme Being (1794). From 1798 there were annual national expositions of crafts and manufactures, which were followed by world's fairs between 1855 and 1900.

Behind the Military Academy stands the headquarters of the United Nations Educational, Scientific and Cultural Organization (UNESCO). The building, erected in 1958, was designed by an international trio of architects and decorated by artists of member nations.

The Invalides. One street to the northeast is the Hôtel des Invalides, founded by Louis XIV to shelter 7,000 aged or invalid veterans. The enormous range of buildings was completed in five years (1671–76). The gold-plated dome (1675–1706) that rises above the hospital buildings belongs to the church of Saint-Louis. The dome was designed by Jules Hardouin-Mansart, who employed a style known in France as "Jesuit" because it derives from the Jesuits' first church in Rome, built in 1568. The churches of the French Academy (Académie Française), the Val-de-Grâce Hospital, and the Sorbonne, as well as three others in Paris, all of the 17th century, followed this style. By using the classical elements more freely than had been done in Rome, the French made it something recognizably Parisian.

In the chapels of Saint-Louis are the tombs of Napoleon's brothers Joseph and Jérôme, of his son (whose body was returned from Vienna in 1940 by Adolf Hitler), and of the marshals of France. Immediately beneath the cupola is a red porphyry sarcophagus that covers the six coffins, one inside the other, enclosing the remains of Napoleon, which were returned from St. Helena in 1840 through the efforts of King Louis-Philippe. Napoleon's uniforms, personal arms, and deathbed are displayed in the Army Museum at the front of the Invalides. A portion of the Invalides still serves as a military hospital; facilities have been modernized since World War II.

Napoleon's tomb

The vast, tree-lined Invalides Esplanade slopes gently to the Quai d'Orsay and the Alexandre III Bridge. The first stone for the bridge, which commemorates the Russian tsar Alexander III, was laid in 1897 by Alexander's son, Tsar Nicholas II. The bridge was finished in time for the International Exposition of 1900, and it leads to two other souvenirs of that year's fair, the Grand Palais and the Petit Palais. The buildings are still used for annual shows and for major visiting art exhibits.

The Louvre. Vikings camped on the Right Bank across from the western tip of the Île de la Cité in their unsuccessful siege of Paris in 885, and in about 1200 King Philip II had a square crusader's castle built on the same site, just outside the new city wall, to buttress the western defenses. Over the following centuries many additions and renovations were made, and from the castle grew one of the world's largest palaces, completed only in 1852. From the original square, known as the Cour Carrée ("Square Court"), two galleries extend westward for 1,640 feet, one along the river, the other along the rue de Rivoli. In 1871, only 19 years after the huge oblong was completed, its western face, the Tuileries Palace (begun 1563), was destroyed by the insurrectionists of the Commune.

The Cour Carrée

Two of the facades of the Cour Carrée had strong influence on French architecture. Pierre Lescot began his inner courtyard facade in 1546, adapting the Renaissance rhythms and orders he had observed in Italy and adding purely French decoration to the classical motifs. The physician and architect Claude Perrault collaborated with Louis Le Vau, architect to the king, to design the outer east face of the palace in 1673. It, too, employs classic elements, making especially graceful use of coupled columns and a pediment.

The Louvre Museum occupies the four sides of the palace around the Cour Carrée as well as the south gallery, which stretches along the river. Among the treasures of the museum are the Victory of Samothrace, the Venus de Milo, and the Mona Lisa. The enormous collections contain works from the 7th century BC to the mid-19th century, with a huge cultural and geographic spread. The north gallery, along the rue de Rivoli, houses a separate museum, the Museum of Decorative Arts, as well as the Ministry of Finance.

Extensive remodeling has been undertaken throughout the Louvre to increase space for art works. Construction began in the early 1980s to create a new main entrance and underground reception hall in the vast Napoleon Courtyard, between the two galleries; the 70-foot-high glass pyramid designed by I.M. Pei to cover the entrance aroused both strong support and spirited criticism.

The Arts Bridge (Pont des Arts), which crosses the Seine from the Louvre to the Left Bank, is one of the most charming of all the Parisian bridges. It was the first (1803) to be made of iron, and it has always been reserved for pedestrians: it provides an intimate view of riverside Paris and of the Seine itself.

The Institute of France. At the point where the Arts Bridge meets the Left Bank stands the Institute of France, which since 1806 has housed the five French academies. The site was originally occupied by the Nesle Tower (Tour de Nesle), a defense work for the Left Bank terminus of the city wall of 1220. Louis Le Vau designed the additional buildings in 1663 to house the College of the Four Nations (Collège des Quatre-Nations), paid for by a legacy from Louis XIV's minister Cardinal Mazarin, who had brought the four entities in question—Piedmont, Alsace, Artois, and Roussillon—under the French crown. Le Vau based his designs on Italian models. The five contemporary academies are the French Academy (Académie Française), founded by Cardinal de Richelieu in 1635, which edits the official French dictionary, awards literary prizes, and has a membership of "40 Immortals"; the Academy of Inscriptions and Belles Lettres, founded in 1663 by Louis XIV's finance minister, Jean-Baptiste Colbert; the Academy of Sciences, founded in 1666, also by Colbert; the Academy of the Fine Arts, two sections formed at different times by Mazarin and Colbert and joined in 1795; and the Academy of Ethics and Political Science, created by the Convention (a governing body during the French Revolution) in 1795 to ponder questions of philosophy, economics, politics, law, and history.

The French Academy

Almost next door is the Mint (Hôtel des Monnaies). In this sober late 18th-century building visitors may watch coins being struck and tour a museum of coins and medals.

Pont-Neuf (New Bridge). Despite its name, the Pont-Neuf, which was built from 1578 to 1604, is the oldest of the Paris bridges (others predate it but have been rebuilt). Its sturdiness has become axiomatic: Parisians still say, "Solid as the Pont-Neuf." The bridge is supported in the middle by the tip of the Île de la Cité, to which it extends five arches from the Left Bank and seven from the Right. The parapet corbels are decorated with more than 250 different grotesque masks. The parapet curves out toward the water at each bridge pier, forming half-moon bays along what was the first sidewalk in Paris; in these bays street vendors set up shop. For 200 years this bridge was the main street and the perpetual fair of Paris. The custom of holding summer fairs on the bridge has been revived to some extent. Although the structure undergoes regular repair, in the main Pont-Neuf as it exists today is the original bridge.

Île de la Cité. Downstream and just below the bridge is the tip of the Île de la Cité, fashioned into a triangular gravel-pathed park bordered by flowering bushes, with rustic benches under the ancient trees. It is surrounded by a wide cobbled quay that is especially popular with sunbathers and lovers. Where the steps come onto the bridge from the park there is a bronze equestrian statue of King Henry IV, who insisted on completion of the Pont-Neuf. The statue is an 1818 reproduction of the 1614 original, which was the first statue to stand on a public way in Paris. Opposite is the narrow entrance to the Place Dauphine (1607), named for Henry's heir, the future Louis XIII. The *place* was formerly a triangle of uniform red-brick houses pointed in white stone, but the row of houses along its base was ripped out in 1871 to make room for construction of part of the Palace of Justice.

Île de la Cité and Île Saint-Louis, on the Seine River at the heart of Paris.
By courtesy of the French Government Tourist Office

The ship-shaped Île de la Cité is 10 streets long and five wide. Eight bridges link it to the riverbanks and a ninth leads to the scow-shaped Île Saint-Louis, which lies to the southeast.

The palace of the early Roman governor (now the Palace of Justice) was rebuilt on the same site by Louis IX (St. Louis) in the 13th century and enlarged 100 years later by Philip IV the Fair, who added the grim, gray-turreted Conciergerie, with its impressive Gothic chambers. The Great Hall, which, under the kings, was the meeting place of the Parlement (the high court of justice), was known throughout Europe for its Gothic beauty. Fires in 1618 and 1871 destroyed much of the original room, however, and most of the rest of the palace was devastated by flames in 1776. The Great Hall now serves as a waiting room for the courts, in one of which, the adjoining first Civil Chamber, the Revolutionary Tribunal sat from 1793, condemning 2,600 persons to the guillotine. After sentencing, the victims were taken back down the stone stairs to the dungeons of the Conciergerie to await the tumbrils. The Conciergerie still stands and is open to visitors.

In the palace courtyards is found one of the great monuments of France, the 13th-century Sainte-Chapelle ("Holy Chapel"). Built at Louis IX's direction between 1243 and 1248, it is a masterpiece of Gothic Rayonnant style. With great daring, the architect (possibly Pierre de Montreuil) poised his vaulted ceilings on a trellis of slender columns, the walls between being made of stained glass. The exquisite chapel was designed to hold the Crown of Thorns, thought to be the very one worn by Jesus at his crucifixion. Louis IX had purchased the relic from the Venetians, who held it in pawn from Baldwin, the Latin king of Byzantium. Other holy relics, such as nails and pieces of wood from the True Cross, were added to the chapel's collection, the remnants of which are now in the treasury of Notre-Dame.

Under King Louis-Philippe (1830–48), the "sanitization"

of the island was begun, and it was continued for his successor, Napoleon III, by Baron Georges Haussmann. The project involved a mass clearing of antiquated structures, widening of streets and squares, and the erection of massive new government offices, including parts of the Palace of Justice. The portion of the palace that borders the Quai des Orfèvres—formerly the goldsmiths' and silversmiths' quay—became the headquarters of the Paris municipal detective force, the Police Judiciaire ("Judicial Police"), which keeps a small museum on the fourth floor.

Across the boulevard du Palais is the Police Prefecture, another 19th-century structure. On the far side of the prefecture is the Place du Parvis-Notre-Dame, an open space enlarged six times by Haussmann, who also moved the Hôtel-Dieu, the first hospital in Paris, from the riverside to the inland side of the square. Its present buildings date from 1868.

Notre-Dame de Paris. At the east end of the square is the cathedral of Notre-Dame de Paris, which is situated on a spot that Parisians have always reserved to the practice of religious rites. The Gallo-Roman boatmen of the *cité* erected their altar to Jupiter there (it is now in the Cluny Museum), and, when Christianity was established, a church was built on the temple site. The first bishop of Paris, St. Denis, became its patron saint. The red in the colours of Paris represents the blood of this martyr who, in popular legend, after decapitation, picked up his head and walked.

When Maurice de Sully became bishop in 1159 he decided to replace the decrepit cathedral of Saint-Étienne and the 6th-century Notre-Dame with a church in the new Gothic style. The style was conceived in France, and a new structural development, the flying buttress, which added to the beauty of the exterior and permitted interior columns to soar to new heights, was introduced in the building of Notre-Dame. Construction began in 1163 and continued until 1345.

After being damaged during the French Revolution, the church was sold at auction to a building-materials merchant. Napoleon came to power in time to annul the sale, and he ordered that the edifice be redecorated for his coronation as emperor in 1804. Louis-Philippe later initiated restoration of the neglected church. The architect Eugène Viollet-le-Duc worked from 1845 to 1864 to restore the monument. Like all cathedrals in France, Notre-Dame is the property of the state, although its operation as a religious institution is left entirely to the Roman Catholic Church.

Restoration of Notre-Dame

A few 16th- and 17th-century buildings survive north of the cathedral. They are what remains of the Cloister of the Cathedral Chapter, whose school was famous long before the new cathedral was built. Early in the 12th century, one of its theologians, Peter Abelard, left the cloister with his disciples, crossed to the Left Bank, and set up an independent school in the open air in the Convent of the Paraclete near the present Place Maubert. After a prolonged struggle with the monks of Saint-Denis the followers of Abelard in 1200 won the right, from both the king and the pope, to form and govern their own community. This was the beginning of the University of Paris.

City walls. After the Roman town on the Left Bank was sacked by barbarians in the 3rd century AD, the fire-blackened stones were freighted across to the Île de la Cité, where a defensive wall was constructed. Neglected in times of peace, it was rebuilt several times over the course of the centuries. The earliest of the bridges to the Left Bank, the Petit Pont (which has been rebuilt several times), was guarded by a fortified gate, the Petit Châtelet, and the bridge to the Right Bank, the Pont au Change, was guarded by the Grand Châtelet, which served as a fort, prison, torture chamber, and morgue until it was demolished in 1801.

From 1180 to 1225 Philip II built a new wall that protected the settlements on both banks. In 1367–70 the Right Bank enclosure was enlarged by Charles V, with the massive Bastille protecting the eastern approaches as the Louvre protected the west. In 1670 Louis XIV had the Charles V extensions transformed into the tree-planted Grands Boulevards, embellished at the Saint-Denis Gate (Porte Saint-Denis) and the Saint-Antoine Gate (Porte Saint-Antoine) with triumphal arches that still stand. (The word *boulevard*, related to "bulwark," originally was a military engineering term for the platform of a defensive wall.)

A century later a new wall was begun. The wall was built with 57 tollhouses to enable the farmers-general, a company of tax "farmers," or collectors, to collect customs duties on goods entering Paris. The tollhouses are still standing at Place Denfert-Rochereau.

The last wall, built by Adolphe Thiers for Louis-Philippe, was a genuine military installation with outlying forts. By the time it was finished it enclosed a number of hamlets outside Paris, among them Auteuil, Passy, Montmartre, La Villette, and Belleville. Post-Revolutionary rebuilding and post-Napoleonic economic recovery, with expansion of employment because of the Industrial Revolution, drew more and more people to Paris, and—as railways developed—with ever-increasing facility. Between 1852 and 1870 Haussmann razed the walls of the farmers-general and built the outer boulevards. The 1845 walls were finally knocked down, and the boulevards were extended in 1925.

The last wall

Île Saint-Louis. In 1627 Louis XIII granted a 60-year lease on two mudbanks behind the Île de la Cité to a contractor, Christophe Marie, and two financiers. It was 37 years before Marie was able to unite the islets, dike the circumference, lay out a central avenue with 10 lateral streets, and rent space to householders. The church of Saint-Louis-en-l'Île was begun the same year, 1664, but one of the finest houses, by Louis Le Vau, had been completed as early as 1640. Another, the Hôtel de Lauzun, a few yards upstream on the Quai d'Anjou, was completed in 1657. The Marie Bridge to the Right Bank, which was completed as part of the contract, is the original span, although it has been modified for modern traffic. The Île Saint-Louis constitutes a tranquil neighbourhood in the centre of the busy city.

The Bastille. The road off the upper end of the Île Saint-Louis leads to the Place de la Bastille on the Right Bank. From the river to the *place* runs a canal, the Arsenal Basin, which formerly supplied water to the moat around the Bastille. At the Place de la Bastille the waterway goes underground for almost a mile, then emerges to form the Saint-Martin Canal, which, with its bridges and locks, and its barges sailing slowly down the centre of city streets, constitutes one of the least known and most picturesque sections of Paris.

The capture of the Bastille on July 14, 1789, was a symbolic blow at tyranny rather than an act of liberation for tyranny's victims. The prison, which had been virtually unused for years and was scheduled for demolition by the monarchy, held on that day only four counterfeiters, two madmen, and a young aristocrat who had displeased his father. The fortress was demolished after its capture.

Napoleon had the *place* laid out in 1803. A railway station was built there in 1859 and was razed in 1984 to allow construction of a new opera house (begun two years later).

The neighbourhood between the Bastille and the Place de la Nation, eastward along the rue du Faubourg Saint-Antoine, has been one of skilled craftsmen since the mid-15th century, when the self-governing royal abbey gave space within its wide domains to those cabinetmakers who refused to abide by the restrictions of Paris guilds as to styles and types of wood to be used. This neighbourhood was always among the first to revolt when revolution was in the air and was noted for the speed with which it raised barricades of impressive height. The character of the area has changed, however, as most of the small workshops have closed.

The Marais. To the west of the Bastille lies a triangular area with its base along the river up to the Hôtel de Ville (City Hall) and its apex just short of the Place de la République to the north. It keeps its name—*le marais* ("the marsh")—from the Middle Ages, and, because it became the market garden of Paris, it gave its name to all market gardens in France (*culture maraîchère*). Extension of the city walls along the Right Bank led to diking of the shore and drainage of the soil. In 1107 the Knights Templar established their Paris Temple, a vast fortified enclosure, at the top of the triangle. In 1360 Charles V moved into his new royal residence in the lower right-hand corner, where the rue des Lions marks the former location of the menageries.

Charles VII preferred to live just behind the Bastille, in the Hôtel des Tournelles, which Henry II had enlarged and beautified by Philibert Delorme in 1550. Great nobles, such as the dukes of Guise and Lorraine, followed the King and had palaces built in the vicinity. When Henry II was killed in a joust on the rue Saint-Antoine in 1559, his widow, Catherine de Médicis, had the Tournelles razed. On the site in 1607 construction began on the first residential square to be designed in Paris. Henry IV had it built and reserved a house there for himself. The three-story houses are made of red brick with white-stone quoins (solid-corner angles) and window surrounds, and the ground floors form arcades over the sidewalks. The square was named Place Royale, but since 1800 it has been called Place des Vosges. Another wave of building by the rich, anxious to be close to a royal project, endowed the Marais with 200 more private palaces.

The first residential square

In 1792 the Knights Hospitaller of St. John of Jerusalem (also known as the Knights of Malta) were turned out of the Temple, which had been given to them in 1313 when the Templar order was dissolved. On Aug. 13, 1792, the royal family was incarcerated in the Temple's tower keep; the King was taken off to his death on Jan. 21, 1793, and the Queen was removed to the Conciergerie on August 2 (and executed on October 16). The Temple's tower was leveled in 1808 to discourage rallies there by royalists.

After the 17th-century construction boom the Marais remained virtually untouched. Three-quarters of the buildings there date from before 1870. Toward the end of the 19th century, while some of the oldest and most imposing of the palaces were being demolished by private developers, other owners managed to restore a few mansions, and the nation and the municipality also restored a handful of fine buildings. Many Jewish refugees from eastern Europe settled in the district. Scores of fine houses were subdivided into tiny apartments to profit from the poverty-stricken newcomers, and workshops were installed on the lower floors and in courtyard sheds. Through centuries of neglect the Marais became one of the worst slums in Paris.

In 1969 the Municipal Council approved an urban renewal scheme for ending slum conditions while preserving the workaday life and animation and restoring the undeniable beauty of the quarter. The scheme has been very successful, and property prices in the Marais have soared.

Among the restored ancient buildings open to the public are the Museum of the History of Paris (Musée Carnavalet), built in 1545 and enlarged by François Mansart in 1645; the Museum of the History of France (National Archives, Hôtel de Soubise), parts of which date from 1375, 1553, and 1704–15; the Museum of Nature and the Hunt (Fondation Somer, Hôtel Guénégaud), built by François Mansart in 1648–51; the National Bureau of Historic Monuments (Caisse Nationale des Monuments Historiques, Hôtel de Sully) by Jean I Androuet du Cerceau; and the Picasso Museum (Hôtel Salé).

Closer to the Hôtel de Ville is the Gothic Hôtel de Sens, built at the end of the 15th century for the bishops of Sens, then also bishops of Paris. It was restored after 40 years of work and now serves as a city library of specialized collections. Nearby, behind facades of a much later date, two half-timbered medieval houses have been uncovered. In the Marais, portions of the 13th-century city wall, including one of the watchtowers, are still to be seen.

Hôtel de Ville. Three city halls have stood on this site, each grander than its predecessor. The present building (1874–82) replaces the Renaissance structure that was in use from the 16th century until it was burned by the insurrectionary Communards in 1871. The first was the House of Pillars (Maison aux Piliers), used by the municipality from 1357 to 1533. The present building contains the official apartments of the mayor of Paris.

The massacre of thousands of Protestants on St. Bartholomew's Day, 1572; the Day of the Barricades, May 12, 1588, when the Catholic League drove Henry III out of Paris; and the civil war known as the Fronde, 1648–53, all involved the Paris masses, but they were palace revolutions rather than popular uprisings. When the people rose in their own cause, the focus of their action was inevitably the Hôtel de Ville, as was indeed the case in 1789, 1830, 1848, 1871, and 1944.

In July 1789, for example, after killing the provost, the revolutionary mob took the Hôtel de Ville as it had already taken the Invalides and the Bastille. Three days later Louis XVI appeared on the balcony, wearing the tricolour cockade (royal white added to municipal red and blue), and was cheered by the crowd. Four years later the building was taken as headquarters for the Commune, which directed mob action to control the Convention. On 9 Thermidor, year II (July 27, 1794), the Convention's guards entered the Hôtel de Ville and seized Robespierre and his Communards; all were executed soon after.

In August 1830 Louis-Philippe appeared on the balcony and was acclaimed by the revolutionary crowd. The name of the square was changed in that year to Place de l'Hôtel de Ville. As the Place de Grève (*grève* meaning "strand," or "bank") it had been the principal port of Paris for centuries. (The refusal of boatmen to put out gave the French worker the phrase for going on strike: *faire la grève.*) From 1310 to 1832 it was Paris' principal place of execution.

In 1871, after Napoleon III's defeat at Sedan, a new republic was declared from the steps of the Hôtel de Ville, but, when the national government, in its turn, capitulated, Parisians refused to accept defeat and in March formed the Commune of Paris. In May troops of the government entered the town and fought sharp engagements with the Communards, who set fire to the Hôtel de Ville, the Tuileries Palace, the Palace of Justice, the Police Prefecture, the Arsenal, and other government buildings. The Communards executed 67 hostages, including the archbishop of Paris. The government subsequently rounded up and executed 20,000 Parisians, shipping thousands of others to penal colonies.

In 1944, as the city was being liberated from German occupation, the National Council of Resistance made the Hôtel de Ville its headquarters. At the climax of the Liberation General Charles de Gaulle appeared on the balcony and was acclaimed by the crowd.

The Halles. On the rue de Rivoli westward from the Hôtel de Ville is the Saint-Jacques bell tower (Tour Saint-Jacques), all that remains of a church in the Flamboyant Gothic style that was torn down in 1797. A few streets farther northwest toward the Louvre is the quarter of the Halles, from 1183 to 1969 the central market of Paris. When the markets moved out to a new location at Rungis, near Orly, the distinctive 19th-century iron-and-glass market halls—10 originals designed by Victor Baltard and built between 1854 and 1866, and two 1936 reproductions—and their neighbourhood were designated for renewal. The renewal projects were delayed for several years, however, by bitter disagreements over how the area—which had been thought of as the heart of Paris—should be used. The old market halls were used temporarily for exhibitions and cultural events, but in 1971 they were torn down. Their demolition left an enormous hole in the ground that became a symbol to many Parisians of the end of an era. Construction at the site began in 1971, and in 1977 a station linking the city's subway system (the Métro) with the regional express system was opened. The Forum des Halles, a partly subterranean, multistoried commercial and shopping centre, was opened in 1979. The nearby streets were converted to a traffic-free zone for pedestrians, and a small formal garden was laid out.

A few of the neighbourhood's old houses have been renovated or restored to keep some of the old flavour, but many buildings have been demolished and the area has been largely transformed. Many of its poorer residents were forced to move as renovation and improvement made the neighbourhood unaffordable. The church of Saint-Eustache (1532–1637) remains, as does the circular Grain Exchange (Halle au Blé; 1811–13), which was burned by the Commune and restored in the 1880s as the Commercial Exchange (Bourse de Commerce).

Another development in the area is the Georges Pompidou National Centre for Art and Culture, popularly called Centre Beaubourg, a vast glass-and-metal structure of distinctive design inaugurated in 1977. It soon proved its popularity and remains a successful attraction for Parisians and tourists alike. The centre houses the National Museum of Modern Art, temporary exhibits, the multimedia Public Information Library, the Industrial Design Centre, the Institute for Acoustic and Musical Research, and workshops for children.

Rue de Rivoli. The Louvre and the Tuileries Gardens take up the south side of this street, and on the other side runs an arcade more than a mile long. Opposite the middle of the Louvre, the Place du Palais-Royal leads to the palace of Cardinal de Richelieu, which he willed to the royal family. Louis XIV lived there as a child, and during the minority of Louis XV the kingdom was ruled from there by the debauched but gifted regent Philippe II, duc d'Orléans from 1715 to 1723. Late in the 18th century Louis-Philippe d'Orléans, who was popularly renamed Philippe-Egalité during the Revolution for his radical opinions, undertook extensive building around the palace garden. It was a commercial operation, and the Prince hoped to pay his debts from the property rents. Around the garden he built a beautiful oblong of colonnaded galleries and at each end of the gallery farthest from his residence a theatre. The larger playhouse has been the home of the Comédie-Française, the state theatre company, since Napoleon's reign. The princely apartments now shelter high state bodies such as the Council of State.

Just behind the courtyard is the Bibliothèque Nationale (National Library), the national library of deposit, with an enormous collection of books and prints.

Haussmann greatly enlarged the Place du Palais-Royal in 1852, and he was careful to preserve the palace when he laid out the avenue de l'Opéra. At the top of the avenue, where the Grands Boulevards crossed an enormous new *place,* the new opera house was built from 1825 to 1898. The Paris Opera House, a splendid monument

The markets of the Halles

The Hôtel de Ville as a centre of revolution

Garnier's Opera

Portion of the multistoried Forum des Halles commercial and shopping centre, with glass-enclosed subterranean stories, a café and carousel at street level, and an elevated promenade.

Nancy Cohen—Black Star

to the Second Empire, was designed in the neo-Baroque style by Charles Garnier. It is known especially for its decorative embellishments, chief among them the Grand Staircase. Just behind the Opera House are various large department stores.

The next *place* along the rue de Rivoli is the Place des Pyramides. The gilded equestrian statue of Joan of Arc stands not far from where she was wounded at the Saint-Honoré Gate (Porte Saint-Honoré) in her unsuccessful attack on Paris (at that time held by the English), on Sept. 8, 1429.

Farther along toward the Place de la Concorde the rue de Castiglione leads to the Place Vendôme, an elegant octagonal *place,* little changed from the 1698 designs of Jules Hardouin-Mansart. In the centre, the Vendôme Column bears a statue of Napoleon. It was pulled down during the Commune and put back up under the Third Republic (1871–1940). The *place* and the rue de la Paix have lost none of their discreet distinction, nor have their shops.

The "Triumphal Way." From the Arc de Triomphe du Carrousel, in the courtyard between the open arms of the Louvre, extends one of the most remarkable perspectives to be seen in any modern city. It is sometimes called la Voie Triomphale ("the Triumphal Way"). From the middle of the Carrousel arch the line of sight runs the length of the Tuileries Gardens, lines up on the obelisk in the Place de la Concorde, and goes up the Champs-Élysées to the centre of the Arc de Triomphe and beyond to the skyscrapers of La Défense, in the western suburbs.

The Louvre's modest triumphal arch stands in the open space where costumed nobles performed in an equestrian display—*carrousel*—to celebrate the Dauphin's birth in 1662. The design of the arch, an imitation of that of the Arch of Septimius Severus in Rome, was conceived in 1808 by Charles Percier and Pierre Fontaine. The flanks of the Carrousel arch are incised with a record of Napoleon's victories.

The Tuileries Gardens, which fronted the Tuileries Palace (looted and burned in 1871 during the Commune), have not altered much since André Le Nôtre redesigned them in 1664. Le Nôtre was born and died in the gardener's

cottage in the Tuileries; he succeeded his father there as master gardener. His design carried the line of the central allée beyond the gardens and out into the countryside by tracing a path straight along the wooded hill west of the palace. On this hilltop, 170 years later, the Arc de Triomphe was erected.

At the western edge of the gardens, Napoleon III erected a hothouse, known as the Orangery, and the Jeu de Paume, an indoor court for court tennis. Both eventually were adapted as museums: the Orangery had a small permanent collection, including a group of 19 of Claude Monet's paintings of waterlilies displayed as panoramas. The Jeu de Paume housed the Louvre's collection of paintings by the Impressionists and their forerunners. The collections of the two museums—with the exception of the Monet panoramas—were moved to the Orsay Museum, which opened in 1986, and the Jeu de Paume and the Orangery were then reserved for occasional exhibitions.

The formal exit gate from the Tuileries is flanked by two winged horses (17th century), and the entrance to the Champs-Élysées across the square is similarly adorned, only by earthbound horses (18th century), both pairs having been removed in turn from the water trough at the Château de Marly.

The Place de la Concorde was designed as a moated octagon in 1755 by Jacques-Ange Gabriel. The river end was left open, and on the inland side two matching buildings were planned. The ground floor was arcaded and the facade was nimbly adapted from the Louvre colonnade, all with a refinement typical of the era. Although Gabriel built eight giant pedestals around the periphery of his *place,* they remained untenanted until Louis-Philippe gave them statues representing provincial capitals. Viewed clockwise starting from the Navy Ministry (Ministère de la Marine), the statues are Lille, Strasbourg, Lyon, Marseille, Bordeaux, Nantes, Brest, and Rouen. Louis-Philippe also had the Luxor Obelisk, a gift from Egypt, installed in the centre and flanked by two fountains. Later, the surrounding moat was filled in.

Louis XVI was decapitated near the statue of Brest on Jan. 21, 1793. Four months later the guillotine was erected

The
Tuileries
Gardens

near the gates of the Tuileries, and the executions continued there for nearly three years, accounting for a total of 1,343 deaths.

The Madeleine

Between the twin buildings on the northeastern side of the *place,* the broad rue Royale mounts to the Church of Sainte-Marie-Madeleine, consecrated in 1842. The church is a stern oblong, fenced with columns 60 feet high. Its design, supposedly that of a Greek temple, is actually closer to the Roman notion of Greek.

The Place de la Madeleine is the western terminus of the Grands Boulevards, which imitate the arch of the river from there north and east to the Place de la République and the Bastille. The glittering chic of the Grands Boulevards, which flavoured Paris life from 1750 to the 1880s, disappeared with the *boulevardiers,* but many of the boulevards' theatres and other entertainments survive. The state-run Opéra-Comique ("Comic Opera") stands fast just off the boulevard des Italiens, the wax museum survives on the boulevard Montmartre, and, a few doors away, the Théâtre des Variétés, founded under the Second Empire by the composer Jacques Offenbach, still operates. The Théâtre de la Renaissance, where the actor Benoît-Constant Coquelin created the role of Cyrano de Bergerac in 1897, remains on the boulevard Saint-Martin, as does the Théâtre de l'Ambigu, where Frédéric Lemaître, the celebrated actor in boulevard melodrama, thrilled all Paris in the mid-19th century. Some of the movie palaces of the 1930s also remain along the boulevards.

To the west off the rue Royale runs the rue du Faubourg Saint-Honoré, which, in addition to the British Embassy and the Élysée Palace (residence of the French president), has on its shop windows some of the most prestigious names in the Paris fashion trade.

Along the first 2,500 feet of the Champs-Élysées, between Concorde and the Rond-Point des Champs-Élysées (a roundabout, or traffic circle), little has changed for a century: the avenue is bordered with chestnut trees, behind which on both sides are gardens, usually full of children at play. The pavilions in the gardens are used as tearooms, restaurants, and theatres.

The Champs-Élysées today

From the Rond-Point up to the Arc de Triomphe, however, the avenue has changed with the times. Under the Second Empire this was a street of luxurious town houses. They were supplanted by cafés, nightclubs, luxury shops, and cinemas, but the street retained its feeling of luxury, and the tree-shaded sidewalks (wide as a normal street) offered promenades that were the pride of Paris. Since the 1950s, however, banks, automobile showrooms, airline offices, and fast-food eateries have taken over much of the space. Automobiles park on the sidewalks and in many places one rank of the double file of trees has been felled.

At the top of the Champs-Élysées is a circular *place* from which 12 imposing avenues radiate to form a star (*étoile*). It was called Place de l'Étoile from 1753 until 1970, when it was renamed Place Charles de Gaulle. In the centre of the *place* is the Arc de Triomphe, commissioned by Napoleon in 1806. It is twice as high and as wide as the Arch of Constantine, in Rome, which inspired it. Jean Chalgrin was the architect and François Rude sculpted the frieze and the spirited group, "The Departure of the Volunteers of 1792" (called "La Marseillaise"). On Armistice Day in 1920, the Unknown Soldier was buried under the centre of the arch, and each evening the flame of remembrance is rekindled by a different patriotic group.

In the 1970s the largest concentration of tall buildings in Europe arose some two miles beyond the arch, on the far side of the suburban wedge of Neuilly. The site, called the Quartier de la Défense, was formerly just a place on the road adjoined by the suburban municipalities of Puteaux, Courbevoie, and Nanterre. Today tall office buildings, heated and air conditioned from a central plant, are the hub of the complex. The "ground level" between buildings is a raised platform reserved to pedestrians, with roads and parking below. There are shops, restaurants, cafés, a shopping centre, hotels, and apartment houses. Before the project was begun, the state had already constructed at La Défense its National Centre for Industries and Technologies, a large exhibition hall. Nanterre became the site of a campus of the University of Paris in the 1960s, and specialized schools at the university level have been installed in the new centre: the National School of Architecture, the National School of Decorative Arts, the National Conservatory of Music, and the Institute of Advanced Cinematographic Studies. The three municipalities have benefited by the acquisition of low-rise public housing in park settings, a large park, day-care centres for children, and new schools.

Urban development at La Défense

Modern business quarters. As a counterbalance to the westward march of office buildings and as part of the effort to limit the obliteration of residential quarters around the business centre, five "poles of attraction" were instituted in other parts of Paris, beginning in the late 1960s. Two of these are directly on the waterfront at each end of Paris: Front de Seine ("Seine Waterfront") in the southwest corner, and Austerlitz-Bercy-Lyon in the southeast corner.

The Front de Seine is located on the Left Bank, between

Fountain and the Luxor Obelisk in the Place de la Concorde.

the Eiffel Tower and the southern city limits. A neighbourhood of factories and substandard housing has been replaced by a spread of 16 towers of 32 stories and four buildings 15 stories high. One-quarter of the space is used for offices and the rest for apartments, some of which are low-cost housing.

The project at the opposite end of the river straddles the Seine, with office buildings around the Austerlitz (Left Bank) and the Lyon (Right Bank) railroad stations. Bercy, which lies directly on the river on the Right Bank, was until this development one of the "secret cities" of Paris. This was the village of vintages, where merchants stored and sold their stocks of wine. Fenced and guarded, its chalets lined cobbled lanes named for the great vineyard districts of France. The great oaks, it was said, flourished because their roots were soaked in wine. The Bercy area is being redeveloped on a large scale, with many large office blocks and a new sports and leisure centre.

Modernization at Bercy

The "Italian sector," near the Place d'Italie in the south of Paris, between the centre and Orly Airport, underwent an extensive renovation during the 1970s. Some 9,000 timeworn dwellings were demolished and replaced by 13,000 new ones capable of housing 45,000 persons. A cultural centre was built, and new green spaces and a sports ground were provided.

The planning achievement that overshadows the others is Maine–Montparnasse, where the centrepiece of the composition is a 56-story office tower on the site of the old Montparnasse railway station. A more compact station has been built one street away on the avenue du Maine, where the rails are hidden on three sides by three buildings 15 to 18 stories high. The units are joined by a raised platform that serves as a "ground level" above the street.

The ministry quarter. The government, both local and national, occupies a vast amount of Paris' office space. The seventh *arrondissement,* a district on the Left Bank that runs along the river from the Eiffel Tower to the Carrousel Bridge, is known as the ministry quarter. Most of the ministries are located there along with the headquarters of the Île-de-France Region and the National Assembly. The *arrondissement* is the old Faubourg Saint-Germain, an impeccable address since the early 18th century. As such, it was subject to heavy expropriation during the Revolution, and ministries are lodged mostly in splendid old mansions and convents. Although imposing, these are never large enough and are always difficult to adapt to the needs of modern administration. When it proves impractical to spread into adjacent buildings or to construct annexes in the garden, branches are installed wherever space can be found. Some of the ministries occupy as many as 25 separate buildings.

Quai d'Orsay

Probably the best known of all ministries is the low-built, ornate Ministry of Foreign Affairs on the Quai d'Orsay between the Invalides Esplanade and the National Assembly. The address "Quai d'Orsay" has become a synonym for the ministry.

The National Assembly is housed in the Bourbon Palace (1722–28), which was seized during the Revolution. Succeeding regimes have added bits and pieces onto the old palace, including the Greek peristyle facing the river as ordered in 1807 by Napoleon.

The old, disused Orsay railway station near the river was renovated and in 1986 was reopened as a museum of 19th-century art and civilization. It contains, among other collections, the Impressionist and Postimpressionist paintings—by Cézanne, Manet, Monet, Renoir, van Gogh, and others—that were formerly in the Jeu de Paume.

The Latin Quarter (Quartier Latin). At the Concorde Bridge the boulevard Saint-Germain begins, curving eastward to join the river again at the Sully Bridge. A little less than halfway along the boulevard is the pre-Gothic church of Saint-Germain-des-Prés. The old church, which belonged to a Benedictine abbey founded in the 8th century, was sacked four times by Vikings and was rebuilt between 990 and 1201. Parts of the present church date from that time.

The area has long been a gathering place for practitioners of the arts. Racine died there in 1699, Delacroix had his studio in the Place Fürstemberg, publishing houses moved in during the 19th century, and the principal cafés have been meeting places for artists, writers, and publishers ever since. From 1945 to about 1955 it was the hub of the existentialist movement and an associated revival of bohemianism. It is still a lively centre for literature, food, and conversation.

Straight north from the Saint-Germain-des-Prés crossroads is the School of Fine Arts (École des Beaux-Arts), the state school of painting and sculpture, on the Quai Malaquais. Two streets south of the crossroads is the church of Saint-Sulpice (1646–1780), the work of six successive architects. The street alongside the church is sprinkled with shops specializing in devotional statuary, much of it on the aesthetic level of tourist souvenirs and known in France as "Saint Sulpicerie." Eastward to the boulevard Saint-Michel, the area toward the river from the boulevard Saint-Germain is a tangle of narrow, animated streets, which typify the tourist's idea of a vivacious and noisy Paris.

Beyond the boulevard Saint-Michel is the university precinct, self-governing under the kings, where, in class and out, students and teachers spoke Latin until 1789. At the junction of the boulevards Saint-Germain and Saint-Michel are the remains of one of the three baths of the Roman city. These are in the grounds of the Cluny Museum, a Gothic mansion built 1485–1500, which now houses a collection of medieval works of art, including the renowned six-panel unicorn tapestry "La Dame à la licorne."

The wide, straight boulevard Saint-Michel is the main street of the student quarter. It is lined with bookshops, cafés, cafeterias, and movie houses. The buildings of the university are found on smaller streets. The university was built up of colleges, each founded and supported by a donor, often a prelate or a religious order. In about 1257 Robert de Sorbon, chaplain to Louis IX, established a college, known as the Sorbonne, that eventually became the centre of theological study in France. The oldest part of the Sorbonne is the chapel (1635–42), the gift of Richelieu, who is buried there. Designed by Lemercier, it was one of a number of new domed Jesuit-style churches of the period.

The Sorbonne

The Sorbonne served for centuries as the administrative seat of the University of Paris. In 1968–71 the university was divided into a number of entirely separate universities, and the Sorbonne building proper continues to serve as premises for some of these. Other faculties, schools, and institutes have moved out of Paris to more spacious sites in the suburbs in an effort to ease the overcrowding of the Paris student milieu.

The independent College of France was set up a few steps from the university by Francis I in 1529 to offer a more liberal, modern curriculum than the narrow theology and Latin of the Sorbonne. Bestowing no degrees, it has always had a superb faculty of well-known specialists, especially in philosophy, literature, and the sciences.

At the top of the hill rising from the river the boulevard skirts the Luxembourg Gardens, the remains of the park of Marie de Médicis' Luxembourg Palace (1616–21), which now houses the French Senate. The gardens are planted with chestnuts and are enhanced with a pond for toy sailboats, a marionette theatre, and statuary.

Across the boulevard at the end of the rue Soufflot stands the Panthéon (1755–92), designed by Jacques-Germain Soufflot. It was commissioned by Louis XV, after his recovery from an illness, as a votive offering to St. Geneviève and was to replace the mouldering 5th-century abbey in her name. Though intended as the principal church in Paris, it was renamed the Panthéon by the Revolutionary authorities, who made it the last resting place for heroes of the Revolution. The walling up of a number of its windows and removal of much interior decoration replaced the intended effect of light interior space with a gloomy dignity. Among those buried under the inscription "Aux grands hommes, la Patrie reconnaissante" ("To great men, [from] their grateful land") are the authors Victor Hugo, Voltaire, Rousseau, and Zola and Jean Moulin, chief of the Resistance in World War II.

The Panthéon

Behind the Panthéon is a steep street named the rue

de la Montagne Sainte-Geneviève. It was the paved road to Italy in Roman times. The hill leads down to the lively market square of Place Maubert and a tangle of ancient, picturesque riverside streets. The best known of these is the medieval rue de la Huchette, from which the rue du Chat-qui-Pêche ("Street of the Fishing Cat") leads to the Quai Saint-Michel. Two churches, Saint-Séverin (1489–94), Gothic and humble, and Saint-Julien-le-Pauvre (1165–1220), which belongs to the transitional period between the Romanesque and the Gothic, rise from the tangle of streets. The square in front of the church offers one of the finest views of Notre-Dame de Paris.

The Buttes. The river valley of Paris is almost entirely circled by high ground. Upon the heights of Passy, on the Right Bank between the western city limits and the Arc de Triomphe, perch the wealthy neighbourhoods of the 16th *arrondissement*. The Butte-Montmartre (18th *arrondissement*) and the Buttes-Chaumont (19th *arrondissement*), which rise along the northern rim of the city, are still working-class. The 18th *arrondissement* has broad avenues, but it also has winding lanes, some of which become stairways on the steeper hills. From the early 19th century until the migration in the 1920s to Montparnasse, Montmartre was the major art colony of Paris. Some sections are highly commercialized for the tourist trade; others, however, are unself-consciously picturesque. Montmartre is known for its nightclubs and entertainment.

The most noted landmark of Montmartre was built only in 1919: the Sacred Heart Basilica (Basilique du Sacré-Coeur), paid for by national subscription after the French defeat by the Prussians in 1870. The work began in 1876 but was delayed by the death of the architect, Paul Abadie, who took inspiration from the 12th-century five-domed Romanesque church of Saint-Front in Périgueux, itself inspired by either Venetian or Byzantine churches. Alongside the monumental terraced stairway of the garden-planted Square Willette below the church entrance runs the only funicular railway in Paris.

On the Buttes-Chaumont just to the east of Montmartre is the Buttes-Chaumont Park, which was created under Haussmann in 1864–67. A bare hill, half hollowed out by abandoned tunnel quarries and filled with the refuse of generations, was turned into a romantic landscape with a lake, a waterfall, a grotto, winding woodland paths, and picturesque bridges. It is the largest park within the walls of Paris.

This portion of the 19th *arrondissement* is known as Belleville, and just below on the slope toward the river is Ménilmontant, in the 20th *arrondissement*. Père-Lachaise Cemetery, on hilly ground in the 20th *arrondissement*, is the site of the Federalists' Wall (Mur des Fédérés), against which the last of the Communard fighters were shot and to which pilgrimages are still made. Chopin, Marshal Ney, Baron Haussmann, Alfred de Musset, Balzac, Delacroix, Bizet, Rossini, Sarah Bernhardt, Isadora Duncan, Colette, and Edith Piaf are among the well-known people buried there. On the northeastern edge of the city proper, at La Villette, the giant structure of the old city abattoirs, out of use since 1974, was reopened in 1986 as a science museum. Nearby are a spherical panoramic cinema building and a large leisure park and culture complex.

Parks and open spaces. The appearance of Paris as a city well-endowed with parks is fostered in part by the garden effect of the Seine's open waters and its tree-lined banks. Some 87,000 trees (mostly plane trees, with a scattering of chestnuts) line the streets as well. But in fact parks and open spaces cover only 11 percent of the area of the City of Paris. Under Mayor Jacques Chirac the municipal government initiated efforts to create new parks, but the results have been modest.

Most of the parks and gardens of the modern central city are on land that formerly was reserved for the kings on the old city's outskirts. Under Napoleon III, who had been impressed by London's parks while living in Britain, two ancient royal military preserves at the approaches to Paris were made into "English" parks—the Bois de Boulogne on the west, and the Bois de Vincennes to the east. Moreover, during his reign a large area of land was laid out in promenades and garden squares. An assortment of

Mont-martre

Abundance of trees

municipal departments care for the public squares, street trees, riverbank trees, and various gardens.

(B.E./J.A.C.A.)

THE PEOPLE

In 1850 Paris had only 600,000 inhabitants. But it then grew rapidly, as industrial expansion attracted a constant stream of people from the provinces. By 1870 the population had surpassed 1,000,000; and by 1931 the conurbation contained some 5,000,000 people, more than half of them living in the City of Paris, the administrative city within the old gates. Since World War II this growth has continued, and Greater Paris by the late 1980s had close to 9,000,000 inhabitants. The population of the City of Paris, however, has steadily declined, from a peak of 2,900,000 in 1931 to 2,200,000 by 1982, so that more than three out of four Parisians are now suburbanites. The shift has taken place in part because massive rehousing has reduced the City's high density, though it remains well above the north European average. Many families have moved out to newer and more spacious homes in the suburbs, leaving the City of Paris with an aging population and one that is curiously solitary: almost half of the households consist of just one person.

Paris-born Parisians are outnumbered by immigrants who keep their provincial ties; hence many shops, restaurants, and neighbourhoods have a regional flavour. For example, there are said to be more Aveyronnais living in Paris than in the Aveyron *département* of central France. Most of the population is nominally Roman Catholic, though only a small percentage attend Mass regularly.

The foreign element has been increasing and now accounts for nearly one-fifth of the total population. The majority are Muslim Arabs from Algeria, Morocco, and Tunisia. In general, the North Africans are badly housed in the poorer quarters and are employed at menial jobs; in the 1980s their presence gave rise to racial tensions and conflicts. The sizable population of blacks is made up mainly of immigrants from the French Caribbean territories of Martinique and Guadeloupe: they tend to have better jobs and living conditions and are better accepted than are the Muslims. The Jewish community, which has long been settled in Paris, is centred on the Rue des Rosiers quarter of the Marais, where there are numerous synagogues, kosher stores, and Hebrew bookshops. In the 1980s encounters with Sephardic Jewish immigrants from North Africa provoked a mild revival of the anti-Semitism rife in prewar Paris.

In the earlier part of the 20th century Paris was favoured by expatriate writers and artists, including Ernest Hemingway from the United States, James Joyce from Ireland, Pablo Picasso from Spain, and Amedeo Modigliani from Italy. The foreign population from Europe and North America is now fairly small, however, consisting mainly of business people and the staffs of the large Paris-based international agencies, notably UNESCO and the Organisation for Economic Co-operation and Development.

THE ECONOMY

Paris is not only the political and cultural capital of France but also its major financial and commercial centre. Even if large French firms have their manufacturing plants in the provinces, they nearly all keep their headquarters in Paris, conveniently close to the major banks and key ministries. As an industrial centre the Paris region is less dominant in France than it was in its heyday in the 1930s, for since World War II most industrial growth has been in the provinces; but it still contains nearly a quarter of French industry. As a financial centre Paris is the base for many large international concerns in commerce and banking, and despite some pockets of poverty it is a very wealthy city, home of many vast private fortunes both French and foreign. After industry and commerce, the main activity is government administration, which employs nearly 700,000 people.

Industry. It was largely because it was already the political capital, with firms thus attracted to it, that Paris became an actively industrial city in the 19th century. Unlike other older French industrial areas, such as Lorraine and the Nord, it was not near mineral resources. But it did have some natural assets of its own, notably the Seine River, which is still used for heavy barge traffic moving downstream to the sea at Le Havre. Traditional industries were devoted mainly to handicrafts and luxury goods, but, when the growth of railways and canals in the 19th century made the northern coalfields more accessible, heavier industries such as engineering and chemicals began to develop. These soon spread beyond the city into the new industrial suburbs.

Since the 1950s the policy of successive French governments has been to limit the industrial growth of the Paris region in favour of the provinces, many of them still underdeveloped. Paris, which is in many ways overcongested, has instead been encouraged in developing commerce, finance, and services, a policy that has achieved some success. Industrial firms were forbidden to expand in the Paris area or were given various cash incentives to transfer their plants to the regions, and many did so. From 1962 to 1973 the Paris region had a net loss of 77,000 industrial jobs (about 5 percent of the total), while the rest of France gained 670,000.

The region, however, still employs well over a million people in industry. The City of Paris itself is still the home of many small-scale but typically Parisian activities: haute couture, notably in the Faubourg Saint-Honoré; the clothing industry, in the Sentier quarter; jewelry, in the Place Vendôme and rue de la Paix; furniture making, in the Faubourg Saint-Antoine. Newer and larger industries have developed in the northern and western suburbs, especially along the Seine valley toward Rouen: located there are several large automobile and aircraft factories. To the northwest, along the Seine's loop from Suresnes to Gennevilliers, are armaments factories, heavy engineering works, and chemical plants. Other firms are located to the northeast, within reach of Charles de Gaulle Airport. To the south and southwest along the valley of the Bièvre River are tanneries, cement works, breweries, tobacco factories, and other traditional concerns. Many light industries have settled in the new towns that now ring the Paris conurbation.

Commerce and finance. The major French banks, insurance companies, and other financial bodies are all centred on Paris, predominantly in the main financial quarter on the Right Bank around the Stock Exchange (Palais de la Bourse) and the state-owned Bank of France. Scores of foreign multiservice banks have branches in Paris, but the city is not a dynamic centre for specialist activities such as merchant banking and venture capital investment. The Paris Stock Exchange, though expanded and modernized in the 1980s, still handles little more than one-fifth of the volume of the London Stock Exchange.

Paris has developed greatly since World War II as a centre for international commerce, especially in the new skyscraper quarter of La Défense, where many large companies are situated. The city is one of the world's most popular sites for international business conferences, often hosting more than 200 a year. It has several major modern convention centres, notably the Palais des Congrès at the Maillot Gate.

It was the French who invented the modern department store, with the opening of the Bon Marché on the Left Bank in 1852. In the 1960s the major food and wine wholesale markets were transferred from their central locations at the Halles on the Right Bank and the Halle aux Vins (the wine market) on the Left Bank to new and more spacious homes in the suburbs.

Transportation. The Paris public transport system, operated by a body that is largely state-controlled, has been superbly modernized and extended since the early 1970s, and it is now regarded by many as the finest of any major world city. Trains on the 16 principal lines of the Métropolitain (Métro) subway system are fast and frequent. The Réseau Express Régional (RER), a high-speed express subway system, extends far into the suburbs, and at some points its lines have been integrated with the mainline railway network. The hub of the system is Châtelet–Les-Halles, said to be the world's largest and busiest underground station. By the 1980s Paris had become a com-

muter city, its Métro carrying 5,000,000 passengers daily. The cost of the Métro is subsidized by the government; passengers pay only about half of the actual cost. The city's bus system also has been modernized.

Such improvements have been part of an official campaign to ease traffic problems by discouraging the daily use of automobiles for commuting. But the campaign has not been entirely successful. The volume of traffic has swelled inexorably, and, although it often moves briskly along the many broad avenues and boulevards, it also can get clogged for hours in the honeycomb of narrow older streets. In a further attempt to decrease congestion the city has created many new underpasses and riverside expressways and has developed an extensive network of one-way streets. Underground garages have been built to provide parking space.

The city of Paris is encircled by an expressway, the boulevard Péripherique. The expressway is linked with suburban highways and with the national highway network, of which Paris is the hub. Similarly, the large Paris railway terminals serve the French railway network, first built in the 19th century. The network has been modernized and operates high-speed trains to Lyon and elsewhere. The main international airport is Charles de Gaulle, to the northeast; the older Orly Airport, to the south, is used mainly for domestic and charter flights. The Seine River carries barges and pleasure traffic; there are commercial ports both upstream and downstream from the city.

ADMINISTRATION AND SOCIAL CONDITIONS

Government. A sharp distinction is drawn between city administration and suburban administration. The City of Paris is a single political unit—a *commune*—governed by an elected mayor and council, like any other French *commune* down to the smallest village. The suburbs consist of more than 1,200 separate *communes,* large and small, which together with the City of Paris form the administrative region of Île-de-France. The Île-de-France region, with an area of about 4,640 square miles (12,000 square kilometres), extends far beyond the Paris conurbation. The urban area of Greater Paris therefore is not a political unit, and coordination is frequently poor between Paris and its inner suburbs. Because of the fierce rivalries between left-wing and right-wing *communes,* it has never been possible to follow the pattern of other major world cities and create a federated urban district.

The Île-de-France is the most populous of France's 22 regions. The region consists of eight *départements:* Hauts-de-Seine, Seine-Saint-Denis, Val-de-Marne, Essonne, Yvelines, Val-d'Oise, Seine-et-Marne, and Paris. Under the socialist government's devolutionary reforms of 1982–86, the Île-de-France, like the other regions, was given a certain degree of autonomy. It has a directly elected assembly with a chairman and executive; it can raise its own taxes; and it has responsibility for adult education and for some aspects of culture, tourism, road building, planning, and aid for industrial development. The directly elected representatives of the eight *départements* have also been given increased responsibilities: they run the welfare and social services, involving large budgets, as well as controlling some matters concerning the infrastructure. The *communes* in turn look after their own town planning and building. Each *département* is supervised by a state-appointed prefect and the Île-de-France by a regional prefect, but the office of prefect has much less power than before the reforms.

The City of Paris itself has a curious history of local government. The Municipal Council of Paris is elected by the people every six years. From 1871 to 1977 the council had no mayor and was controlled directly by the departmental prefect, so that Paris had less autonomy than any village. The national government, worried by memories of the uprisings of 1789, 1848, and 1871, wanted to keep power from the Paris populace. A statute passed in 1975, however, permitted the councillors once again to elect their own mayor. The mayor now has the same status and powers as in other French towns. The first mayoral election was held in 1977. In 1982 a ward system was introduced, whereby each of the 20 *arrondissements* was given its own mayor and local council. In practice, however, these have not proved very effective, and real control remains in the hands of Paris' mayor.

Services. Electricity and gas utilities in Paris are run by the state, as are the fire departments and the telephone service. Paris alone among French cities has no municipal responsibility for the police, who are controlled by the state and have wider powers than in other towns. In addition to dealing with crime, traffic, and public order, the Paris police register all vehicles and drivers; issue passports, identity cards, and aliens' residence permits; and conduct political surveillance. One of the main challenges facing them has been the growing wave of crime, particularly terrorism. Special police agencies in Paris include the detective and counterespionage services and the Republican Security Force, which are used for dispersing demonstrations. The Republican Guard, a mounted squadron of spurred, helmeted, plumed, and breast-plated guardsmen armed with sabres, are used only for ceremonial occasions such as visits by foreign heads of state.

Health. The public hospitals and hospital groups in Paris are run jointly by the city and the national Ministry of Health and are financed largely by a social welfare system. Some other hospitals are run by churches and by private organizations, and there are numerous private clinics. Of the city's many medical research bodies the best known is the Pasteur Institute, founded in 1887.

Education. As in the rest of France, education is largely in the hands of the state, and schools are of three main kinds: primary, junior secondary (*collèges*), and senior secondary (*lycées*). Almost one-fifth of all pupils are in private, nonstate schools, most of them run by the Roman Catholic Church. Some of the best-known *lycées* in central Paris are the Lycée Henri IV, the Lycée Louis-le-Grand, and the Lycée Janson de Sailly; such schools traditionally have educated a large number of the nation's intelligentsia.

Paris has long been an important world centre of higher education. The building known as the Sorbonne housed the arts and science faculties of the University of Paris, one of Europe's oldest universities, until the university was split into 13 autonomous universities (1968–71), some of which still use the Sorbonne for their premises. The 13 universities, overcrowded and under-funded, with a total of some 250,000 students, have lost prestige to a number of much smaller bodies of higher education that are more specialized and more elitist. These include principally the engineering, technical, and business colleges known as the Grand Schools (Grandes Écoles), of which the two best known in the Paris area are the School of Higher Business Studies (École des Hautes Études Commerciales; HEC) and the Polytechnical School (École Polytechnique), both of them now transferred to spacious new homes in the suburbs. The Normal Superior School (École Normale Supérieure) serves mainly to prepare future university and *lycée* teachers. The Institute of Political Sciences (Institut des Sciences Politiques) nurtures many of the bright young people who then go on to the influential postgraduate Normal School for Administration (École Normale d'Administration; ENA) to train as future senior civil servants. This selective structure has served France well in many ways but has also come under heavy criticism and undergone sporadic reform.

CULTURAL LIFE

Paris has for centuries been regarded as the main cultural powerhouse of the Western world, a magnet for artists and intellectuals, a place where new ideas originate and art reigns supreme. There are those who feel that its cultural life has grown stale and is now more a matter of show and dazzle than of true creativity. But the cultural life of Paris is still highly active and distinctive. Parisians love novelty, they have an abounding intellectual curiosity, they know how to dress up the simplest cultural event with flair and elegance, and they are avid patrons of the arts, so that the theatres and concert halls, museums, art galleries, and art cinemas are always well-attended.

The principal state-run theatres are the Comédie-Française, the Odéon Theatre, and the National Theatre of Chaillot, which offer a repertoire of French classics, serious modern plays, and foreign imports. Lighter fare is provided by the many privately owned "boulevard" theatres, which struggle to survive. There are also more than 150 smaller theatres, many of them state-supported, which present a mixed program of experimental "fringe" shows, cabaret, and the like. Many Parisians are film enthusiasts, and in addition to the many multiscreen commercial cinemas there are scores of little "art" houses that show a wide variety of movies, many of them with subtitles. France's main film studios are in the suburbs of Paris.

While the newly remodeled Louvre is the greatest of the classic art museums, Paris has also built major new museums in the past years. Among them are the National Museum of Modern Art in the Pompidou Centre, the Orsay Museum of 19th-century art and civilization opened in 1986, and the new science museum at La Villette. A speciality of Paris is the staging of large and lavishly mounted exhibitions, usually retrospectives of an individual artist or historical period. The city's musical life, once moribund, has become much livelier since the early 1970s, in part because the state has provided much-needed funding. Although the work of the Paris Opera remains uneven in quality and the building ill-suited to modern productions, the city renewed its commitment to opera by beginning construction on a new opera house in 1986. Major annual festivals, with an emphasis on music and drama, are the Marais Festival, held in June and July, and the Autumn Festival, held from mid-September through December.

The main publishing houses and bookshops are located in the Latin Quarter and Saint-Germain-des-Prés. Of the main daily newspapers published in Paris, the best known is the evening *Le Monde,* followed by the daily *Le Figaro* and *Liberation.* The Paris daily press is relatively weak, however, accounting for less than one-third of total daily circulation in France. On the other hand, weekly newsmagazines flourish, notably *L'Express* and *Le Point.* All of the main French national radio and television networks are centred in Paris; some are owned by the state and some are privately owned.   (J.A.C.A.)

History

FOUNDATION AND MEDIEVAL GROWTH

Paris was in existence by the end of the 3rd century BC as a settlement on an island, the modern Île de la Cité, in the Seine River. At that time it was inhabited by a Gallic tribe known as the Parisii. The first recorded name for the settlement was Lutetia (Latin: "Midwater-Dwelling"). When the Romans arrived, the Parisii were already sufficiently organized and wealthy to have their own gold coinage. Julius Caesar wrote in his *Commentaries* (52 BC) that the inhabitants burned their town rather than surrender it to the Romans.

In the 1st century AD Lutetia grew as a Roman town and began to spread onto the left bank of the Seine. The straight streets and the public buildings in this locale were characteristically Roman, including a forum, several baths, and an amphitheatre.

A series of barbarian invasions began in the late 2nd century. The town on the left bank was destroyed by the mid-3rd century, and the inhabitants took refuge on the island, around which they built a thick stone wall. From the early 4th century the place became known as Paris rather than Lutetia.

By this time, Christianity seems to have spread to Paris. A 10th-century sacramentary cites St. Denis (Latin Dionysius) as having been the first bishop of Paris, in about AD 250. A graveyard excavated near the Carrefour des Gobelins shows that there was a Christian community in very early times on the banks of the Bièvre (a left-bank tributary of the Seine); but it was probably under St. Marcel, the ninth bishop (c. 360–436), that the first Christian church, a wooden structure, was built on the island.

By the end of the 5th century the Salian Franks, under Clovis, had captured Paris from the Gauls, making it their own capital. It remained the capital until the end of Chilperic's reign in 584, but succeeding Merovingians carried the crown elsewhere. Charlemagne's dynasty, the

Carolingians, tended to leave the city in the charge of the counts of Paris, who in many cases had less control over administration than did the bishops. After the election of Hugh Capet, a count of Paris, to the throne in 987, Paris, as a Capetian capital, became more important.

The population and the commerce of Paris increased with the gradual return of political stability and public order under the Capetian kings. The maintenance of order was entrusted to a special representative of the king, the provost of Paris (*prévôt de Paris*), first mentioned in 1050. In the 11th century the first guilds were formed, among them the butchers' guild and the river-merchants' guild, or *marchandise de l'eau*. In 1141 the crown sold the principal port (by the site of the Hôtel de Ville) to the *marchandise,* whose ship-blazoned arms eventually were adopted as those of Paris. In 1171 Louis VII gave the *marchandise* a charter confirming its "ancient right" to a monopoly of river trade.

Expansion under Philip II During the reign of Philip II (1179–1223), Paris was extensively improved. Streets were paved, the city wall was enlarged, and a number of new towns were enfranchised. In 1190, when Philip II went on a crusade for a year, he entrusted the administration of the city not to the provost but to the guild. In 1220 the crown ceded one of its own precious rights to the townsmen: the right to collect duty on incoming goods. The merchants were also made responsible for maintaining fair weights and measures. The King's formal recognition of the University of Paris in 1200 was also a recognition of the division of Paris into three parts, corresponding to the natural division of the site. On the Right Bank were the mercantile quarters, on the island was the *cité,* and the Left Bank contained the university and academic quarters. Numerous colleges were also founded, including the Sorbonne (about 1257).

In the 14th century the development of Paris was hindered not only by the Black Death (1348–49) but also by the outbreak of the Hundred Years' War (1337–1453) and by internal disturbances resulting from it. The provost of the merchants in 1356 was Étienne Marcel, who wanted a Paris as rich and free as the independent cities of the Low Countries. It was he who gave the House of Pillars to the municipal government, and it was he who slew the Dauphin's counselors in the palace throne room and took over the city. He showed great executive skill and equally great political stupidity. He allied himself with the revolting peasants (the Jacquerie), with the invading English, and with Charles the Bad, the ambitious king of Navarre. While going to open the city gates to the Navarrese in 1358, Marcel was slain by the citizens.

In 1382 a tax riot grew into a revolt called the "Maillotin uprising" because the rioters armed themselves with mauls (*maillets*). They were ruthlessly put down and the municipal function was suspended for the next 79 years. It was not until 1533, when Francis I ordered the teetering House of Pillars replaced by a new building, that a monarch manifested an encouraging interest in municipal government.

The dynastic and political vendetta between the Burgundian and the Armagnac faction (1407–35) had continual repercussions in Paris; in the course of it, the butchers and skinners, led by Simon Caboche, momentarily seized power there (1413). The resumption of the Hundred Years' War by the English in 1415 made matters worse. After a revolt of the Parisians (1418), the Burgundians occupied Paris; and the Anglo-Burgundian Alliance (1419) was followed by the installation of John Plantagenet, duke of Bedford, as regent of France for the English king Henry VI (1422). Whereas Charles VI had lived in his father's Hôtel Saint-Paul, Bedford lived in the Hôtel des Tournelles, on the southeastern edge of the Marais, which was to be the Paris residence of later kings until 1559. During the reign of Charles VI, construction began on the Notre-Dame Bridge (1413).

In 1429 Joan of Arc failed to capture Paris. Only in 1436 did it fall to the legitimists, who welcomed Charles VII in person in 1437. Successive disturbances had reduced the population, but the Anglo-French truce of 1444 allowed Charles to begin restoring prosperity.

In 1469, during Louis XI's reign (1461–83), the Sorbonne installed the first printing press in Paris. Otherwise this was a period of intellectual stagnation. Churches were rehabilitated and new houses were built, however; from 1480 splendid private mansions began to appear, such as the Hôtel de Sens and the Hôtel de Cluny.

FROM THE RENAISSANCE TO THE REVOLUTION

The influence of the Italian Renaissance on town architecture appeared in the new building for the accounting office and in the reconstruction of the Notre-Dame Bridge (1500–10) in Louis XII's reign. Under Francis I (1515–47) this influence grew stronger, finding notable expression in the new Hôtel de Ville. Furthermore, whereas from Charles VII's time the kings of France had preferred to reside in Touraine, Francis showed himself willing to make Paris the chief seat of royalty again. With this in mind he had extensive alterations made to the Louvre from 1528 onward. The new splendour of the monarchy, which was well on its way toward absolute rule, was reflected in the way Paris developed as the capital of an increasingly centralized state. The population increased and the town expanded again. Rigorous measures were taken to stamp out Protestantism, which first appeared in Paris during Francis I's reign.

The culmination of the Renaissance in Paris came with Henry II, who made his solemn entry into the capital in 1549. The new impulse given to the building of mansions for the nobility and the bourgeoisie began to transform Paris from a medieval city into a modern one. In 1548 the Brothers of the Passion began performing secular plays at the Hôtel de Bourgogne, in the rue Française, thus inaugurating the first theatre in Paris.

The transfer of the royal residence from the Hôtel des Tournelles to the Louvre was completed after the death of Henry II in 1559. This move signaled the development of the western outskirts of Paris, hitherto rather neglected. Catherine de Médicis began to build the Tuileries Palace, the gardens of which were soon to become a meeting place for elegant society. Classical taste was brilliantly exemplified by the Pont-Neuf, begun in 1577.

The Wars of Religion In the mid-16th century the Wars of Religion broke out in France between Roman Catholics and Huguenots. In Paris these conflicts brought about the Massacre of St. Bartholomew's Day (1572); the Day of the Barricades (May 12, 1588), when the Catholic League rose against Henry III; and the long resistance of the Parisians to the Protestant Henry of Navarre, who succeeded as Henry IV in 1589. Henry IV's siege in 1590 was unsuccessful, and it was only after his conversion to Catholicism that Paris submitted to him (March 22, 1594).

In Louis XIII's reign (1610–43) Paris expanded farther. On the Left Bank outside the wall the queen mother, Marie de Médicis, built the Luxembourg Palace, with its spacious gardens; and along the Right Bank, west of the Tuileries, she laid out the Cours-la-Reine as a promenade for carriages. While the Marais north of the Place Royale was being reclaimed and developed, two uninhabited islets east of the *cité* were united to form the Île Saint-Louis. On the western fringe of the town a quarter with straight streets was laid out north of Richelieu's new palace, the Palais-Cardinal (1624–36; later the Palais-Royal), which also had a magnificent garden; and west of this there was more building and a new fortification was erected.

The war of the Fronde (1648–53) was the major event of the first two decades of Louis XIV's reign. From 1661, when Cardinal Mazarin died and Louis started his personal rule, Paris was dedicated to reflecting the glory of the monarch, even though he was early resolved to establish himself and the seat of his government outside of Paris (he eventually chose Versailles). For the planning of the new splendours of Paris, the greatest part of the credit must go to Jean-Baptiste Colbert, the king's superintendent of buildings.

Work on the Louvre had been resumed in 1624 and was completed by Claude Perrault's magnificent colonnade (1667–74). The Tuileries Palace was altered, completed, and sumptuously decorated. Beyond its gardens to the west, outside the walls of Paris, the tree-planted avenues of the Champs-Élysées were laid out (1667); these were complemented, at the opposite end of Paris, by the Cours de Vincennes.

Paris had become very large. In 1702 the Marquis d'Argenson (Marc René de Voyer), who as lieutenant general of police was the successor of the provosts of Paris, raised the number of districts from 16 to 20 (15 on the Right Bank, five on the Left). Paris had nearly 600,000 inhabitants, and from the Left Bank new suburbs were advancing toward the villages on the surrounding hills.

During the 18th century a great deal was done to improve and beautify Paris. Louis XV's temporary residence in the Tuileries during his younger days encouraged development nearby, so that the Faubourg Saint-Honoré expanded and became, like the Faubourg Saint-Germain, an aristocratic quarter. The garden of the Palais-Royal became a centre of elegant society. The Grands Boulevards began to be bordered with houses, including some fine mansions, and the eastern stretch became a fashionable promenade with little theatres and cafés. Villas built by nobles and financiers were scattered around this outlying sector. On the Left Bank the southern course of boulevards was laid out and the routes were lined with trees and houses. Some of the houses that had been built earlier on the bridges were razed in 1786–88; others remained until 1808. Water was supplied to both banks by two fire pumps, developed by Jacques-Constantin Périer and his father, Auguste-Charles. The wall of the farmers-general, built in the 1780s to facilitate the levying of duties on imports, represented the extension and the unity of Paris.

EVOLUTION OF THE MODERN CITY

The Revolution and Napoleon I. The French Revolution of 1789 on the one hand destroyed those vestiges of the seigneurial systems that had remained in Paris and, on the other, consolidated the status of Paris as the capital of a centralized France. The major events of the Revolution took place in Paris. These included the storming of the Bastille (July 14, 1789); the conveying of the King and the National Constituent Assembly from Versailles to Paris (October 1789); the establishment of the numerous clubs in the convents of the old religious orders, Jacobins, Cordeliers, and Feuillants; the insurrection that heralded the abolition of the monarchy (Aug. 10, 1792); the execution of the King in the Place de la Révolution, not yet named Place de la Concorde (Jan. 21, 1793); the most prolonged manifestation of the Terror (1793–94); and the series of coups d'état, from that of 9 Thermidor, year II (1794), to that of 18 Brumaire, year VIII (1799), which preceded the ascendancy of Napoleon Bonaparte.

Under the Thermidorians and the Directory the boulevard des Italiens became a resort of the fashionable and the frivolous, whereas the populace favoured the boulevard du Temple. After the inauguration of the First Empire, Napoleon in 1806 ordered the triumphal arches of the Carrousel and of the Étoile to be erected. The Neoclassical style recalled imperial Rome, but at the same time great works of public utility served to modernize Paris: the Bourse; new quays and bridges (the Arts, Jena, Austerlitz, and Saint-Louis bridges); the Ourcq and Saint-Martin canals; numerous fountains (such as the Palmier Fountain, on the site of the Châtelet); as well as slaughterhouses, marketplaces, the wine market, and the warehouses of Bercy.

The Restoration and the July Monarchy

Industrialization, already in progress in the Napoleonic period, advanced rapidly under the Restoration (1814–30) and the July Monarchy (1830–48). Gas lighting was introduced; omnibus services began in 1828; and Paris got its first railway, which ran to Le Pecq, near Saint-Germain-en-Laye, in 1837. New districts grew up on the outskirts of Paris. Although the wall of the farmers-general was to remain the administrative boundary of Paris until 1859, it was decided in 1840 to refortify the capital with a longer military wall.

Napoleon III and Haussmann. Even by the mid-19th century, however, there remained areas of Paris that had not been improved substantially for hundreds of years. Access from one centre to another and to the railway stations (which had become in effect the gateways of Paris) was difficult; moreover, overpopulation and rapid industrialization had brought squalor and misery, which account in part for the dominant role played by Paris in the revolutions of 1830 and 1848. Napoleon III, emperor from 1852 to 1870, enjoined his prefect of the Seine, Baron Haussmann, to remedy all this.

Haussmann was the creator of modern Paris. A planner on the grand scale, he advocated straight arterial thoroughfares, symmetry, and advantageous vistas. He slashed the boulevards through the tangles of slums (at the same time beginning the modern sewer and water systems), gutted the Île de la Cité, the heart of Paris, rebuilt the ancient market of the Halles, and added four new Seine bridges and rebuilt three old ones. The brilliance and prosperity of Paris under Napoleon III were exemplified in the exhibitions held there in 1855 and 1867.

The Third Republic and after. The Franco-German War (1870–71), which brought the fall of the Second Empire and the siege of Paris, was followed by the Commune (1871). Under the Third Republic, Haussmann's projects were continued. Further international exhibitions (1878, 1889, 1900, and 1937) were the occasions for the building of monuments such as the Trocadéro (1878), the Eiffel Tower (1889), and the Grand Palais and Petit Palais, with the Alexandre III Bridge (1900), and for the reconstruction of the Trocadéro as the Chaillot Palace (1937). The Métro was constructed, commerce and industry annexed formerly residential districts, and the ever-expanding population overflowed the old limits of Paris. After World War I, Louis-Philippe's fortifications were abolished by a law of April 1919.

During the German occupation of Paris in World War II the city was only slightly damaged. It was a centre for the activities of the Resistance movement, which culminated in the liberation of the city in August 1944.

The immediate postwar years were a time of eager intellectual activity but also of poverty and social tension. The housing shortage was grave, the psychological scars of the German occupation were slow to heal, and colonial wars and political instability both lowered morale. Gradually, however, conditions improved, especially after Charles de Gaulle returned to power in 1958. The city's economy improved, old buildings and neighbourhoods were cleaned up and renovated, and new housing and commercial space were built.

In May 1968 Paris was rocked by a great student uprising, which swelled from scattered unrest among students in the Latin Quarter to a nationwide outbreak of labour strikes and protests. Attention was focused on Paris' economic and social problems, and the uprising was later seen to have been useful in hastening the modernization of French society.

By the 1980s Paris, like many other Western cities, was having to come to terms with problems as diverse as high unemployment and politically motivated acts of terrorism. But these were among the few serious blemishes on a city of bright prosperity and dynamic self-confidence.

BIBLIOGRAPHY

General description: PAUL COHEN-PORTHEIM, *The Spirit of Paris* (1937; originally published in German, 1930); JOHN RUSSELL, *Paris* (1983); HAROLD P. CLUNN, *The Face of Paris* (1933, reprinted 1958); B. EHRLICH, *Paris on the Seine* (1962); and ANTHONY GLYN, *The Companion Guide to Paris* (1985). Guide books include IAN ROBERTSON (ed.), *Paris and Environs,* 6th ed. (1985); *Paris,* 6th ed. (1986), from the Michelin Green Guides series; and the detailed CHRISTIAN MILLAU (ed.), *Le Guide de Paris* (1985). IAN LITTLEWOOD, *Paris: A Literary Companion* (1987), is a guide to the literary landmarks of the city. The monumental work of F. DE ROCHEGUDE and MAURICE DUMOLIN, *Guide pratique à travers le vieux Paris,* new rev. ed. (1923), has been adapted by JEAN-PAUL CLÉBERT, *Les Rues de Paris: promenades du marquis de Rochegude à travers tous les arrondissements de Paris parcourus de nouveau,* 2 vol. (1958, reissued 1966). These may be supplemented by GEORGES PILLEMENT, *Paris inconnu,* rev. ed. (1981). JEAN BASTIÉ, *Géographie du Grand Paris* (1984), describes the geography of Greater Paris; FRANÇOIS CHASLIN, *Les Paris de François Mitterrand: histoire des grands projets architecturaux* (1985), describes architectural projects under President Mitterrand; and PIERRE MERLIN, *Les Transports à Paris et Ile-de-France* (1982), discusses transportation in Paris and the Île-de-France region. WILLIAM MAHDER (ed.), *Paris Arts on Seine* (1985), offers a lively view of cultural trends. JOHN ARDAGH, *France Today,* new rev. ed. (1987), contains diverse materials on present-day life in Paris. For information on churches, see AMÉDÉE C.L. BOINET, *Les Églises parisiennes,* 3 vol. (1958–64). Of sentimental interest are LÉON-PAUL FARGUE et al., *Dans les rues de Paris au temps des fiacres* (1950); and R. HÉRON DE VILLEFOSSE, *Histoire et géographie galantes de Paris* (1957).

History: General histories include HENRY BIDOU, *Paris* (1939; originally published in French, 1937); and ROBERT LAFFONT (ed.), *The Illustrated History of Paris and the Parisians* (1958; originally published in French, 1958; U.K. title, *Paris and Its People*). Other major works include MARCEL POËTE, *Une Vie de cité: Paris de sa naissance à nos jours,* 3 vol. and album (1924–31); LUCIEN DUBECH and PIERRE D'ESPEZEL, *Histoire de Paris,* 2 vol. (1931); and PHILIPPE LEFRANÇOIS, *Paris à travers les siècles,* 10 vol. (1948–56). For the history of the city's growth, see particularly R. HÉRON DE VILLEFOSSE, *Construction*

de Paris (1938). Studies of special periods include PAUL M. DUVAL, *Paris antique: des origines au troisième siècle* (1961); and BERNARD CHAMPIGNEULLE, *Paris de Napoléon à nos jours* (1969). Among analytical works are DANIEL ROCHE, *The People of Paris: An Essay in Popular Culture in the 18th Century* (1987; originally published in French, 1981); DAVID GARRIOCH, *Neighbourhood and Community in Paris, 1740–1790* (1986); LENARD R. BERLANSTEIN, *The Working People of Paris, 1871–1914* (1984); ANN-LOUISE SHAPIRO, *Housing the Poor of Paris, 1850–1902* (1985); and JERROLD SEIGEL, *Bohemian Paris: Culture, Politics, and the Boundaries of Bourgeois Life, 1830–1930* (1986). HERBERT R. LOTTMAN, *The Left Bank: Writers, Artists, and Politics from the Popular Front to the Cold War* (1982), gives a picture of intellectual life in Paris during the 20th century. NORMA EVENSON, *Paris: A Century of Change, 1878–1978* (1979), presents the evolution of the city from a planner's point of view.

(B.E./J.A.C.A.)

Particle Accelerators

A particle accelerator is a device that produces a beam of fast-moving, electrically charged atomic or subatomic particles. Physicists use accelerators in fundamental research on the structure of nuclei, the nature of nuclear forces, and the properties of nuclei not found in nature, such as the transuranic (heavier than uranium) elements and other unstable elements. Accelerators are also used for radioisotope production, industrial radiography, cancer therapy, sterilization of biological materials, and polymerization of plastics. The largest accelerators are used in research on the fundamental interactions of the elementary subatomic particles.

This article reviews the development of accelerators and delineates the various types and their distinguishing features. For specific information about the particles accelerated by these devices, see ATOMS and SUBATOMIC PARTICLES.

This article is divided into the following sections:

GENERAL CONSIDERATIONS

The effectiveness of an accelerator usually is characterized by the kinetic energy, rather than the speed, of the particles. The unit of energy commonly used is the electron volt (eV), which is the energy acquired by a particle that has a charge of the same magnitude as that of the electron when it passes between electrodes that differ in potential by one volt. Related larger units are the kiloelectron volt (keV), which is 1,000 eV; the megaelectron volt (MeV; 1,000,000 eV); the gigaelectron volt (GeV; 1,000,000,000 eV); and the teraelectron volt (TeV; 1,000,000,000,000 eV). Compared with the quantities of energy encountered in everyday experience, even the TeV is a very small amount, about that of a mosquito in flight. The masses of the particles accelerated are so small, however, that kinetic energies in this range correspond to very high speeds: the particles in the smallest ion accelerators travel about 8,000 kilometres (5,000 miles) per second, about 3 percent of the speed of light.

The particles that are accelerated are electrons, positrons (positive electrons), or ionized atoms such as protons (ionized hydrogen), deuterons (ionized heavy hydrogen), alpha particles (ionized helium), or heavier ionized atoms. Sometimes the primary beam is used; in other cases, the primary beam is directed onto a target to produce a beam of secondary particles, such as X rays, neutrons, mesons, hyperons, or neutrinos. A few accelerators are operated as sources of the intense radiation, called synchrotron radiation, emitted by electrons moving at almost the speed of light along curved paths.

Every accelerator has three essential parts: a source of the particles to be accelerated, a vacuum chamber in which to accelerate them, and a source of the electric fields needed to effect the acceleration. Thermionic emission (the emission of electrons from the surface of a heated solid) provides electrons. Positrons are produced as secondary particles by an electron accelerator and then further accelerated. Positive and negative ions are produced by electric arc or glow discharges in a gas at low pressure in a chamber; a high-voltage electrode extracts the ions from the gas through a hole in the chamber. The region in which the particles are accelerated must be highly evacuated to keep the particles from being scattered out of the beam, or even stopped, by collisions with molecules of air.

Accelerators are differentiated by the arrangements of the accelerating electric fields. In a linear accelerator, the path of the particles is a straight line, and the final energy of the particles is proportional to the sum of the voltages produced by the accelerating devices along that line. In a cyclic accelerator, the path of the particles is bent by the action of a magnetic field into a spiral or a closed curve that is approximately circular (see ELECTRICITY AND MAGNETISM). In this case, the particles pass many times through the accelerating devices; the final energy depends on the magnitude of the voltages multiplied by the number of times the particles pass through. Because the total distance travelled by the particles in a cyclic accelerator may be more than a million kilometres, the cumulative effect of minute deviations from the desired trajectory would be dissipation of the beam. Therefore, the beam

Basic components

must be continually focussed by the magnetic fields, which are precisely shaped by powerful magnets.

HISTORY

The motivation for most of the development of the various types of particle accelerators has been their application to research into the properties of atomic nuclei and subatomic particles. Starting with Ernest (later Lord) Rutherford's discovery, in 1919, of a reaction between a nitrogen nucleus and an alpha particle, all research in nuclear physics until 1932 was performed with alpha particles from naturally radioactive elements. The natural alpha particles have kinetic energies as high as 8 MeV. It was not possible, however, to form natural alpha particles into a well-defined beam in which all the particles were of equal energy without reducing the number of particles so much that they were useless. Further experimentation required a beam of artificially accelerated ions, but there seemed little hope of generating laboratory voltages sufficient to accelerate ions to the desired energies. A calculation made by George Gamow (then at the University of Göttingen) in 1928, however, indicated that considerably less energetic ions could be useful, and this stimulated attempts to build an accelerator that could provide a beam of particles suitable for nuclear research. The first successful experiments with artificially accelerated ions were performed at the University of Cambridge, England, by J.D. Cockcroft and E.T.S. Walton in 1932. Using a voltage multiplier, they accelerated protons to energies as high as 710 keV and showed that these react with the lithium nucleus, the products being two energetic alpha particles. Other developments of that period demonstrated principles still employed in the design of particle accelerators. For example, Robert J. Van de Graaff had constructed the first belt-charged electrostatic high-voltage generator at Princeton University, in New Jersey, by 1931.

First proton accelerator

The principle of the resonance linear accelerator was demonstrated by Rolf Wideröe in 1928. At the Rhenish-Westphalian Technical University in Aachen he had used alternating high voltage to accelerate ions of sodium and potassium to energies twice as high as those imparted by one application of the peak voltage. In 1931, Ernest O. Lawrence and his assistant David H. Sloan, at the University of California, Berkeley, employed high-frequency fields to accelerate mercury ions to more than 1.2 MeV; this work augmented Wideröe's achievement in accelerating heavy ions, but the ion beams were not useful in nuclear research.

The magnetic resonance accelerator, or cyclotron, was conceived by Lawrence as a modification of Wideröe's linear resonance accelerator. Lawrence's student M.S. Livingston demonstrated the principle of the cyclotron in 1931, producing 80-keV ions; in 1932, Lawrence and Livingston announced the acceleration of protons to more than 1 MeV. Later in the 1930s cyclotron energies reached about 25 MeV, and Van de Graaff generators, about 4 MeV. In 1940 Donald W. Kerst, applying the results of careful orbit calculations to the design of magnets, constructed the first betatron, a magnetic-induction accelerator of electrons, at the University of Illinois.

The rapid advance in the science of accelerating particles to high energies that has occurred since the end of World War II was initiated by E.M. McMillan, at Berkeley, and V.I. Veksler, at Moscow, who in 1945 independently described the principle of phase stability, which removed an apparent limitation on the energy of resonance accelerators for protons (see below *Classical cyclotrons*) and made possible the construction of magnetic-resonance accelerators (called synchrotrons) for electrons. The principle was promptly demonstrated by the construction of a small synchrocyclotron at the University of California and an electron synchrotron in England. The first proton linear resonance accelerator was constructed soon thereafter. The large proton synchrotrons that have been built since then all depend on this principle.

In 1947 William W. Hansen, at Stanford University, California, constructed the first travelling-wave linear accelerator of electrons, exploiting microwave technology that had been developed for radar during World War II.

The progress in research made possible by raising the energies of protons led to the building of successively larger accelerators; the trend was ended only by the cost of fabricating the huge magnet rings required—the largest weighs approximately 40,000 tons. A means of increasing the energy without increasing the scale of the machines was provided by the demonstration, in 1952, by Livingston, E.D. Courant, and H.S. Snyder of the technique of alternating-gradient focussing (sometimes called strong focussing). Synchrotrons incorporating this principle needed magnets only 1/100 the size that would be required otherwise. All recently constructed accelerators make use of alternating-gradient focussing.

Developments since the 1940s

In 1956 Kerst realized that, if two sets of particles could be maintained in intersecting orbits, it should be possible to observe interactions in which one particle collided with another moving in the opposite direction. Application of this idea requires the accumulation of accelerated particles in loops called storage rings. The highest reaction energies now obtainable have been produced by the use of this technique.

Particle storage rings

CONSTANT-VOLTAGE ACCELERATORS

The simplest type of particle accelerator is constructed by mounting a particle source on one end of an insulated, evacuated tube and creating a high voltage between the ends, with the polarity such that the particles are impelled from the source toward the far end of the tube. Such an accelerator is necessarily linear, and the electrostatic field can be applied to a given particle only once (unless, as in the tandem accelerator described below, the charge of the particle undergoes change in sign). The simplicity of concept soon gives way to complexity in execution when the electric potential exceeds 1,000,000 volts (one megavolt, or 1 MV): these high voltages produce corona discharges and lightning-like sparks outside the accelerator, which dissipate the potential needed to accelerate the particles. Even more difficult to control are sparks within the equipment and, in positive-ion accelerators, unwanted secondary beams produced when the accelerated ions strike the end of the tube.

Because these discharges and sparks generally originate at sharply curved or pointed places on the surface of an electrode, the high-voltage electrode of a modern accelerator is made in the shape of a sphere or a cylinder with rounded ends or, in the case of a low-energy device, a box with rounded edges. The insulating columns that support the terminals are meticulously designed to suppress corona or sparking. Care also is devoted to the design of the accelerator tube to ensure the uniform distribution of the voltage along its length. The voltage that a structure will withstand is increased if the pressure of the gas surrounding it is increased, so direct-voltage accelerators commonly are mounted in tanks pressurized with mixtures of nitrogen and carbon dioxide or, in certain cases, the gas sulfur hexafluoride.

Voltage multipliers (cascade generators). The source of the high voltage for Cockcroft and Walton's pioneering experiments was a four-stage voltage multiplier assembled from four large rectifiers and high-voltage capacitors. Their circuit, in effect, combined four rectifier-type direct-voltage power supplies in series. The alternating voltage supplied by a high-voltage transformer was transmitted to the higher stages through an array of capacitors; a second group of capacitors kept the direct voltage constant. The final direct voltage would have been four times the peak voltage available from the transformer (200,000 volts) if corona discharge had not drained away considerable power. Nevertheless, the apparatus did accelerate protons to energies of 710 keV, sufficient to bring about the hoped-for result, a reaction with lithium nuclei. Their achievement, the first nuclear reaction effected by artificially accelerated particles, was recognized by the award of the Nobel Prize for Physics in 1951.

Cockcroft–Walton generator

Cockcroft and Walton's system for building up high direct voltages can be extended to multiplication factors many times that originally demonstrated. Commercially available accelerators that reach 4 MeV are based on this circuitry.

Van de Graaff generators.   In Van de Graaff generators, electric charge is transported to the high-voltage terminal on a rapidly moving belt of insulating material driven by a pulley mounted on the grounded end of the structure; a second pulley is enclosed within the large, spherical high-voltage terminal, as shown in Figure 1. The belt is charged by a comb of sharp needles with the points close to the belt a short distance from the place at which it moves clear of the grounded pulley. The comb is connected to a power supply that raises its potential to a few tens of kilovolts. The gas near the needle points is ionized by the intense electric field, and in the resulting corona discharge the ions are driven to the surface of the belt. The motion of the belt carries the charge into the high-voltage terminal and transfers it to another comb of needles, from which it passes to the outer surface of the terminal. A carefully designed Van de Graaff generator insulated by pressurized gas can be charged to a potential of about 20 megavolts.

Tandem
Van de
Graaff ac-
celerators   In most constant-voltage accelerators, Van de Graaff generators are the source of high voltage, and most of the electrostatic proton accelerators still in use are two-stage (*tandem*) accelerators. These devices provide a beam with twice the energy that could be achieved by one application of the high voltage. Figure 2 is a diagram of a tandem accelerator. An ion source yields a beam of protons, which are accelerated to a low energy by an auxiliary high-voltage supply. This beam passes through a region containing a gas at low pressure, where some of the protons are converted to negative hydrogen ions by the addition of two electrons. As the mixture of charged particles moves through a magnetic field, those with negative charge are deflected into the accelerator tube, and those with positive charge are deflected away. The beam of negative ions is then accelerated toward the positive high-voltage terminal. In this terminal, the particles pass through a thin carbon foil that strips off the two electrons, changing many of the negative ions back into positive ions (protons). These, now repelled by the positive terminal, are further accelerated through the second part of the tube. At the output end of the accelerator the protons are magnetically separated, as before, from other particles in the beam and directed to the target. In three- or four-stage tandem accelerators, two Van de Graaff generators are combined with the necessary additional provisions for changing the charge of the ions.

Van de Graaff and Cockcroft–Walton generators also are utilized for accelerating electrons. The rates at which charge is transported in electron beams correspond to currents of several milliamperes; the beams deliver energy at

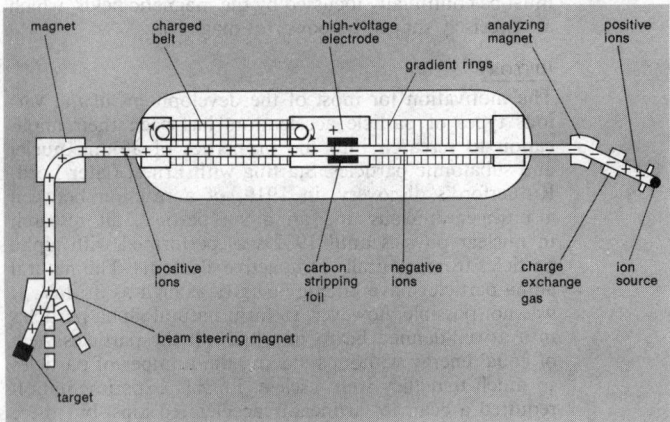

Figure 2: Two-stage tandem accelerator (see text).
Adapted from R.J. Van de Graaff, *Nuclear Instruments and Methods*, vol. 8, p. 195 (1960); North-Holland Publishing Co.

rates best expressed in terms of kilowatts. These intense beams are used for sterilization, industrial radiography, cancer therapy, and polymerization of plastics.

BETATRONS

A betatron is a type of accelerator that is useful only for electrons, which sometimes are called beta particles; hence the name. The electrons in a betatron move in a circle under the influence of a magnetic field that is caused to grow stronger as the electrons' energy is increased. The magnet that produces the field on the electron orbit also produces a field in the interior of the orbit. The increase in the strength of this field with time produces an electric field that accelerates the electrons. If the average magnetic field *inside* the orbit is always twice as strong as the magnetic field *on* the orbit, the radius of the orbit remains constant, so that the acceleration chamber can be made in the shape of a torus, or doughnut, as shown in Figure 3. The poles of the magnet are tapered to cause the field near the orbit to weaken with increasing radius. This focusses the beam by causing any particle that strays from the orbit to be subjected to forces that restore it toward its proper path. The theory of this focussing was first worked out for the betatron; by analogy, the oscillations of particles about their equilibrium orbits in all cyclic accelerators are called betatron oscillations. Betatron
oscillations

Just after the sinusoidally varying strength of the magnetic field has passed through zero and starts increasing in the direction proper to guide the electrons in their circular orbit, a burst of electrons is sent into the doughnut, where—in a 20-MeV betatron—they gain about 100 eV per revolution and traverse the orbit about 200,000 times during the acceleration. The acceleration lasts for one-quarter of the magnet cycle, until the magnetic field has reached its greatest strength, whereupon the orbit is caused to shrink, deflecting the electrons onto a target to produce a beam of intense X rays.

The practical limit on the energy imparted by a betatron is set by the radiation of electromagnetic energy by electrons moving in curved paths. The intensity of this radiation, commonly called synchrotron radiation (see below *Electron synchrotrons*), rises rapidly as the speed of the electrons increases. The largest betatron accelerates electrons to 300 MeV, sufficient to produce pi mesons in its target; the energy loss by its electrons through radiation (a few percent) is compensated by changing the relation between the field on the orbit and the average field inside the orbit. At higher energies this compensation would not be feasible.

Betatrons are now commercially manufactured, principally for use as sources of highly energetic ("hard") X rays for industrial and medical radiography.

CYCLOTRONS

The magnetic resonance accelerator, or cyclotron, was the first cyclic accelerator and the first resonance accelerator that produced particles energetic enough to be useful for nuclear research. For many years the highest particle en-

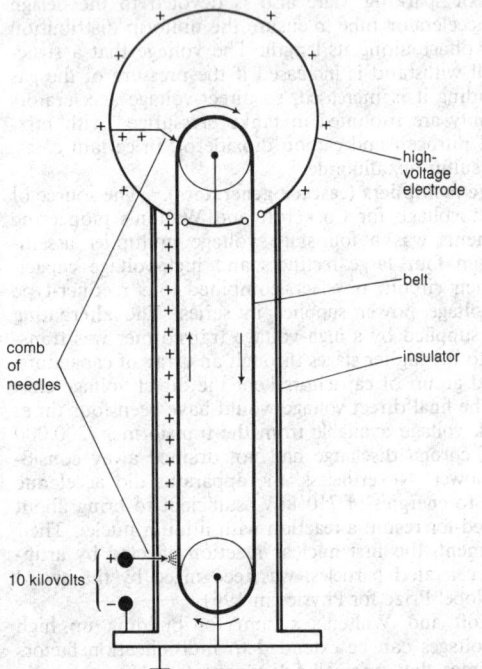

Figure 1: Simplified version of a Van de Graaff high-voltage electrostatic generator (see text).

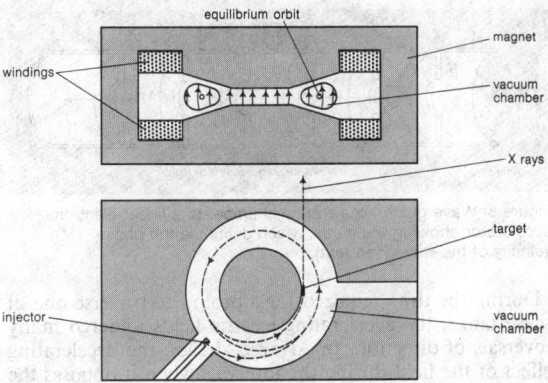

Figure 3: (Top) Cross section and (bottom) plan view of a betatron (see text).
From *Jaderna Energie* (1958)

ergies were those imparted by cyclotrons modelled upon Lawrence's archetype. In these devices, commonly called classical cyclotrons, the accelerating electric field oscillates at a fixed frequency and the guiding magnetic field has a fixed intensity.

Classical cyclotrons. The key to the operation of a cyclotron is the fact that the orbits of ions in a uniform magnetic field are isochronous; that is, the time taken by a particle of a given mass to make one complete circuit is the same at any speed or energy as long as the speed is much less than that of light. (As the speed of a particle approaches that of light, its mass undergoes the increase—predicted by the theory of relativity—that is called relativistic increase.) This isochronicity makes it possible for a high voltage, reversing in polarity at a constant frequency, to accelerate a particle many times. As shown in Figure 4, an ion source is located at the centre of an evacuated chamber that has the shape of a short cylinder, like a pillbox, between the poles of an electromagnet that creates a uniform field perpendicular to the flat faces. The accelerating voltage is applied by electrodes, called dees from their shape: each is a D-shaped half of a pillbox. The source of the voltage is an oscillator—similar to a radio transmitter—that operates at a frequency equal to the frequency of revolution of the particles in the magnetic field. The electric fields caused by this accelerating voltage are concentrated in the gap between the dees; there is no electric field inside the dees. The path of the particle inside the dee is therefore circular. Each time the particle crosses the gap between the dees it is accelerated, because in the time between these crossings the direction of the field reverses. The path of the particle is thus a spiral-like series of semicircles of continually increasing radius.

Some means of focussing is required, as otherwise a particle that starts out in a direction making a small angle with the orbital plane will spiral into the dees and be lost. While the energy of the particle is still low, this focussing is supplied by the accelerating electric fields; after the particle has gained significant energy, focussing is a consequence of a slight weakening of the magnetic field toward the peripheries of the dees as in the betatron.

The energy gained by a particle in a classical cyclotron is limited by the relativistic increase in the mass of the

particle, a phenomenon that causes the orbital frequency to decrease and the particles to get out of phase with the alternating voltage. This effect can be reduced by applying higher accelerating voltages to shorten the overall acceleration time. The highest energy imparted to protons in a classical cyclotron is less than 25 MeV, and this achievement requires the imposition of hundreds of kilovolts to the dees. The beam current in a classical cyclotron operated at high voltages can be as high as 5 milliamperes; intensities of this magnitude are very useful in the synthesis of radioisotopes.

Synchrocyclotrons. Cyclotrons in which the frequency of the accelerating voltage is changed as the particles are accelerated are called synchrocyclotrons, frequency-modulated (FM) cyclotrons, or, in the Soviet Union, phasotrons. Because of the modulation the particles do not get out of phase with the accelerating voltage, so that the relativistic mass increase does not impose a limit on the energy. Moreover, the magnetic focussing can be made stronger, so that the magnetic field need not be so precisely shaped.

Because of the phenomenon of phase stability, it is unnecessary to program the frequency of the accelerating voltage precisely to follow the decreasing frequency of revolution of the particles as they are accelerated. To see how phase stability affects the operation of a cyclotron, consider a particle moving in an orbit. Let the frequency of the accelerating voltage match the orbital frequency of this particle. If the particle crosses the accelerating gap at the time the accelerating voltage is zero, its energy and orbital radius will remain unchanged—it is said to be in equilibrium. There are two such times during each cycle of the accelerating voltage; only one of these (that at which the voltage is falling, rather than rising, through zero) corresponds to *stable* equilibrium. If a particle should arrive a short time before the voltage has fallen to zero, it is accelerated. Its speed therefore increases, but the radius of its orbit increases by an even larger proportion, so that the particle will take longer to reach the gap again and will next cross it at a time closer to that at which it would receive no acceleration. If, on the other hand, the particle reaches the gap a short time *after* the voltage has fallen through zero, its speed is diminished, and the radius of its orbit is diminished even more, so that it takes *less* time to reach the gap again, arriving—like the other particle—at a time closer to that at which it receives no acceleration. This phenomenon, by which the trajectories of errant particles are continually corrected, confers stability on the entire beam and makes it possible to accelerate the particles uniformly, by modulating the frequency, without dispersing them. The small periodic variations of the particles about the equilibrium values of phase and energy are called synchrotron oscillations.

In the operation of a synchrocyclotron, particles are accelerated from the ion source when the frequency of the accelerating voltage is equal to the orbital frequency of the particles in the central field. As the frequency of the voltage falls, the particles, on the average, encounter an accelerating field. They oscillate in phase but around a value that corresponds to the average acceleration. The particles reach the maximum energy in bunches, one for each time the accelerating frequency goes through its program. The intensity of the beam is a few microamperes, much lower than that of a classical cyclotron.

Large synchrocyclotrons have been constructed in many countries. They are used primarily for research with secondary beams of pi mesons. The practical upper limit of the energy of a synchrocyclotron, set by the cost of the huge magnets required, is about 1 GeV.

Sector-focussed cyclotrons. The sector-focussed cyclotron is another modification of the classical cyclotron that also evades relativistic constraint on its maximum energy. Its advantage over the synchrocyclotron is that the beam is not pulsed and is more intense. The frequency of the accelerating voltage is constant, and the orbital frequency of the particles is kept constant as they are accelerated by causing the average magnetic field on the orbit to increase with orbit radius. This ordinarily would cause the beam to spread out in the direction of the magnetic field, but in sector-focussed cyclotrons the magnetic

Phase stability

Synchrotron oscillations

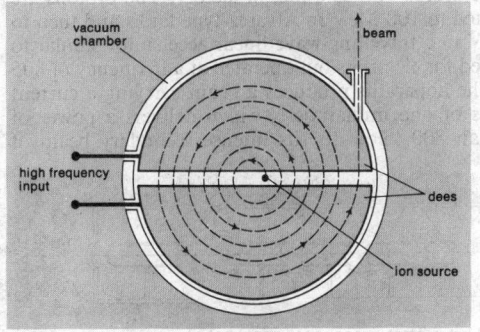

Figure 4: Plan view of the classical cyclotron.

field varies with the angular position as well as with the radius; this produces the equivalent of alternating-gradient focussing (see below *Synchrotrons*). This principle was discovered in 1938 by Llewellyn H. Thomas, then at Ohio State University, but was not applied until the alternating-gradient synchrotron was invented in 1952. Several of these devices, sometimes called azimuthally varying field (AVF) cyclotrons, have been built for use in nuclear and medical research.

LINEAR RESONANCE ACCELERATORS

The technology required to design a useful linear resonance accelerator was not developed until after 1940. These accelerators require very powerful sources of radio-frequency accelerating voltage. Further, a practical linear accelerator for heavy particles, such as protons, must make use of the principle of phase stability.

Types of linear accelerators

Linear accelerators fall into two distinct types: standing-wave linear accelerators (used for heavy particles) and travelling-wave linear accelerators (used to accelerate electrons). The reason for the difference is that after electrons have been accelerated to a few MeV in the first few metres of a typical accelerator, they have speeds very close to that of light. Therefore if the accelerating wave also moves at the speed of light, the particles do not get out of phase, as their speeds do not change. Protons, on the other hand, must reach much higher energies before their speeds can be taken as constant, so that the accelerator design must allow for the prolonged increase in speed.

Linear electron accelerators. The force that acts on electrons in a travelling-wave accelerator is provided by an electromagnetic field with a frequency near 3,000 MHz (1 MHz = 1,000,000 Hertz, or 1,000,000 cycles per second)—a microwave. The acceleration chamber is an evacuated cylindrical pipe that serves as a wave guide for the accelerating field. The phase velocity of an electromagnetic wave in a cylindrical pipe is greater than the velocity of light in free space, so the wave must be slowed down by the insertion of metal irises a few centimetres apart in the pipe, as shown in Figure 5. In the intense field, the electrons gain about two MeV every 30 centimetres or so. The microwaves are produced by large klystrons (high-frequency vacuum-tube amplifiers) with power outputs of 20–30 megawatts. Because sources of radio-frequency power of this magnitude must be operated intermittently (they will not survive continuous service), the beams from these accelerators are delivered in short bursts.

Pulses of electrons are injected at energies of a few hundred keV (that is, speeds about half that of light). The accelerator is so designed that, during the first part of the acceleration, the electrons are caused to gather into bunches, which then are accelerated nearly to the speed of light. Subsequently, the electrons move with the crest of the electromagnetic wave.

Linear electron accelerators are manufactured commercially. They are used for radiography, for cancer treatment, and as injectors for electron synchrotrons.

The 3.2-kilometre- (two-mile-) long linear electron accelerator at Stanford University (called SLAC, an acronym for *S*tanford *l*inear *a*ccelerator *c*entre) is the source of very energetic beams of electrons (almost 25 GeV) and positrons (almost 15 GeV). Electron-beam currents of 50 microamperes and positron-beam currents of more than 1 microampere can be obtained. The accelerator is used for research on subatomic particles and for filling the electron-positron storage ring called SPEAR (*S*tanford *p*ositron-*e*lectron *a*symmetric *r*ing).

Linear electron accelerators constructed of superconducting materials have been developed. The advantage offered by such a device is low power consumption, allowing production of a continuous, rather than a pulsed, beam.

Linear proton accelerators. The design principle applied in linear accelerators for protons was originated by Luis Alvarez at Berkeley in 1946. It is based on the formation of standing electromagnetic waves in a long cylindrical metal tank, or cavity, as it is sometimes called. In the design that has been adopted, the electric field is parallel to the axis of the tank. Most of these accelerators operate at frequencies of about 200 MHz.

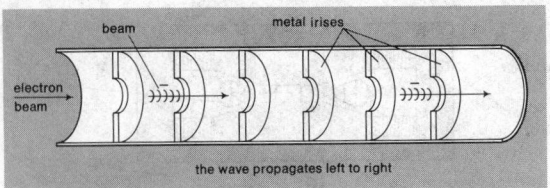

Figure 5: Wave guide acceleration chamber of a linear electron accelerator showing the irises, which decrease the phase velocity of the wave (see text).

During the time required for a proton to traverse one of these tanks, the accelerating electric fields undergo many reversals of direction. In Alvarez' design, the decelerating effect of the field during the intervals when it opposes the motion of the particles is prevented by installing on the axis of the tank a number of "drift tubes," as shown in Figure 6. The electric field is zero inside the drift tubes, and if their lengths are properly chosen, the protons cross the gap between adjacent drift tubes when the direction of the field produces acceleration and are shielded by the drift tubes when the field in the tank would decelerate them. The lengths of the drift tubes are proportional to the speeds of the particles that pass through them.

Use of drift tubes

It would appear that any error in the magnitude of the accelerating voltages would cause the particles to lose the synchronism with the fields needed for proper operation of the device, but the principle of phase stability reduces to a manageable magnitude the need for precision in construction. It also makes possible an intense beam, because protons can be accelerated in a stable manner even if they do not cross the gaps at exactly the intended times. The principle is the same as that of a synchrotron, except that the gap-crossing time for stable phase oscillations coincides with the rise, rather than the fall, of the voltage wave. If a proton arrives at the accelerating gap late, it receives a larger-than-normal increment of energy, enabling it to "catch up."

A very large amount of radio-frequency power is required to produce the accelerating voltages. This makes it necessary for linear proton accelerators to be operated in a pulsed mode. They are supplied with protons accelerated to about 750 keV by a Cockcroft–Walton generator. The entering beam passes through an accelerating radio-frequency cavity a short distance upbeam from the main linear accelerator, so that as the particles pass through the first drift tubes, they are already bunched.

The intense pulses of protons emerging from linear accelerators make these devices ideal as injectors for proton synchrotrons. Their high cost has precluded their construction for other uses except as meson factories. The largest linear accelerators used as injectors are located at the Brookhaven National Laboratory, Upton, New York, and at the Fermi National Accelerator Laboratory ("Fermilab"), Batavia, Illinois. These accelerators are very similar in construction. The beam energy is 200 MeV, and the peak beam current is more than 100 milliamperes. They are needed as injectors only for a short time every few seconds; most of the beams are used for radioisotope production and medical applications.

Injectors for proton synchrotrons

At the Los Alamos Meson Physics Facility in New Mexico, a linear proton accelerator has been constructed for nuclear research and as a meson factory. The protons are accelerated to 100 MeV in Alvarez-type tanks and then to 800 MeV in a travelling-wave linear accelerator similar to those used for electrons but operated at a frequency of 805 MHz. The apparatus produces a beam carrying a current in excess of one milliampere, which delivers a power of more than 800 kilowatts. Its intense secondary beam of

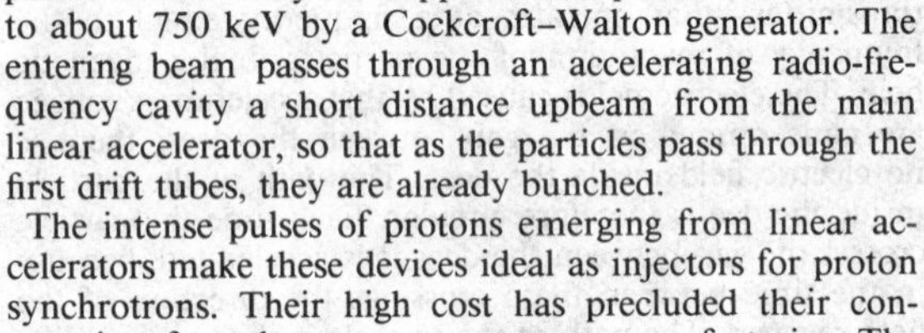

Figure 6: Linear proton resonance accelerator containing *n* metallic drift tubes (see text).

low-energy pi mesons has been applied in experimental cancer therapy.

Heavy-ion linear accelerators. For research with ions more massive than the alpha particle, a relatively high energy per unit of atomic weight is desirable. The production of beams of heavy charged particles at a reasonable cost is practical only if the particles are highly ionized, because the energy gained by an ion is proportional to its charge. The SuperHILAC at Berkeley ("hilac" is an acronym from *heavy-io*n *l*inear *ac*celerator) consists of two Alvarez accelerators operating at 70 MHz. The ions, after acceleration by the first of these machines, have a kinetic energy of 1.2 MeV per unit of atomic weight; this energy corresponds to a speed one-twentieth of the speed of light. These ions then pass through a thin carbon foil, which strips off many electrons. After stripping, the ions (now more highly charged) are accelerated by the second machine to an energy of 8.5 MeV per unit atomic weight, corresponding to a speed about one-seventh of the speed of light. Ions as heavy as those of uranium may be accelerated by the SuperHILAC. Heavy-ion beams have been used in the search for new heavy elements. For example, in 1974 a U.S. research group employed the SuperHILAC to synthesize the element with atomic number 106.

SYNCHROTRONS

As the particles in a synchrotron are accelerated, the strength of the magnetic field is increased to keep the radius of the orbit approximately constant. This technique has the advantage that the magnet required to form the particle orbits is much smaller than that needed in a cyclotron to produce the same particle energies. The acceleration is effected by radio-frequency voltages, while the synchronism is maintained by the principle of phase stability. The rate of increase of the energy of the particles is set by the rate of the strengthening of the magnetic field. The peak accelerating voltage is ordinarily about twice as large as the average energy gain per turn would require, to provide the margin for phase stability. Particles can be stably accelerated with a range of energies and phases with respect to the accelerating voltage, and very intense beams can be produced.

The magnetic field must be shaped so as to focus the beam of particles. In early synchrotrons the field was caused to decrease slightly with increasing radius, as in a betatron. This arrangement resulted in a weak focussing effect that was adequate for machines in which the dimensions of the magnet gap could be appreciable in comparison with the radius of the orbit. The magnitude of the magnetic fields that may be used is limited by the saturation of the iron components that shape the field and provide a path for the magnetic flux. Therefore, if the energy of accelerators is to be increased, their radius must be increased correspondingly. For relativistic particles, the radius is proportional to the kinetic energy. The magnet of a synchrotron with weak focussing, designed to have a reasonable intensity, would have a mass proportional to the cube of the radius. It is clear that increasing the energy beyond some point—in practice, about 10 GeV—would be very expensive.

Alternating-gradient focussing

The introduction of alternating-gradient focussing provided the solution to this problem and made possible the development of synchrotrons with much higher energies. The idea was promptly incorporated in the design of the 33-GeV proton synchrotron at the Brookhaven National Laboratory and the 28-GeV machine at the European Organization for Nuclear Research (CERN), near Geneva, Switzerland.

The magnetic fields in an alternating-gradient synchrotron vary much more strongly with radius than those used for weak focussing. A magnet with pole-tips shaped as shown in cross section *ab* in Figure 7 produces a magnetic field that sharply decreases with increasing radius. To the particle beam, this magnetic field acts like a lens with a very short focal length. In the vertical direction (the orbital plane is horizontal) it focusses the beam, but in the radial direction it is almost equally defocussing. A magnet with the pole-tip shapes shown in cross section *cd* in Figure 7 produces a field that strongly *increases* with increasing ra-

dius. This field is defocussing in the vertical direction and focussing in the radial direction. Although pairing such magnetic fields results in partial cancellation, the overall effect is to provide focussing in both directions. The ring of magnetic field is created by a large number of magnets, with the two types of pole-tips alternating, as shown at the top of Figure 7. The beam, in effect, passes through a succession of lenses as the particles move around the ring, producing a large beam current in a vacuum chamber of small cross section.

Particles accelerated in a large synchrotron are commonly injected by a linear accelerator and are steered into the ring by a device called an inflector. They begin their acceleration in the ring when the magnetic field is small. As the field created by the ring magnets increases, the injection pulse is timed so that the field and the energy of the particles from the linear accelerator are properly matched. The radio-frequency accelerating devices, usually called cavities, operate on the same principle as a short section of a linear accelerator. The useful beam may be either the accelerated particles that have been extracted from the ring by special magnets or secondary particles ejected from a target that is introduced into the beam.

Electron synchrotrons. The invention of the synchrotron immediately solved the problem of the limit on the acceleration of electrons that had been imposed by the radiation of electrons moving in circular orbits. This radiation has been named synchrotron radiation because it was first observed during the operation of a 70-MeV electron synchrotron built at the General Electric Company research laboratory, Schenectady, New York. A betatron can accelerate electrons to 300 MeV only if the radiation is carefully compensated, but a synchrotron needs

Synchrotron radiation

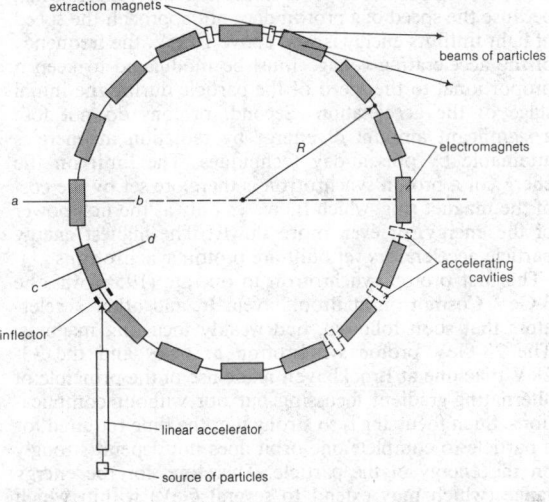

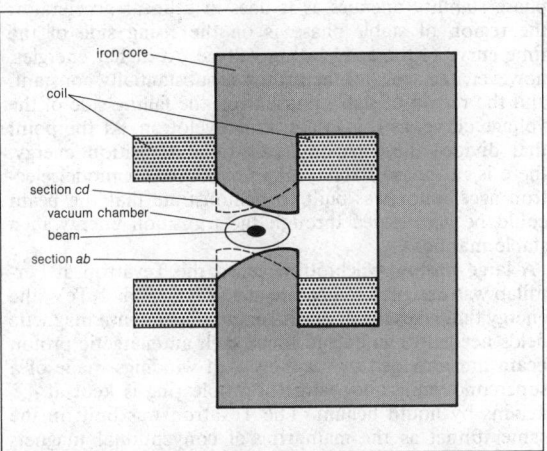

Figure 7: Synchrotron with alternating-gradient focussing, showing the placement of the two types of magnets. Shown at the bottom is a cross section of a typical magnet with the two different types of pole-tips used (see text).

only a modest increase in the radio-frequency accelerating voltage. As the particles lose energy by radiation, their average phase with respect to the accelerating voltage simply shifts slightly so as to increase their average energy gain per revolution.

Several similar electron synchrotrons with energies near 300 MeV were constructed in several countries, the first being the one built in 1949 at Berkeley under McMillan's direction. In these accelerators, the electrons were injected by a pulsed electron gun, and the initial acceleration from 50–100 keV to 2–3 MeV was induced as in a betatron. The magnets were specifically designed to provide the accelerating flux in the initial part of the magnet cycle; during this time, the speed of the electrons increased from about 50 percent of the speed of light to more than 95 percent. At this point, acceleration by the radio-frequency cavity supervened, and the small further change in speed was accommodated by a 5-percent change in the radius of the orbit.

Strong focussing was first applied to the electron synchrotron in the 1.2-GeV device built in 1954 at Cornell University, Ithaca, New York. All large electron synchrotrons now are equipped with linear accelerators as injectors. The practical limit on the energy of an electron synchrotron is set by the cost of the radio-frequency system needed to restore the energy the electrons lose by radiation. To minimize this energy loss, the acceleration time is made as short as possible (a few milliseconds) and the magnetic fields are kept weak. By 1982 superconducting radio-frequency accelerating cavities had been successfully tested in the electron synchrotron.

Proton synchrotrons. The mode of operation of a proton synchrotron is very similar to that of an electron synchrotron, but there are two important differences. First, because the speed of a proton does not approach the speed of light until its energy is well above 1 GeV, the frequency of the accelerating voltage must be modulated to keep it proportional to the speed of the particle during the initial stage of the acceleration. Second, protons do not lose a significant amount of energy by radiation at energies attainable by present-day techniques. The limit on the energy of a proton synchrotron is therefore set by the cost of the magnet ring, which increases only as the first power of the energy, or even more slowly. The highest energy particle accelerators yet built are proton synchrotrons.

The first proton synchrotron to operate (1956) was the 3-GeV Cosmotron at Brookhaven. It, and other accelerators that soon followed, had weakly focussing magnets. The 28-GeV proton synchrotron at CERN and the 33-GeV machine at Brookhaven made use of the principle of alternating-gradient focussing but not without complications. Such focussing is so strong that the time required for a particle to complete one orbit does not depend strongly on the energy of the particle. Therefore, for the energy range (which may extend to several GeV) within which acceleration appreciably affects the speed of the particle, phase stability operates as it does in a linear accelerator: the region of stable phase is on the rising side of the time curve of the accelerating voltage. At higher energies, however, the speed of the proton is substantially constant, and the region of stable phase is on the falling side of the voltage curve, as it is in a synchrocyclotron. At the point that divides these regions, called the transition energy, there is no phase stability. At Brookhaven a model electron accelerator was built to demonstrate that the beam could be accelerated through the transition energy in a stable manner.

Fermilab Tevatron

A large proton synchrotron called the Tevatron at Fermilab was designed to operate at 1,000 GeV or 1 TeV, the energy that gives the device its name. The intense magnetic fields needed to guide and focus such an energetic proton beam are provided by magnets with windings made of a superconducting alloy, and the whole ring is kept at 4.5 kelvins by liquid helium. The Tevatron was built in the same tunnel as the main ring of conventional magnets of the 400-GeV accelerator that went into operation in 1972 and now serves as the injector for the Tevatron. The proton beam originates in a 750-keV Cockcroft–Walton generator and is accelerated to 200 MeV in a linear ac-

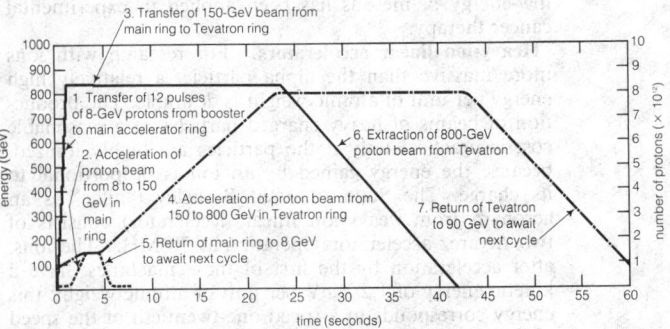

Figure 8: Successive stages comprising one cycle in the operation of the two large accelerating rings at the Fermi National Accelerator Laboratory. The solid line (right-hand scale) shows the number of protons circulating in the rings. The broken lines show the magnet currents, which indicate the energy of the protons (left-hand scale).

By courtesy of John Crawford, Fermilab, Batavia, Illinois

celerator. The protons are then injected into a "booster" synchrotron in which they are accelerated to 8 GeV (99.4 percent of the speed of light). While the magnetic field of the main accelerator ring is held at a strength of 400 gauss, 12 pulses of protons are injected into the ring from the booster. The fields in the bending and focussing magnets are then strengthened as the protons are accelerated to 150 GeV in 1.5 seconds. The protons are then transferred to the ring of superconducting magnets for final acceleration. Figure 8 shows the sequence of processes occurring during one cycle in the operation of the main ring and the superconducting ring to produce and extract a beam of 800-GeV protons. The device completes one cycle per minute, including the extraction of the beam, which occupies about 20 seconds. Prolonging the beam extraction over this extended interval is very important for the proper interpretation of the experiments. In a typical experiment, several particles (called secondary particles) are ejected from a target when an accelerated particle (the primary particle) strikes it. The goal of the experiment is the study of either this production process or the properties of the secondary particles that result from it. These secondary particles produce signals as they pass through many detectors, and it is assumed that all the signals produced at the same time arise from particles coming from the interaction of a single primary particle with the target. If many accelerated particles arrived at the target within too short an interval, numerous interactions would occur at practically the same time, resulting in accidental coincidences that would obscure the effects being searched for.

The two large rings at Fermilab are 1,000 metres in radius; their circumference is 6.3 kilometres (almost 4 miles). In these rings the functions of bending the beam around its orbit and focussing the beam are separated. Each ring has 774 bending magnets; the main ring has 180 focussing magnets, the superconducting ring has 216. Injection, acceleration, and extraction of the beam take place in six straight sections free from magnets. The beam

Adapted from CERN Courier with permission of Fermilab, Batavia, Illinois

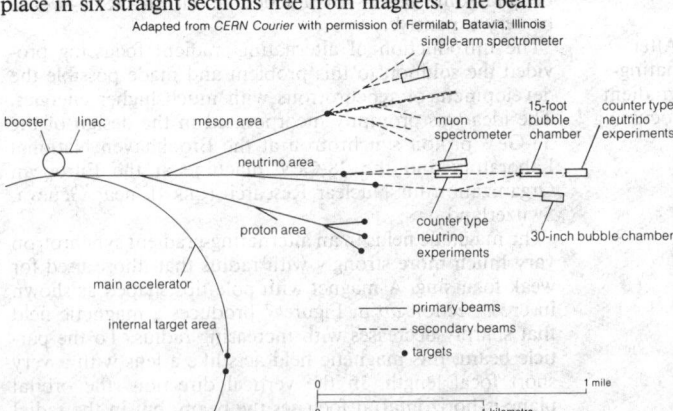

Figure 9: The plan of the Fermi National Accelerator Laboratory accelerator and experimental areas. The angles between the branches of the beam are exaggerated for clarity.

from this accelerator is divided to serve many experimental areas. Figure 9 shows a plan of the accelerator and experimental areas.

An accelerator very similar to the Fermilab 400-GeV synchrotron went into operation in 1976 at CERN, where a 28-GeV proton synchrotron serves as the booster accelerator. In 1981 it was modified to permit operation as a colliding-beam storage ring (see below *Storage rings*). Since then it has been used alternately as a collider, with beams of 315-GeV protons and antiprotons, and as a 450-GeV fixed-target accelerator.

Proton synchrotrons are in operation in laboratories in several countries; they all are used for research into the properties of subatomic particles.

OTHER TYPES OF ACCELERATORS

Inter-
actions of
particle
beams **Storage rings.** Although particles are sometimes accelerated in storage rings, the main purpose of these rings is to make possible energetic interactions between beams of particles moving in opposite directions. When a moving object strikes an identical object that is at rest, at most half of the kinetic energy of the moving object is available to produce heat or to deform the objects: the remainder is accounted for by the motions of the objects after the encounter. If, however, the two objects are in motion in opposite directions with equal speeds, then all the kinetic energy is available to produce heat or deformation at the instant of collision. If the objects stick together, the combination is at rest after the collision. For particles with speeds close to that of light, the effect is accentuated. If a 400-GeV proton strikes a proton at rest, only 27.4 GeV are available for the interaction; the remainder produces motion of the particles. On the other hand, if two 31.4-GeV protons collide, 62.3 GeV are available for the interaction (the collision is not quite "head on").

In a target composed of liquid or solid matter, the number of particles per unit volume accessible to an accelerated beam is very large, but when the target of one beam is another beam, the number of particles interacting is very much smaller: the rate of interactions is proportional to the product of the currents in the two beams. Kerst realized in 1956 that, although the beam current in a high-energy accelerator is small, the currents circulating in the magnet rings are effectively very much larger because of the high orbital frequency of the particles. Colliding
beams of
particles Thus, if the colliding beams are circulating in such rings, useful experiments on the interactions could be carried out. In a colliding-beam apparatus, the two beams may be made up of identical particles (for example, two beams of protons), in which case the installation consists of two separate rings of magnets. In one ring, the magnetic fields guide the particles clockwise; in the other ring, the fields are oriented in the opposite direction so as to guide the particles counterclockwise. The rings intersect at "interaction regions," where the beams collide. In other cases, the two beams are composed of particles of opposite charge (for example, electrons and positrons, or protons and antiprotons). Such beams circulate in opposite directions in the same vacuum chamber, guided by the same magnets. The particles are bunched so that they collide only in the interaction regions.

The highest interaction energies are at present, and will be in the future, achieved in storage rings. This places the research with them at the very forefront of the quest for knowledge, even though many types of experiments cannot be conducted with storage rings. This is true partly because the number of interactions in a storage ring is a small fraction of that occurring in a stationary target and partly because storage beams do not produce intense beams of secondary particles.

Electron storage rings. Many storage rings have been constructed to study the interactions of electrons with positrons. The principal centres of this research are Stanford, California; Orsay, France; Hamburg, West Germany; Frascati, Italy; and Novosibirsk, Russian S.F.S.R.

The manner of operation of a typical electron-positron colliding-beam device is shown in Figure 10. Since the signs of their electrical charges are opposite, electrons and positrons circulate in opposite directions in a magnet ring.

The figure shows a linear electron accelerator for filling the ring; a synchrotron can be used instead. The deflecting magnet sends electrons to an injection point on the ring so that they circulate clockwise. Positrons are created by high-energy electrons in a target, usually called a converter, and then accelerated by the second stage of the linear accelerator. The deflecting magnet sends them to an injection point so that they circulate counterclockwise.

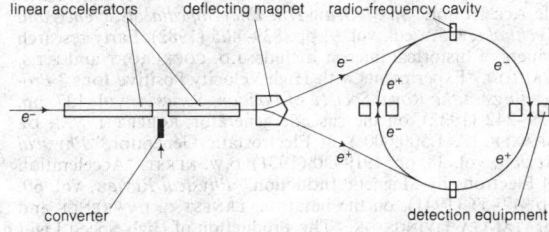

Figure 10: Storage ring with electron-positron colliding beams (see text).

Because of the radiation of energy by the particles, it is necessary to have accelerating cavities if the energy of the particles is to be kept fixed. The accelerating system causes the particles to circulate in bunches so that the collisions take place in only a few (commonly only two) places in the ring. This sparsity of intersections simplifies the operation by minimizing the disruption of each beam caused by interactions with the other, allowing more intense beams to be collected and used in the ring. The detection equipment for the experiments is located near the points where the beams intersect.

The electrons and positrons in a storage ring emit synchrotron radiation at very great rates—more than a megawatt in some installations. From a high-energy storage ring, the wavelength of this radiation extends into the X-ray region. These storage rings now constitute the brightest sources of electromagnetic radiation available in the ultraviolet and X-ray regions. This radiation is increasingly useful for research in solid-state physics, biophysics, and chemical physics; a few electron storage rings of relatively low energy are operated solely for this purpose.

Proton storage rings. The highest interaction energies have been achieved in collisions between protons and antiprotons circulating in opposite directions in a storage ring. The high energy is possible because protons do not dissipate significant energy in the form of synchrotron radiation, as do electrons. Creation of an intense beam of antiprotons required techniques (developed by Simon van der Meer at CERN) to reduce the amplitude of betatron oscillations and to bring all the particles to the same energy. Antiprotons have been produced at CERN by directing protons from a 27-GeV synchrotron onto a copper target. This process is very inefficient: about a million protons must strike the target to produce each antiproton. Furthermore, the antiprotons emerge from the target with random energies and directions. They are collected by magnetic fields into a diffuse beam that is injected into a small storage ring with a large cross-sectional area. As the antiprotons circulate in this ring, electronic devices sense the deviations from the desired orbit and apply corrective forces that focus the particles into a narrow beam of uniform energy. To accumulate enough antiprotons to make up a useful beam in the large storage ring at CERN takes about 24 hours. They then are accelerated to 315 GeV and allowed to collide with 315-GeV protons circulating in the opposite direction; the interaction energy is 630 GeV.

Impulse accelerators. Primarily for use in research on thermonuclear fusion of hydrogen isotopes, several high-intensity electron accelerators have been constructed. One type resembles a string of beads in which each bead is a torus of laminated iron and the string is the vacuum tube. The iron toruses constitute the cores of pulse transformers, and the beam of electrons, in effect, forms the secondary windings of all of the transformers, which are connected in series. The primaries are all connected in parallel and are powered by the discharge of a large bank of capacitors. These accelerators produce beams with energies between 1 and 9 MeV and currents between 200 and 200,000 amperes. The pulses are very brief, lasting about 50 nanoseconds. Besides their application to thermonuclear fusion, such accelerators are utilized for flash radiography, research on collective ion acceleration, microwave production, and laser excitation.

BIBLIOGRAPHY. For physics background see the latest edition of HENRY SEMAT and JOHN R. ALBRIGHT, *Introduction to Atomic and Nuclear Physics,* a college-level text. For an extensive survey for nonspecialists, see H.E. WEGNER *et al.,* "Particle Accelerator," in *McGraw-Hill Encyclopedia of Science and Technology,* 5th ed., vol. 9, pp. 839–865 (1982). Early research papers of historical interest include: J.D. COCKCROFT and E.T.S. WALTON, "Experiments with High Velocity Positive Ions," *Proceedings of the Royal Society of London, Series A,* vol. 137, pp. 229–242 (1932), on the cascade generator; ROBERT J. VAN DE GRAAFF, "A 1,500,000 Volt Electrostatic Generator," *Physical Review,* vol. 38, pp. 1919–20 (1931); D.W. KERST, "Acceleration of Electrons by Magnetic Induction," *Physical Review,* vol. 60, pp. 47–53 (1941), on the betatron; ERNEST O. LAWRENCE and M. STANLEY LIVINGSTON, "The Production of High Speed Light Ions Without the Use of High Voltages," *Physical Review,* vol. 40, pp. 19–35 (1932), on the classical cyclotron: DAVID H. SLOAN and ERNEST O. LAWRENCE, "The Production of Heavy High Speed Ions Without the Use of High Voltages," *Physical Review,* vol. 38, pp. 2021–32 (1931), on the development of the resonance linear accelerator idea; V.I. VEKSLER, "A New Method for Acceleration of Relativistic Particles," *Akademiia Nauk SSSR Doklady,* vol. 43, p. 329 (1944), on phase stability; EDWIN M. MCMILLAN, "The Synchrotron: A Proposed High Energy Particle Accelerator," *Physical Review,* vol. 68, pp. 143–144 (1945); D.W. KERST *et al.,* "Attainment of Very High Energy by Means of Intersecting Beams of Particles," *Physical Review,* vol. 102, pp. 590–591 (1956). For discussions of some modern accelerators see D. ALLAN BROMLEY (ed.), "Large Electrostatic Generators," *Nucl. Instrum. Meth.,* vol. 122, pp. 1–285 (1974); ROBERT R. WILSON, "The Batavia Accelerator," *Scientific American,* vol. 230, pp. 72–83 (Feb. 1974), on the 400-GeV proton synchrotron; MAURICE GOLDSMITH and EDWIN SHAW, *Europe's Giant Accelerator* (1977), a nontechnical history of the CERN 400-GeV proton synchrotron; KJELL JOHNSEN, "The CERN Intersecting Storage Rings," *Nucl. Instrum. Meth.,* vol. 108, pp. 205–223 (1973); ROBERT R. WILSON, "The Next Generation of Particle Accelerators," *Scientific American,* vol. 242, pp. 42–57 (Jan. 1980). More technical works include M. STANLEY LIVINGSTON and JOHN P. BLEWETT, *Particle Accelerators* (1962); JOHN J. LIVINGOOD, *Principles of Cyclic Particle Accelerators* (1961); A.A. KOLOMENSKY and A.N. LEBEDEV, *Theory of Cyclic Accelerators* (1966; originally published in Russian, 1962); R.A. CARRIGAN, F.R. HUSON, and M. MONTH (eds.), *Physics of High Energy Particle Accelerators: Fermilab Summer School, 1981* (1982), American Institute of Physics conference proceedings, no. 87, for modern, advanced accelerator theory; *IEEE Transactions on Nuclear Science* (bimonthly), for new developments in accelerator technology.

(Y.M.A./F.C.S./Ed.)

Pascal

Blaise Pascal, a mathematician, physicist, religious philosopher, and master of French prose, laid the foundation for the modern theory of probabilities, formulated what came to be known as Pascal's law of pressure, and propagated a religious doctrine that taught the experience of God through the heart rather than through reason. The establishment of his principle of intuitionism had an impact on such later philosophers as Jean-Jacques Rousseau and Henri Bergson and also on the Existentialists.

Pascal's life to the Port-Royal years. He was born on June 19, 1623, at Clermont-Ferrand, France, where his father, Étienne Pascal, was presiding judge of the tax court. Pascal's mother died in 1626, and in 1631 the family moved to Paris. Étienne, who was respected as a mathematician, devoted himself henceforth to the education of his children. While his sister Jacqueline (born in 1625) figured as an infant prodigy in literary circles, Blaise proved himself no less precocious in mathematics. In 1640 he wrote an essay on conic sections, *Essai pour les coniques,* based on his study of the now classical work of Girard Desargues on synthetic projective geometry. The young man's work, which was highly successful in the world of mathematics, aroused the envy of no less a personage than the great French Rationalist and mathematician René Descartes. Between 1642 and 1644, Pascal conceived and constructed a calculating device to help his father—who in 1639 had been appointed intendant (local administrator) at Rouen—in his tax computations. The machine was regarded by Pascal's contemporaries as his main claim to fame, and with reason, for in a sense it was the first digital calculator.

Until 1646 the Pascal family held strictly Roman Catholic principles, though they often substituted *l'honnêteté* ("polite respectability") for inward religion. An illness of his father, however, brought Blaise into contact with a more profound expression of religion, for he met two disciples of the abbé de Saint-Cyran, who, as director of the convent of Port-Royal, had brought the austere moral and theological conceptions of Jansenism into the life and thought of the convent. Jansenism was a 17th-century form of Augustinianism in the Roman Catholic Church. It repudiated free will, accepted predestination, and taught that divine grace, rather than good works, was the key to salvation. The convent at Port-Royal had become the centre for the dissemination of the doctrine. Pascal himself was the first to feel the necessity of entirely turning away from the world to God, and he won his family over to the spiritual life in 1646. His letters indicate that for several years he was his family's spiritual adviser, but the conflict within himself—between the world and ascetic life—was not yet resolved. Absorbed again in his scientific interests, he tested the theories of Galileo and Evangelista Torricelli (an Italian physicist who discovered the principle of the barometer). To do so, he reproduced and amplified experiments on atmospheric pressure by constructing mercury barometers and measuring air pressure, both in Paris and on the top of a mountain overlooking Clermont-Ferrand. These tests paved the way for further studies in hydrodynamics and hydrostatics. While experimenting, Pascal invented the syringe and created the hydraulic press, an instrument based upon the principle that became known as Pascal's law: pressure applied to a confined liquid is transmitted undiminished through the liquid in all directions regardless of the area to which the pressure is applied. His publications on the problem of the vacuum (1647–48) added to his reputation. When he fell ill from overwork, his doctors advised him to seek distractions; but what

Contributions to physics and mathematics

By courtesy of the Bibliothèque Nationale, Paris

Pascal, red crayon drawing by Jean Domat, c. 1649. In the Bibliothèque Nationale, Paris.

has been described as Pascal's "worldly period" (1651–54) was, in fact, primarily a period of intense scientific work, during which he composed treatises on the equilibrium of liquid solutions, on the weight and density of air, and on the arithmetic triangle: *Traité de l'équilibre des liqueurs et de la pesanteur de la masse de l'air* (Eng. trans., *The Physical Treatises of Pascal*, 1937) and also his *Traité du triangle arithmétique*. In the last treatise, a fragment of the *De Alea Geometriae*, he laid the foundations for the calculus of probabilities. By the end of 1653, however, he had begun to feel religious scruples; and the "night of fire," an intense, perhaps mystical "conversion" that he experienced on November 23, 1654, he believed to be the beginning of a new life. He entered Port-Royal in January 1655, and though he never became one of the solitaires, he thereafter wrote only at their request and never again published in his own name. The two works for which he is chiefly known, *Les Provinciales* and the *Pensées*, date from the years of his life spent at Port-Royal.

"Les Provinciales." Written in defense of Antoine Arnauld, an opponent of the Jesuits and a defender of Jansenism who was on trial before the faculty of theology in Paris for his controversial religious works, Pascal's 18 *Lettres écrites par Louis de Montalte à un provincial* deal with divine grace and the ethical code of the Jesuits. They are better known as *Les Provinciales*. They included a blow against the relaxed morality that the Jesuits were said to teach and that was the weak point in their controversy with Port-Royal; Pascal quotes freely Jesuit dialogues and discrediting quotations from their own works, sometimes in a spirit of derision, sometimes with indignation. In the two last letters, dealing with the question of grace, Pascal proposed a conciliatory position that was later to make it possible for Port-Royal to subscribe to the "Peace of the Church," a temporary cessation of the conflict over Jansenism, in 1668.

The *Provinciales* were an immediate success, and their popularity has remained undiminished. This they owe primarily to their form, in which for the first time bombast and tedious rhetoric are replaced by variety, brevity, tautness, and precision of style; as Nicolas Boileau, the founder of French literary criticism, recognized, they marked the beginning of modern French prose. Something of their popularity, moreover, in fashionable, Protestant, or skeptical circles, must be attributed to the violence of their attack on the Jesuits. In England they have been most widely read when Roman Catholicism has seemed a threat to the Church of England. Yet they have also helped Catholicism to rid itself of laxity; and, in 1678, Pope Innocent XI himself condemned half of the propositions that Pascal had denounced earlier. Thus, the *Provinciales* played a decisive part in promoting a return to inner religion and helped to secure the eventual triumph of the ideas set forth in Antoine Arnauld's treatise *De la fréquente communion* (1643), in which he protested against the idea that the profligate could atone for continued sin by frequent communion without repentance, a thesis that thereafter remained almost unchallengeable until the French church felt the repercussion of the revocation of the Edict of Nantes (which had granted religious freedom to French Protestants) in 1685. Whereas the Jesuits seemed to represent a Counter-Reformation predominantly concerned with orthodoxy and obedience to ecclesiastical authority, the *Provinciales* advocated a more spiritual approach, emphasizing the soul's union with the Mystical Body of Christ through charity.

Further, by rejecting any double standard of morality and the distinction between counsel and precept, Pascal aligned himself with those who believe the ideal of evangelical perfection to be inseparable from the Christian life. Although there was nothing original in these opinions, Pascal nevertheless stamped them with the passionate conviction of a man in love with the absolute, of a man who saw no salvation apart from a heartfelt desire for the truth, together with a love of God that works continually toward destroying all self-love. For Pascal, morality cannot be separated from spirituality. Moreover, his own spiritual development can be traced in the *Provinciales*. The religious sense in them becomes progressively refined

Association with the Convent of Port-Royal

Morality and spirituality

after the first letters, in which the tone of ridicule is smart rather than charitable.

"Pensées." Pascal finally decided to write his work of Christian apologetics, *Apologie de la religion chrétienne*, as a consequence of his meditations on miracles and other proofs of Christianity. The work remained unfinished at his death. Between the summers of 1657 and 1658, he put together most of the notes and fragments that editors have published under the inappropriate title *Pensées* ("Thoughts"; Eng. trans., *Pensées*, 1962). In the *Apologie*, Pascal shows the man without grace to be an incomprehensible mixture of greatness and abjectness, incapable of truth or of reaching the supreme good to which his nature nevertheless aspires. A religion that accounts for these contradictions, which he believed philosophy and worldliness fail to do, is for that very reason "to be venerated and loved." The indifference of the skeptic, Pascal wrote, is to be overcome by means of the "wager": if God does not exist, the skeptic loses nothing by believing in him; but if he does exist, the skeptic gains eternal life by believing in him. Pascal insists that men must be brought to God through Jesus Christ alone, because a creature could never know the infinite if Jesus had not descended to assume the proportions of man's fallen state.

The second part of the work applies the Augustinian theory of allegorical interpretation to the biblical types (*figuratifs*); reviews the rabbinical texts, the persistence of true religion, the work of Moses, and the proofs concerning Jesus Christ's God-like role; and, finally, gives a picture of the primitive church and the fulfillment of the prophecies. The *Apologie (Pensées)* is a treatise on spirituality. Pascal was not interested in making converts if they were not going to be saints.

Pascal's apologetic, though it has stood the test of time, is primarily addressed to individuals of his own acquaintance. To convert his libertine friends, he looked for arguments in their favourite authors: in Michel de Montaigne, in the Skeptic Pierre Charron, in the Epicurean Pierre Gassendi, and in Thomas Hobbes, an English political philosopher. For Pascal, Skepticism was but a stage. Modernist theologians in particular have tried to make use of his main contention, that "man is infinitely more than man," in isolation from his other contention, that man's wretchedness is explicable only as the effect of a Fall, about which a man can learn what he needs to know from history. In so doing, they sacrifice the second part of the *Apologie* to the first, keeping the philosophy while losing the exegesis. For Pascal as for St. Paul, Jesus Christ is the second Adam, inconceivable without the first.

Finally, too, Pascal expressly admitted that his psychological analyses were not by themselves sufficient to exclude a "philosophy of the absurd"; to do so, it is necessary to have recourse to the convergence of these analyses with the "lines of fact" concerning revelation, this convergence being too extraordinary not to appear as the work of providence to an anguished seeker after truth (*qui cherche en gémissant*).

He was next again involved in scientific work. First, the "Messieurs de Port-Royal" themselves asked for his help in composing the *Élements de géométrie;* and second, it was suggested that he should publish what he had discovered about cycloid curves, a subject on which the greatest mathematicians of the time had been working. Once more fame aroused in him feelings of self-esteem; but from February 1659, illness brought him back to his former frame of mind, and he composed the "prayer for conversion" that the English clergymen Charles and John Wesley, who founded the Methodist Church, were later to regard so highly. Scarcely capable of regular work, he henceforth gave himself over to helping the poor and to the ascetic and devotional life. He took part intermittently, however, in the disputes to which the "Formulary"—a document condemning five propositions of Jansenism that, at the demand of the church authorities, had to be signed before a person could receive the sacraments—gave rise. Finally a difference of opinion with the theologians of Port-Royal led him to withdraw from controversy, though he did not sever his relations with them.

Pascal died on August 19, 1662, after suffering terrible

Pascal's apologetics

pain, probably from carcinomatous meningitis following a malignant ulcer of the stomach. He was assisted by a non-Jansenist parish priest.

Assessment. At once a physicist, a mathematician, an eloquent publicist in the *Provinciales,* and an inspired artist in the *Apologie* and in his private notes, Pascal was embarrassed by the very abundance of his talents. It has been suggested that it was his too concrete turn of mind that prevented his discovering the infinitesimal calculus; and in some of the *Provinciales* the mysterious relations of human beings with God are treated as if they were a geometrical problem. But these considerations are far outweighed by the profit that he drew from the multiplicity of his gifts; his religious writings are rigorous because of his scientific training; and his love of the concrete emerges no less from the stream of quotations in the *Provinciales* than from his determination to reject the vigorous method of attack that he had used so effectively in his *Apologie.*

MAJOR WORKS

MATHEMATICS, LOGIC, AND THE FOUNDATIONS OF SCIENCE: *Essai pour les coniques* (1640); *Lettre sur le sujet de la machine inventée par le sieur B.P. pour faire toutes sortes d'opération d'arithmétique* (1645); *De l'autorité en matière de philosophie,* the first editor's title of Pascal's preface to a projected *Traité du vuide,* consisting of a general statement of the principle of scientific research (written 1647, printed 1779); *Traité du triangle arithmétique avec quelques autres petits traités sur la même matière* (written 1654, printed 1665); *De l'esprit géométrique—de l'art de persuader* (written c. 1658, first printed in two parts 1728 and 1776); *Histoire de la roulette, appellée autrement trochoïde ou cycloïde* (1658); *Lettres de A. Dettonville, contenant quelques-unes de ses inventions de géométrie* (1658–59).

PHYSICS: *Expériences nouvelles touchant le vuide* (1647); *Récit de la grande expérience de l'équilibre des liqueurs* (1648); *Traites de l'équilibre des liqueurs et de la pesanteur de la masse de l'air* (written 1651, printed 1663; *The Physical Treatises of Pascal: The Equilibrium of Liquids and the Weight of the Mass of the Air,* 1937).

RELIGIOUS PHILOSOPHY AND CONTROVERSY: *Abrégé de la vie de Jésus-Christ* (written 1654 or 1655, printed 1846); *Lettre escritte à un Provincial par un de ses amis sur le sujet des disputes présentes de la Sorbonne* (January 1656, followed by 17 more pamphlets on the same themes down to March 1657), all 18 being subsequently republished together as *Les Provinciales* (1657; augmented edition, with supplementary pamphlets, 1659); *Projet de mandement contre l'Apologie pour les casuistes* (written 1658, printed 1779); *Ecrits sur la grâce* (four treatises drafted between 1656 and 1658 and printed from 1779 onward); *Pensées de M. Pascal sur la religion et sur quelques autres sujets* (1670; the first Eng. trans. was *Monsieur Pascal's Thoughts, Meditations, and Prayers,* 1688; numerous new translations and versions have appeared since then); *Prière pur demander à Dieu le bon usages des maladies* (written 1659, printed 1666 and 1670).

OTHER WORKS: *Trois discours sur la condition des grands* (comprised 1660, printed 1670). Collected editions of Pascal's works also include several private letters of mathematical or spiritual interest.

COLLECTED EDITIONS: Considerable editions of Pascal's *Oeuvres complètes* were undertaken by the Abbé Charles Bossut, 5 vol. (1779); and by Léon Brunschvicg, Pierre Boutroux, and Félix Gazier, 14 vol. (1908–25). The handiest edition is by LOUIS LAFUMA, *l'Intégrale* (1960). Collections in English include *The Miscellaneous Writings of Pascal* (1849); *Thoughts, Letters, Minor Works* (1910); and *Provincial Letters, Pensées, Scientific Treatises,* Encyclopædia Britannica "Great Books of the Western World" (1952).

BIBLIOGRAPHY. A standard edition of Pascal's works is that by LÉON BRUNSCHVICG, PIERRE BOUTROUX, and FÉLIX GAZIER, 14 vol. (1908–25); in part replaced by the edition of JEAN MESNARD, 2 vol. (1964–72); and by *Pensées sur la religion,* ed. by LOUIS LAFUMA, 3rd ed., 3 vol. (1960). See also the editions by HUGH F. STEWART of *Pensées* (1950), containing an English translation, and of *Provinciales* (1920, reissued 1951). Biographical and critical studies include: JEAN MESNARD, *Pascal: His Life and Works* (1952; originally published in French, 1951), an excellent biography, with bibliography, *Pascal* (1965), and *Pascal et les Roannez,* 2 vol. (1965); LUCIEN JERPHAGNON, *Le Caractère de Pascal* (1962); PHILIPPE SELLIER, *Pascal et saint Augustin* (1970); ROBERT J. NELSON, *Pascal: Adversary and Advocate* (1982), a biographical study concentrating on linguistics, theology, and personal development; ALBAN J. KRAILSHEIMER, *Pascal* (1980), an introductory biography for the general reader; JAN MIEL, *Pascal and Theology* (1970), a study of his theology of grace; HUGH M. DAVIDSON, *The Origins of Certainty* (1979), an introduction to the *Pensées;* ÉMILE CAILLIET, *The Clue to Pascal* (1943, reprinted 1973); and *Blaise Pascal, l'homme et l'oeuvre* (1956), a collection of articles and discussions from the proceedings of a congress on Pascal held at Royaumont, France, in 1954.

(J.Or./L.J./Ed.)

Pasteur

The scientific contributions of Louis Pasteur, French chemist and microbiologist, were among the most varied and valuable in the history of science and industry. It was he who proved that microorganisms cause fermentation and disease; he who originated and was the first to use vaccines for rabies, anthrax, and chicken cholera; he who saved the beer, wine, and silk industries of France and other countries; he who performed important pioneer work in stereochemistry; and he who originated the process known as pasteurization.

Born December 27, 1822, at Dole in eastern France, Pasteur was the descendant of generations of tanners. His great-grandfather had been an indentured labourer who had purchased his freedom. In his youth Pasteur showed little interest in anything but drawing and produced a number of pastels, portraits of his parents and friends. After attending primary and secondary schools in Arbois, where his family had moved, and then in Besançon, Pasteur earned his *bachelier ès lettres* (bachelor of arts) in 1840 and *bachelier ès sciences* (bachelor of science) at the Royal College in Besançon in 1842. The following year he was admitted to the École Normale Supérieure, the famous teachers' college in Paris. He became *licencié ès sciences* (master of science) in 1845, and, after acquiring an advanced degree in physical sciences, he won his *docteur ès sciences* (doctor of philosophy) in 1847. On May 22, 1848, at the age of 26, he presented before the Paris Academy of Sciences a paper reporting a remarkable discovery he had just made—that certain chemical compounds were capable of splitting into a "right" component and a "left" component, one component being the mirror image of the other. His discoveries arose out of a crystallographic

Stereo-chemical investigations

Archives Photographiques

Pasteur.

investigation of tartaric acid, an acid formed in grape fermentation that is widely used commercially, and racemic acid—a new, hitherto unknown acid that had been discovered in certain industrial processes in the Alsace region. Both acids not only had identical chemical compositions but also had the same structure; yet they showed marked differences in properties. The German chemist Eilhardt Mitscherlich (1794–1863) had shown that while ordinary commercial tartaric acid affects the rotation of plane polarized light, the unknown acid had no such effect. With the help of his own chemical methods Pasteur supplied the clue to this enigma by showing that the salts of the racemic acid consisted of two types of crystals that were mirror images of one another (like right- and left-hand gloves). When separated the two types of crystals rotated plane polarized light to the same degree but in opposite directions (one to the right, or clockwise, and the other to the left, or counterclockwise). One of the two crystal forms of racemic acid proved to be identical with the tartaric acid of fermentation. As Pasteur showed further, one component of the racemic acid (that identical with the tartaric acid from fermentation) could be utilized for nutrition by micro-organisms, whereas the other, which is now termed its optical antipode, was not assimilable by living organisms. On the basis of these experiments, Pasteur elaborated his theory of molecular asymmetry, showing that the biological properties of chemical substances depend not only on the nature of the atoms constituting their molecules but also on the manner in which these atoms are arranged in space.

In 1848 Pasteur was appointed professor of physics at the Dijon Lycée (secondary school) but was shortly called to the University of Strasbourg as professor of chemistry. There, on May 29, 1849, he married the daughter of the rector of the university, Marie Laurent, by whom he was to have five children, only two of whom survived childhood.

In 1854 Pasteur became dean of the new science faculty at the University of Lille, where he initiated a highly modern educational concept: by instituting evening classes for the many young workmen of the industrial city, conducting his regular students around large factories in the area, and organizing supervised practical courses, he demonstrated the relationship that he believed should exist between theory and practice, between university and industry. At Lille, after receiving a query from an industrialist on the production of alcohol from grain and beet sugar, Pasteur began his studies on fermentation. In the course of his analysis he once again encountered—though in liquid form—new "right" and "left" compounds. From studying the fermentation of alcohol he went on to the problem of lactic fermentation, showing yeast to be an organism capable of reproducing itself, even in artificial media, without free oxygen—a concept that became known as the Pasteur effect.

In 1857 he was named Director of Scientific Studies at the École Normale Supérieure. He continued his researches and announced that fermentation was the result of the activity of minute organisms and that when fermentation failed, either the necessary organism was absent or was unable to grow properly. Before this discovery, all explanations of fermentation had lacked experimental foundation; Pasteur showed that milk could be soured by injecting a number of organisms from buttermilk or beer but could be kept unchanged if such organisms were excluded.

He was elected to the Academy of Sciences in 1862, and the following year a chair at the École des Beaux-Arts was established for him for a new and original program of instruction in geology, physics, and chemistry applied to the fine arts.

As a scholar engaged in research, Pasteur eventually found his administrative duties as Director of Scientific Studies at the École Supérieure too irksome. He gave up the post in 1867, and, thanks to the support of Emperor Napoleon III, a laboratory of physiological chemistry was created for him at the same institution. As a logical sequel to his work on fermentation, he began research on spontaneous generation (the concept that bacterial life arose spontaneously), a question which at that time divided scientists into two opposing camps. Pasteur's recognition of

the fact that both lactic and alcohol fermentations were hastened by exposure to air led him to wonder whether his invisible organisms were always present in the atmosphere or whether they were spontaneously generated. By means of simple and precise experiments, including the filtration of air and the exposure of unfermented liquids to the air of the high Alps, he proved that food decomposes when placed in contact with germs present in the air, which cause its putrefaction, and that it does not undergo transformation or putrefy in such a way as to spontaneously generate new organisms within itself.

After laying the theoretical groundwork, Pasteur proceeded to apply his findings to the study of vinegar and wine, two commodities of great importance in the economy of France; his pasteurization process, the destruction of harmful germs by heat, made it possible to produce, preserve, and transport these products without their undergoing deterioration.

In 1865 he undertook a government mission to investigate the diseases of the silkworm, which were about to put an end to the production of silk at a time when it comprised a major section of France's economy. To carry out the investigation, he moved to the south of France, the centre of silkworm breeding. Three years later he announced that he had isolated the bacilli of two distinct diseases and had found methods of preventing contagion and of detecting diseased stock.

In 1870 Pasteur devoted himself to the problem of beer. Following an investigation conducted both in France and among the brewers in London, he devised, as he had done for vinegar and for wine, a procedure for manufacturing beer that would prevent its deterioration with time. British exporters, whose ships at the time had to sail entirely around the African continent, were thus able to send British beer as far as India without fear of its deteriorating.

Although Pasteur was partially paralyzed in 1868 and applied for retirement from the university, he continued his researches. In 1873 he was elected a member of the Academy of Medicine, and in 1874 the French Parliament provided him with an award that would ensure his material security while he pursued his work.

When, in 1881, he had perfected a technique for reducing the virulence of various disease-producing microorganisms, he succeeded in vaccinating a herd of sheep against the disease known as anthrax. Likewise, he was able to protect fowl from chicken cholera, for he had observed that once animals stricken with certain diseases had recovered, they were later immune to a fresh attack. Thus by isolating the germ of the disease and by cultivating an attenuated, or weakened, form of the germ and inoculating fowl with the culture, he could immunize the animals against the malady. In this he was following the example of the English physician Edward Jenner in his method for vaccinating animals against cowpox.

On April 27, 1882, Pasteur was elected a member of the Académie Française, at which point he undertook research that proved to be the most spectacular of all— the preventive treatment of rabies. After experimenting with inoculations of saliva from infected animals, he came to the conclusion that the virus was also present in the nerve centres, and he demonstrated that a portion of the medulla oblongata of a rabid dog, when injected into the body of a healthy animal, produced symptoms of rabies. By further work on the dried tissues of infected animals and the effect of time and temperature on these tissues, he was able to obtain a weakened form of the virus that could be used for inoculation. Having detected the rabies virus by its effects on the nervous system and attenuated its virulence, he applied his procedure to man; on July 6, 1885, he saved the life of a nine-year-old boy, Joseph Meister, who had been bitten by a rabid dog. The experiment was an outstanding success, opening the road to protection from a terrible disease. In 1888 the Pasteur Institute was inaugurated in Paris for the purpose of undertaking fundamental research, prevention, and treatment of rabies. Pasteur, although in failing health, headed the institute until his death on September 28, 1895.

Louis Pasteur brought about a veritable revolution in the 19th-century scientific method. By abandoning his labora-

Pasteurization (margin)

Fermentation research (margin)

Assessment (margin)

tory and by tackling the agents of disease in their natural environments, he was able through his investigations to supply the complete solution to a given question, not only identifying the agent responsible for a disease but also indicating the remedy.

A skillful experimenter, endowed with a great curiosity and a remarkable gift of observation, Pasteur devoted himself with immense enthusiasm to science and its applications to medicine, agriculture, and industry. He was prompt to defend his ideas with courage and often with considerable harshness—in writings as well as in speech—toward his opponents. It was chiefly in his work on spontaneous generation and on rabies that he encountered the strongest opposition to his ideas (which were, for the time, revolutionary) from medical circles and a section of the press. He was happy to accept the glory and honours that came his way, for he was well aware of his own value and of his scientific successes. A great friendship developed between Pasteur and the renowned British surgeon Sir Joseph Lister (1827–1912), who was quick to apply to his own discipline the discoveries of his eminent French colleague.

BIBLIOGRAPHY. ÉMILE DUCLAUX, Pasteur: The History of a Mind (1920, reprinted 1973; originally published in French, 1896), a scientific and philosophical work written by a collaborator of Pasteur; "Le laboratoire de Monsieur Pasteur," in Centième Anniversaire (1922); FRANÇOIS DAGOGNET, Méthodes et doctrine dans l'oeuvre de Pasteur (1967), primarily a detailed work of methodology; RENÉ J. DUBOS, Louis Pasteur: Free Lance of Science (1950, reissued 1976), more philosophical than scientific; ÉLIE METCHNIKOFF, The Founders of Modern Medicine: Pasteur, Koch, Lister (1939, reprinted 1971; originally published in French, 1933), written by an important scholar who worked with Pasteur; JACQUES NICOLLE, Louis Pasteur: A Master of Scientific Enquiry and Louis Pasteur: The Story of His Major Discoveries (both 1961), works giving a complete authoritative review of Pasteur's discoveries, and Pasteur, sa vie, sa méthode, ses découvertes (1969), an account of Pasteur's life and work; E. ROUX, "L'oeuvre médicale de Pasteur," in Centième Anniversaire (1922), written by one of Pasteur's collaborators; RENÉ VALLERY-RADOT, M. Pasteur: Histoire d'un savant par un ignorant (1884), written by Pasteur's son-in-law, who was also his secretary, and The Life of Pasteur (1900, reissued 1975; originally published in French, 1899), a fundamental work on the life of Pasteur but weak from the scientific point of view.

(J.-M.-R.N./Ed.)

The Apostle Paul

The Apostle Paul is an outstanding figure in the history of Christianity. Converted only a few years after the death of Jesus, he became the leading Apostle (missionary) of the new movement and played a decisive part in extending it beyond the limits of Judaism to become a worldwide religion. His surviving letters are the earliest extant Christian writings. They reveal both theological skill and pastoral understanding and have had lasting importance for Christian life and thought.

Sources. There are no reliable sources for Paul's life outside the New Testament. The primary source is his own letters. Of these, Romans, I and II Corinthians, and Galatians are indisputably genuine. Most scholars also accept Philippians, I Thessalonians, and Philemon. Opinion is divided about Ephesians, Colossians, and II Thessalonians. The Pastoral Letters (I and II Timothy and Titus) are held by many scholars to have been written considerably later than the time of Paul. The story of Paul's conversion and missionary career is given in Acts, probably written many years after his death. Some sections dealing with sea journeys may be derived from the diary of a companion of Paul. Traditionally this was thought to be Luke, the evangelist and author of Acts, a view still held by a number of scholars. For further information on the sources for Paul's life, see BIBLICAL LITERATURE AND ITS CRITICAL INTERPRETATION: *New Testament literature*.

Life. *Early life.* Paul was a Jew, born, perhaps in AD 10, at Tarsus, a city in Cilicia on the main trade route between East and West, and the home of famous Stoic philosophers. Like many of the Jews there he inherited Roman citizenship, probably granted by the Romans as a reward for mercenary service in the previous century. This fact explains his two names. He used his Jewish name, Saul, within the Jewish community and his Roman surname, Paul, when speaking Greek. Though he had a strict Jewish upbringing, he also grew up with a good command of idiomatic Greek and the experience of a cosmopolitan city, which fitted him for his special vocation to bring the gospel to the Gentiles (non-Jews). At some stage he became an enthusiastic member of the Pharisees, a Jewish sect that promoted purity and fidelity to the Law of Moses. According to Acts, he received training as a rabbi in Jerusalem under Gamaliel I. His knowledge of the Law and of rabbinic methods of interpreting it is evident in his letters. Like most rabbis he supported himself with a manual trade—tent making—probably learned from his father. It is clear that he never met Jesus while in Jerusalem, if, indeed, he was there before the Crucifixion.

Training as rabbi

He learned enough about Jesus and his followers, however, to regard the Christian movement as a threat to the Pharisaic Judaism that he had embraced so eagerly. Thus he first appears on the scene of history as a persecutor of the newly founded church.

Serious persecution of Christians first arose in connection with converts among the Hellenists (Greek-speaking Jews) in Jerusalem. When one of them, Stephen, was stoned to death, the murderers "laid down their garments at the feet of a young man named Saul" (Acts 7:58). At that time Paul shared the sense of outrage aroused by the Hellenist converts. They had not only proclaimed Jesus as the Messiah and heavenly Lord, a man who had been crucified

The stoning of Stephen

Alinari/Art Resource, NY

St. Paul preaching the gospel, detail of a 12th-century mosaic in the Cappella Palatina, Palermo, Sicily.

and therefore accursed by God (Deut. 21:23), but they also claimed that the temple and its sacrifices were superseded by the sacrificial death of Jesus and that therefore the Law could be disregarded (the subject of another curse, Deut. 27:26). Paul thus joined in the effort to stamp out the Christian movement. The Hellenist converts fled to the foreign cities where they had family connections, while the original Aramaic-speaking group in Jerusalem kept a low profile to avoid giving provocation.

Conversion.   Paul, in Galatians, bears out the impression given in Acts that he was converted as a result of a vision on the road to Damascus, on his way to apprehend some of the scattered converts. His own account is tantalizingly brief: "he who had set me apart before I was born, and had called me through his grace, was pleased to reveal his Son to me, in order that I might preach him among the Gentiles" (Gal. 1:15–16). The longer description in Acts, given three times, dramatizes what may have been essentially an inward experience. It was certainly a moment of revelation, changing Paul from bitter enmity to lifelong dedication to the Christian cause.

Explanations for Paul's conversion

Paul's conversion has often been explained psychologically as the resolution of an inner conflict. But the notion that Paul was tormented by scruples rests on a misunderstanding of Rom. 7. This chapter is concerned not with autobiography but with universal experience seen in the light of mature Christian understanding. Paul would not have spoken in these terms before his conversion. In fact, it is clear from other passages that his early life was free from such struggle. He excelled in zeal for the Law, and by its standards his life was blameless.

Paul's own account is much more in keeping with Old Testament callings of a prophet. Though it is impossible to state exactly what happened, the central feature was certainly his vision of Jesus in glory. It convinced him that Jesus was risen from the dead and exalted as Lord in heaven, as the Christians claimed. It also was proof that Jesus had been crucified wrongfully. Hence the curse did not apply, and his death could be understood as a sacrifice on behalf of others.

To Paul this had universal significance. Believing, like many Jews of his time, that God's final Day of Judgment, on which he would come to free the world from evil and to establish lasting peace and righteousness, was imminent, Paul then saw his vocation to be a missionary to people of every nation to prepare them for God's coming. The new feature of this expectation was the place accorded to Jesus Christ. In agreement with the earliest apostolic preaching, Paul believed that Jesus, having died for the sins of mankind, was now reserved in heaven as God's agent for the judgment. Those that believed in him and acknowledged him as Lord would have him as their deliverer on

The cornerstone of Paul's message

that day. Thus faith in Christ became the foundation of Paul's preaching. Along with this he proclaimed the love of God shown in the sacrificial death of Christ, who "loved me and gave himself for me" (Gal. 2:20). All his devotion was transferred to this new centre. Formerly his energy had been directed to preparing people for God's Kingdom by imposing on them strict Pharisaic interpretation of the Law. Now all that seemed useless in the light of what God himself had done for humanity through Jesus. Henceforth his one aim was to proclaim the faith of Jesus as Lord everywhere.

Immediately after his conversion Paul spent a period of solitude in Arabia. He then took up residence in Damascus. There presumably he established contact with the Christians he had originally planned to harm and received from them information about Jesus and his teaching as well as experience of Christian fellowship. Damascus was the base for his first missionary work, but nothing is known of the effects of his mission in the region.

Paul in Antioch.   After three years his work in Damascus came to an abrupt end. Somehow he had fallen foul of the ethnarch (governor) of the region of Nabataean Arabia. The ethnarch set a watch on the gates of Damascus, but Paul escaped over the wall in a basket and made his way to Jerusalem. There he met Peter, the Apostle, and James, the Lord's brother. This was an important meeting, for it established Paul as a recognized Apostle alongside

the founders of the church at Jerusalem. The visit was brief, and Paul did not meet the Christian communities in the vicinity. Most likely this was due to the danger of reprisals from the Pharisees, who regarded Paul as a renegade. Therefore, after only two weeks, he set out on a new mission to Cilicia and Syria, with a base in his native city of Tarsus. About this mission, again, there is no information.

At some point Paul moved to Antioch, the capital of Syria, to assist Barnabas in his successful mission there. The converts included a large number of Gentiles. This eventually led to a serious crisis, in which Paul emerged as the champion of the Gentiles. The controversy, which lasted several years, stimulated Paul's most important contribution to Christian theology. His stand on behalf of the Gentiles ensured that Christianity became not just a Jewish sect but a universal religion. The point at issue was the relationship between Jewish and Gentile Christians. Primitive Christianity was a closely knit fellowship with the common meal and the Eucharist (thanksgiving for the sacrificial death of Christ) at the heart of it. But the Jewish purity rules made Jews reluctant to eat with Gentiles for fear of transgressing the Law. Jesus had taught that purity of heart was more important than attention to rules, but this did not lead his followers to abandon them. But at Antioch the accession of Gentile converts created a mixed congregation, in which the Jewish members were content to eat with the Gentiles for the sake of Christian fellowship. In Jerusalem, however, since the death of Stephen, the Christians had had to take great care not to offend Jewish susceptibilities, and the prospect of making headway in the mission there depended on their being seen as faithful to the Law. Thus reports of the liberal attitude of the Christians in Antioch were bound to be extremely damaging. Some of the Jerusalem Christians who were converted Pharisees even held the view that Gentile converts should be required to accept circumcision and the obligations of the Law.

Champion of the Gentiles

Paul states in Galatians that he did not revisit Jerusalem for 14 years, and, when he finally did so, it was to deal with the problem of Gentile membership of the church. This conflicts with the information in Acts, which tells of a visit by Paul and Barnabas to bring relief during a famine at some time in AD 47–49. Acts then describes a further visit to deal with the Gentile issue. Most scholars today identify the latter visit with that described in Galatians. This means that Luke, in writing Acts on the basis of various sources, either presented twice what was actually one visit or wrongly included Paul's name in the earlier relief visit.

Antioch continued to be Paul's base for further pioneering work. Acts records three itineraries, generally referred to as missionary journeys, spanning a number of years. The second visit to Jerusalem probably took place at the end of the first of these.

First missionary journey.   Acts describes how Paul and Barnabas, accompanied by Barnabas' cousin John Mark, set out for Cyprus, visiting Salamis and Paphos. They then crossed to the mainland (modern Turkey), landing at Perga (near modern Murtana), but Mark left them and returned to Jerusalem. They worked in Pisidia and Pamphylia, which formed the southern part of the Roman province of Galatia, beginning in Pisidian Antioch (near modern Yalvaç). Acts records a sermon that Paul preached in the synagogue, which is a fine specimen of the presentation of the faith to a Jewish audience in New Testament times. After further stops at Iconium (modern Konya), Lystra (near modern Hatunsaray), and Derbe (unidentified), they retraced their steps to Perga and the port of Attalia (modern Antalya) and then sailed back to Antioch.

It is unclear from this account how many of the new converts were drawn from local Jewish communities and how many were Gentiles. The monotheism and strong morality of the Jews always attracted to the synagogues Gentiles who proved to be receptive to the Christian mission, especially as Paul did not require circumcision and observance of the Law for Christian fellowship. In some places the new congregations may have been entirely composed of Gentiles.

The missionary journeys of St. Paul.

At this time Greek and Roman traditional religion was losing its hold, and a deputation had come from Jerusalem to Antioch to insist that the Gentile converts should be circumcised. This led to Paul's second visit to Jerusalem. Paul says that he and Barnabas went "by revelation," perhaps meaning as a result of a message from a prophet, not in response to a summons from Jerusalem as stated in Acts. The party from Antioch included Titus, a Gentile whom Paul had taken into his mission team.

It is almost impossible to harmonize the information in Acts 15 and Gal. 2, but it is best to regard them as accounts of the same occasion. In Jerusalem there seem to have been three main actions. First, Paul and Barnabas had a private consultation with James, Peter, and John, in which they compared the content of their mission preaching and established that they were in basic agreement. This confirmed Paul's contention that the gospel message did not require the circumcision of Gentile converts. A campaign by the hard-line party to have Titus circumcised was firmly resisted. Second, a larger conference was convened in order to inform all about the Gentile mission so that they should have no doubt that the power of the Holy Spirit had been at work. This resulted in the decision that the Gentile mission should continue without pressure to Judaize converts. Paul would carry this on from Antioch, while Peter would continue the mission among Jews from the base at Jerusalem. Paul, however, was urged to bear in mind the precarious position of the Jerusalem church. Third, a letter was sent to Antioch with minimum rules for Gentile converts: to abstain from meat used in pagan sacrifices, to use only kosher meat according to Jewish custom, and to observe Jewish restrictions on sexual relationships. Later events show that the contents of this letter were unknown to Paul, and it is conjectured that it belongs to a later attempt to regulate relationships with the numerous Jewish Christian congregations of Judaea and Syria after Paul had ceased to have close contact with Antioch.

Paul's view had been endorsed by Peter, who subsequently visited the church in Antioch. Apparently he had no difficulty in sharing in the life of the mixed congregation. Yet when some hard-liners came from Jerusalem, Peter felt compelled to withdraw from meals with Gentile members. Other Jewish members also yielded to the pressure, including even Barnabas. Paul, however, was adamant in his conviction that this was fundamentally wrong. This

Second visit to Jerusalem (margin note)

crisis could never have arisen if the letter from Jerusalem had already been sent; it must have been due to differing views of the implications of what had been agreed. Not only Paul but also Peter and the main body in Jerusalem had assumed that the purity rules would not be allowed to interfere with table fellowship in mixed congregations. But it is clear from the trouble over Titus that the hard-liners would demand separation into two groups and then claim that the unity of the congregation would require Judaizing of the Gentile converts. Paul insisted on his own understanding of the agreement, and the visitors left.

Demands to Judaize Gentile converts (margin note)

Second missionary journey.   Paul then planned to revisit the churches of south Galatia. Barnabas wished to take Mark, but Paul refused in view of his previous failure. Barnabas and Mark went to Cyprus, and nothing more is said about them in Acts. The subsequent account is entirely concentrated on Paul, who took with him Silas, also a Roman citizen (Roman name Silvanus). They went overland to Galatia. At Lystra Paul took into his team Timothy, a Gentile with a Jewish mother, who is mentioned with Silas in Paul's letters. The claim of Acts that Paul circumcised him seems improbable in view of the earlier decisions but is not impossible if the work was mainly among Jewish communities.

Because Paul hoped to establish the church in large centres of influence, he planned to go to Ephesus, the principal city of the province of Asia and a port on the Aegean coast. He was, however, prevented from doing so "by the Holy Spirit" (perhaps another reference to Christian prophecy). Instead he turned toward the large cities of Bithynia in the north. Possibly the Gentile churches of north Galatia, to which the letter to the Galatians is addressed, were founded on the way. Once more his plans were prevented, and so he moved northwest to Troas. From there, in response to a vision, he sailed to Macedonia and founded churches at Philippi, Thessalonica (modern Thessaloníki, Greece), and Beroea. Philippi, a Roman colony on the Via Egnatia, the major route across Greece, produced a loyal group of Gentile converts, who frequently contributed funds to Paul in later years. Acts tells how Paul and Silas were imprisoned there but released when they revealed their Roman citizenship. At Thessalonica and Beroea trouble from hostile Jews compelled Paul to move on to Athens. After a short stay there, during which he is said to have addressed the council of the Areopagus, he went on to Corinth. The speech, as given in Acts, was an attempt to meet the needs of a philosophically trained audience. No church was founded in Athens.

The events of that time are reflected in I Thessalonians, perhaps the earliest of Paul's letters, written after Silas and Timothy had joined Paul at Corinth. The letter expressed his great anxiety for this newly founded church in Thessalonica, which he had had to leave hurriedly, having been accused of treason for proclaiming Christ as a rival emperor. It emerges from the letter that he had taught the Gentile audience to turn "to God from idols, to serve a living and true God, and to wait for his Son from heaven, whom he raised from the dead, Jesus who delivers us from the wrath to come" (1:9–10). This can be taken as a good example of Paul's basic mission preaching. Timothy had reported that the converts were anxious about their fate because some of them had already died. Paul explained that the time of Christ's coming (Parousia) for judgment was unknown, but both living and dead who had faith in him would be claimed by him as his own and saved for the everlasting kingdom. II Thessalonians is regarded by some as a supplementary letter, written shortly afterward, but there is doubt about its authenticity. It contains details of the events that are to precede the Parousia (unfortunately these details are by no means easy to understand).

Paul was in low spirits when he reached Corinth after the failure at Athens. At Corinth he met a Jewish couple, Aquila and Priscilla, tentmakers like himself, who became his lifelong friends. They had recently come from Rome, following an edict of the emperor Claudius expelling all Jews from the capital. Possibly they had already become Christians in Rome. In Corinth Paul at last was able to exercise a long and fruitful ministry in a great trading centre. Acts records an incident in which Paul was brought before the proconsul Gallio. This is important for dating Paul's career because an inscription discovered at Delphi proves that Gallio began his year of office in AD 51. Paul had probably arrived in the previous year. When he left Corinth, Aquila and Priscilla accompanied him to Ephesus, but he went on alone by sea to Caesarea for Jerusalem and from there to Antioch.

Third missionary journey. Paul had by then established churches in Asia Minor and Greece, with a major centre at Corinth, and had begun work in the equally important Ephesus. Then followed a period of consolidation. He went overland to Ephesus, which became his base for the next three years. Acts gives little detail, but he must have founded the churches at Colossae, Hierapolis, and Laodicea in the Lycus Valley during this period. A group of followers of John the Baptist at Ephesus is mentioned, and there were probably other Christian missionaries working in the same region. References in his letters to fighting wild beasts at Ephesus and to imprisonment show that he faced great hazards.

This was the period of Paul's most important letters. His correspondence with Corinth shows the grave difficulties that were liable to arise. I Corinthians refers to a previous letter urging the Christians not to associate with immoral persons, but it has not survived. In I Corinthians Paul tackles a whole array of problems. Rival groups were claiming the authority of different teachers (Peter, Apollos, and Paul himself). A case of incest had gone unrebuked. Paul's teaching on freedom from the Law had been twisted to justify licentiousness. There were problems of marriage and divorce. The question of which foods a Gentile Christian might eat was causing problems of conscience. There was disorderly conduct at the Eucharist (Lord's Supper). In dealing with these matters Paul showed knowledge of Jesus' teaching on marriage, and he gave the account of the Last Supper in its oldest known form. A section on the gifts of the Holy Spirit includes his famous chapter on love (chapter 13) and regulates the practice of speaking with tongues. A long section on resurrection shows that, while teaching that Christian life was already participation in the risen Christ, Paul still thought that the Parousia was near and that the full experience of eternal life lay beyond this event.

Before long, however, there were fresh troubles at Corinth. Intruders from another church were trying to undermine Paul's authority. He dashed to Corinth but failed to restore confidence. He returned to Ephesus and wrote a severe letter (possibly partly preserved in II Cor. 10–13), which he regretted as soon as Titus had left with it. Paul had intended to work at Troas but was so anxious about Corinth that he went on to Macedonia instead in the hope of meeting Titus on his return. Titus returned with the good news that the severe letter had accomplished its purpose. With tremendous relief Paul wrote II Corinthians (perhaps only chapters 1–9), which is full of the theme of reconciliation: "God was in Christ reconciling the world to himself, not counting their trespasses against them, and entrusting to us the message of reconciliation" (5:19). Paul also gave further teaching on the resurrection of the body in terms of renewal and transformation into the state of glory.

Another theme of II Corinthians is a collection for the poor church of Jerusalem, a gift that Paul intended to symbolize the unity between the Jewish and Gentile churches. Behind this project was the continuing problem of the Judaizing party. This comes to the fore in Galatians, probably written during this period. The letter is concerned with the attempt of some Jewish Christians to persuade the Gentile Christians of Galatia to be circumcised and keep the Law. Here Paul lays out his doctrine of justification by faith, generally reckoned his most important contribution to Christian theology, which was to reach its classic expression in Romans.

From Macedonia Paul went to Corinth, and it was during his three months there that he wrote to the Christians in Rome. The letter was written ostensibly to seek their help in his plan to evangelize the far west (Spain is mentioned) after taking the collection to Jerusalem. In fact, he clearly felt the need to win their support for his position on the Judaizing issue, and he presented the case at length. God's plan, he argued, is for universal salvation. This is God's gift available through faith in the sacrificial death of Christ. By itself the Law cannot bring salvation. It can show the nature of human sin but is powerless to make people righteous. Paul's opponents feared that without the Law the Gentile converts would be liable to libertine behaviour (as had happened at Corinth). Paul replied that faith in Christ opens the believer to the sanctifying power of the Holy Spirit. Then the opponents complained that Paul's argument left no room for the privileged position of the Jews as God's chosen people. Paul replied that, though many Jews had failed to respond to the gospel, the success of the mission to the Gentiles would prompt them to seek salvation at the end of time, "and so all Israel [would] be saved" (Rom. 11:26). Then the universe would reach the fulfillment of its purpose, and the final transformation could begin.

Arrest and imprisonment. At the end of the letter Paul expressed his fear of danger from the Jews in Jerusalem and even hinted that the church there might not feel able to accept the collection. It seems that both these fears were realized. Acts tells that Paul was accompanied by delegates from the Gentile churches but does not mention the collection. This omission is best explained on the assumption that Luke did not wish to say that the church in Jerusalem did not dare to accept it. If so, Paul's hope that it would symbolize the gathering of the Gentiles into the one family of God was disappointed. In Jerusalem Paul was mistakenly accused of bringing one of the Gentile delegates into the inner courts of the Temple, beyond the barrier excluding Gentiles. He was arrested, partly to save his life from the mob, but given good treatment on account of his Roman citizenship. When a plot against his life came to light, he was removed to Caesarea, the Roman military headquarters. The governor Felix kept him in prison to avoid antagonizing the Jewish authorities. Two years later Felix's successor, Festus, wanted to send him to Jerusalem for trial, but Paul refused to go and appealed to Caesar.

The journey to Rome began in late autumn, but a shipwreck delayed the travelers for three months at Malta, so that they arrived in Rome in the spring of AD 60. There Paul was kept under house arrest for two years awaiting trial. At this point the narrative of Acts closes, and it is left to the reader to guess what happened. As long as the Pastoral Letters were accepted as genuine, their evidence demanded the hypothesis of acquittal, further work

Marginal notes:

Success in Corinth

Active period of correspondence

Justification by faith

in Greece, Asia Minor, and even Crete, before a second arrest, return to Rome, and sentence to death. Now that these letters are recognized to be pseudonymous, there is no reason to suppose that Paul was acquitted at all.

Paul wrote several letters during captivity. These might have been written during an earlier imprisonment in Ephesus or, perhaps, while he was at Caesarea, but Rome seems most likely. Of the four captivity letters, Philippians and Philemon are generally accepted as genuine; Colossians and Ephesians are questioned. The letter to Philemon, a Christian of Colossae, concerns his runaway slave whom Paul has converted in prison and now sends back to him "no longer as a slave but more than a slave, as a beloved brother" (verse 16). This letter, with its sensitive handling of a delicate situation, is a gem among the Pauline writings. Philippians is a serene acknowledgement of the generosity of the Christians at Philippi. Colossians is concerned with trouble from false teachers at Colossae, conjectured to be an unorthodox fringe sect of Judaism. In response, Christ is presented as the true wisdom of God, embodying his whole plan of salvation. Ephesians is an eloquent, perhaps overly rhetorical, statement of the privilege of the Gentiles, who in Christ enjoy the status of God's chosen people. Through his death Christ "has made us both one, and has broken down the dividing wall of hostility" (2:14).

Achievement and influence. Paul's lasting monument is the worldwide Christian Church. Though he was not the first to preach to the Gentiles, his resolute stand against the Judaizing party was decisive for future progress. It can be justly claimed that it was due to Paul more than anyone else that Christianity grew from being a small sect within Judaism to become a world religion.

Paul's influence continued after his death. The Pastoral Letters to Timothy and Titus were written in Paul's name to promote fidelity to his teaching, probably around the end of the 1st century. At the same time, Paul's surviving letters were collected for general circulation. They quickly became a standard of reference for Christian teaching. In particular, theories of atonement (the reconciliation of mankind to God through the sacrificial death of Christ) have always relied heavily on Paul.

In the Western (Latin) half of Christendom Paul had a profound effect upon the history of the church through the writings of St. Augustine. The Pelagian controversy concerning grace and free will turned on the interpretation of passages in Paul's letter to the Romans. In arguing for the necessity of divine grace for salvation, Augustine built on Paul's idea of predestination, correctly interpreting Paul's idea as a reference to God's predestined plan of universal salvation and as a concept that did not necessarily conflict with the exercise of free will.

The reformers of the 16th century were also deeply indebted to Paul. Martin Luther seized on the doctrine of justification by faith and made the distinction between faith and works the basis of his attack on the late medieval

church. John Calvin drew from Paul his concept of the church as the company of the elect, using the idea of predestination, but with the added corollary that predestination to salvation belongs only to the elect. Thus Paul's teaching came through the influence of Augustine to dominate the Reformation and its legacy in the Lutheran and Calvinist churches of modern Protestantism. These issues, however, never had the same prominence in the Eastern Orthodox churches.

Modern study of Paul has tried to reach behind these controversies and to see Paul in his true context of the rise of Christianity. Once the basis of Paul's thought in the context of Jewish concepts of his time is understood in the light of modern scholarship, uncompromising predestinarian views of some of Calvin's followers can be seen to be an overly rigid interpretation of Paul's meaning. Attempts to derive Paul's ideas from Greek or Gnostic influences have been largely abandoned. Paul stands out more clearly as a Christian Jew, whose conversion experience convinced him that Christ was the universal Lord under God, the agent and leader of God's kingdom. Paul thus maintained that through Christ every barrier is broken down: "There is neither Jew nor Greek, there is neither slave nor free, there is neither male nor female; for you are all one in Christ Jesus" (Gal. 3:28).

BIBLIOGRAPHY. From the immense Pauline bibliography, which includes many commentaries on the Acts and letters, only a representative selection can be chosen. GUSTAV ADOLF DEISSMANN, *St. Paul*, trans. from the German (1912); T.R. GLOVER, *Paul of Tarsus* (1925, reissued 1938); and JAMES S. STEWART, *A Man in Christ* (1935, reissued 1975), are valuable biographical studies. H.J. SCHOEPS, *Paul* (1961, reissued 1979; originally published in German, 1959), is a modern Jewish view of Paul. MICHAEL GRANT, *Saint Paul* (1976, reissued 1982), is an introduction to his life and his writings for the general reader. GÜNTHER BORNKAMM, *Paul* (1971; originally published in German, 1969); and FREDERICK F. BRUCE, *Paul: Apostle of the Heart Set Free* (1978, reprinted 1984), are a critical and a conservative account, respectively, of both his life and thought. WAYNE A. MEEKS, *The First Urban Christians* (1983), is a reinterpretation of Pauline thought in light of new information on its social and political contexts. Other specialized studies include WILLIAM M. RAMSAY, *St. Paul the Traveller and the Roman Citizen* (1896, reissued 1982, with an essay on the author), a valuable contribution to historical geography; ROBERT JEWETT, *A Chronology of Paul's Life* (1979); JOHANNES MUNCK, *Paul and the Salvation of Mankind* (1959; originally published in German, 1954), dealing with various aspects of Paul's relationship with the other Apostles; ALBERT SCHWEITZER, *The Mysticism of Paul the Apostle* (1931, reissued 1968; originally published in German, 1930); W.D. DAVIES, *Paul and Rabbinic Judaism*, 4th ed. (1980); E.P. SANDERS, *Paul and Palestinian Judaism* (1977), and *Paul, the Law, and the Jewish People* (1983), providing a balanced discussion of modern assessments of Paul's relationship to Judaism. D.E.H. WHITELEY, *The Theology of St. Paul*, 2nd ed. (1974); and J. CHRISTIAAN BEKER, *Paul the Apostle* (1980), are both thorough works on Paul's teaching.

(B.L.)

Peking

Peking (Wade–Giles romanization: Pei-ching, Pinyin: Beijing), the capital of the People's Republic of China, is one of the world's great cities. Few cities in the world have served for so long as the political headquarters and cultural centre of a country as immense as China. The city has constituted an integral part of the history of China over the past eight centuries, and there is scarcely a major building of any age in Peking that has not made its contribution toward the evolution of the country as a whole. Thus, it is impossible to understand China without a knowledge of this city.

More than 2,000 years ago, a site near present-day Peking was already an important military and trading centre for the northeastern frontier of China. In 1267, during the Yüan (Mongol) dynasty (1206–1368), a new city built on the site—called Ta-tu—became the administrative capital of China. During the reigns of the first two emperors of the Ming dynasty (1368–1644), Nanking was the capital, and the old Mongol capital was renamed Pei-p'ing ("Northern Peace"); the third Ming emperor, however, restored it as the Imperial seat of the dynasty and gave it a new name, Peking ("Northern Capital"). Peking has remained the capital of China except for a brief period (1928–49) when the Nationalist government again made Nanking the capital (although the capital was removed to Chungking during World War II); during that time Peking once again resumed the old name Pei-p'ing, which is still used by the Nationalist government in Taiwan.

In spite of frequent political changes in China, the city throughout the early decades of the 20th century remained the most flourishing cultural centre in the nation; Peking's importance was fully realized, however, only when the city was chosen as the capital of the People's Republic of China in 1949, and this political status has added much vitality to it. Indeed, few cities have ever had such rapid growth in population and geographic area, as well as in industrial and other activities. Combining both historical relics of an ancient culture and new urban construction under a socialist system, Peking has become the showplace of modern China.

This article is divided into the following sections:

Physical and human geography

CHARACTER OF THE CITY

Although much of Peking's older and more picturesque character has been destroyed in the drive since 1949 to modernize and industrialize, some parts of the city are still redolent of the past. Many fine monumental buildings, old restaurants, and centres of traditional Chinese arts and crafts remain, and the central government has taken measures to prevent Peking's further industrialization. Broad new boulevards have displaced the colourful stalls and markets for which the city was once famous, but the neighbourhood life of old Peking can still be glimpsed in the narrow hu-t'ungs (residential alleys), with their coal-burning stoves, tiny potted-plant gardens, and enclosed courtyards—some of which are still guarded by carved stone lions at their gates.

The pace of life in Peking is slow by Western standards. People commute by bus or bicycle and on hot summer evenings sit outside their apartment blocks to catch cooling breezes and to gossip. The citizenry has a wide range of leisure pursuits, particularly those considered good for health. The ancient art of T'ai Chi ch'uan (Chinese boxing) is widely practiced, singly or in groups, along roadsides and in parks. Young people delight in taking day excursions to such nearby historical sites as the Summer Palace, the tombs of the Ming emperors, and the Great Wall. Older people, especially the men, like to huddle in tiny restaurants and tea shops or to sit alone at the Peking equivalent of corner taverns nursing a glass of beer or mao-t'ai (a strong liquor made from sorghum).

For all of the vicissitudes of its history, Peking continues to be a source of pride for its inhabitants. Their obsessions are, as they have been for centuries, food and knowledge: they eat heartily when they have the means and read voraciously in spite of the limited supply of books. Food stalls on the streets, selling a variety of cooked treats, are well-patronized, as are newspaper and magazine kiosks. The ambition of most families is to provide their offspring with a higher education or, if not that, a secure factory job. Despite the shortage of living space in the city, families still try to accommodate parents and grandparents and to be responsible for the well-being of other elderly relatives.

THE LANDSCAPE

The city site. Peking is situated at the northern apex of the triangular North China Plain and lies at an elevation of between about 100 and 130 feet (30 and 40 metres) above sea level. To the north lies the fringe of the Mongolian Plateau; to the northeast rises the mountain range of the Yen Mountains, part of which forms the eastern part of the concave arc that circles the Peking lowland from the northeast to the southwest and is known to geologists as the "Bay of Peking."

The city was built at the mouth of this embayment, which opens onto the great plain to the south and east, and between two rivers, the Yung-ting and the Ch'ao-pai, which eventually join to empty into the Po Hai (Gulf of Chihli), some 100 miles (160 kilometres) to the southeast of Peking. Peking is a natural gateway on the long-distance land communication route between the North China Plain and the northern ranges, plains, and plateaus.

To the south of the city the plain spreads out for about 400 miles until it merges into the lower valley and the delta of the Yangtze. On the east the plain is bounded by the sea, except for the break caused by the Shantung Hills; on the west it is flanked by the T'ai-hang Mountains, which constitute the eastern edge of the Loess Plateau (loess is loamy material deposited by wind).

Because Peking stands at the apex of the triangle, routes running across the great plain naturally converge on the city. In addition, since the dawn of Chinese history, the Yen range has constituted a formidable barrier between the North China Plain to the south, the Mongolian Plateau to the north, and the Liao River Plain in the southern region of the Northeast (formerly Manchuria). A few passes, however, cut through the ranges—the most important being the Nankow (Chü-Yung), Ku-pei, and Shan-hai—and are so situated that all roads leading from Mongolia and the Northeast to the North China Plain are bound to converge on Peking. For centuries, therefore, Peking has been an important terminus of the caravan routes leading to and from the vast Central Asian hinterland.

Since the early 15th century, the city of Peking and its surrounding territories have been organized as a metropolitan district of enormous size, having a governor—formerly appointed by the emperor himself—equal in rank to a provincial governor. This special district organization was continued by the Ch'ing dynasty and by the People's Republic of China. The present metropolitan boundary was established in 1959 and covers a territory of approximately 6,900 square miles (17,900 square kilometres). The metropolis consists of 10 urban and suburban *ch'u* (districts) and eight annexed *hsien* (counties) in peripheral areas. It may be divided into three concentric zones, based on urban functions. The central zone coincides with the central city; it is mainly occupied by old palaces, government buildings, commercial districts, and old residential areas and makes up roughly 1 percent of the total metropolitan area. Four of the *ch'u* lie within the central city. The second zone, the near suburb, comprises five *ch'u* immediately surrounding the old walled city; it is the site of the newer factories, schools, government buildings, and workers' dormitories. The outer fringe of this zone is intensively cultivated and supplies vegetables and fruits to the population of the central zone. The near suburb accounts for about 8 percent of the metropolitan area. The third zone, the far suburb, consists of one *ch'u* and nine annexed *hsien* and constitutes the remainder of the metropolitan area. This zone functions as the economic base—supplying coal, lumber, construction materials, vegetables and fruits, dairy products, water, and some grain crops to the urban population in the central zone and the near suburb. The far suburb of Peking is mainly under the administration of *hsinang* (country towns).

Climate. Though the distance from Peking to the Po Hai is only about 100 miles, the general air circulation in Peking is mainly from the northwest throughout the year. Maritime effects on Peking's weather are meagre. The climate is clearly of the continental monsoon type that occurs in the temperate zone. Local topography has a great effect on Peking's climate. Being located in the lowland area of the nation and shaded by mountains, the city is a little warmer in winter than other areas of China located on the same latitude; it has only five months each year in which the mean monthly temperature is lower than 50° F (10° C). Wind direction in Peking is also influenced by topography, with changes occurring from day to night. Generally, there are more southerly winds in the day but northerly or northwesterly winds at night.

The annual mean temperature of the city is 53° F (12° C). The coldest month is January, when monthly mean temperatures are 24° F (−4° C), and the warmest month is July, when the monthly mean is 79° F (26° C). In an average year, there are 132 days of freezing temperature in Peking (between October and March); the mean amount of precipitation is 25 inches (635 millimetres), with most of the annual total falling from June to August. July is ordinarily the wettest month of the year, with monthly mean precipitation averaging about nine inches.

One of the characteristics of Peking's rainfall is its vari-

ability. In 1959—an extremely wet year for Peking—the total precipitation amounted to 55 inches, whereas in 1891—an extremely dry year—only seven inches of rainfall was recorded. The average number of rainy days is about 80, and the average relative humidity for the city is 57 percent.

Winter in Peking is long and usually begins in October, when northwesterly winds gradually gain strength. Until March, this seasonal wind system dominates Peking; the Siberian air that passes southward over the Mongolian Plateau and into China proper is cold and dry, bringing little snow or other precipitation. The monthly mean temperature from December to February is below freezing. Spring, the windiest season, is short and rapidly becomes warm. Mainly because of the prevailing high winds, the evaporation rate in spring averages about nine times the total spring precipitation and frequently is sufficient to cause droughts that are harmful to agriculture. In addition to being the season of torrential rains, summer is rather hot, as warm and humid air from the southeast often penetrates into North China. Autumn begins in late September and is a pleasant, though short, season when the sky is clear and the temperature comfortable.

Plant life. The mountain areas of Peking belong to the temperate deciduous forest zone, while the plains area belongs to the wooded steppe zone. Because of continuous deforestation by man for several centuries, however, only the mountain areas in the northeast and the western parts of the metropolitan area are still covered with mixed forests, composed mainly of pine, oak, and Manchurian birch. Different types of forest, divided into vertical zones, can be seen at higher elevations. On the lower slopes of many hills to the west of the city, human activities have resulted in the disappearance of forest cover so that only bushes and shrubs dot the landscape. On sunny slopes at altitudes of between about 2,300 and 5,600 feet, a variety of species occurs, including Manchurian birch (*Betula mandshurica*), Dahurian birch (*B. davurica*), trembling poplar (*Populus tremula*), Mongolian oak (*Quercus mongolica*), and Liaotung oak (*Q. liaotungensis*). Between 5,600 and 6,250 feet above sea level, the mixed forest of truncated maple (*Acer truncatum*) and trembling poplar replaces all other species. Above 6,250 feet, goat willow (*Salix caprea*) becomes the dominant tree.

The larger part of the plain areas of Peking has been either cultivated or occupied by various settlements so that it is for the most part bare of any natural vegetation. Occasionally, some small groves of planted trees may be seen near graveyards or in the vicinity of villages; these are mainly composed of mixed woods consisting of oil pine, Chinese juniper, Chinese cypress, willow, elm, and Chinese locust.

The city layout. The traditional core of Peking essentially consisted of two walled cities (the walls no longer stand), the northern inner city and the southern outer city. The inner city, also known as Tatar City, lay approximately on the site of the Mongol city of Ta-tu; it was in the form of a square, with walls nearly 15 miles in length. The outer city, also known as the Chinese City, was added during the reign of the Ming emperor Chia-ching (1521–66/67); it was in the form of an oblong adjoining the inner city, with walls that were 14 miles in length, including four miles of the southern wall of the inner city. Within the inner city was the former Imperial City, also in the form of a square, which had red plastered walls six and a half miles in length. Within the Imperial City, in turn, is the moated "Forbidden City," with walls two and a quarter miles long. The Forbidden City contains the former Imperial Palaces, which have been converted into a museum.

Peking represents, better than any other existing city, the heritage of Chinese architectural achievement. During each dynasty in which Peking was the capital, care was consistently taken to preserve tradition when the city was rebuilt or remodeled. Few cities in the world can thus rival Peking in the regularity and harmony of its city plan.

The plan was composed about a single straight line, drawn north and south through the centre of Peking, on which the internal coherence of the city hinged. All the city walls, important city gates, main avenues and streets, religious

The metropolitan district

Temperature and rainfall

The north–south axis

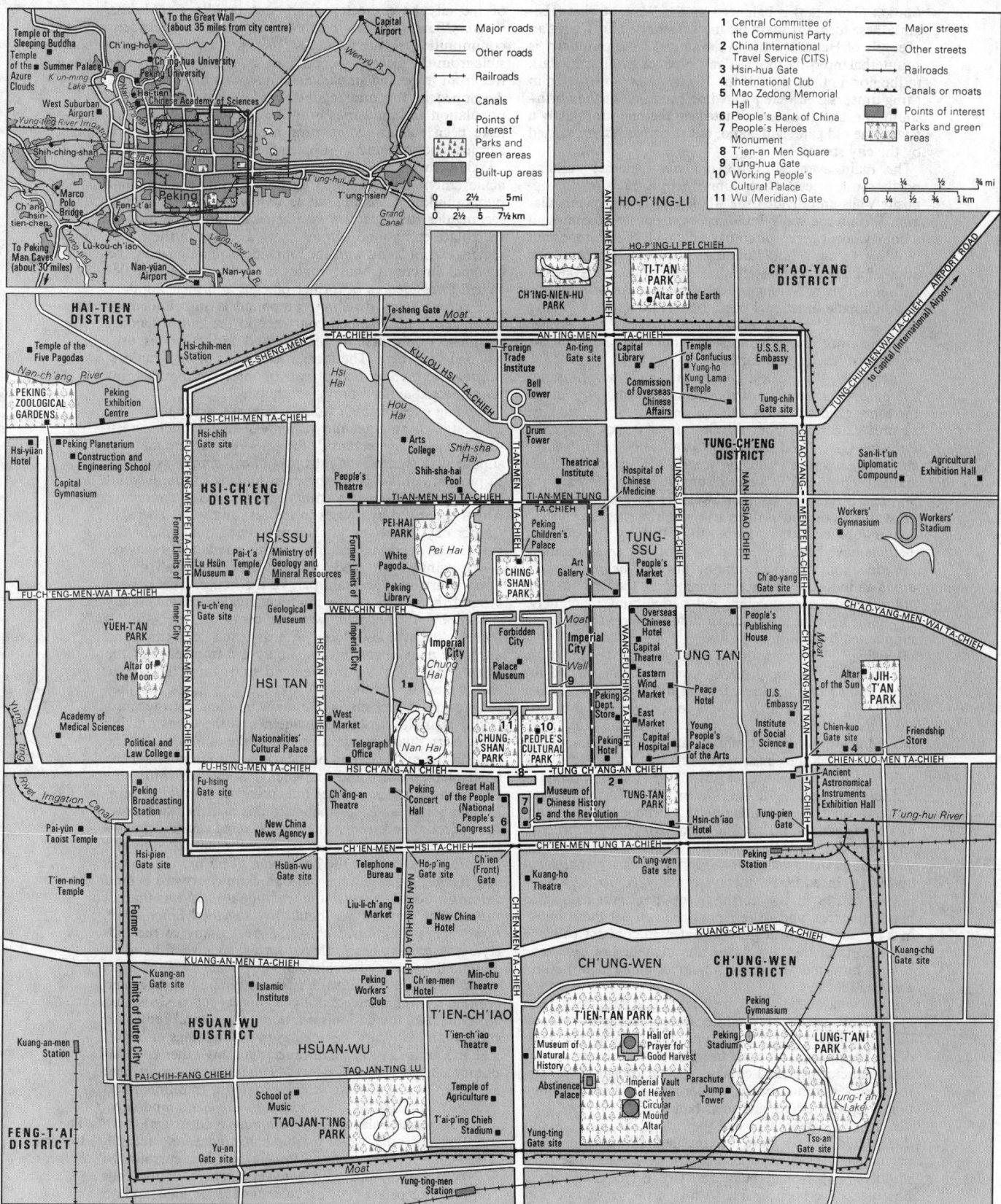

Major roads ═══
Other roads ───
Railroads ┤──┤
Canals ········
Points of interest ■
Parks and green areas
Built-up areas

0   2½   5mi
0 2½ 5 7½km

1 Central Committee of the Communist Party
2 China International Travel Service (CITS)
3 Hsin-hua Gate
4 International Club
5 Mao Zedong Memorial Hall
6 People's Bank of China
7 People's Heroes Monument
8 T'ien-an Men Square
9 Tung-hua Gate
10 Working People's Cultural Palace
11 Wu (Meridian) Gate

Major streets ═══
Other streets ───
Railroads ┤──┤
Canals or moats ····
Points of interest ■
Parks and green areas

0 ¼ ½ ¾ mi
0 ¼ ½ ¾ 1 km

The city of Peking and (inset) its metropolitan area.

buildings, and daily shopping markets were systematically arranged in relation to this central axis. Because the central axis has historically signified the authority of the ruling dynasty, many official buildings, public grounds, and city gates were located along this line. From north to south this line passed through the Bell Tower (Chung-lou); the Drum Tower (Ku-lou); Ching-shan Park; the Forbidden City, including the Imperial Palaces; T'ien-an Men Square;

Ch'ien (Front) Gate; the T'ien-ch'iao neighbourhood; and (no longer standing) Yung-ting Gate.

The symmetrical layout of the city to the east and west of this line is quite striking. In front of the palaces, the Temple of the Imperial Ancestors (now in the People's Cultural Park) on the east side of the axis is balanced by the Altar of Earth and Harvests (now in Chung-shan Park) on the west. Farther away from the palaces, the East

Market (Tung-tan) is balanced by the West Market (Hsi-tan); these form the main business districts. The T'ien-t'an (Temple of Heaven) Park to the south of the inner city is counterbalanced by the Ti-t'an (Altar of the Earth) Park to the north of the city. Of the 16 city gates constructed in Ming times, seven were located on each side of the north–south line, and two were situated on the line itself. Only a few of the old gates still stand, but their names are carried by the city streets.

The main avenues of the old city, whether running north–south or east–west, connected the gates on the opposite walls and divided the whole city into a rectangular grid. Within the walls, buildings were constructed around a courtyard or series of courtyards, with every important building facing south. Buildings often stood behind one another along a north–south line, with small courtyards in between. This prevailing southern orientation of buildings has a climatic functional basis, but it also appears to have been sanctified or conventionalized early in the Bronze Age in connection with ancestral ceremonies and with the worship of heaven and earth.

Since 1949, the greatest change in the city's appearance has been the extension of its streets immediately outside the former old city walls. On the west side of the old city, an area extending about a mile from the spot where the Fu-hsing Gate stood (Fu-hsing Gate site on map) has become an extension of the avenue Hsi Ch'ang-an Ta-chieh and is used primarily for government offices. Toward the Summer Palace, to the northwest, is an area where the most important universities and research institutes of the country are located. To the north of the city, the outlying districts have been developed as a housing area adjoining the educational district in the northwest. The eastern suburb is an industrial district dominated by the manufacture of chemicals, automobiles, and agricultural machinery. Vegetable fields in the southern suburb are gradually being supplanted by industrial plants.

Housing. To cope with the rapid growth of population, a number of housing projects have been constructed for office and factory workers. During the first five-year plan (1953–57), housing projects were concentrated in the western outskirts of the city, where apartment buildings were erected near government offices outside the Fu-hsing Gate site. After 1958 the construction of a large group of multiunit housing estates was begun in the northern outlying districts between the An-ting Gate site and Te-sheng Gate, centring on the residential neighbourhood of Ho-p'ing-li. The Ho-p'ing-li housing development contains primary and secondary schools, nurseries, hotels, and recreational facilities, as well as scores of four- or five-story apartment buildings. In addition, there are many groups of single-family houses in the northern suburbs, with associated parks, theatres, and recreational centres. All these buildings are supplied with gas and water, in contrast with the older parts of the city, where the existence of old stone paving hindered the development of modern structures and facilities.

In the area outside the Chien-kuo Gate site, to the east of the city, apartment buildings accommodate the families of office workers employed in nearby government office buildings. This area has also been selected as the diplomatic district and contains many foreign embassies, together with a number of Western-style houses for diplomatic representatives and their families.

In the older districts inside the former city walls, many dilapidated houses have been pulled down in municipal housing-renewal projects and have been replaced by multistory apartment buildings. Urban-renewal projects, however, have been unable to match the growth of population. As a consequence, many traditional house compounds—originally designed centuries ago to house the families of officials during the Ch'ing, or Manchu, dynasty (1644–1911/12)—have been repaired or renovated and subdivided to provide quarters for three or four families per compound; each family in a compound faces a public courtyard and shares a common front gate with other families.

In order to minimize commuting traffic in the metropolis, many factories in the eastern and southern outskirts of the city have erected apartment buildings to house workers. These workers' residences constitute independent communities and are located so that they are easily accessible from the place of work yet are far enough away to be free from noise and smoke. Satellite towns have also been developed in the rural counties in an effort to disperse population and industries from the central city. Industries have been encouraged in rural areas in order to absorb surplus labourers and to supplement farmers' incomes.

Architecture. Peking's heritage of Chinese architectural achievement is exemplified by both private housing and public buildings. As the whole city was laid out upon a rectangular street pattern symmetrically arranged around the palace compound, almost every dwelling in the city is rectangular in form, with the four sides squarely facing the cardinal directions. Most houses in the inner city were designed as residences of former officials and their families, and almost every dwelling compound is surrounded by high walls, with an open courtyard in the centre flanked by houses on the eastern, western, and northern sides, usually one story high. The former residences of high-ranking officials were composed of two or three compounds, interconnected along a north–south axis.

Stepping over the high wooden gate-sill of the front gate of a large compound, the visitor will find a brick screen wall located a few feet inside the gate—a structure that was supposed to shut off the intrusion of evil spirits, as well as to prevent curious passersby from looking inside. Beyond the screen is the outer courtyard, or service courtyard, which is flanked by houses to the east and west. There, in former days, were the kitchen and living quarters for the gatekeeper, servants, and any visiting guests and relatives. A red-painted gate leads through the north wall of the outer court into the main part of the house. This is built around three sides of the main courtyard, which, usually shaded by a large tree, was the centre of the family's life. All the windows look inward to the courtyard, and a double door opens into the courtyard from each of the three wings. The windows extend from three feet above the ground up to the deep, overhanging eaves. As they face south, the rooms in the main building get the maximum possible sunshine in winter, and the eaves provide a pleasant shade in summer, when the sun is high. The wing at the northern end of the court was intended for the head of the family and his wife. It is divided into three compartments, the central one being the living or community room, and the smaller rooms at either side being the bedroom and study. The rooms facing east and west—three on each side of the court—were for married sons and their families. This is the basic plan of all the old houses in Peking. Larger families built an extra courtyard behind the main house, because the traditional ideal was that all the existing generations should live together. Since 1949, however, as mentioned above, a great many of the old-style houses have been adapted for use by several families.

While the style and architecture of private dwelling units are uniform throughout the city, the public buildings and temples are characterized by a variety of designs and structures. As the nation's political and cultural centre for more than 700 years, Peking has more buildings of historical and architectural significance than any other contemporary city in China. Since 1949 many new government and municipal buildings, combining both traditional and Western architecture, have added to the city's landscape.

The Imperial Palaces (now the Palace Museum), with their golden roofs, white marble balustrades, and red pillars, stand in the heart of Peking and are surrounded by a moat and walls with a tower on each of the four corners. The palaces consist of outer throne halls and an inner court. North of the three tunnel gates that form the front gate, called the Wu (Meridian) Gate, a great courtyard lies beyond five marble bridges. Farther north is the massive, double-tiered Hall of Supreme Harmony (T'ai-ho tien), once the throne hall. A marble terrace rises above the marble balustrades that surround it, upon which stand beautiful, ancient bronzes in the shapes of caldrons, cranes, turtles, compasses, and ancient measuring instruments. The Hall of Supreme Harmony is the largest wooden structure in China.

Workers' community housing

The Imperial Palaces

The Hall of Supreme Harmony (centre), one of the former Imperial Palaces, now part of the Palace Museum complex in the Forbidden City.
Xinhua News Agency

Behind it, beyond another courtyard, is the Hall of Complete Harmony (Chung-ho tien), where the emperor paused to rest before going into the Hall of Supreme Harmony. Beyond the Hall of Complete Harmony is the last hall, the Hall of Preserving Harmony (Pao-ho tien), after which comes the Inner Court (Nei-t'ing). The Inner Court was used as the emperor's personal apartment. It contains three large halls, the Palace of Heavenly Purity (Ch'ien-ch'ing kung), the Hall of Heavenly and Earthly Intercourse (Chiao-t'ai tien), and the Palace of Earthly Tranquillity (K'un-ning kung).

The Palace of Heavenly Purity is divided into three parts. The central part was used for family feasts and family audiences, audiences for foreign envoys, and funeral services; the eastern section was used for mourning rites and the west section for state business. The other two palaces, one behind the other, were Imperial family residences. The three throne halls in the Outer Court and the three main halls in the Inner Court lie along the central axis. On either side are smaller palaces, with their own court-yards and auxiliary buildings. Behind the buildings, before the north gate of the Imperial Palaces is reached, lies the Imperial Garden. Each palace, its courtyard and side halls, forms an architectural whole.

The Temple of Heaven Among the historical and religious structures in Peking, the Temple of Heaven (T'ien-t'an), located in the old outer city, is unique both for its unusual geometric layout and because it represents the supreme achievement of traditional Chinese architecture. Entering from the western gate of the temple, along a path that is about 1,600 feet in length and shaded by ancient cypresses, one comes to a raised passage about 1,000 feet long. This broad walk connects the two sets of main buildings in the temple enclosure. To the north lies the Hall of Prayer for Good Harvests (Ch'i-nien tien) and to the south, the Imperial Vault of Heaven (Huang-ch'iung yü) and the Circular Mound Altar (Huan-ch'iu t'an). The three buildings are built along a straight line. Seen from the air, the wall of the enclosure to the south is square, while the one on the north side is semicircular. This pattern symbolizes the traditional Chinese belief that heaven is round and earth square.

The Hall of Prayer for Good Harvests, built in 1420 as a place of heaven worship for the emperors, is a lofty, cone-shaped structure with triple eaves, the top of which is crowned with a gilded ball. The base of the structure is a large, triple-tiered circular stone terrace. Each ring has balustrades of carved white marble, which gives the effect of lace when seen from a distance. The roof of the hall is deep blue, resembling the colour of the sky. The entire structure, 125 feet high and about 100 feet in diameter, is supported by 28 massive wooden pillars. The four central columns, called the "dragon-well pillars," represent the four seasons; there are also two rings of 12 columns each, the inner ring symbolizing the 12 months and the outer

ring the 12 divisions of day and night, according to a traditional system. The centre of the stone-paved floor is a round marble slab that has a design of a dragon and a phoenix—traditional symbols of king and queen. The hall has no walls, only partitions of open latticework doors.

The Imperial Vault of Heaven, first erected in 1530 and rebuilt in 1752, is a smaller structure some 64 feet high and about 50 feet in diameter. The circular building has no crossbeam, and the dome is supported by complicated span work. Its decorative paintings still retain their fresh original colours.

South of the enclosure lies the Circular Mound Altar, built in 1530 and rebuilt in 1749. The triple-tiered white stone terrace is enclosed by two sets of walls that are square outside and round inside; thus, the whole structure forms an elaborate and integrated geometric pattern. The inner terrace is 16 feet above the ground and about 100 feet in diameter; the middle terrace is about 165 feet across and the lowest terrace some 230 feet across. Each terrace is encircled by nine rings of stones. Both the Imperial Vault of Heaven and the Circular Mound Altar were erected to portray the geometric structure of heaven, as conceived by the architects of the Ming dynasty. After 1949 the whole enclosure of the Temple of Heaven was repaired; it is now a public park.

To the east of T'ien-an Men Square within the People's Cultural Park is found the Working People's Cultural Palace (formerly the Temple of the Imperial Ancestors), where the tablets of the emperors were displayed. The temple, like the Imperial Palaces in style, was built in three stonework tiers, each with double eaves. On either side are two rows of verandas surrounding a vast court-yard large enough to hold 10,000 people. Exhibitions of economic and cultural achievements, both of China and of other countries, are frequently held in the three halls. Lectures by leading scholars on science, literature, and the arts are also held there.

The Great Hall of the People Perhaps the most imposing structure constructed in the heart of the city since 1949 is the Great Hall of the People. The Great Hall is located on the southwestern side of T'ien-an Men Square and is an immense building with tall columns of gray marble set on red marble bases of floral design. It has a flat roof with a golden-yellow tile cornice over green eaves shaped like lotus petals. The base of the building is of pink granite, and its walls are apricot yellow. Its frontage is 1,100 feet long—about the equivalent of two city blocks. The floor space of some 6,060,000 square feet (563,000 square metres) is more than that of all the palaces in the old Forbidden City. Inside the building, the ceiling and walls are rounded. The focus of the lighting system is a red star surrounded by golden sunflower petals. The grand auditorium is where the National People's Congress holds its sessions. Other components are a banquet hall for 5,000, huge lobbies, and scores of meeting rooms and offices for the standing committee of the congress.

Children sweeping the steps at the Hall of Prayer for Good Harvests, central building of the Temple of Heaven.
Emil Schulthess—Black Star

THE PEOPLE

Since 1949 Peking has been one of the most rapidly growing urban centres in China. During the dynastic period, when Peking was the capital, from the 13th to the beginning of the 20th century, the population of Peking seems to have increased very slowly, but in the four decades (1901–49) after the downfall of the Ch'ing dynasty it increased at an accelerating rate. This rapid increase has been attributed to at least three factors: the rural disorder on the North China Plain during the rule of the warlords caused extensive migration to the walled city of Peking; the loss of Manchuria to Japan in 1931 made Peking a shelter for thousands of refugees from the northeastern provinces; and the establishment of numerous institutes of higher education, sponsored by the government or by foreign missionaries, stimulated the growth of the student population in a city that was a cultural as well as a political capital.

The phenomenal increase in Peking's population, however, occurred after the city had resumed its role as the national capital. In 1949 Peking was the fourth largest city in the country; some 10 years later it had become the second largest. This increase resulted primarily from the necessary migration of thousands of government workers to the new capital, the rapid rate of industrial development in the municipality during the 1950s and '60s, and the extension of the municipal boundary in 1959 to include large rural areas. The effect of these circumstances has been that in the four decades since 1949 the population of

Population growth

Peking has more than doubled, with people living in rural areas of the municipality accounting for about two-fifths of the total.

The overwhelming majority of Peking's population is Han (Chinese). Hui (Chinese Muslims), Manchus, and Mongols constitute the largest minority groups. Peking residents speak a dialect that is difficult for outsiders to understand, but all educated citizens can speak Mandarin, or *p'u-t'ung hua* ("common language").

Peking has a small but growing community of foreign residents—mainly diplomats, journalists, business people, and teachers—who have become an important aspect of the city's life. Government authorities have made great efforts to meet the special demands of foreigners and to isolate them as much as possible from local people. Foreigners generally are housed in hotels or in large, enclosed apartment compounds and send their children to Western-style schools (although the children are free to attend Chinese schools); in addition, the government has provided an international club with dining and recreational facilities.

Since the late 1970s efforts have been made to restore the ancient temples, churches, and seminaries of various religions (most prominently Buddhism) that were damaged during the Cultural Revolution (1966–76). Some of the restored structures are again being used by worshipers, monks, and pupils.

THE ECONOMY

Agriculture. Although Peking has been the capital of China for hundreds of years, it is far away from the nation's traditional key economic area, the productive Yangtze Valley. In the past the task of feeding the large urban population in Peking was facilitated by using the Grand Canal and by transporting grain from the south by sea. Since the first decade of the 20th century, railways have played an important role in bringing food supplies to the capital. The city, however, has striven for a high degree of self-sufficiency in secondary food supplies, such

CLICK/Chicago

The People's Heroes Monument, in front of the Great Hall in T'ien-an Men Square.

as vegetables, fruits, fish, and poultry, and in a number of construction materials. The expansion of municipal boundaries in 1958 and 1959 was partially aimed at this goal, and the municipality has succeeded in maintaining an adequate supply of vegetables and fruits. Agricultural reforms in the early 1980s gave individual households greater freedom of production and resulted in greater and more varied food supplies in the city.

Thus, unlike in most of the world's major cities, agriculture forms a significant part of Peking's economy. Vegetables are grown in a belt that encircles the city and is covered by a network of irrigation channels. The channels are supplemented by a large number of electric pumps. These irrigation measures have made intensive farming possible in an area prone to frequent droughts. Vegetables are grown in the winter months in hothouses. This large farm belt is also one of the most highly mechanized agricultural areas in China. The municipal government has encouraged the expanded cultivation of fruit and nut trees, and large areas of wasteland to the north and east of the city have been reclaimed for fruit tree planting. The large-scale planting of fruit and other trees has also reduced considerably the wind erosion of the soil. While the hill areas produce large quantities of pears, persimmons, apples, chestnuts, and walnuts, the reclaimed lowlands are covered with vineyards and peach orchards. Part of the Peking fruit crop is shipped by train to the cities of the Northeast and Inner Mongolia.

Industry. One of the main differences between the Imperial capital of former times and present-day Peking is that the Imperial capital was a consumption rather than a production centre, receiving supplies of all kinds from other parts of the country. Since 1949, however, Peking has emerged as China's most industrial city after Shanghai in terms of total production value. Heavy industries predominate over light industries in the city. Most of the growth took place in the 1950s and 1960s, but concern for the adverse effects of industrialization on the city's environment has since led to a curtailment of industrial expansion.

Zhang Shuyuan—Xinhua News Agency

Agricultural produce market in northern Peking.

Among the large industrial establishments is the Shih-ching-shan Iron and Steel Works, located about nine miles west of the old city. The Shih-ching-shan plant was originally started in 1920, based on local ore and anthracite in the Western Hills; after the Japanese occupation of 1937, it produced a meagre amount of pig iron. Since 1958 the plant has been enlarged and is now one of the largest steel plants in China. Its high-quality steel production supplies such Peking industries as machine building, electrical engineering, and precision instrument manufacturing. A number of smaller finishing mills have also been established to produce such items as cold-drawn bearing steel and flat spring steel for tractor and automobile accessories, seamless tubes for high-pressure boilers, and magnetic steel for machine tools and radios. Peking is also an important centre of machinery manufacture, with plants for manufacturing cranes, locomotives, automobile parts, tractors, wheat harvesters, mining machinery, and printing equipment. Most of these plants were built in the suburbs east and south of the central city, where extensive tracts of level land were available and where the prevailing northwest winds would carry industrial pollutants away from the densely populated areas. With the rapid expansion of cotton cultivation in Hopeh Province in the 1950s and 1960s, Peking also became one of China's major textile centres. Peking's textile industry includes the manufacture of cotton and woolen fabrics and piece goods, serge, and several types of synthetic fabric. Peking's petrochemical industry expanded rapidly when an oil pipeline was constructed in the mid-1970s to link the city with the Ta-ch'ing oil field in the Northeast (formerly Manchuria). The petrochemical industry is dominated by the Yen-shan Petrochemical Corporation, located southwest of the city.

Iron and steel manufacturing

As a former Imperial capital, Peking has a rich accumulation of art treasures, produced by a variety of arts and handicraft industries that were intimately connected with court life and Imperial needs. Much of the traditional handicraft industry has been reorganized and reequipped. Among the city's well-known handicraft products are rugs and carpets, porcelain and chinaware, jade and ivory sculpture, brass ware, enamel and lacquer ware, lace, and embroidery.

Commerce and finance. With the rapid growth of industry and population in the city, many service industries, operated mainly by government agencies, have also greatly expanded.

China has a nationwide and centralized system of banking, in which the state-owned People's Bank of China plays a key role. This bank, with its head office in the inner city, functions as the agent of the national treasury. All funds of state-owned industrial enterprises, as well as of national, provincial, and local governments, the People's Liberation Army, and the network of cooperatives, are deposited with the People's Bank. The bank uses the working capital at its disposal for the operations of the economy and the government. The People's Bank thus acts as cashier of the national budget and of a large part of the nation's financial operations. Through its branch offices and savings account centres, the bank also serves the daily needs of people in the city and in the suburbs. Working in cooperation with the People's Bank and under its supervision are three other banking institutions—the People's Construction Bank, which has the task of financing and supervising all basic construction projects, such as new railways; the Agricultural Bank of China, which specializes in agricultural investment; and the Bank of China, which handles all international trade and foreign exchange. In addition, several foreign-owned banks have representative offices in the city to assist foreign nationals doing business in China.

Banking institutions

Because of the symmetrical layout of the city, Peking lacks the compact central business district that characterizes most cities in the Western world. Historically, the market areas of the city were situated at two street intersections to the southwest and southeast of the Imperial Palace, and the Tung Tan and Hsi Tan neighbourhoods are still major shopping centres. In addition, a number of multistory department stores have been erected along Wang-fu-ching Ta-chieh and in Hsi Tan, supplying a wide

Shopping facilities

variety of goods for daily needs. The Peking Department Store, a state-owned enterprise, is one of the largest department stores in China and has branch stores in major cities throughout the country. The Friendship Store near the San-li-t'un Diplomatic Compound mainly serves foreign visitors, although some Chinese—especially those who receive foreign-currency remittances from relatives living abroad—are allowed to shop there; it specializes in foodstuffs, high-quality clothes, antiques and curios, and other items that are not easily available to most Chinese. In addition to these modern establishments, there are a dozen traditional markets that still serve an important local function. The Peking markets have evolved through a long period of history, and each has developed its own reputation for special commodities and services.

The East Wind Market, located on the busy Wang-fu-ching Ta-chieh, is noted for the traditional handicrafts produced in the city. The market also contains a number of restaurants and cafés serving a variety of Chinese regional foods. The West Market was established in 1932 around Hsi-tan Pei Ta-chieh. It is one of the most diverse markets in the city, composed of several different sections that each offer special commodities or services. There is also a complete department store, as well as a number of recreational establishments.

Two of Peking's more interesting shopping areas are the Liu-li-ch'ang and T'ien-ch'iao markets. The restored Liu-li-ch'ang Market is located just south of the Ho-p'ing Gate site in the old outer city. The area acquired its name (which means "the glazier's shop") from the colourful glazed tiles that were made there during the Ming dynasty, but in the later part of the 18th century it gradually became a market for curios, antiques, old books, paintings, works of ancient Chinese calligraphers, and paper. It is still the centre for traditional art shops. The T'ien-ch'iao Market is located at the south end of the old outer city, near T'ien-t'an Park. As early as the 16th century, poor people of the city began to come to T'ien-ch'iao to buy and sell secondhand goods. Open-air markets were also held there in the evenings. After 1900, when the railway station in the southern suburbs was moved to the vicinity of the Temple of Heaven, peddlers and small traders, folk artists, storytellers, and musicians began to appear in large numbers, and the place became a bustling market for fish, poultry, fruit, and vegetables, as well as a recreational area for poor people. This market has some of the best food shops in the city and remains a folk-entertainment centre for the metropolis.

Tourism

Tourism has become increasingly important to the Peking economy. Tourists are drawn not only to the historical and cultural attractions of the central city but also to such sites in the rural areas as the Great Wall and the tombs of the Ming emperors to the north of the city and the Peking-man caves to the southwest. There has been a steady increase in tourist services provided in Peking. Many hotels and hostels have been built, especially in the 1980s, and old ones have been renovated and enlarged to meet the ever greater demand. The China International Travel Service, which is state-owned, especially serves foreign tourists, while the main function of the Overseas Chinese Travel Service is to take care of overseas Chinese, who constitute the majority of visitors touring China; the general offices of both organizations are located in the inner city, and each has branch offices throughout the country.

Transportation. Peking is the railroad centre of China, forming the terminus of a number of lines in the national railroad network. The major lines radiating from Peking provide connections with Shen-yang (Liaoning Province), Shanghai Municipality, Canton (Kwangtung Province), Pao-t'ou (Inner Mongolia Autonomous Region), and T'ai-yüan (Shansi Province), respectively, each city being a major national industrial and commercial centre. The local lines are of regional importance and serve outlying districts within the metropolitan area. Peking is linked by direct express with several other large urban centres, and it is also periodically connected by express train with Moscow; P'yŏngyang, N. Kor.; and Ulaanbaatar, Mong.

While railroads connect Peking with distant cities, highways are the principal means of communication with

Rail connections

communities within a 125-mile radius. There are about a dozen major highways radiating from the city, along which regular bus services run. Several major bus depots are located in the inner city. Peking's road-transport system, however, is highly inadequate for a city of its size. There are no long-distance express highways. Three-wheeled cycle carts are widely used in the city for short-distance transport, and in the rural areas goods are still commonly hauled by carts drawn by animals or people.

Peking is also the centre of China's civil air transport. The nation's major domestic air routes radiate from Peking to regional centres at Shanghai, Canton, and Wu-lu-mu-ch'i (in Sinkiang Uighur Autonomous Region), as well as to other major cities. Peking's Capital Airport, located northeast of the central city, is the principal international air terminal of the country.

Peking's intracity commuting services are provided primarily by a network of city-owned buses and trolleys. At places to which a large number of people are carried, such as the Shih-ching-shan Iron and Steel Works, bus routes run through the plants themselves. Trolley routes run through the densely populated districts of the city, the pattern much influenced by the symmetrical arrangement of the old city plan. In the early 1970s a subway line—the first in China—was opened, running east–west through the centre of the city; this line was supplemented by a separate loop line opened in the 1980s that follows the old limits of the inner city. There are relatively few taxicabs or private automobiles. Bicycles are very popular for short-distance intracity travel, and they constitute the bulk of street traffic.

ADMINISTRATION AND SOCIAL CONDITIONS

Government. Peking is one of the three centrally administered (*i.e.,* province-level) *shih* (municipalities) in China (the others being Shanghai and Tientsin), and there is no governmental tier between it and the central government. The municipality is divided administratively into four urban and six suburban *ch'u* (districts) and the eight *hsien* (counties) in the peripheral areas. Peking's municipal government is part of the hierarchical structure of the Chinese government—and the parallel structure of the Chinese Communist Party (CCP)—that extends from the national organization, through the provincial apparatus, to the municipal and, ultimately, neighbourhood levels. The principal responsibilities of the People's Congress of Peking Municipality, the major decision-making body, include issuing administrative orders, collecting taxes, determining the budget, and implementing economic plans. A standing committee selected from its members recommends policy decisions and oversees the operation of municipal government. Executive authority rests with the Peking People's Government, the officers of which are elected by the congress; it consists of a mayor, vice mayors, and numerous bureaus in charge of public security, the judicial system, and other civil, economic, social, and cultural affairs.

As a subdivision of the municipality, each district or township has its own mayorality. Below the urban district there are police substations and street mayoralities. Neighbourhood associations have various functions, including mediating disputes, conducting literacy campaigns, supervising sanitation and welfare, and promoting family planning.

As the national capital, Peking houses all of the most important governmental and political institutions in the nation. These include the National People's Congress, nominally the supreme organ of state power; the State Council, the highest executive organ of the state; and the various administrative departments under the jurisdiction of the State Council, including the ministries and commissions in charge of foreign affairs, internal affairs, public security, national defense, justice, finance, culture, health, education, nationality affairs (concerning minority groups in the country), agriculture, and various branches in industry. Peking is also the headquarters of the parallel CCP organizations—the National Party Congress, the Central Committee and Politburo, and the Secretariat. In addition to the above, the highest organ of state concerned with

The State Council

the maintenance of law and order—the Supreme People's Court—is located in Peking.

Public utilities. Peking is not on a river, and most water for municipal consumption has to be brought from elsewhere. Some water, however, comes from shallow wells, which are common throughout much of the region. These provide some villages with drinking water and supply water for irrigation.

From the earliest history of the city, use has been made of local rivers and springs. To the east is the Pai River, which, after being joined by the Ch'ao River at the Mi-yün Reservoir, forms the Ch'ao-pai River, which then flows southward. The tumultuous Yung-ting is a large river, draining the Shansi Plateau and the northwest of Hopeh. After following a twisting course through the mountains, it reaches the Peking plain, passes under the Marco Polo Bridge, nine miles southwest of Peking, and then turns southward to meet the Grand Canal north of Tientsin. The flow of the Yung-ting is irregular; in the rainy season it rises rapidly, carrying with it large quantities of silt, which raise the level of the riverbed considerably. At Marco Polo Bridge it is 50 feet above the level of the city, thus constituting a hazard when the river is in flood but facilitating canalization and irrigation. Several springs rise at the foot of the Hsiang Hills and on Yü-ch'üan Hill, both to the northeast of the city. During the Ch'ing dynasty these springs were tapped by means of an aqueduct that conveyed water for the city moat and for the three lakes near the Imperial Palaces. The moat around the city walls became an important means of water distribution for the municipality.

In the early 1950s, large-scale water-conservation projects were begun to provide more water for the expanding urban area. Two large artificial lakes have since been made: the Mi-yün Reservoir, northeast of the city, and the Kuan-t'ing Reservoir, in the northwestern mountains beyond the Great Wall. These regulate the flow of the Pai and Yung-ting rivers upstream, storing water at times of heavy discharge and releasing it when the rivers are low. Two lesser projects have also been carried out: the construction of the Ming Tombs Reservoir, whose waters feed a hydroelectric power station and irrigate the neighbouring countryside, and a hydroelectric power station near Mo-shih-k'ou, which uses the waters of the Yung-ting and feeds them back into the river through an ancient canal. The hydroelectric station at Kuan-t'ing is the largest source of electricity for the metropolitan area of Peking.

The Peking Water Company, which was originally formed in 1908, is responsible for supplying water for the municipality. Water is obtained from the waterworks within the old city, as well as from several waterworks in the suburbs; the network of mains and pipes extends to every residential and industrial unit, including towns and villages near the Men-t'ou-kou coal mine about seven miles from the city. Public standpipes have also been installed at regular intervals throughout the city, the suburbs, and nearby rural people's communes. The Kuan-t'ing Reservoir, the largest man-made lake in the North China Plain, supplies the metropolitan area of Peking with most of its water.

Peking is one of the few cities in China equipped with a modern sewage system. An underground sewage system was installed as early as the 15th century, which extended nearly 195 miles. Later this network became clogged with effluent and silt. A new system was installed in the early 1950s, which, within the walled area, was partly based on the rehabilitation of the old system. All open sewers, characteristic of many Chinese cities, were eliminated, and new pipes were laid throughout the densely populated areas of the municipality.

The headquarters of the Peking General Post Office is located on the east side of T'ien-an Men Square. It provides more comprehensive services than do post offices in Western cities, handling mail, telegrams, long-distance telephone calls, and the distribution of newspapers and magazines. There are also more than 350 branch offices and stations in the city and the suburbs. The Peking General Post Office also maintains several service centres at certain busy traffic points, such as the Ch'ien Gate and Peking Railway Station, and Wang-fu-ching Ta-chieh.

The service centre on Wang-fu-ching Ta-chieh takes subscriptions to foreign newspapers and magazines and sells single issues.

Health. Chinese medical services employ both the traditional Chinese and the Western systems of medicine. Peking has some of the best hospitals of both systems in the nation.

The Peking Union Hospital, the earliest modern hospital to be established in China, was founded in 1921 as an affiliate of the Peking Union Medical College, which from 1915 onward was supported by the China Medical Board of the Rockefeller Foundation. The hospital, now renamed Capital Hospital, is a large polyclinic combined with an institute of gynecology and pediatrics. It is the largest hospital in Peking. Since 1949 many new hospitals, clinics, and sanitariums have been built. People's Friendship Hospital, a gift of the Soviet Union at the peak of Sino-Soviet friendship in the 1950s, is located in the T'ien-ch'iao neighbourhood in the outer city. Until 1960 the Soviet staff not only treated patients but also gave advanced training to Chinese medical personnel on the latest Soviet methods.

Many hospitals are clinical teaching hospitals attached to medical schools; these include the Fu Wai Hospital of the Chinese Academy of Medical Science, located outside the Fu-ch'eng Gate site; the First Affiliated Hospital of the Peking Medical College, near the Hsi-an Gate site; and the Affiliated Hospital of the Research Institute of Chinese Medicine, located in the western suburban town of Hsiao-yüan. The largest pediatrics hospital in China, the new Peking Children's Hospital, is situated just outside the Fu-hsing Gate site. It was designed to provide a homelike atmosphere for its young patients. In the hills to the west, a sanitarium in the traditional Chinese architectural style has been built for students from Asian countries. The most specialized hospitals are located in the old residential districts of the city and include the Stomatological Hospital (dealing with the mouth and related diseases), the Chest Surgery Hospital, the Hospital of Plastic Surgery, the old Peking Children's Hospital, the Hospital of Chinese Medicine, and the Ji-sui-tan Hospital, which specializes in traumatic (accident-related) and orthopedic surgery.

Chinese traditional medicine comprises prescribing Chinese herb drugs and employing acupuncture (a medical practice encompassing therapeutics and anesthesia that involves inserting needles into various parts of the body). Doctors in both Chinese and Western systems are trained in many universities and institutes in Peking. Students in the Western-style medical schools are taught the essentials of Chinese traditional medicine, and Chinese traditional medical students are expected to be familiar with the essentials of Western medicine. Diagnoses of difficult cases are made only after consultations with specialists of both systems.

For the rural areas of the metropolis, each county has a well-equipped hospital located in the county seat. But the basic unit of the medical service is the health centre in the commune, which is equipped with complete clinical facilities. Medical teams of doctors, nurses, and public health personnel are sent frequently from the teaching centres in the city to the communes to assist in the general medical work and to keep the local medical staff in touch with the latest medical progress and techniques.

Education. The educational system of Peking was massively disrupted by the Cultural Revolution, and throughout the 1980s it was in the process of being restored. Nevertheless, there has been no radical change in the structure of the school system in Peking since 1949; it is still largely composed of six years of primary education, which is universal, and six years of secondary education. For preschool-age children, kindergartens and nurseries are operated by factories, business enterprises, government offices, and city block cooperatives. Their main function is to permit mothers to work, and although some of these facilities are located in the residential neighbourhoods, many are located on the premises of places of employment. In the suburban or rural areas, kindergartens are often temporarily set up during such events as the harvest. In the early 1950s, efforts were made to abolish private

(margin notes)
Water supplies

Traditional medicine

The schools

schools and to put all education in the hands of the state. As a result, all private schools run by missionaries were taken over by the government. It was soon realized, however, that the government could not possibly provide enough schools for the millions who required education. The government then reversed its policy to some degree and decided to encourage the establishment of schools by local organizations, such as factories, business concerns, collectives, and communes. A major part of the finance for elementary education is now met by sources other than the central government, though the government does provide considerable subsidies to schools in difficult financial situations.

The curriculum in the primary school is basic. The early part of primary education is largely devoted to reading, writing, and mathematics, and, in the last two years of primary school, nature study, history, geography, and physical education are added to the curriculum. Closely related to primary education are movements for eliminating illiteracy, phoneticizing Chinese writing, and simplifying Chinese characters.

The secondary schools in Peking are mainly of three types: the general middle school, the normal school, and the vocational and technical school. The general middle school is of the academic type, with a curriculum designed to prepare students for college. The normal school trains teachers for primary schools. The vocational and technical schools, created to provide skilled workers in various fields, have developed most rapidly in the city.

Peking's position as a centre of higher education in China has been further strengthened since 1949, and within the metropolitan area there are numerous institutes of higher learning. A scientific and educational district has emerged in the northwestern outskirts of the city, against the background of K'un-ming Lake, the Summer Palace, and the Western Hills. This area contains such prestigious institutions as Peking University and Ch'ing-hua University. Peking University was founded in 1898 and is one of the largest composite universities in China. In 1953 the university moved from its old site at Sha-t'an, in the inner city, to the present campus, which previously belonged to the missionary-established Yen-ch'ing University. The new campus has been expanded considerably to the east and south. Ch'ing-hua University is the most renowned technical institute in China.

Within the academic district are also found the People's University of China, an institute of ideological training, and the Central Institute of Nationalities, which accepts students from the various autonomous regions and districts. Situated in the same area are the Peking Normal College, the Peking Medical College, and the Central Conservatory of Music. Numerous institutes of higher education are also located in this area; these include the Peking Institute of Steel and Iron, the Peking Institute of Aeronautics and Astronautics, the Peking Petroleum Institute, the Peking Institute of Geological Prospecting, the Peking Institute of Forestry, and the Peking Mechanical Institute of Agriculture. The Chinese Academy of Sciences, the most prestigious research institute in the nation, is also located in this district.

Besides technical colleges, there are a number of foreign-language institutions in Peking where foreigners are employed to teach alongside their Chinese colleagues. The Peking Foreign Language Institute, located on the northwestern outskirts of the city, is the largest institute of its kind in China. The Second Foreign Language Institute was set up in 1964 for training personnel for the New China News Agency. There are also a number of small institutes of language training run by the government and by the Peking Radio Station. The School of Foreign Languages is an institute at the secondary level, which accepts children as young as eight years of age; half of them learn English, while others study French, German, Spanish, Arabic, Russian, and Japanese.

Institutions of higher education

Foreign-language institutions

CULTURAL LIFE

Peking has been the magnificent centre of traditional Chinese culture and learning since the Ming dynasty. Emperors and courtiers patronized the arts, especially painting and calligraphy. Precious objects from other parts of the empire and from foreign countries poured into the capital. This role of cultural centre was continued during the Ch'ing dynasty, although the century of political and social upheaval that began in the mid-19th century led to an overall cultural decline in Peking. This decline continued into the modern period and affected not only Peking but the whole of China. With their defeat in 1949, the Nationalists shipped a huge quantity of art treasures to Taiwan. On the mainland, subsequently, many family heirlooms were purchased by the state for very low prices and were then sold for export or used to enhance museum holdings.

Until the early 1960s traditional arts, crafts, and scholar-

Der Stern—Black Star

May Day rally in T'ien-an Men Square, Peking.

ship were encouraged by the Chinese Communist Party, but the Cultural Revolution swept all before it. Art objects that were not deliberately smashed by the Red Guards were confiscated (some were returned to their former owners during the 1980s). The Cultural Revolution also put a virtual end to traditional Chinese scholarship, as many academics were sent out to the countryside or imprisoned. Since the late 1970s, however, the government has made a concerted effort to restore damaged treasures and to revive the work of traditional artists and scholars. Since much of this activity has taken place in Peking, the capital has undergone something of a cultural renaissance.

Museums and libraries. The Palace Museum, containing the city's greatest collection of art treasures, is housed in the main buildings of the former Imperial Palaces.

The Palace Museum

Many of the halls are kept as they were in dynastic times, each constituting a museum in itself; others are kept for the display of some of the priceless treasures from China's past. Of special interest are the porcelains and enamels, works in embroidery and precious metals, and the stone carvings and scrolls.

The Museum of Chinese History is located on the eastern side of T'ien-an Men Square. There are thousands of historical relics and documents on display, arranged to give a comprehensive survey of the progress of human achievement in China, beginning with the appearance of the prehistoric Peking man some 500,000 years ago, then continuing through the last 6,000 years of Chinese history. The Museum of the Chinese Revolution occupies a wing of the museum building. Its purpose is to trace the history of China since the mid-19th century, laying particular stress on the revolutionary movement and the part played by the Communist Party.

The Peking Planetarium, the first of its kind in China, is located outside the Hsi-chih Gate site. It is an educational centre for the dissemination of general knowledge in astronomy and natural science by means of exhibitions, forums, films, projector demonstrations, and telescopic observations of the heavens. The planetarium proper is situated on the south side of the building. Behind the main building stand an observatory and meteorological station.

The Peking Library

The Peking Library, which holds the historical collections of the National Library of China, is located on the west bank of Pei Hai. The library inherited books and archives from the Imperial Wen-yüan Ko library, a famous collection that has existed for more than 500 years and that, in turn, included books and manuscripts from the Imperial Library of the Southern Sung dynasty, established some 700 years ago. Also in its holdings are other collections from Imperial libraries of the Ch'ing dynasty, Imperial colleges, and private owners. Among them are rare copies of ancient manuscripts and books of five dynastic periods from the Sung to the Ch'ing, including a vast number of manuscript volumes on different subjects, copies of Buddhist sutras dating to the 6th century, old maps, diagrams, and rubbings from ancient inscriptions on metal and stone; in addition, it possesses the *Yung-lo ta-tien* ("Yung-lo Encyclopedia") of the Ming dynasty and a copy of the *Ssu-k'u ch'üan-shu* ("Complete Library of the Four Branches of Literature"), dating from the Ch'ing dynasty. In the late 1980s the collection of modern holdings of the National Library was moved from the Peking Library to a new facility in the western outskirts of the city.

The arts. Traditional Peking opera (*ching-hsi*)—with its elaborate and stylized costumes and makeup, cacophonous music, and spectacular dance and acrobatic routines—has been revived, after an attempt during the Cultural Revolution to adapt the form to modern revolutionary themes. The opera has great appeal to older people but less for the young, who instead prefer motion pictures, television, and popular music. Musical performances of all kinds are given in Peking; the city boasts a symphony orchestra and Western-style opera and ballet companies and hosts visits by foreign orchestras and performers.

A variety of Chinese plays are staged each year, and works by Shakespeare and other Western dramatists have again been playing in Peking. The city's bookshops, almost denuded of cultural works and foreign literature during the Cultural Revolution, are now better stocked. In addition,

calligraphy and the painting of non-revolutionary subjects have again become popular pastimes.

Recreation. As the residence of the Imperial families through several dynastic periods, Peking is well known for its numerous parks and playgrounds; few cities in China have as large a proportion of land within the central city allocated for recreational uses. Among the most popular of Peking's parks are Chung-shan Park, Pei-hai Park, Ching-shan Park, the Summer Palace, and the Peking Zoological Gardens.

Chung-shan Park adjoins the west wall of T'ien-an Men Square; it is the most centrally located park in Peking and encloses the former Altar of Earth and Harvests, where the emperors made offerings to the gods of earth and agriculture. The altar consists of a square terrace in the centre of the park, to the north of which is the 550-year-old Hall of Worship, now the Sun Yat-sen Memorial Hall, which is used for public meetings. The Hall of Worship is the oldest wooden structure in Peking; its simple form, masterly design, and sturdy woodwork bear the characteristic marks of early Ming architecture.

The Water Pavilion, built out over a lotus pond on three sides to provide a gathering place for scholars and poets, is also located in the park. Scattered among the park's pools, goldfish enclosures, rocky hills, weeping willows, pines, cypresses, bamboos, and flowers are pavilions, kiosks, and towers, which are typical of Chinese garden landscape.

Pei-hai Park

Pei-hai Park lies to the northwest of the Forbidden City. It covers some 176 acres (71 hectares), half of which is water. It contains Pei Hai, the most northerly of the three lakes—called "seas" (*hai*)—that lie roughly north and south within the Imperial City. Pleasure grounds, lakes, and buildings have existed on this site for 800 years. As the lakes were deepened and dredged, the excavated earth was used to build hillocks and islands of great beauty. In 1651 a Manchu emperor built the White Pagoda, the most striking landmark in the park, on the top of a hill. Many of the buildings in the park are used for serious pursuits, as well as recreation. They include an Institute of Research on the History of Chinese Classical Literature and a Natural History Museum, as well as the Peking Library. Pei Hai is crowded with rowboats in summer, and it freezes over to become a natural skating rink in winter.

Ching-shan (Prospect Hill) Park, also known as Mei-shan (Coal Hill) Park, is a man-made hill, more than a mile in circumference, located north of the Forbidden City. The hill, from the top of which a spectacular panorama of Peking can be seen, has five ridges, with a pavilion on each. The hill was the scene of a historical tragedy when, in 1644, at the end of the Ming dynasty, the defeated Ming emperor hanged himself on a locust tree on its east slope. In the northern part of the park is Peking Children's Palace, with recreational, athletic, and educational facilities.

The Summer Palace

The Summer Palace, lying close to the Western Hills, is about six miles northwest of the Hsi-chih Gate site. It is the largest park on the outskirts of Peking and is noted for its artificial landscaping, which provides an inimitable blend of woods, water, hills, and architecture. The Summer Palace covers more than 800 acres, four-fifths of which consists of K'un-ming Lake, the remainder being man-made hillocks. More than 100 buildings—halls, towers, pavilions, bridges, and pagodas—lie scattered throughout the park; a marble boat, two stories high and some 80 feet long, located at the northwest corner of the lake, is one of the major attractions. Connecting the buildings and courts along the shore of the lake are a series of richly painted covered promenades.

Peking Zoological Gardens is located on the western outskirts of the city. The zoo was established toward the end of the 19th century and was named the "Garden of Ten Thousand Animals" (Wan-sheng Yuan). Its collection is actually less than half that size, but it is the largest zoo in the country, with animals from all parts of China and the world; one of the zoo's most popular attractions is its collection of giant pandas.

Peking Workers' Stadium, located in the eastern part of the city, seats 80,000 and is the largest sports facility in China. Soccer games and field and track events are

Ta-kuan Park modeled after the garden described in the novel *Dream of the Red Chamber*.

Song Lianfeng—Xinhua News Agency

often held there. The Capital Gymnasium in the western outskirts has facilities for a variety of indoor games; it has enough space for 24 table tennis matches to be held simultaneously. A movable floor facilitates formation of an ice rink for figure skating and ice hockey.

Cuisine

The Chinese love of good food is world-renowned, and Peking is China's culinary showcase. All of the regional cuisines are represented among the city's hundreds of restaurants, although the Peking style predominates. The best-known dish to foreigners is Peking duck, which is the specialty of several establishments.

History

THE EARLY EMPIRES

With but few interruptions, Peking has been the capital of China for some 700 years, and in the number of years as the Imperial capital it is exceeded only by Sian (Ch'ang-an) in Shensi Province and Lo-yang in Honan Province. In prehistoric times the area around Peking was inhabited by some of the earliest known human beings. Between 1918 and 1939 the fossil remains of Peking man (formerly *Sinanthropus pekinensis*; now known as *Homo erectus pekinensis*), who lived about 500,000 years ago, and of Upper Cave man, who lived about 50,000 years ago, were unearthed at Chou-k'ou-tien, a village about 30 miles southwest of Peking.

While long periods in Peking's early history necessarily remain blank, it is certain that, some 3,000 years ago, Neolithic communities settled on or near the site where Peking now stands. During the Chan-kuo (Warring States) period (475–221 BC) of the Chou dynasty (c. 1111–255 BC), one of the powerful feudal states, the kingdom of Yen, established its capital named Chi near the present city of Peking; this was the first capital city to be associated with the site. The city was destroyed by the troops of Shih huang-ti, founder of the Ch'in dynasty (221–206 BC).

Chi—the capital of Yen

During the Ch'in dynasty, the Yen capital was incorporated into one of the 36 prefectures then established throughout the country. A new town was built during the Han dynasty (206 BC–AD 220) and was known as Yen. Throughout the Han dynasty and the turbulent centuries that followed, however, the place remained a provincial town, witnessing most of the time the fateful struggle between the Han Chinese to the south and the nomadic Hsiung-nu, or Huns, to the north.

During the period of San-kuo (Three Kingdoms; AD 220–280), the city was again called Yen. The northern border of ancient China ran close to the present city of

Peking, and northern nomadic tribes frequently broke in from across the border. Thus the area that was to become Peking became an important strategic as well as a local political centre.

For nearly 300 years (from the end of the Hsi [Western] Chin dynasty in 316/317 to the beginning of the Sui dynasty in 581), the northern territory, including the site where Peking now stands, was largely under the control of invading nomads. It was not until the T'ang dynasty (618–907) that it was recovered by the Han people and became known as Yu-chou. By the middle of the T'ang dynasty, measures were taken to prevent the nomadic Tangut tribes of Tibet, the Hsi Hsia and the Khitans (a Manchurian people), from raiding the border lands and the local capital. The position of Yu-chou consequently became increasingly important. On the fall of T'ang China, a number of states emerged in North China. One of these states was established by the Khitans; after destroying the city of Yu-chou, the Khitans established the Liao kingdom (947–1125) and built one of their capitals on approximately the same site, calling it Nanking ("Southern Capital") to distinguish it from other capitals in their Manchurian homeland. The Liao capital was bounded by a square wall, almost 14 miles in circumference and some 32 feet high. It had eight gates and enclosed a fine Imperial palace in the centre, which indicated the strong influence of Chinese city planning.

In the middle of the 12th century, when the Juchen, a Manchurian people from the Amur Valley, defeated the Liao and established the state of Chin, the Liao capital was rebuilt as the new Chin capital and renamed Chung-tu ("Central Capital"). Chung-tu under the rule of the Juchen was constructed on a larger scale, with splendidly decorated palaces and halls.

Between 1211 and 1215 the Mongols, under the leadership of Genghis Khan, one of the great conquerors of history, repeatedly attacked and finally took the city from the Chin. In the battle the palaces of Chung-tu were set on fire and blazed for more than a month. When all China fell to the Mongol hordes, Kublai Khan (1215–94), a successor to Genghis Khan and founder of the Yüan, or Mongol, dynasty (1206–1368), determined to build a new capital at Peking, abandoning the old city of Karakorum in Mongolia. In 1272 he named the new capital Ta-tu ("Great Capital"); under Mongol control it became for the first time the political centre of all China.

The Mongol capital of Ta-tu

Ta-tu was larger than any of its forerunners and was rebuilt slightly northeast of the old site. The square of the outer wall measured about 18 miles in length and enclosed an area of more than 20 square miles. The city walls were built with pounded earth, and once a year labourers were called in to repair them with mud. The Imperial Palace, which was approximately to the west of the existing one, was situated in the southern half of the capital city. The chief palace architect at the time was an Arab, appointed by Kublai Khan. The city of Ta-tu exemplified the imposing and variegated architecture of the Mongol period. The square walls and the 12 gates were all modeled on the Chinese plan, but the inner chambers and living quarters were often in the style of Mongolia or of Central Asia. It was at this time that a canal, the T'ung-hui Canal, was dug and connected to the Grand Canal, so that boats transporting the tribute rice from the provinces south of the Yangtze could sail into one of the new lakes inside the city. Ta-tu, which had magnificent Imperial palaces and treasures drawn from every corner of the country, was the scene of stupendous feasts given by the khan (ruler) on state occasions. These characteristics and the well-organized post-stages on the roads leading to the city astounded Marco Polo, the Venetian traveler who visited Ta-tu in the 1280s.

CENTURIES OF GROWTH

The Ming and Ch'ing dynasties. In the middle of the 14th century, Chu Yüan-chang headed a peasant revolt that overthrew the Mongol dynasty and, as the Hung-wu emperor, established the Ming dynasty (1368–1644). He moved the capital to Chin-ling, near his own hometown in Anhwei Province, and called it Nanking; Ta-tu was renamed Pei-p'ing ("Northern Peace") and was placed under his son's rule. On Chu's death (1398) the throne passed to his grandson in Nanking, but his son, Chu Ti (also called the Yung-lo emperor), who ruled Pei-p'ing, usurped the throne. In consequence, in 1403 the city was renamed Peking ("Northern Capital"), and in 1421 it was officially made the capital city of the Ming dynasty.

Peking in the Ming period grew on a yet grander scale than under the Mongols. The former city walls and the extant moats, palaces, and temples were mostly built in the 15th century. The old city of Ta-tu, including the palaces, was largely demolished. The new city was situated farther south, thus leaving the northern part of the Mongol city derelict while at the same time slicing off one gate from the east and west walls, respectively. In 1553 an outer city wall was begun, to include the increasing number of inhabitants living outside the city, but, when the entire construction was subsequently found to be too costly, the plan was abandoned on the completion of the south wall, thus producing the present shape of the old city. Unlike the city wall of pounded earth of Mongol times, the walls of the Ming city were faced with a layer of bricks, in order to prevent weathering.

In 1644 Peking was taken over by Li Tzu-ch'eng, who led a peasant uprising against the Ming regime. Li's army held it for only 40 days, for the Manchus were simultaneously preparing an incursion south of the Great Wall, and— thanks to the treachery of a Ming general who opened the gate—they swept down on the city. Peking fell intact and in the same year was declared the Manchu capital by Shun-chih, the first emperor of the Ch'ing dynasty (1644–1911/12).

Peking remained superficially the same throughout Ch'ing times. The city plan was unaltered, though many palaces, temples, and pavilions were added outside the walls to the west, notably the Yüan-ming Yüan (old Summer Palace), built in the 17th century, and the I-ho Yüan (new Summer

The 15th-century city

Palace), built in the late 19th century. The old Summer Palace was completely destroyed by fire in 1860 by the allied British and French troops during the "Arrow" War (1856–60). In the same year, as a result of the treaties of Tientsin in 1858, a permanent British embassy was established in the city, and a legation quarter, situated to the southeast of the palace ground, was reserved for British and other embassies. The legation quarter was besieged for nearly two months by the Boxer rebels in 1900.

The modern city. After the revolution of 1911, Peking remained the political centre of the Republic of China until 1928, when the Nationalists moved the capital to Nanking; Peking was again called Pei-p'ing. The city came under increasing pressure from the Japanese, who established the puppet state of Manchukuo in Manchuria in 1931. In July 1937 fighting broke out between Chinese and Japanese troops near the Marco Polo Bridge, southwest of the city; Pei-p'ing was subsequently occupied by the Japanese until 1945. After World War II the city reverted to the Nationalists, who were defeated by the Communists in the ensuing civil war. In 1949, with the establishment of the People's Republic of China, Peking (with its old name restored) was chosen as the capital of the new regime. The city soon regained its position as the leading political, financial, and cultural centre of China.

BIBLIOGRAPHY

General works: ROSS TERRILL, *Flowers on an Iron Tree: Five Cities of China* (1975); FELIX GREENE, *Peking* (1978); and DAVID BONAVIA, *Peking* (1978), describe city life in Peking. A number of important works on scenic and structural aspects of Peking were completed during the 1930s; among them are L.C. ARLINGTON and WILLIAM LEWISOHN, *In Search of Old Peking* (1935, reprinted 1987); and JULIET BREDON, *Peking: A Historical and Intimate Description of Its Chief Places of Interest*, 3rd rev. ed. (1931). OSVALD SIRÉN, *The Walls and Gates of Peking* (1924), and *The Imperial Palaces of Peking* (1926, reprinted 1976), give details on architectural features of the old walled city. HEDDA MORRISON, *A Photographer in Old Peking* (1985), is a record of the city in the 1940s. NORMAN A. CHANCE, *China's Urban Villagers: Life in a Beijing Commune* (1984), provides insight into economic and political factors. For demographic information, see the annual *China Urban Statistics.*

Guidebooks: DAVID BONAVIA et al., *A Guide to Beijing* (1987), is a survey from the China Guide Series. LIU JUNWEN, *Beijing: China's Ancient and Modern Capital* (1982), is a detailed guidebook. There is a chapter on history, development, and life in the city in the comprehensive work by FREDRIC M. KAPLAN, JULIAN M. SOBIN, and ARNE J. DE KEIJZER, *The China Guidebook*, 8th ed. (1987). YU ZHUOYUN (comp.), *Palaces of the Forbidden City* (1984; originally published in Chinese, 1982), is a guide to the Palace Museum.

History: Historical development is covered by RODERICK MACFARQUHAR, *The Forbidden City* (1972); NIGEL CAMERON and BRIAN BRAKE, *Peking: A Tale of Three Cities* (1965); and ZHOU SHACHEN, *Beijing Old and New: A Historical Guide to Places of Interest* (1984; originally published in Chinese, 1982). FRANK DORN, *The Forbidden City* (1970), associates the details of the Imperial Palaces with historical events. Other studies include JOHN S. BURGESS, *The Guilds of Peking* (1928, reprinted 1970); PETER FLEMING, *The Siege at Peking* (1959, reissued 1984); and GEORGE N. KATES, *The Years That Were Fat: The Last of Old China* (1952, reissued 1976), covering the period of the 1930s. Accounts of life in the city in the early decades of the 20th century are found in H.Y. LOWE, *The Adventures of Wu: The Life Cycle of a Peking Man* (1940, reprinted 1983); HAROLD ACTON, *Peonies and Ponies* (1983), a novel set in Peking's expatriate community in the 1930s; and PU YI, *From Emperor to Citizen: Autobiography of Aisin-Gioro Pu Yi*, new ed., trans. from Chinese by W.J.F. JENNER (1987), the memoir of the last Chinese emperor.

(S.-d.C./D.M.Bo.)

Human Perception

Perception, or perceiving, refers to the process whereby sensory stimulation is translated into organized experience. That experience, or percept, is the joint product of the stimulation and of the process itself. Relations found between various types of stimulation (*e.g.*, light waves and sound waves) and their associated percepts suggest inferences that can be made about the properties of the perceptual process; theories of perceiving then can

be developed on the basis of these inferences. Because the perceptual process is not itself public or directly observable (except to the perceiver himself, whose percepts are given directly in experience), the validity of perceptual theories can be checked only indirectly. That is, predictions derived from theory are compared with appropriate empirical data, quite often through experimental research.

This article is divided into the following sections:

General considerations

Historical background

Historically, systematic thought about perceiving was the province of philosophy. Indeed, perceiving remains of interest to philosophers, and many issues about the process that were originally raised by philosophers are still of current concern. As a scientific enterprise, however, the investigation of perception has especially developed as part of the larger discipline of psychology.

Philosophical interest in perception stems largely from questions about the sources and validity of what is called human knowledge (see EPISTEMOLOGY). Epistemologists ask whether a real, physical world exists independently of man's experience, and if so, how man can come to learn its properties and how the truth or accuracy of that experience can be determined. They also ask whether there are innate ideas or whether all experience originates through contact with the physical world, mediated by the sense organs. For the most part, psychology bypasses such questions in favour of problems that can be handled by its special methods. The remnants of such philosophical questions, however, do remain; researchers are still concerned, for example, with the relative contributions of innate and learned factors to the perceptual process.

Such fundamental philosophical assertions as the existence of a physical world, however, are taken for granted among most scientific students of perceiving. Typically, researchers in perception simply accept the apparent physical world particularly as it is described in those branches of physics concerned with electromagnetic energy, optics,

and mechanics. The problems they consider are those relating to the process whereby percepts are formed from the interaction of what is called physical energy (for example, light) with the perceiving organism. Of further interest is the degree of correspondence between percepts and the physical objects to which they ordinarily relate. How accurately, for example, does the visually perceived size of an object match its physical size as measured (*e.g.*, with a yardstick)?

Questions of the latter sort imply that perceptual experiences typically have external referents and that they are meaningfully organized, most often as objects. Meaningful objects, such as trees, faces, books, tables, and dogs, are normally seen rather than separately perceived as the dots, lines, colours, and other elements of which they are composed. In the language of Gestalt psychologists, immediate human experience is of organized wholes (*Gestalten*), not of collections of elements.

A major goal of Gestalt theory in the 20th century was to specify the brain processes that might account for the organization of perception. Gestalt theorists, chief among them the German-U.S. psychologist and philosopher, the founder of Gestalt theory, Max Wertheimer and the German-U.S. psychologists Kurt Koffka and Wolfgang Köhler, rejected the earlier assumption that perceptual organization was the product of learned relationships (associations), the constituent elements of which were called simple sensations. Although Gestaltists agreed that simple sensations logically could be understood to comprise organized percepts, they argued that percepts themselves were basic to experience. One does not perceive so many discrete dots (as simple sensations), for example; the percept is that of a dotted line.

Without denying that learning can play some role in perception, many theorists took the position that perceptual organization reflects innate properties of the brain itself. Indeed, perception and brain functions were held by Gestaltists to be formally identical (or isomorphic), so much so that to study perception is to study the brain. Much contemporary research in perception is directed toward inferring specific features of brain function from such behaviour as the reports (introspections) people give of their sensory experiences. More and more such inferences are gratifyingly being matched with physiological observations of the brain itself.

Many investigators relied heavily on introspective reports, treating them as though they were objective descriptions of public events. Serious doubts were raised in the 1920s about this use of introspection by the U.S. psychologist John B. Watson and others, who argued that it yielded only subjective accounts and that percepts are inevitably private experiences and lack the objectivity commonly required of scientific disciplines. In response to objections about subjectivism, there arose an approach known as behaviourism that restricts its data to objective descriptions or measurements of the overt behaviour of organisms other than the experimenter himself. Verbal reports are not excluded from consideration as long as they are treated strictly as public (objective) behaviour and are not interpreted as literal, reliable descriptions of the speaker's private (subjective, introspective) experience. The behaviouristic approach does not rule out the scientific investigation of perception; instead, it modestly relegates perceptual events to the status of inferences. Percepts of others manifestly cannot be observed, though their properties can be inferred from observable behaviour (verbal and nonverbal).

One legacy of behaviourism in contemporary research on perception is a heavy reliance on very simple responses (often nonverbal), such as the pressing of a button or a lever. One advantage of this Spartan approach is that it can be applied to organisms other than man and to human infants (who also cannot give verbal reports). This restriction does not, however, cut off the researcher from the rich supply of hypotheses about perception that derive from his own introspections. Behaviourism does not proscribe sources of hypotheses; it simply specifies that only objective data are to be used in testing those hypotheses.

Behaviouristic methods for studying perception are apt to call minimally on the complex, subjective, so-called higher mental processes that seem characteristic of adult human beings; they thus tend to dehumanize perceptual theory and research. Thus, when attention is limited to objective stimuli and responses, parallels can readily be drawn between perceiving (by living organisms) and information processing (by such devices as electronic computers). Indeed, it is from this information-processing approach that some of the more intriguing theoretical contributions (*e.g.*, abstract models of perception) are currently being made. It is expected that such practical applications as the development of artificial "eyes" for the blind may emerge from these man–machine analogies. Computer-based machines that can discriminate among visual patterns already have been constructed, such as those that "read" the code numbers on bank checks.

CLASSICAL PROBLEMS

Sensing and perceiving. Many philosophers and psychologists have commonly accepted as fundamental a distinction made on rational grounds between sensing and perceiving (or between sensations and percepts). To demonstrate empirically that sensing and perceiving are indeed different, however, is quite another matter. It is often said, for example, that sensations are simple and that percepts are complex. Yet, only if there is offered some agreed upon (a priori) basis for separating experiences into two categories—sensations and percepts—can experimental procedures demonstrate that the items in one category are "simpler" than those in the other. Clearly, the arbitrary basis for the initial categorization itself cannot be

subjected to empirical test. (See also SENSORY RECEPTION.)

Problems of verification aside, the simplicity–complexity distinction derives from the assumption that percepts are constructed of simple elements that have been joined through association. Presumably, the trained introspectionist can dissociate the constituent elements of a percept from one another, and in so doing, experience them as simple, raw sensations. Efforts to approach the experience of simple sensations might also be made by presenting very simple, brief, isolated stimuli; *e.g.,* flashes of light.

Another commonly offered basis for distinction is the notion that perceiving is subject to the influence of learning while sensing is not. It might be said that the sensations generated by a particular stimulus will be essentially the same from one time to the next (barring fatigue or other temporary changes in sensitivity), while the resulting percepts may vary considerably, depending on what has been learned between one occasion and the next (see below *Perceptual learning*).

Some psychologists have characterized percepts as typically related to external objects and sensations as more nearly subjective, personal, internally localized experiences. Thus, a spontaneous pain in the finger would be called a sensation; however, if the salient feature of experience is that of a painfully sharp, pointed object, such as a pin located "out there," it would be called a percept.

The above definitional criteria all relate to properties of experience; that is, they are psychological. An alternative way of distinguishing between sensing and perceiving that has become widely accepted is physiological-anatomical rather than psychological. In this case, sensations are identified with neural events occurring immediately beyond the sense organ, whereas percepts are identified with activity farther "upstream" in the nervous system, at the level of the brain. This assignment of anatomical locations to sensory and to perceptual processes seems consistent with psychological criteria. That is, the complexity and variability of percepts (both a product of learning) are attributed to the potential for physiological modification inherent in the vastly complex neural circuitry of the brain.

Temporal (time) relations. Clearly, many subjective processes (such as problem solving) take time to run their courses. This is true even for such relatively simple activities as perceptual discriminations in the size of different objects. It is not readily apparent, however, whether

The role of brain function

Perceptual learning

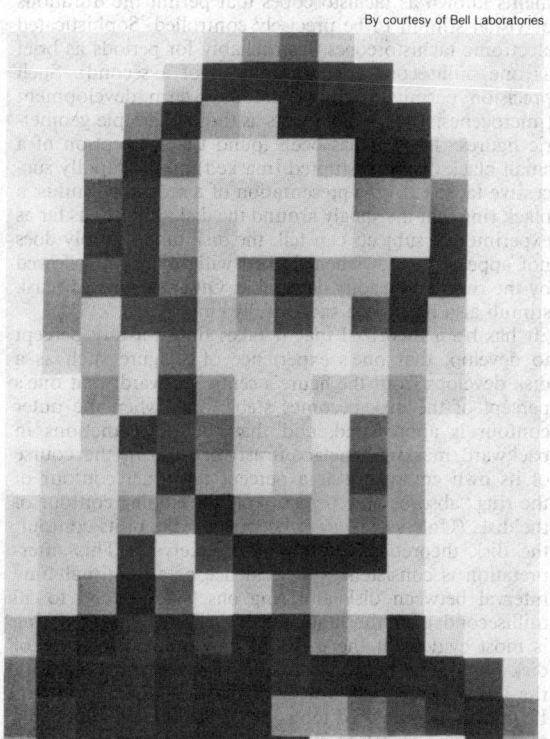

By courtesy of Bell Laboratories

Figure 1: An ambiguous picture. Increasing viewing distance permits more precise perception (see text).

percepts themselves—which, for example, might enter as elements in problem solving—take time to form. To the naïve observer, percepts probably do seem essentially instantaneous: the moment a square is shown, a square seems to be seen. Yet, experimental evidence suggests that percepts, even of simple geometric forms, follow a measurable, developmental time course. In some instances the temporal development of percepts is relatively long (on the order of seconds), and in some it is quite brief (on the order of thousandths of a second).

Pictures that are incomplete or ambiguous provide good examples of relatively long-term temporal development of percepts. Look at Figure 1 and continue looking until you see something more than a pattern of black, gray, and white patches. Abruptly, you probably will perceive a familiar face that, on subsequent viewing, will reappear to you without difficulty. How long it takes for such a percept to develop will vary considerably from one person to another, perhaps revealing fundamental differences among individuals in their speed of perceptual processing. It might be instructive to show Figure 1 to several people, and with the aid of a stopwatch, measure the time it takes each of them to achieve the desired percept, both initially and then on some later occasion. (Figure 1 commonly is seen by most people as the face of Abraham Lincoln.)

A somewhat different way in which percepts may change with time is illustrated in the section *Illusions and hallucinations,* below. On initial viewing of this type of drawing, one will probably immediately see a meaningful picture. After continued gazing at the drawing, the initial percept may abruptly be replaced by another. Thereafter, the two percepts should alternate with the passage of time. Stimuli of this sort (which can yield more than one percept) raise such questions as, for example, what determines the initial percept; why do some people first see a vase whereas others see two profiles; why does the initial percept give way to the alternate; what determines the rate of fluctuation from one percept to the other; do differences from one person to another in the rate of fluctuation of ambiguous figures indicate fundamental differences in perceptual activity? Tentative answers to such questions continue to be proposed.

Instances of slowly developing percepts require relatively simple procedures to uncover. Those percepts with a very rapid time course may be studied with the aid of instruments known as tachistoscopes that permit the durations of visual stimuli to be precisely controlled. Sophisticated electronic tachistoscopes flash reliably for periods as brief as one millisecond (one-thousandth of a second). Such precision permits study of the short-term development (microgenesis) of such percepts as those of simple geometric figures. Thus, it has been found that perception of a small black disk is disrupted (masked) by the rapidly successive tachistoscopic presentation of a second stimulus: a black ring that fits snugly around the disk. Indeed, as far as experimental subjects can tell, the disk target simply does not appear, though when flashed without being followed by the ring, it is readily detectable. Other target and mask stimuli also have been successfully employed.

It has been theorized that it takes time for any percept to develop; that one's experience of a figure such as a disk develops from the figure's centre outward; that one's percept of the disk becomes stable only when the outer contour is appreciated; and that the ring functions in backward masking (metacontrast) because in the course of its own emergence as a percept the inner contour of the ring "absorbs" the perceptually developing contour of the disk. (Unless the viewer becomes aware of its contour, the disk theoretically cannot be perceived.) This interpretation is consistent with evidence of an optimal time interval between disk and ring onsets (about 30 to 50 milliseconds) for the best masking effect. Thus, masking is most evident at the moment developing awareness of disk contour is held to coincide in space and time with the initial perceptual growth of the ring's inner contour. If the ring is presented too soon or too late, theoretically, the contour absorption on which masking presumably depends is ineffective.

While such theories are controversial, masking experiments in general do clearly indicate that in human beings there is a brief period (100 to 200 milliseconds at most) during which a percept is highly vulnerable to disruption. Whatever its exact mechanism, the phenomenon of masking manifestly demonstrates that percepts do not emerge instantaneously and full-blown at the moment of sensory stimulation. Thus, assuming that percepts are synthesized from simpler elements, relatively complex percepts would be expected to take longest to develop and, hence, to be most vulnerable to masking. Yet empirical studies show just the opposite, indicating that the more complex the visual target, the more difficult it is to mask.

Perceiving as synthesizing. The organization apparent in percepts has been attributed by some to learning, as being built up through arbitrary associations of elements that have repeatedly occurred together in the person's experience. Other theorists (particularly Gestaltists) stress the view that perceptual organization is physiologically inborn, being inherent in innate aspects of brain functioning rather than depending on a synthesizing process of learning to combine simpler elements into more complex, integrated wholes. One way of resolving such theoretical disputes would be to deprive people from birth of all visual sensory experience and, hence, of all opportunity for visual perceptual learning. Then at the time normal sensory function was restored, they would need to be tested to determine what perceptual functions, if any, were intact. Such a strategy was proposed in a letter to the British philosopher John Locke by a fellow philosopher William Molyneux in 1690. Molyneux's suggestion waited until the 20th century to be taken seriously, after surgical methods had been found to restore the sight of people born blind because of cataract (clouded lens within the eye).

After removal of their cataracts, such newly sighted people are found to be normally sensitive to changes in intensity of illumination and to colour. Though they are able initially to tell when a figure is present, they cannot at first discriminate one simple shape from another, nor can they readily remember the shape of a just-exposed object. This deficiency extends to such socially important visual stimuli as people's faces. Only after a long and painstaking period of experience—perhaps of several months duration—do such seemingly primitive visual performances as discriminating a square from a triangle come easily. Until then, the person must count corners, for example, to achieve accurate discrimination.

Findings derived from cataract surgery have provided a rich source of hypotheses for further research, including posited neurophysiological mechanisms (*e.g.,* assemblies of brain cells) that might serve as the medium for the structural changes presumed to accompany perceptual learning. This situation led to experimental attempts to show how, through repeated stimulation, the perceptual system could progress from performance of only very primitive functions to the highly complex operations (such as form identification and discrimination) that are characteristic of the mature organism.

A host of experiments using laboratory animals as subjects (*e.g.,* pigeons, rats, cats, dogs, monkeys, and chimpanzees) have been conducted to determine, under rigorous experimental control, the extent to which learning early in life contributes to later perceptual functioning. By analogy with humans born with cataract, such animals were deprived of visual experience from as close to birth (or hatching) as possible; *e.g.,* chimpanzees were reared in darkness. In another type of experiment, animals were reared in environments that provided more than the normal amount and variety of stimulation or were exposed to specific stimuli they might not ordinarily encounter. These research strategies are said to provide impoverished or enriched environments. Experiments of both sorts have consistently provided verification of the general hypothesis that early perceptual experience plays an important role in later perceptual (as well as intellectual and emotional) development, even producing changes in brain weight and biochemistry. This research also offers a strong scientific rationale for efforts to enrich the environments of so-called disadvantaged or culturally deprived children.

Studies of human infants indicate that their early per-

Backward masking, or metacontrast

The use of cataract surgery to study perception

ceptual experiences are not the "blooming, buzzing confusion" postulated by the U.S. psychologist William James late in the 19th and early in the 20th century. Rather, even infants one or two days old are capable of refined visual discriminations. Recording of the infants' visual fixations as their eyes move indicates them to have reliable preference for one paired stimulus over another, giving evidence of visual discrimination. Research employing this technique shows that preferences among various visual patterns or shapes generally are related to the complexity and novelty of the stimuli, for infants and for older human subjects as well. Evidence of this sort seems out of keeping with the findings of cataract surgery, which suggest that figural discrimination is not innate for the visually naïve. It may be, however, that adults who were blind with cataracts at birth suffer more than mere lack of normal visual experience; they are not quite comparable to visually naïve, but otherwise intact, infants. It may be that visual experience is necessary, not to generate pattern perception but to maintain it; that is, the infant's built-in (innate) perceptual abilities may somehow deteriorate through disuse.

The visual cliff technique

Similar research has dealt with visual depth perception in laboratory animals and human babies. One technique (the visual cliff) depends on the evident reluctance of young animals to step off the edge of what seems to be a steep cliff. The so-called visual cliff apparatus in one of its versions consists of a narrow platform on which the subject is placed and two wide platforms on either side of it. Although both flanking platforms are equally and only slightly lower than the central platform, the subject sees visual patterns designed so that one looks much deeper than the other. Typically, the subject explores the central platform and then investigates the flanks, finally stepping down onto the shallow-appearing side. By this response, the subject indicates sensitivity to visual depth cues. To discover if prior visual experience is necessary for the typical avoidance of the flanking platform that looks deepest requires subjects able to locomote well from the start (*e.g.*, chicks) or those deprived of visual experience (*e.g.*, rats) until their locomotor ability has developed. Research with the visual cliff clearly demonstrates the presence of depth perception in visually naïve subjects.

In summary, there is evidence among cataract sufferers of the necessity of early visual experience in human visual pattern discrimination; laboratory animals reared in impoverished or enriched environments demonstrate the importance (if not necessity) of early visual stimulation for perceptual development; human infants and other visually naïve animals behave as if they are innately capable of pattern and depth perception (*i.e.*, without the need for learning). These data together suggest that some basic visual functions, including pattern perception, are built in but that visual experience serves to maintain and elaborate them.

Structuralism

In a theory called structuralism, that everyday perceptual experience is structured or synthesized from "sensations," psychologists such as the English-U.S. introspectionistic psychologist Edward Bradford Titchener even devised a formal method of introspection for experimentally analyzing (or taking apart) percepts in an effort to reveal their constituent elements. The procedure required that the introspecting experimental subjects learn to avoid reporting on their experiences as they naïvely seemed. To establish this way of treating experience required careful training. One consequence of this training is that the observer's introspective reports may be contaminated by his expectations and hence may, in all honesty, reflect little more than his theoretical biases.

But the problem remains interesting: If percepts are indeed syntheses of simpler elements, can those elements be made to appear in experience? If so, what will they turn out to be? Can this problem be investigated without recourse to the structuralist's method of introspection and reliance on the reports of strongly biassed observers?

Evidence that percepts have constituent elements emerged serendipitously from research on stabilized retinal images. The image cast on the retina of the eye by a fixed object normally is continually moving because the perceiver himself is always in motion. Even when dampened by physical restraint, some residual movement will be left, attributable largely to high-frequency tremors (nystagmus) of the eyeballs. If the perceiver functioned as if he were a camera, the normal instability of the retinal image would produce a blurred percept and a concomitant impairment of visual acuity.

It is not feasible to eliminate eye movements, but it is possible to stabilize or fix the location of the retinal image by coupling the source of the image to the eyeball itself. An optical lever system can be so adjusted that when the eye moves the image source moves with it, and potential motion in the retinal image is eliminated. As expected, visual acuity is slightly enhanced when the retinal image is kept motionless. A remarkable, unexpected finding, however, was that such stabilized images rapidly seem to disappear, the perceiver losing awareness of them. It would seem that some movement in retinal image is needed to maintain perception over extended periods of time.

The optical lever system

One limitation of the optical lever system is that it permits the use of only very simple targets, such as straight, vertical lines. With a different device (in effect, a miniature projector attached to the eyeball), stabilized images of complex patterns may be presented. Complex patterns are found to produce percepts that are relatively slow to deteriorate; furthermore, they do not disappear in toto. The manner of the fragmentation is perhaps revealing of the way in which complex percepts are synthesized. Speaking metaphorically, observing how percepts "come apart" under retinal stabilization may be very much like discovering the structure of a rock by striking it with a powerful hammer blow.

Indeed, under retinal stabilization, single lines seem to disappear and reappear in a unitary (altogether) fashion. In a figure comprised of several lines (say, a square), percepts of parallel lines are likely to disappear and reappear together; proximity also affects the joint perceptual fate of pairs of lines. Retinally stabilized segments of such geometric figures as circles and triangles can seem to disappear and reappear without implicating the entire figure. In the disappearance of percepts of triangles, lines rather than angles are the functional units. (This finding is embarrassing to earlier theorizing about the crucial role of angles in the development of the neural network underlying the percept of a triangle.)

Clearly, with stabilized images, the constituent perceptual elements of complex geometric forms are lines, straight or curved; and lines with the same orientation are likely to have similar perceptual fates, as though forming a higher-order component of complex patterns than do individual lines. These conclusions are remarkably similar to those drawn from studies of the effect of visual stimuli on the electrical activity of single neurons in the cerebral cortex. A finding of major theoretical significance is the failure of percepts of circles, squares, and triangles to act as units. Such percepts are treated in classical Gestalt theory, however, as though they are basic and unitary and not readily decomposable.

PRIMARY TENDENCIES IN PERCEPTUAL ORGANIZATION

Gestalt principles. Gestalt theory was meant to have general applicability; its main tenets, however, were induced almost exclusively from observations on visual perception. Whatever their ultimate theoretical significance, these observations have been raised to the level of general principles. It is conventional to refer to them as Gestalt principles of perceptual organization.

The overriding theme of the theory is that stimulation is perceived in organized or configurational terms (*Gestalt* in German means "configuration"). Patterns take precedence over elements and have properties that are not inherent in the elements themselves. One does not merely perceive dots; he perceives a dotted line. This notion is captured in a phrase often used to characterize Gestalt theory: "The whole is more than the sum of its parts."

Of the many principles of organization that have been enunciated by various Gestalt theorists, the most general is referred to as *Prägnanz*. In effect, according to the principle of *Prägnanz*, the particular perceptual configuration achieved, out of a myriad of potential configurations, will be as good as prevailing conditions permit. What constitutes a "good" configuration, or a poor one, is unfortunately not clearly specified, though several properties of good configurations can be listed, chief among them being simplicity, stability, regularity, symmetry, continuity, and unity. What happens when these properties of figures come into conflict is not specified, but should be possible to determine empirically.

The principle of closure often operates in the service of *Prägnanz;* for example, a circular figure with small gaps in it will be seen as a complete or closed circle. Similarly, if a portion of the image of a figure falls on the blind spot of the retina, a complete figure often will still be perceived. Some distortions from good configuration may be so large as to preclude closure; in those cases, the figures may be a source of tension for the observer.

Prägnanz may also be achieved through good continuation; this principle describes a tendency for smooth continuity of contour to be dominant over discrete, irregular, abruptly changing contours. Thus, a figure composed of the overlapping outlines of an ellipse and a rectangle will probably be seen as such rather than as three figures, each with irregular, noncontinuous borders.

Closure and good continuation represent two of the factors that are held to determine what percepts will emerge from a complex stimulus. Implicit in them (and in the general principle of *Prägnanz*) is the assumption that whenever possible some figure will be perceived; more specifically, that the visual field will be articulated into figures and patterns of figures. It is understood that such emerging patterns are not *in* the stimulus. Although they are *permitted by* the stimulus, they are created by the perceptual system; that is, by the perceiver himself.

In the illustrations in Figure 2, in the panel on the left, the vertical distance between elements is less than the horizontal distance. By virtue of this differential proximity, the elements become perceptually organized into columns. In the right-hand panel, similarity, another principle of organization, is operative. Here, by virtue of similarity in brightness, the visual field tends to be perceptually articulated into alternating sets of black and gray rows.

It is not at all obvious why organization by similarity should occur; physical stimulation allows but does not demand it. Clearly in that case the articulation of the visual

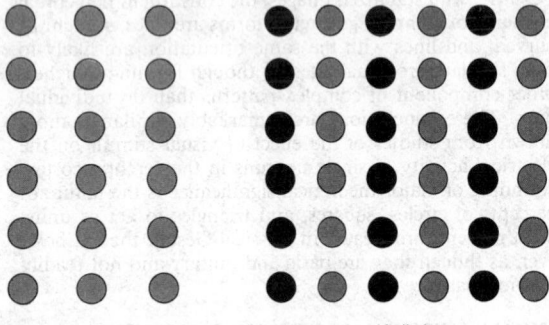

proximity   similarity

Figure 2: *Examples of Gestalt principles of organization.*
(Left) Horizontal distance between dots is greater than vertical distance. (Right) Equal distance between horizontal and vertical.

field into columns reflects a tendency in the perceptual system itself. Organization by proximity may not seem to reveal anything more than a close correspondence between perception and stimulation. (Though as argued by the Gestalt theorist Kurt Koffka, it is not an adequate explanation to say that "things look as they do because they are what they are.") Yet, when a proximity pattern like the one shown in Figure 2 was briefly presented and subjects were asked (under guise of another task) to reproduce what they saw, many people failed to indicate a differentiated percept of columns. Instead, they reproduced a homogeneous matrix of elements. After repeated exposures, some of those subjects began to draw proximity-based columns of elements. Organization according to the principle of

proximity seems to be neither universal nor, for those who achieve it, immediate.

In the latter experiment, people who failed to obtain the differentiated percept of columns scored significantly lower on a test of verbal intelligence than did those who succeeded at some point in the experiment. Perhaps the Gestalt principles of organization apply to perceivers (such as Gestalt theorists) whose intellectual development has reached a high degree of maturity. When organized percepts are easy to come by, gradations in intelligence do not seem to matter; when some barrier to organization is imposed (as by brief stimulus exposure), however, then the effect on perception of such differences among individuals may show up.

If people see a pattern of columns in the left panel of Figure 2 because that is how the stimulus is constructed, then why do some people not see it that way? Both achieving and failing to achieve an organized percept must be explained. Surely, part of the explanation must lie in the nature of the perceptual process itself. Thus, the experimental results indicate that perceptual organization is not universal and immediate; rather, they support the major tenet of Gestalt theory that things look as they do because of the organization imposed by the perceptual process (*i.e.,* by the perceiver).

One Gestalt principle, that of common fate, depends on movement and is quite striking when observed. According to the principle of common fate, stimulus elements are likely to be perceived as a unit if they move together. An illustration of this principle is provided by a well-camouflaged object, such as a military vehicle; when stationary, the elements of the vehicle are integrated, through proximity, similarity, and so on, into patterns of background elements, and the object is difficult to detect. But it is easy to see it once it starts moving; with all of its elements moving in unison, the vehicle is readily perceived as a unitary figure, clearly segregated from its background.

Movement is also at the heart of a set of observations of considerable significance in the historical development of Gestalt theory. These observations concern circumstances in which people perceive movement in the absence of actual physical motion of the stimulus. One familiar instance of this class of events is referred to as the phi phenomenon. In simplest form, the phi phenomenon can be demonstrated by successively turning two adjacent lights on and off. Given appropriate temporal and spatial relations between the two lights, an observer will perceive the first light as if it were moving from its location to that of the second light. The phi phenomenon is basic to the eye-catching displays used on theatre marquees and to cinematic and television presentations. The motion-picture screen, for example, presents a series of briefly flashed, still images; the movement people see is a creation of their own perceptual systems (see below *Perception of movement*).

It is the lack of one-to-one correspondence between stimulation and perception, as dramatically illustrated in the phi phenomenon, that underscores the Gestaltists' dissatisfaction with stimulus-bound models of perception and their insistence on the priority of patterns and relations. What people perceive is determined not only by what is present at the point under direct observation but also by what is occurring in the total stimulus context or display.

Context effects. One of the simplest instance of relational (or context) effects in perception is that of brightness contrast. Thus, the apparent brightness of a stimulus depends not only on its own luminance but also on that of the surrounding stimulation. The same gray square looks whiter against a dark background and blacker when placed in a bright surround. Similarly, a white or gray patch will take on an apparent hue that is complementary to the colour of the surround (*e.g.,* the patch will seem tinged with yellow when it is placed against a blue background).

Analogous context effects are evident in many commonplace experiences. A man of average height seems to be a runt when he is on a basketball court with much taller players; yet the same man looms like a giant when refereeing a game played by little boys. It is known that a typical winter's day seems delightfully balmy when temperatures rise after a week of subfreezing weather.

To the Gestaltist, contrast effects dramatize the relational nature of perception. They also play a significant role in a more recently developed adaptation-level theory, which also provides a general perceptual model. At the core of the model is the notion that the manner in which a stimulus is perceived depends not only on its own physical characteristics but also on those of surrounding stimuli and of stimuli previously experienced by the observer. In other words, the perceiver is said to be perceptually adapted to past sensory stimuli; his adaptation level forms a kind of zero point against which any new stimulus is perceived. An example is provided by the almost overwhelming silence one experiences when the sound of an air conditioner (to which he has adapted) suddenly ceases.

Gestalt theorists also attached significance to the observer's history of stimulation; indeed, some of them interpreted so-called figural aftereffects within a Gestaltist model of brain functioning. Figural aftereffects refer to changes in the perceived shape or location of a figure following its inspection; for example, a curved line will appear to get straighter after prolonged inspection. Or the distance between two parallel lines seems to change as an aftereffect of previous inspection.

In a typical experiment one looks at a point adjacent to a dark vertical bar (the inspection figure) on a screen. Following this inspection period, the dark bar is replaced by two identical pairs of vertical lines, one pair on either side of the region where the bar had been, the second pair alongside in a region not previously exposed to the inspection figure. The subject again fixates the same point. A figural aftereffect shows up as a greater apparent distance between the pair of lines surrounding the region of the inspection figure even though the other pair is actually identical. This distortion is not simply a generalized contrast effect because it occurs only in the small area along the borders of the inspection figure; that is, the effect is localized and restricted.

Localized satiation in the brain It thus has been speculated that visual exposure to a figure induces in the brain a condition of localized satiation. The passage of electrical activity is assumed to be impeded in satiated areas of the brain. Moreover, it is postulated that the perceived distance between two borders of a figure is directly related to the time it takes for electrical currents to pass between them. Thus, it is held that one effect of satiation is to increase the apparent distance between the borders of a figure that straddles a satiated region. Whatever the merits of such physiological speculations, they have stimulated a vast amount of research on figural aftereffects. Good evidence for similar effects in other senses, such as touch, also has been obtained. Clearly, perception can be influenced not only by the context of current background but also by the residues (after-effects) of previous stimulation.

Concurrent visual stimulation may modify one's acuity in detecting auditory stimuli. Similar interactions are claimed to occur for other combinations of senses. Some dentists report success in using audioanalgesia, in which stimulation with sound waves is said to reduce the experience of pain in the mouth. The high specificity of some of the reported sensory interactions seems to preclude an explanation that concurrent stimulation works by changing the subject's general level of alertness. However these intersensory effects might be mediated, they do suggest that the brain does not function as a collection of entirely independent sensory channels. As a physical system, the brain follows physical principles; thus overlapping and spreading or waning fields of neural excitation in the brain have been theorized to underlie such phenomena as closure and audioanalgesia. Köhler referred to these models of neural analogues of perceptual phenomena as physical Gestalten; unfortunately, there is little direct physiological evidence for them.

An alternative to field effects in brain functioning is the assumption that local stimulation gives rise, in one-to-one fashion, to a mosaic of local responses. Implicit in the mosaic hypothesis is a kind of telephone switchboard model of the brain as a machine in which the electrical activity is strictly confined to separate pathways of neurons that are well insulated (isolated) from one another. The Gestaltists

rejected this model because in its early formulations it did not explain intersensory and intrasensory perceptual phenomena. A more sophisticated machine model, however, provides for fieldlike effects through the operation of complex networks of neural elements. It is held that electrical activity remains confined to discrete pathways, but that these pathways do not simply travel straight through the system; that they also interconnect, with both excitatory and inhibitory consequences. Supporting evidence comes from records of the electrical activity in single neurons in the cat brain; when the cat's eye is probed by a small spot of light, a specific area on the retina can be found that serves to excite a given brain neuron.

Further mapping of the cat retina often uncovers inhibitory areas adjacent to the one that is excitatory; that is, when light strikes those retinal areas the activity in the brain neuron being monitored is depressed. The excitatory and inhibitory areas thus comprise the brain neuron's retinal receptive field. Analogous inhibitory effects have also been found in research on the eye of the crab, *Limulus*. Such context effects as brightness contrast could be based on these simple inhibitory mechanisms. It remains to be seen, however, just how many perceptual phenomena that fit Gestalt field theory also can be handled by sophisticated variants of the machine or mosaic model.

Perceptual constancies. Even though the retinal image of a receding automobile shrinks in size, the normal, experienced person perceives the size of the object to remain constant. Indeed, one of the most impressive features of perceiving is the tendency of objects to appear stable in the face of their continually changing stimulus features. Though a dinner plate itself does not change, its image on the retina undergoes considerable changes in shape and size as the perceiver and plate move. What is noteworthy is stability in perception despite gross instability in stimulation. Such matches between the object as it is perceived and the object as it is understood to actually exist (regardless of transformations in the energy of stimulation) are called perceptual constancies.

Dimensions of visual experience that exhibit constancy include size, shape, brightness, and colour. Perceptual constancy tends to prevail for these dimensions as long as the observer has appropriate contextual cues; for example, perception of size constancy depends on cues that allow one a valid assessment of his distance from the object. With distance accurately perceived, the apparent size of an object tends to remain remarkably stable, especially for highly familiar objects that have a standard size. Thus, people's heads all tend to look the same size regardless of distance; similarly, an object identified as a lump of coal tends to look black even when intensely illuminated.

Loss of perceptual constancy The experience of constancy may break down under extreme conditions. If distance is sufficiently great, for example, the perceived size of objects will decrease; thus, viewed from an airplane in flight, there seem to be "toy" houses, cars, and people below. To the extent that they prevail, the constancies lend the perceiver's experience and behaviour relative stability. Imagine an alternative, kaleidoscopic perceptual world in which everything seems to change, solid objects apparently swelling, shrinking, and warping with every movement. Breakdown in perceptual constancy seems to complicate the course of some psychiatric disorders in which the perceptual boundary between the sufferer and the external world is weakened. Normal constancies also can be intentionally overcome, as in paintings of flabby watches and distorted people that apparently depict the unique perceptual world of the artist.

INDIVIDUAL DIFFERENCES IN PERCEIVING

Theoretical assertions about perceiving are often made as though they apply indiscriminately to all organisms, or at least to all people. Perhaps perceptual principles of such great generality eventually will be uncovered. In the meantime it is evident that there are clear differences in perceptual functioning among individuals, among classes of individuals, and within the same individual from one occasion to another.

Perceptual learning. That perceptual functioning should change with the perceiver's age is expected on the grounds that psychological development stems from maturation and learning. Indeed, empirical evidence for age-related changes in perceiving is substantial. There are, for example, reliable data that perceptual constancies are enhanced with the person's increasing age, improvement leveling off at about age ten. Similarly, there is a great deal of evidence for both decreased and increased susceptibility to various optical illusions with increasing age (see *Illusions and hallucinations*). Those illusions that become less pronounced with increasing age probably depend on the subject's changes in scanning and on his increased ability to segregate parts of a pattern from one another; illusions that become more pronounced probably reflect the operation of expectancies that develop through experience. Anatomical and physiological changes in the eye itself also may account for some age-related perceptual changes. (W.N.D.)

Optical illusions among older persons

Historically, the perceptual role of learning was a source of controversy. Vigorous denials that perceiving is influenced by learning are found in arguments of early Gestalt psychologists (*e.g.,* Max Wertheimer, 1880–1943, a German). By contrast, heavy reliance is placed on learning processes in the writings of the German philosopher and scientist H.L.F. von Helmholtz (1821–94). Today, there is virtually full agreement that perceiving is modified by learning. Disputes now focus on the process of perceptual learning itself. Most theoretical alternatives reflect two underlying themes: discovery and enrichment. The discovery thesis is reflected in Eleanor J. Gibson's view that perceptual learning is a process of discovering how to transform previously overlooked potentials of sensory stimulation into effective information. Enrichment theories depict perceptual learning as enriching sensory experience with specific associations and with rules for its interpretation that derive from past experience. Discovery theories propose that perceptual modification results from learning to respond to new aspects of sensory stimuli, while enrichment theories hold that such modification results from learning to respond differently to the same sensory stimuli.

Theories: discovery versus enrichment

Direct confrontations of these positions are rare, their advocates tending to differ in their selection of experimental procedures and learning situations. It may be that discovery and enrichment theories are compatible, simply accounting for different forms of perceptual learning.

General acceptance of the perceptual role of learning should not be taken to endorse the claim that perceiving originally depends on learning. Indeed, studies of human newborn and very young infants indicate highly organized and stable perceptual functions. Learning is to be regarded as supplementary to unlearned factors that mediate perceiving.

Effects of practice. The most direct examination of perceptual learning is provided by investigating the effects of practice. In so-called detection tasks the observer is required to detect the presence or absence of a selected stimulus. For example, effects of practice on visual acuity were studied by requiring observers to detect simple orientation (left or right) in a row of leaning letters; *e.g.,* Ɛ Ɛ Ɛ Ɛ. Practice tended to lower acuity thresholds, defined as the lowest intensity of illumination at which each observer could detect the orientation. Or, observers were asked to say when they just could see that an approaching pair of parallel bars was double. With practice they continued to report seeing the narrow space between the bars at increasing distances. Such improvements suggest that sensitivity to simple (unidimensional) stimuli is not immutable, being modifiable through practice.

Detection of stimuli

Improvement is not limited to simple variables. In one visual-search procedure, subjects scanned a long list of letters to find a single letter that appeared only once. Search time was reduced by a factor of 10 following extensive practice, after which 10 different letters could be detected as quickly as a single letter. Practice effects with complex targets also have been studied. In one experiment, two rows of figures were displayed on each trial, one with four simple outlines of geometrical figures, the other containing three complicated figures. Subjects were to guess or detect which one of the simple figures was concealed (embedded)

in all three of the complex figures. Again, ability to identify the correct simple figure improved with practice.

Tasks involving absolute judgment require much more of the observer than does simple or complex detection. For example, he may be asked to estimate the diameters of circular targets numerically (*e.g.,* in inches or centimetres). In a similar study, two groups of subjects made absolute judgments of widely varying distances outdoors, both before and after interpolated activity. One group spent the interpolated period estimating a large number of other distances, none the same as in the original series. The other group spent the interval on unrelated paper-and-pencil work. In the first (extra-practice) group, judgments became more accurate and less variable than among the pencil-and-paper workers. Increased precision following practice also has been reported for absolute judgments of odour intensities, and of multidimensional visual (colour) and auditory stimuli. Improvement with practice is observed even when the subject remains uninformed of his accuracy; correcting him seems to confer slight benefit.

Many studies have failed to establish a clear basis for observed improvements in altered perceptual sensitivity or discriminability. For example, better performance on an acuity test may result from adopting a new criterion of visual doubleness or from learning how to use characteristics of blur to infer slant among leaning Es. Such uncertainties cloud the theoretical and practical significance of much available data.

U.S. psychologist William James (1842–1910) probably introduced the notion that practice in labelling stimuli can alter their discriminability. Indeed, sometimes vague visual forms that are distinctively named are easier to discriminate (acquired distinctiveness). If several such stimuli have the same verbal label, discriminability may be reduced (acquired equivalence).

Labelling effects in the laboratory have been discouragingly fragile, however, and factors that favour them are poorly understood. Perhaps labelling affects one's efforts to discover distinguishing characteristics of stimuli. Having him learn distinctive labels may encourage him to analyze sensory features more fully. Or it may be that he begins to perceive a compound stimulus that includes the visual form and its associated label. If labels differ, the presumed compound stimuli are different, and discrimination should be enhanced. These hypotheses express both the discovery and enrichment theses.

Effects of perceptual assumptions. According to one version of the enrichment thesis, exposure to recurrent regularities among stimuli prompts one to assume specific relationships between the environment and his sensory experience. For example, one learns that a continuous sequence of projective transformation (*e.g.,* the circular profile of a dinner plate seems to become elliptical) is associated with changing positions of the object in view, or that continuous symmetrical expansion of the retinal image is associated with approach. In addition, one presumably learns to make assumptions about what is called reality; *e.g.,* despite alterations in retinal image, one perceives the plate to stay the same size. Psychologists Adelbert Ames, Jr., and Egon Brunswik proposed that one perceives under the strong influence of his learned assumptions and inferences, these providing a context for evaluating sensory data (inputs). In keeping with enrichment theory, Brunswik and Ames contended that sensory stimuli alone inherently lack some of the information needed for mature, adaptive perceiving; enrichment was held necessary to reduce ambiguity.

Much of the evidence for the contention that all perceiving is modified by one's assumptions comes from investigations in which most of the visual, everyday stimuli are eliminated. Often, the subject may view an isolated target in total darkness or look at a motionless display while keeping his head steady. To show that learned assumptions about physical size affect perceived distance, the observer may be asked to judge how far he is from a rectangle of light displayed against total darkness. He is told at one time that the rectangle is a calling card; at another it is called a business envelope. His assumptions about these objects in relation to the size of his retinal

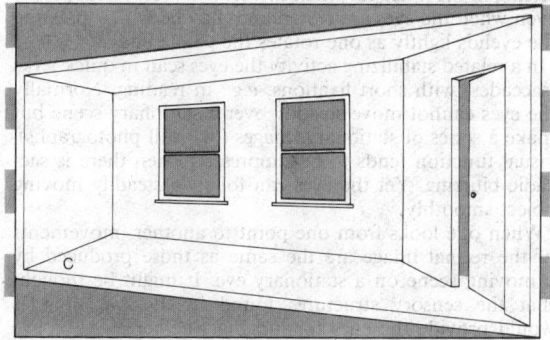

Figure 3: Perception modified by learned assumptions in a distorted room. The same men change places in A and B in a room modelled after C.

image are invoked as prompting him to say that the "envelope" looks more distant than does the "calling card." Dramatic examples of this effect were invented by Ames, including his famous distorted room (see Figure 3).

Ames held that perceiving under unusual conditions (*e.g.*, in a dark room) follows the same principles that govern more ordinary experience. The special conditions are said to permit experimental scrutiny of the same processes that are so difficult to examine under ordinary, uncontrolled conditions.

An opposing view is that such perceptual assumptions and inferences operate *only* under specific experimental conditions. It is asserted that only when commonly available sources of information are eliminated is the subject forced to rely on assumptions.

In the tradition of Helmholtz, Ames and Brunswik seemed to liken perceiving to reasoning, although not as a conscious process. They held that perceptual assumptions, once established, are influenced only slightly by logic. Although the floor and ceiling of the distorted room are sloped and all windows are of different size, it projects the same retinal pattern as a normal room; and a naïve subject will report that he sees an ordinary room. But even after he explores the room he remains likely to say it looks rectangular as before, despite his new informaton. Comparable observations have been reported for a variety of situations. Familiarization or instruction seems to have little effect on long-established perceptual assumptions.
(W.E.)

Psychoanalytic theory explicitly calls for motivational influences on such functions as memory, thinking, and

Reasoning and perceiving

perceiving. In particular, the theory is concerned with unconscious motives and conflicts and with unconscious defenses (such as repression) used to control them. According to the psychoanalytic hypothesis, there should be wide perceptual variation among individuals in response to stimuli that have motivational significance. At any rate, a host of experiments have been designed to show that perceiving is indeed subject to unconscious influences.

In some studies, for example, it seemed that so-called obscene words flashed on a screen had to be exposed longer than apparently neutral (control) words before their meaning could be perceived. In the other studies, children of poor families have been found to overestimate the size of coins as compared with the judgments of children of richer families. One major problem with such research lies in finding or creating appropriate experimental and control stimuli. Considering differences in the use of language, for example, it is most unlikely that what once were widely called obscene words would currently evoke the conflicts and defenses of more than a few subjects.

Assuming suitable stimuli can be found, an even more serious problem arises around the interpretation of the subjects' behaviour; for example, do people really find it more difficult to recognize obscene words or are they simply reluctant to admit recognition? Problems of this sort have plagued researchers, and unambiguously interpretable experiments in this field are most difficult to produce. The hypothesis of such individual influences as motivation on perception remains appealing and viable, but unproved.
(W.N.D.)

Information discrepancy. Striking examples of perceptual learning are observed when one receives sensory data that contradict earlier experiences. For example, spectacles containing a wedge prism will bend light rays to displace images on the retina. An object thus will be seen as if it were somewhere other than its ordinarily perceived position. The subject's initial attempts to touch the target will be misdirected, and there is a discrepancy between its location as seen and as felt. A right-angle prism will tilt the visual scene to any desired degree, altering the customary direction in which retinal images move. Usually, images of stationary objects move parallel to the direction of head movement; now their motion is at an angle to the head's path.

However, if an observer wears such eyeglasses for an extended period, objects no longer seem displaced, nor does the scene continue to appear tilted. The observer has adapted to the prismatic distortions and comes to perceive the environment as he did pre-experimentally. Similarly adaptation to the perceptual aftereffects rapidly occurs after the prism is removed in such experiments.

Adaptation may be interpreted as perceptual learning that results from exposure to discrepancy. People who wear prism spectacles during active, self-initiated movement tend to show a greater degree of adaptation than do those who sit still or who are moved passively. Apparently conditions that heighten exposure to discrepancies facilitate adaptation. It seems likely that adaptation reflects a learning process during which the perceiver re-evaluates one or more sources of sensory information to reduce his experience of discrepancy. For example, information generated by receptors that respond to tension in skeletal muscles may be re-evaluated to resolve a discrepancy between felt and seen position.

It often is suggested that adaptation to prism eyeglasses may involve the same processes that serve perceptual development in infants. Indeed, some conditions that experimentally facilitate adaptation to prism distortion also seem necessary for everyday perceptual development (*e.g.*, active, self-initiated movement). In work reported by Richard Held (*Scientific American*, November 1965), actively moving kittens developed visually guided movements normally. When each of these was yoked to a littermate that was pulled passively over the same path, the passive partner failed to develop normal perceptual function. Yet both kittens apparently received identical visual stimuli.

The effects of learning on perceiving are varied. Most of these involve learning to respond to new stimuli or to

Psychoanalytic theory

Adaptation

make new responses to old stimuli. The one case consists of differentiating previously neglected stimulus characteristics; the other is a matter of re-evaluating stimuli and learning to respond to them differently.

(W.E.)

Sex differences in perceiving. It is difficult to assess the degree to which differences related to the sex of the perceiver are biologically based or are the cultural product of traditional differences in sex role. Biological sex and sex role thus far have been hopelessly confounded in experiments with human subjects.

Sex differences in perceiving, whatever their basis, can be illustrated in research on differences in the style with which people perceive. This stylistic difference emerges in extremes of response to context. If a person perceives the world as highly differentiated, he tends to resist contextual influences and is said to be field independent; the person who perceives in an extremely diffuse style, the field-dependent individual, tends to be highly susceptible to contextual effects. Thus, field-independent people are superior in locating a simple visual figure (*e.g.*, a triangle) embedded in a complex pattern; similarly, field-independent subjects can better adjust a rod in a tilted frame to the true vertical when no other visual cues to verticality are present.

Both age and sex are found to be implicated in these differences in perceptual style. Specifically, field dependence declines with increasing age, as does the closely related susceptibility to optical illusions. In North American studies, female subjects tend to be more field dependent than are males, especially after puberty. Perhaps these results are distinctive of cultures in which females are at least implicitly trained to be passive and perceptually diffuse, and in which males are encouraged to assume an active, perceptually articulated stance. This hypothesis has received some support in studies of the parent–child interactions characteristic of the early years of the two types of subject.

Cultural influences. Beyond sex differences in perceiving that seem to be culturally imposed, there is evidence for more general cultural influences on perception. The burden of much research is to show that the type of physical environment people construct for themselves or choose to inhabit can influence their style of perceiving. There are African groups (*e.g.*, Zulu and San), for example, whose environments are virtually lacking in rectangular forms, by contrast with the carpentered, right-angled world of people in Western cultures. People in these African groups also make no use in their art work of two-dimensional representations of three-dimensional objects. Such differences in visual environments show up in tests of susceptibility to illusions. Zulu and San subjects are relatively resistant to those visual illusions that depend for their effectiveness on the subjects' treating the lines comprising the pictures as borders of three-dimensional, rectangular objects. Analogous effects with different classes of illusion have been shown for other peoples who live in a perceptually unique environment.

(W.N.D.)

Perception of movement

Most animals (including people) move in search of food that itself often moves; they move to avoid predators and to mate. Animals must perceive their own movements to balance themselves and to move effectively; without such perceptual functions the chances for survival would be sharply reduced.

VISUAL CUES TO MOVEMENT

The eye is by far the most effective organ for sensing movement. Some animals are especially sensitive to visual stimuli that move in specific ways. For instance, electrical patterns from the eye of a frog show that some elements in the organ respond only when the stimulus is about the size of a fly moving in the insect's range of speed. Generally the eyes of lower animals seem to respond selectively to what is of importance to survival. In these animals the eye's retina does much of the visual processing. This is an economical arrangement since the animal tends to respond only to essential stimuli, the brain having little to

do but relay signals to the motor system. It is an inflexible mechanism, however; higher animals process visual information in more elaborate ways, the brain being more heavily involved. Thus, some cells in the visual area of the cat's brain respond only to moving stimuli, sets of movement-detector cells functioning specifically for each direction across the field of view. Features of human visual experience also suggest that movement detectors exist in the human brain.

Each retina in most higher animals has a central (foveal) zone for detailed colour and pattern vision and a surrounding peripheral zone that effectively is sensitive only to the grosser features of the outer visual field. The peripheral retina is especially sensitive to movement (often a signal of danger), which induces a reflex turning of the eyes to project the image on the fovea and permit the moving object to be recognized.

Visual stability. Mechanisms have evolved that yield stable, clear visual input despite swaying and other blurring factors. In a reflex mechanism called optokinetic nystagmus, the eyes pursue a moving scene to keep the image stationary on the retina. When they can move no farther, they snap back and pursue the scene again in a to-and-fro alternation of slow pursuit and quick return. These eye movements are readily observed in people who are looking at a moving pattern of stripes or turning their heads, this response being inhibited only when something stationary is visually fixated.

Similar nystagmic movements are triggered by impulses arising in the inner ear when the head moves. These persist even when the eyes are closed and may be felt by pressing the eyelids lightly as one rotates the whole body.

In a related stabilizing activity the eyes scan in quick jerks (saccades) with short fixations; *e.g.*, in reading. Normally the eyes cannot move steadily over a stationary scene but make a series of stationary images (like still photographs); visual function tends to be suppressed when there is saccadic blurring. Yet the eyes can follow a steadily moving object smoothly.

When one looks from one point to another, movements of the retinal image are the same as those produced by a moving scene on a stationary eye. It might be thought that the sensory structures found in the eye muscles would provide the cues for judging whether it is the eye or the scene that has moved. Yet we see the scene as stationary only when we move our eyes voluntarily and not when they are moved passively by the finger. This suggests that motor-nerve signals inform us whether our eyes are moving, rather than the sensory structures in the eye muscles. When the eye is moved by pushing it with the finger there is no normal motor discharge to inform the brain, and changes in retinal image are perceived as movement of the scene. Indeed, people with paralyzed eye muscles experience the scene as moving when they try to move their eyes. When the motor discharge thus generated is not accompanied by the expected image motion, the person falsely perceives the scene and the eye to be moving together.

Relative visual movement. A visual field containing familiar objects provides a stable framework against which relative motion may be judged. People often report that an isolated point of light in a dark room is moving when it is not; the experience is known as autokinetic movement. It was observed in 1799 by Alexander von Humboldt while he was watching a star through a telescope, and he attributed it to movement of the star itself. Not until about 60 years later was the effect shown to be subjective, apparently arising from instability in the sense of eye position without a visual frame of reference.

Similarly, if a small object is presented in a frame with nothing else in view, movement usually is attributed to the object even when only the frame moves. This induced movement effect reflects our tendency to use the larger surround as a stable frame of reference. Recall the illusion that your train is moving when it is really the moving train alongside that, seen through the window, is falsely accepted as the frame of reference.

People cannot perceive very slow movement; below a minimum speed (about that of the minute hand on a

Eye and brain

Nystagmus; saccades

Autokinesis; induced movement

watch) movements become imperceptible and can only be inferred (as in remembering the previous position of the hour hand). At high speeds, one perceives a blurred streak rather than a definite object in motion.

Movement aftereffect. When a parade is interrupted after some minutes, the pavement may seem to move in the opposite direction to the marchers who have passed. Phenomena similar to this movement aftereffect occur in other senses. For instance, after disembarking, a sailor feels the land to be rolling like a ship as the result of kinesthetic and vestibular aftereffects. The visual movement aftereffect probably arises when movement detectors in the brain that respond to the original direction of motion become fatigued, leaving predominant those detectors that respond to contrary movement.

Apparent movement. Motion-picture film is a strip of discrete, still pictures but produces the visual impression of continuous movement. Stationary light bulbs coming on one after the other over the theatre entrance also produce an impression of steady movement. In part, such effects of apparent movement (called the visual phi phenomenon) depend on persistence of vision: visual response outlasts a stimulus by a fraction of a second. When the interval between successive flashes of a stationary light is less than this visual-persistence time, the flicker will appear to fuse into a continuous light. The flicker frequency at which this occurs is called the perceiver's flicker-fusion frequency (or critical flicker frequency) and represents the temporal resolving power of his visual system at the time. Another process on which apparent movement depends is a tendency (called visual closure or phi) to fill in the spaces between adjacent visual objects. This means that the movement detectors of the visual system are triggered as effectively by a closely spaced pair of lights alternately going on and off as by a single light moving back and forth. It would seem that two aspects of visual function (flicker fusion and phi) make the motion-picture industry possible.

Stroboscopic effect. When a rotating electric fan is illuminated by a flashing light source (called a stroboscope) so that a flash arrives whenever a fan blade passes a fixed position, the blades will seem to stand still. This is a useful way of observing fast-moving objects such as machinery or insect wings. If the flashes occur less frequently, the object will seem to move slowly in its actual direction; when the flashes arrive more frequently, the object will seem to move backward, as stagecoach wheels may do in the cinema.

Visual movement in depth. An object moving directly away from an observer provides fewer visual cues of movement than it would be moving across the field of view. However, changes in retinal-image size are produced that give a clue to its movement. Thus a stationary, but shrinking, luminous object in the dark is seen as if it were receding. Other clues to movement in depth are changes in the convergence angle of the two eyes, in the focussing mechanism, and in the haziness and brightness of the object.

NONVISUAL CUES

Auditory. Sound waves travel well in water, and fish are accordingly able to rely heavily on acoustic cues to detect moving objects. Land animals, although typically more visually oriented, also make some use of such cues, including changes in intensity (loudness) and small differences in the time at which the wave reaches each ear. Some animals (*e.g.,* rabbit, horse) have mobile external ears that track moving sound sources. Bats vocalize high-frequency waves and are able to detect objects by sonic reflection (a technique similar to sonar).

Kinesthetic. Kinesthesis here refers to experiences that arise during movement from sense organs in the membranes lining the joints and from the sense of effort in voluntary movement; receptors in muscles seem to have little role in the perception of bodily movements. Depending on speed of motion and the joint involved, blindfolded people can detect a passive joint movement as small as a quarter of a degree. People vary widely in the accuracy with which they can actively produce movement of a given

extent; this ability also varies with direction of movement and the opposing friction, mass, and springiness.

Kinesthetic perception may persist for a limb that has been amputated, giving rise to a hallucinatory experience known as the phantom limb. The patient may experience vividly the "movement" of the absent part; a recent amputee may attempt to stand on his missing leg or to grasp with his missing hand. *(margin: Phantom limb)*

Vestibular system. Vestibular structures, enclosed in a fluid-filled cavity in the region of each inner ear, include the utricle, a small sac containing minute sensitive hairs associated with tiny sandlike granules called otoliths. The utricle functions as a linear accelerometer. When the head tilts relative to gravity or is accelerated, the relatively dense otoliths deflect the hair cells and nerve impulses are transmitted to the brain. At constant velocity the otoliths become stable, stimulation ceases, and a person must rely on other cues (*e.g.,* by observing the passing scene) to detect his motion.

Vestibular structures for each ear also include three fluid-filled semicircular canals, each in a different plane. Each canal has a swelling (ampulla) that contains the cupula, a cluster of sensitive hairs embedded in a jellylike mound. As the head moves in the plane of a given canal, motions of the fluid deflect the cupula to produce nerve impulses. These travel through the brainstem to other brain and spinal centres that mediate equilibrium or balance and that generate nystagmic eye movements. *(margin: Equilibrium)*

Taken together, the semicircular canals serve as a rotary accelerometer. If a person is rotated at constant velocity and then is suddenly stopped, the cupula is redeflected to give a feeling of rotation in the opposite direction; this also gives rise to dizziness and postrotational nystagmus. Dancers and skaters learn to overcome such effects by concentrating on some fixed, visible object; with their eyes closed they are as likely to fall as anyone.

Overstimulation of the vestibular system (*e.g.,* on a ship or airplane) may induce motion sickness. A person with vestibular function totally destroyed is not subject to motion sickness; but if the vestibular mechanism is impaired only on one side, each movement of the head can be nauseating. Such a patient takes a long time to compensate for this imbalance.

In outer space there is no gravitation to mediate feelings of up or down, although these still may arise from visual cues. The utricles and vestibular canals still respond to movements of the head, however, and serve orientation within the spacecraft.   (I.P.H.)

Space perception

Human beings have been interested in the perception of objects in space at least since the question of how a picture or image arises in the human eye was first asked. It was popularly thought in ancient Greece that objects are seen because they emit what was imagined to be a continuous series of extremely thin "membranes" in their own image, which fall upon the eye and there merge into the picture that is perceived. Only after long experimental research was a more tenable conception reached, in which space was described in terms of three dimensions or planes: height (vertical plane), width (horizontal plane), and depth (sagittal plane). These planes all intersect at right angles, and their single axis of intersection is defined as being located within perceived three-dimensional space—that is, in the "eye" of the perceiving individual. Man does not ordinarily perceive a binocular space (a separate visual world from each eye), but sees a so-called Cyclopean space, as if the images from each eye fuse to produce a visual field akin to that of Cyclops, a one-eyed giant in Greek mythology. The horizontal, vertical, and sagittal planes divide space into various sectors: something is perceived as "above" or "below" (the horizontal plane), as "in front of" or "behind" (the vertical plane), or as "to the right" or "to the left" (of the sagittal plane).

GENERAL CONSIDERATIONS

The study of space perception developed rapidly in the second half of the 19th century and still more rapidly

(margin left column: Flicker fusion; phi)

during the 20th. Many modern psychologists who deal with perceptual function hold that the study of space perception is rapidly becoming a distinct branch of psychology in its own right. This special field of investigation within psychology concentrates on the factors contributing to the perceptual articulation (organization) of objects in space (*e.g.*, on cues to depth perception, movement, form, colour, and their interactions), or dwells on particularly interesting special problems such as that of amodal perception (*e.g.*, the question of how one perceives that there are six sides on a cube, even though only three of them can be directly visible at once). Another special problem is the effect of the so-called mirror-ego on perception. It is questioned, for example, whether, when one's skin is touched while he is looking at himself in front of a mirror, he experiences the touch as if it were in the mirror image or perceives it to be in contact with his own body as it actually appears in front of the mirror.

Perception and orientation Space perception research also has tended to become a distinct specialty because of indisputable evidence that behaviour in this area is involved in orienting the individual to his environment. Specifically, man's orientation in space typically seems to reflect his strivings (*e.g.*, to seek food or to avoid injury). He would not be capable of effective orientation behaviour, however, unless the environmental information reaching him through the various sense organs were articulated (perceptually organized) in one way or another, permitting objects in space to be perceived at least approximately in a way that corresponds to their physical "reality" (*i.e.*, to their "actual" condition as stimuli). Such perception is called veridical perception, despite philosophical disputes about perceptual truth or verity (see EPISTEMOLOGY). Without some degree of veridicality of what is perceived to be physical space, one should be unable to efficiently seek food, flee from his enemies, or take part in social interaction. This means that, in service to one's veridical perception (direct perception of stimuli as they exist), one must also experience changing stimuli as if they were stable (invariant); that is, one experiences so-called perceptual invariances. Even though the sensory image of an approaching tiger grows larger, for example, one tends to perceive that the animal's size remains unchanged. One must be capable of perceiving objects in his environment as having relatively constant characteristics (as to size, colour, and so on) despite considerable variations in stimulus conditions.

Primary gravitational effects. Not all perception of space, however, is veridical; *i.e.*, it may fail to correspond to reality. A large number of perceptual effects have been demonstrated in which space as perceived deviates from reality in some systematic way. These are cases of nonveridical perception; for example, it has been demonstrated experimentally that the three basic spatial planes (horizontal, vertical, and sagittal) dominate the ability of the individual to localize visual objects in nearby space. Carefully controlled experiments show that objects tend to be perceived as lying closer to these basic dimensions or planes than they really are. Part of the explanation of these perceptual discrepancies in visual experience may lie in the force of gravity, which undeniably affects the individual from the moment of conception onward, pulling a man's viscera and muscles "down" toward the centre of the earth. The various perceptual phenomena indicative of nonveridical perception nevertheless do not generate chaos in one's perception of space, as might theoretically be expected; indeed, most often they serve to simplify and to articulate the perceived characteristics of surrounding space. If all of the mass of sensory information available at a given moment were perceived veridically, the flood of data might so confuse the perceiver that he would be unable to orient himself appropriately. In other words, some degree of selectivity in perception in general appears to be demanded for the survival of the individual. Ideally, information about the environment is perceived only as it is relevant to the goals, needs, or physiological state of the individual at a given moment.

Selective perception

Visual factors in space perception. On casual consideration, it might be concluded that the perception of space is based exclusively on vision. After closer study, however, this so-called visual space is found to be supplemented perceptually by what are clearly identifiable as cues from auditory (sense of hearing), kinesthetic (sense of bodily movement), olfactory (sense of smell), and gustatory (sense of taste) experience. In addition to these, a number of other spatial cues, such as vestibular stimuli (sense of balance) and other modes for sensing body orientation, must be taken into account. These various (*e.g.*, visual, olfactory) "spaces" are not found to be perceptually independent of one another; powerful experimental evidence shows them to interact in producing unified perceptual experiences.

It is nevertheless undeniable that the individual ordinarily receives the largest part of his information about the environment through the sense of sight; balance or equilibrium (vestibular sense) seems to rank next in importance. It has been shown that in a state of total darkness the orientation of an individual in space is mainly dependent on sensory data deriving from vestibular stimuli. The dominance of visual stimuli in the perception of space becomes particularly understandable when it is noted that vision is a so-called distance sense; it is capable of gathering information from extremely distant points in the environment, reaching out to the stars themselves. Hearing is also considered a distance sense, as is smell, though the space they encompass is considerably more restricted than that of vision. All the other senses, such as touch and taste, are usually considered to be proximal (proximate or direct) senses—*i.e.*, conveying information about the space in direct contact with the perceiving individual's body. Strictly speaking, the latter senses may, on occasion, function over distances. The smell of rotten eggs (produced by hydrogen sulfide gas) several yards away may be associated with a taste experience if the gas dissolves in the perceiver's saliva.

The eye has often been compared to a camera; this is, of course, a very rough comparison, but it is possible to think of the retina (the back surface of the inside of the eye) as if it were the film in a camera and of the lens within the eye as analogous to the single lens of the camera (see SENSORY RECEPTION: *Human vision*). Just as in a portrait photographer's camera, the picture (image) that is projected from the environment onto the retina is upside down. While it might be expected that the perceiver therefore would experience space as turned upside down, normally this does not happen. Some sort of perceptual mechanisms within the individual enable him to see his environment right side up; the exact nature of these mechanisms is under study, yet remains poorly understood. But the process of perception seems to involve at least two inversions: one (optical) inversion of the image on the retina; another (perceptual) associated with nerve impulses in the visual tissues of the brain.

Experiments have been carried out with people who were wearing special optical devices (*e.g.*, as spectacles) that reverse the right–left or up–down dimensions of images as normally received at the surface of the retina. At first the person becomes disoriented, but when he wears such a device all the time, he gradually learns to cope with space correctly while the special glasses are on. Indeed, he reorients himself to his environment to the point that he visually begins to perceive objects as if they were right side up again. This is evidence that the individual can become visually adapted in his perception of space to a new set of stimulus cues that deviate considerably from those previously learned. The process changes direction when the optical distorting device is removed; at first the basic visual dimensions appear reversed to the subject who has adapted to the spectacles. Within a short time, however, a new adaptation occurs; the subject quickly reorients himself to the earlier, well-learned, normal visual cues and perceives his environment as normal once more.

PERCEPTION OF DEPTH AND DISTANCE

The perception of depth and distance depends on information transmitted through various sense organs. Sensory cues indicate the distance at which objects in the environment are located from the perceiving individual and from each other. Such sense modalities as seeing and hearing are known to transmit depth and distance cues and are in substantial degree independent of one another. Each modality by itself can produce consistent perception of the distances of objects. Ordinarily, however, the individual relies on the collaboration of all his senses, (so-called intermodal perception).

Gross tactual–kinesthetic cues. In his perception of the distances of objects located in nearby space, one depends on his tactile (tactual or touch) sense. In tactile experience, however, kinesthesic experience (sensations of muscle movements and of movements of the sense-organ surfaces) normally is so closely associated that investigators lump the two as tactual–kinesthetic cues.

Tactual–kinesthetic sensations enable one to differentiate his own body from the surrounding environment. The body of the individual seems to function as a perceptual frame of reference—that is, as a standard against which the distances of objects are gauged. One's perception of his own body may vary from time to time, and so its role as a perceptual standard is not always consistent. It has been found that the way in which the environment is perceived also affects one's perception of his own body. Thus, for example, it has been shown experimentally that one experiences his own arm as growing longer when he is using it to point at some object off in the environment.

Cues from the eye muscles. When one looks at an object at a distance, the effort arouses activity in two eye-muscle systems called the ciliary muscles and the rectus muscles. The ciliary effect is called accommodation (focussing the lens for near or far vision), and the rectus effect is called convergence (moving the entire eyeball). Each of these muscle systems contracts as a perceived object approaches. The effect of accommodation in this case is to make the jellylike lens more convex, while the rectus muscles rotate the eyes to converge on the object as it comes nearer. One's experience of these muscle contractions provides him with cues to the distance of objects.

Beyond the cues of accommodation and convergence, the size of the retinal image also serves to indicate how far one is from an object. The larger the image on the retina, the closer one judges the object to be. Some workers theorize that these sensory cues activate inherited tendencies immediately to perceive such sensory attributes as size without the need for learning (the so-called nativistic theory). Modern efforts to study these cues have been especially directed toward physiological changes in the body that may be related to depth perception; whether one's perception of depth is totally inborn (nativistic), and thus independent of learning, however, remains most controversial.

Accommodations and convergence provide reliable cues when the perceived object is at a distance of less than about 30 feet (nine metres) and when it is perceived binocularly (with both eyes at once).

Visual cues. Perhaps the most important perceptual cues of distance and depth depend on so-called binocular disparity; that is, since the eyes are imbedded at different points in the skull, they receive slightly different (disparate) images of any given object. The two retinal images of the same object seem to be combined perceptually in the brain into one three-dimensional experience. The degree of disparity between the two retinal images, so-called binocular parallax, depends on the difference between the angles at which an object is fixed by the right eye and by the left eye. Thus, in looking at the indicator needle on a pressure gauge, for example, one will make slightly different readings because of parallax if he uses first the left eye alone and then the right eye. The greater the parallax difference between the two retinal images, the closer the object is perceived to be.

The phenomenon of binocular disparity functions primarily in near space because with objects at considerable distances from the viewer the angular difference between the two retinal images diminishes. Visual disparity nevertheless can be used in estimating greater distances by simply using optical devices that magnify the parallax distance separately for each eye. Such devices include artillery range-finding devices and old-fashioned, three-dimensional picture viewers called stereoscopes.

In what is called visual movement parallax, distance cues are obtained from retinal changes that depend on the interposition of objects in space. Thus, when the individual moves his head either from side to side, or forward and backward, the retinal image of a nearby tree moves more, while that of a distant tree moves less. Unlike binocular disparity, which functions only in binocular vision, movement parallax is especially important for judging distance when only one eye is used (monocular vision).

Another group of visual images called perspective projections provide perceptual cues that are independent of whether there is monocularity or binocularity of vision. Although estimates of distance based on such perspective effects as the apparent distant fusing of railroad tracks in a single point are incompletely understood, they are often considered to depend heavily on learning. Such phenomena illustrate the tendency of the individual to integrate perceptions into consistent and invariant wholes. Experiences of perspective may be generated by putting appropriate lines in an oil painting (linear perspective), by gradations in the tint of the paint (colour perspective), and by viewing the surface of the earth from an airplane (aerial perspective).

Still another group of visual cues of depth and distance consists of apparent differences in object brightness. In experimental studies it is found that the brighter an object appears, the closer it seems to be. Thus, a white card against a dark background seems to recede or to move forward as the level of illumination on the card is experimentally varied. Similar effects can be induced by changing the colour (hue) of an object—*e.g.,* from bright red to dark red.

Auditory cues. Auditory cues for depth perception include sound intensity (loudness), auditory pitch, and the time lapse between visual perception and auditory perception (for example, one hears a distant cannon after seeing the flash and smoke of the explosion).

Changes in pitch function as depth cues because when a moving object (*e.g.,* an automobile) is emitting sound waves (*e.g.,* from its horn), the pitch of the sound seems to rise when the object is approaching the perceiver; to fall when it is moving away.

INTERRELATIONS AMONG THE SENSES

The development of human ability to perceive space normally depends on the interaction of the senses (modalities) of sight and touch. Toward the end of its first year, a child eagerly begins to touch and to explore objects with his hands. Compared with his visual apparatus, which begins to function more efficiently at a later time, the child's sense of touch at this stage of development is delicately and effectively sensitive. By touching objects that are placed at various heights and distances from him, the child learns excellent tactual ways of perceptually evaluating what must be a highly ambiguous world as transmitted by his relatively immature visual apparatus.

The part played by other modalities (*e.g.,* hearing) does not appear to be as fundamental in perceptual learning among young children. By contrast, people are most seriously hampered in learning a detailed, well-articulated perceptual appreciation of space without vision or touch; most people (including those who are blind) may find it difficult to imagine how impoverished an understanding of space one would have if there were only auditory cues. It is well known that people with full sensory endowment learn to locate the sources of sounds by consulting both their visual and tactual experiences. There are subtler forms of sensory interaction as well; for example, one is more accurate in turning a pointer toward a distant source of sound (*e.g.,* a buzzer) if the pointer is simultaneously illuminated whenever there is buzzing. Such anchoring of one sense to another as a basis for spatial perception is vividly illustrated by experiments with laboratory animals.

Young monkeys have been taught to discriminate, on the basis of tactual perception alone, differently shaped objects (balls, cubes, cones, and cylinders, all about the size of a matchbox). That is, each animal was given two of these objects at a time and was allowed to feel them with its hands without seeing them. The animal's choice of one specific shape (say, a cube) and its rejection of another (say, a cone) were rewarded with bits of food. When this selective tactual response had been learned, the animal was given the same tasks of selection, this time to be performed visually (by looking at pictures of the same objects). Under these conditions the animal often was able to discriminate the visually presented figures correctly. This phenomenon (called cross-modal learning) may be explained as a transfer effect based on earlier visual-tactual learning.

Success in orientation, in moving about effectively and without accident in everyday pursuits, is most probable when environmental information at any given time is available through as many senses as possible. When the range of sensory stimuli that forms the usual basis for the experience of perceptual space is experimentally reduced, one's success in orientation is impaired. When visual cues are sharply reduced for sighted people, they complain of disorientation, akin to groping around in a diffuse, undifferentiated fog. Indeed, injuries are all too common even when one seeks in the dark to negotiate such familiar territory as his own bedroom.

Apparently, by learning about systematic relationships that exist among a number of simultaneously available stimuli, people can perceive distances more or less correctly. The retinal image of an object 100 yards (91 metres) away is so much smaller than the image of the same object at a distance of 10 yards (9 metres) that (if they relied solely on the sizes of retinal images) people might perceive moving objects to shrink or grow rather than to recede or approach.

Experiments have shown that the distance (in depth) between selected objects in photographs is most accurately estimated when the objects have been filmed in a richly organized environment—*e.g.,* many people standing at different distances from the camera. On the other hand, it is most difficult indeed to reliably perceive even the relative depth of two vertical rods when they are presented against a background in which other cues have been reduced or eliminated.

Factors of constancy. In general, the considerable range of sensory information offered by isolated local stimuli is typically controlled, sifted, and corrected by the perceiver. The specific nature of these "corrections to conform to reality" generally depends on the unique combination of simultaneously presented stimuli at any given moment. In this way, spatial perception tends to ensure that a person experiences the continually changing circumstances of the environment in which he moves and lives with some degree of stability or constancy.

This "realistic" perception, based on an awareness of the apparently real, physical world, serves as the basis for practical adjustment and survival and appears clearly in a group of perceptual experiences of so-called object constancy. In the experience of size constancy, for example, within a radius of a few hundred yards from the observer, the size of objects is perceived to remain roughly constant no matter where they are. Constancy of form means that an object is perceived to retain its fixed characteristic shape regardless of variation in the angle at which it is observed; for example, a pencil seen end-on only shows a small circular profile but is still perceived as a pencil. Colour constancy clearly illustrates the way in which the brightness and hue experienced over the surface of an object is determined by direct comparison with other objects; a lump of coal still is perceived as black whether the Sun is shining brightly or whether there is a dull, leaden sky.

Path recognition: navigation in space. Different animal species are equipped in various ways for the recognition of their path of movement. Earthbound species of animals often use olfactory (smell) signals in recognizing paths of varying distance; this is encountered both among social insects (*e.g.,* ants) and among many mammals (the dog sniffing from tree to tree). Certain insect larvae can retrace their path of movement by using as guides extremely fine webs or filaments spun during their advance. Many species seem to navigate by the Sun, the angle between the rays of the Sun and the organism's own path being held constant. The ability of migratory birds to orient themselves by stars in twilight or at night is most impressive (see BEHAVIOUR,

Margin note (left): Use of smell to judge distance

ANIMAL: *Migratory behaviour*). In addition to cues offered by the stars and other heavenly bodies, such stimuli as the effects of gravity, temperature changes, and direct visual observation of landmarks such as rivers all seem to contribute to path recognition among animals.

With the burgeoning of aviation and space technology, there has been a growing research effort to increase understanding of the sensory basis for human navigation in space. Reliable perception of the vertical and horizontal dimensions and preservation of perceptual constancy for these dimensions during flight are based on the parallel activity of vision and the vestibular sense (balance, or equilibrium). Even in flying small aircraft it has been shown that the pilot becomes disoriented unless he preserves visual control of the horizontal dimension; he cannot safely rely on the information conveyed by his sense of balance to inform him that a wing tip, for example, is dipping dangerously low. While the sense of balance ordinarily depends on the effect of gravity, the movement of an airplane produces additional (so-called centrifugal and centripetal) forces, particularly as the plane tilts or changes direction, which easily mislead a person's vestibular (balance) receptors. For this reason, in high-altitude flying the horizontal line of the surface of the Earth is simulated for the pilot by an optical display that works on the same principles as does a television screen.

Even greater demands on the human senses of vision and balance are made in space flights, since a person is effectively weightless in outer space. At one laboratory maintained by the U.S. Navy, an enormous, very slowly rotating cylindrical chamber has been constructed. Variations in the perceptual sensitivity of people remaining for variable periods (even days at a time) in this simulated "outer space" environment are studied in an effort to anticipate the short-term and long-term effects of interplanetary flight.

Social and interpersonal aspects of space perception. Many animal species that use nests, lairs, or dens and care for their young act to defend a specifically delimited territory against interlopers. This process is clearly observable in birds and among seals during breeding season. Apparently territorial behaviour depends on a rather precise perception of space, since the animal ceases its defensive manoeuvres when an interloper passes out of the territory by moving across the "border." The social distances maintained by primates (*e.g.,* human beings and apes) are theorized to be the result of territorial groupings. Modern architecture is held to be dominated by an inborn human tendency to divide groups into small, separate family territories (just as birds do), the result being such structures as apartment houses. Geographical distance may also be maintained to separate individuals who belong to different social classes or races, as is observed in the ethnic neighbourhoods or ghettos of large cities.

Margin note (right): Territorial distance

Theories of space perception. An early theory put forth by the Anglican bishop George Berkeley at the beginning of the 18th century was that the third dimension (depth) cannot be directly perceived in a visual way since the retinal image of any object is two-dimensional, as in a painting. He held that the ability to have visual experiences of depth is not inborn (nativistic) but can only result from logical deduction based on empirical learning through the use of other senses (*e.g.,* touch).

Although modern research fails to verify the importance Berkeley placed on reason in perception, contemporary theories still include both nativistic and empiricistic considerations. According to empiricistic theorists, spatial perception develops primarily as the result of learning; indeed, during the early stages of development, the individual gradually does seem to learn something about the significance of observable (empirical) spatial cues. It is just as difficult, however, to deny the nativistic concept that space perception is based on the innate (hereditary) structure of sense receptors and the nervous system; for example, the ability to detect differences in the size of two-dimensional figures seems to be inborn (that is, the differences seem to be immediately recognizable without training or learning).

(K.V.J.v.F./E.J.J./P.Y.K.)

Time perception

The human experience of change is complex. One primary element clearly is that of a succession of events; but distinguishable events are separated by more or less lengthy intervals that are called durations. Sequence and duration are fundamental aspects of what is perceived in change.

Manifestly, duration is relative to the events people isolate in the sequences through which they live: the duration of a kiss, of a meal, of a trip. A given interval always can be subdivided into a sequential chain delimiting briefer durations, as with the regular units that provide empirical measures of time: the second, the day, the year.

Indeed, human experience is not simply that of one single series of events, but of a plurality of overlapping changes. The duration of a radio program, for example, can combine with that of a breakfast, both being inserted within the longer period of an ocean voyage.

Man seems to be unable to live without some concept of time. Ancient philosophies sought to relate the concept of time to some objective reality to which it would correspond. René Descartes (1596–1650) inaugurated a critical era of philosophy by stressing the ancient problem of the origin of ideas, including the idea of time. Immanuel Kant (1724–1804), providing a radical answer to the epistemological problem of time, wrote that we do not appreciate time objectively as a physical thing; that it is simply a pure form of sensible intuition. Other philosophers of the 18th and 19th centuries sought to explain the notion of time as arising from association and memory of successive perceptions.

A move to empirical psychology emerged with the growth of research on the introspective data of experience. From about mid-19th century, under the influence of the psychophysical notions of Gustav Theodor Fechner, psychologists conducted experiments to study the relationship between time as perceived and time as measured in physics. Their work with adults gradually spread to the study of children and of animals. The psychologists then broadened their investigations of time to cover all forms of adaptation to sequence and duration.

(margin: Early philosophical views of time)

SEQUENTIAL ACTIVITIES

Adaptation to successive events. One may respond to stimulation in an immediate way (as in unconditioned reflex action) without taking the element of time into account. Stimulation, however, can also signal an event to follow; then it has meaning only as part of the sequence of which it is the first term: bell announcing dinner, a road sign, or an approaching danger. People react to such stimuli with anticipatory behaviour that is adapted to a stimulus or action that has not yet occurred. The principles that govern such time-binding adaptation are none other than those of conditioning. One event becomes conditioned as the signal for another stimulus that is to be sought or avoided.

The bottle-fed infant who initially reacts to the nipple on his lips with a simple sucking reflex is gradually conditioned to stop crying when he sees the bottle (the signal for feeding). Later he may learn to react to even more secondary signals that announce the arrival of the bottle; *e.g.*, being lifted from the crib or hearing the sounds of his mother warming the milk in the kitchen. His behaviour has come to incorporate the temporal dimension of the events.

According to the principles of instrumental conditioning, one stimulus becomes the signal for an ensuing event only if the second stimulus elicits an adaptive reaction (consummatory or aversive) and only if the order of the sequence is repeated. Conditioning tends to be established most rapidly when the interval between the signal (conditioned stimulus) and the unconditioned stimulus is quite brief. Ivan P. Pavlov estimated that the optimum interval for such a sequence was 0.5 second, which corresponds approximately to the intervals characteristic of sequences that are most accurately discriminable perceptually (see below).

Aside from adapting the individual to the order of a sequence, conditioning also adapts to the duration between signal and immediately effective stimulus. Response to

(margin: Time-binding adaptation as conditioning)

signal tends to occur after about the same interval that separated the two stimuli during conditioning. Thus, an animal may be trained to delay a response for some time after the signal (delayed conditioning).

This form of adaptation is most pervasive in human behaviour, permitting people to anticipate sequences of events in their environment so that they can prepare to cope appropriately with what is yet to happen.

Adaptation to periodic change. In 1912 one of Pavlov's students (I.P. Feokritova) demonstrated that a dog accustomed to being fed every 30 minutes would begin to drool toward the end of each half-hour period. It was clear evidence of conditioning to time; the between-feedings interval itself served as a conditioned stimulus.

That discovery underscores the ever-present periodicity of daily living, especially on the biological level: rhythms of activity and sleep, rhythms of eating and lovemaking. As conditioning intervenes, anticipatory experiences of hunger, fatigue, or arousal serve our adaptation to ecological demands.

Allowance should also be made for the daily, or circadian, rhythms in metabolic activity (*e.g.*, daily cycles of temperature change). There is evidence that these fundamental biological functions can synchronize with the rhythmic phases of environmental (exogenous) change. Thus within a few days after a factory worker has been assigned to the night shift, highs and lows of his daily fluctuations of temperature will be inversed. The rhythmic changes in body temperature persists, nevertheless, suggesting an innate (endogenous) basis for circadian phenomena. Such a hypothesis would mean that the gradual establishment of human circadian rhythms of sleep or temperature results from maturation of the nervous system rather than from conditioning in the strict sense. Experiments begun in 1962, in which men lived in caves or other enclosures for months deprived of temporal cues from the environment, also demonstrated the enduring nature of rhythms in body temperature and in sleep–wakefulness. The rhythmic periods, however, sometimes expanded, the subject beginning to live on an approximately two-day cycle without being aware of it.

Through conditioning to time and by way of circadian rhythms, human physiology provides a kind of biological clock that offers points of reference for temporal orientation.

(margin: Circadian rhythms in metabolic activity)

PERCEPTION OF SEQUENCE AND DURATION

The psychological present. To perceive is to become aware of stimulation. Awareness of sequence or duration may, at first glance, seem inconsistent with the definition of perceiving. In a mathematical sense, certainly, the present is only a point along the continuum of becoming, an instant when future is transformed into past. Nevertheless, there is indeed a more prolonged psychological present, a brief period during which successive events seem to form a perceptual unity and can be apprehended without calling on memory. There is a perceptual field for time just as there is a visual field. The rate or speed of a sequence determines the limits of the time field.

When a metronome tics two or three times a second, one perceives an integral sequence, becoming aware of a rhythmic auditory series characterized by a perceptually distinct frequency. When the ticks come less often, however—at intervals of three seconds, say—the frequency or sequence no longer is perceived. Each physically discrete sound impulse remains an isolated perceptual event; each tick is no longer perceived as belonging to the same temporal field as the one that follows. Similar effects can be achieved by playing a recording of music or speech at a very slow rate. Music or spoken sentences are recognizable only when their elements (melody, rhythmic patterns, phrase) are presented at an optimal speed that permits significant perceptual unity; that is, only when they belong to the relative simultaneity of the psychological present.

The perceived field of time also depends on the number of stimulus elements presented. When a clock strikes three or four times, one knows without counting that it is three or four o'clock. At noon one must count; the first chimes no longer belong to the psychological present that includes the last. Most people also can repeat a series of letters or

(margin: Relation of perceived time to number of elements presented)

numbers they hear, so long as there are no more than seven or eight elements. This ability varies with the degree of perceptual (*e.g.,* semantic) organization among the elements. While most adults can apprehend only about eight letters, they can grasp and repeat without fault sentences of 20 to 25 syllables (see also ATTENTION).

Perception of sequence. A series of physically discrete stimuli that impinge too rapidly on a sensory structure (*e.g.,* flashes of light on the retina) may produce perceptual fusion; the flashes will be indiscriminable and will appear to be uninterrupted light. The experience of fusion yields to one of discontinuity over distinctive critical ranges of frequency for some of the senses: visual flicker appears under prescribed experimental conditions at about 60 flashes per second, auditory flutter at about 1,000 interruptions per second, and tactual vibration at about 4,000 pulses per second. These values depend on differences in the persistence of the receptor systems (*e.g.,* how long an image is seen after removal of the stimulus).

The question of perceiving sequence hardly has meaning for the senses of taste and smell. Hearing appears to be particularly adapted to temporal perception, since the pattern of auditory excitement shows little inertial lag, closely following the physical duration of successive stimuli. Tactual function can give comparable results, but hearing has the practical superiority in everyday experience of reception at a distance.

When two heterogeneous stimuli (*e.g.,* a flash and a click) are successively presented, the critical threshold for passing from perceived simultaneity to an awareness of succession is found for intervals that vary between 0.02 to 0.1 second, depending on the training of the subjects. The maximum interval for perceiving sequence is more difficult to measure. The minimum time intervals are largely determined by the immediate physiological conditions of direct perceiving, while the maximum intervals are obscured by the effects of other cognitive activities. Determining when direct perception ends and when memory takes over is difficult.

At any rate, awareness of unitary sequence ceases for pairs of auditory or visual stimuli when the interval between them increases to approximately two seconds. For perceptually organized stimuli (as in a rhythm, a melody, or a phrase) the interval may reach five seconds, as indicated by one's ability to reproduce the pattern.

Between the upper and lower limits there are optimal values that seem most likely to produce perception of sequence. In the simple case of two homogeneous stimuli the optimum interval seems to be about 0.6 to 0.8 second. This is inferred from a series of clues: the same interval defines the tempo most frequently adopted in spontaneous motor activity (*e.g.,* tapping, walking) and corresponds to the heart rate. It is the interval that is most precisely reproduced by subjects in experiments; shorter intervals tend to be overestimated and longer ones underestimated. Stimuli repeated at that rate are subjectively judged to proceed most comfortably, without appearing to rush each other as in faster tempos and with no tendency to be separately perceived as at slower frequencies.

Perceived duration. Duration, the interval between two successive events, may be distinguished as full or empty (filled or unfilled) in terms of the sensory stimulation that intervenes. An empty interval is bounded by two perceptually discrete stimuli (*e.g.,* two clicks in succession); a duration is full when there is continous stimulation, being delimited by an onset and cessation (*e.g.,* a light stays on throughout the interval). To experience an empty duration is to perceive sequence, while full duration corresponds to the temporal length of a stimulus.

Human subjects need a minimum of about 0.1 second of visual experience or about .01 to .02 second of auditory experience to perceive duration; any shorter experiences are called instantaneous. Direct, unitary perception of duration occurs up to a maximum period of approximately 1.5 to 2 seconds from the beginning to the end of a continuous sensory stimulus.

This roughly two-second maximum for directly perceived duration seems to have a biological basis and can be considered the upper temporal limit of some sort of integrated

(margin left) Full and empty duration

neural mechanism. The immediate physiological process triggered by a stimulus endures beyond the period of stimulation, and may be measured as the duration of electrical impulses (*i.e.,* in the optic nerve) evoked by simple stimulation. This initial activity appears to be integrated subjectively into a cognitive unit that embraces the rapidly ensuing perceptual processes as well. The optimum range of 0.6 to 0.8 second noted earlier seems to represent the typical duration of this integrating mechanism, as inferred from studies of sensory physiology and from reaction-time experiments.

At any rate, only within these limits can the quality and precision of direct human perception (as opposed to estimation and recall) of duration be studied. Such perception can be absolute or relative. Absolute perception corresponds to estimates expressed in subjectively qualitative terms as long or short. In making such estimates, people can discriminate four to five different durations between 0.1 and 1.0 second and six to seven between 0.5 and 5.0 seconds. In studies of relative perception, subjects attempt to reproduce intervals that are presented, or are told either to produce durations of specified length or to compare two successively presented durations. These tasks, especially comparison, give rise to constant time-order errors; that is, errors in estimation that depend on which interval is presented first.

Experimentally, the perception of empty duration is found to vary with the sense that marks the limits. With duration constant, interval estimates tend to be greater (1) when the limits are visual rather than auditory or tactual, (2) when they are of low intensity, or (3) when auditory limits are higher pitched. If the unfilled limits are defined by successive stimuli from different places, duration appears longer when the distance between the two sources is greater; this is called the S effect or kappa effect. The reverse is the tau effect, in which the distance is perceived as being wider when the interval between successive stimuli is longer.

(margin right) Kappa and tau effects

The perception of filled duration also varies with the stimulus. Holding the interval constant, interrupted stimulation (*e.g.,* several successive clicks) appears to last longer than does a continuous stimulus; and auditory stimuli appear to last longer than visual. Filled durations seem longer as stimulus intensity (*e.g.,* loudness) or auditory pitch rises.

One interval can be perceived as longer or shorter than the next when the difference is about 7 to 10 percent (both full and empty durations). This relative difference threshold is lowered by practice. Such studies also reveal that apparent duration remains proportional to the objectively measured length of the interval.

Estimating duration. When an interval lasts more than a few seconds, it no longer is directly perceivable as a whole, but its length can be estimated on the basis of memory function. Since common experience shows how imprecise these estimates are, people generally calculate time from such indicators as the position of the sun or with clocks and watches. Duration then is inferred rather than perceived.

Estimates, however, often are made, including those of absolute duration in which an activity is appreciated as brief or prolonged. Lacking a watch, one may make crude estimates based on such quantitative aspects of activity as distance travelled, number of dishes washed, or number of pages read. Or one may estimate directly as in subjectively counting seconds.

Several important factors influence the subjects estimation of time:

Type of activity. The more often a task is broken up or interrupted, the longer it seems to take. As a corollary, a period of doing nothing appears longer than an equally long period when one is doing something. Similarly, relatively passive activities appear longer than do those requiring active participation; *e.g.,* time passes faster for the student who is taking notes than for one who passively listens.

Level of motivation. The more one is motivated by a given task, the shorter it appears to last. Clearly, motivation and the type of activity pursued are interdependent factors. Lack of motivation tends to interrupt attention to a task; a task in which perceptual focus frequently shifts rarely corresponds to one for which there is strong motivation. The more one notices change during an interval, the longer it is judged to be. More generally, it may be said that time has subjective duration only when one notices it; *e.g.,* in awaiting the arrival of a friend (as opposed to the actual meeting) or in hoping to finish a task (in contrast to working at it).

Change as a factor in judging time

Personality traits. Although inadequacies in quantifying personality traits and difficulties in studying estimates of time spans exceeding a few seconds have hampered scientific study, simple observation reveals marked individual differences in the ability to estimate time. Sex differences have not been reliably established, but the influence of age is well known. Experimental data indicate that children use the same criteria as do adults, but give more variable estimates of duration. One reason for this seems to be that they are less able to compensate for differences in the nature of a task or in personal motivation; also they are inexperienced in making inferences based on the volume of work they have accomplished. Elderly people tend to find time shorter, probably since they are less likely to notice long-accustomed changes less frequently.

Children are as accurate as adults in reproducing various series of metronome clicks that last about two seconds or less. But estimates of longer intervals require processes for organizing experience that develop only with age, and very young children seem to depend only on limited criteria: "It lasts because it's longer; because there's more of it; because it goes faster." According to Jean Piaget, estimates based on more or less explicit comparison with standard units of duration imply concrete cognitive operations that are developed only after about the age of seven or eight. Adolescents typically construct more sophisticated notions of time abstracted from such concrete experimental data.

The influence of body temperature

Physiological effects: drugs. The precision with which time is perceived has not been found to be related to heart rate or to electroencephalographic data. It has been shown, however, that perception of time as in clapping or counting accelerates or decelerates with the rise and fall of body temperature. The precise metabolic basis for such temperature effects awaits further study.

Ethical considerations sharply limit the dosage level of drugs employed for experiments on human beings. Understanding of the interactions between drug effects and personality traits in studies of time estimation is, therefore, quite incomplete. Within the dosage ranges investigated, however, stimulating drugs (*e.g.,* thyroxine, caffeine, amphetamines) produce overestimates of duration, while depressants and anesthetics (*e.g.,* barbiturates, nitrous oxide) promote underestimates. Under the influence of hallucinogens (*e.g.,* marijuana, mescaline, LSD), subjects tend to estimate absolute duration as very long. In addition, a marijuana user may underestimate the speed of a motor vehicle, increasing the chances of accident.

Sensory deprivation and hypnosis. Relatively complete sensory deprivation (such as may be experienced, for example, by persons undergoing prolonged stays in experimental isolation chambers) compresses the experience of time to the point that short or long intervals (from about a minute to a day) seem to pass about twice as fast as usual. Time spent under these unpleasant conditions paradoxically seems shorter than normal time. Thus, the 58 objective days of a subject's first stay in a cave were underestimated as 33 days.

Under hypnosis, durations ordinarily are estimated at least as precisely as ever. Time distortion, however, can be readily induced among hypnotized subjects by simple suggestion. Such a subject, for example, may be exposed to two clicks that delimit an objective, 10-second interval but be told that it lasts 10 minutes. On being asked to count objects for 10 minutes, he may report having counted several hundreds without difficulty over what the experimenter's stopwatch shows to have been 10 seconds. (P.F.)

Illusions and hallucinations

Illusion and hallucination are terms formulated to describe subjective (perceptual) experiences that contradict objective "reality" as it is defined by general agreement among people. Such experiences are not necessarily signs of psychiatric disturbances; they are or have been regularly and consistently reported by virtually everyone. Generally, illusions comprise misinterpretations of "real" sensory stimuli (*e.g.,* the child who perceives tree branches at night as if they are hobgoblins). Hallucinations are experiences that seem to originate when no external source of such stimulation appears (*e.g.,* one's name is called by a voice that no one else seems to hear).

THE NATURE OF ILLUSIONS

Illusions, then, are special perceptual experiences in which information arising from "real" external stimuli leads to an incorrect perception, or false impression, of the object or event from which the stimulation comes.

Causes of illusions

Some of these false impressions may arise from factors beyond an individual's control (such as the characteristic behaviour of light waves that makes a pencil in a glass of water seem bent), from inadequate information (as under conditions of poor illumination), or from the functional and structural characteristics of the sensory apparatus (*e.g.,* distortions in the shape of the lens in the eye). Such visual illusions are experienced by every sighted person.

Another group of illusions results from misinterpretations one makes of seemingly adequate sensory cues. In such illusions, sensory impressions seem to contradict the "facts of reality" or fail to report their "true" character. (For more profound philosophical considerations, see EPISTEMOLOGY.) In these instances the perceiver seems to be making an error in processing sensory information. The error appears to arise within the central nervous system (brain and spinal cord); this may result from competing sensory information, psychologically meaningful distorting influences, or previous expectations (mental set). The driver who sees his own headlights reflected in the window of a store, for example, may experience the illusion that another vehicle is coming toward him even though he knows there is no road there.

TYPES OF ILLUSORY EXPERIENCE

Stimulus-distortion illusions. This type of illusory sense perception, common to mankind, arises when the environment changes or warps the stimulus energy on the way to the person, who efficiently receives it in its distorted pattern (as in the case of the "bent" pencil referred to above).

Auditory illusions. A common phenomenon is the auditory impression that a blowing automobile horn changes its pitch as it passes an observer on a highway. This is known as the Doppler effect, for C. Doppler, an Austrian physicist, who in 1842 noted that the pitch of a bell or whistle on a passing railroad train is heard to drop when the train and the perceiver are moving away from each other and to grow higher when they are approaching each other. The sound heard is also affected by such factors as a wind blowing toward or away from the person.

Uses of the pseudophone

Another auditory illusion was described in 1928 by P.T. Young, an American psychologist, who tested the process of sound localization (the direction from which sound seems to come). He constructed a pseudophone, an instrument made of two ear trumpets, one leading from the right side of the head to the left ear and the other vice versa. This created the illusory impression of reversed localization of sound. While walking along the street wearing the pseudophone he would hear footsteps to his right when they actually came from the left.

When two sources of sound in the same vicinity emit sound waves of slightly different frequencies (*i.e.,* vibrations per second), there will come intervals when waves from both sources arrive at the ear in phase (simultaneously) and produce the experience of a combined, louder sound. These intervals of combined sound will be perceived as "beats," or periodic alternations of sound intensity. When such auditory beats occur too rapidly to be discriminated, the resulting experience may be that of a harsh, continuous noise. These periodic alternations are of two kinds: summation tones (in which the waves reinforce each other), which are weaker and harder to observe, and difference tones (waves cancel each other), which are obvious, distinguishable, and which reinforce each other. Piano tuners depend in part upon their ability to employ these experiences in a reliable way in tightening and loosening the strings of the instruments.

Visual illusions. Numerous optical illusions are produced by the refraction (bending) of light as it passes through one substance to another in which the speed of light is significantly different. A ray of light passing from one transparent medium (air) to another (water) is bent as it emerges. Thus, the pencil standing in water seems broken at the surface where the air and water meet; in the same way, a partially submerged log in the water of a swamp gives the illusion of being bent.

Rainbows result from another characteristic of light waves, called diffraction. As the sun's rays pass through rain, the droplets separate (diffract) the white light into its component colours (see LIGHT). As rays of white light from any source pass through a prism, they are diffracted (broken up) to give the appearance of a spectrum of colour as in the rainbow of a summer morning. Another illusion that depends on atmospheric conditions is the mirage, in which, for example, the vision of a pool of water is created by light passing the layers of hot air above the heated surface of a highway. In effect, cooler layers of air refract the sun's rays at different angles than do less dense strata of heated air, giving the appearance of water where there is none; nearby objects (*e.g.,* barns, telephone poles) may even appear to be reflected in it. Under unusual conditions, more elaborate mirages may appear as cities, forests, "unidentified flying objects," oases, and even as the images of ships in a nearby body of water plying the sky of a desert.

Perceiver-distortion illusions. Some illusions are related to perceiver characteristics such as brain function. When an observer is confronted with a visual assortment of dots, for example, the brain may appear to group the dots that "belong together." These groupings are made on the basis of such things as observed similarity (*e.g.,* red versus black dots), proximity, common direction of movement, perceptual set (the way one is expecting to see things grouped), and extrapolation (one's estimate of what will happen based on an extension of what is now happening).

Time-induced error is an example of a Gestalt illusion that occurs over brief time intervals. Two images of the same line, for example, will appear to differ in length if they are flashed quickly one after the other.

Closure (another Gestalt term) is the illusion of seeing an incomplete stimulus as though it were whole. Thus, one unconsciously tends to complete (close) a triangle or a square with a gap in one of its sides. In watching movies, closure occurs to fill the intervals between what are really rapidly projected still pictures, giving the illusion of uninterrupted motion.

Visual illusion. The "figure and ground" illusion is commonly experienced when one gazes at the illustration of a white vase the outline of which is created by two black profiles (see Figure 4). At any moment one will be able to see either the white vase (in the centre area) as "figure" or the black profiles on each side (in which case the white is seen as "ground"). The fluctuations of figure and ground may occur even when one fails deliberately to shift attention, appearing without conscious effort. Seeing one aspect apparently excludes seeing the other.

Another example of ambiguity and object reversibility is the Necker cube (see Figure 5), which may seem to "flip-flop"; younger people tend to perceive these reversals more readily than do their elders.

The so-called Müller-Lyer illusion (also Figure 5) is based on the Gestalt principles of convergence and divergence: the lines at the sides seem to lead the eye either inward or outward to create a false impression of length. The Poggendorff illusion depends on the steepness of the intersecting lines. As obliqueness is decreased, the illusion

Figure 4: Ambiguous figure seen as either white vase or two black profiles.

becomes less compelling. In the Zöllner illusion, the crosshatching disturbs the perception of parallel lines. A figure seen touching converging lines, as in the Ponzo illusion, creates the impression of size larger than does another figure placed between the lines where they are farther apart. In a related experience, linear perspective creates the illusion that parallel lines or contours (such as railroad tracks) converge as they recede from the viewer. If it were not for these converging lines, a figure in the distant background might appear smaller than would an identical figure in the foreground.

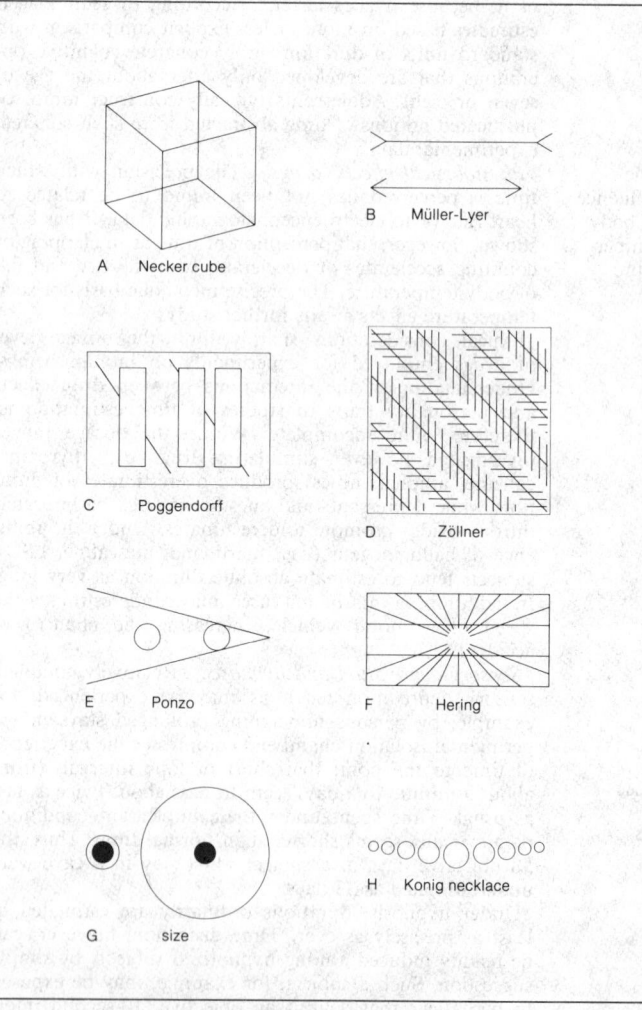

Figure 5: *Examples of optical illusions.*
(A) Cube changes orientation. (B) Lines are equal in length. (C) Lines covered by rectangles are straight. (D) All long lines are parallel. (E) Circles are equal in size. (F) Horizontal lines are parallel. (G) Black dots are equal in size. (H) Tops of circles are on a straight line.

Colour
in visual
illusions

Visual illusions include a variety of contrast colour phenomena. A successive contrast occurs when, after one has stared at a red surface, a green surface looks much brighter. As one enters a dark room from bright sunshine, the room at first seems quite dark by contrast. A simultaneous contrast occurs when an area of brightness is seen against a less intense or a more intense background. If a gray patch of paper is placed on a black background, it looks whiter than it did before; if placed on a white background, it looks darker.

In studies of visual verticality, experimenters investigated the conditions that determine perception of the "upright." A tilted chair that could be mechanically controlled by the subject was placed in a slanted room containing visual indicators of verticals and horizontals. When various persons were asked to sit in the chair and align themselves in a vertical position, some of the subjects aligned themselves with the "true vertical" determined by gravity, while others experienced the illusion of verticality by aligning themselves with the visual directions they saw in the slanted room. Closing the eyes made "true" alignment easier.

Staring at a single bright spot in an otherwise darkened room creates the illusion that the stationary light is moving (autokinetic effect). One theory to account for this is that the impression is caused by minute eye movements of the observer. The so-called phi phenomenon is an illusion of movement that arises when stationary objects, light bulbs for example, are placed side by side and illuminated rapidly one after another. The effect is frequently used on theatre marquees to give the impression of moving lights.

There is a well-known apparent difference in the size of the moon when it is at the horizon and when it is fully risen. The horizon moon, though it is actually farther away from the observer, looks much larger than it does when it is high in the sky and closer. This phenomenon was explained by English physicist S. Tolansky:

> ... we are expecting, like all other objects, that its size should diminish as it nears the horizon. This does not happen. So, because it does not get smaller, as we expect, it therefore appears larger than it should be.

The
illusion of
the size of
the moon

Other explanations have attributed the moon illusion to the fact that the fully risen moon cannot be readily compared to the terrain, as it can at the horizon; to atmospheric haze, which alters the impression of distance and size; to the change in the angle of elevation of the observer's eyes; and to the idea that the moon's increase in altitude (above the horizon) creates an expectation of decrease in size. (This last point seems to be at odds with Tolansky's ideas.) The moon illusion remains a paradox since, although the retinal images (in the eye) of the high moon and the horizon moon are about the same, the perceived size differs grossly.

Other illusory experiences. *Successive-contrast illusions.* Gestalt psychologists have proposed a "fading trace" theory to explain such illusions as occur in successive weight lifting (in which the same object seems to change in weight). It is suggested that, in such contrast illusions (in all the senses), a physical trace (in the form of temporarily excited nerve cells) of the original stimulus is left in the brain even after that stimulus stops; and that this trace influences the estimate or appreciation of a subsequent stimulus.

Recently, it has been suggested that not all people are equally receptive to optical illusions. The thesis is that an aftereffect is a surviving neural "trace" left by the imprint of a visually fixated (stared at) stimulus. The strength of the aftereffect or the speed of its disappearance varies greatly in individual cases. Persons who are field dependent (that is, who tend to observe a field in its totality) are said to show weaker aftereffect traces. Conversely, field-independent subjects (those who, by selective attention, are more likely to consider a specific stimulus apart from its context) show stronger perceptual aftereffects. When experimental subjects viewed a curved line and then the Hering figure (displayed elsewhere in this article), it was found that those who exhibit potent aftereffects (and are field independent) are able to counteract optical illusions, while those who have weaker aftereffects are more prone to experience visual illusions.

Tactual illusions. The skin contains numerous "spots" that respond selectively to either cold or warmth, but generally not to both. It can happen, however, that a very warm stimulus will produce a sensation of cold when placed on a spot that responds to cold. Thus, when a warm stimulus is perceived as cold, the illusion is called that of "paradoxical cold."

Illusions
of hot
and cold

"Paradoxical heat," a less frequent experience, results from stimulating warm and cold spots simultaneously. It appears to be a fusion of warm and paradoxical cold effects, producing a strange, somewhat unpleasant sensation of "heat" that seems to be attended by uneasiness resembling that of pain. The sensation is sometimes called "psychological heat."

Sudden temperature contrasts can play tricks on the senses. If hot water is run over one hand, and cold water over the other long enough for both to adjust to the temperatures and both are then plunged into lukewarm water, the resulting sensation will be that the cold hand will feel warm and the hot, cold. It would seem that in plunging the cold-adapted hand, nerve cells for perceiving cold were suddenly inhibited and those for perceiving hot were suddenly stimulated, while in the hot-adapted hand the reverse took place.

A single pencil may be felt as if it were two when it is held between crossed fingers in such a way that the skin is simultaneously stimulated at two points that would usually require two separate objects to produce such a sensation.

Anchor-effect phenomena. Sensitivity in any sense (sight, hearing, touch, and so on) may be measured as the just-perceptible intensity (threshold, or limen) of the appropriate stimulus. A light too dim to see is said to be subliminal (or below the visual threshold); a sound stimulus that is loud enough to hear is described as being above the auditory threshold (as being supraliminal). The smallest detectable stimulus is called the absolute threshold; the smallest detectable change in the intensity of a stimulus is called the difference threshold. Since such thresholds fluctuate within the same individual under different conditions, they are recognized as statistical (average) values rather than as fixed personal characteristics. At any rate, such thresholds can serve as points of reference, or anchors, against which subsequent stimuli are judged or perceived.

Other colour illusions. The normal human eye can function to detect about 130 gradations of colour in the visible spectrum (as in the rainbow), about 20 barely noticeable differences within a given colour, and about 500 of brightness. When two spots of equally bright light are observed in close succession, the first intensity may seem brighter. (This aftereffect is another example of time error.) The first light may be said to serve the function of brightness adaptation (or adjustment) in the eye, causing the second light to fall on a partly adapted and therefore less sensitive retina. In a brief time such excitement in the retina (or even in the brain) tends to subside, or fade. As a result of what theorists call "fading traces" of excitement (held to produce such aftereffect phenomena), various hues of a given colour may appear to be lighter or darker when looked at successively or in contrast to the background.

Weight illusions. The felt perception of differences in weights received experimental attention in 1899, which experiments indicated that a second weight is felt to be either heavier or lighter than an immediately preceding first one, partially as a result of the expectancy of the person doing the lifting. Having lifted the first weight, the subject is "set" for a certain effort on the next try. If the second weight is lifted quickly and easily, it will feel lighter than the first; if it comes up more slowly, it will feel heavier. Expectancy, or set, is often invoked in efforts to explain the size-weight illusion, in which a large cardboard box feels lighter than a smaller box even though both weigh the same.

Weight
perception

Olfactory intensity. Smell (olfactory) discrimination is influenced by any odour to which the olfactory structures already have adapted. Receptors in the nose, however, adapt quickly and cease to respond to a particular stimulus producing so-called olfactory fatigue. Thus, an odour that is strong at first will gradually become imperceptible, as happens when one becomes unaware of the smell of his own body. There may also be present the phenomenon of masking; this is a decrease in sensitivity to one odour after exposure to another (for example, a strong-smelling disinfectant).

Loudness illusions. The human ear typically serves to distinguish between about 1,500 levels of pitch. For loudness, differential-threshold studies reveal about 325 separately perceived levels in the region of greatest auditory sensitivity (about 1,000 to 4,000 cycles per second). The number of discriminable tones is in the hundred thousands. When two sounds are heard in close succession (time error once more) the intensity or loudness of the second is judged by comparing it with the first. Thus, a murmur may sound loud when compared to a whisper, or a "deafening" noise may make all other sounds inaudible. The hum of an electric fan may help to diffuse the street noises of traffic and thus improve the discrimination of sounds in the room.

Intersensory effects. Normally, the senses combine to produce a kind of common, unitary, or integrated perceptual experience. In dining, for example, the visual array on the table, the conversational tones or background music, the tactile sensations, aromas, and taste of the food, all combine to enhance the gustatory experience with each sense (*e.g.,* sight, hearing) contributing to it. Physiologically, taste and smell appear to be particularly subject to intersensory effects (interdependent). In other situations, seeing, hearing, touching, and often smelling and tasting are all employed in an intersensory way in object identification or location.

Synesthesia. A "crossing" of the senses, analogous to a short circuit in a radio and called synesthesia, has been reported. "Colour-hearing," in which people say that specific sounds evoke in them the actual experience of certain colours, is relatively frequent. Some musicians and others report that they see particular colours whenever they hear given tones and musical passages; poets sometimes claim to hear sounds or musical tones when they see words, images, and colours. Synesthesia may be induced with drugs, and in rare psychiatric disorders the sufferer may not be able to tell whether he is seeing or hearing.

Intersensory rivalry and facilitation. Stimulation through one sense may enhance the function of another. Seeing a boat rocked by waves may activate the sense of balance in an observer on a pier to the point at which it causes seasickness. A painting of an Arctic scene of frost and snow may evoke the sensation of cold or a shiver that produces gooseflesh. An explosion or gunshots may give a bystander the illusion of being struck; and a picture of appetizing food may evoke sensations of taste and smell.

Sensory rivalry, in which one stimulus inhibits the perception of another, may result from a conflict of cues if sensory information is ambiguous or discrepant, as in the tilted-room experiment, during which the visual sense conflicts with cues from the sense of equilibrium. States of pain, panic, monotony, or fatigue may create conditions in which various senses mask or inhibit each other. A witness of a terrifying sight, for example, may become oblivious to all sounds around him. Distraction can elevate the pain threshold, as in the case of wounded soldiers whose injuries become painful only after the stress of combat subsides. In a similar way, some dentists use auditory analgesia (a "masking" of pain by sound).

Illusions of psychiatric significance. Illusions called pseudohallucinations occur at times when feelings of anxiety or fear are projected on external objects, as when a child perceives threatening faces or monsters in shadows at night or sees hobgoblins in trees. A soldier tense with apprehension may, in his fear, perceive inanimate objects as an attacking enemy or one of his own comrades as the foe. In literature, the character Don Quixote perceived windmills as enemy knights. Psychiatric patients have perceived other people as machines, or as teddy bears, or as devils.

The déjà vu phenomenon is a feeling that a past episode is repeating itself in the present; there is a fusion of past and present to create an illusion that one is reliving an experience and that he therefore knows its outcome. It might be called a "hallucination" of familiarity; some theorists interpret the experience as being based on reactivation of old memory traces by stimuli resembling those experienced in the past in the way that a pressed rose discovered in a long-forgotten dance program, for example, may trigger a flood of old memories (see also MEMORY).

Emotions, compelling associations, or strong expectations frequently cause illusional misperceptions in everyday life. The hostile listener hears someone say "wire" and thinks he is being called a "liar"; the self-consciously obese girl misinterprets the word "fate" as "weight." There is also the mistaken identification of strangers as friends in the street. It is as if John thinks Tom is Dick because he is hoping to see Dick or because he definitely wants to avoid Tom.

THE DEVELOPMENT OF MODERN UNDERSTANDING OF HALLUCINATIONS

Traditional psychiatric sources define hallucinations as "perceptions without corresponding stimuli from without" (Swiss psychiatrist E. Bleuler), or as the "apparent perception of an external object when no such object is present" (L.E. Hinsie and J. Shatzky, *Psychiatric Dictionary,* 1940). A historical survey of the subject of hallucinations clearly reflects the development of scientific thought in psychiatry, psychology, and neurobiology. By 1838 the significant relationship between the content of dreams and of hallucinations had been pointed out. In the 1840s the occurrence of hallucinations under a wide variety of conditions (including psychological and physical stress) as well as their genesis through the effects of such drugs as stramonium and hashish had been described.

A.J.F. Brierre de Boismont, a French physician, in 1845 described many instances of hallucinations associated with intense concentration, or with musing, or simply occurring in the course of psychiatric disorder. In the last half of the 19th century, studies of hallucinations continued. Investigators in France were particularly oriented toward abnormal psychological function, and from this came descriptions of hallucinosis during sleepwalking and related reactions. Perhaps the most simple and yet enduring conceptions were those evolved by Sir Francis Galton in the 1880s, and English neurologist John Hughlings Jackson's formulation of the hallucination as being released or triggered by the nervous system was a milestone along the way.

During the first three decades of the 20th century, a spirited interest in hallucinations continued. Freud's concepts of conscious and unconscious activities added new significance to the content of dreams and hallucinations. It was theorized that infants normally hallucinate the objects and processes that give them gratification. Although the notion has recently been disputed, the "regression" hypothesis (*i.e.,* that hallucinating is a regression, or return, to infantile ways) is still widely employed, especially by those who find it clinically useful. During the same period, others put forth theories that were more broadly biological than Freud's but that had more points in common with Freud than with each other.

The medical and scientific literature has continued to contain many references to hallucinatory phenomena, though for 20 years after 1932 there was a surprising decrease of interest. Attention has been revived by the recent upsurge of work on hallucinogenic drugs.

THE NATURE OF HALLUCINATIONS

The general theory of hallucinations here delineated rests upon two fundamental assumptions. One is that life experiences influence the brain in such a way as to leave in that organ enduring physical changes that have variously been called neural traces, templates, or engrams. Ideas and images are held to derive from the incorporation and activation of these engrams in complex circuits involving nerve cells. Such circuits in the cortex (outer layers) of the brain appear to subserve the neurophysiology of memory, thought, imagination, and fantasy. The emotions associated with these intellectual and perceptual functions seem to be mediated through cortex connections with the deeper parts of the brain (the limbic system or "visceral brain,"

Sounds can evoke visual experiences

Déjà vu

Infantile hallucinations

for example), thus permitting a dynamic interplay between perception and emotion through transactions that appear to take place largely at unconscious levels.

Insofar as conscious awareness can be interpreted neurophysiologically, it is found to be regulated through a general arousal process the influence of which is mediated by the ascending midbrain reticular activating system (a network of nerve cells in the brainstem). Analyses of hallucinations reported by sufferers of neurological disorders and by neurosurgical patients in whom the brain is stimulated electrically have shown the importance of the temporal lobes (at the sides of the brain) to auditory hallucinations, for example, and of other functionally relevant parts of the brain in this process.

Interaction of internal and external stimuli

A second basic assumption is that the total human personality is best understood in terms of the constant interplay of forces that continually emanate from inside (as internal physiological activity) and from outside the individual (as sensory stimuli). Such transactions between the environment and the individual may be said to exert an integrating and organizing influence upon memory traces stored in the nervous system and to affect the patterns in which sensory engrams are activated to produce experiences called images, fantasies, dreams, or hallucinations, as well as the emotions associated with these patterns. If such a constantly shifting balance exists between internal and external environmental forces, both physiological considerations (e.g., brain function) and cultural, experiential factors emerge as major determinants of the content and meaning of hallucinations.

The brain is bombarded constantly by sensory impulses, but most of these are excluded from consciousness in a dynamically shifting, selective fashion. The exclusion seems to be accomplished through the exercise of integrative inner mechanisms that permit the limited field of one's awareness to hold selected parts of potential experience in clear focus. (The sound of a ticking clock, for example, fades in and out of awareness.) These mechanisms somehow must simultaneously survey previously stored information within the brain, select tiny samples needed to give adaptive significance to the incoming flow of information from the environment, and bring forth only a few items for actual recall from the brain's enormous "memory banks."   (L.J.W.)

Attention. Thus, the work of concentration or attention may be defined as a scanning and screening process, tending to keep out of consciousness what is not needed or wanted. Theoretically, this work involves an activity akin to information retrieval in digital computers (called "secondary process" thinking by Freud), which employs mainly the associative memory functions of the most recently evolved parts of the brain cortex. It may be contrasted with the way in which unconscious, instinctual, and emotional (analogue) information processing (Freud's "primary process" thinking) primarily involves functions of the parts of the brain that appeared much earlier in evolution. In conditions of psychological health, these primary and secondary functions seem highly integrated with each other. There is evidence that in dreams, delirium, or major psychiatric disorder (e.g., schizophrenia), images, feelings, thoughts, and perceptions become dissociated from each other, and fragments of information arising within the brain itself are confused with information coming in from the external environment.

Primary and secondary functions

During normal wakefulness, the input of information through the sensory pathways serves a basic function in maintaining the organization of scanning and screening activity. As long as it is working well, the brain mechanism of scanning and screening seems to exclude from awareness not only information from the internal and external environments that is undesired or has low priority but also the vast bulk of information already stored within the brain in the form of neural traces, their derivations, and interrelations. Some of this information can be brought deliberately into awareness. (One readily recalls his address when asked, for example.) Many children and a few adults can screen in and scan perceptual memory traces with great clarity, thereby permitting eidetic ("photographic") or near-eidetic imagery.

Reduced sensory activity. When, as in sleep, sensory input is diminished, distorted, or impaired, its organizing effect upon the screening and scanning mechanism tends to decrease. Simultaneously, as a rule, there is a decrease in the stimulating effect of sensory input on the ascending midbrain reticular activating system (through connections from the major incoming sensory pathways, such as tactual structures, passing through the brainstem), and, as a result, arousal and awareness diminish. Under a variety of circumstances, however, great reduction or impairment of sensory input may be accompanied by a residual awareness of considerable degree. In such instances, when the usual information-input level no longer suffices completely to inhibit their emergence, ordinarily quiescent perceptual traces stored in the brain may be activated or "released" and re-experienced. Released perceptions of this sort do not ordinarily become conscious with hallucinatory vividness. In order for them to emerge even into clear awareness, there must be a sufficient general level of arousal for awareness to occur, and the particular perception-bearing brain circuits must trigger and reverberate sufficiently to command awareness.

A sustained level and variety of sensory input normally contributes to the process that inhibits the emergence of reactivated memory traces from within the brain. When effective (attention-commanding) sensory input decreases sufficiently, there may be a release into awareness of previously recorded perceptions through disinhibition of the brain circuits that represent them. If a sufficient level of cortical arousal persists or is stimulated in any one of several ways, these released perceptions can enter awareness and be experienced as fantasies, illusions, visions, dreams, or hallucinations. The greater the level of arousal, the more vivid the hallucinations will be.

INDUCTION OF HALLUCINATIONS

Direct brain stimulation. Hallucinatory experiences can be brought about through direct stimulation of the exposed brain, as in cases of local cortical arousal under the neurosurgeon's stimulating electrode. Under circumstances other than surgery or such situations as, for example, some forms of epilepsy, however, there must be a decrease in the forces that ordinarily dominate consciousness (and inhibit the release of recorded percepts) before hallucinations occur. These inhibiting forces require for their maintenance a relatively high level of sensory input of appropriate quality and frequency.

Sleep. The ways in which the reticular network of cells in the brainstem acts as a regulatory and integrating system for these relationships remain under intensive study. Since levels of brain arousal during sleep and wakefulness also are mediated via reticular formation activity, sleeping and dreaming merit consideration as hallucinatory activities. As a person falls asleep, he passes through a period of "partial sleep" in which awareness of the environment drops rapidly but in which the level of cortical arousal (which falls less rapidly) remains sufficiently high to permit some appreciation of external stimulation. Thus, the so-called hypnagogic phenomena occur.

Dreams and hallucinations

Hypnagogic hallucinations. Common hypnagogic hallucinations may be visual (e.g., scenes from the previous few hours appear) or auditory (e.g., one seems to hear his name called). A frequently occurring hypnagogic hallucination is the sensation of loss of support or balance, perhaps accompanied by a fragmentary "dream" of falling, followed immediately by a jerking reflex recovery movement (the myoclonic jerk) that may jolt the sleeper back into wakefulness.

Dreams. The first stages of sleep appear to be dream free, the sleeper producing large, slow brain waves that may be recorded with a device called the electroencephalograph (EEG.) Sensory stimuli from without (e.g., noise, cold) or stimuli from within the body (e.g., dyspepsia, anxiety), plus a somewhat regular spontaneous fluctuation in the depth of sleep, periodically (perhaps every 90 minutes or so) bring the sleeper into a state that favours perceptual release, in which case dreaming tends to take place. This state (with specific EEG signs and rapid movements of the closed eyes) probably occurs several times every night, so that more than 20 percent of an average person's sleep is taken up with several dreams, each of about 10 to 15 minutes' duration. At the time of awakening, the typical sleeper again passes through a period of perceptual release, often experiencing dreams that increase in intensity, and perhaps may have the hallucinations of "partial sleep," these now being called hypnopompic experiences.

A simplified but perhaps helpful way of characterizing these conditions might be to imagine a person standing at a window opposite a fireplace, looking out at a garden in the sunset. He is so absorbed by the view of the outside world that he fails to visualize the interior of the room at all. As it becomes darker outside, images of the objects in the room behind him are reflected dimly in the window glass. For a time he may see either the garden (if he gazes into the distance) or the reflection of the room's interior (if he focusses on the glass). Night falls, but the fire still illuminates the room. The watcher now sees in the glass a reflection of the interior of the room behind him, which appears to be outside the window. This illusion becomes dimmer as the fire dies down, and, finally, when it is dark both outside and within, nothing more is seen. If the fire flares up from time to time, the visions in the glass reappear.

In an analogous way, hallucinatory experiences such as those of normal dreams occur when the "daylight" (sensory input) is reduced while the "interior illumination" (general level of brain arousal) remains "bright," and images originating within the "rooms" of our brains may be perceived (hallucinated) as though they came from outside the "windows" of our senses.

Another analogy might be that dreams, like the stars, are shining all the time. Though the stars are not often seen by day, since the sun shines too brightly, if, during the day, there is an eclipse of the sun, or if a viewer chooses to be watchful awhile after sunset or awhile before sunrise, or if he is awakened from time to time on a clear night to look at the sky, then the stars, like dreams, though often forgotten, may always be seen.

A more brain-related concept is that of a continuous information-processing activity (a kind of "preconscious stream") that is influenced continually by both conscious and unconscious forces and that constitutes the potential supply of dream content. The dream is an experience during which, for a few minutes, the individual has some awareness of the stream of data being processed. Hallucinations in the waking state also would involve the same phenomenon, produced by a somewhat different set of psychological or physiological circumstances.

Excessive excitation. It is valuable to consider the probable relationship between the level of physiological arousal in the brain and information processing during the waking state. The functions of consciousness apparently reach an optimal point in relation to level of arousal, beyond which they disorganize progressively as arousal increases. The presence of marked arousal (produced, for example, by extreme anxiety or by chemical stimulation of the brain) is accompanied by marked disturbance of concentration. Again, contact with external stimuli is impaired, this time by excessive input that "jams the circuits," in which case spontaneous dissociative experiences may occur. As arousal increases further, the hallucinations of full-blown delirium or psychotic excitement may appear with frightening vividness, intensity, and emotional accompaniment. Greater brain arousal might result in generalized seizure phenomena, as in epilepsy.

Sensory deprivation. When people are kept in isolation (sensory deprivation), information input via the senses (*e.g.,* hearing and sight) is depatterned or reduced. If such a person remains alert, he is likely to experience vivid fantasies and perhaps hallucinations. A slight amount of stimulation of the hallucinated sense may enhance the likelihood of the hallucination's appearance. If stimuli are markedly reduced and the level of arousal is high, the hallucinations can be especially vivid and emotionally charged.

Loss of sleep. Progressive sleep loss appears to decrease one's capacity for integrating perceptions of the external environment. Hallucinations probably will occur in any-

one if wakefulness is sufficiently prolonged; anxiety is likely to hasten or to enhance hallucinatory production. The disorganizing effect of excessive wakefulness has been exploited in extorting confessions from prisoners. Observations suggest that fleeting hallucinations typically begin after two or three days without sleep, and that after 100 to 200 sleepless hours a progressive personality disorganization will develop, marked by periods of hallucinosis or, in some cases, by the reappearance of a previously existing psychiatric disorder.

Hypnosis and trance states. The mystic achieves hallucinations by gaining control of his own dissociative mechanisms; perhaps this is a form of self-hypnosis. Such individuals can accomplish an astonishing withdrawal from the environment by prolonged intense concentration (*e.g.,* by gazing at some object). The hallucinations may be of the type in which the person perceives his "inner self" to leave his body to view himself (autoscopic hallucination) or to be transported to new surroundings. Alternatively, the hallucinations may take the form of unique visual imagery; for example, the *yantra* is a visual hallucination of a coloured, geometrical image that appears at a level of trance of the sort experienced by practitioners of Yoga. The recurrence of certain designs and patterns in human hallucinatory experience is probably related to structural aspects of the visual system. The *yantra*

Ordinary experimental hypnotic and posthypnotic suggestions of hallucinations are well known. The hypnotic subject (who can be described as a person in a controlled dissociative state) may on occasion also experience spontaneous hallucinations in the absence of specific suggestions.

Prolonged monotony or fixation of attention may lead to diminished responsiveness to the environment with a general effect similar to that of absolute reduction of stimulation or of hypnotic trance. Under these conditions such dissociative phenomena as "highway hypnosis" among drivers of motor vehicles may occur. Similar phenomena that occur among aviators have been called fascination or fixation. During prolonged, monotonous flight, pilots may experience visual, auditory, and bodily (kinesthetic) hallucinations; for example, one may suddenly feel that his plane is in a spin or a dive or that it is upside down, even though it is flying level. A kinesthetic hallucination such as this can be so vivid that the pilot will attempt "corrective" manoeuvring of the aircraft, with potentially tragic results.

Sensory defects. Many other examples of hallucinations related to decrease or impairment of sensory input are known in clinical medicine. Visual hallucinations may occur in cases of cataract (opaque lens in the eye) and have been compared with phantom limb experiences (*e.g.,* "pain" in the toes of a missing foot), since there is an absence of normal stimuli from the environment in both cases. Individuals who suffer a progressive loss of hearing may experience auditory hallucinations. A case of combined visual and auditory hallucinations in a patient with progressive blindness (from cataracts) and with deafness from ear disease (otosclerosis) has been observed. Hallucinations of the phantom limb probably arise as the projection of an experientially established set of brain engrams in the absence of long-accustomed sensory input from the missing part. Differences in nerve impulses from those once produced by a missing limb may cause the phantom to be perceived as being distorted in proportion or in size. Hallucination of a phantom limb

Psychological factors. Although the role of expectation (mental set) continues to be studied in relation to perception, there can be no doubt of the significance of psychological factors in determining the nature of hallucinated objects. It may be that the psychophysiologic basis for recognition requires the unconscious preparation of a perceptual engram (the physically stored memory of a previously seen object, for example) against which to match incoming sensory information for identification, significance, and meaning in terms of past experience. If some external object is present but inadequately recognized, an incorrect perceptual engram may be activated to be experienced as an illusion; in the absence of an external stimulus, such an engram is perceived as a hallucination. This may account for the specificity of collective visions *(i.e.,* those shared by more than one person). Among lifeboat survivors at sea, for example, several people who share similar expectancies (mental sets) may see a nonexistent ship projected against the blank screen of empty sea and sky. Such an experience may persist in some of the people even after a logical belief in its impossibility has been communicated to all.

Multiple factors undoubtedly combine in bringing about the psychiatric symptoms of the psychoses; these symptoms often resemble the waking dreams in which hallucinations (usually auditory) may figure prominently. Such additive effects can also be demonstrated among "normal" people in the laboratory; for example, one may readily produce signs of hallucinations among sleep-deprived subjects or among subjects in a state of sensory isolation by administering otherwise subhallucinatory doses of drugs such as LSD or mescaline. In hospital cases of acute psychotic reactions with hallucinosis, combinations of factors clearly can be inferred to be at work: hereditary and cultural predispositions; excessive arousal in anxiety or panic; auto-intoxication (self-poisoning via deranged body physiology) through stress, exhaustion, sleep loss, and dehydration (water loss); and dissociative mechanisms that impair or distort the reception of information from a frightening or threatening social environment.

Chemical factors. Hallucinations may be produced by chemical changes deriving from internal metabolic disturbances that are otherwise engendered inside of the body, or that originate from outside of the body. Some chemicals that produce hallucinatory experiences seem to act by reducing sensory input; for example, dramatic hallucinatory recall of intense experiences from the recent past can be brought about by injections of anesthetic drugs such as sodium amybarbital, which favours the conditions for perceptual release. Hallucinations during induction of (and emergence from) general surgical anesthesia induced by a variety of other chemicals are well-known and can be explained on the same basis.

Such hallucinogenic chemicals seem to impair sensory input by decreasing the transmission of nerve impulses by raising the resistance of the nervous system to their passage. Other hallucinogens increase nerve transmission, disrupting the orderly input of information and "jamming the circuits." Many botanically derived hallucinogens seem to function this way—*e.g.,* LSD (lysergic acid diethylamide) and the ergot (a fungus) that grows on rye, psilocybin from mushrooms, mescaline from the peyote cactus, and tetrahydrocannabinol (THC) from marijuana. Hallucinations also can be induced by jamming the circuits through input overload produced mechanically, bombarding several sensory systems with intense stimuli simultaneously (*e.g.,* with bright flashing lights and loud noises).

Hallucinogenic drugs are substances that, administered in pharmacological doses (not toxic overdoses), create gross distortions in perception without causing loss of consciousness. These distortions frequently include hallucinations. Such compounds also are likely to exert profound effects on mood, thought, and observable behaviour. These resemble (or mimic) the disturbances generated in spontaneously occurring psychoses; indeed some hallucinogens have been termed "psychotomimetic" or "psychotogenic" on this account.

Research scientists and clinicians such as psychiatrists have sometimes deliberately taken these compounds in efforts to understand how it feels to be a severely psychiatric **Self-exper-** patient. It has been hoped that the study of such chemi- **imentation** cally induced "model psychoses" would lead to improved methods of treatment. In addition, some psychiatric workers speak of "psychedelic" (mind-manifesting) substances, controversially held to expand perceptual horizons and insight among a variety of people under treatment for such disorders as alcoholism, rigid personality patterns, and sexual frigidity.

The potentially dangerous psychological changes produced by psychedelic chemicals have sometimes been interpreted as "loosening ego structures," "dissolving ego boundaries," or "disrupting ego defenses." Such changes may include the experiencing of thoughts, feelings, and perceptions that are usually outside the individual's awareness ("unconscious" or "repressed"). Persons who take such drugs (*e.g.,* LSD) may become hypersuggestible, emotionally labile (unstable), and unusually aware of their own reactions and those of others. Feelings of transcendence of ordinary experience, distortions in time perception (*e.g.,* time may seem to slow down), and hallucinations have also been reported.

It appears that all human behaviour and experience (normal as well as abnormal) is well attended by illusory and hallucinatory phenomena. While the relationship of these phenomena to mental illness has been well documented, their role in everyday life has perhaps not been considered enough. Greater understanding of illusions and hallucinations among normal people may provide explanations for experiences otherwise relegated to the uncanny, "extrasensory," or supernatural. Such understanding may also illuminate the remarkable certainty that individuals express in their contrary interpretations of the same basic information. "Reality," like beauty, lies in the eye of the beholder.

(L.J.W./Ed.)

BIBLIOGRAPHY. For a clear presentation of Gestalt theory and its case against structuralism and behaviourism, see w. KOHLER, *Gestalt Psychology* (1959). A comprehensive historical overview is available in E.G. BORING, *Sensation and Perception in the History of Experimental Psychology* (1942). Illustrations and discussions of Gestalt principles of organization along with material on illusions, context effects, and related phenomena are provided in W.N. DEMBER, *The Psychology of Perception* (1960); J.J. GIBSON, *The Perception of the Visual World* (1950); and J.E. HOCHBERG, *Perception* (1964). Implications of research on early experience for perceptual and intellectual development are spelled out in J.M. HUNT, *Intelligence and Experience* (1961). Two excellent collections of technical articles on perception, covering a wide range of topics, have been compiled and edited by R.N. HABER: *Contemporary Theory and Research in Visual Perception* (1968), and *Information-Processing Approaches to Visual Perception* (1969). For a scholarly discussion of depth perception and a lucid description of an elegant series of experiments, see B. JULESZ, *Foundations of Cyclopean Perception* (1971). The potential contributions of neurophysiological research to an understanding of perception are suggested in N. WEISSTEIN, "What the Frog's Eye Tells the Human Brain: Single Cell Analyzers in the Human Visual System," *Psychol. Bull.* 72:157–176 (1969).

P. FRAISSE, *Psychologie du temps* (1957; Eng. trans., *The Psychology of Time,* 1963), provides the most complete synthesis of the psychological works on time. A comparison with M. STURT, *The Psychology of Time* (1925), shows how this problem has developed and evolved. The collective works edited by J.T. FRASER, *The Voices of Time* (1966); and R. FISHER, "Interdisciplinary Perspectives of Time," *Ann. N.Y. Acad. Sci.,* vol. 138, article 2 (1967), present the most varied aspects of the problem of time, ranging from religious conceptions to scientific data from physics and biology. E. BUNNING, *The Physiological Clock* (1964), provides a very sound study of the problems of the temporal regulation of organisms. The point of view of genetic epistemology is developed by JEAN PIAGET, *Le développement de la notion de temps chez l'enfant* (1946; Eng. trans., *The Child's Conception of Time,* 1969).

Descriptive reviews of the literature on perceptual learning have appeared at intervals in the *Annual Review of Psychology,* particularly the articles by J.D. DREVER (1960); E.J. GIBSON (1963); and J.F. WOHLWILL (1966). A more extensive review and evaluation of the diverse phenomena and theoretical formulations may be found in W. EPSTEIN, *Varieties of Perceptual Learning* (1967). A major publication is E.J. GIBSON, *Principles of Perceptual Learning and Development* (1969), an examination of the field from the viewpoint of the discovery theory of perceptual learning.

Works on the psychology of illusion and hallucination include A. BRIERRE DE BOISMONT, *Des hallucinations . . . ,* 2nd ed. (1852; Eng. trans., *Hallucinations: Or, the Rational History of Apparitions, Dreams, Ecstacy, Magnetism, and Somnambulism* (1853), an early classic; S. TOLANSKY, *Optical Illusions* (1964), most of the known visual illusions illustrated, in one of the few modern books on this subject; W. GREY WALTER, *The Neurophysiological Aspects of Hallucinations and Illusory Experience* (1960), visual phenomena viewed by a brain researcher; and L.J. WEST (ed.), *Hallucinations* (1962), an analysis of the subject by contributors from several scientific disciplines.

(L.J.W.)

Personality

Theories of human personality presumably have existed in some form ever since men began to speculate about why people act as they do. The term personality has been given many meanings, but at the core of all of them the reference is to the organization of traits or characteristics within the individual. There are two emphases in this identification of the concept of personality: the individual shares his characteristics (*e.g.*, happiness or ugliness) in common with other people; and each individual is distinguished from all others on the basis of his unique combination of these characteristics and of the degree to which he manifests them.

To suggest that there is a single widely accepted definition of the term personality, however, is misleading. A definition commonly encountered in many textbooks on the subject is comprehensive, defining personality as the sum total of the characteristics of the individual. In contrast, an alternative definition is implied in the everyday practice of suggesting that a person "has a lot of personality," in which usage the reference is to positive, desirable characteristics that give a person social competence and attractiveness. The latter popular definition, which is evaluative, has received relatively little use in the scholarly consideration of theories of personality.

The fullest range of ideas about personality pervades the literary, legal, religious, and philosophical literature about man, just as there are myriad assumptions about what constitutes the nature of man. The notion that whole peoples (*e.g.*, ethnic or racial groups) differ in basic personality characteristics is common; the resulting study of culture and personality in modern times has received attention especially among anthropologists. Fundamental definitions and principles underlying this type of scientific pursuit, however, were clearly enunciated in the writings of the German psychologist Wilhelm Wundt in the mid-19th century. More journalistic forms of ethnic-group personality description are found in earlier writings and essays dating as far back as known history; the ancient Romans, for example, recorded a great variety of personality traits held to be characteristic of the barbarian peoples who lived in the borderlands of the military empire of the Caesars. In more recent journalistic and fictional literature, there are still to be found assertions such as that the French (as an entire people) are volatile, that the Italians are hot-blooded, that the Scandinavians are phlegmatic, and so forth; such statements bear implications that alleged group differences in personality are hereditary rather than being based on culture. Indeed, in the discussion of scientific efforts to establish personality types (which follows below), it should be noted that some human types are defined in terms of heritable bodily characteristics. Since such bodily traits are found to be associated with geographical location, it may be that assertions of ethnic or national tendencies to manifest specific personality traits are not necessarily farfetched.

Assumptions about the nature of man that are commonly found as aspects of religious, moral, and philosophical writings often assume a model of man based on selected qualities; these may be drawn from myths of human origins or from the characteristics attributed to local gods. Thus, in some cultures, humans may be said to have the characteristics of "mother earth," from whom they are believed to spring. Or humans may be portrayed as having both good and evil in them, corresponding to good spirits and bad spirits held to exist in some religions. Often in the religions of technologically advanced peoples, these characteristics are outlined in great detail in sacred writings, and inferences about the nature of men may be drawn from examples and incidents recorded in these writings. Thus, the personality model of a saviour (*e.g.*, the Messiah) may imply both the good example and the bad contrast, with emphasis being placed on the socially important aspects of behaviour. Distinctions among unobservable internal "entities" (*e.g.*, "mind," "spirit," "conscience," "true self") may be contrasted with manifest (observable) behaviour, and there may be considerable controversy about problems of moral and behavioral conflict.

Historically, the precursors of the 19th-century study of personality theory were often concerned with the ultimate or essential nature of man. Drawing from concepts outlined by the ancient Greeks, and from other sources, philosophers of the 1600s and 1700s speculated about human personality and went into theoretical detail at times about human perception and personality traits or dispositions. In the writings of the 18th-century economist Adam Smith, philosophical notions of human personality are postulated with great specificity. Smith's theory of man as an economic creature ("economic man") required him to assert the primacy of particular characteristics of personality (*e.g.*, greed) for his analysis to have any basis.

In the paragraphs that follow, some emphasis is placed on formulations of human personality that have been advanced as theories (that is, as more or less speculative guesses). This does not mean, however, that concern with the objective, nontheoretical aspects of personality is not pervasive in society. The behaviour of every person involves some guessing about associates and family and acting according to these hypotheses. Legal rules, drawn to regulate social behaviour, imply definitions and expectations about "normal" personality, about what may happen in an undesirable ("abnormal") way, and are designed to limit such classes of unwanted behaviour. The nature of man thus is the urgent concern of lawmakers, and in relatively sophisticated legal systems there is considerable concern with defining the personality of a legally accountable, responsible person.

This article is divided into the following sections:

The nature of personality

TYPE THEORIES OF PERSONALITIES

Classical biochemical theories. Theories of personality invariably involve some notions of types (or classes) of people, if only because particular aspects of the person (*e.g.*, his appearance or his mood) are stressed in describing his unique structure and function. Any rigid classification of people into specific personality types might seem to suggest that a given person must fall into one class only, and that he is distinctly, qualitatively unlike others who exhibit different personality types. Such a rigid point of view is an oversimplification of the observable evidence. Though the degree of specificity with which personality types are advanced may vary considerably, the convenience that derives from thinking of persons as being of one distinct personality type or another has been appealing to many theorists. Since there are so many descriptive terms that relate to personality in any given language, the potential variety of type theories is enormous. A theory offered by ancient Greek physicians focussed on the emotional (temperamental) attributes of human personality and was based on a relatively primitive understanding of human biology (specifically, bodily physiology), which prevailed at that time. According to these early theorists, emotional equilibrium (indeed, general health) depended on an appropriate balance among four fluids (humours) within the body: blood, black bile, yellow bile, and phlegm. It was held that an excess of one of the humours would be reflected in bodily illness and in exaggerated personality traits. Thus, if a person had an excess of blood, he was expected to have a sanguine temperament; that is, to be optimistic, enthusiastic, and excitable. The modern term hot-blooded may be a survival of this Greek theory of human personality; the notion was so influential that for many centuries physicians throughout the Western world continued the practice of bleeding people who suffered from medical and psychiatric disorders.

The four humours

Too much black bile (congealed blood from the spleen) was believed to produce a melancholic temperament. The term melancholia literally means black bile, and there are literary allusions to venting one's spleen. When someone was oversupplied with yellow bile (the yellow-green gall secreted by the liver and stored in the gall bladder), he was held to become choleric; that is, to be angry, irritable, and to view his world with a jaundiced eye. Jaundice remains in modern medical language as a disease of the liver or gall bladder in which bile is present in the body to such a degree that the eyeballs and body may turn yellow. Finally, with an abundance of the humour called phlegm, people were supposed to become stolid, apathetic, and undemonstrative; that is, to grow phlegmatic.

As biological science has progressed, these primitive concepts of body chemistry have been replaced by more subtle and complex biological theories of personality. Thus, the chemical factors associated with given psychological dispositions are now more likely to be understood in terms of hormones (as from the thyroid gland), nerve impulses, and so-called psychotropic drugs such as tranquillizers.

Morphological theories. Somewhat less subtle than the biochemical theories of personality are those that distinguish different classes of people through relatively gross characteristics of bodily build (shape or morphology). A morphological theory developed by a German psychiatrist, Ernst Kretschmer (1888–1964), is possibly the most widely known. Kretschmer distinguished three types of bodily structure (somatotypes). What he called the pyknic type was characterized by a thick trunk, short limbs, and a tendency to put on weight, especially with increasing age. According to his observations in the psychiatric hospital where he worked, sufferers of major fluctuations in mood (so-called manic-depressive psychotics, or extreme cyclothymic personalities) were more likely to show the pyknic somatotype than were other inmates. By contrast, Kretschmer delineated an asthenic (leptosomic) body type, characteristically displaying a slim trunk, long legs, and a tendency to be tall and lean. These leptosomes tended to appear temperamentally withdrawn or introverted and seemed more prone than other people to develop symptoms of a group of psychiatric disorders now labelled schizophrenia (see MENTAL DISORDERS). The so-called athletic somatotype, with broad shoulders and slim hips, while no less susceptible to psychiatric disturbance, apparently favoured neither schizophrenia nor the manic-depressive psychosis.

Kretschmer's body types

Despite early hopes that somatotypes might be useful in diagnosing personality characteristics or in identifying psychiatric difficulties, the relationships observed by Kretschmer were not found to be sufficiently clear-cut for practical application. Subsequent and much more elaborate studies reported in the 1940s in the United States also yielded three somatotypes: endomorphy (roughly pyknic

with similar temperament called viscerotonia); ectomorphy (crudely equivalent to Kretschmer's asthenics, and temperamentally characterized as cerebrotonic); and mesomorphy (comparable to the athletic body type, and called somatotonic in temperament).

This system did not serve practical needs any more effectively than had Kretschmer's, even though it had been based on much more painstaking work. Other theories of personality based on physical characteristics such as head shape (physiognomy) and bumps on the skull (phrenology), have not received much serious attention in the 20th century. Nevertheless, structural differences in the body do seem to have some relation to such aspects of personality as intelligence and emotion. In a form of mental deficiency called Down's syndrome, for example, distinctive "Asian" facial features and squat bodily structure are readily recognizable even to untrained observers.

ANALYTIC AND SOCIAL THEORIES

Psychoanalytic theories. *Freud.* Freud's psychoanalytic theories of personality have been among the most influential in the modern era of psychological study. The interest they attract stems in part from Freud's efforts to address himself to the practical problems of dealing with psychiatric disturbances, an orientation quite different from that typically found among academic psychologists. Freud wrote on so many different questions in attempting to explain the origins of psychiatric disorders that it is still difficult to put him in proper historical perspective. Freud's contributions have received many divergent interpretations, and many of his ideas are now viewed as models, suggestions, and intellectual metaphors.

In Freud's view, human personality has three components: the id, the ego, and the superego, each of which is said to have a unity of its own. The behaviour of the individual is said to be the consequence of the interaction of these three components. The id is seen as the original "structure" of the personality system, consisting of inborn, primitive, inherited characteristics or tendencies. It is depicted as the initial source of psychological energy, from which the ego and the superego develop. The id is associated with what Freud called the "pleasure principle," reflected in the tendency of the person to maintain a pleasant, tolerable energy level through the relief of inner tension. The "pleasure principle" may be described as applying to the activities of the individual in achieving pleasure and avoiding pain. Thus, the loud crying of a hungry infant is called an id activity, it being assumed that the baby is responding to his inborn tendency to avoid the discomfort of an empty stomach.

Id, ego, and superego

The ego, associated with the "reality principle," is held to develop from the id so that the individual can negotiate realistically with the objective world. The infant who experiences pain on touching a hot object is said to be developing his ego (reality contact) by learning to avoid the object. Thinking realistically enables one to satisfy his primitive needs and thus serves as a secondary means for tension reduction. The ego is portrayed as controlling intellectual and perceptual functions (the so-called higher mental processes) involved in the control of behaviour. The ego is held to be coordinated to satisfy the inborn instincts (implicit in the id) but primarily to be oriented in a direction that serves to maintain the individual comfortably in relation to his environment.

The superego was theorized by Freud to be the third segment of the personality to develop and to represent the person's adoption (internalization) of social values; *e.g.,* the table manners he learns from his parents. Morality is said to be incorporated into the superego, which is supposed to evaluate the correctness of one's behaviour from the point of view of the standards of society. What is called conscience is held to be manifested by part of the superego. This theoretical division of the personality is seen to function in controlling sexual and aggressive impulses that derive from the id. With regard to the ego, the superego is held to impose "higher" moral goals as substitutes for "lower" realistic (ego) aims. In general, the superego might be said to represent the behavioral ideal. Freud's view of personality rests firmly on his theory of *Triebe* (German: "needs," "drives," "urges," or "instincts"), with biological factors conceived as giving the driving force to the personality through the id. This source of psychic energy is said to be manifested as the person's wishes (corresponding to specific needs). *Triebe* are said to be of two types: (1) so-called life instincts, including the primary drives of sex, hunger, and thirst, are identified with Freud's term libido (or life energy). The orientation of the personality system is theorized to be directed toward satiation of these instincts. The psychic (libidinal) energy involved can also be dissipated by alternate means; expending energy in this substitute way is known as sublimation or displacement. (2) Correspondingly, there are said to be death instincts, of which an important group is labelled the aggressive motives. These id instincts are said to be controlled and harnessed by the ego, which draws psychic energy from them. The ego, as the "manager" of the personality, is crucial in psychoanalytic theory to the understanding of the learning processes involved in identification and displacement.

Critics of Freud's theory of the personality have emphasized its nonexperimental, empirically unverifiable aspects; id, ego, and superego are not observable entities. Some Freudian writings have been criticized as being speculative, imaginative, and unsupportable in any rigorous way.

Jung. Once a follower of Freud's, the Swiss psychiatrist Carl Gustav Jung had a substantial influence in the field of personality theory but did not develop the kind of massive following Freud did. Jung had considerable contact with Freud during the early period of their work, until, beginning in 1914, there were clear signs of a break between them, apparently prompted at least in part by Jung's rejection of Freud's pervasive concern with the sex drive as a basis for psychoanalytic interpretation. Jung agreed with Freud in attaching great importance to unconscious motivations but, unlike Freud, he placed even greater emphasis on interpreting behaviour as consciously purposive and as guided by one's awareness of goals and aspirations.

Jung gave recognition to the biological basis of personality; much in the way of predispositions in human personality is referred to the biological history of man as an animal species. In this context, Jung theorized the inborn existence in each person of a "collective unconscious" that represents one's inherited accumulation of "memories" of ancestral experience dating from the earliest prehistoric man. The emphasis of this concept is on the common biological heritage that a species develops, all men being said to share a similar physical structure and correspondingly similar potential for behaviour.

In Jung's theory of personality, the ego constitutes the conscious "mind," reflected in the person's own feelings of self-identity. In addition (beyond the "collective unconscious"), Jung proposed for each person a "personal unconscious" in which one's unique, individual history of experience resides.

Jung agreed with Freud in holding that the effects of prior experiences that have been pushed back (repressed) out of consciousness may be drawn from the "personal unconscious." Jung's theory is full of historical, speculative, and imaginative references and analogues; his notion of personality as persona, for example, derives from the ancient (Etruscan?) name for the masks worn by actors. In this sense, personality is conceived as the mask the individual advances in maintaining his conventional place in society. As persona, personality is seen to be one's public presentation of himself in a manner likely to be socially acceptable. Jung also held persona to be consistent with the primordial images (archetypes) drawn from the "collective unconscious," which theoretically serve as the repository of ancestral memories. The reappearance of deluge, or flood, myths (*e.g.,* that of Noah and the ark) in many different cultures was offered by Jung as evidence for a common set of archetypes shared by all people.

Adler. While the writings of Freud and Jung may be contrasted with more experimentally grounded, so-called eclectic scientific theories of personality, many other authors were strongly influenced by Freudian and Jungian notions. More recent analytic theories have tended to stress social factors, emphasizing the malleability of the individ-

ual and the effects of social experience on the formation of his personality. Some theories, such as the "Individual Psychology" of Alfred Adler, an Austrian psychiatrist who at one time was an associate of Freud and Jung, gave little or no weight to sexual and archetypal motives. Adler's theory of personality is known for its emphasis on a human "drive to power" (superiority) and on the importance of conscious (rather than unconscious) activities. Adler believed that all individuals must cope with feelings of inferiority, and he stressed compensatory processes (*e.g.,* as exhibited by the short person who compensates by being aggressive). In striving for social acceptance and influence, the person was seen as constantly struggling toward the goal of self-realization.

Social analytic theories. Most of the socially oriented analytic theories of personality are relatively recent; these theories are not basically experimental, having arisen largely in clinical settings and from intuitive thinking. To the extent that they have removed the conceptual rigidities and mysticism of the Freudian fountainhead from which they were largely drawn, such theories have tended to gain acceptance more readily among academic, empirically oriented psychologists such as Henry A. Murray, whose system for defining and measuring the strength of human needs has influenced research extensively. The study of what Murray called need-achievement, for example, is a major emphasis among social psychologists who seek to subject human behaviour to objective, statistical analysis.

Murray's list of human needs shows considerable correspondence to sets of personality characteristics that have been delineated through the painstaking statistical analysis of the responses given by large groups of people to items on personality tests. Theories such as Murray's were generated in much broader investigative contexts than was the case for their Freudian forebear. Thus, Murray sought to adapt his theory to a wide range of research data from psychological, anthropological, and sociological studies. He particularly worked toward the quantitative, empirical validation of his speculative concepts, constructing the *Thematic Apperception Test* (see below *Personality assessment*) in an effort to translate his concerns with unconscious and other subtle motivational aspects of personality into measurable dimensions.

In the view of personality presented by the U.S. psychologist Gordon W. Allport, each individual is seen as a unique, qualitatively different (idiographic) entity. Allport initiated efforts to measure morality or values in personality and helped to develop a well-known personality inventory called the Allport-Vernon-Lindzey Study of Values. He viewed human behaviour as being motivated by relatively stable personality characteristics, or traits; his theorizing tended to be eclectic and to be compatible with clearly defined scientific tradition. Allport also is known for the introduction of such concepts as that of functional autonomy, which describes the tendency of learned motives to be self-sustaining long after the historic reason for them has ceased to exist. Thus, an adult neurotic who suffers from an abnormal fear of heights (acrophobia) may have learned the trait as an infant by responding to the anxious behaviour of oversolicitous parents. Long after the parental signs of alarm have ceased, often long after the parents have died, the acrophobia persists as a functionally autonomous personality characteristic.

RECENT ECLECTIC THEORIES

Contemporary personality study is characterized by a tendency of investigators to interpret their research findings on the basis of the eclectic use of many theories rather than in terms of a single, universally applicable, "grand" theory of personality. This practice may seem to support conclusions that the discipline of personality study suffers from comparative scientific immaturity, even though it has a rich history dating back to the earliest recorded human cultures (see PSYCHOLOGY). Lay people and workers in other fields who are not aware of the various developments in the growth of academic psychology and sociology may not realize that many topics in personality theory were well developed early in the history of these disciplines. Contributions such as those of the U.S.

psychologist William James, concerning the analysis of human instincts and learned behaviour, are reasonably well known.

Role theories. Monumental and incisive work on the development of human personality that was the contribution of an American, James Mark Baldwin, is less known, even among modern investigators and clinicians. Baldwin developed what can be described as a behaviourist theory of personality socialization and had an important influence on the U.S. sociologist Charles Horton Cooley. Cooley's *Human Nature and the Social Order* (1902) provided for a generation an eclectic and more or less scientifically respectable introduction to a social psychology focussed on the individual and his social behaviour. This tradition led to further elaboration and theoretical development in the description of learning processes through which the human infant is brought into society and develops the behavioral characteristics of a socially active person. This particular behaviouristic orientation has been associated with the concept that much social interaction has symbolic meaning to the participants, particularly in the social roles they play. So-called role theory has not yet produced a coherent body of empirically based generalizations; still, proponents of this approach (the study of personality as social role playing, as persona) have the advantage of being relatively free of the constraints imposed by some rigidly dogmatic theories of personality.

Trait theories. An alternative approach to human personality is found in the work of the British psychologist William McDougall and others who have outlined various classifications of personality traits. Though McDougall once was widely criticized for his use of the term instinct in specifying the driving forces of human personality, the notion of instinct has recaptured considerable respectability in scientific circles. McDougall ordered personality characteristics as primary (inherited) propensities and as secondary (acquired or learned) tendencies. Such a stratification of personality characteristics is common to many theoretical attempts to organize personality traits.

McDougall's notion of instinct

Personality theory drawn directly from the empirical study of human traits has attracted the attention of many psychologists. In part, this movement grew from developments in educational psychology, particularly from progress in the construction of psychological tests. The idea of using tests for measuring intellectual characteristics was well established by their successful use in the psychological screening of military personnel during World War I. By the 1930s the statistical technique called factor analysis (a procedure for the examination of the structure of a test) had stimulated this development. Psychologists published masses of empirical data showing the tests to measure sets of statistically distinct "factors" or behavioral dimensions that could be used to define personality traits. Efforts have been made to demonstrate parallel sets of factors derived from empirical biological data and from psychological tests designed to measure personality traits at the level of verbal behaviour. There has been some debate on the quality of evidence offered to demonstrate psychobiological parallelism (or even unity) in human personality, but there is gross evidence that spectacular personality changes can be induced biologically (*e.g.,* by drugs).

Factor analysis

Factor-analytic studies at times may appear to be exploratory and atheoretical, but intrinsically the theory that underlies them is that of all empirical science. In particular, the theory for these approaches rests on the axiom that there are generalizations about human personality that are empirically discoverable and verifiable. Indeed, agreement in repeated factor-analytic studies of personality measures by independent researchers has been considerable. One approach to the description of personality, for example, is through ratings of an individual by others. Factor-analytic studies of such ratings repeatedly have provided evidence for such generalized personality characteristics as assertiveness, sociability, emotionality, and conscientiousness. Traits based on ratings may be described as those ways in which individuals behave and differ from each other that are reliably discernible to others. This is sometimes taken as the focal definition of what one wants to know about a person; namely, how others see him. The structure of personality as defined at this level is related to the theoretically unimportant approach of symbolic social interaction. According to the symbolic-interaction theorists, the identity of a person is defined by his perception of the responses of others to him; that is, by how he perceives his value as a social stimulus.

In factor-analytic studies of formal measures of personality (*e.g.,* pencil-and-paper personality inventories or tests) there has been less agreement among different investigators in delineating specific human traits. In part this results from the great variety of tests available, and from the many different ways of asking questions of the test taker and of scoring and interpreting his responses. Also, it is not possible to measure all the relevant questions about a person's preferences, attitudes, and values in any one test. Thus, different tests do not necessarily sample the same kinds of behaviour. Additionally, personality-test construction has not been performed by equally sophisticated investigators in all circumstances.

One objective of factor analysis and of related techniques is to reduce the number of dimensions required to account for most of the variation in individual responses to all test items. Thus, a personality inventory with three hundred items may yield evidence for only 10 or 15 personality traits (factors or dimensions) that are relatively distinct (*i.e.,* statistically independent of each other). The traits identified by different investigators often seem to differ. Sometimes these discrepancies may be more apparent than fundamental, however, and may simply result from semantic differences in naming the factor. In other studies the differences seem to indicate basically different personality traits, as revealed when the same set of subjects is used to check two sets of earlier findings.

From the point of view of agreement, however, repeated factor-analytic studies with different personality tests do indicate some traits that emerge with at least a degree of consistency. These have commonly been identified as the dimensions of introversion-extroversion and of social adjustment. Particularly interesting in these findings are the suggested ties to earlier work; for example, Jung's early interest in and emphasis on the introversion–extroversion continuum in accounting for such abnormalities of personality as schizophrenia and the manic-depressive psychosis. Personality inventories based heavily on clinical hunches or intuitions (popular before the advent of more sophisticated test-construction techniques) emphasized concepts of the sort offered by Jung.

Statistical procedures used in the study of personality permit the characteristics of a single individual to be charted over periods of time, yielding evidence as to either the stability or transient nature of some traits. Although the technique is fraught with problems, what is called inverted factor analysis is used to examine the degree to which groups of individuals share the same traits. Thus, individual people take the place of tests or test items in the factor analysis. Investigators who use this technique hope to discover with its help more precise ways of grouping people for such purposes as psychiatric diagnosis.

Inverted factor analysis

The present scientific concerns with the study of personality tend to de-emphasize reliance on general theories of personality and to place more stress on the study of specific empirical aspects of human behaviour. Hopes for developing a universal theory of personality probably are no more realizable than is the dream of a global theory to account for the functioning of the human organism as a biological entity. Apparently, the theory can be no less complex than the organism itself. What constitutes personality theory at any point in time thus depends on a cumulative mass of information, segments of which may be understood in great detail while others may remain to be discovered. (E.F.B./Ed.)

Personality assessment

The measurement of personal characteristics is the subject matter of the field of psychology today called personality assessment. Assessment is an end result of gathering information intended to advance psychological theory and research, and to increase the probability that wise decisions will be made in applied settings (*e.g.*, in selecting the most promising people from a group of job applicants). The approach taken by the specialist in personality assessment is based on the assumption that much of the observable variability in behaviour from one person to another results from differences in the extent to which individuals possess particular underlying personal characteristics (traits). The assessment specialist seeks to define these traits, to measure them objectively, and to relate them to socially significant aspects of behaviour.

A distinctive feature of the scientific approach to personality measurement is the effort, wherever possible, to describe human characteristics in quantitative terms. How much of a trait manifests itself in an individual? How many traits are present? Quantitative personality measurement is especially useful in comparing groups of people as well as individuals. Do groups of persons from different cultural and economic backgrounds differ when considered in the light of their particular personality attributes or traits? How large are the group differences?

Overt behaviour is a reflection of interactions among a wide range of underlying factors, including the bodily state of the individual and the effects of his past personal experiences. Hence, a narrowly focussed approach is inadequate to do justice to the complex human behaviour that occurs under the constantly changing circumstances of everyday life. The sophisticated measurement of human personality inescapably depends on the use of a variety of concepts to provide trait definitions and entails the application of various methods of observation and evaluation. Personality theorists and researchers seek to define and to understand the diversity of human traits, the many ways people have of thinking and perceiving and learning and

Personality constructs

emoting. Such human dimensions, types, and attributes are constructs—in this case, inferences drawn from observed behaviour. Widely studied personality constructs include: anxiety, hostility, emotionality, motivation, and introversion-extroversion. Anxiety, for example, is a concept, or construct, inferred from such acts of behaviour as what a person says, the expression on his face, and the manner in which he moves his body.

Efforts to measure personality constructs stem from a variety of sources. Frequently they grow out of theories of personality; anxiety and repression (the forgetting of unpleasant experiences), for example, are among the central concepts of the theory of psychoanalysis. It is understandable that efforts would be made to quantify one's degree of anxiety, for example, and to use the score thus obtained in the assessment of and in the prediction of his future behaviour. Among the major issues in the study of personality measurement is the question of which of the many personality constructs that have been quantified are basic or fundamental and which can be expected to involve wasted effort in their measurement because they represent poorly defined combinations of more elemental constructs; which measurement techniques are most effective and convenient for the purpose of assessment; whether it is better to interview people in measuring personality, or to ask them to say, for example, what an inkblot or a cloud in the sky reminds them of.

Efforts to measure any given personality construct can fail as a result of inadequacies in formulating or defining the trait to be measured and weaknesses in the assessment methods employed. An investigator might desire to specify quantitatively the degree to which individuals are submissive in social and competitive situations. His effectiveness will depend on the particular theory of submissiveness he brings to bear on the problem; on the actual procedures he selects or devises to measure submissiveness; and on the adequacy of the research he performs to demonstrate the usefulness of the measure. Each of these tasks must be considered carefully in evaluating efforts to measure personality attributes.

The methods used in personality description and measurement fall into several categories that differ with regard to the type of information gathered and the methods by which it is obtained. While all should rely on data that come from direct observations of human behaviour if they are to have at least the semblance of scientific value, all may vary with regard to underlying assumptions, validity, and reliability (consistency, in this case).

PERSONALITY EVALUATION WITHOUT TESTS

The interview. In an interview the individual under assessment must be given considerable latitude in "telling his story." Interviews have both verbal and nonverbal (*e.g.*, gestural) components. The aim of the interview is to gather information, and the adequacy of the data gathered depends in large part on the questions asked by the interviewer. In an employment interview the focus of the interviewer is on the job candidate's work experiences and occupational goals. In a diagnostic medical or psychiatric interview considerable attention is paid to the patient's medical history and to any symptoms of behavioral disorder he may have displayed over the years.

Two broad types of interview may be delineated. The interview designed for use in research is directed toward eliciting information that may be relevant to particular practical applications under general study or to those personality theories being investigated. Another type, the clinical interview, is focussed on assessing the status of a particular individual (*e.g.*, a psychiatric patient); such an interview is action oriented (*i.e.*, it may indicate appropriate treatment). Both research and clinical interviews frequently may be conducted to obtain an individual's life history and biographical information, but they differ in the uses to which the information is put.

Although it is not feasible to quantify all of the events occurring in an interview, personality researchers have devised ways of categorizing many aspects of the content of what a person has said. In this approach, called content analysis, the particular categories used depend upon the researchers' interests and ingenuity, but the method of content analysis is quite general and involves the construction of a system of categories that hopefully can be used reliably by an analyst or scorer. The categories may be straightforward (*e.g.*, the number of words uttered by the interviewee during designated time periods), or they may rest on inferences (*e.g.*, the degree of personal unhappiness the interviewee appears to express). Content analysis makes it possible to use frequencies of uttered response to describe verbal behaviour, and it defines behavioral variables for more-or-less precise study in experimental research. It has been used, for example, to gauge how people's attitudes change with the passage of time. Changes in the frequency of hostile reference a neurotic makes toward his parents during a sequence of psychotherapeutic interviews, for example, may be detected and assessed as may the changing self-evaluations of psychiatric hospital inmates in relation to the length of their hospitalization.

Sources of erroneous conclusions that may be drawn from face-to-face encounters stem from the complexity of the interview situation, the attitudes, fears, and expectations of the interviewee, and the interviewer's manner and training. Research has been conducted to identify, control, and, if possible, eliminate these sources of interview invalidity and unreliability. By conducting more than one interview with the same interviewee and by using more than one interviewer to evaluate his behaviour, light can be shed on the reliability of the information derived and may reveal differences in influence among individual interviewers. Standardization of interview format tends to increase the reliability of the information gathered; for example, all interviewers may use the same set of questions. Such standardization, however, may restrict the scope of information elicited; and even a perfectly reliable (consistent) interview technique can lead to incorrect inferences.

Behavioral observation. In every type of assessment situation behaviour is sampled in some way; not every bit of the individual's behaviour can be observed. The behaviour sampled in the interview may be that of self-description in which the individual indicates how he perceives himself. Other behavioral observations (*e.g.*, of facial expression) are also made in interviews. A situational test permits observation of specific aspects of one's behaviour, which may be predictive of his future behaviour. The test takes the form of a miniature life situation; during World War II, for example, situational tests were used by a number of

Erroneous conclusions

governments to select individuals who were judged capable of withstanding the interrogation to which a captured spy might be subjected. The tests typically took the form of stressful situations in which the individual was required to attain specified goals (*e.g.,* completing an assigned project under trying, frustrating conditions).

Another approach to behavioral observations involves the establishment of quantitative base lines against which to compare the future behaviour of individuals. Does the frequency with which a child seeks out other children, for example, increase with the number of play-therapy sessions in which he participates? Such observations permit quantitative description of someone's response repertoire at a given point in time and can provide a basis for measuring therapeutic effectiveness.

Behavioral observations can be treated in different ways. One of these is to keep track of the frequency with which people make designated responses during a given period of time (*e.g.,* the number of times a psychiatric patient makes his own bed or the number of times a child asks for help in a novel situation). Another approach involves asking raters to support their judgments of others by citing specific behaviour (critical incidents); a shop foreman, for example, may rate a worker as depressed by citing incidents when the worker burst into tears. Critical incidents not only add validity to ordinary ratings; they also suggest behavioral details that might be promising predictors of success on the job, response to psychiatric treatment, or level of academic achievement.

Behavioral observations are widely made in interviews and in a variety of workaday settings. Employers, supervisors, and teachers—either formally or informally—make use of behavioral observations in making decisions about people. Unfortunately the subject may know he is being studied or evaluated and, therefore, may behave atypically (*e.g.,* by working harder than usual, or by growing tense). The observer may be a source of error by being biassed in favour of or against the subject. Disinterested observers clearly are to be preferred for research and clinical purposes. The greater the care taken to control for such contributions to error, the greater the likelihood that observations will prove to be reliable.

Rating scales. Some observations do not lend themselves to quantification as readily as do simple counts of motor behaviour (such as the number of times a worker leaves his lathe to go to the bathroom). It is difficult, for example, to quantify how charming an office receptionist is. In such cases, one may fall back on relatively subjective judgments, inferences, and relatively imprecise estimates.

One approach to securing such judgments of the behaviour of others is through the use of rating scales. Rating scales present an observer with scalar dimensions along which those who are observed are to be placed. A teacher, for example, might be asked to rate his students on the degree to which the behaviour of each reflects leadership capacity, shyness, or creativity. Peers might rate each other along dimensions such as friendliness, trustworthiness, and social skills. Several standardized, printed rating scales are used to describe the behaviour of psychiatric hospital patients. Relatively objective rating scales have also been devised for use with other groups; for example, the Fels Parent Behavior Scales are used to assess parental behaviour toward their children in the home situation.

Rating scales are among the oldest and most versatile of the paper-and-pencil methods of personality measurement. They often take a graphic form:

To what degree is John shy?

| | | | | |
| Not at all | Slightly | Moderately | Very | Extremely |

A number of requirements should be met to maximize the usefulness of rating scales. One is that they be reliable: the ratings of the same person by different observers should be consistent. Other requirements are reduction of sources of inaccuracy in personality measurement; the so-called halo effect results in an observer's rating someone favourably on a specific characteristic because the observer has a generally favourable reaction to the person he is rating. One's tendency to say only nice things about others or one's proneness to think of all people as average (to use the midrange of scales) represents other methodological problems that arise when rating scales are used.

Factual information: unobtrusive and physiological measurement. In an interview there is an opportunity for direct observations of expressive behaviour (*e.g.,* speech patterns, poise, gestures) and for gathering the subject's life history and other types of information. While an interviewee usually is aware that he is an object of interest and inquiry, behavioral observations may be recorded whether or not the subject is aware that his behaviour is under study. If he is aware, his behaviour may be influenced significantly by that fact, and he may strive to create a good impression. There are, however, ways of gathering data that are resistant to the biases this creates.

One type of information that is sometimes overlooked because of its very simplicity consists of the subject's life history and present status. Much of this information may be gathered through direct interviews with a subject or with an informant, through questionnaires, and through searches of records and archives. The information might also be gathered by examining the subject's personal documents (*e.g.,* letters, autobiographies) and medical, educational, or psychiatric case histories. The information might concern the individual's social and occupational history, his cultural background, his present economic status, and his past and present physical characteristics. Life-history data can provide clues to the precursors and correlates of present behaviour. This information may help the investigator avoid needlessly speculative or complex hypotheses about the causation of personality traits. Failure on the part of a personality evaluator to be aware of the fact that someone had spent two years during World War II in a concentration camp, for example, could result in misleading conclusions about the subject's present behaviour.

Even if an individual knows he is being evaluated, he may not know which of his personality attributes are of special interest to the assessor. One often unwittingly or uncontrollably reveals feelings and thoughts that he wishes to conceal. Experienced personality assessors (*e.g.,* psychiatric clinicians) become adept at observing expressive nuances (subtleties in behaviour) that an individual either believes are being successfully suppressed or that he is unaware of. Slight variations in gestures, intonations, and mannerisms illustrate these expressive aspects of behaviour.

Along with expressive behaviour, measures of bodily functioning may reveal data that are related to the motivation and behaviour of the individual. Aspects of physique, the levels of hormones or sugar in the blood, tests of neurological functioning (*e.g.,* the knee jerk), and characteristics such as alterations in the resistance of the skin to electric current (the galvanic skin reaction) and changes in the dilation of the pupils of the eyes are among the bodily measures that have been used in personality assessment. With technological advances, it is becoming increasingly feasible and convenient to gauge unobtrusively the internal physical state of the individual. The activity of the sweat glands, the heartbeat, one's total bodily blood volume and blood pressure, and the amount of different substances in his bloodstream can be recorded and used to predict his social behaviour, the intensity of his drives (motivation), and the presence or absence of specified emotionally significant states such as frustration and stress.

One of the challenges confronting assessment psychologists is that personal characteristics are not only not constant but may vary even from moment to moment with changes in the conditions of life. Electronic and mechanical devices designed to monitor changes in bodily functioning that are related to periodic ratings of mood and to other physiological states provide measures of stability and change within the individual.

PERSONALITY TESTS

The aim of personality assessment is to secure accurate and useful statements about persons. While there may be general agreement about the theoretical and practical value of characterizing individuals, it is not immediately obvious how this can be accomplished; disagreements

Marginal notes:

Psychiatric ratings

Searches of records and archives

Physiological measurement

about methodological matters in personality assessment have been widespread. The success that has attended the use of convenient intelligence tests in providing reliable, quantitative (numerical) indices of individual ability has stimulated interest in the possibility of devising similar tests for measuring personality. Procedures now available vary in the degree to which they achieve scorability and convenience. These desirable attributes can be partly achieved by restricting the kinds of responses a subject is free to make. A test that restricts the subject to true-false answers, for example, is likely to be convenient to give and easy to score. So-called personality inventories tend to have these characteristics, in that they are relatively restrictive, objectively scorable, and convenient to administer. Other techniques (such as inkblot tests) for evaluating personality possess these characteristics to a lesser degree.

Personality inventories. In the early history of personality measurement, most tests were constructed on the basis of so-called face validity; that is, they simply appeared to be valid. Items were included because, in the fallible judgment of the person who constructed or devised the test, they were indicative of certain personality attributes. In other words, face validity need not be defined by careful, quantitative study; rather, it typically reflects one's more-or-less imprecise, possibly erroneous, impressions. Personal judgment, even that of an expert, is no guarantee that a particular collection of test items will prove to be reliable and meaningful in actual practice.

Self-report inventories

A widely used early self-report inventory, the Woodworth Personal Data Sheet, was developed during World War I to detect soldiers who were emotionally unfit for combat. Among its ostensibly face-valid items were these: Does the sight of blood make you sick or dizzy? Are you happy most of the time? Do you sometimes wish you had never been born? Recruits who answered the questions in a way that could be taken to mean that they suffered psychiatric disturbance were detained for evaluation. Clearly, however, symptoms revealed by such answers are exhibited by many people who are relatively free of emotional disorder.

Present-day self-report measures that take the form of personality inventories consist of many and varied statements or questions to which the subject is asked to respond in a particular way. His task might be to decide whether or not each of a series of statements is characteristic of his own feelings or behaviour; or he might respond true or false to a series of questions about the world in which he lives. Several inventories require that each of a series of statements be placed on a rating scale in terms of the frequency or adequacy with which the statements are judged by the individual to reflect his tendencies and attitudes. Regardless of the way in which the subject responds, most inventories yield several scores each intended to identify a distinctive aspect of personality.

One of these, the *Minnesota Multiphasic Personality Inventory* (MMPI), is probably the personality inventory in widest use in the English-speaking world. Also available in other languages, it consists in one version of 550 items (*e.g.,* "I like tall women.") to which subjects are to respond "true," "false," or "cannot say." Work on this inventory began in the 1930s, when its construction was motivated by the need for a practical, economical means of describing and predicting the behaviour of psychiatric patients. In its development efforts were made to achieve convenience in administration and scoring and to overcome many of the known defects of earlier personality inventories. Varied types of items were included and emphasis was placed on making these printed statements (presented either on small cards or in a booklet) intelligible even to persons with limited reading ability.

Most earlier inventories lacked subtlety; many people were able to fake or bias their answers since the items presented were easily seen to reflect gross disturbances. In many of these inventories maladaptive tendencies would be reflected in either all true or all false answers. Perhaps the most significant methodological advance to be found in the MMPI was the attempt to measure tendencies to respond, rather than actual behaviour, and to rely but little on assumptions of face validity. The true-false item "I hear strange voices all the time" has face validity for most

people in that to answer "true" to it seems to provide a strong indication of abnormal hallucinatory experiences. But some psychiatric patients who "hear strange voices" can still appreciate the socially undesirable implications of a "true" answer and may therefore try to conceal their abnormality by answering "false." A major difficulty in placing great reliance on face validity in test construction is that the subject may be as aware of the significance of his responses as is the test constructor and thus may be able to put his "best foot" forward and mislead the tester. Nevertheless, the person who hears strange voices and yet answers the item "false" clearly is responding to something—his answer still is a reflection of his personality, even though it may not be the aspect of personality to which the item seems to refer; thus, careful study of responses beyond their mere face validity is often profitable.

Much study has been given to the ways in which response sets and test-taking attitudes influence behaviour on personality inventories. The response set called acquiescence, for example, refers to one's tendency to respond with affirmative answers to questionnaire items regardless of what the item content is. It is conceivable that two people might be quite similar in all respects except for their tendency toward acquiescence. This difference in response set can lead to misleadingly different scores on personality tests. One person might be a "yea-sayer" (someone who tends to answer true to test items); another might be a "nay-sayer"; a third individual might not have a pronounced acquiescence tendency in either direction.

Reactions to the testing environment

There are other test-taking attitudes that may influence personality profiles. One of these is social desirability. A person who has convulsions might say "false" to the item "I have convulsions" because he believes that others will think less of him if they know he has convulsions. The intrusive potentially deceiving effects of the subjects' response sets and test-taking attitudes on scores derived from personality measures can sometimes be circumvented by varying the content and wording of test items. Nevertheless, users of questionnaires have not completely solved problems of bias such as those arising from response sets. Indeed, many of these problems first received widespread attention in research on the MMPI and research on this and similar inventories has significantly advanced understanding of the whole discipline of personality testing.

The MMPI as originally published consists of nine clinical scales (or sets of items), each scale having been found in practice to discriminate a particular clinical group, such as people suffering from schizophrenia, depression, or paranoia. Each of these scales (or others produced later) was developed by determining patterns of response to the inventory that were observed to be distinctive of groups of individuals who had been psychiatrically classified by other means (*e.g.,* by long-term observation). The responses of apparently normal subjects were compared with those of hospital patients with a particular psychiatric diagnosis. Items to which the greatest percentage of "normals" gave answers that differed from those more typically given by patients came to constitute each clinical scale.

In addition to the nine clinical scales and many specially developed scales, there are four so-called control scales on the inventory. One of these is simply the number of items placed by the subject in the "cannot say" category. The L (or lie) scale was devised to measure the tendency of the test taker to attribute socially desirable attributes to himself. In response to "I get angry sometimes" he should tend to mark false; extreme L scorers in the other direction appear to be too virtuous. The F scale was included to provide a reflection of the subjects' carelessness and confusion in taking the inventory (*e.g.,* "Everything tastes the same" tends to be answered true by careless or confused people). More subtle than either the L or F scales is the K scale. Its construction was based on the observation that some persons tend to exaggerate their symptoms because of excessive openness and may obtain high scores on the clinical scales; others may exhibit unusually low scores because of defensiveness. On the K-scale item "I think nearly anyone would tell a lie to keep out of trouble," the defensive person is apt to answer false, giving the same response to "I certainly feel useless at times." The K scale was designed to reduce these biassing factors; by weighting clinical-scale scores with K scores, the distorting effect of defensiveness may be reduced.

It has been found that the greater the number and magnitude of one's unusually high scores on the MMPI, the more likely it is that he is in need of psychiatric care. Most professionals who use the device refuse to make assumptions about the factualness of the subject's answers and about his personal interpretations of the meanings of the items. Their approach does not depend heavily on theoretical predilections and hypotheses. For this reason the inventory has proved popular with those who have doubts about the eventual validity that many theoretical formulations will show in connection with personality measurement after they have been tested through painstaking research. The MMPI also appeals to those who demand firm experimental evidence that any personality assessment method can make valid discriminations among individuals.

In recent years there has been growing interest in actuarial personality description; that is, in personality description based on traits shared in common by groups of people. Actuarial description studies yield rules by which persons may be classified according to their personal attributes as revealed by their behaviour (on tests, for example). Computer programs are now available for diagnosing such disorders as hysteria, schizophrenia, and paranoia on the basis of typical group profiles of MMPI responses. Computerized methods for integrating large amounts of personal data are not limited to this inventory and are applicable to other inventories, personality tests (*e.g.*, inkblots), and life-history information. Computerized classification of MMPI profiles, however, has been explored most intensively.

There are many other personality inventories and paper-and-pencil assessment techniques that are used in applied settings and in research. The *California Psychological Inventory* (CPI), for example, is keyed for several personality variables that include sociability, self-control, flexibility, and tolerance. Unlike the MMPI, it was developed specifically for use with "normal" groups of people. Whereas the judgments of experts (usually psychiatric workers) were used in categorizing subjects given the MMPI during the early item-writing phase of its development, nominations by peers were used in work with the *California Psychological Inventory*. Its technical development has been evaluated by test authorities to be of high order, in part because its developers profited from lessons learned in the construction and use of the MMPI. It also provides measures of response sets and has been subjected to considerable research study.

The *Eysenck Personality Inventory* was created in England and provides measures of neuroticism and extroversion. Its use has been closely linked with English psychologist Hans J. Eysenck's theories of personality. The device is short and easily administered, the neuroticism factor being designed to measure emotional instability and neurotic predispositions to break down under stress. The extroversion items on this inventory are held to sample one's tendency to exhibit sociable, out-going behaviour.

The *Edwards' Personality Preference Schedule* is a so-called forced-choice personality inventory. For each item the subject is required to characterize himself by choosing between paired statements of equal apparent desirability or undesirability. Such a task can be distasteful to many test takers; it may require, for example, being forced to describe oneself as either "stupid" or "ugly." Among others, the *Edwards' Personality Preference Schedule* yields measures of one's needs for achievement, heterosexuality, and social dominance. The strength of each need is not expressed in absolute terms but in relation to the intensity of the individual's other needs.

Beyond personality inventories, there are other self-report approaches to personality measurement. Mention was made earlier of the use of rating scales filled out by observers. An individual also can use rating scales as a vehicle for his own self-description. The so-called semantic differential is a rating-scale technique that permits quantification of an individual's reactions to himself, to others, and, in fact, to any object or concept in terms of a standard set of semantic polarities such as "hot-cold"

Diagnosis with computers

Self-description techniques

or "good-bad." It is a general method for assessing the meanings of these semantic concepts to individuals.

A method called the Q-sort is devised for problems similar to those for which rating scales are used. In a Q-sort a person is given a set of sentences, phrases, or words (usually presented individually on cards) and is asked to use them to describe himself (as he thinks he is or as he would like to be) or someone else. The subject sorts the items on the cards in terms of their degree of relevance so that they can be distributed along what amounts to a rating scale. Examples of descriptive items that might be included are "worries a lot," "works hard," and "is cheerful."

Paper-and-pencil instruments such as personality inventories involve verbal stimuli (words) intended to call forth designated types of responses. There are clearly stated ground rules under which he makes his responses. Paper-and-pencil devices are relatively easy and economical to administer and can be scored accurately and reliably by relatively inexperienced clerical workers. They are generally regarded by professional personality evaluators as especially valuable assessment tools in screening large numbers of people, as in military or industrial personnel selection. Assessment specialists do not assume that self-reports are accurate indicators of personality traits. They are accepted, rather, as samples of behaviour for which validity in predicting one's everyday activities or traits must be established empirically (*i.e.*, by direct observation or experiment). Paper-and-pencil techniques have moved from their early stage of assumed (face) validity to more advanced notions in which improvements in conceptualization and methodology are clearly recognized as basic to the determination of empirical validity.

Projective techniques. One group of assessment specialists holds that the most meaningful path to personality description and classification requires that the person who is assessed be given the opportunity to respond as freely as possible so as to reflect his unique ways of thinking and behaving. Inkblots and other ambiguous stimuli are employed in a number of tests that have been used widely in clinical situations (*e.g.*, in psychiatric hospitals) in this type of assessment. Such stimuli are used to provide so-called projective techniques (since they allow one relative freedom to project his own interests and feelings into them, reacting in any way that seems appropriate).

Personality inventories and projective techniques do have some elements in common; inkblots, for example, are ambiguous, but so also are many of the statements on inventories such as the MMPI. These techniques differ in that the subject is given substantially free rein in responding to projective stimuli rather than merely answering true or false, for example. Another similarity between projective and questionnaire or inventory approaches is that all involve the use of relatively standardized testing situations.

While projective techniques are often lumped together as one general methodology, in actual practice there are several approaches to assessment from a projective point of view. Although projective techniques share the common characteristic that they permit the subject wide latitude in responding, they still may be distinguished broadly as follows: (1) associative techniques, in which the subject is asked to react to words, to inkblots, or to other stimuli with the first associated thoughts that come to mind; (2) construction techniques, in which the subject is asked to create something—for example, make up a story or draw a picture of himself; (3) completion techniques, in which the subject is asked to finish a partially developed stimulus, such as adding his own last words to an incomplete sentence; (4) choice or ordering techniques, in which the subject is asked to choose from among or to give some orderly sequence to stimuli—for example, to choose from or arrange a set of pictures or inkblots; (5) expressive techniques, in which the subject is asked to express himself freely in some manner, as in finger painting.

Because these techniques allow the subject wide latitude in making his responses they are held by some theorists to be sensitive to unconscious dimensions of personality. Hidden personality defense mechanisms, latent emotional impulses, and inner anxieties all have been attributed to test takers by making theoretical inferences from data

Types of projective techniques

gathered as they responded in projective situations. While projective stimuli are ambiguous, they are usually administered under fairly standardized conditions. Quantitative (numerical) measures can be derived from subjects' responses to them. These include the number of responses one makes to a series of inkblots and the number of responses to the blots in which the subject perceives, for example, moving nonhuman animals.

The Rorschach Inkblot Test. The Rorschach inkblots were developed by a Swiss psychiatrist, Hermann Rorschach, in an effort to reduce the time required in psychiatric diagnosis. His test consists of 10 cards, half of which are in colour and half in black and white. The test is administered by showing the subject the 10 blots one at a time; the subject's task is to describe what he sees in the blots or what they remind him of. The subject is usually told that the inkblots are not a test of the kind he took in school and that there are no right or wrong answers.

Rorschach's work was stimulated by his interest in the relationship between perception and personality. He held that a person's perceptual responses to inkblots could serve as clues to basic personality tendencies. Subsequent negative research findings have led many users of projective techniques to become dubious about the role assigned the inkblots in delineating relationships between perception and personality. Emphasis has tended to shift to the analysis of nuances of the subject's social behaviour during the test and to the content of his verbal responses to the examiner; whether, for example, he seeks to obtain the assistance of the examiner in "solving" the inkblots presented to him, sees "angry lions" or "meek lambs" in the inkblots, or is apologetic or combative about his responses.

Over the years, considerable research has been carried out on Rorschach's inkblots; important statistical problems in analyzing data gathered with projective techniques have been identified, and researchers have continued in their largely unsuccessful efforts to overcome them. There is a vast experimental literature to suggest that the Rorschach technique lacks empirical validity.

The *Holtzman Inkblot Test* was developed in an effort to eliminate some of the statistical problems that beset the Rorschach test. It involves the administration of a series of 45 inkblots, the subject being permitted to make only one response per card. The Holtzman has the desirable feature that it provides an alternate series of 45 additional cards for use in retesting the same person.

Research with the Rorschach and Holtzman has proceeded in a number of directions; many studies have compared psychiatric patients and other groups of special interest (delinquents, underachieving students) with ostensibly normal people. Some investigators have sought to derive indices or predictions of future behaviour from responses to inkblots, and have checked, for example, to see if anxiety and hostility (as inferred from content analyses of verbal responses) are related to favourable or unfavourable response to psychotherapy. A sizable area of exploration concerns the effects of special conditions (*e.g.,* experimentally induced anxiety or hostility) on the inkblot perceptions reported by the subject and on the content of his speech.

Thematic Apperception Test (*TAT*). There are other personality assessment devices, which, like the Rorschach, are based on the idea that an individual will project something of himself into his description of an ambiguous stimulus. The *Thematic Apperception Test* presents the subject with pictures of persons engaged in a variety of activities (*e.g.,* someone with a violin). While the pictures leave much to one's imagination, they are more specific, organized visual stimuli than are inkblots. The test consists of 30 black and white pictures and one blank card (to test imagination under very limited stimulation). The subject is asked to make up a story based on each picture, describing the events that led to the scene and the events that will grow out of it. He is also asked to describe the thoughts and feelings of the persons in his story.

Although some content-analysis scoring systems have been developed for the TAT, attempts to score it in a standardized quantitative fashion tend to be limited to research and have been fewer than has been the case for

the Rorschach. This is especially the state of affairs in applied settings in which the test is often used as a basis for conducting a kind of clinical interview; the pictures are used to elicit a sample of verbal behaviour on the basis of which inferences are drawn by the clinician.

Interpretation of a TAT story may begin with an effort to determine who is the hero (*i.e.,* to identify the character with whom the subject seems to have identified himself). The content of the stories is often analyzed in terms of a "need-press system." Needs are defined as the internal motivations of the hero. Press refers to environmental forces that facilitate or interfere with the satisfaction of needs (*e.g.,* in the story the hero may be physically attacked, frustrated by poverty, or suffer the effects of rumours being spread about him). In assessing the importance or strength of a particular inferred need or press, special attention is given to signs of its pervasiveness and consistency in different stories. Analysis of the test may depend considerably on the subjective, personal characteristics of the evaluator, who usually seeks to interpret the subjects' behaviour in the testing situation; the characteristics of his utterances; the emotional tone of the stories; the kinds of fantasies he offers; the outcomes of the stories; and the conscious and unconscious needs inferred from the stories.

Word-association techniques. One of the oldest projective approaches to personality assessment is the so-called word-association test. The Swiss psychiatrist Carl Jung used associations to groups of related words as a basis for inferring personality traits (*e.g.,* the inferiority "complex"). Administering a word-association test is relatively uncomplicated; a list of words is presented one at a time to the subject who is asked to respond with the first word or idea that comes to mind. Many of the stimulus words may appear to be emotionally neutral (*e.g.,* building, first, tree); of special interest are words that tend to elicit personalized reactions (*e.g.,* mother, hit, love). The amount of time the subject takes before he begins each response and the response itself are used to analyze a word association test. The idiosyncratic, or unusual, nature of one's word-association responses may be gauged by comparing them to standard published tables of the specific associations given by large groups of people.

Sentence-completion techniques. The sentence-completion technique may be considered a logical extension of word-association methods. In administering a sentence-completion test, the evaluator asks the subject to finish a series of incomplete sentences in his own words (*e.g.,* "I feel upset when . . . "). Users of sentence-completion methods in assessing personality typically analyze them in terms of what they judge to be recurring attitudes, conflicts, and motives reflected in them. Such analyses, like those of TAT, contain a subjective element.

ASSESSING ASSESSMENT TECHNIQUES

Assessment, whether it is carried out with interviews, behavioral observations, physiological measures, or tests, is intended to permit the evaluator to make meaningful, valid, and reliable statements about individuals. What makes John Doe tick? What makes Mary Doe the unique individual that she is? Whether these questions can be answered depends upon the reliability and validity of the assessment methods used. The fact that a test is intended to measure a particular attribute is in no way a guarantee that it really accomplishes this goal. Assessment techniques must themselves be assessed.

An objective of research in personality measurement is to delineate the conditions under which the methods do or do not make trustworthy descriptive and predictive contributions. One approach to this problem is to compare groups of people known through careful observation to differ in a particular way. It is helpful to consider, for example, whether the MMPI or TAT discriminates significantly between those who show progress in psychotherapy and those who do not, or whether they distinguish between law violators of record and apparent nonviolators. Experimental investigations in which the conditions under which subjects perform are varied systematically also make contributions.

Another area of research on assessment involves the role

Evaluation of Rorschach validity

Word stimulus responses

of the assessor as an evaluator and predictor of the behaviour of others. In most applied settings he subjectively (even intuitively) evaluates and interprets the various assessment data that are available. How successful he is in carrying out this task is critical, as is knowledge of the kinds of conditions under which he is effective in processing such diverse data as impressions gathered in an interview, test scores, and life-history data. The typical clinician usually does not use a statistical formula that weighs and combines test scores and other data. Rather, he integrates the data using impressions and hunches based on his clinical experience and on his understanding of psychological theory and research. The result of this interpretive process usually includes some form of personality description of the person under study and specific predictions or advice for that person; *e.g.*, a recommendation that he consult a surgeon or another specialist.

Evaluating the evaluator

The degree of success an assessor has when he responds to the diverse information that may be available about a particular person is the subject of research that has been carried out on the issue of clinical versus statistical prediction. It is reasonable to ask whether a clinician will do as good a job in predicting behaviour as does a statistical formula or a manual that provides the empirical, statistically predictive aspects of test responses or scores based on the study of large numbers of people. An example would be a book or table of typical intelligence-test scores used to predict how well children perform in school. Another book might offer specific personality diagnoses (*e.g.*, neurotic or psychotic) based on scores such as those yielded by the different scales of the MMPI. Many issues must be settled before the deceptively simple question of clinical versus statistical prediction can be answered definitively.

When statistical prediction formulas (well-supported by research) are available for combining clinical information, however, experimental evidence clearly indicates that they will be more valid and less time-consuming than will a clinician (who may be subject to human error in trying to simultaneously consider and weigh all of the factors in a given case). The clinician's chief contributions to diagnosis and prediction are in situations for which satisfactory formulas and quantified information (*e.g.*, test scores) are not available. Clinicians are especially to be thought of when what are being evaluated are rare and idiosyncratic personality characteristics that have escaped rigorous, systematic empirical study. The greatest confidence obtains when both statistical and subjective clinical methods simultaneously converge (agree) in the solution of specific clinical problems; unfortunately, they often disagree.

Role of the clinician

Although much progress has been made in efforts to measure personality, all available instruments and methods have defects and limitations that must be borne in mind when using them; responses to tests or interview questions, for example, often are easily controlled or manipulated by the subject and thus are readily "fakeable." Some tests, while useful as group screening devices, empirically exhibit only limited predictive value in individual cases, yielding frequent errors. These caveats are especially important when significant decisions about a person are made on the basis of personality measures. Psychiatric institutionalization or discharge, and hiring or firing, are weighty personal matters indeed and can wreak great injustice when based on faulty assessment. In addition, many personality assessment techniques require the probing of highly private areas of the individual's thought and action. Those who seek to measure personality for descriptive and predictive reasons must concern themselves deeply with the ethical and legal implications of their work.

A major methodological stumbling block in the way of establishing the validity of any method of personality measurement is that there always is an element of subjective judgment in selecting or formulating criteria against which measures may be validated. This is not so serious a problem when popular, socially valued, fairly obvious criteria are available that permit ready comparisons between such groups as convicted criminals and ostensible noncriminals, or psychiatric hospital patients and noninstitutionalized individuals. Many personality characteristics, however, cannot be validated in such directly observable ways (*e.g.*, one's inner, private experiences such as anxiety or depression). When such straightforward empirical validation of an untested measure is not possible, efforts at establishing a less impressive kind of validity (so-called construct validity) may be pursued. A construct is a theoretical statement concerning some underlying, unobservable aspect of an individual's characteristics or of his internal state. Constructs refer to private events inferred or imagined to contribute to the shaping of specific public events (observed behaviour). The explanatory value of any construct has been considered by some theorists to represent its validity. Construct validity, therefore, refers to evidence that endorses the usefulness of a theoretical conception of personality. A test designed to measure an unobservable construct (such as "intelligence" or "need to achieve") is said to accrue construct validity if it usefully predicts the kinds of empirical criteria one would expect it to; *e.g.*, achievement in academic subjects.

The degree to which a measure of personality is empirically related to or predictive of any aspect of behaviour observed independently of that measure contributes to its validity in general. A most desirable step in establishing the usefulness of a measure is called cross-validation. The mere fact that one research study yields positive evidence of validity is no guarantee that the measure will work as well the next time; often it does not. It is important to conduct additional, cross-validation studies to establish the stability of the results obtained in the first investigation. Failure to cross-validate is viewed by most testing authorities as a serious omission in the validation process. Evidence for the validity of a full test should not be sought from the same sample of people that was used for the initial selection of individual test items. Clearly this will tend to exaggerate the effect of traits that are unique to that particular sample of people and can lead to high estimates of validity that will not be borne out when other people are studied. Cross-validation studies permit assessment of the amount of "shrinkage" in empirical effectiveness when a new sample of subjects is employed. When evidence of validity holds up under cross-validation, confidence in the general usefulness of test norms and research findings is enhanced. Establishment of reliability, validity, and cross-validation are major steps in determining the usefulness of any psychological test.

Cross-validation

Progress in personality measurement depends upon answers to both methodological and theoretical questions. Scholarly interest in theories of personality, pressing practical problems (such as the need to screen or diagnose patients efficiently), and the intriguing results of incomplete research provide the impetus for those who seek to devise objective, meaningful measures of personal characteristics. In devising these measures a number of frustrating, but crucial, questions remain to be answered. The pursuit of empirical answers to such questions has been partially rewarding and provides reasons to believe that progress will continue to be made in the relatively youthful field of personality measurement.   (I.G.S./Ed.)

BIBLIOGRAPHY. C.S. HALL and G. LINDZEY, *Theories of Personality,* 2nd ed. (1970), surveys the major theories of personality. E.F. BORGATTA and W.W. LAMBERT (eds.), *Handbook of Personality Theory and Research* (1968), integrates several of these theories and the research methods that characterize the discipline. Examples and reviews of personality research are contained in I.G. SARASON, *Personality: An Objective Approach* (1966), and (ed.), *Contemporary Research in Personality,* 2nd ed. (1969). L.J. CRONBACH, *Essentials of Psychological Testing,* 3rd ed. (1970), surveys general approaches of assessment; while O.K. BUROS (ed.), *Personality: Tests and Reviews* (1970), provides a valuable compendium of personality tests and measurement devices. D.N. JACKSON and S. MESSICK (ed.), *Problems in Human Assessment* (1970), deals with selected aspects of personality assessment. See also NANCY CANTOR and JOHN F. KIHLSTROM (eds.), *Personality, Cognition, and Social Interaction* (1981), essays seeking an integration of theories of personality, social psychology, and cognitive psychology.

(E.F.B./I.G.S./Ed.)

Peru

A country that borders the Pacific Ocean, straddles the great Andes Mountain Ranges, and contains the headwaters of the Amazon River, Peru is the third largest nation in South America after Brazil and Argentina. Officially it is called the Republic of Peru (República del Perú). Its name is derived from a Quechua Indian word implying land of abundance, a reference to the economic wealth produced by the highly organized Inca civilization that ruled the region for centuries. The nation's vast mineral, agricultural, and marine resources long have served as the economic foundation of the country.

Except for the Lake Titicaca basin in the southeast, Peru's borders run through sparsely populated zones. The boundaries with Ecuador to the northwest, Bolivia to the southeast, and Chile to the south run across the high Andes, whereas the borders with Colombia to the northeast and Brazil to the east traverse lower ranges or tropical forests. Peru's land area of 496,225 square miles (1,285,-216 square kilometres) is supplemented by territorial waters, reaching 200 miles (320 kilometres) into the Pacific, that are claimed by Peru.

Peru is a tropical country, with its northern tip nearly touching the Equator. A great diversity of climate, of way of life, and of economic activity is brought about, however, by the country's extremes of altitude and by the southwest winds that sweep in across the cold Peru, or Humboldt, Current, which flows along its Pacific shoreline. The immense difficulties of travel posed by the Andes have long impeded national unity. Iquitos, on the upper Amazon, lies only about 600 miles northeast of Lima, the capital, but before the airplane, travelers between the cities often chose a 7,000-mile trip via the Amazon, the Atlantic and Caribbean, the Isthmus of Panama, and the Pacific, rather than the shorter mountain route.

This article is divided into the following sections:

Physical and human geography

THE LAND

Relief. Peru is traditionally described in terms of three broad, longitudinal regions: the arid Costa on the west; the rugged Sierra, or Andes, system in the centre; and, on the east, the wet and forested Montaña of the tropical Amazon Basin.

The Costa. The coastal plain readily divides into three parts—north, central, and south—based on the amount of level land and the distance between the Andean ranges and the sea. Generally speaking, the amount of level coastal land diminishes from north to south. In the northern region, from Ecuador to Chimbote, the plain is typically some 20 to 30 miles wide, with a maximum width of more than 90 miles in the Sechura Desert south of Piura. The central coastal region, which stretches from Chimbote to Nazca, is narrower than the northern region and is characterized by areas of rough hills that extend from the Andes to the shores of the ocean. From Nazca southward to the Chilean border the coast is largely lined by low mountains; the southern valleys are narrow and only in scattered spots are level lands found near the ocean.

The Sierra, or Andean, region. Along the western edge of South America, the Andes Mountains were created by tectonic activity in which the South American Plate overrode the Nazca Plate. Typical of mountain regions of the Pacific rim, the Peruvian Andes are young in geologic terms, with continuing uplift manifested by frequent earthquakes and much instability. Three main backbones protrude from the Peruvian Andes; they are commonly called the cordilleras Occidental, Central, and Oriental, although these designations are not used within Peru.

Slopes are relatively gentle in northern Peru, and maximum elevations seldom exceed 16,000 feet (about 5,000 metres). The Andes in central Peru are higher and more rugged. The ranges of the central zone form particularly difficult barriers to movement. The main pass east of Lima, for instance, is at an elevation of more than 15,000 feet—higher than many of the peaks in the north. Many of the mountains of central Peru are snowcapped and are a popular attraction for climbers and tourists. Of particular fame is the Cordillera Blanca, with the country's highest peak, Mount Huascarán, at 22,205 feet. In southern Peru the character of the Andes changes to that of a high plateau region; this is the Puna, with vast tablelands and elevations between 13,000 and 16,000 feet. Scattered peaks, with elevations of up to about 21,000 feet, protrude

Mount Huascarán

above the broad southern plateaus. Beginning with Misti Volcano, near Arequipa, many of the southern peaks form a volcanic chain that stretches into northern Chile.

The Montaña. The lower slopes of the western Andes merge with the heavily forested tropical lowlands of the Amazon Basin to form the Montaña, which occupies more than three-fifths of the area of Peru. The term *selva* is also used to refer to this area. The physiography of the region is characterized by rolling hills and level plains that extend eastward to the borders with Colombia, Brazil, and Bolivia. Elevations are uniformly low, ranging from about 1,300 feet at the eastern edge of the Andes to about 300 feet above sea level along the Amazon River at the Peru–Brazil border.

Drainage. Distinctive drainage patterns dissect the Costa, Sierra, and Montaña. Of the more than 50 rivers that flow west from the Andes across the Costa, most are short (usually less than 200 miles long) and precipitous, with highly seasonal rates of flow. Most have a period of peak flow (usually during the December to March rainy season) followed by a long dry period; only the largest of the Costa rivers, such as the Santa, have dependable year-round flows.

The Sierra not only contains the headwaters of the streams that flow to both the Pacific and the Amazon but also has a large area of internal drainage. In the south several rivers cross the altiplano in Peru to empty into Lake Titicaca, which is shared with Bolivia and is—at an altitude of 12,500 feet—the world's highest navigable body of water.

The Ama-
zon River

The Montaña region is characterized by great rivers. The Amazon, with the largest volume of flow of any river in the world, has headwaters that rise in several places in the Peruvian Andes; one of the main branches, the Ucayali, originates in southern Peru some 1,700 miles from its juncture with the main branch. The Amazon is navigable, but such large tributaries as the Marañón, Huallaga, and Ucayali can be navigated only for relatively short distances west of the port of Iquitos. These rivers flow northward in long deep valleys before turning east to join the Amazon, forming mostly hindrances to transportation rather than important trade routes.

Soils. Peru has little fertile soil. In the Costa region most of the river valleys have rich soils, derived from silts carried to the coastal plain by rivers flowing out of the Andes. In some areas, however, improper use of the land has led to deposition of salts, thus reducing soil fertility. The soils between valleys, derived largely from windblown sands, are also poorly developed. Sierra soils are fertile in some of the highland basins, but soils on the mountain slopes are often thin and of poor quality. Soils of low fertility covered by heavy forest growth typify the Montaña; they quickly erode when the forests are cut.

Climate. Three broad climatic regions can be readily distinguished in Peru paralleling the three main topographic regions: the Costa, the Sierra, and the Montaña.

The coastal desert. From the Peruvian–Ecuadorian border south to northern Chile, the west coast of South America has one of the Earth's driest climates. This region is dry for three reasons: (1) The Andes block rain-bearing winds from the Amazon Basin, (2) air masses moving toward the coast out of the South Pacific high pressure system produce little rainfall, and (3) northward-flowing cold water off the coast (the Peru, or Humboldt, Current) contributes little moisture to surface air masses. This is not a hot desert, however; average temperatures of the Costa range from 66° F (19° C) in winter to 72° F (22° C) in summer. Despite its dryness some parts of the Costa receive sufficient moisture from winter fogs (locally known as *garúa*) to support some vegetation.

Coastal
aridity

The mountain climates. Within the Sierra are a wide range of climates that vary according to such factors as latitude, altitude, local winds, and rain shadow effects. In general, temperatures decrease as elevation increases and rainfall decreases from north to south and from east to west. During the December–March rainy season, the heaviest precipitation is in the north and along the eastern flanks of the Andes. Temperatures vary little seasonally, but there is a tremendous diurnal range (between daily highs and lows). In Cuzco at 11,152 feet of altitude, for example, the January average temperature is 52° F (11° C), and the July average 47° F (8° C). The diurnal range, however, is frequently more than 40° F (22° C) between the midday maximum and the predawn minimum. Snow falls in the Sierra at higher altitudes, and many peaks have permanent snow.

The tropical forest climates. Hot humid conditions characterize the Montaña climate of eastern Peru. Rainfall throughout the region is high (Iquitos averages more than 90 inches [2,286 millimetres] annually), with precipitation common throughout the year, although it is somewhat heavier from December to March. There is little seasonal variation of temperatures, but the diurnal range again is relatively large. Daytime highs at Iquitos sometimes extend into the mid-90°s F (mid-30°s C), whereas at night temperatures may fall into the 60°s F (below 15° C).

El Niño. The most severe variation in Peruvian weather patterns occurs irregularly, at intervals of about a decade or so. This change, usually called El Niño ("The Child," because it usually begins around Christmas time), is but a small part of what is known as the Southern Oscillation, a pan-Pacific reversal of atmospheric and sea conditions. Although the causes of this phenomenon are not completely understood, the effects in Peru are quite clear: (1) warm water replaces the cold water of the Peru Current, (2) heavy rains fall in the coastal desert, and (3) drought occurs in the southern highlands. Severe occurrences of the El Niño phenomenon, such as those that took place in 1925 and 1983, cause ecological disasters, including widespread loss of bird and fish life and great economic damage.

Plant and animal life. Peruvian plant and animal life can be classified according to the three main physiographic regions: the Costa, the Sierra, and the Montaña.

The Costa. Evidence of plant life is relatively rare in the barren desert of coastal Peru. Where coastal fog is heavy, *lomas* (a mix of grasses and other herbaceous species) are common. In the north coast region, some parts of the desert are covered by epiphytes or by stands of sapote or algarroba (mesquite). The most important feature of the coast, however, is the enormous amount of bird, marine mammal, and fish life that abounds in the coastal waters. The biomass includes such small fish as anchovies and such larger types as corbina (sea bass), tuna, swordfish, and marlin. Sea lions thrive in isolated parts of the coast. Bird life is heavy on islands off the coast. Among the most important bird species are pelicans, cormorants, gannets, and various gulls. Humboldt penguins, an endangered species, are found as far north as the Ballestas Islands near the Paracas Peninsula.

The Sierra. Two plant communities characterize the Peruvian highlands: puna grasslands at elevations from about 13,000 to 16,000 feet, and, at lower elevations, a mixture of native and introduced species. The Puna has an abundance of forage grasses and is home to the llama, alpaca, vicuña, and guanaco, which are native to the region. At lower elevations grow such domesticates as potatoes, quinoa, and corn (maize). Several species of eucalyptus have replaced native tree species.

The Montaña. The eastern slopes of the Andes and the Amazon plains are covered by a heavy growth of tropical forest. In its woods and waters live thousands of plant and animal species. Interesting mammals of this region include the jaguar, capybara, tapir, and several species of monkey. Of special note is the wide and colourful variety of bird and fish life. Reptiles and insects abound. The forests have a broad assortment of hardwood and softwood species that produce a variety of forest products. Scattered in isolated fields in the eastern foothills of the Andes, too, are plantations of coca, the plant from which cocaine is illegally produced.

Amazonian
wildlife

Settlement patterns. The nature of Peruvian life, whether urban or rural, varies by physiographic region. Modern patterns of settlement also reflect three major influences: (1) pan-Andean cultures of pre-Hispanic Peru; (2) colonial settlement of the Costa and the Sierra; and (3) migration to the cities and colonization of the Montaña.

Pre-Hispanic patterns. Diverse groups of indigenous Indians occupied Peru during the pre-Hispanic period. When the first migrants arrived in the Andean area, probably more than 13,000 years ago, they were at a hunting and gathering stage of cultural development. Over a long period of time, however, varied and more sophisticated ways of life were developed. Along the coast, groups became specialized in fishing and shellfish collecting. In the Puna, hunting of vicuña and guanaco was replaced by herding of their related species, the llama and alpaca. Finally, in many parts of Peru agriculture was developed—including the domestication of numerous species of plants, such as beans, quinoa, and potatoes.

At the time of the Spanish arrival, the population of Peru was largely resident in rural areas, with society organized around villages (called by the Incas *ayllus*). The most densely settled areas were the coastal river valleys and some fertile basins in the highlands—for example, those of Cajamarca, the Mantaro Valley near Huancayo, and Cusco, as well as the region around Lake Titicaca. Some urban centres had developed as the capitals of kingdoms or empires—such as the Chimú's Chan Chán near Trujillo

and the Inca's Cuzco—or as religious centres—such as the pre-Incan Pachacamac, south of Lima.

Colonial patterns. The Spanish conquest of the Incas in 1532 was accompanied by several dramatic changes in Andean settlement patterns. First, the Spanish were oriented toward their mother country in Europe. Thus, Spanish cities such as Piura (1532), Lima (1535), and Trujillo (1534) were established near ports that were the sea links to Spain. Second, Spanish settlements focused on the extraction of resources, leading to the establishment of mining centres in Huancavelica and at Potosí, in modern Bolivia. Third, after a period of rapid population decline caused mainly by the introduction of European diseases, the Spanish established new towns that brought together the remnants of the surviving rural population. Finally, the Spanish divided the country into encomiendas, which later formed the basis for haciendas and kept the best agricultural land in the hands of a few wealthy owners. They established feudal systems based on peasant labour that lasted until the sweeping land reforms of the mid-20th century.

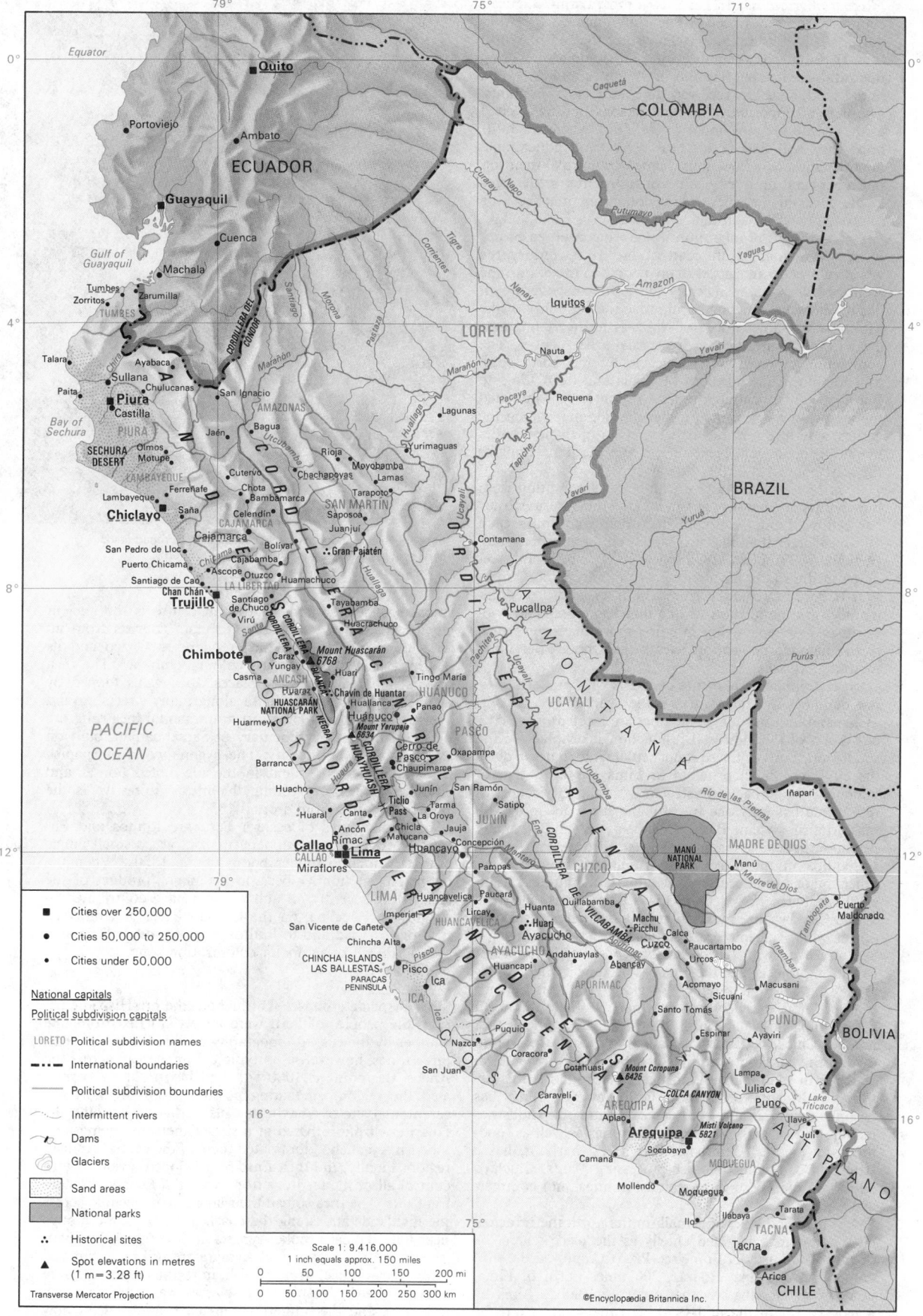

Scale 1: 9,416.000
1 inch equals approx. 150 miles

| 0 | 50 | 100 | 150 | 200 mi |

| 0 | 50 | 100 | 150 | 200 | 250 | 300 km |

©Encyclopædia Britannica Inc.

Legend:

- ■ Cities over 250,000
- ● Cities 50,000 to 250,000
- • Cities under 50,000

National capitals

Political subdivision capitals

LORETO Political subdivision names

-·-·- International boundaries

——— Political subdivision boundaries

Intermittent rivers

Dams

Glaciers

Sand areas

National parks

∴ Historical sites

▲ Spot elevations in metres
(1 m = 3.28 ft)

Transverse Mercator Projection

Recent migrations. In Peru, as in most Latin-American countries, there has been a mass migration to the cities during the 20th century, especially since the end of World War II. Lima has been the principal destination during this rural exodus, but Trujillo in the north and Arequipa in the south have also received large numbers of migrants. The lack of opportunity in rural regions is usually cited as the reason for movement to the cities, where migrants hope they will find better health care and educational opportunities, as well as jobs. Some do improve their lot, but others end up in city slums or in squatter settlements at the edges of the cities, where conditions may be little improved over those in the rural areas.

A second focus of migration in Peru has been eastward, to the Montaña. At the end of the 19th century the world rubber boom caused many people to move into the Amazon Basin; more recently the Peruvian government has developed a program to improve the economy of the Montaña, a main purpose of which is to divert migrants away from the already crowded coastal urban centres. The completion of roads from Chiclayo on the north coast to Tarapoto in the northern Montaña and from Lima to Pucallpa in the central Montaña region have stimulated this eastward movement. Further development along the eastern side of the Andes is designed to open new settlements in this region. Nevertheless, the Montaña remains the least populated of the three regions.

Urban Peru. The massive 20th-century migration from the countryside has brought rapid growth to Peruvian urban centres. Lima has become the urban giant, more than 10 times larger than the next largest city, but other cities, particularly Trujillo and Chimbote in the north and Arequipa in the south, have also grown rapidly. Since World War II Peru has changed from a country with a predominantly rural population to one that has more than two-thirds of its people living in cities; more than one-fourth of the nation's population lives within the greater Lima metropolitan area.

Growth of cities

Ornate colonial architecture contrasts with modern high-rise buildings in Lima, which is the heart of Peru's commerce and industry. Large factories are located in the city, but much of the industrial production takes place in the small workshops of the squatter settlements that surround the city. A difficult problem in Lima has been that of matching the urban infrastructure to the city's growth rate. Lima has only one freeway and lacks an up-to-date mass transit system. Basic public services are, in many neighbourhoods, rudimentary at best. (See LIMA.)

Arequipa in the Sierra and Trujillo in the Costa are other major urban centres. Arequipa is the largest city in southern Peru. Founded in 1540, it is often called the White City because most of its buildings are constructed out of white volcanic rock. Agriculture around Arequipa has improved with the completion of several important irrigation projects, and the area has become a major wool-processing and milk-producing region. Trujillo is a major centre in northern Peru but does not dominate the north as Arequipa does the south. That is because other cities, notably Chiclayo, Chimbote, and Piura, share power in the north, whereas Arequipa is rivaled only by Cuzco, which is in the mountains to the east. Trujillo is the historic power centre in northern Peru, however, and it has become an important commercial centre. Its industries include tractor and diesel motor factories as well as food-processing plants. Chimbote, Peru's best harbour, has a steel mill and numerous fish-processing plants. Chiclayo and Piura mainly serve as regional political and commercial centres.

Most highland cities are small. In the north the principal city, Cajamarca, is noted chiefly as the place where the Spanish conquistador Francisco Pizarro captured the Inca emperor Atahuallpa. Huaraz, 200 miles north of Lima, is a rapidly growing city that was connected to Lima by a paved road in the mid-1970s. To the south, Cerro de Pasco, the nation's largest mining centre, is, at more than 14,200 feet, one of the world's highest cities. Huancayo, about 100 miles due east of Lima, is a farming centre famous for its colourful Sunday market, where Indians sell such handicrafts as llama-wool blankets, ponchos, and

Andean cities

Chachani volcano (highest peak) overlooking terraced fields near Arequipa in the southern Sierra region, Peru.
Chip and Rosa Maria de la Cueva Peterson

sweaters. The best-known Andean centre is the ancient city of Cuzco, once the Inca capital. Tourists from all parts of the world visit Inca remains in Cuzco and its environs, as well as its many colonial churches. The Inca past is apparent in many places. Inca walls topped by Spanish-style structures stand along many streets around Cuzco's main plaza. The most monumental Inca ruins are those of the fortress/sanctuary of Sacsahuamán, built on a hill overlooking the city. The bygone world of Spanish colonial power is evident in the tile-roofed houses and churches of Cuzco. Among the most impressive is the cathedral, dating from around 1550.

The major cities of eastern Peru are Iquitos and Pucallpa. Iquitos, on the upper Amazon, was a small jungle outpost until the rubber boom of the 1880s. When the boom ended, lumber became the major product of the area. More recently oil and tourism have contributed to its growth. Pucallpa, on the Ucayali River, is connected to Lima by road and to Iquitos by river vessels. The area around Pucallpa is a major colonization zone.

Growth of Iquitos

THE PEOPLE

Pre-Hispanic groups. Throughout the pre-Hispanic period, the peoples of Peru were largely isolated from one another by the rugged topography of the country. At least three times, however, a unifying culture spread across the Andes. Beginning *c.* 1000 BC, the Chavín culture permeated the region, emanating possibly from the northern ceremonial site of Chavín de Huántar. After AD 600, the Huari civilization, based at a site of the same name near modern Ayacucho, dominated most of the central Andean region. Finally, the Inca Empire developed, eventually to control all of the territory from northern Ecuador to central Chile. The Inca spread their language, Quechua, across the highlands and along the coast, although some groups near Lake Titicaca spoke Aymara at the time of the Spanish conquest. Quechua and Aymara are still prevalent and have official usage, with Spanish, in regions where they are heavily spoken. Tropical forest areas were outside Incan influence, and the numerous languages and dialects now spoken in the Amazon region reflect the diverse linguistic heritage of the tropical forest peoples.

Ethnic diversity. The Spanish conquerors dominated Peruvian society, including politics, religion, and economics. They brought their European culture and transmitted their racial characteristics, Spanish language, and Roman Catholic religion to their descendants. The Spaniards introduced a few African slaves, but their number did not become significant. Following independence and the prohibition of slavery, Chinese immigrants were imported as farm labourers, and new groups of Spaniards, northern Europeans, and Japanese were among other arrivals. These diverse racial and ethnic groups have tended to intermarry and produce a mix of racial types, which in modern Peru constitute a complex racial mosaic.

Differences in life-styles and attitudes are pronounced. Peruvians of Spanish descent and the mestizos (racially mixed people) live mainly along the coast and control most of the nation's wealth. Typically, a small group of white people hold the main power in government and industry. Mestizo culture is a blend of Indian and European ways known as *criollo*. The Spanish-speaking mestizos make up the middle class of Peruvian society. They hold managerial, administrative, and professional jobs, but some are also small landowners and labourers. The Indians of the Sierra, who make up about one-third of the population, live in extreme poverty in a harsh environment; they remain both indifferent to, and outside of, the mainstream affairs of the country. Land reforms have brought some improvement, but many highland Indians shepherd llama herds and work tiny plots of land to eke out a living. Like their Inca ancestors, the overwhelming number of Indians read neither their own nor another language. The lowland Indians of the Montaña occupy a social position similar to that of the highland Indians.

Religion. Ancient Peru had various polytheistic and pantheistic religions. The most important gods were Viracocha (lord, creator, and father of men) and Pacha Mama (Earth mother). The Sun, Moon, and such phenomena as lightning and mountains were also worshiped. Each culture raised temples to honour its local divinity.

The Hispanic conquest of the Incas brought new religious traditions to the Andean area. The Spanish indoctrinated the Indians and spread Roman Catholicism, built hundreds of churches, and held fiestas for patron saints in each village. The people were not strict in their practices, however. Protestant sects have proliferated during the 20th century, and the Indians have mixed many pagan beliefs into the Roman Catholic rituals to produce a syncretic religion rich in traditions. Although most Peruvians are Roman Catholic, the constitution provides for freedom of religion.

Demography. The population of the Inca Empire at the time of the Spanish conquest in 1532 is commonly estimated to have been around 12,000,000, although estimates vary. Not all of these people, of course, lived within the boundaries of modern Peru, but it is clear that Peru was the most densely settled area in pre-Hispanic South America. During the first century of Spanish domination, the Indian population declined by almost 80 percent—due to overwork, malnutrition, and the introduction of such diseases as smallpox and measles. The country's first accurate census (1791) showed the impact of Hispanic dominance of the Inca: the population had declined to slightly more than 1,000,000 (which included Europeans, people of mixed ancestry, and black slaves). After independence the population gradually increased, mainly as a result of high birth rates. By the mid-1960s the population of Peru was about the same as that of the Inca society at its height—in other words, it had taken more than 300 years to replace the population lost in the first century of Spanish domination.

Since World War II, the population of Peru has grown rapidly and has become predominantly urban. There has been a sharp decline in death rates, caused mainly by improvements in sanitation practices and health care, while at the same time birth rates have remained very high. As a result, there has been a surplus of population in many areas, particularly in the Andean region. Overpopulation of the rural areas has been the root cause of the mass migration to the cities that has occurred in Peru since the 1950s. The high rate of population growth has also placed great pressure on Peru's educational and health care systems.

Population density of Peru.

THE ECONOMY

Peru is a developing country whose economy has long been dependent upon the export of raw materials to the more developed nations of the Northern Hemisphere. It is one of the world's leading fishing countries and ranks among the largest producers of bismuth, silver, and copper. In recent decades, the country has struggled to modernize its economy by developing nontraditional export industries as well as the manufacture of consumer items to meet local needs. Serious economic problems persist, however, in several areas. A shortage of investment capital is paralleled by a loss of university-trained technicians to offers of higher salaries abroad. Extensive destruction of transportation and agricultural systems occurs periodically from earthquakes, landslides, and other natural disasters. The limited agricultural areas do not meet the needs of the rapidly expanding population, resulting in continually rising imports of foodstuffs and difficult attempts to alter the nation's farming and eating habits. To remedy these and other economic deficiencies the government nationalized the petroleum and other industries in the late 1960s and early 1970s and made extensive efforts at agrarian reform. Nationalization, however, created additional economic problems, including massive government debt and a large trade deficit. This caused successive Peruvian governments to reassess the role of the state in the economy and to reopen some economic sectors to private entrepreneurs.

Resources. *Minerals and mining.* Peru has a wealth of mineral resources. Copper, iron, lead, zinc, bismuth, phosphates, and manganese exist in great quantities of high-yield ores. Gold and silver are found extensively, as are other rare metals, and petroleum fields are located along the far north coast. Oil exploration in the eastern tropical forests indicates substantial reserves.

In spite of this potential mineral wealth, exploitation

has lagged for a number of reasons, including diminished foreign investment, world price fluctuations, lack of transportation facilities, a scarcity of processing plants, and the depletion of deposits. Difficulties of geography have also hindered development, because some of the most promising resources are located at elevations above 12,000 feet or in the Amazonian forests.

Hydro-electric development

Power.   The hydroelectric potential of Peru is great, especially on the rivers that flow eastward out of the Andes Mountains to the Amazon Basin. Large power plants have been built on the Santa and Mantaro rivers, and other locations have been selected for future development. Most existing plants, both thermal and hydroelectric, have been connected to a coordinated national electric grid. More than three-fourths of the nation's electrical energy is produced from hydroelectric sources. Much of the nation's production and demand are in the Lima metropolitan area, where there is a heavy concentration of industry.

Agriculture.   The primary economic activity in Peru has long been farming, although since World War II the importance of this sector of the national economy has declined sharply. More than one-third of the work force, however, is still employed in agriculture. Despite the number of farm labourers, harvests have not kept pace with the country's rapid population growth, and since the 1960s the per capita production of food has been declining. Peru must import large amounts of grain (particularly wheat, rice, and corn), vegetable oils, dairy products, and meat to feed its population. Although ambitious development plans have been designed to improve output, the scarcity of arable land is an extremely limiting factor in Peru.

The most productive agricultural areas are the irrigated valleys of the coastal region, where yields are uniformly high. Principal crops include sugarcane, cotton, rice, corn, grapes, olives, and vegetables. In the Sierra, cropland is limited and soil fertility low. The main crops in the Sierra region are potatoes and grains, especially wheat, corn, and quinoa, an extremely high-protein cereal. There is little beyond subsistence agriculture in the Amazon region of Peru, although the Montaña Indians have traditionally harvested the coca leaves for local use and for trade with the Sierra Indians.

Fishing and forestry.   In the 1950s and 1960s Peru's fishing industry expanded rapidly, based on the harvest of enormous schools of anchovy. These fish were converted into fish meal and oil for export as animal feed. By 1963 Peru was the world's leading fishing nation, measured in terms of tonnage caught. The anchovy catch peaked at more than 12,000,000 tons in 1970. Overfishing, combined with a severe occurrence of the El Niño current in 1971–72, sent the fishing industry into decline. Recovery took place during the late 1970s and early 1980s, although the catch did not approach earlier record levels. Increasing emphasis is put on fish for human consumption in the domestic and export markets. Forestry has been mainly concentrated in the Montaña. Many commercial woods are available, but they are often inaccessible and exploitation has been hampered by fears of ecological damage.

Decline of the fishing industry

Industry.   Although the Peruvian government has tried to disperse industrial production, most Peruvian factories are located within the greater Lima area. Many products are imported as partially assembled kits, such as automobiles and appliances, with completion done in local factories using Peruvian labour and some Peruvian components. Much of the production of consumer goods is done in small workshops, outside government regulation and taxation—a disturbing factor for economic planners.

The government has emphasized plans that call for industry to increase its share of the gross national product, and manufacturing has become the fastest growing segment of the economy. To better utilize the nation's natural resources to achieve self-sustained growth, a strong push has been given to industries such as those producing petroleum, textiles, processed food, steel, cement, fertilizer, and chemicals. Many of these industries either were nationalized or benefited from special tax incentives and trade protectionist policies during the 1970s. In general, though, the government's efforts to promote industrial development have not met expected goals.

Finance.   The main institutions dealing with finance in Peru are the large state-owned banks, which control such areas as credit, currency regulation, bank regulation, and foreign exchange. Government financial policies are focused on dealing with inflation and foreign debt, which have become serious problems since the mid-20th century. Major financial institutions include the Central Reserve Bank of Peru, the National Bank, and the Development Finance Corporation.

Trade.   Foreign trade has been a mainstay of the Peruvian economy since colonial times. The country has been historically dependent on imported manufactured products, a situation that has prompted the government to subsidize import substitution industries. The need for imported materials remains, however. Since the 1950s, Peru's imports have consisted primarily of foodstuffs, consumer goods, and component parts for Peruvian industries. Petroleum products formed an expensive share of Peru's imports in the early 1970s, but increased domestic production, particularly from the Amazon area, turned Peru into a net exporter of oil by 1980. Other important exports have been such primary commodities as ores and minerals (copper, silver, lead, and zinc, for example) and such agricultural products as cotton, sugar, and coffee. Fish meal, too, has been a leading export since the 1960s.

The United States is Peru's major trading partner, usually accounting for as much as one-third of imports and exports. Western European countries and Japan are the source for most other manufactured goods, and those countries also buy a large percentage of what Peru exports. Other recipients of Peru's exports include the Soviet Union (particularly for minerals and agricultural commodities) and neighbouring South American countries such as Colombia and Brazil. In 1969 Peru became a charter member of the Andean Common Market (Andean Group), but economic problems have hampered implementation of trade policies.

Major trading partners

Transportation.   Peru's transportation system faces the challenge of the Andes and of the complex Amazon River system. The only truly integrated networks are the roads and the airlines; the country's two railroad systems have not been interconnected, and maritime traffic is primarily dependent on calls from world shipping lines. River traffic in the Amazonian region is unimportant because of the vast distances and low population density of that area. Roadways cross the country from north to south, or they form penetration roads that run east–west over the Andes. The most important road is the Pan American Highway, which parallels the coast from Ecuador to Chile. Another main road connects Lima to Chile through the Andes.

The major Peruvian railroad, the Central Railway, rises from the coast at Callao near Lima to cross the continental divide at about 15,700 feet. It connects with a branch line to Cerro de Pasco, making it of great importance to the mining industry of the central Andes. A longer line, the Southern Railway, serves Cuzco, Arequipa, and other cities; some of its traffic originates in Bolivia. Callao, on the Pacific Ocean, is the largest of Peru's numerous ports. Iquitos, located on the Amazon some 2,300 miles from the river's mouth, is the major river port of eastern Peru.

The rough terrain of Peru compels the use of the airplane, but it also complicates flight. Air transport is especially important in hard-to-reach places of the heavily forested east. Commercial aviation began in 1928, and domestic lines operate in addition to numerous foreign airlines. The Jorgo Chávez International Airport in Callao, which services Lima, is the most important of Peru's airports.

ADMINISTRATION AND SOCIAL CONDITIONS

Government.   Peru has a long history of unstable political life that has been punctuated by numerous military coups and changes of constitution. The 1979 Peruvian constitution decrees a government headed by a popularly elected president who serves as the chief of state and commander of the armed forces. The prime minister, appointed by the president, presides over the Council of Ministers (Cabinet), also appointed by the president. The council approves all presidential law decrees and draft bills sent to the legislature. The bicameral legislature consists of

The legislature

a Senate and Chamber of Deputies. Members of the legislature are elected to five-year terms, running concurrently with the term of the president. All judges are appointed by the president from lists of nominees submitted by the National Justice Council. Appointments are confirmed by the Senate, and, once confirmed, judges may serve until age 70. The Supreme Court has nationwide jurisdiction and hears appeals from lower-court decisions; it also investigates the conduct of lower-court judges.

The country has been politically divided into 24 departments and one constitutional province, Callao; the departments are further divided into provinces and districts. The 1979 constitution calls for each department to be governed by a regional assembly. Considerable powers were given to local governments by the 1979 constitution. In 1987 legislation was passed that provided for the reorganization of departments into 12 regions. A wide spectrum of political parties, ranging from right-wing conservative to left-wing socialist and communist, participate in the political process.

Education. Peru's educational problems are complicated by the steadily increasing percentage of young people in its population. Thus the state must spend a disproportionate share of its resources on education, which is free and compulsory for all children between six and 15. Compulsory education is difficult to enforce, however, especially outside urban centres. Because of extremely large class sizes, inadequate facilities, and poorly trained teachers, the quality of education received by children in public schools is regarded as low. As a result, most middle- and upper-class parents send their children to private schools. Universities in Peru include such large, high-calibre institutions as the Pontifical Catholic University of Peru, the University of Lima, and the National University of San Marcos, which was founded in 1551 and claims to be the oldest university in South America. There are also a number of provincial universities.

Health and welfare. Numerous public agencies in Peru are involved with national health and social security. Nevertheless there is a shortage of doctors, nurses, and health care facilities, particularly outside the Lima urban area, and the nation faces a difficult path to adequate health service for its population. Infant and young-child mortality long has been a major problem, and it is one of the major concerns of the government. Peru has a serious shortage of housing units, especially in the urban squatter settlements, but also in the countryside. Sanitation is another major problem, with most cities lacking adequate sewerage as well as street lighting and paving.

Shortage of health care *(marginal note)*

CULTURAL LIFE

The complex ethnic and cultural mixture of Peru presents an entwining of aboriginal pantheism, Spanish mysticism, and African religious practices manifested in the nation's music, literature, textiles, handicrafts, gold and silver work, and bounteous cuisine.

Heritage. Peru's cultural past is best known in such Inca remains as Machu Picchu, a "lost city" discovered in 1911 on an 8,000-foot-high mountain northwest of Cuzco. Surrounded by lush, green, forested hills and snow-capped peaks, Machu Picchu comprises hundreds of well-built agricultural terraces, a multitude of small stone houses, and several ceremonial temples constructed of carved rock. Research suggests that Machu Picchu was a royal estate of the Inca emperor Pachacuti. Hundreds of archaeological ruins dot the Peruvian countryside, but they are especially impressive around Cuzco, in the region known as the Sacred Valley. Archaeologists have uncovered thousands of decorated jugs and bowls and embroidered textiles; the weavings of the Paracas culture and the ceramics of the Mochica are especially distinguished. The dryness of the coast has preserved many pre-Incan remains.

Machu Picchu *(marginal note)*

The arts. *Folk culture.* Peruvian folk culture is deeply tinged with inheritances from the ancestral races. In both town and countryside notable examples of pre-Hispanic and mestizo lore abound in myths, song, superstitions, and dances. Handicrafts, popular with tourists and collectors, provide a close link with such pre-Hispanic crafts as weaving, ceramics, and metalworking.

Westernized arts. The arts have long occupied positions of esteem among Peru's educated minority. Since the late 19th century, most writers have felt a ceaseless duty to analyze their society. Ricardo Palma was among the first to utilize Peruvian themes. *Aves sin nido* (1889; *Birds Without a Nest*), by Clorinda Matto de Turner, was the first of many books whose authors exposed the conditions of Indian life. César Vallejo is often regarded as Peru's finest poet, and José María Arguedas and Mario Vargas Llosa have received high critical acclaim in the post-World War II era. José María Valle-Riestra's opera *Ollanta* and Vicente Stea's *Sinfonía autóctona* (*Aboriginal Symphony*) were the major musical works of 19th-century Peru. Later, Luis Duncker Lavalle incorporated Peruvian motifs into Western forms.

Literature *(marginal note)*

Painting reached its zenith with the famous Cuzco school during the 17th and 18th centuries. Most of the thousands of paintings and sculptures are anonymous, and the works show resemblances both to Byzantine and to Asian forms. Modern Peruvian art has followed an abstract course, notably in the work of the painter Fernando de Szyszlo and the sculptor Joaquín Roca Rey.

The ancient Peruvians were great builders of houses, temples, palaces, and fortresses, adapting their architecture to the landscape. The oldest colonial work is the cathedral of Lima, and the most important architectural jewel is the convent and church of San Francisco in Lima. Contemporary architecture has been characterized by the so-called neo-Peruvian, or Peruvian Baroque, and by the introduction of modern concrete and steel structures.

The theatre is a popular institution in Peru with a strong tradition dating to colonial times. National professional companies perform in major productions at the Municipal Theatre, which was built in Lima at the site of a colonial theatre dating to 1604. The concerts of the National Symphony Orchestra are also presented there, as are the performances of the main national and touring ballet and folk dance companies. Filmmaking in Peru is not well-developed; most films produced there are short, the full-length features being mostly imports.

Cultural institutions. Much of the country's cultural development is overseen by the National Institute of Culture, which seeks to make cultural activities available to all. The Peruvian museums are especially rich in their archaeological collections representing Peru's pre-Hispanic past. The most noteworthy of these are in Lima and include such institutions as the National Museum of Art, the Museum of Anthropology and Archaeology, and the Gold Museum. The main library collection is housed in the National Library in Lima and in the major university libraries.

Museums and libraries *(marginal note)*

Recreation. Recreational activities vary as widely in Peru as do the social classes, but for everyone there are the fiestas, which are held by numerous communities across the country. These colourful events often celebrate religious themes, but some are held for secular holidays and other events. The most popular spectator sports, as in most other Latin-American nations, are soccer and bullfighting, the latter drawing huge crowds to the renowned Plaza de Acho bullring in Lima. Basketball, horse racing, and cockfighting are among other well-attended events. Sporting and recreational facilities are most prevalent in the large metropolitan areas of the Costa.

Press and broadcasting. Although freedom of the press is guaranteed by the Peruvian constitution, the media has been periodically subjected to government control. The major dailies generally have a tradition of taking strong political stands in support of political parties of their choice. Most of the leading dailies, such as *El Comercio, Expreso,* and *Ojo,* are in Lima; others are published in Arequipa and Chiclayo. Lima's *El Peruano,* one of the oldest dailies in the Americas, was founded in 1825. Electronic media have also been subjected to control, which became especially severe in the early 1970s when the administration assumed 51 percent of the ownership of all television stations and 25 percent of all radio stations. Lima has several television channels, and there are stations in all of the major cities of the Costa.

For statistical data on the land and people of Peru, see

the *Britannica World Data* section in the BRITANNICA WORLD DATA ANNUAL.
(J.P.-V./J.S.K.)

History

Humans have probably lived in Peru for more than 13,-000 years. Beginning about 1250 BC several advanced cultures, such as the Chavín, Chimú, Nazca, and Tiahuanaco, developed in different parts of Peru; however, the area was not unified politically until in AD 1438 the Incas set out from their base in Cuzco on a career of conquest that, during the next 50 years, brought under their control the area of present-day Peru, Bolivia, northern Argentina, Chile, and Ecuador. Within this area the Incas established a totalitarian state that enabled the tribal ruler and a small minority of nobles to dominate an inert population.

THE INCA

Like the Aztec, the Inca came late upon the historical scene; even their legends do not predate AD 1200, with the first emperor. For, like Old World peoples, and unlike other aboriginal Americans, the Inca recounted their history by kingly reigns. Most of the accounts agree on 13 emperors (see PRE-COLOMBIAN CIVILIZATIONS). The first seven emperors were legendary, local, and of slight importance; their traditions are full of impossible or improbable events, especially those of the quasi-mythological founder, Manco Capac. In this period the Inca were a small tribe, one of many, whose domain did not extend many miles around their capital, Cuzco. They were almost constantly at war with neighbouring tribes.

The incredibly rapid expansion of the Inca Empire began with Viracocha's son Pachacuti, one of the great conquerors, and one of the great men, in the history of the Americas. Also with his accession in 1438 reliable history began, almost all the chroniclers being in practical agreement. Pachacuti was called by the British geographer-historian Sir Clements Markham "the greatest man that the aboriginal race of America has produced." He and his son Topa Inca may be aptly compared to Philip and Alexander of Macedon. Pachacuti was evidently a great civic planner as well; tradition ascribes to him the city plan of Cuzco as well as the erection of many of the massive masonry buildings that still awe visitors to this ancient capital.

The sudden great expansion of the Inca Empire was one of the most extraordinary events of history. It covered a little less than a century from the accession of Pachacuti in 1438 to the conquest by Francisco Pizarro in 1532, and most of it was apparently accomplished by Pachacuti and Topa Inca in the 30 years between 1463 and 1493. At its maximum the empire extended from the present Colombia–Ecuador border to central Chile, a coastal distance of more than 2,500 miles, encompassing approximately 380,000 square miles, about equal in area to France, Belgium, The Netherlands, Luxembourg, Switzerland, and Italy combined.

First the Aymara-speaking rivals in the region of Lake Titicaca, the Colla and Lupaca, were defeated, and then the Chanca to the west; the latter attacked and nearly captured Cuzco. After that there was little effective resistance. First the peoples to the north were subjugated as far as Quito, Ecuador, including the powerful and cultured "kingdom" of Chimú on the northern coast of Peru. Topa Inca then took over his father's role and turned southward, conquering all of northern Chile as far as the Maule River, the southernmost limit of the empire. His son, Huayna Capac, continued conquests in Ecuador to the Ancasmayo River, the present border between Ecuador and Colombia.

DISCOVERY AND EXPLORATION BY EUROPEANS

Spanish interest in the west coast of South America grew after Vasco Núñez de Balboa discovered the Pacific in 1513, but it was not until 1524 that Francisco Pizarro, aided by another soldier, Diego de Almagro, and a priest, Hernando de Luque, undertook explorations that led to the conquest of Peru. By 1527 they were convinced of the wealth of the Inca Empire. Failing to win further cooperation from Panama's governor, Pizarro returned to Spain, where he received authorization from Charles I to conquer and govern the area extending 600 miles south from Panama. When Pizarro, accompanied by his brothers, returned to Panama, Almagro was outraged by the vast powers Pizarro had acquired for himself. Nevertheless, he continued to collaborate. Pizarro embarked for Peru in early 1531 with 180 men. Establishing a base at San Miguel on the north coast of Peru, Pizarro crossed the mountains to make contact with the Inca Atahuallpa, who had recently been victorious in civil war against his half-brother Huascar, and who was then residing near Cajamarca with an army of about 30,000. Atahuallpa, scornful of the tiny band of invaders, accepted Pizarro's invitation to meet in Cajamarca. There, after Atahuallpa had refused to accept Spanish suzerainty, he was taken prisoner. After his agents had collected a large ransom for his promised release, Atahuallpa was executed for his presumed responsibility for the murder of Huascar. As a means of controlling the Indians, Pizarro then recognized Manco Capac, Huascar's brother, as emperor. In November 1533 the Spaniards occupied Cuzco, the Inca capital.

Pizarro's base at San Miguel

COLONIAL PERIOD

The consolidation of Spanish control proceeded. The city of Quito was subdued and Diego de Almagro left to conquer his domain of Chile. Pizarro organized a Spanish-type municipal government for Cuzco and in 1535 established a new city, Lima, on the coast, to facilitate communications with Panama. Lands were allotted to the conquerors, who were provided with a labour force by grants of encomiendas, which enabled them to collect tribute from the Indians.

Serious trouble then erupted. An unsuccessful Indian rebellion led by Manco Capac in 1536 was followed by open conflict among the conquerors over the division of the spoils. Almagro, disillusioned by Chile's poverty, sought to seize Cuzco from the Pizarros. Almagro was defeated and executed in 1538, but his adherents continued to conspire with his son, and they succeeded in assassinating Francisco Pizarro in 1541. However, an agent of the Spanish crown, sent to establish order, refused to recognize the younger Almagro, who was captured and executed in 1542.

Difficulties persisted nonetheless. The King of Spain, impelled by humanitarianism and by fear that the encomienda system might promote feudalism, promulgated in 1542 the New Laws. These laws threatened the existence of the encomiendas, which were so important to the conquerors. When Viceroy Blasco Núñez Vela arrived in Peru in 1544 to enforce the New Laws, the conquerors, led by Gonzalo Pizarro, revolted and executed the Viceroy. Pizarro maintained control for two years until Pedro de la Gasca, a Spanish agent, undermined his power.

The New Laws

It was nearly a decade before unruly conquerors were controlled under Viceroy Andrés Hurtado de Mendoza (1555–61), and not until the viceregal administration of Francisco de Toledo (1569–81) was systematic control of the huge Indian population attempted. Toledo adapted Indian institutions to the purposes of Spanish authority. Indian chieftains administered local Indian affairs according to custom but were responsible for collecting tribute and providing forced labour. Spanish agents (corregidors) were appointed to protect the interests of both crown and Indian in the Indian communities. Fearing that Manco Capac's son, Topa Amaru, might prove dangerous to Spanish authority, Toledo ordered him executed in 1571.

By the end of Toledo's administration, the viceroyalty of Peru had assumed the form that it retained into the 18th century. Its territory included all of South America except Venezuela and Portuguese Brazil. Although ranching, agriculture, and commerce were carried on, the mining of precious metals, particularly silver, was the basic industry, making the colony the most important in the Spanish empire. The discovery of the fabulous Potosí mines in 1545 had been followed in 1563 by the opening of the Huancavelica mines, which produced the mercury essential to efficient processing of silver. Because the viceroyalty's mineral resources, except for the gold of New Granada (Colombia), were in Peru proper and Upper Peru (Bolivia), these areas became the most highly developed and richest.

The centre of wealth and power for the entire region was the viceregal capital of Lima. There, during the 16th and 17th centuries, a series of viceroys ruled over most of Spanish South America. The elaborate viceregal court was the apex of a highly stratified society based upon forced Indian labour. It attracted not only the politically oriented but also the wealthy, the artistic, and the intellectual.

Lima was also important as seat of the audiencia, which administered royal justice, and as a religious, cultural, and commercial centre. The archbishop of Lima was head of the church in Peru. Many religious orders established monasteries and convents there, and the tribunal of the Inquisition worked to extirpate religious heresy. In Lima also was the capstone of the educational system—the University of San Marcos. Adding to the wealth and importance of Lima was the privileged position that its merchants enjoyed under the monopolistic Spanish trade system. Lima, with its port of Callao, was the entrepôt for trade between Europe and the commercial centres of South America, ranging from Quito to Chile on the Pacific coast and to Buenos Aires on the Atlantic. Under the Spanish system the bulk of legitimate trade to and from these areas had to pass through merchants in Lima.

During the later 17th century Peru experienced difficulties. Some of these, such as increasing contraband trade with non-Spanish merchants, attacks by pirates, and the growth of venality among government officials, reflected the internal decay of Spain and the decline of its international power. Contributing to Peruvian difficulties was the decline of its production of precious metals.

A series of governmental reforms complicated Peru's problems in the 18th century. The Bourbon dynasty, which in 1700 had replaced the Habsburgs as rulers of Spain, undertook a program of reform during the 18th century, seeking to promote the economic development of their colonies, improve colonial defenses, and provide more efficient government. The first seriously to affect Peru was the establishment of the new Viceroyalty of New Granada, ending Peru's control over northern South America and resulting in its loss to New Granada of the thriving port of Guayaquil (now in Ecuador). For the next few decades Bourbon reforms, together with overall expansion of the economy, improved conditions in Peru. In 1777–78, however, the Spanish government established another viceroyalty, that of Río de la Plata, this time depriving the Peruvian viceroy of authority over Upper Peru and the areas of present-day Argentina, Paraguay, and Uruguay. Chile was reconstituted as a virtually autonomous captaincy general. Following the disastrous loss of the silver mines of Upper Peru, the viceroyalty of Peru was still more weakened by reforms in the trade system, which permitted merchants in ports on the Atlantic and Pacific to trade directly with Spain.

Internal strife created further complications. The Indians, who had from the time of the conquest suffered oppressive taxation and enforced labour, revolted in 1780 under Tupac Amaru II, a descendant of the last Inca emperor and a man of wealth and education. The revolt spread throughout Peru and into Upper Peru and Ecuador. Although Tupac Amaru II was captured and executed in 1781, the Indians continued to fight the Spaniards until 1783, causing considerable disruption.

Nevertheless, in the late 18th and 19th centuries Peru experienced a period of intellectual development that was the result of the influence of the utilitarian ideas of the European Enlightenment, brought to Peru in books and by European participants in scientific expeditions in 1778 and 1793. The chief manifestation of the intellectual development of Peru was the establishment of a literary and scientific club in Lima, the Society of the Lovers of the Country.

ACHIEVEMENT OF INDEPENDENCE

The Napoleonic invasion of Spain in 1808 sparked the Creoles (those of European descent born in America) in other Spanish colonies to struggle for independence between 1810 and 1821. But Peru remained loyal because of the conservative attitude of the Peruvian aristocracy, the presence of many Spaniards in Peru, the concentra-

tion of Spanish military power in Lima, and the effective suppression of Indian uprisings. Peru's independence was, consequently, achieved primarily by outsiders.

Among them was General José de San Martín of Argentina, whose aims were to secure Argentine control of Upper Peru's silver from the Spanish forces that had occupied Upper Peru and to assure Argentina's independence by destroying the remaining Spanish power in South America. Because Argentine forces had previously been defeated in Upper Peru, San Martín determined to surround the Spaniards by liberating Chile and using it as a base for a seaborne attack on Peru. Chile was freed in 1818 and a fleet was readied, which enabled San Martín to occupy the Peruvian port of Pisco in September 1820. When the viceroy withdrew his forces into the interior, San Martín entered Lima. Peruvian independence was declared on July 28, 1821.

Lacking power to attack the strong Spanish forces in the interior, San Martín sought aid from Simón Bolívar, who had liberated northern South America, but Bolívar declined, refusing to share leadership. San Martín then withdrew, and Bolívar assumed power in Peru to carry on the struggle for liberation. At the battles of Junín (Aug. 6, 1824) and Ayacucho (Dec. 9, 1824) Spanish power was broken and Peru's independence assured.

(J.A.Mn./R.N.Bu./T.M.D.)

PERU FROM 1824 TO 1884

The end of Spanish rule did not, however, provide a solution to the many political, social, and economic problems facing the country. The transition from a colonial dependency to a modern state proved difficult.

Struggle for power. At the outset of Peru's national existence, military leaders (caudillos) who had gained prominence in the struggle for independence sought to seize power. The departure of Simón Bolívar in 1826 removed a stabilizing influence. The aims of the caudillos were furthered by the absence of a tradition of self-government, by the prevalence of a feudal society of Creoles and Indians, and by the reluctance of civilians to assume political responsibility. Despite military influences, a liberal constitution was adopted in 1828. This did not prevent General Agustín Gamarra from taking government power by illegal means. He was succeeded in 1835 by another self-seeking caudillo, General Felipe Salaverry.

The ambitions of Gamarra and Salaverry were thwarted by Andrés de Santa Cruz, an intelligent military commander of Spanish-Indian descent, who proposed a confederation of Peru and Bolivia. For three years Santa Cruz, though born in La Paz, obtained the backing of influential groups in Peru and maintained the political union. But his hopes were shattered at the Battle of Yungay in 1839 by a joint force of nationalist-minded Peruvians and of Chileans fearing a threat to the balance of power in the Pacific.

Establishment of order. During the initial period of statehood in Peru, liberal and conservative parties with ill-defined programs emerged. Their rivalry enhanced the political instability of the country.

General Ramón Castilla assumed the presidency in 1845. Castilla dominated the political scene from 1845 to 1851 and from 1855 to 1862, in spite of his mestizo background. His greatest accomplishment for the promotion of national wealth was the exploitation of the guano deposits along the coast and offshore islands. Taxes on this industry, which was controlled by foreign corporations, furnished the principal source of government revenue for several decades. Castilla appealed to liberals by abolishing the payment of tribute by Indians and by emancipating the black slaves. Landowners on the coastal plantations, however, were permitted to import thousands of Chinese coolies in order to have a sufficient labour supply. As an additional concession to the liberals, Castilla established a system of state education at the primary and secondary levels. Through his influence, an assembly in 1860 adopted a constitution that lasted into the 1900s.

In the second half of the 19th century, Peru's history was characterized by many setbacks. In 1864 Spain dispatched a naval force to the Pacific, ostensibly to protect the rights of Basque immigrants but in reality to reestablish domination over its former colony. In 1869, after meeting with the determined opposition of Peru and Chile, Spain withdrew and recognized Peru's independence for the first time, but the conflict was a heavy drain on Peru's treasury.

Dissatisfaction with military rule resulted in 1871 in the formation of the Civilian Party, representing an oligarchy of landowners and merchants. This party, headed by Manuel Pardo (president, 1872–76), approved a costly program of internal development, which included the construction of railroads across the Andes. Corruption on the part of government officials and contractors characterized the work, which decreased the isolation of the Peruvian interior but increased enormously the national debt.

The War of the Pacific (1879–83). Another untoward event was the War of the Pacific with Chile, caused mainly by rivalry over the exploitation of rich nitrate beds in the Atacama Desert (then in Peru, now in Chile). Chile's superior resources and military discipline brought overwhelming defeat to Peru and its ally Bolivia.

At the Battle of Iquique (then in Peru, now in Chile), on May 21, 1879, the Peruvians suffered the loss of one of their best warships, the *Independencia;* the *Huáscar* was then sunk on October 8, and this eventual surrender of control of the sea permitted a Chilean army to land on the Peruvian coast. On Jan. 17, 1881, Chilean forces captured the capital, Lima. Looting and pillaging followed and the National Library was destroyed. According to the terms of the Treaty of Ancón (Oct. 20, 1883), Peru turned over to Chile full possession of the province of Tarapacá and the administration for 10 years of the provinces of Tacna and Arica, after which a plebiscite was to determine their future sovereignty.

PERU FROM 1884 TO 1930

Expenditures for the war, and the consequent loss of revenue from the nitrate fields, created the possibility of imminent bankruptcy. To avert this disaster, the Civilian regime accepted in 1889 a plan proposed by the bondholders for handling the debt. The Peruvian Corporation, representing the creditors, with headquarters in London, was to control the railroads for 66 years, to mine up to 3,000,000 tons of guano, and to receive 33 annual payments of £80,000 each. The plan worked satisfactorily but was hated by the Peruvian people.

Economic recovery program

Social reforms and economic development. The decline in national prestige created an atmosphere conducive to political change. The Democratic Party was formed, and in 1895, under the leadership of Nicolás de Piérola, it won the presidential election. Having a broad, popular base, it championed direct suffrage and the restoration of municipal elections. Public education was fostered, but schools for the children of the poor were lacking.

An orderly political scene, marked by rivalry between the Democratic and Civilian groups, accelerated economic development. There was an increase in the production of minerals, notably copper, and of such agricultural commodities as cotton, sugar, and wool. In the mining of copper, U.S. capital acquired important interests.

Augusto Leguía y Salcedo

Augusto Leguía y Salcedo, chief spokesman for the Civilians, assumed the presidency in 1908. His first term in office (1908–12) was marked by the expansion of sugar and cotton production and the settlement of the boundary dispute with Brazil. During Leguía's second term (1919–30), he embarked upon expensive public works projects, financed by loans from U.S. banks. Rights to the oil fields of La Brea-Pariñas were given to the U.S.-owned International Petroleum Company, which built a refinery to supply the nation with gasoline and oil.

Leguía supported the adoption of a new constitution in 1920. Among its progressive provisions was Article 58, which protected the communal lands of the Indians from sale and seizure. Failure to implement this provision, however, gave rise to a significant development of Indianism. While most intellectuals urged gradual reforms, more radical measures were advocated by the Peruvian Communist Party and others.

Formation of the Aprista movement. The American Popular Revolutionary Alliance (APRA), known as the "Aprista movement," was formed in 1924 in Mexico City by Víctor Raúl Haya de la Torre, an intellectual then in exile. Internationally, it expressed the ideals of the unity of American Indians and the elimination of U.S. imperialism. Internally, it proclaimed the need to end the exploitation of the Peruvian masses through the institution of a planned economy and the nationalization of foreign-owned enterprises. Its anticapitalist and anti-imperialist stand appealed to intellectuals, to the Indians, and to the lower middle class.

By 1930 Leguía had experienced a definite loss in popularity. Final settlement of the long-standing Tacna–Arica dispute with Chile, by which Peru ceded the province of Arica, angered the extreme nationalists, while world depression cost Leguía the support of business groups.

PERU FROM 1930 TO 1968

In 1930 a military junta headed by Colonel Luis Sánchez Cerro overthrew Leguía, and Sánchez Cerro defeated Haya de la Torre, the APRA candidate, in the presidential elections of 1931. APRA claimed that the elections were fraudulent and instigated a campaign to discredit the regime. The threat from the left led to the emergence of a Fascist group, whose chief exponent was the historian José de la Riva Agüero. In July 1932 Apristas organized an uprising in Trujillo, on the northern coast, and Sánchez Cerro was assassinated by an Aprista in 1933. These incidents created an enduring enmity between the military establishment and APRA.

Troubled democracy. Sánchez Cerro's successor (1933–39) was General Oscar Benavides, who restored confidence in the economy. He also settled a dangerous boundary controversy with Colombia over the port of Leticia on the upper Amazon and a finger of land giving access to the river, both of which had been ceded to Colombia in a treaty of 1922. To avoid war Benavides returned the territory to Colombia. Benavides reduced the strength of APRA by declaring the party illegal, by a relentless persecution of its leaders, and by the adoption of social assistance projects. In the presidential election of 1939 the Apristas supported Manuel Prado, a banker and member of an aristocratic family of Lima.

Alignment with the United States

During World War II Peru cooperated with the United States, authorized Allied use of airfields and ports, and arranged to sell the Allies petroleum, cotton, and minerals. In 1942 Peru severed diplomatic relations with the Axis powers, and in 1945 it declared war on them. During the war Peru succeeded, with U.S. support, in getting a favourable settlement of a boundary dispute with Ecuador, which it had invaded.

World War II not only brought economic prosperity but also hope for real democracy. Prado, swayed by public opinion, approved the presidential candidacy in 1945 of José Luis Bustamante y Rivero, a lawyer from Arequipa with liberal leanings, who represented a coalition of middle- and upper-class elements. APRA, again a legal party, obtained a majority of seats in the lower house and half the seats in the Senate. Bustamante generally followed an independent course, and the Apristas withdrew their support. After Apristas staged an abortive insurrection in Callao, near Lima, the President outlawed the party.

The dictatorship of Manuel Odría. In October 1948 General Manuel Odría seized power, protesting the President's lack of firmness in dealing with the radicals, and extreme measures were taken to suppress the Apristas. Haya de la Torre found refuge in the Colombian embassy, where he stayed for five years before leaving Peru.

Odría led an authoritarian regime in which political stability allowed the revival of prosperity. The Korean conflict of the early 1950s benefited foreign trade because of heavy U.S. demand for Peruvian minerals, and a friendly policy toward foreign capital prompted large-scale investments.

Return to elected government. In the election of 1956, Manuel Prado, who was supported by Odría, won a second term, defeating Fernando Belaúnde Terry. A surprising feature of the election was the decline of APRA, some of whose members joined Belaúnde's National Front Party. Prado countered the financial crisis inherited from Odría by appointing as minister of the treasury Pedro Beltrán, whose policies contributed to a 4½ percent annual increase in the gross national product. The fishing industry based on the Peru Current expanded. Beltrán's measures did not, however, lessen the pressure from the landless Indians and the underpaid urban proletariat.

With political tension at a high level in 1962, none of the presidential candidates of the three leading parties received the one-third vote necessary for election. The election went to the congress for a decision, but the military forces seized the government. A new election called in 1963 by the junta permitted Belaúnde's party, now called Popular Action, to be victorious.

Reforms under Belaúnde

Belaúnde promised solutions to the country's economic and social problems. An agrarian act of 1964 provided for more effective use of the land, with expropriation of unused or misused agricultural properties; by 1966 more than 500,000 acres had been distributed. The government also organized community development projects, and Indians were encouraged to colonize land in the foothills east of the Andes. Irrigation schemes were instituted for the arid coastal plain, and a network of roads was planned. Education was promoted with the establishment of new universities and with attacks on illiteracy.

MILITARY RULE (1968–80)

On Oct. 3, 1968, the military forced the resignation of Belaúnde. The junta, headed by Juan Velasco Alvarado, imprisoned opposing politicians and suspended constitutional liberties. On October 9 the government expropriated the holdings of the International Petroleum Company, straining relations with the United States.

Economic nationalism. In 1969 the junta embarked on a program of economic nationalism that would affect U.S. capital investments totaling $600,000,000. In 13 months, three basic reform measures were enacted: the Agrarian Law (June 24, 1969); the Mining Law (April 14, 1970); and the Industrial Law (July 30, 1970). Accordingly, the government seized on Aug. 22, 1969, the Paramonga chemical and paper plant of one of the largest U.S. interests in Peru. It sought also to control essential industries and public services through outright ownership and by "Peruvianization"—insistence that a majority of the stock of a foreign company be held by nationals. The occurrence on May 31, 1970, of a major earthquake in northern Peru partly jeopardized the financial stability of the regime.

Agrarian and fishing reforms

The junta appealed to the peasants by expropriating landed estates. Government-directed collectives operated the large estates, while smaller properties were cultivated by individuals or Indian communes. The opening up of arid lands being part of the new agricultural program, the junta signed in July 1971 a contract with a Yugoslav company for the construction of a canal in the Piura Valley to irrigate 330,000 additional acres, and two more projects were initiated subsequently. Exploitation of fishing as a primary national resource was to be encouraged. The disappearance of the anchovies in 1972 because of El Niño, however, brought about a suspension of fish exports and dealt a serious blow to the economy. In 1973 the government moved to nationalize the fish meal industry, valued at $500,000,000. With the organization of Petroperú, a state-owned company, the petroleum industry expanded.

In order to improve general education, the government promulgated in March 1972 an education reform bill that was to put in force "a system of learning from the cradle to the grave." Major features were recognition of the equality of women, the establishment of rural schools, the granting of autonomy to the universities, and the use of the Indian languages Quechua or Aymara in the schools in the Andes and east of the Sierra.

To prevent criticism of its tight dictatorship, the junta censored the press, and some radio stations and newspapers were closed. In addition the government acquired control of privately owned television stations. In foreign relations the junta initiated a two-China policy, especially hoping to arrange the sale of minerals and fish meal to Peking. As part of an innovative trans-Pacific policy, Japanese investments and contacts were invited to Peru. Friendship with the Soviet Union led to the exchange of ambassadors with Communist-bloc nations.

New junta. Economic factors were primarily responsible for the growth of resentment among many groups toward the Velasco regime. The decline in fish meal exports and in copper prices ended the economic boom, while loans obtained from abroad for agrarian reform and huge copper and petroleum projects increased the foreign debt. On Aug. 29, 1975, a new junta was formed, headed by General Francisco Morales Bermúdez, former minister of finance and economy. Amid increasing economic hardship, Peruvian policies were constantly altered as repeated changes in the Cabinet took place. Morales shifted toward more moderate right-wing policies. The National Agrarian Confederation was dissolved in 1978; Pescaperú, the state fishing enterprise, was returned to private hands; many mining projects were opened to private investors; and more foreign investment was encouraged.

RETURN TO CIVILIAN RULE

The Morales government committed itself to reestablishing constitutional rule, and a popularly elected Constituent Assembly was summoned in June 1978 to draft a new constitution. In this, the first elective assembly in 10 years, the Apristas formed the largest bloc, and Haya de la Torre was elected president of the assembly. After the initial draft was rejected by the Morales regime, the new constitution was signed on July 12, 1979.

Return of Belaúnde

Elections were held in May 1980, and Fernando Belaúnde Terry was returned to the presidency. His party, Popular Action, headed a majority coalition in the legislature. Belaúnde immediately returned to their previous owners newspapers that had been confiscated by the military junta. The legislature issued a package of decrees designed to reorganize the economy with a view toward reducing government involvement and encouraging private enterprise, but these were insufficient to ameliorate the growing economic and political crisis. The economy was hurt by an increase in imports due to Belaúnde's free-market policies, lower world prices for Peru's major export commodities, high international interest rates on the nation's burgeoning foreign debt, and a devastating El Niño in 1982–83. Aggravating the economic problems was the rise of the guerrilla movement, led by the neo-Maoist Sendero Luminoso (Shining Path) and the Tupac Amaru Revolutionary Movement, which forced the government to commit ever-increasing resources to combating the guerrillas and to repairing the damages inflicted in the conflict. When the inflation rate rose a staggering 3,240 percent between July 1980 and June 1985, the economy almost collapsed. Moreover, the sol lost so much of its value that a new currency, the inti, was created in 1986.

Presidency of Alan García Pérez

In the 1985 elections APRA, capitalizing on the nation's plight, had its presidential candidate elected for the first time in its history. He was the young and charismatic Alan García Pérez. The new leader shocked the international community when he announced that Peru would pay no more than 10 percent of its export earnings toward a nearly $14,000,000,000 foreign debt. Adopting a populist stance domestically, García attempted to reactivate the economy, end human rights abuses in the war against the guerrillas, gain control over the drug traffickers, and rally the population. The International Monetary Fund (IMF) added a blow to the country's condition when it declared Peru to be ineligible for future loans and credits until García adopted more orthodox economic and debt repayment measures. Facing a deteriorating economic situation, the president moved to nationalize the banks in 1987, an act that eroded his personal popularity.

The guerrilla movement, in the meantime, continued unabated. The devastating attacks of well-organized and persistent guerrilla groups were rapidly becoming the most disruptive factor in Peruvian society and the most serious threat to the administration's ability to govern.

(J.P.M./T.M.D.)

For later developments in the history of Peru, see the *Britannica Book of the Year* section in the BRITANNICA WORLD DATA ANNUAL.

For coverage of related topics in the *Macropædia* and the *Micropædia*, see the *Propædia*, sections 951, 964, 966, and 974.

BIBLIOGRAPHY

Physical and human geography: An overview of Peru is provided by PICHARD F. NYROP (ed.), *Peru, A Country Study,* 3rd ed. (1981). An analysis of the geography is *Gran geografía del Perú: naturaleza y hombre,* 8 vol. (1986). Other useful studies include DAVID A. ROBINSON, *Peru in Four Dimensions* (1964, reprinted 1971); CARLOS PEÑAHERRERA DEL AGUILA, *Geografía general del Perú: síntesis,* vol. 1, *Aspectos físicos* (1969); and CLAUDE COLLIN DELAVAUD, *Les Régions côtieres du Pérou septentrional: occupation du sol, aménagement régional* (1968), available also in Spanish, *Las regiones costeñas del Peru septentrional* (1984). Peru's natural regions and vegetation are discussed in JAVIER PULGAR VIDAL, *Geografía del Perú: las ocho regiones naturales del Perú,* 8th ed. (1981).

Notable works on the topic of Indians and peasants include HILDEBRANDO CASTRO POZO, *Nuestra comunidad indígena,* 2nd ed. (1979); and MOISÉS SÁENZ, *Sobre el indio peruano y su incorporación al medio nacional* (1933), both early classics; THOMAS M. DAVIES, JR., *Indian Integration in Peru: A Half Century of Experience, 1900–1948* (1974); PAUL L. DOUGHTY, *Huaylas: An Andean District in Search of Progress* (1968), an anthropological study; WILFREDO KAPSOLI E., *Los movimientos campesinos en el Perú, 1879–1965,* 2nd ed. (1982), the best study of peasant uprisings; and PIERRE L. VAN DEN BERGHE and GEORGE P. PRIMOV, *Inequality in the Peruvian Andes: Class and Ethnicity in Cuzco* (1977), a study of Indian domination by the "urban mestizo elite." Good ethnographies include STEPHEN B. BRUSH, *Mountain, Field, and Family: The Economy and Human Ecology of an Andean Valley* (1977); and SUSAN C. BOURQUE and KAY BARBARA WARREN, *Women of the Andes: Patriarchy and Social Change in Two Peruvian Towns* (1981).

General economic studies include ROSEMARY THORP and GEOFFREY BERTRAM, *Peru, 1890–1977: Growth and Policy in an Open Economy* (1978); and E.V.K. FITZGERALD, *The Political Economy of Peru, 1956–78: Economic Development and the Restructuring of Capital* (1979). The economic geography of Peru is discussed in EMILIO ROMERO, *Geografía económica del Perú,* 5th ed. (1966). Labour studies include DAVID CHAPLIN, *The Peruvian Industrial Labor Force* (1967); and DENIS SULMONT S., *Historia del movimiento obrero en el Perú, de 1890 a 1977* (1977). Studies on agriculture and fishing include BALTAZAR CARAVEDO MOLINARI, *Estado, pesca y burguesía, 1939–1973: teoría y realidad* (1979); and ARTHUR J. COUTU and RICHARD A. KING, *The Agricultural Development of Peru* (1969).

Samplings and discussions of Peruvian literature can be found in LUIS ALBERTO SÁNCHEZ, *La literatura peruana: derrotero para una historia cultural del Perú,* 5th ed., 5 vol. (1981); and LYNN A. DARROCH (ed.), *Between Fire and Love: Contemporary Peruvian Writing* (1980). On the political role of the Roman Catholic Church and popular religiosity, see JEFFREY L. KLAIBER, *Religion and Revolution in Peru, 1824–1976* (1977). See also GUSTAVO GUTIÉRREZ, *A Theology of Liberation: History, Politics, and Salvation* (1973; originally published in Spanish, 1972), by a leading theoretician of the liberation theology movement.

(J.S.K./T.M.D.)

History: JORGE BASADRE, *Historia de la república del Perú, 1822–1933,* 6th rev. ed., 17 vol. (1968–70), is the basic point of departure for any study of Peru. HENRY F. DOBYNS and PAUL L. DOUGHTY, *Peru: A Cultural History* (1976), is a sensitive treatment of Peru's historical tradition, with particular emphasis on race relations and ecological adaptation. FREDRICK B. PIKE, *The Modern History of Peru* (1967, reprinted 1969), is competent and comprehensive, while his *United States and the Andean Republics: Peru, Bolivia, and Ecuador* (1977), is a brilliant synthesis of the incompatability of Hispanic and Anglo cultures. DAVID SCOTT PALMER, *Peru: The Authoritarian Tradition* (1980), treats Peruvian history within the context of Latin-American development.

The best accounts of Peru's pre-conquest peoples are EDWARD P. LANNING, *Peru Before the Incas* (1967); LUIS G. LUMBRERAS, *The Peoples and Cultures of Ancient Peru* (1974; originally published in Spanish, 1969); JOHN V. MURRA, *Formaciones económicas y políticas del mundo andino* (1975); and FRANKLIN PEASE G.Y., *Del Tawantinsuyu a la historia del Perú* (1978), which emphasizes the indigenous origins of modern Peruvian culture. Superb ethnohistorical accounts of the impact of conquest and of the early colonial period are NATHAN WACHTEL, *The Vision of the Vanquished: The Spanish Conquest of Peru Through Indian Eyes, 1530–1570* (1977; originally published in French, 1971); KAREN SPALDING, *Huarochirí: An Andean Society Under Inca and Spanish Rule* (1984); and STEVE J. STERN, *Peru's Indian Peoples and the Challenge of Spanish Conquest: Huamanga to 1640* (1982). See also JAMES LOCKHART, *Spanish Peru, 1532–1560: A Colonial Society* (1968); and NOBLE DAVID COOK, *Demographic Collapse: Indian Peru, 1520–1620* (1981), which treats the devastating loss of Indian life due to European contact.

Treatments of Spanish colonial institutions and economy include J.R. FISHER, *Government and Society in Colonial Peru: The Intendant System, 1784–1814* (1970), and *Silver Mines and Silver Miners in Colonial Peru, 1776–1824* (1977); ROBERT G. KEITH, *Conquest and Agrarian Change: The Emergence of the Hacienda System on the Peruvian Coast* (1976); and NICHOLAS P. CUSHNER, *Lords of the Land: Sugar, Wine, and Jesuit Estates of Coastal Peru, 1600–1767* (1980). LEON G. CAMPBELL, *The Military and Society in Colonial Peru, 1750–1810* (1978), studies the origins of Peruvian civil-military relations. TIMOTHY E. ANNA, *The Fall of the Royal Government in Peru* (1979), views independence as an accidental occurrence; while HERACLIO BONILLA et al., *La independencia en el Perú,* 2nd ed. (1981), argues that Peru had to be conquered. HERACLIO BONILLA, *Guano y burguesía en el Perú,* 2nd ed. (1984), analyzes the rise of the guano industry and its impact on capitalist development. FLORENCIA E. MALLON, *The Defense of Community in Peru's Central Highlands: Peasant Struggle and Capitalist Transition, 1860–1940* (1983), treats nascent Peruvian capitalism from a rural perspective. ROBERT N. BURR, *By Reason or Force: Chile and the Balancing of Power in South America, 1830–1905* (1965, reprinted 1974), remains the best diplomatic history of the War of the Pacific.

Excellent political analyses of the 20th century include FRANÇOIS BOURRICAUD, *Power and Society in Contemporary Peru* (1970; originally published in French, 1967); CARLOS A. ASTIZ, *Pressure Groups and Power Elites in Peruvian Politics* (1969); and JULIO COTLER, *Clases, estado y nación en el Perú,* 2nd ed. (1982). The best studies of the crucial period 1919–40 are STEVE STEIN, *Populism in Peru: The Emergence of the Masses and the Politics of Social Control* (1980); and BALTAZAR CARAVEDO MOLINARI, *Clases, lucha política y gobierno en el Perú, 1919–1933* (1977). APRA, one of the most important political movements in Latin America, is the subject of ROBERT J. ALEXANDER (ed. and trans.), *Aprismo: The Ideas and Doctrines of Víctor Raúl Haya de la Torre* (1973); PETER F. KLARÉN, *Modernization, Dislocation, and Aprismo: Origins of the Peruvian Aprista Party, 1870–1932* (1973); and FREDRICK B. PIKE, *The Politics of the Miraculous in Peru: Haya de la Torre and the Spiritualist Tradition* (1986). Economic analyses of Belaúnde's first term include PEDRO-PABLO KUCZYNSKI, *Peruvian Democracy Under Economic Stress: An Account of the Belaúnde Administration, 1963–1968* (1977); and RICHARD C. WEBB, *Government Policy and the Distribution of Income in Peru, 1963–1973* (1977). Guerrilla movements are discussed by members of the movements in HUGO BLANCO, *Land or Death: The Peasant Struggle in Peru* (1972); and HECTOR BÉJAR, *Peru 1965: Notes on a Guerrilla Experience* (1970; originally published in Spanish, 1969).

Civil-military relations are treated in VÍCTOR VILLANUEVA, *Ejército peruano: del caudillaje anárquico al militarismo reformista* (1973), and his seminal study of the Center for High Military Studies, *El CAEM y la revolución de la fuerza armada* (1972); and in BRIAN LOVEMAN and THOMAS M. DAVIES, JR. (eds.), *The Politics of Antipolitics: The Military in Latin America* (1978). The most important literature on the 1968–80 military government includes ABRAHAM F. LOWENTHAL (ed.), *The Peruvian Experiment: Continuity and Change Under Military Rule* (1975), an overly optimistic account; CYNTHIA MCCLINTOCK and ABRAHAM F. LOWENTHAL (eds.), *The Peruvian Experiment Reconsidered* (1983), a scathing postmortem; CYNTHIA MCCLINTOCK, *Peasant Cooperatives and Political Change in Peru* (1981); ALFRED STEPAN, *The State and Society: Peru in Comparative Perspective* (1978), a study of authoritarian rule; GEORGE D.E. PHILIP, *The Rise and Fall of the Peruvian Military Radicals 1968–1976* (1978), an analysis of the reforms undertaken by Velasco; and STEPHEN M. GORMAN (ed.), *Post-Revolutionary Peru: The Politics of Transformation* (1982), an analysis of the successes, failures, and legacy of the military government.

(T.M.D.)

Peter I the Great, of Russia

Peter I the Great (Russian Pyotr I Veliky, in full Pyotr Alekseyevich), tsar of Russia from 1682 and emperor from 1721, was one of his country's greatest statesmen, organizers, and reformers. He was born in Moscow on June 9 (May 30, old style), 1672, the son of Tsar Alexis by his second wife, Natalya Kirillovna Naryshkina. Unlike his half-brothers, sons of his father's first wife, Mariya Ilinichna Miloslavskaya, Peter proved a healthy child, lively and inquisitive. It is probably significant to his development that his mother's former guardian, Artamon Sergeyevich Matveyev, had raised her in an atmosphere open to progressive influences from the West.

Youth and accession. When Alexis died in 1676 Peter was only four years old. His elder half-brother, a sickly youth, then succeeded to the throne as Fyodor III; but, in fact, power fell into the hands of the Miloslavskys, relatives of Fyodor's mother, who deliberately pushed Peter and the Naryshkin circle aside. When Fyodor died childless in 1682, a fierce struggle for power ensued between the Miloslavskys and the Naryshkins: the former wanted to put Fyodor's brother, the delicate and feebleminded Ivan V, on the throne; the Naryshkins stood for the healthy and intelligent Peter. Representatives of the various orders of society, assembled in the Kremlin, declared themselves for Peter, who was then proclaimed tsar; but the Miloslavsky faction exploited a revolt of the Moscow *streltsy*, or musketeers of the sovereign's bodyguard, who killed some of Peter's adherents, including Matveyev. Ivan and Peter were then proclaimed joint tsars; and eventually, because of Ivan's precarious health and Peter's youth, Ivan's 25-year-old sister Sophia was made regent. Clever and influential, Sophia took control of the government; excluded from public affairs, Peter lived with his mother in the village of Preobrazhenskoye, near Moscow, often fearing for his safety. All this left an ineradicable impression on the young tsar and determined his negative attitude toward the *streltsy*.

One result of Sophia's overt exclusion of Peter from the government was that he did not receive the usual education of a Russian tsar; he grew up in a free atmosphere instead of being confined within the narrow bounds of a palace. While his first tutor, the former church clerk Nikita Zotov, could give little to satisfy Peter's curiosity, the boy enjoyed noisy outdoor games and took especial interest

Boyhood influences

in military matters, his favourite toys being arms of one sort or another. He also occupied himself with carpentry, joinery, blacksmith's work, and printing.

Near Preobrazhenskoye there was a *nemetskaya sloboda* ("German colony") where foreigners were allowed to reside. Acquaintance with its inhabitants aroused Peter's interest in the life of other nations, and an English sailboat, found derelict in a shed, whetted his passion for seafaring. Mathematics, fortification, and navigation were the sciences that appealed most strongly to Peter. A model fortress was built for his amusement, and he organized his first "play" troops, from which, in 1687, the Preobrazhensky and Semyonovsky Guards regiments were formed—to become the nucleus of a new Russian Army.

Early in 1689 Natalya Naryshkina arranged Peter's marriage to the beautiful Eudoxia (Yevdokiya Fyodorovna Lopukhina). This was obviously a political act, intended to demonstrate the fact that the 17-year-old Peter was now a grown man, with a right to rule in his own name. The marriage did not last long: Peter soon began to ignore his wife, and in 1698 he relegated her to a convent.

In August 1689 a new revolt of the *streltsy* took place. Sophia and her faction tried to use it to their own advantage for another coup d'état, but events this time turned decisively in Peter's favour. He removed Sophia from power and banished her to the Novodevichy convent; she was forced to become a nun after a *streltsy* rebellion in 1698. Though Ivan V remained nominally joint tsar with Peter, the administration was now largely given over to Peter's kinsmen, the Naryshkins, until Ivan's death in 1696. Peter, meanwhile continuing his military and nautical amusements, sailed the first seaworthy ships to be built in Russia. His games proved to be good training for the tasks ahead.

Peter as sole ruler

External events. At the beginning of Peter's reign, Russia was territorially a huge power, but with no access to the Black Sea, the Caspian, or to the Baltic, and to win such an outlet became the main goal of Peter's foreign policy.

The Azov campaigns (1695–96). The first steps taken in this direction were the campaigns of 1695 and 1696, with the object of capturing Azov from the Crimean Tatar vassals of Turkey. On the one hand, these Azov campaigns could be seen as fulfilling Russia's commitments, undertaken during Sophia's regency, to the anti-Turkish "Holy League" of 1684 (Austria, Poland, and Venice); on the other they were intended to secure the southern frontier against Tatar raids, as well as to approach the Black Sea. The first campaign ended in failure (1695), but this did not discourage Peter: he promptly built a fleet at Voronezh to sail down the Don River and in 1696 Azov was captured. To consolidate this success Taganrog was founded on the northern shore of the Don Estuary, and the building of a large navy was started.

The Grand Embassy (1697–98). Having already sent some young nobles abroad to study nautical matters, Peter, in 1697, went with the so-called Grand Embassy to western Europe. The embassy comprised about 250 people, with the "grand ambassadors" Franz Lefort, F.A. Golovin, and P.B. Voznitsyn at its head. Its chief purposes were to examine the international situation and to strengthen the anti-Turkish coalition, but it was also intended to gather information on the economic and cultural life of Europe. Travelling incognito under the name of Sgt. Pyotr Mikhaylov, Peter familiarized himself with conditions in the advanced countries of the West. For four months he studied shipbuilding, working as a ship's carpenter in the yard of the Dutch East India Company at Saardam; after that he went to Great Britain, where he continued his study of shipbuilding, working in the Royal Navy's dockyard at Deptford, and he also visited factories, arsenals, schools, and museums and even attended a session

Familiarization with the West

By courtesy of the Rijksmuseum, Amsterdam

Peter I the Great, portrait by Aert de Gelder (1645–1727). In the Rijksmuseum, Amsterdam.

of Parliament. Meanwhile, the services of foreign experts were engaged for work in Russia.

On the diplomatic side of the Grand Embassy, Peter conducted negotiations with the Dutch and British governments for alliances against Turkey; but the Maritime Powers did not wish to involve themselves with him because they were preoccupied with the problems that were soon to come to a crisis, for them, in the War of the Spanish Succession.

The destruction of the streltsy (1698). From England, Peter went on to Austria; but while he was negotiating in Vienna for a continuance of the anti-Turkish alliance, he received news of a fresh revolt of the *streltsy* in Moscow. In the summer of 1698 he was back in Moscow, where he suppressed the revolt. Hundreds of the *streltsy* were executed, the rest of the rebels were exiled to distant towns, and the corps of the *streltsy* was disbanded.

The Northern War (1700–21). When it became clear that Austria, no less than the Maritime Powers, was preparing to fight for the Spanish Succession and to make peace with Turkey, Peter saw that Russia could not contemplate a war without allies against the Turks, and he abandoned his plans for pushing forward from the Sea of Azov to the Black Sea. By the Russo-Turkish Peace of Constantinople (Istanbul, 1700) he retained possession of Azov. He was now turning his attention to the Baltic instead, following the tradition of his predecessors.

The Swedes occupied Karelia, Ingria, Estonia, and Livonia and blocked Russia's way to the Baltic coast. To dislodge them, Peter took an active part in forming the great alliance, comprising Russia, Saxony, and Denmark–Norway, which started the Northern War in 1700. This war lasted for 21 years and was Peter's main military **enterprise.** In planning it and in sustaining it he displayed iron willpower, extraordinary energy, and outstanding gifts of statesmanship, generalship, and diplomacy. Mobilizing all the resources of Russia for the triumph of his cause, constantly keeping himself abreast of events, and actively concerning himself with all important undertakings, often at his personal risk, he could be seen sometimes in a sailor's jacket on a warship, sometimes in an officer's uniform on the battlefield, and sometimes in a labourer's apron and gloves with an axe in a shipyard.

Peter's main military enterprise

The defeat of the Russians at Narva (1700), very early in the war, did not deter Peter and, in fact, he later described it as a blessing: "Necessity drove away sloth and forced me to work night and day." He subsequently took part in the siege that led to the Russian capture of Narva (1704) and in the battles of Lesnaya (1708) and of Poltava (1709). At Poltava, where Charles XII of Sweden suffered a catastrophic defeat, the plan of operations was Peter's own: it was his idea to transform the battlefield by works of his military engineers—the redoubts erected in the path of the Swedish troops to break their combat order, to split them into little groups, and to halt their onslaught. Peter also took part in the naval battle of Gangut (Hanko, or Hangö) in 1714, the first major Russian victory at sea.

The treaties concluded by Russia in the course of the war were made under Peter's personal direction. He also travelled abroad again for diplomatic reasons—*e.g.,* to Pomerania in 1712 and to Denmark, northern Germany, Holland, and France in 1716–17.

In 1703, on the banks of the Neva River, where it flows into the Gulf of Finland, Peter began construction of the city of St. Petersburg (now Leningrad) and established it as the new capital of Russia in 1712. By the Treaty of Nystad (September 10 [August 30, O.S.], 1721) the eastern shores of the Baltic were at last ceded to Russia, Sweden was reduced to a secondary power, and the way was opened for Russian domination over Poland.

In celebration of his triumph, the Senate on November 2 (October 22, O.S.), 1721, changed Peter's title from tsar to that of emperor (imperator) of all the Russias.

The popular revolts (1705–08). The peasant serfs and the poorer urban workers had to bear the greatest hardships in wartime and moreover were intensively exploited in the course of Peter's great work for the modernization and development of Russia (see below *Internal reforms*). Their sufferings, combined with onerous taxation, pro-

Other events during the Northern War

voked a number of revolts, the most important of which were that of Astrakhan (1705–06) and that led by Kondraty Afanasyevich Bulavin in the Don Basin (1707–08). These revolts were cruelly put down.

The Turkish War (1710–13). In the middle of the Northern War, when Peter might have pressed further the advantage won at Poltava, Turkey declared war on Russia. In the summer of 1711 Peter marched against the Turks through Bessarabia into Moldavia, but he was surrounded, with all his forces, on the Prut River. Obliged to sue for peace, he was fortunate to obtain very light terms from the inept Turkish negotiators, who allowed him to retire with no greater sacrifice than the retrocession of Azov. The Turkish government soon decided to renew hostilities; but the Peace of Adrianople (Edirne) was concluded in 1713, leaving Azov to the Turks. From that time on Peter's military effort was concentrated on winning his war against Sweden.

The Tsarevich Alexis and Catherine (to 1718). Peter had a son, the tsarevich Alexis, by his discarded wife Eudoxia. Alexis was his natural heir, but he grew up antipathetic to Peter and receptive to reactionary influences working against Peter's reforms. Peter, meanwhile, had formed a lasting liaison with a low-born woman, the future empress Catherine I, who bore him other children and whom he married in 1712. Pressed finally to mend his ways or to become a monk in renunciation of his hereditary rights (1716), Alexis took refuge in the dominions of the Holy Roman emperor Charles VI, but he was induced to return to Russia in 1718. Thereupon proceedings were brought against him on charges of high treason, and after torture he was condemned to death. He died in prison, presumably by violence, before the formal execution of the sentence.

The Persian campaign (1722–23). Even during the second half of the Northern War, Peter had sent exploratory missions to the East—to the Central Asian steppes in 1714, to the Caspian region in 1715, and to Khiva in 1717. The end of the war left him free to resume a more active policy on his southeastern frontier. In 1722, hearing that the Ottoman Turks would take advantage of Persia's weakness and invade the Caspian region, Peter himself invaded Persian territory. In 1723 Persia ceded the western and southern shores of the Caspian to Russia in return for military aid.

Death. The campaign along the parched shores of the Caspian obviously put a great strain on Peter's health, already undermined by enormous exertions and also by the excesses in which he occasionally indulged himself. In the autumn of 1724, seeing some soldiers in danger of drowning from a ship aground on a sandbank in the Gulf of Finland, he characteristically plunged himself into the icy water to help them. Catching a chill, he became seriously ill in the winter but even so continued to work; indeed, it was at this time that he drew up the instructions for the expedition of Vitus Bering to Kamchatka.

Peter died in St. Petersburg on February 8 (January 28, O.S.), 1725, leaving an empire that stretched from Arkhangelsk (Archangel) on the White Sea to Mazanderan on the Caspian and from the Baltic Sea to the Pacific Ocean. Though he had in 1722 issued a decree reserving to himself the right to nominate his successor, he did not in fact nominate anyone. His widow Catherine, whom he had crowned as empress in 1724, succeeded him to the temporary exclusion of his grandson, the future Peter II.

The empire at Peter's death

Internal reforms. At the beginning of Peter's reign, Russia was backward by comparison with the countries of western Europe. This backwardness inhibited foreign policy and even put Russia's national independence in danger. Peter's aim, therefore, was to overtake the developed countries of western Europe as soon as possible, in order both to promote the national economy and to ensure victory in his wars for access to the seas. Breaking the resistance of the boyars, or members of the ancient landed aristocracy, and of the clergy and severely punishing all other opposition to his projects, he initiated a series of reforms that affected, in the course of 25 years, every field of the national life—administration, industry, commerce, technology, and culture.

The towns. At the beginning of Peter's reign there was

already some degree of economic differentiation between the various regions of Russia; and in the towns artisans were establishing small businesses, small-scale production was expanding, and industrial plants and factories were growing up, with both hired workers and serfs employed. There was thus a nascent bourgeoisie, which benefitted considerably from Peter's plans for the development of the national industry and trade. The reform of the urban administration was particularly significant.

Administrative reforms

By a decree of 1699, townspeople (artisans and tradesmen) were released from subjection to the military governors of the provinces and were authorized to elect municipalities of their own, which would be subordinated to the Moscow municipality, or *ratusha*—the council of the great merchant community of the capital. This reform was carried further in 1720, with the establishment of a chief magistracy in St. Petersburg, to which the local town magistracies and the elected municipal officers of the towns (mayors, or *burmistry;* and councillors, or *ratmany*) were subordinated.

All townspeople, meanwhile, were divided between "regulars" and "commons" (inferiors). The regulars were subdivided between two guilds—the first comprising rich merchants and members of the liberal professions (doctors, actors, and artists); the second, artisans (classified according to their vocations) and small tradesmen. A merchant belonged to the first or to the second guild according to the amount of his capital; and those who were also manufacturers had special privileges, coming under the jurisdiction of the College of Manufactures and being exempt from the billeting of troops, from elective rotas of duty, and from military service. The commons were hired labourers, without the privileges of regulars.

Thanks to the reforms, the economic activity and the population of the towns increased. Anyone engaged in trade was legally permitted to settle in a town and to register himself in the appropriate category, and there was a right of "free commerce for people of every rank."

The provinces and the districts. In order to create a more flexible system of control by the central power, Russia was territorially divided in 1708 into eight *guberny,* or governments, each under a governor appointed by the tsar and vested with administrative, military, and judicial authority. In 1719 these *guberny* were dissolved into 50 *provintsy,* or provinces, which in turn were subdivided into districts. The census of 1722, however, was followed by the substitution of a poll tax for the previous hearth tax; and this provoked a wave of popular discontent, against which Peter decided to distribute the army regiments (released from active service by the Peace of Nystad) in garrisons throughout the country and to make their maintenance obligatory on the local populations. Thus came into being the "regimental districts," which did not coincide with the administrative. The regimental commanders, with their own sphere of jurisdiction and their own requirements, added another layer to the already complex system of local authority.

The central government. In the course of Peter's reign, medieval and obsolescent forms of government gave place to effective autocracy. In 1711 he abolished the *boyarskaya duma,* or boyar council, and established by decree the Senate as the supreme organ of state—to coordinate the action of the various central and local organs, to supervise the collection and expenditure of revenue, and to draft legislation in accordance with his edicts. Martial discipline was extended to civil institutions, and an officer of the guards was always on duty in the Senate. From 1722, moreover, there was a procurator general keeping watch over the daily work of the Senate and its chancellery and acting as "the eye of the sovereign."

When Peter came to power the central departments of state were the *prikazy,* or offices, of which there were about 80, functioning in a confused and fragmented way. To replace most of this outmoded system, Peter in 1718 instituted 9 "colleges" (*kollegy*), or boards, the number of which was by 1722 expanded to 13. Their activities were controlled, on the one hand, by the General Regulation and, on the other, by particular regulations for individual colleges, and indeed there were strict regulations for every branch of the state administration. Crimes against the state came under the jurisdiction of the Preobrazhensky Office, responsible immediately to the tsar.

Industry. A secondary purpose of Peter's Grand Embassy to western Europe in 1697 (see above *The Grand Embassy*) had been to obtain firsthand acquaintance with advanced industrial techniques, and the exigencies of his great war against Sweden, from 1700, made industrial development an urgent matter. In order to provide armaments and to build his navy (Russia had virtually no warships at all), metallurgical and manufacturing industries on a grand scale had to be created; and Peter devoted himself tirelessly to meeting these needs. Large capital investments were made, and numerous privileges were accorded to businessmen and industrialists. These privileges included the right to buy peasant serfs for labour in workshops, with the result that a class of "enlisted" serfs came into existence, living in specified areas and bound to the factories. The methods of other countries were further studied, and foreign experts were invited to Russia. The overall result was satisfactory: the army and the navy were supplied with their material needs; a great number of manufacturing establishments were founded (mainly with serf labour); the metallurgical industry was so far advanced that by the middle of the 18th century Russia led Europe in this field; and the foreign-trade turnover was increased sevenfold in the course of the reign.

Europeanization of industry

The armed forces. Peter established a regular army on completely modern lines for Russia in the place of the unreliable *streltsy* and the militia of the gentry. While he drew his officers from the nobility, he conscripted peasants and townspeople into the other ranks. Service was for life. The troops were equipped with flintlock firearms and bayonets of Russian make; uniforms were provided; and regular drilling was introduced. For the artillery, obsolete cannons were replaced with new mortars and guns designed by Russian specialists or even by Peter himself (he drew up projects of his own for multicannon warships, fortresses, and ordnance). The Army Regulations of 1716 were particularly important; they required officers to teach their men "how to act in battle," "to know the soldier's business from first principles and not to cling blindly to rules," and to show initiative in the face of the enemy. For the navy, Peter's reign saw the construction, within a few years, of 52 battleships and hundreds of galleys and other craft; thus a powerful Baltic fleet was brought into being. Several special schools prepared their pupils for military or naval service and finally enabled Peter to dispense with foreign experts.

Cultural and educational measures. From January 1, 1700, Peter introduced a new chronology, making the Russian calendar conform to European usage with regard to the year, which in Russia had hitherto been numbered "from the Creation of the World" and had begun on September 1 (he adhered however to the Julian Old Style as opposed to the Gregorian New Style for the days of the month). In 1710 the Old Church Slavonic alphabet was modernized into a secular script.

Peter was the first ruler of Russia to sponsor education on secular lines and to bring an element of state control into that field. Various secular schools were opened; and since too few pupils came from the nobility, the children of soldiers, officials, and churchmen were admitted to them. In many cases, compulsory service to the state was preceded by compulsory education for it. Russians were also permitted to go abroad for their education and indeed were often compelled to do so (at the state's expense). The translation of books from western European languages was actively promoted. The first Russian newspaper, *Vedomosti* ("Records"), appeared in 1703. The Russian Academy of Sciences was instituted in 1724.

Beside his useful measures, Peter often enforced superficial Europeanization rather brutally; for example, when he decreed that beards should be shorn off and Western dress worn. He personally cut the beards of his boyars and the skirts of their long coats (*kaftany*). The Raskolniki (Old Believers) and merchants who insisted on keeping their beards had to pay a special tax, but peasants and the Orthodox clergy were allowed to remain bearded.

Control
over
church
and
nobility

The church. In 1721, in order to subject the Orthodox Church of Russia to the state, Peter abolished the Patriarchate of Moscow. Thenceforward the patriarch's place as head of the church was taken by a spiritual college, namely the Holy Synod, consisting of representatives of the hierarchy obedient to the tsar's will. A secular official—the *ober-prokuror,* or chief procurator—was appointed by the tsar to supervise the Holy Synod's activities. The Holy Synod ferociously persecuted all dissenters and conducted a censorship of all publications.

Priests officiating in churches were obliged by Peter to deliver sermons and exhortations to make the peasantry "listen to reason" and to teach such prayers to children that everyone would grow up "in fear of God" and in awe of the tsar. The regular clergy were forbidden to allow men under 30 years old or serfs to take vows as monks.

The church was thus transformed into a pillar of the absolutist regime. Partly in the interests of the nobility, the extent of land owned by the church was restricted; Peter disposed of ecclesiastical and monastic property and revenues at his own discretion, for state purposes.

The nobility. Peter's internal policy served to protect the interest of Russia's ruling class—the landowners and the nascent bourgeoisie. The material position of the landed nobility was strengthened considerably under Peter. Almost 100,000 acres of land and 175,000 serfs were allotted to it in the first half of the reign alone. Moreover, a decree of 1714 that instituted succession by primogeniture and so prevented the breaking up of large properties also removed the old distinction between *pomestya* (lands granted by the tsar to the nobility in return for service) and *votchiny* (patrimonial or allodial lands) so that all such property became hereditary.

Moreover, the status of the nobility was modified by Peter's Table of Ranks (1722). This replaced the old system of promotion in the state services, which had been according to ancestry, by one of promotion according to services actually rendered. It classified all functionaries—military, naval, and civilian alike—in 14 categories, the 14th being the lowest and the 1st the highest; and admission to the 8th category conferred hereditary nobility. Factory owners and others who had risen to officer's rank could accede to the nobility, which thus received new blood. The predominance of the boyars ended.

Personality and achievement. Peter was of enormous height, more than six and one-half feet (two metres) tall; he was handsome and of unusual physical strength. Unlike all earlier Russian tsars, whose Byzantine splendours he repudiated, he was very simple in his manners; for example, he enjoyed conversation over a mug of beer with shipwrights and sailors from the foreign ships visiting St. Petersburg. Restless, energetic, and impulsive, he did not like splendid clothes that hindered his movements; often he appeared in worn-out shoes and an old hat, still more often in military or naval uniform. He was fond of merrymaking and knew how to conduct it, though his jokes were frequently crude; and he sometimes drank heavily and forced his guests to do so too. A just man who did not tolerate dishonesty, he was terrible in his anger and could be cruel when he encountered opposition: in such moments only his intimates could soothe him—best of all his beloved second wife, Catherine, whom people frequently asked to intercede with him for them. Sometimes Peter would beat his high officials with his stick, from which even Prince A.D. Menshikov, his closest friend, received many a stroke. One of Peter's great gifts of statesmanship was the ability to pick talented collaborators for the highest appointments, whether from the foremost families of the nobility or from far lower levels of society.

As a ruler, Peter often used the methods of a despotic landlord—the whip and arbitrary rule. He always acted as an autocrat, convinced of the wonder-working power of compulsion by the state. Yet with his insatiable capacity for work he saw himself as the state's servant, and whenever he put himself in a subordinate position he would perform his duties with the same conscientiousness that he demanded of others. He began his own army service in the lowest rank and required others likewise to master their profession from its elements upward and to expect promotion only for services of real value.

Peter's personality left its imprint on the whole history of Russia. A man of original and shrewd intellect, exuberant, courageous, industrious, and iron willed, he could soberly appraise complex and changeable situations so as to uphold consistently the general interests of Russia and his own particular designs. He did not completely bridge the gulf between Russia and the Western countries, but achieved considerable progress in development of the national economy and trade, education, science and culture, and foreign policy. Russia became a great power, without whose concurrence no important European problem could thenceforth be settled. His internal reforms achieved progress to an extent that no earlier innovator could have envisaged.

Peter's
influence
on Russia

BIBLIOGRAPHY. There are numerous studies in Russian on Peter I and his age. *Письма и бумаги Императора Петра Великого,* 11 vol. (1887–1964), contains valuable documents on Russian history up to 1711. Other works particularly recommended include: михаил м. вогословский, *Петр I,* 5 vol. (1940–48, reprinted 1969), a detailed biography of Peter I until 1700; сергей м. соловьев, *Публичныя чтения о Петре Великом* (1872), a famous Russian historian on the role of Peter I; иван и. голиков, *Деяния Петра Великого,* 30 vol. (1788–97), on his reforms; and леонид а. никифоров, *Русско-английские отношения при Петре I* (1950). Peter's military campaigns and his role as the founder of the new Russian army are explored in the works of a prominent Soviet historian, евгений в. тарле, *Русский флот и внешняя политика Петра I* (1949), and *Северная война и шведское нашествие на Россию* (1958). Works in English include benedict h. sumner, *Peter the Great and the Ottoman Empire* (1949, reprinted 1965), and *Peter the Great and the Emergence of Russia* (1950, reprinted 1972); and ian grey, *Peter the Great, Emperor of All Russia* (1960). Peter's reforms aimed at modernizing Russian society are analyzed in james cracraft, *The Church Reform of Peter the Great* (1971); and alexander v. muller (ed. and trans.), *The Spiritual Regulation of Peter the Great* (1972). See also reinhard wittram, *Peter der Grosse: Der Eintritt Russlands in die Neuzeit* (1954), and *Peter I, Czar und Kaiser,* 2 vol. (1964). Other biographies include, matthew s. anderson, *Peter the Great* (1978); alex de jonge, *Fire and Water: A Life of Peter the Great* (1979); and robert k. massie, *Peter the Great: His Life and Work* (1980). xenia gasiorowska, *The Image of Peter the Great in Russian Fiction* (1979), is a study of some 60 historical novels written since Pushkin's time. Works that put Peter the Great and his reign into their historical perspective include martha e. almedingen, *The Romanovs: Three Centuries of an Ill-Fated Dynasty* (1966); john d. bergamini, *The Tragic Dynasty: A History of the Romanovs* (1969); ian grey, *The Romanovs: The Rise and Fall of a Dynasty* (1970); vasili klyuchevsky, *The Rise of the Romanovs,* trans. and ed. by liliana archibald (1970), originally part of Klyuchevsky's comprehensive five-volume history of Russia, published in 1912; j.g. garrard (ed.), *The Eighteenth Century in Russia* (1973); and w. bruce lincoln, *The Romanovs: Autocrats of All the Russias* (1981).

(L.A.N./Ed.)

Pets

Generally, a pet is an animal tamed and kept as a favourite or treated with fondness; however, the range of animals kept by modern man is so wide that the words tamed and fondness must be qualified.

Most pets have been selected from animals that were domesticated early in man's history and have entered into a special, and more or less permanent, relationship with man. They differ from the original forms not only in size, colour, and shape but also in temperament. This inherited capacity to live cooperatively with man may be only potential in some animals, as with horses, which must be individually tamed and trained; others—in particular, the cat—are usually prepared to accept at once their place in the household. In contrast, numerous wild animals are brought into captivity and spend the rest of their lives as captives, some more willingly than others by reason of their temperament or the patience of their masters.

A pet is kept for its own sake and for the pleasure that it gives its owner. For a wide range of higher animals, especially horses, dogs, cats, and primates, this pleasure appears to be mutual. Pet keeping, therefore, is essentially a symbiotic, or mutually beneficial, animal–human relationship. Keeping pets satisfies a deep, universal human need, and pets are found at every cultural level.

The article is divided into the following sections:

General considerations

ORIGIN AND HISTORY OF PETS

The dog as the first pet

The dog, which became domesticated long before any other species, must have been the first true pet. A working relationship probably formed between early man and the wolves that lived around his settlements and gradually evolved until certain individuals became tame and were then regarded as settlement or household dependents as well as partners in hunting and guarding duties. True domestication slowly followed; later came the deliberate selection of a range of breeds illustrated in many ancient carvings and paintings. In Mesopotamia the giant mastiffs were used in the lion hunt; in Egypt the tomb paintings depict greyhound-like dogs and short-legged terriers resembling those of today. In some periods of history man seems to have had a special affinity for animals; this was markedly true in the 12th dynasty in Egypt (1991–1786 BC) when hyenas and lions were tamed and trained and the cat began to be domesticated. This faculty for keeping animals was gradually lost, to be revived some 200 years later, in the time of Queen Hatshepsut.

Of classical references to pet keeping, two in the Bible are well known. In II Sam. 12 Nathan speaks of a ewe lamb brought up in the family of a poor farmer, a practice that is still common. Because of their scavenging habits, house dogs were not kept by the Jews, but in Mark 7:28 a foreign woman spoke of her little pet dogs that sat under the table.

THE RELATIONSHIP OF PETS TO HUMAN BEINGS

Companionship. A wide range of pet–owner relationships is found, the worst of which is little but exploitation. An extreme example of this is the overfed, underexercised dog that has been taught no discipline and whose life contains little of interest or excitement; the selfish owner may keep it alive long after its existence becomes a burden because he or she cannot face losing it. Equally unsatisfactory is a relationship so loose that an animal hardly regards itself as attached to a family, which may feed it but takes little other interest in it.

The emotional relationship between owner and pet is not easy to define, but it seems that most human beings have a latent capacity to seek contact with animals, mostly but not only with furred animals. Modern experience in the pet trade and in zoos suggests that this desire is heightened by living in urban surroundings.

The instructive value of pets

Keeping pets offers the opportunity to teach children the close dependence of privilege on responsibility and also something about sex; the process of mating is soon noticed, followed by such matters as gestation periods and the varied problems involved in the birth and care of young.

Almost by definition, pets kept as companions must also give pleasure and satisfaction. In addition, many animals are kept as personal pets, in the broader sense, to which the description "companion" cannot possibly be given. They are scarcely aware of any relationship with man, for they live in reasonable replicas of their habitats. All invertebrates fall into this class, and, because of their different physiological needs, all fishes and amphibians. This indifference to man is generally true of reptiles as well, but a few snakes, especially captive pythons, appear to seek and enjoy the proximity of humans.

A contrast exists between mammals and birds of domesticated stock and those whose immediate ancestors are truly wild. With the former a more satisfying, complete, and lasting relationship is likely. Such is possible in the latter groups also, but the term companion can be applied properly only to the exceptions. In such cases, which may occur in widely varying groups of mammals and birds, the human, in effect, replaces the mate or, at least, a companion of the same species. Many such animals revert to the wild when they become adult, a pattern particularly true of the large apes. In others, when a mate is accepted, the temperament changes radically, and they can no longer be handled; if the introduction is not made, however, until one or other has long been adult, mate acceptance is unlikely. Moreover, if both animals have been tame, the chance of mating is small and of breeding even less; this is the most likely explanation of the failure to mate many long-term inmates of zoos. The rather vague term humanized is often applied to such animals. From the human side there is some support for this substitute theory; the most extravagant examples of lavish coddling, especially of cats or toy dogs, usually involve unmarried or childless women, often in later life.

Partnership. The relationship between an animal trainer and his animals is a special one, for they form a team to earn money; yet the bond joining them is close, and, although these animals often live in cramped quarters and under artificial conditions, many seem to enjoy a more interesting and satisfying life than the average household pet. This does not consititute an endorsement of all that goes on, especially in the training, but it is clear that most trainers have a deep concern for their animals, which can truly be described as their pets. They are indeed tame animals, whether of wild or domestic stock, in which obedience training has been pursued to an extreme. The training consists largely of noting what individual animals enjoy doing, and developing that habit in an interesting way.

Scientific observation. The margin between keeping pets for their own sake and as objects for serious study is narrow. The wild animals forming the subject of many books often come into human care by accident. The immediate objective, in such instances, is a humanitarian one, providing its own unique satisfaction; this phase is followed by the pleasure of companionship and then the recording of valuable facts about animals hard to observe closely in the wild.

It is doubtful whether any animals used solely for scientific study can truly qualify as pets. Many are subjected to observations and experiments and are unaware that they are being studied (in many cases the development of a personal relationship would invalidate the results).

Pets in studies of animal behaviour

Some aspects of animal behaviour are best studied when the subjects are living free, yet secure and approachable because a special relationship has been built up with the observer. Foremost in this field of ethology is the German zoologist Konrad Lorenz, whose pioneer work is recorded in several popular books (see bibliography). His deep understanding of animal psychology made a family of jackdaws regard him as one of themselves and a flock of greylag geese take him as their leader. Other persons have come to the same terms with wolves, chimpanzees, and gorillas.

KINDS OF PETS AND THEIR NEEDS

It is important to realize that human standards are not of much use in determining the best way to meet the varied needs of the different pets kept by man. This is best illustrated by mentioning certain basic needs for all kinds of pets. Variety in food is largely an invention of civilized man. For most animals, and also for man in many parts of the world, change comes only with the season. A little variety may be useful in keeping some sensitive higher animals interested in food, but the first requirement is a balanced diet appropriate to each species, adjusted when necessary to individual need or whim. Overfeeding is never good; as with humans, it often results in obesity, lethargy, and shortening of the life-span.

Correct design of pet quarters is usually more important than the total area enclosed. Any group of animals, tame or wild, includes bullies and the bullied; a good plan lets the latter keep safely out of the former's way. Many nocturnal pets find security by day in dark holes that other animals would regard with mistrust, and they may be badly upset if disturbed. A dog's kennel gives him a safe feeling; with his rear protected he can be watchful of the area before him.

Some animals carefully deposit waste products away from their immediate living quarters. Others, however, including lorises and bush babies, put urine on their feet to mark their territory; such an odorous condition is necessary to give a sense of security.

Long walks are desirable for some pet animals, such as dogs, whose makeup has been modified by generations of living with man, but few adult wild animals take exercise for its own sake; they run hard when they must—to kill or avoid being killed.

Proper handling is basic in establishing human–pet relationships; some animals enjoy much physical contact, while others dislike even being touched.

Few pets are kept whose needs are not well known; careful study of these should show whether or not an animal will fit into a particular household. Most pets cannot fend for themselves, even for a weekend, and any decision about keeping an animal must take note of the degree of care it requires.

Household pets. *Dog.* The dog is the most variable domestic animal, with more than 100 breeds, ranging in size from two to four pounds (one to two kilograms) for the Chihuahua to over 200 pounds (100 kilograms) for the St. Bernard and the mastiff. Many crossbred, or mongrel, dogs make delightful pets, but their adult size and shape are often unpredictable, and, contrary to popular belief, they are not necessarily of better temperament than a pedigreed dog. As a general rule, a dog becomes attached to people, a cat to premises. (For a more extended treatment of dogs, see below.)

Cat. Partly because of its independent nature and nocturnal wanderings, the cat has comparatively few breeds. Shape and size vary rather little, the differences being mainly in coat length and colour. All cats make good pets, but long-haired breeds should be kept only in homes where they will be groomed daily. (For further treatment of domestic cats, see below.)

Birds. First kept widely in Europe in the 16th century, the canary is still a favourite singing pet. There is much variation of plumage in the show breeds, in which singing is less important. The canary is ideal for a room pet. The wild budgerigar, from Australia, is green, but variants have been selected in many shades and combinations of greens, blues, and yellows, with white and gray. Since they are clean, easily looked after, and cheap to feed, budgerigars (often called parrakeets) make excellent pets, especially for older people living alone. Most individuals of both sexes can be taught to repeat simple phrases. Of the 300 or so parrot species seen in aviaries, the gray parrot of central Africa and the Amazon parrots of South America are the only ones commonly kept as house pets. They are, however, expensive and often noisy, and their powerful beaks make them destructive and capable of severe bites. A member of the starling family, the mynah, is one of the best talking birds. It requires large quantities of soft fruit and may often be messy in its habits.

Other birds kept as house pets include pigeons and doves. There are many varieties of these birds, some of them highly ornamental; they are often kept at liberty, with access to shelter but free to fly in the neighbourhood, where they unfortunately may cause damage.

Poultry and waterfowl are kept primarily for commercial and ornamental purposes, but a few individuals—notably among ducks, geese, and chickens—become unusually tame and are adopted as members of the household.

Vivarium pets. When kept as pets, reptiles and amphibians frequently require special conditions of heat and humidity. For this reason they are best kept in glassed enclosures called vivaria. These animals have no internal temperature regulation and in nature their activity varies with the season. Species of temperate climates can do well at room temperatures and, in the case of some, even outdoors, but they must be allowed to hibernate as winter approaches. The vivaria can be put outdoors in autumn and filled with leaf mold or light soil; when the weather has turned cold, they can be taken in and stored in a cold but frost-free location. Alternatively, early in autumn the animals can be released in suitable places to hibernate.

Tropical snakes, lizards, turtles, frogs, and toads require special treatment. These animals are imported from warm countries, and all are used to being active throughout the year, though not always in the same degree. They need warm quarters at all times, preferably with day and night variation that simulates their native environment. Furthermore, for many people a big difficulty is that snakes, lizards, frogs, and toads eat live animal food. Only experts should keep venomous snakes.

Aquarium pets. Fishes constitute a completely separate section of the pet world, and a worldwide industry exists for catching, breeding, transporting, and supplying stock, as well as for making a great range of equipment and formulating special food. Fishes can be divided into two main groups: cold-water and tropical. Each of these categories may be divided further into freshwater and marine, the largest being the freshwater tropical. Many hundreds of species are available, and there is a rich literature on the subject, with many specialist magazines. (For further treatment of aquarium fish, see below.)

Insect pets. Although enthusiasts in many countries study live insects as a hobby, only a few kinds of insects are of widespread general acceptance as house pets. Stick insects are the easiest to keep; they can be fed privet leaves and do well in simple containers at room temperature. The larvae of silk moths, the semidomesticated form of which yields real silk, can be fed on mulberry or lettuce leaves; they grow to full size before pupating and emerging the following year as silk moths.

It is possible to establish colonies of several kinds of ants in artificial nests in which they can easily be observed under glass.

Hutch pets. Of the common hutch or cage pets, rabbits and guinea pigs perhaps do better when kept in a protected situation out-of-doors, while rats, mice, hamsters, and gerbils thrive under room temperature conditions.

Rabbit. Rabbits are available in many sizes—from the 2½-pound (1-kilogram) Netherland dwarf to the New Zealand and Flemish giant of 12 pounds (5½ kilograms)—and in many colours and patterns, with coats of various lengths and textures. The small and medium sizes are best as pets (the larger are often raised for fur and meat). Rabbits are heavy drinkers and feeders, taking large amounts of roots, leafy shoots, grain products, and hay (modern feeding is based on high protein dried grass pellets and hay).

Guinea pig. There is little variation in size or shape of guinea pigs, but a wide range of colours and three types of coat—short, rosette (Abyssinian), and long (Peruvian). Guinea pigs feed on the same food as rabbits, but not so heavily. They are notably prolific, bearing litter upon litter of young that are fully mobile at birth.

Rat and mouse. Although used mainly in research work, the tame rat, usually white or hooded, makes an excellent and docile pet. It has clean habits and is without a distinctive mousy smell. It tolerates a range of indoor temperatures and is an ideal children's pet that is not easily hurt by handling. Tame mice, domesticated from the house mouse, have certain disadvantages. The adult male's smell is regarded as unpleasant by some. Mice breed rapidly and their small size makes them hard to handle and confine.

Hamster. This small rodent, first tamed from the wild golden variety about 1930, is now available in many colours. The hamster has largely replaced the mouse as a house pet because of its clean habits, lack of odour, and convenient size (six inches long, or about 15 centimetres). Disadvantages are that it is easily injured if dropped and is primarily nocturnal and often bad tempered by day.

Gerbil. Several species of gerbil, mostly from southwestern Asia, became popular pets after having been established as laboratory animals. They are as clean as hamsters and of similar size; however, they are much more active and not as easily handled.

Chinchilla. Originally kept as a fur-producing animal, the chinchilla also makes a charming pet. They enjoy attention, but not all are fond of being picked up and handled.

Paddock pets. This category includes such popular animals as horses and ponies. The high costs of providing for these animals make it increasingly difficult to keep them as personal pets. Space is needed for paddock and stabling, with regular care at all times (see HORSES AND HORSEMANSHIP). In some areas goats are important for their milk and for their wool, and many breeds are kept for show purposes. Some may be suitable as household pets, but they need grazing areas and stabling, with attention twice a day when in milk. The adult male goat is undesirable because of its powerful scent. In farming communities an orphan calf, piglet, or lamb may be adopted by a family, but usually only long enough to rear it safely.

Aviary birds. Many hundreds of species of birds are kept in aviaries, or large enclosures with space for flight. They range from cranes and flamingos to sunbirds and hummingbirds. Jays, magpies, jackdaws, and other members of the crow family are good mimics and make interesting pets. Many are now bred in captivity. The catching of many birds is regulated by governmental agencies.

Unusual mammals. Every year numbers of smaller wild mammals, such as badgers, foxes, otters, hares, and squirrels, are rescued as helpless or wounded young and become hand tamed for varying periods. Only a small minority remain pets all their lives; most of them become difficult to handle after a few months and must be released or sent to the safety of a zoo.

There is much impulse buying of exotic pets; many are offered to zoos after the owners have realized the difficulties of caring for them. The following are some of the most important groups of exotic pets.

Wild animals as pets

Primates. Although apes and monkeys can be kept successfully as house pets, these primates are in general unsuitable for this purpose. With rare exceptions, they cannot be house-trained, they require a great deal of time and attention, and they are potentially dangerous because of their erratic temperament. On the other hand, such primates as bush babies and lorises and other lemurs make interesting pets in warm climates where outside accommodation with some degree of freedom is possible. Their pungent scent, used for marking territory, makes them generally unsuitable as house pets.

Carnivores. Kinkajous, raccoons, coatis, skunks, mongooses, and other small carnivores from many parts of the world are kept in varying numbers, often in large cages, sometimes partly at liberty. Feeding and accommodation are simple, but their temperaments vary widely and only some settle well as pets.

Rodents. Flying squirrels are among the most attractive small rodents. They can do well in pairs in a cage kept indoors. Some enjoy being handled and having occasional freedom of the house so that they may climb and glide.

Jerboas, kangaroo rats, dormice, and other such small rodents make unusual pets and are easy to keep. Because many feed only on seeds and produce dry droppings, they are eminently suitable for keeping indoors.

THE SOURCES OF PETS

Domestic animal sources. Most pets come from domestic stock supplied through breeding and then offered for sale. Small pets going into homes—rodents, budgerigars, etc.—are normally sold through pet shops. The "fancy," or group of enthusiasts interested in a particular pet animal, does most of its business through trade and specialist papers; many dogs and cats are bought and sold in this manner.

Rising costs compel breeders, especially of cats and dogs, to confine themselves to first-class pedigree stock that commands good prices; many buyers go directly to such breeders for their pets. Unfortunately, the standards evolved for some breeds are largely artificial. Attention may be so focussed on details of colour pattern or on small size, for example, that other considerations are ignored and the breed may suffer. This has been particularly marked in dog breeding, in which several breeds have declined in quality since World War I.

Native animal sources. Some local animals are deliberately trapped, netted, or taken from the nest. This is especially true of birds, particularly members of the finch and thrush families, that are valued for their song. Most countries now have strict laws that make it illegal to catch birds other than a few regarded as potential pests. The prohibited species may be kept as pets only when "closed ringed"; *i.e.,* when they have been bred in captivity and ringed as nestlings.

Exotic animal sources. A few exotic animals are brought in by returning travellers, but most are obtained through the normal trade channels, which are usually pet stores stocking a wide range of pets and obtaining less common ones on order.

Fishes, amphibians, snakes, invertebrates, etc. are caught by collectors in many parts of the world. Most mammals and birds are found or caught when young, and are much more likely to survive than wild-caught adults; they are also easier and cheaper to ship to markets.

Attempts to limit animal exports
Restrictions are rightly placed on the traffic in animals. The export of certain animals listed in the Red Data Book (list of species in danger of extinction) of the International Union for the Conservation of Nature is totally forbidden; some countries control trading of additional animals and allow export only to approved institutions such as zoos. It will thus become increasingly difficult to import exotic animals, especially mammals and birds, as pets; other classes of animals are less affected. Increasing water pollution, however, could seriously reduce the supply of wild-caught tropical fish.

DISEASES OF PETS AND THEIR HAZARDS TO HUMAN BEINGS

Many diseases of pets can be transmitted to humans. Some of these ailments are mild and often pass unnoticed for what they are; respiratory diseases and skin rashes are among these zoonoses (diseases common to man and other animals).

Cage birds may harbour trachoma, which may damage eye tissue in man, and psittacosis, a viral disease that may be serious in man. Turtles and perhaps other reptilian pets have been implicated as carriers of viruses and fungi that may infect man. Dogs and cats frequently contract respiratory infections from man and in turn can transmit them to man.

Rabies is one of the most serious animal diseases that can be transmitted to man. It occurs naturally in wild canines such as jackals, foxes, and wolves, and also among the weasels and hyenas. It is widespread in many Asian and European countries where there is always a wild source from which domestic animals may be infected.

External parasites are specific to fairly narrow groups of animals and soon die on other hosts, but some fleas found on cats and dogs may be transferred to man. Suitable insecticides are available that can be used to eradicate these pests. Several serious skin diseases are caused by organisms able to live on various pets as well as on man: most important of these are sarcoptic mange (caused by the mite *Sarcoptes scabei*) and ringworm (caused by the fungus *Microsporum canis*). Among internal parasites, several kinds of parasitic worms of the dog and the cat can be transmitted to man.

Pets obtained from fully reliable sources and well looked after should not endanger human health. Proper care of pets includes sound hygiene, with regular and thorough cleaning of feeding and water bowls, cages or enclosures, and bedding or sleeping area.

It is good practice always to use special bowls for feeding that are kept separate from the utensils used by human members of the household.

PETS IN LAW

Quarantines
Some groups of imported animals are put in quarantine to prevent the spread of serious diseases; in addition, the provision of health certificates from the country of origin may be required. Although details vary with the country and are modified with changing conditions, the most important diseases involving quarantine generally are rabies, foot-and-mouth disease, and psittacosis and other bird diseases.

During outbreaks of some animal diseases, movements within specified areas may be banned and animals such as dogs may be compelled to wear muzzles. Local laws may forbid the keeping of certain types of pets. Animals may be banned from some forms of public transport, and it may be an offense to allow them to run freely on roads or in parks and other public spaces. In many cities, for example, penalties are imposed for the fouling of sidewalks by dogs. In many localities, annual license fees are required for pet animals, especially dogs.

In many countries, societies have been formed that are expressly concerned with the welfare of animals, particularly those in captivity; part of their work may be to help enforce laws that establish minimum standards of care for pets.

(Ge.C.)

Dogs

Dogs, along with wolves, jackals, and foxes, are members of the family Canidae. As such, they share certain features that suit them admirably for a life of active hunting; powerful jaws with teeth adapted to seizing, keen senses of smell and hearing, and a social instinct that maintains and coordinates the efforts of the pack. The family of dogs and their relatives belongs to the mammalian order Carnivora, the "flesh eaters"; for an account of the family and its relationships, see MAMMALS: *Carnivora.* Regardless of superficial differences, all dogs belong to a single species, *Canis familiaris,* and its more than 100 breeds depend entirely on selective breeding and maintenance by man for their continued existence. The dog is an extremely social animal, whose well-being and normal psychological development are products of association with other dogs in a pack. Unlike man's other favourite domesticate, the cat, a dog adjusts with difficulty, if at all, to an independent and wild existence and draws heavily on the mutual exchange of pack members and the guidance of the pack leader, or a human master, who is in fact a surrogate pack leader.

ORIGIN AND HISTORY OF DOGS

The dog has been in the company of man for at least 10,-000 years and originated probably somewhere in Eurasia 12,000 to 14,000 years ago. It belongs to the same genus (*Canis*) as do the coyote, jackal, and wolf, all of which have been considered to be his ancestors. Much farther back in time, about 40,000,000 years ago, lived a tree-climbing carnivorous mammal called *Miacis,* from which the lineage of the canines is traced through *Cynodictis,* from whom the African Cape hunting dog, the Indian wild dog (or dhole), and the South American bush dog ultimately sprang, through *Cynodesmus,* which gave rise to the hyenas, and finally through *Tomarctus,* the progenitor of the fox, wolf, jackal, and dog. The coyote, which lives only in North America, can be eliminated as an ancestor of the early European dog.

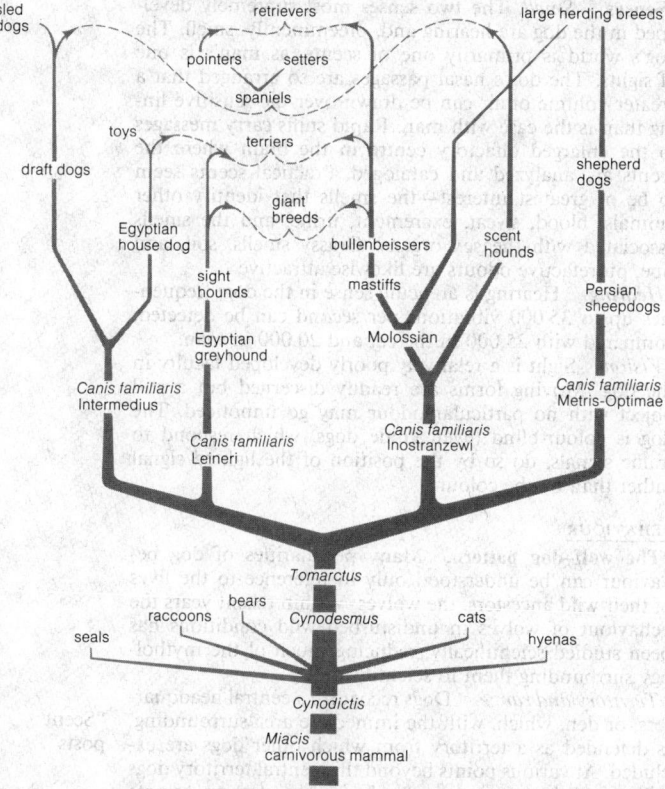

Figure 1: Possible genealogy of the dog.

Probable wolf ancestry The most likely candidate is the gray wolf, which was originally found over all of Europe, Asia, and North America, with a great many highly variable subspecies and local varieties. The wolf is so variable in colour that even individual members of a pack can be easily distinguished. Northern wolves are much larger than southern ones, which makes it probable that dogs came from a smaller central or southern variety. Such a race of small wolves lives in India, and another was formerly found in China. The other possible candidate, the jackal, is primarily an African animal, although its range extends into Mesopotamia, southeastern Europe, and India. The jackal is less social than the dog; it howls in a manner unlike any domestic dog and has a narrow, foxlike head—factors that make it unlikely that it is the dog's ancestor.

Domestication. The wild dog, like the wolf, roams in packs in search of food, and it would seem not unlikely that some primitive dogs found food more readily available near man's encampments, where animal hides and picked-over carcasses were left to rot. The dog apparently was less wary than its canine relatives and may have ventured more boldly into man's settlements to feed. Its

association with man developed gradually; the more docile and tractable dogs were tolerated; the others were run off or killed.

Man may have grown to depend on the dog to warn him of approaching threat, and the dog in turn grew to depend on man for food and shelter. Mutual bonds of benefit and affection probably strengthened gradually over the centuries until by selection for traits and appearance the domesticated dog became man's creation. In time, further attention to breeding resulted in modifications that have led to widely variant breeds.

After dogs became domesticated, certain traits became established that distinguish dogs from their wild relatives. One such trait is the upturned tail, ranging from a sickle shape to a tight curl. This feature probably goes back to the original stock of domestic dog, pointing to a common ancestry for all types of dog. Another characteristic that distinguishes the dog from the wolf is its smaller, less powerful dentition. There must have been an early artificial selection for those animals that were smaller, less toothy, and also more easily tamed and controlled.

Distribution The domesticated dog apparently spread very rapidly all over the world, through both hemispheres and from tropical to Arctic climates. When the Europeans arrived in North America they brought their own dogs with them, but every Indian tribe already had them. At that time there were at least 20 distinct breeds in North and South America. Most of these have disappeared except for the Mexican hairless and the Eskimo dogs.

In Australia there is the dingo, a species separate from the domestic dog. Typically a wild animal, the dingo is sometimes found semidomesticated in the camps of the Aborigines. Its ancestors must have been brought as domestic dogs to Australia by the first immigrants several thousand years ago and later allowed to run wild.

Since the beginning of history dogs have been found all over Africa. One of the surviving native breeds is the African basenji, still used by the pygmy tribes in equatorial regions. The basenji is probably descended from an early breed adapted to tropical living, which spread through southern Asia and the East Indies and eventually to Australia, where it became the dingo. Other varieties of dogs lived throughout Asia and on most of the oceanic islands.

Most is known about the history of European dogs. From the earliest times traders and travellers not only took their favourite dogs on long journeys but often returned with new and exotic varieties. Dogs were nowhere more cultivated than in England.

Origin of breeds. By the time John Caius (the founder of Caius College at Cambridge) wrote a description of English dogs for Konrad von Gesner, a 16th-century naturalist, the English had collected at least six main varieties of dogs—greyhounds, true hounds, bird dogs, terriers, mastiffs, and shepherd dogs. A basic group of dogs not mentioned by Caius includes the sled dogs of the Eskimo, found in the Arctic in both America and Eurasia. These large curlytailed dogs, reputedly crossed with wolves, and similar smaller dogs of northern Eurasia are sometimes called the polar, or spitz, group.

Although the same general types of dogs were found all over the world, many less distinct in their physical and behavioral traits have since disappeared. Many ancient breeds have greatly changed or entirely disappeared, but in Iraq two ancient types of dog, the saluki and the Kurdish herding dog, are still found. The latter of these is a large breed somewhat resembling the mastiffs and war dogs pictured in Babylonian art in 2200 BC.

Historical records indicate that dog breeds have frequently been crossed with each other, so that it is difficult in many cases to determine the ancestors. While conscious human selection has doubtless played a part in producing genetic changes from the earliest times, the dog is also an evolving species. Just as an animal that enters a new physical habitat undergoes rapid change and differentiation, the dog on domestication entered a new biological habitat in association with the human species and underwent a similar rapid evolution assisted by man.

The dog figures prominently in many tales of courage and selfless devotion in the service of humanity, of steadfastness and perseverance, of attentiveness and seeming concern for his master. The romantic stories of Albert Payson Terhune are filled with the heroic deeds of the dog, as are Jack London's *White Fang* (1906) and other novels. The dog has been bred for many special tasks—hunting, guarding, herding, drafting, guiding (for the blind)—but most popularly for companionship and as a household pet.

Because the close social relationship between dogs and human beings appears to many observers to be similar to the human parent–child relationship, dogs have been used to test various theories of child training. Dogs also have important uses in medical research, and the resulting discoveries have helped to improve both animal and human health.

GENERAL FEATURES AND SPECIAL ADAPTATIONS

The wolf-like heritage

The dog, in many of its breeds, is basically a wolflike hunter, with physical features usually identified with such a mode of life: musculature fitting a coursing or running animal, teeth suitable for seizing and holding prey, internal adaptations to a carnivorous habit (short gut and other digestive tract features), and keen senses of smell and hearing.

Coordination and musculature. While the dog is no rival for the cat in fluid movement and balance, it has retained some of the wolflike aspects of deliberate tracking and cautious cunning. It moves the way a horse does when walking but prefers the trot, in which the right foreleg and left hindleg advance together, followed by the other legs; at top speed it breaks into a gallop. The dog is not as agile and foot sure as the cat, nor as flexible in body

construction, but its speed and perseverance are greater than the cat's. The wolflike musculature is still found, though greatly modified in mass and development, in the different breeds. The sheetlike musculature covering the head and main body mass is particularly noticeable by its action in raising the hackles, or back hair, baring the teeth, and cocking the ears. Muscles of the hind back work the tail, which is generally wagged briskly and held high in contentment and waved slowly and in a horizontal position in attentive approach or before attack. The tail aids in balance, as when the dog dashes around a curve.

Teeth. A dog's first, temporary, set of teeth, or milk teeth, is replaced by a permanent set at about five months. The 42 permanent teeth include incisors, which are used to nip and bite; canines, used to tear and shred flesh; and premolars and molars, which shear and crush. The canines are upper and lower fangs for which the dog family was named. As in most carnivores, the teeth are high crowned and pointed, unlike the broad, grinding teeth of many herbivorous animals. Having less manipulative ability than the cat, the dog uses its teeth to catch and hold items, such as food or a toy, as well as to prepare food for digestion.

Senses. *Smell.* The two senses most supremely developed in the dog are hearing and, preeminently, smell. The dog's world is primarily one of scents, as man's is one of sights. The dog's nasal passages are so arranged that a greater volume of air can be drawn over the sensitive lining than is the case with man. Rapid sniffs carry messages to the enlarged olfactory centre in the brain where the scents are analyzed and cataloged. Practical scents seem to be of greatest interest—the smells that identify other animals: blood, sweat, excrement, urine, and the smells associated with the sex organs. Grassy smells, soil, and ripe, putrefactive odours are likewise attractive.

Hearing. Hearing is an acute sense in the dog; frequencies up to 35,000 vibrations per second can be detected, compared with 25,000 in the cat and 20,000 in man.

Vision. Sight is a relatively poorly developed faculty in the dog. Moving forms are readily discerned but a still object with no particular odour may go unnoticed. The dog is colour-blind (even guide dogs, which respond to traffic signals, do so by the position of the lighted signal rather than by the colour).

BEHAVIOUR

The wolf–dog pattern. Many peculiarities of dog behaviour can be understood only in reference to the lives of their wild ancestors, the wolves. Within recent years the behaviour of wolves in undisturbed wild conditions has been studied scientifically, reducing much of the mythology surrounding them to scientific fact.

Territory and range. Dogs recognize a central headquarters, or den, which, with the immediate area surrounding, is defended as a territory from which other dogs are excluded. At various points beyond this central territory dogs will establish "scent posts," where they stop to urinate and defecate. Males lift the leg to urinate and scratch the ground after defecation. Strange dogs passing by will also mark the place in the same manner. These wolflike habits are seen especially in dogs allowed to run loose in town or country: the tendency to defend the immediate areas around the houses of their owners, but to wander much more widely, making certain "scent posts" as they go.

"Scent posts"

Group activities. Wolves are highly social animals. Within the pack, wolves are peaceable and highly cooperative. While feeding, they observe a dominance order, in which the most dominant animal feeds first. Parts of prey animals are often buried, either at the site of the kill or in the vicinity of the den, presumably to save the food from scavengers. Domestic dogs show the same habits, even attempting to bury such things as dry dog food.

Wolves show the same general types of sounds and communication as dogs—barking when a strange animal approaches the den, yelping in fear or distress, growling when threatening another animal, and howling, either alone or, when the pack is together, in unison.

Combative behaviour. Two strange male dogs usually approach each other stiffly, with tails held erect, and appear to identify each other by sniffing in the tail region.

Dominance and subordination behaviour

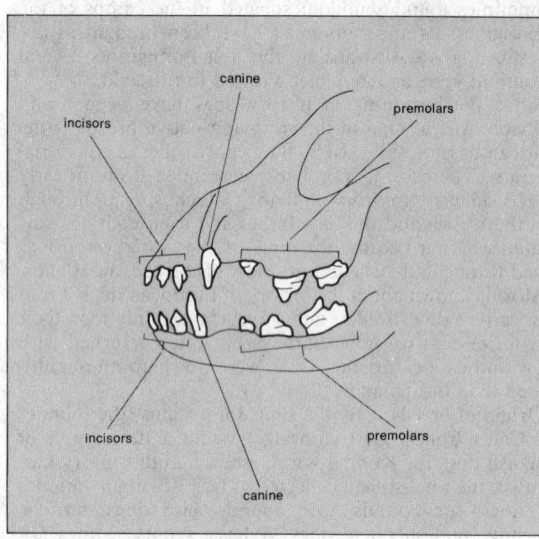

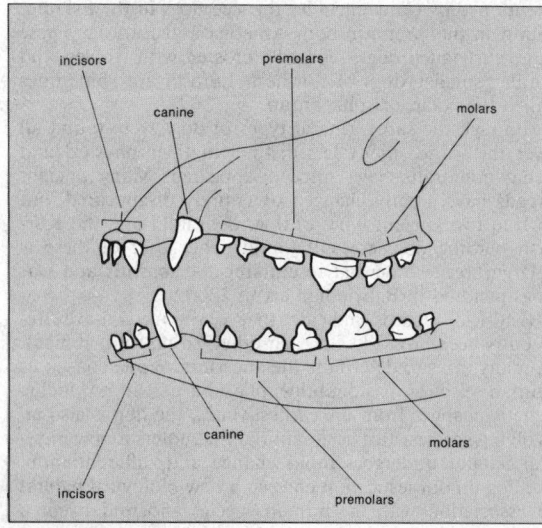

Figure 2: *Dentitions of the dog.*
(Top) Temporary (milk) teeth of a puppy. (Bottom) Adult (permanent) teeth.

If a fight starts, they rush at each other, snapping and snarling, and the fight will last until one runs away or submits. The beaten animal will roll on its back, extending its paws, yelping, and protecting its throat by snapping. The winning animal stands over it, growling and threatening. If dominance has already been established, one dog may indicate this by placing his paws on the other's back and growling while the subordinate animal keeps his tail low. Similar behaviour is seen in wolves.

Courtship and care of young. In courtship dogs show a characteristic pattern of play. They crouch extending their forepaws and cocking their heads to one side, then they throw their forelegs around each other's necks and wrestle. This is followed by running and chasing and eventually mating. Like wolves, dogs show the peculiarity of the sexual tie; after copulation the two animals remain locked together for many minutes.

At first, young puppies are fed exclusively by nursing. After three weeks or so, they begin to take solid food, with final weaning at about seven weeks of age. Wolves feed the young by vomiting. Domestic dogs show this pattern more rarely but vomit readily and, like wolves, frequently eat the vomitus.

Special traits. *Intelligence.* Judging how intelligent a dog is, either in comparison to other dogs or to other animals, is difficult. Obviously, a dog will be unable to perform as well as a monkey any problem involving complex manipulation or colour vision. Intelligence is measured primarily by the ease with which a dog can be trained. This may depend in a large measure, however, on the degree of motivation. In general, when individual dogs are sufficiently motivated there appear to be no wide differences in intelligence between breeds.

There are big differences, however, in the ease with which breeds and individual dogs will accept complex training. Certain breeds, particularly the shepherd dogs and poodles, have reputations for intelligence of this sort. These animals have a high capacity for developing motivation and attention toward their handlers and a similarly high capacity for accepting inhibitory training. Most of the "wonder dogs" famous for their intelligence belong to these groups. A highly trained dog is capable of mastering many different commands.

At the same time there are definite limitations on canine intelligence. Like other mammals (excluding man), dogs do not have the capacity of speech and indeed learn to bark on command only with great difficulty. There is no evidence that dogs are able to recognize the meaning of words when they are used in new combinations (*i.e.,* to understand new sentences); thus the amount of information that actually can be conveyed to a dog is quite limited. A well-trained dog, however, is capable of such attentiveness to his owner's slightest movement and mannerisms that he almost seems to read the owner's mind.

Emotions. Most of a dog's emotional reactions are readily understandable. Growls and snarls are threats, and barking is usually an alarm signal. Rapid horizontal tail wagging indicates a friendly approach and is roughly the social equivalent of the human smile. High-pitched yelping occurs in situations involving pain or terror. The rapid yelps and whines of puppies indicate distress, which may have many causes. Solitary howling usually indicates loneliness or may be a reply to another howling dog.

Some other reactions are less easy to interpret and can be understood only in terms of the behaviour of dogs toward each other. Jumping up and offering the forefeet is usually an attempt to initiate playful fighting so often seen between dogs. A stiff-legged approach with erect and slowly wagging tail indicates aggressiveness and may be followed by an attack. A "worried" dog holds his ears down, so that his forehead is smooth. An attentive dog often displays a wrinkled forehead, usually the result of the erection of the ears.

The external expression, however, is not always a true guide to internal emotional state. A serious prolonged internal emotional disturbance will often show up in depressed activity and loss of appetite.

Abnormal behaviour. It is difficult to interpret any behaviour of a dog as abnormal, because the animal will adapt to a situation in any way that gives him satisfaction, however bizarre this may appear to the onlooker. Unusual behaviour may also result from organic disease. Any marked changes in behaviour, such as convulsions (often called fits), staggering gait, and the like, are usually indications of serious disease.

A neurosis may be defined as a kind of behaviour that gives relief from tension without adaptation to the cause of tension. Dogs confined to small pens for long periods, for example, will often develop the habit of running in circles or jumping from side to side whenever a person approaches. The dog is stimulated to respond to the person but because of confinement can only make what appear to be useless and inappropriate movements. Similarly, a dog left by itself in a house for long periods will often chew furniture and rugs. This behaviour can be understood as a thwarted attempt to escape.

Psychotic behaviour, defined as a general disruption of adaptation to social situations, is seldom seen in dogs. A puppy reared in complete isolation during the period of socialization, however, will avoid all human and canine contacts, showing more severe symptoms than the kennel-dog syndrome that arises from being reared in a limited environment. When dogs closely attached to their masters are separated from them for long periods, they may show symptoms of depression very similar to those exhibited by human beings.

The effect of complete isolation

DOGS AS PETS

The ideal time to acquire an individual puppy is between six and eight weeks of age, in order to permit normal psychological development. Since neither physical nor behavioral development is complete at this time, the best guide to the puppy's future behaviour is that of its parents. As adults, males are usually larger than females, more active, and tend to wander more.

A mongrel is a dog of unknown ancestry. First-generation hybrids between two pure breeds show a great deal of hybrid vigour and are usually more healthy and hardy than either parent breed. Their appearance and behaviour traits may be like one or the other parent, or neither. Some dog breeders regularly produce such hybrids for special purposes when the result can be predicted.

Developmental periods. The early development of a dog is divided into several distinct periods: (1) neonatal, (2) transition, (3) socialization, and (4) juvenile. In the neonatal (newborn) period, the puppy's activity is largely confined to nursing and sleeping.

The newborn puppy is blind and deaf and is consequently largely isolated from the external world. In about 14 days its eyes will open, marking the beginning of the transition period. During the third week the puppy undergoes a rapid change in behaviour and in sensory and motor abilities. Toward the end of the week, when its ears open, the puppy begins to react to sound. At the same time its first teeth appear, and it will attempt to eat solid food if it is offered.

Meanwhile it has begun to walk instead of crawl and to show social responses to humans and to other dogs. This marks the beginning of the period of socialization, at approximately three weeks after birth. The puppy will now slowly approach a strange person, nosing and wagging its tail. Another social response is playful fighting with its littermates. At any time during this period, which lasts up to 12 weeks of age, it is easy to form a close social relationship between a puppy and its owner, the maximum favourable response being obtained between six and eight weeks of age.

Socialization

By removing a puppy from its litter early in the socialization period all social relationships are transferred to human beings. Emotional disturbance and prolonged yelping is a normal reaction to removal from the litter and can be relieved by fondling and companionship. The puppy soon associates its owner with relief from distress. Adopting a puppy late in the period will throw the balance in the opposite direction, so that the puppy's strongest relationships are with dogs rather than with human beings. Puppies raised in large fields apart from human beings will become almost completely wild by 14 weeks of age. This period is therefore a critical one for determining the nature of social relationships and adjustment to the environment. Puppies left in a kennel environment much beyond 12 weeks of age are likely to be permanently shy and timid when brought into the outside world.

Following the period of socialization, the juvenile period lasts up to sexual maturity, usually sometime after six months of age. During this time the puppy is still physically undeveloped and relatively unskillful, and complex training is not advisable.

Punishment versus reward

Trainability. Development of the nervous system is largely completed by eight weeks of age.

Successful training methods vary with the breed of dog and the type of activity desired. Methods that work well with one breed may work only poorly with another. Mild punishment, for example, can easily inhibit undesirable behaviour in many of the shepherd dogs, whereas similar punishment may only stimulate resistance and fighting in the aggressive terrier breeds.

The basis of most training is reward. To be effective the reward must come immediately after the action, so that the dog forms a connection between the two. Good habits formed in this way also help prevent the formation of bad habits, since one interferes with the other. The rewards used vary with breeds and individuals, and the trainer must study the animal to determine which type of prize is most effective. For the hunting breeds food is usually a very strong reward. For many breeds praise and fondling is reward enough.

Punishment is chiefly useful to inhibit activity and is ineffective otherwise. For example, if an owner repeatedly calls a dog to punish it for misdeeds, the dog will soon learn not to come. A general rule is to use punishment sparingly and only in situations that the dog understands. At the same time dominance must be established; it is best accomplished over very young puppies, and by restraint and handling rather than outright punishment.

Breed psychology

Specializations of breeds. The psychology of each breed can be best understood in terms of the work for which it has been selected. Hunting breeds such as hounds have been selected to work independently of human handlers and are therefore somewhat difficult to keep under strict control. They have also been selected to work peaceably in packs or groups; aggressive behaviour is seldom a problem. Shepherd dogs, on the other hand, have been selected for their ability to learn to work under direction and to form firm habits. It is therefore easy to teach them restraint.

Hunting dogs. The hound breeds of dogs have been selected to hunt primarily by sight or by scent and are used to find and run down various sorts of land mammals. Dogs such as the greyhound, which were originally adapted to desert and plains, are representative of the sight hounds, or gazehounds. The bloodhound and related breeds are examples of the scent hounds. Both types track down their quarry.

A different type of hunting is found among bird dogs. When the bird is detected on the ground, the dog, if it is a pointer or setter, is trained to stop and wait; other breeds, such as the spaniels, simply flush the birds so that they can be shot. Another problem in bird hunting is to find the shot and wounded birds and return them to the hunter. For this job several special breeds of retrievers have been developed, some of which are used for both finding and retrieving.

The spaniels appear to have been the original bird dogs, and according to tradition they originated in Spain. They were used for various types of hunting in the Middle Ages. Water spaniels were used for retrieving birds from the water. Land spaniels were used for falconry, being trained to find and flush birds off the ground so that the falcons could attack them. Others were used in setting birds for the net; *i.e.,* on finding birds, they lie flat on the ground while the net is thrown over them and the birds. This was the original meaning of "setter." Later, when shotguns were developed for use in bird hunting, this behaviour trait was useless, and setter breeds were then selected for pointing instead. The original pointers were developed about the same time, probably from a mixture of hound and spaniel breeds.

Hunting game on open plains or deserts is not so much

a problem of finding the game as of catching it. Various greyhounds have been selected and bred for great speed and running down game of different sorts by sight.

The final part of hunting is the attack on the prey, and terrier breeds have been bred as attack dogs. The fox terriers were used to drive foxes out of their dens, and the larger Airedale terriers were, and still are, sometimes used to attack mountain lions and bring them to bay.

Guard dogs and watchdogs. Although guard dogs and watchdogs have had limited uses under modern civilized conditions because their owners are responsible for the damage they do, almost any breed of dog will still sound an alarm when strangers approach. Breeds such as the German shepherd dog (or Alsatian) and the Doberman pinscher are sometimes used in police work and by night watchmen. Dogs find certain use in modern warfare, chiefly in night patrols and in scouting, mine detection, and sentry duty.

Herding dogs. Under primitive conditions herding dogs were used to protect flocks of sheep or goats from predators, and they consequently had to be large and aggressive animals. Many of the modern shepherd breeds, such as the border collies, are now small or medium-size animals that have been selected for the ability to learn commands and obey them from a distance. Dogs are still used for herding cattle.

Sled dogs. One use of dogs that has no counterpart in the behaviour of wolves is as draft animals. With the domestication of larger animals and the development of modern systems of transport, this use has largely disappeared, surviving chiefly in Arctic sled dogs. Before the European carried the horse to North America, Indians used dogs to pull their wheelless vehicles (*travois*).

Companions and pets. An important modern use of dogs is as companions and household pets.

The popularity of dog breeds as pets seems to vary from year to year reflecting a current taste. The most popular are usually small or medium sized. Within the last half-century fox terriers, cocker spaniels, and beagles have been favourites, with some of the working, toy, and hound breeds such as collies, boxers, German shepherds, chihuahuas, Pekingese, miniature schnauzers, dachshunds, and basset hounds being runners-up. Among nonsporting breeds, poodles were registered in numbers more than twice as great as those of the nearest competitor, the German shepherd. Guide dogs for the blind are particularly valuable and devoted companions. Several breeds have been used successfully as guide dogs, but the German shepherd dog is most commonly employed.

Guide dogs

NUTRITION AND GROWTH

Adult dogs. Dogs are basically carnivorous hunting animals and as such are physiologically adapted to going for long periods without food or water. Many adult dogs can go without eating for a week without serious harm. When food is available, a hungry dog will gulp down large quantities as rapidly as possible.

The amount of food a dog needs depends upon the amount of exercise it gets, but a rough guide is one-half pound of dry dog food or its equivalent for a 20-pound dog. Smaller breeds generally require more food per pound of body weight than do larger breeds, and puppies need more food than mature dogs, especially during the period of rapid growth between six weeks and six months of age.

A well-balanced diet for a dog is not too different from that for a human being, except that the dog's intestine is not well equipped for handling roughage, so foods like bran and certain vegetables containing an excess of fibre should be avoided. Dogs digest bones easily and can live almost exclusively upon fresh ones that contain marrow. Splintery bones, such as those of poultry or chops are, however, dangerous. Dogs, because they can produce their own vitamin C, have no need for vegetables and fruits but can eat them if there is nothing else available. They can also readily digest cooked starchy foods.

Puppies. Puppies naturally have special nutritional requirements. In normal development, the young puppy gets all of his food from the mother's milk during the first few weeks of life. The mother then begins to supplement this with vomited food and completely weans the puppies at seven to ten weeks of age. Most mothers are unable to feed their puppies adequately by natural means throughout this whole period, and food supplementation is usually necessary at about three or four weeks of age.

The best supplement is some sort of mash containing milk and meat with large quantities of high-grade protein and also iron. A puppy's diet may be supplemented with vitamin D to prevent rickets. This is particularly important in the large breeds such as the Great Dane.

Rate of growth   A normal rate of growth is the best indication of good health in a young puppy. For the first three weeks puppies gain between 50 and 100 percent of their birth weight each week. Once supplementary feeding is begun they gain weight very rapidly up to four months of age, then more slowly, reaching nearly adult size by six months of age. Growth thereafter is quite slow, and the dog reaches full development at approximately two years. The prime of adult life extends through the fifth year, though many dogs live more than twice that long, and some last well into the teens.

REPRODUCTION

Sexual maturity. The ancestral wolves do not become sexually mature until nearly two years of age. However, females of most breeds of domestic dogs will show their first heat (or estrus) period before they are a year old and sometimes before six months. There is considerable variation both between breeds and individuals. The African basenji has a seasonal cycle, in which the females come into heat in the autumn of each year. A similar cycle is found in the Australian dingo when taken into northern latitudes. Most domestic breeds come into heat at any season of the year, at approximately six-month intervals. The pattern of any individual dog is usually fairly consistent, but longer and shorter cycles are common. Little is known about late-life fertility in bitches; reproductive powers diminish with age, but there is probably no menopause. Heat cycles in the female usually become irregular around the age of 11 or 12. Males usually remain capable of breeding to a more advanced age, but a male of six years is entering middle age.

Heat, or estrus, periods

Spaying the female (removing the ovaries) or castrating a male (removing the testes) before maturity affects the normal pattern of growth; such animals usually become taller and more obese than the average. Spaying terminates the sexual cycle in the female, but castration may have little effect on the sexual behaviour of an experienced male.

Receptivity and gestation. The first sign of estrus in the female is a gradual enlargement of the external genitalia, followed after several days by the discharge of a small amount of blood. At the same time an odorous substance highly exciting to males is secreted in the urine. If the female is not allowed to urinate where males can find it, there will be little trouble, but if she is allowed to run freely, males will gather from miles around. Bleeding may continue for a week or more and at its end the female will accept the male. She may be receptive for a few days or as much as two weeks. Ovulation occurs 72 hours before the last point of receptivity. Conception may occur from matings at any time in the cycle. Many breeders make a practice of repeating matings every other day throughout the receptive period.

The period of gestation is approximately nine weeks counting from the time when the animal is first receptive. The embryos develop quite slowly at first, not becoming implanted until about 21 days after fertilization. The greatest intra-uterine growth of the puppies occurs in the last half of pregnancy, during which the female requires an increased diet. Occasionally a female that has not been bred will show a pseudopregnancy, with swelling of the abdomen and enlargement of the mammary glands.

Litter size   Litter size varies roughly with the size of breed, but there is great individual variation. Some toy breeds rarely have more than one or two puppies, whereas the setters and larger breeds may have eight to ten, with some record litters going much higher. Four to six is a good average; in very large litters the pups are frequently small and weak.

AILMENTS

Parasites. *Worms.* There are many intestinal worms that attack dogs. The most serious one is a variety of *Ascaris,* a roundworm that can cause a high percentage of fatalities in young puppies. Most puppies acquire considerable resistance to them after three months of age, but the majority of dogs have at least light infections. Females about to be bred are usually wormed, bathed, and transferred to thoroughly clean quarters. They can also be wormed as late as seven weeks in pregnancy. If this is not done, the puppies can become infected from the mother, even before birth. Puppies can be given a worm expellant (vermifuge) if symptoms develop. Other parasitic roundworms that attack dogs include heartworms, hookworms, and whipworms.

With the exception of rabies, most diseases of dogs are not transmissible to human beings. A rare exception is a tapeworm, *Echinococcus granulosus,* normally transmitted from dogs to sheep through fecal matter but which can also accidentally be transmitted to human beings, particularly children. The parasite grows as a cyst and may enter the brain or other vital organs and cause severe symptoms. It is found only in places where dogs have access to the bodies or entrails of sheep and cattle. Other less harmful varieties of tapeworms occur commonly in dogs and yield to treatment with appropriate worm expellants, or vermifuges. Dogs may become infected with these tapeworms by eating fleas and the uncooked bodies of food animals in which the tapeworms spend part of their life cycle.

Mange. Mange is caused by two varieties of mites that live in the hair follicles. An afflicted dog loses his hair, and the affected area is itchy and inflamed. The mites are difficult to kill, successful treatment requiring many weeks.

Lice. Lice spend their entire life cycle on the dog and are transferred to new hosts by direct contact. Successful treatment usually requires two or more applications of some oily substance that smothers the lice, or of an insecticide. The developing lice (or nits) are highly resistant, but adult lice are controlled readily, even with soap and water.

Fleas. Fleas present a different problem, since they leave the dog during part of their life cycle in order to breed. Those on the animal are easily eliminated with commercial preparations (sprays and powders), but their breeding areas must also be eliminated for control. Larval fleas live on filth and commonly breed around barnyards or other places where animals deposit feces.

Ticks. Ticks, which breed in grassy or bushy areas, may attach themselves to a dog as it brushes against the vegetation. Individual ticks are easily removed by applying kerosene or some other oily substance to the ticks' bodies, thus suffocating them and causing them to release their hold.

Diseases. *Canine distemper.* One of the most important diseases of domestic dogs is canine distemper, an airborne, highly infectious virus disease that attacks the nervous system. It runs a long course, with a high proportion of fatalities. The disease can be prevented by inoculation with an attenuated virus.

Puppies nursing on immune mothers are protected by the antibodies obtained in the mother's milk for a few weeks after birth and can be successfully vaccinated only after these antibodies have disappeared.

Infectious canine hepatitis. This disease attacks the liver primarily. The early symptom of high fever resembles that of distemper but the disease, which is often fatal, runs a much shorter course. Transmitted by contact through urine, it is less infectious than distemper. Many dogs are carriers, however, and spread the disease long after they have recovered. It can be prevented by inoculation.

Rabies (hydrophobia). Rabies is an invariably fatal disease that is highly dangerous because it can be spread to human beings as well as to other dogs and other mammals. The disease attacks the nervous system, chiefly, causing animals to become highly irritable. Infected dogs are so fearless that they bite anything they come across, spreading the disease through the saliva entering the wounds. Many wild animals, such as foxes and rodents, provide a reservoir for rabies. Dogs can readily be inoculated (see INFECTIOUS DISEASES).

Other ailments. Finally, dogs are susceptible to many other less common bacterial and parasitic diseases, which vary according to the life of the animal and the climate in which it lives. Dogs are also subject to constitutional ailments such as heart disease and cancer. Congenital defects such as crooked legs and cleft palates are common. As in other traits, dogs show hereditary differences in their resistance to disease, but this trait is greatly aided by good nutrition and proper exercise. (See also DISEASE: *Diseases of animals.*)

GENETICS

Not only are there wide differences between breeds but there is also great individual variability within each breed. All traits are genetically determined, but their expression is more or less modified by the environmental circumstances; behavioral traits especially are influenced by training and experience.

Colour. There are certain physical characters the inheritance of which is well-known and highly predictable in breeding experiments. Most of these are based on genes affecting colour. Only a few of the major colour-influencing genes are described below.

The wild-type coat

The basic wolf-gray or wild-type coat consists of long guard hairs, banded with black and red, and a lighter coloured undercoat, which grows heavily in winter and is shed in summer. The colour is distributed in a basic pattern of "countershading": more black hair on the top of the body and more red underneath, becoming almost white on the belly. Thus there are two basic pigments, black and red, with the absence of pigment producing white.

In domestic dogs the original coat has been modified in length, texture, pattern, and colour, in a wide variety of genetic combinations. The A series is the major series of genes that modify colour. Given in order of relative dominance, these genes include: coal black, a^s; red, varying from clear red to red with some dark hair (the so-called sable colouring), a^y; the wild type or wolf gray, a^w; and bicolour (black-and-tan), having a clear black on the upper part of the body and clear red below, with red dots over the eyes, a^t.

Other genes may influence the A series: the recessive *ee* changes all black hair to red, and *bb* changes black hair to brown or liver colour. These pigments may be modified still further by other genes to produce all shades from dark to very light.

Another important series of genes produces various degrees of white spotting, ranging from small spots on the tail, feet, and belly through piebald (heavy mottling over the entire body) to almost completely white animals, as in white bull terriers. The characteristics of hair length and coat texture are also influenced genetically, but less precisely than coat colour. In general, short hair is dominant over long, coarse over fine, straight hair over curly, wire coat is incompletely dominant over smooth, sparse over dense. There are an enormous number of possible combinations, each breed having a limited but often confusing number.

Shape and weight. In body form, there is an ancient mutation for the upcurved tail. This is a physiological trait, since the dog can usually straighten his tail; its inheritance is not well-known. There is major mutation for short legs, seen in such breeds as dachshunds and basset hounds; the first-generation hybrids of a mating of a short-legged dog with a normal-legged one have legs that are intermediate in length. The bulldog mutation chiefly affects the head, producing a short and flattened snout accompanied by an undershot jaw. Again, the first generation of a cross between a bulldog and a normal-faced dog has an intermediate appearance. Still another inherited trait is ear carriage, varying from lop ears to erect ones, the lop-eared condition being dominant.

One of the outstandingly variable characteristics of dogs is body weight, ranging from as little as 0.9 kilograms (two pounds) in dwarf breeds such as the chihuahua, to 68 kilograms (150 pounds) in some of the large breeds such as the mastiff and St. Bernard. Offspring from crosses between large and small breeds tend to be intermediate in size, and the trait is affected by large numbers of genes.

Other traits. The inheritance of behavioral and temperamental characteristics is highly complicated. The behaviour characteristic of a particular breed consists of a combination of several independently inherited traits, each of which is affected by one or two major genes and perhaps other minor ones. The tendency to crouch or sit in cocker spaniels, for example, depends on two independent traits: the crouching posture itself and the tendency to remain quiet.

The danger of preserving unfavourable traits

It is very likely that more than one combination of genes will produce a desirable trait in a dog; therefore, two excellent dogs bred together may produce somewhat inferior offspring, and vice versa. Consequently, most successful dog breeders experiment with matings that give the highest proportion of desirable progeny. Since dogs are long-lived and often fertile, this method of progeny testing can be highly successful. At the same time there is in most pure breeds a large number of undesirable recessive traits of form and behaviour that crop out in certain matings. Many of these are preserved and may be spread throughout a breed if, for instance, a champion male carrying an undesirable recessive trait is widely bred to numerous females. Furthermore, many of the traits desired by dog fanciers, such as the bulldog head, which would be a defect in a wild animal and promptly "selected out" in nature, are perpetuated by man through special care and attention.

BREEDS

The British classification, revised periodically by the Kennel Club of England, set the standard that other countries have followed, with some modifications. The Kennel Club recognizes two major classes of breeds: sporting and nonsporting. The sporting division includes the hound, gundog, and terrier groups; the nonsporting division includes the working, utility, and toy groups.

Variations in breed classification

Classifications of recognized breeds vary widely in other countries. The French list recognizes, in addition to hunting dogs, watchdogs, running dogs, 17 kinds of shepherd dogs, and 24 "ladies' dogs," including toy dogs and lap dogs. The German list emphasizes utility dogs and watch dogs, whereas the Swedish list includes nine different spitz breeds.

The current American classification, devised by the American Kennel Club, is somewhat different from the British. It lists six groups of breeds and embraces most of the breeds of other countries. Some breeds on the British list are not recognized in America and vice versa. The American Kennel Club provides registry service for the more than 100 breeds listed below, with the number still increasing.

Sporting breeds. These are primarily bird dogs or gundogs. The basic breeds were the medieval spaniels, from which the modern setters and pointers were developed—the latter with some admixture of hound ancestry.

Griffon (wirehaired pointing)	Spaniel (American water)
Pointer	Spaniel (Brittany)
Pointer (German shorthaired)	Spaniel (clumber)
Pointer (German wirehaired)	Spaniel (cocker)
Retriever (Chesapeake Bay)	Spaniel (English cocker)
Retriever (curly-coated)	Spaniel (English springer)
Retriever (flat-coated)	Spaniel (field)
Retriever (golden)	Spaniel (Irish water)
Retriever (Labrador)	Spaniel (Sussex)
Setter (English)	Spaniel (Welsh springer)
Setter (Gordon)	Vizsla
Setter (Irish)	Weimaraner

Hound breeds. This group of dogs includes two main types: (1) sight hounds and (2) scent hounds. The greyhounds belong to the first category, and the closely related saluki and Afghan hound are probably nearest to the original type. The borzoi and Irish wolfhound, as well as the Scottish deerhound, are related animals. The second main type comprises the scent hounds, of which the foxhounds and beagles are excellent examples. The basset hound, otter hound, bloodhound, and harrier are closely related. Other animals in the hound group are more miscellaneous.

Afghan hound	Foxhound (English)
Basenji	Greyhound
Basset hound	Harrier
Beagle	Norwegian elkhound
Bloodhound	Otter hound
Borzoi (or Russian wolfhound)	Rhodesian ridgeback
Coonhound (black and tan)	Saluki
Dachshund	Whippet
Deerhound (Scottish)	Wolfhound (Irish)
Foxhound (American)	

Working breeds. The largest number of these breeds are derived from various sorts of herding and farm dogs. The second largest group are the guard dogs, again of miscellaneous origin. Finally there are the sled dogs from various Arctic regions.

Alaskan Malamute	Kuvasz
Belgian Malinois	Mastiff
Belgian sheepdog	Newfoundland
Belgian Tervuren	Old English sheepdog
Bernese mountain dog	Puli
Bouvier des Flandres	Rottweiler
Boxer	St. Bernard
Briard	Samoyed
Bullmastiff	Schnauzer (giant)
Collie	Schnauzer (standard)
Doberman pinscher	Shetland sheepdog
German shepherd dog	Siberian husky
Great Dane	Welsh corgi (Cardigan)
Great Pyrenees	Welsh corgi (Pembroke)
Komondor	

Terrier breeds. These are typically dogs developed to attack vermin living in the terre, or earth.

Airedale terrier	Lakeland terrier
Australian terrier	Manchester terrier
Bedlington terrier	Norwich terrier
Border terrier	Schnauzer (miniature)
Bull terrier	Scottish terrier
Cairn terrier	Sealyham terrier
Dandie Dinmont terrier	Skye terrier
Fox terrier	Staffordshire terrier
Irish terrier	Welsh terrier
Kerry Blue terrier	West Highland White terrier

Toy breeds. These are very small dogs of various origins. Some are merely dwarf editions of larger breeds, in fairly normal form and proportion. Others have heads of the bulldog type, with short flat noses.

Affenpinscher	Pekingese
Chihuahua	Pinscher (miniature)
English toy spaniel	Pomeranian
Griffon (Brussels)	Poodle (toy)
Italian greyhound	Pug
Japanese spaniel	Silky terrier
Maltese	Toy Manchester terrier
Papillon	Yorkshire terrier

Nonsporting breeds. This is a miscellaneous group used entirely for companions and show dogs.

Boston terrier	Keeshond
Bulldog	Lhasa Apso
Chow chow	Poodle (miniature)
Dalmatian	Poodle (standard)
French bulldog	Schipperke

Other breeds. The Kennel Club (Great Britain) greatly expanded its list in the 1960s and recognized the following breeds not found in the American classification. Hounds: dachsbracke, Finnish spitz, Ibiza hound, Pharaoh hound. Gundogs: German longhaired pointer, Italian spinone, kleine Munsterlander. Terriers: Glen of Imaal, miniature bull, Norfolk, soft-coated wheaten terrier. Utility dogs: Iceland dog, Japanese akita, Leonberger, Mexican hairless, Shih Tzu, Tibetan spaniel, Tibetan terrier. Working dogs: Anatolian sheep-dog, Australian kelpie, bearded collie, beauceron, Maremma Italian sheepdog, Norwegian buhund, Polish sheepdog, Portuguese water dog, Tibetan mastiff. Toys: bichon frise, Chinese crested dog, lowchen. Many American breeders have not sought recognition for certain purebred varieties that they have developed. Others have registered their distinct breeds in organizations other than the American Kennel Club. There are many special strains of hounds, often originating from certain famous packs and some named after their owners. Among American foxhounds, the Walker, Trigg, July, Trumbo, and Birdsong strains are well-known, and coonhounds include

the Bluetick, Redbone, Plotthound, and Treeing Walker varieties as well as the black and tan variety recognized by the American Kennel Club.

Other breeds found in various parts of the world include the border collie, Australian cattle dog (or heeler), Drahthaar, Drentsche partrijshond, Catalan sheep dog, Istrian pointer, lurcher, Portuguese pointer, Rumanian sheepdog, Sealydale, Svensk vallhund, and many more.

BREEDERS' ASSOCIATIONS AND DOG SHOWS

In western Europe and North America, dog breeding has been highly developed as a pastime and business. Dog shows and systematic attempts to improve and maintain dog breeds originated in the latter half of the 19th century. The first recorded dog show was held in Newcastle, England, in 1859, and the first large show was held in Chelsea in 1863. About the same time, the showing of dogs became popular in the United States, and by 1880 an annual show in New York featured representatives of about 29 breeds.

As dog shows grew in number, a need was felt for some kind of regulating body. The Kennel Club of England filled this need in Great Britain; it was founded in 1873 and became the supreme governing body of dog breeders' associations in that country. A few years later, in 1884, the American Kennel Club was formed, becoming the ruling body of breeders' associations in the United States. Soon thereafter similar organizations were formed in many other countries.

Dog shows are organized both by local and by national dog clubs. Some dog clubs are devoted to only one breed, whereas others are open to fanciers of any breed. Rules for holding shows in the United States are made and published by the American Kennel Club, and in Britain by the Kennel Club of England.

Show dogs are judged on the basis of breed standards, the various physical characters considered desirable and those considered faults in any particular breed. These standards are not directly concerned with health, vigour, or ability to reproduce; in fact, the quality of the show breeds sometimes suffers in these respects. A popular feature of many shows is the obedience trial, in which dogs are judged on performance rather than appearance.

Field trials, held for hunting breeds, allow dogs to compete against members of their own breeds in the performance of hunting duties such as trailing, pointing, and retrieving. There are also standard field trials for shepherd dogs, in which the dog has to herd a small flock of sheep along a prescribed course, cut sheep out of a flock and drive them in a small pen, relying only on signals given by the shepherd. Other working trials are popular in many parts of the world.

Cats

All cats are grouped in the family Felidae. From the largest, the tiger, to the smallest, the house cat, felids are characterized by supple, low-slung bodies, finely molded heads, long tails that aid in balance, and specialized teeth and claws that adapt them admirably to a life of active hunting. The family of cats belongs to the mammalian order Carnivora, the "flesh-eaters"; for an account of the family and its relationships, see MAMMALS: *Carnivora*.

Domestic cats (*Felis catus*) possess the features of their wild relatives in being basically carnivorous, remarkably agile and powerful, and finely coordinated in movement. It is noteworthy that the ancestors of the other common household pet, the dog (and most other domestic animals as well), were social animals that lived together in packs in which there was subordination to a leader. The dog has readily transferred its allegiance from pack leader to human master. The cat, however, has not yielded as readily to subjugation. Consequently, the house cat is able to revert to complete self-reliance more quickly and more successfully than most other domestic animals.

ORIGIN AND HISTORY OF CATS

The "cat pattern," established very early in the evolution of modern mammals, was a successful one: early cats were

Types of shows

already typical in form at a time when the ancestors of most other modern mammalian types were scarcely recognizable. They first appeared in the early Pliocene Epoch, approximately 7,000,000 years ago, and they have continued with remarkably little change into modern times.

Domestication. Although its origin is hidden in antiquity, the domestic cat has a history that dates nearly 3,500 years to ancient Egypt. There are no authentic records of domestication earlier than 1500 BC, but it may have taken place sooner. Although the cat was proclaimed a sacred animal in the 5th and 6th dynasties (about 2500–2200 BC), it had not necessarily been domesticated at that time. It is probable that the Egyptians domesticated the cat because they realized its value in protecting granaries from rodents. Their affection and respect for this predator led to the development of religious cat cults and temple worship of cats.

Cats have long been known to other cultures. Wall tiles in Crete dating from 1600 BC depict hunting cats. Evidence from art and literature indicates that the domestic cat was present in Greece from the 5th century BC and in China from 500 BC. In India cats were mentioned in Sanskrit writings around 100 BC, while the Arabs and the Japanese were not introduced to the cat until about AD 600. The earliest record of cats in Great Britain dates back to about AD 936 when Howel Dda, prince of south central Wales, enacted laws for their protection. The first domestic cats in the United States date from around 1750.

Ancestry of breeds Even though all cats are similar in appearance, it is difficult to trace the ancestry of individual breeds. Since tabby-like markings appear in the drawings and mummies of ancient Egyptian cats, present-day tabbies may be descendants of the sacred cats of Egypt. The Abyssinian also resembles pictures and statues of Egyptian cats. The Persian, whose colouring is often the same as that of mixed breeds (although the length of hair and the body conformation are distinctive), was probably crossed at various times with other breeds; the tailless Manx cat may be derived from another species or may be a mutation. The ancestry of Persian and Siamese cats may well be distinct from other domestic breeds, representing a domestication of some Oriental wild cat (the ancestor of the Egyptian cat is believed to have come from Africa). In fact, nothing is known of the ancestry of the Siamese types, and there is no living species of Oriental cat that would serve as ancestor.

Associations with human culture. The cat has long played a role in religion and witchcraft. In the Bible "cat" is mentioned only in the apocryphal Letter of Jeremiah. The cat figured prominently in the religion of Egypt, the Norse countries, and various parts of the Orient. The Egyptians had a cat-headed goddess named Bast, whose chief seat of worship was the city of Bubastis. Thousands of cat mummies have been discovered in Egypt, and there were even mouse mummies, presumably to provide food for the

cats. More often, however, the cat has been associated with sorcery and witchcraft, and the superstitions regarding cats, common in all countries, are innumerable. Superstitions often took extremely vicious forms, and throughout the ages cats have been more cruelly mistreated than perhaps any other animal. Black cats in particular have long been regarded as having occult powers and as being the familiars of witches. Cat lovers are called "ailurophiles"; persons in whom cats inspire fear are termed "ailurophobes."

The cat is a familiar figure in nursery rhymes and stories. The English legend of Dick Whittington and his cat is a particular favourite. The writers Théophile Gautier and Charles Baudelaire have paid it homage and, in the 20th century, Rudyard Kipling, Colette, and T.S. Eliot wrote of cats. The influence of the cat also appears most clearly in everyday language where its many-sided character is crystallized in proverbs and sayings.

CATS AS PETS

The cat is of ever-increasing economic importance. There are businesses that manufacture and sell only cat foods or cat accessories, veterinarians who treat only cats, hospitals that cater to sick cats, and cemeteries that bury cats.

Increasing popularity The popularity of the cat continuously grows, especially that of pedigreed breeds. The cat's independent personality, combined with its grace, cleanliness, and subtle signs of affection, are traits that have wide appeal. Typically, cats are creatures of habit; they are inquisitive, but not adventurous, and are easily upset by sudden changes of routine. The ideal household cat has been raised in a clean home, kept away from unhealthy animals, separated from its mother between the ages of two and four months, and inoculated against common infectious cat diseases. The problems of discipline and training may be complicated in a household containing two cats of the same age. A year-old cat, however, may accept a new kitten, other than its own, and teach it, in turn, the disciplines that it has been taught.

A good disposition and overall good health are important criteria for any pet. Disposition varies only slightly between male and female cats. There are, however, distinct differences in intelligence and disposition between the alley cat (or mixed breed) and the pedigree. The mixed breed is a heterogeneous breed of unknown lineage; therefore, its temperament and disposition are difficult to assess. By chance the mixed breed may prove a happier, healthier, and more robust pet than a pedigree. On the other hand, the behaviour and vigour of the direct ancestors of pedigreed cats are indicative of the characteristics the offspring will possess as adults.

GENERAL FEATURES AND SPECIAL ADAPTATIONS

The average weight of the household cat varies from six to 10 pounds, although among nonpedigreed cats weights

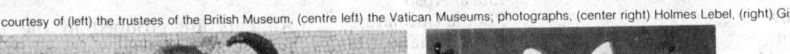

The antiquity and cult of the cat.
(Left) Mummified Egyptian cat of the Roman period. (Centre left) Roman mosaic, c. AD 76–138, depicting a cat killing a chicken. (Centre right) Japanese temple cat from Go-To-Ku-Ji Temple in Tokyo; the raised paw symbolizes ability to attract luck. (Right) Mexican "Judas cat" constructed of papier-mâché inset with firecrackers; in a contemporary Holy Saturday custom, believed to derive from Spain, the figures are burned in effigy of enemies.

up to 28 pounds are not uncommon. Average lengths are 28 inches for males and 20 inches for females. In keeping with a carnivorous habit, the cat has a simple gut; the small intestine is only about three times the length of the body.

The skin of the cat, composed of dermis and epidermis, regenerates and fights off infection very quickly. Tiny erector muscles, attached to all hair follicles, enable the cat to bristle all over. Thus, although the cat is a relatively small animal, it can frighten enemies by arching its back, bristling, and hissing.

Coordination and musculature. Cats are among the most highly specialized of the flesh-eating mammals. Their brains are large and well developed. Cats are digitigrade; *i.e.*, they walk on their toes. Interestingly, the cat, unlike the dog and horse, walks or runs by moving first the front and back legs on one side, then the front and back legs on the other side. Only the camel and the giraffe move in a similar way. The cat's body has great elasticity. The vertebrae of the spinal column are held together by muscles, rather than by ligaments as in man, so the cat can elongate or contract its back, curve it upwards, or oscillate it along the vertebral line. The construction of the shoulder joints permits the cat to turn its foreleg in almost any direction. Cats are powerfully built animals; these animals are so well coordinated that they almost invariably land on their feet if they should happen either to fall or be dropped.

Teeth. One of the most characteristic and specialized features of the cat is its teeth (Figure 3). They are adapted

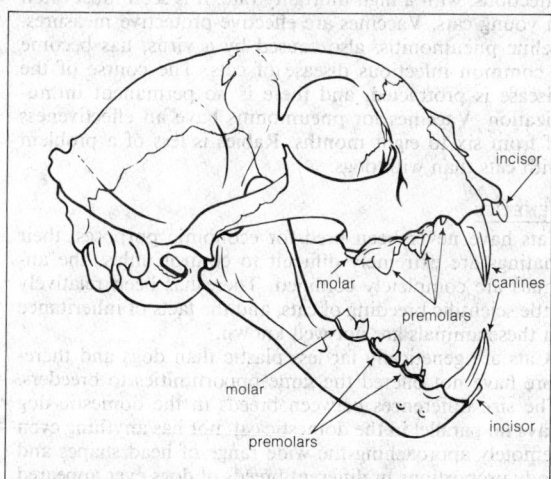

Figure 3: Skull of cat.

to three functions: stabbing (canines), anchoring (canines), and cutting (molars). Cats have no flatcrowned crushing teeth and therefore cannot chew their food; instead, they cut it up. Other than the canines and molars, the teeth are more or less nonfunctional; most of the cheek teeth do not even meet when the mouth is closed. The dental formula in all cats, for either side of both upper and lower jaws, is: incisors 3/3, canines 1/1, premolars 3/2, molars 1/1. The total number of teeth is 16 in the upper jaw and 14 in the lower. Primary or milk teeth number 24; these are replaced by the permanent teeth at about five months in the domestic cat. Each half of the jaw is hinged to the skull by a transverse roller that fits tightly into a trough on the underside of the skull—making grinding movements impossible even if the cat had teeth suitable for grinding.

Retraction of claws

Claws. Another special adaptation is the cat's strong, sharp claws. There is a remarkable mechanism for retracting the claws when they are not in use (Figure 4). The claw is retracted or extended by pivoting the end bone of the toe (which bears the claw) over the tip of the next bone. The action that unsheathes the claws also spreads the toes widely, making the foot more than twice as broad as it normally is and converting it into a truly formidable weapon. This claw-sheathing mechanism is present in all species of the cat family except the cheetah. Although there are no nerve endings in the nail itself, blood capillaries are present in the inner part.

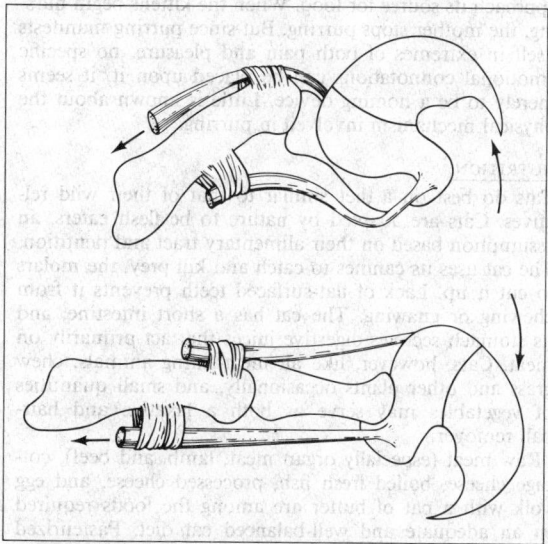

Figure 4: *Movement of retractile claw of a cat.*
(Top) When upper tendon is pulled, claw is retracted. (Bottom) When lower tendon is pulled, claw is unsheathed.

Senses. *Sight.* Cats are generally nocturnal in habit. The retina of the cat's eye is made extra sensitive to light by a layer of guanine, which causes the eye to shine at night in a strong light. The eyes themselves, large with pupils that expand or contract to mere slits according to the density of light, do not distinguish colours clearly. Cats have a third eyelid, or nictitating membrane, commonly called the haw. Its appearance is used frequently as an indicator of the cat's general state of health.

Smell. The cat's sense of smell, well developed particularly in the adult, is crucial to its evaluation of food, so that a cat whose nasal passages become clogged as a result of illness may appear to lose its appetite completely. Cats can distinguish the odour of nitrogenous substances especially keenly (*e.g.*, fish).

Touch. The sense of touch is acute in cats. The eyebrows, whiskers, hairs of the cheek, and fine tufts of hair on the ears are all extremely sensitive to vibratory stimulation. The functions of the whiskers (or vibrissae) are only partially understood; however, it is known that if they are cut off, the cat is temporarily incapacitated. The toes and paws, as well as the tip of the nose, are also very sensitive to touch.

Hearing. Cats also have an acute sense of hearing. Their ears contain almost 30 muscles (compared with six in man); as a result they can turn them many times more quickly in the direction of a sound than can a dog. The ears of cats, although receptive to ultrasonic frequencies up to 25,000 vibrations per second, are slightly inferior to those of dogs, which register 35,000 vibrations per second.

Behaviour. *Grooming and tail-wagging.* The tongue of all cats, which has a patch of sharp, backward-directed spines near the tip, has the appearance and feel of a coarse file; the spines help the cat to lap up liquids and also to groom itself. The disposition to cleanliness is well established in cats; they groom themselves with their rasplike tongues and preen at length, especially after meals. Another peculiarity of behaviour is the nervous tail-wagging common to all cats, from the lion to the house cat; it is believed to be learned from the mother and is associated with early play, a prelude to adult habits of predation.

Purring. While lions and other big cats roar, the domestic cats and other *Felis* species purr. Purring has been described as a low, continuous, rattling hum and has been interpreted as an expression of pleasure or contentment. It has nothing to do with the true voice of the animal; the vibration frequency is far lower than that of the vocal chords. Purring in domestic cats appears to be introduced to the kittens by the mother, who uses it as a means of calling the young to nurse. At birth the kitten's eyes are closed, the ears undeveloped, and the sense of smell absent; purring is felt as a vibration by the kittens, who approach its source for food. When the kittens begin nursing, the mother stops purring. But since purring manifests itself in extremes of both pain and pleasure, no specific emotional connotations can be placed upon it; it seems merely to be a homing device. Little is known about the physical mechanism involved in purring.

NUTRITION

Cats do best on a diet similar to that of their wild relatives. Cats are adapted by nature to be flesh eaters, an assumption based on their alimentary tract and dentition. The cat uses its canines to catch and kill prey, the molars to cut it up. Lack of flat-surfaced teeth prevents it from chewing or gnawing. The cat has a short intestine, and its stomach secretes digestive juices that act primarily on meat. Cats, however, like all meat-eating animals, chew grass and other plants occasionally, and small quantities of vegetables may serve as both a laxative and hairball remover.

Raw meat (especially organ meat, lamb, and beef), cottage cheese, boiled fresh fish, processed cheese, and egg yolk with a pat of butter are among the foods required in an adequate and well-balanced cat diet. Pasteurized cow's milk is not the perfect food for cats and sometimes causes gastric disturbances difficult to remedy. In addition, many other foods important in human nutrition are unacceptable in the cat diet, including most cooked foods, egg whites, pork kidney, horsemeat, vegetables, spicy cold cuts, cereals, ice cream, and sweets.

Polyunsaturates such as corn oil, peanut oil, or safflower oil are important dietary supplements, not only for their nutritive value but also because they act as lubricants to prevent constipation and eliminate hair balls. These oils have been known to arrest formation of kidney stones (*i.e.*, urinary calculi) in cats. On the other hand, mineral oil or preparations with a petroleum base can cause severe harm to cats if given routinely to eliminate hair balls.

REPRODUCTION

As a rule, domestic cats reach reproductive age between seven and 12 months. A breeding female (called a queen) can be in heat or estrus as many as five times a year. During these periods, which last about five days, she "calls," or caterwauls intermittently. The gestation period for cats varies but averages 63–65 days, and the birth usually lasts about two hours. The birth is often known as kittening, and the kittens are known as a litter. The average litter numbers four; however, the Abyssinian usually has fewer, the Siamese more.

Each kitten is born in a separate amniotic sac that is generally broken open at the moment of birth. If it is not, the mother breaks it. She also severs the umbilical cord and eats the placenta (in many cases this stimulates lactation). The kittens are born blind, deaf, and helpless, as are many other carnivores; their senses only begin to function 10 or 12 days after birth. Soon after birth the mother licks her kittens; this action not only cleans them, but also helps stimulate their circulation. Kittens at birth lack distinctive colouring. Their markings are highly deceptive, and many do not acquire their characteristic markings and colour for weeks. For example, Siamese kittens are white at birth, while Blue Persians have tabby markings and Black Persians are brown.

A cat by nature is capable of bearing up to three litters every year. Traditionally, regulation of the cat population was accomplished by the selective killing of the newborn. In modern times, however, sterilization—by means of relatively safe and simple operations, known as spaying, neutering, or altering—became common in affluent societies. Neutering was also viewed as an adaptive measure for indoor life. Cats that roam unsupervised may live eight or nine years; those supervised and cared for live an average of 14–15 years.

Characteristics of newborn

DISEASES AND PARASITES

Until relatively recently little research was concerned directly with cat diseases, their symptoms, or clinical cures. For many years cat treatments were simply extensions of those given dogs. Now, however, cat disorders of the skin, the eyes, the ears, the various systems (circulatory, respiratory, urinary, digestive, nervous, skeletal), and the blood, as well as contagious cat diseases, and external and internal parasites are studied, so that appropriate preventions and treatments can be developed.

Many cats suffer and die because their ailments become serious before their general conditions change sufficiently to reveal symptoms of illness. On the other hand, many symptoms used in diagnosing cat ailments are not definitive for given disorders. For example, signs of possible illness include general symptoms such as a dull coat, lack of appetite, and listlessness. Diarrhea may be a result of serious illness or simply a reflection of a change in diet. Tearing of the eyes may indicate conjunctivitis or a cold, especially when accompanied by sneezing. Since however, sneezing is the cat's only mechanism for blowing its nose, not all sneezing indicates a problem. Open sores, usually at the base of the ear, around the mouth, or on the toes, can point to a ringworm infection or to a fight with another animal.

Symptoms

Cats are attacked by several kinds of external and internal parasites. External parasites are most generally found in kittens, although they occur in adults. The most frequent parasites are fleas, but lice, ticks, and ear mites also occur. Internal parasites include roundworms, tapeworms, and protozoan coccidia. Modern veterinary medicine has made all of these easy to control.

Panleucopenia, often called feline distemper, is the most well-known viral disease in cats. Highly contagious and infectious, with a high mortality rate, it is seen most often in young cats. Vaccines are effective protective measures. Feline pneumonitis, also caused by a virus, has become a common infectious disease of cats. The course of the disease is protracted, and there is no permanent immunization. Vaccines for pneumonitis have an effectiveness of from six to eight months. Rabies is less of a problem with cats than with dogs.

GENETICS

Cats have never been bred for economic purposes; their matings are extremely difficult to control unless the animals are completely confined. There has been relatively little scientific breeding of cats, and the facts of inheritance in these animals are not well known.

Cats are genetically far less plastic than dogs and therefore have not offered the same opportunities to breeders. The size differences between breeds in the domestic dog have no parallel in the domestic cat, nor has anything even remotely approaching the wide range of head shapes and body proportions in different breeds of dogs ever appeared among the cats. In cats the differences between one breed and another are largely differences in colour and texture of the coat. The basic classification is into long-haired and short-haired cats.

Colour. The commonest basic coat colours in nonpedigreed cats are black, yellow, white, and various combinations and dilutions of these colours, such as tabby or striped. Solid white is dominant to all other colours. The mode of inheritance of black is imperfectly understood; the possibility that it is sex-linked is widely accepted. Tortoiseshell, a piebald pattern of black, yellow, and white that results from crossing black and yellow, appears to be sex-linked in some way; male tortoiseshells are born only rarely and are usually sterile.

Dominance of white

Siamese dilution, the typical coloration of Siamese cats, has been described as a case of imperfect albinism and has been compared to the Himalayan pattern in rabbits. Its heredity is not well understood. There are also dilutions of the other ordinary colours: blue is dilute black and cream is dilute yellow. White spotting also occurs and is dominant to uniform or self colour.

Other characters. The long-haired coat of the Persian (the usage Angora is archaic) appears to be a simple unit character. It is recessive to short hair. Eye colour is known to be inherited, but its mode of inheritance is not thoroughly understood. Blue eye colour seems to be associated with dilution in coat colour; blue-eyed white cats are usually deaf, a fact commented on by Charles Darwin. Asymmetry of eye colour is known to be inherited.

Polydactylism, the presence of extra toes, is inherited and behaves as a dominant to the normal condition. It seems to be due to a single gene. The extra toes occur on the inner or thumb side of the foot.

BREEDS

Recognized show breeds and the characteristics valued most highly by show judges include those listed below.

Longhair division. These are the Persian cats. The perfect type should be cobby—low on the legs, deep in the chest, the head round and massive, eyes large and round, the coat long all over the body. The acceptable colour standards are:

White. Pure white, no coloured hairs; eyes deep blue or deep orange.

Black. Dense coal black from roots to tips of hair; eyes copper or deep orange.

Blue. One level shade of blue gray without variation from nose to tip of tail; eyes either brilliant copper or deep orange.

Red. Deep, rich, clear, red orange without shading, marking, or ticking; eyes brilliant copper or deep orange.

Cream. One level shade of cream; eyes brilliant copper or deep orange.

Chinchilla (silver). The undercoat pure white, the coat on back, flanks, head, and tail tipped with black to give the characteristic "sparkling silver" appearance; eyes green; rims of eyes, lips, and nose outlined with black; centre of nose brick red.

Shaded Silver. Pure, unmarked silver; shades gradually down the sides, face, and tail, from dark on the ridge to white on chin, chest, belly, and under the tail; eyes green; rims of eyes, lips, and nose outlined with black, centre of nose brick red.

Smoke. Black, with white undercoat and black points and mask, light silver frill and ear tufts; eyes brilliant copper or deep orange.

Brown Tabby. Ground colour any shade of true brown affording good contrast with markings of dense black with clearly defined and broad pencillings; legs evenly barred, the "bracelets" coming up high to meet the body markings; tail barred; barring on neck and chest, like chains or "necklaces"; head barred with distinct "spectacles" on cheeks; eyes copper.

Silver Tabby. Pale clear silver with broad, dense black markings to conform in pattern to those described for brown tabby; eyes green or hazel.

Blue Tabby. Ground colour pale bluish ivory with fawn overtones; markings deep blue in pattern described for brown tabbies; eyes copper.

Red Tabby. Ground colour red orange, with markings as for brown tabby but in darker red; eyes copper or deep orange.

Tortoiseshell. Black, orange, and cream, the colours bright and well broken; half the nose black, half orange, known as the "blaze"; eyes copper or deep orange.

Calico. Three colours—black, red orange, and cream—well distributed, clearly patched and interspersed with white; white blaze desirable; eyes brilliant deep orange or copper.

Blue Cream. The two colours—blue and cream—bright and well defined, divided and broken into patches; eyes brilliant copper or deep orange.

Shell Cameo. The undercoat pale cream, the coat on the back, flanks, head, and tail tipped with red orange; eyes gold or copper.

Shaded Cameo. Pure, unmarked red orange, with gradual shading down the sides, face, and tail from dark on the ridge to whitish cream on the chin, chest, and stomach; eyes gold or copper.

Smoke Cameo. Deep reddish beige with white or cream undercoat; eyes gold or copper.

Tabby Cameo. Pale cream broken with well-defined reddish or beige tabby markings; eyes gold or copper.

Himalayan. Colour and points same as for Siamese (see below); eyes blue; correctly called a colour-point Persian or a Persian with Siamese marking, not long-haired Siamese.

Shorthair division. *Siamese.* A sleek, smooth coat; straight tail; and eyes that are not crossed; points (face mask, ears, feet, and tail) all the same colour; eyes vivid deep blue. The acceptable colours are:

Seal point: even, pale fawn to cream, shading gradually to a lighter colour on the chest and belly; deep sealbrown points.

Blue point: bluish white, shading gradually to oyster white on the chest and belly; points of definite blue, giving strong contrast.

Chocolate point: ivory all over; milk-chocolate-brown points.

Lilac point: even glacial white without shading; points frosty gray with pinkish tone.

Abyssinian. Larger than Siamese, with regal, alert posture; ruddy brown ticked with shades of darker brown or black; inside of forelegs and belly should harmonize with the main colour (preference is given to orange brown or burnt sienna); lip and chin lightest in colour, off-white or cream; eyes hazel, gold, or green.

Burmese. The ideal Burmese would be of medium size and rich sable-brown colour, with the head rounder than in the Siamese; profile should show visible nose break; fine, glossy, satinlike coat; eyes yellow to gold.

Russian Blue. Bright blue gray even throughout and free from tabby markings and shadings; thick coat, different from that of any other breed of cat; eyes green.

Manx. Completely tailless with decided hollow at the end of the backbone, double coat, back legs to be longer than front giving characteristic hopping gait; all colours of Manx are recognized, including ticked and mackerel tabbies and parti-coloured.

Rex. One of the newly recognized breeds, it has a wavy coat, like Persian lamb to the touch; all coat colours and eye colours acceptable.

Domestic Shorthair. While the domestic shorthairs seen in shows may resemble ordinary mixed breeds, the breeding of the show type is as exacting as for other breeds; recognized in all Persian colours.

BREEDERS' ASSOCIATIONS AND CAT SHOWS

Innumerable societies and associations have been formed to foster interest in cats and to set standards for the recognized breeds. Unrelated organizations, promoting various breeds, have also set up breed standards. None of these organizations has absolute power and occasionally standards conflict.

Cat shows are held annually in many large cities. Shows usually are divided into at least three parts: all breed, shorthair specialty, and longhair specialty. Each shorthaired or long-haired cat may compete in the all-breed and in the appropriate specialty show. Almost any healthy cat may be entered in a show, since often there are classes for kittens, altered cats, and household pets, as well as for pedigreed animals.

In general, an adult, pedigreed, show cat begins its career as a novice, at the age of eight months or older, when it may win its first blue ribbon for its particular breed and colour. It is not thereafter eligible for novice and must compete in the open class. Novice and open classes compete for the winners' ribbons, which designate championship points. Champions, having acquired sufficient ribbons, compete for grand championship status. "Finals" awards are made to best novice, open, etc., in show and "Best Cat in Show" is selected from these finalists.

Fish

The hobby of keeping fishes in the home supports a sizable business in the importation and culturing of exotic fishes, the manufacture of aquariums and apparatus, and the distribution of a variety of publications devoted to the subject, as well as the establishment of clubs or societies in the major cities of the world.

TYPES OF FISH IN HOME AQUARIUMS

Prior to World War I the principal interest of amateur aquarists centred largely on the breeding and development of exceedingly elaborate and fantastic strains of goldfish. Later, the chief interest in fancy-fish rearing transferred to so-called tropical fishes, breeding of which centred chiefly in Germany before 1900 but gradually spread to all parts of the world. Several domesticated forms of wild types have been developed, including the platyfish, swordtail, guppy, and Siamese fighting fish, none of which, however, departs from the wild type to the monstrous degree shown by some goldfish.

Goldfish. Goldfish (*Carassius auratus*) belong to the carp family (Cyprinidae) and are native to eastern Asia. They were first domesticated by the Chinese at least as early as the Sung dynasty (960–1279); they later were introduced into Japan about 1500 and into Europe about 1700.

In the natural state their colour is usually greenish-brown or gray, and the form of the body and of the fins is similar to that of the common carp. This species is extremely plastic, however: individuals occur, for example, in which the brown or black pigment is absent or restricted to spots; some may be golden or all white, or white with silvery patches, and still others may be jet black. Numerous other abnormalities occur: the dorsal fin may be absent; the tail fin may be trilobed; the eyes may protrude excessively. Chinese aquarists, observing these variations, conceived the idea of selecting out such abnormal specimens and breeding them to develop strains having particularly desired qualities. As a result of centuries of careful experiments in China and Japan, more than 125 breeds of fancy goldfishes have been produced.

Tropical fish. Most of the fishes kept in home aquariums in the West may be included in the term tropical, for the vast majority of them come from the areas drained by the Amazon and adjacent lands, from the Indian peninsula, and from southeastern Asia and the islands of the East Indian archipelago. These areas supply many hundreds of species of small freshwater fishes of which 100 or so have found general favour among fish fanciers. A smaller number comes from tropical Africa. Still fewer come from the West Indian islands, Central America, and the southern states of the United States.

The most popular groups of fishes usually found in the tanks of fanciers include representatives of the orders Ostariophysi, Cyprinodontes, Percomorphi, and Labyrinthici, with a liberal sprinkling from the Nematognathi and a few from several other orders and suborders.

Obviously, not all the members of all these orders can be kept in domestic tanks, or in any tank, but a sufficient number have the requisite abilities to live in relatively stagnant water and close quarters and on artificial diets and show sufficiently attractive colours to keep the fancier interested.

Besides attractive colours, some fishes appeal to fanciers by employing odd or unusual means of finding and catching prey. The archer fish (*Toxotes jaculator*), from the brackish waters of the East Indies, has a virtually unerring ability to "shoot down" its prey, insects, by squirting drops of water at them from its mouth. The force of the drops is quite sufficient to knock a large cockroach from a leaf or twig above the water, and the accuracy often is such as to extinguish a glowing cigarette fire at 11-foot (three-metre) distance. (The fish will sometimes "shoot" at the fire of cigarettes at dusk.)

Such fishes as the mudspringers or mud skippers (*Periophthalmus*), species from estuaries and mud flats over a range extending from tropical West Africa to the islands of the South Pacific, always interest fanciers, for they spend more than half their time out of water, hopping about on well-developed pectoral, ventral, and tail fins, catching insects on the wing. It returns to the water to dip first one side of its head, then the other, to replenish storage areas above the gills, and by the constant passage of water from these areas over the gills keeps itself alive and moist.

Odd fishes such as the knife fishes, family Gymnotidae, of which the best known is the electric eel (*Electrophorus electricus*), stir the interest by the habit of swimming backward as easily as forward and by the habit of retiring beneath the sand to sleep. Fishes such as these, once they are brought to the attention of fanciers, readily command a steady market. Even though some of them cannot be safely kept in the same tank, let alone bred, there has developed a considerable trade in these fishes.

Marine fish. The keeping of small seawater fishes offers a constantly recurring problem to fish keepers. Many of these, usually from tropical or subtropical seas, are exceptionally brightly coloured, especially in their early stages. One difficulty is that most of them cannot stand much variation in the chemical constitution of the water in which they live; and, because seawater removed from the ocean starts to deteriorate almost immediately, the fishes have only a limited life before them. Another difficulty is that most of them are used to, and require, much greater quantities of water than is available to them in domestic tanks, even if it is possible to pump the available water into and out of the tank, so that, although this is linked with the other limiting factor, the deterioration of the water, it is a limiting factor in its own right.

These two factors are the main reason for the recurring failure of fanciers to keep marine fishes in domestic tanks, and these are aggravated by the difficulty of obtaining adequate supplies of good seawater. Various formulas for the manufacture of artificial seawater have been produced, all of which are based on analyses of ocean water, but artificial seawater is deficient in many elements that may or may not be necessary to the living of the fishes, and even if these could be provided there are still the organic constituents and the microorganisms of natural seawater which undoubtedly play a vital role in maintaining marine life. For the fanciers who can afford marine fishes there are few more spectacular, however.

Temperate- and cold-water fish. Temperate- or cold-water fishes of freshwater origin can be kept in small aquariums if the water is sufficiently cool and aerated. The usual exotic fishes kept in home aquariums, however, are provided with temperatures of from 72° to 80° F (22° to 26.5° C), which is too warm for many temperate-water fishes. Most of these fishes are also not adjusted to living in stagnant water, even though it is kept cool enough, and are not good candidates for domestic fish tanks. They are usually kept only in public aquariums, which have large tanks and great volumes of water under constant circulation. Aside from such fishes as the live-bearing *Heterandira, Gambusia,* and *Poecilia* and the egg-laying *Fundulus, Jordanella,* and *Chriopeops* from the warmer states of the United States, and the Texas cichlid (*Herichthys cyanoguttatus*), there are virtually no fishes in the temperate zones suitable for aquarium keeping.

CARE AND MAINTENANCE

Home aquariums. A considerable variety of aquatic organisms are accommodated to life in standing water. Caring for standing aquariums is much simpler than caring for public aquariums in which new water is circulated continuously.

A body of standing fresh water such as may be contained in a small, glass-sided aquarium contains in solution the dissolved gases of the air in proportion to their partial pressures. It is the oxygen so dissolved that is available to aquatic organisms unable to use air directly for respiration. Because a fish, under these conditions, uses up the dissolved oxygen in the water, more free oxygen from the air dissolves into the water and so replaces that consumed, according to its partial pressure. From this it follows that the rate at which new oxygen dissolves into the water should be equivalent to the rate at which the fish withdraws the oxygen. If the rate is slower, the fish will eventually suffocate. Concomitantly carbon dioxide is expired by the fish. This escapes into the air through the surface of the water, tending to reach a balance with the partial pressure of that gas in the air. The escape of the exhaled carbon dioxide from the water must be at least equal to the rate at which the fish gives it off or the fish will be suffocated, not from want of oxygen but from inability to pass its continually produced carbon dioxide into the already supercharged water. Other things being equal, the rate at which these gases pass through the interface between air and water is determined by the size of that area. Thus, the greater the surface area of a body of water, the more fish—or larger fish—that body will be able to support. It is for this reason that the globular-shaped bowls with their restricted surface areas were largely abandoned. Because for observation purposes and the swimming needs of fishes there are practical disadvantages in extremely shallow aquariums, the practice of making aquariums as wide as they are high, and twice as long, has reached some degree of standardization. Aquariums with circulating water circumvent this limitation because of the opportunity of aerating the water en route. To offset the limits of the surface available in standing aquariums, air in fine bubbles may be passed through the water by means of an air pump. The surface of each tiny bubble adds to the air exposure of the water; the rising bubbles also induce a slow circulation within the tank which checks any tendency toward stratification.

In addition to exhaling carbon dioxide in the process of respiration, a fish also eliminates various body wastes, which, except for the solids, go into solution, thus modifying the chemical nature of the water in which the fish is bathed. Some species are very sensitive to certain of these wastes and are not able to survive long in standing water. Others are not so affected, and many are evidently positively benefitted. In household aquariums, contrary to popular notions, the water should seldom be completely changed or replenished. Generally, a glass cover should be provided to reduce evaporation and keep the fishes from jumping out.

Aquatic plants

The introduction of some form of aquatic plant life is practically essential, although the presence of plants in such an aquarium further complicates the situation. What has been mentioned about the respiration of fishes is likewise true of submerged aquatic plants. They consume dissolved oxygen and give off carbon dioxide; also, under the influence of bright light, plants consume carbon dioxide and give off oxygen while engaged in photosynthesis. This operates very well so long as light of a certain intensity falls on the plants; the animals give off what the plants can use and vice versa. Aquariums in which the plants and animals are believed to balance each other in a respiratory sense are generally referred to as balanced aquariums. This condition of balance, however, is rarely attained, because when the light falls below a certain value (as at the coming of evening or on cloudy or dull days) the plants are in direct respiratory competition with the animals. Moreover, the atmosphere constantly enters the picture, affecting the exchange of gases through the water surface. Consequently it is best to have the quantities of animal and plant life so related to the surface area that they can survive indefinitely by means of gaseous exchange through the surface film. There is an additional relationship between plants and animals in such an aquarium. The waste products of the fishes form fertilizer or food for the plants and are consumed by them. It is, strictly speaking, such water that aquarists consider conditioned and most suitable for the specimens of their interest. Furthermore, dense, slow-growing plants that consume much of the waste products of relatively few fishes as fast as they are formed usually furnish the most stable and attractive small aquariums. A large variety of plants are suitable for such purposes.

Based on these principles, it is possible to maintain a large variety of freshwater fishes with relatively little attention and inexpensive equipment. Aside from the aquariums themselves it is necessary to provide only sufficient daylight, a suitable and relatively uniform temperature, and the required food.

Feeding. The diet provided for aquarium specimens should approximate the natural diet as closely as possible. In addition to products available from the fish market, several commercially prepared diets and various live foods are available to the professional and home aquarist. As a general rule fishes do better if provided with a varied diet. Brine shrimp (*Artemia*) are a convenient source of food and are available both as newly hatched larvae or adults, either alive, frozen, or freeze dried. It should be noted, however, that they do not fill all of the nutritional requirements of many plankton-feeding fishes.

Disease control. Disease prevention is a constantly strived for goal, since diseases, once introduced into the aquarium, are often difficult to eliminate. Specimens therefore must be provided with water of suitable quality; the proper habitat, including protective cover if necessary; compatible tankmates; and an adequate diet. New speci-

mens are usually quarantined for two or three weeks prior to placement in the display tanks.

Several categories of infectious diseases can occur in aquariums. Protozoans are a common problem, especially those causing freshwater and marine white-spot diseases. Few treatments have thus far been completely successful. The problem in marine aquariums is so severe that many facilities maintain in the water a very low dose of copper sulfate as a preventive measure, despite its undesirability in terms of toxicity. Formalin and insecticides, although both toxic, are common treatments for the larger parasites that attach themselves to fish. Treatments that necessitate handling the specimens are avoided if possible. Large fishes that must be handled are usually anesthetized in order to reduce stress.

Ultraviolet sterilizer units can prevent the spread of disease in aquarium water systems if strategically placed and of sufficient capacity. Antibiotics should be used only if essential for the cure of a specific disease; indiscriminate use can not only result in resistant strains of the disease-causing organisms but also in destruction of nitrifying bacteria.

Categories of infectious diseases

Breeding. Aside from the attractiveness and colourfulness of the specimens and the aquarium as a whole, one of the principal interests of the fancier centres on the breeding of the fishes available, not always from a commercial standpoint but rather as the acceptance of a challenge to find exactly what the creature requires to fulfill its life.

Actually, the breeding behaviour of many fishes is astonishingly complete in its familial aspects. This includes the mating for life of some species of cichlids, with the subsequent choosing of a site for the nest, the preparation of it, the careful placing of the eggs, and the almost fanatical care and protection of them and the resulting young, even to the extent of providing a place of succour for the young in the mouths of the parents. Some go through all the nesting procedures up to the deposition of the eggs but then pick them up and carry them until long after hatching, refusing all food until their offspring are ready to leave for good. Others build elaborate nests, using all sorts of materials that may be available, with the bubble-nest-building labyrinthine fishes such as the two-inch-long Siamese fighting fish, *Betta splendens,* using bubbles of air sealed into capsules of mucus secreted by the mouth and assembled into a raft several inches across and sometimes two inches high. The eggs are caught by the male and thrust into the mass of bubbles immediately after shedding, with the male then standing by beneath the nest until hatching is complete and the young are old enough and active enough to be kept no longer in a compact group.

In a different category is the nest building of the stickleback, not properly a tropical fish but one that is sometimes kept in small aquariums. The males of this group secrete a mucoid substance in long filaments, which harden into a silklike substance. This they wrap around a small cluster of plant stalks until they have an oval mass with a hole running horizontally through it. Into this they coax a waiting female and induce her to deposit her eggs, which she then abandons to the male for further care. A single male may build three or four such nests, one above the other, for the accommodation of the eggs of as many females, all of which he then attends to, cleaning and causing streams of water to flow over them until hatching.

A simpler breeding pattern is the birth of living young to such fishes as guppies (*Poecilia reticulata*), and the platyfishes and swordtails (*Xiphophorus maculatus* and *Xiphophorus helleri*), all small fishes of the family Poeciliidae originating in South or Central America or the West Indian islands. Fishes of this group deliver living young in broods that may number 200, at intervals of about a month or so, after they have reached maturity. Of especial interest is the fact that one fertilization is sufficient for the production of as many as eight separate broods. Such fish are able to look after themselves almost from the instant of birth and receive no parental care at all.

A relative of these species, the mosquito fish (*Heterandria formosa*), from Georgia and Florida, is the smallest live-bearing vertebrate known. This fish follows the general pattern of its relatives, but it is so small (approximately one inch long) and its young so large, relatively, that it spreads the delivery of a single brood over a period of about three weeks.

COMMERCE IN TROPICAL FISH

Many fishes of the live-bearing kinds are bred literally by the millions in suitable climates, such as southern Florida, with a considerable but lesser number coming from greenhouse types of hatcheries scattered throughout the United States, with a fair number being located in Germany and in England. Germany once held the lead in this type of fish culture but lost it during World War II.

A fair number of egg-laying fishes, particularly the Amazon angelfish (*Pterophyllum eimekei*) of the family Cichlidae and the Siamese fighting fish (*Betta splendens*), are raised in commercial establishments, but the majority of the very popular Characidae are caught wild and imported in very large numbers. This is largely a matter of economics, for commercial importers and breeders have found that they can catch and import such fishes as the extremely attractive and popular neon tetra (*Hyphessobrycon innesi*) for less than the cost of feed needed to raise a brood to salable size, with no consideration given to housing or heating.

Other fishes that are imported must of necessity be so, for their breeding requirements are unknown. Others are of use to fanciers only when they are small and less than breeding size, so that these too must be imported in numbers.

The collection and transportation of aquatic specimens in a living state, especially if they are of considerable size, presents a variety of problems. First, they must be caught in such a manner as to be without serious damage. Transportation must be effected as rapidly as possible and with a full continuation of the immediate needs of the aquatic organism. The water in the shipping tank must be kept in suitable condition by circulation, aeration, or chemical treatment throughout the trip. Smaller specimens may be shipped in sealed containers of metal or plastic about half full of water, with the remaining space being filled with air or oxygen under low pressure. Chemicals are now available to render waste products less noxious and to reduce the activity of the animals during their close confinement.

BIBLIOGRAPHY

General: GEORGE S. CANSDALE, *Animals and Man* (1952, reissued 1974), a consideration of all aspects of man's dealings with animals from earliest times, and *Bush Baby Book* (1960), a description of six species of bush babies and other lemuroids kept by the author in Africa and Great Britain, including a chapter on the problems of keeping these animals as house pets; HEINI HEDIGER, *Studies of the Psychology and Behaviour of Captive Animals in Zoos and Circuses* (1955, reprinted 1968; originally published in German, 1954), and *Man and Animal in the Zoo* (1969, reissued 1974), noted animal psychologist; GUSTAVE LOISEL, *Histoire des ménageries de l'antiquité à nos jours*, 3 vol. (1912), published for the Universities Federation for Animal Welfare (UFAW), chiefly valuable for its treatment of rare animals kept in captivity and as pets since ancient Egypt; KONRAD LORENZ, *King Solomon's Ring: New Light on Animal Ways* (1952, reissued 1980; originally published in German, 1952), and *Man Meets Dog* (1953, reprinted 1980; originally published in German, 1950), two popular books by a world-famous authority on animal behaviour; JOHN P. VOLRATH, *Animals in Schools* (1955, enlarged ed. 1956), a useful manual in a series published by the UFAW that covers the complete range of house pets other than cats and dogs. Among the numerous books that acquaint the reader with animal behaviour and serve as reference sources are BERNHARD GRZIMEK (ed.), *Grzimek's Animal Life Encyclopedia*, 13 vol. (1972–75; originally published in German, 1967–72), an authoritative and comprehensive work; and EMIL P. DOLENSEK and BARBARA BURN, *A Practical Guide to Impractical Pets* (1976; reissued as *The Penguin Book of Pets: A Practical Guide to Animal-Keeping*, 1978), information on more than 100 animals, noting which are especially difficult to keep. Useful information and advice is contained in ALFRED LEUTSCHER, *Keeping Reptiles and Amphibians* (1976); CARLA STEVENS, *Insect Pets: Catching and Caring for Them* (1978); WILLIAM J. WEBER, *Care of Uncommon Pets* (1979); STANLEY LEINWOLL, *The Book of Pets* (1980); JULIET CLUTTON-BROCK, *Domesticated Animals from Early Times* (1981), a historical survey; and ERA ZISTEL, *Thistle & Co.* (1982), a vivid account of experiences with animals such as raccoons and skunks as pets.

Dogs as pets: The rules applying to registration and dog shows, lists of registered breeds, and information about specialty breeding clubs may be obtained from the American Kennel Club, New York, and the Kennel Club, London. AMERICAN KENNEL CLUB, *The Complete Dog Book*, 16th ed. (1979); EDUARD C. ASH, *Dogs: Their History and Development*, 2 vol. (1927, reprinted 1972); MARCA BURNS and MARGARET N. FRASER, *Genetics of the Dog: The Basis of Successful Breeding*, 2nd ed. (1966); HENRY P. DAVIS, (ed.), *The New Dog Encyclopedia* (1970, reissued 1974); SPORTS ILLUSTRATED, *Book of Dog Training* (1960); MICHAEL W. FOX, *Canine Behavior* (1965); CLARENCE C. LITTLE, *The Inheritance of Coat Color in Dogs* (1957, reprinted 1973); JOSEPHINE Z. RINE, *The World of Dogs* (1965, reprinted 1973); JOHN P. SCOTT and JOHN L. FULLER, *Genetics and the Social Behavior of the Dog* (1965; reissued as *Dog Behavior: The Genetic Basis*, 1974); RICHARD and ALICE FIENNES, *The Natural History of the Dog* (1968, reprinted 1970); R.F. WALL, *Keeping a Dog*, 5th ed. (1956); LEON F. WHITNEY, *The Complete Book of Dog Care* (1953), and *Dog Psychology: The Basis of Dog Training*, 2nd ed. (1971); and FERNAND MÉRY, *The Life, History, and Magic of the Dog* (1970; originally published in French, 1969). Other general sources are ERICH TYLÍNEK, ISABELLA TYLÍNEK, and PETER TEICHMANN, *The Dog, His World and Ours* (1975; originally published in German); HARRY GLOVER (comp.), *A Standard Guide to Purebred Dogs* (1977, reprinted 1982); M. EUGENE ENSMINGER, *The Complete Book of Dogs* (1977); NANCY DOLENSEK and BARBARA BURN, *Mutt* (1978), on mixed-breed dogs; R.V. DENENBERG, *Dog Catalog* (1978); JOHN HOWE, *Choosing the Right Dog*, rev. ed. (1980), a buyer's guide to breeds approved by the American Kennel Club; ROGER CARAS, *The Roger Caras Dog Book* (1980), and *A Celebration of Dogs* (1982), compilations of facts and stories about dogs; and STEVEN RADBILL and MORRIS KENNEDY, *The Complete Book of Questions Dog Owners Ask Their Vet & Answers* (1980). R.D. LAWRENCE, *The North Runner* (1979), is a story of a wolf/malamute hybrid, written by a naturalist. WILLIAM E. MALONEY and JEAN-CLAUDE SUARÈS (eds.), *The Literary Dog* (1978), is an illustrated anthology of more than 100 selections from poetry and fiction.

Pet ownership: Works that explore the problems of owning pet animals include MICHAEL W. FOX, *Understanding Your Pet: Pet Care and Human Concerns* (1978); LEE EDWARDS BENNING, *The Pet Profiteers: The Exploitation of Pet Owners and Pets in America* (1976); JOHN KEANE, *Sherlock Bones: Tracer of Missing Pets* (1979), a collection of case studies and advice for finding lost animals; and PATRICIA CURTIS, *Animal Partners* (1982), which discusses the training of animals to help people.

Cats as pets: DORIS BRYANT, *Pet Cats: Their Care and Handling* (1963); DOROTHY BEVILL CHAMPION, *Everybody's Cat Book* (1909); ANN CURRAH (ed.), *The Cat Compendium* (1969); MILAN GREER, *The Fabulous Feline, or Dogs Are Passé* (1961); FERNAND MÉRY, *The Life, History, and Magic of the Cat* (1967; originally published in French, 1966); PERCY M. SODERBERG, *Pedigree Cats, Their Varieties, Breeding and Exhibition* (1958); LEON F. WHITNEY, *The Complete Book of Cat Care*, rev. ed. (1980). RICHARD H. GEBHARD, GRACE POND, and IVOR RALEIGH (eds.), *A Standard Guide to Cat Breeds* (1979, reprinted 1982); and MICHAEL WRIGHT and SALLY WALTERS (eds.), *The Book of the Cat* (1980), are detailed reference works. Other works include MURIEL BEADLE, *The Cat: History, Biology and Behavior* (1977), a well-researched study intended for the general reader; MIKE TOMKIES, *My Wilderness Wildcats* (1977), an account of raising wildcats in captivity; PATRICIA MOYES, *How to Talk to Your Cat* (1978), an analysis of the vocal and body language of cats; and MORDECAI SIEGAL, *The Good Cat Book: How to Live with and Take Loving Care of Your Cat* (1981), and *Mordecai Siegal's Happy Pet/Happy Owner Book: How to Recognize and Handle Emotional Problems of Your Pet* (1978), collections of practical advice and case histories. SUSAN MCDONOUGH and BRYNA LAWSON, *The Complete Book of Questions Cat Owners Ask Their Vet* (1979), is a comprehensive work in question-and-answer format. SEON MANLEY and GOGO LEWIS (comps.), *Cat Encounters: A Cat-Lover's Anthology* (1979), is a selection of world literature, both serious and humorous, from classical to modern times. (Ed.)

Philadelphia

Philadelphia has been described either as the elegant but rather jaded great lady or as the overage and sickly spinster of American cities. A more realistic look at Philadelphia, however, shows it to be a very modern and vigorous city, arising in gracious counterpoint to the deep serenity of an older city that has provided gentle but firm intellectual, economic, and humanitarian direction to the nation at whose birth it played midwife.

Philadelphia, the fourth largest city in the United States and the largest in Pennsylvania, displays many characteristics of a small town. Its many trees, parks, and other open spaces and its quiet pace of life reflect in many ways the genteel Quaker heritage bestowed on the city by its founder, William Penn. Nearly everywhere are dignified reminders of the colonial and Revolutionary city and of Benjamin Franklin, a Philadelphian by adoption, who left his imprint on innumerable ongoing institutions, both cultural and commercial, in the city.

Beneath this facade, however, Philadelphia represents an urban cluster of national and international stature. Its harbour, one of the largest freshwater ports in the world, is the major element in the official agglomeration of Delaware River ports known as Ameriport, collectively one of the busiest shipping centres in the world. The enormous industrial production of the city and the surrounding metropolitan area represents a continuation of Philadelphia's early leadership in the Industrial Revolution and in American commerce and finance generally. Lying in the midst of the vast urban community stretching down the Atlantic Seaboard, Philadelphia is an integral part of the turbulent fabric of contemporary social and economic life as well as a tranquil oasis joining together the spirit of America, past and present.

This article is divided into the following sections:

Physical and human geography

THE LANDSCAPE

The city site. Philadelphia spreads over about 129 square miles (334 square kilometres) from the Delaware on the east across the Schuylkill and beyond. The coextensive boundaries of Philadelphia city and county remain essentially as defined by the Consolidation Act of 1854.

The city layout. The gridiron of streets in central Philadelphia, the first U.S. city to be so arranged, follows the original plans of William Penn. Midway between the two rivers, Penn Square, occupied by City Hall, is the centre of the plan. Four shady, fountained squares—Logan, Franklin, Washington, and Rittenhouse—dot the quadrants. Westward from Penn Square along John F. Kennedy Boulevard is Penn Center, a prime symbol of rejuvenated Philadelphia since the 1950s. The multilevel complex comprises high-rise offices and hotels, with interior courts and malls and underground walkways lined with shops and restaurants.

Benjamin Franklin Parkway provides a splendid vista as it cuts diagonally northwestward from Penn Square through the grid, encircling Logan Square and leading into Fairmount Park. The nation's largest landscaped park within city limits and the centre of the Centennial Exposition of 1876, Fairmount is one of the most frequent foregrounds for photographs of Philadelphia's skyline, adding to the city's reputation for shaded, sculpted elegance. Once a section of outlying estates of the wealthy, the park contains many fine old mansions maintained by the city as museums. Through it winds the narrow valley of Wissahickon Creek, whose rugged beauty has inspired generations of poets and painters.

The oldest sections of Philadelphia—Southwark, Society Hill, and the Independence Hall area—lie to the east, along and inland from the Delaware. Southwark is the oldest, having been settled by Swedes in 1643. Those of its ancient and dilapidated houses that have escaped bulldozing for riverfront expressways resemble the edifices of Society Hill before its restoration in the 1950s. This latter area contains some of the city's finest old houses, taverns, and churches, though some high-rise apartment buildings strike a dissonant note in the hearts of many Philadelphians.

Independence National Historical Park, established in 1956 and designated a World Heritage Site in 1979, contains Independence Hall, with the nearby Liberty Bell Pavilion, and many other buildings used by the Revolutionary and early federal governments. Nearby, Elfreth's Alley, dating from 1690, contains 33 houses that make up the oldest continuously inhabited street in the country. Included in the complex are Carpenters' Hall, site of the meeting of the First Continental Congress, and Philosophical Hall, home of the American Philosophical Society.

Throughout these areas and elsewhere, domestic architecture is characterized primarily by two- and three-story red-brick structures fronting directly on the sidewalks and containing impressive examples of colonial design both outside and inside. The Philadelphia Historical Commission has certified about 7,500 buildings and structures, ranging from 17th-century houses to a bridge constructed in 1950. Restoration of the old but habitable has been more characteristic than wholesale demolition and rebuilding throughout most of the city. Even in its downtown section, Philadelphia continues to be a city of shops rather than of huge merchandising outlets. It has nothing approaching New York City's Fifth Avenue as a street of large stores. Chestnut Street is an attractive street of shops but has only one department store, John Wanamaker's. Pine and other streets are noted for such specialties as antique shops. Major features of the skyline are the massive contours of the city's many banking and financial institutions.

The long stretches of Philadelphia north, south, and west of the intersection of Broad and Chestnut streets, a "city hub" of sorts just below Penn Square, contain numerous distinctive sections, often identified for generations with various ethnic groups that have filled the city during its long history. Among the more interesting is the German-

Historic preservations and restorations

town section of North Philadelphia, settled in Penn's time by Germans and the home in the 18th century of wealthy Philadelphians fleeing the periodic yellow-fever epidemics of the riverside city. Much of North Philadelphia comprises a massive black and Puerto Rican community. South Philadelphia contains notable Italian and other sections settled by European immigrants mainly in the 19th century.

THE PEOPLE

Though Philadelphia has had most of the characteristics of an ethnic and racial pot nearly from its start, it lacks the steaming hurly-burly visible everywhere in its behemoth neighbour, New York City, about 90 miles (150 kilometres) northeast. The Philadelphians by and large are not a street people, and their orientation has been so traditionally toward the home that the city became known as a "city of homes." Philadelphians are also great joiners, giving the city more social and other clubs than any other in America. Many of these are based in ethnic neighbourhoods, others are city wide, and still others serve the affluent "Main Liners" who reside in the plush suburbs that grew up in past centuries along the main line of the Pennsylvania Railroad (now Amtrak).

Much of this tradition dates from Philadelphia's early years, from the beliefs and attitudes not only of the Quakers but also of such German pietist sects as the Mennonites, who stressed personal religious experience rather than institutionalized formulations. A basic sobriety underlying these tenets led to many stringent laws that remain in both the city and state. On the other hand, these groups strove for tolerance in all matters. Pennsylvania was among the few colonies admitting Roman Catholics and Jews, and the Quakers long were leaders in seeking justice and the alleviation of inhumanity in racial and other human relations. Philadelphia still has innumerable small, endowed charities of Quaker origin to provide the poor with coal or food—as well as one of the oldest and strongest municipal commissions on human relations.

During the 1800s the Protestant sects were joined by Roman Catholics, initially Irish and German and later Italian, Polish, and Slavic. Eastern European Jews also immigrated, eventually comprising a significant portion of the city's population. Cultural conflicts and competition for housing and jobs created tensions between the oldstock groups and the new arrivals. A series of anti-Catholic nativist riots rocked Philadelphia in the Jacksonian period, with an especially violent riot in 1844. Although immigrants came to Philadelphia in the hundreds of thousands in the late 19th and early 20th centuries, the city had a relatively low proportion of foreign-born when compared with other major cities at that time. Some Irish, Italian, Polish, and Jewish newcomers did find opportunities for considerable economic advancement in Philadelphia; for many, however, hopes never materialized and the urban experience proved rough and oftentimes shattering. The slow progress of these ethnic groups toward full acceptance is represented by the fact that Philadelphia did not elect its first Irish mayor until 1963 and its first Italian mayor until 1971.

Philadelphia has been the focal point of one of the historically most important black communities in the nation. During the early national and antebellum periods, many black leaders came from or centred their activities in Philadelphia, and the free black community there was intensely involved in many efforts to abolish slavery, assist fugitive slaves, and advance the general social and economic well-being of blacks. Between 1829 and 1860, however, the Philadelphia black community was victimized by several antiblack mob actions. At the beginning of the 20th century Philadelphia was the site of the largest black community of any northern city. The migration of Southern-born blacks to the city continued to augment the city's black population throughout the first half of the 20th century. Discrimination in housing resulted in the creation of overcrowded black districts. By the late 20th century about 40 percent of all Philadelphians and well over 50 percent of the public school population were black. The suburbs, by contrast, were about 95 percent white.

During the late 1960s Philadelphia, like other major American cities, was shaken by race riots. This led, in 1971, to a backlash in the election as mayor of Frank Rizzo, a tough former police commissioner oriented toward "law and order." In 1979, however, Philadelphians turned toward more moderate rule by rejecting the attempt of Rizzo to alter the city charter and thereby win permission to seek a third term. In 1983 the city elected its first black mayor, W. Wilson Goode.

Problems of substandard and insufficient housing, delinquency, public health, crime, drug abuse, and other ills, by no means confined to the ghettos, have somewhat dimmed the city's image. Efforts at public housing date back to 1937. Other municipal and federal bodies have continued efforts at urban renewal for both blacks and poor whites, usually following the pattern of rehabilitating neighbourhoods rather than razing them. Unusual is the fact that about two-fifths of the black families own their homes.

THE ECONOMY

Industry. Many of Philadelphia's business enterprises were established in the 1700s, but the city's economy has changed greatly. Such old and once-dominant industries as textile mills met stiff competition from the South. Industry was given a boost by World War II but began to decline later; thousands of jobs were lost in the 1960s. Nonmanufacturing and service industries, however, continue to increase employment. Although such old industries as textiles have declined, new industries, such as electrical products and appliances, have grown. The area is a centre for phonograph and record production, along with radio and television manufacturers. Apparel, food and food products, printing and publishing, and electrical machinery are leaders in manufacturing. A decline has been evident in the migration of both people and business from the city to the suburbs. The Valley Forge area has become a nest of business and industrial locations. Much of this relocation is under the sponsorship of the public Philadelphia Industrial Development Corporation.

Research. George Washington approved the first U.S. patent in 1790, to a Philadelphian named Samuel Hopkins for a better way of making potash. In today's economy research and invention are keys to progress. In West Philadelphia is located the University City Science Center and Institute, a nonprofit project of more than 20 universities and colleges with a multimillion-dollar commitment to research. General Electric, E.I. du Pont de Nemours, Westinghouse, Monsanto, Rohm and Haas, and the Philadelphia Electric Company are other large concerns with extensive research programs within the metropolitan area. U.S. Steel's Fairless Works, on the Delaware at Morrisville, is a fully integrated plant and the largest steel plant in the Delaware River Valley. The area is a centre for research on and refining of petroleum. The computer age was born out of experiments at the University of Pennsylvania, where the first electronic computer was operated in 1945. A unit of the Boeing Company at Eddystone is one of the world's most advanced plants for helicopter research and design.

The unique Food Distribution Center, a nonprofit corporation managed by a board of directors representing city government and private enterprise, is a prime example of how Philadelphia has joined the work of the private and public sectors to serve the best interests of both. Covering more than 400 acres (160 hectares), it is a food-industry park handling in a unified operation every food-marketing facility from ripening bananas to smoking fish; it is composed of more than 100 stores plus warehousing and processing plants.

Finance. From its early days until the 1850s, Philadelphia was the financial capital of the United States, but it then lost this position to New York City. It was the birthplace of American banking, and the first building and loan association was founded there. The city continues to be a major centre of banking, with its financial institutions remaining the oldest and among the most prosperous in the nation. Philadelphia also supplies the stock and exchange services demanded by modern business. The Philadelphia Commercial Exchange was set up in 1868 as

Quaker tradition and ethnic mix

An economic overview

an outgrowth of the older Corn Exchange Association of 1863 to regulate the then-flourishing grain and flour trade. The Philadelphia Bourse was organized in 1891, and the Maritime Exchange was founded in 1875. Philadelphia has the oldest stock exchange (founded in 1790) in the United States. The Philadelphia–Baltimore–Washington Stock Exchange was joined by Pittsburgh in 1969 and in 1976 was renamed the Philadelphia Stock Exchange.

Transportation. A complex system of public and private trolley and bus lines was consolidated in 1963 by the state legislature's creation of the Southeastern Pennsylvania Transportation Authority (SEPTA) to plan, develop, and coordinate a regional transportation system and to fund projects by the sale of bonds. Express buses provide rapid service between the inner and outer city.

A joint New Jersey–Pennsylvania bridge commission operates six toll and 13 tax-supported bridges over the Delaware. Two of these are solely for pedestrian use. The Schuylkill is bridged at a number of points and has a subway tunnel. The New Jersey–Pennsylvania–Delaware port authority administers Ameriport and the Benjamin Franklin and Walt Whitman bridges over the Delaware. The authority has also carried out major improvement and expansion programs throughout the entire port area. Philadelphia International Airport, less than seven miles (11 kilometres) from the city centre, provides nationwide and international flights.

ADMINISTRATIVE AND SOCIAL CONDITIONS

Government. The city–county consolidation in 1854 was a result of the inability of a colonial-type government by committees to adapt to the needs of a growing city for new public services; *e.g.,* better streets, police, transportation, sanitation, and schools. Ironically, Philadelphia had, in fact, led most cities in providing urban improvements, but they were too few and too slow, and the breakdown of law and order in the 1840s forced changes. Until the early 1950s the standard type of U.S. city government prevailed in Philadelphia, comprising an elected mayor and a city council elected from among candidates presented by the political parties in the political divisions, or wards. As in other large cities, this form was subject to pressures for special favours, such as street-railway franchises and public-works contracts; bribery and corruption were both inevitable and rampant.

The reform movement that began in 1939 was joined in 1948 by top business and financial leaders, who organized the Greater Philadelphia Movement, and together they took up the battle for an entirely new city charter. This document effectively removed the city council from its administrative role and increased the staff and powers of the mayor. A strong civil-service commission improved

The Greater Philadelphia Movement

professional employment. The council, seven of whose members were elected by all the voters and 10 by districts, was to review and approve taxes and budgets and enact ordinances. Philadelphia thus had the first modern big-city charter in the United States; its approval by a two-to-one popular vote made it an expression of the desire of Philadelphians for better, more efficient, and honest city government.

The first mayors under the new charter were Joseph S. Clark and Richardson Dilworth, men devoted to making it work. From wealthy Republican families, both were lawyers who revolted against the corruption and inefficiency of city government and became Democrats. Men of the highest qualifications were selected for key positions, planning was made a virtue, and a $150,000,000 plan was launched at once for improvements in sewerage and sanitation, playgrounds, lighting and streets, police and fire protection, and other basic services long neglected. The ambitious plan for a Penn Center involved removal of the old Pennsylvania Railroad "Chinese Wall" of overhead tracks, which ran into the heart of the city at Broad Street, and replacing it and the Broad Street Station.

Renewal planning gave close attention to the need for better housing. The Philadelphia Housing Authority and the Philadelphia Redevelopment Authority, with federal and private aid, approached Philadelphia's housing in terms of improving neighbourhoods rather than total clearance followed by new high-rise apartments. Affected areas included the Independence Hall area, neighbouring Society Hill, and the historic waterfront.

Much of the work of the city government is carried out through housing redevelopment, parking, and other authorities. The Old Philadelphia Development Corporation was organized in 1956 as a quasi-public and private body to aid the new development plans.

Public services. Though the Philadelphia metropolitan area has a per capita income that is the highest of any such area in the state, a large percentage of Philadelphians live below the poverty level. City, state, and federal agencies administer a full range of ameliorative social-service programs. A department of public health operates a variety of services through a number of health districts. With its Quaker tradition, Philadelphia is known for its humanitarian concern and has a great variety of privately supported child-care, hospital, and other social services.

Education. Philadelphia's public school system is an independent governmental unit operating under a board of education appointed by the mayor on the recommendation of a citizens' nominating panel. The city's institutions of higher learning are headed by the privately endowed University of Pennsylvania, which was founded in 1740, opened the nation's first medical school (1765),

The Philadelphia Museum of Art.

Institutions of higher education

and was the first designated "university" in the United States (1779). Temple University (1884) has acquired the reputation of "the people's college" and is known for work in the arts and social sciences. Roman Catholic colleges include LaSalle and St. Joseph's. Philadelphia is also a centre for medical education, with several general schools and specialized schools in pharmacy, podiatry, optometry, and osteopathy. The Curtis Institute of Music (1924) is a leading music school, while the Pennsylvania Academy of Fine Arts (1805) is the oldest art school in the United States.

CULTURAL LIFE

Much of the essence of Philadelphia lies in the features described previously—its small-town atmosphere, its parks and tree-shaded downtown squares and streets, and its innumerable memorials to the American past, as well as its teeming riverside and factories and its diverse business institutions. There are other factors as well that contribute in their way to an understanding of Philadelphia's culture, considered in its broadest implications to comprise the life-styles of its people.

In addition to Fairmount Park, Philadelphia has Pennypack Park in the northeast, a semiwilderness setting with bridle paths, bird-watching trails, and an abundance of deer and other wildlife. More than 100 other parks are located throughout the city.

Philadelphians have always been a sports-loving group, whether passive or participatory, though professional teams have always been the object, like the city itself, of a good-natured deprecation that is tolerated in residents but not in strangers. City baseball fans enjoyed a long-awaited triumph in 1980 when the Philadelphia Phillies won the World Series. Fox hunting in the surrounding countryside is of old Quaker origins, while the Schuylkill is a major rowing site for collegiate and other individuals and crews, and Germantown harbours remnants of a once-lively city-wide enthusiasm for cricket.

In colonial days Philadelphia was known as the "Athens of America," and it retains a high place in the artistic achievement of the nation. The Academy of Music, opened in 1857, is the home of the Philadelphia Orchestra, which is among the finest orchestras of the world and was among the first to broadcast and make recordings. At Fairmount Park are two facilities—the Fredric R. Mann Music Center, which presents classical music, and the Robin Hood Dell, which presents popular music.

Philadelphia was the nation's theatrical centre until well after the Revolution, its stages having hosted the greatest players of Europe and America. The Walnut Street Theatre, opened in 1809, is the oldest playhouse in active use in the English-speaking world. The Playhouse in the Park opened in 1952 as the first city-owned and city-operated theatre of its kind.

Philadelphia was a pioneer in museums of all kinds. Charles Willson Peale's museum was housed in Independence Hall in the 1800s, but the art museums are now led by the Philadelphia Museum of Art. One of the world's great museums, it houses priceless collections of art from the Western Middle Ages onward and from the Orient. Others include the Rodin Museum, featuring the largest collection of sculptures by Auguste Rodin outside of Paris. The Historical Society of Pennsylvania has some 700 portraits by Benjamin West, James Copley, Gilbert Stuart, the four Peales, and other early American painters. The output of visual artists in Philadelphia and vicinity has been by and large conservative, though Thomas Eakins gained fame for work beyond his American contemporaries, and Mary Cassatt was among the few women in the Impressionist school of the late 19th century.

Other museums include the Museum of the Philadelphia Civic Center, originally organized in 1894 as the Commercial Museum to promote trade exhibitions. The Academy of Natural Sciences is the oldest of its kind in the United States. The Franklin Institute Science Museum and Planetarium is full of marvellous things that move and can be moved, while the University Museum is a major feature of the University of Pennsylvania. Among the newer museums in Philadelphia are the Afro-American Historical

and Cultural Museum and the New Year's Shooters and Mummers Museum, both established in 1976, and the Port of History Museum at Penn's Landing. There also are many small museums housed in restored buildings throughout the city.

History

FOUNDATION AND EARLY SETTLEMENT

William Penn acquired the province of Pennsylvania in 1681 from King Charles II of England as a place where his fellow Quakers could enjoy freedom of worship and a chance to govern themselves and develop their own way of life. The King made the grant, signed on March 4, 1681, and proclaimed it a few weeks later, on April 2, partly to settle a debt owed to Penn's father, Adm. Sir William Penn, upon his death and also to complete the settlement of the Middle Atlantic region with Englishmen. Penn sent his cousin William Markham to take charge of affairs of government and also to lay out the city Penn named Philadelphia, city of "brotherly love," the name symbolizing his idealistic concepts. From England, Penn wrote in 1681 asking that "the Rivers and Creeks be sounded on my side of the Delaware River . . . in order to settle a great Towne, and be sure to make your choice where it is most navigable, high, dry, and healthy." He wanted every house to be placed in the middle of its own plot to provide ground about it "that it may be a greene Country Towne, which will never be burnt, and always be wholesome."

Penn arrived in 1682 but had little chance to enjoy his city. He was forced to travel to England in 1684 and was unable to return until 1699. By then, Philadelphia was a flourishing town with many shops and trading houses, as well as several hundred dwellings and about 10,000 people clustered close to the riverfront. Penn's governor declared the city already was the equal of New York "in trade and riches." Penn's policies throughout the colony of religious toleration and the right of the people to take part in the government, in addition to growing prosperity, soon began to attract thousands of English, German, and Scots-Irish settlers, and most came by way of Philadelphia.

Philadelphia by the 1770s had grown to at least 30,000 persons in the central city, and it was the third most important business centre in the British Empire, overshadowed only by Liverpool and London. This position was due in large measure to the city's site at the confluence of the Delaware and Schuylkill rivers, which provided the city access to inland farm regions and to the coal and ore resources that supplied the early iron industry.

A visitor in 1756 wrote that "Everybody in Philadelphia deals more or less in trade," a tribute not merely to Philadelphia's location but also to the shrewd business talents of the Quaker merchants. A large and profitable system of triangular trade involved foodstuffs and wood products, such as lumber and barrel staves, that went from Philadelphia to the West Indies and there were exchanged for sugar, rum, and other West Indian products. These were carried to English ports, where they in turn were exchanged for English manufactures to be brought back to Philadelphia. The prosperous farm country of interior Pennsylvania supplied the Philadelphia merchant with goods for the West Indies, and a profitable coastal trade existed with other colonies and directly with England. By the 1750s Philadelphians had invested heavily in the flourishing charcoal-iron industry. Anthracite coal became an important mineral resource of Pennsylvania 100 years later, and the Philadelphia capital played a leading part in this industry as well as in the mining of bituminous coal farther to the west. Philadelphia continued its leadership in foreign commerce until about 1810, when New York City, with an even more advantageous location, took over this position. Philadelphia surrendered its position as financial capital of the nation in the 1850s.

Shipyards had flourished along the Delaware since colonial days. Most of what came to the city was raw material for manufacture, and Philadelphia became a major centre of the early Industrial Revolution in the United States. In 1785 Oliver Evans invented the first gristmill operated

Penn's plan

Recreational facilities

Museums and galleries

Philadelphia's leadership in commerce and culture

entirely by mechanical power. The city was a pioneer in textile manufacturing and took the raw iron from inland furnaces and made it into tools and implements, such as saws, huge iron castings for cotton-mill machinery, and the first American-built steam locomotives. By 1860 the value of Philadelphia's manufactures ran into several hundred million dollars, about 30 percent of the national total. Textiles, ships, iron products, leather, refined sugar, and boots and shoes were leaders, giving important aid to the Union in the Civil War.

THE GROWTH OF THE CITY

Cultural dominion. Prosperity was translated into personal and community wealth, and with these social and economic advantages Philadelphia assumed early leadership in the arts, in science, and in culture. Benjamin Franklin, who as a young man had migrated from Boston to Philadelphia, became an American leader in scientific and intellectual affairs. Philadelphia had the nation's first free library, its first hospital, and its first learned society, the American Philosophical Society—all founded by Franklin. Along with Franklin, there were men such as Benjamin Rush, the great physician, and David Rittenhouse, an astronomer, mathematician, inventor, and early Philadelphia aristocrat, and many others. The city excelled in printing and publishing: by 1776 there were 23 printers and newspapers with circulations of from 500 to 3,000 copies. Fine private and public buildings were erected. One of them was Andrew Hamilton's Independence Hall, originally—and still—better known by Philadelphians as "the statehouse." Led by Benjamin West, Charles Willson Peale, and Gilbert Stuart, oil painting flourished in the colonial and Federal periods.

The city's strategic location near the midpoint of colonial settlement and its important status as a vital political, economic, and cultural centre—as well as concern that Pennsylvania might not favour the Revolution—brought to Philadelphia the delegates who formed the First Continental Congress in 1774 and a year later the Second Continental Congress, which proclaimed the Declaration of Independence and governed throughout the Revolution. The Constitutional Convention met in Philadelphia in 1787 and framed the federal Constitution, and the city served as the capital of the United States from 1790 to 1800. The nation celebrated its centennial in Philadelphia in 1876.

Political evolution. In the decades just before and following the Civil War, Pennsylvania fell into the hands of Philadelphia-based Republican political machines that, like their counterparts (usually Democratic) in other cities, were becoming increasingly sophisticated in methods of manipulating the political processes, especially through the newer immigrant groups, and profiting from the economic life of the state and city. They were instrumental in electing governors and U.S. senators, and, in the Depression years of the 1930s, the hard-hit city refused aid from the Democratic administration in Washington, D.C. Powerful bankers and industrial and business leaders, living for the most part outside the city, favoured this form of government because it kept taxes low, imposed little or no regulation on business, and maintained an aura of social calm through benign neglect or quiet but forceful repression.

The 20th century. In about 1900 Philadelphia had been described as "corrupt but content," a status quo that

Political machines and civic malaise

Philadelphians were indeed content with until 1939, when a group known as the Young Turks and influenced by the nationwide New Deal of the Democratic Party began to agitate for charter reform and a city planning commission. Women and blacks were brought into the city's political life for the first time. In spite of continued machine domination of the city, the group began to realize its goals—with a "Better Philadelphia Exhibition" in 1947, a coalition of top business and financial leaders the following year, and a new charter in 1951. The election in 1952 of Joseph S. Clark as mayor signalled the moment for a new Philadelphia to leap off the drawing boards.

BIBLIOGRAPHY

General: ROBERT H. WILSON, *Official Handbook for Visitors: Philadelphia*, 300th anniversary ed. (1982), a city guide; *Philadelphia Magazine,* a periodical that often features a sharply critical and satirical approach.

Historical works: CARL and JESSICA BRIDENBAUGH, *Rebels and Gentlemen: Philadelphia in the Age of Franklin* (1942, reprinted 1978), an extremely good picture of colonial and Revolutionary times and people; BROOKE HINDLE, *The Pursuit of Science in Revolutionary America: 1735–89* (1956, reprinted 1974), an excellent source for early science in Philadelphia; AMERICAN PHILOSOPHICAL SOCIETY, *Historic Philadelphia: From the Founding Until the Early Nineteenth Century* (1953), a study in depth; HORACE MATHER LIPPINCOTT, *Early Philadelphia: Its People, Life, and Progress* (1917), a fine study that is both colourful and informative; *Pennsylvania Magazine of History and Biography* (quarterly), the prestigious journal of the Historical Society of Pennsylvania (well indexed); RUSSELL F. WEIGLEY (ed.), *Philadelphia: A 300 Year History* (1982), a collection of scholarly essays; SAM BASS WARNER, JR., *The Private City: Philadelphia in Three Periods of Its Growth* (1968), a prizewinning and provocative interpretation of the impact of urbanization upon the city; WILLIAM W. CUTLER III and HOWARD GILLETTE, JR. (eds.), *The Divided Metropolis: Social and Spatial Dimensions of Philadelphia, 1800–1975* (1980), an insightful anthology of essays. The following provide valuable insights into the texture of working-class life and the nature of interethnic and interracial relations in the city: BRUCE LAURIE, *The Working People of Philadelphia, 1800–1850* (1980); ALLEN F. DAVIS and MARK H. HALLER (eds.), *The Peoples of Philadelphia: A History of Ethnic Groups and Lower-Class Life, 1790–1940* (1973); MICHAEL FELDBERG, *The Philadelphia Riots of 1844: A Study of Ethnic Conflict* (1975); and THEODORE HERSHBERG (ed.), *Philadelphia: Work, Space, Family, and Group Experience in the Nineteenth Century* (1981).

Specialized studies: NATHANIEL BURT, *The Perennial Philadelphians: The Anatomy of an American Aristocracy* (1963, reprinted 1975), an excellent study of Philadelphia society; E. DIGBY BALTZELL, *Puritan Boston and Quaker Philadelphia: Two Protestant Ethics and the Spirit of Class Authority and Leadership* (1979, reprinted 1982), an important comparative history; MAXWELL STRUTHERS BURT, *Philadelphia, Holy Experiment* (1945), a good general description with great feeling for the city; W.E.B. DU BOIS, *The Philadelphia Negro: A Social Study* (1899, reprinted 1971), an excellent monograph on the urban experience of blacks and a landmark in American sociological studies; VINCENT P. FRANKLIN, *The Education of Black Philadelphia* (1979), a solid study of the social and educational history of black Philadelphians during the first half of the 20th century; JEANNE R. LOWE, *Cities in a Race with Time* (1967), an excellent study of urban problems and renewal, including a good history of Philadelphia; GEORGE B. TATUM, *Penn's Great Town: 250 Years of Philadelphia Architecture Illustrated in Prints and Drawings* (1961), a valuable review of the cultural heritage; WILLIAM S. VARE, *My Forty Years in Politics* (1933), a firsthand account of city machine politics.

(S.K.S./J.B.B.T./M.S.Ma.)

Philippines

The Republic of the Philippines (Pilipino: Republika ñg Pilipinas) is an archipelago consisting of some 7,100 islands and islets lying about 500 miles off the southeast coast of Asia. The total land area of the Philippines is 115,800 square miles (300,000 square kilometres). It is bounded by the Philippine Sea to the east, the Celebes Sea to the south, and the South China Sea to the west and north. The Philippines takes its name from Philip II, king of Spain during the Spanish colonization of the islands in the 16th century. Manila, the national capital, is located on Luzon, the largest island, which has a land area of 40,420 square miles.

The archipelago spreads out in the form of a triangle, with the islands south of Palawan, the Sulu Archipelago, and the island of Mindanao forming (west–east) its southern base and the Batan Islands, in the north, its apex. The islands stretch for about 1,150 miles (1,850 kilometres) from north to south and for about 700 miles from east to west at their widest extent. Only about two-fifths of the islands and islets have names, and only some 350 have areas of one square mile or more. The large islands fall into three groups: (1) the Luzon group in the north and west, consisting of Luzon, Mindoro, and Palawan; (2) the Visayan group in the centre, consisting of Bohol, Cebu, Leyte, Masbate, Negros, Panay, and Samar; and (3) Mindanao in the south.

Because it was under Spanish rule for 333 years and under U.S. tutelage for a further 48 years, the Philippines has many cultural affinities with the West. It is, for example, the fourth most populous country in which English is an official language and the only predominantly Roman Catholic country in Southeast Asia. Its peoples, however, are Asian in consciousness and in aspiration. In many ways Filipino society is composed of paradoxes, perhaps the most apparent being the great extremes of wealth and poverty in the nation. The Philippines is a country of rich resources, but it is in the process of developing its full potentialities. It is primarily agricultural, although a high degree of domestic and foreign investment has spurred the rapid development of its industrial potential. Educationally, it is among the most advanced of Asian countries, having a high literacy rate.

This article is divided into the following sections:

Physical and human geography

THE LAND

Relief and drainage. The irregular configuration of the archipelago, the coastline of more than 21,500 miles, the great extent of mountainous country, the narrow and interrupted coastal plains, the generally northward trend of the river systems, and the lakes are the outstanding physical features of the Philippines. The islands are composed of volcanic, coral, and all principal rock formations. The mountain ranges for the most part run in the same general direction as the islands themselves, approximately north to south. The Cordillera Central, the central mountain chain of Luzon, running north to the Luzon Strait from the northern boundary of the central plain, is the most prominent range. It consists of two and in places three parallel ranges, each of which averages 5,900 feet (1,800 metres) in height. The Sierra Madre, extending along the Pacific coast from northern to central Luzon, is the longest mountain range in the country. This range and the Cordillera Central merge in north-central Luzon to form the Caraballo Mountains. To the north of the latter, and between the two ranges, is the fertile Cagayan Valley. The narrow Ilocos, or Malayan, range, lying close along the west coast of northern Luzon, rises in places to

Mountains of Luzon

more than 5,000 feet and is seldom less than 3,500 feet in height; it is largely volcanic. In the southwestern part of northern Luzon are the rugged Zambales Mountains, consisting of more or less isolated old volcanic stocks (rock formed under great heat and pressure deep beneath the Earth's surface).

The central plain of Luzon, about 150 by 50 miles, is only about 100 feet above sea level except near its centre. The greater part of southern Luzon is occupied by isolated volcanoes and irregular masses of hills and mountains. The highest peak is Mayon Volcano (8,077 feet) near Legazpi in Albay province.

Through the island of Palawan, about 25 miles wide and more than 250 miles long, there extends a range with an average height of from 4,000 to 5,000 feet. Each of the Visayan Islands except Samar and Bohol is traversed longitudinally by a single range with occasional spurs. Several peaks in Panay reach an altitude of 6,000 feet or more. Canlaon Volcano, on Negros, is 8,087 feet high, and other peaks reach altitudes of more than 6,000 feet.

There are several important ranges on Mindanao, the Diuata (Diwata) Mountains along the eastern coast being the most prominent. West of this lies the fertile valley of the Agusan River, 20 to 30 miles wide. Farther west and southwest is the Cotabato Valley of the Mindanao River

Relief of Mindanao

(Río Grande de Mindanao), and between its lower course and the southern coast lies a range trending northwest–southeast. On the southeastern border of the basin of the Mindanao River is Mount Apo, at 9,692 feet (2,954 metres) the highest peak in the Philippines. Around Lake Lanao are a number of volcanic peaks, and a low cordillera extends through the Zamboanga Peninsula in the far west.

The plains lying amid the mountains—for example, the central plain of Luzon and the central plain of Panay—have the greatest density of population in the islands, except Cebu, where the people live mostly on the coastal plain because the interior is high and rugged. The most important rivers are the Cagayan, Agno, Pampanga, Pasig,

and Bicol on Luzon and the Mindanao and Agusan on Mindanao. The Pasig, which flows through the city of Manila, is commercially important. The largest lake in the archipelago is Laguna de Bay, located south of Manila.

Volcanoes are a conspicuous feature of the landscape, but there is relatively little volcanic activity. There are altogether about 50 volcanoes, of which more than 10 are known to be active. All gradations of volcanoes can be seen, from the almost perfect cone of Mayon, which has been compared to Mount Fuji in Japan, to old, worn-down volcanic stocks, the present forms of which give little indication of their origin. The several distinct volcanic areas are in south-central and southern Luzon and

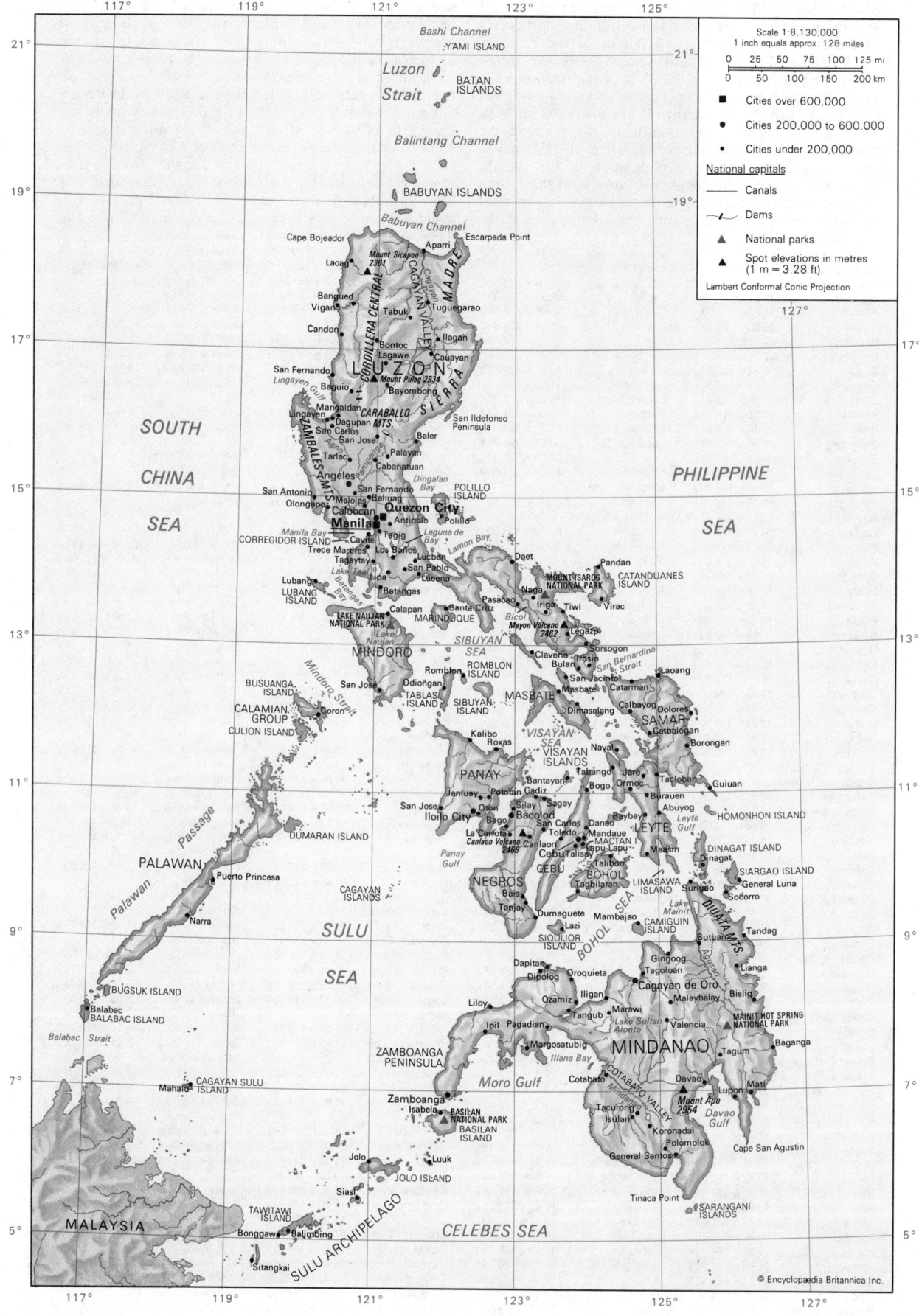

Scale 1:8,130,000
1 inch equals approx. 128 miles

0 25 50 75 100 125 mi
0 50 100 150 200 km

■ Cities over 600,000
● Cities 200,000 to 600,000
· Cities under 200,000

National capitals

—— Canals

⌐ Dams

▲ National parks

▲ Spot elevations in metres
  (1 m = 3.28 ft)

Lambert Conformal Conic Projection

Bashi Channel
Y'AMI ISLAND
Luzon
Strait
BATAN
ISLANDS

Balintang Channel

BABUYAN ISLANDS

Babuyan Channel

Cape Bojeador
Aparri
Escarpada Point
Mount Sicapoo 2361
Laoag
CAGAYAN VALLEY
CORDILLERA CENTRAL
Bangued
Vigan
Tabuk
Tuguegarao
Candon
Ilagan
Bontoc
Cauayan
Lagawe
San Fernando
L U Z O N
Lingayen Gulf
Baguio
Mount Pulog 2934
Bayombong
Mangaldan
Dagupan
San Ildefonso
Peninsula
Lingayen
ZAMBALES MTS.
CARABALLO MTS.
San Carlos
San Jose
Baler
Tarlac
Palayan
Angeles
Cabanatuan
San Antonio
Dingalan
Bay
San Fernando
POLILLO
ISLAND
Olongapo
Malolos
Baliuag
SOUTH
Caloocan
Quezon City
Polillo
CHINA
Manila
Antipolo
CORREGIDOR ISLAND
Cavite
Tagig
Laguna de
Bay
Lamon Bay
SEA
Trece Martires
Los Baños
Daet
Pandan
Tagaytay
Lipa
Lucban
San Pablo
Lucena
Naga
Iriga
Tiwi
CATANDUANES
ISLAND
Lubang
Batangas
Calapan
Santa Cruz
Pasacao
MOUNT ISAROG
NATIONAL PARK
Virac
LUBANG
ISLAND
Bicol
Mayon Volcano 2462
Legazpi
LAKE NAUJAN
NATIONAL PARK
MARINDUQUE
Lake
Naujan
Sorsogon
Claveria
Irosin
San Bernardino
Strait
MINDORO
Bulan
Laoang
SIBUYAN
SEA
Romblon
San Jacinto
Catarman
BUSUANGA
ISLAND
Odiongan
ROMBLON
ISLAND
Masbate
Calbayog
Dolores
CALAMIAN
GROUP
San Jose
TABLAS
ISLAND
MASBATE
Dimasalang
SAMAR
Catbalogan
CULION ISLAND
SIBUYAN
ISLAND
Borongan
Kalibo
VISAYAN
SEA
Naval
Roxas
VISAYAN
ISLANDS
Jaro
Tacloban
Guiuan
PANAY
Bantayan
Tabango
Burauen
Januay
Bogo
Ormoc
Abuyog
HOMONHON ISLAND
San Jose
Pototan
Cadiz
Silay
Sagay
Baybay
Leyte
Gulf
PALAWAN
Iloilo City
Oton
Bago
San Carlos
Danao
LEYTE
Maasin
Passage
La Carlota
Toledo
Mandaue
DINAGAT ISLAND
Canlaon Volcano 2465
Canlaon
MACTAN I.
Dinagat
SIARGAO ISLAND
Puerto Princesa
Cebu
Lapu-Lapu
General Luna
DUMARAN ISLAND
Talibon
Socorro
CAGAYAN
ISLANDS
Talisay
BOHOL
Surigao
NEGROS
CEBU
Tagbilaran
LIMASAWA
ISLAND
Bais
BOHOL
Lake
SEA
Mainit
Narra
Dumaguete
Mambajao
DIATA MTS.
Tanjay
Lazi
CAMIGUIN
ISLAND
Tandag
SULU
SIQUIJOR
ISLAND
Butuan
SEA
Dapitan
Gingoog
Dipolog
Oroquieta
Tagoloan
Lianga
BUGSUK ISLAND
Cagayan de Oro
Balabac
Liloy
Iligan
Malaybalay
Bislig
BALABAC ISLAND
Ozamiz
MAINIT HOT SPRING
NATIONAL PARK
Balabac Strait
Ipil
Tangub
Marawi
Valencia
Pagadian
Lake Sultan
Alonto
Baganga
ZAMBOANGA
PENINSULA
Margosatubig
MINDANAO
Tagum
CAGAYAN SULU
ISLAND
Illana Bay
COTABATO VALLEY
Mahala
Cotabato
Davao
Lupon
Mati
Moro Gulf
Mindanao
Zamboanga
Mount Apo 2954
Isabela
Tacurong
Davao
Gulf
BASILAN
NATIONAL PARK
Isulan
BASILAN
ISLAND
Koronadal
Polomolok
Jolo
Cape San Agustin
Luuk
General Santos
JOLO ISLAND
Siasi
Tinaca Point
SARANGANI
ISLANDS
TAWITAWI
ISLAND
MALAYSIA
Bonggaw
Balimbing
SULU ARCHIPELAGO
CELEBES SEA
Sitangkai

PHILIPPINE

SEA

PALAWAN

Palawan

Panay
Gulf

Moro Gulf

© Encyclopædia Britannica Inc.

on the islands of Negros, Mindanao, Jolo, and elsewhere. Tremors and earthquakes are common.

Climate. The climate of the Philippines is tropical and is strongly affected by monsoon (rain-bearing) winds, which blow from the southwest from approximately May to October and from the northeast from November to February. Thus, temperatures remain relatively constant from north to south during the year, and seasons consist of periods of wet and dry. Throughout the country, however, there are considerable variations in the frequency and amount of precipitation. The western shores facing the South China Sea have marked dry and wet seasons. The dry season generally begins in December and ends in May, the first three months being cool and the second three hot; the rest of the year consists of the wet season. The dry season shortens progressively to the east until it ceases to occur. During the wet season, rainfall is heavy in all parts of the archipelago except for an area extending southward through the centre of the Visayan group to central Mindanao and then southwestward through the Sulu Archipelago; rain is heaviest along the eastern shores facing the Pacific Ocean.

From June to December typhoons often strike the archipelago. Most of these storms come from the southeast, their frequency generally increasing from south to north; in some years the number of typhoons reaches 25 or more. Typhoons are heaviest in Samar, Leyte, eastern Quezon province, and the Batan Islands, and when accompanied by floods or high winds they may cause great loss of life and property. Mindanao is generally free from typhoons.

November through February constitutes the most agreeable season; the air is cool and invigorating at night, and the days are pleasant and sunny. During the hot part of the dry season in most places, and especially in the cities of Cebu, Davao, and Manila, the temperature sometimes rises as high as 100° F (38° C). Overall temperatures decline with altitude, however, and cities and towns located at higher elevations—such as Baguio in northern Luzon, Majayjay and Lucban south of Manila, and Malaybalay in central Mindanao—experience a pleasant climate throughout the year; at times the temperature in these places dips as low as 43° F (6° C).

Plant and animal life. Much of the land area of the islands is covered with forest, and many of the mountains are densely forested. In northern Luzon the principal mountain tree is pine. In many places where the forests have been burned away their place has been taken by tall, coarse cogon grass (genus *Imperata*) or similar grasses. There are about 10,000 known species of flowering plants and ferns. Much of the vegetation resembles that found in Malaysia, and the vegetation of the coastal areas, including the mangrove swamps, is practically identical with that of similar areas throughout the Malay Archipelago. Himalayan elements occur in the mountains of northern Luzon, while a few Australian types are found at various altitudes. A majority of the plant species are indigenous, including the dominant forest species. Lauan (Philippine mahogany) often composes a high percentage of the forest. There are many other valuable hardwoods as well as many softwoods. About 800 species of orchids, some very rare, are found.

There are about 220 species of mammals, among which are carabaos (water buffalo), goats, horses, hogs, cats, dogs, monkeys, squirrels, lemurs, mice, pangolins (scaly anteaters), chevrotains (mouse deer), mongooses, civet cats, and red and brown deer. The tamarau, a very small species of carabao, is found only on Mindoro. There are at least 56 species of bats, many peculiar to the Philippines. Fossil remains show that there were once elephants on the islands.

There are some 500 species of birds, many of which are migrants. Birdlife includes jungle fowl, pigeons, peacocks, pheasants, doves, parrots, hornbills, kingfishers, sunbirds, tailorbirds, weaverbirds, herons, and quails. Many species of birds are unique to the island of Palawan. The rare and endangered monkey-eating eagle is restricted mainly to isolated areas on Mindanao and in the Sierra Madre on Luzon.

The two seasons

Typhoons

Settlement patterns. Before the arrival of the Spanish in the 16th century, the people lived in small independent villages called barangays, each ruled by a petty king called a *datu*. Rural settlement today is centred upon poblaciones, or small towns, originally founded by the Spanish. Roads or trails were built from the poblacion in four to six directions, like the spokes of a wheel, and along the roadsides barrios, or villages, grew up, subdivided into smaller units called sitios. More people now live in the barrios than in the poblaciones. A large barrio may be composed of as many as 1,000 households and have a population of 4,000 or more. The cultivation of rice or corn (maize) and fishing provide the basic subsistence.

Manila, Cebu, Jaro, Vigan, and Nueva Caceres (now called Naga) were granted city charters by the Spanish. More chartered cities were founded under U.S. administration and since independence in 1946. Quezon City was

The barangay

Chartered cities

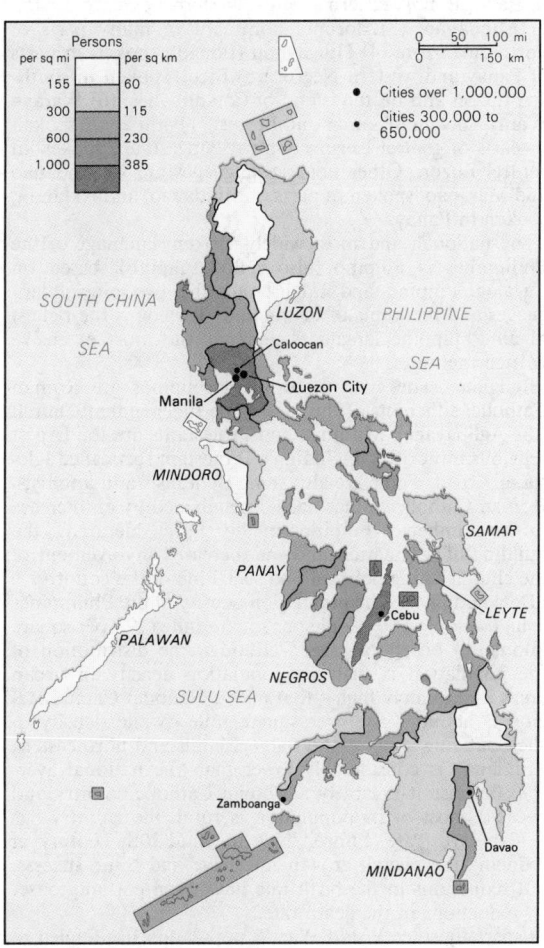

Population density of the Philippines.

chartered in 1939 and became the capital of the Philippines in 1948. In 1975 Manila, Pasay City, Caloocan, and Quezon City and 13 adjoining municipalities were placed under one administrative unit known as Metropolitan, or Metro, Manila. The city proper of Manila was again made the national capital in 1976; Metropolitan Manila is designated the National Capital Region. In addition to the cities there are a great many municipalities and a number of municipal districts.

THE PEOPLE

Ethnic composition. The people of the Philippines are called Filipinos. Their ancestors, who were of Malay stock, came from the southeastern Asian mainland as well as from what is now Indonesia. From the 10th century, contacts with China resulted in a group of mixed Filipino-Chinese descent, who account for a minority of the population. A small percentage of Chinese nationals also live in the country. Spanish-Filipinos and Filipino-Americans may be distinguished by their fairer complexion,

The Filipinos

taller stature, and aquiline nose structure. The relatively small numbers of emigrants from the Indian subcontinent added to the population's racial mixture. There are small numbers of resident U.S. nationals (excluding military personnel) and Spaniards. The aboriginal inhabitants of the islands were the Negritos, or Pygmies, also called Aetas or Balugas; they now constitute only a small percentage of the total population.

Linguistic groups. Estimates of the total number of native languages and dialects spoken in the Philippines differ, but scholarly studies suggest that there are some 70 of them. These languages are all closely related, belonging to the Austronesian (Malayo-Polynesian) family of languages. Traditionally, eight major linguistic groups are identified. These are (1) the Tagalog group, concentrated in Manila, central and south central Luzon, and the islands of Mindoro and Marinduque; (2) Cebuano, in Cebu, Bohol, eastern Negros, western Leyte, and parts of Mindanao; (3) Ilocano, dominant in many parts of northern Luzon; (4) Hiligaynon (Ilongo), spoken in parts of Panay and western Negros; (5) Bicol, spoken in southern Luzon and on the island of Catanduanes; (6) Waray–Waray, spoken in Samar and Leyte; (7) Pampango, spoken in parts of central Luzon; and (8) Pangasinan, spoken in central Luzon. Other notable languages are Magindanao and Maranao, spoken in parts of Mindanao, and Aklanon, spoken in Panay.

The Pilipino language

The national, and most widely spoken, language of the Philippines is Pilipino (also called Filipino), based on Tagalog. Pilipino and English are the two official languages and mediums of instruction. Tagalog is the richest of all Philippine languages and has the most extensive written literature.

Religion. The great majority of Filipinos are Roman Catholic; adherents of the Philippine Independent Church (the Aglipayans), Muslims, and Protestants are the largest religious minorities, including a Protestant sect called Iglesia ni Kristo. There are also some Buddhists and animists. Roman Catholicism has been strengthened by an increase in the number of Filipinos in the church hierarchy, the building of seminaries, and the increased involvement of the church in the political and social life of the country.

Demography. The population density of the Philippines is high—some 500 people per square mile (193 per square kilometre) on the average—although the distribution of the population is uneven. Population density in urban areas is extremely high—that of the National Capital Region is about 30,000 per square mile—while density in such outlying areas as the Batan Islands and northeastern Mindanao is considerably lower than the national average. Because it is largely a Roman Catholic country and because most of its population is rural, the country has a high birth rate. Efforts since the mid-20th century at reducing the overall growth rate have had some success, but reductions in the birth rate have been partially offset by reductions in the death rate.

Demographic trends

Especially since World War II, population has tended to move from rural areas to towns and cities. At the beginning of the 20th century more than 80 percent of the population was rural, but by the late 1980s the number had dropped to less than 60 percent. There is also a considerable amount of Filipino emigration, particularly of manual labourers and professionals. Many emigrants have gone to the United States, Okinawa, Guam, and Canada; in addition, a large number of skilled and semiskilled workers have taken temporary overseas assignments, mainly in the Middle East.

THE ECONOMY

Resources. The Philippines is rich in mineral resources. There are major deposits of gold in northern and southern Luzon; iron ore in northern Mindanao and on nearby islands and in central Luzon; copper in west-central Luzon; lead and zinc in western Mindanao; and high-grade chromium ore (chromite) in west-central and southern Luzon, northern Mindanao, and central Palawan. Deposits of silver, nickel, mercury, molybdenum, cadmium, and manganese occur in several other places. Nonmetallic minerals include limestone for cement, found on Cebu,

Luzon, and Romblon; salt and asbestos on Luzon; marble on Romblon and Panay; asphalt on Leyte; mineral waters on Luzon; gypsum on Luzon; sulfur on Luzon, Leyte, and Mindanao; guano and phosphate rock on Cebu and Bohol; coal and silica on Cebu and Palawan; and petroleum off the northwest shore of Palawan.

At one time about half of the Philippines' total land area was covered with forests. Of this, a large part abounded with trees of commercial value, especially lauan, narra (species of *Pterocarpus,* used in cabinetmaking), ipil (*Intsia bijuga*), molave (*Vitex littoralis*), and *kamagong* (*Diospyros discolor*). Heavy logging and inadequate reforestation measures, however, have reduced considerably the amount of forested land.

No fewer than 2,000 varieties of fish are in the seas surrounding the islands and in lakes, rivers, estuaries, and fish ponds. The most important commercial fishes are milkfish (a herringlike fish), anchovy, herring, sardine, mackerel, grouper, snapper, cavalla, mullet, barracuda, mudfish, and caesio. Fish are raised in ponds in some provinces of Luzon and Panay. There are pearl beds in the Sulu Archipelago to the south, and mother-of-pearl used for making buttons is exported to China, Hong Kong, and elsewhere. Tortoiseshells and shells used for windows are exported to Singapore, Malaysia, and other countries.

Hydro-electric projects

Hydroelectric power in the past has supplied only a small proportion of the country's electrical output, with thermal plants, most of which burn imported oil, supplying the major proportion. But the completion of several dam projects on Luzon and the expansion of another project on Mindanao have increased the percentage of power generated by hydroelectric installations; irrigation and flood control are additional benefits of some of the projects. Dependence on foreign oil has also been reduced by the construction of geothermal and conventional coal-fired thermal plants.

Agriculture. The Philippines is chiefly an agricultural country. Its soil is rich and fertile, and crops grow abundantly throughout the year. The principal farm products are rice, corn (maize), coconut, sugarcane, abaca (Manila hemp), tobacco, maguey (used for making such products as rope), and pineapple. Many tropical fruits are also raised, the most important being banana, mango, lanseh, or lanzon (*Lansium domesticum*), citrus, and papaya. A wide variety of vegetables are raised for domestic consumption.

Rice production

Rice, the principal staple crop, is grown everywhere, but especially in central and north-central Luzon, south-central Mindanao; western Negros and eastern and cen-

Shostal Associates

Mayon Volcano overlooking surrounding rice fields in Albay province, southern Luzon.

tral Panay. Much of the total farmland is used for rice growing. Since the early 1970s rice production in the Philippines has improved considerably, and in some years the country has had surplus rice available for export. Factors contributing to this increase in output include the development and use of higher-yielding strains of rice, the construction of feeder roads and irrigation canals, and the use of chemical fertilizers and insecticides. Use of scientific farming techniques in the Philippines, however, has had its drawbacks. The newer strains of rice have required the application of chemicals that are expensive and that generally must be imported.

Coconut production

The Philippines is one of the world's largest producers of coconuts and a major exporter of coconut products. The area devoted to coconut production is second only to that used for rice and corn. The Philippines also produces more than one-third of the world's copra.

Sugar is one of the country's top exports and earns a substantial amount of foreign exchange. Sugarcane is grown extensively in central and north-central Luzon, western Negros, and on Panay. Much of the sugar crop is exported to the United States. Abaca, or Manila hemp, the source of a useful plant fibre, is also an important export. It is grown extensively in eastern Mindanao, southeastern Luzon, and on Leyte and Samar.

High-quality timber and veneer products traditionally have been leading exports, although their importance has declined. Other forest products include dyewoods, rattan, tanbarks, gutta-percha, beeswax, and rubber. Fishing is also one of the most important of Filipino industries. Canned tuna is the principal fish exported, and fish provides an important proportion of the protein in the Filipino diet. Commercial fishing is carried on primarily off Palawan, Negros, Mindanao, and Panay.

Industry. The principal minerals mined include gold, silver, iron, copper, manganese, zinc, lead, coal, and chromite; some petroleum is also extracted. Many of these minerals—notably copper—are produced for export and thus are vulnerable to fluctuations in world demand. Much industrial growth has taken place in the Philippines, particularly in the 1950s and the 1970s, but the manufacturing sector is still in an early stage of development. Many factories are licensees of foreign companies or act as subcontractors for foreign firms, turning out finished products for export from imported semifinished goods. Major manufactured goods include processed foods and beverages, petroleum products, textiles and wearing apparel, and chemicals.

Finance and trade. In addition to the Central Bank of the Philippines, there are commercial banks, thrift banks, and rural banks. Banking operations are also conducted by such other institutions as the Philippine National Bank and the Development Bank, of the Philippines. The

Exports and imports

principal exports are electronic equipment, coconuts and coconut products, minerals (copper, gold, iron ore), sugar, and garments. The principal imports are fuel, machinery, transport equipment, and electrical equipment. Major trading partners are the United States, Japan, The Netherlands, West Germany, and Hong Kong.

Administration of the economy. The economy of the Philippines is based on free enterprise; individuals and nongovernmental entities are free to participate in its development and management, sometimes with the aid of government credit.

The public sector. The government has assisted the private sector of the economy by exempting certain new industries from taxation for a certain period. Only nominal taxes are imposed on selected industries, and loans on favourable terms are available to others. Government banks, such as the Central Bank of the Philippines, the Philippine National Bank, and the Development Bank, were established to encourage business, agriculture, and industry. Much of the original capital investment of many private rural banks was provided by the government. Private development banks have likewise received government assistance. The National Economic and Development Authority (NEDA) and the Board of Investments were created to help both public and private sectors in planning further economic development.

The government plans national economic development through the NEDA, the National Planning Commission, and other agencies. In so doing, it has sought to increase economic independence; while there have been advantages in the preferential trade relations between the United States and the Philippines, this trade has resulted in the development of industries that would primarily benefit the American rather than the Filipino economy. Although the United States and Japan have continued to be the Philippines' top trading partners, a number of new markets, including those in Communist countries, have been explored. The government has also been engaged in business in its own right. It owns such enterprises as National Development Corporation, the Philippine Ports Authority, and the Philippine National Railways.

Government businesses

Labour relations. The trade-union movement is well-established in Manila and in most other towns and cities. Farmers and tenants are also organized, as are teachers and government employees. The right of all workers to organize unions has been recognized in the constitution promulgated in 1987. Management, for its part, has organized company unions. Relations between trade unions and the employers' union have been generally untroubled. The Bureau of Labor Relations has been effective in settling disputes between labour and management.

Taxation. The government derives its revenue from three major sources: taxation, earnings and other credits, and extraordinary income, including the transfer from special funds (*i.e.,* funds derived mainly from unexpended balances in the budget that are deposited as savings accounts). Revenue is collected primarily through the Bureau of Internal Revenue and the Bureau of Customs. Excise taxes constitute the largest portion of government income; import duties, corporate and individual income taxes, and sales taxes provide much of the remainder. Local governments have only limited taxing powers.

Transportation. Thousands of miles of roads, gravel, asphalt, and concrete, link the towns on the archipelago's many islands, with expressways running north and south from Luzon. Elsewhere on Luzon, most of the road from Manila to Laoag, in the far north of the island, and the greater part of the road to Sorsogon in the extreme south, are hard-surfaced, as are roads branching out from Manila to the city of Baguio and to the heavily populated provinces to the north and south. Thousands of miles of roads of various types have also been constructed on Mindanao, Mindoro, and Palawan and in the Visayas. A major achievement in road construction in the country is the Pan-Philippine Highway (also called the Maharlika Highway), a system of hard-surface roads, bridges, and ferries that connects the islands of Luzon, Samar, Leyte, and Mindanao.

The Pan-Philippine Highway

Two principal railroads operate on Luzon and Panay. The Luzon main line extends from San Fernando in the north to the city of Legazpi in the south. The railroad in Panay connects Iloilo City with Roxas.

The most important port is Manila. Manila North Harbor handles domestic trade, while Manila South Harbor handles shipping from abroad. Other international ports are Cebu (next in importance to Manila), Iloilo City, Davao, Zamboanga, Cagayan de Oro, and Legazpi.

The international airport at Manila, like those at Hong Kong and Singapore, is a focal point for air routes. A separate terminal is used by domestic airlines. The Mactan airport, on Mactan Island near Cebu, also handles international flights. There are a number of other airports for domestic flights, all of which have service to and from Manila.

ADMINISTRATION AND SOCIAL CONDITIONS

Government. *Constitutional framework.* The Philippines has been governed under three constitutions, the first of which was promulgated in 1935, during the period of U.S. administration. It was closely modeled on the U.S. Constitution and included provisions for a bicameral legislative branch, an executive branch headed by a president, and an independent judiciary. During the period of martial law (1972–81) under President Ferdinand E. Marcos, the old constitution was abolished and replaced by a new constitution (adopted in January 1973) that changed the Philippine government from a U.S.-style presidential system to a parliamentary form; the president became head of state, and executive power was vested in a prime minister and Cabinet. President Marcos, however, also served (until 1981) as prime minister and ruled by decree. Subsequent amendments and modifications of this constitution replaced the former bicameral legislature with a unicameral body and gave the president even more powers, including the ability to dissolve the legislature and (from 1981) to appoint a prime minister from among members of the legislature.

Consti-
tution of
1987

After the downfall of Marcos in 1986, a new constitution, similar to the 1935 document, was drafted and was ratified in a popular referendum held in February 1987. Its key provision was a return to a bicameral legislature, called the Congress of the Philippines, consisting of a 250-member House of Representatives and a 24-member Senate. House members are elected from districts, although a number of them are appointed; they can serve no more than three consecutive three-year terms. Senators, elected at large, can serve a maximum of two six-year terms. The first legislative election under the new constitution was held in May 1987. The president, the head of state, can be elected to only a single six-year term, and the vice president to two consecutive six-year terms. The president appoints the Cabinet, which consists of the heads of the various ministries responsible for running the day-to-day business of the government. Most presidential appointments are subject to the approval of a Commission of Appointments, which consists of equal numbers of senators and representatives.

Local government. The country is divided administratively into 73 provinces, which are grouped into 12 regions; the National Capital Region has special status. Each province is headed by an elected governor. Local political subdivisions that also have elected officials include cities and municipalities; during the Marcos regime the ancient barangay was reinstated as the smallest unit of government.

Political parties. Partisan political activity was vigorous before 1972, the principal rivals being the Nacionalista and Liberal parties. Martial-law restrictions all but eliminated partisan politics. Marcos' organization, the New Society Movement (Kilusan Bagong Lipunan; KBL), was created from elements of the Nacionalista Party and other supporters and became predominant. Organized political opposition was revived for legislative elections held in 1978; and since the downfall of Marcos, partisan politics has returned to its pre-1972 level, with a large number of political parties emerging. Certain outlawed political organizations also operate within the country, the two principal ones being the Moro National Liberation Front (MNLF), a group seeking autonomy for Muslim Filipinos (Moros), and the National Democratic Front (NDF), a Communist-led insurgency movement.

Justice. Justices and judges enjoy fixed tenure and reasonably high compensation. The judiciary has consequently been less criticized than other branches of the government; and since 1900 the Supreme Court has retained the trust of the people, although trust in the entire judiciary diminished considerably during the Marcos regime. Judicial independence was reaffirmed by the constitution of 1987.

The extra-
judicial
lupon

In order to reduce the load of the lower courts, local committees of citizens called Pacification Committees (Lupon Tagapayapa) have been organized to effect extrajudicial settlement of minor cases between barangay residents. In each *lupon* there is a Conciliation Body (Pangkat Tagapagkasundo), the main function of which is to bring opposing parties together and effect amicable settlement of differences. The committee cannot impose punishment, but otherwise its decision is binding.

Armed forces. The Department of National Defense is divided into four services: the army, the navy, the air force, and the constabulary (the national police force), each with a commanding officer whose rank is at least that of brigadier general or, in the navy, commodore. Several army battalions served in the Korean and Viet-

nam wars, though in the latter the men performed civic instead of combat duties. The armed forces are responsible for containing the antigovernment military actions of the NDF and the MNLF; for controlling smuggling; and for maintaining order. The armed forces also engages in nonmilitary activities, such as providing disaster relief, constructing civilian housing, and participating in literacy campaigns. The commander in chief of the armed forces (the president of the Philippines) is a civilian.

U.S.
military
bases

Under a series of agreements reached in 1947, the United States maintains several bases in the Philippines and provides the Philippines with military equipment and training. Since the treaty dealing with the bases was revised in 1978, Philippine sovereignty over them has been recognized; all U.S. bases in the country have been placed under the overall command of a Filipino, and the Philippine flag flies over them.

The constabulary is divided into commands in the 12 administrative regions and the National Capital Region. Each province, including the cities within its territorial jurisdiction, is assigned a constabulary unit under a provincial commander. The police throughout the country are integrated under the supervision of the National Police Commission.

Education. The largest governmental ministry is that which administers education as well as such cultural institutions as the Institute of National Language (Surian ng Wilkang Pambansa), the National Library, the National Museum of the Philippines, and the National Historical Institute.

Elementary education lasts for six years, secondary education for four, and college courses for four to nine years. Vocational schools offer specialized training for one to two years. Relatively few students finish high school. In view of this, greater emphasis has been placed on nonformal educational opportunities for adults and out-of-school youths. A Bureau of Continuing Education supervises programs in adult literacy, vocational and technical training, health, and family planning.

There are some four dozen state-run universities and colleges, about one-third of them in Metropolitan Manila, as well as a number of private institutions. The University of Santo Tomas was founded as early as 1611. There are also many technical institutions and community colleges in the provinces, but the tendency of the students is to go to Manila, despite discouragement by the government.

Pilipino is the medium of instruction in all elementary school subjects except science, mathematics, and the English language, which are taught in English. A chronic shortage of supplies and facilities has been partially remedied by a textbook program begun in the mid-1970s and the large-scale manufacture of prefabricated classrooms. A small number of foreign students (mainly from the Middle East, Southeast Asia, and the United States) study annually in the Philippines.

Health and welfare. Health and welfare are the responsibility of the departments of health and social services. The national government maintains a general hospital, a mental hospital, an orthopedic hospital, and a hospital for war veterans and their families. There are also government and private hospitals, as well as rural health units. Incorporated into the Department of Social Services is the Philippine National Red Cross, and a number of private social welfare agencies cooperate with the department.

The rate of mortality has been considerably reduced, particularly among infants and mothers, and there has been a steady increase in average life expectancy. The improvement in health is credited to better prenatal care and the services of more trained midwives, doctors, and nurses, improved housing and sanitation, the provision of health services to government employees and Social Security members, the increasing number of medical and nursing school graduates, and the requirement that a medical graduate render rural service. Nonetheless, the demand for health care continues to outstrip available resources; a large number of trained medical professionals emigrate, particularly to the United States, and many of the poorest people still rely on the services of practitioners of traditional medicine and unlicensed midwives.

Housing   There is a serious housing shortage everywhere, although it is especially acute in Manila. In many places people live in their own dwellings, but the houses are often substandard and lack elementary facilities for health and sanitation. To help meet this problem the government has relocated thousands of squatters from Manila to resettlement areas in nearby provinces. The Marcos regime instituted housing projects in which model communities were built that provided the residents with hygienic dwellings, a number of amenities, and facilities for raising livestock and for pursuing cottage industries and other means of making a living. This program met with some success.

CULTURAL LIFE

Philippine society is an incongruous blend of diversity and homogeneity. Geographically the country is part of the East, but in culture it is strongly Western. Forces of assimilation have constantly worked to overcome differences caused by the relative physical isolation of various groups of people throughout the archipelago who had come over time from disparate ethnic and cultural backgrounds. Nearly four centuries of Western rule, however, left the most indelible imprint on the country, serving as a conduit for the introduction of Western culture and as the catalyst for the emergence of a sense of Philippine political and cultural unity. The Christian churches built by the Spaniards and the mosques in the Muslim areas provided a spiritual anchor, while the educational system established by the United States and expanded by the Filipinos became a strong factor for socioeconomic progress. Nonetheless, traditionally strong family ties and other Asian moorings have remained. The revival of the barangay as the smallest unit of government has contributed to the revival of ancient traditions; and Asian and African history and literature—neglected in the past— have received more attention. Thus, the Philippines has been strengthening its Asian ties without abandoning its Western cultural acquisitions.

Early Spanish chroniclers testified that the Filipinos carved the images of their anitos (gods and goddesses) and ancestors in wood. They also played a variety of musical instruments, including flutes, nose flutes, and guitars. They performed appropriate songs and dances to celebrate courtship, marriage, the harvest, and other occasions. Many of these songs and dances, accompanied by the same musical instruments, have been preserved or reinterpreted and are presented by dance and song groups.

Major dance groups   Some of these groups—among them the Bayanihan, Filipinescas, Barangay, and Hariraya groups, as well as the Karilagan Ensemble and the groups associated with the guilds of the Manila and Fort Santiago theatres—have also performed abroad. Many Filipino musicians have risen to prominence, such as the composer and conductor Antonio J. Molina, the composer Felipe P. de Leon, known for his nationalistic themes, and the opera singer Jovita Fuentes. The Cultural Center of the Philippines, the Folk Arts Theatre, and the restored Manila Metropolitan Theatre (all in Manila) provide homes for the performing arts, featuring local and foreign opera and ballet. To encourage the development of arts the government gives awards of recognition and has established an Arts Center in Los Baños south of Manila.

Filipino painters have included Juan Luna; Fernando Amorsolo, who is known for his traditional rural scenes; the muralists Carlos V. Francisco and Vicente Manansala; and the modernists Victorio Edades and Arturo Rogerio Luz. Among the sculptors, Guillermo Tolentino and Napoleon Abueva are prominent. Tribesmen from mountainous regions in northern Luzon and craftsmen living northwest of Manila and in Paete on the eastern shore of Laguna de Bay are known for wood carving. Romblon and other nearby islands are noted for their marble sculptures. Among Filipino architects, the most notable include Juan F. Nakpil, Otilio Arellano, Fernando Ocampo, Leandro Locsin, Juan Arellano, Carlos Arguelles, and Tomas Mapua.

Folk traditions. Filipinos have a rich folklore tradition. Myths and legends deal with such subjects as the origin of the world, the first man and woman on Earth, why

the sky is high, why the sea is salty, and why there are different races. Other tales are associated with the Spanish conquest. Muslim Filipinos have an epic called *Darangen*, Philippine and the Ilocanos of northern Luzon have another entitled epics *Biag ni Lamang*. Most folktales and popular cultural traits are still to be found in remote barrios and *sitios*. Dean S. Fansler, Maximo Ramos, and Armando and Carolina Malay have compiled collections of Philippine folktales.

Museums. The Bureau of Science and the National Museum, both in Manila, have gathered artifacts connected with many of the folktales and popular beliefs. Several provinces—including Cagayan, Bulacan, Aklan, and Iloilo—have built their own museums. A few universities, such as the University of Santo Tomas, Silliman University in eastern Negros, and Mindanao State University in Lanao del Sur, likewise have added museums to their campuses. Nongovernmental organizations such as the Conservation Society and some historical groups have also sought to preserve the folklore heritage. The Cultural Centre of the Philippines opened in 1970 to encourage interest in the nation's heritage.

The media. A highly independent press developed in the Philippines when it was under U.S. administration, but many newspapers ceased publication during the period of martial law. Limited press freedom was granted in the early 1980s, with full freedoms returning after the change of government in 1986. Newspapers are published in English, Pilipino, and many of the country's vernacular dialects. The major English-language dailies—all published in Manila—include the *Bulletin Today, Times Journal*, and *Manila Times;* the *New Philippines Daily Express* has English and Pilipino editions. Among the major weeklies is *Veritas Weekly*, published by the Roman Catholic Church. The operators of radio and television stations belong to a national organization called the Association of Broadcasters in the Philippines.

For statistical data on the land and people of the Philippines, see the *Britannica World Data* section in the BRITANNICA WORLD DATA ANNUAL.   (Eu.M.A./G.C.B.)

History

In ancient times, the inhabitants of the Philippines were a diverse agglomeration of peoples who arrived in various waves of immigration from the Asian mainland and who maintained little contact with each other. The Philippines is the only nation in Southeast Asia that became subject to Western colonialism before it had had the opportunity to develop either a centralized government ruling over a large territory or an advanced elite culture. Chinese traders were known to have been resident from about AD 1000, and some cultural influences from South Asia, such as a Sanskrit-based writing system, were carried to the islands by the Indonesian empires of Śrivijaya and Majapahit; but in comparison with other parts of the region, the influence of both China and India on the Philippines was of little importance. The peoples of the Philippine archipelago, unlike most of the other peoples of Southeast Asia, never adopted Hinduism or Buddhism.

PRE-SPANISH HISTORY

According to what can be inferred from somewhat later accounts, the Filipinos of the 15th century must have been primarily shifting cultivators, hunters, and fishers. Sedentary cultivation was the exception. Only in the mountains of northern Luzon, where elaborate rice terraces were built in the early centuries AD, were livelihood and social organization linked to a fixed territory. The lowland peoples lived in extended kinship groups known as barangays Barangay under the leadership of a *datu*, or chieftain. The barangay, society which ordinarily numbered no more than a few hundred individuals, was usually the largest stable economic and political unit.

Within the barangay, the status system, though not rigid, appears to have consisted of three broad classes: the *datu* and his family and the nobility, freeholders, and "dependents." This third category consisted of three levels— sharecroppers, debt peons, and war captives—with the last two levels being termed slaves by Spanish observers. The slave status was inherited but, through manumission and interclass marriage, seldom extended over more than two generations. The fluidity of the social system was, in part, the consequence of a bilateral kinship system in which lineage was reckoned equally through the male and female line. Marriage was apparently stable, though divorce was socially acceptable under certain circumstances.

Animism was the religion of the early Filipino, a mixture of monotheism and polytheism in which the latter dominated. The propitiation of evil spirits required numerous rituals, but there was no religious hierarchy. In religion, as in social structure and economic activity, there was considerable variation between—and even within—islands.

This pattern, however, began to change in the 15th century, when Islām was introduced to Mindanao and the Sulu islands through Brunei. Along with changes in religious beliefs and practices came new political and social institutions. By the mid-16th century two sultanates had been established, bringing under their sway a number of barangays. A powerful *datu* as far north as Manila embraced Islām. It was in the midst of this wave of Islāmic proselytism that the Spaniards arrived. Had they come a century later or had their motives been strictly commercial, Filipinos today might be a predominantly Muslim people.

THE SPANISH PERIOD

Spanish colonialist motives were not, however, strictly commercial. The Spanish at first viewed the Philippines as a stepping-stone to the riches of the Spice Islands, but, even after the Portuguese and Dutch had foreclosed that possibility, the Spaniards still maintained their presence in the archipelago.

The Portuguese navigator and explorer Ferdinand Magellan headed the first Spanish foray to the Philippines when he made landfall on Cebu in March 1521; a short time later he met an untimely death on the nearby island of Mactan. After three further expeditions had ended in disaster, Philip II, "the most Catholic of kings," for whom the islands are named, sent out Miguel López de Legazpi, who established the first permanent Spanish settlement, in Cebu, in 1565. The Spanish city of Manila was founded in 1571, and by the end of the 16th century most of the coastal and lowland areas from Luzon to northern Mindanao were under Spanish control. Friars marched with soldiers and soon accomplished the nominal conversion to Roman Catholicism of all the natives under Spanish administration. But the Muslims of Mindanao and Sulu, whom the Spanish called Moros, were never completely subdued by Spain; it took a 20th-century U.S. army to accomplish that task.

Spanish rule for the first 100 years was exercised in most areas through a type of tax farming imported from the Americas known as the encomienda. But abusive treatment of the native tribute payers and neglect of religious instruction by encomenderos, as well as frequent withholding of revenues from the crown, led to the abandonment of the system by the end of the 17th century. The governor general, himself appointed by the king, began to appoint his own civil and military governors to rule directly.

Central government in Manila retained a medieval cast until the 19th century, and the governor general was so powerful that he was often likened to an independent monarch. He dominated the Audiencia, or high court, was captain general of the armed forces, and enjoyed the privilege of engaging in commerce for private profit.

Manila dominated the islands not only as the political capital. The galleon trade with Acapulco, Mex., assured Manila's commercial primacy as well. This exchange of Chinese silks for Mexican silver kept in Manila those Spaniards seeking quick profit, and it also attracted a large Chinese community. The Chinese, despite periodic massacres at the hands of suspicious Spaniards, persisted and soon established a dominance of commerce that they have never relinquished.

Manila was also the ecclesiastical capital of the Philippines. The governor general was civil head of the church in the islands, but the archbishop vied with him for political

The encomienda

supremacy. In the late 17th and 18th centuries, buttressed with the legal status of lieutenant governor, the archbishop frequently won. Augmenting their political power, religious orders, Roman Catholic hospitals and schools, and bishops acquired great wealth, mostly in land. Royal grants and devises formed the core of their holdings, but many arbitrary extensions were made beyond the boundaries of the original grants.

The power of the church derived not simply from wealth and official status. The priests and friars had a command of native languages rare among lay Spaniards, and in the provinces they outnumbered civil officials. Thus, they were an invaluable source of information to the colonial government. The cultural goal of the Spanish clergy was nothing less than the full Christianization and Hispanization of the Filipino. In the first decades of missionary work, native animism was vigorously suppressed; old practices were not tolerated. But as the Christian laity grew in number and the zeal of the clergy waned, it became more and more difficult to prevent the preservation of ancient beliefs and customs under Roman Catholic garb. Thus, even in the area of religion, pre-Spanish Filipino culture was not entirely destroyed.

Power of the church

Economic and political institutions were also altered under Spanish impact but perhaps less thoroughly than in the religious realm. The priests tried to move all the people into pueblos, or villages, surrounding the great stone churches. But the dispersed demographic patterns of the old barangays largely persisted. Nevertheless, the *datu*'s once hereditary position became subject to Spanish appointment.

Agricultural technology changed very slowly until the late 18th century, as shifting cultivation gradually gave way to more intensive sedentary farming, partly under the guidance of the friars. The socioeconomic consequences of the Spanish policies that accompanied this shift reinforced class differences. The *datu*s and other representatives of the old noble class took advantage of the introduction of the Western concept of absolute ownership of land to claim, as their own, fields cultivated by their various retainers, even though traditional land rights had been limited to usufruct. These heirs of pre-Spanish nobility were known as the *principalia* and played an important role in the friar-dominated local government.

THE 19TH CENTURY

By the late 18th century, political and economic changes in Europe were finally beginning to affect Spain and, thus, the Philippines. Important as a stimulus to trade was the gradual elimination of the monopoly enjoyed by the galleon to Acapulco. The last galleon arrived in Manila in 1815, and by the mid-1830s Manila was open to foreign merchants almost without restriction. The demand for Philippine sugar and abaca, or hemp, grew apace, and the volume of exports to Europe expanded even further after the completion of the Suez Canal in 1869.

The growth of commercial agriculture resulted in the appearance of a new class. Alongside the landholdings of the church and the rice estates of the pre-Spanish nobility there arose haciendas of coffee, hemp, and sugar, often the property of enterprising Chinese-Filipino mestizos. Some of the families that gained prominence in the 19th century still play an important part in Philippine economics and politics.

Not until 1863 was there public education in the Philippines, and even then the church controlled the curriculum. Less than 20 percent of those who went to school could read and write Spanish, and far fewer could speak it properly. The limited higher education in the colony was entirely under clerical direction, but by the 1880s many sons of the wealthy were sent to Europe to study. There, nationalism and a passion for reform blossomed in the liberal atmosphere. Out of this talented group of overseas Filipino students arose the so-called Propaganda Movement. Magazines, poetry, and pamphleteering flourished. José Rizal, this movement's most brilliant figure, produced two political novels—*Noli me tangere* (1886; *The Social Cancer*) and *El filibusterismo* (1891; *The Reign of Greed*)—which had a wide impact in the Philippines.

In 1892 Rizal returned home and formed the Liga Filipina, a modest reform-minded society, loyal to Spain, that breathed no word of independence. But Rizal was quickly arrested by the overly fearful Spaniards, exiled to a remote island in the south, and finally executed in 1896. Meanwhile, within the Philippines there had developed a firm commitment to independence among a somewhat less privileged class.

The Katipunan

Shocked by the arrest of Rizal in 1892, these activists quickly formed the Katipunan under the leadership of Andres Bonifacio, a self-educated warehouseman. The Katipunan was dedicated to the expulsion of the Spaniards from the islands, and preparations were made for armed revolt. Filipino rebels had been numerous in the history of Spanish rule, but now for the first time they were inspired by nationalist ambitions and possessed the education that made success a real possibility.

THE PHILIPPINE REVOLUTION

In August 1896, Spanish friars uncovered evidence of the Katipunan's plans, and its leaders were forced into premature action. Revolts broke out in several provinces around Manila. After months of fighting, severe Spanish retaliation forced the revolutionary armies to retreat to the hills. In December 1897 a truce was concluded with the Spaniards. Emilio Aguinaldo, a municipal mayor and commander of the rebel forces, was paid a large sum and was allowed to go to Hong Kong with other leaders; the Spaniards promised reforms as well. But reforms were very slow in coming, and small bands of rebels, distrustful of Spanish promises, kept their arms; clashes grew more frequent.

Meanwhile, war had broken out between Spain and the United States. After the U.S. naval victory at Manila Bay in May 1898, Aguinaldo and his entourage returned to the Philippines with the help of Admiral George Dewey. Confident of U.S. support, he reorganized his forces and soon liberated several towns south of Manila. Independence was declared on June 12, which is now celebrated as Independence Day. In September a constitutional congress met in Malolos, north of Manila, drawing up a fundamental law derived from European and Latin-American precedents. A government was formed on the basis of that constitution in January 1899, with Aguinaldo as president.

Meanwhile, U.S. troops had landed and, with important Filipino help, forced the capitulation in August 1898 of the Spanish commander in Manila. The Americans, however, would not let Filipino forces enter the city. It was soon apparent to Aguinaldo and his advisers that earlier expressions of sympathy for Filipino independence by Dewey and U.S. consular officials had little significance. They felt betrayed.

U.S. commissioners to the peace negotiations in Paris had been instructed to demand the cession of the Philippines to the United States; such cession was confirmed with the signing of the peace treaty on Dec. 10, 1898. Ratification followed in the U.S. Senate in February 1899, but with only one vote more than the required two-thirds. Arguments of "manifest destiny" could not overwhelm a determined anti-imperialist minority.

War against the United States

By the time the treaty was ratified, hostilities had already broken out between American and Filipino forces. Since Filipino leaders did not recognize U.S. sovereignty over the islands and U.S. commanders gave no weight to Filipino claims of independence, the conflict was inevitable. It took two years of counterinsurgency warfare and some wise conciliatory moves in the political arena to break the back of the nationalist resistance. Aguinaldo was captured in March 1901 and shortly thereafter appealed to his countrymen to accept U.S. rule.

The Filipino revolutionary movement had had two goals, national and social. The first goal, independence, though realized briefly, was frustrated by the American decision to continue administering the islands. The goal of fundamental social change, manifest in the nationalization of friar lands by the Malolos Republic, was ultimately frustrated by the power and resilience of entrenched institutions. Share tenants who had rallied to Aguinaldo's cause, partly for economic reasons, merely exchanged one landlord for

another. In any case, the proclamation of a republic in 1898 had marked the Filipinos as the first Asian people to try to throw off European colonialism.

THE PERIOD OF U.S. INFLUENCE

The juxtaposition of U.S. democracy and imperial rule over a subject people was sufficiently jarring to most Americans that, from the beginning, the training of Filipinos for self-government and ultimate independence—the Malolos Republic was conveniently ignored—was an essential rationalization for U.S. hegemony in the islands. Differences between Democratic and Republican policies focused on the speed with which self-government should be extended and the date on which independence should be granted.

In 1899 President William McKinley sent Cornell University president Jacob G. Schurman at the head of a five-man fact-finding commission to the Philippines. Schurman reported back that Filipinos wanted ultimate independence, but this had no immediate impact on policy. McKinley sent out the Second Philippine Commission in 1900, under William Howard Taft; by July 1901 it had established civil government.

In 1907 the Philippine Commission, which had been acting as both legislature and governor general's Cabinet, became the upper house of a bicameral body. The new 80-member Philippine Assembly was directly elected by a somewhat restricted electorate from single-member districts, making it the first elective legislative body in Southeast Asia. When Governor General Francis B. Harrison appointed a Filipino majority to the Commission in 1913, the American voice in the legislative process was further reduced.

Harrison was the only governor general appointed by a Democratic president in the first 35 years of U.S. rule. He had been sent by Woodrow Wilson with specific instructions to prepare the Philippines for ultimate independence, a goal that he enthusiastically supported. During Harrison's term, a Democratic Congress in Washington hastened to fulfill long-standing campaign promises to the same end. The Jones Act, passed in 1916, would have fixed a definite date for the granting of independence if the Senate had had its way, but the House prevented such a move. In its final form the act merely stated that it was the "purpose of the people of the United States" to recognize Philippine independence "as soon as a stable government can be established therein." Its greater importance was as a milestone in the development of Philippine autonomy. Under Jones Act provisions, the Commission was abolished and was replaced by a 24-member Senate, almost wholly elected. The electorate was expanded to include all literate males.

Some substantial restrictions on Philippine autonomy remained, however. Defense and foreign affairs remained exclusive U.S. prerogatives. American direction of Philippine domestic affairs was exercised primarily through the governor general and the executive branch of insular government. There was little more than one decade of thoroughly U.S. administration in the islands, however—too short a time in which to establish lasting patterns. Whereas Americans formed 51 percent of the civil service in 1903, they were only 29 percent in 1913 and 6 percent in 1923. By 1916 Filipino dominance in both the legislative and judicial branches of government also served to restrict the U.S. executive and administrative roles.

By 1925 the only American left in the governor general's Cabinet was the secretary of public instruction, who was also the lieutenant governor general. This is one indication of the high priority given education in U.S. policy. In the first few years of U.S. rule, hundreds of schoolteachers came from the United States. But Filipino teachers were trained so rapidly that by 1927 they constituted nearly all of the 26,200 in public schools. The school population expanded fivefold in a generation; education consumed one-half of governmental expenditures at all levels, and educational opportunity in the Philippines was greater than in any other colony in Asia.

U.S. educational policy

As a consequence of this pedagogical explosion, literacy doubled to nearly 50 percent in the 1930s, and educated

Filipinos acquired a common language and a linguistic key to Western civilization. By 1939, 27 percent of the population could speak English, a larger percentage than for any of the native dialects. Perhaps more important was the new avenue of upward social mobility that education offered. In educational policy was found the only successful U.S. effort to establish a socio-cultural basis for political democracy.

American attempts to create equality of economic opportunity were more modest and less successful. In a predominantly agricultural country the pattern of landownership is crucial. The trend toward greater concentration, which began in the 19th century, continued during the American period, despite some legal barriers. Vast American-owned plantations were forestalled, but legal restrictions had little effect on those politically well-connected Filipinos who were intent on amassing fortunes. The percentage of farmers under share tenancy doubled between 1900 and 1935; and the frustration of the tenants erupted in three small rebellions in central Luzon during the 1920s and 1930s.

Nor was U.S. trade policy conducive to the diffusion of economic power. From 1909 the Payne–Aldrich Tariff Act allowed free entry of Philippine products into the U.S. market; at the same time U.S. products, mostly manufactured, were exempted from tariff in the Philippines. The free flow of U.S. imports was a powerful deterrent to industrial growth. Export agriculture, especially sugar, prospered in the protected U.S. market. Owners of mills and large plantations profited most, thus reinforcing the political dominance of the landed elite.

American preparation of the Philippines for democratic self-government suffered from an inherent contradiction, perhaps not recognized at the time. Transferring governmental responsibility to those capable of undertaking it was not consistent with building a social and economic base for political democracy. Self-government meant, of necessity, assumption of power by those Filipinos who were already in positions of leadership in society. But these men came for the most part from the landed elite; preservation of their political and economic position was incompatible with equalization of opportunity. Even the expansion of an educated middle class did not necessarily result in a transformation of the pattern of power. Most middle-class aspirants for political leadership adjusted to the values and the practices of the existing power elite.

Formation of political parties

Filipino leaders quickly and skillfully utilized the opportunities for self-government that the Americans opened to them. The Filipino political genius was best reflected in an extralegal institution—the political party. The first party, the Federal Party, was U.S.-backed and stressed cooperation with the overlords, even to the point of statehood for the Philippines. But, when openly nationalist appeals were allowed in the 1907 election, the Nacionalista Party, advocating independence, won overwhelmingly. The Federalists survived with a new name, Progressives, and a new platform, ultimate independence after social reform. But neither the Progressives nor their successors in the 1920s, the Democrats, ever gained more than one-third of the seats in the legislature. The Nacionalista Party under the leadership of Sergio Osmeña and Manuel Quezon dominated Philippine politics from 1907 until independence.

More significant than the competition between the Nacionalistas and their opposition was the continuing rivalry between Osmeña and Quezon. In fact, understanding this personality conflict provides more insight into the realities of prewar Philippine politics than any examination of policy or ideology.

In 1933 the U.S. Congress passed the Hare–Hawes–Cutting Act, which set a date for Philippine independence. The act was a fulfillment of the vague pledge in the Jones Act; it was also responsive to the demands of a series of "independence missions" sent to Washington by the Philippine legislature. But this unprecedented transfer of sovereignty was decided upon in the dark days of the Great Depression—and with the help of some incongruous allies. The Depression had caused American farm interests to look desperately for relief, and those who suffered real or imaginary hurt from the competition of Philippine products sought to exclude those products. They had already failed in a direct attempt to amend the tariff on Philippine imports but found that the respectable cloak of the advocacy of independence increased the effectiveness of their efforts. Tied to independence was the end of free entry into American markets of Philippine sugar, coconut oil, rope, and other less important items. That these economic interests were able to accomplish what they did is partly explainable by the fact that their political clout was great compared to that of the small group of American traders and investors in the Philippines.

The Philippine legislature rejected the Hare–Hawes–Cutting Act, apparently as a result of the Osmeña–Quezon feud, much to the displeasure of American officialdom. But, when Quezon came to Washington the following year to work for a new bill, the same alliance of forces in the U.S. Congress obliged by producing the almost identical Tydings–McDuffie Act. It was endorsed by Quezon and accepted with alacrity by the Manila legislature. It provided for a 10-year commonwealth during which the U.S. would retain jurisdiction over defense and foreign affairs. Filipinos were to draft their own constitution, subject to the approval of the U.S. president.

A constitutional convention was quickly elected, a constitution framed (which bore a strong resemblance to its U.S. model), and the document approved by plebiscite and by President Franklin D. Roosevelt. The last governor general, Frank Murphy, became the first high commissioner, with more of a diplomatic than a governing role. The commonwealth was inaugurated on Nov. 15, 1935. The Nacionalista Party patched up its internal quarrels and nominated Quezon for president and Osmeña for vice president. They were elected overwhelmingly.

The commonwealth period was intended to be devoted to preparation for economic and political independence and perfection of democratic institutions. But even before the tragic events of 1941 the transition did not run smooth.

The Common-wealth

WORLD WAR II

Japanese aggression in China prompted much attention to military preparedness. Nearly one-fourth of the national budget was devoted to defense. General Douglas MacArthur, retiring as army chief of staff in Washington, was called by President Quezon to direct plans and preparations. Meanwhile, agrarian unrest festered, and leftist political activity grew. Quezon pushed significant reform legislation through the National Assembly, but implementation was feeble, despite the rapid accumulation of power in his hands.

The Japanese attack of Dec. 8, 1941, came at a time when the U.S. military buildup had hardly begun. Before Christmas, Manila was declared an "open city," while Quezon and Osmeña were evacuated to MacArthur's headquarters on Corregidor. Despite a desire, at one point, to return to Manila in order to surrender, Quezon was persuaded to leave the Philippines in March on a U.S. submarine; he was never to return. Osmeña also went. Filipino and American forces, under General Jonathan M. Wainwright, surrendered in May 1942. An Executive Commission, made up of more than 30 members of the old Filipino political elite, had been cooperating with Japanese military authorities in Manila since January.

The Executive Commission lasted until September 1943, when it was superseded by an "independent Philippine Republic." The president, chosen by the Japanese, was José Laurel, former associate justice of the Commonwealth Supreme Court and the only Filipino to hold an honorary degree from Tokyo Imperial University. More than half of the Commonwealth Senate and more than one-third of the House served at one time in the Japanese-sponsored regime. Yet collaboration with Japan was neither as willing nor as widespread as elsewhere in Southeast Asia.

The "independent Philippine Republic" under the Japanese

Even before the fall of Bataan Peninsula in April 1942, guerrilla units were formed throughout the Philippines. Most were led by middle-class officers and were enthusiastically pro-United States; in central Luzon, however, a major force was the Hukbalahap, which, under Communist leadership, capitalized on earlier agrarian unrest. Though in a number of instances collaborators secretly assisted guerrillas, many guerrillas in the hills were bitter against those who appeared to benefit from the occupation. The differences between the two groups became an important factor in early postwar politics.

Soon after the U.S. landings on Leyte in October 1944, commanded by MacArthur, civil government was returned to the Commonwealth, at least in name. Sergio Osmeña, who had become president in exile on the death of Quezon in August, had few resources to deal with the problems at hand, however. Osmeña's role was complicated by the fact that MacArthur chose to lionize a leading collaborator who had also been in contact with U.S. military intelligence, Manuel A. Roxas. As president of the Senate, Roxas became, in effect, MacArthur's candidate for president. Roxas was nominated in January 1946 in a separate convention of the "liberal wing" of the Nacionalista Party, as it was first called. Thus was born the Philippines' second major political party, the Liberals.

Osmeña, though he had the advantages of incumbency, was old and tired and did not fully use the political tools he possessed. In April, Roxas was elected by a narrow margin. The following month he was inaugurated as the last chief executive of the Commonwealth, and on July 4, when the Republic of the Philippines was proclaimed, he became its first president.

THE EARLY REPUBLIC

Roxas, as expected, extended amnesty to all major collaborators with Japan. In the campaign for the election of 1949 there was an attempt to raise the collaboration issue against José Laurel, the Nacionalista presidential candidate, but it was not effective. In the fluidity of Philippine politics, "guerrillas" and "collaborators" were by that time to be found on both sides of all political fences.

The Philippines had gained independence in the "ashes of victory." Intense fighting, especially around Manila in the last days of the Japanese retreat, had nearly destroyed the capital. The economy generally was in disarray. Rehabilitation aid was obviously needed, and President Roxas was willing to accept some onerous conditions placed implicitly and explicitly by the U.S. Congress. The Bell Act in the United States extended free trade with the Philippines for eight years, to be followed by 20 years of gradually increasing tariffs. The United States demanded and received a 99-year lease on a number of Philippine military and naval bases in which U.S. authorities had virtual territorial rights. And finally, as a specific requirement for release of U.S. war-damage payments, the Philippines had to amend its constitution to give U.S. citizens equal rights with Filipinos in the exploitation of natural resources—the so-called Parity Amendment.

The changing character of Philippine–U.S. relations has been a major theme in postwar Philippine history. The trend has been toward weakening of the link, achieved partly by diversification of Philippine external ties and partly by more articulate anti-American feeling. Economic nationalism, though first directed against the local Chinese community's dominance of retail trade, by the 1950s was focused on the special status of American business firms.

At independence, the military ties with the United States were as strong as the economic ones. Filipino troops fought against Communist forces in Korea, and noncombatant engineers augmented U.S. forces in the Vietnam War. Crucial to U.S. military action in Vietnam were bases in the Philippines. The Military Bases Agreement has been the greatest single cause of friction in relations between the United States and the Philippines. Since 1965, however, a series of agreements between the two countries have reduced the size and number of the U.S. bases and shortened base leases. In 1979 formal jurisdiction over the base areas passed to the Philippine government; and the constitution of 1987 formalized the process by which the bases agreement could be extended beyond the expiration in 1991 of base leases.

The nature and effectiveness of Filipino political institutions since independence has been a special concern of the former colonial power that helped establish them. For Filipinos, those institutions have determined the ability or inability to maintain domestic social order. Clumsy repression of dissent and the fraudulent election of the nation's

Situation at independence

second president, Elpidio Quirino, in 1949 set the stage for an intensification of the Communist-led Hukbalahap (Huk) Rebellion, which had begun in 1946. The rebellion also reflected a growing sense of social injustice among tenant farmers, especially in central Luzon. Suppression of the rebellion five years later, however, was attributable to American military aid as well as to the opening of the political process to greater mass participation, particularly during the campaign of Ramon Magsaysay, a uniquely charismatic figure in Filipino politics who was elected president in 1953. Magsaysay's attempts at social and economic reform failed largely because of the conservative outlook of the legislature and the bureaucracy. When Magsaysay died in a plane crash in 1957, leadership of the country fell to his vice president, Carlos P. Garcia. During Garcia's presidential term, and that of his reform-minded successor, Diosdado Macapagal (1961–65), unrest was usually channeled through the electoral process and peaceful protest.

Hukbalahap Rebellion

THE MARCOS REGIME AND AFTER

In November 1965, Ferdinand E. Marcos was elected to the presidency. His administration faced grave economic problems that were exacerbated by corruption, tax evasion, and smuggling.

In 1969 Marcos became the first elected president of the Philippines to win reelection. His campaign platform included the renegotiation of major treaties with the United States and trade with Communist countries. These promises reflected a change in the self-concept of the nation during the 1960s. The idea of the Philippines as an Asian outpost of Christianity was increasingly rejected in favour of the development of Asian cultural identity. Artists, musicians, and writers began to look to pre-Spanish themes for inspiration. More important was the trend toward seeking cultural identity through the national language, Pilipino. English remained the language of business, of most government documents, and of the greater part of university education. Demands that the government meet the social and economic needs of its citizenry continued.

A short-lived sign that the Filipino political system was again attempting to respond constructively to those needs was the choosing in 1970 of a widely representative Constitutional Convention in one of the most honest and peaceful elections in Philippine history. Large student demonstrations urged the convention to undertake a fundamental restructuring of political power.

Marcos, who was approaching the end of his constitutionally delimited eight years in office, had narrower goals: he pressed for the adoption of the parliamentary style of government, which would allow him to remain in power. He feared that the new constitution would not come into force before he lost the advantages of incumbency. At the same time, foreign investors, predominantly American, felt increased pressure from economic nationalists in the legislature.

Martial law. In September 1972 Marcos declared martial law, claiming that it was the last defense against the rising disorder caused by increasingly violent student demonstrations. One of his first actions was to arrest opposition politicians in Congress and the Constitutional Convention. Under martial law the regime was able to reduce violent urban crime, collect unregistered firearms, and suppress Communist insurgency in some areas. At the same time, a series of important new concessions were given to foreign investors, including a prohibition on strikes by organized labour, and a land-reform program was launched. In January 1973 Marcos proclaimed the ratification of a new constitution based on the parliamentary system, with himself as both president and prime minister. He did not, however, convene the interim legislature that was called for in the constitution.

Initial public reaction to martial law was mostly favourable except in Muslim areas of the south, where a separatist rebellion, led by the Moro National Liberation Front, broke out in 1973. Despite half-hearted attempts to negotiate a cease-fire, the rebellion continued to claim thousands of military and civilian casualties. Communist insurgency spread to new areas.

General disillusionment with martial law and with the consolidation of political and economic control by Marcos, his family, and close associates grew during the 1970s. Despite growth in the gross national product, workers' real income dropped, few farmers benefited from land reform, and the sugar industry was in confusion. The precipitous drop in sugar prices in the early 1980s, coupled with lower prices and demand for coconuts and coconut products—traditionally the most important export commodity—added to the country's economic woes; the government was forced to borrow large sums from the international banking community. Reports of widespread corruption began to surface with increasing frequency.

Elections for an interim National Assembly were finally held in 1978. The opposition—of which the primary group was led by the jailed former senator Benigno S. Aquino, Jr.—produced such a bold and popular campaign that the official results, which gave Marcos' opposition virtually no seats, were widely believed to have been illegally altered. In 1980 Aquino went into exile in the United States, and the following year, after announcing the suspension of martial law, Marcos won a virtually uncontested election for a new six-year term.

The downfall of Marcos and return of democratic government. The assassination of Aquino as he returned to Manila in August 1983 was generally thought to have been the work of the military; it became the focal point of a renewed and more heavily supported opposition to Marcos' rule. By late 1985 Marcos, under mounting pressure both inside and outside the Philippines, called a snap presidential election for February 1986. Corazon C. Aquino, Benigno's widow, became the candidate of a coalition of opposition parties. Marcos was declared the official winner; but strong public outcry over the election results precipitated a revolt that by the end of the month had driven Marcos from power. Aquino then assumed the presidency.

Election of 1986

Euphoria over the ouster of Marcos proved to be short-lived. The new government was faced with an enormous external debt, a severely depleted economy, and a growing threat from Moro and Communist insurgents. The Aquino administration also had to weather considerable internal dissension and repeated coup attempts during its early years in power. Aquino's great personal popularity and widespread international support were instrumental in establishing the new government. Shortly after taking office she abolished the constitution of 1973 and began ruling by decree. A new constitution was drafted and was ratified in February 1987 in a general referendum; legislative elections in May and the convening of a new bicameral congress in July marked the return of the form of government that had been present before the imposition of martial law in 1972.

The resumption of active partisan politics, however, was the beginning of the end of the coalition that had brought Aquino to power. Pro-Aquino candidates had won a sweeping victory in the 1987 legislative elections, but there was less support for her among those elected to provincial and local offices in early 1988.

For later developments in the history of the Philippines, see the *Britannica Book of the Year* section in the BRITANNICA WORLD DATA ANNUAL.

For coverage of related topics in the *Macropædia* and *Micropædia*, see the *Propædia*, sections 969 and 976.

BIBLIOGRAPHY

Physical and human geography: General works include FREDERICK L. WERNSTEDT and J.E. SPENCER, *The Philippine Island World: A Physical, Cultural, and Regional Geography* (1967); KEITH LIGHTFOOT, *The Philippines* (1973); FUND FOR ASSISTANCE TO PRIVATE EDUCATION, *The Philippine Atlas*, 2 vol. (1975); DAVID JOEL STEINBERG, *The Philippines, a Singular and a Plural Place* (1982); and FREDERICA M. BUNGE (ed.), *Philippines, A Country Study* (1984). FREDERICK L. WERNSTEDT et al., *Philippine Studies: Geography, Archeology, Psychology, and Literature* (1974); and DONN V. HART (ed.), *Philippine Studies: History, Sociology, Mass Media, and Bibliography* (1978), and *Philippine Studies: Political Science, Economics, and Linguistics* (1981), provide useful summaries and bibliographies. For current information, see *Philippine Yearbook*, published by the government. SYLVIA MAYUGA, *Philippines*, 6th ed., updated by ALFRED A. YUSON (1986), is a guidebook.

DOMINGO C. SALITA, *Geography and Natural Resources of the Philippines* (1974); and DOMINGO C. SALITA and DOMINADOR Z. ROSELL, *Economic Geography of the Philippines* (1980), contain information on the economic resources of the Philippines. Two studies by the World Bank, *Philippines: Industrial Development Strategy and Policies* (1980), and *Philippines: A Framework for Economic Recovery* (1987), analyze economic conditions in the 1980s. Agricultural development policies are examined in RENE E. OFRENEO, *Capitalism in Philippine Agriculture* (1980); CLAUDIO GONZALEZ-VEGA, *The Rural Banking System of the Philippines and the CB-IBRD Agricultural Credit Program* (1975); and *Vital Documents on Agrarian Reform in the New Society* (1979). For further information on development, see *Philippine Development Report* (irregular), published by the National Economic and Development Authority; and the *Philippine Statistical Yearbook*.

Social and cultural aspects are explored in MARY RACELIS HOLLNSTEINER (ed.), *Society, Culture, and the Filipino* (1979); LEONARD DAVIS, *The Philippines: People, Poverty, and Politics* (1987); ANDREW B. GONZALEZ, *Language and Nationalism: The Philippine Experience Thus Far* (1980); IRENE L. ORTIGAS and FELIX B. REGALADO, *Society and Culture in Rural Philippines*, rev. ed. (1978); ELENA YU and WILLIAM T. LIU, *Fertility and Kinship in the Philippines* (1980); ERIC S. CASINO, *The Filipino Nation* (1982); RENATO CONSTANTINO, *Neocolonial Identity and Counter-Consciousness: Essays on Cultural Decolonization* (1978); and GABRIEL CASAL et al., *The People and Art of the Philippines* (1981).

History: AUSTIN CRAIG and CONRADO BENITEZ, *Philippine Progress Prior to 1898* (1916), provides useful material on the period before the European presence in the archipelago. EUFRONIO M. ALIP, *Philippine History*, 10th rev. ed. (1974), and *Political and Cultural History of the Philippines*, new rev. ed., 2 vol. (1967), offer detailed coverage from the early period to the 20th century. RENATO CONSTANTINO, *The Philippines: A Past Revisited* (1975; U.S. title, *A History of the Philippines: From the Spanish Colonization to the Second World War*), and *The Philippines: The Continuing Past* (1978); and HELEN R. TUBANGUI et al., *The Filipino Nation: A Concise History of the Philippines* (1982), are general histories. A good discussion of the early Spanish period is offered in JOHN L. PHELAN, *The Hispanization of the Philippines: Spanish Aims and Filipino Responses, 1565–1700* (1959, reprinted 1967). See also PEDRO S. DE ACHÚTEGUI and MIGUEL A. BERNAD, *Religious Revolution in the Philippines*, 2 vol. (1960–66), and *Documents Relative to the Religious Revolution in the Philippines* (1971); and ELIODORO G. ROBLES, *The Philippines in the Nineteenth Century* (1969). The Philippines' involvement in World War II is discussed in CLARO M. RECTO, *Three Years of Enemy Occupation: The Issue of Political Collaboration in the Philippines* (1946); and DAVID JOEL STEINBERG, *Philippine Collaboration in World War II* (1967). Studies of the Marcos and post-Marcos eras include PRIMITIVO MIJARES, *The Conjugal Dictatorship of Ferdinand and Imelda Marcos* (1976); MONINA ALLAREY MERCADO (ed.), *People Power: The Philippine Revolution of 1986* (1986); GARY HAWES, *The Philippine State and the Marcos Regime: The Politics of Export* (1987); and JOHN BRESNAN (ed.), *Crisis in the Philippines: The Marcos Era and Beyond* (1986), a comprehensive collection of essays by Filipino and American writers. Relations between the Philippines and the United States are treated in PETER W. STANLEY, *A Nation in the Making: The Philippines and the United States, 1899–1921* (1974); EMILIO AGUINALDO and VICENTE ALBANO PACIS, *A Second Look at America* (1957); and PETER W. STANLEY (ed.), *Reappraising an Empire: New Perspectives on Philippine-American History* (1984).

(D.O.D.W./G.C.B.)

Philosophical Anthropology

The word anthropology was first used in the philosophical faculties of German universities at the end of the 16th century to refer to the systematic study of man as a physical and moral being. Philosophical anthropology is thus, literally, the systematic study of man conducted within philosophy or by the reflective methods characteristic of philosophy; it might in particular be thought of as being concerned with questions of the status of man in the universe, of the purpose or meaning of human life, and, indeed, with the issues of whether there is any such meaning and of whether man can be made an object of systematic study. But what actually falls under the term philosophical anthropology varies with conceptions of the nature and scope of philosophy. The fact that such disciplines, as physics, chemistry, and biology—which are now classified as natural sciences—were until the 19th century all branches of natural philosophy serves as a reminder that conceptions of philosophy have changed. Twentieth-century readings of philosophical anthropology are much narrower than those of previous centuries. Four possible meanings are now accepted: (1) the account of man that is contained in any comprehensive philosophy; (2) a particular philosophical orientation known as humanism (see HUMANISM), in which the study of man provides the foundation for all else—a position that has been prominent since the Renaissance; (3) a distinctive, 20th-century form of humanism that on occasion has claimed the label of "philosophical anthropology" for itself and that has taken the human condition, the personal being-in-the-world, as its starting point; and (4) any study of man that is regarded as unscientific. Philosophical anthropology has been used in the last sense by 20th-century antihumanists for whom it has become a term of abuse; antihumanists have insisted that if anthropology is to be possible at all it is possible only on the condition that it rejects the concept of the individual human subject. Humanism, in their eyes, yields only a prescientific, and hence a philosophical (or ideological), nonscientific anthropology.

By tracing the development of the philosophy of man, it will thus be possible to deal, in turn, with the four meanings of philosophical anthropology. First, however, it is necessary to discuss the concept of human nature, which is central to any anthropology and to philosophical debates about the sense in which and the extent to which man can be made an object of systematic, scientific study.

For coverage of related topics in the *Macropædia* and *Micropædia,* see the *Propædia,* Part Ten, Division V, Section 10/52.

This article is divided into the following sections:

THE CONCEPT OF HUMAN NATURE

The concept of human nature is a common part of everyday thought. The ordinary person feels that he comes to know human nature through the character and conduct of the people he meets. Behind what they do he recognizes qualities that often do not surprise him: he forms expectations as to the sort of qualities possessed by other human beings and about the ways they differ from, for example, dogs or horses. People are proud, sensitive, eager for recognition or admiration, often ambitious, hopeful or despondent, and selfish or capable of self-sacrifice. They take satisfaction in their achievements, have within them something called a conscience, and are loyal or disloyal. Experience in dealing with and observing people gives rise to a conception of a predictable range of conduct; conduct falling outside the range that is considered not to be worthy of a human is frequently regarded as inhuman or bestial whereas that which is exceptional—in that it lives up to standards which most people recognize but few achieve—is regarded as superhuman or saintly.

The common conception of human nature thus implicitly locates man on a scale of perfection, placing him somewhere above most animals but below saints, prophets, or angels. This idea was embodied in the theme, Hellenic in origin, of the Great Chain of Being—a hierarchical order ascending from the most simple and inert to the most complex and active: mineral, vegetable, animal, man, and finally divine beings superior to man. In the Middle Ages these divine beings constituted the various orders of angels, with God as the single, supremely perfect and omnipotent, ever-active being. There was a tendency in this theory to take for granted the commonality among all human beings, something by virtue of which they exhibit those characteristics by which people classify them as fully human, which differentiates them from all other animals, and which gives them their place in the order of things. Yet, as with many notions that are habitually employed, the request for a precise definition of "human nature" proves highly problematic.

The Greeks—most notably Plato and Aristotle—introduced the notion of form, nature, or essence as an explanatory, metaphysical concept. Variations on this concept were central to Western thought until the 17th century. Observation of the natural world raised the question of why creatures reproduced after their kind and could not be interbred at will and of why, for example, acorns grew into oaks and not into roses. To explain such phenomena it was postulated that the seeds, whether plant or animal, must each already contain within them the form, nature, or essence of the species from which they were derived and into which they would subsequently develop. This pattern of explanation is preserved in the modern biological concept of a genetic code that is embodied in the DNA molecular structure of each cell. But there are important differences between the modern concept of a genetic code and the older, Greek-derived concept of form or essence.

First, biologists are now able to locate, isolate, experimentally analyze, and manipulate DNA molecules in what has become known as genetic engineering. Being the structures responsible for physical development, DNA molecules represent the terms by which man can be biologically characterized. Forms or essences, on the other hand, were not observable; if they were granted any independent existence, it was as immaterial entities. The form, nature, or

Great
Chain of
Being

essence of man or of any other kind of being was posited as a principle present in the thing, determining its kind by producing in it an innate tendency to strive to develop into a perfect example of itself—to fulfill its nature and to realize its full potential as a thing of a given kind. This gave rise to a teleological, or purposive, view of the natural world in which developments were explained by reference to the goal toward which each natural thing, by its nature, strives; *i.e.,* by reference to the ideal form it seeks to realize. By contrast, the genetic structure present in each cell is now invoked to explain the subsequent development of an organism in a "mechanistic" and nonpurposive way, in which development is shown to be dependent upon and determined by preexisting structures and conditions.

Second, genetic mutability forms an essential part of modern evolutionary biology. Not only are there genetic differences between individuals of a given species to account for differences between them in features, such as coloration, but random genetic mutation in the presence of changing environmental conditions may result in alterations to the genetic constitution of the species as a whole. Thus, in evolutionary biological theory species are not stable; natural kinds do not have the fixed, immutable forms or essences characteristic of biology before the advent of evolutionary theory.

Within either framework, if human nature is understood simply as man's special form of that which is biologically inherited in all species, there remains the delicate problem of discovering, in any given case, exactly what role environment plays in determining the actual characteristics of mature members of the species. Even in the case of purely physiological characteristics this may be far from straightforward: for example, the extent to which diet, exercise, and conditions of work determine such things as susceptibility to heart disease and cancer remains the subject of intensive scientific investigation. In the case of behavioral and psychological characteristics, such as intelligence, the problems are multiplied to the point where they are no longer problems that can be answered by purely empirical investigation. There is room for much conceptual debate about what is meant by intelligence and over what tests, if any, can be supposed to yield a direct measure of this capacity, and thus provide evidence that an individual's level of intelligence is determined at birth (by nature) rather than by subsequent exposure to the environment (nurture) that conditions the development of all his capacities.

This debate—whether the variation in intelligence levels is a product of the conditions into which people all having the same initial potential are born, or whether it is a reflection of variations in the capacities with which they are born—is very closely related to the question of whether there is such a thing as human nature common to all human beings, or whether there are intrinsic differences among those whom we recognize as belonging to the biological species *Homo sapiens.* This is because, as the name *Homo sapiens* suggests, man is traditionally thought to be distinguished from and privileged above other animals by virtue of his possession of reason, or intellect. When the intellect is positively valued as that which is distinctively human and which confers superiority on man, the thought that different races of people differ by nature in their intellectual capacities has been used as a justification for a variety of racist attitudes and policies. Those of another race, of supposedly lesser intellectual development, are classified as less than fully human and therefore as needing to be accorded less than full human rights. Similarly, the thought that women are by nature intellectually inferior to men has been used as a justification for their domination by men, for refusing them education, and even for according them the legal status of property owned by men. On the other hand, if differences in adult intellectual capacity are regarded as a product of the circumstances in which potentially similar people are brought up, the attitude is to consider all as equally human but some as having been more privileged when growing up than others.

More radically, the evidence for variations in intelligence levels may be questioned by challenging the objectivity of the standards relative to which these levels are assessed. It may be argued that conceptions of what constitutes a ra-

tional or intelligent response to a situation or to a problem are themselves culturally conditioned, a product of the way in which the members of the group devising the tests and making the judgments have themselves been taught to think. Such an argument has the effect of undermining claims by any one human group to intellectual superiority over others, whether these others be their contemporaries or their own forebears. Hence, they may also be used to discredit any idea of a progressive development of human intellectual capacities.

These debates about intelligence and rationality provide an example of the complexity of the impact of evolutionary biology on conceptions of human nature, for the dominant traditions in Western thought about human nature have tended to concentrate attention more on what distinguishes man from other animals than on the strictly biological constitution that he largely shares with them. Possession of reason or intellect is far from being the only candidate considered for such a distinguishing characteristic. Man has been characterized as essentially a tool user, or fabricator (Homo faber), as essentially social, as essentially a language user, and so on. These represent differing views concerning the fundamental feature that gives rise to all the other qualities regarded as distinctively human and which serve to mark man off from other animals. These characteristics all centre on mental, intellectual, psychological—*i.e.,* nonphysiological—characteristics and thus leave scope for debate about the relation between mind and body. So long as this question remains open, and so long as mental or intellectual constitution remains the central consideration in discussions of human nature, the question of changes in—and of the possible evolution of—human nature will remain relatively independent of those devoted to physiological change and hence of strictly biological evolution.

Until the 15th century the standard assumption was that man had a fixed nature, one that determined both his place in the universe and his destiny. The Renaissance humanists, however, proclaimed that what distinguishes man from all other creatures is that he has no nature. This was a way of asserting that man's actions are not bound by laws of nature in the way that those of other creatures are. Man is capable of taking responsibility for his own actions because he has the freedom to exercise his will. This view received two subsequent interpretations.

First, the human character is indefinitely plastic; each individual is given determinate form by the environment in which he is born, brought up, and lives. In this case, changes or developments in human beings will be regarded as the product of social or cultural changes, changes that themselves are often more rapid than biological evolution. It is thus to disciplines such as history, politics, and sociology, rather than to biology, that one should look for an understanding of these processes. But if disciplines such as these must constitute the primary study of man, then the question of the extent to which this can be a strictly scientific study arises. The methods of history are not, and cannot be, those of the natural sciences. And the legitimacy of the claims of the so-called social or human sciences to genuine scientific status has frequently been called into question and remains a focus for debate.

Second, each individual is autonomous and must "make" himself. Assertion of the autonomy of man involves rejection of the possibility of discovering laws of human behaviour or of the course of history, for freedom is precisely not being bound by law, by nature. In this case, the study of man can never be parallel to the natural sciences with their theoretical structures based on the discovery of laws of nature. (M.E.T.)

Human nature (marginal note)

Intelligence (marginal note)

HISTORICAL BACKGROUND OF THE PHILOSOPHY OF MAN

In the tradition of Western thought up to the 20th century, the study of man has been regarded as a part of philosophy. Two sayings that have been adopted as mottoes by those who see themselves as engaged in philosophical anthropology date from the 5th century BC. These are: "Man is the measure of all things" (Protagoras) and "Know thyself" (a saying from the Delphic oracle, echoed by Heraclitus and Socrates, among others). Both reflect the specific orientation of philosophical anthropology as humanism, which takes man as its starting point and treats man and the study of man as the centre, or origin, on which all other disciplines ultimately depend.

Man, the world, and God have constituted three important foci of Western thought from the beginnings of its recorded history; the relative significance of these three themes, however, has varied from one epoch to another. Western thought has laid greater stress on the existence of the individual human being than have the great speculative systems of the East; in Brahmanism, for example, personal identity dissolves in the All. But even so it was not until the Renaissance that man became the primary focus of philosophical attention and that the study of human nature began to displace theology and metaphysics as "first philosophy"—the branch of philosophy that is regarded as forming the foundation for all subsequent philosophy and that provides the framework for all scientific investigation.

Ancient Greece. From late antiquity onward differing views of man were worked out within a framework that was laid down and given initial development by Plato and later by Aristotle. Plato and Aristotle concurred in according to metaphysics the status of first philosophy. Their differing views of man were a consequence of their differing metaphysical views.

Plato

Plato's metaphysics was dualistic: the everyday physical world of changeable things, which man comes to know by the use of his senses, is not the primary reality but is a world of appearances, or phenomenal manifestations, of an underlying timeless and unchanging reality, an immaterial realm of Forms that is knowable only by use of the intellect. This is the view expressed in the *Republic* in his celebrated metaphor of the cave, where the changeable physical world is likened to shadows cast on the wall of a cave by graven images. To know the real world the occupants of the cave must first turn around and face the graven images in the light that casts the shadows (*i.e.*, use their judgment instead of mere fantasy) and, second, must leave the cave to study the originals of the graven images in the light of day (stop treating their senses as the primary source of knowledge and start using their intellects). Similarly, human bodily existence is merely an appearance of the true reality of human being. The identity of a human being does not derive from the body but from the character of his or her soul, which is an immaterial (and therefore nonsexual) entity, capable of being reincarnated in different human bodies. There is thus a divorce between the rational/spiritual and the material aspects of human existence, one in which the material is devalued.

Aristotle

Aristotle, however, rejected Plato's dualism. He insisted that the physical, changeable world made up of concrete individual substances (people, horses, plants, stones, etc.) is the primary reality. Each individual substance may be considered to be a composite of matter and form, but these components are not separable, for the forms of changeable things have no independent existence. They exist only when materially instantiated. This general metaphysical view, then, undercut Plato's body–soul dualism. Aristotle dismissed the question of whether soul and body are one and the same as being as meaningless as the question of whether a piece of wax and the shape given to it by a seal are one. The soul is the form of the body, giving life and structure to the specific matter of a human being. According to Aristotle, all human beings are the same in respect to form (that which constitutes them as human), and their individual differences are to be accounted for by reference to the matter in which this common form is variously instantiated (just as the different properties of golf and squash balls are derived from the materials of which they are made, while their common geometrical properties are related to their similar size and shape). This being so, it is impossible for an individual human soul to have any existence separate from the body. Reincarnation is thus ruled out as a metaphysical impossibility. Further, the physical differences between men and women become philosophically significant, the sex of a person becoming a crucial part of his or her identity.

Although Plato and Aristotle gave a different metaphys-

ical status to forms, their role in promoting and giving point to investigations of human nature was very similar. They both agreed that it is necessary to have knowledge of human nature in order to determine when and how human life flourishes. It is through knowledge of shared human nature that we become aware of the ideals at which we should aim, achieved by learning what constitutes fulfillment of our distinctively human potential and the conditions under which this becomes possible. These ideals are objectively determined by our nature. But we are privileged in being endowed with the intellectual capacities that make it possible for us to have knowledge of this nature. Development of our intellectual capacities is thus a necessary part and precondition of a fulfilled human existence.

Medieval period. Western medieval culture was dominated by the Christian Church. This influence was naturally reflected in the philosophy of the period. Theology, rather than metaphysics, tended to be given primacy, even though many of the structures of Greek philosophy, including its metaphysics, were preserved. The metaphysics of form and matter was readily assimilable into Christian thought, where forms became ideas in the mind of God, the patterns according to which he created and continues to sustain the universe. Christian theology, however, modified the positions, requiring some sort of compromise between Platonic and Aristotelian views. The creation story in the book of Genesis made man a creature among other creatures, but not a creature like other creatures; man was the product of the final act of divine initiative, was given responsibility for the Garden of Eden, and had the benefit of a direct relationship with his creator. The Fall and redemption, the categories of sin and grace, thus concern only the descendants of Adam, who were given a nature radically different from that of the animals and plants over which they were given dominion. Man alone can, after a life in this world, hope to participate in an eternal life that is far more important than the temporal life that he will leave. Thus, belief in a life after death makes it impossible to regard man as wholly a natural being and entails that the physical world now inhabited by man is not the sole, or even the primary, reality. Yet, the characteristically Christian doctrine of the resurrection of the body also entails that the human body cannot be regarded as being of significance only in the mortal, physical world.

Against the background of these constraints, Christian philosophy first, through the writings of St. Augustine, gave prominence to Platonic views. But this emphasis was superseded in the 12th century by the Aristotelianism of St. Thomas Aquinas. Augustine's God is a wholly immaterial, supremely rational, transcendent creator of the universe. The twofold task of the Christian philosopher, a lover of wisdom, is to seek knowledge of the nature of God and of his own soul, the human self. For Augustine the soul is not the entire man but his better part. There remains a Platonic tendency to regard the body as a prison for the soul and a mark of man's fallen state. One of the important consequences of Augustine's own pursuit of these two endeavours was the emphasis he came to place on the significance of free will. He argued that since the seat of the will was reason, when people exercise their will, they are acting in the image of God, the supreme rational being. Thomas Aquinas, while placing less emphasis on the will, also regarded man as acting in the image of God to the extent that he exercises and seeks to fulfill his intelligent nature. But he rejected the Platonic tendency to devalue the body, insisting that it is part of the concept of man that he have flesh and bone, as well as a soul.

But whatever the exact balance struck in the relation between the mind and body, the view of man was first and foremost as a creature of God; man was privileged by having been created in the image of God and given the gift of reason in virtue of which he also has free will and must take the burden of moral responsibility for his own actions. In order to fulfill his distinctively human nature man must thus order his thoughts and actions in such a way as to reflect the supremacy of religious values.

In popular medieval culture there was also, however, a strong undercurrent of thoroughly fatalistic thought. This

Man as a creature of God

was reflected in the popularity of astrology and alchemy, both of which appealed to the idea that events on Earth are governed by the influence of the heavenly bodies.

Renaissance. It was in the cultural context of the Renaissance, and in particular with the Italian humanists and their imitators, that the centre of gravity of reflective thought descended from heaven to earth, with man, his nature, and his capacities and limitations becoming a primary focus of philosophical attention. This gave rise to the humanism that constitutes philosophical anthropology in the second sense. Man did not thereby cease to view himself within the context of the world, nor did he deny the existence of God; he did, however, disengage himself sufficiently from the bonds of cosmic determination and divine authority to become a centre of interest in his own eyes. In ancient literature the educated people of the West rediscovered a clear conscience instead of the guilty conscience of Christianity; at the same time, the great inventions and discoveries suggested that man could take pride in his accomplishments and regard himself with admiration. The themes of the dignity and excellence of man were prominent in Italian humanist thought and can be found clearly expressed in Giovanni Pico della Mirandola's influential *De hominis dignitate oratio* (Oration on the Dignity of Man), written in 1486. In this work Pico expresses a view of man that breaks radically with Greek and Christian tradition: what distinguishes man from the rest of creation is that he has been created without form and with the ability to make of himself what he will. Being without form or nature he is not constrained, fated, or determined to any particular destiny. Thus, he must choose what he will become. (In the words of the 20th-century existentialists, man is distinguished by the fact that for him existence precedes essence.) In this way man's distinctive characteristic becomes his freedom; he is free to make himself in the image of God or in the image of beasts.

This essentially optimistic view of man was a product of the revival of Neoplatonist thought. Its optimism is based on a view of man as at least potentially a nonnatural, godlike being. But this status is now one that must be earned; man must win his right to dominion over nature and in so doing earn his place beside God in the life hereafter. He must learn both about himself and about the natural world in order to be able to achieve this. This was, however, only one of two streams of humanist thought. The other (more Aristotelian) was essentially more pessimistic and skeptical, stressing the limitations on man's intellectual capacities. There is an insistence on the need to be reconciled to the fact of man's humanity rather than to persist in taking seriously his superhuman pretensions and aspirations. These two differently motivated movements to focus attention on man himself, on his nature, his abilities, his earthly condition, and his relation to his material environment became more clearly articulated in the 16th and 17th centuries in the opposition between the rationalist and empiricist approaches to philosophy.

THE 16TH AND 17TH CENTURIES: THE RISE OF SCIENTIFIC THOUGHT

Rationalism versus skepticism. The thought of Michel de Montaigne, the 16th-century French skeptical author of the *Essais* (1580–95; *Essays*), represented one of the first attempts at anthropological reflection (*i.e.,* reflection centred on man, which explores his different aspects in a spirit of empirical investigation that is freed from all ties to dogma). Skepticism, the adoption of an empirical approach, and liberation from dogmatic authority are linked themes stemming from the more pessimistic views of man's capacity for knowledge. The emphasis on man's humanity—on the limited nature of his capacities—leads to a denial that he can, even by the use of reason, transcend the realm of appearances; the only form of knowledge available to him is experimental knowledge, gained in the first instance by the use of the senses. The effect of this skeptical move was twofold. The first effect was a liberation from the dogmatic authority of claims to knowledge of a reality behind appearances and of moral codes based on them; skeptical arguments were to the effect that human beings are so constituted that such knowledge must

always be unavailable to them. The second effect was a renewal of attention to and interest in the everyday world of appearances, which now becomes the only possible object of human knowledge and concern. The project of seeking knowledge of a reality behind appearances must be abandoned because it is beyond the scope of human understanding. And this applies as much to man himself as to the rest of the natural world; he can be known only experientially, as he appears to himself.

The anthropology of Montaigne began with a turning in upon himself; it gave priority to that reality which was within. Montaigne, however, was also witness to a renewal of knowledge brought about by numerous discoveries that made the horizons of the traditional universe expand greatly. For him, self-awareness already reflected an awareness of the surrounding world; it wondered about the "savages" of America and about the cannibals that were so different from him and yet so near; it compared the intelligence of man with that of beasts and accepted the idea of a relationship between animal existence and human existence. The idea that moral codes are the work of man, rather than reflective of an objective order, opened up the possibility of recognizing the legitimate existence of a plurality of codes and thus of the empirical study—rather than an immediate condemnation and rejection—of the customs of others.

Work of Descartes. By contrast, the work of the 17th-century French philosopher René Descartes represented a continuation of the theme of optimism about man's capacities for knowledge. Descartes explicitly set out, in his *Meditations* (first published in 1641), to beat the skeptics at their own game. He used their methods and arguments in order to vindicate claims to be able to have nonexperimental knowledge of a reality behind appearances. The *Meditations* thus also begins with a turning in of Descartes upon himself but with the aim of finding there something that would lead beyond the confines of his own mind.

Cartesianism occupies a key position in the history of modern Western philosophy; Descartes is treated as a founding father by most of its now diverse traditions. His work is characteristic of the philosophical effort of the 17th century, which was engaged in a struggle to achieve a synthesis between old established orders and the newly proclaimed freedoms that were based on a skeptical rejection of the older orders. There are undeniable tensions in the philosophy of this period that are the product of various unsuccessful attempts to reconcile two very different views of man in relation to God and the world.

The first, the authoritarian view, was that inherited from medieval philosophy and from Thomist theology. It derived its ideal of human freedom from the Stoic conception of the wise man, who, in the 17th century was called a man of *honestas* (the French concept of *honnêteté*). The man of *honestas* seeks freedom in the discovery of and obedience to the order and law on which the world is grounded. He believes that there is such a law, that he has a "place" in the scheme of things, and that he is bound to his fellow human beings by that nature through which he participates in this higher order. He tends to look to the authorities—whether these be church, state, or classical texts—for knowledge of this order, for it is not to be found at the level of experience; it is a "higher" order. His worldview is derived from a mixture of Platonic and Aristotelian (realist) metaphysics.

The second, the libertarian view, was that of the skeptical humanists—individualists and freethinkers, skeptical of any preestablished order, or at least of man's ability to know what it is or might be. The skeptical humanist is therefore untrammeled by it. He deploys skeptical arguments to release the individual from the constraints and demands of outer authorities. He is free to do what he wills or desires and to make his own destiny, for there can be no knowledge of objective norms. Human knowledge is limited to experience, to what is sensed, and people must therefore make their own order within experience. His view is descended from the *via moderna* of the medieval philosopher William of Ockham and the nominalists.

The synthesis sought was a position that would incorporate recognition of the individual and of his freedom under

(margin left)
Rise of humanism

(margin left)
The thought of Montaigne

(margin right)
Two views of man in relation to God

universal principles of order, a reconciliation of will with reason. This was sought via a nonauthoritarian conception of objective knowledge, which was the same conception that gave rise to modern science. This required, on the one hand, arguments to combat those of the skeptical freethinkers—arguments that demonstrated that there was an objective order external to human thought and that humans have the capacity not merely to know of its existence but also to discover something of its nature. On the other hand, it was necessary to establish, against the authorities, that each individual, insofar as he is rational, has the capacity to acquire knowledge for himself, by the proper use of his reason. It is this second requirement that produced numerous treatises on the scope and limits of human understanding and on the method of acquiring knowledge. The focus was now firmly fixed on the nature of human thought and on the procedures available to it.

Descartes utilized the skeptic's own arguments to urge a meditative turning inward. This inward journey was designed to show that each human being can come to knowledge of his intellectual self and that as he does so he will find within himself the idea of God, the mark of his creator, the mark that assures him of the existence of an objective order and of the objective validity of his rational faculties. The foundation and starting point of Cartesian knowledge is, for each individual, within himself, in his experience of the certainty that he must have of his own existence and in the idea of a perfect, infinite being, in other words, an idea that he finds within himself, of a being whose essence entails God's existence, and of whose existence man can thus be assured on the basis of his idea of God.

Descartes thus preserved and built on Montaigne's emphasis on self-consciousness, and this is what marks the changed orientation in philosophy that constitutes philosophical anthropology in the stricter, second sense. As the French scientist and religious philosopher Blaise Pascal realized, the question had now become one of whether man finds within himself the basis of loyalty to a universal order of reason and law with which his own thought and will is continuous, or whether he finds, by inner examination, that order, at least insofar as it can be known, is relative to his feeling, desire, and will.

Failure of Descartes's proofs of the existence of God

The attempt to regain an objective order by looking inward apparently fails with the failure of Descartes's proofs of the existence of God, proofs that his contemporaries (even those who, like Gottfried Wilhelm Leibniz, were sympathetic to many aspects of the project) were quick to criticize. Reaction to this failure was twofold. In the work of rationalist philosophers, such as Spinoza, Leibniz, and Malebranche, there is a return to the classical Greek approach to philosophy through metaphysics. Empiricists, such as Locke, Condillac, and Hume, on the other hand, retain the Cartesian, introspective basis seeking what Hume calls a mitigated skepticism. This is a position that recognizes essential limitations placed on human cognitive capacities by assuming that experience is the only source of knowledge, but that affirms the value of the knowledge so gained and seeks to define the project of natural science as a quest for objective order within this domain.

Work of Locke. John Locke, for instance, argued that while man cannot prove that the material world exists, his senses give him evidence affording all the certainty that he needs. Locke's position is, however, essentially dualist: mind and body remain distinct even though pretensions to intellectual transcendence are given up. Moreover, Locke regarded it as in principle impossible for humans to have any understanding of the relation between mind and body. All perceptions of one's own body, as of the rest of the material world, are ideas in one's mind. It is impossible to adopt any vantage point outside oneself from which to observe the correlation between a condition of one's body and one's perception of this condition. Where other people are concerned, their bodies and behaviour can be observed but an observer can have no direct perception of what is going on in their minds. There is thus a bifurcation in the study of man. The mind and its contents are known to each person by introspection; it is presumed that the minds of all people work in basically the same way so that

introspection provides evidence for human psychology. Other people, their bodies, and their behaviour are known by observation in exactly the same way that knowledge of any other natural object is obtained. One infers from their behaviour that they have minds like one's own and on this basis attributes psychological states to them.

In keeping with this bifurcation Locke distinguished between the terms "man" and "person," reserving "man" for the animal species, an object of study for natural historians. "Person" is used to denote the moral subject, the being who can be held responsible for his actions and thus praised, blamed, or punished. According to Locke, what constitutes a person is a characteristic continuity of consciousness, which is not merely rational thought but the full range of mental states accessible to introspection. Just as a tree is a characteristic organization of life functions sustained by exchanges of matter, so a person is a characteristic organization of mental functions continuing through changes in ideas (the matter of thought). A person can be held responsible for an action only if he acknowledges that action as one which he performed; *i.e.,* one of which he is conscious and remembers having performed.

The empiricist position thus opens up the possibility of empirical studies both of man as a natural and as a moral being and puts these studies on a par with the natural sciences. But it does so in such a way that the resulting picture lacks any integral unity, for man is an incomprehensible union of body and mind.

Development of anthropological studies. A renewed study of the natural history of man was stimulated by European encounters with the great anthropoid apes of Africa (Angola) and Asia (the Sunda Islands) at the beginning of the 16th century. Until then Europe had known only the smaller monkeys, which were too far removed from the human species to present any confusion. The discovery of the chimpanzee and the orangutan (meaning "man of the woods" in Malay) raised such questions as whether the anthropoid, who resembles man, is an animal or a man, and why it should be considered an ape and not a man. In the climate of opinion—typified by Locke and fostered by the Royal Society of London, with its enthusiasm for empirical observation—these questions prompted the detailed observational studies of a leading member of the society, Edward Tyson.

Discovery of the anthropoid apes

Work of Tyson. Tyson had the opportunity to study the remains of a young chimpanzee (named Pygmie) from Angola that had died in London several months after its arrival. His research was published by the Royal Society in 1699 under the title *Orang-Outang, sive Homo Sylvestris: or, The Anatomy of a Pygmie Compared with That of a Monkey, an Ape, and a Man.* This treatise, a landmark in anthropology and comparative anatomy, is remarkable for the empirical approach used in the investigation. Tyson's precise measurements, his complete exploration of the external and internal structures of the animal, and his minutely detailed sketches permitted him to pose what is perhaps the central problem of physical anthropology: whether it is possible to find among the anatomical or physiological characteristics of the ape the justification for asserting a radical difference between ape and man, notwithstanding all their similarities. He analyzed in great detail the similarities and dissimilarities between a chimpanzee and a man. He emphasized the fact that the ape is a quadrumane (having four hands) rather than a quadruped (having four feet); unlike the human foot, its foot has an opposable, and thus thumblike, big toe. The arrangement of the internal organs allows the erect posture that makes the ape similar to man. But on an analysis of the form and mass of the brain and speech apparatus, Tyson concluded that he was unable to determine, from a strictly anatomical point of view, why the ape is incapable of thinking and speaking.

Integral to the empiricism that forms the philosophical background to Tyson's work was a rejection of the whole notion of forms or essences as objectively determining fixed and strict demarcations within the natural world. Classification was the work of man imposed upon a natural continuum, which replaced the older ladderlike conception of the Chain of Being. This encouraged a quest for "missing links," examples of intermediary forms between those already recognized. For example, zoophytes (invertebrate animals resembling plants, such as sponges) were said to form the link between the vegetable order and the animal order. For Tyson, the chimpanzee was the missing link between animal and man.

Emergence of cultural anthropology. If physical anthropology was born out of Western man's encounter with the anthropoid apes, cultural anthropology was made necessary by his encounter with people in the rest of the world during the great voyages of discovery begun in the 15th century. Cultural anthropology became the product of the confrontation between the classical values of the West and the opposing values and customs of newly discovered civilizations.

Discovery of other civilizations

The "savage" appeared to manifest a style of humanity that was a contradiction of the certainties that had sustained Europeans for centuries. The shock was such that the naked Indian and the cannibal were at first assumed not to belong to the human race; this approach enabled Europeans to avoid the problem. This solution was, however, rejected by Pope Paul III in 1537 in his bull, or decree, *Sublimus Deus* ("The Transcendent God"), according to which Indian savages were human beings; they had souls and, as such, could be initiated into the Christian religion. This left the problem of how to reconcile the increasingly manifest human diversity with the theological requirement of human unity. One solution was to account for diversity in terms of environment, including cultural environment, and to regard the "savage" as a "primitive," as a "man of nature," who remained close to an initial state from which a privileged part of humanity had been able to remove itself by a continued effort at community and individual advancement. A study of the history of man endeavoured to bring to light the successive stages through which the human species had passed along the way to the present civilized societies. The themes of "civilization" and "progress" were among the principal preoccupations of the Enlightenment.

THE 18TH-CENTURY ENLIGHTENMENT

What has come to be known as the Enlightenment is characterized by an optimistic faith in the ability of man to develop progressively by using reason. By coming to know both himself and the natural world better he is able to develop morally and materially, increasingly dominating both his own animal instincts and the natural world that forms his environment. However, the divergence between rationalist and empiricist traditions continues, giving rise to rather different interpretations of this theme.

The natural history of man. The writings of the Scottish philosopher David Hume give a clear statement of the implications of empiricist epistemology for the study of man. Hume argued first that scientific knowledge of the natural world can consist only of conjectures as to the laws, or regularities, to be found in the sequence of natural phenomena. Not only must the causes of the phenomenal regularities remain unknown but the whole idea of a reality behind and productive of experience must be discounted as making no sense, for experience can afford nothing on the basis of which to understand such talk. Given that this is so, and given that man also observes regularities in human behaviour, the sciences of man are possible and can be put on exactly the same footing as the natural sciences. The observed regularities of human conduct can be systematically recorded and classified, and this is all that any science can or should aim to achieve. Explanation of these regularities (by reference to the essence of man) is not required in the sciences of man any more than explanation of regularities is required in the natural sciences.

Man thus becomes an object of study by natural history in the widest possible sense. All observations—whether of physiology, behaviour, or culture—contribute to the empirical knowledge of man. There is no need, beyond one of convenience, to compartmentalize these observations, since the method of study is the same whether marital customs or skin colour is the topic of investigation; the aim is to record observations in a systematic fashion making generalizations where possible. Such investigations into the natural history of man were undertaken by Linnaeus, Buffon, and Blumenbach, among others.

In his *Systema Naturae* (1735), the Swedish naturalist Carolus Linnaeus (Carl von Linné) gave a very precise description of man, placing him among the mammals in the order of primates, alongside the apes and the bat. But the distinguishing characteristic of man remains his use of reason; something that is not dependent on any physiological characteristics. Moreover, the variations that are to be found within the genus *Homo sapiens* are the product of culture and climate. In later editions of *Systema Naturae,* Linnaeus presented a summary of the diverse varieties of the human species. The Asian, for example, is "yellowish, melancholy, endowed with black hair and brown eyes," and has a character that is "severe, conceited, and stingy. He puts on loose clothing. He is governed by opinion." The African is recognizable by the colour of his skin, by his kinky hair, and by the structure of his face. "He is sly, lazy, and neglectful. He rubs his body with oil or grease. He is governed by the arbitrary will of his masters." As for the white European, "he is changeable, clever, and inventive. He puts on tight clothing. He is governed by laws." Here mentality, clothes, political order, and physiology are all taken into account.

Work of Linnaeus, Buffon, and Blumenbach

The French naturalist Georges Leclerc, comte de Buffon, devoted two of the 44 volumes of his *Histoire naturelle, général et particulière* (1749–1804) to man as a zoological species. Buffon criticized Linnaeus' system and all other systems of classification that depended only on external characteristics; to force individual objects into a rational set of categories was to impose an artificial construct on nature. He was echoing arguments that Locke had used, arguments based on the conception of the Great Chain of Being as a continuum, not as a sequence of discrete steps. An artificial taxonomy came from the mind, not from nature, and achieved precision at the expense of verisimilitude. Buffon's answer was to determine species not by characteristics but by their reproductive history. Two individual animals or plants are of the same species if they can produce fertile offspring. Species as so defined necessarily have a temporal dimension: a species is known only through the history of its propagation. This means that it is absurd to use the same principles for classifying living and nonliving things. Rocks do not mate and have offspring, so the taxonomy of the mineral kingdom cannot be based on the same principles as that of the animal and vegetable kingdom. Similarly, according to Buffon, there is "an infinite distance" between animal and man, for "man is a being with reason, and the animal is one without reason." Thus, "the most stupid of men can command the most intelligent of animals . . . because he has a reasoned plan, an order of actions, and a series of means by which he can force the animal to obey him." The ape, even if in its external characteristics it is similar to man, is deprived of thought and all that is distinctive of man. Ape and man differ in temperament, in gestation period, in the rearing and growth of the body, in length of life, and in all the habits that Buffon regarded as constituting the nature of a particular being. Most important, apes and other animals lack the ability to speak. This is significant in that Buffon saw the rise of human intelligence as a product of development of an articulated language. But this linguistic ability is the primary manifestation of the presence of reason and is not merely dependent on physiology. Animals lack speech not because they cannot produce articulated sound sequences, but because, lacking minds, they have no ideas to give meaning to these sounds.

The German scholar Johann Friedrich Blumenbach is recognized as the father of physical anthropology for his work *De Generis Humani Varietate Nativa* ("On the Natural Variety of Mankind"), published in 1775 or 1776. He also regarded language as an important distinguishing characteristic of man, but added that it is only man who is capable of laughing and crying. Perhaps most important is the suggestion, also made by the American statesman Benjamin Franklin, that it is only man who has hands that make him capable of fashioning tools. This was a suggestion that broke new ground in that it opened up the

The
thought
of Kant

possibility of speculating on a physiological origin for the development of intellectual capacities.

Man the rational subject. The great German philosopher Immanuel Kant credited Hume with having wakened him from his dogmatic slumbers. But while Kant concurred with Hume in rejecting the possibility of taking metaphysics as a philosophical starting point (dogmatic metaphysics), he did not follow him in dismissing the need for metaphysics altogether. Instead he returned to the Cartesian project of seeking to find in the structure of consciousness itself something that would point beyond it.

Thus, Kant started from the same point as the empiricists, but with Cartesian consciousness—the experience of the individual considered as a sequence of mental states. But instead of asking the empiricists' question of how it is that man acquires such concepts as number, space, or colour, he enquired into the conditions under which the conscious awareness of mental states—as states of mind and as classifiable states distinguished by what they purport to represent—is possible. The empiricist simply takes the character of the human mind—consciousness and self-consciousness—for granted as a given of human nature and then proceeds to ask questions concerning how experience, presumed to come in the form of sense perceptions, gives rise to all of man's various ideas and ways of thinking. The methods proposed for this investigation are observational, and thus the study is continuous with natural history. The enterprise overlaps with what would now be called cognitive psychology but includes introspection regarded simply as self-observation. But this clearly begs a number of questions, in particular, how the empiricist can claim knowledge of the human mind and of the character of the experience that is the supposed origin of all ideas.

Even Hume was forced to admit that self-observation, or introspection, given the supposed model of experience as a sequence of ideas and impressions, can yield nothing more than an impression of current or immediately preceding mental states. Experiential self-knowledge, on this model, is impossible. The knowing subject, by his effort to know himself, is already changing himself so that he can only know what he was, not what he is. Thus, any empirical study, whether it be of man or of the natural world, must be based on foundations that can only be provided by a nonempirical, philosophical investigation into the conditions of the possibility of the form of knowledge sought. Without this foundation an empirical study cannot achieve any unified conception of its object and never will be able to attain that systematic, theoretically organized character that is demanded of science.

Use of
critical
reflection

The method of such philosophical investigation is that of critical reflection—employing reason critically—not that of introspection or inner observation. It is here that the origin of what has come to be regarded as philosophical anthropology in the stricter, third sense (*i.e.,* 20th-century humanism) can be identified, since there is an insistence that studies of the knowing and moral subject must be founded in a philosophical study. But there remain questions about the humanity of Kant's subject. Kant's position was still firmly dualist; the conscious subject constitutes itself through the opposition between experience of itself as free and active (in inner sense) and of the thoroughly deterministic, mechanistic, and material world (in the passive receptivity of outer sense). The subject with which philosophy is thus concerned is finite and rational, limited by the constraint that the content of its knowledge is given in the form of sense experience rather than pure intellectual intuition. This is not a differentiated individual subject but a form of which individual minds are instantiations. The ideals regulating this subject are purely rational ideals. This tendency is even more marked in the philosophies of Fichte, Schelling, and Hegel.

Humanist thought is anthropocentric in that it places man at the centre and treats him as the point of origin. There are different ways of doing this, however, two of which are illustrated in the works of Locke and Kant, respectively. The first, realist, position assumes at the outset a contrast between an external, independently existing world and the conscious human subject. In this view man is presented as standing "outside" of the physical world

that he observes. This conception endorses an instrumental view of the relation between man and the nonhuman, natural world and is therefore most frequently found to be implicit in the thought of those enthusiastic about modern technological science. Nature, from this viewpoint, exists for man, who by making increasingly accurate conjectures as to the laws governing the regular succession of natural events is able to increase his ability to predict them and so to control his environment.

The second, idealist position, argues that the world exists only in being an object of human thought; it exists only by virtue of man's conceptualization of it. In the form in which Kant expressed this position the thought that constitutes the material, physical world, is that of a transcendent mind, of which the actual minds of humans are merely vehicles.

There is also a third, dialectical, form of anthropocentrism, which, although it did not emerge fully until the 19th century, was prefigured in the works of Vico and Herder. From this standpoint the relation between man and nature is regarded as an integral part to the dynamic whole of which it is a part. The world is what it is as a result of being lived in and transformed by human beings, while people, in turn, acquire their character from their existence in a particular situation within the world. Any thought about the world is concerned with a world as lived through a subject, who is also part of the world about which he thinks. There is no possibility of transcendence in thought to some external, non-worldly standpoint. Such a position wants both to grant the independent existence of the world and to stress the active and creative role of human beings within it. It is within this relatively late form of humanism—which arose from a synthesis of elements of the Kantian position, with the insights of the Italian Giambattista Vico and the German Johann Gottfried von Herder—that philosophical anthropology in the third sense can be located.

Vico's *Scienza nuova* (1725; *The New Science of Giambattista Vico*) announced not so much a new science as the need to recognize a new form of scientific knowledge. He argued (against empiricists) that the study of man must differ in its method and goals from that of the natural world. This is because the nature of man is not static and unalterable; a person's own efforts to understand the world and adapt it to his needs, physical and spiritual, continuously transform that world and himself. Each individual is both the product and the support of a collective consciousness that defines a particular moment in the history of the human spirit. Each epoch interprets the sum of its traditions, norms, and values in such a way as to impose a model for behaviour on daily life as well as on the more specialized domains of morals and religion and art. Given that those who make or create something can understand it in a way in which mere observers of it cannot, it follows that if, in some sense, people make their own history, they can understand history in a way in which they cannot understand the natural world, which is only observed by them. The natural world must remain unintelligible to man; only God, as its creator, fully understands it. History, however, being concerned with human actions, is intelligible to humans. This means, moreover, that the succession of phases in the culture of a given society or people cannot be regarded as governed by mechanistic, causal laws. To be intelligible these successions must be explicable solely in terms of human, goal-directed activity. Such understanding is the product neither of sense perception nor of rational deduction but of imaginative reconstruction. Here Vico asserted that, even though a person's style of thought is a product of the phase of culture in which he participates, it is nonetheless possible for him to understand another culture and the transitions between cultural phases. He assumed that there is some underlying commonality of the needs, goals, and requirement for social organization that makes this possible.

Herder denied the existence of any such absolute and universally recognized goals. This denial carried the disturbing implication that the specific values and goals pursued by various human cultures may not only differ but also may not all be mutually compatible. Hence, not

Vico's
*Scienza
nuova*

only may cultural transitions not all be intelligible, but conflict may not be an attribute of the human condition that can be eliminated. If this is so, then the notion of a single code of precepts for the harmonious, ideal way of life, which underlies mainstream Western thought and to which—whether they know it or not—all human beings aspire, could not be sustained. There will be many ways of living, thinking, and feeling, each self-validating but not mutually compatible or comparable nor capable of being integrated into a harmonious pluralistic society.

THE 19TH CENTURY

The 19th century was a time of greatly increased activity in the sciences of man. There was a correspondingly rapid development of various disciplines, but this was accompanied by increasing specialization within disciplines. Perhaps the most significant theme, common to all branches of science, was the declining influence of religon. The philosophers of the Enlightenment had concurred in thinking that the transcendence of God doomed to failure any attempt to encompass him within the framework of human discourse. Theological discourse was thus only human discourse. Herder had stated, "It is necessary to read the Bible in a human manner, for it is a book written by men for men." Even so, he insisted, "The fact that religion is integrally human is a profound sign in recognition of its truth." But with human truth the only available truth, such a line was hard to maintain, and by the late 19th century the German philosopher Friedrich Nietzsche had announced that God was dead.

But the death of God also meant that the essence of God in every man was dead—that which was common to all and that in virtue of which the individual transcended the natural, material world and his purely biological nature. Also dead was the part of a person that recognized universal God-given ideals of reason and truth, goodness and beauty. There thus emerged views of man that, while integrating him more thoroughly with the natural world—treating his incarnation as an essential aspect of his condition—had to come to terms with the consequences for science, morality, and the study of man himself of the removal of a transcendent support for belief in absolute standards or ideals.

The presumption of a fixed human nature was undercut at the level of natural history by the emergence and eventual acceptance of evolutionary biology. This added a historical, developmental dimension to the natural history of man, which complimented developmental views of culture and of man as a culturally constituted being. But more importantly, evolutionary biology made man a direct descendant of nonhuman primates and suggested that the gift of reason, which so many had seen as establishing a gulf between man and animal, might too have developed gradually and might indeed have a physiological basis.

Even though Buffon had tied classification to the ability to reproduce, and had thus introduced a temporal dimension into the characterization of species, he had retained the idea of stable species. But a static classification could not explain the dynamic relations between isolated species. A primitive time line of natural history thus developed. The relationship of families led to the idea of filiation between them according to an order of succession. The interpretation of fossils aroused impassioned debates. From them have arisen concepts of mutation (the process by which the genetic material of a cell is altered), transformism (the theory that one species is changed into another), and evolution. These concepts, already being formulated in the 18th century, were clarified in the work of Lamarck and Darwin.

The evolutionary theory of Charles Darwin's *Origin of Species* (1859) differed from that of Jean-Baptiste de Lamarck in that it proposed a mechanistic, nonpurposive account of evolution as the product of the natural selection of randomly produced genetic mutations (survival of the fittest). Advantageous characteristics acquired by an individual were not, as Lamarck had thought, inherited and therefore could not play a role in evolutionary development.

The theme of continuity with the rest of the natural world was one that was also to be found in the very different, antiscientific thought of Romanticism, which was one of the reactions to the rise of the doctrine of mechanism and to the Industrial Revolution for which it was held responsible. The experience of the Industrial Revolution was crucial to most 19th-century thought about man. Reactions to this experience can be put into three broad categories. There were those who saw in industrialization the progressive triumph of reason over nature, making possible the march of civilization and the moral triumph of reason over animal instinct. This was a view that continued the spirit of the Enlightenment, with its confidence in reason and the ability to advance through science. Into this category can be put the English philosopher John Stuart Mill, a stout defender of liberal individualism. Mill's philosophy was in many respects a continuation of that of Hume but with the addition of Jeremy Bentham's utilitarian view that the foundation of all morality is the principle that one should always act so as to produce the greatest happiness of the greatest number. This ethical principle gives a prominent place to the sciences of man (which are conceived as being parallel in method to the natural sciences), their study deemed necessary for an empirical determination of the social and material conditions that produce the greatest general happiness. This is a non-dialectical, naturalistic humanism, which gives primacy to the individual and stresses the importance of his freedom. For Mill, all social phenomena, and therefore ultimately all social changes, are products of the actions of individuals.

The humanist opponents of capitalist industrialization fall into two groups, both presuming some form of dialectical humanism: those who, like Marx, retained a faith in the scientific application of reason and those who, like Goethe and Schiller, fundamentally questioned the humanity of mechanistic science and the technology it spawned.

The Romantics questioned the instrumental conception of the relation between man and nature, which is fundamental to the thinking behind much technological science. They insisted on an organic relation between man and the rest of nature. It is not man's place outside of nature that is emphasized but his situation within it. Equally central to this view was a recognition of the historicity of human culture and a rejection of any conception of a fixed, determined human nature on which a science of man parallel in structure to the natural sciences (*i.e.,* a science with laws, whether empirical or rational, that determine the actions and the historical development of mankind) could be based. There was a continued commitment to the perspective of the individual, and his creative relation with the world, an orientation that was carried over into the philosophical anthropology of 20th-century phenomenologists and existentialists, with their critiques of modern industrial science.

The Marxist opposition to capitalist industrialization is not to industrialization as such but to capitalist forms of it. This opposition is founded on socialism, which stresses the role of social structures; it is at the level of society—its structures and its economic base of production—that the course of history can be understood. Marx emphasized the importance of labour and work in man's relation both to the natural and to the social worlds in which he finds himself and which condition his ability to realize himself through these relationships. He deplored the loss of humanity associated with capitalist industrialization, which was manifest in the alienating conditions under which members of the working class were treated as objects and thus deprived of their full status as human subjects by their industrial masters. Nonetheless, he retained a faith in scientific knowledge and in the possibility of a scientific understanding of history by integrating its economic, social, and political aspects. Marx argued, however, that it was not reason but revolution that would cause the overthrow of the capitalist system.

Common to all of these reactions is that whether they privileged reason or not they did not seek to validate the claims of reason—and hence the claims of science—by reference to a rational God. But with this transcendent guarantor removed, the question of the objectivity of rational standards and of the commonality of human

Declining influence of religion

Reactions to the Industrial Revolution

Marxist opposition to capitalism

thought structures became pressing. The Cartesian starting point focused attention on thought as a sequence of ideas, knowable only to the individual concerned. Animals, even if capable of uttering structured sound sequences, were denied linguistic abilities on the ground that these sound sequences could not be the expressions of thoughts and could not have meaning; lacking minds, animals also lack ideas, the thoughts that give words their meaning. According to this view, words are simply conventionally established vehicles for the communication of thoughts that exist prior to, and independent of, their linguistic expression. However, if it is not assumed that human minds are all instantiations of a single transcendent mind, or that although individual they were created from a common pattern, this account of linguistic communication must appear inadequate. Since according to Cartesianism introspection is the only route to awareness of ideas, each person can only ever be aware of his own ideas, never of those of another. He could never know that his attempts to communicate succeed in calling up in another person's mind ideas similar to those in his own. Some new way of looking at linguistic communication was required, and this could be nothing short of a new starting point, a new way of thinking about thought itself.

THE 20TH CENTURY:
EMERGENCE OF PHILOSOPHICAL ANTHROPOLOGY

The mood of the late 19th century, which has also dominated 20th-century philosophy, can be characterized as anti-psychologistic—a rejection of introspective, idea-oriented ways of thinking about thought, which presume that thought is prior to language. This fundamental reorientation had implications for every other aspect of the study of man. The writers of the late 19th and early 20th centuries who most influenced subsequent philosophical thought about man were Gottlob Frege, Edmund Husserl, Ferdinand de Saussure, and Sigmund Freud. Each helped to transform one of the three reactions to the Industrial Revolution outlined above, to bring it into accord with the new, anti-psychologistic orientation: Frege influenced the empiricist, scientific reaction; Husserl the Romantic; and Saussure and Freud the scientific Socialist.

Frege and empiricist anthropology. Frege argued that if language is to be a vehicle for the expression of objective, scientific knowledge of the world, then the meaning (cognitive content) of a linguistic expression must be the same for all users of the language to which it belongs and must be determined independently of the psychological states of any individual. A word may call up a variety of ideas in the mind of an individual user, but these are not part of its meaning. Such associations may be important to the poet but are irrelevant to the scientist. The function of language in the expression of scientific knowledge is to represent an independently existing world. The meanings of linguistic expressions must thus derive from their relation to the world, not from their relation to the minds of language users. Similarly, logic—embodying the principles of reasoning and the standards of rationality—must be concerned not with laws of human thought, but with laws of truth. The principles of correct reasoning must be justified by reference to the function of language in representing the world correctly or incorrectly rather than by reference to human psychology.

Frege's work on formal logic

It is for his work on formal logic, which stemmed from these ideas, that Frege is renowned, because it opened the way for the mechanical reproduction of reasoning processes, which was crucial to the development of information processing by computers and for devices capable of artificial intelligence. Frege argued that the principles of deductive reasoning are purely formal principles, which means that their correct application does not depend on an ability to understand the sentences involved, so long as they have been put into the correct logical form. To give an account of the meaning of a sentence requires that it be analyzed so as to reveal its logical form. The logical analysis of everyday and scientific language thus becomes a primary focus of philosophical activity, hence the name "analytic philosophy" for the tradition, predominating in Great Britain, North America, and Australasia that can be

regarded as post-Fregean philosophy. In this tradition the focus is on the analysis of rational, human thought, where it is presumed that the only correct way to do this is to analyze the logical structure of language.

Thus language has replaced God as the locus of rationality and of principles of reason; and the language–world relation has taken over many of the roles previously played by the God–world relation. The individual participates in a rationality that is independent of him to the extent that he is a language user. The position assumes that standards of rationality are absolute, since they are seen as necessarily governing the meaning structures of all languages. The linguist Noam Chomsky proposed a thesis that was regarded as being complimentary to this philosophical position, namely that of a universal grammar— a formal structure that underlies all languages, no matter how diverse their grammatical forms seem on the surface. Moreover, he suggested that all humans have the same innate capacity to learn language, which explains why it is that they all structure their languages, and hence their thought, in the same way.

A further assumption (christened the "principle of charity" by the American philosopher Donald Davidson) is that all humans are rational and that the majority of human behaviour is to be explained as rational, given the beliefs and desires of the person concerned. This, together with the view that language is the locus of rationality and the embodiment of thought, leads to the view that the primary objective of the sciences of man is to interpret the language of a community under study so as to attribute beliefs and desires to its members on the basis of what they say, and so give some explanation of their behaviour. The interpretation is deemed incorrect if the attributed beliefs and desires result in too much behaviour being portrayed as irrational. There will then be a mutual adjustment between language interpretation and the explanation of behaviour in which there can be no final separation of the two and no such thing as a uniquely correct interpretation. There is thus no hope of finding laws linking psychological states of belief or desire to physiological states, even though, by maintaining that each mental event is just a physical event under a different description, a dualism of mind and body is denied. What remains is an irreducible dualism between physiological and psychosocial studies of man. The situation is frequently explained by utilizing a computer analogy (for the computer is, in this view, man creating a machine in his own image). The relation between the structures of thought and the body is likened to the relation between computer software and hardware; the same hardware may be used to run different software, and the same software may be run on different hardware. The two descriptions of computer functioning are thus relatively independent.

In this account the consciousness of the individual plays little explicit role, but a model of man is nevertheless implicit in the whole approach. It is still basically the model employed by Hume, with experience consisting of sensory stimuli. Experience of other people is thus limited to observation of their physical and behavioral characteristics. It is on the basis of such observations that we have to make conjectures about their mental states. What has changed is the method of making such attributions. It is not sufficient to argue by analogy from introspection; any attribute of rational or mental faculties must go via an analytic interpretation of the language spoken. But with the assumption that all languages must share a common logical structure in virtue of their function in representing the world, there is also an inbuilt presumption of a uniformity in the rational structure of all human thought.

Husserl and philosophical anthropology. Husserl is regarded as the founder of phenomenology. He, like Frege, wished to avoid the so-called psychologism of idea-based discussions of thought and rejected naturalistic approaches to the study of the mind and of what passes for rational thought. He, too, believed that laws of reasoning needed to be validated by reference to the objects of thought, but he did not agree that logic could be made purely formal and independent of the particular subject matter in hand, nor did he agree that the primary focus should be on language.

Indeed, he rejected the position from which Frege started, namely, the assumption that there is a clear separation between the knowing subject and an independently existing reality that is the object of his knowledge. This assumption, Husserl argued, reveals a blindness to the conditions, or presuppositions, involved in all knowledge and already analyzed in part by Kant. Husserl adopted Kant's strategy but in a more radical form that was designed to restore the in-the-worldness of the human subject.

Husserl's phenomenology

The program of phenomenology aimed at rigorous understanding of the life-world. Kant had explored the conditions of the possibility of experience, and in so doing he had presumed that this experience was always that of an "I," a subject. Husserl also asked after the conditions for the possibility of a consciousness that is always potentially self-conscious. He claimed that all consciousness is intentional; *i.e.,* is consciousness of something. The method pursued was a phenomenal investigation of the "contents of consciousness." This required the investigator to "bracket off" all theories, presuppositions, and evidence of existence, including his own existence. There could be no dogmas. The implication was still that the individual can, in principle, abstract from every influence of culture and environment by abstracting also from that element of consciousness that involves awareness of self. It was presumed that consciousness as such had structures that would then be revealed. It is only self-conscious thought that is culturally constituted; for Husserl, each human individual is by necessity socially and historically conditioned by his environment. But even so it has to be doubted whether the required abstraction from self is possible in the sort of consciousness—*i.e.,* reflective rational thought—that is required of a rigorous phenomenological analysis.

Descartes and his successors had taken the self, the individual subject, for granted and in the process inevitably had assigned to the knowing subject a position outside, beyond, or transcending the world of which he sought knowledge. Husserl, by putting the individual subject into the field of philosophical investigation, paved the way for investigations of the human condition that start with the concrete, with man's being-in-the world. In this respect he can also be regarded as the founder of philosophical anthropology in the narrowest sense of the term: the personal unity of the human being becomes both the point of departure and the goal of philosophical reflection. The use of philosophical anthropology to characterize this approach emerged in the first half of the 20th century with the tendency both in Germany and in France to treat the problems of anthropology as the centre of all philosophical studies. Its emergence at this time may be seen

Reaction to totalitarian ideologies

as a reaction to the totalitarian systems of the 20th century: Italian Fascism, Soviet Communism under Stalin, and German Nazism were powerful ideologies calling for the annihilation of the individual character of the person. The philosophical protests of the German phenomenologist Max Scheler, of the Russian existentialist Nikolay Berdyayev, of the Jewish philosophical theologian Martin Buber, and of the French personalist Emmanuel Mounier offered answers to this challenge; the philosophies of the person and of existence present to each individual the means to centre himself upon himself.

Work of Heidegger. Husserl's work not only gave rise to phenomenology but also to the existentialist ideas of Martin Heidegger and Jean-Paul Sartre. Heidegger adopted the method of phenomenology but rejected Husserl's refusal to allow existence to feature in the phenomenological starting point. Heidegger argued for a philosophy in which man's being-in-the-world is registered, and where this being (existence) precedes any determination of what man is (his essence).

In his *Brief über den "Humanismus"* (1947; *Brief Letter on Humanism*), Heidegger wrote:

Are we really on the right track toward the essence of man as long as we set him off as one living creature among others in contrast to plants, beasts and God? . . . when we do this we abandon man to the essential realm of *animalitas* but attribute a specific difference to him. In principle we are still thinking of *homo animalitas*—even when *anima* (soul) is posited as *animus sive mens,* and this in turn is later posited as subject, person, or spirit (*geist*). Such positing is in the manner of metaphysics.

Naturalistic definitions of man fail, because like all traditional metaphysical definitions they naively assume that we know what we mean when we say of something that it is; *i.e.,* when we ascribe being to it.

Humanity and the world form a whole in which neither is privileged. The focus shifts from intentional objects of consciousness to the world itself, a world of objects that appear (and hence exist as individualized objects) only insofar as they have meaning and significance for human beings, by virtue of the way in which they relate to human projects. A fallen tree branch is noticed as firewood only by one who is in search of fuel. Similarly, events are noticed and recorded and so become historical events but only in the light of the meaning that they have for the historian. This means that neither history nor the study of man can be objective and purely factual history. History is always a story about the past from someone who has a specific vantage point within history.

Work of Sartre and other existentialists. Sartre, in *L'Être et le néant* (1943; *Being and Nothingness*), tried to tread a middle line between Husserl and Heidegger, retaining the concrete in-the-worldness of Heidegger while restoring a place for intentional consciousness. He hoped to provide an account of, as he put it, intentional-consciousness-in-the-world-as-it-is-lived. Sartre's driving belief was in human freedom, the ability to choose not only a course of action but also what one would become. Neither Husserl, with his already structured and regulated consciousness, nor Heidegger, with his world that is already given meaning, left enough room for freedom.

Sartre's belief in human freedom

Sartre insisted on the dualism of being (thingness) and consciousness (no-thingness) and of the individual in itself and for itself. The disjunction between these is absolute: no state of the world can determine human action, even to the extent of providing a motive, or reason, for action. If man is truly free, the world, whether material or social, can place no constraints on him, not even to the extent of determining what would or would not be good reasons for following a given course of action. He must create his own values and his own morality and take responsibility for his choices. Sartre's critics pointed out, however, that this total freedom dissolves into arbitrariness and randomness. An action that is selected at whim, chosen without (or beyond) reason, and that recognizes no rational constraints, is more an abandonment to fate than an assertion of freedom; where there is no basis for decision there is simply the necessity to choose.

In his later writings, and in particular the *Critique de la raison dialectique* (1960; *Critique of Dialectical Reason*), which attempts a reconciliation between existentialism and Marxism, Sartre came to recognize that there are constraints on the exercise of human freedom. He first acknowledged that man is a creature with biological needs, who must eat, drink, shelter, and clothe himself as a condition of being able to engage in other kinds of activity; and, second, he saw the struggle against need as conditioned by the fact that it takes place in conditions of scarcity. This means that there is competition for resources and thus the ever-present likelihood that the realization of an individual's freedom will limit that of another. Each individual in these conditions experiences others as possible threats to his own freedom (*i.e.,* he experiences alienation).

Individuals whose freedom is in this way conditioned, not just by naturally occurring material conditions but by the materiality of human practice, are (as Marx had said) both "subjects" and "objects" of history. But Sartre insisted that history is only intelligible because it records a process brought into being by human action. This rules out an understanding of history based on a "dialectic of nature," adopted by some Marxists whom Sartre criticized as being dogmatists. Sartre thus rejected the idea that there could be any naturalistic science of humanity—a science that proceeds by discovering laws without reference to the consciousness of individuals. History is neither a mere process (without a subject) nor the product of some form of social, collective "subject." But this does not mean that individuals can be treated as wholly independent units that can be understood without taking into account the formative and conditioning role of their material and social situation. It is in this work that Sartre was still facing up to, and grappling with, the problem of the reconciliation of the demands of freedom and reason, but in an altogether more practical and concrete way than was done by his 17th-century predecessors.

Sartre's abandonment of the radical freedom of *Being and Nothingness* owed much to the French phenomenologist Maurice Merleau-Ponty's criticism of it—in *Sens et non-sens* (1948; *Sense and Non-Sense*)—as being still a dualist philosophy of consciousness and for failing to put man truly in the world. In *Sense and Non-Sense* he also expressed his view of the relation between existentialism and Marxism:

> Marx gives us an objective definition of class in terms of the effective position of individuals in the production cycle, but he tells us elsewhere that class cannot become a decisive historical force and revolutionary factor unless individuals become aware of it, adding that this awareness itself has social motives, and so on. As a historical factor, class is therefore neither a simple objective fact, nor is it, on the other hand, a simple value arbitrarily chosen by solitary consciousnesses.

In Merleau-Ponty's writing there is also a clear statement of the human presupposition that forms the basis of philosophical anthropology in this third sense:

> I am not the result or the intersection of multiple causalities that determine my body or my "psychism"; I cannot conceive of myself as nothing but a part of the world, as the simple object of biology, psychology, and sociology, nor close over myself the universe of science. Everything that I know of the world, even through science, I know from a viewpoint that is my own . . .

One effect of the insistence that it is concrete, lived experience that must form the starting point of philosophical anthropology is that not only must class and its experience enter into such accounts, but so too must sex and gender. Once the human subject, as a focus of philosophical attention, is no longer a mind whose relation to a body is at best obscure, is no longer a pure consciousness, but is essentially embodied and immersed in human culture, the biological differences between the sexes and the socially constituted role differentiation between male and female must play a part in the account of humanity.

In Simone de Beauvoir's *Deuxième Sexe* (1949; *The Second Sex*), she used the categories provided by Sartre to argue that to be a woman—as distinct from a man—is to be robbed of one's subjectivity, to be treated as an object by men, and to have one's conception of oneself as female defined by men. To assert her subjectivity a woman must thus negate her femininity, to reject the status of object for men that constitutes the feminine. A woman is thus placed in a condition of self-alienation, with which a man does not have to contend. In this way de Beauvoir revealed the need for a philosophy of "man" that is also a philosophy of "woman," a viewpoint that generally has been acknowledged only by female writers.

Philosophical anthropology and theology. Just as class and gender determine the way in which one lives in the world and is related to the world, so too may religion. Even for those not brought up in any religion, Western culture is still one in which religion is significant. Philosophical anthropology must thus take the phenomenon of religious experience seriously, in a way that empiricist anthropology does not. But its starting point is with the constitution of a religious consciousness, and with the conditions of the possibility of the forms of religion encountered; it does not start with theology. There is room once again for dispute over the possibility of any kind of transcendence. The 19th-century Danish philosopher Søren Kierkegaard thought that man's existence has meaning only in the experience of grace, which inexplicably raises man up from his worthlessness. The anguish and loneliness of mortal existence, the "wretchedness of man without God," is only overcome by a form of experience that confers faith in the existence of God and hence the ultimate possibility of human transcendence.

Philosophical anthropology in its narrowest (third) sense is founded on an insistence that the only knowledge available to man is knowledge from his human perspective, conditioned, as he himself is, by his situation in the world. God cannot be invoked as a source of absolute standards of truth or of absolute values nor to give content to the supposition that there are any. If God exists, then the thought that there are such standards and values, even if we cannot know of them, remains possible. This possibility was denied with Nietzsche's proclamation of the death of God; the attempt to come to terms with this view defines the scope of most philosophical anthropology. The view of religion that reflects the inversion which takes place was expressed by Ludwig Feuerbach in *Das Wesen des Christentums* (1841; *The Essence of Christianity*), when he declared that "man is not a shadow of God; it is God who is the shadow of man, an illusory phantasm that man nourishes out of his own substance."

Saussure, Freud, and antihumanism. There were also those, however, who saw the death of God as heralding the death of man as the focus and starting point for philosophy. Saussure, in his *Cours de linguistique général* (1915; *Course in General Linguistics*), held, like Frege, that the meaning of a linguistic sign, that which gives it a value for the purposes of communication, could not be an idea in the mind of an individual. But unlike Frege he did not concentrate on the relation between language and an external world. Rather, he argued that the meaning of any one linguistic sign is dependent on its relation to other signs in the language to which it belongs; thus, the meaning of one sign is determined by its place in the overall structure that constitutes a language. A consequence of this view is that language becomes a closed, autonomous system. Linguistic signs do not depend for their meaning on anything external to language. Moreover, Saussure argued that the present meaning of a word could not be revealed by tracing its etymology. It is only by reference to present language structures that current meanings are determined. The language structures that become the focus of attention are thus to be treated as autonomous from their history (*i.e.,* as if they had no history).

With this focus on structures and the method of studying them, Saussure can be considered to be one of the founding figures of structuralism. This view of meaning came to be extended from linguistic signs to all kinds of human actions to which a conventional meaning, or significance, is attributed. It has been used as the framework for anthropological investigations of cultures, their customs, etc., as, for example, in the work of Claude Lévi-Strauss or in the interpretation of dreams and the structures of the unconscious in the works of Jacques Lacan.

It is significant that, again, meaning is studied without reference to the consciousness of individual language speakers. Man is treated as essentially not just a language speaker but as a user and interpreter of signs, and the significance of these signs is determined without reference to any relation to the individual. A language, or sign-system, takes over the role of providing the framework of reason in which significance is given, but this framework transcends the individual. Such systems of codification regulate all human experience and activity and yet lie beyond the control of either individual or social groups. Indeed, since there is no meaning or understanding outside of a given sign-system, it is only from the meaning of the signs he "uses" that the individual comes to learn what it is that he means by his action, and hence what he thinks. This is why such views of language can readily be grafted onto Freud's theory of the unconscious.

Freud treated the realm of the mind as one that is as law-governed as is the natural world; nothing that a person does or says is haphazard or accidental, for everything can in principle be traced to causes that are somehow in the person's mind, although many of these are not accessible to consciousness. Freud's view of the human mind is thus very different from Descartes's. For Freud, the part of the mind that is accessible to consciousness is but the tip of a large iceberg; the hidden remainder, which influences the conscious, is the unconscious. Thus, for instance, there are unconscious desires that can cause someone to do things that he cannot explain rationally to others, or even to himself. In this there is a parallel between Freud and

Marginal notes:

Deuxième Sexe of de Beauvoir

Thought of Saussure

Freud's theory of the unconscious

Marx, for both hold views on which human consciousness, far from being perfectly free and rational, is really determined by causes of which man is not aware; but whereas Marx says that these causes are social and economic in nature, Freud claims that they are individual and mental. In both cases the implications for the study of man are anti-psychologistic in that they turn attention away from the individual consciousness. On both views a scientific understanding of man is only to be gained by examining the factors that determine consciousness rather than the level of the individual subject of consciousness.

The id, ego, and superego

In his later expositions (those given in the 1920s) Freud assigned to the mind a tripartite structure: the id, which contains all the instinctual drives seeking immediate satisfaction; the ego, which deals with the world outside the person, mediating between it and the id; and the superego, a special part of the ego that contains the conscience, the social norms acquired in childhood. Whatever can become conscious is in the ego, although even in it there may be things that remain unconscious, whereas everything in the id is permanently unconscious. The instincts or drives contained in the id are the motivating forces in the mental apparatus, and all of the energy of the mind comes from them. Freud included a sexual instinct as one of the basic instincts and thus gave sexuality a much wider scope in psychology and in the study of man than had previously been the case. Freud's account of individual human character is also developmental. He held that particular "traumatic" experiences, although apparently forgotten, could continue to exercise a harmful influence on a person's mental health. The fully fledged theory of psychoanalysis generalizes from this and asserts the crucial importance, for the adult character, of the experiences of infancy and early childhood. Freud also held that the first five or so years of life are the time in which the basis of an individual's personality is laid down; one cannot fully understand a person, therefore, until he comes to know the psychologically crucial facts about that person's early childhood. Freud produced detailed theories of the stages of development that are concerned specifically with the development of sexuality, in which this concept is widened to include any kind of pleasure obtained from parts of the body. Freud's view was that individual well-being, or mental health, depends on a harmonious relationship between the various parts of the mind and between the person and the real world in which he must live. Neurosis results from the frustration of basic instincts, either because of external obstacles or because of internal mental imbalance. The work of the analyst is to interpret the behaviour and speech of a patient in such a way as to give insight into the unconscious, to be able to explain what is inexplicable at the conscious level, and in this way to try to give the patient an understanding of himself. Here there is a need for a theory of signs and of interpretation in which its notion of meaning, or significance, does not rest on either reference to the physical world or on ideas in an individual consciousness; structuralist theories provide one such possibility.

From the point of view of either Freudian theory or of the non-existentialist reading of Marx, any attempt to provide a study of man—of human behaviour and history—that starts from the individual consciousness must seem misguided. This will include the empiricist approaches, which assume that all human behaviour is to be explained in terms of the conscious mental states (*i.e.,* beliefs and desires) of individuals. Such approaches seem to fail to acknowledge that the causes of human actions include factors of which they are not consciously aware. A scientific account, one that is concerned with providing causal explanations, must not be confined to the subjectivity of the individual consciousness but must adopt an objective standpoint, a standpoint from which these factors can be recognized and studied. Equally as important, however, the sort of arguments used by phenomenologists and existentialists to query the availability of objective viewpoints can be reapplied here. Thus, structuralism gives place to the post-structuralism of Derrida and Deleuze, according to which neither a scientific nor a philosophical anthropology is possible.

BIBLIOGRAPHY. General works include LESLIE STEVENSON, *Seven Theories of Human Nature* (1974), which gives short introductory sketches of the views of Plato, Christian philosophers, Marx, Freud, Skinner, Sartre, and Lorenz; BERNARD GROETHUYSEN, *Anthropologie philosophique* (1953, reprinted 1980), a series of historical sketches of human personality from antiquity to the Renaissance; MICHAEL LANDMANN, *De Homine: Man in the Mirror of His Thought* (1979; originally published in German, 1962), philosophical rather than anthropological; J.S. SLOTKIN (ed.), *Readings in Early Anthropology* (1965), a good selection of important historical texts, mainly of Anglo-Saxon thinkers; GEORGES GUSDORF, *Les Sciences humaines et la pensée occidentale* (1966–), a general history of the sciences of man on the basis of an anthropological philosophy—12 of 13 vol. had appeared to 1986; ERNST CASSIRER, *An Essay on Man: An Introduction to the Philosophy of Human Culture* (1944, reprinted 1974), a useful and accurate sketch; and A.L. KROEBER (ed.), *Anthropology Today: An Encyclopedic Inventory* (1953, reissued 1965).

On the history of the philosophy of man in the Western tradition, see PRUDENCE ALLEN, *The Concept of Woman: The Aristotelian Revolution, 750 BC–AD 1250* (1985), which contains an excellent bibliography and numerous quotations from historical sources on human nature and the relation between male and female. Insights into the spirit of Renaissance thinking about man are given by ERNST CASSIRER, *The Individual and the Cosmos in Renaissance Philosophy,* trans. by MARIO DOMANDI (1963, reissued 1972; originally published in German, 1927); and DOROTHY KOENIGSBERGER, *Renaissance Man and Creative Thinking: A History of Concepts of Harmony, 1400–1700* (1979). The problems faced by 17th-century philosophers are outlined in LEROY E. LOEMKER, *Struggle for Synthesis: The Seventeenth Century Background of Leibniz's Synthesis of Order and Freedom* (1972). ERNST CASSIRER, *The Philosophy of the Enlightenment,* trans. by FRITZ C.A. KOELLN and JAMES P. PETTEGROVE (1951, reissued 1979; originally published in German, 1932), provides a general discussion of the Enlightenment. On Hegel's philosophy and its impact, see CHARLES TAYLOR, *Hegel and Modern Society* (1979). A useful comparison of two very different 19th-century views of man and society is provided by GRAEME DUNCAN, *Marx and Mill* (1973, reprinted 1977). CHARLES COULSTON GILLISPIE, *Genesis and Geology: A Study in the Relations of Scientific Thought, Natural Theology, and Social Opinion in Great Britain, 1790–1850* (1951, reissued 1959), discusses the impact of science on religious conceptions of man and his place in the order of nature in the decades before Darwin; and MARY MIDGLEY, *Beast and Man; The Roots of Human Nature* (1978, reissued 1980).

Post-Fregean, analytic philosophical thinking about man is conveyed in SAMUEL GUTTENPLAN (ed.), *Mind and Language* (1975, reprinted 1977); AMÉLIE OKSENBERG RORTY (ed.), *The Identities of Persons* (1976); JOHN SEARLE, *Minds, Brains, and Science* (1984); and DONALD DAVIDSON, *Essays on Actions and Events* (1980). The controversy over whether linguistic ability is a distinctively human trait is discussed in EUGENE LINDEN, *Apes, Men and Language* (1975, reprinted 1981); and NOAM CHOMSKY's *Language and Mind,* enl. ed. (1972).

Post-Hegelian philosophy that constitutes philosophical anthropology in the strict, third sense, together with reactions against it, is discussed in KATE SOPER, *Humanism and Anti-Humanism* (1986); and MARK POSTER, *Existential Marxism in Postwar France* (1975, reprinted 1977). Works with the orientation characteristic of philosophical anthropology in this sense include HANNAH ARENDT, *The Human Condition* (1958, reprinted 1974); EDMUND HUSSERL, *Ideas: General Introduction to Pure Phenomenology,* trans. by W.R. BOYCE GIBSON (1931, reissued 1972; originally published in German, 1913); MARTIN HEIDEGGER, *Being and Time,* trans. by JOHN MACQUARRIE and EDWARD ROBINSON (1962, reissued 1973; originally published in German, 7th ed., 1953); JEAN-PAUL SARTRE, *Being and Nothingness,* trans. by HAZEL E. BARNES (1956, reissued 1978; originally published in French, 1943), and *Critique of Dialectical Reason,* trans. by ALAN SHERIDAN-SMITH (1976, reissued 1982; originally published in French, 1960); M. MERLEAU-PONTY, *Phenomenology of Perception,* trans. by COLIN SMITH (1962, reprinted 1981; originally published in French, 1945); and SIMONE DE BEAUVOIR, *The Second Sex,* trans. by H.M. PARSHLEY (1953, reprinted 1983; originally published in French, 2 vol., 1949).

Opposition to this orientation can be found in, among others, CLAUDE LÉVI-STRAUSS, *The Savage Mind* (1966, reissued 1972; originally published in French, 1962), and *Structural Anthropology,* 2 vol. (1963–76; originally published in French, 1958–73); LOUIS ALTHUSSER, *For Marx,* trans. by BEN BREWSTER (1969, reissued 1979; originally published in French, 1965); and JACQUES LACAN, *The Four Fundamental Concepts of Psycho-Analysis,* trans. by ALAN SHERIDAN (1977, reissued 1981; originally published in French, 1973).

(G.P.G./M.E.T.)

Western Philosophical Schools and Doctrines

It is the purpose of this article to examine in detail major schools of Western philosophy, ancient, medieval, and modern. Several of the ancient schools presented here developed around the philosophical systems of eponymous "founders." In the cases of Platonism and Aristotelianism, the treatments herein exclude the doctrines of Plato and Aristotle themselves, focussing rather on the survival and metamorphosis of these doctrines in subsequent thought; the original Platonic and Aristotelian systems are treated in full, along with the lives of the respective philosophers, in the *Macropædia* articles PLATONISM and ARISTOTELIANISM. While the philosophy of Thomas Aquinas is treated briefly below in the context of medieval Scholasticism, full treatment appears with the biography of Aquinas in the article THOMISM. The central systems of the major modern philosophers are likewise treated in conjunction

with *Macropædia* biographies (namely, CARTESIANISM; HEGELIANISM; KANTIANISM; MARXISM), and the discussion of their philosophies is, therefore, excluded from the present section on modern schools of thought.

It should be noted that several of the schools and doctrines here classified as ancient underwent revivals or reformulations in later periods (*e.g.,* Platonism, Skepticism); further, it could be argued that no philosophical school regarded as modern is without its precedent in the ancient tradition. The present material, therefore, is drawn together to facilitate comparing and contrasting what might be called the careers of these ideas. For chronological, narrative treatment of the development of Western philosophy, see the *Macropædia* article PHILOSOPHY, THE HISTORY OF WESTERN.   (Ed.)

This article is divided into the following sections:

ANCIENT AND MEDIEVAL SCHOOLS

Aristotelianism

Aristotle's work, constituting the ancient world's greatest encyclopaedia, has exerted an immense influence over the succeeding centuries. It is proposed in the context of the present section to trace the course of the several streams of thought which had their source in Aristotle.

THE HELLENISTIC AGE AND NEOPLATONISM

The school founded by Aristotle in the Lyceum in Athens in 335 BC long survived his death. Its members became known as the Peripatetics. Aristotle's immediate disciples, Theophrastus of Eresus and Eudemus of Rhodes, devoted themselves to maintaining and to developing his teaching without altering either its content or its spirit; but after them the school fell rapidly into a decline as far as philosophy was concerned, and thenceforward until the middle or later decades of the 1st century BC no one taught as Aristotle had done. Then at last Andronicus of Rhodes made it his business to bring to light the long-sequestered treatises of Aristotle, to classify them according to their subject matter, and to publish them. His edition started a revival of interest in Aristotelian philosophy, and numerous commentaries on these texts were produced in the last centuries of the Hellenistic Age.

Andronicus of Rhodes

Andronicus himself interpreted a series of Aristotle's treatises, especially those of the *Organon,* and his example was followed. One of the most important commentators was Alexander of Aphrodisias, who taught in Athens from AD 198 to AD 211 and was known as the Second Aristotle because of the clarity of his exposition. Commentaries by him on part of the *Organon,* on *Metaphysics* I–IV, on the *Meteorologica,* and on the treatise *On Sensation and the Sensible* are extant; and in an original work of his, *On the Soul,* he gives a materialist interpretation of Aristotle's psychology of man, at the same time identifying the "active intellect" with God.

After Alexander, the Peripatetic school was absorbed by Neoplatonism, under which Platonic doctrines were resuscitated amid strong currents of Aristotelian influence. The last Greeks of the ancient world to write commentaries on Aristotle were all Neoplatonists, as follows:

Porphyry (234–*c.* 305), a pupil of Plotinus, wrote a very important *Isagoge,* or introduction, to the *Categories,* as well as a commentary on that treatise.

Themistius (*c.* 320–390), who taught in Constantinople, left commentaries on several works of Aristotle's, notably on the treatise *On the Soul.*

Ammonius Hermiae, who after studying under Proclus in Athens was head of the school of Alexandria toward the end of the 5th century, lectured on several of Aristotle's treatises: transcripts are extant of notes taken down at his lectures on the *Categories,* on the treatise *On Interpretation,* on the *Prior Analytics,* and also on Porphyry's *Isagoge.*

Simplicius, who was a pupil of Ammonius in Alexandria, wrote ample commentaries on the *Categories,* on the *Physics,* and on the treatise *On the Heavens.*

Finally John Philoponus, another pupil of Ammonius but a member of the Christian community in Alexandria, wrote against certain doctrinal errors that he detected in Aristotle: fragments of his treatise *Against Aristotle* are extant; so is most of his book *De aeternitate mundi,* which attacks the thesis of the eternity of the world as elaborated by the pagan Neoplatonist Proclus; and a series of Aristotelian commentaries is ascribed to him, some of which consist, however, of notes taken down at Ammonius' lectures and simply filled out by John Philoponus.

To sum up, Aristotle's philosophy can hardly be said to have been maintained in its entirety among the Greeks of the ancient world after the first generation of his disciples. Andronicus launched a revival in the 1st century BC, but from the 4th century AD onward Aristotelianism was submerged in Neoplatonism, which accommodated to its own peculiar view of the universe whatever Aristotelian doctrine it cared to take up.

ARISTOTELIANISM IN ARABIC PHILOSOPHY

Aristotelianism was to have a highly distinguished history in the world of Islām; but the Arabic philosophers, who owed their first acquaintance with it to the Neoplatonists' commentaries, never presented it in its purity or disengaged it from the Neoplatonic context in which it had been transmitted to them. This is readily understandable: whereas Aristotle's own metaphysic was too imperfect to satisfy Islāmic monotheism, the Neoplatonist metaphysic of Plotinus supplied an invaluable complement, to which Muslim thinkers always, to a greater or lesser extent, had recourse. The tendency to combine Aristotelianism proper with Neoplatonism was moreover strengthened by the diffusion of a work known as the *Theology of Aristotle:* this, originally compiled in Syriac by a Christian monk availing himself of extracts from the *Enneads* of Plotinus, was translated into Arabic *c.* 840 and was commonly ascribed to Aristotle himself, with the result that the latter came to be credited with metaphysical doctrines characteristic of Plotinus. Much later, probably in the 12th century, another pseudo-Aristotelian work—of Arabic origin this time—was circulated in Spain, namely the work well known from its prompt translation into Latin as the *Liber de causis* ("On Causes"): a commentary on propositions selected from Proclus' *Elements of Theology,* it was monotheistic in inspiration and served further to confirm the habit of attributing to Aristotle creationist doctrines wholly foreign to him.

The combination of Aristotelianism with Neoplatonism is already realized in the writings of the first Arabic philosopher, al-Kindī, who flourished in 9th-century Baghdad. A century later, al-Fārābī (died *c.* 950), who likewise taught mainly in Baghdad, similarly linked Aristotle's doctrines with the metaphysic of the last Alexandrian Neoplatonists, stressing however the independence of philosophy from religion.

The first major thinker of Islām was the Iranian philosopher and physician Avicenna (properly Ibn Sīnā, 980–1037). Besides his personal writings, many of which are lost, he produced a great encyclopaedia of philosophy, *Kitāb ash-shifā'* ("Book of Healing"), which consists largely of a paraphrase of Aristotelian writings but is capped with an emanationist metaphysic derived from the so-called *Theology of Aristotle* and from other Neoplatonic sources.

Avicenna

Aristotle's influence in the Arabic world reached its zenith with the work of Averroës (properly Ibn Rushd, 1126–98), of Córdoba in Andalusia, who professed a boundless admiration for the Greek master and regarded him as sent by God to teach men true philosophy. Often in reaction against Avicenna, Averroës meant to restore Aristotelianism in its integrity and composed three series of commentaries on Aristotle's treatises: (1) the "little commentaries," short compendiums or epitomes providing a brief analysis of the treatises; (2) the "middle commentaries," explaining the texts literally; and (3) the "great commentaries," a more advanced and more profound literal exegesis. While he is faithful, on the whole, to Aristotle's thought, Averroës nonetheless, perhaps unwittingly, gives it an undue extension by endowing the Aristotelian "prime mover" with the characteristics of the Plotinian and Islāmic transcendent God, the universal First Cause. Furthermore, he often enough supplements Aristotle by advancing his own interpretation of obscure passages or by developing doctrines that Aristotle scarcely considered at all. The typical instance is where he propounds his own "monopsychism": forcing Aristotle to follow his metaphysical principles to their logical conclusion, Averroës maintains that the two human intellects, namely the passive or receptive intellect and the active intellect, being immaterial, cannot be multiplied in individuals; that consequently both are single substances, entering by their own operation into relation with human individuals, as the passive intellect thinks by means of the ideas that the active intellect abstracts from images in the human brain; and that the human individual is only a superior kind of animal, altogether mortal. If Averroës won few followers among the Arabs, his interpretation of Aristotle and, particularly, his monopsychism were taken up with great interest by Jewish and even more so by Christian thinkers.

ARISTOTELIANISM IN JEWISH PHILOSOPHY

Mai-monides' Guide

Jewish speculative thought in the Muslim world was long dominated by Neoplatonism, but all Jewish philosophers from the time of Isaac Israeli (9th–10th century) to the end of the Middle Ages were subject, more or less, to the Aristotelian influence. A firmer orientation toward Aristotelianism is discernible in the famous *Guide of the Perplexed* of Moses Maimonides (1135–1204), a contemporary of Averroës and, like him, a native of Córdoba. But here again there is no occasion to speak of pure Aristotelianism: Maimonides adopts a large measure of Neoplatonic theology (emanation and the *via negativa* or "negative way" to knowledge of God), adopts also much of the Plotinian system of ethics, and furthermore differs from Aristotle on the question of the eternity of the world. Jewish philosophy in Spain, in France, and in Italy was influenced by Maimonides throughout the remainder of the Middle Ages and even longer.

A Jewish opposition to Aristotelianism had already manifested itself most distinctly in the first decades of the 12th century, when Judah ha-Levi denounced the current philosophy. After Maimonides this anti-Aristotelian reaction persisted, notably among the Kabbalists.

THE CHRISTIAN EAST

During the patristic period, some Aristotelian doctrines infiltrated Eastern Christianity through Neoplatonic channels: they can be shown to have affected St. Gregory of Nyssa and Nemesius of Emesa in the 4th century; Pseudo-Dionysius the Areopagite and John Philoponus (whose work as a commentator has already been mentioned) in the 6th; and St. John of Damascus in the 8th. In the 9th century the Byzantine patriarch Photius and his disciple Arethas took an interest in Aristotelian logic, and from the 11th century onward there was a major revival of Aristotelian studies in Constantinople, exemplified particularly by Michael of Ephesus (late 11th century) and by Eustratius of Nicaea (*c.* 1050–1120), who both wrote commentaries on parts of the *Organon* and on the *Nicomachean Ethics.* Further commentaries appeared in the 13th and 14th centuries. In the 15th century Cardinal Bessarion argued for the ultimate concordance of Aristotelianism with Platonism.

THE CHRISTIAN WEST

Aristotle's influence during the patristic period was even more restricted in Western Christianity than in Eastern: St. Augustine of Hippo, for instance, was acquainted with nothing Aristotelian except the *Categories.*

Boethius

The fountainhead of Aristotelianism in the Christian West was the Roman philosopher Boethius (*c.* 480–524). With the intention of demonstrating the profound harmony between Plato and Aristotle, he set himself to translate the works of those two great masters into Latin. He is known to have succeeded at least in translating all the treatises of the *Organon* except the *Analytica posteriora,* together with Prophyry's *Isagoge;* and he also produced commentaries on the *Categories,* on the treatise *On Interpretation,* and on the *Isagoge.* Though his achievement fell short of his project, his work was of capital importance for the transmission of Greek philosophical thought and of Aristotelian logic to Latin Christendom: the *Categories,* the treatise *On Interpretation,* and the *Isagoge* constituted the principal textbooks of logic for the early Middle Ages and so came, later, to be known as the *Ars vetus* or *Logica vetus* ("old technique" or "old logic") when the other parts of the *Organon,* known as the *Ars nova* or *Logica nova,* had been rediscovered and published in Latin versions. Boethius therefore well deserves to be remembered as "the Teacher of the West," particularly because of the essential role played by Aristotelian logic in the intellectual formation of the new peoples who arrived in western Europe as barbarian invaders and remained there to develop a

civilization replacing that of the Roman Empire. With his works on logic Boethius paved the way for the elaboration of the scholastic method, and in his commentary on Porphyry's *Isagoge* he posed the problem of universals, which was to figure so prominently in the controversies of a later age.

Charlemagne's educational policy confirmed the status of Aristotelian logic in the scholastic curriculum during the literary and scientific revival of the Carolingian Renaissance: "dialectic," or logic, was in fact the only philosophic discipline to be admitted among the seven "liberal arts" that represented secular, or "profane," learning in the program of teaching authorized by Charlemagne's capitulary of the year 778. Subsequently, between the 9th and the 12th centuries, more and more work on logic was undertaken; Aristotle's influence grew continuously as the nature of knowledge was discussed; and with Peter Abelard (1079–1142) the moderate realism of the Aristotelians was vindicated against the extreme realism of the Platonists. With Abelard likewise, and especially in his book *Sic et non,* the scholastic method was perfected. The scholastic method, a product of Aristotelian logic, contributed much not only to the development of speculative theology but also to the progress of the deductive sciences and to the grammatical organization of the European languages.

The triumph of Aristotelianism in the epistemology and in the logic of the 12th-century scholastics prepared the ground for the Aristotelian domination of the universities in the 13th century. The middle of the 12th century had seen the start of a massive penetration of Aristotle's works into western Europe, in Latin translations first from Arabic versions, then from Greek texts. Most of Aristotle's treatises were known by the beginning of the 13th century, but it was only gradually, in the course of the next 100 years, that the consequences of this flood of pagan philosophy became clear (Aristotle's works were accompanied by those of other pre-Christian Greeks, as well as by the commentaries of the Muslims). In the universities the "faculties" of arts (successors of the earlier schools of the liberal arts) enlarged their curricula from the start of the 13th century, and Aristotelianism became more and more firmly implanted, both at Paris and at Oxford, despite opposition from some of the ecclesiastical authorities. The Paris faculty of arts decided on March 19, 1255, that its students should attend lectures on every known treatise of Aristotle's, and indeed by that time every faculty of arts was turning into a faculty of philosophy teaching Aristotelianism. Already, moreover, in the 1220s, Aristotelianism had broken into the faculties of theology; and thenceforward until the end of the Middle Ages (or even later in some establishments) it was to remain fundamental to the structure of scholasticism, both philosophically and theologically. Of all the Aristotelian revivals, the most dynamic was that which the 13th century witnessed in the Christian West.

Aristotelianism in the medieval universities

The revived Aristotelianism of the Christian Middle Ages was no purer, however, than that of the Arabs or that of the Jews had been: various complementary or corrective elements were always present, whether religious or philosophical. Philosophically the main influence was derived, once again, from Neoplatonism.

Up to 1250, Latin Aristotelianism remained very eclectic and, for the most part, Avicennian, so that Aristotle's doctrine, albeit preponderant, was compounded with secondary importations. Avicenna's paraphrases were found useful for the interpretation of difficult texts; the Jewish Neoplatonist Ibn Gabirol (Avicebron) was highly esteemed; Proclus was also available; and in the 1230s the work of Averroës became known to Christian Europe. For theology, Aristotelianism was combined with traditional doctrines (derived mainly from St. Augustine and from the Pseudo-Dionysius) or with the teaching of the 12th-century masters.

After 1250, the Aristotelian influence becomes perceptibly stronger, though at the same time it branches out in various directions. The several schools of thought can be distinguished from one another by the differences in their attitude toward Aristotle, but all remain basically Aristotelian (the Augustinian school in the strict sense of the name did not come into existence until *c.* 1270, as a reaction against heterodox Aristotelianism and Thomism). Thus the Aristotelianism of St. Bonaventura is of an Augustinian tendency; that of St. Albertus Magnus is more Neoplatonic, being strongly affected by Proclus, by the Pseudo-Dionysius, and by Avicenna; that of St. Thomas Aquinas is so profoundly recogitated as to be converted into a distinct system, Thomism; and that of Siger of Brabant is heterodox, as it accepts doctrines imcompatible with Christianity.

The great doctrinal controversies of the 13th century were largely disputes between champions of the various sorts of Aristotelianism. Thus, when St. Thomas Aquinas held his ground against the majority of the Paris theologians (*c.* 1270), the conflict was not so much between Aristotelianism and Augustinianism as between the eclectic Aristotelianism for which Alexander of Hales and William of Auvergne had stood and the more consistent and vigorous Aristotelianism which Thomas was maintaining. Similarly the conflict between Thomas and Siger can be regarded as one between the Christian and the heterodox or pagan varieties of Aristotelianism.

From the end of the 13th century Aristotelianism in philosophy was upheld chiefly by the logicians, metaphysicians, psychologists, and ethical theorists teaching in the faculties of arts and was usually "moderate"; *i.e.*, orthodox with respect to Christian doctrines. Thomism became the established system of the Dominicans and even won adherents outside their order. The Neo-Augustinianism that had come into being in the reaction against the nascent Thomism found its definitive expression in Scotism, which in fact was marked by a reversion to Aristotelianism in certain fields and remained in many respects dependent on Aristotle. Finally an Averroist Aristotelianism was launched in Paris by John of Jandun in the first quarter of the 14th century and was taken up in Italy by Taddeo da Parma and by Angelo d'Arezzo. This Latin Averroism was still flourishing in Italy in the 16th century, though it was opposed alike by the Platonism of the humanist Renaissance and by the rival Aristotelianism of the Alexandrists, who revived the doctrines of Alexander of Aphrodisias to interpret Aristotle's psychology.

The 14th century, however, saw also new currents of thought running counter to the influence of Aristotelianism. On the one hand, the Aristotelian system of physics was challenged both at Paris and at Oxford; on the other hand, moderate realism was battered successively by Nominalism, by phenomenalism, by Skepticism, and by agnosticism, which, to a greater or lesser degree, questioned the validity of knowledge and, in particular, the possibility of metaphysics. Failing to disengage itself soon enough from the obsolete physics, Scholasticism was brought farther and farther into disrepute by the successes of the new. One of the reproaches that the men of the humanist Renaissance cast most frequently at the Scholastics was that of being excessively obsequious to Aristotle. Nevertheless, Aristotelianism was still the standard doctrine of some universities down to the end of the 18th century and even longer. In the 19th and 20th centuries there was a great revival of Aristotelian studies, most notably in England (Oxford), in Germany, in France, and in Belgium (Louvain). For some scholars, the interest was chiefly historical: they saw Aristotle as one of the most brilliant products of Greek culture and, indeed, of human culture in general. For the promoters of the Thomist revival, on the other hand, the interest in Aristotelianism was essentially doctrinal, St. Thomas Aquinas having taken him as the main source of his philosophy.

Modern revivals

CONCLUSION

Very different judgments have been passed on Aristotelianism in the course of history, and its value as a philosophy or as an instrument of theological speculation is still debated. Defenders of religion, whether Jewish, Muslim, or Christian, have often denounced Aristotelianism as tending toward empiricism, as defective in its metaphysic, and as limited to earthly life in its ethic, and they have accused its followers of being naturalists or rationalists. Platonists and idealists also object to Aristotelianism on the grounds

that it is empiricist, that it gives a central place to natural philosophy in its scheme of things, and that it makes excessive use of discursive reason and of abstract concepts. Finally, many modern thinkers regard the majority of Aristotle's philosophical categories as out of date. On the contrary side, Thomists maintain that many of the notions advanced by Aristotle, not only in metaphysics but also in physics, in psychology, and in ethics, are still really valuable, quite independently of the evident fact that his "science" is now altogether obsolete.

(F.V.Sn.)

Atomism

In the broadest sense the term Atomism refers to any doctrine that explains complex phenomena in terms of aggregates of fixed particles or units. This philosophy has found its most successful application in natural science: according to the atomistic view, the material universe is composed of minute particles, which are considered to be relatively simple and immutable and too small to be visible. The multiplicity of visible forms in nature, then, is based upon differences in these particles and in their configurations; hence any observable changes must be reduced to changes in these configurations.

THE BASIC NATURE OF ATOMISM

Atomism is in essence an analytical doctrine. It regards observable forms in nature not as intrinsic wholes but as aggregates. In contrast to holistic theories, which explain the parts in terms of qualities displayed by the whole, Atomism explains the observable properties of the whole by those of its components and of their configurations.

In order to understand the historical development of Atomism and, especially, its relation to modern atomic theory, it is necessary to distinguish between Atomism in the strict sense and other forms of Atomism. Atomism in the strict sense is characterized by three points: the atoms are absolutely indivisible, qualitatively identical (*i.e.*, distinct only in shape, size, and motion), and combinable with each other only by juxtaposition. Other forms of Atomism are less strict on these points.

Core concepts

Atomism is usually associated with a "realistic" and mechanistic view of the world. It is realistic in that atoms are not considered as subjective constructs of the mind employed for the sake of getting a better grip upon the phenomena to be explained; instead, atoms exist in actual reality. By the same token, the mechanistic view of things, which holds that all observable changes can be reduced to changes of configuration, is not merely a matter of employing a useful explanatory model; the mechanistic thesis holds, instead, that all observable changes are caused by motions of the atoms. Finally, as an analytic doctrine Atomism is opposed to organismic doctrines, which teach that the nature of a whole cannot be discovered by dividing it into its component parts and studying each part by itself.

VARIOUS SENSES OF ATOMISM

The term Atomism is derived from the Greek word *atoma*—"things that cannot be cut or divided."

Two basic types of Atomism. The history of Atomism can be divided into two more or less distinct periods, one philosophical and the other scientific, with a transition period between them (from the 17th to the 19th century). This historical fact justifies the distinction between philosophical and scientific Atomism.

Philosophical Atomism. In philosophical Atomism, which is as old as Greek philosophy, attention was focussed not on the detailed explanation of all kinds of concrete phenomena but on some basic general aspects of these phenomena and on the general lines according to which a rational explanation of these aspects was possible. These basic aspects were the existence in nature of a manifold of different forms and of continuous change. In what way could these features be explained? Philosophical Atomism offered a general answer to that question. It did not, however, strictly confine itself to the general problem of explaining the possibility of change and multiplicity—not even in

Forces and change

ancient Greek Atomism, for in Greek thought philosophy and science still formed a unity. Consequently, Atomists also tried to give more detailed explanations of concrete phenomena, such as evaporation, though these explanations were meant more to endorse the general doctrine of Atomism than to establish a physical theory in the modern sense of the word. Such a theory was not yet possible, because a physical theory must be based upon indirect or direct information about the concrete properties of the atoms involved, and such information was not then available.

Modern atomic theory. With the development of a scientific atomic theory, the general philosophical problems gradually disappear into the background. All attention is focussed on the explanation of concrete phenomena. The properties of the atoms are determined in direct relationship with the phenomena to be explained. For this reason the chemical atomic theory of the 19th century supposes that each identified chemical element has its own specific atoms and that each chemical compound has its own molecules (fixed combinations of atoms). What particles act as unchanged and undivided units depends upon what kind of process is involved. Some phenomena, such as evaporation, are explained by a process in which the molecules remain unchanged and identical. In chemical reactions, however, the molecules lose their identity. Their structures are broken up, and the composing atoms, while retaining their own identity, are rearranged into new molecules. With nuclear reactions a new level is reached, on which the atoms themselves are no longer considered as indivisible: more elementary particles than the atoms appear in the explanations of nuclear reactions.

Extensions to other fields. Whereas classical Atomism spoke mainly of material atoms (*i.e.,* of particles of matter), the success of the atomic doctrine encouraged the extension of the general principles of Atomism to other phenomena, more or less removed from the original field of application. Rather plausible, for example, was the extension of Atomism to the phenomena of electricity. There were reasons to suppose the existence of an elementary charge of electricity associated with an elementary material particle, the electron (19th century). A second fruitful extension concerned energetic processes (20th century). Some experimental data suggested the hypothesis that energy can exist only in amounts that are whole multiples of an elementary quantity of energy. Extensions of the idea of an atomic structure to amounts of gravitation and even to time have been attempted but have not been sufficiently confirmed.

More removed from the original field of application of Atomism is a theory known as Logical Atomism (developed by the eminent philosopher and logician Bertrand Russell and by the philosopher of language Ludwig Wittgenstein), which supposes that a perfect isomorphism exists between an "atom" of language (*i.e.,* an atomic proposition) and an atomic fact; *i.e.,* that for each atomic fact there is a corresponding atomic proposition. An atomic proposition is one that asserts that a certain thing has a certain quality; *e.g.,* "this is red." An atomic fact is the simplest kind of fact and consists in the possession of a quality by some individual thing.

Another application of Atomism (albeit in a moot sense) lies in the monadology of the philosopher-scientist G.W. Leibniz. According to Leibniz the atoms of Democritus, who provides the paradigm case of ancient Greek Atomism, were not true unities; possessing size and shape, they still were divisible in principle. The ultimate constituents of things must, therefore, be points, said Leibniz—not mathematical but metaphysical points; *i.e.,* points of real existence. They are indeed a kind of soul, which he came to call "monads."

In psychology, Atomism is a doctrine about perception. It holds that what man perceives is a mosaic of atomic sensations, each independent and unconnected with any other sensation. According to the early modern Empiricist David Hume and the pre-World War I father of experimental psychology Wilhelm Wundt, the fact that man nevertheless experiences an ordered whole formed from the unordered "atoms" of perception is caused by the mind's capacity to combine them by "association."

Logical Atomism, monadology, associationism (margin note)

DIVERSE PHILOSOPHICAL CHARACTERIZATIONS OF ATOMISM

The intrinsic nature of the atoms. In 1927 the Belgian astronomer Georges Lemaître formulated the hypothesis that the present high degree of differentiation of matter in space and the complexity of forms displayed by the various astronomical objects must have resulted from a violent explosion and subsequent dispersal of an originally highly compressed homogeneous material, a kind of "primitive atom," containing all of the matter that exists. From the philosophical viewpoint this hypothesis is interesting. By its attempt to reduce the manifold to unity it recalls the beginning of Greek philosophy, which was also inspired by a thesis of the unity of being, propounded by the Eleatic Parmenides. Even apart from their respective contexts, there is, of course, a great difference between Lemaître's and Parmenides' conceptions of the unity of being, for the latter combined the thesis of the unity of being with that of the immutability of being.

Although it would be wrong to classify Parmenides among the Atomists, it is nonetheless appropriate that in an introduction to the diverse forms of Atomism, his conception of reality as just one being should be mentioned. Parmenides' thesis is not only historically but also logically the cornerstone of atomistic thought. Any atomic theory can be interpreted as an attempt to reconcile the thesis of the unity and immutability of being with the fact that the senses observe multiplicity and change. The different ways in which the unity and immutability are understood characterize the different forms of Atomism.

Atoms as lumpish corpuscles. As corpuscles (minute particles), atoms can either be endowed with intrinsic qualities or be inherently qualityless.

The most striking basic differences in the material world, which lead to a first classification of substances in nature, are those between solids, liquids, gases, and fire. These differences are an observed datum that must be accounted for by every scientific theory of nature. It is, therefore, only natural that one of the first attempts to explain the phenomena of nature was based upon these differences and proclaimed that there are four qualitatively different primitive constituents of everything, namely, the four elements: earth, water, air, and fire (Empedocles, 5th century BC)—a theory that dominated physics and chemistry until the 17th century.

Although the theory of the four elements is not necessarily an atomistic theory, it obviously lends itself to interpretation in atomistic terms, namely, when the elements are conceived as smallest parts that are immutable. In this case, all observable changes are reduced to the separation and commingling of the primitive elementary substances. Thus Parmenides' thesis that being is immutable is maintained, whereas the absolute unity of being is abandoned. Yet, the fact that the infinite variety of forms and changes in nature is reduced to just one type of process between only four elementary kinds of atoms shows its affinity with the thesis of the unity of all being.

Notwithstanding the great disparity between the theory of the four elements and modern chemistry, it is clear that modern chemistry with its approximately 100 qualitatively different atoms falls into the same class of atomic theories as that of Empedocles. There are differences, of course, but these will be deferred for later discussion.

More removed from the original thesis of Parmenides was the theory of his contemporary Anaxagoras of Clazomenae, which assumed as many qualitatively different "atoms" as there are different qualitied substances in nature. Inasmuch as these atoms, which Anaxagoras called "seeds," were eternal and incorruptible, this theory still contains an idea borrowed from Parmenides. A special feature of Anaxagoras' theory was that every substance contains all possible kinds of seeds and is named after the kind of seed that predominates in it. Since the substance contains also other kinds of seed, it can change into something else by the separation of its seeds.

Another interesting form of Atomism with inherently qualitied atoms, also based on the doctrine of the four elements, was proposed by Plato. On mathematical grounds he determined the exact forms that the smallest parts of

One being: Lemaître and Parmenides (margin note)

Inherently qualitied atoms (margin note)

the elements must have. Fire has the form of a tetrahedron, air of an octahedron, water of an icosahedron, and earth of a cube. Inasmuch as he characterized the atoms of the four elements by different mathematical forms, Plato's conception can be considered as a transition between the qualitative and quantitative types of Atomism.

Qualityless atoms

The most significant system of Atomism in ancient philosophy was that of Democritus (5th century BC). Democritus agreed with Parmenides on the impossibility of qualitative change but did not agree with him on that of quantitative change. This type of change, he maintained, is subject to mathematical reasoning and therefore possible. By the same token, Democritus also denied the qualitative multiplicity of visible forms but accepted a multiplicity based on purely quantitative differences. In order to reduce the observable qualitative differences to quantitative differences, Democritus postulated the existence of invisible atoms, characterized only by quantitative properties: size, shape, and motion. Observed qualitative changes are based upon changes in the combination of the atoms, which themselves remain intrinsically unchanged. Thus Democritus arrived at a position that was defined above as Atomism in the strict sense. In order to make the motion of atoms possible, this Atomism had to accept the existence of the void (empty space) as a real entity in which the atoms could move and rearrange themselves. By accepting the void and by admitting a plurality of beings, even an infinite number of them, Democritus seemed to abandon—even more than Empedocles did—the unity of being. Nevertheless, there are sound reasons to maintain that, in spite of this doctrine of the void, Democritus' theory remained close to Parmenides' thesis of the unity of being. For Democritus' atoms were conceived in such a way that almost no differences can be assigned to them. First of all, there are no qualitative differences; the atoms differ only in shape and size. Secondly, the latter difference is characterized by *continuity;* there are no privileged shapes and no privileged sizes. All shapes and sizes exist, but they could be placed in a row in such a manner that there would be no observable difference between successive shapes and sizes. Thus not even the differences in shape and size seem to offer any ground explaining why atoms should be different. By accepting an infinite number of atoms, Democritus retained as much as possible the principle that being is *one.* With respect to the acceptance of the void, it must be stressed that the void in the eyes of Democritus is more nonbeing than being. Thus even this acceptance does not seriously contradict the unity of being.

Atoms as sheer extension. Democritus had declared quantitative differences to be intelligible, because they were subject to mathematical reasoning. Precisely this relationship between quantitative differences and mathematics made it impossible for Descartes (17th century) to think along the atomistic lines of Democritus. If the only thing that is clearly understandable in matter is mathematical proportions, then matter and spatial extension are the same—a conclusion that Descartes did not hesitate to draw. Consequently, he rejected not only the idea of indivisible atoms but also that of the void. In his eyes the concept "void" is a contradiction in terms. Where there is space, there is by definition extension and, therefore, matter.

Descartes's vortices

Yet, however strange it may seem in view of his identification of matter with extension, Descartes offered nonetheless a fully developed theory of smallest particles. To the questions that arise immediately as to how these particles are separated and distinct from each other, Descartes answered that a body or a piece of matter is all of that which moves together. In the beginning of the world all matter was divided into particles of equal size. These particles were in constant motion and filled all of space. As, however, there was no empty space for moving particles to move into, they could only move by taking the places vacated by other particles that, however, were themselves in motion. Thus the motion of a single particle involved the motion of an entire closed chain of particles, called a vortex. As a result of the original motion, some particles were gradually ground into a spherical form, and the re-

sulting intermediary space became filled with the surplus splinters or "grindings." Ultimately, three main types of particles were formed: (1) the splinter materials, which form the finest matter and possess the greatest velocity; (2) the spherical particles, which are less fine and have a smaller velocity; and (3) the biggest particles, which originated from those original particles that were not subject to grinding and became united into larger parts.

Thus Descartes could construct an atomic theory without atoms in the classical sense. Although this theory as such has not been of great value for the scientific atomic theory of modern times, its general tendency was not without importance. However arbitrarily and speculatively Descartes may have proceeded in the derivation of the different kind of corpuscles, he finally arrived at corpuscles characterized by differences in mass, velocity, amount of motion, etc.—properties that could be treated mathematically.

Atoms as centres of force: dynamic particles. Most systems of Atomism depict the action between atoms in terms of collision—*i.e.,* as actual contact. In Newton's theory of gravitation, however, action between bodies is supposed to be action at a distance—which means that the body in question acts everywhere in space. As its action is the expression of its existence, it is difficult to confine its existence to the limited space that it is supposed to occupy according to its precise shape and size. There is, therefore, no reason for a sharp distinction between occupied and empty space. Consequently, the mind finds it natural to consider the atoms not as extended particles but as point-centres of force. This conception was worked out by the Dalmatian scientist R.G. Boscovich (1711–87), who attempted to account for all known physical effects in terms of action at a distance between point-particles, dynamic centres of force.

Boscovich's point-centres and Leibniz's monads

Atoms as psychophysical monads. The idea of applying the atomistic conceptions not only to material but also to psychical phenomena is as old as Atomism itself. Democritus had spoken of the atoms of the soul. According to the principles of his doctrine these atoms could differ only quantitatively from those of the body: they were smoother, rounder, and finer. This made it easy for them to move into all parts of the body. Basically, however, the atoms of the soul were no less material than other atoms.

In Leibniz's monadology the situation was quite different. Leibniz did not first conceive of material atoms and then only later interpret the soul in terms of these atoms; from the beginning he conceived his "atoms," the monads, in terms of an analogy with the soul. A monad is much more a spiritual than a material substance. Monads have no extension; they are centres of action but not, first of all, in the physical sense. Each of the monads is gifted with some degree of perception; each mirrors the universe in its own way. Monads differ from each other, however, in the degree of perception of which they are capable.

The immutability of atoms. By their nature all atomic theories accept a certain degree of immutability of the atoms. For without any fixed units no rational analysis of complex phenomena is possible. At least with respect to the stable factors in the analysis involved, the atoms have to be considered as immutable. According to Atomism in the strict sense, this immutability had to be interpreted in an absolute way.

Absolute vs. relative

The same absolute interpretation appeared in classical chemistry, although its atomic theory deviated from Atomism in the strict sense by assuming qualitatively different atoms and by assuming molecules (rather stable aggregates of atoms). The decisive point, however, is that molecules were formed by mere juxtaposition of atoms without any intrinsic change of the qualities of the atoms. Modern atomic theory, in contrast, gives a less rigid interpretation of the immutability of elementary particles: the particles that build up an atom do not retain their identity in an absolute way.

In some philosophical atomistic theories, the immutability of the atoms has been understood in a highly relative sense. This interpretation arose mainly in the circles of those Aristotelian philosophers who tried to combine atomistic principles with the principle of Aristotle that elements changed their nature when entering a chemical compound. The combination of both principles led to the doctrine known as the *minima naturalia* theory, which holds that each kind of substance has its specific *minima naturalia,* or smallest entities in nature. *Minima naturalia* are not absolutely indivisible: they can be divided but then become *minima naturalia* of another substance; they change their nature. In a chemical reaction the *minima* of the reagents change into the *minima* of the substances that result from the reaction.

Other differences. Atomisms also differ regarding the number of atoms, whether they occupy a void, and how they relate to one another.

Number of atoms. As has already been mentioned, Democritus introduced the hypothesis that the atoms are infinite in number. Although one may question whether the term infinite has to be taken in its strict sense, there is no doubt that by using this term Democritus wanted not merely to express the triviality that, on account of their smallness, there had to be an enormous quantity of atoms. Democritus also had a strong rational argument for postulating a strictly infinite quantity of atoms: only thus could he exclude the existence of atoms that specifically differed from each other.

When in modern science the problem of the number of atoms arises, the situation is quite different from that of the Greek Atomists. There is now much more detailed information about the properties of the atoms and of the elementary particles, and there is also in astrophysical cosmology some information about the universe as a whole. Consequently, the attempt to calculate the total number of atoms that exist is not entirely impossible, although it remains a highly speculative matter. In a time (around 1930) when all chemical atoms were supposed to be composed of electrons and protons, the pioneering joint-relativity-quantum astrophysicist A.S. Eddington calculated the number of these elementary particles to be $2 \times 136 \times 2^{256}$, or approximately 10^{79}, arguing that, since matter curves space, this is just the number of particles required barely to close the universe up into a hypersphere and to fill up all possible existence states.

The existence of the void. To Democritus the existence of the void was a necessary element in atomistic theory. Without the void the atoms could not be separated from each other and they could not move. In the 17th century Descartes rejected the existence of the void, whereas Newton's conception of action at a distance was in perfect harmony with the acceptance of the void and the drawing of a sharp distinction between occupied and nonoccupied space.

The success of the Newtonian law of gravitation was one of the reasons that atomic theories came to prevail in the 18th century. Even with respect to the phenomena of light, the corpuscular and hence atomic theory of Newton, which held that light is made of tiny particles, was adopted almost universally, in spite of Huygens' brilliant development of the wave hypothesis.

When in the beginning of the 19th century the corpuscular theory of light in its turn was abandoned in favour of the wave theory, the case for the existence of the void had to be reopened, for the proponents of the wave theory did not think in terms of action at a distance; the propagation of waves seemed to presuppose, instead, a medium with not only geometrical properties but with physical ones as well. At first the physical properties of the medium, the ether, were described in the language of mechanics; later they were described in that of the electromagnetic field theory of J.C. Maxwell. Yet, to a certain extent the old dichotomy between occupied and nonoccupied space continued to exist. For, according to the ether theory, the atoms moved without difficulty in the ether, whereas the ether pervaded all physical bodies.

In contemporary science this dichotomy has lost its sharpness, owing to the fact that the distinction between material phenomena, which were supposed to be discontinuous, and the phenomena of light, which were supposed to be continuous, appears to be only a relative one. In conclusion it can be claimed that although modern theories still speak of space and even of "empty" space, this "emptiness" is not absolute: space has come to be regarded

Edding-
ton's
cosmical
number

as the seat of the electromagnetic field, and it certainly is not the void in the sense in which the term was used by Democritus.

Atoms in external aggregation versus in internal relationship. In most forms of Atomism it is a matter of principle that any combination of atoms into a greater unity can only be an aggregate of these atoms. The atoms remain intrinsically unchanged and retain their identity. The classical atomic theory of chemistry was based upon the same principle: the union of the atoms into the molecules of a compound was conceived as a simple juxtaposition. Each chemical formula (*e.g.,* H_2O, H_2SO_4, NaCl, etc.) reflects this principle through the tacit implication that each atom is still an H, O, or S, etc., even when in combination to form a molecule.

Chemistry had a twofold reason for adopting this principle. One reason was an observational, the other a philosophical one. The fact that some of the properties of a chemical compound could, by simple juxtaposition, be derived from those of the elements (the molecular weight, for example, equals the simple sum of the respective atomic weights) was a strong factual argument in favour of the principle. Many properties of the components, however, could not be determined in this way. In fact, most chemical properties of compounds differed considerably from those of the composing elements. Consequently, the principle of juxtaposition could not be based on factual data alone. It was in need of a more general support. This support was offered by the philosophical idea that inspired all Atomism, viz., that if complex phenomena cannot be explained in terms of aggregates of more elementary factors, they cannot be explained at all.

For the evaluation of this idea, the development of the scientific atomic theory is highly interesting, especially with respect to the interpretation of the concept of an aggregate. Is the only interpretation of this concept that of an assemblage in which the components preserve their individuality—like, for instance, a heap of stones?

Modern atomic theory offers an answer to this question. This theory still adheres to the basic principle that a complex structure has to be explained in terms of aggregates of more elementary factors, but it interprets the term "aggregate" in such a way that it is not limited to a mere juxtaposition of the components. In modern theories atomic and molecular structures are characterized as associations of many interacting entities that *lose* their own identity. The resulting aggregate originates from the converging contributions of all of its components. Yet, it forms a new entity, which in its turn controls the behaviour of its components. Instead of mere juxtaposition of components, there is an internal relationship between them. Or, expressed in another way: in order to know the properties of the components, one has to study not only the isolated components but also the structures into which they enter. To a certain extent modern atomic theory has bridged the gap between atomistic and holistic thought.

Holistic
tendencies

HISTORY AND MAJOR REPRESENTATIVES
OF THE VARIOUS ATOMISMS

Philosophical Atomism. From the ancient Greeks through the 16th century, Atomism remained mainly philosophical.

Ancient Greek Atomism. It is characteristic of the importance of Greek philosophy that, already in the foregoing exposition of the different aspects of Atomism, several Greek philosophers had to be introduced. Not only the general idea of Atomism but also the whole spectrum of its different forms originated in ancient Greece. As early as the 5th century BC Atomism in the strict sense (Leucippus and Democritus) is found, along with various qualitative forms of Atomism: that of Empedocles, based on the doctrine of the four elements, and that of Anaxagoras, with as many qualitatively different atoms as there are different substances.

Yet, in spite of its successful start, Atomism did not gain preeminence in Greek thought. This is mainly because Plato and Aristotle were not satisfied with the atomistic solution of the problems of change as a *general* solution. They refused to reduce the whole of reality, including

Criticisms
by Plato
and
Aristotle

man, to a system that knew nothing but moving atoms. Even with respect to the problems of the material world, Atomism seemed to offer no sufficient explanation. It did not explain the observable fact that, notwithstanding continual changes, a total order of specific forms continued to exist. For this reason Aristotle, with Plato, was more interested in the principle of order than in that of the material elements. In his own analysis of change, which resulted in the matter-form doctrine, Aristotle explicitly rejected the thesis of Democritus that in a chemical reaction the component parts retain their identity. According to Aristotle, the elements that entered into a composite with each other did not remain what they were but became a compound. Although there is some indication that in Aristotle's chemical theory smallest particles played a role, it was certainly not a very important one.

Meanwhile, atomistic ideas remained known in Greek thought. Their opponents paid much attention to them, and there were also a few adherents of Democritean Atomism in later times, such as the Greek hedonist Epicurus (*c.* 341–279 BC) and the Roman poet Lucretius Carus (*c.* 95–55 BC) who, through his famous didactic poem *De rerum natura* ("On the Nature of Things"), introduced Atomism into the Latin world.

The elachista of the early Aristotelian commentators. Empedocles had suggested an Atomism with qualitatively different atoms, based upon the doctrine of the four elements. Aristotle adopted the latter doctrine but without its atomistic suggestion. Certain Greek commentators on the works of Aristotle, however, viz., Alexander of Aphrodisias (2nd century AD), Themistius (4th century AD), and Philoponus (6th century AD), combined the Aristotelian theory of chemical reactions with atomistic conceptions. In their systems the atoms were called *elachista* ("very small" or "smallest"). The choice of this term is connected with the Aristotelian rejection of the infinite divisibility of matter. Each substance had its own minimum of magnitude below which it could not exist. If such a minimum particle were to be divided, then it would become a minimum of another substance.

The minima naturalia of the Averroists. The Latin commentators on Aristotle translated the term *elachista* into its Latin equivalent *minima* or also into *minima naturalia; i.e., minima* determined by the nature of each substance. In fact, for most medieval Aristotelians the *minima* acquired little more reality than the theoretical limit of divisibility of a substance; and in their descriptions of physical and chemical processes, they paid no attention to the *minima*. With the Averroists—followers of the Arab Aristotelian Averroës (1126–98)—an interesting development occurred. Agostino Nifo (1473–1538), for example, explicitly stated that in a substance the *minima naturalia* are present as *parts;* they are physical entities that actually play a role in certain physical and chemical processes. Because the *minima* had acquired more physical reality, it then became necessary to know how the properties of the *minima* could be connected with the sensible properties of a substance. Speculations in this direction were developed by the Italian physician, philosopher, and litterateur Julius Caesar Scaliger (1484–1558).

Modern scientific Atomism: early pioneering work. Modern Atomism arose with the flowering of science in the present sense of the word.

The 17th century. In the history of Atomism the 17th century occupies a special place for two reasons: it saw the revival of Democritean Atomism, and it saw the beginning of a *scientific* atomic theory.

The revival of Democritean Atomism was the work of the ambiguous Epicureo-Christian thinker Pierre Gassendi (1592–1655), who made his contemporaries not only better acquainted with Atomism but also succeeded in divesting it of the materialistic interpretation with which it was hereditarily infected. This reintroduction of Democritus was well timed. Because of its quantitative character Democritus' Atomism invited for its elucidation the application of mathematics and mechanics, which in the 17th century were sufficiently developed to answer this invitation. In point of fact, the 17th century was more interested in the possibilities that Atomism offered for a

Gassendi, Sennert, and Boyle

physical theory than it was in the philosophical differences between the different atomistic systems. For this reason it saw, for example, hardly any difference between the systems of Gassendi and Descartes, although the latter explicitly rejected some of the fundamentals of Democritus, such as the existence of the void and the indivisibility of the atoms, as noted above (see *Atoms as sheer extension*).

In the case of scientists mainly interested in the chemical aspects, the same shift of emphasis from philosophical to scientific considerations can be discerned. According to the physician and philosopher of nature Daniel Sennert (1572–1637), Democritus' Atomism and the *minima* theory really amounted to the same thing. As far as philosophy was concerned, Sennert was only interested in the general idea of Atomism; the precise content of an atomic doctrine in his view ought to be a matter of chemical experimentation. His own experience as a chemist taught him the specific differences existing between the atoms. In this respect Sennert continued the *minima* tradition. His own contribution to the chemical atomic theory lay in the clear distinction that he made between elementary atoms and the *prima mista,* or atoms of chemical compounds.

The early modern experimentalist Robert Boyle (1627–91) followed the same line of thought as Sennert, but he was much more aware of the discrepancy between Democritus' Atomism and an atomic theory suitable for chemical purposes. Boyle's solution to this problem was the thesis that the atoms of Democritus were normally associated into primary concretions, which did not easily dissociate and which acted as elementary atoms in the chemical sense. These primary concretions can combine to form compounds of a higher order, which may be compared to Sennert's *prima mista* and to the molecules of modern chemistry.

Founding of modern Atomism. The 17th century had laid the theoretical foundations for a scientific atomic theory. For its further development it was in need of better chemical insights, especially concerning the problem of what substances should be considered as chemical elements. Boyle had shown conclusively that the traditional four "elements" were certainly not elementary substances, but at the same time he confessed that he did not yet see any satisfactory method to determine which substances were true elements. This method was provided by another of the principal founders of modern chemistry A.-L. Lavoisier (1743–94): a chemical element is a substance that cannot be further analyzed by known chemical methods.

Lavoisier and Dalton

John Dalton (1766–1844), usually regarded as the father of modern atomic theory, applied the results of Lavoisier's chemical work to atomistic conceptions. When Dalton spoke of elementary atoms, he did not have a merely theoretical idea in mind but the chemical elements as determined by Lavoisier. Dalton held that there are as many different kinds of elementary atoms as there are chemical elements. The atoms of a certain element are perfectly alike in weight, figure, etc.; and the same point applies to the atoms of a certain compound. As weight was the decisive characteristic in Lavoisier's theory, Dalton stressed the importance of ascertaining the relative weights of atoms and the number of elementary atoms that constituted one compound "atom." As to the question of the way in which the atoms are combined in a compound, Dalton conceived this combination as a simple juxtaposition with each atom under the influence of Newtonian forces of attraction. The atoms retain their identity through a chemical reaction. In this one point the founder of the chemical atomic theory did not differ from Democritus.

Recent and contemporary scientific Atomism. Until its development in the third decade of the 20th century, the scientific atomic theory did not differ philosophically very much from that of Dalton, although at first sight the difference may appear large. Dalton's atoms were no longer considered to be immutable and indivisible; new elementary particles sometimes appeared on the scene; and molecules were no longer seen as a mere juxtaposition of atoms—when entering into a compound atoms became ions. Yet, these differences were only accidental; the atoms revealed themselves as composed of more elementary particles—protons, neutrons, and electrons—

but these particles themselves were considered then as immutable. Thus the general picture remained the same. The material world was still thought to be composed of smallest particles, which differed in nature and which in certain definite ways could form relatively stable structures (atoms). These structures were able to form new combinations (molecules) by exchanging certain component parts (electrons). The whole process was ruled by well-known mechanical and electrodynamic laws.

In contemporary atomic theory the differences from Dalton are much more fundamental. The hypothesis of the existence of immutable elementary particles has been abandoned: elementary particles can be transformed into radiation and vice versa. And when they combine into greater units, the particles do not necessarily preserve their identity; they can be absorbed into a greater whole.

Atomism in the thought of India.   It is interesting to note that atomistic conceptions are not restricted to Western philosophy and science. Examples of qualitative Atomism, based upon the doctrine of the four elements, are also found in Indian philosophy. In some Indian systems the atoms are not absolutely indivisible but only relatively so. In certain aspects Indian Atomism is, therefore, more related to the *minima* doctrine than to the Atomism of Democritus. Indian Atomism has, however, not developed into a scientific theory.

FOUNDATIONAL ISSUES POSED BY ATOMISM

Atomism as a metaphysical system.   In discussing Atomism, one particular system, that of Democritus, has been here distinguished as Atomism in the strict sense because of the fact that in no other system have the foundational issues of Atomism been so clearly expressed. Atomism in the strict sense is not merely one of the historical forms of Atomism, one of the many possible scientific attempts at explaining certain physical phenomena; it is, first of all, a metaphysical system: it has been presented as the only possible explanation of change and multiplicity. And as a metaphysic it is rationalistic, mechanistic, and realistic.

It is *rationalistic* because it has so much confidence in reason that, in order to explain observed phenomena, it does not hesitate to postulate the existence of unobservable atoms: *i.e.*, of things that are in principle unobservable by the human senses and can be known only by a process of reasoning. Atomists go even further, for they not only are convinced of the existence of atoms but they also think it possible to deduce in a rational way their fundamental properties. Moreover, the description of these properties in *mechanistic* terms is not just a matter of convenience; it is supposed to be the adequate expression of *reality*.

This rationalistic and mechanistic metaphysics is not only characteristic of Democritus' Atomism but also of the early forms of scientific Atomism. The clearest expression of this metaphysics is found in Descartes. For Democritus mechanistic concepts are clear and distinct ideas, so that any further experimental investigation is superfluous. It should be stressed that the atomistic assumption that the human mind, by mere reasoning, can know the properties of the atoms is a necessary consequence of the idea that atoms are not subject to internal change; for the changeless can never be a subject of experimentation. The great weakness of the mechanistic concept of immutable atoms was that it forced the analyzing experiments to stop at the atoms; but this weakness could reveal itself only after, in the course of the further development of science, the fundamentally experimental character of human knowledge had become evident.

This weakness, in fact, was precisely one of the reasons why Aristotle rejected the Atomism of Democritus, viz., that the latter had postulated atoms that were not subject to change. For Aristotle the very essence of matter was its being subject to change; hence to him the concept of immutable atoms was a contradiction in terms.

Aristotle's criticism of Atomism was clearly directed against its mechanistic metaphysics, not against its realism. This latter characteristic was the target, however, of an attack launched by the incomparable 18th-century epistemologist Immanuel Kant. In a famous argument, known as the antinomy of the continuum, Kant tried to prove that the acceptance of the reality of spatial extension, the cornerstone of Atomism, led to contradictions. His argument can be summarized as follows: It is possible to prove that any compound must be composed of simple things (for if not, there would be nothing but composition). On the other hand, it also is possible to prove that no material thing can be simple, for the very reason that a part of an extended being is always extended and is thus open to division. Hence, every allegedly simple part is at once simple and nonsimple. Consequently, spatial extension cannot be real. Extension is therefore not a property of the material world itself; it is a form imposed upon reality by man's perception.

By his argument Kant did not intend to reject atomic theories as such; he rejected only their realistic pretensions. Kant was deeply convinced that man had to *think* of nature by way of analogy with a mechanism, but he denied that knowledge construed in such a fashion could reach reality itself.

In the 19th century, scientists were, as a rule, hardly impressed by Kant's attack on the realistic pretensions of human knowledge. Scientists had already learned to go their own way and no longer worried about philosophical considerations. Only when an internal crisis in science itself arose were they prepared to reflect upon their presuppositions. Such a crisis occurred in the 20th century when science was forced to accept the relativity of both classical models: the wave and the particle models.

To a certain extent, the problem of whether a scientific model is nothing but a subjective construct in which the scientist unites his experience is the same as the problem that Kant had in mind. One of the differences, however, is that in Kant's time science was still rather exclusively *theory*. Its close connection with praxis (practice, doing) had not yet been discovered. For this reason the Kantian epistemological (or human knowledge) problem could centre on such a question as: what guarantee does the *knowing* subject have that his "models" of reality reflect reality itself? Inasmuch as, in an exclusively theoretical science, the only contact that one has with reality is afforded by means of one's knowledge, the problem seems to be insoluble.

The development of science from a theoretical to an experimental discipline forces philosophy to view the epistemological problem in a new way. For in an experimental science man is in a twofold contact with reality, viz., by his knowledge and by his experimental praxis. Modern atomic theory is one of the best examples to illustrate this point. It was this theory that was most directly confronted with the problem of the realistic value of its models. It could take up this challenge because of the theory's effectiveness for experimental praxis, which is the final judge of the realistic value of the theoretical models. It has confirmed the audacious rational speculations of ancient Atomism; but at the same time it has revealed that, in order to be really effective, reason is in need of experimental assistance.

Ancient Greek Atomism versus contemporary scientific Atomism.   In comparing Greek Atomism and modern atomic theories, it should be recalled that in Greek thought philosophy and science still formed a unity. Greek Atomism was inspired as much by the desire to find a solution for the problems of mutability and plurality in nature as by the desire to provide scientific explanations for specific phenomena. While it is true that some of the Greek Atomists' ideas can rightly be considered as precursors of later physics, the main importance of the old atomistic doctrines for modern science does not lie in these primitive anticipations. Much more important is the attempt to take seriously the variety and mutability discerned by sense experience and yet to reconcile it with the thesis of Parmenides about the unity and the immutability of matter. In its search for universal and unchangeable laws, modern science is to a great extent inspired by the same idea as Parmenides, since universal laws presuppose a certain unity in the material world and unchangeable laws cannot be established without the presupposition that something unchangeable must be hidden behind all changes. By the same token, without this latter presupposition experiments would not make any sense at all. For if the diversity of reactions occurring under different conditions is to re-

Rationalistic, mechanistic, realistic

Kant's antirealism and scientific models

Parmenides and the modern quest for laws

veal anything, these reactions must be the expression of an immutable nature. The differences have to indicate something about that which remains the same. The great achievement of the Greek philosophers was, therefore, that they took a general view of nature as a whole that made a scientific attitude possible. To this, both the quantitative and the qualitative forms of Atomism contributed, the former drawing attention to the mathematical aspects of the problem, the latter to the observational.

A comparison of ancient Greek Atomism with scientific Atomism merely on the basis of their respective scientific contents would therefore do a great injustice to Greek Atomism; it would in fact misjudge its main value. Such a comparison would, however, also take too narrow a view of modern scientific Atomism. It would imply the philosophical irrelevance of the latter. It has here been shown, however, that the later development of the scientific atomic theory has clarified many philosophical problems that, as basic issues, divided Atomism in the strict sense from other forms of Atomism. To mention only a few examples: the development of the scientific atomic theory has deepened man's insights into the relationship between a whole and its components, into the relative character of ultimate particles, and into certain fundamental epistemological problems.

Evaluation of Atomism.   The success of the atomic theory shows the value of the general idea of Atomism: the explanation of the complex in terms of aggregates of fixed particles or units. Its history also shows, however, the inherent danger of this idea, viz., that of absolutism. History has corrected this absolutism: the unitary factors have to be conceived as ultimate only with respect to the complex under consideration, and their union into aggregates need not occur only by way of juxtaposition.   (A.G.M.v.M.)

Eleaticism

One of the principal schools of ancient Pre-Socratic philosophy was Eleaticism, so called from its seat in the Greek colony of Elea (or Velia) in southern Italy. This school, which flourished in the 5th century BC, was distinguished by its radical monism; i.e., its doctrine of the One, according to which all that exists (or is really true) is a static plenum of Being as such, and nothing exists that stands either in contrast or in contradiction to Being. Thus, all differentiation, motion, and change must be illusory. This monism is also reflected in its view that existence, thought, and expression coalesce into one.

The sources for the study of Eleaticism are both archaeological and literary. Archaeologists have ascertained that, at the time of Parmenides, the Rationalist who founded the school, Elea was a large town with many temples, a harbour, and a girdle of walls several miles long. They have also unearthed a site presumed to be that of the medical school that Parmenides founded and an inscription bearing Parmenides' name.

The literary sources consist of fragments preserved by later classical authors—19 from Parmenides, four from his pupil Zeno, renowned for his paradoxes of motion, and 10 from another pupil, Melissus, an admiral of Samos—of which all but three from Parmenides and two from Melissus are 10 lines or less in length. The interpretation is also affected by the weight of scholarly opinion that now holds (as against Karl Reinhardt, an early 20th-century philologist and historian of philosophy) that Parmenides reacted to Heracleitus and not vice versa. Moreover, the biases of the citing authors must be weighed. Heracleitans and Parmenideans of the second generation, for example, saw their masters, simplistically, only as the prophets of movement and immobility; and the ancient Skeptic Sextus Empiricus distorted Parmenides' thinking into problems of epistemology (theory of knowledge), because this is what his Skeptical eye saw in his writings.

THE ELEATIC SCHOOL VIS-À-VIS RIVAL MOVEMENTS
Each member of the Eleatic school espoused a distinctive variety of Eleaticism: Parmenides pursued a direct and logical course of thought and viewed Being as finite and timeless; Zeno concurred in Parmenides' doctrines but

employed the indirect methods of reductio ad absurdum and infinite regress (see below); and Melissus modified the doctrines, viewing Being as infinitely extensive and eternally temporal. A fourth thinker, the Sicilian Sophist Gorgias of Leontini, though not an adherent to Eleaticism, employed the methods of the Eleatic Zeno to defend its opposite—a nihilism that affirmed Non-Being instead of Being.

Eleaticism represents a reaction against several tendencies of thought. Methodologically, it spurned the empirical (observational) approach taken by earlier cosmologists, such as the 6th-century Milesians Thales and Anaximenes, who discerned ultimate reality in water and in air (or breath), respectively, for these substances are materializations of Being—analogous to the materialization that occurs in Pythagoreanism in passing from an abstract line or plane or three-dimensional form to a solid perceptible body—rather than Being itself; or, at best (as some scholars hold), the substances are mythological representations of Being. The Eleatics, on the contrary, ignoring perceptual appearances, pursued a rationalistic—i.e., a strictly abstract and logical—approach and thus found reality in the all-encompassing, static unity and fullness of Being and in this alone. Thus Parmenides was the father of pure ontology. Contrasts with other movements

Ontologically—in its view of the nature of Being—the Eleatic school, holding to what Parmenides called the "way of truth" ("what is"), stood opposed to two other "ways of research" that were then current: first, to the "way of opinion" (or seeming; later developed at length by Plato in the *Sophist*), which held that a being comprises or is defined not only by what it is but also by what it is not—i.e., by its contrast with other things; and, second, to a way recognizable as that of Heracleitus, a caustic and often cryptic philosopher then living in Ephesus, who maintained—still more radically—that the essence of a being lies in part in its involvement in, or even its identity with, its opposite. Finally, as an aspect of Parmenides' opposition to the way of opinion, he was in reaction also against Anaximander, another Milesian scientist and philosopher. Though Anaximander's basic principle, the *apeiron* ("boundless"), was duly abstract and not a part of the world itself (as were water and air), his philosophy depended, nonetheless, upon the world's contrast with the infinite *apeiron*, from which all things come and to which they return "in accordance with the ordinance of Time." This contrast—which, in a Pythagorean version, envisioned the world as breathing in voidness from the infinite outer breath in order to keep things apart or discreet—thus spawned "a many" that contradicts the Eleatic One.

THE RIGOROUS ONTOLOGISM
OF PARMENIDES AND MELISSUS
For a long time Xenophanes of Colophon, a religious thinker and rhapsode of the 6th–5th century BC, was considered the founder of the Eleatic school and Parmenides' mentor. This ancient claim, however, has been successfully criticized by Reinhardt. It is even possible that, on the contrary, Xenophanes was an older pupil of Parmenides. In any case, his monistic view of a cosmic God, whom he may have equated pantheistically with Being itself, was Eleatic in its contention that God is one and ungenerated, that his seeing, thinking, and hearing are equally all-pervading (i.e., he is not a composite), and that he "always remains in the same place, not moving at all."

Parmenides' poem *Peri physeōs* ("On Nature") is divided into three parts: (1) a proem (preface), in which his chariot ride through the heavens to the very seat of the goddess Alētheia (Truth) is described and their initial conversation is related, in which he announces that he is "to learn all things, both the unshaken heart of well-rounded truth and also what seems to mortals, in which is no true conviction"; (2) the "Way of Truth," the main part, in which the real and unique Being is depicted; and (3) the "Way of Opinion" (or Seeming), in which the empirical world—i.e., the single things as they appear every day to every man—is presented. Parmenides' poem and the two ways of research

Logical and linguistic approach.   Thus, at the very heart of Parmenides' philosophy lies the distinction made by the goddess (in Fragment 2) between the two "ways of research." As noted earlier, the first is the antinomy (or paradox) of those who think and say that everything is Being and who shun all assertions of Non-Being; and the second is that of those who think and say that something is in a way and is not in another way—that a book is a book, for example, and not a table. There is, however, also a third way that is far more erroneous and fallacious than the second: that of Heracleitus, who acknowledged, just as Parmenides did, the ontological antinomy of is and is not but reversed it, holding that the real way of understanding things is to grasp their essential contradiction, their intrinsic opposition to everything else. In this view, one must say that to be a table is also not to be just a table and that to be a chair is not to be just a chair but to be also a table, because not only opposite things but also things that are merely different are bound to each other. Thus, life is death to Heracleitus, death is life, and justice would be meaningless if it had no injustice to defeat.

In essence, then, the possible ways are three: (1) that of renouncing all contradictions whatsoever (truth); (2) that of contradicting oneself relatively (seeming); and (3) that of contradicting oneself completely and absolutely (Heracleitus). And Eleaticism chose the first, the absolutely noncontradictory way that says that only what is, Being, is really true.

Coalescence of Being, thought, and expression

Not-Being, in fact, can neither be recognized nor expressed, for, as Parmenides then added, "for the same thing can be thought and can exist." And—if one may guess at the words (now lost) that probably followed—what-is-not you can neither know nor say; thus, to think is indeed the same as to say that what you think is. To this coalescence of existing reality and the intellectual grasping of it, Parmenides also added the linguistic communication of such knowledge. Each way of research, in fact, is at the same time a way of speculation and a way of diction; *i.e.,* both a way of searching for truth with one's mental eyes and of expressing it in words. The primal source of the Eleatic philosophy thus lies in the archaic sense of language, according to which one cannot pronounce "yes" and "no" without deciding about the reality or unreality of the objects of the statements. Thus, "yes," or "is," becomes the name of the truth; and "no," or "it is not," becomes that of its opposite.

This Eleatic principle may be illustrated by a passage from Aeschylus, a leading Greek dramatist, who, in his *Septem contra Thebas* (Eng. trans., *Seven Against Thebes*), judged it very appropriate that Helen would have destroyed Troy, because her name—naïvely derived from *helein* ("destroy") and *naus* ("ship")—marked her as a destroyer of ships. Here *nomen est omen:* the language is not merely a symbol; it corresponds to reality in its very structure. Thus, the Eleatic could not imagine a truth that is only expressible but not thinkable nor one that is only thinkable but not expressible.

Monistic theory of Being. From the premise of the essential coalescence of language and reality follows Parmenides' theory of Being, which comprises the heart of his philosophy. The only true reality is Eōn—pure, eternal, immutable, and indestructible Being, without any other qualification. Its characterizations can be only negative, expressions of exclusions, with no pretense of attributing some special quality to the reality of which one speaks.

Conflict with Melissus on the eternity of Being

In Fragment 8, verse 5, Parmenides said that the absolute Being "neither was nor will be, because it is in its wholeness now, and only now." Thus, its presence lasts untouched by any variation in time; for no one can find a genesis for it, either from another being (for it is itself already the totality of Being) or from a Not-Being (for this does not exist at all). Obviously, this Parmenidean conception of the eternal presence of the Being conflicts with Melissus' idea of the perpetual continuation of the Being in the past, in the present, and in the future. Thus, if Eleaticism had been founded by Melissus, no one could have really understood its actual doctrine. One could suspect in it only an aspiration to have things capable of being really enduring. But even then the theory would hardly be understandable, because what one wants is not stable things in general; one wants good things to be firm and stable and bad things

to be ephemeral. The perpetual continuity of existence as espoused by Melissus was despised by Parmenides just because "will be" and "has been" are not the same as "is." Only "is" is the word of the reality—just because it is the right name for the right thinking of the right Being.

Among the consequences of this Eleatic conception is the rejection of every change (birth, movement, growth, death) as pertaining only to the second-rate reality, which is known and expressed through the second "way of research." Thus, the true and noncontradictory reality is extraneous to all of those happenings, great or small, that make the constant stuff of all history.

Secondly, the real Being has no difference, no lack, no variety whatsoever in itself. Melissus is here the true pupil of Parmenides, who said that the Eōn is so closely connected in itself that "all Being is neighbour of all Being": for Melissus developed this theory by the negation of every form of *kenon* ("void"): the Being is an absolute plenum just because every lack in its plentifulness would amount to a presence of some Not-Being.

THE PARADOXES OF ZENO

The position of the other great pupil of Parmenides, Zeno of Elea, was clearly stated in the first part of Plato's dialogue *Parmenides.* There Zeno himself accepted the definition of Socrates, according to which he did not really propose a philosophy different from that of Parmenides but only tried to support it by the demonstration that the difficulties resulting from the pluralistic presupposition of the *polla* (the multiple beings of man's daily experience) were far more severe than those that seemed to be produced by the Parmenidean reduction of all reality to the single and universal Being.

Paradoxes of plurality

The arguments by which Zeno upheld his master's theory of the unique real Being were aimed at discrediting the opposite beliefs in plurality and motion. There are several arguments against plurality. First, if things are really many, everything must be infinitely small and infinitely great—infinitely small because its least parts must be indivisible and therefore without extension and infinitely great because any part having extension, in order to be separated from any other part, needs the intervention of a third part; but this happens to such a third part, too, and so on ad infinitum.

Very similar is the second argument against plurality: if things are more than one, they must be numerically both finite and infinite—numerically finite because they are as many things as they are, neither more nor less, and numerically infinite because, for any two things to be separate, the intervention of a third thing is necessary, ad infinitum. In other words, in order to be two, things must be three, and, in order to be three, they must be five, and so on. The third argument says: if all-that-is is in space, then space itself must be in space, and so on ad infinitum. And the fourth argument says: if a bushel of corn emptied upon the floor makes a noise, each grain must likewise make a noise, but in fact this does not happen.

Paradoxes of motion

Zeno also developed four arguments against the reality of motion. These arguments may also be understood (probably more correctly) as proofs *per absurdum* of the inconsistency of any presupposed multiplicity of things, insofar as these things may be proved to be both in motion and not in motion. The first argument states that a body in motion can reach a given point only after having traversed half of the distance. But, before traversing half, it must traverse half of this half, and so on ad infinitum. Consequently, the goal can never be reached.

The second argument is that of "Achilles and the tortoise." If in a race the tortoise has a start on Achilles, Achilles can never reach the tortoise; for, while Achilles traverses the distance from his starting point to that of the tortoise, the tortoise will have gone a certain distance, and, while Achilles traverses this distance, the tortoise goes still further, ad infinitum. Consequently, Achilles may run indefinitely without overtaking the tortoise. This argument is fundamentally identical to the previous one, with the only difference being that here two bodies instead of one are moving.

The third argument is the strongest of them all. It says

the following: So long as anything is in a space equal to itself, it is at rest. Now, an arrow is in a space equal to itself at every moment of its flight; therefore, even the flying arrow is at rest all of the time. And the final argument says: Two bodies moving at equal speed traverse equal spaces in an equal time. But, when two bodies move at equal speed in opposite directions, one passes the other in half of the time that a moving body needs to pass a body that is at rest.

The difficulty with all these arguments is that of really understanding them in their historical frame, which neither Aristotle—who was mainly concerned to confute Zeno—nor many modern scholars—who are concerned with developing new theories for the calculation of infinitesimal quantities—really tried to do. Moreover, the role of the author of the paradoxes in the history of Greek philosophy is itself paradoxical, for many of the same arguments by which Zeno proved the self-contradictory nature of the unity considered as the smallest element of a pluralistic reality (the Many) were later similarly used by Gorgias and Plato to demolish the Parmenidean One-Totality itself.

THE DECLINE OF ELEATICISM

This problem is also connected with that of the correct interpretation of the second part of Plato's *Parmenides*. Here the discussion to which Zeno submits the young Socrates is meant as a serious exemplification of the logical training that Socrates still needs if he wants to make progress in philosophy. But the result is simply comic—a "fatiguing joke," according to Plato's *Parmenides*—because Zeno always starts from the mere principles of the pure Being or the One and arrives at absurd conclusions: everything is shown to be true as well as false and deducible and not deducible from everything else.

Gorgias'
nihilism
and Plato's
Sophist

Such dialectical futility had been anticipated by the nihilism of Gorgias, presented in a work ironically entitled *Peri tou mē ontos ē peri physeōs* ("On That Which Is Not, or On Nature"), in which he said (1) that nothing exists; (2) that if anything exists, it is incomprehensible; and (3) that if it is comprehensible, it is incommunicable—and in so doing he applied Parmenides' coalescence of Being and thought and expression to Non-Being instead of to Being and thus signalled the decline of Eleaticism.

The serious discussion and criticism of the Eleatic philosophy, however, and the positive interpretation of every Non-Being as a *heteron* (*i.e.*, as a being characterized only by its difference from "another" being) is neither in Gorgias nor in the *Parmenides* but in the *Sophist* of Plato. There Plato argued that the antinomy between *On* and *Mē-On* (Being and Non-Being) does not really exist, the only real antinomy being that of *Tauton* and *Heteron*; *i.e.*, only that of a single object of consciousness in its present determination and all other things from which it is distinguished.

The real story of ancient Eleaticism thus ends with Plato and with Democritus, who said that Being exists no more than Non-Being, the thing no more than the no-thing. But many thinkers, and great thinkers at that—from Aristotle to Kant and from Hegel to Marx—have continued to work or to fight with the antinomy of Being and Non-Being.

(G.C./L.H.St.)

Epicureanism

In a strict sense, Epicureanism is the philosophy taught by Epicurus (341–270 BC); in a broad sense, it is a system of ethics embracing every conception or form of life that can be traced to the principles of his philosophy. In ancient polemics, as often since, the term was employed with an even more generic (and clearly erroneous) meaning as the equivalent of hedonism, the doctrine that pleasure or happiness is the chief good. In popular parlance, Epicureanism thus means devotion to pleasure, comfort, and high living, with a certain nicety of style.

THE NATURE OF EPICUREANISM

Several fundamental concepts characterize the philosophy of Epicurus. In physics, these are Atomism, a mechanical conception of causality, limited, however, by the idea of a spontaneous motion, or "swerve," of the atoms, which interrupts the necessary effect of a cause; the infinity of the universe and the equilibrium of all forces that circularly enclose its phenomena; the existence of gods conceived as beatified and immortal natures completely extraneous to happenings in the world. In ethics, the basic concepts are the identification of good with pleasure and of the supreme good and ultimate end with the absence of pain from the body and the soul—a limit beyond which pleasure does not grow but changes; the reduction of every human relation to the principle of utility, which finds its highest expression in friendship, in which it is at the same time surmounted; and, in accordance with this end, the limitation of all desire and the practice of the virtues, from which pleasure is inseparable, and a withdrawn and quiet life.

Atomism;
pleasure;
friendship

In principle, Epicurus' ethic of pleasure is the exact opposite of the Stoic's ethic of duty. The consequences, however, are the same: in the end, the Epicurean is forced to live with the same temperance and justice as the Stoic. Of utmost importance, however, is one point of divergence: the walls of the Stoic's city are those of the world, and its law is that of reason; the limits of the Epicurean's city are those of a garden, and the law is that of friendship. Though this garden can also reach the boundaries of earth, its centre is always a man.

HISTORY OF EPICUREANISM

Epicurus' predecessors were in physics Leucippus and Democritus and in ethics Antiphon Sophista, Aristippus of Cyrene, and Eudoxus of Cnidus, a geometer and astronomer. Epicurus differed from all of these in his systematic spirit and in the unity that he tried to give to every part of philosophy. In this respect, he was greatly influenced by the philosophy and teachings of Aristotle—taking over the essentials of his doctrines and pursuing the problems that he posed.

Epicurus' own life and teachings. In 306 BC, Epicurus established his school at Athens in his garden, from which it came to be known as The Garden.

His works. In accordance with the goal that he assigned to philosophy, Epicurus' teaching had a dogmatic character, in substance if not in form. He called his treatises *dialogismoi*, or "conversations." Since the utility of the doctrines lay in their application, he summarized them in *stoicheia*, or "elementary propositions," to be memorized. In this respect, Epicurus was the inventor of the catechetical method. The number of works produced by Epicurus and his disciples reveals an impressive theoretical activity. But no less important was the practical action in living by the virtues taught by him and in honouring the obligations of reciprocal help in the name of friendship. In these endeavours, continuous assistance was rendered by Epicurus himself, who, even when old and ill, was occupied in writing letters of admonishment, guidance, and comfort—everywhere announcing his gospel of peace and, under the name of pleasure, inviting to love.

Doctrine of Epicurus. Philosophy was, for Epicurus, the art of living, and it aimed at the same time both to assure happiness and to supply means to achieve it. As for science, Epicurus was concerned only with the practical end in view. If possible, he would have done without it. "If we were not troubled by our suspicions of the phenomena of the sky and about death," he wrote, "and also by our failure to grasp the limits of pain and desires, we should have no need of natural science." But this science requires a principle that guarantees its possibilities and its certainty and a method of constructing it. This principle and this method are the object of the "Canon," which Epicurus substituted for Logic. Since he made the "Canon" an integral introduction to the "Physics," however, his philosophy falls into two parts, the "Physics" and the "Ethics."

His
"Canon"

The name canon, which means "rule," is derived from a special work entitled "On the Criterion, or Canon." It held that all sensations and representations are true and serve as criteria. The same holds for pleasure and pain, the basic feelings to which all others can be traced. Also true, and included among the criteria, are what may be called concepts (*prolēpsis*), which consist of "a recollection of what has often been presented from without . . . ." Man, therefore, must always cling to that "which was originally thought" in relation to every single "term" and which constitutes its background. Since the truth attested by each of the criteria is reflected in the *phainomena,* man must cling to these, employing them as "signs," and must "conjecture" whatever "does not appear." With the use of signs and conjecture, however, the level of judgment is reached, and thought is well advanced into that sphere in which error is possible, a state that begins as soon as single terms are tied into a proposition. Error, which consists of what "our judgment adds" to the evidence, can be of two types, one relative to what is not an object of experience, the other relative to what is such an object but for which the evidence is dubious. Each type has its own method of proof. Following the principles and methods of the "Canon," Epicurus arrived at an Atomism that, like that of the ancient naturalist Democritus, taught that the atoms, the void space in which they move, and the worlds are all infinite. But in contrast to Democritus, who had followed the deductive route of the intellect, considering the knowledge of the senses to be spurious, Epicurus, following an inductive route, assigned truth to sensation and reduced the intellect to it. On the basis of the totality of problems as Aristotle posed them in his "Physics," Epicurus modified entirely the mechanical theory of causes and of motion found in Democritus and added the concept of a natural necessity, which he called nature, and that of free causality, which alone could explain the freedom of motion of man and animals. For this purpose he distinguished three forms of motion in the atoms: a natural one of falling in a straight line, owing to their weight; a forced one due to impacts; and a free motion of declination, or swerving from a straight line. Secondly, he made finite the number of forms of the atoms in order to limit the number of sensible qualities, since each form begets a distinctive quality, and he taught a mathematical as well as a physical Atomism. Lest an infinity of sensible qualities be generated, however, by an infinity of aggregations (if not of atomic kinds), Epicurus developed, from just this concept of infinity, the law of universal equilibrium of all the forces, or "isonomy." Upon it, enclosing the events in a circle, he founded a theory of cyclic returns.

As part of his "Physics," Epicurus' psychology held that the soul must be a body. It is made of very thin atoms of four different species—motile, quiescent, igneous, and ethereal—the last, thinnest and the most mobile of all, serving to explain sensitivity and thought. Thus constituted, the soul is, from another perspective, bipartite: in part distributed throughout the entire body and in part collected in the chest. The first part is the locus of sensations and of the physical affects of pain and pleasure; the second (entirely dissociated from the first) is the *psychē* par excellence—the seat of thought, emotions, and will. Thought is due not to the transmission of sense motion but to the perception of images constituted by films that continuously issue from all bodies and, retaining their form, arrive at the *psychē* through the pores. The full autonomy and freedom of the *psychē* is assured, as, with an act of apprehension, it seizes at every moment the images it needs, meanwhile remaining master of its own feelings.

The object of ethics is to determine the end and the means necessary to reach it. Taking his cue from experience, Epicurus looked to the animal kingdom for his answer. He concluded from this cue that the chief end is pleasure. He distinguished two kinds—a "kinetic" pleasure of sense and a "static" pleasure, consisting in the absence of pain—and taught that the pleasure of sense is good, though it is not good merely as motion but rather as a motion favourable to the nature of the receiving sense organ. In essence, pleasure is the equilibrium of the being with itself, existing wherever there is no pain.

Epicurus concluded that "freedom from pain in the body and from trouble in the mind" is the ultimate aim of a happy life. The damages and the advantages following the realization of any desire must be measured in a calculus

in which even pain must be faced with courage if the consequent pleasure will be of longer duration.

Having thus given order to his life, however, the wise man must also provide himself with security. This he achieves in two ways—by reducing his needs to a minimum and withdrawing, far from human competition and from the noise of the world, to "live hidden"; and by adding the private compact of friendship to the public compact from which laws arise. To be sure, friendship stems from utility; but, once born, it is desirable in itself. Epicurus then added that "for love of friendship one has even to put in jeopardy love itself"; for every existence, being alone, needs the other. "To eat and drink without a friend," he wrote, "is to devour like the lion and the wolf." Thus, the utility sublimates itself and changes into love. But as every love is intrepid, the wise man, "if his friend is put to torture, suffers as if he himself were there" and, if necessary, "will die for his friend." Thus, into the bloody world of his time, Epicurus could launch the cry: "Friendship runs dancing through the world bringing to us all the summons to wake and sing its praises."

If man's unhappiness stemmed only from his own vain desires and from worldly dangers, this wisdom, founded upon prudence alone, would suffice. But besides these sources of unhappiness there are two great fears, fear of death and fear of the gods. If science, however, is effective in revealing the bounds of desire and (as already seen) in quelling the fear of the gods, it can also allay the fear of death. Regarding the soul as a body within another body, science envisions it as dissolving when the body dissolves. Death, then, "is nothing to us, so long as we exist, death is not with us; but when death comes, then we do not exist." But death is feared not only for what may be awaiting man in the beyond but also for itself. "I am not afraid of being dead," said the comic Epicharmus of Cos: "I just do not want to die." The very idea of not existing instills a fear that Epicurus considered to be the cause of all the passions that pain the soul and disorder men's lives. Against it Epicurus argued that if pleasure is perfect within each instant and "infinite time contains no greater pleasure than limited time, if one measures by reason the limits of pleasure," then all desire of immortality is vain. Thus, Epicurus' most distinguished pupil, Metrodorus of Lampsacus, could exclaim, "*bebiōtai*" ("I have lived"), and this would be quite enough. And he who has conquered the fear of death can also despise pain, which "if it is long lasting is light, and if it is intense is short" and brings death nearer. The wise man has only to replace the image of pain present in the flesh with that of blessings enjoyed, and he can be happy even "inside the bull of Phalaris." The most beautiful example was set by Epicurus at the moment of his death:

> A happy day is this on which I write to you . . . . The pains which I feel . . . could not be greater. But all of this is opposed by the happiness which the soul experiences, remembering our conversations of a bygone time.

The ultimate concentration of all his wisdom is the *Tetrapharmacon,* preserved by Philodemus: "The gods are not to be feared. Death is not a thing that one must fear. Good is easy to obtain. Evil is easy to tolerate."

The Epicurean school.   Epicurus' successor in the direction of the Garden was Hermarchus of Mitylene, and he was succeeded in turn by Polystratus, who was the last survivor to have heard Epicurus. Superior to both, however, were Metrodorus and Colotes, against whom a small work by Plutarch was directed. Among the Epicureans of the 2nd century BC, mention must be made of Demetrius of Lacon, of whose works some fragments remain, and Apollodorus, who wrote more than 400 books. Much was also written by his disciple Zeno of Sidon, who was heard by Cicero in 79 BC in Athens. After Zeno, there were Phaedrus, also a teacher of Cicero, who was in Rome in 90 BC, and Patro, the head of the school until 51 BC. Already famous as an epigram writer was Philodemus of Gadara (born 110 BC). In the papyri of Herculaneum, comprising the effects of Philodemus' library, there are sizable remains of almost all of his numerous works. Epicureanism had already been introduced in Rome, in the 2nd century BC. The first person to spread its doctrines in Latin prose was

Natural necessity and free causality

The two kinds of pleasure

The two great fears

Lucretius'
*De rerum
natura*

a certain Amafinius. At the time of Cicero, Epicureanism was in fact the philosophy in vogue; and the number of Romans subscribing to it was, according to Cicero, very large. Among the greatest was Titus Lucretius Carus (*c.* 95–55 BC), who, in the poem *De rerum natura* ("On the Nature of Things"), left an almost complete and amazingly precise exposition of Epicurus' "Physics." The extent to which Epicurus was still popular in the 1st century after Christ is demonstrated by Seneca, who cited and defended him. To the 2nd century AD belongs Diogenes of Oenoanda, who carved Epicurus' works on a portico wall. In the same century should perhaps be mentioned Diogenianus, fragments of whose polemic against the Stoic Chrysippus are found in the church historian Eusebius. Also Epicurean, between the 4th and 5th centuries, was the epigrammatist Palladas.

On account of its dogmatic character and its practical end, the philosophy of Epicurus was not subject to development, except in the polemic and in its application to themes that Epicurus either had treated briefly or had never dealt with at all. To be aware of this, it is sufficient to run through what remains of the representatives of his school and particularly of the works of Philodemus of Gadara. Epicurus' philosophy remained essentially unchanged. Once truth has been found, it requires no more discussion, particularly when it completely satisfies the end toward which man's nature tends. The main thing is to see this end; all of the rest comes by itself, and there is no longer anything to do but follow Epicurus, "liberator" and "saviour," and to memorize his "oracular words."

Epicureanism and egoism in modern philosophy.   In the Middle Ages Epicurus was known through Cicero and the polemics of the fathers. To be an Epicurean at the time of Dante meant to be one who denied Providence and the immortality of the soul. In the 15th century, the notable humanist Lorenzo Valla—following brief hints by Petrarch—wrote, in the dialogue *De voluptate* (1431; "On Pleasure"), the first modern defense of the ethics of Epicurus, maintaining that the true good is pleasure and not virtue but concluding that the supreme pleasure is that which awaits man in heaven, which even the Bible calls *paradisum voluptatis.* In the 16th century, in terms of attitude and direction of thought, the first two great Epicureans were Michel de Montaigne in France and Francesco Guicciardini in Italy. Epicurean in everything, as man and as poet, was the early 16th-century classicist Ludovico Ariosto. But not until the 17th-century Provençal abbot Pierre Gassendi was the system of Epicurus to rise again in its entirety—this time, however, by approaching truth through faith. Gassendi in 1649 wrote a commentary on a book by the 3rd-century (AD) biographer Diogenes Laërtius. This comment, called the *Syntagma philosophiae Epicuri* ("Treatise on Epicurean Philosophy"), was issued posthumously at The Hague 10 years later. At the same time, in England, Thomas Hobbes, a friend of Gassendi, took up again the theory of pleasure and interpreted it in a dynamic sense, which was therefore closer to the doctrine of the ancient Cyrenaics. Starting from the premise that, in the natural state, "man is a wolf to man," he concluded that peace, without which there is no happiness, cannot be guaranteed by anything but force, and that this force must be relinquished, by common agreement, to the power of only one.

During the 17th and 18th centuries, the European nation in which Epicureanism was most active was France, where its representatives were called libertines, among them moralists such as François, duc de La Rochefoucauld, and Charles de Saint-Évremonde; scientists such as Julien de La Mettrie, who believed that man could be explained as a machine, Claude-Adrien Helvétius, who reduced the ethic of the useful to a form of experimental science but who put public above private well-being, and Paul Henri Dietrich, baron d'Holbach, who gave particular importance to the physics of the atoms. The purely sensistic conception of knowledge had its most thoroughgoing theoretician in Étienne de Condillac. In England, Adam Smith, developing the ethical concepts of Hume (founded on sympathy), surmounted the egoism that is the basis of every act by using the principle of the impartial observer invoked to

Gassendi's
revived
Epicu-
reanism

sympathize with one or another of the antagonists. After him, the jurist Jeremy Bentham, eliminating sympathy, reduced ethics to the pure calculus of the useful, which—in an entirely Epicurean formula—he defined as a "moral arithmetic." In the Epicurean stream lay also the Utilitarianism of the 19th century, of which the greatest representative was John Stuart Mill.

Epicureanism in contemporary philosophy.   In contemporary times, the interpretation of pleasure as a psychic principle of action was initiated by Gustav Fechner, the founder of psychophysics, and developed toward the end of the century by Freud on the psychoanalytic level of the unconscious.

Epicureanism and egocentric hedonism have few faithful representatives among 20th-century philosophers, though the viewpoint remains as a residue in some strains of popular thinking.

Pleasure
as a life-
style

CRITICISM AND EVALUATION

In the first half of the 17th century, at a time when Pierre Gassendi was reviving atomistic Epicureanism, René Descartes, often called the founder of modern philosophy, offered arguments that tended to undercut Atomism. Reality is a plenum, he held, a complete fullness; there can be no such thing as a vacuous region, or the void of Atomism. Since matter is nothing but spatial extension, its only true properties are geometrical and dynamic. Because extension is everywhere, motion occurs not as a passage through emptiness, as Epicurus supposed, but as vortices, or "whirlpools," in which every motion sets up a broad area of movement extending indefinitely around itself—a view that has tended to be confirmed in contemporary gravitational and field theory.

Close to the heart of Epicureanism is the principle, which occurred also in Democritus, that denies that something can come from or be rooted in nothing. In a poem composed by an ancient monist, Parmenides of Elea (born *c.* 515 BC), this principle had been expressed in the two formulas: "Being cannot be Non-Being," and "Non-Being must be Non-Being." Though Epicurus had faithfully adhered to this principle almost throughout his system, he has been criticized for abandoning it at one point—in the swerves that he attributed to occasional atoms that take them aside from their normal paths. Epicurus abandoned the principle at this point in order to avoid espousing a physics that was inconsistent with the autonomy that he observed in the physical behaviour of men and animals. But to his Stoic critics, the swerves of the atoms were a scandal, since they implied that an event can occur without a cause. It has seldom been noted, however, that the swerve is merely a special case—a transposition into atomistic terms—of Aristotle's theory of accidents (*i.e.,* of properties that are not essential to the substances in which they occur), inasmuch as an accident, too, as Aristotle himself had stated (*Met.* I 3), is without a cause. Moreover, a similar view has been seriously advanced in modern times under the name of tychism by Charles Sanders Peirce, a philosopher of science.

To the Stoic charge that Epicurus lacked a doctrine of Providence (since he viewed the gods as being lazy), Epicurus answered that "mythical gods are preferable to the fate" posited by the Stoics. It has been suggested that he might equally well have added that the "immobile Prime Mover" of Aristotle's theology was hardly less lazy than Epicurus' gods. Epicurus' way of phrasing this issue, however, must not obscure the fact that the problem of Providence and its secularization has been a crucial one in the philosophy of history ever since ancient times.

The effort of Epicurus to reduce the good to pleasure reflects the only criterion to which he would entrust himself, the "evidence of those passions immediately present," which give man the word of Nature. In the argument of psychological hedonism, here implied, the Epicurean holds that men as a matter of fact do take satisfaction in pleasure and decry pain, and he argues then to an egoistic ethical hedonism that identifies the (objective) good with pleasure. Most moralists, however, have felt that a thoroughgoing psychological hedonism cannot be defended; that desire is often, as a matter of fact, directed toward

Critique
of egoistic
hedonism

an object with no thought at all about the pleasure that it will bring; that a mother's impulse to save her young from danger is more fundamental than any pleasure involved (which usually comes only afterward); that the tendency of a child to imitate his parents can be, in fact, quite painful; and that, as a 19th-century Utilitarian, Henry Sidgwick, has argued, in what he called the "hedonistic paradox," one of the most ineffective ways to achieve pleasure is to deliberately seek it out.

Some scholars have even argued that an Epicurean egoistic hedonism, however foresighted it may be, must logically be self-defeating. If the view is universalized, the egoist must advocate the maximization of his enemy's pleasure as well as of his own, which can lead to actions painful to himself. In consequence, the entire branch of ethics that covers the advising or judging of other agents is banned from consideration, and it may be questioned whether such a view can comprise an ethic at all.

On the other hand, it has been argued that man is subject to antinomies, or contradictions, that no system can escape; there are dimensions in his nature that transcend the rational level. Thus, whatever its rational credentials may be, Epicureanism, as an attitude toward life that was theorized in its purest form by Epicurus, nonetheless remains one of the important forms that human behaviour has often assumed; and, at its best, it has achieved a type of asceticism that, even in retirement and solitude, does not negate company but welcomes it, finding the purest joys of life in the unique richness of human encounters.

(C.D.)

Platonism

Since Plato refused to write any formal exposition of his own metaphysic, our knowledge of its final shape has to be derived from the statements of Aristotle, which are confirmed by scanty remains of the earliest Platonists preserved in the Neoplatonist commentaries on Aristotle. These statements can, unfortunately, only be interpreted conjecturally.

ARISTOTLE'S ACCOUNT OF PLATONISM

According to Aristotle (*Metaphysics* i, 987 b 18–25) Plato's doctrine of forms was, in its general character, not different from Pythagoreanism, the forms being actually called numbers. The two points on which Aristotle regards Plato as disagreeing with the Pythagoreans are (1) that, whereas the Pythagoreans said that numbers have as their constituents the unlimited and the limit, Plato taught that the forms have as constituents the one and the great and small; and (2) that, whereas the Pythagoreans had said that things are numbers, Plato intercalated between his forms (or numbers) and sensible things an intermediate class of mathematicals. It is curious that in connection with the former difference Aristotle dwells mainly on the substitution of the "duality of the great and small" for the "unlimited," not on the much more significant point that the one, which the Pythagoreans regarded as the simplest complex of unlimited and limit, is treated by Plato as itself the element of limit. He further adds that the "great and small" is, in his own technical terminology, the matter, the one, the formal constituent, in a number.

If we could be sure how much of the polemic against number-forms in *Metaphysics* xiii–xiv is aimed directly at Plato, we might add considerably to this bald statement of his doctrine, but unluckily it is certain that much of the polemic is concerned with the teaching of Speusippus and Xenocrates. It is not safe, therefore, to ascribe to Plato statements other than those with which Aristotle explicitly credits him. We have then to interpret, if we can, two main statements: (1) the statement that the forms are numbers; and (2) the statement that the constituents of a number are the great and small and the one.

Light is thrown on the first statement if we recall the corpuscular physics of the *Timaeus* and the mixture of the *Philebus*. In the *Timaeus*, in particular, the behaviour of bodies is explained by the geometrical structure of their corpuscles, and the corpuscles themselves are analyzed into complexes built up out of two types of elementary

Platonic number theory

triangle, which are the simplest elements of the narrative of Timaeus. Now a triangle, being determined in everything but absolute magnitude by the numbers that express the ratio of its sides, may be regarded as a triplet of numbers. If we remember then, that the triangles determine the character of bodies and are themselves determined by numbers, we may see why the ultimate forms on which the character of nature depends should be said to be numbers and also what is meant by the mathematicals intermediate between the forms and sensible things. According to Aristotle, these mathematicals differ from forms because they are many, whereas the form is one, from sensible things in being unchanging. This is exactly how the geometer's figure differs at once from the type it embodies and from a visible thing. There is, for example, only one type of triangle whose sides have the ratios 3:4:5, but there may be as many pure instances of the type as there are triplets of numbers exhibiting these ratios; and again, the geometrical triangles that are such pure instances of the type, unlike sensible three-sided figures, embody the type exactly and unchangingly. A mathematical physicist may thus readily be led to what seems to be Plato's view that the relations of numbers are the key to the whole mystery of nature, as is actually said in the *Epinomis* (990 e).

We can now, perhaps, see the motive for the further departure from Pythagoreanism. It is clear that the Pythagorean parallelism between geometry and arithmetic rested upon the thought that the point is to spatial magnitude what the number 1 is to number. Numbers were thought of as collections of units, and volumes, in like fashion, as collections of points; that is, the point was conceived as a minimum volume. As the criticisms of Zeno showed, this conception was fatal to the specially Pythagorean science of geometry itself, since it makes it impossible to assert the continuity of spatial magnitude. (This, no doubt, is why Plato, as Aristotle tells us, rejected the notion of a point as a fiction.)

Further departure from Pythagoreanism

There is also a difficulty about the notion of a number as a collection of units, which must have been forced on Plato's attention by the interest in irrationals that is shown by repeated allusions in the dialogues, as well as by the later anecdotes that represent him as busied with the problem of doubling the cube or finding two mean proportionals. Irrational square and cube roots cannot possibly be reached by any process of forming collections of units, and yet it is a problem in mathematics to determine them, and their determination is required for physics (*Epinomis* 990 c–991 b).

This is sufficient to explain why it is necessary to regard the numbers that are the physicist's determinants as themselves determinations of a continuum (a great and small) by a limit and why at the same time the one can no longer be regarded as a blend of unlimited and limit but must be itself the factor of limit. (If it were the first result of the blending, it would reappear in all the further blends; all numbers would be collections of one and there would be no place for the irrationals.) There is no doubt that Plato's thought proceeded on these general lines. Aristotle tells us that he said that numbers are not really addable (*Metaphysics* xiii, 1083 a 34), that is, that the integer series is not really made by successive additions of 1; and the *Epinomis* is emphatic on the point that, contrary to the accepted opinion, surds are just as much numbers as integers. The underlying thought is that numbers are to be thought of as generated in a way that will permit the inclusion of rationals and irrationals in the same series. In point of fact there are logical difficulties that make it impossible to solve the problem precisely on these lines. It is true that mathematics requires a sound logical theory of irrational numbers and, again, that an integer is not a collection of units; it is not true that rational integers and real numbers form a single series.

The Platonic number theory was inspired by thoughts that have since borne fruit abundantly but was itself premature. We learn partly from Aristotle, partly from notices preserved by his commentators, that, in the derivation of the integer series, the even numbers were supposed to be generated by the dyad that doubles whatever it lays hold of, the odd numbers in some way by the one that limits or equalizes, but the interpretation of these statements is, at best, conjectural. In the statement about the dyad there seems to be some confusion between the number 2 and the indeterminate dyad, another name for the continuum also called the great and small, and it is not clear whether this confusion was inherent in the theory itself, or has been caused by Aristotle's misapprehension.

Nor, again, is it at all certain exactly what is meant by the operation of equalizing ascribed to the one. It would be improper here to propound conjectures that our space will not allow us to discuss. A collection and examination of the available evidence is given by L. Robin in his *Théorie platonicienne des idées et des nombres d'après Aristote* (1908), and an admirable exposition of the significance of the problem of the irrational for Plato's philosophy by G. Milhaud in *Les Philosophes-géomètres de la Grèce, Platon et ses prédécesseurs,* new ed. (1934). For a conjectural interpretation see A.E. Taylor, "Forms and Numbers," in *Mind,* new series, vol. 35 and 36 (1926, 1927).

THE ACADEMY AFTER PLATO: THE RISE OF NEOPLATONISM

Plato's Academy continued to exist as a corporate body down to AD 529, when the emperor Justinian, in his zeal for Christian orthodoxy, closed the schools of Athens and appropriated their emoluments. Plato's greatest scholar, Aristotle, had finally gone his own way and organized a school of his own in the Lyceum, claiming that he was preserving the essential spirit of Platonism while rejecting the difficult doctrine of the forms. The place of official head of the Academy was filled first by Speusippus, Plato's nephew (c. 347–339 BC), then by Xenocrates (c. 339–314 BC). Under Arcesilaus (c. 276–241 BC) the Academy began its long-continued polemic against the sensationalist dogmatism of the Stoics, which accounts both for the tradition of later antiquity that dates the rise of a New (some said Middle) and purely skeptical Academy from Arcesilaus and for the 18th-century associations of the phrase "academic philosophy."

In the 1st century BC the most interesting episode in the history of the school is the quarrel between its president, Philo of Larissa, and his scholar Antiochus of Ascalon, of which Cicero's *Academica* is the literary record. Antiochus, who had embraced Stoic tenets, alleged that Plato had really held views indistinguishable from those of Zeno of Citium and that Arcesilaus had corrupted the doctrine of the Academy in a skeptical sense. Philo denied this. The gradual rapprochement between Stoicism and the Academy is illustrated from the other side by the work of Stoic scholars such as Panaetius of Rhodes and Poseidonius of Apamea, who commented on Platonic dialogues and modified the doctrines of their school in a Platonic sense.

The history of the Academy after Philo is obscure, but since the late 1st century AD we meet with a popular literary Platonism of which the writings of Plutarch are the best example. This popular Platonism insists on the value of religion, in opposition to Epicureanism, and on the freedom of the will and the reality of human initiative, in opposition to the Stoic determinism; a further characteristic feature, wholly incompatible with the genuine doctrine of Plato, is the notion that matter is inherently evil and the source of moral evil.

Genuine Platonism was revived in the 3rd century AD, in Rome, and independently of the Academy, by Plotinus. His Neoplatonism represents a real effort to do justice to the whole thought of Plato. Two aspects of Plato's thought, however, in the changed conditions inevitably fell into the background: the mathematical physics, and the politics. The 3rd century AD had no understanding for the former, and the Roman Empire under a succession of military chiefs no place for the latter. The doctrine of Plotinus is Platonism seen through the personal temperament of a saintly mystic and with the *Symposium* and the teaching of the *Republic* about the form of good always in the foreground. Plotinus lived in an atmosphere too pure for sectarian polemic, but in the hands of his successors Neoplatonism was developed in conscious opposition to Christianity. Porphyry, his disciple and biographer, was the most formidable of the anti-Christian controversialists;

The Neoplatonism of Plotinus

in the next century, "Platonists" were among the allies and counsellors of the emperor Julian in his attempts to invent an Hellenic counterpart to Christianity.

Early in the 5th century, Neoplatonism flourished for a short time in Alexandria (which disgraced itself by the murder of Hypatia in 415) and captured the Athenian Academy itself, where its last great representative was the acute Proclus (AD 410–485). The latest members of the Academy, under Justinian, occupied themselves chiefly with learned commentaries on Aristotle, of which those of Simplicius are the most valuable. The doctrine of the school itself ends in Damascius with mystical agnosticism.

INFLUENCE OF PLATONISM ON CHRISTIAN THOUGHT

Traces of Plato are probably to be detected in the Alexandrian *Wisdom of Solomon;* the thought of the Alexandrian Jewish philosopher and theologian Philo, in the 1st century AD, is at least as much Platonic as Stoic. There are, perhaps, no certain marks of Platonic influence in the New Testament, but the earliest apologists (Justin, Athenagoras) appealed to the witness of Plato against the puerilities and indecencies of mythology. In the 3rd century Clement of Alexandria and after him Origen made Platonism the metaphysical foundation of what was intended to be a definitely Christian philosophy. The church could not, in the end, conciliate Platonist eschatology with the dogmas of the resurrection of the flesh and the Last Judgment, but in a less extreme form the platonizing tendency was continued in the next century by the Cappadocians, notably St. Gregory of Nyssa, and passed from them to St. Ambrose of Milan. The main sources of the Platonism that dominated the philosophy of Western Christian theologians through the earlier Middle Ages, were, however, Augustine, the greatest thinker among the western Fathers, who had been profoundly influenced by Plotinus read in a Latin version before his conversion to Christianity; and Boethius, whose wholly Platonist vindication of the ways of Providence in his *De Consolatione Philosophiae* was the favourite serious book of the Middle Ages.

Augustine and Boethius

A further powerful influence was exerted by the writings of the Pseudo-Dionysius the Areopagite. These works are, in fact, an imperfectly Christianized version of the speculations of Proclus and cannot date before the end of the 5th century AD at the earliest, but they enjoyed an immense authority based on their attribution to an immediate convert of St. Paul. After their translation into Latin in the 9th century by John Scotus Erigena, they became popular in the West.

Apart from this theological influence, Plato dominated the thought of the earlier Renaissance that dates from the time of Charlemagne in another way. Since the West possessed the philosophical writings of Cicero, with the Neoplatonic comment of Macrobius on the *Somnium Scipionis,* as well as the Latin translation of the first two-thirds of the *Timaeus* by Chalcidius, with his commentary on the text, and versions, also, at least of the *Phaedo* and of the *Meno,* whereas nothing was known of the works of Aristotle except Latin versions of some of the logical treatises, the Middle Age, between Charlemagne and the beginning of the 13th century, when the recovery of Aristotle's physics and metaphysics from Moors, Persians, and Jews began, was much better informed about Plato than about Aristotle; in particular, in the various encyclopaedias of this period, it is the *Timaeus* that forms the regular background.

The 13th century saw a change. Aristotle came to displace Plato as the philosopher, partly in consequence of the immediately perceived value of his strictly scientific works as a storehouse of well-digested natural facts, partly from the brilliant success of the enterprise carried through by St. Thomas Aquinas, the reconstruction of philosophical theology on an Aristotelian basis. Plato is, however, by no means supplanted in the Thomist system; the impress of Augustine on Western thought has been far too deep for that. Augustine's "exemplarism," that is, the doctrine of forms in the version, ultimately derived from Philo of Alexandria, which makes the forms creative thoughts of God, is an integral part of the Thomist metaphysics, though it is now denied that the exemplars are themselves cognizable by the human intellect, which has to collect its forms, as best it can, from the data of sense.

Directly or through Augustine, the influence of Plato, not only on strictly philosophic thought but also on popular ethics and religion, has repeatedly come to the front in ages of general spiritual requickening and shows no signs of being on the wane.

Two revivals in particular are famous. The first is that of the 16th century, marked by the Latin translation of Marsilio Ficino and the foundation of Lorenzo de' Medici's fantastic Florentine Academy. What was revived then was not so much the spirit of Plato as that of the least sober of the Neoplatonists; the influence of the revival was felt more in literature than in philosophy or morals, but in literature its importance may be measured by the mere mention of such names as Michelangelo, Sir Philip Sidney, and Edmund Spenser.

In the 17th century, Plato, seen chiefly through the medium of Plotinus, supplied the inspiration of a group of noble thinkers who were vindicating a more inward morality and religion against the unspiritual secularism and Erastianism of Hobbes: namely the so-called Cambridge Platonists, Benjamin Whichcote, Henry More, Ralph Cudworth, and John Smith. In the 20th century, on the one hand A.N. Whitehead tried to work out a philosophy of the sciences that confessedly connected itself with the ideas of the *Timaeus;* and on the other the rise of totalitarian governments produced a number of publications confronting Plato with the theories (Communist, Fascist, etc.) inherent in their policies. Neo-Kantianism, Existentialism, and analytical philosophy produced their own interpretations of Plato.   (A.E.Ta./Pp.M.)

The "Cambridge Platonists"

Pythagoreanism

The philosophical school and religious brotherhood known as Pythagoreanism is believed to have been founded by Pythagoras of Samos, who settled in Croton in southern Italy about 525 BC.

GENERAL FEATURES OF PYTHAGOREANISM

The character of the original Pythagoreanism is controversial, and the conglomeration of disparate features that it displayed is intrinsically confusing. Its fame rests, however, on some very influential ideas, not always correctly understood, that have been ascribed to it since antiquity. These ideas include those of (1) the metaphysic of number and the conception that reality, including music and astronomy, is, at its deepest level, mathematical in nature; (2) the use of philosophy as a means of spiritual purification; (3) the heavenly destiny of the soul and the possibility of its rising to union with the divine; (4) the appeal to certain symbols, sometimes mystical, such as the *tetraktys,* the golden section, and the harmony of the spheres (to be discussed below); (5) the Pythagorean theorem; and (6) the demand that members of the order shall observe a strict loyalty and secrecy.

By laying stress on certain inner experiences and intuitive truths revealed only to the initiated, Pythagoreanism seems to have represented a soul-directed subjectivism alien to the mainstream of Pre-Socratic Greek thought centring on the Ionian coast of Asia Minor (Thales, Anaximander, Anaxagoras, and others), which was preoccupied with determining what the basic cosmic substance is.

In contrast with such Ionian naturalism, Pythagoreanism was akin to trends seen in mystery religions and emotional movements, such as Orphism, which often claimed to achieve through intoxication a spiritual insight into the divine origin and nature of the soul. Yet there are also aspects of it that appear to have owed much to the more sober, "Homeric" philosophy of the Ionians. The Pythagoreans, for example, displayed an interest in metaphysics (the nature of Being), as did their naturalistic predecessors, though they claimed to find its key in mathematical form rather than in any substance. They accepted the essentially Ionian doctrines that the world is composed of opposites (wet-dry, hot-cold, etc.) and generated from something unlimited; but they added the idea of the imposition of limit upon the unlimited and the

sense of a musical harmony in the universe. Again, like the Ionians, they devoted themselves to astronomical and geometrical speculation. Combining, as it does, a rationalistic theory of number with a mystic numerology and a speculative cosmology with a theory of the deeper, more enigmatic reaches of the soul, Pythagoreanism interweaves Rationalism and irrationalism more inseparably than does any other movement in ancient Greek thought.

MAJOR CONCERNS AND TEACHINGS

The problem of describing Pythagoreanism is complicated by the fact that the surviving picture is far from complete, being based chiefly on a small number of fragments from the time before Plato and on various discussions in authors who wrote much later—most of whom were either Aristotelians or Neoplatonists (see below *History of Pythagoreanism*). In spite of the historical uncertainties, however, that have plagued searching scholars, the contribution of Pythagoreanism to Western culture has been significant and therefore justifies the effort, however inadequate, to depict what its teachings may have been. Moreover, the heterogeneousness of Pythagorean doctrines has been well documented ever since Heracleitus, a classic early 5th-century Greek philosopher who, scoffing at Pythagoras' wide-ranging knowledge, said that it "does not teach one to have intelligence." There probably never existed a strictly uniform system of Pythagorean philosophy and religious beliefs, even if the school did have a certain internal organization. Pythagoras appears to have taught by pregnant, cryptic *akousmata* ("something heard") or *symbola.* His pupils handed these on, formed them partly into *Hieroi Logoi* ("Sacred Discourses"), of which different versions were current from the 4th century on, and interpreted them according to their convictions.

Religion and ethics. The belief in the transmigration of souls provided a basis for the Pythagorean way of life. Some Pythagoreans deduced from this belief the principle of "the kinship of all beings," the ethical implications of which were later stressed in 4th-century speculation. Pythagoras himself seems to have claimed a semidivine status in close association with the superior god Apollo; he believed that he was able to remember his earlier incarnations and, hence, to know more than others knew. Recent research has emphasized shamanistic traits deriving from the ecstatic cult practices of Thracian medicine men in the early Pythagorean outlook. The rules for the religious life that Pythagoras taught were largely ritualistic: refrain from speaking about the holy, wear white clothes, observe sexual purity, do not touch beans, and so forth. He seems also to have taught purification of the soul by means of music and mental activity (later called philosophy) in order to reach higher incarnations. "To be like your Master" and so "to come nearer to the gods" was the challenge that he imposed on his pupils. Salvation, and perhaps ultimate union with the divine cosmos through the study of the cosmic order, became one of the leading ideas in his school.

Significance of belief in transmigration of souls

The advanced ethics and political theories sometimes ascribed to Pythagoreanism may to some extent reflect ideas later developed in the circle of Archytas, the leading 4th-century Pythagorean. But a picture current among the Peripatetics (the school founded by Aristotle) of Pythagoras as the educator of the Greeks, who publicly preached a gospel of humanity, is clearly anachronistic. Several of the Peripatetic writers, Aristoxenus, Dicaearchus, and Timaeus, seem to have interpreted some principles—properly laid down only for esoteric use in the brotherhood—as though these applied to all mankind: the internal loyalty, modesty, self-discipline, piety, and abstinence required by the secret doctrinal system; the higher view of womanhood reflected in the admission of women to the school; a certain community of property; and perhaps the drawing of a parallelism between the macrocosm (the universe) and the microcosm (man), in which (for instance) the Pythagorean idea that the cosmos is an organism was applied to the state, which should thus mix monarchy, oligarchy, and democracy into a harmonic whole—these were all universalized.

Metaphysics and number theory. According to Aristotle, number speculation is the most characteristic feature of Pythagoreanism. Things "are" number, or "resemble" number. To many Pythagoreans this concept meant that things are measurable and commensurable or proportional in terms of number—an idea of considerable significance for Western civilization. But there were also attempts to arrange a certain minimum number of pebbles so as to represent the shape of a thing—as, for instance, stars in a constellation that seem to represent an animal. For the Pythagoreans even abstracted things "have" their number: "justice" is associated with the number four and with a square, "marriage" with the number five, and so on. The psychological associations at work here have not been clarified.

The harmony of the cosmos. The sacred decad in particular has a cosmic significance in Pythagoreanism: its mystical name, *tetraktys* (meaning approximately "fourness"), implies $1 + 2 + 3 + 4 = 10$; but it can also be thought of as a "perfect triangle," as in Figure 1.

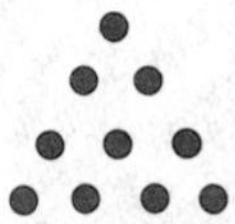

Speculation on number and proportion led to an intuitive feeling of the *harmonia* ("fitting together") of the *kosmos* ("the beautiful order of things"); and the application of the *tetraktys* to the theory of music (see below *Music*) revealed a hidden order in the range of sound. Pythagoras may have referred, vaguely, to the "music of the heavens," which he alone seemed able to hear; and later Pythagoreans seem to have assumed that the distances of the heavenly bodies from the Earth somehow correspond to musical intervals—a theory that, under the influence of Platonic conceptions, resulted in the famous idea of the "harmony of the spheres." Though number to the early Pythagoreans was still a kind of cosmic matter, like the water or air proposed by the Ionians, their stress upon numerical proportions, harmony, and order comprised a decisive step toward a metaphysic in which form is the basic reality.

The doctrine of opposites. From the Ionians, the Pythagoreans adopted the idea of cosmic opposites, which they—perhaps secondarily—applied to their number speculation. The principal pair of opposites is the limit and the unlimited; the limit (or limiting), represented by the odd $(3,5,7,\ldots)$, is an active force effecting order, harmony, "cosmos," in the unlimited, represented by the even. All kinds of opposites somehow "fit together" within the cosmos, as they do, microcosmically, in an individual man and in the Pythagorean society. There was also a Pythagorean "table of ten opposites," to which Aristotle has referred—limit–unlimited, odd–even, one–many, right–left, male–female, rest–motion, straight–curved, light–darkness, good–evil, and square–oblong. The arrangement of this table reflects a dualistic conception, which was apparently not original with the school, however, or accepted by all of its members.

The Pythagorean number metaphysic was also reflected in its cosmology. The unit (1), being the starting point of the number series and its principle of construction, is not itself strictly a number; for, to be a number is to be even or odd, whereas, in the Pythagorean view, "one" is seen as *both* even and odd. This ambivalence applies, similarly, to the total universe, conceived as the One. There was also a cosmogonical theory (of cosmic origins) that explained the generation of numbers and number-things from the limiting-odd and the unlimited-even—a theory that, by stages unknown to scholars, was ultimately incorporated into Plato's philosophy in his doctrine of the derivation of sensed realities from mathematical principles.

Mathematics and science. Pythagorean thought was scientific as well as metaphysical and included specific developments in arithmetic and geometry, in the science of musical tones and harmonies, and in astronomy.

Arithmetic. Early Pythagorean achievements in mathematics are unclear and largely disputable, and the following is, therefore, a compromise between the widely divergent views of modern scholars.

Use of the *gnōmones*

In the speculation on odd and even numbers, the early Pythagoreans used so-called *gnōmones* (Greek: "carpenter's squares"). Judging from Aristotle's account, gnomon numbers, represented by dots or pebbles, were arranged in the manner shown in Figure 2. If a series of odd numbers

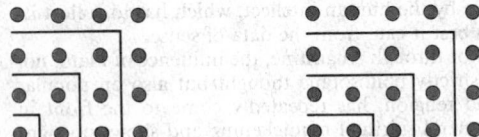

Figure 2: Gnomons of Pythagorean number theory (see text).

is put around the unit as gnomons, they always produce squares; thus, the members of the series 4, 9, 16, 25, . . . are "square" numbers. If even numbers are depicted in a similar way, the resulting figures (which offer infinite variations) represent "oblong" numbers, such as those of the series 2, 6, 12, 20 . . . . On the other hand, a triangle represented by three dots (as in the upper part of the *tetraktys*) can be extended by a series of natural numbers to form the "triangular" numbers 6, 10 (the *tetraktys*), 15, 21. . . . This procedure, which was, so far, Pythagorean, led later, perhaps in the Platonic Academy, to a speculation on "polygonal" numbers.

Probably the square numbers of the gnomons were early associated with the Pythagorean theorem (likely to have been used in practice in Greece, however, before Pythagoras), which holds that for a right triangle a square drawn on the hypotenuse is equal in area to the sum of the squares drawn on its sides; in the gnomons it can easily be seen, in the case of a 3,4,5–triangle for example (see Figure 3), that the addition of a square gnomon number

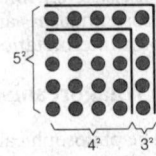

Figure 3: Gnomon for Pythagorean theorem. The marked off "carpenter's square"—comprising 3 groups of 3 dots each (3×3)—thus represents 3^2, which when added to 4^2 yields 5^2 (the total gnomon).

to a square makes a new square: $3^2 + 4^2 = 5^2$, and this gives a method for finding two square numbers the sum of which is also a square.

Some 5th-century Pythagoreans seem to have been puzzled by apparent arithmetical anomalies: the mutual relationships of triangular and square numbers; the anomalous properties of the regular pentagon; the fact that the length of the diagonal of a square is incommensurable with its sides—*i.e.,* that no fraction composed of integers can express this ratio exactly (the resulting decimal is thus defined as irrational); and the irrationality of the mathematical proportions in musical scales. The discovery of such irrationality was disquieting because it had fatal consequences for the naive view that the universe is expressible in whole numbers; the Pythagorean Hippasus is said to have been expelled from the brotherhood, according to some sources even drowned, because he made a point of the irrationality.

The problem of irrational numbers

In the 4th century, Pythagorizing mathematicians made a significant advance in the theory of irrational numbers, such as the-square-root-of-n ($\sqrt{n}$), n being any rational number, when they developed a method for finding progressive approximations to $\sqrt{2}$ by forming sets of so-called diagonal numbers.

Geometry. In geometry, the Pythagoreans cannot be credited with any proofs in the Euclidean sense. They were evidently concerned, however, with some speculation on geometrical figures, as in the case of the Pythagorean theorem, and the concept that the point, line, triangle, and tetrahedron correspond to the elements of the *tetraktys*, since they are determined by one, two, three, and four points, respectively. They possibly knew practical methods of constructing the five regular solids, but the theoretical basis for such constructions was given by non-Pythagoreans in the 4th century.

It is notable that the properties of the circle seem not to have interested the early Pythagoreans. But perhaps the tradition that Pythagoras himself discovered that the sum of the three angles of any triangle is equal to two right angles may be trusted. The idea of geometric proportions is probably Pythagorean in origin; but the so-called golden section—which divides a line at a point such

Figure 1: The *Tetraktys* (see text).

that the smaller part is to the greater as the greater is to the whole—is hardly an early Pythagorean contribution. Some advance in geometry was made at a later date, by 4th-century Pythagoreans; *e.g.*, Archytas offered an interesting solution to the problem of the duplication of the cube—in which a cube twice the volume of a given cube is constructed—by an essentially geometrical construction in three dimensions; and the conception of geometry as a "flow" of points into lines, of lines into surfaces, and so on, may have been contributed by Archytas; but on the whole the numerous achievements of non-Pythagorean mathematicians were in fact more conspicuous than those of the Pythagoreans.

Music. The achievements of the early Pythagoreans in musical theory are somewhat less controversial. The scientific approach to music, in which musical intervals are expressed as numerical proportions, originated with them, as did also the more specific idea of harmonic "means." At an early date they discovered empirically that the basic intervals of Greek music include the elements of the *tetraktys,* since they have the proportions 1:2 (octave), 3:2 (fifth), and 4:3 (fourth). The discovery could have been made, for instance, in pipes or flutes or stringed instruments: the tone of a plucked string held at its middle is an octave higher than that of the whole string; the tone of a string held at the $^2/_3$ point is a fifth higher; and that of one held at the $^3/_4$ point is a fourth higher. Moreover, they noticed that the subtraction of intervals is accomplished by dividing these ratios by one another. In the course of the 5th century they calculated the intervals for the usual diatonic scale, the tone being represented by 9:8 (fifth minus fourth); *i.e.,* $3/2 \div 4/3$, and the semitone by 256:243 (fourth minus two tones); *i.e.,* $4/3 \div (9/8 \times 9/8)$. Archytas made some modification to this doctrine and also worked out the relationships of the notes in the chromatic (12-tone) scale and the enharmonic scale (involving such minute differences as that between A flat and G sharp, which on a piano are played by the same key).

Astronomy. In their cosmological views the earliest Pythagoreans probably differed little from their Ionian predecessors. They made a point of studying the stellar heavens; but—with the possible exception of the theory of musical intervals in the cosmos—no new contributions to astronomy can be ascribed to them with any degree of probability. Late in the 5th century, or possibly in the 4th century, a Pythagorean boldly abandoned the geocentric view and posited a cosmological model in which the Earth, Sun, and stars circle about an (unseen) central fire—a view traditionally attributed to the 5th-century Pythagorean Philolaus of Croton.

HISTORY OF PYTHAGOREANISM

The life of Pythagoras and the origins of Pythagoreanism appear only dimly through a thick veil of legend and semihistorical tradition. The literary sources for the teachings of the Pythagoreans present extremely complicated problems. Special difficulties arise from the oral and esoteric transmission of the early doctrines, the profuse accumulation of tendentious legends, and the considerable amount of confusion that was caused by the split in the school in the 5th century BC. In the 4th century, Plato's inclination toward Pythagoreanism created a tendency—manifest already in the middle of the century in the works of his pupils—to interpret Platonic concepts as originally Pythagorean. But the radical skepticism as to the reliability of the sources shown by some modern scholars has on the whole been abandoned in recent research. It now seems possible to extract bits of reliable evidence from a wide range of ancient authors, such as Porphyry and Iamblichus (see below *Neo-Pythagoreanism*).

Most of these literary sources hark back ultimately to the environment of Plato and Aristotle; and here the importance of one of Aristotle's students has become obvious, viz., the musicologist and philosopher Aristoxenus, who in spite of his bias possessed firsthand information independent of the point of view of Plato's Academy. The role played by Dicaearchus, another of Aristotle's pupils, and by the Sicilian historian Timaeus, of the early 3rd century BC, is less clear. Recently, the reliability of Aristot-

le's account of Pythagoreanism has also been emphasized against the doubts that had been expressed by some modern scholars; but Aristotle's sources, in turn, hardly lead farther back than to the late 5th century (perhaps to Philolaus; see below *Two Pythagorean sects*). In addition, there are scattered hints in various early authors and in some not very substantial remains of 4th-century Pythagorean literature. The mosaic of reconstruction thus has to be to some extent subjective.

Early Pythagoreanism. Within the ancient Pythagorean movement four chief periods can be distinguished: early Pythagoreanism, dating from the late 6th century BC and extending to about 400 BC; 4th-century Pythagoreanism; the Hellenistic trends; and Neo-Pythagoreanism, a revival that occurred in the mid-1st century AD and lasted for two and a half centuries.

Background. The background of Pythagoreanism is complex, but two main groups of sources can be distinguished. The Ionian philosophers (Thales, Anaximander, Anaximenes, and others) provided Pythagoras with the problem of a single cosmic principle, the doctrine of opposites, and whatever reflections of Oriental mathematics there are in Pythagoreanism; and from the technicians of his birthplace, the Isle of Samos, he learned to understand the importance of number, measurements, and proportions. Popular cults and beliefs current in the 6th century and reflected in the tenets of Orphism introduced him to the notions of occultism and ritualism and to the doctrine of individual immortality. In view of the shamanistic traits of Pythagoreanism, reminiscent of Thracian cults, it is interesting to note that Pythagoras seems to have had a Thracian slave.

Pythagorean communities. The school apparently founded by Pythagoras at Croton in southern Italy seems to have been primarily a religious brotherhood centred around Pythagoras and the cults of Apollo and of the Muses, ancient patron goddesses of poetry and culture. It became perhaps successively institutionalized and received different classes of esoteric members and exoteric sympathizers. The rigorism of the ritual and ethical observances demanded of the members is unparalleled in early Greece; in addition to the rules of life mentioned above, it is fairly well attested that secrecy and a long silence during the novitiate were required. The exoteric associates, however, were politically active and established a Crotonian hegemony in southern Italy. About 500 BC a coup by a rival party caused Pythagoras to take refuge in Metapontum, where he died.

During the early 5th century, Pythagorean communities, inspired by the original school at Croton, existed in many southern Italian cities, a fact that led to some doctrinal differentiation and diffusion. In the course of time the politics of the Pythagorean parties became decidedly antidemocratic. About the middle of the century a violent democratic revolution swept over southern Italy; in its wake, many Pythagoreans were killed, and only a few escaped, among them Lysis of Tarentum and Philolaus of Croton, who went to Greece and formed small Pythagorean circles in Thebes and Phlious.

Two Pythagorean sects. Little is known about Pythagorean activity during the latter part of the 5th century. The differentiation of the school into two main sects, later called *akousmatikoi* (Greek: *akousma,* "something heard," viz., the esoteric teachings) and *mathēmatikoi* (Greek: *mathēmatikos,* "scientific"), may have occurred at that time. The acousmatics devoted themselves to the observance of rituals and rules and to the interpretation of the sayings of the master; the "mathematics" were concerned with the scientific aspects of Pythagoreanism. Philolaus, who was rather a mathematic, probably published a summary of Pythagorean philosophy and science in the late 5th century.

4th-century Pythagoreanism. In the first half of the 4th century, Tarentum, in southern Italy, rose into considerable significance. Under the political and spiritual leadership of the mathematic Archytas, a friend of Plato, Tarentum became a new centre of Pythagoreanism, from which acousmatics—so-called Pythagorists who did not sympathize with Archytas—went out travelling as mendicant

Mathematical ratios of tones

Literary sources, especially Aristotelian

Four chief periods

Archytas and his school

ascetics all around the Greek-speaking world. The acousmatics seem to have preserved some early Pythagorean *Hieroi Logoi* and ritual practices. Archytas himself, on the other hand, concentrated on scientific problems, and the organization of his Pythagorean brotherhood was evidently less rigorous than that of the early school. After the 380s there was a give-and-take between the school of Archytas and the Academy of Plato, a relationship that makes it almost impossible to disentangle the original achievements of Archytas from joint involvements (but see above, *Geometry* and *Music*).

The Hellenistic Age. Whereas the school of Archytas apparently sank into inactivity after the death of its founder (probably after 350 BC), the Academics of the next generation continued "Pythagorizing" Platonic doctrines, such as that of the supreme One, the indefinite dyad (a metaphysical principle), and the tripartite soul. At the same time, various Peripatetics of the school of Aristotle, including Aristoxenus, collected Pythagorean legends and applied contemporary ethical notions to them. In the Hellenistic Age, the Academic and Peripatetic views gave rise to a rather fanciful antiquarian literature on Pythagoreanism. There also appeared a large and yet more heterogeneous mass of apocryphal writings falsely attributed to different Pythagoreans, as if attempts were being made to revive the school. The texts fathered on Archytas display Academic and Peripatetic philosophies mixed with some notions that were originally Pythagorean. Other texts were fathered on Pythagoras himself or on his immediate pupils, imagined or real. Some show, for instance, that Pythagoreanism had become confused with Orphism; others suggest that Pythagoras was considered a magician and an astrologist; there are also indications of Pythagoras "the athlete" and "the Dorian nationalist." But the anonymous authors of this pseudo-Pythagorean literature did not succeed in reestablishing the school, and the "Pythagorean" congregations formed in early imperial Rome seem to have had little in common with the original school of Pythagoreanism established in the late 6th century BC; they were ritualistic sects that adopted, eclectically, various occult practices.

Neo-Pythagoreanism. With the ascetic sage Apollonius of Tyana, about the middle of the 1st century AD, a distinct Neo-Pythagorean trend appeared. Apollonius studied the Pythagorean legends of the previous centuries, created and propagated the ideal of a Pythagorean life—of occult wisdom, purity, universal tolerance, and approximation to the divine—and felt himself to be a reincarnation of Pythagoras. Through the activities of Neo-Pythagorean Platonists, such as Moderatus of Gades, a pagan trinitarian, and the arithmetician Nicomachus of Gerasa, both of the 1st century AD, and, in the 2nd or 3rd century, Numenius of Apamea, forerunner of Plotinus (an epoch-making elaborator of Platonism), Neo-Pythagoreanism gradually became a part of the expression of Platonism known as Neoplatonism; and it did so without having achieved a scholastic system of its own. The founder of a Syrian school of Neoplatonism, Iamblichus, a pupil of Porphyry (who in turn had been a pupil of Plotinus), thought of himself as a Pythagorean sage and about AD 300 wrote the last great synthesis of Pythagoreanism, in which most of the disparate post-classical traditions are reflected. It is characteristic of the Neo-Pythagoreans that they were chiefly interested in the Pythagorean way of life and in the pseudoscience of number mysticism. On a more popular level, Pythagoras and Archytas were remembered as magicians. Moreover, it has been suggested that Pythagorean legends were also influential in guiding the Christian monastic tradition.

Amalgamation with Neoplatonism

Medieval and modern trends. In the Middle Ages the popular conception of Pythagoras the magician was combined with that of Pythagoras "the father of the quadrivium"; *i.e.,* of the more specialized liberal arts of the curriculum. From the Italian Renaissance onward, some "Pythagorean" ideas, such as the tetrad, the golden section, and harmonic proportions, became applied to aesthetics. To many Humanists, moreover, Pythagoras was the father of the exact sciences. In the early 16th century, Nicolaus Copernicus, who developed the view that the Earth re-

volves around the Sun, considered his system to be essentially Pythagorean or "Philolaic," and Galileo was called a Pythagorean. The 17th-century Rationalist G.W. Leibniz appears to have been the last great philosopher and scientist who felt himself to be in the Pythagorean tradition.

It is doubtful whether advanced modern philosophy has ever drawn from sources thought to be distinctly Pythagorean. Yet Platonic–Neoplatonic notions, such as the mathematical conception of reality or the philosopher's union with the universe and various mystical beliefs are still likely to be stamped as Pythagorean in origin. Even today a relatively uncritical admiration of Pythagoreanism is common.

EVALUATION

The history of the projection of Pythagoreanism into subsequent thought indicates how fertile some of its core concepts were. Plato is here the great catalyst; but it is possible to perceive behind him, however dimly, a series of Pythagorean ideas of paramount potential significance: the combination of religious esoterism (or exclusivism) with the germs of a new philosophy of mind, present in the belief in the progress of the soul toward the actualization of its divine nature and toward knowledge; stress upon harmony and order, and upon limit as the good; the primacy of form, proportion, and numerical expression; and in ethics, and emphasis upon such virtues as friendship and modesty. The fact that Pythagoras, to later ages, also became alternatively conceived of as a Dorian nationalist, a sportsman, an educator of the people, or a great magician is a more curious consequence of the productivity of his teaching.

(H.T.)

Realism

Understood in its broadest philosophical sense, Realism connotes any viewpoint that accords to the objects of man's knowledge an existence that is independent of whether he is perceiving or thinking about them. Though it may seem strange to the unphilosophical layman that the independent existence of objects "out there" should be questioned, the philosopher, faced with the many profound challenges that Idealists have posed against the independence of objects, knows that the problem of the existence of objects—whether in thought or in concrete form—is far from trivial.

Clearly, Idealists have argued, musical tones such as middle C do not have existence as tones in the air; they appear, instead, to be qualities that the mind itself generates when the appropriate hair cells in the organ of Corti are stimulated. Nor does the colour purple have existence as a quality in the world outside of the mind; there can be, in fact, no such thing as a beam of pure (monochromatic) purple light inasmuch as purple is a unique kind of colour that is perceived when vibrations at the opposite extremes of the visual spectrum (red and violet) are mixed together in the same beam. At least in this one case, the colour seems created by the mind. But if this is so of purple, the Idealists ask, is it not true, also, of all colours? Similarly, under certain circumstances heat is felt as cold and rotation as oscillation. It is not surprising, therefore, that philosophers have asked what, if any, residual properties an object might have in and of itself after due allowance has been made for those qualities that the mind and perspective of the observer have imposed upon it; nor is it surprising that they have asked what, if anything, it would mean to insist on the objective existence of an object of which all of the qualities were mental. Realists, on the other hand, have held that, in spite of the foregoing considerations as proposed by the Idealists, there still remains a sense in which objects can have an existence that is independent of minds.

The Idealist challenge

Realism exists, however, in several strikingly different versions: its objects may be, for example, either individual things (such as "the Moon"), or merely particular qualities of things (such as "roundness," "yellowness"), or species and genera of things (such as "moons," "planetary bodies"). In one way or another, however, whether it regards things from the viewpoint of the things themselves or from that of the human activities related to them, Realism tends to stress some definite function of the independent existence of objects.

NATURE AND SCOPE OF REALISM

Realism and the problem of knowledge. One of the major problems confronting Realism involves the distinction between private, public, and so-called ontological objects.

Private, public, and ontological objects

A private object is a sheer datum (such as a perceived patch of yellow) taken purely as an uninterpreted item in the knower's own inner experience; a public object is one that the mind has projected into an objective conceptual frame of space and time shared in common with other minds, an object that the mind has constituted as a percept (such as the perceived Moon)—though it is still acknowledged to be in part mental (*e.g.,* its yellowness; or its visual size, which is larger when it is near the horizon); and an ontological object is the Kantian "thing-in-itself" (the Moon as it really is), which may as well consist of monads, of God's thoughts, of will, or of action, as of force and matter. Though Realists and Idealists both acknowledge that the knower transcends the private object, they make different assumptions about the relationship between the public and the ontological object: on the one hand, the Realist holds that the physical sphericity, yellowness, and hardness perceived (or perceivable) in the public object are in some degree actual properties of the ontological thing-in-itself; the Idealist, on the other hand, holds that the public object is merely a phenomenon, from which little can be inferred about the underlying *onta* (realities), least of all of their basic qualities, which are probably quite different from the roundness and hardness of the perceived object. The Idealist may, in fact surmise that the nature of the *onta* is conveyed more faithfully in the fundamental mental tone of the public object—in the colours, feelings, and durations (which are of the nature of mind)—than in its specific material properties. (A third contender, that philosopher known as the metaphysical solipsist, would hold to the viewpoint that the ontological object does not exist at all.)

Similarly, if a particular thing regarded in its particularity (such as the Moon) is distinguished from a universal— *i.e.,* an entity comprising the essence of the thing (moonness)—that which it shares with all the other things of the same species or genus (as with the moons of Jupiter)— then a form of Realism can be defined as asserting the independent reality of universals, which it may even exalt above that of particulars.

Contrast with other views

Accordingly, Realism may be variously opposed to the tenets of other philosophical positions. As opposed to Nominalism, which denies that essences (or the specific and generic natures of things) have any reality at all (except as names), and conceptualism, which grants such universals reality only as concepts within the mind, Realism allows to the specific or generic nature of the thing a distinct existence in reality outside the mind. Against Idealism (see above), it asserts that the existence of sense objects (such as the perceived Moon) and that of their qualities is external to thought. In opposition to phenomenalism and sensationalism, which regard objects as comprising mere private volleys or families of disconnected sense fragments, Realism grounds objects in real unified and enduring substances. Unlike conventionalism, a philosophy of science that regards scientific laws and theories as freely chosen constructs that are simply devised by the scientist for the purpose of describing reality, Realism holds that laws and theories have determined and real counterparts in things.

The term Realism first appeared early in the 19th century, though the adjective Realist dates from the late 16th century. These terms have been applied, however— often retroactively—to various systems that have arisen throughout history.

In its broadest scope, the term Realism has application in a number of distinct areas. In literature, art, and aesthetics, in law, and in philosophy, it emphasizes real existence or relation to it. The present article is concerned solely with Realism in the philosophical area.

Philosophical senses of Realism. Even within philosophy Realism has a wide range of applications. Though a definitely modern term, Realism is freely used today for tenets of the Greek and medieval epochs, as well as for the modern period.

Basic kinds of Realism. Among philosophical Realisms, two fundamentally different kinds can be distinguished: the Realism of natures and the Realism of things. In the Realism of natures, that which is viewed as having an existence external to the mind is an entity that, in some sense, is set apart in the world of things—an entity that is variously understood as the Form or Idea in which a thing participates, such as "manness" or "bedness" (Platonic Realism), as the essence or *to ti ēn einai,* "the 'what it is' of a thing" (Aristotelian Realism), or as its nature, either absolute, specific, or generic (medieval Realism or the Realism of universals), or, finally, as laws or theoretical models abstracted from scientific observations. In the Realism of things, on the other hand, that which is viewed as having an existence external to the mind is the total, concrete, and individual object of experience, which the Realist regards as retaining its chief properties at all times, even when left unseen. This Realism, too, can be variously conceived: the externality of the world, for example, can be regarded as simply and obviously given (commonsense Realism); the object itself, though external, can be viewed as the sole entity standing before the mind and grasped by it (neo-Realism); or the object can be conceived as, in some sense, duplicated, so that the mind directly encounters only a counterpart of the external object and not the object itself (critical Realism), a counterpart which was sometimes regarded as a representation of it (representational Realism).

Distinctions among the Realisms. As previously noted, the term Realism has been applied retroactively to the transcendence of the Platonic Forms or Ideas, to the extent that for Plato the natures of things have, in the ideas of them, an existence more real than that of sensible, individual things. Yet from its emphasis on ideal as opposed to concrete existence, this Platonic doctrine would be classed as an Idealism instead of a Realism. In the parallel issue in Aristotelianism, the stand that the universals, or specific and generic natures, exist only in the mind but are nonetheless grounded in the real forms of things has been called a moderate Realism. Aristotle himself, however, vigorously denied that the universals have any substantiality (*Metaphysics,* Z: 13–14; 1038^{b}8–1039^{b}19), which clearly suggests that, for him, the universals have no existence independently of cognition; this tends, in this first context, to invalidate the designation Realism for the Aristotelian doctrine.

Realism of natures

Correspondingly, Realism is used to describe medieval views that allowed species and genera some kind of distinct existence outside of their conception by the mind. There it meant that not only individual men and individual animals and so on exist outside cognition but also that the specific nature of man and the generic nature of animal and the like have an existence of their own in the outside world. For Realism, objects "fall into" such categories as humanness, mountainness, etc., *naturally.* For its opponents, however, this is not always the case: thus, in terms of a modern illustration, graniteness—that which all the granite rocks share in common—does not exist except as an artificial category set up by the mind (conceptualism) because it merges by imperceptible gradations into diorite or felsite as its mineral composition and texture gradually change.

Yet in actual fact the various medieval doctrines do not fit neatly under these divisions. In the philosophies of several medieval Scholastics, for instance, both the particular thing and the universal are distinguished in one way or another from a third entity, the specific or generic nature *taken absolutely* in itself. This so-called absolute nature is given a "being of its own" by the influential Persian Avicenna, an early 11th-century philosopher and physician; and—in the 13th century—by Henry of Ghent, an eclectic Christian Scholastic, and by the voluntarist Duns Scotus, the greatest medieval British Scholastic, who gave the absolute nature a reality that was distinct in form from the individual thing, but unitively contained in it. Thomas Aquinas gave it no being at all. Though these views reflect radically different metaphysical settings, they all variously bar the natures from real existence when separated in any way from the individual.

In its conventional applications to Greek and medieval thought, accordingly, Realism turns out to be an elusive and even confusing notion. It seems to be an inept way of emphasizing difficulties that are significantly present in the philosophies of these epochs, which require understanding and solution. But the granting of extramental existence to the generic and specific natures has raised more difficulties than it has solved.

All of these ancient and medieval doctrines—whether Realistic, conceptualistic, or nominalistic—accept the external existence of individual sensible things. From this viewpoint, they would all be Realisms in the second main sense of the term, that of the Realism of ordinary things, which is the sense in which Realism is predominantly employed in the modern era. Here it means the epistemological (or theory-of-knowledge) view that things taken as individual wholes have an existence that is outside of human cognition.

Realism of things

HISTORY OF WESTERN REALISM

In these and other related ways, modern writers have seen the philosophic attitude called Realism continually surfacing in the stream of Western thought, suggesting that it is a perennial feature.

Ancient Realism. In pre-Socratic thought, even in Parmenides (late 6th century), known for reducing reality to the One, the relevant reality of the objects of cognition was everywhere assumed. In Plato (5th and 4th centuries BC), the separate and more excellent existence of the natures, or Forms, was strongly asserted at times, though quite often the immanence of the form in individuals was just as surely implied without any satisfactory reconciliation of the contradiction. With Philo of Alexandria, a Hellenistic Jewish philosopher in the 1st century AD, the existence of the Platonic Forms was located within the mind of God, a view also found in the early 5th century in Augustine of Hippo (*De diversis quaestionibus,* "On Diverse Questions"). In the medieval Augustinian tradition, for instance in the writings of Anselm of Canterbury, the influence of this interpretation persisted. In the early 6th century, on the other hand, Boethius, perhaps the intellectual founder of the Middle Ages, in transmitting Aristotelian logic to the West, presented the universal notions with a strong cast of Platonic Realism, while acknowledging that the Aristotelian view was different. Among medieval thinkers in the early 12th century, such as William of Champeaux, the Parisian logician and theologian, the Platonizing tradition of Boethius was dominant, though it was brought under fire by such men as Roscelin, founder of nominalism, who saw universals as mere words. With the stormy controversialist Peter Abelard, who was the foremost dialectician of his time, the Boethian Realism was attacked. But according to Abelard, more than mere words were required to justify universality; in his view, universals were concepts signifying real things and had their ultimate basis in the divine ideas, as in the Augustinian tradition.

Medieval Realism. The approach of the early medieval thinkers to the problem of universals was made from the side of logic. But it soon involved theological issues, which, when added to the much deeper study of its metaphysical backgrounds made by Boethius, led the scholars to place the relevant questions in a different setting. The natures or common essences of things came to be scrutinized from a threefold viewpoint: as existent in sensible things, as existent in the mind, and as absolutely existent in themselves. This subjected the problem to metaphysical investigation. In that setting, Aquinas allowed neither being nor unity to be attributed to the nature taken absolutely. Duns Scotus, however, accorded it a lesser unity than that of the individual and gave it a kind of being proportionate to this real specific unity, but which required unitive containment of the nature by the individual. In these different ways the nature, so taken, provided the ground for the universal

Scholastics, Cartesians, and Platonists

Moderate Realism

that existed only in the mind. Views incorporating this feature have been called moderate Realisms, though the designation is open to the same objection as it is in its application to Aristotle (see above, *Distinctions among the Realisms*). In later Scholastic tradition the currents became badly confused, and unending controversy raged on the various kinds of universals and the respective status of each type.

Modern Realism. In the familiar formula *cogito ergo sum* ("I think; therefore, I am") proffered by the first notable modern philosopher, René Descartes, methodical thinking was rooted in thought itself, thus raising the problem of how any material world outside of thought could be reached philosophically. In Descartes and a half century later in the British Empiricist John Locke, an external origin for sensations was accepted, though without any thoroughly philosophical justification. Rather, the denial of an external world was regarded as too absurd to be countenanced. In this perspective Locke's philosophy displayed a commonsense Realism. According to one of Locke's contemporaries, the Cartesian Nicolas Malebranche (known for his claim that God's will is the true cause of motion), religious faith guaranteed the external world. The Cambridge Platonists, a sober group of 17th-century moral and religious Rationalists, in a similar atmosphere of faith and with a Cartesian understanding of sensation, acquiesced in the external existence of sensible things while, against a Neoplatonic background, they accorded a respectively greater reality to the objects of intellectual cognition. For Berkeley, an early 18th-century Empiricist and Idealist, the scriptural guarantee was lacking because matter was nowhere mentioned in the revealed descriptions of the sensible universe; accordingly, in his view, no sensible world outside cognition was left. But in David Hume, whose teachings marked the climax of the Empiricist movement, even the cognitive subject, or soul, vanished.

Facing the impossibility of a genuine philosophical justification for arguing to an external world from the starting point of mind or idea, Claude Buffier, an early 18th-century French Jesuit, and, shortly later, the Scottish Realists leaned explicitly on common sense as the motive for accepting the world's external existence. The most prominent exponent of this school was Thomas Reid, an opponent of paradox and skepticism. And John Witherspoon, who was called from Scotland to the presidency of Princeton University, held that "the impression itself implies and supposes something external that communicates it, and cannot be separated from that supposition." Consequently, the attempt of the viewpoint of Berkeleian immaterialism "to unsettle the principles of common sense by metaphysical reasoning" could, in his view, never produce conviction.

Views based on common sense

20th-century Realism. Around the turn of the 20th century, a strong revolt against Kantian subjectivism and the dominant Idealisms appeared in such thinkers as William James, a psychologist and Pragmatist; Bertrand Russell, perhaps the most influential logician and philosopher of his time; and G.E. Moore, a meticulous pioneering Analyst. Thus it was that very early in the century philosophers came to use Realism, as opposed to Idealism, for their own ways of thinking. In 1904, James signalled the resurrection of natural Realism. In 1910, W.P. Montague of Columbia University and Ralph Barton Perry of Harvard University and several others signed an article entitled "The Program and First Platform of Six Realists," and followed it with a cooperative volume, *The New Realism* (1912). New Realism, or neo-Realism, in defending the independence of known things, explained that in cognition "the content of knowledge, that which lies in or before the mind when knowledge takes place, is numerically identical with the thing known." To other Realists this epistemological monism, as Perry called his theory of knowledge, failed to extricate itself from the egocentric predicament (*i.e.,* from the incapacity of the mind to transcend its private experience) that they all professed to see in the logic of Idealism. Nor could it give a satisfactory explanation of the mind's proneness to error, or even of cognition itself as being significantly different from the things known. Another type of Realism was advanced against neo-Realism in a similarly cooperative volume entitled *Essays in Critical Realism* (1920), by the naturalist George Santayana and several others. To the monism of the neo-Realists such writers opposed an epistemological dualism, in which the object in cognition and the object in reality are numerically two at the time of perception. They divided, however, into a majority group and a minority group on the status of the immediately given object. For the majority group this datum was not an existent but merely an essence; for the others it was an existent—a mental or psychic existent for some and a physical (brain) existent for others. Here agreement failed, and the cooperative effort of the critical Realists soon fell apart.

These and the ensuing discussions left a recognized distinction between the schools of representative Realism and direct Realism: for representative Realism the immediate confrontation of cognition occurred over against a mental representation of the external object; for direct Realism the confrontation was immediately with the thing existent outside of cognition. The critical Realists themselves, in claiming that the datum was not an object as such but only the means of perceiving it, disavowed any representationalism; but in others, who proposed that the sense-datum was the image directly apprehended and was markedly different from the physical object, representative Realism was definitely present. Representationalism may also be seen in the Realism of the Belgian Neoscholastic Désiré Mercier, who founded the school of Louvain, and in the physiological Idealisms of contemporary neurophysiologists. In essence, representationalism was the inferential procedure employed by Descartes and Locke for reaching the external world. Direct Realism, on the other hand—as defended by recent writers—acknowledged no intermediate object between cognition and the external thing perceived.

Naive and tacit Realisms

Within the ambit of contemporary discussions, naive Realism was the label for any unquestioning belief that things in reality correspond exactly to human cognition of them. Expressly meant as a prephilosophical attitude, naive Realism can hardly be included under philosophical procedures. Yet its appropriateness to the man in the street has also been widely challenged; for the ordinary man is keenly interested in distinguishing critically between reality and figments of cognition, and is continually doing so in ordinary life. He does not proceed, however, as did the aforementioned Realisms: he does not first regard the object in terms of its status in cognition and then explore its relation to reality. But to come under the notion as introduced by the Realists, naive Realism must be explained in terms of the cognitional relation— *e.g.*, as one of the "three typical theories of the knowledge relation." It is, accordingly, a philosophical category, though historians and controversialists shun the listing of recognized philosophers under such a title.

Further, a number of philosophies that neither bore the name of Realism nor defined reality in terms of its relation to cognition are frequently regarded as Realisms today. Aristotelianism, for example, explained the reality of things through their substantiality, Thomism through their existence in themselves, Scotism through the metaphysical priority of a nature possessed in common, and contemporary linguistic philosophy, as in John Austin, an important mid-20th-century Oxford Analyst, through a completely ostensive view of language; yet all have been seen as Realisms. The process philosophies of the Pragmatist John Dewey and of Alfred North Whitehead, an influential cosmologist and metaphysician, and—still more controversially—the philosophy of Charles Sanders Peirce, an individualistic American logician and Pragmatist, may also be taken as Realisms, even though they did not stress the basic relation to cognition; for these thinkers agreed that things as a fact do have, or may have, existence outside cognition, even though this existence was not reached from cognition nor defined through its relation to cognition. With them the cognitional relation was only an inessential afterthought. Serious interest in explaining as Realism the traditional tenets of pre-Cartesian philosophies may be seen in the writings of many contem-

Metaphysical Realisms

poraries. Yet for Aristotle and Aquinas, what was meant by the reality of sensible things is already established metaphysically, through their substantiality or ontal (real) existence, before they are compared with cognition; hence to bring in the further notion of Realism for this purpose seems meaningless. The notion is therefore extraneous to the philosophical procedures of thinkers who locate the starting point of their philosophy in some actuality of the real thing itself; for relation to cognition does not play an operative role in their basic procedures. Only by means of entirely extrinsic bonds can they be grouped with the genuine Realisms.

MAJOR ISSUES AND EVALUATION OF REALISM

From the foregoing survey of the historical development of Realistic thought, the major issues upon which Realism focusses attention stand out clearly. For both speculative and practical reasons, men wish to distinguish sharply between what they call reality and what they recognize or suspect to be merely products of their own cognition. Accordingly, the ancient Platonic concentration on specific and generic natures and, in Aristotle, the essential role played by the universal in reasoning led to a close scrutiny of the way in which these natures exist. Undoubtedly, they exist in human thought. For the Realistically inclined thinker, however, their crucial role tends to demand counterparts if human thinking is to bear on what really exists. Still more drastic are the post-Cartesian philosophies in which the existence of external things themselves does not enter human cognition in direct confrontation. Finally, the mathematical and scientific constructs, which have been so fruitful in man's struggle for mastery over nature, seem to require for the Realistically minded thinker some counterpart in the things themselves in order to provide an adequate philosophical explanation of their success.

When the issues are faced in the foregoing manner, some lines of procedure common to the various explicit Realisms emerge upon which it may be possible to base an evaluation. Universals, sensations and perceptions, scientific formulas and laws are all found to be existent in cognition. From that sure starting point, attempts are made to show that objects either corresponding to them or identical with them exist outside the mind. That pattern seems to be the general procedure followed in any way of thinking that has spontaneously given rise to the notion of an epistemological Realism and that can, with historical and philosophical significance, be labelled such. As is likewise apparent from the foregoing survey, this way of thinking follows a dubious procedure: Realism is not primarily a doctrine of the existence of things but rather a doctrine of cognition. In Realism, cognition is regarded as the object most present to itself; *i.e.,* a man knows his own thought processes more intimately than anything else. But the genuine Realist seems unwittingly to take the material thing as his model in conceiving cognition. No external object can be more present to a material thing than that material thing itself. If cognition is conceived after this analogy, it will be what is most present to itself, and will have to be the starting point from which the Realist reasons. This starting point seems to offer no exit. The objects reached from it can be only internal products or occurrences in the mind, for it offers nothing more basic from which to reason than the cognition itself. Any philosophically genuine Realism seems, in consequence, prone to failure in its basic objective.

Problems and current status

Accordingly, Realism, in the senses responsible for the epistemological use of the term, has long since ceased to inspire vigorous debate. In a Platonic tradition that continues in modern thought, however, Realism in respect to the natures of things is by no means dead. In regard to the Cartesian problem of the world's external existence, representative Realism seems to have shared the fate of the sense-datum and to be quite inoperative outside of the wake of neurophysiological writings. But attempts at direct Realism are still made. In the scientific field the opposition to conventionalism and to retaining a merely instrumental status for laws or theories has remained a lively issue. Moreover, modern means, such as the electron microscope (which shows molecules in real existence) and the hope of being able to see atoms foretoken a greater correspondence of scientific constructs with the structure of reality than had previously been demonstrated. But this verification process consists in a comparison of reality with thought rather than in any attempt to reach reality from cognition alone.   (J.O./L.H.St.)

Scholasticism

From the time of the Renaissance until at least the beginning of the 19th century, the term Scholasticism, not unlike the name Middle Ages, was used as an expression of blame and contempt. The medieval period was widely viewed as an insignificant intermezzo between Greco-Roman antiquity and modern times, and Scholasticism was normally taken to describe a philosophy busied with sterile subtleties, written in bad Latin, and above all subservient to the theology of popery. Even the German Idealist Hegel, in his *Vorlesungen über die Geschichte der Philosophie* (1833–36; *Lectures on the History of Philosophy,* 1892–96), declared that he would "put on seven-league boots" in order to skip over the thousand years between the 6th and 17th centuries and, having at last arrived at Descartes, said that now he could "cry land like the sailor." In those same first decades of the 19th century, on the other hand, the Romanticists swung the pendulum sharply to the opposite side, to an indiscriminate overestimation of everything medieval.

Today, scholars seem better able to confront the medieval epoch, as well as Scholasticism—*i.e.,* its philosophy (and theology)—without prejudgments. One reason for this state of affairs is the voluminous research which has been devoted to this era and which has revealed its true nature, not only as a respectable continuation of the genuinely philosophical tradition but also as a period of exemplary personalities quite able to stand comparison with any of the great philosophers of antiquity or of modern times.

NATURE AND SIGNIFICANCE

Scholasticism is so much a many-sided phenomenon that, in spite of intensive research, scholars still differ considerably in their definition of the term and in the emphases that they place on individual aspects of the phenomenon. Some historians, seeming almost to capitulate to the complexity of the subject, confine themselves to the general point that Scholasticism can only be defined denotatively as that kind of philosophy that during the European Middle Ages was taught in the Christian schools. The question of its connotation, however, remains, viz., What kind of philosophy was it?

The answer that Scholasticism was "school" philosophy and, in fact, "Christian" school philosophy can be understood only by examining the historical exigencies that created the need for schools. The search thus leads the inquirer back to the transition from antiquity to the Middle Ages—a point which, according to Hegel, was marked by the symbolic date AD 529, when a decree of the Christian emperor Justinian closed the Platonic Academy in Athens and sealed "the downfall of the physical establishments of pagan philosophy." In that same year, however, still another event occurred, which points much less to the past than to the coming age and, especially, to the rise of Scholasticism, viz., the foundation of Monte Cassino, the first Benedictine abbey, above one of the highways of the great folk migrations. This highly symbolic fact not only suggests the initial shift of the scene of the intellectual life from places like the Platonic Academy to the cloisters of Christian monasteries, but it marks even more a change in the dramatis personae. New nations were about to overrun the Roman Empire and its Hellenistic culture with long-range effects: when, centuries later, for example, one of the great Scholastics, Thomas Aquinas, was born, though he was rightly a southern Italian, his mother was of Norman stock, and his Sicilian birthplace was under central European (Hohenstaufen) control.

It was a decisive and astonishing fact that the so-called barbarian peoples who penetrated from the north into the ancient world often became Christians and set out to master the body of tradition that they found, including the rich harvest of patristic theology as well as the philosophical ideas of the Greeks and the political wisdom of the Romans. This learning could be accomplished only in the conquered empire's language (*i.e.,* in Latin), which therefore had to be learned first. In fact, the incorporation of both a foreign vocabulary and a different mode of thinking and the assimilation of a tremendous amount of predeveloped thought was the chief problem that confronted medieval philosophy at its beginnings. And it is only in the light of this fact that one of the decisive traits of medieval Scholasticism becomes understandable: Scholasticism above all was an unprecedented process of learning, literally a vast "scholastic" enterprise that continued for several centuries. Since the existing material had to be ordered and made accessible to learning and teaching, the very prosaic labour and "schoolwork" of organizing, sorting, and classifying materials inevitably acquired an unprecedented importance. Consequently, the writings of medieval Scholasticism quite naturally lack the magic of personal immediacy, for schoolbooks leave little room for originality. It is therefore misleading, though understandable, that certain polemicists have wrongly characterized Scholasticism as involving no more than the use of special didactic methods or a narrow adherence to traditional teachings.

First of all, if the major historical task of that epoch was really to learn, to acquire, and to preserve the riches of tradition, a certain degree of "scholasticity" was not only inevitable but essential. It is not at all certain that today's historians would have direct intellectual access to Plato, Aristotle, and Augustine had the Scholastics not done their patient spadework. Besides, the progress from the stage of mere collection of given sentences and their interpretation (*expositio, catena, lectio*), to the systematic discussion of texts and problems (*quaestio, disputatio*), and finally to the grand attempts to give a comprehensive view of the whole of attainable truth (*Summa*) was necessarily at the same time a clear progression toward intellectual autonomy and independence, which in order to culminate, as it did in the 13th century, in the great works of Scholasticism's Golden Age, required in addition the powers of genius, of men like Albertus Magnus and Thomas Aquinas.

On the other hand, the moment had to come when the prevalent preoccupation with existing knowledge would give way to new questions, which demanded consideration and answers that could emerge only from direct experience. By the later Middle Ages, procedures for exploiting and discussing antecedent stocks of insight had been largely institutionalized, and it was an obvious temptation to perpetuate the dominion of those procedures—which could lead only to total sterility. It is widely agreed that this is almost exactly what did happen in the 14th century in what is called the "decline" and disintegration of Scholasticism.

HISTORY AND ISSUES

Roots of Scholasticism.   From the beginning of medieval Scholasticism the natural aim of all philosophical endeavour to achieve the "whole of attainable truth" was clearly meant to include also the teachings of Christian faith, an inclusion which, in the very concept of Scholasticism, was perhaps its most characteristic and distinguishing element. Although the idea of including faith was expressed already by Augustine and the early Church Fathers, the principle was explicitly formulated by the pivotal, early 6th-century scholar Boethius. Born in Rome and educated in Athens, Boethius was one of the great mediators and translators, living on the narrow no-man's-land that divided the epochs. His famous book, *The Consolation of Philosophy,* was written while he, indicted for treachery and imprisoned by King Theodoric the Goth, awaited his own execution. It is true that the book is said to be, aside from the Bible, one of the most translated, most commented upon, and most printed books in world history; and that Boethius made (unfinished) plans to translate and to comment upon, as he said, "every book of Aristotle and all the dialogues of Plato." But the epithet that he won as "one of the founders of Scholasticism" refers to

Barbarians' need for school learning

Desirability of Scholasticism

Boethius and Cassiodorus

quite another side of his work. Strictly speaking, it refers to the last sentence of a very short tractate on the Holy Trinity, which reads, "As far as you are able, join faith to reason"—an injunction which in fact was to become, for centuries, the formal foundation of Scholasticism. Instead of "faith," such concepts as revelation, authority, or tradition could be (and, indeed, have been) cited; and "reason," though unambiguously meant to designate the natural powers of human cognition, could also be granted (and, in fact, has been granted) very different meanings. In any case, the connection between faith and reason postulated in this principle was from the beginning and by its very nature a highly explosive compound.

Boethius himself already carried out his program in a rather extraordinary way: though his *Opuscula sacra* ("Sacred Works") dealt almost exclusively with theological subjects, there was not a single Bible quotation in them: logic and analysis was all.

Though called the "first Scholastic," Boethius was at the same time destined to be for almost a millennium the last layman in the field of European philosophy. His friend Cassiodorus, author of the *Institutiones,* an unoriginal catalog of definitions and subdivisions, which (in spite of their dryness) became a source book and mine of information for the following centuries, who, like Boethius, occupied a position of high influence at the court of Theodoric and was also deeply concerned with the preservation of the intellectual heritage, decided in his later years to quit his political career and to live with his enormous library in a monastery. This fact again is highly characteristic of the development of medieval Scholasticism: intellectual life needs not only teachers and students and not only a stock of knowledge to be handed down; there is needed a certain guaranteed free area within human society as well, a kind of sheltered enclosure, within which the concern for "nothing but truth" can exist and unfold. The Platonic Academy, as well as (for a limited time) the court of Theodoric, had been enclosures of this kind; but in the politically unsettled epoch to come "no plant would thrive except one that germinated and grew in the cloister."

The principle of the conjunction of faith and reason, which Boethius had proclaimed, and the way in which he himself carried it out were both based on a profound and explicit confidence in man's natural intellectual capacity—a confidence that could possibly lead one day to the rationalistic conviction that there cannot be anything that exceeds the power of human reason to comprehend, not even the mysteries of divine revelation. To be sure, the great thinkers of Scholasticism, in spite of their emphatic affirmation of faith and reason, consistently rejected any such rationalistic claim. But it must nonetheless be admitted that Scholasticism on the whole, and by virtue of its basic approach, contained within itself the danger of an overestimation of rationality, which recurrently emerged throughout its history.

On the other hand, there had been built in, from the beginning, a corrective and warning, which in fact kept the internal peril of Rationalism within bounds, viz., the corrective exercised by the "negative theology" of the so-called Pseudo-Dionysius, around whose writings revolved some of the strangest events in the history of Western culture. The true name of this protagonist is, in spite of intensive research, unknown. Probably it will remain forever an enigma why the author of several Greek writings (among them *On the Divine Names,* "On the Celestial Hierarchy," and *The Mystical Theology*) called himself "Dionysius the Presbyter" and, to say the least, suggested that he was actually Denis the Areopagite, a disciple of Paul the Apostle (Acts). In reality, almost all historians agree that Pseudo-Dionysius, as he came to be called, was probably a Syrian Neoplatonist, a contemporary of Boethius. Whatever the truth of the matter may be, his writings exerted an inestimable influence for more than 1,000 years by virtue of the some-what surreptitious quasi-canonical authority of their author, whose books were venerated, as has been said, "almost like the Bible itself." A 7th-century Greek theologian, Maximus the Confessor, wrote the first commentaries on these writings, which were followed over the centuries by a long succession of com-

The Pseudo-Dionysius

mentators, among them Albertus Magnus and Thomas Aquinas. The main fact is that the unparalleled influence of the Areopagite writings preserved in the Latin West an idea, which otherwise could have been repressed and lost (since it cannot easily be coordinated with rationality)—that of a negative theology or philosophy that could act as a counter-poise against Rationalism. It could be called an Eastern idea present and effective in the Occident. But after the Great Schism, which erected a wall between East and West that lasted for centuries, Denis the Areopagite, having become himself (through translations and commentaries) a Westerner "by adoption," was the only one among all of the important Greco-Byzantine thinkers who penetrated into the schools of Western Christendom. Thus negative theology was brought to medieval Scholasticism, as it were, through the back door.

The most important book of Denis, which dealt with the names that can be applied to God, exemplified his negative theology. It maintained first of all the decidedly biblical thesis that no appropriate name can be given to God at all unless he himself reveals it. But then Denis showed that even the revealed names, since they must be comprehensible to man's finite understanding, cannot possibly reach or express the nature of God; and that in consequence, every affirmative statement about God requires at once the corrective of the coordinate negation. The theologian cannot even call God "real" or "being," because he derives these concepts from the things to which God has given reality; and the Creator cannot possibly be of the same nature as that which he has created. Thus, *The Mystical Theology* concluded by finally relativizing also the negations, because God surpasses anything that man may possibly say of him, whether it be affirmative or negative.

Scholasticism certainly could have learned all of this also from Augustine, who repeatedly warned that "Whatever you understand cannot be God." But probably an authority of even greater weight than Augustine was needed to counteract a reason that was tending to overrate its own powers; and this authority was attributed, although falsely, to the works of Denis the Areopagite. This impact could, of course, not be restricted to the idea of God; it necessarily concerned and changed man's whole conception of the world and of existence. The influence of Denis is reflected in the noteworthy fact that Thomas Aquinas, for instance, not only employed more than 1,700 quotations from Denis the Areopagite but also appealed almost regularly to his work whenever he spoke, as he often did (and in astonishingly strong terms), of the inexhaustible mystery of being. Thomas Aquinas, however, who also wrote a remarkable commentary on Denis' book *On the Divine Names,* is mentioned here only as an example, albeit a most telling example.

At the very end of the medieval era of Scholasticism, the Areopagite emerged once more in the work of a 15th-century cardinal, Nicholas of Cusa, also known as a mathematician and advocate of experimental knowledge, in whose library there are preserved several translations of the Areopagite writings—replete, moreover, with marginal notes in the Cardinal's handwriting. But even without this concrete evidence, it would be quite plain that Cusanus' doctrine of "knowing nonknowing" is closely linked to the Areopagite's conviction that all of reality is unfathomable.

The translation into Latin of the *Corpus Areopagiticum,* which was made in the 9th century—*i.e.,* some 400 years after the death of its author—by John Scotus Erigena, is itself worthy of mention, especially because the translator was one of the most remarkable figures of early medieval philosophy. After generations of brave and efficient collectors, organizers, and schoolmasters had come and gone, Erigena, in his *De divisione natura* ("On the Division of Nature"), developed the Dionysian Neoplatonism on his own and tried to construct a systematic conception of the universe, a more or less pantheistic world view, which (as Gilson says) for a moment offered the Latin West the opportunity—or the temptation—to choose the way of the East once and for all. The church, though not until centuries later, condemned the book, apparently convinced that any counterpoise to its own position can become dangerous in itself.

Erigena's translation

Early Scholastic period. If there was any philosophical-theological thinker of importance during the Middle Ages who remained untouched by the spirit of the Areopagite, it was the 11th-century Benedictine Anselm of Canterbury, a highly cultivated Franco-Italian theologian who for years was prior and abbot of the abbey Le Bec in Normandy and then became, somewhat violently, the archbishop of Canterbury. In Anselm's entire work there is not a single quotation from Denis; not even the name is mentioned. Consequently, Anselm's thinking, thus freed from the corrective embodied in the Areopagite's negative theology, displayed a practically unlimited confidence in the power of human reason to illuminate even the mysteries of Christian faith; he thus frequently approached a kind of Rationalism, which did not shrink from the attempt to demonstrate, on compelling rational grounds, that salvation (for example) through God incarnate was philosophically necessary. To be sure, a theologian such as Anselm certainly would never have subscribed to the extreme thesis that nothing exists that is beyond the power of human reason to comprehend: the two famous phrases, coined by him and expressing again, in a grandiose formulation, the principle of Boethius, "faith seeking to be understood" and "I believe in order to understand," clearly proclaim his faith in the mysteries of revelation as comprising the very basis of all reasoning. Nevertheless, in the case of Anselm, the very peculiar conjunction of faith and reason was accomplished not so much through any clear intellectual coordination as through the religious energy and saintliness of an unusual personality. It was accomplished, so to speak, rather as an act of violence, which could not possibly last. The conjunction was bound to break up, with the emphasis falling either on some kind of Rationalism or on a hazardous irrationalization of faith.

That this split did actually happen can be read to some extent in the fate of the "Anselmic argument," which Kant, 700 years later, was to reject as the "ontological proof of God"—connecting it, however, not with the name of Anselm but with that of Descartes, the earliest modern philosopher. It is, in fact, significant that Descartes, in his proof of the existence of God, imagined that he was saying the same thing as Anselm, and that, on the other hand, Anselm would scarcely have recognized his own argument had he encountered it in the context of Descartes's *Discours de la méthode* (1637; *Discourse on Method*, 1950), which claims to be "pure" philosophy based upon an explicit severance from the concept of God held by faith. But given Anselm's merely theoretical starting point, that severance was not only to be expected; it was almost inevitable.

But, also within the framework of medieval Scholasticism, a dispute was always brewing between the dialecticians, who emphasized or overemphasized reason, and those who stressed the suprarational purity of faith. Berengar of Tours, an 11th-century logician, metaphysician, and theologian, who was fond of surprising formulations, maintained the preeminence of thinking over any authority holding, in particular, that the real Presence of Christ in the Eucharist was logically impossible. His contemporary the Italian hermit-monk and cardinal Peter Damian, however—who was apparently the first to use the ill-famed characterization of philosophy as the "handmaid of theology"—replied that, if God's omnipotence acts against the principle of contradiction, then so much the worse for the science of logic. Quite analogous to the foregoing controversy, though pitched on a much higher intellectual level, was the bitter fight that broke out almost one century later between a Cistercian reformer, Bernard of Clairvaux, and a logician and theologian, Peter Abelard. Bernard, a vigorous and ambivalent personality, was in the first place a man of religious practice and mystical contemplation, who, at the end of his dramatic life, characterized his odyssey as that of *anima quaerens Verbum,* "a soul in search of the Word." Although he by no means rejected philosophy on principle, he looked with deep suspicion upon the primarily logical approach to theology espoused by Abelard. "This man," said Bernard, "presumes to be able to comprehend by human reason the entirety of God."

Logic was at that time, as a matter of fact, the main battleground of all Scholastic disputations. "Of all philosophy, logic most appealed to me," said Abelard, who by "logic" understood primarily a discipline not unlike certain present-day approaches, the "critical analysis of thought on the basis of linguistic expression." From this viewpoint (of linguistic logic), Abelard also discussed with penetrating sharpness the so-called "problem of universals," which asks, Is there an "outside" and objective reality standing, for example, not only for the name "Socrates" but also for such common names as "man," "canineness," and the like? Or do common concepts ("universals") possess only the reality of subjective thought or perhaps merely that of the sound of the word? As is well known, it has been asserted that this was the principal, or even the only, subject of concern in medieval Scholasticism—a charge that is misleading, although the problem did greatly occupy philosophers from the time of Boethius. Their main concern from the beginning was the whole of reality and existence.

The advance of medieval thought to a highly creative level was foreshadowed, in those very same years before Peter Abelard died, by Hugh of Saint-Victor (an Augustinian monk of German descent), when he wrote *De sacramentis Christianae fidei* ("On the Sacraments of the Christian Faith"), the first book in the Middle Ages that could rightly be called a *summa;* in its introduction, in fact, the term itself is used as meaning a comprehensive view of all that exists (*brevis quaedam summa omnium*). To be sure, its author stands wholly in the tradition of Augustine and the Areopagite; yet he is also the first medieval theologian who proclaims an explicit openness toward the natural world. Knowledge of reality is, in his understanding, the prerequisite for contemplation; each of the seven liberal arts aims "to restore God's image in us." "Learn everything," he urged; "later you will see that nothing is superfluous."

It was on this basic that the university—which was not the least of the achievements of medieval Scholasticism—was to take shape. And it was the University of Paris, in particular, that for some centuries was to be the most representative university of the West. Though there are usually a variety of reasons and causes for such a development, in this case the importance of the university—unlike that of Bologna and also of Oxford—lay mainly in the fact that it was founded in the most radical way upon those branches of knowledge that are "universal" by their very nature: upon theology and philosophy. It is, thus, remarkable, though not altogether surprising, that there seems to have existed not a single *summa* of the Middle Ages that did not, in some way or other, derive from the University of Paris.

Strangely enough, the classical theological-philosophical textbook used in the following centuries at the universities of the West was not the first *summa,* composed by Hugh of Saint-Victor, but was instead a work by Peter Lombard, a theologian who probably attended Abelard's lectures and who became *magister* at the cathedral school of Notre-Dame and, two decades later, bishop of Paris. Lombard's famous *Four Books of Sentences,* which, though written one or two decades later than Hugh's *summa,* belonged to an earlier historical species, contained about 1,000 texts from the works of Augustine, which comprise nearly four-fifths of the whole. Much more important than the book itself, however, were the nearly 250 commentaries on it, by which—into the 16th century—every master of theology had to begin his career as a teacher. In view of this wide usage, it is not astonishing that Lombard's book underwent some transformations, at the hands, for instance, of its most ingenious commentator, Thomas Aquinas, but also (and even more so) at the hands of Duns Scotus in his *Opus Oxoniense,* which, in spite of being a work of extremely personal cast, was outwardly framed as a commentary on the "Master of Sentences."

Maturity of Scholasticism. Clearly, the world view of Western Christendom, on the whole Augustinian and Platonic in inspiration and founded upon Lombard's "Augustine breviary," was beginning to be rounded out into a system and to be institutionalized in the universities.

Anselm's belief in human reason

Bernard and Abelard

Hugh's summa and Lombard's Sentences

The renascence of Aristotle

At the very moment of its consolidation, however, an upheaval was brewing that would shake this novel conception to its foundations: the main works of Aristotle, hitherto unknown in the West, were being translated into Latin—among them his *Metaphysics,* the *Physics,* the *Nichomachean Ethics,* and the books *On the Soul.* These writings were not merely an addition of something new to the existing stock; they involved an enormous challenge. Suddenly, a new, rounded, coherent view of the world was pitted against another more-or-less coherent traditional view; and because this challenge bore the name of Aristotle, it could not possibly be ignored, for Aristotle's books on logic, translated and equipped with commentaries by Boethius, had for centuries been accepted as one of the foundations of all culture. During the lifetime of Abelard the full challenge of the Aristotelian work had not yet been presented, though it had been developing quietly along several paths, some of which were indeed rather fantastic. For instance, most of the medieval Latin translations of Aristotle stem not from the original Greek but from earlier Arabic translations.

Within the Western Christendom of the 2nd millennium, a wholly new readiness to open the mind to the concrete reality of the world had arisen, a view of the universe and life that resembled the Aristotelian viewpoint. The tremendous eagerness with which this new philosophy was embraced was balanced, however, by a deep concern lest the continuity of tradition and the totality of truth be shattered by the violence of its assimilation. And this danger was enhanced by the fact that Aristotle's works did not come alone; they came, in fact, accompanied by the work of Arabic commentators and their heterodox interpretations.

The most influential Arabic commentators were an 11th-century polymath, Avicenna, a Persian by birth, and a 12th-century philosopher, Averroës, born in Spain. Avicenna, personal physician to sovereigns, but also a philosopher and theologian, read—according to his own account— Aristotle's *Metaphysics* 40 times without understanding it, until he learned the text by heart. F.C. Copleston has called him "the real creator of a Scholastic system in the Islāmic world." In the view of Averroës, who was not only a philosopher but also a jurist and a doctor, Aristotle's philosophy represented simply the perfection of human knowledge; and to the West, he himself was to become *the* commentator. A third great commentator was a 12th-century orthodox Jewish philosopher, Moses Maimonides, also born in Spain, who wrote his main works in Arabic. Maimonides was at the same time a vigorous adherent of the Aristotelian world view and was, thus, confronted by the same unending task that preoccupied the great teachers of medieval Christendom. At first sight it appears strange that none of these three thinkers had any appreciable influence within his own world (neither Islām nor Judaism knew of any such thing as a "discovery" of Aristotle), whereas on almost every page of the 13th-century Christian *summae* the names of Avicenna, Averroës, and Maimonides are found.

Albertus Magnus and Aristotelianism

The first theologian of the Middle Ages who boldly accepted the challenge of the new Aristotelianism was a 13th-century Dominican, Albertus Magnus, an encyclopedic scholar. Although he knew no Greek, he conceived a plan of making accessible to the Latin West the complete works of Aristotle, by way of commentaries and paraphrases; and, unlike Boethius, he did carry out this resolve. He also penetrated and commented upon the works of the Areopagite; he was likewise acquainted with those of the Arabs, especially Avicenna; and he knew Augustine. Nevertheless, he was in no wise primarily a man of bookish scholarship; his strongest point, in fact, was the direct observation of nature and experimentation. After having taught for some years at the University of Paris, he travelled, as a Dominican superior, through almost all of Europe. Not only was he continually asking questions of fishermen, hunters, beekeepers, and birdcatchers but he himself also bent his sight to the things of the visible world. But amidst the most palpable descriptions of bees, spiders, and apples, recorded in two voluminous books on plants and animals, Albertus formulated completely new, and even revolutionary, methodological principles: for instance, "There can be no philosophy about concrete things," or, "in such matters only experience can provide certainty."

With Albertus, the problem of the conjunction of faith and reason had suddenly become much more difficult, because reason itself had acquired a somewhat new meaning. "Reason" implied, in his view, not only the capacity for formally correct thinking, for finding adequate creatural analogies to the truths of revelation, but it implied, above all, the capacity to grasp the reality that man encounters. Henceforth, the Boethian principle of "joining faith with reason" would entail the never-ending task of bringing belief into a meaningful coordination with the incessantly multiplying stock of natural knowledge of man and the universe. Since Albertus' nature, however, was given more to conquest than to the establishment of order, the business of integrating all of these new and naturally divergent elements into a somewhat consistent intellectual structure waited for another man, for his pupil Thomas Aquinas.

Thomas Aquinas

To epitomize the intellectual task that Aquinas set for himself, the image of Odysseus' bow, which was so difficult to bend that an almost superhuman strength was needed, is fitting. As a young student at the University of Naples, he had met in the purest possible form both extremes, which, though they seemed inevitably to be pulling away from one another, it was nevertheless his life's task to join: one of these extremes was the dynamic, voluntary poverty movement whose key word was "the Bible"; and the second phenomenon was the Aristotelian writings and outlook, which at that time could have been encountered nowhere else in so intensive a form. And "Aristotle" meant to Thomas not so much an individual author as a specific world view, viz., the affirmation of natural reality as a whole, including man's body and his natural cognitive powers. To be sure, the resulting *Summa theologiae* (which Thomas himself chose to leave incomplete) was a magnificent intellectual structure; but it was never intended to be a closed system of definitive knowledge. Thomas could no longer possess the magnificent naiveté of Boethius, who had considered it possible to discuss the Trinitarian God without resorting to the Bible, nor could he share Anselm's conviction that Christian faith so completely concurred with natural reason that it could be proved on compelling rational grounds.

In the meanwhile, the poles of the controversy—the biblical impulses, on the one hand, and the philosophical and secular ones, on the other—had begun to move vigorously apart, and partisans moving in both directions found some encouragement in Thomas himself. But in his later years he realized that the essential compatibility as well as the relative autonomy of these polar positions and the necessity for their conjunction had to be clarified anew by going back to a deeper root of both; that is, to a more consistent understanding of the concepts of creation and createdness. At Paris, he had to defend his own idea of "a theologically based worldliness and a theology open to the world" not only against the secularistic "philosophism" of Siger of Brabant, a stormy member of the faculty of arts, and against an aggressive group of heterodox Aristotelians around him, but also (and even more) against the traditional (Augustinian) objection that by advocating the rights of all natural things Thomas would encroach upon the rights of God, and that, besides, the theologian needs to know only that part of creation that is pertinent to his theological subject. The latter idea was supported also by the Italian mystical theologian Bonaventura, who, in his earlier days as a colleague of Thomas at the university, had likewise been enamoured of Aristotle, but later, alarmed by the secularism that was growing in the midst of Christendom, became more mistrustful of the capacities of natural reason. Thomas answered this objection in somewhat the following way: The benefit that the theologian may derive from an investigation of natural reality cannot be determined in advance, but, in general, faith presupposes and therefore needs natural knowledge of the world; at times, an error concerning the creation leads men astray also from the truth of faith. This may sound like an optimistic Rationalism; but the corrective of negative theology and philosophy was always present in the mind of Thomas, as well. Not only, as he argued in his treatise on God, does man not know what God is, but he does not know the essences of things either.

Late Scholastic period. Thomas did not succeed in bridging the faith–reason gulf. When he left Paris (1272) and after his death (1274), the gulf became much more radical; and on March 7, 1277, the Archbishop of Paris, in fact, formally condemned a list of sentences, some of them close to what Thomas himself had allegedly or really taught. This ecclesiastical act, questionable though it may have been in its methods and personal motivations, was not only understandable; it was unavoidable, since it was directed against what, after all, amounted in principle to an antitheological, rationalistic secularism. Quite another matter, however, were the factual effects of the edict, which were rather disastrous. Above all, two of the effects were pernicious: instead of free disputes among individuals, organized blocks (or "schools") now began to form; and the cooperative dialogue between theology and philosophy turned into mutual indifference or distrust. Nonetheless, the basic principle itself ("join faith with reason") had not yet been explicitly repudiated. This was to happen in the next generation.

Duns Scotus and William of Ockham

The negative element, as formulated in the theology of the Areopagite, proved to be insufficient as a corrective to counter the overemphasis of reason, for reason seemed to imply the idea of necessity; Anselm's asserted "compelling grounds" for revealed truths, for example, were akin to such a necessitarianism. A second corrective was therefore demanded and this took the name of "freedom"—which indeed was the battle cry of an important Franciscan, Duns Scotus, known as the "subtle doctor," who lived at the turn of the 14th century. Scotus used "freedom" primarily with reference to God; consequently, since redemption, grace, and salvation as well as all of creation were the work of God's groundless, absolute freedom, there could be no "necessary reasons," if indeed any reasons at all, for anything. It was therefore futile to attempt to coordinate faith with speculative reason. Clearly, Scotus' theological starting point made the conjunction of what man believes with what he knows every bit as difficult as it had been in Siger of Brabant's secularistic "philosophism." From both positions there was only one step to the doctrine of a "double truth"—a step that in fact was taken in the 14th century by the Nominalist William of Ockham, also a Franciscan, to whom singular facts alone are "real," and their coherence is not; this mere factuality, he held, can neither be calculated nor deduced, but only experienced; reason therefore means nothing but the power to encounter concrete reality. And upon such soil only a consistently "positive" theology could thrive. Any collaboration with speculative reason must be rejected as untheological. Faith is one thing and knowledge an altogether different matter; and a conjunction of the two is neither meaningfully possible nor even desirable. Inexorably, and justified by reasons on both sides, a divorce was taking place between faith and reason—to the connection of which the energies of almost a thousand years had been devoted. What was occurring was the demise of medieval Scholasticism.

ENDURING FEATURES

But not all of Scholasticism is specifically medieval and therefore definitively belonging to the dead past; there are perennial elements that are meant for every age, the present one included, three of which may be here distinguished. First, not only has Scholasticism held true to the normal historical rule that ideas, once thought and expressed, remain present and significant in the following time; but the medieval intellectual accomplishments have surpassed the rule and exerted, though more or less anonymously, a quite exceptional influence even on philosophers who consciously revolted against Scholasticism. New historical investigations clearly show that the classical modern philosophers Descartes, Locke, Spinoza, and Leibniz owe much to medieval ideas. Of Descartes, for instance, it has been said, contrary to the usual view, that he could quite well have been "included with the later Scholastics"; and even Charles Sanders Peirce, the

originator of 20th-century American Pragmatism, refers not too rarely to Scholastic maxims. Secondly, there have been explicit attempts to go back to Scholastic thinkers and inspire a renascence of their basic ideas. Two chief movements of this kind were the Scholasticism of the Renaissance (called *Barockscholastik*) and the Neoscholasticism of the 19th and 20th centuries, both of which were primarily interested in the work of Thomas Aquinas.

Renaissance and Neoscholasticism

Renaissance Scholasticism received its first impulses from the Reformation. One of its leading figures, a Dominican, Cardinal Thomas de Vio (16th century), commonly known as Cajetan, had some famous disputations with Martin Luther. Cajetan's great commentary on Thomas Aquinas, published again in a late edition of the *Summa theologiae* (1888–1906), exerted for at least three centuries an enormous influence on the formation of Catholic theology. He was much more than a commentator, however; his original treatise on the "Analogy of names," for example, can even pass as a prelude to modern linguistic philosophy. The so-called Silver Age of Scholastic thought, which occurred in the 16th century, is represented by two Spaniards: Francisco de Vitoria of the first half and Francisco Suárez of the last half of the century were both deeply engaged in what has been called the "Counter-Reformation." Though likewise commentators on the works of Thomas Aquinas, the Renaissance Scholastics were much less concerned with looking back to the past than with the problems of their own epoch, such as those of international law, colonialism, resistance to an unjust government, and world community. Though Suárez was for more than a hundred years among the most esteemed authors, even in Protestant universities, Renaissance Scholasticism was eradicated by Enlightenment philosophy and German Idealism. This, in turn, gave rise in due time to the Neoscholasticism of the 19th century, one of the most effective promoters of which was a German Jesuit, Joseph Kleutgen, who published a voluminous scholarly apology of patristic and Scholastic theology and philosophy and was also responsible for the outline of the papal encyclical *Aeterni Patris* of Leo XIII (1879), which explicitly proclaimed the "instauration of Christian philosophy according to St. Thomas." The result, fed of course from many different sources, was that all over the world new centres of Scholastic research and higher learning (universities) arose—some more traditionalistic, some from the start engaged in the dialogue with modern philosophy and science, and some primarily devoted to historical studies and the preparation of critical editions of the great medieval Scholastics—and that a multitude of periodicals and systematic textbooks were produced. It is too early for a competent judgment on this enterprise to be made. Its immeasurable educational benefit for several generations of students, however, is as undeniable as the unique contributions of some Neoscholastic thinkers to current intellectual life. A weak point, on the other hand, seems to be a somewhat "unhistorical" approach to reality and existence. In any case, it is scarcely a matter of mere chance that, after World War II, the impact of Existentialism and Marxism caused a noticeable decline in Neoscholasticism and that the positions of "Scholastic" authors active in the 1970s were already beyond Neoscholasticism.

The third and most important aspect of the enduring significance of the Scholastic movement implies the acceptance of the following fundamental tenets: that there exist truths that man knows, and also revealed truths of faith; that these two kinds of truth are not simply reducible to one another; that faith and theology do not, by means of symbols and sensuous images, merely say the same as what reason and science say more clearly by conceptual argumentation (Averroës, Hegel); that, on the other hand, reason is not a "prostitute" (Luther), but is man's natural capacity to grasp the real world; that since reality and truth, though essentially inexhaustible, are basically one, faith and reason cannot ultimately contradict one another. Those who hold these convictions appear quite unable to refrain from trying to coordinate what they know with what they believe. Any epoch that addresses itself to this interminable task can ill afford to ignore the demand-

Perennial tenets of Scholasticism

ing and multiform paradigm of Scholasticism; but to the problems posed it will have to find its own answer.

(Jf.Pi.)

Skepticism

As a philosophical attitude, skepticism is the doubting of knowledge claims set forth in various areas. Skeptics have challenged the adequacy or reliability of these claims by asking what they are based upon or what they actually establish. They have raised the question whether such claims about the world are either indubitable or necessarily true, and they have challenged the alleged grounds of accepted assumptions. Practically everyone is skeptical about some knowledge claims; but the Skeptics have raised doubts about any knowledge beyond the contents of directly felt experience. The original Greek meaning of *skeptikos* was "an inquirer," someone who was unsatisfied and still looking for truth.

Skepticism in history

From ancient times onward Skeptics have developed arguments to undermine the contentions of dogmatic philosophers, scientists, and theologians. The Skeptical arguments and their employment against various forms of dogmatism have played an important role in shaping both the problems and the solutions offered in the course of Western philosophy. As ancient philosophy and science developed, doubts arose about basic accepted views of the world. In ancient times Skeptics challenged the claims of Platonism, Aristotelianism, and Stoicism, and in the Renaissance those of Scholasticism and Calvinism. After Descartes, Skeptics attacked Cartesianism and other theories justifying the "new science." Later, a Skeptical offensive was levelled against Kantianism and then against Hegelianism. Each Skeptical challenge led to new attempts to resolve the difficulties. Skepticism, especially since the Enlightenment, has come to mean disbelief—primarily religious disbelief—and the Skeptic has often been likened to the village atheist.

VARIOUS SENSES AND APPLICATIONS

Skepticism developed with regard to various disciplines in which men claimed to have knowledge. It was questioned, for example, whether one could gain any certain knowledge in metaphysics (the study of the nature and significance of being as such) or in the sciences. In ancient times a chief form was medical Skepticism, which questioned whether one could know with certainty either the causes or cures of diseases. In the area of ethics doubts were raised about accepting various mores and customs and about claiming any objective basis for making value distinctions. Skepticisms about religion have questioned the doctrines of different traditions. Certain philosophies, like those of Hume and Kant, have seemed to show that no knowledge can be gained beyond the world of experience and that one cannot discover the causes of phenomena. Any attempt to do so, as Kant argued, leads to antinomies, contradictory knowledge claims. A dominant form of Skepticism, the subject of this article, concerns knowledge in general, questioning whether anything actually can be known with complete or adequate certainty. This type is called epistemological Skepticism.

Epistemological Skepticism

Kinds of epistemological Skepticism can be distinguished in terms of the areas in which doubts are raised; that is, whether they be directed toward reason, toward the senses, or toward knowledge of things-in-themselves. They can also be distinguished in terms of the motivation of the Skeptic—whether he is challenging views for ideological reasons or for pragmatic or practical ones to attain certain psychological goals. Among the chief ideological motives have been religious or antireligious concerns. Some Skeptics have challenged knowledge claims so that religious ones could be substituted—on faith. Others have challenged religious knowledge claims in order to overthrow some orthodoxy. Kinds of Skepticism also can be distinguished in terms of how restricted or how thoroughgoing they are—whether they apply only to certain areas and to certain kinds of knowledge claims or whether they are more general and universal.

ANCIENT SKEPTICISM

Historically, skeptical philosophical attitudes began to appear in pre-Socratic thought. In the 5th century BC, the Eleatic philosophers, known for reducing reality to a static One, questioned the reality of the sensory world, of change and plurality, and denied that reality could be described in the categories of ordinary experience. On the other hand, the Ephesian philosopher of change Heracleitus and his pupil Cratylus thought that the world was in such a state of flux that no permanent, unchangeable truth about it could be found; and Xenophanes, a wandering poet and philosopher, doubted whether man could distinguish true from false knowledge.

A more developed Skepticism appeared in some of Socrates' views and in a couple of the Sophists (see below). Socrates, in the early Platonic dialogues, was always questioning the knowledge claims of others; and in the *Apology,* he said that all that he really knew was that he knew nothing. Socrates' enemy, the Sophist Protagoras, contended that man is the measure of all things. This thesis was taken as a kind of skeptical relativism: no views are ultimately true, but each is merely one man's opinion. Another Sophist, Gorgias, advanced the skeptical-nihilist thesis that nothing exists; and if something did exist, it could not be known; and if it could be known, it could not be communicated.

The putative father of Greek Skepticism is Pyrrhon of Elis (c. 360–c. 272 BC), who tried to be a living Skeptic. He avoided committing himself to any views about what was actually going on and acted only according to appearances. In this way he sought happiness or at least mental peace.

Academic and Pyrrhonian schools

The first school of Skeptical philosophy developed in Plato's Academy (see above *Platonism*) in the 3rd century BC and was thus called "Academic" Skepticism. Starting from the skeptical side of Socrates, its leaders, Arcesilaus (316/315–c. 241 BC) and Carneades (214/213–129/128 BC), set forth a series of epistemological arguments to show that nothing could be known, challenging primarily the two foremost schools, those of the Stoics and Epicureans. They denied that any criteria could be found for distinguishing the true from the false; instead, only reasonable or probable standards could be established for knowledge. This limited or probabilistic Skepticism was the view of the Academy until the 1st century BC, when Cicero was a student there. His *Academica* and *De natura deorum* are the main sources for knowledge of this movement. (St. Augustine's *Contra academicos* is an answer to Cicero's views.)

The other major form of ancient Skepticism was Pyrrhonism, apparently developed by medical Skeptics in Alexandria. Beginning with Aenesidemus (1st century BC), this movement, named after Pyrrhon, criticized the Academic Skeptics because they claimed to know too much, namely, that nothing could be known and that some things are more probable than others. The Pyrrhonians advanced a series of tropes, or ways of opposing various kinds of knowledge claims, in order to bring about *epochē* (suspense of judgment). The Pyrrhonian attitude is preserved in the writings of one of its last leaders, Sextus Empiricus (2nd or 3rd century AD). In his *Outlines of Pyrrhonism* and *Adversus mathematicos,* Sextus presented the tropes developed by previous Pyrrhonists. The 10 tropes attributed to Aenesidemus showed the difficulties to be encountered in ascertaining the truth or reliability of judgments based on sense information, owing to the variability and differences of human and animal perceptions. Other arguments raised difficulties in determining whether there are any reliable criteria or standards—logical, rational, or otherwise—for judging whether anything is true or false. To settle any disagreement, a criterion seems to be required. Any purported criterion, however, would appear to be based on another criterion, thus requiring an infinite regress of criteria, or else it would be based upon itself, which would be circular. Sextus offered arguments to challenge any claims of dogmatic philosophers to know more than what is evident; and in so doing he presented in one form or another practically all of the skeptical arguments that have ever appeared in subsequent philosophy.

Sextus said that his arguments were aimed at leading people to a state of *ataraxia* (unperturbability). People who thought that they could know reality were constantly disturbed and frustrated. If they could be led to suspend judgment, however, they would find peace of mind. In this state of suspension they would neither affirm nor deny the possibility of knowledge but would remain peaceful, still waiting to see what might develop. The Pyrrhonist did not become inactive in this state of suspense but lived undogmatically according to appearances, customs, and natural inclinations.

MEDIEVAL SKEPTICISM

Pyrrhonism ended as a philosophical movement in the late Roman Empire, as religious concerns became paramount. In the Christian Middle Ages the main surviving form of Skepticism was the Academic, described in St. Augustine's *Contra academicos.* Augustine, before his conversion, had found Cicero's views attractive and had overcome them only through revelation. With faith, he could seek understanding. Augustine's account of Skepticism and his answer to it provided the basis for medieval discussions.

In Islāmic Spain, where there was more contact with ancient learning, a form of antirational Skepticism developed among Muslim and Jewish theologians. Al-Ghazāli, an Arab theologian of the 11th and early 12th centuries, and his Jewish contemporary Judah ha-Levi (*c.* 1075/*c.* 1085–*c.* 1141), who was a poet and physician as well as a philosopher, offered skeptical challenges (much like those later employed by the occasionalist Nicolas Malebranche and by David Hume) against the contemporary Aristotelians in order to lead people to accept religious truths in mystical faith. This kind of fideism also appears in the late Middle Ages in the German cardinal and philosopher Nicolaus of Cusa's advocacy of learned ignorance as the way to religious knowledge.

MODERN SKEPTICISM

Modern Skepticism emerged in the 16th century, not from medieval views but from the intellectual crises of the Renaissance and Reformation and from the rediscovery of the Skeptical classics. The voyages of exploration; the humanistic rediscovery of the learning of ancient Greece, Rome, and Palestine; and the new science—all combined to undermine confidence in man's accepted picture of the world. The religious controversy between the Protestants and Catholics raised fundamental epistemological issues about the bases and criteria of religious knowledge. At the same time the texts of Cicero and Sextus became available again. (Sextus' *Outlines of Pyrrhonism* [*Hypotyposeis*] was published in Latin in 1562, his *Adversus matematicos* in 1569, and the Greek texts of both in 1621.)

In the Reformation. The fundamental skeptical issues raised by the Reformation appeared in the debate between the outstanding humanist scholar Erasmus and Luther. Erasmus, using Academic skeptical materials, insisted that the issues in dispute could not be resolved, that one should therefore suspend judgment and remain with the church. Luther insisted, on the other hand, that true and certain religious knowledge could and must be gained through conscience. Erasmus' view developed into a Christian Skepticism, accepting traditional Christianity on faith after seeing that no adequate evidence existed. Luther's view, and later that of Calvin, proposed a new criterion—that of inner experience—while the Catholics of the Counter-Reformation employed Pyrrhonian and Academic arguments to undermine the criterion.

Following after Erasmus, another humanist, Giovanni Pico della Mirandola II (nephew of the famous count of the same name) and H.C. Agrippa von Nettesheim, a stormy occult philosopher and physician, employed the skeptical arguments against Scholasticism, Renaissance Naturalism, and many other views to win people to the "true religion." The Catholic scholar Gentian Hervet, in the preface to his 1569 edition of Sextus, saw the Skeptical arguments as the definitive answer to Calvinism and the way to true Christianity.

In the 17th century. The new concern with Skepticism was given a general philosophical formulation by Michel de Montaigne and his cousin Francisco Sanches. Montaigne in *Apology for Raimond Sebond* and Sanches in *Quod nihil scitur,* both written in 1576, explored the human epistemological situation and showed that man's knowledge claims in all areas were extremely dubious. Montaigne recommended living according to nature and custom and accepting whatever God reveals, and Sanches advocated recognizing that nothing can be known and then trying to gain what limited information one can through empirical scientific means.

Montaigne's Skepticism was extremely influential in the early 17th century. His followers, Pierre Charron, J.-P. Camus, La Mothe Le Vayer, and others, further popularized his views. Various French Counter-Reformers used the arguments of Montaigne and Sextus to undermine Calvinism. Montaigne's Skepticism opposed all sorts of disciplines, including the new science, and was coupled with a fideism that many suspected to be insincere.

In the 1620s efforts to refute or mitigate this new Skepticism appeared. A Christian Epicurean, Pierre Gassendi, himself originally a Skeptic, and Marin Mersenne, one of the most influential figures in the intellectual revolution of the times, while retaining epistemological doubts about knowledge of reality yet recognized that science provided useful and important information about the world. The constructive Skepticisms of Gassendi and Mersenne, and later of members of the Royal Society of England like Bishop John Wilkins and Joseph Glanvill, developed the attitude of Sanches into a hypothetical, empirical interpretation of the new science.

René Descartes offered a fundamental refutation of the new Skepticism, contending that, by applying the skeptical method of doubting all beliefs that could possibly be false (due to suffering illusions or being misled by some power), one would discover a truth that is genuinely indubitable, viz., "I think, therefore I am" (*cogito ergo sum*), and that from this truth one could discover the criterion of true knowledge, viz., that whatever is clearly and distinctly conceived is true. Using this criterion, one could then establish: God's existence, that he is not a deceiver, that he guarantees our clear and distinct ideas, and that an external world exists that can be known through mathematical physics. Descartes, starting from Skepticism, claimed to have found a new basis for certitude and for knowledge of reality. Throughout the 17th century Skeptical critics—Mersenne, Gassendi, the reviver of Academic philosophy Simon Foucher, and Pierre-Daniel Huet, one of the most learned men of the age—sought to show that Descartes had not succeeded, and that, if he sincerely followed his skeptical method, his new system could only lead to complete Skepticism. They challenged whether the *cogito* proved anything, or whether it was indubitable; whether Descartes' method could be successfully applied, or whether it was certain; and whether any of the knowledge claims of Cartesianism were *really* true. Nicolas Malebranche, the developer of occasionalism, revised the Cartesian system to meet the Skeptical attacks only to find his efforts challenged by the new Skeptical criticisms of Foucher and by the contention of the Jansenist philosopher Antoine Arnauld that Malebranchism led to a most dangerous Pyrrhonism.

Various English philosophers culminating in Locke tried to blunt the force of Skepticism by appealing to common sense and to the "reasonable" man's inability to doubt everything. They admitted that there might not be sufficient evidence to support the knowledge claims extending beyond immediate experience. But this did not actually require that everything be doubted; by using standards of common sense, an adequate basis for many beliefs could be found. Blaise Pascal, who presented the case for Skepticism most forcefully in his *Pensées,* still denied that there can be a complete Skepticism; for nature prevents it. Lacking rational answers to complete Skepticism, man's only recourse lies in turning to God for help in overcoming doubts.

The culmination of 17th-century Skepticism appears in the writings of Pierre Bayle, especially in his monumental *Dictionnaire historique et critique* (1697–1702). Bayle, a superb dialectician, challenged philosophical, sci-

---

Fideistic views

Christian Skepticism

Cartesian Skepticism

Pierre Bayle

entific, and theological theories, both ancient and modern, showing that they all led to perplexities, paradoxes, and contradictions. He argued that the theories of Descartes, Spinoza, Leibniz, and Malebranche, when skeptically analyzed, cast in doubt all information about the world, even whether a world exists. Bayle skillfully employed Skeptical arguments about such things as sense information, human judgments, logical explanations, and the criteria of knowledge in order to undermine confidence in human intellectual activity in all areas. Bayle suggested that man should abandon rational activity and turn blindly to faith and revelation; he can therefore only follow his conscience without any criterion for determining true faith. Bayle showed that the interpretations of religious knowledge were so implausible that even the most heretical views, like Manichaeism, known for its cosmic dualism of good and evil, and Atheism, made more sense. As a result Bayle's work became "the arsenal of the Enlightenment," and he was regarded as a major enemy of religion.

In the 18th century. Most 18th-century thinkers gave up the quest for metaphysical knowledge after imbibing Bayle's arguments. George Berkeley, an Empiricist and Idealist, fought Skeptical doubts by identifying appearance and reality and offering a spiritualistic metaphysics. He was immediately seen as just another Skeptic since he was denying the world beyond experience.

David Hume

Bayle's chief 18th-century successor was David Hume. Combining empirical and skeptical arguments, Hume charged that neither inductive nor deductive evidence could establish the truth of any matter of fact. Knowledge could only consist of intuitively obvious matters or demonstrable relations of ideas but not of anything beyond experience; the mind can discover no necessary connections within experience nor any root causes of experience. Beliefs about the world are based not upon reason or evidence nor even upon appeal to the uniformity of nature but only on habit and custom. Beliefs cannot be justified. Belief that there is an external world, a self, a God is common; but there is no adequate evidence for it. Although it is natural to hold these convictions, they are inconsistent and epistemologically dubious. "Philosophy would render us entirely Pyrrhonian, were not Nature too strong for it." The beliefs that a man is forced to hold enable him to describe the world scientifically, but when he tries to justify them he is led to complete Skepticism. Before he goes mad with doubts, however, Nature brings him back to common sense, to unjustifiable beliefs. Hume's fideism was a natural rather than a religious one; it is only animal faith that provides relief from complete doubt. The religious context of Skepticism from Montaigne to Bayle had been removed, and man was left with only his natural beliefs, which might be meaningless or valueless.

The central themes in Hume's Skeptical analysis—the basis of induction and causality, knowledge of the external world and the self, proofs of the existence of God—became the key issues of later philosophy. Hume's contemporary Thomas Reid hoped to rebut Hume's Skepticism by exposing it as the logical conclusion of the basic assumptions of modern philosophy from Descartes onward. Such disastrous assumptions should be abandoned for commonsensical principles that have to be believed. As Hume and Kant saw, Reid had not answered Hume's Skepticism but had only sidestepped the issue by appealing to commonsensical living. This provided, however, neither a theoretical basis for beliefs nor a refutation of the arguments that questioned them.

Kant and his critics

Kant saw that Hume had posed a most fundamental challenge to all human knowledge claims. To answer him, it had to be shown not that knowledge is possible but *how* it is possible. Kant combined a Skepticism toward metaphysical knowledge with the contention that certain universal and necessary conditions are involved in having experience and describing it. In terms of these it is possible to have genuine knowledge about the forms of all possible experience, space and time, and about the categories in which all experience is described. Any effort to apply this beyond all possible experience, however, leads into contradictions and Skepticism. It is not possible to know about things-in-themselves nor about the causes of experience.

Though Kant thought that he had resolved the Skeptical problems, some of his contemporaries saw his philosophy as commencing a new Skeptical era. G.E. Schulze (or Schulze-Aenesidemus) a notable critic of Kantianism, insisted that, on Kant's theory, no one could know any objective truths about anything; he could only know the subjective necessity of his views. The Jewish critic Salomon Maimon contended that, though there are such things as a priori concepts, their application to experience is always problematical, and whether they apply can only be found through experience. Hence, the possibility of knowledge can never be established with certainty. Assured truth on the basis of concepts is possible only of human creations, like mathematical ideas, and it is questionable whether these have any objective truth. The thesis that human creativity is the basis of truth, however, was soon to be developed by Johann G. Fichte, a leading German Idealist, as a new way of transcending Skepticism.

Another Skeptical critic of Kant, J.G. Hamann, saw in Hume's and Kant's work a new basis for fideism. If knowledge of reality cannot be gained by rational means, then one must turn to faith. Based on Hume's efforts, Hamann advanced an antirational Skepticism in an effort to convince Kant to become a fideistic Christian. Hamann's kind of fideism was also developed in France by Catholic opponents of the French Revolution and liberalism—like Joseph de Maistre and H.-F.-R. de Lamennais.

Existentialism

In recent and contemporary philosophy. Irrational Skepticism was developed into Existentialism by Søren Kierkegaard in the 19th century. Using traditional Skeptical themes to attack Hegelianism and liberal Christianity, Kierkegaard stressed the need for faith. Only by an unjustified and unjustifiable "leap into faith" could certainty be found—which would then be entirely subjective rather than objective. Modern neo-orthodox and Existentialist theologians have argued that Skepticism highlights man's inability to find any ultimate truth except through faith and commitment. Nonreligious forms of this view have been developed by Existentialist writers like Albert Camus, combining the epistemological Skepticism of Kierkegaard with the religious and value Skepticism of Nietzsche. The rational and scientific examination of the world shows it to be unintelligible and absurd; and if God is dead, as Nietzsche proclaimed, then the world is ultimately meaningless. But it is necessary to struggle with it. It is thus through action and commitment that one finds whatever personal meaning one can, though it has no objective significance.

Other kinds of Skepticism appear in various forms of recent and contemporary philosophy. The English Idealist F.H. Bradley used classical Skeptical arguments in his *Appearance and Reality: A Metaphysical Essay* to contend that the world could not be understood empirically or materialistically; true knowledge could be reached only by transcending the world of appearance.

George Santayana, an American critical Realist, in *Scepticism and Animal Faith,* presented a naturalistic Skepticism. Any interpretation of immediate or intuited experience is open to question. To make life meaningful, however, men make interpretations by "animal faith," according to biological and social factors. The resulting beliefs, though unjustified and perhaps illusory, enable them to persevere and find the richness of life.

Positivism and Analysis

Types of Skepticism also appear in Logical Positivism (see below *Positivism and Logical Empiricism*) and various forms of linguistic philosophy (see below *Analytic and Linguistic Philosophy*). The attack on speculative metaphysics developed by the physicist and early Positivist Ernst Mach, by Bertrand Russell, and by Rudolf Carnap, a leader in the Vienna Circle, where Logical Positivism was nourished, incorporated a Skepticism about the possibility of gaining knowledge beyond experience or logical tautologies. Russell and the important philosopher of science Karl Popper have further stressed the unjustifiability of the principle of induction, and Popper has criticized theories of knowledge based upon empirical verification. A founder of linguistic analysis, Fritz Mauthner, has set forth a Skepticism in which any language is merely relative to its users and thus subjective. Every attempt to tell what is true just leads one back to linguistic formulations, not to objective states of affairs. The result is a complete Skepticism about reality—a reality that cannot even be expressed except in terms of what he called godless mystical contemplation. Mauthner's linguistic Skepticism bears some affinities to the views expressed in Ludwig Wittgenstein's *Tractatus Logico-Philosophicus.*

CRITICISM AND EVALUATION

In Western thought Skepticism has raised basic epistemological issues. In view of the varieties of human experience, it has questioned whether it is possible to tell which are veridical. The variations that occur in different perceptions of what is presumed to be one object raise the question of which is the correct view. The occurrence of illusory experiences raises the question of whether it is really possible to distinguish illusions and dreams from reality. The criteria employed can be questioned and require justification. On what basis does one tell whether one has the right criteria? By other criteria? Then, are these correct? On what standards? The attempt to justify criteria seems either to lead to an infinite regress or to just stop arbitrarily. If an attempt is made to justify knowledge claims by starting with first principles, what are these based upon? Can it be established that these principles cannot possibly be false? If so, is the proof itself such that it cannot be questioned? If it is claimed that the principles are self-evident, can one be sure of this, sure that one is not deceived? And can one be sure that one can recognize and apply the principles correctly? Through such questioning, Skeptics have indicated the basic problems that an investigator would have to resolve before he could be certain of possessing knowledge; *i.e.,* information that could not possibly be false.

Criticisms   Critics have contended that Skepticism is both a logically and a humanly untenable view. Any attempt to formulate the position will be self-refuting since it will assert at least some knowledge claims about what is supposed to be dubious. Montaigne suggested that the Skeptics needed a nonassertive language, reflecting the claim of Sextus that the Skeptic does not make assertions but only chronicles his feelings. The strength of Skepticism lies not in whether it can be stated consistently but upon the effects of its arguments on dogmatic philosophers. As Hume said, Skepticism may be self-refuting, but in the process of refuting itself it undermines dogmatism. Skepticism, Sextus said, is like a purge that eliminates itself as well as everything else.

Critics have claimed that anyone who tried to be a complete Skeptic, denying or suspending all judgments about ordinary beliefs, would soon be driven insane. Even Hume thought that the complete Skeptic would have to starve to death and would walk into walls or out of windows. Hume, therefore, separated the doubting activity from natural practical activities in the world. Skeptical philosophizing went on in theory, while believing occurred in practice. Sextus and the contemporary Norwegian Skeptic Arne Naess have said, on the other hand, that Skepticism is a form of mental health. Instead of going mad, the Skeptic—without commitment to fixed positions—can function better than the dogmatist.

Some recent thinkers like A.J. Ayer and John Austin have contended that Skepticism is unnecessary. If knowledge is defined in terms of satisfying meaningful criteria, then knowledge is open to all. The Skeptics have raised false problems, because it is, as a matter of fact, possible to tell that some experiences are illusory since we have criteria for distinguishing them from actual events. We do resolve doubts and reach a state of knowledge through various verification procedures, after which doubt is meaningless. Naess, in his book *Scepticism,* has sought to show, however, that, on the standards offered by Ayer and Austin, one can still ask if knowledge claims may not turn out to be false and hence that Skepticism has still to be overcome.

Evaluation   Skepticism throughout history has played a dynamic role in forcing dogmatic philosophers to find better or stronger bases for their views and to find answers to the Skeptical attacks. It has forced a continued reexamination of previous knowledge claims and has stimulated creative thinkers to work out new theories to meet the Skeptical problems.

The history of philosophy can be seen, in part, as a struggle with Skepticism. The attacks of the Skeptics also have served as a check on rash speculation; the various forms of modern Skepticism have gradually eroded the metaphysical and theological bases of European thought. Most contemporary thinkers have been sufficiently affected by Skepticism to abandon the search for certain and indubitable foundations of human knowledge. Instead, they have sought ways of living with the unresolved Skeptical problems through various forms of naturalistic, scientific, or religious faiths.   (R.H.P.)

Sophists

The Sophists were certain Greek lecturers, writers, and teachers in the 5th and 4th centuries BC, most of whom travelled about the Greek-speaking world giving instruction in a wide range of subjects in return for fees.

HISTORY OF THE NAME

The term sophist (Greek *sophistes*) had earlier applications. It is sometimes said to have meant originally simply "clever" or "skilled man," but the list of those to whom Greek authors applied the term in its earlier sense makes it probable that it was rather more restricted in meaning. Seers, diviners, and poets predominate, and the earliest Sophists probably were the "sages" in early Greek societies. This would explain the subsequent application of the term to the Seven Wise Men (7th–6th century BC), who typified the highest early practical wisdom, and to Pre-Socratic philosophers generally. When Protagoras, in one of Plato's dialogues (*Protagoras,* 317 a–b) is made to say that, unlike others, he is willing to call himself a Sophist, he is using the term in its new sense of "professional teacher," but he wishes also to claim continuity with earlier sages as a teacher of wisdom. Plato and Aristotle altered the meaning again, however, when they claimed that professional teachers such as Protagoras were not seeking the truth but only victory in debate and were prepared to use dishonest means to achieve it. This produced the sense "captious or fallacious reasoner or quibbler," which has remained dominant to the present day. Finally, under the Roman Empire the term was applied to professors of rhetoric, to orators, and to prose writers generally, all of whom are sometimes regarded as constituting what is now called the Second Sophistic movement (see below).

THE 5TH-CENTURY SOPHISTS

The names survive of nearly 30 Sophists properly so called, of whom the most important were Protagoras, Gorgias, Antiphon, Prodicus, and Thrasymachus. Plato protested strongly that Socrates was in no sense a Sophist—he took no fees, and his devotion to the truth is beyond question. But from many points of view he is rightly regarded as a rather special member of the movement. The actual number of Sophists was clearly much larger than 30, and for about 70 years, until *c.* 380 BC, they were the sole source of higher education in the more advanced Greek cities. Thereafter, at least at Athens, they were largely replaced by the new philosophic schools, such as those of Plato and Isocrates. Plato's dialogue *Protagoras* describes something like a conference of Sophists at the house of Callias in Athens just before the Peloponnesian War. Antimoerus of Mende, described as one of the most distinguished of Protagoras' pupils, is there receiving professional instruction in order to become a Sophist (*Protagoras,* 315 a), and it is clear that this was already a normal way of entering the profession.

The
Sophistic
movement

Most of the major Sophists were not Athenians, but they made Athens the centre for their activities, although travelling continuously. The importance of Athens was doubtless due in part to the greater freedom of speech prevailing there, in part to the patronage of wealthy men like Callias, and even to the positive encouragement of Pericles, who was said to have held long discussions with Sophists in his house. But primarily the Sophists congregated at Athens because they found there the greatest demand for what they had to offer, namely, instruction to young men, and the extent of this demand followed from the nature of the city's political life. Athens was a democracy, and although its limits were such that Thucydides could say it was governed by one man, Pericles, it nonetheless gave opportunities for a successful political career to citizens of the most diverse backgrounds, provided they could impress their audiences sufficiently in the council and the assembly. After Pericles' death this avenue became the highroad to political success.

The
Sophistic
teaching

The Sophists taught men how to speak and what arguments to use in public debate. A Sophistic education was increasingly sought after both by members of the oldest families and by aspiring newcomers without family backing. The changing pattern of Athenian society made merely traditional attitudes in many cases no longer adequate. Criticizing such attitudes and replacing them by rational arguments held special attraction for the young, and it explains the violent distaste which they aroused in traditionalists. Plato thought that much of the Sophistic attack upon traditional values was unfair and unjustified. But even he learned at least one thing from the Sophists—if the older values were to be defended, it must be by reasoned argument, not by appeals to tradition and unreflecting faith.

Seen from this point of view, the Sophistic movement was a valuable function of Athenian democracy in the 5th century BC. It offered an education designed to facilitate and promote success in public life. All of the Sophists appear to have provided a training in rhetoric and in the art of speaking, and the Sophistic movement, responsible for large advances in rhetorical theory, contributed greatly to the development of style in oratory. In modern times the view occasionally has been advanced that this was the Sophists' only concern. But the range of topics dealt with by the major Sophists makes this unlikely, and even if success in this direction was their ultimate aim, the means they used were surely as much indirect as direct, for the pupils were instructed not merely in the art of speaking, but in grammar; in the nature of virtue (*aretē*) and the bases of morality; in the history of society and the arts; in poetry, music, and mathematics; and also in astronomy and the physical sciences. Naturally the balance and emphasis differed from Sophist to Sophist, and some offered wider curricula than others. But this was an individual matter, and attempts by earlier historians of philosophy to divide the Sophistic movement into periods in which the nature of the instruction was altered are now seen to fail for lack of evidence. The 5th-century Sophists inaugurated a method of higher education that in range and method anticipated the modern humanistic approach inaugurated or revived during the Renaissance.

NATURE OF SOPHISTIC THOUGHT

A question still discussed is whether the Sophists in general had any real regard for truth or whether they taught their pupils that truth was unimportant compared with success in argument. Plato's hostile judgment on both counts is still frequently repeated without question. The Platonic writings make frequent reference to what Plato calls "eristic" (Greek *eristikos,* "fond of wrangling") and "antilogic"; the two often have been incorrectly treated as identical. Eristic, for Plato, consists in arguments aimed at victory rather than at truth. Antilogic involves the assignment to any argument of a counterargument that negates it, with the implication that both argument and counterargument are equally true. Antilogic in this sense was especially associated with Protagoras; but Plato, no doubt correctly, attributes its use to other Sophists as well. He regards the use of antilogic as essentially eristic, whether it be used to silence an opponent by making his position seem self-contradictory, or whether it be used mechanically to negate any proposition put forward in debate. He concludes that the widespread use of antilogic is evidence that Sophists had no real regard for the truth, which must itself be free from antilogic.

But Plato himself believed, for much or possibly all of his life, that the phenomenal world was essentially antilogical inasmuch as no statement about it could be made possessing a greater degree of truth than the contradictory of that statement. For example, if a man is tall in relation to one object, he will be short in relation to another object. In so characterizing the phenomenal world, Plato certainly did not wish to be called eristic—he regarded the application of antilogic to the description of the phenomenal world as an essential preliminary to the search for the truth residing in the Platonic Forms, which are themselves free from antilogic.

Seen in this perspective, the Sophistic use of antilogic must be judged less harshly. To the extent that it was used irresponsibly to secure success in debate it was eristic, and the temptation so to use it must often have arisen. But where it was invoked in the sincere belief that antilogic elements were indeed involved, or where it was used for analyzing a complex situation in order to reveal its complexity, then antilogic was in no way inconsistent with devotion to truth. This raises the question to what extent the Sophists possessed any general view of the world or gave expression to any genuine philosophical views, whether original or derived. Ancient writers, influenced by Plato and Aristotle, seem to have excluded the Sophists, apart from Protagoras, for their schematized accounts of early Greek thinkers. Modern writers have frequently maintained that, whatever else they were, the Sophists were in no sense philosophers. Even those who acknowledge the philosophical interest of certain particular doctrines attributed to individual Sophists often tend to regard these as exceptions and claim that, inasmuch as the Sophists were not a school but only independent teachers and writers, as a class they were not philosophers. Two questions are involved: whether the Sophists held common intellectual doctrines and whether some or all of these could actually be termed philosophical.

Philosophy
of the
Sophists

Among moderns, Hegel was one of the first to reinsert the Sophists into the history of Greek philosophy. He did so within the framework of his own dialectic, in which every thesis invokes its own opposite, or antithesis; thus he treated the Sophists as representing the antithesis to the thesis of the group of philosophers known collectively as the Pre-Socratics. Pre-Socratics such as Thales, Heracleitus, and Parmenides sought the truth about the external world with a bold enthusiasm that produced a series of explanations, each claiming to be correct. None of these explanations of the physical world paid attention to the observer and each was driven to reject more and more of the phenomenal world itself as unreal. Finally, with the Eleatics, a 5th-century school at Elea in Italy that held that reality is a static one, of which Parmenides and Zeno are representatives, little or nothing of the phenomenal world was left as real. This trend in turn produced a growing distrust of the power of human beings to attain knowledge of the ultimate basis of natural phenomena. Philosophy had reached an impasse, and there was a danger of complete skepticism. Such an extreme position, according to Hegel's view, provoked the "antithesis" of the Sophistic movement, which rejected the "thesis" of the objectivists and concentrated attention upon man rather than upon nature. To Hegel, the Sophists were subjective Idealists, holding that reality is only minds and their contents, and so philosophy could move forward by turning its attention to the subjective element in knowing. Reflection upon the contrast between the thought of the Sophists and that of their predecessors produced the "syntheses" of Plato and Aristotle.

Whether any of the Sophists actually were subjective Idealists may be doubted. The conclusion depends in part on whether Protagoras held that phenomena had subjective existence only, or whether he thought that all things perceived had objective existence but were perceived differently according to the nature of the percipient and their relation to him—*i.e.,* whether he interpreted phenomena subjectively or relativistically. It is fairly clear, however, that the Sophists did concentrate very largely upon man and human society, upon questions of words in their relations to things, upon issues in the theory of knowledge, and upon the importance of the observer and the subjective element in reality and in the correct understanding of reality.

This emphasis helps to explain the philosophical hostility of Plato and Aristotle. Particularly in the eyes of Plato, anyone who looks for the truth in phenomena alone, whether he interprets it subjectively or relativistically, cannot hope to find it there; and his persistence in turning away from the right direction virtually amounts to a rejection of philosophy and of the search for truth. Many a subsequent thinker for whom metaphysics, or the investigation of the deepest nature of reality, was the crowning achievement of philosophy has felt with Plato that the Sophists were so antimetaphysical that they have no claim to rank as philosophers. But in a period when, for many philosophers, metaphysics is no longer the most important part of philosophy and is even for some no part at all, there is growing appreciation of a number of problems and doctrines recurring in the discussions of the Sophists in the 5th and 4th centuries BC. In the 18th and early 19th centuries the Sophists were considered charlatans. Their intellectual honesty was impugned, and their doctrines were blamed for weakening the moral fibre of Greece. The charge was based on two contentions, both correct: first, that many of the Sophists attacked the traditionally accepted moral code; and second, that they explored and even commended alternative approaches to morality that would condone or allow behaviour of a kind inadmissible under the stricter traditional code.

Much less weight has been attached to these charges since about the mid-19th century. First, many of the attacks on the traditional morality were in the name of a new morality that claimed to be of greater validity. Attacks upon particular doctrines often claimed that accepted views should be abandoned as morally defective. Furthermore, even when socially disfavoured action seemed to be commended, this was frequently done to introduce a principle necessary in any satisfactory moral theory. Thus when Thrasymachus in the first book of Plato's *Republic* argues that justice is unwarranted when it merely contributes to another's good and not to the good of the doer, Plato agrees. Finally, there is no evidence that any of the Sophists were personally immoral or that any of their pupils were induced to immoral actions by Sophistic teaching. The serious discussion of moral problems and the theory of morality tends to improve behaviour, not to corrupt it.

WRITINGS

In addition to their teaching, the Sophists wrote many books, the titles of which are preserved by writers such as Diogenes Laërtius, who probably derived them from library catalogues. It has usually been supposed that the writings themselves hardly survived beyond the period of Plato and Aristotle, but this view requires modification in the light of papyrus finds, admittedly few, that were copied from Sophistic writings in the Christian Era. It also has been possible to identify in the works of later writers certain imitations or summaries of 5th-century Sophistic writers, whose names are unknown. The most important of these are the discussion of law in the *Protrepticus,* or "Exhortation to Philosophy," by the 3rd-century-AD Syrian Neoplationst Iamblichus, and the so-called *Dissoi logoi* found in the manuscripts of Sextus Empiricus (3rd century AD). This evidence suggests that while most later writers took their accounts of the Sophists from earlier writers, especially from Plato, the original writings did in many cases survive and were consulted.

PARTICULAR DOCTRINES

As part of his defense of the Sophists against the charge of immoral teachings, the English historian George Grote (1794–1871) maintained that they had nothing in common with each other except their profession, as paid teachers qualifying young men to think, speak, and act with credit to themselves as citizens. This denial of common doctrines cannot be sustained—the evidence is against it. While the Sophists were not a sect, with a set of obligatory beliefs or doctrines, they had a common interest in a whole series of questions to which they sought to apply solutions along certain clearly defined lines.

There are great difficulties, however, in the precise reconstruction of individual Sophistic doctrines. No complete writings survive from any of the Sophists to check the accounts found in Plato, and later writers were often, but not always, dependent upon what they found in Plato. Plato doubtless knew well the doctrines of individual Sophists; but he was writing for those to whom these doctrines were already well known, and he was always more interested in following the argument where it led than in providing precise statements of other people's views for the sake of posterity. Consequently, almost everything that is said about particular Sophistic doctrines is subject to controversy.

Theoretical issues. Relativism and skepticism have often been regarded as common features of the Sophistic movement as a whole. But it was early pointed out that only in Protagoras and Gorgias is there any suggestion of a radical skepticism about the possibility of knowledge; and even in their case Sextus Empiricus, in his discussion of skepticism, is probably right when he declares that neither was really a skeptic. Protagoras does seem to have restricted knowledge to sense experience, but he believed emphatically that whatever was perceived by the senses was certainly true. This led him to assert that the tangent does not touch the circle at a point only, but along a definite length of the circumference; clearly he was referring to human perception of drawn tangents and circles. Gorgias, who claimed that nothing exists, or if it does exist it cannot be known, or if it exists and is knowable it cannot be communicated to another, has often been accused of denying all reality and all knowledge. Yet he also seems to have appealed in his very discussion of these themes to the certainty of perceived facts about the physical world; *e.g.,* that chariots do not race across the sea. Others dismiss his whole thesis as a satire or joke against philosophers.

Probably neither view is correct. What Gorgias seems to have been attacking was not perceived reality nor one's power to perceive it but the attempt to assign existence or nonexistence (with the metaphysical implications of such an operation) to what we perceive around us. There is evidence that other Sophists (*e.g.,* Hippias) were interested in questions of this kind, and it is likely that they were all concerned to some degree with rejecting claims of any nonsensible existence, such as those of the Eleatics. The Sophists, in fact, were attempting to explain the phenomenal world without appealing to any principles outside of phenomena. They believed that this could be done by including the observer within the phenomenal world. Their refusal to go beyond phenomena was, for Plato, the great weakness in their thinking.

A second common generalization about the Sophists has been that they represent a revolt against science and the study of the physical world. The evidence is against this, inasmuch as for Hippias, Prodicus, Gorgias, and Protagoras there are records of a definite interest in questions of this kind. The truth is rather that they were in revolt against attempts to explain the physical world by appeals to principles that could not be perceived by the senses; and instead of framing new "objective" explanations, they attempted to explain things, where explanation was required, by introducing the perceiver as one element in the perceptual situation.

One of the most famous doctrines associated with the Sophistic movement was the opposition between nature and custom or convention in morals. It is probable that the antithesis did not originate in Sophistic circles but was rather earlier; but it was clearly very popular and figured largely in Sophistic discussions. The commonest form of the doctrine involved an appeal from conventional laws to supposedly higher laws based on nature. Sometimes these higher laws were invoked to remedy defects in actual laws and to impose more stringent obligations; but usually it was in order to free men from restrictions unjustifiably imposed by human laws that the appeal to nature was made. In its extreme form the appeal involved the throwing off of all restraints upon self-interest and the desires of the individual (*e.g.,* the doctrine of Callicles in Plato's *Gorgias* that might, if one possesses it, is actually right), and it was this, more than anything else, that gave support to charges against the Sophists of immoral teaching. On other occasions the terms of the antithesis were reversed and human laws were explicitly acclaimed as superior to

Moral views of the Sophists

Relativism and skepticism

Nature and law

the laws of nature and as representing progress achieved by human endeavour. In all cases the laws of nature were regarded not as generalized descriptions of what actually happens in the natural world (and so not like the laws of physics to which no exceptions are possible) but rather as norms that people ought to follow but are free to ignore. Thus the appeal to nature tended to mean an appeal to the nature of man treated as a source for norms of conduct.

To Greeks this appeal was not very novel. It represented a conscious probing and exploration into an area wherein, according to their whole tradition of thought, lay the true source for norms of conduct. If Callicles in Plato's *Gorgias* represents a position actually held by a living Sophist when he advocates free rein for the passions, then it was easy for Plato to argue in reply that the nature of man, if it is to be fulfilled, requires organization and restraint in the license given to the desires of particular aspects of it; otherwise the interests of the whole will be frustrated. Both Plato and Aristotle, in basing so much of their ethics on the nature of man, are only following up the approach begun by the Sophists.

Religion and society   **Humanistic issues.** The Sophists have sometimes been characterized by their attacks on the traditional religious beliefs of the Greeks. It is true that more than one Sophist seems to have faced prosecution for impiety, as did Socrates also. Protagoras wrote "concerning the gods, I cannot know either that they exist or that they do not exist nor what they are like in form," and Prodicus offered a sociological account of the development of religion. Critias went further when he supposed that the gods were deliberately invented to inspire fear in the evildoer. It is thus probably correct to say that the tendency of much Sophistic thought was to reject the traditional doctrines about the gods. Indeed this follows almost inevitably if the supposition is correct that all the Sophists were attempting to explain the phenomenal world from within itself, while excluding all principles or entities not discernible in phenomena. But in their agnostic attitudes toward the Olympian deities the Sophists were probably at one with most of the Pre-Socratic philosophers of the 6th and 5th centuries and also with most thinking people living toward the end of the 5th century. It is thus probably misleading to regard them as revolutionary in their religious beliefs.

The importance the Sophists attached to man meant that they were extremely interested in the history and organization of human societies. Here again most is known about Protagoras, and there is a danger of treating his particular doctrines as typical of the Sophistic movement as a whole. In the 5th century, human history was very commonly seen in terms of a decline from an earlier golden age. Another view supposed that there were recurring cycles in human affairs according to which a progression from good to bad would give way to one from bad to good. The typical Sophistic attitude toward society rejected both of these views in favour of one that saw human history in terms of progress from savagery to civilization. In a famous myth Protagoras explained how man achieved civilized society first with the aid of arts and crafts and then by gaining a sense of respect and justice in the ordering of his affairs. The general thinking of most of the Sophists seems to have been along similar lines.

One of the most distinctive Sophistic tenets was that virtue can be taught, a position springing naturally from the Sophists' professional claim to be the teachers of young men. But the word virtue (*aretē*) implied both success in living and the qualities necessary for achieving such success, and the claim that *aretē* could be taught by the kind of teaching that the Sophists offered had far-ranging implications. It involved the rejection of the view that *aretē* came only by birth—for example, by being born a member of a noble family—and it involved also the rejection of the doctrine that *aretē* was a matter of the chance occurrence of specified qualities in particular individuals. *Aretē,* in the Sophists' view, was the result of known and controllable procedures, a contention of profound importance for the organization of society. Moreover, what can be taught has some relation to what can be known and understood. The belief that teaching of a high intellectual calibre could produce success both for the individual and

for governments has had a profound influence upon the subsequent history of education. Once again, it is through the acceptance of this doctrine by Plato and Aristotle that the Sophistic position came to be part of subsequent humanist tradition.

THE SECOND SOPHISTIC MOVEMENT

It is a historical accident that the name "Sophist" came to be applied to the Second Sophistic movement. Greek literature underwent a period of eclipse during the 1st century BC and under the early Roman Empire. But Roman dominance did not prevent a growing interest in sophistic oratory in the Greek-speaking world during the 1st century AD. This oratory aimed merely at instructing or interesting an audience and had of necessity no political function. But it was based on elaborate rules and required a thorough knowledge of the poets and prose writers of antiquity. Training was provided by professional teachers of rhetoric who claimed the title of Sophists, just as the 5th-century Sophists had adopted a name already used by others.

The revival of the Greek spirit under Hadrian and other emperors in the 2nd century AD who were also admirers of Greek culture found expression in a fresh flowering of Greek prose following principles developed and applied by the professors of rhetoric in the 1st century AD. Hence a group of Greek prose writers in the 2nd century AD were regarded as constituting the Second Sophistic movement. This was a backward-looking movement that took as its models Athenian writers of the 5th and 4th centuries BC; hence the label "Atticists" (Greek *Attikos,* "Athenian") applied to some of its leading members. The limits of the movement were never clear. It is usually taken to include Polemon of Athens, Herodes Atticus, Aelius Aristides, Maximus of Tyre, and the group of Philostrati. Dio Chrysostom of Prusa is often included, although others would regard him as preparing the way for the main period. Other writers, like Lucian, Aelian, and Alciphron, were influenced by the movement even if not properly members of it; and the writers of prose romances, such as Longus and Heliodorus, and the historians Dio Cassius and Herodian are also associated with the general trend. By the 3rd century AD, however, its impulse was weakening, and it was shortly no longer distinguishable within the general stream of Greek literature.   (G.B.K.)

Stoicism

Stoicism, a school of thought that flourished in Greek and Roman antiquity, was one of the loftiest and most sublime philosophies in the record of Western civilization. In urging participation in the affairs of man, Stoics have always believed that the goal of all inquiry is to provide man with a mode of conduct characterized by tranquillity of mind and certainty of moral worth.

NATURE AND SCOPE OF STOICISM

For the early Stoic philosopher, as for all the post-Aristotelian schools, knowledge and its pursuit are no longer held to be ends in themselves. The Hellenistic Age was a time of transition, and the Stoic philosopher was perhaps its most influential spokesman. A new culture was in the making. The heritage of an earlier period, with Athens as its intellectual leader, was to continue, but to undergo many changes. If, as with Socrates, to know is to know oneself, rationality as the sole means by which something outside of the self might be achieved may be said to be the hallmark of Stoic belief. As a Hellenistic philosophy, Stoicism presented an *ars vitae,* a way of accommodation for people to whom the human condition no longer appeared as the mirror of a universal, calm, and ordered existence. Reason alone could reveal the constancy of cosmic order and the originative source of unyielding value; thus, reason became the true model for human existence. To the Stoic, virtue is an inherent feature of the world, no less inexorable in relation to man than are the laws of nature. The Stoics believed that perception is the basis of true knowledge. In logic, their comprehensive presentation of the topic is derived from perception, yielding not only the judgment that knowledge is possible but also that *certain* knowledge is possible, on the analogy of the incorrigibility of perceptual experience. To them, the world is composed of material things, with some few exceptions (*e.g.*, meaning), and the irreducible element in all things is right reason, which pervades the world as divine fire. Things, such as material, or corporeal, bodies, are governed by this reason or fate, in which virtue is inherent. The world in its awesome entirety is so ruled as to exhibit a grandeur of orderly arrangement that can only serve as a standard for mankind in the regulation and ordering of his life. Thus, the goal of man is to live according to nature, in agreement with the world design. Stoic moral theory is also based on the view that the world, as one great city, is a unity. Man, as a world citizen, has an obligation and loyalty to all things in that city. He must play an active role in world affairs, remembering that the world exemplifies virtue and right action. Thus, moral worth, duty, and justice are singularly Stoic emphases, together with a certain sternness of mind. For the moral man neither is merciful nor shows pity, because each suggests a deviation from duty and from the fated necessity that rules the world. Nonetheless—with its loftiness of spirit and its emphasis on man's essential worth—the themes of universal brotherhood and the benevolence of divine nature make Stoicism one of the most appealing of philosophies.

Rival schools in antiquity

Its chief competitors in antiquity were: (1) Epicureanism, with its doctrine of a life of withdrawal in contemplation and escape from worldly affairs and its belief that pleasure, as the absence of pain, is the goal of man; (2) Skepticism, which rejected certain knowledge in favour of local beliefs and customs, in the expectation that these guides would provide man with the quietude and serenity that the dogmatic philosopher (*e.g.*, the Stoic) could not hope to achieve; and (3) Christianity, with its hope of personal salvation provided by an appeal to faith as an immanent aid to human understanding and by the beneficent intervention of a merciful God.

Along with its rivals, Stoicism enabled the individual to better order his own life and to avoid the excesses of human nature that promote disquietude and anxiety. It was easily the most influential of the schools from the time of its founding through the first two centuries AD, and it continued to have a marked effect on later thought. During the late Roman and medieval periods, elements of Stoic moral theory were known and used in the formulation of Christian, Jewish, and Muslim theories of man and nature, of the state and society, and of law and sanctions— *e.g.*, in the works of Marcus Cicero, Roman statesman and orator; in Lactantius, often called the "Christian Cicero"; and in A.M.S. Boethius, a scholar transitional to the Middle Ages. In the Renaissance, Stoic political and moral theory became more popular to theorists of natural law and political authority and of educational reform— *e.g.*, in Hugo Grotius, a Dutch jurist and statesman, and in Philipp Melanchthon, a major Reformation scholar. More recently, Stoicism has become popular again for its insistence on the value of the individual and the place of value in a world of strife and uncertainty—*e.g.*, in Existentialism and in Neo-orthodox Protestant theology. Stoicism also plays an important role in reassessments of the history of logic—*e.g.*, in Jan Łukasiewicz, a Polish logician, and in William and Martha Kneale, mid-20th-century British logicians.

ANCIENT STOICISM

Historical and philosophical setting

Early Greek Stoicism. With the death of Aristotle (322 BC) and that of Alexander the Great (323 BC), the greatness of the life and thought of the Greek city-state (polis) ended. With Athens no longer the centre of worldly attraction, its claim to urbanity and cultural prominence passed on to other cities—to Rome, to Alexandria, and to Pergamum. The Greek polis gave way to larger political units; local rule was replaced by that of distant governors. The earlier distinction between Greek and barbarian was destroyed; provincial and tribal loyalties were broken apart, first by Alexander and then by Roman legions. The loss of freedom by subject peoples further encouraged a deterioration of the concept of the freeman and resulted

in the rendering of obligation and service to a ruler whose moral force held little meaning. The earlier intimacy of order, cosmic and civic, was now replaced by social and political disorder; and traditional mores gave way to uncertain and transient values.

Stoicism had its beginnings in a changing world, in which earlier codes of conduct and ways of understanding proved no longer suitable. But it was also influenced by tenets of the older schools. The earliest Greek philosophers, the Milesians, had called attention to cosmic order and the beauty of nature. Later, the monist Parmenides of Elea stressed the power of reason and thought, whereas Heracleitus of Ephesus, precursor of the philosophy of becoming, had alluded to the constancy of change and the omnipresence of divine fire, which illumined all things. A deeper understanding of man himself came with Socrates, symbol of the philosophic man, who personified *sophia* and *sapientia* (Greek and Latin: "wisdom"). Of the several schools of philosophy stemming from Socrates, the Cynic and Megarian schools were influential in the early development of Stoic doctrine: the Cynics for their emphasis on the simple life, unadorned and free of emotional involvement; and the Megarians for their study of dialectic, logical form, and paradoxes.

The Early Stoa

Stoicism takes its name from the place where its founder, Zeno of Citium (Cyprus), customarily lectured—the Stoa Poikile (Painted Colonnade). Zeno, who flourished in the early 3rd century BC, showed in his own doctrines the influence of earlier Greek attitudes, particularly those mentioned above. He was apparently well versed in Platonic thought, for he had studied at Plato's Academy both with Xenocrates of Chalcedon and with Polemon of Athens, successive heads of the Academy. Zeno was responsible for the division of philosophy into three parts: logic, physics, and ethics. He also established the central Stoic doctrines in each part, so that later Stoics were to expand rather than to change radically the views of the founder. With some exceptions (in the field of logic), Zeno thus provided the following themes as the essential framework of Stoic philosophy: logic as an instrument and not as an end in itself; human happiness as a product of life according to nature; physical theory as providing the means by which right actions are to be determined; perception as the basis of certain knowledge; the wise man as the model of human excellence; Platonic Ideas—or the abstract Forms that things of the same genus share—as being unreal; true knowledge as always accompanied by assent; the fundamental substance of all existing things as being a divine fire, the universal principles of which are (1) passive (matter) and (2) active (reason inherent in matter); belief in a world conflagration and renewal; belief in the corporeality of all things; belief in the fated causality that necessarily binds all things; cosmopolitanism, or cultural outlook transcending narrower loyalties; and man's obligation, or duty, to choose only those acts that are in accord with nature, all other acts being a matter of indifference.

Cleanthes of Assos, who succeeded Zeno as head of the school, is best known for his *Hymn to Zeus*, which movingly describes Stoic reverence for the cosmic order and the power of universal reason and law. The third head of the school, Chrysippus of Soli, who lived to the end of the 3rd century, was perhaps the greatest and certainly the most productive of the early Stoics. He devoted his considerable energies to the almost complete development of the Zenonian themes in logic, physics, and ethics. In logic particularly, he defended against the Megarian logicians and the Skeptics such concepts as certain knowledge, comprehensive presentation, proposition and argument, truth and its criterion, and assent. His work in propositional logic, in which unanalyzed propositions joined by connectives are studied, made important contributions to the history of ancient logic and is of particular relevance to more recent developments in logic.

In physics, Chrysippus was responsible for the attempt to show that fate and free will are not mutually exclusive conceptual features of Stoic doctrine. He further distinguished between "whole" and "all," or "universe," arguing that the whole is the world, while the all is the external void together with the world. Zeno's view of the origin of man as providentially generated by "fiery reason" out of matter was expanded by Chrysippus to include the concept of self-preservation, which governs all living things. Another earlier view (Zeno's), that of nature as a model for life, was amplified first by Cleanthes and then by Chrysippus. The Zenonian appeal to life "according to nature" had evidently been left vague, because to Cleanthes it seemed necessary to speak of life in accord with nature conceived as the world at large (the cosmos), whereas Chrysippus distinguished between world nature and human nature. Thus, to do good is to act in accord with both human and universal nature. Chrysippus also expanded the Stoic view that seminal reasons were the impetus for animate motion.

He established firmly that logic and (especially) physics are necessary and are means for the differentiation of goods and evils. Thus, a knowledge of physics (or theology) is required before an ethics can be formulated. Indeed, physics and logic find their value chiefly in this very purpose. Chrysippus covered almost every feature of Stoic doctrine and treated each so thoroughly that the essential features of the school were to change relatively little after his time.

The Middle Stoa

Later Roman Stoicism. The Middle Stoa, which flourished in the 2nd and early 1st centuries BC, was dominated chiefly by two men of Rhodes: Panaetius, its founder, and his disciple Poseidonius. Panaetius organized a Stoic school in Rome before returning to Athens, and Poseidonius was largely responsible for an emphasis on the religious features of the doctrine. Both were antagonistic to the ethical doctrines of Chrysippus, who, they believed, had strayed too far from the Platonic and Aristotelian roots of Stoicism. It may have been because of the considerable time that Panaetius and Poseidonius lived in Rome that the Stoa there turned so much of its emphasis to the moral and religious themes within the Stoic doctrine. Panaetius was highly regarded by Cicero, who used him as a model for his own work. Poseidonius, who had been a disciple of Panaetius in Athens, taught Cicero at his school at Rhodes and later went to Rome and remained there for a time with Cicero. If Poseidonius admired Plato and Aristotle, he was particularly interested—unlike most of his school—in the study of natural and providential phenomena. In presenting the Stoic system in the second book of *De natura deorum* (45 BC), Cicero most probably followed Poseidonius. Because his master, Panaetius, was chiefly concerned with concepts of duty and obligation, it was his studies that served as a model for the *De officiis* (44 BC) of Cicero. Hecaton, another of Panaetius' students and an active Stoic philosopher, also stressed similar ethical themes.

If Chrysippus is to be commended for his diligence in defending Stoic logic and epistemology against the Skepticism of the New Academy (3rd–2nd century BC), it was chiefly Panaetius and Poseidonius who were responsible for the widespread popularity of Stoicism in Rome. It was precisely their turning of doctrine to themes in moral philosophy and natural science that appealed to the intensely practical Romans. The times perhaps demanded such interests, and with them Stoicism was to become predominantly a philosophy for the individual, showing how—given the vicissitudes of life—one might be stoical. Law, world citizenship, nature, and the benevolent workings of Providence and the divine reason were the principal areas of interest of Stoicism at this time.

The Late Stoa

These tendencies toward practicality are also well illustrated in the later period of the school (in the first two centuries AD) in the writings of Lucius Seneca, a Roman statesman; of Epictetus, a slave freed by Nero; and of Marcus Aurelius, a Roman emperor. Both style and content in the *Libri morales* (Eng. trans., *Moral Essays*) and *Epistulae morales* (*Moral Letters*) of Seneca reinforce the new direction in Stoic thought. The *Encheiridion* (*Manual*) of Epictetus and the *Meditations* of Marcus Aurelius furthered the sublime and yet personal consolation of the Stoic message and increasingly showed the strength of its rivalry to the burgeoning power of the new Christianity. The mark of a guide, of the religious teacher, is preeminent in these writings. It is difficult to establish with any precision, however, the extent of Stoic influence by the

time of the first half of the 2nd century AD. So popular had these ideas become that many specifically Stoic terms (viz., right reason, comprehension, assent, indifference, *logos,* natural law, and the notion of the wise man) commonly were used in debate and intellectual disputes.

Stoic elements in Pauline and patristic thought. There is much disagreement as to the measure of Stoic influence on the writings of St. Paul, the Apostle of Christ. At Tarsus, Paul certainly had opportunities for hearing Stoic lectures on philosophy. And it may be that his discussion of nature and the teaching of it (I Cor. 11:14) is Stoic in origin, for it has a parallel in the *Manual* of Epictetus 1.16, 10. Although not a Stoic technical term, *syneidēsis,* which Paul used as "conscience," was generally employed by Stoic philosophers. In I Cor. 13 and in the report of Paul's speech at Athens (Acts 17), there is much that is Hellenistic, more than a little tinged by Stoic elements— *e.g.,* the arguments concerning man's natural belief in God and the belief that man's existence is in God.

The assimilation of Stoic elements by the Church Fathers was generally better understood by the 4th century. Stoic influence can be seen, for example, in the relation between reason and the passions in the works of St. Ambrose, one of the great scholars of the church, and of Marcus Minucius Felix, a Christian Apologist. Each took a wealth of ideas from Stoic morality as Cicero had interpreted it in *De officiis.* In general, whereas the emerging Christian morality affirmed its originality, it also assimilated much of the pagan literature, the more congenial elements of which were essentially Stoic.

Stoic concepts in Tertullian and Origen

Earlier, in the 3rd century, Quintus Tertullian, often called the father of Latin Christian literature, seems to have been versed in Stoic philosophy; *e.g.,* in his theory of the agreement between the supernatural and the human soul, in his use of the Stoic tenet that from a truth there follow truths, and in his employment of the idea of universal consent. Even in his polemical writings, which reveal an unrelenting hostility to pagan philosophy, Tertullian showed a fundamental grasp and appreciation of such Stoic themes as the world *logos* and the relation of body to soul. This is well illustrated in his argument against the Stoics, particularly on their theme that God is a corporeal being and identified with reason as inherent in matter— also to be found in his polemics against Marcion, father of a heretical Christian sect, and against Hermogenes of Tarsus, author of an important digest of rhetoric. Yet in his doctrine of the Word, he appealed directly to Zeno and Cleanthes of the Early Stoa. Another important polemic against the Stoics is found in the treatise *Contra Celsum,* by Origen, the most influential Greek theologian of the 3rd century, in which he argued at some length against Stoic doctrines linking God to matter.

Also, St. Cyprian, bishop of Carthage in the 3rd century, revealed the currency of Stoic views; *e.g.,* in his *Ad Demetrianum,* a denunciation of an enemy to Christianity, in which Cyprian castigates the ill treatment of slaves, who, no less than their masters, are formed of the same matter and endowed with the same soul and live according to the same law. The beliefs in the brotherhood of man and in the world as a great city, commonly found in early Christian literature, were current Stoic themes. The Christian attitude appears in what St. Paul said of Baptism: "You are all sons of God through Faith. For as many of you as were baptized into Christ have put on Christ" (Gal. 3:26–27).

STOICISM IN MEDIEVAL AND MODERN PHILOSOPHY

Stoic undercurrents in medieval thought. During the period when Christian institutions and doctrines were developing (AD 230–1450), Stoicism continued to play a popular role. The *De consolatione philosophiae* (524) of Boethius (died AD 524/525) was widely known and appreciated as a discourse on the mysterious questions of the nature of good and evil, of fortune, chance, or freedom, and of divine foreknowledge. If the plan of Boethius was to serve as an interpreter of Plato and Aristotle, he succeeded only in working through some logical theories of Aristotle, together with several commentaries on those theories. In the *Consolatione,* however, the themes are quite different;

Stoic concepts in Boethius and Lactantius

in the fifth book, for example, he attempted to resolve the apparent difficulty of reconciling human freedom with the divine foreknowledge, a problem that among Stoic thinkers—though by no means uniquely among them—had been in general currency for a long time. This work of emancipation from worldly travail through the glories of reason and philosophy, which included Stoic doctrines as found in the writings of Cicero and Seneca, was much more influential for later medieval thought than that of Lactantius, of the late 3rd to early 4th century, who was largely concerned with the writing of a history of religion—a summary statement of Christian doctrine and life from earliest times. Lactantius also wrote a not unimportant work, *De ira Dei* (313), on the possibility of anger in God. It poses a problem of how to deal with the essentially Greek, or philosophic, view that God cannot feel anger because he is not subject to passions and that *apatheia* ("apathy," or "imperturbableness") is not merely the mark of the wise man but is also a divine attribute. This view, which had been most thoroughly developed among Stoic thinkers and particularly by Epictetus, raised a peculiarly Christian problem, the concern of the power of God to reward the righteous and punish the transgressor; thus, it challenged the very idea of Providence. Other manifestations of anthropopathism, the attributing of human feelings to God, had also been charged against the early Christian religionists; and the writers of the time—Lactantius and Tertullian among them—took great pains to refute the largely Stoic formulations of these charges. Although the refutations took the form—in St. Augustine, for example—of denying that the wrath of God is a perturbation of the soul and of holding that it is rather a judgment, the concept of the divine essence excludes all passions. Within the monastic tradition, there remained more than a residue of concern over apathy as a divine attribute and as a model for the truly religious.

Stoicism in legal and political theory Other significant Stoic influences appeared in medieval discussions of the popular origin of political authority, *res publica* and *res populi*, and on the distinctions made in law between *jus naturale, jus gentium, jus civile*—doctrines of Stoic origin—found in 3rd-century Roman juridical texts gathered together by Isidore of Seville (died AD 636), a Spanish encyclopaedist and theologian. The Stoic belief—as against Aristotle—that men are by nature equal was an integral part of the knowledge that certain rules of law are universally recognized, laws that all people might naturally follow. In this way, the Romans—whose genius lay in organization and in law—fostered the conception of natural, or common, law, which reason was supposed to make evident to all men. Thus, in the second half of the 11th century, the Stoic texts of Cicero and Seneca became important doctrinal sources for the initial discussions of social and political philosophy. These early theories of law, of the natural equality of men, and of the rights of prince and populace were to become the basis for 13th-century systems of social and political privilege and obligation.

In the 12th century, John of Salisbury, an English critical scholar, produced, in his *Policraticus* (1159), the first complete attempt at a philosophy of the state since Classical times. Stoic doctrines of natural law, society, state, and Providence were important elements in his effort to construct a social philosophy on ethical and metaphysical principles. The impact of these doctrines and the lengthy history of their use in the earlier Middle Ages can also be found in the views of Thomas Aquinas on the philosophy of the state and of man.

Renascence of Stoicism in modern times. If the influence of Stoic doctrines during the Middle Ages was largely restricted to the resolution of problems of social and political significance, it remained for the Renaissance, in its passion for the rediscovery of Greek and Roman antiquity, to provide a basis for the rebirth of Stoic views in logic, epistemology, and metaphysics, as well as the documentation of the more familiar Stoic doctrines in ethics and **Stoic concepts in Lipsius and certain Skeptics** politics. Late in the 16th century, Justus Lipsius, a Flemish scholar and Latin Humanist, was responsible for the first restatement of Stoicism as a defensible and thoroughgoing (Christian) philosophy of man. His treatises *De constantia* (1584) and *Politicorum sive civilis doctrinae libri V* (1589)

were widely known in many editions and translations. His defense of Stoic doctrine in *Manuductio ad Stoicam Philosophiam* (1604) and *Physiologia Stoicorum* (1604) provided the basis for the considerable Stoic influence during the Renaissance. Around the turn of the 17th century, Guillaume du Vair, a French lawyer and Christian philosopher, made Stoic moral philosophy popular, while Pierre Charron, a French theologian and Skeptic, utilized Stoic themes in *De la sagesse* (1601; Eng. trans., *Of Wisdome*, 1608), as did the Skeptic Michel de Montaigne in his *Essais* (1580; Eng. trans. 1603). Through the work of Lipsius, Stoic doctrines were to influence the thought of Francis Bacon, a precursor of modern philosophy of science, and, later, the *De l'esprit des lois* (1748; Eng. trans., *The Spirit of Laws,* 1750), by the political theorist Charles-Louis, baron de Montesquieu. In the continuing and relentless war against the Aristotelianism of the later Middle Ages, the doctrines of Stoicism influenced many prominent figures of the Renaissance and Reformation periods.

Pietro Pomponazzi, an Aristotelian of early 16th-century Italy, in defending an anti-Scholastic Aristotelianism against the Averroists, who viewed the world as a strictly necessitarian and fated order, adopted the Stoic view of Providence and human liberty. The 15th-century Humanist Leonardo Bruni absorbed Stoic views on reason, fate, and free will. Pantheism, the view that God and nature are unitary in the sense that God is an impersonal being, and naturalism, the view that nothing is supernatural, both of which identify God with the cosmos and ascribe to it a life process of which the world soul is the principle, were widely held Renaissance notions. Such a pantheistic naturalism was advocated—though from diverse standpoints—by Francesco Patrizi, a versatile Platonist, and by Giordano Bruno, defender of an infinite cosmos; and in both authors the inspiration and source were fundamentally Stoic. In the development of a philosophy of public law based upon a study of man, Stoic elements are found in the *Utopia* (1516; Eng. trans. 1551), by Thomas More, and the *De Jure Belli ac Pacis* (1625; Eng. trans. 1682), by Hugo Grotius. This latter work is one of the most famous Renaissance treatises on the theory of natural and social rights.

The foremost Swiss reformer of the early 16th century, Huldrych Zwingli, who regarded justification by subjective belief as the foundation of the new Christianity, utilized Stoic views on the autonomy of the will, on the absolute predestination of the good and evil man, and on moral determinism.

Another Stoic influence of considerable importance in the tradition of Christian Humanism was the view that all religions have a common basis of truths concerning God—a universal Deism. Among those who favoured such a view were Zwingli and Desiderius Erasmus, the great Renaissance Humanist and scholar. More and Grotius also laid special stress on this view, and its influence was felt in the moral, social, and even the artistic life of the 16th century. Later, Herbert of Cherbury, often called the father of Deism, further developed the idea of religious peace and the reduction of opposing religious views to common elements. This view became one of the most popular ideas of the 17th century.

Philipp Melanchthon also cultivated Humanism and the philosophy of antiquity as a basis for a reborn Christianity. Although Aristotle was his chief inspiration, Melanchthon made telling use of the Stoic theory of knowledge, with its notions of innate principles and the natural light of reason, which teach man the great truths of metaphysical and moral order. Stoicism thus became the basis for the natural-law theory, which holds that the state is of immediately divine origin and independent of the church—a Protestant view opposed by Catholic writers.

The Cartesian revolution in thought in the 17th century brought forward several Stoic notions: that morality consists of obedience to the law of reason, which God has deposited within man; that ethics presupposes a knowledge of nature, because man must learn to know his place in the world, for only then may he act rightly; that self-examination is the foundation of ethics; and that the innateness and commonality of truths bespeak the view that **Stoic concepts in Cartesian and Spinozistic thought** only thoughts and the will belong properly to man, for the body is a part of the material world. Such views were particularly developed by René Descartes, often hailed as the father of modern philosophy, in his dualism of mind (or soul) and body.

Benedict de Spinoza, a freethinking Jewish Rationalist, made similar use of Stoic views on the nature of man and the world. That aspect of Spinoza's thought that is debatably labelled pantheist is essentially Stoic in character. Together with the Cartesians, Spinoza insisted upon the importance of internal and right reason as the sole means by which to attain to indubitable truths and to the possibility of human freedom.

Blaise Pascal, a French scientist and religious writer, also was sympathetic to Cartesian conceptions of man and nature. Though he turned his back on philosophy, his religious thought retained the Cartesian and Stoic insistence on the independence of human reason, holding that man is fundamentally a thinking being, innately capable of making right decisions. There is an important and crucial difference and conflict between Pascal's views and those of Spinoza and the Cartesians: for Pascal, though the use of (the Stoic) right reason might result in proofs and demonstrations that lead to the God of truth, it would never lead to the God of love, the one true God. Thus, the Stoic exaltation of reason to an entity in its own right—indeed, to a divine entity—as exemplified among the Cartesians

and in the thought of Spinoza, was rejected by Pascal in the Jansenist Christianity that he finally adopted—a rejection that, because it also repudiated free will, distinguishes Pascal from those who held Stoic as well as alternative conceptions of human freedom and responsibility.

Christianity in general, in spite of striking contrasts with Stoicism, has found elements within it that parallel its own position. As the Stoic, for example, feels safe and protected in the rational care of some immanent Providence, so the Christian senses that a transcendent though incarnate and loving God is looking after him. And in general, Stoicism has played a great part throughout the ages in the theological formulation of Christian thought as well as in the actual realization of the Christian ideals.

Contemporary philosophy has borrowed from Stoicism, at least in part, its conviction that man must be conceived as being closely and essentially connected with the whole universe. And contemporary Humanism still contains some obviously Stoic elements, such as its belief in the solidarity of all peoples based upon their common nature, and in the primacy of reason. It is perhaps just because Stoicism has never become a full-fledged philosophic system that, many centuries after the dissolution of the Stoic school, fundamental themes of its philosophy have emerged again and again, and many have become incorporated into modern thinking.   (Ja.L.S.)

Stoic concepts in Christianity and modern philosophical thought

MODERN SCHOOLS

Analytic and Linguistic philosophy

The methods that have dominated British philosophy for most of the 20th century and American philosophy since somewhat more recently have been called Linguistic and Analytic because language and the analysis of the concepts expressed by language have been a central concern. Though Australia and the Scandinavian countries have also contributed to this movement, it has won a very limited following elsewhere. Although there is a unity of outlook in the tradition, individual philosophers and movements within it have differed, often radically, about the goals and methodology of philosophy. A leading figure prior to the mid-20th century, Ludwig Wittgenstein, an Austrian-born Cambridge philosopher, for example, may have been unique in the history of philosophy in having engaged in two periods of profoundly influential philosophical productivity of which the later work was in large part a renunciation and a sustained argument against the earlier. Yet both the early Wittgenstein (represented by his *Tractatus Logico-Philosophicus,* 1922) and the later (represented by the *Philosophical Investigations,* 1953) are central examples of Analytic philosophy.

Different approaches to the study of language

Moreover, the aims assigned to the philosophical study of language have often been different. Some philosophers, among them Bertrand Russell and the early Wittgenstein, have thought that the underlying structure of language mirrors that of the world—that from an analysis of language a philosopher can grasp important truths about reality. This so-called picture theory of language, though influential, is generally repudiated by current Analytic philosophers. Another important dispute concerns whether everyday language is defective, vague, misleading, and even, at times, contradictory. Some Analytic philosophers have thus proposed the construction of an "ideal" language: precise, free of ambiguity, and clear in structure. The general model for such a language has been symbolic logic, the growth of which in the 20th century has played a central role in Analytic philosophy. An ideal language, it was thought, would resolve many traditional philosophical disputes that have arisen from the misleading structure of natural languages. At the other pole, some philosophers have thought that many philosophic problems have come from paying too little attention to what men say in everyday language about various situations.

Despite such disagreements, Analytic philosophers have much in common. Most of them, for example, have con-

centrated on particular philosophical problems, such as that of induction, or have examined specific concepts, such as those of memory or of personal identity, without attempting to construct any grand metaphysical schemes—an attitude that has roots as ancient as those of the Socratic method exemplified in Plato's dialogues. Almost invariably Plato began with specific questions such as "What is knowledge?" or "What is justice?" and pursued them in a way that can be viewed, without undue strain, as philosophical analysis in the modern sense.

Ideally, a philosophical analysis illuminates some important concept and helps to answer philosophical questions involving the concept. A famous example of such analysis is contained in Bertrand Russell's theory of definite descriptions. In a simple subject–predicate statement such as "Socrates is wise," he said, there seems to be something referred to (Socrates) and something said about it (that he is wise). If, instead of a proper name, however, a "definite description" is substituted, as in the statement "The president of the United States is wise," there is apparently still something referred to and something said about it. But a problem arises when nothing fits the description, as in the statement "The present king of France is wise." Though there is apparently nothing for the statement to be about, one nevertheless understands what it says. Consequently, a pre-World War I philosopher, Alexius Meinong, celebrated for his *Gegenstandstheorie* ("theory of objects"), felt forced by such examples to distinguish between things that have real existence and things that have some other sort of existence; for such statements could not be understood unless they were about something.

Theory of definite descriptions

In Russell's view, philosophers such as Meinong were misled by surface grammatical form into thinking that such statements are simple subject–predicate statements. In reality they are complex; in fact, an analysis of the foregoing example shows that the definite description, "the present king of France," is not an independent unit in the statement at all. Upon analysis, the statement is a complex conjunction of statements: (1) "There is a present king of France"; (2) "There is at most one present king of France"; and (3) "If anyone is a present king of France, he is wise." But, more importantly, each of the three components is a general statement and is not about anything or anyone in particular. There is no phrase in the complete analysis equivalent to "the present king of France," which shows that the phrase is not an expression, like a proper name, that refers to something as the thing that the whole statement talks about. There is no need, therefore, to make Meinong's distinction between things that have real existence and things that have some other kind of existence.

GENERAL VIEWPOINT OF ANALYTIC PHILOSOPHY

Nature, role, and method of analysis. Analytic philosophy is concerned with the close and careful examination of concepts.

Status of philosophy in the Empiricist tradition. In spirit and style Analytic philosophy has strong ties with the Empiricist tradition, which stresses the data received through the senses and which, except for brief periods, has characterized British philosophy for some centuries, distinguishing it from the more Rationalistic trends of continental European philosophy. It is not surprising, therefore, that Analytic philosophy should find its home mainly in the Anglo-Saxon countries. In fact, the beginning of modern Analytic philosophy is generally dated from the time when two of its major figures, Bertrand Russell and G.E. Moore, both Cambridge philosophers, rebelled against an anti-Empiricist Idealism that had temporarily captured the English philosophical scene. The most famous British Empiricists—John Locke, George Berkeley, David Hume, and John Stuart Mill—had many interests, doctrines, and methods in common with contemporary Analytic philosophers. Although many of their particular doctrines are favorite targets of attack by Analytic philosophers today, one feels that this is more the result of a common interest in certain problems than any difference in general philosophical outlook.

Most Empiricists, though admitting that the senses fail to yield the certainty requisite for knowledge, hold nonetheless that it is only through observation and experimentation that justified beliefs about the world can be gained; *i.e.,* a priori reasoning from self-evident premises cannot reveal how the world is. This view has resulted in a sharp dichotomy among the sciences: between the physical sciences, which ultimately must verify their theories by observation, and the deductive or a priori sciences— *e.g.,* mathematics and logic—the method of which is the deduction of theorems from given axioms. Thus, the deductive sciences cannot give justified beliefs, much less knowledge, of the world. This consequence was one of the cornerstones of two important movements within Analytic philosophy, logical atomism and Logical Positivism (see below). In the Positivist's view, for example, the theorems of mathematics are merely the result of working out the consequences of the conventions that have been adopted for the use of its symbols.

Physical versus a priori sciences

The question then arises whether philosophy itself is to be assimilated to empirical or to a priori sciences. Early Empiricists assimilated philosophy to the Empirical sciences. They were less self-reflective about its methods than contemporary Analytic philosophers are. Being preoccupied with epistemology (theory of knowledge) and the philosophy of mind, and holding that fundamental facts can be learned about these subjects from individual introspection, they took their work to be a kind of introspective psychology. Analytic philosophers in the 20th century, on the other hand, have been less inclined to appeal ultimately to direct introspection. Moreover, the development of rigorous methods in formal logic seemed to promise help in solving philosophical problems—and logic is as a priori as a science can be. It seemed, then, that philosophy must be classed with mathematics and logic.

Conceptual, linguistic, and scientific analysis. The question remained, however, what philosophy's function and methodology are. For a great many Analytic philosophers who do philosophy in the minute and meticulous manner of G.E. Moore and, in particular, for those who have made Oxford the centre of Analytic philosophy (see below, *Recent trends in England: Oxford philosophers*), its business is the analysis of concepts. For them, philosophy is an a priori discipline because the philosopher in some sense already possesses the concept in which he is interested and needs no observations in order to analyze it.

Function and methodology of philosophy

Philosophy can be seen either as conceptual or as linguistic analysis. In the analysis of the concept of seeing, for

example, the philosopher is not expressing purely linguistic concerns—with, say, the English verb "to see"—though an investigation of what can be said using that verb may be relevant to his conclusions. For a concept is independent of any particular languages; a concept is something that all languages, insofar as they are capable of expressing the concept, have in common. Thus, philosophers who stress that it is concepts that they analyze attempt to rebut the charge that their problems and solutions are merely verbal.

In contrast, other Analytic philosophers have been concerned with how expressions are used in a particular, nontechnical, everyday language. Thus, the term ordinary language philosophy has been applied by critics as a term of opprobrium to such philosophers. An influential study, *The Concept of Mind* (1949), by Gilbert Ryle, a prominent Oxford Analyst, is an example of a work that some critics took to depend in large part on a trivial appeal to how English speakers talk; but many of Ryle's arguments could equally well have been given by Analytic philosophers who would look upon the term ordinary language with horror.

The problem of perception illustrates how Analytic philosophers who do conceptual analysis think of the goal of philosophy as both different from and complementary to science. Physiologists, psychologists, and physicists— through experiments, observations, and testable theories— have also contributed to man's understanding of perception. There is in the sciences, however, a strong tendency to advance beyond earlier positions, which seems to be absent from philosophy. In philosophy, for example, the account of perception given by such 20th-century Analytic philosophers as G.E. Moore and the Positivist A.J. Ayer has a close connection with that of Locke in the 17th century.

Philosophy as compared with science

The difference between philosophy and science is that, whereas the scientist investigates an actual occurrence, such as seeing, the philosopher investigates a concept that he already possesses quite independently of what he might discover through the occurrence. Whereas the scientist begins by supposing that he can recognize examples of seeing and is already exercising the concept, the philosopher wants to know what is involved in seeing in the sense of what conditions one can use to classify cases as examples of seeing. He may want to know, for example, whether certain conditions are necessary or sufficient. In testing the philosophical theory that, for an observer to see an object, the object must cause a visual experience in him (the causal theory of perception), one does not set up a scientific experiment. It would be of no use to set up situations in which various physical objects are not causing any visual experiences in order to see whether they still can be seen. For if the theory is correct, no such experimental situation will be an instance of seeing; and if it is wrong, merely describing a hypothetical situation would suffice. The question is one about how situations are classified, and for that purpose hypothetical situations are as good as real ones.

Therapeutic function of analysis. For some philosophers in the Analytic tradition, especially those influenced by Wittgenstein, the analysis of concepts has therapeutic value beyond the intrinsic enjoyment of doing it. Even scientists and laymen in their philosophical moments generate problems by not understanding the proper analyses of the concepts that they employ. They are then tempted to formulate theories to explain these difficulties, when instead they should be sorting out the roles of the concepts, which would show them that there was no problem to begin with. Thus, the failure to see how psychological concepts—sensations, emotions, and desires—are employed has led philosophers to such problems as how one can know what is going on in another's mind or how desires and emotions can produce physical changes in the body, and vice versa. Analysis of the concepts involved would, in this way of looking at philosophy, "dissolve" rather than solve the problems, for philosophers would come to see that their formulations of the problem rest on mistakes about the concepts involved.

Dissolving of problems by analysis

This way of looking at philosophy has often been criticized as making it merely a clearing up of the confusions of other philosophers and therefore a sterile enterprise. The confusions, however, need not be only those of other philosophers. Scientists, for example, can also generate philosophical theories that affect how they design their experiments, which may, thus, be subjects for philosophical therapeutics. Behaviorism in psychology—which views emotions, desires, and attitudes as being dispositions to behave in certain ways—seems to be a philosophical theory and perhaps to be based on a confusion about the analysis of psychological concepts. Yet Behaviorism has influenced psychologists in their approach to the science. Thus, in this view, philosophy can have a therapeutic value beyond the sphere of philosophical games.

Philosophy, in spite of its abstractness, has traditionally been concerned with human needs, and the therapeutic model may even fulfill this ideal. Laymen, as well as philosophers, for example, are bothered by the thought that their actions are determined not by themselves but by prior conditions. This is a problem that, if the therapeutic view is correct, rests on the misunderstanding of such concepts as causation, responsibility, and action, which need clarification.

Formal versus ordinary language. The role of language as a central concern of Analytic philosophers is the dimension most involved in disputes about the methodology employed. Philosophers outside the Analytic movement tend to think that its preoccupation with language is a departure from philosophy as classically conceived. Yet Plato and Aristotle, medieval philosophers, the Empiricists—and, in fact, most of the philosophers whose works have been considered important—have found it essential to talk about language. There are serious differences, however, about what role language should play. One such difference concerns the importance of formal languages (in the sense employed in symbolic logic) for philosophical problems.

Development of mathematical logic. Since the time of Aristotle, logic has been allied to philosophy. Until the late 19th century, however, logic was largely confined to formulating elaborate rules for one fairly simple form of argument—the syllogism; and there was a lack of systematic development of the subject along lines that had been taken in mathematics since early times.

Axiomatic method and use of symbols

Almost from the beginning, mathematicians had rigorously exploited two important techniques: (1) the use of the axiomatic method (as in Euclid's geometry) in developing the subject; and (2) the use of schematic letters or variables for stating general truths in the subject (thus, one can write "$A + B = B + A$," in which any names or numbers whatsoever can be substituted for A and B, and the result will still be true).

It is surprising that logicians through the ages failed to grasp the power of the use of schematic letters. When they finally began to employ these and other mathematical techniques, they made great contributions to man's understanding of the subject.

Among the developments that occurred in the 19th century, primarily through the work of mathematicians, those of the Englishman George Boole, creator of Boolean algebra, and of Georg Cantor, the Russian-born creator of set theory, are especially important inasmuch as they gave promise of bringing logic and mathematics closer together. The one figure who was both a mathematician and a philosopher and so might be credited with the marriage of logic as a philosophical subject with the techniques of mathematics was Gottlob Frege (died 1925), of the University of Jena in Germany. Historically, Frege, whose works are now appreciated in their own right, was important principally for his influence on Bertrand Russell, whose monumental work, *Principia Mathematica* (1910–13), written in collaboration with Alfred North Whitehead, together with Russell's earlier *Principles of Mathematics* (1903), awakened philosophers to the fact that the use of mathematical techniques in logic might prove to be of great importance for philosophy. Its symbolism had the advantage of being closely connected with ordinary language, whereas its rules can be precisely formulated. Moreover, work in symbolic logic has produced many distinctions and techniques that can be applied to ordinary language.

Divergence of ordinary language from formal logic. Ordinary language, however, seems to differ from the artificial language of symbolic logic in more respects than its lack of precisely stated rules. On the surface, it often appears to violate the rules of symbolic logic. In the English statement "If this is gold [symbolized by p], then this will dissolve in aqua regia [symbolized by q]," for example, which in symbolic logic is expressed in a form known as the material conditional, $p \supset q$ (in which $\supset$ means "If . . . then . . . "), one of the rules is that the statement is true whenever "This is gold" is false. In ordinary language, on the contrary, one would not count the statement as true merely on formal logical grounds but only if there were some real connection in the world of chemical reactions between being gold and dissolving in aqua regia—a connection that plays no role in symbolic logic.

Divergences between logic and language

Among Analytic philosophers the existence of many such apparent divergences between symbolic logic and ordinary language has generated attitudes ranging from complete mistrust of symbolic logic as relevant to nonartificial languages to the position that ordinary language is not a proper vehicle for the rigorous statement of scientific truths.

Interpretations of the relation of logic to language. Symbolic logic has been viewed by many Analytic philosophers as providing the framework for an ideal or perfect language. This statement can be taken in two ways:

1. Russell and the early Wittgenstein thought of logic as revealing, in a precise fashion, the real structure of any language. Any seeming departure from this structure in ordinary language must therefore be attributed to the fact that its surface grammar fails to reveal its real structure and is apt to be misleading. As a corollary, philosophers who have held this view have often explained philosophical problems as arising from being taken in by the surface features of the language. Because of the similarity of sentences such as "Tigers bite" and "Tigers exist," for example, the verb "to exist" may seem to function, as other verbs do, to predicate something of the subject. It may seem, then, that existence is a property of tigers just as their biting is. In symbolic logic, however, the symbolic equivalent of the two sentences would be quite different; existence would not be represented by a symbol for a predicate but by what is called the existential quantifier, ($\exists x$), which means "There exists at least one x such that . . . ."

2. The other sense in which symbolic logic has been seen as the framework of an ideal language is exemplified in the work of Rudolf Carnap, a 20th-century semanticist, who was concerned with what the best language—especially the best for the purposes of science—is.

One distinctive feature of the formal language of *Principia Mathematica* is that it becomes, when interpreted, a language of true-or-false statements. In ordinary language, on the contrary, one is not restricted to statements of truths; in it one can also issue commands, ask questions, make promises, express beliefs, give permission, and assert necessities and possibilities. Consequently, many philosophers have developed nonstandard logics that incorporate the nonassertoric features of language. Thus, various systems of logic have been formulated and studied (see LOGIC).

Non-assertoric uses of language

On the other side of the coin, many philosophers—most notably the later Wittgenstein and those influenced by him—have thought that attempting to put language into the straitjacket of a formal system is to falsify the way that language works. Language performs a multitude of tasks, and even among expressions that seem to be alike in the way they function—those sentences, for example, that one might think are used simply for expressing facts—examination of their actual use reveals many differences: differences, for instance, in what is counted as showing them to be true or false and in their relationships to other parts of language. Formal systems, according to this view, at best oversimplify and at worst can lead to philosophical problems generated by supposing that all language operates strictly according to a simple set of rules. Accordingly, far from settling philosophical disputes by getting underneath the misleading exterior of ordinary language, formal systems add their own share of confusion.

EARLY HISTORY OF ANALYTIC PHILOSOPHY

Reaction against Idealism. During the last decades of the 19th century, English philosophy was dominated by an absolute Idealism that stemmed from the German philosopher G.W.F. Hegel. For English philosophy this represented a break in an almost solid tradition of Empiricism. The seeds of modern Analytic philosophy were sown when two of the most important figures in its history, Bertrand Russell and G.E. Moore, broke with Idealism at the turn of the 20th century.

Ideal-
ism and
science

Absolute Idealism was avowedly metaphysical in the sense that its adherents thought of themselves as describing, in a way not open to scientists, certain very fundamental truths about the world. Indeed, what pass for truths in the sciences, were, in their view, not really truths at all; for the scientist must, perforce, treat the world as composed of distinct objects and can only describe and state the relationships supposedly holding among them. But the Idealists held that to talk about reality as if it were a multiplicity of objects is to falsify it; in the end only the whole, the absolute, has reality.

In their conclusions and, most importantly, in their methodology, the Idealists were decidedly not on the side of commonsense intuition. Thus, a Cambridge philosopher, J.M.E. McTaggart, argued that the concept of time is inconsistent and cannot therefore be exemplified in reality. British Empiricism, on the other hand, had always thought of common sense as an ally and science as the model of the way in which to find out about the world. Even when their views might seem out of step with common sense, the Empiricists were generally concerned to reconcile the two.

One can hardly claim that Analytic philosophers have universally thought of themselves as on the side of common sense and much less that metaphysical conclusions (on the ultimate nature of reality) are absent from their writings. But there is in the history of the Analytic movement a strong antimetaphysical strain, and its exponents have generally assumed that the methods of science and of everyday life are the authentic ways of finding out the truth.

Founding fathers: Moore and Russell. The first break from the Idealist view that the physical world is really only a world of appearances occurred when Moore, in a paper, "The Nature of Judgment" (1899), argued for a theory of truth that implies that the physical world has the independent existence that, apart from philosophical theories, it is naively supposed to have. Though the theory was soon abandoned, it did represent a return to common sense.

Compari-
son of
the two
founders
of Analytic
philosophy

The influences on Russell and Moore—and thus their methods of dealing with problems—soon diverged, and their different approaches became the roots of two broadly different methodologies in the Analytic tradition.

Russell was a major influence on those who approached philosophical problems armed with the technical equipment of formal logic, who saw the physical sciences as the only means of gaining knowledge of the world, and who regarded philosophy—if a science at all—as a deductive and a priori enterprise on a par with mathematics. Russell's contributions to this side of the Analytic tradition have been important and, in great part, lasting.

Moore, on the other hand, never found much need to employ technical tools nor to turn philosophy into a science. His dominant themes were (1) the defense of commonsensical views about the nature of the world against esoteric, skeptical, or grandly metaphysical views and (2) the conviction that the right way to approach philosophical puzzles is to ask exactly what the question is that generated the puzzle before trying to solve it. Philosophical problems, he thought, are often intractable because philosophers have not stopped to formulate precisely what is at issue.

G.E. Moore. Because of these two themes, Moore enlisted much more sympathy among Analytic philosophers from the 1930s and onward who were followers of Wittgenstein's later writings, of Gilbert Ryle's postwar *The Concept of Mind,* and of John Austin's work (see below *Oxford philosophers*). These philosophers, like Moore, saw little hope in advanced formal logic as a means of solving traditional philosophical problems and believed that philosophical skepticism about the existence of an independent external world or of other minds—or, in general, about what men label as common sense—must be wrong. The followers of Wittgenstein also shared with Moore the belief that it is often more important to look at the questions that philosophers pose than at their proposed answers. Thus, unlike Russell, who was important for his solutions in formal logic and ideal models of language, it was more the spirit of Moore's conception of philosophy than its lasting contributions that makes him a seminal influence.

The Idealists were given to arguing for what, in Moore's eyes, were outrageous positions. Thus, in his essay "A Defence of Common Sense" (1925), as in others, his defense was not only against such Idealist doctrines as the unreality of time but also against any of the forms of skepticism—about the existence of other minds or of a material world—that philosophers have espoused. The skeptic, he pointed out, usually has some argument for his conclusion. Instead of examining such arguments, however, Moore pitted against the skeptic's premises quite everyday beliefs, such as, for example, that he had breakfast that morning (thus time cannot be unreal) or that he does in fact have a pencil in his hand (thus there must be a material world). His challenge to the skeptic is to show that the premises of the skeptic's argument are more certain than the everyday beliefs that form Moore's premises.

Moore's
attack on
Idealism

Although some commentators have seen Moore as an early practitioner of the appeal to "ordinary language," his appeal was really not to what it is proper to say but rather to the beliefs of common sense. His rejection of anything that offends against common sense, however, was influential not only in the release that it afforded from the metaphysical excesses of absolute Idealism but also in its impact on the continuing attitudes of most Analytic philosophers—even though they may have given it a linguistic turn.

Moore was also important for his vision of the proper business of philosophy—analysis. He was puzzled about what is the proper analysis of "*X* sees *Y*," in which *Y* designates a physical object (*e.g.,* a pencil). There must be a special sense of "see," in which one does not see the pencil but only part of its surface. And finally—and most importantly—there is also a sense in which what is directly perceived is not even the surface of the pencil but, rather, what Moore called "sense data" and which earlier Empiricists had called "visual sensations" or "sense impressions." Moore's problem was to discern the relationships among these various elements in perception and, in particular, to discover how a person can be justified, as Moore fully believed he is, in his claims to see physical objects when what he immediately perceives are really sense data. The idea that sense impressions form the immediate objects of perception has played a large role in Analytic philosophy, showing once again its Empiricist roots. It later became an important source of division, however, among the Logical Positivists (see below). Most post-World War II Oxford philosophers, however, together with those closely influenced by Wittgenstein's later work, have found sense data to be as unpalatable and unwarranted as Moore had found McTaggert's doctrine of the unreality of time to be.

Moore's
notion
of "sense
data"

Bertrand Russell. One of the recurring themes in philosophy is the idea that the subject needs to be given a new methodology. Among Empiricists this has often meant making it more scientific. From an early date, Russell enunciated this viewpoint (which was not shared by Moore), finding in the techniques of symbolic logic a measure of reassurance that philosophy might be put on a new basis. Russell did not see the philosopher, however, as merely a logician. Symbolic logic might provide the framework for a perfect language, but the content of that language is something else. The job of the philosopher is—for Russell, as it was for Moore—analysis. But the purpose is somewhat different. In most of Russell's work, analysis has the task of uncovering the necessary assumptions—especially about the kinds of things that exist—for a description of the world as it is. For the most part this description is the one that science gives and is therefore realistic. Thus, Russell's use of analysis was openly metaphysical.

Russell's use of the theory of descriptions

The question then arises of how philosophical analysis, which is concerned with how men talk about the world, can presume to give any answers about how the world is. The search for an answer begins with the above-mentioned theory of descriptions—a theory that seems to be closely tied to linguistic concerns. It will be recalled that Russell considered that such definite descriptions as "the author of 'On Denoting' " are not really expressions used to refer to things in the world but that, instead, they make the statements in which they occur into quite general propositions about the world, to the effect that one and only one thing of a certain sort exists and that it has a certain property. Because there must be some way, however, of directly speaking of the things in the world, Russell turned his attention to proper names. The name Aristotle, for example, does not seem to carry any descriptive content. But Russell argues, on the contrary, that ordinary names are really concealed definite descriptions ("Aristotle" may simply mean "The student of Plato who taught Alexander, wrote the *Metaphysics*, etc."). If a name had no descriptive content, one could not sensibly ask about the existence of its bearer, for one could then not understand what is expressed by a statement involving it. If "Bosco" were a name in this sense (without any descriptive content), then merely to understand the statement that Bosco exists or the statement that Bosco does not exist presupposes that one already knows what the name Bosco refers to. But then there cannot be any genuine question about Bosco's existence, for just to understand the question one must know the thing to which the name refers. Ordinary proper names, however—Russell, Homer, Aristotle, and Santa Claus—as Russell pointed out, are such that it makes sense to question the existence of their bearers. Thus, ordinary names must be concealed descriptions and cannot be the means of directly referring to the particular things in the world.

Names in the strict logical sense, then, are very rare; Russell, in fact, suggests that in English the only possible candidates are the demonstrative pronouns, this and that. Yet, if men are ever to talk about the actual things in the world directly, there must be the possibility of such demonstrative expressions underlying their language—in their private thoughts about the world if not in their public language.

To this point, Russell had concluded that things in the world can be talked about only through the medium of a special kind of name; in particular, one about which no question can arise whether it names something or not. At this point there was a transition from questions about the nature of language to results about the nature of the world. Russell asked what sort of thing it is that can be named in the strict logical sense, that can be known and talked about, and that can tell a man something about the world. The important restriction is that no question can arise about whether it exists or not. Ordinary physical objects and other people seem not to fit this requirement.

The question of what can be known and talked about

In his search for something whose existence cannot be questioned, Russell hit upon present experience and, in particular, upon sense data: one can question whether he is really seeing some physical object—whether, for example, there is a desk before him—but a person cannot question that he has had visual impressions or sense data; thus, what a man can name in the strict logical sense and what things he can actually talk about turn out to be the elements of his present experience. Russell therefore made a distinction between what can be known by acquaintance and what can be known only by description; *i.e.*, between those things the existence of which cannot be doubted and those about which, at least theoretically, doubt can be raised. What is novel about Russell's conclusion is that it was arrived at from a fairly technical analysis of language: to be directly acquainted with something is to be in a position to give it a name in the strict logical sense, and to know something only by description is to know only that something uniquely fits the description.

Russell was not constant in his view about physical objects. At one point he thought that the observer must infer their existence as the best hypothesis to explain his experience. Later he argued that they could be taken as logical constructions out of sense data.

Logical atomism: Russell and the early Wittgenstein. The next important development in Analytic philosophy was initiated when Russell published a series of articles entitled "Philosophy of Logical Atomism" (1918–19), in which he acknowledged a debt to Wittgenstein, who had studied with Russell before the war. Wittgenstein's own work, the *Tractatus Logico-Philosophicus* (1922), which can also justly be said to present a logical atomism, turned out to be not only tremendously influential on developments in Analytic philosophy but also such a deep and difficult text that it has generated a growing body of scholarly interpretation.

Russell's choice of the words logical atomism to describe this viewpoint was, in fact, particularly apt. By using the word logical Russell meant to sustain the position, described earlier, that through analysis—particularly with the aid of the ideal structure provided by symbolic logic—the fundamental truths about how any language functions can be revealed and that this disclosure, in turn, would show the fundamental structure of that which the language is used to describe. And by using the word atomism Russell highlighted the particulate nature of the results that his analyses and those of Wittgenstein seemed to yield.

Simple atomic and molecular propositions

On the linguistic level, the atoms in question are atomic propositions, the simplest statements that it is possible to make about the world; and on the level of what language talks about, the atoms are the simplest atomic facts, those expressible by atomic propositions. More complex propositions, called molecular propositions, can then be built up out of atomic propositions via logical connectives—such as "either . . . or . . . ," "both . . . and . . . ," and "not . . ."—the truth-value of the molecular proposition being in each case a function of the truth values of its component atomic propositions.

Language, then, must break down, upon analysis, into ultimate elements that cannot be analyzed into any other component propositions; and, insofar as language mirrors reality, the world must then be composed of facts that are utterly simple. Atomic propositions are composed, however, of strings of names understood, as Russell had explained it, in the strict logical sense; and atomic facts are composed of simple objects, the things that could be thus named.

The details of the Russell–Wittgenstein view have fascinated philosophers by the way in which they not only formed a coherent view but also seemed to follow inexorably from the central assumptions. There are close connections between this period, which was perhaps the most metaphysical in contemporary Analytic philosophy, and traditional Empiricism. The breakdown of language and the world into atomic elements had been one of the prominent features in the classical Empiricists, John Locke, George Berkeley, and David Hume. There was also a view of the connection between language and the world—adumbrated in Russell but fully evident in the *Tractatus*—which has been important and influential, viz., the picture theory, which holds that the structure of language mirrors that of the world. Analysis is important because ordinary language does not show immediately, for example, that it is founded on the atomic–molecular proposition model. Another theme is that the deductive sciences—mathematics and logic—are based solely on the way that language operates and cannot reveal any truths about the world, not even about a world of entities called numbers. Finally, logical atomism, in Wittgenstein's thought as opposed to Russell's, was at one and the same time metaphysical—in the sense of conveying via pure reasoning something about how the world is—and antimetaphysical. Wittgenstein's *Tractatus* is unique in the history of Empiricism in its acceptance of the fact that it is itself a metaphysic and that part of its metaphysics is that metaphysics is impossible: the *Tractatus* says of itself that what it says cannot be coherently said. Only empirical science can tell a man anything about the world as it is. Yet the *Tractatus* apparently tells him, for example, about the relationship between language and the

Logical atomism as an antimetaphysical metaphysic

facts of the world. For Wittgenstein, the solution of this seeming paradox lies in his distinction between what can be said and what can only be shown. There are certain things that can somehow be seen to be so—in particular, the ways in which language is connected with the world. The *Tractatus* could not straightforwardly tell its readers about these matters—metaphysics cannot be a body of facts expressible in any language—but the attempt to say these things, done in the right way, can show them what it cannot coherently express.

Logical Positivism: Carnap and Schlick. Wittgenstein's *Tractatus* was both a landmark in the history of contemporary Analytic philosophy and perhaps its most aberrant example. It not only contained the most highly sophisticated metaphysics but also was an important influence on the most antimetaphysical of the positions taken by Analytic philosophers, viz., that of Logical Positivism, which was mainly developed by a group of philosophers, scientists, and logicians who were centred in Vienna and came to be known as the Vienna Circle. Among these, Rudolf Carnap and Moritz Schlick have perhaps had the most influence on Anglo-American philosophy, although it was an English philosopher, A.J. Ayer—whose *Language, Truth and Logic* (1936) is still the most widely read work of the movement in America and England—who introduced the ideas of Logical Positivism to English philosophy. Its main tenets have struck sympathetic chords in the Analytic philosophers and are still important today, even if in repudiation.

Above all else, Logical Positivism was antimetaphysical; nothing can be learned about the world, it held, except through the methods of the empirical sciences. The Positivists sought a method for showing both (1) when a theory that seemed to be about the world was really metaphysical and (2) that such a theory was, in fact, meaningless, and this they found in the principle of verification. In its positive form, the principle said that the meaning of any statement that is really about the world is given by the methods employed for verifying its truth or falsity—the only allowable methods being, ultimately, those of observation and experiment. In its negative form, the principle said that no statement could both be a statement about the world and have no method of verification attached to it. Its negative form was the weapon used against metaphysics and for the vindication of science as the only possible source of knowledge about the world. The principle would, thus, class as meaningless many philosophical and religious theories that purport to say something about the world but provide no way of testing the truth of the statements; for example, in religion it would render suspect the statement that God exists, which, being metaphysical, would be, strictly speaking, meaningless.

The principle of verification ran almost immediately into difficulties, most of which were first raised by the Positivists themselves. The attempt to work out these difficulties belongs to a more detailed study of the movement (see below *Positivism and Logical Empiricism*). It is sufficient to note here that these problems were sufficient to make most subsequent Analytic philosophers wary of appealing directly to the principle. It has, however, influenced philosophical work in more subtle ways.

With the principle of verification in hand, the Positivists thought that they could show a great many theories to be nonsense. There were several areas of discourse, however, which failed the test of the principle but which were simply impossible to rule out as concealed nonsense. Foremost among these disciplines were mathematics and ethics. Mathematics (and logic) could hardly be written off as nonsense. Yet their theorems are not verifiable by observation and experiment; they are known, in fact, by pure a priori reasoning alone. The answer seemed to be provided in Wittgenstein's *Tractatus,* which held that the propositions of mathematics and logic are, in Kantian terms, analytic; *i.e.,* true—like the statement "All bachelors are unmarried"—in virtue of the conventions that lie behind the use of the symbols involved.

About ethics or, more precisely, about any statements involving value judgments, the Positivist view was different, yet still of lasting importance. In this view, value

Marginal note: Principle of verification

Marginal note: Emotive theory of ethics

judgments are not, like mathematical truths, necessary adjuncts to science. But they cannot be put off as nonsense; nor, obviously, are they true by definition or linguistic convention. The usual view of the Positivists, called emotivism, is that what look like statements of fact (*e.g.,* that one should not tell lies) are really expressions of one's feelings toward a certain action; thus, value judgments are not really true or false. The Positivist's position was that neither mathematical nor ethical statements could be dismissed, as were metaphysical propositions. Both had then to be exempted from the principle of verification; and this was done by arguing that their statements are not really about the world: mathematical truths are conventions, and ethical statements are merely expressions of feelings. The divorce of ethics from science, once again, reflects an old Empiricist theme, to be seen, for example, in David Hume's dictum that from matters of fact one cannot derive a conclusion about what ought to be nor vice versa.

LATER HISTORY OF THE MOVEMENT

"Philosophical Investigations": the later Wittgenstein. A crucial turn that initiated developments that were destined to have a lasting and profound effect on much of contemporary Analytic philosophy occurred in 1929, when Wittgenstein, after some years in Austria during which he was not philosophically very active, returned to England and established his residence at Cambridge. There, the direction of his thought soon shifted radically away from his *Tractatus,* and his views became in many ways diametrically opposed to those of logical atomism. Because he published none of the materials of this period, his influence on other English philosophers—and ultimately on those in all of the countries associated with Analytic philosophy—spread by way of his students and those who heard him in the small groups to whom he spoke at Cambridge. His style, too, changed from the semi-rigorous and formally organized propositions of the *Tractatus* to sets of loosely connected paragraphs and remarks in which the ideas are often conveyed more by suggestion and example than discursively. The result has been that one of the major splits within the ranks of Analytic philosophy is that between those who derive their methods from the later Wittgenstein and those who have followed the *Tractatus.*

Although Wittgenstein's thoughts ranged over almost the entire field of philosophy, from the philosophy of mathematics to ethics and aesthetics, their impact has been felt most, perhaps, where it has concerned the nature of language and the relationship between the mental and the physical.

Language and following rules. In logical atomism, as shown above, language was conceived as having a certain necessary and fairly simple underlying structure that it was the job of philosophy to expose. Wittgenstein began to tear away at this assumption. Language, he now thought, is like an instrument that can be used for an indefinite number of purposes. Hence, any effort to codify how it must operate by giving some small set of rules would be like supposing that there is some rigid necessity that a screwdriver (for instance) can be used only to drive screws and forgetting that screwdrivers are also, quite successfully, used to open jars and to jimmy windows. Language is a human institution that is not bound by an outside set of rules—only by what men consider to be correct and incorrect. And that, in turn, is not really a matter for a priori theories to consider.

The notion of a rule and what it means to follow a rule was especially prominent in his writings. Several concerns made this point of particular interest to Wittgenstein. In mathematics and logic, emphasis was being placed on the rules for manipulating the symbolism. As has been seen, symbolic logic has also been a model for the underlying structure of language. If this fact is coupled with the fact that Russell and the Wittgenstein of the *Tractatus* saw language as reflecting these rules and with the general Empiricist tradition that explains how language operates by each person following internal rules and standards for the use of his words, the picture of the system that Wittgenstein thought mistaken then emerges, and it becomes clear why he placed the notion of a rule so centrally.

Marginal note: Language as a multi-purpose conventional instrument

Natural languages, however, are significantly different in that one does not first learn the rules and then use the language; indeed, prior to learning the language, one would not know what to do with rules. Mathematics and logic are, in this sense, bad models for language because they aim at setting out before hand the rules and principles that are subsequently to be used. They encourage the belief that language must have a rigid structure and that, without rules, no language would be possible. The "rules" that one might plausibly discern in the language that one speaks are not, as rules, already there, in a ghostly way, guiding what one says; they are either generalizations from the finite data of what is counted as correct or incorrect, or they are rules that, as Wittgenstein metaphorically expressed it, one puts away in the archives—one adopts the rule but only after the fact.

Following a rule, however, was a concept that Wittgenstein saw as wrongly analyzed in many classical views about language. Thus, he cast irrevocable doubt on the prevalent theory—typified best, perhaps, in John Locke's *Essay Concerning Human Understanding* (1690)—that to use an expression meaningfully is to have in one's mind a standard or a rule for applying it correctly. Against this theme, Wittgenstein's point was that a rule by itself is dead—it is like a ruler in the hands of someone who has never learned to use it, a mere stick of wood. Rules cannot compel nor even guide a person unless he knows how to use them; and the same is true about mental images, which have often been thought to provide the standard for using linguistic expressions. But if rules themselves do not give life to words but require a similar explanation for what gives them life, then there is a useless regress and no (philosophical) explanatory value in the whole apparatus of internal rules and standards.

Relation between mental and physical events. In some respects, Wittgenstein made some significant breaks with the Empiricist tradition—in his views about language and the explanation of the rigour of the deductive sciences. His treatment of the relationship between mental events and physical events also represents an important departure. Empiricists generally have started from the important assumption that what a person is immediately acquainted with is his own sensations, ideas, and volitions, and that these are mental and not physical; and, most importantly, that the things he knows immediately are essentially private and inaccessible to others. For both Moore and Russell there then arose the problem of how, in view of the privacy stressed by the sense-datum theory, the world of physical objects could be known. Wittgenstein's attack on this viewpoint, which has come to be known as "the private language" argument, has become well known, partly because it was in this area that Wittgenstein presented what could most easily be picked out as a more or less formal argument—one that could then be analyzed and criticized in an analytic manner. Even in this case, however, his style of writing was such that his precise formulation of the argument has become a main source of controversy. Wittgenstein argued that the notion of an utterly private experience would imply: (1) that what goes on in the mental life of a person could be talked about only in a language that that person alone whose mental life it was could understand; (2) that such a private language would be no language at all (this has been the main source of controversy); and (3) that the widely held doctrine that there are absolutely private mental events cannot be intelligibly stated, because to do so would be to suppose that one can publically say something about what the doctrine itself says cannot be mentioned in a language accessible to more than one person.

The fact that Wittgenstein's argument against private language depends essentially on the question, "What is it to follow a rule?" illustrates a common characteristic of his writings, viz., that themes developed in one area of philosophy continually emerge in apparently quite divorced areas. His extraordinary ability to see a common source of difficulty in philosophical problems that seem to be unrelated helps to explain his style of writing, which seems at first sight to be a somewhat chaotic arrangement of ideas.

Analytic philosophy has also been attracted to a be-

haviouristic view of mental phenomena that holds that such apparently private events as the feeling of fear are not only not really private but also that they can be identified with publicly observable patterns of behaviour. The disposition toward empirical science, with observation as its foundation, united with the observation that the evidence men have of what goes on in the mental lives of other people must come from what they see of their behaviour, has often warred against the other inclination of Empiricism to regard the starting point of all knowledge of the world, for each person, as being essentially private sense experience. Wittgenstein has had tremendous influence, however, in suggesting that these two extremes are not the only alternatives. Yet attempts to state how Wittgenstein could deny the privacy of experience without espousing some form of behaviourism have not been very successful. Sympathetic interpreters have taken up the notion of "criteria," used, but not developed in any detail, by Wittgenstein. For mental states such as fear, outward behaviour (*e.g.,* running away, blanching, or cringing) does not constitute what it is to be in that state, as behaviourism would have it, but neither is it merely evidence of some completely private event. The problem has been to characterize the relation between behaviour and mental states so that the two are neither identical nor evidence one for the other, while still acknowledging that a knowledge of the person's characteristic behaviour is essential to understanding the notion of a certain mental state.

Recent trends in England. Those philosophers who might fairly be labelled "Wittgensteinians," who follow the methods that Wittgenstein employed in his later period, should be distinguished from those who have been influenced more indirectly by the general trends and philosophical atmosphere that arose in large part from Wittgenstein's work.

Wittgensteinians. Close students of his ideas have tended to work chiefly on particular concepts that lie at the core of traditional philosophical problems. As an example of such an investigation, a monograph entitled *Intention* (1957), by G.E.M. Anscombe, an editor of Wittgenstein's posthumous works, may be cited as an extended study of what it is for a person to intend to do something and of what the relationship is between his intention and the actions that he performs. This work has occupied a central place in a growing literature about human actions, which in turn has influenced views about the nature of psychology, of the social sciences, and of ethics. And, as an extension of this British influence into the United States, one of Wittgenstein's students, Norman Malcolm of Cornell University, has investigated such concepts as knowledge, certainty, memory, and dreaming. As these topics suggest, Wittgensteinians have tended to concentrate on Wittgenstein's ideas about the nature of mental concepts and to work in the area of philosophical psychology. Typically, they begin with classical philosophical theories and attack them by arguing that they employ some key concept, such as that of knowledge, in a manner incongruous with the way in which the concept would actually be employed in various situations. Their works thus abound with descriptions of hypothetical, though usually homely, situations and with questions of the form, "What would a person say if . . .?" or "Would one call this a case of X?" In doing so, they are following out Wittgenstein's advice that, instead of trying to capture the essence of a concept by an abstract analysis, the philosopher should look at how it is employed in a variety of situations.

Oxford philosophers. After World War II, Oxford University was the centre of extraordinary philosophical activity; and, although Wittgenstein's general outlook on philosophy—his turning away, for example, from the notion of formal methods in philosophical analysis—was an important ingredient, many of the Oxford philosophers could not be called Wittgensteinians in the strict sense. The method employed by many of these philosophers has often been characterized—especially by critics—as an "appeal to ordinary language," and they were thus identified as belonging to the school of "ordinary language" philosophy. Exactly what this form of argument is supposed to be and what exemplifies it in the writings of these

Side notes (left margin):

Post-factum status of rules

Arguments against private language

Side notes (right margin):

Problem of behaviourism

Concentration on philosophical psychology

Gilbert
Ryle's *The
Concept of
Mind*

philosophers has been by no means clear. Gilbert Ryle, Moore's successor as editor of a leading journal, *Mind*—and especially in his *The Concept of Mind*—was among the most prominent of those analysts who were regarded as using ordinary language as a philosophical tool. Ryle, like Wittgenstein, pointed out the mistake of regarding the mind as what he called "a ghost in a machine"—to defeat the radical dualism of mind and body that has characterized much of philosophical thinking—by investigating how people employ a variety of concepts, such as memory, perception, and imagination, that designate "mental" properties. He tried to show that, when philosophers carry out such investigations, they find that, roughly speaking, it is the way people act and behave that leads to attributing these properties to them, and that there is no involvement of anything internally private. He also attempted to show how philosophers have come to dualistic conclusions—usually from having a wrong model in terms of which to interpret human activities. A dualistic model may be constructed, for example, by wrongly supposing that an intelligently behaving person must be continually utilizing knowledge of facts—knowledge that something is the case. Ryle contended, on the contrary, that much intelligent behaviour is a matter of knowing how to do something and that, once this fact is acknowledged, there is no temptation to explain the behaviour by looking for a private internal knowledge of facts. Though Ryle's objectives were similar to those of Wittgenstein, his results have often seemed more behavioristic than Wittgenstein's.

It is true that Ryle did ask, in pursuit of his method, some fairly detailed questions about when a person would say, for example, that someone had been imagining something; but it is by no means clear that he was appealing to ordinary language in the sense that his was an investigation into how, say, speakers of English use certain expressions. In any case, the charge, often voiced by critics, that this style of philosophizing trivializes and perverts philosophy from its traditional function would probably also have to be levelled against Aristotle, who frequently appealed to "what we would say."

The work
of John
Austin

A powerful philosophical figure among postwar Oxford philosophers was John Austin, who was White's professor of moral philosophy until his death, in 1960. Austin felt that many philosophical theories derive their plausibility from overlooking distinctions—often very fine—between different uses of expressions, and he also thought that philosophers too frequently think that any one of a number of expressions will do just as well for their purposes. (Thus, ignoring the difference between an illusion and a delusion, for example, gives credence to the view that what one immediately perceives are not physical objects, but sense data.) Austin's work was, in many respects, much closer to the ideal of philosophy as comprising the analysis of concepts than was that of Ryle or Wittgenstein. He was also much more concerned with the nature of language itself and with general theories of how it functions. This novel approach, as exemplified in *How to Do Things with Words* (1962), set a trend that has been followed out in a growing literature in the philosophy of language. Austin took the total speech act as the starting point of analysis, which allowed him to make distinctions based not only upon words and their place in a language but also upon such points as the speaker's intentions in making the utterance and its expected effect on the audience. There was also in Austin's approach something of the program of Russell and the early Wittgenstein for laying bare the fundamental structure of language.

Recent trends in the United States. Although the Oxford philosophers and the posthumous publication of Wittgenstein's writings have produced a revolution in Anglo-American philosophy, the branch of Analytic philosophy that emphasized formal analyses by means of modern logic has by no means been dormant. Since the appearance of *Principia Mathematica*, striking new findings have emerged in logic, many of which, though requiring for their understanding a high level of mathematical sophistication, are nevertheless important for philosophy.

W.V.O.
Quine's use
of symbolic
logic

Among those philosophers for whom symbolic logic occupies a central position, W.V.O. Quine, Pierce professor of philosophy at Harvard University, has been especially important. Symbolic logic represented for him, as it did for many earlier Analytic philosophers, the framework for the language of science. There were two important themes in his work, however, that represent significant departures from, say, the positions of the logical atomists and the Logical Positivists. In the first place, Quine rejected the distinction between those statements in which their truth or falsity depends upon the meaning of the terms involved and those in which their truth or falsity is a matter of empirical and observable fact—a distinction that had played an essential role in Logical Positivism and was thought by most Empiricists to be the basis for a division between the deductive and the empirical sciences. Quine, in "Two Dogmas of Empiricism" (1951) and subsequent writings, argued that the sort of distinction intended by philosophers is impossible to draw. In the course of his argument, a similar doubt was cast upon concepts traditional not only to philosophy but also to linguistics—in particular, the concept of synonymy or sameness of meaning. Quine's attack has been a threat not only to some long-held doctrines of the Analytic tradition but also to its conception of the nature of philosophy, which has generally depended upon contrasting it with the empirical sciences.

The second important departure of Quine's philosophy has been his attempt to show that science can be successfully conducted without what he calls "intentional entities." In contrast to "extensional," used above as an essential feature of standard symbolic logic, intentional entities include many of the common items that Analytic philosophers often assume that they can talk about without difficulty, such as the meanings of expressions, propositions, or the property of certain statements (such as those of mathematics) of being necessarily true. Quine's program—as exemplified by *Word and Object* (1960)—is intended in part to show that science can say everything that it needs to say without using concepts that cannot be expressed in the extensional language of standard logic. Quine's work, though by no means widely accepted, has made Analytic philosophers at least wary of uncritically accepting certain of their standard distinctions.

Since the mid-20th century, there has been an interaction between the science of linguistics and Analytic philosophy. This did not occur before because Analytic philosophers had almost always considered their study of language to be a priori and unconcerned with empirical facts about particular languages. Recently, however, a book by Noam Chomsky, a U.S. generative grammarian, entitled *Syntactic Structures* (1957), has produced a theory of grammar that not only has profoundly affected the course of linguistics but also bears striking resemblances to philosophical analysis. At first, some Analytic philosophers saw in Chomsky's theory a technique that could be applied to philosophy. It was subsequently considered, however, that, whereas the possibility of looking at grammar in Chomsky's way had contributed valuable concepts for philosophers, the possibility that it would become a methodology for Analytic philosophy had receded. The interchange between linguists and philosophers, however, has continued.

Noam
Chomsky's
generative
grammar

Analytic philosophy today. It is not possible to forecast in any detail the future trends of Analytic philosophy in Anglo-American and Scandinavian countries. It seems relatively certain, however, that the two conceptions of the subject that stem from Moore and Russell will both continue.

Analytic philosophers, mainly influenced by Oxford philosophy, and those for whom symbolic logic is a touchstone analyze many of the same problems and benefit from each other's work. Analysis in the more rigorous sense that Russell's theory of definite descriptions represents is more frequently an aim, despite the doubts of Wittgenstein and many of the Oxford philosophers. The general idea that the only ultimate explanations of the world are the scientific ones and the usual corollary that philosophy is in the service of science—which was a central idea for Russell, for the Logical Positivists, and (in recent times) for Quine—has apparently lost nothing of its vigour. The opposing tendencies, noted above, among Empiricists in general, and present also in Analytic philosophy, toward behaviourism or Materialism, on the one hand, and toward an Idealism of a phenomenalistic sort (such as that of the Irish bishop George Berkeley), on the other, are not present in the same form—mainly because of the sustained criticisms of Wittgenstein, of his followers, and of the Oxford philosophers. The battleground has shifted to a more subtle level. A substantial number of Analytic philosophers who are styled Materialists or physicalists have proposed a novel technique for reducing mental events and states to physical states. They avoid the well-exposed difficulties of older attempts in which it was held that, when one apparently talks about a separate realm of the mind—speaking of such things as thoughts, emotions, and sensations—the proper analysis of its meaning would be in terms of physical properties and events (usually observable behaviour). The novel idea, on the contrary, is that there is, in fact, an identity between so-called mental events and certain physical events, particularly those occurring in the brain, an identity that it is eventually the task of science to specify—in a way modelled after that in which science discovered that lightning is identical with an electrical discharge. The opposition against this new brand of scientific Materialism does not set up against it a view of the mind as a separate realm coexisting with the physical nor as an essentially private collection of nonphysical events and objects. Rather, the issue has been joined on the question whether the language (or perhaps the concepts) of the psychological and the physical are such as to allow for a scientifically discovered identity between items of the one and items of the other. That there still remains a division among Analytic philosophers concerning the problem of the mental and the physical (though in much altered form) shows both the continuity of the movement and the changes that have occurred. (K.S.D.)

(margin note: The New Materialism*)*

Empiricism

In its most general sense, Empiricism is the name applied to the attitude that beliefs are to be accepted and acted upon only if they first have been confirmed by actual experience—a definition that accords with the derivation of the name from the Greek word *empeiria,* "experience."

More specifically, Empiricism comprises a pair of closely related, but still distinct, philosophical doctrines—one pertaining to concepts and the other to propositions:

1. The first of these doctrines, a theory of meaning, holds that words (*e.g.,* the word substance) can be understood or the concepts requisite for any articulate thought possessed only if they are connected by their users with things that they have experienced or could experience (*e.g.,* pieces of wood, or the gases in a gasoline engine).

2. The second doctrine, a philosophical theory of knowledge, views beliefs, or at least some vital classes of beliefs (*e.g.,* that Jane is kind), as depending ultimately and necessarily on experience for justification (Jane is seen performing acts of kindness).

(margin note: Empiricism of concepts and of beliefs*)*

It is not obvious, however, that either of these two doctrines strictly implies the other. Several recognized Empiricists have admitted that there are a priori propositions but have denied that there are a priori concepts. The reverse disconnection between the two forms of Empiricism, however, has no obvious exponents, since there are hardly any philosophers who totally deny a priori propositions and certainly none who would at the same time accept a priori concepts.

Stressing experience, Empiricism is thus opposed to the claims of authority, intuition, imaginative conjecture, and abstract, theoretical, or systematic reasoning as sources of reliable belief. Its most fundamental antithesis is with the latter (*i.e.,* with Rationalism, also called intellectualism or apriorism). A Rationalist theory of meaning asserts that there are concepts not derived from or correlated with experienceable features of the world, such as "cause," "identity," or "perfect circle," and that these concepts are a priori (Latin: "from the former") in the traditional sense of being part of the mind's innate or natural equipment—as opposed to being a posteriori (Latin: "from the latter"), or grounded in the experience of facts. On the

other hand, a Rationalist theory of knowledge holds that there are beliefs that are a priori (*i.e.,* that depend for their justification upon thought alone), such as the belief that everything must have a sufficient reason or that a process cannot exist by itself but must occur within some substance. Such beliefs can arise either from intellectual intuition, the direct apprehension of self-evident truth, or from purely deductive reasoning.

VARIOUS MEANINGS OF EMPIRICISM

Broader senses. In both everyday attitudes and philosophical theories, the experiences referred to are principally those arising from stimulation of the sense organs, in particular those of sight and touch. Most philosophical Empiricists, however, have maintained that sensation is not the only provider of experience, admitting as empirical the awareness of mental states in introspection or reflection, such as feelings of pain or of fear, often metaphorically described as present to the "inner sense." It is a controversial question whether still further types of experience, such as moral, aesthetic, or religious experience, ought to be acknowledged as empirical.

Two other viewpoints related to but not the same as Empiricism are the Pragmatism of the American philosopher and psychologist William James, an aspect of which was Radical Empiricism, and Logical Positivism, also called Logical Empiricism (see below *Positivism and Logical Empiricism*). Though these philosophies are, indeed, empirical, each has a distinctive focus that warrants its treatment as a separate movement. Pragmatism stresses the involvement of ideas in practical experience and action, whereas Logical Empiricism is more concerned with scientific experience.

When describing an everyday attitude, the word Empiricism sometimes conveys an unfavourable implication of ignorance of or indifference to relevant theory. Thus, to call a doctor an "Empiric" has been to call him a quack—a usage traceable to a sect of medical men who were opposed to the elaborate medical, and in some views metaphysical, theories of Galen, a prominent Greek physician of the 2nd century AD, theories which dominated medicine until the 17th century. The medical Empiricists opposed to Galen preferred to rely on treatments of observed clinical effectiveness, without inquiring into the mechanisms sought by therapeutic theory. But "Empiricism," detached from this medical association, may also be used, more favourably, to describe a hard-headed refusal to be swayed by anything but the facts that the thinker has observed for himself, a blunt resistance to received opinion or precarious chains of abstract reasoning.

(margin note: Popular and medical Empiricism*)*

Stricter senses. As a more strictly defined movement, Empiricism reflects certain fundamental distinctions and occurs in varying degrees.

Fundamental distinctions. If the blurring of the distinction between concepts and propositions has confused discussions of Empiricism, another influence at least equally vexing is that which, embodied in the traditional terminology of the debate, contrasts the empirical not with the a priori but with the innate. Since logical problems are easily confused with psychological problems, it is difficult to disentangle the question of the causal origin of man's concepts and beliefs from that of their meaning and justification.

(margin note: Innate versus a priori*)*

A concept, such as "Five," is said to be innate if a man's possession of it is causally independent of his experience—*e.g.,* of groupings of five objects. A concept, such as "Ought," is a priori, on the other hand, if the logical conditions of its application (or those of the word expressing it) do not include any reference to experienceable states of affairs (thus "Ought" cannot be defined in terms of facts alone). Similarly, a belief is innate if its acceptance is causally independent of the believer's experience; and it is a priori if its justification is logically independent of experience. Propositions could be innate without being a priori: for example, the baby's empirical belief that its mother's breast will nourish it.

Some colour is lent to the confusion of the a priori and the innate by the fact that most empirical concepts are actually acquired through the technique of ostensive definition, in which a concept (such as "long") is conveyed by introducing instances of it (several long pencils) into the experience of the learner. But it is not in virtue of their mode of acquisition that concepts are empirical; it is the way in which they are applied, once they are possessed, that qualifies them as such. Even if a man were born with an instinctive capacity to use the word blue and never had to learn how to use it, it would still be an empirical concept if the occasion for its use were always his sense experience of a blue object. Furthermore, the fact that men learn, postnatally, to use the word cause does not prove that it expresses an empirical concept if its application to something always implies more than the sense which experience of that kind of thing presents to the mind.

Another supposedly identical but in fact more or less irrelevant property of concepts and beliefs is that of the universality of their possession or acceptance—that a priori or innate concepts must be the common possession of all men and that such beliefs must be accepted by everyone. There may be, in fact, some basis for inferring universality from innateness, since many innate characteristics such as the fear of loud noises appear to be common to the whole species.

Formal versus categorial

Two main kinds of concept have been held to be a priori and thus nonempirical. First, there are certain formal concepts of logic and of mathematics that reflect the basic structure of discourse: "not," "and," "or," "if," "all," "some," "existence," "unity," "number," "successor," "infinity," Secondly, there are categorial concepts, such as "substance," "cause," "mind," and "God," so called after the "categories of thought" as listed by Aristotle and Kant, which the mind imposes upon the given data of experience.

A very large variety of different types of proposition has been held to be a priori. Few would deny this status to such definitional truisms or obvious tautologies as "all hairless heads are bald" or "a rose is a rose." There are also the truths of logic, of mathematics, and of metaphysics—whether transcendent, such as the existence of God or things-in-themselves (lying behind appearances), or immanent and thus discernible within reality, such as the principles (presupposed by much natural science) of conservation, causality, and sufficient reason. Some have held that the basic principles of ethics or the causal laws of nature are a priori. Empiricism maintains, however, that some of these are a priori.

Degrees of Empiricism. Empiricism, whether concerned with meaning or knowledge, can be held with varying degrees of strength. On this basis, absolute, substantive, and partial Empiricisms can be distinguished.

Absolute Empiricists hold that there are no a priori concepts, either formal or categorial, and no a priori propositions. Absolute Empiricism about knowledge is less common than that about concepts, and nearly all philosophers admit that at least obvious tautologies and definitional truisms are a priori; but many would add that these represent a degenerate case.

Substantive Empiricism

A more moderate form of Empiricism is that of the substantive Empiricists, who are unconvinced by attempts that have been made to interpret formal concepts empirically and who therefore concede that formal concepts are a priori but deny that categorial concepts, such as "substance," "cause," and "God," are a priori. In this view, formal concepts would be no longer semantical, pertaining to the relation of words to things; they would be, instead, merely descriptive or purely syntactical, pertaining to the relations between ideas. On this basis "God," for example, would not be an entity alongside other entities but a device for arranging a man's factual beliefs about the world; the concept "God" would thus play a structural and not an informative role.

The parallel point of view about knowledge assumes that the truth of logical and mathematical propositions is determined, as is that of definitional truisms, by the relationships between meanings that are established prior to experience. The truth often espoused by moralists, for example, that one is truly obliged to rescue a man from drowning only if it is possible to do so is a matter of meanings and not of facts about the world. On this view,

all propositions that, in contrast to the foregoing example, are in any way substantially informative about the world are empirical. Even if there are a priori propositions, they are all formal or verbal or conceptual in nature, and their necessary truth derives simply from the meanings that man has attached to the words he uses. A priori knowledge is useful because it makes explicit the hidden implications of substantive, factual assertions. But a priori propositions do not themselves express genuinely new knowledge about the world; they are factually empty, "true in all possible worlds." Thus "All bachelors are unmarried" merely gives explicit recognition to the commitment to describe as unmarried anyone who has been described as a bachelor; but it does not add anything new.

Substantive Empiricism about knowledge, which is fundamental to most contemporary Analytical philosophy, regards all a priori propositions as being more-or-less concealed tautologies, or, in Kantian terms, as being analytic. If a person's "duty" is thus defined as that which he should always do, the statement "A person should always do his duty" then becomes "A person should always do what he should always do." Deductive reasoning is conceived accordingly as a way of bringing this concealed tautological status to light. That such extrication is nearly always required means that a priori knowledge is far from trivial.

For the substantive Empiricist, truisms and the propositions of logic and mathematics exhaust the domain of the a priori. Science, on the other hand—from the fundamental assumptions about the structure of the universe to the singular items of evidence used to confirm its theories—is regarded as empirical throughout. The propositions of ethics and those of metaphysics, which deals with the nature of Being as such (for example, "Only that which is not subject to change is real"), are either disguised tautologies or empirical statements or only pseudo-propositions; *i.e.,* combinations of words that, despite their grammatical respectability, cannot be taken as true or false assertions at all.

The least thoroughgoing type of Empiricism here distinguished, ranking third in degree, can be termed partial Empiricism. Many philosophers hold that other concepts besides the formal are a priori and that there are substantially informative propositions about the world that are nevertheless not empirical. The theses of transcendental, or Kantian, metaphysics and those of theology, the general scientific principles of conservation and causality, the basic principles of morality, and the causal laws of nature have all been held to be at once synthetic and a priori—substantial and yet establishable by reasoning alone without recourse to experience. In all versions of this view, however, there remain a great many straightforwardly empirical concepts and propositions: ordinary singular propositions about matters of fact and the concepts that figure in them are held to fall in the empirical domain.

Partial Empiricism

HISTORY OF EMPIRICISM

In ancient philosophy. So-called common sense is inarticulately empiricist; and philosophy, in seeking to correct it, has to start from a rationalistic position. Philosophical Empiricism is thus always critical, a resistance to the pretensions of a more speculative philosophy. The ground was prepared for Plato, the greatest of Rationalist philosophers, by three earlier bodies of thought: the Ionian cosmologies of the 6th century BC—so-called from their concentration along the western coast of Asia Minor—with their distinction between sensible appearance and a reality accessible only to pure reason; the philosophy of Parmenides (early 5th century BC), the important early monist, in which purely rational argument is used to prove that the world is really an unchanging unity; and Pythagoreanism (see above), which, holding that the world is really made of numbers, took mathematics to be the repository of ultimate truth.

The first Empiricists in Western philosophy were the Sophists, who rejected such Rationalist speculation about the world as a whole and took man and society to be the proper objects of philosophical inquiry. Invoking skeptical arguments to undermine the claims of pure reason, they posed a challenge that invited the reaction that comprised

Plato's philosophy (see below, *Criticism and evaluation*).

Plato and to a lesser extent Aristotle were both Rationalists. But Aristotle's successors in the ancient Greek schools of Stoicism and Epicureanism advanced an explicitly Empiricist account of the formation of man's concepts or ideas. For the Stoics the human mind is at birth a clean slate, which comes to be stocked with ideas by the sensory impingement of the material world upon it. Yet they also held that there are some ideas or beliefs, the "common notions," present to the minds of all men; and these soon came to be conceived in a nonempirical way. The Empiricism of the Epicureans, however, was more pronounced and consistent. For them man's concepts are memory images, the mental residues of previous sense experience; and knowledge is as empirical as the ideas of which it is composed.

In medieval philosophy. Most medieval philosophers after St. Augustine (see below, *Criticism and evaluation*) took an Empiricist position, at least about concepts, even if they recognized much substantial but nonempirical knowledge. The standard formulation of this age was: "There is nothing in the intellect that was not previously in the senses." Thus St. Thomas Aquinas (1225–74) altogether rejected innate ideas. Both soul and body participate in perception, and all of man's ideas are abstracted by the intellect from what is given to the senses. Man's ideas of unseen things, like God and angels, are derived by analogy from the seen.

The 13th-century scientist Roger Bacon emphasized empirical knowledge of the natural world and anticipated the polymath Renaissance philosopher of science Francis Bacon (1561–1626) in preferring observation to deductive reasoning as a source of knowledge. The Empiricism of the 14th-century Franciscan Nominalist William of Ockham was more systematic. All knowledge of what exists in nature, he held, comes from the senses, though there is, to be sure, "abstractive knowledge" of necessary truths; but this is hypothetical and does not imply the existence of anything. His more extreme followers extended his line of reasoning toward a radical Empiricism, in which causation is not a rationally intelligible connection but merely an observed regular sequence.

In modern philosophy. In the earlier and unsystematically speculative phases of Renaissance philosophy, the claims of Aristotelian logic to yield substantial knowledge were attacked by several 16th-century logicians, and, in the same century, the role of observation was stressed. One mildly skeptical Christian thinker, Pierre Gassendi (1592–1655), advanced a deliberate revival of the empirical doctrines of Epicurus. But the most important defender of Empiricism was Francis Bacon, who, though he did not deny the existence of a priori knowledge, claimed that, in effect, the only knowledge that is worth having (as contributing to the relief of man's estate) is empirically based knowledge of the natural world, which should be pursued by the systematic, indeed almost mechanical, arrangement of the findings of observation and is best undertaken in the cooperative and impersonal style of modern scientific research. Bacon was, indeed, the first to formulate the principles of scientific induction.

A Materialist and Nominalist, Thomas Hobbes (1588–1679), combined an extreme Empiricism about concepts, which he saw as the outcome of material impacts on the bodily senses, with an extreme Rationalism about knowledge, of which, like Plato, he took geometry to be the paradigm. For him all genuine knowledge is a priori, a matter of rigorous deduction from definitions. The senses provide ideas; but all knowledge comes from "reckoning," from deductive calculations carried out on the names that the thinker has assigned to them. True knowledge is thus not merely a priori but also analytic. Yet it all concerns material and sensible existences: everything that exists is a body.

The most elaborate and influential presentation of Empiricism was made by John Locke (1632–1704), an early Enlightenment philosopher, in the first two books of his *Essay Concerning Human Understanding* (1690). All knowledge, he held, comes from sensation or from reflection, by which he meant the introspective awareness of the workings of man's own mind. Locke confused the two issues of the nature of concepts and the justification of beliefs. His Book I, though titled "Innate Ideas," is largely devoted to refuting innate knowledge. And even so, he later admitted that much substantial knowledge—in particular, that of mathematics and morals—is a priori. He argued that infants know nothing; that if men are said to know innately what they are capable of coming to know, then all knowledge is, trivially, innate; and that no beliefs whatever are universally accepted. Locke was more consistent about the empirical character of all man's concepts and displayed in detail the ways in which simple ideas can be combined to form complex ideas of what has not in fact been experienced. One group of dubiously empirical concepts—those of unity, existence, and number—he took to be derived both from sensation and from reflection. But he allowed one a priori concept—that of substance—which the mind adds, seemingly from its own resources, to its conception of any regularly associated group of perceptible qualities.

Bishop George Berkeley (1685–1753), a theistic Idealist and opponent of Materialism, applied Locke's Empiricism about concepts to refute Locke's account of man's knowledge of the external world. He drew and embraced the inevitable conclusion that material things are simply collections of perceived ideas, a position that ultimately leads to phenomenalism; *i.e.,* to the view that reality is nothing but sensations. He accounted for the continuity and orderliness of the world by supposing that its reality is upheld in the perceptions of an unsleeping God. The theory of spiritual substance involved in Berkeley's position seems to be vulnerable, however, to most of the same objections as those that he posed against Locke.

The Scottish Skeptical philosopher David Hume (1711–76) fully elaborated Locke's Empiricism and used it reductively to argue that there can be no more to man's concepts of body, mind, and causal connection than what occurs in the experiences that he has of them. For Hume all necessary truth is formal or conceptual, determined by the relations of identity and exclusion that hold between ideas.

Voltaire imported Locke's philosophy into France; and its Empiricism, in a very stark form, is the basis of sensationalism, in which all of the constituents of human mental life are analyzed in terms of sensations alone.

A genuinely original and clarifying attempt to resolve the controversy between Empiricists and their opponents was made in the critical philosophy of Immanuel Kant (1724–1804), drawing upon Leibniz and Hume. With the dictum that, although all knowledge begins with experience it does not all arise from experience, he established a clear distinction between the innate and the a priori. He held that there are a priori concepts, or categories—substance and cause being the most important—and also substantial or synthetic a priori truths. Although not derived from experience, the latter apply to experience. A priori concepts and propositions do not relate to a reality that transcends experience; they reflect, instead, the mind's way of organizing the amorphous mass of sense impressions that flow in upon it.

Lockean Empiricism prevailed in 19th-century England until the turn to Hegel occurred in the last quarter of the century. To be sure, the Scottish philosophers who followed Hume but avoided his Skeptical conclusions insisted that man does have substantial a priori knowledge. But the philosophy of John Stuart Mill (1806–73), logician, economist, and Utilitarian moralist, is thoroughly Empiricist. He held that all knowledge worth having, including mathematics, is empirical. The apparent necessity of mathematics, according to Mill, is the result of the unique massiveness of its empirical confirmation. All real knowledge for Mill is inductive and empirical; and deduction is sterile. On similar lines, the philosopher of evolution Herbert Spencer (1820–1903) offered another explanation of the apparent necessity of some of man's beliefs: they are the well-attested empirical beliefs of his ancestors from whom he has inherited them, an evolutionary revival of the doctrine of innateness. Two important mathematicians and pioneers in the philosophy of modern physics,

The Empiricism of William of Ockham

Locke's Empiricism

J.S. Mill and Positivism

W.K. Clifford (1845–79) and Karl Pearson (1857–1936), defended radically Empiricist philosophies of science, anticipating the Logical Empiricism of the 20th century.

In contemporary philosophy. The most influential Empiricist of the 20th century was the great British philosopher and logician Bertrand Russell (1872–1970), who at first was Lockean in his theory of knowledge—admitting both synthetic a priori knowledge and concepts of unobservable entities. Ludwig Wittgenstein (1889–1951), the influential pioneer of the school of Linguistic Analysis, convinced Russell that the truths of logic and mathematics are analytic; and Russell then came to believe, with Hume, that the task of philosophy is to analyze all concepts in terms of what can be directly present to the senses. In this spirit, he tried to show that even the concepts of formal logic are ultimately empirical though the experience that supplies them may be introspective instead of sensory.

Doctrines developed through the collaboration of Russell and Wittgenstein yielded the Logical Positivism of the German philosopher Rudolf Carnap (1891–1970) and of the Vienna Circle, a discussion group in which that philosophy was worked out. The Empiricism of Logical Positivism is especially evident in its restatement of the fundamental thesis of Hume's philosophy in a form known as "the verification principle," which recognizes as meaningful and synthetic only those sentences that are in principle verifiable by reference to sense experience.

CRITICISM AND EVALUATION

The critique of Plato and Aristotle

The earliest expressions of Empiricism in ancient Greek philosophy were those of the Sophists. In reaction to them Plato presented the Rationalistic view that man has only "opinion" about changing, perceptible, existing things in space and time; that "knowledge" can be had only of timeless, necessary truths; and that the objects of knowledge—the unchanging and imperceptible forms or universals (such as "Bed," "Man," etc.)—are the truly real. The circles and triangles of geometrical "knowledge," in this view, are quite different in their perfect exactness from the approximately circular and triangular things present to man's senses. In the *Phaedo,* Plato expounded a theory of literally innate ideas; man, for example, has a conception of exact "equality," which, since it could not have been supplied by the senses, must have been acquired by the soul before it was embodied.

Aristotle agreed with Plato that knowledge is of the universal but held that such universal forms should not be conceived as "separated" from the matter embodying them. This belief does not make Aristotle an Empiricist, although he was certainly a less extreme Rationalist than Plato. Aristotle took the Rationalist view that every science or body of knowledge must resemble Euclidean geometry in consisting of deductions from first principles that are self-evidently and necessarily true and that, although the senses acquaint man with the sensible forms of things, he cannot have knowledge of them unless reason is brought into play to acquaint him with their intelligible forms as well.

The Stoic view of "common notions," or beliefs that are held by all men—a Rationalistic element in an otherwise Empirical school of thought—was expanded during the early medieval period by the Christian Platonist St. Augustine (AD 354–430), a thoroughgoing Rationalist. The Stoic common notions, Augustine held, are truths that God has implanted in the human mind through direct illumination.

Although the early modern expression of Empiricism in the 17th century by Francis Bacon heralded the scientific age, its influence was lessened by his failure to appreciate the revolutionary use of mathematics that comprised the genius of Galileo's new physics and, even more fundamentally, by his underestimation of the need for imaginative conjecture in the formation of scientific hypotheses to restrict the overwhelming number of facts that would otherwise have to be handled. In contrast to Bacon's view, the philosopher and mathematician René Descartes (1596–1650), his contemporary and one of the principal founders of modern thought, developed a comprehensive Rationalism that was more immediately influential. For

Descartes all clear and distinct ideas, and in particular those of philosophy and of geometrical physics, are innate; sense experience is at most the agency that elicits ideas already present in the mind. In principle, all knowledge is a priori and demonstrable by pure reasoning, but in practice, because of man's finite intellect, it is necessary to rely on experience to confirm propositions for which rational proof is beyond reach. In England innate ideas and knowledge were defended by Edward Lord Herbert of Cherbury (1582–1648), precursor of Deism, and by a school of Puritan Humanists known as the Cambridge Platonists. The case for innate ideas, however, is hard to establish; there can be in the nature of the case little actual evidence that one can possess concepts before having had some relevant experience.

In the second half of the 17th century, the Empiricist views of John Locke were similarly controverted by a systematic thinker and man of affairs, G.W. Leibniz, who examined Locke's views in minute detail in his book *Nouveaux essais sur l'entendement humain* (1704, published 1765; Eng. trans., *New Essays,* 1916), arguing that ideas can be virtually innate in a less trivial sense than Locke allowed. Interpreting Locke's notion of reflection as reasoning rather than as introspection, Leibniz supposed that Locke was more of a Rationalist than he really was.

In contemporary philosophy, there are thinkers who, though broadly sympathetic to Positivism, have voiced reservations about its more specifically Empiricist elements. One important philosopher of science, Karl Popper, has rejected the inductivism that views the growth of empirical knowledge as the result of a mechanical routine of generalization. To him it is falsifiability by experience that makes a statement empirical. An influential American philosopher and logician, W.V. Quine, has been critical of the Logical Empiricists' frequent recourse to the concept of meaning and has rejected the sharp distinction they make between analytic and factual truths, on which most of contemporary Empiricism rests. For Quine, both human concepts and beliefs are the joint outcome of experience and conventional decision, and he denies that the role of the two factors can be readily distinguished as Empiricists assert.

The theory of knowledge has been the central discipline in philosophy since the 17th century, and its most basic issue is that between Empiricism and Rationalism, an issue that is still being actively debated. On the one hand, the idea that science rests on substantial but nonempirical presuppositions has been put in question by the fact that in some areas it seems to get along without them: without conservation in cosmology, without causality in quantum physics. On the other hand, the traditional theory of the innate powers of the mind has been reanimated by the considerations underlying the theory of language offered by Noam Chomsky, a generative grammarian, who holds that the learning of language is too rapid and too universal to be attributed entirely to an empirical process of conditioning. The basic strength of Empiricism consists in its recognition that human concepts and beliefs apply to a world outside oneself, and that it is by way of the senses that this world acts upon the individual. The question, however, of just how much the mind itself contributes to the task of processing its sensory input is one that no simple argument can answer.   (A.M.Q.)

Existentialism

The various philosophies (dating from about 1930) that have been referred to by the term Existentialism have in common an interpretation of human existence in the world that stresses its concreteness and its problematic character.

NATURE OF EXISTENTIALIST THOUGHT AND MANNER

According to Existentialism: (1) Existence is always particular and individual—always *my* existence, *your* existence, *his* existence. (2) Existence is primarily the problem of existence (*i.e.,* of its mode of being); it is, therefore, also the investigation of the meaning of Being. (3) This investigation is continually faced with diverse possibilities, from among which the existent (*i.e.*, man) must make a selection, to which he must then commit himself. (4) Because these possibilities are constituted by man's relationships with things and with other men, existence is always a being-in-the-world—*i.e.*, in a concrete and historically determinate situation that limits or conditions choice. Man is therefore called *Dasein* ("there being") because he is defined by the fact that he exists, or is in the world and inhabits it.

Contrasts and directions of thought

With respect to the first point, that existence is particular, Existentialism is opposed to any doctrine that views man as the manifestation of an absolute or of an infinite substance. It is thus opposed to most forms of Idealism, such as those that stress Consciousness, Spirit, Reason, Idea, or Oversoul. Secondly, it is opposed to any doctrine that sees in man some given and complete reality that must be resolved into its elements in order to be known or contemplated. It is thus opposed to any form of objectivism or scientism since these stress the crass reality of external fact. Thirdly, Existentialism is opposed to any form of necessitarianism; for existence is constituted by possibilities from among which man may choose and through which he can project himself. And, finally, with respect to the fourth point, Existentialism is opposed to any solipsism (holding that I alone exist) or any epistemological Idealism (holding that the objects of knowledge are mental), because existence, which is the relationship with other beings, always extends beyond itself, toward the being of these entities; it is, so to speak, transcendence.

Starting from these bases, Existentialism can take diverse and contrasting directions. It can insist on the transcendence of Being with respect to existence, and, by holding this transcendence to be the origin or foundation of existence, it can thus assume a theistic form. On the other hand, it can hold that human existence, posing itself as a problem, projects itself with absolute freedom, creating itself by itself, thus assuming to itself the function of God. As such, Existentialism presents itself as a radical atheism. Or it may insist on the finitude of human existence— *i.e.*, on the limits inherent in its possibilities of projection and choice. As such, Existentialism presents itself as a humanism.

Diversity of interests and sources

From 1940 on, with the diffusion of Existentialism through continental Europe, its directions have developed in terms of the diversity of the interests to which they are subject: the religious interest, the metaphysical (or nature of Being) interest, the moral and political interest. This diversity of interests is rooted, at least in part, in the diversity of sources on which Existentialism has drawn. One such source has been the subjectivism of the 4th–5th-century theologian St. Augustine, who exhorted man not to go outside himself in the quest for truth, for it is within him that truth abides. "If you find that you are by nature mutable," he wrote, "transcend yourself." Another source has been the Dionysian Romanticism of Nietzsche, who exalted life in its most irrational and cruel features and made this exaltation the proper task of the "higher man," who exists beyond good and evil. Still another source has been the nihilism of Dostoyevsky, who, in his novels, presented man as continually defeated as a result of his choices and as continually placed by them before the insoluble enigma of himself. As a consequence of the diversity of these sources, Existentialist doctrines have focussed on several aspects of existence.

They have focussed, first, on the problematic character of the human situation, through which man is continually confronted with diverse possibilities or alternatives, among which he may choose and on the basis of which he can project his life.

Second, the doctrines have focussed on the phenomena of this situation and especially on those that are negative or baffling, such as the concern or preoccupation that dominates man because of the dependence of all his possibilities upon his relationships with things and with other men; the dread of death or of the failure of his projects; the "shipwreck" upon insurmountable "limit situations" (death, the struggle and suffering inherent in every form of life, the situation in which everyone daily finds himself); the guilt inherent in the limitation of choices and in the responsibilities that derive from making them; the boredom from the repetition of situations; the absurdity of man's dangling between the infinity of his aspirations and the finitude of his possibilities.

Third, the doctrines have focussed on the intersubjectivity that is inherent in existence and is understood either as a personal relationship between two individuals, I and thou, such that the thou may be another man or God, or as an impersonal relationship between the anonymous mass and the individual self deprived of any authentic communication with others.

Fourth, Existentialism focusses on ontology, on some doctrine of the general meaning of Being, which can be approached in any of a number of ways: through the analysis of the temporal structure of existence; through the etymologies of the most common words—on the supposition that in ordinary language Being itself is disclosed, at least partly (and thus is also hidden); through the rational clarification of existence by which it is possible to catch a glimpse, through ciphers or symbols, of the Being of the world, of the soul, and of God; through existential psychoanalysis that makes conscious the fundamental "project" in which existence consists; or, finally, through the analysis of the fundamental modality to which all the aspects of existence conform—*i.e.*, through the analysis of possibility.

Approaches to the general meaning of Being

There is, in the fifth place, the therapeutic value of existential analysis that permits, on the one hand, the liberating of human existence from the beguilements or debasements to which it is subject in daily life and, on the other, the directing of human existence toward its authenticity; *i.e.*, toward a relationship that is well-grounded on itself, and with other men, with the world, and with God.

The various forms of Existentialism may also be distinguished on the basis of language, which is an indication of the cultural traditions to which they belong and which often explains the differences in terminology among the various authors. The principal representatives of German Existentialism are Martin Heidegger and Karl Jaspers; those of French personalistic Existentialism are Gabriel Marcel and Jean-Paul Sartre; that of French Phenomenology is Maurice Merleau-Ponty; that of Spanish Existentialism is José Ortega y Gasset; that of Russian Idealistic Existentialism is Nikolay Berdyayev (who, however, lived half of his adult life in France); and that of Italian Existentialism is Nicola Abbagnano. The linguistic differences, however, are not decisive for a determination of philosophical affinities. For example, Marcel and Sartre are farther apart than Heidegger and Sartre; and there is greater affinity between Abbagnano and Merleau-Ponty than between Merleau-Ponty and Marcel.

HISTORICAL SURVEY OF EXISTENTIALISM

Many of the theses that Existentialists defend or illustrate in their analyses are drawn from the wider philosophical tradition.

Precursors of Existentialism. The problem of what man is in himself can be discerned in the Socratic imperative "know thyself," as well as in the work of Montaigne and Pascal, a religious philosopher and mathematician. Montaigne had said: "If my mind could gain a foothold, I would not write essays, I would make decisions; but it is always in apprenticeship and on trial." And Pascal had insisted on the precarious position of man situated between Being and Nothingness: "We burn with the desire to find solid ground and an ultimate sure foundation whereon to build a tower reaching to the Infinite. But our whole groundwork cracks, and the earth opens to abysses."

Socrates, Montaigne, and Pascal

The stance of the internal tribunal—of man's withdrawal into his own spiritual interior—which reappears in some Existentialists (in Marcel and Sartre, for example) already belonged, as earlier noted, to St. Augustine. In early 19th-century French philosophy, it was defended by a reformed *Idéologue*, Marie Maine de Biran, who wrote: "Even from infancy I remember that I marvelled at the sense of my existence. I was already led by instinct to look within myself in order to know how it was possible that I could be alive and be myself." From then on, this posture inspired a considerable part of French philosophy.

The theme of the irreducibility of existence to reason, common to many Existentialists, was also defended by a leading German Idealist, F.W.J. von Schelling, as he argued against Hegel in the last phase of his philosophy, and Schelling's polemic, in turn, inspired the thinker usually cited as the father of Existentialism, the religious Dane Søren Kierkegaard.

The requirement to know man in his particularity and, therefore, in terms of a procedure different from those used by science to obtain knowledge of natural objects was confronted by Wilhelm Dilthey, an expounder of historical reason, who viewed "understanding" as the procedure and thus as the proper method of the human sciences. Understanding, according to Dilthey, consists in the reliving and reproducing of the experience of others. Hence it is also a feeling together with others and a sympathetic participation in their emotions. Understanding, therefore, accomplishes a unity between the knowing object and the object known.

The immediate background and founding fathers. The theses of Existentialism found a particular relevance during World War II, when Europe found itself threatened alternately by material and spiritual destruction. Under those circumstances of uncertainty, the optimism of Romantic inspiration, by which the destiny of man is infallibly guaranteed by an infinite force (such as Reason, the Absolute, or Mind) and propelled by it toward an ineluctable progress, appeared to be untenable. Existentialism was moved to insist on the instability and the risk of all human reality, to acknowledge that man is "thrown into the world"—*i.e.,* abandoned to a determinism that could render his initiatives impossible—and to hold that his very freedom is conditioned and hampered by limitations that could at any moment render it empty. The negative aspects of existence, such as pain, frustration, sickness, and death—which 19th-century optimism refused to take seriously because they do not touch the infinite principle that these optimists believed to be manifest in man—become for Existentialism the essential features of human reality.

The thinkers who, by virtue of the negative character of their philosophy, constituted the exception to 19th-century Romanticism thus became the acknowledged masters of the Existentialists. Against Hegelian necessitarianism, Kierkegaard interpreted existence in terms of possibility: dread—which dominates existence through and through—is "the sentiment of the possible." It is the feeling of what can happen to a man even when he has made all of his calculations and taken every precaution. Despair, on the other hand, discovers in possibility its only remedy, for "If man remains without possibilities, it is as if he lacked air." Karl Marx, in holding that man is constituted essentially by the "relationships of work and production" that tie him to things and other men, had insisted on the alienating character that these relationships assume in capitalistic society, where private property transforms man from an end to a means, from a person to the instrument of an impersonal process that subjugates him without regard for his needs and his desires. Nietzsche had viewed the *amor fati* ("love of fate") as the "formula for man's greatness." Freedom consists in desiring what is and what has been and in choosing it and loving it as if nothing better could be desired.

Emergence as a movement. Contemporary Existentialism reproduces these ideas and combines them in more or less coherent ways. Human existence is, for all the forms of Existentialism, the projection of the future on the basis of the possibilities that constitute it. For some Existentialists (the Germans Heidegger and Jaspers, for example), the existential possibilities, inasmuch as they are rooted in the past, merely lead every project for the future back to the past, so that only what has already been chosen can be chosen (Nietzsche's *amor fati*). For others (such as Sartre), the possibilities that are offered to existential choice are infinite and equivalent, such that the choice between them is indifferent; and for still others (Abbagnano and Merleau-Ponty), the existential possibilities are limited by the situation, but they neither determine the choice nor render it indifferent. The issue is one of individuating, in every concrete situation and by means of

a specific inquiry, the real possibilities offered to man. For all the Existentialists, however, the choice among possibilities—*i.e.,* the projection of existence—implies risks, renunciation, and limitation. Among the risks, the most serious is man's descent into inauthenticity or into alienation, his degradation from a person into a thing. Against this risk, for the theological forms of Existentialism (as in Gabriel Marcel, a Socratic dramatist; Karl Barth, a Swiss Neo-orthodoxist; Rudolf Bultmann, a biblical interpreter), there is the guarantee of the transcendent help from God, which in its turn is guaranteed by faith.

Existentialism, consequently, by insisting on the individuality and nonrepeatability of existence (following Kierkegaard and Nietzsche), is sometimes led to regard one's coexistence with other people (held to be, however, an ineluctable fact of the human situation) as a condemnation or alienation of man. Marcel has said that all that exists in society beyond the individual is "expressible by a minus sign," and Sartre has affirmed in his major work *L'Être et le néant* (1943; *Being and Nothingness,* 1956) that "the Other is the hidden death of my possibilities." For the other forms of Existentialism, however, a coexistence that is not anonymous (as that of a mob) but is grounded on personal communication conditions man's authentic existence.

Existentialism has had ramifications in various areas of contemporary culture. In literature, Franz Kafka, author of haunting novels, walking in Kierkegaard's footsteps, described human existence as the quest for a stable, secure, and radiant reality that continually eludes it (*Das Schloss* [1926; *The Castle,* 1930]); or he described it as threatened by a guilty verdict about which it knows neither the reason nor the circumstances but against which it can do nothing—a verdict that ends with death (*Der Prozess* [1925; *The Trial,* 1937]).

The theses of contemporary Existentialism were then diffused and popularized by the novels and plays of Sartre, by the writings of the French novelists and dramatists Simone de Beauvoir and Albert Camus. In *L'Homme révolté* (1951; *The Rebel,* 1953), Camus described the "metaphysical rebellion" as "the movement by which a man protests against his condition and against the whole of creation." In art, the analogues of Existentialism may be considered to be Surrealism, Expressionism, and in general those schools that view the work of art not as the reflection of a reality external to man but as the free immediate expression of human reality.

Existentialism made its entrance into psychopathology through Karl Jaspers' *Allgemeine Psychopathologie* (1913; *General Psychopathology,* 1965), which was inspired by the need to understand the world in which the mental patient lives, by means of a sympathetic participation in his experience. Later, Ludwig Binswanger, a Swiss psychiatrist of the *Daseinsanalyse* school, in one of his celebrated works, *Über Ideenflucht* (1933; "On the Flight of Ideas"), inspired by Heidegger's thought, viewed the origin of mental illness as a failure in the existential possibilities that constitute human existence (*Dasein*). From Jaspers and Binswanger, the Existentialist current became diffused and variously stated in contemporary psychiatry.

In theology, Barth's *Römerbrief* (1919; *The Epistle to the Romans,* 1933) started the "Kierkegaard revival," the emblem of which was expressed by Barth himself; it is "the relation of this God with this man; the relation of this man with this God—this is the only theme of the Bible and of philosophy." Within the bounds of this current, on the one hand, there was an insistence upon the absolute transcendence of God with respect to man, who could place himself in relationship with God only by denying himself and by abandoning himself to a gratuitously granted faith. On the other hand, there was the requirement to demythologize the religious content of faith, particularly of the Christian faith, in order to allow the message of the eschatological event (of salvation) to emerge from among the existential possibilities of man.

METHODOLOGICAL ISSUES IN EXISTENTIALISM

The methods that the Existentialists employ in their interpretations have a presupposition in common: the imme-

Kierke-gaard, Marx, and Nietzsche

Broader cultural ramifications

diacy of the relationship between the interpreter and the interpreted, between the interrogator and the interrogated, between the problem of being and Being itself. The two terms coincide in existence; for the man who poses the question "What is Being?" cannot but pose it to himself and cannot respond without starting from his own being.

This common ground notwithstanding, each Existentialist thinker has defended and worked out his own method for the interpretation of existence. Heidegger, an Existentialist with ontological (nature of Being) concerns, availed himself of the philosophy of Edmund Husserl, founder of Phenomenology, which, as *logos* of the *phainomenon,* employs speech that manifests or discloses what it is that one is speaking about and that is true—in the etymological use of the Greek word *alētheia* (*i.e.,* the sense of uncovering or manifesting what was hidden). The phenomenon is, from Heidegger's point of view, not mere appearance, but the manifestation or disclosure of Being in itself. Phenomenology is thus capable of disclosing the structure of Being and hence is an ontology of which the point of departure is the being of the one who poses the question about Being, namely man.

Jaspers, an authority in psychopathology as well as in the philosophy of human existence, on the other hand, employed the method of the rational clarification of existence; he maintained that existence, as the quest for Being, is man's effort of rational self-understanding, or universalizing, of communicating—a method that presupposes that existence and reason are the two poles of man's being. Reason is possible existence; *i.e.,* existence that, as Jaspers writes in his *Vernunft und Existenz* (1935; *Reason and Existence,* 1955), becomes "manifest to itself and as such real, if, *with, through* and *by* another existence, it arrives at itself." This activity, however, is never consummated; thus, when the impossibility of its achievement is recognized, it is changed into faith, into the recognition of transcendence as providing the only possibility of its final achievement.

According to the views of Sartre, the foremost philosopher of mid-20th-century France, the method of philosophy is existential psychoanalysis; *i.e.,* the analysis of the "fundamental project" in which man's existence consists. In contrast to the precepts of Freudian psychoanalysis, which stop short at the irreducibility of the libido, or primitive psychic drive, existential psychoanalysis tries to determine the "original choice" through which man constructs his world and decides in a preliminary way upon particular choices (which, however, may place in crisis the primordial choice itself).

According to Marcel, a Christian Existentialist philosopher and dramatist, the method of philosophy depends upon a recognition of the mystery of Being (*Le Mystère de l'être* [1951; *The Mystery of Being,* 1950–51]); *i.e.,* on the impossibility of discovering Being through objective or rational analyses or demonstrations. Philosophy should lead man up, however, to the point of making possible for him "the productive illumination of Revelation."

Finally, according to humanistic Existentialism, as represented by Abbagnano, the leading Italian Existentialist, and by Merleau-Ponty, a French Phenomenologist, the method of philosophy consists of the analysis and the determination—by employing all available techniques including those of science—of the structures that constitute existence; *i.e.,* of the relations that connect man with other beings and that figure, therefore, not only in the constitution of man but in the constitution of the other beings as well.

SUBSTANTIVE ISSUES IN EXISTENTIALISM

Fundamental concepts and contrasts. Both the ontology and manner of human existence are of concern to Existentialism.

Ontic structure of human existence. The fundamental characteristic of Existentialist ontology is the primacy that that study of the nature of existence gives to the concept of possibility. This priority dominated the philosophy of Kierkegaard and also was amply utilized by Husserl, who had explicitly affirmed the ontological priority of possibility over reality. Possibility, however, is not understood by

the Existentialists in the purely logical sense as absence of contradiction nor in the sense of traditional metaphysics as potentiality destined to become actuality but, rather, in the sense of ontic or objective possibility, which is the very structure of human existence; it is thus the specific modality of man's being.

Another way of expressing this thesis is the affirmation of Heidegger and Sartre that "existence precedes essence," which signifies that man does not have a nature that determines his modes of being and acting but that, rather, these modes are simply possibilities from which he may choose and on the basis of which he can project himself. In this sense, Heidegger has said that "*Dasein* is always its own possibility," and Sartre has written: "It is true that the possible is—so to speak—an option on being, and if it is true that the possible can come into the world only through a being which is its own possibility, this implies for human reality the necessity of being its being in the form of an option on its being."

As possibility, human existence is the anticipation, the expectation, the projection of the future. The future is its fundamental temporal dimension, to which the present and the past are subordinate and secondary; existence is always stretched out toward the future. As possibility, existence is also transcendence, being beyond, because all of its constitutive possibilities organize it beyond itself toward the other beings of the world and toward the world in its totality. To transcend thus means to move toward something that is not one's own existence; *i.e.,* toward things and toward other men, with which man is related in every situation in which he finds himself.

Yet for some Existentialists, the being of these other entities has a modality that differs from the being of man's existence: their existence is not possible being but real or factual being. To existence, Heidegger contrasts the presence of the things in the world—a presence that assumes, as man takes notice of these things for his needs, the aspect of utilizability. But utilizability is not a simple quality of things; it is their very being. Analogously, Sartre distinguishes the for-itself—the mode of being of man's existence that he identifies, following Descartes and Husserl, with consciousness—from the in-itself, the being or reality of things that he identifies with their utilizability. According to Jaspers, over against the existence of the possible (man, *Dasein*) stands the world as the infinite horizon that encompasses within itself each possible existence and, therefore, cannot itself be encompassed by any one of them. This is a world that is a reality of fact, at the origin of which there is a Being that is pure transcendence and that, therefore, never reveals itself.

Similarly, the religious forms of Existentialism insist on transcendence, considering it to be the property of the Being that is beyond the existential possibilities and that can enter among them solely under the form of mystery (Marcel) and of the extratemporal revelation of faith (Barth, Jaspers). Marcel, in this regard, has contrasted Being, which is a mystery, with having, which is the condition of man in the world; that is to say, man has objects before him that are foreign to his subjectivity. He tries to organize them and discover the bond that ties them together so as to control and use them.

In all of these doctrines, there is the dominating theme of the contrast between the modality proper to existence, which is possibility, and the modality proper to Being, which is reality or facticity. As a result of this contrast, existence (as possibility) appears as the nothingness of Being, as the negation of every reality of fact. In a brief but famous essay, *Was ist Metaphysik?* (1929), Heidegger affirmed that "Human existence cannot have a relationship with being unless it remains in the midst of nothingness." Rudolf Carnap, a semanticist and leading Logical Positivist, in an equally famous essay, "Überwindung der Metaphysik durch die logische Analyse der Sprache" (1931; "The Elimination of Metaphysics Through Logical Analysis of Language"), criticized this hypostatization (or making real) of Nothingness as one of the grosser fallacies of metaphysics. In truth, Nothingness is, for the Existentialists, possible existence, as the negation of the reality of fact. Sartre has written: "The possible is the *something* which the For-itself lacks *in order* to be itself"; it is what the subject lacks in order to be an object; thus it does not exist except as a lacking.

This is also true of value, which is such insofar as it does not exist. For even when value occurs or is perceived in certain acts, it lies beyond them and constitutes the limit or the goal toward which they aim. Analogously, knowledge, in which the object (the in-itself) presents itself to consciousness (the for-itself), is a relationship of nullification, because the object cannot be offered to consciousness except as that which is not consciousness. Furthermore, another existence is such insofar as it is not mine; thus this negation is "the constitutive structure of the being-of-others."

But this reduction of existence to Nothingness can lead in two directions: it can lead to insisting on the lack of meaning—*i.e.,* on the absurdity of existence and of every possible project—as it does in Sartre, in Camus, and in atheistic Existentialism; or it can lead toward the quest for a more direct relationship of existence with Being, beyond the constitutive possibilities of existence, so that Being reveals itself, at least partly, in existence—through language or through faith or through some mystical form of religiousness, as happens in the later phase of Heidegger's thought, in Jaspers, and in all of the forms of theological Existentialism.

Manner and style of human existence.   Existentialism is never a solipsism in the proper sense of the term (that I alone exist), because every existential possibility relates man to things and to other men. Sometimes it is presented as humanism in the sense that it places human destiny in the hands of men themselves. But this version is rejected by all of the currents of the movement that, starting with Heidegger, insist on the priority and the initiative of Being with regard to human existence. The opposition between these two points of view depends on how the different Existentialists solve the problem of freedom.

Destiny versus freedom of choice

Man always finds himself in a situation in which his constitutive possibilities are rooted. For Heidegger and Jaspers, this situation determines the choice that he makes among these possibilities; for Sartre, conversely, the situation is determined by the choice. Existentialism fluctuates in this way between the concept of a destiny in which, like Nietzsche's *amor fati,* man accepts what has already been chosen and the concept of a radical freedom whereby the choices are offered to man in an absolute indifference. From the first point of view, every project of life falls back on or is reduced to the situation from which it starts; thus the possibility of being, of acting, of willing, of choosing is really, as Jaspers points out in his *Philosophie* (1932), the impossibility of being, acting, willing, and choosing in a manner different from the way things are; *i.e.,* from the factual conditions of the situation. From the second point of view, the fundamental project, which is the primordial choice, has no conditions; as Sartre says: "Since I am free, I project my total possible, but I thereby posit that I am free and that I can always nihilate this first project and make it past." From the first, or deterministic, point of view, the past determines the future and assimilates it to itself; from the second, or libertarian, point of view, the meaning of the past depends upon the present project. In the latter instance, freedom is a kind of damnation: as Sartre affirms: "We said that freedom is not free not to be free and that it is not free not to exist."

A choice, however, is offered to man even from the destinarian point of view: that between understanding and not understanding one's own nothingness. According to Heidegger, a man achieves what he calls "authentic existence" when he understands the impossibility of all of the possibilities of existence—the impossibility of which the sign or term is death. Jaspers affirms, in his turn, that the only choice offered to man is that between accepting or rejecting the situation with which he is identified. The rejection of it, however, is a betrayal that plunges him back into the situation itself.

Existentialist ontology thus fluctuates between Being and Nothingness and concludes by regarding Nothingness as the only possible revelation of Being. In the atheistic version, it is man, as Sartre affirms, who "strives to be God" and consumes himself vainly in the effort. In the cosmological or theological version, it is Being that intervenes, in a way that is more or less mysterious or hidden, to redeem man from Nothingness.

Problems of Existentialist philosophy.   The key problems for Existentialism are those of man himself, of his situation in the world, and of his more ultimate significance.

Man and human relationships.   Existentialist anthropology is strictly connected with its ontology. The traditional distinction between soul and body is completely eliminated; thus the body is a lived-through experience that is an integral part of man's existence in its relationship with the world. According to Sartre, "In each project of the For-itself, in each perception the body is there; it is the immediate Past in so far as it still touches on the Present which flees it." As such, however, the body is not reduced to a datum of consciousness, to subjective representation. Consciousness, according to Sartre, is constant openness toward the world, a transcendent relationship with other beings and thereby with the in-itself. Consciousness is existence itself, or, as Jaspers says, it is "the manifestation of being." In order to avoid any subjectivistic equivocation, Heidegger went so far as to renounce the use of the term consciousness, preferring the term *Dasein,* which is more appropriate for designating human reality in its totality. For the same reasons, the traditional opposition between subject and object, or between the self and the nonself, loses all sense. *Dasein* is always particular and individual. It is always a self; but it is also always a project of the world that includes the self, determining or conditioning its modes of being.

Self, body, and relationship with the world

All of these modes of being thus arise, as Heidegger shows in his masterpiece *Sein und Zeit* (1927; *Being and Time,* 1962), from the relationship between the self and the world. Heidegger has regarded concern (in the Latin sense of the term) to be the fundamental aspect of this relationship, insofar as it is man's concern to obtain the things that are necessary for him and even to transform them with his work as well as to exchange them so as to make them more suitable to his needs. Concern demonstrates that man is "thrown into the world," into the midst of other beings, so that in order to project himself he must exist among them and utilize them. Being thrown means, for man, being abandoned to the whirling flow of things in the world and to their determinism.

This happens inevitably, according to Heidegger, in inauthentic existence—day-to-day and anonymous existence in which all behaviour is reduced to the same level, made "official," conventional, and insignificant. Chatter, idle curiosity, and equivocation are the characteristics of this existence, in which "One says this" and "One does that" reign undisputed. Anonymous existence amounts to a simple "being together" with others, not a true coexistence, which is obtained only through the acceptance of a common destiny (see below).

All of the Existentialists are in agreement on the difficulty of communication; *i.e.,* of well-grounded intersubjective relationships. Jaspers has perhaps been the one to insist most on the relationship between truth and communication. Truths are and can be different from existence. But if fanaticism and dogmatism (which absolutize a historical truth) are avoided on the one hand while relativism and skepticism (which affirm the equivalence of all truths) are avoided on the other, then the only other way is a constant confrontation between the different truths through an always more extended and deepened intersubjective communication.

Difficulty of intersubjective communication

Sartre, however, denies that there is authentic communication. According to him, consciousness is not only the nullification of things but also the nullification of the other person as other. To look at another person is to make of him a thing. This is the profound meaning of the myth of Medusa. Sexuality itself, which Sartre holds to be an essential aspect of existence, fluctuates between sadism and masochism, in which either the other person or oneself is merely a thing. On this basis, the intersubjective relationship is obviously impossible.

The human situation in the world.   Heidegger has pointed to the foundation of the intersubjective relationship in dread. When a man decides to escape from the banality of anonymous existence—which hides the nothingness of existence, or the nonreality of its possibilities, behind the mask of daily concerns—his understanding of this nothingness leads him to choose the only unconditioned and insurmountable possibility that belongs to him: death. The possibility of death, unlike the possibilities that relate him to other things and to other men, isolates him. It is a certain possibility, not through its apodictic evidence but because it continuously weighs upon existence. To understand this possibility means to decide for it, to acknowledge "the possibility of the impossibility of any existence at all" and to live for death. The emotive tonality that accompanies this understanding is dread, through which man feels himself to be *"face to face* with the 'nothing' of the possible impossibility of [his] existence."

But neither the understanding of death nor its emotive accompaniment opens up a specific task for man, a way to transform his own situation in the world. They enable him only to perceive the common destiny to which all men are subject; and they offer to him, therefore, the possibility of remaining faithful to this destiny and of freely accepting the necessity that all men share in common. In this fidelity consists the historicity of existence, which is the repetition of tradition, the return to the possibilities from which existence had earlier been constituted, the wanting for the future what has been in the past. And in this historicity participate not only man but all of the things of the world, in their utilizability and instrumentality, and even the totality of Nature as the locus of history.

Dread, therefore, is not fear in the face of a specific danger. It is rather the emotive understanding of the nullity of the possible, or, as Jaspers says, of the possibility of Nothingness. It has, therefore, a therapeutic function in that it leads human existence to its authenticity. From the fall into factuality into which every project plunges him, man can save himself only by projecting not to project; *i.e.,* either by abandoning himself decisively to the situation in which he finds himself or by being indifferent to any possible project—with regard to which Sartre says, "Thus it amounts to the same thing whether one gets drunk alone or is a leader of nations."

The pivotal point of that conclusion—the conclusion most widely held among the Existentialists and the one in fact often identified with Existentialism—is the antithesis between possibility and reality. On the one hand, existence is interpreted in terms of possibilities that are not purely logical possibilities or manifestations of a man's ignorance of what exists but are, rather, effective, or ontic, possibilities that constitute man as such; on the other hand, contrasted to possibilities in this sense is a reality, a for-itself, a world, a transcendence that is a factual presence, insurmountable and oppressive, with respect to which possibility is a pure Nothingness. The contradiction to which this antithesis leads becomes clear when the same reality is interpreted in terms of possibility: when the being of things, for example, is reduced to their possibility of being utilized; when the being of other men is reduced to the possibility of anonymous or personal relationships that the individual can have with them; and when the being of transcendence, or of God, is reduced to the possibility of the relationship, although ineffable and mysterious, between transcendence, or God, and man.

It has been said that a coherent Existentialism should avoid the constant mortal leap between Being and Nothingness; should not confuse the problematic character of existence with the fall into factuality; should not confuse the finitude of possibilities with resignation to the situation, choice with determinism; freedom conditioned by the limits of the situation with the acknowledgement of the omnipresent necessity of the Whole. In this inquiry, it is held, Existentialism could well benefit from a more attentive consideration of science, which it has viewed until now only as a preparatory, imperfect, and objectifying knowledge in comparison with the authentic understanding of Being, which it considers to be a more fundamental mode of the being of man in the world. Science, it is submitted, offers today the example of an extensive and coherent use of the concept of the possible in the key no-

tions that it employs, especially in those branches that are interdisciplinary—among them such notions as indeterminacy, chance, probability, field, model, project, structure, and conditionality.

Some steps in this direction have been taken by Abbagnano and by Merleau-Ponty. According to the latter, considerations of probability are rooted in the being of man, inasmuch as he is situated in the world and invested with the ambiguity of his events. Merleau-Ponty has written in his *Phénoménologie de la perception* (1945):

> Our freedom does not destroy our situation, but is engaged with it. The situation in which we live is open. This implies both that it appeals to modes of privileged resolution and that it is of itself powerless to obtain one of them.

From this point of view, there is always a certain freedom in situations, although its degree varies from situation to situation.

Significance of Being and transcendence.   Among the thinkers most frequently mentioned here, the concept of the necessity of Being prevails as the basis of their metaphysical or theological orientations. Heidegger has come more and more to insist on the massive presence of Being in the face of human existence, by attributing to Being all initiative and to man only the possibility of abandoning himself to Being and to the things that are the modes of the language of Being. For Heidegger, Being is interpreted better through the etymology of those words that designate the most common things of daily life than through the analysis of existential possibilities. Jaspers has seen the revelation of transcendence in ciphers—*i.e.,* in persons, doctrines, or poems—all of which can be interpreted as symbols of existential situations and above all of limit situations, the insurmountability of which, in provoking the total "shipwreck" of human possibilities, makes man feel the presence of absolute transcendence. In a less philosophically elaborate form, Being has been understood as mystery by Marcel; as the perfect actuality that guarantees the existential possibilities by Louis Lavelle, a leader of the French *philosophie de l'esprit;* and as the absolute value that man encounters in his own spiritual intimacy by René Le Senne, also of the *philosophie de l'esprit.*

Problems of Existentialist theology.   Existentialism has a theological dimension. Though Heidegger rejects the label of atheist, he also denies to the Being of which he speaks the essential qualifications of divinity, inasmuch as it is not the ultimate cause and the Good. But Jaspers, in his last writings, emphasized more and more the religious character of faith in transcendence. Faith is the way to withdraw from the world and to resume contact with the Being that is beyond the world. Faith is life itself, in that it returns to the encompassing Whole and allows itself to be guided and fulfilled by it. Jaspers has even developed a theology of history. He speaks of an axial age, which he places between the 8th and 2nd centuries before Christ, the age in which the great religions and the great philosophers of the Orient arose—Confucius and Lao-tzu, the *Upaniṣads,* Buddha, Zoroaster, the great prophets of Israel—and in Greece the age of Homer and of classical philosophy as well as Thucydides and Archimedes. In this age, for the first time, man became aware of Being in general, of himself, and of his limits. The age in which man now lives, that of science and technology, is perhaps the beginning of a new axial age that is the authentic destiny of man but a destiny that is far off and unimaginable.

For Bultmann, the theologian of the demythologization of Christianity, inauthentic existence is tied to the past, to fact, to the world, while authentic existence is open to the future, to the nonfact, to the nonworld; *i.e.,* to the end of the world and to God. Thus, authentic existence is not the self-projection of man in the world but, rather, the self-projection of man in the love of and obedience to God. But this self-projection is no longer the work of human freedom; it is the saving event that enters miraculously through faith into the future possibilities of man.

In these theological speculations and in others that are comparable, the common presupposition of the Existentialists is recognized—*i.e.,* the gap between human existence and Being. There is either an acknowledgment of that gap, with existence assuming the role of the demonic

The antithesis between possibility and reality

(the alternative that Sartre and others have all illustrated above all in their literary works), or an acknowledgment of the hidden participation of human existence in Being through a gratuitous initiative on the part of Being.

Aesthetic, ethical, and religious levels

Kierkegaard had earlier distinguished three stages of existence between which there is neither development nor continuity but gaps and jumps: the aesthetic stage is the one in which one lives for the pleasure of the moment; the ethical stage is the one based on the stability and continuity of life in work and in matrimony; and the religious stage is the one characterized by faith, which is always a "dreadful certainty"—*i.e.,* a dread that becomes certain of a hidden relationship with God.

The ethical and religious stages correspond roughly to what Heidegger and Jaspers call, respectively, the inauthenticity and the authenticity of existence. Art is not as a rule recognized by contemporary Existentialists as an autonomous stage; it is almost always for them an essential manifestation of existence itself. For Jaspers, it is a mode of reading in nature, in history, and in men the cipher of transcendence; *i.e.,* the negative symbol in which transcendence is revealed. According to Camus, it is an aspect of man's revolt against the world. The artist tries to remake the sketch of the world that is before him and to give it the style—that is to say, the coherence and unity—that it lacks. For this purpose, he selects the elements of the world and freely combines them in order to create a value that escapes man continuously but that the artist perceives and tries to salvage from the flux of history.

From this point of view, art would be a way of reshaping the world beyond its factual forms, in order that it might show their negative and troublesome characteristics. The directions of contemporary art that have deliberately forsaken the imitation of reality find their justification in this point of view.

SOCIAL AND HISTORICAL PROJECTIONS OF EXISTENTIALISM

The metaphysical or theological dimension of Existentialism does not leave man with nothing to do. Once the nullity of the existential possibilities is recognized, man cannot but resign himself to Being, which, in one of its new manifestations in the world or beyond it, conducts him to a new epoch. Even someone like José Ortega y Gasset, the leading Spanish Existentialist and writer, who, in examining the social aspects of existence, has characterized the present epoch by the advent of the masses and the socialization of man, has halted at the recognition of the crisis and the total uncertainty that dominates the future of man (*La rebelión de las masas* [1929; *The Revolt of the Masses,* 1932]).

On the other hand, humanistic Existentialism has recognized the positive and the to-some-degree determining function that man may have in history. It has insisted, as in Merleau-Ponty, on man's duty to assume the responsibility of an effective action for the transformation of society and, in general, of the world that he inhabits.

Sartre's synthesis of Existentialism and Marxism

Along this line of assuming responsibility, Existentialism has moved toward Marxism, with which it shares the diagnoses of existence as the primordial and ineradicable relationship of man with nature and with society. In the *Critique de la raison dialectique* (1960; "Critique of Dialectical Reason"). Sartre attempted a synthesis between Existentialism and Marxism by modifying the notion of "project" that he defended in *L'Être et le néant* and by utilizing the notion of dialectic as understood by Marx. The project of which existence consists is not the result of an arbitrary choice (as Sartre had previously maintained); it is, instead, that of a conditioning by the objective possibilities that Sartre identifies (as does Marx) with "the material conditions of existence." The project remains, however, that of the particular individual of a unique consciousness—but of a consciousness that tries to become totalized; *i.e.,* to enter into relationship with others so as to constitute, with others, human groups that are more and more comprehensive. In this manner it tends toward a complete and definitive totalization without appeals. Dialectical reason would be precisely such a process of growing totalization; and it becomes, moreover, the true protagonist of history and becomes that with which the interior freedom of any individuals who participate in history is identified.

From the defense of the freedom of the individual, Sartre has thus moved to the defense of the absolute dialectical necessity of history despite its being interiorized and lived by individuals. A historical project of human life that tries to remove the characteristics of inauthenticity or of alienation from existence—a project that may bring Existentialism and Marxism close together—thus ends by losing, in this form, its risky and problematic character and the awareness of the conditions and the modalities of its realization. These features are also lost in the "transcendental project" of a new society elaborated by one of the leaders of the New Left, the German-born American Herbert Marcuse. While insisting on the requirement that the "transcendental project" be "in accord with the real possibilities open at the attained level of the material and intellectual culture," Marcuse entrusts its realization to an impersonal and contemplative Reason, which cannot but invite the "great refusal" of contemporary society.

Having developed in different and contrasting directions, Existentialism has furnished philosophy and the whole of contemporary culture with conceptual tools, of which the nature and techniques of employment have still not been clarified—as, for example, terms like "problematicity," "chance," "condition," "choice," "freedom," and "project." Although these tools can be employed usefully for the interpretation of existence—*i.e.,* to orient philosophical inquiry in the fields of epistemology, ethics, aesthetics, education, and politics—it is nonetheless indispensable that the pivot on which they turn, "possibility," be granted its own ontological status that does not reduce it either to Nothingness or to Being. It is indispensable, moreover, that a positive datum be perceived in possibility, a datum that is verifiable with appropriate techniques and that, while not offering infallible guarantees, allows man to project and to act in the world with calculated risks and with a prudent trust.   (N.Ab.)

Idealism

As a philosophical term, Idealism refers to any view that stresses the central role of the ideal or the spiritual in man's interpretation of experience. It may hold that the world or reality exists essentially as spirit or consciousness, that abstractions and laws are more fundamental in reality than sensory things, or, at least, that whatever exists is known to man in dimensions that are chiefly mental—through and as ideas. Thus the two basic forms of Idealism are metaphysical Idealism, which asserts the ideality of reality, and epistemological Idealism, which holds that in the knowledge process the mind can grasp only the psychic or that its objects are conditioned by their perceptibility. In its metaphysics, Idealism is thus directly opposed to Materialism, the view that the basic substance of the world is matter and that it is known primarily through and as material forms and processes; and in its epistemology, it is opposed to Realism, which holds that in human knowledge objects are grasped and seen as they really are—in their existence outside and independently of the mind. As a philosophy often expressed in bold and expansive syntheses, Idealism is also opposed to various restrictive forms of thought: to Skepticism, with occasional exceptions as in the British Hegelian F.H. Bradley (1846–1924); to Positivism, which stresses observable facts and relations as opposed to ultimates and therefore spurns the speculative "pretensions" of every metaphysic; and often to atheism, since the Idealist commonly extrapolates the concept of mind to embrace an infinite Mind. The essential orientation of Idealism can be sensed through some of its typical tenets: "Truth is the whole, or the Absolute"; "to be is to be perceived"; "reality reveals its ultimate nature more faithfully in its highest qualities (mental) than in its lowest (material)"; "the Ego is both subject and object."

Contrasts with opposing schools

APPROACHES TO UNDERSTANDING IDEALISM

What Idealism is may be clarified by approaching it in three ways: through its basic doctrines and principles, through its central questions and answers, and through its significant arguments.

Six core
concepts **Basic doctrines and principles.** Six common, basic conceptions distinguish Idealistic philosophy:

The union of individuality and universality. Abstract universals, such as "canineness," which express the common nature or essence that the members of a class (*e.g.,* individual dogs or wolves) share with one another, are acknowledged by all philosophers. Many Idealists, however, emphasize the concept of a concrete universal, one that is also a concrete reality, such as "mankind" or "literature," which can be imagined as gatherable into one specific thing. As opposed to the fixed, formal, abstract universal, the concrete universal is essentially dynamic, organic, and developing. Thus universality and individuality merge.

The contrast between contemporaneity and eternity. While most philosophers tend to focus on matters of contemporary concern, Idealists always seek a much wider perspective that embraces epochs and eras in the broad sweep of history. In the words of the 17th-century Rationalist Spinoza, they strive to view the contemporary world "under the aspect of eternity." Thus, in spite of the extensive formative influence of culture, Idealists claim that their philosophy transcends the parochialism of a particular culture; and Idealisms are found, in fact, in all of the major cultures of the world.

The doctrine of internal relations and the coherence theory of truth. It seems natural to suppose, as non-Idealists usually do, that the consideration of two things in their relatedness to one another can have no effect on the things themselves—*i.e.,* that a relation is something in addition to the things or terms related and is thus external. On this basis, truth would be defined as a relation of correspondence between a proposition and a state of affairs. The Idealist believes, however, that reality is more subtle than this. The relationship between a mineral deposit and the business cycle, for example, is an internal one: the deposit changes to an ore when prices render it profitable to mine the mineral. Similarly, it is part of the essence of a brick that it is related to a wall or pavement. Thus terms and relations logically determine one another. Ultimate reality is therefore a system of judgments or propositions, and truth is defined in terms of the coherence of these propositions with one another to form a harmonious whole. Thus a successful spy is judged either a hero or a villain only in relation to a total system of international relations, an accepted philosophy of history, and the moral judgments involved. There are therefore degrees of reality and degrees of truth within a system of truth cohering by internal relations, and the truth of a judgment reflects its place in this system.

The dialectical method. Idealism seeks to overcome contradictions by penetrating into the overall coherent system of truth and continually creating new knowledge to be integrated with earlier discoveries. Idealism is thus friendly to all quests for truth, whether in the natural or behavioral sciences or in art, religion, and philosophy. It seeks the truth in every positive judgment and in its contradictory as well. Thus it uses the dialectical method of reasoning to remove the contradictions characteristic of human knowledge. Such removal leads to a new synthetic judgment that incorporates in a higher truth the degree of truth that was present in each of the two lower judgments.

The centrality of mind in knowledge and being. Idealism is not reductive, as are opposing philosophies that identify mind with matter and reduce the higher level of reality to the protons and electrons of mathematical physics. On the contrary, Idealism defends the principle that the lower is explained by the higher—specifically, that matter can be explained by mind but that mind cannot be explained by matter. The word spirit can be substituted for "mind" or even placed above it; and "Spiritualism" is often used, especially in Europe, as a synonym for Idealism.

The transmutation of evil into good. Nearly all Idealists accept the principle that the evils with which man has to deal may become ingredients in a larger whole that overcomes them. The eminent American Hegelian Josiah Royce (1855–1916) held that the larger whole is the Absolute Mind, which keeps evils under control as a man

might hold a viper under the sole of his boot. Along with this doctrine of the sublimation or transmutation of evil, Royce incorporated into his metaphysics a point from the 19th-century irrationalism of Schopenhauer, itself a voluntaristic form of Idealism, viz., that "the world is my idea." Schopenhauer, however, was probably the only Idealist who defended the converse principle that good is transmuted into evil.

Basic questions and answers. In defining philosophical Idealism in its historical development as a technical metaphysical doctrine, three most difficult and irreducible questions arise. From the efforts to answer these questions there has been created an extensive literature that is the corpus of philosophical Idealism.

Ultimate reality. The first of the three questions is metaphysical: What is the ultimate reality that is given in human experience? Historically, answers to this question have fallen between two extremes. On the one hand is the Skepticism of the 18th-century Empiricist David Hume, who held that the ultimate reality given in experience is the moment by moment flow of events in the consciousness of each individual. This concept compresses all of reality into a solipsistic specious present—the momentary sense experience of one isolated percipient. At the other extreme, followers of the 17th-century Rationalist Spinoza adopted his definition of ultimate substance as that which can exist and can be conceived only by itself. According to the first principle of his system of pantheistic Idealism, God, or Nature, or Substance is the ultimate reality given in human experience. Hegel said that this dogmatic absolutism was the lion's den into which all tracks enter and from which none ever returns. In answering the first question, most philosophical Idealists steer between Hume and Spinoza and in so doing create a number of types of Idealism, which will be discussed below. Meta-
physical
and logical
issues

The given. The second question to arise in defining Idealism is: What is given? What results can be obtained from a logical interpretation and elaboration of the given? According to Idealists the result, though it is frequently something external to individual experience, is, nevertheless, a concrete universal, an order system (like the invisible lattice structure of a crystal), or an ideality in the sense explained earlier. In Hegel's words: "What is real is rational, and what is rational is real." Idealists believe that the collective human spirit of intellectual inquiry has discovered innumerable order systems that are present in external, nonhuman reality, or nature, and that this collective creative intelligence has produced the various sciences and disciplines. This production has required a long period of time called history. But history was antedated by the achievements of ancestors who created languages and religions and other primitive institutions. Consequently, the logical interpretation and elaboration of the given is actually the complete transformation of the earth by its various inhabitants; so that the moon flights portend a similar transformation of the planetary system. An inherent part of the collective intelligence is the spiritual force that Idealists call the spirit of philosophy.

Change. The third question is: What position or attitude is a thinker to take toward temporal becoming and change, and toward the presence of ends and values within the given? According to Idealists, reason not only discovers a coherent order in nature but also creates the state and other cultural institutions, which together constitute the cultural order of a civilized society. Idealistic political philosophers recognize the primacy of this cultural order over the private order or family and over the public order—the governing agencies and economic institutions. The conservation and enhancement of the values of all three orders is the basic moral objective of every civilized people. A useful distinction drawn by the German philosopher Ernst Cassier (1874–1946), a member of the late 19th- and 20th-century Marburg school of Neo-Kantianism (see below), between the efficient energies and the formative energies of a people emphaszes the way in which these moral forces function: the efficient energies are the conserving, and the formative are the creative forces in society. It is on the basis of this distinction that Idealists have made a contribution to international ethics, Order and
value in
nature and
society which charges that no nation has a right to use its efficient energies to exercise power over another civilized people except to further the formative energies of that people, to enrich their cultural order. Ethically, then, there can be no power over without power for; economic exploitation is wrong.

Modern Idealists have also created an Idealistic philosophy of history. An eminent early 20th-century Italian Idealist, Benedetto Croce (1866–1952), expressed it in the formula "every true history is contemporary history"; and at the same time in France a subjective Idealist, Léon Brunschvicg (1869–1944), agreed. There are close relations between the philosophy of history and the philosophy of values.

Basic arguments.   Idealists delight in arguments. They agree with Socrates and Plato in thinking that every philosopher should follow the argument wherever it leads, and, like them, they believe that it will eventually lead to some type of Idealism. Four basic arguments found in the literature of Idealism may be briefly summarized.

Epistemological issues *The esse est percipi (to be is to be perceived) argument of Berkeley.*   According to this argument all of the qualities attributed to objects are sense qualities. Thus hardness is the sensing of a resistance to a striking action, and heaviness is a sensation of muscular effort when holding the object in one's hand, just as blueness is a quality of visual experience. But these qualities exist only while they are being perceived by some subject or spirit equipped with sense organs. A classical 18th-century British Empiricist, George Berkeley (1685–1753), rejected the idea that sense perceptions are caused by material substance, the existence of which he denied. Intuitively he grasped the truth that "to be is to be perceived." The argument is a simple one, but it has provoked an extensive and complicated literature, and to some contemporary Idealists it seems irrefutable.

The reciprocity argument.   Closely related to the *esse est percipi* argument is the contention that subject and object are reciprocally dependent upon each other. It is impossible to conceive of a subject without an object, since the essential meaning of being a subject is being aware of an object and that of being an object is being an object to a subject, this relation being absolutely and universally reciprocal. Consequently, every complete reality is always a unity of subject and object—*i.e.,* an immaterial ideality, a concrete universal.

The mystical argument.   In the third argument, the Idealist holds that in man's most immediate experience, that of his own subjective awareness, the intuitive self can achieve a direct apprehension of ultimate reality, which reveals it to be spiritual. Thus the mystic bypasses normal cognition, feeling that, for metaphysical probings, the elaborate processes of mediation interposed between sense objects and their perceptions reduces its reliability as compared to the direct grasp of intuition.

It is significant that the claims of this argument have been made by numerous thinkers, in varying degrees Idealistic and mystical, living in different periods and in different cultures. In ancient Greece, for example, it was made by Plato, to whom the final leap to the Idea of the Good was mystical in nature. In Indian Hindu Vedānta philosophy it was made by the 9th-century monistic theologian Śáṅkara, by the 12th-century dualistic Brahmin theist Rāmānuja, and by the recent philosopher-president of India Sarvepalli Radhakrishnan. In Buddhism the claims were made by the sometimes mystical, extreme subjectivism of the Vijñānavāda school of Mahāyāna (represented by Aśvaghoṣa in the 1st and Asaṅga in the 4th century) and in China by the Ch'an school and by the 7th-century scholar Hui-neng, author of its basic classic *The Platform Scripture.* In Islāmic lands it was made by Ṣūfīs (mystics)—in particular, by the 13th-century Persian writer Jalāl ad-Dīn ar-Rūmī. And in the recent West it was made by several distinguished Idealists: in Germany, by the seminal modern theologian Friedrich Schleiermacher (1768–1834); in France, by the evolutionary intuitionist Henri Bergson (1859–1941), by the philosopher of action Maurice Blondel (1861–1949), and by the Jewish religious Existentialist Martin Buber (1878–1965); and in English-

speaking countries, by the Scottish metaphysician James Frederick Ferrier (1808–64) and the American Hegelian William E. Hocking (1873–1966).

The ontological argument.   This famous argument originated as a proof of the existence of God. It came to the 11th-century Augustinian, St. Anselm of Canterbury, as an intuitive insight from his personal religious experience that a being conceived to be perfect must necessarily exist, for otherwise he would lack one of the essentials of perfection. God's perfection requires his existence. Some Idealist philosophers have generalized the argument to prove Idealism. They distinguish conceptual essences that exist only in the intellect from categorial essences that actually exist *in re* (in the thing). Every actual reality, therefore, is a unity of one or more categorial essences and existence; and again, this means that it is an immaterial ideality or concrete universal. According to Hegel "the ideality of the finite" is "the main principle of philosophy."

TYPES OF PHILOSOPHICAL IDEALISM

Several types of Idealism have already been distinguished. Some modern types should now be mentioned, classified first by cultures and then by branches of philosophy.

Types classed by culture.   Cultural differences suggest a division into Western and Oriental Idealisms.

Western types.   Berkeley's Idealism is called subjective Idealism because he reduced reality to spirits (his name for subjects) and the ideas entertained by spirits. In Berkeley's philosophy the apparent objectivity of the world outside the self was accommodated to his subjectivism by claiming that its objects are ideas in the mind of God. The foundation for a series of more objective Idealisms was laid in the late 18th century by Immanuel Kant, whose epochal work *Kritik der reinen Vernunft* (2nd ed., 1787; *Critique of Pure Reason,* 1929) presented a formalistic or transcendental Idealism, so named because Kant thought that the human self, or "transcendental ego," constructs knowledge out of sense impressions, upon which are imposed certain universal concepts that he called categories. Three systems constructed in the early 19th century by, respectively, the moral Idealist J.G. Fichte, the aesthetic Idealist F.W.J. Schelling, and the dialectical Idealist G.W.F. Hegel, all on a foundation laid by Kant, are called objective Idealisms in contrast to Berkeley's subjective Idealism. The designations, however, are not consistent; and when the contrast with Berkeley is not at issue, Fichte himself is often called a subjective Idealist, inasmuch as he exalted the subject above the object, employing the term Ego to mean God in the two memorable propositions: "The Ego posits itself" and "The Ego posits the non-Ego (or nature)." And in contrast now to the subjective Idealism of Fichte, Schelling's is called an objective Idealism and Hegel's an absolute Idealism. Subjective, transcendental, objective, and absolute Idealisms

All of these terms form backgrounds for contemporary Western Idealisms, most of which are based either on Kant's transcendental Idealism or on those of Fichte, Schelling, and Hegel. Exceptions are those based on other great Idealists of the past—Plato, Plotinus, Spinoza, Leibniz, and others. A revised form of Spinoza's spiritual monism, for example, which held that reality is one Substance to be identified with God, has been formulated by the Idealist logician H.H. Joachim (1868–1938), a follower of the British Hegelian F.H. Bradley.

Unwilling to accept any of the above titles, one school of modern Idealists adopted the motto "Back to Kant" and are thus called Kantian Idealists. Edward Caird (1835–1908), who imported German Idealism into England, and the German philosopher of "As If," Hans Vaihinger (1852–1933), who held that much of man's so-called knowledge reduces to pragmatic fictions, were Kantian Idealists or transcendentalists. On this tradition are based the Idealism of the austerely religious essayist Thomas Carlyle (1795–1881) in *Sartor Resartus* (1833–34) and the New England transcendentalism of Ralph Waldo Emerson (1803–82). It must be stated, however, that Kant preferred the name critical Idealism to that of transcendental Idealism. Kantian and theistic Idealisms

Another group of Idealists, adopting the motto "From Kant forward," founded the so-called Marburg school of Neo-Kantian, or scientific, Idealism. They rejected the

Idealisms of Fichte, Schelling, and Hegel and the classical Newtonian dynamics presupposed by Kant and built instead upon the new quantum and relativity theories of modern physics. Founded by Hermann Cohen (1842–1918), champion of a new interpretation of Kant, and his colleague, the Platonic scholar Paul Natorp (1854–1924), who applied Kant's critical method to humanistic as well as to scientific studies, this school underwent a remarkable development, especially under the leadership of Ernst Cassirer, noted for his profound analyses of man defined as that animal that creates culture through a unique capacity for symbolic representation. The Russian novelist Boris Pasternak, in his *Autobiography,* tells of enrolling in Cohen's graduate seminar on Kant at the University of Marburg. Undoubtedly this type of Idealism continues to wield considerable influence on intellectuals in Soviet Russia.

Theistic Idealism was founded by the medical instructor R.H. Lotze (1817–81), who became a broadly learned metaphysician and whose theory of the world ground, in which all things find their unity, has been widely accepted by theistic philosophers and Protestant theologians. To Lotze, the world ground is the transcendent synthesis of an evolutionary world process, which is both mechanical and teleological (purposive); it is an infinite spiritual being, or God. In England, the absolute Idealism of T.H. Green (1836–82), a philosopher influenced chiefly by Plato and Kant, was shared by his disciple, the more Hegelian thinker Bernard Bosanquet (1848–1923), whose views are based upon Lotze's Idealism, and by the somewhat skeptical metaphysician of the movement, F.H. Bradley (1846–1924).

Theistic absolutism is represented by a pioneer of contemporary philosophical theology, F.R. Tennant (1866–1957), and by the eminent German-American theologian Paul Tillich (1886–1956). It differs from the personalistic form of absolute Idealism in accepting the traditional theological monotheism that is essential to the Jewish, Christian, and Islāmic religions. It revives classic arguments for the existence of God that were rejected by Kant and uses recent advances in the physical, biological, and behavioral sciences to support these revisions. The cosmological argument, for example, is restated as the continuing relation of the cosmos to a world ground that is spiritual in essence; thus the concept of God as a first cause is rejected. The concept of the fitness of the environment to life and to human history and other recent scientific concepts are used to modernize the teleological argument. Nevertheless, all of this revision is kept within the framework of Idealistic metaphysics and epistemology. A theistic spiritual pluralism, which interprets reality in terms of a multitude of interacting psychic monads (elementary units), was developed by the English philosopher James Ward (1843–1925). On the other hand, an atheistic spiritual pluralism, which holds that reality consists entirely of individual minds and their contents, was espoused by the Cambridge Hegelian J.M. Ellis McTaggert (1866–1925).

During the late 19th century a movement known as American Hegelian Idealism arose in the United States. The movement found vigorous early expression in the work of W.T. Harris (1835–1909), central figure in a midwestern group of scholars known as the St. Louis school and editor of its *Journal of Speculative Philosophy,* and finds current expression in the recently organized Hegel Society of America. In its later development, American Idealism split into two branches: one, of the aforementioned Bradley–Bosanquet type, and a second, of the Royce–Hocking type, so called because it was founded by one of America's most distinguished philosophers, the absolute Idealist and personal pantheist Josiah Royce (1855–1916), and developed by his disciple W.E. Hocking (1873–1966). The American philosopher of religion Borden Parker Bowne (1847–1910) founded another important American school, that of Personalism, a Kantian- and Lotzean-based variety of theistic Idealism similar to the spiritual pluralism of Ward. Whereas most previous Idealisms had stressed the rational as the highest category of reality and hence as its paradigm, Personalism saw in the centred structures of personhood, both finite and infinite, an even higher category, displaying dimensions richer than the rational alone. Personalism has had an influential development in America, most notably through the Methodist philosopher E.S. Brightman (1884–1953), known for his defense of the doctrine of a finite God, and through *The Personalist,* edited by one of Bowne's disciples, R.T. Flewelling (1871–1960). Personalism is also found in the French philosopher C.B. Renouvier (1815–1903) and in several Latin American philosophers.

To the above types should be added the vitalism or creative evolutionism of the French anti-intellectualist Henri Bergson (1859–1941), which first found in the apprehension of subjective time a more valid insight into reality than in that of an objective space–time order and then, extending this metaphysics to the cosmic level, discerned there an Idealistic *élan vital* (or vital impetus) that is more fundamental than matter, which subsequently appeared in the role of a husk born of the mechanization of the *élan.* In this same tradition, the voluntarism of Maurice Blondel (1861–1949), a unique theory of belief in God as a live option that must be deliberately willed by the self before it can be found to be true in experience, is an important contribution to Idealistic philosophy. Miguel de Unamuno y Jugo (1864–1936), a Spanish philosopher, developed a unique type of Idealism, more literary than philosophical. He stressed the significance of each individual and argued for personal immortality.

Eastern types. For centuries, philosophical Idealism has dominated the philosophy of India. An Idealism that is quite influential in Japan is that of Nishida Kitarō, a distinguished Berlin-trained philosopher. Prior to World War II, Kitarō created a system of absolute Idealism that employed the dialectical method of Hegel to clarify the Zen Buddhist doctrine of nothingness, which, in his view, is that of which all phenomenal existences are determinations and in which they all appear.

Some classical types of Indian and Chinese Idealism were considered above (see *The mystical argument*). A number of gifted Indian and Chinese scholars have restated and revitalized the principles and arguments of classic Oriental Idealisms in an extensive literature.

Probably the major recent proponent of Indian Idealism has been Radhakrishnan, who has spent a long lifetime expounding and defending its mystical types and has presented authoritative analyses of all of its classical systems. He saw his modernized Idealism as destined to save civilization from exploitation by Western commercial technology. Surendranath Dasgupta, an outstanding Sanskrit and Pāli scholar, in a monumental work, has revived the classic systems of Indian Idealism, concluding that "Idealism has not only been one of the most dominant phases of Indian thought in metaphysics, epistemology, and dialectics, but it has also very largely influenced the growth of the Indian ideal as a whole." Ghose Aurobindo, reinterpreting the Indian Idealistic heritage in the light of his own Western education, rejected the *māyā* doctrine of illusion, replacing it with the concept of evolution. Arguing that the "illumination of individuals will lead to the emergence of a divine community," Aurobindo founded the influential Pondicherry Ashram, a religious and philosophical community, and headed it until his death. Late in the 19th century, Swami Vivekananda, a spiritual monist, promulgated the Idealistic philosophy of mystical Brahmanism in lectures on the Vedānta delivered and published widely.

The inwardness of subjectivity of Indian Idealism has been contrasted with the outwardness of Western objective Idealism, and a synthesis of the two has been advocated in comparative studies made by P.T. Raju, an Indian philosopher who has taught both in Indian universities and in the U.S.

Prior to World War II, Sir Rabindranath Tagore, a distinguished Hindu Idealist poet and Nobel laureate, contributed to what Dasgupta has called the "Indian ideal as a whole." A selection from Tagore's aphorisms will convey its spirit:

Let your life lightly dance on the edges of Time like dew on the tip of a leaf.
Our little heaven, where dwell only two immortals, is too absurdly narrow.

Is it then true that the mystery of the Infinite is written on
this little forehead of mine?
Where is this hope for union except in thee my God?
Raise my veil and look at my face proudly, O Death, my
Death.
All is done and finished in the eternal Heaven. But Earth's
flowers of illusion are kept externally fresh by death.
If my claims to immortal fame after death are shattered, make
me immortal while I live.
This I know that the moment my God has created me he has
made himself mine.

Chinese Idealism

In addition to the Ch'an and Hui-neng schools mentioned
above (see *The mystical argument*), three other notable
Idealistic schools have flourished in China. Representing
one wing of the Neo-Confucian movement of the 11th and
12th centuries, Ch'eng Hao and his disciple, the rationalist
Chu Hsi, developed a dualistic philosophy that has been
compared to Cartesianism. In this view, however, reason
takes precedence over matter and the two together are the
primary cause of the universe or the absolute; thus this
view is essentially Idealistic. At the turn of the 15th century, a more purely Idealistic school arose—forming the
other wing of Neo-Confucianism—under the leadership of
Wang Yang-ming, who, having had an inner experience
of enlightenment, sought to understand the cosmos within
his own mind and heart. The third school is that of the
20th-century Idealist Hsung Shih-li, who, borrowing to
some extent from Wang Yang-ming, proclaimed a "new
doctrine of consciousness only," of which the basic ideas
are the unity of substance and function and the primacy
of the original Mind. To Hsung Shih-li, reality and all of
its manifestations are one, and the original Mind is will
and consciousness as well as reason.

Types classed by branches of philosophy. Another way
of classifying Idealisms is to use branches of philosophy to
distinguish the various types. Such types, however, overlap
those given above.

Metaphysical, epistemological, and axiological Idealisms

A term that covers several of the above types (the
spiritual, theistic, and Hegelian; Personalism; vitalism)
is metaphysical Idealism. A.N. Whitehead (1861–1947),
noted for his collaboration with Bertrand Russell in mathematical logic and for his process metaphysics, who was
profoundly influenced by Bradley, created an original Idealistic philosophy of science, a highly complicated form
of metaphysical Idealism; and the leading metaphysician
Charles Hartshorne (1897–   ) may be regarded as a representative of Whiteheadian Idealism, although rightly
claiming originality. Epistemological Idealism, of which
the Kantian scholar N.K. Smith's (1872–1958) *Prolegomena to an Idealist Theory of Knowledge* is an excellent
example, covers all Idealistic theories of epistemology, or
knowledge. Aesthetic Idealism is devoted to philosophical theories of beauty in nature and in all forms of art.
Because Schelling claimed that art is the best approach
to an understanding of philosophy, his system is designated aesthetic Idealism. Axiological Idealism is a name
referring to such philosophies as those of Wilbur M.
Urban (1873–1952) and others who have developed Idealistic theories of value and valuation. Ethical Idealism
deals with moral values, rights, and obligations. Several
of the above-mentioned philosophers, such as Fichte and
Green, as well as the Plato scholar A.E. Taylor (1864–
1945), the theistic pluralist Hastings Rashdall (1858–
1924), and the absolutist W.R. Sorley (1855–1935), could
be called ethical Idealists in the sense that they have
produced well-thought-out systems of ethics. The writings
of the German philosopher of life and action Rudolf
Eucken (1846–1926) provide an excellent example of ethical Idealism.

These classifications are not exhaustive. The actual existence of so many types of philosophical Idealism, however,
proves its fertility and ubiquity.

CRITICISM AND APPRAISAL

Obviously, some of the types of Idealism in the above
classifications conflict with one another. For example, spiritual monism and spiritual pluralism are opposite types;
Personalism rejects absolute Idealism; and atheistic spiritual pluralism is in sharp conflict with theistic spiritual
pluralism. These and other debatable issues keep Ideal-

ists in dialogue with each other, but each type tends to
preserve itself.

Over against these internal disputes stand the criticisms **Perry,**
of the anti-Idealists. The wide-ranging Realist Ralph Bar- **Moore,**
ton Perry's (1876–1957) article "The Ego-Centric Predica- **Positivism,**
ment" (1910) is a widely discussed criticism. Perry ad- **Marxism**
mitted that the primary approach of every philosopher to
the problem of ultimate reality must be through his own
thought, using his own ideas; but this is a human predicament that has been unjustifiably exploited by the Idealists,
according to Perry, and turned into the "fallacious" *esse
est percipi* argument.

The famous "Refutation of Idealism" prepared by the
meticulous Cambridge philosopher G.E. Moore (1873–
1958) and a similar refutation by the Realist Bertrand
Russell (1872–1970) rest upon the distinction between a
subject's act of perceiving and the perceptual object of this
act, which they both called a "sense datum." They claimed
that Berkeley's *esse est percipi* argument is vitiated by his
failure to make this distinction.

Logical Positivism claims that a basic weakness in Idealism is its rejection of the doctrine of empirical verifiability, according to which every proposition that claims
to be true must be verified by searching out the sense
experience in which its terms originated. Linguistic philosophy attacks Idealism by making a detailed analysis of
its more technical terms in an effort to prove that they
are full of ambiguities and double meanings. Critics have
also severely attacked the ontological and the mystical
arguments for Idealism. Karl Marx (1818–83) and his
followers borrowed and adapted the dialectical argument
of Hegel and used it effectively to develop dialectical Materialism, an archenemy of all Idealisms. Buttressed by
the political endorsements of various Communist regimes,
Marxism (*q.v.*) poses a formidable opposition to Idealism;
and even in the non-Communist countries of Europe it
presents a significant cultural alternative to spiritualism
and Thomism.

Idealists consider all of the foregoing criticisms to be external. Instead of answering them in detail, some Idealists
prefer to challenge the critics to make really constructive
efforts to build an adequate substitute for Idealism—a
system to be reached by seriously working at the problems
from within philosophy. So far a satisfactory substitute has
not been achieved. To produce such a substitute would
require careful reconsideration of the arguments of at least
some of the above Idealistic systems.

In evaluating the effects of these criticisms and attacks, **Prognosis**
the question remains: Will they succeed in eradicating
philosophical Idealism? Although it is now on the wane,
at least in Western culture, the great Idealist tradition
has survived many other historic periods of turmoil and
has often been reborn in prolonged periods of settled and
peaceful social conditions. Will it rise again? Only the
future holds the answer. But Idealism shows evidence of
being, perhaps, a reflection of some permanent aspect of
the human spirit, and it may then be a perennial philosophy. In any case, it seems highly unlikely that such a rich
heritage of philosophical thought will vanish entirely.

(D.S.R.)

Materialism

The word Materialism has been used in modern times to
refer to a family of metaphysical theories (*i.e.,* theories on
the nature of reality) that can best be defined by saying
that a theory tends to be called Materialism if it is felt sufficiently to resemble a paradigmatic theory that will here
be called mechanical Materialism. This section covers the
various types of Materialism and the ways by which they
are distinguished and traces the history of Materialism
from the Greeks and Romans to modern and contemporary Materialisms.

TYPES OF MATERIALIST THEORY

Mechanical Materialism is the theory that the world
consists entirely of hard, massy material objects, which,
though perhaps imperceptibly small, are otherwise like
such things as stones. (A slight modification is to allow

the void—or empty space—to exist also in its own right.) These objects interact in the sort of way that stones do: by impact and possibly also by gravitational attraction. The theory denies that immaterial or apparently immaterial things (such as minds) exist or else explains them away as being material things or motions of material things.

Physicalistic, deistic, emergent, and epiphenomenal types

Types distinguished by departures from the paradigm. In modern physics (if interpreted realistically), however, matter is conceived as made up of such things as electrons, protons, and mesons, which are very unlike the hard, massy, stonelike particles of mechanical Materialism. In it the distinction between matter and energy has also broken down. It is therefore natural to extend the word Materialist beyond the above paradigm case (of mechanical Materialism) to cover anyone who bases his theory on whatever it is that physics asserts ultimately to exist. This sort may be called physicalistic Materialism. Such a Materialist allows the concept of material thing to be extended so as to include all of the elementary particles and other things that are postulated in fundamental physical theory—perhaps even continuous fields and points of space-time. Inasmuch as some cosmologists even try to define the elementary particles themselves in terms of the curvature of space-time, there is no reason why a philosophy based on such a geometricized cosmology should not be counted as Materialist, provided that it does not give an independent existence to nonphysical things such as minds.

Another sort of departure from the paradigm leads in the direction of what might be called a deistic Materialism. In this view it would be allowed that, although there is a spiritual Creator of the universe, he does not interfere with the created universe, which is itself describable in terms of mechanical or physicalist Materialism.

Still another departure from the paradigm is the theory that holds that everything is composed of material particles (or physical entities generally) but also holds that there are special laws applying to complexes of physical entities, such as living cells or brains, that are not reducible to the laws that apply to the fundamental physical entities. (To avoid inconsistency, such a theory may have to allow that the ordinary laws of physics do not wholly apply within such complex entities.) Such a theory, which could be called "emergent Materialism," can shade off, however, into theories that one would not wish to call Materialist, such as hylozoism, which ascribes vital characteristics to all matter, and panpsychism, which attributes a mindlike character to all constituents of material things.

Another common relaxation of the paradigm is that which allows as compatible with Materialism such a theory as epiphenomenalism, according to which sensations and thoughts do exist in addition to material processes but are nonetheless wholly dependent on material processes and without causal efficacy of their own. They are related to material things somewhat in the way that a man's shadow is related to the man. A similar departure from the paradigm is a form of what might be called "double-aspect Materialism," according to which in inner experience men are acquainted with nonphysical *properties* of material processes, though these properties are not causally effective. A form of double-aspect theory in which these properties were allowed to be causally effective would be a species of emergent Materialism.

Of course, more than one of these qualifications might be made at the same time: thus a person might wish to speak of "physicalist deistic epiphenomenalist Materialism." If no other qualifications are intended, it is convenient to use the word extreme and to speak, for example, of "extreme physicalist Materialism"—which is probably the type most discussed among professional philosophers in English-speaking countries.

Dialectical Materialism

Type distinguished by its view of history. In the wider world, however, the word Materialism most commonly brings to mind dialectical Materialism, which is the orthodox philosophy of Communist countries. This is most importantly a theory of how changes arise in human history, though a general metaphysical theory lies in the background. Dialectical Materialists contrast their view with what they call "vulgar" Materialism; and it does, indeed, appear that their theory is not an extreme Mate-

rialism, whether mechanical or physicalist. They seem to hold merely that mental processes are dependent on or have evolved from material ones. Though they might be akin to emergent Materialists, it is hard to be sure; their assertion that something new emerges at higher levels of organization might refer only to such things as that a wireless receiver is different from a mere heap of the same components. And if so, even an extreme physicalistic Materialist could acquiesce in this view. The distinctive features of dialectical Materialism would, thus, seem to lie as much in its being dialectical as in its being Materialist. Its dialectical side may be epitomized in three laws: (1) that of the transformation of quality into quantity, (2) that of the interpenetration of opposites, and (3) that of the negation of the negation. Nondialectical philosophers find it hard, however, to interpret these laws in a way that does not make them into either platitudes or falsehoods.

Perhaps because of the historical determinism implicit in dialectical Materialism, and perhaps because of memories of the mechanical Materialist theories of the 18th and 19th centuries, when physics was deterministic, it is popularly supposed that Materialism and determinism must go together. This is not so. As indicated below, even some ancient Materialists were indeterminists, and a modern physicalist Materialism must be indeterministic because of the indeterminism that is built into modern physics. Modern physics does imply, however, that macroscopic bodies behave in a way that is effectively deterministic, and, because even a single neuron (nerve fibre) is a macroscopic object by quantum mechanical standards, a physicalistic Materialist may still regard the human brain as coming near to being a mechanism that behaves in a deterministic way.

Central-state Materialism and analytical behaviourism

Types distinguished by their account of mind. A rather different way of classifying Materialist theories, which to some extent cuts across the classifications already made, emerges when the theories are divided according to the way in which a Materialist accounts for minds. A central-state Materialist identifies mental processes with processes in the brain. An analytical behaviourist, on the other hand, argues that, in talking about the mind, one is not talking about an actual entity, whether the brain or an immaterial soul, but, rather, one is somehow talking about the way in which people would behave in various circumstances. According to the analytical behaviourist, there is no more of a problem for the Materialist in having to identify mind with something material than there is in identifying such an abstraction as the average plumber with some concrete entity. Analytical behaviourism differs from psychological behaviourism, which is merely a methodological program to base theories on behavioral evidence and to eschew introspective reports. The analytical behaviourist usually has a not too plausible theory of introspective reports according to which they are what are sometimes called "avowals": roughly, he contends that to say "I have a pain" is to engage in a verbal surrogate for a wince. Epistemic Materialism is a theory that can be developed either in the direction of central-state Materialism or in that of analytical behaviourism and that rests on the contention that the only statements that are intersubjectively testable are either observation reports about macroscopic physical objects or statements that imply such observation reports (or are otherwise logically related to them).

Before leaving this survey of the family of Materialistic theories, a quite different sense of the word Materialism should be noted in which it denotes not a metaphysical theory but an ethical attitude. A person is a Materialist in this sense if he is interested mainly in sensuous pleasures and bodily comforts and hence in the material possessions that bring these about. A man might be a Materialist in this ethical and pejorative sense without being a metaphysical Materialist, and conversely. An extreme physicalistic Materialist, for example, might prefer a Beethoven record to a comfortable mattress for his bed; and a person who believes in immaterial spirits might opt for the mattress.

HISTORY OF MATERIALISM

Greek and Roman Materialism. Though Thales of Miletus (*c.* 580 BC) and some of the other Pre-Socratic philosophers have some claims to being regarded as Materialists, the Materialist tradition in Western philosophy really begins with Leucippus and Democritus, Greek philosophers who were born in the 5th century BC. Leucippus is known only through his influence on Democritus. According to Democritus, the world consists of nothing but atoms (indivisible chunks of matter) in empty space (which he seems to have thought of as an entity in its own right). These atoms can be imperceptibly small, and they interact either by impact or by hooking together, depending on their shapes. The great beauty of atomism was its ability to explain the changes in things as due to changes in the configurations of unchanging atoms. The view may be contrasted with that of the earlier philosopher Anaxagoras (c. 480 BC), who thought that when, for example, the bread that a person eats is transformed into human flesh, this must occur because bread itself already contains hidden within itself the characteristics of flesh. Democritus thought that the soul consists of smooth, round atoms and that perceptions consist of motions caused in the soul atoms by the atoms in the perceived thing (see above *Atomism*).

Because Epicurus' philosophy was expounded in a lengthy poem by Lucretius, a Roman philosopher of the 1st century BC, Epicurus (died 270 BC) was easily the most influential Greek Materialist. He differed from Democritus in that he postulated an absolute up–down direction in space, so that all atoms fall in roughly parallel paths. To explain their impacts with one another, he then held that the atoms are subject to chance swerves—a doctrine that was also used to explain free will. Epicurus' Materialism therefore differed from that of Democritus in being an indeterministic one. Epicurus' philosophy contained an important ethical part, which was a sort of enlightened egoistic hedonism (see above *Epicureanism*). His ethics, however, were not Materialistic in the pejorative sense of the word.

Modern Materialism. Materialism languished throughout the medieval period, but the Epicurean tradition was revived in the first half of the 17th century in the atomistic Materialism of the French Catholic priest Pierre Gassendi. In putting forward his system as a hypothesis to explain the facts of experience, Gassendi showed that he understood the method characteristic of modern science, and he may well have helped to pave the way for corpuscular hypotheses in physics. Gassendi was not thoroughgoing in his Materialism inasmuch as he accepted on faith the Christian doctrine that men have immortal souls. His contemporary, the English philosopher Thomas Hobbes, also propounded an atomistic Materialism and was a pioneer in trying to work out a mechanistic and physiological psychology. Holding that sensations are corporeal motions in the brain, Hobbes skirted, rather than solved, the philosophical problems about consciousness that had been raised by another contemporary, the great French philosopher René Descartes. Descartes's philosophy was dualistic, making a complete split between mind and matter. In his theory of the physical world, however, and especially in his doctrine that animals are automata, Descartes's own system had a mechanistic side to it that was taken up by 18th-century Materialists, such as Julien de La Mettrie, the French physician whose appropriately titled *L'Homme machine* (1747; *Man a Machine,* 1750) applied Descartes's view about animals to man himself. Denis Diderot, an 18th-century French Encyclopaedist, supported a broadly Materialist outlook by considerations drawn from physiology, embryology, and the study of heredity; and his friend Paul, baron d'Holbach, published his *Système de la nature* (1770), which expounded a deterministic type of Materialism in the light of evidence from contemporary science, reducing everything to matter and to the energy inherent in matter. He also propounded a hedonistic ethics as well as an uncompromising atheism, which provoked a reply even from the Deist Voltaire.

The 18th-century French Materialists had been reacting against orthodox Christianity. In the early part of the 19th century, however, certain writers in Germany—usually with a biological or medical background—reacted against a different orthodoxy, the Hegelian and Neo-Hegelian tra-

dition in philosophy, which had become entrenched in German universities. Among these were Ludwig Büchner and Karl Vogt. The latter is notorious for his assertion that the brain secretes thought just as the liver secretes bile. This metaphor of secretion, previously used by P.-J.-G. Cabanis, a late 18th-century French Materialist, is seldom taken seriously, because to most philosophers it does not make sense to think of thought as a *stuff*. The Hobbesian view, also espoused by Büchner, that thought is a *motion* in the brain is usually viewed as a more promising one.

The synthesis of urea (the chief nitrogenous end product of protein metabolism), discovered in 1828, broke down the discontinuity between the organic and the inorganic in chemistry, which had been a mainstay of nonmaterialistic biology. Materialist ways of thinking were later strengthened enormously by the Darwinian theory of evolution, which not only showed the continuity between man and other living things right back to the simplest organisms but also showed how the apparent evidences of design in natural history could be explained on a purely causal basis. There still seemed to be a gap, however, between the living and the nonliving, though E.H. Haeckel, a 19th-century German zoologist, thought that certain simple organisms could have been generated from inorganic matter and, indeed, that a certain simple sea creature may well be in process of generation in this way even now. Though Haeckel was wrong, 20th-century biologists have proposed much more sophisticated and more plausible theories of the evolution of life from inorganic matter. Haeckel and his contemporary, the British zoologist T.H. Huxley, did much to popularize philosophical accounts of the world that were consonant with the scientific thought of their time, but neither could be regarded as an extreme Materialist.

Contemporary Materialism. Perhaps because recent developments in biochemistry and in physiological psychology have greatly increased the plausibility of Materialism, there has lately been a resurgence of interest in the philosophical defense of central-state Materialism. Central-state Materialists have proposed their theories partly because of dissatisfaction with the analytical behaviourism of the Oxford philosopher Gilbert Ryle. Ryle himself is reluctant to call himself a Materialist, partly because of a dislike of all "isms" and partly because he thinks that the notion of matter has meaning only by contrast with that of mind, which he thinks to be an illegitimate sort of contrast. Nevertheless, it would seem that analytical behaviourism could be used to support a physicalist Materialism that would go on to explain human behaviour by means of neural mechanisms. (Ryle himself is suspicious of mechanistic accounts of biology and psychology.) Analytical behaviourism has been felt to be unsatisfactory, however, chiefly because of its account of introspective reports as avowals (see above), which most philosophers have found to be unconvincing.

Philosophers have distinguished two forms of central-state Materialism, namely, the translation form and the disappearance form. The translation form is the view that mentalistic discourse can be translated into discourse that is neutral between physicalism and dualism, so that the truth of a man's introspective reports is compatible with the objects of these reports being physical processes. The disappearance form is the view that such a translation cannot be done and that this fact, however, does not refute physicalism but shows only that man's ordinary introspective reports are contaminated by false theories.

Translation central-state theories. Among the philosophers who have advocated the translation form is the U.S. philosopher Herbert Feigl, earlier a member of the Vienna Circle, who, in an influential monograph (see *Bibliography*), did the most to get contemporary philosophers to treat central-state Materialism as a serious philosophical theory. Against the objection that, for example, "visual sensation" does not *mean* "process in the visual cortex," advocates of the translation form point out that "the morning star" does not mean the same as "the evening star," and yet the morning star as a matter of fact *is* the evening star. The objection confuses meaning and reference. Against the objection that a purely physical process (a dance of electrons, protons, and so on) cannot have the sensory quality of greenness that is observed in a visual experience of seeing grass, say, they reply that to talk of the sensory experience of something looking green (or having a green mental image) is not to talk of anything that is literally green, but is simply to report that some internal process is of the sort that normally goes with seeing something, such as a lawn, which really is green. Though an immaterialist might say that the sort of process in question is a spiritual process, the Materialist can equally claim that it is a material process in the brain. The analysis of the introspective report is neutral between these two contentions; the Materialist, however, opts for his contention on various grounds. The British Materialist U.T. Place does so on the ground of normal scientific methodology; and the Australian Materialist J.J.C. Smart does so with a metaphysical application of the principle (called "Ockham's razor") that entities should not be multiplied beyond necessity. A physicalistic Materialist has, of course, an obligation to go on to give a suitable account of such apparently nonphysicalist qualities as the greenness of grass. At one time Smart analyzed colours in terms of the discriminatory behaviour of human beings. Another Australian Materialist, D.M. Armstrong, holds, on the other hand, that colours are as a matter of fact properties of objects, such properties being of the sort describable in the theoretical terms of physics. Feigl, in turn, is to some extent (and rather reluctantly) a double-aspect theorist. He qualifies the position taken by the other translation theorists, conceding that the translations do leave something out, viz., the immediately introspectable properties of "raw feels," such as that of hearing the tone of middle C. He holds, however, that such properties are irrelevant to causal explanations of phenomena. The translation form of central-state Materialism thus has some affinities with the earlier epistemic Materialism of the Positivist philosophers Rudolf Carnap and Hans Reichenbach, Germans who settled in the United States. Thus Carnap has suggested that mental predicates be treated as applying to material entities: for example, "Carnap sees green" could be taken as meaning "the body Carnap is in the state of green-seeing," the state of green-seeing being a purely physical state that explains the behavioral facts that led one to ascribe the predicate "sees green" to Carnap in the first place. David K. Lewis, a United States philosopher of science and language, has developed a translation form of central-state Materialism on the basis of a theory regarding the definition of theoretical terms in science. According to this theory, entities such as electrons, protons, and neutrons are defined in terms of the causal roles that they play in relation to observational phenomena—*e.g.*, phenomena in cloud chambers—but the method of definition is able to do justice to the causal and other interrelations between the theoretical entities themselves. Lewis applies this account to commonsense psychology. Since mental entities, such as pains, are defined in commonsense psychology in terms of their causal roles (in relation to observable behaviour) and since there is empirical reason to ascribe the same causal roles to brain processes, Lewis identifies mental events, processes, and states with brain events, processes, and states.

Disappearance central-state theories. The disappearance form of central-state Materialism is the sort of theory held by P.K. Feyerabend, a U.S. philosopher, who denies that the Materialist can give a neutral analysis of introspective reports. In Feyerabend's view, commonsense introspective reports are irreducibly immaterialist in content. He argues, however, that this admission does not show the untenability of Materialism. Ordinary mentalistic discourse, he holds, is comparable to the medieval discourse about epileptics as being "possessed by the devil." If one now "identified" demon possession with a certain medical condition of the brain, this would really be an assertion that there is no such thing as a demon-possessed state: the medieval way of looking at the matter is thus rejected. It is in this sort of way that Feyerabend wants to "identify" the mind with the brain: he simply rejects the ordinary mentalistic conceptual scheme and so feels no obligation to show its compatibility with Materialism.

The influential American philosophers W.V. Quine and Wilfrid Sellars also hold theories that could be regarded as disappearance forms of physicalistic Materialism, though there is a Kantian twist to Sellars' philosophy that makes it hard to classify. Sellars holds that mentalistic concepts cannot be eliminated from man's commonsense picture of the world, which he calls "the manifest image." In a way reminiscent of Kant he holds that, although the manifest image is inescapable, it does not give metaphysical truth about the world as it really is in itself. This truth is given, instead, by "the scientific image"—*i.e.*, by theoretical science, which is physicalist. In the case of Quine, there is a certain Platonism in that he believes in the objective reality of nonspatiotemporal entities, viz., those that are the subject matter of pure mathematics. Because he holds that the reason for believing mathematics is that it is needed as part of physical theory, his reasons for believing in numbers and the like are not in principle different from those for believing in electrons; thus Quine's Platonism does not really compromise his physicalism.

The Austrian philosopher Ludwig Wittgenstein, who lived to the mid-20th century and was professor of philosophy at Cambridge University, has sometimes been interpreted as a behaviourist, though his insistence that an inner process stands in need of outward criteria could possibly be interpreted as a sort of epistemic and central-state Materialism. Nevertheless, to count Wittgenstein as a Materialist would be to take considerable liberties with him; for, while displaying at times a certain mystical attitude, he also held very strongly that the business of a philosopher is not to put forward any metaphysical theory but to clear up conceptual confusions—to show the fly the way out of the fly bottle.

Eastern Materialism. This historical survey has been concerned with Materialism in Western philosophy. On the whole, Materialism is contrary to the spirit of both Indian and traditional Chinese philosophy, though the Cārvāka school of Materialists flourished from the 6th century BC until medieval times in India. Mention should also be made of the strong naturalistic tendency in Theravāda Buddhism, as also in certain schools of Chinese philosophy that exalt *ch'i* ("ether" or "material force") above principle and mind.

SUBSTANTIVE ISSUES IN MATERIALISM

Reductionism, consciousness, and brain. The main attraction of Materialism today is the way in which it fits in with a unified picture of science—a picture that has become very plausible. Thus, chemistry is reducible to physics inasmuch as there is a quantum-mechanical theory of the chemical bond. Biology is mainly an application of physics and chemistry to the structures described in natural history (including the natural history that one can explore through powerful microscopes). Increasingly, biological explanations resemble explanations in engineering, in which material structures are described and then the laws of physics and chemistry are used to explain the behaviour of these structures. (In the biological case, of course, these structures are often dynamic in the sense that their molecules are continually being replaced.) Through the influence of neurophysiology and also cybernetics (the science of information and control, which can be applied also to artificial automata), scientific psychology is also fitting well into the same mechanistic scheme. The recalcitrant residue appears in the phenomena of consciousness. Here mental events seem, indeed, to be correlated with physical events; but, if the mental events are not the very same as the physical events, one is left with apparently ultimate (or irreducible) physical–mental laws that do not fit happily into unified science, and one is thus faced with a situation unlike that of the rest of science. Looking at science generally, one expects *ultimate* laws to relate simple entities, such as fundamental particles. A physical–mental law, however, would have to refer to something very complex—a brain process involving perhaps millions of neurons, with each neuron being itself an almost fantastically complex entity. There would be a multitude of physical–mental laws, which would look like excrescences on the face of science. Because they would not fit into

Margin note left: Feyerabend, Quine, Sellars, Wittgenstein

Margin note right: Unified science and physical–mental laws the network of scientific laws, Herbert Feigl has called them "nomological danglers." To get rid of these danglers is one of the chief attractions of Materialism. Of course, an immaterialist might assert that mental entities exist and also that there are no physical–mental laws. But it might be hard for him to reconcile this position with the empirical evidence; and in any case he would be faced with the problem of how to distinguish the free exercise of such anomalous physical–mental interaction from mere chance behaviour.

The development of computers and other devices to take over much of the more routine sort of human behaviour has led to attempts on the part of scientists and technologists, such as the American M.L. Minsky, to develop real artificial intelligence. So far, the success that these scientists hoped for has not been achieved. An American linguistic theorist, Noam Chomsky, has argued on the basis of his theories of generative grammar that the brain is quite unlike any already-understood type of mechanism. Indeed, any physicalistic Materialist must certainly concede that there are very deep problems about the brain, which apparently can no longer be thought of as a bundle of conditioned reflex mechanisms or the like, as it often has seemed to be to many psychologists. The physicalist can stress, however, that the investigator's ignorance need not lead him to assume that he will never be able to find an explanation of intelligence and of linguistic abilities in terms consonant with his present notion of a physical mechanism. (There is also the possibility that physical laws not yet discovered might be needed to explain the workings of the brain. So long as these turned out to be basic laws of physics, such discoveries would not imply a shift to emergentist Materialism.)

Artificial intelligence and generative grammar

Logic, intentionality, and psychical research. Some philosophers, such as the Oxford philosopher J.R. Lucas, have tried to produce positive arguments against a mechanistic theory of mind by employing certain discoveries in mathematical logic, especially Gödel's theorem, which implies that no axiomatic theory could possibly capture all arithmetical truths. In general, philosophers have not found such attempts to extract an antimaterialist philosophy from mathematical logic to be convincing. Nevertheless, the problems of mechanizing intelligence, including the mathematical abilities of human beings, do pose unsolved problems that the Materialist is obliged to take seriously.

Perhaps the most common challenge to Materialism comes from philosophers who hold that it cannot do justice to the concept of intentionality, which Franz Brentano, a pre-World War I German philosopher, made the distinguishing mark between the mental and the nonmental. (A related objection is that Materialism cannot do justice to the distinction between behaviour and mere bodily movements.) Brentano held that mental events and states somehow point toward objects beyond themselves (or have a "content"). Many contemporary philosophers agree with Brentano that purely physical entities cannot have this property. If it is said, for example, that punched holes on the tape of a computer can refer beyond themselves in the way that thoughts do, then it is commonly replied that, in themselves, the holes on the tape have no reference or content—for this belongs only to the thoughts in the mind of a person who reads the tape. The Materialist reply may be to argue, however, that there is a fundamental unclarity in the very notion of intentionality (this is roughly Quine's position) or else to argue that purely physical systems can, after all, possess intentionality.

The alleged spiritualistic and other phenomena reported in psychical research are sometimes adduced against Materialism. The Materialist, however, can well afford to postpone discussion of these phenomena until such time as they are accepted by the general scientific community, which on the whole still remains skeptical of them.

At present, there are reputable philosophers who accept Materialism, and there are also reputable philosophers who either reject it as false or hold that it is not the business of a philosopher to propound any sort of metaphysical system. Perhaps Materialists are still in a minority; but at any rate there is much less tendency than there was a generation ago for this type of theory to be thought philosophically naive.

(J.J.C.S.)

Phenomenology

In the 20th century, Phenomenology is mainly used as the name for a philosophical movement the primary objective of which is the direct investigation and description of phenomena as consciously experienced, without theories about their causal explanation and as free as possible from unexamined preconceptions and presuppositions. The word itself is much older, going back at least to the 18th century, when the Swiss-German mathematician and philosopher Johann Heinrich Lambert applied it to that part of his theory of knowledge that distinguishes truth from illusion and error. In the 19th century the word became associated chiefly with the *Phänomenologie des Geistes* (1807; *Phenomenology of Mind,* 2nd ed., 1931), by G.W.F. Hegel, who traced the development of the human spirit from mere sense experience to "absolute knowledge." The so-called Phenomenological movement did not get under way, however, until early in the 20th century. But even this new Phenomenology includes so many varieties that a comprehensive characterization of the subject requires their consideration.

CHARACTERISTICS OF PHENOMENOLOGY

In view of the spectrum of Phenomenologies that have issued directly or indirectly from the original work of the Austrian-born German philosopher Edmund Husserl, it is not easy to find a common denominator for such a movement beyond its common source. But similar situations occur in other philosophical as well as non-philosophical movements.

Essential features and variations. Although, as seen from Husserl's last perspective, all departures from his own views could only appear as heresies, a more generous assessment will show that all those who consider themselves Phenomenologists subscribe, for instance, to his watchword, *Zu den Sachen selbst* ("To the things themselves"), by which they meant the taking of a fresh approach to concretely experienced phenomena, an approach, as free as possible from conceptual presuppositions, and the attempt to describe them as faithfully as possible. Moreover, most adherents to Phenomenology hold that it is possible to obtain insights into the essential structures and the essential relationships of these phenomena on the basis of a careful study of concrete examples supplied by experience or imagination and by a systematic variation of these examples in imagination. Some Phenomenologists also stress the need for studying the ways in which the phenomena appear in men's object-directed ("intentional") consciousness.

"To the things themselves"

Beyond this merely static aspect of appearance, some also want to investigate its genetic aspect, exploring, for instance, how the phenomenon intended—for example, a book—shapes ("constitutes") itself in the typical unfolding of experience. Husserl himself believed that such studies require a previous suspension of belief in the reality of these phenomena, whereas others consider it not indispensable but helpful. Finally, in existential Phenomenology, the meanings of certain phenomena (such as anxiety) are explored by a special interpretive ("hermeneutic") Phenomenology, the methodology of which needs further clarification.

Contrasts with related movements. It may also be helpful to bring out the distinctive essence of Phenomenology by confronting it with some of its philosophical neighbours. In contrast to Positivism and to traditional Empiricism, from which Husserl's teacher at Vienna, Franz Brentano, had started out and with which Phenomenology shares an unconditional respect for the positive data of experience ("We are the true positivists," Husserl claimed in his *Ideen zu einer reinen Phänomenologie und phänomenologischen Philosophie* [1913; "Ideas for a Pure Phenomenology and Phenomenological Philosophy"]), Phenomenology does not restrict these data to the range of sense experience but admits on equal terms such non-sensory ("categorial") data as relations and values, as long as they present themselves intuitively. Consequently, Phenomenology does not reject universals; and, in addition to analytic a priori statements, whose predicates are logically contained in the subjects and the truth of which is independent of experience (*e.g.*, "All material bodies have extension"), and the synthetic a posteriori statements, whose subjects do not logically imply the predicate and the truth of which is dependent on experience (*e.g.*, "My shirt is red"), it recognizes knowledge of the synthetic a priori, a proposition whose subject does not logically imply the predicate but one in which the truth is independent of experience (*e.g.*, "Every colour is extended"), based on insight into essential relationships within the empirically given.

In contrast to phenomenalism, a position in the theory of knowledge (epistemology) with which it is often confused, Phenomenology—which is not primarily an epistemological theory—accepts neither the rigid division between appearance and reality nor the narrower view that phenomena are all that there is (sensations or permanent possibilities of sensations). These are questions on which Phenomenology as such keeps an open mind—pointing out, however, that phenomenalism overlooks the complexities of the intentional structure of men's consciousness of the phenomena.

In contrast to a Rationalism that stresses conceptual reasoning at the expense of experience, Phenomenology insists on the intuitive foundation and verification of concepts and especially of all a priori claims; in this sense it is a philosophy from "below," not from "above."

In contrast to an Analytic philosophy that substitutes simplified constructions for the immediately given in all of its complexity and applies "Ockham's razor," Phenomenology resists all transforming reinterpretations of the given, analyzing it for what it is in itself and on its own terms.

Phenomenology shares with Linguistic Analysis a respect for the distinctions between the phenomena reflected in the shades of meaning of ordinary language as a possible starting point for phenomenological analyses. Phenomenologists, however, do not think that the study of ordinary language is a sufficient basis for studying the phenomena, because ordinary language cannot and need not completely reveal the complexity of phenomena.

In contrast to an Existential philosophy that believes that human existence is unfit for phenomenological analysis and description, because it tries to objectify the unobjectifiable, Phenomenology holds that it can and must deal with these phenomena, however cautiously, as well as other intricate phenomena outside the human existence.

(H.Sp.)

ORIGIN AND DEVELOPMENT
OF HUSSERL'S PHENOMENOLOGY

Basic principles. Phenomenology was not founded; it grew. Its fountainhead was Edmund Husserl, who held professorships at Göttingen and Freiburg im Breisgau and who wrote *Die Idee der Phänomenologie* (*The Idea of Phenomenology,* 1964) in 1906. Yet, even for Husserl, the conception of Phenomenology as a new method destined to supply a new foundation for both philosophy and science developed only gradually and kept changing to the very end of his career. Trained as a mathematician, Husserl was attracted to philosophy by Franz Brentano, whose descriptive psychology seemed to offer a solid basis for a scientific philosophy. The concept of intentionality, the directedness of the consciousness toward an object, which is a basic concept in Phenomenology, was already present in Brentano's *Psychologie vom empirischen Standpunkte* (1874): "And thus we can define psychic phenomena by saying that they are those phenomena which, precisely as intentional, contain an object in themselves." Brentano dissociated himself here from Sir William Hamilton, known for his philosophy of the "unconditioned," who had attributed the character of intentionality to the realms of thought and desire only, to the exclusion of that of feeling.

The point of departure of Husserl's investigation is to be found in the treatise *Der Begriff der Zahl* (1887; "The Concept of Number"), which was later expanded into *Philosophie der Arithmetik: Psychologische und logische*

Untersuchungen (1891). Numbers are not found ready-made in nature but result from a mental achievement. Here Husserl was preoccupied with the question of how something like the constitution of numbers ever comes about. This treatise is important to Husserl's later development for two reasons: first, because it contains the first traces of the concepts "reflection," "constitution," "description," and the "founding constitution of meaning," concepts that later played a predominant role in Husserl's philosophy; and second, because it reflected two events—(1) a criticism of his book by Gottlob Frege, a seminal thinker in logic, who had charged him with confusing logical and psychological considerations, and (2) Husserl's discovery of the *Wissenschaftslehre* (1837; *Logic and Scientific Methods,* 1971) by Bernard Bolzano, a Bohemian mathematician, theologian, and social moralist, and his view concerning "truths in themselves"—which led Husserl to an analysis and critical discussion of psychologism, the view that psychology could be used as a foundation for pure logic, which he clearly felt to be no longer possible.

In the first volume of *Logische Untersuchungen* (1900–01; *Logical Investigations,* 1970), entitled *Prolegomena,* Husserl began with a criticism of psychologism. And yet he continued by conducting a careful investigation of the psychic acts in and through which logical structures are given; these investigations, too, could give the impression of being descriptive psychological investigations, though they were not conceived of in this way by the author. For the issue at stake was the discovery of the essential structure of these acts. Here Brentano's concept of intentionality received a richer and more refined signification. Husserl distinguished between perceptual and categorical intuition and stated that the latter's theme lies in logical relationships. The real concern of Phenomenology was clearly formulated for the first time in his *Logos* article, "Philosophie als strenge Wissenschaft" (1910–11; *Philosophy as Rigorous Science,* 1965). In this work Husserl wrestled with two unacceptable views: naturalism and historicism.

Naturalism attempts to apply the methods of the natural sciences to all other domains of knowledge, including the realm of consciousness. Reason becomes naturalized. Although an attempt is then made to find a foundation for the human sciences (*Geisteswissenschaften*) by means of experimental psychology, it proves to be impossible, because in so doing one is unable to grasp precisely what is at stake in knowledge as found in the natural sciences.

What a philosopher must examine is the relationship between consciousness and Being; and in doing so, he must realize that from the standpoint of epistemology, Being is accessible to him only as a correlate of conscious acts. He must thus pay careful attention to what occurs in these acts. This can be done only by a science that tries to understand the very essence of consciousness; and this is the task that Phenomenology has set for itself. Because clarification of the various types of objects must follow from the basic modes of consciousness, Husserl's thought remained close to psychology. In contradistinction to what is the case in psychology, however, in Phenomenology, consciousness is thematized in a very special and definite way, viz., just insofar as consciousness is the locus in which every manner of constituting and founding meaning must take place. In man's intuition, conscious occurrences must be given immediately in order to avoid introducing at the same time certain interpretations. The nature of such processes as perception, representation, imagination, judgment, and feeling must be grasped in immediate self-givenness. The call "To the things themselves" is not a demand for realism, because the things at stake are the acts of consciousness and the objective entities that get constituted in them: these things form the realm of what Husserl calls the phenomena.

Thus, the objects of Phenomenology are "absolute data grasped in pure, immanent intuition," and its goal is to discover the essential structures of the acts (*noesis*) and the objective entities that correspond to them (*noema*).

On the other hand, Phenomenology must also be distinguished from historicism, a philosophy that stresses the immersion of all thinkers within a particular historical

Marginal notes:

Husserl's earlier development

Antinaturalism

Antihistoricism

setting. Husserl objected to historicism because it implies relativism. He gave credit to Wilhelm Dilthey, author of "Entwürfe zur Kritik der historischen Vernunft" ("Outlines for the Critique of Historical Reason," in *Gesammelte Schriften*, 12 vol. [1914–36], vol. 5, 6), for having developed a typification of world views, but he doubted and even rejected the skepticism that flows necessarily from the relativity of the various types. History is concerned with facts, whereas Phenomenology deals with the knowledge of essences. To Husserl, Dilthey's doctrine of world views was incapable of achieving the rigour required by genuine science. Contrary to all of the practical tendencies found in world views, Husserl demanded that philosophy be founded as a rigorous science. Its task implies that nothing be accepted as given beforehand but that the philosopher should try to find the way back to the real beginnings. This is tantamount to saying, however, that he must try to find the way to the foundations of meaning that are found in consciousness. Just as for Immanuel Kant the empirical has merely relative validity and never an absolute, or apodictic, validity, so for Husserl, too, what is to be searched for is a scientific knowledge of essences in contradistinction to a scientific knowledge of facts.

Basic method. The basic method of all Phenomenological investigation, as Husserl developed it himself—and on which he worked throughout his entire lifetime—is the "reduction": the existence of the world must be put between brackets, not because the philospher should doubt it but merely because this existing world is not the very theme of Phenomenology; its theme is rather the manner in which knowledge of the world comes about. The first step of the reduction consists in the phenomenological reduction, through which all that is given is changed into a phenomenon in the sense of that which is known in and by consciousness; for this kind of knowing—which is to be taken in a very broad sense as including every mode of consciousness, such as intuition, recollection, imagination, and judgment—is here all-important. There are several reasons why Husserl gave a privileged position to intuition: among them is the fact that intuition is that act in which a person grasps something immediately in its bodily presence and also that it is a primordially given act upon which all of the rest is to be founded. Furthermore, Husserl's stress on intuition must be understood as a refutation of any merely speculative approach to philosophy.

This reduction reverses—"re-flects"—man's direction of sight from a straightforward orientation toward objects to an orientation toward consciousness.

Eidetic and transcendental reductions

The second step is to be found in the eidetic reduction. To get hold of consciousness is not sufficient; on the contrary, the various acts of consciousness must be made accessible in such a way that their essences—their universal and unchangeable structures—can be grasped. In the eidetic reduction one must forego everything that is factual and merely occurs in this way or that. A means of grasping the essence is the *Wesensschau*, the intuition of essences and essential structures. This is not a mysterious kind of intuition. Rather, one forms a multiplicity of variations of what is given, and while maintaining the multiplicity, one focusses attention on what remains unchanged in the multiplicity; *i.e.*, the essence is that identical something that continuously maintains itself during the process of variation. Husserl, therefore, called it the invariant.

To this point, the discussion of reduction has remained within the realm of psychology, albeit a new—namely, a phenomenological—psychology. The second step must now be completed by a third, the transcendental reduction. It consists in a reversion to the achievements of that consciousness that Husserl, following Kant, called transcendental consciousness, although he conceived of it in his own way. The most fundamental event occurring in this consciousness is the creation of time awareness through the acts of protention (future) and retention (past), which is something like a self-constitution. To do phenomenology was for Husserl tantamount to returning to the transcendental ego as the ground for the foundation and constitution (or making) of all meaning (German *Sinn*). Only when a person has reached this ground can he achieve the insight that makes his comportment trans-

parent in its entirety and makes him understand how meaning comes about, how meaning is based upon meaning like strata in a process of sedimentation.

Husserl worked on the clarification of the transcendental reduction until the very end of his life. It was precisely the further development of the transcendental reduction that led to a division of the Phenomenological movement and to the formation of a school that refused to become involved in this kind of system of problems (see below *Phenomenology of essences*).

Basic concepts. In an effort to express what it is to which this method gives access, Husserl wrote:

Intentionality and constitution theory

> In all pure psychic experiences (in perceiving something, judging about something, willing something, enjoying something, hoping for something, etc.) there is found inherently a being-directed-toward.... Experiences are intentional. This being-directed-toward is not just joined to the experience by way of a mere addition, and occasionally as an accidental reaction, as if experiences could be what they are without the intentional relation. With the intentionality of the experiences there announces itself, rather, the essential structure of the purely psychical.

The phenomenological investigator must examine the different forms of intentionality in a reflective attitude because it is precisely in and through the corresponding intentionality that each domain of objects becomes accessible to him. Husserl took as his point of departure mathematical entities and later examined logical structures, in order finally to achieve the insight that each being must be grasped in its correlation to consciousness, because each datum becomes accessible to a person only insofar as it has meaning for him. From this position, regional ontologies, or realms of being, develop: for instance, those dealing with the region of "nature," the region of "the psychic," or the region of "the spirit." Moreover, Husserl distinguished formal ontologies—such as the region of the logical—from material ontologies.

In order to be able to investigate a regional ontology, it is first necessary to discover and examine the founding act by which realities in this realm are constituted. For Husserl, constitution does not mean the creation or fabrication of a thing or object by a subject; it means the founding constitution of its meaning. There is meaning only for consciousness. All founding constitution of meaning is made possible by transcendental consciousness. Speaking of this transcendental motif, Husserl wrote:

> It is the motif of questioning back to the last source of all achievements of knowledge, of reflection in which the knower reflects on himself and his knowing life, in which all the scientific constructs which have validity for him, occur teleologically, and as permanent acquisitions are kept and become freely available to him.

In the realm of such transcendental problems, it is necessary to examine how all of the categories in and through which one understands mundane beings or purely formal entities originate from specific modes of consciousness. In Husserl's view, the temporalization must be conceived as a kind of primordial constitution of transcendental consciousness itself.

Understood in this way, Phenomenology does not place itself outside the sciences but, rather, attempts to make understandable what takes place in the various sciences and, thus, to thematize the unquestioned presuppositions of the sciences.

In his last publication, *Die Krisis der europäischen Wissenschaften und die transzendentale Phänomenologie: Eine Einleitung in die phänomenologische Philosophie* (1936; *The Crisis of European Sciences and Transcendental Phenomenology*, 1970), Husserl arrived at the life-world—the world as shaped within the immediate experience of each man—by questioning back to the foundations that the sciences presuppose. In *Die Krisis* he analyzed the grounds that had led to the European crisis of culture and philosophy, which found its immediate expression in the contrast between the great successes of the sciences of nature and the failure of the sciences of man. In the modern era, scientific knowledge had become fragmented into an objectivistic-physicalist and a transcendental knowledge. Until recently this split could not be overcome. It led, rather, to the attempt to develop the sciences of man in

Husserl's notion of the life-world

accordance with the procedures used in the exact sciences of nature (naturalism)—an attempt doomed to failure. In opposition to this attempt, Husserl wished to show that in the new approach one must reflect on the activities of the scientists.

> As the immediately given world, this merely subjective world, was forgotten in the scientific thematization, the accomplishing subject, too, was forgotten and the scientist himself was not thematized.

Husserl demonstrated this point by using the example of Galileo and his mathematization of our world. The truth characteristic of the life-world is by no means an inferior form of truth when compared to the exact, scientific truth but is, rather, always a truth already presupposed in all scientific research. That is why Husserl claimed that an ontology of the life-world must be developed—*i.e.,* a systematic analysis of the constitutive achievements the result of which is the life-world, a life-world that, in turn, is the foundation of all scientific constitutions of meaning. The stimulating change that occurred here consists in the fact that truth is no longer measured after the criterion of an exact determination. For what is decisive is not the exactness but, rather, the part played by the founding act.

It is in this connection that, rather abruptly, historicity, too, became relevant for Husserl. He began to reflect upon the emergence of philosophy among the Greeks and on its significance as a new mode of scientific knowledge oriented toward infinity; and he interpreted the philosophy of René Descartes, often called the father of modern philosophy, as the point at which the split into the two research directions—physicalist objectivism and transcendental subjectivism—came about. Phenomenology must overcome this split, he held, and thus help mankind to live according to the demands of reason. In view of the fact that reason is the typical characteristic of man, mankind must find itself again through Phenomenology.

LATER DEVELOPMENTS

Phenomenology of essences. A different type of Phenomenology, the Phenomenology of essences, developed from a tangential continuation of that of the *Logische Untersuchungen.* Its supporters were Husserl's students in Göttingen and a group of young philosophers in Munich, originally students of Theodor Lipps, a Munich psychologist and philosopher—students who had turned away from Lipp's psychologism and discovered powerful support in Husserl. The Phenomenological movement, which then began to take shape, found its most tangible expression in the publication of the *Jahrbuch für Philosophie und phänomenologische Forschung* (1913–30), a Phenomenological yearbook with Husserl as its main editor, the preface of which defined Phenomenology in terms of a return to intuition (*Anschauung*) and to the essential insights (*Wesenseinsichten*) derived from it as the ultimate foundation of all philosophy.

The 11 volumes of the *Jahrbuch* contained, in addition to Husserl's own works, the most important fruits of the movement in its broader application. Of the co-editors, Alexander Pfänder contributed chiefly to the development of phenomenological psychology and pure logic but developed also the outlines of a complete Phenomenological philosophy. Moritz Geiger applied the new approach particularly to aesthetics and Adolf Reinach to the philosophy of law. The most original and dynamic of Husserl's early associates, however, was Max Scheler, who had joined the Munich group and who did his major Phenomenological work on problems of value and obligation. A Polish philosopher, Roman Ingarden, did major work in structural ontology and analyzed the structures of various works of art in its light; Hedwig Conrad-Martius, a cosmic Realist at the University of Munich, worked intensively in the ontology of nature; and others made comparable contributions in other fields of philosophy. None of these early Phenomenologists, however, followed Husserl's road to transcendental Idealism; and some tried to develop a Phenomenology along the lines of Realism.

Heidegger's hermeneutic Phenomenology. Martin Heidegger, one of Germany's foremost philosophers at the middle of the 20th century, was inspired to philosophy through Brentano's work *Von der mannigfachen Bedeutung des Seienden nach Aristoteles* (1862; "On the Multifarious Meaning of Being According to Aristotle"). While he was still studying theology, from 1910 to 1911, Heidegger encountered Husserl's *Logische Untersuchungen.* From then on he pursued the course of Phenomenology with the greatest interest, and from 1916 he belonged to the narrow circle of students and followers of the movement. The typical character of the Phenomenological intuition was at that time the focus of Husserl's seminar exercises. To be sure, there appeared very early a difference between Husserl and Heidegger. Discussing and absorbing the works of the important philosophers in the history of metaphysics was, for Heidegger, an indispensable task, whereas Husserl repeatedly stressed the significance of a radically new beginning and—with few exceptions (among them Descartes, Locke, Hume, and Kant)—wished to bracket the history of philosophy.

Heidegger's basic work, *Sein und Zeit* (1927; *Being and Time,* 1962), which was dedicated to Husserl, strongly acknowledged that its author was indebted to Phenomenology. In it, Phenomenology was understood as a methodological concept—a concept that was conceived by Heidegger in an original way and resulted from his questioning back to the meanings of the Greek concepts of *phainomenon* and *logos. Phainomenon* is "that which shows itself from itself," but together with the concept of *logos,* it means "to let that which shows itself be seen from itself in the very way in which it shows itself from itself." This conception of Phenomenology, which relied more on Aristotle than on Husserl, constituted a change that was later to lead to an estrangement between Husserl and Heidegger. For in *Sein und Zeit* there is no longer a phenomenological reduction, a transcendental ego, or an intuition of essences in Husserl's sense. Heidegger's new beginning was, at the same time, a resumption of the basic question of philosophy: that concerning the meaning (*Sinn*) of Being. His manner of questioning can be defined as hermeneutical in that it proceeds from the interpretation of man's situation. What he thematized is, thus, the explanation of what is already understood.

At the heart of *Sein und Zeit* lies Heidegger's analysis of the one (the man) who asks the question—who is capable of asking the question—concerning Being, who precisely through this capability occupies a privileged position in regard to all other beings, viz., that of *Dasein* (literally, "being there"). By conceiving of *Dasein* as being-in-the-world, Heidegger made the ancient problem concerning the relationship between subject and object superfluous. The basic structures of *Dasein* are primordial moodness (*Befindlichkeit*), understanding (*Verstehen*), and logos (*Rede*). These structures are, in turn, founded in the temporalization of *Dasein,* from which future, having-been (past), and present originate. The two basic possibilities of man's existing (from the Latin *ex* and *sistere,* "standing out from") are those in which *Dasein* either comes to its self (called authenticity) or loses itself (called inauthenticity); *Dasein* is inauthentic, for example, when it lets the possibilities of the choice for its own "ek-sisting" be given to it by others instead of deciding for itself. Heidegger's concept of care (*Sorge, cura*) has nothing to do with distress (*Bekümmernis*) but includes the unity of the articulated moments of man's being-in-the-world.

The hermeneutic character of Heidegger's thought manifested itself also in his interpretation of poetry, in which he discovered a congenial spirit in Friedrich Hölderlin, one of Germany's greater poets, of whose poetry he inaugurated a completely new interpretation; but it manifested itself equally well in his interpretation of metaphysics, which Heidegger tried to envision as an occurrence determined by the forgottenness of Being, an occurrence in the centre of which man finds himself and of which the clearest manifestation is to be found in "technicity," the attempt of modern man to dominate the earth by controlling beings that are considered as objects.

The concept of transcendental consciousness, which was central for Husserl, is not found in Heidegger—which clearly shows how Heidegger, in *Sein und Zeit,* had already dissociated himself from Husserl's Phenomenology.

Marginal notes:

Fruits of the movement in broader application

Heidegger's return to ontology

Other developments. Eugen Fink, for several years Husserl's collaborator, whose essay "Die phänomenologische Philosophie Edmund Husserls in der gegenwärtigen Kritik" (1933) led to a radicalization of Husserl's philosophical, transcendental Idealism, later turned in another direction, one that approached Heidegger's position and divorced itself at the same time from that of Husserl.

Ludwig Landgrebe, who was Husserl's personal assistant for many years, published in 1938 *Erfahrung und Urteil* ("Experience and Judgment"), the first of Husserl's posthumous works devoted to the genealogy of logic. Among German-language scholars, Landgrebe remained closest to Husserl's original views and has developed them consistently in several works.

DISSEMINATION OF PHENOMENOLOGY

Phenomenology in various countries. Following upon the work of Husserl, Phenomenology spread into a worldwide movement.

In France. One of the first French authors to become familiar with Husserl's philosophy was Emmanuel Lévinas, a pluralistic Personalist, who combined ideas from Husserl and Heidegger in a very personal way. Similarly, Jean-Paul Sartre, the leading Existentialist of France, took his point of departure from the philosophies of Husserl and Heidegger. His first works, *L'Imagination* (1936; *Imagination: A Psychological Critique,* 1962) and *L'Imaginaire: Psychologie phénoménologique de l'imagination* (1940; *The Psychology of Imagination,* 1950), remain completely within the context of Husserl's analyses of consciousness. Sartre explains the distinction between perceptual and imaginative consciousness with the help of Husserl's concept of intentionality, and he frequently employs the method of ideation (*Wesensschau*).

In *L'Être et le néant* (1943; *Being and Nothingness,* 1956), an essay on Phenomenological ontology, it is obvious that Sartre borrowed from Heidegger. Some passages from Heidegger's *Was ist Metaphysik?* (1929; *What Is Metaphysics?,* 1949), in fact, are copied literally. The meaning of nothingness, which Heidegger in this lecture made the theme of his investigations, became for Sartre the guiding question. Sartre departs from Heidegger's analytic of *Dasein* and introduces the position of consciousness (which Heidegger had overcome).

The distinction between being-in-itself (*en-soi*) and being-for-itself (*pour-soi*) pervades the entire investigation. The in-itself is the opaque, matter-like substance that remains the same, whereas the for-itself is consciousness permeated by nothingness. The influence of the Idealist G.W.F. Hegel becomes apparent when the author tries to interpret everything in a dialectical way; *i.e.,* through a tension of opposites. The dialectic of men's being-with-one-another is central: thus, seeing and being-seen correspond to dominating and being-dominated. The basic characteristic of being-for-itself is bad faith (*mauvaise foi*), which cannot be overcome because facticity (being-already) and transcendence (being-able-to-be) cannot be combined.

The Phenomenological character of Sartre's analyses of consciousness consists in the way in which he elucidates certain modes of behaviour: love, hatred, sadism, masochism, and indifference. Although Sartre sees and describes these forms of behaviour strikingly and precisely, he limits himself to those modes that fit his philosophical interpretation. The significance of psychology, recognized by Husserl, emerges again in Sartre and leads to a demand for an Existential psychoanalysis.

Sartre's definition of man as a being of possibilities that finds or loses itself in the choice that it makes in regard to itself refers to Heidegger's definition of *Dasein* as a being that has to materialize itself. For Sartre, freedom is the basic characteristic of man; thus Sartre belongs to the tradition of the great French moralist philosophers.

In his later works, as in his *Critique de la raison dialectique* (1960; *Search for a Method,* 1963), Sartre turned to Marxism, though he developed a method of understanding that was influenced by hermeneutics. Here the choice made by the individual is limited by social and psychological conditions. Sartre's outstanding two-volume interpretation of Flaubert, *L'Idiot de la famille; Gustave Flaubert de 1821–1857* (1971), is an example of this new method of understanding and interpretation, which combines Marxist elements with interpretations of a highly personal nature taken from depth psychology.

Maurice Merleau-Ponty (died 1961), who, together with Sartre and his associate Simone de Beauvoir, a writer and novelist, was an important representative of French Existentialism, was at the same time the most important French Phenomenologist. His works, *La Structure du comportement* (1942; *Structure of Behaviour,* 1963) and *Phénoménologie de la perception* (1945; *Phenomenology of Perception,* 1962), were the most original further developments and applications of Phenomenology to come from France. Merleau-Ponty gave a new interpretation of the meaning of the human body from the viewpoint of Phenomenology and, connected with this, of man's perception of space, the natural world, temporality, and freedom.

Starting from Husserl's later phenomenology of the lifeworld, Merleau-Ponty anchored the phenomena of perception in the phenomenology of the lived body (the body as it is experienced and experiences), in which the perceiving subject is incarnated as the mediating link to the phenomenal world. Such a phenomenology of human "presence" in the world was also to offer an alternative to the rigid dichotomy between Idealism and Realism, in which consciousness and world could be reciprocally related. Phenomenology thus became a way of showing the essential involvement of human existence in the world, starting with everyday perception.

Although it is true that Merleau-Ponty was originally close to Husserl in his thought, he later developed noticeably in the direction of Heidegger, a change that became particularly manifest in *L'Oeil et l'esprit* (1964; "Eye and Mind," in *The Primacy of Perception,* 1964).

Paul Ricoeur, a student of the volitional experience, whose translation of Husserl's *Ideen zu einer reinen Phänomenologie* brought Husserl closer to the younger French generation, writes in a Phenomenological vein but with the intention of further developing Husserl's conception of Phenomenology. Ricoeur's two-volume *Philosophie de la volonté* (1950–60; "Philosophy of the Will") also deals with the problems involved in the theological concept of guilt.

Suzanne Bachelard, who in 1957 translated Husserl's *Formale und transzendentale Logik: Versuch einer Kritik der logischen Vernunft,* has pointed to the significance of Husserl for modern logic; and Jacques Derrida, an original French thinker on the limits of thought and language, has combined Phenomenology and Structuralism in his interpretation of literature.

In Germany. After World War II, interest in Phenomenology sprang up again in its own homeland. The influence of Ludwig Landgrebe in Cologne has been particularly felt, as have the activities of the Husserl Archives in Cologne, with editions by Walter Biemel, who also published *Philosophische Analysen zur Kunst der Gegenwart* (1968; "Philosophical Analyses of Contemporary Art") and essays on the relationships between Husserl and Heidegger. The circle around Gerhard Funke in Mainz, author of *Phänomenologie—Metaphysik oder Methode?* (1966), has also had a positive influence.

In other European countries. In Belgium, at the Catholic University of Louvain, are located the entire posthumous works of Husserl, as well as his personal library. Thanks to the initiative of H.L. Van Breda, founder of the Husserl Archives, several scholars worked intensively on the manuscripts for several decades. By 1972, 12 volumes of collected works had been published. Van Breda was also the director of the *Phaenomenologica* series—totalling 42 volumes by 1972—in which the most important publications in the field of Phenomenology (taken in a very broad sense) have been published. Thus, mainly through Van Breda's efforts, Louvain has become the most important centre for Phenomenology. Van Breda also organized international colloquia on Phenomenology. The influence of Alphonse de Waelhens, a Belgian philosopher of fresh experience and author of *Phénoménologie et vérité* (1953) and *Existence et signification* (1958), also bears mentioning.

Marginal notes:

Jean-Paul Sartre's use of the method

The Phenomenology of Maurice Merleau-Ponty

Husserl scholarship at Cologne and Louvain

In The Netherlands, Stephan Strasser, who is oriented particularly toward phenomenological psychology, is especially influential. And in Italy, the Phenomenology circle centres around Enzo Paci. The Husserl scholar Jan Patocka, a prominent expert in Phenomenology as well as in the metaphysical tradition, is influential in Czechoslovakia; in Poland, Roman Ingarden has represented the cause of Phenomenology; and there are also important representatives in Yugoslavia, Portugal, England, South America, Japan, and India.

In the United States. In the United States, Phenomenology has lived a rather marginal existence for quite some time, notwithstanding the meritorious journal of *Philosophy and Phenomenological Research* founded by Husserl's student Marvin Farber, who is also the author of *The Foundation of Phenomenology* (1943). In recent years, however, a noticeable change has taken place, chiefly because of the work of two scholars at the New School for Social Research in New York, Alfred Schütz, an Austrian-born sociologist and student of human cognition (died 1959), and Aron Gurwitsch, a Lithuanian-born philosopher. Schütz came early to Phenomenology, developing a social science on a phenomenological basis. Gurwitsch, author of *Théorie du champ de la conscience* (1957; *The Field of Consciousness,* 1964), came to Phenomenology through his study of the Gestalt psychologists Adhemar Gelb and Kurt Goldstein. While in Paris, Gurwitsch influenced Merleau-Ponty. The essays on Phenomenology published by Gurwitsch in the United States are among the best. His comprehensive knowledge ranges from mathematics, via the natural sciences, to psychology and metaphysics. The work *The Phenomenological Movement* (2nd ed. 1965), by Herbert Spiegelberg, an Alsatian–American Phenomenologist, is the movement's first encompassing historical presentation.

Phenomenology in other disciplines. Of greater significance is the role of Phenomenology outside of philosophy proper in stimulating or reinforcing phenomenological tendencies in such fields as mathematics and the biological sciences. Much stronger was its impact on psychology, in which Franz Brentano and the German Carl Stumpf had prepared the ground and in which the U.S. psychologist William James, the Würzburg school, and the Gestalt psychologists had worked along parallel lines. But Phenomenology has probably made its strongest contribution in the field of psychopathology, in which the German Karl Jaspers, a foremost contemporary Existentialist, stressed the importance of phenomenological exploration of a patient's subjective experience. Jaspers was followed by the Swiss Ludwig Binswanger and several others. The Phenomenological strand is also very pronounced in American Existential psychiatry and has affected sociology, history, and the study of religion.

CONCLUSION

At the turn of the fourth quarter of the 20th century, it remained to be seen whether Phenomenology could make solid contributions to philosophical knowledge. To this end, it needed to develop rigorous standards, which had not always been observed by some of its most brilliant practitioners, such as Max Scheler, and which were likely to be violated in a philosophy the ultimate appeal of which had to be made to intuitive verification. With this proviso, Phenomenology may well be qualified not only to become a bridge for better international communication in philosophy but also to shed new light on philosophical problems old and new, to reclaim for philosophy parts of man's everyday life-world that have been abandoned by science as too private and too subjective, and, finally, to give access to layers of man's experience unprobed in everyday living, thus providing deeper foundations for both science and life. (W.Bi.)

Positivism and Logical Empiricism

As a philosophical ideology and movement, Positivism first assumed its distinctive features in the work of the French philosopher Auguste Comte, who also named and systematized the science of sociology. It then developed through several stages known by various names, such as Empiriocriticism, Logical Positivism, and Logical Empiricism, and finally, in the mid-20th century, flowed into the movement known as Analytic and Linguistic philosophy.

The basic affirmations of Positivism are (1) that all knowledge regarding matters of fact is based upon the "positive" data of experience, and (2) that beyond the realm of fact is that of pure logic and pure mathematics, which were already recognized by the Scottish Empiricist and Skeptic David Hume as concerned with the "relations of ideas" and, in a later phase of Positivism, were classified as purely formal sciences. On the negative and critical side, the Positivists became noted for their repudiation of metaphysics; *i.e.,* of speculation regarding the nature of reality that radically goes beyond any possible evidence that could either support or refute such "transcendent" knowledge claims. In its basic ideological posture, Positivism is thus worldly, secular, antitheological, and antimetaphysical. Strict adherence to the testimony of observation and experience is the all-important imperative of the Positivists. This imperative is reflected also in their contributions to ethics and moral philosophy, and most Positivists have been Utilitarians to the extent that something like "the greatest happiness for the greatest number of people" was their ethical maxim. It is notable, in this connection, that Auguste Comte was the founder of a short-lived religion, in which the object of worship was not the deity of the monotheistic faiths but humanity.

There are distinct anticipations of Positivism in ancient philosophy. Though the relationship of Protagoras, a 5th-century-BC Sophist, for example, to later Positivistic thought was only a distant one, there was a much more pronounced similarity in the classical Skeptic Sextus Empiricus, who lived at the turn of the 3rd century AD, and in Pierre Bayle, his 17th-century reviver. Moreover, the medieval Nominalist William of Ockham had clear affinities with modern Positivism. An 18th-century forerunner who had much in common with the Positivistic antimetaphysics of the following century was the German thinker Georg Lichtenberg.

Positivism clearly has its proximate roots, however, in the French Enlightenment, which stressed the clear light of reason, and in the 18th-century British Empiricism, particularly that of Hume and of Bishop George Berkeley, which stressed the role of sense experience. Comte was influenced specifically by the Enlightenment Encyclopaedists (such as Denis Diderot, Jean d'Alembert, and others) and, especially in his social thinking, was decisively influenced by the founder of French Socialism, Claude-Henri, comte de Saint-Simon, whose disciple he had been in his early years and from whom the very designation Positivism stems.

THE SOCIAL POSITIVISM OF COMTE AND MILL

Comte's Positivism was posited on the assertion of a so-called law of the three phases (or stages) of intellectual development. There is a parallel, as Comte saw it, between the evolution of thought patterns in the entire history of man, on the one hand, and in the history of an individual's development from infancy to adulthood, on the other. In the first, or so-called theological, stage, natural phenomena are explained as the results of supernatural or divine powers. It matters not whether the religion is polytheistic or monotheistic; in either case, miraculous powers or wills are believed to produce the observed events. This stage was criticized by Comte as anthropomorphic; *i.e.,* as resting on all-too-human analogies. Generally, animistic explanations—made in terms of the volitions of soullike beings operating behind the appearances—are rejected as primitive projections of unverifiable entities.

The second phase, called metaphysical, is in some cases merely a depersonalized theology: the observable processes of nature are assumed to arise from impersonal powers, occult qualities, vital forces, or entelechies (internal perfecting principles). In other instances, the realm of observable facts is considered as an imperfect copy or imitation of eternal ideas, as in Plato's metaphysics of pure Forms. Again, Comte charged that no genuine explanations result; questions concerning ultimate reality,

The work of Farber, Schütz, and Gurwitsch

Affirmations and negations

Comte's law of three phases

first causes, or absolute beginnings are thus declared to be absolutely unanswerable. The metaphysical quest can lead only to the conclusion expressed by the German biologist and physiologist, Emil du Bois-Reymond: *"Ignoramus et ignorabimus"* ("We are and shall be ignorant"); it is a deception through verbal devices and the fruitless rendering of concepts as real things.

The sort of fruitfulness that it lacks can be achieved only in the third phase, the scientific, or "positive," phase—hence the title of Comte's magnum opus: *Cours de philosophie positive* (1830–42; *The Positive Philosophy of Auguste Comte,* 1853)—because it claims to be concerned only with positive facts. The task of the sciences, and of knowledge in general, is to study the facts and regularities of nature and society and to formulate the regularities as (descriptive) laws; explanations of phenomena can consist in no more than the subsuming of special cases under general laws. Mankind reached full maturity of thought only after abandoning the pseudoexplanations of the theological and metaphysical phases and substituting an unrestricted adherence to scientific method.

Classification of the sciences; sociology

In his three stages Comte combined what he considered to be an account of the historical order of development with a logical analysis of the levelled structure of the sciences. By arranging the six basic and pure sciences one upon the other in a pyramid, Comte prepared the way for Logical Positivism to "reduce" each level to the one below it. He placed at the fundamental level the science that does not presuppose any other sciences—viz., mathematics—and then ordered the levels above it in such a way that each science depends upon, and makes use of, the sciences below it on the scale: thus arithmetic and the theory of numbers are declared to be presuppositions for geometry and mechanics, astronomy, physics, chemistry, biology (including physiology), and sociology. Each higher level science, in turn, adds to the knowledge content of the science or sciences on the levels below, thus enriching this content by successive specialization. Psychology is conspicuously missing in Comte's system of the sciences. Anticipating some ideas of 20th-century Behaviourism and physicalism, Comte assumed that psychology should become a branch of biology (especially of brain neurophysiology), on the one hand, and of sociology, on the other. As the "father" of sociology, Comte maintained that the social sciences should proceed from observations to general laws, very much as (in his view) physics and chemistry do. He was skeptical of introspection in psychology, being convinced that, in attending to one's own mental states, these states would be irretrievably altered and distorted. In thus insisting on the necessity of objective observation, he was close to the basic principle of the methodology of 20th-century Behaviourism.

Among Comte's disciples or sympathizers were Cesare Lombroso, an Italian psychiatrist and criminologist, and Paul-Emile Littré, J.-E. Renan, and Louis Weber.

Despite some basic disagreements with Comte, the 19th-century English philosopher John Stuart Mill, also a logician and economist, must be regarded as one of the outstanding Positivists of his century. In his *System of Logic* (1843), he developed a thoroughly Empiricist theory of knowledge and of scientific reasoning, going even so far as to regard logic and mathematics as empirical (though very general) sciences. The broadly synthetic philosopher Herbert Spencer, author of a doctrine of the "unknowable" and of a general evolutionary philosophy, was, next to Mill, an outstanding exponent of a Positivistic orientation.

THE CRITICAL POSITIVISM OF MACH AND AVENARIUS

The influences of Hume and of Comte were also manifest in important developments in German Positivism, just prior to World War I. The outstanding representatives of this school were a philosophical critic of the physics of Newton, an Austrian, Ernst Mach, who was also an original thinker as a physicist and excelled as a historian of mechanics, thermodynamics, and optics, and Richard Avenarius, founder of a philosophy known as Empiriocriticism.

Mach's phenomenalism

Mach, in the introductory chapter of his book *Beiträge zur Analyse der Empfindungen* (1886; *Contributions to the Analysis of the Sensations,* 1897), reviving the Humean antimetaphysics, contended that all factual knowledge consists of a conceptual organization and elaboration of what is given in the elements; *i.e.,* in the data of immediate experience. Very much in keeping with the spirit of Comte, he repudiated the transcendental Idealism of Kant. For Mach, the most objectionable feature in Kant's philosophy was the doctrine of the *Dinge an sich—i.e.,* of the "things-in-themselves"—the ultimate entities underlying phenomena, which Kant had declared to be absolutely unknowable though they must nevertheless be conceived as partial causes of man's perceptions. Hermann von Helmholtz, a wide-ranging scientist and philosopher and one of the great minds of the 19th century, by contrast, held that the theoretical entities of physics are, precisely, the things-in-themselves—a view which, though generally Empiricist, was thus clearly opposed to the Positivist doctrine. Theories and theoretical concepts, according to the Positivist understanding, were merely instruments of prediction. From one set of observable data, theories formed a bridge over which the investigator could pass to another set of observable data. Positivists generally maintained that theories might come and go, whereas the facts of observation and their empirical regularities constituted a firm ground from which scientific reasoning could start and to which it must always return in order to test its validity. In consequence, most Positivists were reluctant to call theories true or false but preferred to consider them merely as more or less useful.

The task of the sciences, as it earlier had been expressed by the German physicist Gustav Kirchhoff, was the pursuit of a compendious and parsimonious description of observable phenomena. Concern with first causes or final reasons was to be excluded from the scientific endeavour as fruitless, or hopeless (if not meaningless). Even the notion of explanation became suspect and was at best taken (as already in Comte) to be no more than an ordering and connecting of observable facts and events by empirically ascertainable laws.

Mach and, along with him, Wilhelm Ostwald, the originator of physical chemistry, were the most prominent opponents of the atomic theory in physics and chemistry. Ostwald even attempted to derive the basic chemical laws of constant and multiple proportions without the help of the atomic hypothesis. To the Positivist the atom, since it could not be seen, was to be considered at best a "convenient fiction" and at worst an illegitimate ad hoc hypothesis. Hans Vaihinger, a subjectivist who called himself an "idealistic Positivist," pursued the idea of useful fictions to the limit, and was convinced that the concept of the atom, along with the mathematical concepts of the infinite and the infinitesimal, and those of causation, free will, the economic man, and the like, were altogether fictitious, some of them even containing internal contradictions.

Antiatomism of Mach and Ostwald

The anti-atomistic strand in the thought of the Positivists was an extreme manifestation of their phobia regarding anything unobservable. With the undeniably great success of the advancing microtheories in physics and chemistry, however, the Positivist ideology was severely criticized, not only by some contemporary philosophers but also by outstanding scientists. The Austrian Ludwig Boltzmann and the German Max Planck, for example, both top-ranking theoretical physicists, were in the forefront of the attack against Mach and Ostwald. Boltzmann and Planck, outspoken Realists, were deeply convinced of the reality of unobservable microparticles, or microevents, and were clearly impressed with the ever-growing and converging evidence for the existence of atoms, molecules, quanta, and subatomic particles. Nevertheless, the basic Positivist attitude was tenaciously held by many scientists, and striking parallels to it appeared in American Pragmatism and instrumentalism; in parts of the work of the Pragmatists Charles Sanders Peirce, William James, and John Dewey, there is a philosophy of pure experience essentially similar to that of Mach.

Though Richard Avenarius has not become widely known, he too anticipated a good deal of what the American Pragmatists propounded. His Positivism, like that of Mach, comprised a biologically oriented theory of knowl-

The Positivism of Avenarius

edge. From the needs of organisms in their adaptation to the exigencies of their environment develop the conceptual tools needed for prediction of future conditions. In Avenarius' view, the raw material of the construction of the concepts of common sense and of the sciences, however, was "the given"; *i.e.,* the data of immediate sensory experience. Just as Mill in the 19th century considered ordinary physical objects as "permanent possibilities of sensation," so Mach and Avenarius construed the concepts pertaining to what men commonsensically regard as the objects of the real world as "complexes of sensations." Thus, it was maintained that a stone, for example, is no more than a collection of such sensory qualities as hardness, colour, and mass. The traditional assumption that there must be an underlying substance that has these properties was repudiated. To the question "What would be left over if all of the perceptible qualities were stripped (in thought) away from an observable object?" these Positivists answered: "Precisely nothing." Thus the concept of substance was declared not only superfluous but meaningless as well.

In similar fashion, the concept of causation was explicated not as a real operating principle but as regularity of succession or as functional dependency among observable or measurable variables. Because these dependencies are not logically necessary, they are contingent and ascertained by observation, and especially by experimentation and inductive generalization.

The Newtonian doctrine according to which space and time are absolute or substantive realities had been incisively criticized by the 17th-century Rationalist Gottfried Leibniz and was subjected by Mach to even more searching scrutiny. While Leibniz had already paved the way for the conception of space and time as exclusively a matter of relations between events, Mach went still further in attacking the arguments of Newton in favour of a dynamic and absolute space and time. In particular, the inertial and centrifugal forces that arise in connection with accelerated or curvilinear motions had been interpreted by Newton as effects of such motions with respect to a privileged reference medium imagined as an absolute Cartesian mesh system graphed upon a real space. In a typically Positivistic manner, however, Mach found the idea quite incredible. How, he asked, could an absolutely empty space have such powerful effects? Mach conjectured that any privileged reference system must be generated not by an imperceptible grid but by material reality—specifically, by the total mass of the universe (galaxies and fixed stars), an idea that later served as an important starting point for Einstein's general theory of relativity and gravitation.

Influence of Mach and Avenarius

The Positivist theory of knowledge, as proposed by Mach and Avenarius, impressed many scholars, most notable among whom was probably the leading British logician and philosopher Bertrand Russell in one of the earlier phases of his thought. In a work entitled *Our Knowledge of the External World* (1914), Russell analyzed the concept of physical objects as comprising classes of (perceptual) aspects or perspectives, an idea that later stimulated the work of Rudolf Carnap, an outstanding philosophical semanticist and Analyst, entitled *Der logische Aufbau der Welt* (1928; *The Logical Structure of the World,* 1967). Mach remained the most influential thinker among Positivists for a long time, though some of his disciples, like Josef Petzoldt, are now largely forgotten. But *The Grammar of Science* (1892), written by Karl Pearson, a scientist, statistician, and philosopher of science, still receives some attention; and in France it was Abel Rey, also a philosopher of science, who, along the lines of Mach, severely criticized the traditional mechanistic view of nature. In the United States, John Bernard Stallo, a German-born American philosopher of science (also an educator, jurist, and statesman), developed a Positivistic outlook, especially in the philosophy of physics, in his book *The Concepts and Theories of Modern Physics* (1882), in which he anticipated to a degree some of the general ideas later formulated in the theory of relativity and quantum mechanics.

LOGICAL POSITIVISM AND LOGICAL EMPIRICISM

A first generation of 20th-century Viennese Positivists began its activities, strongly influenced by Mach, around 1907. Notable among them were a physicist, Philipp Frank, mathematicians Hans Hahn and Richard von Mises, and an economist and sociologist, Otto Neurath. This small group was also active during the 1920s in the Vienna Circle of Logical Positivists, a seminal discussion group of gifted scientists and philosophers that met regularly in Vienna, and in the related Berlin Society for Empirical Philosophy.

The Vienna Circle and the Berlin Society

These two schools of thought, destined to develop into an almost worldwide and controversial movement, were built on the Empiricism of Hume, on the Positivism of Comte, and on the philosophy of science of Mach. Equally important influences came from several eminent figures who were at the same time scientists, mathematicians, and philosophers—G.F. Bernhard Riemann, the author of a non-Euclidean geometry; Hermann von Helmholtz, a pioneer in a broad range of scientific studies; Heinrich Hertz, the first to produce electromagnetic waves in his laboratory; Ludwig Boltzmann, a researcher in statistical mechanics; Henri Poincaré, equally eminent in mathematics and philosophy of science; and David Hilbert, distinguished for his formalizing of mathematics. Most significant, however, was the impact of Albert Einstein, as well as that of the three great mathematical logicians of the past 100 years—the ground-breaking German Gottlob Frege and the authors of the monumental *Principia Mathematica* (1910–13), Bertrand Russell and Alfred North Whitehead.

The earlier Positivism of Viennese heritage. The confluence of ideas from these sources and the impressions that they made upon the Vienna and Berlin groups in the 1920s gave rise to the philosophical outlook of Logical Positivism—a label supplied in 1931 by A.E. Blumberg and the Minnesota philosopher of science Herbert Feigl. The leader of the Vienna Circle between 1924 and 1936 was Moritz Schlick, who in 1922 succeeded to the chair (previously held by Mach and Boltzmann) for the philosophy of the inductive sciences at the University of Vienna. By 1924 an evening discussion group had been formed with Schlick, Hans Hahn, Otto Neurath, Victor Kraft, Kurt Reidemeister, and Felix Kaufmann as the prominent active participants. The most important addition to the circle was Rudolf Carnap, who joined the group in 1926. One of the early activities was the study and critical discussion of the *Tractatus Logico-Philosophicus* (1922) of Ludwig Wittgenstein, a seminal thinker in Analytical and Linguistic philosophy. It seemed at the time that the views of Carnap and Wittgenstein, although they had been formulated and elaborated quite differently, shared a large measure of basic agreement. Parallel, but not completely independent, developments occurred in the Berlin group, in which Hans Reichenbach, Richard von Mises, Kurt Grelling, and Walter Dubislav were the leading spirits.

Scientific, antimetaphysical orientation

Both the Vienna and Berlin groups consisted mainly of philosophically interested scientists or scientifically trained and oriented philosophers. Schlick had already anticipated some of the basic epistemological tenets of the groups in his *Allgemeine Erkenntnislehre* (1918; "General Theory of Knowledge"). But the philosophical outlook was sharpened and deepened when, in the late 1920s, the Viennese Positivists published a pamphlet *Wissenschaftliche Weltauffassung: Der Wiener Kreis* (1929; "Scientific Conception of the World: The Vienna Circle"), which was to be their declaration of independence from traditional philosophy—and, in the minds of its authors (Carnap, Hahn, and Neurath, aided by Waismann and Feigl), a "philosophy to end all philosophies."

Language and the clarification of meaning. The basic ideas of Logical Positivism were roughly as follows: the genuine task of philosophy is to clarify the meanings of basic concepts and assertions (especially those of science)—and not to attempt to answer unanswerable questions such as those regarding the nature of ultimate reality or of the Absolute. Inasmuch as an extremely ambitious Hegelian type of metaphysics, Idealistic and absolutist in orientation, was still prevalent in the German-speaking countries, there were many who believed that the antidote was urgently needed. Moreover, the Logical Positivists also had only contempt and ridicule for the ideas of the German Existentialist Martin Heidegger, whose interminable torment regarding such questions as "Why is there anything at all?" and "Why is what there is, the way it is?" and especially his pronouncements about Nothingness seemed to them to be not only sterile but so confused as to be nonsensical. The Logical Positivists viewed metaphysics as a hopelessly futile way of trying to do what great art, and especially poetry and music, already do so effectively and successfully. These activities, they held, are expressions of visions, feelings, and emotions and, as such, are perfectly legitimate as long as they make no claims to genuine cognition or representation of reality. What Logical Positivism recommended positively, on the other hand, was a logic and methodology of the basic assumptions and of the validation procedures of knowledge and of evaluation.

An adequate understanding of the functions of language and of the various types of meaning is another of the fundamentally important contributions of the Logical Positivists. Communication and language serve many diverse purposes: one is the representation of facts, or of the regularities in nature and society; another is the conveying of imagery, the expression and arousal of emotions; a third is the triggering, guidance, or modification of actions. Thus, they distinguished cognitive–factual meaning from expressive and evocative (or emotive) significance in words and sentences. It was granted that, in most utterances of everyday life (and even of science), these two types of meaning are combined or fused. What the Logical Positivists insisted upon, however, was that the emotive type of expression and appeal should not be mistaken for one having genuinely cognitive meanings. In such expressions as moral imperatives, admonitions, and exhortations there is, of course, a factually significant core; viz., regarding the (likely) consequences of various actions. But the normative element—expressed by such words as "ought," "should," "right," and their negations (as in "Thou shalt not. . . .")—is by itself not cognitively meaningful but has primarily emotional and motivative significance.

Cognitive versus emotive meaning

Early statements about moral value judgments, such as those by Carnap or by A.J. Ayer, a more radical British Positivist, seemed shocking to many philosophers, to whom it seemed that, in their careless formulation, moral norms were to be treated like expressions of taste. Equally shocking was their condemnation as nonsense (really non-sense; *i.e.*, complete absence of factual meaning) of all moral, aesthetic, and metaphysical assertions. More adequate and delicate analyses, such as that of the American Positivist Charles Stevenson, were soon to correct and modify those extremes. By proper allocation of the cognitive and the normative (motivative) components of value statements, many thinkers rendered the originally harsh and implausible Positivist view of value judgments more acceptable. Nevertheless, there is—in every Positivistic view—an ineluctable element of basic, noncognitive commitment in the acceptance of moral, or even of aesthetic, norms.

The verifiability criterion of meaning and its offshoots. The most noteworthy, and also most controversial, contribution of the Logical Positivists was the so-called verifiability criterion of factual meaningfulness. In its original form, this criterion had much in common with the earlier Pragmatist analysis of meaning (as in Charles Sanders Peirce and William James). Schlick's rather careless formulation: "The meaning of a [declarative sentence] is the method of its verification," which was really intended only to exclude from the realm of the cognitively meaningful those sentences for which it is logically inconceivable that either supporting or refuting evidence can be found, was close to the Pragmatist and, later, to the operationalist slogan that may be paraphrased by: "A difference must make a difference in order to be a difference"—or (more fully explicated): only if there is a difference in principle, open to test by observation, between the affirmation and the denial of a given assertion does this assertion have factual meaning. To take the classical example from Hume's analysis of the concept of causation, there is no difference between saying "*A* is always followed by *B*" and saying "*A* is necessarily always followed by *B*." That all *effects* have causes is true by virtue of the (customary) definitions of

Untestability of causation, ether, simultaneity

"cause" and "effect"; it is a purely formal or logical truth. But to say (instead of speaking of effects) that all *events* have causes is to say something factual—and conceivably false. (It should be noted that these rather crude uses of "causality" and "necessity" were later replaced by much more subtle analyses.)

One of the most important examples that stimulated the formulation of the meaning criterion was Einstein's abandonment, in 1905, of the ether hypothesis and of the notion of absolute simultaneity. The hypothesis that there exists a universal ether, as a medium for the propagation of light (and of electromagnetic waves generally), had been quite plausible and was widely accepted by physicists during the second half of the 19th century. To be sure, there were a number of serious difficulties with the idea: the properties that had to be ascribed to the ether were difficult to conceive in a logically compatible manner; and the ether hypothesis in the last stage of its development (by the Dutch physicist Hendrik Lorentz and the Irish physicist George Fitzgerald) had become objectionable in that it sought to provide excuses for the absolute unobservability of that mysterious, allegedly all-pervasive, universal substance. Similarly, it had become impossible, except at the price of intolerably ad hoc hypotheses, to maintain the notions of absolute time and of absolute simultaneity. Thus Einstein, by eliminating these empirically untestable assumptions, was led to his special theory of relativity.

Several important changes in the formulation of the meaning criterion took place in the ensuing decades from 1930 to 1960. The original version formulated in terms of verifiability was replaced by a more tolerant version expressed in terms of testability or confirmability. Obviously, universal propositions, such as "All cats have claws," being only partially supportable by positive instances (one cannot examine every cat that exists), are not conclusively verifiable. Nevertheless, scientists do accept lawlike statements on the basis of only incomplete, as well as indirect, verification—which is what "confirmation" amounts to. It was in coming to this juncture in his critique of Positivism that Karl Popper, an Austro-English philosopher of science, in his *Logik der Forschung* (1935; *The Logic of Scientific Discovery*, 1959), insisted that the meaning criterion should be abandoned and replaced by a criterion of demarcation between empirical (scientific) and transempirical (nonscientific, metaphysical) questions and answers—a criterion that, according to Popper, is to be testability, or, in his own version, falsifiability; *i.e.*, refutability. Popper was impressed by how easy it is to supposedly verify all sorts of assertions—those of psychoanalytic theories seemed to him to be abhorrent examples. But the decisive feature, as Popper saw it, should be whether it is in principle conceivable that evidence could be cited that would refute (or disconfirm) a given law, hypothesis, or theory. Theories are (often) bold conjectures. It is true that scientists should be encouraged in their construction of theories—no matter how far they deviate from the tradition; it is also true, however, that all such conjectures should be subjected to the most severe and searching criticism and experimental scrutiny of their truth claims. The growth of knowledge thus proceeds through the elimination of error; *i.e.*, through the refutation of hypotheses that are either logically inconsistent or entail empirically refuted consequences.

Modifications of the meaning criterion

Despite valuable suggestions in Popper's philosophy of science, the Logical Positivists and Empiricists continued to reformulate their criteria of factual meaningfulness. The Positivist Hans Reichenbach, who emigrated from Germany to California, proposed, in his *Experience and Prediction* (1938), a probabilistic conception. If hypotheses, generalizations, and theories can be made more or less probable by whatever evidence is available, he argued, then they are factually meaningful. In another version of meaningfulness, first adumbrated by Schlick (under the influence of Wittgenstein's thought), the philosopher's attention is focussed on concepts rather than on propositions. If the concepts in terms of which theories are formulated can be related, through chains of definitions, to concepts that are definable ostensibly—*i.e.*, by pointing to or exhibiting items or aspects of direct experience—

then those theories are factually meaningful. This is the version also advocated by Richard von Mises, an Austro-American mathematician and methodologist, in his *Positivism* (1951) and, later, more technically elaborated by Carnap, in *Minnesota Studies in the Philosophy of Science,* vol. 1 (1956).

Other issues. These views of meaningfulness are essentially refinements of the doctrine of so-called protocol sentences, developed in the late 1920s and early 1930s and elaborated especially by Carnap, by Otto Neurath, a polymath sociologist and philosopher, and also (with some differences) by Schlick. Protocol sentences, originally conceived along the lines of an interpretation, developed in the Vienna Circle, of Wittgenstein's elementary propositions, were identified as those sentences that make statements about the data of direct experience. But Neurath—and independently also Popper—warned of the danger that this doctrine might lead to subjective Idealism and recommended that it be given a rational reconstruction on an intersubjective basis. Thus, Neurath and Carnap

Physicalism and the Unity of Science

preferred that a physicalistic thing-language be employed as the starting point and testing ground of all knowledge claims. Propositions in this language would describe objectively existing, directly observable states of affairs or events. Because all objective and intersubjective knowledge was seen, in such a physicalism, to rest on statements representing things and their properties, relations and ongoing processes as they are found in unbiassed, and presumedly theory-free, observation, the physicalists were thus proclaiming a first thesis of the so-called Unity of Science principle. Though Mach had proceeded from the basis of (neutral) immediate experience, his insistence on the unity of all knowledge and all science was retained—at least in general spirit—by the later Positivists. In this view, all classifications of the sciences, or divisions of their subject matter, were seen as artificial, valuable at best only administratively, but without philosophical justification.

Sharply to be distinguished from this first thesis of the Unity of Science is a second that formulates a reductionism of a very different type: whereas the first thesis concerns the unity of the observational basis of all the sciences, the second proposes (tentatively) a unity of the explanatory principles of science. Reductions within physics itself, such as that of thermodynamics to the kinetic theory of heat (statistical mechanics) and of optics to electromagnetics; and, beyond that, the explanation of chemical phenomena, with the help of the quantum theory, in terms of atomic and molecular processes; and, furthermore, the progress that has been made in the physical explanation of biological phenomena (especially in the recent development of molecular biology)—all of these encourage the idea of a unitary set of physical premises from which the regularities of all of reality could be derived. But it must be admitted that, in contrast to the first thesis (which, by comparison is almost trivial), the second, being a bold conjecture about future reductions in the sciences, might well prove to be limited in the scope of its validity. The most controversial part of this reductionist ideology, however, concerns the realms of organic life and especially that of mind; it concerns, in other words, the reducibility of biology to physics and chemistry and of psychology to neurophysiology—and (though this is clearly utopian at present) of both ultimately to basic physics.

The most serious alternative to this reducibility thesis of the Unity of Science movement is the theory of emergent evolution, according to which life or mind (or both) are genuinely novel forms of reality that could not possibly have been derived from, or predicted by, any laws or theories of the lower or earlier levels of existence.

Historically, it may be plausible that the notorious perplexities of the traditional problem of how mind relates to body motivated both the phenomenalistic Positivists as well as the Behaviourists and physicalists. In either view, the mind–body problem conveniently disappears; it is branded as a metaphysical pseudoproblem. The phenomenalism of Mach and the early Russell was expressed in a position called neutral monism, according to which both psychological and physical concepts are viewed as logical constructions on the basis of a neutral set of data of im-

Neutral monism and mental states

mediate experience. There are thus not two realities—the mental and the physical; there are merely different ways of organizing the experiential data. In the Behaviourist–physicalist alternative, on the other hand, the philosopher, considering the concepts that are ordinarily taken to characterize private mental acts and processes, defines them on the basis of publicly (intersubjectively) observable features of the behaviour, including the linguistic behaviour, of man.

The absolute privacy of mental events was first criticized, however, by Carnap and later by an Oxford Analytical philosopher, Gilbert Ryle; and Wittgenstein, in an argument against the very possibility of a private language, maintained that, unless men have objective criteria for the occurrence of mental states, they cannot even begin to communicate meaningfully with each other about their direct experiences. Wittgenstein thus repudiated the traditional view according to which a man's knowledge of other persons' minds must be based on analogical inference from his own case. In a similar vein, an American psychologist, B.F. Skinner, tried to account for man's acquisition of subjective terms in his language by a theory of verbal behaviour. A man learns to describe his mental states, explained Skinner, from the utterances of others who ascribe these states to him by virtue of their observation of his behaviour (*e.g.*, in the social context; or when a certain stimulus situation prevails in his environment).

Both Carnap and Ryle have emphasized that many mental features or properties have a dispositional character. Dispositional terms, whether used in psychology or more broadly, have to be understood as shorthand expressions for test conditions—or test-result conditionals. Thus, even in ordinary life, a man appraises, for example, the intelligence of a person in the light of what he does, how he does it, how fast he does it, when confronted with various tasks or problems. Just as such physical properties as malleability, brittleness, or thermal or electrical conductivity must be defined in terms of what happens when certain conditions are imposed, so also mental dispositions are to be construed as similarly hypothetical; *i.e.*, as (in the simplest case) stimulus–response relationships.

Dispositions as conditionals

The later Positivism of Logical Empiricism. Logical Positivism, essentially the doctrine of the Vienna Circle (*c.* 1924–38), underwent a number of important changes and innovations in the middle third of the century, which suggested the need for a new name. The designation Positivism had been strongly connected with the Comte–Mach tradition of instrumentalism and phenomenalism. The emphasis that this tradition had placed, however, on the positive facts of observation and their negative attitude toward the atomic theory and the existence of theoretical entities in general were no longer in keeping with the spirit of 20th-century science. Nevertheless, the requirement that hypotheses and theories be empirically testable, though it became more flexible and tolerant, could not be relinquished. It was natural, then, that the word "empiricism" should occur in any new name. Accordingly, retaining the term "logical" in roughly its same earlier meaning, the new name "Logical Empiricism" was coined.

The status of the formal and a priori. The intention of the word "logical" was to insist on the distinctive nature of logical and mathematical truth. In opposition to Mill's view, according to which even logic and pure mathematics are empirical (*i.e.*, are justifiable or refutable by observation), the Logical Positivists—essentially following Frege and Russell—had already declared mathematics to be true only by virtue of postulates and definitions. Expressed in the traditional terms used by Kant, logic and mathematics were recognized as a priori disciplines (valid independently of experience) precisely because their denial would amount to a self-contradiction, and statements within these disciplines were expressed in what Kant called analytic propositions; *i.e.*, propositions that are true or false only by virtue of the meanings of the terms they contain. In his own way, the broad-ranging scholar Gottfried Leibniz had seen this in the 17th century long before Kant. The truth of such a simple arithmetical proposition as, for example, "$2 + 3 = 5$" is necessary, universal, a priori, and analytic because of the very meaning of "2," "+,"

The analytic and synthetic in mathematics

"3," "5," and "=." Experience could not possibly refute such truths because their validity is established (as Hume said) merely by the "relation of ideas." Even if—"miraculously"—putting two and three objects together should on some occasion yield six objects, this would be a fascinating feature of those objects (rabbits, perhaps); but it would not in the least tend to refute the purely definitional truths of arithmetic.

The case of geometry is altogether different. Geometry can be either an empirical science of natural space or an abstract system with uninterpreted basic concepts and uninterpreted postulates. The latter is the conception introduced in rigorous fashion by a late 19th-century mathematician, David Hilbert, and, still later, by a United States geometer, Oswald Veblen. In the axiomatizations that they developed, the basic concepts, called primitives, are implicitly defined by the postulates: thus, such concepts as point, straight line, intersection, betweenness, and plane are related to each other in a merely formal manner. The proof of theorems from postulates, and with explicit definitions of derived concepts (such as of triangle, polygon, circle, or conic section), is achieved by strict deductive inference. Very different, however, is geometry as understood in practical life, and in the natural sciences and technologies, in which it constitutes the science of space. Ever since the development of the non-Euclidean geometries in the first half of the 19th century, it has no longer been taken for granted that Euclidean geometry is the only geometry uniquely applicable to the spatial order of physical objects or events. In Einstein's general theory of relativity and gravitation, in fact, a four-dimensional Riemannian geometry with variable curvature was successfully employed, an event that amounted to a final refutation of the Kantian contention that the truths of geometry are "synthetic a priori." With respect to the relation of postulates to theorems, geometry is thus analytic, like any other rigorously deductive discipline; but the postulates themselves, when interpreted—*i.e.,* when construed as statements about the structure of physical space—are indeed synthetic, but also a posteriori; *i.e.,* their adequacy depends upon the results of observation and measurement.

Developments in Linguistic Analysis and their offshoots. Important contributions, beginning in the early 1930s, were made by Carnap, by Kurt Gödel, a Moravian-American mathematical logician, and others to the logical analysis of language. Charles Morris, a Pragmatist concerned with Linguistic Analysis, had outlined the three dimensions of semiotics (the general study of signs and symbolisms): syntax, semantics, and pragmatics (the relation of signs to their users and to the conditions of their use). Syntactical studies, concerned with the formation and transformation rules of language (*i.e.,* its purely structural features), soon required supplementation by semantical studies, concerned with rules of designation and of truth. Semantics, in the strictly formalized sense, owed its origin to Alfred Tarski, a leading member of the Polish school of logicians, and was then developed by Carnap and applied to problems of meaning and necessity. As Wittgenstein had already shown, the necessary truth of tautologies simply amounts to their being true under all conceivable circumstances. Thus the so-called eternal verity of the principles of identity (*p* is equivalent with itself), of noncontradiction (one cannot both assert and deny the same proposition), and the principle of excluded middle (any given proposition is either true or false; there is no further possibility) is an obvious consequence of the rules according to which the philosopher uses (or decides to use) the words "proposition," "negation," "equivalence," "conjunction," "disjunction," and others. Quite generally, questions regarding the meanings of words or symbols are answered most illuminatingly by stating the syntactical and the semantical rules according to which they are used.

Ordinary versus artificial language

Two different schools of thought originated from this basic insight: (1) the philosophy of "ordinary language" Analysis—initiated by Wittgenstein, especially in his later work, and (following him) developed in differing directions in the works of Gilbert Ryle and John Langshaw Austin, both Oxford philosophers, of the Cambridge Analyst John Wisdom, and others; and (2) the ideology, essentially that of Carnap, usually designated as logical reconstruction, which builds up an artificial language. In the procedures of "ordinary language" Analysis, an attempt is made to trace the ways in which a person commonly expresses himself. In this manner, many of the traditional vexatious philosophical puzzles and perplexities are shown to arise out of deviant uses of language. (Lewis Carroll had already anticipated some of these oddities in his whimsical manner in *Alice in Wonderland.*) The much more rigorous procedures of the second school—of Tarski, Carnap, and many other logicians—rest upon the obvious distinction between the language (and all of its various symbols) that is the object of analysis, called the object language, and that in which the analysis is formulated, called the metalanguage. If needed and fruitful, this process can be repeated, in that the erstwhile metalanguage can become the object of a metametalanguage, and so on—without the danger of a vicious infinite regress.

With the help of semantical concepts, an old perplexity in the theory of knowledge can then be resolved. Positivists have often tended to conflate the truth conditions of a statement with its confirming evidence, a procedure which has led to certain absurdities committed by phenomenalists and operationalists, such as the pronouncement that the meanings of statements about past events consist in their (forthcoming future) evidence. Clearly, the objects—the targets or referents—of such statements are the past events. Thus the meaning of a historical statement is its truth conditions; *i.e.,* the situation that would have to obtain if the historical statement is to be true. The confirmatory evidence, however, may be discovered either in the present or in the future. Similarly, the evidence for an existential hypothesis in the sciences may consist, for example, in cloud-chamber tracks, spectral lines, or the like, whereas the truth conditions may relate to subatomic processes or to astrophysical facts. Or, to take an example from depth psychology, the occurrences of unconscious wishes or conflicts are the truth conditions for which the observable symptoms (Freudian lapses, manifest dream contents, and the like) serve merely as indicators or clues; *i.e.,* as items of confirming evidence.

The third dimension of language (in Morris' view of semiotic)—*i.e.,* the pragmatic aspect—has not been as fully and formally analyzed as the other two dimensions. There is even some disagreement as to whether some of the cognitive activities (such as verifying, refuting, or interpreting), in addition to the noncognitive functions (such as the motivative and persuasive appeals), are to be included in studies of pragmatics.

Undecidability; probability

One of the most surprising and revolutionary offshoots of the metalinguistic (formal) analyses was Kurt Gödel's discovery, in 1931, of an exact proof of the undecidability of certain types of mathematical problems, a discovery that dealt a severe blow to the expectations of the Formalistic school of mathematics championed by Hilbert and his collaborator, Paul Bernays. Before Gödel's discovery, it had seemed plausible that a mathematical system could be complete in the sense that any well-formed formula of the system could be either proved or disproved on the basis of the given set of postulates. But Gödel showed rigorously (what had been only a conjecture on the part of the Dutch Intuitionist L.E.J. Brouwer and his followers) that, for a large class of important mathematical systems, such completeness cannot be achieved.

Both Carnap and Reichenbach, in their very different ways, made extensive contributions to the theory of probability and induction. Impressed with the need for an interpretation of the concept of probability that was thoroughly empirical, Reichenbach elaborated a view that conceived probability as a limit of relative frequency and buttressed it with a pragmatic justification of inductive inference. Carnap granted the importance of this concept (especially in modern physical theories) but attempted, in increasingly refined and often revised forms, to define a concept of degree-of-confirmation that was purely logical. Statements ascribing an inductive probability to a hypothesis are, in Carnap's view, analytic, because they merely formulate the strength of the support bestowed upon a hypothesis by a given body of evidence.

Logical Positivism and Logical Empiricism have from their very beginnings been subjected to searching criticisms. At first it was the verifiability criterion of meaningfulness that produced a storm of oppositions. One group of critics asked whether the criterion was meaningful in the light of its own standard. Carnap replied that the criterion itself was not intended as a factual assertion but rather as a proposal for a better and clearer use of language. Nevertheless, the Logical Empiricists felt that the (tolerant–liberal) formulation of the meaning criterion—far from being an arbitrary injunction—came rather close to what enlightened common sense, and especially the scientific attitude, intended by the difference between sense and non-sense.

Scientific explanation

Other recent and current criticisms concern the Logical Empiricist views regarding the nature of scientific explanation, in regard to which matters are not as simple as they were originally conceived to be. Closer attention to the history of scientific theories has revealed important discontinuities, or revolutions, in the conceptual schemes of the sciences. The significant role of statistical (or probabilistic) explanations in most modern sciences, for example, is receiving increasingly sophisticated analyses.

Nevertheless, the prevalence of scientific revolutions and anarchism or subjectivism in scientific method has been exaggerated in differing ways by several scholars. As has been conceded by all competent philosophers of science and even by the greatest scientist-philosophers of the century—Albert Einstein, Niels Bohr, Erwin Schrödinger, and others—there is no straight logical path, no standard recipe, by which to move from the data of observation and arrive at scientific theories. It may also be admitted that, though scientific creativity has psychologically much in common with artistic creation, the criteria of appraisal are certainly quite different. And, although, from the present critical point of view, all and any scientific assertions are in principle subject to revision, it is nonetheless felt to be grotesque to deny the relative stability of the empirical laws that serve as the testing ground of alternative theories.

(H.Fe.)

Pragmatism

In its broadest and most familiar sense, "pragmatism" refers to the usefulness, workability, and practicality of ideas, policies, and proposals as criteria of their merit and claims to attention. Achieving results, "getting things done" in business and public affairs is often said to be "pragmatic." There is a harsher and more brutal connotation of the term in which any exercise of power in the successful pursuit of practical and specific objectives is called "pragmatic." The character of American business and politics is often so described. In these cases "pragmatic" carries the stamp of justification: a policy is justified pragmatically if it is successful. The familiar and the academic conceptions have in common an opposition to invoking the authority of precedents or of abstract and ultimate principles. Thus in law, judicial decisions that have turned on the weighing of consequences and probable general welfare rather than on being deduced from precedents have been called pragmatic.

The word pragmatism goes back to the Greek πραγμα ("action," "affair"). The Greek historian Polybius (died 118 BC) called his writings "pragmatic," meaning thereby that they were intended to be instructive and useful to his readers. In his introduction to the *Philosophy of History,* Hegel commented on this "pragmatical" approach as the second kind of reflective history, and for this genre he cited Johannes von Müller's *History of the World* (Eng. trans. 1840). As the psychologist and leading Pragmatist William James remarked, "the term is derived from the same Greek word πραγμα meaning action, from which our words 'practice' and 'practical' come." Charles Peirce, another pioneering Pragmatist, who may have been the first to use the word to designate a specific philosophic doctrine, had Kant's German term rather than the Greek word in mind: *Pragmatisch* refers to experimental, empirical, and purposive thought "based on and applying to experience." In the philosophy of education the notion

that children learn by doing, that critical standards of procedure and understanding emerge from the application of concepts to directly experienced subject matters, has been called "pragmatic." In semiotics, the general theory of language, that part that studies the relation of the user to the words or other signs that he uses is called pragmatics (as distinct from semantics and syntax).

During the first quarter of the 20th century, Pragmatism was the most influential philosophy in America, exerting an impact on the study of law, education, political and social theory, art, and religion. Six fundamental theses of this philosophy can be distinguished. It is, however, unlikely that any one thinker would have subscribed to them all; and even on points of agreement, varying interpretations mark the thought and temper of the major Pragmatists. The six theses are:

1. Responsive to Idealism and evolutionary theory, Pragmatists have emphasized the "plastic" nature of reality and the practical function of knowledge as an instrument for adapting to reality and controlling it. Existence is fundamentally concerned with action, which some Pragmatists exalted to an almost metaphysical level. Change being an inevitable condition of life, Pragmatists have called attention to the ways in which change can be directed for individual and social benefit. They have consequently been most critical of moral and metaphysical doctrines in which change and action are relegated to the "merely practical," on the lowest level of the hierarchy of values. Some Pragmatists anticipated the more concrete and life-centred philosophy of Existentialism by arguing that only in acting—confronted with obstacles, compelled to make choices, and concerned to give form to experience—is man's being realized and discovered.

2. Pragmatism is a continuation of critical Empiricism in emphasizing the priority of actual experience over fixed principles and a priori reasoning in critical investigation. For James this meant that the Pragmatist

turns away from abstraction and insufficiency, from verbal solutions, from bad *a priori* reasons, from fixed principles, closed systems, and pretended absolutes and origins. He turns towards concreteness and adequacy, towards facts, towards action.... It means the open air and possibilities of nature, as against ... dogma, artificiality, and the pretence of finality in truth.

3. The pragmatic meaning of an idea, belief, or proposition is said to reside in the distinct class of specific experimental or practical consequences that result from the use, application, or entertainment of the notion. As Peirce commented: "Our idea of anything is our idea of its sensible effects." Two propositions for which no different effects can be discerned have merely a verbal appearance of dissimilarity, and a proposition for which no definite theoretical or practical consequences can be determined is pragmatically meaningless. For Pragmatists "there is no distinction of meaning so fine as to consist in anything but a possible difference of practice." Meaning thus has a predictive component, and some Pragmatists came close to identifying the meaning of a term or proposition with the process of its verification.

4. While most philosophers have defined truth in terms of a belief's "coherence" within a pattern of other beliefs or as the "correspondence" between a proposition and an actual state of affairs, Pragmatism has, in contrast, generally held that truth, like meaning, is to be found in the process of verification. Thus truth *is* the verification of a proposition, or the successful working of an idea. Crudely, truth is "what works." Less crudely and more theoretically, truth is in Peirce's words, the "limit towards which endless investigation would tend to bring scientific belief." For John Dewey, founder of the "Instrumentalist" school of Pragmatism, these are beliefs "warranted" by inquiry.

5. In keeping with their understanding of meaning and truth, Pragmatists have interpreted ideas as instruments and plans of action. In contrast to the conception of ideas as images and copies of impressions or of external objects, Pragmatist theories have emphasized the functional character of ideas: ideas are suggestions and anticipations of

possible conduct; they are hypotheses or forecasts of what will result from a given action; they are ways of organizing behaviour in the world rather than replicas of the world. Ideas are thus analogous in some respects to tools; they are efficient, useful, and valuable, or not, depending on the role that they play in contributing to the successful direction of behaviour.

6. In methodology, Pragmatism is a broad philosophical attitude toward the formation of concepts, hypotheses, and theories and their justification. To Pragmatists man's interpretations of reality are motivated and justified by considerations of efficacy and utility in serving his interests and needs; the molding of language and theorizing are likewise subject to the critical objective of maximum usefulness according to man's various purposes.

HISTORY OF PRAGMATISM

Antecedents in modern philosophy. Pragmatism was a part of a general revolt against the overly intellectual, somewhat fastidious, and closed systems of Idealism in 19th-century philosophy. These boldly speculative Idealists had expanded man's subjective experience of mind till it became a metaphysical principle of cosmic explanation. To the Idealist, all of reality was one fabric, woven from parts that cohered by virtue of the internal relations that they bore to one another; and this reality was often interpreted in abstract and fixed intellectual categories. The theory of evolution, then still new, seemed to the Pragmatists, on the other hand, to call for a new, non-Idealist interpretation of nature, life, and reason—one that challenged the long-established conceptions of fixed species. The new emphasis was on the particular variations and struggles of life in adapting to the environment. Philosophically, the fact of growth and the development of techniques for instituting changes favourable to life became the significant factors rather than the Idealist's ambitious rationalistic account of human goals and of the universe in general, and important developments in natural science and logic also encouraged a critical attitude toward earlier systems.

There were two main influences on the early formation of Pragmatism: One was the tradition of British Empiricism in the work of John Stuart Mill, Alexander Bain, and John Venn, which had stressed the role of experience in the genesis of knowledge—and particularly their analyses of belief as being intimately tied in with action and, indeed, as definable in terms of one's disposition and motive to act. The work of George Berkeley, an important 18th-century empirical Idealist, which presented a theory of the practical and inferential nature of knowledge, of sensations as signs (and thus predictive) of future experience, led Peirce to refer to him as "the introducer of Pragmatism." The other major influence came from modern German philosophy: from Kant's analysis of the purposive character of belief and of the roles of will and desire in forming belief and his doctrine of "regulative ideas," such as God or the Soul, which guide the understanding in achieving systematic completeness and unity of knowledge; from Romantic Idealists, for whom all reason is "practical" in expanding and enriching human experience; and from Hegel's historical and social conception of changing and developing subject matters. In sum, Peirce was profoundly impressed by Kant and by the Scottish philosophy of common sense, James by British Empiricism and by the voluntarisms (stressing the role of choice or will) of the genetic epistemologist James Ward and the relativistic French Personalist Charles Renouvier, Dewey by Coleridge's version of Kant's active conception of mind and by neo-Kantian and Hegelian Idealism.

Finally, to these influences must be added that of American social experience in the 19th century: the rapid expansion of industry and trade and a popular optimism, with its roots in Puritan theology, holding that hard work and virtue are bound to be rewarded. Both the precariousness of frontier life, however, and the rapidly expanding economy weakened the prevailing Calvinistic belief in a predestined future and encouraged the emergence of inventiveness, a sense of living still in the New World experiment, and adoption of the ideal of "making good."

The Metaphysical Club. It was in the critical group discussions of the "Metaphysical Club" in the 1870s in Cambridge, Massachusetts, that Pragmatism first received philosophic expression. In addition to Peirce and James, membership in the club included Chauncey Wright, F.E. Abbot, and Justice Oliver Wendell Holmes, Jr. A version of Peirce's now classic paper "The Fixation of Belief" (November 1877) seems to have been presented at the club. But James also published a paper in 1878, "Spencer's Definition of Mind as Correspondence," in which his Pragmatism and analysis of thought and belief are clearly discernible. It was in a lecture delivered 20 years later, however, that James introduced Pragmatism, then fully crediting the idea to Peirce. It was primarily James's exposition that became famous and was received by the world at large.

The classical Pragmatists. The Pragmatic philosophy of Charles Sanders Peirce was part of a more general theory of thought and of signs. Thought, or "inquiry," it was held, results from doubt, a state in which habitual actions are blocked or confused and from which organic irritation and irresolution result. Resolution, unobstructed conduct, on the other hand, are products of belief, which is a form of stability and satisfaction. It is the function of scientific thought to produce true beliefs. In a prolonged effort to embed this analysis of doubt and inquiry within a more comprehensive theory of signs in which communication, thought, knowledge, and intelligent conduct could be fully understood, Peirce achieved a wealth of original insights. A sign is a socially standardized way by which something (a thought, word, object) refers man (the community of sign users) to something else (the interpretant), which, in turn, is itself another sign. Peirce's Pragmatism is thus a method for translating certain kinds of signs into clearer signs in order to surmount linguistic or conceptual confusion. Getting at the interpretant involves determining the "effects" or consequences of the signs or ideas in question.

Peirce's Pragmatism is therefore primarily a theory of meaning that emerged from his first-hand reflections on his own scientific work, in which the experimentalist understands a proposition as meaning that, if a prescribed experiment is performed, a stated experience will result. The method has two different uses:

(1) It is a way of showing that when disputes permit no resolution, the difficulties are due to misuses of language, to subtle conceptual confusions. Such questions as whether the physical world is an illusion, whether man's senses always mislead him, or whether his actions are fated are "not real problems."

(2) The method may be employed for clarification. As Peirce wrote:

Consider what effects, that might conceiveably have practical bearings, we conceive the object of our conception to have. Then our conception of these effects is the whole of our conception of the object.

To say, for example, that an object O is hard means that if the operation of scratching O is performed, O will not be scratched by most substances. One thus achieves clarity when one can supply a conditional statement of this kind.

Similarly, in his theory of truth, one means by truth of belief that if a certain operation is the subject of continuous scientific inquiry by the community of investigators, assent to the belief would increase and dissent decrease "in the long run." Consequently, not only is thought purposive but meaning carries a reference to the future. Peirce's concept of the community of sign users and inquirers also has social and moral relevance, for it is nothing less than the ideal of rational democracy.

Witnessing his doctrine undergo a medley of dubious interpretations, Peirce eventually dissociated himself from these by calling his own view "Pragmaticism," a term he called so ugly as to be safe from uninformed use. Parts of the work of Dewey, of the social Pragmatist G.H. Mead, and of the conceptualistic Pragmatist C.I. Lewis are a further development of the logical Pragmatism of Peirce. The English logician F.P. Ramsey and the Italians Giovanni Vailati and Mario Calderoni also undertook significant extensions of Peirce's Pragmatism.

An alternative, though not wholly different, version of Pragmatism was developed by William James. It took a

James's
Prag-
matism

psychological and moral form largely unforeseen and un-intended by Peirce.

A basic difference between Peirce and James is discernible in their respective conceptions of the direction to be taken by Pragmatic analysis. While Peirce construed meaning in general, conditional schema, and interpretants, James focussed upon the distinct contributions that ideas and beliefs make to specific forms of human experience on the living level of practical wants and purposes. Between the two close friends there persisted a fundamental philosophical difference in outlook that affected even their styles. While James was a Nominalist, holding that the full significance of ideas, meanings, and actions lies in their particular concrete existent occurrence, Peirce—as a scholastic Realist—sharply criticized him at this point, arguing that "a thing in general is as real as in the concrete."

The most conspicuous feature of James's writings on Pragmatism is the dominant place given to considerations of value, worth, and satisfaction—consequences of his teleological (purposive) conception of mind (*cf.* his *Principles of Psychology*). James maintained that thought is adaptive and purposive but also suffused with ideal emotional and practical interests—"should-be's"—which, as conditions of action, work to transform the world and create the future, even to "make the truth which they declare." Consequently, truth and meaning are species of value: "*The true is the name of whatever proves itself to be good in the way of belief.*"

James took meaning to be an intimate part of the use of ideas for expediting action. The notion of the difference that a proposition makes in experience was fundamental in James's Pragmatic methodology. He remarked that "it is a good rule in physiology, when we are studying the meaning of an organ," to look to the specific function that it performs. In like manner, the special difference that the presence of mind makes in observable cases, reflected in its unique functioning, defines the use of "mind"; "In particular, the pursuance of future ends and the choice of means . . . are thus the *mark and criterion of the presence of mentality.*"

With his training in medicine and psychology and the influence of Darwin in the background, James considered that the main function of thought is to help us establish "satisfactory relations with our surroundings." Thus man helps to mold the character of reality according to his needs and desires. Indeed, this is fundamental in James's defense of the right to believe in his famous essay "The Will to Believe" (1897). James argued that we may have a reasonable right to hold a religious or metaphysical belief (*e.g.,* that there is a perfect, eternal, and personal aspect of the universe) when the belief in question would supply a vital psychological and moral benefit to the believer, when evidence for and against the belief is equal, and when the decision to believe is forced and momentous. In James's functional conception of truth, the "working," and hence the truth, of ideas is their role in opening up valuable possible directions of thought and action—"a leading that is worth while."

James's "working" view of truth and of a reality that man in part makes by acting out and realizing ideas, and especially his essay "The Will to Believe," were enthusiastically received by F.C.S. Schiller in England and by Giovanni Papini in Italy, and these doctrines became a cause célèbre for Pragmatists and their critics.

Schiller's
Prag-
matism

An admirer and friend of James, Schiller, now nearly forgotten, was once the most famous Pragmatist in England and Europe. Schiller was initially a humanist in the sense that, for him, both reality and knowledge are reflections of human activity—"the taken" rather than "the given." He first came to appreciate James's "The Will to Believe" in 1897 and subsequently acknowledged its impact on his thinking in an early and important paper, "Axioms As Postulates" (1902). He was a tireless critic of the "closed" systems of Idealism of F.H. Bradley, J.M.E. McTaggart, and Bernard Bosanquet and an advocate of the intellectual freedom that consists in "open," plural, changing, and to some extent never finished philosophical theorizing. According to Schiller, reality and truth are "man-made" rather than eternal verities. The true and the false are basically forms of good and bad and are relative to the private purposes of some particular person. He attempted to describe and analyze the "logic" of the experimental "trying" through which such needs are satisfied. For Schiller, reality is wholly plastic; and, starting out from initial postulates, one proceeds to construct one's schemes for achieving a satisfactory outcome of desire, finally rendering one's unformed possibilities (*hylē*) into a common world of language and action. On this view, all of science derives from and is inescapably guided by the psychological process of human thought; man is the measure of all things.

John Dewey once noted that "Peirce wrote as a logician and James as a humanist." This distinction characterizes not only the course of Pragmatism but also the shaping of Dewey's own thought. Dewey first felt the influence of James in the 1890s, during the period in which he was struggling to free himself from the hold of Hegelian Idealism. Later, he recognized the value of Peirce's work, which clearly prefigured certain ideas that he had developed independently.

Dewey's
Instru-
mentalism

With indefatigable effort and care Dewey reformulated Pragmatism, critically readjusting some of its conflicting doctrines, drawing upon his own work in psychology and education, and finding stimulation in the social Pragmatism of his friend George Herbert Mead. The resulting construction was Instrumentalism, which Dewey conceived as a single coherent theory embracing both the logical and humanistic currents of Pragmatism and thus integrating the methods and conclusions of scientific knowledge with beliefs about values and purposes.

While scientific, moral, and social experiences may differ in subject matter, the method of thought functioning "in the experimental determinations of future consequences" remains the same for all inquiry. Initially provoked by doubtful or problematic conditions, intelligent conduct is addressed to a resolution and settling of these conditions and to a "warranted assertion"—Dewey's version of "truth." Such is the "mediative function" of reason. "Truth" is thus identified with the outcome of competent inquiry. Actions occurring on the organic level, if they be at first confused and obstructed, can then become organized, coherent, and liberated through such inquiry.

Dewey's analysis of the organic, cultural, and formal conditions of intelligent action implies that all reflective conduct issues in an evaluation of a situation with respect to future action and consequences: thus inquiry is essentially an evaluative procedure. This method, most impressively applied in the sciences, is nonetheless a paradigm of moral activity as well. In ethics, "the action needed to satisfy" the situation is not to be found simply by the application of moral codes. The meaning

has to be searched for [since] there are conflicting desires and alternative apparent goods . . . . Hence inquiry is exacted . . . . The good of the situation has to be discovered, projected and attained on the basis of the exact defect and trouble to be rectified.

In general, for Instrumentalism, moral ideals and "ends" function as means and hypotheses in guiding the deliberative process directed to controlling experience and attaining future goods.

Not health as an end fixed once for all, but the needed improvement in health—a continual process—is the end and good . . . . Not perfection as a final goal, but the ever-enduring process of perfecting, maturing, refining is the aim of living . . . . Growth itself is the only moral 'end.'

Inquiry possessed a genuine religious significance for Dewey, and in its functioning as a critical, self-corrective social process of human growth he envisaged the working ethic of democracy.

Other American Pragmatists. Two important contributions to American Pragmatism, which have not yet received the attention that they deserve, came from Mead and Lewis.

Mead's orientation was social psychology. He had studied physiological psychology in Germany, had earlier worked under James and Josiah Royce at Harvard, and was also familiar with Peirce's analyses of thought and signs. Dewey regarded him as one of the most fertile minds in American philosophy.

Mead's social and Lewis' conceptualistic Pragmatism

Mead developed the most comprehensive of the Pragmatist theories of mind. He depicted the evolution of mind and self-consciousness as emerging from social interactions and the use of gestures and "significant symbols" such as words. In contrast to other creatures, an individual regarded as having mind, engaging with others in social acts, can respond to his own gestures as others respond to them—thus taking on social roles and becoming an "other" in respect to himself. It is therefore by means of language, the use of "significant symbols," that mind emerges.

Fundamental to Mead's philosophy is his conception of the social act, in which individuals modify and direct one anothers' activities, work out their purposes, and accordingly transform their environments. In the social act the future controls present conduct, and this is distinctive of consciousness. Since the function of intelligence is to render the world "favourable for conduct," Mead viewed the development of scientific knowledge and the evolutionary process as coinciding.

Lewis's theory of "conceptualistic Pragmatism" was derived partly from his study of modern logic and partly from the influence of Royce and the classic Pragmatists. The critical results of a careful study of Kant are traceable in his work.

Lewis's Pragmatism focusses upon concepts, categories, and principles through which experience is interpreted. Though the sensuously given is "unalterable," how it is taken, how conceptually interpreted, depends on the purposes and initiatives of the mind—the a priori element in knowledge, which, functioning as categorical criteria of reality, is "true no matter what." It is by means of these that a systematic interpretation of reality is developed. However,

> there may be alternative conceptual systems, giving rise to alternative descriptions of experience, which are equally objective and equally valid.... When this is so, choice will be determined ... on pragmatic grounds.

In stressing the purposive character of conceptualization, Lewis is thus in the main course of American Pragmatism.

Pragmatism in Europe. In his preface to *Pragmatism,* James commented that the Pragmatic movement was the focal expression of a number of philosophic tendencies suddenly becoming conscious of themselves and of "their combined mission." He mentioned the French thinkers Maurice Blondel, Édouard Le Roy, and B. de Sailly and the Italian Giovanni Papini. Blondel was the author of *L'Action* (1893) and spokesman for a voluntaristic and activistic theory of knowledge. He was a founder of the "school of action," a liberal Catholic group that was part of the modernist movement (which employed the new historico-critical approach to the Bible and promoted a rationalistic interpretation of the faith). As early as 1888, Blondel appropriated the term *Pragmatisme,* only to abandon it when he learned of American Pragmatism, which was a more naturalistic philosophy than his own. Le Roy, closer to James than other French thinkers, also called his views Pragmatism. In broad respects he was like James in holding that the truth and the full significance of beliefs is found in acting them out. Le Roy was a disciple of Henri Poincaré, who had argued that scientific theories are not mere summaries of data, nor deduced from axioms, but are creative constructions, products of human thought and ingenuity, "conventions." To the question of what limits are imposed on otherwise arbitrary conventions, of what justifies them, Le Roy suggested their convenience in use. James saw similar forms of Pragmatism in Ernst Mach, Wilhelm Ostwald, Pierre Duhem, and Théodore Ruyssen in "the notion that no theory is absolutely a transcript of reality" and that "their great use is to summarize old facts and lead to new ones" so that they are a "man-made language, a conceptual shorthand ... in which we write our reports of nature."

Another French thinker, Georges Sorel, undertook to reformulate James's Pragmatism into a "useful" doctrine of social criticism. Mussolini later cited Sorel and James as two of his philosophic mentors. He claimed to find in

Blondel, Le Roy, Papini, and others

James "that faith in action, that ardent will to live and fight, to which Fascism owes a great part of its success." To the democratic James, no lesson could have been more badly learned.

A more immediate and direct form of James's Pragmatism occurred in Italy with its centre in the journal *Leonardo,* under the leadership of the iconoclastic critic Giovanni Papini. James referred to Papini as "a brilliant, humorous and witty writer." He called him a genius and was addressed in turn by him as "the Master." Papini's Pragmatism, derived from James's "The Will to Believe," became a theory of the will to action. In action, through creative power and passion, man achieves a kind of divinity. This romantic exaltation of action was appealing to artists but also to fanatics. Papini and his associate Giuseppe Prezzolini comprised the "magical" school of Pragmatism (in the sense of seeking "divinely-creative" power) in contrast to the "logical" school inspired by Peirce of G. Vailati and M. Calderoni.

Later tendencies. Certain extensions and applications of Pragmatism are to be found in current American philosophy. Sidney Hook has directed some of the critical techniques of analysis against a number of ideologies. In the tradition of the scientifically oriented Pragmatisms of Peirce and Dewey, he has explored the relation between the logic of experimental inquiry and the ethic of democracy. A converging of Pragmatism and Logical Positivism resulted in the movement of "logical empiricism" which, in addition to Dewey and Lewis, included the top-rank philosophers of science P.W. Bridgman, Rudolf Carnap, and Ernest Nagel, and the philosophical semanticist Charles W. Morris, all of whom were responsive to the Pragmatisms of Peirce, James, and Dewey. More recent and detailed studies of the structure of science, the nature of theories and explanation, by Carnap, Lewis, and Nagel, and a new interest in Instrumentalism deriving from the work of F.P. Ramsey, Ludwig Wittgenstein, W.H. Watson, and Gilbert Ryle (as well, of course, as from Dewey) exhibit a further continuation of Pragmatism.

Maintaining a "more thorough Pragmatism" than that of Carnap and Lewis, who viewed choices made within scientific frameworks as pragmatic decisions, the prominent logician W.V. Quine has argued against the alleged boundary between analytic and synthetic truths. No portion of the conceptual scheme of science is exempt (as analytic truths were supposed to be) from possible revision in the flux of experience and in the light of pragmatic interests in efficacy and comprehension in predicting future experience. In important respects Quine's view of the evolution, organization, and function of the conceptual structure of science is close to that of Schiller, James, and Dewey.

Quine has also defended a methodological Pragmatism and relativism on ontological questions on the nature of being or reality. This position, also taken by another contemporary philosopher of science and language, Nelson Goodman, recalls the earlier Pragmatists' notion of the "plastic" character of reality, now seen as conceptually plastic in the sense of being expressible in a variety of systems of symbols and languages. It is conceptually misguided to seek *the* nature of objects, since what there *is* is not describable *in abstracto* from the particular language in which an ontological question has been put. Objects declared to be real, be they classes, numbers, atoms, or stones, may differ widely. But differences between the "theoretical" and the "factual" entities are basically differences of degree and purpose in evolving conceptualization. Hence reality is anything that it is truly said to be—in any of many linguistic and symbolic systems; and where differences in ways of speaking about objects call for choices, the ensuing adjudications will be pragmatic.

Positivists and Nominalists

EVALUATION OF PRAGMATISM

Pragmatism has been vulnerable to certain criticisms. It has often been portrayed as a rationalization of the American business ethos—a portraiture perhaps inspired, but not by any scrutiny of the writings of the philosophers themselves. Similarly, the Pragmatic theory of truth has been assailed. Concerning an idea or belief, James had held that one can say: " 'It is useful because it is true' or that 'it is true because it is useful.' " "Both phrases," he added, "mean the same thing." Most scholars, however, have denied this equivalence. His position may seem, moreover, to allow for an idea to be true (*i.e.,* useful or expedient) for one person and false (inexpedient) for others. Finally, James was accused of reducing truth to a subjective play of opinions that one happens to relish or find useful to believe. To these charges James replied that "what immediately feels most 'good' is not always most 'true' when measured by the verdict of the rest of experience." He also warned: "Woe to him whose beliefs play fast and loose with the order which realities follow in his experience."

As a single movement, Pragmatism is no longer extant; but as a body of ideas it contributes a heritage that is destined for future analysis and development. Chief among these are the interpretation of thought and meaning as forms of purposive behaviour, of knowledge as evaluative procedure in which normative and descriptive materials are integrally related, and of the logic of scientific inquiry as a norm of intelligent conduct in the affairs of men. Finally, Pragmatism has succeeded in its critical reaction to the 19th-century philosophy from which it emerged. It has influenced the current conception of philosophy as a critical method of investigating problems and clarifying communication rather than as a universal synthesis of knowledge. Pragmatism thus has certain affinities with the critical philosophizing of G.E. Moore and Bertrand Russell, as well as with the thought of the French intuitionist and vitalist Henri Bergson and his disciple Édouard Le Roy, of Blondel, of the early Positivists Mach and Duhem, of the fictionalist Hans Vaihinger, of the Vienna Circle and the philosopher of logic and language Ludwig Wittgenstein, and also of the founder of Phenomenology, Edmund Husserl, and some of the continuing forms of Phenomenology and Existentialism. It has recognized the relative, contingent, and fallible (yet still authentic) character of human reason, rather than perpetuating the dubious ideal of philosophy as a system of eternal truths. In so doing, and in thus altering the philosophical scene, Pragmatism has become vitally implicated in the practices of current intellectual life; and in the light of this fact, a more pragmatic justification of Pragmatism is difficult to imagine. (H.S.T.)

Rationalism

Rationalism is the philosophical view that regards reason as the chief source and test of knowledge. Holding that reality itself has an inherently logical structure, the Rationalist asserts that a class of truths exists that the intellect can grasp directly. There are, according to the Rationalists, certain rational principles—especially in logic and mathematics, and even in ethics and metaphysics—that are so fundamental that to deny them is to fall into contradiction. The Rationalist's confidence in reason and proof tends, therefore, to detract from his respect for other ways of knowing. Rationalism has long been the rival of Empiricism, the doctrine that all knowledge comes from, and must be tested by, sense experience. As against this doctrine, Rationalism holds reason to be a faculty that can lay hold of truths beyond the reach of sense perception, both in certainty and generality. In stressing the existence of a "natural light," Rationalism has also been the rival of systems claiming esoteric knowledge, whether from mystical experience, revelation, or intuition, and has been opposed to various irrationalisms that tend to stress the biological, the emotional or volitional, the unconscious, or the existential at the expense of the rational.

TYPES AND EXPRESSIONS OF RATIONALISM

Rationalism has somewhat different meanings in different fields, depending upon the kind of theory to which it is opposed.

In the psychology of perception, for example, Rationalism is in a sense opposed to the genetic psychology of the Swiss scholar Jean Piaget, who, exploring the development of thought and behaviour in the infant, argued that the categories of the mind develop only through the infant's

experience in concourse with the world. Similarly, Rationalism is opposed to Transactionalism, a point of view in psychology according to which man's perceptual skills are achievements, accomplished through actions performed in response to an active environment. On this view, the experimental claim is made that perception is conditioned by probability judgments formed on the basis of earlier actions performed in similar situations. As a corrective to these sweeping claims, the Rationalist defends a nativism, which holds that certain perceptual and conceptual capacities are innate—as suggested in the case of depth perception by experiments with "the visual cliff," which, though platformed over with firm glass, the infant perceives as hazardous—though these native capacities may, at times, lie dormant until the appropriate conditions for their emergence arise.

In the comparative study of languages, a similar nativism was developed in the 1950s by the innovating syntactician Noam Chomsky, who, acknowledging a debt to Descartes, explicitly accepted the rationalistic doctrine of "innate ideas." Though the 4,000 languages spoken in the world differ greatly in sounds and symbols, they sufficiently resemble each other in syntax to suggest that there is "a schema of universal grammar" determined by "deep structures" or "innate presettings" in the human mind itself. These presettings, which have their basis in the brain, set the pattern for all experience, fix the rules for the formation of meaningful sentences, and explain why languages are readily translatable into one another. It should be added that what Rationalists have held about innate ideas is not that some ideas are full-fledged at birth but only that the grasp of certain connections and self-evident principles, when it comes, is due to inborn powers of insight rather than to learning by experience.

Common to all forms of speculative Rationalism is the belief that the world is a rationally ordered whole, the parts of which are linked by logical necessity and the structure of which is therefore intelligible. Thus in metaphysics it is opposed to the view that reality is a disjointed aggregate of incoherent bits and is thus opaque to reason. In particular, it is opposed to the logical atomisms of such thinkers as David Hume and Ludwig Wittgenstein, who held that facts are so disconnected that any fact might well have been different from what it is without entailing a change in any other fact. Rationalists have differed, however, with regard to the closeness and completeness with which the facts are bound together. At the lowest level, they have all believed that the law of contradiction "A and not-A cannot coexist" holds for the real world, which means that every truth is consistent with every other; at the highest level, they have held that all facts go beyond consistency to a positive coherence; *i.e.,* they are so bound up with each other that none could be different without all being different.

In the field where its claims are clearest—in epistemology, or theory of knowledge—Rationalism holds that some, at least, of man's knowledge is gained through a priori (prior to experience), or rational, insight as distinct from sense experience, which too often provides a confused and merely tentative approach. In the debate between Empiricism and Rationalism, Empiricists hold the simpler and more sweeping position, the Humean claim that all knowledge of fact stems from perception. Rationalists, on the contrary, urge that some, though not all, knowledge arises through direct apprehension by the intellect. What the intellectual faculty apprehends is objects that transcend sense experience—universals and their relations. A universal is an abstraction, a characteristic that may reappear in various instances: the number three, for example, or the triangularity that all triangles have in common. Though these cannot be seen, heard, or felt, Rationalists point out that man can plainly think about them and about their relations. This kind of knowledge, which includes the whole of logic and mathematics as well as fragmentary insights in many other fields, is, in the Rationalist view, the most important and certain knowledge that the mind can achieve. Such a priori knowledge is both necessary (*i.e.,* it cannot be conceived as otherwise) and universal, in the sense that it admits of no exceptions. In critical

Nativism in psychology and linguistics

Metaphysical and epistemological Rationalism

philosophy, epistemological Rationalism finds expression in the claim that the mind imposes its own inherent categories or forms upon incipient experience (see below *Kant and Hegel*).

In ethics Rationalism holds the position that reason, rather than feeling, custom, or authority, is the ultimate court of appeal in judging good and bad, right and wrong. Among major thinkers, the most notable representative of rational ethics is Immanuel Kant, who held that the way to judge an act is to check its self-consistency as apprehended by the intellect: to note, first, what it *is* essentially, or in principle—a lie, for example, or a theft—and then to ask if one can consistently will that the principle be made universal. Is theft, then, right? The answer must be "No," because, if theft were generally approved, no one's property would be his own as opposed to anyone else's and theft would then become meaningless; the notion, if universalized, would thus destroy itself, as reason, by itself, is sufficient to show.

In religion Rationalism commonly means that all of man's knowledge comes through the use of his natural faculties, without the aid of supernatural revelation. "Reason" is here used in a broader sense, referring to man's cognitive powers generally, as opposed to supernatural grace or faith—though it is also in sharp contrast to so-called existential approaches to truth. Reason, for the Rationalist, thus stands opposed to many of the religions of the world, including Christianity, which have held that the divine has revealed itself through inspired persons or writings and which have required, at times, that its claims be accepted as infallible, even when they do not accord with natural knowledge. Religious Rationalists hold, on the other hand, that if the clear insights of man's reason must be set aside in favour of alleged revelation, then human thought is everywhere rendered suspect—even in the reasonings of the theologians themselves. There cannot be two ultimately different ways of warranting truth, they assert; hence Rationalism urges that reason, with its standard of consistency, must be the final court of appeal. Religious Rationalism can reflect either a traditional piety, when endeavouring to display the alleged sweet reasonableness of religion, or an anti-authoritarian temper, when aiming to supplant religion with the "goddess of reason."

HISTORY OF RATIONALISM

Epistemological Rationalism in ancient philosophies. The first Western philosopher to stress rationalist insight was Pythagoras, a shadowy figure of the 6th century BC. Noticing that, for a right triangle, a square built on its hypotenuse equals the sum of those on its sides and that the pitches of notes sounded on a lute bear a mathematical relation to the lengths of the strings, Pythagoras held that these harmonies reflected the ultimate nature of reality. He summed up the implied metaphysical Rationalism in the words "All is number." It is probable that he had caught the Rationalist's vision, later seen by Galileo, of a world governed throughout by mathematically formulable laws.

The difficulty in this view, however, is that, working with universals and their relations, which, like the multiplication table, are timeless and changeless, it assumes a static world and ignores the particular, changing things of daily life. The difficulty was met boldly by the Rationalist Parmenides, who insisted that the world really is a static whole and that the realm of change and motion is an illusion, or even a self-contradiction. His disciple Zeno of Elea further argued that anything thought to be moving is confronted with a row of points infinite in number, all of which it must traverse; hence it can never reach its goal, nor indeed move at all. Of course, perception tells us that we do move; but Zeno, compelled to choose between perception and reason, clung to reason.

The exalting of rational insight above perception was also prominent in Plato (c. 427–347 BC). In the *Meno*, Socrates dramatized the innateness of knowledge by calling upon an illiterate slave boy, and drawing a square in the sand, proceeding to elicit from him, step by step, the proof of a theorem in geometry of which the boy could never have heard (to double the size of a square, draw a square on the

diagonal). Such knowledge, Rationalists insist, is certain, universal, and completely unlearned.

Plato so greatly admired the rigorous reasoning of geometry that he is alleged to have inscribed over the door of his Academy "Let no one unacquainted with geometry enter here." His famous "ideas" are accessible only to reason, not to sense. But how are they related to sensible things? His answers differed. Sometimes he viewed the ideas as distilling those common properties of a class in virtue of which one identifies anything as a member of it. Thus what makes anything a triangle is its having three straight sides; this is its essence. At other times, Plato held that the idea is an ideal, a non-sensible goal to which the sensible thing approximates; the geometer's perfect triangle "never was on sea or land," though all actual triangles more or less embody it. He conceived the ideas as more real than the sensible things that are their shadows and saw that the philosopher must penetrate to these invisible essences and see with the eye of his mind how they are linked together. For Plato they formed an orderly system that was at once eternal, intelligible, and good.

Plato's successor Aristotle (384–322 BC) conceived of the work of reason in much the same way, though he did not view the ideas as independent. His chief contribution to Rationalism lay in his syllogistic logic, regarded as the chief instrument of rational explanation. Man explains particular facts by bringing them under general principles. Why does one think Socrates will die? Because he is a man, and man as such is mortal. Why should one accept the general principle itself that all men are mortal? In human experience such principles have so far held without exception. But the mind cannot finally rest in this sort of explanation. Man never wholly understands a fact or event until he can bring it under a principle that is self-evident and necessary; and he then has the clearest explanation possible. On this central thesis of Rationalism, the three great Greeks were in accord.

Nothing comparable in importance to their thought appeared in Rationalistic philosophy in the next 1,800 years, though the work of Thomas Aquinas in the 13th century was an impressive attempt to blend Greek Rationalism and Christian revelation into a single harmonious system.

Thoroughgoing Rationalism is to be found only in the philosophical tradition that has come down from Greece; the mysticism of India and the practicality of China have offered a less congenial soil for it. The nearest parallels to it in Eastern thought are found in the work of the Indian philosopher Śaṅkara, who flourished about AD 800, and in that of the Chinese sage Chu-Hsi (1130–1200). Both were commentators on the ancient scriptures of their lands; and in ordering the scattered insights of these sources into intelligible systems, they did for their respective peoples something like what Aquinas did for the West in his harmonizing of Greek with Christian thought. Śaṅkara held, as Sir Sarvepalli Radhakrishnan has expressed it, that "the Absolute is the unattainable goal towards which the finite intellect strives." Perception is confined to what is transient and fragmentary; reason rises to truth that is timeless and universal; but even reason falls short of full understanding, which is achieved, if at all, only through mystical vision. Chu Hsi, who has influenced Chinese thought for the past six centuries, was a disciple of Confucius, though he had a stronger speculative interest than his master. He held that in all human minds a single reason was at work, which he called "the Way." All things were in some degree manifestations of it, and hence the understanding of the world lay in more complete identification with it.

Epistemological Rationalism in modern philosophies. The first modern Rationalist was René Descartes (1596–1650), who was an original mathematician whose ambition was to introduce into philosophy the rigour and clearness that delighted him in mathematics. He set out to doubt everything in the hope of arriving in the end at something indubitable. This he reached in his famous *cogito ergo sum,* "I think, therefore I am"; for to doubt one's own doubting would be absurd. Here then was a fact of absolute certainty, rendered such by the clearness and distinctness with which it presented itself to his reason. His task was to build on this as a foundation, to deduce from it a series of other propositions, each following with the same self-evidence. He hoped thus to produce a philosophical system on which men could agree as completely as they do on the geometry of Euclid. The main cause of error, he held, lay in the impulsive desire to believe before the mind is clear. The clearness and distinctness upon which he insisted was not that of perception but of conception, the clearness with which the intellect grasps an abstract idea, such as the number three, or its being greater than two.

His method was adopted in essentials by both Benedict Spinoza (1632–77) and G.W. Leibniz (1646–1716), who agreed that the framework of things could be known by a priori thinking. They differed from him, however, in their starting points. What was most undeniable to Spinoza was not the existence of his self but that of the universe, called by him Substance. From the idea of Substance, and with the aid of a few definitions and axioms, he derived his entire system, which he set forth in his *Ethics* in a formal fashion patterned after Euclid's geometry. Still, for both Spinoza and Leibniz much in nature remained stubbornly opaque. Leibniz distinguished necessary truths, those of which the opposite is impossible (as in mathematics), from contingent truths, the opposite of which is possible, such as "snow is white." But was this an ultimate distinction? At times Leibniz said boldly that if only man knew enough, he would see that every true proposition was necessarily true—that there are no contingent truths, that snow must be white.

Kant and Hegel

How, then, does reason operate and how is it possible to have knowledge that goes beyond experience? A new answer was given by Immanuel Kant (1724–1804) in his *Critique of Pure Reason,* which, as he said, involved a Copernican revolution in philosophy. The reason man can be certain that his logic and mathematics will remain valid for all experience is simply that their framework lies within his own mind; they are forms of arrangement imposed from within upon the raw materials of sensation. Man will always find things arranged in certain patterns because it is he who has unwittingly so arranged them. Kant held, however, that these certainties were bought at a heavy price. Just because a priori insights are the reflection of man's own mind, he cannot trust them as a reflection of the world outside himself. Whether the rational order in which man arranges his sensation—the order, for example, of time, space, and causality—represents an order holding among things-in-themselves (German *Dinge-an-sich*) he cannot hope to know. Kant's Rationalism was thus the counterpart of a profound Skepticism.

Rationalism in non-Western thought

G.W.F. Hegel (1770–1831), the most thoroughgoing of Rationalist thinkers, attempted to break out of this Skepticism. He argued that to think of an unknowable is already to bring it within the sphere of what is known and that it is meaningless to talk of a region in which logic is invalid. Further, to raise the question "Why?" is to presume that there is an intelligible answer to it; indeed the faith of the philosopher must be that the real is the rational and the rational real, for this faith is implicit in the philosophic enterprise itself. As an attempt to understand and explain the world, philosophy is a process of placing something in a context that reveals it as necessary. But this necessity is not, as earlier Rationalists had supposed, an all-or-nothing affair issuing in a self-evident finality. Understanding is a matter of degree. What alone would wholly satisfy thought is a system that is at once all-inclusive and so ordered that its parts entail each other. Hegel believed that the universe constitutes such a whole and, as an idealist, held that it is a single, absolute mind. To the degree that the philosopher embodies and realizes this mind, his own mind will achieve both truth and reality. Indeed, the advance of civilization reflects the enlarging presence and control of such a system in the human spirit. Broadly similar Rationalistic systems were developed in England by F.H. Bradley (1846–1924) and Bernard Bosanquet (1848–1923) and in America by Josiah Royce (1855–1916).

Ethical Rationalism. The views of Kant were presented above as typical of this position (see above, *Types and expressions of Rationalism*). But few moralists have held to ethical Rationalism in this simple and sweeping form. Many have held, however, that the main rules of conduct

are truths as self-evident as those of logic or mathematics. Lists of such rules were drawn up by Ralph Cudworth and Henry More among the Cambridge Platonists of the 17th century, who were noted for holding that moral principles were intrinsic to reality; and in the 18th century Samuel Clarke and Richard Price, defenders of "natural law" ethics, and the "common sense" moralist Thomas Reid also presented such lists. A 20th-century revision of this Rationalism has been offered by the Rational Intuitionists H.A. Prichard and Sir David Ross of Oxford under the name of deontology (Greek *deon,* "duty"), which respects duty more than consequences. Ross provides a list of propositions regarding fidelity to promises, reparation for injuries, and other duties, of which he says: "In our confidence that these propositions are true there is involved the same trust in our reason that is involved in our trust in mathematics." What is taken as self-evident, however, is not specific rules of conduct, but *prima facie* duties— the claims that some types of action have on men because of their nature. If a man is considering whether to repay a debt or to give the money to charity, each act has a self-evident claim on him; and their comparative strengths must be settled by a rational intuition.

Legalistic versus utilitarian ethics

The most influential variety of 20th-century ethical Rationalism has probably been the Ideal Utilitarianism of the British moralists Hastings Rashdall (1858–1924) and G.E. Moore (1873–1958). Both were teleologists (Greek *telos,* "end") inasmuch as they held that what makes an act objectively right is its results (or end) in intrinsic goods or evils. To determine what is right, reason is required in two senses: firstly, the inference to the consequences is an act of inductive reasoning; secondly, the judgment that one consequence is intrinsically better than another is a priori and self-evident. Moore thought that there is a single rule for all conduct—one should so act as to produce the greatest good—and that this is also a principle self-evident to reason.

Religious Rationalism. Stirrings of religious Rationalism were already felt in the Middle Ages regarding the Christian revelation. Thus the skeptical mind of Abelard (1079–1142) raised doubts by showing in his *Sic et Non* ("Yes and No") many contradictions among beliefs handed down as revealed truths by the Church Fathers. The greatest of the Medieval thinkers, Thomas Aquinas (1225–74), was a Rationalist in the sense of believing that the larger part of revealed truth was intelligible to and demonstrable by reason, though he thought that a number of dogmas opaque to reason must be accepted on authority alone.

Expansion of religious Rationalism. Religious Rationalism did not come into its own, however, until the 16th and 17th centuries, when it took two chief forms: the scientific and the philosophic.

Galileo (1564–1642) was a pioneer in astronomy and the founder of modern dynamics. He conceived of nature as governed throughout by laws statable with mathematical precision; the book of nature, he said, is "written in mathematical form." This notion not only ruled out the occasional appeal to miracle; it also collided with dogmas regarding the permanent structure of the world—in particular with that which viewed the Earth as the motionless centre of the universe. When Galileo's demonstration that the Earth moves around the Sun was confirmed by the work of Newton and others, a battle was won that marked a turning point in the history of Rationalism, since it provided a decisive victory in a crucial case of conflict between reason and apparently revealed truth.

Galileo and Descartes

The Rationalism of Descartes, as already shown, was the outcome of philosophic doubt rather than of scientific inquiry. The self-evidence of the *cogito,* seen by his "natural light," he made the ideal for all other knowledge. The uneasiness that the church soon felt in the face of such a test was not unfounded, for Descartes was in effect exalting the natural light into the supreme court even in the field of religion. He argued that man's guarantee against the possibility that even this natural light might deceive him lay in the goodness of the Creator. But then to prove this Creator, he had to assume the prior validity of the natural light itself. Logically, therefore, the last word lay with rational insight, not with any outside divine warrant.

Descartes was inadvertently beginning a Copernican revolution in theology. Before his time, the truths regarded as most certain were those accepted from revelation; afterwards these truths were subject to the judgment of human reason, thus breaking the hold of authority on the European mind.

Four waves of religious Rationalism. The Rationalist attitude quickly spread, its advance forming several waves of general interest and influence. The first wave occurred in England in the form of Deism. Deists accepted the existence of God, but spurned supernatural revelation. The earliest member of this school, Lord Herbert of Cherbury (1583–1648), held that a just God would not reveal himself to a part of his creation only and that the true religion is thus a universal one, which achieves its knowledge of God through common reason. The Deistic philosopher John Toland (1670–1722), in his *Christianity Not Mysterious,* sought to show that "there is nothing in the Gospels contrary to reason, nor above it"; any doctrine that is really above reason would be meaningless to man. Attacking revelation, the freethinking polemicist Anthony Collins (1676–1729) maintained that the prophecies of the Old Testament failed of fulfillment; and the religious controversialist Thomas Woolston (1670–1733) urged that the New Testament miracles, as recorded, are incredible. Matthew Tindall (1657–1733), most learned of the English Deists, argued that the essential part of Christianity is its ethics, which, being clearly apparent to natural reason, leaves revelation superfluous. Thus the Deists, professing for the most part to be religious men themselves, did much to reconcile their public to the free play of ideas in religion.

The second wave of religious Rationalism, less moderate in tone and consequences, was French. This wave, reflecting an engagement with the problem of natural evil, involved a decay in the natural theology of Deism such that it merged eventually with the stream that led to materialistic Atheism. Its moving spirit was Voltaire (1694–1778), who had been impressed by some of the Deists during a stay in England. Like them, he thought that a rational man would believe in God but not in supernatural inspiration. Hardly a profound philosopher, he was a brilliant journalist, clever and humorous in argument, devastating in satire, and warm in human sympathies. In his *Candide* and in many other writings, he poured irreverent ridicule on the Christian scheme of salvation as incoherent and on the church hierarchy as cruel and oppressive. In these attitudes he had the support of Diderot (1713–84), editor of the most widely read encyclopaedia that had appeared in Europe. The Rationalism of these men and their followers, directed against both the religious and the political traditions of their time, did much to prepare the ground for the explosive French Revolution.

The next wave of religious Rationalism occurred in Germany under the influence of Hegel, who held that a religious creed is a halfway house on the road to a mature philosophy, the product of a reason that is still under the sway of feeling and imagination. This idea was taken up and applied with learning and acuteness to the origins of Christianity by David Friedrich Strauss (1808–74), who published in 1835, at the age of 27, a remarkable and influential three-volume work, *Das Leben Jesu* (*The Life of Jesus, Critically Examined,* 1846). Relying largely on internal inconsistencies in the Synoptic Gospels, Strauss undertook to prove these books to be unacceptable as revelation and unsatisfactory as history. He then sought to show how an imaginative people innocent of either history or science, convinced that a Messiah would appear, and deeply moved by a unique moral genius, inevitably wove myths about his birth and death, his miracles, and his divine communings.

Strauss's thought as it affected religion was continued by the philosophical historian Ernest Renan (1823–92) and as it affected philosophy by the humanist Ludwig Feuerbach (1804–72) of the Hegelian left. Renan's *Vie de Jésus* (1863; *Life of Jesus*) did for France what Strauss's book had done for Germany, though the two differed greatly in character. Whereas Strauss's work had been an intellectual exercise in destructive criticism, Renan's was an attempt to reconstruct the mind of Jesus as a wholly human person—a feat of imagination, performed with a disarming admiration and even reverence for its subject and with a felicity of style that gave it a large and lasting audience. Feuerbach's *Wesen des Christentums* (1841; Eng. trans. by George Eliot, *Essence of Christianity,* 1853) applied the myth theory even to belief in the existence of God, holding that "man makes God in his own image."

The fourth wave occurred in Victorian England, following the publication in 1859 of Darwin's *Origin of Species.* This book was taken as a challenge to the authority of Scripture because there was a clear inconsistency between the Genesis account of creation and the biological account of man's slow emergence from lower forms of life. The battle raged with bitterness for several decades but died away as the theory of evolution gained more general acceptance.

STATUS OF RATIONALISM

Religious. With increasing freedom of thought and wider acceptance of scientific views, Rationalism in religion has lost its novelty and much of its controversial excitement. To the contemporary mind, it is too obvious to warrant debate that reason and revelation cannot both qualify as sources of ultimate truth for, were they to conflict, truth itself would become self-contradictory. Hence theologians have sought accommodation through new interpretative principles that discern different grades of authenticity within the Scriptures and through new views of religious truth, existential rather than cognitive, that turn from propositional dogmas to the explication of lived human existence. Criticism of supernaturalism, however, is still carried on by such societies as the Rationalist Press Association, in Great Britain, and the Humanist Association, in the United States.

Ethical. Rationalism in ethics has suffered its share of criticism. Regarding its lists of rules—on the keeping of promises, the return of loaned goods, etc.—it has been argued, for example, that if they were specific enough to be useful (as in the rule against lying or stealing), they would tend to have exceptions—which no rule laid down by reason ought to have. On the other hand, if without exceptions, they would often prove to be tautologies: the rule of justice, for example, that we should give everyone his due would then mean only that we should give him what is justly his. After enduring a period of eclipse, however, during which noncognitive theories of ethics (emotive and existential) and relativism had preempted the field, rationalistic views, which agree in holding that moral standards do not depend upon the varying attitudes of persons or peoples, were receiving renewed attention in the mid-20th century. Prominent among these developments has been the "good-reasons" approach taken by the broadly gauged scholar Stephen Toulmin, by Kurt Baier, and others, which examines the contexts of various moral situations and explores the kinds of justification appropriate for each.

Metaphysical. Typical of the ways of reasoning employed by Rationalists are two approaches taken to the metaphysical doctrine that all things are connected by internal relations: one a logical, the other a causal argument. An internal relation is one that could not be removed without affecting the terms themselves between which the relation holds. The argument runs: Everything is related to everything else at least by the relation "A *is different from* B." But difference is itself an internal relation, since the terms could not remain the same if it were removed. Hence everything is so connected with everything else that it could not be what it is unless they were what they are. The appeal to internal relations played an important part in the philosophies of Hegel, F.H. Bradley, and A.N. Whitehead (1861–1947).

The other line of argument is causal. Every event, it is maintained, is connected with every other, either directly or indirectly. Sir James Jeans argued that if the law of gravitation is valid, a man cannot crook his little finger without affecting the fixed stars. Here the causal relation is direct. It can also be shown that seemingly unrelated events are joined indirectly through their common con-

Deism

Voltaire and Diderot

Hegelianism

Evolution

nection with some remote historical event, by a chain of events leading back, for example, to Columbus' discovery of America. But if this had been different, all of its consequences would presumably have been different; thus an indirect and internal relation proves to have been present.

Many Rationalists have held with Spinoza that the causal relation is really a logical one—that a causal law, if precisely stated, would reveal a connection in which the character of the cause logically necessitates that of its effect; and if this is true, they maintain, the facts and events of the world must thus compose a single rational and intelligible order.

Rationalism and quantum physics

In the 20th century, such Rationalism met with a new and unexpected difficulty presented by quantum physics. According to the indeterminacy principle, formulated in 1927 by the German physicist Werner Heisenberg, it is impossible to discover with precision both the position and the velocity of a moving electron at the same time. This implies that definite causal laws for the behaviour of these particles can never be attained, but only statistical laws governing the behaviour of immense aggregates of them. Causality, and with it the possibility of rational understanding, seemed to be suspended in the subatomic world. Some interpreters of the new physics, however, notably Max Planck, Albert Einstein, and Bertrand Russell, sustained the hopes of the Rationalists by insisting that what was excluded by the indeterminacy principle was not the fact of causality in this realm, but only the precise knowledge of it.

Indeed, some leaders of 20th-century science took the new developments in physics as on the whole supporting Rationalism. Protons and electrons, they contended, though beyond the reach of the senses, can still be known; and their behaviour, at least in groups, is increasingly found to conform to mathematical law. In 1932, Sir James Jeans, an astrophysicist and popularizer of science, said with a curious echo of Galileo, "the universe appears to have been designed by a pure mathematician."

Challenges to epistemological Rationalism. At first glance the claim of Empiricism that knowledge must come from sense experience seems obvious: how else could one hope to make contact with the world around one? Consequently, Rationalism has been sharply challenged—in the 19th century by the Empiricism of John Stuart Mill (1806–73) and in the 20th by that of the Logical Positivists. Mill argued that all a priori certainties are illusory: why does man believe, for example, that two straight lines cannot enclose a space? Is it because he sees it as logically necessary? No; it is because he has experienced so long and so unbroken a row of instances of it—a new one whenever he sees the corner of a table or the bordering rays of a light beam—that he has formed the habit of thinking in this way and is now unable to break it. A priori propositions, Mill claimed, are merely empirical statements of very high generality.

This theory has now been abandoned by most Empiricists themselves. Its implication that such statements as "$2 + 2 = 4$" are only probably true and may have exceptions has proved quite unconvincing. The Rationalist's rejoinder is that one cannot, no matter how hard one tries, conceive $2 + 2$ as making 5; for its equalling 4 is necessary. But a priori knowledge is also universal. Neither of these two characteristics can be accounted for by sense experience. That a crow is black can be perceived, but not that it must be black or that crows will always be black; no run of perceptions, however long, could assure us of such truths. On the other hand, a priori truths can be seen with certainty—that if a figure, for instance, is a plane triangle within a Euclidean space, its angles must and always will equal two right angles.

Perhaps the most formidable challenge to Rationalism has come in the 20th century from such Logical Positivists as the Oxford Empiricist A.J. Ayer (1910–) and Rudolf Carnap (1891–1970), who had been a central figure in the Vienna Circle, where this movement first arose. Unlike Mill, they accepted a priori knowledge as certain; but they laid down a new challenge—the denial of its philosophic importance. A priori propositions, they said, are (1) linguistic, (2) conventional, and (3) analytic: (1) They are

statements primarily of how one proposes to use words; if one says that "a straight line is the shortest line between two points," this merely reports one's definition of "straight" and declares one's purpose to use it only of the shortest. (2) Being a definition, such a statement expresses a convention to which there are alternatives; it may be defined in terms of the paths of light rays if one chooses. (3) The statement is analytic in that it merely repeats in its predicate a part or the whole of the subject term and hence tells nothing new; it is not a statement about nature but about meanings only. And since Rationalistic systems depend throughout upon statements of this kind, their importance is illusory.

To this clear challenge some leading Rationalists have replied as follows: (1) Positivists have confused real with verbal definition. A verbal definition does indeed state what a word means; but a real definition states what an object is, and the thought of a straight line is the thought of an object, not of words. (2) The Positivists have confused conventions in thought with conventions in language. One is free to vary the language in which a proposition is expressed, but not the proposition itself. Start with the concept of a straight line, and there is no alternative to accepting it as the shortest. (3) Some a priori statements are admittedly analytic, but many are not. In "whatever is coloured is extended," colour and extension are two different concepts of which the first entails the second, but is not identical with it in whole or part. Contemporary Rationalists therefore hold that the a priori has emerged victorious from the Empiricists' efforts to discredit such knowledge and the Positivists' attempts to trivialize it.

(B.Bl.)

Utilitarianism

The fundamental principle of Utilitarianism, a tradition in ethics stemming from the late 18th- and 19th-century English philosophers and economists Jeremy Bentham and John Stuart Mill, is that an action is right if it tends to promote happiness and wrong if it tends to produce the reverse of happiness—not just the happiness of the performer of the action but that of everyone affected by it. Such a theory is in opposition to egoism, the view that a man should pursue his own self-interest, even at the expense of others, and to any ethical theory that regards some acts or types of acts as right or wrong independently of their consequences. Utilitarianism also differs from ethical theories that make the rightness or wrongness of an act dependent upon the motive of the agent; for, according to the Utilitarian, it is possible for the right thing to be done from a bad motive.

THE NATURE OF UTILITARIANISM

Utilitarianism is an effort to provide an answer to the practical question "What ought a man to do?" Its answer is that he ought to act so as to produce the best consequences possible.

Basic concepts. In the notion of consequences the Utilitarian includes all of the good and bad produced by the act, whether arising after the act has been performed or during its performance. If the difference in the consequences of alternative acts is not great, some Utilitarians do not regard the choice between them as a moral issue. According to Mill, acts should be classified as morally right or wrong only if the consequences are of such significance that a person would wish to see the agent compelled, not merely persuaded and exhorted, to act in the preferred manner.

In assessing the consequences of actions, Utilitarianism relies upon some theory of intrinsic value: something is held to be good in itself, apart from further consequences, and all other values are believed to derive their worth from their relation to this intrinsic good as a means to an end. Bentham and Mill were hedonists; *i.e.,* they analyzed happiness as a balance of pleasure over pain and believed that these feelings alone are of intrinsic value and disvalue. Utilitarians also assume that it is possible to compare the intrinsic values produced by two alternative actions and to estimate which would have better consequences. Bentham believed that a hedonic calculus is theoretically

Assessment of consequences

possible. A moralist, he maintained, could sum up the units of pleasure and the units of pain for everyone likely to be affected, immediately and in the future, and could take the balance as a measure of the overall good or evil tendency of an action. Such precise measurement as Bentham envisioned is perhaps not essential, but it is nonetheless necessary for the Utilitarian to make some interpersonal comparisons of the values of the effects of alternative courses of action.

Methodologies. As a normative system providing a standard by which an individual ought to act and by which the existing practices of society, including its moral code, ought to be evaluated and improved, Utilitarianism cannot be verified or confirmed in the way in which a descriptive theory can; but it is not regarded by its exponents as simply arbitrary. Bentham believed that only in terms of a Utilitarian interpretation do words such as "ought," "right," and "wrong" have meaning and that whenever anyone attempts to combat the principle of utility, he does so with reasons drawn from the principle itself. Bentham and Mill both believed that human actions are motivated entirely by pleasure and pain; and Mill saw that motivation as a basis for the argument that, since happiness is the sole end of human action, the promotion of happiness is the test by which to judge all human conduct.

One of the leading Utilitarians of the late 19th century, a Cambridge philosopher, Henry Sidgwick, rejected their theories of motivation as well as Bentham's theory of the meaning of moral terms and sought to support Utilitarianism by showing that it follows from systematic reflection on the morality of "common sense." Most of the requirements of commonsense morality, he argued, could be based upon Utilitarian considerations. In addition, he reasoned that Utilitarianism could solve the difficulties and perplexities that arise from the vagueness and inconsistencies of commonsense doctrines.

Most opponents of Utilitarianism have held that it has implications contrary to their moral intuitions—that considerations of utility, for example, might sometimes sanction the breaking of a promise. Much of the defense of Utilitarian ethics has consisted in answering these objections, either by showing that Utilitarianism does not have the implications that they claim it has or by arguing against the moral intuitions of its opponents. Some Utilitarians, however, have sought to modify the Utilitarian theory to account for the objections.

Criticisms. One such criticism is that, although the widespread practice of lying and stealing would have bad consequences, resulting in a loss of trustworthiness and security, it is not certain that an occasional lie to avoid embarrassment or an occasional theft from a rich man would not have good consequences, and thus be permissible or even required by Utilitarianism. But the Utilitarian readily answers that the widespread practice of such acts would result in a loss of trustworthiness and security. To meet the objection to not permitting an occasional lie or theft, some philosophers have defended a modification labelled "rule" Utilitarianism. It permits a particular act on a particular occasion to be adjudged right or wrong according to whether it is in accordance with or in violation of a useful rule; and a rule is judged useful or not by the consequences of its general practice. Mill has sometimes been interpreted as a "rule" Utilitarian, whereas Bentham and Sidgwick were "act" Utilitarians.

Another objection, often posed against the hedonistic value theory held by Bentham, holds that the value of life is more than a balance of pleasure over pain. Mill, in contrast to Bentham, discerned differences in the quality of pleasures that made some intrinsically preferable to others independently of intensity and duration (the quantitative dimensions recognized by Bentham). Some philosophers in the Utilitarian tradition have recognized certain wholly nonhedonistic values without losing their Utilitarian credentials. A British philosopher, G.E. Moore, a pioneer of 20th-century Analysis, regarded many kinds of consciousness—including love, knowledge, and the experience of beauty—as intrinsically valuable independently of pleasure, a position labelled "ideal" Utilitarianism. Even in limiting the recognition of intrinsic value and disvalue

to happiness and unhappiness, some philosophers have argued that those feelings cannot adequately be further broken down into terms of pleasure and pain and have thus preferred to defend the theory in terms of maximizing happiness and minimizing unhappiness. It is important to note, however, that even for the hedonistic Utilitarians, pleasure and pain are not thought of in purely sensual terms; pleasure and pain for them can be components of experiences of all sorts. Their claim is that, if an experience is neither pleasurable nor painful, then it is a matter of indifference and has no intrinsic value.

Another objection to Utilitarianism is that the prevention or elimination of suffering should take precedence over any alternative act that would only increase the happiness of someone already happy. Some recent Utilitarians have modified their theory to require this focus or even to limit moral obligation to the prevention or elimination of suffering—a view labelled "negative" Utilitarianism.

HISTORICAL SURVEY

The ingredients of Utilitarianism are found in the history of thought long before Bentham.

Antecedents of Utilitarianism among the ancients. A hedonistic theory of the value of life is found in the early 5th century BC in the ethics of Aristippus of Cyrene, founder of the Cyrenaic school, and 100 years later in that of Epicurus, founder of an ethic of retirement, and their followers in ancient Greece. The seeds of ethical universalism are found in the doctrines of the rival ethical school of Stoicism and in Christianity.

Growth of classical English Utilitarianism. In the history of English philosophy, some historians have identified Bishop Richard Cumberland, a 17th-century moral philosopher, as the first to have a Utilitarian philosophy. A generation later, however, Francis Hutcheson, a British "moral sense" theorist, more clearly held a Utilitarian view. He not only analyzed that action as best that "procures the greatest happiness for the greatest numbers" but proposed a form of "moral arithmetic" for calculating the best consequences. The Skeptic David Hume, Scotland's foremost philosopher and historian, attempted to analyze the origin of the virtues in terms of their contribution to utility. Bentham himself said that he discovered the principle of utility in the 18th-century writings of various thinkers: of Joseph Priestley, a dissenting clergyman famous for his discovery of oxygen; of the Frenchman Claude-Adrien Helvétius, author of a philosophy of mere sensation; of Cesare Beccaria, an Italian legal theorist; and of Hume. Helvétius probably drew from Hume, and Beccaria from Helvétius.

Another strand of Utilitarian thought took the form of a theological ethics. John Gay, a biblical scholar and philosopher, held the will of God to be the criterion of virtue; but from God's goodness he inferred that God willed that men promote human happiness.

Bentham, who apparently believed that an individual in governing his own actions would always seek to maximize his own pleasure and minimize his own pain, found in pleasure and pain both the cause of human action and the basis for a normative criterion of action. The art of governing one's own actions Bentham called "private ethics." The happiness of the agent is the determining factor; the happiness of others governs only to the extent that the agent is motivated by sympathy, benevolence, or interest in the good will and good opinion of others. For Bentham, the greatest happiness of the greatest number would play a role primarily in the art of legislation, in which the legislator would seek to maximize the happiness of the entire community by creating an identity of interests between each individual and his fellows. By laying down penalties for mischievous acts, the legislator would make it unprofitable for a man to harm his neighbour. Bentham's major philosophical work, *An Introduction to the Principles of Morals and Legislation* (1789), was designed as an introduction to a plan of a penal code.

With Bentham, Utilitarianism became the ideological foundation of a reform movement, later known as "philosophical radicalism," that would test all institutions and policies by the principle of utility. Bentham attracted as his

Meaning, motivation, and commonsense theories

"Rule," "act," and "ideal" Utilitarianisms

From Hutcheson to Bentham

disciples a number of younger (earlier 19th-century) men. They included David Ricardo, who gave classical form to the science of economics; John Stuart Mill's father, James Mill; and John Austin, a legal theorist. James Mill argued for representative government and universal male suffrage on Utilitarian grounds; he and other followers of Bentham were advocates of parliamentary reform in England in the early 19th century. John Stuart Mill was a spokesman for women's suffrage, state-supported education for all, and other proposals that were considered radical in their day. He argued on Utilitarian grounds for freedom of speech and expression and for the noninterference of government or society in individual behaviour that did not harm anyone else. Mill's essay "Utilitarianism," published in *Fraser's Magazine* (1861), is an elegant defense of the general Utilitarian doctrine and perhaps remains the best introduction to the subject. In it Utilitarianism is viewed as an ethics for ordinary individual behaviour as well as for legislation.

Late 19th- and 20th-century Utilitarianism.   By the time Sidgwick wrote, Utilitarianism had become one of the foremost ethical theories of the day. His *Methods of Ethics* (1874), a comparative examination of egoism, the ethics of common sense, and Utilitarianism, contains the most careful discussion to be found of the implications of Utilitarianism as a principle of individual moral action.

The 20th century has seen the development of various modifications and complications of the Utilitarian theory. G.E. Moore argued for a set of ideals extending beyond hedonism by proposing that one imaginatively compare universes in which there are equal quantities of pleasure but different amounts of knowledge and other such combinations. He felt that he could not be indifferent toward such differences. The recognition of "act" Utilitarianism and "rule" Utilitarianism as explicit alternatives was stimulated by the analysis of moral reasoning in "rule" Utilitarian terms by Stephen Toulmin, a British philosopher of science and moralist, and by Patrick Nowell-Smith, a moralist of the Oxford linguistic school; by the interpretation of Mill as a "rule" Utilitarian by another Oxford Analyst, J.O. Urmson; and by the analysis by John Rawls, a Harvard moral philosopher, of the significance for Utilitarianism of two different conceptions of moral rules. "Act" Utilitarianism, on the other hand, has been defended by J.J.C. Smart, a British-Australian philosopher.

EFFECTS OF UTILITARIANISM IN OTHER FIELDS

The influence of Utilitarianism has been widespread, permeating the intellectual life of the last two centuries. Its significance in law, politics, and economics is especially notable.

The Utilitarian theory of the justification of punishment stands in opposition to the "retributive" theory, according to which punishment is intended to make the criminal "pay" for his crime. According to the Utilitarian, the rationale of punishment is entirely to prevent further crime by either reforming the criminal or protecting society from him and to deter others from crime through fear of punishment.

In its political philosophy Utilitarianism bases the authority of government and the sanctity of individual rights upon their utility, thus providing an alternative to theories of natural law, natural rights, or social contract. What kind of government is best thus becomes a question of what kind of government has the best consequences—an assessment that requires factual premises regarding human nature and behaviour.

Generally, Utilitarians have supported democracy as a way of making the interest of government coincide with the general interest; they have argued for the greatest individual liberty compatible with an equal liberty for others on the ground that each individual is generally the best judge of his own welfare; and they have believed in the possibility and the desirability of progressive social change through peaceful political processes.

With different factual assumptions, however, Utilitarian arguments can lead to different conclusions. If the inquirer assumes that a strong government is required to check man's basically selfish interests and that any change

James and J.S. Mill; Sidgwick; Moore

Legal and political theory

may threaten the stability of the political order, he may be led by Utilitarian arguments to an authoritarian or conservative position. On the other hand, William Godwin, an early 19th-century political philosopher, assumed the basic goodness of human nature and argued that the greatest happiness would follow from a radical alteration of society in the direction of anarchistic Communism.

Classical economics received some of its most important statements from Utilitarian writers, especially Ricardo and John Stuart Mill. Ironically, its theory of economic value was framed primarily in terms of the cost of labour in production rather than in terms of the use value, or utility, of commodities. Later developments more clearly reflected the Utilitarian philosophy. William Jevons, one of the founders of the marginal utility school of analysis, derived many of his ideas from Bentham; and "welfare economics," while substituting comparative preferences for comparative utilities, reflected the basic spirit of the Utilitarian philosophy. In economic policy, the early Utilitarians had tended to oppose governmental interference in trade and industry on the assumption that the economy would regulate itself for the greatest welfare if left alone; later Utilitarians, however, lost confidence in the social efficiency of private enterprise and were willing to see governmental power and administration used to correct its abuses.

As a movement for the reform of social institutions, 19th-century Utilitarianism was remarkably successful in the long run. Most of their recommendations have since been implemented unless abandoned by the reformers themselves; and, equally important, Utilitarian arguments are now commonly employed to advocate institutional or policy changes.

Economic and social theory

SUMMARY AND EVALUATION

As an abstract ethical doctrine, Utilitarianism has established itself as one of the small number of live options that must be taken into account and either refuted or accepted by any philosopher taking a position in normative ethics. In contemporary discussion it has been divorced from adventitious involvements with the analysis of ethical language and with the psychological theory with which it was presented by Bentham. Utilitarianism now appears in various modified and complicated formulations. Bentham's ideal of a hedonic calculus is usually considered a practical if not a theoretical impossibility. Present-day philosophers have noticed further problems in the Utilitarian procedures. One of them, for example, is with the process of identifying the consequences of an act—a process that raises conceptual as well as practical problems as to what are to be counted as consequences, even without precisely quantifying the value of those consequences. The question may arise whether the outcome of an election is a consequence of each and every vote cast for the winning candidate if he receives more than the number necessary for election; and in estimating the value of the consequences, one may ask whether the entire value or only a part of the value of the outcome of the election is to be assigned to each vote. There is also difficulty in the procedure of comparing alternative acts. If one act requires a longer period of time for its performance than another, one may ask whether they can be considered alternatives. Even what is to count as an act is not a matter of philosophical consensus.

These problems, however, are common to almost all normative ethical theories since most of them recognize the consequences—including the hedonic—of an act as being relevant ethical considerations. The central insight of Utilitarianism, that one ought to promote happiness and prevent unhappiness whenever possible, seems undeniable. The critical question, however, is whether the whole of normative ethics can be analyzed in terms of this simple formula.   (H.R.W.)

Problems in Utilitarian procedures

BIBLIOGRAPHY. For bibliographies of Platonism and Aristotelianism, see the *Macropædia* articles PLATONISM and ARISTOTELIANISM, respectively.

Atomism: E. CANTORE, *Atomic Order: An Introduction to the Philosophy of Microphysics* (1969); F. COPLESTON, *A History of Philosophy,* 8 vol. (1950–66); E.J. DIJKSTERHUIS, *Die Mecha-*

nisierung des Weltbildes (1956; Eng. trans., *The Mechanization of the World Picture,* 1961), a history of science from antiquity to the 17th century; A.S. EDDINGTON, *The Philosophy of Physical Science* (1939); K. LASSWITZ, *Geschichte der Atomistik vom Mittelalter bis Newton,* 2 vol. (1890, reprinted 1963), a 19th-century classic; A.G.M. VAN MELSEN, *Van atomos naar atoom* (1949; Eng. trans., *From Atomos to Atom: The History of the Concept Atom,* 2nd ed. 1960), including references for the primary sources; L.K. NASH, *The Atomic-Molecular Theory* (1950), a discussion of the first phase of the chemical atomic theory; E.T. WHITTAKER, *History of the Theories of Aether and Electricity,* rev. ed., 2 vol. (1951–54), only for readers with a solid background in science; L.L. WHYTE, *Essay on Atomism: From Democritus to 1960* (1961), a brief introduction to the idea of Atomism and its history. See also MRINALKAUTI GANGOPADHYAYA, *Indian Atomism: History and Sources* (1980).

Eleaticism: The main edition of the fragments of the Eleatic, as of all the Pre-Socratic, philosophers is still HERMANN DIELS, *Die Fragmente der Vorsokratiker* (1903; 11th ed. rev. by WALTHER KRANZ, 3 vol., 1964), which is a critical edition of the Greek fragments with German translations; for English translations see KATHLEEN FREEMAN, *Ancilla to the Pre-Socratic Philosophers* (1948, reprinted 1962); PILO ALBERTELLI, *Gli Eleati: testimonianze e frammenti* (1939), is a good Italian translation with commentary. Much of the best material is in general works on ancient Greek or Pre-Socratic philosophy. The most comprehensive treatment is in EDUARD ZELLER, *Die Philosophie der Griechen,* 6–7th ed., 3 vol., ed. by W. NESTLE (1920–23); in the revised Italian trans. of Zeller, ed. with extensive additions by ROLDOLFO MONDOLFO, the portion on the Eleatic school by GIOVANNI REALE (1967) occupies the whole 3rd volume of the 1st section and contains a good selected bibliography; an English translation of Zeller is entitled *A History of Greek Philosophy, from the Earliest Period to the Time of Socrates,* 2 vol. (1881). See also JOHN BURNET, *Early Greek Philosophy,* 4th ed. (1930, reprinted 1963); GEOFFREY KIRK and JOHN E. RAVEN, *The Presocratic Philosophers,* pp. 263–306 (1957); W.K.C. GUTHRIE, *A History of Greek Philosophy,* vol. 2 (1965); and GUIDO CALOGERO, *Storia della logica antica,* vol. 1, pp. 109–208 (1967).

Epicureanism: The first complete collection of the extant works and fragments of Epicurus is H. USENER (ed.), *Epicurea* (1887, reprinted 1966). A smaller selection, with Eng. trans. and commentary, is CYRIL BAILEY (ed.), *Epicurus: The Extant Remains* (1926), a very useful book that includes the "Vatican Fragments." All of the ethical fragments (and several other items) are published in CARLO DIANO (ed.), *Epicuri Ethica* (1946), with extensive Latin commentaries. CARLO DIANO (ed. and trans.), *Lettere di Epicuro e dei suoi* (1946), contains 14 letters of Epicurus and his friends taken from Pap. Herc. 1418. G. ARRIGHETTI (ed.), *Epicuro, Opere* 2nd ed. (1967), contains all of the works and fragments (including the *Peri Physeos*), with notes and an *index verborum;* to be used with caution. Lucretius can be read in the three volumes prepared, with introduction, translations, and comments, by CYRIL BAILEY, *Lucreti, De Rerum Natura* (1947).

English translations of Epicurus and Lucretius include WHITNEY J. OATES (ed.), *The Stoic and Epicurean Philosophers* (1940), which contains translations by CYRIL BAILEY and by H.A.J. MUNRO. See also *The Philosophy of Epicurus: Letters, Doctrines, and Parallel Passages from Lucretius,* trans. by GEORGE K. STRODACH (1963); DIOGENES LAERTIUS, *Lives of Eminent Philosophers,* bk. 10 on Epicurus, trans. by R.D. HICKS (1925); and LUCRETIUS, *On the Nature of the Universe,* trans. by R.E. LATHAM (1964).

Valuable for its breadth and richness of detail, CYRIL BAILEY, *The Greek Atomists and Epicurus* (1928; new ed., 1964), is a fundamental work. For Epicurus' psychology and his relation to Aristotle, see CARLO DIANO, "La psicologia d'Epicuro e la teoria delle passioni," in *Giornale critico della filosofia italiana* (1939–42). A book that stresses Epicurus' anti-Platonism is N.W. DEWITT, *Epicurus and His Philosophy* (1954). Also important for its perceptive study of Epicurus' religiosity and ethics is A.J. FESTUGIERE, *Épicure et ses dieux* (1946; Eng. trans., *Epicurus and His Gods,* 1956). See also the article "Epikur," by W. SCHMID in the *Reallexikon für Antike und Christentum,* 5:681–819 (1961); L.L. WHYTE, *Essay on Atomism: From Democritus to 1960* (1961); and BENJAMIN FARRINGTON, *The Faith of Epicurus* (1967). G.D. HADZSITS, *Lucretius and His Influence* (1935), traces the influence of Epicurean ideas, especially since Roman times, in a broad perspective. For further bibliography, see PHILLIP DE LACY, "Some Recent Publications on Epicurus and Epicureanism (1937–1954)," in *Classical Weekly,* 48:169–177 (1955). BERNARD FRISCHER, *The Sculpted Word: Epicureanism and Philosophical Recruitment in Ancient Greece* (1982), a discussion of the school's success.

Pythagoreanism: The collection of the fragments in HERMANN DIELS and WALTHER KRANZ, *Die Fragmente der Vor-*

sokratiker, 6th ed., vol. 1 (1951), is insufficient; additions are given in MARIA TIMPANARO CARDINI (ed.), *Pitagorici: Testimonianze e frammenti,* 3 vol. (1958–64); and in CORNELIA J. DE VOGEL, *Pythagoras and Early Pythagoreanism* (1966). For the pseudo-Pythagoreans, see HOLGER THESLEFF (ed.), *The Pythagorean Texts of the Hellenistic Period* (1965).

The best comprehensive introduction to Pythagoreanism is the long chapter "Pythagoras and the Pythagoreans," in W.K.C. GUTHRIE, *A History of Greek Philosophy,* vol. 1, pp. 146–340 (1962). Somewhat different approaches have been taken by DE VOGEL (*op. cit.*); and JAMES A. PHILIP, *Pythagoras and Early Pythagoreanism* (1966), works that demand more active criticism by the reader. Fairly full references to the discussion of Pythagoreanism up to 1960 are in WALTER BURKERT, *Weisheit und Wissenschaft: Studien zu Pythagoras, Philolaos, und Platon* (1962; Eng. trans., *Lore and Science in Ancient Pythagoreanism,* 1972), a highly technical and at times rather overcritical work. Among later technical discussions, likely to become influential, are the articles "Pythagoras" and "Pythagoreer" in *Pauly-Wissowa Realencyclopädie,* vol. 47, (1963), and suppl. vol. 10 (1965)—of the contributors, KURT VON FRITZ and H. DORRIE arrive at less controversial conclusions than B.L. VAN DER WAERDEN.

Hellenistic Pythagoreanism is treated in HOLGER THESLEFF, *An Introduction to the Pythagorean Writings of the Hellenistic Period* (1961); additions and corrections in *Entretiens Fondation Hardt,* vol. 18 (1972). Neo-Pythagoreanism is treated in PHILIP MERLAN, *From Platonism to Neoplatonism* (1953).

For up-to-date bibliographical accession, see *L'Année philologique* (annual), under the subject heading "Pythagorica" and the various Pythagoreans.

Realism: There is no single monograph that covers comprehensively the whole topic of Realism. The following works will be helpful for the study of its particular phases.

For Medieval Realism, see M.H. CARRÉ, *Realists and Nominalists* (1946, reissued 1967). For Neo-realism and critical Realism, see E.B. HOLT *et al., The New Realism* (1912, reprinted 1970); DURANT DRAKE *et al., Essays in Critical Realism* (1920, reprinted 1968); RENÉ KREMER, *La Théorie de la connaissance chez les néo-réalistes anglais* (1928); T.E. HILL, "Realistic Theories," *Contemporary Theories of Knowledge,* pp. 77–205 (1961, reissued 1980), good general coverage of the American and English fields.

Neoscholastic Realisms are treated in LÉON NOËL, *Le Réalisme immédiat* (1938); and works by ÉTIENNE GILSON: *Le Réalisme méthodique* (1936), which presents the author's own views; ch. 5, "Vade Mecum of a Young Realist," trans. by W.J. QUINN, in R. HOUDE and J. MULLALLY (eds.), *Philosophy of Knowledge* (1960); and *Réalisme Thomiste et critique de la connaissance* (1939), a critique of the leading Neoscholastic views. For the linguistic approach, see MARTIN LEAN, *Sense-Perception and Matter* (1953, reprinted 1973); J.L. AUSTIN, *Sense and Sensibilia* (1962).

Universals in contemporary thought are treated in I.M. BOCHENSKI, ALONZO CHURCH, and NELSON GOODMAN, *The Problem of Universals* (1956); FARHANG ZABEEH, *Universals* (1966); PANAYOT BUTCHVAROV, *Resemblance and Identity: An Examination of the Problem of Universals* (1966, reissued 1982); NICHOLAS WOLTERSTORFF, *On Universals: An Essay in Ontology* (1970).

For Scientific Realism, see BERTRAND RUSSELL, *Our Knowledge of the External World,* rev. ed. (1926, various printings); W.H. WERKMEISTER, *The Basis and Structure of Knowledge* (1948, reissued 1968), bibliography, pp. 420–438; MORITZ SCHLICK, "Are Natural Laws Conventions?" in H. FEIGL and MAY BRODBECK (eds.), *Readings in the Philosophy of Science,* pp. 181–188 (1953); ROMANO HARRÉ, *Theories and Things* (1961); GROVER MAXWELL, "The Ontological Status of Theoretical Entities," in *Minnesota Studies in the Philosophy of Science,* 3:3–27 (1962); J.J.C. SMART, *Philosophy and Scientific Realism* (1963); DAVID M. ARMSTRONG, *Universals and Scientific Realism,* 2 vol. (1980).

Other 20th-century Realisms are discussed in G.D. HICKS, *Critical Realism* (1938); JAMES FEIBLEMAN, *The Revival of Realism* (1946, reissued 1972); WILFRID SELLARS, *Science, Perception and Reality* (1963); R.M. CHISHOLM (ed.), *Realism and the Background of Phenomenology* (1961), convenient bibliography, pp. 290–304; J.D. WILD (ed.), *The Return to Reason: Essays in Realistic Philosophy* (1953); E.B. MCGILVARY, *Toward a Perspective Realism* (1956); D.M. ARMSTRONG, *A Materialist Theory of the Mind* (1968); INGEBORG WIRTH, *Realismus und Apriorismus in Nicolai Hartmanns Erkenntnistheorie* (1965); GUSTAV BERGMANN, *Realism: A Critique of Brentano and Meinong* (1967).

Scholasticism: For the latest and most detailed bibliography, see W. TOTOK, *Handbuch der Geschichte der Philosophie,* vol. 2, *Mittelalter und frühe Neuzeit* (1970). Among the most reliable, best grounded presentations of the whole period are: E. GILSON, *History of Christian Philosophy in the Middle Ages* (1955); F. COPLESTON, *A History of Philosophy,* vol. 2, *Mediaeval Philosophy,* vol. 3, *Late Mediaeval and Renaissance Philosophy* (1950, 1953; paperback edition, 1962, 1963); M. DE WULF, *Histoire de la philosophie médiévale,* 6th ed., 3 vol. (1934–47; Eng.

trans. of vol. 1, 1951); and E. BREHIER, *La Philosophie du moyen âge,* 2nd ed. (1949). Still indispensable, though obsolete in some details is: F. UEBERWEG, *Grundriss der Geschichte der Philosophie,* vol. 2, B. GEYER, *Die patristische und scholastische Philosophie,* 11th ed. (1928). Lucidly arranged and divided is the 13th volume of FLICHE-MARTIN, *Histoire de l'Église: Le Mouvement doctrinal de XIᵉ au XIVᵉ siècle* (1951), which includes contributions by A. Forest, F. van Steenberghen, and M. de Gandillac. M. GRABMANN's masterpiece, *Die Geschichte der scholastischen Methode,* 2 vol. (1909–11, reprinted 1956), covers only the time until the first years of the 13th century. For a first introduction for the general reader, see J. PIEPER, *Scholastik* (1960; Eng. trans., *Scholasticism,* 1960). Special problems concerning the continuing influence of medieval Scholasticism are treated in the following monographs: A. KOYRE, *Descartes und die Scholastik* (1923); A. TELLKAMP, *Das Verhältnis John Locke's zur Scholastik* (1927); and J.O. FLECKENSTEIN, *Scholastik, Barock, exakte Wissenschaften* (1949). The following are sources on Neoscholasticism: J.P. GOLINAS, *La Restauration du Thomisme sous Leon XIII et les philosophies nouvelles* (1959); GIOVANNI ROSSI, *Le origini del Neotomismo nell'ambiente del Collegio Alberoni* (1957); A. VIEL, "Le Mouvement thomiste au XIXᵉ siècle," *Revue Thomiste* (1909–10); E. BETTONI, *La Situation actuelle de la philosophie parmi les catholiques dans les divers pays* (1948), a survey of centres of study, institutes, and publications; and J.S. ZYBURA (ed.), *Present-Day Thinkers and the New Scholasticism: An International Symposium* (1926).

Skepticism: The basic statements and arguments of various forms of Skepticism are given in: (Academic Skepticism)—CICERO, *Academica* and *De natura deorum,* both with trans. by H. RACKHAM, Loeb Classical Library (1956). (Pyrrhonian Skepticism)—SEXTUS EMPIRICUS, *Adversus Mathematicos,* with trans. by R.G. BURY, Loeb Classical Library: vol. 1–2, *Against the Logicians* and *Outlines of Pyrrhonism* (1933–36); vol. 3, *Against the Physicists, Against the Ethicists* (1936); vol. 4, *Against the Professors* (1959–60); and *Scepticism, Man and God: Selections from the Major Writings of Sextus Empiricus,* ed. by P. HALLIE, trans. by S.G. ETHERIDGE (1964). (Renaissance Skepticism)—MICHEL DE MONTAIGNE, "L'Apologie de Raimond Sebond," in PIERRE VILLEY (ed.), *Les Essais de Michel de Montaigne,* new ed. (1922). (Skepticism and fideism)—BLAISE PASCAL, *Pensées,* ed. by L. BRUNSCHVICG (1951). (Skepticism in relation to modern philosophy)—PIERRE BAYLE, *Dictionnaire historique et critique,* esp. the articles "Pyrrho" and "Zeno of Elea," both of which appear in BAYLE's *Historical and Critical Dictionary: Selections,* trans. and ed. by RICHARD H. POPKIN (1965); DAVID HUME, *Dialogues Concerning Natural Religion,* ed. by N. KEMP SMITH (1947); *Enquiries Concerning the Human Understanding and Concerning the Principles of Morals,* 2nd ed. (1957), and *A Treatise of Human Nature,* both ed. by L.A. SELBY-BIGGE (1958). The standard studies of ancient Skepticism are: EDWYN R. BEVAN, *Stoics and Sceptics* (1959); VICTOR BROCHARD, *Les Sceptiques grecs* (1887); NORMAN MACCOLL, *The Greek Sceptics from Pyrrho to Sextus* (1869); MARY MILLS PATRICK, *The Greek Sceptics* (1929); LEON ROBIN, *Pyrrhon et le scepticisme grec* (1944); and EDUARD ZELLER, *The Stoics, Epicureans and Sceptics,* trans. by O.J. REICHEL (1880). A recent fine study of the epistemological problems involved in ancient Skepticism is CHARLOTTE L. STOUGH, *Greek Skepticism* (1969). See also RAOUL RICHTER, *Der Skeptizismus in der Philosophie* (1904–08); RICHARD H. POPKIN, "Skepticism," *Encyclopedia of Philosophy,* vol. 7, pp. 449–461 (1967), which contains a bibliography on the subject; these examine Skepticism from ancient times to the 19th century. JOHN OWEN, *The Skeptics of the French Renaissance* (1893), is an interesting discussion of Renaissance and 17th-century Skepticism, though not particularly scholarly. DON CAMERON ALLEN, *Doubt's Boundless Sea: Skepticism and Faith in the Renaissance* (1964); and RICHARD H. POPKIN, *The History of Scepticism from Erasmus to Descartes,* rev. ed. (1968), which contains a lengthy bibliography, are studies of Renaissance Skepticism and its impact on philosophy and religion. RICHARD H. POPKIN, "Berkeley and Pyrrhonism," *Review of Metaphysics,* 5:223–246 (1951–52); "David Hume and the Pyrrhonian Controversy," *ibid.,* 6:65–81 (1952–53); "David Hume: His Pyrrhonism and His Critique of Pyrrhonism," *Philosophical Quarterly,* 1:385–407 (1950–51); "The High Road to Pyrrhonism," *American Philosophical Quarterly,* 2:1–15 (1965); "The Skeptical Crisis and the Rise of Modern Philosophy," *Review of Metaphysics,* 7:132–151, 307–322, 499–510 (1953–54); "The Skeptical Precursors of David Hume," *Philosophy and Phenomenological Research,* 16:61–71 (1955–56); and "Scepticism in the Enlightenment," in T. BESTERMANN (ed.), *Studies on Voltaire and the Eighteenth Century,* 26:1321–1345 (1963), are specialized studies on aspects of Skepticism in relation to modern philosophy. ARNE NAESS, *Scepticism* (1968), is a most interesting attempt to clarify Skepticism in relation to contemporary thought and to defend it as a viable outlook

today. BENSON MATES, *Skeptical Essays* (1981), discusses epistemological problems and free will.

Sophists: Ancient sources and fragments are presented in R.K. SPRAGUE, *The Older Sophists, a Complete Translation* (1972), and in K. FREEMAN, *Ancilla to the Pre-Socratic Philosophers* (1948), to be used together with Freeman's *The Pre-Socratic Philosophers,* 2nd ed. (1949). The original Greek texts are in H. DIELS and W. KRANZ (eds.), *Die Fragmente der Vorsokratiker,* 6th ed., vol. 2 (1952); and are edited with an Italian translation and commentary in M. UNTERSTEINER, *Sofisti,* 4 vol. (1949–62). (*General discussions*): T. GOMPERZ, *Greek Thinkers,* Eng. trans. by L. MAGNUS, vol. 1, bk. 3, ch. 5–7 (1901); M. UNTERSTEINER, *The Sophists,* Eng. trans. by K. FREEMAN (1954); W.K.C. GUTHRIE, *A History of Greek Philosophy,* vol. 3, *The Fifth-Century Enlightenment* (1969). G.B. KERFERD, *The Sophistic Movement* (1981), is a study of the intellectual contributions made by the movement.

The Second Sophistic period is treated in G.W. BOWERSOCK, *Greek Sophists in the Roman Empire* (1969).

Stoicism: HANS VON ARNIM, *Stoicorum Veterum Fragmenta,* 4 vol. (1905–24), is the standard text collection. The following works of classic Stoic authors and substantive issues in Stoicism in antiquity are most conveniently available in the "Loeb Classical Library": MARCUS AURELIUS, *Meditations;* EPICTETUS, *Discourses;* CICERO, *De fato, De finibus, De natura deorum,* and *Academica;* DIOGENES LAERTIUS, *Lives of Eminent Philosophers,* vol. 2, book 7; SENECA, *Epistulae Morales* and *Moral Essays;* SEXTUS EMPIRICUS, *Outlines of Pyrrhonism* and *Against the Dogmatists,* 4 vol.; GEORGE MURRAY, *The Stoic Philosophy* (1915), the classical statement of the grandeur of the Stoic philosophy; MAX POHLENZ, *Die Stoa,* 2 vol. (1948–49); and PAUL BARTH, *Die Stoa* (1903), are representative of scholarly studies of Stoic philosophy; JOHNNY CHRISTENSEN, *An Essay on the Unity of Stoic Philosophy* (1962), is a recent and comprehensive essay; LUDWIG EDELSTEIN, *The Meaning of Stoicism* (1966); and JOSIAH B. GOULD, *The Philosophy of Chrysippus* (1970), are among the best of recent studies of Greco-Roman Stoicism; EDUARD ZELLER, *Die Philosophie der Griechen in ihrer geschichtlichen Entwicklung,* 5 vol. (1856–68; in part translated as *Stoics, Epicureans, and Skeptics,* rev. ed., 1962); EDWYN R. BEVAN, *Stoics and Sceptics* (1913, reprinted 1959); and ROBERT D. HICKS, *Stoic and Epicurean* (1910, reprinted 1962), are illustrations of Stoic philosophy in the Hellenistic period. See also JASON L. SAUNDERS, *Greek and Roman Philosophy After Aristotle* (1966); and HARRY A. WOLFSON, *Philo: Foundations of Religious Philosophy in Judaism, Christianity and Islam,* 2 vol. (1962). EDWARD V. ARNOLD, *Roman Stoicism* (1911, reprinted 1958); and FREDERICK W. BUSSELL, *Marcus Aurelius and the Later Stoics* (1910), are excellent statements of Stoicism in the later Roman period. PIERRE DE LABRIOLLE, *Histoire de la littérature latine chrétienne* (1920; Eng. trans., *History and Literature of Christianity from Tertullian to Boethius,* 1924), an excellent presentation of the influence of Stoic views in late antiquity and the patristic period; ETIENNE GILSON, *History of Christian Philosophy in the Middle Ages* (1955); HARRY A. WOLFSON, *The Philosophy of the Church Fathers,* 3rd ed. rev. (1970); MAURICE DE WULF, *Histoire de la philosophie médiéval,* 2 vol. (1925; Eng. trans., *History of Mediaeval Philosophy,* 2 vol., 1926); and ISAAC HUSIK, *A History of Medieval Jewish Philosophy* (1940), are careful introductions to Stoic influences in patristic and medieval times; JASON L. SAUNDERS, *Justus Lipsius: The Philosophy of Renaissance Stoicism* (1955); HAROLD HOFFDING, *A History of Modern Philosophy,* 2 vol. (1950); and FREDERICK C. COPLESTON, *A History of Philosophy,* rev. ed., vol. 3–6 (1962), trace the Stoic influence from its revival in the Renaissance into modern philosophy. JOHN M. RIST (ed.), *The Stoics* (1978), is an excellent collection of essays covering logic, cosmology, ethics, psychology, and aesthetics.

Stoic logic and physics are treated in BENSON MATES, *Stoic Logic* (1953); SAMUEL SAMBURSKY, *The Physical World of the Greeks,* 2nd ed. (1960; orig. pub. in Hebrew) and *Physics of the Stoics* (1959).

Analytic and Linguistic philosophy: G.J. WARNOCK, *English Philosophy Since 1900* (1958), is a very readable account covering much of the history. J.O. URMSON, *Philosophical Analysis* (1956), is especially good on logical atomism and its demise. BERTRAND RUSSELL, *The Problems of Philosophy* (1959), is a nontechnical account of his views just prior to the period of logical atomism. A collection of Russell's papers, *Logic and Knowledge,* ed. by R.C. MARSH (1956), contains his "Lectures on Logical Atomism," together with more technical papers. G.E. MOORE, *Some Main Problems of Philosophy* (1953), gives a good introduction to his methods and philosophical concerns. Two key papers by Moore are "A Defence of Common Sense," in *Contemporary British Philosophy,* Second Series (1925), and "Proof of an External World," in *Proceedings of the British Academy,* 25:273–300 (1939). Among anthologies are those of A.J. AYER (ed.), *Logical Positivism* (1959), which also includes papers critical of the movement and has an excellent bibliography; BERNARD WILLIAMS and ALAN MONTEFIORE (eds.), *British Analytical Philosophy* (1966); RICHARD RORTY (ed.), *The Linguistic Turn* (1967); J.A. FODOR and J.J. KATZ (eds.), *The Structure of Language* (1964); and LEONARD LINSKY (ed.), *Semantics and the Philosophy of Language* (1952). The 1961 translation of WITTGENSTEIN's *Tractatus Logico-Philosophicus* by D.F. PEARS and B.F. MCGUINESS is superior to the original English version. Wittgenstein's *Philosophical Investigations* (1953) is the best known and historically the most influential of the posthumously published works from his later period. A.J. AYER, *Language, Truth and Logic,* 2nd ed. (1946), remains the best introduction to Logical Positivism. GILBERT RYLE, *The Concept of Mind* (1949), is the most famous example of what has been called "ordinary language" philosophy. J.L. AUSTIN, *How To Do Things with Words* (1962), contains the most discussed features of his views. W.V.O. QUINE, *From a Logical Point of View* (1953), is a collection of fairly nontechnical essays that provide good examples of the continuing influence of formal logic.

Empiricism: Classic texts include JOHN LOCKE, *An Essay Concerning Human Understanding,* 2 vol. (1690); DAVID HUME, *A Treatise of Human Nature,* book 1, pt. 1 (1739); IMMANUEL KANT, *Kritik der reinen Vernunft* (1781; Eng. trans., *Critique of Pure Reason,* 1929); JOHN STUART MILL, *A System of Logic, Ratiocinative and Inductive,* books 1 and 2 (1843).

W.H. WALSH, *Reason and Experience* (1947); and H.H. PRICE, *Thinking and Experience,* 2nd ed. (1969), are good general surveys. For a comprehensive selection of standard works from Locke to J.S. Mill, see A.J. AYER and R. WINCH (eds.), *The British Empirical Philosophers* (1952). Modern works in the Empiricist tradition include BERTRAND RUSSELL, *Human Knowledge* (1948); W.T. STACE, *Theory of Knowledge and Existence* (1932); RUDOLF CARNAP, *Der logische Aufbau der Welt* (1928; Eng. trans., *The Logical Structure of the World,* 1967); and A.J. AYER, *Language, Truth and Logic,* 2nd ed. (1946), a short exposition of the extreme Empiricist position. HAROLD MORICK (ed.), *Challenges to Empiricism* (1980), is a collection of essays.

Existentialism: Fundamental texts include SOREN KIERKEGAARD, *Philosophiske smuler* (1844; *Philosophical Fragments,* 1936); *Afsluttende uvidenskabelig efterskrift til de philosophiske smuler* (1846; *Concluding Unscientific Postscript,* 1941). FRIEDRICH NIETZSCHE, *Also sprach Zarathustra* (1883–84; *Thus Spoke Zarathustra,* trans. by W. KAUFMANN in *The Portable Nietzsche,* 1954); *Zur Genealogie der Moral* (1877; *Toward a Genealogy of Morals,* trans. by W. KAUFMANN in *Basic Writings of Nietzsche,* 1966). KARL JASPERS, *Psychologie der Weltanschauungen* (1919), the first work of contemporary Existentialism, announcing all of the fundamental theses; *Philosophie,* 3 vol. (1932; *Philosophy,* 3 vol., 1969–71); *Vernunft und Existenz* (1935; Eng. trans., *Reason and Existenz,* 1955). MARTIN HEIDEGGER, *Sein und Zeit* (1927; 10th ed., 1963; *Being and Time,* 1962); *Was ist Metaphysik?* (1929; "What Is Metaphysics?" trans. by R.F.C. HULL and A. CRICK in *Existence and Being,* 1949); *Einführung in die Metaphysik* (1953; *An Introduction to Metaphysics,* 1959). GABRIEL MARCEL, *Être et Avoir* (1935; *Being and Having,* 1949); *Le Mystère de l'être,* 2 vol. (1950; *The Mystery of Being,* 1950–51); *The Philosophy of Existence,* (1949). NICOLA ABBAGNANO, *La struttura dell'esistenza* (1939); N. LANGIULLI (ed. and trans.), *Critical Existentialism* (1969). JEAN-PAUL SARTRE, *L'Être et le néant* (1943; *Being and Nothingness,* 1956); *L'Existentialisme est un humanisme* (1946; *Existentialism and Humanism,* 1948). MAURICE MERLEAU-PONTY, *La Structure du comportement* (1942; *The Structure of Behavior,* 1963); *Phénoménologie de la perception* (1945; *The Phenomenology of Perception,* 1962).

Important surveys and analyses include MARJORIE GRENE, *Dreadful Freedom* (1948); HELMUT KUHN, *Encounter with Nothingness: An Essay on Existentialism* (1951); MAURICE NATANSON, *A Critique of Jean-Paul Sartre's Ontology* (1951); JAMES COLLINS, *The Existentialists: A Critical Study* (1952); WILLIAM BARRETT, *What Is Existentialism?* (1964); ADOLPH LICHTIGFELD, *Jaspers' Metaphysics* (1954); MARJORIE GRENE, *Martin Heidegger* (1957); MARY WARNOCK, *Existentialism* (1970); and ROBERT D. CUMMING, *Starting Point* (1979).

Idealism: The two best books on Idealism in English are A.C. EWING, *Idealism: A Critical Survey* (1933); and R.F.A. HOERNLE, *Idealism as a Philosophy* (1927). A.C. EWING (ed.), *The Idealist Tradition from Berkeley to Blanshard* (1957), is a useful volume containing selections from the texts of the major Idealists and selected criticisms of Idealism. Other important collections are C. BARRETT (ed.), *Contemporary Idealism in America* (1932); J.H. MUIRHEAD (ed.), *Contemporary British Philosophy: Personal Statements,* First–Second Series, 2 vol. each (1924); and G.P. ADAMS and W.P. MONTAGUE (eds.), *Contemporary American Philosophy,* 2 vol. (1930). Works on the history and theory of the subject include: B. BLANSHARD, *Reason and Analysis* (1962), a careful critical examination of schools of philosophy

opposed to Idealism; G.W. CUNNINGHAM, *The Idealistic Argument in Recent British and American Philosophy* (1933), a thorough and dependable treatise; S.N. DASGUPTA, *Indian Idealism* (1933); NICOLAI HARTMANN, *Die Philosophie des Deutsches Idealismus,* vol. 1, *Fichte, Schelling, und die Romantik* (1923), vol. 2, *Hegel* (1929), 2nd ed. (1 vol., 1960); A.J.M. MILNE, *The Social Philosophy of English Idealism* (1962); J.H. MUIRHEAD, *The Platonic Tradition in Anglo-Saxon Philosophy: Studies in the History of Idealism in England and America* (1931); P.T. RAJU, *Idealistic Thought of India* (1953); L.S. ROUNER (ed.), *Philosophy, Religion, and the Coming World Civilization: Essays in Honor of William Ernest Hocking* (1966); and A. STERN, *Philosophy of History and the Problem of Values* (1962), a good secondary source.

On the classical systems of Indian philosophy, see S. RADHAKRISHNAN, *Indian Philosophy,* 2 vol. (1923–27), an authoritative exposition; S.N. DASGUPTA, *A History of Indian Philosophy,* 5 vol. (1922–55), an erudite examination of the Sanskrit and Pāli texts; *Indian Idealism* (1933); SRI AUROBINDO, *The Life Divine* (1949), a reinterpretation of the heritage; and SWAMI VIVEKANANDA, *The Yogas and Other Works* (1953), a collection with biography. In *Pragmatism* (1907) and in *The Varieties of Religious Experience* (1902), WILLIAM JAMES quoted Vivekananda at length as a typical representative of spiritual monism. In the *Sacred Books of the East,* 50 vol., ed. by F. MAX MULLER (1879–1910), see especially vol. 1 and 15, *The Upanishads* and vol. 8, *The Bhagavadgîtâ.* In the *Harvard Oriental Series,* 47 vol., ed. by CHARLES ROCKWELL LANMAN (1890–1968), see especially vol. 3, *Buddhism in Translations,* and vol. 17, *The Yoga-System of Patañjali.*

Writings of Idealists are listed in their biographies. P.A. SCHILPP, editor of "The Library of Living Philosophers Series," has issued four important volumes on Idealists: *The Philosophy of Alfred North Whitehead,* 2nd ed. (1951); *The Philosophy of Ernst Cassirer* (1949); *The Philosophy of Sarvepalli Radhakrishnan* (1962); and *The Philosophy of Martin Buber* (1967); and a volume on Brand Blanshard is in preparation. Other works on Idealists include: J.H. COTTON, *Royce on the Human Self* (1954), one of the best books on Royce; D.S. ROBINSON, *Royce and Hocking: American Idealists* (1968); and GABRIEL MARCEL, *La Métaphysique de Royce* (1945; Eng. trans., 1956), which shows the relation of Marcel to Royce and Hocking. H.T. KIM, "Nishida and Royce," *Philosophy East and West,* 1:18–29 (1952), and "The Logic of the Illogical: Zen and Hegel," *ibid.,* 5:19–29 (1955), are informative accounts of Nishida's contributions to Idealism. The following volumes of the *Revue Internationale de Philosophie* contain valuable bibliographies: *Henri Bergson,* vol. 3 (1948); *Léon Brunschvicg,* vol. 5 (1951); *Hegel,* vol. 6 (1952); *George Berkeley,* vol. 7 (1953); *Benedetto Croce,* vol. 7 (1953); *Kant,* vol. 8 (1954); *Whitehead,* vol. 15 (1961); *Leibniz,* vol. 20 (1966); and *Josiah Royce,* vol. 21 (1967). GODFREY VESEY (ed.), *Idealism Past and Present* (1982), includes historical essays on idealistic thought of the past 2,500 years.

Materialism: For the period up to about 100 years ago, see F.A. LANGE, *Geschichte des Materialismus und Kritik seiner Bedeutung in der Gegenwart,* 2 vol. (1902; Eng. trans., *History of Materialism and Criticism of Its Present Importance,* 3rd ed., 3 vol. (1925). For more recent times, see JOHN PASSMORE, *A Hundred Years of Philosophy,* 2nd ed. (1966). There are excellent articles by KEITH CAMPBELL and H.B. ACTON on "Materialism" and "Dialectical Materialism" in the *Encyclopedia of Philosophy,* vol. 5, pp. 179–188 and vol. 2, pp. 389–397 (1967), which also contains excellent articles on nearly all of the noncontemporary philosophers here mentioned. Examples of work by most of the contemporary writers are given in JOHN O'CONNOR (ed.), *Modern Materialism: Readings on Mind-Body Identity* (1969); and C.V. BORST (ed.), *The Mind-Brain Identity Theory* (1970). See also HERBERT FEIGL, *The "Mental" and the "Physical": The Essay and a Postscript* (1967); J.J.C. SMART, *Philosophy and Scientific Realism* (1963); D.M. ARMSTRONG, *A Materialist Theory of the Mind* (1968); and WILFRID SELLARS, *Science, Perception and Reality* (1963), especially ch. 1. A rather difficult book defending Materialism from the difficulties about intentionality is D.C. DENNETT, *Content and Consciousness* (1969). For two very different styles of antimaterialist argument, see J.R. LUCAS, *The Freedom of the Will* (1970); and NORMAN MALCOLM, *Problems of Mind* (1971). Another interesting critique of Materialism is in JOHN BELOFF, *The Existence of Mind* (1962). A mainly mechanistic philosophy of biology is presented by the German biologist B. RENSCH in *Biophilosophie auf erkenntnistheoretischer Grundlage (Panpsychistischer Identismus)* (1968; Eng. trans., *Biophilosophy,* 1971), though Rensch's philosophy is also panpsychist.

Some classic Materialist works are: LUCRETIUS, *On the Nature of the Universe,* trans. by R.E. LATHAM (1951); THOMAS HOBBES, *Body, Mind and Citizen: Selections,* ed. by R.S. PETERS (1962); RENE DESCARTES, *Philosophical Writings,* trans. and ed. by ELIZABETH ANSCOMBE and P.T. GEACH (1954); and A. VARTANIAN,

La Mettrie's "L'Homme Machine": A Study in the Origins of an Idea (1960), which is a critical edition with introductory monograph and notes.

For epistemic Materialism, see RUDOLF CARNAP, "Psychology in Physical Language," in A.J. AYER (ed.), *Logical Positivism* (1959); Carnap's replies to Herbert Feigl and A.J. Ayer in P.A. SCHILPP (ed.), *The Philosophy of Rudolf Carnap* (1964); and H. REICHENBACH, *Experience and Prediction* (1938).

The most relevant and important works by Ryle and Wittgenstein are: GILBERT RYLE, *The Concept of Mind* (1949); and LUDWIG WITTGENSTEIN, *Philosophical Investigations* (1953). For a Materialist critique of Ryle, see BRIAN MEDLIN, "Ryle and the Mechanical Hypothesis," in C.F. PRESLEY (ed.), *The Identity Theory of Mind,* 2nd ed. (1971).

Phenomenology: Most of the classical works on Phenomenology were written by Husserl himself (see the bibliography of the HUSSERL article). In EDMUND HUSSERL, *Logische Untersuchungen,* 2nd ed., 2 vol. (1913–21; Eng. trans., *Logical Investigations,* 2 vol., 1970), one of the fundamental texts on Phenomenology, the phenomenological method is applied in the area of logic. The following works appeared in the journal *Jahrbuch für Philosophie und phänomenologische Forschung* (1913–30); Husserl's *Ideen zu einer reinen Phänomenologie und phänomenologischen Philosophie* (1913; Eng. trans., *Ideas: General Introduction to Pure Phenomenology,* 1931, reprinted 1969), through which Phenomenology established itself as transcendental philosophy and received worldwide reaction; *Vorlesungen zur Phänomenologie des inneren Zeitbewusstseins* (1928; Eng. trans., *The Phenomenology of Internal Time-Consciousness,* 1964); and *Formale und transzendentale Logik* (1929; Eng. trans., *Formal and Transcendental Logic,* 1969); MAX SCHELER, *Der Formalismus in der Ethik* (1916); and MARTIN HEIDEGGER, *Sein und Zeit* (1927; Eng. trans., *Being and Time,* 1962). The following works appeared in Husserl's *Husserliana* (Husserl's collected works): *Cartesianische Meditationen und Pariser Vorträge* (1950; Eng. trans., *The Paris Lectures,* 1964), which contains the text of the Paris lectures of 1929 and the subsequent elaboration; *Die Idee der Phänomenologie* (1950; Eng. trans., *The Idea of Phenomenology,* 1964), an introduction to Phenomenology in five lectures from 1907; *Ideen,* 3 vol. (1950–52); *Die Krisis der europäischen Wissenschaften und die transzendentale Phänomenologie* (1954; Eng. trans., *The Crisis of European Sciences and Transcendental Phenomenology,* 1970), Husserl's later work (1934–37), significant for the problems regarding the life-world; *Erste Philosophie,* 2 vol. (1956–59), a critical history of ideas and a theory of reduction presented in a series of lectures, 1923–24; *Phänomenologische Psychologie* (1962), lectures from 1925, a different wording of the *Encyclopædia Britannica* article of 1927, with remarks by Heidegger and the Amsterdam addresses of 1925; *Zur Phänomenologie des inneren Zeitbewusstseins* (1966), text on the problem of time from 1893–1917 with lectures (in the middle) from 1905 on the inner time-consciousness (first edited by Heidegger); *Analysen zur passiven Synthesis* (1966), a phenomenological analysis having sensation as its subject matter; and *Philosophie der Arithmetik* (1970), early manuscripts from 1890 to 1901. His *The Basic Problems of Phenomenology,* trans. by ALBERT HOFSTADTER (1982; originally published in German., 1975), reproduces a course of lectures given in 1927. See also JOSEPH J. KOCKELMANS, *Edmund Husserl's Phenomenological Psychology* (1967); and RUDOLF BOEHM, *Vom Gesichtspunkt der Phänomenologie* (1968).

In the series "Phaenomenologica" works are published that are written from a Phenomenological perspective, HERBERT SPIEGELBERG, *The Phenomenological Movement,* 2nd ed., 2 vol. (1965), worthy of particular mention, also appeared in this series. Since 1904 MARVIN FARBER has edited the journal *Philosophy and Phenomenological Research* (by no means, however, exclusively dedicated to Phenomenology). In England *The Journal of the British Society for Phenomenology* first appeared in 1970. In the United States the following journals have appeared: *Journal of Phenomenological Psychology* (semi-annual); *Research in Phenomenology* (1971); and *Analecta Husserliana: The Yearbook of Phenomenological Research.*

Positivism and Logical Empiricism: Literature on Classical Positivism includes J. WATSON, *Comte, Mill and Spencer* (1895); W.M. SIMON, *European Positivism in the Nineteenth Century* (1963); JOHN STUART MILL, *Auguste Comte and Positivism* (1865); AUGUSTE COMTE, *Cours de philosophie positive,* 6 vol. (1830–42; Eng. trans. and cond. by H. MARTINEAU, *The Positive Philosophy of Auguste Comte,* 2 vol., 1853). For further references to the ethical views of the classical Positivists, see the bibliography of Utilitarianism in the *Encyclopedia of Philosophy.*

Many of the original classics of Logical Positivism and Logical Empiricism, both books and articles, are listed in the ample bibliography of A.J. AYER (ed.), *Logical Positivism* (1959), an anthology that contains, among other important essays,

RUDOLF CARNAP's "Psychology in Physical Language." The early history of Viennese Positivism is well told in VICTOR KRAFT, *Der Wiener Kreis: Der Ursprung des Neopositivismus* (1950, 2nd ed. 1968; Eng. trans., *The Vienna Circle,* 1953, reprinted 1969). Another important source is J. JOERGENSEN, *The Development of Logical Empiricism,* vol. 2, no. 9 of the *International Encyclopedia of Unified Science* (1951). For a brief account of the European movement of Logical Positivism and its migration and impact in the United States, see H. FEIGL, "The Wiener Kreis in America," in D. FLEMING and B. BAYLIN (eds.), *The Intellectual Migration: Europe and America 1930–1960* (1969). Books, mainly in the foundations of the sciences, but also in philosophy of language and epistemology, many by the leading Logical Empiricists, are listed in the ample *Bibliography and Index,* in HERBERT FEIGL and CHARLES MORRIS (eds.), *International Encyclopedia of Unified Science,* vol. 2, no. 10 (1969). Of direct relevance are the major works of R. Carnap, O. Neurath, M. Schlick, P. Frank, H. Reichenbach, E. Nagel, C.G. Hempel, R. von Mises, and Charles Morris. For criticisms, those of KARL R. POPPER may be used; and the intellectual autobiography of Carnap, the 26 descriptive and critical essays, and his replies, in P.A. SCHILPP (ed.), *The Philosophy of Rudolf Carnap* (1963). For more recent evaluations and reactions, see P. ACHINSTEIN and S.F. BARKER (eds.), *The Legacy of Logical Positivism: Studies in the Philosophy of Science* (1969); and *Minnesota Studies in the Philosophy of Science,* vol. 1–5 (1956–70).

Pragmatism: Classic works include CHARLES SANDERS PEIRCE, "The Fixation of Belief," "How to Make Our Ideas Clear," and "What Pragmatism Is," in *Collected Papers,* vol. 5, ed. by C. HARTSHORNE and P. WEISS (1934); WILLIAM JAMES, *Principles of Psychology,* 2 vol. (1890), *The Will to Believe and Other Essays in Popular Philosophy* (1897), *Pragmatism: A New Name for Some Old Ways of Thinking* (1907), and *The Meaning of Truth* (1909); JOHN DEWEY, *How We Think* (1910), *The Influence of Darwin on Philosophy* (1910), *Democracy and Education* (1916), *Essays in Experimental Logic* (1916), *Reconstruction in Philosophy* (1920, 1948), *Human Nature and Conduct* (1922), *Logic: The Theory of Inquiry* (1938), *Theory of Valuation* (1939), and *Problems of Men* (1946). On F.C.S. Schiller see R. ABEL, *The Pragmatic Humanism of F.C.S. Schiller* (1955), with a bibliography of Schiller's writings; on French and Italian pragmatists, H.S. THAYER, *Meaning and Action: A Critical History of Pragmatism,* part 3 (1968), with further bibliographical references.

For surveys of the movement, see H.S. THAYER, *Meaning and Action: A Critical History of Pragmatism* (1968), with bibliography; "Pragmatism," in D.J. O'CONNOR (ed.), *A Critical History of Western Philosophy,* pp. 437–462 (1964); and H.S. THAYER (ed.), *Pragmatism: The Classic Writings* (1970), the basic writings in the Pragmatism of Peirce, James, Dewey, Mead, and Lewis, and further bibliographical references; John Dewey, "The Development of American Pragmatism," in *Philosophy and Civilization,* pp. 13–35 (1931); and CHARLES W. MORRIS, *The Pragmatic Movement in American Philosophy* (1970). JACQUES BARZUN, *A Stroll with William James* (1983), is an excellent discussion of his ideas.

Rationalism: The classic Ancient Greek work is PLATO, *Meno;* essential modern works are DESCARTES, *Meditationes de Prima Philosophia . . . (Meditations on First Philosophy):* SPINOZA, *Ethics;* LEIBNIZ, *Monadologie (Monadology and Other Philosophical Writings);* KANT, *Kritik der reinen Vernunft (Critique of Pure Reason);* 19th century. Rationalism is epitomized in HEGEL, *Phänomenologie des Geistes (Phenomenology of Mind);* FRANCIS HERBERT BRADLEY, *Appearance and Reality.*

For Rationalism in the theory of knowledge, see BRAND BLANSHARD, *Reason and Analysis* (1962); GEORGE BOAS, *Rationalism in Greek Philosophy* (1961); ERNST CASSIRER, *Die Philosophie der Aufklärung* (1932; Eng. trans., *Philosophy of the Enlightenment,* 1951); M.R. COHEN, *Reason and Nature: An Essay on the Meaning of Scientific Method,* 2nd ed. (1953): A.C. EWING, *Idealism: A Critical Survey* (1934); H.H. JOACHIM, *The Nature of Truth* (1906); A.E. MURPHY, *The Uses of Reason* (1943); H.J. PATON, *In Defence of Reason* (1951); BERTRAND RUSSELL, *Problems of Philosophy* (1912); W.H. WALSH, *Reason and Experience* (1947).

For Rationalism in metaphysics, see the classics listed above. For two outstanding examples from the present century, see J.M.E. MCTAGGART, *The Nature of Existence,* 2 vol. (1921–27), together with the commentary of C.D. BROAD, *Examination of McTaggart's Philosophy,* 2 vol. (1933–38); and ALFRED NORTH WHITEHEAD, *Process and Reality* (1929). For Rationalism in ethics, see WILLIAM WOLLASTON, *The Religion of Nature Delineated* (1722); and KANT, *Die Metaphysik der Sitten* (1785; Eng. trans., *The Metaphysics of Morals,* 1799). For early forms of the appeal to self-evident rules, see RICHARD PRICE, *A Review of the Principal Questions in Morals* (1758). For later types of Rationalism, see G.E. MOORE, *Principia Ethica* (1903); W.D.

ROSS, *The Right and the Good* (1930), and *Foundations of Ethics* (1939); BRIAN ELLIS, *Rational Belief System* (1979).

For Rationalism in religion, excellent standard works are: W.E.H. LECKY, *History of the Rise and Influence of the Spirit of Rationalism in Europe*, 2 vol. (1865); A.D. WHITE, *History of the Warfare of Science with Theology in Christendom*, 2 vol. (1910); J.M. ROBERTSON, *A Short History of Freethought, Ancient and Modern*, 2nd ed., 2 vol. (1906); A.W. BENN, *History of English Rationalism in the Nineteenth Century*, 2 vol. (1906); J.B. BURY, *A History of Freedom of Thought* (1913). SIGMUND FREUD, *Die Zukunft einer Illusion* (1927; Eng. trans., *The Future of an Illusion*, 1928), offers a psychoanalytic study of religious belief.

Utilitarianism: The classical texts are JEREMY BENTHAM, *An Introduction to the Principles of Morals and Legislation* (1789; 2nd ed., 1823); JOHN STUART MILL, *Utilitarianism* (1861; 4th ed., 1871); HENRY SIDGWICK, *The Methods of Ethics* (1874; 7th ed., 1907); G.E. MOORE, *Principia Ethica* (1903) and *Ethics* (1912); D.D. RAPHAEL (ed.), *British Moralists: 1650–1800,* 2 vol. (1969), containing selected readings.

Useful anthologies include MARY PETER MACK (ed.), *A Bentham Reader* (1969); J.B. SCHNEEWIND (ed.), *Mill's Ethical Writings* (1965); SAMUEL GOROVITZ (ed.), *Utilitarianism: John Stuart Mill with Critical Essays* (1971).

Secondary, historical, and contemporary studies include DAVID LYONS, *Jeremy Bentham* (1972) ERNEST ALBEE, *A History of English Utilitarianism* (1902, reprinted 1957); LESLIE STEPHEN, *The English Utilitarians*, 3 vol. (1900, reprinted 1968); ELIE HALEVY, *La Formation du radicalisme philosophique*, 3 vol. (1901–04; Eng. trans., *The Growth of Philosophical Radicalism*, 1928); J.P. PLAMENATZ, *The English Utilitarians* (1949); J.B. SCHNEEWIND (ed.), *Mill: A Collection of Critical Essays* (1968); STEPHEN TOULMIN, *An Examination of the Place of Reason in Ethics* (1950); P.H. NOWELL-SMITH, *Ethics*, ch. 16 (1954); RICHARD BRANDT, *Ethical Theory*, ch. 12–15 (1959); DAVID LYONS, *Forms and Limits of Utilitarianism* (1965); JAN NARVESON, *Morality and Utility* (1967); MICHAEL D. BAYLES (ed.), *Contemporary Utilitarianism* (1968); J.J.C. SMART, *An Outline of a System of Utilitarian Ethics* (1961). DONALD REGAN, *Utilitarianism and Cooperation* (1980), a presentation of a new utilitarian theory with a good survey of disputes among utilitarians.

Philosophies of the Branches of Knowledge

It is no longer possible for any one individual to be a leader in all branches of learning. Perhaps Leibniz, who died in 1716, was the last universal scholar, and his life is a warning rather than an example. In such a situation the enterprise of philosophy is in a sense more difficult than ever before; no one can hope to contribute much to the clarification of ideas in logic who is not himself a logician, or to the clarification of ideas in physics who is not himself a physicist, and so on throughout the fields of specialized knowledge. It thus seems inevitable that there should have evolved philosophical disciplines corresponding to the various branches of study and providing the frameworks upon which they may be studied and evaluated in and of themselves. (Discussions of particular schools of philosophy mentioned in this article will be found in PHILOSOPHICAL SCHOOLS AND DOCTRINES.)

This article, which treats those philosophical disciplines, is divided into the following sections:

Philosophy of science

Taken in a broad sense—*i.e.,* as the progressive improvement of man's understanding of nature—the intellectual enterprise of science originally formed an integral part of philosophy, and the two areas of inquiry have never finally separated. Little more than a hundred years ago, theoretical physics—concerned with the fundamental debate about physical nature—was still described as "natural philosophy," as distinguished from the two other chief divisions of abstract discussion, viz., moral philosophy and metaphysical philosophy—the latter comprising the study of the deepest nature of reality or being, also called ontology. In fact it was only during the 20th century, following on the professionalization and specialization of the natural sciences themselves, that the philosophy of science has become recognized as a separate discipline.

Methodological and epistemological issues—*i.e.,* issues regarding the investigator's manner of approach to nature—are treated in the present section. On the other hand, issues regarding the substantive character of nature as so revealed—*i.e.,* as it is in and of itself—are treated below in *Philosophy of nature.*

NATURE, SCOPE, AND RELATIONS OF THE SUBJECT

As a discipline, the philosophy of science attempts, first, to elucidate the elements involved in the process of scientific inquiry—observational procedures, patterns of argument, methods of representation and calculation, metaphysical presuppositions—and then to evaluate the grounds of their validity from the points of view of formal logic, practical methodology, and metaphysics. In its contemporary form, the philosophy of science is thus a topic for explicit analysis and discussion just as are other subdivisions of philosophy: ethics, logic, and epistemology (the theory of knowledge). The boundaries between these subdivisions are, at certain points, still somewhat arbitrary; it is not easy, for example, to separate completely the philosophical validation of scientific hypotheses from the formal study of inductive logic (which reasons from facts to general principles), or the debate about theory and observation in philosophy of science from that in epistemology.

Throughout the development of philosophy, the preoccupations of those who, if living today, would be called philosophers of science have been of two main kinds: ontological and epistemological, or epistemic. This division reflects a long-standing distinction between object and subject; *i.e.,* between nature, regarded as that about which man sets out to acquire scientific knowledge, and man himself, regarded as the creator, and either discoverer or possessor of that knowledge. Since 1920 new directions within physics itself—particularly in quantum mechanics—have discredited any hard-and-fast distinction between the knower and the known or between the observer and his observation. Nevertheless, the distinction remains relevant on an everyday, or working, level and can be cautiously retained for the purposes of initial exposition.

The ontological preoccupations of philosophers of science (*i.e.,* their concerns with being) have frequently overlapped into the substantive areas of the sciences themselves. For they have been concerned with the general problem,

> What kinds of entities and elements or theoretical terms can properly figure in man's scientific theories? And what sort of existence, or other objective status, do such things possess?

As applied to particular cases, this general problem has inevitably raised questions of substance as well as of intellectual method. An early 20th-century debate between two Austrian physicists, Ernst Mach and Ludwig Boltzmann, and a German physical chemist, Wilhelm Ostwald, about the existence and reality of atoms, for instance, involved both substantive issues of physics and chemistry and philosophical issues of a more strictly analytical kind. Similar overlaps have been unavoidable, also, in the biological and social sciences.

Until recently the epistemic concerns of the subject have been more purely philosophical in character, though this autonomy is now being challenged by developments in psychology that explore and experiment with cognitive processes and others in sociology that study the conditioning of cognition through interpersonal and group relationships. Epistemologically, philosophers of science have analyzed and evaluated the concepts and methods employed in studying natural phenomena and human behaviour, whether individual or collective; and this analysis has covered both the general concepts and methods characteristic of all scientific inquiries and also the more particular ones that distinguish the subject matters and

Ontological versus epistemic concern

problems of different special sciences. In treating the epistemic issues that arise about science and scientific procedures, the emphasis in this article is placed upon their consideration in general terms; the concepts and methods peculiar, say, to sociology, physiology, or quantum physics are discussed elsewhere.

Diverse approaches

Given the vast range of its concerns, the philosophy of science has attracted the attention of men with very different professional backgrounds and interests. At one extreme, as in the writings of Ernest Haeckel, the German Darwinian evolutionist, it has merged into a sweeping kind of popular science; at an opposite extreme, as in 20th-century Logical Positivism or Logical Empiricism (see below), a leading school that holds that knowledge is only what is scientifically verifiable, it has been treated as an extension of formal logic and conceptual analysis. And between these extremes it has drawn in such working scientists as the British astrophysicist Arthur Eddington and the German quantum physicist Werner Heisenberg, whose work has taken them to the frontiers of the subjects and confronted them directly with problems about the existence, status, and validity of the theoretical entities and concepts with which they were dealing.

Correspondingly, different men have approached the philosophy of science in very diverse spirits, ranging from the highly abstract and mathematical to the concrete and historical and from the severely positivistic to the frankly theological. From René Descartes, the first important modern philosopher in the 17th century, to the Logical Positivist Otto Neurath in the 20th, the success of pure mathematics and logic has inspired the mathematically minded to cast the whole of natural science into a single formal system after the pattern of geometry. From John Locke, an 18th-century British Empiricist, to N.R. Hanson, a recent U.S. philosopher of science, their opponents, on the other hand, have sought the proper basis of man's intellectual confidence within the nature of scientific investigation regarded as a human activity. Equally, Positivists such as Hans Reichenbach, a 20th-century German-American philosopher, have looked to philosophy for proof that scientific inquiries alone can provide knowledge worthy of the name; while theists such as Pierre Duhem, a French theoretical physicist, have appealed to it, rather, to demonstrate that the claims of science are inherently limited and so leave room for other, more embracing varieties of metaphysical and religious truth.

Relations with other disciplines

This diversity of concerns and approaches has affected the relations between the philosophy of science and other neighbouring disciplines. On a practical plane, for instance, different philosophical interpretations have implied different procedures for testing and assessing the strength of rival concepts and hypotheses. Thus, no clear dividing line can be drawn between the philosophical analysis of scientific theories and the statistical analysis of scientific procedures and experiments nor between the philosophy of science and the history of scientific ideas. Recent debates about the historiography of science—*i.e.*, about the problems and methods that throw light on its history—indicate that the particular questions that a historian of science brings to his analysis of scientific change inescapably depend on his philosophical attitudes and commitments.

On a more general and abstract level, the philosophy of science has never been definitively separated from metaphysics and epistemology. There are, indeed, some 20th-century philosophers—for instance, the U.S. philosophical logician Willard V. Quine—who effectively restrict the legitimate areas of metaphysics and epistemology to what have here been called the ontal and epistemic aspects of the philosophy of science. In Quine's view, the traditional ontological problem of what there is in the world as man knows it must be attacked by a logical analysis of the claims about what kinds of things exist that are implicit in alternative theoretical systems. Meanwhile, the work of such cognitive psychologists as Switzerland's Jean Piaget, who explore the processes involved in the genesis of knowledge, is eroding the barriers between the logical analysis of conceptual systems, the psychological investigation of thought processes, and the epistemological validation of intellectual procedures. Piaget, for instance,

bases his investigations into the acquisition of concepts on a philosophy akin to that of Kant, who held that all knowledge bears the imprint of the mind's own structure; and, though a psychologist himself, Piaget even refers to certain aspects of his work by the name of "genetic epistemology," a philosophical designation.

The present survey of the philosophy of science, therefore, contains no effort to prejudge the central question, whether the methods of logical analysis alone are legitimate or whether at certain points the subject legitimately overlaps into such neighbouring subjects as cognitive psychology, the history of science, and epistemology. About this question philosophers of science themselves have been sharply divided, some rejecting any alliance except with logic, others cultivating its wider historical and behavioral connections; and both points of view must thus be taken into account.

HISTORICAL DEVELOPMENT

Classical and medieval periods: the beginnings of a philosophy of nature. At the outset the problems of science were as much those of method as of substance and were inseparable from those of what has long been called natural philosophy. The first attempts to move beyond traditional mythologies to a rational account of nature, beginning with the Ionian and south Italian philosophers around 600 BC, involved the sorts of elements or entities that any such account should comprise. Detailed empirical, or observational, considerations favouring one or another of the rival accounts were premature. Were, for example, the diverse phenomena of nature manifestations of one single enduring form of matter or of several elementary substances mixed together, and was the fundamental substance continuous and fluid-like, or discrete and atomic? Alternatively, others asked whether the observed forms of phenomena were evidence, rather, of some universal, underlying mind or of a variety of coexisting kinds of spirit responsible for phenomena having different orders of complexity.

The various Pre-Socratics based their answers at least as much on epistemic grounds—by considering what type of account would be genuinely intelligible—as on ontal or empirical ones by considering what sorts of enduring entities could possibly have, or be found in experience to have, the required kind of existence. Their answers ranged from one extreme, the ontal Realism of Parmenides, foremost philosopher of Eleaticism, a school of southern Italy—according to which all changes are transitory appearances concealing the mutual relations of deeper, unchanging realities—to the critical skepticism of Heracleitus, the Ephesian philosopher of change, at the other extreme, according to which nothing in nature as man knows it can ever have this Parmenidean reality, and everything empirical is in flux.

Though Plato and Aristotle displayed more precise concern for actual cases, their philosophies of science still rested on the same mixture of ontological, epistemological, and empirical considerations. Questions about nature discussed in Plato's *Timaeus* and Aristotle's *Physics,* for instance, were neither purely metaphysical nor purely empirical in character though they had a methodological aspect akin to that of modern philosophy of science. Moreover, Plato's construction of the fundamental theories of science around concepts and patterns borrowed from geometry have had a profound influence in the modern period—upon René Descartes, for example, in the 17th century and upon the founder of modern logic, the German mathematician Gottlob Frege, in the 1880s and after.

Mathematical entities alone, Plato argued, have the sort of enduring intelligibility that Parmenides had rightly demanded of the ultimate constituents in a rational science of nature. Thus, only a physical theory built on a numerical and geometrical framework will reveal the truly permanent structures and relationships behind the evident flux of phenomena. Within such a theory, all inferences will be self-evidently valid at all times and so exempt from the mutability of empirical events; and, correspondingly, the numbers and figures of formal mathematics will have an immutability denied to familiar physical objects.

The Pre-Socratics

Plato and Aristotle

Planetary astronomy and the theory of matter were, in Plato's view, scientific fields within which this mathematical methodology showed immediate promise; the movements of the planets must be explained by constructions drawn from three-dimensional geometry, and the physics of matter seemingly involved atoms with shapes reflecting the geometry of the five regular solids (the tetrahedron, dodecahedron, etc.). In either case, however, the mathematical theories themselves would alone be fully exact and intelligible, whereas empirical objects and processes could be no more than transitory and approximate illustrations of the enduring entities and theoretical relations underlying them.

Given Aristotle's very different scientific preoccupations—which were centred on marine biology rather than planetary movements—he quite naturally developed a very different scientific methodology. In his view, mathematical entities and relations were too completely general and too remote from actual experience to explain the qualitative details of empirical entities. So the ultimate elements of nature must be not Plato's entirely general and abstract mathematical forms—which supposedly existed quite apart from actual phenomena—but rather certain more specific entities, recognizable within the familiar sequences of empirical experience. Instances of such basic essences could be discovered by studying the typical life cycles of different creatures; thus, the morphogenesis of a seed exemplifies the "coming into being" of the corresponding type of animal or plant, of which the mature specific form—as defined by its essence—is the natural destination of its development.

Having recognized the natural destinations toward which natural processes of different kinds were directed, it was then possible to construct a comprehensive classification of essences in terms of which the whole natural world would, in principle, be intelligible. Explanations within such an all-embracing natural history might not be self-evidently general and immutable, as were those of Plato's geometry; but the theoretical inferences involved would be no less deductive or necessary, and it would have the added merit of accounting directly for the specific qualitative characters of different observed objects and processes.

Atomists and Stoics Throughout the subsequent philosophy of science, the themes stated by Plato and Aristotle have recurred repeatedly and are represented even today by two rival approaches to the subject—one (Platonic) based in logic, the other (Aristotelian) based in the history of science. Between them they dominated the subject during the later period of Greek antiquity, which was otherwise notable for only one further debate—that between the Atomist successors of Democritus and Epicurus and the Stoic philosophers, led by Zeno of Citium. This debate provided the first profound analysis of the strengths and weaknesses of atomistic explanation. Epicureans, on the one hand, argued for a purely corpuscular view in which the individual units of matter moved quite independently, except when they were in actual contact. For the Stoics, on the other hand, the empirical world was intelligible only in terms of interactions and stable patterns maintained by harmonies operative at a distance.

These two debates—between Platonists and Aristotelians and between Stoics and Epicureans—presented clearly and for the first time the chief alternative modes of explanation available to science and analyzed their possibilities and limitations in general terms. More than 2,000 years before the rise of modern thermodynamics and field theory, for instance, Aristotle had already recognized the difficulties of explaining changes in physical state (*e.g.,* melting and evaporation) within a purely atomistic theory of matter; whereas, even earlier, Plato had demonstrated the possibility of a unified mathematical explanation of the differences between different kinds of material substance. Indeed, the theoretical physicist Werner Heisenberg was quite ready in the 20th century to cite pre-Socratic arguments regarding the ultimate constitution of nature as relevant to contemporary problems.

Hellenistic through medieval times By contrast with the period before Euclid the geometer (*i.e.,* to 300 BC), the ensuing Hellenistic, Islāmic, and medieval periods added little to the understanding of scientific methodology and explanation. From the Alexandrian astronomer Ptolemy, who detailed the geocentric theory, most natural philosophers deliberately restricted their intellectual claims in an instrumentalist manner; *i.e.,* by endeavouring merely to "save the phenomena" by devising successful mathematical procedures for predicting, for example, lunar eclipses and planetary motions. In this way they disregarded the mechanisms responsible for those phenomena, thus preserving the computational techniques of the sciences from the risk of conflict with theology for the following 1,250 years, until the time of Copernicus.

In the High Middle Ages, accordingly, the possibility that man could make himself the intellectual master of nature was largely neglected. Human understanding was dependent on God's illumination. The guarantees of scientific knowledge lay not in the merits of its methodology but in the divine grace, which assured its reliability. On this interpretation, man had no direct line of access to nature; the only road to knowledge was through the divine mind. Thus, all of the central questions in the philosophy of science were restated as theological issues, as questions about the relationship between God's omniscience and the more limited knowledge of man. In this context the metaphor of "illumination" was taken so seriously in the 13th century that the very subject of optics was cultivated by a distinguished Oxford scholar as much for its theological implications as for its physical content.

The Renaissance and after: from manifesto to critique. Although the intellectual Renaissance of the 16th and 17th centuries was accompanied by a secularization of learning, which shifted the centre of philosophical and scientific debate from monasteries to universities—and even to salons—the link between philosophy and theology was not abruptly snapped. Descartes, Newton, and Leibniz, the leading scholars of the time, were all concerned to demonstrate that their positions were compatible with sound theology; and medieval controversies about human knowledge and divine grace found an echo in such arguments as Descartes's assertion that the rational methods of inquiry can be relied on only provided that God does not deliberately deceive us. Two new factors, however, combined to give the 17th-century debate about scientific methodology a new autonomy: in the first place, philosophy now posed the central questions in the philosophy of science—both those about the origins and functions of scientific concepts and those about the structure and validity of scientific arguments—and faced them directly, instead of only as refracted through a theological prism. And, in the second place, these questions were acquiring an immediate relevance and significance, simply because men were then launching new, empirically based theories of nature with a seriousness unknown for some 1,200 years.

Francis Bacon and Descartes Between 1600 and 1800 the debate in the philosophy of science was barely separable from that within science itself. From Bacon and Galileo by way of Descartes and Leibniz to Laplace and Kant, all of the major participants in the philosophical debate played significant roles on the scientific stage as well. Thus, Francis Bacon, author of the method of exhaustive induction (see below), and René Descartes both conceived the same intellectual goal, that of formulating explicitly a new method for the improvement of the intellect; *i.e.,* codifying the rational procedures of science in a way that would free them from arbitrary and unfounded or superstitious assumptions (Bacon's idols) and ground them in a logically impregnable manner on the properties of "clear and distinct," or self-evidently valid, concepts (as distinguished by Descartes).

To be sure, the two men offered different recipes for a rational science and described the outcome of a properly conducted scientific inquiry in quite different terms. On the one hand, Bacon was preoccupied with empirically observed facts as the starting point for all science and relied on theories only insofar as they were derived from those facts. Ideally, he held that the scientist should provide an exhaustive enumeration of all examples of the empirical phenomenon under investigation as a preliminary to identifying the natural "form" of which they were the manifestation. Though Bacon remained unclear about the exact character of the abstraction involved, he is commonly assumed to have claimed that theoretical propositions in science are justified only if they have been deduced formally from such an enumeration.

In contrast to such so-called "Baconian induction," Descartes focussed upon the problem of constructing self-consistent and coherent deductive systems of theory, within which argument would proceed with the formal security familiar in Euclidean geometry. Whereas Bacon had reacted against the Scholastic reliance on Aristotle's authority by calling for a return to firsthand experience, Descartes reacted against the Skepticism of 16th-century humanists by pointing to mathematics as the pattern to which all genuinely certain knowledge about nature could aspire. Inasmuch as Euclid's axioms, definitions, and postulates had captured the intrinsic characteristics of spatial relations and provided a theoretical starting point from which the whole of geometry could be deductively inferred, the task for 17th-century physics was to extend Euclid's intellectual structure by adding further, equally self-evident axioms, definitions, and postulates. Only in this way could the theories of motion, magnetism, and heat—eventually those of physiology and cosmology, too—achieve the same necessary deductive authority. Descartes set out to show, in the four volumes of his *Principia Philosophiae* ("Principles of Philosophy"), how all of the familiar phenomena of physics could be accounted for by a single, fully comprehensive system of mathematical theory, based on Euclidean foundations and conforming to his own deductivist principles. The very possibility of so interpreting nature was so impressive to Descartes that it lent a "moral certainty" to his conclusions.

Newton's hypo-thetico-deductive method

The arguments of Bacon and Descartes were really manifestos; both offered intellectual programs for a natural science yet to be built, and, while it is true that during the next 150 years, Galileo, Newton, and many others actually constructed the new physical science for which the philosophers had been calling, it is also true that the form of the resulting theories was, nonetheless, not exactly what either man had foreseen. On the one hand, there was little Baconian induction in Newton's intellectual procedures. Those 17th-century scientists, such as Robert Boyle—one of the founders of modern chemistry—who seriously attempted to apply Bacon's maxims found his pedestrian advice to be more of a hindrance than a help in the formulation of illuminating theoretical concepts. (It was said, somewhat unkindly, that Bacon "philosophized like a Lord Chancellor.") On the other hand, though Newton was powerfully influenced by Descartes's mathematical example, he followed his methodological maxims only up to a point. Granted that the theory of motion and gravitation of Newton's *Principia* did indeed conform to Descartes's recipe—adding further dynamical axioms, definitions, and postulates to those of Euclid's geometry—Newton nonetheless made no pretense of proving, in advance of empirical evidence, that these additional assumptions were uniquely self-evident and valid. Instead, he treated them as working assumptions to be accepted hypothetically for just so long as their consequences threw light, in exact detail, on hitherto-unexplained phenomena. Inevitably, the epistemic claims to be made on behalf of such explanations fell short of Descartes's full "deductivist" ambitions. Newton knew of no phenomena, for instance, that evinced the mechanisms of gravitational attraction and saw no point in "feigning hypotheses" about them.

In this way, Newton devised in practice—almost inadvertently—what philosophers of science have since labelled the hypothetico-deductive method, in which, as theorized by Descartes, the proper form of a theory is seen as a mathematical system in which particular empirical phenomena are explained by relating them back deductively to a small number of general principles and definitions. The method, however, abandons the Cartesian claim that those principles and definitions can themselves be established, finally and conclusively, before inquiring what light their consequences throw on actual scientific problems and phenomena.

Empiri-cists, Rational-ists, and Kant

From 1700 on, the terrain of debate in the philosophy of science shifted. At first, attacks on Newton's methods and assumptions by Leibniz, Berkeley, and the remaining Cartesians continued, from different points of view. But by 1740 the time for both manifestos and objections was past; the basic scientific soundness of Newton's concepts was no longer in doubt, and the philosophical question thus became retrospective, viz., How had Newton done it? Over this new question, 18th-century philosophers were divided into three camps: Empiricism, Rationalism, and Kantianism. There were those who believed, like the Scottish Skeptic David Hume, that Newton's philosophy conformed to the Empiricist maxims of Francis Bacon and John Locke. Again, there were those—like the Swiss mathematician Leonhard Euler, one of the founders of modern analysis, and Immanuel Kant in his younger days—who assumed that Newton's physical principles would eventually be put on a fully demonstrative or self-evident basis as required by Cartesian Rationalism. Neither of these positions proved entirely successful, as Kant himself came to recognize: the Empiricists failed to do justice to the deductive rigour of Newton's theoretical arguments; and the Rationalists could not rigorously demonstrate the mathematical uniqueness of Newton's system. As was already known, even Euclidean geometry, which involves the axiom of parallels (according to which one, and only one, line can be drawn through a given point parallel to another line) could no longer claim a formal uniqueness. It had been shown, in 1733 and again in 1766, that alternative geometrical systems can consistently be developed in which the axiom of parallels is replaced by other mathematically acceptable alternatives. Clearly, the authority claimed for Newton's concepts and methodology could no longer be sustained in the old Rationalist way; thus a third alternative, that of Kantianism, arose.

One of the prime goals of Kant's so-called critical philosophy, with its famous so-called transcendental method, in which knowledge reflects the categorial structure of the mind, was to provide an alternative philosophical justification of Newton's results. The system of concepts used in Euclidean geometry and Newtonian physics is uniquely relevant to man's actual experience, Kant argued, not because the empirical applicability of their principles is self-evident—no such self-evidence can tell the inquirer anything about external nature. Still less is it because their inductive support is so strong—no Baconian argument can yield the required kind of certainty. Rather, it is because the scientist can arrive at a coherent, rational system of empirically applicable explanations only by constructing his theories around just those (Euclidean and Newtonian) concepts. He could, in fact, go even further. Euclidean axioms are required, Kant claimed, not merely for science alone; they specify explicitly cognitive structures (of the mind) that are implicitly involved also—as so-called forms of intuition (specifically of space and time)—in the prescientific rational organization of sensory experience into a coherent, intelligible world of substantial objects seen as interacting by causal processes. A grasp of Kant's transcendental method would then enable a thinker to recognize (or so Kant hoped) how and in what respects the use of his established system of rational forms and categories is indispensable alike for any coherent understanding or even for any experience.

Through World War I: philosophy of classical physics. Kant's ambitious philosophical enterprise took a long time to digest. A century later, in the 1880s, philosophers of science as different in other ways as the Austrian phenomenalist Ernst Mach and Heinrich Hertz, pioneer in electromagnetic wave theory, were both pursuing questions opened up by Kant; and some of their implications were still being explored in the 1970s, as, for example, in cognitive psychology. In general terms, Kant's central thesis—*i.e.,* that man confers a structure on his knowledge through the concepts and categories that he brings to the formation and interpretation of experience—has proved extremely fertile: it has helped in the analysis of theory construction, and it has suggested in sensory psychology that man's very capacity for perception can yield effective knowledge only to the extent that his sensory inputs themselves have a cognitive or conceptual structure.

In one respect, to be sure, Kant seems in retrospect to have attempted too much. Including in man's framework

The assimila-tion of Kant

of sensory and intellectual organization all of Euclidean geometry and of fundamental Newtonian physics and the prescientific notions of substance and cause, Kant set out to demonstrate a priori that man's actual current framework is the one and only effective framework—a proof which, as is known today, was misguided, for its thesis is simply not the case. This is so, not merely because alternative systems of geometry and dynamics can be developed consistently in mathematical terms (for Kant himself was aware of that fact); rather, it is so because 20th-century astrophysics and quantum mechanics have succeeded in giving non-Euclidean and post-Newtonian concepts an entirely coherent empirical application in the scientific explanation of natural phenomena—and this was something that Kant was not prepared to contemplate. Pure mathematics aside, indeed, Kant and most of his immediate successors were convinced that Euclid and Newton between them had somehow hit on a uniquely adequate system of geometry and physics—if not on the final mathematical truth about nature.

For about 100 years, then, the epistemic foundations and ontal commitments of this so-called classical science were largely taken for granted. The 19th-century debate in philosophy of science, accordingly, concentrated on peripheral topics and skirted all issues that might have called into question the ascendency of Euclid and Newton. The validity of the classical system having been assumed, the questions remaining for debate involved only its interpretation and implications; and the resulting positions can be classified, with slight oversimplification, under the headings of mechanistic (or Materialist) and Idealist doctrines, respectively.

The Idealists took to heart Kant's thesis that the cognitive structure of experience is imposed upon nature rather than discovered in it and sought to explore its broader consequences. The psychology of sensory perception, for example, previously barred from direct scientific study by Descartes's absolute separation of mind from matter, was now opened up for exploration; thus, by the mid-19th century, Hermann von Helmholtz, pioneer in a broad range of scientific studies, embarked on the remarkable investigations into the production of man's sensory experiences or ideas set out in his monumental *Handbuch der physiologischen Optik* (1856–67; Eng. trans., *Physiological Optics*, 1921–25).

For most of Kant's successors, however, the Idealist road led away from philosophy of science into other areas—particularly, into political ideology, philosophy of history, and sociology. Thus, it was not until well into the 20th century that the distinguished joint relativity–quantum theorist Sir Arthur Eddington, in his *Fundamental Theory* (1946), once again took up seriously the basic task of Kantian Idealism, viz., that of demonstrating, on a priori epistemological principles, that man's physical interpretation of nature embodies certain necessary structures imposed on physics by the character of his theoretical procedures themselves.

Meanwhile, the 19th-century mechanistic Materialists were disregarding Kant's central insights and concentrating instead on the apparent implications of the Newtonian system for other branches of science. A vigorous philosophical debate resulted, particularly in those fields that were just developing effective explanatory methods and theoretical concepts of their own. One good example of such a field was physiology, in which the work of a pioneering experimental physiologist, Claude Bernard, with its striking theoretical analysis of the vasomotor system and other regulatory mechanisms in the body, which anticipated 20th-century ideas about feedback systems, finally broke a long-standing deadlock between two opposed groups of scientists—the extreme mechanists, who recognized no difference at all between organic or physiological processes and the physicochemical phenomena of the inorganic world, and the outright vitalists, who insisted that the two kinds of phenomena were absolutely different. The debate also encouraged an epiphenomenal view of experience—as a kind of subjective mental froth without causal influence on the underlying physical mechanisms—and so sharpened the apparent threat to all claims about human

"free will." Today it seems, indeed, that the sweeping conclusions of such scientific popularizers as the German evolutionist Ernst Haeckel, who wedded the ideas of classical physics with the new Darwinian history of nature to form a comprehensive Materialistic cosmology, or "antitheology," carried more weight at the time than they seem in retrospect to have deserved.

There was one promising exchange about the central epistemic issues in the philosophy of science in mid-century, that which took place between William Whewell, a British philosopher and historian of science noted for his work on the theory of induction, and the political essayist, John Stuart Mill; but this was abortive. The debate ended in cross-purposes, largely on account of differences in temperament and preoccupations. Whewell's knowledge—not merely of contemporary physical science but of its whole historical background—was both broad and detailed. The mathematical necessity of arguments such as those in Newtonian dynamics impressed him quite as much as it had impressed Kant; but he gave a less grandiose account of the reasons for this necessity. Whewell's philosophy, a Kantian variation on Newton's hypothetico-deductive method, was historicized: it was only by a progressive approach that physicists arrived at the most coherent and comprehensive systems of what Whewell called "consilient" hypotheses—or separately derived, yet concordant, sets of laws—that were compatible with the empirical knowledge then at their disposal. Mill, on the other hand, principally concerned with the methodology of the social sciences, concentrated on the observational basis of science to the neglect of its theoretical organization and so emphasized the contingent, or unnecessitated, nature of all genuine empirical knowledge. In due course, certain of his doctrines, such as his account of arithmetical formulas as being a variety of empirical generalization, exposed him to some ridicule; but, for the time being, while the sheer bulk and learning of Whewell's writings muffled the force of his arguments, Mill's more fluent and less technical style of exposition captured the popular attention.

In consequence, it was not until the 1890s and early 1900s that serious doubts grew up about the finality of the Newtonian synthesis; and the writings of Ernst Mach, Heinrich Hertz, the eminent German physicist Max Planck, Pierre Duhem, and others inaugurated the new phase of far-reaching critical reanalysis characteristic of 20th-century philosophy of science. In one way or another, all of these men stood back and looked at the Euclidean and Newtonian systems with fresh and less committed eyes. They had learned Kant's lesson about the constructive character of formal theories, without sharing his belief in the unique rationality of the classical synthesis; and, as a result, the central topics of their discussions turned on the best ways of restating the Kantian problem. Granting that the intellectual activity of theory construction has the effect of building a physical necessity into man's theoretical arguments, they asked, what then follows, ontologically, about the reality or conventionality of the resulting atoms, forces, electrons, etc., and what can be said, epistemologically, about the cognitive status and logical validity of its theoretical principles?

At one extreme, an Austrian physicist and philosopher Ernst Mach, and Richard Avenarius, the author of a philosophy known as empiriocriticism, expounded a sensationalist form of Empiricism reminiscent of David Hume, who had insisted that all ideas be traceable to "impressions" (sensations). On their view, theoretical concepts are intellectual fictions, introduced to achieve economy in the intellectual organization of sensory impressions, or observations, for which alone ontal primacy can be claimed. Correspondingly, all claims to scientific knowledge had epistemic validity for them only insofar as they could be grounded in such sense impressions. As against this instrumentalist or reductionist position, Max Planck, author of the quantum theory, defended a qualified Realism, which, at the least, expressed the ideal toward which all conceptual development in physics proceeds; for, without a belief in the enduring reality of external nature, he argued, all motive for theoretical improvement in science would vanish. Between these two extremes, Henri Poincaré, equally distinguished in mathematics and the philosophy of science, and Pierre Duhem, a French theoretical physicist, occupied a range of intermediate so-called conventionalist positions, which attempted to do justice to the arbitrary elements in theory construction while avoiding the sort of radical doubt about the ontal status of theoretical entities that led Mach into lifelong Skepticism about the reality of atoms.

The 20th-century debate: Positivists versus historians. In the mid-20th century, debate in the philosophy of science became notably detailed, elaborate, and critical; those 50 years, in fact, have seen the subject finally achieving the status of a well-established professional discipline. Not least among the causes of this development have been the profound changes that have taken place since 1900 within theoretical physics and other fundamental branches of natural science. So long as the classical synthesis of Euclid and Newton retained its unquestioned authority, there had been little occasion to probe its ontological and epistemological bases at all deeply; but relativity theory—which qualified earlier geometries and laws in terms of new insights into the tie-ins between space and time—and quantum mechanics—which qualified them in terms of a statistical and indeterministic formulation—posed a frontal challenge to that synthesis and inevitably provoked critical and philosophical questions about the validity of the methods and assumptions on which it had relied. Consequently, between 1920 and 1940 there arose a renewed interaction between theoretical physicists and philosophers of science—especially between the Viennese Positivists and the authors of the new quantum mechanics.

The main themes of the subsequent debate were largely those introduced into discussion in the period around 1900. Mach's critical reductionism, based on his *Beiträge zur Analyse der Empfindungen* (1886; Eng. trans., *Contributions to the Analysis of the Sensations,* 1897), in which he tried to reduce all knowledge to statements about sensations, was a prime source both of the Positivism and Logical Empiricism of the Vienna Circle—a group of eminent philosophers and scientists that met regularly in Vienna during the 1920s and 1930s—and also of the epistemological theories about sense-data and logical constructions developed in Britain about the same time by Bertrand Russell, perhaps the foremost logician and philosopher then in England; by G.E. Moore, a meticulous pioneer in Linguistic Analysis; and by others. Meanwhile, the qualified Realism of Planck and Hertz was carried further by such men as Norman Campbell, an English physicist known for his sharpening of the distinction between laws and theories, and Karl Popper, an Austro-English philosopher recognized for his theory of falsifiability, both of whose views reflect the explicit methodology of many working scientists today. A notable exception would be the Positivistic followers of Niels Bohr in the Copenhagen school of theoretical physics. Finally, there has continued to be substantial support for intermediate, conventionalist compromises, with Kantian overtones, along the general lines developed by Poincaré and Duhem.

From the rich complexity of recent philosophy of science, two main strands may be selected for special mention here. The first is the strand of neo-Humean Positivism, which first developed in the Vienna Circle and has flourished more recently in the United States and has been fundamentally preoccupied with epistemological issues. While largely abandoning Mach's belief that sensations are the sole ultimate ground of knowledge, its proponents have continued, with Mach, to regard theoretical entities as fictions or logical constructs, the validity of which depends entirely on the capacity to give them a basis in empirical observations. This neo-Humean position has derived much encouragement, if not formal confirmation, both from Einstein's emphasis on the essential role of the observer in relativity physics and from the attack from the side of quantum theory made by the German physicist Werner Heisenberg on any sharp distinction, at the subatomic level, between the observer, his observation, and the system observed (see below *Philosophy of nature*).

The Logical Positivists and Empiricists harnessed to these epistemic arguments a formal apparatus taken over from the philosophy of mathematics—specifically, from Russell and Whitehead's *Principia Mathematica* (1910–13). In their view, the activity of theory construction is logically equivalent to the creation of propositional systems, in which groups of propositions are ideally set out in axiomatic form. So interpreted, the hypothetico-deductive method becomes a recipe for devising a succession of progressively more comprehensive axiom systems, based on alternative sets of general postulates (or primitive propositions) posited without proof, from which particular, empirical propositions can be inferred. As in the case of the special theory of relativity, these particular propositions—for instance, that the axis of Mercury's orbital ellipse will precess (or turn) at a certain rate—can then be used to validate the general postulates by comparing them with actual experience thus—directly or indirectly—substantiating the more general primitive propositions as well. The subsequent debate within the Viennese school has been concerned, very largely, with the exact character and force of this substantiation—whether it be verification, confirmation, or corroboration and/or falsification. At its most ambitious extreme, the Viennese school aimed at constructing a single system of unified science, by which the entire corpus of positive knowledge would be embraced in a single, all-embracing axiom system to be constructed around Russell's abstract symbolic logic. According to this program, all truly scientific knowledge must, first of all, be validated by appeal to neutral empirical observations, on pain of being dismissed as meaningless; and it must then be incorporated into the larger scheme of unified science.

The strongest opposition to this Empiricist or Positivist strand has come, correspondingly, from a Neo-Kantian school that has questioned the very possibility of identifying the pool of theoretically neutral observations necessary for substantiating or discrediting alternative theories in a strictly logical manner. This Neo-Kantian strand in 20th-century philosophy of science was inaugurated by the pioneering thinkers Heinrich Hertz (in electromagnetic wave theory) and Ludwig Wittgenstein (in philosophy of language). Rejecting Mach's central epistemological questions about sensations and ideas, these men have started instead from Kantian questions about the use of representations or models in the explanation of phenomena. Hertz's treatise on *The Principles of Mechanics* (1894), for instance, expounded Newtonian dynamics as a formal representation that logically entailed empirical conclusions only insofar as the phenomena concerned were already describable in terms drawn from the theory itself; and Wittgenstein's *Tractatus Logico-Philosophicus* (1922) extended Hertz's analysis to provide a general philosophical theory of language as an instrument for the representation of facts. The implications of this approach for the philosophical analysis and methodology of science have been explored further by some of Wittgenstein's pupils and successors, who have shifted the focus of discussion away from the verification of scientific propositions to the establishment of scientific concepts and theories; by highlighting the problem of conceptual change, they have revived interest in the philosophical significance of the history of scientific ideas. For, from this point of view, logical questions about the structure of propositional systems must be joined by other, equally fundamental rational questions about the manner in which different theoretical systems come to succeed one another (see below *Conceptual change and the development of science*).

During this same period, the remarkable changes taking place within such sciences as theoretical physics, biochemistry, and psychology have been provoking philosophical discussions among scientists themselves. For instance, the displacement of classical Newtonian physics by Heisenberg's quantum mechanics has stimulated a new round of arguments about causality and determinism, with some people hailing Heisenberg's Principle of Indeterminacy—which holds that the location of a particle is intrinsically imprecise in the measure that its momentum is precise (and vice versa)—as giving human free will the toehold that rigorous 19th-century determinism did not seem to allow. Progress in cellular and subcellular physiology, moreover, has given rise to further rounds of debate in

Relativity and quantum mechanics

Logical Positivism versus Neo-Kantianism

Controversy among scientists

the philosophy of biology. Claude Bernard, the foremost experimentalist of 19th-century medicine, had never managed to extend his analysis of regulatory mechanisms, such as those of the nerves that control the size of blood vessels, to cover the processes of embryology and morphogenesis (development of organic forms); and, on this finer level, there had been a renewed deadlock, around the years 1900–20, between the vitalism of Hans Driesch, which posited an almost "soul-like" reality that guides development, and the mechanism of Jacques Loeb, both experimental biologists with philosophical concerns. Once again, supporters of neither extreme position could make out their case entirely; instead, biologists have tended toward the mediating systemic conceptions first introduced by Paul A. Weiss, a distinguished developmental biologist, in the mid-1920s, and subsequently developed in detail as applications of the new theories of cybernetics and feedback, which conduct comparative studies of automatic control systems in the nervous system and in electromechanical engineering. More recently still, the development of molecular biology has compelled scientists to reformulate the problem of morphogenesis yet again—this time as the problem of seeing how the structural patterns of nucleic acid macromolecules in the hereditary genetical material find a structural expression in the developing body as a result of interacting with the environment. At present, this question is still very largely unanswered.

Contro-
versy
in the
behav-
ioral
sciences

Methodologically, since 1940 one new centre of philosophical debate has developed, this time in the behavioral sciences. Ever since Descartes and Hobbes, there has been sharp disagreement about the legitimacy of extending the methods and categories of physical science to the sphere of the higher, distinctively human mental processes; and, even in the 1970s, theoretical psychologists were still far from agreed in their explanations of human behaviour. Some psychologists insist that human actions are subject to laws and mechanisms of the same kind as physical processes; others deny that any direct analogy exists between rules of conduct and laws of nature. Currently, this dispute is most lively in the psychology of language. Behaviorists follow B.F. Skinner, an American psychologist, in rejecting any distinctive class of mental laws and processes, whereas cognitive psychologists and generative grammarians, led by Noam Chomsky, argue that linguistic activities are creative and rule conforming in respects that no behaviorist can explain. In sociology and anthropology, equally, the 20th century has been a period of methodological controversy. Here the unresolved conflict has to do with the significance of history in the explanation of collective human behaviour. On one side, there is, in sociology, a school of so-called structuralists or functionalists that follows another American scholar, Talcott Parsons; or, in anthropology, there are the British ethnologists Arnold Radcliff-Brown and Bronisław Malinowski, students of primitive mentality and behaviour, who regard all of the cultural practices and social institutions that function within a given community at any time as related together systematically within an overall structure: to explain any one of those practices or institutions, they hold, it is enough to show how it connects up with all of the other contemporaneous aspects of the culture. On the other side, a more historically minded school, notably the German "critical Marxists" (such as Jürgen Habermas), emphasizes the dynamic, developing character of social structures and relationships. Here again, the methodological debate is still in progress, and its eventual outcome cannot yet be clearly foreseen.

ELEMENTS OF SCIENTIFIC ENTERPRISE

It is appropriate at this point to define the recurrent problems that have played a central part in the philosphical debate about science and the crucial elements that any adequate philosophy of science must include in its account. From the beginning, scientists themselves have been interested not merely in cataloging and describing the world of nature as they find it but in making the workings of nature intelligible with the help of compact and organized theories. Correspondingly, philosophers of science are obliged to consider not merely nature in isolation—as a mere assemblage of empirical facts, mutely waiting to be discovered by man—but also the manner in which man himself perceives and interprets those facts when bringing them within the grasp of an intelligible theory and the respects in which the validity of the resulting theoretical ideas (or concepts) is affected by that processing of the empirical data.

Historically speaking, the problems posed by this interaction of man and nature have been complex and confused. Though philosophers of science face, even today, many of the same questions that were already being debated in classical Athens, the range and relevance of those questions has been greatly clarified in the meanwhile. For instance, when philosophers in the 17th century analyzed the nature and possible scope of a mathematical and experimental account of nature, they helped to clear the ground for Newton to develop the intellectual program and methodology of modern theoretical physics; while the subsequent philosophical debate about natural and artificial classification similarly cleared the ground for the scientific taxonomy of the Swedish systematist Carolus Linnaeus and the theory of natural selection of Charles Darwin. Methodological clarification in the philosophy of science has, in this way, repeatedly led to creative advance in science itself and so given rise, in turn, to new experience on which philosophers can draw in taking their methodological analyses further.

It is easy enough to list the chief elements that must find a place in any philosophy of science, but problems arise in mapping the relations between them.

Empirical data and their theoretical interpretation. First are the empirical elements. The task of science is to explain actual events, processes, or phenomena in nature; and no system of theoretical ideas, technical terms, and mathematical procedures—or mathematical procedures alone—qualifies as scientific unless it comes to grips with those empirical facts at some point and in some way and helps to make them more intelligible. On the one hand, the facts in question may be discovered by using observational methods—*i.e.*, by recording them as and when they occur naturally, without employing any special contrivances affecting their occurrence. This situation is, of course, the normal case in astronomy, in which the objects of study cannot be influenced or controlled. Alternatively, they may be discovered by using experimental methods—*i.e.*, by devising special equipment or apparatus with the help of which those processes or phenomena are caused to occur on demand and under specially controlled conditions. In that case, the scientist can attack scientific problems—to use Kant's vivid metaphor—by "putting Nature to the question," as in much of physics and fundamental biology. Either way, a philosophical difficulty at once arises about the results of the scientist's empirical studies: for he must ask how such raw empirical facts can be sifted, stated, and described in a way that throws light on the scientist's own theoretical problems. Do all empirical facts whatever serve as raw material for science? Or is this true only of those that have been preselected for their theoretical relevance—or even, to some extent, reshaped to ensure it? Is a scientist concerned with every particular empirical event, as such, or only with general phenomena or regularities recognizable in those events? Different schools of philosophers treat this raw material in very different ways.

Empirical
elements

In the second place, there are conceptual elements. Every science employs its own characteristic abstractions, terminology, and techniques of interpretation and explanation, which can be of very different kinds. They may be ideal types, as in gas theory and parts of sociology; conservation principles, as in dynamics and energetics; taxa, as in biological systematics; particles or constituents, as in genetics and subatomic physics; models or flow diagrams, as in econometric analysis. Such conceptual elements are the intellectual keys by which phenomena are made intelligible, and a most active philosophical debate has turned around the part they play in the interpretation of phenomena. If, for instance, the idea of particles or ultimate constituents of matter is regarded as a concept created by scientists for the purpose of their own theoretical analysis, can an independent existence then be claimed for such

Concep-
tual and
formal
elements

theoretical entities in the world of nature itself? Or must all such ideas be regarded as fictions or constructs for which the claim to reality goes no further than the paper on which the scientific explanations are written? Similarly, if the theoretical descriptions of nature arrived at in science are unavoidably idealized and abstract, does this imply that the necessity attaching to arguments in, say, theoretical physics is itself only an artifact, or by-product, of scientists' own procedures for interpreting phenomena? Or can one, after all, speak of natural events themselves as happening "of necessity"?

Finally, every natural science includes also formal and mathematical elements or mathematical elements alone. These may be mathematical algorithms, or procedures of calculation, like those used in computational astronomy since Babylonian days, or like the computer programs that are their 20th-century counterparts; or geometrical constructions, as in certain branches of optics; or methods of graphical analysis, such as those used in handling statistical data; or the axiomatic systems by which, from classical times on, geometry and physics have been organized into formal schemata of propositions bound together by logical relations. Philosophers in the Platonic tradition give such formal elements special consideration, viewing as authentically intelligible only those theories the content of which can be presented explicitly in formal, and preferably in mathematical, systems of propositions. Theories of this kind alone are capable—as the seminal German logician Gottlob Frege expressed it—of employing "concepts in their pure form." Thus, 20th-century philosophers of science have devoted much time and effort to the question: How far, and on what conditions, can other branches of natural science (e.g., quantum mechanics or genetics) be cast in the same definitive, axiomatic form as classical mechanics and electrical theory? Or is this formal construction itself merely a human convenience, adopted to simplify the handling of the empirical data, which reveals nothing more about the underlying structure of nature itself?

Relation of theory to observation Each of these three groups of elements poses problems about which philosophers of science are still in deep disagreement; and these differences of view can usefully be illustrated by indicating the various approaches adopted by members of rival schools when discussing each of the groups. At one extreme can be cited philosophers of a radically Empiricist frame of mind, who regard it as important, above all, to emphasize the empirical foundations of scientific knowledge; for them, the raw facts of experience are primary and entitled to absolute respect. On this view, general theoretical principles have authentic scientific content only when interpreted as empirical generalizations about directly grasped empirical data; and, correspondingly, abstract theoretical entities must be understood as logical constructions from more fundamental elements that can be directly identified in empirical experience. (This belief, of course, was the basis of Mach's conclusion that submicroscopic atoms were merely intellectual fictions and derived their scientific meaning entirely from the macroscopic sense experiences that they were used to explain.)

At the other extreme, philosophers of a fully Rationalist, or Cartesian, bent can be cited who reject the idea that raw empirical facts, in and of themselves, display any intelligible or law-governed relationships whatsoever—and still less any necessary ones. For them, as for Plato, the scientist's bare experience of nature is a disorganized aggregate, or flux, unless and until he is able to discover some rational structure or principles relating these disconnected facts to a larger, more intelligible whole. Rather than allow equal significance and authority to every passing occurrence, the scientist, on this view, must be highly selective in the observations to which he pays attention; indeed, the very function of a well-designed experiment is now to create phenomena that can illustrate the intelligible relationships that are the true concern of science and so deserve the status of scientifically authenticated facts.

Both of these approaches, the Empiricist and the Rationalist, emphasize valid and important points; but, in their extreme forms, they give rise to difficulties that are probably insuperable. As to the Empiricist approach, the credentials of any scientific concept or theory certainly depend to a substantial extent on its basis in empirical experience. Indeed, much has been learned about statistics, the calculus of probabilities, and the design of scientific experiments from careful analysis of the procedures by which empirical data are actually handled, even before questions of theoretical interpretation were directly raised. Yet it is questionable whether sense impressions alone could ever serve as evidence for any scientific position, as Mach and the sense-data philosophers assumed. All genuine scientific observations, as Kant expressed it, have the form of judgments—i.e., are expressed in statements answering questions formulated beforehand. It is probably an exaggeration to insist that all legitimate theoretical statements in science must be related in a strictly deductive manner to the everyday empirical observations that they are used to explain; and it is a caricature to treat the explanatory power of theoretical laws and principles, as for example in physics, as no different in kind from that of such an elementary generalization as "All robins' eggs are greenish blue."

As to the Rationalist approach, one of the chief tasks for philosophers of science is certainly to account for the rational interconnections that give scientific explanations their characteristic intelligibility. In this respect, such men as Descartes, Kant, and Hertz have deepened the philosopher's understanding of the scientific enterprise by obliging him to recognize the ways in which the intellectual organization of scientific theories rests on the scientist's own constructive activities, rather than on the specific facts. Yet, it would again be misleading to use this fact as an excuse for regarding physical theories—to echo a phrase of Einstein's—as entirely "free creations of the human mind." While the step from observations to theories does not rest on formal entailments alone, it would be an equally serious counter-exaggeration to suggest that theory construction is totally arbitrary or unconstrained by the imperative demands of the specific problems to be solved.

Science as a multiform enterprise The outstanding task for most philosophers of science is, accordingly, to find an acceptable middle way between the Rationalist and Empiricist extremes and thus to do justice both to the empirical foundations of theories and to their internal organization. The different emphases of philosophers commonly reflect, at most, differences in their substantive preoccupations. Those who are interested (as was Mill) in possible methods for developing the human or social sciences naturally place most stress on the empirical basis of scientific knowledge. Those who are familiar (as was Whewell) with the actual outcome of theory construction in established sciences, such as physics, naturally underscore the systematic coherence and structure of scientific understanding. Those who are concerned with the nature and validity of historical understanding (as Giambattista Vico was) likewise end by giving a very different account of certainty and necessity from those (like Descartes) whose ideal of scientific knowledge is a formal, mathematical one.

If the philosopher comes to grips with the full complexity of the scientific enterprise, this approach can lead him to a more exact understanding of the varied intellectual problems of the natural and human sciences. Once it is recognized how different are the kinds of questions arising within such diverse fields as quantum electrodynamics and developmental biology, clinical neurology and historical sociology, the goal of formulating a single scientific method—with a universally appliable set of procedures and criteria for judging new theories or ideas in all fields of science—may come to appear a mirage. Yet the philosopher's legitimate insistence on generality has already helped to promote important extensions and integrations of man's scientific understanding. So again, he must now avoid taking too dogmatic a stand, either for or against complete generality, bearing in mind Kant's warning that the reason can hope to map its own proper boundaries only at the price of occasionally overstepping them.

The empirical procedures of science. Along with the three groups of elements already discussed, each phase in the scientific enterprise—empirical, formal, and conceptual, or interpretative—involves its own characteristic procedures. On the level of empirical observation and description, three topics may be briefly touched upon, all of which are discussed at greater length in other articles (see MEASUREMENT THEORY; CLASSIFICATION THEORY; and articles on the basic sciences).

First, there are the procedures of measurement through which scientists arrive at quantitative estimates of the variables and magnitudes considered in their theories. By now, there is a well-developed body of knowledge upon which scholars are agreed about many of the techniques and precautions to be employed in practice in the measurement of empirical quantities, in the calculation of probable errors or significant deviations, and so on. About the deeper significance of measuring procedures and their outcomes, however, there are still unresolved philosophical disputes. These disagreements reflect the same differences of approach already noted. Thus, some philosophers regard any scientific theory concerned with measurable (or quantifiable) magnitudes as intrinsically superior to a qualitative (or, as they would say, an impressionistic) one, however rich and well organized the latter may be. Others, by contrast, would argue that any insistence on employing numerical measures at all costs, even in such a science as, for example, systematic biology, can only lead the investigator to misconceive the true nature of the problems involved. Again, philosophers of an extremely Empiricist or Positivist persuasion have sometimes interpreted the experimental procedures for measuring theoretical magnitudes in, for example, physics as providing implicit definitions of the associated technical terms—the so-called operational definitions—and have thus felt able to claim that the logical entailments that the scientist is seeking between observations and theories are established by linguistic fiat (see below *Status of scientific propositions and concepts or entities*).

Secondly, there are statistical analytical procedures for the design of scientific experiments. The mathematical techniques employed for this purpose are, in fact, closely related to those involved in the theories of measurement, probable error, statistical significance, and others. In this area, the connection between philosophical discussions of inductive logic and the practical procedures of working scientists is at its closest. Whereas a religious scientist (Blaise Pascal), a Nonconformist minister (Thomas Bayes), and an astronomer (Pierre, marquis de Laplace), all mathematicians as well, analyzed the philosophical foundations of the modern calculus of probabilities in the 17th and 18th centuries, 20th-century mathematicians and inductive logicians have similarly explored the intellectual basis for the design and interpretation of significant experiments; and, by now, the relevant procedures form a full-fledged branch of mathematical statistics with many valuable applications, particularly in fields such as sociology and economics, in which large numbers of variables are involved.

Problems of experimental design, however, can be stated clearly and unambiguously only in situations in which questions of fundamental theoretical interpretations are not actively at issue; *e.g.*, in experiments to determine which of two antibiotics is the more effective against a given infection or to learn whether significant correlation exists between two known physical variables. As soon as more fundamental questions of theory arise, however, the problems of experimental design go beyond the scope of any purely statistical analysis. Moreover, the same is true of computer-programming procedures: the numerical data obtained from a straightforward scientific experiment can in many cases be fed into a computer programmed to select the graph or formula in best statistical accord with the data from among those hypotheses conforming to a predetermined set of conceptual or interpretative requirements; thus, in this sense, a computer can be used to perform inductive inferences. Devising brand-new styles of conceptual or theoretical interpretation, by contrast, involves extending or modifying present explanatory procedures to satisfy novel intellectual requirements; and these tasks call for something more than formal statistical or programming techniques.

Finally, the initial handling of the scientist's empirical data requires him to employ procedures of systematic classification. The nature and validity of scientific classification procedures and of the species, genera, families, and so on into which scientists divide their empirical subject matter have been the subject of a long and contentious debate. A long-standing philosophical deadlock between supporters of natural and artificial classification systems was largely broken—in zoological taxonomy, at any rate—through the success of Darwin's theory of natural selection. As Darwin showed, the species to which organic evolution gives rise are neither eternally unchanging natural entities nor mere fictions of the zoologist's arbitrary creation; considered as coherent, self-isolating populations, they have a genuine though temporary reality that is preserved by the contrary processes of variation and selection perpetuation. In some other areas of thought, however, the preliminary identification and classification of the empirical material still raises contentious philosophical questions. When the sociologist theorizes about social groups or systems in the human sciences, for instance, he has to decide what collections of men and institutions do, or do not, fall under those general headings. Can objective tests be found for identifying natural units of sociological analysis? Or, is this choice of units merely set up for the sociologist's own convenience? This uncertainty about the very subject matter of sociology is itself an obstacle to the creation of an agreed-upon body of social theory; and comparable difficulties can arise in anthropology, linguistics, and psychology as well. It is, therefore, not surprising that some critics have even questioned whether these disciplines can truly be called sciences.

The character of these continuing difficulties underscores one point of general significance about the relation of empirical evidence to scientific theories: though philosophers may find it necessary to distinguish the empirical phases, elements, and procedures of science from the theoretical ones analytically, it does not follow that they can be kept wholly separate in actual practice. Satisfactory measuring procedures, experimental designs, and systematic classification principles are, no doubt, necessary preconditions for effective theorizing; but they themselves are subject, in turn, to revision and refinement in the light of subsequent theoretical considerations. In arriving at his dynamical theories, for example, Newton had to begin by relying on older commonsensical notions of effort, weight, and amount of movement; but he soon replaced these by the more exact, theoretically defined concepts of force, mass, and momentum, and this change reacted back onto the empirical procedures of physics also. Likewise in other fields of science, the decision as to whether or not the outcome of any empirical procedure is scientifically relevant or significant soon ceases to be a purely empirical question, as theoretical changes react back onto those empirical procedures and compel the scientist to modify his manner of collecting and describing the supposedly raw data of science. In this way, the empirical evidence by which his scientific conclusions are justified rapidly loses its pure and theoretically neutral character.

The formal structures of science. In this section and the next, those aspects of the scientific enterprise will be considered that have dominated recent debate in the philosophy of science, viz., the formal structures of scientific theory and the processes of conceptual change. It will soon be clear that the philosophical problems to which these two aspects, respectively, give rise are correlative and complementary—the one being static, the other being dynamic.

Since 1920, most analytical philosophers of science have explicitly based their program on a presupposition inherited from Descartes and Plato, viz., that the intellectual content of any natural science can be expressed in a formal propositional system, having a definite, essential logical structure—what a leading American philosopher of science, Ernest Nagel, concisely called "the structure of science" in his book of that title (1961). One immediate inspiration of this program was the work of David Hilbert, a late 19th-century mathematician. To make the methods of mathematical proof more explicit and more perspicuous and thus more rigorous, Hilbert employed the techniques of formalization, a reduction to relations while disregarding the nature of the relata, and axiomatization, a tracing of entailments back to accepted axioms.

The same techniques were taken over into the philosophy of mathematics by a pioneer German logician, Gottlob Frege, and into symbolic logic by Bertrand Russell and his collaborator Alfred North Whitehead; and, from 1920 on, the Viennese Positivists and their successors attempted to employ them in the philosophy of science also, hoping to demonstrate the validity of formal patterns of scientific inference by the straightforward extension of methods already familiar in deductive logic.

According to the resulting program, the primary task for the philosophy of science was to repeat in quite general terms the kind of analysis by which, in the science of mechanics, Heinrich Hertz, the formulator of electromagnetic wave theory, had already sorted out the formal aspects of science from its empirical aspects. The program was founded on the expectation that it would be possible, first, to demonstrate the existence of formal structures that were essential to any science, properly so-called, and second, to identify the nature of scientific laws, principles, hypotheses, and observations by their characteristic logical functions. Once this had been done, rigorous formal definitions could then be given of validity, probability, degree of confirmation, and all of the other evidential relations involved in the judgment of scientific arguments.

The actual working out of this program has involved complex and highly technical investigations, in the course of which great ingenuity has been displayed—as, for instance, by an outstanding philosophical semanticist and analyst, Rudolf Carnap, in his system of inductive logic, for the criticism of arguments in support of empirical generalizations, and by Hans Reichenbach, an eminent German-American Positivist, in his analysis of probabilistic arguments. So far, however, the program has yielded substantial results only as applied to arguments expressed in an idealized formal symbolism modelled on the lower functional calculus of mathematical logic. By contrast, little has been done to show how one might extend the resulting formal procedures to arguments expressed in the practical terminologies of working science. That extension, in fact, raises difficulties and ambiguities that are so far unresolved and may prove unresolvable. The goal of a purely formal analysis of scientific inference has generated difficulties, for instance, by tempting logicians to play down important differences between mere descriptive generalizations about natural phenomena and the explanatory theories (laws, principles, etc.) that a scientist develops to make those phenomena intelligible; and succumbing to this temptation creates problems both within inductive logic and in its applications.

Problem of generalizations versus laws

One distinguished supporter of this program, Carl Hempel, originally a member of the Berlin group (allied with the Vienna Circle), has discussed what he calls the theoretician's dilemma: if the task of explaining natural phenomena requires a proof that the character of those phenomena is formally entailed by the conditions of their occurrence, taken together with certain straightforward generalizations based on previous empirical experience, and if those empirical generalizations include references to hypothetical entities, then the theorist is faced with an invidious choice: for, in that case, either his generalizations (his laws) do in fact provide a logical link between the conditions of the phenomena and their actual occurrence and the assumption of hypothetical entities is formally superfluous; or else they do not succeed in doing so, and that assumption will not have strictly explained the phenomena. Clearly, this dilemma can be evaded only by challenging the identification of laws with generalizations and insisting that any appeal to laws of nature always involves the scientist in reinterpreting natural phenomena, not in merely generalizing about them.

Looking beyond the internal structure of inductive logic, the dubious equation of scientific laws with empirical generalizations has also been criticized on the ground that it treats the content of those laws as matters of happenstance, far more accidental or contingent than those expressed in any genuine law of nature. In the opposing view, the explanatory force of, say, the physicist's law of inertia is totally different from that of such a generalizing statement as "All swans are white"; and one can learn nothing about the validity of actual physical arguments unless his philosophical analysis respects that crucial difference. It has not proved easy, however, to analyze the formal structure of the sciences in any less abstract manner than that of the Viennese Positivists or to give a true representation of the working language and arguments of science. In his *Essay on Metaphysics* (1940), R.G. Collingwood, a British philosopher and historian, made one striking attempt, in which the formal structure of intellectual systems was explained in terms not of direct entailments between more or less universal propositions but rather of mutual presuppositions between more or less general concepts. In this account, the principle of inertia was not the most universally true assertion in dynamics but was, rather, the most generally applicable presupposition, or principle of interpretation. Such an account has the merit of explaining why, within a particular science, certain formal patterns of argument carry the apparent necessity that they do; but at the same time it lays itself open to the charge of yielding too much to relativism and so of destroying the objectivity of scientific knowledge by giving the impression that the conceptual structures of science are imposed on phenomena by the arbitrary choice of the scientific theorist himself.

Doubts about formalization

The late 1960s, accordingly, saw a renewal of questioning about the original assumption, viz., that the entire intellectual content of a science can be captured in a propositional or presuppositional system. Certain of the doubts about this thesis revive criticisms put forward at the turn of the century by a U.S. Pragmatist, Charles Sanders Peirce, who argued that the logical status of the theoretical terms and statements in a science is—in the nature of the case—subject to historical change as the conceptual organization of the science develops. (This same insight has been explored more recently by a U.S. logician, Willard Quine, who rejects any attempt to classify statements within scientific theories using the traditional hard-and-fast dichotomies—contingent–necessary and synthetic–analytic—as fallacious and dogmatic.) Other criticisms of the thesis go deeper. By focussing his philosophical attention exclusively on the static formal structure of propositional systems and, so, on the intellectual content of the sciences at particular temporal cross sections in their development—they point out—the philosopher is distracted from the complementary questions about the manner in which the conceptual organization of a science changes and, so, from the traditional claims of natural science to be a rational as well as a logical enterprise. At this point in the debate, therefore, the spotlight shifts away from the static problem of analyzing a science in static logical terms to the historical problem of analyzing the dynamic processes of intellectual and conceptual change.

Conceptual change and the development of science. The problem of conceptual change has recently come back to the fore. The crucial question it poses is: "What is a concept?" In the heyday of Logical Empiricism, that question had largely been disregarded. Following the example of Frege, the Viennese Positivists had condemned any tendency to regard the philosophy of science as concerned with scientific thinking—which was in their view a matter for psychologists—and had restricted themselves to the formal analysis of scientific arguments. This preoccupation with logic was also reflected in their view of concepts. To interpret a concept such as force as referring either to a feeling of effort or to a mental image could lead, they argued, only to confusion. Instead, the philosopher must equate concepts with the terms and variables appearing in the propositional systems of science and define them, in part by reference to their roles in the formal structures of those propositional systems—thus fixing their systematic import—and in part by reference to the specific events and phenomena they are used to explain—thus fixing their empirical import. In the 1920s and 1930s, accordingly, all substantive philosophical questions about the concepts of science were dealt with summarily: they were simply translated into logical or linguistic questions about the formal roles and empirical references of technical terms and mathematical variables.

Styles of explanatory procedure

Once the philosophy of science is approached more historically, however, those substantive questions must be faced afresh in their own right. Rival scientific theories will now be distinguished not merely as so many alternative formal systems, based on different primitive terms and axioms, but also as alternative ways of organizing the knowledge of nature, based on different explanatory techniques and modes of representation. The distinctive features of different scientific concepts will lie, as a result, not in their respective formal roles and empirical references but in the styles of explanatory procedure involved in their application. Those procedures may be of many different kinds: *e.g.,* physical conservation calculations, optical-ray diagrams, functional analyses, taxonomic classifications, historico-evolutionary reconstructions, or dynamical axiom systems. Correspondingly, they provide occasions for employing mathematical formulas, or intuitively intelligible models, or genealogical trees, or other styles of representation. In each case, however, the philosopher can describe the conceptual organization of the resulting explanations in terms neither of intuitive models nor of mathematical formulas and variables taken alone: what he must now consider is the entire pattern of theoretical interpretation—models, mathematics, and all.

Viewed from this alternative standpoint, the philosophy of science will begin by identifying the different styles of explanation characteristic of different sciences or of different stages in a given science and will recognize how those differences in explanatory style reflect the characteristic problems of different scientific fields and periods. So considered, empirical generalizations and descriptive classifications will serve to organize the empirical data of science in a preliminary way; but serious theoretical interpretation can begin only after that point. The central philosophical task now is to analyze, clearly and explicitly, (1) the standards by appeal to which scientists have to decide whether or not some interpretation is legitimate, justified, and conclusively established and (2) the considerations that justify giving up one currently accepted interpretation in favour of an alternative, novel one.

The first of these questions is one that the Logical Empiricists set out to answer in their own manner. They treated the empirical data and the theoretical principles of science as being connected by purely logical relations and attempted to define the required standards in terms of a formal theory of confirmation, corroboration, or falsification. The second question is one that they never seriously tackled. Instead, they assumed that one could, first, work out a quantitative index of acceptability for individual theories taken separately and, afterward, use this as a scale for measuring and comparing the merits of rival theoretical interpretations. By now, however, it is evident that, when biophysicists, say, abandon one theoretical approach in favour of another—as being more fruitful from the standpoint of biophysics—the considerations that lead them to do so are by no means analyzable in formal terms alone. On the contrary, the ability of a biochemist, say, to judge whether or not such a change in approach will effectively help to solve his theoretical problems is one of the most severe assessments of his substantive grasp of what biochemistry is about.

Reinterpretation of concepts and principles

In this way, the shift of attention from the propositions of science to its concepts is making philosophers more aware of the extent to which theoretical understanding involves the reinterpretation of empirical results, not merely their formal transformation. Similarly, the problem of conceptual change is raising questions about the processes by which theoretical interpretations succeed one another and about the procedures of conceptual judgment that are applied in the rational development of a science. These questions are currently under active discussion, and several lines of attack are being considered, none of which has finally established itself.

At one extreme, there are some who still regard theoretical concepts and principles as organized into compact, logical systems and who attempt to define the alternative standpoints of different sciences as the consequences of different basic premises or presuppositions. Having adopted this systematic approach, the investigator then discovers that conceptual change at a fundamental level finds adequate scope only through the replacement of one complete formal system by another, distinct and separate successor system. As a result, fundamental theoretical change is, in this view, intelligible only as the outcome of thoroughgoing intellectual revolutions, in which one entire theoretical system—axioms, principles, criteria of relevance, standards of judgment, and all—is swept aside in favour of another.

Alternatively, there are those who distinguish two different kinds of fundamental principles in a science—marking off the basic theoretical assertions such as "Matter consists of atoms combining into molecules" from its methodological maxims and standards of judgment, such as "All physical phenomena are to be explained in mechanical terms"—and who recognize fundamental conceptual changes in the science as legitimate, just so long as they respect the methodological maxims that are definitive of the science in question. In this second view, conceptual changes of any depth in the intellectual substance of a science will continue to be intelligible, provided only that the new views are still governed by the established program and framework concepts of the science in question. There will then be revolutions in science only when some entire intellectual approach is discredited—*e.g.,* that of 16th- and 17th-century iatrochemistry, which studied chemistry as a means of treating disease—or when some entirely new science is created, with its own complete system of interpretation—*e.g.,* molecular biology.

At the other extreme, there are some who doubt whether any sharp distinction can be drawn between substantive theoretical assertions and maxims of methodological procedure and who argue that all aspects of a natural science are alike open to historical reconsideration and modification. The more specific the theoretical doctrines and concepts being considered, the more risky they will be, and the more readily they will be modified or abandoned or both. From this third point of view, however, it is questionable whether any change, however drastic—even the hybridization of crystallography, viral genetics, and biochemistry, which led to the inauguration of molecular biology—is ever as discontinuous or revolutionary as the two former views imply. Instead, the attempt may be made to account for the procedures and processes involved in the historical development of scientific concepts by using the same general form of theory on every level—explaining innovation as requiring a selective choice between intellectual variants of different kinds; and, in this way, the theory of conceptual development can be brought into line with other historically based theories of natural and cultural change.

Developmental nature of science

Whichever alternative is adopted, one point must be kept in mind: the moment that problems about the changing theoretical organization of science begin to be treated in an authentically developmental manner, philosophical inquiries are given a quite new direction. This step compels one to view all questions about the logical structure and propositional systems of science against a broader historical background. In this new context the natural sciences are seen not as static formal structures but as rational enterprises characterized by certain typical intellectual procedures or movements. These basic procedures of intellectual development in science are the topic to which attention is directed in the next section.

MOVEMENTS OF SCIENTIFIC THOUGHT

Discovery and rationality. In analyzing the natural sciences for philosophical purposes as historically developing enterprises, the question "What is it that makes the sciences rational?" is raised in a new form: do the intellectual procedures that scientists actually employ to investigate and explain natural phenomena have definite and objective intellectual merits that make their adoption rationally prudent, wise, and obligatory? In answering this question, philosophical opinion has tended to polarize in recent years toward two extreme positions: on the one hand, a formalist or positivist extreme, on the other, a romantic or irrationalist one.

Given their mathematical inspiration and preoccupations, both the Viennese Empiricists and their successors in Britain and the United States have interpreted the rationality of scientific procedures as depending solely on the formal validity, or logicality, of scientific arguments. In their view, questions of rationality can be raised about the scientist's work only at the final stage in his inquiries—*i.e.,* when he sets out, as the final outcome of his work, the explicit explanatory arguments in support of his novel theories or interpretations—only then, they declare, will there be anything about science that is capable of being criticized in logical or philosophical terms.

Formalist
versus
irrational-
ist

It is therefore a commonplace of recent Empiricist analysis in the philosophy of science that one must distinguish at the very outset between discovery and justification. The term discovery refers to all the stages in a scientific inquiry preceding the formulation of the new explanatory arguments that are its final outcome. The term justification refers, by contrast, to the demonstration that the formal validity or explanatory power of those arguments justifies the scientist in accepting their conclusions as scientifically validated or established. In this view, the rational concerns of the philosopher of science are restricted solely to this final phase of justification. All questions about the earlier stages—*i.e.,* about discovery—are matters of mere psychology, not serious philosophy. As one widely accepted epigram expresses it, "There is no logic of discovery"; and this distinction—given the equation of rationality within logicality—seemingly invalidates all questions about the rationality of the preliminary steps by which a scientist arrives at a discovery.

At the opposite extreme, there are those, such as Michael Polanyi, a Hungarian-born scientist and philosopher, and Arthur Koestler, a novelist and journalist, who emphasize the parts played by intuition, guesswork, and chance in scientific investigation, citing these as evidence that theoretical achievement calls into play an intellectual creativity superior to mere rationality. According to this anti-Positivist argument, the modern scientist is a sleepwalker whose creative insight guides him to intellectual destinations that he could never clearly see or state beforehand: any excessive preoccupation with the rationality of scientific procedures, by contrast, springs from a pedestrian desire to clip the wings of imagination and to confine the scientist to stereotyped procedures, thus destroying the creative fertility of science. Rather than subjecting scientific intuition to the barren intellectual accountancy of the Positivists, the conclusion runs, one should embrace a romantic anti-rationalism.

In each of these extreme cases, however, the initial equation of rationality with logicality demands closer examination. Certainly, the activity of investigation and discovery can be examined with advantage from a psychological point of view as it has been, in fact, by a French mathematician, Jacques Hadamard, as well as from a philosophical point of view. Yet the possibility of such psychological inquiries does not obviously prove, entirely by itself, that procedures of intellectual investigation in science and mathematics are essentially nonrational. Chance, for instance, may help to bring relevant material to a scientist's attention. But chance—as has often been remarked—favours the prepared mind, and it is fair to ask how far the scientist acted rationally, after all, in picking out the items he did as being relevant to his particular problems. Similarly, in the case of creative intuition and the rest: once again, the man with the best trained mind can afford to give the freest rein to his intellectual imagination because he will be best qualified to appraise the rational context of his current problems and to recognize significant clues, promising new lines of analysis, or possible answers to his questions, as they come to mind.

Problemat-
ics of
scientific
inquiry

Neither denigrating the early phases of scientific inquiry as of merely psychological interest nor overpraising them as exercises of creative imagination disposes therefore of the philosophical problem that is here involved, viz., that of showing what makes certain procedures of investigation more rational than others. To find a middle way between

formalism and irrationalism, it is necessary to look more closely at the nature of the problems of scientific inquiry. If the improvement of scientific concepts and theories depends on the development of more powerful explanatory procedures, the philosophical analysis of discovery then requires that one show what is essentially involved in devising such procedures, testing them out, and determining the range of their application. This problem must be dealt with, furthermore, not by a formal analysis of the resulting arguments alone but first and foremost by establishing what tasks any novel explanatory procedure in science can be required to perform, what demands its performance can properly be asked to satisfy, and so what intellectual goals a scientist is expected to be aiming at in all the phases of his investigations. Posed in these alternative terms, the problem of scientific rationality becomes a problem of showing how conceptual changes in science result in the introduction of novel ideas, which are—in a phrase coined by Mach as early as 1910—"better adapted, both to the facts and to one another." It is rational for older scientific theories to be displaced by newer ones that are functionally superior; and the task for philosophers of science is to demonstrate explicitly in what such functional adaptedness consists.

At the present time, many younger philosophers of science are actively analyzing the nature of the problems of science in these terms. Significantly, most of these men have had their own primary training within the natural sciences proper rather than in formal logic or pure mathematics, for the task requires a much more detailed analysis of the processes of intellectual innovation than has been customary hitherto. In place of the simple dichotomy between discovery and justification, for instance, it calls for a subdivision of the innovation process into a more complex sequence of distinct stages; and at each stage both rational and causal considerations are relevant. Thus, at the initial stage in any inquiry, a scientist must decide which among all of the philosophically conceivable variants from the current repertory of explanatory methods are to be taken seriously at all; which, that is, are genuine possibilities. This preliminary sorting of initially plausible from implausible innovations must be dealt with—and dealt with in the most rational manner possible—long before any question of justification arises.

This initial sorting procedure is one about which scientists themselves also speak cogently and eloquently. Far from deciding what novel suggestions are genuinely possible or plausible on a purely psychological basis or by the exercise of some mysterious, nonrational intuition, scientists will commonly explain their reasons for accepting one set of conceptual variants rather than another as deserving serious consideration. At the same time, such microanalyses of scientific innovation must certainly leave room for causal as well as rational questions. During certain periods in the historical development of science, for instance, scientists have notoriously disregarded novel possibilities that later turned out to hold a key to the solution of crucial theoretical difficulties. Looking back at such periods, it is possible to reconstruct with care the rational considerations that might have been advanced at the time to explain this neglect; but even so, one is occasionally forced to conclude that the men involved were prejudiced against those possibilities by factors external to their sciences; *e.g.,* by influences originating in the wider social, cultural, or political framework of their time. Thus, Newton was particularly afraid that his theory of material particles might be accused of supporting Epicureanism, whereas Darwin concealed his private speculations about the cerebral basis of mental activities because of public objections to Materialism.

In analyzing the microstructure of scientific problem solving, it is necessary, accordingly, to resist any temptation to generalize prematurely. Scientific investigators working in different fields, or at different times, apparently face theoretical difficulties of quite different kinds. One must therefore begin by studying the specific needs and tasks of each particular science, at one or another stage in its evolution, separately—seeking to recognize, in each individual case, the particular intellectual demands to be met by any new

Diverse
approaches
in different
fields

concept or theory if it is to be successful. Eventually, the accumulated results of specific microanalyses may bring the investigator to a point at which he can again afford to generalize about all of the assorted theoretical problems confronting, say, physics and about the broader intellectual demands to be met by successful theoretical changes in a variety of scientific situations. At the present stage, however, though philosophers of science still cannot afford to beg these questions, they are compelled to conduct their analyses in a more piecemeal way—building up their picture of scientific innovation and discovery by considering a wide range of sample cases and working their way only gradually toward a more comprehensive account of the problematics of the scientific enterprise.

Validation and justification. If this situation is true of the earlier stages in discovery, it is no less true in the case of justification itself. Here again, from 1920 on, the debate in the philosophy of science focussed predominantly on two sharply opposed positions, both of which appear in retrospect to be excessively narrow. On the one hand, Empiricist philosophers argued for a view that made prediction the crucial test of scientific validity; on the other hand, philosophers of a more Rationalist temperament saw coherence and scope as the crucial requirements.

Empiricist versus constructivist positions

For Empiricists, the fundamental presupposition is that the facts justifying changes in scientific ideas are both intellectually prior to the theories that are, in due course, developed to explain them and also capable of being recognized independently and in advance of all theory construction. Given this presupposition, they regard prediction and validation as the crucial and distinctive steps in scientific procedure, arguing that, to establish the validity of any general scientific proposition, it is necessary to show that the theoretical generalization of which the validity is in question entails particular factual statements that are borne out by independent empirical observations. This validation process then involves two essential steps: (1) the formal step of inferring novel predictions from the theory and (2) the empirical step of comparing those predictions with the facts and so confirming the theory or proving it false.

On closer inspection, both steps in the received Empiricist procedure face serious difficulties, and these have lent strength—by reaction—to the alternative, constructivist position. As to step (1), there appears to be no objection to the idea of deducing particular factual predictions directly from theoretical hypotheses, so long as one accepts the Empiricist interpretation of laws of nature as universal empirical assertions on the same logical level as "All polar bears are white." Once that interpretation is questioned, however, it is less clear that direct deductive inferences from theory to fact are always practicable. On the contrary, if theoretical laws and purely empirical reports are, in the nature of the case, framed in terms of distinct and diverse sets of concepts, no general procedure can be available for passing deductively from one to the other. For the theory will then be a reinterpretation of the facts, not a mere generalization from them. Similarly, with step (2), an empirical confrontation of theories and facts gives rise to a more complex range of choices than those implied by the Empiricist account. When faced with discrepancies between prediction and observation, scientists certainly have to modify their theoretical explanations; but this modification can normally be made in any of several alternative ways. For instance, the theoretical relevance of a particular observation may be questioned; or some alternative theoretical interpretation may be put forward; or further refinements may be made within the structure of the theory concerned—and all of this can be done before any question arises of a direct and necessary conflict between the discordant observation and the general theoretical doctrine under investigation.

The rival, constructivist position derives its attractions from such objections as these. This position follows lines of thought already sketched by the French theoretical physicist Pierre Duhem at the turn of the century. On this account, the essential test of a science is that it should provide coherent, consistent, and wide-ranging theoretical organizations. Empirical facts will then be recognized as

scientifically relevant only to the extent that they exemplify these interpretations and make them more discriminating. Thus, no single factual observation can ever serve as a logically crucial experiment and confirm or refute any one specific doctrine conclusively, taken apart from a whole complex of theory and interpretation. What is at risk in any experiment or observation, therefore, is the whole body of the theory, together with the current conventions governing its empirical application; and the more comprehensive a theory is, the more are scientists free to vary the details of their specific applications of it, rather than to accept any single counter-example as a challenge to its general validity.

Complementarity of the modes of justification

If these two philosophical approaches are reconsidered today against a broader and more historical background, however, they no longer appear to be either as exhaustive or as contradictory as they did in the 1920s and 1930s. By choosing suitable illustrations, of course, one can make each position highly attractive and plausible since, in one situation or another, the rational considerations that carry genuine weight in the actual justification of novel scientific theories include both predictive success and conceptual coherence. But the "Book of Nature," as Galileo called it, is like Holy Scripture: it offers texts to suit all occasions and purposes. And, on second thought, it can be argued that both Empiricist and constructivist philosophers oversimplify the justification process in science and the criteria by which scientists judge the validity of novel concepts and theories. Far from there being any single or simple test of validity, the question whether predictive success or coherence, simplicity, historical authenticity, or mechanical intelligibility is the key consideration—and in what sense of each ambiguous phrase—must be considered afresh from case to case, with an eye to the specific demands of each new scientific problem situation.

Within the historically developing enterprise of science, intellectual problems arise of many different types, depending both upon the kinds of subject matter under investigation and upon the stage of development of the science concerned. In one science and at one stage, particular weight may attach to a single unexpectedly successful prediction: as when the wave theory of light led to the totally unexpected discovery that a perfectly circular obstacle placed in front of a point source of light produces a circular shadow having a bright spot at its centre. In another science or at another time, however, it may be neither practicable nor relevant to infer such specific predictions, and new theories and concepts may be validated by considerations of quite other kinds. Even within a single science such as physics, indeed, scientists are not faced at every stage by problems and judgments of a single, uniform type. Instead, the historical evolution of physics—down the centuries from Nicole Oresme, Galileo, and Newton to Maxwell, Rutherford, and Heisenberg—has generated an entire genealogy of varied problems; and the considerations bearing on the theoretical difficulties facing physicists at different stages have themselves changed, quite legitimately, along with the substantive concepts and theories of the science. So, within the more complex framework of a developing rational enterprise, the philosopher's task is no longer to impose any single or simple criterion of intellectual choice upon scientific judgments of all kinds. Rather, his task is to recognize how the rational considerations and criteria of validity relevant to particular judgments vary with the theoretical problem situations that provide their historical contexts.

Unification, pluralism, and reductionism. As one notable illustration of the tug-of-war between logical and pragmatic issues in the philosophy of science, the "unity of science" movement may be cited. Under the vigorous leadership of Otto Neurath, a polymath sociologist and philosopher, this movement represented the high point in the ambitions of Viennese Positivism between World Wars I and II; for the general philosophical aims that motivated the search for a unified science are in striking contrast with the specific problem-solving considerations that lead working physicists to unify or integrate their theoretical concepts and explanatory procedures in actual scientific practice.

The unity of science philosophy

Aside from the primary test of predictive success, the Positivists of the Vienna Circle also did allow—on their own terms—for the further theoretical virtues of coherence and comprehensiveness. Their logico-mathematical approach to the propositional structure of scientific theories, however, led them to interpret this demand for coherent and comprehensive theories in a formal sense. On their interpretation, a totally unified body of scientific ideas would be a comprehensive, quasi-Euclidean system of scientific theorems, based on a single set of general axioms, postulates, and primitive propositions and applicable to natural phenomena of all kinds. Given sufficiently all-embracing empirical generalizations as the starting points of such a unified science, it would then be possible, in their view, to deduce particular statements about all the phenomena covered by the varied special sciences unified within its axiomatic scope. Taking the symbolic logic of Russell and Whitehead as their formal core, philosophical advocates of the unity of science then set out to construct, on a single axiomatic pattern, a fully comprehensive account of nature capable of explaining (*i.e.,* entailing) all natural phenomena whatsoever.

At first glance, this ambition seemed laudable and legitimate, but once again the Empiricist program subsequently encountered unforeseen entanglements. The reasons for this situation were not merely the discovery that the theoretical ideas employed within different branches of a science (*e.g.,* of mathematical physics) are more resistent to conceptual integration than had originally been hoped (the task of constructing a self-consistent relativistic theory of quantum electrodynamics, for instance, is one that still defeats the physicists); but, what is worse, it has now become apparent that several well-founded and properly respected branches of scientific theory do not lend themselves to exposition in a formal mathematical manner at all. Any satisfactory theory of organic evolution, for instance, has an irreducibly historical dimension; and there is no possibility of putting historical zoology on the sort of predictive basis that Empiricists have demanded, still less of incorporating it into Neurath's larger unified axiom system. Faced with this particular example, indeed, one distinguished Empiricist philosopher, Carl Hempel, has drawn a somewhat extreme conclusion, viz., that the theory of natural selection is not really an explanation of organic evolution at all—not even a bad one—but is merely an elaborate redescription of the historical episodes concerned. Yet this is simply a roundabout way of conceding that neither the historical problems nor the theoretical ambitions of evolutionary zoologists conform to the quasi-mathematical pattern that the Logical Empiricists have set out to impose on all of the natural sciences alike in the interests of a longer term axiomatic unification.

Unification in scientific praxis: reductionism

If, on the other hand, the demand for integration or unification is considered as a practical problem of methodology, it will then be found that the scientists are facing problems of a different and more pragmatic kind. The science of physiology poses an interesting example because, within this field, the problem of reductionism—*i.e.,* of whether all phenomena whatsoever can be reduced to physico-chemical terms alone—has repeatedly drawn active debate. Since the time of Antoine Lavoisier, who first explained correctly the process of combustion—*i.e.,* since the late 18th century and even before—there has been a methodological division of opinion, involving, on the one hand, those chemists and physiologists who dreamed of equating physiological functions with chemical reactions and planned their program for biochemistry around that ambition and, on the other hand, those clinical scientists and functionally minded physiologists who questioned the legitimacy of this so-called physicalist program and insisted that physiological phenomena displayed certain features or aspects inexplicable in physio-chemical terms alone. The scientific issues in debate in this case have never been concerned with formal matters of axiomatization and logical integration alone: once again, they have involved substantive questions of interpretation. Correspondingly, the provisional resolution of this dispute, accomplished by Claude Bernard in the mid-19th century, was not arrived at by constructing a single, unified axiom system of biochemistry-cum-physiology. Rather, Bernard distinguished the proper questions and concerns of the two sciences and demonstrated the substantive character—and limits—of their mutual relevance.

Regarded as specific, localizable processes within the main organs of the body, he argued, all physiological phenomena do, indeed, come within the scope of the same general physico-chemical laws and concepts as govern similar processes in inorganic systems. Within the special micro-environments of the body, however, those same general types of phenomena serve certain unique physiological functions, having no inorganic counterparts; and, to this extent, special problems and questions arise within physiology that cannot be exhaustively translated into the language of inorganic physics and chemistry. Though biochemistry and physiology in no sense conflict, there accordingly remains an essential plurality in the explanatory aims of the two sciences; and this plurality gives rise, in turn, to a corresponding plurality of methods and concepts.

Yet even this example does not yield conclusions from which one can safely generalize. Though in certain respects the explanatory aims of physiology and biochemistry will, most probably, always be distinct and separate, in other cases matters have gone the other way. When, in 1873, the Scottish physicist James Clerk Maxwell, for instance, integrated the previously independent sciences of electricity, magnetism, and optics into the unified physics of electromagnetism, there was no comparable division of opinion and no such methodological peace treaty was needed. In this case it remained possible, after Maxwell's work as before, to distinguish between straightforwardly electrical, magnetic, and optical phenomena on the empirical level; but on a more general, theoretical level such distinctions lost their earlier significance, and it ceased to be necessary to keep the problems, methods, and explanatory categories of the three earlier sciences separated.

Limited scope of unification

To sum up: in the methodological drive toward the unification of the sciences, as in the earlier phases of discovery and validation, the intellectual temptation to generalize prematurely exposes the philosopher to certain real dangers. In practice, the case for unifying the theories and concepts of two or more sciences has to be considered afresh in every instance, and it can rarely be decided in advance whether or not such a unification will achieve anything useful for the sciences. Instead, one has to analyze the practical demands of the current problems in the different fields and see how far those requirements can be met by developing a unified explanatory treatment for all of the special sciences in question. The integration of theoretical concepts achieved in the process will not consist solely in the formal running together of different propositional systems: more typically, it will require the development of a whole new pattern of theoretical interpretation. And, though it may be possible, in certain cases, to expound the resulting theory in axiomatic form, it must be established, in each case separately, whether or not this can be done. In this sense, conceptual and methodological unification represents a genuine movement in the development of scientific thought; but the logical form of the unified science towards which the philosopher is working is not something that he can lay down definitively before the event.

PHILOSOPHICAL STATUS OF SCIENTIFIC THEORY

Status of scientific propositions and concepts or entities. The section of this article entitled *Conceptualization and methodology of science* examined, first, the raw material (or elements) with which scientists have to work in developing their theories about the operations of the natural world and, second, the intellectual steps (or movements) by which they arrive at a scientific understanding of nature. By way of summary, it is appropriate to consider finally the main points of view about the intellectual status of the scientific concepts and doctrines embodying the understanding of nature that have emerged from the philosophical debate about science. Beginning with the epistemic status of theoretical propositions in science, it is well to consider the different claims that are made about the objectivity of their applications or their truth or both.

Then, turning to the ontological status of the scientific concepts or entities, it is likewise necessary to consider the claims that are made about the objectivity of their reference or of their meaning or both. In either case, the purpose of a philosophical critique of science is to establish just how far the content and reference of scientific knowledge can be regarded as a true report about the actual structure and operations of nature and just how far they represent, on the contrary, intellectual constructs or artifacts in terms of which men have chanced, chosen, or found it desirable to organize their thoughts about the structure and operations of nature.

Epistemic aspects

Starting with the epistemic status of scientific theories, three main views can be distinguished: At one extreme is a strict Realist position, which underscores the factual basis of all scientific knowledge and emphasizes the logical contingency that this basis implies for all substantive propositions in science. In this view, all but the most purely formal statements in science make assertions about how the world of nature is constituted and operates in fact—as contrasted with all of those alternative states of affairs that are clearly intelligible and so possible but which turn out not to be true of the actual world. Seen from this Realist standpoint, every proposition in science, from the most particular observational report to the most general theoretical principle, simply reports a more or less comprehensive empirical set of facts about nature and aspires to be an accurate, objective mirror of the more or less universal facts about which it speaks.

At the opposite extreme, there is a strict conventionalist position, which underscores the constructive role of the scientist's own theory articulation and emphasizes the logical necessity that is thereby built into the resulting conceptual structure. In this view, all but the most purely observational statements in science reflect the patterns by which the scientist shapes his conceptual picture of the world of nature—the patterns in terms of which all states of affairs clearly conceivable on the basis of current ideas have necessarily to be formulated. Seen from this conventionalist standpoint, theoretical thermodynamics, say, determines the character of all possible worlds consistent with the principles of energy conservation and entropy (or randomness) increase: a world to which thermodynamics is not applicable will then be not so much factually false as inconceivable in present terms.

Finally, a wide range of intermediate views seeks to evade the central opposition between Realists and conventionalists. One representative view of this kind, first made popular by Mach toward the end of the 19th century, invoked Kant's attack on things-in-themselves, viewing the attack as providing grounds for dismissing all debates about reality and objectivity as inescapably barren and empty. In its most developed form, this so-called operationalist position encourages the philosopher to regard theoretical propositions in science as meaningful only insofar as scientific practice includes specific operations—either manual measuring operations, or computational pencil-and-paper operations—in terms of which those propositions are given operational meaning. Nothing is then to be read into scientific knowledge beyond its operational meaning; in particular, scientists are not to be understood as claiming or disclaiming anything about the reality or conventionality of the states of affairs that they report. The idea of nature as a thing-in-itself is thus eliminated, as being an intellectual superstition and an obstacle to better scientific understanding, which survives from an earlier metaphysical era.

Ontological aspects

Three main views should here be distinguished. The central question is, now, whether the nouns and noun phrases used as technical terms in the theoretical propositions of science rely for meaning on any claim that they refer to objective, external entities; and current approaches to this question parallel existing views about the epistemological issues, viz., whether the propositions themselves rely for their truth on a claim to be mirroring or reporting objective, external facts. Here, too, the Realist interprets all of the chief technical terms of scientific theory as the names of objective entities existing in nature independently of all human theories and interpretations. In this view, entropy,

say—a measure of the increase in randomness that every total system undergoes—is a genuine, objective magnitude that has, at all times, played a crucial part in the operations of nature even though physicists have only recently had the wit to discover it; and it just happens, correspondingly, to be the case—in those parts of the cosmos that can be observed—that the total entropy of an isolated system nowhere decreases.

The instrumentalist, for his part, regards all theoretical notions such as entropy as intellectual fictions or artifacts created by the scientist's own theory construction and quite distinct from the natural world of objects, systems, and phenomena that scientific theories have to explain. No doubt, scientific theory and the external reality of nature do come into contact on the everyday or empirical level of tables and chairs, rocks and flowers. Given the intellectual tasks of scientific theorizing, however, the resulting concepts are essentially abstract; and any grasping after real entities, as the objective external reference of the theoretical terms, reflects a plain misunderstanding of this theoretical enterprise.

Meanwhile, the phenomenalist repeats, in the case of the technical terms of science, the same agnostic criticism as that offered by the operationalist in the case of its theoretical propositions. In this view, it is simply a meaningless waste of time for scientists to debate the existence of enduring theoretical entities, regarded as external, objective things-in-themselves; just as it is similarly wasteful for them to interpret scientific theories as making, or denying, similar claims about the existence of objective, external states of affairs. Instead, the terms and concepts of science are all to be understood as the product of so many logical, or semantic, operations or constructions, and questions about their real existence are to be swept aside as damaging metaphysical superstitions.

Philosophical analysis and scientific practice. The arguments about these rival ontological and epistemological views cannot be safely left or judged without first looking more closely at the complex relationship between the general analytical interests of philosophers and the more specific intellectual concerns of working scientists themselves. For the degree to which each view about the reality of scientific entities and facts can carry conviction depends substantially on what branches of science are at issue. As the focus of phlosophical attention has shifted historically from one scientific terrain to another, so, too, have the relative degrees of plausibility of these rival positions varied.

Quantum mechanics; taxonomy; perception

Since the 1920s, for instance, there has been a marked revival of philosophical discussion among scientists working in several specialized fields—particularly, among physicists concerned with the structure and development of quantum mechanics. In epistemic terms, the statistical character of quantum-mechanical explanations has prompted some fundamental questions about the status and limitations of human knowledge. Clearly, the extent and accuracy of human knowledge about nature are limited by the modes of operation of scientific instruments. Is it not also possible, however, that the significance of this statistical character lies at a deeper level? Perhaps the relevant objective relationships and states of affairs in nature itself are governed intrinsically by a merely probabilistic causality and so are essentially indeterminate. Or is there a point to be reached on the microphysical level at which any such distinction between subjective human knowledge and the objective state of affairs has finally broken down? The ontal implications of quantum mechanics have been as puzzling as the epistemic. Is an electron, say, a discrete particle that just happens to elude man's exact observation; is it an essentially blurred wave bundle having no precise dynamical characteristics; is it a concentration of probability, a mere theoretical symbol, or what? Or must one set all these ontological questions aside as lacking any significance for physics and as standing in the way of the physicist's proper task, that of extending the direct explanatory power of quantum-mechanical explanation itself?

Elsewhere, the philosophical debate about science has taken on other specific forms. Just as in Aristotle's natural philosophy the metaphysical controversy about Ideas and essences was reflected in Aristotle's own methodological approach to biology and to the study of the natural relations and classification of organisms, so once again 20th-century reappraisals of traditional taxonomy—in the light of evolution theory, genetics, and population dynamics—have been an occasion for renewed philosophical debate. As a result, earlier disagreements about natural and artificial classifications have been reformulated and have generated a new dispute, about the possibility of basing taxonomy on a mathematical science of phenetics—in which the defining properties of different species, genera, etc. are all given quantitative numbers or measures—and so harnessing the technical resources of modern computers to its purposes.

Similarly, in the psychology of perception and related fields, the extension of understanding in recent years at last has permitted the framing of authentically empirical questions about perception and cognition, which lend themselves to direct investigation instead of being restricted to general a priori speculations. The result has been a theoretical debate, the final outcome of which will have profound effects on both philosophical epistemology and natural science. In areas of this debate where even Mach was content to pose entirely general questions, in the philosophical tradition of David Hume, about the role of sense impressions as the raw material of all cognition and perception whatsoever, it is now clear that many preliminary differences and complexities must be unravelled before one can hope to recognize the truly operative questions in this field. Far from all modes of knowledge and perception conforming to a single common pattern, man's sensory and practical dealings with the world call into play a variety of perceptual systems of which the operations justify no simple epistemological formula about impressions and ideas, sense-data and logical constructions, or intuitions and schemata. Thus, at the present time, the investigations of some physiologists, psychologists, and cyberneticists are bringing man's sensory and cognitive activities within the scope of natural science while at the same time preserving a feeling for the more general philosophical problems and insights of such philosophers as Locke and Leibniz, Hume and Kant, Helmholtz and Mach.

Pluralism and complementarity

At this point, the alliance between science and philosophy is simply carrying over into fields of science that are areas of methodological perplexity today the same interactions that were fruitful in earlier centuries within sciences having methods by now well understood. These interactions are unlikely to vindicate finally any one of the rival positions in the philosophy of science, whether ontological (Realist, instrumentalist, or phenomenalist) or epistemological (Realist, conventionalist, or operationalist). Probably such a vindication was, in any event, too much to expect. For in all the different special sciences—both natural and social—historical development eventually brings the investigator to a point at which he is ready to operate with a variety of technical terms or entities having very different logical characters and functions and at which his most general theoretical propositions or principles display corresponding differences in their logical status and implications.

So long as philosophical discussion is confined within the limits of an artificial, ideal language or propositional system, it is possible, perhaps, to continue posing purely abstract, general dilemmas about, say, theoretical entities or confirmation theory. But the bearing of such formal dilemmas on the actual content of contemporary scientific thought is becoming increasingly unclear. In debating the ontal status of theoretical entities, for instance, the question must at some stage be faced whether that phrase is intended to cover such notions as gene or pi-meson, species or cold front, momentum or superego, social class or economic market. (Certainly, not all of these terms have identical characters and functions.) In debating the epistemic status of scientific theories, likewise, it must be made clear whether one has in mind, say, the mathematical schema of quantum-mechanical field theory, the populational analysis of natural selection, the microstructures and mechanisms of molecular biology, the developmental sequences of cognitive psychology, the labour theory of economic value, the general regularities of terrestrial meteorology, or what. (Once again, not all of these theories have identical kinds of status or implications.)

Philosophical doctrines and approaches that carry great conviction when applied to the theories and ideas of one science may—not surprisingly—lose all of their plausibility when extended to other fields. Thus, an Empiricist analysis may apply quite straightforwardly to meteorology, yet entirely misrepresent the structure and implications of electromagnetic theory; while, in return, a Neo-Kantian account of theoretical physics may lack any direct relevance, say, to ideas about animal behaviour. Today as in classical Athens, analytical clarification in the philosophy of science goes, in this respect, hand in hand with methodological refinements in the sciences themselves. In retrospect, the methodological insights of Aristotle the marine biologist and of Plato the theoretical astrophysicist can be seen to have been complementary, rather than incompatible. Similarly, today, the philosopher must look at rival positions in the philosophy of science not merely as contradictory answers to technical questions within philosophy itself but equally as complementary contributions to the methodological improvement of theoretical understanding over the whole varied range of different scientific fields.

INTERRELATIONSHIPS OF SCIENCE AND CULTURE

Turn to broader human concerns

This survey has been concerned, almost exclusively, with philosophical problems and arguments about the sciences regarded as sources of theoretical knowledge. In pitting Realism against instrumentalism, mechanistic ideas against organicist ones, divine knowledge against human fallibility, or Platonic Ideas against Aristotelian essences, the philosopher is in each case concerned with the intellectual status, implications, and validity of certain general scientific concepts, methods, or entities. To confine oneself entirely to these intellectual aspects, however, would mean accepting a total abstraction of theory from practice and of scientific ideas from their behavioral expression. Thus, along with the present-day shift of emphasis from the physical to the human and social sciences, one finds that all such abstract approaches are coming once again under criticism, as over-intellectualizing the nature and implications of science.

Some of these attacks come from the neo-Marxist direction and reflect a traditional Marxian insistence on the unity of theory and action. (It was not for nothing that Lenin picked on Ernst Mach as a special target for scorn.) Analogous criticisms, however, are also coming from men with very different intellectual loyalties—e.g., from the urban sociologist Lewis Mumford and from many contemporary Existentialists. In conclusion, therefore, a concise discussion is here given of some of the views about the relations between science and the rest of culture; i.e., about the relevance of scientific knowledge to other spheres of experience and concern and, conversely, about the significance of broader, practical considerations for man's understanding of scientific theory itself.

The variety of these views has always been very great. Their exponents have ranged all the way from those who, like the energeticist Wilhelm Ostwald and the evolutionist Julian Huxley—both of whom rooted ethics in nature—present scientific ideas and procedures as rational panaceas for intellectual and practical problems of all kinds to those who, like Pierre Duhem and Carl von Weizsäcker, physicist and philosopher of nature, both of whom are theists, deliberately limit the claims of science so as to preserve a freedom of manoeuvre for ethics, for example, or theology. At each stage, most advocates of extreme claims for science have been ontological Realists; and, in strengthening their ontal and epistemic claims, they have also staked a claim to overriding intellectual priority on behalf of scientific knowledge, in contrast to other forms of experience. Similarly, those who would restrict the broader cultural claims of science have tended to be phenomenalists; and, in weakening their philosophical claims, they have also attempted to limit the authority of science to its own intellectual concerns as narrowly defined.

Science, technology, and ethical values

Whatever one's general philosophical position with respect to the reality of scientific knowledge and entities may be, however, there are other more practical questions to be faced, questions about the specific implications of different scientific ideas and beliefs for parallel fields of human action and experience. On this point, one particular theme unites a wide range of radical critics of science, including both Lewis Mumford, U.S. social critic, and the Existentialists. Just as the Christian Dane Søren Kierkegaard, an early and seminal figure of Existentialism, condemned Kant's universalized system of ethics for ignoring the individuality of actual ethical problems and decisions, so today there is a widespread reaction against any tendency to treat social or practical decisions as technical matters, which can be left to the judgment of scientific or technological experts. The general methods of technology may, indeed, represent practical applications of the theoretical understanding arrived at by science; but all individual decisions about putting those general techniques to use— e.g., in constructing an airport or power station—must be made not by appealing to any general formula or rule of thumb but by balancing a whole range of diverse considerations—economic and aesthetic, environmental and human, as well as merely technical.

According to another contemporary critique, the theoretical points of view adopted in natural science are general and abstract, but the practical demands of sociopolitical action and, a fortiori, of individual action, are concrete and particular; and, by itself, this contrast places an immediate restriction on the existential relevance of scientific ideas and engineering techniques. Such scholars as Thomas Huxley, a versatile scientist and defender of evolution, or Wilhelm Ostwald, a pioneer in electrochemistry, who viewed reality as essentially energy, might argue in general, abstract terms for interpreting ethical principles in evolutionary or thermodynamical terms if they pleased (so the critics continue); but such abstract speculative arguments have no bearing on the actual tasks of ethical decision and action. Here again, every ethical choice involves a unique constellation of considerations and demands; and this problem cannot be dealt with by appealing to any universal rule but must be appraised on an individual basis, as and when it arises.

Others take a more positive approach toward the contribution of science to an understanding of human values. Without necessarily claiming to transform ethics itself into a "science," they at any rate argue that the personal attitudes needed for effective work in science—adventurous skepticism and critical open-mindedness—have a wider relevance also to human conduct and social affairs. Supposing only that social and political discussion were conducted in this same tentative and critical spirit (they claim), its typical and deplorable passion and confusion could be replaced by the more rational consideration of the means required in order to achieve explicitly stated ends. While specific scientific ideas and doctrines may not be enough to direct social and political action by themselves, the scientific attitude may, nonetheless, have a profound significance for social policy and individual ethics alike.

Social significance of science

This contrast, between existentially minded critics of the claim that science is all-embracing and socially minded believers in the scientific attitude, may be epitomized by referring to contemporary discussions about the social significance of science itself. On the one hand, there has recently been a revival of explicitly anti-scientific views, which had been more or less dormant since the time of Blake, Johann Wolfgang von Goethe, and their successors in the Romantic movement. Supporters of this anti-science position point to the central role of military technology in the financial support of 20th-century scientific research and dismiss the average scientist's plea that he is not responsible for the uses to which his ethically neutral discoveries are put, as pallid and insincere. On the contrary (they argue), there is a long-standing and unholy alliance linking the collective institutions of the scientific and technological professions to the economic, industrial, and political powers that be. Faced with the fruits of this historical union (they conclude), it is time that scientists acknowledged their social responsibilities; and, failing better institutional controls, the outcome of this moral self-scrutiny may well prove to be a moratorium on further scientific research. Perhaps man already knows too much for his own good and needs to digest the significance of his existing stock of knowledge much further before adding to it and so widening yet again the gulf between theoretical knowledge and practical wisdom.

On the other hand, there are those who recognize science as playing a crucial role in modern society, but who go on to draw the opposite conclusion. Rather than putting a stop to science (these men would argue), its scope should be broadened; that is, scholars should be studying and understanding better the manner in which science serves as an element in the larger social order—perhaps by developing more adequate analyses of the social structure or perhaps by a large-scale extension of the methods of operations research. Aside from anything else (they point out), a moratorium on science is as impracticable as a moratorium on sin. It could be enforced only if political unanimity prevailed to an unimaginable degree among scientists. In the absence of such enforcement, liberal-minded countries will merely put themselves at a needless disadvantage—both economic and military—as compared with totalitarian states. Instead of pursuing this will-o'-the-wisp, scholars should put more effort into the task of understanding both the social preconditions of effective scientific development and the economic and political priorities involved in the practical application of scientific research.

Science and religion

As compared with the controversies of earlier centuries, the debate between science and religion is curiously muted today. There seems litle room nowadays for the theological passions that engulfed the discussion of Copernicus' new planetary theory, James Hutton's history of the Earth, or Darwin's theory of natural selection; and one would hesitate to speak any longer, as so many of our forefathers did, of warfare between science and religion as unavoidable. It is true that a few partisan writers can still find it a perplexing problem to decide such issues as whether the existence of life on other worlds would require a re-enactment there of the Christian fall and redemption or can insist—conversely—that the results of astronautical exploration refute any religious belief that God is an Old Man up in the sky. For most people, however, such questions have so far lost their earlier bite that they appear, by now, quite naïve.

What is the reason for this change? In earlier times, the term cosmology embraced not only the structure of the astronomical cosmos and the origins of the human species but also the religious significance of man's place in nature. Contemporary theologians, by contast, see physics and biology as having much less bearing on man's religious attitudes and preoccupations than their predecessors had supposed that they had. As a result, men's earlier ambition to construct a single, comprehensive world view, embracing the essential truths of both science and religion, no longer plays the active part in intellectual life that it formerly did. The only branches of science still capable of provoking vigorous theological debate, even now, are the human, rather than the natural sciences. The implications of Freudian psychology for the doctrine of grace and the use of psychedelic drugs for inducing quasi-mystical experiences are topics for live discussion today, in a way that evolution, astrophysics, and historical geology no longer are.

Limitations of science

This change of focus has been accompanied by a change in ideas about the intrinsic limits of science. It was formerly assumed that the boundaries between science and other aspects of human experience could be defined by marking off certain types of subject matter as essentially closed to scientific investigation. To one generation, the heart of this forbidden territory was the mind; to another, it was life; to a third, the creation. In this view, something in the essential nature of mental or vital activities, or in the origins of the present order of nature, made it impossible to treat these as phenomena open to study and explanation by the rational methods and intellectual procedures available to science. In fact, this view always had defects, from both the scientific and the theological points of view. To scientists, it seemed to impose an arbitrary restriction on their sphere of operations and so acted as a standing challenge and irritation. For theologians, it had the disadvantage of placing the essential claims of religion, so to speak, on a sandbank, where they risked being submerged in time by the rising tide of scientific knowledge. So, by tacit consent, the essential limits of science are now defined in quite different terms. These limits are now identified by recognizing that the character of scientific procedures themselves places restrictions on the relevance of their results. A scholar may choose to study whatever objects, systems, or processes he may please, but only certain of the questions that he asks about them will be answerable in the general, theoretical terms characteristic of science.

This change of approach may not have made the substantive problem—that of delimiting the frontiers of science exactly at all points—very much easier to deal with than it was before, but it has one genuine merit: it respects the crucial fact, to which attention has been drawn at several points in this present survey, that the distinctive features of science lie not in the types of object and event to which the scientist has access but in the intellectual procedures that his investigations employ and so in the kinds of problem that lend themselves to a scientific solution.

(S.E.T.)

Philosophy of nature

The discipline here entitled "the philosophy of nature" consists in the investigation of substantive issues regarding the actual features of nature as a reality and is divided into two parts: the philosophy of physics and the philosophy of biology. In this discipline, the most fundamental, broad, and seminal features of natural reality as such are explored and assessments are made of their implications for man's metaphysics, or theory of reality; for his *Weltanschauung,* or "world view"; for his anthropology, or doctrine of man; and for his ethics, or theory and manner of moral action. These implications are explored on the assumption that man's understanding of the natural setting in which his life is staged strongly conditions his beliefs and attitudes in many fields.

In its German form, *Naturphilosophie,* the term is chiefly identified with Friedrich Schelling and G.W.F. Hegel, early 19th-century German Idealists who opposed it to *Logik* and to the *Phänomenologie des Geistes* ("of the spirit or mind"). Employment of the term spread, in due time, beyond its narrower historical context in German Idealism and came to be used, particularly in Roman Catholic parlance, in the sense that it bears in this article (*e.g.,* the philosophies of physics and biology). Despite a notable decline in its usage in more recent years, the term is here employed, in the interest of the clear delineation of topics, as a complement to the philosophy of science, the discipline to which its subject matter has been allocated by recent philosophers. Thus in this work, the article on the philosophy of science is largely restricted to man's approach to nature, and thus to epistemological (theory of knowledge) and methodological issues, while that on the philosophy of nature encompasses the more substantive issues about nature as it is in itself.

PHILOSOPHY OF PHYSICS

Physics as a field of inquiry. *Essential features.* Physics is concerned with the simplest inorganic objects and processes in nature and with the measurement and mathematical description of them. Inasmuch as the binding forces of chemistry can now, at least in principle, be reduced to the well-known laws of physics, or calculated from quantum mechanics (the theory that all energy is radiated or absorbed in small unitary packets), chemistry can henceforth be considered as a part of physics in theory if not in practice. Moreover, it has become clear, through the general theory of relativity (which formulates nature's laws as viewed from various accelerating perspectives), that there is an aspect of geometry, too, that can be regarded as a part of physics. The fact that, over a wide range of circumstances, Euclidean, or ordinary uncurved, geometry presents a good approximation to reality is considered

Axiomatic versus empirical geometry

today not as a fact stipulated by a necessity of thought, nor a derivative from such a necessity, but as a fact to be established empirically; *i.e.,* by observation. In their application, the laws of Euclidean geometry refer to those experiences that arise with measurements of length and angle and optical sightings as well as with surface and volume measurements. The possibility—already extensively elucidated in antiquity—of deriving geometrical propositions by deduction from a few axioms, assumed without proof to be correct, had given rise in earlier philosophy to the opinion that the truth of these axioms must and could be guaranteed by a kind of knowledge that is independent of experience. The recognition of such a priori knowledge, however, has been superseded by the modern development of physics. While it is granted that a pure geometry is free to posit any axioms that it pleases, a geometry purporting to describe the real world must have true axioms. Today it is considered that, if Euclidean geometry is true of the world, this truth must be established empirically; the axioms would be true because the conclusions drawn from them correspond to experience. Actually, the world appears Euclidean, however, only when this experience is limited to cases in which the distances are not too great (not much greater than 10^9 light-years) and in which gravitational fields are not too strong (as they are in the vicinity of a neutron star).

The possibility of deducing all known laws or regularities as logical inferences from a few axioms, which was discovered in Euclidean geometry, became a model for the construction also of another chapter in the history of physics. The classical physics of Newton, the 17th–18th-century father of modern physics, had employed Euclidean geometry as a foundation and had portrayed the solar system as a system of mass points subject to his mechanical axioms. The laws for falling bodies framed by the 16th–17th-century Italian physicist Galileo are the simplest logical consequences of Newton's axioms, and the laws framed by Johannes Kepler, a 16th–17th-century German astronomer, which precisely describe the motions of the planets, follow from them.

In addition to the laws of mechanics there are those of the broad sphere of electromagnetic phenomena as summarized in the equations of James Clerk Maxwell, a 19th-century Scottish physicist, which describe both the electric and magnetic fields and the laws of their mutual changes, equations that may thus be considered as the axioms of electrodynamics. Because they assume the mathematical form of partial differential equations—which express the rates at which differentials (small or infinitesimal distances or quantities) in several dimensions change with respect to their neighbours—electrodynamics is a local-action theory rather than an action-at-a-distance theory as in older formulations modelled after Newton's law of gravitation. The principle of local action states that the variations of electromagnetic magnitudes at a point in space can be influenced only by the electromagnetic conditions in the immediate vicinity of this point. The finite velocity of propagation for electromagnetic disturbances, which follows from this principle, leads on the one hand to the existence of electromagnetic wave events and on the other hand to conformity with the requirements of special relativity (a theory that formulates nature's laws as viewed from the perspectives of various velocities), which demand a maximum finite velocity for signals—the velocity of light in a vacuum.

The most important division of physics today is one that replaces the traditional distinctions between mechanics, acoustics, and other classical branches of physics with that between macroscopic and microscopic physics, in which the latter investigates the conformity of atoms to law and their reactions in discrete quantum jumps, whereas the former extends from the level of ordinary human experience into astronomy to a total comprehension of the universe, attained through theoretical endeavours in the field of cosmology. Because it is now possible to observe especially bright objects (quasars) that are located perhaps 10^{10} light-years from the Earth, the possibility of empirically testing cosmological models is beginning to arise. In particular, the application of non-Euclidean, or curved,

Macroscopic versus microscopic physics

geometries to the cosmos has suggested the conception of a finite, yet boundless, world space (positively curved), in which the maximum possible distance between two points would no longer be much greater than 10^{10} light-years.

Historical sketch. In the historical development of physics before the 17th century, geometry was the only field in which extensive advances were made; besides geometry, only the rudiments of statics (the laws of levers, the principle of hydrostatics of the 3rd-century BC scientist Archimedes) were clarified. After Galileo had discovered the laws of falling bodies, Kepler's laws describing the motions of the planets and Newton's reduction of them to a set of dynamical axioms established the science of classical mechanics, to which was annexed the investigation of electromagnetism. These developments culminated in the discovery of induction by Michael Faraday, an English physical scientist, the knowledge of local action by Faraday and Maxwell, and the discovery of electromagnetic waves by a German physicist, Heinrich Hertz. It was not until the 19th century that the law of the conservation of energy was first recognized as a general law of nature, through the work of Julius von Mayer in Germany and James Joule in England, and that the concept of entropy (see below *Entropy and the direction of time*) was formulated by Rudolf Clausius, a mathematical physicist. At the beginning of the 20th century, the German physicist Max Planck introduced the so-called quantum of action, $h = 6.626 \times 10^{-27}$ erg-seconds, which, when multiplied by the vibration frequency, symbolized by the Greek letter nu, ν, demarcates a basic packet of energy. Albert Einstein then extended the quantum theory to light. The real existence of atoms was proved by him and other investigators, and the science of microphysics thus arose. The researches of Niels Bohr on the quantum-theoretical significance of atomic spectra paved the way for broader search into the fine details of quantum laws, the final comprehension of which was introduced by Werner Heisenberg in 1924 and then systematically developed by Max Born, Heisenberg, and Pascual Jordan, of Germany, and by P.A.M. Dirac, of England. Moreover, Erwin Schrödinger, an Austrian physicist, pursuing a line of thought pointed out by Einstein and Louis de Broglie, arrived at results that were outwardly quite different from those of Heisenberg *et al.*, but were mathematically equivalent. The quantum mechanics, or wave mechanics, created by these men, which formulated quantum phenomena, were later extended to quantum electrodynamics.

General and special theories of relativity

Einstein's theory of relativity, first formulated in 1905, which was eventually extended from a special to a general formulation, brought about a revolutionary transformation in physics similar to that induced by quantum theory. The Newtonian mechanics of mass points turned out to have been merely an approximation to the more exact relativistic mechanics. The most important consequence of the special theory of relativity, the equivalence of mass (m) and energy (E),

$$E = mc^2, \qquad (1)$$

in which c is the velocity of light, was formulated by Einstein himself.

After 1916 Einstein strove to extend the theory of relativity to the so-called general theory, a formulation that includes gravitation, which was still being expressed in the form imparted to it by Newton; *i.e.*, that of a theory of action at a distance. Einstein did succeed in the case of gravitation in reducing it to a local-action theory, but, in so doing, he increased the mathematical complexity considerably, as Maxwell, too, had done when he transformed electrodynamics from a theory of action at a distance to a local-action theory.

The great importance of physics for the technology that depends upon it—which has become a leading factor in the rapidly increasing development in the conditions of human existence—is shown historically in the close connection of decisive technical developments with basic advances in physical knowledge. Einstein's equivalence of mass and energy—to cite but one example—pointed to the atomic nucleus as an energy source that could be opened up through the study of nuclear physics. More-

over, the intellectual influence proceeding from physics and affecting the development of modern thought has become especially strong through the deepened grasp of the concept of causality that has followed from quantum theory (see below *Modalities of the natural order*).

Basic characteristics and parameters of the natural order. *Framework of the natural order.* Earlier mathematicians and particularly Richard Dedekind, a pre-World War I number theorist, have precisely defined the concept of real numbers, which include both rational numbers, such as $\frac{277}{931}$, expressible as ratios of any two whole numbers (integers), and irrational numbers, such as $\sqrt{27}$, π, or e, which lie between the rationals. By reference to these numbers, the Newtonian concept of space and time, which presupposes a Euclidean geometry of space, may be made precise: the values of the time t, ordered according to the ideas of earlier and later, can be made to correspond to the single real numbers, ordered according to those of smaller and larger. Also, the points on a straight line can be brought into correspondence with the real numbers in such a manner that the location of a point P between two other points P_1 and P_2 corresponds to a number assigned to P that lies between those assigned to P_1 and P_2.

Cartesian analytic geometry

Guided by the wish to find a method that allows the systematic proof of all philosophical truths, René Descartes, often called the founder of modern philosophy, established in the 17th century the analytic geometry of Euclidean planes. In it the points of a plane can be designated by two numbers x, y, their coordinates. One chooses two orthogonal coordinate axes, $x = 0$ and $y = 0$, like those of a graph, and, with any point P, associates its two projections, one upon each coordinate axis, which define the location of P. A curve in the $x - y$ plane is then expressed by an equation $f(x,y) = 0$, shorthand for any equation ("function") containing x's and y's. In the context of analytic geometry, every theorem of plane Euclidean geometry may be expressed by equations and thus be analytically proved.

This procedure can also be extended to three-dimensional Euclidean space by introducing three mutually perpendicular axes x,y,z. In this case, there are two different axis systems—either congruent or mirror reflections—analogous to right-handed and left-handed screws.

Metrology in modern physics

The simple space-time relationships of Newtonian physics have been changed in many ways by modern developments. The concept of simultaneity has been made relative by the special theory of relativity; every time measurement t is thus tied to a definite inertial system or moving frame of reference. It is accordingly appropriate to speak not primarily of points in time but of events, which are defined in each case by giving both a point in space and a point in time.

More specifically, an inertial system is a coordinate system that, relative to the fixed stars, is in uniform, straight-line motion (or at rest) with no rotation. In all inertial systems, Newton's principle of inertia, which states that all mass points not acted upon by some force persist in uniform motion with a constant velocity, is valid.

Hyperspherical space-time: x,y,z,u

Moreover, cosmological theories make it probable that space in the real astronomical universe corresponds only approximately to the relationships of Euclidean geometry and that the approximation can be improved by replacing Euclidean space with a space of constant positive curvature. Such a space can be mathematically defined as a three-dimensional hyperspherical "surface"

$$R^2 = x^2 + y^2 + z^2 + u^2 \qquad (2)$$

in a hypothetical Euclidean space of four dimensions with mutually perpendicular x,y,z, and u coordinate axes.

The assertion that the foregoing statement has no operationally comprehensible content—*i.e.*, no content provable by performable measurements—is designated conventionalism, a view that is based on a remark by a French mathematician, Henri Poincaré, who was also a philosopher of science, that a fixed non-Euclidean space can be mapped point by point on a Euclidean space so that both are suitable for the description of the astronomical reality. The range of this remark is limited, however, in that this mapping, though it can indeed carry over points into points, can in no way carry over straight lines into straight lines. Hence, many philosophers of science have held that, as long as astronomical light rays are held to be straight lines, the question of a possible curvature of space (*i.e.*, a deviation from Euclidean conditions) will by no means be solved by some arbitrary convention; that it signifies, instead, a problem to be solved empirically. If the universe in fact has a positive constant curvature, then every straight line has a length that is only finite, and its points no longer correspond, as in the Euclidean case, to the set of all real numbers.

In a very definite manner, cosmological facts have further indicated that time is by no means unlimited both forward and backward. Rather, it seems that time as such had a beginning about 10^{10} to 2×10^{10} years ago; thus, with an explosive beginning, the cosmic development began as an expansion.

The foregoing discussion has considered only the replacement of Euclidean spatial concepts by an elementary non-Euclidean geometry corresponding to a space with a constant curvature. According to Einstein, however, the fundamental idea of a still more generalized Riemannian geometry, so-called after Bernhard Riemann, a geometer and function theorist, must be brought into play in order to produce a local-action theory of gravitation.

Riemann-ian space: g_{kl}

Riemannian geometry is a further development of the theory of surfaces created by the 18th- and 19th-century German mathematician and astronomer Carl Friedrich Gauss, often called the founder of modern mathematics, a theory that aimed to investigate the curved surfaces of three-dimensional (Euclidean) spaces with exclusive regard to their own inner dimensions and no consideration of their being imbedded in a three-dimensional space.

Gauss thought that the points on such a surface could be specified by reference to two arbitrary coordinates u and v defined with the help of two single-parameter families of curves, $u = $ constant and $v = $ constant. The square of the infinitesimal distance between two adjacent points of the surface, ds^2, is then a quadratic form of the differentials du and dv, belonging to the pair of points, namely,

$$ds^2 = g_{11}du^2 + 2g_{12}dudv + g_{22}dv^2, \qquad (3)$$

in which the coefficients g_{kl} are functions of position. One can then calculate the curvature corresponding to the location of the pair of points according to a prescription given by Gauss, a curvature that measures the deviation from Euclidean plane behaviour that exists at this point. The curvature is a definite function of the g_{kl} and their first derivatives.

Riemann extended Gauss's considerations to the case of a three-dimensional space that can have different curvature properties from place to place (expressed by several functions of position that are collectively called the curvature tensor); and Einstein generalized these ideas still further, applying them to the four-dimensional space–time continuum, and thereby attained a reduction of the Newtonian action-at-a-distance theory of gravitation to a local-action theory.

Contents of the natural order. Among the most basic constituents of the physical world are symmetries, fields, matter, and action.

Symme-tries

Symmetry is one of the chief concepts of modern mathematics, which combines the different symmetries belonging to an object or a concept into groups of relevant symmetries. The a priori investigation of the totality of possible groups, defined with respect to some operation (such as multiplication), comprises a division of modern mathematics called group theory.

Three-dimensional Euclidean space displays several important symmetry properties. It is homogeneous; *i.e.*, arbitrary shifts in the origin or zero point of the coordinate system produce no change in the analytic expression of the geometrical laws. It is also isotropic; that is, rotations of the coordinate system leave all geometrical laws in effect. Further, it is symmetric with regard to mirror reflections. It is tempting to suppose that these symmetry properties of space are also valid for the physical processes that occur in space, and this is indeed true over a wide range of cases,

but not in all cases (for exceptions, see below *Charge/ parity/time symmetry*).

That Newtonian mechanics and Maxwellian electrodynamics display in fact all of the symmetries of Euclidean space is revealed by the fact that they can be formulated in the language of vector analysis. Passing over the more familiar Newtonian mechanics, a few points about Maxwell's theory may be mentioned. This theory can be made to satisfy the requirements of operational thinking by ascribing to the electric and magnetic field strengths the significance of measurable physical realities, which makes it unnecessary to interpret them as states of a mysterious, hypothetical substance or ether, for which, in any case, the special theory of relativity (with the equivalence of all inertial systems) has no place.

Vector fields: directional quantities

Mathematically interpreted, a vector a represents a quantity with both magnitude and direction, which preserves its length or value and its direction when displaced. The vector field—*i.e.*, the association of a vector with every point in space (*e.g.*, electric field strength, or electric current density)—and the line integral (or summation) of a vector field V along a curve K leading from a point P to a point P' are basic concepts in vector analysis. To obtain the line integral, the curve K is divided into infinitesimal elements ds, the scalar (numerical or nonvector) product of ds with the value of V at that point is taken, and the results are summed with an integration.

A small surface area envisioned with a given sense of rotation around its boundary curve can also be described by a vector. In this instance, the vector, dF is perpendicular to the surface and forms, with the sense of rotation about the boundary, a right-handed system. Its magnitude is the area of the surface. The flux of the vector field V through the surface dF is called the scalar product $V \cdot dF$.

If V has the property that the line integral along every closed curve K is equal to zero, then V is said to be irrotational. This property is equivalent to the requirement that the vector field be a so-called gradient field; *i.e.*, that there exist a scalar field quantity W with the property that the difference in the value of W at two points P and P' is equal to the line integral of the vector field V from P to P' (along any arbitrary curve K). If V is, for example, an electrostatic (charged) field, the significance of being irrotational is that one can gain no mechanical work in leading a small test charge around any closed curve; the work involved is equal to zero. For an unclosed curve K, however, the movement of the test charge yields an amount of mechanical work that is proportional to the potential difference between the endpoints of the curve. The components of the gradient of W, expressed in partial derivatives ∂, are

$$\text{grad } W = \frac{\partial W}{\partial x}, \ \frac{\partial W}{\partial y}, \text{ and } \frac{\partial W}{\partial z}. \qquad (4)$$

Curl; divergence; charge; and current density

If the vector field is not irrotational, there can then be constructed from it an adjunct rotational field, called curl V, by considering a small (infinitesimal) surface area dF located at a point P and forming the line integral of V along the boundary curve of dF. Then, when this line integral is divided by the magnitude of the surface area, the component of the curl V parallel to the vector dF is obtained.

On the other hand, the flux of a vector field V out of a closed surface can be formed by integration. If this flux is always zero (for every choice of a closed surface), V is called source-free. Otherwise, there is a so-called divergence of V at a point P, which is defined as follows: one divides the net flux of V out of a small surface that surrounds P by the volume enclosed by the surface. The limit of this quotient for infinitesimally small surfaces is called the divergence of V at P or the source field div V.

The formulation of the basic laws of electrodynamics given by Maxwell is called the Maxwell equations. These equations contain, for example, the statement that, in a vacuum, the source field of the electric field strength is proportional to the spatial electric charge density, symbolized by the Greek letter rho, ρ, and that the magnetic field strength is source-free (divergence equal to zero). Thus, magnetic monopoles having no correlate of opposite sign do not exist. Remembering that every source-free vector field may be expressed mathematically as a rotation field (and vice versa), it is possible to derive the magnetic field strength H as a rotation field from a vector field A, which is usually called the vector potential of H

$$H = c \cdot \operatorname{curl} A. \qquad (5)$$

The fundamental law of the conservation of charge results from Maxwell's equations in the form of the continuity equation

$$\dot{\rho} + \operatorname{div} i = 0, \qquad (6)$$

in which $\dot{\rho}$ is the time derivative of the charge density, and the vector field i is the electric current density.

In the case of a vacuum, the Maxwell equation that expresses Faraday's law of induction takes the form of a proportionality between the rotation field of the electric field strength and the time derivative of the magnetic field strength:

$$H = c \cdot \operatorname{curl} E. \qquad (7)$$

Matter and action

It is a significant fact that Maxwell's theory leads to a localization of energy, which in electromagnetic fields is propagated somewhat in the manner of a substance, with a density that, for the vacuum case, is

$$W = (E^2 + H^2)/8\pi. \qquad (8)$$

There remains also the unsolved problem of clarifying the relation of gravitation to quantum theory, which is much aggravated by the fact that gravitational energy allows of no similar localization.

In both mechanics and electrodynamics, the fundamental equations have such a form that they can be understood as the conditions for a variational or an extremal principle: that, through the fulfillment of these conditions, a certain integral receives an extreme value. This integral, which has the dimensions of action—i.e., of energy times time—is one of the most fundamental quantities of nature. Although the concept of action is less obvious to man's physical intuition than that of energy, it is of even greater significance, as it appears also in connection with the quantum laws. For the basic constant of all of quantum physics, which always occurs in the laws of this domain, is likewise of this dimension: namely, Planck's quantum of action

$$h = 6.626 \times 10^{-27} \text{ erg-seconds.} \qquad (9)$$

Modalities of the natural order. In a purely phenomenalist theory of matter— *i.e.,* a theory that does not go into the details of atomic physics but considers matter only in a first approximation as a spatially extended continuum—numerous material properties are ascribed to every type of matter, properties such as density, electrical conductivity, magnetizability, dielectric constant, thermal conductivity, and specific heat. To be complete, a theory must provide a means of deriving all of these material properties theoretically from the laws of atomic physics.

Causality and statistical approach

The hiatus-free causality envisioned throughout the science of physics before the rise of quantum theory cannot be separated conceptually from the far-reaching assumption that all physical processes are continuous. It had been supposed that continuous changes in antecedent causal processes would issue in continuous changes in the sequence of processes that are causally dependent upon them. Quantum physics, however, has expressly breached the old philosophical axiom that *natura non facit saltūs* ("nature does not make leaps") and has introduced a granularity not only in the matter filling space, but also in the finest processes of nature. It is therefore only logical that, with respect to causality, the quantum theory would arrive at new and modified ideas as well. Renouncing unbroken causality, it speaks only of a probability that is statistical and a predetermination for the discrete saltatory events of which physical processes consist—a view that must now, in spite of Einstein, be regarded as irrevocable.

The special theory of relativity demands that the fundamental validity of the local-action principle be acknowledged: all actions have only finite velocities of propagation, which cannot exceed the velocity of light. Thus, in relativistic cosmology it is quite possible that two partial regions of the total spatial manifold may exist between which no causal interaction can occur: causal influences could then assert themselves only inside the so-called interdependent regions in the space–time manifold. These remarks also apply to the quantum theory, in which, however, instead of a causal dependence of physical processes upon each other, there is only an induction of statistical probabilities for possible quantum transitions.

Levels of the natural order. Moving in quite different directions, the theory of relativity on the one hand and the quantum theory on the other have diverged far from the earlier basic ideas of classical physics, which were considered unalterable. There are also some physical problems, however, that can be thought through only by appealing to both the relativistic and the quantum-theoretical modifications. A so-called joint relativistic and quantum-mechanical theory suitable for such problems is quantum electrodynamics, the development of which, however, is not yet complete. Its development was greatly hindered at first by certain mathematical difficulties (so-called divergences), which it later became possible to mitigate by renormalization; *i.e.,* by a technique of correcting the calculated results. The more generally conceived quantum theory of wave fields finds a broad area of possible application in the physics of the different kinds of elementary, though short-lived, particles produced by the huge high-energy accelerators. In its final form, the theory of elementary particles should not only formulate, in general, the laws valid for all known elementary particles but should also allow a deductive derivation for all possible kinds of elementary particles—analogous to the derivations of elements in the periodic table. Heisenberg has endeavoured to set up this far-reaching problem, which has been called the world formula, for a solution. Imposing mathematical difficulties, however, have arisen in the attempt to clarify its consequences for a quantitative comparison with experience, and considerable further work may still be required.

Special problems in the philosophy of physics. *Problems at the formal level.* Euclidean space, in contrast to imaginable spatial structures that deviate from it, is distinguished by the simplicity of the topological properties (those preserved through rubberlike distortions) that arise from its unusually simple continuity relationships. One may ask, then, whether the empirical knowledge of modern physics gives any cause to consider deviations from the topological relations of Euclidean space. The U.S. physicist John A. Wheeler, author of a new theory of physics called geometrodynamics, has speculated about this question. In particular, he has pointed to the possibility of so-called worm holes in space, analogous to the way in which the cylindrical surface of a smooth tree trunk is changed topologically if a worm bores a hole into the trunk and emerges from it again elsewhere: the surface of the trunk has thus obtained a "handle." Similarly, one can envision certain handles being added to three-dimensional Euclidean space. Whether this hypothesis can be fruitful for the theory of elementary particles is yet to be determined. From the methodological and epistemological standpoints, it is obvious that a geometrical structure is here being assumed, the measurement of which is fundamentally hindered by the lack of rulers with calibrations smaller than the structure itself. Presumably, the practical possibility of appealing to such topological modifications of the ordinary notion of space is to be found in astrophysics rather than in elementary particle physics. Viktor A. Ambartsumian, a Soviet astrophysicist, is convinced that the processes involved in the origins of galaxies are connected with explosions in which the matter of new stellar systems arises from prestellar material; and it has been found tempting to suppose that this prestellar material exists in regions with unusual topological properties.

Special topological properties

The basic idea of the special theory of relativity can also be understood as a statement about the symmetry

Lorentz transformations

properties of the four-dimensional space–time manifold. The special principle of relativity states, in fact, that the same physical laws are valid in all of the various inertial coordinate systems—in particular the law that the velocity of light in a vacuum always has the value c. This equivalence of the space–time coordinates x, y, z, t with other coordinates x', y', z', t' that are linear, homogeneous functions of the unprimed coordinates can be expressed by the equation

$$x^2 + y^2 + z^2 - c^2t^2 = x'^2 + y'^2 + z'^2 - c^2t'^2. \quad (10)$$

In this formulation, the isotropy of space—its sameness in all directions—appears as a special case of a more comprehensive symmetry property of the space–time manifold. When $t = t'$, the special case of a purely spatial rotation of coordinates is obtained; and in the general case, in which the primed coordinates are moving with velocity u with respect to the unprimed, the famous Lorentz transformations are obtained, which, to adjust to the finiteness of c, add a factor, symbolized by the Greek letter gamma, $\gamma = \sqrt{1 - \dfrac{u^2}{c^2}}$, to the ordinary Galilean transformation, $x = x' + ut'$, thus yielding

$$x = (x' + ut')\gamma. \quad (11)$$

The group of symmetries of the four-dimensional space–time manifold thus produced is called Poincaré group.

Problems at the quantum level. Problems of particle theory, complementarity, and symmetry have arisen in studies at the quantum level.

Elementary particle theory   Whereas the atomic nuclei beyond hydrogen-1 (the proton) are compounded structures, consisting of neutrons and protons, modern physics also deals with numerous elementary particles—neutrinos; π (pi), μ (mu), and κ mesons; hyperons; etc.—that are thought of as uncompounded. The elementary particles of each particular kind show no individual differences. Except for light quanta, for each kind of particle a corresponding antiparticle has come to light (which, for charged particles, always carries a charge of opposite sign). For instance, to each of the two known forms of neutrino there corresponds an antineutrino with charge zero and zero rest mass; *i.e.,* with a mass that would be zero were it not moving at a velocity of the order of (in fact, at) that of light. Whether Heisenberg's world formula can provide a complete framework for all possible kinds of elementary particles is undecided.

Every type of elementary particle has a definite value for its spin, either integral (*e.g.,* light quanta) or half-integral (*e.g.,* electrons, protons, neutrinos). Particles with half-integral spin obey Fermi–Dirac statistics; those with integral spin obey Bose–Einstein statistics, which differ in form as $u/(1 + u)$ differs from $u/(1 - u)$—u being any function. The conformity to law that underlies the Fermi–Dirac statistics for electrons was first recognized by Wolfgang Pauli and formulated as the Pauli exclusion principle, which played a decisive role in settling upon the shell structure in the periodic system of the elements.

Heisenberg's uncertainty principle   The basic duality of waves and corpuscles is of universal significance for all kinds of elementary particles, even for composite particles in those experiments that cannot lead to a breakup of the particles into their component parts.

An electron (and analogously any other elementary particle or even, for example, an alpha particle) can appear just as well in the form of a wave as in that of a localized corpuscle. In an idealized thought experiment, one can imagine that the position of an electron can be ascertained with a gamma-ray microscope. If the electron is described in terms of wave processes in the sense of Schrödinger's wave mechanics, a very sharply concentrated wave packet appears at the stated position. In an investigation of this packet by Fourier analysis—a technique that analyzes a function into its sinusoidal components—wave components of quite different wavelengths occur; thus an electron in this condition has no definite value for its de Broglie wavelength and consequently none also for its translational momentum. Then, as stated in the so-called de Broglie relation,

$$\lambda = h/mv, \quad (12)$$

there is for an electron moving free from impinging forces a corresponding wavelength, symbolized by the Greek letter lambda, λ, that is inversely proportional to its momentum mv. And conversely, an electron moving inertially with a definite momentum (which in the limiting case of small velocities is equal to the product of the mass and the velocity vector) has no definite position. If an electron that is moving inertially (especially an electron at rest) is constrained by the use of a gamma-ray microscope to "make up its mind," as it were, on a location, then the probability of its appearance at a point in space is the same for all locations. More precisely stated, the probability of the appearance of the electron in a definite volume is proportional to the magnitude of this volume.

In particular, it will be helpful to consider an electron moving in the x-direction and to suppose that it has a wave amplitude that depends only upon x, an electron in which the most representative wavelengths are confined to a narrow interval while the amplitudes that are discernibly different from zero are likewise confined to a certain interval Δx. If, on the other hand, Δp is the range of discernible momentum values—computed from the discernible wavelengths that represent them according to the de Broglie relation (12)—then the product of the uncertainties Δx and Δp cannot be smaller than Planck's fundamental quantum of action h. This statement comprises the famous Heisenberg uncertainty relation, which expresses the "complementarity" of position and momentum—as Niels Bohr characterized it.

If one assumes, as above, that all physically possible states of an electron can be represented by Schrödinger's wave mechanics, then the complementarity of the position coordinate x and its corresponding conjugate momentum p_x is a simple mathematical fact. When one thinks primarily of physical-measurement experiments, it should be emphasized that stringent limitations are imposed on the simultaneous measurement of the position and momentum of a particle that, according to the uncertainty principle, make it impossible to measure simultaneously both of these complementary quantities with unlimited precision. In an experiment that measures its position, the electron is forced into a sharper localization; and its particle nature comes to light. By contrast, in an experiment that measures its momentum, an interference experiment is involved; the electron must be able to display a certain wavelength, which requires an adequately extended region in space for its reacting. These two complementary and opposing demands can only be brought into harmony in the sense of a compromise; and the Heisenberg uncertainty relation formulates the best possible compromise.

Thus, it becomes at the same time clear that the state of the electron given in the wave-mechanical description before carrying out a new measurement experiment can establish only a statistical prediction for the result. The probability density for the appearance of an electron at a point in space is given by the square of the absolute value of the (complex) Schrödinger wave amplitude; for a definite result in measuring a wavelength or a momentum, the square of the absolute value of the (complex) Fourier coefficient belonging to it provides the standard. The general statistical transformation theory of quantum mechanics (as developed by Dirac and Jordan) gives a complete review of the measurable physical quantities for a microscopic mass point (or a system of such points). According to this theory, two different measurable quantities A and B can be simultaneously determined with unlimited precision only if the operators or matrices that describe A and B commute; *i.e.,* if $AB = BA$.

Charge/ parity/ time symmetry   A transformation in which the nucleus emits an electron and a neutrino is called beta decay, an example of nuclear radioactivity. The forces that thus come to light are those of the so-called weak interactions. It has been experimentally determined that for these forces the symmetry associated with reflections in a mirror does not hold. At least in certain circumstances, however, a remnant of this symmetry continues to hold, in which the so-called CPT (for the initials in charge/parity/time) theorem applies. This theorem states that basic physical laws remain of unaltered validity when a reflection of the space coordinates as in a mirror is combined with an interchange of positive and negative charge (which is largely synonymous with the interchange of particles and antiparticles) and with a reversal of the direction of time. Whether or not this symmetry law is valid without exception is by no means fully clarified at present.

Problems at the macrophysical level. Proceeding from the properties of atoms and molecules that are described in terms of quantum theory, a theory of macrophysical substance aggregates has been built using statistical mechanics. The theories of heat, of gases, and of solid-state aggregates (crystal lattices) have been extensively clarified. Only the liquid state still poses certain unsolved problems for the statistical theory of heat.

In any case, Newtonian mechanics may be derived as a macroscopic consequence of the laws of the mechanics of atoms, and its validity for the motions of astronomical bodies presents no problem. It is not so simple to prove, however, that the statements of Newtonian mechanics for rotating bodies (*i.e.,* the mechanical laws of centrifugal force and the Coriolis force) may be established from Einstein's general theory of relativity. Ernst Mach, a physicist and philosopher of science whose train of thought has substantially fertilized the modern development of physics from the point of view of the theory of knowledge, raised objections against Newton's idea that centrifugal force is a consequence of the absolute rotation of a body; he asserted instead that the rotation of a body relative to the very distant giant mass of the universe was the true cause of centrifugal force. This idea, often referred to as Mach's principle, has been corroborated, though in a different form, within the conceptual framework of Einstein's general theory. An irrotational coordinate system—specifically, a system not rotating with respect to the fixed stars (or, better, to the spiral nebulae)—is distinguished from a rotating system by the difference in the metric field for the two cases (*i.e.,* in the properties of their respective space–times as expressed by the equation—(3) above—for the interval between two events). It is true that the local metric field (in the vicinity of the solar system) is influenced by the distant masses of the universe, but of course only in the sense of a local-action principle and therefore in no way such that the metric in the solar system is directly given as a function of these distant masses and of their motions.

The question of the precise circumstances in which Mach's principle can still be defended on the basis of Einstein's theory is somewhat complicated and thus remains obscure. In any case, it is certain that a deduction of this principle from Einstein's theory can only be given in conjunction with a complete solution of the cosmological problem; *i.e.,* of the problem of what are the overall geometric and dynamic properties of the universe considered in its totality. The remaining problems involved in justifying the application of classical Newtonian mechanics in astronomy by means of Einstein's theory contain, however, no additional fundamental difficulties.

There is one more influence of cosmological relationships upon macroscopic physics, which arises in connection with thermodynamics. The existence of irreversible processes in thermodynamics indicates a distinction between the positive and negative directions in time. As Clausius recognized in the 19th century, this irreversibility reflects a quantity, first defined by him, called entropy, which measures the degree of randomness evolving from all physical processes by which their energies tend to degrade into heat. Entropy can only increase in the positive direction of time. In fact, the increase in entropy during a process is a measure of the irreversibility of that process. In contrast, it is true of the quantum theory of the atom that the positive and negative directions in time are equally justifiable (in the sense of the principle of CPT symmetry). Consequently, it is difficult to understand how statistical mechanics can make possible a thermodynamics in which the entropy grows with time.

It is true that there are fluctuating thermodynamic phenomena, even in a system in overall thermodynamic equilibrium—and here theory and experiment agree. Thus, the states that arise within any small partial volume of the

system may be not only those that are thermodynamically most probable but also transitory deviations from the most probable state. The mention of these fluctuations, however, does not help to remove the above paradox.

Most physicists now hold that, until recently, this problem was treated erroneously in the usual textbook presentations. In the statistical theory of heat, entropy was regarded as proportional to the logarithm of the thermodynamic probability, and students came to regard it as a necessity of thought that nature progresses from states of lower probability to states of higher probability. In truth, however, the increase of entropy is a real physical property of the positive direction in time. Nonetheless, it was supposed that shaking a vessel containing red and white balls (or even grains of sand) in an originally ordered condition with the two colours neatly separated must result in a condition of extreme intermixing of balls. This result does not correspond, however, to some necessity of thought but to an empirical property of the real universe in which men live and experiment.

This interpretation, which was held for a long time and has only quite recently been recognized as erroneous, was allegedly supported by a famous mathematical theorem of Boltzmann, which seemed to show that, in an ideal gas for which the entropy—measured by its number of particles and its total energy—was not yet at its maximum value, the entropy must increase. If collisions of gas molecules are characterized by velocity vectors that are mechanically allowable (both before and after the collision), and if these vectors must satisfy both energy and momentum conservation, then what Boltzmann actually proved is that the entropy increase follows only when a correct count of the collision rate is made, according to which every kind of collision of gas molecules has a frequency of occurrence proportional to the product of the number of collision pairs that were present and the velocities that existed before the impact.

As one can subsequently see, the positive direction in time is already marked out by the collision rate count in a manner that no longer corresponds to the CPT principle. Although it is in fact possible to reason out the continuous increase in entropy on this basis, the paradox is not overcome. The question then remains of how it is physically justifiable—*i.e.,* how it can correspond to reality—to regard this principle of collision rates as valid even though it fundamentally contradicts the CPT principle.

An answer to this paradox can now be given, thanks to the insight of modern theoreticians—among them Hermann Bondi, a mathematician and cosmologist—who have shown that the entropy principle must be understood in the sense that in the universe as a whole, one definite time direction is singled out, namely, the one for which the universe expands. The thermodynamic distinction of a positive direction in time—with increasing entropy on the macroscopic level and with collision rate counts on the microscopic level—results from an expansion of the universe. Surprisingly, the Hubble expansion of the system of all the galaxies—so named after Edwin Hubble, an extragalactic astronomer—thus displays physical effects right down to the level of everyday physics; specifically, when two bodies at different temperatures are brought into thermal contact, the temperature equalization that results is an irreversible process corresponding to an asymmetry of the positive and negative directions in time that depends upon the expansion of the universe.

Problems at the cosmological level. A mathematical discovery by Alexander Friedmann has become of great significance for the mathematical derivation of cosmological models from Einstein's general theory of relativity. According to Friedmann, if the average mass density is constant throughout space, the gravitational field equations can be satisfied by a metric that embraces a three-dimensional space of constant curvature together with a time coordinate t such that the radius of curvature $R(t)$ is a definite function of time; and these cosmologies turn out differently depending upon whether the curvature of space is positive, negative, or zero. Among the models of the universe that are mathematically allowable are models in which the time coordinate may run through all values

---

Marginal notes (left column):

Mach's principle of cosmic influence

Entropy and the direction of time

Marginal notes (right column):

Boltzmann's theorem

from zero to infinity, models in which the time is limited to a finite interval, and models in which it may run from minus infinity to plus infinity.

For a time, many specialists working in the field of cosmology found the so-called steady-state theory, first projected by an astronomer, Sir Fred Hoyle, especially convincing. In a modified version, this theory was adapted to the Friedmann model by Bondi. By adopting the so-called perfect cosmological principle, which holds that the broadest features of the universe are the same at all times as well as at all places, the theory then satisfied the unusually high symmetry or homogeneity requirements not only of a three-dimensional space with constant time but also of the entire space-time manifold. This high-degree homogeneity was so convincing to many authors that, in deference to it, a fundamental deviation from Einstein's field equations was tolerated: Bondi and Hoyle supposed that a small but constant creation of hydrogen occurs in the intergalactic vacuum. This hypothesis was introduced in order to achieve, in spite of the Hubble expansion of space, a mass density that remained constant in the universe.

This theory, which in spite of its deviation from Einstein's field equations certainly advocates an allowable hypothesis worthy of consideration, no longer seems tenable, however, because of the discovery of background radiation with a present temperature of 3° Kelvin, which is interpreted as a remnant of an original "big-bang" beginning of the universe. It thus appears that it is no longer possible to uphold the steady-state theory or the perfect cosmological principle upon which it is based. Instead, one must favour either a Friedmann model, which has a beginning, from which it expands monotonically and without limit; or a Lemaître model, in which a quantity lambda, λ, called the cosmical constant, arises that is, mathematically, a constant of integration, and physically, a force of cosmic repulsion that partially neutralizes that of gravitational attraction, and which lends a curvature to space even in its empty regions. For both of these models the time coordinate increases without limit from some initial value, which would naturally be called zero. For the beginning of time, one thinks, moreover, of a singularity $R(0) = 0$ and thus of a space that at the null point of time is still a mass point. Cyclical models that alternately expand and contract in an endless sequence have also been discussed.

The empirical cosmological data, some of which, indeed, are more estimated than ascertained, seem to suggest that, in the present-day universe, the positive energy corresponding to the total rest mass of all the material existing in the universe may be exactly equal to the negative gravitational energy existing in the universe; thus, the total energy would then be equal to zero. This interesting singularity, however, needs further support. At one time, Dirac advocated the speculation that the total mass of the universe is not constant in time but is increasing—at a rate somewhat slower, however, than that in the steady-state theory. Ambartsumian's notion concerning prestellar material, which was mentioned above (see *Problems at the formal level*), could perhaps be considered support for this idea. Many further discussions have followed another conjecture by Dirac, according to which the gravitational constant G should be liable to change in the course of cosmic development. This constant would thus have to be considered a scalar field quantity, which in a Friedmann universe is approximately independent of the three space variables but dependent on the time variable. In spite of extensive theoretical deliberations on this theme, no decision has yet been reached.

The way has been opened for some fundamental conjectures on certain emerging themes by the fact that the product of the mean mass density in the universe and the gravitational constant has the same order of magnitude as the square of the reciprocal of the radius of curvature of the universe. The aforementioned relation between the mass and gravitational energy in the universe presents a different expression for this ratio. The total mass of the universe divided by the proton mass probably has approximately the order of magnitude 10^{80}, according to present

cosmological notions. The order of magnitude of the radius of curvature of the universe is approximately 10^{40}, when expressed as a multiple of an elementary length of which the order of magnitude is approximately that of the nuclear radius. Whether it is justifiable to presume that there is here a functional dependence—*i.e.*, a proportionality of M to R squared—is a question for the present still undecidable. The speculative attempt of Dirac to find an answer, however, is still—at least provisionally—judged with skepticism by the majority of physicists.   (P.W.J.)

PHILOSOPHY OF BIOLOGY

The sharp increase in man's understanding of biological processes that has occurred in recent years has stimulated philosophical interest in biology to an extent unprecedented since the development of evolutionary theory in the 19th century. Biologists and philosophers alike have devoted much attention to a variety of issues regarding the subject matter and the methodology of biology, resulting in a sizable output of written material, formulating philosophical questions that are still arising and framing answers to acknowledged difficulties. Most of the problems of the philosophy of biology are old questions now being investigated afresh in the light of biological advances and new standards of philosophical rigour. In this account contemporary questions will be stressed.

The range of topics. An investigation of recent writings in biophilosophy reveals a continued preoccupation with unanswered—some say unanswerable—questions about evolutionary theory and a growing concern for a critical reappraisal of the question of whether biology is an autonomous discipline unamenable to reduction to mere physical and chemical underpinnings. Until the mid-20th century the biological sciences suffered from a lack of attention by philosophers; the principles that were generated were far less rigorously examined than were those of the physical sciences. There is now renewed hope, however, for a fresh approach to the age-old puzzles regarding life and its raison d'être. This hope rests on the recrudescence of interest in all biological matters as a direct result of an increased understanding of biological processes, of the changing quality of life, of the growing awareness of man's stewardship of the Earth, and of the exploration of space. Biology has just begun to make the sort of impact that the physical sciences have already made. It has generated a life technology with genetic engineering, organ transplants, and artificial organs. Each innovation, each technical masterstoke, each conceptual knot united emphasizes the need for a definitive philosophy of biology, and developments toward this goal are now under way. Good biological work has been accomplished by investigators with varied philosophical outlooks ranging from Neo-Thomism to skeptical naturalism. No inevitable metaphysics evolves from the study of biology or any other natural science; nevertheless, some of the general conclusions of biology have a philosophical interest, defining the limits of reasonable belief about the nature of the living world.

Categorical discontinuities that are recognized for the purpose of scientific methodology often seem impossible to justify as "natural" distinctions. Many biologists have noted, for example, that it is easier to study life than it is to define it. Properties such as metabolism and reproduction undeniably characterize organisms and might be said to define them, yet such a definition is arbitrary to the extent that such properties are logically independent. What is true of all life forms today may not have been true of the very earliest ones and, what is more, might not be true of extra-terrestrial ones that might be encountered in the future. There is not as yet a set of nonarbitrary characteristics that mark the distinction between living and nonliving systems. Moreover, in the course of analysis, it becomes necessary to arrange all of the phenomena of nature in a more or less linear, continuous sequence of classes and then to describe events occurring in the class of more complex phenomena in terms of events in the classes of less complex phenomena (principle of hierarchical continuity). Within each class, however, there are numerous interrelations observed between events of the same order of complexity. It is thus possible to recognize a number of more or less autonomous disciplines, each permitting generalization, but ordered so that the more complex events treated by one discipline can also be analyzed in terms of less complex events treated by another discipline. It is possible, for example, to establish a body of generalizations about human society independent of the behaviour of individual persons; a number of generalizations about individual behaviour without consideration of the physiology of the sensory, conductor, and effector mechanisms involved; and a large body of generalizations about muscle or nerve physiology without considering the molecular mechanisms involved. A particularly striking feature of the hierarchy is that an increase in complexity is coupled with the emergence of new characteristics. The origin and development of life from small systems that synthesized biochemicals to organisms that perform highly complicated functions suggests that the hierarchical arrangement of nature and the sciences is correlated with the temporal order of evolution. The maintenance of a steady state by metabolism, reproduction, responsiveness, modification of response by experience, tradition, and social phenomena are just some of the more dramatic examples of emergent phenomena. The emergence of new qualities as evolution proceeds might generally characterize the universe.

Moreover, photosynthesis, on the one hand, and reproduction followed by natural selection, on the other, provide a mechanism by which physically less probable systems can emerge locally from physically more probable ones. Though it frequently has been supposed that physical evolution is at an end, there is no reason to suppose that this is true of social development, for which Sir Julian Huxley, a biologist, philosopher, and educator, provided an evolutionary context. In his Romanes Lectures, published in 1943, Huxley wrote:

It is only through social evolution that the world-stuff can now realize radically new possibilities. Mechanical interaction and natural selection still operate, but have become of secondary importance. For good or evil, the mechanism of evolution has in the main been transferred [in man] onto the social or conscious level. . . . The slow methods of variation and heredity are outstripped by the speedier processes of acquiring and transmitting experience. . . .
And in so far as the mechanism of evolution ceases to be blind and automatic and becomes conscious, ethics can be injected into the evolutionary process. Before man that process was merely amoral. After his emergence onto life's stage it became possible to introduce faith, courage, love of truth, goodness—in a word moral purpose—into evolution. It became possible, but the possiblity has been and is often unrealized.

It may well be that social evolution is only in its early stages. These stages, moreover, have for the most part taken place in a period during which systematic knowledge was undeveloped. A Russian mineralogist, Vladimir Vernadsky, the founder of biogeochemistry, regarded the envelope of the Earth as passing from a stage determined primarily by biological processes to one determined by conscious human effort. He called this layer of consciousness the noösphere. The concept was later extended, notably by Pierre Teilhard de Chardin, a French priest and paleontologist, who began the building of a new philosphic bridge between biology and religion.

The nature of biological systems. Questions about the character of biological systems and of the biological world merge with those about the concepts and methods required for their understanding. Although the two cannot be wholly separated, in this account those matters most clearly related to the substantive philosophical aspects of biology will be stressed. Methodological issues will be touched on in respect to the concepts being elucidated.

Origin and definition of life. Space exploration has directly influenced the development of life-detecting devices. This technological need spurred intensive study regarding the kinds of evidence living things display reflecting their aliveness. In his *Chance and Necessity* (1972) Jacques Monod, a biologist, deals with the invariance of genetic endowment, morphological autonomy, reproductive invariance, and teleonomy (the tendency to have a purpose or project written into their molecules) as the major properties of living systems; he considers that they involve the chance and necessity that determine the course and character of the entire biological world.

Philosophers have long deliberated over the definitive features of living systems. The distinction between living and nonliving, which was widely discussed at the turn of the 20th century, has lost much of its interest for current biology. A growing conviction, intuitively felt by many biologists, is that no clear line can be drawn between the living and the nonliving. The bridge between what is and is not obviously alive consists of a range of problematic agents, including viruses and genes, which appear to be living at times and nonliving at other times. *margin: Philosophic views*

Viewpoints on the nature of life. Basically and traditionally, there are three distinct philosophical stands regarding the biological nature of life: vitalism, mechanism, and organicism.

Essentially, vitalism holds that there exists in all living things an intrinsic factor—elusive, inestimable, and unmeasurable—that activates life. In its classic form, as espoused by many biologists at the turn of the 20th century—in particular, by Hans Driesch, a German biologist and philosopher—it has suffered severe criticism. Ernest Nagel, a philosopher of science, rang its death knell in 1951, when he wrote in *Philosophy and Phenomenological Research* (11:327 ff.): *margin: Vitalism*

Vitalism of the substantival type . . . is now a dead issue . . . less, perhaps, because of the methodological and philosophical criticism that has been leveled against the doctrine than because of the infertility of vitalism as a guide in biological research and because of the superior heuristic value of alternative approaches.

And whereas most biologists concur in renouncing this so-called naïve vitalism, some continue to espouse a so--called critical vitalism, perhaps indistinguishable from organicism (see below).

Simply stated, the view of the mechanists is that organisms are no different from subtle machines: the whole is the sum of its parts, which are arranged in such a way that an internal energy source can move them in accordance with a built-in program of purposeful action. In the mechanist's view, advances in molecular biology corroborate this claim and demonstrate that in principle organisms are no more than complicated physical systems. This is, in essence, the reductionist position, which states that biological principles can be reduced to physical and chemical laws. Antireductionists, of course, contend that molecular biology cannot explain all aspects of living forms. *margin: Mechanism*

It has often been said that, whereas biologists may think as vitalists—and hold the conviction that organisms are more than just complex machines—they perforce become practicing mechanists in the laboratory, required by the demands of scientific inquiry to view their experiments in terms of the measurable parameters of physics and chemistry. K.F. Schaffner, an American philosopher, suggested in 1967 that, even though reductionism may be correct, a better strategy may be to strive toward an independent biology.

The basic claim of organicism is that organisms must be interpreted as functioning wholes and cannot be understood by means of physics and chemistry alone. Few scientists today call themselves organismic biologists or endorse the doctrines put forward by such organismic theorists as Ludwig von Bertalanffy and Edward Stuart Russell. Nevertheless, most antireductionists subscribe at least to part of the organismic doctrine, in particular to its wholistic claim. Russell, a foremost proponent of organicism, stated in his work *The Interpretation of Development and Heredity* (1930): *margin: Organicism*

Any action of the whole organism would appear then to be susceptible of analysis to an indefinite degree—and this is in general the aim of the physiologist, to analyze, to decompose into their elementary processes the broad activities and functions of the organism. But . . . by such a procedure something is lost, for the action of the whole has a certain unifiedness and completeness which is left out of account in the process of analysis. . . . In our conception of the organism we must . . . take account of the unifiedness and wholeness of its activities . . . , since . . . the activities of the organism all have reference to one or other of three great ends, and that both the past and the future enter into their determination. . . .
Bio-chemistry studies essentially the *conditions* of action of

cells and organisms, while organismal biology attempts to study the actual modes of action of whole organisms, regarded as conditioned by, but irreducible to, the modes of action of lower unities.

In some special sense, then, an organism is regarded as being more than a simple sum of its parts; an additional "something" has accrued to it as a result of the unique arrangement of its components. As Morton O. Beckner, a philosopher of biology, asserted in an article in *The Encyclopedia of Philosophy* (5:549):

In the history of biology it is difficult to disentangle vitalistic and organismic strands, since both schools are concerned with the same sorts of problems and speak the same sort of language. The distinction between them was drawn clearly only in the twentieth century. Organismic biology may be described as an attempt to achieve the aims of the murky organismic-vitalistic tradition, without appeal to vital entities.

Further (p. 551):

Organismic biology is to be interpreted as a series of methodological proposals, based on certain very general features of the organism—namely, the existence in the organism of levels of organization with the biological ends of maintenance and reproduction. These features are sufficient to justify "a free, autonomous biology, with concepts and laws of its own," whether or not the higher levels are ultimately reducible to the lower ones.

Organisms as systems. The concept of an organism as a cybernetic, or automatic-control, system is currently influential in biology.

Holism and emergence The holistic concept of an organism—*i.e.,* the theory that the determining factors in biology are its irreducible wholes—owes its success primarily to the existence of control and regulation mechanisms operating at the molecular level that determine development and behaviour. The character of such systems at all levels of analysis—molecular through total organism—is nothing other than a sophisticated kind of cybernetics. Holism and reductionism are similar in this respect. Closely allied to organicism is the old problem of emergent properties dealt with earlier: at each successive level of organization, qualities emerge that cannot be anticipated by the components and that confer an added dimension to each hierarchical level in the biological world.

General systems theory A theoretical and methodological program called general systems theory—presented in its fullest and most persuasive form by Bertalanffy—is an extension of the tenets of organismic biology. It is an attempt to provide a common methodological approach for all of the sciences, based upon the idea that systems of any kind—physical, biological, psychological, and social—operate in accordance with the same fundamental principles. Ideally, it should be possible to deduce the principles applying to a particular sort of system from the more general ones. This approach is one still very much in need of development.

Teleology Attributions of purpose (teleology) appear frequently in biological writing. Not only do biologists say that parts of organisms have a purpose with respect to the whole, but some hold that life itself is inherently purposive. But the term purpose is both vague and ambiguous. That every biological system—from self-replicating molecules (DNA) to biotic communities—involves specific and identifiable functions is undeniable. But whether, or in what way, functional ends like the reproduction of a cell resemble human intentions or purposes is a matter of some controversy. Even if this matter were settled, a larger question would still remain, viz., whether a biological system as a whole can have a goal that is in some way similar to a human goal—*i.e.,* whether it is programmed with an ultimate purpose. Although resolution of this matter has long been and will continue to be a critical point in the philosophy of biology, much has been done to clarify the issues involved.

Philosophy in evolution. *Teleology and determinism.* Vitalists and those who subscribe to a Lamarckian view of evolution involving the inheritance of acquired characteristics claim that evolution involves a deterministic finalism, or directedness toward an end. Most evolutionists— among them George Gaylord Simpson—reject that claim and hold that natural selection is the non-random element

in evolution, that which gives evolution direction. Other evolutionists—among them Theodosius Dobzhansky—argue that the chance factors in mutation and selection, in addition to the unpredictability of environmental change, make it impossible to formulate deterministic laws even in experimental populations, let alone in natural populations. Similar considerations by others have led to the claim that evolutionary biology is a paradigm of an after-the-fact exploratory science and that the course of evolution can never be predicted.

The species problem. Whether biological species can be said to have a real existence in the world is a question that has been receiving much consideration. The issue may be posed in the words of Benjamin Burma, a paleontologist, who, writing in *Evolution* (3:369), asked:

What, then, is a species? It would seem thus far to be the whole of any one series of breeding populations. . . . [But the] definition as it stands unfortunately puts all living and fossil animals in one species, since there is a continuity of germ-plasm back from John [an individual animal] to the original primordial cell, and from it forward to every living animal (not to mention plant). Thus, if we ignore time, we end up with only one species. . . .

The temporal difficulty, however, is not the only stumbling block to the question of species reality; for, if the species is redefined as the whole of any one series of breeding populations as it exists at any one time, then there is an infinity of species, since time itself is infinitely divisible. On the basis of these and other objections, some biologists have concluded that species have only a subjective existence merely as convenient labels for arbitrary assemblages and have only a minimum of biological significance. On the other hand, there are proponents of the idea that species have an objective reality. Ernst Mayr, a U.S. evolutionist representing the latter group, has written—also in *Evolution* (3:372):

In all multidimensional situations an inference has to be made (Simpson, 1943) on the basis of the objective species of the non-dimensional system. The subjectivity of this expanded species concept by no means invalidates the species concept per se. The species of the local naturalist or of the paleontologist within a given horizon is clearly delimited against other species and can thus be considered as having objective reality.

Although the controversy is confused by semantic difficulties, one of the chief contributions of the philosophy of biology has, in fact, been to separate mere linguistic puzzles from matters of substance. Many taxonomists are guilty of ambiguity of reference; they often fail to distinguish their entities clearly, with the result that there is widespread befuddlement over just what stand is held by whom. The problems are now clearer than they have ever been, and with few exceptions biologists and philosophers tend to agree about the nature of biological species and the definition of the species category.

Evolutionary theory. Although most of the issues connected with evolution as a theory are methodological ones, two issues go beyond the limits of logic. Some philosophers have tried to demonstrate, for example, that evolutionary theory is circular and offers no real understanding of the process of evolution. Others have argued that the notions of types of organisms must be used to understand evolution and that evolutionary change takes place when a new type emerges.

The views of Simpson and Schindewolf Two clear viewpoints regarding evolutionary theory have come to the fore since 1950. One is expressed in detail by George Gaylord Simpson, in his work *The Major Features of Evolution* (1953), and the other is put forward by a paleontologist, Otto Schindewolf, in his *Grundfragen der Paläontologie* (1950). In 1959, Marjorie Grene, a philosopher of biology, writing in the *British Journal of the Philosophy of Science* (9:11 ff.), summarized their positions as follows:

Professor Simpson is the principal American spokesman of neo-Darwinism. . . . He sees evolution as a continuous series of minute changes in innumerable directions, in which all alterations of any significance, larger as well as smaller, quicker as well as slower, are determined by the great cooperating "pressures" of mutation, geographical isolation, and selection, with adaptation as the universal effect, and criterion, of systematic change. The basic concept, ultimately is variation in the occurrence of genes; out of such variations all the systematic relations of living things have been gradually evolved.

Schindewolf's principles are simpler. He sees typical shapes, and sees again and again what appear to be new shapes. Therefore he assumes that living things are able to originate novel types. Mutation, he agrees, must have been the mechanism by which they originated; but the adaptive control of mutation occurs only within, not between types. The basic pattern is of change from type to type, and always, as we have seen, with the more general appearing before its specialised subdivisions.

The controversy between these two opposing viewpoints is a complex one filled with both philosophical and scientific issues. In the opinion of most biologists, Schindewolf's view is persuasive only with respect to the paleontological evidence and is not supported by the experimental study of evolution in current organisms. Most of them thus tend to accept the synthetic theory in more or less the form expressed by Simpson. It remains possible, however, that the process that Schindewolf is talking about is fundamentally different from that explored in population genetics and that typostrophic mutations are so rare, on the time scale of man, as to be beyond hope of detection in the laboratory.

Evolution as a world view. Very few attempts have been made in recent years to employ the concept of evolution as a scheme for viewing all knowledge and experience. Sir Julian Huxley, who remains one of the best representatives of such an effort, continues to claim that the entire universe is in a process of evolution, which, however, has different aspects, viz., physical, biological, and social. Life and nonlife alike must be understood as part of the process of cosmic evolution, and from this follows a host of metaphysical and ethical implications. The other chief representative of this viewpoint is the evolutionist priest Teilhard de Chardin, who has woven into the fabric of cosmic evolution the panoply of a Christocentric religion that sees the perfection of all things in an "Omega" point toward which evolution is moving.

Metaphysics of the more piecemeal kind—exploring the implications that biological knowledge has on beliefs and attitudes—is fostered by Simpson, a consistent antagonist of Huxley and Chardin. Simpson suggests, for instance, that knowledge of man's origins and of the process that has brought him to his current state in no way threatens belief in his own uniqueness. Man is an animal, but a very special sort of animal. Other matters of a similar kind—purpose in nature and man's evolutionary future—are considerations that constitute the implications of biology in general and of evolutionary biology in particular.

Biology and ethics. *The question of innate aggressiveness.* One of the best known issues threatening accepted beliefs about moral responsibility is probably that raised by the proponents of the theory of innate aggression, in particular by such spokesmen as Konrad Lorenz, an Austrian student of animal behaviour, and Robert Ardrey, a U.S. writer. If there is an instinct for aggressiveness, then the notion that it is acceptable to blame individuals and society for outbreaks of violence or war loses its validity. The thrust must then be elsewhere: not in faultfinding but in shoring up against what is felt to be pedestrian and inevitable. As Ardrey puts the theory in his *African Genesis* (1961):

> But we were born of risen apes, not fallen angels, and the apes were armed killers besides. And so what shall we wonder at? Our murders and massacres and missiles, and our irreconcilable regiments? Or our treaties whatever they may be worth; our symphonies however seldom they may be played; our peaceful acres, however frequently they may be converted into battlefields; our dreams however rarely they may be accomplished. The miracle of man is not how far he has sunk but how magnificently he has risen. We are known among the stars by our poems, not our corpses.

Raymond Dart, a South African anatomist and anthropologist, in an article entitled "The Predatory Transition from Ape to Man," published in the *International Anthropological and Linguistic Review* (1:201–208), expressed the thesis of innate depravity on which Ardrey's more popular presentation is based.

Another aspect of the innate aggression inherited from man's primate forebears is militant enthusiasm,

Views
of the
ethologists

which Lorenz described in *Das sogenanannte Böse: zur Naturgeschichte der Aggression* (1963; Eng. trans., *On Aggression,* 1966):

> In reality, militant enthusiasm is a specialized form of communal aggression, clearly distinct from and yet functionally related to the more primitive forms of petty individual aggression. Every man of normally strong emotions knows, from his own experience, the subjective phenomena that go hand in hand with the response of militant enthusiasm. A shiver runs down the back and, as more exact observation shows, along the outside of both arms. One soars elated, above all the ties of everyday life, one is ready to abandon all for the call of what, in the moment of this specific emotion, seems to be a sacred duty. All obstacles in its path become unimportant; the instinctive inhibitions against hurting or killing one's fellows lose, unfortunately, much of their power. Rational considerations, criticism, and all reasonable arguments against the behavior dictated by militant enthusiasm are silenced by an amazing reversal of all values, making them appear not only untenable but base and dishonorable. Men may enjoy the feeling of absolute righteousness even while they commit atrocities. Conceptual thought and moral responsibility are at their lowest ebb. As a Ukrainian proverb says: "When the banner is unfurled, all reason is in the trumpet."

Equally notable opponents of the theory of innate aggression see it much as M.F. Ashley Montagu, a British–U.S. anthropologist, does, as "original sin revisited," and deplore the tendency to neglect authoritative studies in favour of simplistic popularization. In *Man and Aggression* (1968), he writes:

Montagu's
view

> While the findings of these disciplines [anthropology and the behavioral sciences] are wholly opposed to the deeply entrenched view that man is an innately aggressive creature, most people tend to dismiss these findings out of hand or ridicule them as a rather eccentric idealistic heterodoxy, which do not deserve to become generally known. In preference to examining the scientific findings they choose to cast their lot with such "authorities" as William Golding who, in his novel *Lord of the Flies,* offers a colorful account of the allegedly innate nastiness of human nature, and Robert Ardrey who, in *African Genesis* and more recently in *The Territorial Imperative,* similarly seeks to show that man is an innately aggressive creature....
>
> ... when through the distorting glass of his prejudgments he looks at a tool it becomes not simply a scraper but a weapon, a knife becomes a dagger, and even a large canine tooth becomes "the natural dagger that is the hallmark of all hunting animals," while in "the armed hunting primate" it becomes "a redundant instrument." "With the advent of the lethal weapon natural selection turned from the armament of the jaw to the armament of the hand." But the teeth are no more an armament than is the hand, and it is entirely to beg the question to call them so. Virtually all the members of the order of primates, other than man, have large canine teeth, and these animals, with the exception of the baboons, are predominantly vegetarians, ... that such teeth may, on occasion, serve a protective purpose is entirely secondary to their main function, which is to rip and shred the hard outer coverings of plant foods.

Further responses to Ardrey's and Lorenz' thesis are the interpretations of field studies of primate groups, such as those on the gorilla, chimpanzee, and orangutan. These researches suggest that the majority of such groups are singularly free of belligerence. According to Montagu,

> The myth of the ferocity of "wild animals" constitutes one of Western man's supreme rationalizations, for it not only has served to "explain" to him the origins of his own aggressiveness, but also to relieve him of the responsibility for it—for since it is "innate," derived from his early apelike ancestors, he can hardly, so he rationalizes, be blamed for it! And some have gone so far as to add that nothing can be done about it, and that therefore wars and juvenile delinquents, as Mr. Ardrey among others tells us, will always be with us! From one not-so-minor error to another Mr. Ardrey sweeps on to the grand fallacy.

The matter remains moot; but there appears to be a growing consensus that, given a certain genetic constitution—and within the bounds of that endowment—whatever man is, he learns to be, especially in respect to values, morality, and customs. Baser appetitive needs, however, may have a genetic component that is greater than an environmental one.

New understanding of environmental factors and the consequences of man's actions with respect to them has made it clear that man has acquired responsibilities that he did not recognize before. It has become increasingly accepted that standards and values with respect to the environment must be established; this is perhaps the most dramatic case in which recent biological knowledge has generated a crisis of a moral kind. The classic work *Science and Survival* (1966) by a biologist, Barry Commoner, is particularly noteworthy in connecting theoretical and philosophical issues about reductionism and holism to practical matters of environmental understanding and problem solving.

The metaphysical issue of man's place in nature is now being construed as one that requires that man make value decisions, assign responsibilities, and plan for the future of his planet. Environmental problems have become intertwined with problems of social planning, racial tension, transportation and housing crises, genetic engineering, and a host of other current concerns.

Evolutionary ethics. The question of whether nature provides guides to the actions of humankind has held a fascination for many biologists. Those who call themselves evolutionary ethicists say that it does. The defenders of evolutionary ethics contend that external moral standards exist in the facts and process of evolution.

Toward the end of the 19th century, Herbert Spencer, in England, and others advanced a series of principles that came to be called Social Darwinism. It espoused such ideas as the inevitability of progress, survival of the fittest, and the struggle for existence, expressions that have become bywords although they have since been discredited in their original sense, as applied to social phenomena. Social Darwinism, as C.H. Waddington, a biologist, explains in his book *The Ethical Animal* (1960, has been superseded by

> . . . the more recent phase of evolutionary ethical thought beginning in the early 1940s, [which] comprises a number of rather different methods of approach. At one extreme we have discussions framed in terms of extremely wide scope, which treat of evolution not only in the animal world but throughout the cosmos, and attempt to relate such broad concepts to man's religious and spiritual life. The pre-eminent example of this tendency in recent years is Teilhard de Chardin, but a rather similar approach can be found in the works of several biologists, such as Conklin, Holmes, and Huxley. The opposite tendency, which of course is also found expressed to various extents in these authors, particularly in Julian Huxley, is the attempt to demonstrate, in a logically coherent argument, a real connection between evolutionary processes and man's ethical feelings.

Some biologists continue to insist, therefore, that biological facts can provide a yardstick by which to measure the morality of a given course of action. Julian Huxley, for one, has long claimed that moral principles can be found in nature and in the evolutionary process in particular:

> When we look at evolution as a whole, we find, among the many directions which it has taken, one which is characterized by introducing the evolving world-stuff to progressively higher levels of organization and so to new possibilities of being, action, and experience. This direction has culminated in the attainment of a state where the world-stuff (now moulded into human shape) finds that it experiences some of the new possibilities as having value in or for themselves; and further that among these it assigns higher and lower degrees of value, the higher values being those which are more intrinsically or more permanently satisfying, or involve a greater degree of perfection.

Huxley further asserts that, although the Golden Rule, the policy of action based on sympathy—doing as one would be done to by others—may be an immediate good, it ultimately leads to the suppression of those qualities most needed for survival and the continuation of a species. Rather, he argues:

> The facts of nature, as demonstrated in evolution, give us assurance that knowledge, love, beauty, selfless morality, and firm purpose are ethically good. . . . In the broadest possible terms evolutionary ethics must be based on a combination of a few main principles: that it is right to realize ever new possibilities in evolution, notably those which are valued for their own sake; that it is right both to respect human individuality and to encourage its fullest development; that it is right to construct a mechanism for further social evolution which shall satisfy these prior conditions as fully, efficiently, and as rapidly as possible.

Social Darwinism

Evolution and morality

Simpson, however, contends, in the article "Biological Sciences," in *The Great Ideas Today* (1965):

> The facts and the processes of evolution are neither ethical nor unethical. The questions of good or bad are simply irrelevant to this field, with the important reservation that evolution has produced a species, *Homo sapiens,* concerned with ethics. Denial of man's naturalistic origin and animal nature is flatly false, and any ethic based on such denial is invalid. Evolution controverts primitive creation myths, but it is consistent with higher values in the Judeo-Christian tradition and those in most now-current religions and philosophical systems. One need only think of the brotherhood of mankind—a biological fact, not only an ethical idea.

> Beyond such considerations as those, efforts to combine science and religion may be noble in intention but usually end up distorting or stultifying both. One of the most striking examples at present is the cult, as it may fairly be called, of Pierre Teilhard de Chardin. He preaches—necessarily posthumously, for the Roman Catholic Church suppressed his views during his life—a mystical Christianity ostensibly derived from evolutionary principles. But since the mysticism is primary, the evolutionary principles are distorted and downright falsified for seeming coherence with the nonscientific, nonnaturalistic premises. In turn, the mystical views advanced as having that false basis are thereby vitiated. The result (in my opinion) has been a disservice to true relgion and to true science.

> At the same time, no one can deny the purity of Father Teilhard's intentions or the correctness of his view that evolution and religious feeling should be considered congruent aspects of the nature of man. It is almost as irrational to deny evolution as to deny gravity. The management of life and the goals of aspiration, to be sane, must take account of all such truths of nature. They need not thereby become brutal or earthbound.

> (J.R.Mn./R.C.Y.)

Philosophy of history

The term history may be employed in two quite different senses: it may mean (1) the events and actions that together make up the human past, or (2) the accounts given of that past and the modes of investigation whereby they are arrived at or constructed. When used in the first sense, the word refers to what as a matter of fact happened, while when used in the second sense it refers to the study and description of those happenings. The notion of philosophical reflection upon history and its nature is consequently open to more than one interpretation, and contemporary writers have found it convenient to regard it as covering two main types of undertaking. On the one hand, they have distinguished philosophy of history in the traditional or classical sense; this is conceived to be a first-order enquiry, its subject matter being the historical process as a whole and its aim being, broadly speaking, one of providing an overall elucidation or explanation of the course and direction taken by that process. On the other hand, they have distinguished philosophy of history considered as a second-order enquiry; here attention is not focussed upon the actual sequence of events themselves but, instead, upon the procedures and categories used by practicing historians in approaching and comprehending their material. The former, often alluded to as speculative philosophy of history, has had a long and varied career; the latter, which is generally known as critical or analytical philosophy of history, has only risen to prominence during the 20th century.

SPECULATIVE THEORIES

The idea of an order or design in history. The belief that it is possible to discern in the course of human history some general scheme or design, some all-encompassing purpose or pattern, is very old and has found expression in various forms at different times and places. The reasons for its persistence and vitality are numerous, but two very general considerations may be identified as having exercised a fairly continuous influence. First, it has often been supposed that, if the belief in an overall pattern is abandoned, one is obliged to acquiesce in the view that the historical process consists of no more than an arbitrary succession of occurrences, a mere agglomeration or patchwork of random incidents and episodes. But such a view (it has been contended) cannot be seriously entertained, if only because it conflicts with the basic demand for system

The necessity for a meaningful view of history

and order that underlies and governs all rational enquiry, all meaningful thought about the world. Second, it has frequently been felt that to refuse to allow that history is finally intelligible in the required manner implies a skepticism concerning the value of human life and existence that constitutes an affront to the dignity of human nature. The 18th-century German philosopher Immanuel Kant, for example, spoke of the "repugnance" that is inevitably experienced if the past is viewed

> as if the whole web of human history were woven out of folly and childish vanity and the frenzy of destruction, so that one hardly knows in the end what idea to form of our race, for all that it is so proud of its prerogatives.

In more recent times, a comparable attitude is discernible beneath Arnold Toynbee's uncompromising repudiation of the idea that history is "a chaotic, disorderly, fortuitous flux, in which there is no pattern or rhythm of any kind to be discerned." Thus, it has been the object of a long line of theorists, representative of widely divergent outlooks, to demonstrate that such pessimism is unjustified and that the historical process can, when appropriately viewed, be seen to be both rationally and morally acceptable.

Theological origins. Western speculation concerning the meaning of history derived in the first instance chiefly from theological sources. The belief that history conforms to a linear development in which the influence of providential wisdom can be discerned, rather than to a recurrent cyclical movement of the kind implicit in much Greco-Roman thought, was already becoming prevalent early in the Christian Era. Traces of this approach are to be found *Augustine* in the conception of the past set forth by St. Augustine in *and* his *City of God* and elsewhere; it is, for example, compared *Bossuet* on one occasion to "the great melody of some ineffable composer," its parts being "the dispensations suitable to each different period." Yet the cautious subtlety of Augustine's suggestions and the crucial distinction he drew between sacred and secular history make it important not to confuse his carefully qualified doctrines with the cruder positions advanced by some of his self-proclaimed successors. This applies, *par excellence,* to the work of the most renowned and thorough of these, Jacques-Bénigne Bossuet. Written 1,250 years after Augustine's death, Bossuet's *Discours sur l'histoire universelle* (1681; "Discourse on Universal History") is imbued throughout with a naïve confidence that the entire course of history owes its pervasive character to the contrivance of a "higher wisdom." In the eyes of Bossuet, to grasp and understand the great procession of empires and religions was "to comprehend in one's mind all that is great in human affairs and have the key to the history of the universe." For the rise and fall of states and creeds depended in the end upon the secret orders of Providence, the latter being the source of that manifest historical justice and retribution to which, on nearly every page, the annals of the past bore clear and unmistakable witness. Bossuet's vast survey was, in fact, the last major contribution to its genre. Though it made a considerable impression when it was first published, it appeared just before the discoveries of Sir Isaac Newton effected a massive transformation of the European outlook, and the book's impact was short-lived. Thus, the development of historical speculation in the 18th century was generally marked by a tendency to reject theological and providential interpretations in favour of an approach more closely aligned, in method and aim, to that adopted by natural scientists in their investigations of the physical world.

Secular approaches: the Enlightenment and beyond. For many Enlightenment and post-Enlightenment thinkers, the project of establishing a science of history and society, comprising hypotheses and laws of an explanatory power analogous to that attained by theories in the physical sciences, acquired an almost obsessive importance. The age of religious and metaphysical conjectures concerning the destiny of human affairs had, in their opinion, come to a close. The task that now presented itself was one of constructing, upon the basis of hard observable facts, interpretations that would not only rescue the human studies from ignorance, uncertainty, and primitive superstition but also put into men's hands an instrument for predicting and controlling their fate. Thus, the idea of creating a universally valid social science, capable of accounting for the phenomena of history in terms of causal principles comparable to those employed in the natural sphere, came to be linked with the promotion of reformist and revolutionary ideals. Men such as Condillac and Condorcet in the 18th century and Henri de Saint-Simon, Auguste Comte, John Stuart Mill, and Henry Thomas Buckle in the 19th century all believed that it was feasible to apply scientific procedures to the study of human development. But equally—though in widely different ways—they were men deeply concerned with practical objects and committed to changing existing institutions and ways of life. To these men, theory was complementary to practice; knowledge was power.

Yet even in the 19th century, when speculation of this *19th-* type was at its height, there were informed skeptics— *century* Joseph de Maistre and Arthur Schopenhauer, for example, *skepticism* and later the great Swiss historian Jacob Burckhardt—who challenged the optimistic and rationalistic presuppositions on which it was founded. It was pointed out that notions such as that of the perfectibility of man or of the existence of some foreseeable goal toward which the course of events was inexorably leading were not empirically established truths but mere articles of faith; in subscribing to them, historical theorists often appeared to be tacitly importing into their allegedly scientific interpretations teleological conceptions of a kind that it had been their declared intention to banish forever from social enquiry. These objections have been repeated and amplified by 20th-century critics such as Karl Popper, who have also maintained that the theorists in question were, in any case, working with an unacceptably crude notion of scientific reasoning and that their high-sounding generalities conspicuously failed to measure up to the requisite standards of conceptual precision and observational testability.

Although such strictures have considerable force, they should not obscure the significant contribution that had been made toward extending human knowledge and understanding. The tendency, for example, to insist upon the relevance of scientific modes of procedure to the areas of historical and social investigation at least achieved the salutary effect of throwing into relief the inadequacy of previous work in these domains; moreover, it indirectly brought to the fore the entire question of the status of history as a legitimate form of thought. For, if history should prove resistant to attempts to assimilate it to other accredited branches of enquiry, it would be necessary to show why this was so and to exhibit those features of historical thinking that lent it its distinctive and irreducible character.

The new science: Vico and Herder. Among the 18th-century theorists, two writers can indeed be picked out who—while remaining firmly within the speculative tradition—at the same time possessed sufficient genius and prescience to realize that the solution to the problem of establishing history as a reputable discipline might be found by pursuing a course different from one modelled upon the methodology of the natural sciences. Partly because of the obscure and scholastic manner in which it was written, Giambattista Vico's *Scienza nuova* (3rd ed. 1744; "New Science") was a work whose importance remained for a long time wholly unrecognized, and it is only fairly recently that its significance and originality have been fully appreciated.

Central to the book is the contention that the kind of *Vico's* knowledge that men can achieve of their own actions, *notion* creations, and institutions is of a radically different type *of unique* from the knowledge that is acquired by the observation *historical* and investigation of the nonhuman or natural world; *knowledge* knowledge of the former variety is, moreover, held to be in principle superior to that of the latter. For, in Vico's opinion, in order truly to know something it is necessary in some sense to have made it: it followed that, whereas the reality studied by the physical scientist is the creation of God and therefore only properly known by God, the "world of nations" that forms the subject matter of history is the creation of men and is therefore something that men can "hope to know." Thus, Vico was led to stress the differences rather than the analogies between historical and other forms of enquiry; in particular, he emphasized the need for the historian to enter imaginatively into the spirit of past ages, re-creating the outlooks and attitudes that informed them as opposed to seeking to impose upon them inappropriate or falsifying interpretations—"pseudomyths"—that derived from the cultural ethos of his own time. Vico propounded a cyclical theory of human history, according to which "nations" or societies pass through determinate stages, and he combined this with the idea that a providential principle is in some manner immanent within the various forms of life that men construct. He employed such conceptions, however, in a fashion that underlined man's nature as a historical being, whose powers and capacities do not conform to a fixed or static pattern but are necessarily subject to change and development in the course of time.

In a similar vein, the German writer Johann Gottfried von Herder, in his influential *Ideen zur Philosophie der Geschichte der Menschheit* (4 vol., 1784–91; Eng. trans., *Outlines of a Philosophy of the History of Man,* 1800), implied that it was vital to view human actions and achievements from a standpoint that took proper account of "time, place and national character"—in other words, cultural milieu and the inevitable limits imposed by historical situation and circumstance. In its general direction, Herder's historical thought reflected the Enlightenment preconceptions of man as a progressive being. Herder's chief importance lies, however, in his insistence upon the misconceptions involved in treating the products of past thought and action as if they were the manifestations of an unchanging human consciousness and as if they could be explained by reference to abstract laws eternally valid for men everywhere. According to Herder, such an approach failed to recognize the complex influences that act upon human beings as members of particular historical societies; each of these societies possessed its unique life-style, subtly but inescapably determining the mentalities of those born within its confines in a manner that rendered futile all attempts to reduce human propensities and needs to the terms of some simple set of abstract formulas.

Many of Vico's and Herder's ideas appear familiar today, but it is easy to forget that the emergence of what has come to be known as the "historical sense" is a comparatively recent phenomenon, one that represents a genuine revolution in European thought. It is largely because of this revolution that social and political theories of the kind elaborated by men such as Thomas Hobbes and Benedict de Spinoza in the 17th century seem oddly artificial to 20th-century eyes, so remote are the categories in which they sought to explain human life and behaviour from those that have subsequently found acceptance.

History as a process of dialectical change: Hegel and Marx. The suggestion that there is something essentially mistaken in the endeavour to comprehend the course of history "naturalistically" and within an explanatory framework deriving from scientific paradigms was powerfully reinforced by conceptions stemming from the development of German Idealism in the 19th century. Hegel's "philosophy of the spirit" made its appearance upon the intellectual scene contemporaneously with Saint-Simonian and Comtean Positivism, rivalling the latter in scope and influence and bringing with it its own highly distinctive theory of historical evolution and change. Hegel's stress upon the "organic" nature of social wholes and the incommensurability of different historical epochs owed evident debts to Herderian ideas, but he set these within an overall view that pictured the movement of history in dynamic terms. Regularities and recurrences of the sort that typically manifest themselves in the realm of nature are foreign, Hegel maintained, to the sphere of mind or spirit, which was characterized instead as involving a continual drive toward self-transcendence and the removal of limitations upon thought and action. Man was not to be conceived according to the mechanistic models of 18th-century Materialism; essentially he was free, but the freedom that constituted his nature could only achieve fulfillment through a process of struggle and of overcoming obstacles that were themselves the expression of his own

activity; it was in this sense that Hegel claimed that spirit was "at war with itself"—"it has to overcome itself as its most formidable obstacle" (*Lectures on the Philosophy of History*). In concrete terms, this meant that historical advance did not proceed through a series of smooth transitions. Once the potentialities of a particular society had been realized in the creation of a certain mode of life, its historical role was over; its members became aware of its inadequacies, and the laws and institutions they had previously accepted unquestioningly were now experienced as fetters, inhibiting further development and no longer reflecting their deepest aspirations. Thus, each phase of the historical process could be said to contain the seeds of its own destruction and to "negate" itself; the consequence was the emergence of a fresh society, representing another stage in a progression whose final outcome was the formation of a rationally ordered community with which each citizen could consciously identify himself and in which there would therefore no longer exist any sense of alienation or constraint. Somewhat curiously, the type of community Hegel envisaged as exemplifying this satisfactory state of affairs bore a striking resemblance to the Prussian monarchy of his own time.

The notion that history conforms to a "dialectical" pattern, according to which contradictions generated at one level are overcome or transcended at the next, was incorporated—though in a radically new form—in the theory of social change propounded by Karl Marx. Like Hegel, Marx adopted a "directional" view of history; but, whereas Hegel had tended to exhibit it as representing the unfolding in time of an inner spiritual principle, Marx looked elsewhere for the ultimate determinants of its course and character. Man, according to Marx, was a creative being, situated in a material world that stood before him as an objective reality and provided the field for his activities; this primitive truth, which had been obscured by Hegel's mystifying abstractions, afforded the key to a proper understanding of history as a process finally governed by the changing methods whereby men sought to derive from the natural environment the means of their subsistence and the satisfaction of their evolving wants and needs. The productive relations in which men stood to one another, resulting in such phenomena as the division of labour and the appearance of economically determined classes, were the factors fundamental to historical movement. What he termed the superstructure of society—which covered such things as political institutions and systems of law, ethics, and religion—was in the last analysis dependent upon the shape taken by the "material production" and the "material intercourse" of human beings in their struggle to master nature: "it is not the consciousness of men that determines their being, but, on the contrary, their social being that determines their consciousness." Hence, the inner dynamic of history was held to lie in conflicts arising from changes in the means of production and occurring when modes of social organization and control, adapted to the development of the productive forces at one stage, became impediments to it at another; they were to be resolved, furthermore, not by abstract thought but by concrete action. Thus, the Hegelian conception of spirit as involved in a relentless struggle with itself and with what it had created underwent a revolutionary transformation, explosive in its implications.

Marx's interpretation of the historical process, with its stress upon necessity and the operation of ineluctable laws, has often been portrayed by its proponents as being scientific in character. It has, however, more than one aspect, and it would be an error to identify its underlying methodology with that associated with Comtean Positivism. Generally speaking, the basic categories within which it was framed derived from a theory of human nature that had more in common with the postulates of German romantic thought than with those of British and French Empiricism: to this extent, the logical structure Marx sought to impose upon the data of history belonged to a tradition that stressed the differences rather than the resemblances between the human and the natural world.

Twentieth-century systems. The tendency to detect in history the presence of large-scale patterns and comprehensive uniformities continued into the 20th century in the work of a number of writers, most notably Oswald Spengler and Arnold Toynbee. Spengler's *Decline of the West* (originally published in German, 1918–22), wherein the history of mankind was presented in terms of biologically conceived cultures whose careers conformed to a predetermined course of growth and decay, was widely acclaimed during the years of disillusionment that followed World War I; and a somewhat similar reception was given to Toynbee's massive *A Study of History* (1934–61) immediately after World War II. Toynbee, like Spengler, undertook a comparative study of civilizations, thereby repudiating attempts to treat the past as if it exhibited a single linear progression: at the same time, he diverged from Spengler in suggesting that current Western society might not after all be necessarily doomed to extinction and in tempering a predominantly deterministic mode of thought with reservations that allowed a place for human free will and the possibility of divine intervention. Yet, as some of his critics were quick to point out, such qualifications were not easy to reconcile with his original insistence upon the need to adopt "a scientific approach to human affairs"; nor was it clear that his own use of inductive methods to establish the laws governing the development of civilizations was above logical suspicion or reproach. Toynbee's experiment might have been impressive as an individual achievement; nevertheless, with the multiplication of objections and in a theoretical climate that had become skeptical of speculative system-building of any kind, the very feasibility of engaging upon a project of the type he had undertaken came to be seriously questioned. It was felt increasingly that philosophy of history in the traditional sense—resting largely upon uncriticized assumptions concerning the nature of historical enquiry and its relations with other disciplines—had reached something of an impasse; if history was still to be treated as a proper subject for philosophical examination, it must be along lines quite different from those previously pursued.

Toynbee's system

ANALYTICAL PROBLEMS

The concept of history. The task of trying to delineate the specific character of historical knowledge and understanding, rather than of seeking to construct vast speculative schemes in the earlier manner, first began to attract the attention of philosophers toward the end of the 19th century. To such thinkers as Wilhelm Dilthey and Benedetto Croce, the claim that, in the absence of some all-embracing system of a teleological or quasi-scientific kind, the course of history could be regarded as constituting nothing better than a meaningless chaos appeared to be totally unacceptable. History is intelligible, they believed, in the sense that historians make it so; moreover, this was the only type of intelligibility it was either necessary or legitimate to demand. What could reasonably be looked for was a clearer and deeper insight into the conditions that render historical knowledge possible, an elucidation of the presuppositions upon which historical enquiry is founded and of the principles according to which it proceeds. It was with such an investigation in mind that R.G. Collingwood, a British philosopher who owed much to Crocean ideas, wrote in his *Autobiography* that "the chief business of twentieth-century philosophy is to reckon with twentieth-century history." By contending that the philosopher should eschew the grandiose ambition of providing a synoptic vision of the entire historical process and concern himself, instead, with the articulation and justification of existing historical procedures, Collingwood and his continental precursors made, in effect, a crucial contribution toward setting philosophy of history on a new path. Their proposals were, moreover, given additional impetus by the widespread acceptance of analytical approaches in other branches of philosophy. In consequence, contemporary thinkers have tended to focus attention upon the explication of concepts and terms that perform a key role in historical thought and description as these are actually carried on: among other things, they have been led into discussing the ways in which historians typically divide up and classify the past, the manner in which they argue for and substantiate their interpretations,

The work of R.G. Collingwood

and the logical structure of the explanations they are accustomed to offer.

Explanation and understanding. Both Croce and Collingwood, in their criticisms of earlier theorists, were especially anxious to expose what they believed to be recurrent and fundamental misconceptions regarding the method and subject matter of history: central to these was the assumption that historical occurrences could be subsumed under, and explained in terms of, universal laws of the sort that played an essential part in scientific interpretations of inanimate nature. This assumption was, in their opinion, a gross error. As Collingwood put it, the moment had arrived for history to be released from "its state of pupilage to natural science." With this in mind, he went on to develop an account of historical understanding according to which the historian explains events by exhibiting them as the expressions of past thinking on the part of self-conscious purposive agents—thinking that the historian must imaginatively reconstruct or re-enact in his own mind—rather than by showing the events to be instances of general uniformities or regularities that are established by induction. In propounding this view—which Croce, though he formulated it less clearly and precisely, basically shared—Collingwood set in motion a controversy concerning knowledge and explanation in history that has been central to much subsequent discussion. As Collingwood himself was fully aware, a position similar to his own had been originally advanced (though in a very different context) by Vico; and it is indeed noteworthy that the general division, evident at the speculative level, between those who wished to comprehend historical phenomena in ways suggested by the physical sciences and those who, by contrast, argued for an altogether distinct pattern of interpretation has tended, in recent times, to re-emerge at the level of methodological and conceptual analysis.

Thus, on one side of the dispute, there have ranged philosophers who have taken their stand upon what has been called "the unity of science" and who have insisted that the categories and procedures appropriate to the human studies do not enjoy a unique or privileged status that somehow sets them apart from those characteristic of systematic empirical enquiry in other domains. In a classical 18th-century discussion, David Hume had argued that, if two events were said to be causally related, this could only be in the sense that they instantiated certain regularities of succession that had been repeatedly observed to hold between such events in the past: to presume otherwise was to fall back upon an unacceptable belief in "intuitable" connections that had no warrant either in reason or experience. This doctrine may be said to have been given more rigorous expression among Positivist philosophers of the present century in the shape of what is variously known as the "deductive-nomological" or "covering law" theory of explanation; as originally applied to history by Carl Hempel, it amounted to the claim that explaining a given historical occurrence in terms of some other event or set of events necessarily involves an appeal, which need not be more than tacit, to laws or general propositions correlating events of the type to be explained with those of the kind cited as its causes or conditions. Although the proposed analysis has received a variety of different formulations, each designed to meet specific objections that have been raised against it, its adherents have not wavered from the conviction that some such account must be in principle correct if explanations in history are to be open to rational assessment of the sort properly demanded within any legitimate branch of empirical investigation. It is for this reason, together with others, that they have been strongly opposed to *Verstehen*, or "empathy," theories of historical knowledge, regarding the contention that historical understanding presupposes an allegedly direct identification with the mental processes of past human agents as representing at best a heuristic recommendation of doubtful utility, at worst an obscurantist doctrine that transparently fails to provide an objective criterion whereby divergent historical interpretations can be evaluated.

Resistance to the Positivist approach has come from more than one direction. To a number of practicing historians, for instance, the account offered has appeared implausible

The unity of science approach

The criterion of appropriateness

inasmuch as it overlooks the "irreducible particularity" of historical occurrences and because it postulates an unjustifiably high degree of reliance upon the presence of discernible uniformities in the sphere of human affairs. So far as philosophers are concerned, dissatisfaction has been voiced both by those to whom the Croce-Collingwood notion of historical thinking as the "re-enactment of past experience" has seemed to contain an important element of truth and also by those followers of Ludwig Wittgenstein who have been impressed by the skepticism concerning the adequacy of scientific models apparent in his later discussions of mental concepts. A leading representative of the former group, W.H. Dray, not only constructed a series of arguments to demonstrate the deficiencies of the covering-law theory but further proposed an alternative conception of "rational explanation," which—it was suggested—fitted many of the familiar ways whereby historians seek to render the past intelligible. Thus, Dray has maintained that the function of much historical explanation consists of showing the actions of historical persons to have been "appropriate" when viewed within the perspective of their specific beliefs, aims, and principles: it was this consideration, he claims, that was uppermost in the minds of theorists who were concerned to stress the part played by imaginative or empathetic understanding in historical reconstruction, their point being primarily a "logical" one and not necessarily carrying any of the dubious epistemological implications attacked by Positivist critics. From a different standpoint, Anglo-U.S. writers influenced by Wittgenstein have challenged the entire assumption that explanations involving the notions of human intention and purpose are susceptible to a Humean pattern of causal analysis; they have also (for example, in the work of Peter Winch) stressed the extent to which historical descriptions of past behaviour require to be framed in terms the agents themselves would have recognized as giving meaning to their activities, terms embodying references to ideas and conventions that defined the social reality in which they participated.

Objectivity and evaluation. Fundamental issues concerning the status of historical enquiry of the kind just mentioned have arisen in another crucial area of discussion, centring upon the question of whether—and, if so, in what sense—history can be said to be an objective discipline. Some modern philosophers have inclined to the view that the entirely general problem of whether history is objective cannot sensibly be raised; legitimate questions regarding objectivity are only in place where some particular piece of historical work is under consideration, and in that case there are accepted standards available, involving such matters as documentation and accuracy, by which they can be settled. To others, however, things have not seemed so clear, and they have drawn attention to the doubts that may be felt when history is compared with different branches of investigation, such as chemistry or biology: by contrast with such enquiries, the historian's procedure, including the manner in which he conceptualizes his data and the principles of argument he employs, may appear to be governed by subjective or culturally determined predilections that are essentially contestable and, therefore, out of place in a supposedly reputable form of knowledge. One topic that has been recurrently examined in this connection has been the role of evaluation (specifically, of moral evaluation) in historical writing—a subject, incidentally, about which historians themselves are apt to exhibit a certain uneasiness. Nevertheless, recommendations to the effect that value judgment can and should be totally excluded from history and, indeed, from the social studies as a whole have met with a mixed philosophical reception. Among Positivists and Logical Empiricists, traditionally skeptical of the rationality of value judgments and anxious in any case to reduce the differences between the human and the natural sciences, they have found some measure of support. But that has been by no means a general response. Thus, objectors have pointed out that the language the historian customarily uses, adapted as it is to the assessment and appraisal of human motives and characteristics, makes some degree of evaluation unavoidable; they argue that, even if the possibility of a drastically

The question of value judgments

revised historical vocabulary allows the ideal of a *wertfrei,* or objective history, to be theoretically conceivable, such an ideal can scarcely be seriously entertained as a realizable practical goal. These considerations have been reinforced by the further point that every historian, insofar as he has to select from the mass of material confronting him, is necessarily committed to forming judgments ascribing relative importance and significance; such attributions cannot, however, be simply read off from the facts and must, rather, be said to depend upon the prior acceptance of certain critical standards. To this extent, then, one is required to acknowledge the presence in historical writing of an ineliminable evaluative component, which is liable to obtrude itself into even so "objective" a field as that of causal analysis: it is notorious that disputes between historians as to the "true" causes of occurrences such as wars or revolutions often appear to resist resolution at a purely empirical level, and it has been persuasively maintained by some philosophers that the basic grounds for such disputes may often be traced back to one historian's adherence to a moral or political standpoint not shared by his opponent.

Conclusions. Although the topics discussed above have occupied a central position in 20th-century critical discussion, they represent only a sample of the issues with which analytical philosophers of history have been concerned: other problems that have attracted attention have related to the freedom and responsibility of historical agents, the nature and description of historical events, and the role of narrative in history. Here, as elsewhere, the approach adopted has often produced results of considerable interest, throwing a revealing light on features of historical enquiry that are easily missed or ignored by theorists in the grip of some powerful dogma or ideology. Even so, it has perhaps been accompanied by a too ready acquiescence in the view that history is "in order as it is," the philosopher's function being confined to offering a purely descriptive elucidation of typical modes of historical thought and argument. In accepting this conception of their role, analytical philosophers of history have no doubt been partly, and understandably, influenced by a desire to avoid emulating the heady ambitions of their speculative predecessors. Yet, normative questions regarding the validity or adequacy of established procedures within any domain can always be legitimately raised; in the case of history, there seems to be no compelling reason to assume that such problems necessarily lie beyond the scope of philosophical criticism and appraisal. (P.L.G.)

Philosophy of religion

In addition to treating what is commonly called the philosophy of religion, this section considers a wide spectrum of situations, experiences, and issues recognized as "religious" and endeavours to appraise the characteristic approaches and attitudes not only of the adherents of particular religions but also of those who stand outside any particular religion, whether as sympathizers or caustic critics. Outside the scope of this section, however, are questions relating to the study of religions and its methodology or questions relating to the types of argument by which one interpretation of a religious claim is preferred to another (see also RELIGIONS, THE STUDY AND CLASSIFICATION OF).

RELIGION AS A FACT IN HUMAN EXPERIENCE, CULTURE, AND HISTORY

Evidences of religious attitudes and loyalties exist in every sector of human life—in human experience in general; in "culture," the complex interweaving of attitudes, concerns, and views; and in history, the record of social and personal behaviour.

The findings of psychology. Religion incorporates certain characteristic feelings and emotions such as wonder, awe, and reverence. The religious person tends to show a concern for values, moral and aesthetic, and to seek appropriate action to embody these values. He is likely to characterize behaviour not only as good or evil but also as holy or unholy and people as not only virtuous or unvirtuous but also as godly or ungodly.

Characteristic feelings and emotions of religion

As a feature of human existence, religious life can be studied, for example, in terms of psychology, sociology, and history. Among the first books in the psychology of religion were two by Jonathan Edwards, an 18th-century American theologian: *A Faithful Narrative of the Surprising Work of God* (1737) and *A Treatise Concerning Religious Affections* (1746). About a century later, during a period of religious "revivals," interest developed concerning the age at which conversions most often took place—the period of adolescence. Reflections on such facts, and in this sense the psychology of religion, only came, however, with the works of two American psychologists: Edwin Diller Starbuck's *Psychology of Religion* (1889) and the classical treatment by William James's *Varieties of Religious Experience* (1902). Generally, the psychology of religion has shown that though religion for some is a crisis experience, for others it is a natural growth.

As psychology became more analytical it became more interested in the abnormal, in neuroses and dreams, in the techniques of hypnosis, and in the kinds of experience induced by drugs. When Freud spoke of religion as an illusion, he maintained that it is a fantasy structure from which a man must be set free if he is to grow to maturity; and in his treatment of the unconscious he moved toward atheism. The study of the unconscious by the Swiss psychiatrist Jung, however, suggested that dominant archetypes (implying innate tendencies to form symbolic images) are supplied by a racial unconscious, thus providing a psychological approach to belief in God.

Classifications of individuals

In classifying individuals into different types, psychology has distinguished between religious people who are: "extrovert" or "introvert" (Jung), "healthy minded" or "sick" (William James), and "objective" or "subjective" worshippers (J.B. Pratt). There is always the danger, however, that psychological distinctions may beg too many philosophical questions.

One of the most widely accepted studies of religious experience in regard to feelings was written by the modern German Protestant theologian Rudolf Otto. In his *Idea of the Holy,* Otto analyzed what is distinctively religious in terms of the unique concept of the "numinous"; *i.e.,* something both awesome and appealing, both fearful and attractive.

Psychology, however, is concerned not only with individuals but also with what is known about group behaviour, which can also be of importance in any study of the Christian Church or other religious institutions regarded as communities of religious people. The authority of a religious leader, like that of all leaders, is derived from his symbolic character and the extent to which the leader and his followers share a common ideal.

The findings of sociology. The ideas and images of a religion are much influenced by the social culture in which it emerges. Some of the oldest social institutions and practices, such as those concerning birth and death, marriage and the family, and art and music, have developed in a religious context. Religion has often been a driving force in the reform of social abuses, but also it has been associated with reaction and oppression. More recently, the sociology of religion—influenced by contemporary sociology—has been concerned with making use of sociological criteria and of demographical and statistical studies in planning the church's mission and appraising its significance.

The findings of the history of religions. Conclusions in the history of religions have been largely determined by the particular ideas of man or history with which the study was approached. Some scholars have supposed that at the dawn of human existence there was a belief in a single god and that only later there occurred a development into a belief in many gods as well as animism (a belief in souls or spirits in man and other aspects of nature). Other scholars have supposed an evolutionary development of religion, which only reached monotheism—considered to be the highest form of religious belief—after a long period of purification. The two approaches sponsor, respectively, two contrasting myths about primitive man. According to the one, there was once a golden age of innocence and harmony; according to the other, the life of the earliest man was hasty, brutish, and short.

Granted the ubiquity of religion and its diversity, historians have found no universal essence expressible in terms of common beliefs. What is probably common to all religions is nothing more than the claim that reality is not restricted solely to what is yielded by sense experience itself.

The role of religion in culture. Religion has had a strong but ambiguous cultural influence. The thought that a man depended for his life and existence on a power not his own has encouraged some persons to be lazy, as it has inspired others to greater effort. A conviction about another world has led some religious people to disvalue human life; it has led others to view human life as having the significance of a state of probation. It has been plausibly argued by some (*e.g.,* the German sociologist Max Weber) that Protestantism provided a seedbed for modern capitalism; Catholicism, according to others, easily accommodates a Socialist point of view.

The ambiguity of religion's influence on culture

Because a religious view is generally associated with a conviction about the inadequacy of "things seen and temporal," religion as a cultural influence usually shows itself dissatisfied with things as they are. Often, however, when confronted with novelty, religion has tended to be conservative. Thus, religion has alternately opposed or fostered social and cultural development.

VIEWS WITH TRANSCENDENT REFERENCES

A situation is regarded as religious when through its spatiotemporal features that can be termed depth or another dimension can be disclosed objectively. In this sense, there cannot be such a thing as a religion that is nontranscendent. On the subjective side, there will be a matching self-disclosure, a "coming to one's self" that occurs as a response to a vision of the eternal in and through the temporal.

Relation to an ultimate power or being, to values, or to ideals. Different religious approaches can be distinguished by the different interpretations they give of what is objectively disclosed, of what in this sense is the transcendent. In primitive religion, for example, the transcendent is always interpreted in terms of an ultimate power or activity expressing itself, whether singly (monism) or with multiplicity (pluralism), through the objects and events of the world.

Animism, totemism, and interpretations of cosmic power

Animism views the world as having life, power, and feeling as do men. A monistic view of the universe is conceptually akin to the view according to which people or objects exert the peculiar influence they do and have the strange significance they possess because of mana—a power or force somewhat similar to the scientific concept of energy—that they embody. Animism becomes more diversified and pluralistic when it becomes spiritism, which locates the cosmic life, power, and feeling in particular objects. Totemism involves a highly complex system of beliefs and practices whereby an animal or plant becomes a totem, or a focal symbol for the life and well-being of a tribe. Just as tribal communities are sustained by a power that the totem symbolizes and expresses, so the patterns of tribal behaviour are maintained by taboos. Persons, things, and behaviour are taboo, or are prohibited to members of a society, when they are judged to be so highly charged with sacred power that ordinary "profane" persons must keep their distance.

These primitive viewpoints have a certain conceptual kinship with what the more sophisticated religious viewpoints have labelled with such terms as theism, polytheism, pluralism, and Idealism. Theism interprets the one cosmic, life-giving power in personal terms—different versions varying in their views of the adequacy of those personal terms. Polytheism posits a multiplicity of cosmic personal powers on whose activity (whether in cooperation or conflict) the universe depends. Pluralism views cosmic power as mediated and expressed through a multiplicity of ultimates (*e.g.,* finite persons) or otherwise views the universe as best understood in terms of ultimate atomic units, with no claim made for the absolute supremacy of any one of them. In this way, pluralism—even of a personal kind—differs from theism, which holds that God is a Supreme Person.

Absolute Idealism maintains that activity is an ultimate category but makes no claim, as does theism, for this activity to be personal. Instead, it takes a biological organism as its dominant model. Theism, like deism, has sometimes posited an ultimate personal power or being beyond, above, and certainly separated from the changing scenes of life, whereas absolute Idealism posits an ultimate power or being that is considered to be the whole, of which the changing scenes of life are but a part.

Seeking salvation in a life beyond. Religion is not merely a matter of being aware of a transcendent dimension nor is it merely a claim for a broader and more comprehensive view of the reality. Fundamental to religion is the conviction that through a right relation with a cosmic power or powers, man will find his salvation. Various views of such salvation have been held. Salvation has been regarded as something attainable only after this life. Other views, however, tend to posit a salvation for man through escape rather than fulfillment. Alternatively, salvation may be viewed as something anticipated in the present but fulfilled perfectly after this life. Salvation also has been interpreted in terms of fellowship with God or as a state of bliss needing no God (as by the early 20th-century British philosopher J.M.E. McTaggart), as a state of ultimate peace that arises when man sees his peculiar and rightful place in the whole universe (as by Spinoza), and as a state of bliss in which man cannot properly speak of himself as a self-conscious individual as in the Buddhist state of Nirvāṇa.

VIEWS WITH ANTHROPIC REFERENCES

Inner attitudes and dispositions. A religious view of the universe contends that a new dimension and depth can be disclosed within the person who responds. Though religious faith has its characteristic inner attitudes and dispositions, they must be of a transcendently self-involving kind, and there must be a depth to any attitude or disposition before it can be called religious. Thus, the attitude of awe is related to the feeling of fear. For fear to become awe, however, it must be characterized by a particular depth and self-involvement that come from responding to the presence and activity of God, or of the sacred or holy that call it forth.

Religion relates to the whole of a man's personality and because of this totality of human response, people speak of "conversion" in relation to religious attitudes. Generally, a person who becomes religious or ceases to be religious undergoes a profound transformation. Persons who have become converted to religion speak of the world as having taken on a fuller and richer dimension; those for whom the religious vision has disappeared speak of a world as having become flat, dead, and bleak.

Behavioral discipline with prescribed practices. Many religions bind their adherents to specific practices and particular moral codes. Thus, conversion has often shown itself in radical changes of behaviour; *e.g.*, an alcoholic becoming a total abstainer. Such behaviour as murder, lying, breaking promises, stealing, and commiting adultery have been condemned by the world religions. So strong is the ethical element in Confucianism that some regard it more as an ethical system than a religion. Yet, ethical (and ceremonial) codes can be transformed imperceptibly into no more than current social conventions and mere customs. Whether such codes have changed or not, their range and detail vary widely. Pork is eaten by Christians but is considered to be unclean by Jews and Muslims. Muslims and Buddhists abstain totally from alcohol; Christians and Jews need not. A Sikh will not shave his beard; but Hindus, Christians, and Muslims are free to do so if they wish. In contrast with Christians, Buddhists will not kill animals, and Muslims may practice polygamy.

Participation in a social institution. Whatever the diversities, religious faith is not only self-involving, but it has a social dimension as well. Hermits apart, religion brings people together as children of one family having a common father. For Christians, the significance of the universal religious community, the church, has been variously interpreted. Some, with a Protestant emphasis, have viewed the church as a voluntary institution created ad hoc for the convenience of its members to enable them to gather together to worship, to sing hymns, and to share common interests and beliefs. The Catholic view is that the church is a social institution that is derived from God and whose structure expresses the givenness of God himself.

To be of religious significance, however, social practices and moral codes, like inner experiences must have depth, a transcendent dimension, or they become superficial and dangerous parodies of religion, all the more dangerous for being in their outward features so similar.

THE VIEW FROM WITHIN AS PRIVILEGED

The assertion that the view of religion from within is privileged needs careful analysis.

First, religious faith is logically privileged insofar as it is characterized by a self-involvement, commitment to which partial commitments can only point. A temporary loyalty, however intensive, is at best a distant pointer to a conversion. Further, because religious faith is grounded in a disclosure, there is something logically privileged about it in the same sense that some are "privileged" to understand a joke when others do not. Yet, even though religion has a disclosure basis, it is still true that just as there are techniques for jokes so also are there techniques for meditation, whether in Christianity or in other religions. By virtue of such techniques men can have a reasonable expectation of a view of religion from within. In another sense, the view that religion from within is privileged may merely mean that if a man believes something and is committed, he is more involved than a man who does not believe.

One aspect of the logically privileged position of religion might be called its semantic privilege; *i.e.*, the fact that a religious vision cannot adequately be expressed. One fundamental problem for religious language, according to linguistic analysts, is to discover more reliable rather than less reliable ways of talking. One need not presuppose, however, so fundamental a distinction between the sacred and the secular that men become committed to total silence on religious matters. When St. Paul, for example, wrote of being "caught up" (in II Cor.) he "heard things that cannot be told, which man may not utter." If this statement of Paul's were generally true of religion, however, religious people would be so privileged that they would be living in a segregated silence.

Some scholars have argued that the privileged character of religion makes it unsuitable as a proper study for the philosopher, who must in principle be detached, not committed, and have an openness to all truth. The lack of finality in philosophical thought is contrasted with religious commitment and the final claims sometimes made for religious doctrine. Nevertheless, insofar as anyone has a coherent world view, there will be some degree of commitment.

Religion is not, however, altogether beyond argument, and those who are outside a religion can still have some inkling of what is being discussed within a religion and the manner in which it is being discussed, especially when the social, cultural, historical, and psychological embodiments of the religion are described. For this reason Western Christians and Jews, for example, are able to know something about the primitive religion of an African or Indonesian tribe.

Thus, much about religion can be known by those outside it, however, views about the nature of religion and definitions of religion have a systematic inadequacy about them. Like everything of the spirit, religion cannot be described so as to make clear to the detached observer the characteristic quality and depth of religious awareness and commitment.

THE DIMENSION OF RELIGION FOR INSIDERS

The essence or core of religion. For the insider, the essence of religion is given in a moment of vision and disclosure. Friedrich Schleiermacher, a German philosopher of the 18th and 19th centuries, described the basic religious experience in terms of a kiss or an embrace. Attempts to understand such a unity can only be made in terms of

Interpretations of salvation

The concept of conversion

the particulars into which the unity subsequently breaks, and such particulars then fall broadly into subjective and objective compartments.

The subjective and objective aspects of religion. Faith describes a subjective state that accepts what a disclosure discloses and is akin to personal trustfulness, to a conation or striving that, according to Spinoza, all living things display. Prayer is the utterance of words (rite) with or without some dramatic context (ceremonial) designed either to carry one into the presence of what is worshipped or to express appropriate sentiments in the presence of what is worshipped. Most prayers incorporate words that function in both ways. Ritual is especially concerned with events in human life that have disclosure possibilities and in which mystery is at its highest.

Mystery in the context of religion refers to situations, such as birth, reproduction, death, and suffering, in which there are numerous possibilities for new insights and yet further insights. Public worship must constantly renew and realize in the liturgy the possibilities of the past disclosures. If the outward expressions and forms come to dominate, ritual can become an empty shell, and religious practices can become devoid of religious significance.

Effects of religious beliefs and practices. One of the effects of religious beliefs and practices is sacralization, a process in which certain persons, days, or objects become regarded as sacred. If such objects are granted more than the status of symbols, they may become objects of idolatry or superstition.

Belief in salvation, which often accompanies religious commitment, can have various practical results. If salvation is viewed as something that inspires progress and may be accomplished in the realm of time, such doctrines of salvation encourage social reforms and projects that envision an abundant life for humanity. If, on the other hand, salvation is viewed as something that is beyond the realm of time and set entirely apart from this world—something for which at best this world is a probation and at worst a sink of misery and iniquity from which the sooner man is released the better—such doctrines of salvation can be excessively individualistic and may even encourage oppression and tyranny.

Religious belief has sometimes led men to detailed conclusions about nature and history. Good harvests have been interpreted as due rewards for appropriate worship or good behaviour, or both; calamities have been viewed as the results of sin, either ceremonial or moral. If God is believed to be in control of history, a nation that does what is right and follows his guidance, as expressed through its prophets and other religious personages, is expected to experience national prosperity and success. In previous periods, when this did not occur, the ensuing calamities were attributed to the backslidings of earlier generations.

Many observers of religion claim that in the modern world few would suppose that God intervenes in this direct and predictable way. According to this view, God's activity in the world, apart from being expressed in its constant creativity and conservation, is effective through man's own intellectual and physical activity. Insofar as man's own creativity is exercised, however, within the framework of the order that the world displays, and in no way violates it, one cannot exclude a similar creativity on the part of God. Admittedly, the fact that man expresses his activity through an intermediate organism (his body) indicates that there is no exact parallel between God and man; nevertheless, because God's activity terminates with the universe, the analogy with God's activity might very well be expressed in the number of ways in which man can effect creative development in his own body.

INTERNAL CRITICISMS OF RELIGION

Internal criticisms of religion have their basis in the imbalance that occurs when one aspect or one understanding of religion is allowed to dominate the rest. Heresies have arisen when one way of understanding has been developed without balancing it with another. In the development of doctrines concerning the nature and person of Christ within Christianity, for example, heresies arose when a particular model (*e.g.*, that of fatherhood and sonship)

was believed to be capable of infinite development. The model of the Father–Son relationship was pressed too far, and the Son was subordinated to the Father in a way inconsistent with Christian orthodoxy, thus leading to what became heresy. Sectarianism develops when religious insights are associated exclusively with one particular doctrinal or theological phrase, such as justification by faith, or with one particular theological view regarding religious practices; *e.g.*, baptism. Because religion is at once infinite and mysterious, it is important that religious belief does full justice to a wide variety of approaches.

Another criticism of religion has been that it has tended to be overintellectual; and when this trait has been combined with moral laxity and factional rivalries, it has led to protests about the arrogance of intellectualized religion, often leading to the opposite error of supposing that belief does not matter as long as common sentiments are shared. Religious believers have not always recognized that for the most part their belief explicates metaphors, images, and symbols. Though ways of religious reasoning are appropriately informal and variegated, having their origins in a multitude of images and symbols, it nevertheless is considered a religious duty to produce the most reliable overall discourse based on the various images and models.

The fundamental difficulty of all religious understanding, however, is to balance intelligibility and mystery. If the intelligibility is neglected, religious belief can become dishonest and religious men can lose integrity; if mystery is neglected, there may be splendid controversy and exercises in logical appraisal, but the heart of religion will have disappeared.

The basic difficulty of all religions and of historical religions in particular is to effect a constant rebirth of symbols in changing cultures. In the course of time some of the most powerful images and symbols lose their fertility in promoting ideas that inform a religious community. This might be said of the image of sacrifice in the Christian religion. Religious practices and institutions, though they may have social merits, can all become stereotyped routine, as happens when they fail to preserve a sense of reverence and fail to disclose the givenness of the sacred or holy. Because religious belief is so important and influences all aspects of a society, there is a tendency for religious institutions to become authoritarian and oppressive. If a religious institution becomes interwoven with political views it can become tyrannical. Religion's only compulsion, according to some scholars, must be the compelling power of a vision, as the modern English–American philosopher Alfred North Whitehead expressed it: "The power of God is the worship He inspires." The authority of any religion is the authority of a vision, the authority of that which, in being disclosed, inspires men and leads them to fulfillment in their lives. For a Christian, the final authority is the love of God in Christ, and love is not love if its power is anything but inspiration. For other religions there is the compelling inspiration of that to which—Nirvāna or the Qur'ān, the Buddha or Muḥammad—point.

Internal criticisms of religion usually focus on such themes as narrowness, sectarianism, traditionalism, conventionalism, materialism, and immorality. Some criticism is also reserved for religiosity, which, though granting a dimension of faith, treats faith in an altogether superficial and often unbalanced way. Religiosity represents an excessive preoccupation with religion that is depicted in an incoherent and oversimplified relating of religious faith to intellectual views and social and personal practices.

THE REJECTION OF RELIGION OR RELIGIOUSNESS

Because religious commitment is so all-embracing and tends to influence thought, feelings, and behaviour, it is not surprising that there are many reasons why religious claims have been rejected.

Rejections on the grounds of alleged incoherence. Religious claims have been rejected because of their alleged logical or moral incoherence.

Alleged logical incoherence. Logical incoherence may arise internally or externally and in relation to different issues. In regard to internal coherence, critics have maintained that man should be able to expect that God would

---

Marginal notes (left column):

Faith, prayer, and ritual

Conclusions about nature and history

Marginal notes (right column):

Balancing intelligibility and mystery

see to it that there could be no possibility of ignoring his existence or of making mistakes about religious beliefs and behaviour, if religious convictions are so important. They have also claimed that it is altogether too naïve, though inevitable, to think of God as made in the image of man. Some have rejected theistic belief because of the incoherence of the idea of God, which must—they claim—combine so many incompatible predicates; *e.g.,* God is eternal, yet acts in time, or he is loving and yet incapable of suffering or feeling.

External incoherence, in conflict with other views of world

Religious beliefs have been alleged to be externally, as well as internally, incoherent because of their conflict with other views about the universe, especially scientific views. The doctrines of heaven and hell, in particular, which have given great personal and social significance to religious belief, have been rejected by many critics when these doctrines were viewed literally. Yet it has been the supposed actuality of heaven and hell that has given religious persons their hope and their terror respectively. Absolute Idealism, it has sometimes been alleged, is incoherent insofar as it states that time is not "real" and that evil does not really exist. This is not to say, however, that there is no temporal succession or nothing evil, claims that would be obviously incoherent. What is being claimed is that within a particular interpretation of the universe, time and evil are not left as ultimate categories but are in some sense derivative from other categories.

It has been argued that by far the greatest problem of external incoherence that belief in God has to face is that of the evil and suffering that characterize the world. Critics have stated that if God cannot rid the world of evil and suffering, he is not all-powerful; if he could, but he won't, then he isn't all-good; if he is powerful and good but not all-wise, then, even though he is trying his best, there are bound to be disasters. The most serious classical expression of this problem was given by David Hume, in his *Dialogues Concerning Natural Religion* (1779). With such considerations in mind, some philosophers, such as John Stuart Mill, have been willing to argue for a limited God—*i.e.,* the great fellow-sufferer who understands and has compassionate sympathy.

Alleged moral incoherence. Though religious conviction shows itself in moral behaviour, it has been argued that religious people have not shown outstanding moral qualities. An 18th-century English philosopher and churchman, Bishop George Berkeley, when presented with this objection, remarked that nothing evil can be attributed as such to the Christian religion and that the only legitimate comparison is that between a person who is a Christian and what the same person would have been otherwise. The distinctiveness of the Christian faith, however, has sometimes been supported by arguing a stark contrast with morality. The 19th-century Danish philosophical theologian Søren Kierkegaard, for example, by a too literal misreading of the biblical story of Abraham and Isaac (Gen. 22), supposed that religious obedience must be in radical opposition to moral duty. However that may be, religious men often may be only too well aware of their moral lapses, their sins, and for this very reason they seek the grace and power of God. The good that they would do they do not do, and the evil that they despise they continually do, as St. Paul noted in his letter to the Romans. In this moral predicament, those with a Christian commitment believe that the grace and power of God comes to inspire and release them from the dominion of sin. This does not mean that the Christian never sins, but it does mean that he is assured of ultimate victory over sin. The Christian Church is viewed not as a society of saints but a school for sinners.

The problem of sin and grace

The exclusiveness of religious sects is regarded by those outside the sects as hardly to the sectarians' credit. For Christians, sectarian exclusiveness is viewed as a scandal to the gospel that they preach. On the other hand, the criticisms of Puritanism that hold it as inevitably negative and oppressive sometimes fail to see that it may be neither negative nor oppressive if it is grounded in a spiritual and religious vision.

The doctrine of grace (the view that God grants man abilities that man does not merit by his own efforts) has sometimes appeared to make God himself—interpreted as the spirit dwelling in a man—the actual agent of good behaviour. In this way, some interpretations of the doctrines of grace have compromised man's freedom and come close to denying man responsibility for his actions.

Outside Christianity, critics have pointed to the gap between religious profession and moral action, though within Christianity, with its strong emphasis on moral transformation, the gap has been very wide and the criticism most challenging. In Hinduism for instance, Gandhian reformational and nonviolence ideals have not mixed well with social corruption or with the type of neutralism that allowed China to persecute Tibetan Buddhists. Again, the Buddhist who goes to a temple is not necessarily compassionate as his religion dictates, and the Muslim who attends services in a mosque may be less filled with an inner sense of justice and patience than with thoughts of a holy war. In Sri Lanka (Ceylon) and Vietnam nationalist loyalties have given rise to a violence untypical of Buddhism. In the last resort, however, each religion will appeal to its doctrine of salvation when presented with a gap between its moral ideals and the actual actions and behaviour of its adherents.

Other grounds for the rejection of religion. *Rejection of historical beliefs, practices, and institutions as spurious or irrelevant.* When a religion appeals to historical events, other grounds for its rejection arise. The Old Testament view of history appears to have been exceedingly selective in order to emphasize a particular point about God and his activity. The miracles of Jesus—both those relating to his own person (his birth and Resurrection) and those that he himself performed (especially nature miracles)—conflict with what men experience in the normal course of their natural lives and experience. Prayers requesting favourable weather, plentiful crops, or safety in a journey are characterized by many as spurious and irrelevant. Ideas of God intervening in the universe, according to such critics, satisfy neither science nor religion. From a scientific point of view, "laws" of nature are no longer viewed as divine prescriptions; and the word law becomes, in fact, misleading. Furthermore, in order to allow for miraculous intervention of this kind, God's providential care is viewed as a compromise. He thus becomes the absentee landlord who absented himself from the world, which must take care of itself except for some spectacular visitation. According to this view, the only coherent way to speak of an intervention of God is to interpret it in the context of personal intervention.

Religious institutions have been criticized on the grounds that they conflict with the ideas of the founder and are supported by claims that cannot be historically verified. These claims, according to critics, depend on taking certain historical events on which the religion is founded, and reinterpreting them by theological speculation or a very full imagination, to produce, for example, a doctrine of papal supremacy according to which Christ is believed to have given explicitly to the successors of St. Peter final jurisdiction over the church.

Rejection of religious sentiments or dispositions as valueless. According to some views, anyone who prizes "another world" must despise this world and be uncertain in his attitude toward the world around him. In this way, it is said, religion dries up the sources of its activity and attacks such happiness as this world can provide—though promising happiness hereafter, which has been called "pie in the sky" or "opiate of the people" by critics of religion. A humanist concern to liberalize and relax laws (*e.g.,* on abortion and divorce), to abolish capital punishment, and to encourage birth control has always been opposed, according to humanists, by Christian orthodoxy, which they interpret as having a negative and conservative attitude that has proceeded from a nervous fear of a decline in moral standards. At the same time, humanists would continue, moral standards have hardly been upheld by sectarian strife and persecutions. Further, they point out, too often the church, in its desire to indicate what abides, has confused what is abiding with current social and political institutions and traditions inherited from the

Humanist criticisms of religion

past, generally resulting in an illiberal obscurantism and a reactionary outlook.

Some critics of religion have contended that almost all scientific progress has been hindered by religious beliefs and attitudes. Biology, physics, and geology, they have claimed, only made the rapid progress that they did when they were freed from a context of religious belief by the 17th-century philosopher René Descartes, who devised a metaphysical myth of the separation of mind and body.

Naturalistic or skeptical views of the origin and development of religion. In the matter of the origins and development of religion, many (*e.g.,* the psychologist James Henry Leuba in his *Psychology of Religious Mysticism* [1925]) have argued that there is a close connection between mysticism and hallucination, between hysteria and ecstatic institutionalized inspiration as, for example, in Pentecostal churches. Religious people, according to such views, often have personality weaknesses and are psychologically disturbed. Freud, the founder of psychoanalysis, maintained that inner conflicts—often the result of repression, particularly in relation to sex—become expressed in peculiarities of behaviour and mood, especially in the vivid imagery of dreams that erupt from the unconscious area of one's personality. By comparing the symbolism of dreams and mythology, Freud held that belief in God—in particular, the father image—merely perpetuates in fantasy what the individual must in actual fact overcome as part of his growth to maturity, thus giving religious belief a treatment that not only made belief in God unnecessary but positively unhelpful.

Carl Jung, a former disciple of Freud, gave a different account of the psychology of the unconscious. Each person displays a libido, a fundamental striving that is creative and purposive and of which there is evidence in the symbolic language of dreams. Behind all such symbolic language are archetypes (innate tendencies to form symbolic images), which all humanity shares and which inspire a person to move toward a balanced integration to which the energy of the libido would creatively move, if given proper freedom and encouragement. Thus, Jung posits a racial or impersonal unconscious in which, at the deepest level, all individual human beings share. Jung's archetypes raise the metaphysical question of whether they are symbols of an existent God or gods—a question that psychology leaves open. For many psychologists it is a question of little interest, because for them the archetypes themselves suffice in practice.

In addition to such naturalistic or skeptical views about the origin and development of religion are other claims that religion is merely an infantile reaction to fear, a more or less harmful sublimation of sex, a projection of wishful thinking, or a social device for use in the class struggle. On the other side, however, it is likely to be pointed out that one must be careful not to indulge in the genetic fallacy: no account of the origin and development of anything, of religion in particular, is necessarily a reliable analysis of what that particular phenomenon is now; a single explanation of the origin and development of a phenomenon as complex and variegated as religion is difficult to describe and maintain. It is also necessary to beware of the "really only," or reductionist, fallacy. To say "*x* is really only *y*" is, in effect, denying the significance of *y* language despite the fact that *y*-talk as well as *x*-talk already occurs; *e.g.,* persons are really only "machines," or worship is really only a social occasion. Over-simplification streamlines discourse at the cost of adequacy and truth.

Some have thought of religion as no more than a body of stories designed to encourage a noble attitude toward life and humanity. If, however, one asks why or how these attitudes encourage and why a particular attitude is valued, what begins as a simple account of religion becomes, in the end, as complicated as any. Another criticism of religion, arguing for its redundancy, claims that the progress of man in society can and should be determined by scientific considerations. This contention, however, goes beyond the particular conclusions of the individual sciences; it is to make a philosophy out of science. On the one hand, such a scientific view of man and society would be open to philosophical criticism, not the least if it were sug-

Problem of the genetic and reductionist fallacies

gested that man's subjectivity—that which makes him the unique person he is—has to be analyzed in terms of the objects of science. On the other hand, if science becomes a philosophy, it might be said to have assumed a religious dimension itself.

In the realm of religion in the latter part of the 20th century, in what might still be called the Christian societies of the West, the attitude of very many people lies in an intermediate zone between religious belief and atheism, but the content appears rather to be given to agnosticism. Such persons believe in God but dislike any kind of formal worship, pray only on exceptional occasions, and find it difficult to have a sense of sin but admire saintliness. They are critical of the need for a Christian ministry except insofar as a priest or pastor can show sympathy and act as a vehicle of social concern. They are distrustful of dogma and critical of Christian sectarianism. They may be uncertain of Christ's divinity, but the words and example of Jesus are viewed as a guide to the good life. This outlook has many affinities with the "natural religion" of the 18th century in which the ethical example and teachings of Jesus were emphasized. Though, as in the 18th century, there may be an intent to reject revelation, persons holding such an outlook may rather be rejecting certain stylings of Christian revelation.

Ambiguities in attitudes of persons in Christian societies

Examples of occurrence of such a "natural piety" can also be found in religions other than Christianity, though significantly not in Islām—unless the Baha'i movement be taken as an approximation of this outlook. This attitude, for example, has provided the basic cohesion for the State of Israel in the latter half of the 20th century. Further, the spread of technology has gradually been alienating many Hindus and Buddhists from their traditional beliefs, but the Hindu has continued to treasure his spiritual ideology, which may well give to technological development its needed direction and wider setting. Buddhism in Japan, and perhaps elsewhere in the East, is still valued in the 20th century insofar as it supplies a local religious dimension to a society whose public and industrial life has been increasingly Westernized. Thus, an attitude has arisen that is sympathetic to the broad claims of religion, but has been critical, if not disdainful, of theological dogma and rivalries.

THE ACKNOWLEDGMENT OF RELIGION OR RELIGIOUSNESS AS VALID

Traditional justifications. *Religion as pointing to an ultimate power, being, or value.* More generally, persons who are outside the particular religions and who have nevertheless acknowledged religion as significant often seem to base their views on a fundamental feeling of absolute dependence. The grandeur of the universe, the character of the moral struggle, reflections on human nature, and an awareness of moral values inspiring men to reform society have all joined together to point men to an ultimate power or being—a "power, not ourselves, which makes for righteousness," according to the 19th-century English poet Matthew Arnold.

The fundamental difference in the latter part of the 20th century between the secularist and the religious person most likely has been between someone who takes a narrower and someone who takes a wider view of humanity. That there is an acknowledged need in modern times to give a moral direction to technology seems to many to bring with it the need for a religious view of the universe, even though they may not themselves be adherents of a particular religion.

Religion as producing wholesome spiritual or moral effects. Others point to examples of the wholesome moral and spiritual effects that religion has had. They mention that society has ceased to practice child exposure and there has been a notable development in the status of women in society. Religion, where it is not parodied, misrepresented, or misunderstood, broadens rather than narrows vision. Insofar as human nature is inadequately understood, if no place is granted to the spirit of man, human nature, it is argued, will never find satisfaction except through the self-realization and self-fulfillment that come from responding to the inspiring ideal.

The pragmatic view

Alternatives to traditional beliefs, practices, and institutions. *The quest for authentic existence.* In the 20th century various alternatives to traditional religious beliefs, practices, and institutions have become apparent. Chief among these is the quest for authentic existence. This has been encouraged and portrayed by various Existentialists (those who view man in terms of his existing thoughts and actions rather than in terms of his "essence"), who have been concerned in one way or another with emphasizing the significance of certain situations. In this way, they have given their own versions of salvation—that situation in which a person finds his true significance. For some, such as the German philosopher Martin Heidegger, a sense of authentic existence is given to each person when he realizes his true subjectivity, which his life in the world and his social transactions so often conceal. Authentic existence is often contrasted with cosmic anxiety—*i.e.,* anxiety of a deep and far-reaching kind to which the antidote is to find oneself and one's freedom in a total commitment to what is called the ground of Being.

Existentialists of an atheistic persuasion, such as the philosopher and Nobel laureate Jean-Paul Sartre, regard human existence as absurd and other people as hell, because, though one needs other people, they can never be other than "other people"—their subjecthood, their freedom is inaccessible. Love is, thus, doomed to permanent frustration. The need to know others like oneself is matched by its impossibility. According to Sartre, this condition only reflects the absurdity of man's own existence, which is always attempting to overcome a radical estrangement between man as the object of scientific study and man himself (*en soi*) and the subjectivity man knows in consciousness (*pour soi*). Suicide is the final absurdity, for in getting rid of *en soi,* what man is, *pour soi* disappears at the same time.

Religious Existentialism as a God-given fellowship

This pessimistic estimate of human life and its apparent absurdity, however, has been converted into a religious view by other Existentialists, such as Gabriel Marcel, another French philosopher, who point to a participation—a mysterious self-involvement that persons can have intersubjectively with each other—in a kind of fellowship that is viewed as God-given. According to this view, man needs to open himself to the presence and grace of God for a dynamic transformation in which the mysterious transcends the purely problematic. Common to all Existentialists, however, is the view that the authentic man is not merely satisfied with playing a role, with being a cog in industrial society. One way or another, the quest for authentic existence is to discover the means by which man can recapture and enjoy occasions of self-disclosure. So significant are these occasions that they have been viewed by some theologians to be the paradigm for the kind of situation that the Christian gospels recount.

Secular religion. Another feature of 20th-century development has been society's rediscovery of the significance of the secular. This change has led to an outlook and attitude that has been characterized as "religionless Christianity," a Christianity influenced by its residual social and political ideal, but bereft of its specifically religious practices, doctrines, or institutions. Such practices as traditional intercessory prayer are dismissed as empty approximations to magic; doctrine is condemned as outdated and expressed in terms of past cultures; institutions are criticized as oppressive and conservative.

Behind all this suspicion of structures and doctrinal schemes and practices, however, is a desire to get back to basic principles and origins, to learn again what is distinctive about the religious point of view. According to some proponents, such a goal might be attained by beginning with the secular, with activities in the secular world, not least with compassionate service, by seeing where the need arises for religious conviction and by ascertaining what contribution faith will make to secular endeavour. Though secular religion broadens out into a more sympathetic and a more positive attitude than agnosticism, it is never as explicit or particularized as orthodoxy.

Marxism. Marxism, which provides remarkable evidence of the power of dominant key ideas to inspire and direct man, is undoubtedly one of the greatest challenges to traditional religious belief. Based on the socio-economic philosophical thought of the 19th-century thinker Karl Marx, Marxism can be said to be a quasi-religion on two counts. First, Marxism had connections with the metaphysics of G.W.F. Hegel, an 18th–19th-century German philosopher who interpreted reality in terms of a spiritual Absolute. Furthermore, the thinking of Marx had religious overtones, whether from his own Jewish background or from a Christian atmosphere, not least in Britain where he lived from 1849 to 1883. Second, Marxism can be called a quasi-religion insofar as it calls from its followers a devotion and a commitment that in their empirical character greatly resemble the commitment and devotion that characterize religious people. Marxism has undoubtedly fired the spirit of man and given to revolutions, whether in Russia or China, a powerful direction that has maintained stability and avoided anarchy. Furthermore, like a religion, it has provided themes of fulfillment and hope—a revolution interpreted as the initiation of a Communist world society that would be a final consummation. There are many logical similarities between the doctrine of the Marxist millennium and the Christian doctrine of Christ's Second Coming. Marxism has also stressed the significance of cooperating with the immanent spirit of the times—something comparable to the providence of God—in economic and military struggles that are viewed as the travail by which society would be reborn. The main difference between Marxism and Christianity in the 19th and early 20th centuries, according to some scholars, was that for many the Christian vision encouraged men to endure tyranny, while the Marxist view inspired men to rebel. Yet, once it can be established that religion is not the servant of oppression, is not necessarily linked with an illiberal regime, and does not use concepts of "other worldliness" to make men content with tyranny and injustice, then religion may yet have a place in the Communist state. Such a religion would not have to concern itself with the kind of supernaturalism that Marxism now rejects; it would not have to appeal to an invisible world entirely other than the present world. It is not without significance that Marxism has its own form of public ceremonial and its own language of glorification. If it has to be granted that many religions have a ceremonial, a symbolism, and a moral code that has lost the vision they once had, Marxism is a social program, a doctrine, and a ceremonial searching for a vision that haunts it and that may at some time bring it to fruition. In this regard, Chinese Marxism is particularly significant insofar as Marxism in China cannot escape some interweaving with Chinese Buddhism. Chinese Buddhism brings with it a natural framework of absolute Idealism, which may yet supply Marxism with the spiritual dimension that for many critics appears to be Marxism's main inadequacy, something it lost when it shed its Hegelian metaphysics and became the anti-God Materialistic world-view of the U.S.S.R.

Marxism as a quasi-religion

HISTORY OF THE PHILOSOPHY OF RELIGION

Most philosophies have incorporated religious views in the wide sense of being concerned with a reality beyond appearance, and in this sense they have provided a philosophy of religion.

Developments in the West. *Ancient and medieval concepts.* For the Greek philosophers Plato and Aristotle, wonder was the beginning of philosophy. From such wonder, according to Plato, emerged religious knowledge that was also mediated through Ideas, eternal entities or concepts in which the things of time participate. In performing every good act, man realizes his link with eternity and the Idea of the Good. For the moment, however, man, as in a cave, is chained by his earthly existence so that he cannot see the light outside; he can only see shadows on the wall, which are signs and tokens of the eternal light behind him. This was Plato's way of styling the relationship between time and eternity, between appearance and reality, and it is a styling that found a particular welcome in the Christian tradition and not least by Christian Platonists, whether of the 2nd or 17th centuries. Plato's philosophy also led to belief in God, and his *Timaeus* is a philosophical creation story.

Religious ideas of Plato and Aristotle

Aristotle, impressed with organic life in man and animals, took as his fundamental category growth and development. The nature of anything was thought of as a form by which its movement and development as an organism was to be understood. It was as if the form supplied the driving force. In this context, God was thought of as pure form, as final cause, and as prime mover. Aristotle provided for St. Thomas Aquinas, the great medieval philosopher of Western Christendom, the foundation on which he developed Scholasticism, which has been a distinctive feature of Christian philosophy of religion since the 13th century. Other medieval philosophers, such as Erigena, with his pantheism (God in all); Abelard, with his critical questions; Eckehart, with his mysticism; and Duns Scotus and Bonaventure, with a wider view of reason than could be contained in the Scholastic philosophy, all illustrate the variety and independence of Christian thinkers.

Modern concepts. Descartes, the "father of modern philosophy," is significant in terms of his reacting against external authority in matters of belief, seeking a fresh basis for certainty, and finding it in the existence of his own mind. He must think in order to doubt his existence, hence his famous statement, *Cogito ergo sum* ("I think, therefore, I am"). Henceforward, much significance was given to the individual mind, and the resulting myth of the body–mind separation enabled both physics and biology to develop without the risk of ecclesiastical interference. Only in recent years has the inadequacy of the Cartesian body–mind myth come under general criticism not only because of the metaphysical problems it poses but also because it fails to do justice to the unity of personality that recent developments in medicine, such as those pertaining to psychosomatic disorders, presuppose.

The myth of the body–mind separation

Many of Descartes's 17th- and 18th-century successors can be best understood by reference to him. Nicolas Malebranche, a French Cartesian philosopher, and the occasionalist philosophers, were more radical than Descartes; they dispensed with any unity whatever in man himself and linked together man's mind and body by means of the constant correlation effected by God himself, claiming that mental events were merely "occasions" for God effecting material change. For Spinoza, the whole universe had not only Descartes's two attributes of mentality and materiality but an infinite number of attributes, and it could be alternatively named God or Nature. Each existent in the world could be pictured as a particular whirlpool in an infinitely deep sea made up of endless layers of particular fluids of which man knows only two—mentality and materiality. Gottfried Leibniz viewed Descartes's minds as the only ultimate existents, so that even material things were colonies of souls. God was viewed as the supreme monad (the ultimate substance) that establishes coherence and harmony among all other monads. What appears to men as the external world is, so to speak, the result of blurred vision on the part of those groups of monads that are human beings.

After Descartes there appeared the British Empiricists: John Locke, George Berkeley, Joseph Butler, and David Hume. Locke, though rejecting some of Descartes's characteristic doctrines, nevertheless took over Descartes's view of the human mind and then concerned himself with the philosophical psychology of how the mind comes to have the ideas it possesses. By the time of David Hume (died 1776), the mind was viewed as nothing more than a collection or bundle of ideas thought of as very similar to images, which means, as Hume frankly admitted, that it becomes impossible to do justice to the subjectivity that makes each person distinctively the person he is. The significance of Berkeley (died 1753) in this sequence is that he saw the need for an extended Empiricism that took the notion of personality seriously and that regarded activity as a key concept. Indeed, for Berkeley the fundamental unit for thought was "activity-directed-towards-and-terminating-in ideas," and it was the activity of God directed to those ideas, which make up the external world, that gave to this world its continuous independent existence. His contemporary Butler also argued for a broader Empiricism, which for him centred on the significance of man as a moral agent and on a reasonableness that need

not always conform to a mathematical paradigm. In a matter of great consequence, a man's action can be reasonable even though there may be little supporting evidence for his decision and though, indeed, the evidence may be very much against it. It may, thus, often be a moral duty to act in such problematical circumstances. This led to Butler's famous doctrine of probability—"probability is the very guide of life"—a view that influenced the treatment of belief in *The Grammar of Assent* (1870), by the English theologian John Henry Newman.

Immanuel Kant has been called the second founder of modern philosophy. With Kant, late 18th-century philosophy began to take an interest in human knowledge, its varieties, scope, and limits. In Kant's critical philosophy, which emerged in his old age, he showed how scientific knowledge left room for morality. Though he was inclined to interpret all religious assertions in terms of morality, belief in God was justified as the holding of a regulative idea that brings coherence into all of man's thinking. The foundation of this idea is to be found, in fact, in those experiences of unity to which moral ideals, beauty, and the notion of a purposive universe all point. This idea of unity, largely implicit in Kant, was developed by Hegel, who came to regard the universe and its cultural, social, and political progress as but manifestations in time of an unchanging absolute spirit. In this way, Hegelianism provided a spiritual interpretation of the universe, but it regarded particular religions as no more than visual aids toward understanding Hegelian truths. A century later, the British philosopher F.H. Bradley was able to use a Hegelian approach in a much more empirical and far less intellectual context. Whatever form Hegelianism took and though its spiritual insights seemed on first view to make it a friend to religion, it has proved to be a position in opposition to Christianity, whether by its minimizing the historical element or by the way in which it compromises belief in a personal God.

The Kantian and Hegelian idea of unity

Since the absolute Idealists, there has perhaps been only one philosopher in the mainstream of tradition—Alfred North Whitehead—who, in taking becoming rather than being as the fundamental category, made "process philosophy" possible. This philosophical view maintains a metaphysics that not only provides an interpretative scheme linking God, man, and the world but one that incorporates scientific and historical thinking, though in taking growth and process as fundamental, Whitehead seems, to some, to have an evolutionary God.

There were two main reactions against Hegelianism. The first, initiated by Kierkegaard, viewed Hegelianism as altogether too detached and objective and its ways of reasoning entirely unsuited to the deepest experiences of human life, the tragic situations in which human beings find themselves. From Kierkegaard, the Existentialist movement began. Also, in reaction against Hegel, were the modern Empiricists, such as Bertrand Russell and G.E. Moore from England, whose watchword was clarification in their attempts to create a straightforward, unambiguous language. This movement passed easily into Logical Positivism (a philosophical position that accepts only scientific knowledge as factual and rejects metaphysics), which challenged not only the truth but the meaning of theological assertions.

Developments in the East. *Buddhist concepts.* Among the religious philosophies of the East, the conservative Theravāda (Way of the Elders and another term for Hīnayāna) Buddhism regarded all existence as a succession of transitory states: what alone was permanent was Nirvāṇa, a deathless realm the existence of which was revealed to the Buddha himself in the Enlightenment that came to him while he meditated beneath the bo tree (late 6th century BC). About Nirvāṇa, the wise will say little more except to affirm its existence and to express their conviction that the plurality of individual souls that man knows in this world cannot in the same way exist in that deathless realm where there is no rebirth. Such ideas find a natural home in the philosophical standpoint of absolute Idealism, and Nirvāṇa can be regarded as an alternative word for the Absolute. Broadly speaking, Buddhism is agnostic both about a personal creator and personal im-

The concept of Nirvāṇa

mortality, though Theravāda Buddhism explicitly rejects belief in a creator. Undoubtedly, the dominant theme of Buddhism is the quest for release from the changes and chances of this world, which will lead to the serenity and peace of Nirvāṇa. A Buddhist saint is someone who has indeed become the Absolute, which thus incorporates and transcends all human imperfections and struggles and all the imperfect ideas, ideals, and deities of popular religion and popular ways of thinking. The difference between the *arhat* of Theravāda, and the *bodhisattva* of the Mahāyāna is one between two different routes of realizing Nirvāṇa— the one through self-concentration; the other through self-sacrifice for the welfare of others. The difference is one between two "saintly" routes to the one saintliness—being possessed by and dwelling in the Absolute.

Thus, Buddhism, by embracing what is, in effect, a metaphysical concept of the absolute, not only could but did hold together a complex mythology within a unifying philosophical insight and was able, as in Japan and China, to incorporate a complex popular pantheon of the cult of ancestors. Furthermore, it could combine a popular devotion to a personal lord with a mystical contemplation that had encouraged the development of Buddhist monasteries. In sponsoring such a broad synthetic (all-embracing) view, the philosophical significance of Mahāyāna (Greater Vehicle) Buddhism emerged. Such developments began about 100 BC and lasted for several centuries; it was Mahāyāna Buddhism that spread to China and East Asia to influence and modify the religions native to those areas. In Mahāyāna, the humanitarian saviour notion of the *bodhisattva* has some echoes in Kenotic Christianity (*i.e.,* emptying oneself to become a suffering servant), and attitudes to the Buddhist scriptures have parallels with those of Christians toward the Bible. Common to both is the view that revelation can express itself in developing forms and that it is a mistake to concentrate on the texts themselves, sacred though they are, rather than on that which transcends them and of which they are symbols and to which they point. In this respect, one may contrast the open and exploratory attitudes of many Buddhists and Christians toward their sacred books with the closed and rigid attitudes of most Muslims.

Confucian, Taoist, and Japanese concepts. Prior to the introduction of Buddhism into China in the 1st century AD, the two main strands of religious thought in that country were represented by Confucianism and Taoism. Confucianism displays a reverential propriety that is expressed and developed in social relationships and fulfilled in Heaven. Taoism claims that the wise man will constantly seek harmony and rapport with Tao (the Way), which, at one and the same time, is the way for men to follow if they would reach blessedness and the principle that underlies and sustains the world. As a concept that is both moral and cosmological, Tao has a logical status similar to that of the Logos (or Word, the active principle of God in creation and revelation) in Christian philosophy. The Taoist thinks little of the ways of the world, including the decorum of the Confucianist; his outlook rather encourages a laissez-faire policy toward the world and even withdrawal from its affairs. The immediate mystical experience of Taoism or the inspired behaviour of Confucianism can easily blend with Buddhism, which sets both within a metaphysics of the Absolute.

In Japanese religion are found the same two themes that are found in most religions, though in their extreme forms they are mutually exclusive. On the one hand is mysticism—specifically, nature mysticism, of which the mysticism of the Zen practitioner belonging to an intuitive meditative form of Buddhism is a specific example. In Zen Buddhism, religion is scarcely distinguished from an aesthetic experience in which shrines, gardens, mountains, woods, and streams reveal a mysterious beauty and in which the exercise of the intellect is at a minimum. In contrast to mysticism, there is devotion to a supreme personal lord, at one time symbolized in the emperor as a descendant of Amaterasu, the Sun-Goddess. At other times Shintō ("Way of the gods") devotion focussed on particular shrines and particular deities, just as Zen Buddhism could concentrate on a particular image or on

particular events. In both types of devotions, however, it could be argued that such particularity was fulfilled and transcended in the unity revealed to a mature mystical insight. These different philosophical positions have an interesting reflection in the Christian position in which the Christian claims to find evidence of God's presence and activity in particular places and situations (especially in the incarnation of Christ), though at the same time allowing for God to be omnipresent.

Hindu concepts. This mixture of a mystical contemplation, which sees the divine everywhere, and a personal devotion to a particularized divinity recur in Hinduism. The most characteristic feature of Hinduism, however, is the doctrine of an eternal soul and its rebirth. The universe is pictured as the arena in which the immortal soul engages in a succession of incarnations from which man seeks release, a release that true contemplation can give him, especially when approached through Yoga (a mental, physical, and spiritual meditation technique). At the same time, a sensitivity to the numinous (spiritual) has left open the possibility of and certainly encouraged personal devotion. The most famous of Indian scriptures, the *Bhagavadgītā* ("Song of God") has for its recurrent theme the majesty, glory, and terror of God and the devotion due to him, though as in Christianity these attributes are compatible with a loving God. In the matter of revelation and incarnation, it is an open question as to how far the Hindu conception of revelation is the same or similar to Christian or Muslim conceptions. The Hindu view of *avatāra* ("incarnation"), however, implies many incarnations and in a Christian context would demand many Christs; thus, the concept of *avatāra,* a salient feature of Vaiṣṇavism (centring on the veneration of Vishnu, the preserver), cannot be easily reconciled with the uniqueness attributed to Jesus.

Depending on the particular questions that determine a particular content of discussion, Hinduism can talk of a plurality of souls, when it would concentrate on the theme of reincarnation, but, especially when influenced by Buddhist (and also pre-Buddhist) ideas, it can also sponsor an absolutism, or a monism; yet, again, it can come very close to a traditional Western theism. On the whole, however, it might be said that Hinduism holds together in a creative tension both theism and monism, though often it appears that in conceptual foundations and philosophical discussion the theistic strand predominates. Even in its classical period (600 BC to 450 BC) Hinduism was characterized by an astonishing variety of doctrines and cultures. Indeed, it well illustrates a characteristic of Indian thought that is becoming more acceptable to Western ways of thinking— the notion that there are many different approaches to the truth, which matches the concept of a multiple theology. It was regarded, however, as a retrograde step when these varieties of culture, ritual, and mythology became hardened into social strata and castes.

In the medieval period, Śaṅkara (*c.* 788–820), the leading exponent of Advaita Vedānta, or nondualism, is the most significant Hindu figure in the philosophy of religion. Arguing in a way very reminiscent of absolute Idealism, he claimed that the only existent was an absolute and that all else was an illusion. In this context he equated *ātman* (the individual soul) with Brahman (the universal or absolute soul). Both were viewed as one in a cosmic consciousness. For Śaṅkara, only ignorance or lack of insight into the nature of being prevents a man from realizing his identity with Brahman and thus becoming here and now aware of the freedom that is his. Śaṅkara also allows as permissible, without being accepted as the truth, talk of God as personal and as creator and of men as separate souls related to one another and to him. This, however, is only considered a way of talking—salvation in the Absolute transcends all such imperfect discourse. The same logical problems recur here in the concept of Nirvāṇa in Buddhism. In Hinduism, the *Upaniṣads,* Hindu philosophical treatises, and the *Bhagavadgītā* use the imperfect language of finite man, who has not yet found release, and in this way they can only point beyond themselves to that which they cannot adequately express. Here again are ideas reminiscent of some of those in Western philosophy of religion in the

Doctrine of an eternal soul and rebirth

Concepts of ātman and Brahman

modern world: the importance of theological reticence, the limitations of theological language, and, in another context, the significance of "existential situations."

Twentieth-century Hinduism has been chiefly characterized by attempts to purify and reform the doctrines of its medieval period, to deepen its spirituality, to reassert its moral dimension, and to inspire social reform. Mahatma Gandhi and Sri Aurobindo, the founder of a spiritual community and a Communist, were significant in such ventures. Aurobindo has been compared with the French Jesuit paleontologist and theologian Teilhard de Chardin insofar as both have a repeated experience of cosmic consciousness and a profound belief in evolution, both of which point to a divinization of man.

Islāmic concepts. At the heart of Islām is an experience of awe before the one, all-powerful, mysterious creator Allāh. Thus, its dominant theme has been surrender, though it must not be forgotten that it has nurtured mystics to whom the mysterious and awesome God has revealed himself through created things. Allāh controls man's destiny, whether to salvation or damnation, which points to the ultimacy of God, to his majesty and power. The concept of heaven inspired warriors to fight to the death; the concept of hell encouraged loyalty by showing what terrible punishments awaited the disloyal. The Qur'ān (the Islāmic sacred scriptures) is regarded as an infallible book—a transcript of a tablet that is eternal in the heavens. Islām shows pre-eminently the strength and limitations of a total surrender based on clear-cut beliefs, themselves arising from a basis in infallible texts, the whole being translated into vigorous political and social practices associated with a rigorous ritual and ceremonial discipline. Its mixture of both rigour in theology and vigour in politics in India and the Middle East from the Middle Ages to the 20th century can perhaps be compared with the same mixture as has been seen in the Protestant and Catholic communities in Ireland since the 17th century. However much the concept and practice of holy warfare is repugnant to many minds today, in the context of Islām it implies a sensitivity to evil and a conviction that evil has to be resisted and overcome in a total dedication. In this way the faith of Islām has shaped human history by obedience to a resolute and powerful God. Islām also illustrates the point that predestination need not bring with it a submissive fatalism. Furthermore, it has to be granted that Islām has allowed, within itself, for some allegorical interpretations of the scriptures—explicitly by the Ṣūfīs (mystics)—and it has also allowed for differences of piety and beliefs and even intellectual exploration on the part of particular disciples. Nevertheless, to other religions Islām has shown itself to be very conservative and with a distrust of compromise and a passionate desire to proselytize.

East and West: common ground. In reviewing the different philosophical understandings of religions in both East and West, two points clearly emerge. First, that however great the variety, there is almost universal agreement that "what there is" is not restricted to the facts and features of the world as they are given to or received by man's senses. Secondly, what has been for the philosophy of religion in the East almost a permanent problem is coming to be a crucial problem for the West, viz., how to preserve both the concept of absolute spirit and the significance of personal individuality or, alternatively, how far one can speak reliably of God as a person. The West is becoming aware of the problematic character of religious discourse. If, in such ways, Western philosophy of religion can benefit from some of the insights of the East, so also can the East—as a growing interest in the Empiricists of the West demonstrates—gain from the West. Not least, scientific developments have created Eastern interest in the English Empiricists, particularly John Locke; Eastern philosophers also have been impressed by the political liberalism of some modern Western Empiricists, such as Bertrand Russell. The Empirical philosophy of religion, as it has been recently developed in the West, may provide basic approaches and techniques for a closer mutual study of religions in East and West.

Marginal note: The strength and limitations of a total surrender

BASIC THEMES AND PROBLEMS
IN THE PHILOSOPHY OF RELIGION

The problem of God, the Absolute, or the supreme value. *The existence of God.* The so-called proofs of God's existence are of two kinds: independent logical exercises or particular conclusions set within an overall metaphysics. Either way, the discourse of these independent proofs or metaphysical schemes is best viewed as speech designed to evoke a disclosure. A particular argument recommends, as a way of speaking about what the disclosure discloses, a particular brand of discourse offering an interpretation of the world and man and one that develops from a specific key idea grounded in the disclosure. The existence of an Absolute or a supreme value has never been concluded as a result of an isolated logical exercise but has always arisen in the context of a total metaphysics. Thus, a quasi-mathematical structure, for Spinoza; a dialectic method, for Hegel; and evolutionary considerations, for the modern French philosopher Henri Bergson, determined the discourse that these three philosophers used in order to evoke that situation to which God or Nature, the Absolute Spirit, or the life force became for them respectively key concepts of interpretation. Bradley similarly reached a belief in an Absolute Spirit by reflecting on the logical problems of relatedness.

The following are some traditional arguments for the existence of God restyled along the lines suggested above:

The ontological argument of Anselm of Canterbury (*c.* 1033–1109) takes a phrase "that than which nothing greater can be conceived" and uses it as a technique for disclosure, directing one without limit to an ever-increasing perspective, in the hope that at some point the light will dawn, whereupon the phrase "necessary being" will be used to develop talk of the God.

The cosmological argument uses as a technique for disclosure such questions as "Why is this thus?" or "Why is there anything at all?" In receiving replies to these questions in causal terms, the cosmological argument builds up an ever-increasing causal spread until a disclosure occurs, whereupon the phrase "first cause" specifies what is disclosed and advocates certain ways of talking.

The argument from design takes a story with acknowledged disclosure possibilities—*e.g.,* the interrelated parts of a watch—and uses this as a catalyst to evoke a disclosure around some ever-broadening purpose patterns of the universe, in relation to which one can speak of God in terms, for example, of eternal purpose.

What is, in different ways, implied by these arguments is that the word God is unique in its logic, that it works in discourse as no other word exactly works. Thus, one cannot say "God exists" but rather "God necessarily exists." This is sometimes expressed by remarking that the existence of God is not the existence of a physical object or even the existence of a person, though what can be said about persons is less misleading in speaking about God than in speaking about the logic of things. This point is sometimes made, albeit misleadingly by saying that God does not exist, but this is only a picturesque way of saying that he does not exist in the way that a table exists.

The nature of God. These reflections are of wider applicability in relation to the nature and attributes of God. Such attributes are spoken of in terms of personal models, such as wisdom, goodness, power, love, mercy, righteousness, and so on. These models, however, will always need qualification by words such as infinite, perfect, and all. What is quite clear is that grammar itself is no clue to the logic of phrases such as "infinitely wise." Although that phrase is similar in grammar to one such as "exceedingly wise"—a phrase that is entirely descriptive in its logic—it is logically quite different, because "infinitely wise" has both descriptive and what has been called performative force. In other words, it not only describes some matters of fact—some specimens of wisdom—because of the word wise, which works descriptively as a model, but it also generates something—the word infinite acting as an operator, continually directing persons to expand their understanding until a moment of vision emerges. Alternatively, the point that God is not a being has sometimes been made by saying that God is the ground of Being—

Marginal notes: The kinds of proofs of God's existence

Qualifications for personal models

"the ground of" functioning as a qualifier, operating as the model of beings, or things. The emphasis of such qualifiers is twofold. First, they remind one of the inadequacy of all language used to speak of God—language authorized by particular models that, arising in a moment of vision or disclosure, naturally originate speech about what the disclosure discloses. Secondly, qualifiers constantly point one back through developed discourse to that moment of vision in which the discourse originated and in which alone one knows what the discourse is speaking about. The logic of models and qualifiers is a way of combining the intelligibility and mystery that any philosophy of religion must preserve.

Language about God thus develops as a multiple discourse, having various strands of which each is authorized by a particular model and of which each must, somewhere along the line, be modified by the presence of the others. Thus, theological understanding is a complex interweaving of different strands, and not least is the task of the philosopher of religion to produce the most comprehensive, coherent, consistent, and simple discourse he can. When problems arise that seem to be problems about the nature of God—for example, the conflict between different attributes—these are most profitably translated into problems of language. They then become problems of how to create discourse of the kind that in the end produces the best understanding of a cosmic disclosure with a single individuation, in which all the pertinent discourse originates and about which all the different strands endeavour to speak.

The knowledge of God. Natural theology is the name given to the kind of discourse about God and the world that originates in natural moments of vision without reference to God's revelation of himself in an incarnation, and in this sense "natural theology" is distinguished from "revealed theology." Among some philosophers—*e.g.,* Locke—the distinction is one between general and special revelation. In natural theology are generally included the "proofs" of the existence of God, discussions about the immortality of the soul, and discussions about God's providential control of the world, which provides for man a state of moral probation.

Some have viewed religious experience as affording direct evidence for the existence of God. In any discussion of religious experience, however, it is important at the outset to distinguish religious experience in general—a sense of awe or reverence, or a sense of the numinous—from mystical experience. The language of mystics is notoriously confusing to those not accustomed to the mystical idiom, and a leading question is how far mystical experience can establish the kind of objective reference it claims. Words such as immediate, direct, and intuitive refer rather to the way in which the experience occurs as a disclosure rather than justifying one in taking as guaranteed the interpretation that this disclosure appears to bring with it. If one already has an interpretative scheme, then mystical experience may provide an instance of such a scheme, but this has been rightly described as supporting belief in God "on the way back" rather than "on the way out." The concept of revelation is used by Christians to describe the way in which God's activity is uniquely disclosed in Christ, and faith relates to the human attitude and response that matches revelation subjectively. Revelation is sometimes contrasted with discovery, the former being said to relate to a passive subject, the latter to an active subject, but the distinction is largely one of emphasis. Philosophers of religion are now inclined to view revelation in terms of activity that waits to be interpreted rather than as a revelation of propositions. Revelation thus relates to events rather than to doctrine. According to this view, doctrine could never have the ultimacy and finality that necessarily belongs to the givenness of God in his incarnation or incarnations.

Special problems. *Freedom.* Among the classical problems in the philosophy of religion are those of free will, self-identity, immortality, evil, and suffering. The freedom of the will is a claim for the uniqueness of the subject, known in occasions of activity in which the subject "comes alive" and realizes his subjectivity as that which cannot be reduced to the behaviour patterns and facts— *i.e.,* the objects—of the natural and social sciences. Such freedom is realized in responding to a situation that has equally come alive objectively to inspire a person and call forth such response. Some claim the predictable character of human behaviour rules out man's freedom; others state that the extent to which human behaviour is unpredictable argues for freedom. This controversy, however, does not in any way solve the problem of freedom; it only makes evident what kind of problem the problem of freedom is, viz., how far human nature is capable of being analyzed into behavioral terms without any residue.

Self-identity and immortality. When there has been a self-disclosure of transcendence, of what cannot be characterized in space and time, one cannot say that any self so disclosed entirely comes to an end. In this sense, there is an argument for personal immortality, though one can only talk sensibly about it by expressing immortality in terms of continuing personal life. In Christianity this becomes speech about the resurrection of the body, and in Hinduism it becomes speech about reincarnation in this world or in the universe at large. All detailed talk about a future life, whether in Christianity or other religions, is only a way of spelling out and pointing back to that experience of man's transcendence here and now, in terms of language that expresses the claim that such a transcendent element is not annihilated by death. To be articulate about immortality, emphasis is placed on features of life that, at first view, have high significance and point here and now to experiences in which man's self-disclosure is most often found—*e.g.,* inspiring music or the intimate and deep fellowship of a particularly significant meal. General claims for immortality in relation to an objective disclosure (whether it be spoken of in terms of God or moral ideals) have to be distinguished from, though they have evident similarities to, the Christian claim for eternal life. Eternal life is, according to the Christian view, a subjective self-disclosure alongside the objective disclosure of God's activity in Jesus Christ, and it is as unique as the uniqueness of God in Christ, a uniqueness that is, however, an inclusive, and not exclusive, uniqueness.

Evil and suffering. The problem of evil arises (1) from the loss of a sense of God's presence in the face of evil or suffering and (2) from an apparent conflict between the language used to describe God (*e.g.,* all powerful, all good, and all wise) and that to describe the world as being characterized by evil and suffering. The solution proffered by the Book of Job in the Old Testament is that of evoking such a sense of awe around the created universe that, discovering in this way a renewed sense of God's presence, one accepts both evil and good and contents himself verbally by acknowledging a final incomprehensibility.

Other solutions relate good and evil to God and thus seek consistency by relating good and evil to God's primary and secondary will or to God's willing and permitting, respectively. In demanding some overall purpose to complete such a story, however, these solutions point to others that seek to resolve the conflict between good and evil within some reconciling model, which is then used to specify, with suitable qualification, a purpose or attribute of God. Thus, the conflict necessarily involved in the creation of a community of freely responsible persons is used as a model to illuminate a personal conflict exhibited, for example, by war. Also, the conflicts resulting from general rules imposed for the sake of training are used to provide a model to illuminate the disharmony exhibited in, for example, earthquakes or floods. These models are then developed and amplified in order to lead one to a renewed disclosure of God's presence. These solutions—by raising questions about God's character—perhaps point to another solution that attributes to God redeeming love—something that, as directed to evil, can be creative of personal maturity and fulfillment in a way not otherwise attainable. This attribute must then be appropriately qualified so as to lead to a renewed disclosure of God's presence, in this way enabling one both to face evil and to talk of it more coherently in relation to God.

In the matter of absolute Idealism, which is the kind of metaphysics implied in Eastern religions generally, evil

---

Marginal notes:

Natural and revealed theology

Arguments for personal immortality

and good are transcended in the Absolute Spirit that is beyond good and evil. Logically, this is akin to the solution of the Book of Job.

THE PRESENT SITUATION
IN THE PHILOSOPHY OF RELIGION

Interest in religious language

In the latter part of the 20th century in western Europe and the United States there has been an Empirical philosophy of religion, the interest of which has been in religious language and the kind of Empirical basis there can be for religious discourse. The definitive question has been concerned with what are the patterns of religious reasoning and what is the character of religious language if such discourse points back to and articulates situations of the particular kind that have been discussed above. The approach originated in what has been called Logical Positivism. According to the verification principle, which gave what the Positivists considered to be the touchstone of meaning, an assertion had meaning if and only if it was verifiable at least in principle by sense experience. Logical Positivists were not at all daunted when this seemed to exclude the whole of theology and a good deal of ethics from meaningful discourse.

Since the 1950s, however, there has been a reaction against the Positivist's veto, and the works of the Austrian British philosopher Ludwig Wittgenstein are symptomatic of those who broadened Empiricism so that it has become interested in displaying and elucidating the variegation of language, in setting language in actual contexts, and in relating it to specific situations. Significantly, this mellowing of Empiricism has been accompanied by a growing interest in personality and the self. This newer emphasis of Empiricism unites with Existentialism in suggesting that personal situations may very well provide helpful parallels to religious situations. There has been introduced into the philosophy of religion a renewed sense of the significance of mystery and a new emphasis on theological reticence. With this has come a renewed awareness of the significance of metaphor, myth, and symbol, and there has also emerged a significant use of the concept of the model. The use of terms like myth and mythological, it is important to recognize, does not mean that the assertions so called are false. Myth includes stories that try to articulate what is objectively given in a certain religious situation. Myths also relate to historical events—though the myth may be selective in its choice of such events—when speech about these events is used to articulate a claim of a transcendent kind. In other words, myth, metaphor, symbol, and model are all ways of expressing in ordinary language an extraordinary point.

Questions of reference and criteria

The present stress on metaphors and models in religious language, however, inevitably raises two far-reaching questions: the question of reference and the question of criteria. The former concerns the possibility of the assurance that one is talking about anything at all. The latter concerns what the criteria are for better and worse ways of talking. The question of criteria has been answered in terms of the logical character and the empirical pattern of the multimodel discourse to which the different strands arising from the different metaphors or models give rise. That this discourse talks about something must in the end rest on the claim that, in a disclosure situation, a subject is relatively passive—*i.e.,* aware of an activity bearing on his own and thus aware of something other than himself about which he is talking.

In this context the significance of the Existentialist approach is to underline, as does recent Empiricism, the importance of a wider view of human experience than ordinary scientific experience might allow and to point one to highly significant personal situations that cannot be netted in scientific terms. The phenomenological approach, as developed by the Moravian philosopher Edmund Husserl, represents an attempt to be objective and scientific about experience, an endeavour to set out facts uncompromised and unprejudiced by metaphysical frameworks. As an endeavour to reach agreement on what is being talked about and as an attempt to seek the simplest and clearest interpretations, the phenomenological approach has been applauded by many philosophers of religion and theologians. There can be no question, however, about a purely scientific account of a religious situation—that would be a contradiction in terms, and, though there can be a phenomenological approach to religious situations, there can be no phenomenological explanation of them that claims to be adequate. The main contribution of Phenomenology is that of encouraging scholars to describe situations with as much critical analysis as possible.

Logical Empiricism, it might be said, has absorbed something of the Phenomenologists' concern. It has certainly raised questions about and directed interest toward the way situations are talked about and interpreted, the possibility of there being different interpretations of the same situation, and so on. In this way it has provided the tools for and greatly stimulated contemporary interest in hermeneutics (critical interpretations)—a second order appraisal of interpretations together with an interest in their empirical bases.

The future of the philosophy of religion

As to the future of the philosophy of religion, a merging of the Empirical and Existential strands may well be expected. Metaphysical and religious views of the future most likely will combine conviction with tolerance and commitment with openness. The commitment and the conviction will probably come from moments of vision. Claims to finality, fanaticism, and bigotry will disappear, it is hoped, when it is made obvious that no self-guaranteed translations of what disclosure is are given, and tolerance and openness will arise from the acknowledgment that all understanding of these moments of vision is a multiple exploration, an exploration yielding different strands of discourse. Solutions to contemporary problems, social and intellectual, demand a multiple consideration by scholars from many disciplines of all the issues involved in the problem, a consideration set within a framework of faith and morality in which man is interpreted as distinctively human, characteristically a person. From such interprofessional, interdisciplinary groups may emerge a new metaphysics and a new theology linked with, but by no means prescriptive of, assertions in other subjects. In this way there may be created a new culture—scientific, moral, religious, and technological at the same time. To be involved in such groups would seem to be the main task of the philosopher of religion, as of the metaphysician, today. If he is successful and if these interdisciplinary groups are creative, the modern period will then take its place among those that have marked crucial turning points in the history of mankind and its culture. (I.T.R.)

Philosophy of art

DISTINGUISHING CHARACTERISTICS

Difference between the philosophy of art and art criticism

The philosophy of art is distinguished from art criticism, which is concerned with the analysis and evaluation of particular works of art. Critical activity may be primarily historical, as when a lecture is given on the conventions of the Elizabethan theatre in order to explain some of the devices used in Shakespeare's plays. It may be primarily analytical, as when a certain passage of poetry is separated into its elements and its meaning or import explained in relation to other passages and other poems in the tradition. Or it may be primarily evaluative, as when reasons are given for saying that the work of art in question is good or bad, or better or worse than another one. Sometimes it is not a single work of art but an entire class of works in a certain style or genre (such as pastoral poems or Baroque music) that is being elucidated; and sometimes it is the art of an entire period (such as Romantic). But in every case, the aim of art criticism is to achieve an increased understanding or enjoyment of the work (or classes of works) of art, and its statements are designed to achieve this end.

The test of the success of art criticism with a given person is: has this essay or book of art criticism increased his understanding or enhanced his appreciation of the work of art in question? Art criticism is particularly helpful and often necessary for works of art that are more than usually difficult, so that the average person would be unable adequately to understand or enjoy them if left to himself. The task of the philosopher of art is more fundamental than that of the art critic in that the critic's pronouncements presuppose answers to the questions set by the philosopher of art. The critic says that a given work of music is expressive; but the philosopher of art asks what is meant by saying that a work of art is expressive and how one determines whether it is. In speaking and writing about art, the critic presupposes that he is dealing with clear concepts, the attainment of which is the task of the philosopher of art.

The task of the philosopher of art is not to heighten understanding and appreciation of works of art but to provide conceptual foundations for the critic by (1) examining the basic concepts underlying the critic's activities to enable him to speak and write more intelligibly about the arts, and by (2) arriving at true conclusions about art, aesthetic value, expression, and the other concepts that the critic employs.

The meaning of "art"

Upon what does the philosopher of art direct his attention? "Art," is the ready answer; but what is art and what distinguishes it from all other things? The theorists who have attempted to answer this question are many, and their answers differ greatly. But there is one feature that virtually all of them have in common: a work of art is a man-made thing, an artifact, as distinguished from an object in nature. A sunset may be beautiful, but it is not a work of art. A piece of driftwood may have aesthetic qualities, but it is not a work of art since it was not made by man. On the other hand, a piece of wood that has been carved to look like driftwood is not an object of nature but of art, even though the appearance of the two may be exactly the same. This distinction is being challenged in the 20th century by artists who declare that *objets trouvés* ("found objects") are works of art, since the artist's perception of them as such makes them so, even if the objects were not man-made and were not modified in any way (except by exhibition) from their natural state.

Nevertheless, according to the simplest and widest definition, art is anything that is man-made. Within the scope of this definition, not only paintings and sculptures but also buildings, furniture, automobiles, cities, and garbage dumps are all works of art: every change that human activity has wrought upon the face of nature is art, be it good or bad, beautiful or ugly, beneficial or destructive.

The ordinary usage of the term is clearly less wide. In daily life when works of art are spoken of, the intention is to denote a much narrower range of objects, namely, those responded to aesthetically. Among the things in this narrower range, a distinction, although not a precise one, is made between fine and useful art. Fine art consists of those works designed to produce an aesthetic response or that (regardless of design) function as objects of aesthetic appreciation (such as paintings, sculptures, poems, musical compositions)—those man-made things that are enjoyed for their own sake rather than as means to something else. Useful art has both an aesthetic and a utilitarian dimension: automobiles, glass tumblers, woven baskets, desk lamps, and a host of other handmade or manufactured objects have a primarily useful function and are made for that purpose, but they also have an aesthetic dimension: they can be enjoyed as objects of beauty, so much so that a person often buys one brand of car rather than another for aesthetic reasons even more than for mechanical reasons (of which he may know nothing). A borderline case is architecture: many buildings are useful objects the aesthetic function of which is marginal, and other buildings are primarily objects of beauty the utility of which is incidental or no longer existent (Greek temples were once places of worship, but today their value is entirely aesthetic). The test in practice is not how they were intended by their creators, but how they function in present-day experience. Many great works of painting and sculpture, for example, were created to glorify a deity and not, insofar as can be ascertained, for an aesthetic purpose (to be enjoyed simply in the contemplation of them for their own sake). It should be added, however, that many artists were undoubtedly concerned to satisfy their aesthetic capabilities in the creation of their work, since they were highly perfectionistic as artists; but in their time there was no such discipline as aesthetics in which they could articulate their goals; in any case, they chose to create "for

the greater glory of God" by producing works that were also worthwhile to contemplate for their own sake.

This aesthetic sense of the word "art," whether applied to fine art or useful art, is the one most employed by the majority of critics and philosophers of art today. There are two other senses of "art," however, that are still narrower, and, to avoid confusion, their use should be noted: (1) Sometimes the term "art" is restricted to the visual arts alone or to some of the visual arts. Thus, the art department in 20th-century colleges and universities is usually the department of painting and sculpture (and sometimes architecture). But as philosophers of art use the term (and as it is used here), art is not limited to visual art; music and drama and poetry are as much arts as painting, sculpture, and architecture. (2) Sometimes the term "art" is used in a persuasive sense, to include only those works considered good art. "That's not art!" exclaims the viewer at an art gallery as he examines a painting he dislikes. But if the term "art" is to be used without confusion, it must be possible for there to be bad art as well as good art; the viewer, then, is not really denying that the work in question is art (it is a man-made object presented to be contemplated for its own sake) but only that it is worthwhile.

Other senses of the term "art"

The word "art" is also ambiguous in another way: it is sometimes used to designate the activity of creating a work of art, as in the slogan "Art is expression"; but it is more often used to designate the product of that process, the completed artwork or artifact itself, as in the remark "Art is a source of great enjoyment to me." There will be occasion later to remark on this ambiguity.

Countless proffered definitions of "art" are not definitions at all but theories about the nature of art that presuppose that the ability to identify certain things in the world as works of art already exists. Most of them are highly unsatisfactory even as theories. "Art is an exploration of reality through a sensuous presentation"—but in what way is it an exploration? Is it always concerned with reality (how is music concerned with reality, for example)? "Art is a re-creation of reality"—but is all art re-creation, even music? (It would seem likely that music is the creation of something, namely, a new set of tonal relationships, but not that it is the re-creation of anything at all.) "Art is an expression of feeling through a medium"—but is it always an expression (see below *Art as expression*) and is it always feeling that is expressed? And so on. It appears more certain that Shakespeare's *King Lear* is a work of art than that these theories are true. All that seems to be required for identifying something as a work of art in the wide sense is that it is not a natural object but something made or transformed by man; and all that is required for identifying it as art (not as good art but as art) in the narrower sense is that it functions aesthetically in man's experience, either wholly (fine art) or in part (useful art); it is not even necessary, as has been shown, that it be intended by its creator to function in this way.

THE INTERPRETATION OF ART

Works of art present problems of both interpretation and evaluation. Evaluation is not the concern of this article (see AESTHETICS); but one problem about interpretation deserves to be mentioned. Works of art are often difficult, and how to interpret them properly is far from obvious. The question then arises as to what factors should guide efforts at interpretation.

At one extreme lies the view known as isolationism, according to which a knowledge of the artist's biography, historical background, and other factors is irrelevant to an appreciation of the work of art and usually is harmful in that it gets in the way, tending to substitute a recital of these facts for the more difficult attempt to come to grips with the work of art itself. If the work of art is not understood on first acquaintance, it should be read (or heard, or viewed) again and yet again. Constant re-exposure to it, so that the recipient is totally absorbed in and permeated by it, is the way to maximum appreciation.

Isolationism and contextualism

At the other extreme, contextualism holds that the work of art should always be apprehended in its context or setting and that not merely knowledge about it but total appreciation of it is much richer if it is approached with this knowledge. According to the contextualists, not only literature (ordinarily appreciated contextually) but also the other arts, even nonrepresentational painting and music, should be apprehended in this way.

No critic or art lover need hold to either position in its undiluted form: a person could well be an isolationist about some kinds of art, such as music, a contextualist about others, such as historical dramas and religious paintings. It is essential to be more specific, however, about the factors—other than careful and repeated perusal of the work of art itself—that the contextualist holds are either necessary or extremely helpful in the appreciation of works of art:

1. Other works of art by the same artist. If the artist has created other works, particularly in the same genre, acquaintance with them may enhance appreciation of the work at hand. Quantity of works has no particular merit in itself; but, when, say one of the piano concertos of the 18th-century Austrian composer Wolfgang Amadeus Mozart is heard, the auditor may (often largely unconsciously) compare its mode, thematic material, and method of development and resolution with some of Mozart's 25 other piano concertos. Knowledge of the entire corpus of his work in a certain genre may heighten enjoyment of a particular work.

2. Other works of art in the same genre by other artists, particularly in the same style or tradition. Appreciation of the pastoral poem "Lycidas," by the English poet John Milton, is doubtless enhanced by a study of the pastoral tradition in poetry, with which Milton supposed his readers to be acquainted. To study "Lycidas" in isolation would needlessly deprive the reader of much of the richness of texture of the poem and would even make some of the references in it unintelligible.

3. A study of relevant facts about the artistic medium, such as the instrumental limitations or advantages of pipe organs in the time of the German composer Johann Sebastian Bach (1685–1750) or the modes of presentation of ancient Greek tragedies in the Athenian theatre. An acquaintance with the artistic conventions and idioms in which the artist operated often leads to better understanding of certain aspects of his work and helps to avert misunderstandings of it.

4. A study of the age in which the artist lived—the spirit of the time and its current ideas, the complex influences that molded the artist, even the social, economic, and political conditions of the time and place in which he worked. Sometimes such knowledge is of dubious relevance: it can be argued that no aid to the study of the 82 string quartets and 104 symphonies of the 18th-century Austrian composer Joseph Haydn is provided by reading about the political and economic conditions of his day. It is interesting to study the evolution of the string quartet or symphony from its origin through Haydn to the present; but this would appear to be an evolution traceable entirely within the art form and not dependent on factors outside it. This, however, is not always so: particularly in literature, where a study of such exterior factors seems to be of much more relevance. It would seem important to know, for example, that Milton was aware of the new Copernican astronomy but deliberately chose in *Paradise Lost* to make his cosmos Ptolemaic, the antiquated astronomical system that was already steeped in literature, mythology, and tradition.

5. A study of the artist's life. Anthologists of literature constantly assume that this is an important consideration, since they supply detailed biographies prior to their selections by each author. It is true, of course, that knowledge of the artist's life can distract attention from his work, as with those who cannot hear Beethoven's late quartets without constantly thinking, "What a pity it was that he was deaf at the time!" Yet such knowledge may also heighten experience of a work; some would say, at any rate, that it helps to know that Milton was blind when he wrote the sonnet "On His Blindness." It is the relevance of this kind of knowledge to an appreciation of the poem, as a poem, that is in dispute. In every case, however, it should be kept in mind that acquaintance with the artist's biography is a means toward an end, the enhanced ap-

External influences on the artist

preciation and understanding of the work of art, and that otherwise it is aesthetically irrelevant. The facts about the artist's life are the means and the enhanced appreciation the end, not the other way around, as is often found, for example in psychoanalytic essays attempting to infer facts about the artist's subconscious conflicts from his work; in these cases the work is being taken as the means and the study of his life as the end.

6. A study of the artist's intentions. It is this factor that has prompted the principal controversy in the mid-20th century. When difficulties arise as to what to make of a work of art or when several conflicting interpretations come to mind, how is the difficulty to be resolved? One obvious suggestion is to consult the artist or his records or memoirs or the testimony of people who knew him, to discover what his intentions were with regard to the work or the passage. It is tempting to believe that whichever way he intended it this is the way the work should be interpreted; for in regard to his own work, surely the author's own word should be law.

This temptation is hotly decried by other critics as "the intentional fallacy"—the fallacy (if it is a fallacy) of believing that whichever way the artist intended it is by definition the way it really is. A work of art should stand on its own, without help from the artist; if he has not sufficiently realized his intentions within the work, forcing the recipient to go outside for help, this is held to be an artistic defect. Once the artist has completed his work, moreover, and presented it to the world, it belongs to the world and no longer exclusively to him: in the interpretation of it he now becomes just one critic among many, whose word should be respected but not taken as the final authority. Perhaps other critics can think of better interpretations than he did, which give a greater aesthetic reward in subsequent encounters with the work; perhaps there are even acceptable interpretations (such as the Freudian interpretations of Shakespeare's *Hamlet*) that he could not possibly have thought of himself at the time.

"Intentional fallacy"

In the late 18th and early 19th centuries, Johann Wolfgang von Goethe set forth three criteria for critics to consider in interpreting and evaluating a work of art: (1) What was the artist trying to do? (2) Did he do it? (3) Was it worth doing? The first of the three is intentionalistic; and, says the intentionalist, surely this is plausible: an artist can hardly be blamed for failing to do what he had no intention of doing. It must first be known, then, what he was trying to do.

But the anti-intentionalist points out that the intention makes no difference, only the product does. If the ballerina excuses her fall in the middle of the dance by saying that she intended it, the dance is just as marred aesthetically as if she had fallen accidentally. And if a poet admits that he wrote rubbish and says that this is just what he intended to write, one does not rate the poem any higher because the poet's intention was fulfilled.

The persistent questioner might ask, however, if there are not at least some works of art in which the intentions of the artist have to be known? Suppose that a contemporary critic reads a dull, stodgy, moralistic Victorian novel and says at the end, "What an excellent parody of a Victorian novel!" But it was not a parody; its intentions were deadly serious—and should not this be known in order to interpret and evaluate it properly? Not at all, replies the anti-intentionalist; all the critic has to say is, "As a Victorian novel, this is deadly dull; as a parody of a Victorian novel, it is brilliant; if the author intended it in the former way, so much the worse for him—his work can still be praised for being brilliant parody, even if it wasn't intended as one. He just achieved something better than he knew at the time."

Still, the intentionalist has a point: sometimes the clue to unlock an otherwise intransigent work may come from the author's statement of intention, and a plausible interpretation might be unobtainable without it. Such a suggestion might have come from a reader other than the author; but there is no point in disdaining helpful hints, regardless of their source. If the suggestion does come from the artist himself, that is nothing against it. Perhaps a work is less aesthetically perfect because it requires outside clues to its

The author's statement of intention

interpretation, but few works of art even approach perfection, and they may yet amply repay attention, all the more if some plausible suggestion comes from the outside. The 20th-century Russian composer Sergey Prokofiev intended his *Classical Symphony* to be a parody of the classical symphonies of Mozart and Haydn—and regardless of whether the suggestion that it be construed this way came from Prokofiev (as it did) or from someone else, if it is rewarding to listen to it in this way, then no one gains by refusing to accept the suggestion. A statement of intention is not the only key to unlocking the secrets of works of art, but it is one key among many, and there appears to be no good reason why it should not be used.

THE MEDIUMS OF ART

In the context of every work of art there are three items to consider:

1. The genesis of the work of art.
2. The artifact, or work of art, which is a publicly available object or thing made by the artist and viewed by the audience.
3. The effects of the work of art upon the audience.

The first item comprises all the artist's mental states, both conscious and unconscious, in the creation of the work, including his intention with regard to the work, as well as all the factors that led to these states of mind: for example, the spirit of the age, the socio-economic conditions of the times, his exchange of ideas with other artists, and so forth. Whatever factors helped to form the work of art in the artist's mind fall under this heading. The experiences undergone by the artist in the creation of the work constitute the artistic experience.

The third item includes all the effects of the work of art upon those who experience it, including both aesthetic and nonaesthetic reactions, the influence of the work of art upon the culture, on the state of knowledge, on current morality, and the like. The experience that involves the observer's attention to the work of art for its own sake and not for the sake of some ulterior end is called aesthetic, but of course art has many effects that are not aesthetic. The aesthetic experience belongs to the consumer of art, as opposed to the artistic experience, which belongs to the creator of art.

The second item is what is usually called the work of art itself. According to some writers, such as the Italian philosopher Benedetto Croce (1866–1952), the work of art exists only in the mind of the artist, and the physical artifact then counts as an effect of the work of art. But in ordinary usage, as well as the usage of most philosophers of art, the work of art is identified with the physical artifact, as it exists in the physical medium. What goes on in the creator's mind is already contained in the first item.

Every work of art occurs in a medium; that is, there is some physical object or series of events by which the work is communicated to the recipient (listener, observer, reader) by means of his senses. In painting, the medium is paint; in sculpture, such materials as stone or wood or plastic. It might at first be thought that the medium of music consists of the musical score on which the composer writes the notes; but the written notes are not music, they are a set of visual cues for the production of the tones to be emitted by the various instruments. If every player had a perfect memory, he would have no need for the written score; indeed, music existed long before there were any written scores and was played or sung from memory from one year or generation to the next. It could be said more plausibly that the medium of music consists of the physical sound waves by means of which the sound sensations enter the consciousness of the listener. The medium of literature can truly be said to be words, yet not words as abstract entities conceived in the mind but words as spoken (in oral presentation) or written. The physical medium of literature, then, is either auditory or visual, although what is conveyed through the medium is not.

Classifying arts by their mediums. There are many ways of classifying the arts—by their purpose, by their intentions, by their effects. But the most usual and the most fundamental method of classifying the arts is by their mediums:

The medium of music

Visual art. This includes two-dimensional visual arts such as drawing and painting and also three-dimensional visual arts such as sculpture and architecture. Some of these should doubtless be called visuo-tactual art: buildings are ordinarily touched as well as seen, sculptures could be more fully appreciated if touched as well as seen, and even paintings may sometimes have enough three-dimensionality to repay touch experience. At any rate, all these arts appeal first and foremost, though not exclusively, to the sense of sight; and the artifact is an object in the visual medium.

Auditory art. This includes music in all its forms but not song, opera, and those arts that combine music with literature (see below). Just as the medium of visual art is sight, so the medium of auditory art is sound.

In auditory art there is—unlike visual art—no physical object (other than the score, which as has been seen is not the music). There is only the temporally successive series of sounds: sound waves emanating from the various instruments. While no such tones are being emitted, no sounds exist; only the musical score exists (and the memories of listeners, some of whom might enable the score to be reproduced if it were lost), from which music can be reproduced. Unlike the existence of paintings and sculptures, the existence of musical sounds is intermittent. In what sense, then, does the music exist between performances? It exists only in the sense that it is reproducible from the written score.

Verbal art. The art of literature is clearly different from both visual and auditory art. There are sound values in poetry, particularly when read aloud; but as sound alone, literature would be the most poverty-stricken of arts: what makes the sounds of poetry effective is (at least 99 percent) knowledge of the meanings of the words heard. Listening to the sounds of a poem or play uttered in an unfamiliar language gives some idea of the importance in literature of knowing the meanings of the words. Note that "murmuring," one of the most pleasant sounding words in English, has almost the same sounds as "murdering." It is almost exclusively a knowledge of word meanings that makes it possible to appreciate the art of literature.

The meanings of words

Nor is literature a visual art, although it is customary to read works of literature from a printed page. A critic who said, "I think this poem is a bad one, because it is written in unpleasant small type in double-column pages on yellowed paper," might be giving advice to typesetters and book designers (these two groups are engaged in the practice of visual arts), but he would be saying nothing about the merits of the poem. The printed or written word or for that matter the spoken word is only a vehicle for the meanings. Literature, then, must be placed in a separate class from either auditory or visual arts.

Mixed arts. Other arts variously combine the above three types of arts; this group includes all the arts of performance. Drama combines the art of literature (verbal art) with the visual arts of costuming, stage designing, and so on. Opera combines the art of music (its predominant component) with the art of literature (the libretto) and the visual arts of stage design. Dance combines the visual spectacle of moving bodies (the principal component) with musical accompaniment, sometimes with accompanying words and often with stage design. Song combines words with music. The motion picture combines the visual component (a series of pictures presented in such rapid succession that they appear to be moving) with the verbal component (the script) and usually an intermittent musical background as well.

All the visual arts are also spatial arts, or arts of space; music and literature are both temporal arts, or arts of time. This leads to very great differences in the things each can do. In temporal arts, the parts do not appear together before the audience but appear successively in time, the second moment not beginning until the first one has finished. In spatial arts, the entire work of art is present simultaneously; attention to the parts of it is successive—it is impossible to concentrate on the whole at once, at least on first viewing—but the entire object is nevertheless there, and it is up to the viewer which part he shall examine first. In three-dimensional art, such as

Spatial arts and temporal arts

sculpture and architecture, the entire object is present, but it is impossible even to see (much less to look at) all of it at once: the back of a statue cannot be seen at the same moment as the front and the exterior of a cathedral cannot be viewed by someone inside it.

Temporal arts must be attended to in a certain order: it is impossible to hear the symphony played backward, or the drama, or the movie; even when technically it can be done (as in running a motion picture in reverse), the results usually are an aesthetic catastrophe. The recipient is supposed to attend to the temporal work's various parts in an order predetermined by the artist. For this reason, painting is not capable of telling a story in the way that a novel is; for a story is a series of temporally successive happenings, and a painting can at best take a series of represented persons and objects and show them as they exist at one moment only, one knife-edge of time; whereas a novel can depict the temporally successive happenings in the order of their occurrence (or in a different order, such as flashback).

The German aesthetician and dramatist Gotthold Lessing made this distinction the basis of his study *Laokoon,* contending that the function of visual art is to create beautiful objects and that the artist should select that stance or moment at which the person or object appears most beautiful, to enable the viewer to continue looking at it with pleasure; whereas literature, being temporal, is equipped to tell a story that includes many moments other than pleasing ones (moreover, the scenes in literature are not seen with the eyes but only imagined). Lessing's thesis that each art should restrict itself to what it can do best or is peculiarly equipped by its medium to do is a highly controversial one: it would virtually eliminate program music, for example, and descriptions of nature in novels. The tendency of art today is to attempt to curtail distinctions between time and space rather than to preserve them.

Differences in the arts related to mediums.   Very significant differences among the arts occur because of the differences in their mediums:

Literary and nonliterary.   The greatest difference among the arts is between the literary and the nonliterary. Literature consists of a system of symbols with assigned meanings. A word is not simply a noise (or a mark on a printed page); a word is a noise or a printed mark with an assigned meaning. In different languages, different noises have been assigned meanings, and the language must be learned in order to understand what is being said. To appreciate the work of the 11th-century novelist Lady Murasaki Shikibu, one must learn Japanese; to fully appreciate Molière, the 17th-century playwright, one must learn French. No other art has this problem: the Englishman can appreciate German music as well as a German—or if he does not, it is not for lack of learning a language.

Assigned meanings of words

Shapes, colours, and tones do not have assigned meanings. That is not to say that these elements when present in art cannot be said to have some sense of the term "meaning." There are many meanings of the word "meaning," and a colour, for example, can have meaning in that it may symbolize something, as red symbolizes courage; or it may have strong emotional or other effects upon the viewer, evoking all manner of strong associations. But a colour or a tone has no assigned meaning: if the question were asked, "What does middle C mean?", the answer would be, "It has no assigned meaning at all; in that sense, it means nothing—it just has certain effects." But if the meaning of a certain word in a poem is not known, the reader is to that extent prevented from appreciating the poem; for the medium of poetry is not noises, not printed marks, but words, and the difference between a noise and a word lies in the fact that a word is a noise with a meaning.

This fact makes for an enormous difference between literature and the other arts. A colour in a painting may be the colour of an object represented; a colour may even "mean" something; for example, the white of a white flag that a person depicted in a battle painting is holding up as a sign of surrender. But a colour, as a colour, has no meaning at all; and the same is true of musical tones. A pattern of musical tones may occasionally acquire a mean-

ing (the first four tones of Beethoven's *Fifth Symphony* were used to symbolize victory in World War II), but when this happens it really has very little to do with the music, and in any case most music is appreciated without any such symbolism being present. But a noise, however pleasing to the ear, is only a noise and not a word unless it has an assigned meaning; and one must know what that meaning is in order to appreciate a poem or any other work of literature.

The translation problem.   Because literature consists of conventional symbols, there exists in literature the problem of translation, which does not exist in the other arts. When one seeks to make a work of literature available to a wider audience than that composed of only the native speakers of the language in which the work was written, the process of translation must be resorted to, and, in this process, a great deal of the work's original character is lost.

In a poem there are (1) the sounds, (2) the dictionary meanings of the words, and (3) the connotations of the words—the manifold associations that they evoke (sensory, intellectual, and emotional) in the minds of readers. The sounds are the least important of the three, and many a great poem as sheer sound is hardly even pleasing. The finding of like dictionary meanings is usually a simple matter, and when there is a word that has no rough equivalent in the other language, it may be simply retained in the original language (for example, the German word *Weltanschauung,* meaning something like "world outlook," is often retained in English translations of German works). As for the associations that hover about a word, they may vary from language to language, so that if a work is translated rather literally, the associative values of the words are lost. Thus, "My God!" is a much stronger expletive in English than "mon dieu" is in French, so that if the French expression is translated into the English one, it is, though literally correct, quite unfaithful to the weaker emotive force of the French expression. Words can often be found in the second language that have a roughly equivalent associative value to the original one, but these will usually not provide a literal translation; thus, the translator is faced with the dilemma of being able to provide a literal-meaning translation or a translation that renders the spirit or "feel" of the original but not both.

Difficulties in translating poetry

The question of correspondence to actuality.   The arts also differ from one another, according to their mediums, in whether the items in the medium correspond to items in the world. Objects with colours and shapes are represented on canvas, and objects with colours and shapes also exist in the outside world. Even when a painting is non-representational, it consists of colours and shapes, which are items in the outside world (even though certain individual colours and shapes in the painting may not exist in the outside world). But the case with music is different: though the visual arts may (to varying degrees) convey the sights of nature, music does not convey the sounds of nature. Even when a work of music attempts to represent the sound of an iron foundry or the clattering of horses' hooves, it really does not sound like these things: musical instruments emit tones, and in nature are found largely noises, and between the two there is an enormous auditory difference. Some rhythms of nature can be duplicated by musical instruments but hardly the sounds themselves.

The medium of literature, words, is indeed man created; but of course this feature is far from unique to literature. Words were devised and employed in countless situations of daily life before they were ever embodied in literature; so in literature, as in visual art, a medium is being employed that existed before the art itself.

ART AS IMITATION (REPRESENTATION)

The view that "art is imitation" is at least as old as the Greek philosopher Plato (428–347 BC), and, although not widely held today, its long and distinguished history is evidence of its continuing hold on human beings as an account of the distinctive function of art. A terminological point, however, is in order here: in the interests of clarity, an artist should be spoken of as representing in his work the persons and things and scenes of the world but as imitating the work of other artists. Thus, "In this painting he represents a barn and some wheat fields, and in his style he is imitative of Vincent van Gogh." This distinction will be employed here, with the result that these traditional theories of art will be spoken of as theories of representation rather than of imitation.

At some period in the history of art, aestheticians and critics wrote as if nature should be recorded by the artist with photographic fidelity. The invention of photography (which can do this better than any painter) could plausibly be said to have relieved the artist of any such responsibility. Still, art can represent reality: the representation of a house in a painting may not look exactly like a house—it cannot, since the real house is three-dimensional and the painting is two-dimensional—but it looks enough like one to enable everyone unhesitatingly to identify it as a house.

Distinction between depiction and portrayal

A distinction should be made between depiction and portrayal. A painting may be said to depict a house if it looks more like a house than like anything else. Thus, most persons unhesitatingly classify this as a man, that as a tree, and so on; only when the painter has distorted or abstracted so much that a thing looks somewhat like a wolf and also somewhat like a bobcat, do they hesitate in saying what the object represented is. A picture may depict a rather short man in a French general's uniform of the early 19th century; but it may, in addition, portray Napoleon. It portrays Napoleon if (1) the artist intended it to represent Napoleon (for example, if the title of the painting is "Napoleon") and (2) the painting does look like Napoleon to some degree at least—at any rate it contains no important characteristics known to be incompatible with those of Napoleon. Clearly, if it is a painting that depicts a tree in someone's yard, it cannot be considered a portrait of Napoleon, no matter how much the artist said he intended it to be one. Depiction subjects can ordinarily be recognized at once with a little knowledge of the world and the names of the things in it. Portrayal subjects require knowledge of whomever the artist intended to portray; even when that seems obvious, as in the case of Napoleon (who would be instantly recognized, unlike the portrait of a private in his army), the viewer would have to be told, by the title or otherwise, that not only does the painting depict a man in a French general's uniform but that it was intended by the artist to be a portrait of this particular man. Otherwise, how would the viewer know that it did not actually portray his double, or his stand-in? The word represent, as used in connection with art, can mean either "depict" or "portray."

Analysis of representation. Representation always involves a certain degree of abstraction; that is, the taking away of one characteristic or more of the original. Even a fairly realistic painting of a person, for example, lacks some features that characterize actual persons: the painting is two-dimensional, whereas every actual person is three-dimensional; the surface of a painting is paint, but not so the person; the actual person has very numerous pores and other marks on his face that are lacking (in whole or in part) in the painting, and so on. The depiction of a person in a painting is usually sufficient to enable human viewers to recognize the figure as a person—though it is apparently not sufficient for an animal, who sees only a coloured canvas where people see on the coloured canvas a representation. When the degree of abstraction is so great that it is no longer possible to recognize this shape as a human shape or as the shape of any identifiable object, the painting is then spoken of as non-representational. (In popular parlance such paintings are called abstract; but this is misleading, for abstraction is a matter of degree, and, as has just been shown, all depictions are necessarily abstract—that is, abstracted from reality to some degree.) The actual object with all its millions of qualities is at one end of the spectrum, and the painting so abstracted that a depiction subject is unrecognizable is at the other end; between the two extremes lie all the possible degrees of abstraction.

Representation in literature

Literature can be representational but not in the same way as visual art. It is quite natural to say that in a novel or drama a number of characters and actions are represented. The representation is, of course, not a visual one; it is representation through language. The painter portrays Napoleon by making a portrait of him; the writer does so by describing him in words. The writer, unlike the painter, can also depict action. Not all literature, of course, is representational in this way: a sonnet may contain no characters at all and no action, consisting solely of an expression of feeling by some unspecified speaker.

Any of the mixed arts that include words as part of their medium, such as drama or film, can be, like literature, representational. Indeed, they have a further advantage: they can depict action not only through words but also by showing the characters and exhibiting the action before the spectator. These arts are visual as well as verbal, and since they are not limited to one moment in time, as painting and sculpture are, they are temporal arts as well as spatial. These mixed arts, then, can be doubly representational.

Is it possible for music, too, to be representational? Music cannot visually show characters or objects, nor can it describe them in words; can it "depict them in tones"? Program notes at concerts usually assume without question that it can. The audience is told about the tone poem *Don Quixote,* by the Austrian composer Richard Strauss, "The composer has given us a musical representation of the Don's adventures. The 17th-century Spanish writer Miguel de Cervantes has described them in words, and Strauss has done so in tones." But the claim to representation in music is, to say the least, quite dubious. Without the title, with the music alone, would there be any clue that the music was supposed to be "about" the adventures of Don Quixote? True, there is a passage that resembles the bleating of sheep sufficiently for that much to be guessed; but even to conjecture that this passage is a representation of sheep bleating is a far cry from being able to reconstruct the entire story. Suppose that Strauss had left every note in the score just as it was but changed the title; would the piece then have been a representation of something else? The very fact that this question can be asked shows how different music is from visual art: if a painter has drawn a house but indicated in the title that it was supposed to be a tree, the viewer could still say, on the basis of what he saw in the picture, that it was not a tree but a house. But in music the listener is never in this situation: if he says that this series of tones represents the adventures of Don Quixote, he says this because of the title Strauss used. If the composer had given it no programmatic title, one listener might think of one represented subject, another a different one, and a third none at all, and there would be no way of showing who was right or even whose opinion was to be preferred. The conclusion seems to be that music by itself—without title, without words, without depicted action (as in a combination of music and drama such as opera)—is incapable of representing anything. There is simply a series of musical tones that may suggest differing associations, programmatic or otherwise; but the musical tones by themselves cannot be said to represent anything at all.

This might be objected to as an overstatement. If a picture can represent a house by looking more like a house than like anything else, cannot a work of music represent the sea by sounding more like the sea than any alternative? And is this not the case in, for example, the French composer Claude Debussy's tone poem *La Mer?* Even this, however, is highly questionable; almost no one guesses the title to Debussy's tone poem without first knowing what it is; it may seem obvious enough after the composer has channelled the listener's response by means of his title but not beforehand. And surely this is because the sounds in the tone poem do not sound more like the sea than like anything else: the tone poem consists, after all, of a series of complex musical tones, emitted by violins, cellos, clarinets, flutes, trumpets, and so on; and it would be difficult indeed for these sounds, which are musical tones, to sound very much like the sea, whose sounds consist after all of a series of complex noises. There is no great similarity between any one series of musical tones and any one series of nature's noises. Hence, the first cannot be said to constitute a representation of the second.

The matter is even more obvious in the case of those

Musical attempts to represent the soundless

numerous programmatic titles in which the supposedly represented subject contains no sounds at all. Debussy's *Reflets dans l'eau* (*Reflections in the Water*) is taken by some as a musical representation of reflections in the water. But reflections in the water emit no sounds at all, not even noises. No one, then, could say that the sounds in Debussy's piano composition resemble the sounds of reflections in water. The resemblance, if there is any, is much more remote: it may be that the feeling obtained when Debussy's composition is heard is somewhat like the feeling that arises when reflections in water are seen. This is highly improbable without knowledge of the title, but at most it would provide a mood resemblance, which is far removed from a representation by music of things in the world. The conclusion seems inescapable that music is not to be classified as a representational art, at least not in the same straightforward meaning of "representation" that applies to the other arts.

So much, then, for the capacities of the various arts as far as representation is concerned. But the question remains: in those arts that are properly called representational, what should be the nature of the representation?

That art should be an outright duplication (incorrectly called "imitation") of reality is a view that was put forward by the French novelist Émile Zola in his book *Le Roman expérimental* (*The Experimental Novel*) and has been occasionally held (though not practiced) by painters reacting against Romanticism, such as the 19th-century French artist Gustave Courbet. Zola advocated a novel that resembled a scientific investigation into reality. Plot was to be of no importance, rather an aspect of reality was to be examined searchingly, and from this the story would unfold without imaginative effort. Persons or groups of persons would be depicted, and from them the action would evolve.

Objections to Zola's theory of duplicating reality

It would be impossible, of course, to carry out such an ideal of art as "report" and undesirable even if it were possible. First, the author or painter must select a subject; and, within the subject, he must select which details to treat, for he cannot in a hundred lifetimes describe them all: since every object and event has an indefinitely large array of qualities, there is no point at which a description of it would be completed. Besides, the very language used (no matter how neutral a description is attempted) will colour the account. Even if the words were colourless, the mode of putting them together would yield a style, which would colour the account once again. Indeed, should such an ideal be achieved (as in the verbatim transcription of an actual trial) it would be the deadliest possible bore.

Art, even representational art, is not a reproduction of reality; it is a transformation of reality. How, specifically, is reality transformed in being represented in art? There is probably no general satisfactory answer to this question. Each art, each style of art, and each work of art transforms reality in its own way—the 19th-century French painters Paul Cézanne in one way, Pierre-Auguste Renoir in another; the 19th-century Russian writers Fyodor Dostoyevsky in one way, Leo Tolstoy in another. No set of rules can lead to predictions as to what transformation of reality will be conceived in the mind of the next creative artist. Reality is the common base, but each artist deals with it in his own unique way.

Subject matter. Do all works of art have a subject matter? The answer to this depends on what is meant by the term subject matter, which basically signifies what the work is about. There are several senses of being "about" that may be referred to:

1. "What is the subject matter of the *Odyssey* by the ancient Greek poet Homer?" The most natural answer would be: "The wanderings of Odysseus." This is the "representational content" of the work. A person who read it simply for the story could easily give this answer. There is contained in the work itself an account of the wanderings of a character named Odysseus, who has no counterpart in the outside world (that is, he is a fictional character) but who does resemble people in the outside world in that he is a man, he is away from home, he is beset by many vicissitudes, and so on. If the subject matter were stated in greater detail, the result would be an account of the plot.

Does painting have subject matter in this sense? If "subject matter" is taken to mean representational content, the answer is often yes; representations of people and trees and the like are easily identifiable in the painting. Sometimes the subject could not be ascertained except for the title, which is not strictly a part of the painting (the title is not a piece of visual art, consisting as it does of words). But quite clearly it cannot be said that the subject matter of the painting is whatever the title says it is: if the title says "Clouds" and the painting is obviously a still life with pears and grapes, it can hardly be said that the painting has clouds as its subject matter simply because the title says so. It was long said that the painting called "Sacred and Profane Love" by the 16th-century Italian artist Titian had sacred and profane love as its subject matter; but Titian himself gave it no such title—the title was added more than a century later by someone else. It cannot be said that the subject matter is what whatever title it came to be given says it is (it could be given numerous incompatible titles); the subject matter, in this sense, must be evident from—or at least not incompatible with—what is seen in the painting itself. The same remarks apply to music: music cannot be "about" anything that the composer happens to seize on as a title; if it were, and he changed the title without changing a note of the music, would the subject matter of the music have changed? Strong reasons already have been given to doubt that music can have a subject matter at all.

2. In addition to a subject matter in the sense of representational content, a work of art may have subject matter in the sense of theme, or underlying idea. The subject matter in the sense of representational content of *Jude the Obscure,* by English novelist and poet Thomas Hardy, is the intellectual ambitions of the main character, Jude, and the vicissitudes befalling him along the way; but the subject matter in the sense of theme or underlying idea is man's struggle to realize his ambitions; and the thesis (implicit message) of the novel is (or may be) that man's highest ambitions are doomed to frustration. Not all novels and dramas and poems have a theme or thesis; they may simply tell a story and nothing more. Works of literature do sometimes operate in both dimensions: a story and a theme or thesis underlying the story. Works of representational visual art may also do so: one might allege that the theme of "Guernica," by the 20th-century Spanish artist Pablo Picasso, is the horror of war. Again, it is doubtful whether works of music can be said to have a theme at all (indeed, the term theme applied to music has a very different meaning: it refers to a set of tones around which variations or developments are composed). If someone were to say that the theme of a work of music was the human condition or man's fear of death, how would such a view be supported? Since music is not representational, what musical passages would he take as evidence for his theory, and why? A composer might indeed title his work "The Human Condition," but this would no more show that the music was about the human condition (had the human condition as its subject matter) than giving the programmatic title "Clouds" to a musical composition shows that the composition actually is about clouds.

Thematic subjects

Symbols in art. Works of art may not only have subject matter, they may also contain symbols. Certain elements in a work of art may represent, say, a whale; but the whale thus represented may be (as it is in *Moby Dick* by the 19th-century U.S. writer Herman Melville) a symbol of evil. In Tolstoy's *Anna Karenina* is represented a gallery of characters dominated by Anna herself, and a tremendous number of actions in which these characters engage; but there is a constantly recurring item in the representational content, namely, the train. Time and again the train causes or accompanies frustration, disaster, betrayal, and other evils—so much so that before the novel is ended it becomes apparent that the train here is a symbol of the iron forces of material progress toward which Tolstoy had such great antipathy.

What is it that makes an item in a work of art a symbol? It is something represented in the work of art—an object, an action, or a pattern of objects and actions, or even (less frequently) simply a nonrepresentational item such as a colour or a line—that does the symbolizing; what is symbolized is a characteristic, such as evil or progress or courage. But by virtue of what does the first (A) become a symbol of the second (B)?

The answer is not the same for all symbols, since some are conventional and some are natural. The cross is a symbol of Christianity, and it is a conventional symbol of suffering; in order for it to become a symbol, people had to adopt or accept the cross as standing for suffering. Other symbols are natural—the sun as the symbol of life and strength, a river as the symbol of eternal change and flowing, and so forth; in these cases there was no agreement (convention) as to what would stand for what, for the relation is too obvious—the symbolism is much the same in the tradition of all nations and civilizations.

Various symbols have, to varying degrees, elements of both the conventional and the natural: the eagle on the standard of the United States of America symbolizes strength—this is natural, because the eagle is strong, and conventional, because the eagle was officially adopted as the symbol of the United States. In the case of many symbols, the natural relation between symbol and thing symbolized is not strong enough by itself to achieve the symbolism, and the conventional relation was entered into in order to effect a symbolism that already had a certain natural basis. When A is a symbol of B, there must be some relation, either natural or conventional, between the symbol and what is symbolized. When the natural relation is strong, the conventional is minimal or nonexistent, and vice versa.

But there is another element to symbolism if it is to function with full-bodied effectiveness in a work of art, and that is what has been called a "vital basis" provided by history and tradition. In the U.S. flag there is very little natural basis for symbolism; it is almost wholly conventional. But the fact that it has been saluted for so long, that it has been present on battlefields, that the bodies of military dead have been wrapped in it, and so on—that is, the fact that it has acquired a life, a history—have given it an "affect" (human emotion or mood) it did not have before. Melville and Tolstoy not only represented the whale and the train: they invested these representations with such strong emotional affect that the reader is much more inclined than he would be otherwise to say that these objects are the symbols of the qualities he ascribes to them.

When some item in a work of art is construed as a symbol, it is always infused with these vital qualities. Clearly, not every case of one thing standing for something else is a symbol in this sense: a carrot in a painting does not, just by itself, symbolize growth. But barbed-wire fences do symbolize tyranny, not only because many prisoners have been enclosed in barbed-wire fences (this is the natural basis for the symbolism) but also because of concentration camps and the countless tragic events of recent history that have provided the "vital basis" for the symbolism.

Meaning. Do works of art have meaning? The answer depends once again on how the question is construed: the word "meaning" is an equivocal term that can itself mean many different things.

Clouds mean rain, a falling barometer means that a storm is coming, a twister in the sky means an approaching tornado—that is, the one is a sign of the other; these relations exist in nature and were discovered, not invented, by man. On the other hand, a bell ringing means the end of class, this note on the score means that D sharp is to be played on a certain instrument, and the word cat to someone who knows English means a certain species of domesticated quadruped; these relations are conventional, established by man. But both the natural and the conventional items are examples of meaning in its most general sense—one thing (A) standing for another (B).

Since the medium of literature is words, and words are conventional vehicles of meaning, literature has meaning in a way that the other arts do not, since every word, to be a word at all, must have a meaning. In the sense in which the word cat means something, middle C and an ellipse do not have meanings at all.

When the question is asked about meaning in art, however, it is not usually the individual ingredients in it that are being referred to: if it were, the answer could simply be, "Yes, this word has a meaning and that word has; so does the sentence as a whole; and items in paintings sometimes have meaning; for example, the halo over the Madonna's head symbolizes holiness." What is being asked is whether the work of art as a whole has a meaning. But what does the question itself mean? Several different things can be meant: (1) The inquirer may be asking, "What is it about?" in which case the question is about subject matter, already discussed. (2) He may be asking, "What is its theme?"—for example, is the motion picture *He Who Must Die* really a parable about the life of Christ? (3) He may be asking, "What is its thesis?" For example, what is the message of the Anglo-Irish author Jonathan Swift to the reader in "A Modest Proposal"? (4) The inquiry may be about the effects of a work of art on the recipient—either what these effects are or what they could or should be. In this sense, all works of art have meaning, since they all have effects (whether there is one type of effect that a given work of art should have is another question). This is, however, an extremely misleading use of the word "meaning." Indeed, the entire discussion of "meaning in art" is a most confusing one—and the fault does not lie in art, but in the human users of words. Endless unnecessary mysteries can be created by using such nebulous words as "meaning" as if they were simple, straightforward, and susceptible to one interpretation. It would contribute greatly to the clarification of discussions of philosophy of art if the word meaning were not used in them at all but some conception clearer and more specific.

ART AS EXPRESSION

The view that "art is imitation (representation)" has not only been challenged, it has been moribund in at least some of the arts for more than a century. It has largely been replaced by the theory that art is expression. Instead of reflecting states of the external world, art is held to reflect the inner state of the artist. This, at least, seems to be implicit in the core meaning of "expression": the outer manifestation of an inner state. Art as a representation of outer existence (admittedly "seen through a temperament") has been replaced by art as an expression of man's inner life.

But the terms "express" and "expression" are ambiguous and do not always denote the same thing. Like so many other terms, "express" is subject to the process–product ambiguity: the same word is used for a process and for the product that results from that process. "The music expresses feeling" may mean that the composer expressed his feeling in writing the music or that the music when heard is expressive (in some way yet to be defined) of human feeling. Based on the first sense are theories about the creation of art; founded on the second are theories about the content of art and the completion of its creation.

Expression in the creation of art. The creation of a work of art is the bringing about of a new combination of elements in the medium (tones in music, words in literature, paints on canvas, and so on). The elements existed beforehand but not in the same combination; creation is the re-formation of these pre-existing materials. Pre-existence of materials holds true of creation quite apart from art: in the creation of a scientific theory or the creation of a disturbance. It applies even to creation in most theologies, except some versions of Christian theology, in which creation is *ex nihilo;* that is, without pre-existing matter.

That creation occurs in various art mediums is an obvious truth. But once this is granted, nothing has yet been said about expression; and the expressionist would say that the foregoing statement about creation is too mild to cover what he wants to say about the process of artistic creation. The creative process, he wants to say, is (or is also) an expressive process; and for expression something more is necessary than that the artist is creating something. Great care must be taken at this stage: some say that the creation of art is (or involves) self-expression; others say that it is the expression of feeling, though not necessarily of one's own feeling (or perhaps that and something more, such as the feeling of one's race, or of one's nation, or of all men);

others say that it is not necessarily limited to feelings, but that ideas or thoughts can be expressed, as they clearly are in essays. But the distinctively expressionist view of artistic creation is the product of the Romantic movement, according to which the expression of feelings constitutes the creation of art, just as philosophy and other disciplines are the expression of ideas. It is, at any rate, the theory of art as the expression of feelings (which here shall be taken to include emotions and attitudes) that has been historically significant and developed: art as specially connected with the life of feeling.

When a person is said to be expressing a feeling, what specifically is he doing? In a perfectly ordinary sense, expressing is "letting go" or "letting off steam": man expresses his anger by throwing things or by cursing or by striking the person who has angered him. But, as many writers have pointed out, this kind of "expressing" has little to do with art; as the U.S. philosopher John Dewey said, it is more of a "spilling over" or a "spewing forth" than expression. In art at least, expression requires a medium, a medium that is recalcitrant and that the artist must bend to his will. In throwing things to express anger, there is no medium—or, if the man's body is called the medium, then it is something he does not have to study to use for that purpose. It is still necessary to distinguish a "natural release" from an expression. If poetry were literally "the spontaneous overflow of powerful feelings," as William Wordsworth said, it would consist largely of things like tears and incoherent babblings. If artistic creation can plausibly be said to be a process of expression, something different from and more specific than natural release or discharge must be meant.

Emotional expression in art
One view of emotional expression in art is that it is preceded by a perturbation or excitement from a vague cause about which the artist is uncertain and therefore anxious. He then proceeds to express his feelings and ideas in words or paint or stone or the like, clarifying them and achieving a release of tension. The point of this theory seems to be that the artist, having been perturbed at the inarticulateness of his "ideas," now feels relieved because he has "expressed what he wanted to express." This phenomenon, indeed a familiar one (for everyone has felt relieved when a job is done), must still be examined for its relevance. Is it the emotion being expressed that counts or the relief at having expressed it? If the concern here is with art as therapy or doing art to provide revelations for a psychiatrist, then the latter is what counts; but the critic or consumer of the art is surely not concerned with such details of the artist's biography. This is an objection to all accounts of expression as process: how is any light at all cast upon the work of art by saying that the artist went through any expressive process or through any process whatever in the genesis of it? If the artist was relieved at the end of it, so much the better for him; but this fact is as aesthetically irrelevant as it would be if he had committed suicide at the end of it or taken to drink or composed another work immediately thereafter.

Another problem should be noted: assuming that the artist does relieve his oppressed state of mind through creating, what connection has this with the exact words or score or brushstrokes that he puts on paper or canvas? Feelings are one thing, words and visual shapes and tones are quite another; it is these latter that constitute the art medium, and in it that works of art are created. There is doubtless a causal connection between the feelings of the artist and the words he writes in his poem; but the expression theory of creation talks only about the artist's feelings, while creation occurs within the art mediums themselves; and to speak only of the former is not to tell anything about the work of art—anything, that is, that would be of interest other than to the artist's psychiatrist or biographer. Through what paroxysms of emotion the artist passed does not matter anymore, insofar as one's insight into his work is concerned, than knowing that a given engineer had had a quarrel with his wife the night before he began building his bridge. To speak of anything revelatory of works of art, it is necessary to stop talking about the artist's emotions and talk about the

genesis of words, tones, and so on—items in the specific art mediums.

The expressionists have indeed brought out and emphasized one important distinction: between the processes involved in art and in craft. The activity of building a bridge from the architect's blueprint or constructing a brick wall or putting together a table just like a thousand others the artisan has already made is a craft and not an art. The craftsman knows at the beginning of the processes exactly what sort of end product is wanted: for example, a chair of specific dimensions made of particular materials. He knows at the beginning how much material it will take to do the job, which tools, and so forth, and, if he does not know these things, he is not a good (efficient) craftsman. But the creative artist cannot work in this manner: "The artist doesn't know what he is going to express until he has expressed it" is a watchword of the expressionist. He cannot state in advance what the completed work of art will be like: the poet cannot say what words will constitute the completed poem or how many times the word "the" will occur in it or what the order of the words will be—when he knows that, he has completed the creation of the poem, and until then he cannot say. Nor could he set about working with such a plan: "I shall compose a poem that contains the word 'the' 563 times, the word 'rose' 47 times," and so on. What distinguishes art from craft is that the artist, unlike the craftsman, "does not know the end in the beginning"; he cannot state until his work is finished what the completed product will be like—if he could, he would not have to undergo the "divine agonies" of creation in order to produce it.

Distinction between art and craft

The distinction seems valid enough, but whether it supports the expressionist's view is more dubious; for it can be held regardless of the attitude assumed toward the theory of expression. The open-ended process described as art rather than craft characterizes all kinds of creation: of mathematical hypotheses and of scientific theory, as well as art. What distinguishes creation from all other things is that it results in a new combination of elements, and it is not known in advance what this combination will be. Thus, one may speak of creating a work of sculpture or creating a new theory, but rarely of creating a bridge (unless the builder was also the architect who designed it, and then it is to the genesis of the idea for the bridge, not to its execution, that the word creation applies). This, then, is a feature of creation; it is not clear that it is a feature of expression (whatever is being done in expressing that is not already being done in creating). Is it necessary to talk about expression, as opposed to creation, to bring out the distinction between art and craft?

There does not seem to be any true generalization about the creative processes of all artists nor even of great artists. Some follow their "intuitions," letting their artistic work grow "as the spirit moves" and being comparatively passive in the process (that is, the conscious mind is passive, and the unconscious takes over). Others are consciously active, knowing very much what they want in advance and figuring out exactly how to do it (for example, the 19th-century U.S. writer Edgar Allan Poe in his essay "The Philosophy of Composition"). Some artists go through extended agonies of creation (the 19th-century German composer Johannes Brahms, weeping and groaning to give birth to one of his symphonies), whereas for others it seems to be comparatively easy (Mozart, who could write an entire overture in one evening for the next day's performance). Some artists create only while having physical contact with the medium (for example, composers who must compose at the piano, painters who must "play about" in the medium in order to get painterly ideas), and others prefer to create in their minds only (Mozart, it is said, visualized every note in his mind before he wrote the score). There appears to be no true generalization that can be made about the process of artistic creation—certainly not that it is always a process of expression. For the appreciation of the work of art, no such uniformity, of course, is necessary, greatly though it may be desired by theorists of artistic creation.

Problems
in drawing
con-
clusions
about the
creation
of art

The main difficulties in the way of accepting conclusions about the creative process in art are (1) that artists differ so much from one another in their creative processes that no generalizations can be arrived at that are both true and interesting or of any significance; and (2) that in the present stage of psychology and neurology very little is known about the creative process—it is surely the most staggeringly complex of all the mental processes in man, and even his simpler mental processes are shrouded in mystery. In every arena hypotheses are rife, none of them substantiated sufficiently to compel assent over other and conflicting hypotheses. Some say—for example, Graham Wallas in his book *The Art of Thought*—that in the creation of every work of art there are four successive stages: preparation, incubation, inspiration, and elaboration; others say that these stages are not successive at all but are going on throughout the entire creative process, while still others would produce a different list of stages. Some say that the artist begins with a state of mental confusion, with a few fragments of words or melody gradually becoming clear in his mind and the rest starting from there, working gradually toward clarity and articulation; whereas others hold that the artist sets himself a problem, which he gradually works out during the process of creation, but his vision of the whole guides his creative process from its inception. The first view would be a surprise to the dramatist who sets himself from the beginning to write a drama in five acts about the life and assassination of Julius Caesar; and the second would be a surprise to artists like the 20th-century English artist Henry Moore, who has said he sometimes begins a drawing with no conscious aim but only the wish to use pencil on paper and make tones, lines, and shapes. Again, as to psychological theories about the unconscious motivations of artists during creation, an early Freudian view is that the artist is working out in his creation his unconscious wish fulfillments; a later Freudian view is that he is engaged in working out defenses against superego charges, "proving something to himself." Views based on the ideas of the 20th-century Swiss psychologist Carl Jung reject both these alternatives, substituting an account of the unconscious symbol-making process. Until a great deal more is known about the empirical sciences that bear on the issue, there is little point in attempting to defend one view of artistic creation against another.

The expressive product. Although talk about expression as a process is hedged with difficulties and in any case seems irrelevant to the philosophy of art (as opposed to the psychology of art), there is another way in which talk about expression may be both true and important to the philosophy of art. Mention is made about expressive properties as belonging to works of art: for example, it is said that a certain melody expresses sadness, that there is a feeling of great calm expressed in a particular painting, or that tension is expressed in the thrusts of a tower or the development of the plot of a novel or drama.

The question arises at once of what it means to say such things. Melodies and sentences are not joyous or tense or melancholy; only persons have these qualities. The artist can have them, but how can the work of art? Clearly, to speak of a work of art as having emotions, if it is not to be utter nonsense, must be metaphorical. But what is the meaning of this metaphor? What does it mean to say that the music expresses sadness, if not in the sense of process; *i.e.*, that in writing it the composer expressed his sadness?

Meta-
phorical
expression
of
emotion

The music is heard, the painting is seen; each presents itself to the senses. But there is much more involved in music than simply hearing (or even listening to) the sounds and in visual art than simply seeing (or even looking at) the colours and shapes. Even very simple combinations of sounds and shapes and colours seem to express certain qualities of life: a curved line, it is said, is graceful or sprightly; the drooping willow tree is sad, as are certain passages in music. It is virtually impossible for most persons to view art as a series of sensory stimuli only. Even when a picture contains no story, no plot, no program, the viewer "reads into the script": he attributes to works of art qualities of human moods, feelings, emotions—in short, "affects." It would be safe to say that in all art, every percept is suffused with affect. The problem is: What is it that makes certain percepts expressive of certain affects?

The simplest answer, that "The melody is sad" means no more or less than "Hearing the melody makes me (or other listeners, or most listeners) feel sad," is surely inadequate. (This would be a theory of evocation, not of expression.) "The music expresses whatever feelings it arouses in me when I hear it." But often the listener does not feel emotions at all (he may imagine them), or, if he does, he feels very different emotions from the ones he believes to be expressed in the music. He may consider the rondo delirious with joy, but if he is grief stricken on a given day he hears it without feeling joy; and if he has heard the same rondo 30 times that day he feels only boredom or fatigue, while still believing that the piece is expressive of joy. Nor is it an adequate analysis to say that "The melody expresses joy" means "I am disposed to (or inclined to) feel joy when I hear it," for many people seem to recognize joy as a quality of the music without feeling it at all: or they may imagine it or just recognize the emotion without feeling it or believe that what they hear sounds the way joy feels—or any of a number of other accounts.

The true analysis of expressiveness in art must be more complex than this: it is not that the melody evokes emotion X, but that emotion X is somehow embodied in the music. But this leads back again to the question, how can an emotional quality be in a work of art? There is no single answer to this question that would be accepted by all philosophers of art, but most accounts begin by noting certain similarities, or analogies, between features of music and features of human feeling; so that when X (a passage of music, for example) is said to express Y (a state of feeling), there are certain similarities (for example, of structure) between X and Y. The physical accompaniments to a mood, say, of restlessness, such as rapid breathing and drumming fingers, have their musical equivalents: trills, quavers, increases in tempo, and the like.

When a listener says that a certain melody is sad, he is saying that the music literally has certain qualities A, B, C, D that can be perceived in the music. Slowness is surely one such quality (the same melody played fast would not be called sad); another is the absence of large intervals between tones; another is that the sounds tend to be hushed rather than, for example, strident; another is that the tendency of the musical movement is downward rather than rising. When a listener says that the music is sad, he is saying that it has these qualities.

Emotional
qualities
embodied
in art

But why these qualities rather than others? Why is it said that the music is sad when it has A, B, C, D rather than when it has M, N, O, and P? Because A, B, C, D are the qualities that also characterize people when they are sad, such as slowness and soft and low speaking voices. If this theory or anything like it is true, it explains how emotional characteristics can be attributed to works of art—why it can be said that the melody is sad, that the horizontal lines in a painting make it calm (horizontal being the position of rest and peace, sleep and maximum relaxation, and from which one does not fall), why the lines in a painting are droopy (they are lines similar in shape to that of, say, an old woman with hunched shoulders), and so on. These qualities, it should be noted, are qualities of the work of art, not of the artist (whether he was sad when he wrote sad music is a separate question, to which the answer may sometimes be no) and not of the listener or observer (the melody is sad even if I am not sad when I hear it). They are, so to speak, embodied in the music, quite independently of the state of the artist or of the observer, or listener, though of course it requires the presence of a listener to recognize them and be moved by them.

Talk about artistic expressiveness, then, can be justified. But there is no need to resort to the language of expression in order to state it: instead of saying, "The music expresses sadness," it can simply be said, "The music is sad." But regardless of the terminology employed, it is important to have justified this conclusion.

ART AS FORM

The formalist position. Against all the foregoing accounts of the function of art stands another, which belongs distinctively to the 20th century—the theory of art as form, or formalism. The import of formalism can best be seen by noting what it was reacting against: art as representation, art as expression, art as a vehicle of truth or knowledge or moral betterment or social improvement. Formalists do not deny that art is capable of doing these things, but they believe that the true purpose of art is subverted by its being made to do these things. "Art for art's sake, not art for life's sake" is the watchword of formalism. Art is there to be enjoyed, to be savoured, for the perception of the intricate arrangements of lines and colours, of musical tones, of words, and combinations of these. By means of these mediums it is true that objects in the world can be represented, scenes from life depicted, and emotions from life expressed; but these are irrelevant to the principal purpose of art—indeed, art is much less adapted to the telling of a story or the representation of the world than it is to the presentation of colours, sounds, and other items in the art medium simply for their own sake.

'Art for art's sake'

Most people who claim to enjoy paintings, for example, enjoy them not as presentations but as representations of things and situations in life; and thus their response is not of a kind that is unique to art, but one that takes them back to the emotions of life, from which they came. They could use art to take them into a realm of pure form unknown to anyone who is unacquainted with art; but instead they use it to direct them back to the feelings and situations of life. Thus, according to the formalists, these viewers miss the opportunity of being taken into a fresh world of purely aesthetic experience and get from a work only what they bring to it: familiar experiences and emotions they employ the work to recall.

What, then, should be brought from life to art? Knowledge of life's struggles and emotions? Knowledge at least of what people are like, and what visual objects look like? Not even these things, for even they get in the way. Representation is not bad in itself, it is merely irrelevant. Only if the representation is satisfactory as form and contributes to the general abstract design can it be said to matter aesthetically.

Most formalists have directed their attention primarily to visual art. The prerequisite for appreciating this, they believe, is a sense of form and colour and a knowledge of three-dimensional space (the last required because otherwise a cube, for example, would appear in a painting as a flat pattern and would be unable to play the architectural role intended for it). Armed with this bit of knowledge from life, they have all they need (as far as knowledge of the world outside art is concerned) for appreciating visual art. Armed with more than this, they would find their attention drawn away from the sublimities of art to the more approachable concerns of humanity (such as representation). Shorn of this extraneous knowledge and coming to painting with eyes innocent of extraneous concepts, the viewer could then be in a position to look at what painting presents directly to his vision—complex arrangements of forms and colours—which, for reasons thus far unexplained, have the capacity to move the recipient deeply with emotions utterly alien to the emotions of life.

The formalist's account of music runs along similar lines: not only representation (program music) is excluded but so is the entire realm of human feeling—not the feeling that the contemplation of pure form can give but only the feelings of life, such as love or terror. As to literature and all those arts in which words play a part (song, opera, drama, cinema), the formalist position would seem to be impossible; and indeed formalists have seldom attempted to extend their theory to literature. The medium of literature is words and sentences; and words and sentences are not merely noises but noises with meanings; and these meanings inevitably have to do with the objects, actions, qualities, and situations of life. As sound, literature is a poor thing—as a complex of meanings, it can be profound and beautiful. Take these away, and literature could cease to be. Literature does have formal properties—a drama can be as tightly knit as a fugue or a symphony—but the appreciation of it can never consist of these formal properties alone; and the reason lies in the very nature of the medium. It is the role of words to indicate images and

Inapplicability of the formalist position

meanings and emotions, and these are the stuff of life—therefore verbal art is inescapably humanistic. Whatever sensory beauty words have in their sounds is slight and secondary; not so with painting, where colour, line, and space have a beauty all their own and need stand for nothing outside themselves to satisfy the eye.

Formal principles in art. What, then, are the specific qualities in works of art that the formalist is seeking? Most formalists have held that a partial account can be given of these but that, in the end, the presence of the qualities must be felt intuitively and cannot be described. Accounts of formal qualities in works of art go back as far as Aristotle's *Poetics*, written in the 4th century BC, and usually include (though sometimes in different terminology) the following as principal ingredients:

Organic unity. A work of art must have what Aristotle called "a beginning, a middle, and an end"; it must be unified, it must "hang together" as one entity. Everything, of course, has some degree of unity or other; even a collection of things, such as a woodpile, has some unity inasmuch as it can correctly be called one thing: it is a collection, but it is a single collection. But the unity desired in works of art is much greater than this: it is more like the unity of the higher organisms in which every part functions not independently of the others but interdependently with them; and it is this interdependency of the parts that constitutes an organic unity. Take away one part, and the remainder of the parts fail to function as before. This is only approximately true of organisms: without a heart or a brain a person could not continue to exist, and the activity of the other organs would cease; but without an ear or a toe they surely would. Philosophers of art have often noted that the purest examples of organic unity in the universe are not organisms but works of art: here the interdependency of parts often achieves a state of such perfection that it could often be said, of a melody or a sonnet, that if this note (or word) were not there, in just the place that it is, the effect on the entire remainder of the melody or poem would be disastrous.

Complexity, or diversity. This principle is the natural accompaniment of the first one. A blank wall has unity but no variety and is not long worth contemplating. Nor is there any triumph in achieving unity at so small a price. The work of art must hold in suspension (as it were) a great diversity of elements and unify them—the greater the complexity that is integrated into a unity, the greater the achievement. This fact is so universally recognized that the two criteria are often stated as one, unity-in-diversity, or variety-in-unity.

Very many great works of art are much less than perfect organic unities (which is another way of saying that unity-in-variety is not the only criterion for excellence in works of art). Particularly in long poems or novels or operas, some parts are clearly more important than the others, though contributing to the whole, and some parts may be simply "padding." One could hardly allege that the entire ancient Greek epic the *Iliad* is an organic unity and that if (for example) the catalog of ships were removed the entire epic would be ruined (some even say it would be improved). In Dostoyevsky's novels there are whole chapters that are unnecessary from the point of view of relevance to the rest of the story, and, aesthetically (though perhaps not in other ways), these are a pure excrescence. In most works of art there are high spots and low spots, and there is a great deal of elasticity as to what could follow what. But in spite of this, unity-in-variety is quite universally recognized as a criterion for artistic excellence. If a drama consisted of two plots that never connected with one another, even at the end, such a play would be condemned at once for lack of unity; and a work of art is never praised for being disjointed or disunified, though it might be praised in spite of being disunified.

Unity-in-variety in works of art

Theme and thematic variation. In many works of art there is a dominant theme, or motif, which stands out and upon which the other portions are centred. This theme is then varied in different ways in other portions of the work. This is a special case of unity-in-variety: if every line in a work of music or literature were entirely novel and different from the other ones, there would be enormous diversity but no unifying connecting links; whereas if there were simply a repetition of the initial theme or of entire sections of the work (as sometimes happens when a composer does not know how to develop the thematic material with which he has begun) there is unity but no variety. Both unity and variety are preserved by having central themes, with other material that is related to them (unity) but not identical with them (variety).

Development, or evolution. In works of temporal art, each part develops or evolves into the next, each part being necessary to the succeeding part, so that if an earlier part were altered or deleted, all the subsequent parts would have to be altered in consequence. If a portion of Act IV could be interchanged with a portion of Act II without loss of effect, the principle of development has not been observed, for then the material occurring in between would not have made any difference.

Balance. The arrangement of the various parts should be balanced, usually in contrasting ways (the adagio movement coming between two faster movements, for example). In painting, there should be a balance between the right and left halves of the canvas. The many ways, other than simple mechanical symmetry ("for every item on the left there should be an item on the right," which soon becomes monotonous), in which a painting may have variety and yet retain balance are too complex to be discussed other than in a book of art criticism. But in its simplest essentials, the principle is acknowledged by everyone: the housewife who places all the furniture on one half of the living room while leaving the other half empty finds the arrangement aesthetically displeasing because the room lacks balance.

Generalizations based on formal principles

There are many descriptions of principles of form in art, which differ from one another in their terminology more than in their final outcome. In general, however, few if any of these principles would be denied (only the detail of their formulations might be) by most philosophers of art. Why certain principles of form are found satisfactory and others are not is a fascinating psychological question, leading back to a discussion (necessarily vague in the present state of knowledge) of the nature of the human organism and the discriminatory powers of the human mind. But however obscure the explanation, the facts of the case seem clear enough: certain formal principles in art must be observed, and, to the degree that they are ignored or violated, aesthetic catastrophe occurs: the work of art cannot evoke our interest or sustain it long once it is initiated.

Though a discussion of these formal principles is helpful particularly to those who have little native sense of form and who want "to know what to look for" in art, they are sufficiently vague so that many critics can agree on a formal principle, such as unity, and yet disagree on the degree to which a specific work possesses it.

In addition, these principles are far from complete: a work of art can possess unity and the other requirements in high degree and yet be unsuccessful even as form. The requirements listed seem only to have skimmed the surface. Yet what more is required to distinguish a formally correct but dull work of art from a brilliant one seems to defy precise analysis. Moreover, the majority of critics who have assented to these principles are not formalists: they have acknowledged and even insisted on the great importance of form in works of art, but they have not alleged, as formalists do, that these principles constitute the sole criteria of excellence in works of art. They have held that the fulfillment of formal criteria counts as a necessary condition for artistic excellence but not a sufficient condition.

PRAGMATIC THEORIES OF ART

There are theories of art that differ from one another in what they allege to be the real purpose or function of art but are at one with each other in the belief that art is a means to some end, whether that end be the titillation of the senses or the communization of the nations of the world or the conversion of mankind to belief in God or the improved moral beliefs or moral tone of the reader or viewer. In every case, the work of art is considered as a means to some end beyond itself, and hence what counts in the final analysis is not the nature of the work of art itself but its effects upon the audience—whether those effects be primarily sensory, cognitive, moral, religious, or social.

Hedonistic theories of art. According to one kind of theory, the function of art is to produce just one kind of effect upon its audience: pleasure. It may also inform or instruct, represent or express, but first and foremost it must please. The more pleasure it gives, the better the art.

If the theory is left in this simple form, it yields the result that glossy and superficial works and those containing nothing difficult or obscure are the best works of art: thus, on the hedonistic account, *King Lear* might come out far behind Henry Wadsworth Longfellow's *The Song of Hiawatha,* or Joyce Kilmer's "Trees," in view of the difficulty of comprehending Shakespeare by many people and the pleasant, easy lilting quality of Longfellow's poem; and similarly a simple ditty might come out ahead of Bach's *Mass in B Minor.* True, Shakespeare and Bach might produce more pleasure in the long run since their works have endured through more centuries. But on the other hand, the simple works can be apprehended and enjoyed by vastly more people.

In any case, the theory has often been amended to read "aesthetic pleasure" rather than simply "pleasure"—thus placing great importance on exactly how the term "aesthetic" is to be defined. The definition of this troublesome term is beyond the scope of this article (see AESTHETICS); it will simply be said here that no quick and easy way of distinguishing aesthetic pleasures from other pleasures will suffice for the task at hand. If it is said, for example, that aesthetic pleasure consists in satisfaction taken in the contemplation of sensuous particulars (tones, colours, shapes, smells, tastes) for their own sake—that is, for no further end and without ulterior motive—then one confronts the fact that as much pleasure may be taken in single smells and tastes for their own sakes, without any reference beyond them, as may be taken in the most complex works of art. For that matter, pleasure in playing a game (one not played for money) is pleasure in doing something for its own sake, as is the pleasure of robbing a house if it is done not for money but for "kicks." If something is found pleasurable, ordinarily the pleasure is what one wants from it, not something else beyond it.

The meaning of "aesthetic pleasure"

Moreover, if it is said that a work of art should be a means toward pleasure, that is treading suspiciously near to the opposed view that art should not be a means to an end but an end in itself. If someone says, "Why do you go jogging every morning for three miles? Because you feel the exercise is good for you?" and another person answers, "No, not that at all, I just enjoy doing it," this would ordinarily and quite sensibly be taken as saying that he did not do exercise as a means toward an end but as an end in itself. If something is done just because it is enjoyed, in common parlance this would be taken to be "doing it as an end in itself"; and if one objected, "No, I'm not doing it as an end in itself, I'm doing it as a means toward the enjoyment I'll get out of it," his reply would be considered sophistical, for doing it for enjoyment's sake is precisely what is ordinarily meant (or one thing that is ordinarily meant) by the statement that a thing is being done for its own sake.

In any case, the effect of great works of art upon a reader or viewer or listener can hardly be described as merely hedonistic. No one would presumably wish to deny that art can and should give us pleasure; but few would wish to assert that pleasure is all that it should give us. If one were to ask, "How did viewing Picasso's 'Guernica' affect you?" and the reply was, "I found it pleasant," we would conclude that his reaction to the painting was, to say the least, inadequate. Great art may please; it may also move, shock, challenge, or change the lives of those who experience it deeply. Pleasure is only one of many kinds of effects it produces.

Art as a means to truth or knowledge. One of the things that has been alleged to be the purpose of art is its cognitive function: art as a means to the acquisition of truth. Art has even been called the avenue to the highest knowledge available to man and to a kind of knowledge impossible of attainment by any other means.

Knowledge in the most usual sense of that word takes the form of a proposition, knowing that so-and-so is the case. Thus, it can be learned from sense observation that the sun is setting, and this is knowledge. Is knowledge acquired in this same sense from acquaintance with works of art? There is no doubt that there are some propositions (statements) that can be made after acquaintance with works of art that could not be made before: for example, that this performance of Beethoven's *Eroica Symphony* was 47 minutes long, that this painting predominates in green, that this piece of sculpture originated around 350 BC. The question is whether there is anything that can be called truth or knowledge (presumably knowledge is of truths, or true propositions) that can be found in works of art.

The cognitive function of literature

Literature is surely the most obvious candidate; for literature consists of words, and words are combined into sentences, and sentences (at least declarative sentences) are used to convey propositions; that is, to make assertions that are either true or false. And works of literature do certainly contain many true statements: a novel about the French Revolution conveys facts about the series of events; in a verse of the English scholar and poet A.E. Housman (1859–1936), it is said that "The tears of all that be/ Help not the primal fault." Since literature contains statements, it would be surprising indeed if at least some of them were not true.

But the relevance of this fact to literature as an art is extremely dubious. If an 18th-century novel gives a true picture of English country life of that time, this makes it useful to read as history; does it also make it a better novel? Many, at any rate, would say that it does not: that a tenth-rate novel might give more facts about 18th-century life than a first-rate novel of the same century. For that matter, many of the propositions in a novel are, taken at face value, false; it is false, for example, that there was a foundling named Tom Jones who had an uncle named Squire Western. The thousands of pages of description in novels of fictional characters, ascribing to them thoughts and actions, are all false, since these characters never actually existed. Yet this fact in no way impugns their value as literature. Shakespeare, in *The Winter's Tale*, sets part of the action on the seacoast of Bohemia; but the fact that Bohemia has no seacoast does not damage *The Winter's Tale* as literature, though it would as geography. The fact that Milton used the outdated Ptolemaic astronomy does not make *Paradise Lost* less valuable, nor does the nonexistence of the lands described in *Gulliver's Travels* in any way diminish Swift's work. There is no doubt, then, that works of literature can contain true statements and false ones; but it is tempting to ask, what does their truth or falsity matter? Literature is not astronomy or geography or history or any branch of knowledge, particular or general.

Many would hold that the above statements are indeed irrelevant, as are any that encroach upon the domain of science; but, they would add, there are other assertions that matter a great deal: for example, the statements in which a world view is presented in a poem or drama or novel. The main burden of the ancient Latin poet Lucretius' *De rerum natura* ("On the Nature of Things") is a presentation of the materialism of the Greek philosopher Democritus; and an embodiment of the world view of medieval Catholicism is the very warp and woof of Dante's *Divine Comedy*—and such considerations (it would be contended) are relevant to these works as literature. In reply, however, it might be said that while it is true that these world views must be understood and taken into consideration in the reading of these poems and that they cannot be understood or appreciated without knowing them, the truth or falsity of these views still does matter aesthetically. If Lucretius' view is true, then Dante's must be false, and vice versa, since they are incompatible; but in order to appreciate the poem it is not necessary to know which (if either) is true. Appreciating art, unlike taking a stand for or against a cause in life, does not require a yes or no to statements. It requires only that the viewer look and appreciate, that he experience as richly and fully as possible the feeling and attitudes involved in the

world view that is presented. Philosophers and scientists are concerned with whether the Democritean materialism of Lucretius is true; appreciators of art are concerned only to capture the feeling appropriate to the world view in question.

Explicit and implicit statements in literature

Many statements in works of literature are not explicitly made at all but are implicit: Hardy never tells in his novels what his world view is, but it emerges rather clearly before the reader is halfway through any of them. Probably the most important points made in works of literature that contain a central thesis are implicit rather than explicit. How, in that case, can it be determined what thesis it is that is implied? In a court of law, if someone says, "He didn't say it exactly, he just implied it," the judge would be likely to rule that this was insufficient evidence of slander, since the person did not actually say it. Still, many statements in daily life are not stated but implied—in the sense that they are intended; the trouble lies in proving that the speaker intended them, since no one else is in a comparable position to say what his intentions were; and, in the case of deceased authors, there is no evidence of their intentions other than what they said. One is doubtless on safer ground, therefore, saying that many statements are implied in the sense that they are suggested (whether the speaker intended to do so or not) by the tone of voice and the juxtaposition of the words used. Thus, "They had children and got married" suggests, though it does not state, that they had the children before they were married; any normal user of the English language would tend to construe it thus. And it is surely no overstatement to say that Swift's *Gulliver's Travels* suggests that the author was misanthropic or that the novels of the French author Marcel Proust (1871–1922) suggest a pessimistic view of love and other human relationships close to that of the German philosopher Arthur Schopenhauer (1788–1860). A serious reader of literature will become increasingly sensitive to what is suggested in the works he is reading.

But, once again, the importance of the suggested statements, even when they are true, in no way shows that they must be accepted as true by the reader if he is to value them as works of art. Is the sincere Roman Catholic who finds Dante's world view congenial and Lucretius' repellent committed to saying that Dante's is the better poem? If so, he may be accused of confusing his moral and theological judgments with his aesthetic ones. Still, it should be noted that there are some critics who believe that if two works of literature are both equal in excellence on all counts, yet one presents a true view of reality and the other fails to, the one presenting a true view is better— better even as a work of art—than is the other one.

There is, however, another way of talking about truth in literature that is not or is not as obviously connected to propositions. A characterization in a novel or drama is spoken of as being true to human nature, true to the way people actually speak or behave or feel. No matter that Becky Sharp—in the English novelist William Thackeray's *Vanity Fair*—is a fictional character, it would be said, as long as she is depicted as a person of a certain type would behave, she is being depicted truly; truth in fiction does not mean truth of the statements (for the statements in Thackeray's novel describing her are false), but truth to human nature.

The notion of "truth to human nature" in literature

But what exactly does "truth to human nature" mean? The criterion is as old as Aristotle, who wrote that poetry is more true than history because it presents universal truths whereas history gives only particular truths and that poetry (dramatic fiction) shows how a person of this or that kind probably or necessarily would behave (or think, or feel). This criterion, however, is too vague as it stands: what is probable or plausible behaviour in one person is not in another, and what is probable in one set of circumstances is not so in another. The test of truth to human nature would be roughly as follows: Would a person such as has been described thus far (in the novel or drama) behave (or think or feel or be motivated) in the way that the author depicts this character as behaving in the circumstances described? It is often very difficult to decide this question, because knowledge of human beings is insufficient or because the dramatist himself has not provided enough clues. Still, once readers or critics are convinced that the character described would not have behaved as the novelist depicts him as behaving, they may criticize the characterization (at least with regard to this bit of behaviour or motivation) as implausible. If a character who has been described as spending years working toward a certain goal is represented by the novelist as abandoning it once he is within sight of it, the reader will have considerable reservations about this delineation unless the author has depicted the character as being unstable or masochistic or in some way as being the kind of person who might in these circumstances do this kind of thing. It is true that there are people in the world who abandon their goals within sight of them after years of labour, but the conviction must be implanted that the character already presented by the novelist belongs to this classification or the behaviour will seem reasonless and unmotivated.

Is truth to human nature aesthetically relevant? That is, when present does it make the work of literature better and when absent or flawed does it make the work worse as literature? Here again there would be some difference of opinion, but a very large number of critics and aestheticians, in the tradition of Aristotle, would say that it matters aesthetically a great deal. The novelist does not have to be true to geography or history or astronomy, but he must be, as the 19th-century U.S. author Nathaniel Hawthorne said of all literary artists, true to the human heart. A literary artist may tamper with all the other truths with impunity, but not this one: his characters must be convincing, and they will not be convincing if they are not depicted as having anger, love, jealousy, and other human emotions that real people have and in pretty much the contexts in which real people have them. If a novelist's characters were not motivated in much the way that human beings are motivated, the reader would not even be able to understand them—they would be alien and unintelligible to him. Even when a writer (such as the Englishman Kenneth Grahame in *The Wind in the Willows*) depicts animals as central characters in novels, however much they may differ from human beings in external appearance, they must psychologically be presented as human beings—how else and in what other terms could their behaviour and their motivation be understood? Such, then, are the reasons for saying that whatever else a literary artist does, his depictions must be truthful to human nature.

Truth to human nature in arts other than literature

Can works of art other than literature possess truth to human nature? It would seem that in a limited degree they can. Motion pictures and operas and other mixed arts clearly can, but they employ words, and literature is a principal ingredient in them. But what of arts that employ no words at all? Painting and sculpture, not being temporal arts, cannot depict action, and action is all-important in the representation of human character. These arts contain depictions of persons (real or imaginary) only on a knife-edge of time. Still, sometimes something may be inferred even from a knife-edge. The late self-portraits of the 17th-century Dutch artist Rembrandt do seem to reveal an agonized yet sometimes serene inner spirit, suggesting that there are flashes of human insight to be found in depictions of human beings in visual art. As for musical art (music without the accompaniment of words), it contains nothing that could be called depiction, not even depiction on a knife-edge of time; and, if this is so, there can be no such thing here as true depiction or false depiction. Music may be expressive of human feelings, in the sense already described, but this is a far cry from saying that it contains depictions that are true to human nature.

Even if truth to human nature in the depiction of character is aesthetically relevant (which many would question), to say this is still far from saying that it is the only criterion for excellence in works of art, or even that this is the principal thing that art gives or its main excuse for being. To go so far would be to discount colour and form and expressiveness as criteria for excellence in art; and this virtually no one is willing to do. It would seem, then, that in no case is truth (even truth to human nature) necessary in works of art, seeing that entire genres of art, such as music, exist without it; and that even when it

is present and when its presence increases the merit of a work of art (which again many would deny), it is only one virtue among many. Thus, the view that the purpose or function of art is to provide truth is quite surely mistaken; perhaps the person who wants truth and is indifferent to the presence of anything else had better turn to science or philosophy rather than to the arts.

Art as a means to moral improvement. To say that a work of art is aesthetically good or has aesthetic value is one thing; to say that it is morally good or has a capacity to influence people so as to make them morally better is another. Yet, though the two kinds of judgments differ from one another, they are not entirely unrelated. Three views on the relation of art to morality can be distinguished:

Moralism. According to this view, the primary or exclusive function of art is as a handmaiden to morality—which means, usually, whatever system of morality is adhered to by the theorist in question. Art that does not promote moral influence of the desired kind is viewed by the moralist with suspicion and sometimes with grudging tolerance of its existence. For art implants in people unorthodox ideas; it breaks the molds of provincialism in which people have been brought up; it disturbs and disquiets, since it tends to emphasize individuality rather than conformity; and works of art are often created out of rebellion or disenchantment with the established order. Thus, art may undermine beliefs and attitudes on which, it is thought, the welfare of society rests and so may be viewed with suspicion by the guardians of custom. When art does not affect people morally one way or the other (for example, much nonrepresentational painting), it is considered a harmless pleasure that can be tolerated if it does not take up too much of the viewer's time; but, when it promotes questioning and defies established attitudes, it is viewed by the moralist as insidious and subversive. It is viewed with approval only if it promotes or reinforces the moral beliefs and attitudes adhered to by the moralist.

Plato's moralistic view of art

Plato is the first champion in the Western world of the moralistic view of art—at least in *The Republic* and *Laws.* Plato admired the poets and was himself something of a poet; but, when he was founding (on paper) his ideal state, he was convinced that much art, even some passages in Homer, tended to have an evil influence upon the young and impressionable, and accordingly he decided that they must be banned. Passages that spoke ill or questioningly of the gods, passages containing excessive sexual passion (and all works that would today be described as pornographic), and even passages of music that were disturbing to the soul or the senses were all condemned to the same fate. Plato's concern here was with the purity of soul of the men who would become members of the council of rulers of the state; he was not concerned with censorship for the masses, but, since one could not predict which young people would pass the series of examinations required for membership in the council of rulers and since it was (and is) practically impossible to restrict access to works of art to a certain group, the censorship, he decided, would have to be universal. The objection might be raised, to be sure, that rulers to be should not be hothouse plants separated from the influences of the outside world and that they would be better off facing all of reality, including its evils. But Plato's view was that these influences should be kept from them during their formative years—that during this critical time, when the whole tenor of their lives was being shaped, art could be an influence for evil and had to be sacrificed in the interests of morality. In other dialogues of Plato, such as the *Ion* and the *Phaedrus,* when he was not concerned with building a state, he extolled the virtues of art and even held the artist to be divine (although madly divine); but when it came to a conflict between art and morality, it was art that would have to go.

Tolstoy's moralistic view of art

The most famous champion of the moralistic view of art in modern times is Tolstoy. Long after he had finished writing his novels, he fell under the influence of primitive (prechurch) Christianity, the principal tenet of which was the brotherhood of all mankind. This one idea became such an obsession with him that everything else, including the pursuit of art to which he had devoted his life, became subordinate to it. Almost all the literature of his own time, including all his own novels, he condemned as inimical to the brotherhood of man by emphasizing class distinction and pitting one group of mankind against another. Even art that appealed primarily (in his opinion) to "upper class" tastes, such as the symphonies of Beethoven and the operas of Richard Wagner, both 19th-century German composers, were condemned as "false art." The art that remained after these colossal excisions included such items as folk songs that peasants might sing in the fields as they worked and pictures and stories either illustrating the tenets of primitive Christianity or fostering the spirit of Christianity by promoting the brotherhood of all mankind.

The moralistic view of art is still, on the whole, the unarticulated view of art held by the masses, particularly when they are under the sway of a dominant religious or political doctrine. Historically, Christianity has been suspicious of all art except those works that depicted some aspects of biblical history or could be used to further the spread of Christian belief and practice (although this is no longer strictly true). It would probably be fair to say that the view of art held by the Soviet government is a moralistic one: works of fiction and poems must praise Communism or further its doctrines, and works of music must be melodic and singable (Soviet composers such as Dmitry Shostakovich have often been condemned by the official hierarchy as "too German" or "too materialistic"). Whenever a culture or nation is under the sway of a dominant view, whether moral or religious or political, the tendency of the rulers of that nation is to promote it at all costs—and one of the casualties in the process is art, at any rate that great body of art that is either indifferent or hostile to the reigning dogma.

Aestheticism. Diametrically opposed to the moralistic view is aestheticism, the view that instead of art (and everything else) being the handmaiden of morality, morality (and everything else) should be the handmaiden of art. The proponents of this view hold that the experience of art is the most intense and pervasive experience available in human life and that nothing should be allowed to interfere with it. If it conflicts with morality, so much the worse for morality; and if the masses fail to appreciate it or receive the experience it has to offer, so much the worse for the masses. The vital intensity of the aesthetic experience is the paramount goal in human life. If there are morally undesirable effects of art, they do not really matter in comparison to this all-important experience which art can give. When the son-in-law of the 20th-century Italian dictator Benito Mussolini waxed lyrical in his description of the beauty of a bomb exploding in the midst of a crowd of unarmed Ethiopians, he was carrying to its fullest extent the aestheticist's view of art.

Aesthetic values versus moral values

Few persons would wish to go so far. Even the most ardent lovers of art would stop short of saying that the value of art holds a monopoly over all other values. It may well be that the experience of works of art is the greatest experience available to human beings (though this, too, could be questioned), but at any rate it is not the only one available, and, this being the case, the others should be considered as well. There is a plurality of values; and aesthetic values, although far greater, admittedly, than most persons realize, are still just a few among many. It is therefore necessary to consider the relation of the values derived from art to the values derived from other things, such as the conduct of life apart from art: no one can devote every waking hour to the pursuit of art, even if for no other reason than the need for survival, and thus the values of such mundane things as food and shelter have also to be considered.

Mixed positions. The moralistic and aesthetic positions are extremes, and the truth is likely to be found somewhere between them. Indeed, art and morality are intimately related, and neither functions wholly without the other. But to trace the precise relations between art and morality is far from easy; for want of a better term, "interactionism" could be used to label the view that aesthetic and moral values each have distinctive roles to play in the world but that neither operates independently of the other.

It would be admitted, first of all, that works of literature (which will be examined first, since of all the arts the relation of literature to morality is most obvious) can teach valuable moral lessons through explicit presentation: the genre that has this as its aim is didactic literature, as exemplified by *Pilgrim's Progress* by the English Puritan John Bunyan and *Back to Methuselah* by the Irish dramatist George Bernard Shaw. But most works of literature do not exist to teach a moral lesson: possibly, Shakespeare did not write *Othello* merely to attack racial prejudice or *Macbeth* to prove that crime does not pay. Literature does teach but in a far more important way than by explicit preachment: it teaches, as John Dewey said, by being, not by express intent.

Expression of morality in literature

How does literature achieve this moral effect? It presents characters and situations (usually situations of difficult moral decision) through which the reader can deepen his own moral perspectives by reflecting on other people's problems and conflicts, which usually have a complexity that his own daily situations do not possess. He can learn from them without himself having to undergo in his personal life the same moral conflicts or make the same moral decisions. The reader can view such situations with a detachment that he can seldom achieve in daily life when he is immersed in the stream of action. By viewing these situations objectively and reflecting on them, he is enabled to make his own moral decisions more wisely when life calls on him in turn to make them. Literature can be a stimulus to moral reflection unequalled perhaps by any other, for it presents the moral choice in its total context with nothing of relevance omitted.

Perhaps the chief moral potency of literature lies in its unique power to stimulate and develop the faculty of the imagination. Through literature the reader is carried beyond the confines of the narrow world that most persons inhabit into a world of thought and feeling more profound and more varied than his own, a world in which he can share the experiences of human beings (real or fictitious) who are far removed from him in space and time and in attitude and way of life. Literature enables him to enter directly into the affective processes of other human beings, and, having done this, no perceptive reader can any longer condemn or dismiss en masse a large segment of humanity as "foreigners" or "wastrels," for a successful work of literature brings them to life as individuals, animated by the same passions as he is, facing the same conflicts, and tried in the same crucible of bitter experience. Through such an exercise of the sympathetic imagination, literature tends to draw all men together instead of setting them apart from one another in groups or types with convenient labels for each. Far more than preaching or moralizing, more even than the descriptive and scientific discourses of psychology or sociology, literature tends to unite mankind and reveal the common human nature that exists in everyone behind the facade of divisive doctrines, political ideologies, and religious beliefs.

This is not to say, of course, that those who read great works of literature are necessarily tolerant or sympathetic human beings. Reading literature alone is not a cure for human ills, and people who are neurotically grasping or selfish in their private lives will hardly cease to be so as a result of reading works of literature. Still, wide and serious reading of literature has an observable effect: people who do this kind of reading, no matter what their other characteristics may be, do tend to be more understanding of other people's conflicts, to have more sympathy with their problems, and to be able to empathize more with them as human beings than do people who have never broadened their horizons by reading literature at all. No one who has read great literature widely and for a considerable period, so as to make it an integral part of his life, can any longer share the same provincialism and be dominated by the same narrow prejudices that seem to characterize most people most of the time. Literature, perhaps more than anything else, exercises a leavening influence on the temper of a man's moral life. It looses him from the bonds of his own position in space and time; it releases him from exclusive involvement with his own struggles from day to day; it enables him to see his own local problems and

The leavening influence of literature

trials from the perspective of eternity—he can now view them as if from an enormous height.

To have moral effects, it is not necessary that a work of literature present a system of morality. Its moral potency is perhaps greatest when it presents not systems but human beings in action, so that through the exercise of the imagination the reader can see his own customs and philosophies as he sees theirs: as some among many of the countless adjustments and solutions to human problems that different circumstances and man's endlessly varied and resourceful nature have produced.

Works of literature, then, develop more than anything else the human faculty of the imagination; and the 19th-century English poet Percy Bysshe Shelley said that the imagination is the greatest single instrument of moral good. Perhaps this sounds like an absurd overstatement, but consider what morality is like without the imagination. Consider the average morality of a small community, relatively isolated from centres of culture and unacquainted with any artistic tradition. Its morality is rigid and circumscribed; the details of each member's personal life are hedged about with constant annoyances, and everyone's life is open to the prying eyes of others who are unfailingly quick to judge, with or without evidence. Outsiders are looked upon askance; people of a different religion, race, or culture are viewed with suspicion and distrust; and anyone who does not subscribe to whatever moral code is dominant in the community is condemned or ostracized. No doubt these people are sincere—they are dreadfully sincere, deadly sincere. But sincerity without enlightenment can be as harmful to the achievement of good as intelligence without wisdom when that intelligence is possessed by political leaders playing with hydrogen bombs. Generally speaking, the people of a small community have not known the leavening influence of literature. Their morality is rigid, cramped, and arid. If these same people had been exposed from early youth to great masterpieces of literature and had learned through them to appreciate the tremendous diversity of human mores and beliefs held by other groups, with the same degree of sincerity that they themselves possess, they would be less likely to be as harsh, intolerant, and rigid as they are.

People are usually inclined to separate art and morality into two hermetically sealed compartments. They talk as if morality were already complete and self-sufficient without art, and that art, if it is to be tolerated at all, can grudgingly be permitted, provided that it conforms to the moral customs of the time and place of those judging it. But this view is surely to conceive the relation between art and morality in far too one-sided a manner. If art must take cognizance of morality, equally morality must take congnizance of art. Almost everything that is alive and imaginative about morality comes from the leavening influence of art.

Influence of ancient dramatists

To consider examples from ancient Greece alone, what would morality be today without the influence of the dramatists Aeschylus and Sophocles, without Socrates as described in Plato's dialogues, even without the historians Herodotus and Thucydides with their quiet humour, gentle prodding skepticism, and tolerance for other customs and views? It is through great works of art that the most vivid conceptions of various ways of life are obtained. What is it about other times and places that people most remember? Is it their political squabbles, their wars, their economic upheavals? These events are known in general to intelligent laymen and in detail to historians, but even then such events do not usually make much of a dent in peoples' personal lives in the way that art does. What is alive today about ancient Greece is its sculpture, its poetry, its epic and drama; what is alive today about the Elizabethan period, even more than the defeat of the Spanish Armada and the reign of Queen Elizabeth I, is its poetic drama, with its vivid characterizations and boundless energy. Other civilizations and cultures may be sources of facts and theories that enlighten modern understanding, but what enables contemporary man to share directly their feelings and attitudes toward life is not their politics nor even their religion but their art. Art alone is never out of date. Science is cumulative; even the science

textbooks of ten years ago are now discarded as obsolete; the science of the ancient Greeks and the Elizabethans is studied today primarily for its historical value. But great art is never obsolete; it can still present to modern man its full impact, undiminished by time. Shakespeare will not be out of date as long as human beings continue to feel love, jealousy, and conflict in a troubled world. A biblical statement might be paraphrased and applied to past cultures: "By their arts shall ye know them." The artists whose works are now revered may have died unsung; most of them, even those who were appreciated during their lifetimes, were considered far less important than the latest naval victories or the accession of the current king; yet today these things have all passed into history, but art survives with undiminished vigour. The art of the past molds in countless ways the attitudes, responses, and dispositions of modern man's daily life. Most of what is perceptive and imaginative in morality owes its origin to art, and, when morality loses contact with the tradition of art, it becomes dead and sterile. Yet, in spite of this, some people tell us that art is merely the salve of morality, to soothe its stringency.

Already, in the preceding paragraph, mention has begun of arts other than literature. How, it could be asked, can they have any moral effects on those who view them or listen to them? Yet there are effects of these arts on the observer that, in a broad sense, are moral (as opposed to nonmoral) and that account for the attempts of many people to censor them.

Historically, the most famous supposition about the moral effect of art on its audience is Aristotle's theory of catharsis; Aristotle applied the theory to tragedy only, but many since his day have applied it to art in general. According to this view, art acts as an emotional cathartic and achieves a "purgation of the emotions." Certain emotions man would be better off without (Aristotle limited them to pity and fear, but they could easily be extended) are generated during the course of daily life. Art is the principal agency that should help to dispel these emotions. By observing works of art (witnessing a drama, listening to a powerful symphony, looking at certain works of sculpture or painting) the recipient can work off these emotions rather than let them fester inside him or take them out in unpleasant ways on his fellow men. Art siphons off these disturbing inner states rather than letting them grow rancid within man.

Aristotle's theory of catharsis

As it stands, this view is undoubtedly somewhat crude, especially in the light of modern psychology; and fault could be found in many respects with the Aristotelian doctrine of catharsis. Yet the experience of reading, viewing, or listening to a work of art does give a peculiar release, a feeling of freedom from inner turbulence. The mere act of plunging, for a few hours, into an entirely different world when attending a play or a concert is often enough to transform, however temporarily, the tone of people's daily lives. It is not merely that for a few hours they can forget their troubles—any form of entertainment, however worthless, might do this. It is not merely that art provides a break or interruption in the course of people's lives at the end of which they are exactly what they were before. It is that through the aesthetic process itself, in the very act of concentrating energies on an art object of great unity and complexity and depth, a kind of inner clarification is achieved that was not present before.

It is not true, therefore, that reading novels of crime and detection leads people to indulge in a life of crime; on the whole, those who read such novels are law-abiding people, and, if anything, the reading of such novels is a substitute for aggressive activity (it is aggression vicariously experienced) rather than an incitement to it. Nor do works of art of a licentious nature usually incite people to rape or adultery; far from acting as incitements to action, they are safety valves against action by providing a kind of substitute gratification. It has been said, for example, that Shakespeare's *Antony and Cleopatra* is an immoral work because it celebrates the passionate surrender to an illicit love and the victory of this love over practical, political, and moral concerns. But is there any evidence that people who read this play will behave like the lovers in question because they read the play? On the contrary: it could be argued that reading the play has an instrumental value in that it presents another example of a complex moral situation, the perusal of which provides many avenues for moral reflection, and that the play also possesses the intrinsic value of acute characterization, dramatic power, and poetry whose imagery and intensity are among the most splendid in the English language. Again, it is said that American youth has been demoralized by such 20th-century U.S. writers as Ernest Hemingway and William Faulkner in that these writers set an example of bad behaviour. But to say that they are capable of demoralizing an entire generation is certainly to attribute to them too much moral power, especially over people who have never even heard of them. Even among those who do read serious literature, the effects are probably more beneficial than harmful: through books the horizons of such readers have been expanded to include other ways of life than they would have previously known.

The essential morality of the aesthetic experience

Quite apart from the ultimate effect of a work of art on a man's emotions, it would appear that the very act of experiencing the work may itself have a moral effect. If he is really concentrating on the details of a work of art and not just passively letting it play upon his senses, this effect—the heightening of his sensibilities and the refining of his capacities for perceptual discrimination—will make him more receptive to the world around him, thus raising the tone of his daily life and making his experience of the world richer than before.

Most of what passes for aesthetic appreciation does not begin to have this effect; but its failure is only because it is not aesthetic appreciation at all—it is a kind of tired reverie rather than an intense absorption in the aesthetic object. Most people, when they hear music, simply allow themselves to be inundated by the sheer flow of sound. Such people do not actively listen to the music and are not even aware of the most elementary kind of ebb and flow occurring within it; they only receive it passively, perhaps using it as a springboard for a private reverie or an emotional debauch of their own. Music has for them not an aesthetic effect but an anesthetic effect. It is not just hearing music that will have the required effect. The aesthetic experience, which involves nothing less than a total concentration on the perceptual details of the aesthetic object, is an experience that heightens consciousness, exercises man's capacity for perceptual awareness and discrimination, and helps him come alive to the sight and texture of the world around him. After a viewer has seen an exhibition of landscapes by Cézanne, the entire world may seem to him to have changed its structure and complexion: it may, indeed, take on the look of Cézanne's landscapes. And is not anything that increases awareness and subtlety of discernment and discrimination a potentially moral agent? Art provides the most intense, concentrated, and sharply focussed of the experiences available to man. Because of this, art can have an enormous influence on the tenor of a person's life, more influential no doubt than any particular system of morality. In its ability to do this, it has an effect on man's life that, in an extended sense at least, can surely be called moral. Morality transcends particular systems of morality; and art, by being for many persons the dominant influence in their lives, thus transcends them also.   (Jo.Ho.)

Philosophy of logic

The term logic comes from the Greek word *logos*. The variety of senses that *logos* possesses may suggest the difficulties to be encountered in characterizing the nature and scope of logic. Among the partial translations of *logos*, there are "sentence," "discourse," "reason," "rule," "ratio," "account" (especially the account of the meaning of an expression), "rational principle," and "definition." Not unlike this proliferation of meanings, the subject matter of logic has been said to be the "laws of thought," "the rules of right reasoning," "the principles of valid argumentation," "the use of certain words labelled 'logical constants'," "truths (true propositions) based solely on the meanings of the terms they contain," and so on.

LOGIC AS A DISCIPLINE

Nature and varieties of logic. It is relatively easy to discern some order in the above embarrassment of explanations. Some of the characterizations are in fact closely related to each other. When logic is said, for instance, to be the study of the laws of thought, these laws cannot be the empirical (or observable) regularities of actual human thinking as studied in psychology; they must be laws of correct reasoning, which are independent of the psychological idiosyncrasies of the thinker. Moreover, there is a parallelism between correct thinking and valid argumentation: valid argumentation may be thought of as an expression of correct thinking, and the latter as an internalization of the former. In the sense of this parallelism, laws of correct thought will match those of correct argumentation. The characteristic mark of the latter is, in turn, that they do not depend on any particular matters of fact. Whenever an argument that takes a reasoner from p to q is valid, it must hold independently of what he happens to know or believe about the subject matter of p and q. The only other source of the certainty of the connection between p and q, however, is presumably constituted by the meanings of the terms that the propositions p and q contain. These very same meanings will then also make the sentence "If p, then q" true irrespective of all contingent matters of fact. More generally, one can validly argue from p to q if and only if the implication "If p, then q" is logically true—*i.e.*, true in virtue of the meanings of words occurring in p and q, independently of any matter of fact.

Valid argument and matters of fact

Logic may thus be characterized as the study of truths based completely on the meanings of the terms they contain.

In order to accommodate certain traditional ideas within the scope of this formulation, the meanings in question may have to be understood as embodying insights into the essences of the entities denoted by the terms, not merely codifications of customary linguistic usage.

The following proposition (from Aristotle), for instance, is a simple truth of logic: "If sight is perception, the objects of sight are objects of perception." Its truth can be grasped without holding any opinions as to what, in fact, the relationship of sight to perception is. What is needed is merely an understanding of what is meant by such terms as "if–then," "is," and "are," and an understanding that "object of" expresses some sort of relation.

The logical truth of Aristotle's sample proposition is reflected by the fact that "The objects of sight are objects of perception" can validly be inferred from "Sight is perception."

Many questions nevertheless remain unanswered by this characterization. The contrast between matters of fact and relations between meanings that was relied on in the characterization has been challenged, together with the very notion of meaning. Even if both are accepted, there remains a considerable tension between a wider and a narrower conception of logic. According to the wider interpretation, all truths depending only on meanings belong to logic. It is in this sense that the word logic is to be taken in such designations as "epistemic logic" (logic of knowledge), "doxastic logic" (logic of belief), "deontic logic" (logic of norms), "the logic of science," "inductive logic," and so on. According to the narrower conception, logical truths obtain (or hold) in virtue of certain specific terms, often called logical constants. Whether they can be given an intrinsic characterization or whether they can be specified only by enumeration is a moot point. It is generally agreed, however, that they include (1) such propositional connectives as "not," "and," "or," and "if–then" and (2) the so-called quantifiers "$(\exists x)$" (which may be read: "For at least one individual, call it x, it is true that") and "$(\forall x)$" ("For each individual, call it x, it is true that"). The dummy letter x is here called a bound (individual) variable. Its values are supposed to be members of some fixed class of entities, called individuals, a class that is variously known as the universe of discourse, the universe presupposed in an interpretation, or the domain of individuals. Its members are said to be quantified over in "$(\exists x)$" or "$(\forall x)$." Furthermore, (3) the concept of identity (expressed by =) and (4) some notion of predication

The various branches of logic

(an individual's having a property or a relation's holding between several individuals) belong to logic. The forms that the study of these logical constants take are described in greater detail in the article LOGIC, in which the different kinds of logical notation are also explained. Here, only a delineation of the field of logic is given.

When the terms in (1) alone are studied, the field is called propositional logic. When (1), (2), and (4) are considered, the field is the central area of logic that is variously known as first-order logic, quantification theory, lower predicate calculus, lower functional calculus, or elementary logic. If the absence of (3) is stressed, the epithet "without identity" is added, in contrast to first-order logic with identity, in which (3) is also included.

Borderline cases between logical and nonlogical constants are the following (among others): (1) Higher order quantification, which means quantification not over the individuals belonging to a given universe of discourse, as in first-order logic, but also over sets of individuals and sets of n-tuples of individuals. (Alternatively, the properties and relations that specify these sets may be quantified over.) This gives rise to second-order logic. The process can be repeated. Quantification over sets of such sets (or of n-tuples of such sets or over properties and relations of such sets) as are considered in second-order logic gives rise to third-order logic; and all logics of finite order form together the (simple) theory of (finite) types. (2) The membership relation, expressed by $\in$, can be grafted on to first-order logic; it gives rise to set theory. (3) The concepts of (logical) necessity and (logical) possibility can be added.

This narrower sense of logic is related to the influential idea of logical form. In any given sentence, all of the nonlogical terms may be replaced by variables of the appropriate type, keeping only the logical constants intact. The result is a formula exhibiting the logical form of the sentence. If the formula results in a true sentence for any substitution of interpreted terms (of the appropriate logical type) for the variables, the formula and the sentence are said to be logically true (in the narrower sense of the expression).

Features and problems of logic. Three areas of general concern are the following.

Logical semantics. For the purpose of clarifying logical truth and hence the concept of logic itself, a tool that has turned out to be more important than the idea of logical form is logical semantics, sometimes also known as model theory. By this is meant a study of the relationships of linguistic expressions to those structures in which they may be interpreted and of which they can then convey information. The crucial idea in this theory is that of truth (absolutely or with respect to an interpretation). It was first analyzed in logical semantics around 1930 by the Polish-American logician Alfred Tarski. In its different variants, logical semantics is the central area in the philosophy of logic. It enables the logician to characterize the notion of logical truth irrespective of the supply of nonlogical constants that happen to be available to be substituted for variables, although this supply had to be used in the characterization that turned on the idea of logical form. It also enables him to identify logically true sentences with those that are true in every interpretation (in "every possible world").

The ideas on which logical semantics is based are not unproblematic, however. For one thing, a semantical approach presupposes that the language in question can be viewed "from the outside"; *i.e.,* considered as a calculus that can be variously interpreted and not as the all-encompassing medium in which all communication takes place (logic as calculus versus logic as language).

Furthermore, in most of the usual logical semantics the very relations that connect language with reality are left unanalyzed and static. Ludwig Wittgenstein, an Austrian-born philosopher, discussed informally the "language-games"—or rule-governed activities connecting a language with the world—that are supposed to give the expressions of language their meanings; but these games have scarcely been related to any systematic logical theory. Only a few other attempts to study the dynamics of the representa-

tive relationships between language and reality have been made. The simplest of these suggestions is perhaps that the semantics of first-order logic should be considered in terms of certain games (in the precise sense of game theory) that are, roughly speaking, attempts to verify a given first-order sentence. The truth of the sentence would then mean the existence of a winning strategy in such a game.

Limitations of logic. Many philosophers are distinctly uneasy about the wider sense of logic. Some of their apprehensions, voiced with special eloquence by a contemporary Harvard University logician, Willard Van Quine, are based on the claim that relations of synonymy cannot be fully determined by empirical means. Other apprehensions have to do with the fact that most extensions of first-order logic do not admit of a complete axiomatization; *i.e.,* their truths cannot all be derived from any finite—or recursive (see below)—set of axioms. This fact was shown by the important "incompleteness" theorems proved in 1931 by Kurt Gödel, an Austrian (later, American) logician, and their various consequences and extensions. (Gödel showed that any consistent axiomatic theory that comprises a certain amount of elementary arithmetic is incapable of being completely axiomatized.) Higher-order logics are in this sense incomplete and so are all reasonably powerful systems of set theory. Although a semantical theory can be built for them, they can scarcely be characterized any longer as giving actual rules—in any case complete rules—for right reasoning or for valid argumentation. Because of this shortcoming, several traditional definitions of logic seem to be inapplicable to these parts of logical studies.

These apprehensions do not arise in the case of modal logic, which may be defined, in the narrow sense, as the study of logical necessity and possibility; for even quantified modal logic admits of a complete axiomatization. Other, related problems nevertheless arise in this area. It is tempting to try to interpret such a notion as logical necessity as a syntactical predicate; *i.e.,* as a predicate the applicability of which depends only on the form of the sentence claimed to be necessary—rather like the applicability of formal rules of proof. It has been shown, however, by Richard Montague, an American logician, that this cannot be done for the usual systems of modal logic.

Logic and computability. These findings of Gödel and Montague are closely related to the general study of computability, which is usually known as recursive function theory (see MATHEMATICS, FOUNDATIONS OF: *The crisis in foundations following 1900: Logicism, formalism, and the metamathematical method*) and which is one of the most important branches of contemporary logic. In this part of logic, functions—or laws governing numerical or other precise one-to-one or many-to-one relationships—are studied with regard to the possibility of their being computed; *i.e.,* of being effectively—or mechanically—calculable. Functions that can be so calculated are called recursive. Several different and historically independent attempts have been made to define the class of all recursive functions, and these have turned out to coincide with each other. The claim that recursive functions exhaust the class of all functions that are effectively calculable (in some intuitive informal sense) is known as Church's thesis (named after the American logician Alonzo Church).

One of the definitions of recursive functions is that they are computable by a kind of idealized automaton known as a Turing machine (named after Alan Mathison Turing, a British mathematician and logician). Recursive function theory may therefore be considered a theory of these idealized automata. The main idealization involved (as compared with actually realizable computers) is the availability of a potentially infinite tape.

The theory of computability prompts many philosophical questions, most of which have not so far been answered satisfactorily. It poses the question, for example, of the extent to which all thinking can be carried out mechanically. Since it quickly turns out that many functions employed in mathematics—including many in elementary number theory—are nonrecursive, one may wonder whether it follows that a mathematician's mind in thinking of such functions cannot be a mechanism and whether the possibly nonmechanical character of mathematical thinking

Truth as defined in model theory

Incompleteness of higher-order logics

may have consequences for the problems of determinism and free will. Further work is needed before definitive answers can be given to these important questions.

ISSUES AND DEVELOPMENTS IN THE PHILOSOPHY OF LOGIC

In addition to the problems and findings already discussed, the following topics may be mentioned.

Analytical truth

Meaning and truth. Since 1950, the concept of analytical truth (logical truth in the wider sense) has been subjected to sharp criticism, especially by Quine. The main objections turned around the nonempirical character of analytical truth (arising from meanings only) and of the concepts in terms of which it could be defined—such as synonymy, meaning, and logical necessity. The critics usually do not contest the claim that logicians can capture synonymies and meanings by starting from first-order logic and adding suitable further assumptions, though definitory identities do not always suffice for this purpose. The crucial criticism is that the empirical meaning of such further "meaning postulates" is not clear.

Logical semantics of modal concepts. In this respect, logicians' prospects have been enhanced by the development of a semantical theory of modal logic, both in the narrower sense of modal logic, which is restricted to logical necessity and logical possibility, and in the wider sense, in which all concepts that exhibit similar logical behaviour are included. This development, initiated between 1957 and 1959 largely by Stig Kanger of Sweden and Saul Kripke of the U.S., has opened the door to applications in the logical analysis of many philosophically central concepts, such as knowledge, belief, perception, and obligation. Attempts have been made to analyze from the viewpoint of logical semantics such philosophical topics as sense-datum theories, knowledge by acquaintance, the paradox of saying and disbelieving propounded by the British philosopher G.E. Moore, and the traditional distinction between statements *de dicto* ("from saying") and statements *de re* ("from the thing"). These developments also provide a framework in which many of those meaning relations can be codified that go beyond first-order logic, and may perhaps even afford suggestions as to what their empirical content might be.

Intensional logic. Especially in the hands of Montague, the logical semantics of modal notions has blossomed into a general theory of intensional logic; *i.e.,* a theory of such notions as proposition, individual concept, and in general of all entities usually thought of as serving as the meanings of linguistic expressions. (Propositions are the meanings of sentences, individual concepts are those of singular terms, and so on.) A crucial role is here played by the notion of a possible world, which may be thought of as a variant of the logicians' older notion of model, now conceived of realistically as a serious alternative to the actual course of events in the world. In this analysis, for instance, propositions are functions that correlate possible worlds with truth-values. This correlation may be thought of as spelling out the older idea that to know the meaning of a sentence is to know under what circumstances (in which possible worlds) it would be true.

Logic and information. Even though none of the problems listed seems to affect the interest of logical semantics, its applications are often handicapped by the nature of many of its basic concepts. One may consider, for instance, the analysis of a proposition as a function that correlates possible worlds with truth-values. An arbitrary function of this sort can be thought of (as can functions in general) as an infinite class of pairs of correlated values of an independent variable and of the function, like the coordinate pairs (x, y) of points on a graph. Although propositions are supposed to be meanings of sentences, no one can grasp such an infinite class directly when understanding a sentence; he can do so only by means of some particular algorithm, or recipe (as it were), for computing the function in question. Such particular algorithms come closer in some respects to what is actually needed in the theory of meaning than the meaning entities of the usual intensional logic.

Possible worlds and truth-values

This observation is connected with the fact that, in the usual logical semantics, no finer distinctions are utilized

in semantical discussions than logical equivalence. Hence the transition from one sentence to another logically equivalent one is disregarded for the purposes of meaning concepts. This disregard would be justifiable if one of the most famous theses of Logical Positivists were true in a sufficiently strong sense, viz., that logical truths are really tautologies (such as "It is either raining or not raining") in every interesting objective sense of the word. Many philosophers have been dissatisfied with the stronger forms of this thesis, but only recently have attempts been made to spell out the precise sense in which logical and mathematical truths are informative and not tautologous.

Problems of ontology. Among the ontological problems—problems concerning existence and existential assumptions—arising in logic are those of individuation and existence.

Individuation. Not all interesting interpretational problems are solved by possible-world semantics, as the developments earlier registered are sometimes called. The systematic use of the idea of possible worlds has raised, however, the subject of cross identification; *i.e.,* of the principles according to which a member of one possible world is to be found identical or nonidentical with one of another. Since one can scarcely be said to have a concept of an individual if he cannot locate it in several possible situations, the problem of cross-identification is also one of the most important ingredients of the logical and philosophical problem of individuation. The criticisms that Quine has put forward concerning modal logic and analyticity (see above) can be deepened into questions concerning methods of cross identification. Although some such methods undoubtedly belong to everyone's normal unarticulated conceptual repertoire, it is not clear that they are defined or even definable widely enough to enable philosophers to make satisfactory sense of a quantified logic of logical necessity and logical possibility. The precise principles used in ordinary discourse—or even in the language of science—pose a subtle philosophical problem. The extent to which special "essential properties" are relied on in individuation and the role of spatio-temporal frameworks are moot points here. It has also been suggested that essentially different methods of cross identification are actually used together, some of them depending on impersonal descriptive principles and others on the perspective of a person.

Existence and ontology. Because one of the basic concepts of first-order logic is that of existence, as codified by the existential quantifier "$(\exists x)$," one might suppose that there is little room left for any separate philosophical problem of existence. Yet existence, in fact, does seem to pose a problem, as witnessed by the bulk of the relevant literature. Some issues are relatively easy to clarify. In the usual formulations of first-order logic, for instance, there are "existential presuppositions" present to the effect that none of the singular terms employed is without a bearer (as "Pegasus" is). It is a straightforward matter, however, to dispense with these presuppositions. Though this seems to involve the procedure, branded as inadmissible by many philosophers, of treating existence as a predicate, this can nonetheless be easily done on the formal level. Given certain assumptions, it may even be shown that this "predicate" will have to be "$(\exists x) (x = a)$" (for "*a* exists"—literally, "There exists an x such that x is a") or something equivalent. Furthermore, the logical peculiarities of this predicate seem to explain amply philosophers' apparent denial of its reality.

The interest in the notion of existence is connected with the question of what entities a theory commits its holder to or what its "ontology" is. The "predicate of existence" just mentioned recalls Quine's criterion of ontological commitment: "To be is to be a value of a bound variable"—*i.e.,* of the x in $(\forall x)$ or in $(\exists x)$. According to Quine, a theory is committed to those and only those entities that in the last analysis serve as the values of its bound variables. Thus ordinary first-order theory commits one to an ontology only of individuals (particulars), whereas higher order logic commits one to the existence of sets—*i.e.,* of collections of definite and distinct entities (or, alternatively, of properties and relations). Likewise, if

Entities to which a theory is committed

bound first-order variables are assumed to range over sets (as they do in set theory), a commitment to the existence of these sets is incurred.

The doctrine that an ontology of individuals is all that is needed is known as (the modern version of) nominalism. The opposite view is known as (logical) realism. Even those philosophers who profess sympathy with nominalism find it hard, however, to maintain that mathematics could be built on a consistently nominalistic foundation.

The precise import of Quine's criterion of ontological commitment, however, is not completely clear. Nor is it clear in what other sense one is perhaps committed by a theory to those entities that are named or otherwise referred to in it but not quantified over in it. Questions can also be raised concerning the very distinction between what in modern logic are usually called individuals ("particulars" would be a more traditional designation) and such universals as their properties and relations; and these questions can be combined with others concerning the "tie" that binds particulars and universals together in predication.

An interesting approach to these problems is the distinction made by Gottlob Frege, a pioneer of mathematical logic in the late 19th century, between individuals—he called them objects—and what he called functions (which in his view include concepts) and his doctrine of the unsaturated character of the latter, according to which a function (as it were) contains a gap, which can be filled by an object. Another approach is the "picture theory of language" of Wittgenstein's *Tractatus Logico-Philosophicus,* according to which a simple sentence presents a person with an isomorphic representation (a "picture") of reality as it would be if the sentence were true. According to this view (which was later given up by Wittgenstein), "a sentence [or proposition, *Satz*] is a model of reality such as we think of it as being."

Alternative logics. The natures of most of the so-called nonclassical logics can be understood against the background of what has here been said. Some of them are simply extensions of the "classical" first-order logic—*e.g.,* modal logics and many versions of intensional logic. The so-called free logics are simply first-order (or modal) logics without existential presuppositions.

Intuition- | One of the most important nonclassical logics is intu-
istic | itionistic logic, first formalized by the Dutch mathemati-
logic | cian Arend Heyting in 1930. It has been shown that this logic can be interpreted in terms of the same kind of modal logic serving as a system of epistemic logic. In the light of its purpose to consider only the known, this isomorphism is suggestive. The avowed purpose of the intuitionist is to consider only what can actually be established constructively in logic and in mathematics— *i.e.,* what can actually be *known.* Thus, he refuses to consider, for example, "Either A or not-A" as a logical truth, for it does not actually help one in knowing whether A or not-A is the case. This does not close, however, the philosophical problem about intuitionism. Special problems arise from intuitionists' rejection (in effect) of the nonepistemic aspects of logic, as illustrated by the fact that only a part of epistemic logic is needed in this translation of intuitionistic logic into epistemic logic.

Other new logics are obtained by modifying the rules of those games that are involved in the game-theoretical interpretation of first-order logic mentioned above. The logician may reject, for instance, the assumption that he possesses perfect information, an assumption that characterizes classical first-order logic. One may also try to restrict the strategy sets of the players—to recursive strategies, for example.

Many- | Among the oldest kinds of alternative logics are many-
valued | valued logics. In them, more truth values than the usual
logics | true and false are assumed. The idea seems very natural when considered in abstraction from the actual use of logic. But a philosophically satisfactory interpretation of many-valued logics is not equally straightforward. The interest in finite-valued logics and the applicability of them are sometimes exaggerated. The idea, however, of using the elements of an arbitrary Boolean algebra—a generalized calculus of classes—as abstract truth-values has provided a powerful tool for systematic logical theory.

LOGIC AND OTHER DISCIPLINES

Technical disciplines. The relations of logic to mathematics, to computer technology, and to the empirical sciences are here considered.

Mathematics. It is usually said that all of mathematics can, in principle, be formulated in a sufficiently theorem-rich system of axiomatic set theory. What the axioms of a set theory that could accomplish this might be, however, and whether they are at all natural is not obvious in every case. (The recent development in abstract algebra known as category theory offers the most conspicuous examples of these problems.) The axioms of set theory may be presumed to hold in virtue of the meanings of the terms set, member of, and so on. Thus, in some loose sense all of pure mathematics falls within the scope of logic in the wider sense. This assertion is not very informative, however, as long as the logician has no ways of analyzing these meanings so as to be able to tell what assumptions (axioms of set theory) should be adopted. The definitions of basic mathematical concepts (such as "number") in logical terms proposed by Gottlob Frege (in 1884), by Bertrand Russell (in 1903), and by their successors do not help in this enterprise. It is not clear that more recent insights in logic help very much, either, in the search for strong set-theoretical assumptions. The relationship of mathematics to logic on this level therefore remains ambiguous.

Notwithstanding these deep problems, virtually all normal mathematical argumentation is carried out in logical terms—mostly in first-order terms, but with a generous sprinkling of second-order reasoning and various principles of set theory. Historically speaking, most specific early examples of nontrivial logical reasoning were taken from mathematics.

Often these examples were set in contrast to logical arguments understood in a narrow traditional sense—in a sense narrower still than the idea of logic as being exhausted by quantification theory. According to this traditional view, logic is equated with syllogistic; *i.e.,* with a part of that part of first-order logic that deals with properties and not with relations. Much of what earlier philosophers said of mathematical reasoning must, thus, be understood as applying to relational (first-order) reasoning. The present-day philosophy of logic is therefore as much an heir to traditional philosophy of mathematics as to traditional philosophy of logic.

Specific logical results are applicable in several parts of mathematics, especially in algebra, and various concepts and techniques used by logicians have often been borrowed from mathematics. (Thus one can even speak of "the mathematics of metamathematics.")

Computers. It has already been indicated that recursive function theory is, in effect, the study of certain idealized automata (computers). It is, in fact, a matter of indifference whether this theory belongs to logic or to computer science. The idealized assumption of a potentially infinite | Turing ma-
computer tape, however, is not a trivial one: Turing ma- | chines and
chines typically need plenty of tape in their calculations. | the infinite
Hence the step from Turing machines to finite automata | tape
(which are not assumed to have access to an infinite tape) is an important one.

This limitation does not dissociate computer science from logic, however, for other parts of logic are also relevant to computer science and are constantly employed there. Propositional logic may be thought of as the "logic" of certain simple types of switching circuits. There are also close connections between automata theory and the logical and algebraic study of formal languages. An interesting topic on the borderline of logic and computer science is mechanical theorem proving, which derives some of its interest from being a clear-cut instance of the problems of artificial intelligence, especially of the problems of realizing various heuristic modes of thinking on computers. In theoretical discussions in this area, it is nevertheless not always understood how much textbook logic is basically trivial and where the distinctively nontrivial truths of logic (including first-order logic) lie.

Methodology of the empirical sciences. The quest for theoretical self-awareness in the empirical sciences has led to interest in methodological and foundational problems as well as to attempts to axiomatize different empirical theories. Moreover, general methodological problems, such as the nature of scientific explanations, have been discussed intensively among philosophers of science. In all of these endeavours, logic plays an important role.

By and large, there are here three different lines of thought. (1) Often, only the simplest parts of logic—*e.g.,* propositional logic—are appealed to (over and above the mere use of logical notation). Sometimes, claims regarding the usefulness of logic in the methodology of the empirical sciences are, in effect, restricted to such rudimentary applications. This restriction is misleading, however, for most of the interesting and promising connections between methodology and logic lie on a higher level, especially in the area of model theory. In econometrics, for instance, a special case of the logicians' problems of definability plays an important role under the title "identification problem." On a more general level, logicians have been able to clarify the concept of a model as it is used in the empirical sciences.

Use of first-order versus set-theoretical formulations

In addition to those employing simple logic, two other contrasting types of theorists can be distinguished: (2) philosophers of science, who rely mostly on first-order formulations, and (3) methodologists (*e.g.,* Patrick Suppes, a U.S. philosopher and behavioral scientist), who want to use the full power of set theory and of the mathematics based on it. Both approaches have advantages. Usually realistic axiomatizations and other reconstructions of actual scientific theories are possible only in terms of set theoretical and other strong mathematical conceptualizations (theories conceived of as "set-theoretical predicates"). In spite of the oversimplification that first-order formulations often entail, however, they can yield theoretical insights because first-order logic (including its model theory) is mastered by logicians much more thoroughly than is set theory.

Many empirical sciences, especially the social sciences, use mathematical tools borrowed from probability theory and statistics, together with such outgrowths of these as decision theory, game theory, utility theory, and operations research. A modest but not uninteresting beginning in the study of their foundations has been made in modern inductive logic.

Human disciplines. The relations of logic to linguistics, psychology, law, and education are here considered.

Linguistics. The revival of interest in semantics among theoretical linguists in the late 1960s awakened their interest in the interrelations of logic and linguistic theory as well. It was also discovered that certain grammatical problems are closely related to logicians' concepts and theories. A near-identity of linguistics and "natural logic" has been claimed by the U.S. linguist George Lakoff. Among the many conflicting and controversial developments in this area, special mention may perhaps be made of attempts by Jerrold J. Katz, a U.S. grammarian-philosopher, and others to give a linguistic characterization of such fundamental logical notions as analyticity; the sketch by Montague of a "universal grammar" based on his intensional logic; and the suggestion (by several logicians and linguists) that what linguists call "deep structure" is to be identified with logical form. Of a much less controversial nature is the extensive and fruitful use of recursive function theory and related areas of logic in formal grammars and in the formal models of language users.

Psychology. Although the "laws of thought" studied in logic are not the empirical generalizations of a psychologist, they can serve as a conceptual framework for psychological theorizing. Probably the best known recent example of such theorizing is the large-scale attempt made in the mid-20th century by Jean Piaget, a Swiss psychologist, to characterize the developmental stages of a child's thought by reference to the logical structures that he can master. Elsewhere in psychology, logic is employed mostly as an ingredient of various models using mathematical ideas or ideas drawn from such areas as automata or information theory. Large-scale direct uses are rare, however, partly because of the problems mentioned above in the section on logic and information.

Law. Of the great variety of kinds of argumentation used in the law, some are persuasive rather than strictly logical, and others exemplify different procedures in applied logic rather than the formulas of pure logic. Examinations of "Lawiers Logike"—as the subject was called in 1588—have also uncovered a variety of arguments belonging to the various departments of logic mentioned above. Such inquiries do not seem to catch the most characteristic kinds of legal conceptualization, however—with one exception, viz., a theory developed by Wesley Newcomb Hohfeld, a pre-World War I U.S. legal scholar, of what he called the fundamental legal conceptions. Although originally presented in informal terms, this theory is closely related to recent deontic logic (in some cases in combination with suitable causal notions). Even some of the apparent difficulties are shared by the two approaches: the deontic logician's notion of permission, for example, which is often thought of as being unduly weak, is to all practical purposes a generalization of Hohfeld's concept of privilege.

Hohfeld's theory and deontic logic

Education. After having been one of the main ingredients of the general school curriculum for centuries, logic virtually disappeared from liberal education during the first half of the 20th century. It has made major inroads back into school curricula, however, as a part of the new mathematical curriculum that came into fairly general use in the 1960s, which normally includes the elements of propositional logic and of set theory. Logic is also easily adapted to being taught by computers and has been used in experiments with computer-based education.

(K.J.Hi.)

The nature of mathematics

A chief point of interest that has emerged from modern attempts to characterize philosophy is the importance of distinguishing dialectical or analytical inquiries about meaning from empirical inquiries about fact. A primary, traditional task of the philosopher has been to present things in such a light that human feelings may be reasonably grounded. The need for this is especially obvious in the case of the moral philosopher or the aesthetician, whose work treats explicitly of subjective concerns. But the need remains the same in all philosophical inquiries, including even discussions of the foundations of mathematics. For it is obvious to a careful observer that persons who put forward theses about the nature of mathematics are involved not just intellectually but also emotionally in their pursuits; while it must be supposed that in some cases this involvement stems from or inevitably leads to intellectual confusion, it must also be allowed that a certain emotional commitment may perhaps be a necessary condition for the making of discoveries. Thus it can scarcely be an accident that no great mathematician has ever accepted the conventionalist view according to which mathematical truths are man-made.

The inquiry into the nature, underlying assumptions, and scope of mathematics has emerged in the 20th century as a subdiscipline of mathematics itself, known as the study of foundations. For a full historical treatment of this field, see the *Macropædia* article MATHEMATICS, THE FOUNDATIONS OF. The material below, edited from an article originally written by Alfred North Whitehead for the 11th edition of the *Encyclopædia Britannica,* treats mathematics itself as an object of philosophical investigation.

A cursory definition of mathematics

It has been usual to define mathematics as "the science of discrete and continuous magnitude." Even Leibnitz, who initiated a more modern point of view, follows the tradition in thus confining the scope of mathematics properly so called, while apparently conceiving it as a department of a yet wider science of reasoning. A short consideration of some leading topics of the science will exemplify both the plausibility and inadequacy of the above definition. Arithmetic, algebra, and the infinitesimal calculus, are sciences directly concerned with integral numbers, rational (or fractional) numbers, and real numbers generally, which include incommensurable numbers. It would seem that "the general theory of discrete and continuous quantity" is the exact description of the topics of these sciences. Furthermore, can we not complete the circle of the mathematical sciences by adding geometry? Now geometry deals with points, lines, planes, and cubic contents. Of these all except points are quantities. Also, as the Cartesian geometry shows, all the relations between points are expressible in terms of geometric quantities. Accordingly, at first sight it seems reasonable to define geometry in some such way as "the science of dimensional quantity." Thus every subdivision of mathematical science would appear to deal with quantity, and the definition of mathematics as "the science of quantity" would appear to be justified. We have now to see why the definition is inadequate.

CRITICAL QUESTIONS

Types relating to numbers.   What are numbers? We can talk of five apples and 10 pears. But what are "five" and "10" apart from the apples and pears? Also in addition to the cardinal numbers there are the ordinal numbers: the fifth apple and the 10th pear claim thought. What is the relation of "the fifth" and "10th" to "five" and "10"? "The first rose of summer" and "the last rose of summer" are parallel phrases, yet one explicitly introduces an ordinal number and the other does not. Again, "half a foot" and "half a pound" are easily defined. But in what sense is there "a half," which is the same for "half a foot" as "half a pound"? Furthermore, incommensurable numbers are defined as the limits arrived at as the result of certain procedures with rational numbers. But how do we know that there is anything to reach? We must know that $\sqrt{2}$ exists before we can prove that any procedure will reach it.

Types relating to geometry.   Also in geometry, what is a point? The straightness of a straight line and the planeness of a plane require consideration. Furthermore, "congruence" is a difficulty. For when a triangle "moves," the points do not move with it. So what is it that keeps unaltered in the moving triangle? Thus the whole method of measurement in geometry as described in the elementary textbooks and the older treatises is obscure to the last degree. Lastly, what are "dimensions"? All these topics require thorough discussion before we can rest content with the definition of mathematics as the general science of magnitude; and by the time they are discussed the definition has evaporated. An outline of the modern answers to questions such as the above will now be given. A critical defense of them would require a volume.

Nature of cardinal numbers.   A one–one relation between the members of two classes α and β is any method of correlating all the members of α to all the members of β, so that any member of α has one and only one correlate in β, and any member of β has one and only one correlate in α. Two classes between which a one-one relation exists have the same cardinal number and are called cardinally similar; and the cardinal number of the class α is a certain class whose members are themselves classes—namely, it is the class composed of all those classes for which a one-one correlation with α exists. Thus the cardinal number of α is itself a class, and furthermore α is a member of it. For a one-one relation can be established between the members of α and α by the simple process of correlating each member of α with itself. Thus the cardinal number one is the class of unit classes, the cardinal number two is the class of doublets, and so on. Also a unit class is any class with the property that it possesses a member x such that, if y is any member of the class, then x and y are identical. A doublet is any class which possesses a member x such that the modified class formed by all the other members except x is a unit class. And so on for all the finite cardinals, which are thus defined successively. The cardinal number zero is the class of classes with no members; but there is only one such class, namely—the null class. Thus this cardinal number has only one member. The operations of addition and multiplication of two given cardinal numbers can be defined by taking two classes α and β, satisfying the conditions (1) that their cardinal numbers are respectively the given numbers, and (2) that they contain no member in common, and then by defining by reference to α and β two other suitable classes whose cardinal numbers are

Cardinal numbers as classes

defined to be respectively the required sum and product of the cardinal numbers in question.

With these definitions it is now possible to *prove* the following six premises applying to finite cardinal numbers, from which Peano has shown that all arithmetic can be deduced:—

i. Cardinal numbers form a class. ii. Zero is a cardinal number. iii. If a is a cardinal number, $a + 1$ is a cardinal number. iv. If s is any class and zero is a member of it, also if when x is a cardinal number and a member of s, also $x + 1$ is a member of s, then the whole class of cardinal numbers is contained in s. v. If a and b are cardinal numbers, and $a + 1 = b + 1$, then $a = b$. vi. If a is a cardinal number, then $a + 1 = 0$.

It may be noticed that (iv.) is the familiar principle of mathematical induction. Peano in a historical note refers its first explicit employment, although without a general enunciation, to Maurolycus in his work, *Arithmeticorum libri duo* (Venice, 1575).

But now the difficulty of confining mathematics to being the science of number and quantity is immediately apparent. For there is no self-contained science of cardinal numbers. The proof of the six premises requires an elaborate investigation into the general properties of classes and relations that can be deduced by the strictest reasoning from our ultimate logical principles. Also it is purely arbitrary to erect the consequences of these six principles into a separate science. They are excellent principles of the highest value, but they are in no sense the necessary premises that must be proved before any other propositions of cardinal numbers can be established. On the contrary, the premises of arithmetic can be put in other forms, and, furthermore, an indefinite number of propositions of arithmetic can be proved directly from logical principles without mentioning them. Thus, while arithmetic may be defined as that branch of deductive reasoning concerning classes and relations that is concerned with the establishment of propositions concerning cardinal numbers, the introduction of cardinal numbers makes no great break in this general science. It is merely a subdivision in a general theory.

Nature of ordinal numbers.   We must first understand what is meant by "order," that is, by "serial arrangement." An order of a set of things is to be sought in that relation holding between members of the set that constitutes that order. The set viewed as a class has many orders. Thus the telegraph posts along a certain road have a space-order very obvious to our senses; but they have also a time-order according to dates of erection, perhaps more important to the postal authorities who replace them after fixed intervals. A set of cardinal numbers has an order of magnitude, often called *the* order of the set because of its insistent obviousness to us; if they are the numbers drawn in a lottery, their time-order of occurrence in that drawing also ranges them in an order of some importance. Thus the order is defined by the "serial" relation. A relation (R) is serial when (1) it implies diversity, so that, if x has the relation R to y, x is diverse from y; (2) it is transitive, so that if x has the relation R to y, and y to z, then x has the relation R to z; (3) it has the property of connexity, so that if x and y are things to which any things bear the relation R, or which bear the relation R to any things, then *either x is identical with y, or x has the relation R to y, or y has the relation R to x. These conditions are necessary and sufficient to secure that our ordinary ideas of "preceding" and "succeeding" hold in respect to the relation R. The "field" of the relation R is the class of things ranged in order by it. Two relations R and R' are said to be ordinally similar, if a one-one relation holds between the members of the two fields of R and R', such that if x and y are any two members of the field of R, such that x has the relation R to y, and if x' and y' are the correlates in the field of R' of x and y, then in all such cases x' has the relation R' to y', and conversely, interchanging the dashes on the letters; *i.e.,* R and R', x and x', etc. It is evident that the ordinal similarity of two relations implies the cardinal similarity of their fields, but not conversely. Also, two relations need not be serial in order to be ordinally similar; but if one is serial, so is the other.

Serial relations

The relationship-number of a relation is the class whose members are all those relations that are ordinarily similar to it. This class will include the original relation itself. The relation-number of a relation should be compared with the cardinal number of a class. When a relation is serial its relation-number is often called its serial type. The addition and multiplication of two relation-numbers is defined by taking two relations R and S, such that (1) their fields have no terms in common; (2) their relation-numbers are the two relation-numbers in question, and then by defining by reference to R and S two other suitable relations whose relation-numbers are defined to be respectively the sum and product of the relation-numbers in question. We need not consider the details of this process. Now if n be any finite cardinal number, it can be proved that the class of those serial relations, which have a field whose cardinal number is, n, is a relation-number. This relation-number is the ordinal number corresponding to n; let it be symbolized by $\dot{n}$. Thus, corresponding to the cardinal numbers 2, 3, 4 . . . there are the ordinal numbers $\dot{2}$, $\dot{3}$, $\dot{4}$ . . . The definition of the ordinal number 1 requires some little ingenuity owing to the fact that no serial relation can have a field whose cardinal number is 1; but we must omit here the explanation of the process. The ordinal number $\dot{0}$ is the class whose sole member is the null relation—that is, the relation that never holds between any pair of entities. The definitions of the finite ordinals can be expressed without use of the corresponding cardinals, so there is no essential priority of cardinals to ordinals. Here also it can be seen that the science of the finite ordinals is merely a subdivision of the general theory of classes and relations.

Cantor's infinite numbers. Owing to the correspondence between the finite cardinals and the finite ordinals, the propositions of cardinal arithmetic and ordinal arithmetic correspond point by point. But the definition of the cardinal number of a class applies when the class is not finite, and it can be proved that there are different infinite cardinal numbers, and that there is a least infinite cardinal, now usually denoted by $\aleph_0$, where $\aleph$ is the Hebrew letter aleph. Similarly, a class of serial relations, called *well-ordered* serial relations, can be defined, such that their corresponding relation-numbers include the ordinary finite ordinals, but also include relation-numbers which have many properties like those of the finite ordinals, though the fields of the relations belonging to them are not finite. These relation-numbers are the infinite ordinal numbers. The arithmetic of the infinite cardinals does not correspond to that of the infinite ordinals. It will suffice to mention here that Peano's fourth premise of arithmetic does not hold for infinite cardinals or for infinite ordinals. Contrasting the above definitions of number, cardinals and ordinals, with the alternative theory that number is an ultimate idea incapable of definition, we find that our procedure exacts greater attention and less credulity.

The data of analysis. Rational numbers and real numbers in general can now be defined according to the same general method. If m and n are finite cardinal numbers, the rational number m/n is the relation that any finite cardinal number x bears to any finite cardinal number y when $n \times x = m \times y$. Thus the rational number one, which we will denote by 1_r, is not the cardinal number 1; for 1_r is the relation 1/1 as defined above, and is thus a relation holding between certain pairs of cardinals. Similarly, the other rational integers must be distinguished from the corresponding cardinals. The arithmetic of rational numbers is now established by means of appropriate definitions, which indicate the entities meant by the operations of addition and multiplication. But in order to obtain general enunciations of theorems without exceptional cases, mathematicians employ entities of ever-ascending types of elaboration. These entities are not created but are employed by mathematicians, and their definitions should show the construction of the new entities in terms of the old. The real numbers, including irrational numbers, have now to be defined. Consider the serial arrangement of the rationals in their order of magnitude. A real number is a class (α, say) of rational numbers that satisfies the condition that it is the same as the class of those rationals

each of which precedes at least one member of α. Thus, consider the class of rationals less than 2_r; any member of this class precedes some other members of the class—thus 1/2 precedes 4/3, 3/2 and so on; also the class of predecessors of predecessors of 2_r is itself the class of predecessors of 2_r. Accordingly this class is a real number; it will be called the real number 2_R. Note that the class of rationals less than or equal to 2_r is not a real number. For 2_r is not a predecessor of some member of the class. In the above example 2_R is an integral real number, which is distinct from a rational integer, and from a cardinal number. Similarly, any rational real number is distinct from the corresponding rational number. But now the irrational real numbers have all made their appearance. For example, the class of rationals whose squares are less than 2_r satisfies the definition of a real number; it is the real number $\sqrt{2}$. The arithmetic of real numbers follows from appropriate definitions of the operations of addition and multiplication. Except for the immediate purposes of an explanation, such as the above, it is unnecessary for mathematicians to have separate symbols, such as 2, 2_r and 2_R, or 2/3 and $(2/3)_R$. Real numbers with signs (+ or −) are now defined. If a is a real number, $+a$ is defined to be the relation that any real number of the form $x + a$ bears to the real number x, and $-a$ is the relation that any real number x bears to the real number $x + a$. The addition and multiplication of these "signed" real numbers is suitably defined, and it is proved that the usual arithmetic of such numbers follows. Finally, we reach a complex number of the nth order. Such a number is a "one-many" relation which relates n signed real numbers (or n algebraic complex numbers when they are already defined by this procedure) to the n cardinal numbers 1, 2, . . . n respectively. If such a complex number is written (as usual) in the form $x_1 e_1 + x_2 e_2 + \ldots + x_n e_n$, then this particular complex number relates x_1 to 1, x_2 to 2, . . . x_n to n. Also the "unit" e_1 (or e_s) considered as a number of the system is merely a shortened form for the complex number $(+1)e_1 + 0e_2 \ldots + 0e_n$. This last number exemplifies the fact that one signed real number, such as 0, may be correlated to many of the n cardinals, such as 2 . . . n in the example, but that each cardinal is only correlated with one signed number. Hence the relation has been called above "one-many." The sum of two complex numbers $x_1 e_1 + x_2 e_2 + \ldots + x_n e_n$ and $y_1 e_1 + y_2 e_2 + \ldots + y_n e_n$ is always defined to be the complex number $(x_1 + y_1)e_1 + (x_2 + y_2)e_2 + \ldots + (x_n + y_n)e_n$. But an indefinite number of definitions of the product of two complex numbers yield interesting results. Each definition gives rise to a corresponding algebra of higher complex numbers. We will confine ourselves here to algebraic complex numbers—that is, to complex numbers of the second order taken in connection with that definition of multiplication that leads to ordinary algebra. The product of two complex numbers of the second order—namely, $x_1 e_1 + x_2 e_2$ and $y_1 e_1 + y_2 e_2$, is in this case defined to mean the complex $(x_1 y_1 + x_2 y_2)e_1 + (x_1 y_2 + x_2 y_1)e_2$. Thus $e_1 \times e_1 = e_1$, $e_2 \times e_2 = -e_1$, $e_1 \times e_2 = e_2 \times e_1 = e_2$. With this definition it is usual to omit the first symbol e_1, and to write i or $\sqrt{-1}$ instead of e_2. Accordingly, the typical form for such a complex number is $x + yi$, and then with this notation the above-mentioned definition of multiplication is invariably adopted. The importance of this algebra arises from the fact that in terms of such complex numbers with this definition of multiplication the utmost generality of expression, to the exclusion of exceptional cases, can be obtained for theorems that occur in analogous forms, but complicated with exceptional cases, in the algebras of real numbers and of signed real numbers. This is exactly the same reason as that which has led mathematicians to work with signed real numbers in preference to real numbers, and with real numbers in preference to rational numbers.

DEFINITION OF MATHEMATICS

It has now become apparent that the traditional field of mathematics in the province of discrete and continuous number can only be separated from the general abstract theory of classes and relations by a wavering and inde-

Rational and real numbers

terminate line. Of course a discussion as to the mere application of a word degenerates into the most fruitless logomachy. But on the assumption that "mathematics" is to denote a science well marked out by its subject matter and its methods, and that at least it is to include all topics habitually assigned to it, "mathematics" is employed in the general sense of the "science concerned with the logical deduction of consequences from the general premises of all reasoning."

Kinds of mathematical propositions

Geometry. The typical mathematical proposition is: "If x, y, z . . . satisfy such and such conditions, then such and such other conditions hold with respect to them." By taking fixed conditions for the hypothesis of such a proposition a definite department of mathematics is marked out. For example, geometry is such a department. The "axioms" of geometry are the fixed conditions that occur in the hypotheses of the geometrical propositions. It is sufficient to observe here that they are concerned with special types of classes of classes and of classes of relations, and that the connection of geometry with number and magnitude is in no way an essential part of the foundation of the science.

Classes and relations. We now must deduce the general properties of classes and relations from the ultimate logical premises. In the course of this process, some contradictions have become apparent. That first discovered is known as Burali-Forti's contradiction and consists in the proof that there both is and is not a greatest infinite ordinal number. But these contradictions do not depend upon any theory of number, for Russell's contradiction does not involve number in any form. This contradiction arises from considering the class possessing as members all classes that are not members of themselves. Call this class w; then to say that x is a w is equivalent to saying that x is not an x. Accordingly, to say that w is a w is equivalent to saying that w is not a w. An analogous contradiction can be found for relations. It follows that a careful scrutiny of the very idea of classes and relations is required. Note that classes are here required in extension, so that the class of human beings and the class of rational featherless bipeds are identical; similarly for relations, which are to be determined by the entities related. Now a class in respect to its components is many. In what sense then can it be one? This problem of "the one and the many" has been discussed continuously by the philosophers. All the contradictions can be avoided, and yet the use of classes and relations can be preserved as required by mathematics, and indeed by common sense, by a theory that denies to a class—or relation—existence or being in any sense in which the entities composing it—or related by it—exist. Thus, to say that a pen is an entity and the class of pens is an entity is merely a play upon the word "entity"; the second sense of "entity" (if any) is indeed derived from the first but has a more complex signification. Consider an incomplete proposition, incomplete in the sense that some entity that ought to be involved in it is represented by an undetermined x, which may stand for any entity. Call it a propositional function; and, if φx be a propositional function, the undetermined variable x is the argument. Two propositional functions φx and ψx are "extensionally identical" if any determination of x in φx that converts φx into a true proposition also converts ψx into a true proposition, and conversely for ψ and φ. Now consider a propositional function $F\chi$ in which the variable argument χ is itself a propositional function. If $F\chi$ is true when, and only when, χ is determined to be either φ or some other propositional function extensionally equivalent to φ, then the proposition $F\varphi$ is of the form which is ordinarily recognized as being about the class determined by φx taken in extension— that is, the class of entities for which φx is a true proposition when x is determined to be any one of them.

Classes of classes and of relations

A similar theory holds for relations that arise from the consideration of propositional functions with two or more variable arguments. It is then possible to define by a parallel elaboration what is meant by classes of classes, classes of relations, relations between classes, and so on. Accordingly, the number of a class of relations can be defined, or of a class of classes, and so on. This theory is in effect a theory of the *use* of classes and relations and does not decide the philosophic question as to the sense (if any) in which a class in extension is one entity. It does indeed deny that it is an entity in the sense in which one of its members is an entity. Accordingly, it is a fallacy for any determination of x *to* consider "x is an x" or "x is not an x" as having the meaning of propositions. Note that for any determination of x, "x is an x" and "x is not an x" are neither of them fallacies but are both meaningless, according to this theory. Thus Russell's contradiction vanishes, and the other contradictions vanish also.

APPLIED MATHEMATICS

Selection of topics. The selection of the topics of mathematical inquiry among the infinite variety open to it has been guided by the useful applications, and indeed the abstract theory has only recently been disentangled from the empirical elements connected with these applications. For example, the application of the theory of cardinal numbers to classes of physical entities involves in practice some process of counting. It is only recently that the *succession* of processes that is involved in any act of counting has been seen to be irrelevant to the idea of number. Indeed, it is only by experience that we can know that any definite process of counting will give the true cardinal number of some class of entities. It is perfectly possible to imagine a universe in which any act of counting by a being in it annihilates some members of the class counted during the time and only during the time of its continuance. A legend of the Council of Nicaea illustrates this point: "When the Bishops took their places on their thrones, they were 318; when they rose up to be called over, it appeared that they were 319; so that they never could make the number come right, and whenever they approached the last of the series, he immediately turned into the likeness of his next neighbour." Such a story cannot be disproved by deductive reasoning from the premises of abstract logic. We can only assert that a universe in which such things are liable to happen on a large scale is unfitted for the practical application of the theory of cardinal numbers.

Relation of theory and physical reality

The application of the theory of real numbers to physical quantities involves analogous considerations. In the first place, some physical process of addition is presupposed, involving some inductively inferred law of permanence during that process. Thus in the theory of masses we must know that two pounds of lead when put together will counterbalance in the scales two pounds of sugar, or a pound of lead and a pound of sugar. Furthermore, the sort of continuity of the series (in order of magnitude) of rational numbers is known to be different from that of the series of real numbers. Indeed, mathematicians now reserve "continuity" as the term for the latter kind of continuity; the mere property of having an infinite number of terms between any two terms is called "compactness." The compactness of the series of rational numbers is consistent with quasi-gaps in it—that is, with the possible absence of limits to classes in it. Thus the class of rational numbers whose squares are less than 2 has no upper limit among the rational numbers. But among the real numbers all classes have limits. Now, owing to the necessary inexactness of measurement, it is impossible to discriminate directly whether any kind of continuous physical quantity possesses the compactness of the series of rationals or the continuity of the series of real numbers. In calculations the latter hypothesis is made because of its mathematical simplicity. But the assumption has certainly no a priori grounds in its favour, and it is not very easy to see how to base it upon experience. For example, the continuity of space apparently rests upon sheer assumption unsupported by any a priori or experimental grounds. Thus the current application of mathematics to the analysis of phenomena can be justified by no a priori necessity.

Existence of applied mathematics. In one sense there is no science of applied mathematics. When once the fixed conditions that any hypothetical group of entities are to satisfy have been precisely formulated, the deduction of the further propositions, which also will hold respecting them, can proceed in complete independence of the question as to whether or not any such group of entities can be found in the world of phenomena. Thus rational mechanics, based on the Newtonian Laws and viewed as mathematics, is independent of its supposed application, and hydrodynamics remains a coherent and respected science though it is extremely improbable that any perfect fluid exists in the physical world. But this unbendingly logical point of view cannot be the last word upon the matter. For no one can doubt the essential difference between characteristic treatises upon "pure" and "applied" mathematics. The difference is a difference in method. In pure mathematics the hypotheses that a set of entities are to satisfy are given, and a group of interesting deductions are sought. In "applied mathematics" the "deductions" are given in the shape of the experimental evidence of natural science, and the hypotheses from which the "deductions" can be deduced are sought. Accordingly, every treatise on applied mathematics, properly so-called, is directed to the criticism of the "laws" from which the reasoning starts, or to a suggestion of results that experiment may hope to find. Thus if it calculates the result of some experiment, it is not the experimentalist's well-attested results that are on their trial but the basis of the calculation.   (A.N.W.)

Western philosophy of law

Philosophy of law is concerned with the formulation of concepts and theories to aid in understanding the nature of law, the sources of its authority, and its role in society. In English-speaking countries the term "jurisprudence" is often used synonymously and is invariably used in reference to particular subdivisions of the field.

To the extent that it implies some necessary link or coincidence with general philosophy, the phrase "philosophy of law" may be somewhat misleading, for philosophy of law is mostly untouched by the conflicts of different philosophical schools, and its practitioners may without incongruity draw on diverse philosophical outlooks—on Logical Positivism for some analytical problem of the structure of legal orders and, simultaneously, on Existentialism for a problem of sociological jurisprudence or justice, for example—without commitment in any such instance to an entire philosophical outlook.

Nor can one treat philosophy of law as a specialized branch of philosophy such as ethical or political philosophy, epistemology, or logic, for in philosophy of law all these branches may make contributions. Ideas that may illumine jurisprudential problems must indeed be sought not only in philosophy but in all systematic bodies of thought. Only if "philosophy" is interpreted in its least technical and broadest sense does "philosophy of law" cease to be a misnomer.

PROBLEMS OF THE PHILOSOPHY OF LAW

Three major subdivisions of philosophy of law

Various approaches. For practical reasons, such as to avoid overlappings, it is convenient to organize jurisprudence into three principal branches only: analytical jurisprudence, sociological jurisprudence, and the theory of justice.

Analytical jurisprudence. The analytical questions in jurisprudence are concerned with articulating the axioms, defining the terms, and prescribing the methods that best enable one to view the legal order (or part of it) as a self-consistent system and that maximize awareness of its logical structure. Perhaps the most rigorous solutions are those which, like that of Hans Kelsen, a contemporary Austrian–American legal philosopher, attempt to identify structural or relational features as being necessarily entailed in the meaning of legal norms or in lawyers' intellectual operations with them (see below *Pure theory of law*). Alternatively, the basis for logical structuring may be found in some imputed attribute of law not itself inherently structural. The 19th-century English legal philosopher John Austin, for example, thought it an essential preliminary to his quest for a logical system in law to clarify what was involved in his assumption that law always consists of "commands." This clarification is important, but the claim that such a clarified version of a common assumption necessarily amounts to an analytical model of law seems unwarranted.

On more modest levels, the analyst may seek to infuse clarity and orderliness into some particular branch of a legal system or even into the applications of some particular rule. Such work shades over, on the one hand, into ordinary legal analysis and, on the other, into jurisprudential efforts to clarify the meaning of particular legal terms. Analysis of a particular word or even a particular branch of law will usually, by necessity, be particularist in the sense that it works upon legal materials found only in one particular legal system. In between particularism and universalism lie what are sometimes called comparative approaches, in which analytical jurisprudence is applied to materials drawn from more than one (but not from all) legal systems.

Sociological jurisprudence. The sociological questions in jurisprudence are concerned with the actual effects of the law upon the complex of attitudes, behaviour, organization, environment, skills, and powers involved in the maintenance of a particular society. Conversely, sociological jurisprudence is also concerned with the effects of social phenomena on both the substantive and procedural aspects of law, as well as on the legislative, judicial, and other means of forming, operating, changing, and disrupting the legal order. The fact that men in a given time and place hold particular ideas and values, including ideals of justice, is itself a fact the relation of which to law must be studied; but the focus is sharply different from that in the study of theories of justice. Its focus is descriptive, not normative; it is concerned with what is or with what goes on, not with what ought to be or ought to go on.

The theory of justice. The theory of justice is concerned with the evaluation and criticism of law in terms of the ideals or goals postulated for it. This involves the identification and articulation of the values that the legal order seeks to realize. This aspect of jurisprudence is inextricably interwoven with ethical and political philosophy, and theories of justice thus tend to parallel the full range of ethical and political philosophies.

Law, morality, and natural law. A consideration of fundamental importance in the philosophy of law is that of the distinction between law and morality. The importance of the distinction is illustrated by the main questions to which it gives rise: (1) How far and in what sense should the law of a community seek to give effect to its morality? (2) Is there a moral duty to obey the law even when it does not embody morality, and, if so, are there any limits to this duty? (3) When a legal rule directs conduct that morality forbids, which should the citizen obey? (4) Is there ever (and, if so, when is there) a duty to overthrow an entire legal system because of its conflict with morality?

In all these questions the word "law" refers to the specialized form of social control familiar in modern, secular, politically organized societies. The word "morality" in the four questions may, however, refer to any of the following: (1) the community's relevant factual behaviour patterns (its mores); (2) its socially approved behaviour patterns, as sanctified by some widely held rational or religious ideal, whether observed in practice or not (social morality); or (3) the moral ideals accepted by each individual as binding on himself and on others, whether or not those others agree (individual morality). All these, like law, are means of controlling human conduct by setting normative standards; and all three have a constantly changing interaction with each other, as well as with law.

Definitions of morality

The fact that legal and moral norms vary from place to place and from one historical period to another lies in part behind a persistent theme in the philosophy of law: the search for unchanging norms that are universally valid. Clearly, the most certain way of establishing such norms would be to base them on widely observed facts, such as man's social propensities or the ubiquitous importance of kinship in social organization, which supposedly reveal something fundamental about the nature of man and his adjustment to the world. The attempt to base norms on some such category of facts has for two millennia been associated with the concept of natural law. This concept has many versions, the principal of which are outlined in the historical survey below, but the significance of the topic merits some separate preliminary discussions.

Aristotle's conception of natural law

It has always been possible to trace a mainstream of natural-law thought, flowing from Aristotle's premise that the "nature" of any creature, from which obligations must be derived, is what it will be in its fullest and most perfect development. For man, this means what he is when the powers and qualities distinguishing him from other creatures, namely, his reason and his impulse to social living, are fully developed. Natural law embodies those obligations that will appear if mankind's reason and sociality are fully unfolded.

A major difficulty presented by this attempt to develop normative standards appears to be that it is very difficult to demonstrate, let alone create a sense of obligation toward, values that are only immanent. All theories of natural law, moreover, have found it necessary to rely on what are essentially intuitions or preconceptions as to what man's true nature is. All such theories acknowledge, for instance, that the full development or fulfillment of an entity is not the same as its mere continued existence, that there may be a "warping" or "impeding" of the natural tendencies, so that what exists may then "be said to be unsound or incorrect." Thus, mere factuality is not a sufficient source of obligation. Similarly, St. Thomas Aquinas himself, in identifying the "inclinations" from which men may learn natural law, found it necessary to order these in grades of inclination, so that those inclinations most closely related to reason and sociality take priority over those concerned (for example) with procreation and self-preservation. The criteria by which such a hierarchy is ordered must be drawn from sources other than the factual inclinations themselves. The "lower" grades (such as self-preservation) may well be based on something like instinct; but the question arises at the higher grades whether there is any comparable instinct by which men seek to find moral precepts binding all of them in common. Aquinas here appealed to synderesis, a kind of sympathetic understanding found in men, a disposition (habit) of the practical intellect inclining them to the good and murmuring against evil.

To derive from this synderesis a universal natural law, however, it would be necessary to demonstrate some "universal conscience" of all mankind. But natural lawyers faced with the fact that men's consciences do not coincide explain that conscience may err and reason be corrupt. Invocation of synderesis is in fact helpful not as an account of how one may arrive at factually based normative standards but as an illustration of the psychological tendency of men to assert values.

HISTORICAL SURVEY OF LEGAL THEORIES

The ancient world. *Greek thought.* The major contribution of Greece was a body of philosophical and cosmological ideals about justice, more apt for orators' appeals to popular assemblies than for preceptual application to day-to-day life situations.

Early Greek cosmologies, embedded in some of the earliest myths, had seen the individual as held within a kind of transcending harmony of the universe, emanating from the divine law (*logos*) and expressed in relation to human life in the law (*nomos*) of the polis, the city-state. The later Sophists, however, who examined critically all assumptions relating to life in the city-state, pointed to the wide disparities in human law and morals and rejected the claim that this human law (*nomos*) necessarily reflected any universal law (*logos*). Taking man as "the measure of all things," they rejected any claims of his law (*nomos*) to absolute value and saw law and justice and values generally as created by men's reasons, in their multitudes and generations, in all their individuated, relativistic, and historically changing dimensions.

Plato's idea of law

In the restless intellectual and political climate of 5th-century Athens, Plato was concerned to redefine the nature of justice by relating it to something far more permanent and absolute than the *nomos* of the city-state. He assigned "reality" to the unchanging archetypal forms—*i.e.*, the ideas—of things rather than to the ephemeral phenomena as superficially and confusedly perceived by individual men unenlightened by philosophy. In the utopia described in *The Republic*, Plato defines justice in an architectonic sense: justice prevails when the state is ordered in accordance with the ideal forms ascertained by its philosopher-kings and is thus unrelated to the *nomos* of the city-state. There is no need for human law, since transcendental knowledge rules. In his later thought, however, as revealed in *Politicus* (the "Statesman") and the *Laws,* when he is concerned to describe a more practicable but nevertheless "second best" state, Plato assigns to law a role almost as important as that of knowledge in *The Republic.* A famous classification of states given in *Politicus* is indeed based on the criterion of whether or not they are ruled by law. The law as Plato here conceived it, however, was not mere convention or the imperfect individual judgments of men but a reflection of the common human reason in its full development. To this extent the rule of law might approximate the ideal rule of knowledge envisaged in *The Republic,* for in the inherited law of men is crystallized that much wisdom of which they are capable.

And yet it was difficult for Plato to find justification for such an argument in his basic philosophical position, with its emphasis on the contrast between the mere opinion of ordinary men and the transcendental knowledge of the philosopher. Aristotle, who in common with Plato held a view of nature or reality that transcended the variability of things as perceived by the senses, was, however, able more successfully to defend the validity of a law resulting from the practice of ordinary men. For Aristotle's transcendental reality is more firmly related to things as they are: it comprises that which they will become as their potentialities unfold in nature toward the end that is theirs in nature. Man, in his nature, is moral, rational, and social, and his law may be judged by the extent to which it facilitates the development of these innate qualities.

The Stoic conception of natural law

The Greek conception of natural law underwent further refinement by the Stoic school of philosophy, which became active toward the end of the 4th century BC. The Stoics posited the existence of a natural law, the *jus naturale,* which was an emanation of the *lex aeterna,* the law of reason of the cosmos. The existence of an innate reason in men linked everyone with the cosmic order and subjected all to a universally valid moral law. This latter concept thoroughly infused Roman thinking, largely as a result of the influence of Stoic philosophy on Rome.

Roman thought. Greek law scarcely survived as a system, because it never developed a class of legal specialists or abandoned its lay administrators or its popular tribunals of grotesque size. Roman law, on the other hand, developed through the efforts of expert jurisconsults (learned lawyers) and praetors (magistrates) into a permanent heritage of Western society. By its adoption into works such as Cicero's *De republica* as well as in the work of the great jurisconsults, Stoic speculation concerning reason and nature was brought onto the level of precepts for concrete problem solving. The crude, tribal *jus civile* ("civil law") of the Romans was thus transformed into a natural-law-based *jus gentium* (law applying to all people), a set of principles common to all nations and appropriate, therefore, for application to foreigners as well as Romans.

Hebrew thought. In the Talmud there is an assertion that "Whatever decision of a mature scholar in the presence of his teacher will yet derive from the Law (Torah) that was already spoken to Moses on Mt. Sinai." In theory, this presupposed that the Oral Law must respect every jot and tittle of the revealed written law. Yet the richness, ambivalences, and silences of what was written, in relation to a changing world, still left the widest freedom to the scholarly reason of the rabbinical exegetes into whose care both the written law and the Oral Law finally came.

The operations of the rabbinical schools and courts over many creative centuries, especially during and following the first Babylonian Exile, resembled those of the great Roman jurisconsults and the great judges of the common-law tradition. One Talmudic story tells of a doctrinal rift between the majority of a rabbinical court led by a great rabbi and a dissenting but no less great rabbi, in which the dissenter successfully summoned the authentic voice of God onto his side of the argument. To this intervention the majority of the court responded: "The law is not in heaven, the law has been handed down to us on earth from Mt. Sinai, and we no longer take notice of heavenly voices. . . ." And the story relates that, at that point, God said with a smile to Elijah the prophet, with whom he was walking: "My children have defeated me, my children have defeated me." But this was an indulgent ratification, not an implacably cruel wrath such as the Greek god brought down on the head of Prometheus. Thus, even against divine intervention, the learned stood their ground, relying for the interpretation of the law on their own wisdom and reason.

The Middle Ages. *Augustine.* St. Augustine of Hippo, in attempting to refute the pagan assertion that Christianity was responsible for the decline of Roman power, reintroduced Stoic philosophy alongside Judeo-Christian thought into the stream of modern jurisprudential speculation. He placed God's reason beside God's will as the highest source of the unchangeable, eternal, divine law binding directly on man and all other creatures. The divine law was thus accessible to both man's reason and his faith and was not, as St. Paul had largely concluded, the product of his will alone and hence not rational in terms of human as opposed to divine reason.

At a second level, Augustine placed the no less unchangeable natural law, being the divine law as man is given the reason, heart, and soul to understand it. The third level, of temporal, or positive, law (for him, the Roman law of the Christian Roman Empire), was warranted by the eternal divine law, even though it changed from time to time and from place to place, so long as it respected the limits laid down by the divine and natural law. This rationale of secular power, some have thought, preserved the idea of government under law through the disintegration of the ancient world, for recultivation in the revival of learning of the 12th and 13th centuries.

Scholasticism. Aquinas, like Augustine long before, succeeded in quieting momentarily the competing claims of the will against the reason of God, the struggle between "voluntarism" and "rationalism," as the underlying basis of the eternal and natural law. Aquinas, like Augustine, gave a plausible place to both natural law and temporal (or positive) law under the eternal law. Human, or positive, law is a creation of human reason for the common good, within limits that natural law prescribes, so that even this proceeds from right reason and therefore from the eternal law. Such positive law as violated the natural and thus the eternal law "was not law" or merely was not binding "in conscience."

The tendency to make reason prevail over will (as in Plato's call for philosophers to be kings or the Arab Averroës' call for philosophers to interpret what is revealed) was challenged by a voluntarist countermovement at Paris and Oxford in the quarter of a century after Aquinas' death in 1274. A Franciscan, John Duns Scotus, insisted on the uniqueness of all beings as finally traceable to the uniqueness of God's will. All precepts, even of the divine law, depend on the single precept "Love God," and, since not reason but will gives access to this, there is no natural law accessible to man's reason. All that can be required of human, or positive, law is that it must be "consonant" with the precept "Love God," or with any other precept willed by God.

The Renaissance period to the 18th century. *Machiavelli.* Machiavelli presented himself (on one interpretation, at least) as seeking to escape from both transcendent will and transcendent reason into the empirical, into life as it is, observed through the eyes of a worldly man whose mind is uncluttered with philosophical and theological preconceptions. He can be understood, in his own words, to be seeking "what a principality is, the variety of such States, how they are won, how they are held, how they are lost." This conception was the more remarkable in 1513, since such an approach had then barely been promulgated for study of the physical world. It had still, indeed, to await its major manifesto in that sphere until Francis Bacon's *Advancement of Learning* at the end of the century.

The
normative
element
in
Machia-
velli's
thought

Even on the more favourable view of Machiavelli's aim—*i.e.*, as describing, rather than prescribing, political behaviour—it remains true that he saw this description as ancillary to the art of maintaining the state and its ruler, so that this maintenance is a kind of end in itself. The omnipotence—unrestrained by law or morality—that he both

ascribes and prescribes to the prince is thus a product not so much of his scientific detachment as of his tendency to view political power as a value, as an end in itself.

Natural law and social-contract theory. The supremacy of the human lawgiver, as posited by Machiavelli and in their diverse ways also by the French and English political theorists Jean Bodin and Thomas Hobbes and others, interwove in the following centuries with continued insistence by Grotius and others on the dominance of the divine reason and man's participation in it, by which he has access to the natural law.

The Dutch political and legal philosopher Hugo Grotius, amid the political expediencies and anarchy of the Thirty Years' War (1618–48), sought to introduce a degree of normative restraint among the monarchical rulers of the newly emerged sovereign states of Europe and to establish a basis in natural law for a rejection of *raison d'état* as a just cause for war, as well as for legal limits on the means and modes of violence in war. Even if the wills of sovereign states form the basis of the international order, Grotius argued, "the totality of the relations between States" is still "governed by law." That law he found in an updated version of the Stoic natural law, as naturalized into Roman law and Christian theology.

With Grotius, as with the Stoics, the normative or moral power of the natural law derives from the fact that man's innate nature (itself part of the nature of the cosmos) and his propensities are viewed as ideal or inherently good. In Grotius' own time, however, there arose a skepticism toward such unfounded optimism, a skepticism that underlies the thought of Hobbes.

With Hobbes (1588–1679), as with the Greek Sophists, the nature of man is not the ideal nature of Grotius and the Stoics. It is rather man's supposed actual nature, before sociality and authority have tempered it. Man, in a state of nature, is motivated by desires and aversions and most of all by the desire to preserve his biological existence. This need for security is best met by all men vesting their rights of self-help in a sovereign, whether that sovereign be a single man or an assembly of men, and subjecting themselves to the laws of that sovereign, or "great Leviathan."

The reason why men must obey the law of the sovereign state, which is the only institution capable of protecting men against each other, is thus based firmly in Hobbes's conception of man's nature, albeit a very different conception from the idealist premises of earlier theories of natural law. Natural-law theorizing after Hobbes is thus divided into these two major streams.

Judicial supremacy. By the beginning of the 17th century the idea of applying natural law as a test of the validity of the positive law (the law of the particular human jurisdiction) had passed from the province of speculative writers to courts of law. The English jurist Lord Coke, in Bonham's case in 1610, was already referring to the tradition that "when an act of Parliament is against common right or reason or repugant or impossible to be performed, the common law will control it, and adjudge such act to be void." About a century before that, an English treatise known as "St. Germain, Doctor and Student" had already presented a three-tier hierarchy of the law of God, natural law (the law of reason), and human (positive) law, obviously deriving from Augustine and Aquinas.

In the United States in the next century, constitutional theory became highly infused with ideas of natural rights. The Declaration of Independence, with its assertion of the self-evident rights of life, liberty, and the pursuit of happiness, marked the beginning of a continuing natural-law influence on American constitutional development. The power of the judiciary to "review" legislation for consistency with a written constitution was taken in the United States to import the power to declare it void, constitutional law being analogized to natural law. Indeed, American judicial statements of 1814, 1822, and 1831 asserted the power of the judiciary to strike down statutes for violation not only of explicit constitutional restraints but also of "eternal principles of justice which no government has a right to disregard." The analogy of constitutional and natural law did not necessarily require that the power to strike down legislation should be a judicial power: this was not so in ancient Rome, nor is it always so in modern civil-law countries. It is arguable that such a judicial repository of the power of final review is unavoidable, since the legislature cannot be expected to annul its own acts; and the executive, even if it were not a party to such acts, is scarcely equipped for the tasks of objective interpretation involved. Yet there are real difficulties of policy and principle raised by giving the judiciary the final word. A distinction must first of all be made among diverse constitutional restraints. Safeguards for such rights as free speech and assembly and access to courts, which help to assure the responsibility of rulers and to prevent the fall of democracy into tyranny or demagoguery, may well be placed in the final custody of judges. But, beyond this point, others have argued, judicial supremacy, in enforcing restraints laid down by the Founding Fathers of an earlier generation, may clearly constitute an obstacle to the implementation by the courts of a society's present convictions.

Decline of natural law. If man is the measure of all things, as the Sophists taught, then a given society of men is the measure of its culture, including its moral and legal standards. In the modern period the French jurist and political philosopher Montesquieu's *De l'esprit des lois* (1748) and *Lettres persanes* (1721) offered the thesis that a people's law and justice are determined by the particular factors and environment that operate upon them. They thus could not, as the natural-law theory of the time held, be unchanging from age to age and from people to people. The French sociologist Auguste Comte's *Système de philosophie positive* (1851–54), which set out to explain positive laws, like other social facts, by reference to verified hypotheses concerning cause and effect and interaction, was similarly antithetical to natural-law theory as it had so far developed. To Comte, metaphysical concepts about such abstractions as ideal essences belonged to a past stage in man's intellectual development. And Darwin's *On the Origin of Species by Means of Natural Selection* (1859), the English philosopher Herbert Spencer's positivism, and other related thinking of the period provided a biological model of self-development of organisms and institutions through a struggle in which survival was a function of challenge and response in the given environment. Change and adaptation, rather than constancy and inviolability, were thus at the heart of their system.

Under the leadership of anthropologists, analyses of man's internal process of response to the exigencies of existence within a particular culture—to conscious and subconscious psychic drives and motivations—deeply affected the jurisprudential study of law and society and helped to bring natural-law thinking to a 19th-century nadir. In the anthropologist Bronislaw Malinowski's most mature statement on the matter, he distinguished four major meanings of the word law as important in understanding the growth of civilization. They included "laws of nature" in the scientific sense of rules governing men's conscious adaptations to the environment; rules of "efficiency" and "convenience" according to which the group lives; rules for conflict adjustment; and rules about enforcement of the last two. No conception of natural law, which had engaged earlier thinkers for two millennia and more, was included.

"Idealism" and justice. Another line of thought, which was also divorced from natural-law concepts, was contained in the Idealist philosophy of Immanuel Kant. Fundamental to Kant's ethical and jurisprudential reasoning is the premise that all moral concepts have their basis wholly in a priori thought, that they can be arrived at by reason alone, without reference to experience or recourse to intuition of rules alleged immanent in experience. Man, furthermore, is a free agent whose actions are determined by aims that he is at liberty to select. From such premises Kant deduced the nature of an ideal law, in which is implicit a theory or criterion of justice. This ideal law comprises the conditions under which all members of society can enjoy the maximum freedom from subjection to the arbitrary will of others.

But Kant's supposedly a priori concepts are in fact as

transcendental as anything natural lawyers have offered. It is thus not surprising that later thinkers, such as Johann Fichte, Kant's Idealist successor, had little difficulty in putting the new Kantian wine into natural-law bottles.

The 20th century saw a fresh attempt at the Kantian approach in the work of the German legal philosopher Rudolf Stammler. Adopting the Kantian position that knowledge is independent of sensory experience, Stammler set out to discover pre-experiential categories, or "pure forms," of thinking about law. Stammler arrived at a social ideal of a "community of free-willing men," an ideal that he claimed to have universal validity because of its supposed a priori basis. Having thus arrived at a "pure" ideal of society, untainted by empirical content deriving from sense perception, he felt able to formulate equally pure principles for just law that would regulate his ideal society. Stammler's pure idea of society comprised the harmony of individual and common purposes: his pure idea of just law thus comprised those principles conducive to such harmony—the mutual respect of individuals for each other's purposes and the participation of all in the achievement of the common purposes.

The different stream of Idealism flowing from Hegel's philosophy of history was fed into jurisprudence by Josef Kohler, Stammler's close predecessor in that subject in the Berlin University. His work is still another effort to relate social facts and the norms of justice by exposing the immanence of values in facts—in "civilization" in Kohler's case.

In perspective, these idealisms, despite their formal or philosophical antagonism to "rationalism" and natural-law thinking, seem to have reinforced in the age of the Industrial Revolution the individualist and libertarian trends that natural law had built up successively against medieval church and empire, the shackles of medieval social, political, and economic organization, and 18th-century despotism.

The 19th and 20th centuries. *Analytical Positivism.* The early 19th century witnessed a reaction against both Kantian Idealism and iusnaturalism (natural-law theorizing). The scientific temper of the age, reflected in the practical achievements of the early decades of the Industrial Revolution, was not conducive to deductive reasoning from a priori hypotheses, which appeared an impractical method of solving the problems of complex societies. Such problems might better be approached via a thorough analysis of existing law and institutions. This new climate of opinion came to be known as Positivism.

Among the chief meanings of Positivism in the legal-analytical sphere are the separation of law as it is and law as it ought to be, stress on the analysis of legal concepts, reliance on logical reasoning in the search for applicable law, and denial that moral judgments can be based on observation and rational proof. Anglo-Saxon analytical Positivism has directed itself mainly to the logical dissection, appraisal, and clarification of the precept element of law, ignoring the elements consisting of lawyers' traditional techniques and received ideals. By the nature of its tasks, analytical jurisprudence does not concern itself with either the facts surrounding or the consequences flowing from legal precepts or with their ethical evaluation, though particular analysts may also be interested in those matters.

Analytical Positivism in England began with the work of the philosopher and legal reformer Jeremy Bentham. His work influenced John Austin, the most outstanding figure in English jurisprudence, who set out to analyze the notions pervading English law. In order to delimit his subject, he defined positive law as the commands of a sovereign addressed to political inferiors and backed by threats of evil in the event of disobedience. Positive law might well be derived from moral precepts and other sources, but such precepts become law only when commanded by a sovereign.

The analytical-Positivist attitude has continued to influence thinkers, although the particular approach of Austin is now of historical interest only. Logical analysis is clearly a tool that may be employed in many spheres of jurisprudence, and its importance thus transcends the limits of any one school. Analysis means little in itself; its value

Montesquieu and early social science

Kant's ideal law

Meaning of Positivism in jurisprudence

depends largely on the validity of the premises from which the argument is made and on the relevance of the subject matter that is chosen for analysis. The paramountcy for the analytical Positivist of questions of logical order and consistency represents a permissible deviation, yet still a deviation, from the wider concerns of ordinary lawyers and students of law and society generally. This is not to say that there is a necessary conflict between the requirements of justice among changing social facts and those of logical consistency of precepts. It means only that there is surely no necessary (nor indeed usual) coincidence between them.

Historical Positivism. In discarding speculative cosmology, the a priori, and the self-evident, 19th-century historical jurisprudence opened the way for the search for the realities of law through empirical observation—for a sociodescriptive rather than a logico-analytical-Positivist jurisprudence.

The leading figure in the historical school was the German jurist Friedrich Karl von Savigny, who confronted the natural-law aspiration for a universal human code with the singularity of the law of particular peoples resulting from their unique sociocultural experiences.

For Savigny, law rests on the *Volksgeist,* or innate popular consciousness; law *par excellence* is customary law. He recognized, of course, that the details of a developed legal system do not spring from simple group intuition. With maturity, both life and law become more specialized and artificial, creating a dualism in more mature law. Part of such a system still rests directly on the popular consciousness and way of life ("the political element"); but this becomes elaborated by jurists, be they Roman jurisconsults or common-law judges, who in this respect represent the community ("the technical element").

Savigny's emphasis on the need of legal change to respect the continuity of the *Volksgeist* offers a pre-Darwinian concept of juristic evolution. The *Volksgeist* corresponds to modern notions of social rather than biological inheritance. Savigny's sense of the impotence of legislatures in the face of the restraints imposed by the *Volksgeist* foreshadows modern recognition of the social and psychological limits of effective legal action.

The English legal historian Sir Henry Maine's dual academic concern with both English law and Roman law challenged him to explain their independent yet often parallel growths and may well have redeemed him from Savigny-like overemphasis of national uniqueness. His concern led him to a comparative historical jurisprudence seeking hypothetical "laws" of development controlling all legal systems. He saw changes in substantive law and in the machinery and modes of legal enforcement and growth as moving in pace with certain recognizable stages in social growth, from primitive, kin-organized society to the mature, complex commercial and industrial societies of Europe.

Maine's experience in India after the publication of his *Ancient Law* in 1861 broadened his interests so that he embraced less well known and less developed systems, such as the Brehon, Hindu, Welsh, Germanic, Anglo-Saxon, and Hebrew. His breadth of interest matched the concurrent growth in anthropological study of primitive peoples.

Maine's work shows the strong combined influence of the analogy of biological to social evolution and of the Hegelian philosophy of history. The consequent, somewhat mechanistic tenor of his interpretations resulted in his being accused by many anthropologists and legal historians of making false assumptions concerning the pattern and sequence of social development.

Economic interpretations. Certain residues of the Marxist economic interpretation of history have won a central place in sociological jurisprudence (see below *Sociological jurisprudence*), as indeed in most branches of social science. One such persistent trend of thought is the close interrelatedness of legal, ethical, economic, and psychological inquiries; another is the pre-eminence among these of economic factors. According to Marxist doctrine, the political and judicial systems—the state and the law— represent the superstructure of society, their nature being determined by the economic base—the mode of produc-

The Marxist conception of law

tion and exchange. The state and its repressive law are but instruments of class domination, becoming redundant under Communism, which has no need of coercion. During the transition to full Communism, they would "wither away." There were, of course, softenings of this bold doctrine in its original authors, with admissions that the ethical or legal superstructure should not be seen as a merely passive effect; and Lenin himself pressed to extremes both the passion of the original thesis and its qualifications. Lenin, indeed, saw state power as an essential weapon of the proletarian dictatorship until the movement to a full Communist society should be completed.

The first half-century of the Soviet Union, with its steady consolidation of state power and its attendant law, has imposed the severest strains on the withering-away prediction. The general tenor of explanation is that the "law" the disappearance of which is prophesied refers only to the kind of coercive order manifest in such instrumentalities as the courts, police, and jails of capitalist countries.

Within these sweeping theses of Marxist thinking, more modest subtheses have played a valuable part. The Socialist jurist Karl Renner, for example, in his *Rechts-institute des Privatrechts und ihre soziale Funktion* (1929), was concerned to show that the legal conception of ownership, formulated in early economies, had profound new effects when continued as an institution of the 19th-century economy. It then, through the law of property and contract, alienated into private hands great segments of what should be in the public domain.

Even more notable are the German sociologist Max Weber's studies of the correlations of socioeconomic and ethicojuristic change, freed of the straitjacket of economic determinism. In these, the impact of unique factors or combinations of factors in particular civilizations is taken into account, including the existence of accepted systems of values, immediate and ultimate, which may (and in Weber's view did) have a decisive effect on the emergence of the Western capitalist system.

Sociological jurisprudence. The historical jurisprudence of the earlier part of the 19th century became subject to the influence of the developing social sciences, which attempted to explain law in its social context. The result was the emergence of a sociological school of jurisprudence.

The early decades of sociological jurisprudence combined 19th-century faith in progress, social evolution, rationalism, humanitarianism, and political pluralism with a sanguine belief that the Newtonian model of natural science would also hold for the social sciences. It was affected by questions of whether the social sciences are truly sciences, what their mutual boundaries are, and whether they can be integrated or somehow transcended by some subject such as sociology or anthropology.

An outstanding figure of the early sociological school was a German, Rudolf von Jhering, who in the 1860s contributed to the intellectual stream a theory of justice predicated on a view of law as a social phenomenon. He saw law as an outcome of the struggle of men to fulfill their purposes and of the force that they marshal behind this. Another historical jurist, the German Otto von Gierke, stirred a related interest with his emphasis on the importance of the inner life and activities of groups and associations as sources of binding social norms. This opened up jurisprudence to some psychological issues. Gierke's work also contributed to the later American Neorealism through its influence on Oliver Wendell Holmes, Jr., and to the theory of the "living law" of the Austrian jurist Eugen Ehrlich, in the first decade of the 20th century. Ehrlich insisted on the profuse norm-creating activities of the countless associations in which men are involved.

At the beginning of the 20th century a great variety of psychological hypotheses were brought to bear on law. A theory of dynamic psychic drives, for example, was propounded by an American sociologist, Lester F. Ward, who argued that such drives could be utilized in social planning. Freud's exploration of psychic activity on a subconscious level, as well as studies of the nonrational and the irrational in the social process by the Italian and German sociologists Vilfredo Pareto and Max Weber, were also profoundly influential.

Early 20th-century views

Revival of natural-law theories. Iusnaturalism, in the sense of the assertion of an order of norms for human conduct transcending human will, to which the validity of positive law is subjected, has certainly experienced a 20th-century revival. The massive human delinquencies of the century, such as those of the Nazis, have been important in stimulating these modern natural-law yearnings. The revival, indeed, has rarely overthrown dominant Positivist positions, but it has certainly reopened some questions that Positivists have not adequately faced.

Contributions to this re-emergence have come from varied directions, rather than from a single intellectual movement. They have often avoided explicit reference to natural law and have even expressed hostility or ridicule toward it. The German Stammler and the French jurist François Gény were certainly among its pioneers. Gény's *Méthode d'interprétation* (1899) displayed the inescapably creative (or lawmaking) role of the judiciary even under a comprehensive code such as the Code Napoléon. It led him to the questions of what are "the sources of law" and where does the legislator's prescription fall short. Answers to such questions must be based on the facts of each particular situation to be adjusted—the legislator cannot impose his view on the court. This line of thinking foreshadowed a variety of doctrines about "the nature of things" or "the nature of facts," all of which shared the idea that the decisive nature of a situation has its base in the facts for which men seek governing law. The properties and circumstances of these facts themselves afford immediate guidelines for just regulation. The fact situation, if only its essence will be perceived, has the superior applicable norms immanent within it.

In his *Lehre von dem richtigen Recht* (1902), Stammler sought, as described above, the a priori social principles of just law concerning respect for and participation by all members. His call for "natural law with a changing content" based on these a priori principles quickly became a 20th-century slogan.

Even as this express reinvocation of natural law was proceeding, the French public lawyer Léon Duguit was expressly denouncing it. Duguit's concern was to place law and lawyers within what he saw to be the correct frame. This he found in Émile Durkheim's Positivist sociology. This led him, with some paradox for a contemner of natural law, to insist that law is but "*le produit spontané des faits*" ("the immediate result of the facts"). The observed "facts" of social solidarity arising from economic specialization of functions generated, Duguit argued, the society's norms. Breach of these norms causes social disorder and a spontaneous movement toward readjustment. Even a supreme legislator was bound (Duguit affirmed) by this objective "rule of law," so that his acts violating it are void, even apart from any other constitutional restraint. All this bears the clear iusnaturalist mark of the assumed immanence in observed facts of a transcending and overriding order. It pays cryptic homage to a natural law, fealty to which Duguit denied.

The German legal philosopher Gustav Radbruch's turn toward natural law at the end of a life of great contributions to democratic legal relativism and Positivism was very different. Positivism, Radbruch argued, had encouraged German lawyers to stand by at Nazi barbarism, declaring "*Gesetz ist Gesetz*" ("Law is Law"). Nor was Radbruch's turn to natural law in any way cryptic. He came to declare quite openly that:

> where justice is not even striven for, where equality which is the core of justice is constantly denied in the enactment of positive law, there the law is not only "unjust law" but lacks the nature of law altogether.

The linkage with the revived natural law of the legal institutionalism of the French legal philosopher Maurice Hauriou and the writer and historian Georges Renard is different again. As with Duguit, the linkage is not proclaimed, but no overt hostility disguised their obvious sympathy for Thomist positions. Theirs is a Catholic version of institutionalism (which regards social institutions such as the family or the corporation as expressing the social reality underlying the law). The natural-law assumptions are apparent in the insistence on "the principles of

organization," the "communion" of members in realizing "durable ideals," and the placing of men's powers of organization into the service of such ideals, as essential elements of any institution. For them, as for Duguit, the principles of justice were principles of social organization, immanent and self-evident.

It has been tempting for many to seek kinships between natural law and Existentialism, as was attempted by the German legal philosopher Werner Maihofer. Such efforts seem, however, destined to denature either Existentialism or natural law itself. Even in all their varieties, Existentialist positions approach no nearer to natural law than to assert that the traumas, anxieties, and demands of mere "existence" confront men with fateful value choices. Yet this is far short of asserting that any transcending principles of harmony may be discoverable.

Abstract symbols such as "social solidarity," "the principles of social organization," or "immanence in the facts of social life" are by virtue of their ambiguity susceptible to misappropriation by absolutist governments. The same may be said of Savigny's *Volksgeist* notion, as witness its affinity to the racialism of Nazi law. Thus, while the modern revival of natural law has been in part a revulsion from totalitarianism, it can also be exploited to rationalize totalitarianism.

There is another paradox also: The growth of the social sciences has invited restatement of natural-law traditions in terms of social ideals. Yet the very complexity of the social and economic orders and of their attendant sciences has placed forbidding barriers before the aspiration to base justice or other values on "objective" knowledge. Some have been tempted to hope that natural law may somehow overleap such barriers.

Pure theory of law. In part, at least, the influence of the distinguished legal philosopher Hans Kelsen's "pure theory of law" reflects early 20th-century skepticism about natural law and sociology, to both of which Kelsen opposed his claimed purity of method; *i.e.*, a method free from contamination by values of any sort.

He asserted, first, that legal theory was properly a science in the sense of an uncommitted, value-free, methodical concern with a determined object of knowledge. Second, he argued, legal theory must be isolated from psychological, sociological, and ethical matters. Third, purity of method permits the analyst to see that every legal system is in essence a hierarchy of norms in which every proposition is dependent for its validity on another proposition. The justification for describing any particular rule as law thus depends on whether there is some other proposition standing behind it, imparting to it the quality of law. This regression is continued until the *Grundnorm,* or "basic norm," is arrived at. The basic norm derives its validity from the fact that it has been accepted by some sufficient minimum number of people in the community.

Kelsen's assertion that norms can spring only from other norms seems but another way of stating his rejection of the relevance of facts to values and, therefore, of iusnaturalism and sociology to his pure science of law. Yet finally it has seemed to many dubious whether the Kelsenite theory itself escaped the *liaison fatal* between facts and norms; for, if all legal norms must finally hang on the basic norm, then whatever it is that the basic norm hangs on must be nonlaw. And whether the basic norm hangs on "habitual obedience to determinate persons," as the English legal philosopher John Austin in effect proposed a century before, or on "efficaciousness," as Kelsen proposed, what it hangs on is in fact rather than norm. Critics have complained that, at most points in the creation of norms in Kelsen's system, what is decisive is the intervention of acts of will of persons endowed by higher norms with norm-making authority. The determination whether such acts of will have occurred is a factual inquiry, to the decisiveness of which Kelsen's pure theory gave little weight.

Modern schools of realism. The American jurist Oliver Wendell Holmes's description of law in 1897 as "what the courts will do in fact" and of the "real ground" of decisions as resting often in some "inarticulate major premise" rather than in expressed reasons gave 20th-century legal realism its central theme.

Law in Positivist sociology

Kelsen's hierarchy of norms

Certain features are common to the "realist" jurists. They include (besides the above-mentioned concern with "the law in action") stress on the social purposiveness of law, on the endless flux in both society and law, on the need to divorce the "is" and the "ought" for purposes of study and to question all orthodox assumptions made by lawyers, and in particular on the need to substitute more realistic working categories for current lawyers' generalities. Among the orthodoxies thus challenged, these writers tended to include the works of early sociological jurisprudence. Yet it is clear, from the present perspective, that the concerns common to the realists and the more orthodox sociological jurists were far more important than the ephemeral if bitter conflicts that at first flared up between them. The American realists in their important surviving contributions have for the most part reinforced, clarified, and elaborated a number of main insights, notably about rule uncertainty and fact uncertainty, which they shared with sociological jurisprudence.

Scandi-
navian
realism

Scandinavian realists, while temperamentally akin to their American colleagues, were rather different in intellectual concerns. Methodologically, they invoked a somewhat gross empiricism, leading them to deny that the law could be the subject of scientific inquiry at all, since its concepts and principles are not founded on spatial and temporal data of experience. Taking lawyers' talk of the will of the sovereign very literally, they were concerned to show that there is no such will of common content and that even legislators who enact a code are merely rubber stamping what others drafted.

The Swedish jurist Axel Hägerström insisted that the idea of rules of law as commands is an idea not corresponding with facts. His disciple Karl Olivecrona added that this false idea results from the syntactical imperative form used in modern legislation. Such rules, he urged, were commands only in a depersonalized sense. He preferred to describe them as "independent imperatives." Such "imperative statements about imaginary actions, rights, duties" may not be directed to any particular persons. Yet, even if some legal rules are directed "so to say, into the air," others are certainly directed to particular persons. If any form of imperative notion is to be preserved, it should be one that accommodates both situations.

Some of the problems that these writings address are rather tied to the special experience of their authors' own legal cultures. Others reach out independently toward truths already reached earlier in Anglo-American jurisprudential scholarship, especially as to the merely noetic and conceptual (rather than physical or psychological) nature of rights, duties, and liabilities.

THE STATUS OF CONTEMPORARY PHILOSOPHY OF LAW

By the middle of the 20th century, serious scholars no longer argued for or against the exclusive imperium of either the analytical–logical, the justice–ethical, or the sociological approach. Whether jurisprudence is a single field in some scientific sense or whether its unity lies in the need to serve the intellectual needs of those concerned with making, applying, improving, or generally understanding law, all the above areas are included within it.

The
"revolt
against
formal-
ism"

A characteristic feature of contemporary jurisprudence is what has come to be known as "the revolt against formalism"; that is, against preoccupation with the technical and logical aspects of law. It can be traced back to Savigny's early 19th-century reaction against natural law, to Jhering's attacks on the German Pandectists (commentators on Roman law), and to Maine and the work of the anthropologists and early sociological jurists. Its early pressure was toward broader and deeper history, toward recognition of the organic nature of the processes of cultural growth, and toward problems of social action and the value choices therein entailed.

In the United States the legal philosopher Morton White identified five later contributing strains of thought, including the pragmatism of John Dewey; the economist Thorstein Veblen's institutionalism, rejecting both the abstractions of classical political economy and the fatalism of the Marxist interpretation of history; the revolt within jurisprudence of the American legal realists already de-

scribed; and the approach to history as no mere chronicle of kings and battles but rather as a product of underlying economic forces and a guide to present and future civilizations.

The sometimes-overhasty iconoclasms of this revolt have proved less important than its positive affirmations. It has affirmed, for example, that the evaluating activities of justice must somehow move alongside the describing activities of sociological jurisprudence, that the choices of ethics, social policy, and justice still remain to be made when all the empirics of social science are done. The central question includes not merely what are the facts but also what should be done about the facts. These affirmations reject any regression to simple amoralism, stirring new temptations to return to natural law or other intuitive absolutes.

There are important advantages in the drive, characteristic of much contemporary social science, for overall cognition of the social and legal orders and the identification of key points for social action within them. But there are also dangers, for, especially with subject matters such as the law, systematic theory and overall cognition can rarely be of aid save in the rather long run, for which present decision makers cannot usually wait.

Growth of the sociological school. The most eminent pioneers and champions of modern sociological jurisprudence were Roscoe Pound in the United States and Hermann Kantorowicz in Europe. For both, the task of sociological jurisprudence, though orientated mainly to practical administrative or legislative problems, included that of framing hypotheses (as to the limits of effective legal action, for example) on which to base general laws of the operation of law in society.

Methodology of sociological jurisprudence

As with the social sciences, the principal methods available to sociological jurisprudence are those of survey, statistical analysis, comparative observation, and experimentation. The controls and corrections available usually fall far short of those of the natural-science models. Much work in sociological jurisprudence has merely brought to bear upon the law relevant findings from other social sciences. But it may also generate its own findings, as it has done in relation to traffic laws, control of moneylending, credit unions, bankruptcy laws, the effect of antitrust practices or of poverty on legal rights, the theory of appellate judicial decision making, and a host of other matters. Examinations of the prehistory and aftercareers of convicted criminals and of persons on probation or parole, probings of family and environmental influences bearing on potential deviance, and attempts to identify decisive factors predictive of future deviance are among the staples of sociological jurisprudence.

Sociological jurisprudence is confronted by the questions whether (and, if so, how and how far) it is possible through empirical methods to approach central issues of social action that involve value judgments. The fact that lawyers are necessarily involved with ideas of obligation, values, and norms sharpens this confrontation. A second group of problems arises from the high level of individuality of men, groups, and societies, from the unending variety of their emotions, roles, and expectations, and from the feedback effects on human behaviour that the empirical observation and testing of that behaviour brings about.

These problems give central importance to efforts to develop frames of social knowledge that give due place to both facts and values. Such inquiries show the great complexity of values held and their intricate and dynamic relation to the physical and cultural environments.

The study of law in society thus shares with anthropology and other social sciences a central interest in roles and functions as basic meaningful categories and in certain mechanisms and channels whereby conduct is thought to become socially meaningful. These notions are thought to permit the analysis of complex social situations into more refined terms, such as constituent goals, tasks, expectations, and allocated rights, powers, and duties.

As to the mechanisms or channels through which conduct becomes socially meaningful, earlier thought tended to explain social norms as built up from individual instances through group usages and mores that then crystallize in institutions such as law. Insofar as this suggests a cumulative movement or process, current thought would regard it as oversimplified. The growth of socio-ethical convictions is rather to be seen in terms of symbolic interaction between individuals. A particular society may be seen, in this light, as a collection of individuals with a culture that has been learned by symbolic communication from other individuals back through time, enabling members to gauge their behaviour to each other and to the society as a whole.

The future of sociological jurisprudence. In his famous program of 1911–12, Pound formulated a series of rather practical objectives for the movement, including making studies of the law in action, of the means of more effective legislation and law enforcement (by creation of ministries of justice, for example), of legal and judicial reasoning, of legal history in its social context, and of the role of the legal profession. An early quip against the sociological school was that it was like a great orchestra constantly tuning its instruments but never actually playing. Yet many practical tasks have been performed, and the school continued to show a gathering momentum and a widening range of concerns.

The maladjustments and inadequacies of the law gave to early sociological jurisprudence an intensely activist drive, directed to ad hoc remedies, and a great deal of the relevant work is still of this nature. Especially since 1945, however, juristic work on the relations of law and society has come into more fruitful contact with other social sciences, leading in turn to greater stress on cognition of the social and economic orders in their complex unity. Whatever the difficulties of designs for an overall analysis of the social system, some adjustment toward them is inevitable for sociological jurisprudence. This is in part, no doubt, a result of the waning of interest in many of the kinds of ad hoc problems with which it was initially concerned. But the interest in sociological theory also results from growing awareness that some problems require to be approached on a wider basis. This has created new stirrings of the turn-of-the-century ambition that the study of law in society become a specific branch of social science, concerned with framing and testing general laws governing law as a social phenomenon.   (Ju.S.)

Philosophy of education

Philosophy of education is a field of inquiry, speculation, and application in which philosophical methods are applied to the study of a problem, topic, or issue in education. Characteristic of these methods is the attempt to think as accurately, clearly, coherently, and systematically as possible. Analytical philosophers would say that philosophy of education should end with the attempt to clarify and justify educational statements and arguments. In practice, however, the field includes much more than that. It considers as relevant material much that has been written on education by influential philosophers of the past. There is, therefore, much overlap with the field of history of education, and ultimately no clear demarcation can be drawn between the two fields, which nourish and illuminate each other in their interconnectedness (see ED-UCATION, HISTORY OF). Many philosophers of education also go beyond analysis in being concerned with establishing a commitment to value judgments and substantive positions. They take pains to attempt to clarify and justify those judgments and positions on the grounds that clear and substantiated judgments have greater probability of being sound.

The philosophy of education has a special concern with the *applications* of knowledge and theories. Thus, many philosophers of education are especially interested in the relationship between theory and practice. Moreover, they are often concerned with the ways in which philosophy relates to other fields of study in the attempt to shed light on educational problems and issues. This gives them a wide-angled approach to education, which some philosophers have called "educational theory" to distinguish it from a more narrowly analytical form of philosophy of education.

With regard to the term "education," there is a similar spectrum of views ranging from the narrow view of education as that which goes on in schools and universities to a definition of education as all those experiences that affect the growth and development of a person throughout life. The former view has tended to give way, with increased recognition of the crucially important part that informal experiences and relationships play in determining what and how an individual learns.

COMMON ASSUMPTIONS ABOUT HUMAN LEARNING

Symbolization. First, it is to be noted that human learning is largely dominated by symbolic processes. Much of the learning that man acquires during his lifetime is gained through his growing ability to understand and manipulate symbols—verbal, mathematical, artistic, musical, and so on. This symbolic emphasis gives human learning much of its power. It brings power because symbols enable man to deal abstractly and at a high level of generality with words, data, and ideas. Thus, he can learn to think rapidly, to link varied items in fruitful ways, and to create shortcuts to new knowledge.

The symbolic emphasis also brings dangers. It can trap man into circling around at a high level of generality without ever feeling the need to tie his abstractions to concrete applications. Schooling thus can become an apparently self-justifying cycle, which in fact fails to pay off in terms of improving men's lives. Moreover, since learners assimilate and master these symbolic processes at different rates, it is tempting for educators to identify all education with symbol manipulation, to classify those who take longer to master the process as inferior, and to reserve the privileges of higher schooling for those who master this particular process rapidly. This is to mistake a part for the whole and leads to enormous losses of human power and development.

Human motivation. Motivations to learning are more variable in man than in subhuman species. In other animals learning patterns develop largely through instinctual motivations. This means that lower animals need less training than humans before they are independent and self-reliant. Human beings are the most dependent of creatures when young, and they take longest to educate for independent activity. It is precisely this long period of dependence and education that constitutes man's superiority over lower animals, for it is in this period that the growing human being absorbs much of his culture and develops the skills and knowledge that enable him to build on the work of his predecessors. His lower degree of reliance on innate mechanisms also means that man is more flexible in his responses and is capable of adjusting those responses in the light of previous experiences. Thus, he is not condemned to repeat previous patterns of living and thinking but can create change, both in himself and in his culture.

Educators have often acted as if man were a lower animal, for schooling has often resembled training, with emphasis upon imitation, obedience, repetition, drill, and control, more than it has resembled education, with emphasis upon initiative, creativity, choice, decision making, and freedom. As a result, schooling has been more successful in improving man's skill in mechanical and repetitive activities at the lower end of his capacity scale than in developing higher qualities of intellect, feeling, and will that constitute his peculiar humanness.

Human capacity to learn. So far there have been discovered no limits to man's capacity to learn. From earliest times, however, men in positions of power or influence have suggested that the learning capacity of certain individuals or groups is severely limited and that they should not be expected to profit greatly, if at all, from education. These "ineducable" individuals have usually been members of minority or disadvantaged groups. But, repeatedly, when their cultural disadvantages have been removed, these groups have shown that their previous failure to learn has been due not to incapacity but to lack of fully realized opportunity.

These findings have led educators to be much more modest and less hasty in their labelling and classifying procedures. It has been realized that labels affixed to children tend to become self-fulfilling prophecies, that those who are expected to learn usually do so, and those who are expected to fail to learn also usually do so. Hence, when educators resort to classifying children at all, they increasingly tend to use their labels as temporary rather than permanent, as saying something only about a quality of the child rather than about his person, and as something to be abandoned as soon as the child's performance proves the label wrong.

Similarly, no one has been able to confirm any certain limits to the speed with which man can learn. Schools and universities have usually been organized as if to suggest that all students learn at about the same rather plodding and regular speed. But, whenever the actual rates at which different people learn have been tested, nothing has been found to justify such an organization. Not only do individuals learn at vastly different speeds and in different ways, but man seems capable of astonishing feats of rapid learning when the attendant circumstances are favourable. It seems that, in customary educational settings, one habitually uses only a tiny fraction of one's learning capacities.

Complexity of human learning. Human learning is complex rather than simple. Learners are apt to learn more than one thing at a time. Sometimes this process is conscious, as when one simultaneously or rapidly assimilates many specific items of a whole. More often, the process is entirely or partly unconscious, as when the student learns some "content" consciously but at the same time absorbs unwittingly a great deal more from interrelationships, tones of voice, and so on.

Correlative learning Educators are therefore becoming increasingly concerned with these concomitant learnings. They are aware that the long-term significance of the arithmetical skill that the student consciously learns may be nugatory compared with the importance of what he learns about himself as a learner, about his capacities and limits, about his relationship with his teacher, about power and authority, about his relationships with his fellow students, about equality, collaboration, competition, and friendship. As educators become more knowledgeable about the importance of learning climates, they are impelled to abandon simplified techniques of teaching in favour of a more complex approach that views learning in the context of a matrix of relationships and forces that act upon the student, the teacher, the school, and the community.

Intellectual–emotional–physical–volitional integrity of learning. Human learning concerns the whole person. The intellect is not the only agent of learning. This activity is shared by the body, the emotions, and the will. Moreover, the process cannot be limited to any one of these domains without affecting the others. Educators are most conscious of intellectual learnings, which tend to play the largest part in their plans and intentions. But there is increasing evidence that makes clear the folly of attempting to confine education to the training of intellects. If the teacher does so, he is destined to fare badly, for the child who is emotionally frozen or whose stomach is empty or who is determined to thwart the teacher will not perform intellectually as the teacher intends.

Educators are also becoming more aware of the other side of this coin—that is, that the learner's powers are vastly enhanced when not only is his intellect stimulated but also his feelings are respected, his body is nurtured, and his will to learn is strengthened. Effective education, therefore, is found when the learner is regarded as a person to be respected, nurtured, strengthened, and stimulated, rather than as an intellect to be trained.

DIFFERING CONCEPTIONS OF EDUCATION

Model theories of the educated person. In different historical eras and in different cultures a variety of conceptions has been put forward concerning the nature of mind, of truth, of knowledge, of moral goodness, of aesthetic beauty, and of the purposes of life. These views carry implications for the purpose and nature of the educational process, the ends toward which one should educate, the means by which one can best achieve those ends, the degree of consistency between the ends and the means, and the model, if any, of the ideally educated person that one has in mind when engaging in the educational

process. These relate to some of the perennial questions that concern the philosopher of education. The following represent some of the most influential models that have been presented of the educated person.

Platonic view. The first great attempt to create a philosophically coherent model of the educated person was that of Plato. Reacting against the turbulence and chaos of his own times, Plato envisaged in *The Republic* and the *Laws* a permanent, stable, hierarchical society in which those most adept at education would rule, those moderately adept would become warriors and carry out the orders of the rulers or guardians, and those least adept at education would fill the lowliest worker functions in society. The education that would thus order and segregate the different groups in society would be based upon the ability to understand the perennial, ideal Forms that, Plato maintained, underlie the transient, concrete manifestations of those Forms in everyday life. Since, supposedly, not all people could surmount the difficulties of such an intellectually demanding program of study, it would be justifiable to select, classify, segregate, and reject students at the various stages of the educational process. Intellectually segregated education

The Platonic scheme has been enormously influential, especially in the Western world, during the last 25 centuries. Most educational programs in the West have consistently reflected this hierarchical pattern. Schooling has usually been a process of selection and rejection, with great effort and ingenuity expended on testing, measuring, classifying, and segregating in accordance with the best available knowledge. Similarly, Plato's concept of mind has exerted lasting influence on Western education. Patterns of schooling have reflected the greater prestige accorded to the study of ideas and abstractions and the lower prestige given to practical studies and manual work. There has persisted a dichotomy between the so-called liberal arts, which have been considered suitable educational fare for potential leaders of society, and so-called vocational studies, which have been considered more suitable for potential followers. This pattern has lasted to the present day, not only in Europe and North America, but also in those parts of Asia, Africa, and Latin America greatly influenced by European culture. Thus, one finds in many former colonial societies that students often strongly prefer to follow "liberal" studies, even though the choice may condemn them to genteel unemployment in a society whose economy cries out for people with technological, practical, and manual skills.

Thomist view. In the 13th century, St. Thomas Aquinas made a monumental attempt to reconcile the two great streams of the Western tradition. In his teaching at the University of Paris and in his writings—particularly the *Summa theologiae* and the *Summa contra gentiles*—Aquinas tried to synthesize reason and faith, philosophy and theology, university and monastery, activity and contemplation. In his writings, however, faith and theology ultimately took precedence over reason and philosophy because the former were presumed to give access to truths that were not available through rational inquiry. Hence, Aquinas started with assumptions based on divine revelation and went on to a philosophical explication of man and nature. The model of the educated man that emerged from this process was the Scholastic, a man whose rational intelligence had been vigorously disciplined for the pursuit of moral excellence and whose highest happiness was found in contemplation of the Christian God.

This Scholastic model has greatly affected the development of Western education, especially in fostering the notion of intellectual discipline. Aquinas' theological-philosophical doctrine has been a powerful intellectual force throughout the West and has constituted the official basis of Catholic theology since 1879. Although Aquinas made an important place in his hierarchy of values for the practical uses of reason, later Thomists have often been more exclusively intellectual in their educational emphasis. For Aquinas, the primary agent of education was the learner, and his model was, thus, a person capable of self-education. Intellectually autonomous, he should be able to conduct his own process of research and discovery. The Roman Catholic Church, however, has usually put the learner firmly under the authoritative superordination of the teacher.

Lockean view. John Locke, the 17th-century English philosopher, has been credited with formulating the classical liberal defense of individual freedom against the authorities of state and church. Opposed both to what he deemed the stagnation of unreflective tradition and the perils of enthusiastic radicalism, Locke saw science, reason, and experience as the best safeguards against these dangers. Responding to the rise of the new bourgeoisie and the new science, he became the principal spokesman for the increasingly powerful middle class, who were predominantly skeptical and practical in their intellectual temper. The model of the gentleman had traditionally been the English ideal of the educated person. Locke's achievement was to take this ideal and modify it to a form acceptable to the new bourgeoisie. Originally an aristocratic model, the gentleman ideal became infused, under Locke's influence, with democratic, Puritan, and practical characteristics.

Education of the practical gentleman

Locke's notion of the mind at birth as a *tabula rasa*, a "blank tablet" devoid of innate ideas, gave enormous importance to the role of experience and sense perception in the educational process. In *Some Thoughts Concerning Education* (1693) and the *Conduct of the Understanding* (1706), Locke outlined the heavily experiential education that would be appropriate for a gentleman. His four cardinal aims of education, in order of importance, were virtue, wisdom, breeding, and learning. Some critics have insisted that the order has remained important to the present day in English education, that learning must always be lightly worn and never ostentatious. Not only was Locke's thinking influential in shaping the subsequent development of English educational thought, but his Puritan individualism also had a considerable effect on the growth of American educational ideals. Locke's failure to recognize the possibilities of the uses of institutional power and legislation for interventions that would enhance rather than restrict freedom was an omission that has often bedevilled American educational thinking.

Naturalistic view. Most movements in philosophy and education have seemed to engender their own opposition. Hence, the rationalism and scientific objectivity of the Enlightenment found a reaction in the subjectivity and emotional spontaneity of romantic naturalism, the principal spokesman of which was Jean-Jacques Rousseau. In particular, Rousseau reacted against the excessive formalism and rationalism of 18th-century France. Out of this reaction there came a model of the educated person as the natural man, a figure presented in contrast to what Rousseau saw as the pathetic products of contemporary civilization. Against civilized values like rationalism, conscious reflection, control, complexity, and objectivity, Rousseau offered his own values of romanticism, intuitive spontaneity, freedom, simplicity, and subjectivity.

Subjectivity and spontaneity in learning

In *Émile* (1762), one of the most influential books on education ever written, Rousseau argued that one should protect the child from the corruptions of civilization and carefully nurture his natural, spontaneous impulses, which were always healthy. It was important, he maintained, to avoid premature intellectualization of emotion so that the child's intellectual powers could develop without distortion. Feeling should precede thinking, and the child should be controlled only by things, not by adults' wills. In these ideas lay some of the germs of progressive education, which spread throughout the world during the 19th and 20th centuries. Constantly in tension with the classical demands of reason, discipline, authority, and scholarship, the romantic naturalism of the progressive-education movement has continued to remind educators that their ultimate concern should be the growth of the unique, ultimately unfathomable child.

Marxist view. Probably the most influential writer of recent times was Karl Marx, whose writings, mostly in collaboration with Friedrich Engels, altered the course of history and continue to affect the lives of millions of people in all parts of the world. A central concern of Marx and Engels was to cure the alienation and dehumanization of man caused by what they saw as the exploitative forces of capitalism. In Marx's writings, the material dimension of history appeared as primary. Economic production was deemed the basis of life, and the prevailing ideas (religious, educational, and political) of a society were seen as being determined by its economic structure. The dominant ideas of an epoch or society were considered to be the ideas of its ruling class—that is, the class that controlled the means of material production. In order to find the hidden interest behind an idea, Marx argued, one had to examine its social function rather than its intellectual content. Marx saw the need for a proletarian revolution in order to bring about Communism. Under Communism, he argued, the opposition between the individual and the group would disappear; each man's interests would be seen to be identical with the interests of all, and alienation would be banished.

In Marx's view, what was needed for man's growth toward maturity was genuine community; that is, the voluntary drawing together of autonomous and socially responsible persons. The model of the educated person that Marx put forward was not the irresponsible individualist nor the coerced collectivist but the accountable communal man, who attained his freedom not by fleeing from social relationship but *through* social relationships. Individual freedom required social authority.

Marxist emphasis on social education

Marx's and Engels' writings, particularly *Das Kapital* (1867–94), *The German Ideology* (London ed., 1938) and *The Communist Manifesto* (1848), have reshaped the world. Millions have been inspired by their vision of unalienated work and education. Unfortunately, like many influential ideas, they have been abused and distorted. Several states have tried to bring about a Communist utopia through collectivist coercion and social manipulation in a distortion of Marx's arguments. There is a need for state intervention to remove gross inequalities and to expand opportunities, in Marx's view, but ultimately human regeneration is a task for each individual.

Pragmatist view. Out of the America that was created by immigration, urbanization, and industrialization in the second half of the 19th century came the philosophy of Pragmatism. Associated with such thinkers as C.S. Peirce, William James, and John Dewey, Pragmatism, as the dominant American philosophy, exerted a strong influence on the shape of education in the United States, and affected educational ideas and practices in Europe and Japan. In the hands of Dewey, Pragmatism evolved into a philosophy that saw man as formed through interaction with his natural and social environment. The educated person was always viewed by Dewey in a social context. Neither the individual nor society had any meaning without the other. Dewey created a model of the educated person as the reflective man, one who was critical of the authority of custom and tradition as the determinant of belief and action and who preferred the method of science, of "organized intelligence" as the best way to solve his problems.

In *My Pedagogic Creed* (1897), *How We Think* (1910), *Democracy and Education* (1916), *Human Nature and Conduct* (1922), and a stream of other philosophical and pedagogic writings, Dewey formulated a viewpoint that constituted a rigorous intellectual core of the progressive-education movement, although he criticized many of the manifestations of progressive pedagogy in practice. For example, he viewed the child's interests as vitally important and to be neither repressed nor humoured. To repress them was to commit the fault of much traditional education by ignoring the child's unique bent. But to humour them was to commit the fault of some progressive education by failing to discover the underlying power below the passing whim. Subject matter, Dewey argued, should consist of activities that enabled the child to reflect upon his social experiences. When subject matter preceded or was unrelated to the child's experiences, it was largely meaningless. It gained meaning through being made the medium for continued reflection upon, and reconstruction of, experience.

Progressive emphasis on blending individual and social needs

Behaviourist view. In the 20th century, the use of science has been extended to the study of virtually all aspects of human affairs. The possibilities of scientific control of men and events have brought profound changes in philosophy and education. By studying only the behavioral aspects of man, science has been able to predict and control in ways that have powerful and sometimes frightening implications. The behaviourist view has been most notably represented by the American psychologist B.F. Skinner. In his writings, including the utopian novel, *Walden Two* (1948), *Science and Human Behavior* (1953), and *Beyond Freedom and Dignity* (1971), he has firmly rejected the conventional model of man as a free agent who acts in accordance with the decisions of an inner self that is neither fully explicable nor fully controllable by scientific means. Instead, Skinner envisages the use of scientific knowledge about the control of human behaviour to create a planned man, one who will be conditioned to behave in the way best calculated to achieve society's goals. Behavioral engineering will have removed all of his antisocial tendencies, and he will want only what is good for himself and his society.

Pro-
grammed
learning
and
behavioral
develop-
ment Behaviourism in general and Skinner in particular have exerted considerable influence on Western, and especially American, education through developments that range from the invention of programmed instruction (or the so-called "teaching machine") to the widespread emphasis on behavioral objectives in educational programs. The philosophy of Behaviourism compels one to examine carefully the issue of control in education. Skinner wants to use scientific control to bring about a society in which it will be easy to be good and to bring about an educational process through which it will be easy to be excellent. There is no alternative to control, in his view. It is simply a matter of *who* is to control. One does not grant the child "freedom" merely by leaving him alone. To refuse to use scientific control to shape human behaviour is, for the Behaviourist, a failure in responsibility.

Existentialist view. The application of science to ever more aspects of the study of man has been particularly marked in the West; but, in reaction to this trend, there has developed some criticism of the scientific way of viewing man as an object to be categorized, studied objectively, or subsumed under a generalization. Prominent in this reaction have been Existentialist philosophers, among whom the Jewish philosopher, Martin Buber, played an outstanding role in deepening contemporary understanding of man and education. In such books as *I and Thou* (1923) and *Between Man and Man* (1947), Buber's model of the educated person appeared as one whose life was shaped by existential decision making. Such a person did not determine choices in advance of existential situations. He used principles and traditions only as checks or reminders, not as infallible guides. His values were created in the concrete here and now and were manifested as he related to other men. Thus, each man was seen as a unique person rather than as a member of a category.

Rela-
tionship
between
learning
and life A vital concept for Buber was responsibility, viewed in terms of one's response to another. Thus, the dialogue became a central focus in his educational philosophy. The educated person was one who could listen as well as talk. And since genuine dialogue depended upon authenticity, upon *being* rather than *seeming,* one needed the courage to be oneself in relationships. Buber also urged the recognition of a continuity between learning and life, rather than the encouragement of knowledge for its own sake. He insisted that learning be related to consequent action. Thus, for Buber, the educated person was not one who merely had had his cognitive faculties trained but one whose inmost spirit had been infused by what he had learned.

Areas of disagreement among educational theorists. *Conceptions of what constitutes knowledge.* Although there is wide agreement that the assimilation of knowledge by the learner is a principal goal of education, this agreement is more apparent than real, because there is much disagreement about what constitutes knowledge. Clearly, if one person identifies knowledge with information, his pedagogic approach is likely to differ from that of one who identifies knowledge with a process of thinking. Some philosophers have attempted to clarify a distinction between "knowing that" (something is true or false) and

"knowing how" (to do or learn to discover something). The former emphasis is common in educational programs that focus on the product—that is, on the information that the learner has amassed and can reproduce at the end of his program. The latter emphasis is common in programs that focus on the process—that is, on the skills and attitudes that the learner has adopted that enable him to learn more.

Conceptions of how knowledge should be communicated. Throughout history, the commonest way for knowledge to be communicated has been through what can be loosely called apprenticeship. The one who does not know (the apprentice) watches the one who does (the master); he imitates the master, probably fails, watches again, tries again, and so on until he knows what the master knows. This is primarily the way young people learn role identity, for example—what it means to be a husband or wife, a father or mother, a male or female. It is not an effective method for stimulating the growth of new knowledge. A second method, one that has been time-honoured in institutions of formal schooling, is telling. The one who knows (the teacher) tells the one who does not (the student). The student listens, tries to remember, and is usually required to reproduce his memorizations at some stage so that the teacher can judge whether or not the knowledge has been assimilated. This method is a much less effective way of communicating knowledge than would be guessed from its prevalence as an educational practice. Other methods try to remove the difficulties of human relationships from the act of communication by removing one party from the scene. For example, the apprentice can watch the master on film or videotape. Or the teacher can write his lectures in a book, which the student can then read. Another method is that of the dialogue. Unlike the previous methods, which imply superiority–inferiority relationships, this method implies equality between the members of the dialogue. All may at different moments be teachers or learners. The method assumes that all have some knowledge to give and that all need to learn. Appren-
ticeship,
telling,
and
dialogue

Conceptions of the purpose of education. One of the commonest areas of disagreement among educational theorists concerns what education should be for. Two broad divisions of opinion can be identified. They are, first, that education should serve the needs of the individual and second, that it should serve the needs of society. In industrialized nations it is common for both of these goals to be held but for different classes of the population. For the elite, the needs of the individual tend to prevail, and thus upper-class schooling often tolerates diversity and encourages idiosyncrasy. For the masses, the needs of society tend to dominate, and schooling usually serves to prepare children to become obedient, well-drilled, uncomplaining workers in industry and agriculture. In addition to this dichotomy, there are many national and cultural variations. In France and Germany, for example, there is a strong tendency to see the primary purpose of education as some form of intellectual development, with the French *lycée* and the German *Gymnasium* serving as characteristic institutions. In England, education has usually been seen as primarily serving the purpose of character building. The English public school is sometimes taken as an epitome of this emphasis. In Roman Catholic and Communist countries, moral or religious training is usually the primary purpose of education. Hence, every subject is imbued with religious (or, if it is Marxism–Leninism, quasi-religious) content, and there is a constant attempt to draw moral lessons from educational material. In the United States, where large-scale immigration once brought the fear of social disintegration, preparation for citizenship and development of national consciousness have tended to be emphasized. Even today, nationalistic rituals such as displaying flags and reciting the "Pledge of Allegiance" in classrooms distinguish American schools from those in most other countries. Needs of
the
individual
and of
society

Conceptions of uniform versus differential grouping. One of the controversies that most consistently divides educational theorists is whether students should be clustered together with similar students for instruction or whether

Means of
segregat-
ing
students

instructional groups should be made deliberately diverse. The criteria that are employed for differentiating students are manifold. They include chronological age, mental age, IQ, skin colour, sex, social class, geographical location, parental income, performance ability on various tests, and so on. Some of these criteria, such as skin colour, are used "officially" in some countries, such as South Africa, and "unofficially" in others, such as the United States. Other criteria, such as parental income, are used overtly in some schools (expensive, private schools) and covertly in others (public schools located in expensive suburbs). Some criteria, such as mental age, IQ, and performance ability, often have the effect of separating rich from poor or elites from cultural minorities because of the cultural content of the tests used. The customary arguments used in favour of homogeneous grouping tend to emphasize speed and efficiency in instruction and learning. Arguments in favour of heterogeneous grouping tend to emphasize social outcomes, such as an enhanced understanding of others and tolerance of diversity.

Conceptions of control and discipline. When education is viewed as a transaction between superior (the teacher) and inferior (the student), questions of control invariably arise; *e.g.,* can students be relied upon to do what is best if they are not controlled by teachers? Answers to this question refer back to assumptions about the nature of man as learner. Those theorists who tend to see man as basically untrustworthy will tend to find justification for a regimen of strict control over students, in order to prevent their natural impulses from harming themselves and others. Theorists who view man as basically trustworthy will tend to justify more lenient, loose, and permissive systems of control. Most theorists would agree that an important goal of discipline would be for the student to develop self-discipline. But disagreement arises over whether one best learns self-discipline through practice in obeying others or through practice in commanding oneself.

Conceptions of the need for competition and collaboration. In most cultures of the world, children from an early age seek to compete against and to surpass their fellows. Whether this competitive spirit is innate or whether it is acquired through the culture is at present unverifiable. The question that divides education theorists, however, is whether these existing competitive strivings should be encouraged or reduced. Some argue that, since competition is endemic in the culture and since schooling should assimilate the child to the culture, the school should encourage individual competition and help children to develop the strengths necessary to compete successfully. On the other hand, others argue that competitiveness in the culture is pernicious and that schooling should not serve to adjust children to harmful aspects of the culture but should foster cultural progress. Usually, the school is in conflict over these two attitudes and gives mixed messages to students. As a result, the students often suffer the double strain of trying to compete successfully but to do so without appearing to compete.

Conflict
of aims in
school

Conceptions of the boundaries of formal education. Considerable disagreement exists over what should legitimately be studied in formal institutions of learning. Usually some topics or subjects are considered taboo. These taboos may come about through interpretations of the law, as in the case of the exclusion of religious teaching from public schools in the United States. Or they may come about as a result of pressure from interest groups, as in the attempts to exclude sex education, teaching about Communism, and sensitivity training from American schools. The major considerations are that young children are not well equipped to resist heavy bias in teaching and that they are usually compelled by law to attend school and thus constitute a captive audience. It is sometimes argued, therefore, that they should be protected against religious and political propaganda and against material or experiences that require greater maturity to be handled creatively. On the other side, the danger in such arguments is that they can be used to keep all controversy out of schools and to render them places characterized by dull uniformity of thought.

(Pa.N.)

BIBLIOGRAPHY

Philosophy of science: ERNEST NAGEL, *The Structure of Science* (1961); and M.W. WARTOFSKY, *Conceptual Foundations of Scientific Thought* (1968), together cover the main approaches to the philosophy of science as a general field of study; whereas ARTHUR DANTO and SIDNEY MORGENBESSER (eds.), *Philosophy of Science* (1962), provides a useful anthology of classic papers on the subject; and SAMUEL B. RAPPORT and HELEN WRIGHT (eds.), *Science: Method and Meaning* (1964), is a stimulating anthology of nontechnical papers. W.V. QUINE, *Theories and Things* (1981), is a collection of papers by an eminent philosopher, on topics of ontology, logic, semantics, epistemology, philosophy of mathematics, identity, existence, etc.; W.H. NEWTON-SMITH, *The Rationality of Science* (1981), is an analysis of interpretations of science; V.V. NALIMOV, *Faces of Science* (1981), is a collection of essays on the nature of science, which originally were published in Soviet philosophical journals; LOREN R. GRAHAM, *Between Science and Values* (1981), is an examination of the relationship of science to values; JEREMY CAMPBELL, *Grammatical Man: Information, Entropy, Language, and Life* (1982), is a study of philosophical aspects of information theory.

The origins and development of natural science and the attitudes of philosophers toward scientific explanation in antiquity and the Middle Ages are well treated in SAMUEL SAMBURSKY, *The Physical World of the Greeks,* 2nd ed. (1962; orig. pub. in Hebrew, 1954); and *The Physical World of Late Antiquity* (1962); JOHN H. RANDALL, JR., *Aristotle* (1960); and in ALISTAIR C. CROMBIE, *Medieval and Early Modern Science,* 2nd ed., 2 vol. (1963). For the 17th and 18th centuries, see EDWIN A. BURTT, *The Metaphysical Foundations of Modern Physical Science,* 2nd ed. (1932); ALEXANDRE KOYRE, *Newtonian Studies* (1965); HERBERT BUTTERFIELD, *The Origins of Modern Science: 1300–1800,* rev. ed. (1965); I. BERNARD COHEN, *Franklin and Newton* (1956); and GOTTFRIED MARTIN, *Immanuel Kant: Ontologie und Wissenschaftstheorie* (1951; Eng. trans., *Kant's Metaphysics and Theory of Science,* 1955). For the 19th century, the most significant contributions have come from scientists writing as philosophers: CLAUDE BERNARD, *Introduction à l'étude de la médecine expérimentale* (1865; Eng. trans., *An Introduction to the Study of Experimental Medicine,* 1927, reprinted 1961); HERMANN VON HELMHOLTZ, *Popular Scientific Lectures* (1962; reprint of a selection of lectures from *Popular Lectures on Scientific Subjects,* 1st and 2nd series, 1881); T.H. HUXLEY, *Science and Culture, and Other Essays* (1882); and WILLIAM WHEWELL, *The Philosophy of the Inductive Sciences, Founded upon Their History,* 2nd ed. (1847, reprinted 1966). RYAN D. TWENEY, MICHAEL E. DOHERTY, and CLIFFORD R. MYNATT (eds.), *On Scientific Thinking* (1981), consists of selections from the writings of Bacon, Newton, Descartes, Darwin, and Einstein; EDWARD GRANT, *Much Ado About Nothing: Theories of Space and Vacuum from the Middle Ages to the Scientific Revolution* (1981), is a study of the origins of modern science and scientific thinking; MORRIS BERMAN, *The Reenchantment of the World* (1981), is a controversial analysis of scientific tradition with alternative suggestions for understanding the modern world.

The background to the 20th-century debate in the philosophy of science, as it developed between 1890 and 1920, can be reconstructed from ERNST MACH, *Die Mechanik in ihrer Entwicklung historisch-kritisch Dargestellt,* 9th ed. (1933; Eng. trans., *The Science of Mechanics,* 1960); and *Die Analyse der Empfindungen und das Verhältnis des Physischen zum Psychischen,* 5th ed. (1906; Eng. trans., *The Analysis of Sensations and the Relation of the Physical to the Psychical,* 1959); KARL PEARSON, *The Grammar of Science,* 3rd ed. (1960); PIERRE DUHEM, *La Théorie physique: son objet et sa structure* (1906; Eng. trans., *The Aim and Structure of Physical Theory,* 1954); HENRI POINCARE, *La Science et l'hypothèse* (1903; Eng. trans., *Science and Hypothesis,* 1905); and HEINRICH HERTZ, *Die Prinzipien der Mechanik* (1895; Eng. trans., *The Principles of Mechanics,* 1889, reprinted 1956), especially the Introduction. The subsequent course of the debate, between 1920 and 1960, is illustrated in CARL G. HEMPEL, *Aspects of Scientific Explanation, and Other Essays in the Philosophy of Science* (1965); RUDOLF CARNAP, *Logical Foundations of Probability,* 2nd ed. (1962); KARL R. POPPER, *Logik der Forschung* (1935; 2nd ed., 1966; Eng. trans., *The Logic of Scientific Discovery,* 1959); ROBIN G. COLLINGWOOD, *An Essay on Metaphysics* (1940); NORMAN R. CAMPBELL, *What Is Science?* (1921); and WILLIAM H. WATSON, *On Understanding Physics* (1959). Two significant side-views of the debate from very different formal standpoints may be found in WILLIAM V. QUINE, *From a Logical Point of View,* 2nd ed. rev. (1961); and RONALD A. FISHER, *Statistical Methods for Research Workers,* 14th ed. (1970). PETER ACHINSTEIN and STEPHEN F. BARKER (eds.), *The Legacy of Logical Positivism* (1969), is a first attempt at an historical appraisal of the period. PAUL K. FEYERABEND, *Philosophical Papers,* 2 vol. (1981), is a brilliant examination of historical and philosophical evidence of rationality of science; RICHARD L. GREGORY, *Mind in Science:*

A History of Explanations in Psychology and Physics (1981), is a study of philosophical ideas generated in different historical periods; MANFRED EIGEN and RUTHILD WINKLER, *Laws of the Game: How the Principles of Nature Govern Chance* (1981; trans. from the German), is a discussion of scientific topics from evolution to information theory; LIEBE F. CAVALIERI, *The Double-Edged Helix: Science in the Real World* (1981), deals with sociophilosophical traits of science and technology.

The current debates about conceptual change and the rationale of discovery in science are central topics in KARL R. POPPER, *Conjectures and Refutations,* 2nd rev. ed. (1965); NORWOOD R. HANSON, *Patterns of Discovery* (1958); STEPHEN TOULMIN, *Human Understanding,* vol. 1 (1972); THOMAS S. KUHN, *The Structure of Scientific Revolutions,* 2nd ed. rev. (1970); IMRE LAKATOS and ALAN MUSGRAVE, *Criticism and the Growth of Knowledge* (1970); and MICHAEL POLANYI, *Personal Knowledge* (1958). For broader cultural aspects of the contemporary debate about science, see C.H. WADDINGTON, *The Scientific Attitude,* new ed. (1968); JACOB BRONOWSKI, *Science and Human Values,* rev. ed. (1965); THEODORE ROSZAK, *The Making of a Counter Culture* (1969); and LEWIS MUMFORD, *The Myth of the Machine* (1967). See also PETER B. MEDAWAR, *Pluto's Republic* (1982), a discussion of the relationship between scientists and society; JOHN W. HARRINGTON, *Dance of the Continents* (1983), an explanation of the processes of interpretive scientific thinking; HANS-GEORG GADAMER, *Reason in the Age of Science* (1982; trans. from the German), a collection of essays on hermeneutic philosophy; FRITJOF CAPRA, *The Turning Point: Science, Society, and the Rising Culture* (1982), suggesting a new vision of scientific reality; RICHARD HEALEY (ed.), *Reduction, Time, and Reality: Studies in the Philosophy of the Natural Sciences* (1981), a collection of articles by eminent philosophers; and PETER SMITH, *Realism and the Progress of Science* (1982), examining philosophical foundations of the progress of science.

Philosophy of physics: R. HARRE, "Philosophical Aspects of Cosmology," and W. DAVIDSON, "Philosophical Aspects of Cosmology," *Br. J. Phil. Sci.,* 13:104–119, 120–129 (1962); OTHMAR SPANN, *Naturphilosophie,* 2nd ed. (1963); IVOR LECLERC, *The Nature of Physical Existence* (1972); PASCUAL JORDAN, *Albert Einstein: Sein Lebenswerk und die Zukunft der Physik* (1969), and *Atom und Weltall: Einführung in den Gedankeninhalt der modernen Physik,* 2nd ed. (1960); E.T. WHITTAKER, *From Euclid to Eddington: A Study of Conceptions of the External World* (1949); JACQUES MERLEAU-PONTY and BRUNO MORANDO, *Les Trois Étapes de la cosmologie* (1971; Eng. trans., *The Rebirth of Cosmology,* 1975); LOUIS DE BROGLIE, *La Physique nouvelle et les quanta* (1937; Eng. trans., *The Revolution in Physics,* 1953, reprinted 1969); R.G. COLLINGWOOD, *The Idea of Nature* (1945, reprinted 1960); P.K. FEYERABEND, "Philosophie de la nature," in M.F. SCIACCA (ed.), *Les Grands Courants de la pensée mondiale contemporaine,* part. 2, vol. 2, pp. 901–927 (1961); ERROL E. HARRIS, *The Foundations of Metaphysics in Science* (1965); JAGJIT SINGH, *Great Ideas and Theories of Modern Cosmology,* rev. and enlarged ed. (1970); P.A. SCHILPP (ed.), *Albert Einstein: Philosopher–Scientist,* 2 vol. (1959); PHILIPP FRANK, *Philosophy of Science* (1957); ALFRED NORTH WHITEHEAD, *Process and Reality* (1929, corrected ed. 1978), and *The Concept of Nature* (1920, reprinted 1964); MARY B. HESSE, *Forces and Fields* (1961); CARL FRIEDRICH VON WEIZSAECKER, *Zum Weltbild der Physik,* 12th ed. (1976); ADOLPH GRUENBAUM, *Philosophical Problems of Space and Time,* 2nd enlarged ed. (1973); WERNER HEISENBERG, *Physics and Philosophy* (1958); A.S. EDDINGTON, *The Nature of the Physical World* (1928, reprinted 1958); HENRI POINCARE, *La Science et l'hypothèse* (1903; Eng. trans., *Science and Hypothesis,* 1905); HENRY MARGENAU, *The Nature of Physical Reality* (1950, reprinted 1977), and *Physics and Philosophy* (1978). KARL R. POPPER, *Realism and the Aim of Science* (1983), *The Open Universe: An Argument for Indeterminism* (1982), and *Quantum Theory and the Schism in Physics* (1982), comprise the work of one of the greatest philosophers of the 20th century, who challenges most of the traditional assumptions in modern physics; JEREMY BERNSTEIN, *Science Observed: Essays of My Mind* (1982), is a collection of essays on the process of science; ROGER S. JONES, *Physics as Metaphor* (1982) is an original personal commentary on the nature of physical science; HEINZ R. PAGELS, *The Cosmic Code: Quantum Physics as the Language of Nature* (1982), is a very up-to-date review of modern physics; see also FRITJOF CAPRA, *The Tao of Physics: An Exploration of the Parallels Between Modern Physics and Eastern Mysticism,* 2nd rev. ed. (1983); BENJAMIN GAL-OR, *Cosmology, Physics, and Philosophy* (1983); EDWARD M. MacKINNON, *Scientific Explanation and Atomic Physics* (1982); and P.C.W. DAVIES, *The Accidental Universe* (1982).

Philosophy of biology: FRANCISCO JOSC AYALA and THEODOSIUS DOBZHANSKY (eds.), *Studies in the Philosophy of Biology: Reduction and Related Problems* (1974), a collection of conference papers that discuss definitions and the implications of reductionism; M.O. BECKNER, "Biology," in *The Encyclopedia of Philosophy,* vol. 1, pp. 310–318 (1967), an excellent review of some of the basic philosophical problems in biology; LUDWIG VON BERTALANFFY, *General System Theory* (1968), an attempt to unify the disparate aspects of biology and formulate general principles; BARRY COMMONER, "In Defense of Biology," *Science,* 133:1745–1748 (1961), an argument for the autonomy of biology decrying the emphasis on molecular biology to the neglect of general biology; FRANCIS CRICK, *Of Molecules and Men* (1966), a work that expresses the attitudes and positions taken by many molecular biologists in defense of reductionism; W.M. ELSASSER, *The Chief Abstractions of Biology* (1975), a refutation of reductionist analysis in the life sciences; A.G.N. FLEW, *Evolutionary Ethics* (1967), a significant attempt to relate evolutionary theory to ethics. T.A. GOUDGE, *The Ascent of Life* (1961), a work devoted solely to philosophical problems of evolutionary theory; MARJORIE GRENE, *Approaches to a Philosophical Biology* (1968), a review of the European viewpoints on the philosophy of nature (*Naturphilosophie*); THOMAS H. and JULIAN HUXLEY, *Touchstone for Ethics, 1893–1943* (British title, *Evolution and Ethics, 1893–1943;* 1947, reprinted 1969), opposing views on the same theme by two famous biologists; HANS JONAS, *The Phenomenon of Life: Toward a Philosophical Biology* (1966, reprinted 1979), a collection of essays presenting an existential interpretation of biology in the tradition of *Naturphilosophie;* JACQUES MONOD, *Le Hasard et la nécessité: essai sur la philosophie naturelle de la biologie moderne* (1970; Eng. trans., *Chance and Necessity: An Essay on the Natural Philosophy of Modern Biology,* 1971), a significant addition to the biological literature by a Nobel Prize-winning biologist; ASHLEY MONTAGU (ed.), *Man and Aggression,* 2nd ed. (1973), a collection of essays and reviews critical of the notion of innate aggressiveness as expounded by Konrad Lorenz and Robert Ardrey; RONALD MUNSON (ed.), *Man and Nature: Philosophical Issues in Biology* (1971), a collection of writings that provides an excellent introduction to current thinking in biophilosophy, with incisive commentary by the editor; JEAN PIAGET, *Biologie et connaissance* (1967; Eng. trans., *Biology and Knowledge,* 1971), concerned primarily with the evolution of mental faculties; V.R. POTTER, *Bioethics* (1971), a collection of articles dealing with the influence of biology on practical moral problems. BERNHARD RENSCH, *Biophilosophie auf erkenntnistheoretischer Grundlage* (1968; Eng. trans., *Biophilosophy,* 1971), a work emphasizing the rise and nature of consciousness within the framework of the evolutionary process; MICHAEL A. SIMON, *The Matter of Life* (1971), a good review of the current approaches to the philosophy of biology; GEORGE GAYLORD SIMPSON, *This View of Life: The World of an Evolutionist* (1964), a collection of essays by a renowned scholar, some of which have shaped the direction of philosophical biology today, and the especially pertinent chapter, "Man's Place in Nature," in his *Meaning of Evolution,* pp. 281–294, rev. ed. (1967); PIERRE TEILHARD DE CHARDIN, *Le Phénomène humain* (1956; Eng. trans., *The Phenomenon of Man,* 1959), a controversial attempt to meld science and religion by presenting a mystical viewpoint of cosmic evolution; C.H. WADDINGTON, *The Ethical Animal* (1960), a defense of the claim that biological facts can provide grounds for moral principles. STEVEN ROSE (ed.), *Against Biological Determinism* (1982) and *Towards a Liberatory Biology* (1982), are two volumes of essays collected by the DIALECTICS OF BIOLOGY GROUP, based on proceedings of meetings of philosophers and biologists and exploring alternatives in modern life science; CHARLES BIRCH and JOHN B. COBB, *The Liberation of Life: From the Cell to the Community* (1982), is a survey of philosophical interpretations of problems of ecology; JOHN C. GREENE, *Science, Ideology, and World View: Essays in the History of Evolutionary Ideas* (1981), is a discussion of the role of philosophy of evolution in Western intellectual history; C. LEON HARRIS, *Evolution: Genesis and Revelations: With Reading from Empodocles and Wilson* (1981), is a survey of the history of evolutionary thought; and U.J. JENSEN and R. HARRÉ (eds.), *The Philosophy of Evolution* (1981), is a collection of essays on evolutionary concepts in different fields; see also ERNST MAYR, *The Growth of Biological Thought: Diversity, Evolution, and Inheritance* (1982).

Philosophy of history: ROBIN G. COLLINGWOOD, *The Idea of History* (1946), a classical contribution to the critical theory of history; KARL R. POPPER, *The Poverty of Historicism* (1957), an influential critique of types of historical speculation; WILLIAM H. WALSH, *An Introduction to Philosophy of History* (1951), a lucid, general account; PATRICK L. GARDINER, *The Nature of Historical Explanation,* 3rd ed. (1967); WILLIAM H. DRAY, *Laws and Explanation in History* (1957); PETER WINCH, *The Idea of a Social Science and Its Relation to Philosophy* (1958); and MORTON G. WHITE, *Foundations of Historical Knowledge* (1965), four analytical discussions relating to historical knowledge and understanding; FRANK E. MANUEL, *Shapes of Philosophical History* (1965), a brief but reliable survey of the development of speculative theories. WILLIAM DRAY, *Perspectives in History* (1980), is an explorative collection of essays on particular theorists of history by a prominent contemporary philosopher; ANTHONY GIDDENS, *A Contemporary Critique of Historical Materialism: Power, Property, and the State* (1982), is a work by a leading British sociologist in which he offers an alternative interpretation of history based upon contemporary anthropological research; HILARY PUTNAM, *Reason, Truth and History* (1981), is a discussion of the nature of truth, knowledge, and order, especially the dichotomy between objective and subjective views of truth; LAWRENCE STONE, *The Past and the Present* (1981), is an examination of historiographic methodology; JOHN W. MILLER, *The Philosophy of History with Reflections and Aphorisms* (1981), is an original personal reflection on history as a human science; see also discussions of special issues in MARK BLITZ, *Heidegger's Being and Time and the Possibility of Political Philosophy* (1981); ALFRED SCHMIDT, *History and Structure: An Essay on Hegelian-Marxist and Structuralist Theories of History* (1982; originally published in German, 1971); EDMUND E. JACOBITTI, *Revolutionary Humanism and Historicism in Modern Italy* (1981); EUGENE WEBB, *Eric Voegelin: Philosopher of History* (1981).

Philosophy of religion: General introductions include H.D. LEWIS, *Philosophy of Religion* ("Teach Yourself Book") (1965); and J. HICK, *Philosophy of Religion* (1963). Introductory books that range over a somewhat narrower field include J.L. GOODALL, *An Introduction to the Philosophy of Religion* (1966); I.T. RAMSEY, *Religious Language* (1957 and 1963); and THOMAS FAWCETT, *The Symbolic Language of Religion* (1971). NINIAN SMART, *Philosophers and Religious Truth,* 2nd ed. (1969), centres discussion of some salient issues around particular philosophers. NINIAN SMART, *The Religious Experience of Mankind* (1969); and EDWARD GEOFFREY PARRINDER, *Comparative Religion* (1962), provide general introductions to the comparative study of religions. In *World Religions* (1966), H.D. LEWIS and R.L. SLATER consider issues in the world religions that are highlighted by contemporary approaches in the philosophy of religion and the comparative study of religions respectively. In the psychology of religion, the classic work of WILLIAM JAMES, *The Varieties of Religious Experience* (1902, reprinted 1952), is probably still the best introduction that might then be followed by a comprehensive survey of the contemporary field, such as L.W. GRENSTED, *The Psychology of Religion* (1952). Most of these books contain excellent bibliographies for further reading. NINIAN SMART, *Historical Selections in the Philosophy of Religion* (1962); and I.T. RAMSEY, *Words About God* (1971), are useful sourcebooks for some classic discussions of topics in the philosophy of religion; an excellent survey of recent thought is given in JOHN MACQUARRIE, *Twentieth-Century Religious Thought: The Frontiers of Philosophy and Theology, 1900–1960* (1963). F.R. TENNANT, *Philosophical Theology,* 2 vol. (1928–30); H.H. FARMER, *The World and God: A Study of Prayer, Providence and Miracle in Christian Experience* (1935); and H.D. LEWIS, *Our Experience of God* (1959), represent different general treatments of the subject. WILFRED C. SMITH, *Towards a World Theology: Faith and the Comparative History of Religion* (1980), is an introduction to analysis of the interrelationship of various religious traditions; JOHN B. COBB and W. WIDICK SCHROEDER (eds.), *Process Philosophy and Social Thought* (1981), is a collection of essays on reshaping of social and political thinking; MICHAEL D. CLARK, *Worldly Theologians: The Persistence of Religion in Nineteenth Century American Thought* (1981), is an examination of the relationship between religion and secular thought; SEYYED HOSSEIN NASR, *Knowledge and the Sacred* (1982), is an exposition of neo-traditionalism in philosophy and religion; FREDERICK COPLESTON, *Religion and the One: Philosophies East and West* (1982), is a comparison of various world philosophies in their treatment of human religious experience. For discussion of particular religious philosophers see TERENCE J. GERMAN, *Hamann on Language and Religion* (1982), ROBERT J. VANDEN BURGT, *The Religious Philosophy of William James* (1981); HENRY S. LEVINSON, *The Religious Investigations of William James* (1981); JEFFREY STOUT, *The Flight from Authority: Religion, Morality, and the Quest for Autonomy* (1981).

Books dealing with specific problems of religious belief are: PETER R. BAELZ, *Prayer and Providence* (1968); J. HICK, *Evil and the God of Love* (1966); A. FARRER, *Love Almighty and Ills Unlimited* (1966); I.T. RAMSEY, *The Problem of Evil* (1972); W.T. STACE, *Mysticism and Philosophy* (1960); JOHN HICK, *God Has Many Names* (1982); LESZEK KOLAKOWSKI, *Religion: If There Is No God: On God, the Devil, Sin, and Other Worries of the So-Called Philosophy of Religion* (1982); HARRY J. AUSMUS, *The Polite Escape: On the Myth of Secularization* (1982); and CHARLES F. KEYES and E. VALENTINE DANIEL (eds.), *Karma: An Anthropological Inquiry* (1983).

Philosophy of art: PAUL ZIFF, "The Task of Defining a Work of Art," *Phil. Rev.,* 62:58–78 (1953); DEWITT PARKER, *The*

Analysis of Art (1926); SUSANNE K. LANGER, *Feeling and Form* (1953); JOHN DEWEY, *Art As Experience* (1934); WARREN E. STEINKRAUS, *Philosophy of Art,* rev. ed. (1984); V.A. HOWARD, *Artistry: The Work of Artists* (1982); R.A. SHARPE, *Contemporary Aesthetics: A Philosophical Analysis* (1983); PATRICIA H. WERHANE (ed.), *Philosophical Issues in Art* (1984); and HAROLD ROSENBERG, *The De-definition of Art* (1983).

For a discussion of intention in art interpretation see first the classic attack on intention by WILLIAM K. WIMSATT and MONROE C. BEARDSLEY, "The Intentional Fallacy," in *The Verbal Icon* (1954); for an opposed view see LESLIE A. FIEDLER, "Archetype and Signature: A Study of the Relationship Between Biography and Poetry," *Sewanee Rev.,* 60: 253–273 (1952); and HENRY D. AIKEN, "The Aesthetic Relevance of the Artist's Intentions," *J. Phil.,* 52:742–753 (1955). Classic sources on art as imitation (representation) are ARISTOTLE, *Poetics,* and LONGINUS, *On the Sublime.* Recent works include WALTER ABELL, *Representation and Form* (1936), particularly in visual art; THEODORE M. GREENE, *The Arts and the Art of Criticism* (1940); and STEPHEN C. PEPPER, *The Work of Art* (1955). See also RICHARD KUHNS, *Psychoanalytic Theory of Art: A Philosophy of Art on Developmental Principles* (1983); and HOWARD J. SMAGULA, *Currents, Contemporary Directions in the Visual Arts* (1983).

A classic source on art as expression is LEO TOLSTOY's *What Is Art?* (1898; Aylmer Maude translation in "Oxford World's Classic Library," 1930, reprinted 1960); defense of forms of expression theory are ROBIN G. COLLINGWOOD, *The Principles of Art* (1938); and CURT J. DUCASSE, *The Philosophy of Art,* rev. ed. (1966). An anthology of readings on artistic expression is JOHN HOSPERS (ed.), *Artistic Expression* (1971). Later monographs include R.L. HELD, *Endless Innovations: Frederick Kiesler's Theory and Scenic Design* (1982); and MARCIA MUELDER EATON, *Art and Nonart* (1983).

For a defense of art as form, see CLIVE BELL, *Art* (1914, reprinted 1958); ROGER FRY, *Transformations* (1927); EDUARD HANSLICK, *Vom Musikalisch-Schönen,* 7th ed. rev. (1885; Eng. trans., *The Beautiful in Music,* 1891, reprinted 1957). Moral and societal aspects of the subject are treated in GEORGE SANTAYANA, *Reason in Art* (1910). ROGER TAYLOR, *Beyond Art: What Art Is and Might Become If Freed from Cultural Elitism* (1981), is a discussion of art as an integral part of life; ARTHUR C. DANTO, *The Transfiguration of the Commonplace: A Philosophy of Art* (1981), is an examination of the relationship between philosophy and art, and of the distinction between art works and commonplace objects. DENNIS DUTTON (ed.), *The Forger's Art: Forgery and the Philosophy of Art* (1983), is a collection of original essays on this special topic.

Histories of the subject include ALBERT HOFSTADTER and RICHARD KUHNS (eds.), *Philosophies of Art and Beauty* (1964); ALEXANDER SESONSKE (ed.), *What Is Art?* (1965); and MONROE C. BEARDSLEY, *Aesthetics from Classical Greece to the Present* (1966). See also EUGENIO TRÍAS, *The Artist and the City* (1982; originally published in Spanish, 1976); MICHAEL F. PALMER, *Paul Tillich's Philosophy of Art* (1984); MIKEL DUFRENNE, *Main Trends in Aesthetics and the Science of Art* (1979); and STEPHEN DAVID ROSS (ed.), *Art and Its Significance: An Anthology of Aesthetic Theory* (1984).

Philosophy of logic: W.V. QUINE, *Philosophy of Logic* (1970), is the best compact introductory exposition. HILARY PUTNAM, *Philosophy of Logic* (1971), is useful as a complement to Quine. Much of the important recent literature, however, is in the form of brief papers rather than monographs. The most successful anthologies of such papers are perhaps L.W. SUMNER and JOHN WOODS (eds.), *Necessary Truth* (1969), on logical truth and analyticity; and LEONARD LINSKY (ed.), *Reference and Modality* (1971), on modal concepts and intensional logic. RAYMOND KLIBANSKY (ed.), *Contemporary Philosophy,* vol. 1 (1968), contains several survey articles covering thoroughly the whole field. Still central are the classical writings of the great modern philosophers of logic: PETER GEACH and MAX BLACK (eds.), *Translations from the Philosophical writings of Gottlob Frege,* 2nd ed. (1960); BERTRAND RUSSELL, *Logic and Knowledge* (1956); LUDWIG WITTGENSTEIN, *Tractatus logicophilosophicus* (Eng. trans., 1922) and *Philosophical Investigations* (Eng. trans., 1953); ALFRED TARSKI, *Logic, Semantics, and Metamathematics* (1956); and RUDOLF CARNAP, *Meaning and Necessity* (1947). The period 1879–1931 is also covered in a magnificent volume by JEAN VAN HEIJENOORT (ed.), *From Frege to Gödel: A Source Book in Mathematical Logic, 1879–1931* (1967), which contains valuable introductions to the different selections and comments on them. Of recent literature, especially noteworthy are the writings of Strawson and Quine: P.F. STRAWSON, *Logico-Linguistic Papers* (1971); W.V. QUINE, *From a Logical Point of View* (1953), *Word and Object* (1960), and *Ontological Relativity and Other Essays* (1969). Quine's ideas are discussed critically in DONALD DAVIDSON and JAAKKO HINTIKKA (eds.), *Words and Objections* (1969). A broad spectrum of new work on the borderline of philosophical logic and linguistics is represented in DONALD DAVIDSON and GILBERT HARMAN (eds.), *Semantics of Natural Language* (1972). Several problems mentioned above are discussed in JAAKKO HINTIKKA, *Logic, Language-Games, and Information* (1972); and in J.W. DAVIS, D.J. HOCKNEY, and W.K. WILSON (eds.), *Philosophical Logic* (1969). Later monographs include JOHN MARENBON, *From the Circle of Alcuin to the School of Auxerre: Logic, Theology, and Philosophy in the Early Middle Ages* (1981), an examination of the progress of medieval philosophical logic; RUDY RUCKER, *Infinity and the Mind: The Science and Philosophy of the Infinite* (1982), a book on the interface of philosophy and computer science; GEORGE BEALER, *Quality and Concept* (1982), an appraisal of elementary symbolic logic; and OSWALD HANFLING, *Logical Positivism* (1981), a treatment of the philosophical movement.

Philosophy of law: Leading treatises in English include A. ROSS, *Om ret og retfaerdighed* (1953; Eng. trans., *On Law and Justice*, 1958); W. FRIEDMANN, *Legal Theory*, 5th ed. (1967); H. KELSEN, *General Theory of Law and State* (1945); G.W. PATON, *A Text-Book of Jurisprudence*, 3rd ed. by D.P. DERHAM (1964); R. POUND, *Jurisprudence*, 5 vol. (1959); J. STONE, *Legal System and Lawyers' Reasonings* (1964); *Human Law and Human Justice* (1965); *Social Dimensions of Law and Justice* (1966); LEV S. JAWITSCH, *The General Theory of Law: Social and Philosophical Problems* (1981; trans. from the Russian); ROBERT S. SUMMERS, *Instrumentalism and ──── Legal Theory* (1982).

...s an analysis of the

...phy of law include

...(1950–54); A. VER-

...2nd ed. (1963); R.

...e (1971); G. FASSO,

...66–68; 2nd ed., vol.

...*Ideology in Hume's*

...e survey of Hume's

...r, and government,

...*Analytical jurispru-*

...*nce* (1832); H.L.A.

...IFELD, *Fundamen-*

...*Reasoning* (1923);

...; Eng. trans., *Pure*

...*Relations*, 2nd ed.

...*gal Logic* (1969).

...*f Justice* (1958); J.

...*Morals and Legis-*

...*Justice* (1967); H.

...*N, Justice* (1967);

...(ed.), *The Legal*

...). 47–226 (1950).

...*l jurisprudence*):

...IRLICH, *Grundle-*

...s., *Fundamental*

...FRIEDMAN and

...*ences* (1969); G.

GURVITCH, *Sociology of Law* (1942); K.N. LLEWELLYN, *Jurisprudence* (1962); H. MAINE, *Ancient Law* (1861); F. VON SAVIGNY, *Vom Beruf unsrer Zeit für Gesetzgebung und Rechtswissenschaft* (1830; Eng. trans., *Of the Vocation of Our Age for Legislation and Jurisprudence*, 1831); E.M. SCHUR, *Law and Society* (1968); J. STONE, *Law and the Social Sciences in the Second Half-Century* (1966). See also DONALD DAVIDSON, *Essays on Actions and Events* (1980); HANNU TAPANI KLAMI, *Anti-Legalism* (1980); M.A. STEWART (ed.), *Law, Morality, and Rights* (1983); JOHN D. HODSON, *The Ethics of Legal Coercion* (1983); ANTHONY ALLOTT, *The Limits of Law* (1980); B.R. KRISHNA IYER, *Law Versus Justice* (1981).

Philosophy of education: For an excellent example of the analytical approach to philosophy of education, see ISRAEL SCHEFFLER (ed.), *Philosophy and Education*, 2nd ed. (1966). A representative British example is P.H. HIRST and R.S. PETERS, *The Logic of Education* (1970). Several scholars have attempted to group philosophies of education into schools of thought. The best collections are JOHN PAUL STRAIN (comp.), *Modern Philosophies of Education* (1971); and THEODORE B.H. BRAMELD, *Patterns of Educational Philosophy: Divergence and Convergence in Culturological Perspective* (1971). For examples of attempts to focus on a single problem or issue and to combine clarity and commitment, see PAUL NASH, *Authority and Freedom in Education: An Introduction to the Philosophy of Education* (1966); KENNETH D. BENNE, *Education in the Quest for Identity and Community* (1962); and ROBERT ULICH, *The Human Career: A Philosophy of Self-Transcendence* (1955). A good collection of Existentialist statements on education may be found in MAXINE GREENE (comp.), *Existential Encounters for Teachers* (1967). For selections from the classics on conceptions of the educated person, see PAUL NASH (ed.), *Models of Man: Explorations in the Western Educational Tradition* (1968); and ROBERT ULICH (ed.), *Three Thousand Years of Educational Wisdom*, 2nd ed. enl. (1954). Original essays on all of these major figures may be found in PAUL NASH, ANDREAS M. KAZAMIAS, and HENRY J. PERKINSON (eds.), *The Educated Man: Studies in the History of Educational Thought* (1965). Contemporary problems are treated in BRENDA COHEN, *Education and the Individual* (1982), exploring the concept of freedom of education; MORTIMER J. ADLER, *The Paideia Proposal: An Educational Manifesto* (1982); HENRY A. GIROUX, *Ideology, Culture, and the Process of Schooling* (1981), espousing radical Marxist thought; LLOYD DUCK, *Teaching with Charisma* (1981), analyzing psychology of teaching behaviours; R.F. HOLLAND, *Against Empiricism: On Education, Epistemology, and Value* (1980), a collection of essays of broad concern; LAWRENCE KOHLBERG, *The Philosophy of Moral Development: Moral Stages and the Idea of Justice* (1981), stressing an interdisciplinary approach in education; MICHAEL R. MATTHEWS, *The Marxist Theory of Schooling: A Study of Epistemology and Education* (1981); and DAVID NYBERG, *Power Over Power: What Power Means in Ordinary Life, How It Is Related To Acting Freely, and What It Can Contribute to a Renovated Ethics of Education* (1981).

The History of Western Philosophy

This article has three basic purposes: (1) to provide an overview of the history of philosophy in the West; (2) to relate philosophical ideas and movements to their historical background and to the cultural history of their time; and (3) to trace the changing conception of the definition, the function, and the task of philosophy.

The article is divided into the following sections:

Nature of philosophy and the writing of its history

PHILOSOPHY IN THE WESTERN TRADITION

Various conceptions of what philosophy is

It is a paradox faced by all of those who attempt to write the history of philosophy that the "philosophy" whose history they write probably would not have been defined exactly alike by any two of the major figures whom they judge it fitting to include in their accounts. For throughout its long and varied history in the West, "philosophy" has meant many different things. Some of these have been a search for the wisdom of life (the meaning closest to the Greek words from which the term is derived); an attempt to understand the universe as a whole; an examination of man's moral responsibilities and social obligations; an effort to fathom the divine intentions and man's place with reference to them; an effort to ground the enterprise of natural science; a rigorous examination of the origin, extent, and validity of men's ideas; an exploration of the place of will or consciousness in the universe; an examination of the values of truth, goodness, and beauty; an effort to codify the rules of human thought in order to promote rationality and the extension of clear thinking. Even these do not exhaust the meanings that have been attached to the philosophical enterprise, but they give some idea of its extreme complexity and many-sidedness.

It is difficult to determine whether any common element can be found within this diversity and whether any core meaning can be discovered for philosophy that could serve as a universal and all-inclusive definition. But a first attempt in this direction might be to define philosophy either as "a reflection upon the varieties of human experience" or as "the rational, methodical, and systematic consideration of those topics that are of greatest concern to man." Vague and indefinite as such definitions are, they do suggest two important facts about philosophizing: (1) that it is a reflective, or meditative, activity and (2) that it has no explicitly designated subject matter of its own but is a method or type of mental operation (like science or like history) that can take any area or subject matter or type of experience as its object. Thus, although there are a few single-term divisions of philosophy of long standing—such as logic, ethics, epistemology (the theory of knowledge), or metaphysics (theory of the nature of Being)—its divisions are probably best expressed by phrases that contain the preposition "of"—such as philosophy of nature, philosophy of mind, philosophy of law, or philosophy of art.

Part of what makes it difficult to find a consensus among philosophers about the definition of their discipline is precisely that they have frequently come to it from different fields, with different interests and concerns, and that they therefore have different areas of experience upon which they find it especially necessary or meaningful to reflect. St. Thomas Aquinas (a Dominican friar of the 13th century), George Berkeley (a bishop of the Irish Church in the 18th century), and Søren Kierkegaard (a Danish divinity student in the 19th century) all saw philosophy as a means to assert the truths of religion and to dispel the Materialistic or Rationalistic errors that, in their opinion, had led to its decline. Pythagoras in ancient south Italy, René Descartes in the late Renaissance, and Bertrand Russell in the 20th century have been primarily mathematicians whose views of the universe and of human knowledge have been vastly influenced by the concept of number and by the method of deductive thinking. Some philosophers, such as Plato or the British philosophers Thomas Hobbes and John Stuart Mill, have been obsessed by problems of political arrangement and social living, so that whatever else they have done in philosophy has been stimulated by a desire to understand and, ultimately, to change the social and political behaviour of men. And still others—such as the Milesians (the first philosophers of Greece); Francis Bacon, an Elizabethan philosopher; and, in the 20th century, Alfred North Whitehead, a process metaphysician—have begun with an interest in the physical composition of the natural world, so that their philosophies resemble more closely the generalizations of physical science than those of religion or sociology.

The history of Western philosophy reveals in detail the concentrated activity of a multitude of serious and able men reflecting upon, reasoning about, and considering deeply the nature of their experience. But throughout this diversity certain characteristic oppositions habitually recur, such as the division between monists, dualists, and pluralists in metaphysics; between Materialists and Idealists in cosmological theory; between Nominalists and Realists in the theory of signification; between Rational-

Characteristic oppositions in philosophy

ists and Empiricists in the theory of knowledge; between Utilitarians, self-realizationists, and proponents of duty in moral theory; and between partisans of logic and partisans of emotion in the search for a responsible guide to the wisdom of life.

Many of these fundamental oppositions among philosophers will be treated in the article that follows. But if any single opposition is taken as central throughout the history of Western philosophy at every level and in every field, it is probably that between the critical and the speculative impulses. These two divergent motivations tend to express themselves in two divergent methods: that of analysis and that of synthesis. Plato's *Politeia* (*The Republic*) is an example of the second. The *Principia Ethica* (1903) of G.E. Moore, a founder of linguistic philosophy, is an example of the first. Beginning with a simple question about justice, *Politeia* in its discursiveness slowly but progressively brings more and more areas into the discussion: first ethics, then politics, then educational theory, then theory of knowledge, and finally metaphysics. Starting with one specific question, Plato finally managed to make his discussion as broad as the world. *Principia Ethica* does just the opposite. Beginning with a general question—What is good?—it progressively breaks up this question into a whole series of subordinate questions, analyzing meanings ever more minutely, growing narrower and narrower but always with the utmost modesty and sincerity, striving for increasing simplicity and exactitude.

The analytic, or critical, impulse treats any subject matter or topic by concentrating upon the part, by taking it apart in the service of clarity and precision. It was essentially the method of Aristotle and of Peter Abelard, a medieval Scholastic; of David Hume, a Scottish Skeptic, and of Rudolf Carnap, a 20th-century semantic Positivist; and of Russell and Moore. The synthetic, or speculative, impulse operates by seeking to comprehend the whole, by putting it all together in the service of unity and completeness. It is essentially the method of Parmenides, a Pre-Socratic monist, and of Plato; of St. Thomas and of Benedict de Spinoza, a modern Jewish Rationalist; of G.W.F. Hegel, a German Idealist, and of Whitehead. Throughout philosophy's history, each of the two traditions has made its insistent claim.

There is one philosophical tradition—that of Positivism—that sees philosophy as originating in the obscure mists of religion and coming finally to rest in the pure sunshine of scientific clarity. This represents a necessary progress, because Positivism considers it a scandal when philosophers speak a language that is not accessible to "verification"; it holds that bold and adventuresome philosophical speculation is at best mere self-indulgence, a passing state occurring when philosophical problems are raised prematurely—that is, at a time when philosophy does not possess the means to solve them.

Though Positivism represents a partisan view that it is not necessary to hold, it does express indirectly a basic truth—that the philosophical enterprise has always hovered uncertainly between the lure of religious seriousness and that of scientific exactitude. In the earliest philosophers of Greece it is impossible to separate ideas of divinity and the human soul from ideas about the mystery of being and the genesis of material change, and in the Middle Ages philosophy was acknowledged to be "the handmaiden of theology." But the increased secularization of modern culture has largely reversed this trend, and the Enlightenment emphasis upon the separation of nature from its divine creator has increasingly placed philosophical resources at the disposal of those interested in creating a philosophy of science.

Yet philosophy's continuing search for philosophical truth leads it to hope, but at the same time to profoundly doubt, that its problems are objectively solvable. With respect to a total description of Being or a definitive account of the nature of values, only individual solutions now seem possible; and the optimistic hope for objective answers that secure universal agreement must be given up.

In this respect, philosophy seems less like science than like art and the philosopher more like an artist than a scientist, for his philosophical solutions bear the stamp of his own personality, and his choice of arguments reveals as much about himself as his chosen problem. As a work of art is a portion of the world seen through a temperament, so a philosophical system is a vision of the world subjectively assembled. Plato and Descartes, Immanuel Kant, an 18th-century German Idealist, and John Dewey, a U.S. Pragmatist, have given to their systems many of the quaint trappings of their own personalities.

But if philosophy is not true in the same sense as science, it is not false in the same sense either; and this gives to the history of philosophy a living significance, which the history of science does not enjoy. In science, the present confronts the past as truth confronts error; thus, for science, the past, even when important at all, is important only out of historical interest. In philosophy it is different. Philosophical systems are never definitively proved false; they are simply discarded or put aside for future use. And this means that the history of philosophy consists not simply of dead museum pieces but of ever-living classics—comprising a permanent repository of ideas, doctrines, and arguments and a continuing source of philosophical inspiration and suggestiveness to those who philosophize in any succeeding age. It is for this reason that any attempt to separate philosophizing from the history of philosophy is both a provincial act and an unnecessary impoverishment of its rich natural resources.

GENERAL CONSIDERATIONS

The writing of the history of philosophy. The writing of the history of philosophy is itself controlled by a series of cultural habits or conventions.

Ways of ordering the history. The ensuing article on the history of Western philosophy is divided into three sections—ancient, medieval, and modern—and this division is so pervasive today that it is difficult to remember that the threefold distinction is only as old as the end of the 17th century. This distinction—first employed in the writing of European history proper by Georg Horn of Leiden in his *Arca Noae: Sive Historia Imperiorum et Regnorum a Condito Orbe ad Nostra Tempora* (1666; "Noah's Ark; or, The History of Empires and Kingdoms from the Beginning of the World to Our Times") and a generation later by Christophorus Cellarius, a German historian, in 1696— slowly spread to historical writing in all fields and was given definitive influence in philosophical writing through the series of lectures on *Philosophiegeschichte* ("History of Philosophy") that Hegel delivered first at Jena, then at Heidelberg, and finally at Berlin between 1805 and 1830. Since Hegel, it has been taken for granted as standard practice, although a host of cultural assumptions is implied by its use.

Treatment of the total field of the history of philosophy has been traditionally subject to two types of ordering, according to whether it was conceived (1) as primarily a history of ideas or (2) as a history of the intellectual products of men. In the first ordering, certain ideas, or concepts, are viewed as archetypal (such as matter or mind or doubt); and the condensations occurring within the flow of thought tend to consist of basic types or schools. This ordering has characterized such works as Friedrich Lange's *Geschichte des Materialismus . . .* (1866; *The History of Materialism*), A.C. Ewing's compilation *The Idealist Tradition: From Berkeley to Blanshard* (1957), or Richard H. Popkin's *History of Scepticism from Erasmus to Descartes* (1960). In the second type of ordering, the historian, impressed by the producers of ideas as much as by the ideas themselves—that is, with philosophers as agents—reviews the succession of great philosophical personalities in their rational achievement. This ordering has produced the more customary histories such as Émile Bréhier's *Histoire de la philosophie* (1926–32), Bertrand Russell's *History of Western Philosophy* (1945), and Karl Jaspers' *Die grossen Philosophen* (1957; *The Great Philosophers*).

These two different types of ordering depend for their validity upon an appeal to two different principles about the nature of ideas, but their incidental use may also be influenced by social or cultural factors. Thus the biographers and compilers of late antiquity (among them, Plutarch, Sextus Empiricus, Philostratus, and Clement of Alexandria), impressed by the religious pluralism of the age in which they lived, thought of philosophers, too, as falling into different sects and wrote histories of the Sophists, the Skeptics, the Epicureans, and other such schools; whereas almost 2,000 years later, Hegel—living in a period of Romantic historiography dominated by the concept of the great man in history—deliberately described the history of philosophy as "a succession of noble minds, a gallery of heroes of thought."

Moving between these two ordering principles, the article below will be eclectic (as has come to be the custom), devoting chief attention to outstanding major figures, while joining more minor figures, wherever possible, into the schools or tendencies that they exemplify.

Factors in writing the history of philosophy. The type of ordering suggested above also has some relationship to the more general problems of method in the writing of the history of philosophy. Here there are at least three factors that must be taken into account: (1) the historian must understand how (at least in part) any philosopher's doctrines depend upon those of his predecessors; (2) he must understand that a man's philosophy occurs at a certain point in history and, thus, how it expresses the effects of certain social and cultural circumstances; and (3) he must understand how in part it stems from the philosopher's own personality and situation in life. This is only to say that the history of philosophy, to be at all comprehensive and adequate, must deal with the mutual interplay of ideas, of cultural contexts, and of agents.

Logical, socio-logical, and individual factors

The first factor may be called logical because a given philosophy is, in part, the intellectual response to the doctrines of its forerunners, taking as central the problems given by the current climate of controversy. Thus, many of the details of Aristotle's ethical, political, and metaphysical systems arise in arguments directed against statements and principles of Plato; much of *An Essay Concerning Human Understanding* (1690) by John Locke, an initiator of the Enlightenment, is directed against current Cartesian presuppositions; and the *Nouveaux essais sur l'entendement humain* (1704; *New Essays Concerning Human Understanding*) by Gottfried Wilhelm Leibniz, a broadly learned Rationalist, is, in turn, specifically directed against Locke.

The second factor may be called sociological because it considers philosophy, at least in part, as a direct form of social expression, arising at a certain moment in history, dated and marked by the peculiar problems and crises of the society in which it flourishes. From this perspective, the philosophy of Plato may be viewed as the response of an aristocratic elitism to the immediate threat of democracy and the leveling of values in 5th-century Athens—its social theory and even its metaphysics servicing the thrust toward an aristocratic restoration in the Greek world. Thus, the philosophy of St. Thomas Aquinas may be viewed as an effort toward doctrinal clarification in support of the institution of the medieval Roman Church, as the saint spent his life obediently fulfilling the philosophical tasks set for him by his superiors in the church and the Dominican order. Thus, the philosophy of Kant, with all of its technical vocabulary and rigid systematization, may be viewed as an expression of the new professionalism in philosophy, a clear product of the rebirth of the German universities during the 18th-century Enlightenment.

The third factor may be called biographical, or individual, because, with Hegel, it recognizes that philosophies are generally produced by men of unusual or independent personality, whose systems usually bear the mark of their creators. And what is meant here by the individuality of the philosopher lies less in the facts of his biography (such as the wealth or poverty, the married state or bachelorhood that he shares with other men) than in the essential form and style of his philosophizing. The cool intensity of Spinoza's geometric search for wisdom, the unswerving (if opaque) discursiveness of Hegel's quest for completeness or totality, the relentless and minute analytic search for distinctions and shades of meaning that marks Moore's master passion ("to be accurate—to get everything exactly right"), these qualities mark the philosophical writings of Spinoza, Hegel, and Moore with an unmistakably individual and original character.

Shifts in the focus and concern of philosophy. Any adequate treatment of individual figures in the history of philosophy tries to utilize this threefold division of logical, sociological, and individual factors; but in a synoptic view of the history of philosophy in the West, one is particularly aware of the various shifts of focus and concern that philosophy has sustained and, indeed, of the often profound differences in the way that it defines itself or visualizes its task from age to age or from generation to generation.

Philosophy among the Greeks slowly emerged out of religious awe into wonder about the principles and elements of the natural world. But as the Greek populations more and more left the land to become concentrated in their cities, interest shifted from nature to social living; questions of law and convention and civic values became paramount. Cosmological speculation partly gave way to moral and political theorizing, and the preliminary and somewhat fragmentary questionings of Socrates and the Sophists turned into the great positive constructions of Plato and Aristotle. With the political and social fragmentation of the succeeding centuries, however, philosophizing once again shifted from the norm of civic involvement to problems of salvation and survival in a chaotic world.

Medieval and modern history

The dawn of Christianity brought to philosophy new tasks. Augustine, the philosophical bishop of Hippo, and the Church Fathers used such resources of the Greek tradition as remained (chiefly Platonism) to deal with problems of the creation, of faith and reason, and of truth. New translations in the 12th century made much of Aristotle's philosophy available and prepared the way for the great theological constructions of the 13th century, chiefly those of the Scholastic philosophers Bonaventure, Albertus Magnus, Thomas Aquinas, Roger Bacon, and Duns Scotus. The end of the Middle Ages saw a new flowering of the opposite tendencies in the Nominalist William of Ockham and the mystic Meister Eckehart.

The Middle Ages gave way to the Renaissance. Universalism was replaced by nationalism. Philosophy became secularized. The great new theme was that of the mystery and immensity of the natural world. The best philosophical minds of the 17th century turned to the task of exploring the foundations of physical science, and the symbol of their success—the great system of Newton's physics—turned the philosophers of the Enlightenment to epistemology and to the examination of the human mind that had produced so brilliant a scientific creation. The 19th century, a time of great philosophical diversity, discovered the irrational and in so doing prepared the way for the oppositions between Analysis and Phenomenology and between Positivism and Existentialism that characterize 20th-century philosophy.

Although the foregoing capsule presentation of the history of philosophy in the West follows a strict chronology, it does not do justice to the constant occurrence and recurrence of dominant strands in the history of thought. It would also be possible to write the philosophical history of the Middle Ages simply by noting the complicated occurrence of Platonic and Aristotelian doctrines, of the Renaissance according to the reappearance of Greek Materialism, Stoicism, and Skepticism, and of the 18th century in terms of the competing claims of Rationalist and Empiricist principles. Thus, chronology and the interweaving of philosophical systems cooperate in a history of philosophy. (A.W.L.)

Ancient Greek and Roman philosophy

THE PRE-SOCRATIC PHILOSOPHERS

Cosmology and the metaphysic of matter. Because the earliest Greek philosophers focused their attention upon the origin and nature of the physical world, they are often called cosmologists or naturalists. Though monistic views (which trace the origins of the world to a single substance) prevailed at first, they were soon followed by several pluralistic theories (which trace it to several ultimate substances).

Monistic cosmologies. There is a consensus, dating back at least to the 4th century BC and continuing to the present, that the first Greek philosopher was Thales of

Thales of Miletus

Miletus, who flourished in the first half of the 6th century BC. At that time the word *philosopher* ("lover of wisdom") had not yet been coined. Thales was counted, however, among the Seven Wise Men (Sophoi), whose name derives from a term that then designated inventiveness and practical wisdom rather than speculative insight. Thales showed these qualities by trying to give the mathematical knowledge that he derived from the Babylonians a more exact foundation and by using it for the solution of practical problems—such as the determination of the distance of a ship as seen from the shore or of the height of the Pyramids. Though he was also credited with predicting an eclipse of the Sun, it is likely that he merely gave a natural explanation of one on the basis of Babylonian astronomical knowledge.

Thales was considered the first Greek philosopher because he was the first to give a purely natural explanation of the origin of the world, free from all mythological ingredients. He upheld that everything had come out of water—an explanation based on the discovery of fossil sea animals far inland. His tendency (and that of his immediate successors) to give nonmythological explanations of the origin of the world was undoubtedly prompted by the fact that all of them lived on the coast of Asia Minor surrounded by a number of nations whose civilizations were much farther advanced than that of the Greeks and whose mythological explanations differed greatly both among themselves and from those of the Greeks. It appeared necessary, therefore, to make a fresh start on the basis of what a person could observe and figure out by looking at the world as it presented itself. This procedure naturally resulted in a tendency to make sweeping generalizations on the basis of rather restricted but carefully checked observations.

Anaximander of Miletus

Thales' disciple and successor, Anaximander of Miletus (mid-6th century), tried to give a more elaborate account of the origin and development of the ordered world (the cosmos). According to him, it developed out of the apeiron, something both infinite and indefinite (without distinguishable qualities). Within this apeiron something arose to produce the opposites of hot and cold. These at once began to struggle with each other and produced the cosmos. The cold (and wet) partly dried up (becoming solid earth), partly remained (as water), and—by means of the hot—partly evaporated (becoming air and mist), its evaporating part (by expansion) splitting up the hot into fiery rings, which surround the whole cosmos. Because these rings are enveloped by mist, however, there remain only certain breathing holes that are visible to men, appearing to them as Sun, Moon, and stars. Anaximander was the first to realize that upward and downward are not absolute directions, but that downward means toward the middle of the Earth and upward away from it, so that the Earth had no need to be supported (as Thales had believed) by anything. Starting from Thales' observations, Anaximander tried to reconstruct the development of life in more detail. Life, being closely bound up with moisture, originated in the sea. All land animals, he held, are descendants of sea animals; man, specifically, is the descendant of an oviparous sea animal of the family of the cetaceans, the *Galeus levis,* that carries its young in a pouch after they have come out of the egg or later lets them return to it until they can fend for themselves. Gradually, however, the moisture will be partly evaporated, until in the end all things will have returned into the undifferentiated apeiron, "in order to pay the penalty for their injustice"—that of having struggled against one another.

Anaximenes of Miletus

Anaximander's successor, Anaximenes of Miletus (second half of the 6th century), taught that air was the origin of all things. His position was for a long time thought to have been a step backward because, like Thales, he placed a special kind of matter at the beginning of the development of the world. But this criticism missed the point. Neither Thales nor Anaximander appear to have specified the way in which the other things arose out of the water or apeiron. Anaximenes, however, declared that the other types of matter arose out of air by condensation and rarefaction. In this way, what to Thales had been merely a beginning became a fundamental principle that remained essentially the same through all of its transmuta-

tions. Thus, the term arche, which originally simply meant "beginning," acquired the new meaning of "principle," a term that henceforth played an enormous role in philosophy down to the present. This concept of a principle that remains the same through many transmutations is, furthermore, the presupposition of the idea that nothing can come out of nothing and that all of the comings to be and passings away that men observe are nothing but transmutations of something that essentially remains the same eternally. In this way it also lies at the bottom of all of the conservation laws—those of the conservation of matter, of force, and of energy—that have been basic in the development of physics. Though Anaximenes of course did not realize all of the implications of his idea, its importance can hardly be exaggerated.

The first three Greek philosophers have often been called hylozoists because they seemed to believe in a kind of living matter. But this is hardly an adequate characterization. It is, rather, characteristic of them that they did not clearly distinguish between kinds of matter, forces, and qualities nor between physical and emotional qualities. The same entity is sometimes called fire and sometimes the hot. Heat appears sometimes as a force and sometimes as a quality, and again there is no clear distinction between warm and cold as physical qualities and the warmth of love and the cold of hate. To realize these ambiguities is important to an understanding of certain later developments in Greek philosophy.

Xenophanes and Parmenides

Xenophanes of Colophon (born *c.* 560 BC), rhapsodist and philosophical thinker, who emigrated from Asia Minor to Elea in southern Italy, was the first to bring out more clearly what was implied in Anaximenes' philosophy. He criticized the popular notions of the gods, saying that men made their gods in their own image. But, more importantly, he argued that there could be only one God, the ruler of the universe, who must be eternal. For, being the strongest of all beings, he could not have come out of something less strong, nor could he be overcome or superseded by something else, because nothing could arise that is stronger than the strongest. The argument clearly rested on the axiom that nothing can come out of nothing and that nothing that is can really vanish.

This axiom was made more explicit and carried to its extreme consequences by Parmenides of Elea (first half of the 5th century BC), the founder of the so-called school of Eleaticism, of whom Xenophanes has been regarded as the teacher and forerunner. In a philosophical poem Parmenides insisted that "what is" cannot have come into being and cannot pass away because it would have to have come out of nothing or to become nothing, whereas nothing by its very nature does not exist. There can be no motion either; for it would have to be a motion into something that is—which is not possible since it would be blocked—or a motion into something that is not—which is equally impossible since what is not does not exist. Hence everything is solid immobile being. The familiar world, in which things move around, come into being, and pass away, is a world of mere belief (*doxa*). In a second part of the poem, however, Parmenides tried to give an analytical account of this world of belief, showing that it rested on constant distinctions between what is believed to be positive—*i.e.,* to have real being, such as light and warmth—and what is negative—*i.e.,* the absence of positive being, such as darkness and cold.

It is significant that Heracleitus of Ephesus, a contemporary of Parmenides, whose philosophy was later considered to be the very opposite of Parmenides' philosophy of immobile being, came, in some fragments of his work, near to what Parmenides tried to show: the positive and the negative, he said, are merely different views of the same thing; death and life, day and night, or light and darkness are really one.

Pluralistic cosmologies. Parmenides had an enormous influence on the further development of philosophy. Most of the philosophers of the following two generations tried to find a way to reconcile his thesis that nothing comes into being nor passes away with the evidence presented to men by their senses. Empedocles of Acragas (mid-5th century) declared that there are four material elements

Empedocles and Anaxagoras

(he called them roots of everything) and two forces, love and hate, that did not come into being and would never pass away or increase or diminish. But the elements are constantly mixed with one another by love and again separated by hate. Thus, through mixture and decomposition composite things come into being and pass away. Because he conceived of love and hate as blind forces, Empedocles had to explain how through random motion living beings could emerge. This he achieved by means of a somewhat crude anticipation of the theory of the survival of the fittest. In the process of mixture and decomposition the limbs and parts of various animals would be formed by chance. But they could not survive. Only when by chance they had come together in such a way that they were able to support and reproduce themselves would they survive. It was in this way that the various species were produced and continued to exist.

Anaxagoras of Clazomenae, a 5th-century pluralist, believed that because nothing can really come into being, everything must be contained in everything, but in the form of infinitely small parts. In the beginning all of these particles had been mixed in an even mixture, in which nothing could be distinguished, much like the indefinite apeiron of Anaximander. But then nous, or intelligence, began at one point to set these particles into a whirling motion, foreseeing that in this way they would become separated from one another and then recombine in the most various ways so as to produce gradually the world in which men live. In contrast to the forces assumed by Empedocles, the nous of Anaxagoras is not blind but foresees and intends the production of the cosmos, including living and intelligent beings; but it does not interfere with the process after having started the whirling motion. This is a strange combination of a mechanical and a nonmechanical explanation of the world.

Leucippus and Democritus

By far of greatest importance for the later development of philosophy and physical science was an attempt by the Atomists Leucippus (mid-5th century) and (in the following generation) Democritus to solve the Parmenidean problem. Leucippus found the solution in the assumption that, contrary to Parmenides' argument, the nothing *does* in a way exist, viz., as empty space. There are then, however, only two fundamental principles of the physical world, empty space and filled space—the latter consisting of atoms that, in contrast to those of modern physics, are real atoms; that is, they are absolutely indivisible because nothing can penetrate to split them. On these foundations, laid by Leucippus, Democritus appears to have built a whole system, aiming at a complete explanation of the varied phenomena of the visible world by means of an analysis of its atomic structure. This system begins with elementary physical problems, such as that of why a hard body can be lighter than a softer one. The explanation is that, although the heavier body contains more atoms, they are equally distributed and of round shape; the lighter body, however, has fewer atoms, most of which have hooks by which they form rigid gratings. The system ends with educational and ethical questions. A sound and cheerful man, useful to his fellowmen, is literally well composed. Although destructive passions involve violent long-distance atomic motions, education can help to contain them, creating a better composure. Democritus also developed a theory of the evolution of culture, which influenced later thinkers. Civilization, he thought, is produced by the needs of life, which compel man to work and to make inventions. When life becomes too easy because all needs are met, there is a danger that civilization will decay as men become unruly and negligent.

Epistemology of appearance. All of the post-Parmenidean philosophers, like Parmenides himself, presupposed that the real world is different from the one that men perceive. Thus the problems of epistemology, or theory of knowledge, arose. According to Anaxagoras, everything is contained in everything. But this is not what people perceive. He solved this problem, however, by assuming that, if there is a much greater amount of one kind of particle in a thing than of all other kinds, the latter are not perceived at all. The observation was then made that sometimes different persons or kinds of animals have different perceptions of the same things. He explained this phenomenon by assuming that like is perceived by like. If, therefore, in the sense organ of one person there is less of one kind of stuff than of another, he will perceive the former less keenly than the latter. This reasoning was also used to explain why some animals see better by night and others by daylight. According to Democritus, the atoms have no sensual qualities such as tastes, smells, or colours at all. Thus, he tried to reduce all of them to tactile qualities (explaining a bright white colour, for instance, as sharp atoms hitting the eye like needles), and he made a most elaborate attempt to reconstruct the atomic structure of things on the basis of their apparent sensual qualities.

Zeno of Elea

Also of very great importance in the history of epistemology was Zeno of Elea (mid-5th century), a younger friend of Parmenides. Parmenides had, of course, been severely criticized because of the strange consequences of his doctrine that in reality there is no motion and no plurality either because there is just one solid being. To support him, however, Zeno tried to show that the assumption that there is motion and plurality leads to consequences that are no less strange. This he did by means of his famous paradoxes, saying that the flying arrow rests since it can neither move in the place in which it is nor in a place in which it is not and that Achilles cannot outrun a turtle because when he has reached its starting point, the turtle will have moved to a further point, and so on ad infinitum—that, in fact, he cannot even start running, for, before traversing the stretch to the starting point of the turtle, he will have to traverse half of it and again half of that and so on ad infinitum. All of these paradoxes are derived from the problem of the continuum. Although they have often been dismissed as logical nonsense, many attempts have also been made to dispose of them by means of mathematical theorems, such as the theory of convergent series or the theory of sets. In the end, however, the difficulties inherent in his arguments have always come back with a vengeance, for the human mind is so constructed that it can look at a continuum in two ways that are not quite reconcilable.

Metaphysic of number. All of the philosophies mentioned so far are in various ways historically akin to one another. Toward the end of the 6th century, however, there arose quite independently another kind of philosophy, which only later entered into interrelation with the developments just mentioned: the philosophy of Pythagoras of Samos. Pythagoras traveled extensively in the East and in Egypt and, after his return to Samos, emigrated to southern Italy because of his dislike of the tyranny of Polycrates. At Croton and Metapontum he founded a philosophical society with strict rules and soon gained considerable political influence. He appears to have brought his doctrine of the transmigration of souls from the East. Much more important for the history of philosophy and science, however, was his doctrine that "all things are numbers," which means that the essences and structures of all things can be determined by finding the numerical relations contained in them. Originally, this, too, was a very broad generalization made on the basis of comparatively few observations: for instance, that the same harmonies can be produced with different instruments—strings, pipes, disks, etc.—by means of the same numerical ratios—1:2, 2:3, 3:4—in one-dimensional extensions; the observation that certain regularities exist in the movements of the celestial bodies; and the discovery that the form of a triangle is determined by the ratio of the lengths of its sides. But because the followers of Pythagoras tried to apply their principle everywhere with the greatest of accuracy, one of them—Hippasus of Metapontum—about 450 BC made one of the most fundamental discoveries of the entire history of science, that of incommensurability, viz., that the quantitative relation between the side and diagonal of such simple figures as the square and the regular pentagon cannot be expressed as a ratio of integers. At first sight this discovery seemed to destroy the very basis of the Pythagorean philosophy, and the school thus split into two sections, one of which engaged in rather abstruse numerical speculations while the other succeeded in overcoming the difficulty by ingenious mathematical inven-

Pythagoras of Samos

tions and laid the foundations of all quantitative science. Pythagorean philosophy also exerted a great influence on the development of Plato's thought in his later years.

The speculations described so far constitute in many ways the most important part of the history of Greek philosophy because all of the most fundamental problems of Western philosophy turned up here for the first time and one finds here the formation of a great many concepts that have continued to dominate Western philosophy and science to the present day.

Anthropology and relativism. In the middle of the 5th century BC, Greek thinking took a somewhat different turn The
Sophists through the advent of the Sophists. The name is derived from the verb *sophizesthai,* "making a profession of being inventive and clever," and aptly described the Sophists, who, in contrast to the philosophers mentioned so far, asked money for their instruction. Philosophically they were, in a way, the leaders of a rebellion against the preceding development, which more and more had resulted in the belief that the real world is quite different from the phenomenal world. "What is the sense of such speculations?" they asked, since men do not live in these so-called real worlds. This is the meaning of the pronouncement of Protagoras of Abdera (mid-5th century) that "Man is the measure of all things, of those which are that they are and of those which are not that they are not." For man the world is what it appears to him to be, not something else; and, though he meant man in general, he illustrated it by pointing out that even in regard to an individual man it makes no sense to tell him that it is really warm when he is shivering with cold, because for him it is cold—for him, the cold exists, is there.

His younger contemporary Gorgias of Leontini, famous for his treatise on the art of oratory, made fun of the philosophers in a book *Peri tou mē ontos ē peri physeōs* ("On that which is not, or on Nature"), in which—referring to the "truly existing world," also called "the nature of things"—he tried to prove (1) that nothing exists, (2) that if something existed, man could have no knowledge of it, and (3) that if nevertheless somebody knew it, he could not communicate his knowledge to others.

The Sophists were not only skeptical of what had by then become a philosophical tradition but also of other traditions. On the basis of the observation that different nations have different rules of conduct even in regard to things considered most sacred—such as the relations between the sexes, marriage, and burial—they concluded that most rules of conduct are conventions. What is really important is to be successful in life and to gain influence on others. This they promised to teach. Gorgias was proud of the fact that, having no knowledge of medicine, he was more successful in persuading a patient to undergo a necessary operation than his brother, a physician, who knew when an operation was necessary. The older Sophists, however, were far from openly preaching immoralism. They, nevertheless, gradually came under suspicion because of their sly ways of arguing. One of the later Sophists, however, Thrasymachus of Chalcedon (late 5th century), was bold enough to declare openly that "right is what is beneficial for the stronger or better one"; that is, for the one able to win the power to bend others to his will.

THE SEMINAL THINKERS OF GREEK PHILOSOPHY

Socrates. By many of his contemporaries, Socrates (5th century BC) was also considered to be a Sophist because of his tricky arguments, though he did not teach for money and his aims were entirely different from theirs. Although there is a late tradition according to which Pythagoras invented the word *philosopher,* it was certainly through Socrates—who insisted that he possessed no wisdom but was striving for it—that the term came into general use and was later applied to all earlier serious thinkers. In fact, all of the records of his life and activity left by his numerous adherents and disciples indicate that he never tried to teach anything directly. But he constantly engaged in conversations with everybody—old and young, high and low—trying to bring into the open by his questions the inconsistencies in their opinions and actions. Though he never taught directly, his whole activity rested on two unshakable premises: (1) the principle never to do wrong nor to participate, even indirectly, in any wrongdoing and (2) the conviction that nobody who really knows what is good and right could act against it. He demonstrated his unshakable adherence to the first principle on various occasions and under different regimes. When, after the Battle of Arginusae, the majority of the Athenian popular assembly demanded death without trial for the admirals, Socrates, who on that day happened to be president of the assembly (an office changing daily), refused to put the proposal to the vote because it was wrong to condemn anyone without a fair trial. He refused to do so even though the people threatened him, shouting that it would be terrible if the sovereign people could not do as they pleased.

When, after the overthrow of democracy, the so-called Thirty Tyrants, who tried to involve everybody in their wrongdoings, ordered him to arrest an innocent citizen whose money they coveted, he simply disobeyed. This he did although at that time such disobedience was still more dangerous than disobeying the sovereign people had been at the time of unrestricted democracy. Likewise, in the time of the democracy he pointed out by his questions the inconsistency of allowing oneself to be swayed by the oratory of a good speaker instead of first inquiring into his capability as a statesman, whereas in private life a sensible citizen would not listen to the oratory of a quack but would try to find the best doctor. When, after the overthrow of democracy, the Thirty Tyrants had many people arbitrarily executed, he asked everybody whether a man was a good shepherd who diminished the number of the sheep instead of increasing it and did not cease doing so when Critias, the leader of the Thirty, warned him to take heed not to diminish the number of the sheep by his own, Socrates', person. But the most fundamental inconsistency that he tried to show up everywhere was that most people by their actions showed that they considered what they found to be good, wonderful, and beautiful in others—such as, for instance, doing right at great danger to oneself—not to be good for themselves, and considered to be good for themselves what they despised and condemned in others. Though all of these stands won him the most fervent admiration of many, especially among the young of all classes, it caused also great resentment among leading politicians, whose inconsistencies were shown up publicly by him and his adherents. Though Socrates had survived unharmed through the regime of the Thirty— partly because it did not last long, partly because he was supported by some close relatives of their leader Critias— it was under the restored democracy that he was accused of impiety and of corrupting the youth and finally condemned to death, largely also in consequence of his intransigent attitude during the trial.

After Socrates' death his influence became a dominating one through the greater part of Greek and Roman philosophy down to the end of antiquity and was more or less noticeable even in all of the rest. Many of his adherents—among them Xenophon, a military man and a historian, and Aeschines of Sphettus, one of those present at his death—tried to preserve his philosophical method by writing Socratic dialogues. Some founded schools or sects that perpetuated themselves over long periods of Founding
of schools
and sects time, Eucleides of Megara emphasizing the theoretical aspects of Socrates' thought, and Antisthenes stressing the independence of the true philosopher from material wants. The latter, through his disciple Diogenes of Sinope, who carried voluntary poverty to the extreme and emphasized freedom from all conventions, became the founder of the sect of the Cynics. Aristippus of Cyrene, traditional founder of the Cyrenaic school, stressed man's independence from material needs in a somewhat different way, declaring that there is no reason why a philosopher should not enjoy material goods as long as he is completely indifferent to their loss. Though Aristippus renounced his son because he led a dissolute life, the school that he founded (through his daughter and his grandson) was hedonistic, holding pleasure to be the good.

Plato. By far the most important disciple of Socrates, however, was Plato, a scion of one of the most noble Athenian families, who could trace his ancestry back to the last king of Athens and to Solon, the great social and political reformer.

Life. As a very young man Plato became a fervent admirer of Socrates in spite of the latter's plebeian origin. Contrary to his master, however, who always concerned himself with the attitudes of individuals, he believed in the importance of political institutions. In his early youth he had observed that the Athenian masses, listening to the glorious projects of ambitious politicians, had engaged in foolhardy adventures of conquest, which led in the end to total defeat in the Peloponnesian War. When, in consequence of the disaster, democracy was abolished, Plato at first set great hopes in the Thirty Tyrants—especially since their leader, Critias, was a close relative. But he soon discovered that—to use his own words—the despised democracy had been gold in comparison with the new terror. When the oligarchy was overthrown and the restored democracy, in 399, adopted a new law code—in fact, a kind of written constitution containing safeguards against rash political decisions—Plato again had considerable hope and was even inclined to view the execution of Socrates as an unfortunate incident rather than a logical consequence of the new regime. It was only some years later, when demagogy appeared to raise its head again, that he "despaired and was forced to say that things would not become better in politics unless the philosophers would become rulers or the rulers philosophers." He wrote a dialogue, the *Gorgias,* violently denouncing political oratory and propaganda and then traveled to southern

Visit to
Syracuse Italy in order to study political conditions there. Again, however, he found the much vaunted dolce vita of the Greeks there, in which the rich lived in luxury exploiting the poor, much worse than the democracy at Athens. But at Syracuse he met a young man, Dion, brother-in-law of the ruling tyrant, Dionysius I, who listened eagerly to his political ideas and promised to work for their realization if any occasion should arise. On his return to Athens, Plato founded the Academy, an institution for the education of philosophers, and in the following years elaborated, besides other dialogues, his great work, *Politeia* (*The Republic*), in which he drew the outlines of an ideal state. Because it is the passions and desires of men that cause all disturbances in society, the state must be ruled by an elite governed exclusively by reason and supported by a class of warriors entirely obedient to them. Both ruling classes must have no individual possessions and no families and lead an extremely austere life, receiving the necessities of life from the working population, which alone is permitted to own private property. The elite receives a rigid education to fit it for its task. At the death of Dionysius I, Dion induced Plato to come to Syracuse again to try to persuade Dionysius' successor to renounce his power in favour of a realization of Plato's ideals. But the attempt failed, and in his later political works, the *Politicus* (*Statesman*) and the *Nomoi* (*Laws*), Plato tried to show that only a god could be entrusted with the absolute powers of the philosopher-rulers of his *Politeia.* Human rulers must be controlled by rigid laws, he held—though all laws are inevitably imperfect because life is too varied to be governed adequately by general rules. But the *Nomoi* still placed strict restrictions on the ownership of property.

Philosophy. In the field of theoretical philosophy, Plato's most influential contribution was undoubtedly his theory of Ideas, which he derived from Socrates' method in the following way: Socrates, in trying to bring out the inconsistencies in his interlocutors' opinions and actions, had often asked what it is that makes men say that a certain thing or action is good or beautiful or pious or brave; and he had asked what people are looking at when they make such statements. Plato sometimes made Socrates ask what is the Eidos, or the Idea—*i.e.,* the image—that a person

Theory of
Ideas has before him when he calls something "good." A definite answer is never given, however, because no abstract definition would be adequate, the purpose being rather to make the interlocutor aware of the fact that he somehow does look at something undefinable when making such statements.

What was at first simply a way of somehow expressing something that is difficult to express developed into a

definite theory of Ideas when Plato made the discovery that something similar could be observed in the field of mathematics. No two things in the visible world are perfectly equal, just as there is nothing that is perfectly good or perfectly beautiful. Yet equality is one of the most fundamental concepts not only in mathematics but also in everyday life—the foundation of all measurement. Hence, like the notion of the good and the beautiful, it appears to come from a different world, a world beyond that of the senses, a world that Plato then called the world of Ideas. Further intimations of such a realm beyond the immediate realm of the senses may be found in the fact that men, in construing a system of knowledge, constantly prefer what is more perfect to what is less perfect; *i.e.,* what is formed and thus recognizable to what is not, what is true to what is false, a sound logical conclusion to a logical fallacy, even an elegant scientific demonstration to a clumsy one, without considering the former as good and the latter as bad.

According to Plato, all of the things that men perceive with their senses appear to be but very imperfect copies of the eternal Ideas. The most important and fundamental one of these is the Idea of the Good. It is "beyond being and knowledge," yet it is the foundation of both. "Being" in this connection does not mean existence, but being something specific—a man, a lion, or a house—being recognizable by its quality or shape.

Knowledge begins with a perception of these earthly shapes, but it ascends from there to the higher realm of Ideas, which is approachable to the human mind. In the famous myth of the cave in the seventh book of *Politeia,* Myth of
the cave Plato likened the ordinary person to a man sitting in a cave looking at a wall on which he sees nothing but the shadows of the real things that are behind his back, and he likened the philosopher to a man who has got out in the open and seen the real world of the Ideas. Coming back, he may be less able to distinguish the shades because he has been blinded by the light outside; but he is the only one who knows reality, and he conducts his life accordingly.

In his later thinking, in *Theaetetus,* Plato criticized a sensualist theory of knowledge, anticipating the explanations of the 17th-century English sensualists, such as Thomas Hobbes. In the *Timaeus,* he tried to build up a complete system of physics, partly employing Pythagorean ideas. Most modern Positivists do not take Plato seriously any longer. But one of the greatest physicists of the 20th century, Werner Heisenberg, has insisted that the modern physicist still has to learn a good deal from Plato concerning the foundation of his science.

Aristotle. After Plato's death the Academy continued to exist for many centuries under various heads. When Plato's nephew, Speusippus, was elected as his successor, his greatest disciple, Aristotle, left to go first to Assus and then to the island of Lesbos, where he met Theophrastus, who became his most gifted disciple. But soon thereafter he was called to the Macedonian court at Pella to become the educator of the crown prince, who was later to become Alexander the Great. After the latter had become king, Aristotle returned to Athens and opened there a school of his own, whose members became known as the Peripatetics.

Philosophy. Aristotle had become a member of the Academy at the age of 17, in the year 367 (during Plato's absence in Sicily), under the acting chairmanship of Eudoxus of Cnidus, a great mathematician and geographer. It is a controversial question as to how far Aristotle, during the 20 years of his membership in the Academy, developed a philosophy of his own differing from that of his master. But two things can be considered as certain: (1) that he soon raised certain objections to Plato's theory of Ideas, for one of the arguments against it attributed to him is discussed in Plato's dialogue *Parmenides,* which Plato must have written soon after his return from Sicily, and (2) that it was during his membership in the Academy that Aristotle began and (to a considerable extent) elaborated his theoretical and formal analysis of the arguments used in various Socratic discussions—an enterprise that (when completed) resulted in the corpus of his works on logic, a new science, which Aristotle himself claimed to have originated and about which (until rather recent times) it used to be said that he completed it in such a way that hardly anything could be added.

Certainly quite some time before his return to Athens to open a school of his own, Aristotle declared that it is not necessary to assume the existence of a separate realm of transcendent Ideas of which the individual things that men perceive with their senses are but imperfect copies; that the world of perceived things is the real world; and that it is necessary merely to be able to say that something is generally true of certain types or groups of things in order to build up a system of knowledge about them. Thus, it would be wrong to say that, having abandoned the theory of Ideas, Aristotle was left with a completely contingent world. The last chapters of his *Analytica posteriora* (*Posterior Analytics*) show, on the contrary, that he merely replaced Plato's transcendent Ideas with something (*katholou*) corresponding to them that the human mind can grasp in individual things.

Teleology and perfection

Aristotle retained another important element of the theory of Ideas in his teleology, or doctrine of purposiveness. According to Plato, individual things are imperfect copies of perfect Ideas. Aristotle pointed out, however, that all living beings develop from an imperfect state (from the seed, the semen, through the germinating plant, or embryo, to the child and young adult), to the more perfect state of the fully developed plant or the full grown mature animal or man—after which they again decay and finally die, having reproduced themselves. But not all individuals reach the same degree of relative perfection. Many of them die before reaching it; others are retarded or crippled or maimed in various ways in the process. It is, therefore, of the utmost importance for man to find out what the best conditions are for reaching the most perfect state possible. This is what the gardener tries to do for the plants; but it is even more important for man to do it in regard to himself. The first question, then, is what kind of perfection a human being as human can reach. In answering this question Aristotle observed that man, being the social animal par excellence, can reach as an individual only some of the perfections possible for man as such. Cats are more or less all alike in their functions; thus each can fend for itself. With bees and termites, however, it is different. They are by nature divided into worker bees, drones, and queen bees or worker termites, soldier termites, and queens. With human beings the differentiation of functions is much more subtle and varied. Men can lead satisfactory lives only on the basis of a division of labour and distribution of functions. Some human individuals are born with very great talents and inclinations for special kinds of activity. They will be happy and will make their best possible contribution to the life of the community only if they are permitted to follow this inclination. Others are less one-sidedly gifted and more easily adaptable to a variety of functions. These people can be happy shifting from one activity to another. That this is so is an enormous advantage the human species has over all other animals because it enables it to adapt to all sorts of circumstances. But the advantage is paid for by the fact that no human individual is able to develop all of the perfections that are possible for the race as a whole.

There is another possible and, in its consequences, real disadvantage to such adaptability; the other animals, tightly confined to the limits set by nature, are crippled almost exclusively by external factors; but man, in consequence of the freedom of choice granted to him through the variety of his gifts, can and very often does cripple and harm himself. All human activities are directed toward the end of a good and satisfactory life. But there are many subordinate aims that are sensible ends only as far as they serve a superior end. There is, for example, no sense in producing or acquiring more shoes than can possibly be worn. This is self-evident. With regard to money, however, which has become exchangeable against everything, the illusion arises that it is good to accumulate it without limit. By doing so, man harms both the community and himself because, concentrating on such a narrow aim, he deprives his soul and spirit of larger and more rewarding experiences. Similarly, an individual especially gifted for large-scale planning needs power to give orders to those capable of executing his plans. Used for such purposes, power is good. But coveted for its own sake, it becomes oppressive to those subdued by it and harmful to the oppressor because he thus incurs the hatred of the oppressed. Because of his imperfection man is not able to engage in serious and fruitful activities without interruption. He needs relaxation and play, or amusement. Because the necessities of life frequently force man to work beyond the limit within which working is pleasant, the illusion arises that a life of constant amusement would be the most pleasant and joyful. In reality nothing is more tedious.

Aristotle's teleology seems to be based entirely on empirical observation. It has nothing to do with a belief in divine providence and is not, as some modern critics believe, at variance with the law of causality. It forms the foundation, however, of Aristotle's ethics and political theory. Aristotle was an avid collector of empirical evidence. He induced his students, for instance, to make collections of the laws and political institutions (and their historical developments) of all known cities and nations in order to find out how they worked and at what points their initiators had been mistaken regarding the way in which they would work. In later times, Aristotle came to be considered (and by many is still considered) a dogmatic philosopher because the results of his inquiries were accepted as absolutely authoritative. In reality, however, he was one of the greatest Empiricists of all times.

Disciples and commentators. After Aristotle's death his immediate disciples carried on the same kind of work, especially in the historical field: Theophrastus wrote a history of philosophy and works on botany and on mineralogy, Eudemus of Rhodes wrote histories of mathematics and of astronomy, Meno a history of medicine, and Dicaearchus of Messene a history of civilization and a book on types of political constitutions. The next two generations of Peripatetics spread out in two different directions: literary history, in the form of histories of types of poetry, epic, tragedy, and comedy, and of biographies of famous writers, and physical science, Straton of Lampsacus creating a new kind of physics based on experiments, and the great astronomer Aristarchus of Samos inventing the heliocentric system. The school then went for some time into eclipse until, in the 1st century AD, after the rediscovery of Aristotle's lecture manuscripts, there arose a great school of commentators on his works, which had an enormous influence on medieval philosophy.

HELLENISTIC AND ROMAN PHILOSOPHY

The period after the death of Aristotle was characterized by the decay of the Greek city-states, which then became pawns in the power game of the Hellenistic kings who succeeded Alexander. Life became troubled and insecure. It was in this environment that two dogmatic philosophical systems came into being, the Stoic and the Epicurean, which were destined to give their adherents something to hold onto and to make them independent of the external world.

Zeno of Citium

Stoics. The Stoic system was created by a Syrian, Zeno of Citium (about the turn of the 3rd century BC), who went to Athens as a merchant but lost his fortune at sea. Zeno was consoled by the Cynic philosopher Crates, who taught him that material possessions were of no importance whatsoever for a man's happiness. He therefore stayed at Athens, heard the lectures of various philosophers, and—after he had elaborated his own philosophy—began to teach in a public hall, the Stoa Poikile (hence the name Stoicism).

Zeno's thought comprised, essentially, a dogmatized Socratic philosophy, with added ingredients derived from Heracleitus. The basis of human happiness, he said, is to live "in agreement" (with oneself), a statement that was later replaced by the formula "to live in agreement with nature." The only real good for man is the possession of virtue; everything else (wealth or poverty, health or illness, life or death) is completely indifferent. All virtues are based exclusively on right knowledge—self-control (*sōphrosynē*) being the knowledge of the right choice, fortitude the knowledge of what must be endured and what must not, and justice the right knowledge "in distribution." The passions, which are the cause of all evil, are the result of error in judging what is a real good and what is not. Because it is difficult to see, however, why murder, fraud, and theft should be considered evil if life and possessions are of no value, the doctrine was later modified by making among the "indifferent things" distinctions between "preferable things," such as having the necessities of life and health; "completely indifferent things"; and "anti-preferable things," such as lacking the necessities of life or being ill—while insisting still that the happiness of the truly wise man could not be impaired by illness, pain, hunger, or any deprivation of external goods. In the beginning, Zeno also insisted that a man is either completely wise, in which case he would never do anything wrong and would be completely happy, or he is a fool. Later he made the concession, however, that there are men not completely wise but progressing toward wisdom. Though the latter might even have true insight, they are not certain that they have it, whereas the truly wise man is also certain of having true insight. The world is governed by divine Logos—a word originally meaning "word" or "speech," then (with Heracleitus) also a speech that expresses the laws of the universe, and, finally, "reason." This Logos keeps the world in perfect order. Man can deviate from or rebel against this order, but by doing so he cannot disturb it but can only do harm to himself.

Development of Zeno's philosophy

Zeno's philosophy was further developed by Cleanthes, the second head of the school, and by Chrysippus, its third head. Chrysippus elaborated a new kind of logic, which did not receive much attention, however, outside the Stoic school until in recent times (under the name of "propositional logic") it has been hailed by some logicians as superior to the "conceptual logic" of Aristotle. In the mid-2nd century BC, Panaetius of Rhodes adapted Stoic philosophy to the needs of the Roman aristocracy (whose members were then governing the known world) and made a great impression on some of the leading men of the time, who tried to follow his moral precepts. In the following century, in the time of the decay of the Roman Republic, of civil war, and of slave rebellions, Poseidonius of Apamea, who was also one of the most brilliant historians of all times, taught that the Stoic takes a position above the rest of mankind, looking down on men's struggles as on a spectacle. In the periods of the rising monarchy and of its established rule, Stoicism became the religion of the republican opposition. The most famous Stoic was the younger Cato, who committed suicide after the victory of Julius Caesar. It was also the guiding philosophy of Seneca the Younger, the educator and (for a long time) the adviser of Nero, who tried to keep Nero on the path of virtue but failed and finally had to commit suicide on the orders of the Emperor. In spite of the oddities of Zeno's original doctrine, Stoicism gave consolation, composure, and fortitude in times of trouble to many proud men to the end of antiquity and beyond.

Epicurus and Lucretius Carus

Epicureans. The thought of Zeno's contemporary Epicurus also comprised a philosophy of defense in a troubled world. It has been (and still is) considered—in many respects justly—the opposite of Zeno's. Whereas Zeno had proclaimed that the wise man would try to learn from everybody and would always acknowledge his debt to earlier philosophers, Epicurus insisted that everything he taught was the result of his own thinking, though it is obvious that his physical explanation of the universe is a simplification of Democritus' Atomism. And whereas the Stoics had taught that pleasure and pain are of no importance for a man's happiness, Epicurus made pleasure the very essence of a happy life. Moreover, the Stoics from the beginning had acted as advisers of kings and statesmen. Epicurus, on the other hand, lived in the retirement of his famous Garden, cultivating intimate friendships with his adherents but warning against participation in public life. The Stoics believed in divine providence; Epicurus taught that the gods pay no attention whatsoever to human beings. Yet in spite of these contrasts, the two philosophies had some essential factors in common. Though Epicurus made pleasure the criterion of a good life, he was far from

advocating a dissolute life and debauchery; he insisted that it was the simple pleasures that made life happy. When in his old age he suffered terrible pains from prostatitis, he asserted that philosophizing and the memory and love of his distant friends made pleasure prevail even in the grips of such pain. Nor was Epicurus an atheist. His Roman admirer, the poet Lucretius Carus (c. 95–55 BC), in his poem *De rerum natura* (*On the Nature of Things*), praised Epicurus enthusiastically as the liberator of mankind from all religious fears; and Epicurus himself had affirmed that this had been one of the aims of his philosophy. But although he taught that the gods are much too superior to trouble themselves with paying attention to mortals, he said—and, as his language clearly shows, sincerely believed—that it is important for human beings to look at the gods as perfect beings, since only in this way could men approach perfection. It was only in Roman times that people began to misunderstand Epicureanism, holding it to be an atheistic philosophy justifying a dissolute life, so that a man could be called "a swine from the herd of Epicurus." Seneca recognized the true nature of Epicureanism, however, and in his *Epistulae morales* (*Moral Letters*) deliberately interspersed through his Stoic exhortations maxims from Epicurus.

Skeptics. There was still another Hellenistic school of philosophy, the Skeptic school initiated by another of Zeno's contemporaries—Pyrrhon of Elis—a school that was destined to become of great importance for the preservation of a detailed knowledge of Hellenistic philosophy in general. Pyrrhon had come to the conviction that no man can know anything for certain nor ever be certain that the things he perceives with his senses are real and not illusory. He is said to have carried the practical consequences of his conviction so far that, when walking in the streets, he paid no attention to the vehicles and other obstacles, so that his faithful disciples always had to accompany him to see that he came to no harm. Pyrrhon's importance for the history of philosophy lies in the fact that one of the later adherents of his doctrine, Sextus Empiricus (2nd–3rd century AD), wrote a large work, *Pros dogmatikous* ("Against the Dogmatists"), in which he tried to refute all of the philosophers who had a more positive philosophy and in so doing he quoted extensively from their works, thus preserving much that would otherwise have been lost. It is a noteworthy fact that the British sensualists of the 18th century, such as David Hume, and also Immanuel Kant derived most of their knowledge of ancient philosophy from Sextus.

Pyrrhon of Elis and Sextus Empiricus

Neo-Pythagoreans and Neoplatonists. All of the philosophical schools and sects of Athens that had originated in the 4th century BC continued into late antiquity, most of them until the emperor Justinian I ordered all of them closed in AD 529 because of their pagan character. Within that whole period of nearly 1,000 years only two new schools were added; these, however—the Neo-Pythagorean and the Neoplatonic schools—drew their inspiration from early Greek philosophy, though only the latter was of importance for the history of philosophy. Neoplatonism began with Ammonius Saccas (first half of the 3rd century AD), who had been brought up as a Christian but had abandoned his religion for the study of Plato and developed his own kind of Platonic philosophy. Because he wrote nothing, his philosophy is known only through his famous disciple, Plotinus. But Plotinus did not publish anything either. His philosophy is known, however, through the publication of notes, discussions, and explanations following his lectures by his disciple Porphyry, who also wrote a biography of Plotinus.

The philosophy of Plotinus (and Ammonius) was derived from the study of Plato. It, moreover, used many philosophical terms first coined by Aristotle and adopted some elements of Stoic philosophy as well. Yet it is essentially a new philosophy, agreeing with the religious and mystical tendencies of its time. Plotinus assumed the existence of several levels of Being, the highest being that of the One, or the Good, which are identical but indescribable and indefinable in human language. The next lower level is that of the nous, or pure intellect or reason; the third is that of the soul or souls. There then follows the world

Plotinus and Iamblichus

perceivable by the senses and, finally, at the lowest level there is matter, which is the cause of all evil. The highest bliss for man is union with the One, or Good, attained by contemplation and purification. That this is not a lasting state attained once for all—like the status of the Stoic wise man, who was supposed never to lose his wisdom again—is shown by the fact that Porphyry, in his *Vita Plotini,* said that Plotinus had experienced this supreme bliss seven times in his life, whereas he, Porphyry, had experienced it only once.

The further history of Neoplatonism is extremely complicated. While Porphyry had emphasized the ethical element in Plotinus' philosophy, his disciple Iamblichus of Chalcis in Syria (died *c.* AD 330), founder of a Syrian branch of the sect, mingled Neoplatonism with Neo-Pythagoreanism, writing on the Pythagorean way of life and on number theory. Above all, he multiplied the levels of being, or the emanations from the One, which enabled him to incorporate the traditional Greek gods into his system. Another branch of the school was founded in Pergamum, in western Asia Minor, by his disciple Aedesius, who with his disciple Maximus tried to revive the ancient Greek mystery religions, such as Orphism. All of these developments became of great importance in the 4th century when the emperor Julian attempted to revive paganism. In the following century the Athenian school reached a new high point when Proclus combined ideas of his predecessors into one comprehensive system. When in 529 Justinian closed all of the philosophical schools in Athens, however, a branch continued to exist in Alexandria. The Athenian Neoplatonists found refuge at the court of the Persian king Khosrow, and in 535 they were permitted to return to Athens. But gradually pagan philosophy as such died out, though it continued to exist as an influence in the development of Christian philosophy and theology.

(K.v.Fr.)

Medieval philosophy

Medieval philosophy designates the philosophical speculation that occurred in western Europe during the Middle Ages; *i.e.,* from the fall of the Roman Empire in the 4th and 5th centuries AD to the Renaissance of the 15th century. Philosophy of the medieval period remained in close conjunction with Christian thought, particularly theology, and the chief philosophers of the period were churchmen, particularly churchmen who were teachers. Philosophers who strayed from the close relation were chided by their superiors. Greek philosophy ceased to be creative after Plotinus in the 3rd century AD. A century later Christian thinkers such as Ambrose, Victorinus, and Augustine began to assimilate Neoplatonism into Christian doctrine in order to give a rational interpretation of Christian faith. Thus, medieval philosophy was born of the confluence of Greek (and to a lesser extent of Roman) philosophy and Christianity. Plotinus' philosophy was already deeply religious, having come under the influence of Middle Eastern religion. Medieval philosophy continued to be characterized by this religious orientation. Its methods were at first those of Plotinus and later those of Aristotle. But it developed within faith as a means of throwing light on the truths and mysteries of faith. Thus, religion and philosophy fruitfully cooperated in the Middle Ages. Philosophy, as the handmaiden of theology, made possible a rational understanding of faith. Faith, for its part, inspired Christian thinkers to develop new philosophical ideas, some of which became part of the philosophical heritage of the West.

Toward the end of the Middle Ages, this beneficial interplay of faith and reason started to break down. Philosophy began to be cultivated for its own sake, apart from, and even in contradiction to, Christian religion. This divorce of reason from faith, made definitive in the 17th century by Francis Bacon and René Descartes, marked the birth of modern philosophy.

EARLY MEDIEVAL PHILOSOPHY

The early medieval period, which extended to the 12th century, saw the barbarian invasions of the Roman Empire,

the collapse of its civilization, and the gradual building of a new, Christian culture in western Europe. Philosophy in these troubled and darkened times was cultivated by late Roman thinkers such as Augustine (354–430) and Boethius (*c.* 480–*c.* 525), then by monks such as Anselm (1033–1109). The monasteries became the main centres of learning and education and retained their preeminence until the founding of the cathedral schools and universities in the 11th and 12th centuries.

Augustine. During these centuries philosophy was heavily influenced by Neoplatonism; Stoicism and Aristotelianism played only a minor role. Augustine was awakened to the philosophical life by reading Cicero, but the Neoplatonists most decisively shaped his philosophical methods and ideas. To them he owed his conviction that beyond the world of the senses there is a spiritual, eternal realm of truth that is the object of the human mind and the goal of all man's striving. This truth he identified with the God of Christianity. Man encounters this divine world of truth and beauty not through his senses but by turning inward to his mind, and above his mind to the intelligible light, in which he sees the truth. The Augustinian demonstration of the existence of God coincides with the proof of the existence of necessary, immutable Truth. Augustine considered the truths of both mathematics and ethics to be necessary, immutable, and eternal. These truths cannot come from the world of contingent, changing, and temporal things, nor from the mind itself, which is also contingent, mutable, and temporal. They are due to the illuminating presence in man's mind of eternal and immutable Truth, or God. Any doubt that man knows the truth with certainty was dispelled for Augustine by the certitude that even if he is deceived in many cases, man cannot doubt that he exists and knows and loves.

Augustine conceived of man as a composite of two substances, body and soul, of which the soul is by far the superior. The body, nevertheless, is not to be excluded from human nature, and its eventual resurrection from the dead is assured by Christian faith. The soul's immortality is proved by its possession of eternal and unchangeable Truth.

Augustine's *Confessions* (*c.* 400) and *De Trinitate* (400–416; *On the Trinity*) abound with penetrating psychological analyses of knowledge, perception, memory, and love. His *De civitate Dei* (413–426; *The City of God*) presents the whole drama of human history as a progressive movement of humanity, redeemed by God, to its final repose in its Creator.

Boethius. One of the most important channels by which Greek philosophy was transmitted to the Middle Ages was Boethius. He began to translate into Latin all the philosophical works of the Greeks, but his imprisonment and death by order of Theodoric, king of the Ostrogoths, cut short this project. He translated only the logical writings of Porphyry (a 3rd-century-AD Neoplatonist) and Aristotle. These translations and his commentaries on them brought to the thinkers of the Middle Ages the rudiments of Aristotelian logic. They also raised important philosophical questions, such as the nature of universals (terms that can be applied to more than one particular thing). Are universals real or only mental concepts? If real, are they corporeal or incorporeal; if incorporeal, do they exist in the sensible world or apart from it? Medieval philosophers debated at length these and other problems relating to universals. In his logical works Boethius presents the Aristotelian doctrine of universals, that they are only mental abstractions. In his *De consolatione philosophiae* (*c.* 525; *Concerning the Consolation of Philosophy*), however, he adopts the Platonic notion that they are innate ideas and their origin is in the remembering of knowledge in a previous existence. This book was extremely popular and influential in the Middle Ages. It contains not only a Platonic view of knowledge and reality but also a lively treatment of providence, divine foreknowledge, chance, fate, and human happiness.

Greek Fathers of the Church and Erigena. Another stream from which Greek philosophy, especially Neoplatonic thought, flowed into the Middle Ages was the Greek Fathers of the Church, notably Origen (*c.* 185–*c.* 254),

The question of the nature of universals

Gregory of Nyssa (c. 335–c. 394), Nemesius (c. 400), Pseudo-Dionysius the Areopagite (c. 500), and Maximus the Confessor (c. 580–662). In the 9th century, John Scotus, called Erigena ("belonging to the people of Erin") because he was born in Ireland, a master at the Carolingian court of Charles the Bald, translated into Latin some of the writings of these Greek theologians, and his own major work, *De divisione naturae* (862–866; *On the Division of Nature*), is a vast synthesis of Christian thought organized along Neoplatonic lines. For him, God is the primal unity, unknowable and unnameable in himself, from which the multiplicity of creatures flows. He so far transcends his creatures that he is most appropriately called superreal and supergood. Creation is the process of division whereby the many derive from the One. The One descends into the manifold of creation and reveals himself in it. By the reverse process the multiplicity of creatures will return to their unitary source at the end of time, when everything will be absorbed in God.

Anselm. After the breakdown of the Carolingian Empire in the 10th century, intellectual speculation was at a low ebb in western Europe. In the next century some political stability was achieved by Otto I, who reestablished the empire, and Benedictine monasteries were revitalized by reformers such as Peter Damian. Like Tertullian, a Christian writer of the 2nd and 3rd centuries, Damian mistrusted secular learning and philosophy as harmful to the faith. Other monks showed a keen interest in dialectic and philosophy. Among the latter was Anselm, an Italian who became abbot of the French monastery of Bec and later archbishop of Canterbury.

Anselm's proofs of the existence of God

Like Augustine, Anselm used both faith and reason in his search for truth. Faith comes first, in his view, but reason should follow, giving reasons for what men believe. Anselm's monks asked him to write a model meditation on God in which everything would be proved by reason and nothing on the authority of Scripture. He replied with his *Monologium* (1077; "Monologue"; Eng. trans., *Monologium*), the original title of which was "A Meditation on the Reasonableness of Faith." It contains three proofs of the existence of God, all of which are based on Neoplatonic thought. The first proof moves from the awareness of a multiplicity of good things to the recognition that they all share or participate more or less in one and the same Good, which is supremely Good in itself, and this is God. The second and third proofs are similar: beginning with their awareness of a multiplicity of beings that have more or less of being, and more or less of perfection, men recognize that they share in One who is supremely Being and perfect.

Anselm's later work, the *Proslogium* (1077/78; "Allocution" or "Address"; Eng. trans., *Proslogium*), also entitled "Faith Seeking Understanding," contains his most famous proof of the existence of God. This begins with a datum of faith: men believe God to be the being than which none greater can be thought. Some, like the fool in the Psalms, say there is no God; but even the fool, on hearing these words, understands them, and what he understands exists in his intellect, even though he does not grant that such a being exists in reality. But it is greater to exist in reality and in the understanding than to exist in the understanding alone. Therefore it is contradictory to hold that God exists only in the intellect, for then the being than which none greater can be thought is one than which a greater can be thought, namely, one that exists both in reality and in the understanding. Philosophers still debate the meaning and value of this so-called ontological argument for God's existence.

Bernard of Clairvaux and Abelard. Anselm's inquiry into the existence and nature of God, as also his discussion of truth, love, and human liberty, aimed at fostering monastic contemplation. Other monks, such as the Cistercian Bernard of Clairvaux (1090–1153), were suspicious of the use of secular learning and philosophy in matters of faith. Bernard complained of the excessive indulgence in dialectic displayed by contemporaries such as Peter Abelard (1079–1142) and Gilbert de La Porrée. He himself developed a doctrine of mystical love, the influence of which lasted through the centuries. The monks of the Parisian Abbey of Saint-Victor were no less intent on fostering mystical contemplation, but they cultivated the liberal arts and philosophy as an aid to it. In this spirit, Hugh of Saint-Victor wrote his *Didascalicon* (c. 1127; "Teaching"; Eng. trans., *Didascalicon*), a monumental treatise on the theoretical and practical sciences and the trivium (grammar, rhetoric, dialectic) and the quadrivium (arithmetic, music, geometry, astronomy). During the same period the School of Chartres, attached to the famous cathedral near Paris, was the focus of Christian Neoplatonism and humanism.

Urban development in the 12th century shifted the centre of learning and education from the monasteries to the towns. Abelard founded several urban schools near Paris and taught in them. A passionate logician, he pioneered a method in theology that contributed to the later Scholastic method. His *Sic et non* (1115–17; *Yes and No*) cites the best authorities on both sides of theological questions in order to reach their correct solution. In philosophy his main interest was logic. On the question of universals he agreed with neither the Nominalists nor the Realists of his day. His Nominalist teacher Roscelin held that universals, such as "man" and "animal," are nothing but words, or names (*flatus vocis*). Abelard argued that this does not take into account the fact that names have meaning. His Realist teacher William of Champeaux taught that universals are realities apart from the mind. For Abelard, only individuals are real; universals are indeed names or mental concepts, but they have meaning because they refer to individuals. They do not signify an essence common to individuals, as the Realists maintained (*e.g.*, the essence "humanity" shared by all men), but signify instead the individuals in their common condition, or status, of being in a certain species, which results from God's creating them according to the same divine idea.

TRANSITION TO SCHOLASTICISM

In the 12th century a cultural revolution took place that influenced the whole subsequent history of Western philosophy. The old style of education, based on the liberal arts and emphasizing grammar and the reading of the Latin classics, was replaced by new methods stressing logic, dialectic, and all the scientific disciplines known at the time. John of Salisbury, of the School of Chartres, witnessed this radical change:

> Behold, everything was being renovated: grammar was being made over, logic was being remodeled, rhetoric was being despised. Discarding the rules of their predecessors, [the masters] were teaching the quadrivium with new methods taken from the very depths of philosophy.

Growing interest in Aristotelianism

In philosophy itself, there was a decline in Platonism and a growing interest in Aristotelianism. This change was occasioned by the translation into Latin of the works of Aristotle in the late 12th and early 13th centuries. Until then, only a few of his minor logical treatises were known. Now his *Topica, Analytica priora,* and *Analytica posteriora* were rendered into Latin, giving the schoolmen (the teachers of Western Christian philosophy in the 13th and 14th centuries) access to the Aristotelian methods of disputation and science, which became their own techniques of discussion and inquiry. Many other philosophical and scientific works of Greek and Arabic origin were translated at this time, creating a "knowledge explosion" in western Europe.

Arabic thought. Among the translations from Arabic were some of the writings of Avicenna (980–1037). This Islāmic philosopher had an extraordinary impact on the medieval schoolmen. His interpretation of Aristotle's notion of metaphysics as the science of *ens qua ens* ("being as being"), his analysis of many metaphysical terms, such as "being," "essence," "existence," and his metaphysical proof of the existence of God were often quoted, with approval or disapproval, in Christian circles. Also influential were his psychology, logic, and natural philosophy. His *al-Qānūn fī aṭ-ṭibb* (*Canon of Medicine*) was an authority on the subject until modern times. The *Maqāṣid al-Falāsifah* (1094; "The Aims of the Philosophers") of the Arabic theologian al-Ghazālī, known in Latin as Algazel (died c. 1111), an exposition of Avicenna's philosophy written in order to criticize it, was read as a complement of Avicenna's works. The anonymous *Liber de causis* ("Book of Causes") was also translated into Latin from Arabic. This work, excerpted from Proclus' *Stiocheiōsis theologikē* (*Elements of Theology*), was often ascribed to Aristotle, and it gave a Neoplatonic cast to his philosophy until its true origin was discovered by Thomas Aquinas.

The commentaries of the Arabic philosopher Averroës were translated along with Aristotle's works. As Aristotle was called "the Philosopher" by the medieval philosophers, Averroës was dubbed "the Commentator." These two taught the Scholastics philosophy as a purely rational discipline, divorced from revealed religion. The Christian schoolmen often attacked Averroës as the archenemy of Christianity for his rationalism and his doctrines of the eternity of the world and the unity of the intellect for all men; *i.e.*, the doctrine that intellect is a single, undifferentiated form with which men become reunited at death. This was anathema to the Christian schoolmen because it contravened the Christian doctrine of individual immortality.

Jewish thought. Of considerably less influence on the Scholastics was medieval Jewish thought. Ibn Gabirol, known to the Scholastics as Avicebron or Avencebrol, was thought to be an Arab or Christian, though in fact he was a Spanish Jew. His chief philosophical work, written in Arabic and preserved only in a Latin translation entitled *Fons vitae* (*c.* 1050; *Fountain of Life*), stresses the unity and simplicity of God. All creatures are composed of form and matter, either the gross corporeal matter of the sensible world or the spiritual matter of angels and human souls. Some of the schoolmen were attracted to the notion of spiritual matter and also to Ibn Gabirol's analysis of a plurality of forms in creatures, according to which every corporeal being receives a variety of forms by which it is given its place in the hierarchy of being—for example, a dog has the forms of a corporeal thing, a living thing, an animal, a dog.

Maimonides, or Moses ben Maimon, was known to Christians of the Middle Ages as Rabbi Moses. His *Dalālat al-ḥāʾirīn* (*c.* 1190; *Guide of the Perplexed*) helped them to reconcile Greek philosophy with revealed religion. For Maimonides there can be no conflict between reason and faith because both come from God; an apparent contradiction is due to a misinterpretation of either the Bible or the philosophers. Thus, he showed that creation is reconcilable with philosophical principles and that the Aristotelian arguments for an eternal world are not conclusive because they ignore the omnipotence of God, who can create a world of either finite or infinite duration.

The universities and Scholasticism

While Western scholars were assimilating the new treasures of Greek, Islāmic, and Jewish thought, universities that became the centres of Scholasticism were being founded. Of these the most important were Paris and Oxford (formed 1150–70 and 1168, respectively). Scholasticism is the name given to the theological and philosophical teachings of the schoolmen in the universities. There was no one Scholastic doctrine; each of the Scholastics developed his own, which was often in disagreement with that of his fellow teachers. They had in common a respect for the great writers of old, such as the Fathers of the Church, Aristotle, Plato, Boethius, the Pseudo-Dionysius, and Avicenna. These they called "authorities." Their interpretation and evaluation of the authorities, however, frequently differed. They also shared a common style and method that developed out of the teaching practices in the universities. Teaching was done by lecture and disputation (a formal debate). A lecture consisted of the reading of a prescribed text followed by the teacher's commentary on it. Masters also held disputations in which the affirmative and negative sides of a question were thoroughly argued by students and teacher, before the latter resolved the problem.

THE AGE OF THE SCHOOLMEN

Robert Grosseteste and Roger Bacon. The newly translated Greek and Arabic treatises had an immediate effect on the University of Oxford. Its first chancellor, Robert Grosseteste (*c.* 1168–1253), commented on some of Aristotle's works and translated the *Ethica Nichomachea*

(*Nicomachean Ethics*) from Greek to Latin. He was deeply interested in scientific method, which he described as both inductive and deductive. By the observation of individual events in nature, man advances to a general law, called a "universal experimental principle," that accounts for these events. Experimentation either verifies or falsifies a theory by testing its empirical consequences. For Grosseteste the study of nature is impossible without mathematics. He cultivated the science of optics (*perspectiva*), which measures the behaviour of light by mathematical means. His studies of the rainbow and comets employ both observation and mathematics. His treatise *De luce* (1215–20; *On Light*) embodies a metaphysics of light, presenting light as the basic form of all things and God as the primal uncreated light.

Grosseteste's pupil Roger Bacon (*c.* 1220–*c.* 1292) made the mathematical and experimental methods the key to natural science. The term experimental science was popularized in the West through his writings. For him, man acquires knowledge through reasoning and experience, but without the latter he can have no certitude. Man gains experience through the senses and also through an interior divine illumination that culminates in mystical experience. Bacon was critical of the methods of Parisian theologians such as Albertus Magnus and Thomas Aquinas. He strove to create a universal wisdom embracing all the sciences and organized by theology. He also proposed the formation of a single worldwide society, or "Christian republic," that would unite all men under the leadership of the pope.

William of Auvergne. At the University of Paris, William of Auvergne (*c.* 1180–1249) was one of the first to feel the impact of the philosophies of Aristotle and Avicenna. As a teacher, and then as bishop of Paris, he was concerned with the threat of pagan and Islāmic thought to the Christian faith. He opposed the Aristotelian doctrine of the eternity of the world as contrary to the Christian notion of creation. His critique of Avicenna centred around the latter's conception of God and creation. The God of Avicenna, who creates the universe eternally and necessarily, through the mediation of 10 Intelligences, was opposed by William of Auvergne with the Christian notion of a God who creates the world freely and directly. Creatures are radically contingent and dependent on God's creative will. Unlike God, they do not exist necessarily; indeed, their existence is distinct from their essence and accidental to it. God has no essence distinct from his existence; he is pure existence. In stressing the essential instability and noneternity of the world, he attributed true existence and causality to God alone. William of Auvergne was a follower of Augustine, but, like others at the time, he was compelled to rethink the older Augustinian notions in terms of the newer Aristotelian and Avicennian philosophies.

Opposition to Aristotelianism

Bonaventure. The Franciscan friar Bonaventure (*c.* 1217–74) reacted similarly to the growing popularity of Aristotle and his Arabic commentators. He admired Aristotle as a natural scientist, but he preferred Plato and Plotinus, and, above all, Augustine, as metaphysicians. His main criticism of Aristotle and his followers was that they denied the existence of divine ideas. As a result, Aristotle was ignorant of exemplarism (that is, God's creation of the world according to ideas in his mind) and also of divine providence and government of the world. This involved Aristotle in a threefold blindness: he taught that the world is eternal, that all men share one agent intellect (the active principle of understanding in man), and that there are no rewards or punishments after death. Plato and Plotinus avoided these mistakes, but, because they lacked Christian faith, they could not see the whole truth. For Bonaventure, faith alone enables men to avoid error in these important matters.

Bonaventure did not confuse philosophy with theology. Philosophy is the knowledge of the things of nature and the soul innate in man or acquired by his own efforts, whereas theology is the knowledge of heavenly things based on faith and divine revelation. Bonaventure, however, rejected the practical separation of philosophy from theology. Philosophy needs the guidance of faith; far from being self-sufficient, it is but a stage toward the higher knowledge that culminates in the vision of God.

For Bonaventure, every creature to some degree bears the mark of its Creator. The soul has been made in the very image of God. Thus, the universe is like a book in which the triune God is revealed. His *Itinerarium mentis in Deum* (1259; *The Soul's Journey into God*) follows Augustine's path to God, from the external world to the interior world of the mind, and then above the mind from the temporal to the eternal. Throughout this journey, men are aided by a moral and intellectual divine illumination. The mind has been created with an innate idea of God, so that, as Anselm pointed out, man cannot think that God does not exist. In a terse reformulation of the Anselmian argument for God's existence, Bonaventure states that if God is God, he exists.

Albertus Magnus.   The achievement of the Dominican friar Albertus Magnus (c. 1200–80) was of vital importance for the development of medieval philosophy. A man of immense erudition and intellectual curiosity, he was one of the first to recognize the true value of the newly translated Greco-Arabic scientific and philosophical literature. Everything he considered valuable in it, he included in his encyclopaedic writings. He set out to teach this literature to his contemporaries and in particular to make the philosophy of Aristotle, whom he considered to be the greatest philosopher, understandable to them. He also proposed to write original works in order to complete what was lacking in the Aristotelian system. In no small measure, the triumph of Aristotelianism in the 13th century can be attributed to him.

Albertus' observations and discoveries in the natural sciences advanced botany, zoology, and mineralogy. In philosophy he was less original and creative than his famous pupil Thomas Aquinas. Albertus produced a synthesis of Aristotelianism and Neoplatonism, blending together the philosophies of Aristotle, Avicenna, and Ibn Gabirol, and, among Christians, Augustine and Pseudo-Dionysius.

Thomas Aquinas.   Albertus Magnus' Dominican confrere and pupil Thomas Aquinas (1224/25–1274) shared his master's great esteem for the ancient philosophers, especially Aristotle, and also for the more recent Arabic and Jewish thinkers. He welcomed truth wherever he found it and used it for the enrichment of Christian thought. For him reason and faith cannot contradict each other because they come from the same divine source. In his day conservative theologians and philosophers regarded Aristotle with suspicion and leaned toward the more traditional Christian Neoplatonism. Thomas realized that their suspicion was due, in part, to the fact that Aristotle's philosophy had been distorted by his Arabic commentators; so he wrote his own commentaries on Aristotle to show the essential soundness of his system and to convince contemporaries of its value for Christian theology.

Thomas' own philosophical views are best expressed in his theological works, especially his *Summa theologiae* (1265/66–1273; Eng. trans., *Summa theologiae*) and *Summa contra gentiles* (1258–64; *Summa Against the Gentiles*). In these works he clearly distinguishes between the domains and methods of philosophy and theology. The philosopher seeks the first causes of things, beginning with data furnished by the senses; the subject of the theologian's inquiry is God as revealed in sacred Scripture. In theology, appeal to authority carries most weight; in philosophy, it carries least.

Thomas found Aristotelianism and, to a lesser extent, Platonism useful instruments for Christian thought and communication; but he transformed and deepened everything he borrowed from them. For example, he took over Aristotle's proof of the existence of a primary unmoved mover, but the primary mover at which Thomas arrives is very different from that of Aristotle; it is in fact the God of Judaism and Christianity. He also adopted Aristotle's teaching that the soul is man's form and the body is his matter, but for Aquinas this does not entail, as it does for the Aristotelians, the denial of the immortality of the soul or the ultimate value of the individual. Thomas never compromised Christian doctrine by bringing it into line with the current Aristotelianism; rather, he modified and corrected the latter whenever it clashed with Christian belief. The harmony he established between Aristotelianism

Triumph of Aristotelianism (margin)

and Christianity was not forced but achieved by a new understanding of philosophical principles, especially the notion of being, which he conceived as the act of existing (esse). For him, God is pure being, or the act of existing. Creatures participate in being according to their essence; for example, man participates in being, or the act of existing, to the extent that his humanity, or essence, permits. The fundamental distinction between God and creatures is that creatures have a real composition of essence and existence, whereas God's essence is his existence.

Averroists.   A group of masters in the Faculty of Arts at Paris welcomed Aristotle's philosophy and taught it in disregard of its possible opposition to the Christian faith. They wanted to be philosophers, not theologians, and to them this meant following the Aristotelian system. Because Averroës was the recognized commentator on Aristotle, they generally interpreted his thought in an Averroistic way. Hence, in their own day they were known as "Averroists"; today they are often called "Latin Averroists" because they taught in Latin. Their leader, Siger de Brabant, taught as rationally demonstrated certain Aristotelian doctrines that contradicted the faith, such as the eternity of the world and the oneness of the intellect for all men. They were accused of holding a "double truth"— of maintaining the existence of two contradictory truths: one commanded by faith, the other taught by reason. Although Siger never proposed as true philosophical conclusions contrary to faith, other members of this group upheld the right and duty of the philosopher to follow human reason to its natural conclusions, even when they contradicted the truths of faith.

This growing rationalism confirmed the belief of theologians of a traditionalist cast that the pagan and Muslim philosophies would destroy the Christian faith. They attacked these philosophies in treatises such as Giles of Rome's *Errores philosophorum* (1270; *The Errors of the Philosophers*). In 1277 the Bishop of Paris condemned 219 propositions based on the new trend toward rationalism and naturalism. These included even some of Thomas' Aristotelian doctrines. The same year, the Archbishop of Canterbury made a similar condemnation at Oxford. These reactions to the novel trends in philosophy did not prevent the Averroists from treating philosophical questions apart from religious considerations. Theologians, on their part, were increasingly suspicious of the philosophers and less optimistic about the ultimate reconciliation of philosophy and theology.

Condemnation of Aristotelian doctrines (margin)

PHILOSOPHY IN THE LATE MIDDLE AGES

In the late Middle Ages earlier ways of philosophizing were continued and formalized into definite schools of thought. In the Dominican order, Thomism (theology and philosophy of Thomas Aquinas) was made the official teaching, though the Dominicans did not always adhere to it rigorously. Averroism, cultivated by philosophers such as John of Jandun (died c. 1328), remained a live, though sterile, movement into the Renaissance. In the Franciscan order, the Englishmen John Duns Scotus and William of Ockham developed new styles of theology and philosophy that vied with Thomism throughout the late Middle Ages.

Duns Scotus.   John Duns Scotus (c. 1265–1308) opposed the rationalists' contention that philosophy is self-sufficient and adequate to satisfy man's desire for knowledge. In fact, he claimed, a pure philosopher, such as Aristotle, could not truly understand the human condition because he was ignorant of the Fall of man and his need for grace and redemption. Unenlightened by Christian revelation, Aristotle mistook man's present fallen state, in which all his knowledge comes through the senses, for his natural condition, in which the object of his knowledge would be coextensive with all being, including the being of God. The limitation of Aristotle's philosophy is apparent to Duns Scotus in the Aristotelian proof of the existence of God as the primary mover of the universe. More adequate than this physical proof, he contended, is his own very intricate metaphysical demonstration of the existence of God as the absolutely primary, unique, and infinite being. He incorporated the Anselmian argument into this demonstration. For Duns Scotus, the notion of infinite being, not that of primary mover or being itself, is man's most perfect concept of God.

In opposition to the Greco-Arabic view of the government of the universe from above by necessary causes, Duns Scotus stressed the contingency of the universe and its total dependence on God's infinite creative will. He adopted the traditional Franciscan voluntarism, elevating the will above the intellect in man.

Duns Scotus' doctrine of universals justly earned him the title "Doctor Subtilis." Universals, in his view, exist only as abstract concepts, but they are based on common natures, such as humanity, which exist, or can exist, in many individuals. Common natures are real, and they have a real unity of their own distinct from the unity of the individuals in which they exist. The individuality of each individual is due to an added positive reality that makes the common nature to be this individual; for example, humanity to be Socrates. Duns Scotus calls such a reality an "individual difference," or "thisness" (*haecceitas*). It is an original development of the earlier medieval realism of universals.

William of Ockham. In the late 14th century, Thomism and Scotism were called the "old way" (*via antiqua*) of philosophizing in contrast to the "modern way" (*via moderna*) begun by such men as William of Ockham (*c.* 1285–1347). Ockham, no less than Duns Scotus, wanted to defend the Christian doctrine of the freedom and omnipotence of God and the contingency of creatures against the necessitarianism of Greco-Arabic philosophy. But for him the freedom of God is incompatible with the existence of divine ideas as positive models of creation. God does not use preconceived ideas when he creates, as Duns Scotus maintained, but he fashions the universe as he wishes. As a result, creatures have no natures or essences in common. There are no realities but individual things, and these have nothing in common. They are more or less like each other, however, and on this basis men can form universal concepts of them and talk about them in general terms.

The absolute freedom of God was often used by Ockham as a principle of philosophical and theological explanation. Because the order of nature has been freely created by God, it could have been different: fire, for example, could cool, as it now heats. If he wishes, he can give us the sight, or "intuitive knowledge," of a star without the reality of the star. The moral order could also have been different. God could have made hating him meritorious instead of loving him. It was typical of Ockham not to put too much trust in the power of human reason to reach the truth. For him, philosophy must often be content with probable arguments, for example, in establishing the existence of the Christian God. Faith alone gives certitude in this and in other vital matters. Another principle invoked by Ockham is that a plurality is not to be posited without necessity. This principle of the economy of thought, later stated as beings are not to be multiplied without necessity, is called "Ockham's razor."

Ockhamism was censured by a papal commission at Avignon, Fr., in 1326, and in 1474 it was forbidden to be taught at Paris: it spread widely in the late Middle Ages, nevertheless, and rivaled Thomism and Scotism in popularity. Other Scholastics in the 14th century shared Ockham's basic principles and contributed with him to skepticism and probabilism in philosophy. John of Mirecourt (*c.* 1345) stressed the absolute power of God and the divine will to the point of making him the cause of man's sin. Nicholas of Autrecourt (*c.* 1347) adopted a skeptical attitude regarding such matters as man's ability to prove the existence of God and the reality of substance and causality. Rejecting Aristotelianism as inimical to the Christian faith, he advocated a return to the Atomism of the ancient Greeks as a more adequate explanation of the universe.

Meister Eckehart. The trend away from Aristotelianism was accentuated by the German Dominican Meister Eckehart (*c.* 1260–1327/28), who developed a speculative mysticism of both Christian and Neoplatonic inspiration. Eckehart depicts the ascent of the soul to God in Neoplatonic terms: by gradually purifying itself from the body, the soul transcends being and knowledge until it is ab-

sorbed in the One. The soul is then united with God at its highest point, or "citadel." God himself transcends being and knowledge. Sometimes Eckehart describes God as the being of all things. This language, which was also used by Erigena and other Christian Neoplatonists, leaves him open to the charge of pantheism (the doctrine that the being of creatures is identical with that of God); but for Eckehart there is an infinite gulf between creatures and God. Eckehart means that creatures have no existence of their own but are given existence by God, as the body is made to exist and is contained by the soul. Eckehart's profound influence can be seen in the flowering of mysticism in the German Rhineland in the late Middle Ages.

Nicholas of Cusa. Nicholas of Cusa (1401–64) also preferred the Neoplatonists to the Aristotelians. To him, the philosophy of Aristotle is an obstacle to the mind in its ascent to God because its primary rule is the principle of contradiction, which denies the compatibility of contradictories. But God is the "coincidence of opposites." Because he is infinite, he embraces all things in perfect unity; he is at once the maximum and the minimum. Nicholas uses mathematical symbols to illustrate how, in infinity, contradictories coincide. If a circle is enlarged, the curve of its circumference becomes less; if a circle is infinite, its circumference is a straight line. As for man's knowledge of the infinite God, he must be content with conjecture or approximation to the truth. The absolute truth escapes man; his proper attitude is "learned ignorance."

For Nicholas, God alone is absolutely infinite. The universe reflects this divine perfection and is relatively infinite. It has no circumference, for it is limited by nothing outside of itself. Neither has it a centre; the Earth is neither at the centre of the universe nor is it completely at rest. Place and motion are not absolute but relative to the observer. This new, non-Aristotelian conception of the universe anticipated some of the features of modern theories.

Thus, at the end of the Middle Ages, some of the most creative minds were abandoning Aristotelianism and turning to newer ways of thought. The philosophy of Aristotle, in its various interpretations, continued to be taught in the universities, but it had lost its vitality and creativity. Christian philosophers were once again finding inspiration in Neoplatonism. The Platonism of the Renaissance was in direct continuity with the Platonism of the Middle Ages.

(A.A.Ma.)

Modern philosophy

THE RENAISSANCE AND EARLY MODERN PERIOD

The philosophy of a period arises as a response to social need, and the development of philosophy in the history of Western civilization since the Renaissance has, thus, reflected the process in which creative philosophers have responded to the unique challenge of each stage in the development of Western culture itself.

The career of philosophy—how it views its tasks and functions, how it defines itself, the special methods it invents for the achievement of philosophical knowledge, the literary forms it adopts and utilizes, its conception of the scope of its subject matter, and its changing criteria of meaning and truth—hinges on the mode of its successive responses to the challenges of the social structure within which it arises. Thus, Western philosophy in the Middle Ages was primarily a Christian philosophy, complementing the divine revelation, reflecting the feudal order in its cosmology, devoting itself in no small measure to the institutional tasks of the Roman Catholic Church. It was no accident that the major philosophical achievements of the 13th and 14th centuries were the work of churchmen who also happened to be professors of theology at the universities of Oxford and Paris.

The Renaissance of the late 15th and 16th centuries presented a different set of problems and therefore suggested different lines of philosophical endeavour. What is called the European Renaissance followed upon the introduction of three novel mechanical inventions from the East: gunpowder, block printing from movable type, and the compass. The first was used to explode the massive fortifications of the feudal order and thus became an

Margin notes (left column):

Defense of the doctrine of God's will

Trend away from Aristotelianism

Margin notes (right column):

Cultural impact of new inventions and nations

agent of the new spirit of nationalism that threatened the rule of churchmen—and, indeed, the universalist emphasis of the church itself—with a competing secular power. The second, printing, made the propagation of knowledge widespread, secularized learning, reduced the intellectual monopoly of an ecclesiastical elite, and restored the literary and philosophical classics of Greece and Rome. The third, the compass, increased the safety and scope of navigation, produced the voyages of discovery that opened up the Western Hemisphere, and symbolized a new spirit of physical adventure and a new scientific interest in the structure of the natural world.

Each of these inventions with its wider cultural consequences presented new intellectual problems and novel philosophical tasks within a changed political and social environment. For, as the power of a single religious authority was slowly eroded under the influence of the Protestant Reformation and as the prestige of the universal Latin language gave way to vernacular tongues, philosophers became less and less identified with their positions in the ecclesiastical hierarchy and more and more identified with their national origins. The works of Albertus Magnus, St. Thomas Aquinas, St. Bonaventure, and John Duns Scotus had been basically unrelated to the countries of their birth; but the philosophy of Niccolò Machiavelli was directly related to Italian experience, that of Sir Francis Bacon and Thomas Hobbes was English to the core, and that of René Descartes set the standard and tone of French intellectual life for 200 years.

Dominant strands of Renaissance philosophy. Knowledge in the contemporary world is conventionally divided between the natural sciences, the social sciences, and the humanities. In the Renaissance, however, fields of learning had not yet become so sharply departmentalized: in fact, each of these divisions arose in the comprehensive and broadly inclusive area of Renaissance philosophy. For, as the Renaissance mounted its revolt against the reign of religion and therefore reacted against the church, against authority, against Scholasticism, and against Aristotle, there was a sudden blossoming of interest in problems centring on civil society, man, and nature. These three interests found exact representation in the three dominant strands of Renaissance philosophy: (1) political theory, (2) humanism, and (3) the philosophy of nature.

Political theory. As secular authority replaced ecclesiastical authority and as the dominant interest of the age shifted from religion to politics, it was natural that the rivalries of the national states and their persistent crises of internal order should raise with renewed urgency philosophical problems, practically dormant since pre-Christian times, about the nature and the moral status of political power. This new preoccupation with national unity, internal security, state power, and international justice stimulated the growth of political philosophy in Italy, France, England, and Holland.

Machia-
velli and
power

In early 16th-century Italy, Niccolò Machiavelli, sometime state secretary of the Florentine republic, explored in *Il principe* (written 1512–13; *The Prince*) and in his *Discorsi sopra la prima deca di Tito Livio* (completed by 1521; "Discourses on the First Ten Books of Livy" in *Discourses*) the techniques for the seizure and retention of power in ways that seemed to exalt "reasons of state" above morality and codified the actual practices of Renaissance diplomacy for the next 100 years. In fact, Machiavelli was motivated by patriotic hopes for the ultimate unification of Italy and by the conviction that the low estate of Italian Renaissance morality needed to be elevated by restoring the ancient Roman virtues. More than half a century later in France, Jean Bodin, magistrate of Laon and a member of the Estates-General, insisted that the state must possess a single, unified, and absolute power; he thus developed in detail the doctrine of national sovereignty in all of its administrative consequences and in its role as the source of all legal legitimacy.

In the 17th century in England, Thomas Hobbes, who was to become tutor to the future Charles II, developed the fiction that in the "state of nature" that preceded civilization life was "nasty, brutish, and short" with "every man's hand raised against every other," and that a "social

contract" was thus agreed upon to convey all private rights to a single sovereign in return for general protection and for the institution of a reign of law. Because law is simply "the command of the sovereign," Hobbes at once turned justice into a by-product of power and denied any right of rebellion except when the sovereign becomes too weak to protect the commonwealth and hold it united.

In Holland, a prosperous and tolerant commercial republic in the 17th century, the issues of political philosophy took a different form. Thus, when the Dutch East India Company commissioned a great jurist, Hugo Grotius (1583–1645), to provide a defense of their trade rights and of their free access to the seas, the resulting two treatises, *Mare Liberum* (1609; *The Freedom of the Seas*) and *De Jure Belli ac Pacis* (1625; *On the Law of War and Peace*), were the first significant codifications of international law. Their philosophical originality lay, however, in the fact that, in defending the rights of a small, militarily weak nation against the powerful absolutisms of England, France, and Spain, Grotius was led to a preliminary investigation of the sources and validity of the concept of "natural law"—the notion that inherent in human reason and immutable even against the willfulness of sovereign states are imperative considerations of natural justice and moral responsibility, which must serve as a check against the arbitrary exercise of vast political power.

Ambiv-
alence of
political
philoso-
phers

In general, the political philosophy of the Renaissance was dualistic: it was haunted, even confused, by the conflict between political necessity and general moral responsibility. Machiavelli, Bodin, and Hobbes asserted claims that justified the actions of Italian despotism and the absolutisms of the Bourbon and Stuart dynasties. Yet Machiavelli was obsessed with the problem of human virtue; Bodin insisted that even the sovereign ought to obey the law of nature—that is, to govern in accordance with the dictates of natural justice; and Hobbes himself found in natural law the rational motivation that causes a man to seek for security and peace. In the end, though Renaissance political necessity required that the philosophical doctrines of Thrasymachus (who held that right is what is in the interest of the strong) be implemented, it could never finally escape a twinge of Socratic conscience.

Humanism. The Renaissance was characterized by the renewed study of mathematics, medicine, and classical literature. The first two sparked the scientific revolution of the 16th and 17th centuries; the last became the foundation of the philosophy of Renaissance humanism. From its origin, humanism—suspicious of science and generally indifferent to religion—emphasized anew the centrality of man in the universe, his supreme value and importance. Characteristic of this emphasis was the famous *Oratio de hominis dignitate* (written 1486; *Oration on the Dignity of Man*) of a late 15th-century Platonist, Pico della Mirandola, a leading member of Lorenzo de' Medici's Platonic Academy of Florence. But the new emphasis upon man's personal responsibility and on the possibility of his self-creation as a work of art was in no small part a consequence of the rediscovery of a series of crucial classical texts, which served to reverse the trends of medieval learning. Renaissance humanism was predicated upon the victory of rhetoric over dialectic and of Plato over Aristotle, as Quintilian and Cicero had triumphed over Abelard and as the cramped format of Scholastic philosophical method gave way to a Platonic discursiveness.

Much of this had been prepared by Italian scholarly initiative in the early 15th century. The recently discovered manuscript of Quintilian was used by Lorenzo Valla, an antiauthoritarian humanist, for the creation of modern rhetoric and the principles of textual criticism. But even more important was the rebirth of an enthusiasm for the philosophy of Plato in Medicean Florence and at the cultivated court of Urbino, a dukedom east of Florence. Precisely to service this enthusiasm, Marsilio Ficino, head of the Platonic Academy, had translated the entire Platonic corpus into Latin by the end of the century.

Enthu-
siasm for
Plato

Except for Pico and Giordano Bruno, a late 16th-century Italian philosopher, the direct influence of Platonism upon Renaissance metaphysics is difficult to trace. The Platonic account of the moral virtues, however, was admirably adapted to the requirements of Renaissance education and gave new support to the Renaissance ideal of the courtier and the gentleman. But Plato also represented the philosophical importance of mathematics and the Pythagorean attempt to discover the secrets of the heavens, the earth, and the world of nature in terms of number and exact calculation; and this aspect of Platonism spilled over from humanism into the domain of Renaissance science. The scientists Nicolaus Copernicus, Johannes Kepler, and Galileo owe more to the general climate of Pythagorean confidence in the explanatory power of number than does Renaissance metaphysics.

But Platonism also had the effect of influencing the literary form in which Renaissance philosophy was written. Although the very early medieval Platonists St. Augustine and John Scotus Erigena occasionally had used the dialogue form, later Scholasticism had abandoned it in favour of the formal treatise, of which the great "Summas" of Alexander of Hales and St. Thomas Aquinas are pristine examples. The Renaissance rediscovery of the Platonic dialogues suggested the literary charm of this conversational method to humanists, scientists, and political theorists alike. The humanist philosopher Bruno put forth his central insights in a dialogue, *De la causa, principio e uno* (1584; *Concerning the Cause, Principle, and One*); Galileo presented his novel mechanics in his *Dialogo sopra i due massimi sistemi del mondo, tolemaico e copernicano* (1632; *Dialogue Concerning the Two Chief World Systems—Ptolemaic and Copernican*); and even the politician Machiavelli wrote *Dell'arte della guerra* (1521; *The Art of War*) as a genteel conversation taking place in a quiet Florentine garden.

Renaissance humanism was primarily a moral and a literary, rather than a narrowly philosophical, movement. And it flowered in figures with broadly philosophical interests, such as Erasmus of Rotterdam, the erudite citizen of the world; Sir Thomas More, the learned but unfortunate chancellor of Henry VIII; and, in the next generation, in the great French essayist and mayor of Bordeaux, Michel de Montaigne. But the recovery of the Greek and Latin classics, which was the work of humanism, had profound effects upon the entire field of Renaissance philosophy and science through the ancient schools of philosophy to which it once more directed attention. In addition to Platonism, the most notable of these were Greek Atomistic Materialism, Greek Skepticism, and Roman Stoicism. The discovery of the manuscript of Lucretius (and the Atomistic doctrines of Democritus) finally came to influence Galileo, Bruno, and, later, Pierre Gassendi, a modern Epicurean, through the insights into nature reflected in this work. The recovery of the manuscript of Sextus Empiricus, with its carefully argued Skepticism presented in a printed text in 1562, produced "a skeptical crisis" in French philosophy, which dominated the period from Montaigne to René Descartes. And the Stoicism of Seneca and Epictetus became almost the official ethics of the Renaissance—to appear prominently in the *Essais* (1580–88) of Montaigne, in the letters that Descartes wrote to the princess Elizabeth of Bohemia and to Queen Christina of Sweden, and in the later sections of the *Ethics* (first published 1675) of the Rationalist Benedict de Spinoza.

Philosophy of nature. Philosophy in the modern world is a self-conscious discipline. It has managed to define itself narrowly, so as to differentiate itself on the one hand from religion and on the other from exact science. But this narrowing of focus came about very late in its history—certainly not before the 18th century. The earliest philosophers of Greece were theorists of the physical world; Pythagoras and Plato were at once philosophers and mathematicians; and in Aristotle no clear distinction between philosophy and natural science can be maintained. The Renaissance continued this breadth of conception characteristic of the Greeks. Galileo and Descartes were mathematicians, physicists, and philosophers at once; and physics retained the name of "natural philosophy" at least until the death of Sir Isaac Newton in 1727.

Had the Renaissance been painstakingly self-aware in the matter of definition (which it was not), it might have defined philosophy, on the basis of its actual practice, as

"the rational, methodical, and systematic consideration of man, civil society, and the natural world." The areas of its interests would in no case have been in doubt. But exactly what constitutes "rational, methodical, and systematic consideration" would have been extremely controversial. For knowledge advances through the discovery and advocacy of new philosophical methods; and, because the diverse methods advocated depend for their validity upon the acceptance of different philosophical criteria of truth, meaning, and importance, the crucial philosophical quarrels of the 16th and 17th centuries were at bottom quarrels in the advocacy of methods. It is this issue rather than any disagreement over subject matter or areas of attention that separated the greatest Renaissance philosophers—such as Francis Bacon, René Descartes, and Thomas Hobbes.

The great new fact that confronted the Renaissance was the immediacy, the immensity, and the uniformity of the natural world. But what was of primary importance was the new perspective in which this fact was interpreted. To the Middle Ages the universe was hierarchical, organic, and God-ordained. To the Renaissance it was pluralistic, machinelike, and mathematically ordered. In the Middle Ages scholars thought in terms of purposes, of ends, of divine intentions; in the Renaissance they thought in terms of forces, mechanical agencies, and physical causes. All of this had become clear by the end of the 15th century. Within the early pages of the *Notebooks* of Leonardo da Vinci, the great Florentine artist, scientist, humanist, and mechanical genius, occur the following three propositions:

Leonardo's three theses

(1) Since experience has been the mistress of whoever has written well, I take her as my mistress, and to her on all points make my appeal.
(2) Instrumental or mechanical science is the noblest and above all others the most useful, seeing that by means of it all animated bodies which have movement perform all their actions.
(3) There is no certainty where one can neither apply any of the mathematical sciences, nor any of those which are based upon the mathematical sciences.

Here are enunciated respectively: (1) the principle of Empiricism, (2) the advocacy of mechanistic science, and (3) the faith in mathematical explanation; and it is upon these three formulations, as upon a rock, that the science and philosophy of the Renaissance built their foundations. From each of Leonardo's theses descended one of the great streams of Renaissance philosophy: from the empirical principle the work of Francis Bacon; from mechanism the work of Thomas Hobbes; and from mathematical explanation that of René Descartes.

Any adequate philosophical treatment of scientific method surely contains both an empirical principle and a faith in mathematical explanation; and, in Leonardo's thinking, as in scientific procedure generally, there need be no conflict between them. Yet they do represent two poles of emphasis, each capable of excluding the other. Moreover, the peculiar accidents of Renaissance scientific achievement did present some evidence for their mistaken separation: for the revival of medical studies on the one hand and the novel blooming of mathematical physics on the other emphasized opposite virtues in scientific methodology. This polarity was represented by the opposing figures of Vesalius and Galileo.

In the mid-16th century Andreas Vesalius, a Belgian physician, was astounding all of Europe with the unbelievable precision of his anatomical dissections and drawings. Having invented new tools for this precise purpose, he successively laid bare the vascular, the neural, and the musculature systems of the human body; and this procedure seemed to demonstrate the virtues of empirical method, of physiological experiment, and of the precision and disciplined skill in sensory observation that made his demonstrations classics of inductive procedure.

Only slightly later the Italian physicist Galileo, following in the tradition already established by Copernicus and Kepler, founders of modern astronomy (but without their more mystical and metaphysical eccentricities), attempted to do for terrestrial and sidereal movements what Vesalius had managed for the structure of the human body—creating his experiential dynamics, however, with the help

Galileo's experiential dynamics

Revival of other ancient Greek schools

of hypotheses supplied by the quantitative calculations of mathematics. In Galileo's work all of the most original scientific directions of the Renaissance came to a head: the revival of Alexandrian mathematics, the experimental use of new instruments, like the lens and the telescope, the search for certainty in physics based upon the undoubted applicability of mathematical theory, and the underlying faith that the search for absolute certainty in science was reasonable because matter in motion accorded with a model of mathematical simplicity. Galileo's work also deals with some of the recurrent themes of 16th- and 17th-century philosophy: an atomism that relates changes in the relations of physical bodies to the corpuscular motion of their parts, the reduction of all qualitative differences to quantitative reasons, and the resultant important distinction between "primary" and "secondary" qualities. The former—including shape, extension, and specific gravity—were considered to be in fact a constituent part of nature and therefore "real." The latter—such as colour, odour, taste, and relative position—were taken to be simply the effect of bodily movements upon perceiving minds and therefore ephemeral, "subjective," and essentially irrelevant to the nature of physical reality.

Rise of Empiricism and Rationalism. The scientific contrast between Vesalius' rigorous observational techniques and Galileo's reliance upon mathematical theory received further expression in the contrast between the respective philosophies of Francis Bacon and René Descartes. And, indeed, in its more abstract formulation as the contrast between Rationalism and Empiricism, it was to dominate the philosophical controversies of the 17th and 18th centuries and to present a dilemma hardly to be resolved before the advent of Immanuel Kant.

The Empiricism of Francis Bacon. Flourishing about the turn of the 17th century, Sir Francis Bacon (1561–1626) was the outstanding apostle of Renaissance Empiricism. Less an original metaphysician or cosmologist than the advocate of a vast new program for the advancement of learning and the reformation of scientific method, Bacon conceived of philosophy as a new technique of reasoning that should reestablish natural science upon a firm foundation. In the *Advancement of Learning* (1605) he charted the map of knowledge: history, which depends upon the human faculty of memory; poetry, upon that of imagination; and philosophy, upon man's reason. To reason, however, Bacon assigned a completely experiential

function. Fifteen years later, in his *Novum Organum,* he made this clear: because, he said, "we have as yet no natural philosophy which is pure, . . . the true business of philosophy must be . . . to apply the understanding . . . to a fresh examination of particulars." A technique for "the fresh examination of particulars" thus constituted his chief claim to philosophical distinction.

Bacon's hope for a new birth of science hinged not only upon vastly more numerous and varied experiments but chiefly upon "an entirely different method, order, and process for advancing experience." This method consisted in the construction of what he called "tables of discovery." He distinguished three kinds: tables of presence, of absence, and of degree (*i.e.,* in the case of any two properties, such as heat and friction, instances in which they appeared together, instances in which one appeared without the other, and instances in which their amounts varied proportionately); and the ultimate purpose of these tables was to order facts in such a way that the true causes of phenomena (the subject of physics) and the true "forms" of things (the subject of metaphysics—the study of the nature of Being) could be inductively established.

Bacon's was no raw Empiricism; his profound sense of fact and his belief in the primacy of observation led him to elicit laws and generalizations. Also, his conception of forms was quite un-Platonic: a form for him was not an essence but a permanent geometric or mechanical structure. His enduring place in the history of philosophy lies, however, in his single-minded advocacy of experience as the only source of valid knowledge and in his profound enthusiasm for the perfection of natural science. It is in this sense that "the Baconian spirit" continued as a source of inspiration: his elaborate classification of the sciences

inspiring the French Encyclopaedists of the 18th century and his Empiricism inspiring the English philosophers of science of the 19th century.

The Materialism of Thomas Hobbes. The English political philosopher Thomas Hobbes (1588–1679) was acquainted with both Bacon and Galileo. With the first he shared a strong concern for philosophical method, with the second an overwhelming interest in matter in motion. His philosophical efforts, however, were more inclusive and more complete than those of either of these contemporaries. He was a comprehensive thinker within the scope of an exceedingly narrow set of presuppositions, and he produced one of the most systematic philosophies of the early modern period—an almost completely consistent description of nature, man, and civil society according to the tenets of mechanistic Materialism.

Hobbes's account of what philosophy is and ought to be clearly distinguished between content and method. As method, philosophy is simply reasoning or calculating by the use of words as to the causes of phenomena. When a man reasons forward from causes to effects, he reasons synthetically, and, when he reasons from effects backward to causes, he does so analytically. (His strong deductive and geometric bias favoured the former.) Hobbes's dogmatic metaphysical presupposition was that the basic reality is matter in motion. The real world is a corporeal universe in constant movement, and the phenomena, the causes and effects of which it is the business of philosophy to lay bare, are either the mutual action of bodies or the quaint effects of bodies upon minds. From this assumption follows Hobbes's classification of the fields that form the content of philosophy: (1) physics, (2) moral philosophy, and (3) civil philosophy. Physics is the science of the motions and actions of natural bodies conceived in terms of cause and effect. Moral philosophy (or, more accurately, psychology) is the detailed study of "the passions and perturbations of the mind"—that is, how minds are "moved" by desire, aversion, appetite, fear, anger, and envy. And civil philosophy concerns the concerted actions of men in a commonwealth—how in detail the wayward wills of men are constrained by power (force) in the prevention of civil disorder and the maintenance of peace.

Hobbes's philosophy was a bold Renaissance restatement of Greek Atomistic Materialism with applications to the realities of Renaissance politics that would have seemed strange to its ancient originators. But there are also elements in it that make it characteristically English. For Hobbes's conventionalist account of language led him to a nominalistic position—that is, to a position denying the reality of universals (general or common concepts)—in much the same fashion as did Bacon's exaggerated emphasis on particulars. Moreover, Bacon's general emphasis upon experience also had its analogue in Hobbes's sensationalist theory of knowledge: the notion that all knowledge has its origin in sense impressions and that all sensations are caused by the action of external bodies upon the organs of sense. Empiricism has been a basic and recurrent expression of British mentality, and its nominalistic and sensationalist roots were already clearly evident in both Bacon and Hobbes.

Rationalism of Descartes. But it was not their philosophy that was to dominate the last half of the 17th century but rather that of René Descartes (1596–1650), a French gentleman who signed himself "Lord of Perron" and who lived the 20 most productive years of his life in the tolerant and hospitable Dutch republic. Descartes, a crucial figure in the history of philosophy, combined (however unconsciously or even unwillingly) the influences of the past into a synthesis that was striking in its originality and yet congenial to the scientific temper of the age. In the minds of all later historians he counts as the progenitor of the modern spirit in philosophy.

From the past there seeped into the Cartesian synthesis doctrines about God from Anselm and Aquinas, a theory of the will from Augustine, a deep sympathy with the Stoicism of the Romans, and a skeptical method taken indirectly from the ancient Skeptics Pyrrho and Sextus Empiricus. But Descartes was also a great mathematician, who invented analytic geometry, who made many physical and anatomical experiments, who knew and profoundly respected the work of Galileo, and who withdrew from publication his own cosmological treatise *Le Monde* ("The World") after Galileo's condemnation by the Inquisition in 1633.

Each of the maxims of Leonardo, which compose the Renaissance worldview, found its place in Descartes: the Empiricism of his physiological researches described in his *Discours de la méthode* (1637; *Discourse on Method*), the mechanistic interpretations of the physical world and human action detailed in the *Principia Philosophiae* (1644; *Principles of Philosophy*) and *Traité des passions de l'âme* (1649; *The Passions of the Soul*), and the mathematical bias that dominates his theory of method in the *Regulae ad Directionem Ingenii* (published 1701; *Rules for the Direction of the Mind*) and his metaphysics in the *Meditationes de Prima Philosophia* (2nd ed. 1642; *Meditations on the First Philosophy*). But of these three, it is the mathematical strain that clearly predominates.

Bacon and Descartes, the founders of modern Empiricism and Rationalism, respectively, shared two pervasive Renaissance tenets: an enormous enthusiasm for physical science; and the belief that knowledge means power—that the ultimate purpose of theoretical science is to serve the practical needs of men.

In his *Principia* Descartes defined philosophy as "the study of wisdom" or "the perfect knowledge of all one can know." Its chief utility is "for the conduct of life" (morals), "the conservation of health" (medicine), and "the invention of all the arts" (mechanics). He expressed the relation of philosophy as theoretical inquiry to practical consequences in the famous metaphor of the tree of philosophy whose root is metaphysics, whose trunk is physics, and whose branches are, respectively, morals, medicine, and mechanics. The metaphor is revealing for it indicates that, for Descartes (as for Bacon and Galileo), the major concern was for the trunk (physics) and that he busied himself with the roots only in order to provide a firm foundation for the trunk. Thus the *Discours de la méthode,* which provides a synoptic view of the Cartesian philosophy, shows it to be not (as with Aristotle or Whitehead) a metaphysics founded upon physics but rather—that more characteristic product of the 17th century—a physics founded upon metaphysics.

Elements in Cartesian synthesis

Descartes's mathematical bias was expressed in his determination to ground natural science not in sensation and probability (as did Bacon) but in a principle of absolute certainty. Thus his metaphysics in essence consisted of three principles:

1. To employ the procedure of complete and systematic doubt to eliminate every belief that does not pass the test of indubitability (skepticism);

2. To accept no idea as certain that is not clear, distinct, and free of contradiction (mathematicism);

3. To found all knowledge upon the bedrock certainty of self-consciousness, so that "I think, therefore I am" becomes the only innate idea unshakable by doubt (subjectivism).

From the indubitability of the self, Descartes deduced the existence of a perfect God; and, from the fact that a perfect being is incapable of falsification or deception, he made the inference that those ideas about the corporeal world that he has implanted within man must be true. The achievement of certainty about the natural world was thus guaranteed by the perfection of God and by the clear and distinct ideas that are his gift.

The Cartesian metaphysics is the fountainhead of Rationalism in modern philosophy, for it suggests that the mathematical criteria of clarity, distinctness, and absence of contradiction among ideas are the ultimate test of meaningfulness and truth. This stance is profoundly antiempirical. Bacon, who had said that "reasoners resemble spiders who make cobwebs out of their own substance," might well have said so of Descartes, for the Cartesian self is just such a substance from which the idea of God originates and with which all deductive reasoning begins. Yet for Descartes the understanding is vastly superior to the senses, and, in the question of what constitutes truth in science, only man's reason can ultimately decide.

Cartesianism after Descartes

Cartesianism was to dominate the intellectual life of the Continent until the end of the 17th century. It was a fashionable philosophy, appealing alike to learned gentlemen and highborn ladies; and it was one of the few philosophical alternatives to the decadent Scholasticism still being taught in the universities. Precisely for this reason it constituted a serious threat to established religious authority. In 1663 the Roman Catholic Church placed Descartes's works on the Index of Forbidden Books, and the University of Oxford forbade the teaching of his doctrines. Only in the liberal Dutch universities, such as Groningen and Utrecht, did Cartesianism make serious headway.

Certain features of the Cartesian philosophy made it an important starting point for subsequent philosophical speculation. Being the meeting ground of the medieval and the modern worldviews, it accepted the doctrines of Renaissance science while attempting to ground them metaphysically in the medieval notions of God and the human mind. Thus a certain dualism between God the Creator and the mechanistic world of his creation and between mind as a spiritual principle and matter as mere spatial extension was inherent in the Cartesian position; and a whole generation of French Cartesians (among them Arnold Geulincx, Nicolas Malebranche, and Pierre Bayle) wrestled with the resulting problems of the interaction and reconciliation between the counterposed entities.

Rationalism of Spinoza and Leibniz. Two philosophers of genius carried on the tradition of continental Rationalism: the Dutch Jew Benedict de Spinoza (1632–77) and his younger contemporary Gottfried Wilhelm Leibniz (1646–1716), a Leipzig scholar and polymath. Bacon's philosophy had been a search for method in science, and Descartes's basic aim had been the achievement of scientific certainty; but Hobbes and Spinoza provided the most comprehensively worked out speculative systems of the early modern period. In certain respects they had much in common: a mechanistic picture of the world, with its events guided by a strict determinism, and even a political philosophy in each case looking for political stability based upon centralized power. Yet Spinoza introduced a conception of philosophizing that was new to the Renaissance: Philosophy became a personal and moral quest for the wisdom of life and for the achievement of human perfection.

Spinoza's aim, terminology, and method

In conducting this search, Spinoza borrowed much of the basic apparatus of Descartes: the aim at a rational understanding of principles, the terminology of "substance" and of "clear and distinct ideas," and a mathematical method that seeks to convert philosophical knowledge into a complete deductive system using the geometric model of Euclid's *Elements.* Spinoza viewed the universe pantheistically as a single infinite substance, which he called "God," with the dual attributes (or aspects) of thought and extension, and which he differentiated into plural "modes" (or particular things); and he attributed to this world as a whole the properties of a timeless logical system—of a complex of completely determined causes and effects. In so doing Spinoza was simply seeking for man the series of "adequate" ideas that furnish the intellect and constitute human freedom. For ultimately, for Spinoza, the wisdom that philosophy seeks is achieved when one perceives the universe in its wholeness, through the "intellectual love of God," which merges the finite individual with the eternal unity and provides the mind with the pure joy that is the final achievement of its search.

Whereas the basic elements of the Spinozistic worldview are given in his one great work, the *Ethics,* Leibniz' philosophy has to be pieced together from numerous brief expositions or fragments, which seem to be mere intermissions, or philosophical interludes, in an otherwise busy life. But the philosophical form is deceptive. Leibniz was a mathematician and jurist (inventor of the infinitesimal calculus and codifier of the laws of Mainz), diplomat, historian to royalty, and court librarian in a princely house; yet he was also one of the most original philosophers of the early modern period. His chief contributions were in the fields of logic, in which he was a truly brilliant innovator, and metaphysics, in which he provided a third alternative to the Rationalist constructions of Spinoza and Descartes. Leibniz saw logic as a mathematical calculus.

He was the first to distinguish "truths of reason" from "truths of fact" and to contrast the "necessary" propositions of logic and mathematics (which express identities), which hold for all possible worlds, with the "contingent" (or empirical) propositions of science, which hold only for certain existential conditions; and he saw clearly that, as "the principle of contradiction" controls the first, so "the principle of sufficient reason" governs the second.

A plu-
ralism of
monads

In metaphysics Leibniz espoused pluralism (as opposed to the dualism of Descartes's thought and extension and the monism of Spinoza's single substance, which is God). There were for him an infinite number of spiritual substances (which he called "monads"), each different, each a percipient of the universe around it, and each mirroring that universe from its own point of view. The chief significance of Leibniz, however, lies not in his differences from Descartes and Spinoza but in the extreme Rationalism that all three shared. In the *Principes de la nature et de la grâce fondés en raison* (1714; "Principles of Nature and of Grace Founded in Reason"), he stated the maxim that can stand for the entire school:

> True reasoning depends upon necessary or eternal truths, such as those of logic, numbers, geometry, which establish an indubitable connection of ideas and unfailing consequences.

Literary forms and sociological conditions. The literary forms in which philosophical exposition was couched in the early modern period ranged from the scientific aphorisms of Bacon and the autobiographical meditations of Descartes to the systematic prose of Hobbes and the episodic propositional format of Leibniz. Two basic tendencies, however, can be discerned:

1. The early Renaissance commitment to the dialogue form (already noted), inspired by the rediscovery of the Platonic dialogues;
2. The later prevalence of the systematically ordered treatise, undoubtedly influenced by the enormous prestige of deductive mathematics.

The concept of serial order stressed by geometry, in which the reasoner passes from more universal axioms to more specific derivative propositions, influenced in turn the style of Hobbes, Descartes, and Spinoza. The order of presentation in Hobbes's *Leviathan* and in Descartes's *Principia Philosophiae* reflects this serial concern, while Spinoza's *Ethics* utilizes the Euclidean method so formalistically as almost to constitute an impenetrable barrier to the basic lucidity of his thought.

Medieval philosophy with its texts, readings, learned authorities, Disputed Questions, Quodlibetal Questions (brief academic discussions), and its Summas was characteristically associated with the medieval university. It is a singular fact, therefore, that from the birth of Bacon in 1561 to the death of Hume in 1776—*i.e.,* for 200 years—not one first-rate philosophical mind in Europe was permanently associated with a university.

The fact is that, as the age of the saint passed into that of the gentleman, philosophers too reflected this profound change in their titles, their social status, and their economic situation. Sir Francis Bacon was a lawyer, judge, and attendant upon the royal court. Thomas Hobbes was the tutor and companion of young noblemen. René Descartes, son of a noble family, traveled and studied at leisure, retiring to Holland to live out his life on inherited income. Gottfried Wilhelm Leibniz, courtier, diplomat, and scholar, became a privy councillor and baron of the Holy Roman Empire. Thus philosophers often belonged to the lesser nobility or were closely associated with the nobility, to whom—like poets—they dedicated their works; and they lived not by philosophy but for it—either independently, by pensions, gifts, inherited income, or in the households of the nobility.

Thus, philosophy in the 16th and 17th centuries was clearly the preoccupation of a widely scattered elite; and this meant that, despite the printed essay, much philosophical communication took place within a small but at the same time loose and informal circle. Treatises were circulated in manuscript; comments and objections were solicited; and a vast polemical correspondence was built up. Prior to its publication, Descartes prudently sent his *Meditationes* to the theologians of the Sorbonne for comment; and, after its publication, his friend Mersenne sent it to Hobbes, Antoine Arnauld, and Pierre Gassendi, among others, who returned formal "objections," to which Descartes in turn replied. In addition, the 17th century possessed a rich repository of philosophical correspondence, such as the letters that passed between Descartes and the scientist Christiaan Huygens, between Spinoza and Henry Oldenburg (one of the first secretaries of the Royal Society), and between Leibniz and Arnauld. But philosophers were also familiar with the great monarchs and administrators of the age: Descartes gave philosophical instruction to Queen Christina of Sweden, Leibniz was an intimate of Queen Sophia Charlotte of Prussia, and Spinoza enjoyed the personal friendship of the Dutch politician Johan de Witt.

The chief fact, however, remains the sharp separation of creative philosophers from the formal centres of learning: Hobbes expressed extreme contempt for the decadent Aristotelianism of Oxford; Descartes, despite his prudence, scorned the medievalists of the Sorbonne; and Spinoza refused the offer of a professorship of philosophy at Heidelberg with polite aversion. It was to be another 100 years before philosophy returned to the universities.

THE ENLIGHTENMENT

Although they both lived and worked in the late 17th century, Sir Isaac Newton and John Locke were the true fathers of the Enlightenment. Newton was the last of the scientific geniuses of the age, and his great *Philosophiae Naturalis Principia Mathematica* (1687; *Mathematical Principles of Natural Philosophy*) was the culmination of the entire movement that had begun with Copernicus and Galileo—the first great physical synthesis based upon the application of mathematics to nature in every detail. The basic idea of the authority and autonomy of reason, which dominated all philosophizing in the 18th century, was, at bottom, the consequence of Newton's work.

Seminal
influence
of
Newton's
Principia

Copernicus, Kepler, Bacon, Galileo, and Descartes—scientists and methodologists of science—performed like men urgently attempting to persuade nature to reveal her secrets. Newton's comprehensive mechanistic system made it seem as if at last she had done so. It is impossible to exaggerate the enormous enthusiasm that this assumption kindled in all of the major thinkers of the 18th century from Locke to Kant. The new enthusiasm for reason that they all instinctively shared was based not upon the mere advocacy of propagandists like Descartes and Leibniz but upon the conviction that for the intellectual conquest of the natural world reason had really worked.

Classical British Empiricism and its basic tasks. Two major philosophical problems remained: to account for the genetic origins of the reason that had proved so successful and to shift its application from external nature to man. John Locke's *Essay Concerning Human Understanding* (1690) was devoted to the first; and David Hume's *Treatise of Human Nature* (1739–40), "being an attempt to apply the method of experimental reasoning to moral subjects," was devoted to the second.

These two basic tasks reflect a shift away from the direction in which philosophizing had moved in the late Renaissance. The Renaissance preoccupation with the natural world had represented a certain "realistic" bias. Hobbes and Spinoza had each produced a metaphysics. They had been interested in the real constitution of the physical world. Moreover, the Renaissance bias in favour of mathematics had generated the profound interest in rational principles, necessary propositions, and innate ideas that was so prevalent in the philosophies of Leibniz and Descartes. On the other hand, the Enlightenment, in turning from the realities of nature to account for the structure of the mind that knows it so successfully and in attempting an experiential account of the furnishings of that mind, settled on the sensory components of knowledge rather than on the merely mathematical. Thus the school of so-called British Empiricism (John Locke, George Berkeley, and David Hume) dominated the perspective of Enlightenment philosophy until the time of Kant. And this school philosophized in terms of ideas rather than things

Shift to
epistemo-
logical and
Empiricist
philosophy

and of experience rather than innate necessary principles. Whereas the philosophy of the late Renaissance had been metaphysical and Rationalistic, that of the Enlightenment was epistemological and Empiricist.

Origin and nature of reason in Locke and Berkeley. Locke's *Essay Concerning Human Understanding* thus marked a decisively new direction for modern philosophizing because it proposed what amounts to a new criterion of truth. The design of his essay was "to inquire into the origin, certainty, and extent of human knowledge," which involved three tasks:

1. To discover the origin of men's ideas;
2. To exhibit their certainty and evidential value;
3. To examine the claims of all knowledge that is less than certain.

What was crucial for Locke, however, was that the second task is dependent upon the first. Following the general Renaissance custom, Locke defined an "idea" as a mental content, as "whatever is the object of the understanding when a man thinks"; but, whereas for Descartes and the entire Rationalistic school the certainty of ideas had been a function of their self-evidence—*i.e.,* of their clarity and distinctness—for Locke their validity hinged expressly upon the mode and manner of their origin. A genetic criterion of truth and validity replaced an intrinsic one.

Locke's exhaustive survey of mental contents is useful, if elaborate. Though he distinguished between ideas of sensation and ideas of reflection, the whole thrust of his efforts and those of his Empiricist followers was to reduce the latter to the former, to minimize the originative power of the mind in favour of its passive receptivity to the sensory impressions received from without. Locke's classification of ideas into simple and complex was an attempt to distinguish mental contents such as blueness or solidity, which come from a single sense like sight or touch, and those such as figure, space, extension, rest, and motion, which are the product of several senses combined, on the one hand, from those complicated and compounded (complex) ideas of universals such as triangle or gratitude, of substances, and of relations such as identity, diversity, and cause and effect, on the other.

Locke's *Essay* was a dogged attempt to produce the total world of man's conceptual experience out of a set of elementary sensory building blocks, moving always from sensation toward thought and from the simple to the complex. The basic outcome of his epistemology was therefore:

1. That the ultimate source of men's ideas is sensation;
2. That all mental operations are a combining and compounding of simple sensory materials into complex conceptual tools.

It was a theory of knowledge based upon a kind of sensory atomism, which sees the mind as an agency of discovery rather than of creation and views its ideas as "like" the objects that are the sources of the sensations it receives. But it sees also that an important distinction must still be made between those "primary qualities" such as solidity, figure, extension, motion, and rest, which are the actual characteristics of objects themselves, and those "secondary qualities" such as colour, taste, and smell, which are simply the internal consequences of how the mind is affected by them. This important Lockean distinction (already found in Galileo) was only a mirroring in the theory of knowledge of the physics of Sir Isaac Newton, which was its contemporary.

It was precisely this dualism presupposed by the science of the time between primary qualities, which belong to matter, and secondary qualities, which belong to mind, that Locke's successor George Berkeley (1685–1753) sought to overcome. Though Berkeley was a bishop in the Anglican Church who wanted to combat "atheistic Materialism" and to sustain the power of God and spirituality, his importance for the theory of knowledge lies rather in the way in which he demonstrated that, in the end, primary qualities are reducible to secondary qualities. His Empiricism led to a denial of abstract ideas because he believed that general notions are simply fictions of the mind and vehemently denied that one may validly distinguish between objects and the sensory impressions that repose in the mind. Science, he argued, can easily dispense with

the concept of matter: nature is simply that which men perceive by their senses, and this means that sense data can be considered as "objects for the mind" rather than as "qualities adhering in a substance." A thing is simply a recurrent group of sense qualities. With this important reduction of substance to quality, Berkeley thus became the true father of the epistemological position known as phenomenalism, which has remained an important influence in British philosophizing to the present day.

Basic science of man in Hume. The third, and in many ways the most famous, of the British Empiricists was the Skeptic David Hume (1711–76). Hume's philosophical intention was to reap, humanistically, the harvest sowed by Newtonian physics, to apply the method of natural science to human nature, and to create a basic science of man. The paradoxical result of this admirable purpose, however, was to create a skeptical crisis more devastating than that of the early French Renaissance and to reduce human certainty once more to the state that it was in before Descartes had reached the dogmatic halting point in his procedure of methodical doubt.

Hume followed Locke and Berkeley in approaching the problem of knowledge from a psychological perspective. He too found the origin of knowledge in sense impressions. But whereas Locke had found a certain trustworthy order in the compounding power of the mind, and Berkeley had found mentality itself expressive of a certain spiritual power, Hume's relentless analysis discovered as much contingency in mind as in the external world. All uniformity in perceptual experience, he held, comes from "an associating quality of the mind." The "association of ideas" is a fact, but the relations of resemblance, contiguity, and cause and effect that it produces have no intrinsic validity because they are the product of an inexplicable "mental habit." Thus the causal principle upon which all knowledge rests indicates no necessary connections between things but is simply the accident of their constant conjunction in men's minds. Moreover, the mind itself, far from being an independent power, is simply "a bundle of perceptions" without unity or cohesive quality. Hume's denial of a necessary order of nature on the one hand and of a substantial or unified self on the other precipitated a philosophical crisis from which Enlightenment philosophy was not to be definitely rescued until the work of Kant.

Nonepistemological movements in the Enlightenment. Though the school of British Empiricism represented the mainstream of Enlightenment philosophy until the time of Kant, it was by no means the only type of philosophy that the 18th century produced. The Enlightenment, which was based upon a few great fundamental ideas— such as the dedication to reason, the belief in intellectual progress, the confidence in nature as a source of inspiration and value, and the search for tolerance and freedom in political and social institutions—produced many crosscurrents of intellectual and philosophical expression.

Materialism and scientific discovery. The profound influence of Locke spread to France, where it not only produced the skeptical Empiricism of Voltaire but also united with the mechanistic side of the teachings of Descartes to create an entire school devoted to a sensationalistic Materialism. Julien de La Mettrie in *L'Homme-machine* (1747; *Man a Machine*), Étienne de Condillac in his *Traité des sensations* (1754; *Treatise on the Sensations*), and Paul, baron d'Holbach, in his *Système de la nature* (1770; *The System of Nature*) represented a limited worldview in which matter in motion is the only reality, determining the functioning of the human brain and its sensations according to ironclad and necessary laws. This position even found its way into many of the articles of the great French encyclopaedia edited by Denis Diderot and Jean d'Alembert, which was almost a complete compendium of the scientific and humanistic accomplishments of 18th-century intellectual life.

Though the Middle Ages and the Renaissance had not referred to themselves by these names, the 18th century called itself "the Enlightenment" with self-conscious enthusiasm and pride. It was an age of optimism with a sense of new beginnings. Great strides were made in chemistry and biological science. Jean-Baptiste, chevalier

Margin notes:

Locke's effort to build a total world

Sense impressions and association of ideas

Optimism and the beginning of many disciplines

de Lamarck, Georges Cuvier, and Georges-Louis Leclerc, comte de Buffon, were perfecting a system of animal classification. And, in the eight years between 1766 and 1774, Henry Cavendish discovered hydrogen; Daniel Rutherford, nitrogen; and Joseph Priestley, oxygen. It was the period when foundations were being laid in psychology and the social sciences and in ethics and aesthetics. Anne-Robert-Jacques Turgot, the marquis de Condorcet, and Montesquieu in France, Giambattista Vico in Italy, and Adam Smith in England marked the beginning of history, economics, sociology, and jurisprudence as sciences. Hume, Jeremy Bentham, and the British moral sense philosophers were turning ethics into a specialized field of philosophical inquiry; and Anthony Ashley, 3rd earl of Shaftesbury, Edmund Burke, Johann Gottsched, and Alexander Baumgarten were laying the foundations for a systematic aesthetics.

Social and political philosophy. But, outside of the theory of knowledge, the most significant contribution of the Enlightenment came in the field of social and political philosophy, as Locke's *Two Treatises of Civil Government* (1690) and Jean-Jacques Rousseau's *Du contrat social* (1762; *The Social Contract*) proposed a justification of political association grounded in the newer political requirements of the age. The Renaissance political philosophies of Machiavelli, Bodin, and Hobbes had centred on the absolute power of kings and rulers. But the Enlightenment theories of Locke and Rousseau turned instead to the freedom and equality of citizens. It was a natural historical transformation. The 16th and 17th centuries had constituted the age of absolutism; the political problem had been largely that of internal order, and political theory had been presented in the language of national sovereignty. But the 18th century was the age of the democratic revolutions (including the French Revolution); the political problem was that of freedom and the revolt against injustice, and political theory was expressed in the idiom of natural and inalienable rights.

(margin) Freedom, equality, justice, rights

Locke's political theory was an express denial of the divine right of kings and the absolute power of the sovereign as contained in the doctrines of Hobbes. Instead, he insisted that all men have a natural right to freedom and equality. The state of nature in which men originally live is not, as in Hobbes, intolerable, but it has certain inconveniences. Therefore men band together to form society, as Aristotle had taught, "not simply to live, but to live well." Political power can never be exercised apart from its ultimate purpose, which is the common good; for men enter the political contract in order to preserve life, liberty, and property.

Locke thus stated one of the fundamental principles of the liberal tradition: that there can be no subjection to power without consent, although once political society has been founded, there is an obligation to submit to the decisions of the majority. It is the legislature that makes these decisions, although the ultimate power of choosing the legislature rests with the people; and even the powers of the legislature are not absolute, because the laws of nature remain as a permanent standard and as principles of protection against any arbitrary authority.

Rousseau's more radical political doctrines were built upon Lockean foundations. For him, too, the convention of the social contract formed the basis of all legitimate authority among men, although his conception of citizenship was much more organic and much less individualistic than Locke's. The surrender of natural liberty for civil liberty means that all individual rights (among them property rights) become subordinate to the general will. For Rousseau the state is a moral person whose life is the union of its members, whose laws are acts of the general will, and whose end is the liberty and equality of the citizens. It follows that, when any government usurps the power of the people, the social compact is broken; and not only are the citizens no longer compelled to obey but they also have an obligation to rebel. Rousseau's defiant collectivism was clearly a revolt against Locke's systematic individualism; for him the fundamental category is not "natural person" but "citizen." Nevertheless, however much they differed, in these two social theorists of the

Enlightenment is to be found the germ of all modern liberalism: its faith in representative democracy, in civil liberties, and in the basic dignity of man.

Professionalization of philosophy. In his *Éléments de philosophie* (1759; "Elements of Philosophy"), Jean d'Alembert, an 18th-century French mathematician and Encyclopaedist, wrote:

Our century is the century of philosophy par excellence. If one considers without bias the present state of our knowledge, one cannot deny that philosophy among us has shown progress.

D'Alembert was calling attention to that reflective self-examination for which the 18th century is famous, and he was undoubtedly referring to the activities of mathematicians like himself, jurists, economists, and amateur moralists rather than to narrow philosophical specialists. But the 18th century was clearly the "century of philosophy par excellence" in a more technical sense also. For it was the period in which philosophizing first began to pass from the hands of gentlemen and amateurs into those of true professionals. The chief sign of this shift was the return of reputable philosophy to the universities.

This transformation first occurred in Germany and is chiefly associated with the University of Halle (founded 1694). In the time of the generation that lies between Leibniz (died 1716) and Kant (born 1724), the philosophical climate changed profoundly. The chief representative of this change was Christian Wolff, who taught philosophy at Halle and was the intermediary between the ideas of Leibniz and those of Kant and the profoundly different conceptions of philosophizing for which they stood.

(margin) University of Halle and Christian Wolff

Kant later called Wolff "the real originator of the spirit of thoroughness in Germany"; and Wolff was indeed a pioneer in those techniques that transform philosophy into a professional discipline—the self-conscious adoption of a systematic approach and the creation of a specialized philosophical vocabulary. Wolff carefully distinguished the various fields of philosophy; wrote textbooks in each of them, which were used in the German universities for many years; and created many of the specialized philosophical terms that have survived to the present day.

The German Enlightenment was the first modern period to produce "specialists in philosophy." In England philosophizing in the universities did not become serious until well after the time of Hume, but already philosophical fields had been sufficiently distinguished to be represented by distinct professorships. The titles professor of mental or moral or metaphysical philosophy, as they arose at Oxford and Cambridge, were the product of the late 18th and early 19th centuries.

Two additional factors of the German Enlightenment are relevant: (1) the founding of the first professional journals and (2) the rising concern of philosophy with its own history. The learned journal, like the scientific society, was an innovation of the 17th century. But what had begun as a general intellectual endeavour became in 18th-century Germany a specifically philosophical enterprise. Journals were published in great numbers; *e.g.,* *Acta Philosophorum* (Halle, 1715–26), *Der Philosophische Büchersaal* (Leipzig, 1741–44; "The Philosophical Book Room"), and the short-lived *Neues philosophisches Magazin* (Leipzig, 1789–91), devoted exclusively to the philosophy of Kant.

(margin) Journals and histories of philosophy

More interesting still is the flowering of voluminous German histories of philosophy after 1740. By the 18th century there was already a vast accumulation of historical materials, and the self-conscious feeling that philosophy constitutes a specific field the past of which is worth examination and careful ordering combined with the German spirit of thoroughness to produce a series of massive histories such as Johann Brucker's *Historia Critica Philosophiae,* 6 vol. (1742–44; *The History of Philosophy*); Johann Buhle's *Lehrbuch der Geschichte der Philosophie,* 8 vol. (1796–1804; "Textbook on the History of Philosophy"); Dietrich Tiedemann's *Geist der spekulativen Philosophie von Thales bis Berkeley,* 6 vol. (1791–97; "The Spirit of Speculative Philosophy from Thales to Berkeley"); and Gottlieb Tennemann's *Geschichte der Philosophie,* 11 vol. (1789–1819; excerpted in *A Manual of the History of Philosophy*).

Critical examination of reason in Kant. All of these developments led directly to Immanuel Kant (1724–1804), professor at Königsberg, the greatest philosopher of the modern period, whose works mark the true culmination of the philosophy of the Enlightenment. Historically speaking, Kant's great substantive contribution was to relate both the sensory and the a priori elements in knowledge and thus to mend the breach between the extreme Rationalism of Leibniz and the extreme Empiricism of Hume. But in addition to the brilliant content of his philosophical doctrines, Kant was responsible for three crucial philosophical innovations: (1) a new definition of philosophy, (2) a new conception of philosophical method, and (3) a new structural model for the writing of philosophy.

Kant's definition of philosophy culminated the Enlightenment, for it took reason to be the very heart of the philosophical enterprise. Philosophy's sole task, in his view, is to determine what reason can and cannot do. Philosophy, he said, "is the science of the relation of all knowledge to the essential ends of human reason"; and its true aim is both constructive ("to outline the system of all knowledge arising from pure reason") and critical ("to expose the illusions of a reason that forgets its limits"). Philosophy is thus a calling of great dignity, for its aim is wisdom, and its practitioners are themselves "lawgivers of reason." But in order for philosophy to be "the science of the highest maxims of reason," the philosopher must be able to determine the source, the extent, and the validity of human knowledge and the ultimate limits of reason. And these tasks require a special philosophical method.

The transcendental, or critical, method of examining reason

Sometimes Kant called this the "transcendental method," but more often the "critical method"; for his purpose was to reject the dogmatic assumptions of the Rationalist school, and his wish was to return to the semiskeptical position with which Descartes had begun before his dogmatic pretensions to certainty took hold. Kant's method was to conduct a critical examination of the powers of an a priori judging reason and to inquire what reason can achieve when all experience is removed. The method was based upon a doctrine that he himself called "a Copernican revolution" in philosophy (by analogy with the change from geocentric to heliocentric cosmology): the assumption not that man's knowledge must conform to objects but that objects must conform to man's apparatus of knowing. The question then became: What is the exact nature of that knowing apparatus?

Unlike Descartes, Kant could not question that knowledge exists. Mathematics and Newtonian physics were too real for any Enlightenment mentality to entertain this doubt. Kant's methodological question was rather: How is mathematical and physical knowledge possible? What must be the structure of man's knowing process to have made these sciences secure? The attempt to answer these questions was the task of Kant's great *Kritik der reinen Vernunft* (1781; *Critique of Pure Reason*).

But Kant's great aim was to examine reason not merely in one of its domains but in each of its employments, according to the threefold structure of the human mind that he had taken over from Wolff. Thus the critical examination of reason in thinking (science) is undertaken in the *Kritik der reinen Vernunft,* that of reason in willing (ethics) in the *Kritik der praktischen Vernunft* (1788; *Critique of Practical Reason*), and that of reason in feeling (aesthetics) in *Kritik der Urteilskraft* (1790; *Critique of Judgment*).

Literary forms. The literary format of Enlightenment philosophizing was essentially simple and straightforward. Except for an occasional reversion to the dialogue form, as in Berkeley's *Three Dialogues Between Hylas and Philonous* (1713) and in Hume's *Dialogues Concerning Natural Religion* (1779), it consisted of inquiries, discourses, treatises, dissertations, and essays, generally well written in clear, relatively nontechnical prose. But Kant not only introduced a formidable technical philosophical terminology into his works but was, in fact, the originator of a new philosophical form—the "critique" or "critical examination"—which had its own special architectonics. Each of Kant's three critiques consists of the same division into three parts: (1) an "Analytic," or analysis of reason's right functioning; (2) a "Dialectic," or logic of error, showing the pitfalls into which a careless reason falls; and (3) a "Methodology," which is an arrangement of rules for practice. It is a form that was unique to Kant, but it raised certain problems of "oppositional" thinking, to which 19th-century philosophers such as Hegel, Schopenhauer, and Kierkegaard were subsequently to turn.

THE 19TH CENTURY

The end of the Enlightenment

Kant's death in 1804 formally marked the end of the Enlightenment. The 19th century ushered in new philosophical problems and new conceptions of what philosophy ought to do. It was a century of great philosophical diversity. In the Renaissance the chief intellectual fact had been the rise of mathematics and natural science, and the tasks that this fact imposed upon philosophy determined its direction for two centuries. In the Enlightenment attention had turned to the character of the mind that had so successfully mastered the natural world, and Rationalists and Empiricists had contended for mastery until the Kantian synthesis. As for the 19th century, however, if one single feature of its thought could be singled out for emphasis, it might be called the discovery of the irrational. But many philosophical schools were present, and they contended, one with another, in a series of distinct and powerful oppositions: Pragmatism against Idealism; Positivism against irrationalism; Marxism against liberalism.

Politically the 19th century began with the consulate of Napoleon and ended with the Golden Jubilee of Queen Victoria; but it is the intellectual and social changes that fell in between that have philosophical consequences. These changes were chiefly the Romantic movement of the early 19th century, which was a poetic revolt against reason in favour of feeling; the maturation of the Industrial Revolution, which caused untold misery within society and called forth a multitude of philosophies of social reform; the Revolution of 1848 in Paris, Germany, and Vienna, which symbolized class divisions and first implanted in the European consciousness the concepts of "the bourgeoisie" and "the proletariat"; and, finally, the great surge in biological science with Darwin and the publicizing of the idea of biological evolution. Romanticism influenced both German Idealism and philosophers of irrationalism. Experiences of economic discord and social unrest produced the ameliorative social philosophy of English Utilitarianism and the revolutionary doctrines of Karl Marx. And the developmental ideas of Darwin provided the prerequisites for American Pragmatism.

A synoptic view of philosophy in the 19th century reveals an interesting chronology. The early century was dominated by the German school of absolute Idealism (Johann Fichte, Friedrich Schelling, and G.W.F. Hegel). The mid-century was marked by a rebirth of interest in science and its methods (Auguste Comte in France and John Stuart Mill in England) and by liberal (Mill) and radical (Marx) social theory. The late century saw a second flowering of Idealism, this time in England (T.H. Green, F.H. Bradley, and Bernard Bosanquet) and, with Charles Sanders Peirce and William James, the rise of American Pragmatism. The new philosophies of the irrational in the highly individual thinkers Søren Kierkegaard, Arthur Schopenhauer, and Friedrich Nietzsche ran through the century in its entirety.

German Idealism of Fichte, Schelling, and Hegel. The Enlightenment, inspired by the example of natural science, had accepted certain bounds to the possibility of knowledge; that is, it had recognized certain limits to reason's ability to penetrate ultimate reality because that would require methods that surpass the boundaries of scientific method. In this particular modesty, the philosophies of Hume and Kant were much alike. But the early 19th century marked a resurgence of the metaphysical spirit at its most ambitious and extravagant extreme. German Idealism reinstated the speculative pretensions of Leibniz and Spinoza at their height. This turn was partly a consequence of the Romantic influence but, more importantly, of a new alliance of philosophy not with science but with religion. It was not accidental that all of the great German Idealists were university professors whose fathers were Protestant pastors or who had themselves studied theology: Fichte at Jena and Leipzig (1780–84); Schelling

Resurgence of religiously inspired metaphysics

and Hegel at the Tübingen seminary (1788–95). And it is probably this circumstance that gave to German Idealism its intensely serious, its quasi-religious, and its dedicated character.

The consequence of this religious alignment was that philosophical interest shifted from Kant's *Critique of Pure Reason* (in which he had attempted to account for natural science and denied the possibility of certainty in metaphysics) to his *Critique of Practical Reason* (in which he had explored the nature of the moral self) and his *Critique of Judgment* (in which he had treated of the purposiveness of the universe as a whole). For absolute Idealism was based upon three premises:

1. That the chief datum of philosophy is the human self and its self-consciousness;

2. That the world as a whole is spiritual through and through, that it is, in fact, something like a cosmic Self;

3. That, in both the self and the world, it is not primarily the intellectual element that counts but, rather, the volitional and the moral.

Thus, to understand the self, self-consciousness, and the spiritual universe became for Idealistic metaphysics the task of philosophy.

From the point of view of doctrine, Fichte, Schelling, and Hegel had much in common. Fichte (1762–1814), professor of philosophy at the newly founded University of Berlin (1809–14) and a great symbol of German patriotism through the Napoleonic Wars, combined in a workable unity the subjectivism of Descartes, the cosmic monism of Spinoza, and the moral intensity of Kant. He saw human self-consciousness as the primary metaphysical fact through the analysis of which the philosopher finds his way to the cosmic totality that is "the Absolute." And, just as the moral will is the chief characteristic of the self, so also is it the activating principle of the world. Thus Fichte provided a new definition of philosophizing that made it central in dignity in the intellectual world. The sole task of philosophy is "the clarification of consciousness." And the highest degree of self-consciousness is achieved by the philosopher because he alone recognizes "Mind," or "Spirit," as the central principle of reality.

Hegel: "the rational is the real"

This line of thought was carried further by Georg Wilhelm Friedrich Hegel (1770–1831), Fichte's successor at Berlin and perhaps the single most comprehensive and influential thinker of the 19th century. Kant's problem had been the critical examination of reason's role in human experience. For Hegel, too, the function of philosophy is to discover the place of reason in nature, in experience, and in reality; to understand the laws according to which reason operates in the world. But whereas Kant had found reason to be the form that mind imposes upon the world, Hegel found it to be constitutive of the world itself—not something that mind imposes but that it discovers. As Fichte had projected consciousness from mind into reality, so Hegel projected reason; and the resultant Hegelian dictates—that "the rational is the real" and that "the truth is the whole"—although they express an organic and a totalitarian theory of truth and reality, tend to blur the usual distinctions that previous philosophers had made between logic and metaphysics, between subject and object, and between thought and existence. For the basic tenet of Idealism, that reality is spiritual, generates just such a vague inclusiveness.

To the Fichtean foundations, however, Hegel added one crucial corollary: that the Absolute, or Whole, which is a concrete universal entity, is not static but undergoes a crucial development in time. Hegel called this evolution "the dialectical process." By stressing it, Hegel accomplished two things: (1) he indicated that reason itself is not eternal but "historical," and (2) he thereby gave new meaning and relevance to the changing conditions of human society in history—which added to the philosophical task a cultural dimension that it had not possessed before.

The philosopher's vocation, in Hegel's view, was to approach the Absolute through consciousness, to recognize it as Spirit expressing and developing itself ("realizing itself" was his own phrase) in all of the manifold facets of human life. For struggle is the essence of spiritual existence, and self-enlargement is its goal. For these reasons the various branches of intellect and culture become stages in the unfolding of the World-Spirit:

1. The psychological characteristics of man (habit, appetite, judgment) representing "Subjective Spirit";

2. His laws, social arrangements, and political institutions (the family, civil society, the state) expressing "Objective Spirit";

3. His art, religion, and philosophy embodying "Absolute Spirit."

What began, therefore, in Hegel as a metaphysics of the Absolute ended by becoming a total philosophy of human culture.

Positivism and social theory in Comte, Mill, and Marx. The absolute Idealists wrote as if the Renaissance methodologists of the sciences had never existed. But if in Germany the Empirical and scientific tradition in philosophy lay dormant, in France and in England in the middle of the 19th century it was very much alive. In France, Auguste Comte (1798–1857) wrote his great philosophical history of science, *Cours de philosophie positive* (1830–42; *The Positive Philosophy of Auguste Comte* [abridged]) in six volumes. Influenced by Bacon and the entire school of British Empiricism, by the doctrine of progress put forward by Turgot and Condorcet during the 18th century, and by the very original social reformer Henri de Saint-Simon, Comte called his philosophy "Positivism," by which he meant a philosophy of science so narrow that it denied any validity whatsoever to "knowledge" not derived through the accepted methods of science. But the *Cours de philosophie positive* made its point not by dialectic but by an appeal to the history of thought, and here Comte presented his two basic ideas:

1. The notion that the sciences have emerged as sciences in strict order, beginning with mathematics and astronomy, followed by physics, chemistry, and biology in that order, and culminating in the new science of sociology, to which Comte was the first to ascribe the name;

2. The so-called "law of the three stages," which views thought in every field as passing progressively from superstition to science by first being (*a*) religious, then (*b*) abstract, or metaphysical, and finally (*c*) positive, or scientific. Comte's permanent contribution was to initiate an antireligious and an antimetaphysical bias in the philosophy of science that has passed into the 20th century.

In mid-19th-century England the chief representative of the Empirical tradition from Bacon to Hume was John Stuart Mill (1806–73). Mill's theory of knowledge, best presented in his *Examination of Sir William Hamilton's Philosophy* (1865), was not particularly original but rather a judicious combination of the doctrines of Berkeley and Hume; but it symbolized his mistrust of vague metaphysics, his denial of the a priori element in knowledge, and his determined opposition to any form of intuitionism. It is in his enormously influential *System of Logic* (1843), however, that Mill's chief theoretical ideas are to be found.

This work, as part of its subtitle, *the Principles of Evidence and the Methods of Scientific Investigation,* shows, was concerned less with formal logic than with scientific methodology. Mill made here the fundamental distinction between deduction and induction, defined induction as the process by which men discover and prove general propositions, and presented his "four methods of experimental inquiry" as the heart of the inductive method. These methods were, in fact, only an enlarged and refined version of Francis Bacon's "tables of discovery." But the most significant section of *A System of Logic* was its conclusion: book 6, "On the Logic of the Moral Sciences."

Mill had taken men's experience of the uniformity of nature as the warrant of induction. Here he reaffirmed the belief of Hume that it is possible to apply the principle of causation and the methods of physical science to moral and social phenomena. These may be so complex as to yield only "conditional predictions," but in this sense there are "social laws." Thus Comte and Mill agreed upon the possibility of a true social science.

Mill's *Logic* was extremely influential, and it continued to be taught at Oxford and Cambridge well into the 20th century; but in the end his importance lay less in logic and

Comte's Philosophie positive

theory of knowledge than in ethics and political theory. For Mill was the great apostle of political liberalism in the 19th century, a true follower of John Locke. And, just as Locke and Rousseau had represented the liberal and the radical wings of social theory in the early modern period, so Mill and Karl Marx represented the liberal and the radical approaches to social reform 100 years later.

Mill's political liberalism and ethics

Raised by social reformers (his father, James Mill, and Jeremy Bentham) to be a social reformer himself, Mill's social theory was an attempt, by gradual means arrived at democratically, to combat the evils of the Industrial Revolution. His ethics, expressed in his *Utilitarianism* (1861), followed the formulations of Bentham in finding the end of society to consist in the production of the greatest quantity of happiness for its members, but he gave to Bentham's cruder (but more consistent) doctrines a humanistic and individualistic slant. Thus, the moral self-development of the individual becomes the ultimate value in Mill's ethics.

This trend was also expressed in his essay *On Liberty* (1859) and *Considerations on Representative Government* (1861). In the former he stated the case for the freedom of the individual against "the tyranny of the majority," presented strong arguments in favour of complete freedom of thought and discussion, and argued that no state or society has the right to prevent the free development of human individuality. In the latter he provided a classic defense for the principle of representative democracy, asked for the adequate representation of minorities, urged renewed public participation in political action for necessary social reforms, and pointed up the dangers of class-oriented or special-interest legislation.

Marx and social revolution

A radical counterbalance to Mill's liberal ideas was provided by Karl Marx (1818–83), a German philosopher, social revolutionary, and political economist. Taking over from Hegel the idea of estrangement (which Hegel had used in a metaphysical sense), Marx used this notion prior to 1848 to indicate the alienation of the worker from the enjoyment of the products of his work, the crass treatment of human labour as a mere commodity (and man as a thing), and, in fact, the general dehumanization of man in a selfish, profit-seeking capitalist society.

In the famous *Communist Manifesto* (1848), Marx, yielding to the revolutionary temper of the times, called (as Rousseau had done before the French Revolution) for the violent overthrow of the established order. All of history, Marx said, is the struggle between exploiting minorities and the underlying population, that is, between bourgeois and proletarians; and he advocated the formation of a Communist Party to stimulate proletarian class consciousness toward the seizure of power and the institution of a just and democratically managed Socialist society.

Marx's revolutionary fervour may have tended to dampen his philosophical reputation in the West, and his philosophical achievement remains a controversial point; but certain of his ideas (some Hegelian in inspiration, some original) have endured. Among these are the ideas:

1. That society is a moving balance (dialectic) of antithetical forces that produce social change;
2. That there is no conflict between a rigid economic determinism and a program of revolutionary action;
3. That ideas (including philosophical theories) are not purely rational and thus independent of external circumstance but depend upon the nature of the social order in which they arise.

Independent and irrationalist movements. The end of the 19th century saw a flowering of many independent philosophical movements. After Hegel was almost forgotten in Germany, his influence migrated to England, where T.H. Green, F.H. Bradley, and Bernard Bosanquet initiated a new Hegelian renaissance. Bradley's *Appearance and Reality* (1893) constituted the high-water mark of the rediscovery of Hegel's dialectical method. In America a strong reaction against Idealism led to the beginnings of the Pragmatic movement initiated by Charles Sanders Peirce and William James. Peirce was an exact logician who recognized that the function of all inquiry is to eradicate doubt and that the meaning of a concept consists in the practical consequences that the concept might be said

to have. James transformed Peirce's pragmatic theory of meaning into a pragmatic theory of truth and, in his *Will to Believe* (1897), asserted that men have a right to believe even in the face of inconclusive evidence and that, because knowledge is an instrument for the sake of life, the true test of a belief is the practical consequences that it entails. Meanwhile, in Austria, Franz Brentano, who taught at Vienna from 1874 to 1895, and Alexius Meinong, who taught at Graz, were developing an empirical psychology and a theory of objects, which were to have considerable influence upon the new philosophy of Phenomenology.

Irrationalism in Kierkegaard and Schopenhauer

It was not, however, any of these late 19th-century developments but, rather, the emphasis upon the irrational, which started almost at the century's beginning, that gave the philosophy of the period its peculiar flavour. Hegel, despite his commitment to systematic metaphysics, had, nonetheless, carried on the Enlightenment tradition of faith in human rationality. But soon his influence was challenged from two different directions. The Danish Christian thinker Søren Kierkegaard (1813–55) challenged the logical pretensions of the Hegelian system; and one of his contemporaries, Arthur Schopenhauer (1788–1860), himself a German Idealist and constructor of a bold and imaginative system, contradicted Hegel by asserting that the irrational is the truly real.

Kierkegaard's criticism of Hegel was an appeal to the concrete as against the abstract. He satirized Hegelian Rationalism as a perfect example of "the academic in philosophy"—of detached, objective, abstract theorizing and system building, blind to the realities of human existence, to its subjective, living, emotional character. What a man requires in life, said Kierkegaard, is not infinite inquiry but the boldness of resolute decision and commitment. Man's essence is not contained in thinking but in the existential conditions of his emotional life, in his anxiety and despair. The titles of three of Kierkegaard's books—*Frygt og baeven* (1843; *Fear and Trembling*), *Begrebet angest* (1844; *The Concept of Dread*), *Sygdommen til døden* (1849; *The Sickness unto Death*)—indicate his preoccupation with states of consciousness quite unlike the usual philosophical concentration on cognition and the validity of knowledge.

Schopenhauer, even though, for a short time, he competed unsuccessfully with Hegel at the University of Berlin, soon withdrew and thereafter waged a lifelong battle against academic philosophy. His own system, though orderly and carefully worked out, was written in a vivid and engaging style. Schopenhauer agreed with Kant that the world of appearances, of phenomena, is governed by the conditions of space, time, and causality. But he held that science, which investigates this world, cannot itself penetrate the real world behind appearances, which is dominated by a strong, blind, striving, universal cosmic Will that expresses itself in the vagaries of human instinct, in sexual striving, and in the wild uncertainties of all animal behaviour. Everywhere in nature one sees strife, conflict, and inarticulate impulse; and these, rather than rational processes or intellectual clarity, are man's true contacts with ultimate reality.

Nietzsche's Dionysian irrationalism

Schopenhauer's great work *Die Welt als Wille und Vorstellung* (*The World As Will and Idea*) was published in 1819, and Kierkegaard's uneven masterpieces appeared between 1843 and 1849. But Friedrich Nietzsche (1844–1900), the third of the irrationalist triumvirate, wrote between 1872 and 1889. A prolific but unsystematic writer, presenting his patchwork of ideas in swift atoms of thought, Nietzsche saw the task of the philosopher as that of a man who destroys old values, creates new ideals, and through them a new civilization. He agreed with Schopenhauer that mind is an instrument of instinct to be used in the service of life and power, and he held that illusion is as necessary to man as truth. Nietzsche spent much time in the analysis of such states as resentment, guilt, bad conscience, and self-contempt.

Kierkegaard, Schopenhauer, and Nietzsche provided for the 19th century a new, nonrational conception of human nature, and they viewed the mind not with the rational clarity of Locke and Hume but as something dark, obscure, hidden, deep. But, above all, they initiated a new style of philosophizing. Schopenhauer wrote like an 18th-century essayist; Kierkegaard was a master of the methods of irony and paradox; and Nietzsche used aphorism and epigram with conscious literary intention. For these three, the philosopher should be less a crabbed academician than a man of letters.

THE 20TH CENTURY

Despite the tradition of philosophical "professionalism" established during the Enlightenment by Wolff and Kant, philosophy in the 19th century was still largely created by men outside of the universities. Comte, Mill, Marx, Kierkegaard, and Schopenhauer were not professors. Only the German Idealist school was rooted in academic life. Today, however, it is difficult to find one first-rate philosophical mind outside of the academy. (George Santayana after his early years and Jean-Paul Sartre are the notable exceptions.) The agencies of professionalism—the philosophical congress, the national philosophical societies, the narrowly specialized journals—have become increasingly important. Philosophers more and more employ a technical vocabulary and deal with specialized problems, and they write not for a broad intellectual public but for one another.

Professionalism also has sharpened the divisions between philosophical schools and made the definition of what philosophy is and ought to be, a matter of the sharpest controversy. Philosophy has become extremely self-conscious about its own method and nature. Intellectual competitiveness, moreover, has been further sharpened by geographical and political considerations. The tradition of clear analysis, inaugurated by Locke and Hume, still dominates the Anglo-Saxon world; the Hegelian tradition of speculative metaphysics and the Nietzschean tradition of bold psychological generalization still dominate the Continent. And the special framework of thinking established by Karl Marx still dominates philosophy in the Socialist world.

Individual philosophies of Bergson, Dewey, and Whitehead. Except, then, for philosophical Marxism and a few individual philosophers such as Henri Bergson, John Dewey, and A.N. Whitehead, who evade easy classification, the main currents of contemporary philosophy are (1) Analytic philosophy with its two chief branches, (*a*) Logical Positivism and (*b*) Linguistic Analysis; and (2) Continental philosophy with its two branches, (*a*) Existentialism and (*b*) Phenomenology.

Henri Bergson (1859–1941), John Dewey (1859–1952), and Alfred North Whitehead (1861–1947) have been called the three most important speculative philosophers of the first half of the 20th century. The French Bergson and the American Dewey shared an instrumental theory of mind; that is, influenced by Darwinism, they both held that mind has emerged in the course of biological evolution as an instrument of man's adaptation to his environment and, therefore, that man's mental functions are chiefly utilitarian agencies of action. Bergson and the English Whitehead were both adherents of a process philosophy; that is, each held that actuality is, like a river, fluent, that ultimate reality is mobile and dynamic. Yet, in fact, each of the three defined philosophy differently and saw it as performing a uniquely different task. Bergson's vision of philosophy was intuitional, Whitehead's was speculative, and Dewey's was pragmatic.

Bergson's two ways of knowing

Bergson, in the *Introduction à la métaphysique* (1903; *An Introduction to Metaphysics*) and in his masterpiece, *L'Évolution créatrice* (1907; *Creative Evolution*), distinguished between two profoundly different ways of knowing: the method of analysis, which is that of science; and the method of intuition, which is just that intellectual sympathy by which men enter into objects and persons and identify with them. All basic metaphysical truths, Bergson held, are grasped by philosophical intuition. This is how men know their deepest selves, the duration, which is the essence of all living things, and the vital spirit, which is the mysterious creative agency in the world.

For Whitehead, philosophy was primarily metaphysics (or "speculative philosophy"), the effort "to frame a coherent, logical, necessary system of general ideas in terms of which every element of our experience can be inter-preted." Whitehead's philosophy was, thus, an attempt to survey the world with a large generality of understanding, an end toward which his great trilogy, *Science and the Modern World* (1925), *Process and Reality* (1929), and *Adventures of Ideas* (1933), was directed.

While Bergson and Whitehead were principally metaphysicians and philosophers of culture, Dewey was an all-around philosopher who dominated the fields of ethics, metaphysics, and methodology in the United States for many years and who stressed the unity, interrelationship, and organicity of all forms of philosophical knowledge. He is chiefly notable, however, because his notion of philosophy stressed so powerfully the conceptions of practicality and moral purpose. One of the guiding aims of Dewey's philosophizing was the effort to find the same warranted assertibility for ethical and political as for scientific judgments. Philosophy, he said, should be oriented not to professional pride but to human need.

The social thought of Mill and Marx presented opposed solutions to the social problems of the 19th century; that of Dewey and Lenin presented opposed solutions to the problems of the 20th century. Not revolution but the continuous application of intelligence to social affairs was Dewey's answer. He believed in social planning, in conscious intelligent intervention to produce desirable social change; and he proposed a new "experimentalism" in social affairs as the guide to enlightened public action to promote the aims of a democratic community. His pragmatic social theory is the major social philosophy that liberal democracy has produced in the modern world.

Marxist thought. The framework of 19th-century Marxist thought, augmented by the philosophical suggestions of Vladimir Ilich Lenin, still serves as the starting point of all philosophizing in the Socialist countries of eastern Europe. To Marx's conception of the dialectic (that the social world progresses through the rise and fall of oppositions), Lenin added a strong tinge of metaphysical Materialism (material things and their systems of relations exist independently of mind, and the laws of nature are objective) and a naively Realist theory of knowledge (ideas and sensations are true copies of independently existing things). But much of Lenin's thinking was also devoted to rather practical issues, like the tactics of violence and the role of the Communist Party in bringing about and consolidating the proletarian revolution.

Later Marxism has continued this concern with practical issues, because it represents the basic Marxist conception of what philosophy is and ought to be. For Marxism (like Pragmatism) tries to assimilate theoretical issues to practical needs. It asserts the basic unity of theory and practice by finding that the function of the former is to serve the latter. Marx and Lenin both held that theory is always in fact expressive of class interests; consequently, they wished philosophy to be transformed into a tool for furthering the class struggle: not abstractly to discover the truth but concretely to forge the intellectual weapons of the proletariat is philosophy's dominant task. Thus philosophy becomes inseparable from ideology.

Unity of theory and practice in Marxism

Since the discovery and publication in 1927 and 1932 of some of Marx's early writings, many have sensed a breath of fresh air in Marxist philosophizing outside the Soviet Union. For the concern of the young Marx with alienation, with a theory of the nature of man, and with moral values has given Marxism a new humanistic dimension and has inspired some notable revisionist thinking in Poland, Hungary, and particularly Yugoslavia.

Analytic philosophy. *Logical Positivism.* Logical Positivism, or Logical Empiricism, the earliest branch of modern Analytic philosophy, was jointly inspired by Hume and by the new logic of Russell and Whitehead, authors of the *Principia Mathematica* (3 vol.; 1910–13). The school, formally instituted at the University of Vienna in a seminar of Moritz Schlick in 1923, continued there as the Vienna Circle until 1938. Its great period began in 1926 when Rudolf Carnap, who became a leading semanticist and philosopher of science, arrived at the University. Its manifesto of 1929, *Wissenschaftliche Weltauffassung: Der Wiener Kreis* ("Scientific Conception of the World: The Vienna Circle"), and its journal *Erkenntnis* ("Knowledge"), founded a year later, marked its self-consciousness as a philosophical movement.

Logical Positivism's basic contribution has been a profound alteration in the conception of the role that philosophy itself must play. Philosophy, it claimed, must henceforth be scientific. It should seek less a content than a function: it should produce not complicated pictures of the world but clear thinking. This was best stated by Ludwig Wittgenstein in his *Tractatus Logico-Philosophicus* (1922), first published as *Logische-philosophische Abhandlung* (1921):

> The object of philosophy is the logical clarification of thoughts. Philosophy is not a theory but an activity. A philosophical work consists essentially of elucidations. The result of philosophy is not a number of "philosophical propositions," but to make propositions clear.

Despite this emphasis upon philosophy as a pure activity, Logical Positivism did propound, at the same time, a series of revolutionary theses:

1. All meaningful discourse consists either of (*a*) the formal sentences of logic and mathematics or (*b*) the factual propositions of the special sciences;

2. Any assertion that claims to be factual has meaning only if it is possible to say how it might be verified;

3. Metaphysical assertions, coming under neither of the two classes of (1), are meaningless;

4. All statements about moral, aesthetic, or religious values are scientifically unverifiable and meaningless.

Logical Positivism's radical denial of the meaningfulness of metaphysics and of assertions of value at first produced something of a philosophical scandal. But meanwhile Bertrand Russell and his student Wittgenstein (who had emigrated from Austria) were propounding similar doctrines in England; and, after the Nazis overran Austria and Carnap, Hans Reichenbach (a Berlin Positivist), and many others from the Vienna Circle moved to America, this philosophy proved remarkably influential in the Anglo-American world. The Logical Positivists were mainly interested in three basic themes: logic, language, and perception. Whereas Russell began with logic, turned to problems of perception, and ended with semantics, Carnap, having begun with perception in *Der logische Aufbau der Welt* (1928; *The Logical Structure of the World*), turned to problems of semantics in *Logische Syntax der Sprache* (1934; *The Logical Syntax of Language*) and ended with logic in *Meaning and Necessity* (1947). But of these three themes it was that of language that proved most enduring. This emphasis Logical Positivism shared with its successor, Linguistic Analysis.

Linguistic Analysis. Sometimes called "ordinary language" Analysis or even "Oxford philosophy" from its later stronghold, this movement was, in fact, largely the product of two philosophers of the first half of the 20th century who were associated with the University of Cambridge, G.E. Moore (1873–1958) and Ludwig Wittgenstein (1889–1951). Moore made the examination of the assertions of other men philosophically popular—*i.e.,* the practice of directing the philosopher's critical energies to the mistakes of his contemporaries. The major subjects of his interest were ethics and the theory of knowledge; his thought was always Realistic and commonsensical, and he introduced into philosophy an unbelievably precise and closely applied analytical method. It was Moore's passion for clarity and his infinite pains "to get everything *exactly* right" that served as moral inspiration to a succeeding generation of younger men who had attended his Cambridge lectures over a span of 30 years.

Wittgenstein had begun as a kind of adjunct to the Vienna Circle. There was a time when his philosophical position was much like that of Russell and Carnap; but as he later became more skeptical of the foundations of mathematics and logic, his interest turned from logic and artificial language systems toward a critical examination of ordinary natural language. This change was principally registered in his *Philosophical Investigations,* posthumously published in 1953, which has become the true bible of Linguistic Analysis. For it is here that Wittgenstein showed how a man's entire world is constituted by his linguistic experience and suggested that "all philosophy is critique of language." Wittgenstein thought that to ask "Why do we use this particular word or expression?" was the crucial philosophical question since a focusing of philosophy not upon the world but upon the mechanisms of linguistic use would solve most of the perplexities that have plagued philosophizing. Thus Linguistic philosophy was to perform a therapeutic function.

Wittgenstein's example found many followers in the United States and, particularly, in England. There philosophers Gilbert Ryle, J.L. Austin, and P.F. Strawson have examined "category mistakes," "systematically misleading expressions," "mental-conduct concepts" (such as "other minds"), and all of the major "perception words" such as "looking," "seeing," "sensing," "feeling," and the like. The effect of this concentration not upon things or ideas but upon words has, for members of this school, turned the customary works on ethics, aesthetics, or the philosophy of religion into treatises entitled "The Language of Ethics" or "The Language of Aesthetics" or "The Language of Religion." And these efforts are all, in Wittgenstein's terms, "a battle against the bewitchment of our intelligence by means of language."

Continental philosophy. The Analytic philosophy that by the mid-1970s had come to dominate Anglo-American philosophical thinking for almost half a century has had comparatively little influence on the continent of Europe. There the metaphysical and speculative traditions have remained strong; and in the 1950s and 1960s the interest in both, but particularly in Phenomenology, posed an increasing threat to philosophical Analysis in Britain and the United States. Continental philosophy may be divided into Phenomenology and Existentialism, but the division is not sharp. Thinkers such as Martin Heidegger, Jean-Paul Sartre, and Maurice Merleau-Ponty combine the two strands. And the phenomenological method has been one of the formative forces in Existentialism.

Phenomenology of Husserl and others. Edmund Husserl (1859–1939), a German mathematician turned philosopher, was the true father of Phenomenology. He was an extremely complicated and technical thinker whose views changed considerably over the years. His chief contributions were the phenomenological method, developed early, and the concept of the life-world, appearing only in his later writings. Husserl proposed the phenomenological method as a technique for conducting phenomenological analyses—that is, for making possible "a descriptive account of the essential structures of the directly given." The emphasis here is upon the immediacy of experience, the attempt to isolate it and set it off from all assumptions of existence or causal influence and to lay bare its actual intrinsic structure; for it is this structure that constitutes its essence. Phenomenology restricts the philosopher's attention to the pure data of consciousness uncontaminated by metaphysical theories or scientific assumptions. Husserl's concept of the life-world expressed this same idea of immediacy. It is the individual's personal world as directly experienced, with the ego at the centre and with all of its vital and emotional colourings.

With the appearance of the *Jahrbuch für Philosophie und Phänomenologische Forschung* (1913–30; "Annual for Philosophical and Phenomenological Research"), under Husserl's chief editorship, his personal philosophizing flowered into an international movement. Its two most notable adherents were Max Scheler, a scholar of life-philosophy, whose *Formalismus in der Ethik und die materiale Wertethik* ("Formalism in Ethics and the Material Value-Ethics") was published in the *Jahrbuch* (1913–16), and the ontological Existentialist Martin Heidegger (1889–1976), whose famous *Sein und Zeit (Being and Time)* appeared in the *Jahrbuch* in 1927. Despite the differences in their individual philosophies their work showed clearly the influence of the phenomenological method: in Scheler's careful explorations of the role that emotion plays in men's moral values and in his descriptive analyses of the human attitudes of resentment, sympathy, and love; and in Heidegger's startlingly original investigations of human existence with its unique dimensions of being-in-the-world, dread, care, and being toward death. In all of these painstaking and enormously detailed inquiries, however,

[margin note:] Seminal influence of Moore and Wittgenstein

[margin note:] Husserl's phenomenological method and life-world

[margin note:] Scheler, Heidegger, and Merleau-Ponty

both Scheler and Heidegger held to the phenomenological principle that philosophy is not empirical but is the strictly self-evident insight into the structure of experience. Later, Maurice Merleau-Ponty, a French student of philosophical psychology, in his *Phénoménologie de la perception* (1945; *The Phenomenology of Perception*), took over Husserl's conception of the life-world and used the notions of the lived body and its facticity to build up a hierarchical order of man's lived experience.

Existentialism of Jaspers and Sartre. Continental Existentialism, true to its roots in Kierkegaard and Nietzsche, is oriented toward two major themes: (1) the analysis of human Being and (2) the centrality of human choice. Thus its chief theoretical energies are devoted to ontology and decision. Existentialism as a philosophy of human existence found its best spokesman in the German Karl Jaspers, who came to philosophy from medicine and psychology. As a philosophy of human decision, its spokesman was the French philosopher and playwright Jean-Paul Sartre. These two preoccupations of Existentialism lead to two different conceptions of philosophy's function.

Human existence and choice in Jaspers and Sartre

For Jaspers (1883–1969), as for Dewey, the aim of philosophy is practical; for Dewey, however, it guides human doing, whereas for Jaspers its purpose is the achievement of human Being. Philosophizing is an inner activity by which the individual finds and becomes himself: it is a revelation of Being. It is an attempt to answer the question of what man is and what he can become; and this activity, wholly unlike that of science, is one of mere thought, through the "inwardness" of which a man becomes aware of the deepest levels of Being.

But if, for Jaspers, philosophy is devoted to "the illumination of existence," that illumination is achieved when a person recognizes that human existence is revealed most profoundly in his experience of those "extreme" situations that define the human condition—conflict, guilt, suffering, and death. It is in man's confrontation with these extremes that he achieves his existential humanity.

Sartre (1905–80), too, has some concern for man's Being and his dread before the threat of Nothingness. But Sartre finds the essence of this Being in man's liberty—in his duty of self-determination and his freedom of choice—and therefore spends much time in describing the human tendency toward "bad faith"—reflected in man's perverse attempts to deny his own responsibility and to flee from the truth of his inescapable freedom. Sartre, like Schopenhauer and Nietzsche, considered himself less an academic philosopher than a man of letters and also wrote novels and plays that assert the Existential dogma of human freedom and explore the inexhaustible mechanisms of bad faith. It is not that Sartre overlooks the legitimate series of obstacles to freedom a human being has to face in the givens of place, past, environment, fellowmen, and death; but his Existentialist bias demands that man surmount these limitations by acts of conscious decision. For only in acts of freedom does human existence achieve authenticity.

Concluding comments. It seems clear that, in the 50 years around the mid-20th century, philosophizing has become uncommonly concerned with problems of language, symbolism, and communication. Renaissance philosophy was primarily preoccupied with nature, with an external physical world and the objects contained within it. The Enlightenment turned to the mind that knows the world; its philosophy spoke of the genesis of ideas, the relation of concepts, the quality of appearances. But 20th-century philosophizing largely states its problems in terms of symbolic manipulation and the characteristics of words.

Nor is this merely the preoccupation of Analytical philosophy: Dewey was interested in social communication; Whitehead wrote a little volume on *Symbolism: Its Meaning and Effect* (1927); Heidegger turned to poetry and the etymology of words for the revelation of Being; Ernst Cassirer, a German Neo-Kantian, produced a "philosophy of symbolic forms"; and Jaspers tried to decipher the meanings reflected in human speech and gesture.

Apart from this underlying tendency there seems little prospect for philosophical unification. The scientific and the metaphysical tempers still pursue their opposite courses, and the subjectivity of Existentialism and the objectivity of Logical Positivism still express their opposition in mutual contempt. Thus, in the contemporary philosophical universe, multiplicity and division still reign.

(A.W.L.)

BIBLIOGRAPHY

General histories: G.W.F. HEGEL, *Lectures on the History of Philosophy*, 3 vol. (1892–96, reprinted with the title *Hegel's Lectures on the History of Philosophy,* 1983; originally published in German, 2nd rev. ed., 1840); FRIEDRICH UEBERWEG, *A History of Philosophy, from Thales to the Present Time,* 2 vol. (1872–74, reprinted 1972; originally published in German, 4th ed., 3 vol., 1871–73); WILHELM WINDELBAND, *A History of Philosophy,* 2nd ed. rev. (1901, reissued 1979; originally published in German, 1892), a problems approach, particularly good on Kant and German Idealism; ALFRED WEBER, *History of Philosophy,* rev. ed. (1925; originally published in French, 5th ed. rev., 1892), with supplement by RALPH BARTON PERRY, "Philosophy Since 1860"; FRANK THILLY, *A History of Philosophy,* 3rd ed. rev. by LEDGER WOOD (1957); EMILE BRÉHIER, *Histoire de la philosophie,* new ed., 3 vol. (1981), particularly good on French thinkers, less so on English; JULIÁN MARÍAS, *History of Philosophy* (1967; originally published in Spanish, 22nd ed., 1966); BERTRAND RUSSELL, *A History of Western Philosophy . . .* (1945); WILLIAM T. JONES, *A History of Western Philosophy,* 2nd ed., 5 vol. in 6 (1969–75); FREDERICK C. COPLESTON, *A History of Philosophy,* 9 vol. (1946–74); and JOHN HERMAN RANDALL, *The Career of Philosophy,* 2 vol. (1962–65), an informed, comprehensive, and judicious treatment. The best sources for bibliographic information in philosophy are TERRENCE N. TICE and THOMAS P. SLAVENS, *Research Guide to Philosophy* (1983); and *Répertoire bibliographique de la philosophie* (quarterly), which the Institut Supérieur de Philosophie at Louvain began publishing in 1949. R.J. HOLLINGDALE, *Western Philosophy: An Introduction* (1966, reissued 1983), is for the neophyte.

Ancient Greek and Roman philosophy: (*Studies*): Detailed histories on the whole course of Greek and Roman philosophy can be found in EDUARD ZELLER, *Die Philosophie der Griechen,* 3 vol. in 2 (1844–52), also available in the following translations from parts of various editions: *A History of Greek Philosophy from the Earliest Period to the Time of Socrates,* trans. by SARAH F. ALLEYNE (1881), *Socrates and the Socratic Schools,* trans. by OSWALD REICHEL, 3rd rev. ed. (1885), *Plato and the Older Academy,* trans. by SARAH F. ALLEYNE and ALFRED GOODWIN, new ed. (1888), *Aristotle and the Earlier Peripatetics,* trans. by B.F.C. COSTELLOE and J.H. MUIRHEAD (1897), and *A History of Eclecticism in Greek Philosophy,* trans. by SARAH F. ALLEYNE (1883). Equally thorough and up to date is the great work by W.K.C. GUTHRIE, *A History of Greek Philosophy,* 6 vol. (1962–81). For short introductions to Greek philosophy in English, see MARGARET E.J. TAYLOR, *Greek Philosophy* (1921, reissued 1945); REX WARNER, *The Greek Philosophers* (1958); and the excellent one by W.K.C. GUTHRIE, *The Greek Philosophers: From Thales to Aristotle* (1950, reissued 1975). (*Collections of fragments and works*): An influential source from perhaps the 3rd century AD is LAERTIUS DIOGENES, *Lives of Eminent Philosophers,* trans. from the Greek by R.D. HICKS, 2 vol. (1925, reprinted 1979–80). The best comprehensive collection of the fragments of the pre-Socratic philosophers is still HERMANN DIELS and WALTHER KRANZ, *Die Fragmente der Vorsokratiker,* 11th ed. edited by WALTHER KRANZ, 3 vol. (1951–52, reprinted 1972–73), made more readily accessible for English-speaking readers by KATHLEEN FREEMAN, *Ancilla to the Pre-Socratic Philosophers: A Complete Translation of the Fragments . . .* (1948, reprinted 1983). A good selection of texts from the whole history is CORNELIA J. DE VOGEL, *Greek Philosophy: A Collection of Texts Selected and Supplied with Some Notes and Explanations,* 3rd ed., 3 vol. (1963–67). (*Bibliographies*): The most detailed bibliography to 1925 is in FRIEDRICH UEBERWEG, *Grundriss der Geschichte der Philosophie,* vol. 1, *Die Philosophie des Altertums,* ed. by KARL PRAECHTER, 13th ed. (1953); the most complete bibliography from 1926 to 1963 is WILHELM TOTOK, *Handbuch der Geschichte der Philosophie,* vol. 1, *Altertum* (1964), 353 pages of bibliography, including ancient Indian philosophy.

Medieval philosophy: ETIENNE GILSON, *History of Christian Philosophy in the Middle Ages* (1955, reissued 1980), is the best account of medieval philosophy. AIMÉ FOREST, FERNAND VAN STEENBERGHEN, and MAURICE DE GANDILLAC, *Le Mouvement doctrinal du IXᵉ au XIVᵉ siècle* (1951, reissued 1956), traces doctrinal developments from the 9th to the 14th century. FERNAND VAN STEENBERGHEN, *La Philosophie au XIIIᵉ siècle* (1966), gives a different interpretation of 13th-century philosophy from that of Gilson, and his *Aristotle in the West,* 2nd ed. (1970), is a valuable account of the introduction of Aristotle's works into western Europe. DAVID KNOWLES, *The Evolution of Medieval Thought* (1962, reissued 1964), is the work of an eminent historian of medieval religion. ARMAND A. MAURER, *Medieval Philosophy,* 2nd ed. (1982), sketches medieval philosophy from Augustine to the Renaissance; while NORMAN KRETZMANN, ANTHONY KENNY, and JAN PINBORG (eds.), *The Cambridge History of Later Medieval Philosophy* (1982), covers the period from the rediscovery of Aristotle to the decline of Scholasticism (1100–1600). The following are short accounts of philosophy in the Middle Ages: JOHN MARENBON, *Early Medieval Philosophy (480–1150): An Introduction* (1983); GORDON LEFF, *Medieval Thought: St. Augustine to Ockham* (1958, reissued 1980); PAUL VIGNAUX, *Philosophy in the Middle Ages* (1959, reissued 1975; originally published in French, 3rd ed., 1958); and JULIUS R. WEINBERG, *A Short History of Medieval Philosophy* (1964, reprinted 1974). Useful information about medieval Arab and Jewish philosophy is contained in T.J. DE BOER, *The History of Philosophy in Islam* (1903, reprinted 1970; originally published in German, 1901); GOFFREDO QUADRI, *La filosofia degli arabi nel suo fiore,* 2 vol. (1939); ISAAC HUSIK, *A History of Mediaeval Jewish Philosophy* (1916, reissued 1974); and GEORGES VAJDA, *Introduction à la pensée juive du Moyen Âge* (1947). Collections of translated texts include RICHARD MCKEON (ed.), *Selections from Medieval Philosophers,* 2 vol. (1928, reissued 1958); HERMAN SHAPIRO, *Medieval Philosophy: Selected Readings from Augustine to Buridan* (1964); ARTHUR HYMAN and JAMES J. WALSH (eds.), *Philosophy in the Middle Ages: The Christian, Islamic, and Jewish Traditions,* 2nd ed. (1983); and JOHN F. WIPPEL and ALLAN B. WOLTER (eds.), *Medieval Philosophy: From St. Augustine to Nicholas of Cusa* (1969). See also TIMOTHY C. POTTS (ed.), *Conscience in Medieval Philosophy* (1980), a study of many theories of conscience.

Modern and contemporary philosophy: (*Comprehensive classical studies*): JOHANN EDUARD ERDMANN, *A History of Philosophy,* 3 vol., 6th ed. (1915; originally published in German, 2 vol., 1878); KUNO FISCHER, *History of Modern Philosophy: Descartes and His School* (1887, reprinted 1890; originally published as vol. 1 in his *Geschichte der Neuern Philosophie,* 11 vol., 1878); and HARALD HØFFDING, *A History of Modern Phi-* *losophy,* 2 vol. (1900, reprinted 1958; trans. from the 1895–96 German ed.; originally published in Danish, 1894–95). (*Contemporary works*): RAYMOND KLIBANSKY (ed.), *Philosophy in the Mid-Century: A Survey,* 4 vol. (1958–59, reissued 1976), and *Contemporary Philosophy: A Survey,* 4 vol. (1968–71), broad coverage in essays by leading scholars; ALBERT WILLIAM LEVI, *Philosophy and the Modern World* (1959, reissued 1977), a broad treatment, and *Philosophy as Social Expression* (1974); WOLFGANG STEGMÜLLER, *Main Currents in Contemporary German, British, and American Philosophy* (1969, reissued 1970; originally published in German, 4th ed., 1969), narrower, more technical treatment; WALTER KAUFMANN (ed.), *Existentialism from Dostoevsky to Sartre,* rev. ed. (1975), selections with introductions; and MARVIN FARBER (ed.), *Philosophic Thought in France and the United States: Essays Representing Major Trends in Contemporary French and American Philosophy,* 2nd ed. (1968; originally published in French, 1950). (*Chiefly Anglo-American*): JOHN PASSMORE, *A Hundred Years of Philosophy,* 2nd ed. (1966, reissued 1984), and its supplement, *Recent Philosophers* (1985); G.J. WARNOCK, *English Philosophy Since 1900,* 2nd ed. (1969, reprinted 1982); and HERBERT W. SCHNEIDER, *A History of American Philosophy,* 2nd ed. (1963), standard reference work with excellent bibliographies. (*Chiefly continental*): I.M. BOCHEŃSKI, *Contemporary European Philosophy* (1956, reprinted 1982; originally published in German, 2nd rev. ed., 1951); MICHELE FEDERICO SCIACCA, *Philosophical Trends in the Contemporary World* (1964; originally published in Italian, 3rd ed., 2 vol., 1958); HERMANN NOACK, *Die Philosophie Westeuropas,* 2nd rev. ed. (1976); HERBERT SPIEGELBERG, *The Phenomenological Movement: A Historical Introduction,* 3rd rev. ed. (1982); and ANNA-TERESA TYMIENIECKA, *Phenomenology and Science in Contemporary European Thought* (1962). See also ROGER SCRUTON, *From Descartes to Wittgenstein: A Short History of Modern Philosophy* (1981, reissued as *A Short History of Modern Philosophy: From Descartes to Wittgenstein,* 1984).

(K.v.Fr./A.A.Ma./A.W.L.)

Photography

Photography (from the Greek *photos* ["light"] and *graphos* ["writing"]) is the recording of visible images by light action on light-sensitive materials. The term usually refers to the formation of optical images projected by a lens in a camera onto a film or other material carrying a layer of light-sensitive silver salts and the duplication and reproduction of such images by light action (printing); in an extended sense it also includes the formation of images by certain invisible radiations (ultraviolet and infrared rays) and images recorded in other sensitive materials not containing silver by means of chemical or physical processes or both. Related processes include the recording of images by X rays, electron beams, and nuclear radiations (radiography) and the recording and transmission of light images in the form of electromagnetic signals (television and videotape).

This article treats the historical, technical, and aesthetic aspects of still photography. For a similar treatment of motion-picture photography, or cinematography, see MOTION PICTURES.

For coverage of related topics in the *Macropædia* and *Micropædia*, see the *Propædia*, sections 628 and 735.

The article is divided into the following sections:

The history and art of photography

As a means of visual communication and expression, photography has marked aesthetic capabilities. In order to understand them, the characteristics of the process itself must first be understood. Of these the first is immediacy. Usually, but not necessarily, the image that is recorded is formed by a lens in a camera. Upon exposure to the light forming the image, the sensitive material undergoes changes in its structure; a latent image is formed, which becomes visible by development and permanent by fixing. With modern materials, the processing may take place immediately or may be delayed for weeks or months. But, either way, the elements of the final image are determined at the time of exposure. This characteristic is unique to photography and sets it apart from other ways of picture

Immediacy of the photograph

making. Although the photographer can control the character of the original image he captured upon film by the way he develops the negative and prints it, he cannot alter it except by manual interference.

A second characteristic of the photograph is that it can contain more than the photographer intended it to. The first daguerreotypes, shown to an astounded public in Paris in the winter of 1838–39 by the inventor Louis-Jacques-Mandé Daguerre, were praised because of the amount of detail recorded by them; looking at one with a magnifying glass, it was said, was like looking at nature with a telescope. The rival inventor of photography, William Henry Fox Talbot, after noting this characteristic, commented:

It frequently happens, moreover—and this is one of the charms of photography—that the operator himself discovers on examination, perhaps long afterwards, that he has depicted many things he had no notion of at the time. Sometimes inscriptions and dates are found upon the buildings, or printed placards most irrelevant, are discovered upon their walls: sometimes a distant dial-plate is seen, and upon it—unconsciously recorded—the hour of the day at which the view was taken.

As technological advances have improved photographic equipment, materials, and techniques, the scope of photography has expanded enormously. High-speed photography has made visible certain aspects of motion never before seen; with material sensitive to invisible radiation, hidden aspects of nature can be revealed; and, by a combination of photographic, electronic, and space technology, even the planets can be observed in new ways. Photography pervades every sphere of activity in modern civilization. Its thousandfold applications have made it indispensable in daily life. Photography disseminates information about humanity and nature, records the visible world, and extends human knowledge into areas the eye cannot penetrate. Next to the printed word the image drawn by light is the most important means of communication, and for this reason photography has been aptly called the most important invention since the printing press.

**Authen-
ticity of the
photograph** The seemingly automatic recording of an image by photography has given the process a sense of authenticity shared by no other picture-making technique. The fact that the photograph can show more than the eye can see and that the image is not filtered through the brain of a man and put down by the skill of his hand has given it value as evidence. The photograph has become, in the popular mind, so much a substitute for reality and of such apparent accuracy that the adage "The camera does not lie" has become a cliché.

This intrinsic characteristic is of such strength that it has dominated the evaluation of photography's role in the arts. In the past photography was sometimes belittled as a mechanical art because of its dependence on technology. It has also been used over and over again as a foil by art critics to denounce paintings that rely heavily upon exact representation of subject matter. Indeed, after reviewing the daguerreotype process, the painter and art expert Paul Delaroche, who served on the committee that advised the French government to purchase the rights to the new process, declared: "From today painting is dead."

In truth, photography is not the automatic process that is implied by the use of a camera. A fully automatic camera can produce a correctly exposed and sharp negative, but it cannot distinguish between a banal snapshot and a well-composed picture. The ability to make such a distinction rests solely with the person behind the camera. The creative photographer perceives the essential qualities of the subject and interprets it according to his judgment, taste, and involvement. The mechanical photographer merely reproduces what he sees.

Although the camera does limit the photographer to depicting existing objects rather than imaginary or interpretive views, the skilled photographer has at his command a wide variety of controls that can be used to overcome the constraints of literalness and to introduce creativity into the mechanical reproduction process. The image can be modified by different lenses and filters. The type of sensitive material used to record the image is a further control, and the contrast between highlight and shadow can be changed by variations in development. In printing the negative, the photographer has a wide choice in the physical surface of the paper, the tonal contrast, and the image colour. **Technical
controls**

The most important control is, of course, the photographer's vision. He chooses the vantage point and the exact moment of exposure. Through experience he knows how the camera will record what he sees. He learns to previsualize the final print. If he has visual imagination and perception, he can make more than a passive record. He can express universal qualities. He can extend the vision of the viewer.

So facile a medium is photography that it is difficult to grasp its aesthetic capabilities and accomplishments. Of the billions of photographs that are taken every year, only a relatively small number can be considered art. Few camera users are deliberately concerned with the production of photographs to be judged as art. A far greater number look upon photography as a means of communication. While the aim of the commercial photographer, the photojournalist, and the scientist may not primarily be aesthetic, it is significant and remarkably characteristic of the medium that often in their work can be found memorable pictures that reach beyond the particular to the universal. Recognition plays an overwhelming role in photography: recognition by the creative photographer of the picture possibilities presented to him and recognition by the viewer of aesthetic qualities in photographs that he sees.

THE PIONEERS

The forerunner of the camera was the camera obscura, a dark chamber or room with a hole (later a lens) in one wall through which images of objects outside the room were projected on the opposite wall. The principle was probably known to Aristotle more than 2,000 years ago. The Italian scientist and writer Giambattista della Porta, late in the 16th century, demonstrated and described in detail the use of a camera obscura with a lens. By the 18th

First successful photograph from nature, heliograph on pewter by Nicéphore Niepce, 1826/27.

century artists commonly used various types of camera obscura to trace accurate images from nature. These devices still depended on the artist's drawing skills, however, and the search for a method to reproduce images completely mechanically continued.

In 1727 the German professor of anatomy Johann Heinrich Schulze proved that the darkening of silver salts, known since the 16th century, and possibly earlier, was caused by light and not heat. He demonstrated the fact by using sunlight to record words on the salts, but he made no attempt to preserve the images permanently. His discovery, in combination with the camera obscura, provided the basic technology necessary for photography. It was not until the early 19th century, however, that photography actually came into being, largely through the artistic aspirations of two Frenchmen, Nicéphore Niepce and Louis-Jacques-Mandé Daguerre, and two Englishmen, Thomas Wedgwood and William Henry Fox Talbot.

Contributions of Niepce and Daguerre. Niepce, an amateur inventor living near Chalon-sur-Saône, a city 189 miles southeast of Paris, came to photography through his interest in lithography. In this process drawings were copied by hand onto the lithographic stone. To make the drawings Niepce relied upon his son's artistic skill, but, when his son entered military service, he was left without a draftsman. Not artistically trained, he devised a method by which light drew the pictures he needed. He oiled an engraving to make it transparent, then placed it on a plate coated with a light-sensitive solution and exposed the setup to sunlight. After a few hours the solution under the light areas of the engraving hardened, while that under the dark areas remained soft and could be washed away, leaving a permanent, accurate copy of the engraving. Using a type of asphalt, bitumen of Judea, which changes its solubility in oil of lavender according to its exposure to light, he succeeded from 1822 onward in copying oiled engravings onto lithographic stone, glass, and zinc and from 1826 onto pewter plates. In 1826/27, using a camera obscura fitted with a pewter plate, Niepce produced the first successful photograph from nature, a view of the courtyard of his country estate, Gras, from an upper window of the house. The exposure time was about eight hours, during which the sun moved from east to west so that it appears to shine on both sides of the building. The photograph was rediscovered in 1952 by the historian Helmut Gernsheim and is now preserved in the Gernsheim Collection at the University of Texas.

Niepce produced his most successful copy of an engraving, a portrait of Cardinal d'Amboise, in 1826. It was correctly exposed in about three hours, and in February 1827 he had the pewter plate etched to form a printing plate and had two prints pulled. The plate and prints are the oldest photomechanical reproductions still in existence. (The plate and one print are in the Science Museum, London; the other print is in the Gernsheim Collection.) Paper prints were the final aim of Niepce's heliographic (*i.e.,* sun-drawn) process, yet all his other attempts, whether made using a camera or engravings, were underexposed and too weak to be etched. Nevertheless, Niepce's discoveries showed the path that Daguerre and others were to follow with more success.

Daguerre was a professional scene painter. Between 1822 and 1839 he was co-proprietor of the Diorama in Paris, an auditorium in which he and his partner Charles-Marie Bouton displayed immense paintings, 45½ by 71½ feet (14 by 22 metres) in size, of famous places and historical events. The partners painted the scenes on translucent paper or muslin and by the careful use of changing lighting effects were able to present vividly realistic tableaux. The views provided grand entertainment in the illusionistic style, and the amazing trompe l'oeil effect was purposely heightened by the accompaniment of appropriate music and the positioning of real objects, animals, or people in front of the painted scenery.

Like many other artists, Daguerre made his preliminary sketches by tracing the images produced by a camera obscura. About 1826 he began unsuccessful experiments in recording the camera image "by the spontaneous action of light." Learning of Niepce's work, he wrote to him, and on Dec. 14, 1829, the two men formed a partnership for the express purpose of improving Niepce's invention of heliography. From then on Daguerre worked using the improved materials Niepce had adopted—silvered copper plates and iodine—without achieving any improved results until 1835, two years after the death of his partner. By accident Daguerre discovered that a latent image forms on a plate of iodized silver and that it can be "developed" and made visible by exposure to mercury vapour, which settles on the exposed parts of the image. Exposure times could thus be reduced from eight hours to 30 minutes. The results were not permanent, however; when the developed picture was exposed to light, the unexposed areas of silver darkened until the image was no longer visible. By 1837, though, Daguerre was able to fix the image permanently by using a solution of table salt to dissolve the unexposed silver iodide. That year he produced a photograph of his studio on a silvered copper plate, a photograph that was remarkable for its fidelity and detail. Contrary to his contract with Niepce, Daguerre now called the improved process after himself: daguerreotype.

Niepce's heliographic process

The daguerreotype process

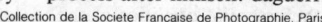
Collection de la Societe Francaise de Photographie, Paris

"Still Life," daguerreotype by Louis-Jacques-Mandé Daguerre, 1837.

In 1839 Daguerre and Niepce's son sold full rights to the daguerreotype and the heliograph to the French government, in return for annuities for life. On August 19 full working details were published. Daguerre wrote a booklet describing the process, *An Historical and Descriptive Account of the Various Processes of the Daguerreotype and the Diorama,* which at once became a best-seller: 29 editions and translations appeared before the end of 1839.

Contributions of Wedgwood and Talbot. In 1802 Thomas Wedgwood, son of the famous potter Josiah Wedgwood, reported his experiments in recording images on paper or leather sensitized with silver nitrate. Although he could record silhouettes of objects placed on the paper, he was not able to make them permanent and, to his disappointment, he failed to record a camera image. Nonetheless, the paper published by Sir Humphry Davy in the *Journal of the Royal Institution,* London, in June 1802, on the experiments of his friend Wedgwood, is the first account of an attempt to produce photographs.

Unaware of the work of Wedgwood and the French pioneers, Talbot, trained as a scientist at Cambridge University, was led to invent a photographic process because of his inability to draw landscapes. On a holiday trip to Italy in 1833, the idea came to him of recording by chemical means the images he observed in his camera obscura. By 1835 he had a workable technique: he made paper light-sensitive by soaking it alternately in solutions of common salt (sodium chloride) and silver nitrate. Silver chloride was thus produced in the fibres of the paper. On exposure to light the silver chloride became finely divided silver, dark in tone. Theoretically, the resulting negative could be used to make any number of positives simply by putting fresh sensitized paper in contact with the negative and exposing it to light. Talbot's method of fixing the print by washing it in a strong solution of sodium chloride was inadequate, however, and the process was not successful until February 1839, when the scientist Sir John F.W. Herschel suggested fixing the negatives with sodium hyposulphite (now called sodium thiosulfate) and waxing them before printing, which reduced the grain of the paper.

When news of Daguerre's process reached England in January 1839, Talbot rushed publication of his "photogenic drawing" process and subsequently explained his technique in complete detail to the members of the Royal Society—six months before the French government divulged working directions for the daguerreotype. There were many others who had similar techniques and who were to claim priority, but to Talbot and Daguerre are owed the two basic processes that were to establish photography as the most facile and convincing way to produce pictures.

First criticism. The two pioneer processes were different in several ways. Daguerreotypes were on metal; photogenic drawings were on paper. Each daguerreotype was unique; photogenic drawings could be duplicated. The aesthetic as well as physical character differed markedly. The daguerreotype rendered detail to a degree that was remarkable; the photogenic drawing, because of the fibrous structure of the paper supporting the silver image, gave a broader, somewhat diffused effect.

The first criticism of photography was necessarily based on a comparison with painting or drawing, since no other standards of picture making existed. Photography's remarkable ability to record a seemingly inexhaustible amount of detail was marveled at again and again. The critics regretted that, because of the great length of exposure, moving objects were not recorded or were rendered blurry and indistinct. The inability of the first processes to record colours was disappointing, but since the critics were already conditioned to black-and-white prints and drawings, this was not as serious a drawback as the harshness of the tonal scale. The technique of photography was at once recognized as a shortcut to art. No longer was it necessary to spend years in art school drawing from sculpture and from life, mastering the laws of linear perspective and chiaroscuro. As Daguerre boasted in a broadsheet in 1838, "with this technique, without any knowledge of chemistry or physics, one will be able to make in a few minutes the most detailed views."

Talbot's photogenic drawing process

Differences between the two pioneer processes

PRE-WORLD WAR I HISTORY

Daguerre's process rapidly spread throughout the world. Before the end of 1839, travelers were bringing back to Paris daguerreotypes of famous monuments in Egypt, Israel, Greece, and Spain; from them engravings were made that were published in two volumes as *Excursions daguerriennes* between 1841 and 1843. Although his process was published "free to the world" by the French government, Daguerre took out a patent for it in England; the first licensee was Antoine-François-Jean Claudet. The first daguerreotypes in America were made on Sept. 16, 1839, just four weeks after the announcement of the process. Exposures were at first of excessive length—a daguerreotype of King's Chapel, Boston, in the International Museum of Photography, Rochester, N.Y., bears a label stating that it was made between 4:40 and 5:30 PM on April 19, 1840. At such exposures moving objects could not be recorded, and portraiture was impractical. Even in blazing sunlight and with the face whitened by flour, a person had to sit immobile for several minutes.

Experiments were started in Europe and the United States to improve the optical, chemical, and practical aspects of the daguerreotype process to make it more feasible for portraiture, the most desired application. Using a camera with a mirror substituted for the lens, Alexander Wolcott opened in New York in March 1840, a "Daguerrean Parlor" for tiny portraits. This was the earliest known photography studio anywhere; the first studio in Europe was opened by Richard Beard in a glasshouse on the roof of the Royal Polytechnic Institution in London on March 23, 1841. Unlike the many daguerreotypists who were originally scientists or miniature painters, Beard had been a coal merchant and patent speculator. Having acquired the exclusive British license for the American mirror camera (he later also purchased the exclusive rights to Daguerre's invention in England, Wales, and the colonies), Beard employed the chemist John Frederick Goddard to try to improve and accelerate the exposure process. Among the techniques Goddard studied were two that Wolcott had tried: increasing the light sensitivity of the silver iodide with bromine vapours and filtering the blindingly bright daylight necessary for exposure through blue glass to ease the portrait sitter's eye strain. By December 1840 Goddard had succeeded well enough to produce tiny portraits ranging in size from one centimetre in diameter to 1.5 by 2.5 inches (four by six centimetres). By the time Beard opened his studio exposure times were said to vary between one and three minutes according to weather and time of day. Daguerreotype portraits were immensely popular, and the studio made considerable profits the first few years, but competition soon appeared and Beard lost his fortune in several lawsuits against infringers of his licenses.

The finest daguerreotypes in Britain were produced by Claudet, who opened a studio on the roof of the Royal Adelaide Gallery in June 1841. He was responsible for numerous improvements in photography, for the discovery that red light did not affect sensitive plates and could therefore be used safely in the darkroom, and for the practical introduction of stereoscopic daguerreotypes in 1851.

The most important advances in photographic lens and camera design came from József Petzval and Friedrich Voigtländer, both of Vienna. Petzval produced an achromatic portrait lens that was about 20 times faster than the simple meniscus lens the Parisian opticians Charles Chevalier and N.M.P. Lerebours had made for Daguerre's cameras. Voigtländer reduced Daguerre's clumsy wooden box to easily transportable proportions for the traveler. These valuable improvements were introduced by Voigtländer in January 1841. That same month another Viennese, Franz Kratochwila, freely published a chemical acceleration process in which the combined vapours of chlorine and bromine increased the sensitivity of the plate five times.

The improvements that had been made in lenses and sensitizing techniques reduced exposure times to approximately 20 to 40 seconds. Daguerreotyping became a flourishing industry, especially in the United States, which, it was generally conceded, led the world in the production of daguerreotypes. In the late 1840s every city had its

Early daguerreotype studios

Early daguerreotypes in the United States

"daguerrean artist," and villages and towns were served by traveling photographers who had fitted up wagons as studios. In New York City alone there were 77 galleries in 1850. Of these, the most celebrated was that of Mathew B. Brady, who began in 1844 to form a "Gallery of Illustrious Americans," and to that end collected portraits of notables taken by his own and other cameramen. Twelve of the portraits were published by lithography in a folio volume. In Boston a studio operated by Albert Sands Southworth and Josiah Johnson Hawes that was advertised as "The Artists' Daguerreotype Rooms" produced the finest portraits ever made by the daguerreotype process. The partners avoided the stereotyped lighting and posing formulas of the average daguerreotypist and did not hesitate to portray their sitters unprettified and "as they were." Lemuel Shaw, a judge of the Supreme Court of Massachusetts, stands with crumpled coat and unruly locks of hair under a glare of sunshine; Lola Montez, adventuress, dancer, actress, lolls over the back of a chair, a cigarette between her gloved fingers. Cities and towns, as well as their inhabitants, were photographed by American daguerreotypists: the rapid growth of San Francisco was documented month by month, and the first history of the city, published in 1855, was illustrated by engravings made from daguerreotypes.

Development and use of the calotype process.   The popularity of the daguerreotype surpassed that of the photogenic drawing, but Talbot continued work to improve his process. On Sept. 21–23, 1840, while experimenting with gallic acid, a chemical he was informed would increase the sensitivity of his prepared paper, Talbot discovered that the acid could be used to develop a latent image. This procedure revolutionized photography on paper as it had photography on metal in 1835. Whereas previously Talbot had needed a camera exposure of one hour to produce a 6.5- by 8.5-inch negative, he now found that one minute was sufficient. Developing the latent image had put photography on paper on a par with the daguerreotype. Talbot named his improved negative process the calotype, from the Greek meaning "beautiful picture," and protected his rights by patent.

The first and most aesthetically satisfying use made of this improved process was in the work of David Octavius Hill, a Scottish landscape painter, and his partner, Robert Adamson, an Edinburgh photographer. In 1843 Hill de-

"John Henning and Alexander Handyside Ritchie," calotype by David Octavius Hill and Robert Adamson, *c.* 1845.
By courtesy of the Art Institute of Chicago

cided to paint a group portrait of the ministers who in that year formed the Free Church of Scotland. There were more than 400 figures to be painted. Sir David Brewster, who knew of Talbot's process from the inventor himself, suggested to Hill that he make use of this new technique. Hill then enlisted the aid of Adamson, and together they made hundreds of photographs, not only of the members of the church meeting but also of people from all walks of life. Although their sitters were posed outdoors in glaring sunlight and had to endure exposures of upward of a minute, Hill and Adamson managed to retain spontaneity. Hill's vision was dominated by the painting style of the period in lighting and posing, particularly in the placement of the hands. Many of the calotypes are strikingly reminiscent of canvases by Sir Henry Raeburn and other contemporary artists. Indeed, William Etty, a Royal Academician, copied in oils the calotype Hill and Adamson made of him in 1844 and exhibited it as a self-portrait. In addition to their formal portraiture, the partners made a series of photographs of fishermen and their wives at Newhaven, in Edinburgh, and architectural studies.

The potential of the calotype for recording great monuments of architecture was shown by a number of Frenchmen, many of whom were trained as painters. In the 1850s they began to photograph historical buildings for the government. Working with cameras making photographs as large as 20 by 29 inches, Henri Le Secq, Charles Marville, and Charles Nègre produced remarkable calotypes of the cathedrals of Notre-Dame in Paris, Chartres, and Amiens, as well as other structures that were being restored after centuries of neglect. An establishment was set up in Lille, Fr., by Louis-Désiré Blanquart-Evrard for bulk printing these paper negatives. Among the products of this firm was a superb volume of photographs by the Parisian writer Maxime Du Camp taken during his travels with the writer Gustave Flaubert in Egypt, Israel, and Syria, from 1849 to 1851.

Calotypes of architectural monuments

Development and use of the collodion process.   Photography was revolutionized in 1851 by the introduction of the collodion process for making glass negatives. This new technique, invented by the English sculptor Frederick Scott Archer, was 20 times faster than all previous methods and was, moreover, free from patent restrictions. The

By courtesy of the Metropolitan Museum of Art, New York, gift of Edward S. Hawes, Alice Mary Hawes, Marion A. Hawes, 1938

"Chief Justice Lemuel Shaw," daguerreotype by Albert Sands Southworth and Josiah Johnson Hawes, 1851.

glass plate negatives recorded detail in a way that rivaled the daguerreotype, and from them paper prints could be made. The process had one serious drawback: the photographer had to sensitize his plate almost immediately before exposure and expose it and process it while the coating was moist. Collodion is a solution of nitrocellulose (guncotton) in alcohol and ether; when the solvents evaporate, a clear plasticlike film is formed. Since it is then impervious to water, the chemicals used for developing the exposed silver halides and removing the unexposed salts cannot penetrate to them. Despite the drawback that the photographer had to have a complete darkroom outfit with him always, the collodion process was almost at once universally adopted. It reigned supreme for more than 30 years and greatly increased the popularity of photography. Some of the most remarkable photographs of all time were produced by this wet-plate process.

At first the positive prints made from the glass plate negatives were produced by Talbot's salt paper method, but from the mid-1850s on they were made on albumen paper, a slow printing-out paper (*i.e.*, paper that produces a visible image on direct exposure, without chemical development) that had been coated with egg white before being sensitized. The egg white gave the paper a glossy surface that improved the picture. Albumen paper was introduced in 1850 by Blanquart-Evrard and remained in general use until World War I.

The new collodion process was also used to produce imitation daguerreotypes called positives on glass or ambrotypes. They were simply underexposed or bleached negatives that appeared positive with a dark coating or backing. In posing and lighting, these popular portraits were identical to daguerreotypes; they were of the same standard sizes, and they were enclosed in the same type of case. They did not approach the brilliancy of the daguerreotype, however. Tintypes, first known as ferrotypes or melainotypes, were cheap variations of the ambrotype. Instead of glass the collodion emulsion was coated on thin iron sheets enameled black. At first they were presented in cases, surrounded by narrow gilt frames, but by the 1860s this elaborate presentation had been abandoned, and the metal sheets were simply inserted in paper envelopes, each with a cutout window the size of the image. Easy to make, inexpensive to purchase, tintypes remained a kind of folk art through the 19th century. Poses were often informal, if not humorous.

Portraiture. A new style of portrait, introduced in Paris by André-Adolphe-Eugène Disdéri in 1854, was universally popular from 1859 onward. It came to be called the carte de visite because the size of the mounted photograph (four by 2½ inches) corresponded to that of a calling card. Disdéri used a four-lens camera to produce eight negatives on a single glass plate. Each picture could be separately posed, or several exposures could be made at once. The principal advantage of the system was its economy: to make eight portraits the photographer needed to sensitize only a single sheet of glass and make one print, which he then cut up into separate pictures. At first cartes de visite almost invariably showed the subjects standing. Backgrounds, which had usually been plain in the days of the daguerreotype, became ornate: furniture and such architectural fragments as papier-mâché columns and arches were introduced, and heavy-fringed velvet drapes were hung within range of the camera. With the advent of the cabinet-size (6½ by four inches) picture in 1866, the baroque tendencies of the photographer became yet more audacious, so that in 1871 a photographer wrote: "One good, plain background, disrobed of castles, piazzas, columns, curtains and what not, well worked, will suit every condition of life." It was at this period that retouching, the use of handwork on the negative, was introduced, as was the practice of painting over the photograph in oil colours.

In contrast to the excessive reliance on accessories and retouching shown by the popular portrait photographers of Europe and America, the work of two Frenchmen and one Englishwoman stands apart. In their portraiture they reached a level unsurpassed since the daguerreotypes of Southworth and Hawes and the calotypes of Hill and Adamson. These photographers were Gaspard-Félix Tour-

nachon, a Parisian writer, editor, and caricaturist who used the pseudonym of Nadar; Étienne Carjat, likewise a Parisian caricaturist; and Julia Margaret Cameron, wife of an eminent British jurist.

Nadar took up photography in 1853 as a means of making studies of the features of prominent Frenchmen for inclusion in a large caricature lithograph, the "Panthéon Nadar." He posed his sitters against plain backgrounds and bathed them with diffused daylight, which brought out every detail of face and dress. He knew most of them, and the powers of observation he had developed as a caricaturist led him to recognize their salient features, which he recorded directly, without the exaggeration that he put in his drawings. When Nadar's photographs were first exhibited, they won great praise in the *Gazette des Beaux Arts,* then the leading art magazine in France. Nadar was a colourful man who had a passion for balloons. He combined his interests by taking a series of aerial photographs, which inspired the French artist Honoré Daumier to produce a cartoon bearing the mocking title "Nadar Élevant la Photographie à la Hauteur de l'Art" ("Nadar Raising Photography to the Height of Art").

Carjat's portraits, more intense perhaps than Nadar's, have the dignity and distinction of those of his contemporary and rival.

Cameron took up photography as a pastime in 1864. Awkward as it was, she used the wet-plate process and began to take portraits of such celebrated Victorians of her acquaintance as Alfred Tennyson, George Frederick Watts, Thomas Carlyle, Charles Darwin, and Sir John F.W. Herschel. A number of her portraits were shown at the Paris International Exhibition of 1867. Cameron used a lens of the extreme focal length of 30 inches to obtain large close-ups. This lens required such long exposures that the subjects frequently moved. The lack of optical definition plus this accidental blurring was universally criticized, yet the very power of her work won her international praise. This can only be explained by the intensity of her vision. "When I have had these men before my camera," she wrote about her portraits of great men,

my whole soul has endeavoured to do its duty toward them in recording faithfully the greatness of the inner man as well as

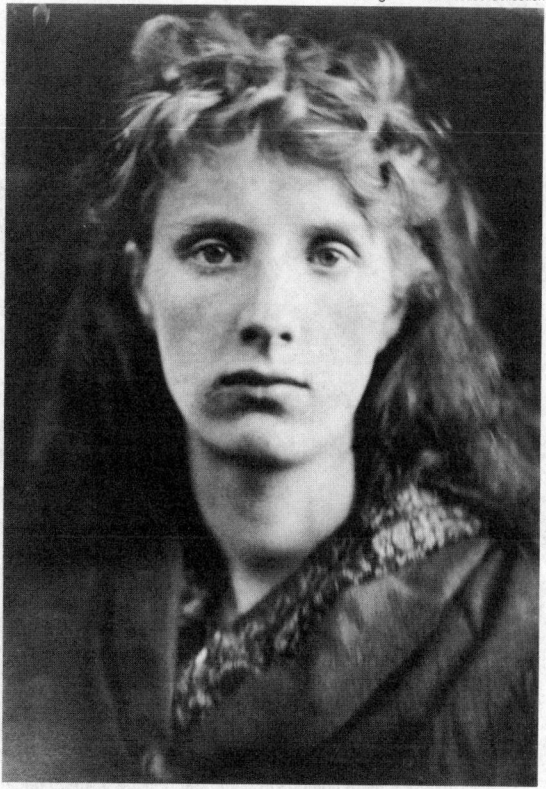

"The Mountain Nymph, Sweet Liberty" by Julia Margaret Cameron, 1867.

[Margin notes]

Development of the tintype

Contributions of Nadar, Carjat, and Cameron

the features of the outer man. The photograph thus obtained has almost been the embodiment of a prayer.

Besides these memorable portraits, Cameron produced a large number of allegorical studies, of children and young women in costume, acting out biblical scenes or themes based on the poetry of her hero, Tennyson. In making these pictures—which today seem weak and sentimental— she was much influenced by the Pre-Raphaelite painters and the photographic work of Oscar G. Rejlander and Henry Peach Robinson (see below), leaders in the production of photographs that emulated paintings.

Influence of painting. Consideration of photography as an aesthetic medium was given impetus by the formation of photographic societies, made up of both professionals and amateurs, who had been attracted to the camera by the popularity of the collodion process. In 1853 the Photographic Society, parent of the present Royal Photographic Society, was formed in London, and in the following year the Société Française de Photographie was founded in Paris.

At the first meeting of the Photographic Society the president, Sir Charles Eastlake (who was then also president of the Royal Academy), invited the miniature painter Sir William Newton to read a paper "Upon Photography in an Artistic View" (*Journal of the Photographic Society,* i, 1853). His argument was that photographs could be useful to the painter so long as they were taken "in accordance [as far as it is possible] with the acknowledged principles of Fine Art." One way by which the photographer could make his results more like works of art, Newton suggested, was to throw the subject slightly out of focus. He also recommended liberal retouching.

Combination printing

An outcome of the urge to create photographs that would fit a priori concepts of what "art" should be was the practice of combining several negatives to make one print in order to achieve painterly compositions of subjects too complicated to be photographed in a straightforward manner. A famous example was by Oscar G. Rejlander, a Swede who had studied art in Rome and was practicing photography in England. He used 30 negatives to produce a 31- by 16-inch print titled "The Two Ways of Life," showing, in allegory as obvious as it was sentimental, that the way of the blessed led through good works and the way of the damned through vice. Rejlander, who described the technique in detail in photographic journals, stated that his purpose was to prove to artists the aesthetic possibilities of photography, which they had generally denied. The photograph was shown in the Manchester Art Treasures Exhibition of 1857 and was purchased by Queen Victoria for Prince Albert.

Rejlander's technique stimulated Henry Peach Robinson, a professional photographer who had been trained as an artist, to produce similar combination prints. He achieved fame with a five-negative print, "Fading Away," produced in 1858. The subject, a dying girl, was considered by critics as too painful a subject to be represented by photography. Perhaps the implied authenticity of the camera bothered them, for painters had long presented subjects of a far more painful nature.

Robinson became a most articulate member of the Photographic Society, and his teaching was even more influential than his photography. In 1869 appeared the first of many editions and translations of his book, *Pictorial Effect in Photography.* From an outmoded handbook on painting, Robinson borrowed compositional formulas the use of which, he claimed, would bring artistic success. The importance of balance was stressed, and the opposition of light against dark was made clear. The fault of the book lay not only in the assumption that rules set up for one art form could be applied to another but also in its intellectual and academic approach to art.

Robinson's rules for photography

Robinson's work is weak and artificial by present standards of taste. Not only did he practice combination printing when it was not technically necessary, but he preferred to work in the studio, against painted backdrops and with props of natural objects, even foliage, mounted on casters. When he did photograph the real world, he took models with him, dressing them up to play the part of country girls.

So long as photographers maintained that the way to art was by the emulation of painting, critics were reluctant to admit the new medium to an independent aesthetic position. Portraits, when done as sensitively and as directly as those produced by Hill and Adamson, Nadar, and Cameron, won the praise of art critics. But sentimental genre scenes, posed and arranged for the camera, lacked the sharp objective truth that is a characteristic of photography. Other photographers, not concerned about producing art for exhibition, were making photographs of the world and man's activities with such extraordinary perception and understanding of the medium that often their work surpassed more consciously artistic works. These men took their cameras to battlefields and to faraway places, often at the risk of their lives.

Combat photography. In 1855 Roger Fenton sailed from London to the Crimea to photograph the war. He was sent to provide visual evidence countering the caustic written reports dispatched by William Russell, war correspondent for *The Times* of London, criticizing military mismanagement and the inadequate, unsanitary living

Contributions of Fenton and Brady

George Eastman House Collection

"The Two Ways of Life," a composite photograph made from 30 negatives taken and assembled by Oscar G. Rejlander, 1857. The tableau is allegorical, showing a young man torn between a life of (left) debauchery and (right) virtuous labour.

"Fading Away," a composite photograph made from five negatives by Henry Peach Robinson, 1858.

George Eastman House Collection

conditions of the soldiers. Fenton had to develop his wet plates in a horse-drawn van that had been converted into a darkroom. It was visible for miles in the bare landscape and a few times attracted enemy fire. Despite the difficulty, during his four-month stay Fenton produced 360 photographs, the first large-scale camera documentation of a war.

When the Civil War broke out in the United States, Mathew Brady, the New York daguerreotypist and portraitist, who had been among the first to adopt the wet-plate process, conceived the bold plan of making a photographic record of the hostilities. When President Lincoln told him the government could not finance such an undertaking, he invested his own savings in the project, expecting to recover his outlay by selling thousands of prints. Brady and his photographers—notably Alexander Gardner and Timothy H. O'Sullivan, who left his employ in the midst of hostilities—produced an amazing record of the battlefield. At his New York gallery, Brady showed pictures of the dead at Antietam. The *New York Times* reported on Oct. 20, 1862:

> Mr. Brady has done something to bring home to us the terrible reality and earnestness of war. If he has not brought bodies and laid them on our dooryards and along the streets, he has done something very like it.... It seems somewhat singular

that the same sun that looked down on the faces of the slain blistering them, blotting out from the bodies all semblance to humanity, and hastening corruption, should have thus caught their features upon canvas, and given them perpetuity for ever. But it is so.

Long prized for their value as historical documents, the Civil War photographs are now valued for their aesthetic qualities as well. Unfortunately for Brady, immediately after the war they were seen as unnecessary reminders of hardship and conflict. Unable to sell the prints as he had planned, Brady died embittered in a charity hospital in New York City. Fenton's Crimean War photographs had similarly lost their audience as soon as the peace treaty was signed. Nevertheless, entrepreneurs hoping to sell prints or commemorative albums continued to finance the photographic documentation of the more important conflicts of the late 19th century. The Boer War and the Russo-Japanese War were also covered by photographers engaged by newspapers and by three American mass producers of stereographs.

Landscape photography. During the collodion period scores of photographers journeyed to the far corners of the world, producing memorable travel views despite the trying conditions of the wet-plate process. Among the most successful was the Englishman Francis Frith. The

By courtesy of the Museum of Modern Art, New York

"Ruins of the Gallego Flour Mills, Richmond, Virginia" by Mathew B. Brady, 1865.

most active of several European photographers working in the Middle East in the late 1850s, he took hundreds of fine pictures of monuments along the Nile from Cairo to Abu Simbel, as well as in Syria and Palestine. Samuel Bourne, Felice Beato, John Thomson, and other British amateurs traveled to Asia, bringing back to England lively images of the nature, people, and customs of India, China, and Japan. Other British photographers concentrated on Europe: Charles Clifford recorded the landscape and architecture of Spain, Robert MacPherson that of Rome, and Thomas Annan of Glasgow and George Washington Wilson of Aberdeen the wildness, castles, and abbeys of Scotland. The Bisson brothers (Louis-Auguste and Auguste-Rosalie), Gustave Le Gray, and Edouard-Denis Baldus depicted the landscape and architecture of France. In the United States Carleton E. Watkins and the English-born Eadweard Muybridge both won recognition for their scenic views of Yosemite, the Columbia River, Alaska, and other wilderness regions of North America.

Landscape photography was usually intended for publication in books or as portfolios of prints to be sold to collectors, but in the United States photographers were often important members of government surveys and were also commissioned by railroad companies to make publicity pictures of track laying, bridge building, and spectacular scenery through which the new lines ran. Of the photographers of the American frontier, two stand out: Timothy H. O'Sullivan, of Civil War fame, and William Henry Jackson. O'Sullivan's photographs of the Southwest are of great beauty, particularly his views of Indian cliff dwellings in the Canyon de Chelly in Arizona, made in 1873. Jackson, self-trained as a painter in Vermont, crossed the plains as a wagon driver. In 1868 he opened a photographic gallery in Omaha, Neb. The Union Pacific Railroad was under construction, and he received an order to produce 10,000 stereographs. The excellence of his work led F.V. Hayden, a geologist, to hire him to photograph the Yellowstone as part of Hayden's government-financed expedition there in

Photography on the American frontier

George Eastman House Collection

"Canyon de Chelly, Arizona" by Timothy H. O'Sullivan, 1873.

1871. The photographs Jackson took were influential in the decision by Congress to create Yellowstone National Park. Later, in 1875, he recorded the immensity of the western landscape, using large glass plates.

Stereoscopic photography. Many of the landscape photographers also took stereographs. These double pictures, taken after 1856 with twin-lens cameras, produce a remarkable effect of three dimensions when viewed through a stereoscope. Stereography, first described in 1832 by the English physicist Charles Wheatstone, is uniquely photographic, since no artist could draw two scenes in exact perspective from viewpoints separated only 2 1/2 inches—the normal distance between human eyes. Wheatstone's mirror stereoscope, however, was not practical for use with photographs, and the invention languished until the Scottish scientist Sir David Brewster designed a simplified viewing instrument, which was exhibited at the 1851 Great Exhibition in the Crystal Palace, London. Queen Victoria was entranced by the stereo daguerreotypes she saw there, and with the introduction of the collodion process, which simplified exposure and printing techniques, three-dimensional photography became a popular craze.

In 1854 the London Stereoscopic Company was formed. Their chief photographer was William England, whose lively street scenes of New York City in rainy weather and views of Niagara Falls taken in 1859 were the wonders of the day. The instantaneous street scenes, which showed pedestrians and vehicles stopped in their tracks, were made possible because the small size of the stereo-camera reduced exposure times to less than half a second. To minimize movement street views were usually taken from a first-floor window with the camera focused directly down the street. (Such views later inspired several Impressionists to paint similar street scenes.) Between 1860 and about 1920 a stereo viewer was as ubiquitous in British and American homes (where a simplified and cheap hand viewer was introduced by Oliver Wendell Holmes [the American physician was a great lover of photography]) as the television set is today. Millions of stereographs were circulated in the years before newspaper reproduction of photographs, and their impact was enormous.

Development of the dry plate. In the 1870s many attempts were made to find a dry substitute for wet collodion so that plates could be prepared well in advance and developed long after exposure. The suggestion casually made in 1871 by Richard Leach Maddox, an English physician, to suspend silver bromide in a gelatin emulsion led, in 1878, to the introduction of factory-produced dry plates coated with gelatin containing silver salts, an event that marked the beginning of the modern era of photography.

Gelatin plates were about 60 times more sensitive than collodion plates. The increased speed freed the camera from the tripod, and a great variety of small hand cameras that allowed photographers to take instantaneous snapshots became available at relatively low cost. Of these, the most popular was the Kodak camera, introduced by George Eastman in 1888. Its simplicity greatly speeded the growth of amateur photography. In place of glass plates, it contained a roll of negative material sufficient for taking 100 circular pictures, each roughly 2 1/2 inches in diameter. After exposing the last negative, the entire camera was sent to one of the Eastman factories (Rochester, N.Y., or Harrow, Middlesex), where the roll was processed and printed. "You Press the Button, We Do the Rest" was Eastman's description of the Kodak system. At first Eastman's so-called "American film" was used in the camera. This film was paper based, and the gelatin layer containing the image was stripped away after development and fixing and transferred to a transparent support. In 1889 it was replaced by film on a transparent plastic base of nitrocellulose that had been developed by the Reverend Hannibal Goodwin of Newark, N.J., in 1887.

Invention of the Kodak camera

Photography of movement. A few years before the introduction of the dry plate, the world was amazed at the photographs of horses taken by Eadweard Muybridge in California. Using a series of 12 to 24 cameras ranged side by side opposite a reflecting screen, with their shutters released by the breaking of threads as the horse dashed by, Muybridge secured sets of sequence photographs of succes-

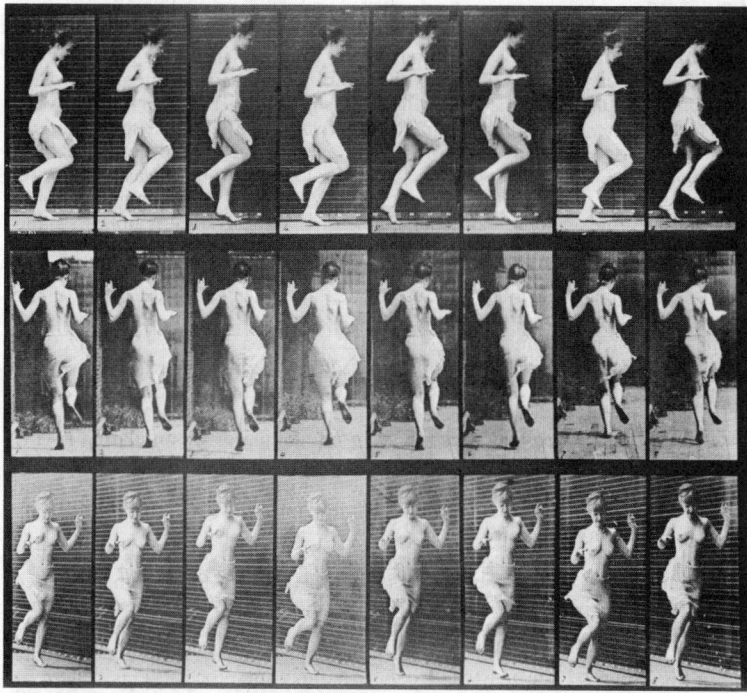

"Figure Hopping" by Eadweard Muybridge, 1887. Sequence of eight stages of movement, simultaneously photographed by multiple cameras at three different positions.

By courtesy of the Cooper-Hewitt Museum of Decorative Arts and Design, Smithsonian Institution

sive phases of the walk, the trot, and the gallop. When the pictures were published internationally in the popular and scientific press, they were so different from the traditional hand-drawn representation of a horse's steps that it was difficult to believe that they were accurate. To prove that his photographs were correct, Muybridge threw them upon a screen one after the other with a lantern-slide projector he had built for the purpose; the result was the world's first motion-picture presentation. This memorable event took place at the San Francisco Art Association in 1880.

Muybridge's early studies were taken with wet plates. With the new gelatin plates, he was able to improve his technique greatly, and in 1884–85, at the invitation of the University of Pennsylvania, he produced 781 sequence photographs of many kinds of animals as well as men and women engaged in a wide variety of activities.

Muybridge's photographic analysis of movement led the French physiologist Étienne-Jules Marey to develop chronophotography. Whereas Muybridge had employed a battery of cameras to record detailed, separate images of successive stages of movement, Marey used only one, recording an entire sequence of movement on a single plate. With Marey's method, the images of various phases of motion sometimes overlapped, but it was easier to see and understand the flow of movement. Marey was also able to record higher speeds at shorter intervals than Muybridge. Both his and Muybridge's work greatly contributed to the field of motion study and to the development of the motion picture.

Naturalistic photography. *Contributions of Emerson.* In the late 19th century the growing number of amateur photographers used the camera to capture daily occurrences

George Eastman House Collection

"Pond in Winter" by Peter Henry Emerson, 1888.

and important moments in their lives, but the members of the societies and clubs concerned with photography as an art became more and more divorced from matters of ordinary life. Subjects in the so-called art photographs were artificially composed in the studio in imitation of 17th-century Dutch paintings. Photographers strove to master complicated printing methods allowing manual interference. Photographing everyday life was considered mere record-making or documentation. Landscape pictures, the strength of British photographers in past decades, found little favour. When similar beliefs prevailed in French academic painting 35 years previously, the French realist painter Gustave Courbet was prompted to call for a "return to nature." So now Peter Henry Emerson, physician by profession and an ardent amateur photographer, attacked the artificiality of the photographs generally accepted as outstanding examples of the artistic use of the camera. Emerson's passionate plea for the return to natural subjects was indeed salutary, but of greater importance was his advice that photographers should respect the photographic process and limit their controls to those that were inherent.

Emerson's photographs of natural subjects

In his book *Naturalistic Photography* (1889) Emerson further developed his theories (some of which he later disclaimed). Although his writings were influential, his photographs of the life of simple country folk presented a far more convincing argument for his beliefs. Emerson's photographs were far removed from the usual artificial genre studies and close to the graphic work of the French painter J.-F. Millet, which Emerson greatly admired. They were published in limited editions in handsome folio volumes and motivated other amateurs to seek inspiration in nature.

The photographs in Emerson's first and finest album, *Life and Landscape on the Norfolk Broads* (1886), were printed on the newly invented platinotype paper. In this printing paper, salts of iron and platinum replaced those of silver as the light-sensitive material. Platinotypes had a long and delicate tonal scale, and they did not fade, unlike the more common silver prints. Emerson helped to popularize the paper, which remained in use until about 1920, when the rising price of platinum made it impractical.

The Linked Ring and the Photo-Secession. The recognition of photography as an art rather than a mechanical process and its evaluation on its own terms rather than according to the traditional rules governing painting were further advanced by the formation in London in 1892 of the Brotherhood of the Linked Ring. The group, which was founded by the prominent pictorial photographer H.P. Robinson, George Davison, a leader of the Art Nouveau movement, and others dissatisfied with the scientific bias of the London Photographic Society, held annual exhibitions, which they called salons. By 1901 it was their proud boast that "through the *Salon* the Linked Ring has clearly demonstrated that pictorial photography is able to stand alone and that it has a future entirely apart from that which is purely mechanical."

Similar groups formed in other countries. One of the most influential was the Photo-Secession, founded in the United States in 1902 by Alfred Stieglitz. Stieglitz, who had previously organized the Camera Club of New York City and served as editor of the club journal, *Camera Notes,* was a strong proponent of "straight" photography. He did not believe in retouching or manipulating in any way his negatives or prints. He had, as early as 1892–93, demonstrated the pictorial possibilities of the hand camera with his photographs of New York under all weather conditions.

Stieglitz's contributions to photography

A few of the Photo-Secession members, including Clarence H. White and Harry C. Rubincam, favoured naturalistic photography like Stieglitz. Many, however, notably Edward Steichen and Alvin Langdon Coburn, were adherents of the impressionistic soft-focus school and of the newly introduced gum print process. This technique gave the photographer the utmost manual control. He coated paper with watercolour pigment of any desired tint mixed with gum arabic and potassium bichromate. On exposure to light beneath a negative, the pigment became insoluble according to the amount of light received. The print was "developed" simply by bathing it in water. If desired, areas could be eliminated by brushing them with hot water or by drawing on them.

Steichen's gum prints

Despite their stylistic differences, the members of the Photo-Secession were united in their disdain for the lack of standards and the general conduct of photographic exhibitions in the United States. They chose the name "secession" to dramatize their rebellion against the status quo, just as avant-garde German and Austrian painters had used the same word to make manifest their independence of officialdom. The record of the Photo-Secession

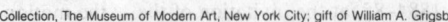

Collection, The Museum of Modern Art, New York City; gift of William A. Grigsby

"Steeplechase Day, Paris: Grand Stand," duogravure by Edward Steichen, 1905; from *Camera Work*, 1913. 15.72 cm × 20.16 cm.

"The Steerage" by Alfred Stieglitz, 1907.

is contained in 50 issues of the much praised *Camera Work,* published by Stieglitz between 1903 and 1917; this quarterly publication contained superb reproductions of photographs but was of uneven quality, partly because of the members' stylistic differences. The photographs were occasionally overly sentimental, artificial, or banal, and indeed, far better work was being produced in New York City at this time by documentary photographers such as

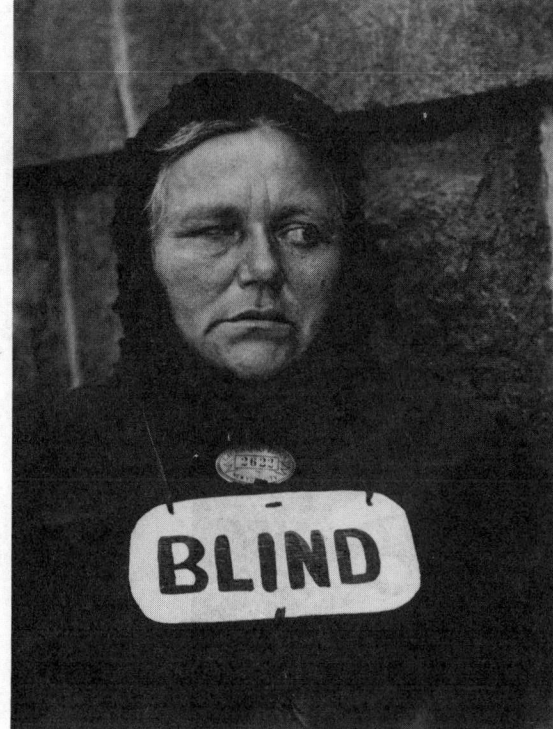

"Blind Woman, New York" by Paul Strand, 1916; from *Camera Work,* 1917.

Jacob Riis and Lewis W. Hine, whose photographs were not then considered art.

In addition to *Camera Work,* the Photo-Secession had a gallery, which came to be known as 291 from the street number on Fifth Avenue, New York City, where it was located. There Stieglitz showed not only pictorial photographs but also, from 1906 on, avant-garde modern art, selected at first by Steichen in Paris. At 291 Americans saw, long before the Armory Show of 1913 made them popular, paintings and sculpture by Rodin, Marin, Toulouse-Lautrec, Cézanne, Van Gogh, Picasso, Brancusi, and Matisse. Stieglitz also organized there the first exhibitions in the world of drawings by children (1912) and of African art (1914).

Other important photographers of the period were Paul Strand and Coburn. The last two issues of *Camera Work* contained photographs by Strand only. They showed an entirely new approach. There were views looking down from unusual angles; there were bowls in quasi-abstract arrangements; there was a group of powerful open-air portraits taken in the streets of the lower East Side of New York City. These portraits had been taken with a 45° prism fitted over the lens, so that the subjects were unaware that they were being photographed. Coburn, one of the first of the Photo-Secessionists, made a series of photographs in 1912 looking down from tall buildings, which he exhibited as "New York from Its Pinnacles"; they were remarkable for the way in which emphasis was placed on form. He pushed this interest in abstraction to the total elimination of recognizable subject matter in his "Vortographs," some of which were published in *Photograms of the Year* in 1917.

POST–WORLD WAR I HISTORY

During the 1920s and '30s, a new, more realistic style of photography gained prominence, a reflection, perhaps, of post-World War I disillusionment. At the close of the war, Steichen, who had been in command of aerial photography for the American Expeditionary Forces, abandoned the broad, impressionistic style he had earlier practiced for sharply focused portraits of celebrities, taken for *Vanity Fair* and *Vogue* magazines. The painter Charles Sheeler used the camera to record the stark beauty of Pennsylvania barns and the forms of industrial structures.

In California, Edward Weston, who had been working as a photographer for more than 15 years, turned in 1923 to a more direct and realistic use of the camera, with a certain emphasis upon abstract form that he never allowed to detract from the recognition of subject matter. "The camera should be used for a recording of *life,*" he wrote in 1924, "for rendering the very substance and quintessence of the *thing itself,* whether it be polished steel or palpitating flesh." He formulated a working method based on the use of the classic view camera for eight- by 10-inch negatives, a high-quality lens, well stopped down to ensure great depth of field, and the complete avoidance of artificial lighting. He printed the negatives by contact on glossy bromide paper to secure maximum detail. Enlarging and retouching of any kind was inadmissable.

To Stieglitz this revaluation of photographic aesthetics was in fact a strengthening of the beliefs he had held since his student days. He produced some of his most powerful work in the 1920s—especially his photographs of cloud forms that he called "Equivalents" because they were equivalent to his thoughts and emotions. Ill health forced him to abandon the camera in 1936, but he continued to maintain an art gallery until his death in 1946.

Paul Strand, whose striking close-ups and semiabstract photographs Stieglitz had first exhibited, developed a style equally rigorous and self-disciplined during the same period. He produced powerful landscapes, direct portraits, and minute details of driftwood and plant life. In 1940 a portfolio of superb photographs Strand had taken in Mexico was issued. After Strand settled in France in 1950, he traveled extensively, producing similar publications on France, Italy, the Hebrides, Egypt, and Ghana, each providing insight into the life in small communities. Asked to define his sphere of interest, Strand once replied that he considered himself a photographer of people.

Realistic photography in the United States

"Dunes, Oceano" by Edward Weston, 1936.

Edward Weston

Viewing the negatives of Strand led Ansel Adams in 1930 to make photography his career. He was then studying the piano and photographing for his own satisfaction. Long interested in nature—his first photographs were of the Sierra Nevada Range and Yosemite National Park—he refined and sharpened his technique. In 1932, with Willard Van Dyke, Edward and Brett Weston, Imogen Cunningham, and Sonya Noskowiak, Adams founded an informal society, Group f.64, so named for the smallest setting of the aperture of the lens that coupled maximum depth of field with maximum sharpness. Adams' great contribution was in what he called "the interpretation of the natural scene." His photographs "Mount Williamson—Clearing Storm" (1944) and "Sierra Nevada from Lone Pine" (1944) are classics.

A major representative of the postwar realistic style, known as the Neue Sachlichkeit ("New Objectivity") in Germany, was Albert Renger-Patzsch, a professional photographer who spent most of his life in Essen. Beginning in 1922, he introduced a completely new approach to photography in Germany. He abhorred the vagueness and falsification of photography of the art nouveau period (1890–1914). A firm believer in straight photography, he was fascinated by the beauty of everyday things. Like Strand before him, Renger-Patzsch considered a purely objective photography to be the true, if unattainable, goal.

New Objectivity in Germany

Ansel Adams

"Mount Williamson—Clearing Storm" by Ansel Adams, 1944.

"Driving Shaft of a Locomotive" by Albert Renger-Patzsch, 1923.
By courtesy of the Gernsheim Collection, The University of Texas at Austin

His photographs are characterized by strong design, factual documentation, and stark realism stressing materials. Like Weston he insisted that the final image should exist, in all its completeness, before the exposure was made and that the print should directly record this image in full detail.

Renger-Patzsch's work was first exhibited in 1925, and three years later his most famous book appeared, *Die Welt ist schön* ("The World Is Beautiful"). The very title set the work apart in a period when artists were more concerned with creating abstractions than interpreting the environment. Renger-Patzsch looked hard at the world. The art historian Heinrich Schwarz wrote in 1929: "If today the photographs of Renger-Patzsch create more pure pleasure than many paintings, it is not an accident, but evidence that the time has found in the photographer a more sensitive instrument for the expression of its artistic needs than in the painter." Renger-Patzsch's subsequent books were largely concerned with regional landscapes and architecture, but his last two publications, *Im Wald* (1958; "Trees") and *Gestein* (1966; "Stones"), have an abstract beauty inspired by their themes.

Neue Sachlichkeit gathered momentum when Karl Blossfeldt's breathtaking, detailed magnifications of plants, which he had taken around 1900 to assist him in modeling plants, were published in *Original Forms of Art* (1928), followed by the *Magic Garden of Nature* (1932). About that time, August Sander, sick of the sweet-looking, posed studio portraits by which he had made his living for nearly 30 years, vowed "From now on I only want the honest truth about our time and people." In *Portrait of an Epoch* (1929) Sander presented such an unflattering portrait of the German middle class that in 1934 the Nazis impounded all unsold copies. Sander's idea of photographing tradespeople in his studio in Cologne inspired the American fashion photographer Irving Penn to shoot a similar series 30 years later. In both cases the portraits are unconvincing because the workers are divorced from their usual surroundings. The finest portraits of the German intelligentsia of the 1920s were taken by Hugo Erfurth of Dresden. They are imbued with strong artistic conception and a sympathetic understanding of the sitter.

Influence of abstract art. In 1919 Christian Schad, a member of the Dada group of modern artists in Geneva, amused himself by arranging small, flat objects directly on photographic paper. Upon exposure to light, the paper darkened more or less or not at all, according to the opacity or transparency of the objects. These "schadographs," as they came to be called, were minor contributions to the Dada movement and would be forgotten except that they inspired the American Surrealist painter Man Ray and the Hungarian constructivist painter László Moholy-Nagy to produce similar, though larger, abstract photographs.

Cameraless photographs

Man Ray had settled in Paris in 1921 and was supporting himself by taking portraits and fashion photographs. One day he accidentally set a glass funnel, a graduate, and a thermometer on a piece of photographic paper, thus producing "rayographs."

I turned on the light; before my eyes an image began to form, not quite a simple silhouette of the objects as in a straight photograph, but distorted and refracted by the glass more or less in contact with the paper.

© AUGUST SANDER ARCHIVE, courtesy Sander Gallery, Inc., New York City

"Bricklayer's Mate" by August Sander, Cologne, 1929.

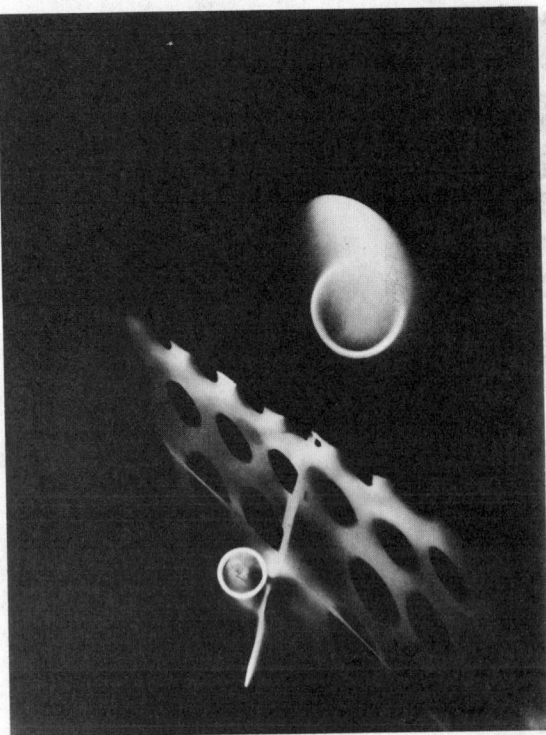

"Photogram," photogram by László Moholy-Nagy, 1926.
George Eastman House Collection

About the same time, in Berlin, Moholy-Nagy (or perhaps his wife, Lucia, a trained photographer) began to use three-dimensional objects to make similar cameraless photographs, which he called "photograms." Although identical in technique, the work of each was quite different. Man Ray emphasized the distorted but recognizable object; Moholy-Nagy the play of light, no matter how abstract. The former brought to photography the vision of the Surrealists; the latter, that of the Constructivists.

As a teacher in the influential Bauhaus art school, Moholy-Nagy explored the potential of the unconventional use of the camera as a means of discovering form. He delighted in the worm's-eye and the bird's-eye view. He considered the negative an end as well as a means. Amazed at the power of the medium to make visible the invisible, he collected X rays, photomicrographs, and astronomical and ultrahigh-speed photographs. When in 1925 he put together a book of these pictures titled *Painting, Photography, Film,* the eyes of the world were opened to the scope and breadth of photography as a tool for vision.

Photomontage. The art of combining photographs with watercolour paintings was a popular pastime in the 1870s. In the first decades of the 20th century the idea of freely combining mediums was revived when Cubist painters began to glue on their abstract canvases words clipped from newspapers, labels from bottles, and even actual objects. The extension of this collage technique (from the French *coller,* meaning "to glue") to photography was logical. The German artist John Heartfield, the greatest master of photomontage, claimed that the origin of the technique lay in postcards that he and his friend the German artist George Grosz sent to friends at the front during World War I. These were

> a mischmasch of advertisements for hernia belts, student song books and dog food, labels from schnaps and wine bottles, and photographs from picture papers, cut up at will in such a way as to say, in pictures, what would have been banned by the censors if we had said it in words.

Heartfield's photomontages, which were published weekly, first in Berlin and later in Prague, between 1929 and 1938, have a savage quality. Violent contrasts of the scale and perspective of the image elements, the ruthless cropping of heads and bodies, the substitution of machine parts for vital organs, and other seeming illogical juxtapositions, were carefully calculated to have a shock effect. Heartfield's anti-Fascist montages were among the strongest protests made by any visual artist.

Excellent montages were also produced in the 1920s by the German artists Hannah Höch, Herbert Bayer, Otto Umbehr, and the Surrealist painter Max Ernst. Most of these combined photographs cut from newspapers with other ephemera to express a specific idea. The montages of the Constructivists are more architectural: space is created with the purely photographic self-portrait of the Russian artist El Lissitzky (1924) and a fantasy world is built by Moholy-Nagy in his "Leda and the Swan." The power of montage lies in the tensions set up by the juxtaposition of disparate visual elements.

Documentary photography. At this same period, the documentary photographs of Eugène Atget first became known to the public. Beginning around 1898, this French photographer produced approximately 10,000 photographs of Paris and its environs that were direct, straightforward, and poetic in their sympathetic rendering of the very fabric of the city. He photographed shop fronts, buildings, wheeled vehicles of all kinds, decorative details, and the

Photo-
montage
technique

By courtesy of Mrs. Gertrud Heartfield

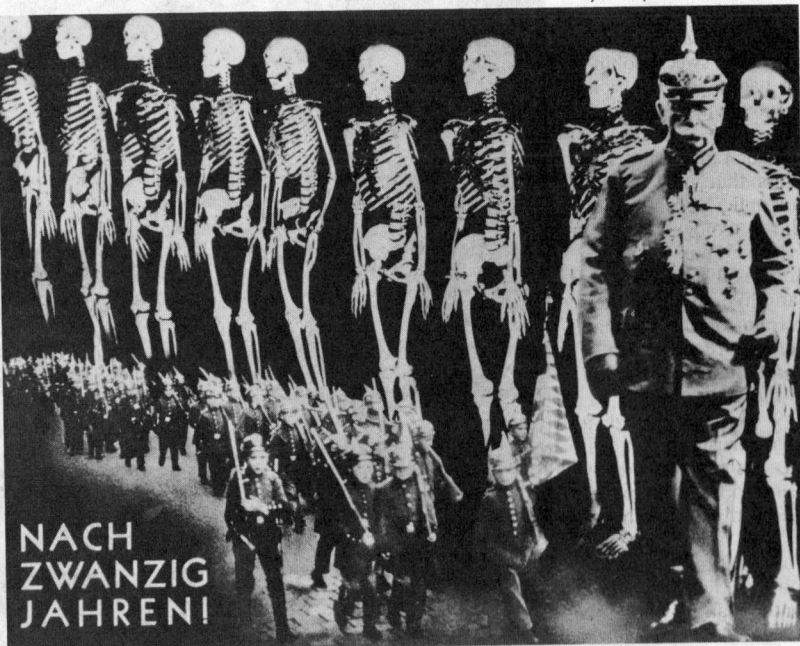

"Twenty Years Later," photomontage by John Heartfield, 1934.

people who earned their living in the streets. Unknown to the photographic world, Atget worked alone, supporting himself by selling prints to architects, painters, and, above all, museums. The beauty of his photographs attracted the attention of Man Ray, who published a few of them in the periodical *La Revolution Surréaliste* in 1926. Upon Atget's death in 1927 his entire collection of prints and negatives was saved for posterity by the U.S. photographer Berenice Abbott (with the help of the New York art dealer Julien Levy); they are now in the collection of the Museum of Modern Art, New York City.

Although Atget was one of the most prominent photographers in the documentary field, he was by no means the first. The value of the photograph as a record of the world and man's conditions and achievements has been evident since the inception of the medium in 1839.

Early uses of documentary photography

Early documentary photographs were used to relay information about important events (*e.g.,* the Brady staff's record of the Civil War) as well as the scenery and people of distant or unexplored lands. They were also used to record the successive stages of significant or complex projects. The English artist Philip Henry Delamotte, for example, was hired to document in weekly photographs the progress of the construction of the Crystal Palace in London, from the laying of its foundation in 1852 to its opening by Queen Victoria two years later. Shortly afterward, by order of the French government, Édouard-Denis Baldus photographed to scale the sculpture, capitals, scrollwork, and other architectural details of the new wing of the Louvre Museum. Valuable work of a similar timely nature was undertaken by the English photographers Alfred and John Bool and Henry Dixon. Between 1875 and 1886 they worked for the Society for Photographing Old London, recording the historic buildings and relics that were gradually disappearing as a result of modernization.

The recognition of the power of photography to persuade as well as to inform came somewhat later. The classic sociological study *London Labour and the London Poor,* by Henry Mayhew (1851–62), was illustrated with drawings partly copied from daguerreotypes taken by Richard Beard; a sequel, patterned upon it, appeared in 1877—*Street Life in London,* by Adolphe Smith and John Thomson. The photographs, taken by Thomson, were moving, straightforward pictures of chimney sweeps, flower sellers, bargemen, and other tradesmen. They were reproduced by the woodburytype process, which gave exact, permanent facsimiles of the original prints. The intent of the publication was to show—as Charles Dickens had shown in his novels—the hardships and problems faced by the ever-growing working-class population of London. Each of the photographs was accompanied by a detailed explicative text by Smith. Oscar G. Rejlander photographed orphan children in the streets of London performing such humble tasks as cleaning boots and sweeping streets.

To Jacob A. Riis, a police reporter in New York City in the 1880s, the camera became the ally of his pen in the personal crusade he was waging to better the lot of the immigrants who then lived and worked in wretched conditions in tenements in Manhattan's Lower East Side. Himself an immigrant—he arrived in New York from Denmark in 1870—he knew at first hand the conditions he was seeking to eradicate. To supplement his written descriptions, he turned to photography. When the cameraman he employed proved unsatisfactory, he learned the process himself and was one of the first to use flash powder, a German invention recently introduced to the United States. His photographs, published in crude facsimile in newspapers and in his now-famous books, *How the Other Half Lives* (1890) and *Children of the Poor* (1892), were instrumental in stimulating legislative reform.

Beginning in 1905, Lewis W. Hine, a teacher at the Ethical Culture School in New York and a trained sociologist, began to make a pictorial record of immigrants passing through Ellis Island. He followed them in New York City, photographing them in their living quarters, at work, and in the streets. Later Hine traveled to textile mills, mines, and other places where young children were employed; largely through the evidence of his photographs, legislation was eventually passed against child-labour abuses.

In England Sir Benjamin Stone, a member of Parliament for Birmingham, was obsessed by the wish to document old English customs and pageants that he rightly feared would gradually disappear. He was the most active member of the National Photographic Record Association, which he had founded for this purpose in 1895, leaving to the city of Birmingham a collection of 22,000 photographs.

The body of photographs produced for the Farm Security Administration during the Great Depression in the United States has been preserved for future generations by the Library of Congress. The pictures cover the period from 1935 until the outbreak of World War II and were taken by a group of dedicated photographers, under the direction of Roy E. Stryker. Stryker, a professor of economics at Columbia University, was invited by the Secretary of Agriculture to form a historical section in the department to document the plight of farmers driven from their land in the dust bowl and who were migrating to the West. This at once took the form of a photographic project. The first photographer to be hired was Arthur Rothstein, a student of Stryker's. From California came Dorothea Lange, who had photographed migratory workers there. Her photographs are notable for their compassionate attitude toward people. In her "Migratory Pea Picker," a destitute young mother, surrounded by her children, peers at the camera with determination and courage. Walker Evans, with a direct uncompromising sense of environment and the beauty of everyday architecture, contributed a notable series. With the writer James Agee he documented the lives of sharecroppers in the book *Let Us Now Praise Famous Men* (1941). Others were documenting America at this time: Berenice Abbott produced a notable series of photographs of New York City, and Margaret Bourke-White with her husband, Erskine Caldwell, did a passionate survey of the South, which appeared in book form as *You Have Seen Their Faces* (1937).

Documenting the Depression in the United States

Photojournalism. From the outset, photography has served the press. Within weeks after the French government's announcement of the process in 1839, magazines were publishing woodcuts or lithographs with the byline "from a daguerreotype." In fact, the two earliest illustrated weeklies—*The Illustrated London News,* which started in May 1842, and *L'Illustration,* based in Paris from its first issue in March 1843—owe their origin to the invention of photography. Early reproductions were generally crude, however, and carried little of the conviction of the original photograph. Regular use of photographs in magazines be-

By courtesy of the Library of Congress, Washington, D.C.

"Migrant Mother, Nipomo, California" by Dorothea Lange, 1936.

"Window Display, Bethlehem, Pennsylvania," gelatin silver print by Walker Evans, 1935.
Library of Congress, Washington, D.C.

gan with the perfection of the halftone process for facsimile reproduction in the 1890s. By 1915 newspapers had also turned to photography for reporting topical events, and the profession of newspaper illustrator gradually became obsolete. Although technical advances improved reproduction quality, the subjects and styles of early journalistic photography were generally unimaginative and dull.

It was not until the appearance of the Ermanox in 1924 and the Leica in 1925 that a new approach to pictorial journalism began to emerge. These two German-made miniature cameras, fitted with wide-aperture lenses, required extremely short exposure times for outdoor work and were even able to photograph indoor scenes by available light. This capability led to photographs whose informality of pose and sense of presence were remarkable. In 1928–29 two of the largest picture magazines in Europe, the *Münchner Illustrierte Presse* and the *Berliner Illustrirte Zeitung,* began to print the new style of photographs. Erich Salomon captured revealing candid portraits of politicians and other personalities by sneaking his camera into places and meetings officially closed to photographers. Felix H. Man was encouraged by Stefan Lorant, editor of the *Münchner Illustrierte,* to take sequences of photographs at interviews and cultural and social events. Lorant then laid out the photographs in imaginative picture essays.

The example of the German picture magazines was followed in other parts of Europe and in the United States. One was the short-lived *Vu,* established in Paris in 1928. An issue of *Vu* devoted entirely to the Spanish Civil War contained memorable photographs by Robert Capa. In 1936 both *Life* and *Look* were conceived in America, and a formula was evolved in which the picture editor, photographer, researcher, and writer constituted a team. The result was the creation of a definite photographic style.

Life's first photographers were Margaret Bourke-White, already famous for her industrial photographs made largely for the magazine *Fortune;* Alfred Eisenstaedt, an experienced photo reporter for the Keystone Picture Agency in Germany; Peter Stackpole, whose photographs of the

Influence of the Ermanox and Leica cameras

Life's first photographers

Golden Gate Bridge in San Francisco attracted much attention; and Thomas D. McAvoy, a news photographer who had pioneered in photographing interior scenes by available light. The concept of *Life* from the start, according to its founder, Henry Luce, was to replace haphazard picture taking and editing with the "mind-guided camera." Photographers were briefed for their assignments and encouraged to take great quantities of photographs, in order that the editors might have a large selection. The visual organization of the picture story was carefully planned for maximum reader impact. The opening photograph of the picture essay established the situation, and like written narration there was a visual climax and a definite conclusion. Usually the photographs were chosen and arranged on the pages before the accompanying text was written. Unlike the illustrated article, the picture essay quite logically is based upon the photographs, and the text is devoted to information that cannot be expressed visually: names, dates, places.

Life and *Look* preferred to use pictures of great sharpness and depth. Thus, instead of unobtrusive miniature cameras, American photographers used large-format cameras requiring slow lenses, large plates, and additional flash light. At first, the photographers made great use of so-called synchroflash; *i.e.,* flash that was synchronized with the camera shutter. The next step was the multiple flash, which made possible more sophisticated and pleasing lighting effects. By duplicating the existing illumination with the flash lighting, photographers could await the moment when people were at their most natural and then make the exposure without the need for posing.

This way of photographing was soon challenged. Lorant, who had left the *Münchner Illustrierte Presse,* moved in 1934 from Germany to London. There, he established the magazines *Weekly Illustrated* (1934) and *Picture Post* (1938). Staff photographers on both magazines included old colleagues from Germany, such as Man and Kurt Hutton. They, as well as other contributors, were encouraged to develop the technique and pictorial style of available-light photographs so brilliantly begun in the 1920s. Their pictures had a remarkable naturalness that brought great reader appeal—so much so that *Life* began to publish sim-

Available-light photography

W. Eugene Smith

"Spanish Village" by W. Eugene Smith, 1951.

"Children in Seville, Spain" by Henri Cartier-Bresson, 1933.
Henri Cartier-Bresson—Magnum

ilar photographs and in 1945 hired a former *Picture Post* photographer, Leonard McCombe, with an extraordinary clause in his contract: he was forbidden to use flash.

Memorable groups of photographs have been taken for the picture magazines. Examples are Man's "A Day with Mussolini," first published in the *Münchner Illustrierte Presse* (1931), and then, with a brilliant new layout, in *Picture Post;* W. Eugene Smith's "Spanish Village" (1951) and "Nurse Midwife" (1951) in *Life;* and Eisenstaedt's informal, penetrating portraits of famous Britons, also in *Life.*

Cartier-Bresson's instantaneous image

The photojournalist's ability to train himself to perceive the significant in the fraction of a second and to use the camera with such speed and precision that the instantaneous perception is preserved forever is a great creative gift. The gift is evident in the work of the Hungarian André Kertész as early as 1915 and in his later work in Paris during the 1920s. The Frenchman Henri Cartier-Bresson began around 1930 to develop the style that he later called the search for the "decisive moment." To him the camera was an "extension of the eye." With extraordinary precision he perceived a fully composed picture of the most fleeting scenes. Unlike many other photographers, he did not crop or recompose his pictures after they had been taken: every detail of a Cartier-Bresson photograph is present in the negative. He preferred the miniature 35-mm-film camera. When he found a picture possibility he stalked his prey unobtrusively, working with his camera to a visual climax.

Colour photography. Photography's transmutation of nature's colours into various shades of black and white had been considered a drawback of the process from its inception. Hence, at the request of a client, many portrait photographers collaborated with artists who hand-tinted daguerreotypes and calotypes or painted over albumen prints in oils. Some artists also copied the photograph onto canvas; others, such as Franz von Lenbach in Munich, had the image projected onto canvas that had been made light-sensitive, whereupon they painted freely over it. In Japan, where hand-coloured woodcuts had a great tradition and labour was cheap, some firms from the 1870s on sold photographs of scenic views and daily life that had been delicately hand-tinted. In the 1880s photochromes, colour prints made from hand-coloured photographs, became fashionable and remained popular until they were gradually replaced in the first decades of the 20th century by Autochrome plates.

The Autochrome process, the first practical colour photography process, was introduced in France in 1907 by Auguste and Louis Lumière. It used a colour screen (a glass plate covered with grains of starch dyed to act as primary-colour filters and black dust that blocked all unfiltered light) coated with a thin film of panchromatic (*i.e.,* sensitive to all colours) emulsion and resulted in a positive colour transparency. The Lumières' success was due in part to the introduction of panchromatic emulsion the previous year by a London firm of photographic plate manufacturers. All previous experimenters trying to solve the problem of colour photography had been seriously impeded by the comparative insensitivity of the earlier negative material to all colours except blue and violet.

Researchers continued to look for improvements and alternative colour processes, and in 1935 Leopold Godowsky, Jr., and Leopold Mannes, two American musicians working with the Kodak Research Laboratories, initiated the modern era of colour photography with their invention of Kodachrome film. With this reversal (slide) film, colour transparencies could be obtained that were suitable both for projection and for reproduction. A year later the Agfa Company of Germany developed the Agfacolor negative–positive process, but due to World War II the film did not become available until 1949. Meanwhile, Kodak had introduced in 1942 the Kodacolor negative–positive film that, 20 years later—after many improvements in quality and speed and a great reduction in price—became the most popular film used for amateur photography. Today about 80 percent of all photographs are shot in colour.

The invention of Kodachrome film

Later trends. Throughout its history, there have been two complementary yet distinct aesthetic approaches to photography. On the one hand, there has been the recognition of the basic qualities of photography and the desire to make use of them in a functional way. On the other hand, there have been those who believe that the most aesthetic use of photography is to relate it to other mediums. Since 1950 both these trends have been pursued with vigour, and to them has been added a third approach, the expressive, emotional use of photography pioneered by Stieglitz with his "equivalents" series.

In the United States, Minor White, through his long career, his writing, his teaching, and his founding and editing of the influential magazine *Aperture,* developed the Stieglitz approach to a highly sophisticated level. For him, the photograph must be transformed in such a manner that the viewer can read an inner message, which is not visible upon the surface, but which is carried by it. White's book *Mirrors, Messages, Manifestations* (1970) is a collection of superb photographs that present his spiritual biography.

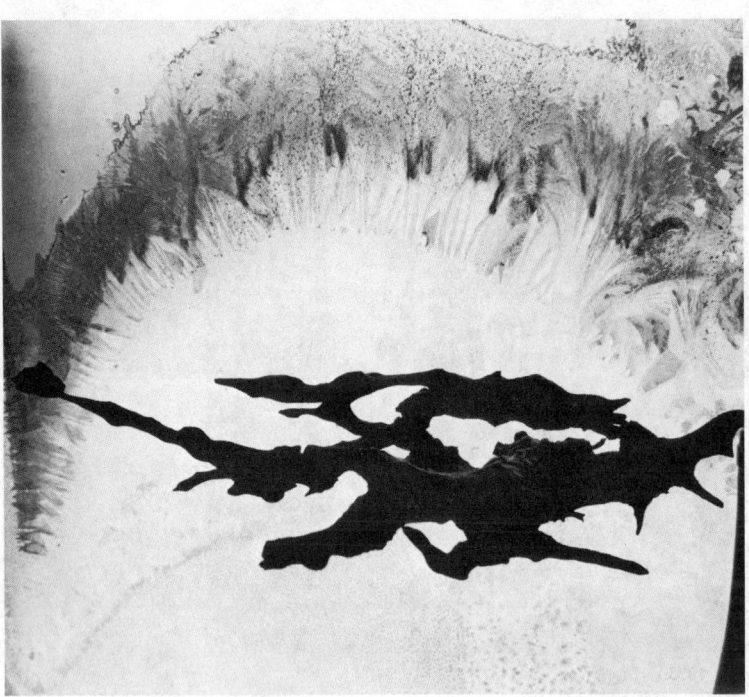

"Ritual Branch" by Minor White, 1958.
George Eastman House Collection

To Aaron Siskind, who worked with wall scrawls, weathered wood and plaster, torn billboards, and what he called "the detritus of our world," the photograph must communicate more than the subject itself. The photographs of Harry Callahan express his highly developed sense of linear form, often by means of sharp contrasts of black and white and multiple images.

One of the finest photographers working after World War II was former *Life* photographer Andreas Feininger. His dramatic close-ups of architecture and nature reveal a thorough understanding of design, composition, and structure, which can perhaps be attributed to his early training as an architect.

Colour photography has become increasingly popular within the ranks of the amateur. Although many professionals have explored the artistic possibilities of colour, which can add intensity and realism to the picture and in-

crease interest in the subject, some prefer black-and-white to colour film for aesthetic reasons. Among professional colour photographers, Eliot F. Porter and Marie Cosindas (one of the first to work with Polaroid instant films) were the leaders in America: both preferred a somewhat realistic approach.

A considerable impediment to a more widespread use of colour in monographs and other publications studying the art of photography is the often prohibitive price of colour reproduction.

The urban social scene viewed objectively without sentiment or moralization—often called the "social landscape"—has been a subject of much interest to photographers in both the United States and Europe. The work of such photographers as Robert Frank, Bruce Davidson, and William Klein takes the form of penetrating sociological observations, somewhat reminiscent of the documentary

"Social landscape" photography

Aaron Siskind

"Chicago 1949" by Aaron Siskind.

"Parade—Hoboken, New Jersey" by Robert Frank, 1955.
Robert Frank

photography of the 1930s. The approach differs in that, rather than presenting problems faced by a certain level of society, emphasis is placed on the effects of the urban environment upon people.

In England and Europe, trends closely parallel those in the United States. Bill Brandt, whose classic social reportage began with the book *The English at Home* (1936) and continued during World War II with trenchant photographs of life in the bomb shelters of London, changed his style during the 1950s. Using an extremely wide-angle lens he created startling abstract studies of nudes, some of which are reminiscent of Henry Moore sculptures. Cecil Beaton, fashion photographer for British *Vogue,* created pictures with exquisite taste. His moving photographs of London during the bombing of World War II and of other scenes of the war stress the human aspect rather than the military. The "social landscape" school is well represented in the work of Tony Ray-Jones and Raymond Moore. The strongest contribution probably lies in the field of photojournalism. George Rodger, one of the founders of the Magnum agency and a former *Life* photographer, and Bert Hardy, a former *Picture Post* photographer, provided a solid tradition for the work of Don McCullin, who—like Robert Capa before him—traveled from war to war, photographing with deep compassion the conflicts that appeared in his book *The Destruction Business* (1971).

The most imaginative photographs in Europe are mostly made for publication, rather than for exhibition or hanging in galleries and homes. Europeans, in general, do not consider the photographic print as an end in itself, but as a step toward reproduction in periodicals and books. Brassaï (the pseudonym of Gyulas Halász) made his name in photography with the publication of *Paris de nuit* (1933), intimate and sympathetic photographs of night life in the more humble quarters of Paris. In the 1950s, like Aaron Siskind, he became fascinated with wall scrawls and graffiti. Robert Doisneau was a master of humour and satire, catching moments of absurdity in everyday life. Lucien Clergue turned to the natural scene and to the nude in surf. The tradition of cameraless abstraction was enriched by the Belgian Pierre Cordier with the introduction in 1958 of his "chimigrammes"—colour images made, not by light, but chemical action on photographic paper.

Steinert's Subjective Photography

In Germany the greatest influence was the teaching of Otto Steinert at Saarbrücken and, since 1959, at the Folkwangschule in Essen. Almost single-handedly he brought back to Germany that spirit of experimentation and boldness of concept that had been suppressed during the Third Reich. An excellent photographer, Steinert was the founder in 1951, together with the art historian J.A. Schmoll gennant Eisenweth, of a movement they named "Subjective Photography." He led the group "Fotoform," which first exhibited its work in 1950, to explore the creative potential of any possible expressive technique. Peter Keetman is one of the strongest representatives of Fotoform's dedication to creating innovative, expressive graphic designs and abstract patterns. Robert Häusser, a student of Steinert, was strongly influenced by Fotoform in his early work. Later he introduced mystifying ele-

"Pipes" by Peter Keetman, 1958.

Salt-encrusted, sand-lined drainage patterns at the fringe of the Etosha Pan, South West Africa/Namibia, aerial photograph by Georg Gerster, 1980–81.

ments into his landscapes, wilfully distorting reality until it bordered on abstract expressionism. Chargesheimer, like Robert Frank in the United States, laid great stress on the unpleasant side of his themes in hard, almost brutal photographs of German cities. Floris M. Neusüss, who teaches at the University of Kassel, in West Germany, is a great exponent of conceptual photography, which uses concepts as material and in which the preconceived idea is more important than the object. Erwin Fieger stands out with such books as *13 Photo-Essays* (1969), *Japan, Sunrise Island* (1971), and *Mexico* (1973) as one of the finest in the field of colour reportage. Horst Baumann specialized in illustration, particularly in colour.

The Austrian Ernst Haas was a master of colour photography, turning toward the abstract in his remarkable photographs of blurred action and bold compositions. A member of the Magnum group, a cooperative formed by Cartier-Bresson and others in 1947, Haas produced work that is international in scope.

Outstanding among Swiss photographers working after World War II was Werner Bischof, who, until his death in 1954, movingly photographed refugees in Europe, the famine in India, Japan, and the Incas of Peru. Superb colour work was produced by Emil Schulthess for his books *Africa* (1959), *The Amazon* (1962), *China* (1966), and others. Georg Gerster revealed in his aerial views, primarily taken in colour, a beauty of design that frequently comes close to modern art.

The Czechoslovakian Josef Sudek is best known abroad for his still lifes, Vilem Heckel for his photographs of industry and mountains, Karel Plicka for his views of Prague, and Josef Koudelka for his impressive work on Gypsies. In Sweden each member of the group of photographers known as TIO ("Ten") has produced outstanding work. Each works in a different field, but all are united by their modern style. The most gifted Russian photographer, Alexander M. Rodchenko, was too modern for Stalin's taste, and his work was banished until the dictator's death. During World War II Dimitri Baltermans produced fine reportage work on the front.

In Italy Franco Fontana, shooting in colour with telelenses, created amazing abstractions of landscapes, fields, and buildings; Mario de Biasi made a fine record of the uprising in Budapest in 1956; and Fulvio Roiter produced a series of travel books, the most sensitive and romantic

Children wearing straw capes to protect them from the cold, Niigata prefecture, Japan, from *The Snow Country* by Hiroshi Hamaya, 1956.

of which focused on his hometown, Venice. The chief concern of most photographers in Italy and elsewhere in Europe, however, is centred upon the recording of the social scene: Mario Giacomelli's series of photographs of nuns and village life is typical and outstanding.

In Japan the extraordinary documentary and landscape photographs by Hiroshi Hamaya parallel the straight photographic approach. Superb photographs were also produced by Takayuki Ogawa, the social realist, and by the imaginative Eikoh Hosoe.

A lively interest in expanding the medium of photography beyond the straight approach was characteristic of much work in the late 20th century. The experimentation took many forms, including the revival of long-obsolete printing techniques such as the gum bichromate process and the platinotype. Perhaps the most startling change to come about after 1960 was an interchange of mediums between photographers and painters. Many photographers made liberal use of manual techniques, such as negative and print retouching and the addition of colour. Simultaneously, painters, who had long utilized photographs as tools for observation, boldly imitated the very quality of photographic vision and sometimes introduced unaltered photographs by collage techniques or silkscreen reproduction directly into their canvases.

Another late 20th-century trend was the photographer's increasing reliance on books for the presentation of his work. Several factors contributed to this practice, among them the demise of many of the major picture magazines, technical developments that provided better printing quality at lower costs, and the complete acceptance of photography as an art worthy of study and preservation.

(Be.N./H.E.R.G.)

The technology of photography

The most widely used photographic process is the black-and-white negative–positive system (Figure 1). In the camera the lens projects an image of the scene being photographed onto a film coated with light-sensitive silver salts, such as silver bromide. A shutter built into the lens admits light reflected from the scene for a given time to produce an invisible but developable image in the sensitized layer, thus exposing the film.

During development (in a darkroom) the silver salt crystals that have been struck by the light are converted into metallic silver, forming a visible deposit or density. The

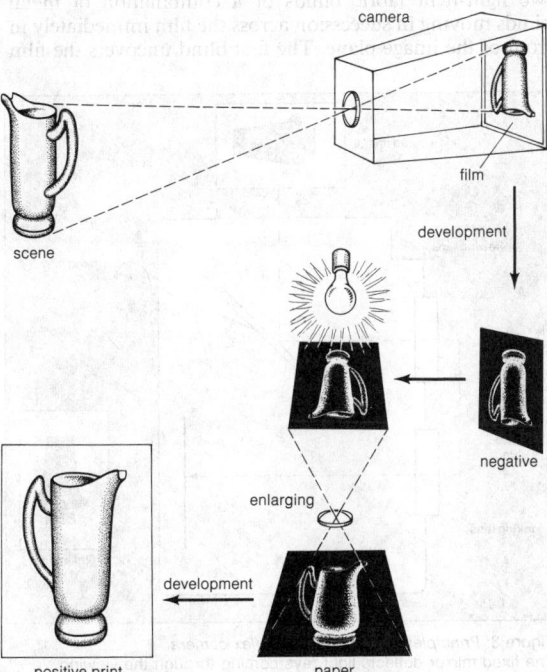

Figure 1: Sequence of negative–positive process, from the photographing of the original scene to enlarged print (see text).

more light that reaches a given area of the film, the more silver salt is rendered developable and the denser the silver deposit that is formed there. An image of various brightness levels thus yields a picture in which these brightnesses are tonally reversed—a negative. Bright subject details record as dark or dense areas in the developed film; dark parts of the subject record as areas of low density; *i.e.,* they have little silver. After development the film is treated with a fixing bath that dissolves away all undeveloped silver salt and so prevents subsequent darkening of such unexposed areas. Finally, a wash removes all soluble salts from the film emulsion, leaving a permanent negative silver image within the gelatin layer.

A positive picture is obtained by repeating this process. The usual procedure is enlargement: the negative is projected onto a sensitive paper carrying a silver halide emulsion similar to that used for the film. Exposure by the enlarger light source again yields a latent image of the negative. After a development and processing sequence the paper then bears a positive silver image. In contact printing the negative film and the paper are placed face to face in intimate contact and exposed by diffused light shining through the negative. The dense (black) portions of the negative image result in little exposure of the paper and, so, yield light image areas; thin portions of the negative let through more light and yield dark areas in the print, thus re-creating the light values of the original scene.

CAMERAS AND LENSES

Basic camera functions. In its simplest form, the camera is a light-tight container carrying a lens, a shutter, a diaphragm, a device for holding (and changing) the film in the correct image plane, and a viewfinder to allow the camera to be aimed at the desired scene.

The lens projects an inverted image of the scene in front of the camera onto the film in the image plane. The image is sharp only if the film is located at a specific distance behind the lens. This distance depends on the focal length of the lens (see below *Characteristics and parameters of lenses*) and the distance of the object in front of the lens. To photograph near and far subjects, all but the simplest cameras have a focusing adjustment that alters the distance between the lens and the film plane to make objects at the selected distance produce a sharp image on the film. In some cameras focusing adjustment is achieved by moving only the front element or internal elements of the lens, in effect modifying the focal length.

The shutter consists of a set of metallic leaves mounted in or behind the lens or a system of blinds positioned in front of the film. It can be made to open for a predetermined time to expose the film to the image formed by the lens. The time of this exposure is one of the two factors controlling the amount of light reaching the film. The other factor is the lens diaphragm, or aperture, an opening with an adjustable diameter. The combination of the diaphragm opening and exposure time is the photographic exposure. To obtain a film image that faithfully records all the tone gradation of the object, this exposure must be matched to the brightness (luminance) of the subject and to the sensitivity or speed of the film. Light meters built into most modern cameras measure the subject luminance and set the shutter or the lens diaphragm to yield a correctly exposed image.

Principal camera types. The simplest camera type, much used by casual amateurs, has most of the features listed in the previous section—lens, shutter, viewfinder, and film-holding system. The light-tight container traditionally had a box shape. Present-day equivalents are pocket cameras taking easy-load film cartridges or film disks. Typically, a fixed shutter setting gives about $\frac{1}{50}$-second exposure; the lens is permanently set to record sharply all objects more than about five feet (1.5 metres) from the camera. Provision for a flash may be built in. Though simple to handle, such cameras are in daylight restricted to pictures of stationary or slow-moving subjects.

The 35-mm miniature camera. Perforated 35-millimetre (mm) film (originally standard motion-picture film) in cartridges holding 12 to 36 exposures with a nominal picture format of 24 × 36 mm is employed in miniature cameras.

Creation of a negative image

The two basic elements of exposure

Smaller image formats down to 18 × 24 mm (half frame) may be used. The 35-mm camera has a lens with a range of apertures and a shutter with exposure times typically from one second to $^1/_{1,000}$ second or shorter, and it can focus on subject distances from infinity down to five feet or less. A winding lever or built-in motor advances the film from one frame to the next and at the same time tensions (cocks) the shutter for each exposure. At the end of the film load the film is rewound into the cartridge for removal from the camera in daylight.

A 35-mm camera usually has a direct-vision viewfinder, often combined with a rangefinder or autofocus system for accurate distance settings. Most current versions incorporate a light meter coupled with the exposure settings on the camera. Advanced models may have interchangeable lenses and an extended accessory system. Many 35-mm cameras are single-lens reflex types (see below).

The ultraminiature or subminiature.   This camera takes narrow roll film (16-mm or 9.5-mm) in special cartridges or film disks. The picture size ranges from 8 × 10 mm to 13 × 17 mm. These formats are used for making millions of snapshooting pocket-size cameras; special versions may be as small as a matchbox for unobtrusive use.

The view, or technical, camera.   For studio and commercial photography the view, or technical, camera takes single exposures on sheet films (formerly plates) usually between 4 × 5 inches and 8 × 10 inches. A front standard carries interchangeable lenses and shutters; a rear standard takes a ground-glass screen (for viewing and focusing) and sheet-film holders. The standards move independently on a rail or set of rails and are connected by bellows. Both standards can also be displaced laterally and vertically relative to each other's centre and swung or tilted about horizontal and vertical axes. These features provide versatility in image control (sharpness distribution, subject distance, and perspective), though not speed in use. The view camera is nearly always mounted on a tripod.

The medium-size hand camera.   This type of camera takes sheet film (typical formats of from $2^1/_2 × 3^1/_2$ inches to 4 × 5 inches), roll film, or 70-mm film in interchangeable magazines; it has interchangeable lenses and may have a coupled rangefinder. Special types use wide-angle lenses and wide picture formats (*e.g.*, $2^1/_4 × 4^1/_2$ to $2^1/_4 × 6^3/_4$ inches [6 × 12 to 6 × 17 centimetres]). The medium-size hand camera was popular with press photographers in the first half of the 20th century. Older versions had folding bellows and a lens standard on an extendable baseboard or strut system. Modern modular designs have a rigid body with interchangeable front and rear units.

The folding roll-film camera.   The folding roll-film camera, now rare, resembles the 35-mm miniature camera in shutter and viewfinder equipment but has bellows and folds up to pocketable size when not in use. Generally it takes roll films holding eight to 16 exposures; typical picture sizes are $2^1/_4 × 2^1/_4$, $2^1/_4 × 3^1/_4$, or $1^3/_4 × 2^1/_4$ inches. Some 35-mm cameras were also produced with bellows.

The single-lens reflex.   The ground-glass screen at the back of the studio, or view, camera slows down picture taking because the screen must be replaced by the film for an exposure. The single-lens reflex camera (Figure 2) has a screen, but the film remains constantly in position. A 45° mirror reflects the image-forming rays from the lens onto a screen in the camera top. The mirror moves out of the way during the exposure and back again afterward for viewing and focusing the next picture. The image on the screen therefore temporarily disappears from view during the exposure. Present-day single-lens reflexes are either 35-mm cameras or advanced roll-film models. Most 35-mm reflexes have optical prism systems for eye-level screen viewing, built-in light-meter and electronic exposure-control systems, interchangeable lenses, and numerous other refinements. Often the camera is part of an extensive accessory system. Advanced roll-film reflexes are even more modular, with interchangeable viewfinders, focusing screens, and lenses.

The twin-lens reflex.   The twin-lens reflex is a comparatively bulky dual camera (Figure 3) with a fixed-mirror reflex housing and top screen mounted above a roll-film box camera. Its two lenses focus in unison so that the top

Reflecting the image through the lens

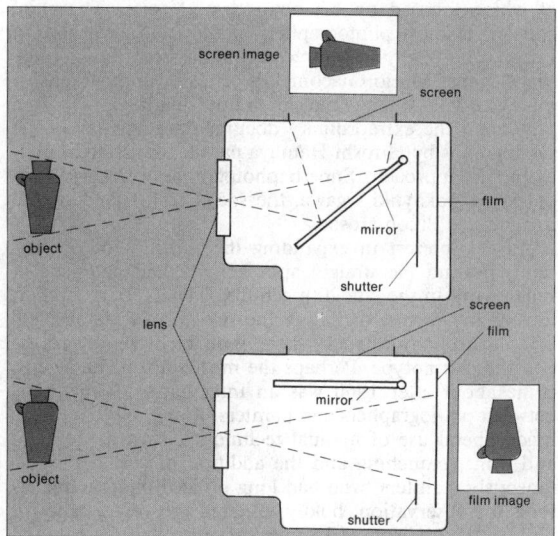

Figure 2: *Single-lens reflex principle.*
(Top) Before exposure, upright but laterally reversed image is visible on top screen. (Bottom) During exposure, with mirror up and shutter open, an upside down but laterally correct image is projected on the film.

screen shows the image sharpness and framing as recorded on the film in the lower section. The viewing image remains visible all the time, but the viewpoint difference (parallax) of the two lenses means that the framing on the top screen is not exactly identical with that on the film.

Shutter and diaphragm systems.   Principal present-day shutters are the leaf shutter and the focal-plane shutter.

The leaf shutter.   The leaf, or diaphragm, shutter consists of a series of blades or leaves fitted inside or just behind the lens. The shutter opens by swinging the leaves simultaneously outward to uncover the lens opening. The leaves stay open for a fixed time—the exposure time—and then close again. A combination of electromagnets or electromagnets and springs drives the mechanism, while an electronic circuit—often coupled with a light metering system—or an adjustable escapement in mechanical shutters controls the open time. This is typically between one second and $^1/_{500}$ second.

Focal-plane shutter.   The focal-plane shutter consists of two light-tight fabric blinds or a combination of metal blinds moving in succession across the film immediately in front of the image plane. The first blind uncovers the film

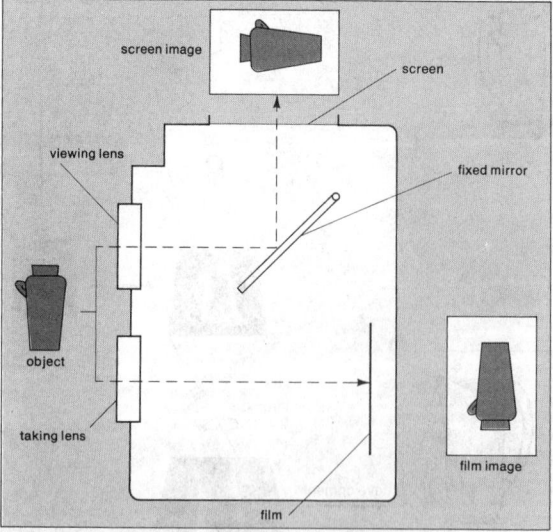

Figure 3: *Principles of the twin-lens reflex camera.*
The fixed mirror deflects light rays coming through the viewing lens to a top screen, which shows the image upright but laterally reversed. Light from the object also goes through the taking lens, which is mounted on a common panel with the viewing lens, and is projected on the film.

and the second blind covers it up again, the two blinds forming a traveling slit the width of which determines the exposure time: the narrower the slit, the shorter the time. The actual travel time is fairly constant for all exposure times. A mechanism or electromagnet and control circuit triggers the release of the second blind. Focal-plane shutters are usually adjustable for exposure times between one second (or longer) and $1/1,000$ to $1/4,000$ second.

Diaphragm and shutter settings. In the lens diaphragm a series of leaves increases or decreases the opening to control the light passing through the lens to the film. The diaphragm control ring carries a scale of so-called *f*-numbers, or stop numbers, in a series: such as 1.4, 2, 2.8, 4, 5.6, 8, 11, 16, 22, and 32. The squares of the *f*-numbers are inversely proportional to the amount of light admitted. In the above international standard series, each setting admits twice as much light as the next higher *f*-number, or stop (giving twice as much exposure).

Shutter settings on present-day cameras also follow a standard double-or-half sequence—*e.g.*, 1, $1/2$, $1/4$, $1/8$, $1/15$, $1/30$, $1/60$, $1/125$, $1/250$, $1/500$, $1/1,000$ second, and so forth. The shorter the exposure time, the "faster" the shutter speed.

Exposure values. An attempt to simplify the mathematics of *f*-number and shutter speed-control functions led to the formulation of exposure values (EV). These run in a simple whole-number series, each step (EV interval) doubling or halving the effective exposure. The lower the EV number, the greater the exposure. Thus, EV 10 gives twice as much exposure as EV 11 or half as much as EV 9. Each EV value covers a range of aperture/speed combinations of the same equivalent exposure; for instance, $f/2.8$ with $1/250$ second, $f/4$ with $1/125$ second, and $f/5.6$ with $1/60$ second. For a time some cameras carried an EV scale and coupled the aperture and speed settings; at a given EV setting in such cameras selecting various speeds automatically adjusted the aperture to compensate and vice versa. Exposure-value setting scales became obsolete with exposure automation, but the notation remains in use to indicate either exposure levels or—at specified film speeds—lighting levels requiring a given exposure.

Automatic-diaphragm systems. On a camera with a viewing screen (view camera or single-lens reflex) viewing and focusing are carried out with the lens diaphragm fully open, but the exposure is often made at a smaller aperture. Reflex cameras (and increasingly also view cameras) therefore incorporate a mechanism that automatically or semiautomatically stops down (reduces) the lens to the working aperture immediately before the exposure.

Methods of focusing and framing. The ground-glass (now mostly grained plastic) screen is the most direct way of viewing the image for framing and for sharpness control. The screen localizes the image plane for observation. The image is also visible without a screen, but then the eye can locate the image plane of maximum sharpness only with a precisely focused high-power magnifier. This aerial focusing method avoids interference of the ground-glass structure with sharpness assessment.

Focusing aids. The eye is not good at recognizing slight unsharpness, so focusing screens (especially in reflex cameras) often incorporate focusing aids such as a split-image wedge alone or with a microprism area, in the screen centre. The split-image wedge consists of a pair of prism wedges that split an out-of-focus image into two sharp halves laterally displaced relative to one another. When the lens is correctly focused the image becomes continuous across the wedge area—a point that the eye can assess more precisely. The microprism area contains several hundred or thousand minute wedges that give a blurred image very ragged outlines and a broken-up texture; these clear abruptly as the image becomes sharp.

The focusing screen is often overlaid by a pattern of fine concentric lens sections. Called a Fresnel screen, it redirects the light from the screen corners toward the observer's eye and makes the image evenly bright.

Cameras without a screen generally are equipped with a distance scale, the lens being set to the estimated object distance. More advanced cameras have an optical rangefinder as a distance-measuring aid; it consists of a viewfinder (see below) and a swinging mirror a few inches

The series of f-numbers

Micro-prism grid of multiple wedges

to one side of the viewfinder axis. As the eye views an image of the object, the mirror superimposes a second image from a second viewpoint. On turning the mirror through the correct angle, which depends on the object distance, the two images are made to coincide. The mirror movement can be linked with a distance scale, or coupled with the lens focusing adjustment. When the lens is incorrectly focused, the rangefinder shows a double or split image. In place of a rotating mirror, the rangefinder may use swinging or rotating optical wedges (prisms).

Autofocus systems. Some cameras evaluate the coincidence (or lack thereof) between two rangefinder images by image analysis with a microchip system. This signals electronically when the lens is set to the correct distance and often carries out the distance setting by a servomotor built into the camera. Such focusing automation makes the camera even simpler to use. Alternative automatic ranging systems used in amateur cameras depend on triangulation with infrared rays or pulses sent out by a small light-emitting diode (LED), or on measurement of the time an ultrasonic signal takes to be reflected back from the subject (sonar).

While these devices measure distance automatically, single-lens reflex cameras may incorporate electronic image-analysis systems to measure sharpness. The signal output of such systems actuates red or green LEDs in the camera finder system to show whether the image is sharp or not. The same signal can control a servomotor in the lens for fully automatic focusing. These devices are limited at low lighting and contrast levels—where the human eye also finds sharpness assessment difficult.

Viewfinders. The sighting devices in cameras lacking screens are called viewfinders; they show how much of the scene will appear on the film. The simplest viewfinder is a wire frame above the camera front, with a second frame near the back to aid the eye in correct centring. Most present-day finders are built into the camera and are compact lens systems. Bright-frame finders show a white frame reflected into the view to outline the field recorded on the film. An alternative form is the reflecting viewfinder in which the photographer looks down into a field lens on top of the camera. The upper section of a twin-lens reflex camera is such a reflecting finder.

As the viewfinder axis in a camera other than a single-lens reflex does not usually coincide with the lens axis, the finder's and the lens's views do not exactly match. This parallax error is insignificant with distant subjects; with near ones it is responsible for the familiar fault of a portrait shot of a head that appears partly cut off in the picture even though it was fully visible in the finder. Camera viewfinders may have parallax-compensating devices.

The optical finder gives a direct upright and right-reading view of the subject with the camera held at eye level. The traditional reflex camera, held at waist level, showed a laterally reversed view. Modern reflexes have a pentaprism arrangement that permits upright, right-reading, eye-level viewing by redirecting the image from the horizontal screen on top of the camera.

Exposure-metering systems. Exposure meters, or light meters, measure the light in a scene to establish optimum camera settings for correct exposures. A light-sensitive cell generates or controls an electric current according to the amount of light reaching the cell. The current may energize a microammeter or circuit controlling LEDs to indicate exposure settings. In most modern cameras the current or signal acts on a microprocessor or other circuit that directly sets the shutter speed or lens aperture. The cell usually is a silicon or other photodiode generating a current that is then amplified. In older cadmium sulfide cells the light falling on the cell changed the latter's resistance to a current passing through it. Selenium cells, still used in some cameras, also generate a current but are larger and less sensitive.

Single-lens reflex cameras have one or more photocells fitted in the pentaprism housing to measure the brightness of the screen image. The exposure reading depends on the light coming through the lens (TTL metering) and so allows for the lens's angle of view, close-up exposure corrections, stray light, and other factors. Some TTL sys-

Parallax problems with close-at-hand subjects

Through-the-lens (TTL) meter systems

tems divert the light from the lens to a photocell before it reaches the screen (*e.g.*, by beam-splitting arrangements or the use of photocells behind a partly reflecting mirror), or they measure the light reflected from the film or from a specially structured first shutter blind at the beginning of, or during, the exposure. Such off-the-film (OTF) measurement is also used for electronic flash control (see below).

View cameras may use a photocell on a probe that can be moved to any point just in front of the focusing screen, thus measuring image brightness at selected points of the image plane. This takes place before the exposure, and the probe is then moved out of the way. Professional photographers also use hand-held separate exposure meters and transfer the readings manually to the camera.

Flash systems. Flash is a widely used artificial light source for photography, providing a reproducible light of high intensity and short duration. It can be synchronized with an instantaneous exposure. Being battery powered, small flash units are self-contained.

Electronic flash. The most common flash system depends on a high-voltage discharge through a gas-filled tube. A capacitor charged to several hundred volts (by a step-up circuit from low-voltage batteries or from the line voltage supply) provides the discharge energy. A low-voltage circuit generating a high-voltage pulse triggers the flash, which lasts typically $1/1,000$ second or less. Small electronic flash units may be built into or clipped onto the camera. Larger units are attached with brackets. Large professional units with floodlight and spotlight fittings are used in studio photography. Even small flashes often have adjustable reflectors, for example, to illuminate an indoor subject by the flash reflected from the ceiling or walls.

Automatic and dedicated flash. Electronic flash units often incorporate a fast-responding photodiode that cumulatively measures the light reflected from the subject and switches off the flash when that light has reached a preselected amount (computer flash). This flash-duration control thus adjusts the flash exposure automatically as long as the subject is within a certain distance range (typically from two to 20 feet). At lower power or near subject distances the duration of a computer flash may drop to $1/50,000$ second.

With certain camera–flash combinations OTF metering inside the camera can control the flash duration by suitable contacts made when the flash is attached to the camera. These "dedicated" flashes (so named because their control circuitry has to match that of specific cameras) may also signal in the camera finder when the flash is ready to operate and to set the camera automatically to its synchronizing shutter speed (see below).

Flashbulbs. An older type of flash is an oxygen-filled glass envelope containing a specific amount of aluminum or zirconium wire and means for igniting the wire in the bulb. The wire burns away with a brilliant flash lasting typically about $1/100$ to $1/50$ second. Each flashbulb can, however, yield only one flash. Current flashbulb systems use four to 10 tiny bulbs, each in its own reflector, arranged in cube or bar carriers that plug into cameras designed for them. The individual flashes are fired in turn by a battery and circuit in the camera through mechanically generated current pulses or other means. In view of the greater convenience of electronic flash, flashbulbs in their various forms are largely obsolescent.

Firing and synchronization. Flash units are usually fired with a switch in the camera shutter to synchronize the flash with the shutter opening. A contact in the camera's flash shoe (hot shoe) or a flash lead connects the unit with this shutter switch. The shutter contact usually closes the instant the shutter is opened. A focal plane shutter must fully uncover the film (generally at a shutter speed of $1/60$ second or slower) for flash synchronization. With flashbulbs the shutter must also stay open while the flash reaches its peak brightness—about $1/50$ second.

System cameras. From the development of the 35-mm miniature camera in the 1930s evolved the concept of the system camera that could be adapted to numerous jobs with a range of interchangeable components and specialized accessories. Today, most moderately advanced 35-mm miniatures take interchangeable lenses, close-up

and photomicrographic attachments, filters, flash units, and other accessories. The most elaborate camera systems also include such accessories as alternative finder systems; interchangeable reflex screens, film backs, and magazines; and remote-control and motor-drive systems. Modular professional roll-film and view cameras are built up from a selection of alternative camera bodies, film backs, bellows units, lenses, and shutters. This is the nearest approach to the universal camera, assembled as required to deal with practically every type of photography.

Modular systems

Characteristics and parameters of lenses. The lens forming an image in the camera is a converging lens, the simplest form of which is a single biconvex (lentil-shaped) element. In theory such a lens makes a light beam of parallel rays converge to a point (the focus) behind the lens. The distance of this focus from the lens itself is the focal length, which depends on the curvature of the lens surfaces and the optical properties of the lens glass. An object at a very long distance (optically regarded as at "infinity") in front of the lens forms an inverted image in a plane (the focal plane) going through the focus. Light rays from nearer objects form an image in a plane behind the focal plane. The nearer the object, the farther behind the lens the corresponding image plane is located—which is why a lens has to be focused to get sharp images of objects at different distances.

Focal length and image scale. The image scale, or scale of reproduction, is the ratio of the image size to the object size; it is often quoted as a magnification. When the image is smaller than the object, the magnification of the object is less than 1.0. If the image is $1/20$ the size of the object, for example, the magnification may be expressed either as 0.05 or as 1:20. For an object at a given distance, the scale of the image depends on the focal length of the lens (Figure 4). A normal camera lens usually has a focal length approximately equal to the diagonal of the picture format covered. A lens of longer focal length gives a larger scale image but necessarily covers less of the scene in front of the camera. Conversely, a lens of shorter focal length yields an image on a smaller scale but—provided the angle of coverage is sufficient (see below)—takes in more of the scene. Many cameras, therefore, can be fitted with interchangeable lenses of different focal lengths to allow varying the image scale and field covered. The focal length of a lens in millimetres (sometimes in inches) is generally engraved on the lens mount.

Aperture. The aperture, or *f*-number, is the ratio of the focal length to the diameter of an incident light beam as it reaches the lens. For instance, if the focal length is 50 millimetres and the diameter of the incident light beam is 25 millimetres, the *f*-number is 2. This incident-beam diameter is often roughly the lens-diaphragm diameter, but it may be appreciably larger or smaller. The maximum

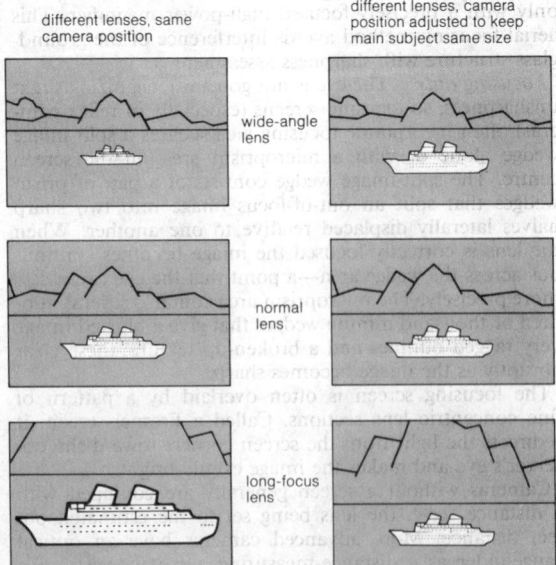

different lenses, same camera position

different lenses, camera position adjusted to keep main subject same size

wide-angle lens

normal lens

long-focus lens

Figure 4: Effects of using lenses of different focal lengths.

aperture (*f*-number at the largest diaphragm opening) is also marked on the lens, usually in the form *f*:2, *f*/2, or 1:2.

Angle of coverage. A lens must cover the area of a camera's film format to yield an image adequately sharp and with reasonably even brightness from the centre to the corners of the film. A normal lens should cover an angle of at least 60°. A wide-angle lens covers a greater angle—about 70° to 90° or more for an ultrawide-angle lens. A long-focus lens covers a smaller angle.

The angle of coverage depends on the lens design. Designations like "wide angle" or "narrow angle" are not necessarily synonymous with "short focus" and "long focus," as the latter terms refer to the focal length of the lens relative to the picture format.

Optical performance. A simple lens produces a very imperfect image, which is usually blurred away from the centre. The image may have colour fringes around object outlines, and straight lines may be distorted. Such defects, called aberrations, can be eliminated—and even then not completely—only by replacing the single lens element by a group of elements of appropriate shape and separation. Aberrations arising from some of the lens elements then counteract opposite aberrations produced by other elements. The larger the maximum aperture, the greater the angle of coverage, and the higher the degree of correction aimed at, the more complex camera lenses become. Lens design for relative freedom from aberrations involves advanced computer programming to calculate the geometric parameters of every lens element. Some aberrations can also be corrected by making one or more of the surfaces of a lens system aspheric; *i.e.,* with the variable curvature of a paraboloid or other surface rather than the constant curvature of a spherical one.

Groups of lens elements for correcting aberrations

Lenses usually consist of optical glass. Transparent plastics also have come into use, especially as they can be molded into elements with aspheric surfaces. They are, however, more sensitive to mechanical damage.

Aberrations. There are a number of lens aberrations, each with its own characteristics. Chromatic aberration is present when the lens forms images by different-coloured light in different planes and at different scales. Colour-corrected lenses largely eliminate these faults. Spherical aberration is present when the outer parts of a lens do not bring light rays into the same focus as the central part. Images formed by the lens at large apertures are therefore unsharp but get sharper at smaller apertures. Curvature of field is present when the sharpest image is formed not on a flat plane but on a curved surface. Astigmatism occurs when the lens fails to focus image lines running in different directions in the same plane; in a picture of a rail fence, for instance, the vertical posts are sharp at a focus setting different from the horizontal rails. Another aberration, called coma, makes image points near the edges of the film appear as irregular, unsharp shapes. Distortion is present when straight lines running parallel with the picture edges appear to bow outward (barrel distortion) or inward (pincushion distortion).

Resolving power and contrast-transfer function. One way of testing lens performance is to observe the image it forms of patterns of increasingly closely spaced black lines separated by white spaces of line width. The closest spacing still recognizable in the image gives a resolving power value, expressed in line pairs (*i.e.,* black line plus white space) per millimetre. Photographs of such line patterns, or test targets, show the resolving power of the lens and film combination. For example, a resolution of 80–100 line pairs per millimetre on a fine-grain film represents very good performance for a normal miniature camera lens.

The visual sharpness of an image depends also on its contrast. Opticians, therefore, often plot the contrast with which the image is reproduced against the line spacing of that image. The resulting contrast-transfer curve, or function, gives a more reliable indication of the lens performance under practical picture-taking conditions.

Special lens types. Apart from general-purpose camera lenses of various focal lengths, there are lenses of special characteristics or design.

Telephoto lenses. Long-focus lenses are bulky, because they comprise not only the lens itself but also a mount or tube to hold it at the appropriate focal distance from the film. Telephoto lenses are more compact; their combinations of lens groups make the back focus (the distance from the rear lens element to the film) as well as the length of the whole lens appreciably shorter than the focal length. Strictly, the term telephoto applies only to a lens of this optically reduced length; in practice long-focus lenses of all types tend to be called indiscriminately telephoto or "tele" lenses.

If a camera lens is interchangeable, an accessory teleconverter lens group can be positioned between the prime lens and the camera. This turns a normal lens into an even more compact telephoto system, which is less costly than a telephoto lens but which reduces the speed of the prime lens and usually impairs sharpness performance.

Tele-converter lenses

Wide-angle and retrofocus lenses. Short-focus, wide-angle lenses are usually mounted near the film. Single-lens reflex cameras need a certain minimum lens-to-film distance to accommodate the swinging mirror. Wide-angle (and sometimes normal-focus) lenses for such cameras therefore use retrofocus designs. In these the back focus is appreciably longer than the focal length. Both a telephoto and a retrofocus lens must be specially designed for its particular use to ensure optimum image performance.

Fish-eye lenses. For image angles greater than 110°, it becomes difficult to bring the lens close enough to the film to allow the rays between the lens and film to diverge sufficiently. The fish-eye lens overcomes this difficulty by making the rays diverge less behind the lens than they do in front. The resulting image shows appreciable distortion, with image details near the edges and corners progressively compressed. Fish-eye lenses usually cover angles between 140° and 210° and are used for unusual wide-angle effects where the distortion becomes a deliberate pictorial element. They also have certain scientific applications, for instance, to cover a horizon-to-horizon view of the sky in recording cloud formations.

Mirror lenses. Images can also be formed by light reflected from curved mirrors. This method, long used in astronomical telescopes, is applied to long-focus lens systems of short overall length by folding the light path back onto itself. A mirror lens or catadioptric system has no chromatic aberrations. Other aberrations are corrected by incorporating one or more appropriate lens elements. The arrangement of the system, with a central opening in the primary mirror, makes stopping down with a customary diaphragm difficult, and neutral-density filters are used to control light transmission.

Variable-focus lenses. In variable-focus lenses the focal length can be varied by movement of some of the elements or groups within the lens system. One lens can thus replace a range of interchangeable lenses.

The variable-focus, or zoom, lens was originally developed for motion-picture photography, in which adjustment of the focal length during a shot produced a zooming-in or zooming-out effect (hence the name). It is now widely used in single-lens reflex cameras where the reflex finder permits accurate continuous assessment of image coverage. In a true zoom lens the image changes in scale but not in sharpness during zooming; some varifocal lenses, however, need refocusing at different focal lengths. Due to correction requirements over a range of focal lengths, zoom lenses are complex systems containing from 12 to 20 elements. Zoom lenses for still cameras have focal-length ratios from 2:1 to 4:1 or more (*e.g.,* 35–135 mm for a 35-mm reflex).

Lens-changing systems. Miniature and roll-film cameras hold interchangeable lenses in screw or quick-change bayonet mounts. In a focal-plane shutter camera the usable range of focal lengths is practically unlimited. In cameras with leaf shutters, either the lens is mounted in front of the shutter or the lens is changed with the shutter. Some designs use convertible lenses with the rear components built into the camera together with the shutter; interchangeable front groups then provide different focal lengths in combination with the fixed rear group. View-camera lenses—usually with their own shutters—are mounted on lens boards that clip into and out of the front camera standard.

Convertible lens with fixed rear component

Afocal attachments provide the effect of alternative focal lengths with a fixed camera lens. They are magnifying or reducing telescopes without a focal length (hence afocal), yielding a virtual image that the camera lens projects onto the film. Their designated magnification factor indicates the effect on the image scale; *e.g.,* a 1.5× tele attachment magnifies the image on the film 1 1/2 times, while a 0.7× wide-angle attachment reduces the image scale to 0.7 times that of the prime camera lens.

Lens coating. When light passes from one optical medium to another (especially from air to glass and vice versa in a lens), about 4 to 8 percent of it is lost by reflection at the interface. This light loss builds up appreciably in complex multielement lenses. Some of the reflected light still reaches the film as ghost images or light spots or as general contrast-reducing scattered light.

To reduce such losses, the air-to-glass surfaces of modern lenses typically carry a microscopically thin coating of metallic fluorides. The coating eliminates most reflected rays. Complete elimination can occur only for light of one wavelength if the coating thickness and refractive index are exactly right. In practice a coated lens surface reflects about 0.5 percent of incident white light—1/10 of the light lost by an uncoated lens. Multiple coatings can reduce reflections over a wider wavelength range.

BLACK-AND-WHITE FILMS

The latent image. The sensitive surface of ordinary film is a layer of gelatin carrying minute suspended silver halide crystals or grains (the emulsion)—typically silver bromide with some silver iodide. Exposure to light in a camera produces an invisible change yielding a latent image, distinguishable from unexposed silver halide only by its ability to be reduced to metallic silver by certain developing agents.

Formation of the latent image

Current theories postulate that silver halide crystals carry minute specks of metallic silver—so-called sensitivity specks—which amount in mass to about 1/100,000,000 part of the silver halide crystal. A silver halide is a compound of silver with fluorine, chlorine, bromine, or iodine, but only the last three are light-sensitive. When light action releases electrons from the silver halide crystal, they migrate to the sensitivity specks. The resulting electric charge on the specks attracts silver ions from the neighbouring silver halide; and as the silver ions accumulate, they become metallic silver, causing the speck to grow. Halogen (*e.g.,* bromine) atoms at the same time migrate to the surface of the silver halide crystal and are there absorbed by the gelatin of the emulsion. When the sensitivity speck is large enough, it provides a point of attack for the developer, which can then reduce the whole silver halide crystal to silver. Developers are selective organic reducing agents that attack only silver halide crystals that have sufficiently large sensitivity specks. The halide grains carrying a developable sensitivity speck make up the latent image.

Sensitometry and speed. The sensitivity or speed of a film determines how much light it needs to produce a given amount of silver on development. Sensitometry is the science of measuring this sensitivity, which is determined by giving the material a series of graduated exposures in an appropriate instrument (the sensitometer). After development under specified conditions, the density of the silver deposit produced by each exposure is measured and the densities are plotted on a graph against the logarithm of the exposure. The resulting characteristic curve, or D/log E curve (see below *Contrast*), shows how the film reacts to exposure changes. A specified point on the curve also serves as a criterion for calculating film speed by methods laid down in various national and international standards.

The internationally adopted scale is ISO speed, written, for example, 200/24°. The first half of this (200) is arithmetic with the value directly proportional to the sensitivity (and also identical with the still widely used ASA speed). The second half (24°) is logarithmic, increasing by 3° for every doubling of the speed (and matching the DIN speeds still used in parts of Europe). A film of 200/24° ISO is twice as fast (and for a given subject requires half as much exposure) as a film of 100/21° ISO, or half as fast as a film of 400/27° ISO.

All-around films for outdoor and some indoor photography have speeds between 80/20° and 200/24° ISO; fine-grain films for maximum image definition between 25/15° and 64/19° ISO; and high-speed and ultraspeed films for poor light from 400/27° ISO up.

Colour sensitivity. Initially, the silver halide emulsion is sensitive to ultraviolet radiation and to violet and blue light. Most films contain sensitizing dyes to extend their colour sensitivity through the whole visible spectrum. Such films, called panchromatic films, were introduced in 1904. They record subject colour values as gray tones largely corresponding to the visual brightness of the colours.

Non-colour-sensitized or blue-sensitive emulsions (without sensitizing dyes) are used for copying monochrome originals and similar applications needing no extended colour sensitivity. At one time orthochromatic films— sensitive to violet, blue, green, and yellow but not to red— were also used for general photography; now they are employed mainly for photographing of phosphor screens, such as cathode-ray tubes, and for other purposes requiring green but not red sensitivity.

Use of ortho-chromatic films

Infrared films, developed in 1919, are sensitized to invisible infrared wavelengths. They are used in aerial photography to cut through atmospheric haze (which scatters blue light but not infrared rays) and for special purposes in scientific and forensic photography.

Filters. Filters can modify the way in which a film records colours as monochrome tone values. They are disks of coloured glass or gelatin with controlled transmission characteristics. Placed in front of the camera lens, they preferentially transmit light of their own colour and hold back light of other colours. A yellow or yellow-green filter is often used in landscape photography to prevent overexposure of the blue sky and to bring out detail in cloud formations. Orange and red filters make the sky still darker and cut through haze by absorbing scattered blue light.

Contrast filters differentiate between the gray values of objects of different colour but of similar brightness. For instance, a red flower and green foliage record in similar shades of mid-gray. A red filter holds back green light to darken the green foliage, making the flower lighter; a green filter absorbs red light, thus darkening the flower. Such deliberate tone distortion is widely used in photomicrography and other fields.

Other filter types used in photography include ultraviolet, infrared, and polarizing filters. Ultraviolet-absorbing filters screen out ultraviolet rays at high altitudes (*e.g.,* in mountain photography). Because camera lenses are not normally corrected for such rays, the rays can reduce image sharpness, even though the lenses allow only a small amount of ultraviolet to be transmitted. Infrared filters are used with infrared film to hold back visible light. Polarizing filters polarize light and can absorb polarized light if suitably oriented. Light reflected at certain angles from shiny surfaces of nonmetallic media (glass, water, varnish) is polarized; a properly oriented polarizing filter subdues such reflections in a picture.

Because a filter screens out part of the light, its use calls for extra exposure, the amount of which is indicated by a filter factor—*e.g.,* 2×, which means the exposure time must be multiplied by 2. For cameras with an exposure-value scale, a filter may specify an exposure value reduction (such as −1 or −1 1/2; *i.e.,* the indicated exposure value must be reduced by this amount). The factor of a given filter depends on the spectral sensitivity of the film, the colour quality of the lighting, the type of subject, the effect aimed at, and other exposure conditions.

Filter factors for proper exposure

Other film characteristics. Of practical interest to the photographer are the graininess, resolving power, and contrast of a film. Although they are characteristics of the film itself, they are influenced by the conditions of development (see below *Black-and-white processing and printing*).

Grain. The image derived from minute silver halide crystals is discontinuous in structure. This gives an appearance of graininess in big enlargements. The effect is most prominent with fast films, which have comparatively large silver halide crystals.

Resolving power and acutance. The fineness of detail

that a film can resolve depends not only on its graininess but also on the light scatter or irradiation within the emulsion (which tends to spread image details) and on the contrast with which the film reproduces fine detail. These effects can be measured physically to give an acutance value, which is preferred to resolving power as a criterion of a film's sharpness performance. Fine-grain films with thin emulsions yield the highest acutance.

Contrast. High-contrast films reproduce tone differences in the subject as great density differences in the image; low-contrast films translate tone differences into small density differences. The characteristic curve of a film obtained by plotting the density against the logarithm of the exposure (mentioned earlier under *Sensitometry and speed*) can be used to express a film's contrast (see Figure 5). The slope of the straight-line section of the

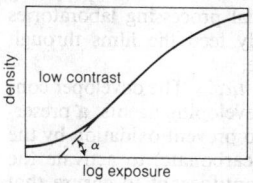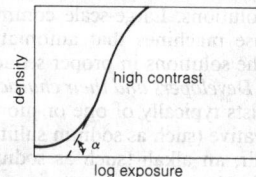

Figure 5: Characteristic curves of low-contrast and high-contrast film (see text).

curve (sometimes called the gamma, actually the tangent of the angle *a*) indicates contrast: the steeper the slope, the higher the contrast rendering. General-purpose films yield medium contrast (gamma 0.7 to 1). High-contrast films (gamma 1.5 to 10) are used for copying line originals and other specialized purposes; low-contrast films for continuous-tone reproduction. Gamma is also used to indicate degree of development, since increased development generally results in a higher gamma.

Film structure and forms. Film consists of a number of layers and components: (1) A supercoat of gelatin, a few micrometres (one micrometre is 0.001 millimetre) thick, protects the emulsion from scratches and abrasion marks. (Pressure and rubbing can produce developable silver densities.) (2) The emulsion layer (silver halide suspended in gelatin) is usually nine to 12 micrometres (up to $1/_{2,000}$ inch) thick but may sometimes reach 25 micrometres. (3) A substrate or subbing layer promotes adhesion of the emulsion to the film base. (4) The film base, or support, is usually cellulose triacetate or a related polymer. The thickness may range from 0.08 to 0.2 millimetre (0.003 to 0.008 inch). Films for graphic arts and scientific purposes are often coated on a polyethylene terephthalate or other polyester support of high dimensional stability. Glass plates—once the most common support for negative materials—are now used only for applications requiring extreme emulsion flatness. (5) A backing layer on the rear of the film base counteracts curling. Usually it contains also a nearly opaque dye to suppress light reflection on the rear support surface. Such reflection (halation) reduces definition by causing halolike effects around very bright image points. Some film bases (especially in 35-mm films) are tinted gray to absorb light that has passed through the emulsion layer.

Sheet film. View and studio cameras generally take sheet film—single sheets (typical sizes range between $2^{1}/_{2} \times 3^{1}/_{2}$ and 8×10 inches) loaded in the darkroom into light-tight film holders for subsequent insertion in the camera.

Roll film. The term roll film is usually reserved for film wound up on a spool with an interleaving light-tight backing paper to protect the wound-up film. The spool is loaded into the camera in daylight, the backing paper leader threaded to a second spool, and the film wound from picture to picture once the camera is closed. This is the classical roll film of roll-film cameras. Common current film widths are 62 mm and 45 mm. The rear of the backing paper carries sets of consecutive numbers spaced at frame intervals for different image formats. In some roll-film cameras these numbers are visible through a viewing window in the camera and show how far the film must be wound to advance it from one picture to the next. Instant-loading cartridges also use paper-backed roll film.

Perforated film. Some film is perforated along its edges and rolled up on its own inside a light-tight cartridge, which can be loaded into the camera in daylight. Once the camera is closed, a transport sprocket engaging the edge perforations draws the film from the cartridge onto a spool and advances it from picture to picture. The most common film width is 35 mm (for 35-mm miniature cameras), and its cartridge typically holds enough film for up to 36 (sometimes 72) exposures. A 70-mm film for larger cameras and 16-mm strips for ultraminiatures are packed and used in a similar way.

In March 1983 the Eastman Kodak Company announced the development of a new coding system for 35-mm film and cartridges. The DX film system employs optical, electrical, and mechanical encoding to transmit to appropriately equipped cameras such information as film type, film speed, and number of exposures. The system also supplies data that enable automatic photofinishing equipment to identify and sort film quickly, simplifying processing and printing. In the interest of uniformity, Kodak freely offered the DX system to all film and camera manufacturers, and within two years it was generally adopted.

Disk film. Some compact mass-market cameras take circular disks of film, 65 millimetres in diameter, in light-tight cartridges and coated on a 0.18-mm polyester base. In the camera the disk rotates as up to 15 exposures (frame size 8×10 millimetres) are recorded around the disk circumference. The disk lies flatter in the camera than rolled-up film and is suitable for more automated photofinishing; the high printing magnification required, however, limits the image quality.

PICTURE-TAKING TECHNIQUE

The main areas of practical camera handling in photography concern sharpness control, exposure, and lighting.

Sharpness control. The image on the film is sharpest when the lens is focused to the exact object distance. Usually, however, a scene includes objects at varying distances from the camera. Various factors affect the sharpness distribution in a picture of such a scene.

Depth of field. The sharpness in the image of objects in front of and behind the focused distance falls off gradually. Within a certain range of object distances this sharpness loss is still comparatively unnoticeable. This range is the depth of field and depends on: (1) the amount of sharpness loss regarded as acceptable: miniature negatives requiring big enlargement must be sharper than larger format negatives, which are enlarged less; (2) the lens aperture used: stopping down the lens (higher *f*-numbers) increases the depth of field; (3) the object distance: the depth of field is smaller for near objects than for more distant ones; and (4) the focal length of the lens: depth of field is reduced with longer focus lenses (and with larger picture formats requiring lenses of longer focal length), and the depth increases with shorter focus lenses. A depth of field indicator, often included on the focusing mounts of lenses, shows on the distance scale how far in front of and behind the focused distance objects will be in focus at different diaphragm openings.

Subject and camera movement. Movement of the subject while the camera shutter is open for the exposure leads to a blurred image. The exposure time must therefore be short enough to keep the blur within acceptable limits. The shutter speed required depends on the movement speed of the object, the scale of the image (movement blur becomes greater the nearer the subject or the longer the focal length of the lens used) and the movement direction; movement across the direction of view produces the most blurring.

Movement blur can be reduced, even with comparatively slow shutter speeds, by moving the camera (panning) to follow the subject during the exposure. This records the moving object comparatively sharply against a blurred background and emphasizes the impression of speed.

Camera shake through unsteady support during the exposure also creates image blur—over the whole picture in such cases. Hand-held shots generally demand shutter speeds of $1/_{30}$ second or shorter. For longer times a firm camera support—such as a tripod—is essential.

Use of anti-halation dye

Factors influencing depth of field

Exposure technique.   The correct exposure (aperture and shutter settings) can be derived from tables or calculators or by direct measurement of the subject luminance with a light meter.

Automatic meter control. Cameras with through-the-lens (TTL) exposure meters—and also hand-held meters pointed at the subject—measure the average reflected light intensity, yielding reliable exposures for subjects of average contrast and brightness distribution. Subjects of extreme contrast or very bright or dark dominant areas need overriding exposure corrections; automatic cameras often have provision for this. Such a TTL measurement is usually centre-weighted (predominantly based on the image centre). Some cameras (and meters) permit spot readings covering a small subject area only and give reliable exposures if this selected area is a medium subject tone.

The selection of an appropriate aperture and shutter speed among equivalent camera exposures depends on depth-of-field and subject-movement requirements. Some automatic cameras simplify this by selecting just one such combination at each exposure level (program automation).

Flash exposures. Most current electronic flash units incorporate a sensor cell that measures the light reflected from the subject and controls the flash duration (and hence the exposure) accordingly. In certain cameras in which photocells measure the light reflected from the film, the same cells can similarly control the flash duration of suitable dedicated flash units. Lacking these provisions, flash exposures may be determined by measurement or by guide-number calculation.

Special meters can measure flash light quantity on a scene during a test firing of flashes; these are used extensively with more elaborate studio setups.

Flash exposure calculations rely on the fact that the exposure depends only on the lens aperture. (The electronic flash is usually much shorter than the synchronizable shutter time.) The light intensity reaching the film is inversely proportional to the square of the diaphragm *f*-number. By basic illumination laws the light intensity on a scene is also inversely proportional to the square of the distance between the light source and subject. For a given flash source and film speed, the exposure is thus constant for a constant product of distance and *f*-number. Flash manufacturers quote this product as a guide number for various flash–film combinations. For rapid exposure calculation, dividing the guide number by the flash-to-subject distance gives the required *f*-number; dividing the guide number by the *f*-number gives the distance at which the flash must be arranged for correct exposure.

Lens aperture as the key to flash exposure

Some cameras use this principle for semiautomatic flash-exposure control: the aperture adjustment is coupled with the distance setting on the lens (or with an automatic rangefinding system) so that the lens aperture gets larger with increasing distance. This coupling is adjustable for different flash guide numbers.

Exposure latitude. The ideal negative exposure records the darkest subject shadows as a just visible density. More exposure yields a denser negative, which, however, can still give an acceptable print by appropriate print-exposure adjustment. This range of usable negative exposures, the exposure latitude, depends on the film and the subject. This latitude is greater the lower the subject contrast and the greater the film's exposure range (and, generally, the lower the film contrast). Because of exposure latitude, simple cameras with limited exposure adjustability can still yield acceptable pictures under differing light conditions.

Lighting technique.   The kind of lighting on the scene governs the way in which the picture reproduces the subject. Orientation of the subject—as in taking a portrait—with respect to the light direction can often control the effect. Lighting from behind the camera gives flat effects, light from one side yields depth and modeling, while the principal light from behind the subject produces dramatic against-the-light effects of high contrast. Artificial light set-ups in the studio, with tungsten lamps or electronic flash, offer the greatest flexibility. Under such conditions the photographer can arrange two or more lamps for various lighting effects.

Flexibility with studio lighting

Directional lighting improves detail contrast and brilliance. Excessive subject contrast, however, makes accurate exposure settings difficult and may lead to loss of picture detail in the highlights or shadows. Fill-in lighting, by a flash or other light source on or near the camera, can illuminate heavy shadows facing the camera.

BLACK-AND-WHITE PROCESSING AND PRINTING

Negative development.   Amateurs usually process films in developing tanks. In this type of development roll or miniature film is wound around a reel with a spiral groove, which keeps adjacent turns separated and allows access by the processing solutions. Once the tank is loaded (in the dark), processing takes place in normal light, the processing baths (developer, intermediate rinse, fixer) being poured into the tank at the appropriate intervals. Sheet films are similarly treated in small tanks or held in hangers and immersed sequentially in the different processing solutions. Large-scale commercial processing laboratories use machines that automatically feed the films through the solutions in proper sequence.

Developers and their characteristics. The developer consists typically of one or more developing agents, a preservative (such as sodium sulfite) to prevent oxidation by the air, an alkali (such as sodium carbonate) to activate the developer, and a restrainer or antifoggant to ensure that the developer acts only on exposed silver halide crystals. A developer's main characteristics are activity, development speed, and effect on film gradation, graininess, and sharpness. Developers may be prepared on the basis of published formulas or bought as ready-mixed powders or concentrates for dilution with water.

The developer is allowed to act for a specific time to build up the image to the required density and contrast. This time depends on the developer, the temperature, the degree of agitation, and the film—as indicated by recommendations from film and developer manufacturers.

Fixing. The fixing bath contains a chemical (sodium or ammonium thiosulfate) that converts the silver halide into soluble, complex silver salts that dissolve in the fixer. During this process the film loses its original silver halide milkiness overlaying the image and becomes clear. The fixer also contains a weak acid (to halt the development process) and a hardening agent to reduce gelatin swelling.

Washing and drying. Washing removes all residual soluble chemicals from the emulsion and must be thorough for image permanence. Films are hung up to dry after removal from the tank.

High-speed processing. Greatly reduced processing times are possible with high-activity developers at elevated temperatures and with fast-acting fixing agents, such as ammonium thiosulfate. Such processes can cut access time to the negative down to less than a minute. One-bath (monobath) processing in a solution containing both a fast-acting developing agent and fixing chemicals also reduces processing time. In special rapid-access processing equipment, films pass through chambers spraying the processing solutions onto the film surface or run in contact with monobath-soaked webs.

Monobath processing with developer and fixer

Printing.   The simplest printing equipment is the contact printing frame in which the negative and printing paper are held together behind a glass plate during exposure to a suitable lamp. A printing box is essentially a printing frame with a built-in light source. Contact printing gives a positive of the same size as the negative.

Enlargers. Negatives usually are enlarged to prints of the desired final size. The enlarger is a projection system on a vertical column mounted on a horizontal baseboard. It has a lens, a film holder (negative carrier), and a lighting system (typically a lamp and condenser lens) for illuminating the negative. Raising or lowering the enlarger head on the column controls the image magnification; adjustment of the lens-to-negative distance focuses the image on the enlarging paper on the baseboard. In enlargers that focus automatically these two adjustments are linked mechanically to keep the image sharp all the time. Enlargers are made in various sizes to take different maximum negative formats.

Printing papers. Papers for enlarging and contact printing are produced in grades of differing exposure range—

i.e., ratios of shortest to longest exposure to produce the lightest tone and a full black, respectively. The various grades yield prints of a normal tone range from negatives of different contrasts: a soft paper grade for a high-contrast negative, a normal paper for a normal negative, a hard paper for soft negatives, and so on. Paper grades are also numbered—typically from 0 to 5—in ascending order of contrast. Variable-contrast papers use a mixture of two emulsions of a different contrast and colour sensitivity; the contribution of each is controlled by filters in the path of the exposing light.

Paper
grades in
order of
contrast

Other characteristics of printing papers are the speed (slower for contact papers, faster for enlarging papers), image colour (blue-black to warm brown), surface texture (glossy, velvet, mat), and base thickness (single or double weight). Most printing materials use a resin-coated (plastic-laminated) paper base that absorbs no water during processing.

Printing exposures. Correct printing exposures are determined by trial and error or by test strips given a series of progressively increasing exposures. More sophisticated exposure control systems measure either the brightness of selected image portions projected on the enlarger baseboard or the average light intensity reaching the paper during the exposure. Printing papers are exposed and processed in a darkroom lit by an olive-green or orange safelight. Printing papers are sensitive to violet, blue, and sometimes green light.

Print processing. The processing of prints consists of development, an intermediate rinse or stop bath, fixing, and washing. The developer and fixer are similar in principle to those used for negative films. In the normal method, dish or tray processing, prints are immersed successively in the solutions in dishes laid out side by side. Development is checked visually, the print remaining in the developer until the image has reached its full density. For drying, the prints may be clipped to a line, placed in a heated print dryer, or squeegeed onto a mirror-finished plate for a high-gloss surface.

Stabilization processing. Certain rapid-processing papers incorporate developing agents in their emulsions and are processed on a roller processor. This processor runs the paper through an activating bath for instant development and then through a stabilizing bath, followed by a pair of squeegeeing rollers from which the print emerges merely damp. This process takes about 10 to 15 seconds; the prints, however, do not keep quite as well as conventional prints, since unexposed silver salts are not removed from the emulsion but only converted into moderately light-stable compounds. Such prints can be made more permanent by subsequent fixing and washing.

Disadvan-
tage of
prints
finished by
stabiliza-
tion
processing

Dry processing. Processing baths can be completely eliminated by incorporating in the emulsion of the paper development and stabilization chemicals that become active on heating. One method is to disperse the processing chemicals in the emulsion in microscopic capsules containing the solution and a blowing agent. On passing the exposed paper over a heated roller, the blowing agent bursts the capsules, and the liberated processing solutions act on the silver halide immediately around each capsule. The liquid solvent instantly evaporates, leaving a dry print. Encapsulation materials are used for such purposes as making proof prints of negatives and reenlarging microfilm images. Certain non-silver processes in photocopying systems also offer dry processing.

COLOUR PHOTOGRAPHY

Colour reproduction. Present-day colour photographic processes are tricolour systems, reproducing different colours that occur in nature by suitable combinations of three primary-coloured stimuli. Each of these primary colours—blue-violet, green, and red—covers roughly one-third of the visible spectrum. Tricolour impressions can be produced by combining coloured lights (additive synthesis) or by passing white light through combinations of complementary filters, each of which holds back one of the primary colours (subtractive synthesis).

In additive synthesis a combination of red and blue-violet light (*e.g.,* light beams of the two colours directed

on the same spot of a white screen) gives a purplish pink (magenta); equal parts of red and green produce yellow, and equal parts of green and blue-violet produce bluish green (cyan). Superimposition of all three light beams on a screen yields white; combinations of varying proportions of two or three of the colours produce virtually all the other hues.

In subtractive synthesis yellow, magenta, and cyan filters or dye layers subtract varying proportions of the primary colours from white light. The yellow filter absorbs the blue component of white light and so controls the amount of blue present in a white-light beam that has passed through the filter. Similarly, the magenta filter controls the amount of green light left, and the cyan controls the amount of the red component. A cyan and a magenta filter superimposed in a white-light beam hold back both the red and the green component, making the emerging beam blue. Similarly, a cyan and a yellow filter together yield green, and a yellow and a magenta filter together yield red. Superimposing such filters or dye images of different densities in a white-light beam can therefore re-create any colour impression in the same way as superimposing light beams of the primary colours.

Subtraction
of primary
colours by
filters or
dye layers

The difference between additive and subtractive synthesis is the approach: in additive synthesis colours are built up by combining different intensities of primary-coloured light, and in subtractive synthesis colours are achieved by removing different proportions of primary-coloured light from white light. Most modern colour films are based on subtractive synthesis. Either method of colour synthesis should be capable of reproducing every existing colour in nature. In practice, the reproduction is imperfect; no filter dyes meet the required ideal specifications. Nevertheless, for most purposes reproduction is adequate.

Colour films. *Reversal (slide) films.* To reproduce colour by subtractive three-colour synthesis (Figure 6), colour films first break down the colours of an image into their primary components by means of three separate sensitized layers, each of which responds exclusively to blue, green, or red light. The image in each layer is reversal-processed to yield a positive dye image in a colour complementary to the layer's spectral sensitivity. Thus, the blue-sensitive layer first yields a negative image of everything blue in the original scene (*e.g.,* the blue sky) and then a positive image of everything that is not blue. This positive image is coloured yellow. Similarly, the green-recording layer yields a magenta positive image of everything that is not green, and the red-recording layer a positive cyan image of everything that is not red. Blue sky, for instance, does not figure in the yellow positive image but does figure in the magenta positive image (not being green) and in the cyan positive image (not being red). The magenta and cyan dyes in the areas that were blue sky are superimposed, and white light passing through the resulting transparency loses its green and red, but not its blue, component; thus, the sky appears blue. Similarly, green subject components end up as positive yellow image density in the blue-recording and positive cyan density in the red-recording layer, combining to green in the transparency. Yellow records as a negative image in the green-recording and red-recording layers, hence leaving a positive yellow image only in the blue-recording layer. All other colours are formed by similar combinations of different densities of the dye images.

Negative (print) films. Negative colour materials work

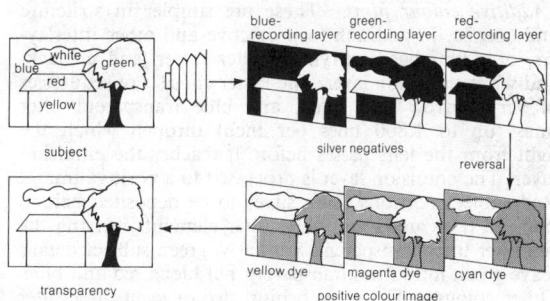

Figure 6: Colour reproduction sequence with subtractive reversal film (see text).

in a similar way but yield a negative dye image by direct development. Blue subject tones record in the blue-sensitive film layer to produce a yellow negative image. Green colour components yield a magenta dye image in the green-responding layer, and red components yield a cyan dye image in the red-recording layer. With respect to the subject, the colour negative therefore reverses the tones in brightness as well as in colour. Printing the colour negative on a colour paper with three differentially responding layers reverses the process once more, reconstituting the original subject colours in a positive print.

Colour-film structure. Reversal colour film has these components: (1) A top layer of plain gelatin, which protects the underlying layers against abrasion and damage. (2) The first emulsion layer, which contains blue-sensitive silver halide plus a yellow-forming colour coupler. This is a colourless substance that reacts with the decomposition products of the developing agent to generate dye in all areas where a silver image is produced and in proportion to the density of that silver image. (3) A yellow filter layer, which holds back blue light from the subsequent emulsion layers. It disappears during the bleaching stage of processing. (4) The second emulsion layer, which contains blue- and green-sensitive silver halide plus a magenta-forming colour coupler. The blue sensitivity is suppressed by the yellow filter layer. (5) The next emulsion, which is blue-and-red sensitive (blue again being suppressed) and contains a cyan-forming colour coupler. (6) A substrate, which ensures optimum adhesion of the emulsion layers to the film base and may also contain light-absorbing silver to prevent the scattering of light by reflection from the support surface (halation). (7) The film base, or support, of clear cellulose acetate derivative (or sometimes polyester), typically about 0.005 inch thick. (8) The back of the support, which carries a light-absorbing layer (an alternative to the antihalation layer in the substrate); on roll film this also acts as an anticurl layer.

Variations in reversal colour films

This scheme can vary. Often one or more of the selectively sensitized layers is duplicated. Some reversal colour films do not incorporate colour couplers in the emulsions but introduce them in the processing solutions. Processing such nonsubstantive colour films is more complex than processing substantive-coupler films containing couplers in the emulsions. Negative colour films are similar, but the couplers are often already coloured yellow or red or both. The unreacted couplers remain as positive images, which compensate for some deviations of the image dyes from the colour characteristics of ideal dyes. Such negatives have an apparently overall reddish or orange tint.

Some colour films come with different combinations of colour sensitivity and dye colour formed in the individual layers for deliberately falsified colour rendering (false-colour films) in special applications.

Colour-positive (print) materials have a paper or white, opaque film base instead of transparent film and have no antihalation layer. The emulsion sequence may be different from the above scheme; their spectral sensitivities may be keyed to the transmission characteristics of the negative dyes for better colour reproduction.

The dye images are reasonably lightfast but fade on prolonged exposure to ultraviolet-rich radiation. Colour transparencies and prints intended for continuous display may be protected by ultraviolet-absorbing coatings or filter layers.

Additive colour films. These are simpler in structure and consist, in addition to protective and other interlayers, of a film base, carrying a filter raster, and a black-and-white emulsion layer. The raster consists of sequences of very narrow red, green, and blue transparent filter lines (up to 1,800 lines per inch) through which the light from the lens passes before it reaches the emulsion layer. The emulsion layer is processed to a positive image. Red subject portions cause silver to be deposited behind non-red (*i.e.*, green and blue) filter elements, leaving the red filter lines transparent. Similarly, green subject details leave green filter lines transparent but block red and blue. Other colours affect areas behind two or even three filter lines—for example, yellow leaves red and green filter lines clear. In such areas the eye cannot resolve the separate

filter elements but gets an additive impression of yellow. Other colours form corresponding additive effects, including white, where all three filter elements are transparent. Because of the presence of the filter elements everywhere in the image, additive colour transparencies are much denser than subtractive ones; at high magnification the filter raster pattern may also become visible. Additive colour transparencies are used only in rapid-access diffusion-transfer systems (see below *Instant-picture photography*).

Colour balance. Colour film reacts to all hue and tone differences, including the prevailing light colour. A film recording approximately natural colours in daylight reproduces scenes photographed by tungsten light with a reddish overall tint—because this lighting is richer in red rays than is daylight. This spectral balance of different "white" light sources may be rated numerically by the colour temperature—a concept of theoretical physics that, with tungsten lighting, corresponds roughly to the absolute lamp-filament temperature. Such absolute temperatures are expressed in kelvins (K). The higher the colour temperature the richer the light is in bluish and the poorer it is in reddish rays and vice versa. Average daylight is rated at about 5,500 K, the light from an overcast sky from 6,500 K up; the colour temperature of tungsten lamps ranges between 2,600 and 3,400 K.

To ensure correct "white-light" colour reproduction with different types of lighting, the sensitivities of the three film layers must be matched to the colour temperature of the light. Colour slide (reversal) films are therefore made in different versions balanced for faithful rendering either with 5,500 to 6,000 K light sources (such as daylight or electronic flash) or with specified tungsten lighting (3,200 to 3,400 K).

"Universal" colour films

Such accurate film balance matching is less vital with negative colour films since the colour rendering of the print can be modified during colour printing. "Universal" amateur negative colour films are usable with any light, from tungsten to daylight. For high quality, professional negative colour films are still preferentially balanced to either daylight or tungsten sources.

Strongly coloured filters are suitable only for special effects; they overlay the colour image with the filter colour. Pale correction filters can match a film to a light source other than that for which it is balanced—*e.g.*, pale blue, with a daylight-type film used in tungsten lighting, to raise in effect the colour temperature. Pale pink or amber filters similarly reduce the colour temperature for using artificial-light-balanced films in daylight. Colour-film manufacturers publish detailed recommendations of actual filters required for such conversion.

In outdoor photography, especially involving distant views, an ultraviolet-absorbing filter is often required, as ultraviolet radiation records in the blue-sensitive layer of the film, producing an overall blue cast in the transparency. A pale pink skylight filter for outdoor subjects lit only by skylight counteracts the cold, bluish colour rendering resulting from such illumination.

Colour-film processing. The processing sequence for colour materials is longer than for black-and-white films and requires more solutions. Development needs very precise timing and temperature control. Colour films can be processed in amateur developing tanks; professionals use sets of tanks in temperature-controlled water jackets with provision for standardized solution agitation.

Reversal colour-film processing. Most colour films use a standard processing sequence and chemistry (usually available in kits). For substantive films (incorporating couplers in the emulsion) the sequence comprises: (1) development to form a negative silver image in each emulsion layer; (2) a reversal bath that renders developable the remaining silver halide in each emulsion layer; (3) colour development to produce a positive silver image in the remaining silver halide plus a coincident dye image by reaction with the colour couplers; (4) bleaching and fixing to reconvert the negative and positive silver images into silver halide and to dissolve the latter out of the emulsion, leaving only the three dye images; (5) a final rinse and stabilizer to remove soluble chemicals and improve light-fastness of the dyes; and (6) drying. There are also intermediate rinse stages.

The complete sequence without drying takes a little longer than 30 minutes.

Processing of nonsubstantive colour films, in which the couplers are in the colour developer, is more complex because each emulsion layer is reexposed by appropriately coloured light and colour-developed separately. This operation requires automated processing machinery.

Negative colour processing. Negative colour films are practically all of the substantive-coupler type. Most again follow a standard processing sequence consisting of colour development (forming a negative silver image in each emulsion layer together with a corresponding dye image), a rinse, and a bleaching and fixing stage to convert the silver image into silver halide and dissolve that (plus residual halide) out of the emulsion. A final rinse and drying conclude the process, which, excluding drying, takes about 12 minutes. Substantially the same procedure is followed for processing positive colour papers.

Colour printing. Colour print processing may be done in dishes or trays or in light-tight drums that are rotated manually or mechanically, processing solutions being poured in and out in succession. Professional colour laboratories use more elaborate versions of such rotating drum systems or roller or other automated machines that transport prints through the different solutions in turn.

Positive prints from colour negatives. Positive prints may be obtained from colour negatives by enlarging the colour negative onto a positive colour paper. Colour control consists of modifying the colour of the printing light by yellow, magenta, and cyan filters (typically by inserting high-density filters of these colours to varying degrees in the light path) to obtain a print of the correct or desired colour balance. The light is thoroughly mixed in a diffusing box before reaching the negative. An alternative method is to have three light sources behind the yellow, magenta, and cyan filters and to adjust their relative intensities or switch them on for different exposure times.

This subtractive, or white-light, printing method depends on subtracting or holding back colour components of white light. Commercial photofinishing printers often use an additive system in which prints are given successive exposures through high-density red, green, and blue filters. Each of these exposures forms the image in one of the emulsion layers of the paper; colour balance depends on the proportions of the individual exposures. In automatic colour printing systems the exposures are controlled by photocells that evaluate the red, green, and blue components of light transmitted by the negative.

Reversal colour printing. Colour transparencies can be printed on a reversal colour paper similar to a reversal film and processed in an analogous way. The same kind of colour control with filters is again possible, but the colour effect of the subtractive filters or of the additive filter exposures is reversed.

Dye-destruction processes. Dye-destruction processes differ from chromogenic colour materials (where colour images are produced during development) in starting off with emulsion layers containing the final dyes. During processing these are bleached in proportion to the silver image formed. Straightforward processing of a dye-destruction or dye-bleach material yields a positive image from a positive original and consists of: (1) development to form a silver image; (2) stop-fixing to arrest development and remove unexposed silver halide; (3) dye bleaching to bleach the dye in the areas containing a silver image; (4) silver bleaching to convert the silver image into silver halide; and (5) fixing to remove residual silver halide. Washing is done between all the processing stages.

Obtaining a positive image from a negative requires a more elaborate processing sequence, analogous to reversal processing in a chromogenic system. Dye-bleach materials use far more light-stable dyes than those produced by colour-coupling development. The positive–positive procedure also yields duplicate transparencies on dye-bleach materials with a transparent film base.

Diffusion-transfer colour prints. Materials derived from instant-picture diffusion-transfer processes (see below *Instant-picture photography*) have been adapted to colour print production. They are more expensive than tradi-tional colour print materials but considerably easier to process. In their simplest form they require only a single highly alkaline activator bath followed by a water rinse, the whole sequence lasting about five to 10 minutes, with considerable processing latitude. Such materials exist for prints from either negatives or transparencies. The colour printing and filter control principles are the same as with the traditional processes described above.

Assembly colour prints. The original method of producing colour prints was based on separation negatives obtained by photographing the original scene on separate black-and-white plates or films through a blue, green, and red filter, respectively. This method analyzes the subject in terms of its tricolour components in the same way as the initial negative images in a three-layer colour film. Positive prints from the separation negatives, converted into colour images (*e.g.*, by toning) and superimposed on top of each other, yield a subtractive tricolour print.

The main surviving assembly print process, dye transfer, uses a set of separation positives on a panchromatic matrix film made either from separation negatives of a colour transparency or by separation (three filtered exposures) from a colour negative. Appropriate processing converts the matrix film into a gelatin relief image whose depth is proportional to the positive silver density. Each matrix is soaked in a dye solution (yellow for the matrix derived from the blue-filter negative and so on), and the dyes from the matrices are transferred in succession to a single sheet of gelatin-coated paper. Elaborate care is required to ensure accurate superimposition (registration) of the dye images; the result is a positive colour print.

Transparency projection. Many amateur colour pictures are in the form of transparencies, particularly on 35-mm film. These are usually mounted in plastic or card frames or bound between glass for projection on a screen in a darkened room. The projector consists of a lens, a holder for the slide, and a lighting system (lamp, reflector, and condenser lenses to concentrate the light onto the slide). Modern slide projectors take the slides in magazines or trays holding 30 to 50 or more slides. An automatic slide transport feeds each slide from the tray into the light path of the projector and may be operated from a remote control unit or by pulses from a tape recorder, which can also record a commentary to the complete slide series. Some projectors feature remote-controlled or automatic focusing to keep each successive slide image sharp on the screen.

The standard miniature slide size is 2×2 inches for transparencies up to $1\frac{5}{8} \times 1\frac{5}{8}$ inches; the most usual transparency format in such slides is 24×36 millimetres. Projectors for larger slides (*e.g.*, $2\frac{3}{4} \times 2\frac{3}{4}$ inches for transparencies up to $2\frac{1}{4} \times 2\frac{1}{4}$ inches) and ultraminiature projectors (*e.g.*, 10×14-millimetre transparencies in 3×3-centimetre slide frames) are suitably scaled-up or scaled-down versions of the standard models.

The size of the projected image depends on the distance of the projector from the screen and the focal length of the projection lens. Projectors may also project from the back onto a translucent screen; such rear-projection setups are more compact, and the image is often bright enough for viewing in daylight. The rear-projection system is used in schools and for commercial displays. Elaborate slide shows are produced by linking two or more projectors aimed at the same or adjacent screen areas. With a suitably assembled slide set, the pictures can be made to change, overlap, and assemble, according to a predetermined program.

INSTANT-PICTURE PHOTOGRAPHY

History and evolution. Cameras with built-in processing facilities, to reduce the delay between exposure and the availability of the processed picture, were proposed from the 1850s onward. The ferrotype process later adapted for "while-you-wait" photography by itinerant street and beach photographers goes back almost as far. Because of the messiness of handling liquid chemicals in or just outside the camera, such systems remained largely impractical. In the 1940s Edwin H. Land, a U.S. scientist and inventor, designed a film configuration that included a sealed pod containing processing chemicals in a viscous jelly or paste form to permit virtually dry processing inside the camera and yield a positive print within a minute or less of exposure. Land demonstrated (1947), and through his Polaroid Corporation marketed (1948), a camera and materials that realized this system. It used a positive sheet and negative emulsion, the latter being discarded after use. An instant-print colour film (Polacolor) was introduced in 1963 and an integral single-sheet colour film in 1972. After the mid-1970s other manufacturers offered similar instant-print processes. In 1977 Polaroid introduced an 8-mm colour movie film, and in 1982 it introduced still transparency films that permit rapid processing outside the camera.

The Polaroid process

Black-and-white diffusion transfer. The Polaroid process is based on negative paper carrying a silver halide emulsion and a nonsensitized, positive sheet containing development nuclei. After the exposure the two sheets are brought into intimate contact by being pulled between a pair of pressure rollers. These rupture a sealed pod (attached to the positive sheet) to spread processing chemicals—in the form of a viscous jelly—between the two sheets. This reagent develops a negative image and causes the silver salts from the unexposed areas to diffuse into the positive layer and deposit metallic silver on the development nuclei. After about 30 seconds to one minute the negative and positive sheets are peeled apart and the negative can be discarded. In special versions of the process the negative may be washed and treated to give a conventional negative for normal enlarging.

In the original Polaroid instant-picture process the material was a dual roll of negative and positive sheets. Later versions of this peel-apart process use film packs and sheet films. They require special cameras incorporating the pressure rollers that operate the spread of processing jelly while the peel-apart sandwich is fed out of the camera. Special camera backs with this mechanism allow the use of Polaroid materials in professional cameras taking interchangeable film holders or magazines. Peel-apart Polaroid systems include high-speed emulsions, high-contrast, process, transparency, and scientific materials.

Silver diffusion-transfer processes were invented in 1939 in Belgium and Germany and were used for a number of years in office copying systems until superseded by dry copying processes.

The Polacolor process. Polaroid colour film has a larger number of active layers, including a blue-sensitive silver halide emulsion backed by a layer consisting of a yellow dye–developer compound, a green-sensitive layer backed by a layer of magenta dye–developer, and a red-sensitive layer backed by a cyan dye–developer. The dye–developer in each case consists of dye molecules (not colour couplers) chemically linked to developing agent molecules.

After exposure and activation by the alkaline jelly, the dye–developer molecules in each layer migrate into the adjacent silver halide layer. Development of exposed silver halide to a negative image anchors the dye–developer molecule in position. Dye–developer molecules in unexposed image areas are not used up by development but migrate into the receiving layer of the positive material. There they are immobilized, remaining as dye images corresponding to a positive of each silver halide layer in the negative film. The dyes thus re-create a full-colour positive image. The process depends on the controlled diffusion of the dye–developer molecules, achieved by spacing layers and balanced exposure and development time. Developing takes about one minute. Polacolor films include an 8 × 10-inch material for regular studio and view cameras (with separate processing machinery) and giant formats of 20 × 24 inches or even larger for special cameras.

Single-sheet process. The Polaroid single-sheet, or integral, films contain all the negative and positive layers in a single preassembled film unit that is exposed through the transparent positive layer. The unit incorporates a viscous processing reagent that acts in principle similarly to the chemistry of the Polacolor process. It includes "opacifying" dyes and a highly opaque white pigment that together protect the negative layers against light during processing outside the camera. The pigment provides a background to the positive image after the dye–developer molecules from the negative layers have migrated into the receiving layer.

Other constituents of the system neutralize residual active chemicals after processing, for all chemistry remains within the single-sheet print. The print size is about $3^1/_2 \times 4^1/_4$ inches, the effective image size about $3^1/_8 \times 3^1/_8$ inches. The Eastman Kodak and Fuji Photo Film companies also have marketed single-sheet films and cameras that accept each other's films. These materials and cameras are not compatible with the Polaroid products.

Autoprocess materials. Because it requires cameras or camera backs with integral processing facilities, the instant-picture process is not suitable for conditions precluding immediate processing of the picture (*e.g.,* in underwater or space photography), nor is it suitable for motion-picture or 35-mm cameras. Alternative procedures suggested to overcome this usually involve some form of semidry rapid-access processing. The Polaroid Autoprocess system uses 35-mm film in standard cartridges to fit any 35-mm camera. After exposure the film is driven through a tabletop processor, which sandwiches the film with a stripping film carrying a thin layer of processing fluid. The latter processes the negative image, causes the formation of a positive image by a diffusion-transfer process, and then releases the negative layers, which are finally removed from the film (together with residual chemicals) by the stripping material. The transparencies remaining on the 35-mm film are immediately ready for viewing and projection. Black-and-white as well as colour systems (by an additive process) are available in this form.

Applications. Instant-picture processes have an advantage in applications that need quick access to a finished print. The initial field of the process was amateur snapshooting and instant portraits, from which evolved the taking of identification pictures for work and security passes. Such passes are made with special cameras that record a portrait together with personal details on a composite print that is then laminated to form a tamper-proof identity card. In studio photography instant prints provide a quick method of making exposure tests and checking the effect of lighting. Large- and giant-format Polacolor prints are used in studio portraiture; normal instant prints have numerous commercial applications. Instant pictures are also widely used in the laboratory to record experimental setups, for photomicrography and for infrared photography; for instant endoscopy and for clinical and forensic records; for rapid copying of normal colour transparencies; and for instant hard copy of oscilloscope, video, and computer graphic displays. Autoprocess transparencies are used for the rapid production of colour or black-and-white slides for lectures and publication and in various fields of scientific photography (including photomicrography) relying on the use of conventional 35-mm (usually single-lens reflex) cameras.

SPECIAL PHOTOSENSITIVE SYSTEMS

The high working speed (efficiency of converting light into permanent images) of silver halides makes them almost the only materials suitable for camera use. Numerous light-sensitive systems not using silver have been known since the beginning of photography. In view of silver's high price, a number of substitute systems have grown in importance, and new ones have appeared. Most of them are limited to office copying, microfilming, the graphic arts, and other applications in which flat copy is reproduced.

Electrophotography. Electrophotography covers a number of processes that rely on photoconductive substances whose electrical resistance decreases when light falls on them. A layer of such a substance with a grounded backing plate is given a uniform electrostatic charge in the dark. When a light image is projected onto the surface, the photoconductor allows the electrostatic charge to leak away in proportion to the exposure. This leaves an "image" charge that can be converted, in various ways, into a visible image.

In xerography the photoconductive layer is selenium, and the image is made visible by dusting the plate with an electrostatically charged powder (toner) having a charge that is the opposite of that of the electrostatic image. The powder adheres to the image portions only and is then transferred to a sheet of plain paper also under the in-

Principles of xerography

fluence of electrostatic fields. A final heat treatment fuses the powder into the paper for a permanent picture. The process usually makes a positive from a positive original. In office copying machines (the main application of xerography) the whole operating sequence is programmed and automated. A zinc oxide-coated paper may replace the selenium plate; if so, the pigment powder deposit is fused directly into the paper surface.

The process is used mainly for line images without intermediate tones between black and white. Modified procedures permit continuous-tone reproduction and—with coloured pigments—also colour printing.

In the electroplastic process a transparent thermoplastic serves as the photoconductive layer. After the plastic is charged and exposed, the residual electrostatic charge forms stresses in the thermoplastic. Controlled heating deforms the surface in the image areas into a grain pattern, which is frozen into the plastic on cooling. The resulting image is light-scattering and is viewed by reflection or in special projection systems.

Colloid and photopolymer processes. A comparatively early non-silver process depended on organic colloid (gum or gelatin) treated with a bichromate. Exposure to light hardened the gelatin, rendering it insoluble, while unexposed portions could be washed away with warm water, leaving a relief image.

Photopolymer systems substitute a plastic precursor in place of the gelatin. The plastic precursor polymerizes to an insoluble plastic when exposed to light, and the unexposed soluble material is washed out by a suitable solvent. Photopolymer processes have been adapted for forming resists (protective coatings) for etching, as, for instance, in the manufacture of printed circuits. In indirect photopolymer systems a light-sensitive substance is mixed with a plastic precursor and on exposure decomposes into compounds that initiate polymerization of the plastic. The polymerizable layer may include a pigment for a final coloured image. Superimposing colour images derived from separation negatives can yield positives; systems of this type are used for quick colour proofing in photomechanical reproduction.

Diazonium processes. A diazo, or dyeline, process depends on the decomposition by light of organic diazonium salts. These salts can also couple with certain other compounds to form dyes. After exposure only the exposed (and decomposed) diazonium salt forms dye, producing a positive image from a positive original.

The materials are usually papers or transparent supports impregnated with the required chemicals. They are mainly sensitive to ultraviolet rays and can therefore be handled by normal tungsten lighting.

The light-decomposition of diazonium compounds also produces gaseous nitrogen. This phenomenon is utilized in vesicular processes that incorporate the diazonium compound in a thermoplastic layer. The nitrogen slowly diffuses out of this layer, but, if heat is applied immediately after exposure, the expanding nitrogen gas forms minute light-scattering bubbles visible as an image. The scattering power corresponds to the exposure. Further general exposure, after the plastic has cooled, decomposes the residual diazonium compound with gradual diffusion of the nitrogen out of the layer, destroying the latter's light sensitivity. This process and thermal dyeline systems are dry-processing instant-access systems and are used for making microfilm duplicates.

Photochromic systems. Certain dyelike substances can exist in a colourless and a coloured state. They are called photochromic compounds. The coloured state is formed by exposure to radiations of a certain wavelength. The compound reverts to its colourless state either in the dark or on treatment with radiation of a different wavelength. This reversibility is a primary characteristic of photochromism, and it is an instant-image system involving no processing.

Photochromic systems are used in microrecording (see below *Microfilming and microreproduction*). As the change of state takes place on a molecular level, the images are practically grain-free, and resolution is limited only by the resolving power of the optical system being used. Pho-

Reversibility of the photochromic systems

tochromic materials can be negative- or positive-working. With some photochromic compounds the dye image can be rendered permanent by optical or other treatment.

Glasses containing certain metal compounds also act as photochromic materials. Exposure to light breaks down the compounds into metal that forms a visible (and permanent) image in the glass. Another type of photochromic glass contains silver halide crystals dispersed in the glass melt. The action of light decomposes the silver halide, forming a visible silver deposit. The halogen cannot escape from the glass, so it recombines with the silver in the dark and the image fades. Such photochromic glasses are incorporated in automatic light-control devices; light transmission decreases as the intensity of the light reaching the glass rises. Such glass has found use in certain types of sunglasses.

Electronic photography. As television cameras and recorders became more compact, home video recording began to replace home movies in the amateur field in the late 1970s. Video recording of still images was incidental to this; it became widely involved in the storage of computer-generated or computer-processed images on magnetic tape or discs, for instance, in satellite photography, radiography, image scanning in picture transmission, and photomechanical reproduction.

A still video camera resembling traditional photographic apparatus (the Sony Mavica single-lens reflex) was first demonstrated in 1981. It uses a fast-rotating magnetic disc, two inches in diameter, recording on it up to 50 separate video images formed in a solid-state device in the camera. The images can be played back through a television receiver or monitor, or converted to paper in a printer that uses the video signals to control a printout device. Apart from being a potential rival to instant-picture photography, electronic records of this type are capable of direct transmission via telephone lines. Thus the process is of interest to press photographers, who can transmit pictures from their cameras directly to newspaper editorial offices without intermediate processing. The magnetic record also is able to directly control halftone engraving machines to engrave printing plates or cylinders.

SPECIAL TECHNIQUES AND APPLIED PHOTOGRAPHY

High-speed and stroboscopic photography. High-speed photography is generally concerned with exposure times shorter than about $1/1,000$ second (one millisecond) and often exposures shorter than $1/1,000,000$ second (one microsecond). This field partly overlaps that of high-speed cinematography—sequences of very short exposures. Exposure times can be reduced by high-speed shutter systems or by short-duration flash sources.

High-speed photography, together with high-speed cinematography, aids in the study of missiles, explosions, nuclear reactions, and other phenomena of military and scientific interest. In industry high-speed pictures show up movement phases of machinery, relays, and switches; dynamic fractures of materials or insulation breakdown; and, in natural science studies, flight movement of birds and insects.

High-speed shutters. The shortest exposure with mechanical shutters is about $1/4,000$ second. Special high-speed shutter systems are magneto-optical, electro-optical, or electronic. A magneto-optical shutter (Faraday shutter) consists of a glass cylinder placed inside a magnetic coil between two crossed polarizing filters; so long as the filters remain crossed, virtually no light can pass through. A brief current pulse through the coil generates a magnetic field that rotates the light's plane of polarization in the cylinder so that during the pulse some light passes through the second polarizing filter. The electro-optical shutter (Kerr cell) is made up of a liquid cell of nitrobenzene fitted with electrodes and again placed between two crossed polarizers. An electric pulse applied to the electrodes changes the polarization properties of the nitrobenzene so that this arrangement again transmits light. Minimum exposure time is around five nanoseconds (5×10^{-9} second). Image converter tubes electronically transmit and amplify an optical image focused on one end of a tube onto a phosphorescent screen at the other end. Electrons flow in the tube only in

Principle of the Kerr cell

the presence of an electric field, which can be controlled by short-time pulses down to a few nanoseconds.

High-speed light sources. The shortest electronic-flash duration is around one microsecond. Spark discharges in air between electrodes yield still shorter exposures; discharge voltage may go up to tens or hundreds of thousands of volts. Short-duration pulses applied to X-ray tubes produce X-ray flashes for high-speed radiography. The shortest exposures are between 20 and 50 nanoseconds. Special switching modes turn lasers into high-speed sources with durations down to a fraction of a nanosecond.

Synchronization. Generally the event photographed is made to trigger the exposure (the current pulse to operate the shutter or flash or spark source) to ensure correct synchronization. Examples are bullets interrupting a light beam to a photocell or self-luminous phenomena (explosions) triggering the system via a photocell circuit. The event and the exposure may be also triggered together by a signal from a common source.

Stroboscopic photography. Electronic-flash units designed to flash in rapid succession (up to several hundred times a second) can photograph a moving subject in front of a stationary camera with its shutter open to yield multiple images of successive movement phases. The technique has been used in pictorial and sports photography (*e.g.,* recording the movement of dancers or golfers) and for analyzing movement cycles without a motion-picture camera. Stroboscopic flash can be synchronized with a selected movement phase of an object in rapid cyclic motion (*e.g.,* a rotating machine component); the moving component illuminated in this way then appears stationary.

Aerial photography. Photographs from airborne or spaceborne vehicles either provide information on ground features for military and other purposes (reconnaissance) or record the dimensional disposition of such features (surveying).

Reconnaissance photographs call for maximum sharpness and detail rendering. Infrared films are often used to bring out details not discernible visually. In nonmilitary applications such photographs may reveal ecological factors (tree diseases, crop variations) and traces of archaeological sites not visible from the ground. Such shots are generally taken with cameras using 5- or 9½-inch roll film in large magazines, built into the aircraft and operated electrically by the pilot or other crew member, or automatically at set intervals. Some systems incorporate a shutterless technique; the film runs continuously past a slit at a rate matched exactly to the image movement in the camera's focal plane as the aircraft flies over the ground (image motion compensation).

Aerial survey is a systematic procedure of photographing the ground for map production; exposures are made at intervals to partly overlap the view of successive pictures. The individual photographs are enlarged to the same degree and then assembled in a precise mosaic. Aerial photographs taken under precisely specified conditions can serve for accurate measurements of ground details by stereoscopic evaluation (see below *Stereoscopic and three-dimensional photography*).

Satellite and space photography. Satellites orbiting the Earth record changing meteorologic features (weather satellites) and broadcast the video images to ground stations where they may be recorded on magnetic tape or converted to hard-copy pictures by suitable printers. Video cameras in spacecraft sent to record surface details of other planets similarly scan electronically the view taken in by a lens and beam the scanning signals back to Earth, where they are recorded and reconverted to visible images. The signals are usually processed electronically to enhance image information and detail. Such enhancement often brings out more information than can be recorded by conventional photography. Similar techniques are used by military satellites monitoring ground features from high orbits above the Earth.

Underwater photography. Underwater photography requires either special watertight cameras or pressure-resistant housings for normal cameras. In both cases camera functions are controlled through pressure-tight glands. A flat glass or plastic window is usually in front of the camera lens. The red and yellow absorption of the water more than a few feet below the surface turns colour photographs taken by daylight into virtually monochrome shots; hence artificial light is essential to show up the full colour range of fish and other underwater subjects. Light sources are battery-powered tungsten or tungsten-halogen lamps or electronic flash units (again in self-contained pressure-proof housings). For comfortable handling the weight of the housing with camera is adjusted to slight negative buoyancy. Complete camera and lighting outfits may be built into sledgelike or torpedo-like units with an electric or compressed-air motor for self-propulsion through the water.

Since the refractive index ratio of glass to water is lower than for glass to air, the light-bending power of a glass lens is less in water than in air. This factor reduces the lens's angle of view and makes objects appear at about three-fourths of their actual distance. This difference must be allowed for in focusing—possibly by a suitably calibrated distance scale or by fitting the housing with a compensating porthole, which acts as a diverging lens.

Underwater cameras with lenses designed for direct contact with the water eliminate the air space between the lens and the porthole. Such lenses can cover wider angles of view without distortion, but they do not give sharp images outside the water.

Close-range and large-scale photography. Near photography to reveal fine texture and detail covers several ranges: (1) close-up photography at image scales between 0.1 and 1 (one-tenth to full natural size); (2) macrophotography between natural size and 10 to 20× magnification, using the camera lens on its own; (3) photomicrography at magnifications above about 20×, combining the camera with a microscope; and (4) electron micrography with an electron microscope at magnifications of 10,000 to 1,000,000×, which involves photography of the electron microscope's phosphor screen or placing a photographic emulsion inside the vacuum chamber of the electron microscope to record directly the image formed by the electron beams.

Close-up and macrophotography. Supplementary close-up lenses or extension tubes (placed between the lens and camera body) allow the camera to focus on near distances for large scales of reproduction. Special close-up rangefinders or distance gauges establish exactly the correct camera-to-subject distance and precise framing of the subject field. Special simple close-up cameras, as in fingerprint recording and certain fields of medical photography, are permanently set to a fixed near distance and have a distance gauge or similar device built in. Screen-focusing cameras (view and single-lens reflex) need no such aids, as the finder screen shows the precise focus and framing.

Extension tubes or extension bellows or both or "macro" lenses of extended focusing range are used for the macro range of distances. For optimum image quality macrophotographic lenses specially corrected for large image scales may be used or the camera lens reversed back to front.

Photomicrography. There are two principal methods of photographing through a microscope. In the first the camera, with its lens focused at infinity, is lined up in the optical axis of the microscope, which is also focused visually on infinity. In the other method the camera without lens is positioned behind the microscope eyepiece, which is focused to project the microscope image directly onto the film.

Special photomicrographic cameras generally employ the second method. Microscope adapters to provide a light-tight and rigid connection between the camera and microscope are available for both systems. Such microadapters may incorporate their own shutter and a beam splitter system for viewing and focusing of the microscope image through a focusing telescope. Photomicrographs are the essential adjunct to all microscopy to record biologic, bacteriologic, physical, and other observations in black-and-white or colour.

Stereoscopic and three-dimensional photography. Visual three-dimensional depth is perceived partly because of the fact that the human eyes see a scene from two viewpoints separated laterally by about 2½ inches. The two views show slightly different spatial relationships between

Reconnaissance photography for capturing detail

Underwater cameras

Basis of depth perception

near and distant objects (parallax); the visual process fuses these stereoscopic views into a three-dimensional impression. A similar impression is obtained by viewing a pair of stereoscopic photographs taken with two cameras or a twin camera with lenses $2\frac{1}{2}$ inches apart, so that the left eye sees only the picture taken by the left-hand lens and the right eye only that of the right-hand lens. Binocular viewers or stereo-selective projection systems permit such viewing.

Stereo photographs can also be combined in a single picture by splitting up the images into narrow vertical strips and interlacing them. On superimposing a carefully aligned lenticular grid on the composite picture, an observer directly sees all the strips belonging to the left-eye picture with the left eye and all the strips belonging to the right-eye picture with the right eye. Such parallax stereograms are seen in display advertising in shop windows or showcases. They also can be reproduced in print, overlayed by a lenticular pattern embossed in a plastic covering layer.

Photogrammetry makes use of stereo photography in measuring dimensions and shapes of ground objects in depth, as from successive exposure pairs made during an aerial survey flight. If all exposure parameters, including flying height, ground separation between exposures, and focal length of the aerial camera lens are known, the height of each ground feature can be measured. Photogrammetric plotting instruments do this and draw height contour curves of all features for aerial maps.

Similar photogrammetric evaluation of stereo photographs of nearby subjects can also be made. For instance, it is possible to reconstruct accurately the scene of a highway accident. In industry a photogrammetric plot of an automobile model can be fed into a computer to program the machine tools that will shape the full-scale motor body components.

Infrared photography. Images formed by infrared and heat radiations can be recorded either directly, on films sensitive to them, or indirectly, by photographing the image produced by some other system registering infrared radiation.

Silver halide emulsions can be sensitized to infrared rays with wavelengths up to around 1,200 nanometres (one nanometre is $\frac{1}{1,000,000}$ of a millimetre). The usual sensitivity range is 800 to 1,000 nanometres. Direct infrared-recording aerial photography shows up ground features of differential infrared reflection but similar light reflection (*e.g.*, different types of foliage) and cuts through haze and mist. Special colour films with an infrared-sensitive layer and processed to colours different from the natural rendering (false-colour films) show up such differences still more clearly. In forensic photography infrared pictures reveal ink alterations in forgeries, differentiate stains, and help to identify specific textiles and other materials. In medicine infrared photographs show subcutaneous blood vessels, as the skin is transparent to infrared.

With suitable equipment it is possible to convert an infrared image into one visible on a fluorescent screen, where it can be photographed. In infrared scanner systems a moving mirror scans the object or scene and focuses the radiation onto an infrared-sensitive cell. The cell generates electric signals to modulate a light source, which, in turn, scans a photographic film or paper synchronously with the mirror. The resulting image records hotter and colder parts of the object as lighter and darker areas and can establish actual temperatures of subject details—sometimes to within a fraction of a degree. This system has been used to record temperature variations in the skin for the diagnosis of cancer.

Ultraviolet photography. Invisible shortwave ultraviolet radiations can be recorded directly or used in fluorescence photography. For direct ultraviolet recording the photographically useful wavelength range lies between 400 nanometres (visible violet) and about 200 nanometres and needs special optical systems transparent to ultraviolet rays (quartz, silica, or fluoride elements or combinations thereof). Light sources rich in ultraviolet such as mercury vapour lamps—with an ultraviolet-transmitting, but visually opaque, filter in front of the camera lens—ensure

Applications of direct infrared photography

that the photograph records only the ultraviolet-reflecting characteristics of the subject.

Fluorescence photography records the glow or visible light given off by certain substances when they are irradiated by ultraviolet rays. The object is illuminated only by ultraviolet rays by screening out the visible light with a filter that transmits only ultraviolet radiation, and another filter that absorbs the ultraviolet rays is placed over the camera lens, permitting only the visible light (fluorescence) to be recorded on the film. Normal lenses and panchromatic or colour materials are used.

Ultraviolet photography can identify or separate pigments and fabrics and can detect forgeries of documents. Fluorescence photography can identify dyes, stains, and markings, specific chemical substances, and fluorescent components in microscopy specimens. Ultraviolet microscopy offers increased resolution through the shorter wavelength radiations employed. Aerial and satellite photography by ultraviolet can show up ultraviolet-reflective ground features.

Radiography and other radiation recording techniques. Silver halide emulsions are sensitive to X rays, gamma rays, and charged particles emitted by radioactive substances. Some of these rays penetrate visually opaque materials to varying degrees to show up internal structures. Radiography covers techniques of recording the subsurface features of objects.

X-ray radiography. X rays (wavelengths between $\frac{1}{100}$ and $\frac{1}{100,000}$ that of visible light) are produced by high-voltage electron streams bombarding an electrode in a vacuum tube. For radiography the object to be recorded is placed between an X-ray tube and the film; the film registers the differential absorption of the X rays by the object's internal structure as a projection shadowgraph.

The most familiar application is in medicine for diagnosis and recording, including dental radiography. Industrial radiography permits nondestructive inspection of castings, welds, and engineering structures.

Gamma radiography. The technique of gamma-ray radiography is similar to that of X-ray radiography but relies on rays emitted by radioactive substances. Gamma rays have wavelengths from 100 to 1,000 times shorter than X rays and correspondingly greater penetrating power. Small gamma-ray sources are placed in areas inaccessible to X-ray tubes such as inside pipelines. In all radiographic applications the exposure occurs under conditions of normal light, from which the radiographic film is protected by a light-tight (but radiation-transparent) wrapping.

Autoradiography. Autoradiography records the distribution of radioactive materials in botanical and histological specimens placed in contact with a photographic emulsion. This technique has been applied to the study of metabolism of plants and animals; it records the activity of organic compounds of radioactive isotopes introduced into the system of the plant or animal. In engineering studies autoradiography can be used to follow the transfer of radioactive substances from one surface to another in lubrication. The technique also has applications in machining and other metal-treatment processes.

Nuclear-track recording. Tracks of subatomic particles, such as protons, electrons, and mesons, produced by nuclear reactions, can be recorded by photographic means. The most common technique is to photograph the visible traces of such tracks in bubble or spark chambers with special camera and lens arrangements. Different arrangements can provide for coverage of large fields or the recording of tracks simultaneously from several directions for three-dimensional reconstruction.

Particle tracks can be recorded directly in thick (up to one millimetre) emulsion layers or in emulsion stacks (up to 20 inches) carried in high-altitude balloons and in spacecraft and satellites. Special processing procedures are required to deal with these emulsion thicknesses.

Astronomical photography. By the cumulative effect of light received over a long period, a photographic emulsion can record celestial objects too faint to be visible. Before radio telescopes (see MEASUREMENT AND OBSERVATION, PRINCIPLES, METHODS, AND INSTRUMENTS OF), photography was the only way of detecting many such objects.

Applications of ultraviolet photography

Astronomical cameras as units of telescopes

Astronomical cameras are film- or plate-holding units built onto high-power telescopes, typically reflecting systems. The telescopes run on precision, clock-driven mounts to keep the optical axis stationary with respect to the sky area as the Earth rotates during an exposure time, which can run into several hours. For increased recording sensitivity, the telescope image may be intensified electronically.

Astronomical photographs taken through narrow-band colour filters—including infrared or ultraviolet transmitting filters—show selective emission characteristics of stars. In the case of the Sun and of planets, such photographs can reveal some surface details not observable by white light. Colour photographs reveal colours not directly visible because the intensity of starlight is too low to stimulate the eye's colour-vision mechanism.

Spectrography records the composition of light emitted by stars and other objects, the star image of the telescope being photographed through a diffraction grating, a device that disperses white light into constituent wavelengths. Elements present in the star or the gas mantle surrounding it can be identified from their characteristic spectral lines. Displacement of such lines from their known wavelength position can indicate the velocity with which the distant stellar systems recede from or approach the Earth.

Microfilming and microreproduction. Microfilming is the copying of documents, drawings, and other such matter at a reduced scale—typically 1:15 to 1:42—for compact storage. Complete microreproduction systems include methods of filing the film copies for easy retrieval and reenlargement.

Documents, periodicals, and other printed matter are usually microfilmed on 16-mm film with an image size between 10×14 and 14×20 mm in a copying camera taking 100-foot lengths of film. Engineering drawings of high information content are microfilmed on 35-mm unperforated film with a standard image size of 32×45 mm. Films of up to 105 mm in width are also used. Automated microfilm cameras run continuously, documents being fed onto a moving band carried past the camera at a steady speed while the film runs past a slit at a matched rate.

Readers and reader printers are desk-top projectors that display the frames reenlarged to about natural size on a back projection screen. In a reader printer the image may also be projected on sensitized paper for full-size enlargements. Advanced readers have elaborate retrieval systems based on frame coding and run the microfilm rolls through at high speed until a specific searched image is reached.

Aperture cards or standard-size transparent jackets store microfilm images as single frames or groups of frames. Such unitized microfilms permit easier indexing and retrieval by classical or punched card indexing systems. Certain 35-mm microfilm cameras photograph the original document directly on film premounted in an aperture card and processed on the spot.

Microfiche system

Widely used is the unitized microfiche system, which carries up to 98 frames, each about 9×12 mm, on a 4×6-inch sheet of film. The microfiche camera repositions the film frame by frame after every exposure. Microfiche with a larger frame can also be produced by jacketing strips of 16-mm microfilm in multichannel plastic jackets 4×6 inches in size.

Various duplication methods allow microfilm records to be extensively distributed.

For still greater space saving, microfilm images may be reduced beyond 1:100 on high-resolution photochromic image materials. Extreme fine-grain silver copies then hold 3,000 to 4,000 individual frames on a single 4×6-inch film. This method, useful for complex catalogs and like purposes, offers easy retrieval of individual frames but requires a high-magnification reader.

THE PHOTOGRAPHY INDUSTRY

Equipment manufacture

Present-day manufacture of cameras and other photographic equipment is concentrated in mass-production plants that make most of the components (camera bodies, lenses, shutters, and other parts) on largely automated machines; the components are then assembled by semiskilled or skilled labour. Smaller manufacturers of low- and medium-priced cameras obtain components for assembly from such specialist suppliers as shutter manufacturers and lens producers. High-quality precision cameras are produced on a smaller scale with automated fabrication of the engineering components but much more extensive manual assembly by highly skilled technicians. Components and functions of every camera are tested at every production stage; less expensive cameras are usually batch-tested by a sampling procedure.

The raw material for lens manufacture covers a range of optical glasses of different optical characteristics. About 10 major worldwide glass producers supply the several dozen optical firms offering lenses of well-known brands. The glass is cast into blanks for specific lens elements and ground and polished to the required exact specifications, with the elements assembled in metal (sometimes plastic) mounts. Extensive production tests and optical performance checks safeguard quality standards.

Silver halide emulsions are made by mixing silver nitrate with a solution of alkali halide—typically potassium bromide and iodide—in gelatin. The silver halide then precipitates out as fine crystals. After cooling to a jelly, shredding, and washing, the emulsion is remelted and treated to increase speed and contrast. Colour sensitizers (and colour couplers for colour emulsions) and additives are introduced, and the gelatin emulsion is machine-coated on wide continuous webs of paper or film. Generally several coatings are applied—up to a dozen for certain colour films. Operations from emulsion mixing onward are carried on in total darkness. After cooling and drying, the material is batch-tested for consistent characteristics and then is cut and packed.

Film base is produced either by coating a solution of the base material on large drums, where it solidifies (film casting), or by extrusion of plastics, such as polyester, in film extruders. For print materials, paper of suitable purity is coated with a barium sulfate emulsion in gelatin, to provide a smooth white surface, and then with the silver halide emulsion.

Photofinishing laboratories process most amateur and some professional photographers' films and prints. In the 1980s, virtually all of the total business of the laboratories in the United States was in colour processing.

Continuous processing of films

Photofinishing laboratories use machines that carry the films in spliced-together lengths or on racks through successive tanks of the processing solutions. Prints are usually made to standard formats on automatic enlargers, taking both the negatives and the paper in continuous rolls. The paper rolls of 250 or 500 feet are processed in continuous-strip processors, which deliver prints dry and ready for automatic cutting. Many printers have automatic exposure measurement based on overall negative density, with automatically controlled colour correction for colour negatives. High-capacity colour printers of this type can produce 2,000 to 3,000 prints per hour. Coding systems identify individual films and corresponding prints by customer or order number for final re-sorting. More exacting processing services grade colour negatives before printing by light transmission measurements through different colour filters; the resulting exposure data may be punched as edge codes in the film itself or programmed on perforated paper tape. When the tape is run through the printer together with the film, the perforations directly control the colour exposures and corrections. Advanced automatic printing systems may involve electronically controlled image enhancement.

Enlargements to special sizes and colour printing for professional photographers require individual enlarging by skilled personnel on conventional enlargers with advanced automation features of focusing, exposure measurement, and colour control. Other processing services include duplication of transparencies, various types of photocopying (partly on coin-operated copiers set up in public places), microfilming, and microfilm processing.

(L.A.Ma./Ed.)

BIBLIOGRAPHY. General reference works on photography include INTERNATIONAL CENTER OF PHOTOGRAPHY, *Encyclopedia of Photography* (1984); and the volumes in the "Life Library of Photography" series by the editors of Time-Life Books, on the art and history of photography, types of photography, and techniques and processes. See also TURNER BROWNE and ELAINE PARTNOW, *Macmillan Biographical Encyclopedia of Photographic Artists & Innovators* (1983); MICHELE AUER and MICHEL AUER, *Encyclopedie internationale des photographes de 1839 a nos jours: Photographers Encyclopaedia International 1839 to the Present* (1985); and COLIN NAYLOR (ed.), *Contemporary Photographers*, 2nd ed. (1988).

The history and art of photography: Historical overviews of the development of the art of photography are provided in ROBERT TAFT, *Photography and the American Scene: A Social History, 1839–1889* (1938, reprinted 1964), the first history of photography in America in the 19th century; HELMUT GERNSHEIM, *Creative Photography: Aesthetic Trends, 1839–1960* (1962); PETER POLLACK, *The Picture History of Photography: From the Earliest Beginnings to the Present Day,* rev. and enl. ed. (1969), especially valuable for its wealth of illustrations; WILLIAM WELLING, *Photography in America: The Formative Years, 1839–1900* (1978, reprinted 1987); PETR TAUSK, *Photography in the 20th Century* (1980; originally published in German, 1977); BEAUMONT NEWHALL, *The History of Photography: From 1839 to the Present,* rev. and enl. ed. (1982), the stylistic development of the art of photography as related to the technological and scientific characteristics of the medium; NAOMI ROSENBLUM, *A World History of Photography* (1984); PETER TURNER (ed.), *American Images: Photography 1945–1980* (1985); and JEAN-CLAUDE LEMAGNY and ANDRÉ ROUILLÉ (eds.), *A History of Photography: Social and Cultural Perspectives* (1987; originally published in French, 1986).

Essays on art and photography can be found in CHARLES H. CAFFIN, *Photography as a Fine Art: The Achievements and Possibilities of Photographic Art in America* (1901, reissued 1972); IRVING PENN, *Moments Preserved: Eight Essays in Photographs and Words* (1960); NATHAN LYONS (ed.), *Photographers on Photography: A Critical Anthology* (1966), essays by photographers from the 1890s to the 1960s; JOHN SZARKOWSKI, *The Photographer's Eye* (1966, reissued 1980), a penetrating examination of photographic aesthetics; AARON SCHARF, *Art and Photography* (1968, reprinted 1986); VOLKER KAHMEN, *Photography as Art* (1974; originally published in German, 1973); JEAN-LUC DAVAL, *Photography, History of an Art* (1982; originally published in French, 1982); BRYAN HOLME (ed.), *Photography as Fine Art* (1983); and ANDY GRUNDBERG and KATHERINE MCCARTHY GAUSS, *Photography and Art: Interactions Since 1946* (1987), photographs from an exhibition.

Studies of particular schools and types of photography include ROBERT DOTY, *Photo Secession: Photography as a Fine Art* (1960, reprinted with title *Photo-Secession: Stieglitz and the Fine-Art Movement in Photography,* 1978), an account of events leading up to and following the founding of the society by Alfred Stieglitz; WILLIAM CULP DARRAH, *Stereo Views: A History of Stereographs in America and Their Collection* (1964); *French Primitive Photography* (1969), a catalog of an exhibition; RICHARD RUDISILL, *Mirror Image: The Influence of the Daguerreotype on American Society* (1971), a thorough survey; VAN DEREN COKE, *The Painter and the Photograph: From Delacroix to Warhol,* rev. and enl. ed. (1972), an exhibition catalog; BEAUMONT NEWHALL, *The Daguerreotype in America,* 3rd rev. ed. (1976), a study of the industry as well as the art of daguerreotyping; BEN MADDOW, *Faces: A Narrative History of the Portrait in Photography* (1977); MARGARET HARKER, *The Linked Ring: The Secession Movement in Photography in Britain, 1892–1910* (1979); VAN DEREN COKE, *Avant-Garde Photography in Germany, 1919–1939,* trans. from German (1982); RAINER FABIAN and HANS-CHRISTIAN ADAM, *Masters of Early Travel Photography* (1983; originally published in German, 1981); and *Bauhaus Photography* (1985; originally published in German, 1982). See also BEAUMONT NEWHALL and NANCY NEWHALL (eds.), *Masters of Photography* (1958, reissued 1982); short biographical sketches of 19 photographers, with representative photographs by each.

Photojournalism as a separate form is discussed in WILSON HICKS, *Words and Pictures: An Introduction to Photojournalism* (1952, reissued 1973); KEN BAYNES (ed.), *Scoop, Scandal, and Strife: A Study of Photography in Newspapers* (1971); and JOHN R. WHITING, *Photography Is a Language* (1946, reprinted 1979). See also STANLEY RAYFIELD, *How Life Gets the Story: Behind the Scenes in Photojournalism* (1955), field experience of photographers from *Life,* presented in the format and photographic essay style of the magazine.

(Be.N./H.E.R.G.)

The technology of photography: General works include *The Focal Encyclopedia of Photography,* rev. ed., 2 vol. (1965, reissued 1977); L.P. CLERC, *Photography: Theory and Practice,* rev. and enl. ed. edited by D.A. SPENCER, 4 vol. (1970–71; originally published in French, 1926), a classic treatise on the technology of photography; *The Theory of the Photographic Process,* 4th

ed. edited by T.H. JAMES (1977), a classic work; C.B. NEBLETTE, *Neblette's Handbook of Photography and Reprography: Materials, Processes, and Systems,* 7th ed. edited by JOHN M. STURGE (1977); *Encyclopedia of Practical Photography,* 14 vol. (1977–79), edited by and published for the Eastman Kodak Company; JOHN HEDGECOE, *The Photographer's Handbook: A Complete Reference Manual of Techniques, Procedures, Equipment, and Styles,* 2nd ed. rev. (1982); and BRUCE PINKARD, *The Photographer's Bible: An Encyclopedic Reference Manual* (1983). See also ALBERT BONI (ed.), *Photographic Literature* (1962), and a supplemental volume, *Photographic Literature, 1960–1970* (1972), an exhaustive and valuable bibliography, listing books and articles, with detailed references to other bibliographies; and BEAUMONT NEWHALL, *Latent Image: The Discovery of Photography* (1967, reissued 1983), helpful for the understanding of the establishment of the medium.

The evolution of photographic techniques is traced in H. FOX TALBOT (WILLIAM HENRY FOX TALBOT), *The Pencil of Nature* (1844–46, reprinted 1969), the inventor's account, illustrated with 24 actual calotypes; GEORGES POTONNIÉE, *The History of the Discovery of Photography* (1936, reissued 1973; originally published in French, 1925), a detailed account of the early days of photography; JOSEF MARIA EDER, *History of Photography* (1945, reprinted 1978; originally published in German, 4th rev. ed., 2 vol., 1932), a pioneer Austrian work that deals primarily with the scientific and technological development of photography; BEAUMONT NEWHALL (ed.), *On Photography: A Sourcebook of Photo History in Facsimile* (1956), an anthology of the inventors' own accounts of various processes; D.B. THOMAS, *The First Negatives: An Account of the Discovery and Early Use of the Negative-Positive Photographic Process* (1964); JOSEPH S. FRIEDMAN, *The History of Color Photography,* 2nd ed. (1968); HELMUT GERNSHEIM, *The History of Photography from the Camera Obscura to the Beginning of the Modern Era,* 2nd ed. (1969), the first part of which was revised as *The Origins of Photography* (1982); and GAIL BUCKLAND, *Fox Talbot and the Invention of Photography* (1980).

See also WOLFGANG BAIER, *Quellendarstellungen zur Geschichte der Fotografie: A Source Book of Photographic History* (1963, reissued 1977), detailed bibliographies and references to the literature on photographic developments, with an introduction in English.

Camera history and technology is outlined in LESLIE D. STROEBEL, *View Camera Technique,* 5th ed. (1986), on the use of studio and field cameras in industrial, commercial, and other applications; MICHEL AUER, *The Illustrated History of the Camera from 1839 to the Present,* trans. from French and adapted by D.B. TUBBS (1975); BRIAN COE, *Cameras: From Daguerreotypes to Instant Pictures* (1978); and EATON S. LOTHROP, JR., *A Century of Cameras from the Collection of the International Museum of Photography at George Eastman House,* rev. and expanded ed. (1982).

Lenses and optical principles are described in C.B. NEBLETTE and ALLEN E. MURRAY, *Photographic Lenses,* rev. ed. (1973); ARTHUR COX, *Photographic Optics: A Modern Approach to the Technique of Definition,* 15th rev. ed. (1974), classic manual of lens principles and use; and SIDNEY F. RAY, *The Photographic Lens* (1979), an introduction.

Film and the techniques of taking pictures are examined in WALTER NURNBERG, *Lighting for Photography: Means and Methods,* 16th rev. ed. (1968, reissued 1971), an analysis of illumination techniques; and MICHAEL LANGFORD, *Basic Photography,* 5th ed. (1986), and *Advanced Photography: A Grammar of Techniques,* 4th ed. (1980), manuals of practical technique for professional photographers.

Film processing and printing are the subject of D.H.O. JOHN and G.T.J. FIELD, *A Textbook of Photographic Chemistry* (1963), basics of chemical reactions in black-and-white processing; C.I. JACOBSON and R.E. JACOBSON, *Developing: The Negative-Technique,* 18th ed. (1972), manual of all aspects of negative technique; C.I. JACOBSON and L.A. MANNHEIM, *Enlarging,* 22nd ed. (1975), manual of positive technique in black and white and colour; L.F.A. MASON, *Photographic Processing Chemistry,* 2nd ed. (1975), detailed treatment of processing mechanisms and reactions; GRANT HAIST, *Modern Photographic Processing,* 2 vol. (1979), chemistry and technology of black-and-white and colour processing; and JAN ARNOW, *Handbook of Alternative Photographic Processes* (1982).

Colour photography is treated in LOUIS WALTON SIPLEY, *A Half Century of Color* (1951); RALPH M. EVANS, W.T. HANSON, JR., and W. LYLE BREWER, *Principles of Color Photography* (1953), principles of colour rendering, response, and reproduction; D.A. SPENCER, *Colour Photography in Practice,* rev. ed. by L.A. MANNHEIM and VISCOUNT HANWORTH (1966, reissued 1975), containing both theory and practical techniques; R.W.G. HUNT, *The Reproduction of Colour,* 3rd ed. (1975), a standard handbook on colour photography, television, and printing, with moderately advanced mathematical treatment; and GERT

KOSHOFER, *Farbfotographie*, 3 vol. (1981), a complete historical review of all colour processes, including a lexicon of equipment and materials.

Special photographic techniques and applications are the focus of HAROLD E. EDGERTON and JAMES R. KILLIAN, JR., *Flash! Seeing the Unseen by Ultra High-Speed Photography*, 2nd ed. (1954), and *Moments of Vision: The Stroboscopic Revolution in Photography* (1979, reprinted 1984); J. BERGNER, E. GELBKE, and W. MEHLISS, *Practical Photomicrography* (1966; originally

published in German, 1961), a comprehensive manual; R.F. SAXE, *High-Speed Photography* (1966), a condensed but comprehensive survey; JOHN BRACKETT HERSEY (ed.), *Deep-Sea Photography* (1967); C.R. ARNOLD, P.J. ROLLS, and J.C.J. STEWART, *Applied Photography* (1971), on scientific applications; H. LOU GIBSON, *Photography by Infrared: Its Principles and Applications*, 3rd ed. (1978); and GJON MILI, *Gjon Mili: Photographs and Recollections* (1980), on stroboscopic photography.

(H.E.R.G./L.A.Ma.)

Photosynthesis

Photosynthesis, which means putting together with light, is the process by which green plants and certain other organisms transform light energy into chemical energy. During photosynthesis in green plants, light energy is captured and used to convert water, carbon dioxide, and minerals into oxygen and energy-rich organic compounds.

It would be impossible to overestimate the importance of photosynthesis in the maintenance of life on Earth. If photosynthesis ceased, there would soon be little food or other organic matter on Earth. Most organisms would disappear, and in time the Earth's atmosphere would become nearly devoid of gaseous oxygen. The only organisms able to exist under such conditions would be the chemosynthetic bacteria, which can utilize the chemical energy of certain inorganic compounds and thus are not dependent on the conversion of light energy.

Photosynthesis also is responsible for the "fossil fuels" (*i.e.,* coal, oil, and gas) that power industrial society. In past ages, green plants and small organisms that fed on plants increased faster than they were consumed, and their remains were deposited in the Earth's crust by sedimentation and other geological processes. There, protected from oxidation, these organic remains were slowly converted to fossil fuels. These fuels not only provide much of the energy used in factories, homes, and transportation, but

they also serve as the raw material for plastics and other synthetic products. Unfortunately, modern civilization is using up in a few centuries the excess of photosynthetic production accumulated over millions of years.

Requirements for food, materials, and energy in a world where human population is rapidly growing have created a need to increase both the amount of photosynthesis and the efficiency of converting photosynthetic output into products useful to people. One response to these needs—the so-called "Green Revolution"—has achieved enormous improvements in agricultural yield through the use of chemical fertilizers, pest and plant disease control, plant breeding, and mechanized tilling, harvesting, and crop processing. This effort has limited severe famines to a few areas of the world despite rapid population growth, but it has not eliminated widespread malnutrition.

A second agricultural revolution, based on plant genetic engineering, may lead to increases in plant productivity and thereby partially alleviate malnutrition. Since the 1970s, molecular biologists have possessed the means to manipulate a plant's genetic material (DNA) to achieve improvements in disease and drought resistance, product yield and quality, frost hardiness, and other desirable properties. In the future, such genetic engineering may result in improvements in the process of photosynthesis.

This article is divided into the following sections:

GENERAL CHARACTERISTICS

Development of the idea. The study of photosynthesis began in 1771, with observations made by the English chemist Joseph Priestley. Priestley had burned a candle in a closed container until the air within the container could no longer support combustion. He then placed a sprig of mint plant in the container and discovered that after several days the mint had produced some substance (later recognized as oxygen) that enabled the confined air to again support combustion. In 1779 the Dutch physician Jan Ingenhousz expanded upon Priestley's work, showing that the plant must be exposed to light if the combustible substance (*i.e.,* oxygen) was to be restored; he also demonstrated that this process required the presence of the green tissues of the plant.

In 1782 it was demonstrated that the combustion-

supporting gas (oxygen) was formed at the expense of another gas, or "fixed air," which had been identified the year before as carbon dioxide. Gas-exchange experiments in 1804 showed that the gain in weight of a plant grown in a carefully weighed pot was the sum of carbon, which came entirely from absorbed carbon dioxide, and water taken up by plant roots. Almost half a century passed before the concept of chemical energy developed sufficiently to permit the discovery (in 1845) that light energy from the sun is stored as chemical energy in products formed during photosynthesis.

Overall reaction of photosynthesis. In chemical terms, photosynthesis is a light-energized oxidation–reduction process. (Oxidation refers to the removal of electrons from a molecule; reduction refers to the gain of electrons by a molecule.) In plant photosynthesis, the energy of light is used to drive the oxidation of water (H_2O), producing oxygen gas (O_2), hydrogen ions (H^+), and electrons. Most of the removed electrons and hydrogen ions ultimately are transferred to carbon dioxide (CO_2), which is reduced to organic products. Other electrons and hydrogen ions are used to reduce nitrate and sulfate to amino and sulfhydryl groups in amino acids, which are the building blocks of proteins. In most green cells, carbohydrates—especially starch and the sugar sucrose—are the major direct organic products of photosynthesis. The overall reaction in which carbohydrates—represented by the general formula (CH_2O)—are formed during plant photosynthesis can be indicated by the following equation:

$$CO_2 + 2H_2O \xrightarrow[\text{green plants}]{\text{light}} (CH_2O) + O_2 + H_2O.$$

This equation is merely a summary statement, for the process of photosynthesis actually involves numerous complex reactions. These reactions occur in two stages: the "light" stage, consisting of photochemical (*i.e.,* light-dependent) reactions; and the "dark" stage, comprising chemical reactions controlled by enzymes (organic catalysts). During the first stage, the energy of light is absorbed and used to drive a series of electron transfers, resulting in the synthesis of the energy-rich compound adenosine triphosphate (ATP) and the electron donor reduced nicotine adenine dinucleotide phosphate (NADPH). During the dark stage, the ATP and NADPH formed in the light reactions are used to reduce carbon dioxide to organic carbon compounds. This assimilation of inorganic carbon into organic compounds is called carbon fixation.

Origin of oxygen gas in photosynthesis

During the 20th century, comparisons between photosynthetic processes in green plants and in certain photosynthetic sulfur bacteria provided important information about the photosynthetic mechanism. Sulfur bacteria use hydrogen sulfide (H_2S) as a source of hydrogen atoms and produce sulfur instead of oxygen during photosynthesis. The overall reaction is

$$CO_2 + 2H_2S \xrightarrow[\text{sulfur bacteria}]{\text{light}} (CH_2O) + S_2 + H_2O.$$

In the 1930s Dutch biologist Cornelis van Niel recognized that the utilization of carbon dioxide to form organic compounds was similar in the two types of photosynthetic organisms. Suggesting that differences existed in the light-dependent stage and in the nature of the compounds used as a source of hydrogen atoms, he proposed that hydrogen was transferred from hydrogen sulfide (in bacteria) or water (in green plants) to an unknown acceptor (called A), which was reduced to H_2A. During the dark reactions, which are similar in both bacteria and green plants, the reduced acceptor (H_2A) reacted with carbon dioxide (CO_2) to form carbohydrate (CH_2O) and to oxidize the unknown acceptor to A. This putative reaction can be represented as:

$$CO_2 + 2H_2A \xrightarrow{\text{light}} (CH_2O) + 2A + H_2O.$$

Van Niel's proposal was important because the popular (but incorrect) theory had been that oxygen was removed from carbon dioxide (rather than hydrogen from water) and that carbon then combined with water to form carbohydrate (rather than the hydrogen from water combining with CO_2 to form CH_2O).

By 1940 chemists were using heavy isotopes to follow the reactions of photosynthesis. Water marked with an isotope of oxygen (^{18}O) was used in early experiments. Plants that photosynthesized in the presence of water containing $H_2{}^{18}O$ produced oxygen gas containing ^{18}O; those that photosynthesized in the presence of normal water produced normal oxygen gas. These results provided strong support for van Niel's theory that the oxygen gas produced during photosynthesis is derived from water.

Basic products of photosynthesis. As has been stated, carbohydrates are the most important direct organic product of photosynthesis in the majority of green plants. The

Glucose

formation of a simple carbohydrate, glucose, is indicated by a chemical equation,

$$6CO_2 + 12H_2O \xrightarrow[\text{green plants}]{\text{light}} C_6H_{12}O_6 + 6O_2 + 6H_2O.$$

carbon water   glucose oxygen water
dioxide

Little free glucose is produced in plants; instead, glucose units are linked together to form starch or are joined with fructose, another sugar, to form sucrose (see BIOCHEMICAL COMPONENTS OF ORGANISMS: *Carbohydrates*).

Synthesis of other organic components

Not only carbohydrates, as was once thought, but also amino acids, proteins, lipids (or fats), pigments, and other organic components of green tissues are synthesized during photosynthesis. Minerals supply the elements (*e.g.,* nitrogen, N; phosphorus, P; sulfur, S) required to form these compounds. Chemical bonds are broken between oxygen (O) and carbon (C), hydrogen (H), nitrogen, and sulfur, and new bonds are formed in products that include gaseous oxygen (O_2) and organic compounds. More energy is required to break the bonds between oxygen and other elements (*e.g.,* in water, nitrate, and sulfate) than is released when new bonds form in the products. This difference in bond energy accounts for a large part of the light energy stored as chemical energy in the organic products formed during photosynthesis. Additional energy is stored in making complex molecules from simple ones.

Evolution of the process. Although life and the quality of the atmosphere today depend on photosynthesis, it is likely that green plants evolved long after the first living cells. When the Earth was young, electrical storms and solar radiation probably provided the energy for the synthesis of complex molecules from abundant simpler ones, such as water, ammonia, and methane. The first living cells probably evolved from these complex molecules (see LIFE). For example, the accidental joining together (condensation) of the amino acid glycine and the fatty acid acetate may have formed complex organic molecules known as porphyrins; these molecules, in turn, may have evolved further into coloured molecules called pigments; *e.g.,* chlorophylls of green plants, bacteriochlorophyll of photosynthetic bacteria, hemin (the red pigment of blood), and cytochromes, a group of pigment molecules essential in both photosynthesis and cellular respiration.

Primitive coloured cells then had to evolve mechanisms for using the light energy absorbed by their pigments. At first, the energy may have been used immediately to initiate reactions useful to the cell. As the process for utilization of light energy continued to evolve, however, a larger part of the absorbed light energy probably was stored as chemical energy, to be used as required in the processes necessary to maintain life. Green plants, with their ability to use light energy to convert carbon dioxide and water to carbohydrates and oxygen, are the culmination of this evolutionary process.

The first oxygenic (oxygen-producing) cells probably were the cyanophytes, or "blue-green algae," which appeared about 2,000,000,000 to 3,000,000,000 years ago. These microscopic organisms are believed to have greatly increased the oxygen content of the atmosphere, making possible the development of aerobic (oxygen-using) organisms. Cyanophytes are prokaryotic cells; that is, they contain no distinct, membrane-enclosed subcellular particles (organelles), such as nuclei and chloroplasts. Green plants, by contrast, are composed of eukaryotic cells, in which the photosynthetic apparatus is contained within membrane-bound chloroplasts. There is a theory that the first photosynthetic eukaryotes were red algae that may have developed when nonphotosynthetic eukaryotic cells engulfed cyanophytes. Within the host cells, these cyanophytes are thought to have evolved into chloroplasts. Alternatively, the ancestors of chloroplasts in green plants may have been another oxygenic prokaryote like *Prochloron,* an organism that has been found only growing symbiotically inside ascidians.

There are a number of photosynthetic bacteria that are not oxygenic (*e.g.,* the sulfur bacteria previously discussed). The evolutionary pathway that led to these bacteria diverged from the one that resulted in oxygenic organisms. In addition to the absence of oxygen production, nonoxygenic photosynthesis differs from oxygenic photosynthesis in two other ways: light of longer wavelengths is absorbed and used by pigments called bacteriochlorophylls, and reduced compounds other than water (such as hydrogen sulfide or organic molecules) provide the electrons needed for the reduction of carbon dioxide.

Bacterial photosynthesis

FACTORS THAT INFLUENCE THE RATE OF PHOTOSYNTHESIS

The rate of photosynthesis is defined in terms of the rate of oxygen production either per unit mass (or area) of green plant tissues or per unit weight of total chlorophyll. The amount of light, the carbon dioxide supply, the temperature, the water supply, and the availability of minerals are the most important environmental factors that directly affect the rate of photosynthesis in land plants. The rate of photosynthesis also is determined by the plant species and its physiological state; *e.g.,* its health, its maturity, and whether or not it is in flower.

Light intensity and temperature. As has been mentioned, the complex mechanism of photosynthesis includes a photochemical, or light-dependent, stage and an enzymatic, or dark, stage that involves chemical reactions. These stages can be distinguished by studying the rates of photosynthesis at various degrees of light saturation (*i.e.,* intensity) and at different temperatures. Over a range of moderate temperatures and at low to medium light intensities (relative to the normal range of the plant species), the rate of photosynthesis increases as the intensity increases and is independent of temperature. As the light intensity increases to higher levels, however, the rate becomes increasingly dependent on temperature and less dependent on intensity; light "saturation" is achieved at a specific light intensity, and the rate then is dependent only on temperature if all other factors are constant. In the light-dependent range before saturation, therefore, the rate of photosynthesis is determined by the rates of photochemical steps. At high light intensities, some of the chemical reactions of the dark stage become rate-limiting. At light saturation, rate increases with temperature until a point is reached beyond which no further rate increase can occur. In many land plants, moreover, a process called photorespiration occurs at high light intensities and temperatures. Photorespiration competes with photosynthesis and limits further increases in the rate of photosynthesis, especially if the supply of water is limited (see below *Photorespiration*).

Carbon dioxide. Included among the rate-limiting steps of the dark stage of photosynthesis are the chemical reactions by which organic compounds are formed using carbon dioxide as a carbon source. The rates of these reactions can be increased somewhat by increasing the carbon dioxide concentration. During the past century, the level of carbon dioxide in the atmosphere has been rising due to the extensive combustion of fossil fuels. The atmospheric level of carbon dioxide climbed from about 0.028 percent in 1860 to 0.0315 percent by 1958 (when improved measurements began), and to 0.034 percent by 1981. This increase in carbon dioxide directly increases plant photosynthesis, but the size of the increase depends on the species and physiological condition of the plant. Furthermore, if increasing levels of atmospheric carbon dioxide result in climatic changes, including increased global temperatures as some meteorologists predict, these changes will affect photosynthesis rates.

Water. For land plants, water availability can function as a limiting factor in photosynthesis and plant growth. Besides the requirement for water in the photosynthetic reaction itself, water is transpired from the leaves; that is, water evaporates from the leaves to the atmosphere via the stomates. These stomates are small openings through the leaf epidermis, or outer skin; they permit the entry of carbon dioxide but also allow the exit of water vapour. The stomates open and close according to the physiological needs of the leaf. In hot and arid climates the stomates may close to conserve water, but this closure limits the entry of carbon dioxide and hence the rate of photosynthesis, while the wasteful process of photorespiration may increase. If the level of carbon dioxide in the atmosphere increases, more carbon dioxide could enter through a smaller opening of the stomates, so that more photosynthesis could occur with a given supply of water.

Minerals. Several minerals are required for healthy plant growth and for maximum rates of photosynthesis. Nitrate or ammonia, sulfate, phosphate, iron, magnesium, and potassium are required in substantial amounts for the synthesis of amino acids, proteins, coenzymes, de-oxyribonucleic acid (DNA) and ribonucleic acid (RNA), chlorophyll and other pigments, and other essential plant constituents. Smaller amounts of such elements as manganese, copper, and chlorine are required in photosynthesis. Some other trace elements are needed for various nonphotosynthetic functions in plants.

Internal factors. Each plant species adapts to a range of environmental factors. Within this normal range of conditions, complex regulatory mechanisms in the plant's cells adjust the activities of enzymes (*i.e.,* organic catalysts). These adjustments maintain a balance in the overall photosynthetic process and control it in accordance with the needs of the whole plant. With a given plant species, for example, doubling the carbon dioxide level might cause a temporary increase of nearly twofold in the rate of photosynthesis; a few hours later, however, the rate might fall to the original level because photosynthesis had made more sucrose than the rest of the plant could use. By contrast, another plant species provided with such carbon dioxide enrichment might be able to use more sucrose and would continue to photosynthesize and to grow faster throughout most of its life cycle.

ENERGY EFFICIENCY OF PHOTOSYNTHESIS

The energy efficiency of photosynthesis is the ratio of the energy stored to the energy of light absorbed. The chemical energy stored is the difference between that contained in gaseous oxygen and organic compound products and the energy of water, carbon dioxide, and other reactants. The amount of energy stored can only be estimated because many products are formed, and these vary with the plant species and environmental conditions. If the equation for glucose formation given earlier is used to approximate the actual storage process, the production of one mole (*i.e.,* 6.02×10^{23} molecules; abbreviated N) of oxygen and one-sixth mole of glucose results in the storage of about 117 kilocalories (kcal) of chemical energy. This amount must then be compared to the energy of light absorbed to produce one mole of oxygen in order to calculate the efficiency of photosynthesis.

Light can be described as a wave of particles known as photons; these are units of energy, or light quanta. The quantity N photons is called an einstein. The energy of light varies inversely with the length of the photon waves; that is, the shorter the wavelength, the greater the energy content. The energy (e) of a photon is given by the equation $e = hc/\lambda$, where c is the velocity of light, h is Planck's constant, and λ is the light wavelength. The energy (E) of an einstein is $E = Ne = Nhc/\lambda = 28,600/\lambda$, when E is in kilocalories and λ is given in nanometres (nm; 1 nm = 10^{-9} metres). An einstein of red light with a wavelength of 680 nm has an energy of about 42 kcal. Blue light has a shorter wavelength and therefore more energy than red light. Regardless of whether the light is blue or red, however, the same number of einsteins are required for photosynthesis per mole of oxygen formed. The part of the solar spectrum used by plants has an estimated mean wavelength of 570 nanometres; therefore, the energy of light used during photosynthesis is approximately 28,600/570, or 50 kilocalories per einstein.

In order to compute the amount of light energy involved in photosynthesis, one other value is needed: the number of einsteins absorbed per mole of oxygen evolved. This is called the quantum requirement. The minimum quantum requirement for photosynthesis under optimal conditions is about nine. Thus the energy used is 9×50, or 450 kilocalories per mole of oxygen evolved. Therefore, the estimated maximum energy efficiency of photosynthesis is the energy stored per mole of oxygen evolved—117 kilocalories—divided by 450; that is, 117/450, or 26 percent.

The actual percentage of solar energy stored by plants is much less than the maximum energy efficiency of photosynthesis. An agricultural crop in which the biomass (total dry weight) stores as much as 1 percent of total solar energy received on an annual area-wide basis is exceptional, although a few cases of higher yields (perhaps as much as 3.5 percent in sugarcane) are reported. There are several reasons for this difference between the predicted maximum efficiency of photosynthesis and the actual energy stored in biomass. First, more than half of the incident sunlight is composed of wavelengths too long to be absorbed, while some of the remainder is reflected or lost to the leaves. Consequently, plants can at best absorb only about 34 percent of the incident sunlight. Second, plants must carry out a variety of physiological processes in such nonphotosynthetic tissues as roots and stems; these processes, as well as cellular respiration in all parts of the plant, use up stored energy. Third, rates of photosynthesis in bright sunlight sometimes exceed the needs of the plants, resulting in the formation of excess sugars and starch. When this happens, the regulatory mechanisms of the plant slow down the process of photosynthesis, allowing more absorbed sunlight to go unused. Fourth, in many plants, energy is wasted by the process of photorespiration. Finally, the growing season may last only a few months of the year; sunlight received during other seasons is not used. Furthermore, it should be noted that if only agricultural products (*e.g.,* seeds, fruits, and tubers, rather than total biomass) are considered as the end product of the energy conversion process of photosynthesis, the efficiency falls even further.

CHLOROPLASTS, THE PHOTOSYNTHETIC UNITS OF GREEN PLANTS

The process of plant photosynthesis takes place entirely within the chloroplasts. Detailed studies of the role of these organelles date from the work of the British biochemist Robert Hill. About 1940 Hill discovered that green particles obtained from broken cells could produce oxygen from water in the presence of light and a chemical compound, such as ferric oxalate, able to serve as an electron acceptor. This process is known as the Hill reaction. During the 1950s Daniel Arnon and other American biochemists prepared plant cell fragments in which not only the Hill reaction but also the synthesis of the energy-storage compound ATP occurred. In addition, the coenzyme NADP was used as the final acceptor of electrons, replacing the nonphysiological electron acceptors used by Hill. His procedures were refined further so that individual small pieces of isolated chloroplast membranes, or lamellae, could perform the Hill reaction. These small pieces of lamellae were then fragmented into pieces so small that they performed only the light reactions of the photosynthetic process. It is now possible also to isolate the entire chloroplast so that it can carry out the complete process of photosynthesis, from light absorption, oxygen formation, and the reduction of carbon dioxide to the formation of glucose and other products.

Structural features. The intricate structural organization of the photosynthetic apparatus is essential for the efficient performance of the complex process of photosynthesis. The chloroplast is enclosed in a double outer membrane, and its size approximates a spheroid about 2,500 nanometres thick and 5,000 nanometres long. Some single-celled algae have one chloroplast that occupies more than half the cell volume. Leaf cells of higher plants contain many chloroplasts, each approximately the size of the one in some algal cells.

When thin sections of a chloroplast are examined under the electron microscope (Figure 1), several features are apparent. Chief among these are the intricate internal membranes (*i.e.,* the lamellae) and the stroma, a colourless matrix in which the lamellae are embedded. Also visible are starch granules, which appear as dense bodies.

The stroma is basically a solution of enzymes and small molecules. The dark reactions occur in the stroma, the soluble enzymes of which catalyze the conversion of carbon dioxide and minerals to carbohydrates and other organic compounds. The capacity for carbon fixation and reduction is lost if the outer membrane of the chloroplast is broken, allowing the stroma enzymes to leak out.

A single lamella, which contains all the photosynthetic pigments, is approximately 10–15 nanometres thick. The lamellae exist in more-or-less flat sheets, a few of which extend through much of the length of the chloroplast. Examination of cross sections of lamellae under the electron microscope shows that their edges are joined to form closed hollow disks that are called thylakoids ("saclike").

The Hill reaction

Size and shape

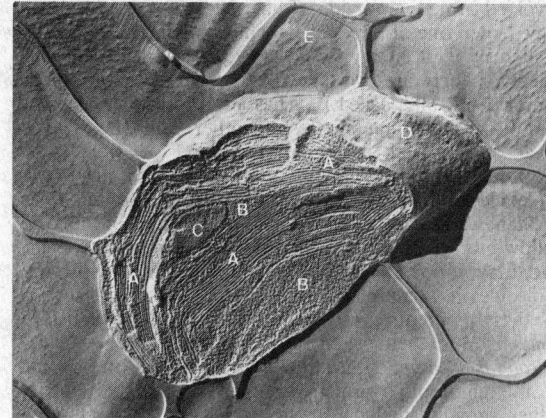

Figure 1: *Electron micrograph of an isolated spinach chloroplast prepared by the freeze-etching method.*
(A) Lamellae, which are layers of lipid and protein with chlorophyll, other pigments, and enzymes, are the sites of light absorption and splitting of the water to give oxygen and hydrogen. (B) Stroma, containing soluble enzymes, is the site of conversion of carbon dioxide and hydrogen to carbohydrates. (C) Starch granule is a storage product of photosynthesis. (D) Surface of the chloroplast, and (E) frozen solution in which the chloroplast was suspended.
By courtesy of the University of California, Lawrence Berkeley Laboratory

The chloroplasts of most higher plants have regions, called grana, in which the thylakoids are very tightly stacked. When viewed by electron microscopy at an oblique angle, the grana appear as stacks of disks. When viewed in cross section (Figure 1), it is apparent that some thylakoids extend from one grana through the stroma into other grana. The thin aqueous spaces inside the thylakoids are believed to be connected with each other via these stroma thylakoids. These thylakoid spaces are isolated from the stroma spaces by the relatively impermeable lamellae.

The light reactions occur exclusively in the thylakoids. The complex structural organization of lamellae is required for proper thylakoid function; intact thylakoids apparently are necessary for the formation of ATP. Thylakoids that have been broken down to smaller units can no longer form ATP, even when the conversion of light into chemical energy occurs during electron transport in these units. Such lamellar fragments can carry out the Hill reaction, with the transfer of electrons from water to $NADP^+$.

Chemical composition of lamellae. *Lipids.* Lamellae consist of about equal amounts of lipids and proteins. About one-fourth of the lipid portion of the lamellae consists of pigments and coenzymes; the remainder consists of various lipids, including polar compounds such as phospholipids and galactolipids. These polar lipid molecules have "head" groups that attract water (*i.e.,* are hydrophilic) and fatty acid "tails" that are oil soluble and repel water (*i.e.,* are hydrophobic). When polar lipids are placed in an aqueous environment, they can line up with the fatty acid tails side by side. A second layer of phospholipids forms tail-to-tail with the first, establishing a lipid bilayer in which the hydrophilic heads are in contact with the aqueous solution on each side of the bilayer. Sandwiched between the heads are the hydrophobic tails, creating a hydrophobic environment from which water is excluded. This lipid bilayer is an essential feature of all biological membranes (see CELLS: *The biological membrane*). The hydrophobic parts of proteins and lipid-soluble cofactors and pigments are dissolved or embedded in the lipid bilayer. Lamellar membranes can function as electrical insulating material and permit a charge, or potential difference, to develop across the membrane. Such a charge can be a source of chemical or electrical energy.

Approximately one-fifth of the lamellar lipids are chlorophyll molecules; one type, chlorophyll *a,* is more abundant than the second type, chlorophyll *b.* The chlorophyll molecules are specifically bound to small protein molecules. Most of these chlorophyll-proteins are "light-harvesting" pigments. These absorb light and pass its energy on to special chlorophyll *a* molecules that are directly

Grana

involved in the conversion of light energy to chemical energy. When one of these special chlorophyll a molecules is excited by light energy (as described later), it gives up an electron. There are two types of these special chlorophyll a molecules: one, called P_{680}, has an absorption spectrum that peaks at 684 nanometres; the other, called P_{700}, shows an absorption peak at 700 nanometres.

Pigments

Although chlorophylls are the main light-absorbing molecules in green plants, other pigments such as carotenes and carotenoids (which are responsible for the yellow-orange colour of carrots) also can absorb light and may supplement chlorophyll as the light-absorbing molecules in some plant cells. The light energy absorbed by these pigments must be passed to chlorophyll before conversion to chemical energy can occur.

Proteins. Many of the lamellar proteins are components of the chlorophyll–protein complexes described above. Other proteins include enzymes and protein-containing coenzymes. Enzymes are required as organic catalysts for specific reactions within the lamellae. Protein coenzymes,

Electron carrier molecules

also called cofactors, include important electron carrier molecules called cytochromes, which are iron-containing pigments with the pigment portions attached to protein molecules. During electron transfer, an electron is accepted by an iron atom in the pigment portion of a cytochrome molecule, which thus is reduced; then the electron is transferred to the iron atom in the next cytochrome carrier in the electron transfer chain, thus oxidizing the first cytochrome and reducing the next one in the chain.

In addition to the metal atoms found in the pigment portions of cytochrome molecules, metal atoms also are found in other protein molecules of the lamellae. In proteins with a total molecular weight of 900,000 (based on the weight of hydrogen as one), there are two atoms of manganese, 10 atoms of iron, and six atoms of copper. These metal atoms are required for the catalytic activity of some of the enzymes important in photosynthesis. The manganese atoms are involved in water-splitting and oxygen formation. Both copper- and iron-containing proteins function in electron transport between water and the final electron-acceptor molecule of the light stage of photosynthesis, an iron-containing protein called ferredoxin. Ferredoxin is a soluble component in the chloroplasts. In its reduced form, it gives electrons directly to the systems that reduce nitrate and sulfate and via NADPH to the system that reduces carbon dioxide. A copper-containing protein called plastocyanin (PC) carries electrons at one point in the electron transport chain. PC molecules are water soluble and can move through the inner space of the thylakoids, carrying electrons from one place to another.

Quinones. Small molecules called plastoquinones are found in substantial numbers in the lamellae. Like the cytochromes, quinones have important roles in carrying electrons between the components of the light reactions. Since they are lipid soluble, they can diffuse through the membrane. They can carry one or two electrons and, in their reduced form (with added electrons), they carry hydrogen atoms that can be released as hydrogen ions when the added electrons are passed on, for example, to a cytochrome.

THE PROCESS OF PHOTOSYNTHESIS: THE LIGHT REACTIONS

Light absorption and energy transfer. The light energy absorbed by a chlorophyll molecule excites some electrons within the structure of the molecule to higher energy levels, or excited states. Light of shorter wavelength (such as blue) has more energy than light of longer wavelength (such as red), so that absorption of blue light creates an excited state of higher energy. A molecule raised to this higher energy state quickly gives up the "extra" energy as heat and falls to its lowest excited state. This lowest excited state is similar to that of a molecule that has just absorbed the longest wavelength light capable of exciting it. In the case of chlorophyll a, this lowest excited state corresponds to that of a molecule that has absorbed red light of about 680 nanometres.

The return of a chlorophyll a molecule from its lowest excited state to its original low-energy state (ground state)

requires the release of the extra energy of the excited state. This can occur in one of several ways. In photosynthesis, most of this energy is conserved as chemical energy by the transfer of an electron from a special chlorophyll a molecule (P_{680} or P_{700}) to an electron acceptor. When this electron transfer is blocked by inhibitors, such as the herbicide dichlorophenylmethylurea (DCMU), or by low temperature, the energy can be released as red light. Such re-emission of light is called fluorescence. The examination of fluorescence from photosynthetic material in which electron transfer has been blocked has proved to be a useful tool for scientists studying the light reactions.

The pathway of electrons. The general features of a widely accepted mechanism for photoelectron transfer, in which two light reactions occur during the transfer of electrons from water to carbon dioxide, were proposed by Robert Hill and Derek Bendall, in 1960. A modified scheme for this mechanism is shown in Figure 2. In this figure the vertical scale represents the relative potential (in volts) of various cofactors of the electron-transfer chain to be oxidized or reduced. Molecules that in their oxidized form have the strongest affinity for electrons (*i.e.,* are strong oxidizing agents) are near the bottom of the scale. Molecules that in their oxidized form are difficult to reduce are near the top of the scale; once they have accepted electrons, these molecules are strong reducing agents.

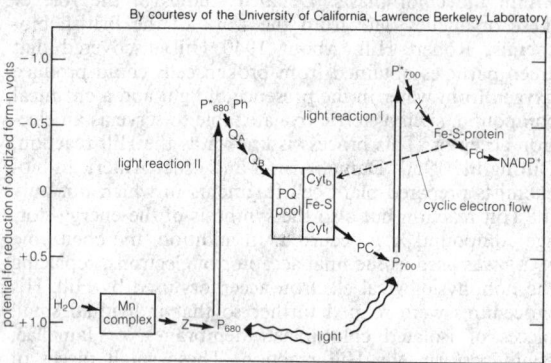

By courtesy of the University of California, Lawrence Berkeley Laboratory

Figure 2: *Flow of electrons during the light reaction stage of photosynthesis.*
Arrows pointing upward represent light reactions that increase the chemical potential; arrows slanting downward represent flow of electrons via carriers in the membrane (see text).

The actual photochemical steps are indicated by the two vertical arrows, which signify that the special pigments P_{680} and P_{700} receive light energy from the light-harvesting chlorophyll-protein molecules and are raised in energy from their ground state to excited states, symbolized as P^*_{680} and P^*_{700}. In their excited state, these pigments are extremely strong reducing agents that quickly transfer electrons to the first acceptor. These first acceptors also are strong reducing agents and rapidly pass electrons to more stable carriers. In light reaction II the first acceptor may be pheophytin (Ph; a molecule similar to chlorophyll), which also has a strong reducing potential and quickly transfers electrons to the next acceptor. Q_A and Q_B are special quinones, similar to plastoquinone. They receive electrons from pheophytin and pass them to the intermediate electron carriers, which include the plastoquinone (PQ) pool and the cytochromes b and f (Cyt_b and Cyt_f) associated in a complex with an iron-sulfur protein (Fe-S).

Electron transfer chains

In light reaction I the identity of the first electron acceptor, X, is not known. It passes electrons on to iron-sulfur proteins (Fe-S-protein) in the lamellar membrane, after which the electrons flow to ferredoxin (Fd), a small, water-soluble iron-sulfur protein. When NADP+ and a suitable enzyme are present, two ferredoxin molecules, carrying one electron each, transfer two electrons to NADP+, which picks up a proton (*i.e.,* a hydrogen ion) and becomes NADPH.

Each time a P_{680} or P_{700} molecule gives up an electron, it returns to its ground (unexcited) state, but with a positive charge due to the loss of the electron. These positively charged ions are extremely strong oxidizing agents that remove an electron from a suitable donor. The P_{680}+ of

Reduction of P_{680}+ and P_{700}+

light reaction II is capable of taking electrons from water in the presence of appropriate catalysts. There is good evidence that two or more manganese atoms complexed with protein are involved in this catalysis, taking four electrons from two water molecules (with release of four hydrogen ions). The manganese-protein complex gives up these electrons one at a time via an unidentified carrier Z to P_{680}^+, reducing it to P_{680}. When manganese is selectively removed by chemical treatment, the thylakoids lose the capacity to oxidize water, but all other parts of the electron pathway remain intact.

In light reaction I, P_{700}^+ recovers electrons from plastocyanin (PC), which in turn receives them from intermediate carriers, including the plastoquinone pool and cytochrome b and cytochrome f molecules. The pool of intermediate carriers may receive electrons from water via light reaction II and Q_A and Q_B. Transfer of electrons from water to ferredoxin via the two light reactions and intermediate carriers is called noncyclic electron flow. Alternately, electrons may be transferred only by light reaction I, in which case they are recycled from ferredoxin back to the intermediate carriers (dashed line, Figure 2). This process is called cyclic electron flow.

Evidence of two light reactions. Many lines of evidence support the concept of electron flow via two light reactions. An early study by the U.S. biochemist Robert Emerson employed the algae *Chlorella,* which was illuminated with red light alone, with blue light alone, and with red and blue light at the same time. Oxygen evolution was measured in each case. It was substantial with blue light alone but not with red light alone. With both red and blue light together, the amount of oxygen evolved far exceeded the sum of that seen with blue and red light alone. These experimental data pointed to the existence of two types of light reactions that, when operating in tandem, would yield the highest rate of oxygen evolution. It is now known that light reaction I can use light of a slightly longer wavelength than red ($\lambda = 680$ nanometres), while light reaction II requires light with a wavelength of 680 nanometres or shorter.

Since those early studies, the two light reactions have been separated in many ways, including separation of the membrane particles in which each reaction occurs. As discussed previously, lamellae can be disrupted mechanically into fragments that absorb light energy and break the bonds of water molecules (*i.e.*, oxidize water) to produce oxygen, hydrogen ions, and electrons. These electrons can be transferred to ferredoxin, the final electron acceptor of the light stage. No transfer of electrons from water to ferredoxin occurs if the herbicide DCMU is present. The subsequent addition of certain reduced dyes (*i.e.*, electron donors) restores the light reduction of $NADP^+$ but without oxygen production, suggesting that light reaction I but not light reaction II is functioning. It is now known that DCMU blocks the transfer of electrons from Q_A to the PQ pool (see Figure 2).

Lamellar fragments

When treated with certain detergents, lamellae can be broken down into smaller particles capable of carrying out single light reactions. One type of particle can absorb light energy, oxidize water, and produce oxygen (light reaction II), but a special dye molecule must be supplied to accept the electrons. In the presence of electron donors, such as a reduced dye, a second type of lamellar particle can absorb light and transfer electrons from the electron donor to ferredoxin (light reaction I).

Photosystems I and II. The structural and photochemical properties of the minimum particles capable of performing light reactions I and II have received much study. Treatment of lamellar fragments with neutral detergents releases these particles, designated photosystem I and photosystem II, respectively. Subsequent harsher treatment (with charged detergents) and separation of the individual polypeptides with electrophoretic techniques has helped identify the components of each photosystem. Each consists of a light-harvesting complex and core complex. Each core complex contains a reaction centre with the pigment (either P_{700} or P_{680}) that can be photochemically oxidized, together with electron acceptors and electron donors. In addition, the core complex has some 40 to 60 chlorophyll molecules bound to proteins. Besides the light absorbed by the chlorophyll molecules in the core complex, the reaction centres receive a major part of their excitation from the pigments of the light-harvesting complex.

Quantum requirements. The quantum requirements of the individual light reactions of photosynthesis are defined as the number of light photons absorbed for the transfer of one electron. The quantum requirement for each light reaction has been found to be approximately one photon. The total number of quanta required, therefore, to transfer the four electrons that result in the formation of one molecule of oxygen via the two light reactions should be four times two, or eight. It appears, however, that additional light is absorbed and used to form ATP by a cyclic photophosphorylation pathway (see next section). The actual quantum requirement, therefore, probably is nine to 10.

THE PROCESS OF PHOTOSYNTHESIS: THE CONVERSION OF LIGHT ENERGY TO ATP

The electron transfers of the light reactions provide the energy for the synthesis of two compounds vital to the dark reactions: NADPH and ATP. The previous section explained how noncyclic electron flow results in the reduction of $NADP^+$ to NADPH. In this section, the synthesis of the energy-rich compound ATP is described.

ATP is formed by the addition of a phosphate group to a molecule of adenosine diphosphate (ADP); or to state it in chemical terms, by the phosphorylation of ADP. This reaction requires a substantial input of energy, much of which is captured in the bond that links the added phosphate group to ADP. Because light energy powers this reaction in the chloroplasts, the production of ATP during photosynthesis is referred to as photophosphorylation.

Unlike the production of NADPH, the photophosphorylation of ADP occurs in conjunction with both cyclic and noncyclic electron flow (see Figure 2). In fact researchers speculate that the sole purpose of cyclic electron flow may be for photophosphorylation, since this process involves no net transfer of electrons to reducing agents. The relative amounts of cyclic and noncyclic flow may be adjusted in accordance with changing physiological needs for ATP and reduced ferrodoxin and NADPH in chloroplasts. In contrast to electron transfer in light reactions I and II, which can occur in membrane fragments, intact thylakoids are required for efficient photophosphorylation. This requirement stems from the special nature of the mechanism linking photophosphorylation to electron flow in the lamellae.

The chemiosmotic theory of ATP formation

The theory relating the formation of ATP to electron flow in the membranes of both chloroplasts and mitochondria (the organelles responsible for ATP formation during cellular respiration) was first proposed by the English biochemist Peter Mitchell. This chemiosmotic theory has been somewhat modified to fit later experimental facts, and there is still debate over many of the details. The general features, however, are widely accepted. A central feature is the formation of a hydrogen ion (proton) concentration gradient and an electrical charge across intact lamellae. The potential energy stored by the proton gradient and electrical charge is then used to drive the energetically unfavourable conversion of ADP and inorganic phosphate (P_i) to ATP and water.

The manganese-protein complex associated with light reaction II is exposed to the interior of the thylakoid. Consequently, the oxidation of water during light reaction II leads to release of hydrogen ions (protons) into the inner thylakoid space. Furthermore, it is likely that photoreaction II entails the transfer of electrons across the lamella toward its outer face, so that when plastoquinone molecules are reduced they can receive protons from the outside of the thylakoid. When these reduced plastoquinone molecules are oxidized, giving up electrons to the cytochrome-iron-sulfur complex, protons are released inside the thylakoid. Because the lamella is impermeable to them, the release of protons inside the thylakoid by oxidation of both water and plastoquinone leads to a higher concentration of protons inside the thylakoid than outside it. In other words, a proton gradient is established across the lamella. The movement of electrons (negatively charged particles) outward across the lamella during both light reactions results in the establishment of an electrical charge across the lamella. (Some scientists believe, however, that the proton gradient and electrical charge required for ATP formation need not be between inner and outer thylakoid space but only within the membrane.)

An enzyme complex located partly in and on the lamellae catalyzes the reaction in which ATP is formed from ADP and inorganic phosphate. The reverse of this reaction is catalyzed by an enzyme called ATP-ase, hence the enzyme complex is sometimes called an ATP-ase complex. It is also called the coupling factor. It consists of hydrophilic polypeptides (F_1), which project from the outer surface of the lamellae, and hydrophobic polypeptides (F_0), which are embedded inside the lamellae. Researchers hypothesize that F_0 forms a channel that permits protons to flow through the lamellar membrane to F_1. The enzymes in F_1 then catalyze ATP formation, using both the proton supply and the lamellar transmembrane charge.

In summary, the use of light energy for ATP formation occurs indirectly: a proton gradient and electrical charge—built up in or across the lamellae as a consequence of electron flow in the light reactions—provide the energy to drive the synthesis of ATP from ADP and P_i.

THE PROCESS OF PHOTOSYNTHESIS: CARBON FIXATION AND REDUCTION

The assimilation of carbon into organic compounds is the result of a complex series of enzymatically regulated chemical reactions—the dark reactions. This term is something of a misnomer, for these reactions can take place in either light or darkness. Furthermore, some of the enzymes involved in the so-called dark reactions become inactive in prolonged darkness.

Elucidation of the carbon pathway. Radioactive isotopes of carbon (^{14}C) and phosphorus (^{32}P) have been valuable in identifying the intermediate compounds formed during carbon assimilation. A photosynthesizing plant does not strongly discriminate between the natural carbon isotopes and ^{14}C. During photosynthesis in the presence of $^{14}CO_2$, the compounds formed become labelled with the radioisotope. During very short exposures, only the first intermediates in the carbon-fixing pathway become labelled. Early investigations showed that some radioactive products were formed even when the light was turned off and the $^{14}CO_2$ was added just afterward in the dark, confirming the nature of the carbon fixation as a "dark" reaction.

The U.S. biochemist Melvin Calvin, a Nobel Prize recipient for his work on the carbon reduction cycle, allowed green plants to photosynthesize in the presence of radioactive carbon dioxide for a few seconds under various experimental conditions. Products that became labelled with radioactive carbon during Calvin's experiments included a three-carbon compound called 3-phosphoglycerate (abbreviated PGA, see Figure 3), sugar phosphates, amino acids, sucrose, and carboxylic acids. When photosynthesis was stopped after two seconds, the principal radioactive product was PGA, which therefore was identified as the first compound formed during carbon dioxide fixation in green plants.

Further studies with ^{14}C as well as with inorganic phosphate labelled with ^{32}P led to the mapping of the carbon fixation and reduction pathway called the reductive pentose phosphate cycle (RPP cycle). An additional pathway for carbon transport in certain plants was later discovered in other laboratories (see below *Carbon fixation via C_4 acids*). All the steps in these pathways can be carried out in the laboratory by isolated enzymes in the dark. Several steps require the ATP or NADPH generated by the light reactions. In addition, some of the enzymes are fully active only when conditions simulate those in green cells exposed to light. In vivo, these enzymes are active during photosynthesis but not in the dark.

The reductive pentose phosphate cycle. *Overall reaction.* The RPP cycle, in which carbon is fixed, reduced, and utilized, involves the formation of intermediate sugar phosphates in a cyclic sequence (Figure 3). One complete RPP cycle incorporates three molecules of carbon dioxide

Margin note: Identification of the first compound formed

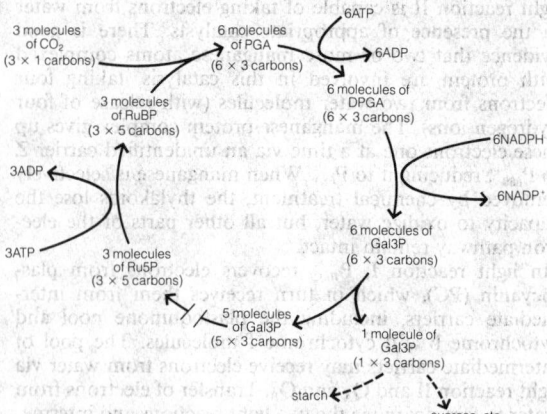

Figure 3: *Pathway of carbon dioxide fixation and reduction in photosynthesis, the reductive pentose phosphate cycle.* The diagram represents one complete turn of the cycle, with the net production of one molecule of Gal3P. The nine molecules of ATP and six molecules of NADPH come from the light reactions (see text).

Adapted from Helena Curtis, *Biology* (1983); reproduced with permission of Worth Publishers, Inc.

and produces one molecule of the three-carbon compound glyceraldehyde-3-phosphate (Gal3P). This three-carbon sugar phosphate usually is either exported from the chloroplasts or is converted to starch (dashed lines).

Figure 3 summarizes the main steps that take place during one complete turn of the RPP cycle. ATP and NADPH formed during the light reactions are utilized for key steps in this pathway and provide the energy and reducing equivalents (*i.e.*, electrons) to drive the sequence in the direction shown. For each molecule of carbon dioxide that is fixed, two molecules of NADPH and three molecules of ATP from the light reactions are required. The overall reaction can be represented as follows:

$$9ATP + 6NADPH + 3CO_2 \longrightarrow Gal3P + 6NADP^+ + 9ADP + 8P_i$$

The cycle is composed of four stages: (1) carboxylation, (2) reduction, (3) isomerization/condensation/dismutation, and (4) phosphorylation.

Carboxylation. The initial incorporation of carbon dioxide, which is catalyzed by the enzyme ribulose 1,5-bisphosphate carboxylase, proceeds by the addition of carbon dioxide to the five-carbon compound ribulose 1,5-bisphosphate (RuBP) and the splitting of the resulting unstable six-carbon compound into two molecules of PGA, a three-carbon compound. As indicated in Figure 3, this reaction occurs three times during each complete turn of the cycle; thus, six molecules of PGA are produced.

Reduction. The six molecules of PGA are first phosphorylated with ATP by the enzyme PGA-kinase, yielding six molecules of 1,3-diphosphoglycerate (DPGA). These then are reduced with NADPH and the enzyme glyceraldehyde-3-phosphate dehydrogenase to give six molecules of Gal3P. These reactions are the reverse of two steps of the process glycolysis in cellular respiration (see METABOLISM).

Isomerization/condensation/dismutation. For every complete RPP cycle, one of the Gal3P molecules, with its three carbon atoms, is the net product and may be transferred out of the chloroplast or converted to starch inside the chloroplast (dashed lines, Figure 3). For the cycle to regenerate, the other five Gal3P molecules (with a total of 15 carbon atoms) must be converted back to three molecules of five-carbon RuBP. The conversion of Gal3P to RuBP begins with a complex series of enzymatically regulated reactions (not shown in Figure 3) that lead to the synthesis of the five-carbon compound ribulose-5-phosphate (Ru5P). The occurrence of this complex series, which entails isomerization, condensation, and dismutation reactions, is indicated by the broken arrow in Figure 3.

Phosphorylation. The three molecules of Ru5P are converted to the carboxylation substrate, RuBP, by the enzyme phosphoribulokinase, using ATP. This reaction, shown below, completes the cycle.

Margin note: Conversion of Gal3P to Ru5P

$$3Ru5P + 3ATP \longrightarrow 3RuBP + 3ADP$$

Regulation of the cycle.

Regulation of the cycle. Photosynthesis cannot occur at night, but the respiratory process of glycolysis—which uses some of the same reactions as the RPP cycle, except in the reverse—does take place. Consequently, some steps in the RPP cycle would be wasteful if allowed to occur in the dark, because they would counteract the reactions of glycolysis and result in the wasteful net consumption of ATP. For this reason, some enzymes of the RPP cycle are "turned off" (*i.e.*, become inactive) in the dark.

Even in the presence of light, changes in physiological conditions frequently necessitate adjustments in the relative rates of reactions of the RPP cycle, so that enzymes for some reactions change in their catalytic activity. These alterations in enzyme activity typically are brought about by changes in levels of such chloroplast components as reduced ferredoxin, acids, and soluble components (*e.g.*, P_i and magnesium ions).

Products of carbon reduction. The most important use of Gal3P is its export from the chloroplasts to the cytoplasm of green cells, where it is used for biosynthesis of products needed by the plant. In land plants, a principal product is sucrose (ordinary table sugar), which is translocated from the green cells of the leaves to other parts of the plant. Other important products include the carbon skeletons of certain primary amino acids, such as alanine, glutamate, and aspartate. To complete the synthesis of these compounds, amino groups are added to the appropriate carbon skeletons made from Gal3P. Sulfur amino acids such as cysteine are formed by adding sulfhydryl groups as well as amino groups. Other biosynthesis pathways lead from Gal3P to lipids, pigments, and most of the constituents of green cells.

Starch synthesis and accumulation in the chloroplasts occurs particularly when photosynthetic carbon fixation exceeds the needs of the plant. Under such circumstances, sugar phosphates accumulate in the cytoplasm, binding cytoplasmic P_i. The export of Gal3P from the chloroplasts is tied to a one-for-one exchange of P_i for Gal3P, so less cytoplasmic P_i results in decreased export of Gal3P and decreased P_i in the chloroplast. These changes trigger alterations in the activities of regulated enzymes, leading to increased starch synthesis. This starch can be broken down at night and used as a source of reduced carbon and energy for the physiological needs of the plant. Too much starch accumulation in the chloroplasts leads to diminished rates of photosynthesis, however. Thus, under the ideal photosynthetic conditions of a bright, warm day, many plants typically have slower rates of photosynthesis in the afternoon.

Photorespiration. Under conditions of high light intensity, hot weather, and water limitation, the productivity of the RPP cycle is limited in many plants by the occurrence of photorespiration. This process converts sugar phosphates back to carbon dioxide; it is initiated by the oxygenation of RuBP (*i.e.*, the combination of gaseous oxygen [O_2] with RuBP). This oxygenation reaction yields only one molecule of PGA and one molecule of a two-carbon acid, phosphoglycollate, which is subsequently converted in part to carbon dioxide. The reaction of oxygen with RuBP is in direct competition with the carboxylation reaction (CO_2 + RuBP) that initiates the RPP cycle and is, in fact, catalyzed by the same protein, ribulose 1,5-bisphosphate carboxylase. The relative concentrations of oxygen and carbon dioxide within the chloroplasts determine whether oxygenation or carboxylation is favoured. The concentration of oxygen inside the chloroplasts may be higher than atmospheric (20 percent) due to photosynthetic oxygen evolution, whereas the internal carbon dioxide concentration may be lower than atmospheric (0.035 percent) due to photosynthetic uptake. Any increase in the internal carbon dioxide pressure tends to help the carboxylation reaction compete more effectively with oxygenation.

Carbon fixation via C_4 acids. Certain plants—including the important crops sugarcane and corn (maize), as well as other diverse species believed to have evolved in the drier tropical areas—have developed a special mechanism of carbon fixation that largely prevents photorespiration. The leaves of these plants have special anatomy and biochemistry. In particular, photosynthetic functions are divided between mesophyll and bundle sheath leaf cells. The carbon fixation pathway begins in the mesophyll cells, where carbon dioxide is added to the three-carbon acid phosphoenolpyruvate (PEPA) by an enzyme called phosphoenolpyruvate carboxylase. The product of this reaction is the four-carbon acid oxaloacetate, which is reduced to malate, another four-carbon acid, in one form of C_4 pathway. Malate then is translocated to bundle sheath cells, which are located near the vascular system of the leaf. There, malate enters the chloroplasts and is oxidized and decarboxylated (*i.e.*, loses CO_2) by malic enzyme. This yields carbon dioxide, which is fed into the RPP cycle of the bundle sheath cells, and pyruvate, a three-carbon acid that is translocated back to the mesophyll cells. In the mesophyll chloroplasts, the enzyme pyruvate orthophosphate dikinase (PPDK) uses ATP and P_i to convert pyruvate back to PEPA, completing the C_4 cycle. There are several variations of this pathway in different species. For example, the amino acids aspartate and alanine can substitute for malate and pyruvate in some species.

The C_4 pathway acts as a shuttle for carrying carbon dioxide into the chloroplasts of the bundle sheath cells, where it is used in carbohydrate synthesis. The resulting higher level of internal carbon dioxide in these chloroplasts serves to increase the ratio of carboxylation to oxygenation, thus minimizing photorespiration. Although the plant must expend extra energy to drive this shuttle, the energy loss is more than compensated by the near elimination of photorespiration under conditions where it would otherwise occur. Sugarcane and certain other plants that employ this pathway have the highest annual yields of biomass of all species.

THE MOLECULAR BIOLOGY OF PHOTOSYNTHESIS

Oxygenic photosynthesis occurs in both prokaryotic cells (cyanophytes) and eukaryotic cells (algae and higher plants). In eukaryotic cells, which contain chloroplasts and a nucleus, the genetic information needed for the reproduction of the photosynthetic apparatus is contained partly in the chloroplast chromosome and partly in chromosomes of the nucleus. For example, the carboxylation enzyme ribulose 1,5-bisphosphate carboxylase is a large protein molecule comprising a complex of eight large polypeptide subunits and eight small polypeptide subunits. The gene for the large subunits is located in the chloroplast chromosome, while the gene for the small subunits is in the nucleus. Transcription of the DNA of the nuclear gene yields messenger RNA (mRNA) that encodes the information for the synthesis of the small polypeptides. During this synthesis, which occurs on the cytoplasmic ribosomes, some extra amino acid residues are added to form a recognition leader on the end of the polypeptide chain. This leader is recognized by special receptor sites on the outer chloroplast membrane; these receptor sites then allow the polypeptide to penetrate the membrane and enter the chloroplast. The leader is removed and the small subunits combine with the large subunits, which have been synthesized on chloroplast ribosomes according to mRNA transcribed from the chloroplast DNA. The expression of nuclear genes that code for proteins needed in the chloroplasts appears to be under control of events in the chloroplasts in some cases; for example, the synthesis of some nuclear-encoded chloroplast enzymes may occur only when light is absorbed by chloroplasts.

Enzymes such as PPDK, which are required for the efficient C_4 cycle described above, are expressed much more in sugarcane than in plants without the C_4 mechanism. One step toward achieving higher productivity in conventional crops like rice and wheat might be to obtain greater expression of C_4-pathway enzymes through methods of molecular genetics.

BIBLIOGRAPHY. Photosynthesis is discussed in chapters 9 and 10 of the text by FRANK B. SALISBURY and CLEON W. ROSS, *Plant Physiology*, 2nd ed. (1978). GOVINDJEE (ed.), *Photosynthesis*, 2 vol. (1982); vol. 1, *Energy Conversion by Plants and Bacteria*, includes comprehensive discussions by specialists of all aspects of the light reactions; vol. 2, *Development, Carbon Metabolism, and Plant Productivity*, discusses the molecular biology of photosynthesis, carbon dioxide assimilation, and photorespiration, as well as aspects affecting crop production. J.A. BASSHAM and MELVIN CALVIN, *The Path of Carbon in Photosynthesis* (1957), reviews mapping the path of carbon in photosynthesis using radiocarbon. JEROME A. SCHIFF (ed.), *On the Origins of Chloroplasts* (1982), studies the possible bacterial origins of chloroplasts. RODERICK K. CLAYTON, *Photosynthesis: Physical*

Mechanisms and Chemical Patterns (1980), is a comprehensive review of research done during the 1970s, with ample discussion of background information; J. KENNETH HOOBER, *Chloroplasts* (1984), is a concise, readable monograph on the structure and function of the photosynthetic organelle.

(J.A.B.)

Physical Principles and Concepts

This article deals with three ideas essential to the structure of the science of physics. Conservation laws and symmetry have to do with the persistence of certain qualities of matter and energy during the course of outwardly drastic transformations in the properties of states of physical systems. The best known of the conservation laws is the statement that, although mass and energy may be converted into one another, their total does not change. An instance of the symmetry pervading physics is the existence of an antiparticle that corresponds to each of the subatomic entities: the electron has its counterpart in the positron, the proton in the antiproton, and so on.

Among the situations covered by field theory are those in which any two material particles exert a weak attrac-

tive force on one another, regardless of how far apart the particles may be. This action at a distance is regarded as the result of an influence—in this case, gravitation—propagated throughout space in all directions from each particle; at any point within this gravitational field, a second particle will be affected by this force.

All of the mathematical formulations of the intensity of physical effects take the form of equations that contain additive constants or constants of proportionality. Examples of these constants are the gravitational constant and the magnitude of the charge of the electron. The quantitative understanding of all physical phenomena depends upon accurate knowledge of the values of these constants.

This article is divided into the following sections:

Conservation laws and symmetry

Conservation laws in physics state that certain measurable quantities, called physical properties, do not change in the course of time within an isolated physical system. Common examples are the conservation laws of electrical charge, mass–energy, and linear and angular momentum. The existence of conservation laws is directly related to the symmetry of the laws of nature; *i.e.*, to their invariance or changelessness under various symmetry operations such as rotations, translations, and reflections of the spatial and temporal coordinates.

GENERAL CONSIDERATIONS

The most familiar law of conservation concerns matter. A clearly stated philosophical recognition that certain aspects of matter might remain unaltered through every conceivable kind of transformation was first made, according to some interpretations of his works, by the Greek philosopher Anaxagoras (*c.* 450 BC). The principle was reiterated from time to time by such natural philosophers as Sir Francis Bacon (1620), but the first scientific statement of it was made toward the end of the 18th century—on the

basis of precise observations of chemical reactions—by Antoine Lavoisier, the French chemist. This law of conservation of matter may be stated as follows: the sum total of matter in the universe cannot be changed; *i.e.*, matter can neither be created nor destroyed. The next concept of conservation concerned energy, which, by the middle of the 19th century, had become mathematically definable. The law of conservation of energy merely substitutes the word energy for the word matter: the sum total of energy in the universe remains unchanged no matter what events take place; *i.e.*, energy cannot be created or destroyed. Eventually, after Einstein posited the equivalence of matter and energy, these two conservation laws had to be restated into the law of conservation of matter and energy: the sum total of matter and energy in an isolated system remains the same.

The concept of symmetry is familiar from such figures as a circle or square in elementary geometry because they can be made to coincide with themselves under the operation of rotation. Other kinds of symmetry are revealed in the behaviour of subatomic particles.

The underlying basis for the existence of all conservation laws in macroscopic physics—*i.e.*, the physics of bulk

Familiar symmetry

matter—can be shown to be the geometric symmetry of space, which can be extended to include time as another dimension. In microscopic physics—*i.e.,* physical phenomena at or below the atomic level of magnitude—the same symmetry-based conservation laws apply, but here they play an even more important role; they account for the transport or propagation of such quantities as energy and electric charge. Finally, in the theory of subatomic particles, which must be treated according to quantum mechanical symmetry operations (a mathematical description of the behaviour of subatomic systems undergoing rotations, reflections, and translations, not only in real space–time but in certain abstract spaces), the application of symmetry operations leads to a classification of the particles and their interactions with each other and to a number of new conserved quantities that have no macroscopic counterparts.

This whole subject, clearly, involves modern physics, and in a brief discussion such as this it is impossible to provide the necessary mathematical background that supports concepts and physical details. Thus, in this section, the nature of conservation laws and symmetry can be treated only generally. (For more detailed and technical treatment, see ATOMS; SUBATOMIC PARTICLES; GEOMETRY; ALGEBRA; MECHANICS; RELATIVITY.)

Geometrical symmetry. Of Greek origin, the word symmetry at first had the meaning "balanced proportions, or beauty of form arising from such proportions," but in later usage, it took on a more precise geometrical meaning. For example, an object is said to have bilateral symmetry if there is a median plane such that the left half of the object is the exact mirror image of the right half. If any two-dimensional curve is rotated about an axis lying in its plane, the resulting three-dimensional figure is said to possess cylindrical symmetry or rotational symmetry about the axis. Other examples of this concept are rotational symmetry about a point (spherical symmetry) and the symmetries possessed by the regular polygons (equilateral triangle, square) in a plane, or the regular solids (polyhedrons) in space.

Geometrical symmetries are characterized by a set of mathematical operations that can shift a figure but leave it undistinguishable from itself in its former position, called the group of symmetry transformations. To illustrate, a *Polygon rotations* regular polygon, a closed plane figure bounded by straight lines, may be considered, with its corners labelled counterclockwise *A, B, C,* etc. If the polygon has *n* sides, then in the symmetry operation, rotating the polygon counterclockwise about its centre will bring the polygon into congruence (coincidence) with itself a certain number of times. For example, if the polygon is a square, there are four sides ($n = 4$), and therefore there will be congruences when the figure is rotated $^0/_4$, $^1/_4$, $^2/_4$, and $^3/_4$ times 360°; *i.e.,* 0°, 90°, 180°, and 270°. In general terms, if *m* is any integer that is equal to 0, or 1, or 2 through $(n - 1)$, then congruence will take place by rotating the polygon (m/n) times 360°. Each rotation is thus a member, or element, of a symmetry group.

Another set of congruences of the regular polygon is obtained by considering reflection, as in a mirror. In such a case, the counterclockwise labelling *A, B, C,* etc., would appear to be clockwise. Thus, reflection in one of the planes of bilateral symmetry is an operation that changes the ordering of the labels *A, B, C,* etc., from counterclockwise to clockwise.

If, instead of the polygon, one considers a circle, any rotation about its centre will bring the circle into itself if one imagines its points to be ordered counterclockwise.

It is possible also to consider translational symmetry, by which a straight line is carried into congruence with itself (*i.e.,* slid along its length), and dilatational symmetry, which results in a consideration of similarities rather than mere congruences, such as a square within a square.

Symmetry in art and nature. Many examples of all these symmetries can be found both in art and in nature. One- and two-dimensional translation symmetry are frequently found in friezes and wallpaper patterns if these are imagined to be continued indefinitely. Columns and rosette decorations possess rotational symmetry, as do some en-

tire buildings and monuments. Biological forms frequently possess bilateral or rotational symmetry and, in the case of such free-floating microscopic animals as the radiolarians, even have the shapes of the regular polyhedrons. Some molecules, as well as the external forms of most minerals, exhibit the symmetries of crystals; *i.e.,* combinations of rotations and reflections. These external crystalline forms arise from the symmetrical arrangements of the atoms within the smallest or unit crystal cell, which, in turn, is repeated three-dimensionally throughout the volume of the crystal in a symmetrical way to form a periodic lattice.

The arrangements of the atoms in the unit crystal cell, and its repetition in the lattice, determine its electrical, optical, acoustical, and other physical properties. In the case of magnetic materials, a given magnetic state can be reversed by reversing all currents, the effect being the equivalent of the exchange of north and south poles of the magnetic crystal. The magnetic crystal can be restored to its original state by a combination of this operation, called time-reversal operation, *T,* and one of the geometrical operations described above. There are 32 types of crystals, or point groups, that exhibit symmetry in the absence of a time-reversal operation and 58 more that require an additional time-reversal operation, giving a total of 90 magnetic-symmetry groups.

SYMMETRY AND THE LAWS OF PHYSICS

From the earliest days of natural philosophy (Pythagoras in the 6th century BC), symmetry has furnished insight into the laws of physics and the nature of the cosmos. The two outstanding theoretical achievements of the 20th century, relativity and quantum theory, involve notions of symmetry in a fundamental way. Einstein's special theory of relativity can be economically stated as the invariance (that is, unchanging form) of the laws of physics under a continuous group of symmetry transformations known as the Poincaré (or inhomogeneous Lorentz) group. It is notable that in quantum theory every symmetry yields a conservation law; *i.e.,* for every symmetry operation that leaves the laws invariant, there exists a measurable physical property (*e.g.,* charge) of an isolated or undisturbed system that does not change during the development of that system in the course of time.

Derivation of conservation laws from symmetry

Some of these conservation laws can also be deduced in classical physics, in which they are closely related to the classical laws of physics. For example, the physics of Galileo and Newton states that the total linear momentum of a system (the sum of the linear momenta, mass times velocity, of each mass point) is constant, providing that the system is not acted upon by an external force. This conservation law is related to the translational symmetry of geometrical space, as can be seen intuitively by considering a two-dimensional analogy: on a huge, flat, smooth, horizontal table, a flat object is sliding without friction; until the edge is reached, nothing will act to change the momentum. If the table is curved, tipped, or rough, however, or if it contains holes, the momentum will not be conserved; for then the system will be acted on by an external force, gravity or friction. Similarly, a three-dimensional space in which the law of conservation of momentum holds contains by analogy no roughness, curvature, edges, or other local features to disturb the motion. That is, each part of empty space is assumed to be like every other part. Similarly, every direction in empty space is assumed to be equivalent to every other direction, a complete rotational symmetry, the consequence of which is the conservation of the quantity called angular momentum, a physical property of a body having magnitude and direction that is related to its mass and angular velocity. These symmetries assumed for the geometrical space are summarized by saying that the space is homogeneous (translational symmetry) and isotropic; *i.e.,* has properties with the same values when measured along axes in all directions (rotational symmetry).

In relativity, and in classical theory as well, time can be imagined as a fourth dimension, distinct from the three dimensions of ordinary space. If the laws of physics are assumed to be the same at different times, they are said to be invariant under translations in time. The consequence of this assumption can be shown to be the conservation of energy. Finally, if it is assumed that the laws of physics are unchanged and that the velocity of light is constant for observers moving with any constant relative velocity, the result is the special theory of relativity in which, for example, moving objects appear contracted in length and their masses appear to increase, and moving clocks appear, to an observer outside the moving frame of reference, to run more slowly (see RELATIVITY).

Conservation of mass and energy. Perhaps the best known result of the special theory is Einstein's relation, which states that the total energy (E) of an isolated system is equal to its mass (m) times the square of the velocity (c) of light: $E = mc^2$. The total energy includes the kinetic energy of the particle so that the mass represents the increased mass caused by the motion; *i.e.*, relativistic effect. Two separate conservation laws of classical physics, that of mass and that of energy, are thus united into a single conservation law—that of mass–energy. Particles held together by mutually attractive forces—*e.g.*, neutrons and protons bound together in the atomic nucleus—have a total mass smaller than that of their separate masses, whereas particles repelling each other have a larger mass. Indeed, the stability of the nucleus is based upon the fact that energy must be supplied to separate it into its parts. In the case of certain nuclei, such as the naturally occurring uranium-235 nuclei, which are heavier than the two parts (other nuclei) into which it can split, the nucleus is unstable and undergoes spontaneous fission with the release of a considerable amount of energy.

The subatomic particles. It will be helpful to review the forces, or interactions, that prevail between subatomic particles, which have symmetries. The most familiar of the subatomic, or elementary, particles are the proton and neutron, constituents of the nucleus of the atom and called nucleons, and the electron. A simple lettering system is used in discussing these: an atom of mass number A (equal to the sum of neutrons and protons) has an atomic

Atomic mass and atomic number

number Z equal to the number of protons in its nucleus, each proton having a single positive electrical charge; the number of electrically neutral neutrons is, then, $A - Z$. In a normal atom, the nucleus is surrounded by electrons, Z in number, each having a single negative electrical charge. The nuclear particles (nucleons) are much heavier than the electron, the proton being 1,836.1 times as heavy and the neutron being slightly heavier than the proton. Many other subatomic particles are known and some are listed in Table 1 with their masses given in energy units as millions of electron volts (MeV) according to the relation $E = mc^2$.

Because every elementary particle has wavelike properties, its size is not well defined but depends upon its mass, its interaction properties, and its state of motion. A measure of the size of one of the massless particles listed in Table 1 is furnished by its wavelength (represented by the Greek lambda, λ), the value of which can be obtained by combining Planck's relation that a quantum of energy (E) is equal to a constant (h) times the frequency (represented by the Greek nu, ν) of the wave that it represents, or $E = h\nu$, with the simple wave equation that the product of a wave's frequency and wavelength is constant, or $\lambda\nu = c$ (E being its energy, h Planck's constant of action, ν the wave frequency, and c the speed of light). This equation yields a wavelength (λ) equal to the product of Planck's constant and the velocity of light divided by the energy of the particle, namely, $\lambda = hc/E$. The same measure applied to the particles with mass of the lepton group (*e.g.*, electron and muon), gives, upon substitution of the mass–energy equivalent (mc^2) for the total energy E in the above equation, a quantity known as the Compton wavelength, $\lambda_c = h/mc$. Although the Compton wavelength is a good measure of the particle size when its velocity is large, at lower velocities the Heisenberg indeterminacy principle (which states that uncertainty in the momentum of a particle multiplied by its uncertainty in position is greater than or equal to $h/4\pi$) prevents specifying its position anywhere within a radius of one de Broglie wavelength; *i.e.*, the wavelength associated with a particle, h/mv, in which v is the speed of the particle and m is its mass. Thus in the hydrogen atom, the "size" of the electron is

Table 1: Some Elementary Particles

particle	symbol	spin (units of $h/2\pi$)	rest mass (mc^2 in MeV)
Graviton	g	2	0
Photon	γ	1	0
Leptons			
Neutrino (electron)	ν_e	$\frac{1}{2}$	0
Neutrino (muon)	ν_μ	$\frac{1}{2}$	0
Electron	e^-	$\frac{1}{2}$	0.5111
Muon	μ^-	$\frac{1}{2}$	105.7
Hadrons			
Mesons (B = 0)			
Pion (S = 0)	π^+, π^-	0	139.6
	π^0	0	135.0
Kaons (S = 1)	K^+	0	493.8
	K^0	0	497.8
Kaons (S = −1)	$\bar{K}^0$	0	497.8
	K^-	0	493.8
Eta (S = 0)	η	0	548.8
Baryons (B = 1)			
Proton (S = 0)	p	$\frac{1}{2}$	938.3
Neutron (S = 0)	n	$\frac{1}{2}$	939.6
Lambda (S = −1)	Λ	$\frac{1}{2}$	1,115.6
3 − 3 resonance (S = 0)	Δ	3/2	1,236.0

roughly the size of the atom itself (about 10^{-8} centimetre in diameter).

In the case of the particles that respond to nuclear forces—that is, strongly interacting particles (called hadrons), including baryons and mesons (see Table 1)—their size is taken as the distance over which they can interact with other particles, about 10^{-13} centimetre. This distance, which can be measured experimentally, is called the Fermi unit. These particles have the ability to emit and reabsorb numbers of other hadrons and may be visualized by thinking of each hadron as having surrounding "clouds" of other hadrons. For example, the proton "size" is nearly the Compton wavelength of the pion, which is equal to h/mc, Planck's constant divided by the velocity of light times the pion's mass, which forms the most extended cloud.

Strong interaction

Quantum statistics. In quantum mechanics a system of particles is described by a mathematical expression known as a wave function. When two or more particles of the system are of identical type, that wave function must remain unchanged or, at most, change sign when the coordinates of the two particles are exchanged in the function. Wave functions, which change sign through exchange, are said to have odd exchange symmetry or to be antisymmetric; if they do not change sign they have even exchange symmetry and are said to be symmetric. If two identical particles have an antisymmetric wave function they are said to obey Fermi–Dirac statistics; if their wave function is symmetric, they are said to obey Bose–Einstein statistics.

Spin properties. Another important property of an elementary particle is its intrinsic angular momentum, or the spin it has about its own axis, measured in units of Planck's constant divided by 2π, or $h/2\pi$, that can be represented by a vector (an arrow symbolizing magnitude and direction). This spin is always one of the values 0, $1/2$, 1, $3/2$ ... (*i.e.*, either integer or half-integer) allowed by quantum mechanics. Identical particles with half-integer spins (leptons and baryons) have what are called Fermi–Dirac statistics and obey the Pauli exclusion principle; *i.e.*, a given quantum state in a system can be occupied by at most one of a set of identical particles. In consequence, these particles form systems having layered or shell structure (neutron and proton shells in atomic nuclei, electron shells in atoms). Particles with integer spins have a different type of statistics, called Bose–Einstein statistics, which tends to concentrate identical particles in the same state (*e.g.*, photons of light in a laser beam). The same distinction as to statistics applies to identical agglomerates of elementary particles. Total spin of an atomic nucleus depends on the spins of the constituent particles; when the total spin is integral (*e.g.*, that of the helium isotope with mass 4, helium-4) the nucleus obeys Bose–Einstein statistics, whereas when the total spin is half-integral (*e.g.*, the isotope of helium with mass 3, helium-3) it obeys Fermi–Dirac statistics.

Shell structures

Magnetic properties. An important property of electrical charges possessing angular momentum is magnetic moment; *i.e.*, magnet-like behaviour. Even electrically neutral spinning hadrons (see Table 1), like the neutron, possess magnetic moments—another indication that they have internal structure. This structure may be due to electrically (but not magnetically) compensating clouds of mesons or, possibly, to the circulation of other more elementary constituents.

Forces within the nucleus. In order to clarify the notions of range and strength of interaction mentioned above, it is necessary to deal with the forces found within the nucleus. They are the electrostatic force between charged particles (like charges repel, unlike attract), also common to macroscopic physics, and two nuclear forces (called strong and weak) found only in subatomic physics. While it is possible to begin with the electrostatic interaction of two point charges (e_1 and e_2), separated by a distance r_{12}—that is, the charges can be said to attract or repel each other with a force equal to the product of the electrostatic charges divided by the square of their distance of separation, or e_1e_2/r_{12}^2—it is more convenient to consider their potential energy (or what is called their Coulomb interaction energy), which is simply the product of the charges divided by the distance to the first power, namely, e^2/r_{12}. If the charges are in motion relative to each other, the force is much more complicated but is always proportional to the charges, which, in that sense, measure the strength of interaction. In the case of the strong nuclear forces, the laws analogous to those of electricity—that is, of moving charges or electrodynamics—are unknown, although they are thought to be at least as complicated as those of electricity. In the following section, interactions are stated mathematically.

Mathematical formulations of interactions. An approximation of the nuclear force between two stationary nucleons, however, can be represented as the product of the strengths of interaction (g_1 and g_2) divided by the distance of separation (r_{12}) between them, times the exponential value of minus the ratio of the separation to the range (λ) of the force; *i.e.*, the approximate distance of separation at which the nuclear force becomes relatively small: g_1g_2/r_{12} exp $(-r_{12}/\lambda)$. This form for the potential energy, known as the Yukawa interaction, was proposed in analogy to the quantum theory of moving charges, or electrodynamics, which considers the electromagnetic interaction as being caused by the exchange of photons (a quantum of energy, or the particle form of electromagnetic radiation) between electric charges. In Yukawa's theory, these field quanta, known as mesons, analogous to the photons in quantum electrodynamics, have a mass m intermediate between that of electron and proton and the range of the force that they carry is λ, equal to their Compton wavelength divided by 2π—that is, equal to Planck's constant divided by the product of 2π times meson mass times the velocity of light, or $\lambda = h/2\pi mc$.

In this last equation, if the mass of Yukawa's meson is set in million electron volts equal to 140 divided by the velocity of light squared ($m = 140/c^2$), the observed mass of the pion (from $mc^2 = E$), a Compton wavelength for the meson equal approximately to 10^{-13} centimetre is obtained, which agrees with the observed range of nuclear forces. Also, if the strengths of interaction are set equal to a coupling constant (g)—that is, $g_1 = g_2 = g$, in which the coupling constant measures the strength of the meson interaction with the nucleon—experiment gives a dimensionless measure of the interaction between nucleons a value ($g^2/2hc$) of approximately 15.

In the electromagnetic theory, from which the meson analogy was drawn, the electric charges measure the strength of coupling of the photon to its source, the charged particle. For two electrons, equating $e_1 = e_2 = -e$, the analogous dimensionless measure of the strength of electrical forces ($e^2/2hc$) of approximately 1/137 is obtained.

Comparison of forces. In comparing the above strengths of interactions, the nuclear forces are seen to be hundreds of times stronger than electrical forces. Because the mass of the photon is zero, the range of force (λ) is infinite, and examination of the Yukawa equation for nuclear interaction shows that it tends to the (Coulomb) interaction equal to the coupling constant squared divided by the sep-

aration (g^2/r_{12}) when the range tends to infinity. (A similar quantum field theory of gravitation can be formulated, the massless field quantum analogous to the photon being called the graviton. The range of force is again infinite and the source of the quanta is the particle's mass. No dimensionless measure of the strength exists, but in the physics of elementary particles, the gravitational forces between particles are about 10^{40} times weaker than the electrical forces and thus negligible.)

In addition to the pion, more than 20 heavier mesons have been identified experimentally, and it is probable that there are many others not yet observed. Each of these mesons can serve as the quantum of a field having shorter range than the pion field, so that the account given in the previous paragraph describes only the longer range part of the nuclear force. In high-energy scattering experiments, which probe the inner nucleon structure, a complicated set of forces is revealed. The mathematical description of this "shape" of the nucleon, revealed by using a beam of high-energy electrons as an electromagnetic probe, is called the nucleon form factor.

Weak interaction. Another type of nuclear force, the weak interaction, has a range so short that the corresponding field quantum is roughly 80 times as massive as the proton. So far, two types of this class of particle, variously called the intermediate vector boson or weakon, have been observed—namely, W^+ and W^-—in high-energy accelerator experiments. Investigators expect to find a third type of weakon, the Z^0, which is electrically neutral, by producing proton–antiproton collisions at extremely high energies. The strength of the weak force is substantially less than that of the strong force. Its influence is confined to a distance on the order of only about 10^{-16} centimetre—approximately a thousandth of the diameter of a proton.

To summarize, three types of force are important in the atomic and subatomic domain: electromagnetic forces, and strong and weak nuclear forces. Their ranges and strengths differ greatly. Particles that participate in strong interactions are called hadrons (mesons and baryons); the others are leptons. The photon is exceptional, being neither a hadron nor a lepton. Both baryons and leptons have weak interactions. All particles that have either electric charge or electric-charge structure (such as the neutron) have electromagnetic interactions. As will be seen below, each type of interaction has its characteristic symmetry properties, and, corresponding to the hierarchy of interactions, there is a remarkable hierarchy of symmetries such that the stronger the interaction the more symmetrical it is.

Relationship of quantum theory to conservation laws. In the elementary particles, quantum theory and the special theory of relativity play preeminent roles. Conservation laws and their related symmetries become most important. Some reasons for this may be briefly stated:

1. The equations of motion from classical mechanics are known; thus while the recognition of the symmetries they imply is aesthetically satisfying and often provides a powerful analytical method, the laws in themselves are already complete and nothing essentially new is added. In those parts of quantum theory in which the laws are only partially known, however, an attempt is often made to find those predictions that follow only from accepted (or assumed) symmetry principles and conservation laws.

2. Quantum theory is usually applied to the simpler systems, such as crystals, molecules, atoms, nuclei, and elementary particles, in which intrinsic symmetries are more readily observable. Also, there are more symmetries in quantum theory than in classical theory.

3. Classical physics can be considered as a special application of quantum physics when the effect of the constant of action h (Planck's constant) is negligible; that is, in the limiting case, when the effect of Planck's constant tends to zero, the separation between states of definite energy tends to zero, so that a classical state is an ensemble of many quantum mechanical states. For example, an elementary magnet in a uniform magnetic field is restricted to one of a finite set of discrete orientations in quantum theory, whereas in classical theory it may have any orientation whatsoever. When the number of possible orientations is small, powerful restrictions can be placed on the internal

complexity of the system because of symmetry principles, whereas in classical theory this is not possible.

Dipole moment of neutron

As an example of this type of reasoning, there is the proof that the neutron cannot have an electric dipole moment (separation of charges to produce effective positive and negative regions), providing time-reversal is a valid symmetry. The neutron, being electrically neutral but possessing an internal structure, may be regarded as an equal mixture of positive and negative charge. If the spin is represented by a vector (an arrow pointing upward along the axis when the sense of the spin is positive and vice versa), a positive electric dipole moment would mean a net separation of the charges, with more of the positive charge near the point of the arrow. The time-reversal transformation, however, would reverse the spin and hence would exchange the point and tail of the arrow but would not change the distribution of the charge. Thus the sign of the electric dipole moment, referred to the sense of the spin, would change. If the time-reversal symmetry is a valid one for the neutron, however, it would mean that an intrinsic static property like the electric dipole moment (static because the electric dipole moment does not depend on rotation) cannot change sign and must therefore be zero.

Dynamical symmetries. Two types of symmetries can be seen to lead to conserved quantities in elementary particle physics. The first type is referred to as dynamical symmetry, associated with properties of the space–time continuum assumed by the special theory of relativity, sometimes called geometrical symmetry. This leads to the absolute conservation (constancy in time for an isolated system) of the vector linear momentum (i.e., the product of mass and its velocity in a certain direction), the tensor of total angular momentum (i.e., the analogous quantity for rotation), and the total energy. The behaviour of the physical laws under the operations of space and time inversion can also be studied as dynamical symmetries.

The term operator as used in theoretical physics represents a symbolic means for changing a mathematical expression that describes a physical entity or system. In quantum mechanics such operators are generally theoretical representations of measurements on the described system. Operations (or measurements) that leave the system unchanged have the special significance of providing numbers that describe the quantum mechanical state called quantum numbers (except for the trivial identity operator that leaves all states unchanged). Tests or measurements of symmetry are, of course, also represented by operators.

Space inversion. The space inversion operator, called the parity operator P, has the meaning of reflection in the origin of the space coordinates of a particle or system; that is, the three space dimensions x, y, and z become, respectively, $-x$, $-y$, and $-z$. A right-handed coordinate system is one in which turning the $+x$-axis into the $+y$-axis, the system advances in the direction of increasing z, just as a right-hand screw would advance when rotated. Under parity change, a right-handed coordinate system changes to a left-handed coordinate system and vice versa. As another example, when a particle is moving along a path and is also spinning about its direction of motion in the same direction that would advance a right-hand screw, it

Helicity

is said to have positive helicity; under the parity operation P it would acquire, instead, negative helicity. If the laws of physics were invariant under parity, the laws and all their predictions could be expressed mathematically in such a way that it would be impossible to tell whether a right-handed or left-handed coordinate system had been employed.

Time inversion. The time inversion, or time reversal operator T, means the reversal of motion. Thus under the time reversal operation T, a particle of positive helicity remains of positive helicity, applying the right-hand rule above, because both the sense of spin and the direction of motion are reversed by the operation. Time-reversal invariance (or symmetry) holds if, whenever a motion is allowed by the laws of physics, the reversed motion is also an allowed one. Thus if a motion picture were taken of the motion of a body and viewed when run backward, it would be possible to say that the observed motion is an allowed motion.

The laws of classical physics are, indeed, invariant under the space-inversion and time-reversal operations P and T, but in the classical case this condition does not lead to any conservation laws. For an example of this invariance under the parity operator, the components of a vector representing electric field change direction (as x, y, and z directions cited earlier), but the components of the magnetic field vector do not; the currents that are the source of the magnetic field and those that are acted upon by magnetic fields, however, also reverse their sense of direction, with the result that there is no observable effect of changing from a right-handed to a left-handed description of magnetic phenomena.

The invariance of physical phenomena under time reversal may seem surprising at first. If, for example, an egg is cracked into a bowl and beaten, a motion picture of these actions shown in reverse would strain one's credulity. It is necessary to go further and to imagine the situation if all the final microscopic motions of the egg episode were reversed. Theoretically, the egg would reform itself; however, this is an operation impossible to achieve in practice, and this is the reason that time appears to be unidirectional.

Violation of conservation laws. Until 1956 the laws of quantum physics were generally assumed to be invariant under parity and time reversal. In that year, however, in order to explain an apparent lack of conservation of the parity quantum number in the decay of K-mesons (kaons) (see Table 1) into two or three π-mesons (pions), two Chinese physicists in the United States, Tsung-Dao Lee and Chen Ning Yang, pointed out that the conservation of parity had not been experimentally tested in the weak nuclear interactions previously observed (e.g., nuclear beta minus decay, symbolized β^-, the emission of negative electrons from a nucleus) and proposed several new experiments. When these experiments were carried out during 1957, the nonconservation of parity was decisively verified. In 1964 when the decay of kaons into pions was investigated by others, another new and surprising result was obtained and was interpreted as being due to a violation of the conservation law associated with time reversal in a new superweak nuclear interaction.

Charge conjugation. The inversion symmetries of space and time are associated in relativistic quantum field theory with another symmetry, that of charge conjugation (C). In theories that conserve parity and time reversal, such as quantum electrodynamics or the strong nuclear interaction, invariance under charge conjugation, which changes the sign of the electric charge, implies that every charged elementary particle has an oppositely charged partner, its antiparticle. The antiparticle of an electrically neutral particle may be identical to the particle, as in the case of the neutral pion, or it may be distinct, as in the case of the antineutron. All of the expected antiparticles have been observed, beginning in 1933 with the discovery of the antielectron, or positron. Weak nuclear interactions, however, do not conserve charge conjugation, a phenomenon that poses a paradox for the theoretical prediction of the existence of antiparticles.

Antiparticles

Time reversal/charge conjugation/parity. The difficulty may be resolved. Physicists have shown that invariance under the combined symmetry time reversal/charge conjugation/parity (TCP) is sufficient to demand the existence of antiparticles. The meaning of a combined symmetry may be illustrated in the case of the weak (but not superweak) nuclear interaction that conserves CP but not C and P separately. In the above discussion of parity, reference was made to the notions of positive and negative helicity. Neutrinos, which enter only into the weak interactions, are found to have negative helicity, whereas antineutrinos have positive helicity. Thus invariance under charge conjugation alone, which would imply the existence of neutrinos and antineutrinos of the same helicity, is violated. The same conclusion would follow if P-invariance were to hold because parity changes the sign of the helicity without changing neutrino to antineutrino. Under the combined inversion CP, however, a neutrino of negative helicity becomes an antineutrino of positive helicity, in accord with observation. Similarly, the existence of antiparticles is predicted even if charge conjugation, parity, and time reversal are violated separately, providing *TCP* is still a valid symmetry.

Internal symmetries. The dynamical symmetries considered so far are related to the properties of space and time, and the continuous symmetry transformations such as translation in space, time, and velocity (or, alternatively, Lorentz transformation) all lead to such absolutely conserved quantities as energy and momentum. In the case of the discrete transformations, charge conjugation, parity, and time reversal, however, it has been seen that certain interactions—the weak nuclear interactions—would not conserve these symmetries separately but would do so in certain combinations. A number of other symmetries in elementary particle physics, some absolute and some approximate, are extremely useful for classifying the particles and lead to selection rules; *i.e.*, rules that tell which reactions among the particles are allowed and which are forbidden.

Absolutely conserved charges. There are four absolutely conserved charges: electric charge Q, baryon number B, and two lepton numbers l_e and l_μ, associated respectively with electrons and muons. In the sense that all known electric charges are integral multiples of the fundamental charge $e = 1.60 \times 10^{-19}$ coulomb, the electric charge Q may be regarded as a quantum number that, like B, l_e, and l_μ, takes on only integer values. In other respects, however, the electric charge is distinguished from the other absolutely conserved quantities, being a property of both leptons and hadrons and being the source of the electromagnetic field. In any elementary particle reaction, if a and b represent reactants and c, d, etc., the products, an equation can be written: $a + b \rightarrow c + d + \ldots$; in this equation, the sum of the charges on the left side of the arrow must equal the sum of the charges of the particles on the right. (Here, and below, the arrow indicates decay or transformation of particles on its left into particles on its right.)

Baryon number
Baryon number B is a property only of the hadrons; those in which B equals zero are called mesons, those in which B equals one are called baryons, whereas antibaryons have B equal to minus one. Protons and neutrons are baryons, and hence the mass number A of the atomic nucleus is identical with its baryon number. It is the absolute additive conservation of baryon number and of energy that makes the free proton absolutely stable because it is lightest of the baryons. The neutron, being slightly heavier than the proton, can undergo the weak nuclear interaction in which the neutron (n) decays into a proton (p), electron (e^-), and antineutrino ($\bar{\nu}$) according to the equation: $n \rightarrow p + e^- + \bar{\nu}_e$. This process is called beta decay. If one did not take into account the energy and momentum carried by the massless neutral particle $\bar{\nu}_e$ (the antineutrino of the electron), the other three quantities would appear to be not conserved. It was on this basis that the neutrino's existence was predicted by Wolfgang Pauli, a German physicist, in 1931. It is sometimes (energetically) possible for protons bound in nuclei to undergo the following decay reaction in which e^+ is the positron (antiparticle of the electron) and ν_e is the neutrino (the massless particle) associated with the production of the positron, $p \rightarrow n + e^+ + \nu_e$.

Additive conservation of the lepton (electrons, neutrinos, and muons; see below) number l_e is also illustrated by the decay processes of the neutron and proton mentioned in the previous paragraph. The leptons (ν_e and e^-) are assigned the lepton number $l_e = +1$, and the antileptons ($\bar{\nu}_e$ and e^+) are assigned the lepton number $l_e = -1$. On both sides of each arrow above (in time: before and after the reaction takes place), the total electron lepton number l_e (the sum of the lepton numbers for each particle) must be the same. In addition to the electron, there is another charged lepton, the muon, which is much heavier than the electron and which occurs typically as a product in the decay of pions or kaons (see Table 1). Free charged pions, for example, undergo the decay processes $\pi^+ \rightarrow \mu^+ + \nu_\mu$, and $\pi^- \rightarrow \mu^- + \bar{\nu}_\mu$. Again, the particles μ^- and ν_μ are assigned (conventionally) the lepton number $l_\mu = +1$, and their antiparticles μ^+ and $\bar{\nu}_\mu$ are assigned $l_\mu = -1$. That the neutrinos associated with electron and muon are different,

implying the existence of two different lepton numbers l_e and l_μ, was established in the early 1960s. One consequence is that whereas the muon decays (in about 10^{-6} second) by the process $\mu^- \rightarrow e^- + \bar{\nu}_e + \bar{\nu}_\mu$, processes such as $\mu^- \rightarrow e^- + e^- + e^+$ are forbidden and do not occur.

Strangeness and hypercharge. Other internal symmetry properties such as strangeness, treated below, belong to hadrons alone (see Table 1). From 1947 on, a number of hadrons, both mesons and baryons, have been observed with the following property: although produced copiously, in strong interactions such as proton–proton collisions, they are unable to decay by strong or electromagnetic interactions even when that is allowed by all the conservation laws considered so far in this article. As a consequence, these particles are relatively stable, with lifetimes of 10^{-10} to 10^{-8} second, characteristic of the weak nuclear interaction. The apparent contradiction between their behaviour in production and decay is resolved by assigning a new quantum number, the strangeness number S, and requiring that it be conserved by strong and electromagnetic interactions. In production, then, two or more particles of nonzero S can be produced, providing their total strangeness adds up to zero. The conservation of strangeness does not hold for the weak interactions by which the particles decay, but it can change by one unit. The strange particles have antiparticles of opposite strangeness. Examples of reactions permitted by the strangeness selection rule are a pion and proton producing a kaon: $\pi^- + p \rightarrow +K^+ + \Lambda$ (associated production), and an antiproton and proton producing antilambda plus lambda particles: $\bar{p} + p \rightarrow \bar{\Lambda} + \Lambda$; as the π^- (pion), and $\bar{p}$ (antiproton) have strangeness numbers $S = 0$, Λ (lambda) has $S = -1$, and K^+ (kaon) and the antilambda $\bar{\Lambda}$ have $S = +1$ (see Table 1).

A quantity closely related to the internal symmetry property strangeness, which is useful in the symmetry classification of hadrons, is the hypercharge Y, defined as equal to the sum of the baryon and strangeness numbers: $Y = B + S$. Because the baryon number is absolutely conserved, the change of strangeness in any reaction is always the same as the change of its hypercharge.

Isospin symmetry. A typical characteristic of the hadrons is that they occur in families of the same spin, intrinsic parity, baryon number, and of closely similar mass. Such groupings of particles, differing in electric charge but not in hypercharge—such as proton and neutron, or such as the three pions—are called charge multiplets, or isospin multiplets. It is believed that the small mass differences that can exist between differently charged members of a charge multiplet would vanish if only the strong nuclear interactions were present and that, except for small electromagnetic and weak interaction corrections, their strong interactions would be identical. In atomic nuclei, for example, the forces between a pair of protons, a pair of neutrons, or a neutron and a proton appear to be the same except for corrections that can be reasonably ascribed to their differing electromagnetic properties. This concept is called the charge independence of nuclear forces.

In this situation, the proton and neutron are regarded as different charge states (of charge $Q = 1$ and $Q = 0$), respectively of a single particle, the nucleon. The pions π^+, π^0, and π^- are regarded as charge states of a single particle, the pion, having charges $Q = 1$, $Q = 0$, and $Q = -1$. In visualizing the symmetry corresponding to the charge independence of the strong nuclear interaction, it is useful to represent the charge states of the nucleons as vectors in an abstract, two-dimensional complex space (one spatial coordinate is complex; *i.e.*, its magnitude is multiplied by the imaginary quantity $\sqrt{-1}$, called the charge space, or isospin space). Charge independence, or isospin invariance, is then the statement that the strong nuclear interaction is invariant under arbitrary rigid rotations of the axes in this abstract space. The three operators that generate these rotations have the same algebra as the three operators that generate the rotations in real space (angular momentum operators), hence the name isospin. One of them, I_3, is related to charge and hypercharge by the relation: $Q = I_3 + \frac{1}{2}Y$. The largest value of I_3 within a multiplet is called I, and there are $2I + 1$ charge states in

Margin notes:

Other internal symmetry properties

Isospin space

the multiplet. The continuous symmetry transformations (called the Lie group, after Marius Sophus Lie, a Norwegian mathematician), which lead to the conservation of angular momentum in the real space and of isospin in the abstract space, belong to the special unitary group in two dimensions, $SU(2)$. As stated, the generator I_3 of this group is related to the value of the charge, whereas I_1 and I_2 are related to the transformation from one charge state to another.

SU(3) and higher symmetries. By considering a three-dimensional abstract complex vector space and the group of rotations in this space, $SU(3)$, larger family groupings can be accommodated, which may be called charge–hypercharge multiplets. In this larger space, there are eight generators of rotations: the three isospin operators I_1, I_2, I_3, the hypercharge Y, and four others related to the change of strangeness. Although isospin multiplets may contain any number of members, $SU(3)$ multiplets are limited to sets, representations of the group, containing prescribed numbers of members. According to the presently accepted $SU(3)$ scheme (proposed in 1962 by a U.S. physicist, Murray Gell-Mann, and an Israeli physicist, Yuval Ne'eman), known as the "eightfold way," the simplest nontrivial representation employed by the hadrons has eight members. For example, a certain meson octet contains three pions, four kaons, and an eighth, a neutral meson, the eta. The baryon octet contains one proton, one neutron, one lambda, and five other strange baryons. About a dozen or more such representations have been identified.

In contrast to the well-established charge independence of the strong nuclear force, $SU(3)$ invariance is not an excellent symmetry, for it appears to be violated not only by the weak and electromagnetic interaction but by a part of the strong interaction force itself. The strong symmetry-breaking interaction is not well understood, but its presence is indicated by the fact that the average mass difference between isospin multiplets that make up an $SU(3)$ representation is far larger than the electromagnetic mass differences within the isospin multiplets. The eta mass, for example, is four times that of the pion.

A great deal of theoretical research has been concerned with the attempt to understand the breaking of $SU(3)$ symmetry and to explore still larger symmetry groups such as $SU(6)$, with the object of relating the properties of larger sets of particles to each other and to understanding the dynamics of the strong interactions. Particular emphasis has been placed upon the algebra of the conserved and partially conserved currents, related to the generators of the symmetry groups just as the electric current is related to the electric charge.

Quark models. As the properties of atomic nuclei are related to the constituent protons and neutrons, so the properties of hadrons would find a natural explanation if they could be regarded as composites of more elementary constituents. $SU(3)$ symmetry would require a triplet of half-spin constituents, called quarks. The quark triplets, q_1, q_2, and q_3, with their quantum numbers, are given in Table 2. There are also postulated three antiquarks, the quantum numbers of which are the negatives (except for I) of those of the quarks. The quarks q_1 and q_2 form an isospin doublet (like proton and neutron) and q_2 is an isospin singlet (like lambda). In the strong nuclear interaction, it is assumed that each variety of quark is separately conserved in the same sense as baryon number and lepton number (*i.e.,* number of quarks minus number of antiquarks of a given variety). Conservation of strangeness is explained as the conservation of the strange quark q_3, whereas weak interactions occur by a transformation of quark type.

Hadrons composed of quarks (margin note)

Because each quark is assigned baryon number $B = 1/3$, baryons ($B = 1$) are made of three quarks, and mesons ($B = 0$) are made of one quark and one antiquark. All hadrons so far observed can be constructed from the three quarks and their antiquarks and their masses, mass differences, and interaction properties can be qualitatively understood in terms of their quark structures. The values of electric charge Q given in Table 2 are derived only from theoretical relationships. Intensive searches for particles of nonintegral electric charge have failed so far to provide conclusive evidence for their existence, which suggests that the quarks may be extremely heavy particles, if indeed they exist.

(L.M.B./Ed.)

Field theory

A field in physics may be defined as a continuous distribution of some observable quantity in space and time. The observable quantity, which must be measurable, may be any of a variety of phenomena, including (but not limited to) such things as the colour in a liquid, the density of dust in the atmosphere, temperature distribution in a body, the flow pattern of a stream, or the magnetic field surrounding the Earth. But under all circumstances, whatever is described as a field must be measurable by some technique.

If the observed quantity varies in space but does not change with time, the field is said to be static. Otherwise it is called a time-varying field. In the examples above, the field was considered in three-dimensional space; *i.e.,* in terms of length, breadth, and depth. The field concept is capable of generalization, however, to spaces of more than three dimensions, as will be indicated later in this article, just as the idea of space can be expanded to any number of dimensions. Though a time-varying field is, strictly speaking, a field in four dimensions, it is customary to describe such a field as a variable three-dimensional field.

MATHEMATICAL TREATMENT OF FIELDS

The mathematical description of the field is in terms of the measurable dimensions of the space under consideration. This means that the field is considered to be a function of the space; *i.e.,* in order to discuss the properties of the field mathematically, it is necessary that points in the field must be discussed. Any point in the field is identified in terms of its position in space relative to other points. To locate any point in the field, several types of three-coordinate systems may be used; for example, *x, y,* and *z* represent three spatial directions and distances of the points from a common point. When the measured property has magnitude but no direction it is called a scalar. When a measured property has direction it is called a vector and the spatial coordinates are, therefore, vectors. In mathematical language, then, a field is a function, signified by *f,* of the three space coordinates, signified by **r**, and the time coordinate, signified by *t.* This is written $f(\mathbf{r},t)$. Ordinarily **r** is a vector designating a point in three-dimensional space with coordinates *x, y, z,* but it may also symbolize a space of any number of dimensions. A field is said to be known when: (1) the function $f(\mathbf{r},t)$ is known, and (2) the observable property to which *f* refers is given.

While the preceding statements formally define a field, they do not fully characterize the kinds of fields that are useful in physical science. Such fields must satisfy one additional requirement: they must be defined by a known law that permits their calculation and prediction. The law is usually expressed as a differential equation (an equation that contains rate of change of variable quantities).

The following sections are devoted to a description of various fields useful in science and the laws that apply to them. The physical disciplines in which the fields occur are treated elsewhere; *e.g.,* under ELECTRICITY AND MAGNETISM; ELECTROMAGNETIC RADIATION; ATOMS; GRAVITATION; THERMODYNAMICS; and MECHANICS: *Quantum mechanics.*

Vectors and scalars (margin note)

CLASSIFICATION OF FIELDS

Material and nonmaterial. There are various ways of classifying fields. One important distinction, that between

Table 2: Quantum Numbers for Quarks

	I	I_3	S	B	Y	Q
q_1	$\frac{1}{2}$	$\frac{1}{2}$	0	$\frac{1}{3}$	$\frac{1}{3}$	$\frac{2}{3}$
q_2	$\frac{1}{2}$	$-\frac{1}{2}$	0	$\frac{1}{3}$	$\frac{1}{3}$	$-\frac{1}{3}$
q_3	0	0	-1	$\frac{1}{3}$	$-\frac{2}{3}$	$-\frac{1}{3}$

material and nonmaterial fields, must be made at the outset but need not be pursued further in its manifold philosophical implications. In a material field, the observable property signified by *f* describes some property of matter, such as the density, pressure, or the temperature of a gas, or the velocity of a portion of liquid. A nonmaterial field is not descriptive of any material property (although it is usually caused by matter) but describes some latent effect that would take place at a point of space under certain circumstances. The electric field is of this kind. Its "observable" is the electrostatic field indicated by *E* and its value at a point defined by the coordinates *x, y, z* is given by the field function. Nothing, however, may actually exist or be evident at that point. What matters is that *if* a charge were placed at the point defined by *x, y, z* it *would* experience a force proportional to the function of the field; *i.e.,* as explained above, *E (x, y, z).* Other nonmaterial fields are the magnetic field, the field of general relativity, and a variety of what are called probability fields, which are discernible as a statistical probability of occurrences, such as the state of an electron in an atom, treated as a function of quantum mechanics.

Non-
material
fields Material fields are introduced into physics because the variables to which they refer are of direct physical interest. Nonmaterial fields are usually introduced to simplify the theoretical description of phenomena by replacing the notion of action at a distance with that of local interactions. By saying that a charge located at *r* (*r* is the resultant vector at a point identified by *x, y, z* coordinates) sets up an electric field designated as *E (r)*, throughout space, one can more simply describe how a second charge at *r*₂ is affected by the first: the second charge interacts locally with the electric field at *r*₂.

Scalars, vectors, and tensors. Fields can be classified according to whether the observable function *f* (*i.e.,* the field quantity) is a scalar, a vector, or a tensor. A scalar is ordinarily defined as a quantity having magnitude but no direction. Examples include mass, density, and temperature.

A vector is said to be a quantity endowed with direction in space, like a force, or the strength of an electric or magnetic field. A vector field is symbolized by *V (r)* and has three space components, as has been explained, and these are symbolized by V_x *(r)*, V_y *(r)* and V_z *(r)*.

When the measurable function of a field cannot be expressed as a simple scalar or vector quantity, but many such quantities must be considered together, and their dependency must also be taken into account, a tensor may be set up. The nature of a tensor can be illustrated by the example of the stress tensor, denoted by **S**. It has nine components, signified as S_{ij}, both *i* and *j* ranging from 1 to 3. This means that *i* and *j* together have three times three, or nine different quantities. Each subscript corresponds to a direction in space; S_{ij} is the component of force along the *j*-direction of a cube of matter due to a deformation along *i*. Thus **S**, when fully written, amounts to an assemblage of nine quantities, as follows:

$$\mathbf{S} = \begin{matrix} S_{11} & S_{12} & S_{13} \\ S_{21} & S_{22} & S_{23} \\ S_{31} & S_{32} & S_{33} \end{matrix}.$$

The idea of a tensor can be generalized in two ways. First, the number of dimensions in space can be increased from three to *n*, as was suggested in the introduction, and the tensor then takes on *n* times *n*, or n^2 components. Second, the rank of the tensor can be raised; *i.e.,* the number of suffixes may be changed from two to *m*. For example, in *n* dimensions, S_{yk}, a tensor of rank 3, has n^3 components.

Given a field of a certain type (*e.g.,* a vector field), it is possible to generate for purposes of study and calculation other vector fields, scalar fields, tensor fields, and so on. Certain transformations between scalar and vector fields are also useful and have their own symbols.

EXAMPLES OF FIELDS IN ORDINARY SPACE

Some examples of different kinds of fields are here given in very general terms. It should be noted that the same differential equation may control the behaviour of quite different fields, and it should be stressed that differential equations have many solutions and, therefore, the field is not specified simply by the equation. Boundary conditions must also be imposed; that is, the field must be specified in certain regions. The differential equation then allows computation of the field at certain points in space and time if the value at some other point has already been specified.

Scalar fields. A simple example is provided by the pressure at different heights in the atmosphere. It is known that pressure exists everywhere in the atmosphere and that it is actually the result of gravitational attraction between the Earth and gas molecules. In other words, pressure is the result of air molecules accelerating toward the Earth in the gravitational field. This movement, however, is then offset by the motion of the molecules due to their heat energy, which makes them bombard one another continuously, with the result that there is a constant tendency in the atmosphere to expand, and the expansion can only be upward. A steady state is achieved between the two tendencies: the gas does not all collect on the surface of the Earth, as a liquid does, nor does it expand and vanish into space against the gravitational attraction (as it does on the Moon, where the gravitational field is not strong enough to counteract the expansion). The atmosphere is most dense closest to the Earth, where the gravitational field is strongest and the tendency of the gas to expand is most effectively balanced by its tendency to move toward the Earth. Thus, the pressure is a function of the height, decreasing with height. Achievement of
steady
state

The differential equation, then, states that the change in pressure over a specific, small difference in height equals the acceleration of gravity times the change in density at that height. With this equation, therefore, the whole field—which is pressure of the atmosphere—can be mapped to its outer limits.

The density of matter in a moving fluid forms a scalar field, which can be said to obey a general law, the factors to be considered being: change in density at a point in the flow over a small period of time, the rate of diffusion, and the variation in density between two points.

An equation of the same form holds for the temperature field (also a scalar field) in a medium that, because its temperature is not uniform, is involved in a temperature readjustment; *i.e.,* heat is being transmitted from one area to another. The differential equation then relates the change in temperature over a small period of time, the coefficient of heat conductivity, the specific heat, the density, and the temperature at the point of observation.

The gravitational potential (*i.e.,* the work done on a unit mass in bringing it from infinity to the point defined by the space coordinates) obeys an equation (known by the name of its originator, Siméon-Denis Poisson) that is also applicable to other fields. It relates the gravitational potential (a scalar quantity), the gravitational constant, and the density of matter there.

Electrostatic potential, the repulsion between like charges or the attraction between unlike charges, is given as a differential equation of the scalar field; it relates the potential to the charge density (the number of charges per unit volume of space). A similar equation is used for the magnetostatic field potential, the magnetostatic field being taken to be the attraction or repulsion between unlike or like magnetic poles.

Any medium pervaded by a wave becomes the site of a wave field that satisfies the wave equation. As an example, with sound, the pressure in an acoustic field is controlled by the wave equation.

Vector fields. In a moving fluid the velocity vector forms a field each of whose components is a function of the *x, y, z* coordinates. They must satisfy the equations of continuity, which include the fluid density, which may vary from place to place. If it is constant (*i.e.,* if the fluid is incompressible) then the full equation asserts that the amount of fluid flowing from a point is equal to the amount flowing into it.

Perhaps the most important vector field of mathematical physics is the electromagnetic field, characterized by vectors for the electric field and for the magnetic field. When these two fields are nonstatic, they interact in characteristic ways, and the law governing them cannot be written for either one alone. It takes the form of equations that, in free space, include the velocity of light in vacuum.

The field quantity in many types of waves (*e.g.*, light waves, elastic disturbances in solids, seismic waves in the Earth's crust) is a vector. It obeys the same form of wave equation but with the proper vector quantity.

Tensor fields. One important example will be considered, namely the pressure field in a hydrodynamic system; *i.e.*, a fluid in complicated motion with different temperatures at different points inside the fluid. In this case the vectors are: the average velocity of particles at a point in the fluid, the heat flow vector (calories changing per second), and the force per unit area in the direction resulting from the motion in the *i*-direction. The tensor appears in numerous important hydrodynamic equations, notably that of energy flow. Its knowledge, together with velocity and heat flow vectors, provides a complete understanding of the behaviour of the hydrodynamic system. The law controlling it consists of five differential equations, known as the Navier-Stokes equations. They contain the coefficient of viscosity and the thermal conductivity.

This example illustrates the interaction of several fields: the pressure, temperature, and flow fields.

FIELDS WITH DISTRIBUTIONS
IN MORE THAN THREE DIMENSIONS

Phase space

Thermodynamic phenomena. In connection with the laws of thermodynamics, a space can be constructed of $6n$ dimensions to account for the behaviour of a system of n particles. It is called phase space, and certain rules of correspondence relate ρ, the field quantity representing density in this space, to such thermodynamic observables as temperature, entropy (a measure of disorder in a system), free energy, and others. To aid visual intuition, ρ is thought of as a cloud of dust of varying density in phase space, and the movement of the cloud (*i.e.*, the field under consideration) determines the values of the quantities measured in thermodynamics.

Relativity. Perhaps the most interesting example of a field in more than three dimensions occurs in the theory of general relativity, where the behaviour of all matter is described in what is called the metric field. It operates in a space of four dimensions, x, y, z, t (see above *Mathematical treatment of fields*). A metric field tensor defines empty space as Euclidean (or flat). The presence of matter causes curvature of the space. Once the tensor is known, the motion of any particle can be calculated. The components of the tensor obey Einstein's law of gravitation, which relates them to the distribution of matter in the universe.

Quantum mechanics. The fundamental constructs (or quantities) of quantum mechanics, the state functions, are also fields. In classical mechanics, the motion of a particle is described by specifying its position as a function of time. In quantum theory, one deals no longer with the particle's position but with the probability of finding it at that position, and that probability forms a field.   (H.Ma.)

Physical constants

Throughout all of the formulations of the basic theories of physics and their application to the real world, there appear again and again certain invariant quantities called the fundamental physical constants. These quantities, all of which are associated with specific and universally used symbols, are of such importance that they must be known with as high an accuracy as is possible. They include the speed of light in vacuum (c); the elementary charge (e), which is the magnitude of the charge on the electron; the mass of the electron (m_e); the Planck constant (h); and the fine-structure constant, symbolized by the Greek letter alpha (a). These will all be considered in detail below.

There are, of course, many other important quantities that can be measured with high accuracy—the density of a particular piece of silver, for example, or the lattice spacing (the distance between the planes of atoms) of a particular crystal of silicon, or the distance from the Earth to the Sun. These quantities, however, are generally not considered to be fundamental constants. First, they are

not universal invariants because they are too specific, too closely associated with the particular properties of the material or system upon which the measurements are carried out. Second, such quantities lack universality because they do not consistently appear in the basic theoretical equations of physics upon which the entire science rests, nor are they properties of the fundamental particles of physics of which all matter is constituted.

DEFINITION, IMPORTANCE, AND ACCURACY

The constants named above, five among many, were listed because they exemplify the different origins of fundamental constants. The speed of light and the Planck constant are examples of quantities that occur naturally in the mathematical formulation of certain fundamental physical theories, the former in James Clerk Maxwell's theory of electric and magnetic fields and Albert Einstein's theories of relativity, and the latter in the theory of atomic particles, or quantum theory. For example, in Einstein's theories of relativity, mass and energy are equivalent, the energy (E) being directly proportional to the mass (m), with the constant of proportionality being the velocity of light squared (c^2)—*i.e.*, the famous equation $E = mc^2$. In this equation, E and m are variables and c is invariant, a constant of the equation. In quantum theory, the energy (E) and frequency, symbolized by the Greek letter nu (v), of a photon (a single quantum unit of electromagnetic energy such as light or heat radiation) are related by $E = hv$. Here, the Planck constant is the constant of proportionality.

Elementary charge and electron mass

The elementary charge and the electron mass are examples of constants that characterize the basic, or elementary, particles that constitute matter, such as the electron, alpha particle, proton, neutron, muon, and pion. Additionally, they are examples of constants that are used as standard units of measurement. The charge and mass of atomic and elementary particles often are expressed in terms of the elementary charge and the electron mass; the charge of an alpha particle, the nucleus of the helium atom, is given as $2e$; whereas the mass of the muon is given as $206.77 \, m_e$.

The fine-structure constant (a) is an example of a fundamental constant that can be expressed as a combination of other constants. The fine-structure constant is equal to a numerical constant times the velocity of light times the electron charge squared divided by twice Planck's constant, or $\mu_0 ce^2/2h$, μ_0 being the so-called permeability of free space, equal to exactly $4\pi \times 10^{-7}$ henry/metre. (The system of measurement units used here is the Système Internationale d'Unités [International System of Units], or SI.) Because this particular combination of constants appears in many theoretical equations in exactly the same way, however, the fine-structure constant is really a fundamental constant in its own right. For example, it is the fundamental constant of quantum electrodynamics, the quantum theory of the interaction (mutual influence) among electrons, muons, and photons, serving as a measure of the strength of these interactions. Another quantity that is a combination of other constants is the Rydberg constant (symbolized R_∞), which is equal to the product $\mu_0^2 c^3 e^4 m_e /8h^3$. It sets the scale (magnitude) of the various allowed electron-energy states or levels in atoms such as hydrogen.

It is important to know the numerical values of the fundamental constants with high accuracy for at least two reasons. First, the quantitative predictions of the basic theories of physics depend on the numerical values of the constants that appear in the theories. An accurate knowledge of their values is therefore essential if people hope to achieve an accurate quantitative description of the physical universe. Second, and more important, the careful study of the numerical values of these constants, as determined from various experiments in the different fields of physics, can in turn test the overall consistency and correctness of the basic theories of physics themselves.

Many of the fundamental constants can be currently measured with an accuracy of a few parts in a million. By accuracy is meant the relative size of the uncertainty that must be assigned to the numerical value of any quantity to indicate how far from the true value it may be because

Uncertainty in measuring constants

of limitations in experiment or theory or both. This uncertainty is a quantitative estimate of the extent of the doubts associated with the value. The most commonly used uncertainty, the standard deviation, symbolized by the Greek letter sigma (σ), is such that there is about a 68 percent chance that the true value differs from the assigned value by less than σ. Furthermore, there is a 95 percent chance that the true value lies between plus and minus two standard deviations, 2σ, and a 99.7 percent chance that it lies between plus and minus 3σ. (All uncertainties quoted in this article will be one standard deviation.)

In practice, an accuracy or uncertainty of one part per million (abbreviated ppm) is rather respectable. It corresponds to determining the length of a United States football field (100 yards, or about 91 metres) to within the thickness of two of these pages (one page is about 0.0022 inch, or 0.000087 millimetre, thick). There are several quantities that have been measured with uncertainties approaching one part in 1,000,000,000,000 (one in 10^{12}); this uncertainty corresponds to determining the distance from New York City to San Francisco to within one-tenth the thickness of this page.

Table 3 displays the best values for the six fundamental constants mentioned above and gives their uncertainties (in ppm). Here, $1/a$, the inverse of the fine-structure constant, is given rather than a. The fine-structure constant is dimensionless; i.e., it is a pure number and, therefore, has no units.

Table 3: Values of Some Selected Fundamental Constants

	symbol	units	value*	uncertainty (ppm)†
Speed of light in vacuum	c	10^8 metres per second	2.99792458(1.2)	0.004
Elementary charge	e	10^{-19} coulomb	1.6021892(46)	2.9
Planck constant	h	10^{-34} joule-second	6.626176(36)	5.4
Electron rest mass	m_e	10^{-31} kilogram	9.109534(47)	5.1
Inverse fine-structure constant	$1/a$	—	137.03604(11)	0.82
Rydberg constant	R_∞	10^7 per metre	1.097373177(83)	0.075

*The numbers in parentheses are the standard-deviation uncertainties in the last digits of the quoted values. †Parts per million.

HISTORICAL MEASUREMENTS

Millikan's oil-drop experiments

One of the earlier experiments to measure a fundamental constant to high accuracy, as well as an example of how the accurate determination of a fundamental constant using different methods can lead to an improved understanding of a particular physical phenomenon, was the measurement of the fundamental unit of charge (e) by Robert A. Millikan, a physicist in the United States. From about 1907 to 1917 he carried out his now-famous oil-drop experiment to determine e. In this method, the displacement of small, charged oil drops (the charge on the drop is usually just a few e) moving in air between two horizontal and parallel metal plates (with and without an applied known voltage) is followed as a function of time. The value of the fundamental constant e is then calculated from many observations on different drops and knowledge of other relevant quantities, especially the viscosity (resistance to flow) of the air. Millikan's final value, reported in 1917, was $(4.774 \pm 0.002) \times 10^{-10}$ esu (esu being the electrostatic unit, one of the units of charge in the centimetre-gram-second [cgs] system of units; this cgs-esu system was in wide use before the general adoption of the SI system).

That this value was significantly in error became clear in the 1930s with the development of a new but indirect method for obtaining the value of e. The technique consisted of separately measuring N_A, the Avogadro constant (the number of atoms or molecules contained in a mole, which is defined as a mass in grams equal to the atomic or molecular weight of a substance), and F, the Faraday constant (the amount of charge that must pass through a solution to cause electrolytic deposition of a mole of a singly charged, or monovalent, element contained in the solution). These two quantities are related by the simple equation that states that the Faraday constant is equal to

the Avogadro constant times unit of charge, or $F = N_A e$. It therefore follows that $e = F/N_A$, so that the constant e can readily be obtained if the two constants, Faraday and Avogadro, are known.

The Avogadro constant was determined by measuring the density, molecular weight, and crystal lattice spacing of a particular crystal species, such as rock salt, using X-ray techniques. The Faraday was determined by measuring the mass of material (e.g., silver) electrolytically deposited onto an electrode when a known current flowing for a known time was allowed to pass through a solution containing the material. The indirect value of the elementary charge deduced in this way was $(4.8021 \pm 0.0009) \times 10^{-10}$ esu, significantly different from the Millikan value. The major source of this disturbing discrepancy was traced in the late 1930s to the use by Millikan of an incorrect value for the viscosity of air. When Millikan's data were recalculated using a corrected value for the viscosity of air, the value of e obtained agreed with the indirect value calculated from the Faraday and the Avogadro constant.

Although this case is an example of the general fact that the experimentally determined value of a constant varies with each determination, it must be realized that it is just these variations from one determination to another in the measured numerical values of the constants that often furnish important clues to errors in experiment and theory.

The fundamental-constants field has advanced rapidly since the mid-20th century. Indeed, few measurements of constants existed before about the turn of the 20th century. Some of the more important historical measurements made before 1940—in addition to Millikan's oil-drop measurement of e, the early measurements of the Faraday made about 1910 to 1915, and the early determinations of the Avogadro constant in the 1930s by the U.S. physicist Joyce A. Bearden and others using X-ray techniques—are described below.

Speed of light. To determine a velocity requires knowledge of both a distance and a time. Attempts to measure the speed of light (c) date back to Galileo, whose *Dialogues Concerning Two New Sciences* (1634) describes an unsuccessful determination of c by having two men stand at a known distance from each other and alternately cover and uncover their hand-held lanterns as soon as each saw the light from the other man's lamp, thus seeking to determine the elapsed time for light to travel the known distance between the two men. A 17th-century Danish astronomer, Ole Rømer, calculated a value of c from the dependence of the period of revolution of a moon of Jupiter on the Earth's orbital position about the Sun. Similarly, in 1726, an English astronomer, James Bradley, determined c from the apparent change in position of a number of stars in the sky as the Earth moved about the Sun.

The problem of overcoming the short time interval associated with light travelling a readily measured distance on the Earth's surface was first solved by a French physicist, Armand-Hippolyte-Louis Fizeau, in the mid-19th century. He did this by having the light pass through a gap between the teeth of a toothed wheel rotating at a known rate, reflect off a fixed mirror a known distance away, and return to the wheel. A related method utilizing a rotating mirror was also employed by another French physicist, Jean Foucault, in 1862.

The classic pre-World War II measurements of the constant c are associated with Albert A. Michelson, a physicist in the United States. From 1924 to 1926, Michelson measured c by reflecting light between a rotating mirror with a number of faces and a fixed mirror some 35 kilometres (22 miles) away. A second measurement using essentially the same method but in a 1.6-kilometre (one-mile) evacuated tube was carried out by Michelson and his associates over the period 1931 to 1935.

Michelson's determinations of c

Ratio of the elementary charge to the electron mass. Numerous direct measurements of the ratio e/m_e were carried out over the period 1897 to 1938. The experiments usually involved the deflection of beams of free electrons by electric and magnetic fields. Many of the experiments required the simultaneous measurement of the velocity of the electrons and of the voltage used to impart kinetic energy (i.e., velocity) to the electrons. Often the electron velocity was determined by a null deflection method in which the magnitudes of crossed electric and magnetic fields, through which the electron beam travelled, were so adjusted that the electric and magnetic deflecting forces just balanced each other. An English physicist, Joseph John Thomson, was the first to use this technique in 1897.

Ratio of the Planck constant to the elementary charge. The very first precise determination of the ratio h/e used the photoelectric effect: the emission of electrons from a metal when light of a particular wavelength is allowed to impinge upon the surface. If a retarding voltage, or potential, is applied to the metal so that the electrons are just prevented from leaving the surface, then a unique relationship exists between the wavelength of the light, the voltage, and the ratio h/e. Millikan, using sodium and lithium, first reported a result from this method in 1916.

A second method to determine the ratio h/e depends on the so-called short wavelength limit of the continuous X-ray spectrum. In this technique, a beam of electrons is accelerated through a known voltage and is allowed to strike a metal target. The maximum-energy X-ray (that is, the one having the highest frequency or shortest wavelength) is emitted when all of the electrical potential energy of an electron in the beam is converted to a single X-ray photon. By measuring the voltage and the wavelength of the emitted X-ray, the ratio h/e can be determined. The first precise measurement of this type was reported in 1921.

The Newtonian gravitational constant. The universal, or Newtonian (after Isaac Newton), gravitational constant (G) is the constant of proportionality in the equation relating the gravitational force between two separated bodies to their masses. Two different classes of experiment have been performed to measure the constant G. The first involves estimating the mass of the Earth and separately determining the radius of the Earth and the acceleration of an object falling toward the Earth because of gravity. Attempts to measure the mass of the Earth have taken two forms. In 1775, a British astronomer, Nevil Maskelyne, used the deflection from the vertical of a plumb line placed on either side of a mountain of known shape and density. In 1854 another astronomer, George Biddell Airy of England, measured the gravitational constant by comparing the period of the swing of a pendulum at the surface of the Earth and at the bottom of a mine shaft of known depth.

The second general class of experiment for determining the gravitational constant, a significantly more accurate one, consists of measuring the gravitational force attracting two masses in the laboratory. In 1798 Henry Cavendish of England, using a torsion balance designed a few years earlier, carried out the first such experiment. He suspended by a thin fibre a light, stiff rod with two solid five-centimetre (two-inch) diameter lead spheres attached at either end. He then brought two 30-centimetre diameter (12-inch) lead spheres near the smaller spheres. The gravitational attraction between them produced a torque, or turning force, that twisted or deflected the suspending fibre. The most accurate value of the gravitational constant known in the mid-1970s was obtained using the same general method during the period 1932–42.

Cavendish's measurement of the gravitational constant

MODERN MEASUREMENTS

The great progress made in determining the numerical values of the fundamental constants after World War II is the direct result of the advances made in the general fields of electronics, microwaves, and other technologies during and after the war. These advances have not only resulted in new and improved measurements of some of the constants listed earlier (for example, a determination of the speed of light, using a microwave interferometer, made in 1957 with uncertainty of 0.33 ppm and another, using lasers, made in 1972 with an uncertainty of 0.004 ppm), but for the first time permitted the direct measurement of a whole new group of constants and related quantities. The more important of these new measurements are summarized below; the first two are concerned with the proton, which has a mass approximately 1,836 times that

of an electron and a charge identical to that of the electron, but positive.

Gyromagnetic ratio of the proton. The axis of the intrinsic rotational motion, or spin, of the proton precesses in a magnetic field at a speed measured by the gyromagnetic ratio, γ_p. This ratio may be determined by first producing a known magnetic field by the passage of a known electric current through a coil, or solenoid, of precisely known dimensions and then measuring by means of standard electronic techniques the precession frequency of the protons in a water sample within the solenoid. This procedure is the low-field method, in which the accurately determined magnetic field is only about 20 times that of the Earth. In the high-field method, the magnetic field, established by an electromagnet, may be 10,000 times larger than that of the Earth. For this case, the field is determined by measuring the force it exerts on a small coil of known dimensions carrying a known current; this apparatus is often called a Cotton balance. The gyromagnetic ratio of the proton was first determined with high accuracy by the high-field method in 1950 and by the low-field method in 1957. In the mid-1970s the most accurate measurements of this ratio by the high-field method had an uncertainty of 1.0 ppm; by the low-field method, 0.42 ppm.

Magnetic moment of the proton. The magnetic moment of the proton, expressed in nuclear magnetons, is the ratio μ_p/μ_N of the above-mentioned frequency with which the spin axis of a proton precesses in a magnetic field to the frequency of the proton's orbital, or circular, motion in the same field, called the cyclotron frequency. The first measurement of this ratio was reported in 1949 by the U.S. physicist John A. Hipple and his associates, using a device called an omegatron. In this method, an adjustable radio-frequency electric field is applied to the omegatron at right angles to the direction of the magnetic field. When the frequency of this electric field is properly adjusted, protons in the omegatron are accelerated by it and spiral outward until they hit a collector and are detected. The frequency of the orbital motion of the proton can then be determined from the adjusted frequency of the electric field. The present best experimental determination of μ_p/μ_N has an uncertainty of 0.43 ppm.

Measuring the magnetic moment

Fine structure of atomic hydrogen. The term fine structure refers to the differences between certain states, or levels, of energy in atoms. The fine structure of atomic hydrogen was first measured with high accuracy by a U.S. physicist, Willis E. Lamb, Jr., and co-workers and reported in a series of classic papers over the period 1950 to 1953. In these experiments, changes in the energy state of particular atoms were induced by irradiating a beam of the atoms with microwaves of a properly adjusted and known frequency as the beam was passed through a known magnetic field. The energy differences, or fine structure, could then be accurately calculated from the field and frequency. The accuracy of 5–10 ppm achieved by Lamb had not been surpassed by the 1970s.

Free electron g factor. Because the electron has an electric charge and an intrinsic rotational motion, or spin, it behaves in some respects like a small bar magnet; that is, it is said to have a magnetic moment. Because the electron also has mass, it behaves in some respects like a spinning top; that is, it is said to have spin angular momentum. The g factor of the electron is defined as the ratio of its magnetic moment to its spin angular momentum. This factor is nominally 2 and was first measured with high accuracy during the period from 1961 to 1963. Electric and magnetic fields can be used to trap electrons with spins prealigned in a particular direction for a known length of time. The g factor is then obtained from the change in spin direction during the trapping period and the magnitude of the trapping magnetic field. By the mid-1970s, improvements in this basic method of measuring the g factor had reduced the uncertainty from its earlier value of 0.027 ppm to 0.0035 ppm.

Ground-state hyperfine splitting in atomic hydrogen. The hyperfine splitting (hfs) in the ground state, or lowest energy state, of spinning hydrogen is basically equal to the energy difference between a hydrogen atom in which the orbital electron is spinning in the same direction as the

quantity	symbol	value*	units	uncertainty (ppm)†
Ratio of twice elementary charge to the Planck constant	$2e/h$	483594.000	10^9 Hz/V$_{B169}$	(definition)
Speed of light in vacuum	c	299792458(1.2)	m/s	0.004
Acceleration of gravity (U.S. National gravity base, Washington, D.C.)	$g(CB)$	980104.30(2)	10^{-5} m/s^2	0.02
Acceleration of gravity (National Physical Laboratory, Teddington, England)	$g(BFS)$	981181.77(2)	10^{-5} m/s^2	0.02
Acceleration of gravity (All Union Institute of Metrology, Leningrad)	$g(VNIIM)$	981916.80(1.00)	10^{-5} m/s^2	1.0
Electron magnetic moment in Bohr magnetons (one-half the free electron g-factor)	μ_e/μ_B	1.0011596567(35)		0.0035
One-half the free muon g-factor	$g_\mu/2$	1.00116616(31)		0.31
Ratio of electron to proton magnetic moments	μ_e/μ_p	658.2106880(66)		0.010
Proton magnetic moment in Bohr magnetons	μ_p/μ_B	0.001521032209(16)		0.011
Proton magnetic moment in Bohr magnetons	μ'_p/μ_B	0.001520993215(100)		0.066
Unity plus diamagnetic shielding constant	$1 + \sigma(p')$	$1 + 25.637(67) \times 10^{-6}$		0.067
Proton atomic mass	M_p	1.007276470(11)	u	0.011
Unity plus ratio of free electron mass to free proton mass	$1 + m_e/m_p$	1.000544617		<0.001
Unity plus ratio of free electron mass to free deuteron mass	$1 + m_e/m_d$	1.000272444		<0.001
Unity plus ratio of free electron mass to free alpha particle mass	$1 + m_e/m_a$	1.000137093		<0.001
Rydberg constant for infinite mass	R_∞	10973731.77(83)	m^{-1}	0.075

*The numbers in parentheses are the uncertainties (standard deviations) in the last digits of the quoted values.
†Parts per million. Abbreviations are as follows: Hz = hertz (cycles per second); m = metre; s = second; u = atomic mass unit (^{12}C = 12); p' = "for protons in a spherical sample of pure water."

central proton and a hydrogen atom in which the electron and proton are spinning in opposite directions. Polykarp Kusch, a physicist working in the United States, reported the first high-accuracy measurement of this quantity in 1955, using a microwave-excitation method resembling that used for fine-structure measurements.

Use of a maser to measure hyperfine splitting

A much more accurate value was obtained in 1963 by a U.S. physicist, Norman F. Ramsey, and co-workers using the so-called hydrogen maser, which is a type of microwave amplifier. In this device, excited hydrogen atoms are focussed by a magnetic field onto an aperture in a Teflon-coated quartz bulb that is located in a radio-frequency-resonant metallic cavity. When the cavity frequency is tuned to the frequency corresponding to the hyperfine-splitting-energy difference, maser-like oscillations are produced. The measurable oscillation frequency then equals the hyperfine splitting. The hydrogen hfs is presently the most accurately measured physical quantity: its uncertainty is about 2 in 10^{13}.

NEW DETERMINATIONS AND
INTERRELATIONSHIPS AMONG THE CONSTANTS

To these important post-World War II measurements must be added the determination of $2e/h$, the ratio of twice the elementary charge to the Planck constant. First reported in 1967 by the U.S. physicists William H. Parker, Barry N. Taylor, and Donald N. Langenberg, this experiment involving low-temperature physics offers what is probably the best example in recent years of the important consequences that can follow from a highly accurate determination of a fundamental constant. Furthermore, its discussion naturally leads to the exploration of other ideas such as the interdependency of the constants, standards of measurement, conversion factors, and least-squares adjustments of the constants.

The $2e/h$ measurement in question is based on a remarkable phenomenon in superconductors (metals that lose their electrical resistance at extremely low temperatures) known as the alternating current (ac) Josephson effect. In 1962, a physicist, Brian Josephson of Cambridge University, England, showed theoretically that, if two su-

Use of the Josephson effect

perconductors are weakly connected together, then an alternating resistanceless current, or ac supercurrent, will flow between them if they are maintained at a finite voltage difference (V). He also showed that the frequency, (v), of the ac supercurrent is proportional to the voltage difference, the constant of proportionality being simply $2e/h$. Thus, $v = (2e/h)V$. Because the Josephson frequency–voltage relation is believed to be exact and independent of a wide variety of experimental variables, the determination of the ratio $2e/h$ is rather straightforward when compared with most other experiments for determining fundamental constants. It is necessary to measure only the voltage difference between the two superconductors and the frequency of the oscillating supercurrent. Indeed, the final result of the original measurements by Parker and his colleagues of the ratio $2e/h$ had an uncertainty of only 2.4 ppm, only $^1/_{20}$ that of the best previous value that had been determined from an X-ray experiment. More recent Josephson-effect measurements of $2e/h$ conducted by several different groups at the various national standardizing laboratories have reduced the uncertainty to a few hundredths of a part per million.

The determination of the constant $2e/h$ by means of the Josephson effect has had its greatest effect in the field of quantum electrodynamics (QED), the quantum theory of interacting electrons, muons, and photons. As previously noted, the fine-structure constant (a) is a measure of the strength of these interactions. Quantum electrodynamics has proven to be one of the most important of the modern theories of physics and one of the few that provide a basis for highly accurate numerical predictions. Such predictions, however, are possible only if an accurate value of a is available, because the theoretical expressions derivable from QED that describe the various physical quantities of interest generally take the form of mathematical expressions involving a.

Heretofore, the most accurate values of the fine-structure constant were obtained from experiment with the aid of theoretical equations containing significant contributions from quantum electrodynamics itself. This situation made it difficult to compare QED theory and experiment unam-

Table 5: QED-Independent Data Considered for Use in the 1973 Adjustment

publication date and author	quantity	symbol	method	value*	uncertainty (ppm)†	item
1964–70, National Measurement Laboratory, Australia	Conversion factor relating International Bureau of Weights and Measures (BIPM) 1 January 1969 as-maintained ohm to SI ohm	Ω_{BI69}/Ω	Thompson-Lampard calculable capacitor	0.99999946(19)	0.19	(1)
1968, Driscoll and Olsen	Conversion factor relating BIPM 1 January 1969 as-maintained ampere to SI ampere	A_{BI69}/A	U.S. National Bureau of Standards Pellat balance	1.0000018(97)	9.7	(2)
1958, Driscoll and Cutkosky	same	same	U.S. National Bureau of Standards current balance	0.9999988(77)	7.7	(3)
1965, 1970, Vigoureux	same	same	National Physical Laboratory, U.K., current balance	1.0000000(55)	5.5	(4)
1960, Craig et al.	Faraday constant	F	silver-perchloric acid coulometer	$9.648672(66) \times 10^4 A_{BI69} \cdot s \cdot mol^{-1}$	6.8	(5)
1968, Marinenko and Taylor	same	same	benzoic and oxalic acid coulometers	$9.648695(93) \times 10^4 A_{BI69} \cdot s \cdot mol^{-1}$	9.6	(6)
1968, Hara et al.	Proton gyromagnetic ratio	γ'_p	low field	$2.6751156(107) \times 10^8 s^{-1} \cdot T^{-1}_{BI69}$	4.0	(7)
1972, Olsen and Driscoll	same	same	same	$2.6751370(54) \times 10^8 s^{-1} \cdot T^{-1}_{BI69}$	2.0	(8)
1965, Vigoureux	same	same	same	$2.6751187(107) \times 10^8 s^{-1} \cdot T^{-1}_{BI69}$	4.0	(9)
1971, Malyarevskaya, Studentsov, and Shifrin	same	same	same	$2.6751100(161) \times 10^8 s^{-1} \cdot T^{-1}_{BI69}$	6.0	(10)
1966, Yagola, Zingerman, and Sepetyi	same	same	high field	$2.675130(20) \times 10^8 A_{BI69} \cdot s \cdot kg^{-1}$	7.4	(11)
1971, Kibble and Hunt	same	same	same	$2.675075(43) \times 10^8 A_{BI69} \cdot s \cdot kg^{-1}$	16	(12)
1972, Mamyrin, Aruyev, and Alekseenko	proton magnetic moment in nuclear magnetons	μ'_p/μ_N	mass spectrometer	2.7927738(12)	0.43	(13)
1972, Petley and Morris	same	same	omegatron	2.7927748(23)	0.82	(14)
1931, Bearden (revised 1964, I. Henins and Bearden)	conversion factor relating kx-unit to angstrom	Λ	plane ruled grating	1.002027(33)	33	(15)
1971, A. Henins	same	same	same	1.0020655(98)	9.8	(16)
1964, Spijkerman and Bearden	same	same	hc/e via short wavelength limit	1.002041(33)	33	(17)
1964, I. Henins and Bearden	product of Avogadro constant and cube of kx-unit angstrom conversion factor	$N_A\Lambda^3$	X-ray crystal density using silicon	$6.059768(95) \times 10^{23} mol^{-1}$	16	(18)
1965, Bearden	same	same	X-ray crystal density using calcite	$6.05961(17) \times 10^{23} mol^{-1}$	28	(19)
1964, Knowles	electronic Compton wavelength	λ_C	electron–positron annihilation via tantalum	$24.21466(37) \times 10^{-3} kxu$	15	(20)
1971, Van Assche	same	same	same	$24.21315(80) \times 10^{-3} kxu$	33	(21)

*The numbers in parentheses are the standard-deviation uncertainties in the last digits of the quoted values. †Parts per million.

Table 6: QED-Dependent Data Considered for Use in the 1973 Adjustment

publication date and author	quantity	symbol	method	value*	uncertainty (ppm)†	item
1971, Wesley and Rich (revised 1972, Granger and Ford)	inverse fine-structure constant	$1/\alpha$	electron anomalous moment, plus theory	137.03563(42)	3.1	(22)
1972, Crowe, Williams et al.	ratio muon magnetic moment to proton magnetic moment	μ_μ/μ_p	muon precession	3.1833467(82)	2.6	(23)
1970, Hutchinson et al.	same	same	same	3.183356(31)	9.6	(24)
1970, DeVoe, Telegdi et al. (revised 1972, Jarecki and Herman)	same	same	muonium Zeeman transitions	3.183350(15)	4.7	(25)
1969–73, Chicago and Yale groups	muonium ground state hyperfine splitting	$\nu Mhfs$	muonium atoms stopped in argon or krypton	4463303.8(1.8) kHz	0.40	(26)
1970, Hellwig et al., 1971, Essen et al.	inverse fine-structure constant	$1/\alpha$	hydrogen maser measurement of hydrogen ground state hyperfine splitting, plus theory	137.03597(22)	1.6	(27)
1972, Baird et al.	same	same	fine structure in hydrogen, plus theory	137.03544(54)	3.9	(28)
1971, Kaufman, Lamb et al.	same	same	same	137.03416(20)	1.5	(29)
1971, Shyn et al.	same	same	same	137.03508(46)	3.3	(30)
1970, Cosens and Vorburger	same	same	same	137.03563(31)	2.3	(31)

*The numbers in parentheses are the standard deviation uncertainties in the last digits of the quoted values. †Parts per million.

biguously. Now, however, by combining the value of $2e/h$ determined from measurements of the alternating-current Josephson effect with the measured values of certain other constants, a highly accurate value of a can be obtained indirectly without any essential use of quantum electrodynamic theory. As a result, definitive comparisons can be made between quantum electrodynamic theory and experimental results.

Among the quantities for which such a comparison was of critical importance in 1967 was the hyperfine splitting in hydrogen, which can be measured experimentally with an accuracy of 2 parts in 10^{13}. In contrast, the theoretical QED equation for the hfs is limited to an accuracy of a few parts per million because of the difficulty of evaluating some of the terms in the equation. One such term—the proton polarizability correction, δ_N—was known to be 1 or 2 ppm at most.

The small theoretical value for the correction δ_N is in marked contrast to that implied by the value of a accepted before 1967. When that value was used to compare theory and experiment, it was found that δ_N had the highly improbable value of 43 ppm with an uncer-

Table 7: Physical Constant Values

quantity	symbol	numerical value*	uncertainty (ppm)	units SI †	units cgs ‡
Speed of light in vacuum	c	299792458(1.2)	0.004	$m \cdot s^{-1}$	$10^2 \, cm \cdot s^{-1}$
Permeability of vacuum	μ_0	4π		$10^{-7} \, H \cdot m^{-1}$	
		$=12.5663706144$		$10^{-7} \, H \cdot m^{-1}$	
Permittivity of vacuum, $1/\mu_0 c^2$	ε_0	8.854187818(71)	0.008	$10^{-12} \, F \cdot m^{-1}$	
Fine-structure constant, $[\mu_0 c^2 / 4\pi](e^2\hbar c)$	a	7.2973506(60)	0.82	10^{-8}	10^{-3}
	a^{-1}	137.03604(11)	0.82		
Elementary charge	e	1.6021892(46)	2.9	$10^{-19} \, C$	10^{-20} emu
		4.803242(14)	2.9		10^{-10} esu
Planck constant	h	6.626176(36)	5.4	$10^{-34} \, J \cdot s$	$10^{-27} \, erg \cdot s$
	$\hbar = h/2\pi$	1.0545887(57)	5.4	$10^{-34} \, J \cdot s$	$10^{-27} \, erg \cdot s$
Avogadro constant	N_A	6.022045(31)	5.1	$10^{23} \, mol^{-1}$	$10^{23} \, mol^{-1}$
Atomic mass unit, $10^{-3} \, kg \cdot mol^{-1} \, N_A^{-1}$	u	1.6605655(86)	5.1	$10^{-27} \, kg$	10^{-24} g
Electron rest mass	m_e	9.109534(47)	5.1	$10^{-31} \, kg$	10^{-28} g
		5.4858026(21)	0.38	$10^{-4} \, u$	$10^{-4} \, u$
Proton rest mass	m_p	1.6726485(86)	5.1	$10^{-27} \, kg$	10^{-24} g
		1.007276470(11)	0.011	u	u
Ratio of proton mass to electron mass	m_p/m_e	1836.15152(70)	0.38		
Neutron rest mass	m_n	1.6749543(86)	5.1	$10^{-27} \, kg$	10^{-24} g
		1.008665012(37)	0.037	u	u
Electron charge to mass ratio	e/m_e	1.7588047(49)	2.8	$10^{11} \, C \cdot kg^{-1}$	10^7 emu $\cdot g^{-1}$
		5.272764(15)	2.8		10^{17} esu $\cdot g^{-1}$
Magnetic flux quantum, $[c]^{-1}(hc/2e)$	Φ_0	2.0678506(54)	2.6	$10^{-15} \, Wb$	$10^{-7} \, G \cdot cm^2$
	h/e	4.135701(11)	2.6	$10^{-15} \, J \cdot s \cdot C^{-1}$	10^{-7} erg $\cdot s \cdot emu^{-1}$
		1.3795215(36)	2.6		10^{-17} erg $\cdot s \cdot esu^{-1}$
Josephson frequency voltage ratio	$2e/h$	4.835939(13)	2.6	$10^{14} \, Hz \cdot V^{-1}$	
Quantum of circulation	$h/2m_e$	3.6369455(60)	1.6	$10^{-4} \, J \cdot s \cdot kg^{-1}$	erg $\cdot s \cdot g^{-1}$
	h/m_e	7.273891(12)	1.6	$10^{-4} \, J \cdot s \cdot kg^{-1}$	erg $\cdot s \cdot g^{-1}$
Faraday constant, $N_A e$	F	9.648456(27)	2.8	$10^4 \, C \cdot mol^{-1}$	10^3 emu $\cdot mol^{-1}$
		2.8925342(82)	2.8		10^{14} esu $\cdot mol^{-1}$
Rydberg constant, $[\mu_0 c^2 / 4\pi]^2(m_e e^4 / 4\pi\hbar^3 c)$	R_∞	1.097373177(83)	0.075	$10^7 \, m^{-1}$	$10^5 \, cm^{-1}$
Bohr radius, $[\mu_0 c^2 / 4\pi]^{-1}(\hbar^2 / m_e e^2) = a/4\pi R_\infty$	a_0	5.2917706(44)	0.82	$10^{-11} \, m$	10^{-8} cm
Classical electron radius, $[\mu_0 c^2 / 4\pi](e^2 / m_e c^2) = a^3/4\pi R_\infty$	$r_0 = a\lambda_C$	2.8179380(70)	2.5	$10^{-15} \, m$	10^{-12} cm
Thomson cross section, $(8/3)\pi r_e^2$	σ_e	0.6652448(33)	4.9	$10^{-28} \, m^2$	$10^{-24} \, cm^2$
Free electron g-factor, or electron magnetic moment in Bohr magnetons	$g_e/2 = \mu_e/\mu_B$	1.0011596567(35)	0.0035		
Free muon g-factor, or muon magnetic moment in units of $[c](e\hbar/2m_\mu c)$	$g_\mu/2$	1.00116616(31)	0.31		
Bohr magneton, $[c](e\hbar/2m_e c)$	μ_B	9.274078(36)	3.9	$10^{-24} \, J \cdot T^{-1}$	10^{-21} erg $\cdot G^{-1}$
Electron magnetic moment	μ_e	9.284832(36)	3.9	$10^{-24} \, J \cdot T^{-1}$	10^{-21} erg $\cdot G^{-1}$
Gyromagnetic ratio of protons in H_2O	γ_p	2.6751301(75)	2.8	$10^8 \, s^{-1} \cdot T^{-1}$	$10^4 \, s^{-1} \cdot G^{-1}$
	$\gamma_p/2\pi$	4.257602(12)	2.8	$10^7 \, Hz \cdot T^{-1}$	$10^3 \, Hz \cdot G^{-1}$
γ_p' corrected for diamagnetism of H_2O	γ_p'	2.6751987(75)	2.8	$10^8 \, s^{-1} \cdot T^{-1}$	$10^4 \, s^{-1} \cdot G^{-1}$
	$\gamma_p'/2\pi$	4.257711(12)	2.8	$10^7 \, Hz \cdot T^{-1}$	$10^3 \, Hz \cdot G^{-1}$
Magnetic moment of protons in H_2O in Bohr magnetons	μ_p'/μ_B	1.52099322(10)	0.066	10^{-3}	10^{-3}
Proton magnetic moment in Bohr magnetons	μ_p/μ_B	1.521032209(16)	0.011	10^{-3}	10^{-3}
Ratio of electron and proton magnetic moments	μ_e/μ_p	658.2106880(66)	0.010		
Proton magnetic moment	μ_p	1.4106171(55)	3.9	$10^{-26} \, J \cdot T^{-1}$	10^{-23} erg $\cdot G^{-1}$
Magnetic moment of protons in H_2O in nuclear magnetons	μ_p'/μ_N	2.7927740(11)	0.38		
μ_p'/μ_N corrected for diamagnetism of H_2O	μ_p/μ_N	2.7928456(11)	0.38		
Nuclear magneton, $[c](e\hbar/2m_p c)$	μ_N	5.050824(20)	3.9	$10^{-27} \, J \cdot T^{-1}$	10^{-24} erg $\cdot G^{-1}$
Ratio of muon and proton magnetic moments	μ_μ/μ_p	3.1833402(72)	2.3		
Muon magnetic moment	μ_μ	4.490474(18)	3.9	$10^{-26} \, J \cdot T^{-1}$	10^{-23} erg $\cdot G^{-1}$
Ratio of muon mass to electron mass	m_μ/m_e	206.76865(47)	2.3		

tainty of 9 ppm. But if one used the value of a derived from measurement of $2e/h$ by the ac Josephson effect, it was found that $\delta_N = 2.5$ ppm with an uncertainty of 4.0 ppm, quite consistent with the theoretical prediction. Thus, acceptance of the Josephson-effect value of the fine-structure constant removed a major discrepancy from quantum electrodynamics. This case illustrates the way in which experiments carried out in one field of physics can have significant implications for other fields, and the way in which accurate measurements of the fundamental constants can illuminate apparent inconsistencies in the physical description of nature.

Although not mentioned above, there are several ways of obtaining an indirect value of the fine-structure constant from the value of $2e/h$. One method involves combining it with some accurately known constants, such as the Rydberg constant (R_∞) and the speed of light (c), and

a value for the proton gyromagnetic ratio (γ_p). Another technique involves combining the value of $2e/h$ with an experimentally derived value obtained for the Faraday (F), again some accurately known constants, and a value for the magnetic moment of the proton in nuclear magnetons (μ_p/μ_N).

In principle, there are also other potential sources of information on the fine-structure constant that do not require the use of either quantum electrodynamic theory or the quantity $2e/h$. For example, a value of a can be obtained from a measurement of the electron Compton wavelength, which is symbolized by λ_C. This value is the wavelength of the radiation emitted by an electron at rest when it annihilates with a positive electron, or positron, also at rest.

The implied equations in the preceding two paragraphs above illustrate not only the complex relationships that

Table 7: Physical Constant Values (continued)

quantity	symbol	numerical value*	uncertainty (ppm)	units SI †	units cgs ‡
Muon rest mass	m_μ	1.883566(11)	5.6	10^{-28} kg	10^{-25} g
		0.11342920(26)	2.3	u	u
Compton wavelength of the electron, $h / m_e c = a^2 / 2R_\infty$	λ_c	2.4263089(40)	1.6	10^{-12} m	10^{-10} cm
	$\lambdabar_c = \lambda_c / 2\pi = a a_0$	3.8615905(64)	1.6	10^{-13} m	10^{-11} cm
Compton wavelength of the proton, $h / m_p c$	$\lambda_{c \cdot p}$	1.3214099(22)	1.7	10^{-15} m	10^{-13} cm
	$\lambdabar_{c \cdot p} = \lambda_{c \cdot p} / 2\pi$	2.1030892(36)	1.7	10^{-16} m	10^{-14} cm
Compton wavelength of the neutron, $h / m_n c$	$\lambda_{c \cdot n}$	1.3195909(22)	1.7	10^{-15} m	10^{-13} cm
	$\lambdabar_{c \cdot n} = \lambda_{c \cdot n} / 2\pi$	2.1001941(35)	1.7	10^{-16} m	10^{-14} cm
Molar volume of ideal gas at s.t.p.	V_m	22.41383(70)	31	10^{-3} m³ · mol⁻¹	10^3 cm³ · mol⁻¹
Molar gas constant, $V_m p_0 / T_0$ ($T_0 \equiv 273.15$ K; $p_0 \equiv 101325$ Pa $\equiv$ 1atm)	R	8.31441(26)	31	J · mol⁻¹ · K⁻¹	10^{-7} erg · mol⁻¹ · K⁻¹
		8.20568(26)	31	10^{-5} m³ · atm · mol⁻¹ · K⁻¹	10 cm³ · atm · mol⁻¹ · K⁻¹
Boltzmann constant, R/N_A	k	1.380662(44)	32	10^{-23} J · K⁻¹	10^{-16} erg · K⁻¹
Stefan-Boltzmann constant, $\pi^2 k^4 / 60 \hbar^3 c^2$	σ	5.67032(71)	125	10^{-8} W · m⁻² · K⁻⁴	10^{-5} erg · s⁻¹ · cm⁻² · K⁻⁴
First radiation constant, $2\pi h c^2$	c_1	3.741832(20)	5.4	10^{-16} W · m²	10^{-5} erg · cm² · s⁻¹
Second radiation constant, hc / k	c_2	1.438786(45)	31	10^{-2} m · K	cm · K
Gravitational constant,	G	6.6720(41)	615	10^{-11} m³ · s⁻² · kg⁻¹	10^{-8} cm³ · s⁻² · g⁻¹
Ratio, kx-unit to ångström, $\Lambda = \lambda(\text{Å}) / \lambda(\text{kxu})$; $\lambda(\text{Cu}K\alpha_1) \equiv 1.537400$ kxu	Λ	1.0020772(54)	5.3		
Ratio, Å* to ångström, $\text{Å*} = \lambda(\text{Å}) / \lambda(\text{Å*})$; $\lambda(\text{W}K\alpha_1) \equiv 0.2090100$ Å*	Λ^*	1.0000205(56)	5.6		

*Note that the numbers in parentheses are the one standard-deviation uncertainties in the last digits of the quoted value computed on the basis of internal consistency, that the unified atomic mass scale ^{12}C $\doteq$ has been used throughout, that u = atomic mass unit, C = coulomb, F = farad, G = gauss, H = henry, Hz = hertz = cycle/s, J = joule, K = kelvin, Pa = pascal = N · m⁻², T = tesla (10^4 G), V = volt, Wb = weber = T · m², and W = watt. In cases where formulas for constants are given (e.g., R_∞), the relations are written as the product of two factors. The second factor, in parentheses, is the expression to be used when all quantities are expressed in cgs units, with the electron charge in electrostatic units. The first factor, in brackets, is to be included only if all quantities are expressed in SI units. We remind the reader that with the exception of the auxiliary constants which have been taken to be exact, the uncertainties of these constants are correlated, and therefore the general law of error propagation must be used in calculating additional quantities requiring two or more of these constants.   ** Parts per million.   † Quantities given in u and atm are for the convenience of the reader; these units are not part of the International System of Units (SI).   ‡ In order to avoid separate columns for the "electromagnetic" and "electrostatic" units, both are given under the single heading "cgs Units." When using these units, the elementary charge e in the second column should be understood to be replaced by e_m or e_0, respectively. Source: Compiled by E.R. Cohen and B.N. Taylor under the auspices of the CODATA Task Group on Fundamental Constants. This set has been officially adopted by CODATA and is taken from J. Phys. Chem. Ref. Data, Vol. 2, No. 4, p. 663 (1973) and CODATA Bulletin No. 11 (December 1973)

exist among the constants but, more important, the fact that a particular constant may be determined by a direct measurement or indirectly by an appropriate combination of several other directly measured constants. Indeed, the indirect value is often so much more accurate than the direct value that the latter is discarded.

This situation is true in the case of the elementary charge (e); the oil-drop determination of the elementary charge has such a low accuracy compared with indirect methods that it is never used. If the direct and indirect values do in fact have comparable accuracy, then both must be taken into account in order to arrive at a best value for that quantity. (By "best value" is meant that numerical value for the quantity that is believed to be closest to the true but unknown value.) Because of the interrelationships existing among the constants and the concomitant existence of indirect values, a new determination of one constant will generally affect the best values of others.

Meaning of best value

Unfortunately, the problem of determining best values for the various fundamental constants is made still more difficult by the existence of conversion factors that relate absolute units to as-maintained units (see below).

STANDARDS OF MEASUREMENT, CONVERSION FACTORS, AND RELATED CONSIDERATIONS

Conversion factors. The magnitude of any quantity must be expressed in terms of certain units. The system of units used throughout most of the world is the Système Internationale d'Unités, or SI. It is based in part on the

SI units

kilogram, metre, second, and ampere. In practice, everyday working standards of mass, length, and time can be constructed that are directly traceable to their fundamental SI definitions and that have an accuracy comparable with that implicit in the definition. This is not true, however, of the ampere; because a current is a flow of charge, it is not easy to construct a storable working standard of current. Instead, standards of voltage and resistance must be separately maintained, and a standard of current must be derived by the application of Ohm's law—i.e., current equals voltage divided by resistance.

In terms of such as-maintained amperes, currents can usually be measured with an accuracy of about 0.1 part per million. No experiment has yet been devised, however, that will allow a given current to be determined in SI units to anything like the 0.01-ppm accuracy inherent in the definition of the SI ampere; present current balances (those that measure the force between current-carrying coils) can at best give a result accurate to between 5 and 10 ppm. This means that the uncertainties of the conversion factors relating the different as-maintained amperes to the defined SI ampere are 5 to 10 ppm. (This uncertainty applies as well to factors for converting the as-maintained volt to the SI volt because the factor for converting the as-maintained ohm to the SI ohm can be determined with an accuracy of a few tenths of a ppm.) Because many fundamental-constants experiments require the accurate measurement of a current, or a voltage, the rather large uncertainty in the current, or voltage, conversion factor is of great significance. Indeed, the conversion factor may be considered equal in importance to the associated fundamental constants, and separate experiments must be undertaken for its determination.

Least-squares adjustments of the constants. In general, each of the many different routes that can be followed, both direct and indirect, in order to obtain a value for a particular constant will give a slightly different value. A situation such as this is best handled by a mathematical technique known as least squares.

The least-squares method provides a self-consistent procedure for calculating best compromise values of the constants from all of the available measurements. For a given set of data, it automatically takes into account all the possible routes for obtaining values of each of the constants being calculated. It then determines a single final value for each constant by automatically weighting the values of the constant obtained from the various routes according to their relative reliability or uncertainty. The uncertainty for each route is determined from the uncertainties of the individual measurements constituting the original set of data. A U.S. physicist, Raymond T. Birge, pioneered

Table 8: Energy Conversion Factors and Equivalents

quantity	symbol	numerical value*	units	uncertainty (ppm) †
1 Kilogram (kg · c^2)		8.987551786(72)	10^{16} J	0.008
		5.609545(16)	10^{29} MeV	2.9
1 Atomic mass unit (u · c^2)		1.4924418(77)	10^{-10} J	5.1
		931.5016(26)	MeV	2.8
1 Electron mass m_e · c^2)		8.187241(42)	10^{-14} J	5.1
		0.5110034(14)	MeV	2.8
1 Muon mass (m_μ · c^2)		1.6928648(96)	10^{-11} J	5.6
		105.65948(35)	MeV	3.3
1 Proton mass (m_p · c^2)		1.5033015(77)	10^{-10} J	5.1
		938.2796(27)	MeV	2.8
1 Neutron mass (m_n · c^2)		1.5053738(78)	10^{-10} J	5.1
		939.5731(27)	MeV	2.8
1 Electron volt		1.6021892(46)	10^{-19} J	2.9
			10^{-12} erg	2.9
	1 eV / h	2.4179696(63)	10^{14} Hz	2.6
	1 eV / hc	8.065479(21)	10^5 m^{-1}	2.6
			10^3 cm^{-1}	2.6
	1 eV / k	1.160450(36)	10^4 K	31
Voltage-wavelength conversion, hc		1.986478(11)	10^{-25} J · m	5.4
		1.2398520(32)	10^{-6} eV · m	2.6
			10^{-4} eV · cm	2.6
Rydberg constant	$R_\infty hc$	2.179907(12)	10^{-18} J	5.4
			10^{-11} erg	5.4
		13.605804(36)	eV	2.6
	$R_\infty c$	3.28984200(25)	10^{15} Hz	0.075
	$R_\infty hc / k$	1.578885(49)	10^5 K	31
Bohr magneton	μ_B	9.274078(36)	10^{-24} J · T^{-1}	3.9
		5.7883785(95)	10^{-5} eV · T^{-1}	1.6
	μ_B / h	1.3996123(39)	10^{10} Hz · T^{-1}	2.8
	μ_B / hc	46.68604(13)	m^{-1} · T^{-1}	2.8
			10^{-2} cm^{-1} · T^{-1}	2.8
	μ_B / k	0.671712(21)	K · T^{-1}	31
Nuclear magneton	μ_N	5.505824(20)	10^{-27} J · T^{-1}	3.9
		3.1524515(53)	10^{-8} eV · T^{-1}	1.7
	μ_N / h	7.622532(22)	10^6 Hz · T^{-1}	2.8
	μ_N / hc	2.5426030(72)	10^{-2} m^{-1} · T^{-1}	2.8
			10^{-4} cm^{-1} · T^{-1}	2.8
	μ_N / k	3.65826(12)	10^{-4} K · T^{-1}	31

*The numbers in parentheses are the standard-deviation uncertainties in the last digits of the quoted value, computed on the basis of internal consistency.   † Parts per million.

least-squares studies of the constants in the late 1920s and continued them into the mid-1940s. Similar studies have been extended to the present by a number of physicists, including Jesse W.M. DuMond and E. Richard Cohen, and Bearden and colleagues. The two most recent least-squares studies of the constants were those published in 1969 and 1973. The 1973 adjustment involved extensive use of the analyses carried out for the 1969 adjustment and was of similar format.

An adjustment of the constants generally is carried out by first dividing the available measurements into two groups. The first group, called the **auxiliary constants**, contains quantities that can be considered as exactly known (see Table 4). An example is the Rydberg constant (R_∞), which has an uncertainty of only 0.075 ppm. The other group of constants contains the less precise input data. An example from this group is the proton gyromagnetic ratio (γ_p), which has a comparatively large uncertainty of 2 to 16 ppm. Next, a subset of constants is chosen in terms of which all the input data can be expressed, with the aid, if necessary, of the auxiliary constants. The constants of this subset are those directly subject to adjustment; they are termed the **adjustable constants**.

In the adjustment carried out by Cohen and Taylor in 1973, the adjustable constants were taken to be a, K, N_A, $\bar{R}$, Λ, and μ. Here, K is A_{BI69}/A, the factor relating the SI ampere to the ampere as maintained on January 1, 1969, by the International Bureau of Weights and Measures (BIPM) in France; $\bar{R}$ is Ω_{BI69}/Ω, the factor converting the ohm, as maintained by the BIPM on January 1, 1969, to the SI ohm; Λ is the factor converting the kilo-x-unit, a unit used to express the length of X-rays, to the SI unit of length, the metre; and μ is μ_μ/μ_p, the ratio of the magnetic moment of the muon to that of the proton. With just these six quantities and the aid of selected auxiliary constants, a series of equations, generally known as the observational equations, was formed for all the input data. The actual data considered for use are summarized in Tables 5 and 6. Table 5 contains the 21 items of data independent of quantum electrodynamic theory, and Table 6, the 10 items that depended on QED theory for their analysis. (All the auxiliary constants listed in Table 4 are essentially independent of QED theory.)

Once the actual numbers are substituted for the auxiliary constants and stochastic data, it is a rather straightforward procedure, with the aid of a computer, to solve the observational equations for the least-squares adjusted values of the adjustable constants, in the case under consideration, a, K, N_A, $\bar{R}$, Λ, and μ. Although numerical values (with uncertainties) for the adjustable constants are the sole result of an adjustment, optimum values for all of the constants are actually obtained, because any constant not chosen for direct adjustment can be calculated from appropriate combinations of those subject to the adjustment—that is (for the present case), from a, K, N_A, $\bar{R}$, Λ, and μ.

One of the main problems in carrying out a least-squares adjustment of the constants is making the critical analysis of the input data and deciding what uncertainty should be assigned to each measurement. Correct assignment of these uncertainties is of the utmost importance, because the weight any particular experiment carries in an adjustment is proportional to the reciprocal of the square of its uncertainty—if one measurement of a particular quantity has half the uncertainty of another, it carries four times as much weight. One reason for the uncertainty problem is that, in most experiments, sufficient data are taken to reduce the so-called random, or statistical, uncertainty to negligible amounts, and the final uncertainty assigned the measurement is determined from estimates of the systematic uncertainties. Systematic uncertainties arise from effects that the experimenter knows little about; their estimation is somewhat subjective and in many instances is what can only be called educated guesses.

Another difficult task associated with the adjusting of constants is deciding what to do with discrepant data— that is, measurements for which the assigned uncertainty seems to be correct but that differ from each other "more than they should." By this phrase is meant that the difference between two values of the same quantity is large compared with the standard deviation of the difference, as obtained by taking the square root of the sum of the squares or root-sum-square of the standard deviations of

Auxiliary constants

Discrepancy in data

Table 9: Comparison of the 1963, 1969, and 1973 Adjustments

quantity*	value, 1973 adjustment, and ppm† uncertainty		value, 1969 adjustment, and ppm uncertainty		change 1973–1969 (ppm)	value, 1963 adjustment, and ppm uncertainty		change 1973–1963 (ppm)	change 1969–1963 (ppm)
$1/a$	137.03604(11)	0.82	137.03602(21)	1.5	+0.15	137.0388(6)	4.4	−20	−20
e	1.6021892(46)	2.9	1.6021917(70)	4.4	−1.6	1.60210(2)	12	+56	+57
h	6.626176(36)	5.4	6.626196(50)	7.6	−3.0	6.62559(16)	24	+88	+91
m_e	9.109534(47)	5.1	9.109558(54)	6.0	−2.6	9.10908(13)	14	+50	+52
N_A	6.022045(31)	5.0	6.022169(40)	6.6	−21	6.02252(9)	15	−79	−58
μ_p/μ_N	2.7928456(11)	0.38	2.792782(17)	6.2	+23	2.79276(2)	7.2	+31	+7.9
F	9.648456(27)	2.8	9.648670(54)	5.5	−22	9.64870(5)	5.2	−25	−3.1

*The units for e are 10^{-19} C; for h, 10^{-34} J · s; for m_e, 10^{-31} kg; for N_A, 10^{23} mol^{-1}; and for F, 10^4 C · mol^{-1}.
Here, C = coulomb, J = joule, kg = kilogram, mol = mole and s = second.   †Parts per million.

the individual measurements. If two measurements differ by between two and three times the standard deviation of their difference, they are inconsistent and one or the other is highly likely to be incorrect. Such data are not to be included in an adjustment uncritically because the inconsistencies imply either fallacious error estimates or the presence of unknown systematic uncertainties.

When faced with inconsistent data, the constants adjuster has two major choices: (1) to use as input data all apparently reliable measurements even though they may be inconsistent, but to expand (increase) the assigned uncertainties sufficiently so that they are compatible; or (2) to decide, on a sound experimental and theoretical basis, which of the inconsistent data are least reliable and discard them, but expand no errors. These two possibilities indicate some of the arbitrariness or subjectiveness in the adjustment of fundamental constants and the possibility that different adjusters might treat the same data differently, thereby arriving at a different set of best values.

Recommended set of fundamental constants. In the adjustment made in 1973, a detailed analysis of the consistency of all the available data as listed in Tables 5 and 6 led Cohen and Taylor to the set of recommended constants given in Table 7. Not all these constants result from the least-squares procedure; for example, the auxiliary constants c, R_∞, and G. Table 8 is a list of best values for certain energy-conversion factors and equivalents.

Some of the pitfalls of discarding data become apparent when the 1969 adjustment is compared with that of 1973. The most critical problem in 1969 was the inconsistency among the five available values of the proton magnetic moment, μ_p/μ_N, and an inconsistency between two of these values and the one available measurement of the Faraday, F. The problem was resolved by discarding the two "high" values of the magnetic moment, retaining the remaining three and that of the Faraday. By 1973, however, two very accurate determinations of μ_p/μ_N (items 13 and 14 of Table 5) not only supplanted the five values available in 1969 but showed that the values discarded in 1969 were more nearly correct than those retained and that the value of the Faraday should have been discarded.

This reassessment accounts for the large changes, apparent in Table 9, in the values recommended for certain constants in 1969 and in 1973. Table 9 also includes values from the 1963 adjustment. The changes that occurred between the 1963 and the 1969 values are due primarily to the change in a resulting from the measurement of $2e/h$ by means of the ac Josephson effect. Table 9 shows that (1) knowledge of the numerical values of the fundamental constants improves as new measurements become available, and (2) the constants are so closely related to one another that a significant shift in one will usually give rise to large shifts in the values of the others.

Recent determinations of fundamental constants. Since the publication of the 1973 least-squares adjustment, several highly accurate determinations have been made. These include a determination of the Avogadro constant with an accuracy of about 1.0 ppm, a measurement of the Faraday with an uncertainty less than 3 ppm, and a determination of the proton gyromagnetic ratio by the low-field method with an accuracy of 0.4 ppm and by the high-field method with an accuracy of 1.0 ppm.

Official adoption of values for the fundamental constants. Until 1961, there existed no national or international body for officially adopting, or endorsing, a particular set of recommended values for the fundamental constants. That year, the National Academy of Sciences–National Academy of Engineering–National Research Council (United States) established the Advisory Committee on Fundamental Constants for the purpose of arriving at best values for the more important constants. The work of the committee led to the 1963 set of adjusted constants, which came into use throughout the world.

In 1966 the International Council of Scientific Unions established the Committee on Data for Science and Technology (CODATA) for the purpose of coordinating and promoting the collection, analysis, and compilation of numerical data for science and technology. Accordingly, in 1968 the CODATA Task Group on Fundamental Constants was appointed to promulgate an internationally accepted set of recommended values for the constants. The 1973 adjustment by Cohen and Taylor was carried out under the auspices of the CODATA Task Group, and their set of recommended values was adopted for international use by the 8th CODATA General Assembly at its meeting in Stockholm in September 1973.   (B.N.T./Ed.)

CODATA

BIBLIOGRAPHY

Conservation laws and symmetry: See HERMANN WEYL, *Symmetry* (1952), a beautifully illustrated book on the mathematical, aesthetic, physical, and biological aspects of symmetry; EUGENE P. WIGNER, *Symmetries and Reflections* (1967), a collection of essays by a Nobel Prize winner, the first five of which discuss conservation laws and symmetry; CHEN NING YANG, *Elementary Particles* (1962), an elegant book by another Nobelist on the symmetries of elementary particles; and OLIVER E. OVERSETH, "Experiments in Time Reversal," *Scient. Am.*, 221:88–94 (1969). Additional references at a more elementary level include: EUGENE P. WIGNER, "Violations of Symmetry in Physics," *Scient. Am.*, 213:28–36 (1965); R.P. FEYNMAN, *The Character of Physical Law* (1965); and M. GARDNER, *The Ambidextrous Universe* (1964).

Field theory: Popular accounts concerning the nature of fields and their uses in physical theories may be found in A. EINSTEIN and L. INFELD, *The Evolution of Physics*, ch. 3 (1938); and in R.E. PEIERLS, *The Laws of Nature*, ch. 2 (1956). For a general account of the types of fields used in physics, the equations they satisfy, and techniques for solution of the equations, see H. MARGENAU and G.M. MURPHY, *The Mathematics of Physics and Chemistry*, 2nd ed., ch. 4, 7, and 12 (1956); and P.M. MORSE and H. FESHBACH, *Methods of Theoretical Physics*, ch. 1–2, 10–11 (1953).

Physical constants: See E. RICHARD COHEN, KENNETH M. CROWE, and JESSE W.M. DUMOND, *The Fundamental Constants of Physics* (1957), a good historical review of the fundamental constants field from its earliest days up to about 1955; B.N. TAYLOR, W.H. PARKER, and D.N. LANGENBERG, *The Fundamental Constants and Quantum Electrodynamics* (1969), a thorough and detailed critical review that brings the field up to 1969; FREDERICK D. ROSSINI, *Fundamental Measures and Constants for Science and Technology* (1974), a general discussion of the field of fundamental constants and related topics; E. RICHARD COHEN and B.N. TAYLOR, "The 1973 Least-Squares Adjustment of the Fundamental Constants," *Journal of Physical and Chemical Reference Data*, vol. 2, pp. 663–734 (1973), a critical review and least-squares adjustment of the constants; and J.H. SANDERS and A.H. WAPSTRA (eds.), *Proceedings of the International Conference on Atomic Masses and Fundamental Constants 4* (1971) and 5 (1975), including numerous papers relating to fundamental constants presented at the National Physical Laboratory, Teddington, England, in 1971 and at Paris in 1975.

(L.M.B./H.Ma./B.N.T./Ed.)

The Physical Sciences

The physical sciences are the ongoing refined and systematic efforts to understand the inorganic world and the results of those efforts. They are generally divided into four broad areas: physics, chemistry, astronomy, and the Earth sciences. The historical development of the first three is surveyed in this article; due attention is also given to their scope, principal concerns, and methods. A complementary treatment of the Earth sciences is provided in a separate article.

Physics, in its modern sense, was founded in the mid-19th century as a synthesis of several older sciences—namely, those of mechanics, optics, acoustics, electricity, magnetism, heat, and the physical properties of matter. The synthesis was based in large part on the recognition that the different forces of nature are related and are, in fact, interconvertible because they are forms of energy.

The boundary between physics and chemistry is somewhat arbitrary. As it has developed in the 20th century, physics is concerned with the structure and behaviour of individual atoms and their components, while chemistry deals with the properties and reactions of molecules. These latter depend on energy, especially heat, as well as on atoms; hence, there is a strong link between physics and chemistry. Chemists tend to be more interested in the specific properties of different elements and compounds, whereas physicists are concerned with general properties shared by all matter.

Astronomy is the science of the entire universe beyond the Earth; it includes the Earth's gross physical properties, such as its mass and rotation, insofar as they interact with other bodies in the solar system. Until the 18th century, astronomers were concerned primarily with the Sun, Moon, planets, and comets. During the last two centuries, however, the study of stars, galaxies, nebulas, and the interstellar medium has become increasingly important. Celestial mechanics, the science of the motion of planets and other solid objects within the solar system, was the first testing ground for Newton's laws of motion and thereby helped to establish the fundamental principles of classical (that is, pre-20th-century) physics. Astrophysics, the study of the physical properties of celestial bodies, arose during the 19th century and is closely connected with the determination of the chemical composition of those bodies. In the 20th century physics and astronomy have become more intimately linked through cosmological theories, especially those based on the theory of relativity.

For coverage of topics related to physics, chemistry, and astronomy in the *Macropædia* and *Micropædia,* see the *Propædia,* sections 111–133, 10/31, and 10/32.

The article is divided into the following sections:

History of the physical sciences

HERITAGE OF ANTIQUITY AND THE MIDDLE AGES

The physical sciences ultimately derive from the rationalistic materialism that emerged in classical Greece, itself an outgrowth of magical and mythical views of the world. The Greek philosophers of the 6th and 5th centuries BC abandoned the animism of the poets and explained the world in terms of ordinarily observable natural processes. These early philosophers posed the broad questions that still underlie science: How did the world order emerge from chaos? What is the origin of multitude and variety in the world? How can motion and change be accounted for? What is the underlying relation between form and matter? Greek philosophy answered these questions in terms that provided the framework for science for approximately 2,000 years.

Ancient Middle Eastern and Greek astronomy. Western astronomy had its origins in Egypt and Mesopotamia. Egyptian astronomy, which was neither a very well-developed nor an influential study, was largely concerned with time reckoning. Its main lasting contribution was the civil

Egyptian and Mesopotamian origins

calendar of 365 days, consisting of 12 months of 30 days each and five additional festival days at the end of each year. This calendar played an important role in the history of astronomy, allowing astronomers to calculate the number of days between any two sets of observations.

Babylonian astronomy, dating back to about 1800 BC, constitutes one of the earliest systematic, scientific treatments of the physical world. In contrast to the Egyptians, the Babylonians were interested in the accurate prediction of astronomical phenomena, especially the first appearance of the new Moon. Using the zodiac as a reference, by the 4th century BC, they developed a complex system of arithmetic progressions and methods of approximation by which they were able to predict first appearances. At no point in the Babylonian astronomical literature is there the least evidence of the use of geometric models. The mass of observations they collected and their mathematical methods were important contributions to the later flowering of astronomy among the Greeks.

The Pythagoreans (5th century BC) were responsible for one of the first Greek astronomical theories. Believing that the order of the cosmos is fundamentally mathematical, they held that it is possible to discover the harmonies of the universe by contemplating the regular motions of the heavens. Postulating a central fire about which all the heavenly bodies including the Earth and Sun revolve, they constructed the first physical model of the solar system. Subsequent Greek astronomy derived its character from a comment ascribed to Plato, in the 4th century BC, who is reported to have instructed the astronomers to "save the phenomena" in terms of uniform circular motion. That is to say, he urged them to develop predictively accurate theories using only combinations of uniform circular motion. As a result, Greek astronomers never regarded their geometric models as true or as being physical descriptions of the machinery of the heavens. They regarded them simply as tools for predicting planetary positions.

Eudoxus of Cnidus (4th century BC) was the first of the Greek astronomers to rise to Plato's challenge. He developed a theory of homocentric spheres, a model that represented the universe by sets of nesting concentric spheres the motions of which combined to produce the planetary and other celestial motions. Using only uniform circular motions, Eudoxus was able to "save" the rather complex planetary motions with some success. His theory required four homocentric spheres for each planet and three each for the Sun and Moon. The system was modified by Callippus, a student of Eudoxus, who added spheres to improve the theory, especially for Mercury and Venus. Aristotle, in formulating his cosmology, adopted Eudoxus' homocentric spheres as the actual machinery of the heavens. The Aristotelian cosmos was like an onion consisting of a series of some 55 spheres nested about the Earth, which was fixed at the centre. In order to unify the system, Aristotle added spheres in order to "unroll" the motions of a given planet so that they would not be transmitted to the next inner planet.

The theory of homocentric spheres failed to account for two sets of observations: (1) brightness changes suggesting that planets are not always the same distance from the Earth, and (2) bounded elongations (*i.e.*, Venus is never observed to be more than about 48° and Mercury never more than about 24° from the Sun). Heracleides of Pontus (4th century BC) attempted to solve these problems by having Venus and Mercury revolve about the Sun, rather than the Earth, and having the Sun and other planets revolve in turn about the Earth, which he placed at the centre. In addition, to account for the daily motions of the heavens, he held that the Earth rotates on its axis. Heracleides' theory had little impact in antiquity except perhaps on Aristarchus of Samos (3rd century BC), who apparently put forth a heliocentric hypothesis similar to the one Copernicus was to propound in the 16th century.

Hipparchus (fl. 130 BC) made extensive contributions to both theoretical and observational astronomy. Basing his theories on an impressive mass of observations, he was able to work out theories of the Sun and Moon that were more successful than those of any of his predecessors. His primary conceptual tool was the eccentric circle, a circle

in which the Earth is at some point eccentric to the geometric centre. He used this device to account for various irregularities and inequalities observed in the motions of the Sun and Moon. He also proved that the eccentric circle is mathematically equivalent to a geometric figure called an epicycle-deferent system, a proof probably first made by Apollonius of Perga a century earlier.

Among Hipparchus' observations, one of the most significant was that of the precession of the equinoxes—*i.e.*, a gradual apparent increase in longitude between any fixed star and the equinoctial point (either of two points on the celestial sphere where the celestial equator crosses the ecliptic). Thus the north celestial pole, the point on the celestial sphere defined as the apparent centre of rotation of the stars, moves relative to the stars in its vicinity. In the heliocentric theory, this effect is ascribed to a change in the Earth's rotational axis, which traces out a conical path around the axis of the orbital plane.

Claudius Ptolemy (fl. AD 140) applied the theory of epicycles to compile a systematic account of Greek astronomy. He elaborated theories for each of the planets, as well as for the Sun and Moon. His theory generally fitted the data available to him with a good degree of accuracy, and his book, the *Almagest,* became the vehicle by which Greek astronomy was transmitted to astronomers of the Middle Ages and Renaissance. It essentially molded astronomy for the next millennium and a half.

Greek physics. Several kinds of physical theories emerged in ancient Greece, including both generalized hypotheses about the ultimate structure of nature and more specific theories that considered the problem of motion from both metaphysical and mathematical points of view. Attempting to reconcile the antithesis between the underlying unity and apparent multitude and diversity of nature, the Greek atomists Leucippus (mid-5th century BC), Democritus (late 5th century BC), and Epicurus (late 4th and early 3rd century BC) asserted that nature consists of immutable atoms moving in empty space. According to this theory, the various motions and configurations of atoms and clusters of atoms are the causes of all the phenomena of nature.

In contrast to the particulate universe of the atomists, the Stoics (principally Zeno, of Citium, bridging 4th and 3rd centuries BC, Chrysippus [3rd century BC], and Poseidonius of Apamea [fl. *c.* 100 BC]) insisted on the continuity of nature, conceiving of both space and matter as continuous and as infused with an active, airlike spirit—pneuma—which serves to unify the frame of nature. The inspiration for the Stoic emphasis on pneumatic processes probably arose from earlier experiences with the "spring" (*i.e.*, compressibility and pressure) of the air. Neither the atomic theory nor Stoic physics survived the criticism of Aristotle and his theory.

In his physics, Aristotle was primarily concerned with the philosophical question of the nature of motion as one variety of change. He assumed that a constant motion requires a constant cause; that is to say, as long as a body remains in motion, a force must be acting on that body. He considered the motion of a body through a resisting medium as proportional to the force producing the motion and inversely proportional to the resistance of the medium. Aristotle used this relationship to argue against the possibility of the existence of a void, for in a void resistance is zero, and the relationship loses meaning. He considered the cosmos to be divided into two qualitatively different realms, governed by two different kinds of laws. In the terrestrial realm, within the sphere of the Moon, rectilinear up-and-down motion is characteristic. Heavy bodies, by their nature, seek the centre and tend to move downward in a natural motion. It is unnatural for a heavy body to move up, and such unnatural or violent motion requires an external cause. Light bodies, in direct contrast, move naturally upward. In the celestial realm, uniform circular motion is natural, thus producing the motions of the heavenly bodies.

Archimedes (3rd century BC) fundamentally applied mathematics to the solution of physical problems and brilliantly employed physical assumptions and insights leading to mathematical demonstrations, particularly in problems

First physical model of the solar system

An early heliocentric hypothesis

The first atomists

The physics of Aristotle

of statics and hydrostatics. He was thus able to derive the law of the lever rigorously and to deal with problems of the equilibrium of floating bodies.

Islāmic and medieval science. Greek science reached a zenith with the work of Ptolemy in the 2nd century AD. The lack of interest in theoretical questions in the Roman world reduced science in the Latin West to the level of predigested handbooks and encyclopaedias that had been distilled many times. Social pressures, political persecution, and the anti-intellectual bias of some of the early Church Fathers drove the few remaining Greek scientists and philosophers to the East. There they ultimately found a welcome when the rise of Islām in the 7th century stimulated interest in scientific and philosophical subjects. Most of the important Greek scientific texts were preserved in Arabic translations. Although the Muslims did not alter the foundations of Greek science, they made several important contributions within its general framework. When interest in Greek learning revived in western Europe during the 12th and 13th centuries, scholars turned to Islāmic Spain for the scientific texts. A spate of translations resulted in the revival of Greek science in the West and coincided with the rise of the universities. Working within a predominantly Greek framework, scientists of the late Middle Ages reached high levels of sophistication and prepared the ground for the scientific revolution of the 16th and 17th centuries.

Mechanics was one of the most highly developed sciences pursued in the Middle Ages. Operating within a fundamentally Aristotelian framework, medieval physicists criticized and attempted to improve many aspects of Aristotle's physics.

The problem of projectile motion was a crucial one for Aristotelian mechanics, and the analysis of this problem represents one of the most impressive medieval contributions to physics. Because of the assumption that continuation of motion requires the continued action of a motive force, the continued motion of a projectile after losing contact with the projector required explanation. Aristotle himself had proposed explanations of the continuation of projectile motion in terms of the action of the medium. The ad hoc character of these explanations rendered them unsatisfactory to most of the medieval commentators, who nevertheless retained the fundamental assumption that continued motion requires a continuing cause.

The most fruitful alternative to Aristotle's attempts to explain projectile motion resulted from the concept of impressed force. According to this view, there is an incorporeal motive force that is imparted to the projectile, causing it to continue moving. Such views were espoused by John Philoponus of Alexandria (fl. 6th century), Avicenna, the Persian philosopher (d. 1037), and the Arab Abū al Barakāt al-Baghdādi (d. 1164). In the 14th century the French philosopher Jean Buridan developed a new version of the impressed-force theory, calling the quality impressed on the projectile "impetus." Impetus, a permanent quality for Buridan, is measurable by the initial velocity of the projectile and by the quantity of matter contained in it. Buridan employed this concept to suggest an explanation of the everlasting motions of the heavens.

During the 1300s certain Oxford scholars pondered the philosophical problem of how to describe the change that occurs when qualities increase or decrease in intensity and came to consider the kinematic aspects of motion. Dealing with these problems in a purely hypothetical manner without any attempt to describe actual motions in nature or to test their formulas experimentally, they were able to derive the result that in a uniformly accelerated motion, distance increases as the square of the time.

Although medieval science was deeply influenced by Aristotle's philosophy, adherence to his point of view was by no means dogmatic. During the 13th century, theologians at the University of Paris were disturbed by certain statements in Aristotle that seemed to imply limitations of God's powers as well as other statements, such as the eternity of the world, which stood in apparent contradiction to scripture. In 1277 Pope John XXI condemned 219 propositions, many from Aristotle and St. Thomas Aquinas, which had clearly theological consequences. Many of these condemned propositions had scientific implications as well. For example, one of these propositions states, "That the first cause (*i.e.*, God) could not make several worlds." Although it is unlikely that anyone in the Middle Ages actually asserted the existence of many worlds, the condemnation led to the discussion of that possibility, as well as other important problems such as the possibility that the Earth moved.

THE SCIENTIFIC REVOLUTION

During the 15th, 16th, and 17th centuries, scientific thought underwent a revolution. A new view of nature emerged, replacing the Greek view that had dominated science for almost 2,000 years. Science became an autonomous discipline, distinct from both philosophy and technology, and it came to be regarded as having utilitarian goals. By the end of this period, it may not be too much to say that science had replaced Christianity as the focal point of European civilization. Out of the ferment of the Renaissance and Reformation there arose a new view of science, bringing about the following transformations: the reeducation of common sense in favour of abstract reasoning; the substitution of a quantitative for a qualitative view of nature; the view of nature as a machine rather than as an organism; the development of an experimental method that sought definite answers to certain limited questions couched in the framework of specific theories; the acceptance of new criteria for explanation, stressing the "how" rather than the "why" that had characterized the Aristotelian search for final causes.

Astronomy. The scientific revolution began in astronomy. Although there had been earlier discussions of the possibility of the Earth's motion, the Polish astronomer Nicolaus Copernicus was the first to propound a comprehensive heliocentric theory, equal in scope and predictive capability to Ptolemy's geocentric system. Motivated by the desire to satisfy Plato's dictum, Copernicus was led to overthrow traditional astronomy because of its alleged violation of the principle of uniform circular motion and its lack of unity and harmony as a system of the world. Relying on virtually the same data as Ptolemy had possessed, Copernicus turned the world inside out, putting the Sun at the centre and setting the Earth into motion around it. Copernicus' theory, published in 1543, possessed a qualitative simplicity that Ptolemaic astronomy appeared to lack. To achieve comparable levels of quantitative precision, however, the new system became just as complex as the old. Perhaps the most revolutionary aspect of Copernican astronomy lay in Copernicus' attitude toward the reality of his theory. In contrast to Platonic instrumentalism, Copernicus asserted that to be satisfactory astronomy must describe the real, physical system of the world.

The reception of Copernican astronomy amounted to victory by infiltration. By the time large-scale opposition to the theory had developed in the church and elsewhere, most of the best professional astronomers had found some aspect or other of the new system indispensable. Copernicus' book *De revolutionibus orbium coelestium, libri VI* (1543; *On the Revolutions of the Celestial Spheres*) became a standard reference for advanced problems in astronomical research, particularly for its mathematical techniques. Thus, it was widely read by mathematical astronomers, in spite of its central cosmological hypothesis, which was widely ignored. In 1551 the German astronomer Erasmus Reinhold published the *Tabulae prutenicae* ("Prutenic Tables"), computed by Copernican methods. The tables were more accurate and more up-to-date than their 13th-century predecessor and became indispensable to both astronomers and astrologers.

During the 16th century the Danish astronomer Tycho Brahe, rejecting both the Ptolemaic and Copernican systems, was responsible for major changes in observation, unwittingly providing the data that ultimately decided the argument in favour of the new astronomy. Using larger, stabler, and better calibrated instruments, he observed regularly over extended periods, thereby obtaining a continuity of observations that were accurate for planets to within about one minute of arc—several times better than any previous observation. Several of Tycho's observations

Revival of Greek science

Criticism of Aristotle

Emergence of a new conception of science

Reception of the Copernican view

contradicted Aristotle's system: a nova that appeared in 1572 exhibited no parallax (meaning that it lay at a very great distance) and was thus not of the sublunary sphere and therefore contrary to the Aristotelian assertion of the immutability of the heavens; similarly, a succession of comets appeared to be moving freely through a region that was supposed to be filled with solid, crystalline spheres. Tycho devised his own world system—a modification of Heracleides'—to avoid various undesirable implications of the Ptolemaic and Copernican systems.

At the beginning of the 17th century, the German astronomer Johannes Kepler placed the Copernican hypothesis on firm astronomical footing. Converted to the new astronomy as a student and deeply motivated by a neo-Pythagorean desire for finding the mathematical principles of order and harmony according to which God had constructed the world, Kepler spent his life looking for simple mathematical relationships that described planetary motions. His painstaking search for the real order of the universe forced him finally to abandon the Platonic ideal of uniform circular motion in his search for a physical basis for the motions of the heavens.

Kepler's laws

In 1609 Kepler announced two new planetary laws derived from Tycho's data: (1) the planets travel around the Sun in elliptical orbits, one focus of the ellipse being occupied by the Sun; and (2) a planet moves in its orbit in such a manner that a line drawn from the planet to the Sun always sweeps out equal areas in equal times. With these two laws, Kepler abandoned uniform circular motion of the planets on their spheres, thus raising the fundamental physical question of what holds the planets in their orbits. He attempted to provide a physical basis for the planetary motions by means of a force analogous to the magnetic force, the qualitative properties of which had been recently described in England by William Gilbert in his influential treatise, *De Magnete, Magneticisque Corporibus et de Magno Magnete Tellure* (1600; *William Gilbert of Colchester . . . on the Great Magnet of the Earth*). The impending marriage of astronomy and physics had been announced. In 1618 Kepler stated his third law, which was one of many laws concerned with the harmonies of the planetary motions: (3) the square of the period in which a planet orbits the Sun is proportional to the cube of its mean distance from the Sun.

Galileo's observation

A powerful blow was dealt to traditional cosmology by Galileo Galilei, who early in the 17th century used the telescope, a recent invention of Dutch lens grinders, to look toward the heavens. In 1610 Galileo announced observations that contradicted many traditional cosmological assumptions. He observed that the Moon is not a smooth, polished surface, as Aristotle had claimed, but that it is jagged and mountainous. Earthshine on the Moon revealed that the Earth, like the other planets, shines by reflected light. Like the Earth, Jupiter was observed to have satellites; hence, the Earth had been demoted from its unique position. The phases of Venus proved that that planet orbits the Sun, not the Earth.

Physics. *Mechanics.* The battle for Copernicanism was fought in the realm of mechanics as well as astronomy. The Ptolemaic–Aristotelian system stood or fell as a monolith, and it rested on the idea of Earth's fixity at the centre of the cosmos. Removing the Earth from the centre destroyed the doctrine of natural motion and place, and circular motion of the Earth was incompatible with Aristotelian physics.

Galileo's contributions to the science of mechanics were related directly to his defense of Copernicanism. Although in his youth he adhered to the traditional impetus physics, his desire to mathematize in the manner of Archimedes led him to abandon the traditional approach and develop the foundations for a new physics that was both highly mathematizable and directly related to the problems facing the new cosmology. Interested in finding the natural acceleration of falling bodies, he was able to derive the law of free fall (the distance, *s*, varies as the square of the time, t^2). Combining this result with his rudimentary form of the principle of inertia, he was able to derive the parabolic path of projectile motion. Furthermore, his principle of inertia enabled him to meet the traditional physical objections to the Earth's motion: since a body in motion tends to remain in motion, projectiles and other objects on the terrestrial surface will tend to share the motions of the Earth, which will thus be imperceptible to someone standing on the Earth.

The 17th-century contributions to mechanics of the French philosopher René Descartes, like his contributions to the scientific endeavour as a whole, were more concerned with problems in the foundations of science than with the solution of specific technical problems. He was principally concerned with the conceptions of matter and motion as part of his general program for science— namely, to explain all the phenomena of nature in terms of matter and motion. This program, known as the mechanical philosophy, came to be the dominant theme of 17th-century science.

The rise of mechanical philosophy

Descartes rejected the idea that one piece of matter could act on another through empty space; instead, forces must be propagated by a material substance, the "ether," that fills all space. Although matter tends to move in a straight line in accordance with the principle of inertia, it cannot occupy space already filled by other matter, so the only kind of motion that can actually occur is a vortex in which each particle in a ring moves simultaneously.

According to Descartes, all natural phenomena depend on the collisions of small particles, and so it is of great importance to discover the quantitative laws of impact. This was done by Descartes's disciple, the Dutch physicist Christiaan Huygens, who formulated the laws of conservation of momentum and of kinetic energy (the latter being valid only for elastic collisions).

The work of Sir Isaac Newton represents the culmination of the scientific revolution at the end of the 17th century. His monumental *Philosophiae Naturalis Principia Mathematica* (1687; *Mathematical Principles of Natural Philosophy*) solved the major problems posed by the scientific revolution in mechanics and in cosmology. It provided a physical basis for Kepler's laws, unified celestial and terrestrial physics under one set of laws, and established the problems and methods that dominated much of astronomy and physics for well over a century. By means of the concept of force, Newton was able to synthesize two important components of the scientific revolution, the mechanical philosophy and the mathematization of nature.

The impact of Newton

Newton was able to derive all these striking results from his three laws of motion:

1. Every body continues in its state of rest or of motion in a straight line unless it is compelled to change that state by force impressed on it;
2. The change of motion is proportional to the motive force impressed and is made in the direction of the straight line in which that force is impressed;
3. To every action there is always opposed an equal reaction: or, the mutual actions of two bodies upon each other are always equal.

The second law was put into its modern form $F = ma$ (where *a* is acceleration) by the Swiss mathematician Leonhard Euler in 1750. In this form, it is clear that the rate of change of velocity is directly proportional to the force acting on a body and inversely proportional to its mass.

In order to apply his laws to astronomy, Newton had to extend the mechanical philosophy beyond the limits set by Descartes. He postulated a gravitational force acting between any two objects in the universe, even though he was unable to explain how this force could be propagated.

The universality of gravitation

By means of his laws of motion and a gravitational force proportional to the inverse square of the distance between the centres of two bodies, Newton could deduce Kepler's laws of planetary motion. Galileo's law of free fall is also consistent with Newton's laws. The same force that causes objects to fall near the surface of the Earth also holds the Moon and planets in their orbits.

Newton's physics led to the conclusion that the shape of the Earth is not precisely spherical but should bulge at the Equator. The confirmation of this prediction by French expeditions in the mid-18th century helped persuade most European scientists to change from Cartesian to Newtonian physics. Newton also used the nonspherical shape of the Earth to explain the precession of the equinoxes, using the differential action of the Moon and Sun on the equatorial bulge to show how the axis of rotation would change its direction.

Optics. The science of optics in the 17th century expressed the fundamental outlook of the scientific revolution by combining an experimental approach with a quantitative analysis of phenomena. Optics had its origins in Greece, especially in the works of Euclid (*c.* 300 BC), who stated many of the results in geometric optics that the Greeks had discovered, including the law of reflection: the angle of incidence is equal to the angle of reflection. In the 13th century, such men as Roger Bacon, Robert Grosseteste, and John Pecham, relying on the work of the Arab Alhazen (d. 1039), considered numerous optical problems, including the optics of the rainbow. It was Kepler, taking his lead from the writings of these 13th-century opticians, who set the tone for the science in the 17th century. Kepler introduced the point by point analysis of optical problems, tracing rays from each point on the object to a point on the image. Just as the mechanical philosophy was breaking the world into atomic parts, so Kepler approached optics by breaking organic reality into what he considered to be ultimately real units. He developed a geometric theory of lenses, providing the first mathematical account of Galileo's telescope.

Descartes sought to incorporate the phenomena of light into mechanical philosophy by demonstrating that they can be explained entirely in terms of matter and motion. Using mechanical analogies, he was able to derive mathematically many of the known properties of light, including the law of reflection and the newly discovered law of refraction.

Many of the most important contributions to optics in the 17th century were the work of Newton, especially the theory of colours. Traditional theory considered colours to be the result of the modification of white light. Descartes, for example, thought that colours were the result of the spin of the particles that constitute light. Newton upset the traditional theory of colours by demonstrating in an impressive set of experiments that white light is a mixture out of which separate beams of coloured light can be separated. He associated different degrees of refrangibility with rays of different colours, and in this manner he was able to explain the way prisms produce spectra of colours from white light.

His experimental method was characterized by a quantitative approach, since he always sought measurable variables and a clear distinction between experimental findings and mechanical explanations of those findings. His second important contribution to optics dealt with the interference phenomena that came to be called "Newton's rings." Although the colours of thin films (*e.g.,* oil on water) had been previously observed, no one had attempted to quantify the phenomena in any way. Newton observed quantitative relations between the thickness of the film and the diameters of the rings of colour, a regularity he attempted to explain by his theory of fits of easy transmission and fits of easy reflection. Notwithstanding the fact that he generally conceived of light as being particulate, Newton's theory of fits involves periodicity and vibrations of ether, the hypothetical fluid substance permeating all space (see above).

Huygens was the second great optical thinker of the 17th century. Although he was critical of many of the details of Descartes's system, he wrote in the Cartesian tradition, seeking purely mechanical explanations of phenomena. Huygens regarded light as something of a pulse phenomenon, but he explicitly denied the periodicity of light pulses. He developed the concept of wave front, by means of which he was able to derive the laws of reflection and refraction from his pulse theory and to explain the recently discovered phenomenon of double refraction.

Chemistry. Chemistry had manifold origins, coming from such diverse sources as philosophy, alchemy, metallurgy, and medicine. It emerged as a separate science only with the rise of mechanical philosophy in the 17th century. Aristotle had regarded the four elements earth, water, air, and fire as the ultimate constituents of all things. Transmutable each into the other, all four elements were believed to exist in every substance. Originating in Egypt and the Middle East, alchemy had a double aspect: on the one hand it was a practical endeavour aimed to make gold from baser substances, while on the other it was a cosmological theory based on the correspondence between man and the universe at large. Alchemy contributed to chemistry a long tradition of experience with a wide variety of substances. Paracelsus, a 16th-century Swiss natural philosopher, was a seminal figure in the history of chemistry, putting together in an almost impenetrable combination the Aristotelian theory of matter, alchemical correspondences, mystical forms of knowledge, and chemical therapy in medicine. His influence was widely felt in succeeding generations.

During the first half of the 17th century, there were few established doctrines that chemists generally accepted as a framework. As a result, there was little cumulative growth of chemical knowledge. Chemists tended to build detailed systems, "chemical philosophies," attempting to explain the entire universe in chemical terms. Most chemists accepted the traditional four elements (air, earth, water, fire), or the Paracelsian principles (salt, sulfur, mercury), or both, as the bearers of real qualities in substances; they also exhibited a marked tendency toward the occult.

The interaction between chemistry and mechanical philosophy altered this situation by providing chemists with a shared language. The mechanical philosophy had been successfully employed in other areas; it seemed consistent with an experimental empiricism and seemed to provide a way to render chemistry respectable by translating it into the terms of the new science. Perhaps the best example of the influence of the mechanical philosophy is the work of Robert Boyle. The thrust of his work was to understand the chemical properties of matter, to provide experimental evidence for the mechanical philosophy, and to demonstrate that all chemical properties can be explained in mechanical terms. He was an excellent laboratory chemist and developed a number of important techniques, especially colour-identification tests.

Effect of
mechanical
theory on
chemistry

SCIENCE FROM THE ENLIGHTENMENT TO THE 20TH CENTURY

Seminal contributions to science are those that change the tenor of the questions asked by succeeding generations. The works of Newton formed just such a contribution. The mathematical rigour of the *Principia* and the experimental approach of the *Opticks* became models for scientists of the 18th and 19th centuries. Celestial mechanics developed in the wake of his *Principia,* extending its scope and refining its mathematical methods. The more qualitative, experimental, and hypothetical approach of Newton's *Opticks* influenced the sciences of optics, electricity and magnetism, and chemistry.

Celestial mechanics and astronomy. Eighteenth-century theoretical astronomy in large measure derived both its point of view and its problems from the *Principia.* In this work Newton had provided a physics for the Copernican worldview by, among other things, demonstrating the implications of his gravitational theory for a two-body system consisting of the Sun and a planet. While Newton himself had grave reservations as to the wider scope of his theory, the 18th century witnessed various attempts to extend it to the solution of problems involving three gravitating bodies.

Early in the 18th century the English astronomer Edmond Halley, having noted striking similarities in the comets that had been observed in 1531, 1607, and 1682, argued that they were the periodic appearances every 75 years or so of but a single comet that he predicted would return in 1758. Months before its expected return, the French mathematician Alexis Clairaut employed rather tedious and brute-force mathematics to calculate the effects of the gravitational attraction of Jupiter and Saturn on the otherwise elliptical orbit of Comet Halley. Clairaut was finally able to predict in the fall of 1758 that Comet Halley would reach perihelion in April of 1759, with a leeway of one month. Its actual return, in March, was an early confirmation of the scope and power of the Newtonian theory.

Newton's
theory of
colours

It was, however, the three-body problem of either two planets and the Sun or the Sun–Earth–Moon system that provided the most persisting and profound test of Newton's theory. This problem, involving more regular members of the solar system (*i.e.*, those describing nearly circular orbits having the same sense of revolution and in nearly the same plane), permitted certain simplifying assumptions and thereby invited more general and elegant mathematical approaches than the comet problem. An illustrious group of 18th-century continental mathematicians (including Clairaut; the Bernoulli family and Leonhard Euler of Switzerland; and Jean Le Rond d'Alembert, Joseph-Louis, comte de Lagrange, and Pierre-Simon, marquis de Laplace, of France) attacked these astronomical problems, as well as related ones in Newtonian mechanics, by developing and applying the calculus of variations as it had been formulated by Leibniz. It is a lovely irony that this continental exploitation of Leibniz' mathematics—which was itself closely akin to Newton's version of calculus, which he called fluxions—was fundamental for the deepening establishment of the Newtonian theory to which Leibniz had objected because it reintroduced, according to Leibniz, occult forces into physics.

In order to attack the lunar theory, which also commanded attention as the most likely astronomical approach to the navigational problem of determining longitude at sea, Clairaut was forced to adopt methods of approximation, having derived general equations that neither he nor anyone else could integrate. Even so, Clairaut was unable to calculate from gravitational theory a value for the progression of the lunar apogee greater than 50 percent of the observed value; therefore, he supposed in 1747 (with Euler) that Newton's inverse-square law was but the first term of a series and, hence, an approximation not valid for distances as small as that between the Earth and Moon. This attempted refinement of Newtonian theory proved to be fruitless, however, and two years later Clairaut was able to obtain, by more detailed and elaborate calculations, the observed value from the simple inverse-square relation.

Certain of the three-body problems, most notably that of the secular acceleration of the Moon, defied early attempts at solution but finally yielded to the increasing power of the calculus of variations in the service of Newtonian theory. Thus it was that Laplace—in his five-volume *Traité de mécanique céleste* (1798–1827; *Celestial Mechanics*)—was able to comprehend the whole solar system as a dynamically stable, Newtonian gravitational system. The secular acceleration of the Moon reappeared as a theoretical problem in the middle of the 19th century, persisting into the 20th century and ultimately requiring that the effects of the tides be recognized in its solution.

Newtonian theory was also employed in much more dramatic discoveries that captivated the imagination of a broad and varied audience. Within 40 years of the discovery of Uranus in 1781 by the German-born British astronomer William Herschel, it was recognized that the planet's motion was somewhat anomalous. In the next 20 years the gravitational attraction of an unobserved planet was suspected to be the cause of Uranus' persisting deviations. In 1845 Urbain-Jean-Joseph Le Verrier of France and John Couch Adams of England independently calculated the position of this unseen body; the visual discovery (at the Berlin Observatory in 1846) of Neptune in just the position predicted constituted an immediately engaging and widely understood confirmation of Newtonian theory. In 1915 the American astronomer Percival Lowell published his prediction of yet another outer planet to account for further perturbations of Uranus not caused by Neptune. Pluto was finally discovered by sophisticated photographic techniques in 1930 and observed visually in 1950.

In the second half of the 19th century, the innermost region of the solar system also received attention. In 1859 Le Verrier calculated the specifications of an intra-mercurial planet to account for a residual advance in the perihelion of Mercury's orbit (38 seconds of arc per century), an effect that was not gravitationally explicable in terms of known bodies. While a number of sightings of this predicted planet were reported between 1859 and 1878—

the first of these resulting in Le Verrier's naming the new planet Vulcan—they were not confirmed by observations made either during subsequent solar eclipses or at the times of predicted transits of Vulcan across the Sun.

The theoretical comprehension of Mercury's residual motion involved the first successful departure from Newtonian gravitational theory. This came in the form of Einstein's formulation of the principle of the general of relativity, one consequence of which was a correction term for a body in motion. The correction involves the square of the ratio of the body's velocity to the enormous velocity of light and hence, among the planets, is appreciable only for the fastest: Mercury. Einstein's theory accounted for the residual effect, which by 1915 was calculated to be 43 seconds. This achievement, combined with the 1919 observation of the bending of a ray of light passing near a massive body (another consequence of general relativity theory), constitutes the main experimental verification of that theory.

Astronomy of the 18th, 19th, and early 20th centuries was not quite so completely Newtonian, however. Herschel's discovery of Uranus, for example, was not directly motivated by gravitational considerations. Nine years earlier, a German astronomer, Johann D. Titius, had announced a purely numerical sequence, subsequently refined by another German astronomer, Johann E. Bode, that related the mean radii of the planetary orbits—a relation entirely outside gravitational theory. The sequence, called Bode's law (or the Bode–Titius law), is given by $0 + 4 = 4$, $3 + 4 = 7$, $3 \times 2 + 4 = 10$, $3 \times 4 + 4 = 16$, and so on, yielding additional values of 28, 52, and 100. If the measured radius of the Earth's orbit is defined as being 10, then to a very good approximation that of Mercury is 4, Venus is 7, Mars is 15 plus, Jupiter is 52, and Saturn is 95 plus. The fit where it can be made is good and continues since the next number in the sequence is 196 and the measured radius for Uranus' orbit is 191, but no planet had been observed to correspond to the Bode–Titius law value of 28. Powerful computational methods finally verified the existence of the asteroid Ceres and confirmed the law. The Bode–Titius law subsequently provided simplifying assumptions for the calculations of the predicted positions, which led to the observations of Neptune and Pluto, while the novel properties of the asteroids (nearly 500 of which had been discovered by the end of the century) stimulated star charts of the zodiacal regions, provided the means for improved measurements of solar-system distances, and forced astronomers, by their very number and variety, to face the question of the allocation of resources.

Regularities in the structure of the solar system, such as the Bode–Titius law, and the fact that all planets move in the same direction around the Sun suggested that the system might originally have been formed by a simple mechanistic process. Laplace proposed that this process was driven by the cooling of the hot, extended, rotating atmosphere of the primitive Sun. As the atmosphere contracted, it would have to rotate faster (to conserve angular momentum), and when centrifugal force exceeded gravity at the outside, a ring of material would be detached, later to condense into a planet. The process would be repeated several times and might also produce satellites. After Herschel suggested that the nebulas he observed in the sky were condensing to stars, the Laplace theory became known as the "nebular hypothesis." It was the favoured theory of the origin of the solar system throughout the 19th century. During this period the associated idea that the Earth was originally a hot fluid ball that slowly cooled down while forming a solid outer crust dominated geologic speculation.

Attempts to detect the motion of the Earth caused investigators of the 18th and 19th centuries observational problems that were directly motivated by the Copernican theory. In 1728 the English astronomer James Bradley attributed annual changes that he observed in stellar positions to a slight tilting of the telescope with respect to the true direction of the star's light, a tilting that compensated for the Earth's motion. This effect, which depends also on the ratio of the Earth's velocity to the velocity of light, is the so-called aberration of light.

In 1838 the long-sought "stellar parallax" effect—the apparent motion of nearby stars due to the Earth's annual motion around the Sun—was discovered by the German astronomer Friedrich Wilhelm Bessel. While anticlimactic as a verification of the Copernican hypothesis, the measurement of parallax provided for the first time a direct quantitative estimate of the distances of a few stars.

While attention has been focused on the more positional aspects of astronomy, mention should be made of two other broad areas of investigation that in their 19th-century form derived largely from the work of William Herschel. These areas, dealing with more structural features of the heavens and with the physical character of the stars, developed in large measure with advancements in physics.

Optics. Since they provided the principal basis for subsequent investigations, Newton's optical views were subject to close consideration until well into the 19th century. From his researches into the phenomena of colour, Newton became convinced that dispersion necessarily accompanies refraction and that chromatic aberration (colour distortion) could therefore be eliminated by employing reflectors, rather than refractors, as telescopes. By the mid-18th century Euler and others had theoretical arguments against Newton, and Euler offered the human eye as an example of an achromatic lens system. Although he was virtually alone in this, Euler also rejected Newton's essentially corpuscular theory of the nature of light by explaining optical phenomena in terms of vibrations in a fluid ether. The dominance of Newton's theory throughout the 18th century was due partly to its successful direct application by Newton and his followers and partly to the comprehensiveness of Newton's thought. For example, Bradley's observations found an immediate and natural explanation in terms of the corpuscular theory that also was supported by the accelerating success of Newton's gravitational theory involving discrete particles of matter.

Criticism of Newton's optics

At the turn of the century, Thomas Young, an English physician studying the power of accommodation of the eye (*i.e.*, its focusing power), was led gradually to extensive investigations and discoveries in optics, including the effect of interference. By means of a wave theory of light, Young was able to explain both this effect, which in its most dramatic manifestation results in two rays of light canceling each other to produce darkness, and also the various colour phenomena observed by Newton. The wave theory of light was developed from 1815 onward in a series of brilliant mathematical and experimental memoirs of the physicist Augustin-Jean Fresnel but was countered by adherents of the corpuscular theory, most notably by a group of other French scientists, Pierre-Simon Laplace, Siméon-Denis Poisson, Étienne Malus, and Jean-Baptiste Biot, and most strikingly in connection with Malus' discovery (1808) of the polarization of light by reflection. Following Young's suggestion in 1817, Fresnel was able to render polarization effects comprehensible by means of a wave theory that considered light to be a transverse rather than a longitudinal wave, as the analogy with sound had suggested.

Wave theory of light

The propagation of a transverse wave, the velocity of which through various media and under a variety of conditions was measured terrestrially with increasing accuracy from mid-century onward, seemed to require an ether having the properties of a highly elastic solid (*e.g.*, such as steel), which, however, offered no resistance to the planetary motions. These bizarre properties stimulated a number of mechanical models of the ether, most notably those of the English physicist William Thomson, Lord Kelvin. In order to encompass the aberration of light by means of his wave theory, Fresnel had assumed that the motionless ether freely permeated the opaque Earth and thus remained unaffected by its motions. Furthermore, he derived as a theoretical consequence (verified experimentally in mid-century by Armand-Hippolyte-Louis Fizeau) that the ether was partially, and only partially, dragged along by a moving transparent substance depending on the index of refraction of the substance. However, all subsequent investigators (most notably the American scientists A.A. Michelson and Edward W. Morley, in 1887) failed in their attempts to measure the required ether drift. It was just to escape this difficulty of a necessary but undetected ether drift that George Francis FitzGerald of England and the Dutch theorist Hendrik Antoon Lorentz independently, at the close of the century, postulated the contraction of moving bodies in the direction of their motion through the ether. The Lorentz–FitzGerald contraction involves the square of the ratio of the velocity of the body to the velocity of light and ensures theoretically the experimental undetectability of the ether drift. It was the seeming necessity of arbitrary postulations of this kind that was eliminated by Einstein's formulation of relativity theory.

Electricity and magnetism. Until the end of the 18th century, investigations in electricity and magnetism exhibited more of the hypothetical and spontaneous character of Newton's *Opticks* than the axiomatic and somewhat forbidding tone of his *Principia*. Early in the century, in England Stephen Gray and in France Charles François de Cisternay DuFay studied the direct and induced electrification of various substances by the two kinds of electricity (then called vitreous and resinous and now known as positive and negative), as well as the capability of these substances to conduct the "effluvium" of electricity. By about mid-century, the use of Leyden jars (to collect charges) and the development of large static electricity machines brought the experimental science into the drawing room, while the theoretical aspects were being cast in various forms of the single-fluid theory (by the American Benjamin Franklin and the German-born physicist F.M.U.T.H. Aepinus, among others) and the two-fluid theory.

Theories of electricity

By the end of the 18th century, in England, Joseph Priestley had noted that no electric effect was exhibited inside an electrified hollow metal container and had brilliantly inferred from this similarity that the inverse-square law (of gravity) must hold for electricity as well. In a series of painstaking memoirs, the French physicist Charles-Augustin de Coulomb, using a torsion balance that Henry Cavendish had used in England to measure the gravitational force, demonstrated the inverse-square relation for electrical and magnetic attractions and repulsions. Coulomb went on to apply this law to calculate the surface distribution of the electrical fluid in such a fundamental manner as to provide the basis for the 19th-century extensions by Poisson and Lord Kelvin.

The discovery of galvanic electricity and the development of voltaic electricity opened whole new areas of investigation for the 19th century by providing convenient sources of sustained electrical current. The Danish physicist Hans Christian Ørsted's discovery, in 1820, of the magnetic effect accompanying an electric current led almost immediately to quantitative laws of electromagnetism and electrodynamics. By 1827, André-Marie Ampère had published a series of mathematical and experimental memoirs on his electrodynamic theory that not only rendered electromagnetism comprehensible but also ordinary magnetism, identifying both as the result of electrical currents. Ampère solidly established his electrodynamics by basing it on inverse-square forces (which, however, are directed at right angles to, rather than in, the line connecting the two interacting elements) and by demonstrating that the effects do not violate Newton's third law of motion, notwithstanding their transverse direction.

Relation of electric and magnetic effects

Michael Faraday's discovery in 1831 of electromagnetic induction (the inverse of the effect discovered by Ørsted), his experimental determination of the identity of the various forms of electricity (1833), his discovery of the rotation of the plane of polarization of light by magnetism (1845), in addition to certain findings of other investigators—*e.g.*, the discovery by James Prescott Joule in 1843 (and others) of the mechanical equivalent of heat (the conservation of energy)—all served to emphasize the essential unity of the forces of nature. Within electricity and magnetism attempts at theoretical unification were conceived in terms of either gravitational-type forces acting at a distance, as with Ampère, or, with Faraday, in terms of lines of force and the ambient medium in which they were thought to travel. The German physicists Wilhelm Eduard Weber and Rudolph Kohlrausch, in order to determine the coefficients in his theory of the former kind, measured the ratio of the electromagnetic and electrostatic units of electrical charge to be equal to the velocity of light.

The Scottish physicist James Clerk Maxwell developed his profound mathematical electromagnetic theory from 1855 onward. He drew his conceptions from Faraday and thus relied fundamentally on the ether required by optical theory, while using ingenious mechanical models. One consequence of Maxwell's mature theory was that an electromagnetic wave must be propagated through the ether with a velocity equal to the ratio of the electromagnetic to electrostatic units. Combined with the earlier results of Weber and Kohlrausch, this result implied that light is an electromagnetic phenomenon. Moreover, it suggested that electromagnetic waves of wavelengths other than the narrow band corresponding to visible light should exist in nature or could be artificially generated.

The nature of light

Maxwell's theory received direct verification in 1886, when Heinrich Hertz of Germany detected the predicted electromagnetic waves. Their use in long-distance communication—"radio"—followed within two decades, and gradually physicists became acquainted with the entire electromagnetic spectrum.

Chemistry. Eighteenth-century chemistry was derived from and remained involved with questions of mechanics, light, and heat as well as with iatrochemistry and notions of medical therapy and the interaction between substances and the formation of new substances. Chemistry took many of its problems and much of its viewpoint from the *Opticks* and especially the "Queries" with which that work ends. Newton's suggestion of a hierarchy of clusters of unalterable particles formed by virtue of the specific attractions of its component particles led directly to comparative studies of interactions and thus to the tables of affinities of the physician Herman Boerhaave and others early in the century. This work culminated at the end of the century in the Swede Torbern Bergman's table that gave quantitative values of the affinity of substances both for reactions when "dry" and when in solution and that considered double as well as simple affinities.

Seventeenth-century investigations of "airs" or gases, combustion and calcination, and the nature and role of fire were incorporated by the chemists Johann Joachim Becher and Georg Ernst Stahl of Sweden into a theory of phlogiston. According to this theory, which was most influential after the middle of the 18th century, the fiery principle, phlogiston, was released into the air in the processes of combustion, calcination, and respiration. The theory explained that air was simply the receptacle for phlogiston, and any combustible or calcinable substance contained phlogiston as a principle or element and thus could not itself be elemental. Iron, in rusting, was considered to lose its compound nature and to assume its elemental state as the calx of iron by yielding its phlogiston into the ambient air.

Theory of phlogiston

Investigations that isolated and identified various gases in the second half of the 18th century, most notably the English chemist Joseph Black's quantitative manipulations of "fixed air" (carbon dioxide) and Joseph Priestley's discovery of "dephlogisticated air" (oxygen), were instrumental for the French chemist Antoine Lavoisier's formulation of his own oxygen theory of combustion and rejection of the phlogiston theory (*i.e.*, he explained combustion not as the result of the liberation of phlogiston, but rather as the result of the combination of the burning substance with oxygen). This transformation coupled with the reform in nomenclature at the end of the century (due to Lavoisier and others)—a reform that reflected the new conceptions of chemical elements, compounds, and processes—constituted the revolution in chemistry.

Lavoisier's revolution

Very early in the 19th century, another study of gases, this time in the form of a persisting Newtonian approach to certain meteorological problems by the British chemist John Dalton, led to the enunciation of a chemical atomic theory. From this theory, which was demonstrated to agree with the law of definite proportions and from which the law of multiple proportions was derived, Dalton was able to calculate definite atomic weights by assuming the simplest possible ratio for the numbers of combining atoms.

For example, knowing from experiment that the ratio of the combining weights of hydrogen to oxygen in the formation of water is 1 to 8 and by assuming that one atom of hydrogen combined with one atom of oxygen, Dalton affirmed that the atomic weight of oxygen was eight, based on hydrogen as one. At the same time, however, in France, Joseph-Louis Gay-Lussac, from his volumetric investigations of combining gases, determined that two volumes of hydrogen combined with one of oxygen to produce water. While this suggested H_2O rather than Dalton's HO as the formula for water, with the result that the atomic weight of oxygen becomes 16, it did involve certain inconsistencies with Dalton's theory.

As early as 1811 the Italian physicist Amedeo Avogadro was able to reconcile Dalton's atomic theory with Gay-Lussac's volumetric law by postulating that Dalton's atoms were indeed compound atoms, or polyatomic. For a number of reasons, one of which involved the recent successes of electrochemistry, Avogadro's hypothesis was not accepted until it was reintroduced by the Italian chemist Stanislao Cannizzaro half a century later. From the turn of the century, the English scientist Humphry Davy and many others had employed the strong electric currents of voltaic piles for the analysis of compound substances and the discovery of new elements. From these results, it appeared obvious that chemical forces were essentially electrical in nature and that two hydrogen atoms, for example, having the same electrical charge, would repel each other and could not join to form the polyatomic molecule required by Avogadro's hypothesis. Until the development of a quantum-mechanical theory of the chemical bond, beginning in the 1920s, bonding was described by empirical "valence" rules but could not be satisfactorily explained in terms of purely electrical forces.

Avogadro's hypothesis

Between the presentation of Avogadro's hypothesis in 1811 and its general acceptance soon after 1860, several experimental techniques and theoretical laws were used by various investigators to yield different but self-consistent schemes of chemical formulas and atomic weights. After its acceptance, these schemes became unified. Within a few years of the development of another powerful technique, spectrum analysis, by the German physicists Gustav Kirchhoff and Robert Bunsen in 1859, the number of chemical elements whose atomic weights and other properties were known had approximately doubled since the time of Avogadro's announcement. By relying fundamentally but not slavishly upon the determined atomic weight values and by using his chemical insight and intuition, the Russian chemist Dmitry Ivanovich Mendeleyev provided a classification scheme that ordered much of this burgeoning information and was a culmination of earlier attempts to represent the periodic repetition of certain chemical and physical properties of the elements.

The significance of the atomic weights themselves remained unclear. In 1815 William Prout, an English chemist, had proposed that they might all be integer multiples of the weight of the hydrogen atom, implying that the other elements are simply compounds of hydrogen. More accurate determinations, however, showed that the atomic weights are significantly different from integers. They are not, of course, the actual weights of individual atoms, but by 1870 it was possible to estimate those weights (or rather masses) in grams by the kinetic theory of gases and other methods. Thus one could at least say that the atomic weight of an element is proportional to the mass of an atom of that element. (M.J.O./J.B.Sp./S.G.B.)

DEVELOPMENTS AND TRENDS OF THE 20TH CENTURY

Astronomy. Some of the most spectacular advances in modern astronomy have come from research on the large-scale structure and development of the universe. This research goes back to William Herschel's observations of nebulas at the end of the 18th century. Some astronomers considered them to be "island universes"—huge stellar systems outside of and comparable to the Milky Way Galaxy, to which the solar system belongs. Others, following Herschel's own speculations, thought of them simply as gaseous clouds—relatively small patches of diffuse matter within the Milky Way Galaxy, which might be in the process of developing into stars and planetary systems, as described in Laplace's nebular hypothesis.

In 1912 Vesto Melvin Slipher began at the Lowell Observatory in Arizona an extensive program to measure the velocities of nebulas, using the Doppler shift of their spectral lines. (Doppler shift is the observed change in wavelength of the radiation from a source that results from the relative motion of the latter along the line of sight.) By 1925 he had studied about 40 nebulas, most of which were found to be moving away from the Earth according to the red shift (displacement toward longer wavelengths) of their spectra.

Although the nebulas were apparently so far away that their distances could not be measured directly by the stellar parallax method, an indirect approach was developed on the basis of a discovery made in 1908 by Henrietta Swan Leavitt at the Harvard College Observatory. Leavitt studied the magnitudes (apparent brightnesses) of a large number of variable stars, including the type known as Cepheid variables. Some of them were close enough to have measurable parallaxes so that their distances and thus their intrinsic brightnesses could be determined. She found a correlation between brightness and period of variation. Assuming that the same correlation holds for all stars of this kind, their observed magnitudes and periods could be used to estimate their distances.

In 1923 the American astronomer Edwin P. Hubble identified a Cepheid variable in the so-called Andromeda Nebula. Using Leavitt's period–brightness correlation, Hubble estimated its distance to be approximately 900,000 light-years. Since this was much greater than the size of the Milky Way system, it appeared that the Andromeda Nebula must be another galaxy (island universe) outside of our own.

In 1929 Hubble combined Slipher's measurements of the velocities of nebulas with further estimates of their distances and found that on the average such objects are moving away from the Earth with a velocity proportional to their distance. Hubble's velocity–distance relation suggested that the universe of galactic nebulas is expanding, starting from an initial state about 2,000,000,000 years ago in which all matter was contained in a fairly small volume. Revisions of the distance scale in the 1950s and later increased the "Hubble age" of the universe to more than 10,000,000,000 years.

The expanding universe

Calculations by Aleksandr A. Friedmann in the Soviet Union, Willem de Sitter in The Netherlands, and Georges Lemaître in Belgium, based on Einstein's general theory of relativity, showed that the expanding universe could be explained in terms of the evolution of space itself. According to Einstein's theory, space is described by the non-Euclidean geometry proposed in 1854 by the German mathematician G.F. Bernhard Riemann. Its departure from Euclidean space is measured by a "curvature" that depends on the density of matter. The universe may be finite, though unbounded, like the surface of a sphere. Thus the expansion of the universe refers not merely to the motion of extragalactic stellar systems within space but also to the expansion of the space itself.

The beginning of the expanding universe was linked to the formation of the chemical elements in a theory developed in the 1940s by the physicist George Gamow, a former student of Friedmann who had emigrated to the United States. Gamow proposed that the universe began in a state of extremely high temperature and density and exploded outward—the so-called big bang. Matter was originally in the form of neutrons, which quickly decayed into protons and electrons; these then combined to form hydrogen and heavier elements.

The big-bang theory

Gamow's students Ralph Alpher and Robert Herman estimated in 1948 that the radiation left over from the big bang should by now have cooled down to a temperature just a few degrees above absolute zero (0 K, or −459° F). In 1965 the predicted cosmic background radiation was discovered by Arno A. Penzias and Robert W. Wilson of the Bell Telephone Laboratories as part of an effort to build sensitive microwave-receiving stations for satellite communication. Their finding provided unexpected evidence for the idea that the universe was in a state of very

high temperature and density sometime between 10,000,-000,000 and 20,000,000,000 years ago.

Evolution of stars and formation of chemical elements. Just as the development of cosmology relied heavily on ideas from physics, especially Einstein's general theory of relativity, so did theories of stellar structure and evolution depend on discoveries in atomic physics. These theories also offered a fundamental basis for chemistry by showing how the elements could have been synthesized in stars.

The idea that stars are formed by the condensation of gaseous clouds was part of the 19th-century nebular hypothesis (see above). The gravitational energy released by this condensation could be transformed into heat, but calculations by Hermann von Helmholtz and Lord Kelvin indicated that this process would provide energy to keep the Sun shining for only about 20,000,000 years. Evidence from radiometric dating, starting with the work of the British physicist Ernest Rutherford in 1905, showed that the Earth is probably several billion years old. Astrophysicists were perplexed: what source of energy has kept the Sun shining for such a long time?

In 1925 Cecilia Payne, a graduate student from Britain at Harvard College Observatory, analyzed the spectra of stars using statistical atomic theories that related them to temperature, density, and composition. She found that hydrogen and helium are the most abundant elements in stars, though this conclusion was not generally accepted until it was confirmed four years later by the noted American astronomer Henry Norris Russell. By this time Prout's hypothesis that all the elements are compounds of hydrogen had been revived by physicists in a somewhat more elaborate form. The deviation of atomic weights from exact integer values (expressed as multiples of hydrogen) could be explained partly by the fact that some elements are mixtures of isotopes with different atomic weights and partly by Einstein's relation between mass and energy (taking account of the binding energy of the forces that hold together the atomic nucleus). The German physicist Werner Heisenberg proposed in 1932 that, whereas the hydrogen nucleus consists of just one proton, all heavier nuclei contain protons and neutrons. Since a proton can be changed into a neutron by fusing it with an electron, this meant that all the elements could be built up from protons and electrons—*i.e.,* from hydrogen atoms.

In 1938 the German-born physicist Hans Bethe proposed the first satisfactory theory of stellar energy generation based on the fusion of protons to form helium and heavier elements. He showed that once elements as heavy as carbon had been formed, a cycle of nuclear reactions could produce even heavier elements. Fusion of hydrogen into heavier elements would also provide enough energy to account for the Sun's energy generation over a period of billions of years. Although Bethe's theory, as extended by Fred Hoyle, Edwin E. Salpeter, and William A. Fowler, is the best one available, there is still some doubt about its accuracy because the neutrinos supposedly produced by the fusion reactions have not been observed in the amounts predicted.

Synthesis and dissemination of heavy elements

According to the theory of stellar evolution developed by the Indian-born American astrophysicist Subrahmanyan Chandrasekhar and others, a star will become unstable after it has converted most of its hydrogen to helium and may go through stages of rapid expansion and contraction. If the star is much more massive than the Sun, it will explode violently, giving rise to a supernova. The explosion will synthesize heavier elements and spread them throughout the surrounding interstellar medium, where they provide the raw material for the formation of new stars and eventually of planets and living organisms.

After a supernova explosion, the remaining core of the star may collapse further under its own gravitational attraction to form a dense star composed mainly of neutrons. This so-called neutron star, predicted theoretically in the 1930s by the astronomers Walter Baade and Fritz Zwicky, is apparently the same as the pulsar (a source of rapid, very regular pulses of radio waves), discovered in 1967 by Jocelyn Bell of the British radio astronomy group under Antony Hewish at Cambridge University.

More massive stars may undergo a further stage of evolu-

The black-hole phenomenon

tion beyond the neutron star: they may collapse to a black hole, in which the gravitational force is so strong that even light cannot escape. The black hole as a singularity in an idealized space-time universe was predicted from the general relativity theory by the German astronomer Karl Schwarzschild in 1916. Its role in stellar evolution was later described by the American physicists J. Robert Oppenheimer and John Wheeler. During the 1980s, possible black holes were thought to have been located in X-ray sources and at the centre of certain galaxies (see below *Study of the stars*).

Solar-system astronomy. This area of investigation, which lay relatively dormant through the first half of the 20th century, was revived in the 1960s under the stimulus of the Soviet and American space programs. Missions to the Moon and planets yielded a wealth of complex information which has yet to be completely assimilated by scientists. A single example of the resulting change in ideas about the history of the solar system will have to suffice here. Before the first manned lunar landing in 1969, there were three competing hypotheses about the origin of the Moon: (1) formation in its present orbit simultaneously with the Earth, as described in the nebular hypothesis; (2) formation elsewhere and subsequent capture by the Earth; and (3) ejection from the Earth by fission (popularly known theory that the Moon emanated from what is now the Pacific Ocean Basin). Following the analysis of lunar samples and theoretical criticism of these hypotheses, lunar scientists came to the conclusion that none of them was satisfactory. Photographs of the surface of Mercury taken by the U.S. Mariner 10 spacecraft in 1974, however, showed that it is heavily cratered like the Moon's surface. This finding, together with theoretical calculations by V.S. Safronov of the Soviet Union and George W. Wetherill of the United States on the formation of planets by accumulation (accretion or aggregation) of smaller solid bodies, suggested that the Earth was also probably subject to heavy bombardment soon after its formation. In line with this, a theory proposed by the American astronomers William K. Hartmann and A.G.W. Cameron has become the most popular. According to their theory, the Earth was struck by a Mars-sized object, and the force of the impact vaporized the outer parts of both bodies. The vapour thus produced remained in orbit around the Earth and eventually condensed to form the Moon. Like the hypothesis proposed by Luis Alvarez that attributes the extinction of the dinosaurs to an asteroid impact, the Hartmann–Cameron theory seemed so bizarre that it could not have been taken seriously until compelling evidence became available.

The Hartmann–Cameron theory

Physics. During the years 1896–1932 the foundations of physics changed so radically that many observers describe this period as a scientific revolution comparable in depth, if not in scope, to the one that took place during the 16th and 17th centuries. The 20th-century revolution changed many of the ideas about space, time, mass, energy, atoms, light, force, determinism, and causality that had apparently been firmly established by Newtonian physics during the 18th and 19th centuries. Moreover, according to some interpretations, the new theories demolished the basic metaphysical assumption of earlier science that the entire physical world has a real existence and objective properties independent of human observation.

The 20th-century scientific revolution

Closer examination of 19th-century physics shows that Newtonian ideas were already being undermined in many areas and that the program of mechanical explanation was openly challenged by several influential physicists toward the end of the century. Yet, there was no agreement as to what the foundations of a new physics might be. Modern textbook writers and popularizers often try to identify specific paradoxes or puzzling experimental results—*e.g.,* the failure to detect the Earth's absolute motion in the Michelson–Morley experiment—as anomalies that led physicists to propose new fundamental theories such as relativity. Historians of science have shown, however, that most of these anomalies did not directly cause the introduction of the theories that later resolved them. As with Copernicus' introduction of heliocentric astronomy, the motivation seems to have been a desire to satisfy aesthetic principles

of theory structure rooted in earlier views of the world rather than a need to account for the latest experiment or calculation.

Radioactivity and the transmutation of elements. The discovery of radioactivity by the French physicist Henri Becquerel in 1896 is generally taken to mark the beginning of 20th-century physics. The successful isolation of radium and other intensely radioactive substances by Marie and Pierre Curie focused the attention of scientists and the public on this remarkable phenomenon and promoted a wide range of experiments.

Ernest Rutherford soon took the lead in studying the nature of radioactivity. He found that there are two distinct kinds of radiation emitted in radioactivity called alpha and beta rays. The alpha rays proved to be positively charged particles identical to ionized helium atoms. Beta rays are much less massive negatively charged particles; they were shown to be the same as the electrons discovered by J.J. Thomson in cathode rays in 1897. A third kind of ray, designated gamma, consists of high-frequency electromagnetic radiation.

Rutherford's investigations of radioactivity

Rutherford proposed that radioactivity involves a transmutation of one element into another. This proposal called into question one of the basic assumptions of 19th-century chemistry: that the elements consist of qualitatively different substances—92 of them by the end of the century. It implied a return to the ideas of Prout and the ancient atomists—namely, that everything in the world is composed of only one or a few basic substances.

Transmutation, according to Rutherford and his colleagues, was governed by certain empirical rules. For example, in alpha decay the atomic number of the "daughter" element is two less than that of the "mother" element, and its atomic weight is four less; this seems consistent with the fact that the alpha ray, identified as helium, has atomic number 2 and atomic weight 4, so that total atomic number and total atomic weight are conserved in the decay reaction.

Using these rules, Rutherford and his colleagues could determine the atomic numbers and atomic weights of many substances formed by radioactive decay, even though the substances decayed so quickly into others that these properties could not be measured directly. The atomic number of an element determines its place in Mendeleyev's periodic table (and thus its chemical properties; see above). It was found that substances of different atomic weight could have the same atomic number; such substances were called isotopes of an element.

Although the products of radioactive decay are determined by simple rules, the decay process itself seems to occur at random. All one can say is that there is a certain probability that an atom of a radioactive substance will decay during a certain time interval, or, equivalently, that half of the atoms of the sample will have decayed after a certain time—*i.e.,* the half life of the material.

The nucleus. At the University of Manchester (England), Rutherford led a group that rapidly developed new ideas about atomic structure. On the basis of an experiment conducted by Hans Geiger and Ernest Marsden in which alpha particles were scattered by a thin film of metal, Rutherford proposed a nuclear model of the atom (1911). In this model, the atom consists mostly of empty space, with a tiny, positively charged nucleus that contains most of the mass, surrounded by one or more negatively charged electrons. Henry G.J. Moseley, an English physicist, showed by an analysis of X-ray spectra that the electric charge on the nucleus is simply proportional to the atomic number of the element.

During the 1920s physicists thought that the nucleus was composed of two particles: the proton (the positively charged nucleus of hydrogen) and the electron. In 1932 the English physicist James Chadwick discovered the neutron, a particle with about the same mass as the proton but no electric charge. Since there were technical difficulties with the proton–electron model of the nucleus, physicists were willing to accept Heisenberg's hypothesis that it consists instead of protons and neutrons. The atomic number is then simply the number of protons in the nucleus, while the mass number, the integer closest to the atomic weight,

Discovery of the neutron

is equal to the total number of neutrons and protons. As mentioned above, this simple model of nuclear structure provided the basis for Hans Bethe's theory of the formation of elements from hydrogen in stars.

In 1938 the German physicists Otto Hahn and Fritz Strassmann found that, when uranium is bombarded by neutrons, lighter elements such as barium and krypton are produced. This phenomenon was interpreted by Lise Meitner and her nephew Otto Frisch as a breakup, or fission, of the uranium nucleus into smaller nuclei. Other physicists soon realized that since fission produces more neutrons, a chain reaction could result in a powerful explosion. World War II was about to begin, and physicists who had emigrated from Germany, Italy, and Hungary to the United States and Great Britain feared that Germany might develop an atomic bomb that could determine the outcome of the war. They persuaded the U.S. and British governments to undertake a major project to develop such a weapon first. The U.S. Manhattan Project did eventually produce atomic bombs based on the fission of uranium or of plutonium, a new artificially created element, and these were used against Japan in August 1945. Later, an even more powerful bomb based on the fusion of hydrogen atoms was developed and tested by both the United States and the Soviet Union. Thus nuclear physics began to play a major role in world history.

Einstein's 1905 trilogy. In a few months during the years 1665–66, Newton discovered the composite nature of light, analyzed the action of gravity, and invented the mathematical technique now known as calculus—or so he recalled in his old age. The only person who has ever matched Newton's amazing burst of scientific creativity— three revolutionary discoveries within a year—was Albert Einstein, who in 1905 published the special theory of relativity, the quantum theory of radiation, and a theory of Brownian movement that led directly to the final acceptance of the atomic structure of matter.

Relativity theory has already been mentioned several times in this article, an indication of its close connection with several areas of physical science. There is no room here to discuss the subtle line of reasoning that Einstein followed in arriving at his amazing conclusions; a brief summary of his starting point and some of the consequences will have to suffice.

In his 1905 paper on the electrodynamics of moving bodies, Einstein called attention to an apparent inconsistency in the usual presentation of Maxwell's electromagnetic theory as applied to the reciprocal action of a magnet and a conductor. The equations are different depending on which is "at rest" and which is "moving," yet the results must be the same. Einstein located the difficulty in the assumption that absolute space exists; he postulated instead that the laws of nature are the same for observers in any inertial frame of reference and that the speed of light is the same for all such observers.

From these postulates Einstein inferred: (1) an observer in one frame would find from his own measurements that lengths of objects in another frame are contracted by an amount given by the Lorentz–FitzGerald formula; (2) each observer would find that clocks in the other frame run more slowly; (3) there is no absolute time—events that are simultaneous in one frame of reference may not be so in another; and (4) the observable mass of any object increases as it goes faster.

Closely connected with the mass-increase effect is Einstein's famous formula $E = mc^2$: mass and energy are no longer conserved but can be interconverted. The explosive power of the atomic and hydrogen bombs derives from the conversion of mass to energy.

In a paper on the creation and conversion of light (usually called the "photoelectric effect paper"), published earlier in 1905, Einstein proposed the hypothesis that electromagnetic radiation consists of discrete energy quanta that can be absorbed or emitted only as a whole. Although this hypothesis would not replace the wave theory of light, which gives a perfectly satisfactory description of the phenomena of diffraction, reflection, refraction, and dispersion, it would supplement it by also ascribing particle properties to light.

Until recently the invention of the quantum theory of radiation was generally credited to another German physicist, Max Planck, who in 1900 discussed the statistical distribution of radiation energy in connection with the theory of blackbody radiation (see below *The methodology of physics*). Although Planck did propose the basic hypothesis that the energy of a quantum of radiation is proportional to its frequency of vibration, it is not clear whether he used this hypothesis merely for mathematical convenience or intended it to have a broader physical significance. In any case, he did not explicitly advocate a particle theory of light before 1905. Historians of physics still disagree on whether Planck or Einstein should be considered the originator of the quantum theory.

Einstein's paper on Brownian movement seems less revolutionary than the other 1905 papers because most modern readers assume that the atomic structure of matter was well established at that time. Such was not the case, however. In spite of the development of the chemical atomic theory and of the kinetic theory of gases in the 19th century, which allowed quantitative estimates of such atomic properties as mass and diameter, it was still fashionable in 1900 to question the reality of atoms. This skepticism, which does not seem to have been particularly helpful to the progress of science, was promoted by the empiricist, or "positivist," philosophy advocated by Auguste Comte, Ernst Mach, Wilhelm Ostwald, Pierre Duhem, Henri Poincaré, and others. It was the French physicist Jean Perrin who, using Einstein's theory of Brownian movement, finally convinced the scientific community to accept the atom as a valid scientific concept.

Quantum mechanics. The Danish physicist Niels Bohr pioneered the use of the quantum hypothesis in developing a successful theory of atomic structure. Adopting Rutherford's nuclear model, he proposed in 1913 that the atom is like a miniature solar system, with the electrons moving in orbits around the nucleus just as the planets move around the Sun. Although the electrical attraction between the electrons and nucleus is mathematically similar to the gravitational attraction between the planets and the Sun, the quantum hypothesis is needed to restrict the electrons to certain orbits and to forbid them from radiating energy except when jumping from one orbit to another.

Bohr's model provided a good description of the spectra and other properties of atoms containing only one electron—neutral hydrogen and singly ionized helium— but could not be satisfactorily extended to multi-electron atoms or molecules. It relied on an inconsistent mixture of old and new physical principles, hinting but not clearly specifying how a more adequate general theory might be constructed.

The nature of light was still puzzling to those who demanded that it should behave either like waves or like particles. Two experiments performed by American physicists seemed to favour the particle theory: Robert A. Millikan's confirmation of the quantum theory of the photoelectric effect proposed by Einstein; and Arthur H. Compton's experimental demonstration that X rays behave like particles when they collide with electrons. The findings of these experiments had to be considered along with the unquestioned fact that electromagnetic radiation also exhibits wave properties such as interference and diffraction.

Louis de Broglie, a French physicist, proposed a way out of the dilemma: accept the wave–particle dualism as a description not only of light but also of electrons and other entities previously assumed to be particles. In 1926 the Austrian physicist Erwin Schrödinger constructed a mathematical "wave mechanics" based on this proposal. His theory tells how to write down an equation for the wave function of any physical system in terms of the masses and charges of its components. From the wave function, one may compute the energy levels and other observable properties of the system.

Schrödinger's equation, the most convenient form of a more general theory called quantum mechanics to which the German physicists Werner Heisenberg and Max Born also contributed, was brilliantly successful. Not only did it yield the properties of the hydrogen atom but it also allowed the use of simple approximating methods for more

Marginal notes (left column):

Splitting of the uranium atom

Relativity of space and time

Quantum theory of radiation

Marginal notes (right column):

Bohr's model of atomic structure

Schrödinger's so-called wave mechanics

Heisen-
berg's inde-
terminacy
principle

complicated systems even though the equation could not be solved exactly. The application of quantum mechanics to the properties of atoms, molecules, and metals occupied physicists for the next several decades.

The founders of quantum mechanics did not agree on the philosophical significance of the new theory. Born proposed that the wave function determines only the probability distribution of the electron's position or path; it does not have a well-defined instantaneous position and velocity. Heisenberg made this view explicit in his indeterminacy principle: the more accurately one determines the position, the less accurately the velocity is fixed; the converse is also true. Heisenberg's principle is often called the uncertainty principle, but this is somewhat misleading. It tends to suggest incorrectly that the electron really has a definite position and velocity and that they simply have not been determined.

Einstein objected to the randomness implied by quantum mechanics in his famous statement that God "does not play dice." He also was disturbed by the apparent denial of the objective reality of the atomic world: Somehow the electron's position or velocity comes into existence only when it is measured. Niels Bohr expressed this aspect of the quantum worldview in his complementarity principle, building on de Broglie's resolution of the wave–particle dichotomy: A system can have such properties as wave or particle behaviour that would be considered incompatible in Newtonian physics but that are actually complementary; light exhibits either wave behaviour or particle behaviour, depending on whether one chooses to measure the one property or the other. To say that it is really one or the other, or to say that the electron really has both a definite position and momentum at the same time, is to go beyond the limits of science.

Bohr's viewpoint, which became known as the Copenhagen Interpretation of quantum mechanics, was that reality can be ascribed only to a measurement. Einstein argued that the physical world must have real properties whether or not one measures them; he and Schrödinger published a number of thought experiments designed to show that things can exist beyond what is described by quantum mechanics. During the 1970s and 1980s, advanced technology made it possible to actually perform some of these experiments, and quantum mechanics was vindicated in every case.

Chemistry. The long-standing problem of the nature of the force that holds atoms together in molecules was finally solved by the application of quantum mechanics. Although it is often stated that chemistry has been "reduced to physics" in this way, it should be pointed out that one of the most important postulates of quantum mechanics was introduced primarily for the purpose of explaining chemical facts and did not originally have any other physical justification. This was the so-called exclusion principle put forth by the Austrian physicist Wolfgang Pauli, which forbids more than one electron occupying a given quantum state in an atom. The state of an electron includes its spin, a property introduced by the Dutch-born American physicists George E. Uhlenbeck and Samuel A. Goudsmit. Using that principle and the assumption that the quantum states in a multi-electron atom are essentially the same as those in the hydrogen atom, one can postulate a series of "shells" of electrons and explain the chemical valence of an element in terms of the loss, gain, or sharing of electrons in the outer shell.

Some of the outstanding problems to be solved by quantum chemistry were: (1) The "saturation" of chemical forces. If attractive forces hold atoms together to form molecules, why is there a limit on how many atoms can stick together (generally only two of the same kind)? (2) Stereochemistry—the three-dimensional structure of molecules, in particular the spatial directionality of bonds as in the tetrahedral carbon atom. (3) Bond length— *i.e.,* there seems to be a well-defined equilibrium distance between atoms in a molecule that can be determined accurately by experiment. (4) Why some atoms (*e.g.,* helium) normally form no bonds with other atoms, while others form one or more. (These are the empirical rules of valence.)

Soon after J.J. Thomson's discovery of the electron in 1897, there were several attempts to develop theories of chemical bonds based on electrons. The most successful was that proposed in the United States by G.N. Lewis in 1916 and Irving Langmuir in 1919. They emphasized shared pairs of electrons and treated the atom as a static arrangement of charges. While the Lewis–Langmuir model as a whole was inconsistent with quantum theory, several of its specific features continued to be useful.

The
quantum-
mechanical
exchange
effect

The key to the nature of the chemical bond was found to be the quantum-mechanical exchange effect, first described by Heisenberg in 1926–27. Resonance is related to the requirement that the wave function for two or more identical particles must have definite symmetry properties with respect to the coordinates of those particles—it must have plus or minus the same value (symmetric or antisymmetric, respectively) when those particles are interchanged. Particles such as electrons and protons, according to a hypothesis proposed by Enrico Fermi and P.A.M. Dirac, must have antisymmetric wave functions. Exchange may be imagined as a continual jumping back and forth or interchange of the electrons between two possible states. In 1927 the German physicists Walter Heitler and Fritz London used this idea to obtain an approximate wave function for two interacting hydrogen atoms. They found that with an antisymmetric wave function (including spin) there is an attractive force, while with a symmetric one there is a repulsive force. Thus two hydrogen atoms can form a molecule if their electron spins are opposite, but not if they are the same.

The Heitler–London approach to the theory of chemical bonds was rapidly developed by John C. Slater and Linus C. Pauling in the United States. Slater proposed a simple general method for constructing multiple-electron wave functions that would automatically satisfy the Pauli exclusion principle. Pauling introduced a valence-bond method, picking out one electron in each of the two combining atoms and constructing a wave function representing a paired-electron bond between them. Pauling and Slater were able to explain the tetrahedral carbon structure in terms of a particular mixture of wave functions that has a lower energy than the original wave functions, so that the molecule tends to go into that state.

Pauling's
valence-
bond
method

About the same time another American scientist, Robert S. Mulliken, was developing an alternative theory of molecular structure based on what he called molecular orbitals. (The idea had been used under a different name by John E. Lennard-Jones of England in 1929 and by Erich Hückel of Germany in 1931.) Here, the electron is not considered to be localized in a particular atom or two-atom bond, but rather it is treated as occupying a quantum state (an "orbital") that is spread over the entire molecule (see below *Studies of molecular structure*).

In treating the benzene molecule by the valence-bond method in 1933, Pauling and George W. Wheland constructed a wave function that was a linear combination of five possible structures—*i.e.,* five possible arrangements of double and single bonds. Two of them are the structures that had been proposed by the German chemist August Kekulé (later Kekule von Stradonitz) in 1865, with alternating single and double bonds between adjacent carbon atoms in the six-carbon ring. The other three (now called Dewar structures for the British chemist and physicist James Dewar, though they were first suggested by H. Wichelhaus in 1869) have one longer bond going across the ring. Pauling and Dewar described their model as involving resonance between the five structures. According to quantum mechanics, this does not mean that the molecule is sometimes "really" in one state and at other times in another, but rather that it is always in a composite state.

The valence-bond method, with its emphasis on resonance between different structures as a means of analyzing aromatic molecules, dominated quantum chemistry during the 1930s. The method was comprehensively presented and applied in Pauling's classic treatise *The Nature of the Chemical Bond* (1939), the most important work on theoretical chemistry in the 20th century. One reason for its popularity was that ideas similar to resonance had been developed by organic chemists, notably F.G. Arndt in Germany and Christopher K. Ingold in England, independently of quantum theory during the late 1920s.

Increasing preference for the molecular-orbital method

After World War II there was a strong movement away from the valence-bond method toward the molecular-orbital method, led by Mulliken in the United States and by Charles Coulson, Lennard-Jones, H.C. Longuet-Higgins, and Michael J.S. Dewar in England. The advocates of the molecular-orbital method argued that their approach was simpler and easier to apply to complicated molecules, since it allowed one to visualize a definite charge distribution for each electron. (S.G.B.)

Physics

Physics is the basic physical science. Until rather recent times the terms physics and natural philosophy were used interchangeably for the science whose aim is the discovery and formulation of the fundamental laws of nature. As the modern sciences developed and became increasingly specialized, physics came to denote that part of physical science not included in astronomy, chemistry, geology, and engineering. Physics plays an important role in all the natural sciences, however, and all such fields have branches in which physical laws and measurements receive special emphasis, bearing such names as astrophysics, geophysics, biophysics, and even psychophysics. Physics can, at base, be defined as the science of matter, motion, and energy. Its laws are typically expressed with economy and precision in the language of mathematics.

Both experiment, the observation of phenomena under conditions that are controlled as precisely as possible, and theory, the formulation of a unified conceptual framework, play essential and complementary roles in the advancement of physics. Physical experiments result in measurements, which are compared with the outcome predicted by theory. A theory that reliably predicts the results of experiments to which it is applicable is said to embody a law of physics. However, a law is always subject to modification, replacement, or restriction to a more limited domain, if a later experiment makes it necessary.

Ultimate aim of physics

The ultimate aim of physics is to find a unified set of laws governing matter, motion, and energy at small (microscopic) subatomic distances, at the human (macroscopic) scale of everyday life, and out to the largest distances (*e.g.,* those on the extragalactic scale). This ambitious goal has been realized to a notable extent. Although a completely unified theory of physical phenomena has not yet been achieved (and possibly never will be), a remarkably small set of fundamental physical laws appears able to account for all known phenomena. The body of physics developed up to about the turn of the 20th century, known as classical physics, can largely account for the motions of macroscopic objects that move slowly with respect to the speed of light and for such phenomena as heat, sound, electricity, magnetism, and light. The modern developments of relativity and quantum theory modify these laws insofar as they apply to higher speeds, very massive objects, and to the tiny elementary constituents of matter, such as electrons, protons, and neutrons.

THE SCOPE OF PHYSICS

The traditionally organized branches or fields of classical and modern physics are delineated below.

Mechanics. Mechanics is generally taken to mean the study of the motion of objects (or their lack of motion) under the action of given forces. Classical mechanics is sometimes considered a branch of applied mathematics. It consists of kinematics, the description of motion, and dynamics, the study of the action of forces in producing either motion or static equilibrium (the latter constituting the science of statics). The 20th-century subjects of quantum mechanics, crucial to treating the structure of matter, subatomic particles, superfluidity, superconductivity, neutron stars, and other major phenomena, and relativistic mechanics, important when speeds approach that of light, are forms of mechanics that will be discussed later in this section.

In classical mechanics the laws are initially formulated for point particles in which the dimensions, shapes, and other intrinsic properties of bodies are ignored. Thus in the first approximation even objects as large as the Earth and the Sun are treated as pointlike—*e.g.,* in calculating planetary orbital motion. In rigid-body dynamics, the extension of bodies and their mass distributions are considered as well, but they are imagined to be incapable of deformation. The mechanics of deformable solids is elasticity; hydrostatics and hydrodynamics treat, respectively, fluids at rest and in motion.

Newton's laws of motion

The three laws of motion set forth by Isaac Newton form the foundation of classical mechanics, together with the recognition that forces are directed quantities (vectors) and combine accordingly. The first law, also called the law of inertia, states that, unless acted upon by an external force, an object at rest remains at rest, or if in motion, it continues to move in a straight line with constant speed. Uniform motion therefore does not require a cause. Accordingly, mechanics concentrates not on motion as such but on the change in the state of motion of an object that results from the net force acting upon it. Newton's second law equates the net force on an object to the rate of change of its momentum, the latter being the product of the mass of a body and its velocity. Newton's third law, that of action and reaction, states that when two particles interact, the forces each exerts on the other are equal in magnitude and opposite in direction. Taken together, these mechanical laws in principle permit the determination of the future motions of a set of particles, providing their state of motion is known at some instant, as well as the forces that act between them and upon them from the outside. From this deterministic character of the laws of classical mechanics, profound (and probably incorrect) philosophical conclusions have been drawn in the past and even applied to human history.

Lying at the most basic level of physics, the laws of mechanics are characterized by certain symmetry properties, as exemplified in the aforementioned symmetry between action and reaction forces. Other symmetries, such as the invariance (*i.e.,* unchanging form) of the laws under reflections and rotations carried out in space, reversal of time, or transformation to a different part of space or to a different epoch of time, are present both in classical mechanics and in relativistic mechanics, and with certain restrictions, also in quantum mechanics. The symmetry properties of the theory can be shown to have as mathematical consequences basic principles known as conservation laws, which assert the constancy in time of the values of certain physical quantities under prescribed conditions. The conserved quantities are the most important ones in physics; included among them are mass and energy (in relativity theory, mass and energy are equivalent and are conserved together), momentum, angular momentum, and electric charge.

Conservation laws

The study of gravitation. This field of inquiry has in the past been placed within classical mechanics for historical reasons, because both fields were brought to a high state of perfection by Newton and also because of its universal character. Newton's gravitational law states that every material particle in the universe attracts every other one with a force that acts along the line joining them and whose strength is directly proportional to the product of their masses and inversely proportional to the square of their separation. Newton's detailed accounting for the orbits of the planets and the Moon, as well as for such subtle gravitational effects as the tides and the precession of the equinoxes (a slow cyclical change in direction of the Earth's axis of rotation) through this fundamental force was the first triumph of classical mechanics. No further principles are required to understand the principal aspects of rocketry and space flight (although, of course, a formidable technology is needed to carry them out).

The modern theory of gravitation was formulated by Albert Einstein and is called the general theory of relativity. From the long-known equality of the quantity "mass" in Newton's second law of motion and that in his gravitational law, Einstein was struck by the fact that acceleration can locally annul a gravitational force (as occurs in the so-called weightlessness of astronauts in an Earth-orbiting

Modern theory of gravitation

spacecraft) and was led thereby to the concept of curved space-time. Completed in 1915, the theory was valued for many years mainly for its mathematical beauty and for correctly predicting a small number of phenomena, such as the gravitational bending of light around a massive object. Only in recent years, however, has it become a vital subject for both theoretical and experimental research. (Relativistic mechanics, discussed below, refers to Einstein's special theory of relativity, which is not a theory of gravitation.)

The study of heat, thermodynamics, and statistical mechanics. Heat is a form of internal energy associated with the random motion of the molecular constituents of matter or with radiation. Temperature is an average of a part of the internal energy present in a body (it does not include the energy of molecular binding or of molecular rotation). The lowest possible energy state of a substance is defined as the absolute zero of temperature. An isolated body eventually reaches uniform temperature, a state known as thermal equilibrium, as do two or more bodies placed in contact. The formal study of states of matter at (or near) thermal equilibrium is called thermodynamics; it is capable of analyzing a large variety of thermal systems without considering their detailed microstructures.

First law. The first law of thermodynamics is the energy conservation principle of mechanics (*i.e.,* for all changes in an isolated system, the energy remains constant) generalized to include heat.

Second law. The second law of thermodynamics asserts that heat will not flow from a place of higher temperature to one where it is lower without the intervention of an external device (*e.g.,* a refrigerator). The concept of entropy involves the measurement of the state of disorder of the particles making up a system. For example, if tossing a coin many times results in a random-appearing sequence of heads and tails, the result has a higher entropy than if heads and tails tend to appear in clusters. Another formulation of the second law is that the entropy of an isolated system never decreases with time.

Third law. The third law of thermodynamics states that the entropy at the absolute zero of temperature is zero, corresponding to the most ordered possible state.

Statistical mechanics. The science of statistical mechanics derives bulk properties of systems from the mechanical properties of their molecular constituents, assuming molecular chaos and applying the laws of probability. Regarding each possible configuration of the particles as equally likely, the chaotic state (the state of maximum entropy) is so enormously more likely than ordered states that an isolated system will evolve to it, as stated in the second law of thermodynamics. Such reasoning, placed in mathematically precise form, is typical of statistical mechanics, which is capable of deriving the laws of thermodynamics but goes beyond them in describing fluctuations (*i.e.,* temporary departures) from the thermodynamic laws that describe only average behaviour. An example of a fluctuation phenomenon is the random motion of small particles suspended in a fluid, known as Brownian motion.

Quantum statistical mechanics — Quantum statistical mechanics plays a major role in many other modern fields of science, as, for example, in plasma physics (the study of fully ionized gases), in solid-state physics, and in the study of stellar structure. From a microscopic point of view the laws of thermodynamics imply that, whereas the total quantity of energy of any isolated system is constant, what might be called the quality of this energy is degraded as the system moves inexorably, through the operation of the laws of chance, to states of increasing disorder until it finally reaches the state of maximum disorder (maximum entropy), in which all parts of the system are at the same temperature, and none of the state's energy may be usefully employed. When applied to the universe as a whole, considered as an isolated system, this ultimate chaotic condition has been called the "heat death."

The study of electricity and magnetism. Although conceived of as distinct phenomena until the 19th century, electricity and magnetism are now known to be components of the unified field of electromagnetism. Particles with electric charge interact by an electric force, while charged particles in motion produce and respond to magnetic forces as well. Many subatomic particles, including the electrically charged electron and proton and the electrically neutral neutron, behave like elementary magnets. On the other hand, in spite of systematic searches undertaken, no magnetic monopoles, which would be the magnetic analogues of electric charges, have ever been found.

Significance of the field concept — The field concept plays a central role in the classical formulation of electromagnetism, as well as in many other areas of classical and contemporary physics. Einstein's gravitational field, for example, replaces Newton's concept of gravitational action at a distance. The field describing the electric force between a pair of charged particles works in the following manner: each particle creates an electric field in the space surrounding it, and so also at the position occupied by the other particle; each particle responds to the force exerted upon it by the electric field at its own position.

Classical electromagnetism is summarized by the laws of action of electric and magnetic fields upon electric charges and upon magnets and by four remarkable equations formulated in the latter part of the 19th century by James Clerk Maxwell. The latter equations describe the manner in which electric charges and currents produce electric and magnetic fields, as well as the manner in which changing magnetic fields produce electric fields, and vice versa. From these relations Maxwell inferred the existence of electromagnetic waves—associated electric and magnetic fields in space, detached from the charges that created them, traveling at the speed of light, and endowed with such "mechanical" properties as energy, momentum, and angular momentum. The light to which the human eye is sensitive is but one small segment of an electromagnetic spectrum that extends from long-wavelength radio waves to short-wavelength gamma rays and includes X rays, microwaves, and infrared (or heat) radiation.

Optics. Because light consists of electromagnetic waves, the propagation of light can be regarded as merely a branch of electromagnetism. However, it is usually dealt with as a separate subject called optics: the part that deals with the tracing of light rays is known as geometrical optics, while the part that treats the distinctive wave phenomena of light is called physical optics. More recently, there has developed a new and vital branch, quantum optics, which is concerned with the theory and application of the laser, a device that produces an intense coherent beam of unidirectional radiation useful for many applications.

Quantum optics

The formation of images by lenses, microscopes, telescopes, and other optical devices is described by ray optics, which assumes that the passage of light can be represented by straight lines, that is, rays. The subtler effects attributable to the wave property of visible light, however, require the explanations of physical optics. One basic wave effect is interference, whereby two waves present in a region of space combine at certain points to yield an enhanced resultant effect (*e.g.,* the crests of the component waves adding together); at the other extreme, the two waves can annul each other, the crests of one wave filling in the troughs of the other. Another wave effect is diffraction, which causes light to spread into regions of the geometric shadow and causes the image produced by any optical device to be fuzzy to a degree dependent on the wavelength of the light. Optical instruments such as the interferometer and the diffraction grating can be used for measuring the wavelength of light precisely (about 500 micrometres) and for measuring distances to a small fraction of that length.

Atomic and chemical physics. One of the great achievements of the 20th century has been the establishment of the validity of the atomic hypothesis, first proposed in ancient times, that matter is made up of relatively few kinds of small, identical parts—namely, atoms. However, unlike the indivisible atom of Democritus and other ancients, the atom, as it is conceived today, can be separated into constituent electrons and nucleus. Atoms combine to form molecules, whose structure is studied by chemistry and chemical physics; they also form other types of compounds, such as crystals, studied in the field of condensed-matter physics. Such disciplines study the most important attributes of matter (not excluding biologic matter) that are encountered in normal experience—namely, those that depend almost entirely on the outer parts of the electronic structure of atoms. Only the mass of the atomic nucleus and its charge, which is equal to the total charge of the electrons in the neutral atom, affect the chemical and physical properties of matter.

Although there are some analogies between the solar system and the atom due to the fact that the strengths of gravitational and electrostatic forces both fall off as the inverse square of the distance, the classical forms of electromagnetism and mechanics fail when applied to tiny, rapidly moving atomic constituents. Atomic structure is comprehensible only on the basis of quantum mechanics, and its finer details require as well the use of quantum electrodynamics (QED) (see below).

Atomic properties are inferred mostly by the use of indirect experiments. Of greatest importance has been spectroscopy, which is concerned with the measurement and interpretation of the electromagnetic radiations either emitted or absorbed by materials. These radiations have a distinctive character, which quantum mechanics relates quantitatively to the structures that produce and absorb them. It is truly remarkable that these structures are in principle, and often in practice, amenable to precise calculation in terms of a few basic physical constants: the mass and charge of the electron, the speed of light, and Planck's constant h, the fundamental constant of the quantum theory named for the German physicist Max Planck.

Condensed-matter physics. This field, which treats the thermal, elastic, electrical, magnetic, and optical properties of solid and liquid substances, has grown at an explosive rate in recent years and has scored numerous important scientific and technical achievements, including the transistor. Among solid materials, the greatest theoretical advances have been in the study of crystalline materials whose simple repetitive geometric arrays of atoms are multiple-particle systems that allow treatment by quantum mechanics. Because the atoms in a solid are coordinated with each other over large distances, the theory must go beyond that appropriate for atoms and molecules. Thus conductors, such as metals, contain some so-called free (or conduction) electrons, which are responsible for the electrical and most of the thermal conductivity of the material and which belong collectively to the whole solid rather than to individual atoms. Semiconductors and insulators, either crystalline or amorphous, are other materials studied in this field of physics.

Other aspects of condensed matter involve the properties of the ordinary liquid state, of liquid crystals, and, at temperatures near absolute zero, of the so-called quantum liquids. The latter exhibit a property known as superfluidity (completely frictionless flow), which is an example of macroscopic quantum phenomena. Such phenomena are also exemplified by superconductivity (completely resistance-less flow of electricity), a low-temperature property of certain metallic and ceramic materials. Besides their significance to technology, macroscopic liquid and solid quantum states are important in astrophysical theories of stellar structure in, for example, neutron stars.

Nuclear physics. This branch of physics deals with the structure of the atomic nucleus and the radiation from unstable nuclei. About 10,000 times smaller than the atom, the constituent particles of the nucleus, protons and neutrons, attract one another so strongly by the nuclear forces that nuclear energies are approximately 1,000,000 times larger than typical atomic energies. Quantum theory is needed for understanding nuclear structure.

Like excited atoms, unstable radioactive nuclei (either naturally occurring or artificially produced) can emit electromagnetic radiation. The energetic nuclear photons are called gamma rays. Radioactive nuclei also emit other particles: negative and positive electrons (beta rays), accompanied by neutrinos, and helium nuclei (alpha rays).

A principal research tool of nuclear physics involves the use of beams of particles (*e.g.*, protons or electrons) directed as projectiles against nuclear targets. Recoiling particles and any resultant nuclear fragments are detected, and their directions and energies are analyzed to reveal details of nuclear structure and to learn more about the strong nuclear force. A much weaker nuclear force, the so-called weak interaction, is responsible for the emission of beta rays. Nuclear collision experiments use beams of higher-energy particles, including those of unstable particles called mesons produced by primary nuclear collisions in accelerators dubbed meson factories. Exchange of mesons between protons and neutrons is directly responsible for the strong nuclear force. (For the mechanism underlying mesons, see below *Fundamental forces and fields*.)

In radioactivity and in collisions leading to nuclear breakup, the chemical identity of the nuclear target is altered whenever there is a change in the nuclear charge. In fission and fusion nuclear reactions in which unstable nuclei are, respectively, split into smaller nuclei or amalgamated into larger ones, the energy release far exceeds that of any chemical reaction.

Particle physics. One of the most significant branches of contemporary physics is the study of the fundamental subatomic constituents of matter, the elementary particles. This field, also called high-energy physics, emerged in the 1930s out of the developing experimental areas of nuclear and cosmic-ray physics. Initially investigators studied cosmic rays, the very-high-energy extraterrestrial radiations that fall upon the Earth and interact in the atmosphere (see below *The methodology of physics*). However, after World War II, scientists gradually began using high-energy particle accelerators to provide subatomic particles for study. Quantum field theory, a generalization of QED to other types of force fields, is essential for the analysis of high-energy physics.

During recent decades a coherent picture has evolved of the underlying strata of matter involving three types of particles called leptons, quarks, and field quanta, for whose existence evidence is good. (Other types of particles have been hypothesized but have not yet been detected.) Subatomic particles cannot be visualized as tiny analogues of ordinary material objects such as billiard balls, for they have properties that appear contradictory from the classical viewpoint. That is to say, while they possess charge, spin, mass, magnetism, and other complex characteristics, they are nonetheless regarded as pointlike. Leptons and quarks occur in pairs (*e.g.*, one lepton pair consists of the electron and the neutrino). Each quark and each lepton have an antiparticle with properties that mirror those of its partner (the antiparticle of the negatively charged electron is the positive electron, or positron; that of the neutrino is the antineutrino). In addition to their electric and magnetic properties, quarks have very strong nuclear forces and also participate in the weak nuclear interaction, while leptons take part in only the weak interaction.

Ordinary matter consists of electrons surrounding the nucleus, which is composed of neutrons and protons, each of which is believed to contain three quarks. Quarks have charges that are either positive two-thirds or negative one-third of the electron's charge, while antiquarks have the opposite charges. Mesons, responsible for the nuclear binding force, are composed of one quark and one antiquark. In addition to the particles in ordinary matter and their antiparticles, which are referred to as first-generation, there are probably two or more additional generations of quarks and leptons, more massive than the first. Evidence exists at present for the second generation and all but one quark of the third, namely the t (or top) quark, which may be so massive that a new higher-energy accelerator may be needed to produce it.

The quantum fields through which quarks and leptons interact with each other and with themselves consist of particle-like objects called quanta (from which quantum mechanics derives its name). The first known quanta were those of the electromagnetic field; they are also called photons because light consists of them. A modern unified theory of weak and electromagnetic interactions, known as the electroweak theory, proposes that the weak nuclear interaction involves the exchange of particles about 100 times as massive as protons. These massive quanta have been observed—namely, two charged particles, W^+ and W^-, and a neutral one, W^0.

In the theory of strong nuclear interactions known as

Spectroscopy

Research on superfluidity and superconductivity

High-energy physics

Quantum
chromo-
dynamics

quantum chromodynamics (QCD), eight quanta, called gluons, bind quarks to form protons and neutrons and also bind quarks to antiquarks to form mesons, the force itself being dubbed the "colour force." (This unusual use of the term colour is a somewhat forced analogue of ordinary colour mixing.) Quarks are said to come in three colours—red, blue, and green. (The opposites of these imaginary colours, minus-red, minus-blue, and minus-green, are ascribed to antiquarks.) Only certain colour combinations, namely colour-neutral, or "white" (*i.e.*, equal mixtures of the above colours cancel out one another, resulting in no net colour), are conjectured to exist in nature in an observable form. The gluons and quarks themselves, being coloured, are permanently confined (deeply bound within the particles of which they are a part), while the colour-neutral composites such as protons can be directly observed. One consequence of colour confinement is that the observable particles are either electrically neutral or have charges that are integral multiples of the charge of the electron. A number of specific predictions of QCD have been experimentally tested and found correct.

Quantum mechanics. Although the various branches of physics differ in their experimental methods and theoretical approaches, certain general principles apply to all of them. The forefront of contemporary advances in physics lies in the submicroscopic regime, whether it be in atomic, nuclear, condensed-matter, plasma, or particle physics, or in quantum optics, or even in the study of stellar structure. All are based upon quantum theory (*i.e.*, quantum mechanics and quantum field theory) and relativity, which together form the theoretical foundations of

Differences
from
classical
physics

modern physics. Many physical quantities whose classical counterparts vary continuously over a range of possible values are in quantum theory constrained to have discontinuous, or discrete, values. The intrinsically deterministic character of classical physics is replaced in quantum theory by intrinsic uncertainty.

According to quantum theory, electromagnetic radiation does not always consist of continuous waves; instead it must be viewed under some circumstances as a collection of particle-like photons, the energy and momentum of each being directly proportional to its frequency (or inversely proportional to its wavelength, the photons still possessing some wavelike characteristics). Conversely, electrons and other objects that appear as particles in classical physics are endowed by quantum theory with wavelike properties as well, such a particle's quantum wavelength being inversely proportional to its momentum. In both instances, the proportionality constant is the characteristic quantum of action (action being defined as energy $\times$ time)—that is to say, Planck's constant h.

In principle, all of atomic and molecular physics, including the structure of atoms and their dynamics, the periodic table of elements and their chemical behaviour, as well as the spectroscopic, electrical, and other physical properties of atoms, molecules, and condensed matter, can be accounted for by quantum mechanics. Roughly speaking, the electrons in the atom must fit around the nucleus as some sort of standing wave (the Schrödinger wave function; see above) analogous to the waves on a plucked violin or guitar string. As the fit determines the wavelength of the quantum wave, it necessarily determines its energy state. Consequently, atomic systems are restricted to certain discrete, or quantized, energies. When an atom undergoes a discontinuous transition, or quantum jump, its energy changes abruptly by a sharply defined amount, and a photon of that energy is emitted when the energy of the atom decreases, or is absorbed in the opposite case.

Although atomic energies can be sharply defined, the positions of the electrons within the atom cannot be, quantum mechanics giving only the probability for the

The inde-
terminacy
principle
as the dis-
tinguishing
feature of
quantum
theory

electrons to have certain locations. This is a consequence of the feature that distinguishes quantum theory from all other approaches to physics, the indeterminacy (or uncertainty) principle of Werner Heisenberg. As was explained earlier in the article, this principle holds that measuring a particle's position with increasing precision necessarily increases the uncertainty as to the particle's momentum, and conversely. The ultimate degree of uncertainty is con-

trolled by the magnitude of Planck's constant, which is so small as to have no apparent effects except in the world of microstructures. In the latter case, however, because both a particle's position and its velocity or momentum must be known precisely at some instant in order to predict its future history, quantum theory precludes such certain prediction and thus escapes determinism.

The complementary wave and particle aspects, or wave–particle duality, of electromagnetic radiation and of material particles furnish another illustration of the uncertainty principle. When an electron exhibits wavelike behaviour, as in the phenomenon of electron diffraction, this excludes its exhibiting particle-like behaviour in the same observation. Similarly, when electromagnetic radiation in the form of photons interacts with matter, as in the Compton effect in which X-ray photons collide with electrons, the result resembles a particle-like collision and the wave nature of electromagnetic radiation is precluded. The principle of complementarity, asserted by Niels Bohr, who pioneered the theory of atomic structure, states that the physical world presents itself in the form of various complementary pictures, no one of which is by itself complete, all of these pictures being essential for our total understanding. Thus both wave and particle pictures are needed for understanding either the electron or the photon.

Although it deals with probabilities and uncertainties, the quantum theory has been spectacularly successful in explaining otherwise inaccessible atomic phenomena and in thus far meeting every experimental test. Its predictions, especially those of QED, are the most precise and the best checked of any in physics; some of them have been tested and found accurate to better than one part per billion.

Relativistic mechanics. In classical physics, space is conceived as having the absolute character of an empty stage in which events in nature unfold as time flows onward independently; events occurring simultaneously for one observer are presumed to be simultaneous for any other; mass is taken as impossible to create or destroy; and a particle given sufficient energy acquires a velocity that can increase without limit. The special theory of relativity, developed principally by Einstein in 1905 and now so adequately confirmed by experiment as to have the status of physical law, shows that all these, as well as other apparently obvious assumptions, are false.

The special
theory of
relativity
and its
ramifica-
tions

Specific and unusual relativistic effects flow directly from Einstein's two basic postulates, which are formulated in terms of so-called inertial reference frames. These are reference systems that move in such a way that in them Newton's first law, the law of inertia, is valid. The set of inertial frames consists of all those that move with constant velocity with respect to each other (accelerating frames therefore being excluded). Einstein's postulates are: (1) All observers, whatever their state of motion relative to a light source, measure the same speed for light; and (2) The laws of physics are the same in all inertial frames.

The first postulate, the constancy of the speed of light, is an experimental fact from which follow the distinctive relativistic phenomena of space contraction, time dilation, and the relativity of simultaneity: as measured by an observer assumed to be at rest, an object in motion is contracted along the direction of its motion, and moving clocks run slow; two spatially separated events that are simultaneous for a stationary observer occur sequentially for a moving observer. As a consequence, space intervals in three-dimensional space are related to time intervals, thus forming so-called four-dimensional space-time.

The second postulate is called the principle of relativity. It is equally valid in classical mechanics (but not in classical electrodynamics until Einstein reinterpreted it). This postulate implies, for example, that table tennis played on a train moving with constant velocity is just like table tennis played with the train at rest, the states of rest and motion being physically indistinguishable. In relativity theory, mechanical quantities such as momentum and energy have forms that are different from their classical counterparts but give the same values for speeds that are small compared to the speed of light, the maximum permissible speed in nature (about 300,000 kilometres per second, or 186,000 miles per second). According to rela-

Equivalence of mass and energy

tivity, mass and energy are equivalent and interchangeable quantities, the equivalence being expressed by Einstein's famous equation $E = mc^2$, where m is an object's mass and c is the speed of light.

The general theory of relativity, as discussed above, is Einstein's theory of gravitation, which uses the principle of the equivalence of gravitation and locally accelerating frames of reference. Einstein's theory has special mathematical beauty; it generalizes the "flat" space-time concept of special relativity to one of curvature. It forms the background of all modern cosmological theories (see COSMOS: *Relativistic cosmologies*). In contrast to some vulgarized popular notions of it, which confuse it with moral and other forms of relativism, Einstein's theory does not argue that "all is relative." On the contrary, it is largely a theory based upon those physical attributes that do not change, or, in the language of the theory, that are invariant.

Conservation laws and symmetry. Since the early period of modern physics, there have been conservation laws, which state that certain physical quantities, such as the total electric charge of an isolated system of bodies, do not change in the course of time. In the 20th century it has been proved mathematically that such laws follow from the symmetry properties of nature, as expressed in the laws of physics. The conservation of mass-energy of an isolated system, for example, follows from the assumption that the laws of physics may depend upon time intervals but not upon the specific time at which the laws are applied. The symmetries and the conservation laws that follow from them are regarded by modern physicists as being even more fundamental than the laws themselves, since they are able to limit the possible forms of laws that may be proposed in the future.

Conservation laws are valid in classical, relativistic, and quantum theory for mass-energy, momentum, angular momentum, and electric charge. (In nonrelativistic physics, mass and energy are separately conserved.) Momentum, a directed quantity equal to the mass of a body multiplied by its velocity or to the total mass of two or more bodies multiplied by the velocity of their centre of mass, is conserved when, and only when, no external force acts. Similarly angular momentum, which is related to spinning motions, is conserved in a system upon which no net turning force, called torque, acts. External forces and torques break the symmetry conditions from upon which the respective conservation laws follow.

In quantum theory, and especially in the theory of elementary particles, there are additional symmetries and conservation laws, some exact and others only approximately valid, which play no significant role in classical physics. Among these are the conservation of so-called quantum numbers related to left-right reflection symmetry of space (called parity) and to the reversal symmetry of motion (called time reversal). These quantum numbers are conserved in all processes other than the weak nuclear interaction.

Internal symmetries

Other symmetry properties not obviously related to space and time (and referred to as internal symmetries) characterize the different families of elementary particles and, by extension, their composites. Quarks, for example, have a property called baryon number, as do protons, neutrons, nuclei, and unstable quark composites. All of these except the quarks are known as baryons. A failure of baryon-number conservation would exhibit itself, for instance, by a proton decaying into lighter non-baryonic particles. Indeed, intensive search for such proton decay has been conducted, but so far it has been fruitless. Similar symmetries and conservation laws hold for an analogously defined lepton number, and they also appear, as does the law of baryon conservation, to hold absolutely.

Fundamental forces and fields. The four basic forces of nature, in order of increasing strength, are thought to be: (1) the gravitational force between particles with mass; (2) the electromagnetic force between particles with charge or magnetism or both; (3) the colour force between quarks; and (4) the weak nuclear interaction by which, for example, quarks can change their type, so that a neutron decays into a proton, an electron, and an antineutrino. The strong nuclear interaction that binds protons and neutrons into nuclei and is responsible for fission, fusion, and other nuclear reactions is in principle derived from the colour force. Nuclear physics is thus related to QCD as chemistry is to atomic physics.

Underlying principles of quantum field theory

According to quantum field theory, each of the four fundamental interactions is mediated by the exchange of quanta, called vector gauge bosons, which share certain common characteristics. All have an intrinsic spin of one unit, measured in terms of Planck's constant h. (Leptons and quarks each have one-half unit of spin.) The term gauge refers to a special type of symmetry they possess. This symmetry was first seen in the equations for electromagnetic potentials, quantities from which electromagnetic fields can be derived. It is possessed in pure form by the eight massless gluons of QCD, but in the electroweak theory, the unified theory of electromagnetic and weak interactions, gauge symmetry is partially broken, so that only the photon remains massless, with the other gauge bosons (W+, W−, and Z) acquiring large masses. At present, theoretical physicists are trying to produce a further unification of QCD with the electroweak theory and, more ambitiously still, to unify them with a quantum version of gravity in which the force would be transmitted by massless quanta of two units of spin called gravitons.

THE METHODOLOGY OF PHYSICS

Physics has evolved and continues to evolve without any single strategy. Essentially an experimental science, refined measurements can reveal unexpected behaviour. On the other hand, mathematical extrapolation of existing theories into new theoretical areas, critical reexamination of apparently obvious but untested assumptions, argument by symmetry or analogy, aesthetic judgment, pure accident, and hunch—each of these plays a role (as in all of science). Thus, for example, the quantum hypothesis proposed by Planck was based on observed departures of the character of blackbody radiation (radiation emitted by a heated body that absorbs all radiant energy incident upon it) from that predicted by classical electromagnetism. P.A.M. Dirac predicted the existence of the positron in making a relativistic extension of the quantum theory of the electron. The elusive neutrino, without mass or charge, was hypothesized by Wolfgang Pauli as an alternative to abandoning the conservation laws in the beta-decay process. Maxwell conjectured that if changing magnetic fields create electric fields (which was known to be so), then changing electric fields might create magnetic fields, leading him to the electromagnetic theory of light. Einstein's special theory of relativity was based on a critical reexamination of the meaning of simultaneity, while his general theory rests on the equivalence of inertial and gravitational mass.

Although the tactics may vary from problem to problem, the physicist invariably tries to make unsolved problems more tractable by constructing a series of idealized models, with each successive model being a more realistic representation of the actual physical situation. Thus, in the theory of gases, the molecules are at first imagined to be particles that are as structureless as billiard balls with vanishingly small dimensions. This ideal picture is then improved on step by step.

Correspondence principle

The correspondence principle, a useful guiding principle for extending theoretical interpretations, was formulated by Niels Bohr in the context of the quantum theory. It asserts that when a valid theory is generalized to a broader arena, the new theory's predictions must agree with the old one in the overlapping region in which both are applicable. For example, the more comprehensive theory of physical optics must yield the same result as the more restrictive theory of ray optics whenever wave effects proportional to the wavelength of light are negligible on account of the smallness of that wavelength. Similarly, quantum mechanics must yield the same results as classical mechanics in circumstances when Planck's constant can be considered as negligibly small. Likewise, for speeds small compared to the speed of light (as for baseballs in play), relativistic mechanics must coincide with Newtonian classical mechanics.

Some ways in which experimental and theoretical physicists attack their problems are illustrated by the following examples.

The modern experimental study of elementary particles began with the detection of new types of unstable particles produced in the atmosphere by primary radiation, the latter consisting mainly of high-energy protons arriving from space. The new particles were detected in Geiger counters and identified by the tracks they left in instruments called cloud chambers and in photographic plates. After World War II, particle physics, then known as high-energy nuclear physics, became a major field of science. Today's high-energy particle accelerators can be several kilometres in length, cost hundreds (or even thousands) of millions of dollars, and accelerate particles to enormous energies (trillions of electron volts). Experimental teams, such as those that discovered the W^+, W^-, and Z quanta of the weak force at the European Laboratory for Particle Physics (CERN) in Geneva can have 100 or more physicists from many countries, along with a larger number of technical workers serving as support personnel. A variety of visual and electronic techniques are used to interpret and sort the huge amounts of data produced by their efforts, and particle-physics laboratories are major users of the most advanced technology, be it superconductive magnets or supercomputers.

Reliance on advanced technology

Theoretical physicists use mathematics both as a logical tool for the development of theory and for calculating predictions of the theory to be compared with experiment. Newton, for one, invented integral calculus to solve the following problem, which was essential to his formulation of the law of universal gravitation: Assuming that the attractive force between any pair of point particles is inversely proportional to the square of the distance separating them, how does a spherical distribution of particles, such as the Earth, attract another nearby object? Integral calculus, a procedure for summing many small contributions, yields the simple solution that the Earth itself acts as a point particle with all its mass concentrated at the centre. In modern physics, Dirac predicted the existence of the then-unknown positive electron (or positron) by finding an equation for the electron that would combine quantum mechanics and the special theory of relativity.

RELATIONS BETWEEN PHYSICS AND OTHER DISCIPLINES AND SOCIETY

Influence of physics on related disciplines. Because physics elucidates the simplest fundamental questions in nature on which there can be a consensus, it is hardly surprising that it has had a profound impact on other fields of science, on philosophy, on the worldview of the developed world, and, of course, on technology.

Indeed, whenever a branch of physics has reached such a degree of maturity that its basic elements are comprehended in general principles, it has moved from basic to applied physics and thence to technology. Thus almost all current activity in classical physics consists of applied physics, and its contents form the core of many branches of engineering. Discoveries in modern physics are converted with increasing rapidity into technical innovations and analytical tools for associated disciplines. There are, for example, such nascent fields as nuclear and biomedical engineering, quantum chemistry and quantum optics, and radio, X-ray, and gamma-ray astronomy, as well as such analytic tools as radioisotopes, spectroscopy, and lasers, which all stem directly from basic physics.

Applied physics

Apart from its specific applications, physics—especially Newtonian mechanics—has become the prototype of the scientific method, its experimental and analytic methods sometimes being imitated (and sometimes inappropriately so) in fields far from the related physical sciences. Some of the organizational aspects of physics, based partly on the successes of the radar and atomic-bomb projects of World War II, also have been imitated in large-scale scientific projects, as, for example, in astronomy and space research.

The impact of physics on philosophy

The great influence of physics on the branches of philosophy concerned with the conceptual basis of human perceptions and understanding of nature, such as epistemology, is evidenced by the earlier designation of physics itself as natural philosophy. Present-day philosophy of science deals largely, though not exclusively, with the foundations of physics. Determinism, the philosophical doctrine that the universe is a vast machine operating with strict causality whose future is determined in all detail by its present state, is rooted in Newtonian mechanics, which obeys that principle. Moreover, the schools of materialism, naturalism, and empiricism have in large degree considered physics to be a model for philosophical inquiry. An extreme position is taken by the logical positivists, whose radical distrust of the reality of anything not directly observable leads them to demand that all significant statements must be formulated in the language of physics.

The uncertainty principle of quantum theory has prompted a reexamination of the question of determinism, and its other philosophical implications remain in doubt. Particularly problematic is the matter of the meaning of measurement, for which recent theories and experiments confirm some apparently noncausal predictions of standard quantum theory. It is fair to say that though physicists agree that quantum theory works, they still differ as to what it means.

Influence of related disciplines on physics. The relationship of physics to its bordering disciplines is a reciprocal one. Just as technology feeds on fundamental science for new practical innovations, so physics appropriates the techniques and instrumentation of modern technology for advancing itself. Thus experimental physicists utilize increasingly refined and precise electronic devices. Moreover, they work closely with engineers in designing basic scientific equipment, such as high-energy particle accelerators. Mathematics has always been the primary tool of the theoretical physicist, and even abstruse fields of mathematics such as group theory and differential geometry have become invaluable to the theoretician classifying subatomic particles or investigating the symmetry characteristics of atoms and molecules. Much of contemporary research in physics depends on the high-speed computer. It allows the theoretician to perform computations that are too lengthy or complicated to be done with paper and pencil. Also, it allows experimentalists to incorporate the computer into their apparatus, so that the results of measurements can be provided nearly instantaneously on-line as summarized data while an experiment is in progress.

Mathematics and electronic computers as invaluable tools

The physicist in society. Because of the remoteness of much of contemporary physics from ordinary experience and its reliance on advanced mathematics, physicists have sometimes seemed to the public to be initiates in a latter-day secular priesthood who speak an arcane language and can communicate their findings to laymen only with great difficulty. Yet, the physicist has come to play an increasingly significant role in society, particularly since World War II. Governments have supplied substantial funds for research at academic institutions and at government laboratories through such agencies as the National Science Foundation and the Department of Energy in the United States, which has also established a number of national laboratories, including the Fermi National Accelerator Laboratory in Batavia, Ill., with the world's largest particle accelerator. CERN, mentioned above, is composed of 14 European countries and operates a large accelerator at the Swiss–French border. Physics research is supported in the Federal Republic of Germany by the Max Planck Society for the Advancement of Science and in Japan by the Japan Society for the Promotion of Science. In Trieste, Italy, there is the International Center for Theoretical Physics, which has strong ties to developing countries. These are only a few examples of the widespread international interest in fundamental physics.

Basic research in physics is obviously dependent on public support and funding, and with this development has come, albeit slowly, a growing recognition within the physics community of the social responsibility of scientists for the consequences of their work and for the more general problems of science and society.   (R.T.We./L.M.B.)

Chemistry

Chemistry is the study of the material substances that occur on Earth and elsewhere in the universe. The great

Principal
concerns

challenge in chemistry is the development of a coherent explanation of the complex behaviour of materials, why they appear as they do, what gives them their enduring properties, and how interactions among different substances can bring about the formation of new substances and the destruction of old ones. From the earliest attempts to understand the material world in rational terms, chemists have struggled to develop theories of matter that satisfactorily explain both permanence and change. The ordered assembly of indestructible atoms into small and large molecules, or extended networks of intermingled atoms, is generally accepted as the basis of permanence, while the reorganization of atoms or molecules into different arrangements lies behind theories of change. Thus chemistry involves the study of the atomic composition and structural architecture of substances, as well as the varied interactions among substances that can lead to sudden, often violent reactions.

Practical
applica-
tions

Chemistry also is concerned with the utilization of natural substances and the creation of artificial ones. Cooking, fermentation, glass making, and metallurgy are all chemical processes that date from the beginnings of civilization. Today, vinyl, Teflon, liquid crystals, semiconductors, and superconductors represent the fruits of chemical technology. The 20th century has seen dramatic advances in the comprehension of the marvelous and complex chemistry of living organisms, and a molecular interpretation of health and disease holds great promise. Modern chemistry, aided by increasingly sophisticated instruments, studies materials as small as single atoms and as large and complex as DNA (deoxyribonucleic acid), which contains millions of atoms. New substances can even be designed to bear desired characteristics and then synthesized. The rate at which chemical knowledge continues to accumulate is remarkable. Over time more than 8,000,000 different chemical substances, both natural and artificial, have been characterized and produced. The number was less than 500,000 as recently as 1965.

Intimately interconnected with the intellectual challenges of chemistry are those associated with industry. In the mid-19th century the German chemist Justus von Liebig commented that the wealth of a nation could be gauged by the amount of sulfuric acid it produced. This acid, essential to many manufacturing processes, remains today the leading chemical product of industrialized countries. As Liebig recognized, a country that produces large amounts of sulfuric acid is one with a strong chemical industry and a strong economy as a whole. The production, distribution, and utilization of a wide range of chemical products is common to all highly developed nations. In fact, one can say that the "iron age" of civilization is being replaced by a "polymer age," for in some countries the total volume of polymers now produced exceeds that of iron.

THE SCOPE OF CHEMISTRY

The days are long past when one person could hope to have a detailed knowledge of all areas of chemistry. Those pursuing their interests into specific areas of chemistry communicate with others who share the same interests. Over time a group of chemists with specialized research interests become the founding members of an area of specialization. The areas of specialization that emerged early in the history of chemistry, such as organic, inorganic, physical, analytical, and industrial chemistry, along with biochemistry, remain of greatest general interest. There has been, however, much growth in the areas of polymer, environmental, and medicinal chemistry during the 20th century. Moreover, new specialities continue to appear, as, for example, pesticide, forensic, and computer chemistry.

Analytical chemistry. Most of the materials that occur on Earth, such as wood, coal, minerals, or air, are mixtures of many different and distinct chemical substances. Each pure chemical substance (*e.g.,* oxygen, iron, or water) has a characteristic set of properties that gives it its chemical identity. Iron, for example, is a common silver-white metal that melts at 1,535° C, is very malleable, and readily combines with oxygen to form the common substances hematite and magnetite. The detection of iron in a mixture of metals, or in a compound such as magnetite, is

a branch of analytical chemistry called qualitative analysis. Measurement of the actual amount of a certain substance in a compound or mixture is termed quantitative analysis. Quantitative analytic measurement has determined, for instance, that iron makes up 72.3 percent, by mass, of magnetite, the mineral commonly seen as black sand along beaches and stream banks. Over the years, chemists have discovered chemical reactions that indicate the presence of such elemental substances by the production of easily visible and identifiable products. Iron can be detected by chemical means if it is present in a sample to an amount of 1 part per million or greater. Some very simple qualitative tests reveal the presence of specific chemical elements in even smaller amounts. The yellow colour imparted to a flame by sodium is visible if the sample being ignited has as little as one-billionth of a gram of sodium. Such analytic tests have allowed chemists to identify the types and amounts of impurities in various substances and to determine the properties of very pure materials. Substances used in common laboratory experiments generally have impurity levels of less than 0.1 percent. For special applications, one can purchase chemicals that have impurities totaling less than 0.001 percent. The identification of pure substances and the analysis of chemical mixtures enable all other chemical disciplines to flourish.

Qualitative
analysis
and quan-
titative
analysis

The importance of analytical chemistry has never been greater than it is today. The demand in modern societies for a variety of safe foods, affordable consumer goods, abundant energy, and labour-saving technologies places a great burden on the environment. All chemical manufacturing produces waste products in addition to the desired substances, and waste disposal has not always been carried out carefully. Disruption of the environment has occurred since the dawn of civilization, and pollution problems have increased with the growth of global population. The techniques of analytical chemistry are relied on heavily to maintain a benign environment. The undesirable substances in water, air, soil, and food must be identified, their point of origin fixed, and safe, economical methods for their removal or neutralization developed. Once the amount of a pollutant deemed to be hazardous has been assessed, it becomes important to detect harmful substances at concentrations well below the danger level. Analytical chemists seek to develop increasingly accurate and sensitive techniques and instruments.

Sophisticated analytic instruments, often coupled with computers, have improved the accuracy with which chemists can identify substances and have lowered detection limits. An analytic technique in general use is gas chromatography, which separates the different components of a gaseous mixture by passing the mixture through a long, narrow column of absorbent but porous material. The different gases interact differently with this absorbent material and pass through the column at different rates. As the separate gases flow out of the column, they can be passed into another analytic instrument called a mass spectrometer, which separates substances according to the mass of their constituent ions. A combined gas chromatograph–mass spectrometer can rapidly identify the individual components of a chemical mixture whose concentrations may be no greater than a few parts per billion. Similar or even greater sensitivities can be obtained under favourable conditions using techniques such as atomic absorption, polarography, and neutron activation. The rate of instrumental innovation is such that analytic instruments often become obsolete within 10 years of their introduction. Newer instruments are more accurate and faster and are employed widely in the areas of environmental and medicinal chemistry.

Gas
chromatog-
raphy and
mass spec-
trometry

Inorganic chemistry. Modern chemistry, which dates more or less from the acceptance of the law of conservation of mass in the late 18th century, focused initially on those substances that were not associated with living organisms. Study of such substances, which normally have little or no carbon, constitutes the discipline of inorganic chemistry. Early work sought to identify the simple substances—namely, the elements—that are the constituents of all more complex substances. Some elements, such as gold and carbon, have been known since antiquity, and many others were discovered and studied throughout the 19th and early 20th centuries. Today, more than 100 are known. The study of such simple inorganic compounds as sodium chloride (common salt) has led to some of the fundamental concepts of modern chemistry, the law of definite proportions providing one notable example. This law states that for most pure chemical substances the constituent elements are always present in fixed proportions by mass (*e.g.*, every 100 grams of salt contains 39.3 grams of sodium and 60.7 grams of chlorine). The crystalline form of salt, known as halite, consists of intermingled sodium and chlorine atoms, one sodium atom for each one of chlorine. Such a compound, formed solely by the combination of two elements, is known as a binary compound. Binary compounds are very common in inorganic chemistry, and they exhibit little structural variety. For this reason, the number of inorganic compounds is limited in spite of the large number of elements that may react with each other. If three or more elements are combined in a substance, the structural possibilities become greater.

After a period of quiescence in the early part of the 20th century, inorganic chemistry has again become an exciting area of research. Compounds of boron and hydrogen, known as boranes, have unique structural features that forced a change in thinking about the architecture of inorganic molecules. Some inorganic substances have structural features long believed to occur only in carbon compounds, and a few inorganic polymers have even been produced. Ceramics are materials composed of inorganic elements combined with oxygen. For centuries ceramic objects have been made by strongly heating a vessel formed from a paste of powdered minerals. Although ceramics are quite hard and stable at very high temperatures, they are usually brittle. Currently, new ceramics strong enough to be used as turbine blades in jet engines are being manufactured. There is hope that ceramics will one day replace steel in components of internal-combustion engines. In 1987 a ceramic containing yttrium, barium, copper, and oxygen, with the approximate formula $YBa_2Cu_3O_7$, was found to be a superconductor at a temperature of about 100 K. A superconductor offers no resistance to the passage of an electrical current, and this new type of ceramic could very well find wide use in electrical and magnetic applications. A superconducting ceramic is so simple to make that it can be prepared in a high school laboratory. Its discovery illustrates the unpredictability of chemistry, for fundamental discoveries can still be made with simple equipment and inexpensive materials.

Many of the most interesting developments in inorganic chemistry bridge the gap with other disciplines. Organometallic chemistry investigates compounds that contain inorganic elements combined with carbon-rich units. Many organometallic compounds play an important role in industrial chemistry as catalysts, which are substances that are able to accelerate the rate of a reaction even when present in only very small amounts. Some success has been achieved in the use of such catalysts for converting natural gas to related but more useful chemical substances. Chemists also have created large inorganic molecules that contain a core of metal atoms, such as platinum, surrounded by a shell of different chemical units. Some of these compounds, referred to as metal clusters, have characteristics of metals, while others react in ways similar to biologic systems. Trace amounts of metals in biologic systems are essential for processes such as respiration, nerve function, and cell metabolism. Processes of this kind form the object of study of bioinorganic chemistry. Although organic molecules were once thought to be the distinguishing chemical feature of living creatures, it is now known that inorganic chemistry plays a vital role as well.

Organic chemistry. Organic compounds are based on the chemistry of carbon. Carbon is unique in the variety and extent of structures that can result from the three-dimensional connections of its atoms. The process of photosynthesis converts carbon dioxide and water to oxygen and compounds known as carbohydrates. Both cellulose, the substance that gives structural rigidity to plants, and starch, the energy storage product of plants, are polymeric

(margin left)
Development of new ceramics

Organometallic chemistry

Bioinorganic chemistry

carbohydrates. Simple carbohydrates produced by photosynthesis form the raw material for the myriad organic compounds found in the plant and animal kingdoms. When combined with variable amounts of hydrogen, oxygen, nitrogen, sulfur, phosphorus, and other elements, the structural possibilities of carbon compounds become limitless, and their number far exceeds the total of all nonorganic compounds. A major focus of organic chemistry is the isolation, purification, and structural study of these naturally occurring substances. Many natural products are simple molecules. Examples include formic acid (HCO_2H) in ants, ethyl alcohol (C_2H_5OH) in fermenting fruit, and oxalic acid ($C_2H_2O_4$) in rhubarb leaves. Other natural products, such as penicillin, vitamin B_{12}, proteins, and nucleic acids, are exceedingly complex. The isolation of pure natural products from their host organism is made difficult by the low concentrations in which they may be present. Once they are isolated in pure form, however, modern instrumental techniques can reveal structural details for amounts weighing as little as one-millionth of a gram. The correlation of the physical and chemical properties of compounds with their structural features is the domain of physical organic chemistry. Once the properties endowed upon a substance by specific structural units termed functional groups are known, it becomes possible to design novel molecules that may exhibit desired properties. The preparation, under controlled laboratory conditions, of specific compounds is known as synthetic chemistry. Some products are easier to synthesize than to collect and purify from their natural sources. Tons of vitamin C, for example, are synthesized annually. Many synthetic substances have novel properties that make them especially useful. Plastics are a prime example, as are many drugs and agricultural chemicals. A continuing challenge for synthetic chemists is the structural complexity of most organic substances. To synthesize a desired substance, the atoms must be pieced together in the correct order and with the proper three-dimensional relationships. Just as a given pile of lumber and bricks can be assembled in many ways to build houses of several different designs, so too can a fixed number of atoms be connected together in various ways to give different molecules. Only one structural arrangement out of the many possibilities will be identical with a naturally occurring molecule. The antibiotic erythromycin, for example, contains 37 carbon, 67 hydrogen, and 13 oxygen atoms, along with one nitrogen atom. Even when joined together in the proper order, these 118 atoms can give rise to 262,144 different structures, only one of which has the characteristics of natural erythromycin. The great abundance of organic compounds, their fundamental role in the chemistry of life, and their structural diversity have made their study especially challenging and exciting. Organic chemistry is the largest area of specialization among the various fields of chemistry.

Biochemistry. As understanding of inanimate chemistry grew during the 19th century, attempts to interpret the physiological processes of living organisms in terms of molecular structure and reactivity gave rise to the discipline of biochemistry. Biochemists employ the techniques and theories of chemistry to probe the molecular basis of life. An organism is investigated on the premise that its physiological processes are the consequence of many thousands of chemical reactions occurring in a highly integrated manner. Biochemists have established, among other things, the principles that underlie energy transfer in cells, the chemical structure of cell membranes, the coding and transmission of hereditary information, muscular and nerve function, and biosynthetic pathways. In fact, related biomolecules have been found to fulfill similar roles in organisms as different as bacteria and human beings. The study of biomolecules, however, presents many difficulties. Such molecules are often very large and exhibit great structural complexity; moreover, the chemical reactions they undergo are usually exceedingly fast. The separation of the two strands of DNA, for instance, occurs in one-millionth of a second. Such rapid rates of reaction are possible only through the intermediary action of biomolecules called enzymes. Enzymes are proteins that owe their remarkable rate-accelerating abilities to their three-dimen-

(margin right)
Isolation, purification, and structural study of material substances

Synthetic chemistry

Probing the molecular basis of life

sional chemical structure. Not surprisingly, biochemical discoveries have had a great impact on the understanding and treatment of disease. Many ailments due to inborn errors of metabolism have been traced to specific genetic defects. Other diseases result from disruptions in normal biochemical pathways.

Frequently, symptoms can be alleviated by drugs, and the discovery, mode of action, and degradation of therapeutic agents is another of the major areas of study in biochemistry. Bacterial infections can be treated with sulfonamides, penicillins, and tetracyclines, and research into viral infections has revealed the effectiveness of acyclovir against the herpes virus. There is much current interest in the details of carcinogenesis and cancer chemotherapy. It is known, for example, that cancer can result when cancer-causing molecules, or carcinogens as they are called, react with nucleic acids and proteins and interfere with their normal modes of action. Researchers have developed tests that can identify molecules likely to be carcinogenic. The hope, of course, is that progress in the prevention and treatment of cancer will accelerate once the biochemical basis of the disease is more fully understood.

Concern with therapeutic agents

The molecular basis of biologic processes is an essential feature of the fast-growing disciplines of molecular biology and biotechnology. Chemistry has developed methods for rapidly and accurately determining the structure of proteins and DNA. In addition, efficient laboratory methods for the synthesis of genes are being devised. Ultimately, the correction of genetic diseases by replacement of defective genes with normal ones may become possible.

Methods of gene synthesis

Polymer chemistry. The simple substance ethylene is a gas composed of molecules with the formula CH_2CH_2. Under certain conditions, many ethylene molecules will join together to form a long chain called polyethylene, with the formula $(CH_2CH_2)_n$, where n is a variable but large number. Polyethylene is a tough, durable solid material quite different from ethylene. It is an example of a polymer, which is a large molecule made up of many smaller molecules (monomers), usually joined together in a linear fashion. Many naturally occurring substances, including cellulose, starch, cotton, wool, rubber, leather, proteins, and DNA, are polymers. Polyethylene, nylon, and acrylics are examples of synthetic polymers. The study of such materials lies within the domain of polymer chemistry, a specialty that has flourished in the 20th century. The investigation of natural polymers overlaps considerably with biochemistry, but the synthesis of new polymers, the investigation of polymerization processes, and the characterization of the structure and properties of polymeric materials all pose unique problems for polymer chemists.

Polymer chemists have designed and synthesized polymers that vary in hardness, flexibility, softening temperature, solubility in water, and biodegradability. They have produced polymeric materials that are as strong as steel yet lighter and more resistant to corrosion. Oil, natural gas, and water pipelines are now routinely constructed of plastic pipe. In recent years, automakers have increased their use of plastic components to build lighter vehicles that consume less fuel. Other industries such as those involved in the manufacture of textiles, rubber, paper, and packaging materials are built upon polymer chemistry.

Besides producing new kinds of polymeric materials, researchers are concerned with developing special catalysts that are required by the large-scale industrial synthesis of commercial polymers. Without such catalysts, the polymerization process would be very slow in certain cases.

Developing special catalysts

Physical chemistry. Many chemical disciplines, such as those already discussed, focus on certain classes of materials that share common structural and chemical features. Other specialties may be centred not on a class of substances but rather on their interactions and transformations. The oldest of these fields is physical chemistry, which seeks to measure, correlate, and explain the quantitative aspects of chemical processes. The Anglo-Irish chemist Robert Boyle, for example, discovered in the 17th century that at room temperature the volume of a fixed quantity of gas decreases proportionally as the pressure on it increases. Thus, for a gas at constant temperature, the product of its volume V and pressure P equals a constant

number—*i.e.*, PV = constant. Such a simple arithmetic relationship is valid for nearly all gases at room temperature and at pressures equal to or less than one atmosphere. Subsequent work has shown that the relationship loses its validity at higher pressures, but more complicated expressions that more accurately match experimental results can be derived. The discovery and investigation of such chemical regularities, often called laws of nature, lie within the realm of physical chemistry. For much of the 18th century the source of mathematical regularity in chemical systems was assumed to be the continuum of forces and fields that surround the atoms making up chemical elements and compounds. Developments in the 20th century, however, have shown that chemical behaviour is best interpreted by a quantum mechanical model of atomic and molecular structure (see above *Quantum mechanics*). The branch of physical chemistry that is largely devoted to this subject is theoretical chemistry. Theoretical chemists make extensive use of computers to help them solve complicated mathematical equations. Other branches of physical chemistry include chemical thermodynamics, which deals with the relationship between heat and other forms of chemical energy, and chemical kinetics, which seeks to measure and understand the rates of chemical reactions. Electrochemistry investigates the interrelationship of electric current and chemical change. The passage of an electric current through a chemical solution causes changes in the constituent substances that are often reversible—*i.e.*, under different conditions the altered substances themselves will yield an electric current. Common batteries contain chemical substances that, when placed in contact with each other by closing an electrical circuit, will deliver current at a constant voltage until the substances are consumed. At present there is much interest in devices that can use the energy in sunlight to drive chemical reactions whose products are capable of storing the energy. The discovery of such devices would make possible the widespread utilization of solar energy.

Electro-chemistry

There are many other disciplines within physical chemistry that are concerned more with the general properties of substances and the interactions among substances than with the substances themselves. Photochemistry is a specialty that investigates the interaction of light with matter. Chemical reactions initiated by the absorption of light can be very different from those that occur by other means. Vitamin D, for example, is formed in the human body when the steroid ergosterol absorbs solar radiation; ergosterol does not change to vitamin D in the dark.

A rapidly developing subdiscipline of physical chemistry is surface chemistry. It examines the properties of chemical surfaces, relying heavily on instruments that can provide a chemical profile of such surfaces. Whenever a solid is exposed to a liquid or a gas, a reaction occurs initially on the surface of the solid, and its properties can change dramatically as a result. Aluminum is a case in point: it is resistant to corrosion precisely because the surface of the pure metal reacts with oxygen to form a layer of aluminum oxide, which serves to protect the interior of the metal from further oxidation. Numerous reaction catalysts perform their function by providing a reactive surface on which substances can react.

Surface chemistry

Industrial chemistry. The manufacture, sale, and distribution of chemical products is one of the cornerstones of a developed country. Chemists play an important role in the manufacture, inspection, and safe handling of chemical products, as well as in product development and general management. The manufacture of basic chemicals such as oxygen, chlorine, ammonia, and sulfuric acid provides the raw materials for industries producing textiles, agricultural products, metals, paints, and pulp and paper. Specialty chemicals are produced in smaller amounts for industries involved with such products as pharmaceuticals, foodstuffs, packaging, detergents, flavours, and fragrances. To a large extent, the chemical industry takes the products and reactions common to "bench-top" chemical processes and scales them up to industrial quantities.

The monitoring and control of bulk chemical processes, especially with regard to heat transfer, pose problems usually tackled by chemists and chemical engineers. The disposal of by-products also is a major problem for bulk chemical producers. These and other challenges of industrial chemistry set it apart from the more purely intellectual disciplines of chemistry discussed above. Yet, within the chemical industry, there is a considerable amount of fundamental research undertaken within traditional specialties. Most large chemical companies have research-and-development capability. Pharmaceutical firms, for example, operate large research laboratories in which chemists test molecules for pharmacological activity. The new products and processes that are discovered in such laboratories are often patented and become a source of profit for the company funding the research. A great deal of the research conducted in the chemical industry can be termed applied research because its goals are closely tied to the products and processes of the company concerned. New technologies often require much chemical expertise. The fabrication of, say, electronic microcircuits involves close to 100 separate chemical steps from start to finish. Thus, the chemical industry evolves with the technological advances of the modern world and at the same time often contributes to the rate of progress.

Applied research

THE METHODOLOGY OF CHEMISTRY

Chemistry is to a large extent a cumulative science. Over time the number and extent of observations and phenomena studied increase. Not all hypotheses and discoveries endure unchallenged, however. Some of them are discarded as new observations or more satisfying explanations appear. Nonetheless, chemistry has a broad spectrum of explanatory models for chemical phenomena that have endured and been extended over time. These now have the status of theories, interconnected sets of explanatory devices that correlate well with observed phenomena. As new discoveries are made, they are incorporated into existing theory whenever possible. However, as the discovery of high-temperature superconductors in 1986 illustrates, accepted theory is never sufficient to predict the course of future discovery. Serendipity, or chance discovery, will continue to play as much a role in the future as will theoretical sophistication.

Studies of molecular structure. The chemical properties of a substance are a function of its structure, and the techniques of X-ray crystallography now enable chemists to determine the precise atomic arrangement of complex molecules. A molecule is an ordered assembly of atoms. Each atom in a molecule is connected to one or more neighbouring atoms by a chemical bond. The length of bonds and the angles between adjacent bonds are all important in describing molecular structure, and a comprehensive theory of chemical bonding is one of the major achievements of modern chemistry. Fundamental to bonding theory is the atomic–molecular concept.

Basic concepts of modern bonding theory

Atoms and elements. As far as general chemistry is concerned, atoms are composed of the three fundamental particles: the proton, the neutron, and the electron. Although the proton and the neutron are themselves composed of smaller units, their substructure has little impact on chemical transformation. As was explained in an earlier section, the proton carries a charge of +1, and the number of protons in an atomic nucleus distinguishes one type of chemical atom from another. The simplest atom of all, hydrogen, has a nucleus composed of a single proton. The neutron has very nearly the same mass as the proton, but it has no charge. Neutrons are contained with protons in the nucleus of all atoms other than hydrogen. The atom with one proton and one neutron in its nucleus is called deuterium. Because it has only one proton, deuterium exhibits the same chemical properties as hydrogen but has a different mass. Hydrogen and deuterium are examples of related atoms called isotopes. The third atomic particle, the electron, has a charge of −1, but its mass is 1,836 times smaller than that of a proton. The electron occupies a region of space outside the nucleus termed an orbital. Some orbitals are spherical with the nucleus at the centre. Because electrons have so little mass and move about at speeds close to half that of light, they exhibit the same wave–particle duality as photons of light. This means that some of the properties of an electron are best described

by considering the electron to be a particle, while other properties are consistent with the behaviour of a standing wave. The energy of a standing wave, such as a vibrating string, is distributed over the region of space defined by the two fixed ends and the up-and-down extremes of vibration. Such a wave does not exist in a fixed region of space as does a particle. Early models of atomic structure envisioned the electron as a particle orbiting the nucleus, but electron orbitals are now interpreted as the regions of space occupied by standing waves called wave functions (see above *Quantum mechanics*). These wave functions represent the regions of space around the nucleus in which the probability of finding an electron is high. They play an important role in bonding theory, as will be discussed later.

Concept of wave functions

Each proton in an atomic nucleus requires an electron for electrical neutrality. Thus, as the number of protons in a nucleus increases, so too does the number of electrons. The electrons, alone or in pairs, occupy orbitals increasingly distant from the nucleus. Electrons farther from the nucleus are attracted less strongly by the protons in the nucleus, and they can be removed more easily from the atom. The energy required to move an electron from one orbital to another, or from one orbital to free space, gives a measure of the energy level of the orbitals. These energies have been found to have distinct, fixed values; they are said to be quantized. The energy differences between orbitals give rise to the characteristic patterns of light absorption or emission that are unique to each chemical atom.

A new chemical atom—that is, an element—results each time another proton is added to an atomic nucleus. Consecutive addition of protons generates the whole range of elements known to exist in the universe. Compounds are formed when two or more different elements combine through atomic bonding. Such bond formation is a consequence of electron pairing and constitutes the foundation of all structural chemistry.

Ionic and covalent bonding. When two different atoms approach each other, the electrons in their outer orbitals can respond in two distinct ways. An electron in the outermost atomic orbital of atom A may move completely to an outer but stabler orbital of atom B. The charged atoms that result, A$^+$ and B$^-$, are called ions, and the electrostatic force of attraction between them gives rise to what is termed an ionic bond. Most elements can form ionic bonds, and the substances that result commonly exist as three-dimensional arrays of positive and negative ions. Ionic compounds are frequently crystalline solids that have high melting points (*e.g.,* table salt).

The second way in which the two outer electrons of atoms A and B can respond to the approach of A and B is to pair up to form a covalent bond. In the simple view known as the valence-bond model, in which electrons are treated strictly as particles, the two paired electrons are assumed to lie between the two nuclei and are shared equally by atoms A and B, resulting in a covalent bond. Atoms joined together by one or more covalent bonds constitute molecules. Hydrogen gas is composed of hydrogen molecules, which consist in turn of two hydrogen atoms linked by a covalent bond. The notation H_2 for hydrogen gas is referred to as a molecular formula. Molecular formulas indicate the number and type of atoms that make up a molecule. The molecule H_2 is responsible for the properties generally associated with hydrogen gas. Most substances on Earth have covalently bonded molecules as their fundamental chemical unit, and their molecular properties are completely different from those of the constituent elements. The physical and chemical properties of carbon dioxide, for example, are quite distinct from those of pure carbon and pure oxygen.

Valence-bond model

The interpretation of a covalent bond as a localized electron pair is an oversimplification of the bonding situation. A more comprehensive description of bonding that considers the wave properties of electrons is the molecular-orbital theory. According to this theory, electrons in a molecule, rather than being localized between atoms, are distributed over all the atoms in the molecule in a spatial distribution described by a molecular orbital. Such orbitals result when the atomic orbitals of bonded atoms combine with each other. The total number of molecular

The molecular-orbital theory

orbitals present in a molecule is equal to the sum of all atomic orbitals in the constituent atoms prior to bonding. Thus, for the simple combination of atoms A and B to form the molecule AB, two atomic orbitals combine to generate two molecular orbitals. One of these, the so-called bonding molecular orbital, represents a region of space enveloping both the A and B atoms, while the other, the anti-bonding molecular orbital, has two lobes, neither of which occupies the space between the two atoms. The bonding molecular orbital is at a lower energy level than are the two atomic orbitals, while the anti-bonding orbital is at a higher energy level. The two paired electrons that constitute the covalent bond between A and B occupy the bonding molecular orbital. For this reason, there is a high probability of finding the electrons between A and B, but they can be found elsewhere in the orbital as well. Because only two electrons are involved in bond formation and both can be accommodated in the lower energy orbital, the anti-bonding orbital remains unpopulated. This theory of bonding predicts that bonding between A and B will occur because the energy of the paired electrons after bonding is less than that of the two electrons in their atomic orbitals prior to bonding. The formation of a covalent bond is thus energetically favoured. The system goes from a state of higher energy to one of lower energy.

Another feature of this bonding picture is that it is able to predict the energy required to move an electron from the bonding molecular orbital to the anti-bonding one. The energy required for such an electronic excitation can be provided by visible light, for example, and the wavelength of the light absorbed determines the colour displayed by the absorbing molecule (*e.g.,* violets are blue because the pigments in the flower absorb the red rays of natural light and reflect more of the blue). As the number of atoms in a molecule increases, so too does the number of molecular orbitals. Calculation of molecular orbitals for large molecules is mathematically difficult, but computers have made it possible to determine the wave equations for several large molecules. Molecular properties predicted by such calculations correlate well with experimental results.

Use of computers to determine wave equations

Isomerism. Many elements can form two or more covalent bonds, but only a few are able to form extended chains of covalent bonds. The outstanding example is carbon, which can form as many as four covalent bonds and can bond to itself indefinitely. Carbon has six electrons in total, two of which are paired in an atomic orbital closest to the nucleus. The remaining four are farther from the nucleus and are available for covalent bonding. When there is sufficient hydrogen present, carbon will react to form methane, CH_4. When all four electron pairs occupy the four molecular orbitals of lowest energy, the molecule assumes the shape of a tetrahedron, with carbon at the centre and the four hydrogen atoms at the apexes. The C–H bond length is 110 picometres (1 picometre = 10^{-12} metre), and the angle between adjacent C–H bonds is close to 110°. Such tetrahedral symmetry is common to many carbon compounds and results in interesting structural possibilities. If two carbon atoms are joined together, with three hydrogen atoms bonded to each carbon atom, the molecule ethane is obtained. When four carbon atoms are joined together, two different structures are possible: a linear structure designated *n*-butane and a branched structure called iso-butane. These two structures have the same molecular formula, C_4H_{10}, but a different order of attachment of their constituent atoms. The two molecules are termed structural isomers. Each of them has unique chemical and physical properties, and they are different compounds. The number of possible isomers increases rapidly as the number of carbon atoms increases. There are five isomers for C_6H_{14}, 75 for $C_{10}H_{22}$, and 6.2×10^{13} for $C_{40}H_{82}$. When carbon forms bonds to atoms other than hydrogen, such as oxygen, nitrogen, and sulfur, the structural possibilities become even greater. It is this great potential for structural diversity that makes carbon compounds essential to living organisms.

Structural isomers

Even when the bonding sequence of carbon compounds is fixed, further structural variation is still possible. When two carbon atoms are joined together by two bonding pairs of electrons, a double bond is formed. A double bond forces the two carbon atoms and attached groups into a rigid, planar structure. As a result, a molecule such as CHCl=CHCl can exist in two nonidentical forms called geometric isomers. Structural rigidity also occurs in ring structures, and attached groups can be on the same side of a ring or on different sides. Yet another opportunity for isomerism arises when a carbon atom is bonded to four different groups. These can be attached in two different ways, one of which is the mirror image of the other. This type of isomerism is called optical isomerism, because the two isomers affect plane-polarized light differently. Two optical isomers are possible for every carbon atom that is bonded to four different groups. For a molecule bearing 10 such carbon atoms, the total number of possible isomers will be $2^{10} = 1,024$. Large biomolecules often have 10 or more carbon atoms for which such optical isomers are possible. Only one of all the possible isomers will be identical to the natural molecule. For this reason, the laboratory synthesis of large organic molecules is exceedingly difficult. Only in the last few decades of the 20th century have chemists succeeded in developing reagents and processes that yield specific optical isomers. They expect that new synthetic methods will make possible the synthesis of ever more complex natural products.

Optical isomers

Investigations of chemical transformations. *Basic factors.* The structure of ionic substances and covalently bonded molecules largely determines their function. As noted above, the properties of a substance depend on the number and type of atoms it contains and on the bonding patterns present. Its bulk properties also depend, however, on the interactions among individual atoms, ions, or molecules. The force of attraction between the fundamental units of a substance dictate whether, at a given temperature and pressure, that substance will exist in the solid, liquid, or gas phase. At room temperature and pressure, for example, the strong forces of attraction between the positive ions of sodium (Na^+) and the negative ions of chlorine (Cl^-) draw them into a compact solid structure. The weaker forces of attraction among neighbouring water molecules allow the looser packing characteristic of a liquid. Finally, the very weak attractive forces acting among adjacent oxygen molecules are exceeded by the dispersive forces of heat; oxygen, consequently, is a gas. Interparticle forces thus affect the chemical and physical behaviour of substances, but they also determine to a large extent how a particle will respond to the approach of a different particle. If the two particles react with each other to form new particles, a chemical reaction has occurred. Notwithstanding the unlimited structural diversity allowed by molecular bonding, the world would be devoid of life if substances were incapable of change. The study of chemical transformation, which complements the study of molecular structure, is built on the concepts of energy and entropy.

Energy and the first law of thermodynamics. The concept of energy is a fundamental and familiar one in all the sciences. In simple terms, the energy of a body represents its ability to do work, and work itself is a force acting over a distance.

Chemical systems can have both kinetic energy (energy of motion) and potential energy (stored energy). The kinetic energy possessed by any collection of molecules in a solid, liquid, or gas is known as its thermal energy. Since liquids expand when they have more thermal energy, a liquid column of mercury, for example, will rise higher in an evacuated tube as it becomes warmer. In this way a thermometer can be used to measure the thermal energy, or temperature, of a system. The temperature at which all molecular motion comes to a halt is known as absolute zero.

The kinetic and potential energy of chemical systems

Energy also may be stored in atoms or molecules as potential energy. When protons and neutrons combine to form the nucleus of a certain element, the reduction in potential energy is matched by the production of a huge quantity of kinetic energy. Consider, for instance, the formation of the deuterium nucleus from one proton and one neutron. The fundamental mass unit of the chemist is the mole, which represents the mass, in grams, of 6.02×10^{23} individual particles, whether they be atoms or molecules.

One mole of protons has a mass of 1.007825 grams and one mole of neutrons has a mass of 1.008665 grams. By simple addition the mass of one mole of deuterium atoms (ignoring the negligible mass of one mole of electrons) should be 2.016490 grams. The measured mass is 0.00239 gram less than this. The missing mass is known as the binding energy of the nucleus and represents the mass equivalent of the energy released by nucleus formation. By using Einstein's formula for the conversion of mass to energy ($E = mc^2$), one can calculate the energy equivalent of 0.00239 gram as 2.15×10^8 kilojoules. This is approximately 240,000 times greater than the energy released by the combustion of one mole of methane. Such studies of the energetics of atom formation and interconversion are part of a specialty known as nuclear chemistry.

Concerns of nuclear chemistry

The energy released by the combustion of methane is about 900 kilojoules per mole. Although much less than the energy released by nuclear reactions, the energy given off by a chemical process such as combustion is great enough to be perceived as heat and light. Energy is released in so-called exothermic reactions because the chemical bonds in the product molecules, carbon dioxide and water, are stronger and stabler than those in the reactant molecules, methane and oxygen. The chemical potential energy of the system has decreased, and most of the released energy appears as heat, while some appears as radiant energy, or light. The heat produced by such a combustion reaction will raise the temperature of the surrounding air and, at constant pressure, increase its volume. This expansion of air results in work being done. In the cylinder of an internal-combustion engine, for example, the combustion of gasoline results in hot gases that expand against a moving piston. The motion of the piston turns a crankshaft, which then propels the vehicle. In this case, chemical potential energy has been converted to thermal energy, some of which produces useful work. This process illustrates a statement of the conservation of energy known as the first law of thermodynamics. This law states that, for an exothermic reaction, the energy released by the chemical system is equal to the heat gained by the surroundings plus the work performed. By measuring the heat and work quantities that accompany chemical reactions, it is possible to ascertain the energy differences between the reactants and the products of various reactions. In this manner, the potential energy stored in a variety of molecules can be determined, and the energy changes that accompany chemical reactions can be calculated.

Measuring the heat and work quantities that accompany reactions

Entropy and the second law of thermodynamics. Some chemical processes occur even though there is no net energy change. Consider a vessel containing a gas, connected to an evacuated vessel via a channel wherein a barrier obstructs passage of the gas. If the barrier is removed, the gas will expand into the evacuated vessel. This expansion is consistent with the observation that a gas always expands to fill the volume available. When the temperature of both vessels is the same, the energy of the gas before and after the expansion is the same. The reverse reaction does not occur, however. The spontaneous reaction is the one that yields a state of greater disorder. In the expanded volume, the individual gas molecules have greater freedom of movement and thus are more disordered. The measure of the disorder of a system is a quantity termed entropy. At a temperature of absolute zero, all movement of atoms and molecules ceases, and the disorder—and entropy— of such perfectly compacted substances is zero. (Zero entropy at zero temperature is in accord with the third law of thermodynamics.) All substances above absolute zero will have a positive entropy value that increases with temperature. When a hot body cools down, the thermal energy it loses passes to the surrounding air, which is at a lower temperature. As the entropy of the cooling body decreases, the entropy of the surrounding air increases. In fact, the increase in entropy of the air is greater than the decrease in entropy of the cooling body. This is consistent with the second law, which states that the total entropy of a system and its surroundings always increases in a spontaneous reaction. Thus the first and second laws of thermodynamics indicate that, for all processes of chemical change throughout the universe, energy is conserved but entropy increases.

Application of the laws of thermodynamics to chemical systems allows chemists to predict the behaviour of chemical reactions. When energy and entropy considerations favour the formation of product molecules, reagent molecules will act to form products until an equilibrium is established between products and reagents. The ratio of products to reagents is specified by a quantity known as an equilibrium constant, which is a function of the energy and entropy differences between the two. What thermodynamics cannot predict, however, is the rate at which chemical reactions occur. For fast reactions an equilibrium mixture of products and reagents can be established in one millisecond or less; for slow reactions the time required could be hundreds of years.

Predicting the behaviour of chemical reactions

Rates of reaction. When the specific rates of chemical reactions are measured experimentally, they are found to be dependent on the concentrations of reacting species, temperature, and a quantity called activation energy. Chemists explain this phenomenon by recourse to the collision theory of reaction rates. This theory builds on the premise that a reaction between two or more chemicals requires, at the molecular level, a collision between two rapidly moving molecules. If the two molecules collide in the right way and with enough kinetic energy, one of the molecules may acquire enough energy to initiate the bond-breaking process. As this occurs, new bonds may begin to form, and ultimately reagent molecules are converted into product molecules. The point of highest energy during bond breaking and bond formation is called the transition state of the molecular process. The difference between the energy of the transition state and that of the reacting molecules is the activation energy that must be exceeded for a reaction to occur. Reaction rates increase with temperature because the colliding molecules have greater energies, and more of them will have energies that exceed the activation energy of reaction. The modern study of the molecular basis of chemical change has been greatly aided by lasers and computers. It is now possible to study short-lived collision products and to better determine the molecular mechanisms that fix the rate of chemical reactions. This knowledge is useful in designing new catalysts that can accelerate the rate of reaction by lowering the activation energy. Catalysts are important for many biochemical and industrial processes because they speed up reactions that ordinarily occur too slowly to be useful. Moreover, they often do so with increased control over the structural features of the product molecules. A rhodium phosphine catalyst, for example, has enabled chemists to obtain 96 percent of the correct optical isomer in a key step in the synthesis of L-dopa, a drug used for treating Parkinson's disease.

Collision theory of reaction rates

Studying the molecular basis of chemical change with lasers and computers

CHEMISTRY AND SOCIETY

For the first two-thirds of the 20th century, chemistry was seen by many as the science of the future. The potential of chemical products for enriching society appeared to be unlimited. Increasingly, however, and especially in the public mind, the negative aspects of chemistry have come to the fore. Disposal of chemical by-products at waste-disposal sites of limited capacity has resulted in environmental and health problems of enormous concern. The legitimate use of drugs for the medically supervised treatment of diseases has been tainted by the growing misuse of mood-altering drugs. The very word chemicals has come to be used all too frequently in a pejorative sense. There is, as a result, a danger that the pursuit and application of chemical knowledge may be seen as bearing risks that outweigh the benefits.

It is easy to underestimate the central role of chemistry in modern society, but chemical products are essential if the world's population is to be clothed, housed, and fed. The world's reserves of fossil fuels (*e.g.,* oil, natural gas, and coal) will eventually be exhausted, some as soon as the 21st century, and new chemical processes and materials will provide a crucial alternative energy source. The conversion of solar energy to more concentrated, useful forms, for example, will rely heavily on discoveries in chemistry.

Practical contributions of chemistry

Long-term, environmentally acceptable solutions to pollution problems are not attainable without chemical knowledge. There is much truth in the aphorism that "chemical problems require chemical solutions." Chemical inquiry will lead to a better understanding of the behaviour of both natural and synthetic materials and to the discovery of new substances that will help future generations better supply their needs and deal with their problems.

Progress in chemistry can no longer be measured only in terms of economics and utility. The discovery and manufacture of new chemical goods must continue to be economically feasible but must be environmentally acceptable as well. The impact of new substances on the environment can now be assessed before large-scale production begins, and environmental compatibility has become a valued property of new materials. For example, compounds consisting of carbon fully bonded to chlorine and fluorine, called chlorofluorocarbons (or Freons), were believed to be ideal for their intended use when they were first discovered. They are nontoxic, nonflammable gases and volatile liquids that are very stable. These properties led to their widespread use as solvents, refrigerants, and propellants in aerosol containers. Time has shown, however, that these compounds decompose in the upper regions of the atmosphere and that the decomposition products act to destroy stratospheric ozone. Limits have now been placed on the use of chlorofluorocarbons, but it is impossible to recover the amounts already dispersed into the atmosphere.

The chlorofluorocarbon problem illustrates how difficult it is to anticipate the overall impact that new materials can have on the environment. Chemists are working to develop methods of assessment, and prevailing chemical theory provides the working tools. Once a substance has been identified as hazardous to the existing ecological balance, it is the responsibility of chemists to locate that substance and neutralize it, limiting the damage it can do or removing it from the environment entirely. The last years of the 20th century will see many new, exciting discoveries in the processes and products of chemistry. Inevitably, the harmful effects of some substances will outweigh their benefits, and their use will have to be limited. Yet, the positive impact of chemistry on society as a whole seems beyond doubt.   (M.C.U.)

Astronomy

Astronomy comprises the study of all extraterrestrial objects. Until the invention of the telescope and the discovery of the laws of motion and gravity in the 17th century, astronomy was primarily concerned with noting and predicting the positions of the Sun, Moon, and planets, initially for calendrical and astrological purposes and later for navigational applications and scientific interest. The catalog of objects now studied is much broader and includes, in order of increasing distances, the solar system, the stars that make up the Milky Way Galaxy, and other more distant stellar objects and galaxies. With the advent of scientific space probes, the Earth also has come to be studied as one of the planets, though its more detailed investigation remains the domain of the geologic sciences.

THE SCOPE OF ASTRONOMY

Astro-
physics and
cosmology
as major
fields of
study

During the 20th century astronomy has expanded to include astrophysics, the application of physical and chemical knowledge to an understanding of the nature of celestial objects and the physical processes that control their formation, evolution, and emission of radiation. Study of the nuclear reactions that provide the energy radiated by stars has shown how the diversity of atoms found in nature can be derived from a universe that originally consisted exclusively of hydrogen. Concerned with phenomena on the largest scale is cosmology, the study of the evolution of the universe. Astrophysics has transformed cosmology from an almost purely speculative activity to a modern science capable of predictions that can be tested.

Its great advances notwithstanding, astronomy is still subject to a major constraint; it is inherently an observational rather than an experimental science. Almost all measurements must be performed at great distances from the objects of interest, with no control over such quantities as their temperature, pressure, or chemical composition. There are a few exceptions to this limitation—namely, meteorites, rock and soil samples brought back from the Moon, and interplanetary dust particles collected in or above the stratosphere. These can be examined with laboratory techniques to provide information that cannot be obtained in any other way. Future space missions may yield samples of comet-tail dust or surface materials from Mars, but much of astronomy appears otherwise confined to Earth-based observations.

Determining astronomical distances.   A central problem in astronomy is the determination of distances. Without a knowledge of distances, sizes would remain nothing more than angular diameters, and stellar brightness could not be converted into true radiated power or luminosity. Astronomical distance measurement began with a knowledge of the Earth's diameter, which provided a base for triangulation. Within the inner solar system, some distances can now be better determined through the timing of radar reflections. For the outer planets, triangulation is still used. Beyond the solar system, distances to the closest stars are determined through triangulation, with the diameter of the Earth's orbit serving as the baseline and shifts in stellar parallax being the measured quantities. Stellar distances are commonly expressed by astronomers in parsecs (pc; 1 pc $= 3.086 \times 10^{18}$ centimetres) or in kiloparsecs. They can be measured out to about 50 parsecs by trigonometric parallax (see STARS AND STAR CLUSTERS: *Determining stellar distances*). Less direct measurements must be used for more distant stars and galaxies.

Use of
radar and
triangula-
tion

Only two general methods for galactic distances are described here. In the first, a clearly identifiable type of star is used as a reference standard because its luminosity (total radiated power) has been well determined. Such a star is termed a "standard candle." The distance to a standard candle can be calculated from its known luminosity and its measured intensity. Identification of the standard candle can be made through its spectrum or regular variations in brightness. (Corrections may have to be made for the absorption of starlight over great distances.) This method forms the basis of measurements of distances to the closest galaxies. It has been found that such distances generally correlate with the speeds of recession (as determined from Doppler-shifted wavelengths; see above). This correlation is expressed in the Hubble law, velocity $= H \times$ distance, with H denoting Hubble's constant, the best value of which is thought to lie between 50 and 100 kilometres per second per megaparsec (km/sec/Mpc). It is currently used to determine distances to remote galaxies in which standard candles have not been found. Application of the Hubble law, however, has been questioned as it relates to some quasars (energetic galactic nuclei), and the value of Hubble's constant cited above is still a subject of disagreement.

Methods
for deter-
mining
distances
to galaxies

Study of the solar system.   The solar system took shape 4,600,000,000 years ago, when it condensed within a large cloud of gas and dust. Gravitational attraction holds the planets in their elliptical orbits around the Sun. Besides the Earth, five major planets (Mercury, Venus, Mars, Jupiter, and Saturn) have been known from ancient times. Since then, only three others have been discovered: Uranus by accident in 1781, and Neptune and Pluto in 1846 and 1930, respectively, after deliberate searches.

The average Earth–Sun distance was originally defined as the astronomical unit (a.u.) and provides a convenient measure for distances within the solar system. The astronomical unit is now defined dynamically (using Kepler's third law), and it has the value $1.49597870 \times 10^{13}$ centimetres. The semimajor axis of the Earth's orbit is $1 + (3.1 \times 10^{-8})$ a.u. Mercury, at 0.39 a.u., is the closest planet to the Sun, while Pluto, at 39.5 a.u., is the farthest. The planes of the planetary orbits (other than that of Pluto) are all within a few degrees of the ecliptic, the plane that contains the Earth's orbit around the Sun. As viewed from far above the Earth's North Pole, all planets move in the same (counterclockwise) direction in their orbits.

All of the planets, apart from those closest to the

Sun (Mercury and Venus), have satellites whose great diversity in appearance, size, and structure has been revealed through closeup observations from long-range space probes. Three planets—Jupiter, Saturn, and Uranus—have rings consisting of small rocks and particles that are confined to disklike systems as they orbit their parent planets.

Most of the mass of the solar system is concentrated in the Sun, with its 1.99×10^{33} grams. Together, all of the planets amount to about 2.7×10^{30} grams, with Jupiter alone accounting for 71 percent of this. The solar system also contains a very large number of much smaller objects. In order of decreasing size, these are the asteroids (also called minor planets), comets, meteoroids, and dust particles.

The four terrestrial planets, Mercury, Venus, Earth, and Mars, along with the Moon, have average densities in the range 3.9–5.5 grams per cubic centimetre (g/cm^3), setting them apart from the outer planets, whose densities are all close to 1 g/cm^3, the density of water. The compositions of these two groups of planets must therefore be significantly different. This is probably attributable to the conditions that prevailed during the early development of the solar system (see below *Theories of origin*). Planetary temperatures now range from about 500° C on Mercury's surface through the typical 20° C on Earth to −135° C on Jupiter and down to −230° C on Pluto.

The surfaces of the terrestrial planets and many satellites show extensive cratering produced by high-speed impacts. On Earth, with its large quantities of water and an active atmosphere, many of these cosmic footprints have eroded, but remnants of very large craters can be seen in satellite and aerial photographs of the terrestrial surface. On Mercury, Mars, and the Moon, the absence of water and any significant atmosphere has left the craters unchanged for billions of years, apart from disturbances produced by infrequent later impacts. Cratering on the largest scale seems to have ceased about 3,000,000,000 years ago, but there is clear evidence for a continued cosmic drizzle of small particles, with the larger objects churning (gardening) the lunar surface and the smallest producing microscopic impact pits in crystals in the lunar rocks.

Lunar exploration. During the U.S. Apollo missions, a total sample weight of 381 kilograms was collected; 300 grams of lunar material also was returned by three unmanned Soviet Luna space vehicles. Less than 10 percent of the samples has so far been distributed for analysis, but planetary science has been revolutionized by these expeditions. A wide range of laboratory techniques has been employed on the lunar samples. The results of the analysis have enabled investigators to determine the composition and age of the lunar surface. Seismic techniques have made it possible to probe the lunar interior. In addition, a retroreflector left on the Moon's surface by Apollo astronauts returns a high-power laser beam emitted from the Earth, enabling researchers to monitor on a regular basis the Earth–Moon distance to an accuracy of a few centimetres. This experiment provides data that can be used in calculations of the dynamics of the Earth–Moon system.

Planetary studies. Mercury is too hot to retain an atmosphere, but Venus' brilliant white appearance is the result of its being completely enveloped by thick clouds of carbon dioxide. Below the upper clouds it has a hostile atmosphere containing clouds of sulfuric acid droplets. The cloud cover shields the planet's surface from direct sunlight, but the energy that does filter through warms the surface, which then radiates at infrared wavelengths. The long waves of infrared radiation are trapped by the dense clouds, resulting in a very high surface temperature of almost 480° C. Radar can penetrate the thick Venusian clouds and has been used to map the planet's surface. The Martian atmosphere is very thin, only about 0.006 that of the Earth, and composed mostly of carbon dioxide (95 percent), with very little water vapour. The outer planets have atmospheres composed largely of light gases. For example, hydrogen and helium, along with some methane and ammonia, have been detected on Jupiter.

Each of the planets rotates on its axis, and nearly all of them rotate in the same (counterclockwise) direction, as viewed from above the ecliptic. The two exceptions are

Venus, which rotates in the clockwise direction beneath its cloud cover, and Uranus, which has its rotational axis very nearly in the plane of the ecliptic.

Some of the planets have magnetic fields. The Earth's field extends outward until it is disturbed by the solar wind, an outward flow of protons and electrons from the Sun that carries a magnetic field along with it. Through processes not yet fully understood, protons and electrons from the solar wind and cosmic rays populate two doughnut-shaped regions called the Van Allen radiation belts, the inner of which extends from about 1,000 to 5,000 kilometres above the Earth's surface and the outer from roughly 15,000 to 25,000 kilometres. In these belts, trapped particles spiral along paths that take them around the Earth while bouncing back and forth between the Northern and Southern hemispheres. During periods of increased solar activity, these regions of trapped particles are disturbed, and some of the particles move down into the Earth's atmosphere where they collide with atoms and molecules to produce auroras.

Jupiter has a stronger magnetic field than the Earth's and many more trapped electrons, whose synchrotron radiation (electromagnetic radiation of the kind produced by electrons in accelerators called synchrotrons) is detectable from Earth. Saturn has a magnetic field that is not quite as strong as Jupiter's, but it, too, has a region of trapped particles. Mercury has a weak magnetic field that is only about 1 percent as strong as the Earth's and contains no discernible trapped particles. No magnetic field has been detected around any of the other planets.

Investigations of the minor bodies. Approximately 3,500 asteroids have now been identified. Most have orbits close to the ecliptic and move in the asteroid belt located between 2.3 and 3.3 a.u. from the Sun. Only about 250 of these objects are larger than 100 kilometres, and their total mass is thought to be roughly $^1/_{2,000}$ that of the Earth.

Comets are considered to come from a vast reservoir, the Oort cloud, which orbits the Sun at distances of 30,000 to 100,000 a.u. More than 600 comets have so far been discovered. Most make only a single pass through the inner solar system, but some are deflected by Jupiter or Saturn into orbits that allow them to return at predictable times. Comet Halley is the best known of these periodic comets, with its next return predicted for AD 2060. About 30 comets have periods of less than 100 years. Comet masses have not been well determined, but most are thought to be less than 10^{18} grams, or 1,000,000,000 times smaller than the Earth.

Even smaller than comets are the meteoroids, lumps of stony material. Meteoroids vary in size from small rocks to large boulders weighing a ton or more. A few have orbits that bring them into the Earth's atmosphere and down to the ground as meteorites. These are classified into three broad groups: stony or chondrites (about 93 percent), iron (5.7 percent), and stony-iron (1.5 percent). Smaller meteoroids that enter the atmosphere may heat up sufficiently to vaporize and appear as meteors. Many, perhaps most, of the meteors occur in showers and follow orbits that seem to be identical with those of certain comets, thus pointing to a cometary origin. For example, each May the Earth crosses the orbit of Comet Halley, and the Eta Aquarid meteor shower becomes visible. Micrometeorites, the smallest meteoroidal particles, can be detected from Earth-orbiting satellites or be sufficiently slowed by atmospheric friction to be collected by specially equipped aircraft flying in the stratosphere and returned for laboratory inspection.

Determinations of age and chemical composition. The age of the solar system, about 4,500,000,000 years, has been derived from measurements of radioactivity in meteorites, lunar samples, and the Earth's crust. Abundances of the isotopes of uranium, thorium, and rubidium and their decay products, lead and strontium, are the measured quantities.

Assessment of the chemical composition of the solar system is based on data from the Earth, Moon, and meteorites, as well as on the spectral analysis of light from the Sun and planets. In broad outline, the solar system abundances of the elements decrease with increasing atomic weight. Hydrogen atoms are by far the most abundant, with 93 percent; helium is next, with 6.7 percent; and all other types of atoms together amount to only 2.3 percent.

Theories of origin. The origin of the Earth, Moon, and solar system as a whole is a problem that has not yet been settled in detail. The Sun probably formed by condensation of the central region of a large cloud of gas and dust, with the planets and other solar-system bodies forming soon after, their composition strongly influenced by the temperature and density gradients in the evolving solar nebula. Less-volatile materials could condense into solids relatively close to the Sun to form the terrestrial planets. The abundant, volatile lighter elements could condense only at much greater distances.

The origin of the planetary satellites is not settled. There is still the question as to the origin of the Moon, and professional opinion has been oscillating between theories that see its origin and condensation simultaneous with the formation of the Earth, to an explanation in terms of a large impact on the Earth resulting in the expulsion of material that subsequently formed the Moon. For the outer planets with their multiple satellites, many very small and quite unlike one another, the picture is even less clear. Some of the objects have icy surfaces, while others are heavily cratered, and at least one, Jupiter's Io, is volcanic. Some of the satellites may have formed along with their parent planets, and others may have formed elsewhere and been captured. (For an in-depth treatment of the solar system and its components, see SOLAR SYSTEM.)

Study of the stars. *Measuring observable stellar properties.* The measurable quantities in stellar astrophyics include the externally observable features of the stars: distance, temperature spectrum and luminosity, composition (of the outer layers), diameter, mass, and variability in any of these. Theoretical astrophysicists use these observations to model the structure of stars and to devise theories for their formation and evolution.

In a system dating back at least to the Greek astronomer-mathematician Hipparchus in the 2nd century BC, apparent stellar brightness (m) is measured in magnitudes. Magnitudes are now defined so that a first-magnitude star is 100 times brighter than a star of sixth magnitude. The human eye cannot see stars fainter than about sixth magnitude, but modern instruments used with large telescopes can record stars as faint as about 26th magnitude. By convention, the absolute magnitude (M) is the magnitude that a star would appear to have if it were located at a standard distance of 10 parsecs. These quantities are related through the expression: $m - M = 5 \log_{10} r - 5$, where r is the star's distance in parsecs.

The magnitude scale is anchored on a group of standard stars. An absolute measure of radiant power is luminosity, usually expressed in ergs per second. This can be calculated when m and r are known. Correction might be necessary for the interstellar absorption of starlight.

There are several methods of measuring a star's diameter. From the brightness and distance, the luminosity (L) can be calculated; and from observations of the brightness at different wavelengths, the temperature (T) can be calculated. As the radiation from many stars can be well approximated by a Planck blackbody spectrum, these measured quantities can be related through the expression $L = 4\pi R^2 \sigma T^4$, thus providing a means of calculating R, the star's radius. In this expression, σ is Stefan's constant, 5.67×10^{-5} erg/cm^{2}deg^{4}sec. (The radius R refers to the star's photosphere, the region where the star becomes effectively opaque to outside observation.) Stellar angular diameters can be measured through interference effects. Alternatively, it is possible to monitor the intensity of the starlight during occultation by the Moon, which produces diffraction fringes whose pattern depends on the angular diameter of the star. Stellar angular diameters of several milliarcseconds can be measured, but so far only for relatively bright and close stars.

Many stars occur in binary systems, with the two partners in orbits around their mutual centre of mass. Such a system provides the best measurement of stellar masses. The period (P) of a binary system is related to the masses of the two stars ($m_1 + m_2$), and the orbital semimajor axis

a via Kepler's third law: $P^2 = 4\pi^2 a^3 / G[m_1 + m_2]$. ($G$ is, as before, the universal gravitational constant.) From diameters and masses, average values of the stellar density can be calculated, and thence the central pressure. With the assumption of an equation of state, the central temperature can then be calculated. Thus, for example, in the Sun the central density is 158 g/cm^3, and the pressure is calculated to be more than 1,000,000,000 atmospheres and the temperature about 15,000,000 K. At this temperature, all atoms are ionized, and so the solar interior consists of a plasma, an ionized gas, with hydrogen and helium nuclei and electrons as major constituents. A small fraction of the hydrogen nuclei possess such high speeds that, upon colliding, their electrostatic repulsion is overcome, resulting in the formation by fusion of helium nuclei and a release of energy. Some of this energy is carried away by neutrinos, but most of it is carried by photons to the surface of the Sun to maintain its luminosity.

Other stars, both more and less massive than the Sun, have broadly similar structures, but the size, central pressure and temperature, and fusion rate are functions of a star's mass and composition. Stars and their internal fusion (and resultant luminosity) are held stable against collapse through a delicate balance between the inward pressure produced by gravitational attraction and the outward pressure supplied by the photons produced in the fusion reactions.

Stars that are in this condition of hydrostatic equilibrium are termed main-sequence stars, and they occupy a well-defined band on the Hertzsprung–Russell (H–R) diagram, in which luminosity is plotted against colour index or temperature. Temperature is deduced from broadband spectral measurements in several standard wavelength intervals. Measurement of apparent magnitudes in the B and V bands (centred on 4350 and 5550 angstroms [Å], respectively) permits calculation of the colour index, $CI = m_B - m_V$, from which the temperature can be calculated.

For a given temperature, there are stars that have luminosity much greater than main-sequence stars. Given the $R^2 T^4$ dependence of luminosity, greater luminosity implies a larger radius, and such stars are called giants or supergiants. Conversely, stars with a luminosity much less than that of main-sequence stars of the same temperature must be smaller and are termed dwarfs. White dwarfs are stars with temperatures that typically range from 10,000 to 12,000 K, and they appear visually as white or blue-white.

Spectral classification, based initially on the colour index, has major spectral types O, B, A, F, G, K, and M, each subdivided into 10 parts. The strength of spectral lines of the more abundant elements in a star's atmosphere allows additional subdivisions within a class. Thus the Sun, a main-sequence star, is classified as G2 V, where the V denotes main sequence. Betelgeuse, a red supergiant with a surface temperature about half that of the Sun but with a luminosity of about 10,000 solar units, is classified as M2 Iab. (For more specific information about stellar spectra and bulk stellar properties, see STARS AND STAR CLUSTERS.)

Stellar formation and evolution. The range of physically allowable masses for stars is very narrow. If the star's mass is too small, the central temperature will be too low to sustain fusion reactions. The theoretical minimum stellar mass is about 0.08 solar mass. An upper theoretical limit of approximately 100 solar masses has been suggested, but this value is not firmly defined. Stars as massive as this will have luminosities about 1,000,000 times greater than that of the Sun.

A general model of star formation and evolution has been developed, and the major features seem to be established. This model shows that a large cloud of gas and dust can contract under its own gravitational attraction if its temperature is sufficiently low. Gravitational energy is released, and the contracting central material heats up until a point is reached where the outward radiation pressure balances the inward gravitational pressure and contraction ceases. Fusion reactions take over as the star's primary source of energy, and the star is then on the main sequence. The time required to pass through these

Basis for theoretical work

Methods of measuring stellar diameter

Determining stellar mass

Use of the Hertzsprung–Russell diagram

Spectral classification

Prevailing conception of star formation and evolution

formative stages and onto the main sequence is less than 100,000,000 years for a star with as much mass as the Sun. It takes longer for less massive stars and a much shorter time for those much more massive.

Once a star has reached its main-sequence stage, it evolves relatively slowly, with the fusion of the hydrogen nuclei in its core to form helium nuclei. Continued fusion not only releases the energy that is radiated but also involves nucleosynthesis, the production of heavier nuclei.

Computer modeling of stellar evolution

Stellar evolution has been followed through computer modeling because the time scales for most stages are generally too extended for measurable changes to be seen even over a period of many years. One exception is the supernova, where major changes have been seen on a scale of hours, and computations have shown that some changes take place on a scale of milliseconds. Calculation of nucleosynthesis during stable and explosive stellar stages has yielded abundances of nuclei in general agreement with observed abundances.

The nature of the terminal products of stellar evolution depend on stellar mass. Some stars pass through an unstable stage in which their dimensions, temperature, and luminosity change cyclically over periods of hours or days. These so-called Cepheid variables serve as standard candles for distance measurements. Some stars may blow off their outer layers to produce planetary nebulas. The expanding material can be seen glowing in a thin shell as it disperses into the interstellar medium, while the remnant core, initially with a surface temperature of as high as 100,000 K, cools to become a white dwarf. The maximum stellar mass that can exist as a white dwarf is about 1.4 solar masses and is called the Chandrasekhar limit. More massive stars may end up as either neutron stars or black holes (see below).

The average density of a white dwarf is calculated to exceed 1,000,000 g/cm³. Further compression is limited by a quantum condition called degeneracy, in which only certain energies are allowed for electrons. Under sufficiently great pressure, the electrons combine with protons to form neutrons. The resulting neutron star will have a density in the range 10^{14}–10^{15} g/cm³, which is comparable to the density within atomic nuclei. The behaviour of large masses having nuclear densities is not yet sufficiently understood to be able to set a limit on the maximum size of a neutron star, but it is thought to be in the region of five solar masses.

Still more massive remnants of stellar evolution would have smaller dimensions and would be even denser than neutron stars. Such remnants are conceived to be black holes, objects so compact that no radiation can escape from their gravitational force within a characteristic distance called the Schwarzschild radius. This critical dimension is defined by $R_S = 2GM/c^2$. (Here, R_S is the Schwarzschild radius, G is the gravitational constant, M is the object's mass, and c is the speed of light.) For an object of three solar masses, the R_S would be about three kilometres.

Search for black holes

Although no light can be detected from a black hole, the presence of such an object may be manifested in the effects of its gravitational field, as, for example, in a binary star system. If a black hole is a member of a double star, it may pull matter from its companion—a normal visible star—toward itself. This matter is accelerated as it approaches the black hole and becomes so intensely heated that it radiates large amounts of X rays from the periphery of the black hole outside the Schwarzschild radius. A few candidates for black holes have been found (*e.g.*, the X-ray source Cygnus X-1). Each of them has an estimated mass clearly exceeding that allowable for a neutron star, a factor crucial in the identification of possible black holes. (For further information on black holes, as well as on stellar evolution, see STARS AND STAR CLUSTERS; COSMOS: *The end states of stars: Black-hole model for active galactic nuclei.*)

Whereas the detection of black holes still needs to be confirmed, the existence of neutron stars was proved in 1968 when they were identified with the then newly discovered pulsars, objects characterized by the emission of radiation at short and extremely regular intervals generally between one and 1,000 pulses per second and stable to better than one part per billion. Pulsars are regarded as rotating neutron stars, the remnants of some supernovas.

Study of the Milky Way Galaxy. *General properties.* Stars are not distributed randomly throughout space. Many stars occur in systems consisting of two or three members with separations of less than 1,000 a.u. On a larger scale, clusters may contain many thousands of stars. Galaxies are much larger systems of stars and usually include clouds of gas and dust.

The solar system is located within the Milky Way Galaxy close to the equatorial plane and about 8.7 kiloparsecs (kpc) from the galactic centre. The galactic diameter is about 30 kiloparsecs, as indicated by luminous matter. There is evidence, however, for nonluminous matter—the so-called dark matter—extending out nearly twice this distance. The entire galactic system is rotating so that, at the position of the Sun, the orbital speed is about 220 kilometres per second, and a complete circuit will take roughly 240,000,000 years. Application of Kepler's third law leads to an estimate of the galactic mass of about 100,000,000,000 solar masses. The rotational velocity can be measured from the Doppler shifts observed in the 21-centimetre emission line of neutral hydrogen and the lines of millimetre wavelengths from various molecules, especially carbon monoxide. At great distances from the galactic centre, the rotational velocity does not drop off as expected but rather increases slightly. This condition appears to require a much larger galactic mass than can be accounted for by the known (luminous) matter. Additional evidence for the presence of dark matter comes from a variety of other observations. The nature and extent of the dark matter (or missing mass) constitutes one of today's major astronomical puzzles.

The problem of dark matter

There are about 100,000,000,000 stars in the Milky Way Galaxy. Star concentrations within the Galaxy fall into three types: open clusters, globular clusters, and associations. Open clusters lie primarily in the disk of the Galaxy and contain from 50 to 1,000 stars within a region of no more than 10 parsecs. Associations tend to have somewhat fewer stars; moreover, the constituent stars are not as closely grouped as those in the clusters and are for the most part hotter. Globular clusters may extend up to about 100 parsecs in size and may have as many as 100,000 stars. The importance of the globular clusters lies in their use as indicators of the age of the Galaxy. Because massive stars evolve more rapidly than do smaller stars, the age of a cluster can be estimated from its H–R diagram. In a young cluster the main sequence will be well populated, but in an old cluster the heavier stars will have evolved away from the main sequence. The extent of the depopulation of the main sequence provides an index of age. In this way, the oldest globular clusters have been found to be about 15,000,000,000 years old, which must therefore be the minimum age of the Galaxy.

Determining the age of the Milky Way with the aid of globular clusters

Investigations of interstellar matter. The interstellar medium (ISM) occupies the regions that lie between the stars. On average, it contains less than one atom per cubic centimetre, with about 1 percent as much mass in the form of minute dust grains. The gas, mostly hydrogen, has been mapped through its 21-centimetre emission line. The gas also contains numerous molecules. Some of these have been detected by the visible-wavelength absorption lines they impose on the spectra of more distant stars, while others have been identified by their own emission lines at millimetre wavelengths. Many of the interstellar molecules occur in giant molecular clouds, wherein complex organic molecules have been discovered.

In the vicinity of a very hot O- or B-type star, the intensity of ultraviolet radiation is sufficiently high to ionize the surrounding hydrogen out to a distance as large as 100 parsecs to produce an HII region known as a Strömgren sphere. Such regions are strong and characteristic emitters of radiation at radio wavelengths, and their dimensions are well calibrated in terms of the luminosity of the central star. Using radio interferometers, astronomers are able to measure the angular diameters of HII regions even in some external galaxies and can thereby deduce the great distances to those remote systems. This method can be used for distances up to about 30 megaparsecs.

Measuring the angular diameters of HII regions

Interstellar dust grains scatter and absorb starlight, with the effect being roughly inversely proportional to wavelength from the infrared to the near ultraviolet. As a result, stellar spectra tend to be reddened. Absorption amounts typically to about one magnitude per kiloparsec but varies considerably in different directions. Some dusty regions contain silicate materials, identified by a broad absorption feature around 10-micrometre wavelengths. Another prominent feature around 2200 angstroms has sometimes but not conclusively been attributed to graphite grains.

Starlight often shows a small degree of polarization (a few percent), with the effect increasing with stellar distance. This is attributed to the scattering of the starlight from dust grains that have been partially aligned in a weak interstellar magnetic field. The strength of this field is estimated to be a few microgauss, very close to the strength inferred from observations of nonthermal cosmic radio noise. This radio background has been identified as synchrotron radiation, emitted by highly relativistic cosmic-ray electrons (*i.e.,* those traveling at nearly the speed of light) that pass through the interstellar magnetic field. The spectrum of the cosmic radio noise is close to what is calculated on the basis of measurements of the cosmic rays near the Earth.

The cosmic rays constitute another component of the interstellar medium. Cosmic rays that are detected in the vicinity of the Earth consist of high-speed nuclei and electrons. Individual particle energies, expressed in electron volts (eV; $1 \text{ eV} = 1.6 \times 10^{-12}$ erg), range with decreasing numbers from about 10^6 to more than 10^{20} eV. Among the nuclei, hydrogen (protons) are the most plentiful at 89 percent, helium next with 9 percent, and all other nuclei at about 1 percent. Electrons are roughly 2 percent as abundant as the nuclear component.

A minority of the cosmic rays are produced in the Sun, especially at times of increased solar activity (as indicated by sunspots and flares). The origin of the galactic cosmic rays has not yet been conclusively identified, but they are thought to be produced in stellar processes such as supernova explosions, perhaps with additional acceleration occurring in the interstellar regions.

Observations of the galactic centre. The central region of the Milky Way Galaxy is so heavily obscured by large quantities of dust that direct observation has become possible only with the development of astronomy for wavelengths that penetrate to or relatively near the Earth's surface—namely, radio, infrared, and more recently X rays and gamma rays. Together, these observations have revealed a nuclear region of intense activity, with a large number of separate sources and a great deal of dust. Detection of gamma-ray emission at a line energy of 511,000 eV, which corresponds to the annihilation of electrons and positrons, along with radio mapping of a region no more than 20 a.u. across, points to a very compact and energetic source at the centre of the Galaxy. Whether this is powered by a black hole or some very close and hot stars remains to be determined. (For more specific information on this matter, see COSMOS: *Galaxies.*)

Study of other galaxies and related phenomena. Galaxies are generally classified into three principal types according to their appearance: spiral, elliptical, and irregular. Galactic dimensions are typically in the tens of kiloparsecs and the distances between galaxies typically in megaparsecs.

Spiral galaxies (of which the Milky Way system is a characteristic example) tend to be flattened, roughly circular systems, with their constituent stars strongly concentrated along spiral arms. These arms are thought to be produced by traveling density waves, which compress and expand the galactic material. (For an explanation of the density-wave theory, see COSMOS: *Dynamics of ellipticals and spirals.*) Between the spiral arms exists a diffuse interstellar medium of gas and dust, mostly at very low temperatures (below 100 K). Spiral galaxies are typically a few kiloparsecs in thickness; they have a central bulge and taper gradually toward the outer edges.

Ellipticals show none of the spiral features. They are more densely packed stellar systems, ranging from the nearly spherical (type E0) to the very flattened (E7), and they contain little interstellar matter. Irregular galaxies

account for only a few percent of all stellar systems and exhibit none of the regular features associated with either spirals or ellipticals.

Properties vary considerably between the different types of galaxies. Spirals generally have masses in the range 10^9–10^{12} solar masses, with ellipticals having values from 10 times smaller to 10 times larger and the irregulars, generally 10 times larger. The visual galactic luminosities show similar spreads, but the irregulars tend to be less luminous. In contrast, at radio wavelengths the maximum luminosity of spirals is usually 100,000 times less than for ellipticals or irregulars.

Quasars are objects whose spectra display very large redshifts, implying that they lie at the greatest distances (see above). They were discovered in 1963, but they remained enigmatic for many years. Quasars are now considered to be the exceedingly luminous cores of distant galaxies.

The Milky Way Galaxy is a member of the Local Group of galaxies, which contains about two dozen members and extends out to a distance of about one megaparsec. Two of the closest members are the Large and Small Magellanic Clouds, irregular galaxies about 50 kiloparsecs away. At 680 kiloparsecs, the Andromeda Galaxy is one of the most distant in the Local Group. Some members of the Local Group are moving toward the Milky Way system, while others are traveling away from it. At greater distances, all galaxies are moving away from the Milky Way Galaxy. Their speeds (as determined from the redshifted wavelengths in their spectra) are proportional to their distances. As explained earlier, the Hubble law relates these two quantities. In the absence of any other method, the Hubble law continues to be used for distance determinations to the farthest objects—that is, galaxies and quasars for which redshifts can be measured. (For a detailed treatment of the properties, structures, and distribution of galaxies, see GALAXIES.)

Cosmology. The currently accepted cosmological model is the big bang. In this picture, the expansion of the universe began with an intense explosion roughly 15,000,000,000 years ago. In this primordial fireball, the temperature exceeded 10^{12} K and most of the energy was in the form of radiation. As the expansion proceeded (accompanied by cooling), the role of the radiation became diminished and other physical processes dominated in turn. Thus, after about one minute, the temperature had dropped to the 1,000,000,000 K range, making it possible for nuclear reactions to take place and produce deuterons and helium nuclei. (At the higher temperatures that prevailed earlier, these nuclei would have been promptly disrupted by high-energy photons.) With further expansion, the time between nuclear collisions would have increased and the proportion of deuterons and helium nuclei would have stabilized. After a few hundred thousand years, the temperature must have dropped sufficiently for electrons to remain attached to nuclei to constitute atoms. Galaxies are thought to have begun forming after a few million years, but this stage is still very poorly understood. Star formation probably started much later, after some billions of years, and the process continues today.

The observational support for this general model comes from several independent directions. The expansion has been documented by the galactic redshifted spectra. The radiation left over from the original fireball would have cooled with the expansion. One of the most striking discoveries of the 20th century came in 1965 with the observation of a widespread cosmic radiation corresponding to a temperature of close to 3 K. The spectrum of this cosmic radio noise peaks at approximately one-millimetre wavelength in the far infrared, a difficult region to observe; however, the spectrum has been well mapped at many wavelengths from that point through the radio region. Additional support for the big-bang theory comes from the observed cosmic abundances of deuterium and helium. Normal stellar nucleosynthesis cannot produce the measured quantities, which fit well with calculations of production during the early stages of the big bang.

Surveys of the cosmic 3 K radiation have indicated that it is extremely uniform in all directions. Calculations have shown that it is difficult to achieve this degree of isotropy

Margin notes:

Observations of nonthermal cosmic radio noise

Classification of galaxies

Identification of quasars

The big-bang model and observational support

unless there was a very early and rapid inflationary period before the expansion settled into its present mode. However, the isotropy poses problems for models of galaxy formation. It has been conjectured that galaxies originate from turbulent conditions that produce local fluctuations of density toward which matter would then be gravitationally attracted. Such density variations are difficult to reconcile with the isotropy required by observations of the 3 K background radiation.

The very earliest stages of the big bang are less well understood. The conditions of temperature and density that prevailed prior to the first microsecond require the introduction of theoretical ideas of subatomic particles. Such particles are usually studied in laboratories with giant accelerators, but the region of particle energies of potential significance to the question at hand lies beyond the range of accelerators currently available. Fortunately, some important conclusions can be drawn from the observed cosmic helium abundance, which is dependent on conditions during the early big bang. This observed helium abundance serves to set a limit to the number of families of certain types of subatomic particles that can exist.

Finally, there is the question of the future behaviour of the universe: Is it open? That is to say, will the expansion continue indefinitely? Or is it closed, so that the expansion will slow down and eventually reverse, resulting in contraction? The outcome hinges on the total mass of the universe. For this reason, the extent of the dark matter (the missing mass) may be decisive. The amount of luminous mass currently known to exist is insufficient to close the universe, but if dark matter is universally present in the quantities suggested by galactic rotation or galactic-cluster dynamics, then the universe will be closed. An additional factor might be the mass of neutrinos. Theoretically postulated to have zero mass, neutrinos are now experimentally known to have a mass less than $1/10{,}000$ that of the electron. Because there are so many neutrinos in the universe, neutrino masses even as small as this might render the universe closed. The issue remains unresolved, although the detection of neutrinos (albeit only 19 of them) associated with a supernova observed in 1987 suggests that neutrino mass is probably less than the critical value postulated. (For a full discussion of the big-bang theory, including conceptions about the ultimate fate of the universe, see COSMOS: *Cosmological models.*)

THE METHODOLOGY OF ASTRONOMY

Astronomical observations involve a sequence of stages, each of which may impose constraints on the type of information attainable. Radiant energy is collected with telescopes and brought to a focus on a detector, which is calibrated so that its sensitivity and spectral response are known. Accurate pointing is required to permit the correlation of observations made with different systems in different wavelength intervals. The radiation must be spectrally analyzed so that the emission processes can be identified.

Telescopic observations. Before Galileo's use of telescopes for astronomical investigations in 1609, all observations were made by naked eye, with corresponding limits on the faintness and degree of detail that could be seen. Since that time, telescopes have become central to astronomy. With apertures much larger than the pupil of the human eye, telescopes permit the study of faint and distant objects. In addition, sufficient radiant energy can be collected in short time intervals to permit rapid fluctuations in intensity to be detected.

Optical telescopes are either refractors or reflectors that use lenses or mirrors, respectively, for their main light-collecting elements (objectives). Refractors are effectively limited to apertures with a diameter of 102 centimetres (40 inches) or less because of problems inherent in the use of large lenses. These distort under their own weight and can be supported only around the perimeter; an appreciable amount of light is lost due to absorption in the glass. Large-aperture refractors are extremely long and require large and expensive domes. The largest modern telescopes are all reflectors. They are not subject to the chromatic problems of refractors, can be better supported mechan-

Optical telescopes

ically, and can be housed in smaller domes because of their more compact dimensions.

The angular resolving power of a single telescope is limited by the wave nature of light. For a telescope having an objective with diameter D and operating at a wavelength λ, the angular resolution (in radians) can be approximately described by the ratio (λ/D). Optical telescopes can have very high intrinsic resolving powers, but in practice, however, these are not attained. Atmospheric effects limit the resolution to about one arc second.

The atmosphere does not transmit radiation of all wavelengths equally well. This restricts ground-based astronomy to the visible and radio regions of the spectrum, with some relatively narrow "windows" in the nearer infrared. Longer infrared wavelengths are heavily absorbed by atmospheric water vapour and carbon dioxide. Atmospheric effects can be reduced by careful site selection and by carrying out observations at high altitudes. Most major optical observatories are now located on high mountains, well away from cities and their reflected lights. Infrared telescopes have been constructed atop Mauna Kea in Hawaii and in the Canary Islands where atmospheric humidity is very low. Airborne telescopes designed mainly for infrared observations, such as the one aboard the Kuiper Airborne Observatory, operate at an altitude of about 12,000 metres (40,000 feet), with flight durations limited to a few hours. Telescopes for infrared-, X-, and gamma-ray observations have been carried to altitudes of more than 30,000 metres by balloons. Higher altitudes can be attained during short-duration rocket flights for ultraviolet observations. Telescopes for all wavelengths from infrared to gamma rays have been carried by remote-controlled Earth-orbiting satellites as well as by some manned space vehicles.

Observations from aircraft, balloons, rockets, and Earth-orbiting spacecraft

Angular resolution better than one milliarcsecond has been achieved at radio wavelengths by using several telescopes in an array. In such an arrangement, the effective aperture (D) becomes the greatest distance between component telescopes. For example, in the Very Large Array (VLA), operated near Socorro, N.M., by the National Radio Astronomy Observatory, 27 movable radio dishes are set out along tracks that extend for nearly 21 kilometres. In a technique called very long baseline interferometry (VLBI), simultaneous observations are made with radio telescopes thousands of kilometres apart.

Very long baseline interferometry

The Earth is a moving platform for astronomical observations. It is important that the specification of precise celestial coordinates be made in ways that correct for telescope location, the position of the Earth in its orbit around the Sun, and the epoch of observation, since the Earth's axis of rotation moves slowly over the years. Time measurements are now based on atomic clocks rather than on the Earth's rotation, and telescopes can be driven continuously to compensate for the planet's rotation so as to permit tracking of a given astronomical object.

Use of radiation detectors. While the human eye remains an important astronomical tool, detectors capable of greater sensitivity and more rapid response are needed at visible wavelengths and especially to extend observations beyond that region of the electromagnetic spectrum. Photography has been used for more than 100 years and continues to be an essential tool. Long time exposures may be needed to reveal faint objects. This integrative property of photography smooths out rapid variations in intensity, for which electronic methods must otherwise be used. Furthermore, photography provides an archival record. A photograph of a particular celestial object may include the images of many other objects that were not of interest when the picture was taken but that become the focus of study years later. When quasars were discovered in 1963, for example, photographic plates dating to before 1900, held by the Harvard College Observatory, were examined to trace possible changes in the position or intensity of quasar 3C273. Also, major photographic surveys, such as those of the National Geographic Society and Palomar Observatory, can provide a historic base for long-term studies.

Photography in astronomical research

Photographic film converts only a few percent of the incident photons into its images, whereas efficiencies of better than 50 percent can be achieved by several electronic methods of detection. The greater sensitivity and intrinsically rapid response of such methods are exploited for tracking exceedingly rapid intensity variations. For example, pulsars that emit their radiation at millisecond intervals can be followed and their pulse shapes monitored. The arrival of individual photons can be recorded with phototubes or more recent devices, such as the charge-coupled device (CCD). Special photographic materials can be employed for the shortest infrared wavelengths, but, for wavelengths longer than a few micrometres, semiconductor detectors that operate at temperatures of liquid nitrogen (77 K) or liquid helium (below 4 K) have to be used. In detectors of this kind, photons are absorbed in small semiconducting crystals to produce a minute temperature increase or a change in electrical resistance. Individual photons are not recorded. Reception of radio waves is based on the production of a small voltage in an antenna rather than on photon counting. Individual X-ray and gamma-ray photons possess sufficient energy to be detected through the ionization they produce.

Spectral analysis
Spectral analysis involves measuring intensity as a function of wavelength or frequency. In some detectors, such as those for X and gamma rays, the energy of each photon can be measured directly. Photographic film is sensitive to photons over a wide range of wavelengths. For low-resolution spectroscopy, broad-band filters suffice. Greater resolution can be obtained with prisms, gratings, and interferometers.

As a departure from the traditional astronomical approach of remote observing, certain more recent lines of research involve the analysis of actual samples under laboratory conditions. These include studies of meteorites, rock samples returned from the Moon, and interplanetary dust particles collected by aircraft in the stratosphere or by Earth-orbiting spacecraft. In all such cases, a wide range of highly sensitive laboratory techniques can be adapted for the often microscopic samples. It is possible to supplement chemical analysis with mass spectroscopy, so that the isotopic composition can be determined. Radioactivity and collisions between cosmic-ray particles can produce minute quantities of gas that remain trapped in crystals. Heating under laboratory conditions releases this gas, which then is analyzed in a mass spectrometer. X-ray spectrometers, electron microscopes, and microprobes are employed to determine crystal structure and composition, from which temperature and pressure conditions at the time of formation can be inferred.

Theoretical approaches. Theory is just as important as observation in astronomy. It is required for the interpretation of observational data, for the construction of models of celestial objects and their properties, and for guiding
Theoretical astrophysics
further observations. Theoretical astrophysics is based on the laws of physics that have been validated with great precision through controlled experiments. Application of these laws to specific astrophysical problems, however, may yield equations too complex for direct solution. Two general approaches are then available. In the traditional method, an idealized description of the problem is formulated, incorporating only the major physical components, to provide equations that can be either solved directly or evaluated numerically. Alternatively, a computer program that will explore the problem numerically can be devised. Computational science is taking its place as a major division alongside theory and experiment.

IMPACT OF ASTRONOMY

No area of science is totally self-contained. Discoveries in one field find applications in others, often unpredictably. There are various notable examples of this involving astronomical studies. Newton's laws of motion and gravity emerged from the analysis of planetary and lunar orbits. Observations during the 1919 solar eclipse provided dramatic confirmation of Einstein's general theory of relativity, which has gained further support with the recent discovery and tracking of the binary pulsar designated PSR 1913 + 16. The behaviour of nuclear matter and of some elementary particles is now better understood as a result of measurements of neutron stars and the cosmological helium abundance, respectively. Study of the

theory of synchrotron radiation was greatly stimulated by its detection in radiation emitted by the Crab Nebula, and machines are now being used to produce synchrotron radiation to probe the structure of materials.

Astronomical knowledge also has had impact outside of science. The earliest calendars were based on astronomical observations of the cycles of repeated solar and lunar positions. Also, for centuries, familiarity with the positions and apparent motions of the stars enabled sea voyagers to navigate with reasonable accuracy. Perhaps the single greatest effect that astronomical studies have had on modern society has been in molding the attitude of its members. The development of what is known as the scientific method was strongly influenced by astronomical observations. The power of science to provide the basis for accurate predictions of such phenomena as eclipses and the positions of the planets and later, so dramatically, of comets has generated an attitude toward science that remains an important social force today.   (M.W.Fr.)

BIBLIOGRAPHY

History of physical sciences: A. RUPERT HALL and MARIE BOAS HALL, *A Brief History of Science* (1964, reprinted 1988), provides a good introduction to the subject; A.E.E. MCKENZIE, *The Major Achievements of Science,* 2 vol. (1960, reprinted 1988), concentrates on developments from the 16th century, with brief extracts from original sources; and CECIL J. SCHNEER, *The Search for Order: The Development of the Major Ideas in the Physical Sciences from the Earliest Times to the Present* (1960, reissued 1984 as *The Evolution of Physical Science*), accounts for the developments from the 17th through the 19th centuries. Comprehensive surveys include STEPHEN F. MASON, *A History of the Sciences,* new rev. ed. (1962); and STEPHEN TOULMIN and JUNE GOODFIELD, *The Architecture of Matter* (1962, reissued 1982). THOMAS S. KUHN, *The Structure of Scientific Revolutions,* 2nd enl. ed. (1970), presents the "paradigm" theory of science, based on historical examples; GERALD HOLTON, *Thematic Origins of Scientific Thought: Kepler to Einstein,* rev. ed. (1988), offers a new interpretation of the history of science, with case studies of the work of Einstein and others; and I. BERNARD COHEN, *Revolution in Science* (1985), is a comparative study. See also STEPHEN G. BRUSH, *The History of Modern Science: A Guide to the Second Scientific Revolution, 1800–1950* (1988). CHARLES COULSTON GILLISPIE (ed.), *Dictionary of Scientific Biography,* 16 vol. (1970–80), is an excellent source for authoritative biographical data. For references to the scholarly literature in the history of science, consult the "Critical Bibliography of the History of Science and Its Cultural Influences," an annual feature in *Isis,* an international review of the history of science. Cumulations of this bibliography appeared as MAGDA WHITROW (ed.), *Isis Cumulative Bibliography: 1913–65,* 6 vol. (1971–84); and JOHN NEU (ed.), *Isis Cumulative Bibliography 1966–1975,* 2 vol. (1980–85).

Physics: I. BERNARD COHEN, *The Birth of a New Physics,* rev. ed. (1985), is an account of the work of Galileo, Newton, and other 17th-century scientists. See also EMILIO SEGRÈ, *From Falling Bodies to Radio Waves: Classical Physicists and Their Discoveries* (1984), and *From X-Rays to Quarks: Modern Physicists and Their Discoveries* (1980; originally published in Italian, 1976). HENRY A. BOORSE and LLOYD MOTZ (eds.), *The World of the Atom,* 2 vol. (1966), is a comprehensive anthology of historical sources on 19th- and 20th-century developments in atomic physics. For recent history, see STEPHEN G. BRUSH, "Resource Letter HP-1: History of Physics," *American Journal of Physics,* 55:683-691 (August 1987). An interesting collection of writings by physicists is presented in JEFFERSON HANE WEAVER (ed.), *The World of Physics: A Small Library of the Literature of Physics from Antiquity to the Present,* 3 vol. (1987).

Reference works surveying the scope and methodology of physics include ROBERT M. BESANÇON (ed.), *The Encyclopedia of Physics,* 3rd ed. (1985); and CESARE EMILIANI, *Dictionary of the Physical Sciences: Terms, Formulas, Data* (1987). Other works include DAVID HALLIDAY and ROBERT RESNICK, *Fundamentals of Physics,* 3rd extended ed., 2 vol. (1988), a good standard text; GERALD HOLTON, *Introduction to Concepts and Theories in Physical Science,* 2nd ed., rev. by STEPHEN G. BRUSH (1973, reprinted 1985), analyzing the physical theories from a historical standpoint; RICHARD P. FEYNMAN, ROBERT B. LEIGHTON, and MATTHEW SANDS, *The Feynman Lectures on Physics,* 3 vol. (1963–65), and RICHARD P. FEYNMAN, *QED: The Strange Theory of Light and Matter* (1985), works by a modern master; FRANK CLOSE, MICHAEL MARTEN, and CHRISTINE SUTTON, *The Particle Explosion* (1987), a discussion of the latest developments in fundamental physics, written for the general reader; STEVEN WEINBERG, *The Discovery of Subatomic Particles* (1983), and *The First Three Minutes: A Modern View of the Origin of the Universe,* updated ed. (1988); P.C.W. DAVIES, *Space and Time in the Modern Universe* (1977); and PETER G. BERGMANN, *The Riddle of Gravitation,* rev. ed. (1987). An unusual social history of the U.S. scientific community is presented in DANIEL J. KEVLES, *The Physicists* (1978, reprinted 1987).

Chemistry: Historical developments in chemistry through the 17th century are explored in ROBERT P. MULTHAUF, *The Origins of Chemistry* (1966). CECIL J. SCHNEER, *Mind and Matter: Man's Changing Concepts of the Material World* (1970, reprinted 1988), gives an interesting account of the history of chemistry in relation to the structure of matter; AARON J. IHDE, *The Development of Modern Chemistry* (1964, reprinted 1984), is a comprehensive history covering the 18th to the middle of the 20th century; and FREDERIC LAWRENCE HOLMES, *Lavoisier and the Chemistry of Life: An Exploration of Scientific Creativity* (1985), is a study of chemical experimentation.

Concise explanations of chemical terms can be found in DOUGLAS M. CONSIDINE and GLENN D. CONSIDINE (eds.), *Van Nostrand Reinhold Encyclopedia of Chemistry,* 4th ed. (1984), a specialized reference work. Comprehensive treatment of chemical theories and reactivity is presented in DONALD A. MCQUARRIE and PETER A. ROCK, *General Chemistry,* 2nd ed. (1987); and in JOHN C. KOTZ and KEITH F. PURCELL, *Chemistry & Chemical Reactivity* (1987). Studies of common applications of chemistry, intended for the general reader, include WILLIAM R. STINE *et al., Applied Chemistry,* 2nd ed. (1981); and JOHN W. HILL, *Chemistry for Changing Times,* 5th ed. (1988). An overview of modern chemistry and discussion of its prospects is found in GEORGE C. PIMENTEL and JANICE A. COONROD, *Opportunities in Chemistry: Today and Tomorrow* (1987). P.W. ATKINS, *Molecules* (1987), is a pictorial examination of chemical structure. LIONEL SALEM, *Marvels of the Molecule,* trans. from French (1987), presents the molecular orbital theory of chemical bonding in simple terms. The extent to which molecular structure has become central to biochemistry is demonstrated in the articles in *The Molecules of Life: Readings from Scientific American* (1985). The fundamental principles governing chemical change and the laws of thermodynamics are presented, with a minimum of mathematics, in P.W. ATKINS, *The Second Law* (1984); and JOHN B. FENN, *Engines, Energy, and Entropy: A Thermodynamics Primer* (1982). Social aspects of developments in chemistry, especially the environmental costs of use of chemical products, are studied in LUCIANO CAGLIOTI, *The Two Faces of Chemistry,* trans. from Italian (1983).

Astronomy: ANTONIE PANNEKOEK, *A History of Astronomy* (1961, reissued 1969; originally published in Dutch, 1951); and STEPHEN TOULMIN and JUNE GOODFIELD, *The Fabric of the Heavens* (1961), are comprehensive surveys. THOMAS S. KUHN, *The Copernican Revolution: Planetary Astronomy in the Development of Western Thought* (1957), discusses the ancient geo-centric theory of the universe and the heliocentric system that replaced it. CHARLES A. WHITNEY, *The Discovery of Our Galaxy* (1971, reprinted 1988), explains theories and observations in stellar astronomy from the 18th through the 20th centuries. OTTO STRUVE and VELTA ZEBERGS, *Astronomy of the 20th Century* (1962), studies the developments and achievements of the first 50 years of the century. The same period is covered in a later study from the ongoing series "The General History of Astronomy": OWEN GINGERICH (ed.), *Astrophysics and Twentieth-Century Astronomy to 1950* (1984).

Literature on current knowledge in astronomy is voluminous. C.W. ALLEN, *Astrophysical Quantities,* 3rd ed. (1973, reprinted 1983), provides a compact compilation of data; and KENNETH R. LANG, *Astrophysical Formulae: A Compendium for the Physicist and Astrophysicist,* 2nd rev. ed. (1980), is a comprehensive reference source, with extensive formulas and background data. ROBERT BURNHAM, JR., *Burnham's Celestial Handbook: An Observer's Guide to the Universe Beyond the Solar System,* rev. ed., 3 vol. (1978), is a guide to stars, nebulas, and galaxies. ARTHUR P. NORTON, *Norton's Star Atlas and Reference Handbook (Epoch 1950.0),* 17th ed., edited by GILBERT E. SATTERTHWAITE (1978, reprinted 1986), is a popular atlas. Introductory texts include GEORGE O. ABELL, DAVID MORRISON, and SIDNEY C. WOLFF, *Exploration of the Universe,* 5th ed. (1987), a comprehensive classic; and A.E. ROY and D. CLARKE, *Astronomy: Principles and Practice,* 3rd ed. (1988), a survey of experimental basics.

The scope and methodology of astronomy are explored in specialized works: J. KELLY BEATTY, BRIAN O'LEARY, and ANDREW CHAIKIN, *The New Solar System,* 2nd ed. (1982); PETER H. CADOGAN, *The Moon: Our Sister Planet* (1981); JOHN C. BRANDT and ROBERT D. CHAPMAN, *Introduction to Comets* (1981); GORDON WALKER, *Astronomical Observations: An Optical Perspective* (1987); R.J. TAYLER, *The Stars: Their Structure and Evolution* (1970, reissued 1981); CARL E. FICHTEL and JACOB I. TROMBKA, *Gamma Ray Astrophysics: New Insights into the Universe* (1981); CLAUS E. ROLFS and WILLIAM S. RODNEY, *Cauldrons in the Cosmos: Nuclear Astrophysics* (1988); DIMITRI MIHALAS and JAMES BINNEY, *Galactic Astronomy: Structure and Kinematics,* 2nd ed. (1981); JOHN D. KRAUS *et al., Radio Astronomy,* 2nd ed. (1986); M.S. LONGAIR, *High Energy Astrophysics: An Informal Introduction for Students of Physics and Astronomy* (1981); MICHAEL ROWAN-ROBINSON, *The Cosmological Distance Ladder: Distance and Time in the Universe* (1985); and EDWARD R. HARRISON, *Cosmology, the Science of the Universe* (1981). For up-to-date reviews of specialized subjects and for current listings of observational information, consult the *Annual Review of Astronomy and Astrophysics, Annual Review of Earth and Planetary Sciences, The Astronomical Almanac* (annual), and *The Observer's Handbook* (annual).

(S.G.B./L.M.B./M.C.U./M.W.Fr.)

Picasso

The enormous body of Picasso's work, including painting, sculpture, works on paper, ceramics, and poetry, remains; and the legend lives on—a tribute to the vitality of the "disquieting" Spaniard with the "sombre . . . piercing" eyes who superstitiously believed that work would keep him alive. For nearly 80 of his 91 years Picasso devoted himself to an artistic production that contributed significantly to and paralleled the whole development of modern art in the 20th century.

LIFE AND CAREER

Early years. Pablo Picasso, son of José Ruiz Blasco, a professor of drawing, and Maria Picasso López, was born in Málaga, Spain, on Oct. 25, 1881. His unusual adeptness for drawing began to manifest itself early, around the age of 10, when he became his father's pupil in La Coruña, where the family moved in 1891. From that point his ability to experiment with what he learned and to develop new expressive means quickly allowed him to surpass his father's abilities. In La Coruña his father shifted his own ambitions to those of his son, providing him with models and support for his first exhibition there at the age of 13.

La Llotja — The family moved to Barcelona in the autumn of 1895, and Pablo entered the local art academy· (La Llotja), where his father had assumed his last post as professor of drawing. The family hoped that their son would achieve success as an academic painter, and in 1897 his eventual fame in Spain seemed assured; in that year his painting "Science and Charity," for which his father modeled for the doctor, was awarded an honorable mention in Madrid at the Fine Arts Exhibition.

The Spanish capital was the obvious next stop for the young artist intent on gaining recognition and fulfilling family expectations. Pablo Ruiz duly set off for Madrid in the autumn of 1897 and entered the Royal Academy of San Fernando. But finding the teaching there stupid, he increasingly spent his time recording life around him, in the cafés, on the streets, in the brothels, and in the Prado, where he discovered Spanish painting. He wrote: "The Museum of paintings is beautiful. Velázquez first class; from El Greco some magnificent heads, Murillo does not convince me in every one of his pictures." Works by these and other artists would capture Picasso's imagination at different times during his long career. Goya, for instance, was an artist whose works Picasso copied in the Prado in 1898 (a portrait of the bullfighter Pepe Illo and the drawing for one of the Caprichos, "Bien tirada está," which shows a Celestina [procuress] checking a young maja's stockings). These same characters reappear in his late work—Pepe Illo in a series of engravings (1957) and

Picasso.
© Rene Burri—Magnum

loved, then turned the gun on himself and died. The impact on Picasso was deep: it was not just that he had lost his loyal friend and perhaps felt a sense of guilt for having abandoned him; more importantly, he had gained the emotional experience and the material that would stimulate the powerful expressiveness of the works of the so-called Blue Period. Picasso made two death portraits of Casagemas several months later in 1901 as well as two funeral scenes ("Mourners" and "Evocation"), and in 1903 Casagemas appeared as the artist in the enigmatic painting "La Vie."

Blue Period. Between 1901 and mid-1904, when blue was the predominant colour in his paintings, Picasso moved back and forth between Barcelona and Paris, taking material for his work from one place to the other. For example, his visits to the Women's Prison of Saint-Lazare in Paris in 1901–02, which provided him with free models and compelling subject matter ("The Soup," 1902), were reflected in his depictions of Barcelona street people—blind or lonely beggars and castaways in 1902–03 ("Crouching Woman," 1902; "Blind Man's Meal," 1903; "Old Jew and a Boy," 1903). The subject of maternity (women were allowed to keep nursing children with them at the prison) also preoccupied Picasso at a time when he was searching for material that would best express traditional art-historical subjects in 20th-century terms.

The move to Paris. Picasso finally made the decision to move permanently to Paris in the spring of 1904, and his work reflects a change of spirit and especially a change of intellectual and artistic currents. The traveling circus and saltimbanques became a subject he shared with a new and important friend, Guillaume Apollinaire. To both the poet and the painter these rootless wandering performers ("Girl Balancing on a Ball," 1905; "The Actor," 1905) became a kind of evocation of the artist's position in modern society. Picasso specifically made this identification in "Family of Saltimbanques" (1905), where he assumes the role of Harlequin and Apollinaire is the strongman (according to their mutual friend, the writer André Salmon).

Picasso's personal circumstances also changed at the end of 1904, when Fernande Olivier became his mistress. Her presence inspired many works during the years leading up to Cubism, especially on their trip to Gosol in 1906 ("Woman with Loaves"), including the sculpture "Head of a Woman" (1909) and several paintings related to it ("Woman with Pears," 1909).

Colour never came easily to Picasso, and he reverted to a generally more Spanish (*i.e.,* monochromatic) palette. The tones of the Blue Period were replaced from late 1904 to 1906 in the so-called Rose Period by those of pottery, of flesh, and of the earth itself ("The Harem," 1906). Picasso seems to have been working with colour in an attempt to come closer to sculptural form, especially in 1906 ("Two Nudes"; "La Toilette"). His "Portrait of Gertrude Stein" (1906) and a "Self-Portrait with Palette" (1906) show this development as well as the influence of his discovery of primitive Iberian sculpture.

Les Demoiselles d'Avignon. Toward the end of 1906 Picasso began work on a large composition that came to be called "Les Demoiselles d'Avignon" (1907). His violent treatment of the female body and masklike painting of the faces (influenced by a study of African art) have made this work controversial. Yet the work was firmly based upon art-historical tradition: a renewed interest in El Greco contributed to the fracturing of the space and the gestures of the figures, while the overall composition owed much to Cézanne's "Bathers" as well as to Ingres's harem scenes. The "Demoiselles," however, named by Picasso's friend Max Jacob (to refer to Avignon Street in Barcelona, where sailors found popular brothels), was perceived as a shocking and direct assault: these women were not conventional images of beauty but prostitutes who challenged the very tradition from which they were born. Although he had his collectors by this date (Leo and Gertrude Stein, the Russian merchant Sergey Shchukin) and a dealer (Daniel-Henry Kahnweiler), Picasso chose to roll up the canvas of the "Demoiselles" and to keep it out of sight for several years.

In 1908 the African-influenced striations and masklike

Celestina as a kind of voyeuristic self-portrait, especially in the series of etchings and engravings known as "Suite 347" (1968).

Picasso fell ill in the spring of 1898 and spent most of the remaining year convalescing in the Catalan village of Horta de Ebro in the company of his Barcelona friend Manuel Pallarès. When Picasso returned to Barcelona in early 1899, he was a changed man: he had put on weight, he had learned to live on his own in the open countryside, he spoke Catalan, and most importantly he had made the decision to break with his art school training and to reject his family's plans for his future. He even began to show a decided preference for his mother's surname, and more often than not he signed his works P.R. Picasso (by late 1901 he had dropped the Ruiz altogether).

In Barcelona Picasso moved among a circle of Catalan artists and writers whose eyes were turned toward Paris. These were his friends at the café Els Quatre Gats ("The Four Cats," styled after the Chat Noir ["Black Cat"] in Paris), where Picasso had his first Barcelona exhibition in February 1900, and they were the subjects of more than 50 portraits (in mixed media) in the show. In addition, there was a dark, moody "modernista" painting, "Last Moments" (later painted over), showing the visit of a priest to the bedside of a dying woman, a work that was accepted for the Spanish section of the Exposition Universelle in Paris in that year. Eager to see his own work in place and to experience Paris firsthand, Picasso set off in the company of his studio-mate Carles Casagemas ("Portrait of Carles Casagemas," 1899) to conquer, if not Paris, at least a corner of Montmartre.

Discovery of Paris. One of Picasso's principal artistic discoveries on that trip (October–December) was colour—not the drab colours of the Spanish palette, the black of the shawls of Spanish women, or the ochres and browns of the Spanish landscape, but colour—the colour of Van Gogh, of new fashion, of a city celebrating a world's fair. Using charcoal, pastels, watercolours, and oils, Picasso recorded life in the French capital ("Lovers in the Street," 1900). In "Moulin de la Galette" (1900) he paid tribute to French artists such as Toulouse-Lautrec and Steinlen as well as his Catalan compatriot Ramon Casas.

After just two months Picasso returned to Spain with Casagemas, who had become despondent about a failed love affair. Having tried unsuccessfully to amuse his friend in Málaga, Picasso took off for Madrid, where he worked as an art editor for a new journal, *Arte Joven*. Casagemas returned to Paris and attempted to shoot the woman he

Margin notes (left column):
Break with art school training

Casagemas

Margin notes (right column):
Friendship with Apollinaire

heads were superseded by a technique that incorporated elements he and his new friend Georges Braque found in the work of Cézanne, whose shallow space and characteristic planar brushwork are especially evident in Picasso's work of 1909. Still lifes, inspired by Cézanne, also became an important subject for the first time in Picasso's career.

Cubism. Picasso and Braque worked together closely during the next few years (1909–12)—the only time Picasso ever worked with another painter in this way—and they developed what came to be known as Analytical Cubism. Early Cubist paintings were often misunderstood by critics and viewers because they were thought to be merely geometric art. Yet the painters themselves believed they were presenting a new kind of reality that broke away from Renaissance tradition, especially from the use of perspective and illusion. For example, they showed multiple views of an object on the same canvas to convey more information than could be contained in a single, limited illusionistic view.

As Kahnweiler saw it, Cubism signified the opening up of closed form by the "re-presentation" of the form of objects and their position in space instead of their imitation through illusionistic means; and the analytic process of fracturing objects and space, light and shadow, and even colour was likened by Apollinaire to the way in which the surgeon dissects a cadaver. This type of analysis is characteristic of Picasso's work beginning in 1909, especially in the landscapes he made on a trip to Spain that summer ("Factory at Horta de Ebro"). These were followed in 1910 with a series of hermetic portraits ("Ambroise Vollard"; "Daniel-Henry Kahnweiler"); and in his 1911–12 paintings of seated figures, often playing musical instruments ("The Accordionist," 1911), Picasso merged figures, objects, and space on a kind of grid. The palette was once again limited to monochromatic ochres, browns, and grays.

Neither Braque nor Picasso desired to move into the realm of total abstraction in their Cubist works, although they implicitly accepted inconsistencies such as different points of view, different axes, and different light sources in the same picture. Furthermore, the inclusion of abstract and representational elements on the same picture plane led both artists to reexamine what two-dimensional elements, such as newspaper lettering, signified. A song title, "Ma Jolie," for instance, could point to events outside the painting; it could refer narratively to Picasso's new mistress, Eva (Marcelle Humbert). But it could also point to compositional elements within the painting, to the function of flat pictorial elements that play off other flat planes or curvilinear motifs. The inclusion of lettering also produced the powerful suggestion that Cubist pictures could be read coming forward from the picture plane rather than receding (in traditional perspective) into it. And the Cubists' manipulation of the picture shape—their use of the oval, for example—redefined the edge of the work in a way that underlined the fact that in a Cubist picture the canvas provides the real space.

Collage. By 1912 Picasso and Braque were gluing real paper (papier collé) and other materials (collage) onto their canvases, taking a stage further the Cubist conception of a work as a self-contained, constructed object. This Synthetic phase (1912–14) saw the reintroduction of colour, while the actual materials often had an industrial reference (e.g., sand or printed wallpaper). Still lifes and, occasionally, heads were the principal subjects for both artists. And in Picasso's works the multiple references inherent in his Synthetic compositions—curves that refer to guitars and at the same time to ears, for instance—introduce an element of play that is characteristic of so much of his work ("Student with a Pipe," 1913) and lead to the suggestion that one thing becomes transformed into another. "Absinthe glass" (1914; six versions), for example, is in part sculpture (cast bronze), in part collage (a real silver sugar strainer is welded onto the top), and in part painting (Neo-Impressionist brushstrokes cover planes of white paint). But the work is neither sculpture, nor collage, nor painting; planes refer to two-dimensionality, while the object indeed possesses three dimensions. The work of art thus hovers between reality and illusion.

By 1915 Picasso's life had changed and so, in a sense, had the direction of his art. At the end of that year his beloved Eva died, and the painting he had worked on during her illness ("Harlequin," 1915; Museum of Modern Art, New York City) gives testimony to his grief—a half-Harlequin, half-Pierrot artist before an easel holds an unfinished canvas against a black background.

Parade. World War I dispersed Picasso's circle; Apollinaire, Braque, and others left for the front, while most of Picasso's Spanish compatriots returned to their neutral homeland. Picasso stayed in France, and from 1916 his friendship with the composer Erik Satie took him into a new avant-garde circle that remained active during the war. The self-appointed leader of this nucleus of talents who frequented the Café de la Rotonde was the young poet Jean Cocteau. His idea to stage a wartime theatrical event in collaboration with Sergey Diaghilev's Ballets Russes resulted in the production of *Parade,* a work about a circus sideshow that incorporated imagery of the new century, such as skyscrapers and airplanes. Cocteau went to Satie for the music and then to Picasso for the sets and costumes. Work began in 1917, and although Picasso intensely disliked travel, he agreed to go with Cocteau to Rome where they joined Diaghilev and the choreographer of *Parade,* Léonide Massine. It was on this occasion that Picasso also met his future wife, Olga Kokhlova, among the dancers.

Parade was first performed in May 1917 at the Théâtre du Châtelet in Paris, where it was considered no less than an attempt to undermine the solidarity of French culture. Satie seems to have been the principal target of abuse (partly because of his inclusion of airplane propellers and typewriters in the score), while Picasso disarmed the public with the contrast between his basically realistic stage curtain and the startling Synthetic Cubist constructions worn by the characters, the sideshow managers, in the ballet.

New Mediterraneanism. Picasso's paintings and drawings of the late teens often seem unexpectedly naturalistic in contrast to the Cubist works that preceded or sometimes coincided with them ("Passeig de Colom," 1917). After his travels to Italy and a return to Barcelona in 1917 (*Parade* was performed there in November), a new spirit of Mediterraneanism made itself felt in his work, especially in the use of classical forms and drawing techniques. This was reinforced by a conscious looking back to Ingres (for example, in Picasso's portrait drawings of Jacob and Vollard, 1915) and to late Renoir. Even the direction of Picasso's Cubist work was affected. By clarifying planes, forms, and colour, the artist imparted to his Cubist paintings a classical expression (Saint-Raphaël still lifes, 1919; two versions of the "Three Musicians," 1921).

Picasso's only legitimate child, Paulo, was born in 1921. As part of his new status as darling of the socialites (encouraged particularly by his wife and Jean Cocteau) Picasso continued his collaborations with the Ballets Russes and produced designs for Manuel de Falla's *Three-Cornered Hat* (1919); Igor Stravinsky's *Pulcinella* (1920); De Falla's *Cuadro Flamenco* (1921); and Satie's ballet *Mercure* (1924). André Breton called Picasso's designs for this ballet "tragic toys for adults" created in the spirit of Surrealism.

Surrealism. Although Picasso never became an official member of the group, he had intimate connections with the most important art movement between the two world wars, Surrealism. The Surrealist establishment, including its main propagandist, André Breton, claimed him as one of their own, and Picasso's art gained a new dimension from contact with his Surrealist friends, particularly the writers. Inherent in Picasso's work since the "Demoiselles" were many elements that the official circle advocated. The creation of monsters, for instance, could certainly be perceived in the disturbing juxtapositions and broken contours of the human figure in Cubist works; Breton specifically pointed to the strange "Woman in a Chemise" (1913). Moreover, the idea of reading one thing for another, an idea implicit in Synthetic Cubism, seemed to coincide with the dreamlike imagery the Surrealists championed.

What the Surrealist movement gave to Picasso were new subjects—especially erotic ones—as well as a reinforce-

Abstract elements in Cubism (margin note)

Jean Cocteau (margin note)

ment of disturbing elements already in his work. The many variations on the subject of bathers with their overtly sexual and contorted forms (Dinard series, 1929) show clearly the impact of Surrealism, while in other works the effect of distortion on the emotions of the spectator can also be interpreted as fulfilling one of the psychological aims of Surrealism (drawings and paintings of the "Crucifixion," 1930–35). In the 1930s Picasso, like many of the Surrealist writers, often played with the idea of metamorphosis. For example, the image of the minotaur, the monster of Greek mythology—half bull and half human—that traditionally has been seen as the embodiment of the struggle between the human and the bestial, becomes in Picasso's work not only an evocation of that idea but also a kind of self-portrait.

Finally, Picasso's own brand of Surrealism found its strongest expression in poetry. He began writing poetry in 1934, and during one year, from February 1935 to the spring of 1936, Picasso virtually gave up painting. Collections of poems were published in *Cahiers d'Art* (1935) and in *La Gaceta de Arte* (1936, Tenerife), and some years later he wrote the Surrealist play *Le Désir attrapé par la queue* (1941, *Desire Caught by the Tail*).

Sculpture. Picasso's reputation as a major 20th-century sculptor came only after his death, because he had kept much of his sculpture in his own collection. Beginning in 1928, Picasso began to work in iron and sheet metal in Julio González's studio in Paris. Then, in 1931, with his new mistress, Marie-Thérèse Walter, he left his wife and moved to a country home at Boisgeloup, where he had room for sculpture studios. There, with Marie-Thérèse as his muse, Picasso began working on large-scale plaster heads. He also began to make constructions incorporating found objects, and until the end of his life Picasso continued working in sculpture in a variety of materials.

The 1930s. The privacy of his life with the undemanding Marie-Thérèse formed a contrast to the hectic pace of life kept by Olga and her bourgeois circle of society friends. Once in Boisgeloup, Picasso lived openly with Marie-Thérèse (with whom he had a child, Maya, in 1935), and she became the subject of his often lyrical, sometimes erotic paintings, in which he combined intense colour with flowing forms ("Girl Before a Mirror," 1932).

Picasso never completely dissociated himself from the women who had shared his life once a new lover occupied his attention. This is evident in his work, in which one mistress often turns into another; for instance, in a private sketchbook (number 99, 1929) Picasso's portrait drawings betray his double life, for the pictures of his then secret mistress evolve into horrific images of screaming Olgas. And in 1936, while money and a certain amount of attention were given to both Olga and Marie-Thérèse, Picasso moved back to Paris and began to live with the Yugoslav photographer Dora Maar. This change in his own life coincided with a period of personal preoccupation with the Spanish Civil War, which had begun in that year.

Although Picasso never returned to his native country after a visit in 1934, his sympathies always lay with Spain (the short-lived Republican government named him honorary director of the Prado), and in early 1937 he produced a series of etchings and aquatints ("Dream and Lie of Franco") to be sold in support of the Republican cause. His major contribution, of course, was the mural painting "Guernica" (named for the Basque town bombed in 1937 by the Fascists) commissioned by the Republican government for the Spanish pavilion at the 1937 World's Fair in Paris. As compensation Picasso was provided with a studio in Paris on rue des Grands Augustins large enough to accommodate the enormous canvas (11.5 × 25.5 feet; 3.49 × 7.77 metres). Dora Maar worked with him to complete the final work, which was realized in just over three weeks. The imagery in "Guernica"—the gored horse, the fallen soldier, and screaming mothers with dead babies (representing the bullfight, war, and female victims, respectively)—was employed to condemn the useless destruction of life, while at the same time the bull represented the hope of overcoming the unseen aggressor, Fascism.

World War II and after. The expressive quality of both the forms and gestures in the basically monochromatic composition of "Guernica" found its way into Picasso's other work, especially in the intensely coloured versions of "Weeping Woman" (1937) as well as in related prints and drawings, in portraits of Dora Maar and Nusch Éluard (wife of Picasso's friend, the French poet Paul Éluard), and in still lifes ("Still Life with Red Bull's Head," 1938). These works led to the claustrophobic interiors and skull-like drawings (sketchbook number 110, 1940) of the war years, which Picasso spent in France with Dora Maar as well as with Jaime Sabartés, a friend of his student days in Barcelona. Thereafter Sabartés shared Picasso's life as secretary, biographer, and companion, and more often than not as the butt of endless jokes ("Portrait of Jaime Sabartés," 1939; "Retour de Bruxelles," sketchbook number 137, 1956).

After the war Picasso resumed exhibiting his work, which included painting and sculpture as well as work in lithography and ceramics. At the Autumn Salon of 1944 ("Salon de la Liberation") Picasso's canvases and sculpture of the preceding five years were received as a shock. This plus the announcement that Picasso had just joined the Communist Party led to demonstrations against his political views in the gallery itself. At the same time Picasso opened up his studio to both new and old writer and artist friends, including Jean-Paul Sartre, Pierre Reverdy, Éluard, the photographer Brassaï, the English artist Roland Penrose, and the American photographer Lee Miller, as well as many American GI's.

Already in 1943 a young painter, Françoise Gilot, had presented herself at the studio, and within months she became the successor to Dora Maar. In 1946 Picasso moved to the Mediterranean with Gilot (with whom he was to have two children, Claude in 1947 and Paloma in 1949). First they moved to Antibes, where Picasso spent four months painting at the Château Grimaldi ("Joie de Vivre," 1946). The paintings of this time and the ceramics he decorated at the studio in nearby Vallauris, beginning in 1947, vividly express Picasso's sense of identification with the classical tradition and his Mediterranean origins. They also celebrate his new-found happiness with Gilot, who is often nymph to Picasso's fauns and centaurs.

Ceramics. Picasso's ceramics are usually set apart from his main body of work and are treated as less important, because at first glance they seem a somewhat frivolous exercise in the decoration of ordinary objects. Plates, jugs, and vases, mostly made by craftsmen at the Madoura pottery in Vallauris, were reshaped or painted, gouged out, scratched, or marked by fingerprints, and, for the most part, were rendered useless. In turning to craft, Picasso worked with a sense of liberation, experimenting with the play between decoration and form (between two and three dimensions) and between personal and universal meaning.

During this period Picasso's fame increasingly attracted numerous visitors, including artists and writers, some of whom (Hélène Parmelin, Édouard Pignon, Éluard, and especially Louis Aragon) encouraged Picasso's further political involvement. Although he contributed designs willingly (his dove was used for the World Peace Congress poster in Wrocław, Pol., in 1949), it was not so much from a commitment to the Communists as from a sincere and lifelong sympathy with any group of repressed people. "War" and "Peace," two panels painted in 1952 to adorn the Temple of Peace attached to an old chapel in Vallauris, reflect Picasso's personal optimism of those years.

The Picasso myth. After World War II an aura of myth grew up around the name of Picasso, and in the last decades of his life his work had, in a sense, moved beyond criticism. Although there were few critics able to keep pace with his latest work, there were few who attacked him. One exception was the British critic John Berger (*The Success and Failure of Picasso,* 1965), who raised questions about Picasso's economic motives and speculated about his inflated public reputation. Picasso's enormous output (especially in printing and drawing) kept his name before the public, even though his work seemed at the time to be far from mainstream, nonfigurative imagery. For example, in the series that characterized the working methods of his late years he used figurative imagery to weave a kind of narrative within each series' numerous variations.

Marie-Thérèse Walter

"Guernica"

Membership in the Communist Party

In 1953 Françoise Gilot with their two children left Picasso, and he spent several years as a bachelor, dividing his time between Paris and his home at La Californie, near Cannes. In 1954 he had met Jacqueline Roque, who worked in the pottery shop in Vallauris, and they married in 1961; she not only became his steadfast companion, but also, as his muse, she became the principal image and source of inspiration for practically all of the late work. They are both buried in the castle at Vauvenargues, which Picasso purchased in 1958. But the years from their marriage to Picasso's death they spent at Mougins.

History of art. In his late work Picasso repeatedly turned toward the history of art for his themes. He seemed at times obsessed with the need to create variations on the works of earlier artists; thus in his many prints, drawings, and paintings of that period, reference is made to artists such as Altdorfer, Manet, Rembrandt, Delacroix, and Courbet. Repeatedly Picasso did a complete series of variations on one particular work, the most famous being perhaps the series on "Las Meninas" of Velázquez consisting of 58 discrete pictures. At times Picasso reworked a specific work because he identified personally with it. For example, he was attracted to Delacroix's "Femmes d'Alger" because the figure on the right bore resemblance to his wife. More often he seemed moved by the challenge to rework in his own way the complex pictorial and narrative problems the older artists had originally posed for themselves. In a sense Picasso was writing himself into the history of art by virtue of such an association with a number of his predecessors.

There is a renewed sense of play in the work of Picasso's later years. He transformed paper cutouts into monumental sculptures, and in Henri-Georges Clouzot's film "Le Mystère Picasso" (1955), the artist, the sole star, behaves like a conjurer, performing tricks with light as well as with his brush. And finally, just as he turned to the paintings of earlier masters, redoing their works in many variations, so he turned to his own earlier oeuvre, prompted by the same impulse. The circus and the artist's studio became once again the stage for his characters, among whom he often placed himself portrayed as an old acrobat or king.

Picasso died in Mougins, Fr., at the age of 91, on April 8, 1973.

ASSESSMENT

Because Picasso's art from the time of the "Demoiselles" was radical in nature, virtually no 20th-century artist could escape his influence. Moreover, while other masters such as Matisse or Braque tended to stay within the bounds of a style they had developed in their youth, Picasso continued to be an innovator into the last decade of his life. This led to misunderstanding and criticism both in his lifetime and since, and it was only in the 1980s that his last paintings began to be appreciated both in themselves and for their profound influence on the rising generation of young painters. Since Picasso was able from the 1920s to sell works at very high prices, he could keep most of his oeuvre in his own collection. At the time of his death he owned some 50,000 works in various media from every period of his career, which passed into possession of the French state and his heirs. Their exhibition and publication has served to reinforce the highest estimates of Picasso's astonishing powers of invention and execution over a span of more than 80 years.

MAJOR WORKS

PAINTINGS: "Girl with Bare Feet" (1895; Picasso Museum, Paris); "Science and Charity" (1897; Picasso Museum, Barcelona); "Portrait of Carles Casagemas" (1899; Picasso Museum, Barcelona); "Lovers in the Street" (1900; Picasso Museum, Barcelona); "Moulin de la Galette" (1900; Solomon R. Guggenheim Museum, New York City); "Mourners" (1901; private collection, United States); "Evocation" (1901; Museum of Modern Art of the City of Paris); "Self-Portrait" (1901; Picasso Museum, Paris); "El Bock (Portrait of Jaime Sabartés)" (1901; State Pushkin Museum of Fine Arts, Moscow); "The Soup" (1902; Art Gallery of Ontario, Toronto); "Crouching Woman" (1902; Art Gallery of Ontario); "The Two Sisters" (1902; Hermitage, Leningrad); "Blind Man's Meal" (1903; Metropolitan Museum of Art, New York City); "Old Jew and a Boy" (1903; State Pushkin Museum of Fine Arts); "La Vie" (1903; Cleve-

land Museum of Art); "The Old Guitarist" (1903; Art Institute of Chicago); "The Tragedy" (1903; National Gallery of Art, Washington, D.C.); "Family of Saltimbanques" (1905; National Gallery of Art); "Girl Balancing on a Ball" (1905; State Pushkin Museum of Fine Arts); "The Actor" (1905; Metropolitan Museum of Art); "The Harem" (1906; Cleveland Museum of Art); "La Toilette" (1906; Albright-Knox Art Gallery, Buffalo); "Portrait of Gertrude Stein" (1906; Metropolitan Museum of Art); "Two Nudes" (1906; Museum of Modern Art, New York City); "Seated Female Nude with Crossed Legs" (1906; National Gallery, Prague); "Self-Portrait with Palette" (1906; Philadelphia Museum of Art); "Woman with Loaves" (1906; Philadelphia Museum of Art); "Les Demoiselles d'Avignon" (1907; Museum of Modern Art); "Three Women" (1908–09; Hermitage); "Bread and Fruit Dish on a Table" (1909; Public Art Collection, Basel, Switz.); "Factory at Horta de Ebro" (1909; Hermitage); "Woman with Pears" (1909; State Pushkin Museum of Fine Arts); "Portrait of Ambroise Vollard" (1910; State Pushkin Museum of Fine Arts); "Portrait of Daniel-Henry Kahnweiler" (1910; Art Institute of Chicago); "The Accordionist" (1911; Solomon R. Guggenheim Museum); "Ma Jolie" (1911–12; Museum of Modern Art); "Still Life with Chair Caning" (1911–12; Picasso Museum, Paris); "Student with a Pipe" (1913; Museum of Modern Art); "Woman in a Chemise" (1913; private collection, United States); "Harlequin" (1915; Museum of Modern Art); "Portrait of Olga" (1917; Picasso Museum, Paris); "Harlequin" (1917; Picasso Museum, Barcelona); "Passeig de Colom" (1917; Picasso Museum, Barcelona); "Three Musicians" (1921; Philadelphia Museum of Art); "Three Musicians" (1921; Museum of Modern Art); "Pipes of Pan" (1923; Picasso Museum, Paris); "Three Dancers" (1925; Tate Gallery, London); "Woman in an Armchair" (1929; Picasso Museum, Paris); "Crucifixion" (1930; Picasso Museum, Paris); "Seated Bather" (1930; Museum of Modern Art); "Bather with Beach Ball" (1932; private collection, United States); "Girl Before a Mirror" (1932; Museum of Modern Art); "The Female Swimmer" (1934; Marina Picasso Collection, Geneva); "Nude Asleep in a Landscape" (1934; Picasso Museum, Paris); "Guernica" (1937; Casón del Buen Retiro, Prado, Madrid); "Weeping Woman" (1937; private collection, England); "Still Life with Red Bull's Head" (1938; Museum of Modern Art); "Portrait of Jaime Sabartés" (1939; Picasso Museum, Barcelona); "Woman Dressing Her Hair" (1940; private collection, United States); "L'Aubade" (1942; National Museum of Modern Art, Beaubourg Centre, Paris); "The Charnel House" (1944–45; Museum of Modern Art); "Joie de Vivre" (1946; Picasso Museum, Antibes, Fr.); "Femme Fleur" (1946; private collection, France); "Peace" (1952; National Picasso Museum, Vallauris, Fr.); "War" (1952; National Picasso Museum); "Women of Algiers, After Delacroix" (series, 1954–55); "Las Meninas, After Velázquez" (series 1957; Picasso Museum, Barcelona); "Rape of the Sabines" (1963; Museum of Fine Arts, Boston); "Man with Pipe and Cupid" (1969; Am Rhyn-Haus, Luzern, Switz.); "The Kiss" (1969; Picasso Museum, Paris); "Young Bather with Sand Shovel" (1971; private collection, France).

SCULPTURE: (Works without ownership identification exist in multiple castings.) "The Jester" (bronze, 1905); "Head of a Woman" (bronze, 1909); "Guitar" (sheet metal and wire, 1912; Museum of Modern Art); "Absinthe Glass" (painted bronze and silver sugar strainer, 1914; six versions); "Guitar" (floorcloth, string, nails, and newspaper, 1926; Picasso Museum, Paris); "Construction" (iron wire, 1928; Picasso Museum, Paris); "Bust of a Woman" (bronze, 1932; Picasso Museum, Paris); "Bull's Head" (saddle and handlebars, 1943; Picasso Museum, Paris); "Death's Head" (bronze, 1942; Picasso Museum, Paris); "Man with a Sheep" (bronze, 1944); "She-Goat" (plaster, later bronze, 1950); "Bathers" (wood, 1956; State Gallery, Stuttgart, W.Ger.); "Head" (steel, 1967; Daley Center Plaza, Chicago).

WORKS ON PAPER: "The Frugal Repast" (etching, 1904); "Portrait of Max Jacob" (pencil, 1915; private collection, France); "Sleeping Peasants" (tempera with coloured pencil, 1919; Museum of Modern Art); "Portrait of Erik Satie" (pencil, 1920; Picasso Museum, Paris); "Portrait of Igor Stravinsky" (pencil, 1920; Picasso Museum, Paris); illustrations for Balzac's *Chef-d'œuvre inconnu* (13 etchings and 67 wood engravings, 1927 [published 1931]); illustrations for Ovid's *Metamorphoses* (30 etchings, 1930 [published 1931]); "Crucifixion, After Grünewald" (india ink series, 1932; Picasso Museum, Paris); cover of *Minotaure* (collage, 1933; Museum of Modern Art); "Model and Surrealist Sculpture" (etching, 1933); "Sculptor's Studio" (etchings, 1933–34); "Minotauromachia" (etching, 1935); "Minotaur" (ink and gouache series, 1936; Picasso Museum, Paris); "Dream and Lie of Franco" (etchings and aquatints, 1937); "David and Bathsheba, After Cranach the Elder" (lithograph series, 1947); "Luncheon on the Grass, After Manet" (sketchbook number 163, 1962; private collection, Paris); "Suite 347" (etchings and engravings, 1968); "Man and Seated Nude, Mougins" (ink, 1970; Ludwig Museum,

Cologne); "Self-Portrait" (crayons, 1972; Fuji TV Company Gallery, Japan).

CERAMICS: "Bullfight" series (plates, 1949); "Centaur" series (plates, 1949); "Visage de Femme" (jug with spout, 1951; private collection, England); "Hands Holding Fish" (plate, 1953; State Pushkin Museum of Fine Arts).

BIBLIOGRAPHY

Biography and criticism: JAIME SABARTÉS, *Picasso: An Intimate Portrait,* trans. from Spanish (1948), is a fundamental biographical source, although many Picasso legends begin here. Picasso himself approved the biography by ANTONINA VALLENTIN, *Picasso* (1963). Other biographies and memoirs are DORE ASHTON (comp.), *Picasso on Art: A Selection of Views* (1972); BRASSAÏ, *Picasso and Company* (1966; U.K. title, *Picasso & Co.,* 1967; originally published in French, 1964), conversations with the artist; PIERRE DAIX, *La Vie de peintre de Pablo Picasso* (1977), a well-documented chronological study of his work; FRANÇOISE GILOT and CARLTON LAKE, *Life with Picasso* (1964, reissued 1981), informative and sometimes biased memoirs; PATRICK O'BRIAN, *Picasso: Pablo Ruiz Picasso: A Biography* (U.K. title, *Pablo Ruiz Picasso,* 1976); FERNANDE OLIVIER, *Picasso and His Friends* (1964; originally published in French, 1933), early memoirs; ROLAND PENROSE, *Picasso: His Life and Work,* 3rd ed. (1981); and GERTRUDE STEIN, *Picasso* (1938). More specific works of criticism are ALFRED H. BARR, JR., *Picasso: Fifty Years of His Art* (1946, reprinted 1984); MARILYN MCCULLY (ed.), *A Picasso Anthology: Documents, Criticism, Reminiscences* (1981, reissued 1982); JOSEP PALAU I FABRE, *Picasso, the Early Years: 1881–1907* (1981; originally published in Catalan, 1980), containing more than 1,500 illustrations; and GERT SCHIFF (ed.), *Picasso in Perspective* (1976), a collection of essays about his work. See also RAY ANNE KIBBEY, *Picasso: A Comprehensive Bibliography* (1977), with limited general coverage through 1976.

Catalogs: GEORGES BLOCH, *Pablo Picasso,* 4 vol. (1968–79), including printed graphic work from 1904 to 1972 and painted ceramics from 1949 to 1971; DOUGLAS COOPER and GARY TINTEROW, *The Essential Cubism 1907–1920: Braque, Picasso & Their Friends* (1983); DOUGLAS COOPER, *Picasso Theatre* (1968; originally published in French, 1967); PIERRE DAIX and GEORGES BOUDAILLE, *Picasso: A Catalogue Raisonné, 1900–1906,* rev. ed. (1967; originally published in French, 1966); PIERRE DAIX, *Picasso: The Cubist Years, 1907–1916: A Catalogue Raisonné of the Paintings and Related Works* (1979; originally published in French, 1979); CHRISTIAN GEELHAAR et al., *Pablo Picasso: Das Spätwerk: Themen 1964–1972* (1981); BERNHARD GEISER (ed.), *L'Oeuvre gravé de Picasso* (1955); JÜRGEN GLAESEMER (ed.), *Der Junge Picasso: Frühwerk und blaue Periode* (1984); ARNOLD GLIMCHER and MARK GLIMCHER (eds.), *Je Suis le Cahier: The Sketchbooks of Picasso* (1986); SEBASTIAN GOEPPERT, HERMA GOEPPERT-FRANK, and PATRICK CRAMER, *Pablo Picasso: The Illustrated Books* (1983; originally published in French, 1983); WILLIAM RUBIN (ed.), *Pablo Picasso: A Retrospective* (1980); GERT SCHIFF, *Picasso: The Last Years, 1963–1973* (1983); WERNER SPIES, *Picasso: Pastelle, Zeichnungen, Aquarelle* (1986); GARY TINTEROW, *Master Drawings by Picasso* (1981); and CHRISTIAN ZERVOS, *Pablo Picasso,* 33 vol. (1932–78), a basic work reproducing the works in black and white.

(M.McCu.)

Planck

Max Planck made many contributions to theoretical physics, but his fame rests primarily on his role as originator of the quantum theory. This theory revolutionized our understanding of atomic and subatomic processes, just as Albert Einstein's theory of relativity revolutionized our understanding of space and time. Together they constitute the fundamental theories of 20th-century physics. Both have forced man to revise some of his most cherished philosophical beliefs, and both have led to industrial and military applications that affect every aspect of modern life.

Early life. Max Karl Ernst Ludwig Planck was born on April 23, 1858, in Kiel, Germany, the sixth child of a distinguished jurist and professor of law at the University of Kiel. The long family tradition of devotion to church and state, excellence in scholarship, incorruptibility, conservatism, idealism, reliability, and generosity became deeply ingrained in Planck's own life and work. When Planck was nine years old, his father received an appointment at the University of Munich, and Planck entered the city's renowned Maximilian Gymnasium, where a teacher, Hermann Müller, stimulated his interest in physics and mathematics. But Planck excelled in all subjects, and after graduation at age 17 he faced a difficult career decision. He ultimately chose physics over classical philology or music because he had dispassionately reached the conclusion that it was in physics that his greatest originality lay. Music, nonetheless, remained an integral part of his life. He possessed the gift of absolute pitch and was an excellent pianist who daily found serenity and delight at the keyboard, enjoying especially the works of Schubert and Brahms. He also loved the outdoors, taking long walks each day and hiking and climbing in the mountains on vacations, even in advanced old age.

Planck entered the University of Munich in the fall of 1874 but found little encouragement there from physics professor Philipp von Jolly. During his *Wanderjahr* (1877–78) at the University of Berlin, he was unimpressed by the lectures of Hermann von Helmholtz and Gustav Robert Kirchhoff, despite their eminence as research scientists. His intellectual capacities were, however, brought to a focus as the result of his independent study, especially of Rudolf Clausius' writings on thermodynamics. Returning to Munich, he received his doctoral degree in July 1879 (the year of Einstein's birth) at the unusually young age of 21. The following year he completed his *Habilitationsschrift* (qualifying dissertation) at Munich and became a *Privatdozent* (lecturer). In 1885, with the help of his father's professional connections, he was appointed *ausserordentlicher Professor* (associate professor) at the University of Kiel. In 1889, after the death of Kirchhoff, Planck received an appointment to the University of Berlin, where he came to venerate Helmholtz as mentor and colleague. In 1892 he was promoted to *ordentlicher Professor* (full professor). He had only nine doctoral students altogether, but his Berlin lectures on all branches of theoretical physics went through many editions and exerted great influence. He remained in Berlin for the rest of his life.

Planck recalled that his "original decision to devote myself to science was a direct result of the discovery . . . that the laws of human reasoning coincide with the laws governing the sequences of the impressions we receive from the world about us; that, therefore, pure reasoning can

EB, Inc.

Planck.

enable man to gain an insight into the mechanism of the [world]. . . ." He deliberately decided, in other words, to become a theoretical physicist at a time when theoretical physics was not yet recognized as a discipline in its own right. But he went further: he concluded that the existence of physical laws presupposes that the "outside world is something independent from man, something absolute, and the quest for the laws which apply to this absolute appeared . . . as the most sublime scientific pursuit in life."

The first instance of an absolute in nature that impressed Planck deeply, even as a *Gymnasium* student, was the law of the conservation of energy, the first law of thermodynamics. Later, during his university years, he became equally convinced that the entropy law, the second law of thermodynamics, was also an absolute law of nature. The second law became the subject of his doctoral dissertation at Munich, and it lay at the core of the researches that led him to discover the quantum of action, now known as Planck's constant h, in 1900.

Development of quantum theory In 1859–60 Kirchhoff had defined a blackbody as an object that re-emits all of the radiant energy incident upon it; *i.e.,* it is a perfect emitter and absorber of radiation. There was, therefore, something absolute about blackbody radiation, and by the 1890s various experimental and theoretical attempts had been made to determine its spectral energy distribution—the curve displaying how much radiant energy is emitted at different frequencies for a given temperature of the blackbody. Planck was particularly attracted to the formula found in 1896 by his colleague Wilhelm Wien at the Physikalisch-Technische Reichsanstalt (PTR) in Berlin-Charlottenburg, and he subsequently made a series of attempts to derive "Wien's law" on the basis of the second law of thermodynamics. By October 1900, however, other colleagues at the PTR, the experimentalists Otto Richard Lummer, Ernst Pringsheim, Heinrich Rubens, and Ferdinand Kurlbaum, had found definite indications that Wien's law, while valid at high frequencies, broke down completely at low frequencies.

Planck learned of these results just before a meeting of the German Physical Society on October 19. He knew how the entropy of the radiation had to depend mathematically upon its energy in the high-frequency region if Wien's law held there. He also saw what this dependence had to be in the low-frequency region in order to reproduce the experimental results there. Planck guessed, therefore, that he should try to combine these two expressions in the simplest way possible, and to transform the result into a formula relating the energy of the radiation to its frequency.

Planck's formulation was hailed as indisputably correct. To Planck, however, it was simply a guess, a "lucky intuition." If it was to be taken seriously, it had to be derived somehow from first principles. That was the task to which Planck immediately directed his energies, and by December 14, 1900, he had succeeded—but at great cost. To achieve his goal, Planck found that he had to relinquish one of his own most cherished beliefs, that the second law of thermodynamics was an absolute law of nature. Instead he had to embrace Ludwig Boltzmann's interpretation, that the second law was a statistical law. In addition, Planck had to assume that the oscillators comprising the blackbody and re-emitting the radiant energy incident upon them could not absorb this energy continuously but only in discrete amounts, in quanta of energy; only by statistically distributing these quanta, each containing an amount of energy $h\nu$ proportional to its frequency, over all of the oscillators present in the blackbody could Planck derive the formula he had hit upon two months earlier. He adduced additional evidence for the importance of his formula by using it to evaluate the constant h (his value was 6.55×10^{-27} erg-second, close to the modern value), as well as the so-called Boltzmann constant (the fundamental constant in kinetic theory and statistical mechanics), Avogadro's number, and the charge of the electron. As time went on physicists recognized ever more clearly that—because Planck's constant was not zero but had a small but finite value—the microphysical world, the world of atomic dimensions, could not in principle be described by ordinary classical mechanics. A profound revolution in physical theory was in the making.

Planck's concept of energy quanta, in other words, conflicted fundamentally with all past physical theory. He was driven to introduce it strictly by the force of his logic; he was, as one historian put it, a reluctant revolutionary. Indeed, it was years before the far-reaching consequences of Planck's achievement were generally recognized, and in this Einstein played a central role. In 1905, independently of Planck's work, Einstein argued that under certain circumstances radiant energy itself seemed to consist of quanta (light quanta, later called photons), and in 1907 he showed the generality of the quantum hypothesis by using it to interpret the temperature dependence of the specific heats of solids. In 1909 he introduced the wave–particle duality into physics. In October 1911 he was among the group of prominent physicists who attended the first Solvay conference in Brussels. The discussions there stimulated Henri Poincaré to provide a mathematical proof that Planck's radiation law necessarily required the introduction of quanta—a proof that converted James (later Sir James) Jeans and others into supporters of the quantum theory. In 1913 Niels Bohr also contributed greatly to its establishment through his quantum theory of the hydrogen atom. Ironically, Planck himself was one of the last to struggle for a return to classical theory, a stance he later regarded not with regret but as a means by which he had thoroughly convinced himself of the necessity of the quantum theory. Opposition to Einstein's radical light quantum hypothesis of 1905 persisted until after the discovery of the Compton effect in 1922.

Einstein's role

Later life. Planck was 42 years old in 1900 when he made the famous discovery that in 1918 won him the Nobel Prize for Physics and that brought him many other honours. It is not surprising that he subsequently made no discoveries of comparable importance. Nevertheless, he continued to contribute at a high level to various branches of optics, thermodynamics and statistical mechanics, physical chemistry, and other fields. He was also the first prominent physicist to champion Einstein's special theory of relativity (1905). "The velocity of light is to the Theory of Relativity," Planck remarked, "as the elementary quantum of action is to the Quantum Theory; it is its absolute core." In 1914 Planck and the physical chemist Walther Hermann Nernst succeeded in bringing Einstein to Berlin, and after the war, in 1919, arrangements were made for Max von Laue, Planck's favourite student, to come to Berlin as well. When Planck retired in 1928, another prominent theoretical physicist, Erwin Schrödinger, the originator of wave mechanics, was chosen as his successor. For a time, therefore, Berlin shone brilliantly as a centre of theoretical physics—until darkness enveloped it in January 1933 with the ascent of Adolf Hitler to power.

In his later years, Planck devoted more and more of his writings to philosophical, aesthetic, and religious questions. Together with Einstein and Schrödinger, he remained adamantly opposed to the indeterministic, statistical worldview introduced by Bohr, Max Born, Werner Heisenberg, and others into physics after the advent of quantum mechanics in 1925–26. Such a view was not in harmony with Planck's deepest intuitions and beliefs. The physical universe, Planck argued, is an objective entity existing independently of man; the observer and the observed are not intimately coupled, as Bohr and his school would have it.

Worldview

Planck became permanent secretary of the mathematics and physics sections of the Prussian Academy of Sciences in 1912 and held that position until 1938; he was also president of the Kaiser Wilhelm Society (now the Max Planck Society) from 1930 to 1937. These offices and others placed Planck in a position of great authority, especially among German physicists; seldom were his decisions or advice questioned. His authority, however, stemmed fundamentally not from the official appointments he held but from his personal moral force. His fairness, integrity, and wisdom were beyond question. It was completely in character that Planck went directly to Hitler in an attempt to reverse Hitler's devastating racial policies, and that he chose to remain in Germany during the Nazi period to try to preserve what he could of German physics.

Planck was a man of indomitable will. Had he been less stoic, and had he had less philosophical and religious conviction, he could scarcely have withstood the tragedies that entered his life after age 50. In 1909, his first wife, Marie Merck, the daughter of a Munich banker, died after 22 years of happy marriage, leaving Planck with two sons and twin daughters. The elder son, Karl, was killed in action in 1916. The following year, Margarete, one of his daughters, died in childbirth, and in 1919 the same fate befell Emma, his other daughter. World War II brought further tragedy. Planck's house in Berlin was completely destroyed by bombs in 1944. Far worse, the younger son, Erwin, was implicated in the attempt made on Hitler's life on July 20, 1944, and in early 1945 he died a horrible death at the hands of the Gestapo. That merciless act destroyed Planck's will to live. At war's end, American officers took Planck and his second wife, Marga von Hoesslin, whom he had married in 1910 and by whom he had had one son, to Göttingen. There, on October 4, 1947, in his 89th year, he died. Death, in the words of James Franck, came to him "as a redemption."

BIBLIOGRAPHY. Technical books that treat Planck's work and the history of quantum physics include MAX JAMMER, *The Conceptual Development of Quantum Mechanics* (1966); EDMUND T. WHITTAKER, *A History of the Theories of Aether and Electricity*, rev. and enlarged ed., vol. 2, *The Modern Theories: 1900–1926* (1954); HANS KANGRO, *Early History of Planck's Radiation Law* (1976); ARMIN HERMANN, *The Genesis of Quantum Theory (1899–1913)* (1971); THOMAS S. KUHN, *Black-Body Theory and the Quantum Discontinuity: 1894–1912* (1978); JAGDISH

MEHRA and HELMUT RECHENBERG, *The Historical Development of Quantum Theory*, 4 vol. (1982); and ROGER H. STUEWER, *The Compton Effect: Turning Point in Physics* (1975). Nontechnical books include BARBARA LOVETT CLINE, *The Questioners: Physicists and the Quantum Theory* (1965); EMILIO SEGRÈ, *From X-Rays to Quarks: Modern Physicists and Their Discoveries* (1980); and ALEX KELLER, *The Infancy of Atomic Physics: Hercules in His Cradle* (1983). Especially noteworthy are three articles by MARTIN J. KLEIN, "Max Planck and the Beginnings of Quantum Theory," *Archive for History of Exact Sciences*, 1:459–479 (1962), "Planck, Entropy, and Quanta, 1901–1906," *The Natural Philosopher*, 1:83–108 (1963), and "Thermodynamics and Quanta in Planck's Work," *Physics Today*, 19:23–32 (1966). Planck described his life and work in his *Scientific Autobiography, and Other Papers* (1949). Valuable insights may be found in the obituary notices of Planck by MAX BORN, *Obituary Notices of Fellows of the Royal Society of London*, 6:161–188 (1948–49); JAMES FRANCK, *Science*, 107:534–537 (1948); WALTER MEISSNER, *Science*, 113:75–81 (1951); and LISE MEITNER, "Max Planck als Mensch," *Naturwissenschaften*, 45:406–408 (1958). The short biography by HANS KANGRO in the *Dictionary of Scientific Biography*, vol. 11, pp. 7–17 (1975), is excellent. There are two valuable biographies in German: ARMIN HERMANN, *Max Planck in Selbstzeugnissen und Bilddokumenten* (1973); and HANS HARTMANN, *Max Planck als Mensch und Denker* (1953). See also HENRY LOWOOD (comp.), *Max Planck: A Bibliography of His Non-Technical Writings* (1977), a listing of more than 600 articles published between 1879 and 1976; and ILSE ROSENTHAL-SCHNEIDER, *Reality and Scientific Truth: Discussions with Einstein, von Laue, and Planck* (1980).

(R.H.St.)

Plate Tectonics

Plate tectonics is a theory dealing with the dynamics of the Earth's outer shell, the lithosphere. Resting on a broad synthesis of geological and geophysical data, it dominates current thinking in the Earth sciences. According to the theory, the lithosphere consists of about a dozen large plates and several small ones. These plates move relative to each other and interact at their boundaries, where they diverge, converge, or slip relatively harmlessly past one another. Such interactions are thought to be responsible for most of the seismic and volcanic activity of the Earth, although earthquakes and volcanoes are not wholly absent in plate interiors. While moving about, the plates cause mountains to rise where they push together and continents to fracture and oceans to form where they pull apart. The continents, sitting passively on the backs of plates, drift with them and thereby bring about continual changes in the Earth's geography.

The theory of plate tectonics, formulated during the late 1960s, is now almost universally accepted and has had a major impact on the development of the Earth sciences. Its adoption represents a true scientific revolution, analogous in its consequences to the Rutherford and Bohr atomic models in physics or the discovery of the genetic code in biology. Incorporating the much older idea of continental drift, the theory of plate tectonics has made the study of the Earth more difficult by doing away with the notion of fixed continents, but it has at the same time provided the means of reconstructing the past geography of continents and oceans. While its impact has, to a considerable degree, run its course in marine geology and shows signs of reaching the limits of usefulness in the study of mountain-building processes, its influence on the scientific understanding of the Earth's history, of ancient oceans and climates, and of the evolution of life is only beginning to be felt.

For details on the specific effects of plate tectonics, see EARTHQUAKES; VOLCANISM; and GEOMORPHIC PROCESSES. For a detailed treatment of the various land and submarine relief features associated with plate motion, see CONTINENTAL LANDFORMS: *Tectonic landforms* and OCEANS: *The ocean basins*.

This article is divided into the following sections:

PRINCIPLES OF PLATE TECTONICS

The plate tectonics theory has a long and tortuous history. Yet, the theory itself is elegantly simple.

The surface layer of the Earth, from 50 to 100 kilometres (31 to 62 miles) thick, is assumed to be composed of a set of large and small plates, which together constitute the rigid lithosphere. The lithosphere rests on and slides over an underlying, weaker layer of partially molten rock known as the asthenosphere. The constituent lithospheric plates move across the Earth's surface, driven by forces as yet not fully agreed upon, and interact along their boundaries, diverging, converging, or slipping past each other. While the interiors of the plates are presumed to remain essentially undeformed, their boundaries are the sites of many of the principal processes that shape the terrestrial surface, including earthquakes, volcanism, and orogeny.

The most conspicuous feature of the Earth's surface is its division into continents and ocean basins, a division that owes its existence to differences in thickness and composition between the continental and the oceanic crust. The continents have a crust of granitic composition and hence are somewhat lighter than the basaltic ocean floor. Also, they are 30–40 kilometres thick as compared to the oceanic crust, which measures only six to seven kilometres in thickness. Their greater buoyancy causes them to float much higher in the mantle than does the oceanic crust, thus accounting for the difference between the two principal levels of the Earth's surface. The boundary between the continental or oceanic crust and the underlying mantle, the Mohorovičić Discontinuity, has been clearly defined by seismic studies.

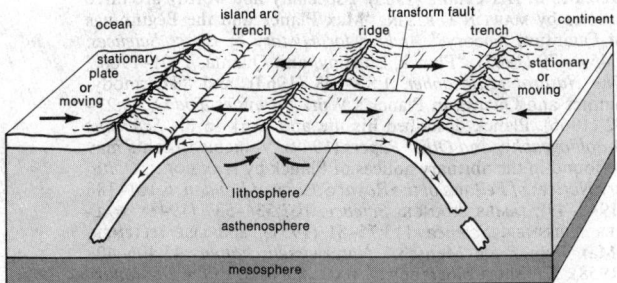

Figure 1: Three-dimensional diagram showing crustal generation and destruction according to the theory of plate tectonics; included are the three kinds of plate boundaries—divergent, convergent (or collision), and strike-slip (or transform).

As conceived by plate tectonics, the lithospheric plates are much thicker than the oceanic or the continental crust; their boundaries do not usually coincide with those between oceans and continents; and their behaviour is only partly influenced by whether they carry oceans, continents, or both. The Pacific plate, for example, is purely oceanic, but most of the others contain continents.

Divergent plate boundaries At a divergent plate boundary, magma wells up from below as the release of pressure produces partial melting of the underlying mantle and generates new crust. Because the partial melt is basaltic in composition, the new crust is oceanic. Consequently, diverging plate boundaries, even if they originate within continents, eventually come to lie in ocean basins of their own making. In fact, most divergent plate boundaries seem to have formed within continents rather than in oceans, probably because a hot, weak layer, sandwiched at a depth of about 15 kilometres between two stronger ones, renders the continental crust more vulnerable to fragmentation than its oceanic counterpart. The creation of the new crust is accompanied by much volcanic activity and by many shallow tension earthquakes as the crust repeatedly rifts, heals, and rifts again.

Convergent plate boundaries The continuous formation of new crust produces an excess that must be disposed of elsewhere. This is accomplished at convergent plate boundaries where one plate descends—i.e., is subducted—beneath the other. At depths between 300 and 700 kilometres, the subducted plate melts and is recycled into the mantle. Because the plates form an integrated system that completely covers the surface of the Earth, it is not necessary that new crust formed at any given divergent boundary be completely compensated at the nearest subduction zone, as long as the total amount of crust generated equals that destroyed.

It is in subduction zones that the difference between plates carrying oceanic and continental crust can be most clearly seen. If both plates have oceanic edges, either one may dive beneath the other; but, if one carries a continent, the greater buoyancy prevents this edge from sinking. Thus, it is invariably the oceanic plate that is subducted. Continents are permanently preserved in this manner, while the ocean floor continuously renews itself. If both plates possess a continental edge, neither can be subducted and a complex sequence of events from crumpling to under- and overthrusting raises lofty mountain ranges. Much later, after these ranges have been largely leveled by erosion, their remains continue as a reminder that this is the "suture" where continents were once fused.

The subduction process, which involves the descent into the mantle of a slab of cold rock about 100 kilometres thick, is marked by numerous earthquakes along a plane inclined 30°–60° into the mantle—the Benioff zone. Most earthquakes in this planar dipping zone result from compression, and the seismic activity extends 300–700 kilometres below the surface. At a depth of 100 kilo-

metres or more the subducted oceanic sediments, together with part of the upper basaltic crust, melt to an andesitic magma, which rises to the surface and gives birth to a line of volcanoes a few hundred kilometres behind the subducting boundary. This boundary is usually marked by an oceanic deep, or trench, where the overriding plate scrapes off the upper crust of the lower plate to create a zone of highly deformed, largely sedimentary rock. If both plates are oceanic, the deformed sediments and volcanoes form two island arcs parallel to the trench. If one plate is continental, the sediments are usually accreted against the continental margin and the volcanoes form inland, as they do in Mexico or western South America.

Along the third type of plate boundary, two plates move laterally and pass each other without creating or destroying crust. Large earthquakes are common along such strike-slip, or transform, boundaries. Also known as fracture zones, these plate boundaries are perhaps best exemplified by the San Andreas fault in California and the North Anatolian fault system in Turkey.

Strike-slip plate boundaries

Most of the seismic and volcanic activity on Earth is therefore concentrated along plate boundaries where mid-ocean ridges, trenches with island arcs, and mountain ranges are generated. Some seismic and volcanic activity also occurs within plates. Interesting examples of this interplate activity are linear volcanic chains in ocean basins, such as the Hawaiian Islands and their westward continuation as a string of reefs and submerged seamounts. An active volcano usually exists at one end of an island chain of this type, with progressively older extinct volcanoes occurring along the rest of the chain. Such topographic features have been explained by J. Tuzo Wilson of Canada and W. Jason Morgan of the United States as the product of "hot spots," magma-generating centres of controversial origin located deep in the mantle far below the lithosphere. A volcano builds at the surface of a plate positioned above a hot spot. As the plate moves on, the volcano dies, is eroded, and eventually sinks below the surface of the sea, while a new one forms above the hot spot. Hot spot volcanism is not restricted to the ocean basins; other manifestations occur within continents, as in the case of Yellowstone National Park in western North America.

The movement of a plate across the surface of the Earth can be described as a rotation around a pole, and it may be rigorously described with the theorem of spherical geometry formulated by the Swiss mathematician Leonhard Euler during the 18th century. Similarly, the motions of two plates with respect to each other may be described as rotations around a common pole, provided that the plates retain their shape. The requirement that plates are not internally deformed has become one of the postulates of plate tectonics. It is not totally supported by evidence,

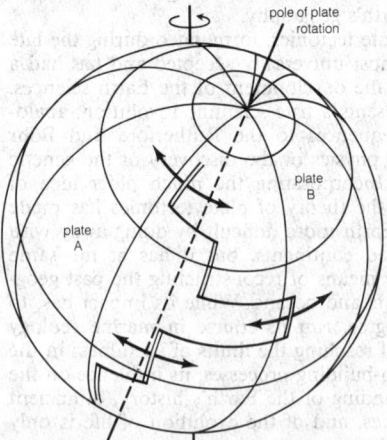

Figure 2: Movement on a sphere of two plates, A and B, can be described as a rotation around a common pole. Circles around that pole correspond to transform faults (single lines connecting divergent plate boundary marked by double line). Note that the pole of rotation of the two plates is not the same as the pole of rotation (spin axis) of the sphere.

but it appears to be a reasonable approximation of what actually happens in most cases. It is needed to permit the mathematical reconstruction of past plate configurations.

The joint pole of rotation of two plates can be determined from their transform boundaries, which are by definition parallel to the direction of motion and so form small circles around the pole. The rate of motion can be computed from the increase in age of the crust away from the divergent plate boundary usually by means of magnetic anomalies (see below *Seafloor spreading*). Because all plates form a closed system, all movements can be defined by dealing with them two at a time.

It is, of course, conceivable that the entire lithosphere might slide around over the asthenosphere like a loose skin, altering the positions of all plates with respect to the spin axis of the Earth and the Equator. To determine the true geographic positions of the plates in the past, which is so important in paleoclimatology and paleoceanography, investigators have to define their motions, relative not to each other, but rather to this independent frame of reference. The hot spot island chains serve this purpose, their trends providing the direction of motion of a plate; the speed of the plate can be inferred from the increase in age of the volcanoes along the chain. It is assumed, of course, that the hot spots themselves remain fixed with respect to the Earth, an assumption that appears to be reasonably accurate for at least some hot spots.

Hot spot island chains as a frame of reference

Quite another method of determining absolute plate movements relies on the fact that the equatorial waters of the ocean are, and always have been, very fertile. The high biological productivity yields an enormous quantity of calcareous microfossils, which, like a gigantic natural chalk line, marks a narrow equatorial zone. The displacement of the equatorial deposits over time, traced by means of deep-sea drill cores, enables investigators to determine the direction and rate of plate movement.

Because the plates all interlock, any change in motion anywhere must reverberate throughout the entire system. If two continents collide, their edges will crumple and shorten, but eventually all motion must stop at this boundary and large parts of the system elsewhere will have to adjust. Earth scientists are thus able to reconstruct the positions and movements of plates in the past so long as they have the ancient oceanic crust to provide them with plate speeds and directions. Since old oceanic crust is continuously consumed to make room for new crust, this kind of evidence is eventually exhausted. Little oceanic crust of Lower Cretaceous age (about 100,000,000 to 136,000,000 years old) remains, and none is older than the Jurassic—the geologic period that began approximately 190,000,000 years ago. Consequently, this method fails for the history of drifting continents during earlier geologic periods (*i.e.*, the Paleozoic and Precambrian eras), making it necessary for investigators to turn to another, less effective technique (see below *Paleomagnetism, polar wandering, and continental drift*).

HISTORICAL OVERVIEW

Precursors. Any major new idea in science appears to lead instantly to a search of the past for those who might once have proposed similar concepts and with whom the current proponents should therefore share the credit. In the case of plate tectonics, the primary candidate is obvious: Alfred Wegener of Germany, who explicitly presented the concept of continental drift for the first time at the outset of the 20th century. Though plate tectonics is by no means synonymous with continental drift, it encompasses this idea and derives much of its impact from it.

There might have been predecessors even to Wegener. The outlines of the continents bordering the Atlantic Ocean are so similar that many probably noticed the correspondence, and some might have drawn the conclusion that the lands on both sides were once joined together. The earliest reference to this peculiar geographic feature was made by the English philosopher Francis Bacon. In his *Novum Organum* (1620), Bacon pointed out the correspondence but did not go beyond that. Such was also the extent of the contribution of the great French naturalist Georges-Louis Leclerc, comte du Buffon, a century later.

Neither can François Paget qualify as a forerunner of continental drift theorists: even though he stated in 1666 that an undivided continent existed before Noah's flood, he explained the creation of the Atlantic Ocean by having part of that continent sink into the sea.

The first credible proponent of continental drift was Antonio Snider-Pellegrini, a belated advocate of catastrophism (the view that geological history consists of a sequence of numerous violent catastrophic events), who in 1858 ascribed the biblical flood to the former existence of a single continent that was torn apart to restore the balance of a lopsided Earth. More recent and much more sophisticated was the work of the American geologist Frank B. Taylor, who, disdaining the then-prevailing contraction model of mountain building, postulated in 1908 that the arcuate mountain belts of Asia and Europe resulted from the equatorward creep of the continents. His analysis of tectonic features foreshadowed in many ways modern thought regarding plate collisions, and he anticipated Wegener's publications by only a few years. Curiously, however, his work instantly sank into oblivion.

Alfred Wegener and the concept of continental drift. Wegener was by training and profession a meteorologist (he was highly respected for his work in climatology and paleoclimatology), but he is best remembered for the foray into geology that led to his formulation of the concept of continental drift. In 1910, again because of the geography of the Atlantic coastlines, Wegener came to consider the existence of a single supercontinent during the late Paleozoic Era (about 350,000,000 to 225,000,000 years ago) and named it Pangaea. He searched the geological and paleontological literature for evidence attesting to the continuity of geological features across the Indian and Atlantic oceans, which he assumed had formed during the Mesozoic Era (about 225,000,000 to 65,000,000 years ago). His efforts proved rewarding, and he presented the idea of continental drift and some of the supporting evidence in a lecture in 1912. This was followed in 1915 by his major work, *Die Entstehung der Kontinente und Ozeane* (*The Origin of Continents and Oceans*).

The super-continent Pangaea

The idea of large ancient continents composed of several of the present-day smaller ones had been put forth in the late 19th century by the Austrian geologist Eduard Suess. Suess, however, was not thinking of continental drift. In the spirit of his day, he assumed that portions of a single enormous southern continent—designated Gondwana, or Gondwanaland—foundered to become the Atlantic and Indian oceans. Such sunken lands, along with vanished land bridges, were frequently invoked in the late 1800s to explain sediment sources apparently present in the ocean and to account for floral and faunal connections between continents. They remained popular until the 1950s, stimulated believers in ancient Atlantis, and even made their way into literary works.

Yet, it was already known that the concept of isostasy rendered large sunken continental blocks geophysically impossible, and Wegener characteristically introduced his continental drift proposal by pointing this out. Only then did he proceed to conclude that, if the continents had been once joined together, drift of their fragments rather than their foundering would have been the consequence. The assumption of a former single continent could be tested geologically, and Wegener next displayed a large array of data. Even today his evidence, ranging from the continuity of fold belts across oceans and similarities of sequences of strata on their opposite sides to paleobiogeographic and paleoclimatological arguments, would be judged worthy of serious consideration. He further argued that, if continents could move up and down in the mantle as a result of buoyancy changes produced by, say, erosion or deposition, they should be able to move horizontally as well. The driving forces he considered, however, were unconvincing: both pole fleeing and the westward tidal force appeared to most to be entirely inadequate.

Wegener's proposition was attentively received by many European geologists, and in England Arthur Holmes pointed out that the lack of a driving force was hardly sufficient grounds to scuttle the entire concept. As early as 1929, Holmes proposed an alternative mechanism—

namely, convection of the mantle, which remains today a serious candidate for the force driving the plates. Wegener's ideas also were appreciated by geologists in the Southern Hemisphere. One of them, the South African Alexander Du Toit, remained a lifelong believer. After Wegener's death, Du Toit continued to amass further evidence in support of continental drift.

Evidence supporting the hypothesis.   Much was thus to be said for the idea that the continents were joined together in the Paleozoic, and supporting evidence has continued to accumulate to this day. The opposing Atlantic shores match well, especially at the 1,000-metre (3,300-foot) depth contour, which is a better approximation of the edge of the continental block than the present shoreline, as Sir Edward Bullard demonstrated in 1964 with the aid of computer analysis. Similarly, the structures and stratigraphic sequences of Paleozoic mountain ranges in eastern North America and northwestern Europe can be matched in detail. This fact was already known to Wegener and has been strengthened in subsequent years.

Often cited as evidence have been the strikingly similar Paleozoic sequences on all southern continents and also in India. This Gondwana sequence—so called after one of Suess's large continents—consists of glacial tillites, followed by sandstones and finally coal measures. Placed on a reconstruction of Gondwana, the tillites mark two ice ages that occurred during the long march of this continent across the South Pole from its initial position north of Libya about 500,000,000 years ago until its final departure from southern Australia 250,000,000 years later. The first of these ice ages left its glacial deposits in the southern Sahara during the Silurian Period (which extended from about 430,000,000 to 395,000,000 years ago), and the second did the same in southern South America, South Africa, India, and Australia from 380,000,000 to 250,000,000 years ago. At each location the tillites were subsequently covered by desert sands of the subtropics, and these in turn by coal measures, indicating that the region had arrived near the Equator.

During the 1950s and 1960s, patient work in isotopic dating showed that the massifs of Precambrian time (from about 4,600,000,000 to 570,000,000 years ago) found on opposite sides of the South Atlantic did indeed closely correspond in age and composition, as Wegener had surmised. It is now evident that they originated as a single assemblage of Precambrian continental nuclei later torn apart by the breakdown of Pangaea.

Disbelief and opposition.   More common than interest or approval, however, was a disbelief so strong that it often bordered on indignation. One of the strongest opponents was the British geophysicist Sir Harold Jeffreys, who spent years attempting to demonstrate that continental drift is impossible because the strength of the mantle should be far greater than any conceivable driving force. He refused to abandon this viewpoint in spite of the massive evidence in favour of plate tectonics. It was in North America, however, that opposition to Wegener's ideas was vigorous to the point of excess and very nearly unanimous. Wegener was attacked from virtually every possible vantage point, his paleontological evidence attributed to land bridges, the similarity of strata on both sides of the Atlantic called into question, the fit of Atlantic shores declared inaccurate, and his very competence doubted. It also did not escape attention that he did not possess proper credentials as a geologist.

What might have been the cause of this overwhelmingly negative response in the light of such a substantial amount of supporting evidence? The unsatisfactory quality of Wegener's driving mechanism has commonly been cited as the reason, but that seems too simple, especially since the absence of a mechanism did not delay the acceptance of plate tectonics. The roots of the resistance most certainly reached far deeper. It would be unusual for the practitioners of any science to flock to a new concept—particularly a revolutionary one of such profound consequences—before the need for a thorough overhaul of the existing conceptual edifice had become compelling and obvious to most, its supporting evidence daily crumbling, and its explanatory power reduced below any acceptable level.

Gondwana sequence

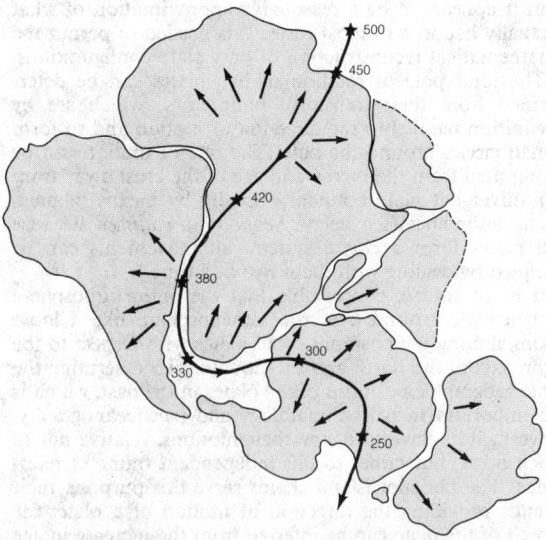

Figure 3: The trail of the South Pole across Gondwanaland during the Paleozoic Era. The numbers indicate its progress by giving the dates of pole positions in millions of years. The arrows show the flow directions of ice caps appearing twice during the long march as ice ages overtook the Earth.

From T.H. van Andel, *New Views on an Old Planet* (1985); Cambridge University Press

Whatever the cause, continental drift, having been rejected by the vast majority of geologists the world over, retreated into obscurity and remained there for roughly three decades. Ironically, though, Du Toit so successfully kept the fires burning in the Southern Hemisphere that it remained quite respectable there to profess oneself an adherent of continental drift during the very years that such a confession north of the Equator would have exposed one to ridicule and disbelief.

Renewed interest in continental drift.   *Paleomagnetism, polar wandering, and continental drift.* The fact that some rocks are strongly magnetized has been known for centuries, and geologists recognized more than 100 years ago that many rocks preserve the imprint of the Earth's magnetic field as it was at the time of their formation. Volcanic rocks such as basalt are especially good recorders of paleomagnetism, but some sediments also align their magnetic particles with the Earth's field at the time of deposition. Investigators therefore have at their disposal fossil compasses that indicate, like any magnet suspended in the Earth's field, the direction to the magnetic pole and that yield the latitude of their origin.

During the 1950s paleomagnetic studies, notably those of Stanley K. Runcorn and his coworkers in England, showed that in the late Paleozoic the north magnetic pole—as seen from Europe—seems to have wandered from a Precambrian position near Hawaii to its present location by way of Japan. This, of course, might mean that the magnetic pole itself had migrated or that Europe had moved relative to a fixed pole. Either continental drift or polar wandering was therefore a reasonable explanation. Paleomagnetic data from other continents, however, soon yielded apparent polar wandering paths different from the European one. Separate wanderings of many magnetic poles are not acceptable, but the paths could be brought to coincide by joining the continents in the manner and at the time suggested by Wegener.

Impressed by this result, Runcorn became the first of a new generation of geologists and geophysicists to accept continental drift as a serious proposition worthy of careful testing. Yet, the band of the converted remained small, and most geologists found sufficient reason to doubt the paleomagnetic results, which were often conflicting due to the primitive nature of the early techniques. Since then, more sophisticated methods capable of removing the overprint of later magnetizations have made paleomagnetic data strong supporting evidence for continental drift and a major tool for reconstructing the geography of the past. In the meantime, however, much progress had been made on an entirely different and quite independent front. It

The paleomagnetic studies of Runcorn

was from evidence extracted from the oceanic crust that plate tectonics would be born.

Gestation and birth of plate tectonics. When Wegener developed his ideas, and for many years thereafter, relatively little was known regarding the nature of the ocean floor. After World War II, however, rapid advances were made in the study of the relief, geology, and geophysics of the ocean basins. Due in large part to the efforts of Bruce C. Heezen and Henry W. Menard of the United States, these features, which constitute more than two-thirds of the Earth's surface, became well enough known to permit serious geological analysis.

Signifi-
cance
of ocean
basin
studies

Several major topographic and tectonic features distinguish the ocean basins from the continents. The first of these is the mid-ocean ridge system. Mid-ocean ridges are broad, elongated elevations of the ocean floor rising to about 2.5 or three kilometres below sea level, with widths ranging from a few hundred to more than 1,000 kilometres. Their crests tend to be rugged and are often endowed with a longitudinal rift valley where fresh lava flows, high heat flow, and shallow earthquakes of the extensional type are found. Mid-ocean ridges nearly girdle the globe.

Trenches constitute another type of seafloor feature. In contrast to mid-ocean ridges, they are long, narrow depressions containing the greatest depths of the ocean basins. Trenches virtually ring the Pacific; a few also occur in the northeastern part of the Indian, and some small ones are found in the Atlantic. Trenches have low heat flow, are often filled with thick sediments, and lie at the upper edge of the Benioff zone of compressive earthquakes. Trenches border continents, as in the case of western Central and South America; but they also may occur in mid-ocean, as, for example, in the southwestern Pacific.

Mid-ocean ridges and, more rarely, trenches are offset by fracture zones—transverse features consisting of linear ridges and troughs approximately perpendicular to the ridge crest that they offset by a few to several hundred kilometres. Fracture zones often extend over long distances in the ocean basins but generally end abruptly against continental margins. They are not volcanic, and their seismic activity is restricted to the area between offset ridge crests where earthquakes indicating horizontal slip are common.

The existence of these three types of striking, large seafloor features, which had gradually become evident during the late 1940s and 1950s, clearly demanded a global rather than local tectonic explanation. The first comprehensive attempt at such an explanation was made by Harry H. Hess of the United States in a widely circulated manuscript that he had written in 1960 but not formally published for several years. In this paper Hess, drawing on Holmes's model of convective flow in the mantle, suggested that the mid-ocean ridges were the surface expressions of rising and diverging convective flow while trenches and Benioff zones with their associated island arcs marked descending limbs. At the ridge crests new oceanic crust would be generated and then carried away laterally to cool, subside, and finally be destroyed in the nearest trenches. Consequently, the age of the oceanic crust should increase with distance away from the ridge crests and, because recycling was its ultimate fate, very old oceanic crust would not be preserved anywhere. This, incidentally, took care of an old and troubling paradox: only rocks younger than Mesozoic had ever been encountered in the oceans, whereas the continents bear ample evidence of the presence of oceans for more than 3,000,000,000 years.

Hess's
seafloor
spreading
model

Hess's model, later dubbed seafloor spreading by the American oceanographer Robert S. Dietz, appeared to account for most observations and was received with interest by many marine geologists. Confirmation of the production of oceanic crust at ridge crests and its subsequent lateral transfer was not long in coming. Fracture zones had thus far been widely regarded as transcurrent faults that gradually displaced one crustal block to the right or left relative to the other. Given this interpretation, the abrupt termination of many fracture zones against continental margins raised intractable problems. The aforementioned Canadian geologist J. Tuzo Wilson solved these problems in 1965 with a single ingenious stroke. Suppose, he argued, that the offset between two ridge crest segments is present

at the outset. Each segment generates new crust, which moves laterally away. Along that part of the fracture zone lying between crests, the crustal slabs move in opposite directions, even though the axes or rift valleys themselves remain stationary. Beyond the crests, adjacent portions of crust move in parallel and are eventually absorbed in a trench. Wilson called this a transform fault and noted that on such a fault the seismicity should be confined to the part between ridge crests, as is indeed the case. Shortly afterward Lynn R. Sykes, an American seismologist, showed that the motions deduced from earthquakes on transform faults conform to the directions of motion postulated by Wilson and are opposite those observed on a transform fault.

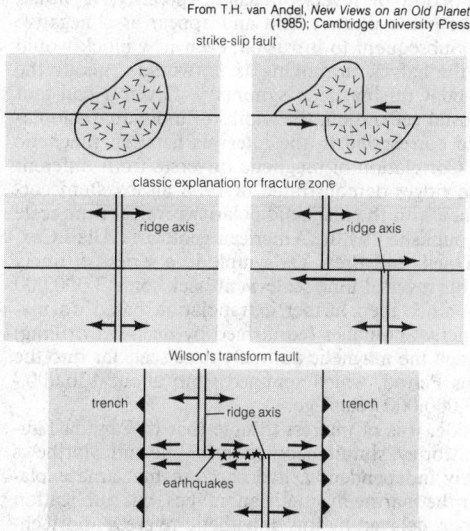

From T.H. van Andel, *New Views on an Old Planet* (1985); Cambridge University Press

Figure 4: Faults that horizontally offset two pieces of crust are called strike-slip faults (top). Fracture zones were initially regarded as classic strike-slip faults until J. Tuzo Wilson demonstrated that they result from the generation of new crust at already offset mid-ocean ridges. The concentration of earthquakes is in the axial part only, and the directions of motion confirm the hypothesis.

The seafloor spreading model also required that the oceanic crust should increase in age with distance from the ridge axis, and Wilson had already pointed out that volcanic islands in the Atlantic indeed show this pattern. Such islands are few, however, and it is in the nature of these piles of lava and ash that the moment of their birth is difficult to ascertain. Additional evidence was needed, and it soon came from magnetic surveys of the oceanic crust.

A magnetic survey of the eastern Pacific floor off the coast of Oregon and California had been published in 1961 by two geophysicists, Arthur D. Raff and Ronald G. Mason. The results were puzzling and gave rise to many farfetched interpretations. Unlike on the continents, where magnetic anomaly patterns tend to be confused and seemingly random except on a fine scale, the seafloor possesses a remarkably regular set of magnetic bands alternately higher and lower than the average Earth field. These positive and negative anomalies are strikingly linear and parallel with the mid-ocean ridge axis, show distinct offsets along fracture zones, and, when displayed in black and white, generally resemble the pattern of a zebra skin. The axial anomaly tends to be higher and wider than the adjacent ones, and in most cases the sequence on one side is the approximate mirror image of that on the other.

Magnetic
anomalies

In his convection/seafloor-spreading model, Hess had attributed the formation of the oceanic crust mainly to the hydration of a peridotitic mantle, a process not judged likely to produce such regular magnetic anomalies. Alternatively, it seemed possible that partial melting of the mantle might yield a basaltic magma, which, after congealing, would be a much better medium for retaining a strong imprint of the Earth's magnetic field. This second hypothesis has since been amply confirmed by deep-sea dredging and drilling.

It had further been known since early in the century

that the polarity of the Earth's magnetic field reverses from time to time. Studies of the remanent magnetism of stacks of basalt lavas extruded in rapid succession on land had, since the late 1950s, begun to establish a sequence of reversals dated by isotopic methods.

Assuming that the oceanic crust is indeed made of basalt intruded in an episodically reversing geomagnetic field, Drummond H. Matthews of Cambridge University and a research student, Frederick J. Vine, postulated in 1963 that the new crust would assume a magnetization aligned with the field at the time of its formation. If the field were normal, as it is today, the magnetization of the crust would be added to that of the Earth and produce a positive anomaly. If intrusion had taken place during a period of reverse magnetic polarity, it would subtract from the present field and appear as a negative anomaly. Subsequent to intrusion, each new block would split and the halves, in moving aside, would generate the observed bilateral magnetic symmetry. Given a constant rate of crustal generation, the widths of individual anomalies should correspond to the intervals between magnetic reversals. Correlation of magnetic traverses from different mid-ocean ridges demonstrated in 1966 an excellent correspondence with the magnetic polarity reversal time scale just then published by the American geologists Allan Cox, Richard Doell, and Brent Dalrymple in a series of timely papers. This reversal time scale went back some 3,000,000 years, but since then further extrapolation based on marine magnetic anomalies (confirmed by deep-sea drilling) has extended the magnetic anomaly time scale far into the Cretaceous Period, which spanned from about 136,000,000 to 65,000,000 years ago.

As an aside, it is of interest to note that in Canada Laurence W. Morley, simultaneously with Vine and Matthews but entirely independently, had come to the same explanation for the marine magnetic anomalies, but publication of his paper, delayed by unsympathetic referees and technical problems, occurred long after Vine's and Matthews' work had already firmly taken root.

These confirmations persuaded a large number of marine geologists that seafloor spreading was a reality. Continental drift, however, was not much in their minds, as they focused mainly on the explanations that the concept provided for a host of oceanic features. Land geologists were disinterested, viewing the affair as primarily an issue for their marine colleagues.

Two concerns, however, remained. The spreading seafloor

was generally seen as a thin skin most likely having its base at the Mohorovičić Discontinuity—*i.e.,* boundary between the crust and mantle considered of such major importance in the early 1960s that plans were undertaken to sample it by deep drilling in the oceans. If only oceanic crust were involved, as seemed to be the case in the Pacific Ocean, the thinness of the slab was not disturbing, even though the ever-increasing number of known fracture zones with their close spacing implied oddly narrow, long convection cells. More troubling was the fact that the Atlantic Ocean, though it had a well-developed mid-ocean ridge, lacked trenches adequate to dispose of the excess oceanic crust. There, the adjacent continents needed to travel with the spreading seafloor, a process that, given the thin but clearly undeformed slab, strained credulity.

Working independently but along very similar lines, Dan P. McKenzie and Robert L. Parker of Britain and W. Jason Morgan of the United States resolved these issues. McKenzie and Parker showed with a geometric analysis that, if the moving slabs of crust were thick enough to be regarded as rigid and thus to remain undeformed, their motions on a sphere would lead precisely to those divergent, convergent, and transform boundaries that are indeed observed. Morgan demonstrated that the directions and rates of movement had been faithfully recorded by magnetic anomaly patterns and transform faults. He also proposed that the plates extended approximately 100 kilometres to the base of a rigid lithosphere, which had long been known to be underlain by a weaker asthenosphere marked by strong attenuation of earthquake waves. In 1968 the French geophysicist Xavier Le Pichon refined these propositions with a computer analysis of all plate data and proved that they did indeed form an integrated system where the sum of all crust generated at mid-ocean ridges is balanced by the cumulative amount destroyed in all subduction zones. That same year, the American geophysicists Bryan Isacks, Jack Oliver, and Lynn R. Sykes showed that the theory, which they enthusiastically labeled the "new global tectonics," was capable of accounting for the larger part of the Earth's seismic activity. Almost immediately others began to consider seriously the ability of the theory to explain mountain building and sealevel changes.

Only a few years later, details of the processes of plate movement and of boundary interactions, along with much of the plate history of the Cenozoic Era (the past 65,000,000 years), had been worked out. Yet, the driving forces—

The
Vine–
Matthews
hypothesis

The
"new
global
tectonics"

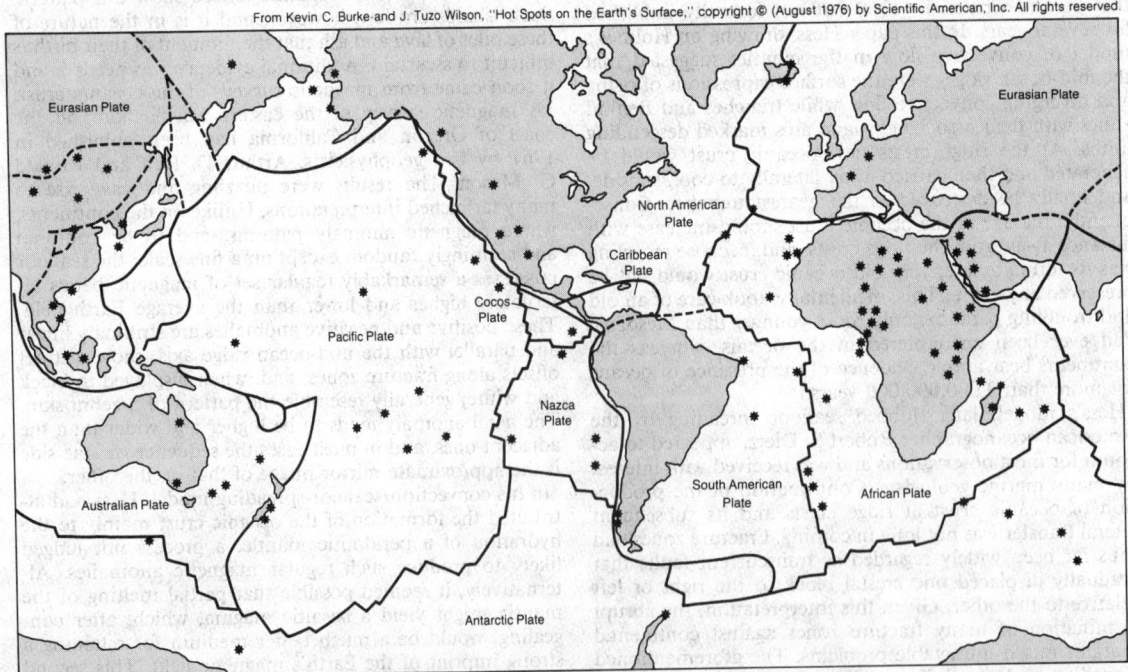

Figure 5: Principal plates that make up the Earth's lithosphere. Very small plates ("microplates") have been omitted. The stars indicate intraplate volcanoes, many of which are thought to be hot spots.

notwithstanding a brief flurry of discussion around 1970—remained mysterious and continue as such. The vast accumulation of data bearing on plate history and plate processes has yielded surprisingly little information about what happens beneath them. Pull by the subducting slab, push at the spreading ridge, convection in the asthenosphere, and even tidal forces have been considered, but in every case the evidence has to be admitted as inconclusive. Many favour convection, but, if this indeed is the driving force, the flow pattern at depth is clearly not reflected in the surface movements of the plates, constrained as they are by each other.

PLATE TECTONICS AS AN EXPLANATION FOR EARTH PROCESSES

Since its inception in 1967–68, plate tectonics has had a pervasive impact on the Earth sciences. If it has not fully lived up to the proud name "new global tectonics," it has nevertheless exerted enormous influence by clarifying areas of obscurity, reconciling seemingly conflicting evidence, unifying to a remarkable degree events occurring in distant parts of the globe, establishing new pathways toward knowledge, and opening the door to new subjects of investigation, all the while raising a myriad of new and important issues. A few examples may suffice to illustrate the dimensions of the revolution it has wrought.

Pangaea and its breakup. Magnetic anomalies, transform faults, and hot spot trails permit rigorous geometric reconstructions of past plate shapes, configurations, and movements. As previously noted, reasonable agreement on such reconstructions can be achieved as far back as the late Cretaceous, but beyond that time little oceanic crust remains. Much effort in reconstructing the geography of the past 100,000,000 years or so has shown that, though some reconstructions are straightforward, others imply that the strict application of the assumption that plates are not internally deformed is not justified. Such is the case, for example, for the Pacific basin as opposed to the simple history of the Atlantic.

Recon-struc-tions of ancient geography

When dealing with geological time beyond the Cretaceous, other means have to be applied in reconstructing ancient geography. Geological data, for instance, can be used in the time-honoured manner to determine the proper fit of continents to make Pangaea. Only minor controversy continues here, such as in the vexing case of the position of Madagascar or of the many fragments that now constitute the Mediterranean, southeastern Europe, and the Middle East. Old collision boundaries are marked by sutures—*i.e.,* zones of deformation that betray points of contact between formerly separate continents even after much erosion. Good examples include the Urals between the old Central European and Siberian continental blocks, and the Indus suture north of the Himalayas between India and Asia. Some sutures, on the other hand, are well concealed, as, for example, the one in northern Florida and southern Georgia that marks a collision between North America and northwestern Africa during the Paleozoic.

Having reconstructed Pangaea and identified the pieces that came together to form it through largely traditional means, investigators are able to trace continental migrations using paleomagnetic data to obtain their paleolatitudes and orientations for appropriate instants in time. What cannot be determined are their paleolongitudes so that knowledge about the widths of intervening oceans remains limited. Paleolongitudes can be estimated only by relatively crude means such as faunal and floral affinities. Accordingly, Earth scientists will never know as much about the geography of the Precambrian, Paleozoic, or early Mesozoic as they do about the last 100,000,000 years of Earth history. Yet, enough information has become available to permit some undoubtedly flawed but fascinating and useful reconstructions.

A widely used Paleozoic reconstruction by a group of geologists at the University of Chicago shows that throughout the Paleozoic, and probably for some time before then, Gondwana existed, consisting of South America, Africa, and Australia. It was surrounded by an ever-shifting array of landmasses, some large—about the size of North America, China, or Siberia—and others small, though numerous and destined eventually to become parts of Europe and Asia.

Paleoclimates and ancient oceans. For Gondwana itself, geological data suffice to recreate in broad outline form not only its coasts, plains, and mountain ranges but also its deserts, polar ice caps, and tropical jungles. These reflect broad climatic zones, which were themselves controlled mainly by insolation, seasonality, and the rotating of the Earth. Large landmasses may sometimes have modified climate to produce monsoons. Given the positions and sizes of continents, paleoclimatic zones may be inferred and then checked against climatic conditions deduced from the fossil record of sedimentary rocks. The results show a satisfactory correspondence between expectations and record, much better than the one obtained by plotting paleoclimatic data on the present-day configuration of continents. They leave little doubt that it is better to accept that the continents have drifted about than to assume that they have remained stationary.

The supercontinent Pangaea was completely surrounded by a world ocean extending from pole to pole and spanning 80 percent of the circumference of the Earth at the Equator. The equatorial current system, driven by the trade winds, resided in warm latitudes much longer than it does today, and its waters were therefore warmer. The gyres that occupy most of the Southern and Northern hemispheres were also warmer, and consequently the temperature gradient from the Equator to the poles was much reduced in comparison to the present.

Early in the Mesozoic, the equatorial current became circumglobal when the Tethys seaway split Gondwana from its northern counterpart, Laurasia. The equatorial surface waters, now able to circumnavigate the world one or more times, became even warmer; but whether the return flows continued to keep the high latitudes warm or diminished in strength and therefore somewhat increased the latitudinal temperature gradients is not certain. Nevertheless, in the middle and later Mesozoic the Arctic and Antarctic surface water temperatures were at or above 10° C (50° F), and the polar regions were warm enough to support forests. As the dispersal of continents following the breakup of Pangaea continued, however, the surface circulation of the oceans became much more complex. During the middle Cenozoic, the northward drift of Australia and South America created a new circumglobal seaway around Antarctica that remained centred on the South Pole. A vigorous circum-Antarctic current developed, isolating the southern continent from the warmer waters to the north. At the same time, the equatorial current system became blocked, first in the Indo-Pacific region, next in the Middle East and eastern Mediterranean, then at Gibraltar, and finally, about 5,000,000 years ago, by the emergence of the Isthmus of Panama. As a result, the equatorial waters were heated less and the mid-latitude ocean gyres were not as effective in keeping the high latitudes warm. Because of this, an ice cap began to form on Antarctica some 20,000,000 years ago and grew to roughly its present size about 5,000,000 years later. This ice cap cooled the waters of the adjacent ocean to such a low temperature that the waters sank and initiated the north-directed abyssal flow that marks the present deep circulation. The Quaternary Ice Age arrived in full when the first ice caps appeared in the Northern Hemisphere about 2,000,000 years ago.

The dispersal of continents and its impact on oceanic current systems

There is no certainty that the changing configuration of continents and oceans can be held solely responsible for the onset of the Quaternary Ice Age, even if such factors as the drift of continents across the latitudes (with the associated changes in vegetation) and reflectivity for solar heat are included. There can be little doubt, however, that it was a major contributing factor and that recognition of its role has profoundly altered all concepts of paleoclimatology.

Plate tectonics and mountain building. Subduction and continental collision raise mountain ranges. Consequently, the implications of plate tectonics for the processes of mountain building have attracted much attention. One of the earliest to apply the new theory was the Cambridge geologist John Dewey, who analyzed the Appalachian and Alpine orogenies. Many other researchers have sub-

The signi-ficance of plate conver-gence in orogeny

sequently undertaken similar work in the Mediterranean system and the American Cordilleran ranges, as well as in the Appalachians.

The collisions that gradually joined North America to Pangaea during the Paleozoic exemplify the role of plate convergence in mountain building. Some 500,000,000 years ago, a subduction zone existed along what is now the eastern seaboard of North America. During the course of the next 70,000,000 years—the Ordovician Period—this region underwent a major phase of mountain building. When it was over, the direction of sediment transport had reversed, indicating that a large source area had appeared to the east of the subduction zone. The thick sequence of deposits from this source in eastern North America bears witness to its size, which is incommensurable with the island arcs that normally accompany a subduction zone. Subduction, sedimentation, and volcanism then continued until a small continent comprising what is today northwestern Europe collided with the northeastern tip of North America. This collision raised a major chain of folded mountains, the remains of which are now found from New England through eastern Canada and Scotland into Norway. This Caledonian range shed sediments to both sides, forming the Catskill delta in eastern North America and the Old Red Sandstone in northwestern Europe. Subsequently, the southern edge of North America collided with South America, and a little later Africa arrived, producing the southern Appalachians. Miscellaneous fragments, today part of central Europe and the western Mediterranean, filled in the gap and completed this portion of Pangaea.

This account fits the plate model fairly well except for two things: (1) the occurrence of paroxysms of mountain building when no continental collision can be assumed; and (2) the need for sizable landmasses, presumably small continents, floating offshore to provide a necessary sediment source. Both problems appear quite often wherever plate movements are used to explain the details of the formation of major mountain ranges. Yet, the model itself is simple. It allows for three possible cases: ocean–ocean collisions; ocean–continent collisions; and continent–continent collisions. In the first two situations, oceanic crust is subducted either under other oceanic crust or under a continent—a steady process presumably accompanied by an equally steady scraping off and deforming of sediments and basaltic crust at the plate edge and by volcanism farther away. The New Hebrides trench and island arcs in the southwestern Pacific exemplify an ocean–ocean collision, while the Andes Mountain Ranges of South America represent a long-lasting collision of oceanic crust and continental crust at the leading edges of plates.

Even in these cases the process appears to be more complicated than the theory suggests, demanding modifications that, though eminently plausible and often proven, are ad hoc and thus diminish its value as a unifying principle. The South American Andes, for example, have had an episodic history not readily matched to the evidently uneventful spreading of the seafloor in the adjacent Pacific. The volcanism of the segments of the Cascade Range in Oregon and Washington in the northwestern United States is only a few million years old in its present form, whereas subduction along the Pacific coast dates back much farther than that. All along the west coast of North America, mountain building has occurred in distinct major phases, ultimately in all probability by changes in the rate and direction of plate movements that complicate the basically simple subduction process.

One of the complicating factors is much in evidence in the coast ranges that extend from California to southern Alaska. Large sections of these mountains fit poorly with the geology of the surrounding terrain and are thought to have originated in the ancient Pacific. Perhaps they once were oceanic plateaus, island arcs, or other thick pieces of oceanic crust that would not subduct but instead lodged against the continental edge, and so disturbed the processes of subduction and mountain building. Some of these "exotic terranes" have been shown by their paleomagnetic properties to have come a long way from their points of origin, perhaps as far as the Southern Hemisphere.

The Indus–Himalayan–Tibetan region in northern India and China represents a continent–continent collision that began 40,000,000 years ago when all of the oceanic crust between northward-drifting India and south central Asia had been consumed and the continent-bearing edges of the two plates met. The suture of this collision, the site of the former subduction zone, lies inconspicuously in the high plateau region north of the Himalayas. This lofty mountain range itself formed long after the collision as India—its momentum not fully spent even today—drove another 2,000 kilometres into the underbelly of Asia. In doing so, Asian lithosphere was displaced laterally along enormous transcurrent faults, which are the sites of the numerous devastating earthquakes in Iran, Afghanistan, and western China. The Himalayas themselves are the product of the northward, low-angle underthrusting of the upper slice of the Indian plate under the Asian plate, making it clear that a continent–continent collision involves a good deal more than the crumpling of opposing front edges.

Plate tectonics and life. Inevitably the continuous rearrangement over time of the size and shape of ocean basins and continents, followed by changes in ocean circulation and climate, have had a major impact on the development of life on Earth. Active interest in these aspects of the Earth science revolution has lagged behind that in other areas, even though as early as 1970 the American geologists James W. Valentine and Eldridge M. Moores attempted to show that the diversity of life increased as continents fragmented and dispersed and diminished when they were joined together.

Subsequently, however, the study of plate activity as a force in the evolution of life has leaped forward. A few simple examples of such research must suffice to illustrate the impact of the plate theory. Toward the end of the Paleozoic, during the Permian Period (about 280,000,000 to 225,000,000 years ago), there was a drastic drop in the variety of animal forms inhabiting the shallow seas around Pangaea. Well over half of the total number of known families became extinct. This drop can be attributed in large part simply to the decrease in biogeographic variety that marks a world consisting of a single continent rather than one comprising many widely dispersed landmasses. Other factors, such as a sharp decrease in the area of shallow-water habitats or a change in ocean fertility due to upwelling, have also been invoked. Moreover, the extinction had a complex history. High latitudes were affected first as a result of the waning of the Permian ice age when the South Pole slipped beyond the southern edge of Pangaea. The equatorial and subtropical zones appear to have been affected somewhat later by a global cooling. On the other hand, the extinctions were not felt so strongly on the continent itself. Instead, the vast semiarid and arid lands that emerged on so large a continent, the shortening of its moist coasts, and the many mountain ranges remaining from the collisions that led to the formation of the supercontinent provided strong incentives for evolutionary adaption to dry or high-altitude environments.

The impact of plate movements and interactions on life is perhaps most clearly demonstrated by what happens when continents diverge or collide. When the Atlantic Ocean began to open during the middle Mesozoic, the similarity between the faunas of opposite shores gradually decreased in almost linear fashion—the greater the distance, the smaller the number of families in common. The difference increased more rapidly in the South Atlantic than in the North Atlantic, where a land connection between Europe and North America persisted until well after the middle Cenozoic. The inverse, the effect of a collision between two hitherto separate landmasses, is illustrated by the consequences of the Pliocene emergence of the Isthmus of Panama. In South America a highly specialized fauna had evolved, rich in marsupials but with few predators. After the emergence of the isthmus had made it possible for land animals to cross, numerous herbivores migrated from north to south. They adapted well to the new environment and were more successful than the local fauna in competing for food. The invasion of highly adaptable carnivores from the north contributed to the extinction of no fewer than four orders of South American land

The effect of plate activity on the evolution of life

mammals. Only a few species, notably the armadillo and the opossum, managed to migrate in the opposite direction. Ironically, many of the invading northerners, such as the llama and tapir, subsequently became extinct in their country of origin and found their last refuge in the south.

Early plate activity. Whatever the forces may be that drive the plates, they consume energy. By far the largest part of this energy is derived from the decay of radioactive isotopes within the Earth, and the energy flow has therefore declined through the 4,500,000,000 years of the Earth's history—rapidly at first and then at a slowly diminishing though not negligible rate. Accordingly, it is quite likely that the behaviour of the lithospheric plates on the early, more energetic Earth was different from what it is today, and what prevails at present will certainly differ from what will prevail in the future. A thickening lithosphere, a decreasing heat flow, a temperature gradient that decreases with depth within the Earth, and enlarging—though perhaps less vigorous—convection cells in the mantle have all been postulated as unidirectional changes that affected the behaviour of the lithosphere. It is possible, for example, that the initial plates were too small, too hot, and hence too light to be subducted. In this case, the first subduction would mark the coming of age of classical plate tectonics, and, indeed, clear evidence is lacking for subduction until rather late in the Precambrian.

The evidence that bears on the existence, nature, and movements of possible lithospheric plates during the first several billion years of Earth history is very limited. The continental nuclei of the early and middle Precambrian seem to have been small and might be regarded as small plates on a more vigorously convecting mantle. These nuclei are thought to have been embedded in strongly deformed complexes of sediments and basic igneous rocks, the greenstone belts reminiscent of the sutures that mark the closure of ancient oceans. In most cases, however, paleomagnetic data do not leave room for the existence of sizable oceanic areas between such nuclei. Investigators are thus forced to contemplate the possibility that in the Precambrian intensive deformation took place within plates, perhaps commensurate with the postulated thinner lithosphere and higher flow of heat toward the surface. On the other hand, current knowledge of this long but obscure portion of Earth history is so deficient that some geologists have emphatically denied that there might have been a remote past to which classical plate tectonics could not be applied.

DISSENTING OPINIONS AND UNANSWERED QUESTIONS

The dissenters. Scientific revolutions as far-reaching in their consequences as the plate tectonics revolution cannot be expected to be easily, or ever completely, accepted. Nevertheless, once the theory had fully emerged, acceptance was quick and widespread and by the late 1960s its influence in the West was pervasive. Such was, however, not the case in the Soviet Union, a country located largely in the continental interior far from present-day plate boundaries. Soviet scientists viewed as central to any issue of global tectonics the vertical movements of continental interiors, phenomena not satisfactorily dealt with by the plate tectonics theory. A leading spokesman for the Soviet position, the academician Vladimir Vladimirovich Belousov, strongly defended a model of the Earth that postulated stationary continents affected almost exclusively by vertical motions. The model, however, only vaguely defined the forces supposedly responsible for the motions. In recent years, a younger generation of Soviet geologists has very gradually come to regard plate tectonics as an attractive theory and a viable alternative to the concepts of Belousov and his followers.

Opposition to plate tectonics was by no means limited to the Soviet Union. Sir Harold Jeffreys continued his lifelong rejection of continental drift on grounds that his estimates of the properties of the mantle indicated the impossibility of plate movements. He did not, in general, deign to take note of the mounting geophysical and geological arguments that were in favour of a mobile outer shell of the Earth.

Others proffered different explanations of the accumu-

Early opposition to plate tectonics

lating evidence, most of which were rather farfetched, as, for instance, the suggestion that new crust was formed at trenches and destroyed on mid-ocean ridges. Still others, notably the American geologists A.A. Meyerhoff and Howard A. Meyerhoff, attempted to assemble data that contradicted the theory and thereby show that the supporting evidence was wrong, insufficient, or simply misconstrued. Demonstrating a remarkable command of often quite obscure literature, they issued a series of negative commentaries in the early 1970s; but they failed to convince the majority of their colleagues, partly because they did not offer alternative explanations for the evidence.

The only serious alternative had been proposed in 1958 by the Australian geologist S. Warren Carey in the form of a new version of an old idea—namely, the expanding Earth model. Carey accepted the existence and early Mesozoic breakup of Pangaea and the subsequent dispersal of its fragments and formation of new ocean basins, but he attributed it all to the expansion of the Earth, the planet presumably having had a much smaller diameter in the late Paleozoic. In his view, the continents represented the pre-expansion crust, and the enlarged surface was to be entirely accommodated within the oceans. This model accounted for a spreading ocean floor and for the young age of the oceanic crust; however, it failed to deal adequately with the evidence for subduction and compression. Carey's model also did not explain why the process should not have started until some 4,000,000,000 years after the Earth was formed, and it lacked a reasonable mechanism for so large an expansion. Finally, it disregarded the evidence for continental drift before the existence of Pangaea.

Carey's version of the expanding Earth model

Unanswered questions. As the philosopher Thomas J. Kuhn has pointed out, science does not always advance in the gradual and stately fashion commonly attributed to it. Major breakthroughs often come from a leap forward that is at least in part intuitive and may fly in the face of conventional wisdom and widely accepted evidence while strict requirements for verification and proof are temporarily relaxed. Revolutions thus often become widely accepted before the verdict from rigorous analysis of evidence is completely in. Such was certainly the case with the geological revolution, which also confirms Kuhn's view that a new paradigm is unlikely to supersede an existing one until there is little choice but to acknowledge that the conventional theory has failed. Thus, while Wegener did not manage to persuade the world, the successor theory was readily embraced 40 years later, even though it remained open to much of the same criticism that had caused the downfall of continental drift. What is the state of the new paradigm? Is it likely to suffer sooner rather than later the same fate that inevitably awaits all scientific theories?

In 1974, almost alone among the doubters who tried to discredit the new theory with contrary evidence, the American geologist John C. Maxwell, in a closely reasoned paper, enumerated all the points on which he believed plate tectonics had failed to offer an explanation. Many of these points have since been resolved, but more than a few remain to suggest that the theory, though in essence valid, may be incomplete.

The greatest successes of plate tectonics have been achieved in the ocean basins where additional decades of effort have confirmed its postulates and enabled investigators to construct a credible history of past plate movements. Inevitably in less rigorous form, the reconstruction of early Mesozoic and Paleozoic continental configurations has provided a powerful tool with which to resolve many important questions. On the other hand, the new paradigm has proved less useful in deciphering mountain-building processes or in offering explanations for the complex history of sea-level fluctuations. The American geologist L.L. Sloss has devoted much effort to demonstrating that continents do indeed rise and fall in unison, but the possible mechanisms for such a process remain elusive.

Where plate boundaries adjoin continents, matters often become very complex and have demanded an ever denser thicket of ad hoc modifications and amendments to the theory and practice of plate tectonics in the form of microplates, obscure plate boundaries, and exotic terranes.

A good example is the Mediterranean, where the collisions between Africa and a swarm of microcontinents have produced a tectonic nightmare that is far from resolved. More disturbingly, some of the present plate boundaries, especially in the eastern Mediterranean, appear to be so diffuse and so anomalous that they cannot be compared to the three types of plate boundaries of the basic theory. There is evidence, as held by the American geophysicist Thomas H. Jordan, that the base of the plates extends far deeper into the asthenosphere below the continents than below the oceans. How much of an impediment this might be for the movement of plates and how it might affect their boundary interactions remain open questions. Others have postulated that the lower layer of the lithosphere peels off and sinks late in any collision sequence, producing high heat flow, volcanism, and an upper lithospheric zone vulnerable to contraction by thrusting.

It is understandable that any simple global tectonic model would work better in the oceans, which, being young, retain a record of only a brief and relatively uneventful history. On the continents, almost 4,000,000,000 years of growth and deformation, erosion, sedimentation, and igneous intrusion have produced a complex imprint that, with its intricate zones of varying strength, must directly affect the application of plate forces. Seismic reflection studies of the deep structure of the continents have demonstrated just how complex the events that form the continents and their margins may have been, and their findings sometimes are difficult to reconcile with the accretionary structures one would expect to see as a result of subduction and collision.

Notwithstanding these cautions and the continuing lack of an agreed-upon driving mechanism for the plates, one cannot help but conclude that the plate tectonics revolution has been fruitful and has immensely advanced scientific understanding of the Earth. Like all paradigms in science, it will most likely one day be replaced by a better one; yet there can be little doubt that, whatever the new theory may state, continental drift will be part of it.

BIBLIOGRAPHY. J. TUZO WILSON (ed.), *Continents Adrift and Continents Aground* (1976), contains an excellent and readable set of articles on the plate tectonics revolution drawn from *Scientific American,* many written by its protagonists, with fine introductions by the editor. Similarly, ALLAN COX (ed.), *Plate Tectonics and Geomagnetic Reversals* (1973), offers a well-chosen selection of the original classical papers that produced this revolution in the Earth sciences, from Holmes's work in the early 1900s to contributions in the late 1960s. An excellent explanation of the new Earth science is SEIYA UYEDA, *The New View of the Earth: Moving Continents and Moving Oceans* (1978), which discusses plate theory and its application to the study of the Earth's surface structures. Scholarly, but written for a lay audience, is TJEERD H. VAN ANDEL, *New Views on an Old Planet: Continental Drift and the History of Earth* (1985), an application of plate theory to the climatic, oceanographic, and geographic history of the Earth, and the relation of the theory to the history of life. The history of ideas pertaining to continental drift and plate tectonics has been thoughtfully analyzed in ANTHONY HALLAM, *A Revolution in the Earth Sciences: From Continental Drift to Plate Tectonics* (1973). A summary of the revolution, mostly in a critical vein by many of its principal opponents, is CHARLES F. KAHLE (ed.), *Plate Tectonics: Assessments and Reassessments* (1974), a bit dated but a good substantive statement on the subject. More technical, though not forbiddingly so, are three books rich in detail and substance: PETER J. WYLLIE, *The Way the Earth Works: An Introduction to the New Global Geology and Its Revolutionary Development* (1976); ROBERT H. DOTT, JR., and ROGER L. BATTEN, *Evolution of the Earth,* 3rd ed. (1981), for the impact of the plate theory on research in Earth history; and STEPHEN STANLEY, *Earth and Life Through Time* (1985), a newer and more advanced treatment.

(T.H.v.A.)

Plato and Platonism

Plato was the second of the great trio of ancient Greeks—Socrates, Plato, and Aristotle—who between them laid the philosophical foundations of Western culture. Building on the life and thought of Socrates, Plato developed a profound and wide-ranging system of philosophy. His thought has logical, epistemological, and metaphysical aspects; but its underlying motivation is ethical. It sometimes relies upon conjectures and myth, and it is occasionally mystical in tone; but fundamentally Plato is a rationalist, devoted to the proposition that reason must be followed wherever it leads. Thus the core of Plato's philosophy is a rationalistic ethics.

For coverage of related topics in the *Macropædia* and *Micropædia,* see the *Propædia,* Part Ten, Division V, especially Sections 51 and 53.

This article deals with the man, his works and influence, and the subsequent history of Platonism. It is divided into the following sections:

Plato and his thought

LIFE

Plato was born, the son of Ariston and Perictione, in Athens, or perhaps in Aegina, in about 428 BC, the year after the death of the great statesman Pericles. His family, on both sides, was among the most distinguished in Athens. Ariston is said to have claimed descent from the god Poseidon through Codrus, the last king of Athens; on the mother's side, the family was related to the early Greek lawmaker Solon. Nothing is known about Plato's father's death. It is assumed that he died when Plato was a boy. Perictione apparently married as her second husband her uncle Pyrilampes, a prominent supporter of Pericles;

Distinguished family

and Plato was probably brought up chiefly in his house. Critias and Charmides, leaders among the extremists of the oligarchic terror of 404, were, respectively, cousin and brother of Perictione; both were friends of Socrates, and through them Plato must have known the philosopher from boyhood.

Plato, Roman herm probably copied from a Greek original, 4th century BC. In the Staatliche Museen, Berlin.

His own early ambitions—like those of most young men of his class—were probably political. A conservative faction urged him to enter public life under its auspices, but he wisely held back. He was soon repelled by its members' violent acts. After the fall of the oligarchy, he hoped for better things from the restored democracy. Eventually, however, he became convinced that there was no place for a man of conscience in Athenian politics. In 399 BC the democracy condemned Socrates to death, and Plato and other Socratic men took temporary refuge at Megara with Eucleides, founder of the Megarian school of philosophy. The next few years are said to have been spent in extensive travels in Greece, in Egypt, and in Italy. Plato himself (if the *Seventh Letter* is his; see below) states that he visited Italy and Sicily at the age of 40 and was disgusted by the gross sensuality of life there but found a kindred spirit in Dion, brother-in-law of Dionysius I, the ruler of Syracuse.

The Academy and Sicily. In about 387 Plato founded the Academy as an institute for the systematic pursuit of philosophical and scientific teaching and research. He presided over it for the rest of his life. The Academy's interests were not limited to philosophy in a narrow sense but also extended to the sciences: there is evidence that Plato encouraged research in such diverse disciplines as mathematics and rhetoric. He himself lectured (on at least one occasion he gave a celebrated public lecture "On the Good"), and he set problems for his pupils to solve. The Academy was not the only such "school" in Athens— there are traces of tension between the Academy and the rival school of Isocrates.

Political activity in Sicily

The one outstanding event in Plato's later life was his intervention in Syracusan politics. On the death of Dionysius I in 367, Dion conceived the idea of bringing Plato to Syracuse as tutor to his brother-in-law's successor, Dionysius II, whose education had been neglected. Plato was not optimistic about the results; but because both Dion and Archytas of Tarentum, a philosopher-statesman, thought the prospect promising, he felt bound to risk the adventure. The plan was to train Dionysius II in science and philosophy and so to fit him for the position of a constitutional king who might hold Carthaginian encroachment

on Sicily at bay. The scheme was crushed by Dionysius' natural jealousy of the stronger Dion, whom he drove into virtual banishment. Plato later paid a second and longer visit to Syracuse in 361–360, still in the hope of effecting an accommodation; but he failed, not without some personal danger. Dion then captured Syracuse by a coup de main in 357, but he was murdered in 354. Plato himself died in 348/347.

Of Plato's character and personality little is known, and little can be inferred from his writings. But it is worth recording that Aristotle, his most able pupil, described Plato as a man "whom it is blasphemy in the base even to praise," meaning that Plato was so noble a character that bad men should not even speak about him.

To his readers through the ages Plato has been important primarily as one of the greatest of philosophical writers; but to himself the foundation and organization of the Academy must have appeared to be his chief work. The *Seventh Letter* contrasts the impact of written works with that of the contact of living minds as a vehicle of philosophy, and it passes a comparatively unfavourable verdict on written works. Plato puts a similar verdict into the mouth of Socrates in the *Phaedrus.* He perhaps intended his dialogues in the main to interest an educated outside world in the more serious and arduous labours of his school.

Influence of the Academy

All of the most important mathematical work of the 4th century was done by friends or pupils of Plato. The first students of conic sections, and possibly Theaetetus, the creator of solid geometry, were members of the Academy. Eudoxus of Cnidus—author of the doctrine of proportion expounded in Euclid's *Elements,* inventor of the method of finding the areas and volumes of curvilinear figures by exhaustion, and propounder of the astronomical scheme of concentric spheres adopted and altered by Aristotle— removed his school from Cyzicus to Athens for the purpose of cooperating with Plato; and during one of Plato's absences he seems to have acted as the head of the Academy. Archytas, the inventor of mechanical science, was a friend and correspondent of Plato.

Nor were other sciences neglected. Speusippus, Plato's nephew and successor, was a voluminous writer on natural history; and Aristotle's biological works have been shown to belong largely to the early period in his career immediately after Plato's death. The comic poets found matter for mirth in the attention of the school to botanical classification. The Academy was particularly active in jurisprudence and practical legislation. As Plutarch testifies,

Plato sent Aristonymus to the Arcadians, Phormion to Elis, Menedemus to Pyrrha. Eudoxus and Aristotle wrote laws for Cnidus and Stagirus. Alexander asked Xenocrates for advice about kingship; the man who was sent to Alexander by the Asiatic Greeks and did most to incite him to his war on the barbarians was Delios of Ephesus, an associate of Plato.

The Academy survived Plato's death. Though its interest in science waned and its philosophical orientation changed, it remained for two and a half centuries a focus of intellectual life. Its creation as a permanent society for the prosecution of both humane and exact sciences has been regarded—with pardonable exaggeration—as the first establishment of a university.

Formative influences. The most important formative influence to which the young Plato was exposed was Socrates. It does not appear, however, that Plato belonged as a "disciple" to the circle of Socrates' intimates. The *Seventh Letter* speaks of Socrates not as a "master" but as an older "friend," for whose character Plato had a profound respect; and he has recorded his own absence (through indisposition) from the death scene of the *Phaedo.* It may well be that his own vocation to philosophy dawned on him only afterward, as he reflected on the treatment of Socrates by the democratic leaders. Plato owed to Socrates his commitment to philosophy, his rational method, and his concern for ethical questions. Among other philosophical influences the most significant were those of Heracleitus and his followers, who disparaged the phenomenal world as an arena of constant change and flux, and of the Pythagoreans, with whose metaphysical and mystical notions Plato had great sympathy.

Plato had family connections with Pyrilampes, a Periclean politician, and with Critias, who became one of the most unscrupulous of the Thirty Tyrants who briefly ruled Athens after the collapse of the democracy.

Plato's early experiences covered the disastrous years of the Deceleian War, the shattering of the Athenian empire, and the fierce civil strife of oligarchs and democrats in the year of anarchy, 404–403. He was too young to have known anything by experience of the imperial democracy of Pericles and Cleon or of the tide of the Sophistic movement. It is certainly not from memory that he depicted Protagoras, the earliest avowed professional Sophist, or Alcibiades, a brilliant but unreliable Athenian politician and military commander. No doubt these early experiences helped to form the political views that were later expounded in the dialogues.

GENERAL FEATURES OF THE DIALOGUES

The canon and text of Plato was apparently fixed at about the turn of the Christian Era. By reckoning the *Letters* as one item, the list contained 36 works, arranged in nine tetralogies. None of Plato's works has been lost, and there is a general agreement among modern scholars that a number of small items—*Alcibiades I, Alcibiades II, Theages, Erastae, Clitopho, Hipparchus,* and *Minos*—are spurious. Most scholars also believe that the *Epinomis,* an appendix to the *Laws,* was written by the mathematician Philippus of Opus. The *Hippias Major* and the *Menexenus* are regarded as doubtful by some, though Aristotle seems to have regarded them as Platonic. Most of the 13 *Letters* are certainly later forgeries. About the authenticity of the *Seventh Letter,* which is by far the most important from the biographical and the philosophical points of view, there exists a long and unsettled controversy.

Order of composition. Plato's literary career extended over the greater part of a long life. The *Apology* was probably written in the early 380s. The *Laws,* on the other hand, was the work of an old man, and the state of its text bears out the tradition that Plato never lived to give it its final revision. Since there is no evidence that Plato began his career with a fully developed system, and since there is every reason to believe that his thoughts changed, the order in which the various dialogues were written takes on importance. Only through it can the development of Plato's thought be adequately charted. Unfortunately, Plato himself has given few clues to the order: he linked the *Sophist* and the *Statesman* with the *Theaetetus* externally as continuations of the conversation reported in that dialogue. Similarly, he seems to have linked the *Timaeus* with the *Republic.* And Aristotle noted that the *Laws* was written after the *Republic.*

Modern scholars, by the use of stylistic criteria, have argued that the *Sophist, Statesman, Philebus, Timaeus* (with its fragmentary sequel *Critias*), and *Laws* form a distinct linguistic group, belonging to the later years of Plato's life. The whole group must be later than the *Sophist,* which professes to be a sequel to the *Theaetetus.* Since the *Theaetetus* commemorates the death of the eminent mathematician after whom it is named (probably in 369 BC), it may be ascribed to *c.* 368, the eve of Plato's departure for Syracuse.

The earlier group of dialogues is generally believed to have ended with the *Theaetetus* and the closely related *Parmenides.* Apart from this, perhaps all that can be said with certainty is that the great dialogues, *Symposium, Phaedo,* and *Republic* (and perhaps also *Protagoras*), in which Plato's dramatic power was at its highest, mark the culmination of this first period of literary activity. The later dialogues are often thought to lack the dramatic and literary merits of the earlier but to compensate for this by an increased subtlety and maturity of judgment.

Persons of the dialogues. One difficulty that initially besets the modern student is that created by the dramatic form of Plato's writings. Since Plato never introduced himself into his own dialogues, he is not formally committed to anything asserted in them. The speakers who are formally bound by the utterances of the dialogues are their characters, of whom Socrates is usually the protagonist.

Since all of these are real historical persons, it is reasonable to wonder whether Plato is reporting their opinions or putting his own views into their mouths, and, more generally, to ask what was his purpose in writing dialogues.

Some scholars have suggested that Plato allowed himself to develop freely in a dialogue any view that interested him for the moment without pledging himself to its truth. Thus Plato can make Socrates advocate hedonistic utilitarianism in the *Protagoras* and denounce it in the *Gorgias.* Others argue that some of Plato's characters, notably Socrates and Timaeus, are "mouthpieces" through whom he inculcates tenets of his own without concern for dramatic or historical propriety. Thus it has often been held that the theory of Ideas, the doctrine of recollection, and the notion of the tripartite soul were originated by Plato after the death of Socrates and consciously fathered on the older philosopher.

Thought of the earlier and later dialogues. There are undeniable differences in thought between the dialogues that are later than the *Theaetetus* and those that are earlier. But there are no serious discrepancies of doctrine between individual dialogues of the same period. Plato perhaps announced his own personal convictions on certain doctrines in the second group of dialogues by a striking dramatic device. In the *Sophist* and *Statesman* the leading part is taken by a visitor from Elea and in the *Laws* by an Athenian. These are the only anonymous, indeed almost certainly the only imaginary, personages of any moment in the whole of Plato's writings. It seems likely, therefore, that these two characters were left anonymous so that the writer could be free to use them as mouthpieces for his own teaching. Plato thus took on himself the responsibility for the logic and epistemology of the *Sophist* and of the *Statesman* and for the ethics and the educational and political theory of the *Statesman* and of the *Laws.*

Doctrine of Forms. There is a philosophical doctrine running through the earlier dialogues that has as its three main features the theory of knowledge as recollection, the conception of the tripartite soul, and, most importantly, the theory of Forms. The theory that knowledge is recollection rests on the belief that the soul is not only eternal but also preexistent. The conception of the tripartite soul holds that the soul consists of reason, appetite, and spirit (or will). Each part serves a purpose and has validity, but reason is the soul's noblest part; in order for man to achieve harmony, appetite and spirit must be subjected to the firm control of reason. The theory of Forms has as its foundation the assumption that beyond the world of physical things there is a higher, spiritual realm of Forms, or Ideas, such as the Form of Beauty or Justice. This realm of Forms, moreover, has a hierarchical order, the highest level being that of the Form of the Good. Whereas the physical world, perceived with the senses, is in constant flux and knowledge derived from it restricted and variable, the realm of Forms, apprehensible only by the mind, is eternal and changeless. Each Form is the pattern of a particular category of things in this world; thus there are Forms of man, stone, shape, colour, beauty, and justice. Yet the things of this world are only imperfect copies of these perfect Forms.

In the *Phaedo* Socrates is made to describe the theory of Ideas as something quite familiar that he has for years constantly canvassed with his friends. In the dialogues of the second period, however, these tenets are less prominent, and the most important of them all, the theory of Forms, is in the *Parmenides* subjected to a searching set of criticisms. The question thus arises as to whether Plato himself had two distinct philosophies, an earlier and a later, or whether the main object of the first group of dialogues was to preserve the memory of Socrates, the philosophy there expounded being, in the main, that of Socrates—coloured, no doubt, but not consciously distorted, in its passage through the mind of Plato. On the second view, Plato had no distinctive Platonic philosophy until a late period in his life.

Socrates and Plato. It may be significant that the only dialogue later than the *Theaetetus* in which Socrates takes a leading part is the *Philebus,* the one work of the second group that deals primarily with the ethical problems on which the thought of Socrates had concentrated. This is usually explained by supposing that Plato was unwilling to make Socrates the exponent of doctrines that he knew to be his own property. It would, however, be hard to understand such misgivings if Plato had already been employing Socrates in that very capacity for years. It is notable, too, that Aristotle, who apparently knew nothing of an earlier and a later version of Platonism, attributed to Plato a doctrine that is quite unlike anything to be found in the first group of dialogues. It was also the view of Neoplatonic scholars that the theory of Ideas of the great earlier dialogues really originated with Socrates; and the fact that they did not find it necessary to argue the point may show that this had been the standing tradition of the Academy.

Few modern scholars, however, support this view. The differences between the early and late periods are not as great as they have sometimes been represented: although Plato's thought developed from the early to the late dialogues, it underwent no sudden dislocation. The ideas of the early period may have been inspired by Socrates, but they were Plato's own—for example, the theory of Forms could not have arisen with Socrates. Plato nevertheless attributed it to him because he saw it as the theoretical basis of what Socrates did teach.

THE EARLIER DIALOGUES

Three main areas of thought

In the *Republic,* the greatest of all the dialogues that precede the *Theaetetus,* there are three main strands of argument deftly combined into an artistic whole—the ethical and political, the aesthetic and mystical, and the metaphysical. Other major dialogues belonging to this period give special prominence to one of these three lines of thought: the *Phaedo* to the metaphysical theme; the *Protagoras* and the *Gorgias* to the ethical and political; the *Symposium* and the *Phaedrus* to the aesthetic. But it should be noted that Plato's dialogues are not philosophical essays, let alone philosophical treatises, and they do not restrict themselves to a single topic or subject.

Dialogues of search. The shorter dialogues, dealing with more special problems, generally of an ethical character, mostly conform to a common type: a problem in moral philosophy, often that of the right definition of a virtue, is propounded, a number of tentative solutions are considered, and all are found to be vitiated by difficulties that cannot be dispelled. The reader is left, at the end of the conversation, aware of his ignorance of the very things that it is most imperative for a man to know. He has formally learned nothing but has been made alive to the confusions and fallacies in what he had hitherto been content to take as knowledge. The dialogues are "aporetic" and "elenctic": they pose puzzles (*aporiai* in Greek) without solving them, and Socrates' procedure consists in the successive refutation (*elenchos*) of the various views presented by his interlocutors.

The effect of these dialogues of search is thus to put the reader in tune with the spirit of Socrates, who had said that the one respect in which he was wiser than other men was in his keen appreciation of his own ignorance of the most important matters. The reader learns the meaning of Socrates' ruling principle that the supreme business of life is to "tend" the soul and his conviction that "goodness of soul" means knowledge of good and evil. The three dialogues directly concerned with the trial of Socrates have a further purpose. They are intended to explain to a puzzled public, as a debt of honour to his memory, why Socrates thought it a matter of conscience neither to withdraw from danger before his trial, nor to make a conciliatory defense, nor, after conviction, to avail himself of the opportunity of flight.

The *Apology,* or *Defense,* purports to give Socrates' speeches at his trial for impiety. In the *Crito* Socrates, in the condemned cell, explains why he will not try to escape paying the death penalty; the dialogue is a consideration of the source and nature of political obligation. The *Euthyphro* is represented as taking place just before Socrates' trial. Its subject is the virtue of "piety," or the proper attitude for men to take toward the gods. The *Hippias*

Themes of the shorter dialogues

Major propounds the question "What is the 'fine' (or 'beautiful')?" The *Hippias Minor* deals with the paradox that "wrongdoing is involuntary." The *Ion* discredits the

poets, who create not "by science" but by a nonrational inspiration. The *Menexenus,* which professes to repeat a funeral oration learned from Aspasia, Pericles' mistress, is apparently meant as a satire on the patriotic distortion of history. The *Charmides, Laches,* and *Lysis* are typical dialogues of search. The question of the *Charmides* is what is meant by *sōphrosunē,* or "temperance," the virtue that is shown in self-command, in dutiful behaviour to parents and superiors, in balance, and in self-possession amid the turns of fortune. It seems that this virtue can be identified with the self-knowledge that Socrates had valued so highly. The *Laches* is concerned with courage, the soldier's virtue; and the *Lysis* examines in the same tentative way friendship, the relation in which self-forgetting devotion most conspicuously displays itself.

The question of whether words have meaning by nature or by convention is considered in the *Cratylus*—whether there is some special appropriateness of the sounds or forms of words to the objects they signify, or whether meaning merely reflects the usage of the community. Plato argues that, since language is an instrument of thought, the test of its rightness is not mere social usage but its genuine capacity to express thought accurately. The dialogue *Euthydemus* satirizes the "eristics"—those who try to entangle a person in fallacies because of the ambiguity of language. Its more serious purpose, however, is to contrast this futile logic chopping with the "protreptic," or hortatory, efforts of Socrates, who urges that happiness is guaranteed not by the possession of things but by the right use of them—and particularly of the gifts of mind, body, and fortune.

Ethical and political dialogues. The *Gorgias,* the *Protagoras,* and the *Meno,* like several of the lesser dialogues, give prominence to ethical and political themes. The *Gorgias* begins ostensibly as an inquiry into the nature and worth of rhetoric, the art of advocacy professed by Gorgias, and develops into a plea of sustained eloquence and logical power for morality—as against expediency—as the sovereign rule of life, both private and public. It ends with an imaginative picture of the eternal destinies of the righteous and of the unrighteous soul.

Gorgias holds that rhetoric is the queen of all "arts." If the statesman skilled in rhetoric is clever enough, he can, though a layman, carry the day even against the specialist. Socrates, on the other hand, declares that rhetoric is not an art but a mere "knack" of humouring the prejudices of an audience. There are two arts conducive to health of soul, those of the legislator and of the judge. The Sophist counterfeits the first, the orator the second, by taking the pleasant instead of the good as his standard. The orator is thus not the wise physician of the body politic but its toady. This severe judgment is disputed by Polus, an ardent admirer of Gorgias, on the ground that the successful orator is virtually the autocrat of the community, and to be such is the summit of human happiness because he can do whatever he likes.

Disputes as to the nature of rhetoric

Socrates rejects this view. He does so by developing one of the "Socratic paradoxes": to suffer a wrong is an evil, but to inflict one is much worse. Thus if rhetoric is of real service to men, it should be most of all serviceable to an offender, who would employ it to move the authorities to inflict the penalties for which the state of his soul calls. All of this is in turn denied by Callicles, who proceeds to develop the extreme position of an amoralist. It may be a convention of the herd that unscrupulous aggression is discreditable and wrong, but "nature's convention" is that the strong are justified in using their strength as they please, while the weak "go to the wall." To Socrates, however, the creators of the imperialistic Athenian democracy were no true statesmen; they were the domestic servants of the democracy for whose tastes they catered; they were not its physicians. That would be a condition like that of the Danaids of mythology, who are punished in Hades by being set to spend eternity in filling leaking pitchers. A happy life consists not in the constant gratification of boundless desires but rather in the measured satisfaction of wants that are tempered by justice and *sōphrosunē.*

The *Meno* is nominally concerned with the question of what virtue is and whether it can be taught. But it is further interesting for two reasons: it states clearly the doctrine that knowledge is "recollection"; and it introduces as a character the democratic politician Anytus, the main author of the prosecution of Socrates.

Whether virtue can be taught Whether virtue can be taught depends on what virtue is. But the inquiry into virtue is difficult—indeed, the very possibility of inquiry is threatened by Meno's paradox concerning the quest for knowledge. If a person is ignorant about the subject of his inquiry, he could not recognize the unknown, even if he found it. If, on the other hand, the person already knows it, inquiry is futile because it is idle to inquire into what one already knows. But this difficulty would vanish if the soul were immortal and had long ago learned all truth, so that it needs now only to be reminded of truths that it once knew and has forgotten. To advance this argument, Socrates shows that a slave boy who has never studied geometry can be brought to recognize mathematical truths. He produces the right answer "out of himself." In general, knowledge is "recollection." Socrates next produces the hypothesis that virtue is knowledge and infers that it is teachable. But if virtue is knowledge, there must be professional teachers of it. Anytus insists that the Sophists, who claim to be such professionals, are mischievous impostors; and even the "best men" have been unable to teach it to their own sons. The *Meno* ends with a distinction between knowledge and true belief, and with the suggestion that virtue comes not by teaching but by divine gift.

The *Protagoras* gives the most complete presentation of the main principles of Socratic morality. In this dialogue Socrates meets the eminent Sophist Protagoras, who explains that his profession is the "teaching of goodness"— *i.e.,* the art of making a success of one's life and of one's city. Socrates urges, however, that both common opinion and the failure of eminent men to teach "goodness" to their sons suggest that the conduct of life is not teachable. But the problem arises as to whether the various commonly recognized virtues are really different or all one. Protagoras is ultimately ready to identify all of the virtues except courage with wisdom or sound judgment. Socrates then attempts to show that, even in the case of courage, goodness consists in the fact that, by facing pain and danger, one escapes worse pain or danger. Thus all virtues can be reduced to the prudent computation of pleasures and of pains. Here, then, is a second "Socratic paradox": no one does wrong willingly—wrongdoing is a matter of miscalculation. It is a puzzling feature of this argument that Socrates appears to embrace a form of hedonism.

Metaphysical foundation of Plato's doctrine: "Phaedo." In the works so far considered, the foundation of a Socratic moral and political doctrine is laid, which holds that the great concern of man is the development of a rational moral personality and that this development is the key to man's felicity. Success in this task, however, depends on rational insight into the true scale of good. The reason **Need for insight into Good** men forfeit felicity is that they mistake apparent good for real. If a man ever knew with assurance what the Good is, he would never pursue anything else; it is in this sense that "all virtue is knowledge." The philosophical moralist, who has achieved an assured insight into absolute Good, is thus the only true statesman, for he alone can tend to the national character. These moral convictions have a metaphysical foundation and justification. The principles of this metaphysics are expounded more explicitly in the following dialogues, in which a theory of knowledge and of scientific method is also discernible.

The object of the *Phaedo* is to justify belief in the immortality of the soul by showing that it follows from a fundamental metaphysical doctrine (the theory of Ideas, or the doctrine of Forms), which seems to afford a rational clue to the structure of the universe. Socrates' soul is identical with Socrates himself: the survival of his soul is the survival of Socrates—in a purified state. For his life has **Arguments for immortality of the soul** been spent in trying to liberate the soul from dependence on the body. In life, the body is always interfering with the soul's activity. Its appetites and passions interrupt the pursuit of wisdom and goodness.

There are four arguments for thinking that the soul survives death.

First, there is a belief that the soul has a succession of many lives. The processes of nature in general are cyclical; and it is reasonable to suppose that this cyclicity applies to the case of dying and coming to life. If this were not so, if the process of dying were not reversible, life would ultimately vanish from the universe.

Second, the doctrine that what men call "learning" is really "recollection" shows, or at least suggests, that the soul's life is independent of the body.

Third, the soul contemplates the Forms, which are eternal, changeless, and simple. The soul is like the Forms. Hence it is immortal.

The fourth argument is the most elaborate. Socrates begins by recalling his early interest in finding the causes of being and change and his dissatisfaction with the explanations then current. He offers instead the Forms as causes. First, and safely, he says that something becomes, say, hot simply by participating in Heat. Then, a little more daringly, he is prepared to say that it becomes hot by participating in Fire, which brings Heat with it. Now if Fire brings Heat, it cannot accept Cold, which is the opposite of Heat. All this is then applied to the soul. Human beings are alive by participating in Life—and, more particularly, by having souls that bring Life with them. Since the soul brings Life, it cannot accept Death, the opposite of Life. But in that case the soul cannot perish and is immortal. (For further discussion of the theory of Forms, see METAPHYSICS.)

Aesthetic and mystical dialogues. Both the *Symposium* and the *Phaedrus* present the Forms in a special light, as objects of mystical contemplation and as stimuli of mystical emotion.

The immediate object of the *Symposium,* which records several banquet eulogies of *erōs* (erotic love), is to find the highest manifestation of the love that controls the world in the mystic aspiration after union with eternal and supercosmic beauty. It depicts Socrates as having reached the goal of union and puts the figure of Alcibiades, who has sold his spiritual birthright for the pleasures of the world, in sharp opposition to him.

The main argument may be summarized thus: *Erōs* is a **Ascent to the supreme Form of Good** reaching out of the soul to a hoped-for good. The object is eternal beauty. In its crudest form, love for a beautiful person is really a passion to achieve immortality through offspring by that person. A more spiritual form is the aspiration to combine with a kindred soul to give birth to sound institutions and rules of life. Still more spiritual is the endeavour to enrich philosophy and science through noble dialogue. The insistent seeker may then suddenly descry a supreme beauty that is the cause and source of all of the beauties so far discerned. The philosopher's path thus culminates in a vision of the Form of the Good, the supreme Form that stands at the head of all others.

Though the immediate subject of the *Phaedrus* is to show how a truly scientific rhetoric might be built on the double foundation of logical method and scientific study of human passions, Plato contrives to unite with this topic a discussion of the psychology of love, which leads him to speak of the Forms as the objects of transcendent emotion and, indeed, of mystical contemplation. The soul, in its antenatal, disembodied state, could enjoy the direct contemplation of the Forms. But sense experience can suggest the Form of Beauty in an unusually startling way: through falling in love. The unreason and madness of the lover mean that the wings of his soul are beginning to grow again; it is the first step in the soul's return to its high estate.

The "Republic." In the *Republic* the immediate problem is ethical. What is justice? Can it be shown that justice benefits the man who is just? Plato holds that it can. Justice consists in a harmony that emerges when the various parts of a unit perform the function proper to them and abstain from interfering with the functions of any other part. More specifically, justice occurs with regard to the individual, when the three component parts of his soul— reason, appetite, and spirit, or will—each perform their appropriate tasks; with regard to society, justice occurs when its component members each fulfill the demands of their allotted roles. Harmony is ensured in the individual when the rational part of his soul is in command; with regard to society, when philosophers are its rulers because philosophers—Platonic philosophers—have a clear understanding of justice, based on their vision of the Form of the Good.

In the ethical scheme of the *Republic* three roles, or "three lives," are distinguished: those of the philosopher, of the votary of enjoyment, and of the man of action. The end of the first is wisdom; of the second, the gratification of appetite; and of the third, practical distinction. These reflect the three elements, or active principles, within a man: rational judgment of good; a multitude of conflicting appetites for particular gratifications; and spirit, or will, manifested as resentment against infringements both by others and by the individual's own appetites.

This tripartite scheme is then applied to determine the structure of the just society. Plato develops his plan for a just society by dividing the general population into three classes that correspond to the three parts of man's soul as well as to the three lives. Thus there are: the statesmen; the general civilian population that provides for material needs; and the executive force (army and police). These three orders correspond respectively to the rational, appetitive, and spirited elements. They have as their corresponding virtues wisdom, the excellence of the thinking part; temperance, that of the appetitive part (acquiescence of the nonrational elements to the plan of life prescribed by judgment); and courage, that of the spirited part (loyalty to the rule of life laid down by judgment). The division of the population into these three classes would not be made on the basis of birth or wealth but on the basis of education provided for by the state. By a process of examination each individual would then be assigned to his appropriate rank in correspondence with the predominant part of his soul.

The state ordered in this manner is just because each of the elements vigorously executes its own function and, in loyal contentment, confines itself within its limits. Such a society is a true aristocracy, or rule of the best. Plato describes successive deviations from this ideal as timocracy (the benign military state), oligarchy (the state dominated by merchant princes, a plutocracy), and democracy (the state subjected to an irresponsible or criminal will).

The training of the philosophical rulers would continue through a long and rigorous education because the vision of the Good requires extensive preparation and intellectual discipline. It leads through study of the exact sciences to that of their metaphysical principles. The central books of the *Republic* thus present an outline of metaphysics and a philosophy of the sciences. The Forms appear in the double character of objects of all genuine science and formal causes of events and processes. Plato expressly denied that there can be knowledge, in the proper sense, of the temporal and mutable. In his scheme for the intellectual training of the philosophical rulers, the exact sciences—arithmetic, plane and solid geometry, astronomy, and harmonics—would first be studied for 10 years to familiarize the mind with relations that can only be apprehended by thought. Five years would then be given to the still severer study of "dialectic." Dialectic is, etymologically, the art of conversation, of question and answer; and according to Plato, dialectical skill is the ability to pose and answer questions about the essences of things. The dialectician replaces hypotheses with secure knowledge, and his aim is to ground all science, all knowledge, on some "unhypothetical first principle."

The Form of the Good

This principle is the Form of the Good, which, like the Sun in relation to visible things, is the source of the reality of all things, of the light by which they are apprehended, and also of their value. As in the *Symposium,* the Good is the supreme beauty that dawns suddenly upon the pilgrim of love as he draws near to his goal.

Dialogues of critical reconstruction. The two works that probably anticipate the dialogues of Plato's old age, the *Parmenides* and *Theaetetus,* display a remarkable difference of tone, clearly the result of a period of fruitful reconstruction.

The theory expounded in the *Phaedo* and *Republic* does not allow enough reality to the sensible world. These dialogues suppose that an entity capable of being sensed is a complex that participates in a plurality of Forms: what else it may be they do not say. Clearly, however, the relation between a thing and a Form (*e.g.,* beauty), which has been called participation, needs further elucidation. In these dialogues truths of fact, of the natural world, have not yet had their importance recognized.

Plato clearly had an external motive for the reexamination of his system as well. The *Parmenides,* the *Theaetetus,* and the *Sophist* all reveal a special interest in the Eleatic philosophy, of which Parmenides was the chief representative. The doctrine of his friend Eucleides of Megara, like that of Parmenides, was that phenomena which can be apprehended by the senses are illusions with no reality at all. Continued reflection on this problem led straight to the discussion of the meaning of the copula "is" and the significance of the denial "is not," which is the subject of the *Sophist.*

Formally the *Parmenides* leads to an impasse. In its first half the youthful Socrates expounds the doctrine of the participation of things in Forms as the solution of the problem of the "one and many." ("How can this, that, and the other cat all be one thing—*e.g.,* black?" "Each distinct cat participates in the unique Form of Blackness.") Parmenides raises what appear to be insoluble objections and hints that the helplessness of Socrates under his criticism arises from insufficient training in logic.

In the second half Parmenides gives an example of the logical training that he recommends. He takes for examination his own thesis, "The one is," and constructs upon it as basis an elaborate set of contradictions.

Objections to the doctrine of Forms

The Eleatic objections to the doctrine of participation are, first, that it does not really reconcile unity with plurality since it leads to a perpetual regress. It says that the many things that have a common predicate, or characteristic, participate in, or imitate, a single Form. But the Form itself also admits of a common predicate, and therefore a second Form must exist, participated in alike by the sensible things and the first Form, and so on, endlessly. Second, a graver difficulty is that the relations between Forms must belong to the realm of Forms, and those between sensible things to the realm of things. Thus men, belonging to the second, can know nothing of the true realities, the Forms. Scholars disagree over the precise interpretation of these objections. They also disagree about how Plato should have reacted to them—and about how he did react.

The *Theaetetus* is a discussion of the question of how knowledge should be defined. It is remarkable that the dialogue treats knowledge at length without making any reference to the Forms or to the mythology of recollection. It remains to this day one of the best introductions to the problem of knowledge. The main argument is as follows:

Efforts at defining knowledge

It seems plausible to say that knowledge is perception, which appears to imply that "What seems to me is so to me; what seems to you is so to you" (Protagoras). This relativistic doctrine is, rather oddly, claimed by Plato to be equivalent to the view held by the late 6th-century-BC Greek philosopher Heracleitus that "everything is always and in all ways in flux." But these views imply that there is no common perceived world and therefore nothing of certainty can be said or thought at all.

As for the thesis that knowledge is perception, one must first distinguish what the soul perceives through bodily organs from what it apprehends by itself without organs—such as number, sameness, likeness, being, and good. But because all knowledge involves truth and therefore being, perception, which cannot grasp being, is not identical with knowledge.

Is knowledge, then, true belief? The reference to true belief leads Plato into a discussion of false belief, for which he can discover no satisfactory analysis. False belief is belief in what is not, and what is not cannot be believed. But the example of verdicts in the law courts is enough to show that there can be true belief without knowledge.

Finally, is knowledge true belief together with an "account"? The concept of an account (*logos*) is not a simple one. No satisfactory definition of knowledge emerges, and the dialogue ends without a conclusion.

Because Plato's argument nowhere appeals to his favourite doctrine of Forms and because the dialogue ends so inconclusively, some scholars have suggested that Plato wanted to show that the problem of knowledge is insoluble without the Forms.

THE LATER DIALOGUES

Formally the important dialogues the *Sophist* and the *Statesman* are closely connected, both being ostensibly concerned with a problem of definition. The real purpose of the *Sophist,* however, is logical or metaphysical; it aims at explaining the true nature of negative predication, or denials that something is so. The object of the *Statesman,* on the other hand, is to consider the respective merits of two contrasting forms of government, personal rule and constitutionalism, and to recommend the second, particularly in the form of limited monarchy. The *Sophist* thus lays the foundations of all subsequent logic, the *Statesman* those of all constitutionalism. A second purpose in both dialogues is to illustrate the value of careful classification as a basis for scientific definition.

The *Sophist* purports to investigate what a Sophist really is. The definitions all lead to such notions as falsity, illusion, nonbeing. But these notions are puzzling. How can there be such a thing as a false statement or a false impression? For the false means "what is not," and what is not is nothing at all and can neither be uttered nor thought. Plato argues that what is not in some sense also is, and that what is in some sense is not; and he refutes Parmenidean monism by drawing the distinction between absolute and relative nonbeing. A significant denial, *A* is not *B*, does not mean that *A* is nothing, but that *A* is other than *B;* every one of the "greatest kinds," or most general, features of reality—being, identity, difference, motion, and rest—is other than every other feature. Motion, say, is other than rest; and thus motion is not rest—but it does not follow that motion is not. The true business of dialectic is to treat the Forms themselves as an interrelated system, with relations of compatibility and incompatibility among themselves.

Absolute versus relative nonbeing

In the *Statesman* the conclusion is reached that government by a benevolent dictator is not suitable to the conditions of human life because his direction is not that of a god. The surrogate for direction by a god is the impersonal supremacy of inviolable law. Where there is such law, monarchy is the best and democracy the least satisfactory form of constitution; but where there is no law, this situation is inverted.

The *Philebus* contains Plato's ripest moral psychology. Its subject is strictly ethical—the question of whether the Good is to be identified with pleasure or with wisdom. Under the guidance of Socrates a mediating conclusion is reached: the best life contains both elements, but wisdom predominates.

Philosophically most important is a classification adopted to determine the formal character of the two claimants to recognition as the Good. Everything real belongs to one of four classes: (1) the infinite or unbounded, (2) the limit, (3) the mixture (of infinite and limit), (4) the cause of the mixture. It emerges that all of the good things of life belong to the third class, that is, are produced by imposing a definite limit upon an indeterminate continuum.

The *Timaeus* is an exposition of cosmology, physics, and biology. Timaeus first draws the distinction between eternal being and temporal becoming and insists that it is only of the former that one can have exact and final knowledge. The visible, mutable world had a beginning; it is the work of God, who had its Forms before him as eternal models in terms of which he molded the world as an imitation. God first formed its soul out of three constituents: identity, difference, being. The world soul was placed in the circles of the heavenly bodies, and the circles were animated with movements. Subsequently the various subordinate gods and the immortal and rational element in the human soul were formed. The human body and the lower components of its soul were generated through the intermediacy of the "created gods" (*i.e.,* the stars).

The forming of the world

The *Timaeus* combines the geometry of the Pythagoreans with the biology of Empedocles by a mathematical construction of the elements, in which four of the regular solids—cube, tetrahedron, octahedron, and icosahedron—are assumed to be the shapes of the corpuscles of earth, fire, air, and water. (The fifth, the dodecahedron, comprises the model for the whole universe.)

Among the important features of the dialogue are its introduction of God as the "demiurge"—the intelligent cause of all order and structure in the world of becoming—and the emphatic recognition of the essentially tentative character of natural science. It is also noteworthy that, though Plato presents a corpuscular physics, his metaphysical substrate is not matter but *chōra* (space). The presence of space as a factor requires the recognition, over and above God or mind, of an element that he called *anankē* (necessity). The activity of the demiurge ensures that the universe is in general rational and well-ordered, but the brute force of material necessity sets limits to the scope and efficacy of reason. The details of Plato's cosmology, physiology, and psychophysics are of great importance for the history of science but metaphysically of secondary interest.

The *Laws,* Plato's longest and most intensely practical work, contains his ripest utterances on ethics, education, and jurisprudence, as well as his one entirely nonmythical exposition of theology. The immediate object is to provide a model of constitution making and legislation to assist in the actual founding of cities. The problem of the dialogue is thus not the construction of an ideal state as in the *Republic* but the framing of a constitution and code that might be successfully adopted by a society of average Greeks. Hence the demands made on average human nature, though exacting, are not pitched too high; and the communism of the *Republic* is dropped.

The practical level of the *Laws*

Purely speculative philosophy and science are excluded from the purview of the *Laws,* and the metaphysical interest is introduced only so far as to provide a basis for a moral theology. In compensation the dialogue is exceptionally rich in political and legal thought and appears, indirectly, to have left its mark on the great system of Roman jurisprudence.

In the ethics of the *Laws* Plato is rigid and rigorous—for example, homosexuality shall be completely suppressed and monogamous marriage with strict chastity shall be the rule. (In the *Republic* the guardian class enters into temporary unions or "sacred marriages," with a community of wives and children, to foster a concern for the common good.) In politics, Plato favours a mixed constitution, one with elements of democratic freedom and autocratic authoritarianism, and he suggests a system for securing both genuine popular representation and the proper degree of attention to personal qualifications. The basis of society is to be agriculture, not commerce. What amounts to a tax of 100 percent is to be levied on incomes beyond the statutory limits. Education is regarded as the most important of all the functions of government. The distinction between the sexes is to be treated as irrelevant.

Careful attention is to be paid to the right utilization of the child's instinct for play and to the demand that the young shall be taught in institutions where expert instruction in all of the various subjects is coordinated. Members of the supreme council of the state shall be thoroughly trained in the supreme science, which "sees the one in the many and the many in the one"; *i.e.,* in dialectic. In the *Laws* Plato instituted regulations which would ensure that trials for serious offenses would take place before a court of highly qualified magistrates and would proceed with due deliberation. Also, provision was made for appeals, and a foundation was laid for a distinction between civil and criminal law.

The *Laws* also creates a natural theology. There are three false beliefs, Plato holds, that are fatal to moral character: atheism, denial of the moral government of the world, and the belief that divine judgment can be bought off by offerings. Plato claims that he can disprove them all. His refutation of atheism turns on the identification of the soul with the "movement which can move itself." Thus all motion throughout the universe is ultimately initiated by souls. It is then inferred from the regular character of the great cosmic motions and their systematic unity that

Plato's natural theology

the souls which originate them form a hierarchy with a best soul, God, at their head. Since some motions are disorderly, there must be one soul that is not the best, and there may be more. (There is no suggestion, however, that there is a worst soul, a devil.) The other two heresies can be similarly disposed of. Plato thus becomes the originator of the view that there are certain theological truths that can be strictly demonstrated by reason; *i.e.*, of philosophical theology. Plato goes on to enact that the denial of any of his three propositions shall be a grave crime.

The *Laws* strikes many readers as a dull and depressing work. Its prose lacks the sparkle of the early dialogues; and Socrates, the hero of those works, would not have been tolerated under a government of the repressively authoritarian style that the *Laws* recommends.   (J.B./Ed.)

Platonism after Plato

The term Platonism can be applied to any philosophy that derives its ultimate inspiration from Plato. Though there was in antiquity a tradition about Plato's "unwritten doctrines" (much discussed by German scholars since 1959), Platonism then and later was based primarily on a reading of the dialogues. But these can be read in many different ways, often very selectively, and it may be that all that the various kinds of Platonism can be said to have in common is an intense concern for the quality of human life—always ethical, often religious, and sometimes political, based on a belief in unchanging and eternal realities, independent of the changing things of the world perceived by the senses. Platonism sees these realities both as the causes of the existence of everything in the universe and as giving value and meaning to its contents in general and the life of its inhabitants in particular. It is this belief in absolute values rooted in an eternal world that distinguishes Platonism from the philosophies of Plato's immediate predecessors and successors and from later philosophies inspired by them—from the immanentist naturalism of most of the pre-Socratics (who interpreted the world monistically in terms of nature as such), from the relativism of the Sophists, and from the correction of Platonism in a this-worldly direction carried out by Plato's greatest pupil, Aristotle.

GREEK PLATONISM FROM ARISTOTLE THROUGH MIDDLE PLATONISM: ITS NATURE AND HISTORY

Plato as construed by Aristotle
Since Plato refused to write his own metaphysics, knowledge of its final shape has to be derived from hints in the dialogues and statements by Aristotle and, to a far lesser extent, other ancient authorities. According to these, Plato's doctrine of Forms was, in its general character, highly mathematical, the Forms being somehow identified with, or explained in terms of, numbers. Here may be seen the influence of the Pythagoreans, though, as Aristotle says, the details of Plato's views on the mathematical constituents of being were not the same as theirs. In addition Aristotle states that Plato introduced a class of "mathematicals," or "intermediates," positioned between sensible objects and Forms. These differ from sensible objects in being immaterial (*e.g.*, the geometer's triangles *ABC* and *XYZ*) and from the Forms in being plural, unlike the Triangle itself.   (H.J.Bl./Ed.)

Aristotle himself had little use for this sort of mathematical metaphysics and rejected Plato's doctrine of transcendent eternal Forms altogether. Something of Platonism, nonetheless, survived in Aristotle's system in his beliefs that the reality of anything lay in a changeless (though wholly immanent) form or essence comprehensible and definable by reason and that the highest realities were eternal, immaterial, changeless self-sufficient intellects which caused the ordered movement of the universe. It was the desire to give expression to their transcendent perfection that kept the heavenly spheres rotating. Man's intellect at its highest was akin to them. This Aristotelian doctrine of Intellect (nous) was easily recombined with Platonism in later antiquity.

Aristotle, however, was not reacting only against Plato but also against Plato's associates and immediate successors as head of the Academy, namely Plato's nephew

Speusippus (*c.* 410–339 BC) and Xenocrates (396–314 BC). Speusippus, in particular, accented the mathematical tendencies of the late Plato and abolished Forms in favour of numbers. He also posited different principles for different sorts of entities and so was accused by Aristotle of breaking the connections in reality. Xenocrates identified Forms and numbers and began the long process of finding firm doctrines in Plato by laying down that Forms were only of those things that exist in nature. Xenocrates was also the first, as far as is known, to turn his attention to what continued to be a subject of controversy throughout the history of Platonism, namely whether the account of creation offered in the *Timaeus* was to be taken as chronological or merely expository. He took the latter view, which turned out to be the most favoured one in antiquity; Aristotle was on the other side. Whether Xenocrates' three successors as head of the Academy (Polemon, Crates, and Crantor) developed Platonism is uncertain. Crantor (*c.* 330–270 BC) was allegedly the first to write commentaries on Plato, particularly on the *Timaeus*. After Crantor the Academy was preoccupied for about two centuries with the serious questioning of man's claims to knowledge. This began with Arcesilaus (316/315–*c.* 241 BC), who is described as the founder of the Middle Academy. There was a genuine desire to recover the critical, questioning, and agnostic attitude of the Socrates of Plato's early dialogues as well as philosophical exasperation with the dogmatism of some of the contemporary Hellenistic philosophers, especially the Stoics. It is likely that Arcesilaus was influenced to some extent by Pyrrhon (*c.* 360–*c.* 272 BC), founder of the tradition to which the name Skeptic was applied in antiquity. The Skeptical Academics denied that certainty on any subject was possible and worked out a sophisticated theory of probability as a guide to practical decision making. Their critical dialectic and probability theory were best expounded by Carneades (214/213–129/128 BC). Though he wrote nothing, he was regarded as the founder of the New Academy. A return to dogmatic and positive philosophical teaching was effected by Philo of Larissa (died *c.* 79 BC) and his pupil Antiochus of Ascalon, who was head of the school in 79–78 BC.

The next important phase of Platonism, Middle Platonism or pre-Neoplatonism, was significant through the influence that it exerted in more than one direction. In the direction of Jewish culture (further described in a later section), it formed the Greek philosophical background of the efforts of Philo Judaeus (Philo of Alexandria) to create a philosophical system on the basis of the Old Testament heritage. Though the origins of Middle Platonism are obscure, its main direction became clear in the 1st century AD. It seems to have been linked from the beginning with the closely related revival of Pythagoreanism (a philosophy holding that reality is number, and sometimes showing, after the revival, a tendency to superstitious occultism). The somewhat Platonized Stoicism of Poseidonius (*c.* 135–*c.* 51 BC), whose dualism of matter and reason enhanced the roles of emotion and will, may have influenced its beginnings, as did the Stoicized Platonism of Antiochus; and Stoic influence, especially in the ethical field, remained important in its later developments. There was also a strong Aristotelian influence, though a minority of 2nd-century Platonists, notably Atticus and, to a lesser extent, Gaius Calvenus Taurus, objected to certain Aristotelian doctrines. Atticus was particularly offended by Aristotle's failure to provide for providence. The general characteristics of this revised Platonic philosophy (and the closely related Neo-Pythagoreanism) were the recognition of a hierarchy of divine principles with stress on the transcendence of the supreme principle, which was already occasionally called "the One"; the placing of the Platonic Forms in the divine mind; a strongly otherworldly attitude demanding a "flight from the body," an ascent of the mind to the divine and eternal; and a preoccupation with the problem of evil, attributed either to an evil world soul or to matter. The best known of the Middle Platonists is the biographer and essayist Plutarch of Chaeronea (*c.* AD 46–120). More important philosophically were other 2nd-century figures: Gaius and two men possibly influenced by him, Albinus and Apuleius (better known as author

The Academy through the Hellenistic Age

Transition to Neoplatonism

of the prose narrative *The Golden Ass*); Atticus; and Numenius of Apamea. It was from the thought of these and other Middle Platonists, combined with his own reading of Alexander and other Peripatetic commentators on Aristotle, that the foremost Neoplatonist, Plotinus, started constructing his own interpretation of Platonism, which was both profoundly original and firmly rooted in an established school tradition.

NEOPLATONISM: ITS NATURE AND HISTORY

Neoplatonism is the modern name given to the form of Platonism developed by Plotinus in the 3rd century AD and modified by his successors. It came to dominate the Greek philosophical schools and remained predominant until the teaching of philosophy by pagans ended in the second half of the 6th century AD. It represents the final form of pagan Greek philosophy. It was not a mere syncretism (or combination of diverse beliefs) but a genuine, if one-sided, development of ideas to be found in Plato and earlier Platonism—though it incorporated important Aristotelian and Stoic elements as well. There is no real evidence for Oriental influence. A certain Gnostic (relating to intuitive knowledge acquired by privileged individuals and immune to empirical verification) tone or colouring sometimes may be discerned in the thought of Plotinus. But he was consciously a passionate opponent of Gnosticism, and in any case there was often a large element of popular Platonism in the Gnostic systems then current. Moreover, the theosophical works of the late 2nd century AD known as the *Chaldean Oracles,* which were taken as inspired authorities by the later Neoplatonists, seem to have been a hodgepodge of popular Greek religious philosophy.

Core concepts of Neoplatonism

Neoplatonism began as a complex (and in some ways ambiguous) philosophy and grew vigorously in a variety of forms over a long period; it is therefore not easy to generalize about it. But the leading ideas in the thought of philosophers who can properly be described as Neoplatonists seem always to have included the following:

1. There is a plurality of levels of being, arranged in hierarchical descending order, the last and lowest comprising the physical universe, which exists in time and space and is perceptible to the senses.

2. Each level of being is derived from its superior, a derivation that is not a process in time or space.

3. Each derived being is established in its own reality by turning back toward its superior in a movement of contemplative desire, which is implicit in the original creative impulse of outgoing that it receives from its superior; thus the Neoplatonic universe is characterized by a double movement of outgoing and return.

4. Each level of being is an image or expression on a lower level of the one above it. The relation of archetype and image runs through all Neoplatonic schemes.

5. Degrees of being are also degrees of unity; as one goes down the scale of being there is greater multiplicity, more separateness, and increasing limitation—until the atomic individualization of the spatiotemporal world is reached.

6. The highest level of being, and through it all of what in any sense exists, derives from the ultimate principle, which is absolutely free from determinations and limitations and utterly transcends any conceivable reality, so that it may be said to be "beyond being." Because it has no limitations, it has no division, attributes, or qualifications; it cannot really be named, or even properly described as being, but may be called "the One" to designate its complete simplicity. It may also be called "the Good" as the source of all perfections and the ultimate goal of return, for the impulse of outgoing and return that constitutes the hierarchy of derived reality comes from and leads back to the Good.

7. Since this supreme principle is absolutely simple and undetermined (or devoid of specific traits), man's knowledge of it must be radically different from any other kind of knowledge. It is not an object (a separate, determined, limited thing) and no predicates can be applied to it; hence it can be known only if it raises the mind to an immediate union with itself, which cannot be imagined or described.

Plotinus and his philosophy. As far as is known, the originator of this distinctive kind of Platonism was Plotinus (AD 205–270). He had been the pupil at Alexandria of a self-taught philosopher called Ammonius, who also taught the Christian Origen and the latter's pagan namesake, and whose influence on his pupils seems to have been deep and lasting. But Ammonius wrote nothing; there are few reports of his views, and these are unreliable so that nothing is actually known about his thought. A number of distinguished scholars have made attempts to reconstruct it, but their speculations go far beyond the evidence. Plotinus must thus be regarded as the first Neoplatonist, and his collected works, the *Enneads* (Greek *enneas,* "set of nine"—six sets of nine treatises each, arranged by his disciple Porphyry), are the first and greatest collection of Neoplatonic writings.

Plotinus, like most ancient philosophers from Socrates on, was a religious and moral teacher as well as a professional philosopher engaged in the critical interpretation of a long and complicated school tradition. He was an acute critic and arguer, with an exceptional degree of intellectual honesty for his, or any, period; philosophy for him was not only a matter of abstract speculation but also a way of life in which, through an exacting intellectual and moral self-discipline and purification, those who are capable of the ascent can return to the source from which they came. His written works explain how from the eternal creative act—at once spontaneous and necessary—of that transcendent source, the One, or Good, proceeds the world of living reality, constituted by repeated double movements of outgoing and return in contemplation; and this account, showing the way for the human self—which can experience and be active on every level of being—to return to the One, is at the same time an exhortation to follow that way.

Metaphysics: system of emanation

Plotinus always insisted that the One, or Good, is beyond the reach of thought or language; what he said about this supreme principle was intended only to point the mind along the way to it, not to describe or define it. But though no adequate concept or definition of the Good is possible, it was, nonetheless, for Plotinus a positive reality of superabundant excellence. Plotinus often spoke of it in extremely negative language, but his object in doing so was to stress the inadequacy of all of man's ways of thinking and speaking to express this supreme reality or to clarify the implications of the claim that the Good is absolutely one and undetermined, the source of all defined and limited realities.

The original creative or expressive act of the One is the first great derived reality, nous (which can be only rather inadequately translated as "Intellect" or "Spirit"); from this again comes Soul, which forms, orders, and maintains in being the material universe. It must be remembered that, to Plotinus, the whole process of generation is timeless; Nous and Soul are eternal, while time is the life of Soul as active in the physical world, and there never was a time when the material universe did not exist. The "levels of being," then, though distinct, are not separate but are all intimately present everywhere and in everyone. To ascend from Soul through Intellect to the One is not to travel in space but to awake to a new kind of awareness.

Intellect for Plotinus is at one and the same time thinker, thought, and object of thought; it is a mind that is perfectly one with its object. As object, it is the world of Forms, or Ideas, the totality of real being in the Platonic sense. These Forms, being one with Intellect and therefore with each other, are not merely objects but are living, thinking subjects, each not only itself but, in its contemplation, the whole. They are the archetypes and causes of the necessarily imperfect realities on lower levels, souls and the patterns or structures that make bodies what they are. Men at their highest are intellects, or souls perfectly conformed to Intellect; they become aware of their intellectual nature when, passing not only beyond sense perception but beyond the discursive reasoning characteristic of the life of Soul, they immediately grasp eternal realities.

Intellect, Soul, world

Soul for Plotinus is very much what it was for Plato, the intermediary between the worlds of Intellect and Sense and the representative of the former in the latter. It is produced by Intellect, as Intellect is by the One, by a double movement of outgoing and return in contemplation, but the relationship between the two is more intimate and the frontier less clearly defined. For Plotinus, as for Plato, the characteristic of the life of the Soul is movement, which is the cause of all other movements. The life of the Soul in this movement is time, and on it all physical movement depends. Soul both forms and rules the material universe from above; and in its lower, immanent phase, which Plotinus often calls nature, it acts as an indwelling principle of life and growth and produces the lowest forms, those of bodies. Below these lies the darkness of matter, the final absence of being, the absolute limit at which the expansion of the universe—from the One through diminishing degrees of reality and increasing degrees of multiplicity—comes to an end. Because of its utter negativity, such matter is for Plotinus the principle of evil; and although he does not really believe it to be an independent principle forming, with the Good, a dualism, his language about it often has a strongly dualistic flavour.

He was not, however, really dualistic in his attitude toward the material universe. He strongly maintained its goodness and beauty as the best possible work of Soul. It is a living organic whole, and its wholeness is the best possible (though very imperfect) reflection on the space–time level of the living unity in diversity of the world of Forms in Intellect. It is held together in every part by a universal sympathy and harmony. In this harmony external evil and suffering take their place as necessary elements in the great pattern, the great dance of the universe. Evil and suffering can affect men's lower selves but can only exceptionally, in the thoroughly depraved, touch their true, higher selves and so cannot interfere with the real well-being of the philosopher.

Ethics and religion: purification

As souls within bodies, men can exist on any level of the soul's experience and activity. (The descent of souls into bodies is for Plotinus—who had some difficulty in reconciling Plato's various statements on this point—both a fall and a necessary compliance with universal law.) Man can ascend through his own intellect to the level of universal Soul, become that whole that he already is potentially, and, in Soul, attain to Intellect itself; or he can isolate himself on the lower level, shutting himself up in the experiences, desires, and concerns of his lower nature. Philosophical conversion—the beginning of the ascent to the One—consists precisely in turning away, by a tremendous intellectual and moral effort, from the life of the body, dominating and rising above its desires, and "waking to another way of seeing, which everyone has but few use." This, Plotinus insisted, is possible while one is still in an earthly body and without neglecting the duties of one's embodied state. But the body and bodily life weight a man down and hamper him in his ascent. Plotinus' language when speaking of the body and the senses in this context is strongly dualistic and otherworldly. Platonists in general think much more dualistically about their own bodies than about the material universe as a whole. The physical world is seen positively as a noble image of the intelligible; the individual, earthly, animal body, on the contrary, tends to be regarded negatively as a hindrance to the intellectual and spiritual life.

When a man's philosophical conversion is complete and he has become Intellect, he can rise to that mystical union in which the One manifests his continual presence, carried on the surging current of the impulse of return to the source (in its strongest and final flow), the pure love of Intellect for the Good from which it immediately springs. There is no consciousness of duality in that union; the individual is not aware of himself; but neither is he destroyed or dissolved into the One—because even in the union he is still Intellect, though Intellect "out of itself," transcending its normal nature and activity. This mystical union for Plotinus was the focus of much of his effort and, for those of similar inclination, the source of the continuing power of his teaching. Philosophy for him was religion, the effort to actualize in oneself the great impulse of return to the Good, which constitutes reality on all its levels; and religion for him was philosophy. There was no room in his thought and practice for special revelation, grace, and repentance in the Christian sense, and little for

external rites or ceremonies. For him the combination of moral purification and intellectual enlightenment, which only Platonic philosophy as he understood it could give, was the only way to union with the Good.

The later Neoplatonists. Porphyry (c. AD 234–c. 305), a devout disciple of Plotinus and a careful editor of his works, occupied a special position in the development of later Neoplatonism. In some ways his thought paralleled that of the later pagan Neoplatonists, but in others it quite opposed them. The most distinctive features of his thought seem to have been an extreme spiritualism, an insistence, even sharper than that of Plotinus, on the "flight from the body" and—more philosophically important—a greater sympathy with the less sharply defined vertical hierarchies of the Platonists who had preceded Plotinus. Porphyry did not always clearly distinguish the One from Intellect. On the other hand one may see in him the beginnings of the late Neoplatonic tendency to structure reality in both vertical and "horizontal" triads. Thus Being, Life, and Intellect are phases in the eternal self-determination of the ultimate reality. This triad became one of the most important elements in the complex metaphysical structures of the later Neoplatonists. But perhaps Porphyry's most important and influential contribution was the incorporation into Neoplatonism of Aristotle's logic, in particular the doctrine of the categories, with the characteristic Neoplatonic interpretation of them as terms signifying entities. Also of interest is his declaration of ideological war against the Christians, whose doctrines he attacked on both philosophical and exegetical grounds in a work of 15 books entitled *Against the Christians*.

Porphyry and Iamblichus

Iamblichus (c. AD 250–c. 330) seems to have been the originator of the type of Neoplatonism that came to dominate the Platonic schools in the 5th and 6th centuries AD. This kind of Neoplatonism sharpened and multiplied the distinctions between the levels of being. The basic position underlying its elaborations is one of extreme philosophical Realism: it is assumed that the structure of reality corresponds so exactly to the way in which the mind works that there is a separate real entity corresponding to every distinction that it can make. In the fully developed late Neoplatonic system the first principle of reality, the ultimate One, was removed to an altogether ineffable transcendence, mitigated by two factors: the presence of the expressions or manifestations of its unifying power, the "henads"—identified with the gods of paganism—at every level of reality; and the possibility of return to absolute unification through the henad with which one is linked. Below the One a vast structure of triads, or trinities, reached down to the physical world; this was constructed by combining Plotinus' vertical succession of the levels of Being, Intellect, and Soul (much complicated by internal subdivision and the interposition at every stage of mediating hypostases, or underlying orders of nonmaterial reality) with another horizontal triadic structure, giving a timeless dynamic rhythm of outgoing and return, such as that already encountered in Porphyry.

Nearly all of Iamblichus' works have been lost, and his thought must be recovered from other sources. At present the main authority for this type of Platonism, and also for some of the later Neoplatonists, is Proclus (AD 410–485). Proclus appears to have codified later Platonism, but it is often impossible to tell which parts of his thought are original and which derive from his teachers Plutarch (see below) and Syrianus on the one hand and Porphyry and Iamblichus, from whom he quotes copiously but not always identifiably, and other earlier Platonists on the other hand. A carefully argued summary of the basic metaphysics of this kind of Neoplatonism may be found in Proclus' *Elements of Theology,* which exhibits the causal relationships of the several hierarchies that constituted his intelligible universe.

This later Neoplatonism aspired to be not only a complete and coherent metaphysical system but also a complete pagan theology, which is perhaps best seen in Proclus' *Platonic Theology.* The maintenance and defense of the old religion in a world more and more intolerantly dominated by its triumphant rival, Christianity, was one of the main concerns of the Platonists after Plotinus. By

Neoplatonism as a pagan theology

the study and sometimes forced exegesis of Aristotle and then Plato, culminating in the *Timaeus* and *Parmenides,* of which they offered a variety of highly metaphysical interpretations totally unacceptable to Plato scholars, they believed it possible to arrive at a complete understanding of divine truth. This truth they held to be cryptically revealed by the gods themselves through the so-called theologians—the inspired authors of the Orphic poems and of the *Chaldean Oracles,* published in the second half of the 2nd century AD. Porphyry first gave some guarded and qualified recognition to them, but they were inspired scripture to Iamblichus, who wrote a work of at least 28 books on the subject, and his successors. Their view of the human soul was a humbler one than that of Plotinus. It was for them a spiritual being of lower rank, which had descended altogether into the material world, while for Plotinus a part remained above; they could not therefore aspire, like Plotinus, through philosophy alone, to that return to and unification with the divine that remained for them the goal of human life. Help from the gods was needed, and they believed that the gods in their love for men had provided it, giving to all things the power of return in prayer and implanting even in inanimate material things—herbs and stones and the like—sympathies and communications with the divine, which made possible the secret rites of theurgy, through which the divine gave the needed spiritual help by material means. Theurgy, though its procedures were generally those of late Greek magic, was thus not thought of merely as magic; in fact a higher and more intellectual theurgy was also practiced. The degree of attention paid to external rites varied considerably from philosopher to philosopher; there seem to have been men even in the last generation of pagan Neoplatonists who had little use for or interest in such things and followed a mystical way much like that of Plotinus.

Neo-platonic schools

The different schools of late Neoplatonism seem to have differed less from each other than has sometimes been supposed. The school of Pergamum, founded by Aedesius, a pupil of Iamblichus, made perhaps the least contribution to the philosophical development of Neoplatonism, but it was not entirely given over to theurgy. Its greatest convert was the emperor Julian, called by Christians the "Apostate"; in that capacity he achieved great notoriety, but philosophically he is of no importance. By the end of the 4th century AD the Platonic Academy at Athens had been reestablished and had become an institute for Neoplatonic teaching and research following the tradition of Iamblichus. It was particularly fervent and open in its paganism and attracted Christian hostility. Though maintaining itself for a surprisingly long time against this hostility, it eventually yielded to it and was probably closed by Justinian in AD 529. In the interim, however, it had produced the greatest and most influential systematic expositor of later Neoplatonism, Proclus (see above). The head of the school at the time of its closing, Damascius, was also a notable philosopher. Another centre of Neoplatonism flourished at Gaza during the 5th and early 6th centuries; it was already Christian in its inspiration, though some of its members studied with the pagan Ammonius (see below). The school of Alexandria in the 5th and 6th centuries does not seem to have differed very much from that of Athens, either in its fundamental philosophical outlook or in the main outline of its doctrines. In fact there was much interchange between the two. The Athenian Syrianus taught the Alexandrian Hermias, whose son Ammonius was taught by Proclus. Ammonius (died *c.* 520) was the most influential of the Alexandrian Platonists. His expositions of Aristotle were published mainly in the commentaries of the Christian heretic John Philoponus (late 5th to mid-6th century). Simplicius, the other great Aristotelian commentator, worked at Athens but, like Damascius, had studied with Ammonius. The Alexandrian concentration on Aristotle, which produced a vast body of learned but Neoplatonically coloured commentary on his treatises, has often been attributed to Christian pressure and attempts to compromise with the church; it may equally well have been due to the quality and extent of Proclus' published work on Plato. Though Philoponus' later philosophical work contains important

Christian modifications, an openly pagan (and very inferior) philosopher, Olympiodorus, was still teaching at Alexandria well into the second half of the 6th century. Finally, in the 7th century, under Heraclius, after philosophical teaching had passed peacefully into Christian hands, the last known Alexandrian philosopher, the Christian Stephanus, was called to teach in the University of Constantinople.

PLATONISM IN THE WORLD OF REVEALED RELIGIONS

Early Jewish Platonism. Well before the beginning of the Christian Era, Jews with some Greek education had begun to make casual use of popular Greek philosophy in expounding their revealed religion: there are traces of this in the wisdom literature of the Old Testament. In Paul's speech to the Areopagus in Acts 17, commonplaces of Stoic philosophy were employed for apologetic purposes. But, as far as is known, the first Jew who was really well-read in Greek philosophy and used it extensively in the exposition and defense of his traditional religion was Philo Judaeus (Philo of Alexandria [*c.* 15 BC–after AD 45]), an older contemporary of St. Paul. Philo expressed his philosophical religion in the form of lengthy allegorical commentaries on the Jewish Scriptures, especially on Genesis. In these he showed to his own satisfaction that the ancient revelation given to Moses accorded with the teaching of the best Greek philosophers, which, in his view, was later and derivative. The Greek philosophy that he preferred and found to be most in accordance with revelation was an early form of Middle Platonism. Philo was neither approved of nor read by later orthodox Jews, but his influence on Greek-speaking and Greek-educated Christians from the 2nd century AD was great; and in important ways he determined the tone of their religious speculation.

Philo of Alexandria

Ancient and medieval Christian Platonism. Like Philo, the Christian Platonists gave primacy to revelation and regarded Platonic philosophy as the best available instrument for understanding and defending the teachings of Scripture and church tradition. But, also like Philo, they did not believe that truth could conflict with truth and were confident that all that was rationally certain in Platonic speculation would prove to be in perfect accordance with the Christian revelation. Their unhistorical approach and unscholarly methods of exegesis of texts, both pagan and Christian, facilitated this confidence. The general attitude of Christian Platonists was one of relatively moderate and humane otherworldliness (the cruder sorts of Christian otherworldliness and hatred of the body seem to derive from non-Platonic and non-Greek sources). They stressed the transcendence of God though, by insisting that it is a transcendence that is also the deepest immanence, they acknowledged his intimate presence within the world as well. They took a dualistic view of soul and body (though accepting bodily resurrection) and emphasized the primacy of the spiritual, while insisting on the goodness of God's material creation.

Patristic Platonism. From the middle of the 2nd century AD Christians who had some training in Greek philosophy began to feel the need to express their faith in its terms, both for their own intellectual satisfaction and in order to convert educated pagans. The philosophy that suited them best was Platonism. Though Stoicism had exerted a considerable influence on Christian ethical thinking (which has persisted to modern times), Stoic corporealism—the belief that God and the soul are bodies of a subtle and peculiar kind—repelled most Christians, and Stoic pantheism was incompatible with Christianity. The Platonism that the first Christian thinkers knew was of course Middle Platonism, not yet Neoplatonism. Its relatively straightforward theism and high moral tone suited their purposes excellently; and the influence of this older form of Platonism persisted through the 4th century and beyond, even after the works of Plotinus and Porphyry began to be read by Christians.

The first Christian to use Greek philosophy in the service of the Christian faith was Justin Martyr (martyred *c.* 165), whose passionate rejection of Greek polytheism, combined with an open and positive acceptance of the

Justin, Origen, the Cappadocians

essentials of Platonic religious philosophy and an unshakable confidence in its harmony with Christian teaching, was to remain characteristic of the Christian Platonist tradition. This was carried on in the Greek-speaking world by Clement of Alexandria (c. 150–c. 215), a persuasive Christian humanist, and by the greatest of the Alexandrian Christian teachers, Origen (c. 185–254). Although Origen was consciously more hostile to and critical of Platonic philosophy than either Justin or Clement, he was, nonetheless, more deeply affected by it. He produced a synthesis of Christianity and late Middle Platonism of remarkable originality and power, which is the first great Christian philosophical theology. In spite of subsequent condemnations of some of his alleged views, his influence on Christian thought was strong and lasting. The Greek philosophical theology that developed during the Trinitarian controversies over the relationships among the persons of the Godhead, which were settled at the ecumenical councils of Nicaea (325) and Constantinople (381), owed a great deal to Origen on both sides, orthodox and heretical. Its most important representatives on the orthodox side were the three Christian Platonist theologians of Cappadocia, Basil of Caesarea (c. 329–379), Gregory of Nazianzus (c. 330–c. 389), and Basil's brother Gregory of Nyssa (c. 335–c. 394). Of these three, Gregory of Nyssa was the most powerful and original thinker (as well as the closest to Origen). He was the first great theologian of mystical experience, at once Platonic and profoundly Christian, and he exerted a strong influence on later Greek Christian thought.

Pseudo-Dionysius and others At some time between the period of the Cappadocian Fathers and the early years of the 6th century, a new turn was given to Christian Platonism by the remarkable writer who chose to publish his works under the name of St. Paul's convert at Athens, Dionysius the Areopagite. The kind of Platonism that the Pseudo-Dionysius employed for his theological purposes was the 5th-century Neoplatonism that is best represented by Proclus (see above). Almost everything about this mysterious author is vigorously disputed by scholars. But there can be no doubt about the influence that his system of the hierarchic universe exerted upon later Christian thought; his vision of man's ascent through it—carried up by divine love, to pass beyond all hierarchy and all knowledge into the darkness of the mystical union with God—had its impact both in the East, where one of the greatest of Greek Christian Platonist thinkers, Maximus the Confessor (c. 580–662), was deeply influenced by the Dionysian writings and commented extensively upon them, and in the West, where they became known and were translated into Latin in the 9th century. In the Latin West there was more than one kind of Christian Platonism. An impressive and extremely difficult philosophical theology, employing ideas approximating Porphyry's version of Neoplatonism to explain and defend the orthodox doctrine of the Trinity, was produced in the second half of the 4th century by the rhetorician and grammarian Marius Victorinus. A strong and simple Platonic theism and morality, which had a great influence in the Middle Ages, was nobly expressed in the final work of the last great philosopher-statesman of the ancient world, Boethius (c. 470–524). This was the *Consolation of Philosophy,* written in prison while its author was under sentence of death. Boethius was also influential in the medieval West through his translations of Aristotle's logical works, especially the *Categories* together with Porphyry's *Isagoge* ("Introduction"), on which he in turn produced two commentaries. But the Christian Platonism that had the widest, deepest, and most lasting influence in the West was that of St. Augustine of Hippo (354–430).

Augustinian Platonism. Each of the great Christian Platonists understood Platonism and applied it to the understanding of his faith in his own individual way, and of no one of them was this truer than of Augustine with his extremely strong personality and distinctive religious history. Augustine's thought was not merely a subspecies of Christian Platonism but something unique—Augustinianism. Nonetheless, the reading of Plotinus and Porphyry (in Latin translations) had a decisive influence on his religious and intellectual development, and he was more deeply and directly affected by Neoplatonism than any of his Western contemporaries and successors.

Teachings of Augustine In his anthropology Augustine was firmly Platonist, insisting on the soul's superiority to and independence of the body. For him, as for Plotinus and Porphyry, it was axiomatic that body could not act on soul, for soul was superior in the hierarchy of reality, and the inferior cannot act on the superior. This affected both his ethical doctrine and his epistemology. On the other hand, he differed from the philosophers who influenced him in his insistence that not only man but higher spiritual beings as well are mutable and peccable, liable to sin and fall, and in his consequent stress on the necessity of divine grace. His crucial doctrine that man's destiny is determined by the right direction of love, though profoundly original, was a development rather than a contradiction of Platonism. His very original theology of history and his view of human society, however, owed little to Plotinus and Porphyry, whose interests lay elsewhere.

In his epistemology Augustine was Neoplatonic, especially in the subjectivity of his doctrine of illumination—in its insistence that in spite of the fact that God is exterior to man, men's minds are aware of him because of his direct action on them (expressed in terms of the shining of his light on the mind, or sometimes of teaching) and not as the result of reasoning from sense experience. For a Platonist, as has been said, body cannot act upon soul. Sense experience, therefore, though genuinely informative on its own level, cannot be a basis for metaphysical or religious thinking. This must be the result of the presence in the soul of higher realities and their action upon it. In Plotinus the illumination of the soul by Intellect and the One was the permanent cause of man's ability to know eternal reality; and Augustine was at this point very close to Plotinus, though for him there was a much sharper distinction between Creator and creature, and the personal relationship between God and the soul was much more strongly stressed.

In his theology, insofar as Augustine's thought about God was Platonic, he conformed fairly closely to the general pattern of Christian Platonism; it was Middle Platonic rather than Neoplatonic in that God could not be the One beyond Intellect and Being but was the supreme reality in whose creative mind were the Platonic Forms, the eternal patterns or regulative principles of all creation. Perhaps the most distinctive influence of Plotinian Neoplatonism on Augustine's thinking about God was in his Trinitarian theology. He started with the unity of God and continually insisted upon it, unlike Greek Christian thinkers, who started with the Three Persons perfectly united; and because he thought that something like the Christian doctrine of the Trinity was to be found in Plotinus and Porphyry, he tended to regard it as a philosophical doctrine and tried to make philosophical sense of it to a greater extent than the Greek Fathers did. His last and most important and influential attempt to do so was in his treatise *On the Trinity,* with its discovery of analogies to the divine mystery in the self-directed, internal activities of the soul.

Medieval Platonism. With the gradual revival of philosophical thinking in the West that began in the Carolingian period (late 8th–9th centuries), the history of Platonism becomes extremely complex. Only a sketch distinguishing the main streams of a more or less Platonic tradition is given here.

Influence of the *Timaeus* In the 4th century the Christian exegete Calcidius (Chalcidius) prepared a commentary on Plato's *Timaeus,* which exerted an important influence on the medieval interpretation of the *Timaeus.* A Christian Platonic theism of the type of which Boethius is the finest example thus arose; based on a reading of the *Timaeus* with Christian eyes, it continued to have a strong influence in the Middle Ages, especially in the earlier period. This kind of theism, issuing in a strongly positive view of God's creation and a nobly austere but humane view of man's duty and destiny, was particularly apparent in the Christian humanism of the School of Chartres (12th century).

The widest, deepest, and most persistent Christian Platonist influence in the Latin West was that of Augustine (see above *Augustinian Platonism*). Augustinianism in a variety of forms—often stiffened, exaggerated, or distorted—persisted throughout the Middle Ages and survived the "recovery of Aristotle" (see below). In the later Middle Ages Augustine's influence was particularly strong in the Franciscan school, though not confined to it. But the greatest and most influential of medieval thinkers deeply influenced by Augustine was Anselm of Canterbury (1033/34–1109), the originator (probably on the basis of suggestions in Augustine) of the still much discussed "ontological argument" for the existence of God (see PHILOSOPHIES OF THE BRANCHES OF KNOWLEDGE: *Philosophy of religion*) and a philosopher whose humility, openness, and readiness to consider objections had a genuinely Socratic quality.

John Scotus Erigena

One of the boldest and most original thinkers of medieval Europe was John Scotus Erigena (810–*c.* 877), who introduced to the West the Greek Christian Platonist tradition (see above *Patristic Platonism*), as it had been developed by Gregory of Nyssa, the Pseudo-Dionysius, and Maximus the Confessor. His views were much disapproved of by the Western church; and his great philosophical work, the *Periphyseon* (usually known as *De divisione naturae* [*On the Division of Nature*]), was not much read and ceased to be copied after his condemnation in 1210. But a considerable part of the text circulated in the form of anonymous glosses to the Latin translations of the Pseudo-Dionysius (of which the first adequate translation was by Erigena himself); and in this way his thought influenced both the tradition of Western mysticism, which derived from the Pseudo-Dionysius, and 13th-century Scholasticism, for which St. Paul's supposed disciple was still a major authority.

The Platonism in "Aristotelian" Scholasticism

There is no more superficial and misleading generalization in the history of philosophy than that which sharply opposes "Christian Platonism" and "Christian Aristotelianism." To be sure, the recovery of the authentic thought of Aristotle through Latin translations of his works in the 12th and 13th centuries was indeed a major event in the history of philosophy. But Platonism and Aristotelianism have never been tidily separated in the history of European thought. There was already a strong Aristotelian element in Middle Platonism and Neoplatonism. Byzantine theologians (in the East) from the 6th century AD onward were as Aristotelian as anybody in western Europe in the 13th century. Thirteenth-century "Aristotelian" Scholastics, though much preoccupied with the new translations of Aristotle and their philosophical and theological implications, were still deeply influenced by Augustine, Boethius, and the Pseudo-Dionysius (with glosses derived from Erigena). And the Islāmic philosophy, to be mentioned below, with which they had to grapple, was as much Neoplatonist as it was Aristotelian. Further, they also were influenced by Latin translations of two pseudo-Aristotelian works in Arabic, based on Neoplatonic sources (see below) as well as by those of some of the shorter works of Proclus (see above). It has been said that "Aquinas is closer to Plotinus than to the real Aristotle," and there is some truth in this judgment.

Islāmic and medieval Jewish philosophy. After the Muslim conquest of Syria and Egypt, there began a great work of translation of the texts that had been studied in the late Greek philosophical schools—including a number of dialogues of Plato and Neoplatonic treatises, as well as the works of Aristotle and a number of the Alexandrian Neoplatonist commentaries on them. The translations—partly from Greek, partly from Syriac versions of the Greek texts—were made between about 800 and 1000. On the basis of these translated texts an impressive development of Islāmic theology and philosophy took place, strongly influenced by Neoplatonism, though Aristotelian influence also became increasingly important. An interesting feature of this Islāmic philosophy, which distinguished it from the familiar Neoplatonism, was the reappearance in al-Fārābī and Averroës of an interest in the political and social side of Plato's thought. The tradition may be seen in four great Muslim philosophers, the Arab al-Kindī (*c.* 800–870), the Turk al-Fārābī (*c.* 878–*c.* 950), and two who deeply influenced the medieval West, Avicenna (Ibn Sīnā, 980–1037) from Persia and Averroës (Ibn Rushd, 1126–98) from Muslim Spain. Of these, Avicenna was perhaps the

more Platonist, and Averroës, whose fame and influence rested primarily on his commentaries on Aristotle, was the more Aristotelian although the latter's commentaries were written on the basis of Greek ones, some of whose authors had used them as a vehicle for Neoplatonism. Medieval Jewish philosophy, which also developed within this Muslim intellectual tradition, reflected—at least in its earlier phases—strong Neoplatonic influence. This is especially true of the thought of the early figure Isaac Israeli (mid-9th–mid-10th century), whose Platonism was pervasive, though derivative and less than fully coherent, and the first great Jewish philosopher of Muslim Spain, Avicebron (Ibn Gabirol, *c.* 1022–*c.* 1058/70), whose Platonism may have been derived from Israeli's. Avicebron's *Fons vitae* (*Fountain of Life*) was also a major influence on scholastic philosophers.

PLATONISM FROM THE RENAISSANCE TO MODERN TIMES

From the 15th century onward the dialogues of Plato and a large number of Middle Platonist and Neoplatonist works, above all the *Enneads* of Plotinus, became available in the original Greek in western Europe and were studied by scholars, philosophers, and theologians. As a result of this new acquaintance with the original texts, Platonic influences on Renaissance and post-Renaissance thought became even more complex and difficult to recognize than those on medieval thought. Older Neoplatonically influenced traditions (notably Augustinianism) persisted, and new ones developed from the direct reading of the Neoplatonic texts. And, at least from the time of Leibniz (1646–1716), European thinkers realized that the Neoplatonic interpretation of Plato was in some ways a distorted and one-sided one; hence they sometimes developed their own allegedly more authentic understandings of Plato on the basis of direct readings of such of his varied works as they found to be philosophically congenial. Only a few of the more interesting Platonic influences can be indicated here.

The persistence of Christian Platonism

In spite of its deep influence on Greek Christian thinkers, Platonism was regarded with profound suspicion by the Byzantine Orthodox Church. The suspicion reflected its association in the Byzantine ecclesiastical mind with the militant paganism of the Athenian Neoplatonists (see above). Nonetheless, it survived in the Byzantine world—generally underground but with an overt revival in the 11th century, in which the most notable figures were the broadly erudite Michael Psellus, who did much to enhance the prestige of philosophy, and his rival, the syncretistic Aristotelian commentator John Italus. In the following century Eustratius, metropolitan of Nicaea, and Michael of Ephesus continued the tradition of writing Neoplatonic commentary on Aristotle, plugging some of the gaps left by the Alexandrian commentators. In the 15th century the last known Byzantine philosopher, George Gemistus Plethon, a passionate pagan Platonist in the manner of Proclus, traveled to Italy (1438–39) and persuaded Cosimo de' Medici to sponsor a Platonic Academy at Florence, of which the greatest figures to emerge were its founder, Marsilio Ficino (1433–99), who translated all of Plato and Plotinus into Latin, the first complete version of either in a Western language, and the humanist Pico della Mirandola (1463–94), author of the influential *Oration on the Dignity of Man*. Ficino's *Platonic Theology: On the Immortality of Souls* contains not only Platonic and Neoplatonic philosophy but also elements drawn from medieval Aristotelianism, Cicero, Augustine, and Italian humanist writers. In spite of the paganism of Plethon, the Platonism of the Florentine Academy was a Christian one of a humane and liberal kind. This was probably at least partly due to the influence in Italy of Nicholas of Cusa (1401–64), who worked out his own very original version of Christian Platonism, influenced by the Pseudo-Dionysius, Erigena, and the German mystical tradition (as in Meister Eckehart).

The influence of the Platonism of the Florentine Academy was quite extensive; it may be seen not only in the writings of later Italian philosophers but also in the iconography of Italian Renaissance painting and in 16th-century French literature and was particularly marked in England.

Perhaps the most impressive development of this post-Renaissance movement lay in the works of the Cambridge Platonists (late 17th century). Since their time a tradition of liberal Christian Platonism has persisted in England. Moreover, there have been other notable traditions of Platonically influenced Christian thought in Europe. One that deserves to be better known is that of the outstanding French philosopher of "action" Maurice Blondel (1861–1949), who found a prominent place in his system for the formation of ideas—interpreted as an important species of action that faithfully reflects the eternal order of reality. Blondel's philosophy has had a widespread influence, mainly among Catholic philosophers dissatisfied with Neoscholasticism. Another French philosopher much influenced by Platonism, in its Plotinian form, was Henri Bergson (1859–1941), whose thought attracted much attention during and just after his lifetime but has been largely neglected since.

Pagan Neoplatonic influence on German Idealism and on English literature

The rediscovery of Proclus by the great German Idealist G.W.F. Hegel (1770–1831) had an important influence on his thought and so on the whole history of 19th-century Idealist philosophy. His contemporary F.W.J. von Schelling (1775–1854) was also strongly influenced by Neoplatonism, in his case that of Plotinus. Idealism, however, should not be interpreted as revived Neoplatonism, nor Neoplatonism as an anticipation of Idealism. But the historical influence of Neoplatonism on Idealist thought is indisputable. There was a strong reaction against Hegel's influence in some quarters, and this reaction led to a corresponding depreciation of Neoplatonism though the tradition of Idealism continued in the work of F.H. Bradley and John Ellis McTaggart in England and Josiah Royce in the United States. But 20th-century continental European philosophers and scholars were, until the 1960s, readier than English-speaking ones to take a serious interest in Neoplatonism. The latter, with some notable exceptions, maintained a hostile attitude toward that philosophy which they wrongly regarded not only as "decadent" but also as "mystical," and thus outside the true tradition of Greek philosophy.

The influence of the sort of Christian Platonism mentioned above on English literature, and especially on English poetry, has been wide and deep. But there has also been a strongly anti-Christian Neoplatonic influence, that of Thomas Taylor "the Platonist" (1758–1835), who published translations of Plato, Aristotle, and a large number of Neoplatonic works in the late 18th and early 19th centuries. Taylor was as militant in his pagan Platonism as was Gemistus Plethon. His ideas had a strong influence on the English Romantics. In the poetry of William Blake, who eventually succeeded in reconciling Taylor's paganism with his own very original version of Christianity, much of the symbolism is Neoplatonic. The Platonism of the English Romantic poets Coleridge and Shelley also derives from Taylor, although both were able to read the original texts. Taylor also deeply influenced Emerson and his circle in America. Later, in the early 20th century, the influence of Taylor's writings was again apparent in the Irish poet and dramatist William Butler Yeats, who in his later poems made use of Stephen MacKenna's then new translation of Plotinus.

The foremost process philosopher (an adherent of a view emphasizing the elements of becoming, change, and novelty in experienced reality), Alfred North Whitehead (1861–1947), perhaps because of his original and abiding concern with mathematical philosophy, was interested in Plato (though not, apparently, in the Neoplatonists); and his reading of the *Timaeus* in particular contributed something to the metaphysical system of his last period and especially to his concept of a God who does not timelessly transcend process but is in some way involved in it. Whitehead is an excellent example of a Platonically influenced thinker whose development of Plato's own thought proceeded along lines completely opposed to Neoplatonism.

EVALUATION OF PLATONISM

The essential point at issue between Platonists and their opponents through the centuries has been the existence (in some sense) of a spiritual or intelligible reality that is in-dependent of the world, and is the ultimate origin of both existence and values. This is a very rough generalization that does not apply to the Skeptical Academy (see above *Greek Platonism from Aristotle through Middle Platonism*) or do full justice to the thought of the modern skeptical Platonist George Santayana. Platonists have understood this central doctrine in a great variety of ways and defended it with a great variety of arguments. But whenever it has been strongly held, it seems to have been by a faith depending on some sort of experience rather than simply on the conclusion of an argument. Its opponents have generally followed the lines of attack laid down by Aristotle (and to some extent anticipated by Plato in the first part of his *Parmenides*), that the doctrine involves the duplication of reality and the postulation of entities for the existence of which no sufficient evidence or arguments can be offered and the relationship of which to the world of sense experience cannot be intelligibly stated. The argument continues and will perhaps never finally be settled, but there can be no doubt about the central importance of Platonism in the history of European thought.

(A.H.A./H.J.Bl.)

MAJOR WORKS

WORKS: Plato's works are here listed in their traditional order, certain spurious items being omitted: *Euthyphrōn (Euthyphro); Apologia Sōkratous (Apology); Critōn (Crito); Phaedōn (Phaedo); Cratylos (Cratylus); Theaetētos (Theaetetus); Sophistēs (Sophist); Politikos (Statesman); Parmenidēs; Philēbos (Philebus); Symposion (Symposium); Phaedros (Phaedrus); Alkibiadēs (Alcibiades); Hipparchos (Hipparchus); Erastai (Lovers); Charmidēs; Lachēs; Lysis; Euthydēmos (Euthydemus); Prōtagoras; Gorgias; Menōn (Meno); Hippias Meizōn (Hippias Major); Hippias Elattōn (Hippias Minor); Iōn; Menexenos (Menexenus); Politeia (Republic); Timaeos (Timeaus); Critias; Nomoi (Laws);* and *Epinomis.*

TEXTS: The standard Greek text is the edition by Ioannes (John) Burnet, *Platonis Opera,* 5 vol. (1900–07, reprinted 1973 from various printings). All of the major works were translated into English by Benjamin Jowett, and the latest revisions of the Jowett translations are still the best available English versions of Plato. The Loeb Classical Library also contains the whole of Plato (in Greek and English); and several of the dialogues are published in the Penguin Classics series, including *Philebus,* trans. by Robin A.H. Waterfield (1982); *Protagoras and Meno,* trans. by W.K.C. Guthrie (1956, reissued 1966); and *Plato's Symposium,* trans. by W. Hamilton (1956).

RECOMMENDED LATER EDITIONS: Numerous English translations are available, including David Gallop (trans.), *Phaedo* (1975, reprinted 1983); John McDowell (trans.), *Theaetetus* (1973); Francis Macdonald Cornford (trans.), *Plato's Theory of Knowledge: The Theaetetus and the Sophist of Plato* (1935, reprinted 1973); J.B. Skemp (trans.), *Statesman* (1957, reissued 1977); R.E. Allen (trans.), *Plato's Parmenides* (1983); J.C.B. Gosling (trans.), *Philebus* (1975); R. Hackforth (trans.), *Phaedo* (1955, reprinted 1972); C.C.W. Taylor (trans.), *Protagoras* (1976); Terence Irwin (trans.), *Gorgias* (1979); R.W. Sharples (ed. and trans.), *Meno* (1985); Paul Woodruff (trans.), *Hippias Major* (1982); and James Adam (ed.), *The Republic,* 2nd ed., 2 vol. (1963, reprinted 1969).

BIBLIOGRAPHY

Plato. *Life and thought:* There are several good brief introductions to Plato, including C.J. ROWE, *Plato* (1984); J.E. RAVEN, *Plato's Thought in the Making: A Study of the Development of His Metaphysics* (1965, reprinted 1985); G.M.A. GRUBE, *Plato's Thought* (1935, reprinted 1980); G.C. FIELD, *The Philosophy of Plato,* 2nd ed. (1969, reprinted 1978); and A.E. TAYLOR, *Plato, the Man and His Work,* 7th ed. (1960, reprinted 1969). On Plato's life, see also G.C. FIELD, *Plato and His Contemporaries: A Study in Fourth-Century Life and Thought* (1930, reprinted 1975); ALICE SWIFT RIGINOS, *Platonica: The Anecdotes Concerning the Life and Writings of Plato* (1976); and the old but still valuable work by GEORGE GROTE, *Plato, and the Other Companions of Sokrates,* new ed., 4 vol. (1888, reprinted 1974). On the history of the Academy, see HAROLD CHERNISS, *The Riddle of the Early Academy* (1945, reprinted 1980); and JOHN GLUCKER, *Antiochus and the Late Academy* (1978). A full and scholarly account of Plato's philosophy can be found in W.K.C. GUTHRIE, *A History of Greek Philosophy,* vol. 4, *Plato: The Man and His Dialogues: Earlier Period* (1975), and vol. 5, *The Later Plato and the Academy* (1978), while vol. 3, *The Fifth-Century Enlightenment* (1969), contains a full account of what is known about Socrates. Other general accounts include PAUL FRIEDLÄNDER, *Plato,* 3 vol. (1958–69; originally published in German, 2nd ed., 1954–60); I.M. CROMBIE, *An Ex-*

amination of *Plato's Doctrines,* 2 vol. (1962–63; reissued 1979); and J.C.B. GOSLING, *Plato* (1973, reissued 1983). GILBERT RYLE, *Plato's Progress* (1966), is idiosyncratic. Much contemporary scholarly work has appeared in articles. GREGORY VLASTOS, *Platonic Studies,* 2nd ed. (1981), contains several classic papers. There are two useful anthologies: GREGORY VLASTOS (ed.), *The Philosophy of Socrates* (1971, reprinted 1980), and *Plato,* 2 vol. (1970–71, reprinted 1978).

On Plato's ethics, see in particular JOHN GOULD, *The Development of Plato's Ethics* (1955, reprinted 1972); PAMELA HUBY, *Plato and Modern Morality* (1972); and TERENCE IRWIN, *Plato's Moral Theory: The Early and Middle Dialogues* (1977, reissued 1979). On his political theory, see R.H.S. CROSSMAN, *Plato Today,* rev. 2nd ed. (1959, reissued 1971); K.R. POPPER, *The Open Society and Its Enemies,* vol. 1, *The Spell of Plato,* 5th ed. (1966, reprinted 1971); RONALD B. LEVINSON, *In Defense of Plato* (1953, reissued 1970); RENFORD BAMBROUGH (ed.), *Plato, Popper and Politics: Some Contributions to a Modern Controversy* (1967); and ROBERT W. HALL, *Plato* (1981). See also MARY MARGARET MACKENZIE, *Plato on Punishment* (1981); and RICHARD KRAUT, *Socrates and the State* (1984). For Plato's views on aesthetics, see IRIS MURDOCH, *The Fire and the Sun: Why Plato Banished the Artists* (1977); and JULIUS MORAVCSIK and PHILIP TEMKO (eds.), *Plato on Beauty, Wisdom, and the Arts* (1982).

For Plato's view of the soul, see T.M. ROBINSON, *Plato's Psychology* (1970). On the physical theory of the *Timaeus,* see GREGORY VLASTOS, *Plato's Universe* (1975); and on his attitude to science, see JOHN P. ANTON (ed.), *Science and the Sciences in Plato* (1980).

On epistemology, see W.F.R. HARDIE, *A Study in Plato* (1936); NORMAN GULLEY, *Plato's Theory of Knowledge* (1962, reprinted 1973); W.G. RUNCIMAN, *Plato's Later Epistemology* (1962); NICHOLAS P. WHITE, *Plato on Knowledge and Reality* (1976); and JON MOLINE, *Plato's Theory of Understanding* (1981). The standard study of Plato's ideas on logic and dialectic is RICHARD ROBINSON, *Plato's Earlier Dialectic,* 2nd ed. (1953, reprinted 1984). See also JULIUS STENZEL, *Plato's Method of Dialectic* (1940, reprinted 1973; originally published in German, 2nd ed., 1931); and KENNETH M. SAYRE, *Plato's Analytic Method* (1969).

On metaphysics and the theory of Forms there is a comprehensive survey by W.D. ROSS, *Plato's Theory of Ideas* (1951, reissued 1976); and a useful collection of essays, R.E. ALLEN (ed.), *Studies in Plato's Metaphysics* (1965, reprinted 1968). See also FRIEDRICH SOLMSEN, *Plato's Theology* (1942, reissued 1967); ANDERS WEDBERG, *Plato's Philosophy of Mathematics* (1955, reprinted 1977); RENFORD BAMBROUGH (ed.), *New Essays on Plato and Aristotle* (1965); J.N. FINDLAY, *Plato: The Written and Unwritten Doctrines* (1974); and WILLIAM J. PRIOR, *Unity and Development in Plato's Metaphysics* (1985).

Commentaries: Among the more useful commentaries are R.E. ALLEN, *Plato's Euthyphro and the Earlier Theory of Forms* (1970), and *Socrates and Legal Obligation* (1980); A.D. WOOZLEY, *Law and Obedience: The Law of Plato's Crito* (1979); ROSAMUND KENT SPRAGUE, *Plato's Use of Fallacy: A Study of the Euthydemus and Some Other Dialogues* (1962); B.A.F. HUBBARD and E.S. KARNOFSKY, *Plato's Protagoras: A Socratic Commentary* (1982, reissued 1984); N.R. MURPHY, *The Interpretation of Plato's Republic* (1951, reprinted 1967); R.C. CROSS and A.D. WOOZLEY, *Plato's Republic: A Philosophical Commentary* (1964, reissued 1980); NICHOLAS P. WHITE, *A Companion to Plato's Republic* (1979); JULIA ANNAS, *An Introduction to Plato's Republic* (1981); and GLENN R. MORROW, *Plato's Cretan City: A Historical Interpretation of the Laws* (1960).

(J.B.)

Platonism. There are few modern English translations of the basic works of Neoplatonism, though more will appear as a result of a project sponsored by the National Endowment for the Humanities. PLOTINUS, *The Enneads,* trans. by STEPHEN MACKENNA, 3rd ed. rev. by B.S. PAGE (1962), is not entirely satisfactory; it is being replaced by the Loeb Classical Library edition, A.H. ARMSTRONG (trans.), *Plotinus* (1966–   ), 5 vol. having appeared to 1986. Other basic works include PROCLUS, *The Elements of Theology,* trans. by E.R. DODDS, 2nd ed. (1963), *A Commentary on the First Book of Euclid's Elements,* trans. by GLENN R. MORROW (1970), and *Proclus: Alcibiades I,* trans. by WILLIAM O'NEILL, 2nd ed. (1971). French translations of Proclus' commentaries have been made by A.J. FESTUGIÈRE, *Commentaire sur le Timée,* 2 vol. (1966–68), and *Commentaire sur la République,* 3 vol. (1970). See also PROCLUS, *Théologie platonicienne,* trans. by H.D. SAFFREY and L.G. WESTERINK (1968–   ), 4 vol. having appeared to 1986; JULIANUS, *Oracles chaldaïques,* trans. by ÉDOUARD DES PLACES (1971); and IAMBLICHUS, *Les Mystères d'Egypte,* trans. by ÉDOUARD DES PLACES (1966). A good source of information on the Platonic and Neoplatonic philosophers up to and including Anselm is *The Cambridge History of Later Greek and Early Medieval Philosophy,* ed. by A.H. ARMSTRONG (1967; reprinted with revised bibliographies,

1970). The bibliographies of this work include a list of the editions of ancient and medieval sources (complete and fragmentary), with the more important translations and modern works. PAUL SHOREY, *Platonism, Ancient and Modern* (1938), remains an excellent introduction, but much of the important work on the period between Plato and Plotinus is still confined to technical articles; this is also true of later Neoplatonism. J.N. FINDLAY, *Plato and Platonism: An Introduction* (1978), argues that Plato developed a complete metaphysical system. JOHN DILLON, *The Middle Platonists: 80 B.C. to A.D. 220* (U.K. title, *The Middle Platonists: A Study of Platonism, 80 B.C. to A.D. 220,* 1977), offers a clear and comprehensive account of its subject; it gives the background to the best general book on ancient Neoplatonism, R.T. WALLIS, *Neo-Platonism* (1972). Many of the important problems in Plotinus are discussed by J.M. RIST, *Plotinus: The Road to Reality* (1967, reprinted 1977). Certain key ideas are traced in RICHARD SORABJI, *Time, Creation, and the Continuum: Theories in Antiquity and the Early Middle Ages* (1983). JAMES A. COULTER, *The Literary Microcosm: Theories of Interpretation of the Later Neoplatonists* (1976), is a study of Neoplatonic literary theory. A collection of articles on pagan and early Christian Neoplatonism may be found in H.J. BLUMENTHAL and R.A. MARKUS (eds.), *Neoplatonism and Early Christian Thought* (1981); a similar collection, extending to modern times, is DOMINIC J. O'MEARA (ed.), *Neoplatonism and Christian Thought* (1982). For the earlier Judeo-Christian tradition, see ERWIN R. GOODENOUGH, *An Introduction to Philo Judaeus,* 2nd ed. rev. (1963); and HARRY CHADWICK, *Early Christian Thought and the Classical Tradition: Studies in Justin, Clement, and Origen* (1966, reprinted 1984). An excellent short summary of the thought of St. Augustine, with due attention to the Platonist elements, is Chadwick's *Augustine* (1986), and his *Boethius: The Consolations of Music, Logic, Theology, and Philosophy* (1981), gives an account of the further development of Western Neoplatonism and includes a study of the development of Neoplatonic logic. For medieval Platonism, see FRIEDRICH UEBERWEG, *Grundriss der Geschichte der Philosophie,* vol. 2, *Die patristische und scholastische Philosophie,* ed. by BERNHARD GEYER, 12th ed. (1951); ÉTIENNE GILSON, *History of Christian Philosophy in the Middle Ages* (1955, reissued 1980), with valuable bibliographical material; DAVID KNOWLES, *The Evolution of Mediaeval Thought* (1962); GORDON LEFF, *Mediaeval Thought: St. Augustine to Ockham* (1958, reprinted 1983); and WERNER BEIERWALTES (ed.), *Platonismus in der Philosophie des Mittelalters* (1969), a collection of important articles. All these works to some extent cover the later medieval period. On Islāmic philosophy see the brief account in W. MONTGOMERY WATT, *Islamic Philosophy and Theology: An Extended Survey,* 2nd ed. (1985). There is no satisfactory longer treatment in English, but for Avicenna, see SOHEIL M. AFNAN, *Avicenna: His Life and Works* (1953, reprinted 1980). A sample of the Platonist contribution to Islāmic thought may be seen in FRANZ ROSENTHAL, *The Classical Heritage in Islam* (1975; originally published in German, 1965). The best survey of Platonism in medieval Jewish philosophy is GEORGES VAJDA, "Le Néoplatonisme dans la pensée juive du moyen âge," in G.E. WEIL (ed.), *Mélange Georges Vajda* (1982), pp. 407–422. For Neoplatonic movements in Jewish Hellenistic and medieval philosophy, see JULIUS GUTTMANN, *Philosophies of Judaism: The History of Jewish Philosophy from Biblical Times to Franz Rosenzweig,* trans. from Hebrew (1964, reissued 1973). D.P. WALKER, *The Ancient Theology: Studies in Christian Platonism from the Fifteenth to the Eighteenth Century* (1972), reviews the Christian apologetic tradition of the Renaissance.

On Byzantine Platonism, see J.M. HUSSEY, *Church & Learning in the Byzantine Empire, 867–1185* (1937, reissued 1963); and BASILE TATAKIS, *La Philosophie byzantine,* 2nd ed. (1959). A good short general account of Renaissance Platonism in English is that by FREDERICK C. COPLESTON, *History of Philosophy,* vol. 3, ch. 12 and 15 (1953); see also the essays in PAUL OSKAR KRISTELLER, *Renaissance Thought: The Classic, Scholastic, and Humanistic Strains* (1961, reprinted 1980). A good short introduction to Renaissance Platonism in England is ERNST CASSIRER, *The Platonic Renaissance in England* (1953, reissued 1970; originally published in German, 1932). GERALD R. CRAGG (ed.), *The Cambridge Platonists* (1968, reprinted 1985), is an excellent anthology, with good introductions and notes; see also C.A. PATRIDES (ed.), *The Cambridge Platonists* (1969, reissued 1980). On English Christian Platonism, see WILLIAM RALPH INGE, *The Platonic Tradition in English Religious Thought* (1926, reprinted 1977). On the influence of Thomas Taylor, see *Thomas Taylor, the Platonist: Selected Writings,* ed. by KATHLEEN RAINE and GEORGE MILLS HARPER (1969); and F.A.C. WILSON, *W.B. Yeats and Tradition* (1958). RICHARD D. MCKIRAHAN, JR., *Plato and Socrates: A Comprehensive Bibliography, 1958–1973* (1978), contains 4,600 unannotated entries.

(A.H.A./H.J.Bl.)

Poisons and Poisoning

Poisons are substances that in small amounts are capable of producing serious injury or death. In truth, however, the poison is in the dose. It is a commonplace that drugs of unchallenged benefit in appropriate doses may become seriously poisonous when such doses are exceeded. It must not be forgotten, also, that the variation in response of different individuals may be so great that an average dose can induce serious adverse reactions in the susceptible. Toxins are poisons of natural origin, whether bacterial, plant, or animal, and comprise some of the most lethal materials known; *e.g.*, aconite, botulinus toxin, and fish poisons. Toxins are also referred to as biotoxins, or biological poisons, and the science concerned with such substances is called biotoxicology.

The sciences of pharmacology and toxicology, the latter of which has poisons and poisoning in its province, share common principles, common procedures, and a common vocabulary; they have so much in common that university departments of pharmacology and toxicology grant advanced degrees in either or both disciplines, and pharmacology–toxicology research centres have been created under government sponsorship. The differences, practical and important, are based on points of view. Toxicology may be defined as the science of the injurious effects of chemicals on living systems or simply as the science of poisons; pharmacology, as the science of the useful, advantageous effects of drugs and chemicals on living systems, especially the effects related to disease, whether preventive, curative, or diagnostic. Material relevant to this subject may also be found in DRUGS AND DRUG ACTION.

In the adaptive struggle for survival, members of every kingdom—unicellular forms, fungi, plants, and animals alike—evolved chemical agents to discourage competition, to defend themselves, and to secure prey. Primitive chemical-warfare agents are well known to humans; for example, the antibiotics produced by bacteria and fungi, the growth inhibitors that suppress competitors of higher plants, and the venoms of bacteria, parasites, insects, and predatory animals. Some of these chemicals are synthesized by the organism—*e.g.*, the nicotine formed in the tobacco root—and some are obtained from the food—*e.g.*, the toxic cardiac glycosides (carbohydrates that affect the heart) in the monarch butterfly that come from the milkweed diet of its caterpillar; these are apparently the reason that birds shun the monarch. Presumably, curiosity led prehistoric man to touch, to taste, and to rub on his skin everything that came to hand and to discover the irritating, emetic, and purging properties of certain earths, molds, plants, and animal tissues. Sorcerers, shamans, and others with special knowledge of natural poisons used these substances both to kill and to heal. Through hallucinations, they established rituals and ordeals; through illness or death, they punished enemies or tribal wrongdoers; they tipped arrows with malignant extracts. A survival of this practice is our word "toxic," from the Greek words *toxon* ("bow") and *toxikon* (*pharmikon*), "arrow (poison)." Poisons, like infectious diseases, may inflict their injuries subtly. It is easy to imagine that, long ago, witch doctors also employed toxins against disease, an image repeated by Shakespeare, "In poison there is physic." Into medieval times, medical remedies included many of these physiologically potent substances, and some remain today as irreplaceable. The extent of the fear and hatred of poisons can be judged from the pronouncement in 1450 by James II forbidding all persons to bring home poisons "Under pain of treason." The persistence into modern times of the king's taster attests to the grim success of poison as a political weapon.

Organisms also developed defenses against the poisons of everyday life. Painful experience (man and poison ivy) teaches individuals, and instinct (birds and monarch butterflies, horses and rattlesnakes) guides species to avoid exposures. Rejection mechanisms (regurgitation, purgation) expel noxious matter. Inside the cells of the organism, special metabolic processes under genetic control detoxify life-endangering molecules.

Modern man has borrowed practices and, in some instances, chemical substances from other species (see below for a full treatment of poisonous animals and plants). In addition, man has developed a broad array of specialized chemicals to protect himself, to enhance his health, and to reduce competition for food or for living space. The remedies made use of by today's physician include many substances with astonishing healing powers in therapeutic doses but also capable of devastating injury. Highly-irritant substances disperse mobs. Agriculture uses millions of pounds annually of compounds selectively toxic for pests of many sorts, from bacteria, molds, and weeds to insects and coyotes.   (H.C.Ho./Ed.)

This article is divided into the following sections:

The nature and action of toxic substances

CLASSIFICATIONS OF TOXICITY

It is virtually impossible to assign a precise meaning to the term toxic. Obviously, almost any substance may be toxic if used in sufficient quantity. One property of a toxin that permits it to be so categorized, however, is that it is harmful to sensitive hosts in relatively small amounts. The relationship between the amount of toxin administered and its effect on a host, or experimental subject, can be depicted by a graph called the dose–response curve. A potent toxin produces a steep slope in the linear portion of the curve (*i.e.*, a small amount of toxin has a great effect), whereas a less toxic substance results in a shallow-sloped linear portion of the curve.

Results of the various methods used to measure the dose response of a given host to a toxin depend upon a statistical treatment of one type or another. In most instances the effect measured is the death of the host. The response is greatest in the region of 50 percent mortality; the 50 percent lethal dose (LD_{50}), or the dosage that will result in the death of 50 percent of the tested animals, thus has been established as the most useful way to estimate toxicity. Unfortunately, animal hosts do not act as completely homogeneous populations, and considerable variation between groups usually occurs, even when homogeneous groups of animals are used. Individual variation in response to toxins is encountered from such factors as the health of the individual host.

(B.W.H./Ed.)

Table 1: Selected Household Products and Drugs of Significant Toxicity

	supertoxic (class 6)	extremely toxic (class 5)	very toxic (class 4)	moderately toxic (class 3)	slightly toxic (class 2)	practically nontoxic (class 1)
Probable lethal dose (human) For a 70 kg (154 lb) man	less than 5 mg/kg a taste (less than 7 drops)	5–50 mg/kg 7 drops–1 tsp	50–500 mg/kg 1 tsp–1 oz	0.5–5 g/kg 1 oz–1 pt	5–15 g/kg 1 pt–1 qt	more than 15 g/kg more than 1 qt
Household products and farm chemicals	a few insecticides, fungicides, rodenticides	drain and sewer cleaners (caustics), fireplace flame colours, some pesticides	disinfectants, degreasers, rust removers, some depilatories, fire extinguishing liquids, many agricultural chemicals	polishes, hair dyes, permanent waves, motor fuels, antifreeze, bleaches, turpentine	most cosmetics, lubricating oils, soap products, waxes, incense, some insecticides	foods, candles, mucilage, pure soap, lead pencils, modelling clay
Drugs	digitoxin atropine cyanide heroin nicotine strychnine	amphetamines antihistamines morphine mercury bichloride ephedrine amobarbital (Amytal) ergot	aspirin phenobarbital boric acid fluoride quinidine chlorpromazine	ether kerosene isopropyl alcohol meprobamate methanol Enovid Dilantin	ethyl alcohol milk of magnesia saccharin	kaolin liquid petrolatum talc aluminum silicate

Several levels of effect may, however, be defined: (1) doses that produce no detectable effects—*i.e.,* cause no symptoms; (2) doses that produce useful or therapeutic effects; (3) doses that produce toxic or injurious effects; and (4) lethal doses. As a rule of thumb, toxicologists assume that doses increase about tenfold between each of the four levels. Such a prediction holds fairly well for morphine and for salicylates, for example, but is by no means universally applicable. Many substances are less lethal than predicted—*e.g.,* the sulfonamide drugs, atropine, and especially penicillin—and others are more lethal; *e.g.,* digitalis. Quantitative toxicity must be measured specifically for each individual substance, however; toxicity is unpredictable even in comparing substances that have nearly identical chemical structures.

Degrees of toxicity

To permit rapid estimates of the chances for recovery of poisoned patients when the ingested material has been identified, systems of toxicity ratings have been proposed. One such system defines toxicity classes based on six commonly-used measures, such as a taste, a mouthful, and an ounce. Substances so poisonous that a taste (less than seven drops) probably would kill a man are rated 6, "supertoxic." At the other end of the scale are found substances in class 1, "practically nontoxic," with probably lethal doses of a quart or more. Examples of selected household products and farm chemicals and of drugs are offered in Table 1.

A few household products warrant ratings of 5 to 6; *e.g.,* concentrated caustic cleaners, some insecticides, and other pesticides. About 70 percent of the consumer products considered in one survey were rated 3 or lower. Most cosmetics and toiletries are found in class 2 (slightly toxic); others—*e.g.,* those with high concentrations of alcohol— were given toxicity ratings of 3. Among drugs, many well-known natural products are rated 5 and 6, including digitoxin, nicotine, morphine, and strychnine. The toxicity of aspirin (rating, 4) and its ready availability in many homes confers on aspirin a special hazard for children. The distinction between toxicity and hazard should be noted. Toxicity is the ability of a substance to injure; hazard is the probability that the chances of exposure are such as to produce injury.

The search for increasingly effective pesticides, antipersonnel agents, and drugs that has included efforts to isolate and identify naturally occurring toxins, has also revealed substances (Table 2) more toxic than any cited in Table 1. These toxicities can be contrasted with those of the insecticide parathion, the oral lethal dose of which is three or more milligrams per kilogram in rats, and the fungicide, methyl mercury dicyandiamide, the intraperitoneal lethal dose of which is 0.4 milligram per kilogram in mice.

Poisons are sometimes classified on the basis of origins, of form, of chemical nature, of activity, and of use. With respect to origins: (*a*) toxins of plant and animal origin are of special interest to veterinary toxicologists, medicinal herbalists, chemists, metabolic biochemists, and nutritionists; (*b*) industrial chemicals and minerals are of concern to occupational physicians and industrial hygienists; and (*c*) drugs are the focus of pharmacologists and clinical toxicologists. With respect to form: (*a*) radiation: radioactive nuclides (*e.g.,* radioactive iodine); (*b*) gases: carbon monoxide, hydrogen sulfide, war gases; (*c*) liquids: solvents; (*d*) solids: asbestos, metals. With respect to chemical nature: (*a*) acids: oxalic; (*b*) alkalies: lye, ammonia; (*c*) alcohols: ethyl, methyl; (*d*) amines: aniline; (*e*) heavy metals: mercury, lead, cadmium; (*f*) hydrocarbons: kerosene, benzene; (*g*) chlorinated hydrocarbons: dichlorodiphenyltrichloroethane (DDT), dieldrin, carbon tetrachloride, polychlorinated biphenyls; (*h*) organic phosphates: parathion, malathion, and others. With respect to activity: (*a*) corrosives: acids, alkalies, phenols; (*b*) irritants: (this class formerly comprised toxic elements but is now obsolete); (*c*) systemic poisons: convulsants, central-nervous-system stimulants and depressants, peripheral-nerve poisons, muscle poisons, metabolic poisons, blood poisons. With respect to use: (*a*) pesticides or economic poisons: herbicides, rodenticides, insecticides, acaricides, fungicides, fumigants, germicides; (*b*) chemotherapeutic agents: antibiotics, anthelminthics, and parasiticides in general; (*c*) homicidal agents: chemicals used in executions (cyanide), in homicide (arsenic, strychnine), in suicide (barbiturates, etc.), in war gases (organic phosphates, mustards); (*d*) riot-control agents: chlorobenzylidine malononitrile, chloracetophenone—"tear gas."

Five types of classification

ACUTE AND CHRONIC POISONING

Acute poisoning is characterized by a sudden onset and a rapid rise to intense effect; the symptoms run a short course that does not necessarily terminate in death. Acute poisonings frequently follow a single, relatively large dose. Chronic poisoning, in contrast, is characterized by a gradual and unnoticed development, a gradual onset of symptoms, and a slowly increasing weakness. The illness may appear in any one or more of a number of ways; for example, it may involve the nervous system, the blood and blood-forming tissues, or the gastrointestinal (digestive) tract. Chronic poisonings, often with frequent remissions and recurrences, as a rule develop from protracted or repeated exposures to small doses. The danger of chronic poisoning is high with some compounds, low with others;

Table 2: Some Extremely Toxic Substances

	estimated average lethal dose (mg/kg)	species	route
Botulinus toxin	0.00015	man	oral
Palytoxin*	0.00015	mouse	intravenous
Tetrodotoxin	0.01	mouse	intravenous
Aflatoxin	0.03–3	duckling	oral
Sarin	0.05	mouse	intravenous

*From a plant growing on coral.

a few compounds never cause it. Identification of the causes of chronic poisonings may be exceedingly difficult.

In both acute and chronic poisoning, the size of the dose required to elicit a toxic response depends on many factors: (1) the physical form; whether the substance is a gas, a liquid, or a solid; (2) certain chemical properties; especially solubility in water or in oil; (3) the chemical nature of the substance; *e.g.*, whether it is a hydrocarbon, an alcohol, or an amine; (4) the route of exposure; *e.g.*, the skin, eye, lung, gastrointestinal tract, or by way of the veins or the muscles; (5) the species exposed; (6) the characteristics of the individual; *e.g.*, age, sex, state of health, susceptibility, heredity; (7) the kind of biological response; *e.g.*, local or systemic, characteristic or not, whether tolerance develops, whether there is interaction with other agents.

Acute poisoning. *Incidence.* The susceptibility of some individuals and the toxic potentialities of many drugs combine to make drug-induced illness so common that one out of 20 acute medical hospital admissions for acute disease is for a poisoning. In addition, in some hospitals there are as many admissions for acute alcoholic intoxication. One in 10 hospitalized persons is treated for drug-induced disease during hospitalization. Although most of the 1,600,000 incidents of ingesting possible poisons that occur annually in the United States are of little moment, more than 80,000 are serious enough to appear in the records of the National Clearinghouse for Poison Control Centers. Drugs are the substances most frequently involved, with cleaning and polishing agents, pesticides, cosmetics, solvents, various botanicals, and miscellaneous agents listed in order of frequency of ingestion. The Poisoning Treatment Centre of the Royal Infirmary of Edinburgh found that most (80 percent) of the acutely poisoned persons treated there suffered from "self-poisoning," defined as "a conscious, often impulsive manipulative act, undertaken to secure redress of an intolerable situation." The remaining 20 percent were distributed evenly between accidental poisonings and determined suicidal attempts; only a few cases were instances of homicidal poisonings. Fifty percent or more of the Edinburgh patients had psychiatric problems that were severe enough to require subsequent treatment.

Poisonings, now considered a common emergency, are most frequent in the young adult, 18–25 years of age; there is an equal distribution between males and females. Fatal poisonings often follow overdoses of the nonbarbiturate sedatives, the hypnotics, the tranquillizers and antidepressants (sedatives allay excitement; hypnotics induce sleep; tranquillizers have a quieting and calming effect), the widely prescribed barbiturates, aspirin and other salicylates, and the drugs taken for cultural or social reasons—ethyl alcohol and, more recently, morphine and other opium derivatives. Carbon monoxide and other gases account for at least half of all fatal poisonings.

Recognition that an acute illness is a poisoning may come by testimony or by circumstantial evidence; for example, a suicide note or a partially empty container; in general, specific diagnostic features are rare. In the absence of head injury, poisoning is the commonest cause of unconsciousness from adolescence to middle age. An acute poisoning is always an emergency.

Treatment. When the poisoned person is brought to the medical centre, the physician immediately assesses the status of the patient, the degree of impairment of consciousness, of respiratory failure, of circulatory failure, or of other injuries. Respiration and circulation of the blood must be maintained so that other emergency measures can be effective. Measures to prevent further absorption of swallowed poisons traditionally include gastric lavage (washing out the stomach), inducing vomiting, or administration of an adsorbing substance, such as activated charcoal.

Lavage is dangerous after the ingestion of nonirritating, deceptively bland hydrocarbons (*e.g.*, kerosene) or of corrosive agents (*e.g.*, concentrated acids or lye). Certain studies have questioned the practice of stomach lavage (1) as potentially dangerous in unconscious persons, and (2) as a strenuous and traumatic experience of variable but usually limited efficacy. Instead, inducing of vomiting by administration of syrup of ipecac is recommended.

Life-saving treatment depends primarily on intensive supportive theraphy; *i.e.*, on expert nursing and on vigilance in maintaining vital functions. Since the mid-1940s, deaths from ingesting potentially lethal quantities of barbiturates have decreased from 25 percent to less than 1 percent as a result of combatting shock, maintaining respiration, and placing patients under the expert and conservative care of nurses and physicians in teams and special facilities analogous to the intensive care units for heart patients. The role of antidotes is often exaggerated, there being specific antidotes available in less than 2 percent of all poisonings.

The most effective measures for reducing incidence of poisoning are those of prevention: the keeping of medicines under lock and key, the physician's giving thought to limiting the prescribing and stocking of sedatives and to watching for side effects of drugs and drug combinations; and the segregation and guarding of dangerous pesticides and household chemicals.

Beginning in 1953, under the leadership of the American Academy of Pediatrics, certain hospitals in the United States began collecting and furnishing information on poisonings through units called poison-control centres. Over 500 such centres are now registered with the National Clearinghouse for Poison Control Centers established in 1957 by the Public Health Service. In many cities, the telephone directory lists a poison-control centre. Government-sponsored poison information services are maintained in several cities in Great Britain and elsewhere in Europe. These services and the National Clearinghouse serve as central repositories for information on new and old products and for case reports of poisonings from local centres and from other government agencies. Statements of product composition and toxicity and of treatment are distributed in the United States to poison-control centres.

Sophisticated drug-information services are being developed in certain teaching hospitals under the supervision of drug specialists; *e.g.*, clinical pharmacists. These services furnish information and advice to physicians not only on poisonings and on adverse drug reactions but also on any aspect of drug use in patient care.

Chronic poisoning. Chronic poisoning frequently develops gradually after long-continued exposures to relatively small, repeated doses; there is characteristically a symptom-free latent period. This type of poisoning represents cumulative effects, usually from repeated undetectable injuries that are not completely repaired in the intervals between exposures. In exceptional circumstances these injuries may follow a single dose; *e.g.*, of a radioactive element, of a cancer-causing substance, or of a toxic metal. Even rarer are chronic effects that suddenly appear when an effective acute dose is given in divided portions; an example is the paralytic response to tri-*o*-cresyl phosphate in chicks when one-thirtieth of the acute paralytic dose is given daily for a month. Cumulative effects are often but not necessarily associated with a buildup of the poisonous substances in the body. The body burden of lead is increased in chronic lead poisoning; chronic carbon monoxide poisoning, on the other hand, does not bring accumulation of carbon monoxide; and there may be scarcely any concentration of beryllium in the tissues in chronic beryllium disease with widespread pulmonary granulomatosis—formation in the lungs of the type of connective tissue that develops in the process of wound healing and scar formation. Furthermore, accumulation is not synonymous with illness; witness the slow but demonstrable increase in skeletal fluoride during the first five or six decades of life in persons with low fluoride intakes who show no functional evidence of any fluoride effect. Certain delayed, long-lasting effects of exposures to substances foreign to the body, such as sensitizations or immune responses, are not usually classed as chronic poisoning.

The group of symptoms in a chronic poisoning may be entirely different from that in an acute poisoning by the same agent. Acute and chronic mercury poisoning furnish classic examples. Fatal, acute inorganic mercury poisoning, such as follows the ingestion of mercury bichloride (corrosive sublimate) runs a catastrophic course of nausea, vomiting, and diarrhea, leading to a shocklike, circulatory collapse, either with death in a few hours or, for survivors

Factors affecting toxicity

Poison-control centres

of this phase, to death in a few days from kidney failure. Chronic mercurialism sometimes takes the form of progressive kidney disease, but the affected person may instead show profound personality changes, sometimes other mental effects (drowsiness, confusion) or predominantly nervous-system signs (tremour, pain, or fever) or may develop muscle weakness and tenderness or may show abnormalities of the heart and circulatory system.

Types of treatment
Treatment cannot be generalized. For some important poisonings, specific antidotes of variable efficacy are available. Chronic lead poisoning in adults yields, on occasion, to treatment with ethylenediaminetetraacetic acid (EDTA); in children afflicted with the preventable effects of lead on the brain (one-half of all chronic cases) EDTA and dimercaprol (BAL) may be life-saving. Unfortunately, of the 75 percent who survive, a third suffer permanent brain damage with mental retardation and sometimes blindness.

In most chronic poisonings, treatment is supportive rather than specific. Removal from further exposure, good nursing care, and the remarkable restorative potential of the body favour recovery. Irreversible alterations in structures or in functions of susceptible parts of the body may cause crippling, even when the poison no longer is present and undamaged tissues function normally.

METABOLISM OF POISON BY THE BODY

A poisonous effect, acute or chronic, whether discerned as an impairment of function or as a derangement of structure, usually can be traced to the presence of the toxic agent in the affected area. The degree and kind of injury is often dependent (1) on the amount as well as (2) on the form in which the agent reaches the tissue, (3) on what happens to the agent there, and (4) on how long it remains. One of the keys to understanding how poisons injure lies in discovering what the body does to the poison (variously described as its fate, its metabolism, or its biotransformation).

Introduced into the stomach or gut, toxic substances may be absorbed or they may be destroyed by digestive action (as is rattlesnake toxin, a mixture of proteins). Insoluble substances, when swallowed, may pass through the body virtually unchanged and be lost in the feces.

The speed with which a poison swallowed, inhaled, spread on the skin, or injected enters the body tissues depends on (1) its solubility in fat or water, (2) its degree of irritancy, (3) its chemical reactivity, (4) the toxicologic reactivity, and other factors. In the bloodstream, portions are carried in greater or lesser amounts to all parts of the body. Gaseous substances stable in the body are usually exhaled. Some substances are tightly bound by (enter into stable combination with) blood constituents, especially proteins, and are slowly released. Particulates are apt to be engulfed by scavenger cells, the macrophages, and carried to the special trapping cells of the spleen, liver, bone marrow, or lymph nodes. Insoluble particulates may thereby create special hazards if their properties are dangerous (e.g., if they are radioactive) and if mobilization (release from the tissues) is slow. Toxic substances with high fat solubility pose special problems. Membranes contain fatty layers across which fat-soluble substances are readily transported during initial absorption as well as during reabsorption from newly formed urine in the kidney tubule. Reabsorption tends to retard excretion and to build up the body load, obviously increasing the hazard of poisoning. Water-soluble substances generally pass out in the urine; some, like penicillin, are swiftly excreted (half is gone in 30 minutes). In contrast, substances of high fat solubility, such as alcohol, tend to remain longer; in the case of alcohol, until it is oxidized.

The body has some chemical defenses. Metabolic machinery in the cytoplasm (cell substance outside the nucleus) alters foreign molecules by various methods, including oxidizing, reducing, or hydrolyzing them (breaking them down by adding of water). All of these chemical changes tend to form products that are less fat-soluble, more water-soluble, frequently more acidic or basic than the original molecule, and therefore less resorbable and much more readily excreted in the urine. In these ways, such processes detoxify the foreign molecule and have long been known as detoxication mechanisms. Natural foodstuffs may contain traces of biologically active substances that, if retained unchanged, may be poisonous. The various detoxifying processes therefore have survival value.

The products of the chemical reactions within the body are occasionally more poisonous than the original molecules. A famous example is the transformation of fluoroacetate (inherently not toxic) into the extremely toxic fluorocitrate, which blocks a key enzyme, aconitase, of an important energy-producing mechanism (the citric-acid cycle) of the mitochondria (the energy-producing structural elements of cytoplasm).

Toxic substances may be stored in the body, sometimes briefly (carbon monoxide as carboxyhemoglobin for hours), sometimes for years (uranium dioxide particles in lymph nodes of the lung, strontium-90 in the skeleton, DDT in fatty tissue, silver in the skin).

Manner of excretion
Excretion occurs mainly by way of the urine or the feces, or both. Some solvents (certain chlorinated hydrocarbons, for example) are exhaled in detectable traces over periods of weeks. Traces of lead, mercury, and arsenic are deposited in hair. Sweat contains detectable quantities of certain poisons. Excretion in milk, though uncommon, is known; epidemics of sometimes fatal milk sickness have afflicted those drinking milk from cows feeding on white snakeroot (*Eupatorium rugosum*).

MECHANISM OF TOXIC ACTION

Although most poisons act at several sites in the body, simultaneously or in sequence, not infrequently the injury to one organ or system is predominantly responsible for serious illness or death. Cyanide blocks a basic energy-providing mechanism (cytochrome oxidase) in most cells. Many substances in overdose injure the liver; the list includes such diverse materials as carbon tetrachloride, *Amanita phalloides* (death cap mushroom) toxins, and elemental phosphorus. Carbon tetrachloride also destroys kidney tissue, as do mercury and arsenic.

Substances that break down red blood cells (hemolysis), such as primaquine and a number of other drugs, are more likely to cause trouble to individuals anemic because of hereditary deficiency in the enzyme glucose-6-phosphate dehydrogenase. Hemolysis can secondarily produce acute kidney failure by blockage of the tubules. Carbon monoxide acts primarily in the blood, combining with hemoglobin to form carboxyhemoglobin in a combination 200 times tighter than with oxygen, thereby effectively preventing the transport of vitally essential oxygen to the brain, heart, muscles and other tissues. Squill can fatally affect the heart by overexciting it. Sudden deaths from inhaling a variety of substances (gasoline and fluorocarbon propellants, for example) have been traced to another kind of heart injury, a loss of coordination of muscle contraction so that individual muscle fibres beat at random; the heart fails to propel blood, and death swiftly ensues. Intoxications prominently involving the central nervous system are commonplace: drunkenness with alcohol, the "high" of marihuana, the ecstasy or the terror of lysergic acid diethylamide (LSD), convulsions from cocaine, poisoning with strychnine, organic phosphate, or dieldrin, destruction of brain tissue by methyl mercury or by severe exposure to carbon monoxide. Injuries to bone tissues are rare but not unknown; the bone cancers of the radium-dial painters of World War I are a frequently cited example.

The dislocations and distortions induced by poisons into the normal workings of organs and tissues can be useful in revealing secrets of the life processes. The inhibitory role of recurrent nerve branches in the spinal cord, for example, was made clear by the effect of strychnine in blocking their normal function. The neurohormone (acetylcholine) was discovered when the enzyme that normally inactivates acetylcholine in seconds was inhibited by a primitive ordeal poison (eserine).

Despite a multitude of experiments and the availability of immensely powerful new tools, only a few mechanisms of toxic action have been described in detail. The limit is often ignorance of the normal action that is disturbed by the poison. From the volumes of experimental work, a few

Queen hornet *(Vespa crabro)*.

Black widow *(Latrodectus mactans)*.

Poisonous plants and animals

Poison hemlock
(Conium maculatum).

Toadstool *(Amanita pantherina)*.

Laportea gigas, an Australian nettle tree, (left) entire tree,
(below) underside of a leaf showing stinging hairs.

Plate 1: (Top left) S.C. Bisserot—Bruce Coleman Inc., (top right) J.A.L. Cooke, (bottom left, bottom right) K. Gillett, World Life Research Institute, (centre left) Kitty Kahout from Root Resources—EB Inc., (centre right) L. Hugh Newman from The Natural History Photographic Agency—EB Inc.

Plate 2   Poisons and Poisoning

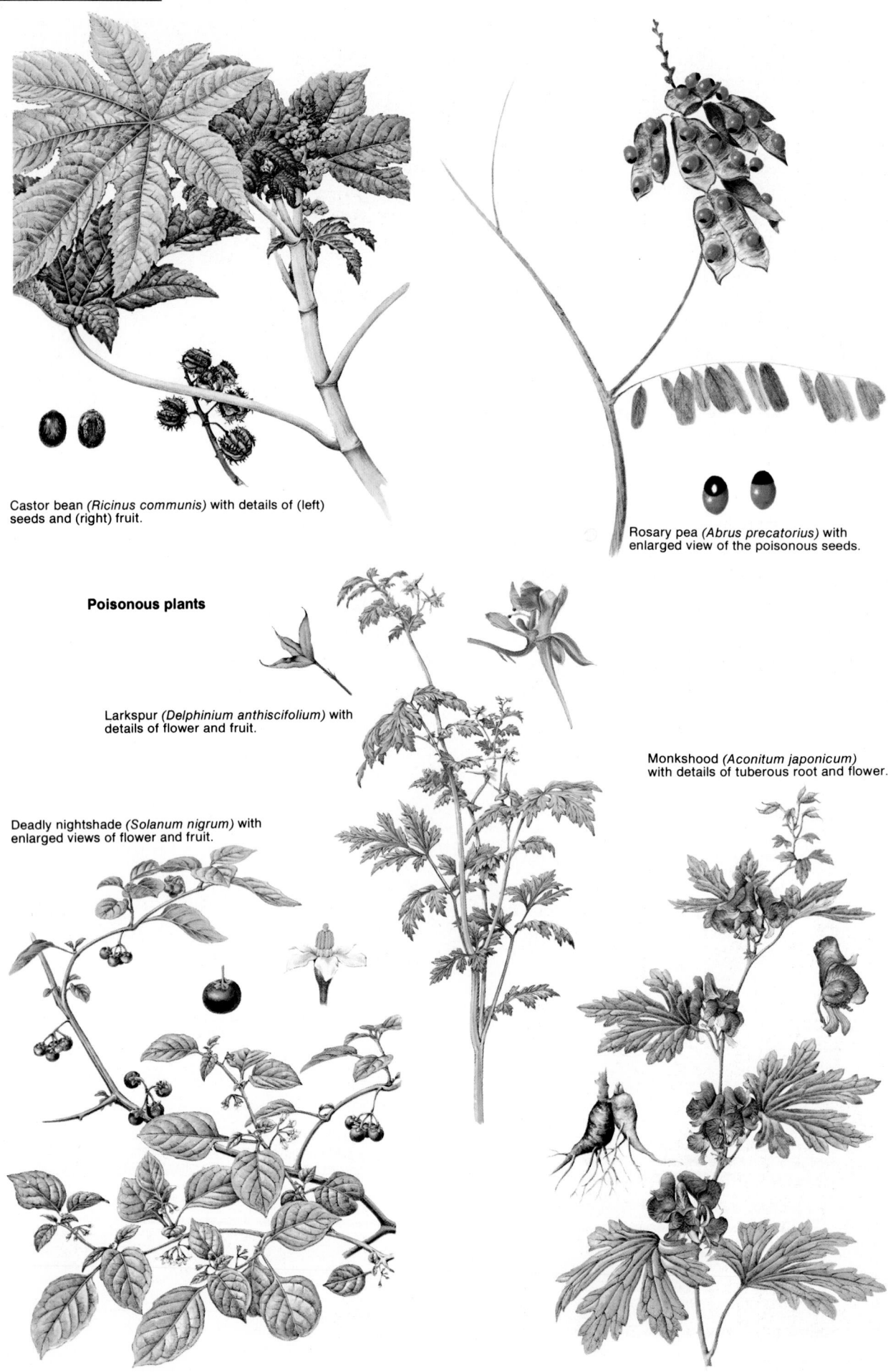

Castor bean *(Ricinus communis)* with details of (left) seeds and (right) fruit.

Rosary pea *(Abrus precatorius)* with enlarged view of the poisonous seeds.

Poisonous plants

Larkspur *(Delphinium anthiscifolium)* with details of flower and fruit.

Monkshood *(Aconitum japonicum)* with details of tuberous root and flower.

Deadly nightshade *(Solanum nigrum)* with enlarged views of flower and fruit.

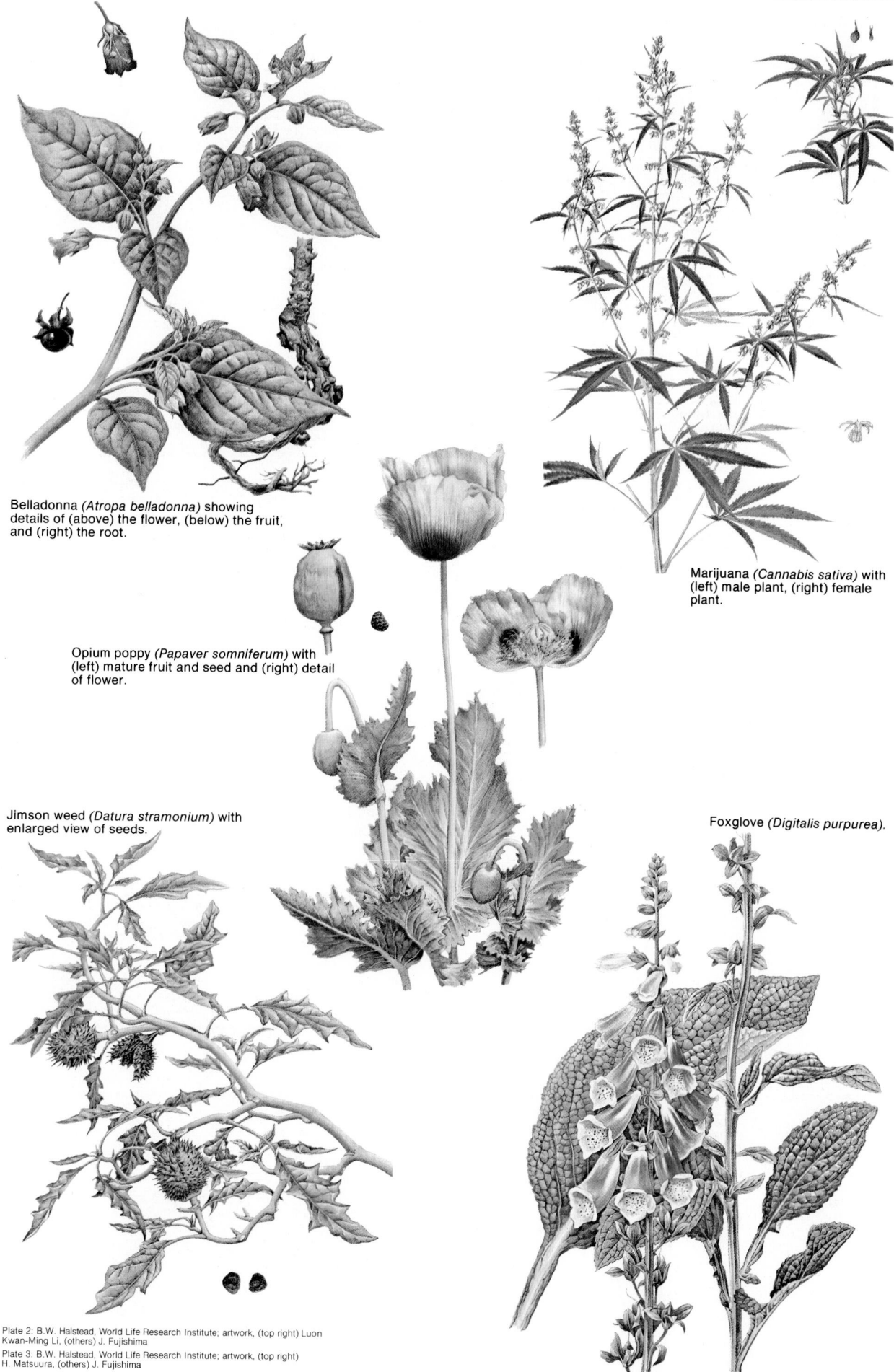

Belladonna *(Atropa belladonna)* showing details of (above) the flower, (below) the fruit, and (right) the root.

Marijuana *(Cannabis sativa)* with (left) male plant, (right) female plant.

Opium poppy *(Papaver somniferum)* with (left) mature fruit and seed and (right) detail of flower.

Jimson weed *(Datura stramonium)* with enlarged view of seeds.

Foxglove *(Digitalis purpurea)*.

Plate 2: B.W. Halstead, World Life Research Institute; artwork, (top right) Luon Kwan-Ming Li, (others) J. Fujishima

Plate 3: B.W. Halstead, World Life Research Institute; artwork, (top right) H. Matsuura, (others) J. Fujishima

Plate 4 Poisons and Poisoning

Crab (*Zozymus aeneus*).

Lionfish (*Pterois volitans*).

Poisonous aquatic and land animals

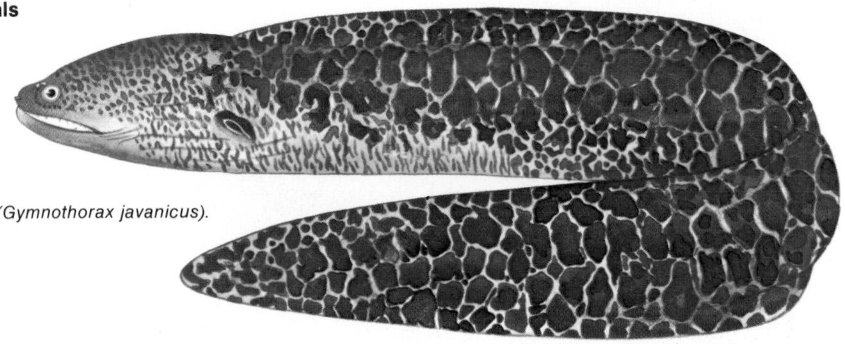

Moray eel (*Gymnothorax javanicus*).

Puffer
(*Fugu rubripes*).

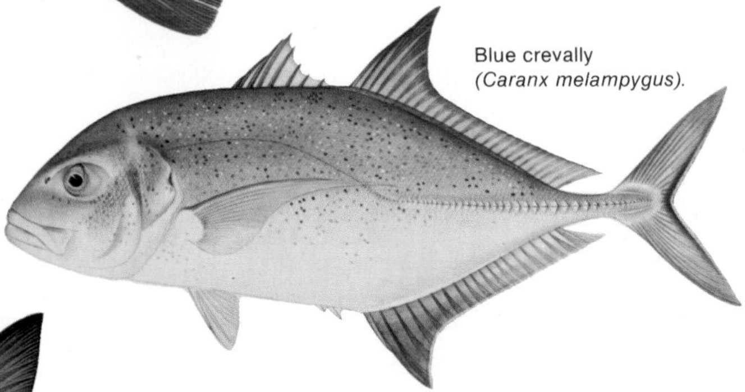

Blue crevally
(*Caranx melampygus*).

Red snapper
(*Lutjanus bohar*).

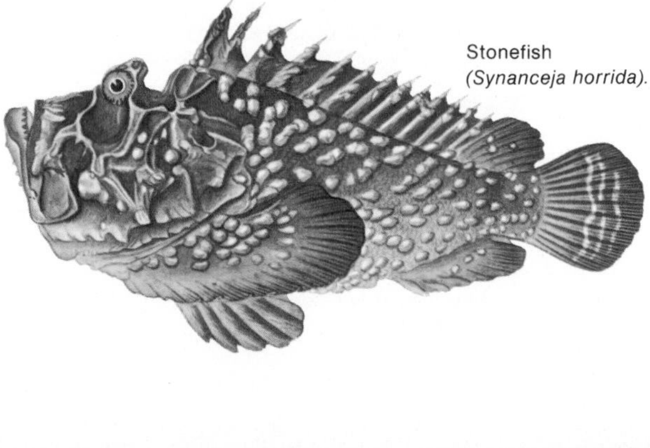

Stonefish
(*Synanceja horrida*).

Plate 4: B.W. Halstead—World Life Research Institute; artwork, (centre right above)
T. Kumada, (centre right below) K. Tomita, (bottom right) S. Arita, (others) M. Shirao
Plate 5: B.W. Halstead—World Life Research Institute; artwork, (centre left) L. Barlow,
(bottom right) L. Barlow and M. Shirao, (others) K. Fogassy

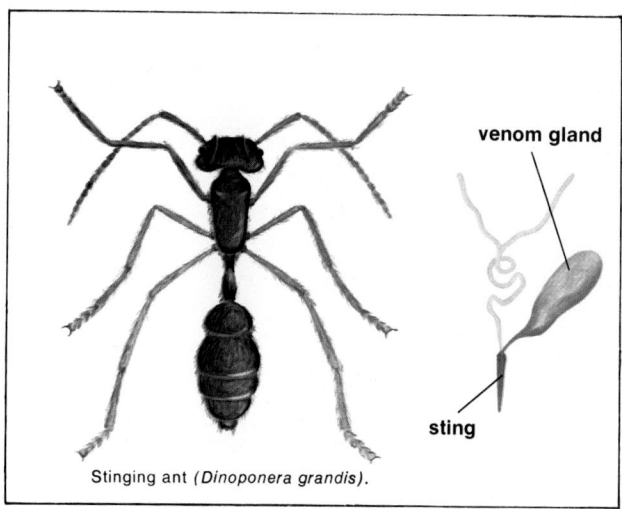

Stinging ant *(Dinoponera grandis)*.

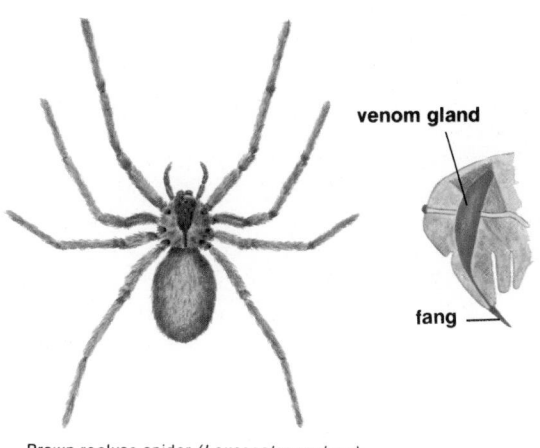

Brown recluse spider *(Loxosceles reclusa)*.

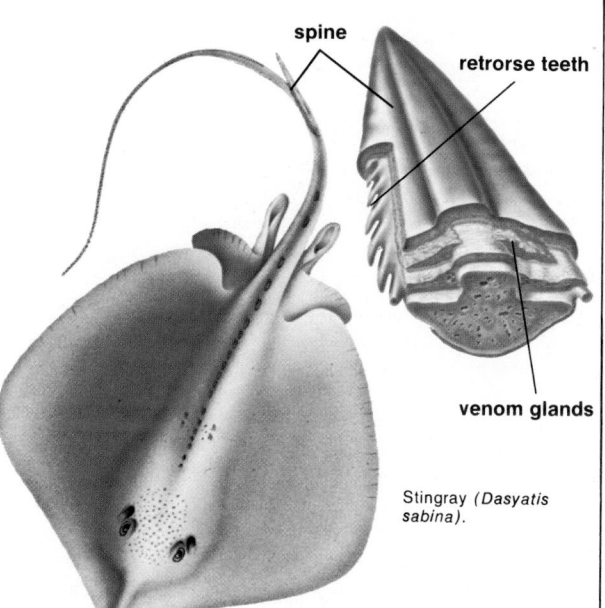

Stingray *(Dasyatis sabina)*.

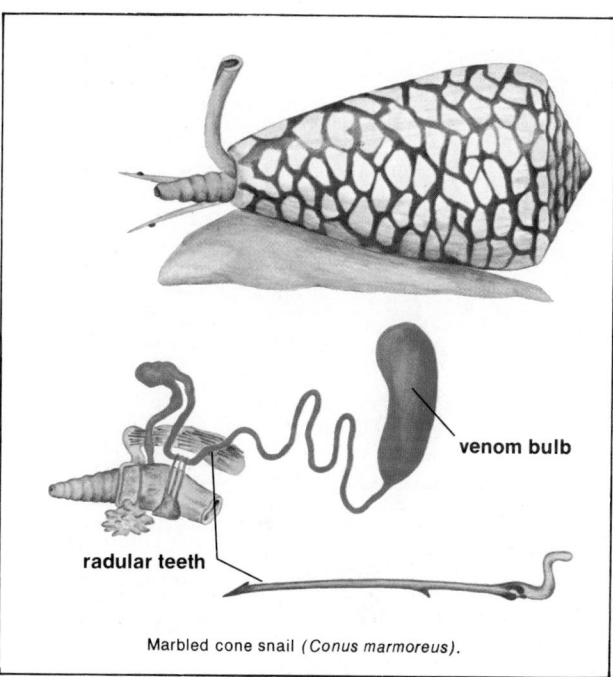

Marbled cone snail *(Conus marmoreus)*.

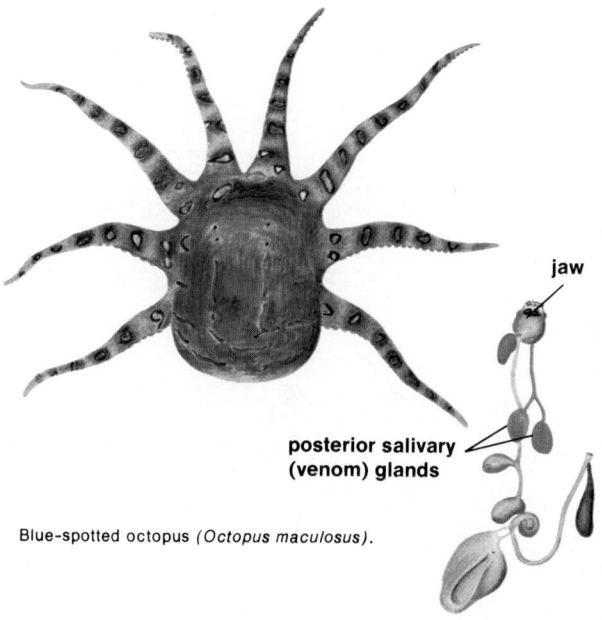

Blue-spotted octopus *(Octopus maculosus)*.

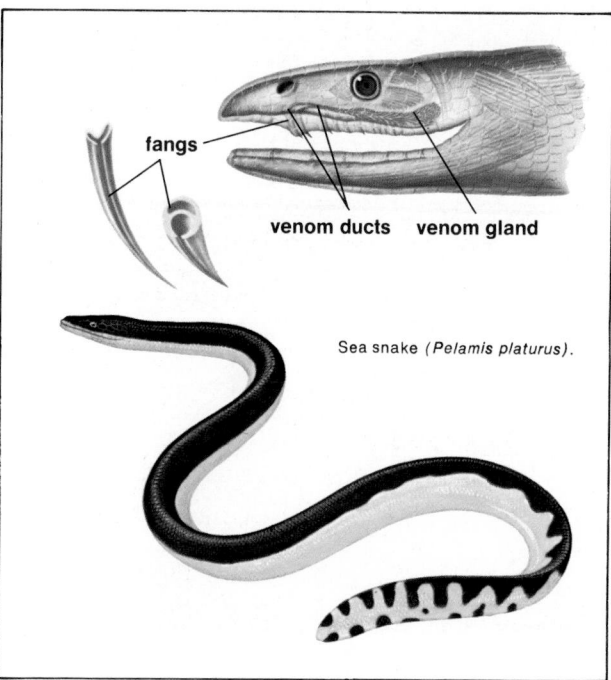

Sea snake *(Pelamis platurus)*.

Plate 6   Poisons and Poisoning

Crown of thorns starfish *(Acanthaster planci).*

Sea wasp *(Chironex fleckeri).*

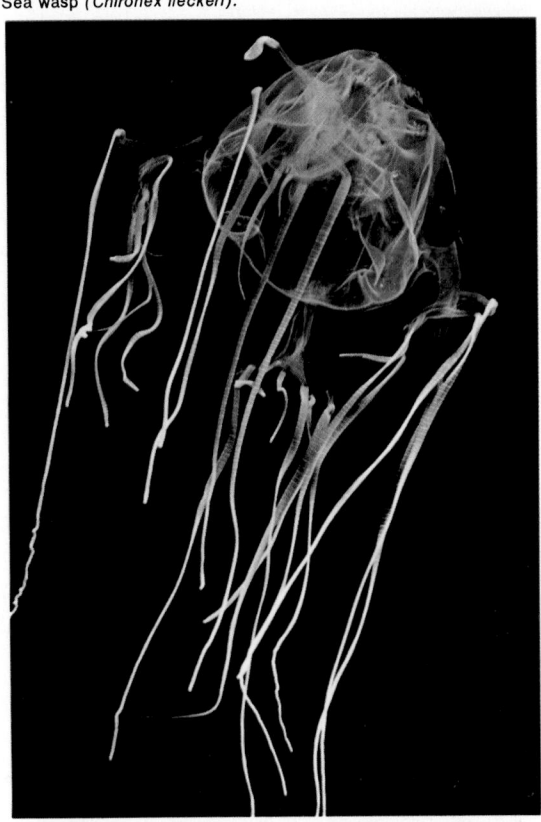

Red tide, Tampa Bay, Florida, showing fish kill and red coloration caused by dinoflagellates.

Poisonous aquatic and land animals

Green mamba *(Dendroaspis viridis).*

Kokoa frog or South American arrow poison frog *(Dendrobates* species).

Gila monster *(Heloderma suspectum).*

Plate 6: (Top left, centre left) World Life Research Institute, (top left) K. Gillett, (top right, bottom left) The National Audubon Society Collection/Photo Researchers, (top right) R.F. Head, (bottom left) George Porter, (centre right) N. Myers—Bruce Coleman Inc., (bottom right) Richard Weymouth Brooks—Photo Researchers

Table 3: Various Toxic Reactions

site	nature of toxic effect	example of poison
Cell membrane	destruction	lye; phenol; heat
	altered permeability	mercury; squill, carbon tetra-chloride, hydrocarbons
	formation prevented	penicillin in susceptible bacteria
Blood	interference with circulation by clotting	some snake venoms
	interference with oxygen access in lung	chlorine, nitrous oxides, ozone
	interference with oxygen transport	carbon monoxide, nitrites
	clotting prevented	warfarin
Nerve	transmission blocked along fibre	cocaine
	release of neurohormone blocked	botulinus toxin
	access to receptor blocked	strychnine, atropine, curare
	enzyme inactivating neurohormone inhibited	organic phosphates
Cell function	growth interference	colchicine, nitrogen mustard
	DNA structure or function altered	nitrosamine, radiation, actinomycin D
	energy-supplying cycle blocked	fluoroacetate
	antimetabolite	methotrexate

examples of the varied natures of toxic actions have been selected and are listed (Table 3), more to illustrate the diversity than to claim detailed knowledge, and certainly not to suggest that the mechanisms of all or even of many are fully understood.

Synergism Interactions between similar or dissimilar compounds can be important. Two organic phosphates, for example, may be synergistic (each may enhance the effect of the other) in their insecticidal action. For this reason, when several chemically-related pesticides are used as mixtures, the amounts permitted as food residues are set for the class and not for individual pesticides.

Another kind of interaction has been identified. Some pesticides (DDT, for example) and some drugs are able to stimulate the production by the liver cells of enzymes that account for much of the detoxication of foreign molecules (including drugs). While the traces of pesticides in foods as consumed are insufficient to stimulate these enzymes, occupational exposures either in manufacture or use may possibly do so. By this type of interaction, certain drugs (*e.g.,* barbiturates) are known to increase the rate of destruction of other drugs, thereby necessitating increase in dosage to maintain therapeutic efficacy. (H.C.Ho./Ed.)

Poisonous animals and plants: biotoxins

GENERAL FEATURES

Properties and occurrence of biotoxins. Numerous microorganisms, plants, and animals produce a vast array of toxic chemical substances, most of which have not yet been adequately characterized as to their chemical nature or biological effects. The classical definition of the term toxin referred only to poisons of microbial origin with high molecular weights (based on the weight of a hydrogen atom as 1) and antigenic properties (*i.e.,* substances to which the body reacts by producing antibodies, proteins that attack and neutralize the antigens). Later, the definition was expanded to include poisons derived from higher plants and animals.

Biotoxins can be conveniently grouped into three major categories: (1) microbial toxins, poisons produced by bacteria, blue-green algae, dinoflagellates, golden-brown algae, etc.; (2) phytotoxins, poisons produced by higher plants; and (3) zootoxins, poisons produced by animals. The term phytotoxin is also commonly used by plant pathologists to refer to substances that are toxic to plants. The term as used in this article, however, is restricted to poisons derived from plants that are toxic to animals and particularly to man. The geographical distribution of poisonous organisms varies greatly; poison-producing microorganisms tend to be ubiquitous in their distribution. Poisonous plants and animals are found in greatest abundance and varieties in warm-temperate and tropical regions. Relatively few toxic organisms of any kind are found in polar latitudes.

Knowledge of the evolutionary significance and development of most biotoxins is largely speculative and poorly understood. In some instances they may have developed during the evolution of certain animal species as part of the food procurement mechanism (*e.g.,* in snakes; cnidarians, jellyfishes, and their relatives; mollusks, octopuses, and others; and spiders). Biotoxins may also function as defensive mechanisms, as in some snakes, fishes, arthropods (*e.g.,* insects, millipedes), and others. The defense may be quite complex—as in the protection of territorial rights for reproductive purposes—and inhibitory or antibiotic substances may be produced that result in the exclusion of competitive animal or plant species. Certain marine organisms and terrestrial plants may release into the water, air, or soil inhibitory substances that discourage the growth of other organisms; well-known examples include the production of antibiotic substances by microorganisms. Similar chemical-warfare mechanisms are used in battles for territorial rights among the inhabitants of a coral reef, a field, or a forest. Thus biotoxins play important roles in the regulation of natural populations. Of increasing interest has been the discovery that certain substances, which may be toxic to one group of organisms, may serve a vital function in the life processes of the source organism.

Evolutionary aspects of biotoxins

The complex ecological relationships between some of the more toxic marine invertebrates and fishes are as yet poorly understood. Interactions between species may, in the presence of certain chemical substances, contribute directly to the production of highly toxic biochemical products, an interaction that is sometimes referred to as ecological biogenesis.

Importance to man. Toxic plants and animals are of importance to man in a variety of ways. Many biotoxins are potent agents capable of adversely affecting man directly by causing disease, pain, or death or indirectly by damaging his plants or animals. Toxic organisms thus constitute a potential public-health problem with economic and sociological implications.

Venom-producing animals and stinging and dermatogenic (*i.e.,* skin-poisoning) plants capable of inflicting pain and sometimes death by means of parenteral contact (*i.e.,* by bringing poisons into the body other than through the digestive tract) constitute environmental hazards. Biotoxic agents may produce their injurious effects by becoming involved in man's food supply; ingestion of a poisonous microbial organism, plant, or marine animal or one of their toxic by-products may cause intoxication. An example is that of the shore fishes of many tropical islands; otherwise valuable food fishes are frequently contaminated by a poison called ciguatoxin. The poison, a potent neurotoxin (nerve poison), is accidentally ingested by the fishes in their food; such fish can no longer be used for either human or animal consumption.

Entry methods for biological poisons

Some of the effects produced by biotoxins on humans are of an acute nature, and the injuries they cause are readily discernible. The effects of some of the mycotoxins (poisons produced by fungi) and poisons produced by higher plants, however, are long-term and chronic; they result in the development of cancerous growths and other chronic degenerative changes that are sometimes difficult to detect.

The scientific importance of biotoxicology is frequently misunderstood. One popular attitude is that, because poisons are potentially lethal substances capable of causing intoxication and death, they are therefore to be avoided and that research is justified to determine their pharmacological and chemical properties with the hope of ultimately developing useful antitoxins. Another aspect equally deserving of consideration, however, is the exploration of biologically active substances and chemical structures in order to determine their physical nature and biological properties. Many of the biotoxins studied even in a cursory manner have been found to have diverse biological properties, some of which have application to medicine: fungicidal, growth inhibitory, antiviral, antibiotic, antitumour, hemolytic (red-blood-cell destroying), anti-inflammatory, analgesic (pain controlling), cardioinhibitory (heart arresting), psychopharmacological (affecting mental processes), and others. Toxicity thus provides important information regarding valuable pharmacological properties of biotoxins. In the area of natural-products research, of which biotox-

icology is an important segment, ethnobotanical and eth-
nozoological studies reveal the way in which plants and
animals have been utilized by primitive peoples. Crude
data of this type serve as useful indicators of the general
pharmacological properties of biotoxins. Biotoxins also offer a spectrum of new or little-known chemical substances,
which the chemist may be able to synthesize and manipulate into useful products. Highly active biotoxins may
also be useful in neurophysiological research, especially in
elucidating the nature of both nervous activity and muscular function.

HISTORICAL BACKGROUND

The recorded story of poisonous plants and animals and
their relationship to mankind dates to the dawn of man's
written language; poisons and poisonous organisms played
a dominant role in the affairs of mankind, especially
in those of ancient magician-physicians and priests. Not
only was it of value for them to know the means of
treating a poisonous sting but it was equally useful that
they be familiar with the biological poisons capable of
causing death of an enemy. Because of the profound and
little-understood physiological effects resulting from contact with plant and animal poisons, ancient cultures often
surrounded biotoxins with an aura of mystery, superstition, and religion. The pre-Grecian era of Mesopotamian
medicine was dominated by magicians and priests. Little is known about their knowledge of specific poisonous
animals, but they were keen observers of natural history
and were undoubtedly aware of the existence of many
noxious pests.

Medical records of ancient Egypt include a practicing
physician's formulary containing about 260 prescriptions,
some of which are for various kinds of animal stings,
including the poisonous puffer fish. The Bible and Talmudic records document the toxic effects of dinoflagellates
(a group of algae). Other records list some 760 medicinal
plants and mention venomous animals and antidotes for
bites and stings.

Out of ancient Chinese science, which was based on
plant and animal lore, demoniac beliefs, and faith healing,
arose a legendary emperor, Sheng Nung, revered as god
of medicine and father of agriculture and herbal therapy; he is credited with the authorship of the predecessor
of Chinese pharmacopeias. Ancient Chinese phytotoxicology was a comparatively well-developed science, and
poisonous plants and their antidotes were described in
elaborate detail.

In the Western world, the ancient Greeks were probably
the first to dissociate medicine from magic and religion.
Aristotle was familiar with the venom of jellyfishes and
scorpion fishes. Mithradates VI, king of Pontus in the
2nd century BC, experimented with the giving and taking
of poisons and is said to have been one of the first to
study intensively the art of poisoning and the preparation
of antidotes. He aspired to develop a universal antidote,
which became known as mithridates and theriacs. In the
1st century AD, Pedanius Dioscorides, a Greek army surgeon, wrote on many terrestrial plants used as drugs and
also recorded the toxic nature of sea hares, polychaete
worms, stingrays, and sea vipers. Pliny the Elder, the Latin
naturalist, dealt with poisonous plants and animals in his
Historia naturalis (*Natural History*) and wrote about the
dangerous wounds inflicted by the venomous spines of the
weever fishes and stingrays and about the toxicity of the
sea hare. He also recommended that a powder of the sting
of the stingray be used as a potion to treat toothache.

From the 5th to the 8th century AD, the centre of medical culture was Constantinople; Paul of Aegina wrote the
Epitomae, a medical encyclopaedia of seven books, one
of which was concerned with venomous stings, bites, and
toxicology. During the early years of the 7th century, the
Arabs wrote extensively about poisons, the effect of venoms, and antidotal remedies.

From the 9th through the 15th century, when there
was neither induction nor experiment, biotoxicology languished along with most other sciences. One of the few
important works was that of the Persian physician Avicenna. His *Qānūn fī aṭ-ṭibb* (*Canon of Medicine*) was a

compilation of his experiences in the practice of medicine
and a compendium of all that was known about medicine
at the time. The *Canon* is concerned with, among other
things, the composition and preparation of drugs. He recognized both oral and parenteral poisons, discussed venomous stings and their treatment, and dealt with animal,
plant, and mineral poisons. For more than 500 years his
work was considered the outstanding authority on poisons
and their antidotes.

Many printed herbals, which began to appear around
1470, included discussions about poisonous plants. The
great work in biotoxicology of the Renaissance was that of
the father of modern biotoxicology, the French physician
Jacques Grévin, who published his book *Deux livres des
venins* (*Two Books of Poisons*) in 1568. Another important
work that appeared in the latter half of the 17th century
dealt with various types of poisonous plants.

In 1702 the British physician Richard Mead published
his *Mechanical Account of Poisons,* in which he described
snake poisoning and his swallowing of the venom, thereby
proving that parenteral administration was in this case
essential to produce intoxication. Other important works
of this period were influential because they paid particular
attention to poisonings resulting from the injudicious use
of medicinal plants and to some of the effects of poisons
on animals.

The important toxicological contributions of the French
physician M.-J.-B. Orfila, who has been designated the father of experimental toxicology, came at the beginning of
the 19th century. His *Traité de toxicologie,* first published
in 1814, went through many editions and translations.
Most of his investigations were concerned with inorganic
agents and plant poisons and, to a lesser extent, with the
venoms of snakes, spiders, bees, wasps, and poisonous
fishes. In 1888 it was demonstrated that the disease-
producing mechanism of a microorganism in human beings could be explained in terms of a toxic substance released by bacteria. Tetanus toxin was discovered in 1890.

Experimental research based on sophisticated analytical
procedures accelerated in the early 20th century. This period also saw the discovery of hypersensitivity reactions
and a better understanding of anaphylaxis and allergies.
During World War II, environmental biological poisons
became medically important in many military operations.
A rapidly expanding world population in the postwar years
further pointed up the need for the utilization of food resources in heavily populated tropical regions in which oral
biotoxins are most likely to be encountered. There have
also been increased demands for new therapeutic agents,
and biotoxins have served as a rich and varied resource.

MAJOR CATEGORIES OF BIOTOXINS

Microbial toxins. Microbial poisons are produced by
the so-called Monera (bacteria and blue-green algae) and
Protista (fungi, dinoflagellates, golden-brown algae, and
others). Various classifications have been proposed for the
microbial poisons, but none is entirely satisfactory. The
problems encountered when dealing with these organisms
result from a lack of precise knowledge concerning their
biological nature and their phylogenetic relationships; in
addition, their poisons show great diversity and chemical
complexity. The following outline, however, is useful in
dealing with this subject.

Bacterial toxins. The prefixes "exo-" and "endo-" are
retained in classifying the bacterial toxins mainly for historical reasons rather than because they are found either
outside or inside the bacterial cell. The main differences
in these toxins lie in their chemical structure. A list of
representative species of toxic bacteria and their toxins is
given in Table 4.

Poisonous proteins from bacteria are sometimes referred
to as bacterial exotoxins. The exotoxins are generally
produced by gram-positive organisms (*i.e.,* bacteria that
react in certain ways to the staining procedure known as
gram staining); at least two bacteria, *Shigella dysenteriae*
and *Vibrio cholerae,* that produce exotoxins are gram-
negative, however. The exotoxins usually do not contain
any nonprotein substances, and most are antigenic; *i.e.,*
they stimulate the formation of antibodies. The exotoxins

Table 4: Representative Toxic Bacteria and Their Toxins

	toxin	chemical nature	comments
Gram-positive bacteria			
Corynebacterium diphtheriae	diphtheria toxin	protein	involved in diphtheria in man
Staphylococcus aureus	α-toxin, β-hemolysin, enterotoxins, leukocidin	protein	causes pyogenic (pus-forming) infections in animals and in man
Clostridium botulinum	botulinus toxin	protein	involved in botulism in man
Clostridium perfringens	α-toxin, θ-toxin	protein	causes gas gangrene in man
Clostridium tetani	tetanospasmin	protein	causes tetanus in man
Streptococcus pyogenes	streptolysin O, erythrogenic toxin	protein	causes scarlet fever and other streptococcal infections in animals and man
Gram-negative bacteria			
Shigella dysenteriae	neurotoxin	protein	causes bacillary dysentery in man
Vibrio cholerae	cholera toxin	protein	causes cholera in man
Escherichia coli, *Salmonella* species, *Shigella* species, *Brucella* species, and others	"conventional endotoxins"	complex of protein, lipid, and polysaccharide	most gram-negative bacteria produce toxic complex chemical mixtures that are categorically referred to as "endotoxins"

may appear in the culture medium in which the bacteria are growing during the declining phases of growth; in some cases they are released at the time of normal destruction of the cells after death (autolysis). The exotoxins are less stable to heat than are the endotoxins, and they may be detoxified by agents that do not affect endotoxins. They are more toxic than endotoxins, and each exotoxin exerts specific effects which are collectively known as pharmacological properties. Exotoxins are neutralized by homologous antibodies—*i.e.,* the active agents in blood serum produced by a process involving the bacteria against which the serum is to be used.

Endotoxins are antigens composed of complexes of proteins, polysaccharides (large molecules built up of numerous sugars), and lipids (fats). The protein part determines the antigenicity, or quality of being reacted against as a foreign substance in a living organism. The polysaccharide part determines the immunological specificity, or limitations on the types of antibodies that can react with the endotoxin molecule and neutralize it (the immunological reaction). Some of the lipids possibly determine the toxicity. Endotoxins are derived from the bacterial cell wall and, when cells are grown in culture, are released only on autolysis. Endotoxins are not neutralized by homologous antibodies and are relatively stable to heat; all of them have the same pharmacological properties.

Mycotoxins. Fungi are plantlike members of the phylum Mycota that do not contain any chlorophyll. It has been estimated that there are about 85,000 species of fungi, about 55,000 of which are microscopically small in size. A significant number are known to produce poisons of various types. Toxic fungi can be roughly divided into two main categories on the basis of their size: the smaller microfungi and the larger mushrooms. The toxic microfungi are members of one of two classes: Ascomycetes, or the sac fungi, and the Deuteromycetes, or the imperfect fungi (*i.e.,* fungi in which no sexual reproductive stages are known). The large toxic mushrooms, or toadstools, are mostly members of the class Basidiomycetes, although some Ascomycetes, such as the poisonous false morel (*Gyromitra esculenta*), may attain a size as large as some of the mushrooms.

The ability of certain fungi, such as ergot (*Claviceps purpurea*) and some mushrooms, to produce intoxication has long been known. During the 19th century it was recognized that molds are responsible for such diseases as yellow-rice toxicoses in Japan and alimentary toxic aleukia in Russia. The eruption of so-called turkey X disease in England in 1960 and the resulting discovery of the substance known as aflatoxin (see Table 5) stimulated study of the subject of mycotoxicology. Despite the vast amount of research on mycotoxins, much remains to be done. New mycotoxins are continuously being discovered, and their chemical and biological properties, which vary greatly from one poison to the next, are being studied with great interest. Because mycotoxins have now been recognized as potential cancer-producing agents (carcinogens) that can become involved in man's food supply, they have become important in the study of environmental carcinogenesis.

Poisonous mushrooms, or toadstools as they are commonly called, are the widely distributed members of the class Basidiomycetes. Although there are more than 30,-000 species of large mushrooms, only a few are known to be poisonous when eaten (see Table 6); some of the poisons, however, are deadly. About 90 percent of the deaths attributed to mushroom poisoning result from eating members of the genus *Amanita.* When eating wild mushrooms, they should be accurately identified by an experienced person; the safest procedure is to eat only cultivated species. The problem of toxicity in mushrooms is complex; no single rule or test method exists by which the toxicity of a mushroom can be determined. The most poisonous species closely resemble some of the most prized edible species; in addition, toxicity within a given wild species may vary from one set of ecological conditions or from one geographical locality to the next. Moreover, although some mushrooms that are poisonous when fresh are edible when cooked, dried, salted, or preserved in some other way, others remain poisonous in spite of all preparation procedures. It has also been observed that some people may become poisoned by eating mushrooms that apparently do not affect others. As with microfungi, the mushroom poisons vary

Poisonous mush-rooms

Table 5: Representative Toxic Microfungi

	toxin	comments
Claviceps purpurea (ergot)	"ergotoxine," a complex of toxic alkaloids, ergocryptine, ergocornine, ergocristine, and others	causes ergot poisoning in animals and humans; produces vomiting, abdominal pain, numbness, nervous disorders, convulsions, gangrene, and abortion
Stachybotrys alternans	stachybotryotoxin	causes a toxicosis in animals and humans; produces stomatitis (inflammatory diseases of the mouth), rhinitis (inflammation of the mucous membranes of the nose), conjunctivitis (inflammation of the inner surface of the eyelid); failure of blood to clot, blood abnormalities, neurological disturbances, and death
Aspergillus flavus and other species *Penicillium* species	aflatoxin complex (16 or more known toxins)	causes toxicosis in animals and possibly man; toxins damage liver and kidneys; aflatoxin is one of the most potent liver-cancer producing agents known
Fusarium sporotrichioides and other *Fusarium* species	fusariogenin, epicladosporic acid, fagicladosporic acid	causes alimentary toxic aleukia in animals and man; produces burning sensation of the mouth, tongue, throat, and stomach, nausea, vomiting, headache, cold extremities, hemorrhagic spots, convulsions, anemia, gangrene, death
Cladosporium epiphyllum and other species of *Cladosporium*	same as *Fusarium* species	
Pithomyces chartarum (*Sporidesmium bakeri*)	sporidesmin	causes facial eczema (an eruptive severe rash) in cattle; produces sensitization of the skin to sunlight resulting in scab formation and sores; there may also be severe liver damage
Fusarium species, *Rhizopus* species, *Aspergillus* species, *Penicillium islandicum*, and others	luteoskyrin, "islanditoxin," citrinin, citreoviridin, and others; a large complex of poisons involved	causes moldy or yellowed rice, which is toxic to animals and man; the effects in man have not been well defined; may cause nausea, vomiting, diarrhea, prostration, liver damage, and death; the effects vary greatly because of the various poisons involved

Table 6: Representative Poisonous Mushrooms

	toxin	type of poisoning
Lorchel, or false morel (*Gyromitra esculenta*)	gyromitrin	toxicity to people is variable; causes severe liver damage accompanied by nausea, vomiting, abdominal pain, jaundice, enlarged and tender liver, coma, convulsions; fatality rate about 15 percent
Fly mushroom, or fly agaric (*Amanita muscaria*)	muscarine	symptoms develop rapidly, are severe, consisting of severe gastrointestinal disturbances, delirium, hallucinations, convulsions; rarely causes death
Panther mushroom (*Amanita pantherina*)	muscarine	symptoms are similar to *A. muscaria* poisoning
Destroying angel, or death cup (*Amanita phalloides*)	amanitine, phalloidine	symptoms develop slowly, about 6–15 hours after eating: extreme abdominal pain, nausea, vomiting, excessive thirst, anuria (absence or defective excretion of urine), prostration, weakness, jaundice, cyanosis, convulsion, death; fatality rate up to 90 percent; no known antidote
Boletus miniato-olivaceus	muscarine (?)	causes gastrointestinal and visual disturbances
Jack-o'-Lantern fungus (*Clitocybe illudens*)	muscarine	causes gastrointestinal upset, not fatal
Inky cap (*Coprinus atramentarius*)	unknown	some people experience a peculiar type of intoxication after eating this mushroom then drinking an alcoholic beverage: giddiness, gastrointestinal upset, prostration, and tachycardia (rapid heart action); the alcohol is believed to increase the solubility and absorption of the poison
Entoloma lividum	unknown	causes gastrointestinal upset, usually not fatal
Inocybe patouillardi	muscarine	symptoms are similar to *A. muscaria* poisoning
Lepiota morgani	unknown	causes gastrointestinal upset; fatalities have been reported
Mexican hallucinogenic mushroom (*Psilocybe mexicana*)	psilocybin, psilocin	causes euphoria, loss of sense of distance and size, and hallucinations

in their chemical and biological properties from species to species.

Algal poisons. The study of poisonous algae is known as phycotoxicology. Two major groups of algae produce toxic substances: the Cyanophyta, or blue-green algae, and the Pyrrophyta, or dinoflagellates.

Algae comprise some of the smallest forms of chlorophyll-bearing organisms. The approximately 1,500 species of blue-green algae are among the most primitive organisms; they resemble the bacteria in their mode of reproduction and in certain physiological functions. The blue-green algae, among the most widely distributed of all organisms, live in all parts of the aquatic environment that receive light, including the exceedingly saline waters of the Dead Sea. They have extreme temperature tolerances and inhabit waters whose temperatures vary from near the freezing point to those of thermal springs as hot as 82° C (180° F). Blue-green algae have a remarkable ability to survive drying for years under desert conditions. About twice as many species are found inhabiting marine waters as freshwaters. Some strains of a species are toxic; other strains of the same species are not. Water blooms of blue-green algae have been responsible for the death of fishes, waterfowl, cattle, horses, swine, and other animals. Blue-green algae have also been implicated as causes of human intoxications. A list of representative poisonous blue-green algae and their poisons appears in Table 7.

The approximately 1,100 species of dinoflagellates, important producers of the primary food supply of the sea, are microscopic one-celled organisms that are dependent upon various inorganic nutrients in the water and upon radiant energy for photosynthesis, the process by which they produce their own food supplies. Although dinoflagellates inhabit both marine waters and freshwaters, most species are marine. Dinoflagellates are most often found in cool or temperate waters. During periods of planktonic blooms (times of high concentrations of microscopic organisms in the water) dinoflagellates multiply in large numbers. These planktonic blooms, sometimes referred to as red tide because they discolour the water, are often associated with weather disturbances that may bring about changes in water masses or upwellings. During periods of bloom large numbers of toxic dinoflagellates may be ingested by shellfish; the poisons accumulate in their digestive glands. Man and animals may in turn be poisoned by eating poisoned shellfish. Certain species of dinoflagellates are capable of producing some of the most toxic substances known. The two species of dinoflagellates most commonly involved in human intoxications have been *Gonyaulax catenella* along the Pacific coast of North America and *G. tamarensis* along the eastern coast of North America. Intoxications from these organisms are known as paralytic shellfish poisoning. The symptoms, which begin with a tingling or burning sensation, then numbness of the lips, gums, tongue, and face, gradually spread. Gastrointestinal upset may be present. Other symptoms include weakness, joint aches, and muscular paralysis; death may result. There is no specific treatment nor antidote. The poison, variously called paralytic shellfish poison, mussel poison, and saxitoxin, is a complex nonprotein nitrogen-containing compound. Paralytic shellfish poisoning is best avoided by following local public-health quarantine regulations. Despite the numerous folk tales as to methods for differentiating poisonous from edible mussels, there is no reliable substitute for laboratory toxicity tests.

Respiratory irritation may result from the inhalation of toxic products in the windblown spray from red-tide areas containing the toxic dinoflagellate *Gymnodinium breve,* which is found in the Gulf of Mexico and Florida; the nature of the poison is unknown. Deaths of large numbers of brackish-water pond fishes because of *Prymnesium parvum* have been reported in Israel; the poison is known as prymnesin.

Plant poisons (phytotoxins). The study of plant poisons is known as phytotoxicology. Most of the poisonous higher plants are angiosperms, or flowering plants. Of the 300 families of angiosperms representing about 200,000 species, only a small percentage are recognized as poisonous. Several systems have been devised for the classification of poisonous plants, none of which is completely satisfactory. Poisonous plants may be classified according to the chemical nature of their toxic constituents, their phylogenetic relationship, or their botanical characteristics. The following classification, which is based on their toxic effects, has been found to be useful: (1) plants that are poisonous to eat; (2) plants that are poisonous upon contact; (3) plants that produce photosensitization; and (4) plants that produce airborne allergies (see Table 8).

Plant poisons, or phytotoxins, comprise a vast range of biologically active chemical substances, such as alkaloids, polypeptides, amines, glycosides, oxalates, resins, toxalbumins, and a large group of miscellaneous compounds whose chemical structure has not yet been determined.

Margin notes:

Environmental extremes for blue-green algae

Symptoms of paralytic shellfish poisoning

Chemical variability of plant poisons

Table 7: Representative Blue-Green Algae and Their Poisons

	toxin	toxic effects
Anacystis cyanea (also called *Microcystis aeruginosa*), a freshwater alga	neurotoxin (a polypeptide)	ingestion causes mass mortality of fish; strychnine-like convulsions in cattle and death; respiratory distress, convulsions and death in laboratory animals; gastroenteritis (inflammation of intestinal tissues) in humans; poison is rapid acting
Anabaena flos-aquae, a freshwater alga	neurotoxin (a polypeptide)	toxic effects are similar to those above; poison is rapid acting
Aphanizomenon flos-aquae, a freshwater alga	neurotoxin (a polypeptide ?)	toxic effects are similar to above, but the poison is usually slower acting
Lyngbya majuscula, a marine and freshwater blue-green alga	dermatogenic toxin, chemistry unknown	causes an acute inflammatory reaction when brought in contact with human skin; toxin has antiviral, antibacterial, and antifungal activity

Alkaloids, most of which are found in plants, are characterized by the presence of nitrogen and their ability to combine with acids to form salts. They are usually bitter in taste. It has been estimated that about 10 percent of the plant species contain some type of alkaloid. Only a few of the 5,000 alkaloids characterized thus far do not produce any biological activity; most cause a strong physiological reaction when administered to an animal. Amines are organic compounds containing nitrogen. A polypeptide is a string of three or more amino acids. A few polypeptides and amines are toxic to animals. Some glycosides, which are compounds that yield one or more sugars and one or more other compounds—aglycones (nonsugars)—when hydrolyzed (chemically degraded by the introduction of water molecules between adjacent subunits), are extremely toxic to animals. Toxicity resides in the aglycone component or a part of it. Oxalates are salts of oxalic acid, which under natural conditions is not toxic but becomes so because of the oxalate ion. Resins, a heterogeneous assemblage of complex compounds, differ widely in chemical properties but have certain similar physical properties. Some resins are physiologically very active, causing irritation to nervous and muscle tissue. Toxalbumins are highly toxic protein molecules that are produced by only a small number of plants. Ricin, a toxalbumin from the castor bean (*Ricinus communis*), is one of the most toxic substances known.

Under certain ecological conditions plants may become

Table 8: Representative Poisonous Plants

name and distribution	toxic principle	toxic effects and comments
Plants poisonous to eat		
Rosary pea, or jequirity bean (*Abrus precatorius*); tropical regions	abrin (*N*-methyltryptophan) and abric acid	onset of symptoms may be delayed several hours to two days, vomiting, diarrhea, acute gastroenteritis, chills, convulsions, death from heart failure; one seed chewed may be fatal to a child
Aconite, or monkshood (*Aconitum napellus*); North America, Europe	aconite and a complex of other alkaloids	tingling, burning sensation in tongue, throat, skin, restlessness, respiratory distress, muscular uncoordination, vomiting, diarrhea, convulsions, possible death; an extremely poisonous plant
Corn cockle (*Agrostemma githago*); North America, Europe	githagin, agrostemmic acid (saponins)	dizziness, diarrhea, respiratory distress, vomiting, headache, sharp pains in spine, coma, death; frequent ingestion of small amounts results in chronic githagism (a disease similar to lathyrism, that results in pain, burning and prickling sensations in lower extremities, and increasing paralysis); milled seeds may be found in wheat flour
Purple loco weed (*Astragulus mollissimus*); Northern Hemisphere	locoine	dullness, weakness, irregular behaviour, impaired vision, edema of eyelids, loss of muscular control, loss of appetite, emaciation, starvation, death in sheep, horses, and cattle
Belladonna (*Atropa belladonna*); United States, Europe, Asia	hyoscyamine, atropine, hyoscine, and a complex of other alkaloids	dryness of the skin, mouth, throat, difficulty in swallowing, flushing of the face, cyanosis (a bluish discoloration of skin due to insufficient oxygen), nausea, vomiting, slurred speech, coma, death; children and animals frequently poisoned by eating fruit
Akee (*Blighia sapida*)	hypoglycin A, B	sudden vomiting, drowsiness, muscular and nervous exhaustion, prostration, coma, death
Rape (*Brassica napus*)	glycosides (isothiocyanates)	pulmonary emphysema, respiratory distress, anemia, constipation, irritability, blindness in cattle
Marijuana (*Cannabis sativa*); United States, Mexico, tropical America	cannabinol, canabidiol, and related compounds	exaltation, inebriety, confusion, followed by central nervous system depression; prolonged, frequent use may produce dullness or mania; ingestion in large quantities or injection in the purified extract may produce death by cardiac depression
Water hemlock (*Cicuta maculata*); northern temperate regions	cicutoxin	abdominal pain, nausea, vomiting, diarrhea, respiratory distress, hypersalivation, convulsions, death; among the most poisonous plants
Poison hemlock (*Conium maculatum*); temperate United States, South America, northern Africa, Asia	coniine, conhydrine, *N*-methyleoniine, coniceine, and other alkaloids	muscular weakness, paralysis of extremities, blindness, respiratory paralysis, death; responsible for many human fatalities; leaves most toxic when plant is flowering
Purging croton (*Croton tiglium*); Asia, Pacific Islands, Africa	croton, croton resin, ricinine	vomiting, violent purging, collapse, death; croton oil is also a skin irritant, causing reddening, swelling, and pustules
Daphne (*Daphne mezereum*); temperate regions	glycoside involving aglycone dihydroxycoumarin	vomiting, burning sensation of the mouth, ulceration of the oral mucosa, diarrhea, stupor, weakness, convulsions, and death
Jimson weed or thornapple (*Datura stramonium*); temperate and tropical regions	hyoscine, hyoscyamine, atropine	headache, nausea, vomiting, dizziness, thirst, dry and burning sensation in skin, mental confusion, mania, loss of memory, convulsions, death; children are often poisoned by eating seeds or sucking flowers
Larkspur (*Delphinium* species); northern temperate regions	delphinine, delphinoidine, delphisine, and other alkaloids	burning and inflammation of mouth, nausea, vomiting, respiratory distress, itching, cyanosis; one of the greatest causes of death in grazing livestock
Dumbcane (*Dieffenbachia seguine*); widely cultivated in temperate regions, tropical regions	protoanemonine, calcium oxalate	irritation and burning of the mouth, tongue, and lips, hypersalivation, swelling of the tongue, difficulty in swallowing and breathing
Foxglove (*Digitalis purpurea*); Europe, North America	glycosides, digitoxigenin, and others	loss of appetite, nausea, vomiting, slow pulse and irregular heartbeat, diarrhea, abdominal pain, headache, fatigue, drowsiness, convulsions, death
Wild yam (*Dioscorea hispida*); southern Asia, Pacific Islands	dioscorine	discomfort, then burning of the throat, giddiness, vomiting of blood, respiratory distress, drowsiness, exhaustion, paralysis of the nervous system, death; raw tubers are a frequent cause of death in the Philippines
Huanuco cocaine (*Erythroxylon coca*); tropics of both hemispheres	cocaine and other alkaloids	central nervous system stimulation followed by depression, numbness of tongue, paralysis of respiratory centres, cyanosis, respiratory distress, death; leaves are commonly chewed by Indians of Peru and Bolivia as a stimulant
Manchineel (*Hippomane mancinella*); Florida, Central America, South America, West Indies	physostigmine or a similar alkaloid plus a sapogenin	fruit causes gastroenteritis, which may be fatal, and causes ulceration of intestinal tract; sap causes burning of skin, swelling and hemorrhage of the eyes; sap is used as an arrow poison
Black henbane (*Hyoscyamus niger*); North America, Europe, Asia, Oceania	hyoscyamine, hyoscine, atropine, and other alkaloids	similar to belladonna poisoning caused by *Atropa belladonna*; children are poisoned by eating seeds and pods
Barbados nut (*Jatropha curcas*); tropics	curcin	burning of the throat, bloating, dizziness, vomiting, diarrhea, drowsiness, dysuria, leg cramps, violent purgative action; may be fatal to children
Mountain laurel (*Kalmia latifolia*); North America	andromedotoxin	hypersalivation, tears, impaired vision, tingling of skin, dizziness, vomiting, muscular paralysis, convulsions, coma, death; children are poisoned by eating leaves
Grass peavine (*Lathyrus sativus*); North America, Europe, northern Africa, Asia	β-aminopropionitrile	back pain, weakness in legs, paralysis; has caused death in children

Table 8: Representative Poisonous Plants (cont.)

name and distribution	toxic principle	toxic effects and comments
Cassava (*Manihot esculenta*); tropics	cyanophoric glycosides	nausea, respiratory distress, twitching, staggering, convulsions, coma, death
Chinaberry (*Melia azedarach*); North America, southern Africa, Asia	azadarin	stomatitis with violent and bloody vomiting, paralysis
Opium poppy (*Papaver somniferum*); Europe, Asia, tropics	morphine, codeine, thebaine, papavarine, narcotine	central nervous system depression, pinpoint pupils, depressed respiration, cyanosis, coma, death
Pokeberry (*Phytolacca americana*); North America, Europe, southern Africa	phytolaccine	burning, bitterness in mouth, vomiting, purging, spasms, convulsions, death
Castor bean (*Ricinus communis*); United States, tropics	ricin, a toxalbumin	burning of mouth, throat, and stomach, vomiting, diarrhea, abdominal cramps, dulled vision, convulsions, respiratory distress, paralysis, death; one to three seeds may be fatal in children
Deadly nightshade (*Solanum nigrum*); North America, Europe	solanine, a glycoalkaloid	nausea, vomiting, abdominal pain, diarrhea, trembling, paralysis, coma, death
Nuxvomica tree (*Strychnos nux-vomica*); India, Hawaii	strychnine, brucine, and other alkaloids	extreme irritability, tonic convulsions, exhaustion, sweating, muscular rigidity, respiratory distress, death
Thevetia (*Thevetia peruviana*); tropics	thevetin, thevetoxin, neriifolin	vomiting, diarrhea, high blood pressure, erratic heartbeat, respiratory distress, heart paralysis, death
False hellebore (*Veratrum viride*)	protoveritrine, germerine, jervine, and other alkaloids	vomiting, abdominal pain, muscular weakness, convulsions, respiratory distress, coma, death
Death camas (*Zigadenus* species)	zygadenine	vomiting, hypersalivation, staggering, paralysis, convulsions, coma, death
Plants poisonous by contact		
Euphorbia, spurge (*Euphorbia* species); worldwide	a complex of substances including alkaloids, glycosides, and others	eye irritation, blindness, blistering of the skin, swelling around the mouth, burning of the mouth, unconsciousness, death; milky sap is used as an arrow poison
Spurge nettle (*Jatropha stimulosus*); North America, Europe, Asia	toxin unknown	contact produces instant, intense stinging and itching due to an irritating substance injected into the skin by the stinging hairs; results in a skin eruption of minute red papular (small conical elevations of the skin) rash, which wears off in about 30 minutes; a dull purplish discoloration of the skin may remain for several weeks
Shiney-leaf stinging tree, tree nettle (*Laportea photiniphylla*); Australia	5-hydroxytryptamine (and other toxic substances?)	contact with the stinging hairs of this plant produces intense rapidly spreading pain, reddened rash, and later a severe skin eruption; severe stings may result in the victim dashing about, rolling on the ground, and crying out with pain; fatalities have been reported; dried leaves may cause intense sneezing
Poisonwood (*Metopium toxiferum*); West Indies, Florida	similar to poison ivy	contact with any part of the tree, especially sap, turns the skin black, causes a rash, blisters, etc; smoke from a burning tree is very irritating causing illness and temporary blindness
Strophanthus (*Strophanthus* species); Florida, tropical America, Africa	an alkaloid, trigonelline, and a large number of cardiac glycosides and aglycones	vomiting, slow and irregular pulse, blurred vision, delirium, circulatory failure, death; used as an arrow poison
Curare (*Strychnos toxifera*); Central America and northern South America	toxiferines, caracurines, and other alkaloids	haziness of vision, relaxation of facial muscles, inability to raise head, loss of muscle control of arms, legs, and respiratory muscles, death; used as a poison for arrows and for blow-gun darts
Poison ivy (*Toxicodendron radicans*, also called *Rhus toxicodendron*); North America	urushiol	skin irritation, swelling, blistering, itching; may be fatal to young children; smoke from burning plant is toxic
Plants that produce photosensitization		
Buckwheat (*Fagopyrum sagittatum*); North America, Europe	fagopyrin, a naphthodianthrone derivative	ingestion of the leaves by animals causes liver dysfunction, thereby resulting in deposition of a photosensitizing pigment in the skin; sunlight then causes redness of the skin, nervousness, swelling of the eyelids, convulsions, and prostration in farm animals
St. Johnswort (*Hypericum perforatum*); North America, Europe	hypericin, a naphthodianthrone derivative	similar to buckwheat
Plants that produce airborne allergies		
Box elder (*Acer negundo*); Northern Hemisphere	oleoresin and a water soluble antigen	hay fever (respiratory allergy) may also cause an eczematous dermatitis of the exposed parts of the body
Poplar, cottonwood (*Populus* species); almost worldwide	similar to box elder	
Ash (*Fraxinus* species); temperate regions	similar to box elder	
Elm (*Ulmus* species); Northern Hemisphere, tropics	similar to box elder	

poisonous as a result of the accumulation of toxic inorganic minerals such as copper, lead, cadmium, fluorine, manganese, nitrates, or selenium. Photosensitization, an unusual toxic reaction resulting from the ingestion of certain plants, may be of two types. The toxic substance may be obtained directly from the plant, which thereupon acts on the skin (primary photosensitivity), or the toxicity may result from liver damage caused by the metabolism of a toxic plant and failure of the breakdown products to be eliminated by the liver (hepatic photosensitivity). In either case the animal reacts by becoming restless; in addition, the skin reddens, and a severe sloughing of the skin develops. Death seldom occurs.

A large number of poisonous plants occur throughout the world; a few representative species and their poisons are listed in Table 8.

Animal poisons (zootoxins). Poisonous animals are widely distributed throughout the approximately 1,000,000 species of animals, ranging from protozoans to polar bears; the only major group that seems to be exempt is the birds. The percentage of organisms that produces toxic substances is not known, but a significant number are poisonous. There are probably many more poisonous animals inhabiting the marine environment than are found on land.

Zootoxins can be divided into several categories: (1) oral poisons—those that are poisonous when eaten; (2) parenteral poisons, or venoms—those that are produced by

Categories of zootoxins

Table 9: Representative Animals Poisonous When Eaten

name and distribution	toxic principle	toxic effects and comments
Protozoans—one-celled animals		
Dinoflagellate (*Gymnodinium breve*); Gulf of Mexico, Florida	unknown	irritation of mucous membranes of nose and throat; causes sneezing, coughing, respiratory distress due to inhalation of windblown spray from red tide areas
Dinoflagellate (*Gonyaulax catenella*); Pacific coast of North America	paralytic shellfish poison, saxitoxin ($C_{10}H_{15}N_7O_3 \cdot 2\ HCl$)	tingling, burning sensation and numbness of lips, tongue, face, spreading elsewhere to the body; weakness, dizziness, joint aches, hypersalivation, intense thirst, difficulty in swallowing, muscular paralysis, and death; extremely toxic; usually involved with the eating of shellfish
Dinoflagellate (*Gonyaulax tamarensis*); east coast of North America	same as *Gonyaulax catenella*	that have been feeding on toxic dinoflagellates
Cnidarians—jellyfish, sea anemones, and relatives		
Matamalu samasama, a sea anemone (*Radianthus paumotensis*); southern Polynesia to Micronesia	poison unknown	nausea, vomiting, abdominal pain, cyanosis, prostration, coma, death; this species of sea anemone eaten raw or cooked is poisonous
Echinoderms—starfishes, sea cucumbers, and relatives		
Sea cucumber (*Holothuria* species); tropical Pacific	holothurin	little is known concerning the symptoms produced by poisonous sea cucumbers; ingestion of toxic sea cucumbers may be fatal; sea cucumbers under most circumstances are safe to eat, but some species are toxic; species are difficult to identify
Mollusks—octopus, squid, shellfish, and others		
California mussel (*Mytilus californianus*); Pacific coast of North America	paralytic shellfish poison, saxitoxin	these mollusks become poisonous to eat because of feeding on toxic dinoflagellates; symptoms same as for dinoflagellates (*Gonyaulax* species)
Butter clam (*Saxidomus giganteus*); Alaska to California	same as California mussel	
Surf clam (*Spisula solidissima*); Labrador to North Carolina	same as California mussel	
Whelk (*Neptunea* species); Europe, Pacific region	tetramine	nausea, vomiting, diarrhea, weakness, fatigue, dizziness, photophobia (intolerance to light), impaired vision, and dryness of the mouth; poison is believed to be restricted to the salivary glands of the whelk
Turban shell (*Turbo argyrostoma*); tropical Pacific Ocean	poison believed to be related to ciguatoxin	diarrhea, weakness of the legs, fatigue, cold water produces a painful stinging sensation, itching; the illness closely resembles ciguatera fish poisoning
Callista shellfish (*Callista brevisiphonata*); Japan	a histamine-like substance, choline	flushing of the face, itching, urticaria (stinging sensation of skin), sensation of constriction of the chest, abdominal pain, nausea, respiratory distress, asthmatic attacks, paralysis, hypersalivation, numbness of the tongue, throat; recovery usually within 10 days
Japanese dosinia (*Dosinia japonica*); Japan	venerupin	nausea, vomiting, nervousness, bleeding from the mucous membranes of the nose, mouth, and gums, halitosis, hemorrhages into the skin, enlarged liver, delirium, coma, death
Japanese littleneck cockle (*Tapes semidecussata*); Japan	same as Japanese dosinia	
Arthropods—joint-legged animals: crabs, spiders, and others		
Shore crab (*Demania toxica*); Philippines	unknown	nausea, vomiting, diarrhea, muscular weakness, respiratory distress, difficulty in speaking, hypersalivation, muscular paralysis, convulsions, death
Crab (*Zozymus aeneus*); Indo-Pacific	similar to tetrodotoxin; toxicity of these crabs variable	tingling about the mouth, nausea, vomiting, muscular paralysis, coma, convulsions, death
Crab (*Eriphia sebana*); tropical Pacific Ocean	same as *Z. aeneus*	
Asiatic horseshoe crab (*Tachypleus tridentatus*); Southeast Asia	unknown	dizziness, headache, nausea, vomiting, abdominal pain, cardiac palpitation, numbness of the lips, weakness, muscular paralysis, hypersalivation, loss of consciousness, death
Sharks, eels, and other fish		
Greenland shark (*Somniosus microcephalus*); Arctic	unknown; flesh toxic; liver of tropical sharks very toxic and may also cause death	nausea, vomiting, diarrhea, abdominal pain, tingling and burning sensation of the tongue, throat, and esophagus, muscular cramps, respiratory distress, coma, death
Moray eel (*Gymnothorax javanicus*); Indo-Pacific†	ciguatoxin*	symptoms may develop rapidly or slowly; tingling about the lips, tongue, and throat, followed by numbness, nausea, vomiting, abdominal cramps, muscular weakness, paralysis, convulsions, teeth feel loose, visual impairment, skin rash, hot objects feel cold and vice versa ("Dry Ice" or "electric shock" sensation); loss of muscular coordination, coma, death in about 12 percent of the cases; known as ciguatera fish poisoning, this is one of the most common forms of fish poisoning
Blue crevally (*Caranx melampygus*); Indo-Pacific†	same as Moray eel	
Red snapper (*Lutjanus bohar*); Indo-Pacific†	same as Moray eel	
Spotted grouper (*Cephalopholis argus*); Indo-Pacific†	same as Moray eel	

*Fish poisoning is categorically referred to as "ichthyosarcotoxism," but there are several different forms of fish poisoning such as ciguatera fish poisoning, clupeotoxism, scombrotoxism, and others. †More than 400 species of tropical reef fishes have been involved in ciguatera fish poisoning. These fish are normally edible, but under certain conditions may become toxic.

a specialized poison gland and administered by means of a venom apparatus; and (3) crinotoxins—those that are produced by a specialized poison gland but are merely released into the environment, usually by means of a pore.

Oral zootoxins (see Table 9) are generally thought to be small molecules; most venoms (Table 10) are believed to be large molecules, usually a protein or a substance in close association with one. Venoms, which are produced by specialized poison glands, are injected by means of a mechanical device that is able to penetrate the flesh of the victim. Little is known about the biological or chemical properties of most crinotoxins (Table 11). The term poisonous may be used in the generic sense to refer to all three categories of zootoxins.

It is difficult to generalize when dealing with poisonous animals because they involve such a complex assemblage of unrelated organisms. Although there are poisonous animals in polar regions, by far the greatest number and variety inhabit warm temperate or tropical areas. One of the most dangerous of all toxic organisms probably is a

Table 9: Representative Animals Poisonous When Eaten (cont.)

name and distribution	toxic principle	toxic effects and comments
Yellowfin grouper (*Mycteroperca venenosa*); west tropical Atlantic†	same as Moray eel*	
Emperor sea bass (*Variola louti*); Indo-Pacific†	same as Moray eel	
Great barracuda (*Sphyraena barracuda*); tropical seas†	same as Moray eel	
Triggerfish (*Balistes vetula*); tropical Atlantic†	same as Moray eel	
Trunkfish (*Lactoria cornutus*); Indo-Pacific†	same as Moray eel	
Thread herring (*Clupanodon thrissa*); Indo-Pacific	clupeotoxin, chemical nature unknown	metallic taste, nausea, vomiting, abdominal pain, vascular collapse, hypersalivation, numbness, muscular paralysis, convulsions, coma, death; this form of poisoning develops rapidly and violently; mortality rate is about 50 percent and death may come within a few minutes; this form of fish poisoning is known as clupeotoxism; no known antidote
Atlantic thread herring, or yellow-billed sprat (*Opisthonema oglinum*); West Indies	same as thread herring	
Red-ear sardine, also called yellow-billed sprat (*Harengula humeralis*); West Indies	same as thread herring	
Castor-oil fish (*Ruvettus pretiosus*); tropical Atlantic, Indo-Pacific	oleic acid	produces a painless diarrhea; poisoning known as gempylotoxism; no treatment needed
Skipjack tuna (*Euthynnus pelamis*); tropical seas Bluefin tuna (*Thunnus thynnus*); subtropical and temperate seas	saurine, a histamine-like substance; scombroid fishes (mackerals, tunas, swordfishes, and allies), contain a chemical constituent in their flesh called histidine; when histidine is acted upon, it forms a histamine-like substance called saurine; this occurs when the fishes are permitted to stand at room temperature for several hours; scombroid fishes are more susceptible to the development of saurine poison than most other kinds of fishes	the symptoms of acute scombroid poisoning resemble those of a severe allergy: sharp, peppery taste, headache, throbbing of the large blood vessels of the neck, nausea, vomiting, massive red welts, and intense itching; recovery after 8–12 hours; this is probably the most common and cosmopolitan form of fish poisoning; antihistamines are used for treatment
Deadly death puffer (*Arothron hispidus*); tropical Pacific, Indian Ocean, Red Sea	tetrodotoxin ($C_{11}H_{17}O_8N_3 \pm y\ H_2O$)	tingling of lips and tongue, loss of motor coordination, floating sensation, hypersalivation, numbness of the entire body, muscular paralysis, difficulty in swallowing, weakness, nausea, vomiting, convulsions, about 60 percent fatality in humans; no known antidote
White-spotted puffer (*Arothron meleagris*); tropical Pacific	same as deadly death puffer	
Amphibians		
California newt (*Taricha torosa*); California	tarichatoxin; poison said to be identical to tetrodotoxin; the eggs of this newt are extremely toxic	effects in man are unknown; no known antidote
Reptiles		
Hawksbill turtle (*Eretmochelys imbricata*); tropical seas Leatherback turtle (*Dermochelys coriacea*); temperate and tropical seas	chelonitoxin, chemistry unknown; the flesh of some species of marine turtles is extremely poisonous	nausea, vomiting, diarrhea, burning sensation of lips, tongue, mouth, tightness of the chest, difficulty in swallowing, hypersalivation, foul breath, skin rash, sloughing of the skin, enlargement of the liver, coma, death; fatality rate is high; no known antidote
Mammals		
Sei whale (*Balaenoptera borealis*); North Pacific and North Atlantic oceans	unknown; livers of many marine mammals are toxic	intense headache, neck pain, photophobia, desquamation (peeling in scales) around the mouth and face, flushing of the face; antihistamines are used in treatment
White whale (*Delphinapterus leucas*); Arctic seas	unknown	flesh is poisonous and has caused fatalities in humans; no known antidote
Polar bear (*Thalarctos maritimus*); Arctic	vitamin A, and possibly other toxic substances	intense throbbing headaches, nausea, vomiting, diarrhea, abdominal pain, dizziness, drowsiness, irritability, muscle cramps, visual disturbances, collapse, coma, rarely death

*See footnote for *ciguatoxin*.   †See footnote for *Moray eel*.

sea wasp (*Chironex fleckeri*) that inhabits the northeast coastal waters of Australia. In less than one minute this jellyfish is able to inflict death in an adult human being by means of its nematocyst, or stinging apparatus.

Some of the most complex relationships in biotoxicology are found in the marine environment. Certain marine biotoxins, such as ciguatera fish poison, apparently originate in marine plants, are ingested by herbivores and then passed on to carnivores and eventually to man. The extremely complex mechanism by which this is accom-

plished has eluded scientists for many years. With the buildup of toxic industrial chemical pollutants in the marine environment, the problems of toxicity in marine organisms are becoming increasingly more serious. There is evidence that under certain conditions chemical pollutants may trigger biotoxicity cycles in marine organisms. The outbreaks in Japan of Minamata disease were the result of such a cycle: microorganisms, algae, shellfishes, and fishes ingested or absorbed industrial wastes with highly toxic organic compounds containing mercury and were in turn

Table 10: Representative Venomous Animals That Inflict a Sting

name and distribution	toxic principle	toxic effects and comments
Cnidarians*		
Fire coral (*Millepora* species); tropical seas	unknown	skin irritation, mild prickly or stinging sensation similar to a nettle (plant) sting
Portuguese man-of-war (*Physalia* species); tropical seas	tetramine, 5-hydroxytryptamine	immediate, intense stinging, throbbing, or burning sensation, shooting sensation, inflammatory rash, blistering of the skin, shock, collapse, in very rare cases death
Sea wasp (*Chironex fleckeri*); northern and northeast Australia	cardiotoxin	immediate extreme painful stinging sensation, seared reddened lines wherever the tentacles touch the skin, large indurated wheallike lesions, prostration, dizziness, circulatory failure, respiratory distress, rapid death in a high percentage of cases
Sea anemone (*Actinia equina*); Mediterranean, Black Sea, etc.	nature of venom unknown	burning, stinging sensation, itching, swelling, redness, ulceration, nausea, vomiting, prostration; no specific antidote available
Mollusks		
Cone shell (*Conus* species); tropical Indo-Pacific region	quaternary ammonium compounds and others	blanching at the site of injection, cyanosis of the surrounding area, numbness, stinging or burning sensation, blurring of vision, loss of speech, difficulty in swallowing, nausea, extreme weakness, coma, and death in some cases; no specific antidote
Spotted octopus (*Octopus maculosus*); Indo-Pacific, Indian Ocean	cephalotoxin, a neuromuscular poison	sharp burning pain, similar to a bee sting, numbness of the mouth and tongue, blurring of vision, loss of tactile sensation, difficulty in speech and swallowing, paralysis of legs, nausea, prostration, coma, and death in a high percentage of cases
Insects		
Kissing bug (*Triatoma* species); Latin America, United States	unknown	bite usually painless; later itching, edema about the bite, nausea, palpitation, redness; the bite is of relatively minor importance but spreads Chagas disease caused by a trypanosome (protozoan)
Hawkmoth (*Acanthosphinx guessfelotii*)	unknown	tibial spurs are capable of inflicting a painful scratch; a poison may be present
Moth (*Anaphe* species); Europe	unknown	female moth possesses hollow barbed setae or hairs in the anal tuft which are released at time of egg laying; during the breeding season they become so numerous they are released in the atmosphere and produce a severe dermatitis; the hairs contain a poison
Puss caterpillar (*Megalopyge* species); United States, Latin America	unknown	stinging hairs of the caterpillar associated with poison-secreting glands; contact with the hairs produces an intense burning pain, itching, pustules, redness, nausea, fever, numbness, swelling, and paralysis; recovery usually within about six days
Honeybee (*Apis* species); worldwide	neurotoxin, hemolytic, melittin, hyaluronidase, phospholipase A, histamine, and others	sting produces acute local pain or burning sensation, blanching at the site of the sting surrounded by zone of redness, and itching; local symptoms usually disappear after 24 hours; severe cases may develop massive swelling, redness, shock, prostration, vomiting, rapid heart beat, respiratory distress, trembling, coma, and death; it is estimated that 500 stings delivered in a short period of time can provide a lethal dose to a human; bees kill more people in the United States than do venomous reptiles
Bumblebee (*Bombus* species); temperate regions	similar to honeybee (*Apis*) venom	stings are similar to honeybee (*Apis*) stings; bumblebees are not as vicious as honeybees
Carpenter bee (*Xylocopa* species); temperate regions	similar to honeybee venom	similar to honeybee stings
Wasp (*Seliphron* species); temperate regions	similar to honeybee venom	similar to honeybee stings; stings may be fatal
Yellow jacket, hornet (*Vespula* species); temperate regions	similar to bee venom; also acetylcholine	they can both bite and sting; the sting is similar to that of the honeybee but more painful; yellow jackets are quite aggressive; stings may be fatal
Wasp (*Polistes* species and *Vespa* species); worldwide	similar to bee venom; also acetylcholine	wasps are less aggressive than hornets and their sting is similar to the honeybee but generally less painful than hornets; stings may be fatal
Velvet ant (*Dasymutilla* species); United States	similar to wasp venom	velvet ants are actually female wingless wasps; stings are similar to other wasp stings
Harvester ant (*Pogonomyrmex* species); United States	bradykinin, formic acid, hyaluronidase, hemolytic, phospholipase A, and others.	ant stings cause immediate intense burning, pain, blanched area at site of sting surrounded by redness, ulceration, fever, blistering, itching, hemorrhaging into the skin, eczematoid dermatitis, pustules, respiratory distress, prostration, coma, and death in some instances
Fire ant (*Solenopsis* species); United States, Latin America	similar to harvester-ant venom	similar to above; stings are very painful, burning sensation, etc.
Ponerine ant (*Paraponera clavata*); Latin America	same as fire ant	
Spiders		
Brown spider (*Loxosceles* species); United States, South America, Europe, Asia	cytotoxic, hyaluronidase, hemolytic, and others	bite causes stinging sensation or burning pain, blanching at site of bite surrounded by redness, blistering, hemorrhages into the skin and internal organs, ulceration, vomiting, fever, cardiovascular collapse, convulsions, sometimes death
Black widow (*Latrodectus* species); tropical and temperate regions	neurotoxic	bite may or may not be painful, two tiny red dots at site of bite, localized swelling after a few minutes; intense cramping pain of abdomen, legs, chest, back; pain may become agonizing causing patient to scream; rigidity of muscles, lasting 12–48 hours, nausea, sweating, respiratory distress, priapism (abnormal, painful erection of the penis) in males, chills, skin rash, restlessness, fever, numbness, tingling, about 4 percent are fatal; antiserum is available
Tarantula (*Dugesiella* and *Lycosa* species); temperate and tropical regions	venom varies, usually mild	most of the large tarantulas found in the United States, Mexico, and Central America are harmless to man; their bites are similar to a pin prick and relatively mild; their danger to man has been grossly exaggerated; some of the large tropical species may be more poisonous, but their effects are largely localized
Scorpions†		
Scorpion (species of *Centruroides*, *Tityus*, and *Leiurus*); warm temperate and tropical regions	neurotoxin, cardiotoxin, hemolytic, lecithinase, hyaluronidase, and others	symptoms vary depending upon the species of scorpion; sting from the tail stinger causes a sharp burning sensation, swelling, sweating, restlessness, salivation, confusion, vomiting, abdominal pain, chest pain, numbness, muscular twitching, respiratory distress, convulsions, death; the mortality rate from stings from certain species of scorpions is very high; antiserum is available

*About 9,000 species of jellyfish, sea anemones, etc.; stings are produced by means of nematocysts, specialized stinging cells.   †About 650 species.

Table 10: Representative Venomous Animals That Inflict a Sting (cont.)

name and distribution	toxic principle	toxic effects and comments
Echinoderms‡		
Crown-of-thorns starfish (*Acanthaster planci*); Indo-Pacific	nature of poison unknown	penetration of the spines produces a painful wound, redness, swelling, vomiting, numbness, and paralysis
Long-spined sea urchin (*Diadema setosum*); Indo-Pacific	nature of poison unknown	penetration of the spines produces an immediate and intense burning sensation, redness, swelling, numbness, muscular paralysis
Sea urchin (*Toxopneustes pileolus*); Indo-Pacific	nature of poison unknown	bites from the stinging jaws or pedicellariae (small pincer-like organs) produce an immediate intense radiating pain, faintness, numbness, muscular paralysis, respiratory distress, and occasionally death
Sharks and rays		
Stingray (*Dasyatis* species); warm temperate and tropical seas	stingray venom, cardiotoxin, chemistry unknown	penetration of the tail spines inflicts jagged painful wounds that produce sharp, shooting, throbbing pain, fall in blood pressure, nausea, vomiting, cardiac failure, muscular paralysis, rarely death; no known antidote; stingrays are among the most common causes of envenomations in the marine environment
Bony fishes		
Weever fish (*Trachinus draco*); Mediterranean Sea	weeverfish venom, chemistry unknown	opercular and dorsal fin spines can produce instant pain, burning, stabbing or crushing sensation; pain spreads and becomes progressively more intense causing the victim to scream with anguish, suffer loss of consciousness, numbness about the wound, swelling, redness, nausea, delirium, difficulty in breathing, convulsions, and death; no known antidote
Scorpion fish (*Scorpaena* species); temperate and tropical seas	scorpionfish venom, chemistry unknown	fin spines can inflict painful stings and intense immediate pain that may cause victim to scream followed by redness, swelling, loss of consciousness, ulceration of the wound, paralysis, cardiac failure, delirium, convulsions, nausea, prostration, and respiratory distress, but rarely death; no known antidote
Stonefish (*Synanceja* species); Indo-Pacific region	stonefish venom, chemistry unknown	produces an extremely painful sting by means of the dorsal fin spines; symptoms similar to other scorpionfish stings but more serious
Reptiles		
Gila monster (*Heloderma suspectum*); southwestern United States	heloderma venom, primarily a neurotoxin	all of the teeth are venomous; bite causes local pain, swelling, weakness, ringing of the ears, nausea, respiratory distress, cardiac failure, may cause death; no antiserum available
Rear-fanged snakes		
Boomslang (*Dispholidus typus*); Africa	coagulates the blood; proteolytic and other enzymes are present	local pain, swelling, hemorrhages, bleeding from nose, mouth, and skin, headache, vomiting, collapse, death; antiserum is available
Front-fixed-fanged snakes		
Death adder (*Acanthophis antarcticus*); Australia, New Guinea	coagulates blood; proteolytic and other enzymes present	effects of envenomation develop slowly (15–60 minutes); nausea, vomiting, faintness, drowsiness, staggering, slurred speech, respiratory distress, hemorrhages, death; antiserum available
Indian krait (*Bungarus candidus caeruleus*); India, Burma, Malaya, Indonesia	cholinesterase, protease, and other enzymes present	little pain or local reaction, latent period up to 12 hours; abdominal pain, staggering gait, difficulty in swallowing, stiffness of jaws, coma, respiratory distress, cardiac failure, death; antiserum available
Brown snake (*Demansia textilis*); Australia	cholinesterase, ophio-adenosinetri-phosphatase, phospholipase, and other enzymes	latent period up to 12 hours; abdominal pain, vomiting, headache, dizziness, blood in the urine, weakness, respiratory and circulatory collapse, death; antiserum available; this snake is responsible for most of the deaths due to snake bite in Australia; very dangerous
Black mamba (*Dendroaspis polylepis*); Ethiopia, Somalia, Natal, southwest Africa	cholinesterase, L-amino-acid oxidase, ophio-adenosine, triphosphatase, and other substances	local pain, swelling, salivation, paralysis of vocal cords, sweating, vomiting, restlessness, drowsiness, collapse, coma, respiratory distress, death; one of the most dangerous of all living snakes; antiserum available; a large black mamba secretes enough venom to kill ten men
Ringhals (*Hemachatus hemachatus*); South Africa	coagulates blood; cholinesterase, L-amino-acid oxidase, 5-nucleoti-dase, lecithinase, protease, and other enzymes	pain, weakness, respiratory distress, may cause blindness, cyanosis, collapse, death; venom sprayed at eyes; this is one of the spitting cobras; antiserum available
Coral snake (*Micrurus corallinus*); subtropical South America	cholinesterase, hyaluronidase, L-amino-acid oxidase, and other enzymes	numbness without pain at bite, headache, swelling of face and lips, hyperesthesia (unusual sensitivity of skin), sore throat, drooping of eyelids, photophobia, vomiting, rapid heart rate, backache, irritability, salivation, death; there are about 40 species in the genus *Micrurus*; all are dangerous; antiserum available for some species but not others
Indian cobra (*Naja naja*); southern Asia, Indonesia, Taiwan, Philippines	carboxypolypeptidase, cholinesterase, diastase, dipeptidase, polypeptidase, protease, and other enzymes; one of the most complex snake venoms	pain radiating from site of bite, edema, numbness, drooping of the eyelids, head, salivation, difficulty in speech, muscular incoordination, weakness, respiratory distress, blindness, incontinence, convulsions, death; antiserum available
Black-necked cobra (*Naja nigricollis*); Africa	cholinesterase, L-amino-acid oxidase, phospholipase, protease, and other enzymes	similar to poisonings by the Indian cobra; venom sometimes sprayed at eyes; produces an intense irritation but permanent damage to eyes is rare; antiserum available
Tiger snake (*Notechis scutatus*); Australia	coagulates blood; cholinesterase, hyaluronidase, ophio-adenosine-triphosphatase, phosphatase, and other enzymes	latent period of 15–60 minutes; nausea, vomiting, faintness, sweating, drowsiness, staggering, slurred speech, difficulty in swallowing, drooping of eyelids, respiratory distress, death; antiserum available
King cobra (*Ophiophagus hannah*); India, Burma, Philippines, Thailand	cholinesterase, L-amino-acid oxidase, ophio-adenosinetriphosphotase	symptoms similar to those produced by other cobras; symptoms develop rapidly, death often occurs in 30–60 minutes; one of the largest of venomous snakes—obtains a length of 16 feet; antiserum available
Taipan (*Oxyuranus scutellatus*); Australia, New Guinea	lecithinase, phospholipase	symptoms similar to those produced by the tiger snake; its long fangs and potent venom make this one of the world's most dangerous snakes; produces flaccid paralysis, respiratory paralysis, often rapidly fatal; antiserum available
Australian black snake (*Pseudechis porphyriacus*); Australia	L-amino-acid oxidase, lecithinase, phospholipase	local pain and swelling, vomiting, hemorrhages from nose and mouth, prostration, hematuria (presence of blood in the urine), and sometimes death; usually the bites are nonfatal; antiserum available
Sea snakes		
Beaked sea snake (*Enhydrina schistosa*); Indo-Pacific; all sea snakes are venomous, but only a few species have caused death in man	lecithinase	no local reaction; latent period minutes to hours; giddiness, muscle ache, muscular weakness, drooping of the eyelids, lockjaw, respiratory failure, acute renal (kidney) failure, death

‡Sea urchins, starfish, etc., about 4,000 species.

Table 10: Representative Venomous Animals That Inflict a Sting (cont.)

name and distribution	toxic principle	toxic effects and comments
Erectile-fanged snakes		
Copperhead (*Ancistrodon contortrix*); eastern and southern United States	cholinesterase, L-amino-acid oxidase, phosphodiesterase, and other enzymes	local pain, swelling, necrosis, nausea, vomiting, shock, petechiae (minute bleeding spots), bloody stools, death; antiserum available
Eastern cottonmouth (*Ancistrodon piscivorus*); southeastern United States to central Texas	cephalinase, cholinesterase, hyaluronidase, lacithinase, and other enzymes	similar to poisoning by the copperhead but more severe; local necrosis more marked; death; antiserum available
Fer-de-lance (*Bothrops atrox*); central Mexico, south into South America	cholinesterase, deoxyribonuclease, L-amino-acid oxidase, protease, and other enzymes	local pain, bleeding from bite, gums, nose, mouth, rectum, blood fails to clot, shock, respiratory distress, hemorrhages into muscles and nervous system, death; antiserum available
Eastern diamondhead rattlesnake (*Crotalus adamanteus*); southeastern United States	cephalinase, cholinesterase, hyaluroindase, and other enzymes	local pain, edema, hemorrhaging into the tissues, dryness of the mouth, vomiting, shock, anemia, tingling sensation, blood in feces, difficulty in speech, yellow vision, loss of consciousness, death; antiserum available
Western diamondback rattlesnake (*Crotalus atrox*); southwestern United States	bradykininogen, cholinesterase, hyaluroindase, L-amino-acid oxidase, and other substances	symptoms similar to poisoning by *C. adamanteus*, but neurological symptoms less marked; antiserum available
Cascabel (*Crotalus durissus terrificus*); southern Mexico south to Argentina	cholinesterase, deoxyribonuclease, hyaluronidase, lecithinase, and other enzymes	symptoms similar to cobra bites, except that no edema occurs; antiserum available
Bushmaster (*Lachesis muta*); Costa Rica to northern South America	protease	very few bites recorded and little is known concerning the effects of its venom; severe prostration, rapid death; antiserum available
Taiwan habu (*Trimeresurus mucrosquamatus*); southeastern China, Taiwan	neurotoxin, amino-acid oxidase, hemorrhagin, and other substances	local pain, blistering, bleeding into the tissues, shock, death; antiserum available
True vipers		
Puff adder (*Bitis arietans*); Africa, Saudia Arabia	fibrinolytic, bradykininogen, cholinesterase, L-amino-acid oxidase, protease, and other substances	severe local edema, necrosis and sloughing of the tissues, restlessness, respiratory distress, gastrointestinal hemorrhages, death; antiserum available
Saw-scaled viper (*Echis carinatus*); India, Iraq, Saudia Arabia, Africa	carboxypolypeptidase, cholinesterase, dipeptidase, endopeptidase, and other enzymes	local pain and edema, hemorrhages into the skin, mucous membranes, and gastrointestinal tract, liver damage, shock, death; antiserum available
European viper (*Vipera berus*); Europe, Asia, Japan	bradykininogen, L-amino-acid oxidase	local pain and edema, hemorrhages along lymphatics, very little general reaction, vomiting, abdominal pain, shock, death; antiserum available
Russell's viper (*Vipera russelli*); Asia, Indonesia	carboxypolypeptidase, cholinesterase, dipeptidase, lipase, lecithinase, protease, and other enzymes	rapidly spreading edema with hemorrhages into the tissues, abdominal pain, vomiting, blood does not clot, loss of consciousness, circulatory failure, shock, death; antiserum available
Mammals		
Duck-billed platypus (*Ornithorhynchus anatinus*); Australia	protease and other enzymes	may inflict envenomation by means of the spurs on the hindlegs of the male platypus; immediate intense pain, swelling, redness in the area of the sting, faintness, numbness about the wound, restlessness, prostration; no death recorded; recovery is uneventful after a few days
Short-tailed shrew (*Blarina brevicauda*); North America	neurotoxic, proteolytic	the lower incisor teeth are associated with submaxillary poison glands; bites produce localized pain, redness in the area of the bite, shooting pains, and general discomfort of the affected part; gradual recovery after several days; no fatalities recorded
Solenodon (*Solenodon paradoxus*); Haiti	same as short-tailed shrew	
European water shrew (*Neomys fodiens*); Europe, Asia	same as short-tailed shrew	

consumed by humans, causing a number of deaths among the population.

The relationships of representative poisonous animals and their position in the total framework of the animal kingdom can best be appreciated by categorizing them according to the group in which they belong. They are further grouped as to whether they are poisonous to eat, venomous, or crinotoxic in Tables 9, 10, and 11.

(B.W.H./Ed.)

BIBLIOGRAPHY

Poisons and poisoning: F.A. PATTY (ed.), *Industrial Hygiene and Toxicology,* vol. 2, *Toxicology,* 2nd ed. (1963), systematic coverage by classes, by compounds, and by elements of important occupational exposures; R.H. WHITTAKER and P.P. FEENEY, "Allelochemics: Chemical Interactions Between Species," *Science,* 171:757–770 (1971), a review of allomones by function and by chemical nature; M.W. MILLER and G.G. BERG (eds.), *Chemical Fallout: Current Research on Persistent Pesticides* (1969), includes biologic and ecologic details; UNITED STATES DEPARTMENT OF HEALTH, EDUCATION AND WELFARE, FOOD AND DRUG ADMINISTRATION, *Appraisal of the Safety of Chemicals in Foods, Drugs and Cosmetics* (1959), descriptions of basic methods of toxicological evaluation; UNITED STATES DEPARTMENT OF HEALTH, EDUCATION AND WELFARE, *Report of Secretary's Commission on Pesticides and Their Relationship to Environmental Health,* 2 pt. (1969), compilations of factual material, with critical summaries on the status of problems, use, benefit, and risk; R.T. WILLIAMS, *Detoxication Mechanisms,* 2nd ed. rev. (1959), an encyclopaedic compilation of biochemical information; NATIONAL RESEARCH COUNCIL, FOOD PROTECTION COMMITTEE, *Evaluating the Safety of Food Chemicals* (1970), an up-to-date, authoritative statement of purposes and values of current procedures; *Use of Human Subjects in Safety Evaluation of Food Chemicals* (1967), a broad and searching inquiry into a major problem of safety evaluation, discussing experimental, legal, ethical, and philosophical aspects; *Toxicants Occurring Naturally in Foods* (1966), summaries of information on classes of toxic substances naturally present in foods; J.M. KINGSBURY, *Poisonous Plants of the United States and Canada* (1964), descriptions of poisonous plants, algae, and fungi; S.M. HERSH, *Chemical and Biological Warfare: America's Hidden Arsenal* (1968), the history, uses, and some of the implications of chemical and biological warfare.

Poisonous animals and plants: S.J. AJL et al., *Microbial Toxins,* 8 vol. (1970–72), the most comprehensive series of review articles ever assembled on the subject of bacterial protein toxins, bacterial endotoxins, and algal and fungal toxins; G. BRESADOLA, *Funghi mangerecci e velenosi,* 2 vol. (1932–33), one of the great classical works on poisonous mushrooms—although primarily European, most of the species discussed have a somewhat cosmopolitan distribution (magnificently illustrated); W. BUCHERL, E. BUCKLEY, and V. DEULOFEU, *Venomous Animals and Their Venoms,* vol. 1 (1968), and W. BUCHERL and E. BUCKLEY, vol. 2–3 (1971), a comprehensive series of review articles on venomous animals, their biology, effects of the venom, and treatment; UNITED STATES NAVY, BUREAU OF MEDICINE AND SURGERY, *Poisonous Snakes of the World: A Manual for Use by U.S. Amphibious Forces* (1968), a valuable, well-illustrated compendium on the poisonous snakes of the world, including their identification, distribution, habits, and first-aid measures and treatment for their bites; C.A. FRAZIER, *Insect Allergy* (1969), one of the most complete works avail-

Table 11: Representative Crinotoxic Animals*

name and distribution	toxic principle	toxic effects and comments
Sponges		
Red moss (*Microciona prolifera*); eastern United States coastal waters	unknown	contact with the sponge produces a chemical irritation of the skin, redness, stiffness of the finger joints, swelling, blisters, and pustules
Flatworms		
Flatworm (*Leptoplana tremellaris*); European coastal waters	unknown	poison is produced by epidermal skin glands; no human intoxications recorded; extracts from the skin of these worms injected into laboratory animals produces cardiac arrest
Arthropods—joint-legged animals		
Blister beetles (*Cantharis vesicatorea*); United States	cantharidin	toxic substance does not seem to be produced by special glands but is found throughout the body of the beetle; no discomfort at time of initial contact; after about 8–10 hours large blisters develop on the skin accompanied by slight burning or tingling sensation; swallowing of the beetles may cause kidney damage; cantharidin is used as an aphrodisiac known as Spanish fly—a very dangerous substance to use; ingestion can cause severe gastroenteritis, kidney damage, blood in the urine, priapism, profound collapse, and death
Millipedes (species of *Orthoporus, Rhinocrichus, Julus,* and *Spirobolus*); temperate and tropical regions	unknown	repugnatorial (distasteful to enemies) fluid may be exuded or forcefully squirted from body pores a distance up to 30 inches or more; contact with the skin causes mild to moderately intense burning pain, redness, and pigmentation of the skin; toxic fluid squirted in the eyes may cause temporary blindness, an inflammatory reaction, and pain
Venomous ticks (species of *Ixodes* and *Ornithodoros*); temperate and tropical regions	unknown	tick bites result in swelling, redness, intense pain, headache, muscle cramps, loss of memory, etc.
Fishes		
Sea lamprey (*Petromyzon marinus*); Atlantic Ocean	unknown	slime of the lamprey is toxic, ingestion may cause diarrhea
Pacific sea bass (*Grammistes sexlineatus*); Indo-Pacific	antibiotic, neurotoxic	slime of fish is toxic; effects on man not known
Soapfish (*Rypticus saponaceus*); tropical and subtropical Atlantic	neurotoxic	slime of fish is toxic; produces an irritation of the mucous membrane
Amphibians†		
European earth salamander (*Salamandra maculosa*); Europe	skin glands of the salamander are poisonous; contains the alkaloids samandarine, samandenone, samandine, samanine, samandarone, samandaridine, and others	effects on humans not known; affects the heart and nervous system; causes in animals convulsions, cardiac irregularity, paralysis, and death
Toads (*Bufo* species); temperate and tropical regions	bufotoxin, bufogenins, and 5-hydroxytryplanime; poison includes a complex of many substances	produces a poisonous secretion in the parotid glands and skin; handling of some toads may cause a skin irritation; ingestion causes nausea, vomiting, numbness of the mouth and tongue, and tightness of the chest; the poison has a digitalis-like action
Frogs (some species of *Dendrobates, Physalaemus,* and *Rana*); northern South America and Central America	skin secretions are poisonous; histamine, bufotenine, physalaemin, serotonin, and other substances; composition varies with the species	skin secretions produce a burning sensation when handled; used by Indians as an arrow poison
Tree frogs (some species of *Hyla* and *Phyllobates*); northern South America, Central America	skin secretions are poisonous; batrachotoxin, steroidal alkaloids, serotonin, histamine, and other substances; bufotenine varies with the species	some frog species produce a burning sensation and a skin rash when handled; skin secretions in the eye may produce a severe inflammatory reaction; if ingested poison causes vomiting and abdominal pain; batrachotoxin is extremely toxic if injected; used by Indians as an arrow poison

*Animals in which poison glands are present and poison is released into environment through a pore.   †Poisonous amphibians are sometimes referred to as "venomous," but they do not possess a true venom apparatus. They possess only poison glands.

able concerning allergies and the poisonous effects of terrestrial arthropods; B.W. HALSTEAD, *Poisonous and Venomous Marine Animals of the World*, 3 vol. (1965–70), an exhaustive and profusely illustrated compendium on the toxic marine animals of the world from protozoans to polar bears, including their historical background, names, geographical distribution, biology, mechanism of intoxication, and medical, toxicological, pharmacological, and chemical aspects; R. HEIM, *Les Champignons toxiques et hallucinogènes* (1963), a valuable handbook on poisonous and hallucinogenic mushrooms, their biology, and poisonous effects; H.L. KEEGAN and W.V. MACFARLANE, *Venomous and Poisonous Animals and Noxious Plants of the Pacific Region* (1963), a useful compendium of technical data on poisonous organisms of the Pacific area, including their biology, poisons, and toxic effects; J.M. KINGSBURY, *op cit.*; L.M. KLAUBER, *Rattlesnakes: Their Habits, Life Histories, and Influence on Mankind*, 2 vol. (1956), the most comprehensive work ever written on North American rattlesnakes, containing valuable information on their identification, venom apparatus, snake bites, and treatment; M. PHISALIX-PICOT, *Animaux venimeux et venins*, 2 vol. (1922), one of the great classical works on poisonous animals and their toxins.

Poland

Poland is situated on the North European Plain between the Baltic Sea and the Carpathian Mountains. Over the past 1,000 years political frontiers have expanded and contracted dramatically, and the name Poland (in Polish, Polska) has been applied to a shifting territorial base, which has repeatedly changed its boundaries. At one time, in the mid-16th century, Poland was the largest state in Europe. At other times there was no Polish state at all.

The contemporary Polish state, the Polish People's Republic (Polska Rzeczpospolita Ludowa), lies at the physical centre of the European continent, approximately between latitude 49° and 55° N and longitude 14° and 24° E. Its area is 120,727 square miles (312,683 square kilometres). Among the states of the Soviet bloc in Europe,

Poland ranks second after the Soviet Union in both area and population.

The frontiers of the Polish People's Republic stretch for 2,198 miles (3,538 kilometres). In the west, they run along the Oder (Odra) and Lusatanian Neisse (Nysa Łużycka) rivers, which border East Germany. In the north, they run along the Baltic shore facing Sweden, from the estuary of the Oder to the Gulf of Gdańsk (Zatoka Gdańska). In the south, they mainly follow the watershed of the Sudeten (Sudety), Beskid, and Carpathian mountain ranges, separating Poland from Czechoslovakia. In the northeast and east, they run along the border of the Soviet Union.

This article is divided into the following sections:

Physical and human geography

THE LAND

Relief.   Poland has a largely lowland character. The average elevation of the whole country is only 568 feet (173 metres); more than 75 percent of the land lies below 650 feet (200 metres). Poland's relief was formed by the actions of Ice Age glaciers, which advanced and receded over the northern part of the country a number of times during the

Pleistocene Epoch (2,500,000 to 10,000 years ago). The great and often monotonous expanses of the Polish lowlands, part of the Central European Plain, are composed of geologically recent deposits that lie over a vast structural basin. In the southern portion of the country, by contrast, older and more diverse geological formations are exposed, and the topography is dominated by the mountainous arc of the Carpathians, dating from the Tertiary mountain-building period of about 25,000,000 years ago. Around the

Carpathian
Mountains

POLAND

MAP INDEX

Political subdivisions

Biała	
Podlaska	52 00 N 23 00 E
Białystok	53 00 N 23 15 E
Bielsko-Biała	49 45 N 19 15 E
Bydgoszcz	53 00 N 18 00 E
Chełm	51 15 N 23 30 E
Ciechanów	53 00 N 20 15 E
Częstochowa	50 45 N 19 00 E
Elbląg	54 00 N 19 15 E
Gdańsk	54 15 N 18 15 E
Gorzów	52 45 N 15 15 E
Jelenia Góra	51 00 N 15 30 E
Kalisz	51 45 N 18 00 E
Katowice	50 15 N 19 00 E

Kielce	50 45 N 20 30 E
Konin	52 15 N 18 15 E
Koszalin	54 00 N 16 00 E
Kraków	50 00 N 20 00 E
Krosno	49 30 N 22 00 E
Legnica	51 15 N 16 00 E
Leszno	51 45 N 16 45 E
Łódź	51 45 N 19 30 E
Łomża	53 15 N 22 15 E
Lublin	51 15 N 22 30 E
Nowy Sącz	49 35 N 20 30 E
Olsztyn	53 45 N 20 30 E
Opole	50 30 N 18 00 E
Ostrołęka	53 00 N 21 30 E
Piła	53 15 N 16 45 E
Piotrków	51 30 N 19 45 E
Płock	52 30 N 19 45 E

Poznań	52 30 N 17 00 E
Przemyśl	50 00 N 22 45 E
Radom	51 30 N 21 00 E
Rzeszów	50 00 N 22 00 E
Siedlce	52 15 N 22 00 E
Sieradz	51 30 N 18 45 E
Skierniewice	52 00 N 20 00 E
Słupsk	54 15 N 17 15 E
Suwałki	54 00 N 22 30 E
Szczecin	53 00 N 15 00 E
Tarnobrzeg	50 45 N 22 00 E
Tarnów	50 00 N 21 00 E
Toruń	53 15 N 19 00 E
Wałbrzych	50 30 N 16 45 E
Warszawa	52 13 N 21 00 E
Włocławek	52 45 N 19 00 E
Wrocław	51 15 N 17 00 E

Zamość	50 45 N 23 15 E
Zielona Góra	52 00 N 15 30 E

Names of the provinces are not shown on the map. Each is identical with the name, or the first word of the name, of its capital city.

Cities and towns

Aleksandrów	
Kujawski	52 52 N 18 42 E
Augustów	53 51 N 23 00 E
Bartoszyce	54 15 N 20 48 E
Bełchatów	51 22 N 19 23 E
Biała	
Podlaska	52 02 N 23 08 E
Białogard	54 00 N 16 00 E
Białystok	53 08 N 23 09 E

northern rim of the Carpathians lies a series of structural basins, separating the mountain belt proper from a much older structural mass, or foreland, that appears in the relief patterns of the region as the Bohemian Massif, the Sudeten, and the Little Poland Uplands (Wyżyna Małopolska).

This structure helps to explain the division of the country into a series of east–west zones. To the north lie the swamps and dunes of the Baltic coast; south of these is a belt of morainic terrain with thousands of lakes, the southern boundary of which marks the limit of the last ice sheet. The third zone consists of the central lowlands, whose minimal relief was created by streams issuing from the retreating glaciers. This zone is the Polish heartland, the site of agriculture in places where loess has been deposited over the relatively infertile fluvioglacial deposits. The fourth zone is made up of the older mountains and highlands to the south; though limited in extent, it offers spectacular scenery. The Little Poland Uplands protect the Little Poland Lowlands (Nizina Małopolska), in which Kraków lies, from the colder air of the north. In the extreme south are the Carpathians and their foothills.

Climate. Varying types of air masses collide over Poland, a process that strongly influences the character of both weather and climate. The major elements involved are oceanic air masses from the west, cold polar air from Scandinavia or from Russia, and warmer, subtropical air from the south. A series of barometric depressions moves eastward along the polar front year-round, dividing the subtropical from the colder air, bringing to Poland, as to other parts of northern Europe, cloudy, wet days. In winter, polar-continental air often becomes dominant, bringing crisp, frosty weather, with still colder Arctic air following in its wake. Warm, dry, subtropical-continental air often brings pleasant days in late summer and autumn.

These elements combine to give the overall climate of Poland a transitional—and highly variable—character, between oceanic and continental types. Six seasons may *Six seasons* be clearly distinguished: a snowy winter of one to three months; an early spring of one or two months, characterized by alternating wintry and springlike conditions; a predominantly sunny spring; a warm summer with plenty of rain and sunshine; a sunny, warm autumn; and a foggy, humid period signifying the approach of winter. Sunshine reaches its maximum over the Baltic in summer and the Carpathians in winter, and mean annual temperatures range from 46° F (8° C) in the southwestern lowlands to 43° F (6° C) in the colder northeast. The climate of the mountains is determined by altitude.

The annual average precipitation is about 24 inches (600 millimetres), but in the mountains the figure approaches 31 to 47 inches, dropping to about 18 inches in the central lowlands. In winter, snow makes up about half the total in the plains and almost all of it in the mountains.

Drainage and soils. No less than 99.7 percent of Poland drains to the Baltic, more than half via the Vistula (Wisła) River and a third via the Oder. Polish rivers experience two periods of high water each year: in spring, the lowland rivers are swollen by melted snow, the effect intensified both by ice dams (which block the rivers for one to three months) and by the fact that the thaw first strikes the upper reaches of the northward-flowing rivers; the summer rains bring a second maximum around the beginning of July.

There are some 9,300 Polish lakes with areas of more than 2½ acres (one hectare), and their total area is about 1,200 square miles (3,200 square kilometres), or 1 percent of the national territory. The majority, however, are found in the northern glaciated belt, where they occupy more than a 10th of the surface area.

Polish soils are varied and without clearly marked regional types. The greatest area is covered by podzol and pseudopodzol types, followed by the less widely distributed brown-earth soils, which are richer in nutrients. In the south are patches of the fertile loess-based soils, especially in the Little Poland Lowlands. The rendzinas, formed on limestone rocks, are a unique type. Alluvial soils filling the river valleys and peaty swamp soils found in the lake area and in poorly drained valleys are also of importance.

Plant and animal life. The vegetation of Poland has developed over the 10,000 years that have elapsed since the last Ice Age and consists of some 2,250 species of seed plants, 630 mosses, 200 liverworts, 1,200 lichens, and 1,500 fungi. Holarctic elements (*i.e.,* those appertaining to the temperate belt of the Northern Hemisphere) are dominant among the seed plants.

The northeastern limits of certain trees—notably beech, *Trees* fir, and the variety of oak known as pedunculate—run through Polish territory. There are few endemic species: the Polish larch (*Larix polonica*) and the Ojców birch (*Betula oycoviensis*) are two examples. Some relics of tundra vegetation have been preserved in the peat bogs and mountains. About 28 percent of the country is wooded. Poland lies in the zone of mixed forests, but in the southeast a fragment of the forest–steppe vegetation zone intrudes, while in the northeast there are portions of the east European subtaiga, with spruce as a characteristic component. In the mountains, the vegetation, like the climate, is determined by altitude. Fir and beech woods give way to the spruce of the upper woods, which in turn fade into subalpine, alpine, and snowline vegetation.

Poland's animal life belongs to the European–West Siberian zoogeographic province, itself part of the Palearctic subregion, and is closely linked with the vegetation cover. The vertebrate fauna includes nearly 400 species, including many types of mammals and more than 200 native birds. Deer and wild pig roam the woods; the elk is found in the coniferous forests of the northeast; and steppe rodents, such as the brindled gopher, are found in the south. Brown bear and wildcat live in the mountain woods, and the chamois and marmot are found at the highest levels. The great Białowieża Forest (Puszcza Białowieska), a national park contiguous with the Belovezhskaya Pushcha in Belorussian S.S.R., provides shelter for a small herd of wisent, or European bison, all that remain of the vast numbers that once roamed the continent.

Settlement patterns. The natural landscape of Poland can be divided broadly into three groups: the lowlands, the highlands, and the mountains. The eastern extremes of Poland display characteristics common to eastern Europe, but the rest of the country is linked by structure, climate, and the character of its vegetation to western Europe.

The coastal plain. The Baltic Coastal Plain stretches across northern Poland from East Germany to the Soviet border, forming a low-lying region built of various sediments. It is largely occupied by the ancient province of Pomerania (Pomorze), the name of which means "along the sea." The scarcely indented Baltic coastline was formed by wave action after the retreat of the ice sheet and the raising of sea levels. The Pomeranian Bay (Zatoka Pomorska) in the west and the Gulf of Gdańsk in the east are the two major inlets. In the southern portion of the former, two islands block off the Szczecin Lagoon (Zalew Szczeciński), into which the Oder discharges its waters. In the Gulf of Gdańsk, the Vistula forms a large delta. Sandbars, on which the winds have created large dunes, line much of the coast, separating the coastal lakes and lagoons from the sea. The main urban centres are the ports of Szczecin (German Stettin) on the lower Oder and Gdańsk (Danzig) and Gdynia in the east. The central portion of the Baltic Coastal Plain is scantily populated—there are only small fishing ports, of which Kołobrzeg is the most important—and the landscape has a desolate beauty.

Coastal settlements

The lake region. The belt immediately to the south of the coastal plain presents, with its many lakes, a varied, hilly landscape of glacial origin. Wide river valleys divide the region into three parts: the Pomeranian Lakeland (Pojezierze Pomorskie); the Masurian Lakeland (Pojezierze Mazurskie), east of the lower Vistula; and the Great Poland Lakeland (Pojezierze Wielkopolskie). The larger settlements and the main communications routes of this zone lie in and along the river valleys; the remainder of the area is mostly wooded and thinly populated. Only the eastern portion of the Great Poland Lakeland has a developed agriculture.

The central lowlands. The extensive central lowlands contain isolated relief features shaped by the oldest glaciations, but their character is generally flat and monotonous. The postglacial lakes have long since been filled in, and glacial outwash masks the weakly developed meltwater valley channels. The basins of the main rivers divide the area into the Silesian Lowlands (Nizina Śląska), which lie in the upper Oder; the southern Great Poland Lowlands (Nizina Wielkopolska), which lie in the middle Warta basin; and the Mazovian and Podlasian lowlands, which lie in the middle Vistula basin. Lower Silesia and Great Poland are important agricultural areas, but large industrial centres are found in many parts of the central lowlands. Warsaw (Warszawa), the capital, situated on the middle Vistula, is most prominent.

The Little Poland Uplands. These uplands, south of the central lowlands, extend from east to west, but they are folded transversely. In the west is the Silesian–Cracovian upthrust, with rich deposits of coal. A second upthrust is formed by the ancient rocks of the Góry Świętokrzyskie ("Holy Cross Mountains"), which reach a maximum height of 2,008 feet (612 metres). Between these two regions lies the Nida Basin, with an average height of 650 to 1,000 feet. East of the Góry Świętokrzyskie, the uplands are cut by the valley of the Vistula, beyond which lie the Lublin Uplands (Wyżyna Lubelska). In the south occur patches of loess on which fertile brown- and black-earth soils have developed. The older geological regions contain valuable minerals: in the Silesian–Cracovian uplands there are coal, iron, zinc, and lead deposits. These mineral resources have made possible the rise of Poland's most important industrial region, and the landscape of Upper Silesia is highly urbanized. Katowice is the largest centre, and the region is closely linked with that around Kraków. To the north the Staropolski (Old Polish) Basin, situated in the foothills of the Góry Świętokrzyskie, has a long history of industrial production. Kielce is the area's urban centre.

The industrial region

The Sudeten. The Sudeten and its foreland, part of the larger Bohemian Massif, have a long and complex geological history. They owe their present rugged form, however, to earth movements that accompanied the Carpathian uplift, and the highest portion, the Karkonosze ("Giant Mountains"; German Riesengebirge, Czech Krkonoše), reach 5,256 feet (1,602 metres) above sea level. The region contains rich mineral deposits, notably coking coal, which has occasioned the growth of an industrial centre around Wałbrzych. The region has many small towns; resorts and spas are found in more secluded areas. The foreland of the Sudeten is separated by a large fault from the larger mass. The foreland contains many granite quarries.

The Carpathians. The southernmost and also most scenic portion of Poland embraces the Carpathian Mountains and their associated chains and basins, created in the geologically recent mountain-building Tertiary Period (about 65,000,000 to 2,500,000 years ago). Within the Polish frontiers lie the Oświęcim and Sandomierz basins; a portion of the Beskid Mountains; the Orawka–Podhale Basin; and the Tatry (Tatra Mountains). The sub-Carpathian basins contain deposits of salt, sulfur, natural gas, and some petroleum. There is a large rural population and many towns of medium size. The highest peak of the Beskidy, Babia Góra, reaches 5,659 feet (1,725 metres); the high Tatry, the highest portion of the Polish Carpathians, with a maximum elevation of 8,199 feet (2,499 metres), have a unique character. Zakopane, the largest tourist and resort centre in Poland, lies at their feet. The Bieszczady Mountains, rolling, carpeted in beech woods, and sparsely inhabited, lie in the extreme southeast.

Environment. Rapid industrialization has threatened the natural environment in Poland, and pollution is severe in many areas. Upper Silesia and Kraków, in particular, are severely afflicted.

THE PEOPLE

Ethnic composition. Before World War II, the Polish lands were noted for the richness and variety of their ethnic communities. In the western and northern provinces of Silesia, Pomerania, and Masuria (then in Germany) there was a preponderance of Germans. In the southeast, Ukrainian settlements predominated in the regions east of Chełm and in the Carpathians east of Nowy Sącz. In all the towns and cities there were large concentrations of Yiddish-speaking Jews. The Polish ethnographic area stretched eastward: in Lithuania, Belorussia, and the western Ukraine, all of which had a mixed population, Poles were predominant not only in the great cities but also in numerous rural districts. There were significant Polish minorities in Daugavpils (in Latvia), Minsk, and Kiev.

The war resulted, however, in severe loss of lives, in massive migrations of peoples, and in radically altered borders, and as a consequence the population of the Polish People's Republic became one of the most ethnically homogeneous in the world. More than 98 percent declare themselves to be of Polish nationality, with Polish as their mother tongue. Ukrainians, the largest minority group, are scattered in various northern districts. Lesser numbers of Belorussians and Lithuanians live in areas adjoining the Soviet frontier. The Jewish community, almost entirely Polonized, has been significantly reduced. In Silesia (southwestern Poland) a significant segment of the population, of mixed Polish and German ancestry, tends to declare itself as Polish or German according to political circumstances.

Language. The Polish language, together with Czech, Slovak, and Sorbian (Wendish or Lusatian), belongs to the West Slavic group of languages, as distinct from the East Slav Group (Russian and Ruthenian) and the South Slav Group. It has numerous dialects that correspond in the main to the old tribal divisions of Great Poland, Little Poland, Pomerania, and Mazovia. In some instances—among the Kashubs of Pomerania and the Górale, or "highlanders," of Podhale, for example—the distinctive features of the regional dialects are so strong as to suggest separate linguistic classification. Elsewhere, Polish has been influenced by contact with foreign languages. In Silesia the inimitable regional patois contains a mixture of Polish and German elements. Since 1945, as the result of

West Slavic language group

mass education and mass migrations, standard Polish has become far more homogeneous, although regional dialects persist. In the western and northern territories, resettled in large measure by Poles from the Soviet Union, the older generation often speaks a language characteristic of the former eastern provinces.

Literary Polish developed from the medieval period onward, on the basis of the dialects of Great Poland and Little Poland. By the 19th century Polish was well established both as a literary vehicle and as the dominant language of common speech in Poland, despite attempts of the partitioning powers to Germanize or Russify the population. Indeed, quite the opposite happened, and the Polish language became the main touchstone of national identity.

Religion. The overwhelming majority of the Polish population is Roman Catholic, and a large number are practicing Catholics. Poland is among the most uniformly Catholic nations in the world, and the Roman Catholic Church in Poland enjoys immense social prestige and political influence.

All religious institutions are subject to the control of the state office for religious denominations. In practice, however, the Roman Catholic Church wields a full measure of independence, partly through the sheer force of the faithful, and partly because in all important matters it answers to the Pope in Rome and not to the government in Warsaw.

The
Roman
Catholic
Church

The religious minorities, though encouraged by the anti-Roman Catholic policies of the Communist state, are barely visible except in local areas. There are two Protestant strongholds—that of the Polish Lutherans in Masuria (Mazury; formerly East Prussia) and the Polish Calvinists (Augsburg Confession) in Cieszyn, Silesia. There is an autocephalous Polish Orthodox Church, partly linked with the small Belorussian minority, and a Ukrainian Uniate community, which survives unofficially in southeastern districts. Poland has residual communities of Polish Jews, whose synagogues and religious activities have official sanction. The Polish National Catholic Church, a schismatic offshoot of Roman Catholicism, was strongly patronized by the government in the early years after the war but has never won popular support. Small groups representing fundamentalist sects such as the Seventh-day Adventists and the Jehovah's Witnesses operate in a few cities.

Demographic trends. The population of Poland was transformed during and immediately after World War II. Of the 34,800,000 people who had been living within the Polish frontiers in 1939, only 23,900,000 were to be found within the new frontiers by 1946. The decrease of almost 11,000,000 can be accounted for mainly by war losses but also in part by changes in frontiers and by the migration of former Polish citizens whose homelands were incorporated into the Soviet Union.

War
losses and
postwar
migrations

Polish war losses are the subject of some controversy. The official figure, issued in 1947, was 6,028,000, although this referred exclusively to losses within the postwar frontiers. As a result of the changes in frontiers, millions of Germans were forcibly expelled in 1946–47, and millions of Poles were transferred from the Soviet Union in the same period. An estimated 500,000 Ukrainians and Belorussians also were transferred into the Soviet Union. At the same time, there were vast internal movements into the new northern and western territories annexed from Germany.

Population losses and movements on this scale introduced permanent distortions into demographic structures and trends. At the end of the war there were huge deficiencies in certain categories, especially males, urban dwellers, and the educated classes as a whole. Although the immediate postwar generation had an unprecedented birthrate, the gaps created by the war could never be filled.

Emigration has been a permanent feature of Polish life for most of the last 200 years, and roughly one Pole in three lives abroad. Wave after wave of political émigrés has left Poland since the mid-18th century. By far the greatest numbers of people have left, however, for economic reasons. Starting in the mid-19th century, Polish emigrants moved into the new industrial areas of Europe and later to America.

Social structures. In the official view, Polish society entered the socialist stage of development in July 1944, and since then it has been engaged in the building of Communism. Official sources do not deny, however, that present-day society is far from the Communist ideal. Although the principal means of production are said to be under state control and Polish society is held to be classless, some private ownership of the means of production and remnants of the former class-based society do, in fact, persist. The presence in Poland of a large private, land-owning sector among the peasantry is a case in point. Another example is the rise of a distinct group of party elite, who in the official view are the best representatives of the working class. In the eyes of their critics the elite constitute instead a new privileged ruling class.

Polish society since the war has been transformed by two great movements—by the growth of a dominant, urban, industrialized working class and by the continuing drift of peasants from the rural areas into towns and cities. One group that has contrived to benefit from both movements is that of the so-called peasant workers, who tend to live on the fringe of industrial regions, with one part of the family maintaining the farm while other family members earn wages in the local factory.

THE ECONOMY

Management of the economy. Since 1948, when the Communist government was initiated, Poland's economic system has been a command economy of the Soviet type. All economic activity is subordinated to the dictates of the state's plans, which aim to regulate the details of production, labour, trade, prices, and social priorities. Party planners and the state planning commission are responsible for the successive five-year plans. Managers of state enterprises have very little freedom to deviate from the dictates of the plans. Most sectors of the economy are state-owned and party-controlled; but even in the relatively extensive private sector the farmers, artisans, and retailers must operate within a rigidly fixed economic framework. Poland is a member of the Council for Mutual Economic Assistance (Comecon), which lays down the general framework within which Poland's own national plan has to operate.

Planning
the
economy

Employment. In Poland, as in other countries of the Soviet bloc, state enterprises act as the main employer. The principal branches of industry, services, and trade are directly owned by the state. As a result, the average worker has no option but to accept the work, pay, and conditions offered. The legal self-employed sector, however, is surprisingly large, and small-scale private workshops, services, restaurants, and businesses have proliferated.

Unemployment does not officially exist, and no unemployment benefits are payable. In reality, there is considerable hidden unemployment or nominal employment of people who appear on the state payroll but do not actually have any work to do.

Wages and cost of living. For 30 years prior to the economic crisis that came to a head in 1980, wages in Poland were stable, inflation was low, and extravagant food subsidies ensured minimum costs of subsistence. In 1980 both wages and prices began to inflate wildly. Since then shortages of food supplies and consumer goods have alternated with shortages of wage flows. By Western standards, the percentage of income spent on housing, heating, and services is minimal, while the relative cost of food, clothing, furniture, domestic appliances, and automobiles is colossal.

Trade unions. Unions registered with the Central Council of Trade Unions are approved by state and party organs. Inasmuch as the government is a monopoly employer in all important branches of industry, and inasmuch as the trade union organization is run by the party, it can be argued that the trade unions are employer unions. Each union is organized on the basis of an individual industry, and links between employees in different trades or different enterprises are not possible. There is no free bargaining over wages or conditions.

The Independent Self-Governing Trades Union, known as Solidarność (Solidarity), was founded in September 1980, shortly after widespread strikes organized by the

Founding
of
Solidarity

Interfactory Strike Committee had forced the government to sanction free and independent unions with the right to organize and to strike. Solidarity broke the monopoly of the official party unions, causing them to collapse. Solidarity quickly gained mass support, even among many party members, and extended its activities far beyond narrow syndicalist concerns.

After December 1981, Solidarity and its various dependent organizations, such as Rural Solidarity (Wiejska Solidarność), were officially suppressed, and the leaders of the independent labour movement were denounced as "criminals." The party ordered its managers and ministers to create new trade unions along the old lines of party control. Much of the membership of the re-created unions consisted of former Solidarity sympathizers, however, and the new unions were not entirely uncritical of party policy.

Resources. *Mineral resources.* Poland is relatively well endowed with natural resources. Its principal mineral asset is bituminous coal. Almost all the output is derived from the rich Upper Silesian coalfield. Brown coal (lignite) is mined as well. Other fuel resources include small amounts of petroleum and moderately large deposits of natural gas.

Sulfur is Poland's second most important mineral, and reserves are among the largest in the world. Other important nonmetallic minerals include barite, salt, kaolin, limestone, chalk, gypsum, and marble.

Metals

Among metallic minerals, copper and zinc are the most important. Reserves of zinc and lead ores are believed to be among the largest in the world. Iron ore is mined in small quantities, although most of Poland's steelworks import ore directly from the Soviet Union. Nickel and other metals such as vanadium, cobalt, and silver are also produced.

Other resources. The quality of the soil varies, but there are large fertile areas, including Lower Silesia and the Little Poland Lowlands, the Kujawy, the Vistula delta, and the Lublin area. The soil is somewhat poorer in large parts of central and northern Poland. Some 80 percent of the country's wooded lands is occupied by coniferous timbers, with pine, larch, and spruce the most important as resources. The bulk of the country's hydroelectricity comes from the Carpathians, the Sudeten region, and the Brda and Vistula rivers.

Agriculture. Polish agriculture is unique in the Soviet bloc in that private farms still account for the greater part of its total output. Following the abandonment of the collectivization campaign in the period 1949–55, more than 80 percent of Poland's farmland returned to private ownership. State farms on the Soviet model remained only on large-scale former German estates in the west and north. Cooperatives account for less than 2 percent of the land.

The state has not promoted modern private farming. Controls on land transfers, on prices and deliveries, and on the supply of fertilizers and machinery have undermined incentives. Mechanization began in the 1970s, but efforts have proved inadequate. Poland's peasants, still working in 19th-century conditions, often with horse and cart on a tiny plot, are unable or unwilling to produce surplus food for the state market. As a result, food shortages, bread queues, and rationing have been a regular feature.

The aging agricultural population has experienced great distress. The drift from the countryside has left the villages without young people to work the farms, while the demands on agricultural production have steadily risen.

Industry. Impressive quantitative advances in industrial production have been overshadowed to some extent by grave shortcomings in quality and by problems of organization. Following the first six-year and five-year plans of the Stalinist era, industrial production surged dramatically until the mid-1970s. Growth was most marked in heavy industry: iron and steel, mining, chemicals, and machinery. In 1972 a new industrial strategy was launched with the aims of improving the consumer sector—especially by producing more automobiles and domestic appliances—and, on the basis of foreign loans, of greatly expanding modern technology and export production. Only five or six years later, with a hard currency debt approaching $30,000,000,000 and no signs of expanded trade or success in introducing high technology, Polish industry sank

into a crisis. From 1979 to 1983 industrial production declined sharply.

All but a small portion of the total electrical power output is derived from bituminous coal and lignite. Natural gas has largely replaced manufactured gas. Power shortages have been a constant feature of the economic crisis that began in the late 1970s. Domestic crude oil production contributes less than 5 percent to the annual consumption of petroleum, most of which has to be imported.

Finance. All financial institutions have been owned by the state since 1944–45 and have formed an integral part of centralized economic planning since 1949. The National Bank of Poland (Narodowy Bank Polski) acts as the main agent of the government's financial policy, managing everything from the currency and money supply to wages and prices, credit, investment, and the detailed business of all state enterprises. Other important banks include the Commercial Bank of Warsaw (Bank Handlowy w Warszawie) for foreign trade; the Investment Bank (Bank Inwestycyjny); the Agrarian Bank (Bank Rolny); and the General Savings Bank (Bank Polska Kasa Opieki). There are no stock exchanges.

Internal monetary operations are conducted in inconvertible local currency, while external operations are conducted either in foreign currency, especially U.S. dollars, or, for the Soviet bloc, in special units of account such as convertible rubles. Local currency cannot be exported and can only be changed by special permission. Exchange rates against foreign hard currency are flexible according to the needs of the State Bank. The official rate as seen by the foreign tourist or visitor is fixed arbitrarily and bears no relation to the real purchasing power of the Polish zloty.

An elaborate black market in hard currency thrives; without it private citizens can rarely travel abroad or purchase foreign goods. Polish citizens are permitted to keep dollar accounts in the state banks. Special shops that sell betterquality goods exclusively for hard currency help dispel the shortages of supplies.

Trade. Although Poland has about one-fourth of eastern Europe's population, it accounts for only slightly more than one-tenth of its foreign trade. Imports exceeded exports by a considerable margin for several decades until 1982, when a nominal trade surplus was achieved by a radical reduction in imports.

Balance of payments

A large measure of Poland's exports consists of machinery and transport equipment, with complete plants, power and electrical machinery, and vessels the most important items. Many of these go to Communist and developing countries. Fuels and raw materials such as coal, coke, iron, and steel also figure prominently as exports.

(E.I.U./A.H.D./N.D.)

Transportation. *Railways.* The communications system in Poland developed in the 19th and early 20th centuries, in a period when the country was divided between Russia, Germany, and Austria. The three areas thus developed in different economic and political conditions, and the main railway lines were centred on the capital cities of the three empires. The density of the railway networks in the three sectors was uneven. In 1918 independent Poland took over the system and began to redesign and rebuild it according to the standard European gauge. Among the most important railway lines built after that date were those linking Warsaw with Poznań and Kraków and a coal trunk line linking Upper Silesia with the newly built seaport of Gdynia.

After the devastation of World War II the railway system was reconstructed once again, and the most used lines were converted to electric power. The railways are administered by the Polish State Railways (Polskie Koleje Państwowe). Because of the location of the country, Polish railway lines are important in the carriage of transit freight between member countries of Comecon, notably between the Soviet Union and East Germany and between Czechoslovakia and the Polish ports.

Highways. The highway system originally showed disproportions similar to those of the railways; that is, the densest network was on lands belonging to Germany and the least dense on lands belonging to Russia. An attempt to remedy this situation was made between 1918 and 1938 and again, but more intensively, after 1945. Modern multilane highways adapted to mass traffic requirements have been built in Warsaw, and projects have been undertaken to link Warsaw to provincial centres.

Inland waterways and merchant shipping. The middle course of the main Polish river, the Vistula, is not regulated, and thus the Vistula is of less importance as a waterway than the smaller Oder. The Oder is linked by the modern Gliwice Canal (Kanał Gliwicki) to the Upper Silesian industrial region and carries coal to the port of Szczecin. The Oder basin is also linked to the lower Vistula by the Bydgoszcz Canal (Kanał Bydgoski). Inland navigation is of little importance in Poland, however, less than 1 percent of Polish freight being carried on rivers and canals. Shipping is well developed, and there are three large seaports—Szczecin (the leader), Gdynia, and Gdańsk—as well as smaller fishing and coastal navigation ports.

Air transport. Domestic and international air transport is provided by a state enterprise, LOT (from Polskie Linie Lotnicze). There are numerous international routes, centred on the airport at Warsaw.

ADMINISTRATION AND SOCIAL CONDITIONS

Government. *The party-state.* The governance of the Polish People's Republic is based on a dual system whereby the constitutional organs of the state are duplicated and controlled by the parallel organs of the ruling Polish Communist party, the United Workers' Party (Polska Zjednoczona Partia Robotnicza, or PUWP), which was founded in 1948. The PUWP, modeled on the Communist Party of the Soviet Union (CPSU), is in effect the executive branch of government. The state, in contrast, is the administrative branch of the party. The party's first secretary is the chief executive, the head of government who controls both the party and the state. The chairman of the Council of State (called the president) and the chairman of the Council of Ministers, although officially described as positions of highest authority, are in fact subordinate to the party leader.

State constitution. The constitution of the Polish People's Republic, as passed in 1952 and amended in 1976, applies only to the state and cannot be invoked to limit the party. An amendment of 1976 declares that the Polish People's Republic is a socialist state and that the PUWP is the leading political force in the construction of socialism. Another amendment underscores Poland's perpetual alliance with the Soviet Union. By virtue of this clause, any attempt to abandon the Soviet alliance can be declared illegal, and any action by the Soviet Union to preserve the status quo in Poland can be declared constitutional in terms of Polish law.

Party structure. The structure of the ruling party is highly centralized. The central organs—the Political Bureau, the Party Secretariat, and the Central Committee—oversee the work of the province, city, and local committees in every detail. The political bureau, or Politburo, which is chaired by the first secretary, maintains effective control over everything else. Members of the Central Committee meet periodically to approve the work of both the Politburo and the secretariat. In addition they prepare the program of the unicameral state legislature, known as the Sejm.

The *nomenklatura* system, the existence of which is not generally acknowledged by official sources, ensures complete party control over all offices and appointments. The *nomenklatura,* a list of names of the politically reliable, is managed by the party secretariat, which matches offices to be filled in the party and state hierarchies with approved people qualified to fill them.

The Patriotic Movement of National Rebirth (Patriotyczny Ruch Odrodzenia Narodowego; PRON), founded in 1982 to replace the National Unity Front, is a party-run organization for managing all non-party political organizations, including the PUWP's two subsidiaries: the United Peasants' Party (Zjednoczone Stronnictwo Ludowe; ZSL) and the Democratic Party (Stronnictwo Demokratyczne; SD). No political bodies are permitted to exist unless they accede in advance to the PRON statute.

State institutions. The main institutions of the Polish

People's Republic are democratic in form and elective in character. State elections are held to determine the composition of the Sejm, for example, and the Sejm in turn elects the Council of State and the Council of Ministers. The party, however, has the right to nominate all candidates and to exclude all true independents.

The state organs carry out policy as laid down by the party. The Council of State acts as a collective presidency. The Council of Ministers directs the work of the state ministries under the guidance of the party secretariat. State council members and ministers only possess senior rank in the system when they serve simultaneously in the Politburo or secretariat.

Judicial system. Judges are appointed by the same party *nomenklatura* that appoints state prosecutors and other court officials. Like the constitution, the law codes are products of party policy. Despite constant political pressure, however, the Polish bar has maintained a lack of subservience unique in the Soviet bloc, and defense counsels have repeatedly produced a spirited defense in periodic political trials.

Regional administration. The regional administrative system is on two levels. The largest units are the *województwa* (provinces), of which there are 49 (including three self-governing cities). Each province is responsible for the submission of proposals for plans for the local economy and land use to the Central Planning Commission. It is also responsible for achieving the targets that are eventually approved by the Sejm. There are also eight *makroregiony* (macro-regions), which have a consultative role only and are not able to compel changes in provincial proposals. The *gminy* (rural communes) are responsible for the provision of some cultural and social services and for local land-use planning. The four largest cities are also divided into districts, called *dzielnice,* which have similar responsibilities.

The armed forces. Poland's armed forces consist of four services—the army, the air force, the navy, and air defense. The armed forces are highly politicized. The military command is controlled by the party's Main Political Administration, which also oversees the political indoctrination and supervision of all units. Officers are trained in the party's Academy of Political and Military Sciences, and most are party members. Senior officers normally are graduated from Soviet academies.

The Polish People's Republic became a founding member of the Warsaw Pact in 1955 and provides the second largest contingent after the Soviet Union. Poland's national defense is the responsibility of the 10 divisions of a separate structure called the National Territory Defense.

State legislature

Relationship of state and party

Shostal Associates

Roman Catholic church at Wambierzyce, Pol., containing a shrine of the Holy Virgin.

Security services. Internal security agencies are large and complex. There are two fully militarized formations: the Frontier Defense Force (known by its Polish initials, WOP), charged with regular defense of the frontiers and the restricted border zones, and the Internal Security Service (WSW), which is the elite guard of the party and state leadership.

The Motorized Detachments of the Citizens' Militia (ZOMO) act as a mobile, paramilitary riot squad and strike-breaking force. Normal civilian police duties are undertaken by the uniformed and nonuniformed branches of the Citizens' Militia (MO). The Security Service (SB), the secret political police organization, operates in conjunction with the Ministry of Internal Affairs.

Education. Schools of all types and on all levels are free, the system of schooling is standard, and attendance throughout the eight-year primary school course and at supplementary study until the age of 18 is obligatory. The system contains nursery schools, primary schools, and Secondary schools secondary schools. There are several types of secondary schools offering basic vocational training, vocational and technical training, and general college-preparatory education. Basically, all schools are subject to the Ministry of Education, but medical schools and colleges are subject to the Ministry of Health and Social Welfare, army colleges to the Ministry of National Defense, and higher schools of art to the Ministry of Art and Culture.

Prominent among Poland's universities are the University of Warsaw (founded 1818), the Jagiellonian University (1364) in Kraków, and the Catholic University of Lublin (1918). The highest academic institution is the Polish Academy of Sciences (Polska Akademia Nauk), with numerous research institutes. The academy represents Polish learning abroad.

Health and welfare. Health care in Poland is largely handled by the Ministry of Health and Social Welfare, which has authority over the health departments of *województwa* People's Councils. Health service facilities include clinics; hospitals; sanatoriums, rest homes, and spas; ambulance services; and the national sanitary inspection. Private medical and dental practices operate with varying degrees of official approval. The pharmaceutical industry is state-owned, but many medicines are only available with a special prescription or from abroad. Medical services are seriously strained in periods of general economic crisis, and medical aid from foreign countries has played a valuable supportive role.

Health insurance Social insurance for the health service covers free treatment for all workers and the members of their families, as well as for pensioners, invalids, students, and certain others. Apart from the health service there is also a social service whose purpose is to ensure a suitable means of support for the elderly and invalids. There are homes for social care, catering to pensioners, the chronically sick, and the mentally retarded.

As a result of the program of urbanization that has been pursued since the 1940s, Polish cities have been overwhelmed by migrant workers from the countryside, and the demand for housing vastly exceeds supply. In urban areas, various cooperative housing schemes have been put into operation by the local government authorities. But the standard family apartment is inadequate for many families, and waiting lists for a newly married couple can stretch for 10 or even 20 years. As a result, a great deal of private building goes on, legally or illegally, especially on the urban periphery.

CULTURAL LIFE

The culture of Poland has been nurtured on a great variety of traditions. Until World War II, because Poland was an area of multinational settlement, it could draw not only on the dominant Polish culture but also on that of the minorities, especially the Germans, Jews, and Ruthenians. The common Slavic element is weak, although aspects of it can be identified in language, literature, and folklore. The formative experience, undoubtedly, was the adoption of Roman Catholic Christianity in the 10th century and the resultant millennium of involvement in "Western" civilization. German, French, and Italian influences have been particularly strong. Unlike Russia, Poland was deeply immersed in all the great movements of Western culture—such as humanism, the Renaissance, the Reformation, the Baroque, the Enlightenment, and Romanticism—and its cultural identity was already very strong before the series of partitions of Polish territory began in 1773. With the loss of political independence, the 19th and 20th centuries have seen an unrelenting struggle to preserve the national culture and its values from foreign impositions and government policy.

The Roman Catholic Church in Poland plays a social and cultural role far beyond the religious sphere. Catechism lessons, conducted with great zeal in the parishes, expose children to a nonofficial view of the world. Church-sponsored societies, such as the Catholic Intellectual Clubs, provide adults with a unique forum for free public discussion. Parish halls provide shelter for a wide variety of uncensored exhibitions, plays, films, and meetings.

Folk culture. Because of rapid industrialization and urbanization, Poland's traditional folk culture has been seriously undermined in the postwar era. Regional dress, regional forms of speech, peasant arts and crafts, and religious and folk festivals have all been swamped by mass culture deriving from the new cities and the official media. In an effort to compensate, the Roman Catholic Church has tried to preserve the religious elements of folk culture, Religious elements of folk culture notably in the large annual pilgrimages to shrines such as Częstochowa, Kalwaria, Lanckorona, or Piekary Śląskie, while the Communist authorities have supported folk music and folk dancing. The colourful and stylized repertoire of the State Folk Ensemble, Mazowsze, for example, has won international acclaim. Several regional communities, including the Górale ("Highlanders") of Podhale, the Kurpie in the northeast, and the inhabitants of Łowics, near Warsaw, have created an authentic blend of the old and the new.

Literature. Polish literature developed long ago into the main vehicle of national expression. For many Poles, their literature stands beside their religion as one of the twin pillars of their heritage. It provides one of their most cherished links with Western civilization and one of the main safeguards of their national identity. The close relationship between local political events and literary trends, however, together with a necessary resort to elaborate allegories, allusions, and symbols, has rendered many excellent Polish works inaccessible to the foreign public. (For detailed discussion, see POLISH LITERATURE.)

The first half of the 19th century witnessed the flowering of the three greatest Polish poets (Adam Mickiewicz, Polish poetry and prose Juliusz Słowacki, and Zygmunt Krasiński), while in the second half, and at the beginning of the 20th century, the great Polish prose writers—including the Nobel prizewinners Henryk Sienkiewicz and Władysław Reymont—were active. Among the postwar Polish poets are Zbigniew Herbert and the Nobel prizewinner Czesław Miłosz.

Music. Polish music, like Polish literature, has a continuous tradition reaching back into the Middle Ages. As the least political of the arts it has suffered less in recent times from official constraints. Founded on the inimitable rhythms and melodies of folk music—the *krakowiak, mazur,* and *polonez*—its native characteristics developed early, and a distinctive school of Polish church music already flourished during the Renaissance. The first major Polish opera, *Cud mniemany czyli Krakowiacy i Górale* ("The Pretended Miracle or the Krakovians and the Highlanders"), by Jan Stefani and Wojciech Bogusławski, was staged in 1794. In the 19th century Stanisław Moniuszko wrote a series of popular operas, including *Halka, Straszny dwór,* and *Hrabina.* Frédéric Chopin is usually considered to have created the quintessence of Polishness in music. In addition to his renown as one of the supreme master composers, he was the first of a constant stream of instrumentalists from Polish lands, among them many prominent Jewish performers who have conquered the international scene. Pianists such as Ignacy Paderewski and Artur Rubinstein and violinists such as Henryk Szeryng or Isaac Stern attest to the vitality of Polish musical life. Contemporary Polish composition has been dominated by the names of Karol Szymanowski, Witold Lutosławski, and

Krzysztof Penderecki. All branches of classical music—opera, symphony, chamber, and choral—are well represented in Poland, and several orchestras and choirs appear regularly on the international circuit. Popular music in Poland is largely derived from Western styles, although Polish jazz has earned a reputation for experiment and excellence.

Visual arts. From the Middle Ages many fine examples of Romanesque and Gothic architecture, both secular and religious, have been preserved, together with outstanding sculptures, among which the wooden altar triptych of Wit Stosz (Veit Stoss), in the Church of the Virgin Mary in Kraków, is the most famous. The vast red-brick castle of Malbork (Marienburg), once the headquarters of the Teutonic Knights, is among the most impressive in Europe.

Architecture, sculpture, and painting

The architecture and sculpture of the Renaissance and Baroque periods were formed under Italian influence but nevertheless developed individual Polish forms, as in the town hall of Poznań or the decorated granaries at Kazimierz Dolny. Zamość, a model Renaissance city built in the 1580s, has survived virtually intact. The best preserved urban architecture of the late Middle Ages and Renaissance is that of the old town and Wawel Castle in Kraków. The classicism of the end of the 18th century and the beginning of the 19th left its most valuable monuments in some of the great palaces, like that of the Radziwiłłs at Nieborów or at Łazienki in Warsaw. There are many examples of imperial German and Russian architecture from the 19th century, among them Lublin Castle.

Painting attained its greatest development in the second half of the 19th century, representing styles developing at that time in western Europe, but again with specific national characteristics. The greatest fame was achieved by Jan Matejko, creator of monumental, romantic historical canvases, by Henryk Siemiradzki, and by a number of landscape and genre painters. The greatest sensitivity was shown in portraits by Stanisław Wyspiański, an artist active also in drama and design.

Theatre and motion pictures. The Polish national theatre, as distinct from earlier religious, court, and foreign plays that had circulated since the Middle Ages, dates from the end of the 18th century. The great pioneer was Wojciech Bogusławski, an actor, director, and author. Political conditions during the period of partition (1772–1914) inhibited theatrical development, however, and most of the Romantic masterworks of Adam Mickiewicz or Juliusz Słowacki were never staged during their lifetime. The comedian and satirist Aleksander Fredro earned a less exalted but no less lasting reputation. Kraków in Austrian Galicia became a centre of lively theatre at the turn of the century. Between World Wars I and II, Juliusz Osterwa in Warsaw and Leon Schiller in Łódź launched the experimental tradition. After 1956, once the era of socialist realism had passed, the avant-garde came into its own. The Theatre of the Absurd was explored alongside the revival of the classical repertoire. During the 1960s the Laboratory Theatre of Jerzy Grotowski gained international acclaim. Grotowski's theories and methods, which emphasized the nonverbal aspects of theatre, had a broad impact, especially in the United States. Henryk Tomaszewski's Mime Theatre saw parallel success. Tadeusz Kantor, a painter and designer, has been an important influence.

Cinema

The origins of Polish cinema go back to 1909, but it was only in the late 1950s that its products began to attract worldwide attention. Just as the State Film School at Łódź earned high standing in the filmmaking profession, so the work of individual directors who broke free of official preferences achieved great success both at home and abroad. Undoubtedly, the leading name is that of Andrzej Wajda, whose films and theatre productions have set precedents for independence and excellence in exploring the conflicts in Polish society. Among other distinguished directors are Andrzej Munk, Roman Polanski, Aleksander Ford, Tadeusz Konwicki, Krzysztof Zanussi, and Agnieszka Holland. Historical epics have enjoyed great popularity, while official taste continues to support war films and themes connected with the Nazi occupation.

Museums. In part because of colossal wartime destruction, and in part also because historiography in Poland has long been subject to official controls, the need to preserve and cherish the records and artifacts of the past is felt with special urgency. Archives and museums of art, ethnography, archaeology, and natural history can be found in many Polish cities. The Czartoryski Museum in Kraków dates to 1805, the Mełżyński Museum in Poznań to 1857, the National Museum in Warsaw to 1862. In the postwar period, official policy has concentrated on the creation of new regional museums in each of the cities of the ex-German recovered territories, on museums connected with the history of the Communist movement, on former private palaces and collections acquired by the state, and on sites connected with Nazi war crimes, such as Oświęcim (Auschwitz) or Majdanek. The Roman Catholic Church is active in preserving and exhibiting the art treasures and records connected with Poland's religious heritage.

Sport and recreation. Group sports and spectator sports are encouraged in Poland. Professional football teams, nominally attached to state enterprises, attract large crowds in the towns, while local authorities provide facilities for athletics and swimming. Skiing and mountaineering in the Tatry and sailing on the Baltic or the Masurian Lakes are well developed. Individual or small-team sports such as tennis or golf are less available.

The media. With very few exceptions, the mass media are either owned or controlled by the state or the party. The state television and radio stations broadcast regularly. The Polish press includes the official organs of the party and state, such as *Trybuna ludu* ("People's Tribune"), the organ of the PUWP; a wide band of less closely controlled semi-party newspapers and journals, such as *Życie Warszawy* ("Warsaw Life"), *Polityka* ("Politics"), a lively weekly, or *Twórczość* ("Creativity"), an intellectual monthly; the independent sector, headed by the respected Kraków *Tygodnik powszechny* ("Universal Weekly"), and by the Roman Catholic journals *Znak* ("The Sign") and *Więź* ("The Link"); and the underground "free sector," in which local newssheets circulate.

The press

Censorship. The government controls all means of publication. The Main Office for the Control of Presentations and Public Performances (GUKPIW), with its headquarters in Warsaw, controls the media, publishing, films, theatres, exhibitions, advertising, and related activities. The bureau maintains an office in all television and radio stations, press and publishing houses, film and theatre studios, and printing works throughout the country. Plans as well as prepared material must be authorized before being made public. Private citizens require an official license to commission printed items such as wedding invitations, obituary notices, or printed stationery. All photocopiers and printing machines must be registered, even in state institutions, and access to them is closely controlled. All purchases of paper in bulk require a permit. Censorship of the foreign mail is routine. No sphere of information is immune, however distant it may be from immediate political concerns: censors, practicing a form of censorship that not only suppresses material but also aims to mold all information at its source, review information on archaeology, environmental issues, and social conditions; poetry; children's literature; scientific journals; government statistics; dictionaries; encyclopaedias; and reference works.

Despite the official controls, the spoken word is not generally suppressed in Poland, and the highly literate Poles are masters at writing and reading "between the lines." Also, unofficial information is available from the foreign media, from within the Roman Catholic Church, and in the vast realm of underground publishing.

For statistical data on the land and people of Poland, see the *Britannica World Data* section in the BRITANNICA WORLD DATA ANNUAL.   (J.A.K./A.H.D./N.D.)

History

ANCIENT AND MEDIEVAL POLAND

Early origins. The Poles belong to the North Indo-European language group comprising the Slavs, the Balts, and the Germans. The primordial homeland of the Slavs can be located in the immediate vicinity of the most ancient settlements of the Germans and Balts, the area occupied by the "Poles" lying in the basins of the Oder and Vistula rivers. The Polish nation originated from a union of such West Slavic tribes as the Polanians (Polanie), Vistulans (Wiślanie), Silesians (Ślęzanie), East Pomeranians (Pomorzanie), and Mazovians (Mazowianie). These "Polish" tribes shared a basically common culture and language and were much more closely related to each other than, for example, the Germanic tribes who founded the Franconian or German kingdom about 800–1024. Chronicles and geographical descriptions of Carolingian, Saxonian, Arabian, and Byzantine origin have described in some detail these Polish tribes, their names, and the regions where they lived. The Polanie tribe (open-country dwellers) lived in the fertile Polish heartland crossed by the Warta River, and this was the group after which the later Polish nation was named. Besides the Polanie tribe, there were approximately 20 Polish tribes that formed small states between the years 800 and 960. The individual tribes owed allegiance to regional leaders, chosen from an assembly of all free Polish males as commanders in case of war. Each tribe commanded several well-fortified castles or fortresses, the larger castles developing into principalities or "castle districts." There were usually fortified city-settlements (*suburbia*) near all the larger castles even in very early times. As early as 900–1025, along the Baltic Sea coast, there were large trading centres with between 6,000 and 10,000 inhabitants; these included Wolin (Wollin) and Szczecin (Stettin), on the mouth of the Oder River, and Truso (later Elbląg) and Gdańsk (Danzig), founded before 990 on the mouth of the Vistula River. The ancient foreign trade routes linking this area with distant regions stimulated the founding and development of small states. The most significant trade route from East to West connected Ratisbon (now Regensburg)–Vienna and Kraków with Kiev and Byzantium (now Istanbul). A well-developed monetary exchange system made it possible for the individual dukes to raise tariffs and tributes, in this manner exerting their sovereign rights on the monetary economy. Mining of precious metals and iron ores probably took place in Upper Silesia and in the Polish Central Highlands at that time.

The region grew into a larger state under the dynasty of the Wiślanie (or Vistulans), as early as 875, extending over the Lędzianie (who lived either on the upper Vistula or the upper Warta River) and perhaps even over some of the East Slavonic tribes on the Bug and San rivers. Around 875 to 880 the state and Silesia came under the sovereign rule of Great Moravia, led by Prince Svatopluk (ruled 870–894). Under his reign, Christianity was introduced in both its Latin and Greek forms through the disciples of "the apostles of the Slavs," Cyril and Methodius. Destroying Great Moravia, the Magyars conquered and settled the Hungarian lands from about 896 to 907. This restored the independence of southern Poland for a short time until it came under the control of the Bohemian dukes Boleslav I (died 967) and Boleslav II (ruled from about 973 to 999).

Both the Latin and Eastern Orthodox faiths were already well established in the area by this time, and the first bishopric of Kraków was established in 969. A territorial association was formed a few decades later, consisting of the tribes of southern Poland, commonly known as Little Poland (Małopolska). Little Poland, with the exception of a few border regions, covered the same area as the bishopric of Kraków.

The Piast dynasty. The second and politically more important founding of a state took place under the Polanie dynasty. The descendants of "Piast," the legendary founder of the dynasty—Siemowit (Ziemowit), Leszek (Lestko), and Siemomysł (Ziemomysł)—united the lands around Poznań, Kruszwica, Gniezno, and Kalisz, and this region later became known as Great Poland (Wielkopolska).

Mieszko I, c. 963–992. Siemomysł's son, Mieszko I, was the first of the Piast dukes to have his biography recorded in detail in the chronicles of that time. Through his desire to conquer Western Pomerania along the Oder River to the trading cities of Szczecin and Wolin, Mieszko I came into contact with the German kingdom, whose ruler Otto I the Great (the Holy Roman emperor) had conquered and subjugated Bohemia in 950 and all the

Polabic tribes (between the Elbe and the Oder rivers) between 936 and 955. This extended the sovereignty of the German king to the Oder River, and, for the time being, Mieszko acknowledged Otto's supremacy and entered into a close trade and cultural relationship with the Duchy of Saxony, Otto's homeland. To counter the German threat, Mieszko I entered into an alliance with the Bohemian duke Boleslav II, marrying his sister, Dubravka (Dąbrówka), in 965. Baptized in 966, he promoted the general spread of Christianity in his lands. In consequence, the year 966 is considered to be the year that marks the founding of Poland. The bishopric of Poznań was established in 968 and placed under the sovereignty of the archbishopric of Magdeburg. During the Great Slav Rebellion in 983, Germany lost its territory east of the Elbe and Saale rivers. In tacit agreement with Germany, Mieszko I conquered the entire coastal region of the Baltic Sea, including Szczecin, during 967 to 990. After dissolving his treaty with Bohemia, he further added Silesia and Little Poland to his other conquests. This established Mieszko as the ruler of an empire covering about 96,500 square miles (250,000 square kilometres) and populated by 1,250,000 people. Of decisive importance for the later development of internal unity was the fact that Mieszko submitted to the formal supremacy of the Holy See in Rome around 990. He took this step in order to avoid being subjected to the authority of the German Church.

Bolesław I the Brave, 992–1025. The eldest son of Mieszko I, Bolesław, further enlarged his empire, going beyond the ethnic boundaries of the Polish tribes. With Bolesław's help, the Holy Roman emperor Otto III set up his own Polish metropolitanate (church province), with the bishoprics of Kraków, Wrocław, and Kołobrzeg and the archbishopric of Gniezno, at the Congress of Gniezno (1000). The first bishop of Prague, Adalbert (Vojtěch), became the national patron saint of Poland in that year, following his martyrdom in 997 during his missionary work with the pagan Prussians in Samland in east Prussia. When Otto III died, Bolesław I conquered Bohemia, Moravia, the German borderlands in Lusatia (Lausitz), west of the Oder River, and probably also Slovakia between 1003 and 1004. But the new king of Germany, Henry II (ruled 1002–24), reconquered Bohemia and also led three campaigns against Bolesław I, without success. In 1018 Bolesław turned east, occupying Kiev for a short period and regaining the borderland at the Bug and San rivers, which had belonged to Poland before 981. Bolesław I was crowned king (presumably with the consent of the Holy See in Rome) on Dec. 25, 1024, and the new kingdom gradually became known under the name of Poland (Polonia) even during his reign. After his death the Polish monarchy came to be the secular symbol of the country's unity, in spite of all the partitions and divisions that the future held in store.

Attempts to expand Polish domination. *Mieszko II Lambert, 1025–34.* One of the younger sons of Bolesław I, Mieszko II Lambert was well educated but did not possess the strategic and statesmanlike talents of his father. After victorious campaigns against the barbarian Polabs in 1030, he attacked the German king Conrad II, who, in alliance with the grand duke Yaroslav of Kiev, attacked Poland (1031), further supported by rebellions within the country. Eventually, about 1033, Mieszko was forced to recognize German supremacy. His death in 1034 thus came at the height of a crisis. The boom in foreign trade that had been a factor in the establishment of the Piast empire had come to a close; the regional overlords were in a state of rebellion, and the barbarian insurrections deeply affected the barely established organization of the church. Chaos followed for the next few years (1034–39), the Bohemian duke Bretislav I occupying Silesia, totally devastating Great Poland, and resettling many of its inhabitants in Bohemia. The coastal regions from Szczecin to Gdańsk seceded from the Polish crown for about a century. The bishopric of Kołobrzeg—and with it the entire Christian movement in Western Pomerania—foundered again.

Casimir I the Restorer, 1039–58. A former monk, Casimir (Kazimierz) I slowly restored Poland with the help of the German king Henry III. Both Great Poland and

Margin notes (left column):
The Polanie tribe

Introduction of Christianity

Margin notes (right column):
Defeat of Mieszko II

Little Poland recognized Casimir I as their duke in 1039–40. Mazovia followed in 1047 and Silesia recognized him in 1050, but Casimir had to pay tribute to Bohemia for Silesia.

Bolesław II the Bold, 1058–79. Casimir's successor, Bolesław II, continued the power politics of Bolesław I, leading many successful campaigns into Hungary (1060–77) and Kiev (1068–77). He also maintained the independence of Poland from Germany by skillfully taking advantage of a controversy between the German king Henry IV and Pope Gregory VII. With the help of the Pope he also renewed the crown of Poland. But after Henry IV had regained power (1077), a party of Polish nobles rebelled in his favour against Bolesław. For reasons unknown, Bolesław had decreed the execution of Bishop Stanisław of Kraków in 1079, and this led to open rebellion. Bolesław was forced to flee to Hungary, where he died in exile in 1081. His younger brother Władysław I Herman (1079–1102) sided with the imperial party and in 1088/89 married Judith, Henry's sister, and relinquished all claims to the Polish crown.

Exile of Bolesław II

Bolesław III the Wry-Mouthed, 1102–38. Władysław's younger son, Bolesław III, again strengthened the position of the Polish monarchy, expelling his elder brothers and his half brother Zbigniew (1107). Two years later he drove back a campaign of the German king Henry V into Silesia. He reconquered all of the Western Pomeranian lands during 1113–22 and incorporated Eastern Pomerania and Gdańsk into Poland. Bolesław then ordered the final and complete Christianization of Western Pomerania and forced Polish rule on the land of Lubusz (Lebus), on the Oder, thus restoring the previous boundaries of the empire of Mieszko I. But the German emperor Lothair finally pushed the German frontier to the banks of the Oder and the western shores of the Neisse (Nysa) River. Bolesław was forced to swear allegiance to Lothair in return for Western Pomerania and the island of Rügen in 1135.

The period of division. Endeavouring to reconcile the separatist demands of the provinces with the needs of national unity, Bolesław III divided Poland among his sons, with the result that Poland ceased to be a united state for two centuries. The eldest son, who was already prince of Silesia and also owned Pomorze (Pomerania), was to have seniority over his brothers and rule over "the land of the senior," with its capital in Kraków; this territory stretched from western Little Poland to central Poland and on to the Baltic shore (eastern Pomerania and Gdańsk). His brothers ruled over Great Poland with Poznań and western Kujavia, Mazovia (in the basin of the middle Vistula) and eastern Kujavia (within the Vistula bend), and Sandomierz (east of Little Poland).

The seniority system. A "seniority constitution" was also introduced with this arrangement, but the plan immediately led to strife. The first "senior," Władysław II the Exile (1138–46), was forced into exile and fled to Germany. His brother Bolesław IV the Curly, hereditary duke of Mazovia, asserted himself as senior between 1146 and 1173, but this led to conflict with the German emperor Frederick I Barbarossa, who intervened twice (1163 and 1172) to secure Silesia for the sons of Władysław II. Władysław's sons divided it among themselves and founded the lineage of the Silesian Piasts; yet another son became the third senior. Of these sons, Mieszko III the Old (1173–77) was exiled from Kraków during a rebellion in 1177 but succeeded in retaining his hereditary land, Great Poland. His youngest brother, Casimir II the Just (1177–94), succeeded as senior after him and, in 1186, also acquired Mazovia, thus becoming the ancestor of the Mazovian line of the Piasts. After the Congress of Łęczyca in 1180, the land of the senior—Little Poland with its capital, the city of Kraków—became a hereditary land like the other lands. Both Pope Alexander III and the emperor Frederick I recognized this decision, but one of its great disadvantages was that the internal unity of Poland would be constantly exposed to foreign hereditary claims as a result. Leszek the White was the last duke who claimed the honour of senior with some success, but he was assassinated together with other Piast dukes in 1227.

The reign of Mieszko the Old

Territorial losses. The internal disintegration of Poland led to the secession of the lands along the Baltic Sea and other border regions. Bogusław I (who ruled about 1156–87), the son of Warcisław I, was forced to yield Western Pomerania to the Danish crown. Even the reigning governor of Eastern Pomerania and Gdańsk, Świętopełk I (died 1266), took advantage of the weakness of the Piasts. Instrumental in the assassination of Leszek the White, he asserted his country's independence and styled himself sovereign duke of Eastern Pomerania, though regarded as a usurper by the Piasts.

The Teutonic Order. The establishment of the Order of the Teutonic Knights, a German crusading organization that had lost a sphere for its activities in Palestine, was of dangerous consequence for Poland. His lands harried by pagan Lithuanians, Jatvingians, and Prussians, Duke Konrad I of Mazovia (died 1247) called for help from the Teutonic Order in 1225–26, leaving them the lands of Chełmno (Kulm) east of the lower Vistula River as a territorial base for combat and control of the Prussians in 1228–30. The grand master of the Teutonic Knights, Hermann von Salza, received sovereign rights over the "masterless heathen country" of the Prussians in the Golden Bull of Rimini (1226) from the emperor Frederick II and in the Privilegium of Rieti (1234) from Pope Gregory IX. In spite of Konrad I's claim to sovereignty over the land, the Order established a system of local government in Chełmno and in Prussia. The subjugation and Christianization of Prussia was completed by 1283. The Teutonic Order soon became the principal military power in Europe.

Supremacy of the Teutonic Order

Internal developments. In the era of knighthood, from about 1025 to 1241, the Polish aristocracy owned large landed estates and also occupied the most important administrative positions at court and in the provinces. With the continuous partition of the country from 1138 on, similar posts were also established within each individual duchy. The internal unity of the Polish nation remained intact, and, in accordance with Polish law, the dukes exercised no personal power but a collective sovereignty. From about 1058 Kraków was considered the common capital for about five centuries. A Latin church organization emerged, and the most important protector of the unity of Poland was the metropolitanate of Gniezno. The archbishopric of Gniezno held the largest estates in Poland (1136), controlling 149 cities and villages. The oldest monastery of Poland was established about 1044 in Tyniec (near Kraków) by the Benedictines, and the order of the Cistercians led the second wave. When Bishop Stanisław was canonized in 1253, Poland acquired a new national patron saint whose cult spread rapidly in the church province of Gniezno. As part of the community of the Holy See, Polish church members contributed the special levy, Peter's Penny, to Rome. The Synod of Łęczyca (1285) further promoted unity by demanding the advancement of the Polish language.

The Mongol invasions and attempts at reunification. The Mongol invasion (1241–42), in Poland's period of division, turned the tide of Poland's history. The Mongol leader Batu Khan first conquered Kiev and most of the Russian principalities before defeating the Polish army at Chmielnik and the Silesian knights of the Teutonic Order at Legnica (Liegnitz; 1241). This frustrated the attempt of the two Silesian dukes Henry I and Henry II to unite all the Polish lands. The Mongols retired in 1242 to elect a new great khan in Mongolia but still remained masters, for another 50 years, of Red Ruthenia, east of Little Poland; from this base their repeated raids devastated Poland. Meanwhile, Great Poland and especially Mazovia suffered from raids by the pagan Lithuanians (1246–1307) and Jatvingians (1248–82). The Mazovian border region around Drohiczyn on the Bug River was lost to Mongol Red Ruthenia around 1241–52, and the land of Lubus with its river passage across the Oder River to the Ascanians of Brandenburg, in about 1249–52. The Bohemian king Wenceslas II (1278–1305) attempted a new dynastic reunification of Poland. Establishing his sovereignty over most of the Silesian duchies around 1289–91, he also gained supremacy over the Duchy of Kraków in 1291–92.

The Mongol raids

Przemysł II. His opponent was Przemysł II (1279–96),

who had reunited Great Poland (including Gniezno) in 1279 and Eastern Pomerania in 1294. His coronation by the archbishop in 1295 in Gniezno reestablished the kingdom of Poland. He was assassinated in 1296, presumably at the instigation of the Margrave of Brandenburg.

Wenceslas II. Wenceslas (Wacław) II of Bohemia, who succeeded him as king (1300–05), ruled over about two-thirds of all Polish territory. He considered these lands as an extension of Bohemia and, consequently, as part of the Holy Roman Empire. His death in 1305 and the assassination of his son Wenceslas III the following year left both the Polish and the Bohemian thrones vacant.

Władysław I the Short, 1314–33. The minor Piast prince Władysław the Short availed himself of the support of Hungary and the traditional protection of the Holy See. He occupied Little Poland in 1305 and sought the help of the Teutonic Order to regain Eastern Pomerania in 1308. The Teutonic Knights, however, bought the interests to these lands from the Brandenburg rulers and established themselves as the legal authority, incorporating Eastern Pomerania into Prussia. By 1314 Władysław had secured Great Poland, and in 1320 he was crowned king of Poland as Władysław I with the consent of the Roman Curia. This act restored the Polish Crown through a national dynasty, and for the next 475 years the crown was to remain the symbol of unity for Poland. The Piast dukes welcomed immigrant Germans and Flemings into Polish territories, and resettlement took place according to the municipal law of Magdeburg, based on German law.

Władysław I faced the opposition of a coalition between Bohemia and the Teutonic Order. The new Bohemian king, John of Luxemburg, laid claim to the Polish crown, and almost all of the Piast dukes in Silesia had recognized him as their feudal lord by 1327–29. Only the little principality of Wieluń (1321–29) was loyal to Władysław I. He instituted lawsuits against the Teutonic Order for the sovereignty of Eastern Pomerania but without success. The Teutonic Knights and the Bohemians terribly devastated Great Poland, especially in the war of 1328–32. At the Battle of Płowce (1331), however, Władysław drove them back and, in alliance with Hungary and Lithuania, secured Poland. Ties with Hungary were strengthened by the marriage of Władysław's daughter Elizabeth (Elżbieta) to the new Angevin king of Hungary, Charles I, in 1320, and the Polish crown prince Casimir (Kazimierz) was married to the Lithuanian princess Anna (Aldona) in 1325, thus creating a pact with Lithuania.

Casimir III the Great, 1333–70. Władysław's son Casimir was a talented statesman and administrator. During the congresses of Trenčin and Vyšehrad in Upper Hungary (Slovakia), he persuaded John I of Luxemburg to relinquish his claims to the Polish crown. In return, after an unsuccessful campaign in 1348 and in face of the Silesian Piast dukes' support of the Bohemian crown, Casimir was forced to renounce finally all demands on Silesia, the country's most densely populated and wealthiest region.

In the Treaty of Kalisz in 1343, Casimir relinquished all claims to Eastern Pomerania in favour of the Teutonic Order—for the time being. Instead, he coerced the Piast dukes of Mazovia to recognize him as their overlord and seized parts of Mazovia. He also regained some of the lands in the west that had been annexed by Brandenburg. Between 1340 and 1352 Casimir won Red Ruthenia with the cities of Przemyśl, Lwów (Lvov), and Halicz; and in 1366 he extended his rule over the Ruthenian principalities of Chełm, Bełz, Włodzimierz, and Podolia. Casimir died in 1370 without a male heir, but in his will he appointed his grandson Casimir to be prince of Pomerania and awarded him parts of the Polish territory to tie Western Pomerania to Poland.

Louis I of Hungary, 1370–82. Poland nevertheless remained a unified kingdom under Casimir's successor, his nephew Louis I of Hungary. Louis, however, regarded Poland as his secondary kingdom, and a governor took over the administration of Halicz Ruthenia. The Polish aristocracy, a deciding factor in the succession to the throne of Poland in 1370 and 1382, obtained from Louis the grant of special privileges at Košice (Kaschau; 1374), which formed the basis of a Polish "Magna Carta."

Internal developments and reform. The years from 1320 to 1382 marked the founding of many new cities, especially during the reign of Casimir the Great. Castles and fortifications, town halls, and merchant houses also were erected. Casimir also established local courts of justice for the cities of Little Poland (1356) and Great Poland (1365), in order to separate his country from the jurisdiction of Magdeburg and the need for its appellate court.

Even though a new social class of burghers and merchants evolved in the cities of Poland, the aristocracy remained the most influential group in politics. The first confederation of nobles in Polish history was founded in Great Poland in 1352–56. Since the previous official positions in the separate palatinates of Poland had long before become the benefices of the aristocracy, Casimir and Louis appointed a governor (*starosta capitaneus*) for each section of the country, after the example set by Wenceslas II (1291). The office of *starosta* remained the most important branch of executive power during the next 470 years. In the Statute of Wiślica (about 1346) Casimir codified the law that was in force in Little Poland. This *jus Polonicum*—the law of the nobility (as opposed to the *jus Teutonicum,* which was the law for the burgher-peasant population of Poland)—was later extended and applied throughout Poland.

The Roman Catholic Church influenced the character of public life in Poland. Poland had lost Silesia in 1348, but the Silesian bishopric of Wrocław remained under the church authority of Gniezno for another 400 years. The Dominican, Franciscan, and Augustine mendicant preaching orders had already built 80 monasteries in the metropolitanate of Gniezno by 1382. Yet, in spite of the power of the Roman Catholic Church, the ideal of religious tolerance became entrenched in the consciousness of the Polish people. In addition to Gniezno, the metropolitanate of Halicz–Lwów was established; and a separate Eastern Orthodox metropolitanate in Halicz (later Lwów), and an Armenian bishopric (later archbishopric) of Lwów were founded. Casimir's kingdom was the only continental European country where several Christian creeds were able to live side by side for any length of time two centuries before the Reformation.

Casimir the Great also provided, with the Statute of Wiślica (1346), protection for the Jews from pogroms and ritual murders at the hands of the Christians. When the Black Death raged through the German lands between 1348 and 1352, more than 300 Jewish communities were either destroyed or expelled from their homelands. The survivors migrated to Poland. Ever since, the majority of Polish Jews has consisted of Ashkenazim (from Germany). Retaining their own Middle High German language—later evolved into Yiddish—most of the Jews rejected any language assimilation until their near extermination by the Nazis during World War II. The Poland of Casimir thus developed into a cosmopolitan empire: Poles, Germans, Ruthenians, Flemings, Walachians, Jews, Armenians, and even Tatars and Karaites living together. Religious and political tolerance was reflected in the founding in 1364 of the University of Kraków, after Prague the second oldest university in Central or Eastern Europe, whose brilliant faculty of law prepared for the later juridical thinking during the Renaissance in Europe.

THE JAGIELLON DYNASTY, 1382–1572

Jadwiga and Władysław II Jagiełło. The union between Poland and Hungary was broken with the death of Louis because the Hungarian aristocracy chose his eldest daughter, Maria, to be their queen, whereas the Polish aristocracy gave preference to his 10-year-old daughter Jadwiga (1384). This was the first step in the direction of developing an elected Polish monarch. The Polish aristocracy favoured a dynastic alliance with Lithuania, especially in order to regain Red Ruthenia and Podolia, which had become estranged from Poland under Louis' regime.

Union of Poland and Lithuania. The grand duke of Lithuania (from 1377 to 1401), Jagiełło (Jogaila), was still a heathen; but after adoption by the widow queen Elizabeth in the Union of Krewo (1385), he was married to the crown princess Jadwiga. Jagiełło thus accepted the

Catholic faith and became the recognized "Master and King of Poland" under the assumed name of Władysław II Jagiełło in 1386. This procedure created a Polish-Lithuanian union that continued under the Jagiełło dynasty during the following 183 years. But the effect was that Poland was able to incorporate, during 1385–86, a state about four times as large as the original Polish realm. The bishopric of Wilno was established in 1387 to convert the Lithuanian people to the Catholic faith. Another area belonged to the Eastern Orthodox Church. The polyethnic, multireligious, and legal-constitutional structure of the Jagiełło empire was more complicated than ever before. The authority of Władysław II also included the old Russian capital Kiev, which had come under Lithuanian suzerainty in 1366 and was now reduced to the status of a residential border town. To the southeast of these lands stretched more than 58,000 square miles of almost uninhabited steppe country, which belonged to Lithuania in name only. The annexation of Lithuania secured the eastern boundaries of Poland against the attacks of the Mongol and Tatar tribes as well as against those from the great principality of Moscow, then under Mongol and Tatar control. It meant also, however, that Poland had to defend Lithuania against the incursions of the Teutonic Order. With the help of the Lithuanians (1387), Poland was able to renew the incorporation of Red Ruthenia and Podolia and to assert its authority over the principality of Moldavia (1387–1497), until then a minor country under Hungarian rule. This gave Poland access to the rich Oriental commerce that flowed via the cities of Kaffa (Feodosia, in the Crimea) and Akkerman (now Belgorod–Dnestrovsky).

Władysław II and Vytautas. Władysław II and Jadwiga reigned together until Jadwiga's death in 1399. Władysław then ruled as the sole king of Poland until 1434. In Lithuania, Władysław found it expedient to acknowledge his cousin Vytautas (Witold; 1392–1430), first as governor, then as duke (1401), and finally as grand duke of Lithuania (1413). But he himself kept supreme command. To free his hands to attack the Tatars and annex Moscow, Vytautas surrendered the Duchy of Samogitia (Żmudź), which linked the Teutonic Order lands of Prussia and of Courland, to the Teutonic Order in 1398 in return for the cessation of all hostilities between them. He suffered

Defeat
by the
Mongols

a grave defeat in 1399, however, on the Vorskla River against the Mongols of the Golden Horde, which ended Lithuania's eastward expansion. Vytautas also supported rebellions in the still pagan Samogitia (1401 and 1409), which prompted the Teutonic grand master Ulrich von Jungingen to declare war against Władysław II in 1409. The Teutonic Knights suffered a decisive defeat in the Battle of Grunwald (Tannenberg) in 1410. The first Treaty of Toruń (1411) returned Samogitia to Lithuania; the return of Eastern Pomerania to Poland was discussed at the Council of Constance (1414–18) and was a factor in two later wars (1421–22 and 1431–35), but the Order remained in possession of the territory. When the Protestant Hussite rebellion broke out in 1419, Władysław II favoured the Hussites, even promoting his relative Sigismund (Zygmunt) as the Hussite candidate for the Bohemian throne in 1422. Because this brought him under suspicion of being a heretic and friend of the heathens, Władysław

Edict of
Wieluń

felt obliged to issue the strong Edict of Wieluń in 1424, against Hussite trends among the Polish nobility, and he crushed a pro-Hussite confederation of the lower Polish nobility in 1438–39. Władysław had obtained 16 mainly German mountain cities in the Spisz (south of the High Tatra Mountains) in 1412, thus giving Poland a share in the rich mining activities of upper Hungary.

Władysław III, 1434–44. Władysław II was succeeded on his death by his 10-year-old son, Władysław III, the chief position in the realm being held by the most eminent of the Kraków magnates, Zbigniew Oleśnicki, bishop of Kraków and one of the previous king's chief advisers. Władysław III renewed the Polish-Hungarian union with the help of the Hungarian commander in chief János Hunyadi. Under the influence of the strongly Roman Catholic Oleśnicki, he organized a crusade to save Byzantium, which was threatened by the Ottoman Empire.

Władysław died when only 20 in the catastrophic defeat of Varna (1444) on the Black Sea coast. The Ottoman troops conquered Byzantium in 1453 and marched immediately against Hungary. The threat was delayed for some decades, however, when Hunyadi defeated the Ottomans in 1456. But the Hungarian imperial administration of Hunyadi terminated the Polish-Hungarian union.

Casimir IV, 1447–92. The younger brother of Władysław III, Casimir, had been ruling as the grand duke of Lithuania since 1440, but it was only after a long interregnum in Poland that he was finally recognized as the king. He signed a treaty with Moscow that established the Lithuanian boundary about 90 miles west of Moscow. This secured the eastern boundary for 37 years. The peace in the east became important when, in 1454, uprising against the rule of the Teutonic Knights broke into the open, led by the cities of Gdańsk, Toruń, and Elbląg, which requested Casimir IV to integrate the Prussian-Eastern Pomeranian lands of the Teutonic Knights with Poland (1454). This marked the start of the Thirteen Years' War against the Teutonic Order. The second Treaty of Toruń (1466) recovered for Poland the former Eastern Pomerania (which received the new name of Royal Prussia), along with the bishopric of Warmia (Ermland). The rest of the territory of the Teutonic Knights acknowledged the king of Poland, and Königsberg became the new residence of the Order's grand master. Poland won back the access to the Baltic Sea that it had lost in 1308–09, and Polish rule stretched from the Baltic Sea to the Black Sea for a period of 32 years.

Extension
of Polish
rule

The King's main interest still lay with the so-often-attempted union with Bohemia and Hungary. Casimir IV succeeded in temporarily acquiring the Kingdom of Bohemia in 1471 (finally acquired 1478–79), for his oldest son Władysław (Vladislas). The smaller Bohemian lands, Moravia and Silesia, remained under the rule of Matthias I Corvinus, the son of János Hunyadi. But after the death of Matthias, even Moravia, Silesia, and Hungary recognized Władysław as their king (1491–92). The result of this dynastic union was the creation of one of the largest empires in Europe. By 1491–92 Casimir IV controlled an area of at least 336,000 square miles, while his son Władysław ruled the Bohemian lands of the crown of Wenceslas and the Hungarian lands of the crown of Stephen, an area of at least 174,000 square miles. This agglomeration of states was, however, as much torn by internal strife as it was exposed to external danger—the greatest external threat coming from the Ottoman Empire and its ally, the tsar of Moscow.

Political changes. Political authority in Poland was gradually taken over by the aristocracy. Aided by the mechanism of the election of kings, the many wars, and the tax exemptions, they were able to slowly reorganize the kingdom into a monarchy of the estates. The main organ of aristocratic authority was the Privy Council (1385–1493), which became the Senate after 1493. The rights and privileges of the nobility were successively established between 1422 and 1433, securing for them the right to a voice in political matters, their factual exemption from taxation, and finally the political and judicial maxim of habeas corpus, or no imprisonment without trial. After the Union of Horodło (1413), the regional assemblies slowly grew into provincial diets (*sejmiki*), becoming recognized as standing establishments in all parts of the country with the Privilegium of Nieszawa (1454). In addition to the Polish diet (Sejm), the Prussian diet held a special position with its own particular law. The lower nobility represented its own interests (usually directed against the hegemony of the aristocracy) through elected delegates.

Privileges
of the
nobility

These delegates marked the beginning of parliamentarianism in Poland when they assembled for the first time in a House of Legates at Piotrków (1493). After this, the Polish Senate became the upper house and the House of Legates became the lower house of the Polish parliament, again called the Sejm. Lithuania also absorbed the culture and the system of government of Poland through the German municipal laws, introduced by the Polish burghers. According to the statutes of 1386–87, at first only the newly converted Roman Catholic nobles were equal to the nobility of Poland, excluding the Eastern Orthodox Boyars, many of whom seceded to the Tsar of Russia. But the Lithuanian and Ruthenian nobles were gradually assimilated into the Polish sphere of interests, and in 1447–93 the first diets of the great principality were formed.

After the death of Casimir IV, his second son, John I Albert (1492–1501), ascended the throne of Poland, and the two countries were temporarily separated, his third son, Alexander, becoming grand prince of Lithuania. Alexander succeeded John Albert as king of Poland (1501–06) through the Union of Mielnik (1501), and Poland and Lithuania were thus united again. A statute of 1499 called the combined kingdoms a "republic" for the first time, terming the Union of Mielnik an indivisible body. The union became even further consolidated under the reign of the fourth of the Jagiellon brothers (Casimir IV's sons), King Sigismund I the Old (1506–48). Ruled by the eldest of the Jagiellons, Władysław (1491–1516) and his son Louis II (1516–26), the combined Kingdom of Bohemia and Hungary remained only loosely connected with the unified Kingdom of Poland-Lithuania.

The Ottoman and Russian incursions. The Ottoman Empire directed its attacks mainly against the unified states of the Jagiellons, conquering the commercial trading cities of Kaffa (1475), Kilia, and Akkerman (1484). Poland was cut off entirely from the trade with the Orient. In addition, Poland found yet another enemy in the Tatars in the Crimea. These had come under Ottoman rule in 1475, and from 1492 they undertook pillaging and slave raids into Red Ruthenia and Little Poland. The Tatars of the Crimea pushed into Polish territory with the aid of the Ottomans, reaching Kraków in 1498–99. Moldavia had also come under the influence of the Ottomans and Tatars. John Albert, the brilliant Polish commander in chief, had always been victorious against the Tatars, but he suffered a heavy defeat at the hands of the Moldavians in the forests of Suceava in 1497.

Tsar Ivan III the Great took advantage of the situation, and, allying himself with the Tatars of the Crimea, he attacked Lithuania twice (1486–94 and 1500–03), capturing all the principalities on the Oka and Desna rivers as far as the middle of the Dnepr River. Another ally of Russia, the German emperor Maximilian I, laid claim to Bohemia and Hungary and prompted the states of the Teutonic Order to rebel against Poland. The result was that the grand master Frederick of Saxony (1498–1510) refused to swear his oath of allegiance, and his successor, Albert (Albrecht) of Hohenzollern, a cousin of the Elector of Brandenburg, went so far as to enter into an alliance with Russia (1517). Poland supplied armed help to Lithuania, but in spite of this Russia took the city of Smoleńsk (1514) in the course of two wars (1507–08 and 1512–22). After this, at the First Congress of Vienna (1515), Maximilian changed sides, renouncing the help of both Russia and the Teutonic Order. Instead, he entered into a mutual hereditary agreement with the Jagiellon kings with respect to the succession in Bohemia and Hungary.

The Ottoman troops advanced through Little Poland (1524), under the leadership of their sultan Süleyman I the Magnificent, and at the first Battle of Mohács (1526) they conquered the greater part of Hungary, killing King Louis II, the last Hungarian Jagiellon. The Ottomans next threatened Vienna (1529), and Poland found it wise to conclude a perpetual peace agreement with them in 1533. This did not, however, prevent the Muslims from threatening Poland's southern boundaries from bases in Hungary—a threat that was to last for about 140 years.

Renewed Moldavian and Russian attacks were repelled by the Polish troops under the brilliant leadership of Jan Tarnowski. Sigismund I the Old was able to incorporate the Duchy of Mazovia into his empire after the death of the last of the Piasts in Mazovia (1524–29). His campaign from 1519 to 1522 also secured Polish sovereignty over Prussia. Albert of Hohenzollern became the first secular duke of Prussia to swear an oath of allegiance to Sigismund (1525), and the land came to be known as Ducal Prussia.

Sigismund II Augustus, 1548–72. The son of Sigismund the Old, Sigismund Augustus, was the last Polish Jagiellon. Trying to secure his country against the Ottoman and Russian empires, he sought alliances with the emperor Charles V and the Roman king Ferdinand I (1549). This at least brought him Charles's final renunciation of any intervention in settling the question of the constitutional position of both Royal and Ducal Prussia. For 24 years Tsar Ivan IV the Terrible had led a war of conquest to obtain the remains of the lands of the Teutonic Order in Livonia (1558–82), and he succeeded in occupying part of the territory. This prompted Sigismund Augustus to enter into an agreement (the Union of Wilno [1561]), with the last grand master of the Order, Wilhelm Ketteler, integrating Livonia directly with Poland while Courland (now a secular duchy) had to recognize the authority of Poland. This antagonized Russia, which invaded Poland and conquered the lands of Połock on the Dvina River in the first Nordic War (1563–70). Under pressure of the Russian threat and the lack of an heir to the throne, the Sejm combined the former crown lands, Lithuania, Royal Prussia, and Livonia in the Union of Lublin, creating a unified and indivisible republic (1569).

Political changes. The Polish population now began to integrate the nobility, the burghers, and a large part of the peasantry in the Lithuanian–Ruthenian regions in the east. From about 1420, but in particular between 1540 and 1580, the people of densely populated Mazovia began to migrate. Resettling, they colonized the enormous virgin forests in the west of Lithuania—particularly Podlasie. Moving south, they also settled in the Duchy of Prussia. As early as 1582, there were more than 150,000 Jews among the many nationalities of the Polish Commonwealth, more than in all the rest of Europe. The two main parts of the country that composed the Polish Republic—the crown lands and Lithuania—each retained its own ministers, treasury, and army. Unification was finally accomplished by the consolidation of a common elective kingdom with a diet consisting of two houses. The upper house seated about 100 senators, and the lower house about 150 delegates. This arrangement created a Royal Republic in 1569, with a constitution that was similar to the constitutions of England and Hungary, and it remained basically unchanged for the next 226 years.

Between 1493 and 1569 the Polish Estate Kingdom slowly evolved into a parliamentary monarchy, which was governed almost entirely by the nobility. The Sejm of Piotrków, in 1493, was the first of about 200 diets that would be convened in the course of the next 300 years. From the assembly of the Sejm of Mielnik in 1501, the king was regarded as the president of the Senate, and in 1505 the constitutional act Nihil Novi ("No innovations") decreed the making of laws to be the sole right of the parliament. The supreme authority of the aristocracy led to a growing opposition from the ranks of the lower nobility, who were incensed at the aristocracy's virtual escape from the burdens of taxation. The lower nobility at last secured their own appointment to the supervision of the highest courts of appeal and secured the formal recognition of their equality with the aristocracy, together with the prohibition of titles (*e.g.,* duke, prince, margrave, count). The superiority of the aristocracy over the lower nobility continued, however, since the aristocracy remained in possession of the wealthiest estates, while the lower nobility were very often poor and propertyless.

Economic changes. The "Golden Age" of Poland expressed itself in the wealth of the country and a favourable boom in its foreign trade. The autonomous free republic of Gdańsk (Danzig) controlled about 80 percent of Poland's foreign trade and became the most important trading city of central and eastern Europe by 1576. The production of raw materials was in the hands of the propertied Polish nobles, now turned into farming entrepreneurs.

The nobles extended their previous manorial domination over the peasant class with statutes passed in 1496, 1518–20, 1532, and 1543 that reduced the peasants to virtually the same status as property; they came under the jurisdiction of the nobles and, as a result, lived under conditions of virtual slavery as cheap labour for the nobles' farmstead economy. The discovery of the Americas paved the way to the second feudal system in Poland, made possible by the imports of gold and silver from the American conti-

Margin notes:

Union of Mielnik

Rebellion of the Teutonic Order

Ducal Prussia

Importance of Gdańsk

nent. In contrast, the same era led to the establishment of modern manufacturing plants and industrial enterprises in western Europe, ushering in the period of early capitalism.

Cultural developments. The Renaissance and the Age of Humanism set their stamp for ever after on the spiritual and intellectual life in Poland. The first Polish books were printed between 1514 and 1524; the art of book printing spread, as did general school education. Young Poles studied at major foreign universities, particularly at Padua, at Bologna, and at the Sorbonne, as well as at the Protestant universities of Wittenberg, Leipzig, Königsberg, Tübingen, and Basel. The department of astronomy at the University of Kraków achieved renown through Nicolaus Copernicus (Mikołaj Kopernik; 1473–1543) and his work on the motions of the planets. Polish literary language came into its own, supplanting the use of Latin alone by scholars.

High level of education

The Reformation. The Reformation came to Poland from Germany, Italy, France, and Bohemia between 1523 and 1526. Lutheran and Calvinist denominations were established alongside the originally Hussite Bohemian Brethren and the Anti-Trinitarians, or Arians (from about 1562–65). Under the leadership of Laelius Socinus (1525–62) and Faustus Socinus (1539–1604) the Arians strove for both a rational secularization of religious life and a radical change in society, including the liberation of the peasantry. In spite of the first suppressive edicts of 1520–26, the Reformation gained strength, particularly after the Sejm suspended the secular execution of ecclesiastical sentences (1552). After this, Poland was the only country in Europe without religious persecutions for about the next 130 years. The Lutheran, Calvinist, and Hussite denominations consolidated in 1570 at the Concord of Sandomierz, but this soon disintegrated because of dogmatic differences. The Compact of Warsaw in 1573 removed the Catholic Church from its dominant position, introducing the constitutional equality of all religions—the first enactment in Europe of complete religious tolerance.

THE ROYAL REPUBLIC AND THE VASA DYNASTY, 1572–1697

The Interregnum and reform of the monarchy. The Interregnum, or period without a ruler, lasted from 1572 to 1575. During this time the republican constitution was further improved and extended. The election of Henry III of Valois (1573–74)—King Henry III of France from 1574—established the basic rule that not only the council of the aristocracy but also all nobles and squires should elect the king. This meant a formal victory for the lower nobility and the founding of the Polish rule by the nobility. The fundamental basis of the constitution, the "Henrician Articles" of 1573, required the king to swear an oath reducing his authority to no more than that of a contract partner in a sovereign nation of nobles. The king was also obliged to convoke the Sejm every two years; and between the sessions he was to be advised by a group of senators. Should the king fail to observe any of these articles, the nation was ipso facto absolved from its allegiance.

The next elected king was Stephen Báthory (Stefan Batory; 1576–86), who had defeated the emperor Maximilian II. During his reign Jan Zamoyski, who had helped to gain the victory for the lower nobility during the Interregnum, rose to the positions of grand chancellor (1578) and grand hetman (commander in chief; 1580). Stephen Báthory and Zamoyski defeated Tsar Ivan IV with three brilliant campaigns (1578–81), forcing the Russians to return the occupied territories of Livonia and Połock by 1582.

Successful campaigns against Tsar Ivan IV

Sigismund III Vasa, 1587–1632. Báthory was succeeded by Sigismund III Vasa, who defeated Maximilian of Austria. Since he was also the legitimate king of Sweden—as the son of John III Vasa of Sweden and of Catherine, daughter of Sigismund I—Sigismund established a brief Polish-Swedish union, but this soon fell apart as the result of Swedish-Lutheran opposition to the Catholic faith of their king.

Revolting against Sigismund III in 1599–1600, Sweden pursued the Swedish–Polish war for 35 years, but Sigismund never relinquished his demands for the Swedish crown. The Polish grand hetmans Zamoyski and Jan Chodkiewicz were at first able to repel the attacks of the Swedes against Livonia (1600–09). They won a famous victory in the Battle of Kirkholm (1605), although outnumbered four to one by the Swedes. In the meantime, a Polish volunteer corps helped the False Dmitry to gain the tsar's throne in 1605–06. Sigismund found it necessary to openly intervene in Russia (1609–13) when a coup d'état took place there. Under the leadership of Stanisław Żółkiewski, the Polish army won a brilliant victory at Kłuszyn (1610) against a sixfold Russian-Swedish majority. Polish troops occupied Moscow (1610–12), but they were driven out by the new tsar, Michael Romanov. The important fort of Smoleńsk remained with Poland.

At the outbreak of the Thirty Years' War (1618), Sigismund remained officially neutral but favoured the Austrian side. The Prince of Transylvania had advanced and besieged Vienna, but a decisive victory by the Polish army in 1619 prepared the way for the Austrian victory at the Bila Hora (Weisser Berg, or White Mountain) in 1620. Although the Poles won a decisive victory against the Turks also at the Battle of Chocim on the Dnestr River in 1621, the Turkish attacks did not cease for another decade. Taking advantage of this Polish predicament, Sigismund's cousin, Gustav II Adolf of Sweden, occupied Livonia and its important Baltic seaport Riga (1621). At the Peace of Altmark, the Swedes temporarily gained possession of Livonia as well as of some Royal Prussian port cities (1629–35).

Władysław IV Vasa, 1632–48. A highly talented field marshal, Sigismund's son Władysław IV (1632–48) assured the existence of Poland when he repelled the renewed attacks of the Turks, Russians, and Swedes (1633–34). He also reconquered, in 1635, the Prussian ports on the Baltic Sea that Sweden had occupied. But his plans to establish a Polish navy that would hold its own against the Swedish domination of the Baltic, to regain sovereign rights over Livonia (1639), and to prepare for an extensive war against the Ottoman Empire (1646–47) were all frustrated by the disinclination of the Polish nobles to wage wars. They wanted peace at any price in order to take advantage of the splendid opportunities opening up on the European market in the wake of the Thirty Years' War.

The prominent powers in northern, eastern, and southeastern Europe had attacked Poland constantly and had forced the republic into repeated compromises on the question of sovereign rights over the Ukraine and the Duchy of Prussia. Meanwhile, the nomadic Ruthenian-Eastern Orthodox farmers—the Cossacks—had established themselves in the Ukraine, and their number was steadily growing with the addition of escaping peasants from Poland and Russia. The Polish landed estate owners could hardly keep them under control over the vastness of the barely populated steppe that the Cossacks inhabited. The Cossacks eventually rebelled against the constant attempts of the Polish estate owners to reduce them to the state of bonded peasants, and their leaders demanded a position of equality with the Polish nobility. The Cossacks remained the foremost social danger in the republic, allying themselves with the Tatars in 1648.

The Cossack revolt

In 1618 John Sigismund, elector of Brandenburg (1608–20), also became duke in Prussia, and thus the two crowns were in personal union, though the sovereignty over Ducal Prussia remained with the Polish crown. His grandson, however, the Great Elector Frederick William (1640–88), by clever maneuvering between Sweden and Poland, succeeded in removing Ducal Prussia from Polish sovereignty by the Treaty of Welawa (Wehlau) in 1657. From then on, the Brandenburg state of Prussia became the most dangerous of Poland's neighbours, not least because Frederick William intended to establish a territorial connection between Western Pomerania and the Duchy of Prussia, henceforth a leading aim of Brandenburg-Prussian politics until the First Partition of Poland about 115 years later. It threatened to cut off Poland from its connections with the Baltic Sea.

Economic and political changes. The booming years between 1577 and 1654 became the high point in the history of Polish economics. At that time, Poland was considered, appropriately, the "granary of Europe." Polish grain was exported to France, England, Spain, and sometimes even to Italy and the Middle East via Amsterdam, the most important grain stock exchange. Gdańsk soared in importance to the rank of a trade city of world renown. As a result of this foreign-trade boom, the landowners pushed the farmsteading economy to its very limits, developing estates into tremendous areas. In many cases the servitude of the peasantry became actual slavery. This caused a number of small rebellions by the peasants, many of whom escaped into the Ukraine.

The economic power of the magnates encouraged the forming of groups of supporters among propertyless voters who would keep their votes at the disposal of one particular aristocrat, thus enabling the magnate to command entire districts of the provincial Sejm and, if necessary, even to paralyze it. In this way the original, formal "democracy of nobles" based on about 150,000 voters had evolved into an oligarchy of about 300 families. This was to prove a decisive factor in the later disintegration of the Polish republic. The undermining of the power of the Sejm culminated in a procedure that made it possible for just one delegate to disrupt it through the liberum veto. The liberum veto was based on the assumption of the political equality of every Polish gentleman, with the corollary that every measure introduced into the Sejm must be adopted unanimously. Consequently, if any single deputy believed that a measure already approved of by the rest of the house might be injurious to his constituency, he had the right to exclaim "Nie pozwalam" ("I disapprove"), the measure in question falling at once to the ground. All efforts toward increasing the power of the central government were held to be against traditional freedom and were opposed. This principle was extended still further until a deputy, by interposing his individual veto, could at any time dissolve the Sejm, and all measures previously passed had to be resubmitted for the consideration of the following Sejm. The liberum veto was used for the first time during the Sejm of 1652, but before the end of the 17th century it was used so recklessly that all business was frequently brought to a standstill. It thus became the chief instrument of foreign ambassadors or native magnates for dissolving inconvenient sessions, as a deputy could always be bribed to exercise his veto.

The Counter-Reformation. Poland experienced the effects of the Counter-Reformation after the Council of Trent (1545–63). Led by prominent scholars such as Cardinal Stanislaus Hosius (Stanisław Hozjusz), who introduced the Society of Jesus, or Jesuits, in Poland in 1564, a total of approximately 50 Jesuit establishments were founded in the republic between 1564 and 1654. The Jesuit colleges in Połock, Smoleńsk, and Černigov and the Jesuit Academy of Wilno (founded in 1578–80) were mainly intended for the conversion of Eastern Orthodox Russia to Catholicism. Through their colleges and schools, the Jesuits established a dominant influence on the education of the Polish people that would last for about two centuries. Piotr Skarga was the most prominent theologian and politician among the Jesuits. The Order of the Camaldolese also supported the Counter-Reformation. The Counter-Reformation led to religious disorders; many of the Protestant churches were closed, especially in the large royal cities (particularly between 1574 and 1612); and the number of Protestant parishes diminished as many of the aristocratic dynasties reverted to Catholicism. By 1650 there were not more than 270 non-Catholic parishes left in the country. Only the established German-Lutheran Church in the city republics of Prussia and the Calvinist Church in Lithuania (approximately 140 churches) remained important. The most significant result of the Counter-Reformation was the Synod of Brześć in 1596, whereby six of the 10 Eastern Orthodox eparchies acknowledged the authority of the Holy See in Rome. Declared illegal and schismatic in 1595, the Eastern Orthodox faith was again recognized in 1635. Its spiritual centre became the Academy of Kiev, modeled after the colleges of the Jesuit order. The Protestant academies of Gdańsk and Leszno retained their European distinction, however, and John Amos Comenius, the philosopher and pedagogue, taught in Leszno.

John II Casimir Vasa, 1648–68. The reign of the last of the Vasa kings in Poland, John II Casimir, is remembered in history as a period of bloody wars and disasters.

The era began with a rebellion of the Ukrainian Cossacks, led by Bohdan Khmelnitsky, who heavily defeated the Polish troops in 1648 and 1651 and established their own military state (1651–54) with the armed assistance of the Tatars of the Crimea and the Ottomans. In the Union of Pereyaslavl, in 1654, the Cossacks acknowledged the authority of the Russian tsar Alexis Mikhaylovich. On the strength of Cossack aid, Alexis attacked Poland, conquering almost the entire eastern part of the country, as far as Lwów, in 1654–55.

Charles X Gustav of Sweden took advantage of the Polish predicament and occupied the Polish and Lithuanian lands of the republic in 1655, receiving some support from the native aristocrats and from Frederick William of Brandenburg. John Casimir fled to Silesia, and the majority of the nobles (among them the future king John III Sobieski) recognized Charles as their king, particularly after he had promised to reconquer the eastern part of Poland from the Russians and Cossacks. The extraordinary brutality of the Swedish army, however, gave rise to a general revolt against Charles, and the Swedes were not able to take the two largest cities of Poland (Gdańsk and Lwów). The brilliant grand hetman Stefan Czarniecki eventually destroyed the Swedish and defeated Frederick William's Brandenburg army between 1655 and 1657. In the treaties of Welawa (Wehlau), Bromberg (Bydgoszcz), and Oliwa (Oliva, 1660), Poland recognized the "superior power of government" of Frederick William over the Duchy of Prussia but reserved the right to reversion with regard to the duchy and did not relinquish this right until 1773.

The Swedish invasion

The Ukraine again entered into a union with Poland in 1658, and Russia was decisively defeated in 1660–62. Nevertheless, Russia obtained Smoleńsk and the eastern half of the Ukraine in the truce of Andruszów (Andrusovo; 1667), after the rebellion of Jerzy Lubomirski against the King of Poland. Having been instrumental in bringing about the greatest catastrophe in the history of Poland, John II Casimir finally abdicated in 1668. The war, the bubonic plague, slave raids, and mass murders had reduced the total population to approximately 4,000,-000 people, or 45 percent of the former total population. The cities suffered worst of all, losing all manufacturing establishments and industrial enterprises along with three-quarters of all their inhabitants. The tremendous costs of the war caused the greatest inflation in the history of Poland. Religious feeling was fanatically inflamed since the war had been conducted in the spirit of a religious struggle, and the Protestant parishes almost totally disappeared. The constitutional maxim of religious tolerance was finally abandoned in 1648–58.

Michael (Korybut) Wiśniowiecki, 1669–73. The short reign of Michael (Korybut) Wiśniowiecki was dominated by internal fighting between the Habsburgs, led by the King, and the French-oriented faction that had gathered around John Sobieski, a military commander of rising fame. The Cossacks seceded again in 1667, allying themselves with the Ottoman Empire (1668), and in the succeeding Turkish attack in 1672–73, the Poles lost Podolia and two-thirds of the Ukraine.

John III Sobieski, 1674–96. A brilliant victory in 1673 established John Sobieski as the "vanquisher of the Turks" and brought him the crown of Poland in 1674. In spite of his many successes in the fight against the Ottomans (1675–76) and despite his liberation of Vienna in 1683—a crucial factor in the development of European history—John III Sobieski was not able to regain the regions in the southeast of the republic held by the Ottomans. He also failed in his attempts to secure the return of the Duchy of Prussia to Poland through treaties with France (1675) and Sweden (1677). Poland's participation in the Holy Alliance against the Ottoman Empire (1684) and the many Turkish campaigns of John III Sobieski (1684–92) eventually aided the development of Austria and Russia as new great European powers. With the Peace of Carlowitz (Karlowice, 1699), Poland again received Podolia and the Ukraine west of the Dnepr River. Given to Russia for two years in 1667 but never returned to Poland, the city of

Peace of Carlowitz

The Jesuits

Kiev was recognized as part of Russia in the "perpetual peace" in 1686.

THE SAXONIAN ERA AND THE RUSSIAN PROTECTORATE, 1697–1763

Augustus II the Strong, 1697–1733. On the death of John III, no fewer than 18 candidates for the vacant Polish throne presented themselves. The successful competitor was Frederick Augustus I, elector of Saxony, who renounced Lutheranism for the crown. Under his reign as Augustus II the Strong, Poland experienced a new wave of wars and catastrophes. The planned union between the industrially developed Saxony and raw material-producing Poland would have been advantageous for the economy of both countries, but that did not materialize because the King, as ambitious as he was lacking in talent, became involved in a war with Sweden through his alliances with Peter I the Great of Russia and King Frederick IV of Denmark.

The Northern War. These allies attacked Sweden and began the Northern War (1700–21). The Swedish king Charles XII repelled Denmark and Russia in 1700 and marched from Livonia into Poland (1701–02), the latter serving him as the base for his future military operations. Appointing Stanisław Leszczyński (Stanisław I) as puppet king (1704), Charles XII invaded Saxony in 1706 and forced Augustus to abdicate. During the civil war of 1704–10, Swedish troops totally devastated Poland, and the Saxonian and Russian armies fared little better. Cultural losses were enormous, and one-third of all Polish cities lay in ruins. Although by 1702 the population had recovered again, reaching about 8,000,000, war and then the bubonic plague of 1709 took their toll, and other disasters reduced the population to about 6,400,000. Poland was spared any further Swedish occupation when the Swedish troops advanced into the Ukraine, where they suffered a decisive defeat at the Battle of Poltava (1709). Stanisław Leszczyński escaped from Poland in 1710, and Augustus II again assumed the crown with the particular support of Peter the Great of Russia. Breaking all agreements with Poland, the Tsar annexed Swedish-held Livonia (1710), the very land that had given Augustus II the pretext to start the war. Then the Tsar turned east and put down the last Cossack rebellion in the Polish Ukraine (1702–04), which the Polish Sejm had provoked by despotically deciding to disband the Cossacks in 1699.

The Prussian situation. The Hohenzollern prince Frederick III had assumed the title of king of Prussia in 1701, with consent of Augustus but without the approval of the republic, which alone had the power to grant this title. In 1715 King Frederick William I tried to acquire the Polish Prussian territory, again with the approval of Augustus. The intervention of Peter the Great, who resided in Gdańsk at the time, frustrated this attempt in 1716, and the Russian troops remained in control of the southern coast of the Baltic Sea. Peter thus assumed the role of protector of the territorial integrity of the Polish republic. From then on, Poland was to all intents and purposes a protectorate of Russia, and this relationship lasted until the dissolution of the republic in 1795.

Augustus III, 1733–63. The French-supported candidate, Stanisław Leszczyński, was elected king for the second time after the death of Augustus II in 1733. The Russian and Saxonian armies interfered, however, forcing the election of his opponent, Augustus III, the son of Augustus II. It was in his reign that Prussia conclusively achieved the position of a European power under its king, Frederick II the Great (1740–86). He annexed Silesia between 1740 and 1745, securing control of the western boundaries of Poland as well as of Polish foreign trade at the points where it was shipped overland to central and western Europe. Inhabited mainly by Poles, the southeastern half of Silesia retained political and cultural ties with Poland, but the Prussian annexation ended the church sovereignty of the metropolitanate of Gniezno over Silesia.

The Seven Years' War. During the Seven Years' War (1756–63), the Russian army used the territories of Gdańsk, Toruń, and Poznań as operational bases in their war against Prussia. Frederick II ordered the counterfeiting

margin note: Civil war of 1704–10

of Polish money, a measure that severely damaged and inflated the monetary system of the republic.

Social, religious, and political change. During the peaceful era between 1716 and 1768, the population grew rapidly, due to both the steady immigration of Germans and the mass exodus of an enslaved peasantry from Russia. By 1772 Poland's population numbered approximately 11,420,000. Comprising more than one-half of all the Jews in the world, the Jewish population of Poland lived in all parts of the country. The Counter-Reformation reached its zenith under the Jesuits, who trained students of noble birth in their greater colleges and other educational institutions. In 1717 and 1733 laws were passed that restricted the spiritual and secular rights of the non-Catholic population. Popular education fell to its lowest level. Spreading through all the other parts of Europe, the Age of Reason affected Poland only by virtue of some individual achievements. Parliamentary life came to an almost complete standstill. Under the reign of Augustus II only four of a total of 13 diets came to an orderly conclusion; under Augustus III only one out of 13 did so, as the result of the use of the liberum veto.

margin note: Population growth

REFORM AND PARTITION

Stanisław II August Poniatowski, a former diplomat, gained the crown of Poland with the help of Russian troops in 1764. Aided by his relatives, the Czartoryski, he tried to introduce political reforms, among other things the temporary abolition of the liberum veto in 1764–66, but his plans failed because of the objections of Catherine II the Great, the Russian empress. Taking advantage of the religious quarrels in Poland, the Empress sent Prince Nikolai V. Repnin as Russian minister to Warsaw with instructions that led to further discord in Polish affairs. Of Poland's population of 11,500,000, about 1,000,000 were dissidents, one-half Protestant and one-half Orthodox. For these people, who had been largely deprived of their rights by the laws of 1717 and 1733, Repnin, in the name of the Russian empress, demanded absolute religious and political equality with the Catholic population of Poland. He was well aware that an aristocratic and Catholic assembly like the Sejm would never concede such a demand.

margin note: Intervention by Catherine the Great of Russia

Early in 1767 a confederation was formed at Repnin's instigation to send a deputation to Catherine, petitioning her to guarantee the liberties of the republic. Subsequently, but not without a stubborn resistance, the Sejm accepted Catherine's authority, and the so-called fundamental laws were enacted, guaranteeing the liberum veto and all the other ancient abuses as unalterable parts of a Polish constitution ensured by Russia. All the restrictions against the dissidents were repealed at the same time.

These events led to a Catholic uprising known as the Confederation of Bar, aided by the Turks. After four years of fighting (1768–72), the Russian troops were able to gain the upper hand. Frederick II of Prussia tried to use this civil war to achieve a partition of Poland, but he met with the resistance of Catherine II. Only the threat of Austrian troops advancing against Russia and the Austrian annexation of some Polish territory in the Carpathian Mountains forced Catherine to seek help from the Prussian king on his terms—namely, the partition of Poland.

The First Partition and reform efforts. With the First Partition of Poland in 1772, the republic lost about 28 percent of its territory, the Livonian and White Ruthenian regions north of the Dvina River and east of the Druć River falling to Russia. Austria received Little Poland south of the Vistula River and almost all of the Red Ruthenian territory under the name of the Kingdom of Galicia. Prussia obtained the smallest but most valuable property, namely, Royal Prussia, comprising Warmia (Ermland) and a part of Great Poland on both sides of the Noteć River, though without the cities of Gdańsk and Toruń. Through this annexation Prussia had not only acquired the desired land connection between Western Pomerania and East Prussia that it had tried to secure for almost 120 years, but it had also gained control over approximately four-fifths of the total foreign trade of Poland. By levying enormous custom duties on the Polish foreign trade going via this route, Prussia made this its most important source of income.

margin note: Prussian control of foreign trade

Prussia was now able to shake off the last vestiges of the old Polish sovereign rights; the treaty of 1773 established the full and complete sovereignty of Prussia over its lands.

The shock of the First Partition caused political and economic reforms in Poland—as far as Russia would permit. The taxation system and the army were thoroughly reorganized, and with the Permanent Council, in 1775, Poland installed its first real central government. Many landed estate owners carried out individual peasant emancipations, and almost 200,000 Germans and at least 300,000 Russians emigrated to Poland, a land that was considered free. Slowly, the cities began to flourish again, and the beginnings of an industrial revolution could be observed with the rise in mining activities, the advances of the textile industry, the founding of the first joint-stock companies, and the employment of the first machine equipment. Polish intellectual pursuit and reasoning received fresh impetus when the Age of Reason was finally accepted. The King promoted the political theories of such men as Edmund Burke and George Washington, while the educated Poles advanced the political theories of Montesquieu and Rousseau. But whatever the theory, the concept of modern democracy, including all ranks and classes of society, quickly became established in Poland.

Improvements in education

The first governmental department for public education in Europe was established in conjunction with the appointment of an education commission in Poland in 1773. Its task was the reorganization of the universities of Kraków and Wilno, as well as the supervision of approximately 80 gymnasiums. The printing of books and the publication of magazines and journals also flourished.

The first codified constitution in Europe since antiquity and the second in the world after the United States, the new Polish constitution passed by the "Four Years Sejm" embodied the following ideas: first, the precept of a "people's sovereignty," which included the nobility as well as the metropolitan bourgeoisie; second, the constitutional separation of powers between the executive, legislature, and judiciary; and third, the responsibility of the cabinet to parliament. The liberum veto and all the obstructive machinery of the anomalous old system were abolished. According to its own rules, this constitution had to be revised after 25 years at the latest. But Catherine II considered such a constitution dangerous to the existence and continuation of her own autocratic governmental system; she therefore ordered her troops to invade Poland in 1792, and the reforms were destroyed by force.

The Second and Third Partitions. The Russo-Prussian treaty of 1793 (the Second Partition) placed almost all the Red Ruthenian and White Ruthenian lands under Russian rule, while Prussia received Gdańsk, Toruń, Great Poland, and part of Mazovia. In 1794 a general popular insurrection broke out under the leadership of Tadeusz Kościuszko against this latest Russo-Prussian humiliation. Kościuszko achieved a partial liberation of the peasant class and began a general armament of the people, mobilizing more than 150,000 men. At first the Polish forces were almost universally successful; but ultimately Kościuszko was defeated by the Russian troops under Aleksandr Suvorov at the Battle of Maciejowice, and Warsaw capitulated at the end of 1794. Russia and Austria—joined later also by Prussia—agreed to the Third Partition of Poland in 1795. Russia annexed the territory east of the Niemen and Bug rivers, Austria took almost all of Little Poland, including Kraków, and Prussia received the remaining lands, including Warsaw. Stanisław II abdicated officially in 1795. For all official purposes, at least, this was the end of the Republic of Poland, which was eradicated from the map of Europe for the next 123 years.

Kościuszko

POLAND UNDER PARTITION, 1795–1914

The Russian, Prussian, and Austrian sectors. With the Third Partition of Poland in 1795, the largest part of the territory fell to Russia. Officially, Catherine II called these partitions a return of Russian territory, even though such a claim dated back 450 years. Proclaiming the unity of all Russians, the largest part of the Uniate Church returned to the fold of the Eastern Orthodox faith. In spite of this, the Polish constitution and culture remained fairly unaffected at first in these "Russian" parts, where Poles still held positions of influence.

Because Russia's level of civilization was still extremely low under the reign of the tsars Paul I (1796–1801) and Alexander I (1801–25), the government was unable to administer the area without Polish help. The land had been divided into eight governmental units in 1801; and since the Poles retained basic administrative control, the municipal rights, control of the Polish county courts and of the Polish diets remained in force for a number of years (1796–1831). This region had the highest standard of civilization, culture, and education within the realm of the Russian Empire—with the exception of the Baltic Sea provinces—and the fundamental principles of the Russian educational system were based on the essential features of the Polish educational institutions of this region.

The Prussian area consisted of the three provinces of West Prussia, South Prussia, and New East Prussia. Together with the province of East Prussia, which had not been under Polish rule since 1657, the country came to be known officially as the Kingdom of Prussia, a part of the Prussian monarchy. Of its population of almost 4,000,000, however, about three-quarters were ethnic Poles.

The Kingdom of Galicia, as the Austrian section was known, was repeatedly reorganized administratively. Most of the native intellectuals in both the Prussian and the Austrian sections were replaced by German administrators who governed in autocratic fashion. In these areas numerous nationalist secret societies were established.

The struggle of the patriots. As early as 1768, Polish emigrant groups were formed in Hamburg, Dresden, Constantinople, and particularly in Paris. The group of Polish Jacobins organized in Warsaw and Wilno (1792–94) had established connections with the French Revolution, especially through Józef Sułkowski, who had politically supervised Napoleon Bonaparte in his capacity as secret police inspector (1796) of the French Directoire. Branching out from their Jacobin origins, the conspiratorial Society of Polish Republicans, formed in Warsaw around 1798–1800, and the Warsaw Society of the Friends of Science, founded in Warsaw in 1800, served partially as a cover organization for Jacobin activities. The centre of the conspiratorial network was in Paris, but it gained a particularly strong hold in Galicia after the French-Austrian War of 1792–1801. Gen. Jan Henryk Dąbrowski, who had gained his fame from the defense of Warsaw in 1794, established Polish legions in northern Italy in 1797, recruiting men from Austrian prisoners of war of Polish nationality. The legions fought without any political success against Austria between 1797 and 1801.

Patriotic and conspiratorial societies

Prince Adam Jerzy Czartoryski, the Russian foreign minister, tried to reestablish the Polish Republic from the sector occupied by Russia. He was aided in this by the tsar Alexander I. The plan was designed to create a buffer zone against Prussia, then allied with France. The idea lost its rationale, however, when Napoleon I of France attacked Prussia in 1806 and Russia came to the aid of Prussia. The French advance against Poznań and Warsaw paved the way for a general Polish insurrection against Prussia, led mainly by Jan Dąbrowski and Józef Wybicki.

Napoleon's Duchy of Warsaw. Taking some purely Polish areas of the Kingdom of Prussia, Napoleon I created the Duchy of Warsaw, placing it under the rule of the king of Saxony, Frederick Augustus (1807). The constitution dictated by Napoleon I and the introduction of the Code Napoléon called for the personal liberation of the peasants. But the soil remained fundamentally with the landed nobility, and therefore this liberation promoted rather than alleviated the agrarian population surplus in Central Poland. Józef Poniatowski (1763–1813), the nephew of the last king, distinguished himself as field marshal during the war of 1809, when the Duchy of Warsaw acquired the Austrian part of the Second Partition, including Kraków, as well as Zamość, annexed with Galicia in 1772. Thus, the Duchy of Warsaw had by this time grown to almost the same size as the Prussian monarchy. The failure of Napoleon's war against Russia in 1812, however, meant that by 1813 the Duchy of Warsaw had come under Russian administration.

Government under Napoleon

Repartition and repression.   The Congress of Vienna (1814–15) established the territorial division of Poland (within the boundaries of 1772) until 1918. In accordance with the Prussian demands, the Grand Duchy of Poznań was detached from the authority of the Duchy of Warsaw and incorporated into the Prussian monarchy. Cut off from the Duchy of Warsaw as well, the "Free City of Kraków" was designated to be the "symbolic capital of the divided Poland," though these intentions came to an end when Austria annexed the city in 1846. Galicia remained an Austrian hereditary land.

The Kingdom of Poland.   The main part of the Duchy of Warsaw was given the title of Kingdom of Poland in 1815. Approximately four-fifths of its population (more than 4,000,000 in 1827) were ethnic Poles, of whom as many as 325,000 were nobles. This area thus came to be considered as the Polish nucleus. After the Congress of Vienna, in 1815, this Congress Kingdom of Poland, or Congress Poland, as it often came to be called, was united

with the Russian Empire, though it retained its own governmental system, its own Sejm, and its own army. Tsar Alexander I was now in command of about three-quarters of all the historically Polish territories and, being not only the tsar of Russia but also the king of Poland, he was well advised to try to win the loyalty of the Polish people.

The constitution of the Kingdom of Poland, passed between 1815 and 1831, was considered the most liberal in all of Europe. The population of the Congress Kingdom of Poland included more voters than France, whose population was six times greater. A severe impediment, however, was the fact that Alexander I reigned with the harshness of an absolute monarch from 1819 on, breaking the constitution several times. This again promoted the creation of secret societies, the most consequential of which was the National Freemasonry (1819–25) under the leadership of Walerian Łukasiński. Similar secret societies were founded in Kraków, Poznań, and especially in the University of Wilno, where the Society of the Philomats functioned

The constitution of the Kingdom

Adapted from N. Davies, *God's Playground: A History of Poland* (1982); Columbia University Press

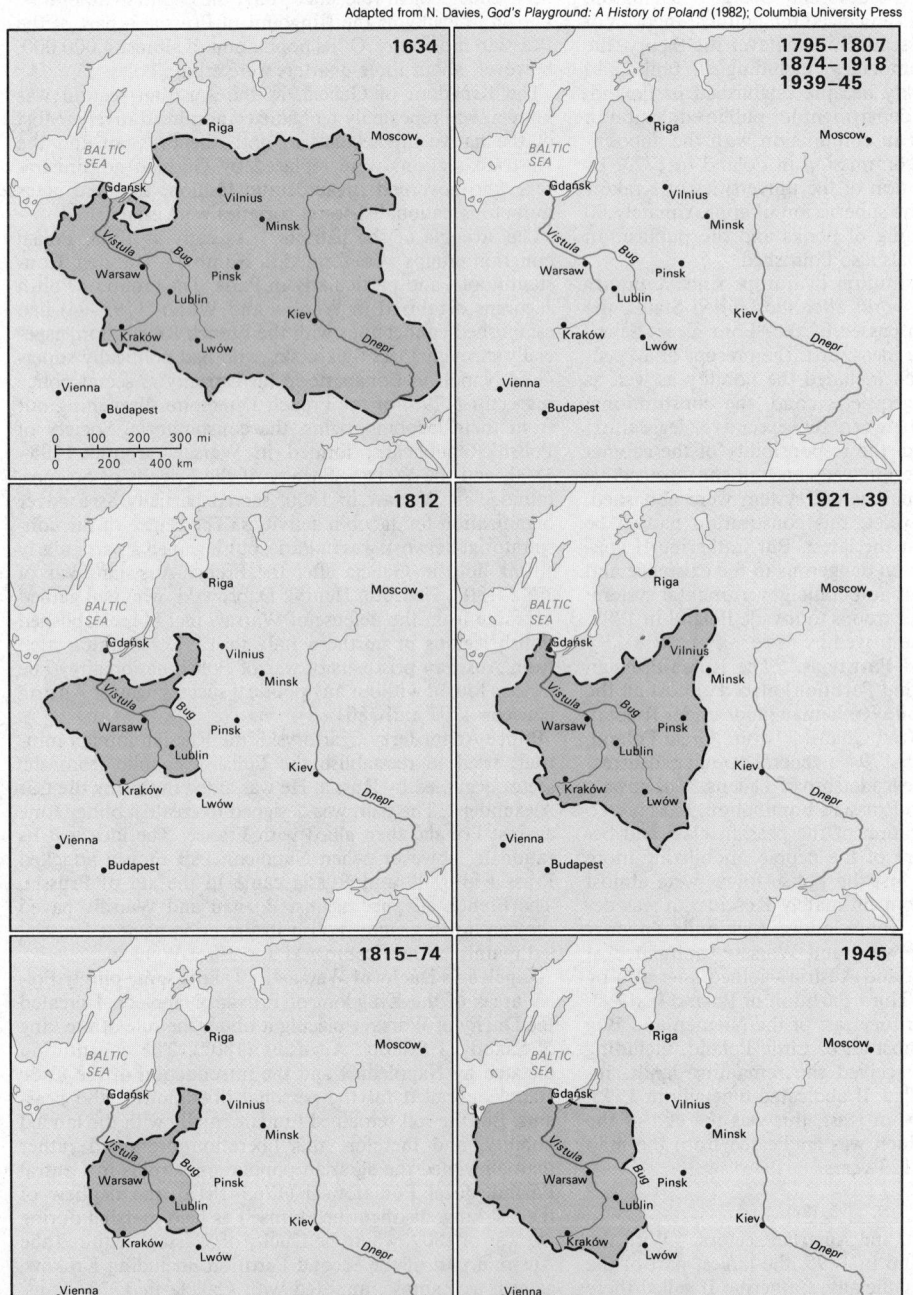

Changes in Poland's territory from 1634 to 1945.

as a front for several conspiratorial groups. Even Adam Mickiewicz, the greatest Polish Romantic poet, became involved in the affairs of the Philomats and was sent into exile for some time. The secret societies continued and flourished, despite repression at the hands of the Russians.

The Rising of 1830 and the aftermath. Alexander's successor, the autocratic tsar Nicholas I (1825–55), planned a military campaign against France and Belgium after the revolution in France in July 1830. He was going to send a Polish army to accomplish this, but most of the Polish ensigns banded together to create the November Insurrection on Nov. 29, 1830, under their leader Piotr Wysocki. Almost the entire army and the majority of all Polish politicians joined in the insurrection, and the Sejm proclaimed the ousting of Tsar Nicholas I on Jan. 25, 1831, an act that led to a formal war between Russia and Congress Poland. The war lasted from January to September 1831, the superior Russian forces finally defeating the Poles, who received no response to their appeal for western European protection. About 6,000 leaders of the rising were forced into exile during 1831–32, most of them emigrating to France in what has become known as the Great Emigration.

The suppression of the November Insurrection meant heavy reprisals in the Russian as well as in the Prussian Polish areas, even though the latter had no actual part in it. Extensive confiscations of estates, deportations, and enforced recruiting were designed to break the national patriotism of the Poles. The universities of Warsaw and Wilno were suppressed, and Polish students were compelled to go to St. Petersburg (now Leningrad) and Kiev in Russian Poland. The remainder of the Uniate Church was abolished and converted to Eastern Orthodoxy between 1831 and 1839, though continuing to exist in Congress Poland until 1875 and in Galicia until 1945. The Organic Statute of 1832 replaced the constitution, the Sejm, and the army in the Kingdom of Poland; and the land was united with the Russian Empire in a true union, although officially the kingdom retained a few autonomous rights.

The Organic Statute

The conservative group of emigrants led by Adam J. Czartoryski, the "king in exile," tried to solve the Polish question through legal and diplomatic means. His minimum goal was the restoration of the legal status of 1815, which had been violated from the very beginning. The radicals had splintered into many factions, but the Polish Democratic Society founded in 1832 soon emerged as the leading organization. Its Manifesto of Poitiers of 1836 was less realistic than the program set up by the conservative side, because its revolutionary agenda demanded an independent Poland within the borders of 1772. But the Manifesto proclaimed the idea of a land reform without compensation to the present owners, and this drew many supporters. In the years between 1833 and 1846, emissaries and leaders of the partisans of the "left" established secret revolutionary cells in all parts of Poland. These cells were persistently traced down by the authorities, and thousands of their members were deported or imprisoned.

The 1846 insurrection. The Polish Democratic Society gained a certain influence in the country with the installation of a committee in Poznań between 1839 and 1846. This committee drew up a plan for a general revolution, but the Prussian police discovered it in 1846. In spite of this, a central government in Kraków, under the revolutionary leaders Jan Tyssowski and Edward Dembowski, tried to get an insurrection started. The uprising spread to Galicia, where Austrian troops soon put it down, at the same time inciting the local population so that many Galician peasants turned against the revolutionaries. The failure of the 1846 revolt severely weakened Polish participation when a general revolutionary wave swept through Europe during the early spring of 1848–49. Originally, Prussia and Austria had nominally supported Polish demands for independence, but now attempts by the Poles to establish a real independence were resisted by armed force in both countries. The course of this revolutionary struggle showed clearly that the fight was no longer only about the ideal of a unified republic based on the boundaries of 1772 but also about the Romantic Idealism of the time, which favoured individualistic, linguistically and cultur-

Romantic revolutionary Idealism

ally separated nationalities. On the other hand, nationalist ambitions now extended beyond the borders of 1772 for the first time. The Polish question also gained more impetus on the international scene. Adam Mickiewicz founded a new Polish legion in Italy and a little later published the moderate socialist newspaper *La Tribune des Peuples* in Paris (1848–49). The landed gentry of Poznań financed the *Neue Rheinische Zeitung* ("The Newspaper of the Rhineland"), the journal through which Karl Marx and Friedrich Engels in 1849 proclaimed the national liberation of Poland to be one of the most important tasks of the workers' movement of Europe.

Alexander II and the rising of 1863. The Eastern Question and the Crimean War (1853–56) caused violent upheavals within the Russian Empire, which motivated Alexander II (1855–81) to take a more conciliatory stand toward the Kingdom of Poland. A series of reforms were implemented, in their later stages by the autocratic count Aleksander Wielopolski, who was installed in high office and stood for a national policy of loyal union with Russia. His methods and character lost him the support of the moderate gentry, however, and aroused the outright enmity of the young patriotic radicals, who were influenced by ideas expressed by Napoleon III of France and by the national reunification of Italy (1859–60). (The left wing of these radicals became linked with the Russian liberal movement and the international emigrants in London centred around Karl Marx and Aleksandr Herzen.) Religious ceremonies became occasions of political demonstrations, rioting broke out in Warsaw, and the situation culminated in the widespread insurrection of Jan. 22, 1863, sparked off by Wielopolski's plans to press the revolutionary youth of the cities into the Russian army. The revolutionaries had relied on French and Austrian support, but these hopes proved to be in vain; and to make matters worse, Prussia again cooperated with Russia. As before, the ethnic groups in the Russian sectors—Poles, Lithuanians, and the Catholic White Ruthenians—united in a common war against the Tsar that lasted for 15 months, though the insurrection was finally crushed when the rebel "National Government" was detected by the Russian administrative authorities on April 10–11, 1864. The defeat was followed by executions, confiscations, and deportations, and all hopes for the Polish people to establish an autonomous national state were ended for the next half century. The Russian government did proclaim, however, the liberation of its peasants on March 13, 1861, and it extended this to the Kingdom of Poland on March 2, 1864. By so doing, it took the most important traditional premise for the revolution out of the hands of the revolutionaries. The agrarian policy, however, was expressly calculated to stir up ill feeling between the peasants and the country gentry, whom Russia was determined to punish in every way for their leading part in the insurrection. Yet the agrarian reforms accelerated the growth of towns and industry and the new social structure produced both financiers who exploited the great possibilities of the Russian market and a new working class, among whom the first socialist organizations began their secret activity.

Liberation of the peasants

The founding of modern Poland, 1864–1914. After the failure of the January Insurrection, a policy of harsh repression fell upon the Poles remaining in the Russian and Prussian sectors. The Russian sector was now offically named the Western Region of the Russian Empire, and its governor general, Mikhail Nikolayevich Muravyov (who became known as the "hangman of Wilno"), made every effort to stamp out Polish culture altogether.

Russification. The Kingdom of Poland was reorganized as the Land of the Vistula under a purely Russian administration. The University of Warsaw became a Russian university in 1869. Russification of all secondary schools was implemented from 1869 to 1874 and of all other public schools after 1885: the Russians accomplished their aim of keeping illiteracy among the common people at as high a level as possible. Consequently, by 1905 there were relatively fewer schools and students in the Land of the Vistula than there had been in 1815. Nearly all private schools and all social and political activities were prohibited.

Prussian and Austrian Poland. Following the Russian example Otto von Bismarck, the German chancellor, instituted a similar policy, and the Prussian sector was incorporated into the newly founded German Reich. In 1872 the entire school system was Germanized. The Colonization Law of 1886 tried to integrate German peasants into the native Polish population. Polish autonomy was able to achieve some success only in the Austrian sector, where its most important agency was the Galician provincial Sejm. The Poles in Austria became the country's second nationality, and they were allowed to participate in the government at Vienna and retained sovereignty over the Ruthenians in Galicia. Galicia itself became the haven of **Galicia** Polish culture, with the University of Kraków, the University of Lwów, and the Academy of Sciences attracting many Polish intellectuals.

Industrial growth and social change. The development of modern industry, notably the textile and metal manufacturing industries, as well as mining, made Congress Poland after the abolition of the customs barrier with Russia the most dynamic, industrialized part of the Russian Empire until about 1890. In Congress Poland alone there were more than 400,000 industrial workers by 1910. It was mainly Polish intellectuals who stimulated industrialization in the Russian and Austrian sections, whereas German intellectuals led the industrialization program of the Prussian part—particularly in Upper Silesia, with its 200,000 Polish miners. Due to the many agrarian crises between 1846 and 1892, most of the 3,200,000 descendants of the former nobility moved to the cities in the Russian sector, where they formed the majority of the liberal professions. In the Polish regions of eastern Germany, Congress Poland, and West Galicia, the intellectual classes were mostly without property and therefore dependent on wages, whereas the Poles in the Western Region of the Russian Empire and in East Galicia were mainly wealthy landowners or belonged to the city bourgeoisie. One of the main features of the period was the mass emigration of Poles from their native lands into the more industrialized parts of Germany, a movement that was to continue for **Mass** decades to come. Thus, by 1910 more than 100,000 min- **emigration** ers of Polish descent were working in the industrial Ruhr **to** district. The rural population of Congress Poland and **Germany** Galicia was mostly illiterate, and poverty increased there to such an extent that at least 3,500,000 people emigrated between 1890 and 1914, mainly to the United States.

Development of political parties. The first permanent political parties were established in Congress Poland and in exile between 1891 and 1893. The Polish League (LP), founded in 1886–87, was reorganized as the National League (LN) by Roman Dmowski in 1892–93 and later became the nucleus of National Democracy (ND), which was the strongest bourgeois party between 1905 and 1939. The Polish Socialist Party (PPS) was founded in 1892–93 under the patronage of Bolesław Limanowski and subsequently, under the leadership of Józef Piłsudski, became the strongest socialist party in the entire Russian Empire during the Russian Revolution of 1905. The left-wing socialist party (SDKP; from 1900 SDKPiL, Social Democracy of the Kingdom of Poland and Lithuania), founded in 1893 and led by Rosa Luxemburg and Junian Marchlewski, remained a minor party in comparison. The 1905 revolution, which swept over Russia, changed political life in all the Polish regions. The National Democracy, led by Roman Dmowski and supported by the majority of the landed gentry and the bourgeoisie, restricted its national platform to the demand for Polish autonomy. For this reason it was allowed to operate legally not only in Congress Poland but in Russian Poland, too, after 1905. The same party also controlled the Polish faction in the Russian Duma, or parliament (1905–17). The PPS split in 1905–06: the patriotic wing under Józef Piłsudski and Tomasz Arciszewski retained its "radical program for independence," in accordance with the teachings of Friedrich Engels, and took part in the abortive revolution of 1905 against the Russian government; the left wing adjusted its program to an internationalist standpoint and so found it easy later on to merge with the SDKPiL, on the extreme left. The introduction of universal suffrage in Austria,

including the Austrian sector of Poland (Galicia), for the parliament in Vienna in 1907 promoted the founding of the agrarian Polish Peasant Party (PSL). This party soon spread its influence to southern Congress Poland, but it split in 1913 into a moderate majority and a radical left. Only in Prussia was the repression of Polish cultural and political life continued, and after 1905 this policy was pursued in an even severer form. For this reason the Polish National Democrats regarded the German Reich rightfully as their main opponent from 1905 on.

THE FOUNDING OF THE SECOND REPUBLIC, 1914–21

Events during World War I. At the outbreak of World War I the governments of Austria and Russia tried to use the Polish question as a political weapon. On Aug. 16, 1914, the Austrian government allowed the formation of a Supreme National Committee (NKN) in Galicia and the organization of a Polish legion recruited mainly from the membership of the followers of Józef Piłsudski. The **Piłsudski** ultimate goal of Austrian policy was the incorporation of **and** Congress Poland into Galicia. On Aug. 14, 1914, the Rus- **Dmowski** sian government recognized the basic right of the Poles to autonomy, particularly in the lands that the Russian troops hoped to conquer. The Polish National Committee (KNP) was formed in Warsaw in November 1914—its chief members coming from the National Democrats, led by Roman Dmowski. The KNP supported the Russian war effort, and Russian forces conquered almost all of Galicia in 1914.

Division of Congress Poland. The troops of the Central Powers—Germany and Austria-Hungary—were able subsequently not only to retake Galicia but to advance deep into Congress Poland. The Central Powers divided it into two military occupation zones, with a German governor general in Warsaw and an Austro-Hungarian one in Lublin. The political groups in both of these zones separated into those who believed in adopting a passive stance and the activists. With the majority of the PPS and the left-wing intellectuals on their side, the activists established the Central National Committee (CKN) in December 1915, their goal being to reestablish a Polish republic with the help of the Central Powers.

Creation of a Kingdom of Poland. At the request of the German commander, Gen. Erich Ludendorff, and the German governor general, Hans Hartwig von Beseler, the German and Austrian emperors proclaimed a new Kingdom of Poland on Nov. 5, 1916. The kingdom consisted of both occupied zones but constituted only about one-sixth of the territory established in 1772. The hopes of both monarchs for more support among the Polish volunteer troops in the Austro-German fight against Russia were in vain, for German aspirations did not match the expectations of the Poles, who had envisioned an eastward expansion of the Kingdom of Poland. Ludendorff, in turn, tried to establish what he himself termed "a national kingdom of Lithuania" in the eastern regions. All these elements now gave the first incentive to an internationalization of the Polish question.

The Russian Revolution. The Russian Revolution in March 1917 brought about the two Poland proclamations of the Soviet of Petrograd and the provisional government of Russia. These recognized Poland's right to independence, while the latter insisted on a military alliance with Russia. After this, three Polish army corps were formed from the ranks of the Russian army between May 1917 and May 1918, and France also recruited a Polish volunteer army. The Polish National Committee, reestablished by Dmowski in Lausanne on Aug. 15, 1917, worked closely with the governments of the Western Allies. In the Kingdom of Poland, Piłsudski and the Polish Legion, now reorganized as the Polish Auxiliary Corps, with about 20,000 men, clashed with the Central Powers. Piłsudski and the majority of his corps were interned in July 1917. The grant of a limited Polish self-government in the Kingdom of Poland and the installation of a Regency Council on Sept. 12, 1917, came too late to overcome the distrust that now divided the Central Powers and the Poles.

The fight for self-determination. The October Revolution in Russia, as well as the proclaimed principle of the "right for self-determination of all nations" as stated by both Lenin and the U.S. president Woodrow Wilson (though both with very different interpretations), gave the Polish question international significance. Wilson demanded the creation of an "independent Polish state" with a free and secured access to the sea in his well-known "14-points speech" of Jan. 8, 1918. This program was ratified as an integral part of the future peace settlement by the governments of France, Great Britain, and Italy on June 3, 1918. The Central Powers used the "right for self-determination of all nations" in the peace negotiations of Brest-Litovsk (now Brest, Belorussian S.S.R.) in February–March 1918 as a pretext for the separation of the Kingdom of Poland from the Russian Empire, but they apportioned the Chełm province, with its predominantly Polish population, to the Ukraine on Feb. 9, 1918. This infuriated Polish opinion.

Reestablishment of the state. The military collapse of Austria in October 1918 led to the formation of a Polish Liquidation Commission in Kraków on Oct. 28, 1918, which assumed power in Western Galicia. On November 7 a Provisional Government of the Polish Republic was established in Lublin. With the collapse of the German Reich in November 1918, Piłsudski was freed from his internment in Germany. Returning to Warsaw, he took control of the whole of Poland on Nov. 11, 1918. The administrations for the regions of Kraków and Lublin also put themselves under his command. Nov. 11, 1918, has thus been generally recognized as the day of the founding of the Second Polish Republic.

The Second Polish Republic. To begin with, the Second Polish Republic consisted of the Kingdom of Poland as it existed in 1916, the Duchy of Cieszyn, and West Galicia. Poland's losses during World War I numbered about 800,000 dead as well as the destruction of the majority of industrial plants and communications and the serious disruption of the Polish monetary system and economy.

Internal developments. Piłsudski secured his position of power in the country by reaching an agreement, in January 1919, with the KNP in Paris, headed by Roman Dmowski. The KNP was the recognized official Polish delegation at the Paris Peace Conference. Ignacy Jan Paderewski, a close associate of Dmowski, formed a government in Warsaw in 1919, but the executive power remained in the hands of Piłsudski, as the Polish "chief of state," from Nov. 22, 1918, until Dec. 14, 1922. The succeeding democratic elections led to the formation of a constitutional Sejm, which operated as both the constituent and legislative assembly (1919–22) after the passing of the "Little Constitution" on Feb. 20, 1919. The strongest parties in the country were the National Democrats and the Peasants (PSL), the latter for the most part cooperating with the National Democrats. The left-wing parties commanded only about one-quarter of the votes. The Communist Workers' Party of Poland was founded on Dec. 16, 1918, and Workers' Councils were set up in November 1918. The Councils were broken up by the government in June 1919, and this established and secured a "bourgeois democracy" in Poland as opposed to the "Soviet democracy" in Russia.

The Treaty of Versailles. At the Paris Peace Conference the Polish delegation demanded the surrender of the formerly Prussian sector, Upper Silesia, and southern East Prussia (Mazuria) from Germany. The largest part of the province of Poznań was already under Polish authority because the December 1918 Polish uprising against the Germans in Poznań had engulfed almost the entire province. The Treaty of Versailles, signed on June 28, 1919, awarded Poland the main part of the Prussian sector, providing the desired direct access to the Baltic Sea, even though the port of Gdańsk (Danzig), to which the Poles had laid claim, became a "Free City." The plebiscite in Mazuria, held on July 11, 1920, resulted in a heavy defeat for Poland, partly because of the Polish-Soviet war, and it brought only a few border regions under Polish authority. The Polish population in Upper Silesia rebelled three times against the German administration. In the plebiscite of March 20, 1921, 682 communes voted for Poland and 792 for Germany, but the Poles secured preponderance in the southeastern plebiscite area, which was industrially

the most important. The new frontier of Oct. 20, 1921, divided this area: Poland was awarded 76 percent of the coal production, 22 out of 37 blast furnaces, and nine out of 14 steelworks, with about 990,000 people. Populated by Poles, Czechs, and Germans, the former Duchy of Cieszyn was the subject of controversy between Poland and Czechoslovakia. On July 28, 1920, it was divided, but in a manner that left a considerable Polish minority in the Czechoslovakian sector.

Territorial disputes. Poland owed its rapid eastward expansion to its quickly recruited and effective army. Evacuation of the territories occupied in the east by the German troops had to be completed by the beginning of February 1919, but every strip of land left by the Germans was promptly taken over by the Red Army. Thus, between November 1918 and February 1919, that army moved westward from the Dnepr to the Bug River line. Piłsudski decided that it was imperative to throw back eastward the forces aiming at imposing a foreign form of government on restored Poland. The central part of historic Lithuania was occupied by the Poles in April 1919. On July 27 the Supreme Council approved a demarcation line between Poland and Lithuania, leaving Wilno (Lithuanian Vilnius) on the Polish side. In eastern Galicia the West Ukrainian People's Republic had been established in November 1918, but Polish troops occupied it in June–July 1919. In addition, the Polish Army extended its sphere of influence over the largest part of White Ruthenia and over the western Ukraine—far beyond the boundary lines of the Second Partition of 1793—without meeting any serious resistance from the Red Army until December 1919, because the Russians were still embroiled in civil war. The Soviets launched a military offensive against Poland between February and May 1920. The militarily and politically ill-advised Polish advance against Kiev in June 1920 led to the Polish-Soviet war that had been brewing for the past one and a half years. The Red Army, under the command of Mikhail Tukhachevsky, advanced, reaching the vicinity of Toruń, Warsaw, and Lwów by July and August 1920. The Polish forces led by Piłsudski defeated the Red Army decisively, however, in a battle on the Vistula between August 16 and 28. This victory crushed the Bolsheviks' last chance of a widespread revolution in central and western Europe. The Polish Army reconquered Central Lithuania with Vilnius (ceded to the Lithuanians by the Red Army), western White Ruthenia, western Wolhynia, and East Galicia before the armistice of Oct. 12, 1920. The Soviet government finally recognized this boundary unconditionally in the Peace of Riga on March 18, 1921.

POLAND FROM 1921 TO 1945

The constitution of March 17, 1921, established a parliament consisting of two houses, the Senate and the Sejm. The political forces in the country had splintered up into numerous parties and groups, and this proved a hindrance to the development of a stable, unified parliamentary government.

Domestic policy. Between 1922 and 1926 Poland was governed by frequently changing cabinets that were based mainly on a coalition between the National Democrats, the Christian Democrats, and the moderate Peasant Party. The primary task of these governments was to attempt to eliminate the inflation that the destruction of World War I and the subsequent conflicts had caused. The government stabilized the situation through the introduction of a new currency, the zloty, on Feb. 1, 1924. But the new currency was in danger again by 1925, mainly as the result of a tariff war instigated by the Germans. The financial crisis that followed led to high unemployment and severe unrest among the working people. This, in turn, gave the Communist Party a steadily rising influence, even though it had been declared illegal in 1923. Piłsudski had not been active on the political scene since 1923, but these new developments compelled him to organize a military coup on May 12–15, 1926, in order to take power. Supporting their former leader with a general strike, the PPS played a decisive role in Piłsudski's victory.

Piłsudski headed the government from 1926 to 1930.

(marginal notes)

Piłsudski's return to Poland

Defeat of the Red Army

The Piłsudski coup

His rule was a moral dictatorship with only a formal preservation of parliamentary authority. His administration aimed at the "moral cleansing" of society in Poland and at eliminating corruption. Piłsudski relied mainly on the army and the conservative nobility of eastern Poland for his support. Between 1926 and 1927 a right-wing opposition emerged, led by Dmowski. Piłsudski confronted them with his Non-Party Block for Cooperation with the Government (BBWR), which was a loose organization held together only by Piłsudski's personality. At any rate, in the elections to the Sejm held on March 4, 1928, the BBWR obtained one-quarter of all the parliamentary seats, though a contributing factor for this political success was the increasing economic prosperity of 1926–29.

The Great Depression

The crisis in the world economy began to affect Poland in October 1929. Unemployment hit about 893,000 workers, excluding agricultural workers—or approximately one-third of those employed in 1931. Production sank between 1931 and 1933 to only 46 percent of the 1913 level. Under the pressure of the general misery and need, the PPS, the Polish Peasant Party (PSL), and some others united on Nov. 1, 1929, to form a left-wing opposing coalition (Centrolew, or Centre-Left). Piłsudski used harsh measures against his opponents, ordering the arrest of about 70 politicians. The Sejm elections of November 1930 gave the BBWR its desired majority, but the genuine political parties now practically disappeared from the political scene. Piłsudski governed from 1930 to 1935 without holding an official public political office. His authority was based on the support of the civil service and of his officers' corps and, in particular, the support of the colonels trained in the legions. Piłsudski tried to master the economic crisis through a program of nonintervention and thrift, but he was largely unsuccessful.

A constitutional reform was introduced on April 23, 1935, strengthening the executive branch of government and giving the head of state the power to enact important laws without the approval of Parliament.

Piłsudski's successors. Piłsudski died on May 12, 1935, and the resulting struggle for power, complicated by strikes and demonstrations, soon reduced all parliamentary activity to a complete farce.

Opposition groups. The elections held in September 1935 and November 1938 showed this only too well, and a large part of the population and most of the opposition parties boycotted them. There were violent demonstrations and strikes in 1936 and 1938, and the beginnings of a popular front, bringing left and left-centre parties together, could be noted. The established radical workers' parties, the PPS and the KPP, found a new ally in the Peasant Party, which had now also become radical under its new leader Stanisław Mikołajczyk. Joseph Stalin's reaction to these signs of national unity was to have the Comintern dissolve the Communist Party of Poland in 1938, branding its leaders as provocateurs and capitalist agents. On the right wing, the National Radical Camp (ONR) generated some Fascist groups, but they were dissolved in 1934 and received hardly any support. Founded by the government on March 1, 1937, the Camp of National Unity (OZN) remained an authoritarian association that—like the BBWR—had no real social or political platform.

Dissolution of the Communist Party of Poland

Social problems. The important social questions of Poland remained unsolved in the time between World Wars I and II. Any permanent solution was beyond the reach of the country's economic resources. The surplus in the agrarian population could only have been eliminated by a comprehensive program of industrialization, but there was no capital to do this. Nevertheless, the agrarian reform based on the laws of July 15, 1920, started the distribution of approximately one-tenth of all arable land. Industrialization made some progress with, for example, the energetic promotion of the chemical industry and the building of the "coal-railroads" from Upper Silesia to the Baltic Sea coast, but the funds necessary for investment in these enterprises stretched Poland's national economy to its limits. The entire 1938 production barely reached the 1913 level. Poland remained an agrarian country, and about two-thirds of its total population depended either directly or indirectly on its agricultural produce. Only one-quarter of the country's inhabitants received their income from industry.

Foreign policy. In its foreign policy, Poland attempted to strengthen its position through alliances with France and Romania (1921). Endangered by political and military cooperation between Germany and the Soviet Union, as well as by their concerted policy aiming at the revision of existing frontiers, Poland found itself in a hazardous position after the treaties of Locarno (1925) and the April 1926 treaty negotiated by Gustav Stresemann and Georgy Vasilyevich Chicherin of the Soviet Union stating that German–Soviet relations should continue to be based on the 1922 Treaty of Rapallo. Acting under Piłsudski's instruction, Józef Beck, Poland's foreign minister, concluded a nonaggression pact with the Soviet Union in 1932 and a similar one with Germany in 1934—the latter preserving both Poland's alliance with France and its freedom of action as a member of the League of Nations. This safeguarded Poland's position, at least for a short time. But the German Reich had by now annexed Austria and the largest part of Czechoslovakia, and it established control over the Slovakian republic and seized Lithuanian Memelland. This placed it in such a strategically favourable position toward Poland that Adolf Hitler dispensed with all caution. His proposals for a global solution were aimed at making Poland completely dependent on Germany so that he would be able to use it as a base for his planned attack on the Soviet Union. Observing the guarantee of March 31, 1939, the British government under Neville Chamberlain gave Poland diplomatic, but no military or financial, assistance. This did nothing to prevent the Germans from attacking Poland or to stop the outbreak of World War II. Hitler, on Aug. 23, 1939, concluded with Stalin a nonaggression pact containing a secret protocol dividing Poland into German and Soviet spheres of interest, circumscribed by the Narew, Vistula, and San rivers. This "Fourth Partition of Poland" proved to be the decisive factor leading to the outbreak of World War II.

Beck's nonaggression pacts

World War II. The fall of Poland came unexpectedly fast during the September campaign of 1939. Warsaw capitulated on Sept. 27, 1939, after the defeat of the Polish Army. The last organized Polish resistance ended on Oct. 5, 1939. Following German demands, the Soviet Union ordered two army corps to invade eastern Poland on Sept. 17, 1939, breaking its earlier agreements of 1921 and 1932. On Sept. 28, 1939, Hitler and Stalin again agreed on a new partition of Poland along the Narew, Bug, and San rivers. Hitler's plans for the creation of a Polish puppet state did not materialize because no collaborator could be found. On Oct. 12, 1939, Hitler gave the order to annex outright the former Prussian section, parts of Mazovia, eastern Great Poland with Łódź, and a border strip in Little Poland.

The division of Poland

Soviet annexations. The regions in the Soviet sphere of interest were incorporated into the Soviet Union with the help of supervised plebiscites held between Oct. 22 and Nov. 2, 1939. The Soviet Union based its decisions, at least formally, on the "right for self-determination of the nationalities," hoping in this way to get its demands internationally legalized. The annexation put the British government into an embarrassing situation. On the one hand, it had guaranteed the security of Poland, while, on the other hand, it did not want to risk a conflict with the Soviet Union. For this reason, on Oct. 26, 1939, the British foreign minister Lord Halifax pointed to the fact that the westward extension of the Soviet boundary approximated the Curzon line of Dec. 8, 1919, and of July 11, 1920. He was the first European statesman to do so, but this explanation became the basis for the later establishment of the boundary between Poland and the Soviet Union at the end of World War II.

Polish government-in-exile. The forming of a Polish government-in-exile in France, based on the 1935 constitution, assured the survival of the Polish Republic. Its leading statesman and supreme commander was Władysław Sikorski. The Polish government-in-exile moved to the United Kingdom after the defeat of France in June 1940. A civil and military resistance movement was also formed in occupied Poland in September 1939.

German repression. From the very beginning, in October 1939, the occupational policy of the Germans was designed to completely eradicate Polish culture. Almost the entire Polish school system was suppressed. Mass executions of Polish intellectuals were carried out, and the infamous concentration camp of Oświęcim (Auschwitz) was set up. The intention was to Germanize the territory, and mass deportations of Poles and mass settlings of Germans in their place were supposed to accomplish this. Germans from the Baltic states and eastern Poland were transferred to the western Polish lands incorporated into the German Reich. The Soviet government also participated in mass deportations of the Polish inhabitants from the eastern parts of their country incorporated into the Soviet Union.

Alliance with the Soviet Union. The German attack on the Soviet Union on June 22, 1941, changed the situation drastically for Poland. Stalin agreed to the annulment of the "Fifth Polish Partition" agreement between the German and the Soviet governments of 1939, but he declined the restitution of the Polish–Soviet border of 1921. In his debate with the British foreign minister, Anthony Eden, on Dec. 16, 1941, he proposed the Curzon Line as the basis for the future Polish–Soviet boundary.

German policy of extermination. The extermination of the Polish intellectuals and the mass deportation of Poles from western Poland continued to be vigorously pursued. Polish citizens of Jewish descent were deported to extermination camps, such as Auschwitz and Treblinka, where they were killed, along with the Jewish population of the greater part of Europe. Neither the belated ghetto risings of Warsaw, Białystok, and Wilno (April–September 1943) nor the special actions taken by the Polish underground were effective enough to halt this extermination.

The ghetto risings

(Ha.Ro./Ed.)

Stalin's Polish policy. In September 1939 both Hitler and Stalin hoped that a Polish national state would never rise again. When the Germans invaded the Soviet Union, however, Stalin had to reverse his Polish policy. On July 30, 1941, he reestablished diplomatic relations with the Polish government-in-exile in London. A military convention was signed in Moscow on August 14 on organizing a Polish army in Russia.

There were at that time hundreds of thousands of Polish deportees on Soviet territory; in addition, in September and October 1939 the Red Army had captured about 230,670 Polish soldiers, from privates to generals. To command the new Polish army, Stalin freed from imprisonment a Polish officer, Gen. Władysław Anders. Both Sikorski and Anders knew that some 15,000 Polish prisoners, including 8,400 officers, were interned at the Soviet prison camps at Kozelsk, Starobelsk, and Ostashkov. Great, however, was Anders' surprise and anxiety when he was told that he could count on only 448 officers picked from the three camps and grouped in April 1940 at Gryazovets.

By December 1941 Anders had put together two divisions. Finding that he could not organize a truly national Polish army, Anders suggested to Sikorski that his units be transferred to the West. During 1942, as a result of an agreement between Stalin and Churchill, 75,000 Polish soldiers were evacuated from the Soviet Union to the Middle East.

As early as November 1941 a small group of Polish Communists was parachuted into German-occupied Poland, where they contacted a few members of the old KPP (dissolved in March 1938); Władysław Gomułka was one of them. In January 1942 the Communist Party of Poland was revived in Warsaw under the name Polish Workers' Party (Polska Partia Robotnicza, or PPR), which in May 1942 formed a nucleus of the People's Army (AL).

The Katyn Massacre

On April 13, 1943, the Germans announced the discovery in the Katyn Forest, on the upper Dnepr River, of mass graves of Polish officers with their personal papers in their pockets. The officers' names published by the Germans were those of inmates of the Kozelsk prison camp, and the Germans accused the Soviets of having executed the prisoners in May 1940. Two days later the Soviet government alleged instead that the Polish prisoners had been engaged in construction work west of Smolensk in 1941 and had been executed by the Germans. On April

17, 1943, the Polish government asked the International Committee of the Red Cross to examine the situation on the spot. Eight days later the Soviet government, accusing the Poles of "contact and accord with Hitler," severed diplomatic relations with the Polish government in London for the second time.

During these fateful weeks Sikorski was in the Middle East inspecting the 2nd Polish Army Corps under Anders. Returning to London, Sikorski was killed on July 4 in an aircraft crash at Gibraltar. Stanisław Mikołajczyk, leader of the PSL, succeeded him as premier. Ignoring the Polish government's views concerning the territorial problems, Franklin D. Roosevelt and Winston Churchill agreed at the Tehrān Conference (Nov. 28–Dec. 1, 1943) to Stalin's demand that the Curzon Line be the new Soviet–Polish frontier.

To consolidate his diplomatic victory at the Tehrān Conference, Stalin instructed the PPR (of which Gomułka became secretary general in November 1943) to form the National Home Council (Krajowa Rada Narodowa, or KRN), which would become the government of the Polish People's Republic with Bolesław Bierut, an old Comintern hand, as president. That was done during the night of December 31.

Even before the severing of diplomatic relations with the legal Polish government, Stalin ordered the organization of a new Polish army, and by March 1944 the 1st Army came into existence. Its first commander was Gen. Zygmunt Berling, a Polish officer who refused to follow Anders, but the majority of officers in command of divisions, regiments, and battalions were detailed from the Red Army. On July 21, 1944, a Polish Committee of National Liberation (PKWN), commonly referred to as the Lublin Committee, was established as an executive branch of the KRN. On July 21 the 1st Belorussian Army Group under Marshal Konstantin Rokossovsky, into which the 1st Polish Army was incorporated, crossed the Curzon Line. Two days later it liberated Lublin, where the Lublin Committee launched a manifesto in which it declared itself to be "the sole legal Polish executive power." A week later Rokossovsky approached the Vistula River near Warsaw. At the same time Radio Moscow was broadcasting in Polish to the population of Warsaw and calling for a general uprising against the Germans. Foreseeing such an eventuality, Gen. Kazimierz Sosnkowski, who had succeeded Sikorski as commander in chief of the Polish armed forces, on July 7 warned Gen. Tadeusz Komorowski (called General Bór), commander of the 300,000-strong Home Army (Armia Krajowa, or AK), that considering its poor armament he should not order a general anti-German insurrection but that it was imperative that the Poles gain control of an important city before the entry of Soviet troops. On July 25, however, Mikołajczyk informed Jan Stanisław Jankowski, delegate general of the Polish government in German-occupied Poland, that he had full powers to order an uprising in Warsaw. Under this decision, General Komorowski ordered his Warsaw units (40,000 men in all) to start fighting on August 1. As soon as Stalin learned of the uprising, he ordered Rokossovsky to stop the offensive and let the Poles feel their dependence on the actions of the Soviet army. After 63 days of struggle, Komorowski had to surrender on October 2. The AK lost 10,200 men in combat and 13,900 were missing. Of the 950,000 civilian population of Warsaw, about 700,000 were evacuated by the Germans and some 200,000 perished in the fighting. Immediately after surrender Hitler ordered the total destruction of the Polish capital. On Jan. 17, 1945, the Red Army "liberated" Warsaw's empty ruins.

The Warsaw uprising

The winter offensive of three Soviet army groups, including two Polish armies of five divisions each, liberated by March 1945 almost all of the lands east of the Oder–Neisse Line. In the meantime, at the Yalta Conference (February 4–11), Roosevelt and Churchill sacrificed the legitimacy of the Polish government-in-exile in London to Stalin by consenting to the formation of a Provisional Polish Government of National Unity, which should include the members of the Lublin administration as well as "other Polish democratic leaders from within Poland and from abroad."

COMMUNIST POLAND

Formation of the People's Republic. On Dec. 31, 1944, the Lublin Committee was reorganized as a provisional government. On April 21 its chairman, Edward Osóbka-Morawski, a left-wing Socialist, signed in Moscow a Polish–Soviet alliance treaty. The Polish Government of National Unity was finally constituted in Moscow on June 28, 1945. Among its 21 members there were only five newcomers, the most important being Mikołajczyk, who became vice premier. The acting president of the republic was Bierut. This government was transferred to Warsaw, and on July 5 the British and U.S. governments recognized it and withdrew recognition from the government in London.

On Aug. 2, 1945, at Potsdam, U.S. Pres. Harry S. Truman, the new British prime minister, Clement (later Lord) Attlee, and Stalin issued a declaration establishing a de facto western frontier of Poland along the Oder–Neisse Line. Poland took over the administration of lands held by Germans to the east of that line, with the exception of the northern part of East Prussia with Königsberg (renamed Kaliningrad), which was incorporated in the Soviet Union. Gdańsk was again a part of Poland. The Potsdam agreement authorized Poland to transfer to the zones of Allied occupation about 3,300,000 Germans (about 4,000,000 had fled westward earlier, dreading the advancing Soviet armies). On Aug. 16, 1945, in Moscow, a Polish–Soviet treaty confirmed Poland's eastern frontier along the Curzon Line. In the east Poland lost 69,290 square miles (179,460 square kilometres) to the Soviet Union. In the west it gained at Germany's expense 39,596 square miles (102,555 square kilometres).

Poland's new frontiers

The Bierut era. The Sovietization of Poland was Stalin's constant aim, and Bierut was his obedient servant. First, he postponed the general elections while the secret police, supervised by the Soviet general Ivan V. Serov, made mass arrests of prominent political and military leaders. Farms of more than 124 acres (50 hectares) were expropriated and at a stroke the landed gentry was pauperized. All industrial establishments employing more than 50 workers were nationalized.

The PPR, PPS, and the Democratic Party were combined in the Democratic Bloc. As Mikołajczyk's PSL refused to join the bloc, Bierut started a ruthless intimidation campaign against its supporters. Nevertheless, at the general elections of Jan. 19, 1947, the PSL received about 84 percent of all votes; the "official" results, however, gave the Communist-controlled bloc 382 seats out of a total of 444. The new Sejm elected Bierut president of the republic, and Józef Cyrankiewicz, a pragmatic Socialist, became premier. Mikołajczyk, accused of being "an ally of foreign imperialists," fled to England. In December 1948 the PPS was eliminated by its compulsory merger with the PPR, and the Polish United Workers' Party (PUWP; Polska Zjednoczona Partia Robotnicza, or PZPR) was born.

During 1948 Gomułka opposed the collectivization of agriculture in Poland, and in consequence he was dismissed from the party and the government and later (1951) arrested. Bierut, now both president and party leader, asked Marshal Michał Żymierski, a prewar Polish officer, to resign as minister of defense and commander in chief because Stalin wanted this post for Rokossovsky (who held it from November 1949 until 1956).

On July 22, 1952, the Sejm approved a Soviet-type constitution. The president of the republic was replaced by a Council of State, and Bierut became premier. In September 1953 he ordered the internment of Stefan Cardinal Wyszyński, Roman Catholic primate of Poland, who opposed the government's interference in church affairs. Bierut abandoned the premiership in March 1954, and Cyrankiewicz returned to that post. In February 1956 Bierut attended the 20th congress of the Communist Party of the Soviet Union in Moscow, at which Nikita Khrushchev denounced Stalin's crimes. This speech fell on Bierut like a thunderbolt. He died on March 12 in Moscow.

The Gomułka era. On March 20, 1956, the PUWP Central Committee elected as its first secretary Edward Ochab, who, apparently immediately, and in conjunction with Cyrankiewicz, began to plan for the return of Gomułka. While they were still in the planning stage, an event of historic significance overtook them on June 28: industrial workers in Poznań started a general strike, and a procession of 50,000 persons demanded bread, freedom, free elections, and the departure of the Russians. On Rokossovsky's order the revolt was crushed by tanks, and more than 70 people were killed.

The Poznań general strike

When the Central Committee met on October 19 to elect a new Politburo, Khrushchev arrived in Warsaw uninvited. At the same time Soviet divisions were marching on Warsaw. Having elected Gomułka a member, the Central Committee decided that the old Politburo— but with Gomułka—would discuss Polish–Soviet relations with Khrushchev. The meeting took place during the night of October 19–20. Gomułka succeeded in convincing Khrushchev that the PUWP Politburo wished to keep Poland within the Communist camp but as an equal member, and Khrushchev returned to Moscow. On October 21 a new Politburo was elected and Gomułka became first secretary again. He promised to end the compulsory collectivization of agriculture and to reduce the rigour of press censorship. He also released Cardinal Wyszyński from confinement. In November Rokossovsky returned to Moscow with 12 other Soviet officers.

During his 14-year reign Gomułka abandoned the principle of collective leadership, becoming an authoritarian martinet. He picked fresh quarrels with the Roman Catholic Church and imposed economic measures that the workers resented as exploitative. To balance the investments expenditure for the years 1971–75, he announced on Dec. 12, 1970, considerable price increases on 46 items of basic foodstuffs, fuel, and clothing. Two days later workers from Gdańsk, Gdynia, and Szczecin shipyards went on strike, and riots occurred. Gomułka used force against the "counterrevolution": about 100 workers were killed by militia and more than 1,100 workers and militiamen were injured.

Baltic riots

Ironically, this bloody tragedy occurred shortly after a great success in the field of foreign policy. On Dec. 7, 1970, Chancellor Willy Brandt of West Germany signed in Warsaw a treaty declaring that the existing German–Polish border along the Oder–Neisse Line "forms the western state frontier of Poland" (East Germany had recognized this reality in June 1950).

The Gierek era. On Dec. 20, 1970, at a session of the Central Committee, Gomułka and his supporters were ejected from the Politburo. Edward Gierek, the party first secretary in the highly industrialized province of Katowice, assumed the party's leadership as first secretary of the Central Committee. Three days later Piotr Jaroszewicz, a deputy premier from 1952, succeeded Cyrankiewicz as chairman of the Council of Ministers.

The new government started well. Gierek's decision to rebuild the Warsaw Royal Castle, destroyed in 1944 on Hitler's order, roused the patriotic feelings of the nation. The West German Bundestag on May 17, 1972, ratified the Oder–Neisse treaty, and the Holy See soon afterward adjusted the external borders of the new western and northern Polish bishoprics with the internationally recognized frontier. The years 1971–73 were the years of Gierek's "specific economic maneuver." Assuming that prosperity in the West would continue, he sought foreign credits to finance the long overdue modernization of Polish industry. Because wages in Poland were lower than in the West, and energy and raw materials were abundant and cheaper, it seemed reasonable to expect a competitive edge for Polish exports in Western markets and repayment of the debts from hard currency profits. Unfortunately a severe recession that affected the developed market economy in 1974 reduced the chances for success of Gierek's imaginative plan.

Higher prices had become an economic necessity, but when on June 24, 1976, Jaroszewicz announced in the Sejm increases averaging 60 percent on many staples, industrial workers went on strike. The protest movement was so strong that the following day Jaroszewicz told the nation on television that the bill was being withdrawn. There was no bloodbath similar to that of December 1970,

Protest strike

but the regime was shaken. Hundreds of protesters were summarily tried and sentenced to prison. A group of Polish intellectuals appealed to the Sejm for clemency and for a free flow of information to avert further such disasters.

In 1978 Karol Cardinal Wojtyła, archbishop of Kraców, was elected pope and took the name John Paul II. His first papal visit to his native country, in June 1979, was a triumph for him and for the Catholic faithful of Poland, while the Communist government garnered some praise for civility and restraint. During the nine days of his visit the Pope spoke on 32 separate occasions, sometimes to gatherings of more than 1,000,000 enthusiastic people.

Revolt and repression. By 1980 the Polish people were facing food shortages, rationing of electric power, and insufficient housing. At the eighth congress of the PUWP, held in February, Jaroszewicz was dropped from the Politburo and replaced as premier by Edward Babiuch. On August 14 the entire work force of 17,000 stopped production at Gdańsk's Lenin Shipyard. The strike, led by Lech Wałęsa, an electrician by trade, spread to other industrial plants on the Baltic coast as well as to the coal mines of Silesia. On August 24 Gierek dismissed Babiuch, and Jozef Pinkowski was nominated as premier. Having sought guidance from the Soviets, who advised him to reach a compromise with the strikers, Gierek appointed Mieczysław Jagielski, a Politburo member and first deputy premier, to begin negotiations with Wałęsa, the charismatic leader and cofounder of the independent trade

Solidarity formed union called Solidarity (Solidarność). On August 31 in Gdańsk, Jagielski and Wałęsa signed an agreement stating that the new self-governing trade unions would "adhere" to the constitution and recognize the central role of the PUWP. All of Solidarity's major demands were granted.

The Soviets warned the Polish party that elements in the country were attempting to overthrow the Communist system. It was reported on Sept. 5, 1980, that Gierek was suffering from ill health, and on the following day the Central Committee elected Stanisław Kania first secretary. On October 24 the government formally recognized Solidarity, by then numbering 10,000,000 members. Rural Solidarity, with about 3,000,000 small farmers, was legalized by the parliament in May 1981. Solidarity held its first national congress in the fall, and on October 2 Wałęsa was elected president of its governing commission.

Pinkowski resigned as premier in February 1981, and Gen. Wojciech Jaruzelski, minister of defense, became the head of the radically revamped government. Under the term *odnowa* ("renewal") the ninth congress of the PUWP met in mid-July and, for the first time in a Soviet-bloc country, elected the Central Committee in a free vote. Kania was confirmed as first secretary, and a new Politburo was elected by the Central Committee. Of the new membership only Kania and Jaruzelski had belonged to that body before February 1980. Gierek, Jaroszewicz, and 10 of their associates were stripped of their party memberships and state medals and decorations. On October 19, after criticism by the Soviets for irresolution in dealing with Solidarity, Kania resigned from his post as first secretary. He was succeeded by Jaruzelski.

Poland's archbishop Jozef Glemp and Solidarity leader Wałęsa had an unprecedented two-hour meeting with Jaruzelski on November 4 concerning creation of a Council of National Understanding. In mid-November talks were held between the leaders of the government and Solidarity. The government appealed for cooperation, but instead the conflict intensified. Meeting in Gdańsk on December 12, Solidarity leaders proposed a nationwide referendum on establishing a non-Communist government and defining Poland's military relationship with the Soviet Union if the government did not agree to a series of union demands by the end of the year. These demands included access to the mass media and free and democratic elections to local councils in the provinces.

Imposition of martial law On Dec. 13, 1981, the government struck back. In a nationwide radio address, General Jaruzelski imposed martial law on the nation. Censorship and restrictions of personal freedoms were imposed throughout Poland. Lech Wałęsa and other leaders and supporters of Solidarity became the targets of a government program of periodic arrests and detentions.

The economy continually worsened, giving rise to greater hardships among the people. The situation was only partially relaxed by the lifting of martial law in July 1983. The government continued to exercise tight control over the domestic situation and maintained its close relationship with the Soviet Union.

For later developments in the political history of Poland, see the *Britannica Book of the Year* section in the BRITANNICA WORLD DATA ANNUAL.

For coverage of related topics in the *Macropædia* and *Micropædia,* see the *Propædia,* Part Nine, Division II, Sections 921 and 923; Division VI, Sections 962 and 963; and Division VII, Sections 971 and 972.   (K.M.S./Ed.)

BIBLIOGRAPHY. *Poland: A Handbook* (1977), is a comprehensive reference source written by Polish authors and published in Poland for readership outside the country. For balanced treatment, see *Poland: A Country Study,* ed. by HAROLD D. NELSON (1983). NORMAN DAVIES, *Poland, Past and Present: Select Bibliography of Works in English* (1977), is useful for further research. R.H. OSBORNE, *East-Central Europe: A Geographical Introduction to Seven Socialist States* (1967), includes a chapter on Poland; and DEAN S. RUGG, *Eastern Europe* (1985), includes a study of the rural and urban landscape of Poland. For statistical information, see *Concise Statistical Yearbook of Poland* (annual). On the economy, see ZBIGNIEW LANDAU and JERZY TOMASZEWSKI, *The Polish Economy in the Twentieth Century,* trans. from Polish (1985). Postwar ideological developments are the subject of DAVID LANE and GEORGE KOLANKIEWICZ (eds.), *Social Groups in Polish Society* (1973). For aspects of cultural life, see BOLESŁAW KLIMASZEWSKI (ed.), *An Outline History of Polish Culture,* trans. from Polish (1984), covering the main cultural trends from medieval times to 1982; JULIAN KRZYŻANOWSKI, *A History of Polish Literature* (1978; originally published in Polish, 1953; 5th ed., 1973); CZESŁAW MIŁOSZ, *The History of Polish Literature,* 2nd ed. (1983); BOGDANA CARPENTER, *The Poetic Avant-Garde in Poland, 1918–1939* (1983); and JANUSZ BOGUCKI, *The Fine Arts in Poland Today* (1967), and *Contemporary Polish Painting* (1958). For current cultural events, see *Polish Perspectives* (monthly); and *The Polish Review* (quarterly). See also JERZY Z. ŁOZIŃSKI and ADAM MIŁOBĘDZKI, *Guide to Architecture in Poland* (1967; originally published in Polish, 1967); BRIAN KNOX, *The Architecture of Poland* (1971); and STANISŁAW LORENTZ, *Guide to Museums and Collections in Poland* (1974; originally published in Polish, 1971).

The history of Poland is presented in the following studies: *The Cambridge History of Poland,* ed. by W.F. REDDAWAY et al., 2 vol. (1941–50, reprinted 1971); NORMAN DAVIES, *God's Playground: A History of Poland,* 2 vol. (1981; U.K. title, *A History of Poland, God's Playground*), and *Heart of Europe: A Short History of Poland* (1984); O. HALECKI and A. POLONSKY, *A History of Poland,* new ed., trans. from Polish (1983); PAUL W. KNOLL, *The Rise of the Polish Monarchy: Piast Poland in East Central Europe, 1320–1370* (1972); PIOTR S. WANDYSZ, *The Lands of Partitioned Poland, 1795–1918* (1974); *A Republic of Nobles: Studies in Polish History to 1864,* ed. and trans. from Polish by J.K. FEDOROWICZ (1982); and R.F. LESLIE (ed.), *The History of Poland Since 1863* (1980). See also ANDRZEJ WALICKI, *Philosophy and Romantic Nationalism: The Case of Poland* (1982); TITUS KOMARNICKI, *Rebirth of the Polish Republic: A Study in the Diplomatic History of Europe, 1914–1920* (1957); ANTHONY POLONSKY, *Politics in Independent Poland 1921–1939: The Crisis of Constitutional Government* (1972); and JÓSEF GARLIŃSKI, *Poland in the Second World War* (1985). For current historical research see *Acta Polonia Historica* (semiannual). IRENA GIEYSZTOROWA et al., *The Historical Atlas of Poland* (1981), is a useful companion to historical readings.

The political situation in the Poland of the 1980s is discussed in MICHAEL CHECINSKI, *Poland: Communism, Nationalism, Anti-Semitism,* trans. from Polish (1982); ABRAHAM BRUMBERG (ed.), *Poland, Genesis of a Revolution* (1983); PETER RAINA, *Poland 1981: Towards Social Renewal* (1985); JANE LEFTWICH CURRY (ed. and trans.), *The Black Book of Polish Censorship* (1984); JADWIGA STANISZKIS, *Poland's Self-Limiting Revolution* (1984); LAWRENCE WESCHLER, *The Passion of Poland: From Solidarity Through the State of War* (1984); NEAL ASCHERSON, *The Polish August: The Self-Limiting Revolution* (1982); and TIMOTHY GARTON ASH, *The Polish Revolution: Solidarity, 1980–82.*

(Ha.Ro./K.M.S./N.D.)

Police

The term police is now used primarily to denote a body of people organized to maintain civil order and public safety, to enforce the law, and to investigate breaches of the law.

All societies need some means of maintaining order. In the smallest societies lacking written laws, informal sanctions discourage deviation. In the simplest forms of state organization, informal sanctions are supplemented by agents of the ruler who enforce his decisions. Although the police function is universal in society, it is only in the larger and more complex states of modern times that full-time officials are appointed with special police responsibilities regulated by politics, tradition, and law. In modern industrial societies most police are enrolled in state, provincial, or municipal forces concerned with criminal investigation, traffic regulation, and preventive patrol. A central government generally has special sections of personnel responsible for the collection of political information, counterespionage, and so forth; and not all of this work is considered policing in its modern connotation.

This article is divided into the following sections:

Police and society

THE DIVERSITY OF POLICE ACTIVITIES

There is a remarkable historical, geographical, and organizational diversity in the activities of persons who are, or have been, counted as police. Within any one country the work of police today is very different from what it was 200 years ago. There are also major differences between countries—policing New York City is bound to have little in common with policing the Solomon Islands. The diversity is so great that the onlooker may wonder if the different kinds of activity and organization have sufficient in common to be classified together.

Police accountability and adaptation

The principle of police accountability is helpful in explaining the diversity. The problem is summarized in a Latin question: *Quis custodiet ipsos custodes?* ("Who guards the guardians?"). From one point of view, it is desirable that a police force be as efficient as possible. This consideration favours the establishment of national police forces, which can take advantage of the economies of scale in training, promotion, organization, and so on. But it often has been felt that the existence of a national force places too much power in the hands of those who direct it; that there is a danger that the government will use its control of the police to keep itself in office; and that the police will not be accountable to the public. Therefore, some countries favour a local basis for police organization.

A second principle that helps explain the diversity of police activities in different societies is that of police adaptation to cultural traditions. If the society is agricultural, as in rural India, the police will be concerned with the state of the crops, the irrigation of fields, the conditions of roads and paths, private feuds and quarrels, the registration of births and deaths, feasts, fairs, and all manner of private and public events. If local landowners are influential, as they were in 19th-century England, much police effort will be expended in the enforcement of laws against poaching and much less in the investigation of ways in which the behaviour of employers infringes the rights of employees. If some offenses are committed by criminals using vehicles, the police must be partially motorized. If criminals use firearms, the police are likely to be armed. Police activity must be adapted to the society that is being policed.

Social control in small communities. Most people obey most laws willingly, whether or not there is a police officer looking on. They comply with the laws because they believe them right and perceive that in the long run it is in everybody's interest to observe them. In small communities in which everyone knows everyone else, people who live up to the shared ideals are rewarded by the esteem of their fellows. If they fall short of other people's expectations, life is made more difficult because others are no longer so ready to help them in times of trouble. This pattern of informal rewards and punishments is, in all kinds of society, the most potent force in law enforcement, but it is stronger in the small community. The forces that order the life of the small community make the task of the police much easier. Instead of imposing requirements, they have only to lubricate the mechanisms inherent in social relations, and police action is needed only when the informal controls have proved insufficient.

Social control in large societies. The bigger a society becomes, the weaker its self-policing elements are likely to be and the stronger the legal means of social control becomes. In the first place, when people are involved with those whom they are unlikely ever to meet again, there may seem to be less reward for honest dealing. In the second place, with technological progress there comes a need for new laws. With the growth of automobile traffic, for example, many new laws governing vehicle construction, licensing, and manner of driving become necessary. Because many such laws do not have the same moral significance as laws penalizing personal violence or dishonesty, the reporting of offenses cannot be left to members of the public. Controls are needed in the form of trained inspectors, officials, and traffic police. When the legislature declares that certain actions are in the future to count as offenses, it increases the amount of crime. There is a danger that people who are convicted of one offense—say, a motoring offense—may feel aggrieved and in the future be less willing to cooperate with the police or to obey the law when they are not being observed. In the third place, as societies grow it becomes more difficult to relate public and private interests. If an employer catches a group of employees committing an offense within the workplace, he may not wish to call in the police. He may believe that, if he deals with it in his own way, production and profit may suffer less; the public interest, however, may not be served thereby.

CENTRALIZATION VERSUS DECENTRALIZATION

For these and other reasons, a tension exists between the forces of society that tend to centralize the public police and those that tend to decentralize it. On the one hand, it would appear that communities cannot wholly be left to police themselves, and that a central government should impose its standards upon local communities. On the other hand, if the central government itself is corrupt or self-seeking, the outcome will be worse than if communities were left to enforce law and order according to their own rights. Moreover, good intentions on the part of the central government are in themselves obviously not sufficient. Much depends upon whether it can induce its agents to use their powers in desired ways.

Although the belief still persists that decentralization favours police accountability, some centralization is required for economic and operational efficiency. As the period of training needed for effective police work has grown longer and work hours have been reduced, police manpower has become more expensive; and it has become important to see that police are not employed on tasks for which less highly trained employees could be used. Consequently, police in most industrial countries are now assisted by a host of auxiliaries: photographers, mechanics, fingerprinting technicians, forensic scientists, and so on. It has become advantageous to have national schemes for fixing the pay scales of both police and auxiliaries; for recruiting; for seeing that similar standards are employed throughout the nation; for establishing a common system of criminal records; for developing national facilities for higher training and the selection of top administrators; for forming specialist squads to investigate particular kinds of crime; for research; and, generally, for seeing that the police service keeps abreast of the changing pattern of criminal activity. Such tendencies make for increased centralization, and they operate in a similar fashion in all industrialized countries. As a result, regardless of the way in which police services have started out—whether, like the French, they have been highly centralized or, like the British, have taken community policing as their model—all have tended to develop some common features.

The classification of police as centralized or decentralized organizations is a relative concept. The English police, for example, are generally considered to be a decentralized force; however, when they are compared to police forces in the United States, they appear quite centralized. The organization of police forces around the world forms a wide spectrum, in which the police of the United States represent the decentralized end and the secret police of totalitarian states the centralized extreme.

(M.P.B./Ed.)

The history of policing

Forms of policing have existed for several thousand years, with religious, political, or military police wielding power as early as the time of Babylon. Early police were usually either military or semi-military organizations that developed from the personal bodyguards of rulers and warlords or from community organizations in which citizens banded together for mutual protection.

The duties of the military type of police usually consisted of keeping the public order and enforcing the religious or political mandates of those in power. Rome, under the emperor Augustus, had one of the earliest forms of organized policing. In 7 BC Augustus divided Rome into 14 *regiones* (wards), each divided into *vici* (precincts) overseen by *vicomagistri* responsible for fire protection, among other administrative and religious duties. In AD 6, after a particularly bad fire, Augustus expanded the city's fire brigade into a corps of *vigiles,* consisting of seven squads, or cohorts, of 1,000 freedmen each. Each cohort was responsible for fire and, especially at night, police protection in two *regiones.* To further impose order on the often violent streets of his city of nearly 1,000,000, Augustus created three cohorts of police, part of the army of the state, who were placed under the command of the urban prefect. These cohorts could, in turn, call upon the emperor's own bodyguard (the Praetorian Guard) for assistance.

Military and semi-military police forces developed independently in many countries of the world. For example, the shogun, ruler of 17th-century feudal Japan, devised an elaborate police system in which each castle town had a military samurai warrior who served as town magistrate, judge, and chief of police. He appointed other sword-carrying samurai (*yoriki* and *dōshin*) to serve as a patrolling police force.

In the early 1700s the Russian tsars also established a police system to enforce their laws. Tsar Nicholas I later expanded the powers of this police force and turned it into an early form of state political police—the dreaded Okhranka. After the Russian Revolution, this force gave rise to V.I. Lenin's powerful and highly organized Cheka, the political police that served as a model for Mussolini's OVRA and Hitler's Gestapo.

The other system of early policing, consisting of citizens banding together for mutual protection, was best evidenced by the frankpledge system of early England. This beginning in communal policing eventually led to the development of the Metropolitan Police Act and a British police system that served as the model for most modern police forces.

ANGLO-SAXON BEGINNINGS

As ubiquitous as the contemporary Western police system may seem, it has existed in its present organizational form only for the past 150 years. The earliest policing system in England predates the Norman Conquest. The Saxon frankpledge was a private system of social obligation in which all adult males were responsible for the good conduct of all others. To formalize this social obligation, all males were grouped into tithings headed by a tithingman. Each tithing, in turn, was grouped into a hundred. The hundred was headed by a hundredman, who served as both administrator and judge.

When crimes were observed, citizens were expected to raise an alarm, gather their countrymen, and pursue and capture the criminal. All citizens were obliged to pursue wrongdoers, and those who refused were subject to punishment. If a crime was committed with no witnesses, efforts to identify the criminal after the fact were the responsibility of the victim alone: no governmental agency existed for the investigation and solution of crimes.

The frankpledge method of policing continued unchanged until the Norman Conquest in 1066, when the Normans added the office of constable to the system. The office of constable was originally a post in the royal court, but by the late 13th century the position had evolved into a local office of individual manors and parishes. In addition to their frankpledge obligations, constables were responsible for overseeing the "watch-and-ward" system (the nightwatch). The primary responsibility of the watch and ward was to guard the city gates at night. Later, the duties of watchmen were expanded to include lighting lamps, calling time, watching for fires, and reporting other conditions. Despite the addition of constables, however,

Police specialists

The frankpledge system

the investigation and prosecution of crimes remained a private mattter to be handled by the victims.

The Statute of Winchester of 1285 codified this system of social obligation. It provided that (1) it was everyone's duty to maintain the king's peace, and any citizen could arrest an offender; (2) the unpaid, part-time constable had a special duty to do so, and in towns he would be assisted by his inferior officer, the watchman; (3) if the offender was not caught red-handed, a hue and cry must be raised; (4) everyone was obliged to keep arms and to follow the cry when required; and (5) the constable had a duty to present the offender at court tests.

In one form or another, this system remained in place in Anglo-Saxon countries until the 19th century. Essentially, it was an unpoliced system in which police functions were fulfilled by citizens who held rotating local offices. Constables and watchmen were supported by citizens, posses, and, in the case of riots, by the military or the yeomanry (a cavalry force largely composed of landowners). Victims who could not recover their property offered rewards for its return and often resorted to hiring "thieftakers." These precursors to modern bounty hunters were private citizens who, for a fee or reward, attempted to identify wrongdoers and return stolen property to its rightful owners.

The stipendiary police. The system of private rewards grew until the payment of fees to justices of the peace and constables was firmly established. When communities began paying private citizens for the capture and conviction of thieves, a standard set of fees was established and a "stipendiary" police system evolved. Sources of fees for this system included public rewards, insurance companies, commercial houses, prosecuting associations, and funds raised by subscription. Any citizen, not only constables and justices, could earn those fees and rewards by becoming a thieftaker or "common informer."

Jonathan Wild

Jonathan Wild is a notorious example of a private citizen who abused the system and turned it into a gigantic racket. He organized the London underworld and systematically arranged to have goods stolen so that he could sell them back to the original owners. Any thief wishing to remain independent of Wild's crime ring was delivered to the authorities (and ultimately the gallows). Finally, after a seven-year reign as the "Thief-Taker General," Wild, too, ended up on the gallows.

The stipendiary system was supported by a legal system that decreed Draconian punishments for crimes that, by today's standards, would be considered petty, and capital punishment and serious mutilation were prescribed for almost every conceivable crime. Such harsh punishments were handed out for two reasons—to deter wrongdoers from committing crimes and, failing that, to provide criminals with the opportunity to repent through punishment and save their souls.

The decline of constabulary police. Although the system of social obligation remained in place for more than 800 years and was transplanted to countries like Australia, Canada, and the United States, it had serious weaknesses that were amplified by industrialization and urbanization. The system had become corrupted, specially in the cities. The status of constables deteriorated through the years, and eventually the position became one of subservience to justices of the peace. As the office was degraded, persons of high social status no longer were willing to serve as constables. As a consequence, laws were established allowing persons to hire replacements to serve their terms as constables. While this did not create serious problems in small towns and agrarian areas, only the poor, aged, and infirm were willing to be constables in cities such as London, Boston, and New York City.

Although riots were an established means of political protest in agrarian England, they were an intolerable disruption of economic life in the urbanized England of the Industrial Revolution. The military and yeomanry, therefore, were called upon to quell rioting with increasing regularity. This presented two problems. First, calling in the military was seen as an easing of the restrictions on the political authority of the crown, and it was feared that once in place, the military could extend the king's political jurisdiction. Second, use of the yeomanry to control rioting exposed propertied classes to attack and created another threat to political stability.

The constable system ultimately failed because it was inefficient. Serious crimes and disorders in cities had reached intolerable levels, and the current system was under constant attack from political leaders and writers like Henry Mayhew and Charles Dickens.

Powerful forces opposed reform, however. Every alternative to the stipendiary system required substantial public funding, and raising taxes was not popular. Also, the idea of government becoming actively involved in policing violated the basic tenets of the dominant political philosophy of the era, which posited that the government that governed least governed best. Political opposition to the idea of a standing police force was substantial. Concerned about the threat of political centralization and aware of the political abuses of the French, or "continental," police, political leaders envisioned the political misuse of a standing police force. Finally, provincial leaders saw inefficiency and corruption as "London" problems and believed that the constable system worked satisfactorily in their areas.

THE FRENCH POLICE SYSTEM

Pre-Revolutionary French police. The pre-Revolutionary French police system was totally different from the English system. Organized, financed, and controlled by the government, the French police were actually the personal political police of the king. The system serves as a striking example of action by a central government to enforce its own standards of behaviour. One fact, however, is certain—the 18th-century citizen of Paris was far better protected from crime than the citizen of London. Police in Paris were controlled by the *lieutenant-général de police,* an appointee of the king. Officially under the control of the minister of Paris, the lieutenant general included in his authority the scrutiny of social, political, and economic activities of Paris, as well as a responsibility for controlling crime and maintaining order.

Paris' 20 districts were policed by 48 *commissaires de police,* officials holding both local administrative and judicial authority in the districts; 20 *inspecteurs de police,* investigators responsible for collecting and collating information from each of the districts; 50 *exempts de police,* officials responsible for maintaining order and who were supported by *sentinelles* (foot soldiers) dispersed throughout the city; 10 brigades of 10 archers each who patrolled throughout the city; a watch guard consisting of 220 horsemen and 400 foot soldiers who also patrolled the city; and *mouchards,* irregular spies, or secret police, who obtained information on the activities of all citizens. The police system also was supported by the military, which could be called upon at any time by the lieutenant general.

Despite its use of preventive patrols, the system was characterized (and made infamous) by its undercover intelligence-gathering activities. *Inspecteurs de police* and *mouchards* gathered enormous amounts of criminal and personal information from spies, brothel keepers, employers, and interdicted mail. Indeed, at one time it was estimated that one-quarter of all the housemaids and lackeys in Paris were receiving money from the police in return for information about their employers and acquaintances. The police chief Sartine once boasted to Louis XV, "Sire, whenever three people speak to one another in the street, one of them will be mine." Each day this information was passed on to the king through the *bulletin moral* and was further distributed to political officials through the *bulletin politique ou d'espionnage.* The king could issue a *lettre de cachet* ordering the imprisonment of persons even if there was insufficient evidence to bring them to trial. Such letters allowed police to detain people without charge and to exercise a kind of summary justice.

At the same time the ordinary police took an active part in many aspects of the city's life. The lieutenants general of police built markets, paved and constructed streets, founded the Bourse (stock exchange), moved a cemetery, provided street lighting, established a system of state pawnshops, created a hospital for children, founded a veterinary college, built schools for children of the poor, sought work for the unemployed, and organized fire and

Political abuse of the early French police

river rescue services. The police took stock of the city's food supplies and forbade wine sellers to have leaden counters and milkmen to use copper vessels. They censored posters and regulated the employment of foster mothers. They persecuted Protestants, controlled the sale of lottery tickets, and inspected drains. They had the streets cleaned. They supervised cabdrivers, made regulations about dogs, checked food prices, surveyed dangerous buildings, read people's letters in the course of post, and even stopped fishmongers from selling oysters between April 30 and September 10. The police inspected prisons, read theological works for signs of heresy, and had a financial agency for the encouragement of overseas trade.

National police (*maréchaussée*), originally created to control crimes committed by patrolling soldiers, eventually were used to deter civilian crimes as well. Immediately before the Revolution, the *maréchaussée* consisted of 3,000 men organized into 30 patrolling companies. Officers had both the privileges of soldiers and the powers of civil arrest.

Post-Revolutionary French police. After the Revolution, the Paris police was reconstructed, and its direction was entrusted to a conglomeration of Parisian committees. The clumsy committee arrangement failed, and in March 1800 control of the police was centralized in the *prefet de police,* an office with administrative but no judicial authority.

The French Ministry of Police was created in 1796 with a mandate to enforce laws and forestall challenges to the Revolution. When Joseph Fouché was appointed director in 1799, he consolidated police administrative powers into four *arrondissements,* each directed by a *conseiller d'État.* His councillors operated with his authority and had few legal restrictions on their power. Ultimately, Fouché's power in France became second only to Napoleon's.

In Paris, Fouché maintained the pre-Revolutionary orientation of the police by recruiting more than 300 spies, including many ex-convicts, into the *regulators de l'opinion à Paris.* Spying was so ubiquitous that private individuals, the military, and even the Jesuits organized their own secret police forces. Eighteenth-century Parisians believed that police agents and spies were everywhere, listening for the smallest hints of discontent. They may have been right, but the belief that nothing that happened in Paris would go unnoticed by the police was far more helpful to the authorities than a host of paid undercover agents. The potential of this system to be politically misused, to stifle dissent, was enormous. Police regularly disrupted, controlled, and even shaped political thought, until corruption and injustice had riddled every phase of the system.

Vidocq and the Sûreté

Perhaps the most famous manifestation of the French detective orientation of policing, at least with crimes of robbery and theft, was the Sûreté. The Sûreté was founded by François-Eugène Vidocq in 1810. A convict and a daredevil jailbreaker, Vidocq approached the police and offered to use his knowledge of the criminal world in exchange for his freedom. The police agreed, and eventually Vidocq became chief of the criminal police. Running the Sûreté with the philosophy that to know and capture criminals one had to be a criminal oneself, Vidocq directed a network of spies and informers in a war against crime that was completely successful. His knowledge of the underworld and his reliance on criminals to catch criminals were the reasons for his success. In 1817, with only 12 full-time assistants, he was responsible for more than 800 arrests.

THE FORMATION OF THE ENGLISH POLICE

The creation of the Thames River Police was one of the most significant police reform experiments of the time. The first regular professional police force in London, the Thames River Police was organized to curb the thefts that plagued the world's largest port. The West India Trading Company created these marine police in June 1798 and installed police reformer Patrick Colquhoun as director of a permanent staff of 80 men and an on-call staff of 1,120. Two features of the marine police were unique. First, patrols were preventive; officers patrolled visibly to prevent thefts. Second, officers were not stipendiary police; they were salaried and were prohibited from taking fees.

The venture was a complete success, and reported crimes dropped appreciably. In July 1890 the House of Commons passed a bill making the marine police a publicly financed organization, which ushered in a new era of policing.

Debate about the creation of a standing police force in England raged during the early part of the 19th century. Confronted with political objections and fears of potential abuse Robert Peel (later Sir Robert Peel) sponsored the first successful bill creating a bureaucratic police force in England.

The Metropolitan Police Act was passed in 1829 as a political compromise. The jurisdiction of the bill was limited to the metropolitan London area, excluding the City of London and provinces. All police were to be uniformed; crime and disorder were to be controlled by preventive patrols; police were to be paid regular salaries; and no stipends were permitted for successful solutions of crimes or the recovery of stolen property. But crime prevention was not the only business of the new police force: they inherited many functions of the watchmen, such as lighting lamplights, calling time, watching for fires, and providing other public services. "Bobbies," named after Peel, were not immediately popular. Most citizens viewed constables as an infringement on English social and political life, and people often jeered the police.

The preventive tactics of the early metropolitan police were successful, and crime and disorder declined. Their pitched battles with (and ultimate street victory over) the Chartists in Birmingham and London proved the ability of the police to deal with major disorders and street riots.

Despite the early successes of the metropolitan police, the expansion of police forces to rural areas was gradual. The Municipal Corporations Act of 1835 ordered all incorporated boroughs to set up police forces under the control of a watch committee, but it was not until 1856 that Parliament mandated that provinces establish police forces.

The Metropolitan Police Act established the principles that shaped modern English policing. First, policing was to be preventive, and the primary means of policing was conspicuous patrolling by uniformed police officers. Second, command and control were to be maintained through a centralized, quasi-military organizational structure. Third, police were to be patient, impersonal, and professional. Finally, the authority of the English constable derived from three official sources—the crown (not the political party in power), the law, and the consent and cooperation of the citizenry.

The origin of modern English policing

EARLY POLICE IN THE UNITED STATES

The United States inherited England's Anglo-Saxon common law as well as its system of social obligation and constables. As both countries moved from rural agrarian to urban industrialized economies, urban riots, crime, and disorder followed. Yet Americans, like the English, were wary of creating standing police forces.

In the early 1800s, as the United States became more urban, patterns of ethnic diversity began to erode the social and political hegemony of the original English and Dutch settlers. Not only did rioting, crime, and disorder begin to flourish, but the basic life-styles of new German and Irish immigrants offended the moral and social sensitivities of the original settlers. Immigrant and urban behaviour was perceived as a threat to the social, economic, and political fabric of American life.

The American response to growing urban unrest was twofold. Versions of the constable and nightwatch system were tried, and voluntary citizens' groups were encouraged to try to solve urban problems. Reformers distributed religious tracts and Bibles, started Sunday schools, created organizations such as the Young Men's Christian Association, and presented themselves as moral examples to immigrants and the poor. By the mid-19th century, middle-class frustration with the deterioration of the cities led to the passage of laws regulating public behaviour and creating new public institutions of social control and coercion—penitentiaries, asylums, and police forces.

In 1844 New York City created the first police department in the United States, using the London Metropolitan Police as a model. Boston and Philadelphia followed. The idea of police spread quickly, and in 10 years cities as far west as Milwaukee had created police departments. The model for American police originated in England: police were organized in a quasi-military command structure; there were no detectives; their task was the prevention of crime and disorder; and they provided a wide array of public services.

Each city created its own police department. Since Americans lacked a unifying symbol like the English crown, local politics and laws became the primary bases of police authority. The decentralization of the authority for policing was extended to political wards and neighbourhoods, which developed relatively autonomous police units. The police established intimate relations with neighbourhoods and neighbourhood leaders and initially did not even wear uniforms. Middle- and upper-class reformers believed that one of the primary tasks of the police was to reestablish political and social control over a population wracked by ethnic and economic rivalries. This tension between being closely linked to communities and being perceived of as an instrument for reform of those same communities inevitably resulted in struggle for political control of the police. This struggle for political control is one of the dominant themes in the history of police in the United States.

DETECTIVE POLICING IN ENGLAND AND THE UNITED STATES

The investigation of crimes was not a central function of the newly formed preventive police departments in England and the United States. In both countries, thief-takers, stipendiary police, and constables continued their investigations of criminal activities. Despite the high hopes of reformers when they created the police, the number of preventable crimes was limited. As victimizations continued, police were pressured into accepting public responsibility for investigations and creating detective units. The London Metropolitan Police created the first criminal investigation division (CID) in 1842. Many American cities followed with detective units: Boston in 1846; New York City in 1857; and Chicago in 1861.

Investigators usually were recruited from former thief-takers or constables who had continued their stipendiary investigative activities after the creation of police departments. Although they brought investigative skills to the police, they also brought the bane of stipendiary police—corruption. In 1877, when three of the four chief inspectors of the CID were found guilty of corruption, the CID was eliminated although later reorganized. Chicago disbanded its unit in 1864 and Boston its unit in 1870, and New York City suffered major scandals in 1877—all as a consequence of corruption. All of these cities soon reconstructed their investigative units, but improvement of the status of detectives had to wait until well into the 20th century.

LATE 19TH-CENTURY ENGLISH AND AMERICAN POLICING

After the Act of 1856 mandated police in the provinces, police departments spread throughout England. Provincial police were funded by both local and central governments. After the Home Office certified the quality of a provincial police department, the central government paid half of the cost of local policing, and local taxes paid the rest. The dominant methods of provincial policing were foot patrols and criminal investigations.

Policing in the United States during the late 19th century, however, was complicated by migration and immigration, which continually reshaped the ethnic and cultural makeup of cities, and by the radical decentralization of police authority within the cities. Decentralized policing had one major strength: it gave police close contact with the public. Police knew the local citizens, and often they were recruited from the very neighbourhoods they policed. Such close communities allowed police to spot troublemakers, identify local problems, and provide an array of public services to the residents, such as manning soup lines and providing overnight lodging in police stations for immigrants.

The decentralization of police jurisdictions to individual cities also created problems. Crime did not respect jurisdictional lines, but police organizations had to. Thus, al-

Strengths and weaknesses of decentralized policing

though serious crimes were rife on the American frontier, no national or state police organization had jurisdiction over crimes committed there. A second problem arose from the lack of a national organization. Since no binding ideology of policing existed, each police organization was an entity unto itself. Each department formed local policy and had little or no communication or coordination with other police organizations. Unlike English policing, for which Sir Robert Peel had articulated a unifying vision, American policing was atomistic and without a coherent identity.

In response to the intra-jurisdictional crime waves of the latter half of the 19th century, states enacted laws giving many corporations the authority to create their own private police forces or to contract with established police agencies. The Coal and Iron Police of Pennsylvania was an example of a company police force that later became notorious for its antilabour vigilantism. The most famous independent police force was the Pinkerton National Detective Agency. Created by Allan Pinkerton, a political fugitive from Scotland, the Pinkerton agency provided a wide array of private detective services, specializing in protecting trains, apprehending train robbers, and participating in anti-labour union activities.

Attempts in the late 19th century to develop a coherent vision of an intercity police system were largely unsuccessful; the police theory that did develop, however, was formulated mainly in local political halls. As ethnic residents gradually gained political control of city wards and neighbourhoods, the link between the police and neighbourhood politics became closer. In some instances the relationship became so close that the police were actually seen as adjuncts of the local political machines. The linking of police and politics bred political and financial corruption and injustice. Police became involved in partisan political activity to ensure election of particular candidates; they received "gratuities" for not enforcing unpopular vice laws; and they excluded strangers from social and political life.

By the end of the 19th century, middle- and upper-class citizens attempted to centralize political power to end the ward-level political control of ethnic minorities. Reformers attempted to centralize services on a citywide basis, create a civil service to end political patronage, and transfer control of police to cities-at-large, or, if all else failed, transfer control of the police to the state government.

DEVELOPMENTS IN AUSTRALIA AND CANADA

Australia. Settled as a penal colony in 1788, Australia first used the British constabulary and watch-and-ward systems. Problems plagued these systems, however, because both constables and watchmen were often recruited from the ranks of convicts. Modeled after England's Metropolitan Police Act, the Sydney Police Act of 1833 led to the establishment of urban police forces. Police coverage was extended to rural areas in 1838 when each of the country's six states created its own state police agency.

Although the state police encountered a lack of public acceptance and many of the same problems of police in England and the United States, their task was complicated by additional responsibilities. Not only were they mandated to capture villains, but they also were responsible for inflicting corporal punishment on convicted criminals. Moreover, from their inception, Australian police duties included the enforcement of health and welfare provisions of the law.

Canada. Canada's earliest legal traditions can be traced to both French and English origins. Quebec City followed French traditions and created a watchman system in 1651. Upper Canada, later renamed Ontario, adopted English traditions and established both a constabulary and a watch-and-ward system. The English system was imposed on French areas after 1759. Using England's Metropolitan Police Act as a model, Toronto created a police department in 1835, Quebec City in 1838, and Montreal in 1840. Provincial police forces were established in 1867 to provide police coverage for the vast rural areas in eastern Canada.

The North West Mounted Police (renamed the Royal

The North West Mounted Police

Canadian Mounted Police in 1920) were created in 1873 to police the vast western plains. The original 300 officers initially were assigned the task of eliminating incursions of whiskey-trading Americans who were inciting Canadian Indians to acts of violence; later the force spearheaded attempts to mold the Canadian frontier into an integral part of Canada.

The North West Mounted Police represented a significant departure from Anglo-Saxon policing traditions. Reminiscent of continental policing in organization, style, and method, they operated more like a military organization than the traditional police force. Strong leadership ensured that they operated with restraint and within Canadian political traditions. The Royal Canadian Mounted Police, along with city and provincial police forces, constitute the three-tier police system now in place in Canada.

20TH-CENTURY POLICING

The struggle for political control of police in the United States gave rise to a distinctive strategy of policing that was to influence policing throughout the Western democracies. This new style of policing integrated managerial techniques, sources of authority, innovative tactics, and a narrowed definition of police work.

The first two decades of the 20th century were tumultuous times for American police: progressives battled entrenched ward and "machine" leaders for political control; labour unrest and concerns about Communist influences preoccupied many politicians and local police organizations; political and economic corruption were widespread at all levels of government; and, the Prohibition movement was becoming a political force. Riots, mass demonstrations, and bombings were not unusual. Arrayed against these vast social problems were scattered local police forces and private detective agencies. So limited was their ability to handle such diverse national and local problems that federal and state governments were forced to create additional police agencies.

Federal and state police. The United States Secret Service was created in 1865 to prevent counterfeiting. Never numbering more than 30 or 40 agents during the 19th century, the agency was operated in the traditions of the previous century. During the 1890s the Secret Service occasionally was called upon to guard the president, but that was not made a permanent duty until 1901.

Federal Bureau of Investigation

The Bureau of Investigation—later the Federal Bureau of Investigation (FBI)—was created in 1908. In debates reminiscent of those in the British Parliament a century earlier, the U.S. Congress opposed the creation of a secret investigatory agency. In this case the concern was more than ideological—the Secret Service had been investigating corruption in Congress as well as in governmental agencies, and many congressmen were wary of increasing the president's investigatory powers. At Pres. Theodore Roosevelt's direction, Charles J. Bonaparte bypassed the reluctant politicians and created the bureau by executive order after Congress had adjourned. The Bureau of Investigation began with a modest mandate to investigate antitrust cases, several types of fraud, and certain crimes committed on government property or by government officials.

In 1920 the Treasury Department created the first sizable federal police agency. Charged with enforcing Prohibition, T-Men, as they came to be known, grew to a force of approximately 4,000 during the peak of the crusade against alcohol.

During the early 1900s states also began creating police forces. Although some states, such as Texas and Massachusetts, had small police forces earlier, in 1905 Pennsylvania established the first modern state police department. Formed with the professed purpose of fighting rural crime, state police in Pennsylvania (and later other states) were used primarily to circumvent corrupt or inefficient local police forces and to control strikes where city police were considered to be sympathetic to the unionists. Other states followed Pennsylvania's lead: New York in 1917; Michigan, Colorado, and West Virginia in 1919; and Massachusetts in 1920. Regarded as models of efficiency and honesty, state police were the prototypes of

what came to be known as professional police organizations: highly disciplined, narrow in focus, and organized along rigid military lines of command and control.

Municipal police reform in the United States. Most efforts to reform the police system during the late 1800s originated from reformers who were outside the occupation of policing. During the early 1900s, pressures for reform started within the police system itself. The most notable and representative police reformer was August Vollmer. Beginning his career in 1905 as the head of a six-person police department in Berkeley, Calif., Vollmer ultimately offered a vision of policing around which the nation's police rallied.

Prohibition was the worst of times for police: corruption flared, fueled by vast amounts of bootlegging profits; public confidence declined; and the profession came to be symbolized by Hollywood's Keystone Kops, who portrayed police as inept and venal. Vollmer and his colleagues were concerned about the broad social issues of policing. Changes in morals, increases in crime and corruption, and, later, the Great Depression, all were seen by reform-minded police as symptoms of the erosion of the authority of basic social institutions like the family, church, schools, and neighbourhoods.

Vollmer saw the police as the vanguard for socializing America's youth. In his view police should continue their traditional law enforcement role, and when necessary they should arrest and process delinquent youths through juvenile and adult courts. Arrest, however, was an undesirable outcome. Special juvenile bureaus should be created to handle problems of children and families; police should take a more active role in casework for social agencies; police should exploit their intimate knowledge of the community and place themselves at the hub of community activities with youth and families.

The police reforms of August Vollmer

In addition to giving police an ideal to strive for, Vollmer also helped consolidate the International Association of Chiefs of Police (IACP) into a truly national police organization. Under its auspices he created the Uniform Crime Reports, which became an important indicator of the health of society and of the performance of police departments. Finally, through his work on the Wickersham Commission, Vollmer exposed many unconstitutional police practices to public scrutiny, especially the practice of detectives using the "third degree" in questioning suspects.

New models of policing. When J. Edgar Hoover took over the Bureau of Investigation in 1924, he laid the groundwork for a strategy that was to make the FBI one of the most prestigious police organizations in the world. The public's opinion of detectives was ready for change. Inspired by detective-heroes in the novels and short stories of Charles Dickens, Edgar Allan Poe, and Sir Arthur Conan Doyle, readers developed a new interest in real-life accounts of detectives' exploits. Hoover set out to make the fictional image of the detective into reality. He eliminated corruption by suspending bureau investigations requiring considerable undercover or investigative work (e.g., vice and, later, organized crime) and by creating a strong bureaucratic organization that emphasized accountability. Educational requirements were established for new agents, and to ensure that they were well trained in police procedures, Hoover created the FBI Academy. He concentrated his resources on crimes that received great publicity and were relatively easy to solve, such as bank robberies and kidnappings. But most of all, Hoover assiduously cultivated publicity to create an image of the "G-Man" as the nation's incorruptible crime fighter.

Vollmer's idealistic vision of police work, with its strong elements of social work, was soon replaced by Hoover's strategy. Ironically, Vollmer's protégé, O.W. Wilson, became the architect of the new police model. Instead of broadening police responsibilities as Vollmer had proposed, the new reformers narrowed them to concentrate on fighting serious street crimes. They also moved to sever the close ties between police and neighbourhoods: assignments were changed often; police no longer patrolled areas in which they lived; and, most importantly, police began to use automobiles to patrol. To insulate police from political influences, reformers created a civil service to hire and

O.W. Wilson's new police model

promote officers and modified the basic police authority from law and politics to law only (especially criminal law). Finally, administrative decentralization within cities was abandoned, and police departments developed centralized citywide bureaucracies that restricted discretion at all levels of the organization. Since its introduction this model has dominated American policing. As the political influence of the United States grew after World Wars I and II, American policing methods spread to other nations.

Until the 1930s and '40s, police tactics were based on crime prevention by conspicuous foot patrol. As automobiles became a more important part of American life, and as reform-minded chiefs broke police officers' ties to neighbourhoods, more officers were assigned to automobile duty. The full motorization of American police was largely accomplished after the end of World War II.

The rationale for using automobiles in anticrime patrols was manifold. Police cars moving randomly and quickly through city streets would create a feeling of police omnipresence to deter criminals and reassure citizens of their safety. Rapidly patrolling police also would be able to spot and intercept crimes in progress. The use of radios in police cars increased the value of automobile patrols. The rapid response to calls for assistance would either deter criminals or help in their immediate apprehension. Police throughout the United States set an optimum goal to arrive at the scene of a crime within three minutes of its first being reported.

Contemporary policing. Wilson's strategy of policing came into fruition during the 1960s. Indeed, in 1967 the President's Commission on Law Enforcement and Crime, which was critical of the strategies of other criminal justice agencies, endorsed both preventive patrol and rapid response to calls. They agreed that improvement of policing would come as a result of fine-tuning police organizations, equipment, and personnel and that the basic strategy of policing was satisfactory. The commission noted that preventive patrol elicited hostility from some, especially minority, communities, but that its anticrime potential was so great that it had to be maintained. Police community-relations programs were proposed to offset the negative results of preventive patrol.

British police strategy

In Britain the police strategy of Sir Robert Peel was successful during the 20th century. Although influenced to some extent by the tactics of American police, the British approach appealed to the public and remained effective. Foot patrols continued in most cities, which lacked the suburban "sprawl" of American cities. Although "fire brigade" policing, as many British characterized the rapid-response orientation of American police, had some influence in Britain, it was counterbalanced by the continued emphasis on the neighbourhood bobby.

Aside from terrorism, which confronts police in all countries, the most serious contemporary problem facing British police surfaced during the 1980s—urban rioting by youths, often minorities, who believed that police tactics were brutal and unjust. The Scarman Report, which resulted from an official inquiry, suggested that police had become too remote from their communities, that local citizens should have more input into police policy-making, and that police tactics should be more sensitive to the growing cultural pluralism of Britain's major cities.

Research and new developments in policing. American policing strategy underwent a crisis during the 1960s. Crime continued to rise despite massive financial outlays for increased numbers of police. The depth of hostility that minority communities felt toward police surfaced during the riots and civil disturbances of the decade. Minority leaders not only resented the police tactics used to suppress civil disturbances, but many also believed that police actions actually caused the riots. With the fear of crime escalating more rapidly than crime itself, citizens refrained from using public and private facilities, took self-defensive measures, and abandoned city streets and parks; many fled the cities completely. Research studies were initiated to find a means of reversing these trends.

In the 1950s and '60s, both civilian and police groups assumed that the primary activity of police officers was dealing with crime and doing so with little discretion. Research on police functions conducted during this period, however, showed that when police activities, calls, and dispatches were analyzed, anticrime activities constituted less than 20 percent of patrol activities. The remaining patrol functions included resolving conflicts, providing emergency services, maintaining order, and providing other public services. Moreover, it was discovered that police officers regularly used discretion in handling events, criminal or otherwise, and that the use of discretion was an essential ingredient of police functions.

One of the earliest and most sophisticated research efforts concerning the effectiveness of police patrol was the Bright Foot Patrol Experiment in Britain in 1970. Although this experiment indicated that crime declined in areas covered by officers on foot patrol, efforts to further decrease crime by using additional foot patrols in the same neighbourhoods did not have a measurable impact.

American studies on the efficacy of preventive automobile patrols found that, despite the commitment of substantial amounts of police time to patrol, relatively little crime-related activity resulted from police initiatives. The vast majority of arrests (93 percent) resulted from citizens' requests for police action. Later studies suggested that preventive patrol by automobile did not effectively attain its goals to reduce crime, increase the public's satisfaction with police, or decrease citizens' fear of crime. Moreover, research studies on the efficacy of rapid response to calls for service suggest that it has little impact on crime prevention or criminal apprehension and that alternative approaches might produce greater levels of citizen satisfaction.

Introduced in the New York City Police Department by Patrick V. Murphy, team policing emphasizes decentralized patrol decisions by teams of officers policing a limited geographical area. Patrol decisions are made on the basis of relatively close communication with local leaders and residents.

Another promising area of police activity focuses on eliminating the opportunities for crime. Certain conditions, such as leaving one's keys in a car, invite crime. By identifying conditions that increase the likelihood of criminal activity, police can help develop policies and procedures to alter conditions and thereby make crimes more difficult to commit. Automobile thefts can be reduced, for example, by making automobiles more difficult to steal.

Eliminating opportunities for crime

In the 1970s and '80s strong community anticrime efforts also were developed in many countries, including the United States, Canada, and Britain. In a sense, these groups represented a return to the ancient tradition of social obligation, with each citizen obliged to come to the aid of others. Although police were instrumental in developing such groups, in cities such as Boston, Philadelphia, and Chicago, which had traditions of strong neighbourhoods, many groups developed on their own. Research suggests they are relatively effective in reducing crime and fear in neighbourhoods. Police experience and research suggests that police action, in itself, is limited in its ability to prevent and investigate crime. Police can be successful only to the extent that they work closely with citizens.

Indeed, the most promising development in American policing during the 1980s was community policing. Incorporating many of the ideas of team policing with research on foot patrols, community policing is an attempt to reintegrate the police officer into the community. Community policing has since proved so effective that most major U.S. cities, including New York City, Los Angeles, Chicago, Houston, and others, have either implemented the procedure or experimented with it.   (G.L.Ke.)

CENTRALIZED POLICE ORGANIZATIONS

The United States and Britain typify countries that have developed decentralized police organizations. France and Italy, on the other hand, are examples of countries with highly centralized police forces.

France. The centralized police force of France's Revolutionary period gradually developed into two national police organizations: the Police Nationale and the Gendarmerie Nationale. The Police Nationale was formed in July 1966 by the amalgamation of the Prefecture of Police of Paris and the Sûreté Nationale, which had been responsible for policing the provincial towns and for certain specialized work. The director general's headquarters includes divisions covering general intelligence, judicial police, public safety, security, regulations, training, and personnel.

The Gendarmerie Nationale is composed of soldiers formed in strictly disciplined units and quartered in barracks. In the larger towns there are Gardiens de la Paix who serve as municipal police, responsible for preventive patrol and the control of traffic.

The mayors of certain communes have communal or rural policemen at their disposal; but, as a rule, police work in country districts and in towns with less than 10,000 inhabitants is undertaken by gendarmes.

These divisions within the French police service, and the separate ties that units have with local administrators, suggest that, though centralized, the French police is far from monolithic. There are many opportunities for one police body to check upon the activities of another to prevent corruption.

Italy. Italy, too, has several national police forces. The Public Security Guards (Guardia di Pubblica Sicurezza), which is part of the armed forces, is charged with the maintenance of internal public security and order, with the protection of life and property, and with preventing and checking crime and gathering evidence in criminal matters. Although the force is of a semi-military character, it performs all normal police functions and is responsible to the minister of the interior. The Corps of Carabinieri is a military-like body housed in barracks; it is responsible to the minister of defense in certain matters but to the minister of the interior in regard to police duties. As an executive organization for the detection of crime, the corps carries out duties assigned to it by law, under the direction of judicial authorities to whom it reports on investigated crimes. At every level, commanders of the corps must maintain liaison with the army and with political, judicial, and police authorities. A Guardia di Finanza is charged principally with protecting the national frontiers from activities connected with smuggling, counterfeiting, illegal entry, and tax evasion. In addition to the national forces, municipalities maintain their own police, the Vigili Urbani, which undertake certain kinds of municipal administration but are increasingly concerned with traffic control. Frequent attempts have been made to amalgamate the Vigili with the Public Security police, but the municipalities have resisted such proposals.

Carabinieri [left margin]

DECENTRALIZED POLICE ORGANIZATIONS

United States. The United States provides a picture of what may be the most decentralized police system in the world, accompanied by an extraordinary degree of duplication and conflicting jurisdiction. Since there is no federal government control to ensure uniform standards, every community is entitled to run its own police department but cannot exclude federal or state officials from investigating offenses over which they have jurisdiction. There are five major types of police agency: (1) the federal system, consisting of police officers attached to the Department of Justice (the Federal Bureau of Investigation, together with 700 U.S. marshals), the Bureau of Internal Revenue (investigating tax evasion), the U.S. Secret Service, the Drug Enforcement Administration, the Postal Inspection Service, and many others; (2) police forces and criminal investigation agencies established by each of the 50 states of the union; (3) sheriffs and deputy sheriffs in more than 3,000 counties, plus a few county police forces that either duplicate their police jurisdictions or displace them; (4) the police forces of about 1,000 cities and more than 20,000 townships and New England towns; and (5) the police of some 15,000 villages, boroughs, and incorporated towns. To this list must be added special categories, such as the police of the District of Columbia; various forces attached to authorities governing bridges, tunnels, parks, and parkways; university, or "campus," police forces; and some units for policing special districts formed for fire protection, soil conservation, and other diverse purposes. The usual estimate is that there are about 20,000 separate

Major types of U.S. police agencies [left margin]

public police agencies in the United States and that the majority of them consist of one, two, or three men who are not employed full-time. Many are not paid wages but are compensated by the payment of fees for duties undertaken.

These police forces are controlled in different ways. The federal bodies are responsible to the federal authorities, and the state forces to the governors of their states. At local levels there are variations. States are divided into counties, and every county has its sheriff, usually elected and with responsibilities for the investigation of crime and the supervision of the custody of prisoners. He may have deputies performing duties as uniformed policemen. In some states there are county police forces under the control of county boards, whereas elsewhere, appointments are made by state governors on the recommendation of the county authorities. In some places county police forces are completely independent of the sheriff's office.

The existing American police structure to some extent reflects public opposition to any concentration of police power. It has been argued that the nation would suffer should all offenses become federal offenses and should power be transferred to Washington, D.C., and local government be enfeebled. Local problems require local remedies, and the weaknesses of big government are all too apparent. On the other hand, it is argued that the integration and consolidation of police forces could result in an improved service that would reduce costs, increase efficiency, and eliminate the problems of overlapping jurisdictions. The first steps in this direction have been taken in respect to training. Since 1960 no police officer in the state of New York has been able to assume his duties until he has received a certificate for successfully completing basic training. California has introduced grants-in-aid for training that are so attractive that most municipalities are taking advantage of them. Other states have adopted similar schemes. The federal government has made available to the police, through the Law Enforcement Assistance Administration, substantial funds for improving police resources and their management.

Australia. Certain other countries with a federal political structure have federal police forces complementing state forces, but the principles involved are no different from those exemplified by the United States. In Australia, for example, each of the six states has its own laws but does not legislate in matters pertaining to federal organizations and cannot pass laws at variance with those of the commonwealth. Each state has its police force. The minister of administrative services oversees the Australian Federal Police who are responsible for the enforcement of federal legislation. Other police forces under federal control are responsible for overseas territories, the Northern Territory of the subcontinent, and the capital territory.

The U.S.S.R. In many countries, changes in the structure of police administration have been in the direction of greater centralization; and it is of interest to consider a country where the change has been in the reverse direction. After the death of Joseph Stalin the police force of the Ministry of State Security of the Soviet Union was absorbed into the force of the Ministry of Internal Affairs (MVD) under Lavrenty Beria, who was arrested less than a year later. This force was then divided. The organization dealing with state security was transferred to the Committee of State Security under the Council of Ministers of the U.S.S.R.; known by the initials KGB, it is understood to be primarily a counterintelligence agency. The body that carries out duties performed elsewhere by the normal uniformed police is the militia. Prior to 1956 it was centralized under the Ministry of the Interior, but in December of that year the administration was decentralized. Units are now subject to control by the higher organizations of the militia, by the soviet of the local administrative area, by the local representative of the procurator general of the U.S.S.R., and by the courts. In 1960 the MVD was abolished, and in some areas the militia was itself replaced by Public Order Detachments made up of workers, builders, farmers, teachers, and students. Two and a half million citizens were enrolled into these detachments as voluntary militia. Two years later these new detachments were being criticized in the Soviet press for using their powers in too high-handed a way. To the outsider it would seem as if the Soviet Union found that a highly centralized police service was not accountable to the public and that better responsiveness required drastic decentralization, even to the extent of occasionally relying upon citizen volunteers.

(M.P.B./Ed.)

SECRET POLICE

Secret police are a special category of police. Established by national governments to maintain political and social orthodoxy, they are generally clandestine organizations that operate independently of regular civil police.

Abuses of secret police

Two notorious 20th-century secret police forces, the Nazi Gestapo and the Russian NKVD, were formed during the early days of unstable regimes. The Nazis, a minority party elected to power, quickly moved to cement their political control by taking control of the civil police and the military with their secret police organization. Their tactics included the arrest, imprisonment, torture, or assassination of political foes, as well as subversive activities aimed at discrediting political enemies and contenders for power.

Russian Communists, after a surprisingly successful political revolution, used secret police (then known as the Vecheka or Cheka) to intimidate and eliminate political enemies. Later Stalin used the force to eradicate all competing political forces and contenders for authority both inside and outside the Communist party.

Secret police not only have the traditional police authority to arrest and detain, but in some cases they are given unsupervised control of the length of detention, assigned to mete out punishments independent of the judiciary, and allowed to administer those punishments without external review. Civil police or militia may continue their traditional common policing roles and may even, at times, restrain secret police, but the tactics of investigation and intimidation permit secret police to accrue so much power that they usually operate with little practical restraint.

In the Soviet Union, Nikita Khrushchev's public revelations of the horrors of Stalin's NKVD is thought to have greatly reduced the organization's powers. However, even though the Soviet secret police have come to operate with more restraint, the potential for serious abuses still exist.

On occasion some police agencies in liberal democracies, like the CIA in the United States or the DGSE in France, also take on characteristics of secret police when they move to discredit political or social deviants. However, since most democracies establish governmental agencies to scrutinize and control secret police organizations, there is little comparison between their excesses and those of genuinely secret police like the Gestapo.

(G.L.Ke.)

Police work and law enforcement

ROUTINE POLICE ACTIVITIES

Watchman, legalistic, and service styles of law enforcement

Earlier reference was made to the way in which police activity is adapted to the kind of society that is to be policed. There are features common to the work of police in differing societies that are founded upon similar technology. Yet within the same society, at times within the same police force, there are variations in the policies of police chiefs. One police administrator, because of his personal beliefs or because of his perception of public opinion, may allocate more officers for the investigation of vice than of fraud, may allocate more or fewer officers for traffic control or crime prevention. A police chief may instruct officers not to bother about prostitution, provided it is confined to a given locality. Thus, the police in different neighbourhoods may follow different patterns of policing.

Within the framework of enforcement policy, police work is divided into various branches. The largest number of officers is usually allocated to uniformed patrol, either on foot or with motor transport. Studies of the activities of police on patrol indicate that only a small portion of their time goes to the making of arrests or to initiating formal actions under the criminal law. Moreover, whether one examines the types of calls for service that police receive, the calls to which police are dispatched, or the activities that police initiate on their own, it is clear that the majority of police activities consist of providing emergency services, maintaining order, resolving disputes, and providing other services.

POLICE AND COURTS

One of the most important ways in which police are held accountable for the manner in which they perform their duties is through the courts. In France (and in countries with similar juridical procedures) the police making inquiries are under the direction of the investigating magistrate, whose task it is to decide whether there is a case for trial and, if so, what it is. The French think it improper that police should inquire into a citizen's activities without his knowledge that they are doing so and without these investigations being under judicial control. The British and American procedure is very different. Anyone may prosecute. The judge listens to the prosecution's argument and evidence that the accused has broken a particular law, and he listens to the defense. Then he decides between them. If he finds the case proved, he then inquires into the accused's previous record and determines the sentence. Should it transpire that the defendant has broken a law but not the one he is accused of having broken, the case must be dismissed.

If the accusatorial system is to function justly, the police must bring all cases of lawbreaking before the courts. It is for the court to decide whether they merit punishment. But, in practice, the police exercise considerable discretion as to whom they will prosecute.

Police discretion in arrest and prosecution

There are three chief arguments in favour of police discretion. First, it has not been possible to draft and keep up-to-date a criminal code that unambiguously encompasses all conduct intended to be made criminal and none other; there are technical offenses or offenses that public opinion no longer regards as culpable. Second, those charged with enforcing the law do not have sufficient resources to enforce all the laws all the time, so that enforcement must be selective. Third, to bring a technical offender to court may, in practice, unduly damage that person's reputation.

The courts control police activities in other ways. In Britain a set of publicized "Judges' Rules" outlines safeguards for accused persons while under investigation. If in court it can be proved, for example, that the police failed at the proper points to warn a person that he was under suspicion of having committed a particular offense and that any statement he might make could be given in evidence, then the prosecution might fail. In the United States the Supreme Court has held that an accused need not answer police questions and that he has a right to consult a lawyer before questioning; if he cannot afford to hire a lawyer, one must be provided. In other decisions, police have been prevented from submitting at a trial any evidence that was obtained by unreasonable search and seizure.

CROWDS AND RIOTS

The London police have developed skillful methods of crowd control but have had little experience of urban rioting on the scale with which American police were confronted in the 1960s. Both crowds and riots require patrol officers to adopt a very different approach from that to which they are accustomed. Normally, police are free to handle members of the public in an individual manner. But the control of civil disturbances requires large numbers of disciplined personnel working as a team under unified command.

British methods of crowd control

From their beginnings in 1829, the English metropolitan police were careful not to overreact when handling crowds. In Britain, if the police fail to control a riot, recompense for the damage has to be paid by the police authority for the district. Were the police to use, say, water cannon, an injured onlooker could sue the police for assault. The London police use no riot squads, no protective clothing, no arms, no riot gas, and no barriers for crowd control. The police line has always to be in close contact with the crowd, preventing the stone throwing and violence that occurs when there is a gap between them and the citizenry. The advantages of the passive police stance encouraged by their legal accountability were exemplified by four

London demonstrations in 1967–68 against U.S. policy in Vietnam. At the fourth of these, in an atmosphere made tense by press apprehensions of revolution, some 50,000 people marched through the city. In February 1971 a demonstration of some 140,000 individual workers passed without an arrest.

Disturbances that erupted in more than 50 American cities in 1967 posed serious problems for the police. Most of these disturbances began during the evening watch, when a police department normally has about 13 percent of its uniformed force on duty. At this time, a city with a population of about 500,000, for example, would have had about 95 uniformed police officers on duty. The National Advisory Commission on Civil Disorders found that many of the disturbances began when allegedly abusive or discriminatory police actions set sparks among the grievances of blacks. In some cases the police were unable to control the resulting situation, and the National Guard, composed of private citizens who undertake part-time military duty, was summoned. The commission concluded that the National Guardsmen were inadequately trained for riot duties and that their performance in 1967 raised doubts about their capabilities for such assignments. Whereas in some cities National Guardsmen and police fired thousands of rounds of ammunition, in others regular troops restored order by calm discipline and little use of firearms. The experience of the 1967 disorders suggests that giving the police more destructive weapons is not sufficient to maintain order when a substantial section of the population is disaffected.

POLICE WORK AS AN OCCUPATION

As has been seen, some police bodies are constituted as part of the armed services. In some European countries it has been normal to recruit as police those who have served as regular soldiers or sailors. It has been even more common to appoint retired army, navy, or air force officers to command police forces. Since World War II the trend has been in the opposite direction.

Police work is seen as a specialist career, and it is argued that the senior positions should go to those who have learned the work by experience. This poses certain problems of recruitment. It is argued that the police should be able to offer appointments as cadets to young persons who want to become policemen. If they have to wait until they are 21 years or so before they are eligible for appointment, they may be lost to the police. On the other hand, it is said that a youth who has come straight into the police from secondary school has had too little experience of life and is likely to be too narrow in his outlook. Cadet training schemes therefore seek to give such entrants a wider experience by sending them to social-service agencies and other bodies.

Officer entry

A similar problem is that of officer entry. The French recruit graduates to the Police Judiciaire by examination, and in Norway only those with legal qualifications are eligible for appointment as police chiefs. In the United States many universities offer courses in police science, and those who obtain qualifications in this field have a certain but limited career advantage. In Britain, graduates are welcomed but have to compete with other entrants for promotion. The most able among the younger officers are selected for a 12-month course at the national Police College at Bramshill; they divide their time so that half is devoted to professional and half to general studies, by contrast with the rather shorter courses at the Federal Bureau of Investigation Academy at Quantico, Va., where all the teaching concentrates on police subjects.

INTERNATIONAL ORGANIZATION

The International Criminal Police Organization (Interpol) has a history going back to 1914, though its present constitution dates from 1956. Each member nation has established a bureau that maintains relations with the General Secretariat in Paris. The bureaus transmit criminal information that may be of interest to other countries; they undertake, within their own countries, inquiries, searches, and arrests requested by other countries; and they take steps to implement resolutions voted by the annual as-

sembly. Interpol can act only within the framework of national laws; criminals can be returned only if an extradition treaty is in force and the offender is a national of the country requesting return. The International Association of Chiefs of Police, with headquarters near Washington, D.C., draws its members largely from the United States and is the leading voice in the United States for professional police standards. It is active in training, research, and public relations. The International Police Association was founded in Britain in 1950 as a social organization. Although it is most active in Europe, its members come from dozens of nations worldwide. The association grants scholarships for study travel and arranges annual conferences.

(M.P.B./Ed.)

Police technology

Police technology covers the methods and techniques of, and the equipment available to, police agencies. Throughout the 20th century, improvements and innovations have been made in police transportation, communications, weaponry, laboratory facilities, and other areas, but these have scarcely more than kept pace with the pressures generated by denser urban populations, greater sophistication on the part of criminals, social disturbances, and new types of crime made possible by economic and technological developments—*e.g.,* aircraft hijacking and computer fraud.

Police technology increasingly involves borrowings from the physical and social sciences, as well as from the fields of jurisprudence and education. Although it was only in the 1960s that police technology became recognized as a distinct academic and scientific discipline, the proliferation of professional publications, educational programs, workshops, and international conferences of police reveals the growing importance attached to the technical aspects of police work.

Two influences serve to restrict the application of technology to police work. First, technical problems themselves may arise when the technology of one discipline is transferred to a different application in police science. Second, in the United States and other democracies, constitutional and legal issues may limit or prevent the use of feasible technologies in police work.

Many examples of an incipient police technology can be found in the ancient and medieval world. Long before the beginning of the Christian Era, Egyptians used detailed word descriptions of individuals, a concept known in modern times as "portrait parle." The Babylonians pressed fingerprints into clay to identify the author of cuneiform writings and to protect against forgery. Fingerprints were also used by the Chinese at an early date for purposes of identification. The concept of comparison and identification of handwriting was established in Roman times, as is evidenced by the Code of Justinian of the Eastern Roman Empire, first enacted in AD 529. Branding and mutilation were used from time immemorial to identify convicted criminals. Trial by ordeal and trial by combat were medieval methods of interrogation of suspects, with the survivors judged innocent. A more humane medieval method, and a step toward modern concepts, was compurgation, in which the friends and families of the disputant took oaths not on the facts but on the disputant's character.

An Asian interrogation method involved scientific principles based on the lessening of salivation under nervous tension. The mouths of several suspects were filled with dry rice; the suspect exhibiting the greatest difficulty in spitting out the rice was judged guilty. Another precursor of the modern lie detector was employed in India. Suspects were sent into a dark room where a sacred ass was stabled and directed to pull the animal's tail. They were warned that if the ass brayed it was a sign of guilt. The ass's tail had been dusted with black powder; those with a clear conscience pulled the tail, whereas the guilty person did not, and an examination of the suspects' hands revealed the person with the guilty conscience.

Modern police methods were beginning to develop in Europe by the 18th century and in the 19th century were reinforced by a great number of technological advances.

Precursors of the modern lie detector

When the British Parliament enacted the reforms of Robert Peel in 1829, the importance of keeping comprehensive police records was recognized. In principle, Peel stated that police records were indispensable for the proper distribution of police strength. His reforms laid the foundation for the development of the modern police communications system and provided for a coherent police organization.

Until the mid-19th century, however, police signal systems consisted of whistles, raps on the pavement with a nightstick or baton, and flashing of lights. In 1849 the central police station at Scotland Yard and the district police stations of London were connected by a telegraph line. Other cities followed, and telegraph boxes placed at points on patrolmen's beats permitted swift calls to headquarters when assistance was needed. The telephone was first installed in a police station in Washington, D.C., in 1878. Two years later Chicago took the important step of installing telephone boxes on patrolmen's beats.

Important advances in identification occurred in the late 19th century. In 1882, Alphonse Bertillon of France introduced a means of identifying suspects by using measurements of the body, head, and limbs. This system was largely supplanted by modern fingerprinting, which dates from about the same period. The Henry system of classifying fingerprints (by patterns and shapes) was adopted by Scotland Yard in 1901, and this system, or variants of it, soon became standard throughout the world.

The idea of tracing and identifying an individual typewriter by means of the peculiarities of its type characters probably first appeared in Arthur Conan Doyle's story "A Case of Identity," written in 1891, three years before the first mention of the subject in technical literature.

First use of the automobile

The automobile, first used in police work in Akron, Ohio, in 1899, became the basis of police transportation in the 20th century. Closely linked with it was the adoption of radio communication. Other innovations in communications were the teletypewriter and facsimile. The teletypewriter evolved from printing telegraphs and developed rapidly during World War I; by the 1920s it was used in police communications in most countries. Facsimile transmission (telephotography) dates from the early 1900s, and in 1908 a criminal was captured as a result of his photo being transmitted by facsimile from Paris to London. After World War I the use of this technique became widespread.

Perhaps the single most important invention in the development of police communications was the transistor, which, in the 1950s, led to the development of small, lightweight, reliable radio transmitter-receivers.

In the 1920s the technique of identifying firearms by the striated markings on bullet jackets was introduced. As these and other new techniques became available, the first police crime laboratories were instituted in Europe and the United States. One of the earliest was established in Lyon, Fr.

There have been few innovations in weaponry. The nightstick (club) and firearm, invariably adaptations of military weapons, remained virtually unchallenged in the police arsenal until the 1960s, when chemicals, tranquilizing darts, light- and sound-energy techniques, and other devices began appearing.

MODERN SURVEILLANCE SYSTEMS

Police use a number of surveillance techniques, but their chief reliance is almost universally placed on patrolling.

Patrol systems. Patrols vary in methodology, assignments, structure, and mobility. Their flexibility has been significantly enhanced by improved methods of communication, especially the two-way radio, and by the availability of numerous types of vehicles such as the automobile, the motorcycle, and, in many countries, the bicycle. The mobility provided by modern communication and transportation techniques is particularly useful in dealing with civil disorders.

The areas covered by metropolitan police patrols vary enormously in population density, character of commerce and industry, terrain, and roads. The initial enthusiasm for using helicopters in routine patrol work lessened when cost analyses showed that the true cost of helicopters was much higher than expected. High maintenance costs and excessive downtime because of a lack of pilots, aircraft disrepair, and poor flying weather resulted in helicopters being rarely used in routine patrols. Helicopters have come to be used primarily for rescue work and special tactical situations requiring surprise or high mobility. In some countries short takeoff and landing aircraft have been adopted for patrol and rescue work.

Police dogs. The training of dogs for police work was originally developed in Ghent, Belg., about 1900 and was soon copied elsewhere. Though certain breeds with especially keen senses are used for special purposes, such as detecting caches of illegal drugs or for tracking fugitives and missing persons, the most widely trained dog for regular patrol work is the German shepherd, or Alsatian. Other breeds that are sometimes used include boxers, Doberman pinschers, Airedale terriers, rottweilers, schnauzers, and bloodhounds. Selection involves the use of standard criteria related to breeding and physical measurements, and training is rigorous.

Electrical protection systems. Electrical protection (alarm) systems substantially reduce burglaries and contribute to the capture of many criminals. The development of alarm equipment and the evolution of operating procedures in the United States, Canada, and western Europe have been significantly influenced by the published standards of Underwriters Laboratories (UL). Central-station systems and local-alarm systems are the two basic categories of UL-regulated burglar-alarm systems.

Central stations

Central stations are commercially operated control centres serving metropolitan and surrounding areas. Burglar-alarm protective circuits and devices automatically transmit signals to these centres. Armed guards are on duty at all times and are dispatched to conduct immediate investigations of unauthorized entry of protected properties. Central stations generally have direct communication channels to police control centres. Some centralized operations in large European cities control several completely automatic satellite stations in nearby cities; the local police are dispatched by the central station.

Local burglar-alarm systems consist of sensitive warning mechanisms that are connected to loud alarms and, often, to a signal system in local police stations. Originally local burglar-alarm systems were used primarily in small towns where central station services were not available, but technological improvements and lower prices have led to their use in homes and small businesses in all types of cities. Many police departments discourage the use of these systems, however, because up to 95 percent of the alarms given by them are false.

Technical surveillance. The application of technology to surveillance operations has greatly expanded the capabilities of law-enforcement agencies and has led to the creation of a special field of police technology known as technical surveillance.

Audial surveillance. Audial surveillance, or electronic eavesdropping, became practical for obtaining evidence and investigative leads as a result of the intensive development of the magnetic tape recorder and solid-state electronic components during World War II and subsequent years. The field has two technically and legally distinct areas: the surreptitious interception of oral communications, commonly known as "bugging," and the surreptitious interception of wire communications, commonly known as "wiretapping." Typical devices used include miniature microphones, miniature radio transmitters, and a variety of radio-receiving and voice-recording equipment.

Microphones, of course, are always required for the interception of oral communications and may be connected by cables directly to recorders located at remote locations or may be connected to transmitters. Excellent quality microphones of very small size are available throughout the world. Some microphones located in the handsets of telephones can be modified to intercept nearby conversations.

Radio transmitters the size of a cigarette package, equipped with integral batteries and microphones, are commonly known as "wireless mikes." Most radio transmitters used for audio surveillance operate within the very high frequency (VHF) range.

The most common type of interception of wire communications consists of monitoring telephone conversations. Equipment used for telephone tapping ranges from the telephone repairman's handset to automatic voice recorders connected to target telephone lines.

Optical surveillance. Optical surveillance makes use of such devices as binoculars and telescopes; cameras with long-focal-length, or telephoto, lenses; closed-circuit television; and video tape recorders. Closed-circuit television is a versatile surveillance method that has become widely used both by police and by private security systems. From a central location, a supervisor can monitor events at one or several remote locations. Cameras may be fixed or they may oscillate to sweep a large area.

Optical surveillance is sometimes used as an evidence-gathering technique. In arrests involving driving and the use of alcohol, the physical condition of the driver is filmed or videotaped and later used as evidence. In an effort to reduce lawsuits concerning interrogation methods, some police agencies also film or videotape interrogation.

Low-light-level devices have greatly extended passive optical-surveillance capabilities. Practical low-light-level television systems are manufactured for optical surveillance operations under light intensities as low as 10^{-8} lumens per square metre, or virtual darkness. Night-vision telescopes using two and three light-amplification stages are also used.

Tagging and tracking. Object tagging and signal tracking are a third category of police technical-surveillance operations. Devices emitting a unique signal are attached to vehicles or implanted in targeted objects. Compatible receiving or activating equipment is used to track the tagged objects. A typical device used in tracking is a miniature radio transmitter using distinctive tone modulation, commonly known as a "bumper beeper," which is surreptitiously attached to a vehicle. The target is discreetly tracked with one or more surveillance vehicles equipped with appropriate receiving equipment.

CRIME REPORTING AND RECORDS

The efficiency and effectiveness of a police department depend in large degree on complete, readily available, and up-to-date record keeping.

Information must be reported, collected, classified, analyzed, processed, and stored. Numerous files must be kept, of which the most important include fingerprints, modus operandi of criminals, and various investigation and reference files. There should be as much cross-filing as possible.

Fingerprint classification. Fingerprint records are among the most significant files that are maintained. Inked fingerprints from all 10 fingers of an individual person can be classified; *i.e.*, be put into narrow categories for file purposes and ultimate retrieval. Most countries use the Henry extension system, a modification of the Henry system, which was developed prior to 1900 in England. In the Henry extension system, each of the 10 individual fingerprints of a person is classified as to arches, loops, whorls, or composite style prints. The type of design, plus subclassification based on locating certain fixed points and counting the ridges lying between the points, is used to make the classification.

Fingerprints obtained from individuals are classified and compared with the fingerprints of other individuals having the same classification. With this system, personnel in a police centre need not compare a set of fingerprints with the millions of cards on file but only with the few in the same classification. (For the technique of fingerprint identification, see below *Laboratory procedures.*)

Modus operandi. If a criminal has been successful using certain methods and techniques, he tends to repeat the same procedure. Thus, evidence of characteristic behaviour and procedure at the crime scene can serve to identify the offender if the pattern is recognized by the police. Although classification of criminals according to operational methods and manners has lost a good deal of its effectiveness in the investigation of burglaries, large law-enforcement agencies still maintain modus operandi files to recognize patterns of behaviour, to associate a group of crimes with a single perpetrator, and to enable

them to predict the next target of the criminal. The modus operandi file is most effective in crimes involving personal contact, such as felonies against persons, confidence games, and forgery. Enhanced computer storage and search capabilities have rekindled interest in modus operandi methods of investigation, even in such cases as burglaries and robberies.

Investigation and reference files. Informational files are maintained by law-enforcement agencies. The primary purpose of these records is to identify the source of evidence discovered in connection with a crime. For example, a file of automotive paint samples can assist in identifying the make and model of a vehicle involved in a hit-and-run case. Automotive registrations and records of firearms assist in establishing ownership. In addition to their own files, the police have access to the records of many governmental agencies that record titles, contracts, vital statistics, significant events, and official acts in general. Among other files maintained by the police the following prove exceptionally useful.

Missing persons. Each year many thousands of persons are reported missing to the police. In addition, the police must investigate cases of unidentified persons, living and dead. Descriptive files are maintained of missing persons under the age of approximately 19, unidentified dead, and unidentified persons who are physically and mentally afflicted.

Laundry and dry cleaners' marks. A valuable clue to the identity of an unknown person can be found in the mark or marked tag placed in his clothing by a laundry, dry cleaner, or tailor. The mark usually consists of a set of numbers or letters identifying the retail store or the wholesale processor. Samples of these marks are filed systematically by larger police departments for the purpose of tracing a lost, dead, or wanted person.

Lost or stolen property. Many cases of burglary and larceny are solved simply by tracing stolen property to the possession of the criminal. For this purpose, police maintain a central cross-indexed file of property lost or stolen and of articles pledged to pawnbrokers or sold to second-hand dealers. The common objects of larceny—automobiles, watches, jewelry, furs, and cameras—are identified by means of an accurate physical description, including serial marks and personal inscriptions.

Computerized records. The record-keeping tasks of police work were long handled by using a diversity of manual systems. Quick nationwide or international utilization of records and files was impossible. Now, however, electronic data processing has revolutionized information-handling techniques. Manual filing systems have been superseded by computers that operate from central geographic points, storing data and making it instantaneously and accurately available to many police constituents. Advances in computer networking permit the linking of many police and investigative data bases and make possible the development of national criminal investigation systems. Interpol is an example of an international computer network that coordinates the exchange of criminal intelligence to aid police agencies in searching for fugitives or missing persons or property.

In addition to serving as a depository and dispenser of information, the computer can provide statistical analysis for research and management, develop intelligence data bases and analysis systems, assist in the analysis of physical evidence, facilitate swift document retrieval, and help in such areas as identification of fingerprints. Using traditional manual methods, fingerprint examiners, for example, have to make visual comparisons of thousands of individual 10-digit fingerprint cards in order to make a positive identification. The development of a computerized fingerprint search system took more than 20 years of industry-wide research. Although the Federal Bureau of Investigation was a pioneer in the development of automated fingerprint files, the vast size of its collection of fingerprint cards and the high cost of converting its files delayed the completion of a high-speed fingerprint search system. The Japanese National Police Agency established the first practical system in Tokyo in the early 1980s. A second generation of the Japanese system focused on

(margin note: Devices for low light levels)

(margin note: Electronic data processing)

individual images instead of 10-digit cards. Since its introduction, this system has been used as a prototype for several computerized systems in the United States, including those in police agencies in Alaska, Massachusetts, San Francisco, and Suffolk County, N.Y. An interactive system established by the California Bureau of Criminal Identification is one of the largest, linking several major police departments and covering more than 90 percent of the population of the state.

COMMUNICATIONS

A total police communications system can be extremely complex, but its complexity varies with the needs associated with particular police organizations and their operational environmental situations. Each police function or situation calls for its own subsystem of communication.

In a large city the sources of information that must be fed into the central system are remarkably varied. Police may be on foot or motorcycles, in patrol cars, in patrol boats, or in aircraft. In addition, the system must encompass links to fire stations, ambulance services, traffic-control systems, rescue teams, alarm systems, emergency utility services, crime-information systems, and crime laboratories. A variety of fixed and mobile systems are used, including radios, television (including closed-circuit), telephone, teletypewriters, and facsimile transmission.

Police radio-communications systems, which profited considerably from the advances in electronics during and after World War II and from developments in the U.S. space program, also benefited from the development of computers, which made possible the quick retrieval of information on stolen property, wanted persons, and other police intelligence. Many urban centres now use police cars that have direct access to departmental computers and contain equipment capable of receiving printouts of orders and lists of wanted persons or missing property. The augmented flow of information has placed an added burden on existing communications systems, which have consequently grown more complex. Among numerous technological innovations, the development of the modern police communications centre merits particular mention.

Functions of a police communications centre

A communications centre performs several functions: (1) receives and processes police calls from the public; (2) audits and dispatches police resources in response to police calls; (3) receives and responds to information inquiries as well as to calls for assistance from police patrols; (4) maintains moment-to-moment information on police resources for command and control purposes.

The geographic distribution of police communications centres has been broadened to include locations in many countries of the world. These centres facilitate police work needed to deal with the international mobility of modern criminals. The extensive radio network maintained through Interpol serves to promote international cooperation among world police organizations.

INTERROGATION METHODS AND EQUIPMENT

Police and other investigators depend on interrogation as a principal means of determining facts and resolving issues. Reliance on interrogation, however, involves certain problems: ascertaining when a suspect or witness is telling the truth, evaluating memory, allowing for the physical and mental condition of a witness or suspect, and understanding the problems created by an individual's perspective.

Interrogation methods and equipment have evolved in response to these problem areas. The psychological, psychophysical, and physical sciences have played vital roles in police interrogation techniques.

The most dramatic gains in interrogation technology have come through the polygraph, or so-called lie detector. The polygraph monitors and records selected body changes that are affected by a person's emotional condition. The recorded changes are then studied, analyzed, and correlated in respect to specific questions or other stimuli.

The first modern polygraph was constructed in 1921 by John A. Larson, a medical student at the University of California, working with a member of the local police department. Larson's instrument was capable of continuously recording blood pressure, pulse, and respiration; since it recorded these conditions simultaneously, it was called a polygraph. A later development provided for the recording of the psychogalvanic skin reflex (electrodermal response), the flow of current between two different parts of the body. Research has continued on both the instrumentation and the psychological techniques necessary for its effective use by the police.

Even though the polygraph has been formally and successfully used in police intelligence and security investigation since 1924, there is still no complete agreement by psychologists on its validity. Furthermore, the results of a polygraph test are not always judicially acceptable. Despite these qualifications, the polygraph has proved an invaluable aid to police interrogation and the development of investigative leads.

WEAPONS AND RELATED DEVICES

To contend with the wide diversity of criminal situations, police require a variety of weapons and restraining and protective devices.

Standard weapons. Standard equipment varies. London police carry only a small baton; New York City police carry a large-calibre revolver and a baton; Paris police carry a small-calibre semiautomatic pistol, a baton, and a leaded cape; and Cairo police carry a submachine gun or automatic rifle.

The most universal physical weapon and certainly the most frequently used weapon over the years has been the baton, nightstick, truncheon, or billy. The baton has been the subject of study and research, and there now exists a family of batons that include, in addition to the original wood or plastic baton, devices that contain firearms, aerosols or tear-gas cartridges, and electric-shock systems. Some batons are made to break at a certain degree of impact in order to avoid serious injury.

Pistols, including the automatic pistol and the revolver, are the second most widely used police weapons. In the United States the revolver (.38 special to .45 calibre) is the primary pistol, whereas in Europe and Asia the automatic (.25 to .38 calibre 9 mm) is extensively used. Shotguns, rifles, and automatic weapons are usually included in the police arsenal but are issued only when essential.

Lacrimators and nauseators

Chemical and other nonlethal weapons. Universally used chemical weapons are those that deliver compounds that cause either severe weeping or tearing at the eyes (lacrimators) or extreme discomfort or sickness (nauseators). The three most commonly used chemicals are known by the initials CN and CS, both lacrimators, and DM, a nauseator. Among the systems used to dispense the chemicals are riot shotguns, fog generators, and grenades. The most commonly used modern weapon is the handheld aerosol tear-gas projector (Mace). Of convenient size, it can be carried in a holster; it is easily aimed and instantly effective. Its range is 15 feet, and it delivers about 40 one-second bursts.

Other nonlethal weapons include sound and light devices that cause confusion, pain, or temporary blindness, as well as stun guns. Stun guns emit a high-voltage charge that temporarily renders a person unconscious. (Because some physicians object to its use, the stun gun must undergo widespread testing and evaluation before it is added to the standard police arsenal.) The water cannon is used, especially in Europe, for crowd control. Nonlethal projectiles include plastic shot and bullets made of rubber, wood, or fabric.

Restraining and protective devices. Criminal restraining and police protective systems have been subjects of much study and research. The developments in restraining devices and systems include lighter, more effective handcuffs with improved locking systems, lightweight thumb cuffs, pressure-twisting devices that are applied to wrists, lighter and stronger straitjackets, and lighter and stronger leg irons.

A modern restraining device is the disposable handcuff. It consists of a nylon plastic strap with a slotted head at one end and a tapered tail at the other. A stainless steel barb in the head allows the tail to be pulled through the head in one direction and locks the strap so that it cannot be withdrawn. To remove plastic cuffs, the police officer merely cuts them off. This device is particularly useful in mass arrests, as in riots.

Significant developments in the technology of protective devices include heavy plastic shields to ward off rocks and other missiles, lightweight nylon clothing resistant to pistol bullets, bulletproof shields, and bulletproof armour made of nylon and ceramic materials, which can withstand high-powered rifle bullets. Studies show that in their first five years of use in the United States, bulletproof vests saved the lives of more than 700 police personnel. Of all the police killed by guns during that period, only 10 percent were wearing vests, and virtually all of that number suffered head wounds.

LABORATORY PROCEDURES

Crime laboratories may be either specialized, such as those that handle principally documentary evidence, or broad in coverage, as is the case with most national police laboratories. The fundamental purposes include the collection and preservation of physical evidence, its examination, and the preparation and presentation of accurate, objective testimony regarding it.

Personnel include specialists such as document examiners, generalists such as criminologists, and technicians and other supporting personnel. They are usually employed by a government unit and must pass rigid examinations.

Facilities and equipment. Crime laboratories usually are equipped with an array of scientific instruments and facilities. Instruments are constantly being developed, and the resources of individual laboratories vary. Some are equipped with expensive and sophisticated analytical instruments, such as the mass spectrograph, the electron microprobe, and the scanning electron microscope. Close cooperation among laboratories makes possible the sharing of specialized equipment when needed.

The largest category of laboratory equipment is related to photography. The usefulness of the medium extends from straightforward photography of, for example, automobile accidents and sites of crimes to specialized work of various kinds. Colour photography is commonly used to obtain more realistic and informative representations of the crime scene. Ultraviolet and infrared photography aid in detecting stains, invisible writing, and alterations on documents. Radiography is also used to provide details that would otherwise be invisible. Photography through a microscope (photomicrography) is a common technique, a special case being the examination of bullets. Fingerprint photography is an area of specialization that may involve conventional methods or any of a number of special techniques to recover useful prints from different types of surfaces.

Value of photography

Among the more common facilities are chemical laboratories, with a range of reagents and analytical instruments, including spectrographs and chromatographs. Optical equipment includes a full range of magnifying devices, from magnifying glasses to specialized microscopes of various kinds, including stereomicroscopes and comparison microscopes.

Evidence and its examination. An investigation at the scene of a crime, particularly in crimes of violence, is the first phase of the laboratory function. Many jurisdictions have mobile crime laboratories, in which some of the regular laboratory tests can be performed by specially trained police personnel called evidence technicians.

Crime sites must be searched to locate pertinent physical evidence, which may range from latent fingerprints to bloodstains to pieces of a broken automobile headlight. Evidence must be marked for identification, preserved, and protectively packaged for transportation to the laboratory. In addition, records (written or photographic) must be made of each piece of evidence and its exact location with respect to the crime. The law requires that the "chain of evidence" remain unbroken and makes police accountable for every item of evidence from the time of its discovery to its ultimate presentation in court.

Certain laboratory procedures and tests are carried out in the field when time is limited or when there is a possibility that the evidence might be disturbed. Among such procedures or tests are dusting for fingerprints, making casts of footprints and automobile tracks, making blood tests, and collecting specimens of organic and inorganic materials from the environment.

Hypnosis. In the 1970s police began experimenting with hypnosis as a means of interviewing witnesses to certain crimes. Hypnosis is reported to be particularly effective in helping witnesses give descriptions of criminals, relate the details of violent sexual attacks, and recall the scenarios immediately preceding certain accidents.

Drug and alcohol testing. Portable field chemical kits have been developed to help police detect narcotics and dangerous drugs. These kits are designed to provide a practical method for initial tests in the field and are not intended to replace the more thorough laboratory examinations.

Tests for determining if a suspect has taken a narcotic or dangerous drug must be performed in a forensic laboratory. These tests require the taking of a urine or blood sample from the suspect and require close medical supervision. Many new techniques for the detection of drugs, including specially trained police dogs, are used.

For many years the basic test for legally determining a driver's blood-alcohol content involved taking a blood sample and sending it to a laboratory for analysis. This method, although accurate, is not practical for law-enforcement purposes because many people object to having a blood sample taken and because test results are not immediately available. The development of the breath analyzer for the determination of blood-alcohol content has given the police a more practical tool. This instrument permits a precise amount of the suspect's breath to pass through a chemical solution (potassium dichromate and sulfuric acid), resulting in a colour density change that is proportional to the amount of alcohol in the air sample. The percentage of alcohol in a given air sample is determined, and from this the percentage of blood-alcohol content can be derived. In cases where the suspect is not conscious or requires serious medical attention, a blood test may be the only recourse.

The breath analyzer

Classes of evidence. Evidence can be categorized according to its potential value as proof. Certain types of evidence can be individualized, or associated with a unique source, whereas other types cannot be pinpointed but can aid in identification because they fall into particular classes. Types of evidence that can be individualized are handwriting, typewriting, fingerprints, footprints, tire marks, impressions or casts of nonstandard items, striated markings on bullets, tool marks, objects with random fractures or tears, and substances that have undergone an alteration that makes them unique among others of the same class. Among evidence that only identifies a certain class are blood and other body fluids, narcotics, toxicological materials, fibres, soils, inks, and many kinds of materials produced in batches.

Examinations can be either "unilateral" or comparative in nature. Blood-typing and establishing the distance from which a weapon was fired are unilateral examinations, whereas studies of handwriting or spent bullets involve comparisons with other examples.

Pathological examinations. Although pathological examinations are not ordinarily conducted by a crime laboratory, they are part of forensic science. Definitive statements relating to the cause of death and time of death are made by the coroner or medical examiner of the jurisdiction in which the death took place. Observations by crime laboratory personnel of the conditions at a crime scene, plus toxicological analysis by a crime laboratory, are used in concluding whether a death was by accident, suicide, or murder. In most jurisdictions an autopsy is conducted if a physician was not in attendance or if the cause of death is not obvious, as in cases involving poisoning, electrocution, asphyxiation, heart attack, or stroke. In cases involving identification of a decedent, crime laboratory personnel may work with a coroner or medical examiner to establish identity by comparison of fingerprints or other methods.

Fingerprints, palm prints, and footprints. Fingerprints found at the scene of a crime can be evidence connecting an individual with a crime. Fingerprints can be either visible or latent. Visible prints—formed by dirt or blood, for example—or three-dimensional prints formed in soft matrices, can be photographed directly. Latent fingerprints, which are not ordinarily visible, can be brought out by dusting techniques when the surface is hard and by chemical techniques when the surface is porous. In dusting for fingerprints, a fine powder of contrasting colour is applied with a fine brush. The powder clings to the residual oils and fats in the print and the excess powder is removed with the brush. On porous surfaces such as paper, fuming iodine, silver nitrate, or ninhydrin solutions are used to develop the latent fingerprints. The most effective developer of latent fingerprints is ninhydrin, which can reveal prints that are several years old.

Finger-
print
"points"

Fingerprints are identified on the basis of agreements in a significant number of individualities, commonly known as "points." These are the bifurcations, ending ridges, and dots in the fingerprint pattern. If sufficient points are found with spatial relationship to other points, a basis exists for identifying a fingerprint. It was formerly considered necessary to have 12 points to identify a fingerprint, but in current practice, a lesser number is often used. Palm prints and footprints are identified in the same manner as fingerprints.

Document examination. The work of the "questioned document examiner" encompasses the examination of handwriting, typewriting, ink, paper, and typography and covers such problems as the identification of handwriting and typewriting, the sequence of events involved in the preparation and handling of a document, the alteration of a document, and the age of a document.

Handwriting, like all other evidence, is identified on the basis of individuality. Children are taught specific ways of forming letters, but they rapidly begin to inject their own individuality into letter forms and writing execution. By the time a person reaches maturity, his writing has acquired peculiarities that serve to identify him.

A forged signature presents other problems. Simulated signatures based upon recollection contain a combination of the forger's own writing habits and his recollection of the victim's habits. In many cases, such simulations can be identified. On the other hand, when the perpetrator makes a careful drawing of the victim's signature or traces an authentic signature, the forgery can be exposed but cannot be identified with the handwriting of the perpetrator. Two individuals making careful tracings of the same signature can produce virtually identical drawings.

Typewriter
identifica-
tion

The make and model of typewriter used to prepare a document can be determined by examining typeface designs and comparing them with information contained in reference files and differentiation charts. The work of a specific typewriter can be identified if it contains sufficient identifying individuality, based on broken or tilting characters, badly aligned characters, characters that print more heavily on one side than on another, and rebounding characters. Mechanical conditions affecting the type basket or the escapement may also have identifying value. Since it is impossible to reinsert a document into a typewriter in its exact former position, it is possible, using a ruled screen, to determine if a document has been prepared at one sitting or has been reinserted.

Ink comparisons provide class evidence that is frequently of value, but it is not possible to individualize ink; *i.e.,* identify it as coming from a unique source. Chemical tests of various kinds are used for ink comparisons.

Papers can be differentiated on the basis of fibre, filler, and sizing constituents. Fibres can be identified by differential staining and microscopic examination. Fillers can be identified by X-ray diffraction because they are crystalline substances. Chemical tests are used for the identification of sizing constituents. Research with neutron activation analysis, a technique involving chemical analysis by radioactivity, indicates that it may even be possible to identify paper by batches.

Questions concerning the sequence of writing—*e.g.,* whether the ink signature is over or under the typewritten portion of a document—can be important in proving the authenticity of a document. In this and related problems, such as deciphering and restoration of eradicated or erased writing, examinations are carried out using stereomicro-

scopes, ultraviolet and infrared techniques, or chemical tests, depending on the specific problem.

Ballistics techniques. Firearms examinations involve such problems as ascertaining the type of weapon and the specific weapon used to fire a bullet, determining the distance between the weapon and the target, and establishing whether or not a particular individual fired a weapon.

The identification of a particular weapon is based upon the comparison of minute striations, or striae, left on bullets as they pass through the rifled barrel. Each barrel leaves a different combination of striae on the side of bullets. A bullet recovered from the scene of a crime can be compared with a test bullet fired from a suspect weapon. The striated markings on both bullets are brought into juxtaposition under a comparison microscope. If there is agreement in the width, depth, and spacing of a significant number of striae in both bullets, an identification can be made. (The same principle is used in the identification of tool marks.) The extractor and ejector markings on rifle and automatic-pistol cartridges can be identified in the same manner. In some cases the firing pins and breechblocks leave individual markings on the face of a cartridge.

The distance from which a weapon was fired can be determined, up to several feet, by examination of the form and size of the hole in a target, the extent of the burned area around the hole, the amount of embedded powder grains, and the presence of mercury or lead from primers. The effects vary with the weapon and the type of ammunition. Such information can be vital in determining whether or not a gunshot wound was self-inflicted. Infrared, X-ray, and chemical tests are used in determining the extent of powder residues.

The best means of determining whether or not an individual has recently fired a gun has been the subject of much controversy. In the dermal nitrate test, melted paraffin is used to pick up traces of nitrates and nitrites on the hand, after which a chemical test is made for such compounds. This method has been discredited because it can give incorrectly positive test results. Use of the neutron-activation technique to detect the presence on the hand of antimony and barium from cartridge primers is much more definitive.

Paint. Under certain circumstances, paint evidence can be individualized. If a jagged edge of a paint fleck found on a suspect can be matched with the edges of the matrix from which it came, a basis exists to connect a suspect with a crime scene. Multilayered paint chips can sometimes be individualized if the discrete layers possess sufficient individuality. Under other circumstances, paint must be considered class evidence. Examination of paint for class characteristics involves the use of chemical tests to determine constituency, as well as examination with instruments such as the infrared spectrophotometer, emission spectrograph, or electron microprobe.

Individu-
ualization
of paint

Inorganic materials. Soil, safe insulation, and other inorganic evidence can also be compared to determine common origin. It is not possible to individualize the evidence, but the fact that the same type of mineral matter was found on a suspect and at a crime scene is usually considered significant. Inorganic materials can be compared in terms of metallic element constituents, density of constituents, and microscopic structure.

Blood, blood spots, and semen. Bloodstains are a natural consequence of many crimes of violence; examinations usually concern the position, extent, and nature of suspected bloodstains. In most cases, the blood is dry. The Teichmann and Takayama tests, both of which rely on a reaction with hemoglobin, are confirmatory tests for blood. Human blood can be differentiated from the blood of other species by the precipitin test, which involves the reaction between blood and antihuman rabbit serum.

Forensic scientists have worked to individualize blood samples. For many years blood analysis was limited to simple groupings (A, B, O, or AB) and a few traits like Rh, Lewis, and Kell factors. Advances in serology now permit the isolation and identification of additional blood factors, including histocompatibility antigens, blood enzymes, and serum proteins. These advances also point to the possibility of individualizing other body fluids.

The shape, position, and extent of bloodstains often give valuable information about the circumstances surrounding the commission of a crime. Blood falling from different heights forms stains of different shapes, which are further modified by the angle at which the blood drop hits the surface. Rough estimates can be made as to the age of bloodstains.

Ultraviolet light and the acid phosphatase test are used for the presumptive identification of semen. Positive identification for semen relies on identifying spermatozoa in the suspected sample.

Hairs and fibres. Hairs and fibres found at the scene of a crime can also be important evidence. It is not possible to trace hair to a specific individual, but narrow classes having probative value can be established. Human hair can be distinguished microscopically from other animal hairs. Hairs from different portions of the body vary in structure. Microscopic examination can reveal if hair has been recently cut, burned, or split. Chemical tests can demonstrate the presence of bleached or tinted hair. Neutron activation analysis has come to be used to identify specific trace elements in hair and to measure the quantities of such trace elements.

Human
hair

The various fibres used in clothing, rope, and furniture are of vegetable, animal, or synthetic origin. They can be differentiated by microscopic study and by simple chemical tests for solubility and other properties. Colour comparisons can be conducted using a comparison microscope or by spectrophotometric evaluation. Because they are mass-produced, fibres cannot be individualized.

Toxicology. Toxicological examinations concern the identification of drugs and poisons, either in the form of pills and powders or as materials recovered from body organs. Among the drugs and narcotics of interest to crime laboratories are marijuana, morphine, heroin, and other narcotic alkaloids, cocaine, amphetamines, barbiturates, tranquillizers, and LSD. These substances must be differentiated from nonprescription drugs. In the case of pills, the exact shape, colour, and external marking may serve as aids in identification. Laboratory test methods for specific chemical substances include colour reaction tests, crystal tests, chromatography, and infrared spectrophotometry. Normally, several tests are performed for the sake of confirmation.

Examination of body organs for the presence of poisonous material requires an involved extraction procedure with a series of tests to confirm or eliminate the presence of toxic materials. In addition to the drugs previously mentioned, other poisonous substances include gaseous and liquid poisons, metallic and inorganic poisons, organic poisons, vegetable and animal poisons, and bacterial poisons.

Voice identification. The use of the sound spectrograph for voice identification is a relatively new development. The sound spectrograph is an instrument that graphically presents the time, frequency, and intensity of speech sound waves. The graphic forms for a sound, as spoken by one person, can be compared with those produced by the speech of a second person and thus differentiated. The accuracy of the technique in identifying individuals remains in doubt among speech scientists, even though voicegraphs, or voiceprints, have been used in court.

(W.B.McM./G.E.Mi.)

BIBLIOGRAPHY. Comparative works include JAMES CRAMER, *The World's Police* (1964), a comprehensive survey of modes of police administration; ROY D. INGLETON, *Police of the World* (1979); and JOHN M. ANDRADE, *World Police and Paramilitary Forces* (1985), later works; HAROLD K. BECKER, *Police Systems of Europe,* 2nd ed. (1980), a survey of police organizations in 10 European countries; RICHARD J. TERRILL, *World Criminal Justice Systems* (1984), a cross-cultural study of five countries, including Japan and the Soviet Union; DAVID H. BAILEY, *Forces of Order: Police Behavior in Japan and the United States* (1976), a comparative work; R.V.G. CLARKE and J.M. HOUGH (eds.), *The Effectiveness of Policing* (1980), a collection of research reports on Canadian, English, Dutch, and American police; and PETER K. MANNING, *Police Work: The Social Organization of Policing* (1977, reprinted 1979), a comparison of British and American systems. THE INTERNATIONAL POLICE ASSOCIATION has published a useful *International Bibliography of Selected Police Literature,* 2nd ed. (1968). Additional sources of information may be found in JACK E. WHITEHOUSE, *A Police Bibliography: Published and Unpublished Sources Through 1976* (1980). For further study, see the same author's *Research Guide for Law Enforcement and the Criminal Justice System: A Bibliography of Bibliographies, Journals, Research, and Reference Materials* (1982); and GEORGE T. FELKENES and HAROLD K. BECKER, *Law Enforcement,* 2nd ed. (1977), an extensive bibliography containing resource articles.

There are histories of the police forces of many countries: T.A. CRITCHLEY, *A History of the Police in England and Wales,* rev. ed. (1978); MARCEL LE CLÈRE, *Histoire de la police,* 4th ed. (1973); JAMES F. RICHARDSON, *Urban Police in the United States* (1974); PAUL RIEGE, *Kleine Polizei-Geschichte,* 3rd ed. (1966); ALAN WILLIAMS, *The Police of Paris, 1718–1789* (1979); ROBERT CONQUEST (ed.), *The Soviet Police System* (1968); WILLIAM KELLY and NORA KELLY, *Policing in Canada* (1976); and KERRY L. MILTE, *Police in Australia* (1977). SAMUEL WALKER, *Popular Justice: A History of American Criminal Justice* (1980), gives an analysis of the criminal justice process in the United States.

For popular accounts of police work and the problems of accountability, two British books deserve mention: BEN WHITAKER, *Police in Society* (1979); and PETER LAURIE, *Scotland Yard* (1970). MICHAEL BANTON, *The Policeman in the Community* (1964), is a sociological comparison of the police role in Scotland and the United States. JOHN ALDERSON, *Policing Freedom* (1979), discusses the responsibilities of the police in democratic societies; and HERMAN GOLDSTEIN, *Policing a Free Society* (1977), analyzes the problems of discretion, accountability, and the application of technology in American policing. JAMES Q. WILSON, *Varieties of Police Behavior* (1968; reprinted 1978), compares the enforcement policies of eight American police departments. ROBERT M. FOGELSON, *Big-City Police* (1977), concentrates on reform in the American police; THOMAS A. REPPETTO, *The Blue Parade* (1978), is a readable history of both federal and state forces; and MARK M. MOORE and GEORGE L. KELLING, "To Serve and Protect: Learning from Police History," *Public Interest,* 70:49–65 (Winter 1983), is an analysis of police strategy. JEROME H. SKOLNICK, *Justice Without Trial,* 2nd ed. (1975), discusses the detective's role in California and is sensitive to the legal as well as the sociological issues. LOUIS A. RADELET, *The Police and the Community,* 3rd ed. (1980), examines police attempts to incorporate management principles and technological advances into their work.

The problems of police operations and accountability are also featured in the reports of the UNITED STATES. PRESIDENT'S COMMISSION ON LAW ENFORCEMENT AND ADMINISTRATION OF JUSTICE, *The Challenge of Crime in a Free Society* (1967), and *Task Force Report: The Police* (1967); and the *Report of the National Advisory Commission on Civil Disorders,* 6 vol. (1968). See also UNITED STATES. PRESIDENT'S COMMISSION ON LAW ENFORCEMENT AND ADMINISTRATION OF JUSTICE, *Task Force Report: Science and Technology* (1967), a study of the application of science and technology to control crime and to solve related sociological problems; PAUL L. KIRK and LOWELL W. BRADFORD, *The Crime Laboratory* (1965), a basic guide to establishing a crime laboratory; EDWARD CLINTON EZELL, *Small Arms of the World,* 12th rev. ed. (1983), a compilation of photographs, technical descriptions, and specifications as well as operational comments; DONALD O. SCHULTZ and LORAN A. NORTON, *Police Operational Intelligence* (1968), a basic guide for the establishment of police intelligence systems; and GEORGE B. JOHNSON and HANS BERT LOCKHOVEN, *International Armament,* 2 vol. (1965), a source for information on small arms, their specifications, and manufacture. EDWARD J. IMWINKELRIED (ed.), *Scientific and Expert Evidence,* 2nd ed. (1981), provides a comprehensive review of forensic science and analyzes the utility and the legal issues of physical evidence. *Crime and Justice* (irregular) is a periodical collection of articles on research and developments in criminal justice. For discussion of the use of computers and automation in police work, see V.A. LEONARD, *The New Police Technology* (1980). The following references are significant and comprehensive texts pertaining to the establishment, management, and operation of a modern forensic laboratory: H.J. WALLS, *Forensic Science,* 2nd ed. (1974); WILSON R. HARRISON, *Suspect Documents, Their Scientific Examination* (1958, reprinted 1981); DAVID A. CROWN, *The Forensic Examination of Paints and Pigments* (1968); JAMES W. OSTERBURG, *The Crime Laboratory* (1982); ARNE SVENSSON, OTTO WENDEL, and BARRY A.J. FISHER, *Techniques of Crime Scene Investigation,* trans. from the Swedish, 3rd ed. (1981); LEWIS C. NICKOLLS, *The Scientific Investigation of Crime* (1956); P.L. KIRK, *Crime Investigation,* 2nd ed. (1974, reprinted 1985); CHARLES E. O'HARA and JAMES W. OSTERBURG, *An Introduction to Criminalistics* (1949, reissued 1972); CHARLES E. O'HARA and GREGORY L. O'HARA, *Fundamentals of Criminal Investigation,* 5th ed. (1980); RICHARD H. WARD, *Introduction to Criminal Investigation* (1975); and DONALD O. SCHULTZ, *Criminal Investigation Techniques* (1978).

(M.P.B./W.B.McM./G.E.Mi./G.L.Ke.)

Polish Literature

Poland acquired a literary language in Latin when it became a Christian land in the 10th century, and thereafter literature in the Polish language was slow to emerge. Its development as a national literature was restrained in part by Poland's remoteness from cultural centres and the difficulties that assailed the young state, frequently attacked by plundering invaders and weakened by division into small principalities, and in part by the domination of foreign priests (when Mieszko I, prince of Poland, accepted Christianity in 966, in effect he placed his lands in the hands of the pope). This article reviews the literary history of Poland from its origins to the present day.

The article is divided into the following sections:

THE MIDDLE AGES

Religious writings. As in other European countries, Latin was at first the only literary language of Poland, and early writings included saints' lives and annals and chronicles written by monks and priests. Two among these works are most important: the *Chronicon,* compiled in about 1115 by a Benedictine known only as Gallus Anonymous, and the *Annales seu cronicae inclyti Regni Poloniae,* written in about 1480 by Bishop Jan Długosz. The two works introduced Polish history and literature into the culture of Europe. Use of the vernacular was allowed by the church where Latin could not meet particular needs—in prayers, sermons, and songs; and the oldest surviving text of poetry in Polish is a song in honour of the Virgin Mary, "Bogurodzica," in which language and rhythm are used with high artistic craftsmanship. The earliest extant copy of the text dates from 1407, but its origins are much earlier. Preaching in Polish became established toward the end of the 13th century; the earliest known example of Polish prose, the *Kazania świętokrzyskie* ("Sermons of the Holy Cross"), dating from the end of the 13th or the beginning of the 14th century, was discovered in 1890. Part of a translation of the Bible, made in about 1455 for Queen Sofia, widow of Władysław II Jagiełło, has also survived.

Early secular literature. Secular works began to appear toward the second part of the 15th century. There was a poem criticizing the papacy (c. 1449) by Jędrzej Gałka, a follower of reformers John Wycliffe and Jan Hus, and a high literary standard was achieved in a morality verse dialogue, *Rozmowa mistrza Polikarpa ze Śmiercią* ("Dialogue Between Master Polycarp and Death"). The style of the medieval period lasted late in Poland. Marcin Bielski represented this late medievalism in his *Kronika wszyst-*

kiego świata (1551; "Chronicle of the Whole World"), the first general history in Polish.

The best examples of Polish literature imply a continuous literary tradition. Although its themes were those of the common European heritage, Polish writing of this period could be intensely personal within its anonymous framework. The groundwork for a leap into the ranks of major literatures was laid during the reign of Casimir III the Great, who in 1364 founded the University of Kraków.

THE RENAISSANCE PERIOD

Although the Renaissance reached Poland comparatively late, it was the golden age of Polish literature. External security, constitutional consolidation, and the Reformation contributed to this flowering.

The first generation of writers that were influenced by the Italian humanists wrote in Latin. Included among this group were Jan Dantyszek (Johannes Dantiscus), author of incidental verse, love poetry, and panegyric; Andrzej Krzycki (Cricius), an archbishop who wrote witty epigrams, political verse, and religious poems; and Klemens Janicki (Janicius), a peasant who studied in Italy, won there the title of poet laureate, and was the most original Polish poet of the age.

Mikołaj Rej of Nagłowice was notable for combining medieval and Renaissance aspects. Self-educated, he was the first idiomatically Polish talent and widely read writer of his time, being known as "the father of Polish literature." He wrote satirical epigrams, but of more importance were his prose works, especially *Świętych słów a spraw Pańskich kronika albo Postilla* (1557; "Chronicle or Comments on the Holy Words and Matters of the Lord"), a collection of Calvinist sermons, and the *Żywot człowieka poczciwego* (1568; "Life of an Honest Man"), a description of an ideal nobleman.

Kochanowski and his disciples. The second generation of humanist poets, and indeed the whole Renaissance period, was dominated by Jan Kochanowski. The son of a country squire, he wrote in the vernacular and was the first Polish writer to attempt both satirical poetry and classical tragedy, but his lyrical works surpassed these experiments. His crowning achievement, the first Polish work to equal the great poems of western Europe, was *Treny* (1580; *Laments*), inspired by despair after the death in 1579 of his young daughter, to be succeeded by a final recovery of his spiritual harmony. In Kochanowski's poetry the archaisms still apparent in Rej's work had almost disappeared; language and idiom were modern. The flexibility and assurance of his poetic genius were immediately recognized as a sign that the literary language had attained its maturity.

The most notable of Kochanowski's followers was Szymon Szymonowic (Simonides). He introduced in his *Sielanki* (1614; "Idylls") a poetic genre that was to retain its vitality until the end of the 19th century. These pastoral poems exemplified the processes of imitation, adaptation, and assimilation by means of which writers of the Renaissance period brought foreign models into the native tradition.

The numerous poems, in Latin and Polish, of Sebastian Klonowic were of interest for their description of contemporary life. *Worek Judaszów* (1600; "Judas' Sack") was a satirical poem on the plebeian life of Lublin, of which he was mayor.

Achievements in prose writing. The prose of the 16th century ranked with its poetry in vitality and range. The most eminent writer in Latin was Andrzej Frycz-Modrzewski. In *Commentariorum de republica emendanda libri quinque* (1554; "Commentary on Reforming the Republic in Five Books"), he evolved a bold social and political system, based on the principle of equality before God and the

The humanist poet Jan Kochanowski

law. Another notable writer in Latin was Marcin Kromer, scholar, humanist, historian, and Catholic apologist. Of his controversial works, most interesting is the Polish *Rozmowy dworzanina z mnichen* (1551–54; "Dialogues of a Courtier and a Monk"), a defense of Catholicism. Many historical and polemical writings and translations of the Bible were also published during this period; the Catholic translation by Jakub Wujek is an outstanding literary work.

Polish literature had become a national literature, reflecting the country's position as a great power with far-flung boundaries, the evolution of the nobility as a ruling class, and the nation's economic prosperity. Its influence spread east, above all to Moscow, while to the west its culture was represented by men of such high repute as the scientist and astronomer Nicolaus Copernicus (Mikołaj Kopernik).

THE BAROQUE PERIOD

The Baroque period began very early in Poland. In 1564 Poland invited the Jesuits to settle in the country, and from about 1570 Protestant influence began to wane. The Baroque style and outlook were congenial to the Polish spirit; the period was one of considerable literary output, in spite of almost incessant wars. Indeed, perhaps it mirrored, in its stylistic tension, the external strife characteristic of the 17th century.

Poetry. A forerunner of Baroque poetry was Mikołaj Sęp Szarzyński, who wrote predominantly religious poetry akin to that of the English Metaphysical poets. In this period satire and pastoral were the most popular forms. Foremost among satirists was Krzysztof Opaliński. His *Satyry albo przestrogi do naprawy rządu i obyczajów w Polszcze należące* (1650; "Satires or Warnings on the Reform of the Government and Customs in Poland") is bitter, pessimistic, and wide-ranging. The pastoral was represented by Samuel Twardowski, author of *Daphnis drzewem bobkowym* (1638; "Daphne into Laurel Tree") and a romance *Nadobna Pasqualina* (1655; "Fair Pasqualina"), a tale of sacred and profane love, in which Polish Baroque achieves its most finely wrought splendour. The *Roxolanki* (1654), a collection of love songs by Szymon Zimorowic, and the *Sielanki nowe ruskie* (1663; "New Ruthenian Idylls"), written by his brother Józef Bartłomiej Zimorowic, introduced topical dramatic elements into the traditional pastoral lyric; images of war and death are superimposed upon the pastoral background, with macabre effect and typical Baroque incongruity.

A parallel but less formalized rustic genre produced much verse celebrating rural life. One of the more successful examples is the *Votum* by Zbigniew Morsztyn, whose finest achievement, however, was in religious poetry. In contrast was the work of his cousin, Jan Andrzej Morsztyn, whose language was marked by the extravagant style of 16th-century Italian. The formal complexity and skill of his verse were unsurpassed; and his translation of the French dramatist Pierre Corneille's *Le Cid* has remained the standard Polish version.

Polish epics

The age was characterized by ambition to write heroic epics—a preoccupation to be explained perhaps by historical events: wars with Sweden, Russia, and Turkey, internal revolts, and attempts to introduce constitutional reforms. The Italian poet Torquato Tasso's *Gerusalemme liberata* (1581; "Jerusalem Liberated"), brilliantly translated by Piotr Kochanowski, inspired attempts at epics on national themes, notably the vigorous *Wojna chocimska* (written 1670, published 1850; "The War of Chocim") by Wacław Potocki. Another epic, the *Psalmodia polska* (1695; "Polish Psalmody"), by Wespazjan Kochowski, was written under the impact of John III Sobieski's victory over the Turks at Vienna in 1683, at which Kochowski was present. The work was the first example of a theme developed by writers of the Romantic movement—the messianic interpretation of Poland's destiny.

Other literary forms. The prose of the period did not rise to the level of its poetry, though there was a wealth of diaries and memoirs. Outstanding were the memoirs of Jan Chryzostom Pasek, a country squire and soldier. The period was also notable for the emergence of the letter as a literary form. The letters of John III Sobieski to his wife are remarkable for their passion and tenderness and for their day-by-day account of his experiences of battles and diplomacy. Another interesting development was the rise of a popular anonymous literature, exemplified by the *komedia rybałtowska* ("ribald comedies"). These were generally popular satiric comedies and broad farces written mainly by playwrights of plebeian birth. One of the few whose names are known was Piotr Baryka, author of a carnival comedy, *Z chłopa król* (performed 1633; "From Peasant to King"), which developed the theme of the introduction to Shakespeare's *Taming of the Shrew*. Some 30 anonymous examples of this type of comedy survive, and they include realistic depictions of popular customs and grotesquely humorous situations, parodying the lofty themes of "official" literature and so expressing an indirect protest against social inequality.

The last stage of Baroque literature (c. 1675–c. 1750) displayed a long process of decline, marked only by the emergence of the first women writers and by the major figure of Stanisław Konarski, a reformer of education, literature, and the political system, who wrote poetry in Latin, a tragedy in Polish (*Tragedia Epaminondy* [1880]), and political treatises.

It was not until the mid-20th century that the literature of the Baroque period was fully appreciated. It may well be regarded as the most enduring of Polish styles, for many of its features have recurred in the Romantic period and in modern writing.

THE ENLIGHTENMENT

Close contact with western Europe, especially France and England, characterized literature of the Enlightenment period in Poland, whose writers were imbued with a desire to save the national culture from effects of partition and foreign rule. Literary developments included the rise of drama; introduction of the periodical and the novel; publication of the first Polish dictionary; and, in poetry, the introduction of *dumy* (ballads).

The literary developments of the Polish Enlightenment

Rise of the Polish drama. Drama was established late in Poland. The earliest significant event was the inauguration of a national theatre in Warsaw in 1765. There were three principal dramatists: Franciszek Bohomolec, who satirized the aristocracy in adaptations of Molière; Wojciech Bogusławski, who wrote a popular national comic opera, *Cud mniemany czyli Krakowiacy i górale* (1794; "The Pretended Miracle or Krakovians and Highlanders"); and Franciszek Zabłocki, important for *Fircyk w zalotach* (1781; "The Dandy's Courtship") and *Sarmatyzm* (1785; "Sarmatian Ways"). Aleksander Fredro's comedies appeared when the Romantic movement was under way, and in them the influences of Molière and Carlo Goldoni were assimilated, as *Zemsta* (1834; "Vengeance") illustrated. They were remarkable for brilliant "type" characterization, ingenious construction, and metrical facility.

Didactic element in prose writing. Didacticism permeated most of the period's prose writing. Modern periodicals appeared at this time (*e.g.*, *Monitor*, 1765–85), and a Polish dictionary was published between 1807 and 1814. Bishop Adam Naruszewicz wrote early in the Enlightenment. His poetic works, considered chronologically, reflected the transition from Baroque to Classical, and he also wrote a history of Poland in which modern methods of scholarship were used. The most important poet, Bishop Ignacy Krasicki, of European outlook and skeptical intellect, wrote two mock-heroic poems, *Myszeis* (1775; "The Idylls of the Mice") and *Monachomachia* (1778; "War of the Monks"), as well as *Satyry* (1779; "Satires") and *Bajki i przypowieści* (1779; "Fables and Moral Tales"), and was remarkable for concise expression, formal elegance, and wit. Krasicki also introduced the novel *Mikołaja Doświadczyńskiego przypadki* (1776; "The Adventures of 'Nicholas Try-all'"), written in diary form and showing the influence of Swift and Rousseau. Two other outstanding poets were Stanisław Trembecki, whose works had an important place in Polish classicism as models of stylistic fluency, and Kajetan Węgierski, a freethinker and admirer of Voltaire, best known for his notorious lampoons.

Continued development of lyric poetry. Lyrical poetry continued to develop. Franciszek Karpiński developed features of the Baroque style in popular pastorals and religious songs, while Franciszek Dionizy Kniaźnin, a conscious experimenter, rewrote much of his earlier work to achieve stylistic uniformity; his verse, cool and intellectual in quality, anticipated Romantic themes of folk poetry, popular superstition, and gypsy life.

Julian Ursyn Niemcewicz's writings were inspired by patriotism and concern for reform. He knew English literature thoroughly and made early translations of English Romantic ballads, his original *dumy* being the first in Poland; he introduced the historical novel to Poland with *Jan z Tęczyna* (1825; "Jan of Tęczyn"), which showed Sir Walter Scott's influence. His comedy *Powrót posła* (1790; "The Return of the Deputy") was one of the best dramatic works of the period, and *Śpiewy historyczne* (1816; "Historical Songs") was widely read.

After loss of national independence, with the third partition of the country between Russia, Austria, and Prussia in 1795–96, the tradition of patriotic poetry was continued by émigré soldier-poets in the Polish legions of Napoleon's army, among them Józef Wybicki, whose popular patriotic song "Mazurek Dąbrowskiego" (1797; "Dąbrowski's Mazurka") was adopted as the national anthem in 1918.

THE 19TH CENTURY

A second distinct period of Polish classicism, called pseudoclassicism, occurred in the early 19th century. In general, pseudoclassicist writing lacked freshness. During the Enlightenment period, literature had reestablished contact with the West and become the voice of national consciousness. Although it was the literature of a community undergoing a severe political crisis, it exercised an influence on neighbouring countries.

Romanticism. The Romantic period began later in Poland than in England or Germany, and it lasted longer. It has been regarded as the greatest period in Polish literature. The rise of Romanticism coincided with the loss of independence, and great writers found in it an expression of their own mood. A need to interpret their country's destiny gave the work of the three great Romantic poets—Adam Mickiewicz, Juliusz Słowacki, and Zygmunt Krasiński—visionary power and moral authority. Writing in exile, they kept faith in the restoration of Polish independence alive, and their concern gave the literature of the Polish Romantic movement its strength and passion. Mickiewicz was the greatest Polish poet and leader of the Romantic period. His *Poezye* (2 vol., 1822–23; "Poetry") was the first major literary event of the period. In its second volume were included parts two and four of *Dziady* (*Forefathers' Eve*), in which he combined folklore and mystic atmosphere to create a new kind of Romantic drama. Mickiewicz' greatest works were written after 1824, when he was deported to Russia for revolutionary activities as a student; they included *Sonety krymskie* (1826; *Sonnets from the Crimea*); a visionary third part of *Dziady* (1832); a messianic interpretation of Poland's past and future destiny, *Księgi narodu polskiego i pielgrzymstwa polskiego* (1832; *The Books of the Polish Nation and of the Polish Pilgrimage*), written in biblical prose; and a great epic, *Pan Tadeusz* (1834; *Master Thaddeus*).

The poets in exile

The suppression of the insurrection of 1830–31 drove the cultural elite into exile in France; among poets whom Mickiewicz joined there were Słowacki, Krasiński, and Cyprian Kamil Norwid. Słowacki, a Romantic in the fullest sense, who in all his work showed genius, wrote verse narratives in the style of Byron and accomplished lyric poetry. He was inspired by patriotic themes: *Kordian* (1834) was a drama of conspiracy and problems of commitment. His subtle *W Szwajcarii* (1839; "In Switzerland") is probably the finest lyrical work in Polish. Much of Słowacki's work was in dramatic form, and although written for an imaginary stage rather than for an intended production, it laid the foundations of Polish tragic drama. His plays showed the influence of French Romantic drama, Shakespeare, classical tragedy, and Calderón. The last years of Słowacki's life were devoted to writing *Król-Duch* (1847; "The Spirit King"), an unfinished lyrical and symbolic epic describing the history of a people as a series of incarnations of the essential spirit of the nation.

Zygmunt Krasiński, when 23, published (anonymously, as with all his works) *Nieboska komedia* (1835; *The Undivine Comedy*), which presented, for the first time in Europe, a struggle between opposed worlds of aristocracy and disinherited masses. *Irydion* (1836; *Iridion*), his second play, was an allegory of Poland's fate. In *Przedświt* (1843; "Daybreak") he developed a messianic interpretation of Polish history, and this conception of Poland as "the Christ among the nations" was also expounded in *Psalmy przyszłości* (1845; "Psalms of the Future"). The introduction of fantastic or supernatural elements into a realistic setting was characteristic of many Polish Romantic works.

The genius of Cyprian Norwid was not fully recognized until the 20th century. During his lifetime he was misjudged and remained obscure, partly because he accepted some ideas of Romanticism while criticizing others but even more because of his ironic intellectual reserve. Among the most important works published in his lifetime was a verse dialogue on aesthetics, *Promethidion* (1851), which expounded a theory of the social and moral function of art anticipating that of John Ruskin. An authentic text of his most important lyrical collection, *Vade-mecum,* was first published in 1947. Norwid experimented with free verse and with the rhythms of speech, and, furthermore, he foreshadowed the French Symbolists in his analogical method of presenting the poetic concept.

The lesser talents of early Romanticism formed the Polish Ukrainian school, of whom Antoni Malczewski was outstanding as the author of a single poem, the Romantic verse narrative *Maria* (1825), a tale of love and treachery remarkable for original diction, dramatic tension, and unity of mood.

There were fewer prose writers than poets among the exiles. Zygmunt Miłkowski (pseudonym Teodor Tomasz Jeż) wrote on a wide range of subjects, including folklore and the history of the Balkan countries. The literary criticism of Maurycy Mochnacki, a passionate advocate of Romanticism and the first Polish critic to link literature with Poland's political progress, exercised a strong and not wholly beneficial influence on literary theory. The historical works of Joachim Lelewel, a great, many-sided scholar, were an impressive example of the prose of the period.

As a result of partition, Romantic poetry in Poland was limited to closed provincial circles. In Warsaw a group of young poets was formed, but its activities were restricted by political pressure. Its most fully developed talent was that of Teofil Lenartowicz. Ryszard Wincenty Berwiński, a poet of social radicalism, wrote *Poezje* (1844) and *Studia o literaturze ludowej* (1854; "Studies on Folk Literature"), which marked a step away from Romantic nationalist interpretations and stressed the international community of folk tradition.

Prose was more popular with writers in Poland than with those in exile. Henryk Rzewuski belonged spiritually to the 18th century: *Pamiątki J. Pana Seweryna Soplicy* (1839; "Memoirs of Mister Seweryn Soplica") evoked the atmosphere of the Baroque tradition. As the century progressed, signs of a Realistic tendency were discernible in Józef Korzeniowski's novels *Spekulant* (1846; "The Speculator") and *Kollokacja* (1847; "The Collocation"). A woman novelist, Narcyza Żmichowska (pseudonym Gabryella), produced *Poganka* (1846; "The Pagan"), a psychological allegory anticipating 20th-century sensibility in its subtle analysis of feeling. The dominant figure among prose writers was Józef Ignacy Kraszewski, whose output ran into hundreds of volumes of fiction, history, ethnography, criticism, and so on. His imaginative writings reflected a change of literary styles during his long career. Banished in 1863, he continued to influence Polish writers at home and in exile, maintaining the Polish cause by his manifold activities.

Polish Romanticism, conscious of its role as the torch of national spirit, retained its force as a mode of thinking beyond the period of the political circumstances that fostered it. It produced works of highest artistic value, which excited the interest of foreign writers. Mickiewicz influenced Slavonic literatures and was compared by George Sand with Goethe and Byron. Słowacki's poetic technique

The influence of Polish Romanticism

proved of fundamental importance to writers at the end of the 19th century, whereas Norwid's influence grew steadily stronger in the 20th century. The political implications of the Romantic movement led to the insurrection of 1863, which ended in Poland's becoming a province of Russia.

Positivism. The literary trend of the period following the 1863 uprising was called positivism and reflected a practical mood and reaction against Romanticism, the rise in Russian and Austrian Poland of an urban intelligentsia acting as a leaven in this ferment. Periodicals were of particular importance in disseminating new ideas, especially the *Tygodnik llustrowany* ("Illustrated Weekly"), founded in 1859. The natural consequence of a positivist outlook was a predominance of prose. With other writers of the Warsaw school, Aleksander Świętochowski voiced anticlerical and anti-aristocratic views in his weekly *Prawda* ("Truth"). Bolesław Prus (Aleksander Głowacki), a journalist, ranked high among Polish novelists: *Lalka* (1890; *The Doll*) gave a complex picture of bourgeois life in Warsaw, and *Faraon* (1897; *The Pharaoh and the Priest*) was an ambitious evocation of ancient Egypt, masking political problems that could not be published in the form of a modern novel.

Eliza Orzeszkowa, a campaigner for social reform, wrote about women's emancipation, the ignorance of the peasants, and the Jewish problem. Her books showed psychological penetration and a fine sense of style.

In 1905 Henryk Sienkiewicz was a winner of the Nobel Prize for Literature; his early critical works propounded positivist aesthetic theories, and his early short stories showed an acute awareness of the contemporary situation and a stark Realism. His famous *Quo Vadis?* (1896; Eng. trans. 1898), a historical novel of Rome under Nero, has been widely translated.

A more flexible Naturalism gained ground toward the end of the period, as seen in the stories of Adolf Dygasiński, famous for portrayals of animal life—such as *Zając* (1900; "The Hare")—which could be compared with those of Rudyard Kipling. Gabriela Zapolska, a critic of social hypocrisy in Naturalistic novels and lively comedies, excelled in dialogue and dramatic situations, in such plays as *Moralność Pani Dulskiej* (1906; "The Morality of Mrs. Dulska").

The period produced two important positivist poets: Adam Asnyk, a reflective lyricist of formal dexterity; and Maria Konopnicka, who wrote of the plight of the oppressed.

THE 20TH CENTURY

The "Young Poland" movement. The "Young Poland" movement describes several different groups and tendencies united by opposition to positivism, and a desire to return to imagination in literature; hence its other name, Neoromanticism. Among its pioneers were Antoni Lange, a poet, and Zenon Przesmycki (pseudonym Miriam), editor of a Symbolist review, *Chimera*. Both made translations from a number of other languages and expressed aesthetic theories in critical essays. Przesmycki's most influential contribution to a development of modern literature was his discovery of Cyprian Norwid.

Kazimierz Tetmajer achieved popularity with his nostalgic *Poezje* (1891–1924), but his prose had greater vigour and precision of observation, *Na skalnym Podhalu* (1903–10; *Tales of the Tatras*) containing some effectively stylized folk material. An interesting poet, Jan Kasprowicz, was of peasant origin. His principal contribution to Polish literature lay in the structure of his longer lyrical poems; those in the volume *Ginącemu światu* (1901; "To a Dying World") employed a technique of association, quotation, musical repetition, and free metre that anticipated the early style of such poets as T.S. Eliot. Tadeusz Miciński, a forerunner of Expressionism and Surrealism, wrote philosophical and mystical poems and plays, notably a collection of poems, *W mroku gwiazd* (1902; "In the Twilight of the Stars"), and a play, *Kniaź Patiomkin* (1906; "Prince Potemkin"). The lyrical poet Leopold Staff, whose work shows great variety and technical dexterity, was at this period associated with the "Young Poland" movement, although some of his finest work was written later.

Stanisław Przybyszewski was a leading exponent of the movement's new aesthetic theories and edited a literary magazine, *Życie* ("Life"). Stefan Żeromski expressed passionate concern for social justice and national freedom in widely read works, but an excess of Realist documentation frequently vitiated the power of his later work. Władysław Stanisław Reymont, of peasant stock, adapted the Naturalistic technique to create a vision of peasant life in an epic novel cycle, *Chłopi* (4 vol., 1904–09; *The Peasants*), for which he received the Nobel Prize for Literature for 1924. One of the most effective novels of the period, *Żywot i myśli Zygmunta Podfilipskiego* (1898; "The Life and Thoughts of Zygmunt Podfilipski"), by Józef Weyssenhoff, presented an ironical portrait of the egoist in society. Wacław Berent's *Próchno* (1903; "Rotten Wood") portrayed with biting irony the late 19th-century decadence of life and art. His *Ozimina* (1911; "Winter Corn"), a Symbolist novel, foreshadowed the associative structure and narrative technique of James Joyce's *Ulysses* (1922). His *Żywe kamienie* (1918; "The Living Stones") stressed the unity of medieval culture and Poland's place within it. A bold experiment antedating by several years the psychoanalytical novel in western Europe was *Pałuba* (1903; "The Hag") by Karol Irzykowski. In it, motivation and behaviour were presented from different viewpoints, ingeniously cemented by the author's own analyses, as in a scientific study. Irzykowski was also a critic and, in *Dziesiąta muza* (1924; "The 10th Muse"), the first to give attention to the cinema as an art form.

Stanisław Brzozowski, an outstanding critic, insisted that a critic must represent the moral consciousness of his age; in *Legenda Młodej Polski* (1909; "The Legend of Young Poland") he analyzed the weakness of the period's literature and expounded his view of the unity of all work—physical, technical, intellectual, and artistic.

Stanisław Wyspiański was an artist and dramatist of genius. In his plays he reforged elements from classical tragedy and mythology, Polish Romantic drama, and national history in a complex whole. *Wesele* (1901; "The Wedding") was a visionary parable of Poland's past, present, and problematical future, cast in the form of the traditional puppet-theatre play. It was a masterpiece of evocative allusion, tragedy, and humour.

The literature of the period was characterized by close contact with western European literatures, but writers such as Wyspiański turned back to the Polish Romantics in a search for new poetic language.

Literature in restored Poland. The restoration of independence in 1918 decisively affected Polish literature. The period between 1918 and 1939 was characterized by richness and variety and increasing contact with other European literatures, especially through publication of many translations. For nearly a decade after 1918 lyrical poetry predominated. A periodical, *Zdrój* ("The Fountainhead"), showed affinities with German Expressionism. In Warsaw several poets formed a group called Skamander, from the name of their monthly publication; it was united by a desire to forge a poetic language, attuned to modern life. Julian Tuwim, a poet of emotional power and linguistic sensitivity, headed the group, and during World War II, in exile in Brazil and the United States, wrote a long, discursive, autobiographical poem, *Kwiaty polskie* (1949; "Polish Flowers"). Among Skamander members were Jan Lechoń, Kazimierz Wierzyński (both died abroad after World War II), Antoni Słonimski, and Jarosław Iwaszkiewicz, who was also a prolific prose writer; among sympathizers of the group were two eminent woman poets, Maria Pawlikowska-Jasnorzewska and Kazimiera Iłłakowiczówna, and Władysław Broniewski, a poet with strong left-wing sympathies, who became a master of the revolutionary lyric, expressing involvement in current social and ideological problems.

A writer of importance was Bolesław Leśmian, whose symbolic, Expressionist poetry was remarkable for the inventiveness of its vocabulary, sensuous imagery, and philosophic content, all anticipating Existentialism. He published only three notable collections—*Łąka* (1920; "The Meadow"), *Napój cienisty* (1936; "The Shadowy Drink"), and *Dziejba leśna* (posthumous, 1938; "Wood-

The Skamander poets

land Tale")—but has been recognized by his admirers as the most outstanding 20th-century Polish lyrical poet.

Other experimental movements, such as Futurism, followed revolutionary trends in poetry—particularly in Italy and Russia. More original was a group called Awangarda Krakowska ("Vanguard of Kraków"). Led by Tadeusz Peiper, it produced few works but had widespread influence in the regeneration of poetic technique. Two of its adherents, Julian Przyboś and Adam Ważyk, who was loosely connected with the movement, ranked among the outstanding poets of the post-World War II period. Also noteworthy was Józef Czechowicz, who assimilated traditional and regional elements to the new style.

Prose writing reached its ascendancy in the second decade of independence. Early stories by Zofia Nałkowska belonged to the "Young Poland" movement and aimed to expose the feminine psyche; later she turned to other themes, striving for narrative objectivity and technical simplicity. Two other women writers of distinction were Zofia Kossak-Szczucka, noted for historical novels, and Maria Kuncewiczowa, who wrote psychological novels. Juliusz Kaden-Bandrowski used experimental Realism in *Czarne skrzydła* (1928–29; "Black Wings") and *Mateusz Bigda* (1933), which treated social and political themes. Michał Choromański's *Zazdrość i medycyna* (1933; *Jealousy and Medicine*) used experimental methods of narrative sequence and was remarkable for its clinical analysis of character. A writer skilled in reflecting subtleties of perception was Bruno Schulz, author of *Sklepy cynamonowe* (1934; *Cinnamon Shops*), whose prose was reminiscent of that of Kafka.

Tadeusz Żeleński (pseudonym Boy), witty, irreverent, and widely read, was a leading literary critic and one of Poland's best interpreters of French literature. The essay form was represented by Jan Parandowski, whose main theme was the classical culture of Greece and Rome. A subversive attack on intellectual and social conventions was launched in *Ferdydurke* (1937; Eng. trans., *Ferdydurke*) by Witold Gombrowicz, who displayed in it a satirical talent reminiscent of Alfred Jarry. The taste for the cyclic novel was satisfied by Maria Dąbrowska with *Noce i dnie* (4 vol., 1932–34; "Nights and Days"), an outstanding modern Polish example of a chronicle novel in epic style, about the development of the Polish intelligentsia of upper-middle-class origin.

The drama was the weakest of the literary forms during this period and returned to the Young Poland's especially symbolic form (Karol Hubert Rostworowski, Jerzy Szaniawski). The experimental dramas of Stanisław Ignacy Witkiewicz were of interest chiefly for their expression of anti-Realist aesthetic theories; he developed many ideas of the Awangarda, applied the principles of "pure form" to painting and drama, and was the main exponent of a movement in Polish literature known as "catastrophism." Obsessed with the idea of a disintegration of European culture, endangered by totalitarian ideologies, and an attempt to impose the uniformity of a "mass society," he developed his ideas in plays combining elements of Surrealism, grotesque misrepresentation, and what later became known (in the plays of Eugène Ionesco, for example, whose work Witkiewicz to some extent foreshadowed) as the Theatre of the Absurd. His novels *Pożegnanie jesieni* (1927; "Farewell to Autumn") and *Nienasycenie* (1930; "Insatiability") expressed the same philosophy. After World War II his work attracted interest abroad and appeared in translation (*e.g., The Madman and the Nun and Other Plays,* 1968).

Literature after 1945. The impact of World War II, the experience of occupation, and the establishment in 1945 of the People's Republic decisively affected the character of literature in Poland and also produced a number of émigré writers who had become famous between World Wars I and II: lyrical poets of the Skamander group and former associates of the Awangarda movement. Among them was Czesław Miłosz, who emigrated to France in 1951 and moved to the United States a decade later. He was awarded the Prix Littéraire Européen for *Zdobycie władzy* (1955; first published in French, as *La prise du pouvoir,* 1953; *The Seizure of Power*), and he received

the Nobel Prize for Literature for 1980. Many émigrés wrote of experiences in enemies' prisons and forced-labour camps. The most accomplished as literature were *Inny świat* (1953; *A World Apart*) by Gustaw Herling-Grudziński and *Sprawa Józefa Mosta* (1953; "The Affair of Józef Most") by Herminia Naglerowa. Jerzy Pietrkiewicz, whose early work was published in Poland during World War II, later wrote mainly in English (the novels *The Knotted Cord,* 1953; *Isolation,* 1959). Witold Gombrowicz, who died in France after a long stay in Argentina, also published his postwar work abroad and became famous with the novels *Trans-Atlantyk* (1953), *Pornografia* (1960; Eng. trans., *Pornografia*), and *Kosmos* (1965; *Cosmos*), which won him the 1967 International Prize for Literature. He also published abroad the plays *Ślub* (1953; *The Marriage*) and *Operetka* (1966; "Operetta"); three volumes of diaries (*Dziennik,* 1953–66); and a book of recollections and reflections, *Wspomnienia polskie* (1977; "Polish Reminiscences"). In all these works, especially the novels, Gombrowicz treated philosophical and psychological themes in a satirical narrative style in which, by emphasizing the grotesque and irrational elements in human nature, he presented an exposé of the conventions of modern life and culture.

In Poland the years immediately after the war saw publication of works written during the occupation or by writers who had been in concentration camp or prison. A frequent theme was the attempt to come to terms with Fascism and war. This was exemplified in the short stories of Tadeusz Borowski, a prisoner at Auschwitz, who, in collections published in 1948, *Pożegnanie z Marią* ("Farewell to Mary") and *Kamienny świat* ("The World of Stone," published in *This Way for the Gas, Ladies and Gentlemen, and Other Stories,* 1967), explored human depravity and degradation; and in those of Adolf Rudnicki, who treated moral and philosophical themes in lyrical prose and described, in *Szekspir* (1948; "Shakespeare") and *Ucieczka z Jasnej Polany* (1949; "Flight from Jasna Polana"), the wartime fate of the Jewish community in Poland. Another theme, shown, for example, by a novel *Popiół i diament* (1948; *Ashes and Diamonds*) by Jerzy Andrzejewski, was the examination of the moral controversies that accompanied political and social changes of the postwar period, especially the tragic situation of young conspirators involved in the struggle against the new regime.

During 1949–54 the literature of Socialist Realism gained ground, and writers attempted to emulate the great 19th-century Realists. A new type of hero was created—the ordinary man or woman actively engaged in "productive" work, and those elements in the social scene that served to present an idea of revolutionary progress were accentuated. The main writer was Leon Kruczkowski, a prewar exponent of the Marxist novel whose outstanding plays *Niemcy* (1949; "The Germans") and *Pierwszy dzień wolności* (1960; "The First Day of Freedom") were successfully performed abroad. Kazimierz Brandys, whose development typified postwar tendencies in Polish literature, published an epic novel cycle, *Między wojnami* (1948–52; "Between the Wars"), and a Socialist Realist novel, *Obywatele* (1954; "Citizens").

Among writers of the period who stood aside from political involvement were Konstanty Ildefons Gałczyński, who combined lyricism with grotesque fantasy, and the reflective Mieczysław Jastrun, who in later work—for example, the essay collection *Mit śródziemnomorski* (1962; "The Mediterranean Myth")—moved toward Existentialism. A group of Catholic writers opposed to Socialist Realism included Antoni Gołubiew, author of an epic novel cycle, *Bolesław Chrobry* (1947–54), the prose writer and dramatist Jerzy Zawieyski, and a historical novelist, Hanna Malewska. Teodor Parnicki used a background of conflict between cultures for an analysis of contemporary problems in experimental and semi-historical novels set mainly in the early Christian period: *Koniec "Zgody Narodów"* (1955; "End of the Covenant of Nations"), *Nowa baśń* (6 vol., 1962–70; "A New Fairytale"), and others.

The weakness of the Socialist Realist movement—its attempt to impose a political pattern on creative writing, its avoidance of themes arising from contemporary

Witkiewicz and "catastrophism"

The literature of Socialist Realism and the reaction against it

conflicts—resulted partly from the stranglehold of the Stalinist regime. In the period beginning in 1954–55, writers began to criticize these weaknesses and to oppose them. Andrzejewski, for example, presented contemporary ideas and problems in two novels combining historical and metaphorical treatment, *Ciemności kryją ziemie* (1957; *The Inquisitors*) and *Bramy raju* (1960; *The Gates of Paradise*), and Brandys criticized Stalinism in the novel *Matka królów* (1957; *Sons and Comrades*).

The political "thaw" after 1956 made it possible for writers to renew contacts with the West. As a result, a period of development and experiment began in which the essay was a vehicle for philosophical and intellectual discussion and comment, and there was an increase of satire. Tadeusz Breza analyzed contemporary life and ideas in a prose of Proustian subtlety in, for example, *Spiżowa brama* (1959; "The Bronze Gate"), a keen description of life in the Vatican. Writers continued to be concerned with World War II, as shown by such novels as *Czarny potok* (1954; *Black Torrent*) by Leopold Buczkowski, *Kolumbowie-rocznik 20* (1957; "The Columbuses-Generation of 1920") by Roman Bratny, and *Tren* (1961; "Threnody") by Bohdan Czeszko. Many chose as their theme consequences of wartime experience, as, for example, Tadeusz Konwicki in *Sennik współczesny* (1963; *A Dreambook for Our Time*). His later novels *Wniebowstąpienie* (1967; "Ascension") and *Nic albo nic* (1971; "Nothing or Nothing") project those themes on contemporary problems. In *Głosy w ciemności* (1956; "Voices in the Dark") and *Austeria* (1966; "The Inn"), Julian Stryjkowski restated the feeling of the Orthodox Jewish Polish community that the world has already ended and gave it universal application.

A number of prewar Polish writers continued to publish: the poets Leopold Staff and Kazimiera Iłłakowiczówna; Maria Dąbrowska, who enhanced her reputation with a collection of short stories, *Gwiazda zaranna* (1955; "Morning Star"), and a series of critical essays on Joseph Conrad; the novelist Maria Kuncewiczowa; and the novelist, poet, and dramatist Jarosław Iwaszkiewicz, who published the epic novel *Sława i chwała* (1956–62; "Fame and Glory").

Many writers of the 1950s and 1960s wrote prose works, ranging from the political novels of Jerzy Putrament to the psychological novels of manners of Stanisław Dygat, while the novels of Stanisław Lem, the leading Polish representative of serious science fiction, looked to the future. Young writers such as Marek Hlasko (died in his early years in Germany after some years spent abroad as an émigré writer) and Marek Nowakowski, in their search for a moral basis for life, often looked into the worlds of those on the fringes of society—outcasts and misfits. An interesting younger writer, Sławomir Mrożek, both in his plays—*Policja* (1958; "The Police"), *Na pełnym morzu* (1961; *Out at Sea*), *Striptease* (1962; Eng. trans., *Striptease*), and above all *Tango* (1964; Eng. trans., *Tango*), his most widely known work—as well as in stories collected in *Słoń* (1957; *The Elephant*), displayed an acute sense of satire and the grotesque, which he used to express a philosophy of life both topical and timeless. His comedy belonged partly to the Theatre of the Absurd and was distinguished by a subtlety of parody and highly stylized language.

New trends in poetry and drama Poetry of the "second" postwar period was notable for expression of philosophical thought. Stanisław Jerzy Lec was a satirical poet noted for skeptical philosophical aphorisms in *Myśli nieuczesane* (published in series from 1957; *Unkempt Thoughts*). Zbigniew Herbert, whose most notable collection was *Studium przedmiotu* (1961; "Study of an Object"), was a representative of intellectual poetry (Eng. trans., *Selected Poems*). Perhaps the most interesting, however, was Tadeusz Różewicz, who had a profound influence on younger lyrical poets; from *Niepokój* (1947), his first collection, to *Głos anonima* (1961; "The Nameless Voice"), his work was occupied with moral themes. He also wrote plays resembling those of Ionesco: *Świadkowie albo nasza mała stabilizacja* (1962; "The Witnesses, or Our Little Stabilization"; translated in *The Witnesses and Other Plays*), and one published with poems in *Kartoteka* (1961; *The Card Index and Other Plays*). Modern problems also dominated the intellectual, ironic poetry of

Wisława Szymborska, collected in *Sól* (1962; "Salt") and *Sto pociech* (1967; "A Barrel of Laughs").

The lyrical poetry of the generation of poets born about 1930 was characterized by a variety of aims and styles. The controversial work of such poets as Miron Białoszewski showed extreme experimentalism; on the other hand, a poet such as Ernest Bryll reasserted traditional poetic forms. Some poets—Tadeusz Nowak and Jerzy Harasymowicz—turned for inspiration to the peasant culture; others, among them Jarosław M. Rymkiewicz, an outstanding translator of English and American poetry, based their poetic program upon the example of T.S. Eliot, in a return to Baroque and Neoclassical forms, and developed an erudite, allusive poetry. Most representative of the poets of this new generation was perhaps Stanisław Grochowiak, who created an expressive poetic style based on sudden contrasts and deliberate emphasis on grotesque aspects of life.

Critics and essayists included Artur Sandauer; Jan Kott (who emigrated to the United States), whose *Szkice o Szekspirze* (1961; *Shakespeare, Our Contemporary*) was widely translated and discussed; Kazimierz Wyka; Jan Błoński; and Andrzej Kijowski.

Political events in 1968 forced some writers to emigrate and publish abroad. Others, such as Paweł Jasienica and Stefan Kisielewski, were temporarily blacklisted. In the 1970s and early 1980s, Polish life was dominated by social tensions, political upheavals, and economic crises. Major outbreaks of unrest, in particular the workers' riots and strikes that led to the creation of the independent trade union Solidarity, encouraged writers to challenge the authorities and the official aesthetic. Censorship still forced many of them to publish abroad, but independent publishing houses emerged that allowed their works to be circulated in Poland and thus opened the way for hitherto proscribed foreign authors, such as George Orwell, and émigré authors, such as Miłosz and Gombrowicz. Books appeared that analyzed the political situation and delved into the recesses of Polish life and history. Among the most important and widely discussed books of the period were Konwicki's novels *Kompleks polski* (1977; *The Polish Complex*) and *Mała apokalipsa* (1979; *A Minor Apocalypse*); Andrzejewski's long-suppressed novel *Miazga* (1981; "Pulp"); and the ironic reflections recorded in a monthly diary called *Miesiące* (1981; *A Warsaw Diary 1978–1981*) by Kazimierz Brandys, who left Poland in 1981. Also important were the volumes of poetry and essays of Ryszard Krynicki and Stanisław Barańczak, who emigrated to the United States; the diaries of Gombrowicz; and two additional volumes of Herbert's poems, *Pan Cogito* (1974; "Mr. Cogito"; partially translated in *Selected Poems*), the poetic meditations of a kind of intellectual Everyman, and *Raport z oblężonego miasta* (1983; "A Report from a Town Besieged").

BIBLIOGRAPHY. The best modern survey of Polish literature in English is CZESŁAW MIŁOSZ, *The History of Polish Literature,* 2nd ed. (1983). JULIAN KRZYŻANOWSKI, *A History of Polish Literature* (1978; originally published in Polish, 1972), is also useful. For the various aspects of Polish literature, see MANFRED KRIDL, *A Survey of Polish Literature and Culture,* trans. from the Polish (1956; reprinted 1967); JULIAN KRZYŻANOWSKI, *Polish Romantic Literature* (1931; reprinted 1968); WACLAW LEDNICKI, *Life and Culture of Poland as Reflected in Polish Literature* (1944); MADELINE G. LEVINE, *Contemporary Polish Poetry, 1925–1975* (1981); W.J. STANKIEWICZ (ed.), *The Tradition of Polish Ideals: Essays on Polish History and Literature* (1981); and TYMON TERLECKI, *Literatura polska na obczyźnie, 1940–1960,* 2 vol. (1964–65), on Polish literature written abroad. For anthologies of texts, see DANIEL GEROULD (ed. and trans.), *Twentieth-Century Polish Avant-Garde Drama: Plays, Scenarios, Critical Documents* (1977); ADAM GILLON and LUDWIK KRZYŻANOWSKI (eds.), *Introduction to Modern Polish Literature: An Anthology of Fiction and Poetry,* 2nd ed. (1982); MARIA KUNCEWICZOWA, *The Modern Polish Mind: An Anthology* (1962), a collection of stories and essays; VASA D. MIHAILOVICH et al. (eds.), *Modern Slavic Literatures,* vol. 2 (1976); and JERZY PETERKIEWICZ and BURNS SINGER, *Five Centuries of Polish Poetry, 1450–1970,* 2nd ed. (1970, reprinted 1979). A useful guide in Polish is JULIAN KRZYŻANOWSKI et al., *Literatura polska,* 2 vol. (1984).

(J.Kr./Ja.W./B.W.Ma.)

Political Parties
and Interest Groups

A political party is a group organized for the purpose of achieving and exercising power within a political system. It may seek political power either by election or by revolution. An interest group (or special-interest group) is any aggregate of individuals who, bound by one or more shared concerns or wants, makes claims upon other groups in society or upon society in general in order to maintain or promote its position or objectives.

An interest group that attempts to influence government becomes a "pressure group." It is distinguished from a political party in that, whereas a party puts up candidates for election to public office and has a structure and carries out activities to secure their election, a pressure group seeks to influence both the government and the parties. The Catholic interest in Italy, for instance, is served both by the Christian Democratic Party and also by the Catholic Action Society. The first is unquestionably a party with its own program, mode of operation, and structures; and the second is unquestionably a pressure group. Again the "natural" group of Swedes in Finland serves itself by the Swedish People's Party; this is clearly a special-interest group, yet it puts up candidates and is represented in the legislature because it thinks its members' interest is best served by exerting pressure as part of a governmental coalition.

Thus, it may be that what begins as a pressure group winds up as a political party. The British Labour Party had its origins in 1900, when a collection of trade unionists formed a Labour Representation Committee in order to secure the election of working-class MP's to Parliament; later it broadened its membership and program to become the Labour Party of today. Again, in France, Pierre Poujade's pressure group, the Union of Small Shopkeepers, was involved in the 1956 elections and won over 40 seats, thus becoming a political party before retiring from the electoral arena in 1958 and reverting to pressure-group status. The reverse process can also occur, as when a political party engenders pressure groups; thus, the Communist parties in France and Italy have set up interest groups for women, youth, workers, and the like.

The article is divided into the following sections:

Political parties

Political parties originated in their modern form in Europe and the United States in the 19th century, along with the electoral and parliamentary systems whose development is reflected in their own evolution. The term party has since come to be applied to all organized groups seeking political power, whether by democratic elections or by revolution.

In earlier, prerevolutionary, aristocratic and monarchical regimes, the political process unfolded within restricted circles in which cliques and factions, grouped around particular noblemen or influential personalities, were opposed to one another. The establishment of parliamentary regimes and the appearance of parties at first scarcely changed this situation. To cliques formed around princes, dukes, counts, or marquesses there were added cliques formed around bankers, merchants, industrialists, and businessmen. Regimes supported by nobles were succeeded by regimes supported by other elites. These narrowly based parties were later transformed to a greater or lesser extent, for in the 19th century in Europe and America there emerged parties depending on mass support.

Ubiquity of parties in the 20th century — The 20th century saw the spread of political parties throughout the entire world. In Africa large parties have sometimes been formed in which a modern organization has a more traditional ethnic or tribal basis; in such cases the party leadership is frequently made up of tribal chiefs. In certain areas of Asia, membership in modern political parties is often determined largely by religious factors or by affiliation with ritual brotherhoods. Many political parties in the developing countries are partly political, partly military. Certain Socialist and Communist parties in Europe earlier experienced the same tendencies.

These last-mentioned European parties have demonstrated an equal aptitude for functioning within multiparty democracies and as the sole political party in a dictatorship. Developing originally within the framework of liberal democracy in the 19th century, political parties have been used in the 20th century by dictatorships for entirely undemocratic purposes.

TYPES OF POLITICAL PARTY

A fundamental distinction can be made between cadre parties and mass-based parties. The two forms coexist in many countries, particularly in western Europe, where Communist and Socialist parties have emerged alongside the older conservative and liberal parties. Many parties do not fall exactly into either category but combine some characteristics of both.

Cadre parties. Cadre parties—*i.e.,* parties dominated by politically elite groups of activists—developed in Europe and America during the 19th century. Except in some of the states of the United States, France from 1848, and the German Empire from 1871, the suffrage was largely restricted to taxpayers and property owners, and, even when the right to vote was given to larger numbers of people, political influence was essentially limited to a very small segment of the population. The mass of people were limited to the role of spectators rather than that of active participants.

The cadre parties of the 19th century reflected a fundamental conflict between two classes: the aristocracy on the one hand and the bourgeoisie on the other. The former, composed of landowners, depended upon rural estates on which a generally unlettered peasantry was held back by a traditionalist clergy. The bourgeoisie, made up of industrialists, merchants, tradesmen, bankers, financiers, and professional people, depended upon the lower classes of clerks and industrial workers in the cities. Both aristocracy and bourgeoisie evolved its own ideology. Bourgeois liberal ideology developed first, originating at the time of the English revolution of the 17th century in the writings of John Locke, an English philosopher. It was then developed by French philosophers of the 18th century. In its clamouring for formal legal equality and acceptance of the inequities of circumstance, liberal ideology reflected the interests of the bourgeoisie, who wished to destroy the privileges of the aristocracy and eliminate the lingering economic restraints of feudalism and mercantilism. But, insofar as it set forth an egalitarian ideal and a demand for liberty, bourgeois classical liberalism expressed aspirations common to all men. Conservative ideology, on the other hand, never succeeded in defining themes that would prove as attractive, for it appeared to be more closely allied to the interests of the aristocracy. For a considerable period, however, conservative sentiment did maintain a considerable impact among the people, since it was presented as the expression of the will of God. In Catholic countries, in which religion was based upon a hierarchically structured and authoritarian clergy, the conservative parties were often the clerical parties, as in France, Italy, and Belgium.

Conservative and liberal cadre parties dominated European politics in the 19th century. Developing during a period of great social and economic upheaval, they exercised power largely through electoral and parliamentary activity. Once in power, their leaders used the power of the army or of the police; the party itself was not generally organized for violent activity. Its local units were charged with assuring moral and financial backing to candidates at election time, as well as with maintaining continual contact between elected officials and the electorate. The national organization endeavoured to unify the party members who had been elected to the assemblies. In general, the local committees maintained a basic autonomy and each legislator a large measure of independence. The party discipline in voting established by the British parties—which were older because of the fact that the British Parliament was long established—was imitated on the Continent hardly at all.

United States parties in the 19th century The first United States political parties of the 19th century were not particularly different from European cadre parties, except that their confrontations were less violent and based less on ideology. The first United States form of the struggle between the aristocracy and the bourgeoisie, between conservative and liberal, was carried out in the form of the Revolutionary War, in which Great Britain embodied the power of the king and the nobility, and the insurgents that of bourgeoisie and liberalism. Such an interpretation is, of course, simplified. There were some aristocrats in the South and, in particular, an aristocratic spirit based on the institutions of slaveholding and paternalistic ownership of land. In this sense, the Civil War could be considered as a second phase of violent conflict between the conservatives and the liberals. Nevertheless, the United States was from the beginning an essentially bourgeois civilization, based on a deep sense of equality and of individual freedom. Federalists and Anti-Federalists, Republicans and Democrats—all belonged to the liberal family since all shared the same basic ideology and the same system of fundamental values and differed only in the means by which they would realize their beliefs.

In terms of party structure, United States parties in the beginning differed little from their European counterparts. Like them, the United States parties were composed of local notables. The ties of a local committee to a national organization were even weaker than in Europe. At the state level there was some effective coordination of local party organizations, but at the national level such coordination did not exist. A more original structure was developed after the Civil War—in the South to exploit the vote of the blacks and along the East Coast to control the votes of immigrants. The extreme decentralization in the United States enabled a party to establish a local quasi-dictatorship in a city or county by capturing all of the key posts in an election. Not only the position of mayor but also the police, finances, and the courts came under the control of the party machine, and the machine was thus a development of the original cadre parties. The local party committee came typically to be composed of adventurers or gangsters who wanted to control the distribution of wealth and to ensure the continuation of their control. These men were themselves controlled by the power of the boss, the political leader who controlled the machine at the city, county, or state levels. At the direction of the committee, each constituency was carefully divided, and every precinct was watched closely by an agent of the party, the captain, who was responsible for securing votes for the party. Various rewards were offered to voters in return for the promise of their votes. The machine could offer such inducements as union jobs, trader's licences, immunity from the police, and the like. Operating in this manner, a party could frequently guarantee a majority in an election to the candidates of its choosing, and, once it was in control of local government, of the police, the courts, and public finances, etc., the machine and its clients were assured of impunity in illicit activities such as prostitution and gambling rings and of the granting of public contracts to favoured businessmen.

The degeneration of the party mechanism was not without benefits. The European immigrant who arrived in the United States lost and isolated in a huge and different world might find work and lodging in return for his commitment to the party. In a system of almost pure capitalism and at a time when social services were practically nonexistent, machines and bosses took upon themselves responsibilities that were indispensable to community life. But the moral and material cost of such a system was very high, and the machine was often purely exploitative, performing no services to the community.

By the end of the 19th century the excesses of the machines and the bosses and the closed character of the parties led to the development of primary elections, in which party nominees for office were selected. The primary movement deprived party leaders of the right to dictate candidates for election. A majority of the states adopted the primary system in one form or another between 1900 and 1920. The aim of the system was to make the parties more democratic by opening them up to the general public in the hope of counterbalancing the influence of the party committees. In practice, the aim was not realized, for the committees retained the upper hand in the selection of candidates for the primaries.

The British Labour Party In its original form the British Labour Party constituted a new type of cadre party, forming an intermediate link with the mass-based parties. It was formed with the support of trade unions and left-wing intellectuals. At the base, each local organization sent representatives to a district labour committee, which was in turn represented at the national congress.

The early (pre-1918) Labour Party was thus structured of many local and regional organizations. It was not possible to join the party directly; membership came only through an affiliated body, such as a trade union. It thus represented a new type of party, depending not upon highly political individuals brought together as a result of their desire to acquire and wield power but upon the organized representatives of a broader interest—the working class. Certain Christian Democrat parties—the Belgian Social Christian Party between the two world wars and the Austrian Popular Party, for example—had an analogous structure: a federation of unions, agricultural organizations, middle class movements, employers' associations, etc. After 1918, the Labour Party developed a policy of direct membership on the model of the continental Socialist parties, individual members being permitted to join local-constituency branches. The majority of its membership, however, continued to be affiliated rather than direct.

Mass-based parties.   Cadre parties normally organize a relatively small number of party adherents. Mass-based parties, on the other hand, unite hundreds of thousands of followers, sometimes millions. But the number of members is not the only criterion of a mass-based party. The essential factor is that such a party attempts to base itself on an appeal to the masses. It attempts to organize not only those who are influential or well known or those who represent special interest groups but rather any citizen who is willing to join the party. If such a party succeeds in gathering only a few adherents, then it is mass based only in potential. It remains, nevertheless, different from the cadre-type parties.

Socialist mass-based parties

At the end of the 19th century the Socialist parties of continental Europe organized themselves on a mass basis in order to educate and to organize the growing population of labourers and wage earners, which industrialization was making increasingly large and which was becoming more important politically because of extensions of the suffrage, and to gather the money necessary for propaganda by mobilizing in a regular fashion the resources of those who, although poor, were numerous. Membership campaigns were conducted, and each member paid party dues. If its members became sufficiently numerous, the party emerged as a powerful organization, managing large funds and diffusing its ideas among an important segment of the population. Such was the case with the German Social Democratic Party, which by 1913 had more than 1,000,000 members.

Such organizations were necessarily rigidly structured. The party required an exact registration of membership, treasurers to collect dues, secretaries to call and lead local meetings, and a hierarchical framework for the coordination of the thousands of local sections. A tradition of collective action and group discipline, more developed among workers as a result of their participation in strikes and other union activity, favoured the development and centralization of party organization.

A complex party organization tends to give a great deal of influence to those who have responsibility at various levels in the hierarchy, resulting in certain oligarchical tendencies. The Socialist parties made an effort to control this tendency by developing democratic procedures in the choice of leaders. At every level those in responsible positions were elected by members of the party. Every local party group would elect delegates to regional and national congresses, at which party candidates and party leaders would be chosen and party policy decided.

The type of mass-based party described above was imitated by many non-Socialist parties. Some cadre-type parties in Europe, both conservative and liberal, attempted to transform themselves along similar lines. The Christian Democrat parties often developed organizations copied even more directly from the mass-based model. But non-Socialist parties were generally less successful in establishing rigid and disciplined organizations.

The first Communist parties were splinter groups of existing Socialist parties and at first adopted the organization of these parties. After 1924, as a result of a decision of the Comintern (the Third International, or federation of working class parties), all Communist parties were transformed along the lines of the Soviet model, becoming

Communist mass-based parties

mass parties based on the membership of the largest possible number of citizens, although membership was and is limited to those who embraced and espoused the ideology of Marxism–Leninism.

The Communist parties developed a new structural organization: whereas the local committees of cadre and Socialist parties focussed their organizing efforts and drew their support from a particular geographical area, Communist groups formed their cells in the place of work. The workplace cell was the first original element in Communist party organization. It grouped together all party members who depended upon the same firm, workshop, or store or the same professional institution (school or university, for example). Party members thus tended to be tightly organized, their solidarity, resulting from a common occupation, being stronger than that based upon residence. The work-place-cell system proved to be effective, and

other parties tried to imitate it, generally without success. Such an organization leads each cell to concern itself with problems of a corporate and professional nature rather than with those of a more political nature. These basic groups, however, smaller and, therefore, more numerous than the Socialist sections, tend to go their separate way. It is necessary to have a very strong party structure and for party leaders to have extensive authority if the groups are to resist such centrifugal pressure.

This has resulted in a second distinctive characteristic of the Communist parties: a high degree of centralization. Although all mass-based parties tend to be centralized, Communist parties are more so than others. There is, in principle, free discussion, which is supposedly developed at every level before a decision is made, but afterward all must adhere to the decision that has been made by the central body. The splintering that has from time to time divided or paralyzed the Socialist parties is forbidden in Communist parties, which have generally succeeded in maintaining their unity. A further distinctive characteristic of Communist parties is the importance given to ideology. All parties have a doctrine or at least a platform. The European Socialist parties, which were doctrinaire before 1914 and between the two wars, later became more pragmatic, not to say opportunistic. But, in Communist parties, ideology occupies a much more fundamental place, a primary concern of the party being to indoctrinate its members with Marxism.

The Fascist model

The 1920s and '30s saw the emergence of Fascist parties that attempted, as do the Communist and Socialist parties, to organize the maximum number of members but that did not claim to represent the great masses of people. Their teaching was authoritarian and elitist. They thought that societies should be directed by the most talented and capable people—by an elite. The party leadership, grouped under the absolute authority of a supreme head, constituted such an elite. Party structure had as its goal the assurance of the obedience of the elite.

This structure resembled that of armies, which are also organized in such a way as to ensure, by means of rigorous discipline, the obedience of a large number of men to an elite leadership. The party structure, therefore, made use of a military-type organization, consisting of a pyramid made up of units that at the base were very tiny but that, when joined with other units, formed groups that got larger and larger. Uniforms, ranks, orders, salutes, marches, and unquestioning obedience were all aspects of Fascist parties. This similarity rests upon another factor; namely, that Fascist doctrine taught that power must be seized by organized minorities making use of force. The party thus made use of a militia intended to assure victory in the struggle for control over the unorganized masses.

Large parties built upon the Fascist model developed between the two wars in Italy and Germany, where they actually came into power. Fascist parties appeared also in most other countries of western Europe during this period but were unable to achieve power. The less-developed nations of eastern Europe and Latin America were equally infected by the movement. The victory of the Allies in 1945, as well as the revelation of the horrors of Nazism, stopped the growth of the Fascists and provoked their decline, but Fascist-type party organization and doctrine remain a potent means of exercising power.

PARTIES AND POLITICAL POWER

Whether they are conservative or revolutionary, whether they are a union of notables or an organization of the masses, whether they function in a pluralistic democracy or in a monolithic dictatorship, parties have one function in common: they all participate to some extent in the exercise of political power, whether by forming a government or by exercising the function of opposition, a function that is often of crucial importance in the determination of national policy.

The struggle for power.   It is possible in theory to distinguish revolutionary parties, which attempt to gain power by violence (conspiracies, guerrilla warfare, etc.), from those parties working within the legal framework of elections. But the distinction is not always easy to make, because the same parties may sometimes make use of both procedures, either simultaneously or successively, depending upon the circumstances. In the 1920s, for example, Communist parties sought power through elections at the same time that they were developing an underground activity of a revolutionary nature. In the 19th century, liberal parties were in the same situation, sometimes employing the techniques of conspiracy, as in Italy, Austria, Germany, Poland, and Russia, and sometimes confining their struggles to the ballot box, as in Great Britain and France.

Revolutionary methods vary greatly. Clandestine plots by which minority groups seize the centres of power presuppose monarchies or dictatorships in which the masses of people have little say in government. But terrorist and disruptive activity can serve to mobilize citizens and to demonstrate the powerlessness of any government. At the beginning of the 20th century leftist trade unionists extolled the revolutionary general strike, a total stoppage of all economic activity that would paralyze society completely and put the government at the revolutionaries' mercy. Rural guerrilla activity has often been used in countries with a predominantly agrarian society; urban guerrilla warfare was effective in the European revolutions of the 19th century, but the development of techniques of police and military control has made such activity more difficult.

Functions of parties within a democracy   Revolutionary parties are less numerous than parties that work within the law: the contest at election time is the means normally used in the struggle for power. Such activity corresponds, moreover, to the original nature of political parties and involves three factors: the organization of propaganda, the selection of candidates, and the financing of campaigns. The first function is the most visible. The party first of all gives the candidate a label that serves to introduce him to the voters and to identify his position. Because of this party label the voters are better able to distinguish the candidates. The promises and declarations of individuals are seldom taken with too much seriousness, and it means more to indicate that one candidate is a Communist, another a Socialist, a third a Fascist, and a fourth a liberal. Finally, the party also furnishes the candidate with workers to raise funds, put up his posters, distribute his literature, organize his meetings, and canvass from door to door.

The function of selecting candidates is exercised in three ways. In cadre parties, candidates are selected by committees of the party activists who make up the party—the caucus system, as it is known in the United States. In general, local committees play essential roles in this regard. In some countries, however, the selection is centralized by a national caucus, as, for example, by the Conservative Party in Britain and the Union of Democrats in France. In mass-based parties, selection is made by members of the regional and national congresses according to apparently democratic procedures; in actual practice, the governing committees play an essential role, the local constituency members generally ratifying their choice. Thirdly, in the United States the mechanism of primary elections has established a system for selecting candidates by means of the votes of all party members or all voters within a particular electoral district.

The various processes of selecting candidates do not, however, differ significantly in their results, for it is almost always the party leaders who play the essential role. This introduces an oligarchical tendency into party politics, a tendency that has not been overcome by the congresses of the mass-based parties or the United States primaries, which provide only a partial limitation on the power of the governing committees.

An important aspect of the struggle for power between political parties is the financing of campaigns. Cadre parties always have in their committees some key figure having connections with businessmen who is responsible for collecting gifts from them. In mass-based parties, rather than looking for large sums of money from a few people, leaders gather smaller sums from a large number of people who usually give on a monthly or annual basis. This method has been viewed as one of the distinguishing characteristics of mass-based parties. Sometimes the law intervenes in the financing of elections and of parties. Laws often limit campaign expenses and attempt to restrict the resources of the parties, but they are generally inoperative because it is quite easy to circumvent them. In some countries the state contributes public funds to the parties. At first, such financial participation was limited to expenses for campaigns and was based on the uniform treatment of candidates (as in France), but in Sweden and Finland the state contributes to the general finances of parties.

Participation in power.   Only the functions of parties in democratic regimes will be considered at this time. The role of the single party in a dictatorship will be analyzed separately.

Once a political party has achieved electoral victory, the question arises of how much influence the party is to have on the government. The influence of the party on members in elective office is frequently quite weak. It defines the general lines of their activity, but these lines can be quite hazy, and few decisions are taken in the periodic meetings between officeholders and their party. Each member of the legislature retains personal freedom of action in his participation in debates, in his participation in government, and, especially, in his voting. The party may, of course, attempt to enforce the party line, but parliamentary or congressional members cannot be compelled to vote the way the party wants them to. Such is the situation in the United States, within most of the liberal and conservative European parties, and within cadre parties in general.

The question of how disciplined a party is, of the extent to which it will always present a united front, enables a distinction to be made between what may be termed rigid and flexible parties; that is, between those that attempt always to be united and disciplined, following what is most often an ideologically based party line, and those that, representing a broader range of interests and points of view, form legislatures that are assemblies of individuals rather than of parties.

Flexible and rigid parties

Whether the parties operating within a particular system will be rigid or flexible depends largely on the constitutional provisions that determine the circumstances in which a government may continue in office. This is clearly illustrated by comparing the situation in the United States with that in Great Britain. In the United States the president and his government continue in office for the constitutionally defined period of four years, regardless of whether a majority in the legislature supports him or not. Since a united party is thus not crucial to the immediate survival of the government, both major parties are able to contain broad coalitions of interests, and votes on issues of major importance frequently split each party. In the United Kingdom the situation is quite different. There, government can continue in office only so long as it commands a majority in the legislature. A single adverse vote can result in the dissolution of Parliament and a general election. Party discipline and unity are thus of crucial importance, and this fact has far-reaching consequences for the composition, organization, and policies of each party. The consequences of party disunity within such a constitutional framework are well illustrated by the weakness and instability of the governments of the Third and Fourth French republics.

The distinction between flexible and rigid parties applies equally to parties in power and to those forming the opposition. Votes of censure or of lack of confidence, votes on proposed legislation or on the budget, questions put to ministers or challenges made to them—in short, all the functions of an opposition party—are worked out differently in flexible and rigid party systems.

In flexible party systems the absence of strong discipline is often of great consequence to the opposition party because only rigid parties can constitute an opposition force sufficiently strong to counterbalance the strength of the party in power. At the same time, party discipline permits the opposition to present the public with an alternative to the majority party; the logical consequence of such a situation is Britain's "shadow cabinet," which accustoms the electorate to the idea that a new group is ready to take over the reins of government.

Parties provide, moreover, a channel of communication

between opposition legislators and the public. The governing party performs a similar service for the government, although it is less necessary, since the government has at its disposal numerous means of communicating with the public. Opposition parties thus provide a means of expressing negative reaction to decisions of government and proposing alternatives. This role justifies the official recognition given to opposition parties, as is the case in Great Britain and Scandinavia.

Power and representation. It is difficult to envisage how representative democracy could function in a large industrialized society without political parties. In order for citizens to be able to make an intelligent choice of representative or president, it is necessary for them to know the real political orientation of each candidate. Party membership provides the clearest indication of this. The programs and promises of each individual candidate are not too significant or informative, because most candidates, in their attempt to gain the most votes, try to avoid difficult subjects; they all tend to speak the same language; that is, to camouflage their real opinions. The fact that one is a Socialist, another a conservative, a third a liberal, and a fourth a Communist provides a far better clue as to how the candidate will perform when in office. In the legislature the discipline of the party limits the possibility that elected representatives will change their minds and their politics, and thus the party label acts as a sort of guarantee that there will be at least some correspondence between promise and performance. Parties make possible the representation of varying shades of opinion by synthesizing different positions into a stance that each representative adopts to a greater or lesser extent.

Individual candidates and the party

But parties, like all organizations, tend to manipulate their members, to bring them under the control of an inner circle of leaders that often perpetuates itself by cooptation. In cadre parties, members are manipulated by powerful committees containing cliques of influential party leaders. In mass-based parties, leaders are chosen by the members, but incumbents are very often re-elected because they control the party apparatus, using it to ensure their continuation in power.

Democratic political systems, while performing the function of representation, thus rest more or less on the competition of rival oligarchies. But these oligarchies consist of political elites that are open to all with political ambition. No modern democracy could function without parties, the oligarchical tendencies of which are best regarded as a necessary evil.

PARTY SYSTEMS

Party systems may be broken down into three broad categories: two-party, multiparty, and single-party. Such a classification is based not merely on the number of parties operating within a particular country but on a variety of distinctive features that the three systems exhibit. Two-party and multiparty systems represent means of organizing political conflict within pluralistic societies and are thus part of the apparatus of democracy. Single parties usually operate in situations in which genuine political conflict is not tolerated. This broad statement is, however, subject to qualification, for, although single parties do not usually permit the expression of points of view that are fundamentally opposed to the party line or ideology, there may well be intense conflict within these limits over policy within the party itself. And even within a two-party or a multiparty system, debate may become so stymied and a particular coalition of interests so entrenched that the democratic process is seriously compromised.

The distinction between two-party and multiparty systems is not as easily made as it might appear. In any two-party system there are invariably some tiny parties in addition to the two major parties, and there is always the possibility that such small parties might prevent one of the two main parties from gaining a majority of seats in the legislature. This is the case with regard to the Liberal Party in Great Britain, for example. Other countries do not fall clearly into either category; thus, Austria and the Federal Republic of Germany only approximate the two-party system. It is not simply a question of the number

of parties that determines the nature of the two-party system; many other elements are of importance, the extent of party discipline in particular.

Multiparty systems. In Anglo-Saxon countries there is a tendency to consider the two-party system as normal and the multiparty system as the exceptional case. But, in fact, the two-party system that operates in Great Britain, the United States, and New Zealand is much rarer than the multiparty system, which is found in almost all of western Europe.

In western Europe, three major categories of parties have developed since the beginning of the 19th century: conservative, liberal, and Socialist. Each reflects the interests of a particular social class and expounds a particular political ideology. After World War I other categories of parties developed that were partly the result of divisions or transformations of older parties. Communist parties began as splinter groups of Socialist parties, and Christian Democrat parties attempted to weld together moderate Socialists and conservatives and some liberals. Other distinctive types of party emerged in some countries. In Scandinavia, liberal rural parties developed in the 19th century, reflecting a long tradition of separate representation of the rural population. In many countries ethnic minorities formed the basis of nationalist parties, which then either joined existing parties or divided them.

The appearance of Socialism in the 19th century upset the earlier lines of battle between conservatives and liberals and tended to throw the latter two groups into a common defense of capitalism. Logically, this situation should have led to the fusion of conservatives and liberals into one bourgeois party that would have presented a united stand against Socialism. This is, in fact, what happened in Great Britain after World War I.

One of the most important factors determining the number of parties operating within a particular country is the electoral system. Proportional representation tends to favour the development of multiparty systems because it ensures representation in the legislature for even small parties. The majority, single-ballot system tends to produce a two-party system, because it excludes parties that may gain substantial numbers of votes but not the majority of votes necessary to elect a representative within a constituency. The majority system with a second ballot favours a multiparty system tempered by alliances between parties. Such a system is very rare, found only in the German Empire (1871–1914) and in the French Third (1870–1940) and Fifth (since 1958) republics. Voters choose between the parties that did best in a first ballot. This leaves small parties at a disadvantge but, nevertheless, gives them opportunity to strengthen their role during the second balloting as long as they are willing to enter into alliances with the leading parties.

Influence of the electoral system on the number of parties

Another factor producing multiparty systems is the intensity of political conflicts. If, within a given political movement, extremists are numerous, then it is difficult for the moderates in that party to join with them in a united front. Two rival parties are likely to be formed. Thus, the power of the Jacobins among 19th-century French liberals contributed to the inability of the moderates to form one great liberal party, as was successfully achieved in Great Britain. Likewise, the power of the extremists among the conservatives was an obstacle to the development of a strong conservative party.

The distinction between the multiparty system and the two-party system corresponds largely to a distinction between two types of Western political regime. In a two-party situation the administration has, in effect, an assurance of a majority in the legislature, deriving from the predominance of one party; it has, therefore, a guarantee of continuance and effectiveness. Such a system is often referred to as majority parliamentarianism. In a multiparty situation, on the other hand, it is quite rare for one party to have a majority in the legislature; governments must, therefore, be founded on coalitions, which are always more heterogeneous and more fragile than a single party. The result is less stability and less political power. Such systems may be referred to as nonmajority parliamentarianism.

In practice, majority and nonmajority parliamentary systems do not coincide exactly with two-party systems and multiparty systems. For, if each of the two parties is flexible and does not control the voting patterns of its members (as is the case in the United States), the numerical majority of one of the parties matters little. It can happen, moreover, that one party in a multiparty system will hold an absolute majority of seats in the legislature so that no coalition is required. Such a situation is unusual but has occurred in West Germany, Italy, and Belgium at various times since 1945.

Ordinarily, however, a coalition will be the only means of attaining a parliamentary majority within the framework of the multiparty system. Coalitions are by nature more heterogeneous and more unstable than a grouping made up of one party, but their effectiveness varies greatly according to the discipline and organization of the parties involved. In the case of flexible parties that are undisciplined and that allow each legislator to vote on his own, the coalition will be weak and probably short-lived. The instability and weakness of governments is at its maximum in such situations, of which the Third French Republic provides a good example.

If, on the other hand, the parties involved in a coalition are rigid and disciplined, it is possible for a system quite similar to the two-party system to develop. This is often the case when two opposing alliances are formed, one on the left and one on the right, and when both are strong enough to endure through the legislative session. This type of coalition, referred to as bipolarized, introduces elements of the two-party system into a multiparty framework. A situation of this type has developed in Sweden, where conservative, liberal, and agrarian parties have been aligned against the Social Democrat Party, which eventually allied itself with the Communist Party (1970).

The system of bipolar alliances may be contrasted with the system of a centrist alliance. Rather than the parties on the right forming a centre–right coalition to oppose a centre–left coalition, there is the possibility that the centre–left and the centre–right will join forces and reject the extremes at both ends of the political spectrum. Such a situation occurred in Germany during the Weimar Republic, when the government rested on a majority formed of a coalition of Catholic Centrists and Social Democrats, with opposition coming from the Communists and the nationalists on the extreme left and right.

Benefits and disadvantages of coalition politics

Centrist coalitions all tend to give the average citizen a sense of political alienation. In rejecting both extremes, coalitions may well be isolating the radical, unstable elements, but the governing coalition may tend to be unresponsive to new ideas, uninspiringly pragmatic, and too ready to compromise. This situation gives rise to a more or less permanent breach between practical politics and political ideals. An advantage of bipolarization or of the two-party system is that the moderates of both sides must collaborate with those who are more extreme in their views, and the extremists must be willing to work with those who are more moderate; the pressure from the extremists prevents the moderates from getting bogged down, while collaboration with the moderates lends a touch of realism to the policies of the extremists.

Two-party systems.   A fundamental distinction must be made between the two-party system as it is found in the United States and as it is found in Great Britain. Although two major parties dominate political life in the two countries, the system operates in quite different ways.

The American two-party system.   The United States has always had a two-party system, first in the opposition between the Federalists and the Anti-Federalists, then in the competition between the Republicans and the Democrats. There have been frequent third-party movements in the history of the country, but they have always failed. Presidential elections seem to have played an important role in the formation of this type of two-party system. The mechanism of a national election in so large a country has necessitated very large political organizations and, at the same time, relatively simplified choices for the voter.

American parties are different from their counterparts in other Western countries. They are not tied in the same way to the great social and ideological movements that have so influenced the development of political life in Europe during the last two centuries. There have been Socialist parties at various times in the history of the United States, but they have never challenged the dominance of the two major parties. It can be argued that the main reason for the failure of Socialist parties in America has been the high degree of upward mobility permitted by a rich and continually expanding economy. The consequence of this mobility has been that class consciousness has never developed in the United States in a manner that would encourage the formation of large Socialist or Communist parties.

In comparison with European political movements, therefore, American parties have appeared as two varieties of one liberal party, and within each party can be found a wide range of opinion, going from the right to the left.

The American parties have a flexible and decentralized structure, marked by the absence of discipline and rigid hierarchy. This was the structure of most of the cadre-type parties of the 19th century, a structure that most liberal parties have retained. Federalism and a concern for local autonomy accentuate the lack of rigid structure and the weakness of lines of authority in the parties. Organization may be relatively strong and homogeneous at the local level, but such control is much weaker on the state level and practically nonexistent on the national level. There is some truth to the observation that the United States has not two parties but 100—that is, two in each state. But it is also true that each party develops a certain degree of national unity for the presidential election and that the leadership of the president within his party gives the victorious party some cohesion.

Coalition voting patterns in the U.S. Congress

In voting, Republicans and Democrats are usually found on both sides. An alliance between liberal Republicans and Democrats against conservative Republicans and Democrats tends to develop. But neither bloc is stable, and the alignment varies from one vote to another. As a consequence, despite the existence of a two-party system, no stable legislative majority is possible. In order to have his budget adopted and his legislation passed, the president of the United States must patiently try to gather the necessary votes on every question; like Penelope, he has the wearisome task of beginning anew each day. The American two-party system is thus a pseudo-two-party system, because each party provides only a loose framework within which shifting coalitions are formed.

The British two-party system.   Another form of the two-party system is operative in Great Britain and in New Zealand. The situation in Australia is affected somewhat by the presence of a third party, the Country Party. A tight alliance between the Australian Liberal Party and the Country Party introduces, however, a rather rigid bipolarization with the Labour Party. The system thus tends to operate on a two-party basis. Canada also possesses what is essentially a two-party system, Liberals or Conservatives usually being able to form a working majority without the help of the small, regionally based parties.

Great Britain has had two successive two-party alignments: Conservative and Liberal prior to 1914 and Conservative and Labour since 1935. The period from 1920 to 1935 constituted an intermediate phase between the two. Britain's Conservative Party is actually a Conservative–Liberal Party, resulting from a fusion of the essential elements of the two great 19th-century parties. Despite the name Conservative, its ideology corresponds to political and economic liberalism. A similar observation could be made about the other major European conservative parties, such as the German Christian Democratic Party and the Belgian Social Christian Party.

Importance of rigid party lines in the British system

The British two-party system depends on the existence of rigid parties; that is, parties in which there is effective discipline regarding parliamentary voting patterns. In every important vote, all party members are required to vote as a bloc and to follow to the letter the directives that they agreed upon in common or that were decided for them by the party leaders. A relative flexibility may at times be tolerated, but only to the extent that such a policy does not compromise the action of the government. It may be admissible for some party members to abstain from voting if their abstention does not alter the results of the vote. Thus, the leader of the majority party (who is at the same time the prime minister) is sure to remain in power throughout the session of Parliament, and the legislation he proposes will be adopted. There is no longer any real separation of power between the executive and legislative branches, for the government and its parliamentary majority form a homogeneous and solid bloc before which the opposition has no power other than to make its criticisms known. During the four or five years for which a Parliament meets, the majority in power is completely in control, and only internal difficulties within the majority party can limit its power.

Since each party is made up of a disciplined group with a recognized leader who becomes prime minister if his party wins the legislative elections, these elections perform the function of selecting both the legislature and the government. In voting to make one of the party leaders the head of the government, the British assure him of a disciplined parliamentary majority. The net result is a political system that is at once stable, democratic, and strong; and many would argue that it is more stable, more democratic, and stronger than systems anywhere else in the world.

This situation presupposes that both parties are in agreement with regard to the fundamental rules of a democracy. If a Fascist party and a Communist party were opposed to one another in Great Britain, the two-party system would not last very long. The winner would zealously suppress the opponent and rule alone.

The system, of course, does have its weak points, especially insofar as it tends to frustrate the innovative elements within both parties. But it is possible that this situation is preferable to what would happen if the more extreme elements within the parties were permitted to engage in unrealistic policies. The risk of immobility is in fact a problem for any party in a modern industrial society, and not just for those in a two-party situation. The problem is related to the difficulties involved in creating new organizations capable of being taken seriously by an important segment of the population and in revitalizing long-standing organizations encumbered by established practices and entrenched interests.

Single-party systems. There have been three historical forms of the single-party system: Communist, Fascist, and that found in the developing countries.

The Communist model. In Communist countries the party is considered to be the spearhead of the urban working class and of other workers united with it (peasants, intellectuals, etc.). Its role is to aid in the building of a Socialist regime during the transitory phase between capitalism and pure Socialism, called the dictatorship of the proletariat. An understanding of the exact role of the party requires an appreciation of the Marxist conception of the evolution of the state. In countries based on private ownership of the means of production, the power of the state, according to the Marxist point of view, is used to further the interests of the controlling capitalists. In the first stage of revolution the power of the state is broken. Power, however, still has to be wielded to prevent counterrevolution and to facilitate the transition to Communism, at which stage coercion will no longer be necessary. Thus, the party, in effect, assumes the coercive functions of the state during the dictatorship of the proletariat or, to be more accurate, during the dictatorship of the party in the name of the proletariat.

It is thus the party hierarchy and not the official state hierarchy that has the real power. The first secretary of the party is the most important figure of the regime, and, whether the party leadership is in the hands of one man or several, the party remains the centre of political power.

In China the role of the party has been modified to some extent. The Great Cultural Revolution (1966–69) seems to have been a device used by Mao Tse-tung to reduce the power of the party, over which he was losing control. He sought support instead from the masses of fanatical youth and the army. Since then, the party has been gradually reorganized, but it is no longer as dominant as it was or as is usual within Communist states. The role of the army

(margin note) Role of the party in Communist states

appears to be preponderant; moreover, it is an army that has been very politicized and that has always maintained close contact with the population.

In all Communist countries, the structure of the party has been determined largely by the need for it to govern firmly while at the same time maintaining its contact with the masses of the people. Party members are a part of the general public, of which they are the most active and most politically conscious members. They remain in contact with the masses by means of a network of party cells that are present everywhere. Party leaders are thus always "listening in on the masses," and the masses are always informed of decisions of party leaders, as long as the communication network is working in both directions.

The party is not only a permanent means of contact between the people and party leaders; it is also a propaganda instrument. Political indoctrination is essential to the survival of Communist parties, and many resources are devoted to it. Indoctrination is accomplished in training schools, by means of "education" campaigns, carefully censored newspapers, periodicals, and books, and the untiring efforts of militants, who play a role similar to that of the clergy in organized religion. The party is thus the guardian of orthodoxy and has the power to condemn and to excommunicate.

The Fascist model. Fascist parties in a single-party state have never played as important a role as Communist parties in an analogous situation. In Italy, the Fascist party was never the single most important element in the regime, and its influence was often secondary. In Spain the Falange never played a crucial role, and in Portugal the National Union was a very weak organization even at the height of dictator António Salazar's strength. Only in Germany did the National Socialist Party have a great influence on the state. But, in the end, Hitler's dictatorship was dependent on his private army, the SS (Schutzstaffel), which formed a separate element within the party and which was closed to outside influences, and on the Gestapo, which was a state organization and not an organization of the party. The Fascist party in the single-party state has a policing or military function rather than an ideological one.

After their rise to power, the Fascist parties in both Germany and Italy gradually ceased to perform the function of maintaining contact between the people and the government, a function that is usually performed by the party in a single-party situation. It was possible to observe a tendency for the party to close in upon itself while suppressing its deviant members. The renewal of the party was then assured through recruitment from youth organizations, from which the most fanatical elements, the products of a gradual selection process starting at a very early age, entered the party. The party tended, therefore, to constitute a closed order.

The single party in the developing countries. Some of the Communist parties in power in developing countries do not differ significantly from their counterparts in industrialized countries. This is certainly true of the Communist Party of the Socialist Republic of Vietnam and the Communist Party of North Korea. There are, however, countries in Africa, Asia, and Latin America in which the single party in power cannot be characterized in terms of a European counterpart. This observation applies to, for example, the Arab Socialist Union in Egypt, the Neo-Destour Party in Tunisia, and the National Liberation Front in Algeria, as well as many parties in black Africa.

Most of these parties claim to be more or less Socialist or at least progressive, while remaining far removed from Communism and, in some cases, ardent foes of Communism. President Nasser attempted to establish a moderate and nationalistic Socialism in Egypt. In Tunisia the Neo-Destour Party is more republican than Socialist and is inspired more by the example of the reforms in Turkey under Kemal Atatürk than by Nasserism. In black Africa, single parties often claim to be Socialist, but with few exceptions they rarely are in practice. But, while they may not be revolutionary, they are reform oriented.

Single parties in developing countries are rarely as well organized as Communist parties. In Turkey the Republican People's Party was more a cadre party than a mass-based party. In Egypt it has been necessary to organize a core of professional politicians within the framework of a pseudoparty of the masses. In black Africa the parties are most often genuinely mass based, but the membership appears to be motivated primarily by personal attachment to the leader or by tribal loyalties, and organization is not usually very strong. It is this weakness in organization that explains the secondary role played by such parties in government.

Some regimes, however, have endeavoured to develop the role of the party to the fullest extent possible. The politics of Atatürk in Turkey were an interesting case study in this regard. It was also Nasser's goal to increase the influence of the Arab Socialist Union, thereby making it the backbone of the regime. This process is significant in that it represents an attempt to move away from the old-fashioned dictatorship, supported by the army or based on tribal traditions or on charismatic leadership, toward a modern dictatorship, supported by one political party. Single-party systems can institutionalize dictatorships by making them survive the life of one dominant figure.

FUTURE OF POLITICAL PARTIES

The necessity of parties in democratic systems

It has often been said in the West that political parties are in a state of decline. Actually, this has been a long-standing opinion in certain conservative circles, arising largely out of a latent hostility to parties, which are viewed as a divisive force among citizens, a threat to national unity, and an enticement to corruption and demagoguery. In certain European countries—France, for example—right-wing political organizations have even refused to call themselves parties, using instead such terms as movement, union, federation, and centre. And it cannot be denied that to some extent the major European and American parties of the late 20th century do appear old and rigid in comparison with their condition at the turn of the century or immediately following World War I. Even relatively new parties, such as the Christian Democratic parties of Germany and Italy (founded in 1945), seem somewhat lifeless.

In terms of size and number, however, political parties are not declining but growing. At the turn of the century they were confined mainly to Europe and North America; elsewhere they were quite weak or nonexistent. In the late 20th century, parties are found practically everywhere in the world. And in Europe and North America there are generally far more people holding membership in parties than prior to 1914. Parties of the late 20th century are larger, stronger, and better organized than those of the late 19th century. In the industrialized nations, especially in western Europe, parties have become less revolutionary and innovative, and this factor may explain the rigid and worn-out image that they sometimes present. But even this phenomenon is found only in a limited area and may, perhaps, pass.

The growth of parties into very large organizations may be responsible for the feelings of powerlessness on the part of many individuals who are involved in them. This is a problem experienced by people who find themselves part of any large organization, whether it be a political party, business enterprise, corporation, or union. The difficulties involved in reforming or changing political parties that have become large and institutionalized, coupled with the next-to-impossible task of creating new parties likely to reach sufficient strength to be taken seriously by the electorate, have resulted in much frustration and impatience with the party system. But it is difficult to imagine how democracy could function in a large industrialized country without political parties. In the modern world, democracy and political parties are two facets of the same reality, the inside and outside of the same fabric.   (M.Du./Ed.)

Interest groups

TYPES OF INTEREST GROUP

Categories defined by motivation. Within the broad definition of interest groups, two polar types are recognizable: first, interest groups proper, such as trade unions, farmers' unions, and employers' associations, which have as their primary purpose the enhancement of the advantage of their members; and, second, promotional groups, such as the societies for the prevention of cruelty to children or various voluntary relief agencies, which exist primarily or entirely to enhance the advantage not of their own members but of the population, even perhaps to the discomfort or disadvantage of their own members. Some of these, such as churches or various evangelizing groups, exist to promulgate a distinctive set of values to be applied to society as a whole. The distinction between interest groups proper and promotional groups is not sharp for two reasons. In the first place, most interest groups proper sincerely believe that in furthering their own material advantage they are also serving that of society as a whole—by promoting "free enterprise" or a healthy and wealthy body of farmers or a well-paid and enthusiastic corps of school teachers. But the propagation of such beliefs is certainly not the primary purpose of such organizations, thus distinguishing them from promotional groups. The second reason is that some groups—for instance, organized churches—fall between the two types; they can simultaneously pursue advantages for their own sect and seek to inculcate a distinctive set of values in a whole society.

Categories defined by structure. In primitive or developing societies, the most prominent type of interest group is the natural (*i.e.,* primordial or communal) one—that is, one based on kinship, lineage, neighbourhood, or religious confession. In Western, industrialized societies, though such groups do sometimes retain influence (as do the nationalities in Yugoslavia or Czechoslovakia), the most prominent interest group is the associational (*i.e.,* secondary or factitious) type, like the trade union or Campaign for Nuclear Disarmament, which is deliberately created to serve defined purposes. Often, associational (or factitious) groups are created for the sake of the specialized purposes of the first type; the Indian Workers Union, for instance, was created from the community of Indian persons in Britain.

Within the class of associational groups, further qualifications must be made:

1. Not all associational groups possess formal structure. "Wall Street" in the United States, or the "City" in London, though consisting of a loose network of persons or functions, may nevertheless exert powerful collective pressures.

2. Some associational groups are collectivities; but others are single, discreet organizations. Thus General Motors Corporation exerts its own strong influence vis-à-vis the U.S. government irrespective of the influence of the more general employers' organization to which it possibly belongs, like the National Association of Manufacturers.

3. Some associational groups are temporary or *ad hoc.* Such are the so-called anomic groups, such as enraged French farmers who come together briefly to put logs across roads in order to draw governmental attention to their grievances.

4. Some associational groups are "latent." There may be a common interest among certain members of the public even though these individuals may not have combined into a formal or informal organization. The individuals may be unaware that they have a common interest or, if aware, see no reason to defend or promote it. Or, even if the members consciously wish to defend or promote an interest, the laws may restrict or control their ability to associate for such a purpose.

Categories defined by political activity. If or when any interest group tries to influence the government in the pursuit of its aims, it becomes a "pressure group." Not all interest groups proper try to exert influence on governments; many (such as businesses and trade unions) do so only as a part of their more general activities of promoting their own interests. Promotional groups, on the other hand, spend much or all their time precisely in trying to influence the government to favour their aims. Groups such as an anglers' association may, therefore, turn into pressure groups for a time—the time when they seek to influence the government for one of their purposes—and then revert to simple interest-group status. A pressure group is therefore definable as "any interest group that

Natural and associational groups

Pressure groups

is not a part of the government and does not itself seek to govern the country in its own name, but does seek to influence that government for its own purposes."

Difficulties of definition arise, however. Some groups are neither a governmental agency nor entirely a private group. In autocratic states, Communist or otherwise, for instance, trade unions are often controlled by the government or the governing party. In the Western liberal democracies, again, agencies like the Tennessee Valley Authority (in the U.S.) or the British Broadcasting Corporation, though subject to the overriding control of the government, enjoy substantial autonomy in certain broad areas.

Also, as noted at the beginning of this article, some pressure groups eventually turn into political parties, or vice versa.

CHARACTERISTICS OF PRESSURE GROUPS

Power elements. Even in the most pluralistic of the Western liberal democratic states, it is wrong to picture public policy as simply the result of a parallelogram of group forces. The groups are themselves restrained by institutions, procedures, and public beliefs. Among the *institutions,* the most important are the public bureaucracy, the political parties, and the independent branches of the government (the executive, legislature, and judiciary—or some combination of these, depending on the structure of government). To the extent that each or all of these institutions have strong traditions, no interest group supplants them but instead has to deal with them. The governmental procedures in force also affect groups' performance. To the extent that public issues are traditionally subject to publicity and wide discussion, groups are limited in the kind of activities that they can pursue. They are constrained by public *beliefs* as to what is in "the public interest," by what is a proper or improper procedure, or by what causes are respectable and what are not. If any of these three entities—institutions, procedures, or public beliefs—become feeble, interest groups can intrude into them. By allying with or gaining power over the parties, the legislature, or the bureaucracy, for instance, groups can tend to substitute themselves for such organs in the decision-making process.

Inside every country the power that pressure groups wield against the government and that each group wields relative to its rivals depends on a combination of the following variables, some of which are mutually dependent:

1. Density is the ratio of actual membership to potential membership. The higher the density, the more "representative" is the group of all the people whose interests it purports to represent and the greater will be the inclination for governments to recognize and consult it. On the other hand, too wide a membership brings with it internal cleavages, so that on certain issues the organization may not be able to tender clear-cut advice or, indeed, may have to refrain from offering advice altogether.

2. Wealth not only helps a group to develop a skilled management and bureaucracy but also enables it to propagandize and to finance political parties.

3. Prestige lends a group the ability to get a favourable initial hearing from government and public, even though its numbers may be small and its wealth meagre.

4. Organization consists notably of the ability to brief legislators and administrators well and quickly, to mobilize members and the public rapidly, and to receive advance intelligence of likely trends in policy.

5. Socioeconomic leverage is strong among some groups (such as trade unions) that can disrupt social life and low among others (such as consumers associations).

6. Militancy consists of making an effective nuisance of oneself, so that, hopefully, governments will be willing to "buy" time or peace.

7. Specialized information and skills add the weight of authority.

8. Electoral strength refers to the power of some groups that, though poorly organized or having a low density, nevertheless command wide support in the electorate and so find themselves courted by rival political parties.

Strategy and tactics. Although all groups seek out the most influential agencies of government, the most influential may not be accessible; and resort must be had to the next most influential organ that *is* accessible. Because the Communist trade unions in Italy, for instance, are not welcome at the Roman Catholic controlled Ministry of Labour, they try to penetrate the legislature through political election. Indeed, in any system the influence of the various organs of government varies. In France the president and bureaucracy are more influential than the majority party and Parliament; in the United States, the president and Congress balance each other, with control of the bureaucracy shared between the two. Strategy, for an interest group, consists of determining and going to the most influential organ that is accessible.

The tactics of an interest group range from the constitutional to the unconstitutional (or "direct action"), the legal to the illegal—all subject, as noted above, to the restraints of institutions, public procedures, and public beliefs. When the target of the tactics is the executive and the governmental bureaucracy, the following are the prime methods: *Constitutional operations* include (1) advice via advisory bodies attached to the ministries (as in Britain and France), (2) official hearings outside the ministries (as in Royal Commissions in the U.K. and presidential commissions in the U.S.) or inside the ministries (as in Germany or Sweden), and (3) ad hoc consultations and cooperation. *Semiconstitutional operations* include (1) recruitment of state civil servants into the private bureaucracies of the interest groups, or vice versa, and (2) bribery and favours, which need not necessarily mean passing of money but can take the form of providing entertainment, gifts, or meals. *Semidirect operations* include such measures as refusing to provide information or to cooperate in administering legislation and thus generally withdrawing from advisory functions. *Direct action* includes such measures as the withdrawal of labour (the British Medical Association, for instance, advised its members to withdraw from the state medical service in 1965 unless its demands were met) or even violence such as the roadblocking activities of enraged French farmers in the 1960s).

When the target is the legislature, the following are the chief kinds of tactics used by interest groups: *Constitutional operations* include (1) testimony before legislative committee hearings (extremely important in the U.S. and somewhat important in Sweden, the German Federal Republic, Japan, and Italy); (2) direct representation in the legislature, which involves having individual businessmen, financiers, farmers, school teachers, journalists, and other professionals representing the larger interests of their profession or sponsoring group (in Great Britain in 1955 some 30 percent of Labour's MP's were trade-union sponsored); and (3) lobbying, which refers to the activities of salaried or nonsalaried persons who try to promote their interest groups' aims by seeking personal contacts with legislators, by sending communications or information to legislators or persuading others to do so, and by rendering campaign assistance to favoured legislators. (In the U.S., lobbying is conducted not only by private interest groups but also by certain members of the executive branch and the bureaucracy.) *Semiconstitutional operations* include subvention or payment of retainers as well as providing campaign contributions, secretarial help, office accommodations, and the like, which are restricted but not forbidden by law. *Semidirect action* includes mass lobbying, such as promoting mass demonstrations before legislators, ostensibly to relate grievances but in fact to impress public opinion. *Direct action* includes threatening legislators with a withdrawal of financial assistance, with physical violence, or with riots (as in Japan, where snake dances and riots become a means of protest).

When political parties are powerful, they may prove a highly preferred target. Tactics in such cases include the following: *Constitutional operations,* such as, (1) exacting election pledges, which is most important and fruitful in countries (such as the U.S.) where there is relatively little national-party discipline, where representatives owe a certain allegiance to local-party groups and constituents, and where, most important, representatives do possess legislative power; (2) financing the party, which in all systems is perhaps the most effective operation and which in most

Tactics to affect the executive

Tactics to affect the legislative

Western parliaments—and in Western-style parliaments like Japan's—is systematically done by trade unions, employers associations, and individual firms; and (3) lobbying the party machinery, a method that is virtually nonexistent in the United States but is significant in such countries as Great Britain and Germany.

A final target of interest groups is public opinion. The general opinion of the public at large can be of importance in issues where questions of "fairness" or "justice" arise (on which most people feel they can pronounce). These questions involve such matters as capital punishment, the use of nuclear weapons, or certain wars, about which large numbers of people feel very strongly.

ROLE OF INTEREST GROUPS IN VARIOUS POLITICAL SYSTEMS

The Anglo-American and Swedish patterns. In the United States, Great Britain, and Sweden, the general population is not irreparably divided on ideological or cultural lines. Although there arise from time to time some small extremist groups, the population at large is not split into irreconcilable blocks. Given this situation, the most influential and prominent groups are "secondary" associations that have highly specialized objectives, form freely without the requirement of prior governmental permission, and carry out their activities autonomously. With the exception of the affiliation of the trade-union movement to the Labour Party in Britain and in Sweden, the groups are politically neutral; and even the alignment of British and Swedish trade unions and cooperatives does not prevent them from cooperating with other parties nor hinder their free access to government departments. Latent groups are few, since freedom of speech and association and the right to petition the government permit most interests to organize, while good communication media facilitate such organization. Public participation in such groups is, by world standards, high. The pressure groups play highly specialized roles and are sharply differentiated from the political parties.

Although American and British means of influencing the executive are similar (by advisory committees, special inquiries, and day-to-day consultation and mutual assistance), these relations are more institutionalized in Britain than in the U.S. British groups seek to influence the parties by affiliation or by securing their members' nomination as candidates, neither mode being employed in the U.S., and by financial assistance, which occurs in both states but in quite different ways owing to the very different legislation on this matter in the two countries. British groups seek to influence the legislature by securing direct representation through participation in party caucuses and by promoting amendments in the committee stage. In the U.S. the methods employed consist of lobbying influential congressmen and appearing at committee hearings, which are far more important in Congress than in the House of Commons. In influencing public opinion, American groups spend far more than their British counterparts—one reason being that purchase of time on radio and television networks is permissible in the U.S., whereas in Britain it is not. In addition, access to the presidency can prove decisive in the U.S.; and some groups such as the National Association for the Advancement of Colored People have scored notable successes by seeking court action.

In Sweden the tactics are somewhat different, owing to three factors: the existence of a multiparty system and the existence of coalition cabinets, the structure of the bureaucracy, and the much greater institutionalization of pressure groups. Sweden, Denmark, and Norway each possess a multiparty system; but when coalitions are formed, they are highly stable. Consensus is achieved in a three-tier operation—first at interparty (electoral) level, then at the interparty-coalition (legislative) level, and finally at the bureaucratic level. In Sweden groups seek to influence the parties by affiliation (the trade unions being affiliated to the Labour Party), by financing them (trade unions giving to the Labour Party, employers groups to the antisocialist parties), and by securing direct representation through the nomination of members as parliamentary candidates. The parties respond by trying to compose a balanced ticket of the spectrum of interests. Hence the groups can affect

the legislature through their representatives inside each of the parties and may, on occasion, form a cross-party legislative pressure group in defense of their common interest; and they also seek access to the party caucus and influence the committee stage of legislation. In the latter case they are assisted by the standard Swedish procedure by which the "comments" of outside interests are attached to the government's bill, even if they contradict the bill's purposes. Groups have ready access to the legislature in the same ways that Anglo-American groups do, except that the procedure is highly institutionalized; the "Royal Commission" with representatives of the bureaucracy, the parties, and the interest groups seek to reach initial agreement on a bill to be presented to the legislature; and when this device is not used, "comments" appended to the bill serve to put the measure in the context of the avowed interests of various groups.

Not unlike the system in Britain, the U.S., and Sweden is the system in Japan, which, despite sharp ideological divisions, has a strong and stable two-party arrangement. This has led to the emergence of a pattern of highly institutionalized pressure groups of the "secondary" type, the most influential of these being business and organized labour. Business, on the whole, is aligned with the conservative Liberal-Democratic party, supplies the bulk of its funds, and has a large say in policy formation. Organized labour constitutes a powerful element within the Japanese Socialist Party. In an earlier day, rural farm groups carried considerable political weight—for the conservatives—but the increasing industrialization and urbanization of the country have tended to reduce its importance.

The French and Italian patterns. In France and Italy the political pattern is characterized by deep ideological cleavages. The Roman Catholic Church, for example, operates through both its own political party and its own interest groups, such as the Catholic Action Society and Catholic youth and women's group. By the same token, the highly ideological and sectarian Commmunist Party establishes its own pressure groups, such as trade unions, farmers associations, and youth movements. Several rival groups thus compete for the same clientele aligned or affiliated with rival political parties.

Under France's Fifth Republic, the executive branch currently controls the majority party in the legislature, and the role of the legislature has been reduced; whereas, under Italy's current system, feeble and fragile coalition cabinets have weakened executive leadership of the legislature, and the legislature itself is highly fragmented among numerous parties. Because contacts between interest groups on the one hand and the parties, civil service departments, and legislature on the other are poorly institutionalized, semidirect action or even direct action against the executive and the legislature are more common, and lawless activities of crowds and violent organizations have proved more widespread.

The means of influencing the chosen targets also vary. In France attention has shifted from the legislature (under the Fourth Republic) to the president and bureaucracy (under the Fifth); interest groups now act through the numerous advisory bodies, private contacts, and such official institutions as the Economic and Social Council. Interest groups secure contacts by putting former civil servants on their own payrolls. The fact that many civil servants and business executives come from the same schools facilitates private collusion.

In Italy interest groups direct their attention mainly to three targets. First, the bureaucracy, even though it is highly fragmented and provides few formal advisory channels of communication, is open to ad hoc and personal consultations (except to groups deemed ideologically distasteful, such as the Communists). Second, the parties are often twinned to interest groups, as noted earlier; and thus the groups seek and achieve direct representation in the legislature. Third, the legislature, because it is composed of interest groups, is heavily influenced in specialized legislative committees. In general, therefore, interest groups have tended to "intrude" into the organs of government, forming close alliances with certain departments and legislative commissions and inserting themselves into others via their membership in political parties. In short, interest groups are not "contained" as they are in Anglo-American and Scandinavian countries—political institutions are fragmented and weak, procedures are irregular or personal and not formal, and public beliefs are polarized into uncompromising ideologies.

Patterns in developing countries. Although there is no one typical pattern for all underdeveloped countries, which of course embrace over two-thirds of the world's sovereign states, there are a few common characteristics that can be suggested. First, political culture in each of these countries is fragmented, sometimes because of ideological differences, sometimes because of the mutual hostility of "natural" groupings based on kinship, lineage, tribe, or language. Second, nascent interest groups representing new modernizing and industrializing forces tend to range against rural natural groupings. The modernizers have defined and specialized objectives, whereas the traditionalists usually represent a spectrum of attitudes, beliefs, values, and interests. Both, in any case, tend to sponsor or generate their own political parties. Third, during preindependence days in some countries, trade unions and other movements (such as the Somali Youth League) carried on activities that would otherwise have been carried on by political parties; when independence came, these groups continued such activities, thus blurring the functional distinctions between parties and interest groups. Fourth, associations in these countries tend to have low membership densities; and in most of these countries the principal "interest"—that is, the peasantry—is hardly organized at all. Attempts to develop widely represented peasant movements have had only limited success. Fifth, although organization and established procedures may be poor, latent interest is usually high. In a particularly divisive and administratively feeble country, this interest latency may reveal itself in lawless and violent group activity—such as strikes, riots, guerrilla movements, and assassinations.

Countries with one-party or military governments

In some countries "parties" in elections are not really parties but simply electoral coalitions of various interest groups—the most influential groups consisting of cliques of landlords; leaders of religious, ethnic, or linguistic groups; and the like. Legislatures tend to reflect these divisions and temporary arrangements in society and so enjoy only feeble authority.

In countries with single-party regimes, such as Kenya, Tanzania, and Tunisia, the parties tend to lose their mass following and fairly well-defined organization in the years following independence. (A notable exception, however, is India with its Congress Party.) To enhance their authority, the party leaders try to limit or abolish the autonomy of such factitious interest groups as trade unions, cooperative movements, and youth and women movements and try to turn these groups into ancillaries of the party.

In some countries the military has taken over, either alone or with civilian elements, and imposed an authoritarian rule. In such cases, the most prominent groups are governmental—the military and the executive. Unless factitious interest groups enjoy a long history of organization (as does the Catholic hierarchy in Latin America), they are often turned into governmental ancillaries or suppressed. In these countries ruled by the military or single parties, the political process turns into a highly informal medley of pressures and personal contacts between the government, the military forces, the various "natural" groups, and some of the more strategically placed factitious groups (such as the church hierarchy or private industry). The "system" is constantly threatened with government coercion or violent outbreaks by sections of the population.

Patterns in Communist states. Like Western states, but unlike developing countries, Communist countries contain various associational groups (trade unions, cooperatives, and the like) but few, if any, promotional groups. In addition, such countries as the U.S.S.R., Czechoslovakia, Yugoslavia, Romania, and the People's Republic of China contain many ethnic groups; and Poland, Hungary, and East Germany contain influential organized churches. But unlike the Western states and like a good many of the developing countries, Communist countries grant such groups very little autonomy. The government is firmly controlled by a single party, is highly centralized, and tries to control a great deal of life. The Communist Party may allow other parties to exist in coalition under conditions that the party itself lays down; in Poland, for instance, the controlling party is the (Communist) United Polish Workers' Party, and it permits the peasant interest to be represented by the minor United Peasant Party and the professions by the even smaller Democratic Party. The leading party assures its power, however, by controlling the nomination (in all but minor cases tantamount to election) of the leadership of all minor parties and interest groups, and the only great interest group that is excluded is the leadership of the Catholic Church. In any event, no interest group or party can be legally constituted in a Communist country without the express permission of the authorities. And even when an interest is allowed to formally organize, it rarely can exert any influence on the government, for governmental leaders, having been nominated by the Communist Party, are responsible to the party alone, not to various interests.

One consequence of these restrictions is a high degree of interest latency in certain sectors; this latency is attested by the fact that within six months of the fall of Antonín Novotný in Czechoslovakia in January 1968 over 70 groups were petitioning the government for legalization.

In the U.S.S.R.

In the U.S.S.R. there exist large trade unions, cooperative associations, and professional societies; many scientific, defense, and sports societies, as well as some 100,000 house committees, sanitary teams, parent-teacher associations, and the like. All are party led and controlled; and they purportedly serve, in Stalin's words, as "transmission belts from the party to the masses." One must not infer, however, that such associations are entirely without other significance. In the first place, the party is not identical with the state bureaucracy, though it controls the latter; hence divergences and collisions can occur between an interest group (such as the trade unions) and a concerned ministry regarding the interpretation or implementation of a party's directive. The result often is a triangular meeting of interest group, officials, and party functionaries, with the latter mediating. Second, the constitution provides that these so-called mass organizations should be consulted on selected issues, as they indeed were in regard to the education act of 1958.

In other Communist states

Poland's groups include such economic interests as the trade unions and the Peasant Self-Aid and such professional ones as the General Technical Organization and the Writers' Union, as well as the Socialist Youth League; the Rural Youth League; the Women's League; and various cultural-ethnic associations for minorities. In all of them, party leadership is assured (with minor exceptions), and they have relations with the bureaucracy and party mediators similar to those in the U.S.S.R. In Poland, however, there is the exceptional role of the Catholic Church, which has established some kind of equipoise with the party and has its own press, organizations, and clubs, even though its electoral freedom is severely restricted (only certain pro-Socialist Catholics are allowed to form "parties," such as the Znak, Pax, and the Christian Socialist Association, which participate in elections on the joint list with the Communist and other parties).

Yugoslavia has gone furthest in recognizing interest groups. The society contains many conflicting interests—nationalities; religious communities; a free-enterprise peasant sector; a decentralized network of workers' councils; and a large number of cultural, economic, and professional associations. The 1963 constitution gives institutional expression to these groups: in the five-chamber legislature, legislation is processed through the Federal Chamber, representing the population at large and individual republics; the Politico-Economic Chamber, representing management agencies and sociopolitical organizations; and the Chambers of Economics, of Education, and of Social Welfare and Health, representing their respective fields. The current factionalism inside the ruling "National Alliance," the centrifugal pulls of the peasant sector and the workers' councils, and the rivalry of the nationalities have combined to make these legal provisions much more than a formality.

(S.E.F./Ed.)

BIBLIOGRAPHY

Political parties: ROBERT MICHELS, *Les Partis politiques: essai sur les tendances oligarchiques des democraties* (1914; Eng. trans., *Political Parties: A Sociological Study of the Oligarchical Tendencies of Modern Democracies,* 1915), provides the first modern theory of political parties, stemming from the doctrines of the "elite," or "ruling class," of Gaetano Mosca. The book is based largely on the example of German social democracy. MAURICE DUVERGER, *Les Partis Politiques* (1951; Eng. trans., *Political Parties: Their Organization and Activity in the Modern State,* 2nd ed., 1964), gives a comparative and systematic study of political parties, emphasizing the experience of the European countries. JOSEPH G. LA PALOMBARA and MYRON WEINER (eds.), *Political Parties and Political Development* (1966), is a collection of contributions by various authors and is the best recent comparative explication of problems concerning political parties. D.W. RAE, *The Political Consequences of Electoral Laws* (1967), provides, on the basis of an examination of the balloting in numerous countries since 1945, an analysis of the relationship between the electoral system and political parties. It is a model of comparative study. Works about American parties are very numerous. Recommended are SAMUEL J. ELDERSVELD, *Political Parties: A Behavioral Analysis* (1964); and WILLIAM N. CHAMBERS and WALTER D. BURNHAM (eds.), *The American Party Systems* (1967). There are very few works that study European political parties comparatively. STANLEY HENIG and JOHN PINDER (eds.), *European Political Parties* (1969), however, provides much factual information in a concise and systematic format. On Great Britain, SAMUEL H. BEER, *Modern British Politics: A Study of Parties and Pressure Groups* (1965); and R.T. MCKENZIE, *British Political Parties: The Distribution of Power Within the Conservative and Labour Parties,* 2nd rev. ed. (1963), are particularly useful. D.E. APTER, *The Politics of Modernization* (1965); THOMAS L. HODGKIN, *African Political Parties* (1961); and A. MAHIOU, *L'Avenement du parti unique en Afrique noire* (1969), provide informative accounts of the operations of political parties in developing countries. JEROME M. CLUBB, W.H. FLANIGAN, and N.H. ZINGALE, *Partisan Realignment: Voters, Parties, and Government in American History* (1980), a study of voter realignment as effected by government performance.

Interest groups: G.A. ALMOND and J.S. COLEMAN (eds.), *The Politics of the Developing Areas* (1960), a synoptic view of government in Latin America, Asia, and Africa that places special-interest groups in the setting of the politics of developing countries; K. VON BEHME, *Interessengruppen in der Democratie* (1969), a classification of the types, strategies, and tactics of groups in the Western democratic states; A.F. BENTLEY, *The Process of Government,* ed. by P.H. ODEGARD (1967, orig. pub. in 1908), the major theoretical source for all subsequent Western democratic writing, advocating the theory by which all political activity is reduced to group activity; D.C. BLAISDELL, *American Democracy under Pressure* (1957), one of the best of many surveys of the role of groups in American society; S.E. FINER, *Anonymous Empire: A Study of the Lobby in Great Britain,* 2nd ed. (1966), a brief analysis of the types, strategies, and tactics of groups in Britain; H.W. EHRMANN, *Organized Business in France* (1957), a highly detailed account of the typical methods of groups in France, and (ed.), *Interest Groups on Four Continents* (1958), a collection of papers, together with summaries of the discussions based upon them, that is one of the best country-by-country accounts of the operation of groups; J. MEYNAUD, *Les Groupes de pression en France* (1958), a detailed analysis of group activity in France; J.G. LA PALOMBARA, *Interest Groups in Italian Politics* (1964), a detailed analysis, much of it based upon interview and behavioral data; ALEC BARBROOK and CHRISTINE BOLT, *Power and Protest in American Life* (1980), a study of women, ethnic minority, and public interest groups.

(M.Du./S.E.F./Ed.)

The History of Western Political Philosophy

The central problem of political philosophy is how to deploy or limit public power so as to maintain the survival and enhance the quality of human life. Like all aspects of human experience, it is conditioned by environment and by the scope and limitations of mind; and the answers given by successive political philosophers to perennial problems reflect the knowledge and the assumptions of their times. Political philosophy, as distinct from the study of political and administrative organization, is more theoretical and normative than descriptive. It is inevitably related to general philosophy and is itself a subject of social anthropology, sociology, and the sociology of knowledge. As a normative discipline it is thus concerned with what ought, on various assumptions, to be and how this purpose can be promoted, rather than with a description of facts—although any realistic political theory is necessarily related to these facts. The political philosopher is thus not concerned so much, for example, with how pressure groups work or how, by various systems of voting, decisions are arrived at, as with what the aims of the whole political process should be in the light of a particular philosophy of life.

There is thus a distinction between political philosophy, which reflects the world outlook of successive theorists and which demands an appreciation of their historical settings, and modern political science proper, which, insofar as it can be called a science, is empirical and descriptive. Political philosophy, however, is not merely unpractical speculation, though it may give rise to highly impractical myths: it is a vitally important aspect of life, and one that, for good or evil, has had decisive results on political action; for the assumptions on which political life is conducted clearly must influence what actually happens. Political philosophy may thus be viewed as one of the most important intellectual disciplines, for it sets standards of judgment and defines constructive purposes for the use of public power. Such consideration of the purposes for which power should be used are in a very real sense more urgent today than they have been in any earlier historical period, for mankind has at its disposal the power either to create a world civilization in which modern technology can immeasurably benefit the human race, or to destroy itself in pursuit of political myths. In this situation the scope for political philosophy is great, the clarification of its purpose and limitations urgent—an aspect, indeed, of civilization's survival.

Despite this unique aspect of the contemporary situation and although ancient political philosophies were formulated under very different conditions, their study still illuminates questions vital today. Questions concerning the aims of government, the grounds of political obligation, the rights of individuals against the state, the basis of sovereignty, the relation of executive to legislative power, and the nature of political liberty and social justice have been asked and answered in many ways over the centuries. They are all fundamental to political philosophy and demand answers in terms of modern knowledge and opinion.

The central purpose of this article is to describe how these questions have been asked and answered by representative and influential political philosophers, from Greco-Roman antiquity through the Middle Ages, early modern times, and the 19th and early 20th centuries. During so long a time span the historical context of these formulations has changed profoundly, and an understanding of the political philosophers selected demands some account of their background. Because of limitations of space, only political philosophers of outstanding importance have been at all fully described, although many minor figures also are briefly discussed.

The article is divided into the following sections:

The history of political philosophy in the West to the end of the 19th century

ANTIQUITY

Although in antiquity great civilizations arose in Egypt and Mesopotamia, in the Indus Valley, and in China, there was little speculation about the problems of political philosophy as formulated in the West and since predominant. The laws of Hammurabi of Babylon (c. 1750 BC) are rules propounded by the monarch as a representative of God on Earth and are mainly concerned with order, trade, and irrigation; the *Admonitions* of the Egyptian vizier Ptahhotep (c. 2300 BC) are shrewd advice on how to prosper in a bureaucracy; and the *Arthaśāstra* of Kauṭilya, grand vizier to the Indian Candragupta Maurya in the late 4th century BC, are Machiavellian precepts on how to survive under an arbitrary power. To be sure, the Buddhist concept of *dharma* (social custom and duty), which inspired the Indian emperor Aśoka in the 3rd century BC, implies a moralization of public power, and the teachings of Confucius in the 6th century BC are a code of conduct designed to stabilize society; but there is not, outside Europe, much speculation about the basis of political obligation and the purpose of the state, with both of which Western political philosophy is mainly concerned. An authoritarian society is taken for granted, backed by religious sanctions, and a conservative and arbitrary power is generally accepted.

In contrast to this overwhelming conservatism, paralleled

by the rule of custom and tribal elders in most primitive societies, the political philosophers of ancient Greece question the basis and purpose of government; and, though they do not separate political speculation from shrewd observations that today would be regarded as empirical political science, they created the vocabulary of Western political thought.

Plato. The first elaborate work of European political philosophy is *The Republic* of Plato (*c.* 378 BC), a masterpiece of insight and feeling, superbly expressed in dialogue form and probably meant for recitation. Further development of Plato's ideas is undertaken in his *Statesman* and *Laws,* the latter prescribing the ruthless methods whereby they might be imposed. Plato grew up during the great war between Athens and Sparta in which Athens suffered defeat and, like many political philosophers, tried to find remedies for prevalent political injustice and decline. Indeed, *The Republic* is the first of the utopias, though not one of the more attractive; and it is the first classic attempt of a European philosopher to moralize political life.

Cast as a lively discussion between Socrates, whose wisdom Plato is recounting, and various leisured Athenians, Books V, VII–VIII, and IX of *The Republic* state the major themes of political philosophy with poetic power. Plato's work has been criticized as static and class bound, reflecting the moral and aesthetic assumptions of an elite in a slave-owning civilization and bound by the narrow limits of the city-state. The work is indeed a classic example of a philosopher's vivisection of society, imposing by relatively humane means the rule of a high-minded minority.

Epistemological assumptions in *The Republic*

The Republic is a criticism of current Hellenic politics— often an indictment. It is based upon a metaphysical act of faith, for Plato believes that a world of permanent Forms exists beyond the limitations of human experience and that morality and the good life, which the state should promote, are reflections of these ideal Forms (see PLATONISM). The point is best made in the famous simile of the cave, in which men are chained with their faces to the wall and their backs to the light, so that they see only the shadows of reality. So constrained, they shrink from what is truly "real" and permanent and need to be forced to face it. This idealistic doctrine, known misleadingly as Realism (in nontechnical language it is hardly realistic), pervades all Plato's philosophy: its opposite doctrine, Nominalism, declares that only particular and observed "named" data are accessible to the mind. On his Realist assumption, Plato, who was perhaps influenced by Indian thought, regards most ordinary life as illusion and the current evils of politics as the result of men pursuing brute instinct. It follows that

unless philosophers bear kingly rule in cities or those who are now called kings and princes become genuine and adequate philosophers, and political power and philosophy are brought together . . . there will be no respite from evil for cities.

Only philosopher-statesmen can apprehend permanent and transcendant Forms and turn to "face the brightest blaze of being" outside the cave, and only philosophically minded men of action can be the saviours and helpers of the people.

Plato is thus indirectly the pioneer of modern beliefs that only a party organization, inspired by correct and "scientific" doctrines, formulated by the written word and interpreted by authority, can rightly guide the state. His rulers would form an elite, not responsible to the mass of the people. Thus, in spite of his high moral purpose, he has been called an enemy of the open society and the father of totalitarian lies. But he is also an anatomist of the evils of unbridled appetite and political corruption and insists on the need to use public power to moral ends.

Having described his utopia, Plato turns to analyze the existing types of government in human terms with great insight. Kingly government is the best but impracticable; in oligarchies the rule of the few and the pursuit of wealth divide societies—the rich become demoralized and the poor envious, and there is no harmony in the state. In democracy, in which the poor get the upper hand, demagogues distribute "a peculiar kind of equality to equals and unequals impartially," and the old flatter the young, fawning on their juniors to avoid the appearance of be-

ing sour or despotic. The leaders plunder the propertied classes and divide the spoils among themselves and the people until confusion and corruption lead to tyranny, a worse form of government. For the tyrant becomes a wolf instead of a man and "lops off" potential rivals and starts wars to distract the people from their discontent. "Then, by Zeus," Plato concludes, "the public learns what a monster they have begotten."

Plato's *Statesman* and *Laws*

In the *Statesman* Plato admits that, although there is a correct science of government, like geometry, it cannot be realized, and he stresses the need for the rule of law, since no man can be trusted with unbridled power. He then examines which of the current forms of government is the least difficult to live with, for the ruler, after all, is an artist who has to work within the limits of his medium. In the *Laws,* purporting to be a discussion of how best to found a polis in Crete, he presents a detailed program in which a state with some 5,000 citizens is ruled by 37 curators of laws and a council of 360. But the keystone of the arch is a sinister and secret Nocturnal Council to be "the sheet anchor of the state," established in its "central fortress as guardian." Poets and musicians will be discouraged and the young subjected to a rigid, austere, and exacting education. The stark consequence of Plato's political philosophy here becomes apparent. He had, nonetheless, stated, in the dawn of European political thought, the normative principle that the state should aim at promoting the good life and social harmony and that the rule of law, in the absence of the rule of philosopher-kings, is essential to this purpose.

Aristotle. Aristotle, who was a pupil in the Academy of Plato, remarks that "all the writings of Plato are original: they show ingenuity, novelty of view and a spirit of enquiry. But perfection in everything is perhaps a difficult thing." Aristotle was a scientist rather than a prophet, and his *Politics* (*c.* 335–322 BC), written while he was teaching at the Lyceum at Athens, is only part of an encyclopaedic account of nature and society, in which he analyzes society as if he were a doctor and prescribes remedies for its ills. Political behaviour is here regarded as a branch of biology, as well as of ethics; in contrast to Plato, Aristotle was an empirical political philosopher. He criticizes many of Plato's ideas as impracticable, but, like Plato, he admires balance and moderation and aims at a harmonious city under the rule of law. The book is composed of lecture notes and is arranged in a confusing way—a quarry of arguments and definitions of great value but hard to master. The first book, though probably the last written, is a general introduction; Books II, III, and VII–VIII, probably the earliest, deal with the ideal state; and Books IV–VII analyze actual states and politics. The treatise is thus, in modern terms, a mixture of political philosophy and political science. (See also ARISTOTELIANISM.)

Like Plato, Aristotle naturally thinks in terms of the city-state, which he regards as the natural form of civilized life, social and political, and the best medium in which men's capacities can be realized. Hence his famous definition of man as a "political animal," distinguished from the other animals by his gift of speech and power of moral judgment. "Man, when perfected," he writes,

is the best of animals, but when separated from law and justice he is the worst of all, since armed injustice is the most dangerous, and he is equipped at birth with the arms of intelligence and wit, moral qualities which he may use for the worst ends.

Since all nature is pervaded by purpose and since men "aim at the good," the city-state, which is the highest form of human community, aims at the highest good. Like sailors with their separate functions, who yet have a common object in safety in navigation, citizens, too, have a common aim—in modern terms survival, security, and the enhancement of the quality of life. In the context of the city-state, this high quality of life can be realized only by a minority, and Aristotle, like Plato, excludes those who are not full citizens or who are slaves; indeed, he says that some men are "slaves by nature" and deserve their status. Plato and Aristotle aim at an aristocratic and exacting way of life, reflecting, in more sophisticated forms, the ideas of the warrior aristocracies depicted by Homer.

Aristotle's
view
of the
role of
law in
the
city-state

Having stated that the aim of the city-state is to promote the good life, Aristotle insists that it can be achieved only under the rule of law.

> The rule of law is preferable to that of a single citizen; if it be the better course to have individuals ruling, they should be made law guardians or ministers of the laws.

The rule of law is better than that even of the best men, for "he who bids law rule may be deemed to bid God and reason alone rule, but he who bids men rule adds the element of the beast; for desire is a wild beast, and passion perverts the minds of rulers, even if they are the best of men." This doctrine, which distinguishes between lawful government and tyranny, survived the Middle Ages and, by subjecting the ruler to law, became the theoretical sanction of modern constitutional government.

Aristotle also vindicates the rule of custom and justifies the obligations accepted by members of society: the solitary man, he writes, "is either a beast or a God." This outlook at once reflects the respect for custom and solidarity that have promoted survival in primitive tribal societies, even at the price of sacrificing individuals, and gives a theoretical justification for the acceptance of political obligation.

Like Plato, Aristotle analyzes the different kinds of city-states. While states are bound, like animals, to be different, he considers a balanced "mixed" constitution the best—it reflects the ideal of justice (*dikē*) and fair dealing, which gives every man his due in a conservative social order in which citizens of the middle condition preponderate. And he attacks oligarchy, democracy, and tyranny. Under democracy, he argues, demagogues attain power by bribing the electorate and waste accumulated wealth. But it is tyranny that Aristotle most detests; the arbitrary power of an individual above the law who is "responsible to no-one and who governs all alike with a view to his own advantage and not of his subjects, and therefore against their will. No free man can endure such a government."

The *Politics* contains not only a firm statement of these principles but also a penetrating analysis of how city-states are governed, as well as of the causes of revolutions, in which "inferiors revolt in order that they may be equal, and equals that they may be superior." The treatise concludes with an elaborate plan for educating the citizens to attain the "mean," the "possible," and the "becoming." The first implies a balanced development of body and mind, ability and imagination; the second, the recognition of the limits of mind and the range and limitations of talent; the third, an outcome of the other two, is the style and self-assurance that come from the resulting self-control and confidence.

While, therefore, Aristotle accepts a conservative and hierarchic social order, he states firmly that public power should aim at promoting the good life and that only through the rule of law and justice can the good life be attained. These principles were novel in the context of his time, when the great extra-European civilizations were ruled, justly or unjustly, by the arbitrary power of semidivine rulers and when other peoples, though respecting tribal custom and the authority of tribal elders, were increasingly organized under war leaders for depredation.

Cicero and the Stoics. Both Plato and Aristotle had thought in terms of the city-state. But Aristotle's pupil Alexander the Great swamped the cities of old Greece and brought them into a vast empire that included Egypt, Persia, and the Levant. Though the civilization of antiquity remained concentrated in city-states, they became part of an imperial power that broke up into kingdoms under Alexander's successors. This imperial power was reasserted on an even greater scale by Rome, whose empire at its greatest extent reached from central Scotland to the Euphrates and from Spain to eastern Anatolia. Civilization itself became identified with empire, and the development of eastern and western Europe was conditioned by it.

Since the city-state was no longer self-sufficient, universal philosophies developed that gave men something to live by in a wider world. Of these philosophies, Stoicism and Epicureanism were the most influential. The former inspired a rather grim self-sufficiency and sense of duty, as exemplified by the writings of the Roman emperor Marcus Aurelius; the latter, a prudent withdrawal from the world of affairs.

The setting for political philosophy thus became much wider, relating individuals to universal empire, thought of, as in China, as coterminous with the civilization itself. Its inspiration remained Hellenic; but derivative Roman philosophers reinterpreted it, and Roman legists enclosed the old concepts of political justice in a carapace of legal definitions, capable of surviving their civilization's decline.

Cicero lived in a time of political confusion during which the old institutions of the republic were breaking down before military dictators. His *De republica* and *Laws* are both dialogues and reflect the classical sense of purpose: "to make human life better by our thought and effort." Cicero defined the *res publica* (commonwealth) as an association held together by law; he further asserted, as Plato had maintained with his doctrine of Forms manifest in the just city, that government was sanctioned by a universal natural law that reflected the cosmic order. Cicero expresses the pre-Christian Stoic attempt to moralize public power, apparent in the exacting sense of public responsibility shown by Hadrian and Marcus Aurelius in the 2nd century AD.

St. Augustine. With the conversion of the emperor Constantine (AD 312), when Christianity, long influential, became the predominant creed of the empire, and, under Theodosius (379–395), the sole official religion, political philosophy changed profoundly. St. Augustine's *City of God* (413–426), written when the empire was under attack by barbarians within and without, sums up and defines a new division between church and state and a conflict between "matter" and "spirit" resulting from the Fall of man and original sin.

St. Augustine, whose *Confessiones* are a record of a new sort of introspection, combined a classical and Hebraic dualism. From the Stoics and Virgil he inherited an austere sense of duty, from Plato and the Neoplatonists a contempt for the illusions of appetite, and from the Pauline and patristic interpretation of Christianity a sense of the conflict between Light and Darkness that reflects Zoroastrian and Manichaean doctrines emanating from Iran. In this context worldly interests and government itself are dwarfed by the importance of attaining salvation and of escaping from an astrologically determined fate and from the demons who embody the darkness. Life becomes illuminated for the elect minority by the prospect of eternal salvation or, for those without grace, shrivels under the glare of eternal fires.

St. Augustine regarded salvation as predestinate and the cosmic process as designed to "gather" an elect to fill the places of the fallen angels and so "preserve and perhaps augment the number of the heavenly inhabitants." The role of government and indeed of society itself becomes subordinated into a "secular arm," part of an earthly city, as opposed to the "City of God." The function of government is to keep order in a world intrinsically evil.

Augus-
tine's
view
of the role
of
govern-
ment

Since Christianity had long played the main role in defense of the veneer of a precarious urban civilization in antiquity, this claim is not surprising. Constantine came of crude Balkan origins, a soldier putting to rights a breakdown in government that would continue in the West with the abdication of the last Western emperor in 476, though in the East the empire would carry on with great wealth and power, centred in the new capital of Constantinople (Byzantium).

St. Augustine thus no longer assumed, as did Plato and Aristotle, that a harmonious and self-sufficient good life could be achieved within a properly organized city-state; he projected his political philosophy into a cosmic and lurid drama working out to a predestinate end. The normal interests and amenities of life became insignificant or disgusting, and the Christian Church alone exercised a spiritual authority that could sanction government. This outlook, reinforced by other patristic writings, would long dominate medieval thought, for with the decline of civilization in the West the church became more completely the repository of learning and of the remnants of the old civilized life.

THE MIDDLE AGES

The decline of ancient civilization in the West was severe; not, indeed, in technology, for the horse collar, the stirrup, and the heavy plow now came in; but political philosophy, like other intellectual interests, became elementary. In the Byzantine Empire, on the other hand, Justinian's lawyers in 529–533 produced the Codex Constitutionum, the Digest, the Institutes, which defined and condensed Roman law, and the Novels. The Byzantine *basileus,* or autocrat, had moral responsibility for guarding and harmonizing an elaborate state, a "colony" of heaven in which reason and not mere will ought to rule. And this autocracy and the orthodox form of Christianity were inherited by the Christianized rulers of the Balkans, of Kievan Russia, and of Muscovy.

In the West, two essential principles of Hellenic and Christian political philosophy were transmitted, if only in elementary definitions, in rudimentary encyclopaedias. Isidore of Seville in his 7th-century *Etymologiae,* for example, asserts that kings rule only on condition of doing right and that the rule reflects a Ciceronic law of nature "common to all people and mankind everywhere by natural instinct." Further, the barbarians respected the civilization they took over and exploited. When converted, they revered the papacy, and in 800 the Frankish Charlemagne even revived the Western Empire as holy and Roman. The idea of Christian empire coterminous with civilization thus survived in Western as well as Eastern Christendom.

John of Salisbury. After Augustine, not until the 12th-century Renaissance did another full-length speculative work of political philosophy appear in the West. The *Policraticus* of John of Salisbury (*c.* 1159) is the work of a man experienced in politics who became bishop of Chartres. Based on wide classical reading, it centres on the ideal ruler, who represents a "public power." John admired Augustus and the Roman emperor Trajan, and, in a still predominantly feudal world, his book carried on the Roman tradition of centralized authority, though without its Byzantine autocracy. The prince, he insists, is he who rules in accordance with law, while a tyrant is one who oppresses the people by irresponsible power. This distinction, which derives from the Greeks, Cicero, and St. Augustine, is fundamental to Western concepts of liberty and the trusteeship of power.

John did not know Aristotle's *Politics,* but his learning is nevertheless remarkable, even if his political similes are unsophisticated. His favourite metaphor for the body politic is the human body: the place of the head is filled by the prince, who is subject only to God; the place of the heart by the senate; the eyes, ears, and tongue are the judges, provincial governors, and soldiers; and the officials are the hands. The tax gatherers are the intestines and ought not to retain their accumulations too long; and the farmers and peasants are the feet. John also compares a commonwealth to a hive and even to a centipede.

This vision of a centralized government, more appropriate to the memory of the Roman Empire than to a medieval monarchy operating in a still semifeudal world, is a landmark of the 12th-century revival of speculative thought and reflects the better organized monarchy that Henry II was then building up.

Aquinas. It is a far cry from this practical 12th-century treatise by a man of affairs to the elaborate justification of Christian kingship and natural law created by St. Thomas Aquinas in the 13th century, during the climax of medieval Western civilization. His political philosophy is only part of a metaphysical construction of Aristotelian range—for Aristotle had now been assimilated from Arabic sources and given a new Christian content, with the added universality of the Stoic and Augustinian world outlook. Aquinas' *Summa theologiae* purports to answer all the major questions of existence, including those of political philosophy. Like Aristotle, Aquinas thinks in terms of an ethical purpose. Natural law is discussed in the first part of the second book as part of the discussion of original sin and what would now be termed psychology, while war comes under the second part of the second book as an aspect of virtue and vice. Law is defined as "that which is regulation and measure." It is designed to

Aquinas' political views in the Summa theologiae

promote the "felicity and beatitude" that are the ends of human life. Aquinas agrees with Aristotle that "the city is the perfection of community" and that the purpose of public power should be to promote the common good. The only legitimate power is from the community, which is the sole medium of man's well being. In his *De regimine* he compares society to a ship in need of a helmsman and repeats Aristotle's definition of man as a social and political animal. Again following Aristotle, he considers oligarchy unjust and democracy evil. Rulers should aim to make the "life of the multitude good in accordance with the purpose of life which is heavenly happiness." They should also create peace, conserve life, and preserve the state—a threefold responsibility. Here is a complete program for a hierarchical society within a cosmic order. It combines the Hellenic sense of purpose with Christian aims and asserts that, under God, power resides in the community, embodied in the ruler but only for so long as he does right. Hence the comment that "St. Thomas Aquinas was the first Whig"—a pioneer of the theory of constitutional government. The society he envisages, however, is medieval, static, hierarchical, conservative, and based on limited agriculture and even more limited technology. Nonetheless, Thomism remains the most complete and lasting political doctrine of the Catholic Church, since modified and adapted but not in principle superseded.

Dante. By the early 14th century the great European institutions, empire and papacy, were breaking down through mutual conflict and the emergence of national realms. But this conflict gave rise to the most complete political theory of universal and secular empire formulated in the medieval West. Dante's *De monarchia* (*c.* 1313), still in principle highly relevant, insists that only through universal peace can human faculties come to their full compass. But only "temporal Monarchy" can achieve this: "a unique princedom extending over all persons in time." The aim of civilization is to actualize human potentialities, and to achieve that "fullness of life which comes from the fulfillment of our being."

Monarchy, Dante argues, is necessary as a means to this end. The imperial authority of the Holy Roman emperor, moreover, comes direct from God and not through the pope. The empire is the direct heir of the Roman Empire, a legitimate authority, or Christ would not have chosen to be born under it. In subjecting the world to itself, the Roman Empire had contemplated the public good.

This high-flown argument, part of the political warfare between the partisans of the emperor and pope that was then affecting Italy, drives to essentials: that world peace can be secure only under a world authority. That Dante's argument was impractical did not concern this medieval genius, who was writing more the epitaph than the prospectus of the Holy Roman Empire; he was concerned, like St. Thomas, to create a political philosophy with a clear-cut aim and a universal view.

Out of the grand but impractical visions of the High Middle Ages in the 13th-century climax of Christian civilization there emerged by early modern times the idea of a well-governed realm, its authority derived from the community itself, with a program designed to ensure the solvency and administrative efficiency of a secular state. In spite of the decline of the civilization of antiquity in the West, the Greco-Roman sense of purpose, of the rule of law, and of the responsibility of power survived in Christian form.

THE 16TH TO THE 18TH CENTURIES

Machiavelli. In the thought of the Italian political philosopher Niccolò Machiavelli may be seen a complete secularization of political philosophy. Machiavelli was an experienced diplomat and administrator, and, since he stated flatly how the power struggle was conducted in Renaissance Italy, he won a shocking reputation. He was not, however, without idealism about the old Roman republic, and he admired the independent spirit of the German and Swiss cities. This idealism made him all the more disgusted with Italian politics, of which he makes a disillusioned and objective analysis. Writing in retirement after political disgrace, Machiavelli states firmly that,

Machiavelli's view of human nature

Since this is to be asserted in general of men, that they are ungrateful, fickle, false, cowards, covetous, and as long as you succeed they are yours entirely: they will offer you their blood, property, life, and children . . . when the need is far distant; but when it approaches they turn against you.

And again,

since the desires of men are insatiable, nature prompting them to desire all things and fortune permitting them to enjoy but few, there results a constant discontent in their minds, and a loathing of what they possess.

This view of human nature, already expressed by Plato and St. Augustine, is here unredeemed by Plato's doctrine of form and illusion or by St. Augustine's dogma of salvation through grace. Machiavelli accepts the facts and advises the ruler to act accordingly. The prince, he states, must combine the strength of the lion with the cunning of the fox: he must always be vigilant, ruthless, and prompt, striking down or neutralizing his adversaries without warning. And when he does an injury it must be total. For "men ought to be either well treated or crushed, because they can avenge themselves of lighter injuries, of more serious ones they cannot." Moreover, "irresolute princes who follow a neutral path are generally ruined." He advises that it is best to come down at the right moment on the winning side and that conquered cities ought to be either governed directly by the tyrant himself residing there or destroyed. Princes, furthermore, unlike private men, need not keep faith: since politics reflects the law of the jungle, the state is a law unto itself, and normal moral rules do not apply to it.

Machiavelli had stated with unblinking realism how, in fact, tyrants behave; and, far from criticizing their conduct or distinguishing between the just prince who rules by law and the tyrant whose laws are in his own breast, he considers that the successful ruler has to be beyond morality since the safety of and expansion of the state are the supreme objective. In this myopic view, the cosmic visions of Aquinas and Dante are disregarded, and politics becomes a fight for survival. Within his terms of reference, Machiavelli made a convincing case, although as an experienced diplomat he might have realized that dependability in fact pays and that systematic deceit, treachery, and violence usually bring about their own nemesis.

Hobbes. The 17th-century English political philosopher Thomas Hobbes, who spent his life as a tutor and companion to great noblemen, was a writer of genius with a greater power of phrase than any other English political philosopher. He was not, as he is sometimes misrepresented, a prophet of "bourgeois" individualism, advocating free competition in a capitalistic free market. On the contrary, he was writing in a preindustrial, if increasingly commercial, society and did not much admire wealth as such but rather "honours." He was socially conservative and anxious to give a new philosophical sanction to a hierarchical, if businesslike, commonwealth in which family authority was most important.

Philo-
sophical
influences
on
Hobbes

Philosophically, Hobbes was influenced by nominalist scholastic philosophy, which had discarded Thomist metaphysics and had accepted a strict limitation of mind. He therefore based his conclusions on the rudimentary mathematical physics and psychology of his day and aimed at practical objectives—order and stability. He believed that the fundamental physical law of life was motion and that the predominant human impulses were fear and, among those above the poverty level, pride and vanity. Men, Hobbes argued, are strictly conditioned and limited by these laws, and he tried to create a science of politics that would reflect them. "The skill of making, and maintaining Common-wealths," therefore, "consisteth in certain Rules, as doth Arithmetique and Geometry; not (as Tennis play) on Practise onely: which Rules, neither poor men have the leisure, nor men that have had the leisure, have hitherto had the curiosity, or the method to find out."

Hobbes ignores the classical and Thomist concepts of a transcendent law of nature, itself reflecting divine law, and of a "chain of being" whereby the universe is held harmoniously together and, following Descartes's practical method of investigation, states plainly that power creates law, not law power. For law is law only if it can be en-

forced, and the price of security is one supreme sovereign public power. For, without it, such is the competitive nature of men, that once more than subsistence has been achieved they are actuated by vanity and ambition, and there is a war of all against all. The true law of nature is self-preservation, he argues, which can be achieved only if the citizens make a compact among themselves to transfer their individual power to the "leviathan" (ruler), who alone can preserve them in security. Such a commonwealth has no intrinsic supernatural or moral sanction: it derives its original authority from the people and can command loyalty only so long as it succeeds in keeping the peace. He thus uses both the old concepts of natural law and contract, often invoked to justify resistance to authority, as a sanction for it.

Hobbes, like Machiavelli, starts from an assumption of basic human folly, competitiveness, and depravity, and contradicts Aristotle's assumption that man is by nature a "political animal." On the contrary, he is naturally antisocial; and, even when men meet for business and profit, only "a certain market-fellowship" is engendered. All society is only for gain or glory, and the only true equality among men is their power to kill each other. Hobbes sees and desires no other equality. Indeed, he specifically discouraged "men of low degree from a saucy behaviour towards their betters."

The *Leviathan* horrified most of his contemporaries; Hobbes was accused of atheism and of "maligning the Human Nature." But, if his remedies were tactically impractical, in political philosophy he had gone very deep by providing the sovereign nation-state with a pragmatic justification and directing it to utilitarian ends.

Signifi-
cance
of the
Leviathan

Spinoza. The 17th-century Dutch philosopher Benedict de Spinoza also tried to make a scientific political theory, but it was more humane and more modern. Hobbes assumes a preindustrial and economically conservative society, but Spinoza, a Portuguese Jew born in Amsterdam, assumes a more urban setting. Like Hobbes, he is Cartesian, aiming at a scientific basis for political philosophy; but, whereas Hobbes was dogmatic and authoritarian, Spinoza desired toleration and intellectual liberty, by which alone human life achieves its highest quality. Spinoza, reacting against the ideological wars of religion and skeptical of both metaphysics and religious dogma, was a scientific humanist who justified political power solely by its usefulness. If state power breaks down and can no longer protect him or if it turns against him, frustrates, or ruins his life, then any man is justified in resisting it, since it no longer fulfills its purpose. It has no intrinsic divine or metaphysical authority.

In *Tractatus Theologico-Politicus* and the *Tractatus Politicus* Spinoza develops this theme. He intends, he writes, "not to laugh at men or weep over them or hate them, but to understand them." In contrast to St. Augustine, he glorifies life and holds that governments should not try to "change men from rational beings into beasts or puppets, but enable them to develop their minds and bodies in security and to employ their reason unshackled." The more life is enjoyed, he declares, the more the individual participates in the divine nature. God is immanent in the entire process of nature, in which all creatures follow the laws of their own being to the limit of their powers. All are bound by their own consciousness, and man creates his own values.

It seems that Spinoza thought good government approximated to that of the free burgesses of Amsterdam, a city in which religious toleration and relative political liberty had been realized. He is thus a pioneer of a scientific humanist view of government and of the neutrality of the state in matters of belief.

Richard Hooker's adapted Thomism. While out of the breakup of the medieval social order there emerged the humanist but sceptical outlook of Machiavelli, then the scientific humanist principles of Descartes, Hobbes, and Spinoza, from which the utilitarian and pragmatic outlook of modern times derives, another influential and politically important strain of political philosophy also emerged. During the Reformation and Counter-Reformation, Protestant and Catholic dogmatists denounced each other and even attacked the authority of princes who, from interest or conviction, supported one side or the other. Political assassination became endemic, for both Protestant and Catholic divines declared that it was legitimate to kill an heretical ruler. Appeal was made to rival religious authority as well as to conscience. Men would resist authority and suffer execution rather than risk damnation, and in the resulting welter Hobbes and Spinoza advocated a sovereign state as the remedy. But other political philosophers salvaged the old Thomist concept of a divine cosmic order and of natural and human laws sanctioning the state. They also put forth the classical and medieval idea of the derivation of public power from the commonwealth as a whole and the responsibility of princes to the law. When Hobbes wrote that might makes right, he outraged such critics, who continued to assert that public power was responsible to God and the laws and that it was right to resist a tyrant who declared that the laws were in his own breast. This political theory was most influentially developed in England, where it inspired the constitutionalism that would also predominate in the United States.

Richard Hooker, an Anglican divine who wrote *Of the lawes of ecclesiasticall politie* (1593–1662), reconciled Thomist doctrines of transcendent and natural law, binding on all men, with the authority of the Elizabethan Anglican Church, which he defended against the Puritan appeal to conscience. Society, he argued, is itself the fulfillment of natural law, of which human and positive law are reflections, adapted to society. And public power is not something personal, for it derives from the community under law. Thus,

> The lawful power of making laws to command whole politic societies of men belongeth so properly unto the same entire societies, that for any prince . . . to exercise the same of himself . . . is no better than mere tyranny.

Such power can derive either directly from God or else from the people. The prince is responsible to God and the community; he is not, like Hobbes's ruler, a law unto himself. Law makes the king, not the king law.

Hooker, indeed, insisted that "the prince has a delegated power, from the Parliament of England, together with the convocation (of clergy) annexed thereto . . . whereupon the very essence of all government doth depend." This is the power of the crown in parliament in a balanced constitution. Hence an idea of harmonious government by consent. The Thomist medieval universal harmony had been adapted to the nation-state.

Locke. It was John Locke, politically the most influential English philosopher, who further developed this doctrine. His *Two Treatises of Government* (1690) were written to justify the Glorious Revolution of 1688–89, and his *Letter Concerning Toleration* (1689) was written with a plain and easy urbanity, in contrast to the baroque eloquence of Hobbes. Locke was a scholar, physician, and man of affairs, well-experienced in politics and business. As a philosopher he accepted strict limitations for mind, and his political philosophy is moderate and sensible, aimed at a balance among executive, judicial, and legislative powers, although with a bias toward the last.

His first *Treatise* was devoted to confuting the Royalist doctrine of patriarchal divine right by descent from Adam, an argument then taken very seriously and reflecting the idea of government as an aspect of a divinely ordained chain of being. If this order were broken, chaos would come about. The argument was part of the contemporary conflict of the ancients and the moderns.

Locke's view of the role and limits of public power

Locke tried to provide an answer by defining a limited purpose for political power, which purpose he considered to be "a right of making laws with penalties of death, and consequently all less penalties, for the regulating and preserving of property, and of employing the force of the community in execution of such laws, and in the defense of the commonwealth from foreign injury, and all this only for the public good." The authority of government derives from a contract between the rulers and the people, and the contract binds both parties. It is thus a limited power, proceeding according to established laws and "directed to no other end but the peace, safety, and public good of the people."

Whatever its form, government, to be legitimate, must govern by "declared and reasoned laws," and, since every man has a "property" in his own person and has "mixed his labour" with what he owns, government has no right to take it from him without his consent. It was the threat of attack on the laws, property, and the Protestant religion that had roused resistance to James II. Locke is expressing the concerns and interests of the landed and moneyed men by whose consent James's successor, William III, came to the throne, and his commonwealth is strictly conservative, limiting the franchise and the preponderant power to the propertied classes. Locke was thus no democrat in the modern sense and was much concerned to make the poor work harder. Like Hooker, he assumes a conservative social hierarchy with a relatively weak executive power and defends the propertied classes both against a ruler by divine right and against radicals. In advocating toleration in religion he was more liberal: freedom of conscience, like property, he argued, is a natural right of all men. Within the possibilities of the time, Locke thus advocated a constitutional mixed government, limited by parliamentary control of the armed forces and of supply. Designed mainly to protect the rights of property, it was deprived of the right of arbitrary taxation or imprisonment without trial and was in theory responsible to all the people through the politically conscious minority who were thought to represent them.

Though he was socially conservative, Locke's writings are very important in the rise of liberal political philosophy. He vindicates the responsibility of government to the governed, the rule of law through impartial judges, and the toleration of religious and speculative opinion. He is an enemy of the totalitarian state, drawing on medieval arguments and deploying them in practical, modern terms.

Burke. The Irishman Edmund Burke, while elaborating Whig constitutional doctrine expressed with such common sense by Locke, wrote with more emotion and took more account of time and tradition. While reiterating that government is responsible to the governed and distinguishing between a political society and a mere mob, he thought that governments were trustees for previous generations and for posterity. He made the predominant political philosophy of the 18th-century establishment appear more attractive and moral, but he wrote no great single work of political philosophy, expressing himself instead in numerous pamphlets and speeches.

In his early *Vindication of Natural Society* Burke is critical of the sufferings imposed by government, but his "Thoughts on the Cause of the Present Discontents" defines and defends the principles of the Whig establishment. He invoked a transcendent morality to sanction a constitutional commonwealth, but he detested abstract political theories in whose name men are likely to vivisect society. He set great store by ordered liberty and denounced the arbitrary power of the Jacobins who had captured the French Revolution. In his *Reflections on the Revolution in France* (1790) and *An Appeal from the New to the Old Whigs* (1791), he discerned in the doctrine of sovereignty of the people, in whose name the revolutionaries were destroying the old order, another and worse form of arbitrary power. No one generation has the right to destroy the agreed and inherited fabric of society, and "Neither the few nor the many have the right to govern by their will." A country is not a mere physical locality, he argued, but a community in time into which men are born, and only within the existing constitution and by the consent of its representatives can changes legitimately be made. Once the frame of society is smashed and its law violated, the people become a "mere multitude told by the head," at the mercy of any dictator who can seize power. He was realistic in predicting the consequences of violent revolution, which usually ends up in some kind of dictatorship. Burke, in sophisticated accents, spoke for the ancient and worldwide rule of custom and conservatism and supplied a needed romanticism to the calculating good sense of Locke.

Burke's concept of an obligation to posterity

Vico. The political philosophies hitherto surveyed contained little idea of progress. In antiquity the idea of cyclic recurrence predominated, and even 18th-century Christians believed that the world had been created in 4004 BC and would end in the Second Coming of Christ and a judgment. The 14th-century Arab philosopher of history Ibn Khaldūn of Tunis, in the *Muqaddimah* to his *Kitāb al-ʿibar,* had pioneered a vast sociological view of the historical process; but in western Europe it was a neglected Neapolitan philosopher, Giambattista Vico (1668–1744), who first interpreted the past in terms of the changing consciousness of mankind. His *Scienza nuova* (1725; revised edition 1744) interpreted history as an organic process involving language, literature, and religion and attempted to reveal the mentality or ethos of earlier ages: the age of the gods, the heroic age, and the human age, its climax and decadence. These ages recur, and each is distinguished by mythology, heroic poetry, and rational speculation respectively. In contrast to the legalistic, contractual, and static political philosophies then prevalent, Vico had discerned new horizons.

Montesquieu. This sort of vision was developed and elegantly popularized by the cosmopolitan French savant Montesquieu, whose work *The Spirit of Laws* (Eng. trans. 1750) won immense influence. It was an ambitious treatise on human institutions and a pioneer work of anthropology and sociology. Believing in an ordered universe—for "how could blind fate have produced intelligent beings?"—Montesquieu examined the varieties of natural law, varying customs, laws, and civilizations in different environments. He made the pedestrian good sense of Locke seem provincial, although he admired him and the British constitution. Unfortunately, he overemphasized the separation of executive, judicial, and legislative powers, considerable in Locke's day but by his own time tending to be concentrated in the sovereignty of Parliament. This doctrine much influenced the founders of the United States and the early French Revolutionaries.

Rousseau. The revolutionary romanticism of the Swiss-French philosopher Jean-Jacques Rousseau may be interpreted in part as a reaction to the analytic rationalism of the Enlightenment. He was trying to escape the aridity of a purely empirical and utilitarian outlook and attempting to create a substitute for revealed religion. Rousseau's *Émile* (1762) and *Du contrat social* (1762) proved revolutionary documents, and his posthumous *Considérations sur le gouvernement de Pologne* ("Considerations on the Government of Poland") contains desultory but often valuable reflections on specific problems.

There had been radical political slogans coined in medieval peasant revolts and in the 17th century, as in the Putney debates (1647) in the Cromwellian army, when a Puritan officer declared that "the poorest hee that is in England hath a life to live as the greatest hee," but the inspiration of these movements had been religion. Now Rousseau proclaimed a secular egalitarianism and a romantic cult of the common man. His famous sentence, "man is born free, but he is everywhere in chains," called into question the traditional social hierarchy: hitherto, political philosophers had thought in terms of elites, but now the mass of the people had found a champion and were becoming politically conscious.

Rousseau was a romantic, given to weeping under the willows on Lake Geneva, and the *Social Contract* and *Discourses* are hypnotically readable, flaming protests by one who found the hard rationality of the 18th century too exacting. But man is not, as Rousseau claims, born free. Man is born into society which imposes restraints on him. Casting about to reconcile his artificial antithesis between man's purported natural state of freedom and his condition in society, Rousseau utilizes the old theories of contract and transforms them into the concept of the "general will." This general will, a moral will that aims at the common good and in which all participate directly, reconciles the individual and the community by representing the will of the community as deriving from the will of moral individuals, so that to obey the laws of such a community is in a sense to follow one's own will, assuming that one is a moral individual.

Similar ideas to that of the general will became accepted as a basis for both the social-democratic welfare state and for totalitarian dictatorships. And, since the idea was mis-

Rousseau's idea of the general will

applied from small village or civic communities to great sovereign nation-states, Rousseau was also a prophet of a nationalism that he never advocated. Rousseau himself wanted a federal Europe. He never wrote the proposed sequel to the *Du contrat social* in which he meant to deal with international politics, but he declared that existing governments lived in a state of nature, that their obsession with conquest was imbecilic, and that "if we could realize a European republic for one day, it would be enough to make it last for ever" (*Political Writings* I, pp. 365–388). But, with a flash of realism, he thinks the project impracticable, owing to the folly of men.

The incursion of this revolutionary romantic into political philosophy changed the climate of political opinion, for it coincided with the breakdown of the old dynastic order and the emergence first of the middle classes and then of the masses to political consciousness and power.

That the concept of general will was vague only increased its adaptability and prestige: it would both make constitutionalism more liberal and dynamic and give demagogues and dictators the excuse for "forcing people to be free" (that is, forcing people to follow the general will, as interpreted by the ruling forces). Rousseau could inspire liberals, such as the 19th-century English philosopher T.H. Green, to a creative view of a state helping people to make the best of their potential through a variety of free institutions. It could also play into the hands of demagogues claiming to represent the general will and bent on molding society according to their own abstractions.

THE 19TH CENTURY

Utilitarianism. A major force in the political and social thought of the 19th century was Utilitarianism, the doctrine that the actions of governments should be judged simply by the extent to which they promoted the "greatest happiness of the greatest number." The founder of the Utilitarian school was Jeremy Bentham, an eccentric Englishman trained in the law.

Bentham judged all laws and institutions by their utility thus defined. "The Fabric of Felicity," he wrote, "must be reared by the hands of reason and Law."

Bentham's *Fragment, on Government* (1776) and *Introduction to the Principles of Morals and Legislation* (1789) elaborated a Utilitarian political philosophy. Bentham was an atheist and an exponent of the new laissez-faire economics of Adam Smith and David Ricardo, but he inspired the spate of legislation that, after the Reform Bill of 1832, had tackled the worst consequences of 18th-century inefficiency and of the Industrial Revolution. His influence, moreover, spread widely abroad. At first a simple reformer of law, Bentham attacked notions of contract and natural law as superfluous, "The indestructible prerogatives of mankind," he wrote, "have no need to be supported upon the sandy foundation of a fiction." The justification of government is pragmatic, its aim improvement and to release the free choice of individuals and the play of market forces that will create prosperity. Bentham thought men far more reasonable and calculating than they are and brushed aside all the Christian and humanist ideas rationalizing instinctive loyalty and awe. He thought society could advance by calculation of pleasure and pain, and his *Introduction* even tries to work out "the value of a lot of pleasure and pain, how now to be measured." He compared the relative gratifications of health, wealth, power, friendship, and benevolence, as well as those of "irascible appetite" and "antipathy." He also thought of punishment purely as a deterrent, not as retribution, and graded offenses on the harm they did to happiness, not on how much they offended God or tradition.

Bentham's calculation of pain and pleasure

If Bentham's psychology was naïve, that of his disciple James Mill was philistine. Mill postulated an economic man whose decisions, if freely taken, would always be in his own interest, and he believed that universal suffrage, along with Utilitarian legislation by a sovereign parliament, would produce the kind of happiness and well-being that Bentham desired. In his *Essay on Government* (1828) Mill thus shows a doctrinaire faith in a literate electorate as the means to good government and in laissez-faire economics as a means to social harmony.

This Utilitarian tradition was humanized by James Mill's son, John Stuart Mill, one of the most influential of mid-Victorian liberals.

Whereas James Mill had been entirely pragmatic, his son tried to enhance more sophisticated values. He thought that civilization depended on a tiny minority of creative minds and on the free play of speculative intelligence. He detested conventional public opinion and feared that complete democracy, far from emancipating opinion, would make it more restrictive. Amid the dogmatic and strident voices of mid-19th-century nationalists, utopians, and revolutionaries, the quiet, if sometimes priggish, voice of mid-Victorian liberalism proved extremely influential in the ruling circles of Victorian England.

Accepting democracy as inevitable, J.S. Mill expressed the still optimistic and progressive views of an intellectual elite. Without complete liberty of opinion, he insisted, civilizations ossify. The quality of progress results not merely from the blind forces of economic competition but from the free play of mind. The worth of the state in the long run is only the worth of the individuals composing it, and without men of genius society would become a "stagnant pool." This militant humanist, unlike his father, was aware of the dangers of even benevolent bureaucratic power and declared that a state that "dwarfs its men" is culturally insignificant.

Mill also advocated the legal and social emancipation of women, holding that ability was wasted by mid-Victorian conventions. He believed that the masses could be educated into accepting the values of liberal civilization, but he defended private property and was as wary of rapid extensions of the franchise as of bureaucratic power.

Tocqueville. Mill's friend Alexis de Tocqueville, whose *De la démocratie en Amérique* (*Democracy in America*) appeared in 1835–40, was a French civil servant also concerned with maintaining the standards and creativeness of civilization in face of the rising tide of mass democracy. Since the United States was then the only large-scale democracy extant, Tocqueville decided to go there, and as a result of his visit wrote a classic account of early 19th-century American civilization. "We cannot," he wrote, "prevent the conditions of men from becoming equal, but it depends upon ourselves whether the principle of equality will lead them to servitude or freedom, to knowledge or barbarism, to prosperity or wretchedness." He feared the possible abuse of power by centralized government, unrestrained by the power of the old privileged classes, and thought it essential to "educate democracy" so that, although it would never have the "wild virtues" of the old regimes, it would have its own dignity, good sense, and even benevolence. Tocqueville greatly admired American representative institutions and made a penetrating analysis of the new power of the press. He realized, as few people then did, that the United States and Russia would become world powers, and he contrasted the freedom of the one and the despotism of the other. He also foresaw that under democracy education would be respected more as a ladder to success than for its intrinsic content and might thus become mediocre. He was alive to the dangers of uniform mediocrity but believed, like Mill, that democracy could be permeated by creative ideas.

T.H. Green. This kind of humanism was given a more elaborate philosophical content by the English philosopher T.H. Green, whose *Lectures on the Principles of Political Obligation* (1895; reprinted from *Philosophical Works,* vol. 2, 1885) greatly influenced the Liberals in the British governments of the period 1906–15. Green, like J.S. Mill and Tocqueville, wished to extend the minority culture to the people and even to use state power to "hinder hindrances to the good life." He had absorbed from Aristotle, Spinoza, Rousseau, and Hegel an organic theory of the state. The latter, by promoting the free play of spontaneous institutions, ought to help individuals both to "secure the common good of society [and] enable them to make the best of themselves."

While hostile to the abuse of landed property, Green was not a Socialist. He accepted the idea that property should be private and unequally distributed and thought the operation of the free market the best way to benefit the whole society; for free trade would, he thought, diminish the inequalities of wealth in a common prosperity. But Green would have extended the power of the state over education, health, housing and town planning, and the relief of unemployment—a new departure in Liberal thought. These recommendations are embedded in the most elaborate and close-knit intellectual construction made by any modern British political philosopher, and they laid the foundation of the British welfare state.

Liberal nationalism. Whereas Green shirked the extension of liberal and constitutional principles into international affairs, the Italian patriot and revolutionary prophet Giuseppe Mazzini made it his vision and became the most influential prophet of liberal nationalism. In his *The Duties of Man* and *Essays* he envisaged a harmony of free peoples—a "sisterhood of nations," in which the rule of military empires would be thrown off, the destruction of clerical and feudal privileges accomplished, and in which the emancipated peoples would be regenerated by means of education and universal suffrage. This vision inspired the more idealistic aspects of the Italian Risorgimento (national revival or resurrection) and of nationalistic revolts in Europe and beyond. Though, in fact, fervid nationalism often proved destructive, Mazzini advocated a united Europe of free peoples, in which national singularities would be transcended in a pan-European harmony. This sort of liberal democratic idealism was catching, and even if it frequently inspired Machiavellian policies, it also inspired President Woodrow Wilson of the United States, who, had he not been thwarted by domestic opposition, might well have made a Mazzinian-type League of Nations a success. Moreover, the Europe of the Common Market owes much to the apparently impractical liberal idealism of Mazzini.

American constitutionalism. The United States was founded by men deeply influenced by republicanism, by Locke, and by the optimism of the French Enlightenment. George Washington, John Adams, and Thomas Jefferson all concurred that laws, rather than men, should be the final sanction and that government should be responsible to the governed. But the influence of Locke and the Enlightenment was not entirely happy. John Adams, who followed Washington as president, prescribed a constitution with a balance of executive and legislative power checked by an independent judiciary. The federal constitution, moreover, could be amended only by a unanimous vote of the states. Anxious to safeguard state liberties and the rights of property, the founding fathers gave the federal government insufficient revenues and coercive powers, as a result of which the constitution was stigmatized as being "no more than a Treaty of Alliance." Yet the federal union was preserved. The civil power controlled the military, and there was religious toleration and freedom of the press and of economic enterprise. Most significantly, the concept of natural rights had found expression in the Declaration of Independence and was to influence markedly political and legal developments in the ensuing decades, as well as inspire the French Declaration of the Rights of Man.

Anarchism and utopianism. While a liberal political philosophy within a framework of capitalistic free trade and constitutional self-government dominated the greatest Western powers, mounting criticism developed against centralized government itself. Radical utopian and anarchist views, previously expounded mainly by religious sects, became secularized in such works as William Godwin's *Political Justice* (1793), Robert Owen's *New View of Society* (1813), and Pierre-Joseph Proudhon's voluminous and anticlerical writings.

The English philosopher William Godwin, an extreme individualist, shared Bentham's confidence in the reasonableness of mankind. He denounced the wars accepted by most political philosophers and all centralized coercive states. The tyranny of demagogues and of "multitudes drunk with power" he regarded as being as bad as that of kings and oligarchs. The remedy, he thought, was not violent revolution, which produces tyranny, but education and freedom, including sexual freedom. His was a program of high-minded, atheistic anarchy.

The English Socialist Robert Owen, a cotton spinner who had made a fortune, also insisted that bad institu-

Green's writing on social reform

Natural rights in American constitutional thought

tions, not original sin or intrinsic folly, caused the evils of society, and he sought to remedy them by changing the economic and educational system. He thus devised a scheme of model cooperative communities that would increase production, permit humane education, and release the naturally benevolent qualities of mankind.

The French moralist and advocate of social reform Pierre-Joseph Proudhon attacked the "tentacular" nation-state and aimed at a classless society in which major capitalism would be abolished. Self-governing producers, no longer slaves of bureaucrats and capitalists, would permit the realization of an intrinsic human dignity, and federation would replace the accepted condition of war between sovereign states. Proudhon tried to transform society by rousing the mass of the people to cooperative humanitarian consciousness.

Saint-Simon and Comte. Another revolt against the prevalent establishment, national and international, was made by the French social philosopher Henri de Saint-Simon. Saint-Simon wanted to develop the Industrial Revolution so as to ameliorate the condition of the poorest class. This would be achieved not through political revolution, but through a government of bankers and administrators who would supersede kings, aristocrats, and politicians. If France were suddenly deprived of three thousand leading scientists, engineers, bankers, painters, poets, and writers, he argued, the result would be catastrophic; but if all the courtiers and bishops and 10,000 landowners vanished, the loss, though deplorable, would be much less severe. Saint-Simon also demanded a united Europe, superseding the warring nation-states, with a European parliament and a joint development of industry and communication. He also invented a synthetic religion appropriate to a scientific phase of history, with a cult of Newton and the great men of science.

Saint-Simon's disciple Auguste Comte went further. His *Course of Positive Philosophy* (1830–42) and *System of Positive Polity* (1851–54) elaborated a "religion of humanity," with ritual, calendar, and a priesthood of scientists, and secular saints, including Julius Caesar, Dante, and Joan of Arc. Society would be ruled by bankers and technocrats and Europe united into a Western republic. This doctrine, backed by pioneering sociology, won much influence among intellectuals. Comte, like Saint-Simon, tackled the essential questions: how to deploy the power of modern technology for the benefit of all mankind; how to avoid wars between sovereign states; and how to fill the void left by the waning of Christian beliefs.

Comte's "religion of humanity"

Hegel. Whereas the utopian reformers had discarded metaphysical arguments, the German philosopher G.W.F. Hegel claimed to apprehend the totality of the cosmos by speculative cognition. Like Vico, he saw the past in terms of changing consciousness, but he viewed the historical process as one of "becoming" rather than as one of eternal recurrence. Hegel had no adequate historical data for his intuitions, since the whole of world history was even less known then than it is today, but his novel sweep and range of theory proved an intoxicating substitute for religion. He divided world history into four epochs: the patriarchal Eastern empire, the brilliant Greek boyhood, the severe manhood of Rome, and the Germanic phase after the Reformation. The "Absolute," like a conductor, summons each people to their finest hour, and neither individuals nor states have any rights against them during their historically determined period of supremacy. Many felt some sense of anticlimax, however, when he claimed that the Prussian state embodied the hitherto highest self-realization of the "Absolute" (see HEGELIANISM). Not since St. Augustine had so compelling a drama been adumbrated. Hegel's drama, moreover, culminates in this world, for "the state is the divine idea as it exists on earth."

Marx and Engels. Hegel was a conservative, but his influence on the revolutionaries Karl Marx and his collaborator Friedrich Engels was profound. They inherited the Hegelian claim to understand the "totality" of history and life as it progressed through a dialectic of thesis, antithesis, and synthesis. But, whereas Hegel envisaged a conflict of nation-states, Marx and Engels thought that the dynamism of history was generated by inevitable class conflict economically determined. This was an idea even more dynamic than Hegel's and more relevant to the social upheavals that were a consequence of the Industrial Revolution. Marx was a formidable prophet whose writings lead up to an apocalypse and redemption. A deeply learned humanist, his ideal was the fullest development of the human personality. But, whereas Plato was concerned with an elite, Marx cared passionately for the elevation of whole peoples.

The Marxist credo was all the more effective as it expressed with eloquent ferocity the grievances of the poor, while prophesying retribution and a happy ending. For the state, once captured by the class-conscious vanguard of the proletariat, would take over the means of production from the capitalists, and a brief "dictatorship of the proletariat" would establish a truly communist society. The state would then wither away and man at last become "fully human" in a classless society.

The powerful slogans of Marx and Engels were a natural result of the unbridled capitalism of laissez-faire, but politically they were naïve. In classical, medieval, and humanistic political philosophy the essential problem is the control of power, and to imagine that a dictatorship, once established, will wither away is utopian. As even Marx's fellow revolutionary the Russian anarchist M.A. Bakunin observed,

> The revolutionary dictatorship of the doctrinaires who put science before life would differ from the established state only in external trappings. The substance of both are a tyranny of the minority over the majority—in the name of the many and the supreme wisdom of the few.

Marx's naïveté regarding the dictatorship of the proletariat

The revolutionaries would vivisect society in the name of dogmas and "destroy the present order, only to erect their own rigid dictatorship among its ruins." For a full account of Marxist philosophy, see MARXISM.

Political philosophy in the 20th century

Nineteenth-century European civilization had been the first to dominate and pervade the whole world and to create a new self-sustaining productivity in which all eventually might share. But, as Saint-Simon had pointed out, this civilization had a fatal flaw. The rule of law, accepted within the politically advanced states, had never been achieved among them. Heavily armed nations and empires remained in a Hobbesian "posture of war," and classical and medieval ideals of world order had long been discarded. Within states, also, laissez-faire capitalism had exacerbated class conflicts, while the decline of religious belief had undermined traditional solidarity. And in 1914, when a general European war broke out, the peoples, contrary to the hopes of cosmopolitan revolutionaries, rallied behind their national governments. When the victorious powers failed to promote world order through the League of Nations, a second global conflict followed, during which were developed weapons so destructive as to threaten life everywhere.

In the aftermath of these catastrophes and the worldwide revulsion they occasioned, not least against the European colonial powers, three mainstreams of mid-20th-century political philosophy may be discerned.

In liberal-constitutional states, with modified, managerial capitalism and various degrees of public welfare, a political pragmatism has emerged, still maintaining the Aristotelian distinction between the rule of law and government by consent, on the one hand, and tyranny on the other. Second, there has been a reaffirmation of religious or quasi-religious values appealing to conscience and the inner man, expressed persuasively in Existentialist writings. Third, revolutionary ideas have also developed, most of them along Marxist lines. Other revolutionary doctrines appeal to anarchist traditions and are elaborated with neo-Marxist and neo-Freudian insights. Within these categories many shades of opinion are expressed, and only a sampling of representative views is presented here.

POLITICAL PRAGMATISM

The first, pragmatist approach probably has been most powerfully asserted in the United States and Great Britain.

The American writer Lewis Mumford, for example, has advocated a militant humanism, defending people against the alienations of megalopolitan life and attacking mechanization and materialism. Like the Greek philosophers and like Tocqueville, whom he admires, Mumford declares, "In the end, all our contrivances have but one object; the continued growth of human personalities and the cultivation of the best life possible." The American philosopher and educationist John Dewey, on the other hand, sought to counteract the dehumanization of industrial mass society by a freer form of education, liberating the personality.

Both these writers criticize the existing structure of society and its modified capitalism, but try to work within it. Another humanist, the English philosopher Bertrand Russell, was more radical. Russell carried into political philosophy an aristocratic individualism, campaigning for toleration, sexual freedom, compassion, and common sense. He broadcast elite values to a mass society and attacked materialism, crass bureaucracy, and war. He twice went to prison in pacifist protest and was obsessed with the universal menace of nuclear weapons. He denounced warlike political theories: "Remember your humanity," he said, "and forget the rest." On political tactics often inept, Russell won wide influence as a man of principle, concerned to adapt archaic institutions to the changed environment of mankind.

The Austrian-born British philosopher Sir Karl Popper has demonstrated the pretensions of the 19th-century determinist philosophies such as those of Hegel and Marx, while an English historian and philosopher, Sir Isaiah Berlin, has ridiculed the idea of a supposedly objective march of histoy. Berlin also rejects the Marxist belief that all values are conditioned by the place men occupy on the "moving stair of time." Marx, he points out, was as romantic as Hegel in envisaging a "world which moves from explosion to explosion in order to fulfil the great cosmic design." Moral values, he insists, are not just a "subjective gloss unworthy of consideration on the great hard edifice of historical construction." No single formula can be found, Berlin argues, whereby the various objectives of men can be harmoniously realized. There are many human goals, which may well be in conflict with one another.

This empirical, pluralist, and liberal political philosophy has much in common with the approach of the Frenchman Émile Durkheim and the Englishman Graham Wallas, both founding fathers of modern sociology. Statesmen and political philosophers, they contend, should not play the part of prophets but rather confine themselves to investigating social patterns and the ideas that are part of them. Ways might thus be found of promoting the survival and vitality of a given society in its particular setting.

Scientific humanism of Graham Wallas

Graham Wallas was concerned to adapt constitutional societies by consent. He wanted to nationalize many essential means of production, including transport and communications, and through increased taxation strengthen social democracy by greater economic and social equality. He was not a revolutionary but a reformer, who understood the precariousness of civilization and the dangers of nationalism, which could only bring, he prophesied, centuries of warfare and regression. He advocated a worldwide and constitutionalist scientific humanism, inspired by the idea of the solidarity of the whole species, for "the master task of civilized mankind is to promote the conditions leading to the good life."

Other political sociologists who accepted the established order did not expect to improve it. The Italian Vilfredo Pareto, and Gaetano Mosca, a Sicilian-born lawyer, set themselves not to state what they wanted but to record what occurs in society. Pareto's *Mind and Society* (1916) is an elaborate, quasi-mathematical classification of nonlogical political myths. Its form is daunting, but its insights are penetrating, especially a hilarious dissection of Rousseau's *General Will,* of which, Pareto concludes, "the intrinsic logico-experimental value . . . is zero." Ranging sardonically over history, Pareto insists that elites will always manipulate society, power merely shifting from one set of rulers to another.

Mosca, in *The Ruling Class* (1939), analyzed how political myths are exploited. He also concluded that elites everywhere are bound to rule and that the least bad government occurs when abuse of power is checked by legal means; that is, by the rule of law. Mosca admired the liberal constitutionalism of the 19th century, although he was aware of its precariousness and limitations. He argued that there is no total explanation of history, which has always been the unpredictable outcome of competing and interacting interests. One thing is certain, nevertheless: in various forms there will always be a struggle for predominance. Mosca's views, more clearly set out than Pareto's, have a salutary realism.

The American philosopher and critic James Burnham also analyzed shifts of power. In *The Managerial Revolution* (1941) he propounded a theory of bureaucratic revolution: the rulers of the new society, the class with power and privilege, will be the bureaucratic managers of "super states." In *The Machiavellians, Defenders of Freedom* (1943), he reinterprets Machiavelli and cites Mosca as a modern Machiavellian. Following Pareto's idea of the "circulation of elites," he asserts that, when a ruling class becomes inadequate, frivolous, or bored, loses confidence in itself and its myths, and becomes irresolute in deploying necessary force, new elites are bound to take over—as in the managerial revolution of the 20th century.

RELIGIOUS AND EXISTENTIALIST APPROACHES

In the second religious and quasi-religious group of political philosophies, the Catholic hierarchy has reiterated its ancient neo-Thomist doctrine of original sin and redemption. Pope Leo XIII, in the encyclicals *Inscrutabili Dei Consilio* (1878), *Immortale Dei* (1885), and *Rerum Novarum* (1891), dismissed all anthropocentric political philosophies as new versions of old heresies. The world, "through an insatiable craving for things perishable," was "rushing wildly upon the straight road to destruction." Society is intelligible only in the light of the Christian revelation and a future life:

exclude the idea of futurity and forthwith the very notion of what is good and right would perish, nay, the whole scheme of the universe would become a dark and unfathomable mystery.

Such is the human condition that visionary innovations are fruitless, and "venomous" teachings can only bring "death-bearing fruit." Society, as St. Augustine had declared, if organized without God, can only be a present hell. Hierarchy, authority, and censorship can alone "control the excesses of the unbridled intellect, which unfailingly end in the oppression of the untutored multitude." Property is essential to the family, on which the social order depends, and inequality is inherent in all human societies. Only a harmonious Christian commonwealth can assuage the consequences of sin, and within that social order the state should therefore encourage Christian trade unions and promote the welfare of the poor. Thus, with these views the papacy, maintaining its monopoly of revelation, tried to come to terms with the demands of industrial civilization.

During the rise of 19th-century nationalism and of Communist, Fascist, and Nazi dictatorships, and in face of the increasing dominance of governments and large-scale industry in all mass societies, the importance of individual responsibility with regard to moral issues was emphasized by a divergent group of thinkers who have come to be described as Existentialists. Søren Kierkegaard (died 1855), a Danish philosopher, declared that "truth is subjectivity" and that only by means of inward revelation can man know God. Jean-Paul Sartre, a brilliant French Existentialist, tried to come to terms with dialectical Materialism. His *Existentialism and Humanism* (1948) comprises an affirmation of human dignity. "If," he writes, "I have excluded God the Father, there must be someone to invent values." Man, who has abandoned God, "must liberate himself by some practical commitment," for only then can he become fully human. Sartre's elaborate *L'Être et le néant* (1943; Eng. trans., *Being and Nothingness,* 1956) is at once Cartesian and laborious, complete with a "key" to its special and pedantic terms. It investigates the loneliness of the human condition, attitudes to others, love,

Sartre's view of human dignity

masochism, indifference, desire, and hate. This intense introspection is even more vividly expressed in his fiction and drama. The Algerian-born Albert Camus in *The Myth of Sisyphus* (1942) and *The Rebel* (1951) also agonizes brilliantly over the current human condition, and in *Man in Revolt* he discards hope of pragmatic improvement.

REVOLUTIONARY DOCTRINES

The third stream of contemporary political philosophy is Marxist–Leninist totalitarian and neo-Marxist anarchist. Many of Marx's original insights into the socio-economic process and its effect on ideas are now generally accepted. His prophecies, on the other hand, have not been fulfilled. The proletarian revolution, for example, came not in an economically advanced country but in one of the most backward; and the state, far from withering away or being diminished by inexorable economic trends, has in fact become more powerful both in Communist and in social-democratic countries. Those who have accepted the total Marxist revelation as superseding all else have had thus to adapt and revise it. Hence, much tortuous and artificial debate has ensued. All orthodox Marxists accept the Hegelian position that one can get beyond empirical knowledge and perceive the historically revealed installments of a total explanation. They also start from Marx's 19th-century belief that economically determined conflicts among feudal, bourgeois, and proletarian classes are the dynamic of history and that the rule of law is not a safeguard for the whole society against arbitrary power but merely the expression of class interest.

Lenin. The first and by far the most significant interpretation of Marx's doctrine as realized in the Soviet Union was made by Lenin and developed by Stalin and is entirely authoritarian. According to Marx and Engels, the revolution could occur only after the bourgeois phase of production had "contradicted" the tsarist order, but Lenin determined to take advantage of the opportunities provided by World War I and settle accounts directly with the "accursed heritage of serfdom, of Asiatic barbarism . . . an insult to mankind," and in 1917 he engineered a coup that secured the support of the peasantry and the industrial workers. He also adopted the revolutionary theorist Leon Trotsky's idea of a "permanent revolution" from above by a small revolutionary elite.

Already in *What Is To Be Done?* (1902), Lenin had argued that an educated elite must direct the proletarian revolution, and when he came to power he dissolved the constituent assembly and ruled through a "revolutionary and democratic dictatorship supported by the state power of the armed workers." In asserting the need for an elite of professional revolutionaries to seize power, Lenin reverted to Marx's program in *The Communist Manifesto,* rather than conforming to the fated pattern of economic development worked out in *Das Kapital.*

In 1921 he further adapted theory to the times. His new economic policy sanctioned the development of a class of prosperous "kulak" peasantry to keep the economy viable. For Lenin thought always in terms of world revolution; and in spite of the failure of the Marxists in central Europe and the defeat of the Red armies in Poland, he died in the expectation of a global sequel. Thus, in *Imperialism, the Highest Stage of Capitalism* (1917), he had extended the class war into an inevitable conflict between European imperialism and the colonial peoples involved. He had been influenced by the English historian J.A. Hobson's *Imperialism, a Study* (1902), which alleged that decadent capitalism was bound to turn from glutted markets at home to exploit the toil of "reluctant and unassimilated peoples."

But, as observed by classical, medieval, and modern constitutionalist political philosophers, authoritarian regimes suffer the tensions of all autocracies. Marx himself might have thought that such planned autocracies had made the worst of his revelation.

Other Marxist approaches. Many Marxist revisionists tend toward anarchism, stressing the Hegelian and utopian elements of his theory. The Hungarian György Lukács, for example, and the German Herbert Marcuse, who fled from the Nazis to the United States, have won some following among those in revolt against both authoritarian "peoples' democracies" and the diffused capitalism and meritocracy of the managerial welfare state. Lukács' *Geschichte und Klassenbewusstsein* (1923; Eng. trans., *History and Class Consciousness,* 1971), a neo-Hegelian work, claims that only the intuition of the proletariat can properly apprehend the totality of history. But world revolution is contingent, not inevitable, and Marxism is an instrument, not a prediction. Lukács renounced this heresy after residence in the Soviet Union under Stalin, but he maintained influence through literary and dramatic criticism. After Khrushchev's denunciation of Stalin, Lukács advocated peaceful coexistence and intellectual rather than political subversion. In *The Meaning of Contemporary Realism* (trans. 1963), he again relates Marx to Hegel and even to Aristotle, against the Stalinist claim that Marx made a radically new departure. Lukács' neo-Marxist literary criticism can be tendentious, but his neo-Hegelian insights, strikingly expressed, have appealed to those anxious to salvage the more humane aspects of Marxism and to promote revolution, even against a modified capitalism and social democracy, by intellectual rather than by political means.

Marcuse also reached back to the more utopian Marx. Now that most of the proletariat has been absorbed into a conformist managerial capitalism or has been regimented into bureaucratic peoples' democracies, freedom, argues Marcuse, is in retreat. In Western affluent societies most employers and workers are equally philistine, dominated by the commercialized mass media, or "cogs in a culture machine." The Soviet Union has reverted to an even more philistine monolithic repression, distorting art and literature. This enslavement of man by his own industrial productivity has been clinched by the colossal power of governments, which renders the old brief and brisk class warfare a romantic, impracticable idea. Marcuse attacked all establishments and transferred the redeeming mission of the proletariat to a fringe of alienated minorities— radical students and the exponents of the "hippie" way of life—as well as to Viet Cong guerrillas and Black Power militants. Such groups, he declared, could apparently form liberating elites and destroy the managerial society. Thus reappeared the old Marxist–Hebraic pattern of redemption through struggle by a chosen people.

The Italian Communist Antonio Gramsci deployed a vivid rhetorical talent in attacking existing society. Like Marcuse, Gramsci was alarmed that the proletariat was being assimilated by the capitalist order. He took his stand on the already obsolescent Marxist doctrine of irreconcilable class war between bourgeois and proletariat. He aimed to unmask the bourgeois idea of liberty and to replace parliaments by an "implacable machine" of workers' councils, which would destroy the current social order through a dictatorship of the proletariat. "Democracy," he wrote, "is our worst enemy. We must be ready to fight it because it blurs the clear separation of classes."

Not only would parliamentary democracy and established law be unmasked, but culture, too, would be transformed. A workers' civilization, with its great industry, large cities, and "tumultuous and intense life," would create a new civilization with new poetry, art, drama, fashions, and language. Gramsci insisted that the old culture should be destroyed and that education should be wrenched from the grip of the ruling classes and the church.

But this militant revolutionary was also a utopian. He turned bitterly hostile to Stalin's regime, for he believed, like Engels, that the dictatorship of the workers' state would wither away. "We do not wish," he wrote, "to freeze the dictatorship." Following world revolution, a classless society would emerge, and mankind would be free to master nature instead of being involved in a class war.

Since World War II, Gramsci's notions have enjoyed a minor revival. They appeal to the fringe of revolutionaries who admire Marcuse and detest the embourgeoisement of an idealized proletariat. But, in a civilization in which, if total war can be avoided, material prospects are good, the destruction of the old culture out of rage, envy, and naïve idealism appears to be a pointless program. Like Marcuse's doctrine, it is a cry of pain, typical of the 1920s in Italy.

Doctrinal assumptions of latter-day Marxists

Marcuse's assessment of revolutionary prospects

Conclusion

The history of political philosophy from Plato until the present day makes plain that modern political philosophy is still faced with the basic problems defined by the Greeks. The need to redeploy public power in order to maintain the survival and enhance the quality of human life, for example, has never been so essential. And if the opportunities for promoting well-being are now far greater, the penalties of the abuse of power are nothing less than the destruction or gross degradation of all life on the planet.

In these circumstances it is of no great importance that some analytical philosophers have declared themselves neutral; they have at least often discredited pretentious metaphysical myths. On the empirical evidence, constitutionalism and the rule of law, with the ancient classic, medieval, and humanist traditions behind them, have proved themselves a more successful response to the environment than tyranny and repression. In the current and more sophisticated view, there are no shortcuts to the millennium. As Mosca points out, utopian ideas become

dangerous when they succeed in bringing a large mass of intellectual and moral energies to bear upon an end that can never be achieved, and that in the day of purported achievement can mean nothing more than the triumph of the worst people and distress and disappointment for the good.

There will perhaps always be a struggle for preeminence in any society, and public laws are necessary to regulate it. Too much cannot be hoped of government, and the best society is that in which tyranny and caprice of power are prevented and in which men are free to create diverse and spontaneous institutions within the framework of law. Only within such a framework of a tolerably well-organized constitutionalism, gradually extended to relations between states, can the swiftly mounting opportunities provided by applied science be taken and the pattern of social life adjusted, so that the human species, instead of being thwarted and deformed by its institutions, can realize its full potentialities.

BIBLIOGRAPHY. The following editions of standard works and commentaries may be consulted.

Classical: PLATO: *The Republic,* trans. with an introduction by A.D. LINDSAY (1957); *The Statesman* (Loeb edition, 1925); *The Laws,* ed. by A.E. TAYLOR (1934). *The Politics of Aristotle,* trans. with introduction by ERNEST BARKER is still the best edition (1946). For the social background of Greek thought, see MAURICE BOWRA, *The Greek Experience* (1957). CICERO, *On the Commonwealth (De re publica)* is available in translation by G.H. SABINE and S.B. SMITH (1929). For *De legibus,* see the Loeb edition (1928, reprinted 1966). ST. AUGUSTINE, *The City of God* has been translated by JOHN HEALEY, with an introduction by ERNEST BARKER (1931). For the background, see PETER BROWN, *Augustine of Hippo* (1967) and *The World of Late Antiquity* (1971). C.N. COCHRANE, *Christianity and Classical Culture* (1940), is worth consultation; and H. OSBORN TAYLOR, *The Medieval Mind,* 4th ed., vol. 2 (1925), is still valuable for patristic and medieval thought. See also JULIA ANNAS, *An Introduction to Plato's Republic* (1981).

Medieval: The most convenient edition of John of Salisbury is *The Statesman's Book of John Salisbury,* trans. and selected by J. DICKSON (1927). For St. Thomas Aquinas, see the *Selected Political Writings,* ed. by A.P. D'ENTREVES (1959). The full texts are in The *"Summa Theologiae" of St. Thomas Aquinas,* 2nd ed., 22 vol., trans. by the FATHERS OF THE ENGLISH DOMINICAN PROVINCE (1921–32). For DANTE'S *Monarchia,* see P.H. WICKSTEED'S translation in *The Latin Works of Dante* (1904), and that by D. NICHOLL (1954). See also A.P. D'ENTREVES, *Dante As a Political Thinker* (1952). The best general survey is R.W. and A.J. CARLYLE, *A History of Medieval Political Theory in the West,* 6 vol. (1903–36). A.L. SMITH, *Church and State in the Middle Ages* (1913); and C.H. MCILWAIN, *The Growth of Political Thought in the West, from the Greeks to the End of the Middle Ages* (1932), are still valuable.

16th–18th centuries: NICCOLO MACHIAVELLI, *The Prince* and *Discourses on the First Decade of Titus Livius* are edited with an introduction by MAX LERNER (1950); his *Literary Works* are edited and translated by J.R. HALE (1961). See also ALLAN H. GILBERT, *Machiavelli's Prince and Its Forerunners* (1938); HERBERT BUTTERFIELD, *The Statecraft of Machiavelli* (1962); and FELIX RAAB, *The English Face of Machiavelli* (1964). THOMAS HOBBES, *The Leviathan, or the Matter, Forme and Power of a Commonwealth, Ecclesiastical and Civil* is edited by A.D. LINDSEY (1950); see also *The Complete Works,* ed. by WILLIAM MOLESWORTH, 11 vol. (1839–45). K.V. THOMAS, "The Social Origins of Hobbes's Political Thought," in *Hobbes Studies,* ed. by K.C. BROWN (1965), is the best account. JOHN BOWLE, *Hobbes and His Critics* (1951), describes Hobbes's political impact and the contemporary reaction to it. SPINOZA'S *Tractatus Theologico-Politicus* (in part) and the full *Tractatus Politicus* have been edited by A.G. WERNHAM (1958). See also STUART HAMPSHIRE, *Spinoza* (1951). For general background, see ALFRED NORTH WHITEHEAD, *Science and the Modern World* (1925). RICHARD HOOKER, *The Laws of Ecclesiastical Polity,* ed. by JOHN KEBLE, 3 vol. (1836), was revised by R.W. CHURCH and F. PAGET (1888). See also C.J. SISSON, *The Judicious Marriage of Mr. Hooker and the Birth of The Laws of Ecclesiastical Polity* (1940). JOHN LOCKE, *Two Treatises on Civil Government* has been edited by PETER LASLETT (1960); *The Second Treatise of Civil Government and A Letter Concerning Toleration* by J.W. GOUGH (1947). For EDMUND BURKE, see his *Complete Works* (Bohn's Classics, 1853) and *Selected Writings,* ed. by R.J.S. HOFFMAN and P. LEVACK (1949). See also PHILIP MAGNUS, *Edmund Burke: A Life* (1939); and ALFRED COBBAN, *Edmund Burke and the Revolt Against the Eighteenth Century,* 2nd ed. (1960). GIOVANNI BATTISTA VICO, *The New Science* is translated by T.G. BERGIN and M.A. FISCH (1961). See HENRY P. ADAMS, *The Life and Writings of Giambattista Vico* (1935); and BENEDETTO CROCE, *The Philosophy of Giambattista Vico,* trans. by T.G. COLLINGWOOD (1964); also CHARLES LOUIS DE SECONDAT, *Oeuvres choisis,* trans. by J. CHAIX-RUY (1946). MONTESQUIEU, *The Spirit of the Laws* is translated by THOMAS NUGENT, with an introduction by FRANZ NEUMAN (1949). For the French Enlightenment generally, see J.B. BURY, *The Idea of Progress* (1921); and CARL BECKER, *The Heavenly City of the Eighteenth Century Philosophers* (1933). The best translation of JEAN-JACQUES ROUSSEAU'S *Social Contract,* with an introduction, is that of ERNEST BARKER (1947). See also *The Political Writings of Jean Jacques Rousseau,* ed. by C.E. VAUGHAN, 2 vol. (1915). WILLIAM H. BLANCHARD, *Rousseau and the Spirit of Revolt* (1967); and J. MCMANNERS, *The Social Contract and Rousseau's Revolt Against Society* (1968), are both illuminating. DAVID HUME, "Of the Original Contract" is available in *Social Contract,* ed. by BARKER (*op. cit.*).

The 19th century: JEREMY BENTHAM, *A Fragment on Government* and *An Introduction to the Principles of Morals and Legislation* are edited by WILFRED HARRISON (1948). See also JOHN PLAMENATZ, *The English Utilitarians,* 2nd rev. ed. (1948), particularly for Mill. J.S. MILL, *On Liberty* and *Considerations on Representative Government* are edited by R.B. MCCALLUM (1946). ALEXIS DE TOCQUEVILLE, *De la démocratie en Amérique* (Eng. trans., *Democracy in America*), ed. by PHILIPS BRADLEY, 2 vol. (1945), is the best edition. For a good abridgment, see H. REEVES'S translation, ed. by H.S. COMMAGER (1946). *L'Ancien Régime* was edited by G.W. HEADLAM (1904). AUGUSTE COMTE, *Système de politique positive (System of Positive Polity)* is translated by J.H. BRIDGES, 4 vol. (1875–77). See J.S. MILL, *Auguste Comte and Positivism* (1865); and EDWARD CAIRD, *The Social Philosophy and Religion of Comte* (1885). BASIL WILLEY in *Nineteenth Century Studies* (1949), has a good essay. *Hegel's Philosophy of Right* is translated by T.M. KNOX (1942); his *Philosophy of History* by J. SIBREE, rev. ed. (1944). HERBERT MARCUSE, *Reason and Revolution: Hegel and the Rise of Social Theory,* 2nd ed. (1960), makes a new interpretation. ROBERT OWEN, *A New View of Society and Other Writings* are edited by G.D.H. COLE (1927). PIERRE-JOSEPH PROUDHON, *Qu'est-ce que la propriété? (What Is Property? An Enquiry into the Principles of Right and Government)* is edited by J.A. LANGLOIS (1966). See his *Oeuvres complètes,* ed. by C. BOUGLE and H. MOYSSET, 15 vol. (1923–36)—also D.W. BROGAN, *Proudhon* (1934). KARL MARX, *A Contribution to the Critique of Political Economy* was translated by N.T. STONE, 2nd rev. ed. (1904). See also KARL MARX, *The Communist Manifesto,* ed. by HAROLD J. LASKI (1948); *Capital: A Critique of Political Economy,* trans. by E. and C. PAUL (1928); *Capital: The Process of Capitalist Production As a Whole* and *The Process of Circulation of Capital,* trans. by ERNEST UNTERMANN (1909); *The Holy Family* (1956); and *Selected Writings in Sociology and Social Philosophy,* ed. by T.B. BOTTOMORE and M. RUBEL (1964). Studies of Marx particularly recommended are FRANZ MEHRING, *Karl Marx: Geschichte seines Lebens* (1933; Eng. trans., *Karl Marx: The Story of His Life,* 1948); and ISAIAH BERLIN, *Karl Marx: His Life and Environment,* 4th ed. reprinted with corrections (1960). JOHN PLAMENATZ, *German Marxism and Russian Communism* (1954), is illuminating. FRIEDRICH ENGELS' works in translation include *The Condition of the Working Classes in England in 1844* (1958); *The Anti-Dühring: Herr Eugen Dühring's Revolution in Science* (1959); and *The Origin of the Family, Private Property and the State* (1884). The standard biography is by GUSTAV MAYER, *Friedrich Engels,* 2 vol. (1934; Eng. trans. 1936). GEORGES SOREL, *Réflexions sur la violence* (1912; *Reflections on Violence*), was translated by T.E. HULME (1915), and by J. ROTH

(1950). See also *Les Illusions du progrès* (1908; 5th ed., 1947); and P.L. PERRON, *Les Ideés sociales de George Sorel* (1935).

The 20th century: ISAIAH BERLIN, *Historical Inevitability* (1954) and *Two Concepts of Liberty* (1958); EMILE DURKHEIM, *The Rules of Sociological Method,* trans. by S.A. SOLVAY and J.H. MUELLER, ed. by C.E.G. CATLIN (1938); VILFREDO PARETO, *Trattato di sociologia generale,* 2nd ed. (1923; Eng. trans., *The Mind and Society,* ed. by A. LIVINGSTON, trans. by A. BONGIONNO and A. LIVINGSTON, 4 vol., 1935); GAETANO MOSCA, *Elementi di scienza politica,* 2nd ed. (1923; Eng. trans., *The Ruling Class,* ed. by A. LIVINGSTON and trans. by H.D. KHAN, 1939); LEO XIII, *The Pope and the People: Select Letters and Addresses on Social Questions* (1929); JEAN-PAUL SARTRE, *L'Être et le néant (Being and Nothingness: An Essay in Phenomenological Ontology),* trans. and ed. by H.E. BARNES (1957); *Existentialism and Humanism,* trans. and ed. by PHILIP MAIRET (1948); LENIN, *The Development of Capitalism in Russia* (1899); *Collected Works,* 4th ed. (1960), vol. 3, *What Is To Be Done?,* vol. 5, *The State and Revolution,* vol. 25, *Imperialism: The Highest Stage of Capitalism* (1916); see also his *Selected Works,* 12 vol. (1936–39). GEORGE LICHTHEIM, *Marxism: An Historical and Critical Study,* 2nd rev. ed. (1964), is a good short account. See also HERBERT MARCUSE, *Reason and Revolution: Hegel and the Rise of Social Theory,* 2nd ed. (1960), *Eros and Civilization* (1955), *Soviet Marxism: A Critical Analysis* (1958), and *One Dimensional Man* (1964); ALASDAIR MACINTYRE, *Marcuse* (1970); GYORGY

LUKACS, *Goethe und seine Zeit* (1947; *Goethe and His Age,* trans. by ROBERT ANCHOR, 1968); *Der historische Roman* (1955; *The Historical Novel,* trans. by H. and G. MITCHELL, 1962); and JAMES JOLL, *The Anarchists* (1965). For A. Gramsci, see *The Modern Prince and Other Writings,* trans. and introduced by L. MARKS (1957); J.M. CAMMETT, *Antonio Gramsci and the Origins of Italian Communism* (1967); A. POZZOLINI, *Antonio Gramsci: An Introduction to His Thought* (1970). See also MARK BLITZ, *Heidegger's 'Being and Time' and the Possibility of Political Philosophy* (1981); GEORGE FRIGOMAN, *The Political Philosophy of the Frankfurt School* (1981).

General histories of political philosophy: G.H. SABINE, *A History of Political Theory,* 3rd ed. (1961), is the most comprehensive survey. W.A. DUNNING, *A History of Political Theories,* vol. 1, *Ancient and Medieval,* vol. 2, *From Luther to Montesquieu,* vol. 3, *From Rousseau to Spencer* (1902–20, reprinted 1936–38), is still valuable. See also KARL POPPER, *The Open Society and Its Enemies,* 5th rev. ed., vol. 1, *The Spell of Plato* and vol. 2, *The High Tide of Prophecy: Hegel, Marx and the Aftermath* (1966). ERNEST BARKER, *The Principles of Social and Political Theory* (1951), analyses essential problems. JOHN BOWLE, *Politics and Opinion in the Nineteenth Century* (1954, paperback 1964); and WILLIAM EBENSTEIN, *Modern Political Thought: The Great Issues,* 2nd ed. (1960), are valuable, as is HAROLD D. LASSWELL, *The Future of Political Science* (1963).

(J.E.B.)

Political Systems

The term political system may be used either narrowly or broadly. Narrowly defined, it is the set of formal legal institutions that constitute a "government" or a "state." This is the definition adopted by many studies of the legal or constitutional arrangements of advanced political orders. More broadly defined, it comprehends actual as well as prescribed forms of political behaviour, not only the legal organization of the state but also the realities of political life. Still more broadly defined, the political system is seen as a set of "processes of interaction" or as a subsystem of the social system interacting with other nonpolitical subsystems, such as the economic system. This usage guides attention to the importance of informal sociopolitical processes and emphasizes the study of political development.

None of these approaches may be neglected. Traditional legal or constitutional analysis, using the first definition, has produced a huge body of literature on governmental structures, many of the specialized terms that are a part of the traditional vocabulary of political science, and several classifying schemes that are still instructive. Similarly, empirical analysis of political processes and the effort to identify the underlying realities of governmental forms have yielded a rich store of data and an important body of comparative theory. The third definition has inspired much recent scholarly work, particularly on non-Western states, that employs new kinds of data, new terms, and some new concepts and categories of analysis. The discussion that follows will draw upon all three approaches to the study of political systems. (See also SOCIAL SCIENCES: *Political science.*)

The article is divided into the following sections:

Typologies of government

The most important type of political system in the modern world is the nation-state. The world today is divided territorially into more than 150 states, in each of which a national government claims to exercise sovereignty—or the power of final authority—and seeks to compel obedience to its will by its citizens. This fact of the world's political organization suggests the distinction employed in the following section among supranational, national, and subnational political systems.

SUPRANATIONAL POLITICAL SYSTEMS

A principal result of the division of the world into a number of separate national entities, or states, that have contact with one another, share goals or needs, and face common threats is the formation of supranational relationships. In some cases, as in many alliances, these relationships are short-lived and fail to result in significant institutional development. In other cases, they lead to interstate organizations and supranational systems. The discussion below examines several types of supranational political systems, together with historical and contemporary examples of each.

Empires. All empires, since they are composed of peoples of different cultures and ethnic backgrounds, are ultimately held together by coercion and the threat of forcible reconquest. Imposing their rule on diverse political structures, they are characterized by the centralization of power and the absence of effective representation of their component parts. Although force is thus the primary instrument of imperial rule, it is also true that history records many cases of multi-ethnic empires that were governed peaceably for considerable periods and were often quite successful in maintaining order within their boundaries. The history of the ancient world is the history of great empires—Egypt, China, Persia, and imperial Rome—whose autocratic regimes provided relatively stable government for many subject peoples in immense territories over many centuries. Based on military force and religious belief, the ancient despotisms were legitimized also by their achievements in building great bureaucratic and legal structures, in developing vast irrigation and road systems, and in providing the conditions for the support of high civilizations. Enhancing and transcending all other political structures in their sphere, they could claim to function as effective schemes of universal order.

In contrast to the empires of the ancient world, the colonial empires of recent times fell far short of universal status. In part, these modern European empires were made up of "colonies" in the original Greek sense; peopled by immigrants from the mother country, the colonies usually established political structures similar to those of the metropolitan centre and were often able to exercise a substantial measure of self-government. In part, also, the European empires were composed of territories inhabited by native populations and administered by imperial bureaucracies. The government of these territories was generally more coercive than in the European colonies and more concerned with protection and supervision of the commercial, industrial, and other exploitative interests of the imperial power. The disintegration of these empires occurred with astonishing speed. The two world wars of the 20th century sapped the power of the metropolitan centres, while their own doctrines of democracy, equality, and self-determination undermined the principle of imperial rule. Powers such as Britain and France found it increasingly difficult to resist claims to independence couched in terms of the representative concepts on which their home governments were based, and they lacked the military and economic strength to continue their rule over restive native populations. In the two decades after 1945 nearly all the major colonial territories won their independence; the great colonial empires that had once ruled more than half the world were finally dismembered.

Leagues. One of the commonest forms of supranational organization in history is that of leagues, generally composed of states seeking to resist some common military or economic threat by combining their forces. This was the case with the early city leagues, such as the Achaean and Aetolian leagues in ancient Greece and the Hanseatic and the Swabian leagues in Europe; and to a great extent it was the case with the League of Nations. Other common features of leagues include the existence of some form of charter or agreement among the member states, an assembly of representatives of the constituent members, an executive organ for the implementation of the decisions of the assembly of representatives, and an arbitral or judicial body for adjudicating disputes.

The League of Nations was one of the great experiments in supranational organization of the 20th century and the predecessor in several important respects of the United Nations. The Covenant of the League was drafted by a special commission of the Peace Conference after World War I, with Pres. Woodrow Wilson of the United States as its leading advocate, and approved by a plenary conference of the victorious powers in 1919. The initial membership of the League consisted of 20 states. The United States failed to take membership in the League, but by 1928 the organization had a total membership of 54. The machinery of the League consisted of an Assembly of all the member nations, acting through agents of their governments; a council on which the great powers were permanently represented and to which the other member powers were elected by the Assembly for three-year terms; a Secretariat to administer the internal affairs of the League; and a number of specialized agencies, such as the International Labour Organisation, that were responsible for implementing various economic and humanitarian programs on an international basis. The Covenant required that international disputes be submitted to peaceful settlement with a provision for adjudication or arbitration by the Permanent Court of International Justice or for intervention by the Council of the League. The Covenant also provided for the use of financial and economic penalties, such as embargoes, to enforce the decisions of the League and for joint military action against convicted aggressors. In practice, however, the League failed its most important tests and was unable to master the crises that led to World War II and its own collapse.

Confederations. Confederations are voluntary associations of independent states that, to secure some common purpose, agree to certain limitations on their freedom of action and establish some joint machinery of consultation or deliberation. The limitations on the freedom of action of the member states may be as trivial as an acknowledgment of their duty to consult with each other before taking some independent action or as significant as the obligation to be bound by majority decisions of the member states. Confederations usually fail to provide for an effective executive authority and lack viable central governments; their member states typically retain their separate military establishments and separate diplomatic representation; and members are generally accorded equal status with an acknowledged right of secession from the confederation. Historically, confederations have often proved to be a first or second step toward the establishment of a national state, usually as a federal union. Thus, the federal union of modern Switzerland was preceded by a confederation of the Swiss cantons; West Germany's modern federal arrangements may be traced to the German Confederation of the 19th century (the Deutsche Bund); and the federal constitution of the United States is the successor to the government of the Articles of Confederation. In some other cases confederations have replaced more centralized arrangements, as, for example, when empires disintegrate and are replaced by voluntary associations of their former colonies. The British Commonwealth, or Commonwealth of Nations, and the French Community are cases of this type.

An example of confederal arrangements that gave birth to a federal union is the Articles of Confederation (1781–89) that preceded the Constitution of the United States. The Articles established a Congress of the confederation as a unicameral assembly of ambassadors from the 13 states, each possessing a single vote. The Congress was authorized to appoint an executive committee of states

Ancient and modern empires

The League of Nations

The Articles of Confederation

to execute, in the recess of Congress, such of the powers of Congress as the United States, in Congress assembled, by the consent of nine States, shall from time to time think expedient to vest them with;

in turn, the committee of states could appoint a presiding officer or president for a term of one year. The Congress could also appoint such other committees and "civil officers as may be necessary for managing the general affairs of the United States," and was given the authority to serve as "the last resort or appeal in all disputes and differences, now subsisting or that hereafter may arise between two or more states." Although the Congress was given authority in important areas such as the regulation of foreign affairs, the establishment of coinage and weights and measures, the appointment of officers in the confederation's land and naval forces, and the issuance of bills of credit, all its powers were in fact dependent for their enforcement upon the states. The Congress lacked both an independent source of revenue and the executive machinery to enforce its will directly upon individuals. As the language of the Articles summarized the situation,

each State retains its sovereignty, freedom and independence, and every power, jurisdiction and right, which is not by this Confederation expressly delegated to the United States in Congress assembled.

The Commonwealth of Nations

The Commonwealth of Nations is an example of a confederation born as the result of the decentralization and eventual disintegration of an empire. A number of former British colonies and dominions, together with the United Kingdom, composed the commonwealth in 1972: Australia, Barbados, Botswana, Canada, Cyprus, Fiji, The Gambia, Ghana, Guyana, India, Jamaica, Kenya, Lesotho, Malaŵi, Malaysia, Malta, Mauritius, Nauru, New Zealand, Nigeria, Sierra Leone, Singapore, Sri Lanka (Ceylon), Swaziland, Tanzania, Tonga, Trinidad and Tobago, Uganda, Western Samoa, and Zambia. Ireland and South Africa had seceded from the commonwealth, and Rhodesia's status was unclear after a lengthy dispute with Britain and the other member nations. All Commonwealth states recognized the Queen as the head of the commonwealth. Barbados, Canada, Jamaica, Malta, and Trinidad and Tobago were monarchies in which the Queen was represented by a governor general appointed on the recommendation of the government of the country concerned and acting in accord with its own constitutional practice; Botswana, Cyprus, Ghana, India, Kenya, Nigeria, Sri Lanka, Tanzania, and Zambia were republics; Malaysia and Lesotho had their own sovereigns; and Uganda had a prime minister who was head of state. Commonwealth governments were represented in the capitals of other commonwealth countries by high commissioners equal in status to ambassadors. The nations of the commonwealth rarely acted in concert on the international scene, and, despite fairly regular meetings of the commonwealth prime ministers, there were at times severe strains in the relations among several of the member states. The fairly general use of the English language and of English common law, together with some common symbols and remaining cultural affinities, appeared to be the major ties binding together this loose association of former British imperial possessions.

Federations. The term federation is used to refer to groupings of states, often on a regional basis, that establish central executive machinery to implement policies or to supervise joint activities. In some cases such groupings are motivated primarily by political or economic concerns; in others, military objectives are paramount. Examples of the former include the association of Belgium, France, The Netherlands, Italy, Luxembourg, and West Germany in what is usually referred to as the Western European Community but is actually a combination of three main structures—the European Coal and Steel Community, established in 1952; the European Economic Community (Common Market), established in 1958; and the European Atomic Energy Community (Euratom), established in 1958. The Community quickly developed executive machinery exercising significant regulatory and directive authority over the governments and private business firms of the member countries. Although each of the member governments retains a substantial measure of sovereignty,

The Western European Community

and a systematic effort by one or more of the governments to resist the authority of the Community's agencies could endanger the whole fabric of cooperative effort, the Community has developed significant supranational features. These include the staffing of executive organs with persons other than governmental representatives, the making of binding decisions on important matters by majority vote, and the capability of the Community agencies to deal directly and authoritatively with individuals and companies within the member states. For example, the high authority of the Coal and Steel Community acts by majority vote of its members, without instruction from any of the governments, to "assure the achievement of the purposes stated in the Treaty"; and in pursuing this function it involves itself deeply in the economies of each of the member nations.

The North Atlantic Treaty Organization (NATO), established in April 1949, is an example of a modern military alliance endowed with complex and permanent executive machinery, employing multilateral procedures, and involving the continuous elaboration of plans for the conduct of joint military action by its member states (Belgium, Canada, Denmark, Greece, Iceland, Italy, Luxembourg, The Netherlands, Norway, Portugal, Turkey, the United Kingdom, the United States, and West Germany; France is associated with the NATO nations for some purposes). As stated in its treaty, the purpose of NATO is to maintain the security of the North Atlantic area by exercise of the right of collective security recognized in the Charter of the United Nations. An impressive array of institutional mechanisms was established, including a secretary general and a permanent staff, a council, a network of committees, a military command structure, various study groups, and liaison staffs; and an ongoing system of collaboration in planning and joint military exercises was brought into being. With the continued development of its organization, NATO gradually added a number of economic and cultural activities to its functions until it came to possess several of the features of multipurpose supranational organization.

The United Nations organization. A supranational political system that does not fit precisely any of the conventional classifications of such systems is the United Nations, a voluntary association of most of the world's nation-states. Its membership had grown from an original 51 states to a total of 130 in 1971, when the government of the People's Republic of China was admitted in place of the government of the Republic of China (Taiwan). Founded at a conference in San Francisco in 1945 attended by representatives of all the nations that had declared war on Germany or Japan, the purposes of the organization are declared in its Charter to be the maintenance of international peace and security, the development of friendly relations among states, and international cooperation in solving the political, economic, social, cultural, and humanitarian problems of the world. Its organizational structure consists of a Security Council of five permanent members (China, France, the Soviet Union, the United Kingdom, and the United States) and ten nonpermanent members elected for two-year terms, a General Assembly, a Secretary General and a Secretariat, an Economic and Social Council, a Trusteeship Council, and the International Court of Justice. Attached to the United Nations are a number of specialized agencies, including the Food and Agriculture Organization, the International Atomic Energy Agency, the International Civil Aviation Organization, the International Labour Organisation, the International Monetary Fund, the International Telecommunications Union, the Universal Postal Union, the United Nations Educational, Scientific and Cultural Organization, the World Health Organization, and the International Bank for Reconstruction and Development (World Bank).

The present world association

Aside from the rather generally stated and decidedly elusive aims of the Charter, the member states of the United Nations cannot be said to have any common goal; they lack even the unity that a common external threat to security brings to many supranational organizations. There is also difficulty in reaching and implementing decisions. Two different formulas are employed for voting in the two principal organs, the General Assembly and the Security Council. In the General Assembly a two-thirds majority decides on important matters; but, since the Assembly's decisions are not binding and are merely recommendations, this qualified majority principle must be viewed as of little significance. Although, on the other hand, the decisions of the Security Council may be binding, a unanimous vote of all five of the permanent members joined by the votes of at least four of the nonpermanent members is required; whenever important questions of peace and security are at stake, it is rarely possible to achieve agreement among the five great powers of the council. These difficulties, which might be fatal to the survival of many supranational organizations, are not in fact totally debilitating. The United Nations continues to serve as a very important forum for international debate and negotiation, and its specialized agencies play an important role in what is sometimes referred to as "the functional approach to peace."

NATIONAL POLITICAL SYSTEMS

The term nation-state is used so commonly but defined so variously that it will be well to indicate its usage in this article with some precision and to give historical and contemporary examples of nation-states. To begin with, there is no single basis upon which such systems are established. Many states were formed at a point in time when a people sharing a common history, culture, and language discovered a sense of identity. This was true in the cases of England and France, which were the first nation-states to emerge in the modern period, and of Italy and Germany, which were established as nation-states in the 19th century. In contrast, however, other states, such as India, the Soviet Union, and Switzerland, have come into existence without a common basis in race, culture, or language. It must also be emphasized that contemporary nation-states are creations of different historical periods and of very varied circumstances. Before the close of the 19th century the effective mobilization of governmental powers on a national basis had occurred only in Europe, the United States, and Japan. It was not until the 20th century and the collapse of the Ottoman, Habsburg, French, and British empires that the world could be fully organized on a national basis. In 1920 the League of Nations recognized seven nation-states as "Great Powers" (Britain, France, the United States, Germany, Italy, Japan, and Russia) and eventually admitted more than 40 other states to membership; in 1946 the United Nations admitted 51 states to membership, but the number had grown to 130 by 1971. The nation-states in today's world include the three "superpowers," the United States, the Soviet Union, and China; the established powers of second rank, Britain, France, Japan, and West Germany; emerging powers such as India and Indochina; and a host of old and new lesser states, such as Denmark, The Gambia, Switzerland, Cyprus, Belgium, Malaysia, Norway, Chile, and others.

The characteristics that qualify these variously composed and historically differing entities as nation-states and distinguish them from other forms of social and political organization amount in sum to the independent power to compel obedience from the populations within their territories. The state is, in other words, a territorial association that may range in size from the Soviet Union to Singapore, in population from China to Luxembourg, and that claims supremacy over all other associations within its boundaries. As an association, the state is peculiar in several respects: membership is compulsory for its citizens; it claims a monopoly of the use of armed force within its borders; and its officers, who are the government of the state, claim the right to act in the name of the land and its people.

A definition of the state in terms only of its powers over its members is not wholly satisfactory, however. Although all states make a claim to supremacy within their boundaries, they differ widely in their ability to make good their claims. States are, in fact, often challenged by competing associations within their boundaries; their supremacy is often more formal than real; and they are sometimes unable to maintain their existence. Moreover, a definition in

terms of power alone ignores the fact that there are great differences among states in the structures they employ for the exercise of power, in the ways they use power, and in the ends to which they turn their power. Some of these differences are explored in the discussion that follows of two general categories of nation-states: the unitary state and the federal state. Partly from administrative necessity and partly because of the pressures of territorial interests, nearly all modern states provide for some distribution of governmental authority on a territorial basis. Systems in which power is delegated from the central government to subnational units and in which the grant of power may be rescinded at the will of the central government are termed unitary systems. Systems in which a balance is established between two autonomous sets of governments, one national and the other provincial, are termed federal. In federal systems, the provincial units are usually empowered to grant and take away the authority of their own subunits in the same manner as national governments in unitary systems. Thus, although the United States is federally organized at the national level, each of the 50 states is in a unitary relationship to the cities and local governments within its own territory.

Unitary nation-states. A majority of all the world's nation-states are unitary systems, including Belgium, Bulgaria, France, Great Britain, The Netherlands, Japan, Poland, Romania, the Scandinavian countries, Spain, and many of the Latin American and African countries. There are great differences among these unitary states, however, in the institutions and procedures through which their central governments interact with their territorial subunits.

In one type of unitary system, decentralization of power among subnational governments goes so far that in practice, although not in constitutional principle, they resemble federal arrangements. In Britain, for example, there are important elements of regional autonomy in the relationship between Northern Ireland, Wales, and Scotland and the national government in London; and the complex system of elected local governments, although in constitutional theory subject to abrogation by Parliament, is in practice a fixed and fairly formidable part of the apparatus of British government. In other unitary systems of this type, decentralization on a territorial basis is actually provided for constitutionally, and the powers of locally elected officials are prescribed in detail. Thus, the Japanese constitution specifies certain autonomous functions to be performed by local administrative authorities.

A second type of unitary system makes substantially less provision for territorial decentralization of authority and employs rather strict procedures for the central supervision of locally elected governments. The classic example of this type is France. The French administrative system is built around 95 *départements,* each headed by a *préfet,* and 322 subdivisions of the *départements,* termed *arrondissements,* each headed by a *sous-préfet.* The *préfets* and *sous-préfets* are appointed by the government in Paris to serve as agents of the central government and also as the executives of the divisional governments or councils, which are composed of elected officials. The system thus combines central supervision of local affairs through appointed officers with territorial representation through locally elected governments.

A third type of unitary system provides for only token decentralization. In such cases, the officials responsible for managing the affairs of the territorial subdivisions are appointees of the central government, and the role of locally elected officers is either minimal or nonexistent. Examples of this kind of arrangement include Germany under Adolf Hitler and also several Communist countries. The Third Reich was divided into 42 *Gaue,* each headed by a gauleiter chosen for his personal loyalty to Hitler; in eastern Europe, the people's councils or people's committees are named by the centrally organized Communist parties; their appointment is confirmed by elections in which one slate of candidates is presented.

Federal systems. In federal systems, political authority is divided between two autonomous sets of governments, one national and the other subnational, both of which operate directly upon the people. Usually a constitutional

The nation-state defined

Decentralization of power in unitary states

division of power is established between the national government, which exercises authority over the whole national territory, and provincial governments that exercise independent authority within their own territories. Of the eight largest countries in the world, seven—Argentina, Australia, Brazil, Canada, India, the Soviet Union, and the United States—are organized on a federal basis. Federal states also include Austria, Cameroon, Czechoslovakia, Libya, Malaysia, Mexico, Nigeria, Switzerland, Tanzania, Venezuela, West Germany, and Yugoslavia.

The governmental structures and political processes found in these federal systems show great variety. One may distinguish, first, a number of systems in which federal arrangements reflect rather clear-cut cultural divisions. A classic case of this type is Switzerland, where the people speak four different languages—German, French, Italian, and Romansh—and the federal system unites 26 historically and culturally different entities, known as cantons and demicantons. The Swiss constitution of 1848, as modified in 1874, converted a confederation originally formed in the 13th century by the three forest cantons of Uri, Schwyz, and Unterwalden into the modern federal state. The principal agencies of federal government are a bicameral legislature, composed of a National Council representing the people directly and a Council of States representing the constituent members as entities; an executive branch (Bundesrat) elected by both houses of the legislature in joint session; and a supreme court that renders decisions on matters affecting cantonal and federal relations. The Soviet Union's federal arrangements, although of a markedly different kind, also reflect underlying cultural and linguistic differences among the 15 union republics. The member republics of the Union of Soviet Socialist Republics are constitutionally endowed with territorial autonomy, a "right to secession," and equal representation in the Supreme Soviet. Ethnic subdivisions within the 15 union republics are also granted territorial autonomy and direct representation in the upper chamber of the Supreme Soviet. These arrangements, however, are rather more important in Soviet constitutional theory than in practice, since, in addition to the virtual monopoly of military, economic, and social controls vested in the central government, more than half the population and territory of the Soviet Union lies within one member republic, the Russian Socialist Federated Soviet Republic.

In other systems, federal arrangements are found in conjunction with a large measure of cultural homogeneity. The Constitution of the United States delegates certain activities that concern the whole people, such as the conduct of foreign relations and war and the regulation of interstate commerce and foreign trade to the federal government; certain other functions are shared between the federal government and the states; and the remainder are reserved to the states. Although these arrangements require two separate bodies of political officers, two judicial systems, and two systems of taxation, they also allow extensive interaction between the federal government and the states. Thus, the election of Congress and the President, the process of amending the Constitution, the levying of taxes, and innumerable other functions necessitate cooperation between the two levels of government and bring them into a tightly interlocking relationship.

SUBNATIONAL POLITICAL SYSTEMS

Although national government is the dominant form of political organization in the modern world, an extraordinary range of political forms exists below the national level—tribal communities, the intimate political associations of villages and towns, the governments of regions and provinces, the complex array of urban and suburban governments, and the great political and administrative systems of the cities and the metropolises. These subnational entities are, in a sense, the basic political communities—the foundation on which all national political systems are built.

Tribal communities. The typical organization of mankind in its early history was the tribe. Today, in many parts of the world, the tribal community is still a major form of human political organization. Even in advanced

systems, traces can still be found of its influence. Some of the *Länder* of modern Germany, such as Bavaria, Saxony, or Westphalia, have maintained their identity since the days of the Germanic tribal settlements. In England, too, many county boundaries can be explained only by reference to the territorial divisions in the period after the end of the Roman occupation.

In many of the new states of Africa, the tribe is still the effective community and a principal vehicle of political consciousness. Most of these states are the successors to the administrative units established by colonial regimes and owe their present boundaries to the often arbitrary decisions of imperial bureaucracies or to the territorial accommodations of rival colonial powers. The result was often the splintering of the tribal communities or their aggregation in largely artificial entities. That the force of tribalism is far from exhausted is suggested by the experience of Nigeria and other new states where a resurgence of tribal rivalries has presented great obstacles to the process of nation building.

In its primary sense, the tribe is a community organized in terms of kinship, and its subdivisions are the intimate kindred groupings of moieties, gentes, and totem groups. Its territorial basis is rarely defined with any precision, and its institutions are typically the undifferentiated and intermittent structures of an omnifunctional social system. The leadership of the tribe is provided by the group of adult males, the lineage elders acting as tribal chiefs, the village headmen, or the shamans, or tribal magicians. These groups and individuals are the guardians of the tribal customs and of an oral tradition of law. Law is thus not made but rather invoked; its repository is the collective memory of the tribal council or chief men. This kind of customary law, sanctioned and hallowed by religious belief, nevertheless changes and develops, for each time it is declared something may be added or omitted to meet the needs of the occasion.

Rural communities. The village has traditionally been contrasted with the city: the village is the home of rural occupations and tied to the cycles of agricultural life, while the inhabitants of the city practice many trades, and its economy is founded on commerce and industry; the village is an intimate association of families, while the city is the locus of a mass population; the culture of the village is simple and traditional, while the city is the centre of the arts and sciences and of a complex cultural development. The village and the city offer even sharper contrasts as political communities. Historically, the village has been ruled by the primitive democracy of face-to-face discussion in the village council or by a headman whose decisions are supported by village elders or by other cooperative modes of government; urban government has never been such a simple matter, and monarchical, tyrannical, aristocratic, and oligarchic forms of rule have all flourished in the city. In the village, the boundaries among political, economic, religious, and other forms of action have not been as clearly drawn as in cities.

The origins and development of the apparatus of government can be seen most clearly in the simple political society of the rural community. The transformation of kinbound societies with their informal, folk-sustained systems of sociopolitical organization into differentiated, hierarchical societies with complex political structures began with the enlargement of the rural community—an increase in its population, the diversification of its economy, or its interaction with other communities. The rudimentary organs of communal government were then elaborated, the communal functions received more specialized direction, and leadership roles were institutionalized. This was sometimes a process that led by gradual stages to the growth of cities. Elsewhere, however, as in the case of ancient Attica, the city was established as the result of a process of *synoikismos,* or the uniting of a number of tribal or village communities. This was undoubtedly the origin of Athens, and, according to its legendary history, Rome also was established as a result of the forcible unification of the tribes that dwelt on the hills surrounding the Palatine Hill.

Even in the nation-states of today's world, the contrasts between the village or the town and the city as centres of

Margin notes:

The Swiss and Soviet systems

Basic political communities

Importance of kinship in tribal societies

human activity are readily apparent. In the country, life is more intimate, the human contacts more informal, the structure of society more stable. In the city, the individual becomes anonymous, the contacts between people are mainly formal, and the standing of the individual or the family in society is subject to rapid change. In many contemporary systems, however, the differences in the forms of government of rural and urban communities appear to be growing less pronounced. In the United States, for example, rural institutions have been seriously weakened by the movement of large numbers of people to the city. The township meeting of New England and other forms of direct citizen participation in the affairs of the community have declined in importance and have often been displaced by more formal structures and the growth of local governmental bureaucracies.

Cities. Cities first emerged as complex forms of social and political organization in the valleys of the Euphrates and the Tigris, the Nile, the Yellow River, and the Yangtze. These early cities broke dramatically with the patterns of primitive life and the rural societies from which they sprang. Kinship as the basis of society was replaced with status determined by class and occupation; the primitive magical leaders of the tribe were displaced by temple priesthoods presiding over highly developed religious institutions and functioning as important agencies of social control; earlier systems of rule by the tribal chieftains and the simple forms of communal leadership gave way to kingships endowed with magical powers and important religious functions; and specialized functionaries in the royal courts became responsible for supervising new kinds of governmental activity. Many other developments contributed to the growing centralization of power in these city civilizations. Barter was replaced by more effective systems of exchange, and the wealth generated in commerce and the specialized city trades became both an object of taxation and an instrument of power. Class distinctions emerged as the result of a division of labour and advances in technical development. A military order and a professional soldiery were created and trained in new techniques of warfare, and a slave class provided the work force for large-scale projects of irrigation, fortification, and royal architecture. As these developments proceeded, the city was able to project its power even further into the surrounding countryside, to establish its rule over villages and other cities in its sphere, and finally to become the centre of such early empires as those of Sumeria, Egypt, China, Babylonia, Assyria, and Persia.

The Greek polis A very different form of city life emerged among the Greeks. The Greek polis also broke with the folkways of primitive society, but its political development was in striking contrast to the despotism of the Oriental city empires and their massive concentrations of power in the hands of king and priest. As the polis transcended its origins in village life, the powers of the tribal chief dwindled and passed into the hands of aristocratic families. The kingship of Homeric tradition vanished, the "kings" who remained became mere dignitaries in the religious and ceremonial life of the city, and new magistracies and other civic offices were founded. These offices became the focus of factional struggle among the aristocratic families and, later, with the weakening of aristocratic rule, the chief prizes in a contest of power between the nobility and the common citizens. Eventually, these developments issued in the characteristic form of Greek city government. A citizen body, always a much narrower group than the total population but often as numerous as the population of freeborn males, acquired power in the direction of the city government through the election of its officers and direct participation in the city councils. Although often interrupted by episodes of oligarchic or tyrannical rule and by periods of civic dissension and class rivalry, the main theme of governmental development in the Greek city was the elaboration of structures that permitted the control of political affairs by its citizens.

The medieval city Autonomous cities also sprang up in Europe in the later Middle Ages. Medieval city life, although it differed from that of the polis and was coloured by the forms of feudal society, also emphasized the principle of cooperative association. Indeed, for the first time in the history of city civilization, the majority of the inhabitants of the city were free. The development of trades, the growth of commerce, and the mobilization of wealth emancipated the city from its feudal environment, and the merchant and craft guilds became the matrices of a new kind of city democracy. In time, the guilds were transformed into closed corporations and became a basis for oligarchic control; and the city's independence was threatened by the rise of the new nation-states. Tempting targets for the ambition of kings, Venice, Genoa, Florence, Milan, Cologne, Amsterdam, Hamburg, and other free cities of Europe eventually succumbed to monarchical control. Theirs was an important legacy, however, for the political order of the medieval city was a powerful influence in the development of the constitutional structures of the modern democratic state.

Modern cities Although cities are no longer independent, the almost universal increase in urban population has made them more important than ever before as centres of human activity. The political organization of modern cities differs from country to country. Even within the same nation-state, there are often important contrasts in the structures of city government. In the United States, for example, three principal types of city government are usually distinguished: the council–manager form, the mayor–council form, and the commission form.

More than half of all American cities with populations of between 25,000 and 250,000 operate under council–manager governments. In council–manager systems the council is generally small, elected at large on a nonpartisan ballot for overlapping four-year terms; no other offices are directly elected, and the mayor, who presides at council meetings and performs mainly ceremonial functions, is chosen by the council from among its members. The manager, a professional city administrator, is selected by the council, serves at the council's pleasure, and is responsible for supervising the city departments and municipal programs, preparing the budget, and controlling expenditures.

Mayor–council governments are found in two basic forms, the "weak" mayor and the "strong" mayor. The former was typical of the 19th-century municipal organization and is now mainly confined to cities of less than 25,000 population; the latter is a common arrangement in cities with populations of more than 5,000,000. In weak-mayor–council governments, a number of officials, elected or appointed for lengthy terms, wield important administrative powers; the council, typically elected by divisions of the city called wards, is responsible for the direction of the major city agencies; and the mayor's powers of appointment and removal and his control over the city budget are severely limited. In many cases, strong-mayor–council governments evolved from weak-mayor–council systems as an independently elected mayor won the power of veto over council ordinances, strengthened his control over appointment and removal, and established himself as the city's chief budgetary officer; at the same time, also, the elective administrative officers and the semi-autonomous appointive boards and commissions were often eliminated and the number of councilmen reduced.

The commission plan, which is now found in fewer than 200 cities of more than 10,000 population, concentrates legislative and executive powers in the hands of a small group of commissioners. The commissioners serve individually as the heads of administrative departments and choose one of their number to act as a ceremonial mayor without executive authority.

The variety in the governmental structures of American cities is paralleled in many other countries, for everywhere in the modern world the government of the city continues to challenge man's political invention. Although no longer sovereign, cities are the centres of modern civilization and, both in terms of the services demanded of them and the range and importance of the functions they exercise, the most important of contemporary subnational political systems. Moreover, it is in the cities that most of the problems of modern industrial society seem to have their focus. These problems are not only governmental but also technological, cultural, and economic. They are found in their most acute form in the great metropolitan centres and in that vast urban agglomeration known as the megalopolis. In political terms, the issue that is posed appears to be whether these huge centres of population can continue as effective communities with democratically manageable governments.

Regions. In many contemporary national political systems the forces of history and administrative necessity have joined to produce regional communities at an intermediate level between the local and the national community. In some cases—the Swiss canton, the English county, the German *Land,* and the American state—these regional communities possess their own political institutions and exercise governmental functions. In other cases, however, the territorial community is a product of ethnic, cultural, linguistic, physiographic, or economic factors and maintains its identity without the support of political structures.

Regional communities

As subnational political systems, regional communities are sometimes based in tradition, even tracing their origin to a period prior to the founding of the nation; in other cases, they are modern administrative units created by national governments for their own purposes. Examples of both types may be found in the history of regionalism in France and its complex pattern of internal territorial divisions. Before the French Revolution, France was divided into ancient provinces—Burgundy, Gascony, Brittany, Normandy, Provence, Anjou, Poitou, and others. After the Revolution, in what seems to have been an effort to discourage regional patriotism and threats of separatism, the Napoleonic government superimposed a new regional structure of *départements* on the old provincial map. More than a century and a half later, in the era of rapid communications and national economic planning, the French national government announced a regrouping of the Napoleonic *départements* into much larger Gaullist *régions.* Recognizing, perhaps, the continuing strength of the provincial attachments of Gascon, Breton, Norman, and Provençal and the survival of old regional folk cultures with their distinctive patterns of speech, the new *régions* were given boundaries similar in many cases to the traditional provincial boundaries of pre-republican France.

The history of the French regional communities is not a special case, for political, administrative, economic, and technical forces have led many other national governments to replace traditional territorial divisions with new regional units. In England, for example, the traditional structure of county governments (52 in number) was replaced by a system of administrative counties (61 plus London); and, in 1969, a royal commission proposed a further reform that would abolish 39 counties. Attempts have also been made to use older regional communities as the infrastructure for new systems of regional government. Thus, the Italian constitution provides for semi-autonomous government in five special regions—Valle d'Aosta, Sardinia, Sicily, Trentino-Alto Adige, and Friuli-Venezia Giulia—which, in different ways, are historically distinct from the rest of Italy. In yet other cases the fear of competition from regional governments or of separatist movements has led national governments to make various efforts to resist the development of regional political structures. Again, Italy provides a convenient example, for its constitution requires the establishment of 14 other autonomous regions, but Italian governments refused to implement this provision of the 1947 constitution until recently. It should be noted that the Italian republic of 1870–1922 and its Fascist successor state also made similar efforts to combat regional political development, the former by the creation of a large number of administrative provinces and the latter by establishing *corporazione* to represent occupations regardless of geographic location.

In several modern states the growth of vast conurbations and the rise of the megalopolis have prompted the development of new kinds of regional governmental structures. The Port of London Authority, the Port of New York Authority, and the San Francisco Bay Area Transit Authority are examples of regional systems designed to serve the needs of urban communities that have outgrown the boundaries of existing city governments. New regional structures have also resulted from the increased responsibility of national governments for the administration of comprehensive social and economic programs. The Tennessee Valley Authority, for example, is both a national agency and a regional government whose decisions affect the lives of the inhabitants of all the states and cities in its sphere. Other examples of new regional administrative structures include the zonal councils established in India for social and economic planning purposes, the districts of the Interstate Commerce Commission in the United States, and the governmental and economic units established in Britain to deal with the problems of industrially depressed areas.

ISSUES OF CLASSIFICATION

The almost infinite range of political systems has been barely suggested in this brief review. Confronted by the vast array of political forms, political scientists have attempted to classify and categorize, to develop typologies and models, or in some other way to bring analytic order to the bewildering variety of data. Many different schemes have been developed. There is, for example, the classical distinction between governments in terms of the number of rulers—government by one man (monarchy or tyranny), government by the few (aristocracy or oligarchy), and government by the many (democracy). There are schemes classifying governments in terms of their key institutions (for example, parliamentarism, cabinet government, presidentialism). There are classifications that group systems according to basic principles of political authority or the forms of legitimacy (charismatic, traditional, rational–legal, and others). Other schemes distinguish between different kinds of economic organization in the system (the laissez-faire state, the corporate state, and Socialist and Communist forms of state economic organization) or between the rule of different economic classes (feudal, bourgeois, and capitalist). And there are modern efforts to compare the functions of political systems (capabilities, conversion functions, and system maintenance and adaptation functions) and to classify them in terms of structure, function, and political culture.

Approaches to the analysis of political systems

Although none is comprehensive, each of these principles of analysis has some validity, and the classifying schemes that are based on them, although in some cases no longer relevant to modern forms of political organization, have often been a major influence on the course of political development. The most influential of such classifying schemes is undoubtedly the attempt of Plato and Aristotle to define the basic forms of government in terms of the number of power holders and their use or abuse of power. Plato held that there was a natural succession of the forms of government: an aristocracy (the ideal form of government by the few) that abuses its power develops into a timocracy (in which the rule of the best men, who value wisdom as the highest political good, is succeeded by the rule of men who are primarily concerned with honour and martial virtue), which through greed develops into an oligarchy (the perverted form of government by the few), which in turn is succeeded by a democracy (rule by the many); through excess, the democracy becomes an anarchy (a lawless government), to which a tyrant is inevitably the successor. Abuse of power in the Platonic typology is defined by the rulers' neglect or rejection of the prevailing law or custom (*nomos*); the ideal forms are thus *nomos* observing (*ennomon*), and the perverted forms are *nomos* neglecting (*paranomon*). Although disputing the character of this implacable succession of the forms of government, Aristotle also based his classification on the number of rulers and distinguished between good and bad forms of government. In his typology it was the rulers' concern for the common good that distinguished the ideal from perverted forms of government. The ideal forms in the Aristotelian scheme are monarchy, aristocracy, and polity (a term conveying some of the meaning of the modern concept of "constitutional democracy"); when perverted by the selfish abuse of power, they are transformed respectively into tyranny, oligarchy, and ochlocracy (or the mob rule of lawless democracy). The concept of the polity, a "mixed" or blended constitutional order, fascinated political theorists for another millennium. To achieve its advantages, innumerable writers from Polybius to St. Thomas

Aquinas experimented with the construction of models giving to each social class the control of appropriate institutions of government.

Another very influential classifying scheme was the distinction between monarchies and republics. In the writings of Machiavelli and others, the tripartism of classical typologies was replaced by the dichotomy of princely and republican rule. Sovereignty in the monarchy or the principality is in the hands of a single ruler; in republics, sovereignty is vested in a plurality or collectivity of power holders. Reducing aristocracy and democracy to the single category of republican rule, Machiavelli also laid the basis in his analysis of the exercise of princely power for a further distinction between despotic and nondespotic forms of government. In the work of Montesquieu, for example, despotism, or the lawless exercise of power by the single ruler, is contrasted with the constitutional forms of government of the monarchy and the republic. As a result of the decline of monarchies and the rise of new totalitarian states terming themselves republics, this traditional classification is now, of course, of little more than historical interest.

The usefulness of all the traditional classifications has been undermined by the momentous changes in the political organization of the modern world. Typologies based on the number of power holders or the formal structures of the state are rendered almost meaningless by the standardization of "democratic" forms, the deceptive similarities in the constitutional claims and governmental institutions of regimes that actually differ markedly in their political practices, and the rise of new political orders in the non-Western world. A number of modern writers have attempted to overcome this difficulty by constructing classifying schemes that give primary importance to social, cultural, economic, or psychological factors. The most influential of such schemes is the Marxist typology, which classifies types of rule on the basis of economic class divisions and defines the ruling class as that which controls the means of production in the state. A monistic typology that also emphasized the importance of a ruling class was developed by an Italian theorist of the early 20th century, Gaetano Mosca. In Mosca's writings all forms of government appear as mere facades for oligarchy or the rule of a political "elite" that centres power in its own hands. Another classification, which distinguishes between "legitimate" and "revolutionary" governments, was suggested by Mosca's contemporary Guglielmo Ferrero. Using a sociopsychological approach to the relations between rulers and ruled, Ferrero held that a legitimate government is one whose citizens voluntarily accept its rule and freely give it their loyalty; in revolutionary systems, the government fears the people and is feared by them. Legitimacy and leadership are also the basis of a typology developed by the German sociologist Max Weber. In Weber's scheme there are three basic types of rule: charismatic, in which the authority or legitimacy of the ruler rests upon some genuine sense of calling and in which the followers submit because of their faith or conviction in the ruler's exemplary character; traditional, in which, as in hereditary monarchy, leadership authority is historically or traditionally accepted; and rational–legal, in which leadership authority is the outgrowth of a legal order that has been effectively rationalized and where there is a prevailing belief in the legality of normative rules or commands. The Weberian typology has been elaborated by a number of recent writers who have found it particularly useful for comparing and classifying the emergent political orders of the non-Western world.

A serviceable classification of political systems must penetrate beneath formal appearances to underlying realities; these realities, however, do not consist only of the facts of social and economic organization. Important differences often exist between political systems having very similar socioeconomic structures. That is why some recent sociological classifications and schemes of analysis fail as tools of political inquiry: they cannot effectively distinguish between certain societies whose political orders are full of contrasts. The political system itself must be the primary focus of inquiry and the phenomena of politics

the principal facts of investigation. Such an approach may involve many different kinds of analysis, but it must begin with an examination of the ways in which power is acquired and transferred, exercised, and controlled. This is important for comparing advanced political orders and also for drawing important distinctions between regimes in the underdeveloped areas of the world.

GOVERNMENTS CLASSIFIED BY MODE OF SUCCESSION

A key problem of all political orders is that of succession. "The king is dead; long live the king" was the answer, not always uncontested, of European hereditary monarchy to the question of who should rule after the death of the king. A second, closely related problem is in what manner and by whom a present ruler may be replaced or deprived of power. To this second question hereditary monarchy gave no definite answer, although the concept of *diffidatio*, or the severance of the bond of allegiance between king and feudal lord, was invoked more than once in the medieval period. Political systems, even those of primitive tribal societies, have approached both problems in a variety of ways. Anthropological records show that tribal chiefs or kings were sometimes selected as a result of ritual tests or the display of magical signs and proofs of divine origin, usually as determined by the tribal elders or magical leaders; in other cases, a principle of heredity, often diluted by a choice among heirs in terms of physique or warrior ability, was applied; in still other cases, the chief was elected, often from among the adult males of a select group of families. Techniques for the removal of tribal rulers were equally varied. Sometimes the ruler would be killed after a specified period or when his magical powers weakened or when his physical prowess or health failed; in other cases the chief was exposed to periodic tests of his magical powers or required to accept challenges to combat from other qualified candidates for rule; and in some cases the elders could remove him from office.

Techniques for assuring the succession are also varied in the modern world. Succession procedures range from the complex hieratic process of identifying a reincarnated Dalai Lama, which was practiced until quite recently in Tibet, to the subtle, informal procedures by which parliamentary majorities choose a successor to the office of prime minister in Britain. In fact, however, the succession practices of modern political systems appear to be of four main types: (1) heredity, (2) constitutional prescription, (3) election, and (4) force.

Hereditary succession. Although dictators still occasionally seek to establish their sons as their heirs, they usually rely on force rather than the claims of heredity to achieve their object. Apart from a few states, mostly in the Arab world, where the dynastic ruler is the effective head of the government, the hereditary principle of succession is now almost exclusively confined to the constitutional monarchies of western Europe. There is some irony in the fact that the line of succession is more securely established in these monarchies now than at any point in their earlier history: intradynastic struggle, it appears, is much less likely when kingship is mainly ceremonial. Heredity may be reinforced or modified by constitutional prescription: this was the case, for example, of the famous Act of Settlement that secured the Hanoverian succession in Britain.

Succession by constitutional prescription. A leading example of succession by constitutional prescription is the United States. Article II, Section 1, of the Constitution of the U.S. provides:

In case of the removal of the President from office, or of his death, resignation, or inability to discharge the powers and duties of the said office, the same shall devolve on the Vice President, and the Congress may by law provide for the case of removal, death, resignation, or inability, both of the President and Vice President, declaring what officer shall then act as President, and such officer shall act accordingly, until the disability be removed, or a President shall be elected.

A constitutional amendment was ratified in 1967 elaborating these procedures to include further arrangements for dealing with the problem of presidential disability. The original language of the Constitution has been the basis for the peaceful succession of Vice Presidents John

Modern classifying systems (margin note)

Tyler, Millard Fillmore, Andrew Johnson, Chester Arthur, Theodore Roosevelt, Calvin Coolidge, Harry S. Truman, and Lyndon Johnson. Constitutionally prescribed arrangements for assuring the succession are not always so successful, and many states whose constitutions contain very similar provisions have experienced succession crises that were resolved only by violence.

Succession by election. Election is a principle of succession also frequently combined with force. In cases of closely contested elections or where there is doubt as to the validity or proper form of the election, the result is often a disputed succession. The Great Schism in the papacy in the 14th century and the disputed succession to the elective kingship of Hungary in the 16th century are instructive examples of the failure of elective systems to assure an orderly succession. Force is also the effective basis of succession in several contemporary states in which *pro forma* confirmation by electoral majorities is given to the ruler who seizes power.

The problem of succession imposes great strains on any political order: the continuity of rule is broken, established patterns of action are interrupted, and the future suddenly becomes uncertain. This political crisis tests the character of regimes in ways that are of some importance for comparative political analysis. A number of interesting comparisons may be drawn from the study of succession practices, but perhaps the most important is the distinction between those systems in which the problem is resolved primarily by force and those systems in which heredity, constitutional prescription, or election assure a peaceful and orderly succession.

The transfer of power

Political orders are subjected to another kind of strain when the rule of their present power holders is challenged and the question arises of depriving them of authority. This is the problem of the transfer of power: whether, in what way, and by whom a present ruler may be displaced. Like succession, it is a recurrent problem in all political systems, and, as in the case of succession practices, the ways in which political systems respond to the strains involved offer important clues to their character. It is, in a sense, the fundamental political crisis, for all systems are in some way shaken, often violently, sometimes to the point of destruction, by the struggles between established rulers and their rivals.

Succession by force. Revolutions, which are the result of the crisis in its most extreme form, involve the overthrow not merely of the government but of the political order itself. Typically, a revolution is preceded by a series of strains within the system: challenges to the authority of the government mount, and its legitimacy is increasingly questioned; the exercise of power becomes coercive, and the challenge to rule assumes ever more violent forms; eventually, the struggle comes to a dramatic climax in the destruction of the old order. The coup d'etat is another form of violent response to the crisis of rule, but it is distinguished from the revolution in that it involves the overthrow only of the government: the political order is not immediately affected, for the coup is managed by an individual or group within the government or within the ruling class. In some cases, however, the coup d'etat is merely a preliminary stage to revolution. Sometimes this happens when the new ruler leads a governmentally imposed revolution: this was the role played by Napoleon I, Napoleon III, Mussolini, and Hitler. At other times, coups are actually prompted by fear of revolution but succeed only in further weakening the claims to legitimacy of the existing order: this has recently been the case in some countries in the non-Western world where conservative-led coups were quickly overthrown by revolutionary movements. In addition to revolutions and coups d'etat, the crisis of rule may prompt other forms of violent political reaction, including civil war and secession, resistance movements and rebellions, guerrilla warfare and terrorism, class warfare, and peasant revolts.

Causes of the overthrow of governments

The causes of internal conflict leading to the forcible overthrow of governments are extremely varied. They include tensions created by rapid social and economic development; the rise of new social classes and the refusal of established elites to share their power; problems of the distribution of wealth and the grievances of different economic groups and interests; the rise of corrosive social and political philosophies and the estrangement of intellectuals; conflict of opinions over the ends of government; factional struggles among power holders or within the ruling class; the rise of a charismatic leader; oppressive rule that alienates powerful groups; weak rule that tolerates antigovernmental or revolutionary movements; and many different combinations of these and other social, economic, and political factors. All political systems experience some of these conditions with some frequency. Yet there are a number of modern states that have avoided internal wars and the forcible overthrow of their governments for considerable periods.

It appears that rulers in the contemporary world are generally safe from violent challenges if they possess an effective monopoly of military, economic, and political power, linked with certain important social controls; or, alternatively, if they are obliged to exercise limited powers for specified periods and are required to yield office to rivals who meet certain qualifications. The first is the definition of a modern totalitarian regime, fully and efficiently organized; the second describes the governments of several contemporary constitutional democracies. In the first case, the government secures itself by force combined with social and psychological means of preventing the formation of opposition. In the second case, alternatives to internal war are provided by the opportunities for oppositions to influence the exercise of power and ultimately to replace the government. The great achievement of constitutional democracy has been to give reasonable security to governments from forcible overthrow by compelling them to accept limitations on their power, by requiring them to forgo the use of force against rivals who agree to accept the same limitations, and by establishing well-known legal procedures through which these rivals may themselves constitute the government.

Autocratic versus nonautocratic rule. The foregoing discussion has suggested a distinction among political systems in terms of the role played by force in the acquisition and transfer of power. The role of force is vital, also, in distinguishing among political systems in terms of the exercise and control of power. Here the contrast is essentially between "autocratic" and "nonautocratic" governments, for totalitarianism is only a recent, although very successful, species of autocracy, to which constitutionalism is the principal contemporary antithesis. Autocracy is characterized by the concentration of power in a single centre, be it an individual dictator or a group of power holders such as a committee or a party leadership. This centre relies on force to suppress opposition and to limit social developments that might eventuate in opposition. The power of the centre is not subject to effective controls or limited by genuine sanctions: it is absolute power. In contrast, nonautocratic government is characterized by the existence of several centres, each of which shares in the exercise of power. Nonautocratic rule allows the development of social forces that generate a variety of interests and opinions. It also subjects the power holders to reciprocal controls and to effective sanctions of law.

In appearance, autocracy may sometimes be difficult to distinguish from nonautocratic rule. Often, autocracies attempt to borrow legitimacy by adopting the language of the constitutions of nonautocratic regimes or by establishing similar institutions. It is a common practice, for example, in many modern totalitarian states to establish institutions—parliaments or assemblies, elections and parties, courts and legal codes—that differ little in appearance from the institutional structures of constitutional democracies. Similarly, the language of totalitarian constitutions is often couched in terms of the doctrines of popular rule or democracy. The difference is that in totalitarian regimes neither the institutions nor the constitutional provisions act as effective checks on the power of the single centre: they are essentially facades for the exercise of power through hierarchical procedures that subject all the officials of the state to the commands of the ruling individual or group. The underlying realities of autocratic rule are always the concentration of power in a

Autocracy

single centre and the mobilization of force to prevent the emergence of opposition.

Totalitarianism, as already noted, is the most successful of contemporary forms of autocratic rule; it is distinguished from previous forms in its use of state power to impose an official ideology on its citizens. Nonconformity of opinion is treated as the equivalent of resistance or opposition to the government, and a formidable apparatus of compulsion, including various kinds of state police or secret police, is kept in being to enforce the orthodoxy of the proclaimed doctrines of the state. A single party, centrally directed and composed exclusively of loyal supporters of the regime, is the other typical feature of totalitarianism. The party is at once an instrument of social control, a vehicle for ideological indoctrination, and the body from which the ruling group recruits its members.

Constitutional democracy

In the modern world, constitutional democracy is the chief type of nonautocratic government. The minimal definition in institutional terms of a constitutional democracy is that it should provide for a regularized system of periodic elections with a free choice of candidates, the opportunity to organize competing political parties, adult suffrage, decisions by majority vote with protection of minority rights, an independent judiciary, constitutional safeguards for basic civil liberties, and the opportunity to change any aspect of the governmental system through agreed procedures. Two features of constitutional democracy require emphasis in contrasting it with modern totalitarian government: the constitution, or basic law, and the political party. A constitution, as the example of British constitutional democracy suggests, need not be a single written instrument; indeed, the essence of a constitution is that it formalizes a set of fundamental norms governing the political community and determining the relations between the rulers and the people and the interaction among the centres of power. In most modern constitutional democracies, however, there is a constitutional document providing for fixed limitations on the exercise of power. These provisions usually include three major elements: an assignment of certain specified state functions to different state organs or offices, the delimitation of the powers of each organ or office, and the establishment of arrangements for their cooperative interaction; a list of individual rights or liberties that are protected against the exercise of state power; and a statement of the methods by which the constitution may be amended. With these provisions a concentration of power in the hands of a single ruler is prevented, certain areas of political and social life are made immune to governmental intervention, and peaceable change in the political order is made possible. The political party is the other chief instrument of constitutional democracy, for it is the agency through which the electorate is involved in both the exercise and transfer of power. In contrast with the centralized, autocratic direction of the totalitarian single-party organization, with its emphasis on ideological conformity and restricted membership, the political parties of constitutional democracy are decentralized, concerned with the integration of many interests and beliefs, and open to public participation. In constitutional democracies there is usually some measure of competition among two or more parties, each of which, if it cannot hope to form a future government, has some ability to influence the course of state action. The party in a constitutional democracy is at once a means of representing a mass electorate in the exercise of power and also a device for allowing the peaceful replacement of one set of power holders with another.

The distinction between autocratic and nonautocratic rule should not conceal the existence of a number of intermediate types of government that combine elements of both. In these cases, also, the best procedure for comparative purposes is to investigate the power configurations underlying the formal structures and to examine the extent to which power is concentrated in a single centre or the role that is played by force in the maintenance of the regime. It is a type of analysis that, by guiding attention to the relative weight of coercive and consensual power and the scope of individual freedom in the political order, allows comparisons between systems in terms of their most important attributes.

GOVERNMENTS CLASSIFIED BY STAGE OF DEVELOPMENT

The difficulties of analyzing political change

Political life is shaped by a wide variety of factors, including social and cultural conditions, economic organization, intellectual and philosophical influences, geography or climate, and historical circumstance. Recurrent attempts have been made to reduce this range of variables to analytically manageable dimensions. This is partly the motive, for example, of Marxist and other efforts to relate specific types of political systems to stages of economic development or particular kinds of socioeconomic organization. Although interesting interrelations between political and economic development have been discovered, such monistic, or single-factor, approaches are inadequate to the task of explaining political change. The problem is not only that there are many factors that should be examined but also that they are found in different combinations from one society to another. All political orders are unique as products of history and creations of the peculiar forces and conditions of their environment. A second problem that confronts comparative analysis is the difficulty of devising measures of political development. The definition of what is modern or what constitutes an advanced or developed political system has troubled many recent writers. Clearly, the older notions of development toward the goals of constitutionalism or democracy must now be seriously questioned, and to judge the maturity of a political system in terms of the extent to which it adopts any particular set of institutions or techniques of rule is an equally doubtful procedure. Another difficulty is that political change is not simply a reaction to "objective" factors such as economic forces but also the product of conscious manipulation. In explaining the growth and development of political systems it is impossible to ignore the fact that men, having considered the advantages and disadvantages of different forms of government, often decide to adopt one form rather than another. A similar problem arises from the fact that the nature of the interaction between political systems and their environment is extremely complex. For example, to treat the political system as merely the outgrowth of particular patterns of social or economic organization is to ignore the fact that changes in social and economic structures are often the product, sometimes the intended product, of governmental action.

These difficulties of analysis have prevented the emergence of any satisfactory theory to explain the processes of political change or growth. In the absence of such a theory, however, several writers have recently attempted to identify certain basic phases in the development of national political systems. For example, five major steps in the emergence of the advanced nation-states of the modern world are often distinguished: (1) unification and independence or autonomy; (2) development and differentiation of political institutions and political roles; (3) transfer of power from traditional elites; (4) further institutional and political role differentiation accompanied by the development of a number of organized social interests and growth in governmental functions; and (5) use of state power in attempts to guide or control social and economic activity, extensive exploitation of resources as the result of technological development, and full participation in the international political system.

Steps in the emergence of advanced nation-states

Other writers distinguish among "traditional," "transitional," and "modern" societies in an effort to identify differences and regularities in social, economic, cultural, and political development. The social structure of the traditional society is described as hierarchical, class bound, based on kinship, and divided into relatively few effectively organized social groupings; its economic basis is primarily agricultural, and industry and commerce are relatively undeveloped; its political institutions are those of sacred monarchy, rule by a nobility, and various forms of particularism. The social system of the transitional society is typified by the formation of new classes, especially a middle class and a proletariat, and conflict among ethnic, religious, and cultural groupings; its economic system experiences major tensions as the result of technological development, the growth of industry, urbanization, and the use of rapid communications; its political institutions are typically authoritarian, although constitutional forms also make their appearance. Modernity is seen as the age of high social mobility, equality, universal education, mass communications, increasing secularism, and sociocultural integration; in its economic system, the modern society experiences a further technological revolution, massive urbanization, and the development of a fully diversified economy; its political institutions are those of democracy and modified totalitarianism, and, in either case, a specialized bureaucracy is used to carry on the expanding functions of government.

These efforts to identify stages of "modernization" are poor substitutes for a general theory of political change, but they serve to emphasize the increasing complexity of all the structures—social, economic, and political—of the modern state. The elaboration of the institutions and procedures of modern government appears to be partly a reflection of the social and economic forces at work in the contemporary world and partly the result of efforts to control these forces through governmental action. The complex structures of advanced political orders are treated in the discussion that follows.

The structure of government

The study of governmental structures must be approached with great caution, for political systems having the same kind of legal arrangements and using the same type of governmental machinery often function very differently. A parliament, for example, may be an important and effective part of a political system; or it may be no more than an institutional facade of little practical significance. A constitution may provide the framework within which the political life of a state is conducted; or it may be no more than a piece of paper, its provisions bearing almost no relationship to the facts of political life. Political systems must never be classified in terms of their legal structures alone: the fact that two states have similar constitutions with similar institutional provisions and legal requirements should never, by itself, lead to the conclusion that they represent the same type of political system.

To be useful, the study of governmental structures must always proceed hand in hand with an investigation of the actual facts of the political process: the analyst must exercise the greatest care in distinguishing between form and reality and between prescription and practice. Approached in this way, an examination of the organizational arrangements that governments use for making decisions and exercising power can be a valuable tool of political inquiry.

CONTEMPORARY FORMS OF GOVERNMENT

The rapidity of change

Few states in the modern world have constitutional arrangements that are more than a century old. Indeed, the vast majority of all the world's states have constitutions written in the 20th century. This is true of states, such as Germany, Italy, and Japan, that were defeated in World War II and of other states, such as the Soviet Union, Spain, and China, that have experienced civil war and revolutions in the course of the century. Great Britain and the United States are almost alone among major contemporary nation-states in possessing constitutional arrangements that predate the 20th century.

Even in Britain and the United States, the 20th century has seen much change in the governmental system. In the United States, for example, the relationship of legislature and executive at both the national and the state levels has been significantly altered by the growth of bureaucracies and the enlargement of the executive's budgetary powers. In Britain, even more far-reaching changes have occurred in the relationship between the prime minister and Parliament and in Parliament's role in supervising the executive establishment. In both countries, the appearance of the welfare state, the impact of modern technology on the economy, and international crises have resulted in major alterations in the ways in which the institutions of government function and interact.

The modern student of constitutional forms and institutional arrangements confronts an endlessly changing world. In many parts of the world, in countries as different as France, Pakistan, Argentina, Tanzania, and South Vietnam, there are continuing experiments with new constitutions. All systems, moreover, even without formal constitutional change, undergo a continual process of adjustment and mutation as their institutional arrangements respond to and reflect changes in the social order and the balance of political forces.

Monarchy. The ancient distinction among monarchies, tyrannies, oligarchies, and constitutional governments, like other traditional classifications of political systems, is no longer very descriptive of political life. A king may be a ceremonial dignitary in one of the parliamentary democracies of western Europe, or he may be an absolute ruler in one of the emerging states of North Africa, the Middle East, or Asia. In the first case his duties may be little different from those of an elected president in many republican parliamentary regimes; in the second his role may be much the same as that of countless dictators and strong men in autocratic regimes throughout the underdeveloped areas of the world.

Decline of traditional monarchy

It may be said of the reigning dynasties of modern Europe that they have survived only because they failed to retain or to acquire effective powers of government. Royal lines have been preserved only in those countries of Europe in which royal rule was severely limited prior to the 20th century or in which royal absolutism had never firmly established itself. More successful dynasties, such as the Hohenzollerns in Germany, the Habsburgs in Austria-Hungary, and the Romanovs in Russia, which continued to rule as well as to reign at the opening of the present century, have paid with the loss of their thrones. Today, in countries such as Great Britain or The Netherlands or Denmark, the monarch is the ceremonial head of state, an indispensable figure in all great official occasions and a symbol of national unity and of the authority of the state; but he is almost entirely lacking in power. Monarchy in the parliamentary democracies of modern Europe has been reduced to the status of a dignified institutional facade behind which the functioning mechanisms of government—cabinet, parliament, ministries, and parties—go about the tasks of ruling.

The 20th century has also seen the demise of most of the hereditary monarchies of the non-Western world. Thrones have toppled in Turkey, in China, in most of the Arab countries, in the principates of India, in the tribal kingdoms of Africa, and in several countries of Southeast Asia. The kings who maintain their position do so less by the claim of legitimate blood descent than by their appeal as popular leaders responsible for well-publicized programs of national economic and social reform or as national military chieftains. In a sense, these kings are less monarchs than monocrats, and their regimes are little different from several other forms of one-man rule found in the modern world.

Dictatorship. While royal rule, as legitimized by blood descent, has almost vanished as an effective principle of government in the modern world, monocracy—a term that comprehends the rule of the remaining non-Western royal absolutists, of the generals and strong men of Latin America and Asia, of the messianic leaders of postcolonial Africa, and of the totalitarian heads of Communist and Fascist states—still flourishes. Indeed, the 20th century, which has witnessed the careers of Kemal Atatürk, Benito Mussolini, Adolf Hitler, Joseph Stalin, Francisco Franco, Mao Tse-tung, Juan Perón, Tito, Gamal Abdel Nasser, Sukarno, Kwame Nkrumah, and Charles de Gaulle, could appear in history as the age of plebiscitary dictatorship.

The contemporary world provides examples of several types of monocratic or dictatorial rule. In many of the new states of Africa and Asia, for example, dictators quickly established themselves on the ruins of constitutional arrangements inherited from Western colonial powers. In some of these countries, presidents and prime ministers captured personal power by banning opposition parties and building primitive replicas of the authoritarian one-party systems of the Communist world. In other new countries the armies seized power, and military dictator-

Monocratic rule

ships were established. Whether as presidential dictatorships or as military dictatorships, the regimes that came into being appear to have had common roots in the social and economic problems of the new state. The constitutional systems inherited from the colonial powers proved unworkable in the absence of a strong middle class; local traditions of autocratic rule retained a powerful influence; the army, one of the few organized forces in society, was also often the only force capable of maintaining order; and a tiny intellectual class was impatient for economic progress, frustrated by the lack of opportunity, and deeply influenced by the example of authoritarianism in other countries. The dictatorships that resulted proved highly unstable, and few of the individual dictators were able to satisfy for long the demands of the different groups that supported their bids for power.

Although similar in some respects to the dictatorships of the new nations, the caudillos of 19th- and 20th-century Latin America represent a very different type of monocratic rule. In its 19th-century form, *caudillismo* was the result of the breakdown of central authority. After a brief period of constitutional rule, each of the former Spanish colonies in the Americas experienced a collapse of effective national government. A self-proclaimed leader, usually an army officer, heading a private army typically formed from the peasantry with the support of provincial landowners, established his control over one or more provinces, and then marched upon the national capital. The famous 19th-century caudillos—Antonio López de Santa Anna of Mexico or Juan Manuel de Rosas of Argentina, for example—were thus essentially provincial leaders who seized control of the national government to maintain the social and economic power of provincial groups. The 20th-century dictatorships in Latin-American countries have had different aims. The modern caudillo is less a provincial than a national leader. The Perón regime, for example, was established by nationalistic army officers committed to a program of national reform and various ideological goals. Often, too, the dictators of contemporary Latin America have allied themselves with a particular social class, attempting either to maintain the interests of established economic groupings or to press far-reaching social reforms.

Dictatorship in the technologically advanced, totalitarian regimes of modern Communism or Fascism is distinctively different from the authoritarian regimes of either Latin America or the new states of Africa and Asia. Nazi Germany under Hitler and the Soviet Union under Stalin are the leading examples of modern totalitarian dictatorships. The crucial elements of both were the identification of the state with the single mass party and of the party with its charismatic leader, the use of an official ideology to legitimize and maintain the regime, the employment of a terroristic police force and a controlled press, and the application of all the means of modern science and technology to control the economy and individual behaviour. The two systems of dictatorship, however, may be distinguished in several ways. Fascism, in its National Socialist form, was primarily a counterrevolutionary movement that mobilized middle and lower middle class groups to pursue nationalistic and militaristic goals and whose sole principle of organization was that of obedience to the Führer. By contrast, Soviet Communism grew out of a revolutionary theory of society, pursued the goal of revolutionary overthrow of capitalist systems internationally, and employed the complex bureaucratic structures of the Communist Party as mechanisms of governmental organization.

Western constitutional democracies have provided examples of another type of contemporary dictatorship. At various points in the 20th century, during periods of domestic or foreign crisis, most constitutional regimes have conferred emergency powers on the executive, suspending constitutional guarantees of individual rights or liberties, or declaring some form of martial law. Indeed, the constitutions of some Western democracies explicitly provide for the grant of emergency powers to the executive in a time of crisis in order to protect the constitutional order. In many cases, of course, such provisions have been

the instruments by which dictators have overthrown the regime. Thus, the proclamation of emergency rule was the beginning of the dictatorships of Mussolini in Italy, of Kemal Atatürk in Turkey, of Józef Piłsudski in Poland, of António de Olveira Salazar in Portugal, of Franz von Papen and Hitler in Germany, and of Engelbert Dollfuss and Kurt von Schuschnigg in Austria. In other democracies, however, constitutional arrangements have survived quite lengthy periods of crisis government. After World War II, for example, in both the United States and Britain, the use of extraordinary powers by the executive came to a halt with the end of the wartime emergency. Similarly, although the 1958 constitution of the Fifth Republic of France contained far-reaching emergency powers conferred on the president—"when the institutions of the Republic, the independence of the nation, the integrity of its territory or the fulfillment of its international obligations are threatened with immediate and grave danger, and when the regular functioning of the constitutional authority is interrupted"—their implicit threat to the constitutional order has not been realized.

Many forces at work in the 20th century appear to lend impetus to the rise of monocratic forms of rule. In nearly all political systems, the powers of chief executives have increased in response to the demanding social, economic, and military crises of the age. The complex decisions required of governments in a technological era, the perfectionist impulses of the great bureaucratic structures that have developed in all industrialized societies, and the imperatives of national survival in a nuclear world continue to add to the process of executive aggrandizement. The question for many constitutional regimes is whether the limitation and balance of power that are at the heart of constitutional government can survive the growing enlargement of executive power.

Oligarchy. In the Aristotelian classification of government there were two forms of rule by the few: aristocracy and its debased form, oligarchy. Although the term oligarchy is rarely used to refer to contemporary political systems, the phenomenon of irresponsible rule by small groups has not vanished from the world.

Many of the classical conditions of oligarchic rule were found until recently in those parts of Asia in which governing elites were recruited exclusively from a ruling caste—a hereditary social grouping set apart from the rest of society by religion, kinship, economic status, prestige, and even language. In the contemporary world, in some countries that have not experienced the full impact of industrialization, governing elites are still often recruited from a ruling class—a stratum of society that monopolizes the chief social and economic functions in the system. Such elites exercise power in the interests of their class.

The simple forms of oligarchic rule associated with pre-industrial societies are, of course, rapidly disappearing. Industrialization produces new, differentiated elites that replace the small leadership groupings that once controlled social, economic, and political power in the society. The demands of industrialization compel recruitment on the basis of skill, merit, and achievement, rather than on the basis of inherited social position and wealth. New forms of oligarchic rule have also made their appearance in many advanced industrial societies. Although governing elites in these societies are no longer recruited from a single class, they are often not subjected to effective restraints on the exercise of their power. Indeed, in some circumstances, the new elites may use their power to convert themselves into a governing class whose interests are protected by every agency of the state. This is the criticism that is made, for example, of the Communist Party bureaucracy in the Soviet Union and in some eastern European states.

Oligarchic tendencies of a lesser degree have been detected in all the great bureaucratic structures of advanced political systems. The growing complexity of modern society and its government thrusts ever greater power into the hands of administrators and committees of experts. Even in constitutional regimes, no fully satisfactory answer has been found to the question of how these bureaucratic decision makers can be held accountable and their powers effectively restrained without, at the same time,

Small leadership groups

jeopardizing the efficiency and rationality of the policy-making process.

Constitutional government. Constitutional government is defined by the existence of a constitution—which may be a legal instrument or merely a set of fixed norms or principles generally accepted as the fundamental law of the polity—that effectively controls the exercise of political power. The essence of constitutionalism is the control of power by its distribution among several state organs or offices in such a way that they are each subjected to reciprocal controls and forced to cooperate in formulating the will of the state. Although constitutional government in this sense flourished in England and in some other historical systems for a considerable period, it is only recently that it has been associated with forms of mass participation in politics. In England, for example, constitutional government was not harnessed to political democracy until after the Reform Act of 1832 and subsequent 19th-century extensions of the suffrage. In the contemporary world, however, constitutional governments are also generally democracies, and they are usually referred to as constitutional democracies or constitutional–democratic systems.

The contemporary political systems that combine constitutionalism and democracy share a common basis in the primacy they accord to the will of the majority of the people as expressed in free elections. In all such systems, political parties are key institutions, for they are the agencies by which majority opinion in a modern mass electorate is mobilized and expressed. Indeed, the history of the political party in its modern form is coincidental with the development of contemporary constitutional–democratic systems. In each case, the transition from the older forms of constitutionalism to modern constitutional democracy was accompanied by the institutionalization of parties and the development of techniques of party competition. The essential functions of political parties in a constitutional democracy are the integration of a multitude of interests, beliefs, and values into one or more programs or proposals for change and the nomination of party members for elective office in the government. In both functions, the party serves as a link between the rulers and the ruled: in the first case by allowing the electorate to register an opinion on policy and in the second by giving the people a chance to choose their rulers. Of course, the centralized, autocratically directed, and ideologically orthodox one-party systems of contemporary totalitarian regimes perform neither of these functions.

The British and U.S. systems compared

The two major types of constitutional democracy in the modern world are exemplified by the United States and Great Britain. The United States is the leading example of the presidential system of constitutional democracy; Britain, although its system is sometimes referred to as a cabinet system, in recognition of the role of the Cabinet in the government, is the classic example of the parliamentary system. The U.S. presidential system is based on the doctrine of separation of powers and distinguishes sharply between the personnel, although not between the functions, of the legislature and the executive; the British parliamentary system provides for the integration or fusion of legislature and executive. In the U.S. system the separation of legislature and executive is reinforced by their separate election and by the doctrine of checks and balances that provides constitutional support for routine disagreements between the branches; in the British system the integration of legislature and executive is reinforced by the necessity for their constant agreement, or for a condition of "confidence" between the two, if the normal processes of government are to continue. In the U.S. system, reciprocal controls are provided by such devices as the presidential veto of legislation (which may be overridden by a two-thirds majority in Congress), the Senate's role in ratifying treaties and confirming executive nominations, congressional appropriation of funds, and judicial review of legislation; in the British system, the major control device is the vote of "no confidence" or the rejection of legislation that is considered vital.

The prestige of constitutional democracy was once so great that many thought all the countries of the world would eventually accede to the examples of the United States or Britain and establish similar arrangements. Recent history, however, has confounded this expectation. The collapse of the Weimar Constitution in Germany in the 1930s and the recurrent political crises of the Fourth Republic in France after World War II suggested that constitutional democracy, even in advanced systems, carries no guarantee of stability. The failure of both presidential and parliamentary systems to work as expected in less advanced countries that modelled their constitutions on those of the United States and Britain resulted in a further diminution in the prestige of both systems. Successful examples of established constitutional democracies are now limited to a dozen or so northwest European and North American countries, together with New Zealand and Australia in the Pacific. Systems in which experiments are being made in the use of constitutional–democratic arrangements with some degree of success include Mexico, Uruguay, Chile, the Philippines, India, and Malaya. In all these countries, constitutionalism and democracy have combined to produce political change under conditions of relative stability.

CONTEMPORARY LEVELS OF GOVERNMENT

Feudalism

Most national societies have passed through a stage in their social and political development, usually referred to as feudalism, in which a weak and ineffectively organized national government competes for territorial jurisdiction with local power holders. In medieval England and France, for example, the crown was perennially threatened by the power of the feudal nobles, and a protracted struggle was necessary before the national domain was subjected to full royal control. Elsewhere, innumerable societies continued to experience this kind of feudal conflict between local magnates and the central government well into the modern era. The warlords of 19th- and 20th-century China, for example, were just as much the products of feudal society as the warring barons of 13th-century England and presented the same kind of challenge to the central government's claim to exercise sovereign jurisdiction over the national territory. By the 1970s, feudalism was almost extinct. The social patterns that had formerly supported the power of local landowners were rapidly disappearing, and central governments had generally acquired a near monopoly of communications and military technology, enabling them to project their power into areas once controlled by local rulers.

In nearly all national political systems, central governments are better equipped than ever before to exercise effective jurisdiction over their territories. In much of the underdeveloped world, nationalist political movements and a variety of modern economic forces have swept away the traditional structures of local government, and the quasi-autonomous governments of village and tribe and province have been replaced by centrally directed systems of subnational administration. Even in the heavily industrialized states of the modern world, there has been an accelerating tendency toward greater centralization of power at the national level. In the United States, for example, the structure of relationships among the governments at the national, state, and local levels has changed in a number of ways to add to the power of the federal government in Washington. Even though the system of national grants-in-aid appears to have been designed as a means of decentralizing administration, the effect has been decidedly centralist, for the conditional character of the grants has allowed the federal government to exercise influence on state policies in fields that were once invulnerable to national intervention.

The nation-state

National government. The nation-state is the dominant type of political system in the contemporary world, and nationalism, or the creed that centres the supreme loyalty of the people upon the nation-state, is the dominating force in international politics. The national ideal triumphed as a result of the wars of the 19th and 20th centuries. The Napoleonic Wars, which spread the doctrines of the French Revolution, unleashed nationalism as a force in Europe and led to the Risorgimento in Italy and the emergence of Bismarck's Germany. The two world wars of the 20th century carried the principles of national self-determination and liberal democracy around the world and gave birth to the independence movements that resulted in the foundation of new states in eastern Europe in 1919 and the emergence from colonial status of countries in Asia and Africa after 1945.

All the major forces of world politics—war and the threat of war, the development of national economies, the demand for social services, and many others—have reinforced the national state as the primary focus of people's loyalties. Wars have played the major part in strengthening national governments and weakening political regionalism and localism. The attachments that people have to subnational political communities are loosened when they must depend for their security on the national power. Even in the new age of total war—which few nations are capable of waging and even fewer of surviving—people look for their security to national governments rather than to international organizations. In nearly all contemporary states, the national budget is dominated by expenditures for defense, the military employs the largest fraction of the work force, and questions of national security pervade the discussion of politics.

The lesson of the last three decades is that national sovereignty remains the most important obstacle to the emergence of new forms of supranational government and to effective international cooperation. Almost everywhere, attempts to achieve federation and other forms of multinational communication have foundered on the rocks of nationalism. The collapse of the Federation of Rhodesia and Nyasaland and the Federation of Malaya are paralleled by the failure of the Organization of American States and the Arab League: in all cases, nationalism has been the divisive force. National sovereignty has been successfully limited in only two major areas of the contemporary world: in eastern Europe, where, as a result of Soviet occupation, a number of formerly independent states were subjected to a form of centralized control from Moscow; and in western Europe, where several nation-states joined in a loose confederation (the European Economic Community) to achieve certain economic goals. Even in these cases, nationalism has been a major threat to continued unity. Several of the countries of eastern Europe have recently declared their independence of Moscow, and France under President de Gaulle made clear its hostility to any form of supranational union of the countries belonging to the European Economic Community.

At the international level, anarchy is the principal form of contemporary rule, for the nation-state's freedom of action is limited only by its power. Some forces are at work, however, that may eventually lead to a lessening of the role of the nation-state and to the emergence of effective supranational governments. The first of these is industrial and commercial development. The development of national industries in the 19th and early 20th centuries played a major part in strengthening national as against regional and local political entities, but the scale of economic activity has now outgrown national markets. Industrial combines and commercial groupings have emerged that cross national frontiers and require international markets. This integrative influence of economic development may be assisted by the threat of nuclear war. Many national frontiers can no longer be adequately defended in the era of the intercontinental missile, and many states, even some that were until recently great powers, are incompetent to preserve themselves. Together these forces may assist the progress of efforts to develop new kinds of cooperative union among nation-states.

Although the failure of efforts to achieve world government and to develop an effective system of international law may be regretted, it should perhaps be remembered that the nation-state continues to function as an extremely effective system for maintaining order within its boundaries. In some cases, this is achieved with remarkably little coercion and in such a way that the progress of civilization is encouraged. In the conditions of our age, world government might well involve much higher levels of coercion and much less civilization.

Regional and state government. The 18th-century political philosopher Montesquieu wrote that governments are likely to be tyrannical if they are responsible for administering large territories, for they must develop the organizational capacity characteristic of despotic states. It was partly this fear that led the American founding fathers to provide for a federal system and to divide governmental functions between the government in Washington and the state governments. Modern technology and mass communication are often said to have deprived Montesquieu's axiom of its force. Yet the technology that makes it possible for large areas to be governed democratically also holds out the spectre of an even greater tyranny than Montesquieu foresaw.

In all political systems the relationships between national and regional or state governments have been affected by technology and new means of communication. In the 18th century Thomas Jefferson, in arguing that local government, or the government closest to the people, was best, could claim that citizens knew most about their local governments, somewhat less about their state governments, and least about the national government. In the present-day United States, however, the concentration of the mass media on the issues and personalities of national government has made nonsense of this proposition. As several recent studies have demonstrated, people know much less about local government than national government and turn out to vote in much larger numbers in national elections. The necessity for employing systems for the devolution of political power is reduced when a central government can communicate directly with citizens in all parts of the national territory, and the vitality of subnational levels of government is sapped when public attention is focussed on national problems.

Another general development that has lessened the importance of regional or state government is the rise of efficient national bureaucracies. In nearly all political systems, there has been some tendency toward bureaucratic centralization, and in some cases national bureaucracies have almost completely replaced older systems of regional and provincial administration. In the United States, for example, complex programs of social security, veterans' benefits, income taxes, agricultural subsidies, and many others that bear directly on individuals are centrally administered; and great agencies of government, such as the Department of Health and Human Services, maintain regional and local offices for the supervision of other national activities.

Even in systems in which a division of functions between national and subnational governments is constitutionally prescribed, the prevailing trend in intergovernmental relations is toward increasing involvement of the national government in areas once dominated by regional or state governments. Thus, the original constitutional arrangements prescribed by the Allied powers for the West German republic in 1949 won general acclaim at the time because they provided for greater decentralization than had the Weimar Constitution; but, as soon as Germany was free to amend its own constitution, several state functions were reassigned to the national government. In the United States, also, the collapse of the doctrine of "dual federalism," according to which the powers of the national government were restricted by the powers reserved to the states, signalled the end of an era in which the states could claim exclusive jurisdiction over a wide range of functions. Today, forms of cooperative federalism involving joint action by national and state governments are increasingly common. Such cooperative relationships in the United States include programs of public assistance, the interstate-highway system, agricultural extension programs, and aid to education. In some areas, such as school desegregation, the national government has used broad powers to compel states to conform to national standards.

Efforts made to halt the trend toward centralization and to re-invigorate regional or state governments have met with little success. In the U.S. a Commission on Intergovernmental Relations established by President Eisenhower in 1953 concluded that it could recommend no major reversion of functions to state governments. Similarly, efforts in France and Italy to decentralize parts of the national administrations have had few practical results.

Decline of regional and state government

Political regionalism appears to be in steep decline almost everywhere, whether in China or in the American South. The attachments that bind people to localities and allow the growth of genuine subnational political communities have weakened under the impact of technology and the growth of national economies. Only where political regionalism has always been a cloak for movements of national independence—for example, in Scotland, Wales, Northern Ireland, Quebec, and Brittany—are there popular attempts to reverse the trend toward national centralization.

The urban metropolis
City and local government. Political scientists since Aristotle have recognized that the nature of political communities changes when their populations grow larger. One of the central problems of contemporary government is the vast increase in urban population and the progression from "polis to metro-polis to mega-polis." The catalog of ills that have resulted from urban growth includes political and administrative problems of extraordinary complexity.

The rise of great urban centres has had a major impact on the politics of all advanced industrial societies. In the United States, for example, the issues of metropolitan politics have become key political issues at the national level. Programs relating to urban renewal, mass-transit systems, school desegregation, and air and water pollution have become of pressing national importance, along with other social problems of the metropolis, such as urban crime, juvenile delinquency, the disorganization of the family, ghetto conditions, and unemployment. The growing involvement of the national government with such issues is in part a consequence of the impoverishment of the cities and the collapse of effective municipal government. The tax base of U.S. cities has dwindled with the flight of the middle classes to the suburbs and the relocation of industry; at the same time, although "bossism" and machine politics have almost vanished, newer forms of city governments have failed to establish effective systems of administration or to win support from stable majorities of city voters. In part, too, the national government gives priority to such issues because of the political power of the urban areas: cities have become the focuses of national politics, for they are rich in the votes that decide national campaigns. Aside from such fiscal and political pressures, the national government is inevitably concerned with the threat posed by racial conflict, ghetto violence, and other kinds of social chaos in the city.

The metropolis suffers from several acute governmental and administrative failures. Responsibility for the issues that transcend the boundaries of local governments has not been defined, for representative institutions have failed to develop at the metropolitan level. In most cases, there are no effective governmental structures for administering area-wide services or for dealing comprehensively with the common problems of the metropolitan community. The result has been the appearance of a new class of problems created by government itself, including uneven levels of service for metropolitan residents, inequities in financing government services and functions, and variations in the democratic responsiveness of the governments scattered through the metropolitan area. The tangled pattern of local governments, each operating in some independent sphere, does not allow the comprehensive planning necessary to deal with the escalating problems of urban life.

Efforts to create new governing structures for metropolitan communities are among the most interesting developments in contemporary government. In the United States these efforts include the creation of special districts to handle specific functions, area-wide planning agencies, interstate compacts, consolidated school and library systems, and various informal intergovernmental arrangements. Although annexation of outlying areas by the central city and city–county consolidations have been attempted in many cases, the reluctance of urban areas to surrender their political independence or to pay for central-city services has been an obstacle. The Los Angeles plan, by which the county has assumed responsibility for many area-wide functions, leaving the local communities with substantial political autonomy, may represent a partial solution to the problem of urban–suburban tensions. In other cases, "metropolitan federation" has been attempted. One of the earliest and most influential examples of a federated system of metropolitan government is the Greater London Area in Britain, which encompasses 32 London boroughs and places effective governing powers in the hands of an elected city council. In Canada the city of Toronto and its suburbs adopted a metropolitan "constitution" in 1953 under which mass transit, highways, planning, and several other functions are controlled by a council composed of elected officials from the central city and surrounding governments. In 1957 Miami and Dade counties in Florida chose "metro" government: Miami and 27 suburban cities retained control of local functions, while area-wide functions such as fire and police protection and transportation were allocated to the new federal structure. In 1962 Nashville, Tennessee, combined with Davidson County to form a single metropolitan government; and in 1968 Jacksonville, Florida, joined with Duval County in a similar arrangement. Other examples of various degrees of area-wide consolidation in the United States include Baton Rouge, Louisiana; Seattle, Washington; Portland, Oregon; and Indianapolis, Indiana.

Most of the major problems of contemporary politics seem to have found their focus in the metropolis, and there is almost universal agreement that new governing systems must be devised for the metropolitan community if the problems are ever to be resolved.

CONTEMPORARY DIVISIONS OF GOVERNMENT

Legis-lative, executive, and judicial functions
In his *Politics,* Aristotle differentiated three categories of state activity—deliberations concerning common affairs; decisions of executive magistrates, and judicial rulings—and indicated that the most significant differences among constitutions concerned the arrangements made for these activities. This threefold classification is not precisely the same as the modern distinction among legislature, executive, and judiciary. Aristotle intended to make only a theoretical distinction among certain state functions and stopped short of recommending that they be assigned as powers to separate organs of government. Indeed, since Aristotle held that all power should be wielded by one man, pre-eminent in virtue, he never considered the concept of separated powers. In the 17th century the English political philosopher John Locke also distinguished the legislative from the executive function but, like Aristotle, failed to assign these to separate organs or institutions. Montesquieu was the first to make the modern division among legislative, executive, and judiciary. Arguing that the purpose of political association is liberty, not virtue, and that the very definition of liberty's great antagonist, tyranny, is the accumulation of all power in the same hands, he urged the division of the three functions of government among three separate institutions. After Montesquieu, the concept of separation of powers became one of the principal doctrines of modern constitutionalism. Nearly all modern constitutions, from the document written at Philadelphia in 1787 through the French Declaration of the Rights of Man and of the Citizen of August 1789 up to the constitutions of the new states of Africa and Asia, provide for the separate establishment of legislative, executive, and judiciary. The functional division among the branches of government is never precise. In the American system, for example, the doctrine of checks and balances justifies several departures from the strict assignment of functions among the branches. Parliamentary forms of government depart even further from the concept of separation and integrate both the personnel and the functions of the legislature and the executive. Indeed, the principle of shared rather than separated powers is the true essence of constitutionalism. In the constitutional state, power is controlled because it is shared or distributed among the divisions of government in such a way that they are each subjected to reciprocal checks and forced to cooperate in the exercise of political power. In the nonconstitutional systems of totalitarianism or autocracy, although there may be separate institutions such as legislatures, executives, and judiciaries, power is not shared but rather concentrated in a single organ. Because this organ is not subjected to the checks of shared power, the exercise of political power is uncontrolled or absolute.

The legislature.   The characteristic function of all legislatures is the making of law. In most systems, however, legislatures also have other tasks, such as selection and criticism of the government, supervision of administration, appropriation of funds, ratification of treaties, impeachment of executive and judicial officials, acceptance or refusal of executive nominations, determination of election procedures, and public hearings on petitions. Legislatures, then, are not simply lawmaking bodies. Neither do they monopolize the function of making law. In most systems the executive has a power of veto over legislation, and, even where this is lacking, the executive may exercise original or delegated powers of legislation. Judges, also, often share in the lawmaking process, through the interpretation and application of statutes or, as in the U.S. system, by means of judicial review of legislation. Similarly, administrative officials exercise quasi-legislative powers in making rules and deciding cases that come before administrative tribunals.

Legislatures differ strikingly in their size, the procedures they employ, the role of political parties in legislative action, and in their vitality as representative bodies. In size, the British House of Commons, with 630 members, is among the largest; the Icelandic lower house, with 40, the New Zealand House of Representatives, with 80, and the Senate of Nevada, with 17 members, are among the smallest. Most legislatures are bicameral, although New Zealand, Denmark, the state of Queensland, in Australia, and Nebraska, in the United States, have all abolished their second chambers. The procedures of the United States House of Representatives, which derive from a manual of procedure written by Thomas Jefferson, are among the most elaborate of parliamentary rules, requiring study and careful observation over a considerable period before members become proficient in their manipulation. Voting procedures range from the formal procession of the division or teller vote in the British House of Commons to the electric voting methods employed in the California legislature and in some other American states. Another point of difference among legislatures concerns their presiding officers. These are sometimes officials who stand above party and, like the speaker of the British House of Commons, exercise a neutral function as parliamentary umpires; sometimes they are the leaders of the majority party and, like the speaker of the United States House of Representatives, major political figures; and sometimes they are officials who, like the vice president of the United States in his role as presiding officer of the Senate, exercise a vote to break ties and otherwise perform mainly ceremonial functions.

Legislative parties are of various types and play a number of roles or functions. In the United States House of Representatives, for example, the party is responsible for assigning members to all standing committees; the party leadership fills the major parliamentary offices, and the party membership on committees reflects the proportion of seats held by the party in the House as a whole. The congressional party, however, is not disciplined to the degree found in British and some other European legislative parties, and there are relatively few "party line" votes in which all the members of one party vote against all the members of the other party. In the House of Commons, party-line voting is general; indeed, it is very unusual to find members voting against their party leadership, and, when they do, they must reckon with the possibility of penalties such as the "withdrawal of the whip" or the loss of their official status as party members.

It is often said that the 20th century has dealt harshly with legislatures and that this is an age of executive aggrandizement. Certainly, executives in most countries have assumed an increasingly large role in the making of law, through the initiation of the legislation that comes before parliaments, assemblies, and congresses, through the exercise of various rule-making functions, and as a result of the growth of different types of delegated legislation. It is also true that executives have come to predominate in the sphere of foreign affairs and, by such devices as executive agreements, which are frequently used in place of treaties, have freed themselves from dependence upon legislative approval of important foreign-policy initiatives. Moreover, devices such as the executive budget and the rise of specialized budgetary agencies in the executive division have threatened the traditional fiscal controls of legislatures. This decline in legislative power, however, is not universal. The United States Congress, for example, has preserved a substantial measure of its power. Indeed, congressional oversight of the bureaucracy is an area in which it has added to its power and has developed new techniques for controlling the executive. The difficulties of recent presidents with legislative programs of foreign aid and the insistent congressional criticism of executive policies in Southeast Asia also suggest that Congress continues to play a vital role in the governing process.

The executive.   Political executives are government officials who participate in the determination and direction of government policy. They include heads of state and government leaders—presidents, prime ministers, premiers, chancellors, and other chief executives—and many secondary figures, such as cabinet members and ministers, councillors, and agency heads. By this definition, there are several thousand political executives in the U.S. national government, including the president, dozens of political appointees in the Cabinet departments, in the agencies, in the commissions, and in the White House staff, and hundreds of senior civil servants. The same is true of most advanced political systems, for the making and implementation of government policy require very large executive and administrative establishments.

The crucial element in the organization of a national executive is the role assigned to the chief executive. In presidential systems, such as in the United States, the president is both the political head of the government and also the ceremonial head of state. In parliamentary systems, such as in Great Britain, the prime minister is the national political leader, but another figure, a monarch or elected president, serves as the head of state. In mixed presidential–parliamentary systems, such as that established in France under the constitution of 1958, the president serves as head of state but also wields important political powers, including the appointment of a prime minister and Cabinet to serve as the government.

The manner in which the chief executive is elected or selected is often decisive in shaping his role in the political system. Thus, although he receives his seals of office from the monarch, the effective election of a British prime minister usually occurs in a private conclave of the leading members of his party in Parliament. Elected to Parliament from only one of 630 constituencies, he is tied to the fortunes of the legislative majority that he leads. By contrast, the American president is elected by a nationwide electorate, and, although he leads his party's ticket, his fortunes are independent of his party. Even when the opposition party controls the Congress, his fixed term and his independent base of power allow him considerable freedom of manoeuvre. These contrasts explain many of the differences in the roles of the two chief executives. The British prime minister invariably has served for many years in Parliament and has developed skills in debate and in political negotiation. His major political tasks are the designation of the other members of the Cabinet, the direction of parliamentary strategy, and the retention of the loyalty of a substantial majority of his legislative party. The presidential chief executive, on the other hand, often lacks prior legislative and even national-governmental experience, and his main concern is with the cultivation of a majority in the electorate through the leadership of public opinion. Of course, since the president must have a legislative program and often cannot depend on the support of a congressional majority, he may also need the skills of a legislative strategist and negotiator.

Another important area of contrast between different national executives concerns their role in executing and administering the law. In the U.S. presidential system, the personnel of the executive branch are constitutionally separated from the personnel of Congress: no executive officeholder may seek election to either house of Congress, and no member of Congress may hold executive office. In parliamentary systems the political management of gov-

Varieties of legislatures

Varieties of executives

ernment ministries is placed in the hands of the party leadership in parliament. In the U.S. system the president often appoints to Cabinet positions persons who have had little prior experience in politics, and he may even appoint members of the opposition party. In the British system, Cabinet appointments are made to consolidate the prime minister's personal ascendancy within the parliamentary party or to placate its different factions. These differences extend even further into the character of the two systems of administration and the role played by civil servants. In the U.S. system a change in administration is accompanied by the exodus of a very large number of top government executives—the political appointees who play the vital part in shaping day-to-day policy in all the departments and agencies of the national government. In Britain, when political control of the House of Commons changes, only the ministers, their parliamentary secretaries, and one or two other top political aids are replaced. For all practical purposes, the ministries remain intact and continue under the supervision of permanent civil servants.

In nearly all political systems, even in constitutional democracies where executive responsibility is enforced through free elections, the 20th century has seen an alarming increase in the powers of chief executives. The U.S. presidency, like the office of prime minister in Britain, has greatly enlarged the scope of its authority. One of the future tasks of representative government is to develop more constitutional restraints on the abuse of executive powers while retaining their advantages for effective rule.

The judiciary. Like legislators and executives, judges are major participants in the policy-making process; and courts, like legislatures and administrative agencies, promulgate rules of behaviour having the nature of law. The process of judicial decision making, or adjudication, is distinctive, however, for it is concerned with specific cases in which an individual has come into conflict with society by violating its norms or in which individuals have come into conflict with one another, and it employs formal procedures that contrast with those of parliamentary or administrative bodies.

Varieties of court systems

Established court systems are found in all advanced political systems. Usually there are two judicial hierarchies, one dealing with civil and the other with criminal cases, each with a large number of local courts, a lesser number at the level of the province or the region, and one or more courts at the national level. This is the pattern of judicial organization in Britain, for example. In some countries—for example, in France—although there is a double hierarchy, the distinction is not between courts dealing with criminal cases and other courts dealing with civil cases but rather between those that handle all civil and criminal cases and those that deal with administrative cases or challenges to the administrative authority of the state. Reflecting the federal organization of its government, the United States possesses two court systems: one set of national courts and 50 sets of state courts. By contrast, West Germany and the Soviet Union, both of which are federal in governmental organization, each possess only one, integrated court system.

Local courts are found in all systems and are usually of two types. The first type deals with petty offenses and may include a traffic court, a municipal court, a small-claims court, and a court presided over by a justice of the peace or a local magistrate. The second type, sometimes called trial courts, are courts of first instance in which most cases of major importance are begun. These are the state superior courts in the United States, the county courts and quarter sessions in Britain, the *tribunal de grande instance* in France, and the district courts, or *Landgerichte,* in Germany. In some systems there is a level above the local court, usually referred to as assize courts, in which exceptionally serious crimes, such as homicide, are tried. Courts of appeal review the procedures and the law in the lower court and either reverse or affirm its judgment or, in some cases, return the case for a new trial. In all systems there are national supreme courts that hear appeals and exercise original jurisdiction in cases of the greatest importance, such as those involving conflict between a state and a national government. Outside the regular court systems, there are sometimes found specialized judicial tribunals, such as administrative courts, or courts of claims that deal with special categories of cases.

The functions of government

In all modern states, governmental functions have greatly expanded with the emergence of government as an active force in guiding social and economic development. In Communist countries, government has a vast range of detailed controls over all types of social and economic behaviour. Even in the United States, where there remains a much greater attachment than in most societies to the idea that government should be only an umpire adjudicating the rules by which other forces in society compete, such governmental activities as the Tennessee Valley Authority or the use of credit controls to prevent economic fluctuations are now accepted with relatively little question. Government has thus become the major or even the dominant organizing power in all contemporary societies.

The historical stages by which governments have come to exercise their contemporary functions make an interesting study in themselves. The scope of government in the ancient polis involved the comprehensive regulation of the ends of human existence. As Aristotle expressed it, what was not commanded by government was forbidden. The extent of the functions of government in the ancient world was challenged by Christianity and its insistence on a division of those things that belong separately to Caesar and to God. When the feudal world succeeded the Roman Empire, however, the enforcement of the sanctions of religion became one of the first objects of political authority. The tendencies that began in the 18th century separated church from state and state from society, and the modern concept of government came into being. The American Colonies' Declaration of Independence expresses the classic modern understanding of those ends that governmental functions exist to secure. The first aim of government is to secure the right to life; this comprehends the safety of fellow citizens as regards one another and the self-preservation of the nation as regards foreign powers. Life exists for the exercise of liberty, in terms of both natural and civil rights, and these, along with other specific functions of government, provide those conditions upon which men may pursue happiness, an end that is finally entirely private and beyond the competence of government.

With the advent of the Marxist conception of the state, the ends of human existence once again became the objects of comprehensive government regulation. Marxism sees the state as a product of class warfare that will pass out of existence in the future age of perfect freedom. Aristotle believed human perfection to be possible only within political society; Marx believed that the perfection of man would follow upon the abolition of political society. Before the final disposal of the state, however, many Marxists believe that forceful use of governmental power is justified in order to hasten mankind's progress toward the last stage of history.

THE TASKS

Self-preservation. The first right of men and nations is self-preservation. The task of maintaining the nation, however, is more complex than the individual's duty of self-preservation, for the nation must seek to command the attachment of a community of citizens as well as to preserve itself from external violence. As Thomas Hobbes insisted, civil war constitutes the greatest threat to governments, for it represents the dissolution of the "sovereign power." In modern terms, civil war signifies that the government has lost one of the basic attributes of political authority: its monopoly of force and its control over the use of violence. In a fundamental sense, political authority may be preserved from the threat of civil war only when there exists in the political community an agreement on the basic principles of the regime. Such a consensus is the result, among other things, of a shared "ideology" that gives fellow citizens a sense of communal belonging and recognizes interlocking values, interests, and beliefs. Ideology, in this sense, may be the product of many

The maintenance of authority

different forces. Sometimes it is associated with ancient customs, sometimes with religion, sometimes with severe dislocations or the sort of common need that has led to the formation of many nation-states, and sometimes with the fear of a common enemy. The ideological commitment that people call patriotism is typically the product of several of these forces.

Governments neglect at their peril the task of strengthening the ideological attachment of their citizens to the regime. In this sense, civic education should be counted among the essential functions of the state, for it is primarily through systems of education that citizens learn their duties. Indeed, as a number of recent sociological studies have shown, the process of political socialization that transforms men into citizens begins in kindergarten and grade school. Even more than this, education is the instrument by which governments further the cohesion of their societies and build the fundamental kinds of consensus that support their authority. It is not surprising, therefore, that national systems of education are often linked to central elements of the regimes. The educational system of the Soviet Union emphasizes political indoctrination; in France, public education is traditionally mixed with the teachings of the Roman Catholic Church; in Great Britain, until very recently, a private system of education supported the class divisions of society; and in the United States a primarily secular form of public education has traditionally used constitutional documents as the starting point of children's training in patriotism.

The preservation of the authority of the state also requires a governmental organization capable of imposing its jurisdiction on every part of the national territory. This involves the maintenance of means of communication, the use of administrative systems, and the employment of police forces capable of controlling domestic violence. The police function, like education, is often a key to the character of a regime. In Nazi Germany, Hitler's Brownshirts took over the operation of local and regional police systems and often supervised the administration of law in the streets. In the Soviet Union, the security police acts to check any deviation from the policy of the party or state. In the United States the police powers are left in the hands of the 50 states and the local agencies of government. They serve to check civil and criminal offenses; with the exception of certain offenses created by the McCarran Act and some parallel statutes, political crimes as such are unknown. In addition, there are state militias that act, under the control of the governors of the various states, in moments of local emergency, such as riots or natural catastrophes. The Federal Bureau of Investigation (FBI), the only equivalent of a national police force, is an agency established to carry out specific assignments dealing with a limited but important class of crimes. Since there is no comprehensive federal criminal code, there is not, strictly speaking, a federal police.

Governments must preserve themselves against external as well as domestic threats. For this purpose they maintain armed forces and carry on intelligence activities. They also try to prevent the entry of aliens who may be spies or saboteurs, imprison or expel the agents of foreign powers, and embargo the export of materials that may aid a potential enemy. The ultimate means of preserving the state against external threats, of course, is war. In war, governments usually enlarge the scope of their domestic authority; they may raise conscript forces, imprison conscientious objectors, subject aliens to internment, sentence traitors to death, impose extraordinary controls on the economy, censor the press, compel settlement of labour disputes, impose internal-travel limitations, withhold passports, and provide for summary forms of arrest.

Many forces generate clashes between nations, including economic rivalry and disputes over trade, the desire to dominate strategic land or sea areas, religious or ideological conflict, and imperialistic ambition. All national governments develop organizations and policies to meet these and other situations. They have foreign ministries for the conduct of diplomatic relations with other states, for representing them in the United Nations and other international organizations, and for negotiating treaties.

Some governments conduct programs such as foreign aid, cultural exchange, and other activities designed to win goodwill abroad.

In the 20th century, relationships among governments have been affected by a developing awareness that world peace depends upon multinational and international cooperation. The League of Nations and the United Nations, together with their associated agencies, represent major efforts to establish substitutes for traditional forms of diplomacy. Regional alliances and joint efforts, such as the Organization of American States, the North Atlantic Treaty Organization, the European Economic Community, and the Organization of African Unity, represent another type of cooperation among nations.

Supervision and resolution of conflicts. The conflict of private interest is the leading characteristic of the political process in constitutional democracies, and the supervision, mediation, arbitration, and adjudication of such conflicts are among the key functions of their governments. Representative institutions are themselves a device for the resolution of conflict. Elections in constitutional democracies provide opportunities for mass participation in a process of open debate and public decision; assemblies, congresses, and other parliamentary institutions provide for public hearings on major issues of policy and require formal deliberative procedures at different stages of the legislative process; and political parties integrate a variety of interests and effect compromises on policy that win acceptance from many different groups.

If the interests that compete in the political process are too narrow or restricted, efforts may be made to control or change the rules of competition. Thus, laws have been enacted that seek to prevent discrimination from locking racial and other minorities out of the democratic process; the franchise has been extended so as to permit all groups, including minorities such as women, blacks, and 18-year-olds, to have a voice in elections; and government bodies such as courts and administrative agencies enforce legislation against groups considered to be too large or monopolistic.

Judicial processes offer a means by which some disputes in society are settled according to rule and legal authority, rather than by political struggle. In all advanced societies, law is elaborated in complex codes governing rights and duties and procedural methods; and court systems are employed that adjudicate disputes in terms of the law. In constitutional systems such as the United States, the judiciary is deeply involved in the process of public decision making; the courts actually produce much of the substantive law that bears on private individuals and economic groups in society.

Regulation of the economy. Government regulation of economic life is not a new development. The national mercantilist systems of the 18th century provided for regulation of the production, distribution, and export of goods by government ministries; even during the 19th century, governments continued to intervene in the economy. The government of the United States, for example, from its inception in 1789, allotted funds or subsidies for the support of agriculture, maintained a system of tariffs for its own revenue and the support of domestic manufacturers, patronized the arts and sciences, and engaged in various kinds of public works to advance commerce and promote the general welfare. In France, even more elaborate governmental schemes of economic regulation were practiced throughout the 19th century, including a variety of Socialist experiments such as the Public Workshops that Louis Blanc established in Paris in 1848. In Britain, the various factory acts of the 19th century represented an effort by government to control working conditions in industry.

After World War II the ability of a government to regulate or control the economy became one of the chief tests of its success, and regulatory agencies multiplied to the point at which they are now often referred to as "the fourth branch of government." The extent of the controls imposed on the economy is one of the principal distinctions among capitalist, Socialist, and Communist systems. In Communist countries it is a matter of doctrine that the means of production should be owned and therefore controlled by the state; in the 1960s and 1970s, however, some Communist countries experimented with various ways of decentralizing economic decision making in an effort to increase flexibility and reduce the weight of the central bureaucracy. In Britain the Labour governments nationalized some major industries, including coal, steel, and the railroads, prompted partly by Socialist doctrine and partly by the failure of British industry to remain competitive in international markets. In the United States the government has involved itself in the economy primarily through its regulatory powers. In France the government has gone further and has engaged in national economic planning in cooperation with private business organizations.

The regulation of industrial conditions and of labour–management relations has been a major concern of most Western governments. In the United States the first regulatory efforts in this field were made during the Progressive era at the turn of the 20th century, when the wages, hours, and working conditions of women and children in industry became a matter of public scandal. A little later, the conditions, hours, food, and wages of merchant seamen were brought under government regulation; an eight-hour day was set for railway crews; and workmen's compensation laws were instituted. With the Depression of the 1930s, minimum wages were introduced for workers in many industries, hours of work were set, and the right to collective bargaining was given legal sanction.

Regulation of transportation has been another major activity in most Western political systems, beginning with the railroads. In the United States their monopolistic practices attracted the criticism of agricultural interests and led eventually to the Interstate Commerce Act of 1887, which regulated railroad rates; subsequent legislation covered the hours, conditions, and wages of railroad employees, among other things. Other modes of land and air transportation have since been brought under regulatory controls implemented by government agencies.

In most European countries, facilities of communication—the telegraph, telephone, radio, and television—are owned and operated by the government. In the United States most of these facilities have remained in private ownership, although they are regulated by the Federal Communications Commission. The regulation by government of important instruments of public opinion such as radio, television, and newspapers has important implications for the freedoms of speech and press and other individual rights. In the United States and Great Britain, government censorship of the press and other media has been restricted to matters of national security. This is also generally true of other Western constitutional democracies, although the celebrated *Der Spiegel* affair in Germany in 1962 and some extraordinary controls imposed on the media in France have been widely criticized. In Communist countries and in many of the new states of Africa and Asia, very extensive controls are imposed on the press, and government-owned newspapers are often the principal sources of political news.

Other forms of government regulation of the economy involve the use of taxes and tariffs, the regulation of weights and measures, and the issuance of money.

Protection of political and social rights. To some extent, all modern governments assume responsibility for protecting the political and social rights of their citizens. The protection of individual rights has taken two principal forms: first, the protection of liberty in the face of governmental oppression; second, the protection of individual rights against hostile majorities and minorities. Even Communist governments recognize certain rights of individuals and minorities in the ordinary spheres of life, if not in matters touching the interests of the state. Beginning in the 1960s there appeared to be a broadening of the sphere of private rights in the Soviet Union. Authors, artists, and scientists were able to engage in criticism of official policies, not with impunity but with much greater freedom than in the Stalin era; and there were some signs that the Soviet state had begun to recognize the rights of the Jewish minority and the claims of some other national groups. In the United States the Supreme Court expanded the rights of the criminally accused; and, after 1954, the

national government acted to bar legal discrimination against ethnic minorities. Indeed, almost all the freedoms detailed in the first ten amendments to the Constitution have been extended since World War II.

Another type of government regulation bearing on the individual concerns the law of immigration and emigration. The great mass migrations of the 19th and early 20th centuries came to an abrupt halt after 1914 with the proliferation of government controls on the freedom of movement across national boundaries.

Provision of goods and services. All modern governments participate directly in the economy, purchasing goods, operating industries, providing services, and promoting various economic activities. One of the indispensable functions of government—national defense—has made governments the most important consumers of goods, and they have not hesitated to use their resulting pricing, purchasing, and contracting powers to achieve various economic aims. In efforts to avoid dependence on private sources of strategic goods and defense materials, some governments have taken a further step and established their own military production plants. In wartime, governments have assumed control over entire industries and have subjected the work force to military direction.

In nearly all political systems, certain functions are recognized as public, or belonging to the government. In addition to national defense, these include the maintenance of domestic peace, public education, fire protection, traffic control, aid to the indigent, conservation of natural resources, flood control, and postal services. But governments have assumed responsibility for many other commercial operations, even in non-Socialist countries. The sale of electric power, for example, is one of the established enterprising functions of national, state, and local governments in the United States and Canada. Municipally owned power utilities exist in about 2,000 cities in North America; 14 states of the U.S. have public power districts; and the U.S. government markets power through the Tennessee Valley Authority, the Bureau of Reclamation, the Bonneville Power Administration, and the Southwestern and Southeastern Power administrations. Another range of functions is performed by other national agencies, including the Rural Electrification Administration, which loans money to rural cooperatives to finance local power projects; the Export–Import Bank of Washington, which makes loans to finance export and import trade; the Maritime Administration, which holds mortgages on ships; and the Veterans Administration, which makes loans for farm or home purchases to military veterans. The United States government, acting through agencies such as the Social Security Board, the Federal Deposit Insurance Corporation, and the Federal Housing Administration, is also the largest insurer in the nation. Through other agencies, such as the Housing and Home Finance Agency, the Urban Renewal Administration, and the Public Works Administration, the national government has also developed a major role in the construction and rental of residential housing for low-income persons.

Other miscellaneous enterprises in which governments are involved include the provision of health care, the operation of public transport facilities, the development of public works, airport and port maintenance, and water-supply systems. In Great Britain the government operates hospitals and provides medical care under the National Health Service. In the United States, many state and local governments operate hospitals on a commercial basis, although providing some charity care. At the local level in the United States, the Port of New York Authority constructs and operates bridges, terminals, and airports. The states in the Delaware Basin recently joined in a compact to establish an agency to control the use of water from the basin, institute programs to prevent pollution, provide recreation facilities, transmit and sell hydroelectric power, and provide watershed management. Cities in the United States and Canada operate more than 70 urban transit systems, 600 municipal gas utilities, and more than 4,000 water-supply systems. Cities are also generally responsible for garbage disposal and sometimes operate commercial slaughterhouses, coal yards, laundries, ice plants, and golf courses. Finally, packaged liquor sales are often made by the state governments, at either wholesale or retail or both.

PUBLIC ADMINISTRATION

Civil
service
While the functional objectives of government administration vary from system to system, all countries that are technologically developed have evolved systems of public administration. A number of common features may be detected in all such systems. The first is the hierarchical, or pyramidal, character of the organization by which a single chief executive oversees a few subordinates, who in turn oversee their chief subordinates, who are in turn responsible for overseeing other subordinates, and so on, until a great structure of personnel is integrated and focussed on the components of a particular program. A second common feature is the division of labour or specialization within the organization. Each individual in the hierarchy has specialized responsibilities and tasks. A third feature is the maintenance of detailed official records and the existence of precise paper procedures through which the personnel of the system communicate with each other and with the public. Finally, tenure of office is also characteristic of all public bureaucracies.

The various national civil services, despite their similarities, also show important differences, particularly in the way in which individuals are recruited and in the status accorded them in the political system. The British civil service, for example, has traditionally been composed of three classes, or grades—clerical, executive, and administrative. Administrative civil servants, the highest grade, are recruited by examination from among recent university graduates. The top managers of the different government ministries are drawn from this elite group. They remain in office despite changes in government and are accorded immense prestige in the British political system. The U.S. civil service is organized into 18 grades. Although promotion from the lower grades is the typical means by which positions in the top grades are filled, there is also a flow of individuals into senior positions from private business and the professions. The U.S. equivalent of the administrative civil servant in Britain is usually a political appointee recruited by each new administration from private life or from a position in politics.

Development and change in political systems

The student of political systems grapples with a subject matter that is today in constant flux. He must deal not only with the major processes of growth, decay, and breakdown but also with a ceaseless ferment of adaptation and adjustment. The magnitude and variety of the changes that occurred in the world's political systems between the second and eighth decades of the 20th century suggest the dimensions of the problem. Great empires disintegrated; nation-states emerged, flourished briefly, and then vanished; world wars twice transformed the international system; new ideologies swept the world and shook established groups from power; all but a few nations experienced at least one revolution and many nations two or more; domestic politics in every system were contorted by social strife and economic crisis; and everywhere the nature of political life was changed by novel forms of political activity, new means of mass communication, the enlargement of popular participation in politics, the rise of new political issues, the extension of the scope of governmental activity, the threat of nuclear war, and innumerable other social, economic, and technical developments.

CAUSES OF STABILITY AND INSTABILITY

Although it is possible to identify a number of factors that obviously have a great deal to do with contemporary development and change in the world's political systems—industrialization, population growth, the "revolution of rising expectations" in the less developed countries, and international tensions—there is no agreed theory to explain the causes of political change. Some social scientists have followed Aristotle's view that political instability is generally the result of a situation in which the distribution of wealth fails to correspond with the distribution of

political power and have echoed his conclusion that the most stable type of political system is one based on a large middle class. Others have adopted Marxist theories of economic determinism that view all political change as the result of changes in the mode of production. Still others have focussed on governing elites and their composition and have seen in the alienation of the elite from the mass the prime cause of revolutions and other forms of violent political change.

In the discussion that follows, a distinction is drawn between unstable and stable political systems, and an attempt is made to suggest ways of understanding the processes of political development and change.

Unstable political systems. In modern times the great majority of the world's political systems have experienced one form or another of internal warfare leading to violent collapse of the governments in power. Certain crisis situations seem to increase the likelihood of this kind of breakdown. Wars and, more particularly, national military defeats have been decisive in prompting many revolutions. The Paris Commune of 1871, the Russian revolutions of 1905 and 1917, Hitler's overthrow of the Weimar Constitution in Germany, and the revolutions in China all occurred in the aftermath of national military disasters. Many factors in such a situation, including the cheapening of human life, the dislocation of population, the ready availability of arms, the disintegration of authority, the discrediting of the national leadership, material scarcities, and a sense of wounded national pride, contribute to the creation of an atmosphere in which radical political change and violent mass action are acceptable to large numbers of people. Economic crises are another common stimulus to revolutionary outbreaks, for they produce not only the obvious pressures of material scarcity and deprivation but also a threat to the individual's social position, a sense of insecurity and uncertainty as to the future, and an aggravation of the relationships among social classes. A severe national economic crisis works, in much the same way as a military disaster, to discredit the existent leadership and the present regime. Another triggering factor is the outbreak of revolutions in other political systems. Revolutions have a tendency to spread: the Spanish Revolution of 1820 had repercussions in Naples, Portugal, and Piedmont; the French Revolution of July 1830 provoked similar outbreaks in Poland and Belgium; the Russian Revolution of 1917 was followed by a dozen other revolutions; and the colonial liberation movements after World War II appear to have involved a similar chain reaction.

Crisis
situations

Crisis situations test the stability of political systems in extremely revealing ways, for they place extraordinary demands on the political leadership and the structure and processes of the system. Since the quality of the political leadership is often decisive, those systems that provide methods of selecting able leaders and replacing them possess important advantages. Although leadership ability is not guaranteed by any method of selection, it is more likely to be found where there is free competition for leadership positions. The availability of established methods of replacing leaders is equally, if not more, important, for the result of crises is often to disgrace the leaders in power, and, if they cannot be replaced easily, their continued incumbency may discredit the whole regime. The stamina and resolve of the ruling elite are also important. It is often said that a united elite, firmly believing in the justice of its own cause and determined to employ every measure to maintain its power, will not be overthrown. Most revolutions have gotten under way not when the oppression was greatest but only after the government had lost confidence in its own cause.

Other conditions of the survival of political systems relate to the effectiveness of the structures and processes of government in meeting the demands placed on them. Political systems suffer violent breakdown when channels of communication fail to function effectively, when institutional structures and processes fail to resolve conflicts among demands and to implement acceptable policies, and when the system ceases to be viewed as responsive by the individual and groups making demands on it. Usually, a system has failed over a period of some time to satisfy persistent and widespread demands; then, exposed to the additional strains of a crisis situation, it is unable to maintain itself. Revolutions and other forms of violent collapse are thus rarely sudden catastrophes but rather the result of a process of considerable duration that comes to its climax when the system is most vulnerable.

Unstable political systems are those that prove vulnerable to crisis pressures and that break down into various forms of internal warfare. The fundamental causes of such failures appear to be the lack of a widespread sense of the legitimacy of state authority and the absence of some general agreement on appropriate forms of political action. Governments suffer their gravest handicap when they must govern without consent or when the legitimacy of the regime is widely questioned. This is often the case in systems that have experienced prolonged civil war, that are torn by tensions among different national or ethnic groups, or in which there are divisions along sharply drawn ideological or class lines. The problem is often most acute where there is a pretender to the throne, a government in exile, a neighbouring state sympathetic to a rebel cause, or some other focus for the loyalty of dissidents. To some degree, also, the problem of legitimacy confronts all newly established regimes. Many of the new states of Africa and Asia, for example, have found it a source of great difficulty. Often they have emulated the form of Western institutions but failed to achieve their spirit: borrowing eclectically from Western political philosophies and systems of law, they have created constitutional frameworks and institutional structures that lack meaning to their citizens and that fail to generate loyalty or a sense that government exercises rightful powers.

Closely related to the problem of legitimacy as a cause of the breakdown of political systems is the absence of a fundamental consensus on what is appropriate political behaviour. A regime is fortunate if there are well-established, open channels of political action and settled procedures for resolving grievances. Although the importance of such "rules of the game" is that they allow change to occur in mainly peaceful ways, stable political systems often show surprising tolerance for potentially violent forms of political behaviour, such as strikes, boycotts, and mass demonstrations. Such forms of political behaviour are not permitted in systems where there are no agreed limits to the role of violence and where there is a high risk that violence may escalate to the point of actual warfare. If the government cannot count upon widespread support for peaceful political procedures, it must restrict many kinds of political action. Such restriction, of course, inhibits still more the development of open methods of citizen participation in politics and adds to tension between the government and the people.

Stable political systems. The simplest definition of a stable political system is one that survives through crises without internal warfare. Several types of political systems have done so, including despotic monarchies, militarist regimes, and other authoritarian and totalitarian systems. After 1868, in the period of the restoration regime under the Meiji emperor, Japan succeeded, without major political breakdowns, in building an industrial state and developing commercial structures that transformed traditional Japanese society. This achievement was based on the development of centralized patterns of political control and the growth of a type of authoritarianism involving the rule of a military elite. Similarly, some of the totalitarian regimes of the contemporary world have demonstrated an impressive capability for survival. The key to their success is their ability to control social development, to manage and prevent change, and to bring under governmental direction all the forces that may result in innovations that are threatening to the system.

In some systems, survival does not depend on the detailed management of the society or close governmental control over social processes but is the result of sensitive political response to the forces of change, of flexible adjustment of the structures of the system to meet the pressures of innovation, and of open political processes that allow gradual and orderly development. Much of the Western democratic world has achieved peaceful progress

Causes of the breakdown of political systems

Managed and evolutionary systems

in this way, despite new political philosophies, population increases, industrial and technological innovations, and many other social and economic stresses.

Such evolutionary change is possible when representative institutions provide effective channels for the communication of demands and criticisms to governments that rely upon majority support. The election of legislators and executive officials, competition between political parties, constitutional guarantees of freedom of speech and press, the right of petition, and many other structures and procedures perform this function in contemporary constitutional democracies. In such systems, social and economic problems are quickly transformed into issues in the open arenas of politics; governments are obliged to shape policies that reflect a variety of pressures and effect compromises among many conflicting demands.

The representative mechanisms that have produced evolutionary change in Western constitutional democracies are themselves subject to a continuous process of adjustment and mutation. Indeed, representative institutions must develop in ways that reflect social and economic developments in the society or they will lose their legitimacy in the minds of the people. In political systems such as the United States, for example, subtle shifts in the function and relative power of different institutions are continuously being made and, over time, produce entirely new structures and very different patterns of institutional behaviour. It is as a result of this process that the presidency has accumulated a range of new powers that have given it primacy among the branches of American government. This process also explains the growth of administrative agencies that perform both legislative and judicial functions. This process of dynamic adjustment is crucial, for institutions that remain static in a changing society are unable to serve as agencies of evolutionary change.

TYPES OF POLITICAL CHANGE

The study of political change is difficult, for change occurs in many different ways and at many different points in the political system. One may distinguish several major types of change.

Radical revolution. First are changes of the most fundamental type—transformations not only of the structure of government but of the whole polity. Such change is not limited to political life but transforms also the social order, the moral basis, and the values of the whole society. Drastic change of this kind occurred in the four great revolutions of the modern era—the English Revolution of the 17th century, the American Revolution, the French Revolution, and the Russian Revolution. These movements had the most profound effect on social and political life, permanently altering the beliefs by which men live. Their consequences were felt not only in the societies in which they occurred but also in many other political systems, in which, as a result of their example, revolutions of an equally fundamental character occurred.

Each of these major revolutions was something of a world revolution, for it resulted in a basic change in the ways in which men in all political systems viewed the nature of politics and the purpose of political life. The independence movements in the colonial empires after World War II, for example, were fuelled by those principles of individual liberty and representative government that were once the slogans of 18th-century American and French revolutionaries. Marxist revolutionary concepts emphasizing economic progress and radical social change have shaped the development of many of the new nations. The continuing impact of such ideas is an example of another way in which fundamental political change occurs. The nature of a political system may be transformed not suddenly or violently in the course of revolution but by the gradual, corrosive influence of ideas and by the accumulating impact of different political philosophies.

Structural revision. A second type of change involves alterations to the structure of the political system. Such change is not fundamental, in the sense of a basic transformation of the nature of the regime, but it may produce great shifts in policy and other political outcomes. Because the structure of a political system—that is, its formal and informal institutional arrangements—is a major determinant of policy outcomes, it is frequently the target of political action of various kinds. The political activist, the reformer, and the revolutionary share the recognition that the policies of a government may be effectively changed by adjusting the institutional forms through which the government acts. In some systems, structural change has been accomplished by legal means. In the United States, for example, such major institutional reforms as the direct election of the Senate and the limitation on presidential terms were made by constitutional amendment; and in Britain the various reforms of Parliament were accomplished by statute. In other systems, structural changes are often achieved by revolution and other violence.

Change of leaders.   A third type of political change involves the replacement of leaders. Again, the recognition that to change the personnel of a government may be an effective way of changing government policy prompts many kinds of political action, ranging from election contests to political assassination and various forms of coup d'etat. In some systems the existence of established means of changing political leaderships works to prevent violent types of political action. In the United States the quadrennial contests for the presidency afford a constitutional opportunity to throw the whole executive leadership out of office. At the other extreme, the coup d'etat leads to the abrupt, often violent replacement of national executives. Although it is a type of revolution, the coup d'etat usually does not involve prolonged struggle or popular participation; after seizing office, the principal aim of the leaders of the coup is usually the restoration of public order. The coup d'etat occasionally develops into much more than the replacement of one set of governmental leaders by another and may prove to be the initial stage of a truly revolutionary process; *e.g.,* the coups d'etat that initiated Communist rule in Czechoslovakia in 1948 and ended King Farouk I's regime in Egypt in 1952.

Change of policies.   Government policy itself may be an important agency of political change. The social and economic policies of Franklin D. Roosevelt's New Deal and the Socialist programs implemented by the British Labour Party after 1945 are examples. In both cases, government policies resulted in far-reaching modifications to the functioning of the political system: a vast expansion in the role of government in the economy, the use of taxes to redistribute wealth, an increase in the political influence of organized labour, and the implementation of national programs of social welfare. Major policy change of this type, of course, is often a response to widespread pressures and demands that, if not satisfied by the system, may intensify and lead to various forms of violent political action. At other times, however, policy changes are imposed by a government to achieve the political, social, and economic goals of a single class, of an elite, or of the political leadership itself.

Many important questions remain as to the reasons for change, the ways in which change occurs, and the effects of change. Political scientists are still not completely certain, for example, why some systems have managed to avoid violent political change for considerable periods, while in other systems change is typically accomplished through coups d'etat, revolutions, and other forms of internal warfare. As suggested above, the explanation may have much to do with the existence in countries such as the United States and Great Britain of well-established political institutions that permit peaceful change, the presence in the population of widely shared attitudes toward the government, and the existence of basic agreement on the legitimacy of state authority. Clearly, however, other factors are also involved. Perhaps one of the chief goals of the study of political systems should be to determine as exactly as possible the conditions and prerequisites of those forms of change that permit the peaceful and evolutionary development of human society.   (D.A.He.)

ELECTORAL PROCESSES

Elections are means of making political choices by voting. They are used in the selection of leaders and in the determination of issues. This conception of elections implies that the voters are presented with alternatives, that they can choose among a number of proposals designed to settle an issue of public concern. The presence of alternatives is a necessary condition, for although electoral forms may be employed to demonstrate popular support for incumbent leaders and their policies, the absence of alternatives disqualifies such devices as genuine elections.

The widespread use of elections in the modern world is due largely to the gradual emergence of representative government from the 17th century on. For proper appraisal, however, it is important to distinguish between the form and substance of elections. Electoral forms may be present but the substance may be missing. The substance is, of course, that the voter has a free and genuine choice between at least two alternatives. In a purely formal sense, the great majority of the approximately 150 contemporary nations have what are called "elections," but probably only a third of these have more or less competitive elections; perhaps a fifth have one-party elections; and in some others the electoral situation is highly ambiguous.

The discovery of the individual as the unit to be counted was, from the 17th century on, the critical factor in the emergence of modern electoral processes. The counting of individuals, in turn, was a by-product of the change from the holistic conception of representation in the Middle Ages to an individualistic conception. The British Parliament, for instance, was no longer seen as representing estates, corporations, and vested interests, but as standing for actual human beings. The movement abolishing "rotten boroughs"—boroughs of small population controlled by one person or family—that culminated in the Reform Act of 1832 was a direct consequence of the individualistic conception of representation. Once governments were not only believed to derive their powers from the consent of the governed but were expected to seek consent, the only remaining problem was to decide who was to be included among the governed whose consent was to be sought. The democratic answer was, of course, universal adult suffrage.

Although it is common to equate representative government, elections, and democracy, and although competitive elections under universal suffrage are in many respects a defining characteristic of political democracy, universal suffrage is not a necessary condition of competitive electoral politics. An electorate may be limited by formal legal requirements—as was the case before universal adult suffrage—or it may be limited by citizens' failure to take advantage of the vote, as is often the case in American municipal and other elections. Although such legal or self-imposed exclusion affects the democratic quality of elections and may ultimately affect the legitimacy of government, it does not impede decision-making by election, provided the voter is presented with alternatives among which to choose.

Access to the political arena during the 18th century depended largely on membership in some aristocracy, and participation in elections was regulated mainly by local customs and arrangements. With the American and French revolutions every citizen was declared formally equal to every other citizen, but the vote remained an instrument of political power possessed by very few.

Even with the arrival of universal suffrage, the ideal of one man, one vote was not achieved. Systems of plural voting were maintained in some countries giving certain social groups an electoral advantage. In Great Britain, for example, university graduates and owners of businesses in constituencies other than those in which they lived continued to have an extra vote until 1948. Before World War I, both Austria and Prussia had three classes of weighted votes that effectively kept electoral power in the hands of the upper social strata.

Whereas in the Western nations of the 19th and 20th centuries the increasing use of competitive mass elections in selecting governments had the purpose and the effect of institutionalizing the diversity of modern societies, in the Eastern, one-party, Communist regimes, mass elections came to have quite different purposes and consequences. Elections in these nations were not designed to offer choice of leadership or to influence policy formation. They differ from competitive elections in that only one team of

Elections in authoritarian systems

candidates is presented, and the voter has only the choice of voting for the official candidate. They are in the nature of the 19th century Napoleonic plebiscites, intended to demonstrate the unity rather than the diversity of the people, and, above all, they do not make or unmake governments.

Although the Soviet Union's constitution of 1936 provided for elections on the Western model, the election mechanism is manipulated to produce almost universal turnout and unanimous support of the regime. Elections are dramatic occasions for Communist agitation and propaganda to strengthen the citizen's identification with the Soviet way of life.

Because voting is considered a pledge of loyalty, it is easier to vote against the official candidate than to abstain. Although nonparticipation is not a legal offense, it may be socially punished. Although an unmarked ballot is considered a "yes" vote, dissent may be registered by crossing out the name of the candidate on the ballot, as some 2,000,000 Soviet citizens do in each election. These voters are easily identified because they are likely to choose voting booths that make secret voting possible. Perhaps for this reason less than 5 percent of the voters risk public scrutiny by secret voting. it may well be that dissenting votes are cast not so much because of dislike of Communism, but because of grievances involving the conduct of minor officials who stand for election to one of the numerous village, town, republic, or oblast soviets.

Not all elections under authoritarian governments follow the Soviet model. In Poland, for instance, more names appear on the ballot than there are offices to fill, and some degree of electoral choice is possible. Electoral participation is usually over 90 percent, but effective dissent is minimal. It is difficult to appraise election results in the Eastern, one-party, Communist nations because published data are unreliable and cannot be easily compared.

In the non-Communist authoritarian regimes of the world a variety of means is employed to eliminate free electoral choice, ranging from suppression of the opposition to the physical intimidation of voters.

Functions of elections. Fundamental to the use of elections is the contribution that they make to democratic government. Where the members of the body politic cannot themselves govern and must entrust government to representatives, elections serve not only to select leaders acceptable to the voters but also to hold the leaders accountable for their performance in office. Accountability, however, is greatly jeopardized in electoral situations in which elected leaders, for want of ambition, do not care whether or not they are re-elected or in situations in which, for historical or other reasons, one party is so predominant as to preclude effective choice among alternate candidates or policies. Nevertheless, the possibility of controlling leaders by requiring them to submit to regular and periodic elections contributes to solving the problem of succession in leadership and, thereby, to the continuation of democracy. Moreover, where the electoral process is competitive and forces candidates or parties to expose their record of accomplishment and future intentions to popular scrutiny in election campaigns, elections serve as forums for the discussion of public issues, facilitate the expression of public opinion, and, more generally, permit an exchange of influence between governors and governed.

Elections also serve to reinforce the stability and legitimacy of the political community in which they take place. Like national holidays commemorating common experiences, elections serve to link the members of a body politic to each other and thereby confirm the viability of the political community. By mobilizing masses of voters in a common act of governance, elections lend authority and legitimacy to the acts of those who wield power in the name of the people.

Elections can also confirm the worth and dignity of the individual citizen as a human being. Whatever other needs he may have, participation in an election serves to gratify the voter's sense of self-esteem and self-respect. It gives him an opportunity to have his say, and he can, through expressing partisanship and even through nonvoting, satisfy his sense of belonging to or alienation from the polit-

ical community. It is for just this reason that the age-long battle for the right to vote and the demand for equality in electoral participation can be seen as the manifestation of a profound human craving for personal fulfillment.

In all forms of government, from the most democratic to the most totalitarian alike, elections have a ritualistic aspect. Elections and the campaigns preceding them are dramatic events which, depending on cultural or historical circumstances, may exude the gay atmosphere of a circus or the sombre atmosphere of a funeral. Rallies, banners, posters, buttons, headlines, and television call attention to the importance of participation in the event. Candidates and parties, from right to left, in addition to propagating their policy objectives through rhetoric and slogans, invoke the symbols of nationalism or patriotism, reform or revolution, past glory or future promise. Whatever the peculiar national, regional, or local variations, elections are events that, by arousing emotions and channelling them toward collective symbols, break the monotony of daily life and focus attention on the common fate.

Systems of counting votes. Individual votes are totalled into collective decisions by rules of counting that voters and leaders have accepted as legitimate prior to the election. These decision rules may call for plurality voting, which requires that, among three or more alternatives, the winner need have only the highest number of votes; simple majority voting, which requires that the winner receive more than 50 percent of the vote; extraordinary majority voting, which requires some higher proportion for the winner, such as a two-thirds vote; or unanimity.

Plurality and majority decision. The simplest means of deciding an election is the plurality rule. To win, a candidate need only poll more votes than any other single opponent; he need not, as required by the majority formula, poll more votes than the combined opposition. The more candidates contesting a constituency seat, the greater the probability that the winning candidate will receive less than 50 percent of the vote. The plurality formula is used in the national elections of such countries as Great Britain, Canada, and New Zealand. One half of the West German Bundestag is elected according to the plurality system, while the other half is elected according to a proportional representation formula (see below).

Under the majority rule, the party or candidate winning over 50 percent of the vote in a constituency is awarded the contested seat. The winning party or candidate must poll more votes than the combined opposition. This system thus ensures that the elected representative has the support of the majority of the voters. The majority formula is employed in the election of the Australian House of Representatives, and of the French National Assembly. It is usually applied only within single-member electoral constituencies.

Both the plurality and the majority-decision rules are employed in the election of U.S. presidents. The composition of the electoral college, which actually elects the president, is determined by a plurality vote taken within each state. Voters choose between the names of the presidential candidates, but they are in effect choosing the electors who will elect the president by means of a majority vote in the electoral college. All of a state's electoral votes (which are equal in number to its seats in Congress) are given to the presidential candidate who gains a plurality of the vote in the state election. It is thus possible for a president to be elected on the basis of a minority of the popular vote.

A critical difficulty with the majority formula is that in a multiparty political system, the formula may produce an electoral deadlock if no candidate secures 50 percent of the total vote. In order to break such deadlocks a second round of elections (second ballot) is required, if no candidate obtains a majority on the first round. In Australia, voters rank the candidates on an alternate preference ballot. If a majority is not achieved on the first round of elections, the weakest candidate is eliminated, and the votes he accrued are distributed to the other candidates according to the second preference on the ballot. This redistributive process is repeated until one candidate collects a majority of the votes. If no candidate secures a majority in the first round of the French National As-

Margin notes:

Democratic functions

Plurality voting

sembly elections, another round of elections is required. In this second round, the candidate securing a plurality of the popular vote is declared winner.

Neither the majority nor the plurality formulas distribute legislative seats in proportion to the share of the popular vote won by the competing parties. Both formulas tend to award the strongest party disproportionately and to handicap the weaker parties. The latter is particularly true if small parties are rooted in ethnic, religious, or social minorities; small parties escape the inequities of the electoral system only if they have a regionally concentrated base. The plurality formula distorts the distribution of seats more than the majority system.

Proportional representation. Proportional representation requires that the distribution of offices be proportional to the distribution of the popular vote among competing political parties or candidates. It seeks to overcome the distribution imbalances that result from majority and plurality formulas, and to create a representative body that reflects the distribution of opinion within the electorate. Because of the use of multimember constituencies in proportional representation, parties with neither a majority nor a plurality of the popular vote can still win legislative representation.

Proportional representation is an ideal that is sought after, but only approximated: the size of electoral districts is the critical factor; the larger the electoral district in terms of seats, the more proportional the representation will be. The number of seats assigned to a constituency is in fact a greater determinant of the proportionality of the outcome than is the specific type of proportional formula used. The different formulas of proportional representation are basically similar in their effect on the conversion of votes to political representation.

Developed in the 19th century in Denmark and in Britain, the single transferable vote formula—or Hare system (after one of its English developers, T. Hare)—employs a ballot that allows the voter to rank the competing candidates in order of preference. When the ballots are counted, any candidate receiving the necessary quota of first preference votes is awarded a seat. In the electoral calculations, votes received by a winning candidate in excess of the quota are transferred to other candidates according to the second preference marked on the ballot. Any candidate who then has the necessary quota is also awarded a seat. This process is repeated, with subsequent surpluses also being transferred, until all the remaining seats have been awarded. Five members constituencies are considered optimal for the working of the Hare system.

The single transferable vote formula, because it involves the aggregation of ranked preferences, necessitates complex electoral computations. This factor, plus the fact that the Hare system limits the influence of political parties, probably accounts for its infrequent use; at present it is used only in Eire and in the selection of the Australian and South African senates. The characteristic of the Hare formula, which distinguishes it from other proportional representation formulas, is its emphasis on candidates, not parties. The party affiliation of the candidates has no bearing on the computations.

The basic difference between the transferable vote formula and the list systems is that, in the latter, voters choose among party-compiled lists of candidates rather than among individual candidates. Although voters may have some limited choice among individual candidates, electoral computations are on the basis of party affiliation; seats are awarded in respect to party rather than candidate totals. The seats that a party wins are allocated to its candidates in the order in which they appear on the party list. Several types of electoral formulas are used, although they fall into two main categories; largest average formulas and greatest remainder formulas. All employ some type of electoral quota.

Largest average formula

In the largest average formula, the number of votes won by each party is divided by the number of seats held by the party, plus one. The first seat is awarded to the party with the highest number of votes, since, no seats yet having been allocated, the initial denominator is 1. When a party wins a seat, its formula denominator is increased by one

and hence the party's chances of winning the next seat are reduced. The available seats are awarded one at a time to the party with the greatest average. Party totals, not candidate totals, are used in the calculations. No transfer of ballots takes place. Frequently named after its Belgian inventor, Victor d'Hondt, the largest average formula is used in Austria, Belgium, Finland, and Switzerland, and in the proportional representation half of the West German Bundestag elections.

The d'Hondt formula has a slight tendency to over reward large parties and to reduce the chance of small parties gaining legislative representation. The so-called Lague variation of the d'Hondt formula—used in Denmark, Norway, and Sweden—reduces the reward to large parties but increases further the handicap to small parties. By adjusting the denominator of the d'Hondt formula, the Lague formula increases the cost of both the initial seat of a party and that of additional seats. The Lague formula thus aids middle-size political parties and reduces the number of legislatively represented small parties.

The greatest remainder method establishes a vote quota for each seat in an electoral district by dividing the total vote in the district by the number of competing parties. The total popular vote won by each party is then divided by the quota, and a seat is awarded as many times as the party total contains the full quota. If all the seats are awarded in this manner, the election is complete. Such an outcome is unlikely, however. Seats that were not won by full quotas are subsequently awarded to the parties with the largest remainder of votes after the quota has been subtracted from each party's total vote for each seat it was awarded. Seats are awarded sequentially to the parties with the largest remainder until all the district's allocated seats have been awarded.

Of all the proportional representation formulas, the greatest remainder formula, given large enough constituencies, yields results closest to the proportional ideal. Small parties fare better when the greatest remainder formula is used than when the largest average formula is employed. The greatest remainder formula is used in Israel, Italy, and Luxembourg and in some elections in Denmark. Italy, however, uses a special variety of the formula, called the Imperiali formula, whereby the electoral quota is established by dividing the total popular vote by the number of parties plus two. This modification increases the legislative representation of small parties, but leads to a greater distortion of the proportional ideal than the unaltered formula.

The choice of majority and plurality or proportional systems is, of course, not simply a matter of pure theory. Different methods of counting, just as different conceptions of representation, usually reflect cultural, social-structural, and political circumstances in a particular jurisdiction. Majority or plural methods of voting are most likely to be acceptable in relatively stable political cultures. In such cultures, fluctuations in electoral support, given to one party or another from one election to the next, reduce polarization and make for political centrism. Thus the "winner take all" implications of the majority or plurality formulas are not experienced as unduly deprivational or restrictive. Proportional representation, on the other hand, is more likely to be found in societies with traditional ethnic, linguistic, and religious cleavages or in societies experiencing pervasive class and ideological conflicts.

Types of elections. *Election of officeholders.* Rather than deciding public policy, election to public office bestows the right to decide on a small group of elected officials. The elections grant officials the authority to make public policy decisions, and thereby legitimize the decisions that are made. The policy voice of the electorate in these elections may be weak. An electoral mandate results not so much in the implementation of the abstract preferences of the majority of the citizens, but rather in the implementation of the policy of those leaders who come to power in elections.

Most officeholder elections are interpretable only in terms of the role of political parties in the political process. Parties are tied so closely to the democratic functions of elections that their competition for the electorate's sup-

Role of parties

port is considered the main criterion by which democratic elections are distinguished from nondemocratic elections. Because of the difficulty in fixing individual responsibility in the complexity and vastness of modern governments, political parties, rather than representatives, have become the vehicle of democratic accountability.

Political parties shape the nature of the electoral decision. The selection and nomination of candidates, a vital first stage of the electoral process, lies in the hands of the political parties; the election serves only as the final process in the recruitment to political office. The party system can thus be regarded in a true sense as an extension of the electoral process. Political parties provide the pool of talent from which candidates are drawn, and they simplify and direct the electoral choice and mobilize the electorate at the registration and election stage. Political parties have transformed elections from a choice of men to a choice of governments.

But the fusion of political parties with the electoral process has not gone unchallenged. In North America a number of modifications have been made in the electoral structure to limit the influence of political parties. Nonpartisan elections (elections in which party affiliations are not formally indicated on ballots) are the norm for some municipalities in the United States and Canada and represent an attempt to remove political parties from the electoral scene. Nonpartisanship started as a reform movement in the early part of the 20th century and was designed to put local government on a more businesslike basis and to isolate local politics from state and national politics. The exclusion of party labels from the ballot, however, does not guarantee that political parties will be inactive or without influence in nonpartisan elections.

Recall. The practice of recalling officeholders was, like most populist innovations, an attempt to minimize the influence of political parties on representatives. The recall was an electoral modification designed to ensure that an elected representative would act as a spokesman for his constituency rather than for his political party or the dictates of his own conscience or interests. It enabled constituents to recall their elected representative before the end of his term of office if, in their opinion, he was no longer acting in accord with the best interests of the constituency. The actual instrument of recall was often a letter of resignation signed by the elected representative *before* assuming office. During the term of office this letter could be evoked by a quorum of constituents if the representative's legislative performance failed to meet their expectations. In practice the recall is not often or widely used today, even where it is provided for constitutionally.

Referendum. A referendum is an election, held either at the initiative of the governors or the governed, in which the preferences of the community regarding a particular issue are assessed. The use of the referendum reflects a reluctance to entrust full decision-making power to elected representatives. Because of the small voting turnout for referendum elections, and the absence of affixed party labels to the referendum alternatives, voting in referendum elections is more open to leadership and interest group influence than is voting in officeholder elections.

Referenda usually concern the raising and spending of public money, although they are occasionally used to decide moral issues in which the elected bodies are deemed to possess no special competence. They may be legislatively binding, or merely consultative, but even consultative referenda are likely to be considered legislative mandates.

Plebiscite. Plebiscites are elections held to decide two paramount types of political issue: the form of government and the national boundaries adopted by the state. In the first case, the plebiscite is a means of establishing the legitimacy to rule, not a means of providing a choice among alternate governmental teams or legislative proposals. The incumbent government, seeking a popular mandate as a basis for legitimacy, employs a plebiscite to establish its right to speak for the nation. The incumbent rulers seek a single identity with the nation, and thus a vote for the nation is interpreted as a vote for the incumbent regime. Plebiscites of this nature are thought to establish a direct linkage between the rulers and the ruled; intermediaries

such as political parties are bypassed in plebiscites, and in this respect they are antithetical to pluralism and competitive politics. Following the Revolution of 1789, the plebiscite had a great appeal in France, rooted as it was in the ideas of nationalism and popular sovereignty. In more recent times totalitarian regimes have employed plebiscites to legitimize their power.

Plebiscites have also been used as a device for establishing the boundaries of political units according to criteria of nationality. After World War I the plebiscite was employed as a means of fitting political boundaries to boundaries of nationality. Eleven plebiscites, based on universal suffrage, were proposed by the League of Nations, the most successful of which was held in 1935 in the Saar (which chose to remain a German territory rather than go to France). The potential of plebiscites for establishing or changing political boundaries is, however, severely limited, because they entail the prior agreement of two governments over what is usually a very contentious issue.

Constituencies: districting and apportionment. The drawing up of constituencies—those subdivisions of the total electorate that send representatives to the local or central assembly—is inextricably linked with questions concerning the nature of representation and methods of voting. Of these questions, that of representation is primary. The problem of electoral representation turns on the question of what is to be represented. In this connection the functions of constituencies and the problem of determining them (districting) become relevant. The central problem is that the constituency, as a geographical area, may contain within its boundaries diverse, and sometimes incompatible, social, economic, religious, or ethnic interests, all of which seek to be represented.

The solution to this problem has been largely historically determined. Where the interests of electors have not been totally incompatible, and where ethnic, religious, social, and economic differences have been relatively free of passionate conflict, as in the Anglo-American countries, geographical areas (electoral districts) have usually been considered the constituency, and the method of counting has been some system of majority or plurality voting. The elected person represents the geographical unit as a whole, irrespective of internal divisions. In general, the district is a single-member constituency, although multimember constituencies are also possible.

On the other hand, where the electorate is composed of several minorities, none of which can hope to obtain a majority, or perhaps even a plurality sufficiently large to obtain representation, the geographical district can only be regarded as an administrative unit for counting votes. The effective constituency is the group of electors that can be identified as having voted for a given candidate. In this case, election is usually by some method of proportional counting whereby any candidate, party, or group receiving a requisite number of votes is entitled to a proportionate number of representatives.

The drawing up, or delimitation, of electoral districts is inextricably linked with differing conceptions of representation; and conceptions of representation are inextricably linked with alternate methods of vote counting. The virtues and vices of different electoral arrangements are still debated by constitution makers, but the arguments advanced in favour of any one set of arrangements remain inconclusive. Although proportional systems treating electoral districts as merely administrative conveniences and providing for multiple representation are believed to approximate more closely the one man, one vote principle of democratic theory than do single-member geographic constituencies providing for majority or plurality voting, they are probably conducive to governmental instability, and they place an inordinately heavy burden of conflict resolution on representative bodies. This often makes for political stalemate or immobilism, as has been the case at times in France and Italy. But it is doubtful that in nations with many interests seeking representation any other method of electoral districting and vote counting would be satisfactory.

Representation of geographic constituencies with majority or plurality voting, on the other hand, disguises many

Districting

differences in the electorate's composition and preferences. In single-member, majority-vote electoral districts, the minority losing at the polls may feel unrepresented. But it is often a precarious assumption that the majority itself is truly represented, since it is likely to be a loose coalition of diverse interests, and no single representative can usually do justice to the diversity of interests involved. In general, therefore, the representative, in so far as he is responsive, is more likely to play the role of broker among his district's diverse interests, rather than the role of spokesman for the district as a whole.

Whatever the role of representative, and however electoral units are conceived—as geographic areas with stable, compatible interests, or as purely administrative areas for the purpose of vote counting—districting must be distinguished from apportionment. In general, if the district is considered as only an administrative unit for counting votes, its boundaries can be drawn rather arbitrarily without injustice. The district as such has no stakes of its own to be represented. On the other hand, if the district is considered a true constituency, in the sense that it has unique interests that can be geographically and, as a result, socially defined, districting should not be arbitrary. The area involved should at least be contiguous and compact so that its presumed interests can be fairly recognized.

The difficulty in treating geographic areas as genuine constituencies is, of course, that internal transformations in their economy and social structure may make their historical boundaries obsolete. As a result, historical areas serving as electoral districts (such as provinces, states, or counties), which once served as genuine communities of interest to be represented, may no longer do so. As these districts become increasingly diverse, making it difficult to identify particular constituency interests, representatives find it increasingly impossible to be responsive to constituency wishes or needs.

Apportionment Problems of apportionment, in contrast to problems of districting, stem from efforts to reconcile the territorial and population bases of representation. If geographic areas, for instance, are assumed to have an equal right to be represented because the area is considered to be a viable constituency, malapportionment in terms of population size is inevitable. New York with a population of nearly 20,000,000 has, in the U.S. Senate, the same number of representatives as Nevada with a population of less than 1,000,000. This kind of "constitutional malapportionment" must not be confused with the kind of "electoral malapportionment" that defies the one man, one vote principle of equal representation. The latter is usually the result of population shifts. Under modern conditions of increasing urbanization, failure to reapportion the number of seats in representative bodies to take account of population changes has largely benefitted rural electoral districts. More recently, the shift of city people to the suburbs has led to possible underrepresentation of suburban vis-à-vis urban populations.

From a political rather than a legal perspective, malapportionment is usually considered "undemocratic" because it results in overrepresentation and underrepresentation of certain sectors of the population and, as a result, may culminate in public policies not acceptable to the true majority.

Apportionment is not a simple matter. In particular, the definition of the population among which a specified number of legislative seats is to be apportioned is not easy to arrive at. Total population, number of citizens of voting age, number of registered voters, or number of actual voters can serve as bases of apportionment. If there were a constant relation between these groupings, apportionment would not be a problem, and any one of them could serve as a basis. In fact, however, the relation is not constant because of variations in registration and voting turnout.

Gerrymandering Malapportionment, whether of the constitutional or electoral sort, must not be confused with gerrymandering— a form of arbitrary districting used to benefit the party that at a given time controls the apportionment process. Gerrymandering is named after governor of Massachusetts Elbridge Gerry (1744–1814), who recognized the possibility of influencing electoral outcomes by manipulating

the boundaries of electoral districts. The practice involves concentrating large percentages of the opposite party's votes into a few districts, and drawing the boundaries of the other districts in such a way that the gerrymandering party wins in them all, even though the majority, or, in three-cornered elections, the plurality, is relatively small.

Gerrymandering comes to politicians easily. Party managers prefer "safe" districts to those that are competitive. By not contesting seriously in the other party's safe districts, by maintaining one's own safe districts, and by carving competitive districts up in such a way that one's own party is favoured, party managers use gerrymandering to create artificial district boundaries that, though advantageous to the parties, may harm other social, economic, and political interests that need representation.

Voting practices. There is a direct relation between the size of an electorate and the formalization and standardization of its voting practices. In very small voting groups, in which political encounters are face-to-face and the members are bound together by ties of friendship or common experience, voting is mostly informal and may not even require counting, because the "sense of the meeting" emerges from the group's deliberations. The consensus of the Quaker meeting is of this order. An issue is discussed until a solution emerges to which all participants can agree or, at least, from which any one participant will not dissent.

By way of contrast, in modern mass electorates, in which millions of individual votes are aggregated into the collective choice, formalization and standardization of voting practices and vote counting are the rule. This is necessary in order to guarantee that the outcome can be considered valid, reliable, and legitimate. Validity means that the collective choice in fact expresses the sense of the electorate. Reliability means that each vote is accurately recorded and effectively counted into the total. Legitimacy means that the criteria of validity and reliability have been met, so that the result of the voting is acceptable and provides authoritative guidelines in subsequent political conduct.

The development of routinized and standardized electoral practices in mass electorates is a surprisingly recent phenomenon, not much older than 100 years. It is as much a corollary of the growth of rapid communication through telephone and telegraph as of the growth of the electorate and rational insistence on making electoral processes fair and equitable. Nevertheless, even today electoral practices around the world differ a great deal, depending not just on formal institutional arrangements, but even more on a country's political culture.

Secret voting. Once suffrage rights had been extended to masses of voters who, in theory, were assumed to be equal but who, in fact, were unequal (in order of birth, in intellectual endowment and educational accomplishment, in social status and the possession of property, and so on), open voting was no longer tolerable precisely because it could and often did involve undue influence, ranging from hidden persuasion and bribery to intimidation, coercion, and punishment. Equality, at least in voting, was not something given but something that had to be engineered; the secrecy of the vote was a first and necessary administrative step toward the one man, one vote principle. Equality in voting was possible only if each vote was formally independent of every other vote, and this suggested the need for strict secrecy.

The slow progress made in introducing secret voting, from the French Revolution well into the 20th century, attests to the fact that social engineering, no matter how desirable or lofty in purpose, depends on favourable conditions for success. One need not assume that the obstacles placed in the way of secret voting were the result of some conspiracy on the part of those who recognized, quite accurately, that the mobilization of large numbers of voters fundamentally changed the distribution of political power and who, through opposing the secret vote, hoped to maintain a stranglehold on the newly enfranchised electorates. Rather, the success of secret voting depended on the reduction of illiteracy and, at the cultural level, on the spread of the individualistic norms of privacy and anonymity to certain classes of the population, notably peasants and workers. Traditionally these groups took their cues from those accepted as superior in status, or from their peers. Secret voting required learning to free oneself as a citizen from one's customary associations and from pressures for conformity. The difficulty of introducing and practicing the secret vote in today's politically and economically less developed nations mirrors the tortuous advance of the secret ballot in the Western nations during the 19th and early 20th centuries.

Benefits
of secret
voting

Secret voting reduces drastically the possibility of undue influence on the voter. Without it, influence can range from outright purchase of votes to social chastisement or economic sanctions. This is not to say that bribery in voting is automatically eliminated by secret voting. Laws prohibiting and punishing the purchase of votes are on the statute books of many countries and undoubtedly contribute to discouraging the practice.

Although informal social pressures on the voter are probably unavoidable and, in some respects, useful in reducing political rootlessness and contributing to political stability, secrecy in voting permits voters to break away from their social moorings and gives them a considerable degree of independence if they wish to take advantage of this electoral freedom. As a result it becomes ever more difficult for interest groups, whether labour unions, farmers' organizations, commercial or industrial associations, ethnic leadership groups, or even criminal syndicates, to "deliver the vote." The extent to which "deviant voting" occurs depends partly on the degree of rigidity in the social structure. In countries where caste or class barriers are high or where traditional social, economic, religious, or regional cleavages remain strong, deviant voting is less likely than in countries where social mobility is possible and where political conflicts cut across traditional social cleavages. In Western nations the increasing difficulties of labour, farm, religious, or ethnic leaders in influencing the voter attests to the success that secret voting seems to have had on freeing the individual from electoral bondage to his traditional or economic affiliations.

Balloting. The ballot makes secret voting possible. Its initial use seems to have been a means to reduce irregularities and deception in elections. This objective, however, could be achieved only if the ballot was not supplied by the voter himself, as was the case in much early voting by secret ballot, or by political parties, as is still the case in some countries. Ballot procedures differ widely, ranging from marking the names of preferred candidates to crossing out those not preferred or writing in the names of persons who are not formal candidates. Ballots also differ according to the type of voting system employed. Where plurality or majority voting is practiced, most elections employ classified ballots whereby the voter casts his vote for only one candidate or list of candidates. Where proportional methods are used, election is by ballots that enable the voter to rank the candidates according to his preferences.

Though evidence is hard to come by, it is commonly believed that the nature of the ballot influences the voter's choice. In jurisdictions where electors are called upon to vote not only for higher offices but also for a multitude of local positions and where, in addition, the election may include propositions in the nature of referenda, the length of the ballot seems to be a factor affecting vote outcomes. Overwhelmed by the length of the ballot, voters may be discouraged from expressing their preferences for candidates of whom they have not heard, or from deciding on propositions that they do not understand. Breaking up of the single ballot into separate short ballots helps overcome this problem but does not eliminate it. Election data show a rapid decline from votes cast for higher offices to those cast for lower offices and referendum-type propositions.

Ballot position also seems to have an effect on the votes cast for particular candidates, especially in the absence of cues as to party affiliation or other identifications. The first position on the ballot may be favoured, and in the case of a long ballot both first and last names may benefit, with candidates in the middle of the ballot suffering a slight handicap. Ballot position is likely to have its greatest

impact in nonpartisan elections, primaries, and elections for minor offices.

Finally, the manner in which candidates are listed—by party column or office bloc—is likely to affect election outcomes. On party-column ballots it is possible to vote a "straight ticket" for all of a party's candidates by entering a single mark, although voting for individual candidates is usually possible. On the other hand, on the office-bloc ballot, voting is for individual candidates grouped by office rather than party. This discourages, though it does not eliminate, voting exclusively for members of one party. This can have important consequences for the structure of government, especially in systems with separated powers and federal territorial organization. If different offices are controlled by different parties, the governmental process may be marked by greater conflict than would otherwise be the case, and governmental decision-making often will be more difficult.

The introduction of voting machines has not substantially changed the balloting process, although it has made it faster, more accurate and economical, and virtually tamper-proof. The voting machine is not without some minor problems of its own, in that it may marginally depress the level of voting. In candidate elections the dampening effect is accounted for by improper use of the machine, a problem that is being overcome through improved machines and voter education.

Compulsory voting. In some nations, notably Australia and Belgium, electoral participation is legally required of all citizens, and nonvoters without legitimate excuses face money fines. The concept of compulsory voting reflects a strain in democratic theory in which voting is considered not merely a right but a duty. Its purpose is to ensure the electoral equality of all social groups.

Whether made compulsory in law or through social pressure, it is doubtful that high voter turnout as such is a good indication of an electorate's capability for intelligent social choice. On the other hand, high rates of abstention or differential rates of abstention by different social classes are not necessarily signs of satisfaction with governmental processes and policies and may in fact indicate the contrary.

Electoral abuses. Corruption of electoral practices is, of course, not limited to bribery or intimidation of the individual voter. The possibilities are endless, ranging from the dissemination of scurrilous rumours about candidates, and deliberately false campaign propaganda, to tampering with the election machinery by stuffing the ballot box with fraudulent returns, dishonest counting or reporting of the vote, and total disregard of electoral outcomes by incumbent officeholders. The existence of these practices depends more on a population's adherence to political civility and the democratic ethos than on the prohibitions and sanctions written into the law.

The integrity of the electoral process is maintained by a variety of devices and practices. Permanent and up-to-date registries of voters are maintained to guarantee easy identification of those eligible to participate in elections, and procedures are designed to make the registration process as simple as possible. In most jurisdictions, elections are now held on a single day rather than staggered. Polling hours in all localities are the same, and opening and closing hours are fixed and announced, so that voters have an equal opportunity to participate. Polling stations are manned by presumably disinterested government officials or polling clerks under governmental supervision; and political party agents or party workers are given an opportunity to observe the polling process, enabling them to challenge irregularities and prevent abuses. Efforts are made to maintain order in polling stations, directly through police protection or indirectly through such practices as closing bars and liquor stores. The act of voting itself takes place in voting booths that protect privacy. Votes are counted and often recounted by tellers, watched by party workers to assure an honest count. The transmission of voting results from local polling stations to central election headquarters is safeguarded and checked.

Participation in elections. The rate at which individuals participate in the electoral process depends on many factors, including the type of electoral system, the social groupings to which voters belong, the voters' personality and beliefs, their place of residence, and a host of other idiosyncratic factors.

Effect of level and type of election

The level and type of election has a great impact on the rate of electoral participation. Electoral turnout is greater in national than in state or provincial elections, and greater in the latter than in local elections. Because of this, scheduling has an impact on the turnout for local elections. If local elections are held concurrently with provincial or national elections, a higher voter turnout is achieved than for nonconcurrent elections.

Whether an election is partisan or nonpartisan also affects voter turnout—lighter participation occurring in the nonpartisan elections. Participation is also greater in candidate elections than in noncandidate elections such as referenda. There is some evidence that elections based on proportional representation, in which in some cases every vote counts, have higher electoral turnouts than majority or plurality elections. Noncompetitive or safe electoral districts tend to depress the level of voter turnout, whereas marginal elections increase the turnout.

Technicalities in electoral law involuntarily disenfranchise many potential voters. As a result of moving, people may temporarily lose their vote because of residence requirements for voters in their new electoral district. Complicated voter registration procedures, combined with a high level of geographical mobility, significantly reduce the size of the active electorate in the United States, whereas in Canada and Great Britain the size of the electorate is maximized by government-initiated registration immediately prior to elections. Voter registration in the United States is left to the initiative of individuals and political parties.

Group differences

Relatively low levels of electoral participation are associated with rural residence, and also with low levels of education, occupational status, and income. The groups in society that have been most recently enfranchised also tend to vote less. Hence women vote less than men, American blacks less than whites, and working class people less than those of the middle class. Young people who have just turned of age, and have therefore just been enfranchised, are less likely to vote than people who are middle-aged. It is important to note that the nonparticipation of certain groups in elections has important implications; if everyone were to vote, the balance of electoral power would shift toward the recently enfranchised and less privileged members of the society.

Some people are conscientious nonvoters, although such people are rare. Others, perceiving the vote more as an instrument of censure than of support, may not vote because they are satisfied with the present government. This group of voluntary nonvoters is also small, however. In fact, nonvoters have been shown to be generally less satisfied with the political status quo than are voters. The vote is a rather blunt and ineffectual instrument for expressing dissatisfaction, and nonvoting is more likely to be symptomatic of alienation from, than of satisfaction with, the political system.

Supporters of political parties vote more frequently than nonsupporters; to party supporters the vote becomes a pledge of their party loyalty as well as a political instrument.

Those who feel that government policies have some direct relevance to their lives are more likely to vote than those who are disinterested or who sense the government as being more remote.

Finally, a great number of random factors may determine individual participation in specific elections. Election campaigns vary in their intensity. A crisis atmosphere may induce an unusually large number of people to vote, on one occasion, whereas on another the chance to vote for an extremist candidate may increase the participation of the normally disinterested. Even the weather has a substantial impact on election turnout.

Influences on the direction of voting. The electoral choice of voters is largely influenced by their membership in social groups or by the social groups with which they identify, and, to a much lesser extent, by campaign issues and party promises. The determinants of party membership or party identification are the most crucial factors behind the voting decision. Membership in social and occupational classes, regional, religious or ethnic groupings, and so on, are thus important influences on the direction of the vote.

Because the electoral choice appears to be largely determined by long-standing group and party identifications, the voting decision may appear to be irrational, in that it is not based on a careful calculation of the immediate benefits expected to accrue to the voter from each electoral outcome. Group-determined voting does not preclude rationality, however, for individual self-interest may well be tied to the destiny of the social groups to which the voter belongs.

The independent voter, contrary to much common belief, is likely to be poorly informed politically and relatively uninterested and uninvolved in politics. Paradoxically, however, by switching their support, independent voters represent an important factor in democratic politics.

Independent voting

In most countries the relatively permanent party alignments are based on social and cultural cleavages. But if elections are to be competitive, and if control of the government is to alternate between parties or coalitions of parties, then some voters must switch party support from election to election. New voters and independent voters, therefore, provide a vital source of change in democratic politics.

(H.E./R.G./Ed.)

BIBLIOGRAPHY

General works: Perhaps the best single introduction to the subjects covered in this article is CARL J. FRIEDRICH, *Man and His Government: An Empirical Theory of Politics* (1963). Other excellent general works include KARL LOEWENSTEIN, *Political Power and the Governmental Process*, 2nd ed. (1965); and R.M. MACIVER, *The Modern State* (1926) and *The Web of Government* (1947). A good introductory text is JOHN C. WAHLKE and ALEX N. DRAGNICH (eds.), *Government and Politics* (1966); and some carefully selected readings are available in HARRY ECKSTEIN and DAVID E. APTER (eds.), *Comparative Politics* (1963). For many subjects, *The International Encyclopedia of the Social Sciences*, 17 vol. (1968), is an excellent reference.

Supranational political systems: The history of the empires of the ancient world may be studied in a number of monumental works, including ARNOLD J. TOYNBEE, *A Study of History*, 1st–2nd ed., 12 vol. (1948–61); OSWALD SPENGLER, *Der Untergang des Abendländes*, 2 vol. (1918–23; Eng. trans., *The Decline of the West*, 2 vol., 1926–28); and EDUARD MEYER, *Geschichte des Altertums*, 5 vol. (1884–1902, reprinted 1910–39). Among other general works, S.N. EISENSTADT, *The Political Systems of Empires* (1963), compares the ancient empires in terms of bureaucracy; and KARL WITTFOGEL, *Oriental Despotism: A Comparative Study of Total Power* (1957), traces the origins of their political orders. Treatments of the major empires of the ancient world include JAMES H. BREASTED, *Development of Religion and Thought in Ancient Egypt* (1912); A.T. OLMSTEAD, *History of Assyria* (1923, reprinted 1960); JOHN A. WILSON, *The Culture of Ancient Egypt* (1956); WILLIAM C. HAYES, *The Scepter of Egypt* (1953); R.E.M. WHEELER, *The Indus Civilization* (1953); OTTO FRANKE, *Geschichte des chinesischen Reiches*, 5 vol. (1930–52); WOLFRAM EBERHARD, *Chinas Geschichte* (1948; Eng. trans., *A History of China*, 3rd ed. rev., 1969); ETIENNE BALAZS, *Chinese Civilization and Bureaucracy* (1964); MIKHAIL ROSTOVTSEV, *The Social and Economic History of the Roman Empire* (1963); A.E.R. BOAK, *History of Rome to 565 A.D.* (1921); GEORGE OSTROGORSKI, *Geschichte des byzantinischen Staates* (1965; Eng. trans., *History of the Byzantine State*, 2nd ed., 1968). Histories of modern colonial empires are found in J. HOLLAND ROSE et al. (eds.), *The Cambridge History of the British Empire*, 9 vol. (1929–59; 2nd ed., 1963–); RICHARD KOEBNER and HELMUT D. SCHMIDT, *Imperialism: The Story and Significance of a Political World, 1840–1960* (1964); CHARLES DE LANNOY and HERMAN V. LINDEN, *Histoire de l'expansion coloniale des peuples européens*, 3 vol. (1907–21); STEPHEN H. ROBERTS, *The History of French Colonial Policy, 1870–1925* (1963); ROBERT L. SCHUYLER, *The Fall of the Old Colonial System* (1945); MARY E. TOWNSEND, *The Rise and Fall of Germany's Colonial Empire, 1884–1918* (1930); CLARENCE H. HARING, *The Spanish Empire in America* (1947). A discussion of the post-imperial era in Asia and Africa is provided by RUPERT EMERSON in *From Empire to Nation* (1960). An excellent discussion of modern supranational political institutions is available in INIS L. CLAUDE, *Swords into Ploughshares*, 4th ed. (1971); the same author discusses the conditions for the development of different types of international organization in his *Power and International Relations* (1962). GERARD J. MANGONE, *A Short History of International Organization* (1954), is a convenient reference for the development of most contemporary supranational political institutions. Standard treatments of the League of Nations and the United Nations are available in FRANCIS P. WALTERS, *A History of the League of Nations* (1960); ALFRED E. ZIMMERN, *The League of Nations and the Rule of Law, 1918–1935* (1938); and HERBERT G. NICHOLAS, *The United Nations As a Political Institution,* 2nd ed. (1962). More specialized works that may be consulted include THOMAS HOVET, *Bloc Politics in the United Nations* (1958); STEPHEN M. SCHWEBEL, *The Secretary-General of the United Nations* (1952); and ALEXANDER DALLIN, *The Soviet Union at the United Nations* (1962). The development of supranational institutions in Europe is discussed in ERNST B. HAAS, *The Uniting of Europe* (1958); MICHAEL CURTIS, *Western European Integration* (1965); WALTER HALLSTEIN, *United Europe: Challenge and Opportunity* (1962); and UWE W. KITZINGER, *The Politics and Economics of European Integration* (1963). Good discussions of the political and constitutional organization of the British Commonwealth are found in WILLIAM S. LIVINGSTON (ed.), *Federalism in the Commonwealth* (1963); J.D.B. MILLER, *The Commonwealth in the World* (1958); and K.C. WHEARE, *The Constitutional Structure of the Commonwealth* (1960). An extremely useful commentary on various forms of supranational political organization is provided in IVO D. DUCHACEK, *Comparative Federalism: The Territorial Dimension of Politics* (1970). A journal published since 1947 by the World Peace Foundation, *International Organization* (quarterly), contains informative articles on current developments in international organization and also provides selective bibliographies. J.D.B. MILLER, *The World of States* (1981), is a pessimistic discussion of the likelihood that an internation political system could replace the national systems.

National political systems: The phenomenon of nationalism is treated in HANS KOHN, *The Idea of Nationalism* (1961); and EUGEN LEMBERG, *Nationalismus,* 2 vol. (1964); and a historical sketch of the emergence of the idea and its reality is provided in CARLTON J.H. HAYES, *The Historical Evolution of Modern Nationalism* (1931, reprinted 1968). Among the many works on federal and unitary systems that the student should consult are ARTHUR W. MACMAHON (ed.), *Federalism, Mature and Emergent* (1955); WILLIAM S. LIVINGSTON, *Federalism and Constitutional Change* (1956); VALERIE EARLE (ed.), *Federalism* (1968); CARL J. FRIEDRICH, *Trends of Federalism in Theory and Practice* (1968); PETER HAY, *Federalism, and Supranational Organizations* (1966); K.C. WHEARE, *Federal Government,* 4th ed. (1963); and GEORGE C.S. BENSON *et al., Essays in Federalism* (1961). IVO D. DUCHACEK (*op. cit.*) should also be consulted. Works on individual nation-states are so numerous that the student may wish to consult some standard texts that include selected bibliographies: HAROLD ZINK, *Modern Governments,* 2nd ed. (1962); HERMAN FINER, *The Major Governments of Modern Europe* (1960); and GWENDOLEN M. CARTER and JOHN H. HERZ, *Major Foreign Powers,* 5th ed. (1967). Comparative studies of different aspects of contemporary national government are also numerous. The bureaucracies and administrative procedures of different modern governments are treated in BRIAN CHAPMAN, *The Profession of Government: The Public Service in Europe* (1959); JOSEPH G. LA PALOMBARA (ed.), *Bureaucracy and Political Development* (1963); FRITZ MORSTEIN MARX, *The Administrative State* (1957); WILLIAM J. SIFFIN (ed.), *Toward the Comparative Study of Public Administration* (1957); ERICH STRAUSS, *The Ruling Servants: Bureaucracy in Russia, France and—Britain?* (1960); and J.D. THOMPSON *et al.* (eds.), *Comparative Studies in Administration* (1959). Constitutions, courts, and other judicial institutions are comparatively treated in LESLIE WOLF-PHILLIPS (ed.), *Constitutions of Modern States* (1968); K.C. WHEARE, *Modern Constitutions,* 2nd ed. (1966); WILLIAM GEORGE ANDREWS (ed.), *Constitutions and Constitutionalism,* 3rd ed. (1968); HENRY J. ABRAHAM, *Courts and Judges* (1959) and *The Judicial Process: An Introductory Analysis of the Courts of the United States, England, and France,* 2nd ed. rev. (1968); FREDA CASTBERG, *Freedom of Speech in the West: A Comparative Study of Public Law in France, the United States, and Germany* (1960); RUSSELL F. MOORE (ed.), *Modern Constitutions* (1957); DOROTHY PEASLEE XYDIS, *Constitutions of Nations,* rev. 3rd ed., 4 vol. (1965–70); and CHARLES F. STRONG, *A History of Modern Political Constitutions* (1964). National legislatures are discussed in LORD CAMPION and D.W.S. LIDDERDALE, *European Parliamentary Procedure* (1953); PAUL EINZIG, *The Control of the Purse* (1959); JOHN E. KERSELL, *Parliamentary Supervision of Delegated Legislation* (1960); and K.C. WHEARE, *Legislatures* (1963). Political parties, elections, and interest groups are comparatively treated in ROBERT R. ALFORD, *Party and Society: The Anglo-American Democracies* (1963); DAVID E. BUTLER (ed.), *Elections Abroad* (1959); ROBERT A. DAHL (ed.), *Political Oppositions in Western Democracies*

(1966); MAURICE DUVERGER, *Les Partis politiques,* 5th ed. (1964; Eng. trans., *Political Parties,* 2nd ed. rev., 1959); HENRY W. EHRMANN (ed.), *Interest Groups on Four Continents* (1958); JOSEPH G. LA PALOMBARA and MYRON WEINER (eds.), *Political Parties and Political Development* (1966); W.J.M. MACKENZIE, *Free Elections* (1958); SIGMUND NEUMANN (ed.), *Modern Political Parties* (1956); and T.E. SMITH, *Elections in Developing Countries* (1960). General comparative studies of national political systems include GABRIEL ALMOND and SIDNEY VERBA, *The Civic Culture: Political Attitudes and Democracy in Five Nations* (1965); GABRIEL ALMOND and JAMES S. COLEMAN (eds.), *The Politics of the Developing Areas* (1960); GABRIEL ALMOND and G. BINGHAM POWELL, JR., *Comparative Politics: A Developmental Approach* (1966); ZBIGNIEW BRZEZINSKI and SAMUEL P. HUNTINGTON, *Political Power: USA/USSR* (1964); JAMES S. COLEMAN (ed.), *Education and Political Development* (1965); ROBERT C. FRIED, *Comparative Political Institutions* (1966); LUCIAN W. PYE (ed.), *Communications and Political Development* (1963); LUCIAN W. PYE and SIDNEY VERBA (eds.), *Political Culture and Political Development* (1965); and KENNETH H.F. DYSON, *The State Tradition in Western Europe* (1980).

Subnational political systems: Excellent general treatments of local and city government are found in WILLIAM A. ROBSON, *The Development of Local Government,* 3rd rev. ed. (1954); and (ed.), *Great Cities of the World: Their Government, Politics, and Planning,* 2nd ed. rev. (1957); and in LEWIS MUMFORD, *The City in History* (1961). On early forms of city government, the student should consult HENRI PIRENNE, *Les Villes du moyen âge* (1927; Eng. trans., *Medieval Cities,* 1956); and FUSTEL DE COULANGES, *La Cité antique* (1864; Eng. trans., *The Ancient City,* 1873, many reprints). A useful comparative study of local government is found in G.M. HARRIS, *Comparative Local Government* (1949). City and local governments in contemporary Western systems are treated in D.N. CHESTER, *Central and Local Government* (1951); HERMAN FINER, *English Local Government,* 4th ed. rev. (1950); and BRIAN CHAPMAN, *Introduction to French Local Government* (1953). Political and sociological analyses of the local community include ROBERT A. DAHL, *Who Governs?* (1961); DONALD J. BOGUE, *The Structure of the Metropolitan Community* (1949); FLOYD HUNTER, *Community Power Structure* (1953); ROBERT S. and HELEN M. LYND, *Middletown: A Study in Contemporary American Culture* (1929); and H.D. MALAVIYA, *Village Panchayats in India* (1966). For tribal forms of government, see J.A. NOON, *Law and Government of the Grand River Iroquois* (1949); and ISAAC SCHAPERA, *The Khoisan Peoples of South Africa* (1930) and *Government and Politics in Tribal Societies* (1956).

Types and models: The student of classical typologies of political systems will first refer to Book IV of Aristotle's *Politics* and then perhaps consult Book VIII of Plato's *Republic* together with a number of passages in *The Laws.* Leading modern efforts to develop types and models of political systems may be found in GAETANO MOSCA, *Elementi di scienza politica,* 2nd ed. (1923; Eng. trans., *The Ruling Class,* rev. ed., 1939); GUGLIELMO FERRERO, *Pouvoir* (1942; Eng. trans., *The Principles of Power,* 1942); and MAX WEBER, *Wirtschaft und Gesellschaft* (1922; Eng. trans. of pt. 1, *The Theory of Social and Economic Organization,* 1947). The Marxist typology, of course, is set forth in the writings of KARL MARX, FRIEDRICH ENGELS, LENIN, and their disciples. Contemporary efforts to develop typologies may be studied in DAVID E. APTER, "A Comparative Method for the Study of Politics," *American Journal of Sociology,* 64:221–237 (1958); DAVID EASTON, *A Systems Analysis of Political Life* (1965); GABRIEL ALMOND and G. BINGHAM POWELL, JR. (*op. cit.*); and ALEXANDER J. GROTH, *Comparative Politics: A Distributive Approach* (1971).

Development and change: There is a large contemporary literature centring on the question of modernization and political development. In addition to works by Gabriel Almond noted above, the student should consult PETER H. MERKL, *Modern Comparative Politics* (1970), which includes an excellent bibliography; and DAVID E. APTER, *The Politics of Modernization* (1965). Other works are CYRIL E. BLACK, *The Dynamics of Modernization* (1966) and (ed.), *The Transformation of Russian Society: Aspects of Social Change Since 1861* (1960); S.N. EISENSTADT, *Modernization: Protest and Change* (1966); JASON FINKLE and RICHARD W. GABLE (eds.), *Political Development and Social Change* (1966); EVERETT E. HAGEN, *On the Theory of Social Change* (1962); ROBERT T. HOLT and JOHN E. TURNER, *The Political Basis of Economic Development* (1966); SAMUEL P. HUNTINGTON, *Political Order in Changing Societies* (1968); JOHN H. KAUTSKY (ed.), *Political Change in Underdeveloped Countries* (1962); DANIEL LERNER, *The Passing of Traditional Society* (1958); MAX F. MILLIKAN and DONALD L.M. BLACKMER (eds.), *The Emerging Nations* (1961); DANKWART RUSTOW, *A World of Nations: Problems of Political Modernization* (1967); EDWARD A. SHILS, *Political Development in the New States* (1962); I. ROBERT SINAI, *The Challenge of Modernisation* (1964);

FRED VON DER MEHDEN, *Politics of the Developing Nations* (1964); IMMANUEL WALLERSTEIN, *Social Change: The Colonial Situation* (1966); BARBARA WARD, *The Rich Nations and the Poor Nations* (1961); and ARISTIDE R. ZOLBERG, *Creating Political Order: The Party-States of West Africa* (1966).

Forms, levels, and divisions of government: One of the best introductions to the study of different forms of government and an excellent review of the differences between constitutionalism and autocracy, democracy and totalitarianism, is KARL LOEWENSTEIN, *Political Power and the Governmental Process,* 2nd ed. (1965). Also excellent are CARL J. FRIEDRICH, *Constitutional Government and Politics* (1937); and with ZBIGNIEW BRZEZINSKI, *Totalitarian Dictatorship and Autocracy,* 2nd rev. ed. (1965). On totalitarianism, other books that should be consulted are ZBIGNIEW BRZEZINSKI, *The Soviet Bloc,* rev. ed. (1967), and *Ideology and Power in Soviet Politics,* rev. ed. (1967); MILOVAN DJILAS, *The New Class* (1957); MERLE FAINSOD, *How Russia Is Ruled,* rev. ed. (1963); ALEX INKELES and R.A. BAUER, *The Soviet Citizen: Daily Life in a Totalitarian Society* (1959); ERNST NOLTE, *Der Faschismus in seiner Epoche* (1963; Eng. trans., *The Three Faces of Fascism,* 1966); J.L. TALMON, *The Rise of Totalitarian Democracy* (1952); ALEXANDER DALLIN and ALAN F. WESTIN (eds.), *Politics in the Soviet Union* (1966); and HERBERT MCCLOSKY and JOHN E. TURNER, *The Soviet Dictatorship* (1960). On constitutional forms, the student should refer to WALTER BAGEHOT, *The English Constitution,* rev. ed. (1911, reprinted 1966); JAMES BRYCE, *The American Commonwealth,* rev. ed., 2 vol. (1931–33); D.L. KEIR, *The Constitutional History of Modern Britain, 1485–1951,* 9th ed. (1969); IVOR JENNINGS, *Cabinet Government,* 3rd ed. (1969), and *Parliament,* 2nd ed. (1957); C.S.W. CASSINELLI, *The Politics of Freedom* (1961); V.O. KEY, *Politics, Parties, and Pressure Groups,* 5th ed. (1964), and *Public Opinion and American Democracy* (1961); A.D. LINDSAY, *The Modern Democratic State* (1943); C.H. MCILWAIN, *Constitutionalism, Ancient and Modern,* rev. ed. (1947); HERBERT MORRISON, *Government and Parliament,* 3rd ed. (1964); CLINTON ROSSITER, *Constitutional Dictatorship* (1948); and HERBERT J. SPIRO, *Government by Constitution: The Political Systems of Democracy* (1959). A good general introduction to the major European forms of constitutional and totalitarian governments is available in SAMUEL H. BEER and ADAM B. ULAM (eds.), *Patterns of Government: The Major Political Systems of Europe,* 2nd ed. rev. (1962). CARL J. FRIEDRICH offers an excellent introduction to the problem of the relationship between different levels of government in *Man and His Government* (1963)—see especially pt. 5, "Ranges and Levels of Government." Other books to consult on this subject are CLAUDE AKE, *A Theory of Political Integration* (1967); HAROLD ALDERFER, *Local Government in Developing Countries* (1964); REINHARD BENDIX, *Nation-Building and Citizenship* (1964); BRIAN CHAPMAN, *Introduction to French Local Government* (1953); L.G. COWAN, *Local Government in West Africa* (1958); RICHARD COX, *Pan-Africanism in Practice* (1964); KARL W. DEUTSCH, *Nationalism and Social Communication* (1953) and *The Nerves of Government* (1963; with new introd., 1966); RUPERT EMERSON, *From Empire to Nation* (1960); RICHARD R. FAGEN, *Politics and Communication* (1966); JAMES FESLER, *Area and Administration* (1949); HERMAN FINER, *English Local Government* (1933); J.A.G. GRIFFITH, *Central Departments and Local Authorities* (1966); LUCIAN W. PYE (ed.), *Communications and Political Development* (1963); WILLIAM A. ROBSON, *Local Government in Crisis* (1966); and MARC J. SWARTZ (ed.), *Local-Level Politics* (1968). Short introductions to the divisions of government, suitable for the beginning student, are available in ROBERT C. FRIED, *Comparative Political Institutions* (1966); and JOHN C. WAHLKE and ALEX N. DRAGNICH (*op. cit.*). On the legislative division of government, in addition to the books listed in an earlier section of this bibliography, the student should consult BERTRAM GROSS, *The Legislative Struggle* (1953); WILLIAM J. KEEFE and MORRIS S. OGUL, *The American Legislative Process,* 2nd ed. (1968); D.W.S. LIDDERDALE, *The Parliament of France* (1951); STEPHEN KING-HALL and R.K. ULLMANN *German Parliaments* (1954); JOHN C. WAHLKE and HEINZ EULAU (eds.), *Legislative Behaviour* (1959); and JOHN C. WAHLKE *et al., The Legislative System* (1962). Additional reading on executives should include C.G. BROWNE and T.S. COHN (eds.), *The Study of Leadership* (1958); EDWARD S. CORWIN, *The President: Office and Powers, 1787–1957,* 4th rev. ed. (1957); ALVIN W. GOULDNER (ed.), *Studies in Leadership* (1950); HOOVER INSTITUTE STUDIES, *Elites,* 5 vol. (1951–55); RICHARD E. NEUSTADT, *Presidential Power* (1960); and ERIC STRAUSS (*op. cit.*). Further reading on courts and systems of law is available in HAROLD J. BERMAN, *Justice in the U.S.S.R.* (1963); FELIX S. COHEN, *Ethical Systems and Legal Ideals* (1933); RENE DAVID and HENRY DE VRIES, *The French Legal System* (1957); JEROME FRANK, *Courts on Trial* (1949); RICHARD M. JACKSON, *The Machinery of Justice in England,* 3rd ed. (1960); HANS KELSEN, *The Communist Theory of Law* (1955); W.F. MURPHY and C.H. PRITCHETT, *Courts, Judges, and Politics* (1961); J.W. PELTASON, *Federal Courts in the Political Process* (1955); J.R. SCHMIDHAUSER, *The Supreme Court: Its Politics, Personalities, and Procedures* (1960); GLENDON SCHUBERT (ed.), *Judicial Decision-Making* (1963); and BERNARD SCHWARTZ, *French Administrative Law and the Common-Law World* (1954).

The functions of government: The functions of government may be studied in many works dealing with each of the world's advanced political systems. For the United States, the student should consult JAMES E. ANDERSON, *The Emergence of the Modern Regulatory State* (1962); MELVIN ANSHEN and FRANCIS D. WORMUTH, *Private Enterprise and Public Policy* (1954); MORROE BERGER, *Equality by Statute* (1952); RICHARD E. CAVES, *Air Transport and Its Regulators* (1962); ROBERT A. DAHL and CHARLES E. LINDBLOM, *Politics, Economics, and Welfare* (1953); KENNETH CULP DAVIS, *Administrative Law* (1951); ERNST FREUND, *Administrative Powers over Persons and Property* (1928); D.E. HATHAWAY, *Government and Agriculture: Public Policy in a Democratic Society* (1963); CARL KAYSEN and DONALD F. TURNER, *Antitrust Policy* (1959); JAMES M. LANDIS, *The Administrative Process* (1938); AVERY LEISERSON, *Administrative Regulation* (1942); JOHN H. LEEK, *Government and Labor in the United States* (1952); MICHAEL D. REAGAN, *The Managed Economy* (1963); EMMETTE S. REDFORD, *American Government and the Economy* (1965) and *Administration of National Economic Control* (1952); GEORGE A. STEINER, *Government's Role in Economic Life* (1953); GEORGE W. TAYLOR, *Government Regulation of Industrial Relations* (1948); and DONALD S. WATSON, *Economic Policy: Business and Government* (1960). For Great Britain, the student should consult PATRICK ABERCROMBIE, *Town and Country Planning,* 3rd ed. (1959); W.P. ALEXANDER, *Education in England: The National System—How It Works,* 2nd ed. (1964); MAX BELOFF, *New Dimensions in Foreign Policy* (1961); A.M. CARTTER, *The Redistribution of Income in Postwar Britain* (1955); HARRY ECKSTEIN, *The English Health Service* (1958); PETER GOLDMAN, *The Welfare State* (1964); F.A. JOHNSON, *Defense by Committee* (1960); T.H. MARSHALL, *Social Policy* (1965); and HAROLD E. RAYNES, *Social Security in Britain,* 2nd ed. (1960). On France there are WARREN C. BAUM, *The French Economy and the State* (1958); JOHN S. HARLOW, *French Economic Planning* (1966); MARIO EINAUDI, MAURICE BYE, and ERNESTO ROSSI, *Nationalization in France and Italy* (1955); W.R. FRASER, *Education and Society in Modern France* (1963); JOHN and ANNE-MARIE HACKETT, *Economic Planning in France* (1963); WALLACE C. PETERSON, *The Welfare State in France* (1960); and JOHN B. SHEAHAN, *Promotion and Control of Industry in Postwar France* (1963).

The changing of government: Further reading on the politics of change should include DAVID E. APTER (ed.), *Ideology and Discontent* (1964); ROBERT N. BELLAH, *Religion and Progress in Modern Asia* (1965); CRANE BRINTON, *The Anatomy of Revolution,* rev. ed. (1952); HARRY ECKSTEIN (ed.), *Internal War* (1964); SAMUEL E. FINER, *The Man on Horseback: The Role of the Military in Politics* (1962); CLIFFORD GEERTZ (ed.), *Old Societies and New States* (1963); MANFRED HALPERN, *The Politics of Social Change in the Middle East and North Africa* (1963); CHALMERS JOHNSON, *Revolutionary Change* (1966); JOSEPH LOPREATO, *Peasants No More* (1967); PAUL E. SIGMUND (ed.), *The Ideologies of the Developing Nations* (1962); KALMAN H. SILVERT (ed.), *Churches and States: The Religious Institution and Modernization* (1967); ROBERT E. WARD and DANKWART RUSTOW (eds.), *Political Modernization in Japan and Turkey* (1964); and J.L. TALMON, *The Myth of the Nation and the Vision of the Revolution* (1982).

Electoral systems: DUNCAN BLACK, *The Theory of Committees and Elections* (1958), a rigorous analysis of the logic of voting based on elementary arithmetic and geometry; C.F. CNUDDE and D.E. NEUBAUER (eds.), *Empirical Democratic Theory* (1969), a useful collection of theoretical and empirical studies of modern voting behaviour and electoral processes; H.F. GOSNELL, *Democracy: The Threshold of Freedom* (1948), a survey of problems connected with electoral processes, in a historical perspective; J.A.O. LARSEN, *Representative Government in Greek and Roman History* (1955), an historical study of the relationship between representative institutions and electoral processes; CHARLES SEYMOUR and D.P. FRARY, *How the World Votes: The Story of Democratic Development in Elections,* 2 vol. (1918), still the most complete review of the history of elections in the English language; R.R. ALFORD, *Party and Society: The Anglo-American Democracies* (1963), a comparative study of the impact of elections on party formations in the United States, Canada, Great Britain, and Australia; S.M. LIPSET and STEIN ROKKAN (eds.), *Party Systems and Voter Alignments: Cross-National Perspectives* (1967), studies of electoral outcomes in Italy, France, Spain, West Germany, Finland, Norway, Japan, Brazil, and West Africa; W.J.M. MACKENZIE, *Free Elections: An Elementary Textbook* (1958), a simple introduction to electoral politics in a cross-national perspective; M.E. MOTE, *Soviet Local and Republic Elections* (1965), a useful survey in an area in which reliable information is difficult to obtain; T.E. SMITH, *Elections in Developing Countries* (1960), an examination of many of the problems besetting the introduction of elections in countries with limited democratic experience; DAVID BUTLER and D.E. STOKES, *Political Change in Britain* (1969), a recent study of voting behaviour in Great Britain based on sample surveys in 1963, 1964, and

1966; ANGUS CAMPBELL *et al., The American Voter* (1960), an authoritative study of numerous aspects of individual voting behaviour in the United States, and *Elections and the Political Order* (1966), studies of voting behaviour in the United States, Norway, and France; RICHARD S. KATZ, *A Theory of Parties and Electoral Systems* (1980), a study emphasizing campaigns and elections in Britain, Ireland, and Italy.

(D.A.He./H.E./R.G./Ed.)

Popular Arts

Each of the popular arts discussed in this article is now dependent on the technology of the present era. The means and methods to reproduce and distribute graphics, music, and the printed word in almost unlimited quantities that are easily available to the general public is unique to the 20th century. The word popular

can be used to refer to a passing fad or fashion, but it can also be used to exclude a specific form of an art. How this is so will be treated with respect to art, dance, literature, music, and theatre.

This article is divided into the following sections:

Popular art

DEFINITION OF POPULAR ART

As might be gathered from countless books, articles, and conversations, it is not likely that art officials, critics, historians, and ordinary appreciators will soon be using "popular" in a very limited sense. Since the word can mean merely "commonly approved, or widely liked," it may be applied to the "Mona Lisa," the ballad "Barbara Allen," Pueblo pots, and television shows. It, or its Romance-language equivalent, has been employed frequently by English scholars and quite regularly by French, Italian, Spanish, and Portuguese scholars to designate what is called "folk" art. In Germany the situation has been somewhat reversed, the word for "folk" being employed to embrace what many Americans are inclined to think of as "popular." Style-term coinage has added to the confusion: in about 1960 the expression "Pop art" became current in the United States and Europe for what, in spite of an iconography derived from such sources as billboards and comic strips, was distinctly a phase of elite modernism, not a whit more "commonly approved, or widely liked" than any other avant-garde movement. Cultural improvers have contributed: in many places "popular" theatre means simply a lowering of admission prices. Politicians also

have intervened: in some totalitarian regimes "popular" means what is "commonly approved" by the government.

The examples could be multiplied. In the realm of common usage, there is not any point in even attempting to limit the sense of such a term. But there is indeed a point in the context of serious discussion of art. For there is clearly a kind of art that is neither elite nor primitive nor folkish. It is a kind whose central characteristics can be discerned, however foggy its remote frontiers may be. And the best adjective for it, in the long perspective of history, is certainly "popular."

Popular art, in this restricted sense, has probably existed ever since people began to crowd into cities and to form readily accessible mass markets; temple figurines of ancient Mesopotamia might be classified as popular, if one knew a little more about the economics of their production and distribution. But the category emerges into prominence and becomes easily distinguishable from the folk category only with the progress of reproductive technology, first with the invention of printing and then with the development of engraving, lithography, photography, the phonograph, motion pictures, radio, television, and the latest audiovisual equipment. Thus popular art can be summarily described as art intended to be popular in the usual sense—commonly approved or widely liked—

Description of popular art

among the common people in a literate, technologically advanced society dominated by urban culture. That excludes, on one ground or another, elite, primitive, and folk art. In the qualification "intended" lies the heart of the matter. The actual audience may not count at all in determining how a particular work should be classified. The sale of 1,000,000 records cannot transform a Beethoven sonata into popular art, in this restricted sense; and the box-office failure of a film concocted for millions of viewers does not transform it into elite art.

Typical productions. Although among the older surviving genres of popular art one must cite dancing, fireworks, street spectacles, circus routines, and several other sorts of almost wordless entertainment, the long-term popular trend, at least in Western countries, has been noticeably literary. This is evident not only in the success of popular fiction but also in the directions taken by nonliterary disciplines once they enter the popular category. Painting as such, for example, is relatively unimportant; what the popular audience wants are pictures that tell stories—in woodcuts, lithographs, photographs, comic strips, films, and television dramas. Music as such cannot, of course, be called unimportant; during the 20th century it has become, with the help of records, perhaps the most popular of the popular arts. But it is predominantly music with words.

Artists and patrons. There have been popular artists, including many in the 20th century, who have expressed deeply felt private convictions about the meaning of ordinary human experience; there have been not a few who have employed their talents in defense of what they believed to be justice or the cause of the common man. There have been some who have refused to grant that the customer was always right. A generalization that leaves such artists out of consideration is unfair. Nevertheless, Role of the popular it can be said that on the whole the popular artist is less artist committed, both to his work and to any particular set of beliefs, than are his opposite numbers in the elite, primitive, and folk categories. Unlike elite artists, he seldom starves in an attic for the sake of his art. Unlike primitive and folk artists, he is not necessarily integrated with his cultural context, and he is not encumbered with a duty to propitiate occult forces and to preserve tribal or community continuity. He is primarily a professional entertainer. He is constantly tempted to express not what he himself thinks but what he—or his immediate employer—thinks the intended audience thinks.

Materials and techniques. In the fairly remote past the materials of popular art were about the same as those of folk art, and surviving works suggest that popular artists often had a folkish lack of the primitive and elite concern to adopt specific techniques for specific materials. But the popular artist of more recent times, if he happens to be of the visual sort, is seldom in direct contact with the material of his finished creation; he is merely the first stage in a process of multiplication for a large market. He does not normally engrave the plate, run the press, or cast the statuette. Something similar to this distancing of actual execution occurs in other sorts of popular art, particularly those that have flourished in the 20th century. The singer's material and technique are partly his own and partly those of amplifying or recording equipment; the film maker's are partly people and processes beyond his firm control. The same situation may occur, naturally, in elite art, but there the creator is usually in a better position to assert himself, and so the aesthetic consequences are apt to be different.

MEANINGS AND FUNCTIONS

Since popular art exists in a pluralistic society quite unlike the unified contexts of primitive and folk art and since it is normally intended as light entertainment or simply as a means of making money, all attempts to generalize about its meanings and social or cultural functions may seem futile as well as humourless. Yet it is perhaps almost as "functional" as primitive and folk art and hence notably different, at least in this respect, from elite "contemplative" art. Popular love stories have been one of the bulwarks of monogamy in the Western world for several centuries.

There can be little doubt that certain varieties of popular music, powerfully helped by modern publicity, provide young people with a satisfying conviction of belonging to an ingroup and that this conviction makes the intrinsic quality of the music a secondary matter (which is not to say that the quality is always poor). Nor can there be much doubt that a popular television show, like a Melanesian tribal ceremony, may function as a ritual to promote community cohesiveness (which is not to reflect adversely on television viewers or on Melanesians).

Styles. The "functionalism," however, of popular art differs radically from that of the primitive kind, as well as from that of folk art, by being tied, especially under modern technological conditions, to comparatively rapid changes in period style—often to short-lived fashions. In primitive Africa, America, and Oceania and in the backcountry of such a folk province as 19th-century Brittany or Pomerania, there was little that could be properly called fashion; styles might change over long periods, but they were essentially matters of tribe, race, or locality, with variations according to sex, age, class, and occupation. In popular art the situation is more or less reversed; styles are essentially matters of time. And, if 20th-century trends in mass communications, politics, sexuality, and social stratification continue, style differences other than the temporal may disappear entirely from popular art. By the 1970s the styles of popular music were already nearly universal.

Special problems. The majority of commentators would probably agree that all the special problems of popular art concern quality: how an artist can aim at a large market without aiming at the lowest common denominator; how the distancing of execution can be reconciled with the personal touch that is a usual requirement for good art; how local flavour can be preserved as globalism grows; how change itself can be kept from becoming the principal popular style as world history accelerates; and where the point is at which popular art ceases to be art and becomes an instrument for something else. By the last third of the 20th century, these perhaps too familiar, but nonetheless pressing, questions were being regularly discussed by intellectuals, by enlightened public officials, and in what was often significantly referred to as "the industry." Answers, none of which were very confidently offered, ranged from resigned proposals to let-consumers-work-things-out to exhortations to launch a cultural and hence partly economic and political revolution. Sometimes the reformers apparently overlooked the plain fact that good popular art—the good song hit, cowboy-and-Indian film, comic strip, television series, advertisement (if that qualifies as art), social dance, magazine story, or item of house decoration—might be less rare than pessimists had alleged.

Unlike primitive and folk art, the popular kind thrives Sources on technological advances (to which it partly owes its of popular existence), on imported ideas, and on influences from the art other aesthetic categories; and it does so not only in the sense of being able to continue an ample production. It has successfully borrowed, for instance, a large number of ideas from both traditional and modern elite painting, for use in illustrations, cartoons, magazine layouts, printed advertisements, and window displays. The latest device of an avant-garde film director is almost certain to appear, after a delay of a few years, in family movies and on the television screen. Perhaps the most effective tricks in the popular fiction of a given decade are borrowings from the elite fiction of a generation or two earlier. But the best example of this sort of aesthetic appropriation is the already mentioned incorporation and transformation of folk music; there is a vast amount of popular song and popular dance music that owes its charm and vitality to old ballads, exotic traditional tunes, and rustic rhythms. Often the content as well as the form may be adopted and adapted; thus a peasant's complaint about the Hundred Years' War may turn up as a protest song of the 20th century.

Scholarly interest in popular art is much more recent than that in the primitive and folk kinds, and much of it has been strictly sociological. Collecting has been neglected, for the evident reason that the material has seemed, until too late, to be everywhere. Many museums of folk visual art, however, have preserved examples of early popular art, usually from the 18th or 19th century. Old popular songs have been recorded or re-recorded. And of course the serious student of contemporary popular art has only to look and listen. (R.McMu.)

Popular dance

The term popular dance refers to dance performed in public or in private solely for the enjoyment of the dancers. Such dance requires no audience nor any special occasion. Its movements are usually simple, but they are sometimes complex in rhythm. It is at times described as social dance, although that term may also embrace folk dances, which are social in function and the forms of which are ancestral to many popular dances. In strictest definition, popular dance developed entirely within the West until, in the 20th century, its forms were carried around the world.

DEFINITION OF POPULAR DANCE

Unlike folk dance, popular dance is neither ritual nor functional, although it has developed or borrowed from traditional sources and may be danced on occasions that were once a part of folk rites. Unlike ballet and other theatrical forms of dance, popular dance requires no strict physical or mental discipline. Its movements usually require little or no training, nor do they express mood, emotion, or action. From the 13th to the 18th century, however, many popular dances originated in court ballrooms, where niceties of behaviour and of dress were, like the dances themselves, subject to rules of the dancing masters. These dances required much training and practice, and dance was an important part of the education of the young nobles.

Bases. The bases of popular dance are numerous. First, popular dance helps to fulfill the need for identity with communal activities. Second, it is related to courting, in which the male displays his ability to move his partner in harmony with himself. In much social dance the male role is dominant, the female that of a follower. Third, some popular dancing, especially before the 20th century, was to celebrate such events as weddings, harvests, or merely the end of a working day.

Change. The forms of popular dance are susceptible to change from many sources. The migration of the performers or the adoption of a dance by a different nation or social class may subject it to new social situations and political institutions. The process of urbanization, the broadening of education, and the ease of communication not only altered traditional forms but also disseminated new dances rapidly. The primary vehicle for change in popular dance, however, always has been youth.

Youth always has tended to rebel against the dancing masters, whose insistence on correctness and uniformity of execution are contrary to the spontaneous responses to rhythm sought by the young. The teaching of these dancing masters led to concentration on performance, to a kind of studied dance that became largely an entertainment for onlookers. Since popular dance has always been, at base, for the participants, demands for correctness of performance rather than enjoyment caused youth continually to seek less conventionalized forms, often from among the dances of another nation or social group.

Music. Unlike the ritual dancer, who guides the music or actually supplies it, the ballroom dancer follows the music. The timing of dance rhythms has varied as fashions have changed or as wars and political upheavals have altered the structure of society. No matter how the rhythms may be beaten out, the dancers have always responded to the lilt of the melody with moving feet and body until they are caught up in the spirit of the dance.

HISTORY OF POPULAR DANCE

The concept "popular dance" cannot properly be applied to most of the dancing of prehistoric or ancient societies, even in the West, because of the ritual elements that pervaded it. Even the Greek Dionysiac dancing at the grape harvest and the Roman floralia at the advent of spring were essentially ritual, despite their popular and orgiastic nature. There was some secular dancing in Greece, but its forms and its festivities placed it in the tradition of the folk dance. Some of these dances persisted into the 20th century and spawned such other dances as the Provençal farandole and the Catalan sardana. A dance of sacrificial ritual survived as a dance by men in Greek seaport taverns. The Cornish Furry Dance, a flower dance, is believed to be descended from the Roman floralia. In ancient Greece, as in later centuries, dance had a place in educating youth. Plato's dictum "dance begets a healthy mind in a healthy body" was echoed by the Greek slave Lucian to his Roman masters. The Romans, however, contributed little to dance and tended to regard it with disfavour.

The dances of the early Middle Ages were often thinly disguised pre-Christian forms that included animal dances, fertility rites, and the like. The church countenanced dancing on social occasions because this popular means of celebrating could not be ignored, but it tried to eradicate the pagan elements.

Early court dances. The court dance, from which the ballroom dance was to develop, evolved about the 13th century from the common chain and circle dances of the townsfolk and peasants. These traditional dances were consciously changed by such mentors as the troubadours, who imposed codes of courtly behaviour onto the dances. These dances followed the codes by emphasizing the strength of the male and the delicacy of the lady. They contained elaborate displays of courtesy between the sexes and indicated the order of social precedence, from the lord and his lady to the squires and ladies-in-waiting. In addition, the dances accommodated the robust peasant steps to the court costumes, with their greater weight and ornament. The "Lay of Robin and Marion" (1285) mentions such new dances as the carole, a solemn stepping in triple time in which ladies and gentlemen, standing alternately hand in hand, circled about gracefully; and the stately courtesia, in which the couples interrupted their slow procession to express their affections through a stylized sequence of mimetic gestures. Such dances usually were accompanied by religious songs of grave tone and measure suited to the slow, gliding steps and the gentle rise and fall of the bodies. A musical setting for the 109th Psalm, of folk origin, was a favourite tune for these dances.

(margin note: Chivalry in dancing*)*

The troubadours may be considered the first of the dancing masters, who subsequently became an institution of importance in the development of the court and, later, the ballroom dance. The earliest of these masters were fiddlers and men of considerable learning. They would frequently accompany their young pupils when the latter married into foreign courts. Such travels made the dancing masters instrumental in the spread of dance forms across Europe, from court to court, as well as in regularizing dance and social decorum. They also made social dancing into an entertainment for spectators, eventually transforming it into staged dances.

In 1416, Domenico da Piacenza, dancing master to the ruling Este family of Ferrara in Italy, wrote the first known treatise on social dance. It indicated that a definite technique had been established for upper class social dance. Originated at the courts of Provence in southeastern France, it was penetrating into the Spanish, English, and other European courts. The caroles and the courtesia were gradually giving place to the branles and *basses danses*. These were similar in quality but were often danced to especially written secular tunes that gave them a livelier movement.

From 1500 to 1650. The period in dance from 1500 to 1650 has been called the "age of the galliard," but this lively couple dance, or jig, with its *cinq pas* ("five steps"), or "sink-a-pace" as Shakespeare called it, was by no means the only quick dance to be performed by the aristocracy. By 1500 youthful courtiers had revolted against the solemn caroles and branles. They again sought change later in the century after the pavane, a slow, procession-like dance from Padua, and the Spanish sarabande, requiring elegant pointing of the toes, were introduced at court. It became fashionable to follow these slow steppings with a faster "after dance." The galliard was the first of these. It included the mimed gestures of courtship that had been eliminated from the slower dances, and its more complex hops and capers allowed the male dancers to show off their agility.

With the increased amount of court entertainment, social dance became more varied, particularly in France after the Fêtes of Bayonne in 1565, staged by the former queen, Catherine de Médicis. At this fete, groups of dancers from various provinces introduced a host of folk dances to the court. Among them were the bourrée from Auvergne, the courante from Périgord, the volta from Provence, and the gavotte and the rigaudon from Dauphiné. The bourrée, with its neatly executed steps, later became the most popular court dance, and the courante was a favourite with Louis XIV (1643–1715). The vigorous volta, in which the male lifted his partner off the floor and swung her, shocked the Spanish ambassador to England when he saw it danced by Elizabeth I, who wore skirts shorter than most noble ladies. The gavotte, one of the first dances in which the feet were lifted from the floor, remained popular for three centuries.

These dances became popular in the courts only after dancing masters evolved techniques that enabled the nobles to perform the rapid and intricate steps with ease and dignity and to display the graceful turnings of their legs or wrists. These subtleties were the marks of ladies and gentlemen aware of the figure they were cutting in society. The book *Orchésographie* (1588) by Thoinot Arbeau (pseudonym of Jehan Tabourot) was an important record of contemporary dances. In it, Arbeau insisted that the dancer pay greater attention to the display of his figure, manner, and style than to his enjoyment of the dance.

From 1650 to 1750. In 1653 the *branle du Poitou* was introduced at the French court under the name "minuet." This dance, of folk origin, became the most popular of aristocratic social dances at European courts until the French Revolution in 1789. It often was revived until the beginning of the 20th century. Characterized by its tiny steps (*pas menus*), it had many different forms, every dancing master altering or adding to the figures made, the exact placing of the feet, the angle of the partners' bodies in relation to each other, and other details. The minuet allowed the couples, who no longer held hands as in the earlier caroles and branles, to woo one another with their glances.

From the accession of Louis XIV in 1643 until just before the beginning of the Revolution in 1789, the fashionable dances of the French court dominated aristocratic ballrooms in western Europe. But in England another kind of group dance became a permanent part of popular dance. These English "country dances," derived from traditional folk sources, were arranged by John Playford and published as *The English Dancing Master,* first in 1650 (dated 1651) and in 17 subsequent expanded editions in the following 80 years. Dances for social occasions always had been easily exchanged between court and common people in England. Contemporary accounts of the dances at the Elizabethan court and of the masques by John Milton, Ben Jonson, and others, as well as numerous references in Shakespearean plays, show the country dances and the various jigs taking their place alongside the fashionable French court dances.

These country dances served the purposes of the middle-class-dominated Commonwealth government in the 1650s. Its puritanical ethic tolerated dancing, provided it was seemly and showed good manners and style. The steps were simple and patterns were intricate and "occupied the mind." The dancers constantly changed partners, giving no occasion for flirtatious behaviour. Everyone stood equal in circular, square, or longways sets, and as many as wished could join in. Moreover, because such dances belonged to tradition and to all classes, a person could step more easily from one rank of society to another without having to be groomed by some foreign dancing master, whose artificialities frequently annoyed Englishmen. These country dances, notably the Scottish and Irish reels and jigs, had already been taken by emigrants to the various colonies, where they continue to be practiced. Many underwent sea changes and came to be known as square dances.

After the Restoration of the English monarchy in 1660, the country dances retained their popularity, both at court

New peasant dances

Minuet

Dance democratized

and in the lower class dance halls that began to spring up in cities. These dances became popular also on the Continent, where they were introduced at the French court in 1710. They found favour quickly among the aristocracy, and, under the name contredanses, they were enlivened with steps from minuets, bourrées, and courantes. The popularity of these dances was due in large measure to the ease with which they could be learned.

The English public dance halls originated at spas, after the Restoration, as entertainments for the upper and middle class patrons who were "taking the waters." Soon they had spread into the cities and across the Channel. Among these were such dance halls and "pleasure gardens" as the Parthenon, Vauxhall, Ranelagh, Mrs. Cornelys', and Almacks, all in London. Their dances were derived from traditional or court dances, but their popularity lay in the rousing tunes played by military or town bands. The musicians made up for any lack of finesse by the robust beat and the lilt of their music. By 1789 Paris alone had 684 public ballrooms. They offered one avenue of youthful escape and allowed the court to maintain its decorum.

The dancing masters who ran these commercial ballrooms assumed the old court title master of ceremonies. As such, they introduced couples to one another and directed each dance, often calling out the steps and figures to be performed. But when the French dancing masters elaborated their contredanses and developed the cotillons, their insistence on formal behaviour and technical precision once again made aristocratic youth look elsewhere for entertainment.

From 1750 to 1900. The allemande, a lively, turning couple dance of German origin, had become the most popular dance at open-air balls and fetes by 1760. It required skill, for the man turned his woman under his arm as they progressed around the ballroom. It was soon popular in aristocratic society, for practically alone among couple dances it allowed partners to keep close contact throughout.

The allemande did not retain its ascendancy long, however, for an exciting new dance began to appear in public ballrooms before the French Revolution. Mozart was one of the first to note the growing popularity of the Austrian Ländler, also known as the Deutsche. It was based on a simple, traditional courtship dance in which the man strutted around the woman like a mountain cock at the mating season. To music in $\frac{3}{4}$ time, the couple spun around in each other's arms with a step and hop. Such steps could not be danced on a slippery ballroom floor nor in the dress of the day, so Austrian musicians gradually smoothed out the lively tunes into a swift, lilting $\frac{3}{4}$ measure. Thus the waltz swept into the people's dance halls and was taken up by aristocratic society.

Waltz

At the Napoleonic court there was an attempt to emulate the grandeur and dignity of the court of Louis XIV by giving pride of place to the more formal figure dances. The quadrille became a favourite in fashionable society of the empire, particularly in the more expensive ballrooms. It provided an excellent opportunity for displays of skill. But once the waltzes of the Strauss family and of other Viennese composers became known throughout western Europe, this swirling dance became queen of the ballroom and remained so into the 20th century.

In 1840 the polka, a lively peasant dance from Bohemia with a bouncing, turning step and strongly rhythmic measure, began to rival the waltz in European ballrooms. It was followed by the even faster and simpler galop in 1845, but neither could surpass the waltz. Goethe's description of the hero of his novel *The Sorrows of Young Werther* (1774) dancing with his beloved suggests the intoxicating quality of that dance:

And never have I moved so lightly. I was no longer a human being. To hold the adorable creature in one's arms and fly round with her like the wind so that everything around us fades away.

The ballrooms of England were among the last to succumb to the waltz. True to tradition, English dancers preferred the older group dances, and at first the middle classes eagerly adopted the cotillons and quadrilles. These in turn, were replaced by the lancers, a quadrille which contained familiar figures from traditional English dances and Scottish and Irish reels. But by the end of the 19th century, with the number of public ballrooms growing even larger, the waltz had become the dance for all.

The 20th century. Dance forms had always moved between social classes with relative ease. In the 20th century differences in dance styles related to the "who" and "where" of performance were virtually eliminated. So-called pop music from phonograph records or the radio and the examples of dance stars performing on the stage, television, and film became available to nearly everyone. These conditions produced at first a uniformity of dances across society. The Official Board of Ballroom Dancing, an association of dance teachers, was founded in England in 1929 to standardize dance techniques and regulate dance competitions. At the same time, social dance, now rightly called popular dance, increasingly defied regimentation. Dancers, especially the young, found improvised steps and patterns preferable to following prescribed routines. In seeking different forms of expression they embraced new dances, quickly exhausted their interest in them, and discarded them for even newer forms. The popular dance became a phenomenon in rapid flux.

A major innovation was the lead taken by the Americas in providing dances to the world. The main sources were the dances of the American Negro, largely by way of the stage, and of Latin America. The latter dances were based on a blend of indigenous and Iberian music and rhythmic elements brought from Africa. The first major break with the older European forms came in 1910 with the arrival of the tango in North American and European ballrooms.

Latin-American dance

It became extremely popular in middle and upper class European ballrooms when managers of hotels and other gathering places began to stage their "tango teas." At these, the dance was first demonstrated by a professional couple, then danced by the clientele, who enjoyed its new hesitant rhythm and seemingly daring steps. The dance could be mastered fairly easily. It provided an excuse, as had the waltz, for close contact with a single partner.

An even more powerful beat began to sound through ballrooms at about the same time. Jazz musicians of the U.S., South America, and the Caribbean gradually brought the sound of their spirituals and "blues," with their syncopated rhythms and improvised playing, into the world of social dance. The original fox-trot was devised by a dancer-comedian, Harry Fox, for the Ziegfeld Follies revue in 1913. The unique syncopation of its music, and the simplicity of its steps, immediately aroused the audience's enthusiasm. Its potentialities were quickly recognized by ballroom-dance teachers, and it spread rapidly before the outbreak of World War I in 1914. The steps were gradually standardized, largely by the famous U.S. dance team of Vernon and Irene Castle, and the fox-trot remained popular for many years.

Throughout World War I the popularity of jazz increased in Europe, especially through the influence of American soldiers. When peace came in 1918, American films, musicals, and revues, as well as dancers and bandsmen, found engagements throughout Europe. The fox-trot, the Boston (a variety of waltz), and the one-step (a fast fox-trot) required little training. But others demanded the services of dancing masters before they became popular or were even countenanced in European ballrooms; *e.g.*, the shimmy of 1923, with its shaking body; the Charleston of 1925, with its wildly flailing legs; and the black bottom and the blues of 1926, the former with its distinctively twisted contortions and the latter with its close embraces.

These dances, too, had originated with the American Negro. They had been given theatrical form without losing their spontaneity. The musicians and dancers used the printed music or the prescribed steps only as the starting point for the improvisation that gave individuality to their performances. Such individuality had no place, however, in English and other European ballrooms. There, decorous behaviour was still expected, and many dancers were still too self-conscious to break into spontaneous movement. The jazz dances were therefore swept aside by new Cuban rhythms, exemplified by a craze for the rumba in 1930. After some sophistication and regularization, the rumba,

like the tango before it, was introduced in public ballrooms by exhibition dancers, who then gave the floor to the spectators.

In the early 1930s some dance halls attempted to revive group dancing to counter the decline of the ballroom as a social meeting place. In these dances a number of couples performed a popular dance while following carefully prescribed patterns over the floor, much in the manner of a corps de ballet. But the idea found favour only among expert dancers, leading to the "formation dancing" performed in ballrooms or on the screen by professionals. The man in the street had no wish to be regimented in this way.

The tradition of the dancing master continued, however, especially in Europe, where he acted as master of ceremonies at dance halls or in hotel ballrooms. Many of the masters developed large and fashionable followings. In the early decades of the century, many dancing studios sprang up in cities in the U.S. and in England, but they made little headway on the Continent. The heads of such studios eventually persuaded local authorities to license and regulate all dancing sessions and thus give their ballrooms a more respectable status in their communities.

The so-called English style of the Official Board of Ballroom Dancing became ascendant with the first international match, between English and Danish dancers, in 1934. It was recognizable for its elegance, grace, and comparative simplicity. Wherever dancers, teachers, and managers felt that the formal techniques of ballroom dancing were the only things that mattered, it became an accepted standard and was used by trained dancers in the major dance halls of the five continents. National and international competitions were fierce, and the ballroom championship of the world was highly prized. But such dancing, like formation dancing, can no longer be considered popular dance.

The English style

Dancers seeking enjoyment rather than the regimentation of the average ballroom took new pleasure in the Lambeth walk, introduced in England in 1937. Originated by the comedian Lupino Lane in his popular musical *Me and My Girl*, it rapidly became popular throughout the British Isles. It was little more than a parade with mimetic passages and friendly, even familiar, gestures that allowed the couple to do more than hold each other sedately. Moreover, the music had all the elements of old London street songs. This friendly familiarity first endeared it to cockney Londoners, then to their mates in the armed forces, and finally to foreigners living in the British Isles during World War II. Three similar cockney dances, "boomps-a-daisy," "under the spreading chestnut tree," and the "hokey-cokey," the last based on a children's game, also became popular.

Just before World War II, in 1939, the jitterbug found its way across the Atlantic. A favourite in the U.S. during the 1930s, it featured improvised spins, twists, lifts, and other athletic interchanges between the youthful partners. It evolved also into the less acrobatic "swing" and "jive" characteristic of the "era of the big bands." True jazz dance, from which jitterbug was derived, was repugnant to European dance-hall managers, because of its unrestrained and improvised movements. Another feature of the 1930s in the U.S. was the dance marathon, in which couples competed for prize money by trying to outlast all others in nonstop dancing. Threats to dance halls that they would lose their licenses kept the phenomenon out of Europe.

World War II led to the final breakdown in class distinctions within popular dance. It also weakened the hold that the dancing master and the ballroom manager had exerted on social dancing since the first Provençal troubadours demanded propriety in the performance of caroles. In Germany all social dance was prohibited, as it had been in World War I, but in England dance became a release for persons living under stress, often in cramped underground shelters. A tune blared out of a radio often broke tensions and brought on spontaneous dancing. In such circumstances, dance became again a communal activity.

Dance in wartime

Since World War II. After 1945, popular dance became increasingly without, and perhaps without need of, aesthetic theory or formal technique. The dances were learned by direct observation of other dancers on the dance floor or on stage, film, or television. As if in revolt against the restrictions of the war as well as of social dancing, youth asserted its own ideas in the dance halls, discothèques, cafés, and wherever else they joined in social activities. They improvised as the music or their spirits moved them. They had danced like that during the war and thus they continued to dance—to the deep-throated Negro singers, to the crooners whispering into their microphones, or to the throbbing beat of electric guitars. Whether it was jive, rock 'n' roll, the twist, the frug, or any other newly fashionable dance, and whether the musicians were some of the dozens of "rock" or "pop" groups or folk singers with their songs of protest, the dancers sought eagerly for new ways to enjoy themselves, to forget their troubles. The flashing stroboscopic lights in many of the teen-age dance halls appeared to freeze their writhing forms in space and time.

DIFFUSION OF EUROPEAN POPULAR DANCE

Influence of colonization and conquest

Beginning with the voyages of exploration and colonization in the 16th and 17th centuries, popular dances found their way from Europe to other parts of the globe. The emigrants from the British Isles to North America, South Africa, and Australia brought their country dances to those areas. These dances often contained elements from other nations as well. In South Africa, for example, the country dances and reels exhibited both the English love of pattern and the Dutch feature of stamping the feet. The do-si-do (dos-à-dos, "back to back") pattern of the North American square dance clearly showed a French influence.

The influence of the Spanish explorers and conquistadors was everywhere evident in Latin America, where the mixture of European, Amerindian, African, and Asian cultures spawned the tangos, sambas, congas, and other popular dances of the 20th century. Mexico and Brazil offer striking examples of the mixtures of peoples and dances. The Mexican Indians were overwhelmed by Spanish, who brought with them not only African but also Asian slaves, from the Philippines and Malaya. With them came the syncopated rhythms that were to make Latin-America dances so popular. In the 1860s came the French armies, led by Archduke Maximilian of Austria. From the early 16th century until the revolution of 1911, Mexico was continually infiltrated by popular tunes and dances from different European countries. First came the Spanish zarabanda and later the fandango. Later, opera became the rage of the Spanish-French upper classes; and the waltzes, mazurkas, and polkas acquired a Spanish flavour and were given fresh colour and new African and Asiatic rhythmic elements.

Brazil offered a similar picture. The case of the samba indicates how the shifting and intermingling of races produced different results. In northern Brazil, *samba* was the place where social dances were—and still are—held. Until recently, these were waltzes, polkas, and fox-trots. In Bahia, in east central Brazil, the *samba* was a communal round dance performed at carnival time with a soloist turning and leaping in the centre of the circle. In the northwest the "samba" was a type of unsyncopated tune in $\frac{2}{4}$ time. In Rio de Janeiro, the popular ballroom *samba* made its debut in 1917 as a reckless couple dance.

Effects of technology

During the 20th century, the phonograph, the motion picture, the radio, and the television set made the latest Western rhythms the property of the world, nearly as familiar in Japan, Africa, India, or the Philippines, as in London and New York. The traveller from the West encountered familiar tunes and saw the same shuffling, shaking, and stepping that he had known at home. He was not, as he might have been a century earlier, an outsider to the fashionable local dances. The transistor radio became a status symbol for many persons in more primitive areas of the globe. Its sounds, together with other elements of Western civilization, weakened the hold of indigenous dances, which as the 20th century progressed, were in danger of becoming museum pieces in many areas.   (Jo.L.)

Popular literature

The term popular literature has several connotations: it may mean literature intended for the masses, or literature that finds favour with large numbers of people, or it may be a literature of the people. The types may overlap, or they may remain distinct. Thus, "popular literature" can describe ballads, verse, tales realistic and picaresque, romances and confessions, jest books and chapbooks, westerns and thrillers, science fiction and fantasy literature, allegory and satire, emblem books, strip cartoons, comics, and even picture postcards; it may be applied to pamphlets and certain kinds of journalism; and it encompasses a whole range of dramatic literature, from monologue and comic turn to full-length play.

THE DEVELOPMENT OF POPULAR LITERATURE

Modest in achievement though so much of it is, popular literature can boast that the origins of journalism and the novel are to be found in it. A vast number of tales and romances of a popular nature were published in Great Britain before 1740, the date Richardson's *Pamela* appeared, and the date used by many critics to mark the beginning of the English novel.

Before some of the attempts to define popular literature are described, it might be useful to examine examples from one particular cultural context—that of English literature—which have proved to be popular or which have been said by scholars with different interests to be expressions of popular culture. The examples and the evaluations are not comprehensive and are not intended to be typical. They may, however, illustrate how differently understood is the expression popular literature and warn against taking too uncritically the generalizations about it.

With the advent of printing, literary popularity of a new magnitude became possible. Early evidence of the extent of such popularity is usually incomplete: the number of copies printed of 16th-century books is not known and often whole editions are lost. Thomas Deloney's tale, *Jacke of Newberie,* was evidently published in some ten or a dozen editions between 1597 and 1637, but no copies of the earlier editions have survived. Deloney's popularity extended beyond his own age, for there were at least another half-dozen editions of *Jacke of Newberie* in the later 17th century, and his *The Gentle Craft* was even more popular, if the number of surviving editions is an indication of the number printed. Furthermore, it was turned into a play by Thomas Dekker a year or two after it first appeared and it survived in chapbook form in the 18th century.

Sermons, chapbooks, and broadsides

Even more popular in Shakespeare's time were the sermon and such moral tales as Richard Bernard's *The Isle of Man* (of which 16 editions are recorded up to 1683). The appetite for sermons, at least in towns, seems to have been insatiable. There are at least 128 known editions of the works of Henry, or "silver-tongued," Smith in various combinations, published between 1589 and 1637; and 128 editions of the works of the Puritan preacher William Perkins (1558–1602) are recorded before 1640. The equivalent editions of Shakespeare for this period number about 90, Marlowe 31, and Spenser 19. "Popular" may justly be associated with Smith and Perkins in ways other than that assessed by counting editions. Sermons were more than instruments of the salvation of mankind; they were the chief source of political information and political ideas for most Englishmen, and their "popular" significance in prerevolutionary England is considerable.

Another source for the history of popular literature is the chapbook, a wood-block illustrated pamphlet of tales, tracts, and rhymes circulated by peddlers in the 18th century. A rival to the chapbook would be the broadside ballad. The variety of subjects of broadsides was considerable. Subjects might be topical, political, or loyal; they might deal with calamities—shipwrecks, fires, or even the collapse of a building; but those that sold in largest numbers in the early 19th century (as many as 2,500,000 copies of a single broadside are reported) were those issued by James Catnach and John Pitts that reported trials and executions.

Although figures for the sale of broadsides in the early

19th century—and thereafter those for the novels of Dickens and Mrs. Henry Wood, and, outstandingly, Harriet Beecher Stowe's *Uncle Tom's Cabin*—are impressive evidence of this kind of popularity, the 19th century is even more significant in terms of popular literature for the birth of popular journalism. Though the origins of the popular press go back to the pamphleteers of the 16th century, it was the success of *Tit-Bits,* launched in 1881, and the *Daily Mail,* in 1896, that ushered in what has come to be called the "post Northcliffe" era of mass culture, after one of the most influential newspaper publishers, Viscount Northcliffe (1865–1922). Television now plays an even more significant part in popular journalism than the newspaper.

This highly selective—and almost arbitrary—list of what has proved popular in terms of sales, or of what has been described by scholars as being of the people, or influenced by them, over the centuries, will indicate how varied is the range of literature which can be described as popular. It will be apparent how loosely the term is used and how broad, and unsure, generalizations about popular literature are likely to be.

FUNCTIONS AND EFFECTS

Popular literature can be approached theoretically in two sharply distinct ways. It can be thought of as deriving *from* the people, or it can be thought of as directed *at* them—with greater or lesser degrees of conscious calculation on the part of its originators. Those who attempt to define the first approach are likely to insist on the importance of the oral tradition. This tradition does not exclude the work of known authors, but it does require that it be refashioned by the community in order to make it a part of the culture of that community.

In discussions of this kind of popular literature, class and community distinctions are important for some scholars. Folk literature may be seen to be associated with agricultural communities or it may be rather more broadly defined as being associated with all the lower classes.

Popular literature, it has been suggested, is designed to entertain; it is immediate and demands spontaneous response. High, or elite literature, in contrast, is said to be formal and composed, an art for contemplation and *intended* to endure. It has also been argued that high literature may be judged by its ability to disturb and challenge, whereas the popular arts confirm known experience and values, seeking to reassure. This is an extremely useful distinction, but it attracts two comments.

Though there is no doubt that much contemporary critical evaluation regards highly the capacity to disturb and to challenge, this is nevertheless a limited approach. It fails, for example, to assign much merit to the capacity to delight (and to create delight without being trivial is, perhaps, more difficult to achieve—and much more difficult to explain—than to challenge or disturb), and it disregards certain aspects of the expression of individuality and independence through language. Popular literature *can* give delight without being trivial and in its use of language, in, say, the absurd and the bad pun, its cultural contribution may be significant and lasting, awkward though it may be to assess in terms of high art.

Second, though it may do so infrequently, popular literature can disturb and challenge. This can be experienced in some of the earliest English dramatic literature that has roots in the community (as in the Crucifixion plays, which are a remarkable mixture of pathos and farce), in some ballads and music-hall songs and acts, and even in film and television comedy. When popular art is accepted by critics of high art, however, it is elevated hierarchically—it becomes work attributed, say, to the "Wakefield Master" or is lifted above the mass, as was the English music-hall art of Dan Leno (1860–1904) by Max Beerbohm, or the works of such detective story writers as Dashiell Hammett in America or Georges Simenon in France were by a variety of critics.

In Germany in the 1930s, then in America, and later in Britain, attention has been paid to the way in which popular literature has been affected—some would say corrupted—by mass media: newspapers, films, radio, and television. Many people express concern at the situation in which nations of the Western world find themselves in this respect. Alongside the fear of the corrupting effect of the mass media is an awareness of the progressive alienation of elite art from popular art. Yet the situation is not, perhaps, quite so desperate, nor so completely distinct as it may seem to modern man, confronted as he has been by three new media—films, radio, and television—in the space of half a century. Furthermore, the alienation of popular and high art forms is not uniform, and in some areas, this trend is being reversed.

Changing contexts of popularity. Elizabethan drama has been called a "popular form" not so much because it was a drama of the streets but because the plays had a *substructure* of the popular in works of high seriousness and in their use of popular attitudes and forms (such as revenge tragedy). It should be noted that "popular" is being used here in both of its principal meanings: popular *of* the people and popular *with* the people.

There are undoubtedly close links between popular dramatic forms and the plays of Shakespeare and many of his contemporaries. That these plays were popular in that they reflected attitudes popularly held, and that they enjoyed wide esteem is well established. But it is also clear that such plays are no longer "popular" either *of* the people or *with* the people. Full houses for Shakespeare in seasons at Stratford-on-Avon are not a true indication of either kind of popularity, and his contemporaries never fare as well.

Although their work has not fallen into the virtual oblivion suffered by the sermons of Smith or Perkins, it has nevertheless become representative of high art. Furthermore, the popular elements of the writing of these dramatists have to be searched out by scholars.

Thus, what was popular (in both major senses) in those dramatists has become, for today, something different, and much else that was popular—whether sermons or pamphlets or plays—can hardly be said to excite the attention of anyone but the specialist scholar. What was popular in the Elizabethan period, a modern scholar's understanding of what then was popular, and the response of a modern popular audience to such works are by no means coincidental.

The "threat" of popular literature. Those who are most sensitive to the high cultural tradition tend to see a threat to it from the popular arts of their own time, especially from the popular arts involving mass media: mass journalism, film, radio, and television. It is difficult to understand the effects of the new media while fully exposed to their innovations. Objective evaluations are complicated by inherited traditions of high culture, fears for their survival, the difficulty of detecting popular traditions in the new media, and perhaps, too, elements of Puritanism. Above all, it is impossible to predict how the human intellect and spirit will respond to these new media. Grounds for optimism may be found in the human response to the advent of printing, a challenge in its time no less remarkable than those occurring in the 20th century.

In the study of popular literature, the present is felt much more sharply than even the recent past. False comparisons with this past can easily result from this sensitive awareness of the present. Popular literature presents a much more difficult problem than any form of high art, which is, by its very nature, selective. In popular literature, some estimate of the whole, the mass, must be made. This presents physical difficulties and there must then arise the inadequacy and inaccuracy of data.

FORMS AND TECHNIQUES

It may seem to a modern scholar, studying the new media of the 20th century, that there has been a sudden shift from popular art to mass art and that this has led to depersonalization and the destruction of style. Mass art, in this use of the term, is not simply the art conveyed to a large audience through one of the mass communications media, but rather an art that is distinct from popular art in its relation to its audience. Popular art is seen as retaining the vital link between artist and audience that folk culture enjoys but mass culture relinquishes. Both appeal to large audiences, but the popular writer respects both his art and his audience, whereas the maker of mass art is ruled by his audience, which he is anxious to please—no matter how. The popular writer knows his audience as he knows himself. Although he may use a mass medium, he still expresses something essential to his own nature, and from the depth of this nature he brings up memories and feelings to which his audience, being of the same background as he, can respond.

That much of the literature fabricated for the mass media of today is depersonalized and lacks style is undeniable: but so, of course, was much of the literature created for large audiences of preceding generations (see, for example, the description of serial writing in Charles Manby Smith's *The Working Man's Way in the World,* 1853). Again, it is impossible to conclude with certainty that the proportion of mediocre writers to genuine artists is higher in the mass art of today than in the popular arts of the 19th century.

The romance probably has the longest and fullest tradition in popular fiction, extending from the early Middle Ages to the present. It is found in verse, prose, and dramatic forms. In popular literature, though it shows countless differences, its mainspring is some kind of forbidden love. The censure may apply in the world outside but not in the fictional world (this is notably so in pornographic literature, which frequently depicts societies freed from civil, and sometimes physical, restrictions and limitations). The censure also can be represented in the story, directly or indirectly; it may be legal or religious, or very frequently social (a class barrier, for example). A characteristic of such romance is that even when it appears to be realistic, it presents a world from which certain normal restrictions are removed.

Another principal kind of fiction is the realistic tale. Though the terms suggest a general difference between the worlds of romance and realism, it should not be assumed that realism necessarily reproduces the actualities of real existence, however carefully verisimilitude may be suggested. It is not actuality with which writers of popular realistic literature are chiefly concerned, still less with "real" issues or "real" relationships. Their aim (though there are exceptions), like that of the writers of popular romance, is to provide their readers with wish fulfillments, and in this respect it can be hard to differentiate between the two kinds.

Of the many other forms favoured by popular literature, fantasy is one of the most significant. Fantasy literature can be conceived of as an extension of the romance except that love is not the object of the inhibition. Utopian literature and science fiction are the two most obvious forms of fantasy writing and the latter is particularly intriguing in this context for two reasons. In the first place, though its worlds may not be our known world, it is often at pains to be "realistic" within its own fantasy—for example, the careful, as well as imaginative, use of technological paraphernalia by the pioneer French science fiction writer Jules Verne. Secondly, while being in most of its manifestations a popular literary form normally disregarded by critics of high literature, it makes use of archetypal myths and gives expression to deep-seated urges and fears, which relate it not only to the popular subconscious but also to high art. The Soviet novelist Yevgeny Zamyatin, for example, using the science-fiction form in his novel *We* (1924), expressed fears of totalitarianism so effectively that he was forced to leave the U.S.S.R.

Values espoused. The prime aim of the writer of popular literature is immediate entertainment, and, in this, the tradition is as limited and as worthy as is the ancient craft of which it is a part: storytelling. The most serious criticism of popular literature (indeed, of all literature) concerned primarily with immediate effect—with wish-fulfillment—is not that its "literary standard" may be low, or its ideas stereotyped, but that its representation of human relationships and the values it espouses are false. The more seemingly in accord with verisimilitude it is, the more will its readers be encouraged to make unreal demands on life and the more frustrated may they become if their expectations are disappointed. Though this would seem to be true of most, if not all, products of formula literature, it ought to be borne in mind that most literature

is mediocre or worse and that these criticisms can also be levelled at literature that is intended to be sophisticated, profound, complex, and enduring.

Nowhere is the difference between popular and high literature more striking in the latter half of the 20th century than in fiction dealing with relations between the sexes. Avant-garde literature and the fiction that gains critical recognition from the serious literary journals reflect an attitude to sexual relationships generally in accord with what has come to be termed the permissive society: frank, open, uninhibited. Yet at the same time there is a steady output of the novel and short story devoted to romantic love. Here, the standard set—the code of behaviour—not only is different at all points from that espoused in high literature, and *seemingly* acceptable in daily life itself, but has at no time come very near to actuality. In this genre (if two manifestations so utterly different can be comprehended in a genre) there is virtually no interaction between high and low, unless it be for the occasional parody of the popular by the high. Attitudes toward love and sex

Qualities beyond literary analysis. On close verbal analysis of what is said and the way it is said, almost all popular literature will seem inferior to high literature. In its manipulation of words, in sophistication and complexity, in the use of irony, and so on, high literature will respond more readily and more satisfyingly to analytical techniques. It is apparent, however, that some popular literature, which is unresponsive to analysis of this kind, is not without artistic and human virtues. This is true of some folk poetry, of some ballads, and, of some of the tradition of nonsense and the absurd in music-hall entertainment. This last tradition fostered imagination and verbal delight when high literary art was concerned with realism and naturalism, and its significance is far greater than what is judged to be its literary merit. In English literature, especially popular literature, the irrational has played an important role: its expression of nonsense is tantamount on occasion to a poetical faculty of a kind quite distinct from that found on the Continent. This quality is also unresponsive to the kind of literary criticism appropriate to high literature.

In its inability to deal with the bad pun, the inadequacy of such criticism can be seen to be particularly acute. The frequent use of the bad pun by the greatest of all English writers, Shakespeare, makes it difficult to dismiss out of hand. The delight afforded to those of all classes by the bad pun cannot be explained in high literary terms. It may be that this play on words, and the distortion of language that is frequently involved, is a means whereby individuality is expressed, due order and the rational are subverted, and personal independence asserted, while at the same time—in the response it evokes—a sense of community is shared. Though the bad pun cannot be accounted for in the terms of high art, its cultural importance (in the anthropological sense), and its popularity—transcending class distinctions—are of great significance. Criticism and the bad pun

The paradox of the bad pun epitomizes some of the peculiarities and problems posed by popular literature. Thus, although by high-literary standards the language of popular literature is often weak, analysis appropriate to high literature may not reveal its essential qualities, and what is different is not necessarily inferior.

INFLUENCE ON FORMAL LITERATURE

As significant as the differences between the characteristics of popular and high literary forms are the ways in which high forms develop from popular beginnings. The influence of the popular on the high is familiar enough in music but less obvious in literature.

One of the most interesting characteristics of certain popular genres of the 20th century has been the way in which they have shown signs of developing higher literary forms. Western novels, for example, have been largely third- and fourth-rate, but the works of such writers as Walter van Tilburg Clark and A.B. Guthrie are something more than "popular entertainment." More subtle has been the indirect effect on dramatists, such as Arthur Miller in America, and the Australian Ray Lawler, of that cliché of the Western, the isolation and independence of the frontier hero; both writers have used it, switching their locales Popular into high literature not merely superficially to the city, but to the frontiers of national attitudes to life.

Without question, the clearest, though not necessarily the most significant, evidence for the growth of a high art form out of the popular is to be found in science fiction. The origins of science fiction, if the term is interpreted broadly, go back many centuries and the names of men of high ability have been associated with the literature of fantastic voyages and Utopian worlds. Nevertheless, it can be shown that in the form in which science fiction has proved so immensely successful in the 20th century, its sources are truly popular—of the people. Modern science fiction has sprung from the passionate enthusiasm of its fans, who exerted strong influence on the editors of science-fiction periodicals to ensure that the literature developed as its readers—its participants, indeed—wished. The way in which ordinary readers in this way played a part in the development of science fiction suggests that the concept of popular literature as being no more than a shadowy imitation of high art is not inevitably true.

Although the literature of science fiction may seem at first homogeneous, it is not only diversified but quite strikingly reflects the cultures supporting it. Thus, American science fiction is much concerned with what has been called the breaking of a culture (seeking new worlds in which man can develop further owing to the decline foreseen in Earth's civilization), while British science fiction is dominated by impending disaster.

The influence of popular art on high art can be seen most clearly in dramatic literature. It is a commonplace that popular drama has burlesqued the greatest art (Shakespeare, for example, by innumerable television comedy writers), and a little less obvious that popular elements have been used by serious creative writers (John Osborne's use of the music hall in *The Entertainer*). But the influence of popular drama on legitimate drama goes much deeper and further.

An examination of two of the most persistent dramatic traditions—the comic monologue and the two-man comic turn—tell much about this influence. The two occur in the earliest English drama, they are much in evidence in the plays of Shakespeare and his contemporaries, and they are to be found in the popular tradition up to the present. What distinguishes these forms from drama, in which disbelief must be suspended, is their continuous breaking of the continuity of the audience's involvement. In drama in which disbelief must be suspended, an actor who forgets his lines embarrasses his audience and the integrity of the play-world is broken. In popular drama, the performer can use such an error as a source of comedy; furthermore, the effect is not to break the dramatic world but, paradoxically, to involve the audience in the performer's world more fully and more willingly. There are, too, differences between the relationship of the actor to his role in the two kinds of drama. The actor is involved in a legitimate role: he takes a part. In popular drama, the performer stands apart, retaining his own personality.

Many forces combined to separate the high and popular dramatic forms. In post-World War II English drama, however, they were reunited in the work of such playwrights as Harold Pinter and Samuel Beckett. What is so fascinating about this new relationship is that it makes intellectual use of popular dramatic material and forms as well as the popular dramatic relationship of performer to audience.

(P.H.D.)

Popular music

Popular music is music inhabiting the broad domain that lies between folk music and fine art music. It is a domain with no clearly defined frontiers, and at one extreme it merges into folk music; at the other, into art music. But for the most part, the distinction between folk, popular, and fine art music is clear enough.

In general, popular music—unlike folk music proper—is produced by professionals and mainly in the towns. At the same time—unlike fine art music—it is in many cases diffused by oral means. In some important examples, such as Spanish flamenco, central European gypsy music, and a great deal of jazz, it flourished without the aid of print. These three considerations, professionalism, urbanism, and the relative degree of its oral transmission, have for centuries affected the nature of popular music in many parts of eastern and western Europe, North and South America, and much of Asia. After the mid-20th century, with the global expansion and dominance of Western music from Los Angeles to Laos, from Prague to Peking, a worldwide uniformity of popular music began to be apparent, derived in large part from U.S. models.

EARLY HISTORY

Antiquity to the Middle Ages. In antiquity another layer of music was interposed between the music of the peasantry and that of the upper classes. Cities such as Rome and Alexandria attracted Greek minstrels, Syrian dancers, Negro musicians, singers from the Italian countryside, and former slaves or smallholders who made a living by providing music for the urban crowds at circuses or in theatres, in processions or dances. The phenomenon of the popular "hit" song, spreading from the theatre into the streets, was already familiar in Roman times. The Roman writer Suetonius reports that when Galba was made emperor in AD 68, the entire audience in a theatre roared out a song in vogue at that moment, satirizing Galba's avarice.

When, in 6th-century Europe, the by then degenerate theatre of antiquity finally disappeared during the barbarian invasions, dispossessed professional musicians were driven afoot to mingle with the bards of various peoples—Teutonic, Celtic, Slav—in that miscellaneous body of entertainers who haunted the towns and thoroughfares of the Middle Ages. Before long, a general European popular music idiom began to show itself, in which the national differences between music of Spanish, Italian, German, and Polish origin, for example, were to some extent masked by a stylization that resulted from the cosmopolitanism of the professional musicians' calling—but to some extent only. It is true that the popular performances of medieval Europe were far more "international" in character than those of folk music, which often varied enormously in style from country to country and even from province to province. Yet there were characteristic differences between the analogous melody forms and utterances of such varieties of poet-musician as the northern French trouvères, Provençal troubadours, German minnesingers, Spanish juglares, and English minstrels. A 14th-century proverb of French origin indicates the manner of popular singing among various nations: "The French sing, the English carol, the Spaniards wail, the Germans howl, the Italians bleat." In the high and late Middle Ages, popular music covered a wide social and artistic range. Minstrels might be of the court or the tavern, they might be large landowners or beggars, wandering scholars or illiterates, virtuosos or strummers. The repertory ranged from aristocratic hero ballads through lyrical songs, courtly or crude, to rustic dance tunes. Musicians' earnings varied as widely as their grades, and the wealthy troubadours were as scornful of the ragged jongleurs (French minstrels) as minnesingers and meistersingers were of the itinerant *Spielleute* of the German countryside and back streets. The fortunes of popular musicians in the Middle Ages were subject to the same ups and downs as those experienced by the star performers today. Thus the talented jongleur Bernard de Ventadour (flourished late 12th century), a baker's son, attained the courtly rank of troubadour and entered the aristocracy; on the other hand, his contemporary, the equally gifted Raimbaut de Vaqueyras, a dispossessed nobleman, sank down into the ranks of the juglares, playing and singing on fairgrounds and in market squares.

International traffic in popular music, exemplified in modern times in the worldwide spread of jazz and rock and roll, was already foreshadowed in the Middle Ages by itinerant professional musicians who might wander anywhere within a territory bounded by Edinburgh (Scotland); Santiago de Compostela (Spain); Cyprus; and Tallinn (Estonia) on the Baltic. Paris-based minstrels would operate in France between Roncesvalles and Metz; German mu-

National differences

sicians based in Nürnberg might be in Cracow (Poland) for the summer and in Verona (Italy) for the winter. French, Italian, Spanish, and Portuguese minstrels were frequent guests in England. In the towns on the Adriatic coast, Serbian, Greek, and Croatian musicians played alongside instrumentalists from the German principalities and from Transylvania (Romania). French popular musicians, settled in the Hungarian wine-growing districts, accompanied the annual Tokay caravans through Slovakia and across the Carpathians into central Poland. All these musicians exchanged melodies, musical ideas, and instrumental techniques.

Near
Eastern
influence

Nor was the influence of the Near East unimportant. Urban popular music of Arabic-Persian origin was early spread over parts of southwest Europe by the Moors in Spain, southern France, and southern Italy. From this culture came the short-necked lute with bent-back pegbox, the instrument now popularly associated with medieval minstrels. Later, with the Turkish invasions and occupations, music of similar provenance was spread among occupational musicians in the towns of southeast Europe, notably Bulgaria, Romania, Serbia, Bosnia, and Albania. It was carried, mainly by gypsy professional entertainers, into Central Europe, where it mingled with the local musical stock to create the peculiar, hybrid, semi-Oriental kind of popular music of which, in the 18th century, Mozart availed himself in his *alla turca* (Turkish-style) compositions.

The Renaissance. As feudalism merged into early capitalism (in western Europe in the 15th and 16th centuries, later elsewhere), popular musicians became more settled, and generally only those in the lowest reaches of the profession remained itinerant. An active traffic between town and country culture became the normal condition of popular song. Some of the agents of this process were amateur composers among the rural middle class, making formalized arrangements of folk tunes; domestic servants bringing village music into towns and taking town music back into the villages with them; fairground and marketplace singers; street showmen; booth-theatre actors; peddlers of cheap songbooks and broadsides (from the 16th century onward).

Various institutions helped in the formation of popular-music idioms. In England, from Tudor times, the municipalities employed "town waits," instrumentalists who combined the functions of perambulating night watchmen and town bandsmen. They played for official visits, for the mayor on market days, and for summer-evening concerts from the guildhall roof or a roadside scaffolding. In Coventry, for instance, they also played softly at various corners of the city five days a week between midnight and 4 AM, for the reassurance of citizens. Their repertory consisted mainly of adapted folk melodies, humble amateur compositions, popular dance tunes, theatre music, and marches. In France, from the time of François Villon and Rabelais onward—*i.e.*, from the early 15th to the mid-16th century—popular city cabarets were putting into circulation a large number of songs, sentimental, satirical, or comic, most of which enjoyed only a brief vogue, though some proved lasting.

An even more powerful source of popular music was the secular theatre that established itself firmly in France, Spain, and Italy during the 15th and 16th centuries. The theatres performed short plays, often four pieces in an evening, acted usually on open platforms of a movable kind by companies consisting partly of professionals and partly of amateurs, including women and at times children. Many of these plays began and ended with a song, in the manner of an overture-finale frame, and most of them were punctuated with chansons, villancicos, and villanelle during the course of the action. Some of the actors played instruments and at times would perform pieces from the regular minstrel repertory, in the absence of music especially written for the theatre.

In Germany, where, following the Reformation, printed music, the popular choral movement, and the activities of educated amateur musicians, parsons, and schoolmasters worked with especially powerful effect on lower class music making, a vast amount of folk song was transformed into popular song by the imposition of the conventions and usages of art music. This was accomplished by simplifying rhythms, converting old modes into modern scales, tidying up the structure of melodies, and encouraging a standard kind of voice production. A characteristic institution of the early capitalist period in Germany was that of the meistersingers—mostly small merchants, artisans, and tradesmen—who assembled, usually in the guildhall on Sunday afternoons, to practice their new often homemade songs that belonged firmly to the realm of popular music, being neither folk song nor fine-art compositions.

The Baroque. In 17th-century England, the powerful expansion of bourgeois ways of life and manners of thought was accompanied by a flourishing of urban popular music that became equally as important as folk music and art music. Significant landmarks were the extremely successful publication of John Playford's *The English Dancing Master,* a collection of contredanse tunes, many of them based on popular song and ballad airs, that ran into 18 editions between 1650 and 1728, and Henry Playford's *Wit and Mirth. An Antidote against Melancholy,* published in 1682, gained great fame when it was re-edited in 1699 with the subtitle of *Pills to Purge Melancholy.* Rather unjustly, Thomas D'Urfey (*c.* 1653–1723) gets the most credit for this collection of popular songs, serious or saucy, of aristocratic, bourgeois, or lower class, origin. New volumes were added over the years and reprintings constantly ordered. By 1720, the work had grown to six volumes and contained more than 1,000 songs, giving a wide view of the popular music of the time in parlour and kitchen, tavern, and pleasure garden.

The pleasure gardens that sprang up, notably during the 18th century, in the cities and spas, or watering-places, gave an important stimulus to popular music through their evening entertainments. Thousands of songs were written specifically for performance in these places and, at least from the middle of the century, were profusely printed on leaflets or in books. In London, between 1769 and the early years of the 19th century, at least one, sometimes two or three, books of Vauxhall Gardens songs were published annually, as were songs from Marylebone Gardens. One composer, James Hook, wrote more than 2,000 songs mainly for the "gardens crowd," and another, Charles Dibdin, wrote nearly 1,000; several other composers were scarcely less diligent. A comparable flood of lyrical popular music flowed at a slightly later time from the beer-garden entertainments of the German and Austrian towns.

Influence
of British
pleasure
gardens

Meanwhile, in most of the larger towns of 18th-century continental Europe, popular comedies with music could be seen in the puppet and marionette tents and on the fairground or back-street stages, often with stereotyped figures derived from the Italian *commedia dell'arte,* such as Pantaloon, Harlequin, and Pulcinella. A report from 1711 tells that at the fairs of Saint-Germain and Saint-Laurent in Paris (held on the respective saints' days), the theatre audiences habitually joined with the actors in singing the favourite songs of the day; the actors had only to sing the opening bars of the song, and the audience knew the rest.

Later in the century, when the French royal opera forbade actors to sing in the popular theatres on grounds of its exclusive privilege for such performance, the actors would cause a scroll to unfurl each time they came to a song, the instrumentalists would introduce the melody, and the entire audience would roar out the song, reading the words from the scroll. Usually, in this kind of performance, the text was more important than the music, which more often than not was derived or adapted from well-known tunes, similar to the ballad opera. Probably the most important of the ballad operas and one that had great effect internationally was *The Beggar's Opera,* by John Gay, an aggressively satirical piece and a huge favourite with the populace. It was first staged in 1728 and was an immediate success; within a few years it had been played on countless stages in England, Ireland, and Scotland. In 1733 it was performed in Jamaica and in 1750, in Paris and New York. Its triumph encouraged others. By the end of 1729 London had seen 15 ballad operas and by 1733, 70. Some 700 popular tunes were

Ballad
opera

used in these works, with librettos sometimes written by hack writers, sometimes by such eminent literary men as Jonathan Swift, Henry Fielding, and Richard Sheridan. In later years, this form of light Baroque lyrical theatre was to have considerable influence on continental popular music, notably in Germany.

The French Revolution. The years of the French Revolution comprise a singular period in the history of popular music. Admired singers would set up their little platforms in the squares or near the bridges of Paris to amuse the public by singing topical songs. In many parts of the city the audiences were so large that coach-and-wagon traffic was seriously hindered, and the municipal authorities were at length obliged to provide special vantage points where the singers might perform. During the height of revolutionary enthusiasm there was hardly a gathering of any kind where patriotic, satirical, or general popular song was not heard. In his compendious work, *Les Hymnes et chansons de la Révolution* (1904), the musicographer of the French Revolution, Constant Pierre, reports:

Political songs

> For a certain period the theatres were literally invaded and treated as an annexe of the public highway; the audiences displayed their opinions by themselves singing songs of political tendency or by demanding performances, there and then, of their preferred ditties.

Singing invaded the National Convention itself, with one deputation after another announcing its revolutionary fervour and then singing its favourite song to the accompaniment of drums and other instruments brought along for the purpose. Deputies had the habit of standing up in the Convention and intoning lengthy ballads written on some topical point or other until, at last, in March 1794, Georges Danton, a prominent revolutionary leader, proposed a resolution "That henceforth this platform hears nothing but reason in prose." The motion was carried, and from then on singers were rarely heard in the Convention hall, unless by invitation. The course of the torrent of revolutionary popular songs is not without interest. In 1789 a mere 100 songs on political or social themes were published. In the enthusiasms of 1793 the number rose to 590, and the next year, 701 such songs were issued. With the reaction that set in after the execution of the revolutionary leader Robespierre, the numbers declined steeply. Only 137 new songs on topical themes were issued in 1795; and by the end of the century the flow of directly political songs had to all intents ceased. This example serves to remind that popular music is far more sensitive to the important moments of history than either fine-art music or folk music, at least in the Western tradition. Thus, the American Revolution and the Civil War both produced a flood of popular songs but only a few occasional pieces for the concert hall, while—contrary to general belief—the reflection of these events in folk song proper was minimal.

The 19th century. The period of industrial capitalism saw the greatest spread of specifically popular music. The growth of large towns meant bigger audiences, which, in turn, gave rise to an entertainment industry of vast scope; at first in Europe, later in the Americas, and then in Africa and Asia. Conditions favouring an oral culture weakened, and the immense mass of working people evolved away from self-made folk song toward the products of music hall, dance hall, and popular theatre.

Particularly in the early part of the 19th century in western and central Europe and the Americas, popular social song developed enormously in all its forms—sentimental, patriotic, comic, satirical. The remarkable evidence of the democratization on musical life, after the period of the French Revolution and with the growth of the industrial proletariat, was the appearance of the British music hall, which was to have an even more decisive influence on the trends of popular music than the cabarets of Paris or the operetta theatres of Vienna. The music halls first sprang up in the big industrial cities as workingmen's beer halls with entertainment. Gradually, during the second half of the 19th century, the entertainment became more important than the drinking, and the beer halls evolved into theatres-with-a-bar, providing shows that largely consisted of humorous, satirical, or sentimentally emotional

Music halls

songs, mainly of lower class life. In the earlier years of the 19th century, visiting entertainers from the British music halls were instrumental in stimulating the American entertainment industry that in a later time, in the domain of popular music as in other fields, was to become the dominant influence throughout the world.

During the whole of the 19th century the process by which music "from below" in the social scale is taken over and formalized by educated composers for the benefit of a middle and even upper class audience was vigorously under way. Out of the topical songs and festive dances (the carmagnole, for example) of the French Revolution emerged the tradition of Parisian cabaret song and such boisterous gallops as the can-can. Describing these songs and dances as he experienced them in lower class city dives, the German poet Heinrich Heine wrote:

> They make fun not only of sexual relations but of bourgeois relations too, and of everything else that seems good and fair . . . patriotism, faith, belief, family relations, heroism and godliness in every shape and form.

This originally proletarian satirical tradition was transformed to provide the basis for the lively bourgeois operettas of Jacques Offenbach, Hervé, Charles Lecocq, and others.

Also powerful in its effect on the popular musical theatre was the less mordant, more sentimental Viennese tradition represented by the younger Johann Strauss and by Franz von Suppé. This tradition had derived much from the *Liedertafel* (sociable-song) movement of popular harmony-singing clubs and from waltz music that had grown out of the Ländler dances of the Austrian and Bavarian peasantry put into evening dress and performed amid the glitter of high bourgeois candelabra. This style even invaded the realm of fine-art music and reached its peak in Richard Strauss's opera *Der Rosenkavalier*.

Even in the less developed parts of Europe and in Central and South America, popular music was expanding and undergoing transformation. In Spain, flamenco music was growing away from its folk origins, becoming progressively more showy and exotic in the cabarets and small theatres that sprang up around the middle of the century, notably in the Andalusian seaports. In Lisbon, the fado developed in much the same way. About the same time in the Balkans, the emancipation of serfs and the weakening of the Turks' grip meant that many private orchestras belonging to nobles and officials—playing an orientally tinged music—were broken up. This released a flood of popular instrumentalists seeking employment in the restaurants and night spots of the towns and cities. The result was the stylized, urbanized idiom loosely called "gypsy music," in which—as with flamenco—the exotic aspects were often exaggerated to satisfy the customers.

In Latin America the great developments in popular music were in the domain of the dance. Fashionable travellers from Europe brought to Havana, Rio de Janeiro, Buenos Aires, and Lima the minuets, gavottes, schottisches, polkas, and waltzes of Paris and Vienna. In the upper class ballrooms, these dances would be performed as received, but as they seeped down to the lower classes—which, from the Caribbean to Brazil, were mainly comprised of Negroes and mulattoes—the dances and the music accompanying them became altered with the choreography, melody, and rhythm current among the working people, producing the rumbas, sambas, and congas that were later to invade the ballrooms and dance halls of North America and Europe and were to have great influence on urban popular music over some parts of Africa.

In the United States, an important development toward the middle of the 19th century was the emergence of the blackface minstrel shows, with white performers disguised as Negroes presenting mainly a burlesque of Negro song and humour. Touring groups, such as Daniel Emmett's Virginia Minstrels, who made their debut in 1843, and the Christy Minstrels, who followed shortly after, gave widespread currency to a vast number of popular songs, some of which are still sung. Companies such as these, as well as the growing number of vaudeville theatres in the U.S. towns, promoted on a vast scale the compositions of such songwriters as Stephen Foster, the composer of

"Black" minstrel shows

"Oh! Susanna" and "Old Folks at Home"; Henry Clay Work (1832–84), who wrote "Marching Through Georgia" and "The Year of Jubilo"; and George F. Root, whose best known songs are "The Battle Cry of Freedom" and "Tramp, Tramp, Tramp." A more peripheral but ultimately influential development was the emergence of a stratum of rural musicians who became entertainers with medicine shows and on the country-town vaudeville circuits, playing a stylized music of folklore origin. It was these minstrels who laid the foundations for the powerful hillbilly "industry" and its subsequent analogues, country and western and bluegrass in the mid-20th century.

THE 20TH CENTURY

Operetta and musical comedy. In the early years of the 20th century, the upper, more genteel reaches of popular music were still dominated by European operetta and opéra bouffe (French light opera). This tradition, characterized by Jacques Offenbach and even more by Johann Strauss the Younger, was prolonged in the 20th century by such composers as the American Victor Herbert, who wrote some 40 operettas including *Babes in Toyland* (1903) and *Naughty Marietta* (1910). Prominent among Herbert's rivals were Rudolf Friml, born in Prague in 1879, and the Hungarian-born Sigmund Romberg (1887–1951), both of whom had emigrated to the United States in the early years of the century. Among Friml's greatest successes were *Rose Marie* (1924) and *The Vagabond King* (1925). Romberg is best remembered for *The Student Prince* (1924) and *The Desert Song* (1926).

At the same time that these talented composers were producing their European-style works—sweetly lyrical, making heavy use of waltz time, and in the main presenting unrealistic and exotic subjects—a new kind of musical play known as musical comedy or just "musical," was emerging in the United States. It is a genre that is somewhat brash in character, with breezy rhythms, usually offering scenes of American life in relatively realistic terms. Representatives of this vigorous trend were Jerome Kern, whose *Show Boat* became a classic; and George Gershwin, who had a brilliant run of successes from *Lady Be Good* (1924) to the quasi-opera *Porgy and Bess* (1935). The boisterous folkways of the American frontier provided two outstanding successes in Richard Rodgers' and Oscar Hammerstein's *Oklahoma!* (1943) and Irving Berlin's *Annie Get Your Gun* (1946). More sophisticated and silken were the works of the composer-lyricist Cole Porter, whose urbane musical comedies skillfully combined the traditions of New York, Paris, and Vienna. Leonard Bernstein's *West Side Story* (1957) was a continuation of the tradition of realistic American urban musical comedy, begun in the opening years of the century by the vaudeville performer George M. Cohan, with such works as *Little Johnny Jones*.

Throughout the first half of the 20th century and to an ever increasing degree, the popular music of the cities and towns in a great part of the Western world (and ultimately, beyond) was nourished mainly from the United States, with songs from the musical shows and other lyrical pieces composed by such well-known musicians as those named above. Although most of these compositions, following the common fate of much commercial popular music, proved brittle and ephemeral, certain of them have lingered on over the years to become standard songs in the popular repertory.

Jazz. Most of the creations of the musical-comedy composers leaned heavily on the conventions of "serious" music for their idiom and the manner of their performance. Nevertheless, as the half-century progressed, they were more and more influenced by the world of jazz. Indeed, the most powerful development in the field of popular music in the 20th century has been the emergence of jazz as a commercially viable entertainment for a public of the broadest social range. Jazz developed first of all as a synthesis of European ballroom dance music (via ragtime), brass-band music, and the songs of black labourers (especially folk blues) and—to a lesser extent—white workers. It became such a powerful trend in mass music because conditions in post-slavery America favoured a synthesis of black African and white European music,

attractive through its exotic colouring and informal atmosphere. Moreover, the growing drift of country workers into urban areas meant that a new current began to flow into the culture of the cities, always avid for novelty. At the same time, from the beginning of the 20th century the most propitious economic and technical conditions developed in America for the marketing of this new music, for adapting it to suit the tastes of various layers of society, and for stimulating its mass production, dissemination, and global export.

Significantly, the first kind of jazz to make an impact on the broad popular music market was precisely the genre lying closest to conventional "serious" music, namely ragtime. The ragtime composers were mostly Negro pianists trained in European music, often men of considerable artistic pretensions. The structures of ragtime derived largely from French or American light-music models rather mechanically infused with syncopations from Negro tradition. Prominent among ragtime composers were Scott Joplin and James P. Johnson. With its basically conventional idiom, ragtime was easily absorbed into the mainstream of commercial popular music, and by 1900 Tin Pan Alley—the professional purveyors of U.S. popular music—had taken it over. As early as 1899, a writer in *Musical Record* forecast "Ragtime will find its way into the works of some great genius and will thereafter be canonized," as if he foresaw Debussy's "Gollywog's Cakewalk" and Stravinsky's "Ragtime."

Only a few years later a deeper, more spontaneous and folk-rooted component of jazz, the blues, entered the popular music market by way of professional women performers on the music-hall stage. The pioneer blues singer "Ma Rainey" (Gertrude Pridgett) obtained her first engagements in 1902, and subsequently, in company with such singers as Bessie Smith and Bertha Hill, established a bold, expressive, essentially professional style that some call "classic blues." Eventually, however, in diluted and polished forms, with its realistic passions replaced by the poetry of bourgeois dreams, the blues was adapted for general show-business exploitation, whether in the most expensive night clubs or in the cheapest suburban dance halls. For all that, it was the lyrical dance music of small jazz bands rather than the piano rags or vocal blues that attracted the attention of large-scale commercial promoters. After 1910, as jazz music and jazz musicians moved northward from such centres as New Orleans to the large cities such as Chicago, Kansas City, and New York, elements of jazz flowed easily and to an increasing extent, into the "sweet" popular music that was the dominant product of the entertainment industry. Prominent among Negro composers who profited from the discoveries and inventions of a great army of nameless jazzmen, black or white, is Duke Ellington (1899–1974), whose compositions over the last half century have moved progressively closer to the realm of "serious" music. As far as the mainstream of popular music is concerned, the vitalizing effect of jazz was most felt on the standard popular lyrical song, with its 32-bar AABA chorus, the great mainstay of the 20th-century light-music industry.

It should be recognized that jazz is not a single category but a whole sphere of popular music, ranging from light salon music (Glenn Miller), "big band" dance music (Count Basie), popular symphonic (certain works of Gershwin and Ellington), to a kind of chamber music (Modern Jazz Quartet) or even to a form of musical Dadaism (Charles Mingus).

Folk- and jazz-derived styles. Jazz was not the only music coming up "from below" to mingle with and ultimately to affect the direction taken by popular music in the 20th century. Just as, in the lowland South, the rapid industrialization of the post-Civil War period in the United States had resulted in the emergence of the predominantly Negro hybrid music called "jazz," so in the upland South—primarily in the Appalachian and Ozark Mountain regions—similar factors produced the predominantly white hybrid music called "hillbilly."

For much of the 20th century this music played but a small part on the general scene of popular music. Shortly after World War I a number of the newly established

Ragtime and blues [marginal note]

Transformation into the "musical" [marginal note]

"Country music" [marginal note]

U.S. country radio stations began to draw on the growing tradition of hillbilly musicians, interspersing local advertising with brief musical interludes provided, often free, by performers appearing in the neighbourhood. By 1924 it was realized that there was even a Northern market for this music; the first successful Barn-Dance program was established on WLS in Chicago, mainly using country musicians from Kentucky. Around the same time the recording industry began to interest itself in the music, intending to issue discs mostly for sale in rural crossroads stores. To their surprise, they soon found there was some national demand, at first modest, for the product. Unlike jazz, which was based chiefly on wind instruments, hillbilly music relied on strings. Instruments such as violin, guitar, and banjo had become widely available in rural areas through urban contact and mail-order houses and were found to be relatively cheap, easy to combine in ensemble, and well-suited for a repertory that had grown to a large extent out of folk-fiddle music.

By the 1930s the place of "country music" was consolidated in the mainstream of popular music. The repertory of performers of "country music" represented a jumble of music deriving from folk-dance tunes, white adaptations of Negro blues, the sacred songs of fundamentalist Protestant sects contrasted with lyrics of drink and violence, ballad-like accounts of railroad disasters and hard times in the cotton mills, and, above all, a range of songs of commercialized pathos treating of dying mothers, orphaned children, bereft lovers, and lonely men far from home. During World War II "country music" expanded enormously through intense promotion by the popular entertainment industry, probably because the strong nostalgic bias of the music was particularly appealing during a time of wide-scale shifts of population into urban industrial plants and the armed forces.

By the mid-1950s, two contrasting styles of "country music" had become dominant: on the one hand, the Southeastern tradition had hardened into the impetuous "bluegrass" forms, giving prominence to a virtuoso five-string banjo style (perfected from North Carolina folk tradition by Earl Scruggs). On the other hand, the Southwestern tradition, less folkloric, more pliant, happily accepted elements from a metronomic, jazz-influenced city Negro blues backed by a heavy thumping bass (called "rhythm and blues"), and from this amalgam, rock and roll emerged.

During the 1950s, the growth of a profitable market among adolescents, combined with the invention of electronic instruments allowing the easy production of a powerful and impetuous sound, stimulated the enormous diffusion of rock and roll music, which relies largely on amplification for its exciting effects and which proved irresistible to many young people throughout the world. Subsequent modifications of "pop" music have retained the metronomic quality present in the music of Elvis Presley and later rock and roll performers, but these modifications have also reinforced its blues ingredient. Rather paradoxically, what was originally an intensely American kind of popular music was to find some of its most characteristic modifications and its greatest commercial successes in England with such performers as the Rolling Stones and most notably and influentially with the four young men who comprised the group that became known worldwide as the Beatles.

Toward the end of the 1960s, a new force began to enter the world of professional popular music, coming mainly from the white middle class, particularly the more libertarian fringes of the intelligentsia. This music was derived in large measure from a parody of the blues, with the old Negro slum preoccupation transposed into bourgeois terms, complaining of spiritual rather than material deprivation and commenting, at times frenetically, on the general dilemmas of the world rather than on personal domestic tragedies. In its various nuances such as folk, acid, and hard rock, this form of music, sometimes called "Progressive Pop," existed successfully alongside the more conventional popular music, at times approaching the aleatory fragmentation characteristic of some present-day "serious" music.

Concurrently, the folk-rooted blues tradition persisted in the cities, reflecting the culture of the Negro ghetto-dweller, yet appealing also to audiences beyond the ghetto. The older city blues evolved into the urban blues style, marked by freer vocal phrasing and, often, larger, more electronically amplified ensembles; and, through urban blues, into "soul" music, which fuses blues with jazz and gospel music influences. Urban blues and "soul" music

Initially formed mainly in the south and west of Europe, Western popular music has gradually spread throughout the entire world, at first to the ends of Europe, then to the colonized Americas, then to the cities of the Orient, and now into the maize and paddy fields and even the jungles of peoples who had hitherto remained primitive. The rise of the United States to a position of economic and political power accelerated the process by which Western popular music was replacing the proper musical arts of Asians, Africans, and other peoples, a process already begun with the weakening of tribal and feudal traditions and the introduction of formal education through Western colonialism. Missions, schools, trade, radio, films, and development aid projects have all played a part in encouraging a taste for Western popular music. At the same time, throughout the Communist world, sovietization carried the more formal idioms of popular European music across a vast area of the globe, acclimatizing it by means of political rather than commercial propaganda.

Throughout the Communist world, popular music has become mainly identified—at least officially—with stylized folk music performed in a diluted manner, while in the Western world and throughout the sphere of Western influence, jazz music has seemed progressively to shrink into an intellectually rarefied atmosphere, replaced in the affections of the younger mass audiences by the emotional and musical simplifications of rock and roll and its successors. Musical comedy, in theatre and in motion pictures, was still vital in the 1970s, but salon music was fading. For the global intrusion of Western popular music, the Orient extracted a mild revenge, with the introduction in the 1970s of one or two Eastern instruments (such as the sitar) and a few tentative Oriental intonations into popular instrumental ensembles of both the U.S. and Europe. (A.L.Ll.)

Popular theatre

To engage in an act of theatre, a living performer does not need a specially designed building nor elaborate equipment nor a written text nor a high artistic aim; all he needs is a place, a time, an audience, and himself. Performers in music hall, vaudeville, burlesque, follies, revue, extravaganza, circus and sideshow, musical comedy, and the like are as much a part of the theatre as those who appear in what is sometimes—rather grandly—called the "legitimate," "high," or "artistic" theatre. The singers, dancers, comedians, clowns, puppeteers, jugglers, acrobats, conjurers, ventriloquists, and others who make up their number refer to their profession as show business, or "show biz," and their unashamed intention is to please and astonish their audiences by the display of some special visual, vocal, or physical skill. They provide what the director Sir Tyrone Guthrie called the "theatre of delight," and they are part of a popular theatre that has at times itself been of the highest importance in the history of world theatre, reaching its peaks in the theatre of ancient Greece, in that of Renaissance England and Spain, and in the commedia dell'arte tradition of 16th- to 18th-century Italy. Outside the West, the Japanese Kabuki theatre, various kinds of puppetry throughout Asia, and certain other forms of Oriental dance or of dance-drama are examples of popular theatre that also achieve the status of high art. Popular theatre is here considered in terms of its impulse to generate exuberance and joy, the nature of its audiences, and its capacity for change. Popular theatre is set within the larger context of theatre art in the article THEATRICAL PRODUCTION, and its history side-by-side with "high" theatre is sketched in the article THEATRE, THE HISTORY OF WESTERN. See also PAGEANTRY AND SPECTACLE and the section Puppetry below. The people of "show biz"

SCOPE AND CHARACTER

Popular theatre adheres to the core of theatrical tradition in three crucial ways. First, it involves performances by one group of persons for another; second, it demands that the performers acquire at least a minimum of skills relevant to their activities on stage; and third, it usually follows an agreed-upon sequence and reaches a set conclusion. The last of these factors eliminates athletic or sporting events, which otherwise are skilled performances—a kind of "theatre of improvisation" or chance. With the almost certain outcome of the bullfight, however, an approximation of ceremony is achieved. (Religious ceremony may involve all three of the conditions, though a close analysis of the relation between religion and art will distinguish performance from ceremony, as well as the impulse to create a work of art from the impulse to worship.)

The notion of popular theatre should also be examined with reference to its basic impulses, its audiences, and its proclivity to change. Popular theatre has almost always involved an expression of physical pleasure and exuberance—indeed, of joy—that can be distinguished from the pleasure of the intellect or spirit. The harvest songs of praise and thanksgiving from which a primitive "theatrical" activity emerged were, among other things, expressions of joy that physical labours were finished and that physical needs were provided for. With regard to the makeup of its audience, popular theatre, in general, continues to be as broadly based as the theatres of Shakespeare or Classical Athens. Peasants doubtless used to watch the jugglers and comedians at a local fair in order to find momentary release from their toil, much as the intellectual today finds recreation in the circus or in the basement café, with its guitarists and folk singers. In the matter of change, fashion and taste prevail here as elsewhere in the arts: such forms as music hall, burlesque, and vaudeville have largely been replaced by various kinds of nightclub and television entertainment. Another kind of change occurs when a popular form is transformed into a more sophisticated brand of entertainment, less appealing to a broad public. The once widely popular art of the mime has been brought to a brilliant polish by such practitioners as Marcel Marceau in France, yet its audience has become restricted to a relatively small coterie. Puppetry, often a joy to persons of all ages, is now almost exclusively a children's entertainment in the West. On the other hand, the musical comedy, as it is understood in the mid-20th century, has drawn upon a long tradition of song, dance, and narrative to emerge as an art form in its own right while yet retaining its popularity and drawing its audience from a broad cross section of society (although the costliness of its presentation and the consequently high admission prices often exclude less affluent patrons).

THE INGREDIENTS OF POPULAR THEATRE

Throughout its history popular theatre has made use of physicality and music as direct means of communication. The two are not always distinct; the movements of the dance, for example, are both physically and musically expressive.

The physical element. The physical element in popular theatre most often presents itself through eroticism, through distortion, or through the acrobatic.

Eroticism. The pre-theatrical ceremonies, characterized by excess, that accompanied spring and harvest festivals appear to have influenced the development of comedy in Classical Greece, where indecency and lewdness were integral parts of comic performances. In Roman times, the highly popular mime made such play of gross indecency that after the triumph of Christianity in the West during the 5th century AD this and all other forms of theatrical activity were officially banned. Theatrical traditions, however, were kept alive by itinerant bands of players, whose repertories undoubtedly made use of eroticism, though probably in humorous form. It was probably also eroticism, disguised as temporary lunacy, that was responsible for the dance manias that sometimes seized entire communities during the Middle Ages; and, as sentiment, it certainly pervaded the cult of chivalry and informed the songs of the troubadours and other wandering minstrels.

Court entertainments in the 15th and 16th centuries, which evolved into ballet, tried to achieve in living form the idealized image of the human body that was represented in ancient Greco-Roman statuary. But the general direction taken by ballet tended away from the erotic. In spite of the glorification of the ballerina throughout the 19th century and the introduction of erotic themes in modern ballet, the form has virtually desexualized dance or else has taken sexuality into a rarefied realm outside that of popular theatre.

It is the female figure in rhythmic motion, however, that has epitomized the erotic element from earliest times. In the 19th century, female dancing became an essential ingredient of popular theatre in four similar manifestations: revue, vaudeville, music hall, and burlesque. The first two, almost identical in form, go back in spirit to medieval France: the revue to street fairs, during which the past year was reviewed in satiric song and skit; vaudeville to similar sources that, in the 18th century, were adapted to accompany the production of short pantomime plays by itinerant players. Revue and vaudeville had as many variants as there were companies performing them; their many offshoots tended either toward greater vulgarity or else toward greater refinement. Whereas the revue became most closely associated with France (though it provided the model for the "follies" type of show in most Western countries), vaudeville became most associated with the United States, in which it passed from a condition of low repute in the early 19th century to that of respectable family entertainment.

In England, the traditional music hall was virtually identical with vaudeville, originating in the "music annex" of working class alehouses but becoming standard fare for all classes of society. All three forms generally offered a variety of short pieces—sentimental and patriotic songs, dances of all kinds, comedians, humorous or pathetic skits, magicians and jugglers, tightrope walkers, and other acrobats. In burlesque, however, there was an insistent emphasis on the female dancer, and in the 1920s striptease became part of the entertainment.

Distortion. The gross deformity of a malformed body has often been used as a source of entertainment: theatrical wonder resides in the body itself rather than in anything it may do. People flock to such sights, perhaps as a means of alleviating their personal sorrows through a reminder of the greater misfortunes of others.

Fascination with deformity has a long history, social as well as theatrical. Primitive societies might either destroy or deify their defectives; barbarian people of odd appearance were herded along, strangely garbed, in the triumphal processions of the ancient world; dwarfish or humpbacked jesters, whether clever or dull-witted, provided kings with entertainment or served as butts for derision; genetic or birth defects resulted in people being called "village idiots" or in their being exhibited in circuses and sideshows; and the humour of "differentness" is still exploited by comedians who caricature, for example, a foreign accent or ethnic cliché. At the fullest artistic exploitation of distortion, Shakespeare often made his fools speak with greater understanding or compassion than did their masters.

Humour itself may be a distortion of reality—sometimes crude, as in the pratfall and the slapstick, sometimes kindly, as in the satires of a revue sketch, and sometimes corrosive, as in the barbed mockery of a modern-day "stand-up comic." Although at times humour reaches so far past the physical that it attains the sophistication of wit, it retains a basically physical impact. Its effect—earthy, ribald laughter—has been sought in all kinds of theatre, no matter how "serious," while the greatest playwrights have been able to blend the humorous and the serious in their reflection of life.

On another level, distortion has served to generalize, to wipe out what is particular to the individual personality and to substitute a universal face that can be funny, pathetic, tragic, or anything else. The mask is the traditional means: wearing it, the performer is depersonalized, his character more obviously seen as symbolic. The Greek tragic and comic actor, the ancient mime, the Nō actor in Japan, the Harlequin and Columbine and Capitano

Marginal notes:

Expressions of exuberance and joy

Influence of Greek spring and harvest festivals

Revue, vaudeville, music hall, and burlesque

Use of the mask

of the commedia dell'arte all used the mask to diminish themselves and to extend their significance. Perhaps the ultimate mask is that of the puppet, where the individual is abandoned altogether. Sometimes a performer, playing in the popular tradition, adopts a private mask of such universal significance that the gap between popular theatre and high art is bridged. Outstanding examples in this connection are Charlie Chaplin's Little Tramp and Buster Keaton's deadpan mask of Everyman.

The acrobatic. The West seems to have lost almost all touch with the experience of magic, especially that of the shaman, the prophet-priest-medicine man whose intense and disciplined training allowed him to mediate between the people of his tribe and the mysterious, invisible forces of nature and who was also a physical and spiritual healer. His skills probably included almost the entire repertory of a modern circus. Many qualities invested in him survive in the West in a fragmented form. All artists, to a greater or lesser degree, follow a regimen such as that of the shaman, disciplining body and mind to the unique demands of their art, and all art may be said to reveal characteristics of the old magic: it excites wonder. Ballet dancers, opera singers, and musicians must keep their various instruments in fine tune, and actors must keep alive the openness that allows many voices to speak through them.

Nowhere, however, is there a greater and more conscious attempt to transcend the limits of the body, to attain an ever more astonishing level of accomplishment than in the art or craft of the acrobat, whether he is a juggler, a tumbler, a trapeze or high-wire artist, a knife thrower, an equestrian, an ice skater, or even a magician-prestidigitator. The shaman, whose maskings and whirlings were a precursor of drama and dance, was not, of course, a performer in the theatrical sense. Nor were his actions and feats carried out as demonstrations of prowess, as ends in themselves. Yet, in the desire to perform an act far beyond the reach of the average person or at least to create the appearance of stretching the human body beyond its capacities into some unknown new area, the acrobat and the prestidigitator retain some small element of the shaman's magical powers of casting spells. Like the shaman, the acrobat must punish his body to attain his skill, and his concentration must be absolute; for one inexpert move or one flicker of inattention can destroy him. And the drumbeats of the shaman to get the attention of the gods might be compared, in their effect on their human audience, to the drum rolls that intensify the suspense surrounding the acrobat's preparation for his next astounding feat of skill and daring.

Such displays of physical skill have been a mainstay of theatre from its earliest days, though they have been granted little esteem as artistic endeavour. With the demise of vaudeville and the music hall, they have retreated to the circus, the sideshow of the carnival or county fair, the ice show, and the television studio.

The importance of music. Few experiences in the theatre can equal the uncomplicated and unabashed enjoyment of "singing along" with the entertainer, whether in a crowded taproom with only an upright piano or in a gilded auditorium with a large orchestra. Indeed, there is little else that can encourage interaction between audience and performers as can music, the very presence of which tends to remove any pretense of realism, thereby joining performer and viewer even more closely in a shared event. Apart from its occasional function as a background accompanying other skills, music in the popular theatre has been employed chiefly in various kinds of musical-dramatic performances, from which today's musical comedy has evolved; in song-and-dance routines characteristic especially of the minstrel show and of vaudeville and its relatives; and in the stage singing and instrumental playing of cabaret, jazz, country-western, folk, rock and roll, and other "pop" performers who have gained favour at various times in the 20th century.

Musical drama. Musical comedy, as it is known today in the West, has had no straight line of development but has emerged from a wide variety of musical, dramatic, and dance styles. The use of relatively simple ballads to reinforce the narrative or dramatic structure of a play

The effect of music

was known to the Elizabethan dramatists and was very popular during the early 18th century in works like John Gay's *The Beggar's Opera.* The tradition of Viennese operetta and that of the English comic operas of Gilbert and Sullivan was exploited in the United States in the early 20th century and Americanized in the musicals of Jerome Kern and others. *Oklahoma!,* in 1943, saw the introduction of balletic dancing and a tighter unity of song, dance, humour, and narrative, while in the late 1950s a more serious vein began to appear in such works as *West Side Story* (1957), *Man of La Mancha* (1965), *Hair* (1968), and *Company* (1970).

Song and dance. The entertainer known as a "hoofer," who could satisfy an audience by executing a good song-and-dance routine, was thought especially important in vaudeville and the music hall and on the showboats that carried live entertainment down the rivers of the U.S. Middle West and South during the 19th century. Also in demand were sentimental and patriotic singers, including much-loved personalities such as Yvette Guilbert and Maurice Chevalier in France; Florrie Forde, Sir Harry Lauder, and Marie Lloyd in Britain; and George M. Cohan and Al Jolson in the United States. The work of such performers is inextricably linked with the history of show business in the late 19th and early 20th centuries, when entertainment became big business. In these decades, with improved communications in most Western nations, professional entertainment became widely available, most of it under the control of a few great theatrical empires that were created around 1900. London, Paris, New York, and other centres became the hubs from which variety and dramatic companies toured provincial theatres. Internecine warfare was practiced to control both talent and theatres: finally, one circuit tottered, then another, until the motion-picture industry began to grow, restricting the living theatre to urban areas.

The heyday of show business

Songs and instruments. "Pop" singer-guitarists and nightclub crooners are part of "show biz"—the latest in a line of singing entertainers that stretches back for centuries to the balladeer. Remnants of very ancient ballad traditions still exist, mainly in isolated regions of less industrialized nations. The urbanized West, however, has received watered-down versions of the old or musical materials manufactured to order (and to formula) through a commercial and competitive branch of show business once known as "Tin Pan Alley."

The advent of the phonograph and its major allies, radio and the jukebox, has increased demand for this kind of popular theatre in live form. In a small town, it is easier to bring together a number of players and a singer than to gather the diverse talents needed for a vaudeville show or a play, and such a group has an assured appeal, especially among the young. The modern balladeers, however much their art may fall short of the epics of Homer or the lyrics of the troubadours, continue to sing of love and peace as their ancestors sang tales of tribal wars, heroes, and heroes' loves. The erotic is often brought into play here, as, sometimes, is humour, while not infrequently the listeners respond with dance—as in those pretheatrical tribal ceremonies when performer and audience were one.

CONTINUITIES AND IMPACTS

Remnants of the popular theatre. Throughout much of the West and in other regions of the world in which Western (especially U.S.) influences have been strong, traditions and instances of live theatre seem to be on the wane despite public and private efforts to inject new life onto its stages. The traditional face-to-face confrontation of performer and audience has generated spontaneity and joy, however shopworn the materials. But the sweeping technological advances of the 20th century have altered, in a few decades, the centuries-old traditions of popular theatre. Circuses and ice shows may visit large cities once or twice a year; a vigorous puppet theatre may help to enliven the arts in a few areas of the world; various entertainments in cabarets, clubs, discotheques, and theatres still may be quite widely available. But the overwhelming proportion of what was the live popular theatre, both physical and musical, now comprises a major part of television's grist.

Popular theatre as the grist of television

Whether audiences and performers experience the same spontaneity and joy is doubtful. No matter how physically rambunctious, suggestive, or broadly satirical television may aspire to be, it remains hobbled by various kinds of censorship in ways the live theatre outside the family living room rarely was.

Popular and literary theatre. Of the countless thousands of performers who have worked in the theatre, the great majority have done so only to make a living or to satisfy some personal drive to showmanship. Their displays of acting, singing, or acrobatics that have been given today must be repeated tomorrow. Before the arrival of film, only the playwright could survive in anything more than reputation. Popular theatre, with little or no literary base, has had to rely on tradition passed from one generation of performers and audiences to the next.

In his book *The Empty Space*, English director Peter Brook has linked popular theatre with what he calls the "Rough" theatre, saying of it that in the many forms it has taken there has been one constant factor:

> . . . a roughness. Salt, sweat, noise, smell: the theatre that's not in a theatre, the theatre on carts, on wagons, on trestles, audiences standing, drinking, sitting round tables, audiences joining in, answering back: theatre in back rooms, upstairs rooms, barns; the one-night stands, the torn sheets pinned up across the hall, the battered screen to conceal the quick changes—that one generic term, *theatre*, covers all this . . . .

Brook relates it to the freedom of Shakespeare's theatre, and contrasts it, by implication, with the respectable sterility that stifles much of today's legitimate theatre (which he dubs "deadly"). The "Rough" theatre, however, has consistently given refreshment and inspiration to the more "serious" theatre with which it exists side-by-side. In the present century, for example, such a director as Joan Littlewood in England has made uninhibited use of its sometimes vulgar but always vigorous current, borrowing its immediacy and excitement. Toward the end of his life Bertolt Brecht in Germany urged that the theatre must rediscover its naivety: his work had already borne witness to his point of view. The small and deliberately tinny orchestra that accompanied his *Threepenny Opera*, for example, was reminiscent of the limitations that a small cabaret might impose, and the format of this and many other of his works had much in common with a series of loosely linked vaudeville skits. Brecht's theory of dramatic alienation, formulated with the aim of forcing his audience into an objective analysis of the drama, owes a good deal of inspiration to fairground entrepreneurs, whose frank and unabashed methods of presentation are far removed from the comfortable theatre of illusion, where audiences are encouraged to sink back into a world of make-believe and think it "real." The clown and the jester of popular theatre, too, their comic images and antics turned to grimly serious purpose in the works of such playwrights as Samuel Beckett and Eugène Ionesco, still play a significant part in modern dramatic theatre, just as they did in the plays of Shakespeare and of Molière. (G.W.W.)

Puppetry

A puppet is an inanimate object moved by human agency in some kind of theatrical show, and the puppet theatre includes any kind of theatrical show that is presented through the medium of puppets. These definitions are wide enough to include an enormous variety of shows and an enormous variety of puppet types, but they do exclude certain related activities and figures. A doll, for instance, is not a puppet, and a girl playing with her doll as if it were a living baby is not giving a puppet show; but, if before an audience of her mother and father she makes the doll walk along the top of a table and act the part of a baby, she is then presenting a primitive puppet show. Similarly, automaton figures moved by clockwork that appear when a clock strikes are not puppets, and such elaborate displays of automatons as those that perform at the cathedral clock in Strasbourg or the town hall clock in Munich must be excluded from consideration, but a dancer gyrating by clockwork that is introduced by the hand of a manipulator into a show *is* a puppet.

Puppet shows seem to have existed in almost all civilizations and in almost all periods. In Europe, written records of them go back to the 5th century BC (*e.g.,* the *Symposium* of the Greek historian Xenophon). Written records in other civilizations are less ancient, but in China, in India, in Java, and elsewhere in Asia there are ancient traditions of puppet theatre, the origins of which cannot now be determined. Among the American Indians, there are traditions of puppet-like figures used in ritual magic. In Africa, records of puppets are meagre, but the mask is an important feature in almost all African magical ceremonies, and the dividing line between the puppet and the masked actor, as will be seen, is not always easily drawn. It may certainly be said that puppet theatre has everywhere antedated written drama and, indeed, writing of any kind. It represents one of the most primitive instincts of the human race.

CHARACTER OF PUPPET THEATRE

It may well be asked why such an artificial and often complicated form of dramatic art should possess a universal appeal. The claim has, indeed, been made that puppet theatre is the most ancient form of theatre, the origin of the drama itself. Claims of this nature cannot be substantiated, nor can they be refuted; it is improbable that all human dramatic forms were directly inspired by puppets, but it seems certain that from a very early period in man's development puppet theatre and human theatre grew side by side, each perhaps influencing the other. Both find their origins in sympathetic magic, in fertility rituals, in the human instinct to act out that which one wishes to take place in reality. As it has developed, these magical origins of the puppet theatre have been forgotten, to be replaced by a mere childlike sense of wonder or by more sophisticated theories of art and drama, but the appeal of the puppet even for modern audiences lies nearer a primitive sense of magic than most spectators realize.

Appeal of puppetry

Granted the common origin of human and puppet theatre, one may still wonder about the particular features of puppet theatre that have given it its special appeal and that have ensured its survival over so many centuries. It is not, for instance, simpler to perform than human theatre; it is more complicated, less direct, and more expensive in time and labour to create. Once a show has been created, however, it can provide the advantage of economy in personnel and of portability; one man can carry a whole theatre (of certain types of puppet) on his back, and a cast of puppet actors will survive almost indefinitely. These are clear advantages, but it would be a mistake to imagine that they can explain the whole popularity of puppet theatre. They do not apply to every kind of puppet—some puppets need two or even three manipulators for each figure, and many puppets need one manipulator for each figure. The company employed by a major puppet theatre, whether it be a traditional puppet theatre from Japan or a modern one from eastern Europe, will not be fewer than for an equivalent human theatre. The appeal of the puppet must be sought at a deeper level.

The essence of a puppet is its impersonality. It is a type rather than a person. It shares this characteristic with masked actors or with actors whose make-up is so heavy that it constitutes a mask. Thus, the puppets have an affinity with the stock characters of ancient Greek and Roman drama, with the masked characters of the Renaissance commedia dell'arte, with the circus clown, with the ballerina, with the mummers, and with the witch doctor and the priest.

In an impersonal theatre, where the projection of an actor's personality is lacking, the essential rapport between the player and his audience must be established by other means. The audience must work harder. The spectators must no longer be mere spectators; they must bring their sympathetic imagination to bear and project upon the impersonal mask of the player the emotions of the drama. Spectators at a puppet show will often swear that they saw the expression of a puppet change. They saw nothing of the kind; but they were so wrapped up in the passion of the piece that their imaginations lent to the puppets their own fears and laughter and tears. The union between

An English Punch and Judy show. Detail from "Punch or May Day," oil painting by Benjamin Robert Haydon, 1829. In the Tate Gallery, London.

the actor and the audience is the very heart and soul of the theatre, and this union is possible in a very special way, indeed in a specially heightened way, when the actor is a puppet.

The impersonality of the puppet carries other characteristics. There is the sense of unreality. In the traditional English Punch and Judy puppet shows, for instance, no one minds when Punch throws the Baby out of the window or beats Judy till she is dead; everyone knows that it is not real and laughs at things that would horrify him if they were enacted by human actors. Psychologists agree that the effect is cathartic—one's innate aggressive instincts are released through the medium of these little inanimate figures.

The puppet also carries a sense of universality. This, too, springs from its impersonality. A puppet Charlemagne in a Sicilian puppet theatre is not merely an 8th-century Frankish king but a symbol of royal nobility; and the leader of his rear guard dying on the pass of Roncesvalles is not merely a petty knight ambushed in a skirmish but a type representing heroism and chivalry. Similarly, in the Javanese puppet theatre, a grotesque giant is a personification of the destructive principle, while an elegantly elongated local deity is a personification of the constructive principle. Here the puppet theatre reveals its close relationship with the whole spirit of folklore and legend.

The puppet achieves its elemental qualities of impersonality, unreality, and universality through the stylizations imposed upon it by its own limitations. It is a mistake to imagine that the more lifelike or natural a puppet can be, the more effective it is. Indeed, the opposite is often the case. A puppet that merely imitates nature inevitably fails to equal nature; the puppet only justifies itself when it adds something to nature—by selection, by elimination, or by caricature. Some of the most effective puppets are the crudest: at Liège, Belgium, for instance, there is a tradition of puppets whose arm and leg movements are not

The unreality and universality of puppets

controlled but purely accidental. The Rajasthani puppets of India have no legs at all. Even less naturalistic and even more stylized are the hunchbacked grotesques of the European tradition, the birdlike profiles of the Indonesian shadow figures, and the intricately shaped leather cutouts of Thailand, but it is precisely among these most highly stylized types of puppets that the art reaches its highest manifestations.

While admiring these puppets that exist furthest from nature, it cannot be denied that there is a charm and a fascination in the miniaturization of life. Much of the appeal of the puppet theatre has come from the spectators' delight in watching a world in miniature. This can be appreciated best of all in a toy theatre, in which a tiny stage on a drawing room table can be filled with choruses of peasants, troops of banditti, or armies locked in combat, while the scenery behind them depicts far vistas of beetling cliffs or winding rivers. A toy theatre, more than any other type of puppet theatre, is the human theatre on a miniature scale, but even here there is something more than a mere arithmetical reduction in scale; there is a something special that belongs to the world of the puppet.

And to the appreciation, often instinctive, of these characteristics that mark the puppet theatre, there must be added admiration for the sheer human skill that has gone into the making and manipulation of the figures. The manipulator is usually unseen; his art lies in hiding his art, but the audience is aware of it, and this knowledge adds an element to the dramatic whole. In some kinds of presentation—for instance, in a type of cabaret floor show that became popular in the mid-20th century—the manipulator works in full view of the audience, who may, if they wish, study his methods of manipulation. This is a far cry from the philosophy of the traditional European puppet players of earlier generations, who guarded the secrets of their craft as if they were conjuring tricks. It is, indeed, fair to say that any presentation that deliberately draws attention to the mechanics of how it is done is distorting the art of puppetry, but the realization, nevertheless, of the expertise involved in a performance and some knowledge of the technical means by which it is achieved do add an extra dimension to the appreciation of this difficult and highly skilled art.

Manipulation—seen and unseen

TYPES OF PUPPETS

There are many different types of puppets. Each type has its own individual characteristics, and for each there are certain kinds of suitable dramatic material. Certain

An English toy theatre, 1850. In Pollock's Toy Museum, London.

types have developed only under specific cultural or geographical conditions. The most important types may be classified as follows:

Hand or glove puppets. These have a hollow cloth body that fits over the manipulator's hand; his fingers fit into the head and the arms and give them motion. The figure is seen from the waist upward, and there are normally no legs. The head is usually of wood, papier mâché, or rubber material, the hands of wood or felt. The most common way to fit the puppet on the hand is for the first finger to go into the head, and the thumb and second finger to go into the arms. There are, however, many variants of this. In the puppets of Cataluña, Spain, for instance, the first three fingers fit into a wooden shoulder piece, carved in one with the head, while the thumb and the little finger fit into extensions running to the arms. The usual "first-two-fingers-and-thumb" method is used for Punch-type figures; it allows the puppet to pick up and grasp small props very well and is obviously useful when wielding the stick that plays a big part in the show, but it tends to produce a lopsided effect, with one arm higher than the other. The Catalan method produces a larger and more impressive figure. The performer normally holds his hands above his head and stands in a narrow booth with an opening just above head height. Most of the traditional puppet folk heroes of Europe are hand puppets; the booth is fairly easily portable, and the entire show can be presented by one person. This is the typical kind of puppet show presented in the open air all over Europe and also found in China. But it need not be limited to one manipulator; large booths with three or four manipulators provide excellent scope for the use of these figures. The virtue of the hand puppet is its agility and quickness; the limitation is small size and ineffective arm gestures.

Rod puppets. These figures are also manipulated from below, but they are full-length, supported by a rod running inside the body to the head. Separate thin rods may move the hands and, if necessary, the legs. Figures of this type are traditional on the Indonesian islands of Java and Bali, where they are known as *wayang golek.* In Europe, they were for a long time confined to the Rhineland; but in the early 20th century Richard Teschner in Vienna developed the artistic potentialities of this type of figure. In Moscow, Nina Efimova carried out similar experimental productions, and these may have inspired the State Central Puppet Theatre in Moscow, directed by Sergey Obraztsov, to develop this type of puppet during the 1930s. After World War II Obraztsov's theatre made many tours, especially in eastern Europe, and a number of puppet theatres using rod puppets were founded as a result. Today, the rod puppet is the usual type of figure in the large state-supported puppet theatres of the U.S.S.R., Poland, Bulgaria, Romania, Hungary, and East Germany.

Prevalence in eastern Europe

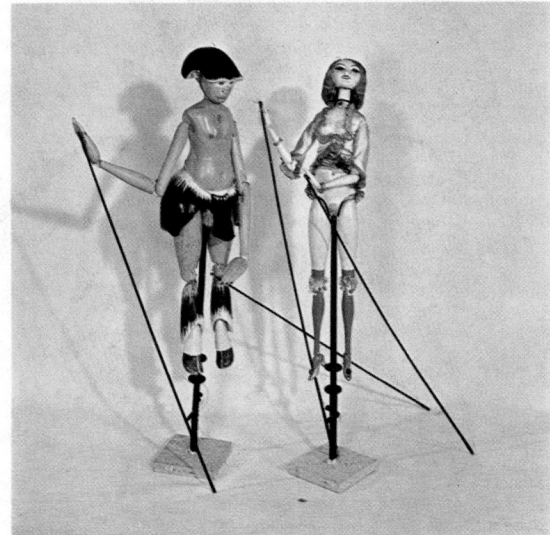

"Faun" and "Nymph," rod puppets by Richard Teschner, 1914. In the Puppentheatersammlung, Munich.

In a similar movement in the United States, largely inspired by Marjorie Batchelder, the use of rod puppets was greatly developed in school and college theatres, and the hand-rod puppet was found to be of particular value. In this figure the hand passes inside the puppet's body to grasp a short rod to the head, the arms being manipulated by rods in the usual way. One great advantage of this technique is that it permits bending of the body, the manipulators' wrist corresponding to the puppet's waist. Although, in general, the rod puppet is suitable for slow and dignified types of drama, its potentialities are many and of great variety. It is, however, extravagant in its demands on manipulators, requiring always one person, and sometimes two or three, for each figure on stage.

Marionettes or string puppets. These are full length figures controlled from above. Normally they are moved by strings or more often threads, leading from the limbs to a control or crutch held by the manipulator. Movement is imparted to a large extent by tilting or rocking the control, but individual strings are plucked when a decided movement is required. A simple marionette may have nine strings—one to each leg, one to each hand, one

Chinese children playing with marionettes, detail from "The Hundred Children," a handscroll of the 17th century. In the British Museum.

to each shoulder, one to each ear (for head movements), and one to the base of the spine (for bowing); but special effects will require special strings that may double or treble this number. The manipulation of a many-stringed marionette is a highly skilled operation. Controls are of two main types—horizontal (or aeroplane) and vertical—and the choice is largely a matter of personal preference.

The string marionette does not seem to have been fully developed until the mid-19th century, when the English marionettist Thomas Holden created a sensation with his ingenious figures and was followed by many imitators. Before that time, the control of marionettes seems to have been by a stout wire to the crown of the head, with subsidiary strings to the hands and feet; even more primitive methods of control may still be observed in certain traditional folk theatres. In Sicily there is an iron rod to the head, another rod to the sword arm, and a string to the other arm; the legs hang free and a distinctive walking gait is imparted to the figures by a twisting and swinging of the main rod; in Antwerp, there are just rods to the head and to one arm; in Liège, there are no hand rods at all, merely one rod to the head. Distinctive forms of marionette control are found in India: in Rajasthani a single string passes from one shoulder over the manipulator's hand and down to the other shoulder; in southern India there are marionettes whose weight is supported by strings attached to a ring on the manipulator's head, rods controlling the hands.

Primitive and developed forms

In European history the marionette represents the most advanced type of puppet; it is capable of imitating almost every human or animal gesture. By the early 20th century,

A scene from a 19th-century Sicilian puppet theatre enacting the Battle of Roncesvalles. The Sicilian puppets were moved from above by both strings and rods. In the Puppentheatersammlung, Munich.

By courtesy of the Puppentheatersammlung, Munich

however, there was a danger that it had achieved a sterile naturalism that allowed no further artistic development; some puppeteers found that the control of the marionette figure through strings was too indirect and uncertain to give the firm dramatic effects that they required, and they turned to the rod puppet to achieve this drama. But, in the hands of a sensitive performer, the marionette remains the most delicate, if the most difficult, medium for the puppeteer's art.

Flat figures. Hitherto, all the types of puppets that have been considered have been three-dimensional rounded figures. But there is a whole family of two-dimensional flat figures. Flat figures, worked from above like marionettes, with hinged flaps that could be raised or lowered, were sometimes used for trick transformations; flat jointed figures, operated by piston-type arms attached to revolving wheels below, were used in displays that featured processions. But the greatest use of flat figures was in toy theatres. These seem to have originated in England by a printseller in about 1811 as a kind of theatrical souvenir; one bought engraved sheets of characters and scenery for popular plays of the time, mounted them and cut them out, and performed the play at home. The sheets were

Toy
theatres

sold, in a phrase that has entered the language, for "a penny plain or twopence coloured," the colouring by hand in rapid, vivid strokes of the brush. During a period of about 50 years some 300 plays—all originally performed in the London theatres—were adapted and published for toy-theatre performance in what came to be called the "Juvenile Drama," and a hundred small printsellers were engaged in publishing the plays and the theatrical portraits for tinselling that often went with them. It was always a home activity, never a professional entertainment, and provided one of the most popular and creative fireside activities for Regency and Victorian families. Although few new plays written for the toy theatre were issued after the middle of the 19th century, a handful of publishers kept the old stock in print until the 20th century. After World War II this peculiarly English toy was revived. Toy theatres also flourished in other European countries during the 19th century: Germany published many plays; Austria published some extremely impressive model-theatre scenery; in France toy-theatre sheets were issued; in Denmark a line of plays for the toy theatre remains in print. The interest of these toy-theatre plays is largely social, as a form of domestic amusement, and theatrical, as a record of scenery, costume, and even dramatic gesture in a particular period of stage history. As genuine performances by flat figures, they represent one aspect of the puppet theatre.

Shadow figures. These are a special type of flat figure, in which the shadow is seen through a translucent screen. They may be cut from leather or some other opaque material, as in the traditional theatres of Java, Bali, and Thailand, in the so-called *ombres chinoises* (literally "Chinese shadows") of 18th-century Europe, and in the art theatres of 19th-century Paris; or they may be cut from coloured fish skins or some other translucent material, as in the traditional theatres of China, India, Turkey, and Greece, and in the recent work of several European theatres. They may be operated by rods from below, as in the Javanese theatres; by rods held at right angles to the screen, as in the Chinese and Greek theatres; or by threads concealed behind the figures, as in the *ombres chinoises* and in its successor that came to be known as the English galanty show. Shadow theatre need not be limited to two-dimensional figures; rounded figures may be used effectively and the blurring of the sharp edge of a shadow that comes when the figure is not pressed sharply against the screen can provide an additional artistic element in the presentation. A particular type of shadow show that was conceived in terms of film is the silhouette films first made by the German film maker Lotte Reiniger in the 1920s;

By courtesy of the Puppentheatersammlung, Munich

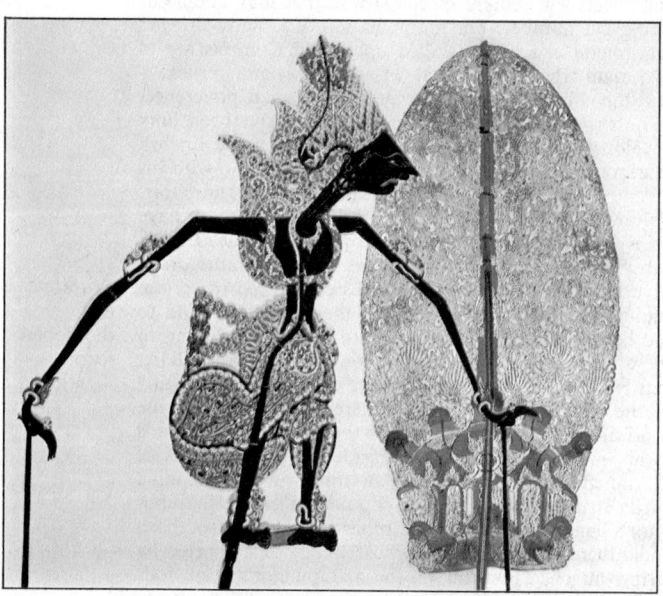
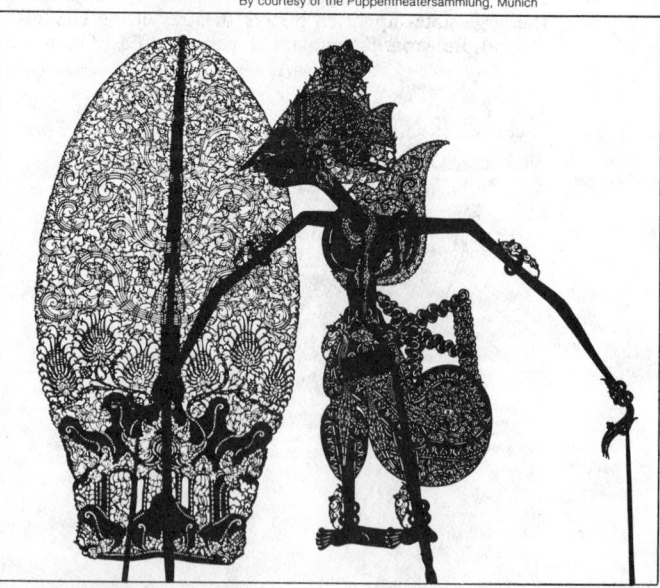

Indonesian *wayang* shadow puppet and decoration. (Left) Spectators may sit on the same side of the screen as the performer, watching the performance as presented by colourful rod puppets. (Right) Connoisseurs of the *wayang* art usually prefer to sit on the other side of the screen, viewing the performance as a shadow play.

for these films, the screen was placed horizontally, like a table top, a light was placed beneath it, the camera was above it, looking downward, and the figures were moved by hand on the screen, being photographed by the stop-action technique. Her early films were in black and white, with figures made from thin sheet lead and card, but she made a few colour films in the 1950s. The shadow theatre is a medium of great delicacy, and the insubstantial character of shadow puppets exemplifies all the truest features of puppetry as an art form.

Other types.   These five types by no means exhaust every kind of figure or every method of manipulation. There are, for instance, the puppets carried by their manipulators in full view of the audience. The most interesting of these are the Japanese *bunraku* puppets, which are named for a Japanese puppet master, Uemura Bunrakuken, of the 18th century. These figures, which are about two-thirds life size, may be operated by as many as three manipulators: the chief manipulator controls with one hand head movements by means of strings inside the body, which may raise the eyebrows or swivel the eyes, while with his other hand he moves the right arm of the puppet; the second manipulator moves the left arm of the puppet; and the third moves the legs; the coordination of movement between these three artists requires long and devoted training. The magnificent costumes and stylized carving of the *bunraku* puppets establish them as among the most striking figures of their kind in the world.

Somewhat similar figures, though artistically altogether inferior, are the dummies used by ventriloquists; ventriloquism, as such, has no relation to puppetry, but the ventriloquists' figures, with their ingenious facial movements, are true puppets. The technique of the human actor carrying the puppet actor on to the stage and sometimes speaking for him is one that has been developed a great deal in some experimental puppet theatres in recent years. Sometimes the human actor is invisible through the lighting technique of "black theatre," but sometimes he is fully visible. This represents a total rejection of much of the traditional thinking about the nature of puppetry, and it remains to be seen how widely the practice will become accepted.

Another minor form of puppet representation is provided by the jigging puppets, or *marionnettes à la planchette,* that were, during the 18th and 19th centuries, frequently performed at street corners throughout Europe. These small figures were made to dance, more or less accidentally, by the slight variations in the tension of a thread passing through their chests horizontally from the performer's knee to an upright post. Similar were puppets held by short rods projecting from the figures' backs, which were made to dance by bouncing them on a springy board on the end of which the performer sat. The unrehearsed movements of figures like these, when loosely jointed, have a

Bunraku puppets

Marionnettes à la planchette, or jigging puppets, being operated by a young puppeteer who provides his own accompaniment on his drum and whistle. "Les Petites Marionnettes," engraving from *Le Bon Genre,* published in France in 1820.
Lalance—Ziolo

spontaneous vitality that more sophisticated puppets often miss. Another interesting, if elemental, type of puppet, the "scarecrow puppets," or *lileki,* of Slovenia, is constructed from two crossed sticks draped with old clothes; two of these figures are held up on either side of a bench draped with a cloth, under which the manipulator lies. The puppets talk with each other and with a human musician who always joins in the proceedings. The playlets usually end with a fight between the two puppets.

Still another minor puppet form is the finger puppet, in which the manipulator's two fingers constitute the limbs of a puppet, whose body is attached over the manipulator's hand.

The giant figures that process through the streets of some European towns in traditional festivities are puppets of a kind, though they do not normally enact any plays. The same applies to the dragons that are a feature of street processions in China and are to be found in some places in Europe—as, for example, at Tarascon, France. Indeed, when a man hides himself within any external frame or mask, the result may be called a puppet. Many of the puppet theatres in Poland today also present plays acted by actors in masks; the Bread and Puppet Theatre in the United States is another example of the same tendency. The divisions between human actors and puppet actors are becoming increasingly blurred; if, in the past, many puppets tried to look and act like humans, today many human actors are trying to look and act like puppets. Clearly, puppetry is being recognized not merely as a particular form of dramatic craft but as one manifestation of total theatre.

Humans as puppets

STYLES OF PUPPET THEATRE

Puppet theatre has been presented in many diverse styles and for many different kinds of audience. Throughout history, the chief of these has been the performance of folk or traditional plays to popular audiences. The most familiar examples are the puppet shows that have grown up around a number of national or regional comic heroes who appear in a whole repertory of little plays. Pulcinella, for example, was a human character in the Italian commedia dell'arte who began to appear on the puppet stages early in the 17th century; he was carried around Europe by Italian puppet showmen and everywhere became adopted as a new character, hunchbacked and hook-nosed, in the native puppet plays. In France he became Polichinelle, in England Punch, in Russia Petrushka, and so on. In England alone did this wide repertory of plays based on popular legend become limited to the one basic pattern of the Punch and Judy show. At about the time of the French Revolution, at the end of the 18th century, a great many local puppet heroes displaced the descendants of

By courtesy of the Puppentheatersammlung, Munich

Japanese *bunraku* theatre; woodblock print by Utashige, 19th century. The puppeteers appear on stage with their puppets; the narrator is shown at the right.

Amusement with a simple finger puppet; lithograph by an unknown artist, c. 1850.

By courtesy of the Puppentheatersammlung, Munich

Pulcinella throughout Europe: in France it was Guignol, in Germany Kasperl, in the Netherlands Jan Klaassen, in Spain Christovita, and so on. All of these characters are glove puppets; most speak through a squeaker in the mouth of the performer which gives a piercing and unhuman timbre to their voices; and all indulge in the fights and other business typical of glove-puppet shows. It is a mistake, however, to regard them all as the same character; they are distinct national types. In Greece, the comic puppet hero is Kararkiózis, a shadow puppet, who originally came from Turkey, where he is known as Karagöz.

Dramatic styles

The dramatic material in which these popular puppets play is sometimes biblical, sometimes based on folk tales, and sometimes from heroic sagas. A play on the Passion of Christ, for instance, is still presented by the Théâtre Toone in Brussels; the Faust legend has provided the classic theme for the German puppet theatre; the Temptation of St. Anthony for the French; and the poems of the Italian Renaissance poet Ariosto, handed on through many popular sources, provide the themes of crusading chivalry for the puppet theatres of Sicily and Liège. More specifically dramatic or literary sources were used by the travelling marionette theatres of England and the United States in the 19th century, when popular plays such as *East Lynne* and *Uncle Tom's Cabin* were played to village audiences almost everywhere.

In Asia, the same tradition of partly religious and partly legendary sources provides the repertory for the puppet theatres. Perhaps the most interesting of these is the *wayang purwa* of Java, from the Indian epics *Rāmāyaṇa* and *Mahābhārata,* in which a deposed deity (Semar) and his grotesque sons (Gareng and Petruk) provide the comic relief.

In distinction to these essentially popular shows, the puppet theatre has, at certain periods of history, provided a highly fashionable entertainment. In England, for instance, Punch's Theatre at Covent Garden, London, directed by Martin Powell from 1711 to 1713, was a popular attraction for high society and received many mentions in the letters and journalism of the day. In the 1770s to the 1790s, several Italian companies attracted fashionable audiences and the commendation of Dr. Samuel Johnson. In Italy, a magnificent puppet theatre was established in the Palazzo della Cancelleria in Rome in 1708, for which Alessandro Scarlatti, with other eminent composers, composed operas. In Austria-Hungary, Josef Haydn was the resident composer of operas for a puppet theatre erected by Prince Esterházy about 1770. In France, the *ombres chinoises* of François-Dominique Seraphin had been es-

tablished at the Palais-Royal, in the heart of fashionable Paris, by 1781. The Italian scene designer Antonio Bibiena painted the scenery for a marionette theatre belonging to a young Bolognese prince, which performed in London in 1780. Exquisite Venetian marionette theatres preserved in the Bethnal Green Museum in London and the Cooper-Hewitt Museum in New York indicate the elegance of these fashionable puppet theatres of the 18th century.

During the 18th century English writers began to turn to the puppet theatre as a medium, chiefly for satire. The novelist Henry Fielding presented a satirical puppet show, under the pseudonym of Madame de la Nash, in 1748. The caustic playwright and actor Samuel Foote used puppets to burlesque heroic tragedy in 1758 and sentimental comedy in 1773. In a similar vein, the dramatist Charles Dibdin presented a satirical puppet revue in 1775, and a group of Irish wits ran the Patagonian Theatre in London from 1776 to 1781 with a program of ballad operas and literary burlesques. In France there was a great vogue for the puppet theatre among literary men during the second half of the 19th century. This seems to have begun with the theatre created in 1847 at Nohant by George Sand and her son Maurice, who wrote the plays; well over a hundred plays were produced during a period of 30 years. These productions were purely for guests at the house; they are witty, graceful, and whimsical. Some years later another artistic dilettante conceived the idea of presenting a literary puppet show, but this time for the public; Louis Duranty opened his theatre in the Tuileries Gardens in Paris in 1861, but it lacked popular appeal and did not survive in its original form for very long. The next year Duranty's experiment inspired a group of literary and artistic friends to found the Theatron Erotikon, a tiny private puppet theatre, which only ran for two years, presenting seven plays to invited audiences. The moving spirit, however, was Lemercier de Neuville, who went on to create a personal puppet theatre that played in drawing rooms all over France until nearly the end of the century.

National preferences

All these literary puppet theatres in France had made use of hand puppets, while the English literary puppeteers of the previous century had used marionettes. In 1887 a French artist, Henri Rivière, created a shadow theatre that enjoyed considerable success for a decade at the Chat Noir café in Paris; Rivière was joined by Caran d'Ache and other artists, and the delicacy of the silhouettes was matched by especially composed music and a spoken commentary. Another type of puppet was introduced to Paris in 1888 when Henri Signoret founded the Petit Théâtre; this theatre used rod puppets mounted on a base that ran on rails below the stage, the movement of the limbs being controlled by strings attached to pedals. The plays presented were pieces by classic authors—Cervantes, Aristophanes, Shakespeare—and new plays by French poets. The Petit Théâtre, like all the 19th-century French literary puppet theatres, performed infrequently to small audiences in a bohemian milieu; as a movement, this lit-

By courtesy of Felix Klee. © Cosmopress, Geneva, and permission of S.P.A.D.E.M. 1971, by French Reproduction Rights, Inc.; photograph, Bil Baird Collection

Hand puppets made by Paul Klee (1879–1940); the centre puppet is a self-portrait. In the collection of Felix Klee.

erary enthusiasm for the puppet theatre had little popular influence, but it served as a witness to the potential qualities of puppet theatre.

The puppet theatre in Japan entered literature with the plays of Chikamatsu (1653–1724). This writer, known as the Shakespeare of Japan, took the form of the existing crude Japanese puppet dramas and developed it into a great art form with over a hundred pieces, many of which remain in the repertory of the *bunraku* theatre today. In this form of theatre the text is chanted by a *jŏruri* who is accompanied by a musician on a three-stringed instrument called a *samisen*.

20th-century styles

In Europe, the art-puppet movement was continued into the 20th century by writers and artists associated with the Bauhaus, the highly influential German school of design, which advocated a "total" or "organic" theatre. One of its most illustrious teachers, the Swiss painter Paul Klee, created figures of great interest for a home puppet theatre, and others designed marionettes that reflected the ideas of Cubism. The eminent English man of the theatre Gordon Craig campaigned vigorously for the puppet as a medium for the thoughts of the artist. Between World Wars I and II and through the 1950s and 1960s, a number of artists endeavoured, in difficult economic conditions, to demonstrate that puppets could present entertainment of high artistic quality for adult audiences. The marionettes of the Art Puppet Theatre in Munich, for instance, were striking exemplars of the German tradition in deeply cut wood carving. A marionette theatre in Brunswick introduced a somewhat lighter and more satirical element. Both these theatres presented impressive productions of the traditional German puppet play of *Doktor Faustus*. In Austria, the Salzburg Marionette Theatre specializes in Mozart operas and has achieved a high degree of naturalism and technical expertise. In Czechoslovakia—a country with a fine puppet tradition—a marionette theatre presented musical turns interspersed with witty satirical sketches introducing the two characters who gave their names to the theatre: Hurvínek, a precocious boy, and Špejbl, his slow-witted father. In France, the prominent artists who designed for Les Comédiens de Bois included the painter Fernand Léger. Géza Blattner, a Hungarian living in Paris, created a theatre with ingenious, sophisticated rod puppets controlled by pedals and keys from below. Yves Joly stripped the art of the puppet to its bare essentials by performing hand puppet acts with his bare hands, without any puppets. The same effect was achieved by the Russian puppeteer Sergey Obraztsov, whose performance has a charm and a wit that are quite different from those of the great rod-puppet theatre that he directs. In England, the fine craftsman Waldo Lanchester played an important part in the marionette revival; his productions included the early madrigal opera *L'Amfiparnaso*. Jan Bussell, with the Hogarth Puppets, achieved an international reputation with his marionette ballets and light operas and also with his shadow-theatre productions designed by Lotte Reiniger.

In the United States, the artistic puppet revival was largely inspired by Ellen Van Volkenburg at the Chicago Little Theatre with productions that included *A Midsummer Night's Dream* in 1916. She later directed plays for Tony Sarg, who became the most important influence in American puppetry, with such large-scale marionette plays as *Rip Van Winkle, The Rose and the Ring,* and *Alice in Wonderland*. The Tatterman Marionettes, founded by William Duncan and Edward Mabley, followed the Sarg tradition with a wide repertory of plays, mostly commercially sponsored, and their touring production of *Peer Gynt* in 1937 represented an important artistic achievement. An important step in the development of puppetry in the United States was taken in 1967 with the opening of a permanent marionette theatre, the Bil Baird Theatre, in Greenwich Village, New York City; Bil Baird's marionettes were already well known from tours and television programs.

Meanwhile, the puppet theatre was continuing on a less exalted plane to demonstrate that it could still provide enjoyable entertainment for popular audiences. From the 1870s a number of English marionette companies had developed the technique of their art to an extraordinarily high level, and their influence was widely spread through Europe, Asia, and America by a series of world tours. Their performances made a great feature of trick effects: there was the dissecting skeleton, whose limbs came apart and then came together again; the Grand Turk, whose arms and legs dropped off to turn into a brood of children while his body turned into their mother; the crinolined lady, who turned into a balloon; the Scaramouch, with three heads; and a host of jugglers and acrobats. The last of the great touring marionette theatres in this tradition was the Teatro dei Piccoli of Vittorio Podrecca, which introduced the marionette pianist and the soprano with heaving bosom that have been widely copied ever since; this theatre closed down shortly after the founder's death in 1959.

During the 20th century there has been an increasing tendency to regard the puppet theatre as an entertainment for children. One of the first people to encourage this development was Count Franz Pocci, a Bavarian court official of the mid-19th century, who wrote a large number of children's plays for the traditional marionette theatre of Papa Schmid in Munich. Important also was Max Jacob, who developed the traditional folk repertory of the German Kasperltheater, between the 1920s and 1950s, into something more suited to modern ideas of what is suitable for children's entertainment. Almost all contemporary puppeteers have created programs for audiences of children.

In this survey of the various styles of puppet theatre in different countries and in different cultures, there are certain features that are common to many otherwise differing forms. In many forms of puppet theatre, for instance, the dialogue is not conducted as if through the mouths of the puppets, but instead the story is recited or explained by a person who stands outside the theatre to serve as a link with the audience. This technique was certainly in use in England in Elizabethan times, when the "interpreter" of the puppets is frequently referred to; this character is well illustrated in Ben Jonson's *Bartholomew Fair,* in which one of the puppets leans out of the booth (they were hand puppets) and hits him on the head because it does not like the way he is telling the story. The same technique of the reciter outside the theatre is found in the Japanese *bunraku* theatre, in which the chanter contributes enormously to the full effect and is, indeed, regarded as the star of the company. The same technique is found in the French shadow theatre at the Chat Noir, and its imitators and successors, which depended to a great extent upon the chansonnier. Many recent puppet productions utilize the same technique. In traditional puppet theatres of Java, Greece, Sicily, and elsewhere, all the speaking is done by the manipulator. The plays consist of a mixture of narration and dialogue, and, though the performer will certainly vary his voice for the different characters, the whole inevitably acquires a certain unity that is one of the most precious attributes of the puppet theatre.

The "interpreter"

Musical accompaniment is an important feature of many puppet shows. The gamelan gong and cymbal orchestra that accompanies a Javanese *wayang* performance is an essential part of the show; it establishes the mood, provides the cadence of the puppets' movements, and gives respite between major actions. Similarly, the Japanese samisen supports and complements the chanter. In the operatic puppet theatre of 18th-century Rome, the refined musical scores of Scarlatti and the stilted conventions and long-held gestures of the opera of that time must have been admirably matched by the slow, contrived but strangely impressive movements of the rod puppets. When, in 1662, Samuel Pepys visited the first theatre to present Punch in England, he noted in his famous diary that "here among the fiddlers I first saw a dulcimer played on with sticks knocking of the strings, and it is very pretty." Even an old-fashioned Punch and Judy show had a drum and panpipes as an overture. Puppets without music can seem rather bald. At one time the gramophone was used extensively by puppeteers, and more recently the tape recorder has provided a more adaptable means of accompanying a puppet performance with music and other sound effects.

Lighting effects can also play an important part in a pup-

Music and lighting

pet production. The flickering oil lamp of the Javanese *wayang* enhances the shadows of the figures on the screen; as long ago as 1781, the scene painter Philip James de Loutherbourg used a large model theatre called the Eidophusikon to demonstrate the range of lighting effects that could be achieved with lamps. Modern methods of dimming electric lamps have enabled directors of puppet productions to achieve astonishing and spectacular effects.

PUPPETRY IN THE CONTEMPORARY WORLD

Opportunities and problems

The puppet theatre in the contemporary world faces great difficulties and great opportunities. The audiences for the traditional folk theatres have almost disappeared. Punch and Judy on the English beaches and Guignol in the parks of Paris still draw a crowd, but the indoor theatres that once attracted humble audiences survive with difficulty, usually with the aid of a sympathetic town council or in the shelter of a local museum. Puppets are increasingly regarded as an entertainment only for children. They certainly do provide a kind of theatre to which children respond with great enthusiasm, and, in the general development of children's theatre, the puppet theatre has a part to play. Some puppeteers are happy to play only for children. But others are eager, today as in the past, to play also on an adult level; and for these, audiences are few. No professional puppet theatre can exist, in the West, on a purely adult repertory. Even those theatres that do play for children face great economic difficulties from the small size of audience to which puppets can play and from the modest admission charges that can be charged to children. If a few companies do continue to present performances of quality, this is a tribute to their dedication to their art.

There are some possible means of performance beyond the children's theatre. There are cabarets or night clubs, which provide an opportunity for slickly presented short turns but obviously no scope for serious drama. And there is television. At first sight, television would seem an ideal medium for puppetry, and many puppet shows have in fact appeared on it, but the great possibilities that it once seemed to offer have not been fully realized. Some puppets, indeed, have become national idols. In England, for instance, Muffin the Mule and his animal friends, manipulated by Ann Hogarth, appeared from 1946 on the top of a piano at which Annette Mills played and sang. Sooty is an endearing little animal whose adventures are guided by his friend and manipulator, Harry Corbett. In the United States, the Kuklapolitans were created by Burr Tillstrom in 1947; Kukla, a small boy, had a host of friends, including Ollie the Dragon, Beulah Witch, Fletcher Rabbit, and Madame Ooglepuss, who exchanged repartee with Fran, a human actress standing outside the booth. The show had enormous popularity for some ten years and presented a social message based upon friendliness and cooperation. The same spirit lies behind the puppets introduced into the more specifically educational "Sesame Street" show; some of the monsters, for instance, do all the wrong things, but, because they are such monsters, the moral is clearly that these things should *not* be done. It must be noted, however, that all these phenomenally successful television puppet characters appeared in association with human actors, whose personalities were an important constituent in the program. Pure puppet programs have not, in general, made quite the same impact. The truth would seem to be that a puppet theatre, more than any other kind of theatre, needs audience response to bring it alive, and this the television screen cannot provide.

State subsidies

The economic difficulties facing puppet companies in western Europe and the United States have been lifted in eastern Europe and China, where the state provides generous subsidies for puppet theatres. Whereas in the West a puppet theatre is lucky if it can afford to pay a company of five or six performers, it is not unusual for a puppet theatre in the East to employ 50 or 60 performers, artists, and technicians. There has been an extraordinary surge of interest in puppet theatre in eastern Europe since World War II, and while the state supports these theatres, there is very little sign of any direct political propaganda in their programs. The results of all this aid have often been impressive in the sheer weight of numbers and scenic

effects, and the productions have often been experimental and imaginative. Mere size, however, does not necessarily guarantee artistic success, and some of the best of these theatres would seem to feel a lack of confidence in their medium by their restless searching for new methods of presentation through "black theatre," mask theatre, and other techniques.

Puppetry in schools

A great feature of education during the 20th century has been the introduction of puppet making into schools as a craft activity. The difficulties facing professional puppet theatre are entirely absent here, and a puppet performance can synthesize many of the arts and skills of a group of children in making, costuming, and manipulating puppets, in writing plays for them, and in acting them. When this activity was first introduced, undue importance was often placed upon the mere construction of figures according to certain set methods and upon the painstaking preparation of a showing, so that the creative release of the performance was long delayed and sometimes never reached. Today the tendency is to create puppets quickly from scrap materials or from natural objects and to perform them impromptu, without rehearsal, as a form of dramatic self-expression. It is from such activities that the therapeutic potentialities of puppets have been utilized by psychiatrists working with disturbed children.

The future of the puppet theatre will certainly be greatly influenced by the cross-fertilization between different traditions in puppetry that will result from puppeteers meeting each other and seeing each other's performances at international festivals of the puppet theatre. These festivals now take place almost every year and are usually sponsored by Unima, the Union Internationale des Marionnettes, an international society of puppeteers. This body was originally founded in 1929 and was reconstituted in 1957; it has members in more than 50 countries and provides a common meeting ground for professional and amateur performers, critics, and enthusiasts. In the past the differing local traditions of puppet theatre have provided a rich variety for this minor but fascinating art. In the future

By courtesy of (top) WTTW-TV, Chicago—Public Broadcasting Service, (bottom) Children's Television Workshop

Puppetry for television.
(Top) Fran Allison with Kukla and Ollie, two puppets created by Burr Tillstrom for the series *Kukla, Fran and Ollie.* (Bottom) Actors Loretta Long and Matt Robinson with two of Jim Henson's Muppets in a scene from the children's series *Sesame Street.*

the local traditions may need some form of self-conscious protection to preserve them, but an even richer variety will surely spring from the interplay of artistic experiment and achievement on an international level. (G.St.)

BIBLIOGRAPHY

Popular art: NORMAN JACOBS (ed.), *Culture for the Millions?* (1964), presents opinions expressed in a wide-ranging symposium on the situation in the United States. MARSHALL MCLUHAN, *Understanding Media* (1964), probes in a controversial way the effects of technology. Of general interest but with a British slant are the chapters on the 20th-century best-seller and on mass communications, respectively by P.N. FURBANK and RICHARD HOGGART, in BORIS FORD (ed.), *The Modern Age* (1963). For more specific treatments, see STUART HALL and PADDY WHANNEL, *The Popular Arts* (1964); and DAVID EWEN, *History of Popular Music* (1961). Particularly useful reading lists will be found in the above studies by, or edited by, Wingert, Otten, Harmon, and Hall and Whannel. PHILIPPE GARNER, *Contemporary Decorative Arts from 1940 to the Present* (1980), is an overview of popular culture via examination of its decorative arts.

Dance: *The Dancing Times* (monthly), and *The Ballroom Dancing Times* (monthly), contain articles on all types of social dances at all periods, as well as articles by expert teachers on all past and present forms of social dance; *Journal of the International Folk Music Council* (annual), contains articles on the relation between folk and popular dance, the development of contemporary popular dance, and the relation of popular dance to its music; P.J.S. RICHARDSON, *A History of Ballroom Dancing, 1910–45* (1946); and CURT SACHS, *Eine Weltgeschichte des Tanzes* (1933; Eng. trans., *A World History of Dance*, 1938, reprinted 1963), both give comprehensive surveys of all types of social dance.

Literature: The number of books and articles on popular literature and the mass arts is vast. The selection below will serve only as an introduction. Most of the books listed contain bibliographies and these should also be consulted. Volume 4 of the *New Cambridge Bibliography of English Literature* (1972), contains a fairly lengthy selection of titles on the cultural debate, mass communications, reading and readership, journalism and the press, popular genres, content analysis, and the relations of literature to film, radio, and television, for the period 1900–50. HELMUT BONHEIM (ed.), *The English Novel Before Richardson* (1971), is a useful checklist of texts and criticism. HERBERT F. SMITH, *The Popular American Novel: 1865–1920* (1980), is a study of popular culture through minor writers.

The best introduction to the common reader is R.D. ALTICK, *The English Common Reader* (1957), containing an extensive bibliography. Q.D. LEAVIS, *Fiction and the Reading Public* (1932), should also be consulted. RAYMOND WILLIAMS, *Culture and Society 1780–1950* (1958), and his *Long Revolution* (1961), are illuminating discussions of the interrelation of artistic and social developments. Undoubtedly the most stimulating and most moving account of popular culture is RICHARD HOGGART, *The Uses of Literacy* (1957). CHRISTOPHER PULLING, *They Were Singing* (1952), not only gives a good account of the music hall, but relates it in a significant way to the social life of the 19th and early 20th centuries. *The Popular Arts* (1964), by STUART HALL and PADDY WHANNELL is a pioneering critical study of the mass media; it is significant not only for what it says but for its attempt to stimulate further discussion by means of a series of projects intended for use in schools and adult education centres. S.L. BETHELL, *Shakespeare and the Popular Dramatic Tradition* (1944), is essential reading for an understanding of the relationship of popular and high dramatic art forms. It served as the starting point for P. DAVISON, "Contemporary Drama and Popular Dramatic Forms," in *Aspects of Drama* (1965). GEORGE ORWELL, *Collected Essays*, 4 vol. (1968), brings together much that has influenced later writers on popular literature in England; P. DAVISON, *Songs of the British Music Hall* (1971), gives words and music of 50 songs, with individual and general critical and social comment.

Five collections of readings are of special interest: B. ROSENBERG and D.M. WHITE (eds.), *Mass Culture: The Popular Arts in America* (1957); E. LARRABEE and R. MEYERSOHN (eds.), *Mass Leisure* (1958); D. THOMPSON (ed.), *Discrimination and Popular Culture* (1964); N.F. CANTOR and M.S. WERTHMAN (eds.), *The History of Popular Culture* (1968); and JEREMY TUNSTALL (ed.), *Media Sociology* (1970).

Finally reference should be made to those centres specializing in the popular arts which issue communications from time to time: The Centre for Contemporary Cultural Studies, University of Birmingham; the Centre for Mass Communication Research, University of Leicester; L'institut de littérature et de technique artistiques de masse, Bordeaux; and the Popular Culture Association (which publishes the *Journal of Popular Culture*), at Bowling Green University, Ohio.

Music: WATER WIORA, *Die vier Weltalter der Musik* (1961; Eng. trans., *The Four Ages of Music,* 1965), a concise and penetrating account of the evolution of music through four great periods—prehistory, antiquity, the growth of Western music, and the era of global industry—that sets the development of popular music clearly within the framework of general musical culture; REGINALD NETTEL, *Seven Centuries of Popular Song* (1956), a social history of English popular (as distinct from folk) song from the Middle Ages to the era of ballroom jazz (handy for the layman); S.G. SPAETH, *A History of Popular Music in America* (1948), a broad panorama of popular songs and the musical theatre from colonial times to the mid-20th century; RICHARD MIDDLETON and DAVID HORN (eds.), *Popular Music I: Folk or Popular?* (1982), scholarly essays examining popular music in its social and historical contexts.

Specialized works are WALTER SALMEN, *Der fahrende Musiker im europäischen Mittelalter* (1960), a comprehensive social-historical study of the way of life of itinerant professional minstrels throughout Europe in the late Middle Ages, with a musicological account of their vocal and instrumental repertory—the best account of this important and little-understood class of popular musicians; C.M. SIMPSON, *The British Broadside Ballad and Its Music* (1966), a monumental reference work that relates some thousands of broadsides from the mid-16th to the early 18th century to the 500-odd tunes for which they were designed; ANDRE HODEIR, *Hommes et problèmes du jazz* (1954; Eng. trans., *Jazz: Its Evolution and Essence,* 1956), an analytical work for the musically educated—brilliant, if a little overbalanced toward the modernist viewpoint; M.W. STEARNS, *The Story of Jazz* (1956, reprinted 1970), a serious study, regarded by some informed critics as the only history of jazz worthy of the name; B.C. MALONE, *Country Music U.S.A.* (1968), a broadbased account of the development of white rural professional music from its humble origins to its present state as large-scale commercial entertainment; CHARLES GILLETT, *The Sound of the City* (1970), an exhaustive survey and acute analysis of the emergence and growth of rock and roll, and the consequent global changes in commercial popular music.

Theatre: Since popular theatre as discussed in this article is not a generally recognized genre, no critical study has been applied to the area as a whole; the closest is ABEL GREEN and JOE LAURIE, JR., *Show Biz* (1951, reprinted 1971), the story of show business in the United States for most of the 20th century as seen through the eyes of the industry's "bible," the weekly newspaper *Variety*. M. WILLSON DISHER has written extensively on aspects of popular theatre, especially *Music Hall Parade* (1938), *Blood and Thunder: Mid-Victorian Melodrama and Its Origins* (1949), and *Pleasures of London* (1950). ENID WELSFORD, *The Fool: His Social and Literary History* (1935); and DOUGLAS GILBERT, *American Vaudeville* (1940), remain valuable. *The Journal of Popular Culture* (quarterly) is a rich resource. Numerous motion pictures have probed into facets of show business; especially perceptive are *The Blue Angel* (German, 1930) and *The Entertainer* (English, 1960). Books containing more general discussions include MARTIN ESSLIN, *The Theatre of the Absurd,* rev. ed. (1968); PETER BROOK, *The Empty Space* (1968); and THEODORE ROSZAK, *The Making of a Counter Culture* (1969), especially ch. 8, "Eyes of Flesh, Eyes of Fire."

Puppetry: A.R. PHILPOTT, *Dictionary of Puppetry* (1969), a brief but comprehensive guide to every aspect of the subject; *The Rosalynde Stearn Puppet Collection,* McGill University Library Special Collections IV (1961), contains a useful bibliography; CHARLES MAGNIN, *Histoire des marionnettes en Europe depuis l'antiquité jusqu'à nos jours,* rev. ed. (1862), the classic history, not yet superseded; ERNEST MAINDRON, *Marionnettes et guignols* (1900), valuable for chapters on East Asia and for carrying the French history up to the end of the 19th century; BIL BAIRD, *The Art of the Puppet* (1965), a magnificently illustrated general survey; MARGARETA NICULESCU (ed.), *The Puppet Theatre of the Modern World* (1967), an international presentation sponsored by the Union Internationale des Marionnettes; GEORGE SPEAIGHT, *The History of the English Puppet Theatre* (1955), includes European puppets up to the 17th century (*Punch and Judy: A History,* 1970, is largely abstracted from this work, but contains some additional material); and *The History of the English Toy Theatre* (1969; a revised edition of *Juvenile Drama,* 1946); PAUL MCPHARLIN, *The Puppet Theatre in America: A History, 1524–1948,* rev. ed. (1969), with a supplement covering developments since 1948 by MARJORIE BATCHELDER MCPHARLIN, including a select bibliography; OLIVE BLACKHAM, *Shadow Puppets* (1960), a description of these figures all over the world.

Population

Few aspects of human societies are as fundamental as the size, composition, and rate of change of their populations. Such factors affect economic prosperity, health, education, family structure, crime patterns, language, culture—indeed, virtually every aspect of human society is touched upon by population trends.

The study of human populations is called demography—a discipline with intellectual origins stretching back to the 18th century, when it was first recognized that human mortality could be examined as a phenomenon with statistical regularities. Demography casts a multidisciplinary net, drawing insights from economics, sociology, statistics, medicine, biology, anthropology, and history. Its chronological sweep is lengthy: limited demographic evidence for many centuries into the past, and reliable data for several hundred years are available for many regions. The present understanding of demography makes it possible to project (with caution) population changes several decades into the future.

This article is divided into the following sections:

THE BASIC COMPONENTS OF POPULATION CHANGE

Closed and open populations

At its most basic level, the components of population change are few indeed. A closed population (that is, one in which immigration and emigration do not occur) can change according to the following simple equation: the population (closed) at the end of an interval equals the population at the beginning of the interval, plus births during the interval, minus deaths during the interval. In other words, only addition by births and reduction by deaths can change a closed population. The notion of a closed population is not an abstraction; unless one believes that there has been substantial migration to and from this planet, the world population as a whole is closed.

Populations of nations, regions, continents, islands, or cities, however, are rarely closed in the same way. If the assumption of a closed population is relaxed, in- and out-migration can increase and decrease population size in the same way as do births and deaths; thus, the population (open) at the end of an interval equals the population at the beginning of the interval, plus births during the interval, minus deaths, plus in-migrants, minus out-migrants. Hence the study of demographic change requires knowledge of fertility (births), mortality (deaths), and migration. These, in turn, affect not only population size and growth rates but also the composition of the population in terms of such attributes as sex, age, ethnic or racial composition, and geographic distribution.

Fertility. Demographers distinguish between fecundity, the underlying biological potential for reproduction, and fertility, the actual level of achieved reproduction. (Confusingly, these English terms have opposite meanings from their parallel terms in French, where *fertilité* is the potential and *fécondité* is the realized; similarly ambiguous usages also prevail in the biological sciences, thereby increasing the chance of misunderstanding.) The difference between biological potential and realized fertility is determined by several intervening factors, including the following: (1) most women do not begin reproducing immediately upon the onset of puberty, which itself does not occur at a fixed age; (2) some women with the potential to reproduce never do so; (3) some women become widowed and do not remarry; (4) various elements of social behaviour restrain fertility; and (5) many human couples choose consciously to restrict their fertility by means of sexual abstinence, contraception, abortion, or sterilization.

Potential and realized fertility

The magnitude of the gap between potential and realized fertility can be illustrated by comparing the highest known fertilities with those of typical European and North American women in the late 20th century. A well-studied high-fertility group is the Hutterites of North America, a religious sect that views fertility regulation as sinful and high fertility as a blessing. Hutterite women who married between 1921 and 1930 are known to have averaged 10 children per woman. Meanwhile, women in much of Europe and North America averaged about two children per woman during the 1970s and 1980s—a number 80 percent less than that achieved by the Hutterites. Even the highly fertile populations of developing countries in Africa, Asia, and Latin America produce children at rates far below that of the Hutterites.

The general message from such evidence is clear enough: in much of the world, human fertility is considerably lower than the biological potential. It is strongly constrained by cultural regulations, especially those concerning marriage and sexuality, and by conscious efforts on the part of married couples to limit their childbearing.

Dependable evidence on historical fertility patterns in Europe is available back to the 18th century, and estimates have been made for several earlier centuries. Such data for non-European societies and for earlier human populations are much more fragmentary. The European data indicate that even in the absence of widespread deliberate regulation there were significant variations in fertility among different societies. These differences were heavily affected by socially determined behaviours such as those concerning marriage patterns. Beginning in France and Hungary in the 18th century, a dramatic decline in fertility took shape in the more developed societies of Europe and North America, and in the ensuing two centuries fertility declines of fully 50 percent took place in nearly all of these countries. Since the 1960s fertility has been intentionally diminished in many developing countries, and remarkably rapid reductions have occurred in the most populous, the People's Republic of China.

There is no dispute as to the fact and magnitudes of such declines, but theoretical explanation of the phenomena has proved elusive. (See below *Population theories*.)

Biological factors affecting human fertility. Reproduction is a quintessentially biological process, and hence all fertility analyses must consider the effects of biology. Such factors, in rough chronological order, include:

the age of onset of potential fertility (or fecundability in demographic terminology);

the degree of fecundability—*i.e.,* the monthly probability of conceiving in the absence of contraception;

the incidence of spontaneous abortion and stillbirth;

the duration of temporary infecundability following the birth of a child; and

the age of onset of permanent sterility.

The age at which women become fecund apparently declined significantly during the 20th century; as measured by the age of menarche (onset of menstruation), British data suggest a decline from 16–18 years in the mid-19th century to less than 13 years in the late 20th century. This decline is thought to be related to improving standards of nutrition and health. Since the average age of marriage in western Europe has long been far higher than the age of menarche, and since most children are born to married couples, this biological lengthening of the reproductive period is unlikely to have had major effects upon realized fertility in Europe. In settings where early marriage prevails, however, declining age at menarche could increase lifetime fertility.

Variations in fecundability

Fecundability also varies among women past menarche. The monthly probabilities of conception among newlyweds are commonly in the range of 0.15 to 0.25; that is, there is a 15–25-percent chance of conception each month. This fact is understandable when account is taken of the short interval (about two days) within each menstrual cycle during which fertilization can take place. Moreover, there appear to be cycles during which ovulation does not occur. Finally, perhaps one-third or more of fertilized ova fail to implant in the uterus or, even if they do implant, spontaneously abort during the ensuing two weeks, before pregnancy would be recognized. As a result of such factors, women of reproductive age who are not using contraceptive methods can expect to conceive within five to 10 months of becoming sexually active. As is true of all biological phenomena, there is surely a distribution of fecundability around average levels, with some women experiencing conception more readily than others.

Spontaneous abortion of recognized pregnancies and stillbirth also are fairly common, but their incidence is difficult to quantify. Perhaps 20 percent of recognized pregnancies fail spontaneously, most in the earlier months of gestation.

Following the birth of a child, most women experience a period of temporary infecundability, or biological inability to conceive. The length of this period seems to be affected substantially by breast-feeding. In the absence of breast-feeding, the interruption lasts less than two months. With lengthy, frequent breast-feeding it can last one or two years. This effect is thought to be caused by a complex of neural and hormonal factors stimulated by suckling.

A woman's fecundability typically peaks in her 20s and declines during her 30s; by their early 40s as many as 50 percent of women are affected by their own or their husbands' sterility. After menopause, essentially all women are sterile. The average age at menopause is in the late 40s, although some women experience it before reaching 40 and others not until nearly 60.

Contraception.   Contraceptive practices affect fertility by reducing the probability of conception. Contraceptive methods vary considerably in their theoretical effectiveness and in their actual effectiveness in use ("use-effectiveness"). Modern methods such as oral pills and intrauterine devices (IUDs) have use-effectiveness rates of more than 95 percent. Older methods such as the condom and diaphragm can be more than 90-percent effective when used regularly and correctly, but their average use-effectiveness is lower because of irregular or incorrect use.

The effect upon fertility of contraceptive measures can be dramatic: if fecundability is 0.20 (a 20-percent chance of pregnancy per month of exposure), then a 95-percent effective method will reduce this to 0.01 (a 1-percent chance).

Abortion.   Induced abortion reduces fertility not by affecting fecundability but by terminating pregnancy. Abortion has long been practiced in human societies and is quite common in some settings. The officially registered fraction of pregnancies terminated by abortion exceeds one-third in some countries, and significant numbers of unregistered abortions probably occur even in countries reporting very low rates.

Sterilization.   Complete elimination of fecundability can be brought about by sterilization. The surgical procedures of tubal ligation and vasectomy have become common in diverse nations and cultures. In the United States, for example, voluntary sterilization has become the most prevalent single means of terminating fertility, typically adopted by couples who have achieved their desired family size. In India, sterilization has been encouraged on occasion by various government incentive programs and, for a short period during the 1970s, by quasi-coercive measures.

Mortality.   As noted above, the science of demography has its intellectual roots in the realization that human mortality, while consisting of unpredictable individual events, has a statistical regularity when aggregated across a large group. This recognition formed the basis of a wholly new industry—that of life assurance, or insurance. The basis of this industry is the life table, or mortality table, which summarizes the distribution of longevity—observed over a period of years—among members of a population. This statistical device allows the calculation of premiums—the prices to be charged the members of a group of living subscribers with specified characteristics, who by pooling their resources in this statistical sense provide their heirs with financial benefits.

Life table

Overall human mortality levels can best be compared by using the life-table measure life expectancy at birth (often abbreviated simply as life expectancy), the number of years of life expected of a newborn baby on the basis of current mortality levels for persons of all ages. Life expectancies of premodern populations, with their poor knowledge of sanitation and health care, may have been as low as 25–30 years. The largest toll of death was that exacted in infancy and childhood: perhaps 20 percent of newborn children died in their first 12 months of life and another 30 percent before they reached five years of age.

In the developing countries by the 1980s, average life expectancy lay in the range of 55 to 60 years, with the highest levels in Latin America and the lowest in Africa. In the same period, life expectancy in the developed countries of western Europe and North America approached 75 years, and fewer than 1 percent of newborn children died in their first 12 months.

For reasons that are not well understood, life expectancy of females usually exceeds that of males, and this female advantage has grown as overall life expectancy has increased. In the late 20th century this female advantage was seven years (78 years versus 71 years) in the industrial market economies (comprising western Europe, North America, Japan, Australia, and New Zealand). It was eight years (74 years versus 66 years) in the nonmarket economies of eastern Europe.

Greater longevity of females

The epidemiologic transition.   The epidemiologic transition is that process by which the pattern of mortality and disease is transformed from one of high mortality among infants and children and episodic famine and epidemic affecting all age groups to one of degenerative and man-made diseases (such as those attributed to smoking) affecting principally the elderly. It is generally believed that the epidemiologic transitions prior to the 20th century (*i.e.,* those in today's industrialized countries) were closely associated with rising standards of living, nutrition, and sanitation. In contrast, those occurring in developing countries have been more or less independent of such internal socioeconomic development and more closely tied to organized health care and disease control programs developed and financed internationally. There is no doubt that 20th-century declines in mortality in developing countries have been far more rapid than those that occurred in the 19th century in what are now the industrialized countries.

Infant mortality.   Infant mortality is conventionally measured as the number of deaths in the first year of life per 1,000 live births during the same year. Roughly speaking, by this measure worldwide infant mortality approximates 80 per 1,000; that is, about 8 percent of newborn babies die within the first year of life.

This global average disguises great differences. In certain countries of Asia and Africa, infant mortality rates exceed 150 and sometimes approach 200 per 1,000 (that is, 15 or 20 percent of children die before reaching the age of

Variations in infant mortality

one year). Meanwhile, in other countries, such as Japan and Sweden, the rates are well below 10 per 1,000, or 1 percent. Generally, infant mortality is somewhat higher among males than among females.

In developing countries substantial declines in infant mortality have been credited to improved sanitation and nutrition, increased access to modern health care, and improved birth spacing through the use of contraception. In industrialized countries in which infant mortality rates were already low the increased availability of advanced medical technology for newborn—in particular, prematurely born—infants provides a partial explanation.

Infanticide. The deliberate killing of newborn infants has long been practiced in human societies. It seems to have been common in the ancient cultures of Greece, Rome, and China, and it was practiced in Europe until the 19th century. In Europe, infanticide included the practice of "overlaying" (smothering) an infant sharing a bed with its parents and the abandonment of unwanted infants to the custody of foundling hospitals, in which one-third to four-fifths of incumbents failed to survive.

In many societies practicing infanticide, infants were not deemed to be fully human until they underwent a rite of initiation that took place from a few days to several years after birth, and therefore killing before such initiation was socially acceptable. The purposes of infanticide were various: child spacing or fertility control in the absence of effective contraception; elimination of illegitimate, deformed, orphaned, or twin children; or sex preferences.

With the development and spread of the means of effective fertility regulation, infanticide has come to be strongly disapproved in most societies, though it continues to be practiced in some isolated traditional cultures.

Mortality among the elderly. During the 1970s and 1980s in industrialized countries there were unexpectedly large declines in mortality among the elderly, resulting in larger-than-projected numbers of the very old. In the United States, for example, the so-called frail elderly group aged 85 years and older increased nearly fourfold between 1950 and 1980, from 590,000 to 2,461,000. Given the high incidence of health problems among the very old, such increases have important implications for the organization and financing of health care.

Marriage. One of the main factors affecting fertility, and an important contributor to the fertility differences among societies in which conscious fertility control is uncommon, is defined by the patterns of marriage and marital disruption. In many societies in Asia and Africa, for example, marriage occurs soon after the sexual maturation of the woman, around age 17. In contrast, delayed marriage has long been common in Europe, and in some European countries the average age of first marriage approaches 25 years. Another aspect of historical marriage patterns in Europe is the high incidence of permanent celibacy: as many as 10 percent of women never marry. In contrast, nearly all women marry in most traditional developing countries of Asia and Africa.

Disruption of marriage

In the 20th century dramatic changes have taken place in the patterns of marital dissolution caused by widowhood and divorce. Widowhood has long been common in all societies, but the declines of mortality (as discussed above) have sharply reduced the effects of this source of marital dissolution on fertility. Meanwhile, divorce has been transformed from an uncommon exception to an experience terminating a large proportion (sometimes more than a third) of marriages in some countries. Taken together, these components of marriage patterns can account for the elimination of as little as 20 percent to as much as 50 percent of the potential reproductive years.

Many Western countries have experienced significant increases in the numbers of cohabiting unmarried couples. In the 1970s some 12 percent of all Swedish couples living together aged 16 to 70 were unmarried. When in the United States in 1976 the number of such arrangements approached 1,000,000, the Bureau of the Census formulated a new statistical category—POSSLQ—denoting persons of the opposite sex sharing living quarters. Extramarital fertility as a percentage of overall fertility accordingly has risen in many Western countries, accounting

for one in five births in the United States, one in five in Denmark, and one in three in Sweden.

Migration. Since any population that is not closed can be augmented or depleted by in-migration or out-migration, migration patterns must be considered carefully in analyzing population change. The common definition of human migration limits the term to permanent change of residence (conventionally, for at least one year), so as to distinguish it from commuting and other more frequent but temporary movements.

Human migrations have been fundamental to the broad sweep of human history and have themselves changed in basic ways over the epochs. Many of these historical migrations have by no means been the morally uplifting experiences depicted in mythologies of heroic conquerors, explorers, and pioneers; rather they frequently have been characterized by violence, destruction, bondage, mass mortality, and genocide—in other words, by human suffering of profound magnitudes.

Early human migrations. Early humans were almost surely hunters and gatherers who moved continually in search of food supplies. The superior technologies (tools, clothes, language, disciplined cooperation) of these hunting bands allowed them to spread farther and faster than had any other dominant species; humans are thought to have occupied all the continents except Antarctica within a span of about 50,000 years. As the species spread away from the tropical parasites and diseases of its African origins, mortality rates declined and population increased. This increase occurred at microscopically small rates by the standards of the past several centuries, but over thousands of years it resulted in a large absolute growth to a total that could no longer be supported by finding new hunting grounds. There ensued a transition from migratory hunting and gathering to migratory slash-and-burn agriculture. The consequence was the rapid geographical spread of crops, with wheat and barley moving east and west from the Middle East across the whole of Eurasia within only 5,000 years.

Growth of migratory populations

About 10,000 years ago a new and more productive way of life, involving sedentary agriculture, became predominant. This allowed greater investment of labour and technology in crop production, resulting in a more substantial and securer food source, but sporadic migrations persisted.

The next pulse of migration, beginning around 4000 to 3000 BC, was stimulated by the development of seagoing sailing vessels and of pastoral nomadry. The Mediterranean Basin was the centre of the maritime culture, which involved the settlement of offshore islands and led to the development of deep-sea fishing and long-distance trade. Other favoured regions were those of the Indian Ocean and South China Sea. Meanwhile, pastoral nomadry involved biological adaptations both in humans (allowing them to digest milk) and in species of birds and mammals that were domesticated. Once completed, these adaptations allowed humans to consume the meat of most male newborn animals and the maternal milk thereby made available.

Both seafarers and pastoralists were intrinsically migratory. The former were able to colonize previously uninhabited lands or to impose their rule by force over less mobile populations. The pastoralists were able to populate the extensive grassland of the Eurasian Steppe and the African and Middle Eastern savannas, and their superior nutrition and mobility gave them clear military advantages over the sedentary agriculturalists with whom they came into contact. Even as agriculture continued to improve with innovations such as the plow, these mobile elements persisted and provided important networks by which technological innovations could be spread widely and rapidly.

That complex of human organization and behaviour commonly termed Western civilization arose out of such developments. Around 4000 BC seafaring migrants from the south overwhelmed the local inhabitants of the Tigris–Euphrates floodplain and began to develop a social organization based upon the division of labour into highly skilled occupations, technologies such as irrigation, bronze metallurgy, and wheeled vehicles, and the growth of cities

Urban cultures

of 20,000–50,000 persons. Political differentiation into ruling classes and ruled masses provided a basis for imposition of taxes and rents that financed the development of professional soldiers and artisans, whose specialized skills far surpassed those of pastoralists and agriculturalists. The military and economic superiority that accompanied such skills allowed advanced communities to expand both by direct conquest and by the adoption of this social form by neighbouring peoples. Thus migration patterns played an important role in creating the early empires and cultures of the ancient world.

By about 2000 BC such specialized human civilizations occupied much of the then-known world—the Middle East, the eastern Mediterranean, South Asia, and the Far East. Under these circumstances human migration was transformed from unstructured movements across unoccupied territories by nomads and seafarers into quite new forms of interaction among the settled civilizations.

These new forms of human migration produced disorder, suffering, and much mortality. As one population conquered or infiltrated another, the vanquished were usually destroyed, enslaved, or forcibly absorbed. Large numbers of people were captured and transported by slave traders. Constant turmoil accompanied the ebb and flow of populations across the regions of settled agriculture and the Eurasian and African grasslands. Important examples include the Dorian incursions in ancient Greece in the 11th century BC, the Germanic migrations southward from the Baltic to the Roman Empire in the 4th to 6th centuries AD, the Norman raids and conquests of Britain between the 8th and 12th centuries AD, and the Bantu migrations in Africa throughout the Christian Era.

Modern mass migrations. Mass migrations over long distances were among the new phenomena produced by the population increase and improved transportation that accompanied the Industrial Revolution. The largest of these was the so-called Great Atlantic Migration from Europe to North America, the first major wave of which began in the late 1840s with mass movements from Ireland and Germany. These were caused by the failure of the potato crop in Ireland and in the lower Rhineland, where millions had become dependent upon this single source of nutrition. These flows eventually subsided, but in the 1880s a second and even larger wave of mass migration developed from eastern and southern Europe, again stimulated in part by agricultural crises and facilitated by improvements in transportation and communication. Between 1880 and 1910 some 17,000,000 Europeans entered the United States; overall, the total amounted to 37,000,-000 between 1820 and 1980.

Since World War II equally large long-distance migrations have occurred. In most cases groups from developing countries have moved into the industrialized countries of the West. Some 13,000,000 migrants have become permanent residents of western Europe since the 1960s. More than 10,000,000 permanent immigrants have been admitted legally to the United States since the 1960s, and illegal immigration has almost surely added several millions more.

Forced migrations. Slave migrations and mass expulsions have been part of human history for millennia. The largest slave migrations were probably those compelled by European slave traders operating in Africa from the 16th to the 19th century. During that period perhaps 20,000,-000 slaves were consigned to American markets, though substantial numbers died in the appalling conditions of the Atlantic passage.

The largest mass expulsion is probably that imposed by the Nazi government of Germany, which deported 7,000,-000–8,000,000 persons, including some 5,000,000 Jews later exterminated in concentration camps. After World War II, 9,000,000–10,000,000 ethnic Germans were more or less forcibly transported into Germany, and perhaps 1,000,000 members of minority groups deemed politically unreliable by the Soviet government were forcibly exiled to Central Asia. Earlier deportations of this type included the movement of 150,000 British convicts to Australia between 1788 and 1867 and the 19th-century exile of 1,000,000 Russians to Siberia.

European settlement of America

Forced migrations since World War II have been large indeed. Some 14,000,000 persons fled in one direction or the other at the partition of British India into India and Pakistan. Nearly 10,000,000 left East Pakistan (now Bangladesh) during the fighting in 1971; many of them stayed on in India. An estimated 3,000,000–4,000,000 persons fled from the war in Afghanistan during the early 1980s. More than 1,000,000 refugees have departed Vietnam, Cuba, Israel, and Ethiopia since World War II. Estimates during the 1980s suggested that approximately 10,000,000 refugees had not been resettled and were in need of assistance.

Internal migrations. The largest human migrations today are internal to nation-states; these can be sizable in rapidly increasing populations with large rural-to-urban migratory flows.

Early human movements toward urban areas were devastating in terms of mortality. Cities were loci of intense infection; indeed, many human viral diseases are not propagated unless the population density is far greater than that common under sedentary agriculture or pastoral nomadism. Moreover, cities had to import food and raw materials from the hinterlands, but transport and political disruptions led to erratic patterns of scarcity, famine, and epidemic. The result was that cities until quite recently (the mid-19th century) were demographic sinkholes, incapable of sustaining their own populations.

Urban growth since World War II has been very rapid in much of the world. In developing countries with high overall population growth rates the populations of some cities have been doubling every 10 years or less (see below *Population composition*).

Natural increase and population growth. *Natural increase.* Put simply, natural increase is the difference between the numbers of births and deaths in a population; the rate of natural increase is the difference between the birthrate and the death rate (see Figure 1). Given the fertility and mortality characteristics of the human species (excluding incidents of catastrophic mortality), the range of possible rates of natural increase is rather narrow. For a nation, it has rarely exceeded 4 percent per year; the highest known rate for a national population—arising from the conjunction of a very high birthrate and a quite low death rate—is that experienced in Kenya during the 1980s, in which the natural increase of the population approximated 4.1 percent per annum. Rates of natural increase in other developing countries generally are lower; these countries averaged about 2.5 percent per annum during the same period. Meanwhile the rates of natural increase in industrialized countries are very low: the highest is approximately 1 percent, most are in the neighbourhood of several tenths of 1 percent, and some are slightly negative (that is, their populations are slowly decreasing).

Population growth. The rate of population growth is the rate of natural increase combined with the effects of migration. Thus a high rate of natural increase can be offset by a large net out-migration, and a low rate of natural increase can be countered by a high level of net in-migration. Generally speaking, however, these migration effects on population growth rates are far smaller than the effects of changes in fertility and mortality.

Population "momentum." An important and often misunderstood characteristic of human populations is the tendency of a highly fertile population that has been increasing rapidly in size to continue to do so for decades after the onset of even a substantial decline in fertility. This results from the youthful age structure of such a population, as discussed below. These populations contain large numbers of children who have still to grow into adulthood and the years of reproduction. Thus even a dramatic decline in fertility, which affects only the numbers at age zero, cannot prevent the continuing growth of the number of adults of childbearing age for at least two or three decades.

Eventually, of course, as these large groups pass through the childbearing years to middle and older age, the smaller numbers of children resulting from the fertility decline lead to a moderation in the rate of population growth. But the delays are lengthy, allowing very substantial additional

Political refugees

population growth after fertility has declined. This phenomenon gives rise to the term population momentum, which is of great significance to developing countries with rapid population growth and limited natural resources. The nature of population growth means that the metaphor of a "population bomb" used by some lay analysts of population trends in the 1960s was really quite inaccurate. Bombs explode with tremendous force, but such force is rapidly spent. A more appropriate metaphor for rapid population growth is that of a glacier, since a glacier moves at a slow pace but with enormous effects wherever it goes and with a long-term momentum that is unstoppable.

By courtesy of the Population Reference Bureau, Inc., Washington, D.C.

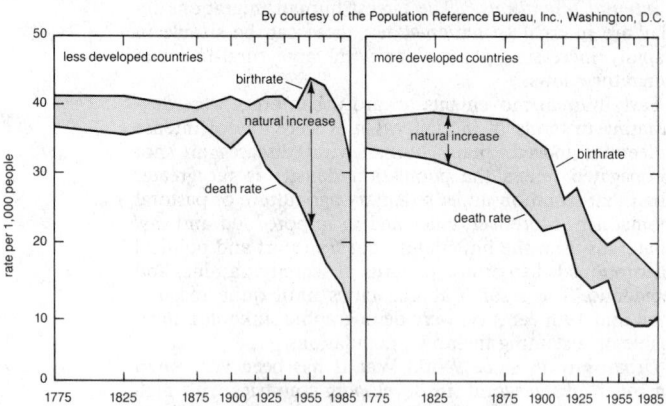

Figure 1: Population growth through natural increase in the less developed and more developed countries, 1775–1985.

POPULATION COMPOSITION

The most important characteristics of a population—in addition to its size and the rate at which it is expanding or contracting—are the ways in which its members are distributed according to age, sex, ethnic or racial category, and residential status (urban or rural).

Age distribution. Perhaps the most fundamental of these characteristics is the age distribution of a population. Demographers commonly use population pyramids to describe both age and sex distributions of populations. A population pyramid is a bar chart or graph in which the length of each horizontal bar represents the number (or percentage) of persons in an age group; for example, the base of such a chart consists of a bar representing the youngest segment of the population, those persons less than, say, five years old. Each bar is divided into segments corresponding to the numbers (or proportions) of males and females. In most populations the proportion of older persons is much smaller than that of the younger, so the chart narrows toward the top and is more or less triangular, like the cross section of a pyramid; hence the name. Youthful populations are represented by pyramids with a broad base of young children and a narrow apex of older

Population pyramids

people, while older populations are characterized by more uniform numbers of people in the age categories. Figure 2 presents population pyramids for three nations that have markedly different characteristics: high fertility and rapid population growth (Mexico), low fertility and slow growth (United States), and very low fertility and negative growth (West Germany).

Contrary to a common belief, the principal factor tending to change the age distribution of a population—and, hence, the general shape of the corresponding pyramid—is not the death or mortality rates, but rather the rate of fertility. A rise or decline in mortality generally affects all age groups in some measure, and hence has only limited effects on the proportion in each age group. A change in fertility, however, affects the number of people in only a single age group—the group of age zero, the newly born. Hence a decline or increase in fertility has a highly concentrated effect at one end of the age distribution and thereby can have a major influence on the overall age structure. This means that youthful age structures correspond to highly fertile populations, typical of developing countries. The older age structures are those of low-fertility populations, such as are common in the industrialized world.

Sex ratio. A second important structural aspect of populations is the relative numbers of males and females who compose it. Generally, slightly more males are born than females (a typical ratio would be 105 or 106 males for every 100 females). On the other hand, it is quite common for males to experience higher mortality at virtually all ages after birth. This difference is apparently of biological origin. Exceptions occur in countries such as India, where the mortality of females may be higher than that of males in childhood and at the ages of childbearing because of unequal allocation of resources within the family and the poor quality of maternal health care.

The general rules that more males are born but that females experience lower mortality mean that during childhood males outnumber females of the same age, the difference decreases as the age increases, at some point in the adult life span the numbers of males and females become equal, and as higher ages are reached the number of females becomes disproportionately large. For example, in Europe and North America, among persons more than 70 years of age in 1985, the number of males for every 100 females was only about 61 to 63. (According to the Population Division of the United Nations, the figure for the Soviet Union was only 40, which may be attributable to high male mortality during World War II as well as to possible increases in male mortality during the 1980s.)

The sex ratio within a population has significant implications for marriage patterns. A scarcity of males of a given age depresses the marriage rates of females in the same age group or usually those somewhat younger, and this in turn is likely to reduce their fertility. In many countries, social convention dictates a pattern in which males at marriage are slightly older than their spouses. Thus if there is a dramatic rise in fertility, such as that called the "baby boom" in the period following World War II, a "marriage squeeze" can eventually result; that is, the number of males of the socially correct age for marriage is insufficient for the number of somewhat younger females. This may lead to deferment of marriage of these women, a contraction of the age differential of marrying couples, or both. Similarly, a dramatic fertility decline in such a society is likely to lead eventually to an insufficiency of eligible females for marriage, which may lead to earlier marriage of these women, an expansion of the age gap at marriage, or both. All of these effects are slow to develop; it takes at least 20 to 25 years for even a dramatic fall or rise in fertility to affect marriage patterns in this way.

Ethnic or racial composition. The populations of all nations of the world are more or less diverse with respect to ethnicity or race. (Ethnicity here includes national, cultural, religious, linguistic, or other attributes that are perceived as characteristic of distinct groups.) Such divisions in populations often are regarded as socially important, and statistics by race and ethnic group are therefore commonly available. The categories used for such groups differ from nation to nation, however; for example, a person

Sex differences in natality and mortality

By courtesy of the Population Reference Bureau, Inc., Washington, D.C.

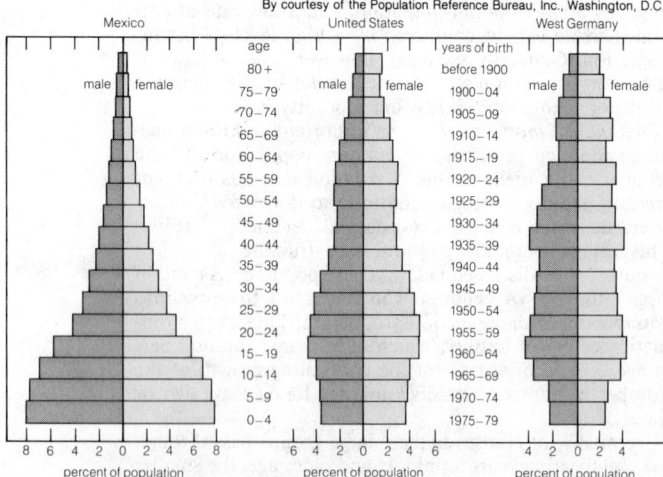

Figure 2: Population pyramids, showing age and sex distributions of the populations of Mexico, the United States, and West Germany in 1980.

of Pakistani origin is considered "black" or "coloured" in the United Kingdom but would probably be classified as "white" or "Asian" in the United States. For this reason, international comparisons of ethnic and racial groups are imprecise, and this component of population structure is far less objective as a measure than are the categories of age and sex discussed above.

Geographical distribution and urbanization. It goes without saying that populations are scattered across space. The typical measure of population in relation to land area, that of population density, is often a meaningless one, since different areas vary considerably in their value for agricultural or other human purposes. Moreover, a high population density in an agrarian society, dependent upon agriculture for its sustenance, is likely to be a severer constraint upon human welfare than would the same density in a highly industrialized society, in which the bulk of national product is not of agricultural origin.

Also of significance in terms of geographical distribution is the division between rural and urban areas. For many decades there has been a nearly universal flow of populations from rural into urban areas. While definitions of urban areas differ from country to country and region to region, the most highly urbanized societies in the world are those of western and northern Europe, Australia, New Zealand, temperate South America, and North America; in all of these the fraction of the population living in urban areas exceeds 75 percent, and it has reached 85 percent in West Germany. An intermediate stage of urbanization exists in the countries making up much of tropical Latin America, where 50 to 65 percent of the population lives in cities. Finally, in many of the developing countries of Asia and Africa the urbanization process has only recently begun, and it is not uncommon to find less than one-third of the population living in urban areas.

Growth
of
cities

The rapidity of urbanization in some countries is quite astonishing. The population of Mexico City in 1960 was around 5,000,000; it was estimated to be about 17,000,000 in 1985 and was projected to reach 26,000,000 to 31,000,000 by 2000. A rule of thumb for much of the developing world is that the rate of growth of urban areas is twice that of the population as a whole. Thus in a population growing 3 percent annually (doubling in about 23.1 years), it is likely that the urban growth rate is at least 6 percent annually (doubling in about 11.6 years).

POPULATION THEORIES

Population size and change play such a fundamental role in human societies that they have been the subject of theorizing for millennia. Most religious traditions have had something to say on these matters, as did many of the leading figures of the ancient world.

In modern times the subject of demographic change has played a central role in the development of the politico-economic theory of mercantilism; the classical economics of Adam Smith, David Ricardo, and others; the cornucopian images of utopians such as the Marquis de Condorcet; the contrasting views of Malthus as to the natural limits imposed on human population; the sociopolitical theories of Marx, Engels, and their followers; the scientific revolutions engendered by Darwin and his followers; and so on through the pantheon of human thought. Most of these theoretical viewpoints have incorporated demographic components as elements of far grander schemes. Only in a few cases have demographic concepts played a central role, as in the case of the theory of the demographic transition that evolved during the 1930s as a counter to biological explanations of fertility declines that were then current.

Population theories in antiquity. The survival of ancient human societies despite high and unpredictable mortality implies that all societies that persisted were successful in maintaining high fertility. They did so in part by stressing the duties of marriage and procreation and by stigmatizing persons who failed to produce children. Many of these pronatalist motives were incorporated into religious dogma and mythology, as in the biblical injunction to "be fruitful and multiply, and populate the earth," the Hindu laws of Manu, and the writings of Zoroaster.

The ancient Greeks were interested in population size, and Plato's *Republic* incorporated the concept of an optimal population size of 5,040 citizens, among whom fertility was restrained by conscious birth control. The leaders of imperial Rome, however, advocated maximizing population size in the interest of power, and explicitly pronatalist laws were adopted during the reign of Augustus to encourage marriage and fertility.

Greek
and
Roman
views

The traditions of Christianity on this topic are mixed. The pronatalism of the Old Testament and the Roman Empire was embraced with some ambivalence by a church that sanctified celibacy among the priesthood. Later, during the time of Thomas Aquinas, the church moved toward more forceful support of high fertility and opposition to birth control.

Islāmic writings on fertility were equally mixed. The 14th-century Arab historian Ibn Khaldūn incorporated demographic factors into his grand theory of the rise and fall of empires. According to his analysis, the decline of an empire's population necessitates the importation of foreign mercenaries to administer and defend its territories, resulting in rising taxes, political intrigue, and general decadence. The hold of the empire on its hinterland and on its own populace weakens, making it a tempting target for a vigorous challenger. Thus Ibn Khaldūn saw the growth of dense human populations as generally favourable to the maintenance and increase of imperial power.

On the other hand, contraception was acceptable practice in Islām from the days of the Prophet, and extensive attention was given to contraceptive methods by the great physicians of the Islāmic world during the Middle Ages. Moreover, under Islāmic law the fetus is not considered a human being until its form is distinctly human, and hence early abortion was not forbidden.

Mercantilism and the idea of progress. The wholesale mortality caused by the Black Death during the 14th century contributed in fundamental ways to the development of mercantilism, the school of thought that dominated Europe from the 16th through the 18th century. Mercantilists and the absolute rulers who dominated many states of Europe saw each nation's population as a form of national wealth: the larger the population, the richer the nation. Large populations provided a larger labour supply, larger markets, and larger (and hence more powerful) armies for defense and for foreign expansion. Moreover, since growth in the number of wage earners tended to depress wages, the wealth of the monarch could be increased by capturing this surplus. In the words of Frederick II the Great of Prussia, "the number of the people makes the wealth of states." Similar views were held by mercantilists in Germany, France, Italy, and Spain. For the mercantilists, accelerating the growth of the population by encouraging fertility and discouraging emigration was consistent with increasing the power of the nation or the king. Most mercantilists, confident that any number of people would be able to produce their own subsistence, had no worries about harmful effects of population growth. (To this day similar optimism continues to be expressed by diverse schools of thought, from traditional Marxists on the left to "cornucopians" on the right.)

Physiocrats and the origins of demography. By the 18th century the Physiocrats were challenging the intensive state intervention that characterized the mercantilist system, urging instead the policy of laissez-faire. Their targets included the pronatalist strategies of governments; Physiocrats such as François Quesnay argued that human multiplication should not be encouraged to a point beyond that sustainable without widespread poverty. For the Physiocrats, economic surplus was attributable to land, and population growth could therefore not increase wealth. In their analysis of this subject matter the Physiocrats drew upon the techniques developed in England by John Graunt, Edmond Halley, Sir William Petty, and Gregory King, which for the first time made possible the quantitative assessment of population size, the rate of growth, and rates of mortality.

Laissez-
faire
economics

The Physiocrats had broad and important effects upon the thinking of the classical economists such as Adam Smith, especially with respect to the role of free markets unregulated by the state. As a group, however, the classical economists expressed little interest in the issue of population growth, and when they did they tended to see it as an effect rather than as a cause of economic prosperity.

Utopian views. In another 18th-century development, the optimism of mercantilists was incorporated into a very different set of ideas, those of the so-called utopians. Their views, based upon the idea of human progress and perfectibility, led to the conclusion that once perfected, mankind would have no need of coercive institutions such as police, criminal law, property ownership, and the family. In a properly organized society, in their view, progress was consistent with any level of population, since population size was the principal factor determining the amount of resources. Such resources should be held in common by all persons, and if there were any limits on population growth, they would be established automatically by the normal functioning of the perfected human society. Principal proponents of such views included Condorcet, William Godwin, and Daniel Malthus, the father of the Reverend Thomas Robert Malthus. Through his father the younger Malthus was introduced to such ideas relating human welfare to population dynamics, which stimulated him to undertake his own collection and analysis of data; these eventually made him the central figure in the population debates of the 19th and 20th centuries.

Malthus and his successors. In 1798 Malthus published *An Essay on the Principle of Population as It Affects the Future Improvement of Society, with Remarks on the Speculations of Mr. Godwin, M. Condorcet, and Other Writers.* This hastily written pamphlet had as its principal object the refutation of the views of the utopians. In Malthus' view, the perfection of a human society free of coercive restraints was a mirage, because the capacity for the threat of population growth would always be present. In this, Malthus echoed the much earlier arguments of Robert Wallace in his *Various Prospects of Mankind, Nature, and Providence* (1761), which posited that the perfection of society carried with it the seeds of its own destruction, in the stimulation of population growth such that "the earth would at last be overstocked, and become unable to support its numerous inhabitants."

Critics
of
Malthus

Not many copies of Malthus' essay, his first, were published, but it nonetheless became the subject of discussion and attack. The essay was cryptic and poorly supported by empirical evidence. Malthus' arguments were easy to misrepresent, and his critics did so routinely.

The criticism had the salutary effect of stimulating Malthus to pursue the data and other evidence lacking in his first essay. He collected information on one country that had plentiful land (the United States) and estimated that its population was doubling in less than 25 years. He attributed the far lower rates of European population growth to "preventive checks," giving special emphasis to the characteristic late marriage pattern of western Europe, which he called "moral restraint." The other preventive checks to which he alluded were birth control, abortion, adultery, and homosexuality, all of which as an Anglican minister he considered immoral.

In one sense, Malthus reversed the arguments of the mercantilists that the number of people determined the nation's resources, adopting the contrary argument of the Physiocrats that the resource base determined the numbers of people. From this he derived an entire theory of society and human history, leading inevitably to a set of provocative prescriptions for public policy. Those societies that ignored the imperative for moral restraint—delayed marriage and celibacy for adults until they were economically able to support their children—would suffer the deplorable "positive checks" of war, famine, and epidemic, the avoidance of which should be every society's goal. From this humane concern about the sufferings from positive checks arose Malthus' admonition that poor laws (*i.e.,* legal measures that provided relief to the poor) and charity must not cause their beneficiaries to relax their moral restraint or increase their fertility, lest such humanitarian gestures become perversely counterproductive.

Having stated his position, Malthus was denounced as a reactionary, although he favoured free medical assistance for the poor, universal education at a time that this was a radical idea, and democratic institutions at a time of elitist alarums about the French Revolution. Malthus was accused of blasphemy by the conventionally religious. The strongest denunciations of all came from Marx and his followers (see below). Meanwhile, the ideas of Malthus had important effects upon public policy (such as reforms in the English Poor Laws) and upon the ideas of the classical and neoclassical economists, demographers, and evolutionary biologists, led by Charles Darwin. Moreover, the evidence and analyses produced by Malthus dominated scientific discussion of population during his lifetime; indeed, he was the invited author of the article "Population" for the supplement (1824) to the fourth, fifth, and sixth editions of the *Encyclopædia Britannica.* Though many of Malthus' gloomy predictions have proved to be misdirected, that article introduced analytical methods that clearly anticipated demographic techniques developed more than 100 years later.

The latter-day followers of Malthusian analysis deviated significantly from the prescriptions offered by Malthus. While these "neo-Malthusians" accepted Malthus' core propositions regarding the links between unrestrained fertility and poverty, they rejected his advocacy of delayed marriage and his opposition to birth control. Moreover, leading neo-Malthusians such as Charles Bradlaugh and Annie Besant could hardly be described as reactionary defenders of the established church and social order. To the contrary, they were political and religious radicals who saw the extension of knowledge of birth control to the lower classes as an important instrument favouring social equality. Their efforts were opposed by the full force of the establishment, and both spent considerable time on trial and in jail for their efforts to publish materials—condemned as obscene—about contraception.

Neo-
Malthu-
sians

Marx, Lenin, and their followers. While both Karl Marx and Malthus accepted many of the views of the classical economists, Marx was harshly and implacably critical of Malthus and his ideas. The vehemence of the assault was remarkable. Marx reviled Malthus as a "miserable parson" guilty of spreading a "vile and infamous doctrine, this repulsive blasphemy against man and nature." For Marx, only under capitalism does Malthus' dilemma of resource limits arise. Though differing in many respects from the utopians who had provoked Malthus' rejoinder, Marx shared with them the view that any number of people could be supported by a properly organized society. Under the socialism favoured by Marx, the surplus product of labour, previously appropriated by the capitalists, would be returned to its rightful owners, the workers, thereby eliminating the cause of poverty. Thus Malthus and Marx shared a strong concern about the plight of the poor, but they differed sharply as to how it should be improved. For Malthus the solution was individual responsibility as to marriage and childbearing; for Marx the solution was a revolutionary assault upon the organization of society, leading to a collective structure called socialism.

The strident nature of Marx's attack upon Malthus' ideas may have arisen from his realization that they constituted a potentially fatal critique of his own analysis. "If [Malthus'] theory of population is correct," Marx wrote in 1875 in his *Critique of the Gotha Programme* (published by Engels in 1891), "then I can*not* abolish this [iron law of wages] even if I abolish wage-labor a hundred times, because this law is not only paramount over the system of wage-labor but also over every social system."

The anti-Malthusian views of Marx were continued and extended by Marxians who followed him. For example, although in 1920 Lenin legalized abortion in the revolutionary Soviet Union as the right of every woman "to control her own body," he opposed the practice of contraception or abortion for purposes of regulating population growth. Lenin's successor, Joseph Stalin, adopted a pronatalist argument verging on the mercantilist, in which population growth was seen as a stimulant to economic progress. As the threat of war intensified in Europe in the 1930s, Stalin promulgated coercive measures to increase Soviet population growth, including the banning of abortion despite its status as a woman's basic right. Although contraception

Stalin's
pro-
natalism

is now accepted and practiced widely in most Marxist-Leninist states, some traditional ideologists continue to characterize its encouragement in Third-World countries as shabby Malthusianism.

The Darwinian tradition. Charles Darwin, whose scientific insights revolutionized 19th-century biology, acknowledged an important intellectual debt to Malthus in the development of his theory of natural selection. Darwin himself was not much involved in debates about human populations, but many who followed in his name as "social Darwinists" and "eugenicists" expressed a passionate if narrowly defined interest in the subject.

In Darwinian theory the engine of evolution is differential reproduction of different genetic stocks. The concern of many social Darwinists and eugenicists was that fertility among those they considered the superior human stocks was far lower than among the poorer—and, in their view, biologically inferior—groups, resulting in a gradual but inexorable decline in the quality of the overall population. While some attributed this lower fertility to deliberate efforts of people who needed to be informed of the dysgenic effects of their behaviour, others saw the fertility decline itself as evidence of biological deterioration of the superior stocks. Such simplistic biological explanations attracted attention to the socioeconomic and cultural factors that might explain the phenomenon and contributed to the development of the theory of the demographic transition.

Theory of the demographic transition. The classic explanation of European fertility declines arose in the period following World War I and came to be known as demographic transition theory. (Formally, transition theory is a historical generalization and not truly a scientific theory offering predictive and testable hypotheses.) The theory arose in part as a reaction to crude biological explanations of fertility declines; it rationalized them in solely socioeconomic terms, as consequences of widespread desire for fewer children caused by industrialization, urbanization, increased literacy, and declining infant mortality.

Changing role of the family

The factory system and urbanization led to a diminution in the role of the family in industrial production and a reduction of the economic value of children. Meanwhile, the costs of raising children rose, especially in urban settings, and universal primary education postponed their entry into the work force. Finally, the lessening of infant mortality reduced the number of births needed to achieve a given family size. In some versions of transition theory, a fertility decline is triggered when one or more of these socioeconomic factors reach certain threshold values.

Until the 1970s transition theory was widely accepted as an explanation of European fertility declines, although conclusions based on it had never been tested empirically. More recently careful research on the European historical experience has forced reappraisal and refinement of demographic transition theory. In particular, distinctions based upon cultural attributes such as language and religion, coupled with the spread of ideas such as those of the nuclear family and the social acceptability of deliberate fertility control, appear to have played more important roles than were recognized by transition theorists.

TRENDS IN WORLD POPULATION

Before considering modern population trends separately for developing and industrialized countries, it is useful to present an overview of older trends. It is generally agreed that only 5,000,000–10,000,000 humans (*i.e.*, one one-thousandth of the present world population) were supportable before the agricultural revolution of about 10,000 years ago. By the beginning of the Christian era, 8,000 years later, the human population approximated 300,-000,000, and there was apparently little increase in the ensuing millennium up to the year AD 1000. Subsequent population growth was slow and fitful, especially given the plague epidemics and other catastrophes of the Middle Ages. By 1750, conventionally the beginning of the Industrial Revolution in Britain, world population may have been as high as 800,000,000. This means that in the 750 years from 1000 to 1750, the annual population growth rate averaged only about one-tenth of 1 percent.

The reasons for such slow growth are well known. In the absence of what is now considered basic knowledge of sanitation and health (the role of bacteria in disease, for example, was unknown until the 19th century), mortality rates were very high, especially for infants and children. Only about half of newborn babies survived to the age of five years. Fertility was also very high, as it had to be to sustain the existence of any population under such conditions of mortality. Modest population growth might occur for a time in these circumstances, but recurring famines, epidemics, and wars kept long-term growth close to zero.

From 1750 onward population growth accelerated. In some measure this was a consequence of rising standards of living, coupled with improved transport and communication, which mitigated the effects of localized crop failures that previously would have resulted in catastrophic mortality. Occasional famines did occur, however, and it was not until the 19th century that a sustained decline in mortality took place, stimulated by the improving economic conditions of the Industrial Revolution and the growing understanding of the need for sanitation and public health measures.

Modern increase in world population

The world population, which did not reach its first 1,000,-000,000 until about 1800, added another 1,000,000,000 persons by 1930. (To anticipate further discussion below, the third was added by 1960, the fourth by 1974, and the fifth before 1990; see Figure 3.) The most rapid growth in the 19th century occurred in Europe and North America, which experienced gradual but eventually dramatic declines in mortality. Meanwhile, mortality and fertility remained high in Asia, Africa, and Latin America.

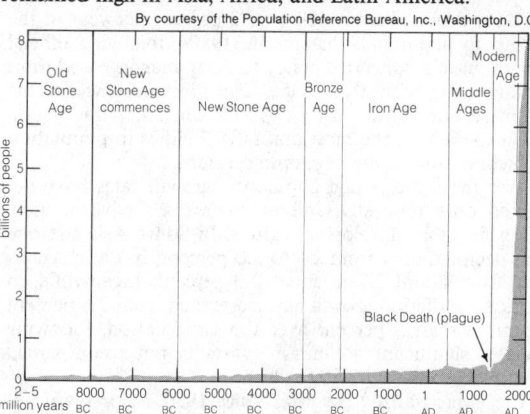

By courtesy of the Population Reference Bureau, Inc., Washington, D.C.

Figure 3: World population growth since 8000 BC.

Beginning in the 1930s and accelerating rapidly after World War II, mortality went into decline in much of Asia and Latin America, giving rise to a new spurt of population growth that reached rates far higher than any previously experienced in Europe. The rapidity of this growth, which some described as the "population explosion," was due to the sharpness in the falls in mortality that in turn were the result of improvements in public health, sanitation, and nutrition that were mostly imported from the developed countries. The external origins and the speed of the declines in mortality meant that there was little chance that they would be accompanied by the onset of a decline in fertility. In addition, the marriage patterns of Asia and Latin America were (and continue to be) quite different from those of Europe; marriage in Asia and Latin America is early and nearly universal, while that in Europe is usually late and significant percentages of people never marry.

These high growth rates occurred in populations already of very large size, meaning that global population growth became very rapid both in absolute and in relative terms. The peak rate of increase was reached in the early 1960s, when each year the world population grew by about 2 percent, or about 68,000,000 people. Since that time both mortality and fertility rates have decreased, and the annual growth rate has fallen moderately, to about 1.7 percent. But even this lower rate, because it applies to a larger population base, means that the number of people added each year has risen from about 68,000,000 to 80,000,000.

The developing countries since 1950. After World War

II there was a rapid decline in mortality in much of the developing world. In part this resulted from wartime efforts to maintain the health of armed forces from industrialized countries fighting in tropical areas. Since all people and governments welcome proven techniques to reduce the incidence of disease and death, these efforts were readily accepted in much of the developing world, but they were not accompanied by the kinds of social and cultural changes that had occurred earlier and had led to fertility declines in industrialized countries.

The reduction in mortality, unaccompanied by a reduction in fertility, had a simple and predictable outcome: accelerating population growth. By 1960 many developing countries had rates of increase as high as 3 percent a year, exceeding by two- or threefold the highest rates ever experienced by European populations. Since a population increasing at this rate will double in only 23 years, the populations of such countries expanded dramatically. In the 25 years between 1950 and 1975, the population of Mexico increased from 27,000,000 to 60,000,000; Iran from 14,000,000 to 33,000,000; Brazil from 53,000,000 to 108,000,000; and China from 554,000,000 to 933,000,000.

The greatest population growth rates were reached in Latin America and in Asia during the mid- to late 1960s. Since then, these regions have experienced variable but sometimes substantial fertility declines along with continuing mortality declines, resulting in usually moderate and occasionally large declines in population growth. The most dramatic declines have been those of the People's Republic of China, where the growth rate was estimated to have declined from well over 2 percent per year in the 1960s to about half that in the 1980s, following official adoption of a concerted policy to delay marriage and limit childbearing within marriage. The predominance of the Chinese population in East Asia means that this region has experienced the most dramatic declines in population growth of any of the developing regions.

Population control in China

Over the same period population growth rates have declined only modestly, and in some cases have actually risen, in other developing regions. In South Asia the rate has declined only from 2.4 to 2.0 percent; in Latin America, from about 2.7 to about 2.3 percent. Meanwhile, in Africa population growth has accelerated from 2.6 percent to more than 3 percent over the same period, following belated significant declines in mortality not accompanied by similar reductions in fertility.

The industrialized countries since 1950. For many industrialized countries, the period after World War II was marked by a "baby boom." One group of four countries in particular—the United States, Canada, Australia, and New Zealand—experienced sustained and substantial rises in fertility from the depressed levels of the prewar period. In the United States, for example, fertility rose by two-thirds, reaching levels in the 1950s not seen since 1910.

A second group of industrialized countries, including most of western Europe and some eastern European countries (notably Czechoslovakia and what is now East Germany), experienced what might be termed "baby boomlets." For a few years after the war, fertility increased as a result of marriages and births deferred during wartime. These increases were modest and relatively short-lived, however, when compared to those of the true baby-boom countries mentioned above. In many of these European countries fertility had been very low in the 1930s; their postwar baby boomlets appeared as three- to four-year "spikes" in the graph of their fertility rates, followed by two full decades of stable fertility levels. Beginning in the mid-1960s, fertility levels in these countries began to move lower again and, in many cases, fell to levels comparable to or lower than those of the 1930s.

A third group of industrialized countries, consisting of most of eastern Europe along with Japan, showed quite different fertility patterns. Most did not register low fertility in the 1930s but underwent substantial declines in the 1950s after a short-lived baby boomlet. In many of these countries the decline persisted into the 1960s, but in some it was reversed in response to governmental incentives.

By the 1980s the fertility levels in most industrialized countries were very low, at or below those needed to maintain stable populations. There are two reasons for this phenomenon: the postponement of marriage and childbearing by many younger women who entered the labour force, and a reduction in the numbers of children born to married women.

POPULATION PROJECTIONS

Demographic change is inherently a long-term phenomenon. Unlike populations of insects, human populations have rarely been subject to "explosion" or "collapse" in numbers. Moreover, the powerful long-term momentum that is built into the human age structure means that the effects of fertility changes become apparent only in the far future. For these and other reasons, it is by now conventional practice to employ the technology of population projection as a means of better understanding the implications of trends.

Population projections represent simply the playing out into the future of a set of assumptions about future fertility, mortality, and migration rates. It cannot be stated too strongly that such projections are not predictions, though they are misinterpreted as such frequently enough. A projection is a "what-if" exercise based on explicit assumptions that may or may not themselves be correct. As long as the arithmetic of a projection is done correctly, its utility is determined by the plausibility of its central assumptions. If the assumptions embody plausible future trends, then the projection's outputs may be plausible and useful. If the assumptions are implausible, then so is the projection. Because the course of demographic trends is hard to anticipate very far into the future, most demographers calculate a set of alternative projections that, taken together, are expected to define a range of plausible futures, rather than to predict or forecast any single future. Because demographic trends sometimes change in unexpected ways, it is important that all demographic projections be updated on a regular basis to incorporate new trends and newly developed data.

A standard set of projections for the world and for its constituent countries is prepared every two years by the Population Division of the United Nations. These projections include a low, medium, and high variant for each country and region. To illustrate the nature of such projected futures, Figure 4 presents these alternatives for the world as a whole and for its developed and developing regions.

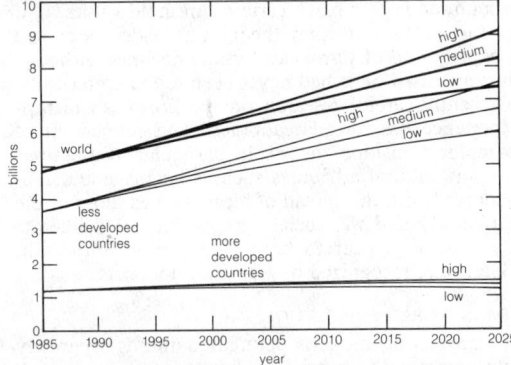

Figure 4: Projected population of the world, less developed countries, and more developed countries (high, medium, and low variants, AD 1985–2025).

BIBLIOGRAPHY

General works: ROLAND PRESSAT, *The Dictionary of Demography* (1985; originally published in French, 1979); JOHN A. ROSS (ed.), *International Encyclopedia of Population,* 2 vol. (1982), a comprehensive reference work that contains articles on topics ranging from classic demography to current problems and that provides coverage of world regions and countries as well as organizations and agencies active in the field; PETER R. COX, *Demography,* 5th ed. (1976), an examination of methods used in the study of population; DENNIS H. WRONG, *Population and Society,* 4th ed. (1977), an introduction to the main aspects of the population dilemma; and WARREN S. THOMPSON and DAVID T. LEWIS, *Population Problems,* 5th ed. (1965), a comprehensive sociological study.

Population change: ARTHUR A. CAMPBELL, *Manual of Fertility Analysis* (1983), a methodological study: GERRY E. HENDERSHOT and PAUL J. PLACEK (eds.), *Predicting Fertility: Demographic Studies of Birth Expectations* (1981), a survey of the concepts, knowledge, and methods of fertility; NORMAN E. HIMES, *Medical History of Contraception* (1936, reissued 1970), a classic historical treatise; JOHN BONGAARTS and ROBERT G. POTTER, *Fertility, Biology, and Behavior: An Analysis of the Proximate Determinants* (1983), a scholarly examination of such aspects of the population problem as family planning, family size, birth intervals, and fertility; ANSLEY J. COALE and SUSAN COTTS WATKINS (eds.), *The Decline of Fertility in Europe* (1985), a summary of studies of fertility transition in Europe during the 1970s; MICHAEL S. TEITELBAUM and JAY M. WINTER, *The Fear of Population Decline* (1985), the history and bases of past and current concerns about low fertility, with special emphasis on major Western countries; PRANAY GUPTE, *The Crowded Earth: People and the Politics of Population* (1984), a study of the effects of Western development programs on overpopulation; SAMUEL H. PRESTON, *Mortality Patterns in National Populations: With Special Reference to Recorded Causes of Death* (1976), a discussion of the determinants and consequences of national mortality patterns, with attention to the role of standards of living, sex differences, and major causes of death; ALAN A. BROWN and EGON NEUBERGER (eds.), *Internal Migration: A Comparative Perspective* (1977), a collection of scholarly articles; *International Migration Policies and Programmes: A World Survey* (1982), a study of immigration and refugee programs, one of the series of population studies conducted by the United Nations; DAVID GRIGG, *Population Growth and Agrarian Change: An Historical Perspective* (1980), a study of the relationship between demography and economics; ELI S. MARKS, WILLIAM SELTZER, and KAROL J. KRÓTKI, *Population Growth Estimation: A Handbook of Vital Statistics Measurement* (1974), an examination of methods for demographic estimates; and NATHAN KEYFITZ, *Population Change and Social Policy* (1982), a compendium of insightful essays. The 1984 issue of the annual *World Development Report* of the World Bank focuses on population changes in underdeveloped countries.

Population composition: COLIN MCEVEDY and RICHARD JONES, *Atlas of World Population History* (1978), comparisons of population statistics; NATHAN KEYFITZ and WILHELM FLIEGER, *World Population: An Analysis of Vital Data* (1968), a statistical analysis of demographic data for different countries; NATHAN KEYFITZ (ed.), *Population and Biology: Bridge Between Disciplines* (1984), a collection of papers on biological aspects of demography; DOROTHY L. NORTMAN, *Population and Family Planning Programs: Compendium of Data Through 1983,* 12th ed. (1985), including an analysis of demographic and social characteristics; DAVID M. HEER, *Society and Population,* 2nd ed. (1975), a brief study of the population of nation-states; PHILIP M. HAUSER et al., *Population and the Urban Future* (1982), which examines various demographic topics, including the quality of life of urbanized populations; RAYMOND F. DASMANN, *Environmental Conservation,* 5th ed. (1984), a study of the human influence on nature and its consequences for human population; and COLIN CLARK, *Population Growth and Land Use,* 2nd ed. (1977), an analysis of specific problems.

Population theories: RONALD FREEDMAN (ed.), *Population: The Vital Revolution* (1964), is a collection of authoritative essays on major aspects of contemporary demographic analysis. The history of population theory is presented in CHARLES EMIL STANGELAND, *Pre-Malthusian Doctrines of Population: A Study in the History of Economic Theory* (1904, reprinted 1967); JOSEPH J. SPENGLER, *French Predecessors of Malthus: A Study in Eighteenth-Century Wage and Population Theory* (1942, reprinted 1980); WILLIAM PETERSEN, *Malthus* (1979); PATRICIA JAMES, *Population Malthus, His Life and Times* (1979); E.P. HUTCHINSON, *The Population Debate: The Development of Conflicting Theories up to 1900* (1967); and J. DUPÂQUIER, A. FAUVE-CHAMOUX, and E. GREBENIK (eds.), *Malthus Past and Present* (1983). Other works include ALFRED SAUVY, *General Theory of Population* (1969; originally published in French, 1952–54), a study of the relationship between the demographic-biological characteristics of societies and their economic and social circumstances; PHILIP M. HAUSER (ed.), *The Population*

Dilemma, 2nd rev. ed. (1969), a collection of papers by leading theoreticians; GARRETT HARDIN, *Population, Evolution, and Birth Control: A Collage of Controversial Ideas,* 2nd ed. (1969), a survey of the history of views and opinions; JONAS SALK and JONATHAN SALK, *World Population and Human Values: A New Reality* (1981), which traces changes in attitudes to developments in population; and JULIAN L. SIMON, *The Ultimate Resource* (1981), an optimistic perspective for the world's population.

Development trends: The spatial distribution of population characteristics is studied in GLENN T. TREWARTHA, *The Less Developed Realm: A Geography of Its Population* (1972), and GLENN T. TREWARTHA (ed.), *The More Developed Realm: A Geography of Its Population* (1978). ALFRED SAUVY, *Fertility and Survival: Population Problems from Malthus to Mao Tse-Tung* (1961; originally published in French, 1959), presents an analysis of problems and proposes solutions. Other works include *The Determinants and Consequences of Population Trends: New Summary of Findings of Interaction of Demographic, Economic, and Social Factors,* 2 vol. (1973–78), a monumental compendium of theory and evidence on population trends compiled by the United Nations; the *Demographic Yearbook,* published by the Statistical Office of the United Nations, a basic source for more than 200 countries and territories; and BERNARD BERELSON (ed.), *Family Planning Programs: An International Survey* (1969), and *Family Planning and Population Programs: A Review of World Developments* (1966), comprehensive assessments of data. Later sources on trends in population development include ESTER BOSERUP, *Population and Technological Change* (1981); GAVIN W. JONES, *Population Growth and Educational Planning in Developing Nations* (1975); JOHN CLELAND and JOHN HOBCRAFT (eds.), *Reproductive Change in Developing Countries: Insights from the World Fertility Survey* (1985); GAVIN W. JONES (ed.), *Demographic Transition in Asia* (1984); C. ALISON MCINTOSH, *Population Policy in Western Europe: Responses to Low Fertility in France, Sweden, and West Germany* (1983); DONALD J. BOGUE, *The Population of the United States: Historical Trends and Future Projections* (1985); JOHN L. ANDRIOT (ed.), *Population Abstracts of the United States* (1980); RICHARD L. RUBENSTEIN, *The Age of Triage: Fear and Hope in an Overcrowded World* (1983); JANE MENKEN (ed.), *World Population & U.S. Policy: The Choices Ahead* (1986), papers by leading experts prepared for the second American Assembly on population issues; and NATIONAL RESEARCH COUNCIL, COMMITTEE ON POPULATION, *Population Growth and Economic Development: Policy Questions* (1986).

Population projections: *World Population Prospects: Estimates and Projections as Assessed in 1982* (1985), and *Patterns of Urban and Rural Population Growth* (1980), are publications of the United Nations Department of International Economic and Social Affairs. See also JUST FAALAND (ed.), *Population and the World Economy in the 21st Century* (1982), a collection of papers with economic and demographic forecasts; and MICHAEL D. BAYLES, *Morality and Population Policy* (1980), and *Reproductive Ethics* (1984), which discuss the moral aspects of long-term population policies.

For current discussions of relevant topics and reports of recent research the following periodicals may be recommended: *Contraception* (monthly); *Demography* (quarterly); *Economic Development and Cultural Change* (quarterly); *Economic History Review* (quarterly); *Family Planning Perspectives* (bimonthly); *Human Biology* (quarterly); *International Labour Review* (bimonthly); *International Migration Review* (quarterly); *Journal of Biosocial Science* (quarterly); *Journal of Economic History* (quarterly); *Journal of Interdisciplinary History* (quarterly); *Monthly Labor Review*; *Population and Development Review* (quarterly); *Population Bulletin* (quarterly); *Population Index* (quarterly); *Population Studies* (three times a year); *Science* (weekly); and *Social Biology* (quarterly). Many non-English periodicals in the field appear with systematic summaries in English: *Annales: Économies, Sociétés, Civilisations* (France, bimonthly); *Demografia* (Hungary, quarterly); *Demografía y economía* (Mexico, quarterly); *Demografie* (Czechoslovakia, quarterly); *Genus* (Italy, weekly); *Journal of Population Problems* (Japan, quarterly); and *Population* (France, bimonthly).

(M.S.T.)

Portugal

One of the oldest countries in Europe, with established frontiers since 1297, Portugal lies on the extreme western rim of the European continent. It is bordered on the east and north by Spain and on the west and south by the Atlantic Ocean. Occupying about 15 percent of the Iberian Peninsula, Portugal has a total area of 34,170 square miles (88,500 square kilometres). Despite its small size, the country displays a great diversity of geographical features and rises to 6,539 feet (1,993 metres) at its highest point in the Serra da Estrela. To the west and southwest lie the Atlantic islands of the Azores and Madeira, which are part of metropolitan Portugal.

Until the 1970s, Portuguese overseas territories included the Cape Verde Islands, São Tomé and Príncipe, Portuguese Guinea, Angola, and Mozambique, all in Africa; Macau in Asia; and Timor in Oceania. Of these, by the late 20th century only Macau (Macao) remained.

As a member of the European Free Trade Association (EFTA) and the North Atlantic Treaty Organization (NATO), Portugal plays a greater role in both European and world affairs than its size would suggest. Nonetheless, it is one of the poorest countries in western Europe.

The article is divided into the following sections:

Physical and human geography

THE LAND

Relief. Most of Portugal consists of lowlands, only 11.6 percent of its area lying above 2,300 feet and most of that north of the Tagus River (Rio Tejo), which, flowing northeast to southwest, cuts the country in two. Southern Portugal is a region of plains and low tablelands, broad river basins, and gently undulating country, with few hills and only one mountain range rising higher than 3,280 feet. In the north, however, more than 90 percent of the land rises above 1,300 feet. Only 30 miles from the sea are mountains more than 3,280 feet high, and large plateaus are cut by deep valleys.

Minho and Douro Litoral. In the northwest, the mountains of Minho province, surmounted by the Serra do Larouco, 5,003 feet (1,525 metres) high, form an amphitheatre facing the Atlantic Ocean. The area is composed of metamorphic rocks (crystalline schists, slates, and quartzites) and intrusive or granitic rocks, marked by fault lines and hot springs. Parallel to the mountainous ridges, rivers such as the Lima and Cávado flow through deep gorges and flat-floored valleys. Along the coast a narrow beach rises gradually to meet the low hills, which lie just a few miles inland.

Trás-os-Montes e Alto Douro. Behind the mountains of Minho is the province of Trás-os-Montes e Alto Douro, bordered on two sides by Spain. It is an extension of the Spanish Meseta, a high, partly fractured plateau (from 2,000 to 2,600 feet high) composed largely of ancient Precambrian rock, such as granites, schists, and slates, marked by rivers that have carved canyons as deep as 1,600 feet. The plateau is surmounted by the Serra de Nogueira (4,324 feet [1,318 metres] high), one of the remnants of the ancient mountains.

The Beira provinces. The rocks and landscape of Minho extend southward beyond the Rio Douro into the Beira Litoral, to a point north of Coimbra on the Rio Mondego. Most of central Portugal is included in the Beira provinces. The heart of Beira Alta is an elevated peneplain, partly dissected by the Mondego and Vouga river systems. Like Trás-os-Montes e Alto Douro, this high plain is an extension of the Meseta of Spain. The low, protected valleys, which are subject to climatic conditions very different from those of the high plateau directly above them, are called the *terra quente* ("hot country"). The high plain of the Beira is bounded on the northwest by the Serra do Caramulo (3,514 feet [1,071 metres]) and the Serra de Montemuro (4,534 feet [1,382 metres]) and their foothills. To the south and southeast it is bordered by the great escarpment of the Serra da Estrela, a granite and schist block that acts as a barrier between the northern and southern parts of Portugal. To the southwest, the mountain chain extends to the Serra de Açor (4,623 feet [1,409 metres]) and the Serra da Lousã (3,950 feet [1,204 metres]). To the south of Beira Alta and to the east of the Serra da Estrela lies the plateau of Guarda, which has an average height of 3,000 feet. Farther south the eroded plateau of Beira Baixa drops from an altitude of 1,600 feet to 700 feet, sloping toward the Tagus River in the south and merging almost imperceptibly into the highlands of Alto Alentejo.

Beira Litoral and Estremadura. North of Lisbon, the western provinces of Estremadura and Beira Litoral form a region totally without crystalline rocks. A narrow band of Triassic sandstones runs north and south from Coimbra to Tomar. To the west and southwest of the sandstones

The
Serra da
Estrela

ATLANTIC

OCEAN

ATLANTIC

OCEAN

ARQUIPÉLAGO
DA MADEIRA
MADEIRA ISLANDS
(Port.)

PORTO SANTO

Pico da Vara
1861△ MADEIRA
Funchal⊙ Machico

ILHAS DESERTAS

ATLANTIC

OCEAN

ILHAS SELVAGENS
(Mad. Is.)

0   50km
0   50mi

CORVO
FLORES
Santa Cruz
das Flores

GRACIOSA
Santa Cruz
da Graciosa
TERCEIRA
Praia da Vitória
FAIAL   Velas   SÃO JORGE
Horta   2351△
São Mateus   Ponta do Pico
Lajes
PICO   Angra do Heroísmo

A   Z   O   R   E   S
(Port.)

SÃO MIGUEL
Ribeira
Grande
Ponta
Delgada   Povoação

SANTA
MARIA
Vila do Porto

0   50   100km
0   50   100mi

ATLANTIC

OCEAN

SPAIN

PORTUGAL

Monção
Melgaço
Valença
Caminha
Ponte
da Barca   Montalegre   Chaves   Vinhais   SERRA DE NOGUEIRA   **Bragança**
Viana do Castelo   MINHO   Boticas   Venda Nova   TRÁS-OS-MONTES   Macedo de
Cavaleiros   Miranda
do Douro
Esposende   Barcelos   Vila Verde   Vieira
do Minho   Pedras
Salgadas   Mirandela   Mogadouro
Póvoa de Varzim   **Braga**   Fafe   Arco de
Baúlhe   Murça   E ALTO DOURO
Vila do Conde   Guimarães   Vila Nova
de Famalicão   Vila Real   Vila
Flor   Torre de
Moncorvo
Maia   Santo Tirso   DOURO   Peso da
Régua   Vila Nova de
Foz Côa
Matosinhos   Valongo   LITORAL   Cinfães   Lamego   Penedono
Porto   São Pedro
da Cova   Gondomar   Tarouca   Meda
Vila Nova de Gaia   Sobrado   Pejão   1302△   Castro Daire   Trancoso   Pinhel
Espinho   São João
da Madeira   São Pedro
do Sul   Sátão   Almeida
Ovar   Estarreja   Viseu   BEIRA ALTA   Vilar Formoso
Murtosa   Rio de Aveiro   Albergaria-
a-Velha   Mangualde   Ceforico
da Beira   Guarda
Aveiro   Águeda   Seia
Ílhavo   BEIRA   Santa   Belmonte   Sabugal
Mira   Comba Dão   Estrela   1993
Mealhada   Bussaco   Covilhã
Cantanhede   Lousã   Fundão
LITORAL   Montemor-
o-Velho   **Coimbra**   BEIRA
CABO MONDEGO   Góis   Idanha-
a-Nova
Figueira
da Foz   Soure   Penela   Foz
Giraldo   BAIXA
Pombal   Pedrógão
Grande   Castelo Branco
Alvaiázere   Sertã   Proença-
a-Nova
Marinha Grande   **Leiria**   Vila Nova
de Ourém   Vila
de Rei   Vila Velha de Ródão
Batalha   Fátima   Mação   Nisa   1027△
Nazaré   Porto
de Mós   Tomar   Abrantes
FARILHÕES   Alcobaça   Torres
Novas   Constância
BERLENGA   Caldas   Entroncamento
CABO CARVOEIRO   da Rainha   ESTREMADURA   RIBATEJO   Portalegre
Peniche   Óbidos   Santarém   Chamusca   Alter do Chão
Bombarral   Cartaxo   Alpiarça   Ponte
de Sor   Arronches
Lourinhã   666△   Almeirim   ALTO
Torres
Vedras   Azambuja   Avis   Monforte   Campo Maior
Salvaterra
de Magos   Montargil   Sousel
Ericeira   Vila Franca
de Xira   Coruche   Estremoz   Elvas
Mafra   Alverca   Benavente   Mora   Borba
Colares   Sintra   Loures   ALENTEJO   Vila
Viçosa
CABO DA ROCA   Sacavém   **LISBON**   Vendas
Novas   Montemor-o-Novo   Redondo
Cascais   **Almada**   Montijo   **Évora**
Cacilhas   Moita   Pinhal Novo
Seixal   **Barreiro**   Reguengos
de Monsaraz
SERRA DA   **Setúbal**   Torrão   Viana do
Alentejo   Portel
Sesimbra   NATIONAL PARK
OF ARRÁBIDA   Alcácer do Sal   Alvito   Amareleja
CABO DE ESPICHEL   Baía de   Vidigueira   Moura
Setúbal   Grândola   Cuba   Barrancos
Ferreira do Alentejo   Beja
Santiago do Cacém   Aldeia Nova
Sines   Ermidas   BAIXO   Serpa de São Bento
ALENTEJO   SPAIN
Santa   Aljustrel
Luzia   Castro   Mértola
Odemira   Verde
Ourique   Almodôvar
Aljezur   Monchique   577△   Barranco
do Velho   Castro
Foia 902△   ALGARVE   Aljortel   Marim
Silves   Loulé   Tavira   Vila Real
de Santo
Lagos   Portimão   Albufeira   António
CABO
DE SÃO   Vila do Bispo   Faro   Olhão
VICENTE   Sagres   CABO DE SANTA MARIA   Golfo de

Cádiz

Cádiz

© Rand McNally & Co.
A-552600-257   -1 -2 -2

PORTUGAL   Size of symbol indicates relative size of town   • ∘ ⊙ ⊡ ▣

Elevations in metres

0   25   50   100   150 km
0   25   50   100 mi

lies a broad band of Jurassic limestones, interspersed with large areas of Cretaceous sandstones and conglomerates. Erosion has produced a landscape of rolling, sandy hills, plateaus of basalt, steep escarpments, and arid slopes.

Alto Alentejo. The south of Portugal is characterized by the rolling countryside of the Alentejo, formed from ancient schistose, granitic, and marble rocks. With an average height of between 700 and 1,600 feet, Alto Alentejo slopes downward toward the west and south.

Ribatejo. Between Beira Baixa, Estremadura, and Alentejo lies the Ribatejo, part of a large sedimentary basin forming the lower section of both the Tagus and Sado river systems.

Baixo Alentejo and the Algarve. The southern edge of the plain of Baixo Alentejo rises into the schistose mountains of the Serra do Caldeirão (1,893 feet [577 metres]) in the east. To the west lie the more extensive scarps and hills of the Algarve, composed of Mesozoic limestones and sandstones. The Serra de Monchique is a dissected massif of syenite, an igneous rock; its highest peak, at 2,959 feet (902 metres), is Foia.

Madeira. Composed of the islands of Madeira and Porto Santo, along with six uninhabited islets, Madeira lies in the Atlantic about 600 miles (1,000 kilometres) southeast of continental Portugal. It has an area of 307 square miles (796 square kilometres). Mountainous Madeira island rises to 6,109 feet (1,862 metres) in the interior, dropping steeply to the north coast, more gently to the south. Porto Santo is flat, formed basically of basalt and trachyte.

The Azores. The nine islands that compose the Azores archipelago lie in the Atlantic, in three widely separated groups, the island nearest to Portugal, São Miguel, being 740 miles (1,190 kilometres) from Cabo da Roca. With a total area of 902 square miles (2,305 square kilometres), they range in size from the 288 square miles of São Miguel to the 6.6 square miles of Corvo. They are characterized by great beauty, variety, and contrasts of landscape, with many lakes lying in craters of extinct volcanoes and constant volcanic activity.

Drainage and harbours. All the main rivers of Portugal flow from Spain over the edge of the Meseta in a series of defiles and gorges. Consequently none of them is navigable between the two countries (with the possible exception of the lower Minho and Guadiana). The longest river crossing Portugal is the Douro (200 miles, or 320 kilometres), whereas the longest river solely in the country is the Mondego (137 miles), rising in the Serra da Estrela. The principal exclusively Portuguese rivers, all of which are partly navigable, include the Vouga (85 miles), the Mondego, the Sado, and the Zêzere (a tributary of the Tagus). North of the Tagus, most of the rivers flow from the northeast to the southwest, whereas most of those in the south flow from the southeast to the northwest.

The coast has only a few natural harbours, the most important at the mouths of rivers: Lisbon, at the mouth of the Tagus; and Setúbal, on the Sado. Other harbours depend on the protection of headlands. North of the mouth of the Douro the artificial harbour of Leixões was built, and another is being constructed at Sines, south of Setúbal. Sandbars at the entrances of many rivers block passage of ships. Lisbon, with its fine harbour, was the only obvious choice for a large port.

Climate. The extreme southwesterly position of Portugal on the continent of Europe accounts for its mild, humid winters and relatively equable, dry summers. The effect of the ocean and the contrasts of relief offer an extremely varied climate marked by transitional features between Marine West Coast and Mediterranean conditions. In winter the northern half of Portugal is dominated by the North Atlantic cyclones, and in summer the Azores high-pressure system advances northward.

In January the average temperatures range from 52° F (11° C) in the southwest to about 45° F (7° C) in the northeast. Severe cold is usually associated with the incursion of high-pressure conditions from the Spanish Meseta or from Siberian anticyclones. The highest areas of the Serra da Estrela and of the region of Bragança (in the northeastern part of Trás-os-Montes e Alto Douro) registers temperatures of less than 32° F (0° C), and snow lies on the mountain summits for several months. Evening breezes off the sea cool the coastal zones in summer. August is usually the hottest month, with an average temperature of 68° F (20° C).

Northern Portugal receives considerable rainfall, and everywhere on the coast humidity is relatively high for the latitude. In the northwest, annual rainfall is more than 40 inches (1,000 millimetres), and a large part of Minho receives between 40 and 80 inches, with up to 100 inches recorded on mountain slopes. Near the northwestern frontier, the summer drought is not pronounced, but toward the northeast and south of the Tagus it is marked.

The climate of Madeira, influenced by the trade winds, is mild, of the Mediterranean type, with relatively high temperatures. Precipitation, rare in summer, seldom exceeds 25 inches (640 millimetres). The Azores also have a mild climate, moderated by the Gulf Stream. Precipitation in the archipelago averages 45 inches annually.

Plant life. Portugal exhibits a mixture of Atlantic deciduous flora and Mediterranean and African evergreens. About two-thirds are species common to Europe and about one-third Iberian and African.

Two species of pine (*Pinus pinaster* and *P. pinea*) and three species of oak (*Quercus robur,* or English oak; *Q. toza,* or Pyrenean oak; and *Q. lusitanica,* or Portuguese oak) predominate in the northern half of Portugal, with notable concentrations of maritime pine (*P. pinaster*) on the predominantly siliceous coastal soils. The chestnut, linden, elm, and poplar, like the olive, are widespread. South of the Tagus is a quite different vegetation region. Maritime pine is replaced in the western Alentejo by the European stone pine (*P. pinea*). The dominant trees, however, are the cork (*Q. suber*) and holm (*Q. ilex*) oaks. Both cultivated and wild olives grow well.

The far southern Algarve is renowned for its groves of carob (locust, or St. John's bread), almond, and fig, but there are also figs near Tomar and almonds in the upper valley of the Douro in the north. The olive, once concentrated in the south, is now widespread, especially in the Algarve, central Portugal, and the Douro Valley. The eucalyptus flourishes in the poorly drained valleys of the Tagus and Sado systems. Notable specialized flora include the aquatic plants of the Ria de Aveiro lagoons, the beautiful woodlands of the Serra da Arrábida, Serra de Sintra, and Serra do Buçaco, and the alpine flora of the Serra da Estrela.

The vegetation of Madeira has a distinctly south European character. There are about 100 plants that are peculiarly Madeiran, either as distinct species or as strongly marked varieties. Much of the indigenous vegetation has been crowded out by plants of foreign origin and now may be found only in virtually inaccessible areas.

The general character of the flora of the Azores is decidedly European, and vegetation in most of the islands is remarkably rich, especially in grasses, mosses, ferns, heath, juniper, and a variety of shrubs. There are almost no tall-growing trees native to the Azores.

Animal life. The fauna of Portugal is largely a mixture of central European and North African types, but there are some species that are indigenous to the Iberian Peninsula. Of the larger wild animals, only wild goat, wild pig, and deer are found in the mountains, the wolf in the remote parts of the Serra da Estrela, and the lynx in Alentejo. The fox, rabbit, and Iberian hare are ubiquitous.

Fish are plentiful in the Atlantic waters, especially the European sardine. Crustaceans are common on the northern rocky coasts, and oyster beds are found in the Ria de Aveiro and the estuaries of the Tagus and Sado. Birdlife is rich, since the peninsula lies on the winter migration routes of western and central European species.

The mammals of the Azores are limited to the rabbit, weasel, ferret, rat (brown and black), mouse, and bat. Game birds include woodcock, red partridge, quail, and snipe. There are valuable tunny, mullet, and bonito fisheries, and the porpoise, dolphin, and whale are common.

No species of land mammal is indigenous to Madeira, but monk seals (*Monachus albiventer*) are native and may still be seen on some of the islands. Among the 40 species

The Douro

Temperature ranges

Trees of Algarve

Azores animal life

of birds that breed in the islands, only one, a wren, is endemic. Many kinds of fish are found in the surrounding waters, but the only freshwater fish is the eel. Beetles are the major form of indigenous Madeiran wildlife, an astonishing 695 species, a large proportion of them endemic, having been identified. Of the more than 100 species of moth collected, about a fourth are peculiar to Madeira.

THE PEOPLE

Although western Iberia has been occupied for a long time, relatively few human remains of the Paleolithic Period have been found. Neolithic and Bronze Age discoveries are commoner, among them many dolmens. Some of the earliest permanent settlements were the northern *citanias,* or *castros,* hill villages first built by Neolithic farmers who began clearing the forests. Incoming peoples, Phoenicians, Greeks, and Celts, intermingled with the settled inhabitants, and Celticized natives occupied the fortified *citanias.* For 200 years these were centres of resistance to the Roman legions. Subsequently the Romans, Suebi, Visigoths, Moors, and Jews exerted influence on the territory. Portugal's situation at the western extremity of Europe made it a gathering place for invaders by land, and its long coastline invited settlement by seafarers.

Although formed of such different elements, the population of Portugal is one of the most homogeneous in Europe, having physical characteristics common to circum-Mediterranean peoples. Most Portuguese are of slightly lower than average stature, with brown eyes, dark wavy hair, and a pallid or brunet skin.

Most Portuguese are Roman Catholic. Though freedom of worship is permitted, followers of other creeds are few. The church is separated from the state, and a concordat regulates the relations of Portugal with the Holy See.

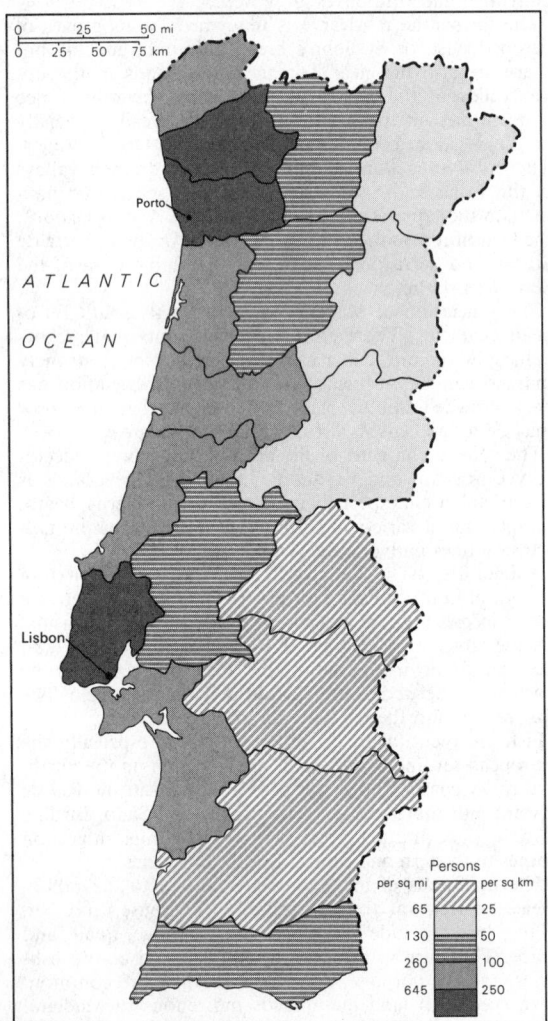

Population density of Portugal.

Population distributions within Portugal reveal striking contrasts between the more densely populated north and the more sparsely populated south. A number of rural areas have suffered considerable population losses, resulting in economic and social depression, particularly in parts of the north, the central east, and the southern coastal areas. The coastal zones between Braga and Setúbal, with their low-lying plains and urban development, have attracted a large proportion of the population. Only the industrial areas of Lisbon and Porto are able to absorb their own working populations. Other areas that are currently going through the process of industrialization are Aveiro, Coimbra, Setúbal, and Faro. Areas such as Minho, the central plains, and the coastal areas of the Algarve are seriously overpopulated.

In the main, rural settlement is dispersed, the inhabitants living in small villages under a system of open-field farming. The Beira Litoral and Estremadura have settlements varying between dispersed and clustered farmsteads. In the region of Aveiro, clusters of farmsteads and other dwellings are strung along roads in strips, often of considerable length and density. Fishing, one of the earliest occupations of the Portuguese, still plays an important role in coastal settlements.

The decolonization process that took place after the revolution of April 25, 1974, inevitably had demographic repercussions on metropolitan Portugal because of the large number of people (mostly Portuguese) who left the former overseas provinces. According to official figures, incoming refugees totalled about 700,000, most of whom (approximately 90 percent) came from Angola because of the civil war between the liberation movements. The majority of the repatriates crowded into Portuguese cities and towns.

Portugal has one of the highest rates of emigration in Europe. Before 1960, most of its émigrés went to Brazil and a few other Latin-American countries. In the late 20th century, however, the industrialized countries of western Europe became the major destination of emigrants whenever work was to be found there. Clandestine emigration, once much greater than legal, was basically channelled to France after the mid-1950s. It is said that, after Lisbon, Paris is the city with the largest Portuguese population.

THE ECONOMY

Even before the revolution of 1974, the economic situation in Portugal was considered to be poor, because of structural deficiencies that were felt in everyday life and that were bringing about increased inflation. After the revolution, the economy was very badly affected by such moves as the nationalization of banks, insurance companies, and heavy and basic industries, which led to the retraction of private initiative and investment; by a drop in emigrants' remittances, in part because of the decrease in the number of emigrants; and by the worsening of the economic situation of enterprises, both nationalized and public, and the small and medium-sized firms of the private sector.

Agriculture, forestry, and fishing. Portuguese agriculture is in persistent decline, chiefly because of the predominance of antiquated techniques. The main crops are cereals, including wheat, barley, maize (corn), and rice; potatoes; grapes; and olives. The country has to import wheat, maize, and meat.

Small farms predominate, particularly in the north, where they are too small and made up of too many dispersed holdings to allow integrated farming and rational crop rotation. In the south (except Algarve) the system of latifundios, or large estates, before 1975 prevented intensive cultivation because the latifundios were owned by absentee landlords who had no interest in making capital investment in machinery, fertilizers, and other items that would increase productivity. After the revolution (from March 1975) an agrarian reform got under way south of the Tagus, where about 3,200,000 acres (1,300,000 hectares) of land in large holdings was expropriated (with compensation) and nationalized. The policy adopted was aimed, among other things, at destroying the latifundio system, changing the tenancy system, handing uncultivated land back to the people, abolishing quitrent, increasing the irri-

Incoming refugees

Types of farms

gated area, introducing new crops, intensifying the output of fodder and cereals, and developing livestock. A large part of the nationalized land was turned over to collective and cooperative production units. To help these and the owners of small and medium-sized farms, agricultural credit was expanded.

The ownership structure was thus profoundly changed. The process took place hastily, however, and accumulated errors, allied to the disturbance typical of such an undertaking, caused political tension, instability, and crisis.

Forestry
One-third of Portugal is wooded. Most of the mountainous areas are well suited to forestry, and forest products (cork, resins, and pine and eucalyptus timber), the market value of which has increased, find a growing demand in industry. For this reason, considerable reforestation has been conducted since the last quarter of the 19th century in areas where crop yields are low and erosion severe.

Portugal's long coastline and the abundance of fish in the surrounding waters have favoured the development of the fishing industry. Sardines, anchovies, and tuna caught near the coasts, together with other species such as codfish from the North Atlantic, make a large contribution to food supplies. The fishing industry has prospered, and its products are exported all over the world. Matosinhos in the north, Setúbal, and Portimão and Olhão and other ports in the Algarve are among the main fishery centres. But even the fishing industry is not able to feed the population; a quarter of the fish consumed in Portugal must be imported, mainly from Iceland (stockfish), Norway (dried cod), and the Soviet Union (sardines).

Mining and industry. Mineral production in Portugal is negligible. Portugal has to import coal, petroleum, and petroleum products.

In its level of industrial development, Portugal had an intermediate but fairly favourable position among southern European countries. Three main groups of industries—foodstuffs and beverages, textiles and footwear, and metals—together accounted for more than half of the country's total industrial product and employed more than half of the industrial labour force. Capital intensity varied widely among the industries included in these broad groups. Industrial centres are unevenly distributed, the more prosperous and rapidly growing industries being concentrated around the larger towns, especially Lisbon and Porto.

In the wake of the revolution, deep alterations have occurred. There were basic labour questions, chiefly claims for better wages, which in many sectors were very low indeed; strikes and occupations took place. After the political crisis of March 1975, heavy industry, basic industries (cement, petrochemical, shipbuilding, electricity, etc.), and even some light industries were nationalized. One of the sectors that was most seriously affected by the unrest was the construction industry, in which activity was almost stopped; the government tried to revitalize it through public housing schemes.

Manufacturing could make a large contribution to equilibrium in the balance of payments. But to do so, Portuguese manufacturing would have to become more export-oriented, since the possibilities for import substitution are limited by the relatively small size of the domestic market. Access to the markets of the European Economic Community (EEC) and the European Free Trade Association (EFTA) augments Portugal's possibilities for increasing exports of manufactured goods, but larger exports would require improvement in the competitiveness of Portuguese industry.

Most electricity in Portugal is produced by hydroelectric plants, despite the relatively low and unevenly distributed rainfall, which constitutes a serious obstacle.

Trade deficits
Trade. Portugal has a large foreign trade relative to its population, and its composition changed considerably after about 1960. The trade balance reflects to a certain extent the deficiencies of the Portuguese economic structure: total imports (the most important being food products, raw materials, and equipment) have been greater than exports, which show little diversification. Until 1973, foreign trade (both imports and exports) was largely distributed among the European countries of the Organization for Economic Co-operation and Development (OECD), especially those belonging to the EEC and the EFTA, and the United States. Transactions with the eastern European countries were very restricted under the system of compensation agreements, since Portugal had no diplomatic relations with those nations.

Portuguese products are insufficiently competitive in foreign markets, mostly because of their higher costs when compared to those of similar products from the OECD countries. Since the revolution of 1974, small and medium-sized firms have experienced rapid increase in production costs brought about by wage increases. In addition there was decreased demand for imports in the OECD countries, which are the destination of 80 percent of Portuguese exports.

Transportation. Although transport and communications were seriously neglected in the past, there has been a strong effort to improve the transport situation.

Several of the country's main roads date back to ancient times, but now main roads connect the largest towns and extend to the border and ports. Secondary roads link the towns with almost every part of the interior, and the total road network is being extended.

The Portuguese railroad network consists of some 3,000 miles (4,800 kilometres) of track; the main Lisbon-Porto line was electrified in 1965. The merchant fleet is of considerable size.

The Portela de Sacavém airport at Lisbon, an important junction for intercontinental flights, is the base of the Portuguese airline, Transportes Aéreos Portugueses (TAP), which provides regular services. The loss of the overseas territories of course caused difficulties for TAP. Other important airports are at Porto and Faro. (I.M.P. do A./Ed.)

ADMINISTRATIVE AND SOCIAL CONDITIONS

Government. Portugal has been a republic since the overthrow of the monarchy in 1910, and its status as a democratic state began with the so-called Captains' Revolution of April 25, 1974, which overthrew the conservative regime of Marcelo Caetano. According to the postrevolution constitution of 1976, the chief of state is the president of the republic, elected by universal suffrage for a five-year term. He is president of the Council of the Revolution and supreme commander of the armed forces. The president appoints the chairman of the Council of Ministers (the prime minister), fixes election dates, represents the nation and directs foreign policy, makes and adjusts international treaties, and promulgates the laws and resolutions of the Assembly of the Republic. In addition, he presides over the Council of the Revolution and, on the advice of the council, convokes and dissolves the Assembly of the Republic and regional organs. He appoints one of the members of the Constitutional Commission and also the chairman of the Advisory Commission on the autonomous regions (the Azores and Madeira) and appoints and dismisses other members of the government at the proposal of the prime minister.

The president of the republic is advised when necessary by the Council of the Revolution, which is composed of the president (both in his civilian capacity and that of supreme commander of the armed forces), the prime minister (if he is a military officer), and 14 officers (eight from the army, three from the air force, and three from the navy), all appointed by the respective services. A Constitutional Commission, operating in conjunction with the Council of the Revolution, pronounces upon the constitutional worth of acts submitted to the consideration of the Council of the Revolution. It reports any violation of the constitutional norm and gives its opinion on questions of unconstitutionality.

Council of the Revolution

The prime minister forms the Council of Ministers (Cabinet) with the president's approval. The duties of the Council of Ministers consist of defining the general lines of government policy, approving decree laws, approving the budget and government acts involving increase or decrease in public revenue or expenditure, and deliberating upon government affairs submitted to it.

The parliamentary body is the Assembly of the Republic, with a minimum of 240 and maximum of 250 deputies, elected every four years under a system of proportional representation. Its duties include discussing and voting upon basic legislation, authorizing the government to raise loans, approving treaties concerning Portugal's membership in international organizations, and approving the politico-administrative statutes of the Azores and Madeira. It may also confer legislative authority upon the government.

Portugal is divided into 22 administrative districts (*distritos;* 18 on the mainland, three in the Azores, and one in Madeira), each with a civil governor who is appointed by and responsible to the central government through the Ministry of the Interior. He is assisted by a board. The country is also divided traditionally (though not officially since 1959) into provinces: Minho, Trás-os-Montes e Alto Douro, Douro Litoral, Beira Alta, Beira Baixa, Beira Litoral, Estremadura, Ribatejo, Alto Alentejo, Baixa Alentejo, and Algarve.

The districts are divided into municipalities (*concelhos*) and parishes (*freguesias*). Local government is in the hands of parish assemblies, municipal assemblies, municipal chambers, and municipal councils. There are about 4,000 parishes, whose assemblies are elected by the local citizens. The assembly elects an executive body, the parish committee. The municipal assemblies consist of the chairmen of the parish committees and at least an equal number of members elected by the voters in the municipal areas. The municipal chambers are the corporate executive organs, and the municipal councils are advisory.

The Portuguese police are under the control of the Ministry of Internal Administration and are divided into two main categories: the Public Security Police (Polícia de Segurança Pública, or PSP) and the National Republican Guard (Guarda Nacional Republicana, or GNR). The GNR includes the road police and is also responsible for rural armed police, who patrol the countryside and have outposts in the larger towns and villages. The duties of the PSP are the general maintenance of public order, direction of city traffic, and prevention of crime. The naval police are in charge of the ports.

Literacy   **Education.** Private schools supplement the state schools that provide free education for the majority of people. There are five long-established universities: the University of Coimbra, one of the oldest in Europe; the University of Lisbon and the Technical University of Lisbon; the University of Oporto; and the Portuguese Catholic University (Universidade Católica Portuguesa), founded in 1968 in Lisbon.

Welfare services. The Portuguese welfare system is composed of several types of institutions that insure workers against sickness, disablement, and old age and provide for the payment of pensions and family allowances. Compulsory insurance by employers is in force in most sectors of business and industry, the employee paying into the fund as well. Trade-union provident funds and welfare funds for other employees take care of most categories of workers, and there are voluntary mutual assistance associations and provident institutions for the military forces and civil servants. Many big companies conduct their own welfare and sick benefit schemes and pensions for their employees.

Workers have the choice of belonging to one of two trade-union federations. One is the Intersindical, which is Communist-controlled. The other is the União Geral de Trabalhadores (UGT; General Union of Workers), which is democratic.

Hospitals   Portugal has both public and private hospitals. Regional hospitals are located in the main provincial centres and subregional hospitals in smaller centres. Charity hospitals (the *santas casas da misericórdia*) give free treatment to the underprivileged. The civil hospitals, mainly run by the municipalities with state support and funds from welfare and social organizations, charge according to the means of the patient. There are dispensaries and clinics all over the country to deal with mothers and infants. Special institutions include a cancer hospital and research unit in Lisbon, a school of tropical medicine, a sanatorium in the northern mountains, and a modern rehabilitation centre for the disabled near Lisbon.

CULTURAL LIFE

Portuguese culture is based on a past that dates from prehistoric times into the eras of Roman and Moorish invasion. All have left their traces in a rich patrimony of archaeological remains, including prehistoric cave paintings at Escoural, the Roman township of Conimbriga, the Temple of Diana in Évora, and the typical Moorish architecture of such southern towns as Olhão and Tavira. Throughout the centuries Portugal's arts have been enriched by foreign influences, including Flemish, French, and Italian. The voyages of the Portuguese discoverers opened the country to Oriental influences, and the revelation of Brazil's wealth of gold and jewels fed the Baroque flame in decoration.

Folk and popular culture. Folk traditions still survive, and old songs and dances grace local religious festivals. Much has been done to preserve them as a tourist attraction. Some of the best examples of the regional dances are the *vira, chula, corridinho, tirana,* and fandango, many of which express the courting and matrimonial traditions of the area. National dress is still seen in the northern Minho province at weddings and other festivals. Traditional garments such as the red and green stocking cap of the Alentejo cattleman still exist, and the *samarra* (a short jacket with a collar of fox fur) and *cifões* ("chaps") survive. In Trás-os-Montes e Alto Douro the shepherd wears a straw cloak.

Regional dances

Regional fairs abound throughout the year, many of them combined with religious festivals. Religious customs in this Catholic country include the burning of the yule log in the atrium of the village church at Christmas, so that the poor may warm themselves; and the fight between St. George and the Dragon in the streets of Monção at Corpus Christi.

Architecture. Romanesque and Gothic influences have given the country some of its greatest cathedrals, and in the late 16th century a national style (Arte Manuelina) was synthesized by adapting several forms into a luxuriantly ornamented whole. Outstanding examples of Portuguese architecture include the Jerónimos monastery in Lisbon, in ornate Manueline style; the Sé (cathedral) of Lisbon, in part of the facade of which the remains of Roman construction may still be seen; the Palace of Justice in Lisbon, a fine, soaring example of austere modern architecture; the castle and church of the Order of Christ (Ordem de Cristo) in Tomar; the late Portuguese Gothic abbey of Santa Maria da Vitória in Batalha; the granite Torre dos Clérigos (Tower of the Clerics) in Porto; and Braga's Romanesque cathedral.

Visual and decorative arts. Sculpture found rich expression in the magnificent tombs of the 12th and 13th centuries, and late 18th-century Baroque wood sculptures, of which the Christmas cribs of Joachim Machado de Castro are the finest, also are outstanding. A school of primitive painters headed by Nuno Gonçalves was prominent in the 15th century, and subsequently Flemish artists influenced the native style, decorating palaces and convents and leaving a rich heritage of religious art. The 19th century saw another rebirth of national art with a late Romantic period. An era of naturalist realism that followed gave way to the experimental 20th century. Maria Helena Vieria da Silva is the country's finest contemporary abstract painter, and Carlos Botelho is noted for his street scenes of Lisbon.

Among the decorative arts, the Portuguese glazed tiles (*azulêjos*) are outstanding. Many 16th- and 17th-century buildings are faced with tiles, and the rooms and halls of palaces and mansions exhibit blue and white tiled panels or motifs in other soft colours. Exceptionally fine examples are found in the Pátio da Carranca (*pátio,* "courtyard") of the Paço do Sintra (*paço,* "palace") at Sintra, São Roque church in Lisbon, and the Quinta da Bacalhoa at Vila Fresca de Azeitão near Setúbal.

Music. Portuguese music reached a peak of achievement during the Renaissance. Its modern revival was primarily the work of Luís de Freitas Branco, whose Neoclassic tradition has been perpetuated by Joly Braga Santos. Early Portuguese music was shaped by liturgical music, but it was accompanied by fine development of the troubadour art. Polyphonic music was developed in the 15th century, with an upsurge of the art of music following in the 17th. The Calouste Gulbenkian Foundation (founded by the oil magnate) continues to inspire the country's musical life. A group of young composers is acquiring prestige both at home and in international competitions, among them Filipe Pires, A. Vitorino de Almeida, Alvaro Cassuto, and Jorge Peixinho. There is an active National Broadcasting Symphony Orchestra, and Porto has had its own symphony orchestra since 1962, the year in which the Chamber Orchestra was set up by the Gulbenkian foundation. In 1971 the Lisbon Municipal Orchestra was created, and the Teatro São Carlos also has its own orchestra and ballet company. Folk music and dancing and the traditional *fado,* a song form that expresses the sad, romantic mood of the nation, remain the country's fundamental forms of musical expression.

Literature. The Portuguese language became synthesized in the 12th century, when a lyrical quality was outstanding in both poetry and prose. A soldier-poet, Luis de Camões, gave expression to the nation's epic genius in the 15th century, as the poet Fernando Pessoa expressed its decadence in the 19th. Lyric poetry still flourishes. The tendency of fiction has been away from the Romanticism of the 19th and early 20th centuries and toward Realism. José Maria Eça de Queirós was the outstanding Realist novelist, his works including *Os Maias* (1888; *The Maias,* 1965) and *A Cidade e as Serras* (1901; *The City and the Mountains,* 1955). In the 20th century Aquilino Ribeiro was the outstanding regional novelist, whose works include *Jardim dos Tormentos* (1913; "Garden of Torments") and *O Homem que Matou o Diabo* (1930; "The Man Who Killed the Devil"), while José Maria Ferreira de Castro has been the outstanding Realist, with *A Selva* (1930; *The Jungle,* 1934) and *Os Emigrantes* (1928; "The Emigrants"). The novelist, essayist, and poet Vitorino Nemésio was outstanding with his novel *Mau Tempo no Canal* (1944; "Bad Weather in the Channel").

Theatre and motion pictures. While the theatre is rapidly picking up after a period of stagnation, the Portuguese film industry is still inactive. With the rebuilding of the classic drama theatre, the National Theatre of Dona Maria II in Lisbon (gutted by fire), there is a revival of the serious play. State and Gulbenkian foundation aid has given new life to the "little theatre" not only in Lisbon but in the provinces. International opera, theatre, and ballet are prominent in regular seasons in the Teatro Nacional São Carlos, in Lisbon, and other theatres.

Museums, libraries, and art galleries. In Lisbon, in addition to the Calouste Gulbenkian Foundation, which houses Gulbenkian's collections, the most outstanding are the National Art Museum, the National Museum of Coaches, with Europe's finest collection of ancient vehicles; the National Museum of Contemporary Art; and the Museum School of Decorative Arts, which trains craftsmen in furniture restoration, bookbinding, repair of ancient tapestries, and other fine handicrafts. Provincial museums include the Soares dos Reis National Museum in Porto, Machado de Castro National Museum in Coimbra, and the Regional Museum of Aveiro. The Biblioteca Nacional (National Library) and Biblioteca da Ajuda (Ajuda Library) in Lisbon have fine collections, while the National Archives of Torre do Tombo contain valuable national documents. Outside Lisbon, the library of the Convento de Mafra in Mafra and that of the University of Coimbra have historical importance. For statistical data, see the "Britannica World Data" section in the current *Britannica Book of the Year.* (J.Sh./Ed.)

History

Portugal became an independent monarchy in the 12th century AD. Its name derives from Portus Cale, a pre-Roman or Roman settlement near the mouth of the Douro River. The southern part of the Roman province of Gallaecia was occupied by the Germanic Suebi in AD 411, and Portucale (Porto) was held by them. They were subdued by the Visigoths, whose state was overthrown by the Muslim invasions in the 8th century. A Christian territory of Portugal was constituted in 868; it later became a

county and was extended to Coimbra. Afonso Henriques assumed the title of king (1139) and annexed Lisbon. His successors took Alentejo and Algarve from the Muslims (by 1252). Portugal now includes the "adjacent islands" of Madeira and the Azores, first settled in the 15th century.

PRE-ROMAN, ROMAN, GERMANIC, AND MUSLIM PERIODS

The earliest human remains found in Portugal are Neanderthal-type bones from Furninhas. Most peninsular Paleolithic industries are represented, but a distinct culture first emerges in the Mesolithic middens of the lower Tagus Valley, dated *c.* 5500 BC. Neolithic cultures entered from Andalusia. There are varied types of beehive huts and passage graves: agriculture, pottery, and the working of soft metals followed by the same route. In the first millennium BC, Celtic peoples entered the peninsula by the Pyrenees, and many groups were projected westward by natural pressure. Hallstatt cultures brought ironworking to the Tagus Valley. Phoenician and later Carthaginian influence reached southern Portugal in the same period. By 500 BC, Iron Age cultures predominated in the north. Celtic hilltop settlements (*castros, citânias*) retained their vitality after the Roman conquest.

After the Second Punic War (218–201 BC), Rome dominated the eastern and southern seaboards of the peninsula, and Celtic peoples who had partially absorbed the indigenous population occupied the west. A Celtic federation, the Lusitani, resisted Roman penetration under the brilliant leadership of Viriathus; but after his assassination (*c.* 140 BC), Decius Junius Brutus was able to march northward through central Portugal, cross the Douro River, and subdue the Gallaeci. Julius Caesar governed the territory for a time. In 25 BC Augustus founded Augusta Emerita (Mérida) as capital of Lusitania, which incorporated the present central Portugal. Gallaecia, to the north of the Douro, became a separate province under the Antonines. In Roman times the region of Beja and Évora was a wheat belt. The valley of the Tagus was famous for its horses and farms, and there were important mines in Alentejo. Notable Roman remains include the "Temple of Diana" at Évora and the site of Conimbriga (Condeixa). Christianity reached Lusitania in the 3rd century and in the 4th Gallaecia, where the heretical and ascetic teaching of Priscillian long held sway.

With the collapse of the Rhine frontier (AD 406), barbarian peoples forced their way into Gaul and crossed the Pyrenees. A Germanic tribe, the Suebi, was settled in southern Gallaecia, their rulers residing at or near Bracara Augusta (Braga) and Portucale. They annexed Lusitania and for a time overran the rest of the peninsula, but the Visigoths were sent to subdue them and extinguished their monarchy (AD 469). The records are silent until *c.* 550, when the Suebic monarchy had been restored and was reconverted to Catholicism by St. Martin of Braga. The Visigoth Leovigild again overthrew the Suebic monarchy and annexed the territory, but it remained distinct from Gothic Spain. St. Martin's church grouped together the bishoprics of the Suebic territory until *c.* 660, when the ecclesiastical divisions were adjusted to the old Roman provincial system and the region to the south of the Douro was restored to Lusitania. With the Muslim invasion of 711, the only serious Gothic resistance was made at Mérida; on its fall the northwest submitted. Berber troops were placed in central Portugal and Galicia, but with the revolt of the Berbers and famine (740–750) the latter was evacuated. Braga was abandoned, but the rural population remained or was restored. When 'Abd ar-Raḥmān I set up the Umayyad monarchy at Córdoba (756), there was some resistance in the west, and he perhaps stationed Berber allies at Mérida and Coimbra. Lisbon was independent for a few years (*c.* 805). The restoration of the Christian sees of Galicia, the discovery of the supposed tomb of St. James, and the erection of his shrine at Santiago de Compostela were followed by the organization of the frontier territory of Portucale (868) by Vimara Peres; Coimbra was annexed by the Christians but later lost again.

THE COUNTY AND KINGDOM OF PORTUGAL (TO 1383)

By the 10th century the county of Portugal (north of the Douro) was held by Mumadona Dias and her husband

Hermenegildo Gonçalves and their descendants, one of whom was tutor and father-in-law to the Leonese ruler, Alfonso V. But when this dynasty was overthrown by the Navarrese-Castilian house of Sancho III the Great, the western county lost its autonomy. Sancho's son, Ferdinand I of Castile, reconquered Coimbra in 1064 but entrusted it to a Mozarabic governor. When the African Almoravids annexed Muslim Spain, Alfonso VI of León (1065–1109) and Castile (1072–1109) provided for the defense of the west by calling on Henry, brother of Duke Eudes (Odo) of Burgundy, whom he married to his illegitimate daughter Teresa and made count of Portugal. From 1095, therefore, Henry and Teresa (who used the title of queen) ruled Portugal and Coimbra. On the death of Alfonso VI, his realms passed to his legitimate daughter Urraca and her little son Alfonso (VII). Henry of Portugal sought power but had achieved little when he died in 1112, leaving Teresa with an infant son, Afonso Henriques. Teresa's intrigues with her Galician favourite, Fernando Peres of Trava, lost her the support of the Portuguese barons, and in 1128 followers of her son defeated and drove her into exile. Thus Afonso Henriques became count of Portugal.

Afonso Henriques Though at first obliged to submit to his cousin Alfonso VII, he began to use the title of king, traditionally because of a victory over the Muslims at Ourique (July 25, 1139; but perhaps a symbolic legend). In 1143 his cousin accepted his autonomy, but the title of king was formally conceded only in 1179, when Afonso Henriques placed Portugal under the direct protection of the Holy See, promising an annual tribute. He had captured Santarém (March 1147) and Lisbon (October 1147), the latter with the aid of English, French, German, and Flemish crusaders bound for Palestine. An English priest, Gilbert of Hastings, became first bishop of the restored see of Lisbon. Although the new Moroccan dynasty of the Almohads struck back (1179–84), when Afonso I died (December 6, 1185) the Portuguese frontier was firmly established on the Tagus. The new military orders, the Templars, those of Calatrava (from c. 1156), and of Santiago (from c. 1170), etc., governed castles and territory on the frontier, and the Cistercians were responsible for the introduction of agriculture and architecture in central Portugal (Alcobaça).

The kingdom and the Reconquista. Although Afonso Henriques began to grant charters to new settlements, it was his son Sancho I (1185–1211) who enfranchised many municipalities (concelhos), especially in eastern and central Portugal. The privileges of these communities were embodied in charters (forais), which attracted settlers from the more feudal north. Even Muslims were enfranchised, though on the other hand many of them were enslaved. Assisted by passing crusaders, Sancho captured Silves in Algarve (1189); but in 1190 an al-Muwāḥḥidūn army from Africa advanced to the Tagus and, although Lisbon, Santarém, and Tomar stood firm, the Muslims recovered Silves in 1191, together with most of the land south of the Tagus. In his later years Sancho was involved in a quarrel with Pope Innocent III over the payment of tribute due to the Holy See and with the bishop of Porto, who received Innocent's support. But peace was made before his death, and it was left to his son Afonso II, the Fat (1211–23), to endeavour to strengthen the power of the throne at the expense of the church.

Though Afonso II was an unwarlike king, his followers were beside the Castilians at the great Christian victory of Las Navas de Tolosa in 1212 and, again assisted by crusaders, recovered Alcácer do Sal in 1217. Meanwhile Afonso repudiated the bequests of large estates made by his father to his brothers and accepted those to his sisters only after a war with León and in a form, settled by the pope, that recognized Afonso's sovereignty. In the first year of his reign, Afonso called a meeting of the Cortes at Coimbra, to which the nobility and prelates were summoned (representatives of the commoners were not to appear until 1254). Both estates obtained important concessions; in fact, the position of the church and the orders was now so strong that Afonso II and his successors were involved in recurrent conflicts with Rome. Afonso himself instituted (from 1220) inquirições, or royal commissions, to investigate the nature of holdings and recover whatever

The Cortes

Portugal in the 12th and 13th centuries.

Adapted from R. Treharne and H. Fullard (eds.), *Muir's Historical Atlas: Medieval and Modern*, 9th ed. (1964); George Philip & Son Ltd., London

had been illegally taken from the crown. In his last years, Afonso quarrelled with the archbishop of Braga, who supported by Pope Honorius III, defied the papacy, and was excommunicated.

Little is known of the reign of his son Sancho II (1223–c. 1246), but the reconquest of Alentejo was now completed and much of Algarve was reduced. On his accession, Sancho found the church in full ascendancy as a result of the agreement made before his father's death. Conflicting reports exist of Sancho's own government, but in his later years the kingdom seems to have slipped into anarchy. At all events, his younger brother Afonso, who had become count of Boulogne by his marriage (1238) with Matilde, daughter of Count Raynald I of Dammartin, was granted a papal commission (1245) to take over the government, and Sancho was ordered to be deposed by papal bull. When Afonso reached Lisbon (late 1245 or early 1246), he received the support of the church and of the inhabitants of Lisbon and other towns. After a civil war lasting two years, Sancho II retired to Toledo, dying there in January 1248.

On his arrival, the count of Boulogne had already declared himself king as Afonso III, and the death of Sancho without issue gave his usurpation the mantle of legality. He brought together the divided kingdom, completed the reconquest of Algarve, transferred the capital from Coimbra to Lisbon, and, fortified by the support of the towns, summoned the Cortes at Leiria at which for the first time commoners representing the municipalities made their appearance (1254). His conquest of Algarve aroused the jealousy of Castile. Two campaigns were fought (1250 and 1252), Afonso probably being worsted, and peace was made by means of a marriage pact. Although still the husband of Matilde of Boulogne, Afonso married Beatriz, illegitimate daughter of Alfonso X of Castile, holding the disputed territory of Algarve as a fief of Castile until such time as the eldest son of the marriage should reach the age of seven, when Algarve was to return to Portugal. This

First representation of commons

marriage led to a dispute with the Holy See, in which Afonso was placed under an interdict. Despite his early connection with Rome, Afonso refused to give way; and in 1263 the bigamous marriage was legalized and his eldest son, Dinis, legitimized. Shortly afterward, Afonso launched *inquirições,* as a result of which the church was deprived of much property. The prelates protested these actions of the royal commissions, and most of them subsequently left the country. Although Afonso was excommunicated and threatened with deposition, he continued to defy the church until shortly before his death early in 1279.

The achievements of Afonso's reign—the completion of the reconquest, the assertion of royal power before the church, and the incorporation of the commoners in the Cortes—indicate important institutional advances. Under his son Dinis (1279–1325), Portugal was to come into closer touch with western Europe and to acquire a university, the elements of a national literature, and a navy. The chartering of fairs and the increased use of minted money bear witness to the growth of commerce, and the planting of pine forests to hold back the sand dunes near Leiria illustrates Dinis' concern for shipbuilding and agriculture. In 1317 Dinis engaged a Genoese admiral, Emmanuele Pessagno, to build up his navy, having already adopted various measures to stimulate foreign trade. He founded the University of Coimbra (at first in Lisbon) in 1290 and was both a poet and patron of literature. Yet he was especially famed as the "farmer king" (*rei lavradór*) for his interest in the land.

Despite Dinis' attachment to the arts of peace, Portugal was several times involved in strife during his reign. In 1297 the Treaty of Alcañices with Castile confirmed Portugal's possession of Algarve and provided for an alliance between Portugal and Castile. In the later years of Dinis' reign, his son, the future Afonso IV, rebelled more than once, being persuaded to submit by the influence of his mother Isabel, daughter of Peter III of Aragon. This remarkable woman, later canonized as St. Elizabeth of Portugal and popularly known as the Rainha-Santa (the Holy Queen), successfully exercised her influence in favour of peace on several occasions.

Disputes with Castile. Afonso IV (1325–57) was also involved in various disputes with Castile. Isabel, who had retired to the Convent of Santa Clara at Coimbra, continued to intervene in favour of peace; but on her death in 1336 war broke out, and terms were not made till 1340, when Afonso himself with a Portuguese army joined Alfonso XI of Castile in the great victory over the Muslims on the Salado River in Andalusia. Afonso's son Peter (Pedro) was married (1336) to Constança (died 1345), daughter of the Castilian infante Juan Manuel; but soon after the marriage he fell in love with one of her ladies, Inês de Castro, by whom he had several children. Afonso was persuaded to countenance the assassination of Inês in 1355, and one of Peter I's earliest acts on his accession was to take vengeance on her murderers. During his short reign (1357–67), Peter devoted himself to the dispensation of justice; his judgments, which he executed himself, were severe and often violent, and his iron rule was tempered only by fits of revelling.

Peter's son by Constança, Ferdinand (1367–83), inherited a wealthy throne almost free of external entanglements; but the dispute between Peter the Cruel and Henry of Trastamara (later Henry II) for the Castilian throne was raging; and, on the murder (1369) of the former, several Castilian towns offered Ferdinand their allegiance, which he was unwise enough to accept. Henry II duly invaded Portugal in 1369, and by the Peace of Alcoutim (1371) Ferdinand was constrained to renounce his claim and to promise to marry Henry's daughter; however, he instead took a Portuguese, Leonor Teles, although she was already married and in spite of the protests of the commoners of Lisbon. He also made alliance (1372) with the English in the person of John of Gaunt, duke of Lancaster, who had married the elder daughter of Peter the Cruel and claimed the Castilian throne. In 1372 Ferdinand provoked Henry II, who invaded Portugal and besieged Lisbon. Unable to resist, Ferdinand was forced to repudiate his alliance with John of Gaunt and to act as an ally of Castile, surrender-

ing various castles and persons as hostages. It was only on the death (1379) of Henry that Ferdinand dared openly to challenge Castile again. In 1380 the English connection was resumed, and in the following year John of Gaunt's brother, Edmund of Langley, earl of Cambridge (afterward duke of York), took a force to Portugal for the invasion of Castile and betrothed his son Edward to Ferdinand's only legitimate child, Beatriz. In mid-campaign, Ferdinand came to terms with the enemy (August 1382), agreeing to marry Beatriz to a Castilian prince. She did, in effect, become the wife of John I of Castile; and when Ferdinand died, prematurely decrepit, Leonor Teles became regent and Castile claimed the Portuguese crown.

Leonor had long been the paramour of the Galician João Fernandes Andeiro, count of Ourém, who had intrigued with both England and Castile and whose influence was much resented by Portuguese patriots. Opponents of Castile chose as their leader an illegitimate son of Peter I, John, master of Aviz, who killed Ourém (December 1383) and, being assured of the support of the populace of Lisbon, assumed the title of defender of the realm. The regent fled to Alenquer and thence to Santarém, and the king of Castile came to her aid, soon however, relegating her to a Spanish convent. Lisbon was besieged for five months (1384), but an outbreak of plague obliged the Castilians to retire.

THE HOUSE OF AVIZ, 1383–1580

The legitimate male line of Henry of Burgundy ended at Ferdinand's death, and when the Cortes met at Coimbra (March–April 1385), John was declared king and became the founder of a new dynasty. This result was not unopposed, for many of the nobility and clergy still considered the queen of Castile the rightful heiress; but popular feeling was strong, and John I had valuable and trusted allies in Nuno Álvares Pereira, "the Holy Constable," his military champion, and in João das Regras, his chancellor and jurist.

Independence assured. A number of towns and castles still held out for Castile when in August 1385 John I of Castile and a considerable army made their appearance in central Portugal. Although much outnumbered, the Portuguese won the great Battle of Aljubarrota (August 14, 1385), in which the Castilian chivalry was dispersed and John of Castile himself barely escaped. The victory, followed by secondary successes won by Nuno Álvares, assured John I of his kingdom and made him a desirable ally. A small force of English archers had been present at Aljubarrota. Now the Treaty of Windsor (May 9, 1386) raised the Anglo-Portuguese connection to the status of a firm, binding, and permanent alliance between the two crowns. John of Gaunt duly went to the Peninsula (July 1386) and attempted an invasion of Castile in conjunction with John I. This was not successful, but the Portuguese king married Gaunt's daughter Philippa of Lancaster (1387), who introduced various English usages into Portugal. The truce arranged with Castile in 1387 was prolonged at intervals until peace was finally concluded in 1411.

The victory of John of Aviz may be regarded as a victory of the national spirit against the feudal attachment to established order. As much of the older nobility had adhered to Castile, John rewarded his followers at their and at the crown's expense. Meanwhile, commerce prospered, and the marriage of John's daughter Isabella to Philip the Good of Burgundy was to be followed by the growth of close trading relations between Portugal and Philip's County of Flanders. With the conclusion of peace with Castile, John found an outlet for the activities of his frontiersmen and of his own sons in the conquest of Ceuta (1415), from which may be dated the great age of Portuguese expansion.

During the short reign of John's eldest son, Edward (Duarte; 1433–38), an unsuccessful attempt was made to conquer Tangier in 1437 by John's third son, Prince Henry the Navigator, and his younger brother Ferdinand, who was captured by the Moors and died, still unransomed, in 1443. On Edward's death, his son Afonso V was still a child, and his brother Pedro, duke of Coimbra, had himself made regent (1440) instead of the widow, Leonor

St.
Elizabeth
of
Portugal

Alliance
with the
English

Trade with
Flanders

of Aragon. But Pedro's own regency was later challenged by the powerful Bragança family, descended from Afonso, illegitimate son of John of Aviz and Beatriz, daughter of Nuno Álvares Pereira. This family continued to set the young king against his uncle, who was forced to resign the regency, driven to take up arms, and killed at Alfarrobeira (May 1449). Afonso V (1438–81) proved unable to resist the demands of the Braganças, who now became the wealthiest family in Portugal. Having married Joan, daughter of Henry IV of Castile, Afonso laid claim to the Castilian throne and became involved in a lengthy struggle with Ferdinand and Isabella in the region of Zamora and Toro, where he was defeated in 1476. He then sailed to France to entreat the aid of Louis XI, in which he failed, and on his return concluded with Castile the Treaty of Alcáçovas (1479), abandoning the claims of his wife Joan. Afonso never recovered from his reverse, and during his last years his son John administered the kingdom.

Consolidation of the monarchy. John II (1481–95) was as cautious, firm, and jealous of the royal power as his father had been openhanded and negligent. At the first Cortes of his reign, he exacted a detailed oath of homage that displeased his greatest vassals. A suspicion of conspiracy enabled him to arrest Fernando II, duke of Bragança, and many of his followers; the duke was sentenced to death and executed (1484) at Évora, and John himself stabbed James (Diogo), duke of Viseu (1484). As well as attacking the power of the nobility, John lessened the effects of the unfavourable treaty with Castile. Calculating and resolute, he later received the epithet "the Perfect Prince."

John II was predeceased by his legitimate son and therefore succeeded by his cousin, the duke of Beja, as Manuel I (1495–1521), known as "the Fortunate." Manuel, who assumed the title of "lord of the conquest, navigation, and commerce of India, Ethiopia, Arabia, and Persia," inherited, because of the work of John II, a firmly established autocratic monarchy and a rapidly expanding overseas empire. Drawn toward Spain by the common need to defend their overseas interests as defined by the Treaty of Tordesillas (1494), Manuel nourished the hope of joining the whole peninsula under the house of Aviz; he married Isabella, eldest daughter of Ferdinand and Isabella, who, however, died (1498) in giving birth to a son, Miguel da Paz. This child was recognized as heir to Portugal, Castile, and Aragon but died in infancy. Manuel then married Isabella's sister Maria (died 1517) and thirdly Eleanor, sister of the emperor Charles V.

As a condition of the marriage with Isabella, Manuel was required to "purify" Portugal of Jews. John II had admitted many Jewish refugees expelled from Spain (1492) and had taxed them heavily but was also to supply ships for them to leave Portugal. This was not done, and Manuel now ordered all Jews to leave within 10 months, by October 1497. On their assembly in Lisbon, every effort was made to secure their conversion by promises or by force. Some who resisted were allowed to go, but the rest were "converted" under promise that no inquiry should be made into their beliefs for 20 years. As "Christians" they could not be forced to emigrate, and they were indeed prohibited from leaving Portugal. In April 1506 a large number of these "new Christians," or *marranos,* were massacred in Lisbon during a riot, but Manuel afterward protected them and allowed many to emigrate to Holland, where their experience of Portuguese trade was put at the service of the Dutch.

If Manuel failed to realize his dream of ruling Spain, his son John III (1521–57) lacked the power to resist Castilian influence. A pious, retiring man, he was ruled by his wife, Catherine, sister of the emperor Charles V, and encouraged the installation of the Inquisition (1536); the first auto-da-fé was held in 1540. The Society of Jesus, established in 1540, soon controlled education in Portugal. In 1529 the settlement by the Treaty of Saragossa (Zaragoza) of a dispute over the possession of the Moluccas removed an obstacle to Portuguese-Spanish understanding, and the line of Tordesillas was matched by a similar line in the Pacific; all the territories of the New World were in theory divided between Spain and Portugal, while the Reformation (as well as the discoveries) had come between the latter and its English ally.

Forced conversion of Jews

John III was succeeded by his grandson Sebastian (1557–78), then a child of three. As a boy, Sebastian became obsessed with the idea of a crusade against Morocco. Fanatically religious, he had no doubts of his own powers and listened only to flatterers. He visited Ceuta and Tangier in 1574 and began in 1576 to prepare a large expedition against Larache: this departed in June 1578 and on August 4 was utterly destroyed by the Moors in the Battle of the Three Kings near Alcazarquivir (Ksar el-Kebir). Sebastian himself was killed, 8,000 of his men are said to have died, and 15,000 were captured. Only a handful escaped.

The disaster of Larache

Sebastian was succeeded by his great-uncle, Cardinal Henry (1578–80), a brother of John III. His age and celibacy made it certain that the Portuguese throne would soon pass from the direct line of Aviz. Philip II of Spain, nephew of John III and husband (by his first marriage) of John's daughter Maria, had already made his preparations and, on the death of the cardinal-king (January 31, 1580), summoned the authorities to obey him. An army under the great duke of Alba entered Portugal in 1580; the resistance of António the prior of Crato (illegitimate son of John III's brother Luís), acclaimed António I at Santarém, collapsed; and Philip II of Spain became Philip I of Portugal (1580–98). The claims of the duchess of Bragança (Catherine, daughter of John's brother Edward) were disregarded.

MEDIEVAL SOCIAL AND ECONOMIC DEVELOPMENT

Medieval Portugal comprised regions of considerable diversity. In the north, the old aristocracy of Leonese descent owned large estates worked mainly by serfs. In the southern territory that had been reconquered from Muslim rule, there were many towns, often separated by districts almost barren and depopulated. The initiative in settling these areas was taken by Cistercian monks, who had reached Portugal by 1143; later kings such as Sancho I and Afonso III established *concelhos* (municipalities), granting to them by the issue of *forais* (charters) many privileges designed to attract population. Tax concessions were often given, and freedom was promised to serfs or to Christian captives after a year's residence. But in the south, the *concelhos* were burdened with defense duties, the *cavaleiros-vilãos* (villein knights) being obliged to horse and arm themselves, and the *peões,* or less substantial men, being obliged to serve as foot soldiers in defense of the country and perhaps also on a *fossado* (raid) into Muslim territory.

At court, the king was advised by his *curia regis* (court or council), comprising the *majordomus curiae,* the head of the administration, the military chief or *signifer,* the *dapifer curiae* (steward of the household), the chancellor (an official whose origins in Portugal were Burgundian rather than Visigothic), and any members of the greater aristocracy, the *ricos-homens,* who might be at court. This class also comprised the bishops and abbots and masters of the orders of knighthood; many held private civil or military authority. The lesser nobility were without such rights. Below them came various classes of free commoners, such as the *cavaleiros-vilãos* and the *malados,* men who had commended themselves to protectors. There were numerous serfs and slaves.

Court officials

By the end of the medieval period several shifts in the social structure had occurred. Many of the old aristocracy lost their position at the advent of the House of Aviz, and the new nobility, exemplified in the House of Bragança, was often of bureaucratic or ministerial origin. The privileges granted to *concelhos* forced landlords to compete for labour, and by the time of Afonso III money payments had largely replaced labour services on the estates. Representatives of the commoners, first attending the Cortes in 1254 on behalf of the *concelhos,* took an increasing part in politics. The Cortes were very frequently called in the reigns of John I, Edward, and Afonso V; but the avenues of power had become wider by the 16th century, and John III's proposal (1525) to call them only every 10 years aroused no opposition. Although the trade guilds were slow in developing, they took some part in determining local taxation in the 13th century. Trade increased, Portuguese merchants having had connections with the Low Countries from the time of Afonso Henriques and with England from the early 13th century. The political crisis of 1385 was followed by intense inflation and many debasements: there was thereafter no national gold currency until 1435, when West African sources began to be tapped.

THE DISCOVERIES AND THE EMPIRE

Henry the Navigator

The idea of expansion into Africa was a logical result of the completion of the reconquest in the peninsula, and the conquest of Ceuta in North Africa (1415) probably provided the impulse toward further expansion. The simple idea of fighting the Muslims on their own soil was linked with more complicated motives: the desire to explore in a scientific sense, the hope of finding a way to the rich spice trade of the Indies, and the impulse to spread the Christian faith. These purposes were gradually molded together into a national enterprise, though at first they represented the hopes and aspirations of one man, Prince Henry. The third son of John I and Philippa of Lancaster, known rather inaccurately as "the Navigator" (he himself never went farther afield than Tangier), Henry became (1420) master of the Order of Christ, which King Dinis had founded (1319). The resources of the Order were used to draw together skilled geographers and navigators and to equip a series of expeditions that only gradually began to bear fruit.

The date of Prince Henry's earliest expedition is not exactly known but appears to have been about 1418, when the island of Porto Santo was visited; the first call at Madeira probably dates from 1419. An attempt was made to settle in the Canaries, and between 1427 and 1431 the Azores were visited by Portuguese seamen. Both the Azores and Madeira were then uninhabited, and their colonization proceeded fairly rapidly from *c.* 1445. Sugar was exported to Europe and gave the islands great economic importance. Meanwhile, Prince Henry's ships were probing the African coast, passing Cape Bojador in 1434 and Rio de Oro in 1436. The unsuccessful expedition against Tangier (1437) was followed by a break in the discoveries, but in 1439 Prince Henry was authorized to colonize the Azores; and from 1440 further expeditions equipped with a new and lighter ship, the caravel, reached the Bay of Arguin (1443), Cape Verde (1444), and by Henry's death (1460) had explored the coast as far south as Sierra Leone.

Under Afonso V, three military expeditions were sent against Morocco (1458, 1463, and 1471); by the last of them, Tangier and Arzila were captured. The African explorations were not entirely neglected, but it remained for John II, with his sharp sense of the national interest, to found a fortress and trading post in the Gulf of Guinea at Elmina (São Jorge da Mina, 1481–82). Diogo Cão (Cam) discovered the mouth of the Congo in 1482 and then advanced to Cape Cross, 200 leagues southward (1486). A native monarchy, the Manikongo, sought conversion and alliance with the Portuguese: its first Christian king, Afonso I (*c.* 1506–43), made Mbanza a centre of Portuguese influence, but the Kongo kingdom fell into internal strife and Portuguese interests were transferred to the

Bartolomeu Dias rounds Cape of Good Hope

neighbouring kingdom of Angola. Paulo Dias de Novais founded Luanda, the first city in West Africa south of the Equator, in 1576. In 1488, Bartolomeu Dias at length rounded the Cape of Good Hope and reached the East African coast, and the seaway to India lay open. His return was followed in 1493 with the news that Christopher Columbus had, as he thought, discovered the "Indies" by sailing across the Atlantic. Much as this news must have perturbed the Portuguese, Columbus brought no news of the spiceries or the cities of the East; and John II ordered the preparation of an expedition to India by way of the Cape of Good Hope, though this sailed only after his death. John also contested the Spanish claim to all lands discovered west of the Atlantic, and by the Treaty of Tordesillas (June 7, 1494), Spain's rights were limited to what lay more than 370 leagues west of the Cape Verde Islands. Thus the territory that was to become Brazil was reserved for Portugal.

The Treaty of Tordesillas had confirmed Portugal's rights to the exploration of Africa and the seaway to India. In July 1497 Vasco da Gama set sail with four ships on the first expedition to India. They reached Calicut (Ko-

zhikode) the following spring, and the survivors put into Lisbon in the autumn of 1499 with specimens of Oriental merchandise. A second fleet was prepared under Pedro Álvares Cabral, who touched the Brazilian coast (April 22, 1500) and claimed it for Portugal. One of Cabral's ships, under Diogo Dias, discovered Madagascar in 1500; João da Nova discovered Ascension in the following year and St. Helena in 1502. Tristão da Cunha sighted the island named after him in 1506 and went on to explore Madagascar. Meanwhile, trading posts in India had been established by Cabral at Cochin and Calicut (1501) and by João da Nova at Cannanore. In 1502 Vasco da Gama made tributary to Portugal the ruler of Kilwa (Quiloa) in East Africa.

Settlements in the Far East

In 1505 Francisco de Almeida arrived as viceroy of India, strengthening the African station at Kilwa and supporting the ruler of Cochin against the *zamorin* of Calicut. The control of sea trade now instituted became the chief source of Portuguese wealth in the East. It was assured by the defeat of Muslim naval forces off Diu in 1509. Almeida's successor, Afonso de Albuquerque, conquered Goa (1510), which he made the seat of Portuguese power, and Malacca (1511); sent two expeditions to the Moluccas (1512 and 1514); and captured Hormuz in the Persian Gulf (1515). Soon after, Fernão Peres de Andrade reached Canton in China; in 1542 Portuguese merchants were permitted to settle at Liampo (Ning-po), and in 1557 they founded the colony of Macao (Macau).

Albuquerque was responsible for this conception of a system of strong points that secured the trade of the Orient to Portugal for nearly a century. Goa soon became the chief port of western India; Hormuz controlled the Persian Gulf, and Malacca the gateway from the Indian Ocean to the South China Sea, while a string of fortified trading posts secured the coast of East Africa and the gulf and shores of India and Ceylon. Farther east, less fortified settlements were set up with the consent of the native rulers from Bengal to China, and the trade of the principal spice islands was in Portuguese hands. The preservation of the whole system was entrusted to a governor, who sometimes held the rank of viceroy, at Goa; and although Portuguese arms had both triumphs and reverses, their control of the Oriental trade remained substantial, if never complete, until the 17th century, when the Dutch, at war with the joint crown of Portugal and Spain and deprived of their traditional trade with Lisbon, began to seek spices from their source and effectively demolished the Portuguese monopoly.

UNION OF SPAIN AND PORTUGAL, 1580–1640

After Philip II of Spain had occupied Portugal in 1580, the island of Terceira in the Azores held out for António of Crato, who himself sought alliances in England and France. In 1582 a French expedition to establish him in the Azores was defeated, and in 1589 an English attempt upon Lisbon, led by Sir Francis Drake and Sir John Norris, failed dismally. But although António died in Paris in 1595, the true symbol of Portuguese independence was not the prior of Crato but King Sebastian himself. The Portuguese people refused to belive that he was dead and nourished a messianic faith in his reappearance, of which four pretenders sought to avail themselves, the last as late as 1600 and as far afield as Venice.

Meanwhile, Philip arrived in Portugal and was accepted as King Philip I (1580–98) by the Cortes held at Tomar (1581). He undertook to preserve Portuguese autonomy, to consider the union as a personal one like that of Aragon and Castile under Ferdinand and Isabella, to appoint only Portuguese to the administration, to summon Cortes frequently, and to be accompanied by a Portuguese council in Madrid. These undertakings were, however, neglected by Philip II (III of Spain, 1598–1621) and completely violated by Philip III (IV of Spain, 1621–40).

Exploitation by the Spanish

Portuguese resentment against Spanish rule was increased by the failure of these kings to visit Portugal, the appointment of Spaniards to Portuguese offices, the loss of trade consequent on Spain's foreign wars, and the levying of taxation to sustain these wars. In 1624 the Dutch seized Bahia in Brazil, only to be expelled by a joint Spanish and

Portuguese expedition (1625). But in 1630 they occupied Pernambuco and the adjoining sugar estates, which they held for a generation. The final straw was the conde-duque de Olivares' plan (1640) of using Portuguese troops against the equally discontented Catalans. Two Portuguese insurrections, in 1634 and 1637, had failed to attain dangerous proportions, but in 1640 Spain's powers were extended to the utmost by war with France and revolt in Catalonia. The French minister, Cardinal de Richelieu, already had agents in Lisbon, and a leader was found in John, duke of Bragança, a grandson of the duchess Catherine (niece of John III) whose claims had been overridden in 1580 by Philip II of Spain. Taking advantage of the unpopularity of the governor, Margaret of Savoy, duchess of Mantua, and her secretary of state Miguel de Vasconcelos, the leaders of the party of independence carried through a nationalist revolution on December 1, 1640. Vasconcelos was almost the only victim; the Spanish garrisons were driven out; and on December 15 the Duke of Bragança was crowned as John IV (1640–56).

THE HOUSE OF BRAGANCA, 1640–1910

Although the Cortes confirmed the accession of the dynasty of Bragança and John's coronation on January 28, 1641, the success of the new regime was not finally assured until 1668, when Spain at last recognized Portuguese independence. Faced with the threat of a Spanish invasion, John had sent missions to the courts of Europe in quest of alliances. France now refused a formal treaty. The Dutch, having seized northern Brazil, accepted a truce in Europe and proceeded to capture Angola from Portugal. John made a treaty (1642) with Charles I of England, which was made void by Charles's execution (1649). Meanwhile, the Portuguese defeated the Spaniards at Montijo (May 26, 1644) and warded off several invasions. In 1654 they negotiated a treaty with the English Commonwealth, obtaining aid in return for commercial concessions. The Dutch were now finally expelled from Pernambuco in northern Brazil. By a secret article of the Treaty of the Pyrenees (1659), France promised Spain to give no further aid to Portugal, but in 1661 Portugal signed a treaty of alliance with the restored English monarchy. In 1662 Charles II of England married John's daughter Catherine of Bragança and, in return for a large dowry, including the cession of Bombay and Tangier, provided arms and men for the war with Spain. Portuguese defense was organized by the German soldier Friedrich Hermann von Schönberg (later duke of Schomberg); in June 1663 Sancho Manuel, count of Vila Flor, defeated Don John of Austria at Ameixial, and in June 1665 von Schönberg won the important victory of Montes Claros. Peace was finally made by the Treaty of Lisbon early in 1668.

On the death of John IV, his second son Afonso VI (1656–83) was 13 years of age. Afonso's mother, Luísa de Gusmão, acted as regent until, in June 1662, he began to rule. Afonso himself was feebleminded, but the country was capably governed by Luiz de Vasconcelos e Sousa, conde de Castelo Melhor, until 1667. The French princess, Maria Francesca of Savoy, who married Afonso in the previous year, now entered into an intrigue with his more personable brother Pedro (afterward Peter, or Pedro, II). They contrived to dismiss Castelo Melhor and to have Maria Francesca's marriage annulled. She at once married Pedro (1668), who was declared regent. Afonso was imprisoned until his death. During the reign of Peter II (1683–1706), Portugal recovered from the strain of the Spanish wars and began to benefit from the discovery of gold and precious stones in Brazil. The first strike of gold in Minas Gerais took place in 1693, and in the last years of the 17th century, considerable wealth was being extracted; however, it was not until 1728 that diamonds were discovered: the mineral wealth of Brazil then formed a very substantial part of the revenue of the Portuguese crown.

The 18th century. The War of the Spanish Succession (1701–13) saw Portugal's recent friends, England and France, on opposing sides; and although Pedro sought at first to remain neutral, Portugal joined the Anglo-Austrian Grand Alliance in 1703, by which it afforded a base for the archduke Charles (later the emperor Charles VI) to

conduct his war for the Spanish throne. In the same year (December 27) the English envoy, John Methuen, also concluded the treaty that bears his name, by which the exchange of port wine for English woollens became the basis for Anglo-Portuguese trade. Although the treaty of 1654 had secured great privileges for English merchants in Lisbon, neither it nor the treaties of 1642 and 1661, by which the traditional alliance was restored, had created trade. This was now done, and by reason of the wealth that soon poured into Lisbon from Brazil, the English merchants gained a commanding position in the trade of Portugal. The political treaties of 1703 proved less fruitful. The Portuguese general António Luís de Sousa, marquess of Minas, entered Madrid in 1706; but French and Spanish forces were victorious at Almansa (1707), and in 1711 the French admiral René Duguay-Trouin sacked Rio de Janeiro. At the conclusion of the war Portugal negotiated a peace treaty with France (April 1713) but did not conclude peace with Spain until 1715.

Under Peter's son John V (1706–50), Portugal attained a degree of prosperity unknown since the restoration. The tax of a royal fifth levied on the precious metals and stones of Brazil gave the monarchy an independent source of wealth. The Cortes, which had met irregularly since 1640, was no longer summoned, and government was carried out by ministers appointed by the king. John V desired the absolute authority enjoyed by Louis XIV. He did not fail to convert his wealth into papal and other dignities: the archbishop of Lisbon became a patriarch (1716), and Pope Benedict XIV in 1749 gave John the title "his most faithful majesty"; and royal academies, palaces, and libraries were inaugurated. But in his later years his ministers proved inadequate and the kingdom sank into stagnation. On John's death, his son Joseph (1750–77) appointed as minister Sebastião José de Carvalho e Melo, later conde de Oeiras and marquês de Pombal, who soon gained a complete ascendancy over the king and endeavoured to replace the stagnant absolutism with a more active type of despotism that, with some qualifications, deserves the epithet enlightened. His full powers date from his efficient handling of the crisis caused by the disastrous Lisbon earthquake of November 1755; but even before this he had reformed the sugar and diamond trades, set up a national silk industry (1750), and formed one chartered company to control the sardine and tunny-fishing industry of Algarve and another to trade with northern Brazil. In 1756 he founded the Junta do Comércio, a board of trade with powers to limit the privileges enjoyed by the English merchants under the treaties of 1654 and 1661, and set up the General Company for Wines of Alto Douro (Companhia dos Vinhos do Alto Douro) to control the port wine trade. Industries for the manufacture of hats (1759), cutlery (1764), and other articles were set up with varying success.

Pombal's methods were arbitrary and his enemies numerous. His reform of the wine industry provoked a riot in Porto (1757) that was savagely repressed; but his principal victims were the Jesuits, expelled in 1759 from all the Portuguese dominions, and the nobility, in particular José Mascarenhas, duque de Aveiro, and the Távora family, who were accused of an attack on the King (September 3, 1758), condemned, and executed (January 12, 1759). Having eliminated the Jesuits from the educational system, Pombal applied regalist principles in the reform of the University of Coimbra (1772) and the royal board of censorship (1768), which supervised the system of lower education from 1771.

While Pombal succeeded in modifying the ascendancy of the British merchants in Portugal, he invoked the English alliance in 1762 when Spain, prompted by the renewal of the Bourbon Family Compact alliance with France, invaded Portugal. The Portuguese Army was reformed by Wilhelm von Schaumburg-Lippe, and an English force was led by James O'Hara, 2nd Baron Tyrawley, and John Campbell, 4th earl of Loudoun. Peace was signed in February 1763 at Fontainebleau. On the death of Joseph (February 24, 1777), his daughter Maria I (1777–1816), who had married his brother, her uncle (Peter III), acceded; Pombal was dismissed (1777) and eventually found

Marginal notes (left column):
Treaties with England

Mineral wealth from Brazil

Marginal notes (right column):
Enlightened despotism of Pombal

Expulsion of Jesuits

guilty on several charges. His successors made peace with Spain by the Treaty of San Ildefonso (1777).

The French Revolutionary and Napoleonic Wars. Maria I suffered from melancholia after the loss of her consort (1786) and eldest son John (1788). In 1792 her mental balance was further disturbed, probably by the news of the French Revolution, and she ceased to reign. Her son, who on her death became John VI (1816–26), then ruled in her name and in 1799 became prince regent. In 1793 Portugal joined England and Spain against France, sending a naval division to assist the English Mediterranean fleet and an army to the Catalan front. The Peace of Basel (July 1795), by which Spain abandoned its allies, left Portugal still at war. Although subjected to pressure from the French Directory and from the Spanish minister, Manuel de Godoy, Portugal remained unmolested until 1801, when Godoy sent an ultimatum and invaded Alentejo. By the Peace of Badajoz (June 1801), Portugal lost the town of Olivenza and paid an indemnity.

From the Peace of Amiens (1802) until 1807, Portugal was once more immune from attack, though subjected to continuous pressure to break off the English connection. By the Berlin decree of November 21, 1806, Napoleon sought to close all continental ports to British ships. Portugal endeavoured to maintain neutrality, but the secret Franco-Spanish Treaty of Fontainebleau (October 1807) provided for its eventual dismemberment by Napoleon I and Godoy. Already Gen. Andoche Junot was hastening

Flight of royal family to Brazil

across Spain with a French army, and on November 27, the prince regent and the royal family and court embarked on a fleet lying in the Tagus River and were escorted by British vessels to Brazil; the court remained 14 years at Rio de Janeiro. Junot declared the Braganças deposed, but his occupation of Portugal was challenged in August 1808 by the arrival of Sir Arthur Wellesley (later duke of Wellington) and 13,500 British troops in Mondego Bay. Winning the victories of Roliça (August 17) and Vimeiro (August 21), Wellesley enabled his superiors to negotiate the Convention of Sintra (August 31), by which Junot was allowed to evacuate Portugal with his army. A second French invasion (1808–09) led to Sir John Moore's death at La Coruña (January 1809) and the reembarkation of the British forces. In February, William Carr (later Viscount) Beresford was placed in command of the Portuguese Army, and in March Marshal N.J. de Dieu Soult advanced from Galicia and occupied Porto. Wellesley returned to Portugal in April, drove Soult from the north, and after his victory of Talavera de la Reina in Spain (July), withdrew to Portugal. The third French invasion followed in August 1810 when Marshal André Masséna with Marshal Michel Ney and Junot entered Beira province. Defeated by Wellington at Bussaco (September 27) near Coimbra,

Lines of Torres Vedras

the French found themselves facing the prepared lines of Torres Vedras, north of Lisbon, where they wintered amid great privations. By the spring of 1811 they could only retreat and, on March 5, began the evacuation of Portugal, harassed all the way by English and Portuguese attacks and crossing the frontier after a defeat at Sabugal (April 3).

Portugal made peace with France on May 30, 1814. It was represented at the Congress of Vienna but played little part in the settlement. The series of Anglo-Portuguese treaties concluded between the years 1809 and 1817, however, was important insofar as it extended many of the conditions of the Anglo-Portuguese alliance to Brazil and had an influence on the future of Africa. England's efforts to get Portuguese collaboration in suppressing the slave trade resulted in the treaty of January 22, 1815, and in the additional convention of 1817, by reason of which Portugal's claims to a considerable part of Africa were formally recognized.

Constitutionalism. The Napoleonic campaigns had caused great devastation in Portugal, and the absence of the royal family and the presence of a foreign commander (Beresford) combined with revolutionary agitation and the influence of Spanish liberalism to produce an atmosphere of discontent and restlessness. On December 16, 1815, Brazil was raised to the rank of a kingdom united with Portugal, and John VI, who succeeded in March 1816, showed no desire to return to Portugal. In 1817 Beres-

ford suppressed a conspiracy in Lisbon, and the Masonic leader Gen. Gomes Freire de Andrade was executed. Unrest increased, and when Beresford himself went to Brazil (March 1820) to press John to return, a constitutionalist revolution began in Porto (August 24, 1820), spread over the country, and led to the formation of a junta in Lisbon (October 4). On Beresford's return (October 10) he was not allowed to land, and British officers were expelled from the army. A constituent assembly was summoned that drew up a very liberal constitution, thus confronting John VI with an accomplished fact.

John's reluctance to return was at last overcome, and he left his elder son Pedro to govern Brazil, landing at Lisbon on July 3, 1821. He swore to uphold the constitution, but his wife, Carlota Joaquina, and their second son, Dom Miguel, refused to take the oath and were sentenced to banishment, though this was not carried out. The Portuguese constitutionalists, not appreciating the determination of Brazil not to yield up its status as a kingdom, sought to compel Pedro to return; but he, rather than sacrifice the rule of the Braganças in Brazil, declared for Brazilian independence (September 7, 1822) and became emperor of Brazil as Pedro I. This enabled his brother Miguel (Michael) to appeal to absolutist forces in Portugal to overthrow the constitutionalists, and an insurrection led by Miguel almost succeeded (April 30, 1824); but through the action of the foreign ministers, John VI was restored and Miguel went into exile in Vienna (June 1824).

Independence of Brazil

War of the Two Brothers. John VI acknowledged the independence of Brazil in 1825, assuming *pro forma* the imperial title and then yielding it to Pedro; but when John died (March 10, 1826), no provision had been made for the succession except that his daughter Maria Isabel was now named regent. Pedro, as Pedro, or Peter, IV of Portugal, issued from Brazil a charter providing for a parliamentary regime by the authorization of the monarchy and not based on the sovereignty of the people. He then made a conditional abdication (May 1826) of the Portuguese throne in favour of his daughter Maria da Glória, aged seven, provided that she should marry her uncle Miguel and that he should swear to accept the charter. This compromise could not be effective. The absolutists had hoped that Pedro would resign all rights to the Portuguese crown, and the council of regency hesitated to publish the charter until Gen. João Carlos de Saldanha (later duque de Saldanha) forced their hand. In 1827 Miguel took the oath and was appointed regent, landing in Lisbon in February 1828. His supporters at once began to persecute the liberals. A form of Cortes met in Lisbon, and in July 1828 repudiated Pedro's claims and declared Miguel rightful king.

Only the island of Terceira in the Azores sustained the liberal cause. In June 1829, however, a regency on behalf of Maria da Glória was set up in Terceira; and in 1831 Pedro, having abdicated the Brazilian throne, went to Europe and began to raise money and men for the conquest of Portugal. In February 1832 the expedition sailed to Terceira, and in July the liberals, led by Pedro, disembarked at Mindelo near Porto, which city they soon occupied. The rest of the country, however, stood by Miguel, who besieged the liberals in Porto for a year (July 1832–July 1833). By now, Miguelite enthusiasm had waned; and António José de Sousa Manuel, duque de Terceira, and Capt. (later Sir) Charles Napier, who had taken command of the liberal navy, made a successful landing in Algarve (June 1833). Terceira advanced on Lisbon, which fell in July 1833, and Miguel capitulated at Evora-Monte in May 1834.

Further political strife. The War of the Two Brothers ended with the exile of Miguel (June) and the death of Pedro (September 24, 1834). Maria da Glória became queen as Maria II (1834–53) at the age of 15. While Maria necessarily came under the influence of the successful generals of the civil war, her principal aim was to defend her father's charter (which had been granted by the crown) from those who demanded a "democratic" constitution like that of 1822, asserting the ultimate sovereignty of the nation.

In September 1836 the latter, thenceforth called Septembrists, seized power. The chartist leaders rebelled and were exiled, but by 1842 the Septembrist front was no longer united, and António Bernardo da Costa Cabral restored the charter. In 1846 the movement of Maria da Fonte, a popular rising against higher taxation to improve roads and reforms in public health in which almost all parties joined, put an end to Costa Cabral's government but left Portugal divided between the Septembrists, who held Porto, and Saldanha, now in Queen Maria's confidence, in Lisbon. Saldanha negotiated for the intervention of other members of the Quadruple Alliance (formed in April 1834 by England, France, Spain, and Portugal), and a combined British and Spanish force received the surrender of the Porto junta in June 1847 and ended the war with the Convention of Gramido (June 29, 1847). Saldanha governed until 1849, when Costa Cabral resumed office only to be overthrown in April 1851. Saldanha then held office for five years (1851–56), and the period of peace at length permitted the country to settle down. The "Regeneration" ended civil strife and established party government.

Maria II was succeeded by her eldest son by her second husband, Ferdinand of Saxe-Coburg, Peter, or Pedro, V (1853–61), who married Stephanie of Hohenzollern-Sigmaringen in 1858. He gave promise of being a capable and conscientious monarch but died of typhoid fever on November 11, 1861. His brother Louis (Luís; 1861–89) seemed to have inherited a country that had recovered from the Napoleonic invasions and from civil wars, political strife, and *pronunciamentos.* But although the main parties were now defined as Historicals (*i.e.,* radicals) and Regenerators (or moderates), the alternation of governments gradually ceased to reflect any semblance of popular feeling, and in the last years of Luís' reign republicanism was already beginning to gain ground.

Colonial policies. With the accession of Charles (Carlos; 1889–1908), a serious dispute with Great Britain occurred. Portugal's possessions in Africa had been recognized by Great Britain in the treaty of 1815, but more recently Germany and Belgium had entered the colonial field; and at the Conference of Berlin (1885), the definition of "effective occupation" was adopted as the basis for possession of colonial territories. A colonial movement had gained momentum in Lisbon, and a Portuguese scheme, known as the "Rose-Coloured Map," which laid claim to a colony stretching across Africa from Angola to Mozambique, was recognized by France and Germany (1886). Although the Marquess of Salisbury registered a protest (1888), the Portuguese foreign minister Henrique de Barros Gomes sent Maj. Alexandre Alberto da Rocha de Serpa Pinto to the Shire Highlands (modern Malawi), with a view to their annexation. He became involved in a fight with the Makololos, who were under British protection, and a series of communications between London and Lisbon ended in the dispatch of the British ultimatum of January 11, 1890, demanding the withdrawal of all Portuguese from the Shire. Amid great popular excitement, Barros Gomes had no alternative but to comply, and the government resigned. The incident caused the deepest resentment in Portugal, not only against the ancient ally but also against the monarchy, which was menaced by an attempted republican revolution in Porto (January 31, 1891).

During the following years, the Portuguese African colonies were defined as a result of the Anglo-Portuguese treaty of July 1891, but the financial position of the country was so bad that it seemed unlikely that the efforts to consolidate the African colonies would succeed. In 1897 it became clear that Portugal would require a considerable loan, and Germany demanded to partake in any assistance that was offered. On August 30, 1898, A.J. (later the earl of) Balfour, temporarily in charge of the British Foreign Office, concluded a secret Anglo-German convention assigning spheres of influence in the Portuguese colonies to Great Britain and Germany in the event of such a loan. This was, however, denounced by the prime minister, Lord Salisbury, and in 1899, when the Germans endeavoured to persuade the Portuguese to accept a loan, Salisbury's action and the imminent danger of a conflict in the Transvaal caused an Anglo-Portuguese approximation. On October 14, 1899, the ancient treaties of alliance

were reaffirmed in a secret declaration, later made public (the so-called Windsor Treaty).

Meanwhile, the financial situation showed little improvement, and the republicans continued to progress. In 1906 João Franco, formerly a Regenerator, came to power as champion of the failing monarchist cause. Unable to obtain the support of the other monarchists, he began to govern by decree. Although Franco bravely undertook to reform the finances and administration, he was accused of illegally advancing money to the King. These scandals were followed by rumours of plots, and on February 1, 1908, Charles and his heir, Luís Filipe, were assassinated as they rode in an open carriage in Lisbon. Whether or not the regicides were isolated fanatics or agents of a hidden organization such as the Carbonária, a republican secret society, the deed was applauded by the republicans, who immediately began their preparations for a final attack on the monarchy.

King Manuel II (1908–10) found no unity among the monarchist politicians. The general election of August 1910 showed republican majorities in Lisbon and Porto, and on October 3 the murder by a madman of one of the republican leaders, the distinguished physician Miguel Bombarda, offered the pretext for a rising that was already organized. Armed civilians, soldiers, and the men aboard some ships in the Tagus began the republican revolution on October 4 and, after faltering, their movement, in which António Machado Santos played the predominant part, succeeded on October 5. Manuel escaped to Ericeira and thence by sea to Gibraltar and to England. On his death in 1932 his body was returned to Portugal.

Social and economic conditions. From the time of the Portuguese overseas conquests, the flow of wealth from the new territories and trading posts, if it sustained the court and capital, did little to improve the domestic economy, still largely rural. The favourable financial position of the late 15th century, derived from trade in slaves, gold, and spices, did not long survive into the 16th century, when the expenses of maintaining far-flung and unproductive foreign stations and the depredations of pirates quickly absorbed any surpluses. There were few native industries. Not only were manufactured goods such as cloth, tapestry, and metalware imported but also basic foodstuffs, salt meat, cured fish, and dairy produce. Agriculture was little regarded, and insufficient land was available for small holdings. During the years of Spanish domination, the ports were closed to English merchants; and by the time they were reopened after 1640 the flow of trade had found new channels, and the Dutch and English had outstripped Portugal as colonial powers. The discovery of gold in Brazil at the end of the 17th century brought about a revival in the country's economy, but gold production was in decline by 1750, while the diamond market was saturated. The later 18th century saw a series of protectionist measures, many introduced by Pombal. The Methuen Treaty with England (1703) had strengthened the port wine trade at the expense of Portuguese cloth; later further attempts were made to improve the export value of port wine. Support was also given for the production of woollen goods, linen, paper, porcelain, and cutlery and to the tunny and sardine fisheries. Pombal attempted to create an educated bourgeoisie, but the Portuguese textile industry could not withstand mechanized competition. After 1850 public works, railways, and ports were given priority, but Portugal had to wait until the 20th century for any sustained attack upon its economic difficulties.

THE REPUBLIC (FROM 1910)

The new regime formed a provisional government under the presidency of Teófilo Braga, a well-known writer. This in turn issued a new electoral law giving the vote to adult Portuguese males and presided over the election of a constituent assembly, which opened on June 19, 1911. The constitution was passed by the assembly on August 20, and the provisional government surrendered its authority a few days later (August 24) to the new president, Manuel José de Arriaga.

Evolutionists, Unionists, and Democrats. Although a monarchist invasion was unsuccessfully attempted by

Roman
Catholic
Church
disestab-
lished

Henrique de Paiva Couceiro in October 1911, the main danger to the new regime came from its internal divisions. For the moment, it was fairly united in denouncing monarchism and persecuting the church. The religious orders were expelled (October 8, 1910) and their property confiscated. The teaching of religion in primary schools was abolished and the Roman Catholic Church disestablished. The conditions under which Catholics and monarchists were imprisoned attracted attention abroad, and it was only gradually that this legislation was modified. New universities were founded at Lisbon and Porto; but the task of destruction proved easier than that of construction, and before long the republicans were divided into Evolutionists (moderates), led by António José de Almeida; Unionists (centre party), led by Manuel de Brito Camacho; and Democrats (the left wing), led by Afonso Augusto da Costa. A number of prominent republicans had no specific party. The whirligig of republican political life offered little improvement on the monarchist regime, and in 1915 the army showed signs of restlessness. Gen. Pimenta de Castro formed a military government and permitted the monarchists to reorganize, but a Democratic revolution (May 14) led to his arrest and consignment to the Azores. President Arriaga resigned and was succeeded by Braga and then by Bernardino Machado (August 5, 1915–December 8, 1917). The Democratic regime, in which Costa was paramount, was ended by the revolution (December 1917) of Maj. Sidónio Pais, who established a "New Republic" of a right-wing tendency, supported at first by the Unionists. On their withdrawal (March 1918), a new National Republican Party gained control. Sidónio Pais' "presidentialist" regime was abruptly ended with his assassination on December 14, 1918, when, after the provisional presidency of Adm. João do Canto e Castro, power passed gradually back to the Democrats.

Meanwhile, on the outbreak of World War I, Portugal had proclaimed its adhesion to the English alliance (August 7, 1914) and on November 23 committed itself to military operations against Germany. On September 11 a first expedition left to reinforce the African colonies, and there was fighting in northern Mozambique, on the Tanganyika frontier, and in southern Angola, on the frontier of German South West Africa. In February 1916 Portugal seized German ships lying in Portuguese ports, and Germany declared war (March 9). A Portuguese expeditionary force went to the western front in 1917, under Gen. Fernando Tamagnini de Abreu; on April 9, 1918, they were under heavy German attack in the Battle of Lys. By the Treaty of Versailles (1919) Portugal received 0.75 percent of the indemnity payable by Germany and the Quionga (Kionga) area of Mozambique captured by Portuguese forces in East Africa.

Fighting
during
World
War I

Almeida completed his term as president (October 5, 1919–October 5, 1923), but, with economic confusion reigning, ministers followed one another in rapid succession. In the violence of 1921, the founder of the republic, Machado Santos, and others were murdered. The Democratic Party, led by António Maria da Silva, governed for 21 months, but da Silva's fall in November 1923 was followed by short-lived ministries. In 1925 the Democrats won a clear majority. Pres. Manuel Teixeira Gomes (1923–25) was succeeded by Bernardino Machado. A military revolt on February 2, 1926, was quelled, but on May 28 a successful revolution was launched at Braga. Machado was deposed, and a provisional military government was formed by Commander José Mendes Cabeçadas and Gen. Manuel de Oliveira Gomes da Costa.

The "New State." The provisional government was shortly (July 9, 1926) taken over by Gen. (later Marshal) António Oscar de Fragoso Carmona, who favoured sweeping changes. He was elected president in March 1928 and re-elected until his death in April 1951. The military leaders attempted to overcome the financial crisis with a loan from the League of Nations, but the conditions included fiscal supervision, which was rejected, and Carmona called on António de Oliveira Salazar to take over the Ministry of Finance with full powers over expenditure.

Salazar's
first years

Salazar, then professor of economics at the University of Coimbra, controlled expenditures from 1928 to 1948,

producing budgetary surpluses (the hallmark of his regime) and devoting the proceeds to development plans. Becoming prime minister in 1932, he promulgated the new constitution of 1933; as minister of colonies in 1930, he prepared the Colonial Act, assimilating the administration of the overseas territories to his system; and as minister for foreign affairs (1936–47), he guided Portugal through the difficulties caused by the Spanish Civil War and World War II. He maintained neutrality until Britain invoked the Anglo-Portuguese alliance to obtain bases in the Azores.

On the death of Carmona (April 18, 1951), Salazar assumed the attributes of the presidency until Gen. Francisco Craveiro Lopes was elected (August). Craveiro Lopes was not re-elected in 1958 but was succeeded by Rear Adm. Américo de Deus Tomás, elected by a large majority on a limited franchise. Salazar's New State (Estado Novo) provided for a National Assembly, with deputies elected quadrennially as a bloc and meeting for at least three months annually, and a Corporative Chamber. All seats in the assembly went to government supporters. The Corporative Chamber did not come into being until employers' and workers' syndicates were formed. Collective contracts were negotiated under government supervision, and strikes were forbidden.

Under the development plans, electrification, afforestation, and industrialization were pressed ahead. In the postwar period the railways were re-equipped, roads were improved, and the national airline was developed. Steel manufacture was introduced, as were the assembly of motor vehicles and repair of tankers. The economies of Angola and Mozambique were integrated.

The determination of the Indian government to annex Portuguese India led to India's severing of diplomatic relations (August 1955) and to mass invasions of the Portuguese possessions by Indian passive resisters. Portugal effectively lost Dadrá and Nagar Haveli to India (despite a ruling by the International Court of Justice in April 1960 favouring Portugal), and on December 19, 1961, India took over Goa, Diu, and Damão.

Salazar had made it plain that decolonization was not part of his plan for Portugal, and when Angola was the scene of disturbances in which a number of lives were lost, he reinforced the troops in the African territories and took over the Ministry of Defense. In 1964 there was a recrudescence of independence movements.

In September 1968 Salazar was incapacitated by a stroke, and on July 27, 1970, he died. After his stroke, President Tomás invited Marcelo Caetano, one of the architects of the New State, to form a government. Caetano pledged himself to continuity and also to "evolution," which included the admission of an opposition to the National Assembly and the relaxation of economic controls in favour of expansionism. Under the Third Development Plan, large enterprises were undertaken, but the general economic crisis led to inflation, and emigration from the countryside to the cities and to other parts of Europe was accelerated. Caetano's moderate liberalization divided his supporters and stimulated the Socialist and Communist opposition.

After
Salazar

Portugal after 1974. *The Captains' Revolution.* The African policy entrenched in the constitution became a bone of contention, and oppositionist decolonization policies were conveyed to discontented younger military officers. Gen. António de Spínola, who had forged a reputation in Guinea while attempting a negotiated settlement there, entered the government as assistant chief of staff and precipitated a crisis with his book *Portugal e o Futuro* ("Portugal and the Future"), which argued that the wars in Africa could not be settled by force of arms and advocated negotiated autonomy for the colonies. On April 25, 1974, Tomás and Caetano were removed by a military coup, which became known as the Captains' Revolution because it was brought about by a group of some 200 service captains who had grown dissatisfied, especially with long, drawn-out wars to maintain Portuguese control of the African colonies. These captains constituted the Armed Forces Movement (Movimento das Forças Armadas, or MFA), led by the chiefs of staff, Francisco da Costa Gomes and Spínola. The latter became head of a figurehead junta.

The institutions of the New State were abolished, and the MFA, dominated by Marxists, obtained control of the press, radio, and education. Then the hitherto small Portuguese Communist Party seized control of organized labour and took possession of land, especially in the Alentejo. The armed and civil services were purged, and Spínola was driven from office and replaced by Costa Gomes, who appointed Col. Vasco Gonçalves to form a government, supported by the Marxist wing of the MFA. Elections for a constituent assembly (April 25, 1975) showed that this regime had little support, but Gonçalves attempted to impose a Marxist program.

Independence was granted to Portuguese Guinea (as Guinea-Bissau) almost immediately after the revolution, and in 1975 both Mozambique and Angola became sovereign states, as did the other Portuguese territories in Africa. Thus ended a Portuguese colonial involvement in that continent that had begun in 1415. From the former African colonies, nearly a million people fled to Portugal, adding a refugee problem to the serious political and economic crisis. (H.V.L.)

In April 1976 a new constitution was approved, which committed Portugal to making a transition to socialism. A transitional government under Adm. José Pinheiro de Azevedo held general elections in which the Socialists obtained 107 seats, the popular Democrats 73, the Social Democratic Centre Party (conservative) 41, and the Communists 40. The leader of the Socialists, Mário Soares, formed a minority government. The chief of staff (since November 1975, after he had put down a left-wing rebellion in the armed forces), Gen. António Ramalho Eanes, was elected president of the republic with 61.5 percent of valid votes in June 1976. (H.V.L./Ed.)

Soares' minority government resigned in December 1977, primarily because it was unable to enact an effective austerity program. In January 1978 Soares formed a new coalition government with the Social Democratic Centre Party, which, however, collapsed after only six months. A number of short-lived centre-left governments followed, until in 1980, in the general election scheduled by the constitution, a centre-right alliance, the Aliança Democrática, swept into power. It was headed first by Francisco Sá Carneiro and, after his death in an airplane crash in December 1980, by Francisco Pinto Balsemão. It was this government that succeeded in revising the character of the 1976 constitution. The Assembly of the Republic approved a series of reforms that included abolishing the Council of the Revolution and reducing the powers of the president. These constitutional reforms completed Portugal's transition to full civilian rule.

The alliance faltered in 1982, propelling the country into yet another crisis. President Eanes called an early general election for April 1983, in which the Socialists, headed by Soares, scored an inconclusive victory. Because Portugal urgently needed a stable, broadly based government to tackle its severe economic problems, Soares formed a coalition government with the Social Democrats (formerly the Democrats). It successfully implemented an 18-month emergency program and a four-year modernization program as a means of gaining admittance to the EEC, a goal Portugal was to achieve on January 1, 1986.

The coalition, although precarious, lasted until June 13, 1985. It survived several internal crises caused predominantly by a division within the Social Democrats between a left wing favouring the coalition and a right wing disagreeing with the coalition's economic policies. In 1985 Anibal Cavaço Sílva, leader of the right wing, became head of the party. He called into question the viability of the coalition, voicing doubts especially on subjects of labour and agrarian reform.

This crisis, which ended the coalition, had been intensified by nationwide strikes in the industrial and transport sectors, led by Communist unions, and by demonstrations from parties on both the left and the right of the political spectrum calling for an end to the coalition government. Soares resigned, and in the elections held in October 1985 the Social Democrats, campaigning on a platform advocating a free-market economy, became the largest single party, able to form a minority government with Cavaço

Sílva as prime minister. In the election of February 16, 1986, Soares became Portugal's first civilian president in 60 years.

For later developments in the political history of Portugal, see the *Britannica Book of the Year* section in the BRITANNICA WORLD DATA ANNUAL. (Ed.)

BIBLIOGRAPHY

General: HERMANN LAUTENSACH, *Bibliografia Geográfica de Portugal* (1948; reprinted 1973), a useful bibliography; ARISTIDES DE AMORIM GIRAO, *Atlas de Portugal*, 2nd ed. (1958), the standard atlas; PIERRE BIROT, *Le Portugal: Étude de géographie régionale* (1950), an excellent concise source; ARISTIDES DE AMORIM GIRAO, *Geografia de Portugal*, 3rd ed. (1960), a handbook; HERMANN LAUTENSACH, *Portugal auf Grund eigener Reisen und der Literatur*, 2 vol. (1932–37), the first major survey of Portugal; ORLANDO RIBEIRO, *Portugal*, vol. 5 of *Geografia de España y Portugal* (1955), the best general survey; *Portugal, o Mediterrâneo e o Atlântico*, 3rd ed. (1967), a synthesizing treatment emphasizing the originality of Portugal; DAN STANISLAWSKI, *The Individuality of Portugal: A Study in Historical-Political Geography* (1959; reprinted 1969); *Portugal Divulgação* (bimonthly), published by the OFFICE OF THE SECRETARY OF STATE FOR MASS COMMUNICATION, is useful. EUGENIO DE CASTRO CALDAS, *Modernização da Agricultura Portuguesa* (1960); A. HUBERT, *Le Portugal et son économie* (1961); J.L. PINTO MACHADO, *Alguns Problemas do Mundo Rural Português* (1965); VALENTIM X. PINTADO, *The Structure and Growth of the Portuguese Economy* (1964); ORLANDO RIBEIRO, *A Evolução Agrária no Portugal Mediterrâneo* (1970); *Alguns Elementos Sobre a Economia Portuguesa* (1963); *III° Plano de Fomento para 1968–1973*, 4 vol. (1968); *Portugal*, OECD Annual Economic Surveys; *Constitution of the Portuguese Republic* (1977), issued by the OFFICE OF THE SECRETARY OF STATE FOR MASS COMMUNICATION; "Any More Questions?" (1970), an informative booklet on Portuguese institutions and culture, published by the Secretariat of State for Information and Tourism; RODNEY GALLOP, *A Book of Folkways* (1961), intensive research on old customs and usage; ANN BRIDGE and SUSAN LOWNDES, *The Selective Traveller in Portugal*, rev. ed. (1967), an intelligent guide to the architecture, art, and culture of Portugal.

History: Histories of Portugal in English include H.V. LIVERMORE, *A History of Portugal* (1947) and *A New History of Portugal*, 2nd ed. (1976); and A.H. DE OLIVEIRA MARQUES, *History of Portugal*, 2 vol. (1972–76). The standard histories in Portuguese are FORTUNATO DE ALMEIDA, *História de Portugal*, 6 vol. (1922–29); and DAMIAO PERES (ed.), *História de Portugal*, 7 vol. (1928–35). For prehistory, see H.N. SAVORY, *Spain and Portugal* (1968). For Roman Portugal, see J. ALARCAO, *Portugal Romano* (1973); for the Germanic invasions, H.V. LIVERMORE, *Origins of Spain and Portugal* (1971). A.H. DE OLIVEIRA MARQUES' guide to medieval Portugal is *Sociedade Medieval Portuguesa* (1964; Eng. trans., *Daily Life in Portugal in the Late Middle Ages*, 1971). The period of the discoveries is dealt with in B.W. DIFFIE and G.D. WINIUS, *Foundations of the Portuguese Empire* (1977); see also V. DE MAGALHAES GODINHO, *L'Économie de l'empire portugais* (1969); DAMIAO PERES, *História dos Descobrimentos Portugueses* (1959; Eng. trans., *A History of the Portuguese Discoveries*, 1960); C.R. BOXER, *The Portuguese Seaborne Empire, 1415–1825* (1969); and F. MAURO, *Le Portugal et l'Atlantique au XVIIe siècle, 1570–1670* (1960). On the Inquisition, see ALEXANDRE HERCULANO DE CARVALHO E ARAUJO, *Da Origem e Estábelecimento da Inquisição em Portugal*, 3 vol. (1854–59; Eng. trans., *History of the Origin and Establishment of the Inquisition in Portugal*, 1 vol., 1926); and A.J. SARAIVA, *Inquisição e Cristãos-Novos*, 2nd ed. (1969). A.D. FRANCIS, *The Methuens and Portugal, 1691–1708* (1966), discusses the famous treaties; and H.E.S. FISHER, *The Portugal Trade* (1971), the commerce of the 18th century. The best study of Pombal remains J. LUCIO D'AZEVEDO, *O Marquês de Pombal e a Sua Época*, 2nd ed. (1922). A. SILBERT, *Le Portugal méditerranéen à la fin de l'Ancien Régime, XVIIIe–début du XIXe siècle*, 2 vol. (1966), is a study of underlying agrarian conditions. An outline of the 19th century is given in R.J. HAMMOND, *Portugal and Africa* (1966). E.V. AXELSON covers *Portugal and the Scramble for Africa, 1875–1891* (1967). Statistics on the last half of the century are included in M. HALPERN PEREIRA, *Livre-câmbio e Desenvolvimento Económico* (1971). The story of the republic is told by the Spanish historian JESÚS PABÓN in *La revolución portuguesa*, 2 vol. (1941–45). Works on Salazar include F. CLEMENT C. EGERTON, *Salazar, Rebuilder of Portugal* (1943). An account of *The Portuguese Revolution, 1974–76* (1976), from *Facts on File*, is ed. by L. SOBEL. The essential documents are in H. BARRILARO RUAS, *A Revolução das Flores*, I, II, III, for 1974–76. See also CARL A. HANSON, *Economy and Society in Baroque Portugal: 1668–1703* (1981); and DOUGLAS L. WHEELER, *Republican Portugal: A Political History, 1910–1926* (1978).

(I.M.P. do A./J.Sh./H.V.L./Ed.)

Portuguese Literature

The literature of Portugal is distinguished by a wealth and variety of lyric poetry, which has characterized it from the beginning; by its medieval lack of and later achievement in the national epic; by its wealth of historical writing; and by its relative slightness in drama, biography, and the essay. The early *cancioneiros* ("song-books") evidence a school of love poetry that spread, with the language, to Spain at a time when Spanish was as yet undeveloped for lyrical purposes. The *romanceiro,* or balladry, on the other hand, was much influenced by that of Spain, though not sharing the latter's predilection for the heroic. In its primitive version *Amadís de Gaula* (14th century; *Amadis of Gaul*), prototype of the romance of chivalry, probably was written in Portuguese, as was, later, *La Diana* (1559) of Jorge de Montemor (Montemayor), the masterpiece of the pastoral novel. *Os Lusíadas* (1572; *The Lusiads*), a history of the Portuguese (the name Lusiads deriving from the ancient Lusitania), by Luís de Camões, may be at once the most successful of the many Renaissance epics cast in the classical mold and the most national of great poems in any modern literature, and many works of history and travel of the 16th and 17th centuries are outstanding. Though Gil Vicente, in the early 16th century, was a dramatist of great gifts, no other appeared until João Baptista de Almeida Garrett in the 19th, and Portugal never developed a national drama.

This literature, which until the 19th century lay largely unstudied and unknown, has from the beginning been exposed to foreign influences. The earliest was Provençal, and Provençal taste ruled for more than a century. Then came Castilian, with a court poetry that provided models until the Renaissance saw the triumph of that form in Italy and in the classics of antiquity. In the 17th century with political domination Spain again imposed its literary standards, followed in the 18th century by France. The Romantic movement reached Portugal from both France and England, two countries whose influence, joined in a lesser degree by that of Germany, persisted long after. The closeness of contacts with Spain, reinforced by dynastic marriages that often brought to the court at Lisbon a predominantly Spanish atmosphere, explains why for two centuries and more after 1450 nearly every Portuguese writer of note was bilingual and wrote also in Spanish, so that some, like Montemor and Francisco Manuel de Melo, are numbered among the classics too of Spanish letters. Portuguese literature retains, nonetheless, a distinct individuality that contrasts strikingly with that of Spain. The medieval lyric, the plays of Gil Vicente, the bucolic verse and prose of the 16th century, and, above all, *Os Lusíadas,* are expressions of a clearly defined national temperament.

This article is divided into the following sections:

WRITINGS OF THE EARLY PERIOD

Poetry. Though no literary documents belonging to the first century of Portugal's history as a nation have survived, there is evidence of the existence of an indigenous popular poetry. A few compositions from before 1200 survive; one, attributed to Sancho I, is the earliest extant parallelistic song, a brief, repetitive lyrical poem marked by a wistful sadness that is never wholly absent from Portuguese literature. Of the many later poems that survive, most belong to the major categories of *cantigas de amor* ("songs of love"; sung by a man to the woman he loves in vain), *cantigas de amigo* ("songs of the lover"; sung by a woman to express her yearning for her lover), and *cantigas de escárnio e maldizer* (satirical songs). This body of lyrics, represented in three great *cancioneiros,* shows the vitality of a school of poetry in Galician-Portuguese (the dialect of northern Portugal) that, while essentially inspired by the sophisticated French and Provençal songs of the troubadours, is also anchored in the popular tradition.

This poetry reached the peak of its creativity in the first half of the 13th century, coinciding with the reign of Afonso III (1248–79). His son, Dinis, had a deep interest in literature and was considered to be the best poet of his age in the Iberian Peninsula. Dinis founded his country's first university at Lisbon in 1290 (it later was moved to Coimbra) and encouraged translation into Portuguese of outstanding works from Spanish, Latin, and Arabic. To his court came troubadours from Leon, Castile, and Aragon to enjoy the last of a cult dying elsewhere, and about 2,000 poems by its 200 poets were preserved in the three great repositories of verse, *Cancioneiros da Ajuda, Cancioneiros da Vaticana,* and *Cancioneiros Colocci-Brancuti* (or *da Biblioteca Nacional de Lisboa*). · *Dinis' encouragement of literature*

In contrast with the restricted horizons of courtly verse, themes of adventure, war, and chivalry mingled with love, religion, and the sea in a collection of ballad poetry known as the *romanceiro.* Few of these ballads can be dated earlier than the 15th century; they belonged to an anonymous poetry kept alive by oral transmission, with a late artificial flowering from known poets in the 16th and 17th centuries.

Prose. Prose literature in Portugal took much longer than verse to perfect. Religious writings, brief annals of the early kings, and books of descent formed the earliest texts. The *Livro de Linhagens* ("Book of Genealogy") of Pedro Afonso, count of Barcelos (the natural son of Dinis), constituted a landmark by going beyond genealogy to history and legend. The work contains short epic narratives, romances, and tales of adventure and fantasy. Pedro was also responsible for the compilation in 1344 of the *Crónica Geral de Espanha* ("General Chronicle of Spain"), interesting, within the peninsular tradition of the general chronicle genre, for its original version of well-known episodes.

The early popularity of subject matter based on Celtic tradition is attested in the five songs based on Breton lays with which the *Cancioneiro Colocci-Brancuti* opens. The ideals of chivalry and the spirit of sentimental adventure associated with the knights of the Round Table made strong appeal to the Portuguese imagination: a *História dos Cavaleiros da Távola Redonda* ("History of the Knights of the Round Table") and the *Demanda do Santo Graal* ("Search for the Holy Grail"), adapted from the French, are the chief relics of considerable activity in this field.

DEVELOPMENTS OF THE 15TH AND 16TH CENTURIES

Literature of the 15th century. Under King John (João) I, founder of the new dynasty of Avis, the Portuguese court became once again a literary centre. The King himself wrote a treatise on hunting. His son Duarte (Edward) collected a rich library of the ancients and of medieval poems · *The influence of the Avis dynasty* and histories and composed a moral treatise, *Leal Conselheiro* (1437/38; "Loyal Counselor"), which revealed a conscious stylist. But the historical chronicle distinguished the age, with credit to King Edward, who in 1434 created the office of *cronista mor do reino,* or "chief chronicler of the realm," and appointed Fernão Lopes, author of chronicles of the first 10 kings of Portugal. The *Crónica dos Sete Primeiros Reis do Portugal,* a chronicle of the first seven kings, discovered in 1947 and published in 1952–53, is almost certainly the first part of that work. Until its discovery only the chronicles of Pedro I, Ferdinand I, and John I were known. Vividness of style combined with serious documentation to produce in Lopes the finest writer of medieval Portuguese prose.

His successor in office, Gomes Eanes de Zurara, continued the chronicle on a lower level of artistry. His chief works are the *Crónica da Tomada de Ceuta* (*Conquests and Discoveries of Henry the Navigator*) and the *Crónica do Descobrimento e Conquista da Guiné* (*The Chronicle of the Discovery and Conquest of Guinea*).

Poetry was cultivated in the mid-15th century after a long eclipse, but much had changed. The dominant influence came now from Spain, and Portuguese poets initiated the long chapter of allegiance to Spain. Apart from the ballads, popular poetry had disappeared along with that of the troubadours. The constable Dom Pedro de Portugal initiated the fashion of writing in Castilian. As one of the first to adopt the new Spanish trend toward allegory and the cult of classical antiquity derived from Italy, his influence on his compatriots was doubly important. His own poems were inspired by deep feeling and much reflection on life, and he was one of almost 200 poets represented in an anthology of poetry, the *Cancioneiro Geral* (1516; "General Songbook"), of the chronicler Garcia de Resende, covering the preceding three-quarters of a century. The main subjects of these 1,000-odd poems, in Portuguese and Castilian, were love, satire, and epigram. Resende was a better poet than most of his contributors.

The
Cancio-
neiro
Geral

Gil Vicente and early drama. The emergence of the modern play may be traced in the works of the court dramatist Gil Vicente. Eleven of his 44 plays were written wholly, and another 17 partly, in Spanish. The *Barcas* (1517–19), a group of *autos,* or religious plays, revealed his dramatic power and a fondness for comic relief; in this lay his strength, and in construction lay his weakness. The phenomenon of a potential national theatre, however, died with its founder, and his real influence was felt in Spain. The Inquisition, introduced into Portugal in 1536, early declared war on the popular theatre on the charge of grossness. Vicente's own plays, which figured on the Spanish Index of 1559, were reduced in number to 35 and were sadly mutilated in the second edition of 1586.

The Renaissance in Portugal. The Renaissance reached Portugal both indirectly through Spain and directly from Italy, with which country there had been close cultural relations through the 15th century. In the following century many famous humanists took up residence in Portugal. In 1532 the historian and humanist João de Barros published the *Rópica Pnefma* ("Spiritual Merchandise"), the most important philosophical dialogue of the time in Portugal.

In 1547 John III reformed the University of Coimbra, and distinguished Portuguese teachers returned from abroad to assist the King in his task. At home Portugal produced scholars of note, including André de Resende, author of *De antiquitatibus Lusitaniae* (1593; "Of the Antiquities of Portugal"), and Francisco de Holanda, painter, architect, and author of the *Diálogos da Pintura Antiga* ("Dialogues on Ancient Painting").

The Italianate school of poetry and drama. The return in 1526 of the poet Francisco de Sá de Miranda after a six years' stay in Italy initiated a literary reform of far-reaching effect. Like his contemporary Garcilaso de la Vega in Spain, he introduced the new poetic forms of sonnet, canzone, ode, and epistle, and he gave fresh vigour to the national verse forms, mainly through his *Satires.* His chief disciple, António Ferreira, a convinced classicist, wrote sonnets superior in form and style. Other poets continued the erudite school, which triumphed with Luís de Camões, author of *Os Lusíadas.* In Camões, a profound

Luís de
Camões

classical education combined with perfect mastery of his instrument and a lifetime of varied experience to produce in sonnets, eclogues, odes, elegies, and *canções* the greatest poetry in the language.

In the drama Sá de Miranda and his followers substituted prose for verse. Taking the Roman dramatist Terence as their model, they produced not Portuguese characters but Romano-Italian types. This revived classical comedy was to be short-lived. Sá de Miranda, avowedly to combat the school of Vicente, wrote *Os Estrangeiros* (*c.* 1528; "The Strangers"), the first prose comedy, and *Os Vilhalpandos* (*c.* 1528), both actions being set in Italy. Ferreira, a greater dramatist, likewise attempted both kinds: *O Cioso,* Italian even to the names of the personages, came nearer to being a comedy of character, but his fame rests chiefly on *Castro* (*c.* 1557; *Ignez de Castro*), which treated one of the most moving tragic themes in the nation's history—the execution of Inês de Castro—by reference to the ancient Greek dramatists Sophocles and Euripides. From the comic playwright Jorge Ferreira de Vasconcelos came a "new invention" of another kind with *Comédia Eufrosina* (1555), written under the influence of the Spanish novel *La Celestina.* This and his other plays, *Comédia Ulissipo* (1618) and *Comédia Aulegrafia* (1619; "Life at Court"), resembled novels in dialogue and contained a treasury of popular lore and wise and witty sayings introduced with a moral purpose.

The 16th-century history. Discovery and conquest in Africa, Asia, America, and on the ocean inspired historians as well as poets. Their records gained in vividness what they might have lost in scientific detachment. In the three "Decades" of his *Décadas da Ásia* (1552–63), João de Barros told in vigorous language the deeds of compatriots overseas down to 1526. His first "Decade" undoubtedly influenced Camões, and together, one by his prose and the other by his verse, these two fixed the written language. This work, continued by the more critical and inclusive Diogo do Couto, can rank as the noblest historical monument of the century. In his *Soldado Prático* (written before 1578, published in 1790; "Experienced Soldier"), Diogo do Couto added acute observations on the causes of Portuguese decadence in the East. Ten years of investigation in India underlay the *História do Descobrimento e Conquista da Índia Pelos Portugueses* (1551–61; "History of the Discovery and Conquest of India by the Portuguese") of the chronicler and notary Fernão Lopes de Castanheda, a work that ranks close to those of Barros and do Couto.

From this spate of writing on expansion overseas, attention returned, by way of chronicles of the monarchs who presided over the work, to the history of Portugal itself. Damião de Góis, diplomat, traveler, humanist, and intimate friend of Erasmus, possessed an encyclopaedic mind and was one of the most critical spirits of the age: his *Chronica do Felicissimo Rey Dom Emanuel* (1566–67; "Chronicle of the Most Happy King, Dom Emanuel") was most valuable where the author's own feelings of experience came into play.

Works of travel abounded, and their authors were often the first Europeans to visit the countries in question. Among the more noteworthy was a much-translated classic, *História da Vida do Padre Francisco Xavier* (1600; "History of the Life of Father Francis Xavier"), by Padre João de Lucena. Important both as history and as human documents were the *cartas,* or "letters," written home by Jesuits in China and Japan. An anonymous *Descobrimento da Florida* ("Discovery of Florida") and a *Tratado Descritivo do Brasil em 1587* ("Descriptive Treatise of Brazil in 1587") of Gabriel Soares de Sousa were reminders that Portugal was also present and active in the New World to the west. A work notable for its curious interest is the *Peregrinacam* (1614; *The Voyages and Adventures of Ferdinand Mendez Pinto, of Portugal*), which Fernão Mendes Pinto, prince of adventurers throughout the East, composed in his old age, and another, known for tragic pathos, is the *História Trágico-Marítima* ("Tragical Maritime History"), a collection of contemporary narratives, told by survivors or based on their accounts, of the more notable disasters that befell Portuguese ships between 1552 and 1604.

Literature of the Portuguese Empire

The novel and other prose. The poet Bernardim Ribeiro, whose five eclogues introduced pastoral poetry to Portugal, was equally an innovator in the pastoral novel with his *Hystoria de Menina e Moça* (1554; "The Story of Menina and Moça"). This tale of rustic love and melancholy with chivalric elements adopted themes and emotions previously found only in poetry. From it a musician and poet, Jorge de Montemor, drew some part of his inspiration for *La Diana*, which, written in Spanish, started a fashion subscribed to by Cervantes and Lope de Vega among many others and represented one of the outstanding contributions of Portugal to the neighbouring literature. The first romance of chivalry in Portuguese was João de Barros' *Crónica do Imperador Clarimundo* (1520; "Chronicle of the Emperor Clarimundo"), concerning the adventures of a fictitious progenitor of the kings of Portugal.

Among moralists and theologians, three ranked as masters of prose style: Frei Heitor Pinto, for his *Imagem da Vida Cristã* (part I, 1563, part II, 1572; "Image of the Christian Life"); Bishop Amador Arrais for 10 *Diálogos* (1589; "Dialogues") on religious and other topics; and Frei Tomé de Jesus for a mystic and devotional treatise, *Trabalhos de Jesus* (1602–09; "Works of Jesus"). The work of scientists included that of a cosmographer and mathematician, Pedro Nunes, and of a botanist, Garcia de Orta, whose *Colóquios dos Simples e Drogas* (1563; *Colloquies on the Simples and Drugs of India*) was the first Portuguese book to be printed in the East (at Goa in India).

THE 17TH CENTURY

From a literary and political point of view, the 17th century found Portugal in a state of decadence. Before the loss of independence to Spain in 1580, Spanish influence had introduced the Inquisition and, with it, censorship of books and the preparation of an Index of Forbidden Books. Between 1552 and 1555 the Jesuits gained control of higher education. The cult of classical Latin was already present, in the work of Camões and others, before the example of the Spanish poet Luis de Góngora y Argote was felt; but with the exhaustion of the national spirit that underlay political eclipse the influence of Góngora penetrated deeply. Its extent may be seen in the five volumes of the *Fénix Renascida* (1716–28; "Phoenix Reborn"), which anthologizes the poetry of the preceding century and reveals the futilities to which good talents could devote themselves. The trend survived the throwing-off of the Spanish yoke in 1640; Portuguese editions of Góngora continued to appear.

The foremost literary figure of the age was the encyclopaedic Francisco Manuel de Melo, a classic of Spanish and—with his series of historical episodes, *Epanáforas de Vária História Portuguesa* (1660; "Anaphoras of Diverse Portuguese History"), and dialogues on literary and social topics, *Apólogos Dialogais* (1721)—of Portuguese literature who strove, more successfully in prose than in verse, to free himself from subservience to Spanish form and style. Most lyricists of the period remained steeped in Gongorism. Epic poets continued active, but few of their productions were more than rhymed chronicles.

Frei Luís de Sousa, a monastic chronicler, won fame as a stylist with his *Vida do Arcebispo D. Frei Bartolomeu dos Mártires* (1619; "Life of Archbishop D. Frei Bartolomeu dos Mártires") and the *História de São Domingos* (three parts, 1623, 1662, 1678; "History of São Domingos"). A Jesuit, António Vieira, missionary and diplomatist, was highly regarded for his *Cartas* (1925–28; "Letters") and *Sermões* (1679–1748; "Sermons").

The popular theatre lived on obscurely with mostly anonymous plays that were never printed. Those that survived were mainly religious and showed the common Gongoristic abuse of metaphor and simile. All through the century most dramatists who aspired to be heard wrote in Spanish. The court after 1640 preferred Italian opera, French plays, and Spanish operettas—to the detriment of native drama and of acting.

THE 18TH CENTURY

The 18th century, in Portugal as in Spain, was predominantly prosaic, even in poetry. Yet signs gradually appeared of a literary revolution that developed eventually into the Romantic movement. Luís António Verney poured scorn on prevailing methods of education in *Verdadeiro Método de Estudar* (1746; "True Method of Studying"). Men of liberal ideas traveled to France and England, and to their example were largely due the reforms that invaded every branch of letters. Among the most influential were Alexandre de Gusmão, Francisco Xavier de Oliveira, António Ribeiro Sanches, José Correia da Serra, Avelar Brotero, and Francisco Manuel do Nascimento. New literary societies called *arcádias* cooperated in the task of reform. In 1720 King John V established the Academia Real da História Portuguesa, which counted among its members such men as Manuel Caetano de Sousa, author of a colossal *História Genealógica de Casa Real Portuguesa* (1735–49; "Genealogical History of the Portuguese Royal House"). The Academia Real das Ciências (Royal Academy of Sciences), founded in 1779, initiated research into the study of Portuguese literary history. In its ranks were found nearly all the scholars of note at the end of the century, such as the ecclesiastical historian Frei Manuel do Cenáculo; a scientist, António Ribeiro dos Santos; João Pedro Ribeiro, perhaps his country's first modern historian; and critics Francisco Alexandre Lobo and Frei Fortunato de São Boaventura.

Establishment of the Portuguese academies

In 1756 António Dinis da Cruz e Silva established the Arcádia Lusitana (or Ulissiponese), its first aim being the uprooting of Spanish influence. The bucolic verse of Dómingos dos Reis Quita signified a return to the native tradition of two centuries earlier. Sincerity and suffering spoke in the justly more famous *Marília de Dirceu* (1792), love lyrics in a pastoral setting, by Tomás António Gonzaga. In 1790, a Brazilian Nova Arcádia came into being, its two most distinguished members being the rival poets Manuel Maria Barbosa du Bocage and José Agostinho de Macedo.

Outside the Arcádias stood the "Dissidents," among whom were at least two writers of distinction. These were the satirist Nicolau Tolentino de Almeida, who painted the customs and follies of his day with devastating accuracy, and Francisco Manuel do Nascimento (pseudonym Filinto Elísio), who addressed himself perseveringly to purifying the language and to restoring the cult of the 16th-century poets.

Early in the century popular authors attempted a revival of the drama in Lisbon. The *Óperas Portuguesas* (1733–41) of Antônio José da Silva owe their name to the interspersing of the prose dialogue with arias, minuets, and *modinhas* (popular light songs).

The attempted revival of drama in Lisbon

THE 19TH CENTURY

Romanticism and after. The 19th century witnessed a general revival of Portuguese letters. The chief exponents of Romanticism were, in poetry and drama, João Baptista de Almeida Garrett and, in prose, Alexandre Herculano; both lived for some years in exile, the price of their political liberalism. Almeida Garrett read literature in English and French and introduced Portugal to nationalistic Romanticism through two epics, *Camões* (1825) and *Dona Branca* (1826). António Feliciano de Castilho, half-Romantic, half-Classicist, exercised much influence over a younger generation of poets: João de Lemos, Soares de Passos, Tomás Ribeiro (who won fame with the ardently patriotic *Dom Jaime*, 1862). In 1865 Antero de Quental, a student of German philosophy and poetry, and Teófilo Braga, disciple of Auguste Comte, led a revolt against the primacy of Castilho, much to the benefit of literature, and of poetry in particular. The *Campo de Flores* (1893; "Field of Flowers") of João de Deus contained some of the finest short poems in the language, marked by a spontaneous simplicity. Abílio Manuel Guerra Junqueiro, heir to Victor Hugo, was a would-be social revolutionary excessively prone to grandiloquence. In *Os Simples* (1892) he turned to the portrayal of peasant life, and this work constituted his finest poetry. Akin to him was António Duarte Gomes Leal, author of *Claridades do Sul* (1875; "Clarities of the South") and *O Anti-Cristo* (1884; "The Anti-Christ"), who could likewise achieve quiet sincerity when dealing with humble themes.

António Cândido Gonçalves Crespo stood out as the first of his country's Parnassians. By contrast Cesário Verde, considered to be the greatest poet of the century, addressed himself to the poetic essence of common realities. The *Só* (1892; "Alone") of António Nobre was intensely Portuguese in themes, mood, and rhythms; he and Teixeira de Pascoais developed a cult of *saudosismo* ("yearning," "nostalgia") that inspired a whole school of poets. French Symbolism found an enthusiastic adept in Eugénio de Castro.

Drama, the novel, and history. Almeida Garrett, seeking to reinvigorate drama, found he had to create alike theatre, plays, actors, and audience. In *Um Auto de Gil Vicente* (1838; "An *Auto* of Gil Vicente"), *O Alfageme de Santarém* (1841; "The Swordsmith of Santarém"), and especially in *Frei Luís de Sousa* (1843; *Brother Luiz de Sousa*), he proved himself to be, after Vicente, his country's most notable dramatist. João da Câmara was the outstanding dramatist of his day, and his works included *Afonso VI* (1890), *Rosa Enjeitada* (1901; "Rose Abandoned"), and *Os Velhos* (1893; "The Old Ones"). Herculano, returning from exile with an enthusiasm for Sir Walter Scott, launched the historical romance with *O Monasticon: Eurico, o presbitero* (1844; "The Monastic: Eurico, the Presbyter") and *Lendas e Narrativas* (1851; "Legends and Narratives"). Many followed suit, including Oliveira Marreca, Arnaldo da Gama, and Pinheiro Chagas, popular successes being *A Mocidade de D. João V* (1852; "The Youth of D. João V"), by Luís António Rebelo da Silva, and João de Andrade Corvo's *Um Ano na Côrte* (1850–51; "A Year in the Court"). This was the great age of the novel: Camilo Castelo Branco, Joaquim Gomes Coelho (better known as Júlio Dinis), and especially José Maria Eça de Queirós were names that would stand high in any country. The first was a master of the language and of dramatic, or melodramatic, plot; Júlio Dinis depicted country life, as in *As Pupilas do Senhor Reitor* (1867; "The Pupils of Senhor Reitor"); while Eça de Queirós introduced Realism with a powerful novel, *O Crime do Padre Amaro* (1876; *The Sin of Father Amaro*).

With his magnum opus, the *História de Portugal* (1846–53; "History of Portugal"), and the *História da Origem e Estabelecimento da Inquisição em Portugal* (1854–59; *History of the Origin and Establishment of the Inquisition in Portugal*), Herculano established himself as a leader of modern Spanish and Portuguese historians. Historiography flourished with the Visconde de Santarém, historian of the Cortes; José Simão da Luz Soriano (of constitutionalism); Rebelo da Silva (of the period of Spanish rule under the Philips); and José Maria Latino Coelho (of the dictatorship of Pombal). Henrique da Gama Barros and António da Costa Lôbo followed in the footsteps of Herculano. The works of Joaquim Pedro de Oliveira Martins gave proof of psychological imagination, a notable capacity for general ideas, and a gift of picturesque narration. He left in his numerous writings a vast portrait gallery of great figures of his country, particularly in the *Portugal Contemporâneo* (1881; "History of Contemporary Portugal").

THE 20TH CENTURY

The passage from monarchy to republic in Portugal in 1910 saw a revisionary urge in literature associated chiefly with Oporto and the *Renascença Portuguesa* ("Portuguese Renaissance"). Leonardo Coimbra was its philosopher, and António Sérgio its critic and historian. Its poets—Mário Beirão, Augusto Casimiro, and João de Barros—adopted the *saudosismo* of Teixeira de Pascoais as the key to the nation's recovery of greatness, though the inadequacy of this nostalgia was soon realized. The "Integralist" school reacted from 1913 onward in favour of the Roman Catholic monarchist tradition, led by António Sardinha, a historian and poet. Fernando Pessoa, author of *Mensagem* (1934; "Message"), was posthumously regarded as the most brilliant poet of his generation.

Among novelists of the first half of the century, Aquilino Ribeiro was a prolific writer whose themes often were centred on his native Beira; his delight in life was combined with awareness of decay and death. Miguel Torga, a poet, storyteller, and author of autobiography, showed a

radical individualism that took its strength from his peasant roots. The psychological novel, which had attained a sophisticated form with José Régio, also an outstanding dramatist and a religious poet, took new directions with Carlos de Oliveira. *Casa na Duna* (1943; "A House on a Sandhill"), his first novel, combines an acute perception of human motivation with social awareness, leading up to *Finisterra* (1978), his last book and a masterpiece. Vergílio Ferreira added a metaphysical dimension to the novel of social concern in *Alegria Breve* (1965; "Brief Joy") and explored the evanescent moods of the past and the idea of death in *Para Sempre* (1983; "Forever").

After the overthrow of the Salazar regime on April 25, 1974, poetry and fiction found a new freedom of expression. Jorge de Sena, a poet and novelist of outstanding quality, published *Sinais de Fogo* (1978; "Signs of Fire"), an impressive novel about the effects in Portugal of the Spanish Civil War. J. Cardoso Pires wrote his best novel, *Balada da Praia dos Cães* (1983; "Ballad of the Beach of the Dogs") based on the account of a political assassination. Women novelists have also brought a new voice to fiction. Agustina Bessa Luís, a most prolific writer, first came to notice in 1955. She extended the psychological insight evident in her drawing of fictional characters to enhance her portraits of historical figures, as in her work *Fanny Owen* (1979). Maria Velho da Costa, one of the authors of *Novas Cartas Portuguesas* (1971; *The Three Marias: New Portuguese Letters*)—a book that became a cause célèbre because its authors were put on trial by the state—explored with great subtlety the condition of women in a repressive society in *Lúcialima* (1983; "Lemon Verbena"). José Saramago came to the fore in the 1980s. His novels combine an acute observation of reality with flights of poetic fancy. In *Memorial do Convento* (1982; "Memorial of the Convent") the story of the building of a magnificent convent is also the allegory of human suffering in history, told in the form of an epic tale.

Notable work also came out in history and literary criticism, and through this Portugal's history and literature have become more adequately known.

BIBLIOGRAPHY

Histories: THEOPHILO BRAGA, *História de Literatura Portugueza*, 11 vol. (1896–1907); J. MENDES DOS REMÉDIOS, *História da Literatura Portuguesa*, 6th ed. (1930), with anthology; FIDELINO DE FIGUEIREDO, *História Literária de Portugal (Seculos XII–XX)*, 3rd ed. (1966); ALBINO FORJAZ DE SAMPAIO (ed.), *História da Literatura Portuguesa Ilustrada*, 4 vol. (1928–42); GEORGES LE GENTIL, *La Littérature portugaise*, 2nd rev. ed. (1951); ANTONIO JOSÉ SARAIVA and OSCAR LOPES, *História da Literatura Portuguesa*, 12th rev. ed. (1982); JACINTO DO PRADO COELHO (ed.), *Dicionário das Literaturas Portuguesa, Galega e Brasileira* (1956–60); AUBREY F.G. BELL, *Portuguese Literature* (1922, reprinted 1970), a standard work, with extensive bibliography.

Critical studies: FIDELINO DE FIGUEIREDO, *Characteristics of Portuguese Literature* (1916; originally published in Portuguese, 1915); *Estudos de Litteratura*, 5 vol. (1917–51), and *A Epica Portuguesa no Seculo XVI*, rev. ed. (1950); AUBREY F.G. BELL, *Studies in Portuguese Literature* (1914, reprinted 1975); EDWARD GLASER, *Portuguese Studies* (1976); M. RODRIGUES LAPA, *Das Origens da Poesia Lírica em Portugal na Idade-Média* (1929), and *Lições de Literatura Portuguesa: Época Medieval*, 9th rev. ed. (1977); PIERRE LE GENTIL, *La Poésie lyrique espagnole et portugaise à la fin du moyen âge*, 2 vol. (1949–52, reprinted in 1 vol., 1981); FREDE JENSEN, *The Earliest Portuguese Lyrics* (1978); JOLE RUGGIERI, *Il canzoniere di Resende* (1931); MARCEL BATAILLON, *Études sur le Portugal au temps de l'humanisme*, 2nd ed. (1974); HERNANI CIDADE, *Tendências do Lirismo Contemporâneo do "Oaristos" às "Encruzilhadas de Deus,"* 2nd ed. (1939), with an anthology of modern poetry; *Lições de Cultura e Literatura Portuguesas*, 2 vol., 6th rev. ed. (1975); *O Conceito de Poesia Como Expressão da Cultura*, 2nd rev. ed. (1957), and *A Literatura Portuguesa e a Expansão Ultramarina*, 2 vol., 2nd rev. ed. (1963–64); H.V. LIVERMORE and W.J. ENTWISTLE (eds.), *Portugal and Brazil: An Introduction* (1953, reprinted 1963), which contains a literary bibliography of studies and of translations from Portuguese to English. Studies of individual authors include EDGAR PRESTAGE, *D. Francisco Manuel de Mello* (1922); AUBREY F.G. BELL, *Diogo do Couto* (1924), *Fernam Lopez* (1921), *Gaspar Corrêa* (1924), *Gil Vicente* (1921), and *Luis de Camões* (1923).

(W.C.A./N.J.L./L.de S.R.)

Postal Systems

In the modern world, the term "postal system" may be defined as the institution—almost invariably under the control of a government agency—that makes it possible for any person to send a letter, packet, or parcel to any addressee, in his own country or abroad, in the expectation that it will be conveyed according to certain established standards of regularity, speed, and security. The service is paid for in advance by the sender according to a relatively simple scale of fees based on weight and, in some countries, on speed of service required. Prepayment is ordinarily made by means of postage stamps, franking machine impression, or printed indication of postage paid; payment is not usually required of the addressee.

It may seem tedious to catalog at such length characteristics that are familiar to everyone. Their very familiarity, however, and the consequent unthinking acceptance of them make it important to emphasize that until recently postal systems lacked many of these features. Though the basic need for a system to exchange written communications has been felt by all human societies and has been met in many ways, the evolution of varied postal systems adopted by different societies through the centuries into the basically similar pattern of today's state monopoly service has been a long and difficult process.

Today the governments of many countries use their postal systems to provide a range of services that often have no direct connection with the traditional function of exchanging letters. To provide for the collection, transport, and delivery of letters throughout a country, it has been necessary to establish a network of post offices extending into the remotest areas. Such a network of offices, staffed by agents of the state, provides an efficient banking service in areas in which it would be uneconomic for a commercial or state bank to establish a branch office. Many governments also pay various social security benefits—such as pensions and family allowances—through vouchers that can be cashed at post offices. In some countries post offices also collect certain taxes, normally through the sale of licenses and revenue or tax stamps. In fact, a wide range of ancillary services is provided through the postal system. In some African and Asian countries, for instance, the postal system helps distribute antimalarial drugs. While the variety of such services significantly indicates the ever-increasing use made of postal systems throughout the modern world, they lie outside the scope of this article, which concentrates on the traditional postal or mail services.

This article is divided into the following sections:

POSTAL OPERATIONS AND MANAGEMENT

The raw material of the postal services, always a single object that demands individual treatment, is something sent by one person or entity to another who may be anywhere else in the world. Letters and parcels go in all shapes and sizes, subject only to the limits of weight and dimensions prescribed by postal legislation. Yet if postal services are to be efficient and economical, these items must be mass-processed, as far as is possible. Thus, the basic function of postal organization is to convert the individual item as rapidly as possible into something that can be handled on a bulk basis, ensuring, however, that it finally regains its individual status.

The The collection and sorting of individual items by the
sorting most economic method, concentrating together all items
process that are going to the same place or in the same direction, involves the use of local transport, usually operated by the postal services themselves, and sorting offices. The size of the sorting office depends on local requirements, but some are, in fact, large centres that handle several million items a day and employ thousands of personnel. Certain ancillary operations are involved, such as the canceling (by machine in all except the smallest offices) of stamps that have served to prepay the postal charge.

The next stage is to transport the grouped items to different destinations that may be intermediate sorting offices, perhaps a railway sorting car. Items are combined by further sorting with mail from other sources to permit grouping the mails for final destinations.

The third stage is the arrival of the mail at the sorting office of the final destination, where it is sorted systematically. The items finally recover their identity and are grouped for delivery to the individual address. In most countries, delivery is on a house-to-house basis, although boxes at a local post office are sometimes used.

All stages have to be planned and dovetailed to meet an overall standard of performance. The transport of mail between sorting offices is normally by services not necessarily directly operated by the post office—*i.e.,* by truck, bus, train, marine shipping, or air services. In some countries, however, the administration operates its own air service, usually by night, to supplement the public services. Post-office counter services (*i.e.,* the public offices that existed originally as depots where the public could buy stamps, make inquiries, and post and collect correspondence) have in many countries gone beyond the role of accessory to the postal service proper and pose their own problems of organization.

Postal services require extensive manpower. Many countries are striving to mechanize or even automate sorting, transport, and counter processes. Postal organization depends largely on geography; large agglomerations of population present the greatest problems. Furthermore, geography usually determines the routing of mails and the intermediate steps between the posting and destination offices. Traffic problems have forced postal managers, through the years, to develop their own approach to the operational aspects of postal organization. They developed their own work-study methods and operational research techniques long before these terms were invented. Apart from postal operations as such, postal management is concerned with the efficient administration and deployment of large bodies of manpower, the organization of large transport fleets, many aspects of property management, and financial and economic problems, particularly in an increasing number of countries where the postal services are expected to depend on their postal revenue in order to meet all of their costs (including those related to capital expenditure). Computer technology is increasingly exploited as a management aid.

In this connection, many of the developed and developing countries have come to realize that postal services often operate within a commercial market where competition can be fierce and efficiency is the watchword. With the adoption of marketing and sales techniques, new services emphasizing speed, convenience, and reliability have been introduced. One such service is express mail, known under different service names according to the country (Express Mail in the United States, Datapost in Great Britain and Germany). At additional cost, this service, in which about half the UPU membership participates, provides expedited conveyance and individualized priority handling of correspondence and goods.

HISTORY

Message-relay systems of the ancient world. Since good communications were clearly essential for governing the extensive empires of the ancient world, it is not surprising that among the earliest historical references to postal systems were those concerning Egypt about 2000 BC and China under the Chou dynasty 1,000 years later. It was probably in China that a posthouse relay system was first developed and was brought to a high state of development under the Mongol emperors. The great Persian Empire of Cyrus in the 6th century BC also employed relays of mounted messengers, served by posthouses. The system was favourably described by the Greek historians Herodotus and Xenophon. The admiration of the Greeks was natural since their political divisions inhibited the growth of a coherent postal system, although each city-state possessed its corps of messengers.

The development of Rome from a small city-state into a vast empire embracing most of the known world brought with it the necessity for reliable and speedy communications with the governors of distant provinces. This need was met by the *cursus publicus,* the most highly developed postal system of the ancient world. The relay stages of the *cursus publicus,* established at convenient intervals along the great roads of the empire, formed an integral part of its complex military and administrative system. The speed with which messengers were able to travel during the peak of the administration was not to be rivaled in Europe until the 19th century: it has been claimed that more than 170 miles (270 kilometres) could be covered in a day and a night. The maintenance of the *cursus publicus* required a high degree of organization; an inspectorial system existed to control its operation and prevent abuse for private ends.

The fall of the Roman Empire in the west during the 5th century did not completely destroy the *cursus publicus.* Its advantages were evident to the new barbarian rulers; some, such as Theodoric, king of the Ostrogoths, who ruled Italy from AD 493 to 526, are known to have maintained the essentials of the Roman postal system within their own domains. Even in the early 9th century, under the Carolingian Empire, the vestiges of the *cursus publicus* appear to have persisted, and posthouses were maintained. While the service did not follow a regularly organized pattern, it was at least reasonably frequent. The continued decay of the Roman roads, the increasing unwillingness of communities bordering the roads to support the expenses of the system, and the progressive political fragmentation of Europe, however, caused all traces of the Roman postal system to disappear.

The *cursus publicus* fared better in the Byzantine Empire because its provinces were eventually absorbed into the Islāmic Empire. The substitution of one centralized imperial regime for another meant that the *cursus publicus*

could be incorporated into a similar Arabian postal system based in Baghdad.

The pre-Columbian civilizations of America, responding to the same needs as the imperial states of Asia and Europe, also evolved relay systems, limited to foot messengers. In the Inca Empire, posthouses were maintained at frequent intervals along the remarkable road network, and a like system probably served the Mayan civilization for more than 1,000 years.

Growth of business correspondence in the Middle Ages. The end of the reign of the last Carolingian king in 987 marked the beginning of several centuries of confusion in Europe, in which it is difficult to trace any postal system worthy of the title. Since the kings of the period were constantly struggling to assert their authority over their unruly feudal vassals, the strong central authority that sustained most postal systems was lacking. The uncertain political situation did not favour the creation of a regulated postal service, though it necessitated frequent contact between the kings and vassals and among the great princes. They, along with other powerful institutions—the municipalities, the religious orders, and the universities (notably in Paris)—started to maintain corps of messengers to serve their particular needs.

One of the more significant trends of the later Middle Ages was the development of international commerce and, with it, the growth of business correspondence. Many corporations or guilds established messenger systems to allow their members to maintain contacts with customers. Notable among these was the so-called Butcher Post (Metzger Post), which was able to combine the carrying of letters with the constant traveling that the trade required.

The mercantile corporations of Italy provided the most extensive and regular postal system of this period. Of particular importance were the links maintained from the mid-13th century between the great Italian commercial centres, such as Florence, Genoa, and Siena, and six important annual fairs held in the Champagne area of northern France. Two fixed dispatches were made to each of these fairs: the first to carry orders and commissions and the second to effect settlements. The service was carefully regulated. Conditions of acceptance, scales of payment, and timetables were laid down; the route was fixed, and hostels were maintained along the route. Since the Champagne fairs were attended by merchants from all over Europe, the postal system provided a valuable international link.

Italian business interests were also responsible for the only regular extra-European postal link of this period, between Venice and Constantinople. The extent and importance of Venetian business correspondence may be gauged from the fact that in 1320 the king of Persia accorded its couriers the right of free passage throughout his domains.

Russia shared in the general European trend toward the development of postal services in the 13th century. Horses and drivers for the transport of couriers were kept at regular staging posts to provide the so-called carriage express, which gradually developed into an organized system for the exchange of letters.

Growth of the post as a government monopoly. Institutional postal systems that developed during the later Middle Ages also conveyed letters between private persons, with or without official sanction and for a substantial fee in either case. Initially, such letters were relatively few. Outside the institutions with their own postal services, the number of literate people having interests that ranged beyond their own neighbourhoods was small.

In the late 15th century, however, the trend toward improved postal services was reinforced by Gutenberg's printing press (*c.* 1450) and the expansion of education. The growth of demand made letter carrying a profitable business, leading to the rise of private undertakings—the majority, like the Swiss Stumpelbotten, purely local in scope. Some, like the Paar family in Austria, developed postal organizations on a national scale. By far the most famous and extensive of such systems was that built up by the Thurn and Taxis family, who originally came from Bergamo near Milan, Italy. Under the patronage of the Habsburg emperors, they became the organizers of an

(margin notes)
Problems of postal management

Express mail

The *cursus publicus*

Early postal links between Italy and France

The Thurn and Taxis postal operation

extensive network of postal routes linking the imperial possessions. Their system developed throughout the 16th century until it covered most of Europe, using 20,000 couriers to operate a relay system that was speedy, efficient, and highly profitable.

Although the remnants of the Thurn and Taxis postal system survived in Germany up to 1867, it was essentially out of keeping—like the empire and the petty German states it served—with the main trend of development in Europe, the rise of nation-states with strong central governments. The first reflection of this trend in the postal sphere was the establishment of efficient national systems of relay posts under the control of the state. In France, Louis XI set up a Royal Postal Service in 1477 employing 230 mounted couriers. In England, a Master of the Posts was appointed by Henry VIII in 1516 to maintain a regular postal service along the main roads radiating from London. Neither of these systems was comprehensive, nor were they intended to serve the public. The security and regularity of the service along certain routes, however, inevitably resulted in an increasing amount of unofficial correspondence being carried. After initial attempts to

Legalizing private mails

prevent this practice in France, its fiscal advantages were realized, and the carrying of private mails was legalized about 1600. The basis of a real public service was not created until 1627, when fees and timetables were fixed and post offices established in the larger cities. In Britain, a separate public service was set up in 1635 by a royal proclamation "for the settling of the letter-office of England and Scotland." Thomas Witherings, a London merchant, was given the task of organizing regular services to run by day and night along the great post roads.

In both countries, these state systems naturally began to develop into monopolies since such an evolution was seen by rulers as advantageous both to the security and to the revenues of the state. In England, the establishment of state posts along the principal roads was accompanied by the suppression, under the royal monopoly, of private and municipal posts, although "common carriers" were still permitted to convey letters on routes not covered by the royal system.

In 1672 France declared postal services to be a state monopoly under which operating rights were sold. Private undertakings that had established legal rights in this field were allowed to continue, but private messenger systems were eventually forced out of business by state competition or were bought out. In 1719 the University of Paris, the most important private competitor, gave up its last postal privileges in return for substantial compensation.

There was still opportunity for private enterprise to succeed by introducing services that were not at that time provided by the state systems. It was in this way that an important step in postal history, the establishment of local collection and delivery services in the great cities of London and Paris, was taken. London was the first city to benefit from an urban service when one William Dockwra set up his Penny Post in 1680. Striking features of the scheme were that letters were prepaid and stamped to indicate place of posting and the time they had been sent out for delivery. Deliveries were made almost hourly. Dockwra's scheme was so successful that he was prosecuted for infringing the state monopoly, and his service was closed down in November 1682, only to be reopened by the government. Not until 1759 was a similar local service introduced in Paris. It too was quickly absorbed by the state postal system; but its originator, Claude-Humbert Piarron de Chamousset, was paid compensation. Thus, the state monopolies expanded their scope, happily combining an improved service to the public with greater profitability.

The pace of postal progress in England during the later 18th century was accelerated by remarkable economic growth and a consequent demand for better mail services to the growing commercial and manufacturing centres. The most striking improvements came as the result of an extensive program of road building that began about 1765, paving the way for the era of the stagecoach. These were

The stagecoach

first used by the post office in 1784 and rapidly superseded the mounted postboys on the main routes. They began by averaging six or seven miles an hour, but continuing improvements in the roads and in the design of the vehicles pushed this up to 10 miles an hour in the 1830s. With the stagecoaches making possible a general reorganization of the entire system of mail circulation, letters could be delivered the morning after posting in towns more than 120 miles from London. A carefully regulated postal service—unprecedented for its standards of speed, frequency, and security—was evolved during this period.

Despite the disruptive effects of the Revolutionary and Napoleonic wars, great progress was made throughout Europe in the late 18th and early 19th centuries in improving the speed and regularity of postal service and in providing internal delivery services for most of the larger cities. In the United States, too, postal services expanded at a remarkable rate: in 1789 only 75 post offices existed, but 40 years later there were more than 8,000.

Rowland Hill's reforms. The publication in 1837 of *Post Office Reform: Its Importance and Practicability,* by Rowland Hill (later Sir Rowland Hill), a British educator and tax reformer, is justly regarded as one of the most important milestones in postal progress. Based on an exhaustive study of the cost structure of postal operations, it demonstrated conclusively that conveyance charges were an insignificant factor in the total cost of handling a letter. The then current intricate charging scales based on distance were shown to be irrelevant: they inflated operating costs by requiring a host of clerks to apply them and to prepare complicated interoffice accounts. He also realized that another major item in the current cost structure—the collection of money payments on delivery—was easily avoidable. Hill's solution was a uniform rate of postage, regardless of distance, and prepayment of postage by means of adhesive stamps sold by the post office. Hill proposed a basic rate of one penny for each half ounce, calculating the "natural cost of distribution" to be slightly less than this. The cheapest current rate of postage was fourpence, and the average charge 6¼ pence (11.56 cents).

Foundation of modern postal systems

Not surprisingly, Hill's proposals rapidly gained strong support: popular agitation for the "penny post" overcame initial political disinterest, and the uniform rate and a system of prepayment by stamps were introduced in 1840. The originality of Hill's proposal for an adhesive postage stamp has been questioned but is irrelevant in considering the overall merits of his work. The significance of his reforms lies not only in the fact that they brought the post within the means of the mass of the people but also in the less obvious way in which they gave the postal system the technical capacity to deal with the vastly increased demand for postal service that ensued. The radical simplification of postal organization and methods characterizing Hill's reforms are the key to the speed and economy with which modern postal systems in many countries handle tens of millions of letters daily.

The chief features of Hill's system were gradually adopted in varying degrees by other countries throughout the world, first among which were Switzerland and Brazil in 1843.

The introduction of uniform cheap rates of postage for letters was accompanied by the establishment of even lower tariffs for newspapers (carried free in some countries) and for printed matter (*e.g.,* the British "Book Post" of 1848). These reduced rates were perhaps originally intended to favour the spread of education but quickly expanded, under the vigorous pressure of vested interests, to cover all sorts of commercial documents, advertising matter, magazines, etc. An inexpensive form of correspondence, the postcard, first introduced by Austria in 1869, was soon adopted by most other countries.

The general postal reforms of the mid-19th century ensured maximum benefit from the technological progress in transport in the great age of the railway and the steamship. These new modes of conveyance permitted a far speedier, more regular, and more reliable mail service, both internally and internationally. Railways in particular had a marked effect on the organization of postal work: instead of merely using trains to carry mailbags more speedily, postal administrations soon introduced the practice of sorting the letters in transit, using specially adapted railway cars. This greatly multiplied the advantages of railway

Effect of railways

conveyance. The first traveling, or railway, post offices ran in 1838 between Birmingham and Liverpool and London and Preston. By the end of the century, Britain, many continental European countries, the United States, and India had built up a complex network of such services, allowing the delivery of letters the day after mailing at distances three or four times as great as had been possible with the stagecoach, exceeding 400 miles in some cases.

International postal reform: the Universal Postal Union. The advent of the steamship and the railway had provided the opportunity for speedier international postal services, and the expansion of commerce ensured a growing demand for such facilities. Unfortunately, serious obstacles to the free exchange of international mails existed. Postal relations between states were the subject of bilateral postal treaties that had multiplied alarmingly during the 19th century. Most large European states were party to at least a dozen treaties by the 1860s. Such treaties necessitated the maintenance of detailed accounts between the countries concerned. Owing to the bewildering variety of currencies and units of weight and measurement then in use, the accounts attained a complexity described by a contemporary postmaster general of the United States as "almost beyond belief." Understandably, the users of the post suffered from this chaotic situation and from the high international postage rates that were its natural result.

The first practical step toward reform did not come until May 1863, when the delegates of 15 European and American postal administrations met at the Paris Postal Conference, convening at the suggestion of the U.S. postmaster general. The conference established important general principles for the simplification of procedures, which were adopted as a model for subsequent bilateral treaties by the countries concerned.

The Paris Postal Conference

The final step required the embodiment of these principles in a formal international treaty and the creation of an organization to administer them. An example was set by another conference at Paris two years later, which established the International Telegraph Union. Similar developments in the postal field were delayed by the advent of the American Civil War and the Franco-German War.

In 1868, however, a plan for a general postal union was put forward by the director of posts of the North German Confederation. Eventually, an international postal congress met, on Sept. 15, 1874, in Bern. It was attended by representatives of 22 states, all European except for Egypt and the United States. On October 9 a "Treaty concerning the Establishment of a General Postal Union" was signed. It was implemented on July 1, 1875, when the General Postal Union came into being. This title was changed in 1878 to the Universal Postal Union (UPU), and the basic treaty was renamed the Universal Postal Convention. The treaty provides a uniform framework of rules and procedures for the exchange of international mails. The union grew rapidly, increasing its membership to 55 within 10 years. By 1914, when China was admitted, it included almost all independent countries. The scope of the union's activities also expanded. In addition to its primary role, it gradually extended its functions to cover other international services provided by postal administrations, such as money orders (1878), parcel post (1885), postal checks (1920), cash on delivery (1947), and savings banks (1957). The UPU has been a specialized agency of the United Nations since 1948.

Activities of the UPU

Development of airmail. Balloon posts, apart from those organized during the sieges of Paris (1870) and Przemyśl (1915), for the most part only carried souvenir mail, owing to the balloons' uncontrollability. Airships overcame this problem but, again, did not establish themselves as a regular means of mail transport. It was only through the development of the airplane in the early decades of the 20th century that airmail truly came into its own. Certain experiments had been undertaken before World War I, such as airmail service between Hendon, on the northwestern outskirts of London, and Windsor in 1911 to mark the coronation of George V and flights between Paris and Bordeaux in 1913. Regular flights did not begin in the United States until 1918, and it was not until 1919, when the reliability of airplanes had considerably improved, that the

first regular international service was introduced—between London and Paris. Other European links soon followed. On the long-distance continental and intercontinental routes airmail demonstrated its clear superiority over all surface transport. Technical factors delayed progress in opening up longer routes. The first American transcontinental airmail flight took place in 1920, but regular service did not begin until 1924. In 1926 a service between Egypt and Karāchi began and was linked to London in 1929. It was extended to Singapore by 1933 and to Australia in 1934. It was not until 1939 that a regular air service across the North Atlantic was launched with the takeoff of the *Yankee Clipper,* an American seaplane, on May 20.

While the growing availability of air flight did not affect basic postal organization as profoundly as the railways, its advantages of speed and operational reliability have been exploited in different ways since the 1920s. Prior to World War II, a number of European countries adopted the practice of forwarding letters to distant destinations at no extra cost to the sender (such as British mails sent to most parts of the British Empire). The consistently high costs of airmail curtailed this trend after the war. During the mid-1960s the UPU, in response to the continuing increase of aircraft capacity, adopted the policy of maximizing air conveyance of mail. In the mid-1970s, the concept of "surface air-lifted" (SAL) mails was developed in conjunction with the International Air Transport Association (IATA). This arrangement allows some mails to receive, for little or no surcharge, speedier transmission than by surface, but without the priority of fully surcharged mails. Use of SAL varies from country to country.

For individual correspondence, the most practical and inexpensive form of airmail remains the compact aerogram, which was introduced in Britain during World War II as a convenient way of writing to overseas military personnel. It consists of a sheet of lightweight paper suitably folded and gummed on all sides. Recognized by the UPU, the aerogram is available in most countries.

The aerogram

Advanced communications technology. Rapidly advancing computer and data transmission technologies of the late 20th century are being felt far more widely within the postal sector than were previous advances, such as improved roads, the railway, and the airplane. Although the latter enabled postal services to reform or enhance existing services, today's technologies go further by providing alternatives to the letter in the form of electronic messaging networks and electronic data-processing techniques to improve administrative efficiency.

NATIONAL POSTAL SYSTEMS

United States. Although the first official reference to overseas mail arrangements (concerning the receipt of overseas mail at Fairbanks' Tavern in Boston) dates to 1639, little real progress was made in building a postal system in colonial America until the appointment of Benjamin Franklin, formerly postmaster at Philadelphia, as deputy postmaster general for the American Colonies in 1753. Through diligent personal survey and inspection, he provided a more extensive, frequent, and speedier mail service, both within the Colonies and to England. Franklin built a sound foundation for the postal service in the United States, and, fittingly, he became its first postmaster general in 1775.

Postal service expanded rapidly after independence: annual revenue increased from $37,935 in 1790 to $1,707,-000 by 1829, when the postmaster general first became a member of the Cabinet. The heavy cost of establishing a postal structure to keep pace with the remarkable economic progress of the country and the accelerating extension of its settled area caused expenditure to rise even faster than revenue. The trend toward annual postal deficits, which began in the 1820s, often exceeded an annual figure of $5,000,000 later in the 19th century.

By 1901, however, this expenditure had produced remarkable results. The accessibility, quality, and range of services provided had improved immeasurably. The number of post offices stood at a peak of 76,945. Postage rates had been considerably reduced with the gradual adoption of the principles of Rowland Hill: a single uniform rate regardless of distance was adopted in 1863 (after an interim period with two rates since 1845), and postage stamps were introduced in 1847. Free collection services came with the provision of street letter boxes in 1858. A free delivery service was established in 1863, covering

Growth of services

49 cities and employing 440 letter carriers. By 1900 the service was provided at 796 offices by 15,322 carriers. The rural free delivery (RFD) service was introduced in 1896 and town delivery in 1912. These delivery services have greatly expanded their scope. The vast majority of mail is delivered by carriers, about one-tenth through post-office boxes, and only a small fraction at windows or counters.

The range of services available to the public has also grown steadily since the first supplementary postal service, registered mail, was introduced in 1855. The major milestones in this progress were postal money order service (1864); international money orders (1867); special delivery (1885); parcel post, with its accessory collect on delivery (COD) and insurances services (1913); and certified mail (1955), which provides proof of posting for items without intrinsic value. In 1911 a postal savings system was inaugurated, reaching a peak of more than 4,000,000 accounts in 1947. A decline to less than 1,000,000 depositors caused

Division of mail into four classes

the service to be discontinued in 1966. Mail was formally divided into three classes in 1863, and a fourth was added in 1879. First-class, or letter, mail (called letter post in the United Kingdom) is the basis of the postal service monopoly and, as the class of mail most commonly used by the public, has generally had a simplified rate structure. The other classes were established according to mail content: second-class consists of newspapers and magazines, third-class encompasses other printed matter and merchandise weighing less than one pound, and fourth-class mail is either merchandise or printed matter that weighs one pound or more. The addition of these classes allowed the post office to adopt more complicated rate structures that would take into account factors affecting handling costs—such as the weight of the piece and the distance it would be conveyed. Second-class mail receives preferential rates because the dissemination of information through newspapers and other publications is considered to serve the public interest.

The post office has played a vital role as a pioneer and major user of all systems of transport as each was developed: the stagecoach, steamboat, canals, and railroads; the short-lived pony express; and airlines and motor vehicles. It also helped subsidize their development. A traveling post-office system, in which mail could be sorted in transit, was introduced experimentally in 1862, and it made railway mail service the dominant form of mail conveyance well into the 20th century. The gradual reduction of passenger train services during the 1930s led to the birth of a highway post-office service in 1941. Both of these services declined rapidly in the 1950s and 1960s. Railway post-office mileage was reduced from 96,400,000 in 1965 to 10,100,000 in 1969, and the number of highway post offices in operation during that period fell from 163 to none. Conversely, annual ton-miles of airmail flown grew from 188,103,000 in 1965 to more than 1,000,000,000 by the 1980s, indicating the significant trend toward air transportation of regular mail without surcharge.

The United States maintains the largest postal system in the world, handling almost half the world's volume of postal traffic. To deal with the problem of increasing deficits and to improve the overall management and efficiency of the post office, the U.S. Congress approved the Postal Reorganization Act of 1970, signed into law Aug.

Postal Reorganization Act of 1970

12, 1970. The act transformed the Post Office Department into a government-owned corporation, called the United States Postal Service. Congress no longer retains power to fix postal tariffs (although changes may be vetoed) or to control employees' salaries, and political patronage has been virtually eliminated. Government subsidies continued on a declining basis until 1982, after which the U.S. Postal Service itself no longer received a direct subsidy from Congress. An indirect subsidy is still paid for certain mailers, however. These mailers, primarily nonprofit organizations or small publishers, pay lower rates than others, with Congress making up the difference in cost. The cor-

poration has authority to raise capital to modernize its equipment and buildings. It is also subject to competition from private companies, a situation that in 1977 led to the introduction of Express Mail, which guaranteed overnight delivery.

The availability of adequate funds for its mechanization and automation program has allowed the post office to benefit considerably from its sustained effort in research and development. More than half of all letter mail is handled by preparation and sorting machines, a trend greatly assisted by the ZIP (Zone Improvement Plan) Code program, which has come to be almost universally used.

Great Britain. The development of the British Post Office up to the reforms introduced by Rowland Hill has already been described. After 1840 the volume of postal traffic increased enormously and by 1870 had reached 10 times its prereform level. The growth was fostered by the introduction of new facilities, such as registration and postcards, and of preferential rates for books, printed papers, and samples. Financial services were also expanded: a savings bank was established in 1861, and postal orders were introduced in 1881 to supplement the money order service taken over from private interests in 1838. In 1883 a parcel post service was established.

The sweeping social reforms of the 20th century have given the post office an additional role as the chief payment agency for social security benefits, beginning with old-age pensions in 1908. This has been expanded to provide a variety of payments and also to collect large sums for state insurance schemes. The scale and range of financial transactions have been further boosted by the establishment in 1968 of the post office's banking arm, National Girobank, which provides an improved money transfer arrangement for the settlement of bills, as well as an account banking system and loan facilities.

British Post Office social services

Another important 20th-century trend has been the gradual recognition of the post office's role as a commercial enterprise rather than a government revenue department. The process of achieving full commercial status took an important step forward in October 1969, when the post office became a public corporation. The British Telecommunications Act of 1981 divided the post office into two corporations, one for postal and banking operations and the other for telecommunications. This law also has provisions for the suspension of the post office's monopoly in certain categories of mail, allowing private companies to compete with it.

To maintain quality of service economically by removing the need to handle nonpriority mail at peak periods, a change to a two-tier system of letter classification was started in September 1968. The system abolished the complex preferential rate structure for printed papers and similar material—based on the contents of correspondence—and substituted the more relevant criterion of priority. The sender indicates the urgency of the item as being high (first-class) or lower (second-class) and pays on this basis, which simplifies the work of accepting the mail.

As in a number of other postal administrations, the sorting of mail has been gradually mechanized since the mid-1960s, with some 80 mechanized offices replacing more than 600 offices. The key to mechanization is an alphanumeric postal code that provides for sorting by machine at every stage of handling, including the carrier's delivery route. The coding equipment translates the postal code into a pattern of dots by means of which machines can sort mail at eight times the speed of manual sorting.

The post office transports mail by road, rail, and increasingly by air. More than half still travels by rail, using an extensive network of railway traveling post offices. To improve service and to enable next-day delivery for remote areas, letters are flown each night either by scheduled or chartered aircraft. New services based on communications and computer technology have been introduced. The Intelpost facsimile service operates nationally and with many other countries. An electronic mail system enables data for large mailings to be transmitted to local centres for enveloping and delivery.

France. The chief stages in the pre-Revolutionary development of postal services in France have already been described. With the Revolution the system of farming, or selling the right to operate a postal service, was abolished. In the years following the 1789 Revolution, the postal and stagecoach services were reorganized into a Directorate of Posts, which became a national monopoly organization on June 16, 1801. After a brief return to the farming system a general Directorate of Posts attached to the Ministry of Finance was created in 1804. During the 19th century, the service developed to keep pace with the Industrial Revolution, notably through improvements in administration and transportation. The first French postage stamp was issued on Jan. 1, 1849, thereby introducing the principle of prepayment as well as simplifying the rate structure. The scope and range of the postal administration's activities widened in the 19th century to include postal money orders (1817), registered letters (1829), parcel post (1881), the savings bank (1881), and postal checks (giro; 1918). During these years the post also took advantage of the newly developing methods of transport. Rail transport, for example, introduced in 1841, was so successful that by 1892 it had become an established means of conveyance; postal steamships served more than 100 ports; and bicycles and, later, motor vehicles were provided for postmen's collection rounds. In the early 1900s a full motor vehicle service was set up for the conveyance of mails in Paris.

French airmail service

The knack of turning technological innovation to good account was repeated with the airplane. The first airmail flights within France began in 1918, and in 1919 an irregular route was established between Avignon and Nice; by 1935 a network of routes linked the main French cities. During that period, the exploits of Antoine de Saint-Exupéry, Juan Mermoz, and other pilots of the Aéropostale airline, founded by Pierre Latécoère, served to establish an overseas network with French West Africa and Latin America.

World War II severely disrupted the postal service, and the German occupation forces exerted strict control over mail conveyed within a homeland that had been divided into virtually separate zones. The reinstatement of night airmail service in 1945 marked the beginning of a period of rapid reorganization for the postwar French postal service. Eventually the propeller-driven aircraft was replaced by relatively quiet turbojets, carrying 20 times the amount of airmail dispatched in 1948. Additionally, the postal service acquired its own custom-built rolling stock, which is used on the high-speed train run between Paris and Lyon. Daily mail traffic has grown by some two and a half times since the early postwar years, and, to cope with the increased volume, work began in the late 1970s on a network of mechanized sorting centres.

To speed up and reduce the cost of processing this huge quantity of mail traffic, the French postal service introduced a two-tier system in January 1969, thus enabling the customer to choose the priority of service desired by paying an appropriate charge. The postal service also entered the express mail market with the Postadex service, which operates with more than 50 other countries, and a national and international facsimile transmission service (Postéclair) has been established. An electronic mail printing and delivery service is being developed. The banking and savings service has also embarked upon a comprehensive program involving the microcomputerization of virtually every aspect of local office operation, as well as actively exploiting memory-card technology.

West Germany. Postal organization in Germany remained on a relatively small scale until the latter half of the 19th century because of the numerous and fragmented sovereign states. The need for a more widely based postal system had been met, to a certain degree, since the 16th century, when the Thurn and Taxis postal service was begun. The fragmented political state of Germany, in fact, allowed the Thurn and Taxis organization to survive until 1867, when its last privileges were acquired by the postal service of the North German Confederation.

Establishment of the German postal service

The unification of Germany under Prussia during the second half of the 19th century, culminating in the establishment of the German Empire in January 1871, was followed by the creation of a German postal service in the same year, under a law establishing a state monopoly for conveying letters and newspapers. In 1924 the postal administration was accorded a considerable degree of financial autonomy, which allowed it to conduct business in a semicommercial manner, while still taking account of national economic and social factors in determining rate structure and pattern of service. The post office has developed a complete range of normal postal and financial services and an extensive postal passenger transport network and carries out various social security, revenue, and other agency functions.

Mail is transported chiefly by rail, but there is also an extensive complementary postal road network and an important night airmail service. The air service, inaugurated in 1961, carries letters and postcards without surcharge.

The present-day operation of the West German post office has been affected by two major factors. The first of these has been increased competition, which has brought about the adoption of customer-oriented business policies, along with appropriate reorganization. As a result, the post office entered the express mail market with overseas (Datapost) and inland services and introduced the surface air-lifted (SAL) parcel service to overseas destinations. The second factor has been the rapid technological development that has taken place over the same period. This has been an agent of change in a number of ways: a new general messaging service, incorporating different forms of electronic mail and the traditional letter mail, is under development; entirely new services such as cash dispensing, interactive videotext, and money services based on memory cards have been introduced; and the post office has exploited modern technology to increase its administrative efficiency and ability to compete.

Introduction of new mail services

Italy. A long history of organized postal systems in Italy began with the *cursus publicus* of the Romans, but a modern national postal system was not established until 1862, when the long process of unifying the former small sovereign states into the new Kingdom of Italy had been completed. The new state postal service was given a monopoly for the collection, conveyance, and delivery of letters, printed papers, and newspapers, and a uniform tariff was established. The monopoly was surrendered for printed papers and newspapers in 1873 but was extended to cover parcels up to 20 kilograms in 1923. A registration service also began in 1862, and postal orders were introduced, extending on a national scale a service that had been made available to the public in the former Kingdom of Sardinia as early as 1845. The Post Office Savings Bank, set up in 1875, and the postal check service, founded in 1917, are other important aspects of the postal service. The post office also acts as an agency for the payment of such social security benefits as state pensions and various other grants.

Railways are the chief means of mail transport, although their use has declined since 1965, while road and particularly air transport have increased significantly, with the need for next-day service between major cities, such as Milan and Palermo. The Italian postal mechanization program moved forward significantly after the late 1970s. In the larger cities mechanized centres have been constructed in which electronic address-reading equipment processes mail for delivery, provided certain physical specifications are met.

Soviet Union. Following the October Revolution of 1917, postal services in the Soviet Union underwent important development, particularly in what are now the Central Asian republics of Kazakh, Kirgiz, Tadzhik, Turkmen, and Uzbek, where the number of post offices is now 30 to 40 times that of the 1913 figure. Today, state enterprises and individual customers alike are served by a network of some 90,000 post offices, about three-fourths of which are located in rural areas that prior to 1917 had little or no service.

For a country with an area of 8,600,400 square miles (22,000,000 square kilometres), air transport is singularly significant among the available types of transport. It accounts for about 60 percent of all postal traffic, which totals some 54,500,000,000 items annually, about 80 percent of which consists of newspapers and magazines. Prompt delivery of central press publications is now achieved by facsimile transmission of text, in some cases by satellite, for decentralized printing. These facilities contributed, in the early 1980s, to a significant increase in the volume of periodicals handled.

All types of mail can be processed by a national network of large sorting centres, which is constantly being improved. Work in public offices is being mechanized in various ways, an example being the national automation of postal order operations. Increasing use is being made of computers at all levels of administration, particularly on mail handling and transport. Postal research efforts aim toward improving productivity, staff working conditions, and service to the public.

China. The first use of a postal system in China was under the Chou dynasty (*c.* 1111–255 BC). A reference by Confucius in the late 6th century demonstrates that it was already renowned for its efficiency: "The influence of the righteous travels faster than a royal edict by post-station service."

By the late 3rd century BC the postal network consisted of relays of couriers, who changed their mounts at staging posts about nine miles apart. This network was considerably enlarged following the opening of new territories in Central Asia under the Han dynasty (206 BC–AD 220), during which time contacts were made with the Romans, who, it was observed, maintained a postal system similar to that of the Han. Further improvements were made under the T'ang dynasty (618–907). During this period the number of staging posts increased, and correspondence could be conveyed by road or by river. Administered centrally by the secretary for transport under the Ministry of War, the postal service underwent periodic checks for quality of service. It was possible for urgent documents to be conveyed up to 93 miles in a day. The Sung dynasty (960–1279) instituted a parallel express service for military correspondence, its couriers regularly traveling as far as 124 miles in a day and even more in cases of extreme urgency. The postal network that had evolved under the T'ang and the Sung was to prove a valuable base for organizing the posts under later dynasties. In the late 13th century Marco Polo revealed to Europe the quality of the Chinese postal system under the Yüan, or Mongol, dynasty (1206–1368). Nothing comparable existed in Europe at the time.

Improvements under the Han dynasty

Until the end of the 14th century the post was used purely for the conveyance of official documents. At the beginning of the 15th century private post offices for the use of traders appeared, conveying private correspondence and arranging payment transfers. During the middle years of the Ch'ing dynasty (1644–1911/12) there were several thousand of these private post offices. In 1896 the Imperial Post was created and organized along European lines, and the old staging points that had functioned for more than 3,000 years were phased out. The new state system gradually absorbed the business of the private companies, although the last one did not close its doors until 1935. The last of the foreign post offices (maintained by Britain, the United States, France, Germany, and the Soviet Union) was withdrawn by the end of 1922.

The Imperial Post

When the Republic was proclaimed after the 1911 Revolution had overthrown the Ch'ing dynasty, the service was renamed the Chinese Post. In 1914 China joined the UPU. Development of services was extremely slow, however, because of internal strife and eight years of resistance to the Japanese invasion. Thus, on the eve of the founding of the People's Republic, there were only 4,868 postal establishments throughout the whole of China, of which 463 alone were in country areas. Postal transport was minimal by present-day standards.

One month after the proclamation of the People's Republic of China on Oct. 1, 1949, the Ministry of Posts and Telecommunications was established. On the mainland this administration reorganized the postal service, known thereafter as the People's Post of China. Much was accomplished in the years that followed. The mainland postal network grew to more than 3,000,000 miles of roads, railways, and air routes centred upon the capital, Peking. It reached into every corner of the land to serve remote towns and villages where prior to 1949 the postal service was hardly known. Letter mail has increased fourfold since the late 1940s.

Postal research centres set up during the 1950s have actively exploited new technology in the design and manufacture of specialized equipment for the postal service. Notable examples include sorting machines using optical character or bar recognition (OCR or OBR) and computer- and microprocessor-controlled sorting machines.

India. The earliest reference to an official postal system in India was made in the 14th century by the Arab traveler and historian Ibn Baṭṭūṭah, remarking upon the organized official service of mounted couriers and runners. The system was brought to its height during the 16th century under the great Mughal emperor Akbar, with a network of 2,000 miles of post roads. Two centuries of political turmoil, without a strong central authority, destroyed this courier system. It was not until 1766 that an official post was reestablished to serve a new ruling power. It was made available for public use in 1774.

In 1837 the Imperial Post was established and granted a monopoly to provide efficient postal communications between the seat of government at Calcutta and the principal provincial towns. Within the provincial districts a complementary local service was maintained. In 1854 the basis of the modern Indian Post Office was established when these parallel systems were merged under a director general. A uniform postage rate was then introduced, a step of particular significance in so vast a country.

Establishment of the Indian Post Office

International postal relations developed rapidly after the establishment of a weekly steamer service between Bombay and England in 1867, with India becoming a member of the UPU by 1876. At the same time, the post office began to expand the range of services provided to the public: COD in 1877, an insured service in 1878, and money orders in 1880.

Internal communications were improved to keep pace with the progress made in these other fields. The "bullock train"—the Indian equivalent of the mail coach—gave way to the growing network of railways. A regular traveling post-office service was introduced in 1870. Although experiments with airmail conveyance started in 1911, a regular inland service did not begin until 1932. Rapid expansion followed in 1949. A complex night airmail network connects all major cities, carrying a growing percentage of the mail. Railways have retained much of the traffic as a result of speedier train services, although motor vehicles have become the dominant carrier of mail.

More traditional forms of transport—the foot runner, horse, mule, camel, bullock cart, and bicycle—still help distribute mail to many of India's villages. More than one-half of these now have daily delivery of letters, and almost all have at least weekly delivery.

Pakistan. Although Pakistan did not exist as an independent sovereign state until 1947, its postal history extends to the official postal systems established by Muslim emperors. Particularly noteworthy was the network of post relays at caravansaries (inns) established by the emperor Shēr Shāh of Sūr in the early 16th century. Under British rule in 1852, the province of Sind had the distinction of being the first region in the subcontinent to adopt a uniform letter postage rate.

On becoming independent, Pakistan was faced with a particularly difficult problem of postal communications because its eastern and western regions were separated by 1,000 miles of Indian territory. The growth of civil aviation services and maritime links overcame the initial difficulty. In 1952 an airmail service was introduced between East and West Pakistan in which letters and postcards were carried without payment of surcharge. This concessionary airmail system was extended to cover the internal mail service of both regions in 1959. The post office made use of the entire network of the national airline to connect 29 key points throughout the country. The service for printed paper and parcel mail was improved in 1962 by the introduction of direct sea-mail links between Karāchi and Chittagong.

Pakistan airmail service

The creation of Bangladesh out of East Pakistan in 1971 allowed Pakistan to improve its internal mail services, especially in rural areas, where three-fourths of the post offices are located. Postal facilities were greatly expanded throughout the country.

The post office is run on a commercial accounting basis but with strong emphasis on its function as a public utility. Postal traffic has grown rapidly. To improve its capacity to deal efficiently with the continuing growth, the postal administration has pursued a carefully considered and moderate policy of mechanization. At some of the busiest offices, machines designed to facilitate the acceptance of registered mail have been introduced. To speed up the handling of mail in sorting offices, electromechanical sorting machines have been installed at Karāchi and Lahore. All major post offices now use electrically operated stamp-canceling machines, as well as franking machines.

Japan. Although official and private systems of communications had existed in Japan from ancient times, it was not until 1870 that the creation of a comprehensive government-operated postal service was proposed. The idea was put forward by Hisoka Maejima, often called "the Father of the Post" in Japan. It was rapidly accepted by the government, which set up a service between Tokyo and Ōsaka on April 20, 1871, and extended it throughout the country in July 1872. In 1873 the postal service was proclaimed a monopoly and private courier systems were prohibited, a uniform postal tariff scale was adopted, and postage stamps and postcards were introduced. The first official overseas mail service was established in 1875 with the United States. International postal relations expanded rapidly, and in 1877 Japan became a member of the UPU.

Other landmarks include the introduction of a parcel post service in 1892, express delivery in 1911, airmail in 1929, and the achievement of a special accounting status on semicommercial lines in 1934.

A distinctive feature of the postal scene in Japan is the special New Year's Mail Service, introduced in 1900. Operating partly for the benefit of charities, this provides for the timely delivery of billions of New Year greetings.

Japan's postal code address system
The shortage of manual labour and the growth in postal business resulting from the country's rapid economic development have also led to the adoption of an extensive mechanization policy. To facilitate this process, a postal code address system was introduced in July 1968. Japanese-produced segregating and sorting equipment, including automatic postal code reader-sorters, has been installed at major post offices throughout the country.

POSTAL SERVICES IN THE DEVELOPING COUNTRIES

The establishment of efficient and comprehensive postal systems in the developing countries is important internationally as well as from the purely domestic viewpoint. Successful maintenance and progressive improvement of international postal service require the effective cooperation of all member countries of the UPU.

The internal need for a good postal service is sufficient in itself, however, to justify a high priority. A country-wide network of post offices provides government with many points of contact with its people for implementing administrative programs in such fields as social security, taxation, and public information. When its operation is properly developed, the post office may also become one of the principal employers in a country; it may help to promote economic growth through its need for buildings, vehicles, and equipment; and it has the potential to become a major user of transport services. The employment potential of a postal system is evident from the fact that the percentage of the working population engaged in providing postal services is generally several times higher in developed than in developing countries.

Importance to national economies
An efficient postal service, in addition to promoting national cohesion, provides an essential infrastructure for the expansion of industry and commerce. Postal money transfer and savings services are particularly valuable in developing economies, where banking facilities are limited. They may generate large resources that can be used for public investment.

Postal administrations in developed countries have long appreciated the importance of collaborating in the improvement of postal services throughout the world, and this participation in postal technical assistance is an aim embodied in the constitution of the Universal Postal Union. In addition to fostering bilateral assistance between members, the UPU itself has, since 1964, taken part as a specialized agency in the United Nations Development Programme (UNDP). UPU activities in this field are monitored and realigned as necessary at each postal congress.

In view of the rapid expansion of postal business in most developing countries, the training of staff is a most urgent need. The UPU's initial activity has, therefore, been largely devoted to this field. The needs of individual countries are evaluated by traveling postal experts attached to the International Bureau in Bern. In addition, expert aid is provided for the establishment of national training schools for postal workers and regional centres for middle and higher management staff, such as those set up in Abidjan, Ivory Coast, and in Bangkok and Damascus. Special instructor-training courses are conducted in Britain and France, as well as in multinational schools in Africa, Asia, and Latin America, where seminars are also held for higher grade officials. Specialist aid is also provided to evaluate operational and organizational needs and subsequently to enlist UNDP assistance in meeting them. The missions of experts are thus directed either to the postal services in general or to a certain sector of postal activity. Some larger projects may include overall postal organization as well as postal training; such projects have been undertaken in Ethiopia and Niger. Fellowships are awarded for overseas study of specialized subjects, such as international mails, philately, and, in particular, instructor training. Although the UNDP provides the major share of technical assistance funds, the UPU has increasingly supplemented these from its own resources to meet the increasing demand for assistance from its members. Moreover, a considerable amount of aid is given directly by developed countries within the framework of their own bilateral technical assistance arrangements.

Many developing countries are not able to provide even the minimum scale of postal facilities. To underline the pressing need for improvement and to provide a yardstick for future progress, the UPU has adopted, for the Second and Third United Nations Development Decades, certain key planning objectives, covering management, quality of service, promotion of its financial services, and improved public information. These are to be carried out to favour, in particular, the least developed countries. *UPU planning objectives*

THE INTERNATIONAL SYSTEM

International mail is a key means of furthering economic, social, and cultural links between nations. The international postal system is in itself an outstanding example of worldwide organization and mutual trust. A postal administration relies completely upon the postal authorities of other countries to play their parts in ensuring that its foreign mails reach their destination.

International cooperation in this field has been greatly facilitated by the Universal Postal Union since 1875. It has built a comprehensive international organization, with a membership composed of numerous sovereign states and several dependent territories. The postal administrations that are not represented generally follow the rules of the UPU.

These fundamental rules of the international postal service are to be found in the Universal Postal Convention and General Regulations and have been little changed since adoption of the Bern Treaty. The first basic principle is that all member countries form "a single postal territory for the reciprocal exchange of correspondence." From it is derived the principle of freedom of transit: every member country guaranteeing to respect the inviolability of transit mails and to forward them by the most rapid transport used for its own mails.

Another important principle is that the charges for letter-post items are not shared. Since 1875 each country has retained the postage it collects on international mail. Although intermediate countries are paid for transit service, the country in which the mail is delivered receives no payment. This principle was adopted in order to minimize the need for complex international accounts and was justified on the supposition that a letter normally generates a reply. Certain developing countries, however, have found themselves at a considerable disadvantage under this rule, due to an excessive imbalance between incoming and outgoing mail. To remedy this, the 1969 Congress of Tokyo provided for compensatory payments in such cases.

Provisions of the Universal Postal Convention

As a further measure of simplification, the convention prescribes international postal charges, as well as agreed tolerances, and specifies weight steps, limits of size, and conditions of acceptance for letter-post items. Disputes between postal administrations, which usually concern allocation of liability for the loss of registered or insured items, are to be settled by arbitration. The convention is completed by two other basic documents: the Final Protocol, which allows member countries to register certain general and specific reservations to the provisions of the convention; and the Detailed Regulations for implementing the convention. Apart from these obligatory documents, there are a number of optional agreements concerning services, such as parcel post and cash on delivery. The provision of a registration service is compulsory under the convention.

Mention should also be made of the constitutive acts of the union that prescribe its general aims, its organization, its financial structure, and the rules of membership, namely, the constitution and its general regulations.

This comprehensive framework of international regulations is regularly revised to take account of changing circumstances and technical advances. This is the chief function of the union's quinquennial congress. Between congresses, the continuity of the union's work is ensured by its elected Executive Council and its permanent office in Bern, the International Bureau. The bureau acts as a clearinghouse for the settlement of international accounts and for the exchange of information between members, especially notifications of important operational and organizational changes. Problems arising in the technical, operational, and economic fields are studied by another permanent organ, the Consultative Council for Postal Studies (CCPS). Regular contact is also maintained with other international bodies, such as the International Telecommunications Union and the International Standards Organisation.

The UPU Constitution authorizes member countries to establish restricted unions, a provision that enables regional groups such as the Arab, African, and Asian–Pacific postal unions to conclude agreements aimed at improving postal services between their members by such means as reduced rates of postage or the elimination of transit fees. These agreements are more easily achieved on a limited regional basis than on a worldwide scale, and the restricted unions have a valuable role in the task of the UPU, which is, basically, to improve international postal service by simplifying its organization and reducing its cost.

POSTAL TECHNOLOGY

Technological progress in postal transport. Postal administrations have been among the first to utilize new forms of transport. They have often applied considerable technical skill in maximizing the benefits to be derived from progress in this field, particularly in originating the traveling post-office concept and apparatus enabling express trains to pick up and discharge mails without slowing. They have also developed their own transport systems to combat traffic congestion in certain busy cities, such as the pneumatic tubes of Paris, New York, and other cities and the automatic underground railway, opened in 1927, that links London's chief mail centres to railway terminals.

The advent of aerospace and telecommunications technology in the mid-20th century gave rise to research aimed at adapting this technology to postal systems. Experiments

Experiments with missilery

have been conducted using ballistic missiles to transport mail, but this remains a novelty because of costs and the problems of reusability and accuracy. Advances in computer and message transmission technologies are, however, being utilized by postal administrations.

Since 1980 public facsimile services have been available in a number of advanced postal administrations in various parts of the world. The United States, Great Britain, France, and Sweden were among the first countries to introduce tele-impression services, whereby bulk correspondence in electronic form is transmitted to regional postal printing centres for enveloping and delivery.

Automation of mail handling. Since the 1950s there has been a marked intensification of research and development efforts to apply technology to the handling of mails, especially in countries faced with manpower problems and higher labour costs. The wide variety of projects undertaken in many countries and the progress made have been summarized in CCPS studies.

Actual implementation has generally been slower than expected. There have been good reasons for this. Primarily, most postal administrations, being government agencies, are subject to strict control of their capital investment programs. Second, mail traffic patterns—with marked peaks of work—make economic utilization of machines difficult: the introduction of measures to counteract this problem takes considerable time. Similarly, the introduction of postal address codes and the standardization of sizes of envelopes and cards, which are prerequisites for mechanical handling, are relatively slow because of difficulties inherent in the change of procedures.

Materials-handling equipment. Postal systems continue to rely heavily on human labour for bulk materials handling and distribution, both at loading bays and between work processes within sorting centres. New mail centres, however, are normally built in the style of factories and include all appropriate materials-handling equipment.

Equipment used for loading and unloading sacks of mail, rigid containers, and loose parcels includes mobile belt conveyors, roller conveyors, forklift trucks, mobile and fixed cranes, and table lifts. Handling equipment within buildings includes chain conveyors; horizontal and rising belt conveyors of all types, for the transport of loose letters, packets, and trays of letters (notably used for continuous clearance of public posting boxes); tow conveyors, which allow wheeled containers to be hooked onto a fixed-path underfloor traction system; bucket or pan elevators; and chutes and other gravity devices.

The use of a wide range of equipment is necessitated by the varied handling characteristics of different types of mail at particular stages. Buffer-storage facilities, in the form of ramps, hoppers, and moving belts, have to be incorporated to compensate for normal postal traffic fluctuations. The smooth distribution of traffic through the system is often monitored by closed-circuit television, which allows effective centralized control. Automatic regulation and recording, using a variety of sensing and counting devices linked to a computer, are the ideal. Modern systems-engineering techniques are thus able to ensure a carefully planned continuous mechanized mail flow with maximum productivity benefits.

Buffer-storage facilities

Segregating machines. Mail collected from branch post offices and street mailboxes, although for the most part made up of ordinary letters and cards, also contains small parcels, newspapers, magazines, and large envelopes. These items, because of their size or shape, cannot be handled on machinery designed for the normal-sized letter and have to be segregated from the majority of standard "machinable" letters. Owing to its varied characteristics, most packet mail has to be manually stamped and sorted, although its movement between work processes may be fully mechanized. So-called packet sorting machines are, in fact, essentially conveyor systems for distributing manually sorted mail.

A commonly adopted type of segregator consists of a laterally inclined rotating drum, into the upper end of which a regulated flow of "mixed" mail is fed from a storage conveyor. Letters within a thickness standard, but of excessive length or breadth, are picked out by various simple mechanical devices installed on the conveyor belt that eventually delivers machinable letters to the storage stacks of the facer–canceler equipment.

Facing and canceling equipment. Facing is the process of aligning letters so that all will have the address side facing the canceler, with stamps in a uniform position. The process is normally combined with a separation of the mail into at least two streams, letter and printed-paper rate or first- and second-class, to allow priority handling for one of the streams.

Facer–canceler machines perform these processes by passing letters through sensing or stamp-detecting units, which identify the presence or absence of a stamp on the side of the envelope facing them, and, when present, its position. Sensing units are also designed to separate mail in the priority class from nonpriority mail by identifying the stamp or commonly used combination of stamps representing the basic postage rate and manipulating selector gates accordingly. This identification is usually achieved by printing distinctive indexes on the stamps in normally invisible, phosphorescent or luminescent inks that are sensitive to ultraviolet radiation emitted by the sensing unit.

Coding and sorting machines. For manual sorting of letters, each operator normally uses a device with between 40 and 50 pigeonholes. This has been found by most administrations to be the optimum arrangement in view of the limited arm span and "memory" of the sorter. The

Mechanization by postal code

development of various types of postal codes was aimed at making the sorting of a coded letter a mechanical process for the operator by dispensing with the need to memorize a sorting plan. To be totally effective these schemes need complete public cooperation, a requirement that has been difficult to achieve.

Postal administrations have responded to this dilemma by concentrating research on using an operator only to impress the postal code on each letter, employing phosphorescent or magnetic ink patterns that can be read by a sensing unit attached to a sorting machine. After the code has been impressed, the letter can be sorted at any subsequent stage by high-speed automatic machines, which are no longer utilized at the pace of a single operator and indeed can take the output of several operators. Furthermore, any second sortation required—even at an intermediate office or where the code includes the necessary information to letter carriers' routes at the delivery office—does not need further manual operations. Another potential advantage of this method is that letters may be directly encoded by the mail-processing machines used by large-volume mailers.

Optical character recognition. The ultimate aim in automated sorting has been to perfect a machine that can read some or all elements of the address on letters. Research in this field has been conducted in most of the industrial nations with sophisticated postal services. The immediate aims of these national research programs vary insofar as the type of character to be recognized is concerned: printed, typewritten, or addressing-machine characters; stylized handwritten scripts; and even ordinary

Advanced machine sorting

handwriting. Some administrations require the machine to read a purely numeric code, others an alphanumeric code, and others the names of towns or regions. Several different techniques are used for the basic task of pattern matching in identifying the characters. For example, the observed character as a whole may be compared with matrices registered in the memory of the machine. Or the different traits of the character observed—vertical or horizontal strokes, curves, etc.—may be analyzed and their combination successively compared with a series of models registered by the computer.

An optical character reader (OCR) can be designed to either directly sort mail or mark it with a machine-readable code so that sorting at subsequent stages can be carried out by high-speed automatic machines. In 1965 the U.S. Postal Service began experimenting with an alphanumeric OCR. By the early 1980s the service had developed a machine capable of scanning up to three lines of an address, verifying the postal code, and imprinting the letter with a routing code.

Research in the United States subsequently has concentrated on various systems that print a machine-readable bar code to allow for high-speed automatic processing to individual carrier routes or blocks of addresses within carrier routes. In 1983 the U.S. Postal Service began deploying OCR's with this capability to major post offices throughout the country. The postal service regards this application of automation, combined with the use of ZIP+4

(a nine-digit postal code) by business mailers, as a major means of keeping postal costs under control as mail volumes expand.

Numerical speech translator. Another line of research being pursued in the United States is the development of equipment that translates five- and nine-digit ZIP codes and sorting-code numbers spoken by an operator into instructions for a sorting machine. Since this system obviates the need for a keyboard, it leaves the operator's hands free, making it particularly valuable in the operation of parcel- and sack-sorting machines. It also eliminates the need for keyboard training of operators. The testing of the equipment includes determination of the effects of regional speech variations, background noise, and operator speech fatigue.

BIBLIOGRAPHY. Postal services are treated in official publications, such as legislative texts, manuals, working instructions, postal guides, annual reports, and commission reports; much of this material is available to the public. Many postal administrations publish periodical reviews or bulletins informing employees and users of recent events and trends. ROWLAND HILL, *Post Office Reform: Its Importance and Practicability,* 4th ed. (1838), is a work by an expert whose reforms affected subsequent worldwide postal development; ROWLAND HILL and GEORGE BIRKBECK HILL, *The Life of Sir Rowland Hill and the History of Penny Postage,* 2 vol. (1880), provides a fuller account of Sir Rowland's innovations. Detailed studies of specific postal service aspects are A.D. SMITH, *The Development of Rates of Postage* (1917); A.D. LITTLE, *The Market for Postal Services* (1968); and MICHAEL E. CORBY, *The Postal Business 1969–79: A Study in Public Sector Management* (1979). International mail services are treated in GEORGE A. CODDING, JR., *The Universal Postal Union* (1964); and L. ZILLIACUS, *Mail for the World: From the Carrier to the Universal Postal Union* (1953), a popular treatment; both F. STAFF, *Transatlantic Mail* (1956, reissued 1980); and HOWARD ROBINSON, *Carrying British Mails Overseas* (1964), provide detailed treatment of the expansion of international mail conveyance.

General and historical literature includes HANS RACKOW (ed.), *Handwörterbuch des Postwesens,* 2nd ed. (1953), a small but comprehensive encyclopaedia; HMSO, *The Post Office: An Historical Summary* (1911); IVIE G.J. HAMILTON, *An Outline of Postal History and Practice with a History of the Post Office of India* (1910); HOWARD. ROBINSON, *The British Post Office* (1948, reissued 1970); and D. NORONA (ed.), *Cyclopedia of United States Postmarks and Postal History* (1933–35, reprinted 1975). Studies concerning the United States include PRESIDENT'S COMMISSION ON POSTAL ORGANIZATION, *Towards Postal Excellence,* 5 vol. (1968), also known as the Kappel Commission Report; CARL H. SCHEELE, *A Short History of the Mail Service* (1970); G. CULLINAN, *The Post Office Department* (1968); ROBERT J. MYERS, *The Coming Collapse of the Post Office* (1975); ALAN L. SORKIN, *The Economics of the Postal System: Alternatives and Reform* (1980); RICHARD J. MARGOLIS, *At the Crossroads: An Inquiry into Rural Post Offices and the Communities They Serve* (1980); JOHN T. TIERNEY, *Postal Reorganization: Managing the Public's Business* (1981); and *Evaluation of The United States Postal Service* (1982), a report by a panel of the National Academy of Public Administration. Somewhat dated but still useful are WILLIAM SMITH, *The History of the Post Office in British North America, 1639–1870* (1920, reprinted 1973); and WAYNE E. FULLER, *R.F.D.: The Changing Face of Rural America* (1964, reprinted 1966). The postal history of France is extensively described in EUGÈNE VAILLÉ, *Histoire générale des postes françaises,* 6 vol. (1947–53), and *Histoire des postes françaises,* 2 vol. (1946–47). Postal services in developing countries are treated in UNION POSTALE UNIVERSELLE, *Memorandum on the Role of the Post as a Factor in Economic and Social Development* (1969).

The origins, development, and procedures of the Universal Postal Union are treated in GEORGE A. CODDING, JR., *The Universal Postal Union* (1964); see also the bimonthly review *Union Postale,* which is devoted to a wide range of questions concerning the UPU and various general aspects of postal activities; and "Collection of Postal Studies," a series by the UPU's CONSULTATIVE COUNCIL FOR POSTAL STUDIES, comprising more than 150 reports on postal service modernization, mechanization, economics, transport, and working methods, available in French with much of the material also available in English.

(An.C.B./Ed.)

Prague

One of the finest cities of Europe, Prague (Czech: Praha), the capital of Czechoslovakia and that nation's major economic and cultural centre, lies at the heart of the Continent. The city has a rich architectural heritage that reflects both the uncertain currents of history in Bohemia and an urban life extending back more than 1,000 years. The physical attractions and landmarks of the city are many. Among the finest is the Charles Bridge (Karlův most), which stands astride the Vltava River. The winding course of the Vltava, with its succession of bridges and changing vistas, contrasts with the ever-present backdrop of the great castle of Hradčany (Prague Castle), which dominates the left-bank region of the city from behind massive walls set high on a hill. The narrow streets and little taverns and restaurants of the older quarters contrast with the broad sweep of Wenceslas Square and modern parks and housing developments, while the great 18th-century Baroque palaces have their own elegance and splendour. Seen from the surrounding hills, the many church towers make up a unique perspective, giving

Prague its description as the "city of a hundred spires." This architectural harmony has been enhanced by post-1945 planning, which has preserved the ancient core of the city as a major monument and has carefully supervised all modern building.

Prague is famous for its cultural life: Wolfgang Amadeus Mozart lived there, and his *Prague Symphony* and *Don Giovanni* were first performed in the city; the lyric music of the great Czech composers Bedřich Smetana, Antonín Dvořák, and Leoš Janáček is commemorated each year in a spring music festival. The U kalicha ("At the Chalice") beer parlour, still popular with local residents and tourists alike, provided the setting for the humorously anti-authoritarian activities of Schweik, immortalized by the novelist Jaroslav Hašek in *The Good Soldier Schweik*. The writings of Franz Kafka, dwelling in a different way on the dilemmas and predicaments of modern life, also seem indissolubly linked with life in this city.

This article is divided into the following sections:

Physical and human geography

THE LANDSCAPE

From its original small riverside settlements Prague has spread over its hills, up river valleys, and along riverside terraces. The Prague metropolitan area covers 192 square miles (496 square kilometres).

The city's core, with its historic buildings, bridges, and museums, is a major centre of employment and traffic congestion. Around the core is a mixed zone of industrial and residential areas, containing about half the city's population and nearly half its jobs. Surrounding this area is the outer city development zone and beyond this yet another zone of development containing new industrial areas, parks and recreation areas, and sports facilities. Finally, there is a belt of agricultural land and open countryside, where state farms and market gardening projects satisfy Prague's demand for food.

The lowest point in the city is 623 feet (190 metres) above sea level and the highest is 1,247 feet, on White Mountain (Bílá hora). The climate of Prague is typically mid-continental, with a July average temperature of 67° F (19.3° C), while that of January averages 31° F (−0.6° C).

THE PEOPLE

Prague has a homogeneous population. There is a small Slovak community, but the overwhelming majority of residents are Czechs. The city has a number of demographic peculiarities stemming mainly from the effects of World War II; there are more women than men, and a sizable proportion of the female population is past the age of fertility. The natural rate of population increase is very small. A tendency toward small families is a reflection of both difficulties in housing and increased participation by both parents in the work force. Migration into the city has continued.

THE ECONOMY

Industry and employment. Though Prague is renowned for its cultural life and monuments, it has also played an important role in the economic life of Czechoslovakia since the early and intensive development in the 19th century of such industries as those producing textiles and machinery. Industry is the largest employer, followed by commerce, construction, education, culture, administration, and transport and communications. Nearly half the labour force is female; the proportion of women in manufacturing is almost one-half, but in education and culture, in trade, and in the health field, it is considerably higher.

In manufacturing, production of machinery occupies the majority of workers, followed, in about equal numbers, by the production of food, electronics, and chemicals. A large portion of manufactured products are consumer goods.

As part of a decentralization plan for the city's growth, since the 1950s industrial districts and warehouses have been located or relocated on the outskirts of Prague. The aim is to provide increased job opportunities in the vicinity of new residential areas, thereby reducing the pressure on the city's central core.

Transportation. Much of the inner-city transportation is handled by bus, tram, and subway (metro) systems, which are inexpensive and subsidized. Despite the efforts to meet the demands of the growing population with an adequate public transportation system, the number of passenger cars and commercial vehicles has increased, resulting in plans for a major urban motorway system to include 10 radial arteries connecting Prague with the national road network.

Prague is one of the nation's major railway junctions, with three main stations and three freight transport circuits. The international airport at nearby Ruzyně was expanded and modernized in the 1960s to serve as a hub at the centre of the Continent. A new port has been built

Women in
the labour
force

Statue of Jan Hus in the Old Town Square.
Robert Harding Picture Library

at the confluence of the Vltava and Berounka rivers. The passenger boats that ply the Vltava during the summer are a popular tourist attraction.

ADMINISTRATION AND SOCIAL CONDITIONS

Government. Prague is one of two cities (the other is Bratislava) that have equal rank with the 10 regions that constitute the Czechoslovak federation. The city is the administrative centre for the Central Bohemian Region, of which the conurbation occupies about one-third. The Prague Municipal National Committee and the Central Bohemian Regional National Committee coordinate town planning, environmental control, and other projects. Prague city is divided into districts, each with its own district national committee, while the settlements included in Prague since the late 1940s have retained their own local national committees.

Public services. The standard municipal services—the supply of natural gas, electricity, and water and the treatment and disposal of sewage and refuse—have been consolidated under state control since World War II and have been considerably modernized and expanded as part of overall urban planning. The high percentage of employed women has caused municipal authorities to turn attention toward the provision of nurseries for the children of working mothers. Other facilities include swimming pools, often run in conjunction with sports organizations. On the river the city provides mooring positions for pleasure boats.

Housing shortage

Like cities in other Socialist-bloc countries, Prague has difficulties with the supply and maintenance of housing. Much of the housing in the inner city consists of small apartments in need of renovation and modernization, while the rate of construction of apartments in the newer zones lags behind the need. Privately owned houses constitute less than 15 percent of all Prague's housing units. In response to the problem, new housing developments have been built in the peripheral areas. Referred to as "towns," they include North Town (Severní město), South Town (Jižní město), and Southwest Town (Jihozápadní město).

All retail establishments—food stores, department stores, and self-service establishments—are publicly owned and are part of the municipal system. There are numerous small restaurants and taverns, many of which—especially in the Malá Strana (Lesser Quarter)—have an intimate and historic atmosphere and offer fine views over the city and the winding river.

Education. There are several institutions of higher education in Prague, but by far the most famous is Charles University, founded in 1348 and the oldest in central Europe. The Academy of Arts and the Academy of Music (with a conservatory founded in 1811) are also important. The activity of the Czechoslovak Academy of Sciences, founded in 1952, is supplemented by many specialized institutions; the academy sponsors a number of international congresses. Higher education in the city benefits from a tradition that can count among its scholars and teachers the great 17th-century astronomers Tycho Brahe and Johannes Kepler and the noted modern physicist Albert Einstein, who taught in Prague in 1911–12.

Health. As the capital city, Prague contains some of the country's main health facilities. These include hospitals, specialized medical clinics, and outpatient clinics. The most noted facilities are those that specialize in plastic surgery, orthopedics, and urology.

CULTURAL LIFE

Prague has a renowned and active musical life, which reaches a high point each year in the internationally known spring music festival. The city's fine orchestras—the Prague Symphony and the Czech Philharmonic—have won reputations abroad. Theatrical traditions are also strong, with more than 20 well-attended theatres in the city. There are also many museums and galleries, and a Palace of Culture was completed in 1981.

Architecture

Perhaps the greatest treasures of the city, however, are the 2,000 officially recognized architectural and artistic monuments, ranging in period from the Romanesque through the Gothic to the Baroque, Rococo, Classical, and Neoclassical. The interiors of the buildings, which often house major art collections, have been restored since 1945. The most notable Romanesque monument is probably the 10th-century Church of St. George, behind the north wall of Hradčany. To the west is its more massive successor, the basically Gothic St. Vitus' Cathedral, the twin spires of which dominate the city skyline. Other Gothic monuments include the Týn Church on Staroměstské Square; the elegant Powder Tower, marking the former city walls in what is now the busy Příkopy shopping area; the restored Bethlehem Chapel, where Jan Hus preached in the 15th century; and the St. Agnes Convent, built in 1234 and notable for its collection of 14th-century paintings. The Old-New Synagogue and the tumbling, crowded gravestones of the Old Jewish Cemetery—Europe's oldest—betoken the strong Jewish tradition in Prague life.

Baroque buildings are the city's greatest single artistic treasure, among them the splendid Valdštejn and Clam-Gallas palaces, St. Nicholas Church, and the Antonín Dvořák Museum. The geometric tiling of the Golz-Kinský Palace facade provides a distinctive glimpse of the Rococo style. Classical buildings include the Bedřich Smetana Museum on the riverside and the elegant Belvedere Palace (the former Royal Summer Palace). The National Museum and the National Theatre are the main Neoclassical buildings.

The beauty of the city is enhanced by its many parks and gardens, including a major cultural, entertainment, and sports centre in the park named for Julius Fučík (a resistance leader of World War II) and a large zoo in suburban Troja. Recreational facilities also include the vast Strahov sports complex—containing three stadiums, the largest of which, Spartakiáda Stadium, holds 250,000 spectators and is used for the mass gymnastic display known as the Spartakiáda—as well as numerous other sports and cultural centres, with emphasis on facilities for youth. The film studios at Barrandov, on the city outskirts, have produced a number of high-quality motion pictures, and there is a museum of modern sculpture at Zbraslav.

History

THE EARLY PERIOD

The foundation of the city. For thousands of years that portion of the Vltava's course where Prague was to rise was crossed by trade routes linking northern and southern Europe. The region is replete with Paleolithic relics, and Neolithic farmers inhabited the region from around 5000 to 2700 BC. Celts had settlements in the region from about 500 to 200 BC, including the fortified Závist, to the south of Prague. From the 4th to the 6th century AD, Slavs appeared on the Vltava banks, followed by the Avars.

The first settlement at what is now Prague has been traced to the second half of the 9th century. The oldest building was Vyšehrad (*hrad,* "castle"), set on a commanding right-bank hill. It was followed by what was to become Hradčany, set on an equally commanding left-bank site a little downstream. Legend (stirringly told in Smetana's opera *Libuše*) ascribes the foundation of Prague to a Princess Libuše and her husband, Přemysl, founder of the Přemyslid dynasty; legend notwithstanding, the Přemyslids, in power from about 800 to 1306, consolidated a political base centred on Prague that was to be the nucleus of the Bohemian state and that enabled the natural trade advantages of the city site to develop under defensive protection. The dynasty included St. Wenceslas (Václav), who was murdered by his brother Boleslav in about 939 and whose statue now looks down upon the square to which his name has been given; and Boleslav I, whose reign (*c.* 936–967) witnessed the consolidation of power against a German threat. The little community flourished, and in 965 the Jewish merchant and traveler Ibrāhīm ibn Yaʿqūb was able to describe it as a "busy trading centre." In 973 the bishopric of Prague was founded.

Medieval growth. The economic expansion of the community was reflected in the topography of the city. A market centre on the right bank, opposite Hradčany, developed into the Old Town (Staré město), particularly after the construction of the first stone bridge, the Judith Bridge, over the river in 1170. By 1230 the Old Town had been given borough status and was defended by a system of walls and fortifications. On the opposite bank, under the

The National Theatre off the Vltava River and the 1st of May Bridge.

walls of Hradčany, the community known as Malá Strana (literally, "Small Side") was founded in 1257. Following the eclipse of the Přemyslids, the House of Luxembourg came to power when John of Luxembourg, son of the future emperor Henry VII, became king of Bohemia. His son, Charles IV, Bohemian king and Holy Roman emperor, had his capital at Prague from 1346 to 1378 and took considerable personal interest in the development of

The role of Charles IV in planning the city

the city. In 1348 he founded Charles University, the first in central Europe, which was later to attract scholars and students from throughout the Continent. His reign also saw the growth of the planned New Town (Nové město) adjacent to the Old Town; construction of the Charles Bridge (1357, reconstructed in 1970) linking the Old Town and the Malá Strana; and the beginning (1344) of the great St. Vitus' Cathedral, which was not completed until 1929. Other buildings included the Carolinum (the central hall of the university), the town hall (destroyed in 1945), and several churches and monasteries in the New Town. The Jewish ghetto was also developed, and the bishopric was raised to an archbishopric in 1344.

By the 14th century Prague had become a major central European city, with the Czech money minted at nearby Kutná Hora serving as the hard currency of the entire region. Foreign merchants, notably Germans and Italians, became economically and politically powerful in uneasy alliance with the kings. The social order, however, became less stable because of the emergent guilds of craftsmen, themselves often torn by internal conflicts. The town paupers added a further volatile element.

The Reformation and the Thirty Years' War. Prague played a significant role in the Reformation. The sermons of Jan Hus, a scholar at the university, begun in 1402 at the now-restored Bethlehem Chapel and carrying forward the criticisms of the church developed by the English reformer John Wycliffe, endeared him to the common people but brought him into conflict with Rome; he was burned at the stake in the town of Constance (Konstanz, W.Ger.) in 1415. Popular uprisings in 1419, led by the Prague priest Jan Želivský, included the throwing of city councillors from the windows of the New Town Hall in the incident known as the first Defenestration of Prague. The next year Hussite peasant rebels, led by the great military leader Jan Žižka, joined forces with the Hussites of Prague to win a decisive victory over the Roman Catholic king (later emperor) Sigismund at nearby Vítkov Hill.

During the next 200 years, the wealthy merchants became ascendant once more, and the late Gothic architectural style flourished in many churches and buildings, reaching a peak in the fine Vladislav Hall of Hradčany. In 1526, however, the Roman Catholic Habsburgs became rulers of Bohemia and attempted to crush Czech Protestantism. The second Defenestration of Prague (1618), when the governors of Bohemia were thrown from the windows of the council room in Hradčany—one of the major events precipitating the Thirty Years' War—was followed by the decisive defeat of Protestant forces at the Battle of the White Mountain, near the city, in 1620. Twenty-seven Prague commoners and Czech noblemen were executed on the Staroměstské Square in 1621; the city ceased to be the capital of the empire, was occupied by Saxons (1631) and Swedes (1648), and went into a decline hastened by two outbreaks of plague.

EVOLUTION OF THE MODERN CITY

The return of more settled conditions in central Europe was marked by renewed economic growth, and Prague's population grew from 40,000 in 1705 to more than 80,000 by 1771. In 1784 the Old Town, the New Town, the Malá Strana, and the Hradčany complex were administratively united into one city. The merchants and the mostly German, Spanish, and Italian nobility who were active in and around Prague in this period had an enormous effect on both architecture and cultural life. Outstanding architects created magnificent palaces and gardens, and churches in the Prague version of the Baroque style sprang up throughout the city.

The onset of the Industrial Revolution had major effects in Prague. The first suburb (Karlín) was established in 1817, and in the next 20 years many factories sprang up, often in association with the coal mines and ironworks at Kladno and Králův Dvůr, not far away. The population passed 100,000 by 1837, and expansion continued after the city received its first railway eight years later. The rise of a working class and of strong nationalistic sentiments had a profound effect on the city; students, artisans, and workers took to the barricades against the ruling Austrians when revolution flared briefly in 1848. Within 20 years Czechs had won a majority on the City Council, and Czech cultural life was experiencing a renascence centred on Prague. The Neoclassical building of the National Museum and the National Theatre are only two examples of the building that took place in this period. By the 1890s the first electric streetcars (trams) were running in the city, urban services were being reorganized, and a replica of the Eiffel Tower overlooked the city from Petřín Hill.

Effects of the Industrial Revolution

In 1918 Prague became the capital of the newly independent Czechoslovak republic, and a Greater Prague of 19 districts had been established within two years. By 1930 the population had reached 850,000. The city suffered a severe setback following the surrender of large parts of Bohemia and Moravia to Germany under the Munich Agreement of 1938. The citizens rose in revolt on May 5, 1945, and held the city until the Red Army arrived four days later. The post-World War II period was marked by economic reconstruction and by careful planning with a view to restoring and preserving the historic monuments of the city centre. From the 1970s there was an increasing emphasis on the development of new satellite communities and of a regional plan for the entire Prague conurbation. The city continued to grow, although most of its population growth was attributable to annexation. The so-called Prague Spring of 1968, a short-lived excursion into liberalized social and governmental controls attempted by the government of Alexander Dubček, was terminated by Soviet military action in August of that year. In spite of the political vicissitudes of the 20th century, Prague has established a growing international reputation and has become a major tourist centre.

After World War II

BIBLIOGRAPHY. GEOFFREY MOORHOUSE, *Prague* (1980), offers information on all aspects of the city. Guidebooks, with information on history, include ALOIS SVOBODA, *Prague* (1965, reissued 1968), in English; EMANUEL POCHE, *The Golden Lane on Prague Castle* (1969; originally published in Czech, 1969), a description of the picturesque street of Hradčany; and FRANTIŠEK KAFKA, *Baedeker's Prague*, trans. from German (1987). Photographic views of the city are presented in JIŘÍ DOLEŽAL and EVŽEN VESELÝ, *Památky staré Prahy* (1966), a survey of historical Prague, with brief commentary; EUGEN VASILIAK, *Nad Prahou: Prague Seen from Above* (1966), a book of aerial photographs of old and new Prague with text in six languages; MIROSLAV KORECKÝ, *Prague in Colour* (1976; originally published in Czech, 1975), which portrays the city's many architectural styles and major landmarks; and BOHUMIL LANDISCH and VÍT PALOCH, *Praha: Praga: Prague* (1982), with annotations in Czech, English, German, and Russian. A study of the city from the perspective of urban sociology is provided by F.W. CARTER, "Prague and Sofia: An Analysis of Their Changing Internal City Structure," ch. 15 in R.A. FRENCH and F.E. IAN HAMILTON (eds.), *The Socialist City: Spatial Structure and Urban Policy* (1979), pp. 425–459. See also JIŘÍ HRŮZA and BLAHOMÍR BOROVIČKA, *Prague: A Socialist City* (1985). F.W. CARTER, "Kafka's Prague," ch. 2 in J.P. STERN (ed.), *The World of Franz Kafka* (1980), pp. 30–43, is an essay on Prague in Kafka's lifetime. Works describing the history of the city include COUNT (FRANZ) LÜTZOW, *The Story of Prague* (1902, reprinted 1971); JOSEF JANÁČEK (ed.), *Dějiny Prahy* (1964), a comprehensive publication covering the development and history of the city from the earliest times to 1960; JOSEPH WECHSBERG, *Prague: The Mystical City* (1971), short essays on Prague's history; and JOSEF JANÁČEK, *Malé dějiny Prahy*, 3rd rev. ed. (1983), on the history and architecture of the city.

(Ja.K./R.H.O./F.W.C.)